PENAL CODE - PEN

TITLE OF THE ACT

(Heading enacted 1872.)

1.

This Act shall be known as The Penal Code of California, and is divided into four parts, as follows:

I.—OF CRIMES AND PUNISHMENTS.
II.—OF CRIMINAL PROCEDURE.
III.—OF THE STATE PRISON AND COUNTY JAILS.
IV.—OF PREVENTION OF CRIMES AND APPREHENSION OF CRIMINALS.

(Amended by Stats. 1985, Ch. 367, Sec. 1.)

PRELIMINARY PROVISIONS

(Preliminary Provisions enacted 1872.)

2.

This Code takes effect at twelve o'clock, noon, on the first day of January, eighteen hundred and seventy-three.

(Enacted 1872.)

3.

No part of it is retroactive, unless expressly so declared.

(Enacted 1872.)

4.

The rule of the common law, that penal statutes are to be strictly construed, has no application to this Code. All its provisions are to be construed according to the fair import of their terms, with a view to effect its objects and to promote justice.

(Enacted 1872.)

5.

The provisions of this Code, so far as they are substantially the same as existing statutes, must be construed as continuations thereof, and not as new enactments.

(Enacted 1872.)

6.

No act or omission, commenced after twelve o'clock noon of the day on which this Code takes effect as a law, is criminal or punishable, except as prescribed or authorized by this Code, or by some of the statutes which it specifies as continuing in force and as not affected by its provisions, or by some ordinance, municipal, county, or township regulation, passed or adopted, under such statutes and in force when this Code takes effect. Any act or omission commenced prior to that time may be inquired of, prosecuted, and punished in the same manner as if this Code had not been passed.

(Enacted 1872.)

7.

Words used in this code in the present tense include the future as well as the present; words used in the masculine gender include the feminine and neuter; the singular number includes the plural, and the plural the singular; the word "person" includes a corporation as well as a natural person; the word "county" includes "city and county"; writing includes printing and typewriting; oath includes affirmation or declaration; and every mode of oral statement, under oath or affirmation, is embraced by the term "testify," and every written one in the term "depose"; signature or subscription includes mark, when the person cannot write, his or her name being written near it, by a person who writes his or her own name as a witness; provided, that when a signature is made by mark it must, in order that the same may be acknowledged or serve as the signature to any sworn statement, be witnessed by two persons who must subscribe their own names as witnesses thereto.

The following words have in this code the signification attached to them in this section, unless otherwise apparent from the context:

(1) The word "willfully," when applied to the intent with which an act is done or omitted, implies simply a purpose or willingness to commit the act, or make the omission referred to. It does not require any intent to violate law, or to injure another, or to acquire any advantage.

(2) The words "neglect," "negligence," "negligent," and "negligently" import a want of such attention to the nature or probable consequences of the act or omission as a prudent man ordinarily bestows in acting in his own concerns.

(3) The word "corruptly" imports a wrongful design to acquire or cause some pecuniary or other advantage to the person guilty of the act or omission referred to, or to some other person.

(4) The words "malice" and "maliciously" import a wish to vex, annoy, or injure another person, or an intent to do a wrongful act, established either by proof or presumption of law.

(5) The word "knowingly" imports only a knowledge that the facts exist which bring the act or omission within the provisions of this code. It does not require any knowledge of the unlawfulness of such act or omission.

(6) The word "bribe" signifies anything of value or advantage, present or prospective, or any promise or undertaking to give any, asked, given, or accepted, with a corrupt intent to influence, unlawfully, the person to whom it is given, in his or her action, vote, or opinion, in any public or official capacity.

(7) The word "vessel," when used with reference to shipping, includes ships of all kinds, steamboats, canalboats, barges, and every structure adapted to be navigated from place to place for the transportation of merchandise or persons, except that, as used in Sections 192.5 and 193.5, the word "vessel" means a vessel as defined in subdivision (c) of Section 651 of the Harbors and Navigation Code.

(8) The words "peace officer" signify any one of the officers mentioned in Chapter 4.5 (commencing with Section 830) of Title 3 of Part 2.

(9) The word "magistrate" signifies any one of the officers mentioned in Section 808.

(10) The word "property" includes both real and personal property.

(11) The words "real property" are coextensive with lands, tenements, and hereditaments.

(12) The words "personal property" include money, goods, chattels, things in action, and evidences of debt.

(13) The word "month" means a calendar month, unless otherwise expressed; the word "daytime" means the period between sunrise and sunset, and the word "nighttime" means the period between sunset and sunrise.

(14) The word "will" includes codicil.

(15) The word "writ" signifies an order or precept in writing, issued in the name of the people, or of a court or judicial officer, and the word "process" a writ or summons issued in the course of judicial proceedings.

(16) Words and phrases must be construed according to the context and the approved usage of the language; but technical words and phrases, and such others as may have acquired a peculiar and appropriate meaning in law, must be construed according to such peculiar and appropriate meaning.

(17) Words giving a joint authority to three or more public officers or other persons, are construed as giving such authority to a majority of them, unless it is otherwise expressed in the act giving the authority.

(18) When the seal of a court or public officer is required by law to be affixed to any paper, the word "seal" includes an impression of such seal upon the paper alone, or upon any substance attached
seal of a private person may b
writing the word "seal" agains

(19) The word "state," when
the District of Columbia and t
the district and territories.

(20) The word "section," whenever hereinafter employed, refers to a section
code, unless some other code or statute is expressly mentioned.

(21) To "book" signifies the recordation of an arrest in official police records, and the taking by the police of fingerprints and photographs of the person arrested, or any of these acts following an arrest.

(22) The word "spouse" includes "registered domestic partner," as required by Section 297.5 of the Family Code.

(Amended by Stats. 2016, Ch. 50, Sec. 65. (SB 1005) Effective January 1, 2017.)

7.5.

Whenever any offense is described in this code, the Uniform Controlled Substances Act (Division 10 (commencing with Section 11000) of the Health and Safety Code), or the Welfare and Institutions Code, as criminal conduct and as a violation of a specified code section or a particular provision of a code section, in the case of any ambiguity or conflict in interpretation, the code section or particular provision of the code section shall take precedence over the descriptive language. The descriptive language shall be deemed as being offered only for ease of reference unless it is otherwise clearly apparent from the context that the descriptive language is intended to narrow the application of the referenced code section or particular provision of the code section.

(Added by Stats. 1998, Ch. 162, Sec. 1. Effective January 1, 1999.)

8.

Whenever, by any of the provisions of this Code, an intent to defraud is required in order to constitute any offense, it is sufficient if an intent appears to defraud any person, association, or body politic or corporate, whatever.

(Enacted 1872.)

9.

The omission to specify or affirm in this Code any liability to damages, penalty, forfeiture, or other remedy imposed by law and allowed to be recovered or enforced in any civil action or proceeding, for any act or omission declared punishable herein, does not affect any right to recover or enforce the same.

(Enacted 1872.)

10.

The omission to specify or affirm in this Code any ground of forfeiture of a public office, or other trust or special authority conferred by law, or any power conferred by law to impeach, remove, depose, or suspend any public officer or other person holding any trust, appointment, or other special authority conferred by law, does not affect such forfeiture or power, or any proceeding authorized by law to carry into effect such impeachment, removal, deposition, or suspension.

(Enacted 1872.)

11.

This code does not affect any power conferred by law upon any court-martial, or other military authority or officer, to impose or inflict punishment upon offenders; nor, except as provided in Section 19.2 of this code, any power conferred by law upon any public body, tribunal, or officer, to impose or inflict punishment for a contempt.

(Amended by Stats. 1989, Ch. 897, Sec. 4.)

12.

The several sections of this Code which declare certain crimes to be punishable as therein mentioned, devolve a duty upon the Court authorized to pass sentence, to determine and impose the punishment prescribed.

(Enacted 1872.)

13.

Whenever in this Code the punishment for a crime is left undetermined between certain limits, the punishment to be inflicted in a particular case must be determined by the Court authorized to pass sentence, within such limits as may be prescribed by this Code.

(Enacted 1872.)

14.

The various sections of this Code which declare that evidence obtained upon the examination of a person as a witness cannot be received against him in any criminal proceeding, do not forbid such evidence being proved against such person upon any proceedings founded upon a charge of perjury committed in such examination.

(Enacted 1872.)

15.

A crime or public offense is an act committed or omitted in violation of a law forbidding or commanding it, and to which is annexed, upon conviction, either of the following punishments:

1. Death;
2. Imprisonment;
3. Fine;
4. Removal from office; or,
5. Disqualification to hold and enjoy any office of honor, trust, or profit in this State.

(Enacted 1872.)

16.

Crimes and public offenses include:

1. Felonies;
2. Misdemeanors; and
3. Infractions.

(Amended by Stats. 1968, Ch. 1192.)

17.

(a) A felony is a crime that is punishable with death, by imprisonment in the state prison, or notwithstanding any other provision of law, by imprisonment in a county jail under the provisions of subdivision (h) of Section 1170. Every other crime or public offense is a misdemeanor except those offenses that are classified as infractions.

(b) When a crime is punishable, in the discretion of the court, either by imprisonment in the state prison or imprisonment in a county jail under the provisions of subdivision (h) of Section 1170, or by fine or imprisonment in the county jail, it is a misdemeanor for all purposes under the following circumstances:

(1) After a judgment imposing a punishment other than imprisonment in the state prison or imprisonment in a county jail under the provisions of subdivision (h) of Section 1170.

(2) When the court, upon committing the defendant to the Division of Juvenile Justice, designates the offense to be a misdemeanor.

(3) When the court grants probation to a defendant and at the time of granting probation, or on application of the defendant or probation officer thereafter, the court declares the offense to be a misdemeanor.

(4) When the prosecuting attorney files in a court having jurisdiction over misdemeanor offenses a complaint specifying that the offense is a misdemeanor, unless the defendant at the time of his or her arraignment or plea objects to the offense being made a misdemeanor, in which event the complaint shall be amended to charge the felony and the case shall proceed on the felony complaint.

(5) When, at or before the preliminary examination or prior to filing an order pursuant to Section 872, the magistrate determines that the offense is a misdemeanor, in which event the case shall proceed as if the defendant had been arraigned on a misdemeanor complaint.

(c) When a defendant is committed to the Division of Juvenile Justice for a crime punishable, in the discretion of the court, either by imprisonment in the state prison or

imprisonment in a county jail under the provisions of subdivision (h) of Section 1170, or by fine or imprisonment in the county jail not exceeding one year, the offense shall, upon the discharge of the defendant from the Division of Juvenile Justice, thereafter be deemed a misdemeanor for all purposes.
(d) A violation of any code section listed in Section 19.8 is an infraction subject to the procedures described in Sections 19.6 and 19.7 when:
(1) The prosecutor files a complaint charging the offense as an infraction unless the defendant, at the time he or she is arraigned, after being informed of his or her rights, elects to have the case proceed as a misdemeanor, or;
(2) The court, with the consent of the defendant, determines that the offense is an infraction in which event the case shall proceed as if the defendant had been arraigned on an infraction complaint.
(e) Nothing in this section authorizes a judge to relieve a defendant of the duty to register as a sex offender pursuant to Section 290 if the defendant is charged with an offense for which registration as a sex offender is required pursuant to Section 290, and for which the trier of fact has found the defendant guilty.
(Amended by Stats. 2018, Ch. 18, Sec. 1. (AB 1941) Effective January 1, 2019.)
17.5.
(a) The Legislature finds and declares all of the following:
(1) The Legislature reaffirms its commitment to reducing recidivism among criminal offenders.
(2) Despite the dramatic increase in corrections spending over the past two decades, national reincarceration rates for people released from prison remain unchanged or have worsened. National data show that about 40 percent of released individuals are reincarcerated within three years. In California, the recidivism rate for persons who have served time in prison is even greater than the national average.
(3) Criminal justice policies that rely on building and operating more prisons to address community safety concerns are not sustainable, and will not result in improved public safety.
(4) California must reinvest its criminal justice resources to support community-based corrections programs and evidence-based practices that will achieve improved public safety returns on this state's substantial investment in its criminal justice system.
(5) Realigning low-level felony offenders who do not have prior convictions for serious, violent, or sex offenses to locally run community-based corrections programs, which are strengthened through community-based punishment, evidence-based practices, improved supervision strategies, and enhanced secured capacity, will improve public safety outcomes among adult felons and facilitate their reintegration back into society.
(6) Community-based corrections programs require a partnership between local public safety entities and the county to provide and expand the use of community-based punishment for low-level offender populations. Each county's Local Community Corrections Partnership, as established in paragraph (2) of subdivision (b) of Section 1230, should play a critical role in developing programs and ensuring appropriate outcomes for low-level offenders.
(7) Fiscal policy and correctional practices should align to promote a justice reinvestment strategy that fits each county. "Justice reinvestment" is a data-driven approach to reduce corrections and related criminal justice spending and reinvest savings in strategies designed to increase public safety. The purpose of justice reinvestment is to manage and allocate criminal justice populations more cost-effectively, generating savings that can be reinvested in evidence-based strategies that increase public safety while holding offenders accountable.
(8) "Community-based punishment" means correctional sanctions and programming encompassing a range of custodial and noncustodial responses to criminal or noncompliant offender activity. Community-based punishment may be provided by local public safety entities directly or through community-based public or private correctional service providers, and include, but are not limited to, the following:
(A) Short-term flash incarceration in jail for a period of not more than 10 days.
(B) Intensive community supervision.
(C) Home detention with electronic monitoring or GPS monitoring.
(D) Mandatory community service.
(E) Restorative justice programs such as mandatory victim restitution and victim-offender reconciliation.
(F) Work, training, or education in a furlough program pursuant to Section 1208.
(G) Work, in lieu of confinement, in a work release program pursuant to Section 4024.2.
(H) Day reporting.
(I) Mandatory residential or nonresidential substance abuse treatment programs.
(J) Mandatory random drug testing.
(K) Mother-infant care programs.
(L) Community-based residential programs offering structure, supervision, drug treatment, alcohol treatment, literacy programming, employment counseling, psychological counseling, mental health treatment, or any combination of these and other interventions.
(9) "Evidence-based practices" refers to supervision policies, procedures, programs, and practices demonstrated by scientific research to reduce recidivism among individuals under probation, parole, or post release supervision.
(b) The provisions of this act are not intended to alleviate state prison overcrowding.
(Amended (as added by Stats. 2011, Ch. 15) by Stats. 2011, Ch. 39, Sec. 5. (AB 117) Effective June 30, 2011. Addition and amendment operative October 1, 2011, pursuant to Secs. 68 and 69 of Ch. 39.)
17.7.
The Legislature finds and declares the following:
(a) Strategies supporting reentering offenders through practices and programs, such as standardized risk and needs assessments, transitional community housing, treatment, medical and mental health services, and employment, have been demonstrated to significantly reduce recidivism among offenders in other states.
(b) Improving outcomes among offenders reentering the community after serving time in a correctional facility will promote public safety and will reduce California's prison and jail populations.
(c) Establishing a California reentry program that encompasses strategies known to reduce recidivism warrants a vigorous short-term startup in the 2014–15 fiscal year using readily available resources in the community, and a comprehensive long-term development plan for future budget years designed to expand the availability, impact, and sustainability of these strategies as further community partnerships are identified and developed.
(Added by Stats. 2014, Ch. 26, Sec. 11. (AB 1468) Effective June 20, 2014.)
18.
(a) Except in cases where a different punishment is prescribed by any law of this state, every offense declared to be a felony is punishable by imprisonment for 16 months, or two or three years in the state prison unless the offense is punishable pursuant to subdivision (h) of Section 1170.
(b) Every offense which is prescribed by any law of the state to be a felony punishable by imprisonment or by a fine, but without an alternate sentence to the county jail for a period not exceeding one year, may be punishable by imprisonment in the county jail not exceeding one year or by a fine, or by both.
(Amended (as amended by Stats. 2011, Ch. 15, Sec. 230) by Stats. 2011, 1st Ex. Sess., Ch. 12, Sec. 7. (AB 17 1x) Effective September 21, 2011. Operative October 1, 2011, by Sec. 46 of Ch. 12.)
18.5.
(a) Every offense which is prescribed by any law of the state to be punishable by imprisonment in a county jail up to or not exceeding one year shall be punishable by imprisonment in a county jail for a period not to exceed 364 days. This section shall apply retroactively, whether or not the case was final as of January 1, 2015.
(b) A person who was sentenced to a term of one year in county jail prior to January 1, 2015, may submit an application before the trial court that entered the judgment of conviction in the case to have the term of the sentence modified to the maximum term specified in subdivision (a).
(Amended by Stats. 2016, Ch. 789, Sec. 1. (SB 1242) Effective January 1, 2017.)
19.
Except in cases where a different punishment is prescribed by any law of this state, every offense declared to be a misdemeanor is punishable by imprisonment in the county jail not exceeding six months, or by fine not exceeding one thousand dollars ($1,000), or by both.
(Amended by Stats. 1983, Ch. 1092, Sec. 231. Effective September 27, 1983. Operative January 1, 1984, by Sec. 427 of Ch. 1092.)
19.2.
In no case shall any person sentenced to confinement in a county or city jail, or in a county or joint county penal farm, road camp, work camp, or other county adult detention facility, or committed to the sheriff for placement in any county adult detention facility, on conviction of a misdemeanor, or as a condition of probation upon conviction of either a felony or a misdemeanor, or upon commitment for civil contempt, or upon default in the payment of a fine upon conviction of either a felony or a misdemeanor, or for any reason except upon conviction of a crime that specifies a felony punishment pursuant to subdivision (h) of Section 1170 or a conviction of more than one offense when consecutive sentences have been imposed, be committed for a period in excess of one year; provided, however, that the time allowed on parole shall not be considered as a part of the period of confinement.
(Amended by Stats. 2011, Ch. 15, Sec. 231. (AB 109) Effective April 4, 2011. Operative October 1, 2011, by Sec. 636 of Ch. 15, as amended by Stats. 2011, Ch. 39, Sec. 68.)
19.4.
When an act or omission is declared by a statute to be a public offense and no penalty for the offense is prescribed in any statute, the act or omission is punishable as a misdemeanor.
(Added by Stats. 1989, Ch. 897, Sec. 11.)
19.6.
An infraction is not punishable by imprisonment. A person charged with an infraction shall not be entitled to a trial by jury. A person charged with an infraction shall not be entitled to have the public defender or other counsel appointed at public expense to represent him or her unless he or she is arrested and not released on his or her written promise to appear, his or her own recognizance, or a deposit of bail.
(Added by renumbering Section 19c by Stats. 1989, Ch. 897, Sec. 8.)
19.7.
Except as otherwise provided by law, all provisions of law relating to misdemeanors shall apply to infractions including, but not limited to, powers of peace officers, jurisdiction of courts, periods for commencing action and for bringing a case to trial and burden of proof.
(Added by renumbering Section 19d by Stats. 1989, Ch. 897, Sec. 9.)
19.8.
(a) The following offenses are subject to subdivision (d) of Section 17: Sections 193.8, 330, 415, 485, 490.7, 555, 602.13, and 853.7 of this code; subdivision (c) of Section 532b, and subdivision (o) of Section 602 of this code; subdivision (b) of Section 25658 and Sections 21672, 25661, and 25662 of the Business and Professions Code; Section 27204 of the Government Code; subdivision (c) of Section 23109 and Sections 5201.1, 12500, 14601.1, 27150.1, 40508, and 42005 of the Vehicle Code, and any other offense that the Legislature makes subject to subdivision (d) of Section 17. Except where a lesser maximum fine is expressly provided for a violation of those sections, a violation that is an infraction is punishable by a fine not exceeding two hundred fifty dollars ($250).
(b) Except in cases where a different punishment is prescribed, every offense declared to be an infraction is punishable by a fine not exceeding two hundred fifty dollars ($250).
(c) Except for the violations enumerated in subdivision (d) of Section 13202.5 of the Vehicle Code, and Section 14601.1 of the Vehicle Code based upon failure to appear, a conviction for an offense made an infraction under subdivision (d) of Section 17 is not grounds for the suspension, revocation, or denial of a license, or for the revocation of probation or parole of the person convicted.
(Amended by Stats. 2015, Ch. 303, Sec. 383. (AB 731) Effective January 1, 2016.)
19.9.
For purposes of this code, "mandatory supervision" shall mean the portion of a defendant's sentenced term during which time he or she is supervised by the county probation officer pursuant to subparagraph (B) of paragraph (5) of subdivision (h) of Section 1170.
(Added by Stats. 2012, Ch. 43, Sec. 14. (SB 1023) Effective June 27, 2012.)
20.
In every crime or public offense there must exist a union, or joint operation of act and intent, or criminal negligence.
(Enacted 1872.)
21a.
An attempt to commit a crime consists of two elements: a specific intent to commit the crime, and a direct but ineffectual act done toward its commission.
(Added by Stats. 1986, Ch. 519, Sec. 1.)
23.
In any criminal proceeding against a person who has been issued a license to engage in a business or profession by a state agency pursuant to provisions of the Business and Professions Code or the Education Code, or the Chiropractic Initiative Act, the state agency which issued the license may voluntarily appear to furnish pertinent information, make recommendations regarding specific conditions of probation, or provide any other assistance necessary to promote the interests of justice and protect the interests of the public, or may be ordered by the court to do so, if the crime charged is substantially related to the qualifications, functions, or duties of a licensee.
For purposes of this section, the term "license" shall include a permit or a certificate issued by a state agency.
For purposes of this section, the term "state agency" shall include any state board, commission, bureau, or division created pursuant to the provisions of the Business and Professions Code, the Education Code, or the Chiropractic Initiative Act to license and regulate individuals who engage in certain businesses and professions.
(Amended by Stats. 2002, Ch. 545, Sec. 3. Effective January 1, 2003.)
24.
This Act, whenever cited, enumerated, referred to, or amended, may be designated simply as The Penal Code, adding, when necessary, the number of the section.
(Enacted 1872.)

PART 1. OF CRIMES AND PUNISHMENTS [25 - 680]

(Part 1 enacted 1872.)

TITLE 1. OF PERSONS LIABLE TO PUNISHMENT FOR CRIME [25 - 29.8]

(Title 1 enacted 1872.)

25.

(a) The defense of diminished capacity is hereby abolished. In a criminal action, as well as any juvenile court proceeding, evidence concerning an accused person's intoxication, trauma, mental illness, disease, or defect shall not be admissible to show or negate capacity to form the particular purpose, intent, motive, malice aforethought, knowledge, or other mental state required for the commission of the crime charged.

(b) In any criminal proceeding, including any juvenile court proceeding, in which a plea of not guilty by reason of insanity is entered, this defense shall be found by the trier of fact only when the accused person proves by a preponderance of the evidence that he or she was incapable of knowing or understanding the nature and quality of his or her act and of distinguishing right from wrong at the time of the commission of the offense.

(c) Notwithstanding the foregoing, evidence of diminished capacity or of a mental disorder may be considered by the court only at the time of sentencing or other disposition or commitment.

(d) The provisions of this section shall not be amended by the Legislature except by statute passed in each house by rollcall vote entered in the journal, two-thirds of the membership concurring, or by a statute that becomes effective only when approved by the electors.

(Added June 8, 1982, by initiative Proposition 8, Sec. 4. Note: Prop. 8 is titled The Victims' Bill of Rights.)

26.

All persons are capable of committing crimes except those belonging to the following classes:

One—Children under the age of 14, in the absence of clear proof that at the time of committing the act charged against them, they knew its wrongfulness.

Two—Persons who are mentally incapacitated.

Three—Persons who committed the act or made the omission charged under an ignorance or mistake of fact, which disproves any criminal intent.

Four—Persons who committed the act charged without being conscious thereof.

Five—Persons who committed the act or made the omission charged through misfortune or by accident, when it appears that there was no evil design, intention, or culpable negligence.

Six—Persons (unless the crime be punishable with death) who committed the act or made the omission charged under threats or menaces sufficient to show that they had reasonable cause to and did believe their lives would be endangered if they refused.

(Amended by Stats. 2007, Ch. 31, Sec. 3. Effective January 1, 2008.)

27.

(a) The following persons are liable to punishment under the laws of this state:

(1) All persons who commit, in whole or in part, any crime within this state.

(2) All who commit any offense without this state which, if committed within this state, would be larceny, carjacking, robbery, or embezzlement under the laws of this state, and bring the property stolen or embezzled, or any part of it, or are found with it, or any part of it, within this state.

(3) All who, being without this state, cause or aid, advise or encourage, another person to commit a crime within this state, and are afterwards found therein.

(b) Perjury, in violation of Section 118, is punishable also when committed outside of California to the extent provided in Section 118.

(Amended by Stats. 1993, Ch. 611, Sec. 2. Effective October 1, 1993.)

28.

(a) Evidence of mental disease, mental defect, or mental disorder shall not be admitted to show or negate the capacity to form any mental state, including, but not limited to, purpose, intent, knowledge, premeditation, deliberation, or malice aforethought, with which the accused committed the act. Evidence of mental disease, mental defect, or mental disorder is admissible solely on the issue of whether or not the accused actually formed a required specific intent, premeditated, deliberated, or harbored malice aforethought, when a specific intent crime is charged.

(b) As a matter of public policy there shall be no defense of diminished capacity, diminished responsibility, or irresistible impulse in a criminal action or juvenile adjudication hearing.

(c) This section shall not be applicable to an insanity hearing pursuant to Section 1026.

(d) Nothing in this section shall limit a court's discretion, pursuant to the Evidence Code, to exclude psychiatric or psychological evidence on whether the accused had a mental disease, mental defect, or mental disorder at the time of the alleged offense.

(Amended by Stats. 2002, Ch. 784, Sec. 528. Effective January 1, 2003.)

29.

In the guilt phase of a criminal action, any expert testifying about a defendant's mental illness, mental disorder, or mental defect shall not testify as to whether the defendant had or did not have the required mental states, which include, but are not limited to, purpose, intent, knowledge, or malice aforethought, for the crimes charged. The question as to whether the defendant had or did not have the required mental states shall be decided by the trier of fact.

(Repealed and added by Stats. 1984, Ch. 1433, Sec. 3.)

29.2.

(a) The intent or intention is manifested by the circumstances connected with the offense.

(b) In the guilt phase of a criminal action or a juvenile adjudication hearing, evidence that the accused lacked the capacity or ability to control his or her conduct for any reason shall not be admissible on the issue of whether the accused actually had any mental state with respect to the commission of any crime. This subdivision is not applicable to Section 26.

(Added by renumbering Section 21 by Stats. 2012, Ch. 162, Sec. 118. (SB 1171) Effective January 1, 2013.)

29.4.

(a) No act committed by a person while in a state of voluntary intoxication is less criminal by reason of his or her having been in that condition. Evidence of voluntary intoxication shall not be admitted to negate the capacity to form any mental states for the crimes charged, including, but not limited to, purpose, intent, knowledge, premeditation, deliberation, or malice aforethought, with which the accused committed the act.

(b) Evidence of voluntary intoxication is admissible solely on the issue of whether or not the defendant actually formed a required specific intent, or, when charged with murder, whether the defendant premeditated, deliberated, or harbored express malice aforethought.

(c) Voluntary intoxication includes the voluntary ingestion, injection, or taking by any other means of any intoxicating liquor, drug, or other substance.

(Added by renumbering Section 22 by Stats. 2012, Ch. 162, Sec. 119. (SB 1171) Effective January 1, 2013.)

29.8.

In any criminal proceeding in which a plea of not guilty by reason of insanity is entered, this defense shall not be found by the trier of fact solely on the basis of a personality or adjustment disorder, a seizure disorder, or an addiction to, or abuse of, intoxicating substances. This section shall apply only to persons who utilize this defense on or after the operative date of the section.

(Added by renumbering Section 25.5 by Stats. 2012, Ch. 162, Sec. 120. (SB 1171) Effective January 1, 2013.)

TITLE 2. OF PARTIES TO CRIME [30 - 33]

(Title 2 enacted 1872.)

30.

The parties to crimes are classified as:

1. Principals; and,
2. Accessories.

(Enacted 1872.)

31.

All persons concerned in the commission of a crime, whether it be felony or misdemeanor, and whether they directly commit the act constituting the offense, or aid and abet in its commission, or, not being present, have advised and encouraged its commission, and all persons counseling, advising, or encouraging children under the age of fourteen years, or persons who are mentally incapacitated, to commit any crime, or who, by fraud, contrivance, or force, occasion the drunkenness of another for the purpose of causing him to commit any crime, or who, by threats, menaces, command, or coercion, compel another to commit any crime, are principals in any crime so committed.

(Amended by Stats. 2007, Ch. 31, Sec. 4. Effective January 1, 2008.)

32.

Every person who, after a felony has been committed, harbors, conceals or aids a principal in such felony, with the intent that said principal may avoid or escape from arrest, trial, conviction or punishment, having knowledge that said principal has committed such felony or has been charged with such felony or convicted thereof, is an accessory to such felony.

(Amended by Stats. 1935, Ch. 436.)

33.

Except in cases where a different punishment is prescribed, an accessory is punishable by a fine not exceeding five thousand dollars ($5,000), or by imprisonment pursuant to subdivision (h) of Section 1170, or in a county jail not exceeding one year, or by both such fine and imprisonment.

(Amended by Stats. 2011, Ch. 15, Sec. 232. (AB 109) Effective April 4, 2011. Operative October 1, 2011, by Sec. 636 of Ch. 15, as amended by Stats. 2011, Ch. 39, Sec. 68.)

TITLE 3. OF OFFENSES AGAINST THE SOVEREIGNTY OF THE STATE [37 - 38]

(Title 3 enacted 1872.)

37.

(a) Treason against this state consists only in levying war against it, adhering to its enemies, or giving them aid and comfort, and can be committed only by persons owing allegiance to the state. The punishment of treason shall be death or life imprisonment without possibility of parole. The penalty shall be determined pursuant to Sections 190.3 and 190.4.

(b) Upon a trial for treason, the defendant cannot be convicted unless upon the testimony of two witnesses to the same overt act, or upon confession in open court; nor, except as provided in Sections 190.3 and 190.4, can evidence be admitted of an overt act not expressly charged in the indictment or information; nor can the defendant be convicted unless one or more overt acts be expressly alleged therein.

(Amended by Stats. 1989, Ch. 897, Sec. 12.)

38.

Misprision of treason is the knowledge and concealment of treason, without otherwise assenting to or participating in the crime. It is punishable by imprisonment pursuant to subdivision (h) of Section 1170.

(Amended by Stats. 2011, Ch. 15, Sec. 233. (AB 109) Effective April 4, 2011. Operative October 1, 2011, by Sec. 636 of Ch. 15, as amended by Stats. 2011, Ch. 39, Sec. 68.)

TITLE 5. OF CRIMES BY AND AGAINST THE EXECUTIVE POWER OF THE STATE [67 - 77]

(Title 5 enacted 1872.)

67.

Every person who gives or offers any bribe to any executive officer in this state, with intent to influence him in respect to any act, decision, vote, opinion, or other proceeding as such officer, is punishable by imprisonment in the state prison for two, three or four years, and is disqualified from holding any office in this state.

(Amended by Stats. 1976, Ch. 1139.)

67.5.

(a) Every person who gives or offers as a bribe to any ministerial officer, employee, or appointee of the State of California, county or city therein, or political subdivision thereof, any thing the theft of which would be petty theft is guilty of a misdemeanor.

(b) If the theft of the thing given or offered would be grand theft the offense is a felony punishable by imprisonment pursuant to subdivision (h) of Section 1170.

(Amended by Stats. 2011, Ch. 15, Sec. 234. (AB 109) Effective April 4, 2011. Operative October 1, 2011, by Sec. 636 of Ch. 15, as amended by Stats. 2011, Ch. 39, Sec. 68.)

68.

(a) Every executive or ministerial officer, employee, or appointee of the State of California, a county or city therein, or a political subdivision thereof, who asks, receives, or agrees to receive, any bribe, upon any agreement or understanding that his or her vote, opinion, or action upon any matter then pending, or that may be brought before him or her in his or her official capacity, shall be influenced thereby, is punishable by imprisonment in the state prison for two, three, or four years and, in cases in which no bribe has been actually received, by a restitution fine of not less than two thousand dollars ($2,000) or not more than ten thousand dollars ($10,000) or, in cases in which a bribe was actually received, by a restitution fine of at least the actual amount of the bribe received or two thousand dollars ($2,000), whichever is greater, or any larger amount of not more than double the amount of any bribe received or ten thousand dollars ($10,000), whichever is greater, and, in addition thereto, forfeits his or her office, employment, or appointment, and is forever disqualified from holding any office, employment, or appointment, in this state.

(b) In imposing a restitution fine pursuant to this section, the court shall consider the defendant's ability to pay the fine.

(Amended by Stats. 2002, Ch. 664, Sec. 169. Effective January 1, 2003.)

69.

(a) Every person who attempts, by means of any threat or violence, to deter or prevent an executive officer from performing any duty imposed upon the officer by law, or who knowingly resists, by the use of force or violence, the officer, in the performance of his or her duty, is punishable by a fine not exceeding ten thousand dollars ($10,000), or by imprisonment pursuant to subdivision (h) of Section 1170, or in a county jail not exceeding one year, or by both such fine and imprisonment.

(b) The fact that a person takes a photograph or makes an audio or video recording of an executive officer, while the officer is in a public place or the person taking the

photograph or making the recording is in a place he or she has the right to be, does not constitute, in and of itself, a violation of subdivision (a).
(Amended by Stats. 2015, Ch. 177, Sec. 1. (SB 411) Effective January 1, 2016.)
70.
(a) Every executive or ministerial officer, employee, or appointee of the State of California, or any county or city therein, or any political subdivision thereof, who knowingly asks, receives, or agrees to receive any emolument, gratuity, or reward, or any promise thereof excepting such as may be authorized by law for doing an official act, is guilty of a misdemeanor.
(b) This section does not prohibit deputy registrars of voters from receiving compensation when authorized by local ordinance from any candidate, political committee, or statewide political organization for securing the registration of voters.
(c) (1) Nothing in this section precludes a peace officer, as defined in Chapter 4.5 (commencing with Section 830) of Title 3 of Part 2, from engaging in, or being employed in, casual or part-time employment as a private security guard or patrolman for a public entity while off duty from his or her principal employment and outside his or her regular employment as a peace officer of a state or local agency, and exercising the powers of a peace officer concurrently with that employment, provided that the peace officer is in a police uniform and is subject to reasonable rules and regulations of the agency for which he or she is a peace officer. Notwithstanding the above provisions, any and all civil and criminal liability arising out of the secondary employment of any peace officer pursuant to this subdivision shall be borne by the officer's secondary employer.
(2) It is the intent of the Legislature by this subdivision to abrogate the holdings in People v. Corey, 21 Cal.3d 738, and Cervantez v. J.C. Penney Co., 24 Cal.3d 579, to reinstate prior judicial interpretations of this section as they relate to criminal sanctions for battery on peace officers who are employed, on a part-time or casual basis, by a public entity, while wearing a police uniform as private security guards or patrolmen, and to allow the exercise of peace officer powers concurrently with that employment.
(d) (1) Nothing in this section precludes a peace officer, as defined in Chapter 4.5 (commencing with Section 830) of Title 3 of Part 2, from engaging in, or being employed in, casual or part-time employment as a private security guard or patrolman by a private employer while off duty from his or her principal employment and outside his or her regular employment as a peace officer, and exercising the powers of a peace officer concurrently with that employment, provided that all of the following are true:
(A) The peace officer is in his or her police uniform.
(B) The casual or part-time employment as a private security guard or patrolman is approved by the county board of supervisors with jurisdiction over the principal employer or by the board's designee or by the city council with jurisdiction over the principal employer or by the council's designee.
(C) The wearing of uniforms and equipment is approved by the principal employer.
(D) The peace officer is subject to reasonable rules and regulations of the agency for which he or she is a peace officer.
(2) Notwithstanding the above provisions, a peace officer while off duty from his or her principal employment and outside his or her regular employment as a peace officer of a state or local agency shall not exercise the powers of a police officer if employed by a private employer as a security guard during a strike, lockout, picketing, or other physical demonstration of a labor dispute at the site of the strike, lockout, picketing, or other physical demonstration of a labor dispute. The issue of whether or not casual or part-time employment as a private security guard or patrolman pursuant to this subdivision is to be approved shall not be a subject for collective bargaining. Any and all civil and criminal liability arising out of the secondary employment of any peace officer pursuant to this subdivision shall be borne by the officer's principal employer. The principal employer shall require the secondary employer to enter into an indemnity agreement as a condition of approving casual or part-time employment pursuant to this subdivision.
(3) It is the intent of the Legislature by this subdivision to abrogate the holdings in People v. Corey, 21 Cal. 3d 738, and Cervantez v. J. C. Penney Co., 24 Cal. 3d 579, to reinstate prior judicial interpretations of this section as they relate to criminal sanctions for battery on peace officers who are employed, on a part-time or casual basis, while wearing a police uniform approved by the principal employer, as private security guards or patrolmen, and to allow the exercise of peace officer powers concurrently with that employment.
(e) (1) Nothing in this section precludes a peace officer, as defined in Chapter 4.5 (commencing with Section 830) of Title 3 of Part 2, from engaging in, or being employed in, other employment while off duty from his or her principal employment and outside his or her regular employment as a peace officer of a state or local agency.
(2) Subject to subdivisions (c) and (d), and except as provided by written regulations or policies adopted by the employing state or local agency, or pursuant to an agreement between the employing state or local agency and a recognized employee organization representing the peace officer, no peace officer shall be prohibited from engaging in, or being employed in, other employment while off duty from his or her principal employment and outside his or her regular employment as a peace officer of a state or local agency.
(3) If an employer withholds consent to allow a peace officer to engage in or be employed in other employment while off duty, the employer shall, at the time of denial, provide the reasons for denial in writing to the peace officer.
(Amended by Stats. 2003, Ch. 104, Sec. 1. Effective January 1, 2004.)
70.5.
Every commissioner of civil marriages or every deputy commissioner of civil marriages who accepts any money or other thing of value for performing any marriage pursuant to Section 401 of the Family Code, including any money or thing of value voluntarily tendered by the persons about to be married or who have been married by the commissioner of civil marriages or deputy commissioner of civil marriages, other than a fee expressly imposed by law for performance of a marriage, whether the acceptance occurs before or after performance of the marriage and whether or not performance of the marriage is conditioned on the giving of such money or the thing of value by the persons being married, is guilty of a misdemeanor.
It is not a necessary element of the offense described by this section that the acceptance of the money or other thing of value be committed with intent to commit extortion or with other criminal intent.
This section does not apply to the request or acceptance by any retired commissioner of civil marriages of a fee for the performance of a marriage.
This section is inapplicable to the acceptance of a fee for the performance of a marriage on Saturday, Sunday, or a legal holiday.
(Amended by Stats. 1992, Ch. 163, Sec. 100. Effective January 1, 1993. Operative January 1, 1994, by Sec. 161 of Ch. 163.)
71.
(a) Every person who, with intent to cause, attempts to cause, or causes, any officer or employee of any public or private educational institution or any public officer or employee to do, or refrain from doing, any act in the performance of his duties, by means of a threat, directly communicated to such person, to inflict an unlawful injury upon any person or property, and it reasonably appears to the recipient of the threat that such threat could be carried out, is guilty of a public offense punishable as follows:
(1) Upon a first conviction, such person is punishable by a fine not exceeding ten thousand dollars ($10,000), or by imprisonment pursuant to subdivision (h) of Section 1170, or in a county jail not exceeding one year, or by both that fine and imprisonment.
(2) If the person has been previously convicted of a violation of this section, such previous conviction shall be charged in the accusatory pleading, and if that previous conviction is found to be true by the jury, upon a jury trial, or by the court, upon a court

trial, or is admitted by the defendant, he or she is punishable by imprisonment pursuant to subdivision (h) of Section 1170.
(b) As used in this section, "directly communicated" includes, but is not limited to, a communication to the recipient of the threat by telephone, telegraph, or letter.
(Amended by Stats. 2011, Ch. 15, Sec. 236. (AB 109) Effective April 4, 2011. Operative October 1, 2011, by Sec. 636 of Ch. 15, as amended by Stats. 2011, Ch. 39, Sec. 68.)
72.
Every person who, with intent to defraud, presents for allowance or for payment to any state board or officer, or to any county, city, or district board or officer, authorized to allow or pay the same if genuine, any false or fraudulent claim, bill, account, voucher, or writing, is punishable either by imprisonment in the county jail for a period of not more than one year, by a fine of not exceeding one thousand dollars ($1,000), or by both that imprisonment and fine, or by imprisonment pursuant to subdivision (h) of Section 1170, by a fine of not exceeding ten thousand dollars ($10,000), or by both such imprisonment and fine.
As used in this section "officer" includes a "carrier," as defined in subdivision (a) of Section 14124.70 of the Welfare and Institutions Code, authorized to act as an agent for a state board or officer or a county, city, or district board or officer, as the case may be.
(Amended by Stats. 2011, Ch. 15, Sec. 237. (AB 109) Effective April 4, 2011. Operative October 1, 2011, by Sec. 636 of Ch. 15, as amended by Stats. 2011, Ch. 39, Sec. 68.)
72.5.
(a) Every person who, knowing a claim seeks public funds for reimbursement of costs incurred in attending a political function organized to support or oppose any political party or political candidate, presents such a claim for allowance or for payment to any state board or officer, or to any county, city, or district board or officer authorized to allow or pay such claims, is punishable either by imprisonment in the county jail for a period of not more than one year, by a fine of not exceeding one thousand dollars ($1,000), or by both such imprisonment and fine, or by imprisonment pursuant to subdivision (h) of Section 1170, by a fine of not exceeding ten thousand dollars ($10,000), or by both such imprisonment and fine.
(b) Every person who, knowing a claim seeks public funds for reimbursement of costs incurred to gain admittance to a political function expressly organized to support or oppose any ballot measure, presents such a claim for allowance or for payment to any state board or officer, or to any county, city, or district board or officer authorized to allow or pay those claims is punishable either by imprisonment in the county jail for a period of not more than one year, by a fine of not exceeding one thousand dollars ($1,000), or by both that imprisonment and fine, or by imprisonment pursuant to subdivision (h) of Section 1170, by a fine of not exceeding ten thousand dollars ($10,000), or by both that imprisonment and fine.
(Amended by Stats. 2011, Ch. 15, Sec. 238. (AB 109) Effective April 4, 2011. Operative October 1, 2011, by Sec. 636 of Ch. 15, as amended by Stats. 2011, Ch. 39, Sec. 68.)
73.
Every person who gives or offers any gratuity or reward, in consideration that he or any other person shall be appointed to any public office, or shall be permitted to exercise or discharge the duties thereof, is guilty of a misdemeanor.
(Enacted 1872.)
74.
Every public officer who, for any gratuity or reward, appoints another person to a public office, or permits another person to exercise or discharge any of the duties of his office, is punishable by a fine not exceeding ten thousand dollars ($10,000), and, in addition thereto, forfeits his office and is forever disqualified from holding any office in this state.
(Amended by Stats. 1983, Ch. 1092, Sec. 234. Effective September 27, 1983. Operative January 1, 1984, by Sec. 427 of Ch. 1092.)
76.
(a) Every person who knowingly and willingly threatens the life of, or threatens serious bodily harm to, any elected public official, county public defender, county clerk, exempt appointee of the Governor, judge, or Deputy Commissioner of the Board of Prison Terms, or the staff, immediate family, or immediate family of the staff of any elected public official, county public defender, county clerk, exempt appointee of the Governor, judge, or Deputy Commissioner of the Board of Prison Terms, with the specific intent that the statement is to be taken as a threat, and the apparent ability to carry out that threat by any means, is guilty of a public offense, punishable as follows:
(1) Upon a first conviction, the offense is punishable by a fine not exceeding five thousand dollars ($5,000), or by imprisonment pursuant to subdivision (h) of Section 1170, or in a county jail not exceeding one year, or by both that fine and imprisonment.
(2) If the person has been convicted previously of violating this section, the previous conviction shall be charged in the accusatory pleading, and if the previous conviction is found to be true by the jury upon a jury trial, or by the court upon a court trial, or is admitted by the defendant, the offense is punishable by imprisonment pursuant to subdivision (h) of Section 1170.
(b) Any law enforcement agency that has knowledge of a violation of this section involving a constitutional officer of the state, a Member of the Legislature, or a member of the judiciary shall immediately report that information to the Department of the California Highway Patrol.
(c) For purposes of this section, the following definitions shall apply:
(1) "Apparent ability to carry out that threat" includes the ability to fulfill the threat at some future date when the person making the threat is an incarcerated prisoner with a stated release date.
(2) "Serious bodily harm" includes serious physical injury or serious traumatic condition.
(3) "Immediate family" means a spouse, parent, or child, or anyone who has regularly resided in the household for the past six months.
(4) "Staff of a judge" means court officers and employees, including commissioners, referees, and retired judges sitting on assignment.
(5) "Threat" means a verbal or written threat or a threat implied by a pattern of conduct or a combination of verbal or written statements and conduct made with the intent and the apparent ability to carry out the threat so as to cause the person who is the target of the threat to reasonably fear for his or her safety or the safety of his or her immediate family.
(d) As for threats against staff or immediate family of staff, the threat must relate directly to the official duties of the staff of the elected public official, county public defender, county clerk, exempt appointee of the Governor, judge, or Deputy Commissioner of the Board of Prison Terms in order to constitute a public offense under this section.
(e) A threat must relate directly to the official duties of a Deputy Commissioner of the Board of Prison Terms in order to constitute a public offense under this section.
(Amended by Stats. 2011, Ch. 15, Sec. 239. (AB 109) Effective April 4, 2011. Operative October 1, 2011, by Sec. 636 of Ch. 15, as amended by Stats. 2011, Ch. 39, Sec. 68.)
77.
The various provisions of this title, except Section 76, apply to administrative and ministerial officers, in the same manner as if they were mentioned therein.
(Amended by Stats. 1982, Ch. 1405, Sec. 2.)

TITLE 6. OF CRIMES AGAINST THE LEGISLATIVE POWER [85 - 88]

(Title 6 enacted 1872.)
85.

Every person who gives or offers to give a bribe to any Member of the Legislature, any member of the legislative body of a city, county, city and county, school district, or other special district, or to another person for the member, or attempts by menace, deceit, suppression of truth, or any corrupt means, to influence a member in giving or withholding his or her vote, or in not attending the house or any committee of which he or she is a member, is punishable by imprisonment in the state prison for two, three or four years.

(Amended by Stats. 2006, Ch. 435, Sec. 1. Effective September 24, 2006.)

86.

Every Member of either house of the Legislature, or any member of the legislative body of a city, county, city and county, school district, or other special district, who asks, receives, or agrees to receive, any bribe, upon any understanding that his or her official vote, opinion, judgment, or action shall be influenced thereby, or shall give, in any particular manner, or upon any particular side of any question or matter upon which he or she may be required to act in his or her official capacity, or gives, or offers or promises to give, any official vote in consideration that another Member of the Legislature, or another member of the legislative body of a city, county, city and county, school district, or other special district shall give this vote either upon the same or another question, is punishable by imprisonment in the state prison for two, three, or four years and, in cases in which no bribe has been actually received, by a restitution fine of not less than four thousand dollars ($4,000) or not more than twenty thousand dollars ($20,000) or, in cases in which a bribe was actually received, by a restitution fine of at least the actual amount of the bribe received or four thousand dollars ($4,000), whichever is greater, or any larger amount of not more than double the amount of any bribe received or twenty thousand dollars ($20,000), whichever is greater.

In imposing a fine under this section, the court shall consider the defendant's ability to pay the fine.

(Amended by Stats. 2014, Ch. 881, Sec. 2. (AB 1666) Effective January 1, 2015.)

88.

Every Member of the Legislature, and every member of a legislative body of a city, county, city and county, school district, or other special district convicted of any crime defined in this title, in addition to the punishment prescribed, forfeits his or her office and is forever disqualified from holding any office in this state or a political subdivision thereof.

(Amended by Stats. 2006, Ch. 435, Sec. 3. Effective September 24, 2006.)

TITLE 7. OF CRIMES AGAINST PUBLIC JUSTICE [92 - 186.34]

(Title 7 enacted 1872.)

CHAPTER 1. Bribery and Corruption [92 - 100]

(Chapter 1 enacted 1872.)

92.

Every person who gives or offers to give a bribe to any judicial officer, juror, referee, arbitrator, or umpire, or to any person who may be authorized by law to hear or determine any question or controversy, with intent to influence his vote, opinion, or decision upon any matter or question which is or may be brought before him for decision, is punishable by imprisonment in the state prison for two, three or four years.

(Amended by Stats. 1976, Ch. 1139.)

93.

(a) Every judicial officer, juror, referee, arbitrator, or umpire, and every person authorized by law to hear or determine any question or controversy, who asks, receives, or agrees to receive, any bribe, upon any agreement or understanding that his or her vote, opinion, or decision upon any matters or question which is or may be brought before him or her for decision, shall be influenced thereby, is punishable by imprisonment in the state prison for two, three, or four years and, in cases where no bribe has been actually received, by a restitution fine of not less than two thousand dollars ($2,000) or not more than ten thousand dollars ($10,000) or, in cases where a bribe was actually received, by a restitution fine of at least the actual amount of the bribe received or two thousand dollars ($2,000), whichever is greater, or any larger amount of not more than double the amount of any bribe received or ten thousand dollars ($10,000), whichever is greater.

(b) In imposing a restitution fine under this section, the court shall consider the defendant's ability to pay the fine.

(Amended by Stats. 2001, Ch. 282, Sec. 3. Effective January 1, 2002.)

94.

Every judicial officer who asks or receives any emolument, gratuity, or reward, or any promise thereof, except such as may be authorized by law, for doing any official act, is guilty of a misdemeanor. The lawful compensation of a temporary judge shall be prescribed by Judicial Council rule. Every judicial officer who shall ask or receive the whole or any part of the fees allowed by law to any stenographer or reporter appointed by him or her, or any other person, to record the proceedings of any court or investigation held by him or her, shall be guilty of a misdemeanor, and upon conviction thereof shall forfeit his or her office. Any stenographer or reporter, appointed by any judicial officer in this state, who shall pay, or offer to pay, the whole or any part of the fees allowed him or her by law, for his or her appointment or retention in office, shall be guilty of a misdemeanor, and upon conviction thereof shall be forever disqualified from holding any similar office in the courts of this state.

(Amended by Stats. 1993, Ch. 909, Sec. 13. Effective January 1, 1994.)

94.5.

Every judge, justice, commissioner, or assistant commissioner of a court of this state who accepts any money or other thing of value for performing any marriage, including any money or thing of value voluntarily tendered by the persons about to be married or who have been married by such judge, justice, commissioner, or assistant commissioner, whether the acceptance occurs before or after performance of the marriage and whether or not performance of the marriage is conditioned on the giving of such money or the thing of value by the persons being married, is guilty of a misdemeanor.

It is not a necessary element of the offense described by this section that the acceptance of the money or other thing of value be committed with intent to commit extortion or with other criminal intent.

This section does not apply to the request for or acceptance of a fee expressly imposed by law for performance of a marriage or to the request or acceptance by any retired judge, retired justice, or retired commissioner of a fee for the performance of a marriage. For the purposes of this section, a retired judge or retired justice sitting on assignment in court shall not be deemed to be a retired judge or retired justice.

This section does not apply to an acceptance of a fee for performing a marriage on Saturday, Sunday, or a legal holiday.

(Amended by Stats. 1987, Ch. 753, Sec. 2.)

95.

Every person who corruptly attempts to influence a juror, or any person summoned or drawn as a juror, or chosen as an arbitrator or umpire, or appointed a referee, in respect to his or her verdict in, or decision of, any cause or proceeding, pending, or about to be brought before him or her, is punishable by a fine not exceeding ten thousand dollars ($10,000), or by imprisonment pursuant to subdivision (h) of Section 1170, if it is by means of any of the following:

(a) Any oral or written communication with him or her except in the regular course of proceedings.

(b) Any book, paper, or instrument exhibited, otherwise than in the regular course of proceedings.

(c) Any threat, intimidation, persuasion, or entreaty.

(d) Any promise, or assurance of any pecuniary or other advantage.

(Amended by Stats. 2011, Ch. 15, Sec. 240. (AB 109) Effective April 4, 2011. Operative October 1, 2011, by Sec. 636 of Ch. 15, as amended by Stats. 2011, Ch. 39, Sec. 68.)

95.1.

Every person who threatens a juror with respect to a criminal proceeding in which a verdict has been rendered and who has the intent and apparent ability to carry out the threat so as to cause the target of the threat to reasonably fear for his or her safety or the safety of his or her immediate family, is guilty of a public offense and shall be punished by imprisonment in a county jail for not more than one year, or by imprisonment pursuant to subdivision (h) of Section 1170, or by a fine not exceeding ten thousand dollars ($10,000), or by both that imprisonment and fine.

(Amended by Stats. 2011, Ch. 15, Sec. 241. (AB 109) Effective April 4, 2011. Operative October 1, 2011, by Sec. 636 of Ch. 15, as amended by Stats. 2011, Ch. 39, Sec. 68.)

95.2.

Any person who, with knowledge of the relationship of the parties and without court authorization and juror consent, intentionally provides a defendant or former defendant to any criminal proceeding information from records sealed by the court pursuant to subdivision (b) of Section 237 of the Code of Civil Procedure, knowing that the records have been sealed, in order to locate or communicate with a juror to that proceeding and that information is used to violate Section 95 or 95.1, shall be guilty of a misdemeanor. Except as otherwise provided by any other law or court order limiting communication with a juror after a verdict has been reached, compliance with Section 206 of the Code of Civil Procedure shall constitute court authorization.

(Added by Stats. 1992, Ch. 971, Sec. 5. Effective January 1, 1993.)

95.3.

Any person licensed pursuant to Chapter 11.5 (commencing with Section 7512) of Division 3 of the Business and Professions Code who, with knowledge of the relationship of the parties and without court authorization and juror consent, knowingly provides a defendant or former defendant to any criminal proceeding information in order to locate or communicate with a juror to that proceeding is guilty of a misdemeanor. Conviction under this section shall be a basis for revocation or suspension of any license issued pursuant to Section 7561.1 of the Business and Professions Code. Except as otherwise provided by any law or court order limiting communication with a juror after a verdict has been reached, compliance with Section 206 of the Code of Civil Procedure shall constitute court authorization.

(Added by Stats. 1992, Ch. 971, Sec. 6. Effective January 1, 1993.)

96.

Every juror, or person drawn or summoned as a juror, or chosen arbitrator or umpire, or appointed referee, who either:

One—Makes any promise or agreement to give a verdict or decision for or against any party; or,

Two—Willfully and corruptly permits any communication to be made to him, or receives any book, paper, instrument, or information relating to any cause or matter pending before him, except according to the regular course of proceedings,

is punishable by fine not exceeding ten thousand dollars ($10,000), or by imprisonment pursuant to subdivision (h) of Section 1170.

(Amended by Stats. 2011, Ch. 15, Sec. 242. (AB 109) Effective April 4, 2011. Operative October 1, 2011, by Sec. 636 of Ch. 15, as amended by Stats. 2011, Ch. 39, Sec. 68.)

96.5.

(a) Every judicial officer, court commissioner, or referee who commits any act that he or she knows perverts or obstructs justice, is guilty of a public offense punishable by imprisonment in a county jail for not more than one year.

(b) Nothing in this section prohibits prosecution under paragraph (5) of subdivision (a) of Section 182 of the Penal Code or any other law.

(Amended by Stats. 1999, Ch. 853, Sec. 7. Effective January 1, 2000.)

98.

Every officer convicted of any crime defined in this Chapter, in addition to the punishment prescribed, forfeits his office and is forever disqualified from holding any office in this State.

(Enacted 1872.)

99.

The Superintendent of State Printing shall not, during his continuance in office, have any interest, either directly or indirectly, in any contract in any way connected with his office as Superintendent of State Printing; nor shall he, during said period, be interested, either directly or indirectly, in any state printing, binding, engraving, lithographing, or other state work of any kind connected with his said office; nor shall he, directly or indirectly, be interested in any contract for furnishing paper, or other printing stock or material, to or for use in his said office; and any violations of these provisions shall subject him, on conviction before a court of competent jurisdiction, to imprisonment pursuant to subdivision (h) of Section 1170 and to a fine of not less than one thousand dollars ($1,000) nor more than ten thousand dollars ($10,000), or by both that fine and imprisonment.

(Amended by Stats. 2011, Ch. 15, Sec. 243. (AB 109) Effective April 4, 2011. Operative October 1, 2011, by Sec. 636 of Ch. 15, as amended by Stats. 2011, Ch. 39, Sec. 68.)

100.

If the Superintendent of State Printing corruptly colludes with any person or persons furnishing paper or materials, or bidding therefor, or with any other person or persons, or has any secret understanding with him or them, by himself or through others, to defraud the state, or by which the state is defrauded or made to sustain a loss, contrary to the true intent and meaning of this chapter, he, upon conviction thereof, forfeits his office, and is subject to imprisonment in the state prison, and to a fine of not less than one thousand dollars ($1,000) nor more than ten thousand dollars ($10,000), or both such fine and imprisonment.

(Amended by Stats. 1983, Ch. 1092, Sec. 238. Effective September 27, 1983. Operative January 1, 1984, by Sec. 427 of Ch. 1092.)

CHAPTER 2. Rescues [102- 102.]

(Chapter 2 enacted 1872.)

102.

Every person who willfully injures or destroys, or takes or attempts to take, or assists any person in taking or attempting to take, from the custody of any officer or person, any personal property which such officer or person has in charge under any process of law, is guilty of a misdemeanor.

(Enacted 1872.)

CHAPTER 3. Escapes and Aiding Therein [107 - 110]

(Chapter 3 enacted 1872.)

107.
Every prisoner charged with or convicted of a felony who is an inmate of any public training school or reformatory or county hospital who escapes or attempts to escape from such public training school or reformatory or county hospital is guilty of a felony and is punishable by imprisonment pursuant to subdivision (h) of Section 1170, or by a fine not exceeding ten thousand dollars ($10,000), or by both that fine and imprisonment.
(Amended by Stats. 2011, Ch. 15, Sec. 244. (AB 109) Effective April 4, 2011. Operative October 1, 2011, by Sec. 636 of Ch. 15, as amended by Stats. 2011, Ch. 39, Sec. 68.)

109.
Any person who willfully assists any inmate of any public training school or reformatory to escape, or in an attempt to escape from that public training school or reformatory is punishable by imprisonment pursuant to subdivision (h) of Section 1170, and fine not exceeding ten thousand dollars ($10,000).
(Amended by Stats. 2011, Ch. 15, Sec. 245. (AB 109) Effective April 4, 2011. Operative October 1, 2011, by Sec. 636 of Ch. 15, as amended by Stats. 2011, Ch. 39, Sec. 68.)

110.
Every person who carries or sends into a public training school, or reformatory, anything useful to aid a prisoner or inmate in making his escape, with intent thereby to facilitate the escape of any prisoner or inmate confined therein, is guilty of a felony.
(Amended by Stats. 1976, Ch. 1139.)

CHAPTER 4. Forging, Stealing, Mutilating, and Falsifying Judicial and Public Records and Documents [112 - 117]

(Chapter 4 enacted 1872.)

112.
(a) Any person who manufactures or sells any false government document with the intent to conceal the true citizenship or resident alien status of another person is guilty of a misdemeanor and shall be punished by imprisonment in a county jail for one year. Every false government document that is manufactured or sold in violation of this section may be charged and prosecuted as a separate and distinct violation, and consecutive sentences may be imposed for each violation.
(b) A prosecuting attorney shall have discretion to charge a defendant with a violation of this section or any other law that applies.
(c) As used in this section, "government document" means any document issued by the United States government or any state or local government, including, but not limited to, any passport, immigration visa, employment authorization card, birth certificate, driver's license, identification card, or social security card.
(Added by renumbering Section 113 (as added by Stats. 1994, 1st Ex., Ch. 17) by Stats. 2001, Ch. 854, Sec. 19. Effective January 1, 2002. See similar subject matter in Section 113 (which was added on Nov. 8, 1994, by Prop. 187).)

113.
Any person who manufactures, distributes or sells false documents to conceal the true citizenship or resident alien status of another person is guilty of a felony, and shall be punished by imprisonment pursuant to subdivision (h) of Section 1170 for five years or by a fine of seventy-five thousand dollars ($75,000).
(Amended by Stats. 2011, Ch. 15, Sec. 246. (AB 109) Effective April 4, 2011. Operative October 1, 2011, by Sec. 636 of Ch. 15, as amended by Stats. 2011, Ch. 39, Sec. 68. Note: This section was added on Nov. 8, 1994, by initiative Prop. 187.)

114.
Any person who uses false documents to conceal his or her true citizenship or resident alien status is guilty of a felony, and shall be punished by imprisonment pursuant to subdivision (h) of Section 1170 for five years or by a fine of twenty-five thousand dollars ($25,000).
(Amended by Stats. 2011, Ch. 15, Sec. 247. (AB 109) Effective April 4, 2011. Operative October 1, 2011, by Sec. 636 of Ch. 15, as amended by Stats. 2011, Ch. 39, Sec. 68. Note: This section was added on Nov. 8, 1994, by initiative Prop. 187.)

115.
(a) Every person who knowingly procures or offers any false or forged instrument to be filed, registered, or recorded in any public office within this state, which instrument, if genuine, might be filed, registered, or recorded under any law of this state or of the United States, is guilty of a felony.
(b) Each instrument which is procured or offered to be filed, registered, or recorded in violation of subdivision (a) shall constitute a separate violation of this section.
(c) Except in unusual cases where the interests of justice would best be served if probation is granted, probation shall not be granted to, nor shall the execution or imposition of sentence be suspended for, any of the following persons:
(1) Any person with a prior conviction under this section who is again convicted of a violation of this section in a separate proceeding.
(2) Any person who is convicted of more than one violation of this section in a single proceeding, with intent to defraud another, and where the violations resulted in a cumulative financial loss exceeding one hundred thousand dollars ($100,000).
(d) For purposes of prosecution under this section, each act of procurement or of offering a false or forged instrument to be filed, registered, or recorded shall be considered a separately punishable offense.
(e) (1) After a person is convicted of a violation of this section, or a plea is entered whereby a charge alleging a violation of this section is dismissed and waiver is obtained pursuant to People v. Harvey (1979) 25 Cal.3d 754, upon written motion of the prosecuting agency, the court, after a hearing described in subdivision (f), shall issue a written order that the false or forged instrument be adjudged void ab initio if the court determines that an order is appropriate under applicable law. The order shall state whether the instrument is false or forged, or both false and forged, and describe the nature of the falsity or forgery. A copy of the instrument shall be attached to the order at the time it is issued by the court and a certified copy of the order shall be filed, registered, or recorded at the appropriate public office by the prosecuting agency.
(2) (A) If the order pertains to a false or forged instrument that has been recorded with a county recorder, an order made pursuant to this section shall be recorded in the county where the affected real property is located. The order shall also reference the county recorder's document recording number of any notice of pendency of action recorded pursuant to paragraph (2) of subdivision (f).
(B) As to any order, notice of pendency of action, or withdrawal of notice of pendency of action recorded pursuant to this section, recording fees shall be waived pursuant to Section 27383 of the Government Code.
(f) A prosecuting agency shall use the following procedures in filing a motion under subdivision (e):
(1) Within 10 calendar days of filing a criminal complaint or indictment alleging a violation of this section, the prosecuting agency shall provide written notice by certified mail to all parties who have an interest in the property affected by the false or forged instrument, or in the instrument itself, including those described in paragraph (5).
(2) (A) Within 10 calendar days of filing a criminal complaint or indictment alleging a violation of this section, the prosecuting agency shall record a notice of pendency of action in the county in which the affected real property is located.
(B) Within 10 calendar days of the case being adjudicated or dismissed without obtaining an order pursuant to subdivision (e), the prosecuting agency shall record a withdrawal of the notice of pendency of action in the county where the affected real property is located.
(3) The written notice and notice of pendency of action described in paragraphs (1) and (2) shall inform the interested parties that a criminal action has commenced that may result in adjudications against the false or forged instrument or the property affected by the false or forged instrument, and shall notify the interested parties of their right to be heard if a motion is brought under subdivision (e) to void the false or forged instrument. The notice shall state the street address, if available, and the legal description of the affected real property.
(4) Failure of the prosecuting agency to provide written notice or record a pendency of action as required under paragraphs (1) and (2) within 10 calendar days shall not prevent the prosecuting agency from later making a motion under subdivision (e), but the court shall take the failure to provide notice or record a pendency of action as required under paragraphs (1) and (2) as reason to provide any interested parties additional time to respond to the motion. Failure of the prosecuting agency to so notify interested parties under this subdivision or record a pendency of action as required under paragraphs (1) and (2) within 10 calendar days shall create a presumption that a finding as described in paragraph (9) is necessary to protect the property rights of the interested party or parties.
(5) If the instrument sought to be declared void involves real property, "interested parties" include, but are not limited to, all parties who have recorded with the county recorder in the county where the affected property is located any of the following: a deed, lien, mortgage, deed of trust, security interest, lease, or other instrument declaring an interest in, or requesting notice relating to, the property affected by the false or forged instrument as of the date of the filing of the criminal complaint or indictment.
(6) Any party not required to be noticed under paragraph (1) or (5) who nonetheless notifies the prosecuting agency in writing of the party's desire to be notified if a motion is brought under subdivision (e) to void the false or forged instrument shall be treated as an interested party as defined in paragraph (1) or (5).
(7) The court shall set a hearing for the motion brought by the prosecuting agency under subdivision (e) no earlier than 90 calendar days from the date the motion is made. The prosecuting agency shall provide a copy by certified mail of the written motion and a notice of hearing to all interested parties described in paragraphs (1), (5), or (6), and all other persons who obtain an interest in the property prior to recordation of notice of pendency of action no later than 90 days before the hearing date set by the court. The notice shall state the street address, if available, and the legal description of the affected real property.
(8) At a hearing on a motion brought by the prosecuting agency under subdivision (e), the defendant, prosecuting agency, and interested parties described in paragraphs (1), (5), or (6), shall have a right to be heard and present information to the court. No party shall be denied a right to present information due to a lack of notice by the prosecuting agency or failure to contact the prosecuting agency or the court prior to the hearing.
(9) (A) At a hearing on a motion brought by a prosecuting agency under subdivision (e), if the court determines that the interests of justice or the need to protect the property rights of any person or party so requires, including, but not limited to, a finding that the matter may be more appropriately determined in a civil proceeding, the court may decline to make a determination under subdivision (e).
(B) If, prior to the hearing on the motion, any person or party files a quiet title action that seeks a judicial determination of the validity of the same false or forged instrument that is the subject of the motion, or the status of an interested party as a bona fide purchaser of, or bona fide holder of an encumbrance on, the property affected by the false or forged instrument, the court may consider that as an additional but not dispositive factor in making its determination under subdivision (e); provided, however, that a final judgment previously entered in that quiet title action shall be followed to the extent otherwise required by law.
(g) As used in this section, "prosecuting agency" means a city attorney, a district attorney, the Attorney General, or other state or local agency actively prosecuting a case under this section.
(h) An order made pursuant to subdivision (e) shall be considered a judgment, and subject to appeal in accordance with, paragraph (1) of subdivision (a) of Section 904.1 of the Code of Civil Procedure.
(Amended by Stats. 2014, Ch. 455, Sec. 1. (AB 1698) Effective January 1, 2015.)

115.1.
(a) The Legislature finds and declares that the voters of California are entitled to accurate representations in materials that are directed to them in efforts to influence how they vote.
(b) No person shall publish or cause to be published, with intent to deceive, any campaign advertisement containing a signature that the person knows to be unauthorized.
(c) For purposes of this section, "campaign advertisement" means any communication directed to voters by means of a mass mailing as defined in Section 82041.5 of the Government Code, a paid television, radio, or newspaper advertisement, an outdoor advertisement, or any other printed matter, if the expenditures for that communication are required to be reported by Chapter 4 (commencing with Section 84100) of Title 9 of the Government Code.
(d) For purposes of this section, an authorization to use a signature shall be oral or written.
(e) Nothing in this section shall be construed to prohibit a person from publishing or causing to be published a reproduction of all or part of a document containing an actual or authorized signature, provided that the signature so reproduced shall not, with the intent to deceive, be incorporated into another document in a manner that falsely suggests that the person whose signature is reproduced has signed the other document.
(f) Any knowing or willful violation of this section is a public offense punishable by imprisonment in a county jail not exceeding 6 months, or pursuant to subdivision (h) of Section 1170, or by a fine not to exceed fifty thousand dollars ($50,000), or by both that fine and imprisonment.
(g) As used in this section, "signature" means either of the following:
(1) A handwritten or mechanical signature, or a copy thereof.
(2) Any representation of a person's name, including, but not limited to, a printed or typewritten representation, that serves the same purpose as a handwritten or mechanical signature.
(Amended by Stats. 2011, Ch. 15, Sec. 248. (AB 109) Effective April 4, 2011. Operative October 1, 2011, by Sec. 636 of Ch. 15, as amended by Stats. 2011, Ch. 39, Sec. 68.)

115.2.
(a) No person shall publish or cause to be published, with actual knowledge, and intent to deceive, any campaign advertisement containing false or fraudulent depictions, or false or fraudulent representations, of official public documents or purported official public documents.
(b) For purposes of this section, "campaign advertisement" means any communication directed to voters by means of a mass mailing as defined in Section 82041.5 of the

Government Code, a paid newspaper advertisement, an outdoor advertisement, or any other printed matter, if the expenditures for that communication are required to be reported by Chapter 4 (commencing with Section 84100) of Title 9 of the Government Code.

(c) Any violation of this section is a misdemeanor punishable by imprisonment in the county jail, or by a fine not to exceed fifty thousand dollars ($50,000), or both.
(Added by Stats. 1991, Ch. 1051, Sec. 2.)

115.25.

(a) No person or entity shall authorize the production or distribution, or participate in the authorization of the production or distribution, of any document, including, but not limited to, any campaign advertisement, as defined in subdivision (d), that the person or entity knows contains inaccurate emergency service phone numbers for various emergency services, including, but not limited to, police, fire, or ambulance services.

(b) A violation of subdivision (a) shall be an infraction, punishable by a fine not exceeding two hundred fifty dollars ($250).

(c) A violation of subdivision (a) resulting in the serious injury or death of persons who innocently rely on the erroneous phone numbers contained in the document is a misdemeanor, punishable by a fine not exceeding ten thousand dollars ($10,000), by imprisonment in a county jail not exceeding one year, or by both that fine and imprisonment.

(d) For purposes of this section, "campaign advertisement" means any communication directed to voters by means of a mass mailing, as defined in Section 82041.5 of the Government Code, a paid television, radio, or newspaper advertisement, an outdoor advertisement, or any other printed matter, if the expenditures for that communication are required to be reported by Chapter 4 (commencing with Section 84100) of Title 9 of the Government Code.
(Added by Stats. 1992, Ch. 1010, Sec. 1. Effective January 1, 1993.)

115.3.

Any person who alters a certified copy of an official record, or knowingly furnishes an altered certified copy of an official record, of this state, including the executive, legislative, and judicial branches thereof, or of any city, county, city and county, district, or political subdivision thereof, is guilty of a misdemeanor.
(Added by Stats. 1984, Ch. 874, Sec. 1. Effective September 5, 1984.)

115.5.

(a) Every person who files any false or forged document or instrument with the county recorder which affects title to, places an encumbrance on, or places an interest secured by a mortgage or deed of trust on, real property consisting of a single-family residence containing not more than four dwelling units, with knowledge that the document is false or forged, is punishable, in addition to any other punishment, by a fine not exceeding seventy-five thousand dollars ($75,000).

(b) Every person who makes a false sworn statement to a notary public, with knowledge that the statement is false, to induce the notary public to perform an improper notarial act on an instrument or document affecting title to, or placing an encumbrance on, real property consisting of a single-family residence containing not more than four dwelling units is guilty of a felony.
(Added by Stats. 1984, Ch. 1397, Sec. 9.)

116.

Every person who adds any names to the list of persons selected to serve as jurors for the county, either by placing the names in the jury box or otherwise, or extracts any name therefrom, or destroys the jury box or any of the pieces of paper containing the names of jurors, or mutilates or defaces the names so that they cannot be read, or changes the names on the pieces of paper, except in cases allowed by law, is guilty of a felony.
(Amended by Stats. 1989, Ch. 1360, Sec. 104.)

116.5.

(a) A person is guilty of tampering with a jury when, prior to, or within 90 days of, discharge of the jury in a criminal proceeding, he or she does any of the following:

(1) Confers, or offers or agrees to confer, any payment or benefit upon a juror or upon a third person who is acting on behalf of a juror in consideration for the juror or third person supplying information in relation to an action or proceeding.

(2) Acting on behalf of a juror, accepts or agrees to accept any payment or benefit for himself or herself or for the juror in consideration for supplying any information in relation to an action or proceeding.

(3) Acting on behalf of himself or herself, agrees to accept, directly or indirectly, any payment or benefit in consideration for supplying any information in relation to an action or proceeding.

(b) Any person who violates this section is guilty of a misdemeanor.

(c) In the case of a juror who is within 90 days of having been discharged, otherwise lawful compensation not exceeding fifty dollars ($50) in value shall not constitute a criminal violation of this section.

(d) Upon conviction under this section, in addition to the penalty described in subdivision (b), any compensation received in violation of this section shall be forfeited by the defendant and deposited in the Victim Restitution Fund.
(Added by Stats. 1994, Ch. 869, Sec. 2. Effective January 1, 1995.)

117.

Every officer or person required by law to certify to the list of persons selected as jurors who maliciously, corruptly, or willfully certifies to a false or incorrect list, or a list containing other names than those selected, or who, being required by law to write down the names placed on the certified lists on separate pieces of paper, does not write down and place in the jury box the same names that are on the certified list, and no more and no less than are on such list, is guilty of a felony.
(Enacted 1872.)

CHAPTER 5. Perjury and Subornation of Perjury [118 - 131]

(Chapter 5 enacted 1872.)

118.

(a) Every person who, having taken an oath that he or she will testify, declare, depose, or certify truly before any competent tribunal, officer, or person, in any of the cases in which the oath may by law of the State of California be administered, willfully and contrary to the oath, states as true any material matter which he or she knows to be false, and every person who testifies, declares, deposes, or certifies under penalty of perjury in any of the cases in which the testimony, declarations, depositions, or certification is permitted by law of the State of California under penalty of perjury and willfully states as true any material matter which he or she knows to be false, is guilty of perjury.

This subdivision is applicable whether the statement, or the testimony, declaration, deposition, or certification is made or subscribed within or without the State of California.

(b) No person shall be convicted of perjury where proof of falsity rests solely upon contradiction by testimony of a single person other than the defendant. Proof of falsity may be established by direct or indirect evidence.
(Amended by Stats. 1990, Ch. 950, Sec. 2.)

118.1.

Every peace officer who files any report with the agency which employs him or her regarding the commission of any crime or any investigation of any crime, if he or she

knowingly and intentionally makes any statement regarding any material matter in the report which the officer knows to be false, whether or not the statement is certified or otherwise expressly reported as true, is guilty of filing a false report punishable by imprisonment in the county jail for up to one year, or in the state prison for one, two, or three years. This section shall not apply to the contents of any statement which the peace officer attributes in the report to any other person.
(Amended by Stats. 1992, Ch. 427, Sec. 124. Effective January 1, 1993.)

118a.

Any person who, in any affidavit taken before any person authorized to administer oaths, swears, affirms, declares, deposes, or certifies that he will testify, declare, depose, or certify before any competent tribunal, officer, or person, in any case then pending or thereafter to be instituted, in any particular manner, or to any particular fact, and in such affidavit willfully and contrary to such oath states as true any material matter which he knows to be false, is guilty of perjury. In any prosecution under this section, the subsequent testimony of such person, in any action involving the matters in such affidavit contained, which is contrary to any of the matters in such affidavit contained, shall be prima facie evidence that the matters in such affidavit were false.
(Added by Stats. 1905, Ch. 485.)

119.

The term "oath," as used in the last two sections, includes an affirmation and every other mode authorized by law of attesting the truth of that which is stated.
(Amended by Stats. 1905, Ch. 485.)

120.

So much of an oath of office as relates to the future performance of official duties is not such an oath as is intended by the two preceding sections.
(Enacted 1872.)

121.

It is no defense to a prosecution for perjury that the oath was administered or taken in an irregular manner, or that the person accused of perjury did not go before, or was not in the presence of, the officer purporting to administer the oath, if such accused caused or procured such officer to certify that the oath had been taken or administered.
(Amended by Stats. 1905, Ch. 485.)

122.

It is no defense to a prosecution for perjury that the accused was not competent to give the testimony, deposition, or certificate of which falsehood is alleged. It is sufficient that he did give such testimony or make such deposition or certificate.
(Enacted 1872.)

123.

It is no defense to a prosecution for perjury that the accused did not know the materiality of the false statement made by him; or that it did not, in fact, affect the proceeding in or for which it was made. It is sufficient that it was material, and might have been used to affect such proceeding.
(Enacted 1872.)

124.

The making of a deposition, affidavit or certificate is deemed to be complete, within the provisions of this chapter, from the time when it is delivered by the accused to any other person, with the intent that it be uttered or published as true.
(Amended by Stats. 1905, Ch. 485.)

125.

An unqualified statement of that which one does not know to be true is equivalent to a statement of that which one knows to be false.
(Enacted 1872.)

126.

Perjury is punishable by imprisonment pursuant to subdivision (h) of Section 1170 for two, three or four years.
(Amended by Stats. 2011, Ch. 15, Sec. 249. (AB 109) Effective April 4, 2011. Operative October 1, 2011, by Sec. 636 of Ch. 15, as amended by Stats. 2011, Ch. 39, Sec. 68.)

127.

Every person who willfully procures another person to commit perjury is guilty of subornation of perjury, and is punishable in the same manner as he would be if personally guilty of the perjury so procured.
(Enacted 1872.)

128.

Every person who, by willful perjury or subornation of perjury procures the conviction and execution of any innocent person, is punishable by death or life imprisonment without possibility of parole. The penalty shall be determined pursuant to Sections 190.3 and 190.4.
(Amended by Stats. 1977, Ch. 316.)

129.

Every person who, being required by law to make any return, statement, or report, under oath, willfully makes and delivers any such return, statement, or report, purporting to be under oath, knowing the same to be false in any particular, is guilty of perjury, whether such oath was in fact taken or not.
(Added by Stats. 1905, Ch. 485.)

131.

Every person in any matter under investigation for a violation of the Corporate Securities Law of 1968 (Part 1 (commencing with Section 25000) of Division 1 of Title 4 of the Corporations Code), the California Commodity Law of 1990 (Chapter 1 (commencing with Section 29500) of Division 4.5 of Title 4 of the Corporations Code), Section 16755 of the Business and Professions Code, or in connection with an investigation conducted by the head of a department of the State of California relating to the business activities and subjects under the jurisdiction of the department, who knowingly and willfully falsifies, misrepresents, or conceals a material fact or makes any materially false, fictitious, misleading, or fraudulent statement or representation, and any person who knowingly and willfully procures or causes another to violate this section, is guilty of a misdemeanor punishable by imprisonment in a county jail not exceeding one year, or by a fine not exceeding twenty-five thousand dollars ($25,000), or by both that imprisonment and fine for each violation of this section. This section does not apply to conduct charged as a violation of Section 118 of this code.
(Added by Stats. 2003, Ch. 876, Sec. 14. Effective January 1, 2004.)

CHAPTER 6. Falsifying Evidence, and Bribing, Influencing, Intimidating or Threatening Witnesses [132 - 141]

(Heading of Chapter 6 amended by Stats. 1985, Ch. 962, Sec. 2.)

132.

Every person who upon any trial, proceeding, inquiry, or investigation whatever, authorized or permitted by law, offers in evidence, as genuine or true, any book, paper, document, record, or other instrument in writing, knowing the same to have been forged or fraudulently altered or ante-dated, is guilty of felony.
(Enacted 1872.)

132.5.

(a) A person who is a witness to an event or occurrence that he or she knows, or reasonably should know, is a crime or who has personal knowledge of facts that he or she knows, or reasonably should know, may require that person to be called as a witness in a criminal prosecution shall not accept or receive, directly or indirectly, any payment or benefit in consideration for providing information obtained as a result of witnessing the event or occurrence or having personal knowledge of the facts.

(b) A violation of this section is a misdemeanor and shall be punished by imprisonment in a county jail for not exceeding six months, by a fine not exceeding one thousand dollars ($1,000), or by both that imprisonment and fine.

(c) Upon conviction under this section, in addition to the penalty described in subdivision (b), any compensation received in violation of this section shall be forfeited by the defendant and deposited in the Victim Restitution Fund.

(d) This section shall not apply if more than one year has elapsed from the date of any criminal act related to the information that is provided under subdivision (a) unless prosecution has commenced for that criminal act. If prosecution has commenced, this section shall remain applicable until the final judgment in the action.

(e) This section shall not apply to any of the following circumstances:

(1) Lawful compensation paid to expert witnesses, investigators, employees, or agents by a prosecutor, law enforcement agency, or an attorney employed to represent a person in a criminal matter.

(2) Lawful compensation provided to an informant by a prosecutor or law enforcement agency.

(3) Compensation paid to a publisher, editor, reporter, writer, or other person connected with or employed by a newspaper, magazine, or other publication or a television or radio news reporter or other person connected with a television or radio station, for disclosing information obtained in the ordinary course of business.

(4) Statutorily authorized rewards offered by governmental agencies for information leading to the arrest and conviction of specified offenders.

(5) Lawful compensation provided to a witness participating in the Witness Protection Program established pursuant to Title 7.5 (commencing with Section 14020) of Part 4.

(f) For purposes of this section, "information" does not include a photograph, videotape, audiotape, or any other direct recording of events or occurrences.

(Amended (as amended by Stats. 2002, Ch. 210, Sec. 1) by Stats. 2003, Ch. 62, Sec. 222. Effective January 1, 2004. See similar subject matter in Section 132.5, as amended by Stats. 2015, Ch. 303. Note: Originally, this section was added by Stats. 1994, Ch. 869.)

132.5.

(a) The Legislature supports and affirms the constitutional right of every person to communicate on any subject. This section is intended to preserve the right of every accused person to a fair trial, the right of the people to due process of law, and the integrity of judicial proceedings. This section is not intended to prevent any person from disseminating any information or opinion.

The Legislature hereby finds and declares that the disclosure for valuable consideration of information relating to crimes by prospective witnesses can cause the loss of credible evidence in criminal trials and threatens to erode the reliability of verdicts.

The Legislature further finds and declares that the disclosure for valuable consideration of information relating to crimes by prospective witnesses creates an appearance of injustice that is destructive of public confidence.

(b) A person who is a witness to an event or occurrence that he or she knows is a crime or who has personal knowledge of facts that he or she knows or reasonably should know may require that person to be called as a witness in a criminal prosecution shall not accept or receive, directly or indirectly, any money or its equivalent in consideration for providing information obtained as a result of witnessing the event or occurrence or having personal knowledge of the facts.

(c) A person who is a witness to an event or occurrence that he or she reasonably should know is a crime shall not accept or receive, directly or indirectly, any money or its equivalent in consideration for providing information obtained as a result of his or her witnessing the event or occurrence.

(d) The Attorney General or the district attorney of the county in which an alleged violation of subdivision (c) occurs may institute a civil proceeding. Where a final judgment is rendered in the civil proceeding, the defendant shall be punished for the violation of subdivision (c) by a fine equal to 150 percent of the amount received or contracted for by the person.

(e) A violation of subdivision (b) is a misdemeanor punishable by imprisonment for a term not exceeding six months in a county jail, a fine not exceeding three times the amount of compensation requested, accepted, or received, or both the imprisonment and fine.

(f) This section does not apply if more than one year has elapsed from the date of any criminal act related to the information that is provided under subdivision (b) or (c) unless prosecution has commenced for that criminal act. If prosecution has commenced, this section shall remain applicable until the final judgment in the action.

(g) This section does not apply to any of the following circumstances:

(1) Lawful compensation paid to expert witnesses, investigators, employees, or agents by a prosecutor, law enforcement agency, or an attorney employed to represent a person in a criminal matter.

(2) Lawful compensation provided to an informant by a prosecutor or law enforcement agency.

(3) Compensation paid to a publisher, editor, reporter, writer, or other person connected with or employed by a newspaper, magazine, or other publication or a television or radio news reporter or other person connected with a television or radio station, for disclosing information obtained in the ordinary course of business.

(4) Statutorily authorized rewards offered by governmental agencies or private reward programs offered by victims of crimes for information leading to the arrest and conviction of specified offenders.

(5) Lawful compensation provided to a witness participating in the Witness Relocation and Assistance Program established pursuant to Title 7.5 (commencing with Section 14020) of Part 4.

(h) For purposes of this section, "information" does not include a photograph, videotape, audiotape, or any other direct recording of an event or occurrence.

(i) For purposes of this section, "victims of crimes" shall be construed in a manner consistent with Section 28 of Article I of the California Constitution, and shall include victims, as defined in subdivision (3) of Section 136.

(Amended (as amended by Stats. 2003, Ch. 62, Sec. 223) by Stats. 2015, Ch. 303, Sec. 384. (AB 731) Effective January 1, 2016.)

133.

Every person who practices any fraud or deceit, or knowingly makes or exhibits any false statement, representation, token, or writing, to any witness or person about to be called as a witness upon any trial, proceeding, inquiry, or investigation whatever, authorized by law, with intent to affect the testimony of such witness, is guilty of a misdemeanor.

(Enacted 1872.)

134.

Every person guilty of preparing any false or ante-dated book, paper, record, instrument in writing, or other matter or thing, with intent to produce it, or allow it to be produced for any fraudulent or deceitful purpose, as genuine or true, upon any trial, proceeding, or inquiry whatever, authorized by law, is guilty of felony.

(Enacted 1872.)

135.

A person who, knowing that any book, paper, record, instrument in writing, digital image, video recording owned by another, or other matter or thing, is about to be produced in evidence upon a trial, inquiry, or investigation, authorized by law, willfully destroys,

erases, or conceals the same, with the intent to prevent it or its content from being produced, is guilty of a misdemeanor.

(Amended by Stats. 2015, Ch. 463, Sec. 1. (AB 256) Effective January 1, 2016.)

135.5.

Any person who knowingly alters, tampers with, conceals, or destroys relevant evidence in any disciplinary proceeding against a public safety officer, for the purpose of harming that public safety officer, is guilty of a misdemeanor.

(Added by Stats. 1998, Ch. 759, Sec. 1. Effective January 1, 1999.)

136.

As used in this chapter:

(1) "Malice" means an intent to vex, annoy, harm, or injure in any way another person, or to thwart or interfere in any manner with the orderly administration of justice.

(2) "Witness" means any natural person, (i) having knowledge of the existence or nonexistence of facts relating to any crime, or (ii) whose declaration under oath is received or has been received as evidence for any purpose, or (iii) who has reported any crime to any peace officer, prosecutor, probation or parole officer, correctional officer or judicial officer, or (iv) who has been served with a subpoena issued under the authority of any court in the state, or of any other state or of the United States, or (v) who would be believed by any reasonable person to be an individual described in subparagraphs (i) to (iv), inclusive.

(3) "Victim" means any natural person with respect to whom there is reason to believe that any crime as defined under the laws of this state or any other state or of the United States is being or has been perpetrated or attempted to be perpetrated.

(Repealed and added by Stats. 1980, Ch. 686, Sec. 2.)

136.1.

(a) Except as provided in subdivision (c), any person who does any of the following is guilty of a public offense and shall be punished by imprisonment in a county jail for not more than one year or in the state prison:

(1) Knowingly and maliciously prevents or dissuades any witness or victim from attending or giving testimony at any trial, proceeding, or inquiry authorized by law.

(2) Knowingly and maliciously attempts to prevent or dissuade any witness or victim from attending or giving testimony at any trial, proceeding, or inquiry authorized by law.

(3) For purposes of this section, evidence that the defendant was a family member who interceded in an effort to protect the witness or victim shall create a presumption that the act was without malice.

(b) Except as provided in subdivision (c), every person who attempts to prevent or dissuade another person who has been the victim of a crime or who is witness to a crime from doing any of the following is guilty of a public offense and shall be punished by imprisonment in a county jail for not more than one year or in the state prison:

(1) Making any report of that victimization to any peace officer or state or local law enforcement officer or probation or parole or correctional officer or prosecuting agency or to any judge.

(2) Causing a complaint, indictment, information, probation or parole violation to be sought and prosecuted, and assisting in the prosecution thereof.

(3) Arresting or causing or seeking the arrest of any person in connection with that victimization.

(c) Every person doing any of the acts described in subdivision (a) or (b) knowingly and maliciously under any one or more of the following circumstances, is guilty of a felony punishable by imprisonment in the state prison for two, three, or four years under any of the following circumstances:

(1) Where the act is accompanied by force or by an express or implied threat of force or violence, upon a witness or victim or any third person or the property of any victim, witness, or any third person.

(2) Where the act is in furtherance of a conspiracy.

(3) Where the act is committed by any person who has been convicted of any violation of this section, any predecessor law hereto or any federal statute or statute of any other state which, if the act prosecuted was committed in this state, would be a violation of this section.

(4) Where the act is committed by any person for pecuniary gain or for any other consideration acting upon the request of any other person. All parties to such a transaction are guilty of a felony.

(d) Every person attempting the commission of any act described in subdivisions (a), (b), and (c) is guilty of the offense attempted without regard to success or failure of the attempt. The fact that no person was injured physically, or in fact intimidated, shall be no defense against any prosecution under this section.

(e) Nothing in this section precludes the imposition of an enhancement for great bodily injury where the injury inflicted is significant or substantial.

(f) The use of force during the commission of any offense described in subdivision (c) shall be considered a circumstance in aggravation of the crime in imposing a term of imprisonment under subdivision (b) of Section 1170.

(Amended by Stats. 1997, Ch. 500, Sec. 1. Effective January 1, 1998.)

136.2.

(a) (1) Upon a good cause belief that harm to, or intimidation or dissuasion of, a victim or witness has occurred or is reasonably likely to occur, a court with jurisdiction over a criminal matter may issue orders, including, but not limited to, the following:

(A) An order issued pursuant to Section 6320 of the Family Code.

(B) An order that a defendant shall not violate any provision of Section 136.1.

(C) An order that a person before the court other than a defendant, including, but not limited to, a subpoenaed witness or other person entering the courtroom of the court, shall not violate any provision of Section 136.1.

(D) An order that a person described in this section shall have no communication whatsoever with a specified witness or a victim, except through an attorney under reasonable restrictions that the court may impose.

(E) An order calling for a hearing to determine if an order as described in subparagraphs (A) to (D), inclusive, should be issued.

(F) (i) An order that a particular law enforcement agency within the jurisdiction of the court provide protection for a victim or a witness, or both, or for immediate family members of a victim or a witness who reside in the same household as the victim or witness or within reasonable proximity of the victim's or witness' household, as determined by the court. The order shall not be made without the consent of the law enforcement agency except for limited and specified periods of time and upon an express finding by the court of a clear and present danger of harm to the victim or witness or immediate family members of the victim or witness.

(ii) For purposes of this paragraph, "immediate family members" include the spouse, children, or parents of the victim or witness.

(G) (i) An order protecting a victim or witness of violent crime from all contact by the defendant, or contact, with the intent to annoy, harass, threaten, or commit acts of violence, by the defendant. The court or its designee shall transmit orders made under this paragraph to law enforcement personnel within one business day of the issuance, modification, extension, or termination of the order, pursuant to subdivision (a) of Section 6380 of the Family Code. It is the responsibility of the court to transmit the modification, extension, or termination orders made under this paragraph to the same agency that entered the original protective order into the Domestic Violence Restraining Order System.

(ii) (I) If a court does not issue an order pursuant to clause (i) in a case in which the defendant is charged with a crime involving domestic violence as defined in Section 13700 or in Section 6211 of the Family Code, the court on its own motion shall consider issuing a protective order upon a good cause belief that harm to, or intimidation or dissuasion of, a victim or witness has occurred or is reasonably likely to occur, that provides as follows:

(ia) The defendant shall not own, possess, purchase, receive, or attempt to purchase or receive, a firearm while the protective order is in effect.

(ib) The defendant shall relinquish any firearms that he or she owns or possesses pursuant to Section 527.9 of the Code of Civil Procedure.

(II) Every person who owns, possesses, purchases, or receives, or attempts to purchase or receive, a firearm while this protective order is in effect is punishable pursuant to Section 29825.

(iii) An order issued, modified, extended, or terminated by a court pursuant to this subparagraph shall be issued on forms adopted by the Judicial Council of California that have been approved by the Department of Justice pursuant to subdivision (i) of Section 6380 of the Family Code. However, the fact that an order issued by a court pursuant to this section was not issued on forms adopted by the Judicial Council and approved by the Department of Justice shall not, in and of itself, make the order unenforceable.

(iv) A protective order issued under this subparagraph may require the defendant to be placed on electronic monitoring if the local government, with the concurrence of the county sheriff or the chief probation officer with jurisdiction, adopts a policy to authorize electronic monitoring of defendants and specifies the agency with jurisdiction for this purpose. If the court determines that the defendant has the ability to pay for the monitoring program, the court shall order the defendant to pay for the monitoring. If the court determines that the defendant does not have the ability to pay for the electronic monitoring, the court may order electronic monitoring to be paid for by the local government that adopted the policy to authorize electronic monitoring. The duration of electronic monitoring shall not exceed one year from the date the order is issued. At no time shall the electronic monitoring be in place if the protective order is not in place.

(2) For purposes of this subdivision, a minor who was not a victim of, but who was physically present at the time of, an act of domestic violence, is a witness and is deemed to have suffered harm within the meaning of paragraph (1).

(b) A person violating an order made pursuant to subparagraphs (A) to (G), inclusive, of paragraph (1) of subdivision (a) may be punished for any substantive offense described in Section 136.1, or for a contempt of the court making the order. A finding of contempt shall not be a bar to prosecution for a violation of Section 136.1. However, a person so held in contempt shall be entitled to credit for punishment imposed therein against a sentence imposed upon conviction of an offense described in Section 136.1. A conviction or acquittal for a substantive offense under Section 136.1 shall be a bar to a subsequent punishment for contempt arising out of the same act.

(c) (1) (A) Notwithstanding subdivision (e), an emergency protective order issued pursuant to Chapter 2 (commencing with Section 6250) of Part 3 of Division 10 of the Family Code or Section 646.91 shall have precedence in enforcement over any other restraining or protective order, provided the emergency protective order meets all of the following requirements:

(i) The emergency protective order is issued to protect one or more individuals who are already protected persons under another restraining or protective order.

(ii) The emergency protective order restrains the individual who is the restrained person in the other restraining or protective order specified in clause (i).

(iii) The provisions of the emergency protective order are more restrictive in relation to the restrained person than are the provisions of the other restraining or protective order specified in clause (i).

(B) An emergency protective order that meets the requirements of subparagraph (A) shall have precedence in enforcement over the provisions of any other restraining or protective order only with respect to those provisions of the emergency protective order that are more restrictive in relation to the restrained person.

(2) Except as described in paragraph (1), a no-contact order, as described in Section 6320 of the Family Code, shall have precedence in enforcement over any other restraining or protective order.

(d) (1) A person subject to a protective order issued under this section shall not own, possess, purchase, or receive, or attempt to purchase or receive, a firearm while the protective order is in effect.

(2) The court shall order a person subject to a protective order issued under this section to relinquish any firearms he or she owns or possesses pursuant to Section 527.9 of the Code of Civil Procedure.

(3) A person who owns, possesses, purchases, or receives, or attempts to purchase or receive, a firearm while the protective order is in effect is punishable pursuant to Section 29825.

(e) (1) In all cases in which the defendant is charged with a crime involving domestic violence, as defined in Section 13700 or in Section 6211 of the Family Code, or a violation of Section 261, 261.5, or 262, or any crime that requires the defendant to register pursuant to subdivision (c) of Section 290, the court shall consider issuing the above-described orders on its own motion. All interested parties shall receive a copy of those orders. In order to facilitate this, the court's records of all criminal cases involving domestic violence or a violation of Section 261, 261.5, or 262, or any crime that requires the defendant to register pursuant to subdivision (c) of Section 290, shall be marked to clearly alert the court to this issue.

(2) In those cases in which a complaint, information, or indictment charging a crime involving domestic violence, as defined in Section 13700 or in Section 6211 of the Family Code, or a violation of Section 261, 261.5, or 262, or any crime that requires the defendant to register pursuant to subdivision (c) of Section 290, has been issued, except as described in subdivision (c), a restraining order or protective order against the defendant issued by the criminal court in that case has precedence in enforcement over a civil court order against the defendant.

(3) Custody and visitation with respect to the defendant and his or her minor children may be ordered by a family or juvenile court consistent with the protocol established pursuant to subdivision (f), but if ordered after a criminal protective order has been issued pursuant to this section, the custody and visitation order shall make reference to, and, if there is not an emergency protective order that has precedence in enforcement pursuant to paragraph (1) of subdivision (c), or a no-contact order, as described in Section 6320 of the Family Code, acknowledge the precedence of enforcement of, an appropriate criminal protective order. On or before July 1, 2014, the Judicial Council shall modify the criminal and civil court forms consistent with this subdivision.

(f) On or before January 1, 2003, the Judicial Council shall promulgate a protocol, for adoption by each local court in substantially similar terms, to provide for the timely coordination of all orders against the same defendant and in favor of the same named victim or victims. The protocol shall include, but shall not be limited to, mechanisms for ensuring appropriate communication and information sharing between criminal, family, and juvenile courts concerning orders and cases that involve the same parties, and shall permit a family or juvenile court order to coexist with a criminal court protective order subject to the following conditions:

(1) An order that permits contact between the restrained person and his or her children shall provide for the safe exchange of the children and shall not contain language either printed or handwritten that violates a "no-contact order" issued by a criminal court.

(2) The safety of all parties shall be the courts' paramount concern. The family or juvenile court shall specify the time, day, place, and manner of transfer of the child, as provided in Section 3100 of the Family Code.

(g) On or before January 1, 2003, the Judicial Council shall modify the criminal and civil court protective order forms consistent with this section.

(h) (1) In any case in which a complaint, information, or indictment charging a crime involving domestic violence, as defined in Section 13700 or in Section 6211 of the Family Code, has been filed, the court may consider, in determining whether good cause

exists to issue an order under subparagraph (A) of paragraph (1) of subdivision (a), the underlying nature of the offense charged, and the information provided to the court pursuant to Section 273.75.

(2) In any case in which a complaint, information, or indictment charging a violation of Section 261, 261.5, or 262, or any crime that requires the defendant to register pursuant to subdivision (c) of Section 290, has been filed, the court may consider, in determining whether good cause exists to issue an order under paragraph (1) of subdivision (a), the underlying nature of the offense charged, the defendant's relationship to the victim, the likelihood of continuing harm to the victim, any current restraining order or protective order issued by any civil or criminal court involving the defendant, and the defendant's criminal history, including, but not limited to, prior convictions for a violation of Section 261, 261.5, or 262, a crime that requires the defendant to register pursuant to subdivision (c) of Section 290, any other forms of violence, or any weapons offense.

(i) (1) In all cases in which a criminal defendant has been convicted of a crime involving domestic violence as defined in Section 13700 or in Section 6211 of the Family Code, a violation of subdivision (a) of Section 236.1, Section 261, 261.5, 262, subdivision (a) of Section 266h, or subdivision (a) of Section 266i, a violation of Section 186.22, or a crime that requires the defendant to register pursuant to subdivision (c) of Section 290, the court, at the time of sentencing, shall consider issuing an order restraining the defendant from any contact with a victim of the crime. The order may be valid for up to 10 years, as determined by the court. This protective order may be issued by the court regardless of whether the defendant is sentenced to the state prison or a county jail or subject to mandatory supervision, or whether imposition of sentence is suspended and the defendant is placed on probation. It is the intent of the Legislature in enacting this subdivision that the duration of any restraining order issued by the court be based upon the seriousness of the facts before the court, the probability of future violations, and the safety of a victim and his or her immediate family.

(2) In all cases in which a criminal defendant has been convicted of a crime involving domestic violence as defined in Section 13700 or in Section 6211 of the Family Code, a violation of Section 261, 261.5, or 262, a violation of Section 186.22, or a crime that requires the defendant to register pursuant to subdivision (c) of Section 290, the court, at the time of sentencing, shall consider issuing an order restraining the defendant from any contact with a percipient witness to the crime if it can be established by clear and convincing evidence that the witness has been harassed, as defined in paragraph (3) of subdivision (b) of Section 527.6 of the Code of Civil Procedure, by the defendant.

(3) An order under this subdivision may include provisions for electronic monitoring if the local government, upon receiving the concurrence of the county sheriff or the chief probation officer with jurisdiction, adopts a policy authorizing electronic monitoring of defendants and specifies the agency with jurisdiction for this purpose. If the court determines that the defendant has the ability to pay for the monitoring program, the court shall order the defendant to pay for the monitoring. If the court determines that the defendant does not have the ability to pay for the electronic monitoring, the court may order the electronic monitoring to be paid for by the local government that adopted the policy authorizing electronic monitoring. The duration of the electronic monitoring shall not exceed one year from the date the order is issued.

(j) For purposes of this section, "local government" means the county that has jurisdiction over the protective order.

(Amended (as amended by Stats. 2017, Ch. 270, Sec. 1) by Stats. 2018, Ch. 805, Sec. 1. (AB 1735) Effective January 1, 2019.)

136.3.

(a) The court shall order that any party enjoined pursuant to Section 136.2 be prohibited from taking any action to obtain the address or location of a protected party or a protected party's family members, caretakers, or guardian, unless there is good cause not to make that order.

(b) The Judicial Council shall promulgate forms necessary to effectuate this section.

(Added by Stats. 2005, Ch. 472, Sec. 4. Effective January 1, 2006.)

136.5.

Any person who has upon his person a deadly weapon with the intent to use such weapon to commit a violation of Section 136.1 is guilty of an offense punishable by imprisonment in the county jail for not more than one year, or in the state prison.

(Added by Stats. 1982, Ch. 1101, Sec. 1.)

136.7.

Every person imprisoned in a county jail or the state prison who has been convicted of a sexual offense, including, but not limited to, a violation of Section 243.4, 261, 261.5, 262, 264.1, 266, 266a, 266b, 266c, 266f, 285, 286, 287, 288, or 289, or former Section 288a, who knowingly reveals the name and address of any witness or victim to that offense to any other prisoner with the intent that the other prisoner will intimidate or harass the witness or victim through the initiation of unauthorized correspondence with the witness or victim, is guilty of a public offense, punishable by imprisonment in the county jail not to exceed one year, or by imprisonment pursuant to subdivision (h) of Section 1170.

Nothing in this section shall prevent the interviewing of witnesses.

(Amended by Stats. 2018, Ch. 423, Sec. 41. (SB 1494) Effective January 1, 2019.)

137.

(a) Every person who gives or offers, or promises to give, to any witness, person about to be called as a witness, or person about to give material information pertaining to a crime to a law enforcement official, any bribe, upon any understanding or agreement that the testimony of such witness or information given by such person shall be thereby influenced is guilty of a felony.

(b) Every person who attempts by force or threat of force or by the use of fraud to induce any person to give false testimony or withhold true testimony or to give false material information pertaining to a crime to, or withhold true material information pertaining to a crime from, a law enforcement official is guilty of a felony, punishable by imprisonment pursuant to subdivision (h) of Section 1170 for two, three, or four years. As used in this subdivision, "threat of force" means a credible threat of unlawful injury to any person or damage to the property of another which is communicated to a person for the purpose of inducing him to give false testimony or withhold true testimony or to give false material information pertaining to a crime to, or to withhold true material information pertaining to a crime from, a law enforcement official.

(c) Every person who knowingly induces another person to give false testimony or withhold true testimony not privileged by law or to give false material information pertaining to a crime to, or to withhold true material information pertaining to a crime from, a law enforcement official is guilty of a misdemeanor.

(d) At the arraignment, on a showing of cause to believe this section may be violated, the court, on motion of a party, shall admonish the person who there is cause to believe may violate this section and shall announce the penalties and other provisions of this section.

(e) As used in this section "law enforcement official" includes any district attorney, deputy district attorney, city attorney, deputy city attorney, the Attorney General or any deputy attorney general, or any peace officer included in Chapter 4.5 (commencing with Section 830) of Title 3 of Part 2.

(f) The provisions of subdivision (c) shall not apply to an attorney advising a client or to a person advising a member of his or her family.

(Amended by Stats. 2011, Ch. 15, Sec. 251. (AB 109) Effective April 4, 2011. Operative October 1, 2011, by Sec. 636 of Ch. 15, as amended by Stats. 2011, Ch. 39, Sec. 68.)

138.

(a) Every person who gives or offers or promises to give to any witness or person about to be called as a witness, any bribe upon any understanding or agreement that the person shall not attend upon any trial or other judicial proceeding, or every person who attempts by means of any offer of a bribe to dissuade any person from attending upon any trial or other judicial proceeding, is guilty of a felony.

(b) Every person who is a witness, or is about to be called as such, who receives, or offers to receive, any bribe, upon any understanding that his or her testimony shall be influenced thereby, or that he or she will absent himself or herself from the trial or proceeding upon which his or her testimony is required, is guilty of a felony.

(Amended by Stats. 1987, Ch. 828, Sec. 5.)

139.

(a) Except as provided in Sections 71 and 136.1, any person who has been convicted of any felony offense specified in Chapter 3 (commencing with Section 29900) of Division 9 of Title 4 of Part 6 who willfully and maliciously communicates to a witness to, or a victim of, the crime for which the person was convicted, a credible threat to use force or violence upon that person or that person's immediate family, shall be punished by imprisonment in the county jail not exceeding one year or by imprisonment pursuant to subdivision (h) of Section 1170 for two, three, or four years.

(b) Any person who is convicted of violating subdivision (a) who subsequently is convicted of making a credible threat, as defined in subdivision (c), which constitutes a threat against the life of, or a threat to cause great bodily injury to, a person described in subdivision (a), shall be sentenced to consecutive terms of imprisonment as prescribed in Section 1170.13.

(c) As used in this section, "a credible threat" is a threat made with the intent and the apparent ability to carry out the threat so as to cause the target of the threat to reasonably fear for his or her safety or the safety of his or her immediate family.

(d) The present incarceration of the person making the threat shall not be a bar to prosecution under this section.

(e) As used in this section, "malice," "witness," and "victim" have the meanings given in Section 136.

(Amended (as amended by Stats. 2010, Ch. 178) by Stats. 2011, Ch. 15, Sec. 253. (AB 109) Effective April 4, 2011. Amending action operative October 1, 2011, by Sec. 636 of Ch. 15, as amended by Stats. 2011, Ch. 39, Sec. 68. Amended version operative January 1, 2012, pursuant to Stats. 2010, Ch. 178, Sec. 107.)

140.

(a) Except as provided in Section 139, every person who willfully uses force or threatens to use force or violence upon the person of a witness to, or a victim of, a crime or any other person, or to take, damage, or destroy any property of any witness, victim, or any other person, because the witness, victim, or other person has provided any assistance or information to a law enforcement officer, or to a public prosecutor in a criminal proceeding or juvenile court proceeding, shall be punished by imprisonment in the county jail not exceeding one year, or by imprisonment pursuant to subdivision (h) of Section 1170 for two, three, or four years.

(b) A person who is punished under another provision of law for an act described in subdivision (a) shall not receive an additional term of imprisonment under this section.

(Amended by Stats. 2011, Ch. 15, Sec. 254. (AB 109) Effective April 4, 2011. Operative October 1, 2011, by Sec. 636 of Ch. 15, as amended by Stats. 2011, Ch. 39, Sec. 68.)

141.

(a) Except as provided in subdivisions (b) and (c), a person who knowingly, willfully, intentionally, and wrongfully alters, modifies, plants, places, manufactures, conceals, or moves any physical matter, digital image, or video recording, with specific intent that the action will result in a person being charged with a crime or with the specific intent that the physical matter will be wrongfully produced as genuine or true upon a trial, proceeding, or inquiry, is guilty of a misdemeanor.

(b) A peace officer who knowingly, willfully, intentionally, and wrongfully alters, modifies, plants, places, manufactures, conceals, or moves any physical matter, digital image, or video recording, with specific intent that the action will result in a person being charged with a crime or with the specific intent that the physical matter, digital image, or video recording will be concealed or destroyed, or fraudulently represented as the original evidence upon a trial, proceeding, or inquiry, is guilty of a felony punishable by two, three, or five years in the state prison.

(c) A prosecuting attorney who intentionally and in bad faith alters, modifies, or withholds any physical matter, digital image, video recording, or relevant exculpatory material or information, knowing that it is relevant and material to the outcome of the case, with the specific intent that the physical matter, digital image, video recording, or relevant exculpatory material or information will be concealed or destroyed, or fraudulently represented as the original evidence upon a trial, proceeding, or inquiry, is guilty of a felony punishable by imprisonment pursuant to subdivision (h) of Section 1170 for 16 months, or two or three years.

(d) This section does not preclude prosecution under both this section and any other law.

(Amended by Stats. 2016, Ch. 879, Sec. 1. (AB 1909) Effective January 1, 2017.)

CHAPTER 7. Other Offenses Against Public Justice [142 - 181]

(Chapter 7 enacted 1872.)

142.

(a) Any peace officer who has the authority to receive or arrest a person charged with a criminal offense and willfully refuses to receive or arrest that person shall be punished by a fine not exceeding ten thousand dollars ($10,000), or by imprisonment in a county jail not exceeding one year, or pursuant to subdivision (h) of Section 1170, or by both that fine and imprisonment.

(b) Notwithstanding subdivision (a), the sheriff may determine whether any jail, institution, or facility under his or her direction shall be designated as a reception, holding, or confinement facility, or shall be used for several of those purposes, and may designate the class of prisoners for which any facility shall be used.

(c) This section shall not apply to arrests made pursuant to Section 837.

(Amended by Stats. 2011, Ch. 15, Sec. 255. (AB 109) Effective April 4, 2011. Operative October 1, 2011, by Sec. 636 of Ch. 15, as amended by Stats. 2011, Ch. 39, Sec. 68.)

145.

Every public officer or other person, having arrested any person upon a criminal charge, who willfully delays to take such person before a magistrate having jurisdiction, to take his examination, is guilty of a misdemeanor.

(Enacted 1872.)

145.5.

(a) (1) Subject to paragraph (2), notwithstanding any law to the contrary, no agency of the State of California, no political subdivision of this state, no employee of an agency, or a political subdivision, of this state acting in his or her official capacity, and no member of the California National Guard on official state duty shall knowingly aid an agency of the armed forces of the United States in any investigation, prosecution, or detention of a person within California pursuant to (A) Sections 1021 and 1022 of the National Defense Authorization Act for Fiscal Year 2012 (NDAA), (B) the federal law known as the Authorization for Use of Military Force (Public Law 107-40), enacted in 2001, or (C) any other federal law, if the state agency, political subdivision, employee, or member of the California National Guard would violate the United States Constitution, the California Constitution, or any law of this state by providing that aid.

(2) Paragraph (1) does not apply to participation by state or local law enforcement or the California National Guard in a joint task force, partnership, or other similar cooperative agreement with federal law enforcement if that joint task force, partnership, or similar cooperative agreement is not for the purpose of investigating, prosecuting, or detaining any person pursuant to (A) Sections 1021 and 1022 of the NDAA, (B) the federal law known as the Authorization for Use of Military Force (Public Law 107-40), enacted in 2001, or (C) any other federal law, if the state agency, political subdivision, employee, or member of the California National Guard would violate the United States Constitution, the California Constitution, or any law of this state by providing that aid.

(b) It is the policy of this state to refuse to provide material support for or to participate in any way with the implementation within this state of any federal law that purports to authorize indefinite detention of a person within California. Notwithstanding any other law, no local law enforcement agency or local or municipal government, or the employee of that agency or government acting in his or her official capacity, shall knowingly use state funds or funds allocated by the state to local entities on or after January 1, 2013, in whole or in part, to engage in any activity that aids an agency of the armed forces of the United States in the detention of any person within California for purposes of implementing Sections 1021 and 1022 of the NDAA or the federal law known as the Authorization for Use of Military Force (Public Law 107-40), enacted in 2001, if that activity would violate the United States Constitution, the California Constitution, or any law of this state.

(Amended by Stats. 2014, Ch. 71, Sec. 116. (SB 1304) Effective January 1, 2015.)

146.

Every public officer, or person pretending to be a public officer, who, under the pretense or color of any process or other legal authority, does any of the following, without a regular process or other lawful authority, is guilty of a misdemeanor:

(a) Arrests any person or detains that person against his or her will.

(b) Seizes or levies upon any property.

(c) Dispossesses any one of any lands or tenements.

(Amended by Stats. 1990, Ch. 350, Sec. 11.)

146a.

(a) Any person who falsely represents himself or herself to be a deputy or clerk in any state department and who, in that assumed character, does any of the following is guilty of a misdemeanor punishable by imprisonment in a county jail not exceeding six months, by a fine not exceeding two thousand five hundred dollars ($2,500), or both the fine and imprisonment:

(1) Arrests, detains, or threatens to arrest or detain any person.

(2) Otherwise intimidates any person.

(3) Searches any person, building, or other property of any person.

(4) Obtains money, property, or other thing of value.

(b) Any person who falsely represents himself or herself to be a public officer, investigator, or inspector in any state department and who, in that assumed character, does any of the following shall be punished by imprisonment in a county jail not exceeding one year, by a fine not exceeding two thousand five hundred dollars ($2,500), or by both that fine and imprisonment, or by imprisonment pursuant to subdivision (h) of Section 1170:

(1) Arrests, detains, or threatens to arrest or detain any person.

(2) Otherwise intimidates any person.

(3) Searches any person, building, or other property of any person.

(4) Obtains money, property, or other thing of value.

(Amended by Stats. 2011, Ch. 15, Sec. 256. (AB 109) Effective April 4, 2011. Operative October 1, 2011, by Sec. 636 of Ch. 15, as amended by Stats. 2011, Ch. 39, Sec. 68.)

146b.

Every person who, with intent to lead another to believe that a request or demand for information is being made by the State, a county, city, or other governmental entity, when such is not the case, sends to such other person a written or printed form or other communication which reasonably appears to be such request or demand by such governmental entity, is guilty of a misdemeanor.

(Added by Stats. 1959, Ch. 2135.)

146c.

Every person who designates any nongovernmental organization by any name, including, but not limited to any name that incorporates the term "peace officer," "police," or "law enforcement," that would reasonably be understood to imply that the organization is composed of law enforcement personnel, when, in fact, less than 80 percent of the voting members of the organization are law enforcement personnel or firefighters, active or retired, is guilty of a misdemeanor.

Every person who solicits another to become a member of any organization so named, of which less than 80 percent of the voting members are law enforcement personnel or firefighters, or to make a contribution thereto or subscribe to or advertise in a publication of the organization, or who sells or gives to another any badge, pin, membership card, or other article indicating membership in the organization, knowing that less than 80 percent of the voting members are law enforcement personnel or firefighters, active or retired, is guilty of a misdemeanor.

As used in this section, "law enforcement personnel" includes those mentioned in Chapter 4.5 (commencing with Section 830) of Title 3 of Part 2, plus any other officers in any segment of law enforcement who are employed by the state or any of its political subdivisions.

(Amended by Stats. 1994, Ch. 202, Sec. 1. Effective January 1, 1995.)

146d.

Every person who sells or gives to another a membership card, badge, or other device, where it can be reasonably inferred by the recipient that display of the device will have the result that the law will be enforced less rigorously as to such person than would otherwise be the case is guilty of a misdemeanor.

(Added by Stats. 1963, Ch. 1180.)

146e.

(a) Every person who maliciously, and with the intent to obstruct justice or the due administration of the laws, or with the intent or threat to inflict imminent physical harm in retaliation for the due administration of the laws, publishes, disseminates, or otherwise discloses the residence address or telephone number of any peace officer, nonsworn police dispatcher, employee of a city police department or county sheriff's office, or public safety official, or that of the spouse or children of these persons who reside with them, while designating the peace officer, nonsworn police dispatcher, employee of a city police department or county sheriff's office, or public safety official, or relative of these persons as such, without the authorization of the employing agency, is guilty of a misdemeanor.

(b) A violation of subdivision (a) with regard to any peace officer, employee of a city police department or county sheriff's office, or public safety official, or the spouse or children of these persons, that results in bodily injury to the peace officer, employee of the city police department or county sheriff's office, or public safety official, or the spouse or children of these persons, is a felony punishable by imprisonment pursuant to subdivision (h) of Section 1170.

(c) For purposes of this section, "public safety official" is defined in Section 6254.24 of the Government Code.

(Amended by Stats. 2011, Ch. 15, Sec. 257. (AB 109) Effective April 4, 2011. Operative October 1, 2011, by Sec. 636 of Ch. 15, as amended by Stats. 2011, Ch. 39, Sec. 68.)

146f.

No inmate under the control or supervision of the Department of Corrections or the Department of the Youth Authority shall be permitted to work with records or files containing peace officer personnel information or be allowed access to the immediate area where that information is normally stored, except for maintenance services and only after those records or files have been secured and locked.

(Added by Stats. 1983, Ch. 399, Sec. 2.)

146g.

(a) Any peace officer, as defined in Chapter 4.5 (commencing with Section 830) of Title 3 of Part 2, any employee of a law enforcement agency, any attorney as defined in Section 6125 of the Business and Professions Code employed by a governmental agency, or any trial court employee as defined in Section 71601 of the Government Code, who does either of the following is guilty of a misdemeanor punishable by a fine not to exceed one thousand dollars ($1,000):

(1) Discloses, for financial gain, information obtained in the course of a criminal investigation, the disclosure of which is prohibited by law.

(2) Solicits, for financial gain, the exchange of information obtained in the course of a criminal investigation, the disclosure of which is prohibited by law.

(b) Any person who solicits any other person described in subdivision (a) for the financial gain of the person described in subdivision (a) to disclose information obtained in the course of a criminal investigation, with the knowledge that the disclosure is prohibited by law, is guilty of a misdemeanor, punishable by a fine not to exceed one thousand dollars ($1,000).

(c) (1) Any person described in subdivision (a) who, for financial gain, solicits or sells any photograph or video taken inside any secure area of a law enforcement or court facility, the taking of which was not authorized by the law enforcement or court facility administrator, is guilty of a misdemeanor punishable by a fine not to exceed one thousand dollars ($1,000).

(2) Any person who solicits any person described in subdivision (a) for financial gain to the person described in subdivision (a) to disclose any photograph or video taken inside any secure area of a law enforcement or court facility, the taking of which was not authorized by the law enforcement or court facility administrator, is guilty of a misdemeanor punishable by a fine not to exceed one thousand dollars ($1,000).

(d) Upon conviction of, and in addition to, any other penalty prescribed by this section, the defendant shall forfeit any monetary compensation received in the commission of a violation of this section and the money shall be deposited in the Victim Restitution Fund.

(e) Nothing in this section shall apply to officially sanctioned information, photographs, or video, or to information, photographs, or video obtained or distributed pursuant to the California Whistleblower Protection Act or the Local Government Disclosure of Information Act.

(f) This section shall not be construed to limit or prevent prosecution pursuant to any other applicable provision of law.

(Added by Stats. 2007, Ch. 401, Sec. 2. Effective January 1, 2008.)

147.

Every officer who is guilty of willful inhumanity or oppression toward any prisoner under his care or in his custody, is punishable by fine not exceeding four thousand dollars ($4,000), and by removal from office.

(Amended by Stats. 1983, Ch. 1092, Sec. 240. Effective September 27, 1983. Operative January 1, 1984, by Sec. 427 of Ch. 1092.)

148.

(a) (1) Every person who willfully resists, delays, or obstructs any public officer, peace officer, or an emergency medical technician, as defined in Division 2.5 (commencing with Section 1797) of the Health and Safety Code, in the discharge or attempt to discharge any duty of his or her office or employment, when no other punishment is prescribed, shall be punished by a fine not exceeding one thousand dollars ($1,000), or by imprisonment in a county jail not to exceed one year, or by both that fine and imprisonment.

(2) Except as provided by subdivision (d) of Section 653t, every person who knowingly and maliciously interrupts, disrupts, impedes, or otherwise interferes with the transmission of a communication over a public safety radio frequency shall be punished by a fine not exceeding one thousand dollars ($1,000), imprisonment in a county jail not exceeding one year, or by both that fine and imprisonment.

(b) Every person who, during the commission of any offense described in subdivision (a), removes or takes any weapon, other than a firearm, from the person of, or immediate presence of, a public officer or peace officer shall be punished by imprisonment in a county jail not to exceed one year or pursuant to subdivision (h) of Section 1170.

(c) Every person who, during the commission of any offense described in subdivision (a), removes or takes a firearm from the person of, or immediate presence of, a public officer or peace officer shall be punished by imprisonment pursuant to subdivision (h) of Section 1170.

(d) Except as provided in subdivision (c) and notwithstanding subdivision (a) of Section 489, every person who removes or takes without intent to permanently deprive, or who attempts to remove or take a firearm from the person of, or immediate presence of, a public officer or peace officer, while the officer is engaged in the performance of his or her lawful duties, shall be punished by imprisonment in a county jail not to exceed one year or pursuant to subdivision (h) of Section 1170.

In order to prove a violation of this subdivision, the prosecution shall establish that the defendant had the specific intent to remove or take the firearm by demonstrating that any of the following direct, but ineffectual, acts occurred:

(1) The officer's holster strap was unfastened by the defendant.

(2) The firearm was partially removed from the officer's holster by the defendant.

(3) The firearm safety was released by the defendant.

(4) An independent witness corroborates that the defendant stated that he or she intended to remove the firearm and the defendant actually touched the firearm.

(5) An independent witness corroborates that the defendant actually had his or her hand on the firearm and tried to take the firearm away from the officer who was holding it.

(6) The defendant's fingerprint was found on the firearm or holster.

(7) Physical evidence authenticated by a scientifically verifiable procedure established that the defendant touched the firearm.

(8) In the course of any struggle, the officer's firearm fell and the defendant attempted to pick it up.

(e) A person shall not be convicted of a violation of subdivision (a) in addition to a conviction of a violation of subdivision (b), (c), or (d) when the resistance, delay, or obstruction, and the removal or taking of the weapon or firearm or attempt thereof, was committed against the same public officer, peace officer, or emergency medical technician. A person may be convicted of multiple violations of this section if more than one public officer, peace officer, or emergency medical technician are victims.

(f) This section shall not apply if the public officer, peace officer, or emergency medical technician is disarmed while engaged in a criminal act.

(g) The fact that a person takes a photograph or makes an audio or video recording of a public officer or peace officer, while the officer is in a public place or the person taking the photograph or making the recording is in a place he or she has the right to be, does not constitute, in and of itself, a violation of subdivision (a), nor does it constitute reasonable suspicion to detain the person or probable cause to arrest the person.

(Amended by Stats. 2015, Ch. 177, Sec. 2. (SB 411) Effective January 1, 2016.)

148.1.

(a) Any person who reports to any peace officer listed in Section 830.1 or 830.2, or subdivision (a) of Section 830.33, employee of a fire department or fire service, district attorney, newspaper, radio station, television station, deputy district attorney, employees of the Department of Justice, employees of an airline, employees of an airport, employees of a railroad or busline, an employee of a telephone company,

occupants of a building or a news reporter in the employ of a newspaper or radio or television station, that a bomb or other explosive has been or will be placed or secreted in any public or private place, knowing that the report is false, is guilty of a crime punishable by imprisonment in a county jail not to exceed one year, or pursuant to subdivision (h) of Section 1170.

(b) Any person who reports to any other peace officer defined in Chapter 4.5 (commencing with Section 830) of Title 3 of Part 2 that a bomb or other explosive has been or will be placed or secreted in any public or private place, knowing that the report is false, is guilty of a crime punishable by imprisonment in a county jail not to exceed one year or pursuant to subdivision (h) of Section 1170 if (1) the false information is given while the peace officer is engaged in the performance of his or her duties as a peace officer and (2) the person providing the false information knows or should have known that the person receiving the information is a peace officer.

(c) Any person who maliciously informs any other person that a bomb or other explosive has been or will be placed or secreted in any public or private place, knowing that the information is false, is guilty of a crime punishable by imprisonment in a county jail not to exceed one year, or pursuant to subdivision (h) of Section 1170.

(d) Any person who maliciously gives, mails, sends, or causes to be sent any false or facsimile bomb to another person, or places, causes to be placed, or maliciously possesses any false or facsimile bomb, with the intent to cause another to fear for his or her personal safety or the safety of others, is guilty of a crime punishable by imprisonment in a county jail not to exceed one year, or pursuant to subdivision (h) of Section 1170.

(Amended by Stats. 2011, Ch. 15, Sec. 259. (AB 109) Effective April 4, 2011. Operative October 1, 2011, by Sec. 636 of Ch. 15, as amended by Stats. 2011, Ch. 39, Sec. 68.)

148.2.

Every person who willfully commits any of the following acts at the burning of a building or at any other time and place where any fireman or firemen or emergency rescue personnel are discharging or attempting to discharge an official duty, is guilty of a misdemeanor:

1. Resists or interferes with the lawful efforts of any fireman or firemen or emergency rescue personnel in the discharge or attempt to discharge an official duty.

2. Disobeys the lawful orders of any fireman or public officer.

3. Engages in any disorderly conduct which delays or prevents a fire from being timely extinguished.

4. Forbids or prevents others from assisting in extinguishing a fire or exhorts another person, as to whom he has no legal right or obligation to protect or control, from assisting in extinguishing a fire.

(Amended by Stats. 1973, Ch. 471.)

148.3.

(a) Any individual who reports, or causes any report to be made, to any city, county, city and county, or state department, district, agency, division, commission, or board, that an "emergency" exists, knowing that the report is false, is guilty of a misdemeanor and upon conviction thereof shall be punishable by imprisonment in a county jail for a period not exceeding one year, or by a fine not exceeding one thousand dollars ($1,000), or by both that imprisonment and fine.

(b) Any individual who reports, or causes any report to be made, to any city, county, city and county, or state department, district, agency, division, commission, or board, that an "emergency" exists, who knows that the report is false, and who knows or should know that the response to the report is likely to cause death or great bodily injury, and great bodily injury or death is sustained by any person as a result of the false report, is guilty of a felony and upon conviction thereof shall be punishable by imprisonment pursuant to subdivision (h) of Section 1170, or by a fine of not more than ten thousand dollars ($10,000), or by both that imprisonment and fine.

(c) "Emergency" as used in this section means any condition that results in, or could result in, the response of a public official in an authorized emergency vehicle, aircraft, or vessel, any condition that jeopardizes or could jeopardize public safety and results in, or could result in, the evacuation of any area, building, structure, vehicle, or of any other place that any individual may enter, or any situation that results in or could result in activation of the Emergency Alert System pursuant to Section 8594 of the Government Code. An activation or possible activation of the Emergency Alert System pursuant to Section 8594 of the Government Code shall not constitute an "emergency" for purposes of this section if it occurs as the result of a report made or caused to be made by a parent, guardian, or lawful custodian of a child that is based on a good faith belief that the child is missing.

(d) Nothing in this section precludes punishment for the conduct described in subdivision (a) or (b) under any other section of law providing for greater punishment for that conduct.

(e) Any individual convicted of violating this section, based upon a report that resulted in an emergency response, is liable to a public agency for the reasonable costs of the emergency response by that public agency.

(Amended by Stats. 2013, Ch. 284, Sec. 1. (SB 333) Effective January 1, 2014.)

148.4.

(a) Any person who does any of the following is guilty of a misdemeanor and upon conviction is punishable by imprisonment in a county jail, not exceeding one year, or by a fine, not exceeding one thousand dollars ($1,000), or by both that fine and imprisonment:

(1) Willfully and maliciously tampers with, molests, injures, or breaks any fire protection equipment, fire protection installation, fire alarm apparatus, wire, or signal.

(2) Willfully and maliciously sends, gives, transmits, or sounds any false alarm of fire, by means of any fire alarm system or signal or by any other means or methods.

(b) Any person who willfully and maliciously sends, gives, transmits, or sounds any false alarm of fire, by means of any fire alarm system or signal, or by any other means or methods, is guilty of a felony and upon conviction is punishable by imprisonment pursuant to subdivision (h) of Section 1170 or by a fine of not less than five hundred dollars ($500) nor more than ten thousand dollars ($10,000), or by both that fine and imprisonment, if any person sustains as a result thereof, any of the following:

(1) Great bodily injury.

(2) Death.

(Amended by Stats. 2011, Ch. 15, Sec. 261. (AB 109) Effective April 4, 2011. Operative October 1, 2011, by Sec. 636 of Ch. 15, as amended by Stats. 2011, Ch. 39, Sec. 68.)

148.5.

(a) Every person who reports to any peace officer listed in Section 830.1 or 830.2, or subdivision (a) of Section 830.33, the Attorney General, or a deputy attorney general, or a district attorney, or a deputy district attorney that a felony or misdemeanor has been committed, knowing the report to be false, is guilty of a misdemeanor.

(b) Every person who reports to any other peace officer, as defined in Chapter 4.5 (commencing with Section 830) of Title 3 of Part 2, that a felony or misdemeanor has been committed, knowing the report to be false, is guilty of a misdemeanor if (1) the false information is given while the peace officer is engaged in the performance of his or her duties as a peace officer and (2) the person providing the false information knows or should have known that the person receiving the information is a peace officer.

(c) Except as provided in subdivisions (a) and (b), every person who reports to any employee who is assigned to accept reports from citizens, either directly or by telephone, and who is employed by a state or local agency which is designated in Section 830.1, 830.2, subdivision (e) of Section 830.3, Section 830.31, 830.32, 830.33, 830.34, 830.35, 830.36, 830.37, or 830.4, that a felony or misdemeanor has been committed, knowing the report to be false, is guilty of a misdemeanor if (1) the false information is given while the employee is engaged in the performance of his or her duties as an agency employee and (2) the person providing the false information knows or should have known that the person receiving the information is an agency employee engaged in the performance of the duties described in this subdivision.

(d) Every person who makes a report to a grand jury that a felony or misdemeanor has been committed, knowing the report to be false, is guilty of a misdemeanor. This subdivision shall not be construed as prohibiting or precluding a charge of perjury or contempt for any report made under oath in an investigation or proceeding before a grand jury.

(e) This section does not apply to reports made by persons who are required by statute to report known or suspected instances of child abuse, dependent adult abuse, or elder abuse.

(f) This section applies to a person who reports to a person described in subdivision (a), (b), or (c), that a firearm, as defined in subdivision (a) or (b) of Section 16520, has been lost or stolen, knowing the report to be false.

(Amended by Stats. 2016, Ch. 47, Sec. 1. (AB 1695) Effective January 1, 2017.)

148.6.

(a) (1) Every person who files any allegation of misconduct against any peace officer, as defined in Chapter 4.5 (commencing with Section 830) of Title 3 of Part 2, knowing the allegation to be false, is guilty of a misdemeanor.

(2) A law enforcement agency accepting an allegation of misconduct against a peace officer shall require the complainant to read and sign the following advisory, all in boldface type:

YOU HAVE THE RIGHT TO MAKE A COMPLAINT AGAINST A POLICE OFFICER FOR ANY IMPROPER POLICE CONDUCT. CALIFORNIA LAW REQUIRES THIS AGENCY TO HAVE A PROCEDURE TO INVESTIGATE CIVILIANS' COMPLAINTS. YOU HAVE A RIGHT TO A WRITTEN DESCRIPTION OF THIS PROCEDURE. THIS AGENCY MAY FIND AFTER INVESTIGATION THAT THERE IS NOT ENOUGH EVIDENCE TO WARRANT ACTION ON YOUR COMPLAINT; EVEN IF THAT IS THE CASE, YOU HAVE THE RIGHT TO MAKE THE COMPLAINT AND HAVE IT INVESTIGATED IF YOU BELIEVE AN OFFICER BEHAVED IMPROPERLY. CIVILIAN COMPLAINTS AND ANY REPORTS OR FINDINGS RELATING TO COMPLAINTS MUST BE RETAINED BY THIS AGENCY FOR AT LEAST FIVE YEARS.
IT IS AGAINST THE LAW TO MAKE A COMPLAINT THAT YOU KNOW TO BE FALSE. IF YOU MAKE A COMPLAINT AGAINST AN OFFICER KNOWING THAT IT IS FALSE, YOU CAN BE PROSECUTED ON A MISDEMEANOR CHARGE.

I have read and understood the above statement.	
Complainant _____	

(3) The advisory shall be available in multiple languages.

(b) Every person who files a civil claim against a peace officer or a lien against his or her property, knowing the claim or lien to be false and with the intent to harass or dissuade the officer from carrying out his or her official duties, is guilty of a misdemeanor. This section applies only to claims pertaining to actions that arise in the course and scope of the peace officer's duties.

(Amended by Stats. 2016, Ch. 99, Sec. 2. (AB 1953) Effective January 1, 2017.)

148.7.

Every person who, for the purpose of serving in any county or city jail, industrial farm or road camp, or other local correctional institution any part or all of the sentence of another person, or any part or all of a term of confinement that is required to be served by another person as a condition of probation, represents to any public officer or employee that he is such other person, is guilty of a misdemeanor.

(Added by Stats. 1963, Ch. 577.)

148.9.

(a) Any person who falsely represents or identifies himself or herself as another person or as a fictitious person to any peace officer listed in Section 830.1 or 830.2, or subdivision (a) of Section 830.33, upon a lawful detention or arrest of the person, either to evade the process of the court, or to evade the proper identification of the person by the investigating officer is guilty of a misdemeanor.

(b) Any person who falsely represents or identifies himself or herself as another person or as a fictitious person to any other peace officer defined in Chapter 4.5 (commencing with Section 830) of Title 3 of Part 2, upon lawful detention or arrest of the person, either to evade the process of the court, or to evade the proper identification of the person by the arresting officer is guilty of a misdemeanor if (1) the false information is given while the peace officer is engaged in the performance of his or her duties as a peace officer and (2) the person providing the false information knows or should have known that the person receiving the information is a peace officer.

(Amended by Stats. 1998, Ch. 760, Sec. 3. Effective January 1, 1999.)

148.10.

(a) Every person who willfully resists a peace officer in the discharge or attempt to discharge any duty of his or her office or employment and whose willful resistance proximately causes death or serious bodily injury to a peace officer shall be punished by imprisonment pursuant to subdivision (h) of Section 1170 for two, three, or four years, or by a fine of not less than one thousand dollars ($1,000) or more than ten thousand dollars ($10,000), or by both that fine and imprisonment, or by imprisonment in a county jail for not more than one year, or by a fine of not more than one thousand dollars ($1,000), or by both that fine and imprisonment.

(b) For purposes of subdivision (a), the following facts shall be found by the trier of fact:

(1) That the peace officer's action was reasonable based on the facts or circumstances confronting the officer at the time.

(2) That the detention and arrest was lawful and there existed probable cause or reasonable cause to detain.

(3) That the person who willfully resisted any peace officer knew or reasonably should have known that the other person was a peace officer engaged in the performance of his or her duties.

(c) This section does not apply to conduct that occurs during labor picketing, demonstrations, or disturbing the peace.

(d) For purposes of this section, "serious bodily injury" is defined in paragraph (4) of subdivision (f) of Section 243.

(Amended by Stats. 2011, Ch. 15, Sec. 262. (AB 109) Effective April 4, 2011. Operative October 1, 2011, by Sec. 636 of Ch. 15, as amended by Stats. 2011, Ch. 39, Sec. 68.)

149.

Every public officer who, under color of authority, without lawful necessity, assaults or beats any person, is punishable by a fine not exceeding ten thousand dollars ($10,000), or by imprisonment in a county jail not exceeding one year, or pursuant to subdivision (h) of Section 1170, or by both that fine and imprisonment.

(Amended by Stats. 2011, Ch. 15, Sec. 263. (AB 109) Effective April 4, 2011. Operative October 1, 2011, by Sec. 636 of Ch. 15, as amended by Stats. 2011, Ch. 39, Sec. 68.)

150.

Every able-bodied person above 18 years of age who neglects or refuses to join the posse comitatus or power of the county, by neglecting or refusing to aid and assist in taking or arresting any person against whom there may be issued any process, or by neglecting to aid and assist in retaking any person who, after being arrested or confined, may have escaped from arrest or imprisonment, or by neglecting or refusing to aid and assist in preventing any breach of the peace, or the commission of any criminal offense, being thereto lawfully required by any uniformed peace officer, or by any peace officer described in Section 830.1, subdivision (a), (b), (c), (d), (e), or (f) of Section 830.2, or subdivision (a) of Section 830.33, who identifies himself or herself

with a badge or identification card issued by the officer's employing agency, or by any judge, is punishable by a fine of not less than fifty dollars ($50) nor more than one thousand dollars ($1,000).

(Amended by Stats. 1998, Ch. 760, Sec. 4. Effective January 1, 1999.)

151.

(a) Any person who advocates the willful and unlawful killing or injuring of a peace officer, with the specific intent to cause the willful and unlawful killing or injuring of a peace officer, and such advocacy is done at a time, place, and under circumstances in which the advocacy is likely to cause the imminent willful and unlawful killing or injuring of a peace officer is guilty of (1) a misdemeanor if such advocacy does not cause the unlawful and willful killing or injuring of a peace officer, or (2) a felony if such advocacy causes the unlawful and willful killing or injuring of a peace officer.

(b) As used in this section, "advocacy" means the direct incitement of others to cause the imminent willful and unlawful killing or injuring of a peace officer, and not the mere abstract teaching of a doctrine.

(Added by Stats. 1971, Ch. 1248.)

152.

(a) Every person who, having knowledge of an accidental death, actively conceals or attempts to conceal that death, shall be guilty of a misdemeanor punishable by imprisonment in a county jail for not more than one year, or by a fine of not less than one thousand dollars ($1,000) nor more than ten thousand dollars ($10,000), or by both that fine and imprisonment.

(b) For purposes of this section, "to actively conceal an accidental death" means any of the following:

(1) To perform an overt act that conceals the body or directly impedes the ability of authorities or family members to discover the body.

(2) To directly destroy or suppress evidence of the actual physical body of the deceased, including, but not limited to, bodily fluids or tissues.

(3) To destroy or suppress the actual physical instrumentality of death.

(Added by Stats. 1999, Ch. 396, Sec. 1. Effective January 1, 2000.)

152.3.

(a) Any person who reasonably believes that he or she has observed the commission of any of the following offenses where the victim is a child under 14 years of age shall notify a peace officer, as defined in Chapter 4.5 (commencing with Section 830) of Title 3 of Part 2:

(1) Murder.

(2) Rape.

(3) A violation of paragraph (1) of subdivision (b) of Section 288 of the Penal Code.

(b) This section shall not be construed to affect privileged relationships as provided by law.

(c) The duty to notify a peace officer imposed pursuant to subdivision (a) is satisfied if the notification or an attempt to provide notice is made by telephone or any other means.

(d) Failure to notify as required pursuant to subdivision (a) is a misdemeanor and is punishable by a fine of not more than one thousand five hundred dollars ($1,500), by imprisonment in a county jail for not more than six months, or by both that fine and imprisonment.

(e) The requirements of this section shall not apply to the following:

(1) A person who is related to either the victim or the offender, including a spouse, parent, child, brother, sister, grandparent, grandchild, or other person related by consanguinity or affinity.

(2) A person who fails to report based on a reasonable mistake of fact.

(3) A person who fails to report based on a reasonable fear for his or her own safety or for the safety of his or her family.

(Amended by Stats. 2016, Ch. 50, Sec. 66. (SB 1005) Effective January 1, 2017.)

153.

Every person who, having knowledge of the actual commission of a crime, takes money or property of another, or any gratuity or reward, or any engagement, or promise thereof, upon any agreement or understanding to compound or conceal that crime, or to abstain from any prosecution thereof, or to withhold any evidence thereof, except in the cases provided for by law, in which crimes may be compromised by leave of court, is punishable as follows:

1. By imprisonment in a county jail not exceeding one year, or pursuant to subdivision (h) of Section 1170, where the crime was punishable by death or imprisonment in the state prison for life;

2. By imprisonment in a county jail not exceeding six months, or pursuant to subdivision (h) of Section 1170, where the crime was punishable by imprisonment in the state prison for any other term than for life;

3. By imprisonment in a county jail not exceeding six months, or by fine not exceeding one thousand dollars ($1,000), where the crime was a misdemeanor.

(Amended by Stats. 2011, Ch. 15, Sec. 264. (AB 109) Effective April 4, 2011. Operative October 1, 2011, by Sec. 636 of Ch. 15, as amended by Stats. 2011, Ch. 39, Sec. 68.)

154.

(a) Every debtor who fraudulently removes his or her property or effects out of this state, or who fraudulently sells, conveys, assigns or conceals his or her property with intent to defraud, hinder or delay his or her creditors of their rights, claims, or demands, is punishable by imprisonment in the county jail not exceeding one year, or by fine not exceeding one thousand dollars ($1,000), or by both that fine and imprisonment.

(b) Where the property so removed, sold, conveyed, assigned, or concealed consists of a stock in trade, or a part thereof, of a value exceeding two hundred fifty dollars ($250), the offense shall be a felony and punishable as such.

(Amended by Stats. 2009, 3rd Ex. Sess., Ch. 28, Sec. 6. (SB 18 3x) Effective January 25, 2010.)

155.

(a) Every person against whom an action is pending, or against whom a judgment has been rendered for the recovery of any personal property, who fraudulently conceals, sells, or disposes of that property, with intent to hinder, delay, or defraud the person bringing the action or recovering the judgment, or with such intent removes that property beyond the limits of the county in which it may be at the time of the commencement of the action or the rendering of the judgment, is punishable by imprisonment in a county jail not exceeding one year, or by fine not exceeding one thousand dollars ($1,000), or by both that fine and imprisonment.

(b) Where the property so concealed, sold, disposed of, or removed consists of a stock in trade, or a part thereof, of a value exceeding two hundred fifty dollars ($250), the offenses shall be a felony and punishable as such.

(Amended by Stats. 2009, 3rd Ex. Sess., Ch. 28, Sec. 7. (SB 18 3x) Effective January 25, 2010.)

155.5.

(a) Any defendant who is ordered to pay any fine or restitution in connection with the commission of a misdemeanor and who, after the plea or judgment and prior to sentencing, or during the period that a restitution fine or order remains unsatisfied and enforceable, sells, conveys, assigns, or conceals his or her property with the intent to lessen or impair his or her financial ability to pay in full any fine or restitution which he or she may lawfully be ordered to pay, or to avoid forfeiture of assets pursuant to the California Control of Profits of Organized Crime Act (Chapter 9 (commencing with Section 186) of this title), is guilty of a misdemeanor.

(b) Any defendant who is ordered to pay any fine or restitution in connection with the commission of a felony and who, after the plea or judgment and prior to sentencing for the same felony offense, or during the period that a restitution order remains unsatisfied

and enforceable, sells, conveys, assigns, or conceals his or her property with the intent to lessen or impair his or her financial ability to pay in full any fine or restitution which he or she may lawfully be ordered to pay or to avoid forfeiture of assets derived from either criminal profiteering pursuant to Chapter 9 (commencing with Section 186) of this title or trafficking in controlled substances pursuant to Chapter 8 (commencing with Section 11470) of Division 10 of the Health and Safety Code, is guilty of a felony.
(Amended by Stats. 1996, Ch. 629, Sec. 1. Effective January 1, 1997.)

156.
Every person who fraudulently produces an infant, falsely pretending it to have been born of any parent whose child would be entitled to inherit any real estate or to receive a share of any personal estate, with intent to intercept the inheritance of any such real estate, or the distribution of any such personal estate from any person lawfully entitled thereto, is punishable by imprisonment pursuant to subdivision (h) of Section 1170 for two, three or four years.
(Amended by Stats. 2011, Ch. 15, Sec. 265. (AB 109) Effective April 4, 2011. Operative October 1, 2011, by Sec. 636 of Ch. 15, as amended by Stats. 2011, Ch. 39, Sec. 68.)

157.
Every person to whom an infant has been confided for nursing, education, or any other purpose, who, with intent to deceive any parent or guardian of that child, substitutes or produces to that parent or guardian another child in the place of the one so confided, is punishable by imprisonment pursuant to subdivision (h) of Section 1170 for two, three or four years.
(Amended by Stats. 2011, Ch. 15, Sec. 266. (AB 109) Effective April 4, 2011. Operative October 1, 2011, by Sec. 636 of Ch. 15, as amended by Stats. 2011, Ch. 39, Sec. 68.)

158.
Common barratry is the practice of exciting groundless judicial proceedings, and is punishable by imprisonment in the county jail not exceeding six months and by fine not exceeding one thousand dollars ($1,000).
(Amended by Stats. 1983, Ch. 1092, Sec. 246. Effective September 27, 1983. Operative January 1, 1984, by Sec. 427 of Ch. 1092.)

159.
No person can be convicted of common barratry except upon proof that he has excited suits or proceedings at law in at least three instances, and with a corrupt or malicious intent to vex and annoy.
(Enacted 1872.)

160.
(a) No bail licensee may employ, engage, solicit, pay, or promise any payment, compensation, consideration or thing of value to any person incarcerated in any prison, jail, or other place of detention for the purpose of that person soliciting bail on behalf of the licensee. A violation of this section is a misdemeanor.
(b) Nothing in this section shall prohibit prosecution under Section 1800 or 1814 of the Insurance Code, or any other applicable provision of law.
(Added by Stats. 2004, Ch. 165, Sec. 1. Effective January 1, 2005.)

165.
Every person who gives or offers a bribe to any member of any common council, board of supervisors, or board of trustees of any county, city and county, city, or public corporation, with intent to corruptly influence such member in his action on any matter or subject pending before, or which is afterward to be considered by, the body of which he is a member, and every member of any of the bodies mentioned in this section who receives, or offers or agrees to receive any bribe upon any understanding that his official vote, opinion, judgment, or action shall be influenced thereby, or shall be given in any particular manner or upon any particular side of any question or matter, upon which he may be required to act in his official capacity, is punishable by imprisonment in the state prison for two, three or four years, and upon conviction thereof shall, in addition to said punishment, forfeit his office, and forever be disfranchised and disqualified from holding any public office or trust.
(Amended by Stats. 1976, Ch. 1139.)

166.
(a) Except as provided in subdivisions (b), (c), and (d), a person guilty of any of the following contempts of court is guilty of a misdemeanor:
(1) Disorderly, contemptuous, or insolent behavior committed during the sitting of a court of justice, in the immediate view and presence of the court, and directly tending to interrupt its proceedings or to impair the respect due to its authority.
(2) Behavior specified in paragraph (1) that is committed in the presence of a referee, while actually engaged in a trial or hearing, pursuant to the order of a court, or in the presence of any jury while actually sitting for the trial of a cause, or upon an inquest or other proceeding authorized by law.
(3) A breach of the peace, noise, or other disturbance directly tending to interrupt the proceedings of the court.
(4) Willful disobedience of the terms as written of any process or court order or out-of-state court order, lawfully issued by a court, including orders pending trial.
(5) Resistance willfully offered by any person to the lawful order or process of a court.
(6) The contumacious and unlawful refusal of a person to be sworn as a witness or, when so sworn, the like refusal to answer a material question.
(7) The publication of a false or grossly inaccurate report of the proceedings of a court.
(8) Presenting to a court having power to pass sentence upon a prisoner under conviction, or to a member of the court, an affidavit, testimony, or representation of any kind, verbal or written, in aggravation or mitigation of the punishment to be imposed upon the prisoner, except as provided in this code.
(9) Willful disobedience of the terms of an injunction that restrains the activities of a criminal street gang or any of its members, lawfully issued by a court, including an order pending trial.
(b) (1) A person who is guilty of contempt of court under paragraph (4) of subdivision (a) by willfully contacting a victim by telephone or mail, or directly, and who has been previously convicted of a violation of Section 646.9 shall be punished by imprisonment in a county jail for not more than one year, by a fine of five thousand dollars ($5,000), or by both that fine and imprisonment.
(2) For the purposes of sentencing under this subdivision, each contact shall constitute a separate violation of this subdivision.
(3) The present incarceration of a person who makes contact with a victim in violation of paragraph (1) is not a defense to a violation of this subdivision.
(c) (1) Notwithstanding paragraph (4) of subdivision (a), a willful and knowing violation of a protective order or stay-away court order described as follows shall constitute contempt of court, a misdemeanor, punishable by imprisonment in a county jail for not more than one year, by a fine of not more than one thousand dollars ($1,000), or by both that imprisonment and fine:
(A) An order issued pursuant to Section 136.2.
(B) An order issued pursuant to paragraph (2) of subdivision (a) of Section 1203.097.
(C) An order issued after a conviction in a criminal proceeding involving elder or dependent adult abuse, as defined in Section 368.
(D) An order issued pursuant to Section 1201.3.
(E) An order described in paragraph (3).
(F) An order issued pursuant to subdivision (j) of Section 273.5.
(2) If a violation of paragraph (1) results in a physical injury, the person shall be imprisoned in a county jail for at least 48 hours, whether a fine or imprisonment is imposed, or the sentence is suspended.
(3) Paragraphs (1) and (2) apply to the following court orders:
(A) An order issued pursuant to Section 6320 or 6389 of the Family Code.

(B) An order excluding one party from the family dwelling or from the dwelling of the other.
(C) An order enjoining a party from specified behavior that the court determined was necessary to effectuate the orders described in paragraph (1).
(4) A second or subsequent conviction for a violation of an order described in paragraph (1) occurring within seven years of a prior conviction for a violation of any of those orders and involving an act of violence or "a credible threat" of violence, as provided in subdivision (c) of Section 139, is punishable by imprisonment in a county jail not to exceed one year, or in the state prison for 16 months or two or three years.
(5) The prosecuting agency of each county shall have the primary responsibility for the enforcement of the orders described in paragraph (1).
(d) (1) A person who owns, possesses, purchases, or receives a firearm knowing he or she is prohibited from doing so by the provisions of a protective order as defined in Section 136.2 of this code, Section 6218 of the Family Code, or Section 527.6 or 527.8 of the Code of Civil Procedure, shall be punished under Section 29825.
(2) A person subject to a protective order described in paragraph (1) shall not be prosecuted under this section for owning, possessing, purchasing, or receiving a firearm to the extent that firearm is granted an exemption pursuant to subdivision (h) of Section 6389 of the Family Code.
(e) (1) If probation is granted upon conviction of a violation of subdivision (c), the court shall impose probation consistent with Section 1203.097.
(2) If probation is granted upon conviction of a violation of subdivision (c), the conditions of probation may include, in lieu of a fine, one or both of the following requirements:
(A) That the defendant make payments to a battered women's shelter, up to a maximum of one thousand dollars ($1,000).
(B) That the defendant provide restitution to reimburse the victim for reasonable costs of counseling and other reasonable expenses that the court finds are the direct result of the defendant's offense.
(3) For an order to pay a fine, make payments to a battered women's shelter, or pay restitution as a condition of probation under this subdivision or subdivision (c), the court shall make a determination of the defendant's ability to pay. In no event shall an order to make payments to a battered women's shelter be made if it would impair the ability of the defendant to pay direct restitution to the victim or court-ordered child support.
(4) If the injury to a married person is caused in whole, or in part, by the criminal acts of his or her spouse in violation of subdivision (c), the community property shall not be used to discharge the liability of the offending spouse for restitution to the injured spouse required by Section 1203.04, as operative on or before August 2, 1995, or Section 1202.4, or to a shelter for costs with regard to the injured spouse and dependents required by this subdivision, until all separate property of the offending spouse is exhausted.
(5) A person violating an order described in subdivision (c) may be punished for any substantive offenses described under Section 136.1 or 646.9. A finding of contempt shall not be a bar to prosecution for a violation of Section 136.1 or 646.9. However, a person held in contempt for a violation of subdivision (c) shall be entitled to credit for any punishment imposed as a result of that violation against any sentence imposed upon conviction of an offense described in Section 136.1 or 646.9. A conviction or acquittal for a substantive offense under Section 136.1 or 646.9 shall be a bar to a subsequent punishment for contempt arising out of the same act.
(Amended by Stats. 2016, Ch. 342, Sec. 1. (SB 883) Effective January 1, 2017.)

166.5.
(a) After arrest and before plea or trial or after conviction or plea of guilty and before sentence under paragraph (4) of subdivision (a) of Section 166, for willful disobedience of any order for child, spousal, or family support issued pursuant to Division 9 (commencing with Section 3500) of the Family Code or Section 17400 of the Family Code, the court may suspend proceedings or sentence therein if:
(1) The defendant appears before the court and affirms his or her obligation to pay to the person having custody of the child, or the spouse, that sum per month as shall have been previously fixed by the court in order to provide for the minor child or the spouse.
(2) The defendant provides a bond or other undertaking with sufficient sureties to the people of the State of California in a sum as the court may fix to secure the defendant's performance of his or her support obligations and that bond or undertaking is valid and binding for two years, or any lesser time that the court shall fix.
(b) Upon the failure of the defendant to comply with the conditions imposed by the court in subdivision (a), the defendant may be ordered to appear before the court and show cause why further proceedings should not be had in the action or why sentence should not be imposed, whereupon the court may proceed with the action, or pass sentence, or for good cause shown may modify the order and take a new bond or undertaking and further suspend proceedings or sentence for a like period.
(Added by Stats. 1999, Ch. 653, Sec. 20. Effective January 1, 2000.)

167.
Every person who, by any means whatsoever, willfully and knowingly, and without knowledge and consent of the jury, records, or attempts to record, all or part of the proceedings of any trial jury while it is deliberating or voting, or listens to or observes, or attempts to listen to or observe, the proceedings of any trial jury of which he is not a member while such jury is deliberating or voting is guilty of a misdemeanor.
This section is not intended to prohibit the taking of notes by a trial juror in connection with and solely for the purpose of assisting him in the performance of his duties as such juror.
(Amended by Stats. 1959, Ch. 501.)

168.
(a) Every district attorney, clerk, judge, or peace officer who, except by issuing or in executing a search warrant or warrant of arrest for a felony, willfully discloses the fact of the warrant prior to execution for the purpose of preventing the search or seizure of property or the arrest of any person shall be punished by imprisonment in a county jail not exceeding one year or pursuant to subdivision (h) of Section 1170.
(b) This section shall not prohibit the following:
(1) A disclosure made by a district attorney or the Attorney General for the sole purpose of securing voluntary compliance with the warrant.
(2) Upon the return of an indictment and the issuance of an arrest warrant, a disclosure of the existence of the indictment and arrest warrant by a district attorney or the Attorney General to assist in the apprehension of a defendant.
(3) The disclosure of an arrest warrant pursuant to paragraph (1) of subdivision (a) of Section 14207.
(Amended by Stats. 2014, Ch. 437, Sec. 7. (SB 1066) Effective January 1, 2015.)

169.
Any person who pickets or parades in or near a building which houses a court of this state with the intent to interfere with, obstruct, or impede the administration of justice or with the intent to influence any judge, juror, witness, or officer of the court in the discharge of his duty is guilty of a misdemeanor.
(Added by Stats. 1970, Ch. 1444.)

170.
Every person who maliciously and without probable cause procures a search warrant or warrant of arrest to be issued and executed, is guilty of a misdemeanor.
(Enacted 1872.)

171.
Every person, not authorized by law, who, without the permission of the officer in charge of any reformatory in this State, communicates with any person detained therein, or

brings therein or takes therefrom any letter, writing, literature, or reading matter to or from any person confined therein, is guilty of a misdemeanor.
(Amended by Stats. 1941, Ch. 106.)

171b.
(a) Any person who brings or possesses within any state or local public building or at any meeting required to be open to the public pursuant to Chapter 9 (commencing with Section 54950) of Part 1 of Division 2 of Title 5 of, or Article 9 (commencing with Section 11120) of Chapter 1 of Part 1 of Division 3 of Title 2 of, the Government Code, any of the following is guilty of a public offense punishable by imprisonment in a county jail for not more than one year, or in the state prison:
(1) Any firearm.
(2) Any deadly weapon described in Section 17235 or in any provision listed in Section 16590.
(3) Any knife with a blade length in excess of four inches, the blade of which is fixed or is capable of being fixed in an unguarded position by the use of one or two hands.
(4) Any unauthorized tear gas weapon.
(5) Any taser or stun gun, as defined in Section 244.5.
(6) Any instrument that expels a metallic projectile, such as a BB or pellet, through the force of air pressure, CO2 pressure, or spring action, or any spot marker gun or paint gun.
(b) Subdivision (a) shall not apply to, or affect, any of the following:
(1) A person who possesses weapons in, or transports weapons into, a court of law to be used as evidence.
(2) (A) A duly appointed peace officer as defined in Chapter 4.5 (commencing with Section 830) of Title 3 of Part 2, a retired peace officer with authorization to carry concealed weapons as described in Article 2 (commencing with Section 25450) of Chapter 2 of Division 5 of Title 4 of Part 6, a full-time paid peace officer of another state or the federal government who is carrying out official duties while in California, or any person summoned by any of these officers to assist in making arrests or preserving the peace while he or she is actually engaged in assisting the officer.
(B) Notwithstanding subparagraph (A), subdivision (a) shall apply to any person who brings or possesses any weapon specified therein within any courtroom if he or she is a party to an action pending before the court.
(3) A person holding a valid license to carry the firearm pursuant to Chapter 4 (commencing with Section 26150) of Division 5 of Title 4 of Part 6.
(4) A person who has permission to possess that weapon granted in writing by a duly authorized official who is in charge of the security of the state or local government building.
(5) A person who lawfully resides in, lawfully owns, or is in lawful possession of, that building with respect to those portions of the building that are not owned or leased by the state or local government.
(6) A person licensed or registered in accordance with, and acting within the course and scope of, Chapter 11.5 (commencing with Section 7512) or Chapter 11.6 (commencing with Section 7590) of Division 3 of the Business and Professions Code who has been hired by the owner or manager of the building if the person has permission pursuant to paragraph (5).
(7) (A) A person who, for the purpose of sale or trade, brings any weapon that may otherwise be lawfully transferred, into a gun show conducted pursuant to Article 1 (commencing with Section 27200) and Article 2 (commencing with Section 27300) of Chapter 3 of Division 6 of Title 4 of Part 6.
(B) A person who, for purposes of an authorized public exhibition, brings any weapon that may otherwise be lawfully possessed, into a gun show conducted pursuant to Article 1 (commencing with Section 27200) and Article 2 (commencing with Section 27300) of Chapter 3 of Division 6 of Title 4 of Part 6.
(c) As used in this section, "state or local public building" means a building that meets all of the following criteria:
(1) It is a building or part of a building owned or leased by the state or local government, if state or local public employees are regularly present for the purposes of performing their official duties. A state or local public building includes, but is not limited to, a building that contains a courtroom.
(2) It is not a building or facility, or a part thereof, that is referred to in Section 171c, 171d, 626.9, 626.95, or 626.10 of this code, or in Section 18544 of the Elections Code.
(3) It is a building not regularly used, and not intended to be used, by state or local employees as a place of residence.
(Amended by Stats. 2010, Ch. 178, Sec. 45. (SB 1115) Effective January 1, 2011. Operative January 1, 2012, by Sec. 107 of Ch. 178.)

171c.
(a) (1) Any person who brings a loaded firearm into, or possesses a loaded firearm within, the State Capitol, any legislative office, any office of the Governor or other constitutional officer, or any hearing room in which any committee of the Senate or Assembly is conducting a hearing, or upon the grounds of the State Capitol, which is bounded by 10th, L, 15th, and N Streets in the City of Sacramento, shall be punished by imprisonment in a county jail for a period of not more than one year, a fine of not more than one thousand dollars ($1,000), or both such imprisonment and fine, or by imprisonment pursuant to subdivision (h) of Section 1170.
(2) Any person who brings or possesses, within the State Capitol, any legislative office, any hearing room in which any committee of the Senate or Assembly is conducting a hearing, the Legislative Office Building at 1020 N Street in the City of Sacramento, or upon the grounds of the State Capitol, which is bounded by 10th, L, 15th, and N Streets in the City of Sacramento, any of the following, is guilty of a misdemeanor punishable by imprisonment in a county jail for a period not to exceed one year, or by a fine not exceeding one thousand dollars ($1,000), or by both that fine and imprisonment, if the area is posted with a statement providing reasonable notice that prosecution may result from possession of any of these items:
(A) Any firearm.
(B) Any deadly weapon described in Section 21510 or in any provision listed in Section 16590.
(C) Any knife with a blade length in excess of four inches, the blade of which is fixed or is capable of being fixed in an unguarded position by the use of one or two hands.
(D) Any unauthorized tear gas weapon.
(E) Any stun gun, as defined in Section 244.5.
(F) Any instrument that expels a metallic projectile, such as a BB or pellet, through the force of air pressure, CO2 pressure, or spring action, or any spot marker gun or paint gun.
(G) Any ammunition as defined in Sections 16150 and 16650.
(H) Any explosive as defined in Section 12000 of the Health and Safety Code.
(b) Subdivision (a) shall not apply to, or affect, any of the following:
(1) A duly appointed peace officer as defined in Chapter 4.5 (commencing with Section 830) of Title 3 of Part 2, a retired peace officer with authorization to carry concealed weapons as described in Article 2 (commencing with Section 25450) of Chapter 2 of Division 5 of Title 4 of Part 6, a full-time paid peace officer of another state or the federal government who is carrying out official duties while in California, or any person summoned by any of these officers to assist in making arrests or preserving the peace while he or she is actually engaged in assisting the officer.
(2) A person holding a valid license to carry the firearm pursuant to Chapter 4 (commencing with Section 26150) of Division 5 of Title 4 of Part 6, and who has permission granted by the Chief Sergeants at Arms of the State Assembly and the State Senate to possess a concealed weapon upon the premises described in subdivision (a).
(3) A person who has permission granted by the Chief Sergeants at Arms of the State Assembly and the State Senate to possess a weapon upon the premises described in subdivision (a).
(c) (1) Nothing in this section shall preclude prosecution under Chapter 2 (commencing with Section 29800) or Chapter 3 (commencing with Section 29900) of Division 9 of Title 4 of Part 6 of this code, Section 8100 or 8103 of the Welfare and Institutions Code, or any other law with a penalty greater than is set forth in this section.
(2) The provisions of this section are cumulative, and shall not be construed as restricting the application of any other law. However, an act or omission punishable in different ways by different provisions of law shall not be punished under more than one provision.
(Amended by Stats. 2013, Ch. 76, Sec. 145.5. (AB 383) Effective January 1, 2014.)

171d.
Any person, except a duly appointed peace officer as defined in Chapter 4.5 (commencing with Section 830) of Title 3 of Part 2, a full-time paid peace officer of another state or the federal government who is carrying out official duties while in California, any person summoned by that officer to assist in making arrests or preserving the peace while he or she is actually engaged in assisting the officer, a member of the military forces of this state or of the United States engaged in the performance of his or her duties, a person holding a valid license to carry the firearm pursuant to Chapter 4 (commencing with Section 26150) of Division 5 of Title 4 of Part 6, the Governor or a member of his or her immediate family or a person acting with his or her permission with respect to the Governor's Mansion or any other residence of the Governor, any other constitutional officer or a member of his or her immediate family or a person acting with his or her permission with respect to the officer's residence, or a Member of the Legislature or a member of his or her immediate family or a person acting with his or her permission with respect to the Member's residence, shall be punished by imprisonment in a county jail for not more than one year, by fine of not more than one thousand dollars ($1,000), or by both the fine and imprisonment, or by imprisonment pursuant to subdivision (h) of Section 1170, if he or she does any of the following:
(a) Brings a loaded firearm into, or possesses a loaded firearm within, the Governor's Mansion, or any other residence of the Governor, the residence of any other constitutional officer, or the residence of any Member of the Legislature.
(b) Brings a loaded firearm upon, or possesses a loaded firearm upon, the grounds of the Governor's Mansion or any other residence of the Governor, the residence of any other constitutional officer, or the residence of any Member of the Legislature.
(Amended (as amended by Stats. 2010, Ch. 178) by Stats. 2011, Ch. 15, Sec. 270. (AB 109) Effective April 4, 2011. Amending action operative October 1, 2011, by Sec. 636 of Ch. 15, as amended by Stats. 2011, Ch. 39, Sec. 68. Amended version operative January 1, 2012, pursuant to Stats. 2010, Ch. 178, Sec. 107.)

171e.
A firearm shall be deemed loaded for the purposes of Sections 171c and 171d whenever both the firearm and unexpended ammunition capable of being discharged from such firearm are in the immediate possession of the same person.
In order to determine whether or not a firearm is loaded for the purpose of enforcing Section 171c or 171d, peace officers are authorized to examine any firearm carried by anyone on his person or in a vehicle while in any place or on the grounds of any place in or on which the possession of a loaded firearm is prohibited by Section 171c or 171d. Refusal to allow a peace officer to inspect a firearm pursuant to the provisions of this section constitutes probable cause for arrest for violation of Section 171c or 171d.
(Added by Stats. 1967, Ch. 960.)

171f.
No person or group of persons shall willfully and knowingly:
1. Enter or remain within or upon any part of the chamber of either house of the Legislature unless authorized, pursuant to rules adopted or permission granted by either such house, to enter or remain within or upon a part of the chamber of either such house;
2. Engage in any conduct within the State Capitol which disrupts the orderly conduct of official business.
A violation of this section is a misdemeanor.
As used in this section, "State Capitol" means the building which is intended primarily for use of the legislative department and situated in the area bounded by 10th, L, 15th, and N Streets in the City of Sacramento.
Nothing in this section shall forbid any act of any Member of the Legislature, or any employee of a Member of the Legislature, any officer or employee of the Legislature or any committee or subcommittee thereof, or any officer or employee of either house of the Legislature or any committee or subcommittee thereof, which is performed in the lawful discharge of his official duties.
(Amended by Stats. 1975, Ch. 548.)

171.5.
(a) For purposes of this section:
(1) "Airport" means an airport, with a secured area, that regularly serves an air carrier holding a certificate issued by the United States Secretary of Transportation.
(2) "Passenger vessel terminal" means only that portion of a harbor or port facility, as described in Section 105.105(a)(2) of Title 33 of the Code of Federal Regulations, with a secured area that regularly serves scheduled commuter or passenger operations.
(3) "Sterile area" means a portion of an airport defined in the airport security program to which access generally is controlled through the screening of persons and property, as specified in Section 1540.5 of Title 49 of the Code of Federal Regulations, or a portion of any passenger vessel terminal to which, pursuant to the requirements set forth in Sections 105.255(a)(1), 105.255(c)(1), and 105.260(a) of Title 33 of the Code of Federal Regulations, access is generally controlled in a manner consistent with the passenger vessel terminal's security plan and the MARSEC level in effect at the time.
(b) It is unlawful for any person to knowingly possess, within any sterile area of an airport or a passenger vessel terminal, any of the items listed in subdivision (c).
(c) The following items are unlawful to possess as provided in subdivision (b):
(1) Any firearm.
(2) Any knife with a blade length in excess of four inches, the blade of which is fixed, or is capable of being fixed, in an unguarded position by the use of one or two hands.
(3) Any box cutter or straight razor.
(4) Any metal military practice hand grenade.
(5) Any metal replica hand grenade.
(6) Any plastic replica hand grenade.
(7) Any imitation firearm as defined in Section 417.4.
(8) Any frame, receiver, barrel, or magazine of a firearm.
(9) Any unauthorized tear gas weapon.
(10) Any taser or stun gun, as defined in Section 244.5.
(11) Any instrument that expels a metallic projectile, such as a BB or pellet, through the force of air pressure, CO2 pressure, or spring action, or any spot marker gun or paint gun.
(12) Any ammunition as defined in Section 16150.
(d) Subdivision (b) shall not apply to, or affect, any of the following:
(1) A duly appointed peace officer, as defined in Chapter 4.5 (commencing with Section 830) of Title 3 of Part 2, a retired peace officer with authorization to carry concealed weapons as described in Article 2 (commencing with Section 25450) of Chapter 2 of Division 5 of Title 4 of Part 6, a full-time paid peace officer of another state or the federal government who is carrying out official duties while in California, or any person

summoned by any of these officers to assist in making arrests or preserving the peace while he or she is actually engaged in assisting the officer.

(2) A person who has authorization to possess a weapon specified in subdivision (c), granted in writing by an airport security coordinator who is designated as specified in Section 1542.3 of Title 49 of the Code of Federal Regulations, and who is responsible for the security of the airport.

(3) A person, including an employee of a licensed contract guard service, who has authorization to possess a weapon specified in subdivision (c) granted in writing by a person discharging the duties of Facility Security Officer or Company Security Officer pursuant to an approved United States Coast Guard facility security plan, and who is responsible for the security of the passenger vessel terminal.

(e) A violation of this section is punishable by imprisonment in a county jail for a period not exceeding six months, or by a fine not exceeding one thousand dollars ($1,000), or by both that fine and imprisonment.

(f) The provisions of this section are cumulative, and shall not be construed as restricting the application of any other law. However, an act or omission that is punishable in different ways by this and any other provision of law shall not be punished under more than one provision.

(g) Nothing in this section is intended to affect existing state or federal law regarding the transportation of firearms on airplanes in checked luggage, or the possession of the items listed in subdivision (c) in areas that are not "sterile areas."

(Amended by Stats. 2010, Ch. 178, Sec. 48. (SB 1115) Effective January 1, 2011. Operative January 1, 2012, by Sec. 107 of Ch. 178.)

171.7.

(a) For purposes of this section:

(1) "Public transit facility" means any land, building, or equipment, or any interest therein, including any station on a public transportation route, to which access is controlled in a manner consistent with the public transit authority's security plan, whether or not the operation thereof produces revenue, that has as its primary purpose the operation of a public transit system or the providing of services to the passengers of a public transit system. A public transit system includes the vehicles used in the system, including, but not limited to, motor vehicles, streetcars, trackless trolleys, buses, light rail systems, rapid transit systems, subways, trains, or jitneys, that transport members of the public for hire.

(2) "Sterile area" means any portion of a public transit facility that is generally controlled in a manner consistent with the public transit authority's security plan.

(3) "Firearm" has the same meaning as specified in subdivision (a) of Section 16520.

(b) It is unlawful for any person to knowingly possess within any sterile area of a public transit facility any of the following, if the sterile area is posted with a statement providing reasonable notice that prosecution may result from possession of these items:

(1) Any firearm.

(2) Any imitation firearm as defined in Section 417.4.

(3) Any instrument that expels a metallic projectile, such as a BB or pellet, through the force of air pressure, CO2 pressure, or spring action, or any spot marker gun or paint gun.

(4) Any metal military practice hand grenade.

(5) Any metal replica hand grenade.

(6) Any plastic replica hand grenade.

(7) Any unauthorized tear gas weapon.

(8) Any undetectable knife, as described in Section 17290.

(c) (1) Subdivision (b) shall not apply to, or affect, any of the following:

(A) A duly appointed peace officer, as defined in Chapter 4.5 (commencing with Section 830) of Title 3 of Part 2.

(B) A retired peace officer with authorization to carry concealed weapons as described in Article 2 (commencing with Section 25450) of Chapter 2 of Division 5 of Title 4 of Part 6.

(C) A full-time paid peace officer of another state or the federal government who is carrying out official duties while in California.

(D) A qualified law enforcement officer of another state or the federal government, as permitted under the Law Enforcement Officers Safety Act pursuant to Section 926B or 926C of Title 18 of the United States Code.

(E) Any person summoned by any of the officers listed in subparagraphs (A) to (C), inclusive, to assist in making arrests or preserving the peace while he or she is actually engaged in assisting the officer.

(F) A person who is responsible for the security of the public transit system and who has been authorized by the public transit authority's security coordinator, in writing, to possess a weapon specified in subdivision (b).

(2) Paragraph (1) of subdivision (b) does not apply to or affect a person who is exempt from the prohibition against carrying a handgun pursuant to Section 25400 if the carrying of that handgun is in accordance with the terms and conditions of the exemption specified in Article 2 (commencing with Section 25450) of Chapter 2 of Division 5 of Title 4 of Part 6 or Sections 25615 to 25655, inclusive.

(3) Paragraph (7) of subdivision (b) shall not apply to or affect the possession of a tear gas weapon when possession is permitted pursuant to Division 11 (commencing with Section 22810) of Title 3 of Part 6.

(d) A violation of this section is punishable by imprisonment in a county jail for a period not exceeding six months, or by a fine not exceeding one thousand dollars ($1,000), or by both that fine and imprisonment.

(e) The provisions of this section are cumulative, and shall not be construed as restricting the application of any other law. However, an act or omission that is punishable in different ways by this and any other provision of law shall not be punished under more than one provision.

(f) This section does not prevent prosecution under any other provision of law that may provide a greater punishment.

(g) This section shall be interpreted so as to be consistent with Section 926A of Title 18 of the United States Code.

(Amended by Stats. 2011, Ch. 285, Sec. 11. (AB 1402) Effective January 1, 2012.)

172.

(a) Every person who, within one-half mile of the land belonging to this state upon which any state prison, or within 1,900 feet of the land belonging to this state upon which any Youth Authority institution is situated, or within one mile of the grounds belonging to the University of California, at Berkeley, or within one mile of the grounds belonging to the University of California at Santa Barbara, as such grounds existed as of January 1, 1961, or within one mile of the grounds belonging to Fresno State College, as such grounds existed as of January 1, 1959, or within three miles of the University Farm at Davis, or within 1½ miles of any building actually occupied as a home, retreat, or asylum for ex-soldiers, sailors, and marines of the Army and Navy of the United States, established or to be established by this state, or by the United States within this state, or within the State Capitol, or within the limits of the grounds adjacent and belonging thereto, sells or exposes for sale, any alcoholic beverage, is guilty of a misdemeanor, and upon conviction thereof shall be punished by a fine of not less than one hundred dollars ($100), or by imprisonment for not less than 50 days or by both such fine and imprisonment, in the discretion of the court.

(b) The provision of subdivision (a) of this section prohibiting the sale or exposure for sale of any alcoholic beverage within 1,900 feet of the land belonging to this state upon which any Youth Authority institution is situated shall not apply with respect to the Fred C. Nelles School for Boys.

(c) Except within the State Capitol or the limits of the grounds adjacent and belonging thereto, as mentioned in subdivision (a) of this section, the provisions of this section

shall not apply to the sale or exposing or offering for sale of ale, porter, wine, similar fermented malt or vinous liquor or fruit juice containing one-half of 1 percent or more of alcohol by volume and not more than 3.2 percent of alcohol by weight nor the sale or exposing or offering for sale of beer.

(d) Distances provided in this section shall be measured not by airline but by following the shortest highway or highways as defined in Section 360 of the Vehicle Code connecting the points in question. In measuring distances from the Folsom State Prison and the eastern facilities of the California Institution for Men at Chino and Youth Training School, the measurement shall start at the entrance gate.

(e) The provision of subdivision (a) prohibiting the sale or exposure for sale of any alcoholic beverage within 1½ miles of any building actually occupied as a home, retreat, or asylum for ex-soldiers, sailors, and marines of the Army and Navy of the United States shall not apply to the Veterans' Home at Yountville, Napa County, California.

(f) The prohibition in subdivision (a) on the sale or exposure for sale of any alcoholic beverage within the State Capitol or within the limits of the grounds adjacent and belonging thereto does not apply with respect to an event that is held on those grounds if all of the following conditions are met:

(1) The event is organized and operated by a nonprofit organization that is located in the City of Sacramento for purposes of increasing awareness of the Sacramento region and promoting education about the food and wine of the Sacramento region.

(2) Tickets for the event are sold on a presale basis only and are not available for sale at the event.

(3) Each attendee has purchased a ticket for the event, regardless of whether the attendee consumes any food or alcohol at the event.

(4) Alcohol is not sold at the event, and any orders or any other activities that would constitute exposure for sale of alcoholic beverages do not occur at the event, except as authorized by this subdivision.

(Amended by Stats. 2017, Ch. 224, Sec. 1. (AB 400) Effective September 11, 2017.)

172a.

Every person who, within one and one-half miles of the university grounds or campus, upon which are located the principal administrative offices of any university having an enrollment of more than 1,000 students, more than 500 of whom reside or lodge upon such university grounds or campus, sells or exposes for sale, any intoxicating liquor, is guilty of a misdemeanor; provided, however, that the provisions of this section shall not apply to nor prohibit the sale of any of said liquors by any regularly licensed pharmacist who shall maintain a fixed place of business in said territory, upon the written prescription of a physician regularly licensed to practice medicine under the laws of the State of California when such prescription is dated by the physician issuing it, contains the name of the person for whom the prescription is written, and is filled for such person only and within 48 hours of its date; provided further, that the provisions of this section shall not apply to nor prohibit the sale of any of said liquors for chemical or mechanical purposes; provided further, that the provisions of this section shall not apply to nor prohibit the sale or exposing or offering for sale of ale, porter, wine, similar fermented malt, or vinous liquor or fruit juice containing one-half of 1 percent or more of alcohol by volume and not more than 3.2 percent of alcohol by weight nor the sale or exposing or offering for sale of beer.

In measuring distances from the university grounds or campus of any such university, such distances shall not be measured by airline but by following the shortest road or roads connecting the points in question. With respect to Leland Stanford Junior University measurements from the university grounds or campus shall be by airline measurement.

Any license issued and in effect in the City and County of San Francisco on the effective date of the amendment of this section enacted at the 1961 Regular Session of the Legislature may be transferred to any location in the City and County of San Francisco.

(Amended by Stats. 1965, Ch. 1588.)

172b.

1. Every person who, within one and one-half miles of the boundaries of the grounds belonging to the University of California at Los Angeles on which the principal administrative offices of the university are located, as such boundaries were established as of July 1, 1959, sells or exposes for sale any intoxicating liquor, is guilty of a misdemeanor, and upon conviction thereof shall be punished by a fine of not less than one hundred dollars ($100), or by imprisonment for not less than 50 days, or by both such fine and imprisonment, in the discretion of the court.

2. The provisions of this section shall not apply to the sale or exposing or offering for sale of ale, porter, wine, similar fermented malt or vinous liquor or fruit juice containing one-half of 1 percent or more of alcohol by volume and not more than 3.2 percent of alcohol by weight nor the sale or exposing or offering for sale of beer.

3. Distances provided in this section shall be measured not by airline but by following the shortest road or roads connecting the points in question.

(Amended by Stats. 1965, Ch. 1588.)

172c.

Section 172a shall not apply to the sale at auction of alcoholic beverages by a nonprofit organization at the California Science Center premises located at Exposition Park, Los Angeles, California.

(Amended by Stats. 1996, Ch. 841, Sec. 15. Effective January 1, 1997.)

172d.

1. Every person who, within one mile of that portion of the grounds at Riverside (hereinafter described) belonging to the University of California, that will be used by the College of Letters and Sciences, sells, or exposes for sale, any intoxicating liquor, is guilty of a misdemeanor, and upon conviction thereof shall be punished by a fine of not less than one hundred dollars ($100), or by imprisonment for not less than 50 days or by both such fine and imprisonment in the discretion of the court.

2. The provisions of this section shall not apply to the sale or exposing or offering for sale of ale, porter, wine, similar fermented malt or vinous liquor or fruit juice containing one-half of 1 percent or more of alcohol by volume and not more than 3.2 percent of alcohol by weight nor the sale or exposing or offering for sale of beer.

3. Distances provided in this section shall be measured not by air line but by following the shortest vehicular road or roads connecting the points in question.

4. The portion of the grounds of the University of California referred to in paragraph 1 are situated in the County of Riverside and more particularly described as follows: beginning at the intersection of Canyon Crest Drive and U.S. Highway 60, thence southeasterly along said highway to a point opposite the intersection of said U.S. Highway 60 and Pennsylvania Avenue, thence northeasterly following centerline of present drive into University campus, thence continuing north along said centerline of drive on west side of Citrus Experiment Station buildings to a point intersecting the present east-west road running east from intersection of Canyon Crest Drive and U.S. Highway 60, thence east 500 feet more or less, thence north 1,300 feet more or less, thence east to intersection of east boundary of the Regents of the University of California property (Valencia Hill Drive), thence north along said east boundary to the north boundary of the Regents of the University of California property (Linden Street), thence west along said north boundary to the west boundary of the Regents of the University of California property (Canyon Crest Drive) thence south along said west boundary to the point of beginning.

(Amended by Stats. 1972, Ch. 1241.)

172e.

The provisions of Sections 172, 172a, 172b, 172d, and 172g of this code shall not apply to the sale or the exposing or offering for sale of alcoholic beverages by an on-sale licensee under the Alcoholic Beverage Control Act within premises licensed as a bona fide public eating place as provided in the Constitution and as defined in the

Alcoholic Beverage Control Act (commencing at Section 23000, Business and Professions Code), or within premises licensed as a club as defined in Articles 4 and 5 of Chapter 3 of the Alcoholic Beverage Control Act, provided that such club shall have been in existence for not less than 5 years, have a membership of 300 or more, and serves meals daily to its members, or by the holder of a caterer's permit under the provisions of Section 23399 of the Business and Professions Code in connection with the serving of bona fide meals as defined in Section 23038 of the Business and Professions Code, and the provisions of such sections shall not be construed so as to preclude the Department of Alcoholic Beverage Control from issuing licenses for bona fide public eating places within the areas prescribed by the sections. The provisions of this section shall not permit the issuance of licenses to fraternities, sororities, or other student organizations.
(Amended by Stats. 1973, Ch. 599.)
172f.
The provisions of Sections 172, 172a, 172b, 172d, and 172g of this code shall not apply to the sale or the exposing or offering for sale of any intoxicating liquor in any premises within the areas prescribed by said sections for which a license was issued under the Alcoholic Beverage Control Act (Division 9 (commencing with Section 23000), Business and Professions Code) and is in effect on the effective date of this section or on the effective date of any amendment to Section 172g specifying an additional institution, or in any licensed premises which may become included in such a prescribed area because of the extension of the boundaries of any of the institutions mentioned in said sections or because of the increased enrollment or number of resident students at any of such institutions.
Any such licenses may be transferred from person to person, and may be transferred from premises to premises if the premises to which the license is transferred are not located nearer to the boundaries of the institution, as they exist on the date of the transfer, than the premises from which the license is transferred, except that such license may be transferred once from premises to premises located nearer by not more than 300 feet to the boundaries of the institution as they exist on the date of transfer than the premises from which the license is transferred. If a license is transferred pursuant to this section from premises to premises located nearer by not more than 300 feet to the boundaries of the institution as they exist on the date of the transfer than the premises from which the license is transferred, such license shall not be thereafter transferred to any other premises located nearer to the boundaries of the institution as they exist on the date of the transfer than the premises from which the license is transferred.
(Amended by Stats. 1976, Ch. 778.)
172g.
(a) Every person who, within one-half mile by air line from the intersection of Sierra Vista, Pierce, and Campus Drive streets at the entrance to La Sierra College in the City of Riverside, or within one mile of the grounds or campus of Loma Linda University in the County of San Bernardino, or within one mile of the grounds of the University of Santa Clara in the City of Santa Clara, sells, or exposes for sale, any intoxicating liquor, is guilty of a misdemeanor, and upon conviction thereof shall be punished by a fine of not less than one hundred dollars ($100), or by imprisonment in the county jail of not less than 50 days nor more than one year, or by both that fine and imprisonment in the discretion of the court.
(b) The provisions of this section shall not apply to the sale or exposing or offering for sale of ale, porter, wine, similar fermented malt or vinous liquor or fruit juice containing one-half of 1 percent or more of alcohol by volume and not more than 3.2 percent of alcohol by weight nor the sale or exposing or offering for sale of beer.
(c) Distances provided in this section shall be measured not by air line but by following the shortest road or roads connecting the points in question except those applying to La Sierra College.
(Amended by Stats. 2013, Ch. 43, Sec. 1. (SB 120) Effective June 28, 2013.)
172h.
The provisions of Sections 172, 172a, 172b, 172d and 172g of this code shall not be applied to prohibit the sale or the exposing or offering for sale of any intoxicating liquor in, or the issuance of an alcoholic beverage license for, any premises because a university has constructed and occupied since January 1, 1960, or in the future constructs, dormitories for its students which has resulted or results in the premises being prohibited by the foregoing sections from selling, exposing or offering such liquor for sale because the premises are or become thereby within the area prescribed by these sections.
(Added by Stats. 1965, Ch. 1309.)
172j.
The provisions of Sections 172, 172a, 172b, 172d, and 172g shall not apply to the sale or exposing for sale of any intoxicating liquor on the premises of, and by the holder or agent of, a holder of a retail package off-sale general license or retail package off-sale beer and wine license issued under the Alcoholic Beverage Control Act (Division 9 (commencing with Section 23000), Business and Professions Code).
(Added by Stats. 1973, Ch. 210.)
172l.
The provisions of Section 172a shall not apply to the sale or offering for sale of any intoxicating liquor on the premises of, and by the holder or agent of a holder of, a retail off-sale license, as defined in Section 23394 of the Business and Professions Code, outside one mile of the closest building of the Claremont Colleges to these premises; nor shall the provisions of Section 172a apply to the sale or offering for sale of any beer, or wine, or both, on the premises of, and by the holder or agent of a holder of, a retail package off-sale beer and wine license, as defined in Section 23393 of the Business and Professions Code, outside 2,000 feet of the closest building of the Claremont Colleges to these premises.
Distance provided in this section shall be measured not by air line but by following the shortest road or roads connecting the points in question.
(Amended by Stats. 1973, Ch. 224.)
172m.
The provisions of Section 172a shall not apply to the sale or the exposing or offering for sale of alcoholic beverages at premises licensed under any type of on-sale license issued pursuant to Division 9 (commencing with Section 23000) of the Business and Professions Code, which premises are located off of the grounds or campus of Leland Stanford Junior University near the City of Palo Alto.
(Added by Stats. 1970, Ch. 1442.)
172n.
The provisions of Sections 172a and 172b shall not apply to the sale or exposing or offering for sale of alcoholic beverages by any off-sale licensee under the Alcoholic Beverage Control Act situated more than 2,000 feet of the boundaries of the grounds belonging to the University of California at Los Angeles on which the principal administrative offices of the university are located, as such boundaries were established as of July 1, 1959, provided the licensee has conducted a retail grocery business and has held an off-sale beer and wine license at the same location for at least 15 years.
Distances provided in this section shall be measured not by airline but by following the shortest road or roads connecting the points in question.
(Added by Stats. 1973, Ch. 210.)
172o.
The provisions of Sections 172, 172a, 172b, 172d, and 172g shall not apply to the sale of wine for consumption off the premises where sold when the wine is sold at a bona fide public eating place by the holder of an on-sale general alcoholic beverage license or an on-sale beer and wine license issued under the Alcoholic Beverage Control Act (Division 9 (commencing with Section 23000) of the Business and Professions Code).
(Added by Stats. 1985, Ch. 267, Sec. 1.)
172p.
The provisions of Section 172a shall not apply to the sale or exposing or offering for sale of beer or wine by any on-sale licensee under the Alcoholic Beverage Control Act whose licensed premises are situated more than 1,200 feet from the boundaries of Whittier College in the City of Whittier.
(Added by Stats. 1997, Ch. 774, Sec. 6. Effective January 1, 1998.)
172.1.
No provision of law shall prevent the possession or use of wine on any state university, state college or community college premises solely for use in experimentation in or instruction of viticulture, enology, domestic science or home economics.
(Amended by Stats. 1970, Ch. 102.)
172.3.
The provisions of Section 172a shall not apply to the sale or exposing or offering for sale of any alcoholic beverages on the premises of, and by the holder or agent of a holder of, any off-sale license situated within 1 1/2 miles from the grounds of the University of Redlands.
(Added by Stats. 1977, Ch. 760.)
172.5.
The provisions of Sections 172 and 172a of this code shall not apply to the sale or exposing or offering for sale of alcoholic beverages by a licensee under the Alcoholic Beverage Control Act within the premises occupied by any bona fide club which is situated within one mile of the grounds belonging to the University of California at Berkeley, if the club meets all of the following requirements:
(a) The membership in the club shall be limited to male American citizens over the age of 21 years.
(b) The club shall have been organized and have existed in the City of Berkeley for not less than 35 years continuously.
(c) The club shall have a bona fide membership of not less than 500 members.
(d) The premises occupied by the club are owned by the club, or by a corporation, at least 75 percent of whose capital stock is owned by the club, and have a value of not less than one hundred thousand dollars ($100,000).
(Amended by Stats. 1967, Ch. 138.)
172.6.
The provisions of Section 172 of this code shall not apply to the sale, gift, or exposing or offering for sale of alcoholic beverages by a licensee under the Alcoholic Beverage Control Act within the premises occupied by any bona fide club which is situated within 2,000 feet of San Quentin Prison in Marin County, provided the club meets all the following requirements:
(a) The club shall have been organized and have existed in the County of Marin for not less than 25 years continuously.
(b) The club shall have a bona fide membership of not less than 1,000 persons.
(c) The premises occupied by the club are owned by the club or by club members.
(Added by Stats. 1965, Ch. 1452.)
172.7.
The provisions of Section 172a shall not apply to the sale, gift, or exposing or offering for sale of alcoholic beverages by a licensee under the Alcoholic Beverage Control Act within the premises occupied by any bona fide club which is situated within one mile of the campus of Whittier College in the City of Whittier, or one mile or more from the campus of Leland Stanford Junior University near the City of Palo Alto, provided the club meets all the following requirements:
(a) The club shall have been organized and have existed for not less than 10 years continuously.
(b) The club shall have a bona fide membership of not less than 350 persons.
(c) The club shall own the building which it occupies.
(Amended by Stats. 1970, Ch. 1285.)
172.8.
The provisions of Section 172a shall not apply to the sale of alcoholic beverages for consumption on the premises, by a nonprofit organization at a municipally owned conference center located more than one but less than 1 1/2 miles from the California Institute of Technology in Pasadena.
(Added by Stats. 1975, Ch. 88.)
172.9.
The word "university," when used in this chapter with reference to the sale, exposing or offering for sale, of alcoholic beverages, means an institution which has the authority to grant an academic graduate degree.
(Amended by Stats. 1965, Ch. 1588.)
172.95.
Sections 172 to 172.9, inclusive, do not apply to sales to wholesalers or retailers by licensed winegrowers, brandy manufacturers, beer manufacturers, distilled spirits manufacturers' agents, distilled spirits manufacturers, or wholesalers.
(Added by Stats. 1965, Ch. 710.)
173.
Every Captain, Master of a vessel, or other person, who willfully imports, brings, or sends, or causes or procures to be brought or sent, into this State, any person who is a foreign convict of any crime which, if committed within this State, would be punishable therein (treason and misprision of treason excepted), or who is delivered or sent to him from any prison or place of confinement in any place without this State, is guilty of a misdemeanor.
(Enacted 1872.)
175.
Every individual person of the classes referred to in Section 173, brought to or landed within this state contrary to the provisions of such section, renders the person bringing or landing liable to a separate prosecution and penalty.
(Amended by Stats. 1972, Ch. 637.)
181.
Every person who holds, or attempts to hold, any person in involuntary servitude, or assumes, or attempts to assume, rights of ownership over any person, or who sells, or attempts to sell, any person to another, or receives money or anything of value, in consideration of placing any person in the custody, or under the power or control of another, or who buys, or attempts to buy, any person, or pays money, or delivers anything of value, to another, in consideration of having any person placed in his or her custody, or under his or her power or control, or who knowingly aids or assists in any manner any one thus offending, is punishable by imprisonment pursuant to subdivision (h) of Section 1170 for two, three or four years.
(Amended by Stats. 2011, Ch. 15, Sec. 271. (AB 109) Effective April 4, 2011. Operative October 1, 2011, by Sec. 636 of Ch. 15, as amended by Stats. 2011, Ch. 39, Sec. 68.)

CHAPTER 8. Conspiracy [182 - [185.]]

(Chapter 8 enacted 1872.)
182.
(a) If two or more persons conspire:
(1) To commit any crime.

(2) Falsely and maliciously to indict another for any crime, or to procure another to be charged or arrested for any crime.
(3) Falsely to move or maintain any suit, action, or proceeding.
(4) To cheat and defraud any person of any property, by any means which are in themselves criminal, or to obtain money or property by false pretenses or by false promises with fraudulent intent not to perform those promises.
(5) To commit any act injurious to the public health, to public morals, or to pervert or obstruct justice, or the due administration of the laws.
(6) To commit any crime against the person of the President or Vice President of the United States, the Governor of any state or territory, any United States justice or judge, or the secretary of any of the executive departments of the United States.
They are punishable as follows:
When they conspire to commit any crime against the person of any official specified in paragraph (6), they are guilty of a felony and are punishable by imprisonment pursuant to subdivision (h) of Section 1170 for five, seven, or nine years.
When they conspire to commit any other felony, they shall be punishable in the same manner and to the same extent as is provided for the punishment of that felony. If the felony is one for which different punishments are prescribed for different degrees, the jury or court which finds the defendant guilty thereof shall determine the degree of the felony the defendant conspired to commit. If the degree is not so determined, the punishment for conspiracy to commit the felony shall be that prescribed for the lesser degree, except in the case of conspiracy to commit murder, in which case the punishment shall be that prescribed for murder in the first degree.
If the felony is conspiracy to commit two or more felonies which have different punishments and the commission of those felonies constitute but one offense of conspiracy, the penalty shall be that prescribed for the felony which has the greater maximum term.
When they conspire to do an act described in paragraph (4), they shall be punishable by imprisonment in a county jail for not more than one year, or by imprisonment pursuant to subdivision (h) of Section 1170, or by a fine not exceeding ten thousand dollars ($10,000), or by both that imprisonment and fine.
When they conspire to do any of the other acts described in this section, they shall be punishable by imprisonment in a county jail for not more than one year, or pursuant to subdivision (h) of Section 1170, or by a fine not exceeding ten thousand dollars ($10,000), or by both that imprisonment and fine. When they receive a felony conviction for conspiring to commit identity theft, as defined in Section 530.5, the court may impose a fine of up to twenty-five thousand dollars ($25,000).
All cases of conspiracy may be prosecuted and tried in the superior court of any county in which any overt act tending to effect the conspiracy shall be done.
(b) Upon a trial for conspiracy, in a case where an overt act is necessary to constitute the offense, the defendant cannot be convicted unless one or more overt acts are expressly alleged in the indictment or information, nor unless one of the acts alleged is proved; but other overt acts not alleged may be given in evidence.
(Amended by Stats. 2011, Ch. 15, Sec. 272. (AB 109) Effective April 4, 2011. Operative October 1, 2011, by Sec. 636 of Ch. 15, as amended by Stats. 2011, Ch. 39, Sec. 68.)
182.5.
Notwithstanding subdivisions (a) or (b) of Section 182, any person who actively participates in any criminal street gang, as defined in subdivision (f) of Section 186.22, with knowledge that its members engage in or have engaged in a pattern of criminal gang activity, as defined in subdivision (e) of Section 186.22, and who willfully promotes, furthers, assists, or benefits from any felonious criminal conduct by members of that gang is guilty of conspiracy to commit that felony and may be punished as specified in subdivision (a) of Section 182.
(Added March 7, 2000, by initiative Proposition 21, Sec. 3. Note: Prop. 21 is titled the Gang Violence and Juvenile Crime Prevention Act of 1998.)
183.
No conspiracies, other than those enumerated in the preceding section, are punishable criminally.
(Enacted 1872.)
184.
No agreement amounts to a conspiracy, unless some act, beside such agreement, be done within this state to effect the object thereof, by one or more of the parties to such agreement and the trial of cases of conspiracy may be had in any county in which any such act be done.
(Amended by Stats. 1919, Ch. 125.)
[185.]
Section One Hundred and Eighty-five. It shall be unlawful for any person to wear any mask, false whiskers, or any personal disguise (whether complete or partial) for the purpose of:
One—Evading or escaping discovery, recognition, or identification in the commission of any public offense.
Two—Concealment, flight, or escape, when charged with, arrested for, or convicted of, any public offense. Any person violating any of the provisions of this section shall be deemed guilty of a misdemeanor.
(Amended by Code Amendments 1873-74, Ch. 614.)

CHAPTER 9. Criminal Profiteering [186 - 186.8]

(Chapter 9 added by Stats. 1982, Ch. 1281, Sec. 1.)
186.
This act may be cited as the "California Control of Profits of Organized Crime Act."
(Added by Stats. 1982, Ch. 1281, Sec. 1.)
186.1.
The Legislature hereby finds and declares that an effective means of punishing and deterring criminal activities of organized crime is through the forfeiture of profits acquired and accumulated as a result of such criminal activities. It is the intent of the Legislature that the "California Control of Profits of Organized Crime Act" be used by prosecutors to punish and deter only such activities.
(Added by Stats. 1982, Ch. 1281, Sec. 1.)
186.2.
For purposes of this chapter, the following definitions apply:
(a) "Criminal profiteering activity" means any act committed or attempted or any threat made for financial gain or advantage, which act or threat may be charged as a crime under any of the following sections:
(1) Arson, as defined in Section 451.
(2) Bribery, as defined in Sections 67, 67.5, and 68.
(3) Child pornography or exploitation, as defined in subdivision (b) of Section 311.2, or Section 311.3 or 311.4, which may be prosecuted as a felony.
(4) Felonious assault, as defined in Section 245.
(5) Embezzlement, as defined in Sections 424 and 503.
(6) Extortion, as defined in Section 518.
(7) Forgery, as defined in Section 470.
(8) Gambling, as defined in Sections 337a to 337f, inclusive, and Section 337i, except the activities of a person who participates solely as an individual bettor.
(9) Kidnapping, as defined in Section 207.
(10) Mayhem, as defined in Section 203.
(11) Murder, as defined in Section 187.
(12) Pimping and pandering, as defined in Section 266.
(13) Receiving stolen property, as defined in Section 496.
(14) Robbery, as defined in Section 211.
(15) Solicitation of crimes, as defined in Section 653f.
(16) Grand theft, as defined in Section 487 or subdivision (a) of Section 487a.
(17) Trafficking in controlled substances, as defined in Sections 11351, 11352, and 11353 of the Health and Safety Code.
(18) Violation of the laws governing corporate securities, as defined in Section 25541 of the Corporations Code.
(19) Offenses contained in Chapter 7.5 (commencing with Section 311) of Title 9, relating to obscene matter, or in Chapter 7.6 (commencing with Section 313) of Title 9, relating to harmful matter that may be prosecuted as a felony.
(20) Presentation of a false or fraudulent claim, as defined in Section 550.
(21) False or fraudulent activities, schemes, or artifices, as described in Section 14107 of the Welfare and Institutions Code.
(22) Money laundering, as defined in Section 186.10.
(23) Offenses relating to the counterfeit of a registered mark, as specified in Section 350, or offenses relating to piracy, as specified in Section 653w.
(24) Offenses relating to the unauthorized access to computers, computer systems, and computer data, as specified in Section 502.
(25) Conspiracy to commit any of the crimes listed above, as defined in Section 182.
(26) Subdivision (a) of Section 186.22, or a felony subject to enhancement as specified in subdivision (b) of Section 186.22.
(27) Offenses related to fraud or theft against the state's beverage container recycling program, including, but not limited to, those offenses specified in this subdivision and those criminal offenses specified in the California Beverage Container Recycling and Litter Reduction Act, commencing at Section 14500 of the Public Resources Code.
(28) Human trafficking, as defined in Section 236.1.
(29) Any crime in which the perpetrator induces, encourages, or persuades a person under 18 years of age to engage in a commercial sex act. For purposes of this paragraph, a commercial sex act means any sexual conduct on account of which anything of value is given or received by any person.
(30) Any crime in which the perpetrator, through force, fear, coercion, deceit, violence, duress, menace, or threat of unlawful injury to the victim or to another person, causes a person under 18 years of age to engage in a commercial sex act. For purposes of this paragraph, a commercial sex act means any sexual conduct on account of which anything of value is given or received by any person.
(31) Theft of personal identifying information, as defined in Section 530.5.
(32) Offenses involving the theft of a motor vehicle, as specified in Section 10851 of the Vehicle Code.
(33) Abduction or procurement by fraudulent inducement for prostitution, as defined in Section 266a.
(34) Offenses relating to insurance fraud, as specified in Sections 2106, 2108, 2109, 2110, 2110.3, 2110.5, 2110.7, and 2117 of the Unemployment Insurance Code.
(b) (1) "Pattern of criminal profiteering activity" means engaging in at least two incidents of criminal profiteering, as defined by this chapter, that meet the following requirements:
(A) Have the same or a similar purpose, result, principals, victims, or methods of commission, or are otherwise interrelated by distinguishing characteristics.
(B) Are not isolated events.
(C) Were committed as a criminal activity of organized crime.
(2) Acts that would constitute a "pattern of criminal profiteering activity" may not be used by a prosecuting agency to seek the remedies provided by this chapter unless the underlying offense occurred after the effective date of this chapter and the prior act occurred within 10 years, excluding any period of imprisonment, of the commission of the underlying offense. A prior act may not be used by a prosecuting agency to seek remedies provided by this chapter if a prosecution for that act resulted in an acquittal.
(c) "Prosecuting agency" means the Attorney General or the district attorney of any county.
(d) "Organized crime" means crime that is of a conspiratorial nature and that is either of an organized nature and seeks to supply illegal goods or services such as narcotics, prostitution, pimping and pandering, loan-sharking, counterfeiting of a registered mark in violation of Section 350, the piracy of a recording or audiovisual work in violation of Section 653w, gambling, and pornography, or that, through planning and coordination of individual efforts, seeks to conduct the illegal activities of arson for profit, hijacking, insurance fraud, smuggling, operating vehicle theft rings, fraud against the beverage container recycling program, embezzlement, securities fraud, insurance fraud in violation of the provisions listed in paragraph (34) of subdivision (a), grand theft, money laundering, forgery, or systematically encumbering the assets of a business for the purpose of defrauding creditors. "Organized crime" also means crime committed by a criminal street gang, as defined in subdivision (f) of Section 186.22. "Organized crime" also means false or fraudulent activities, schemes, or artifices, as described in Section 14107 of the Welfare and Institutions Code, and the theft of personal identifying information, as defined in Section 530.5.
(e) "Underlying offense" means an offense enumerated in subdivision (a) for which the defendant is being prosecuted.
(Amended by Stats. 2016, Ch. 86, Sec. 221. (SB 1171) Effective January 1, 2017.)
186.3.
(a) In any case in which a person is alleged to have been engaged in a pattern of criminal profiteering activity, upon a conviction of the underlying offense, the assets listed in subdivisions (b) and (c) shall be subject to forfeiture upon proof of the provisions of subdivision (d) of Section 186.5.
(b) Any property interest whether tangible or intangible, acquired through a pattern of criminal profiteering activity.
(c) All proceeds of a pattern of criminal profiteering activity, which property shall include all things of value that may have been received in exchange for the proceeds immediately derived from the pattern of criminal profiteering activity.
(Added by Stats. 1982, Ch. 1281, Sec. 1.)
186.4.
(a) The prosecuting agency shall, in conjunction with the criminal proceeding, file a petition of forfeiture with the superior court of the county in which the defendant has been charged with the underlying criminal offense, which shall allege that the defendant has engaged in a pattern of criminal profiteering activity, including the acts or threats chargeable as crimes and the property forfeitable pursuant to Section 186.3. The prosecuting agency shall make service of process of a notice regarding that petition upon every individual who may have a property interest in the alleged proceeds, which notice shall state that any interested party may file a verified claim with the superior court stating the amount of their claimed interest and an affirmation or denial of the prosecuting agency's allegation. If the notices cannot be given by registered mail or personal delivery, the notices shall be published for at least three successive weeks in a newspaper of general circulation in the county where the property is located. If the property alleged to be subject to forfeiture is real property, the prosecuting agency shall, at the time of filing the petition of forfeiture, record a lis pendens in each county in which the real property is situated which specifically identifies the real property alleged to be subject to forfeiture. The judgment of forfeiture shall not affect the interest in real property of any third party which was acquired prior to the recording of the lis pendens.
(b) All notices shall set forth the time within which a claim of interest in the property seized is required to be filed pursuant to Section 186.5.

(Amended by Stats. 1983, Ch. 208, Sec. 1.)

186.5.

(a) Any person claiming an interest in the property or proceeds may, at any time within 30 days from the date of the first publication of the notice of seizure, or within 30 days after receipt of actual notice, file with the superior court of the county in which the action is pending a verified claim stating his or her interest in the property or proceeds. A verified copy of the claim shall be given by the claimant to the Attorney General or district attorney, as appropriate.

(b) (1) If, at the end of the time set forth in subdivision (a), an interested person, other than the defendant, has not filed a claim, the court, upon motion, shall declare that the person has defaulted upon his or her alleged interest, and it shall be subject to forfeiture upon proof of the provisions of subdivision (d).

(2) The defendant may admit or deny that the property is subject to forfeiture pursuant to the provisions of this chapter. If the defendant fails to admit or deny or to file a claim of interest in the property or proceeds, the court shall enter a response of denial on behalf of the defendant.

(c) (1) The forfeiture proceeding shall be set for hearing in the superior court in which the underlying criminal offense will be tried.

(2) If the defendant is found guilty of the underlying offense, the issue of forfeiture shall be promptly tried, either before the same jury or before a new jury in the discretion of the court, unless waived by the consent of all parties.

(d) At the forfeiture hearing, the prosecuting agency shall have the burden of establishing beyond a reasonable doubt that the defendant was engaged in a pattern of criminal profiteering activity and that the property alleged in the petition comes within the provisions of subdivision (b) or (c) of Section 186.3.

(Added by Stats. 1982, Ch. 1281, Sec. 1.)

186.6.

(a) Concurrent with, or subsequent to, the filing of the petition, the prosecuting agency may move the superior court for the following pendente lite orders to preserve the status quo of the property alleged in the petition of forfeiture:

(1) An injunction to restrain all interested parties and enjoin them from transferring, encumbering, hypothecating or otherwise disposing of that property.

(2) Appointment of a receiver to take possession of, care for, manage, and operate the assets and properties so that such property may be maintained and preserved.

(b) No preliminary injunction may be granted or receiver appointed without notice to the interested parties and a hearing to determine that such an order is necessary to preserve the property, pending the outcome of the criminal proceedings, and that there is probable cause to believe that the property alleged in the forfeiture proceedings are proceeds or property interests forfeitable under Section 186.3. However, a temporary restraining order may issue pending that hearing pursuant to the provisions of Section 527 of the Code of Civil Procedure.

(c) Notwithstanding any other provision of law, the court in granting these motions may order a surety bond or undertaking to preserve the property interests of the interested parties.

(d) The court shall, in making its orders, seek to protect the interests of those who may be involved in the same enterprise as the defendant, but who were not involved in the commission of the criminal profiteering activity.

(Added by Stats. 1982, Ch. 1281, Sec. 1.)

186.7.

(a) If the trier of fact at the forfeiture hearing finds that the alleged property or proceeds is forfeitable pursuant to Section 186.3 and the defendant was engaged in a pattern of criminal profiteering activity, the court shall declare that property or proceeds forfeited to the state or local governmental entity, subject to distribution as provided in Section 186.8. No property solely owned by a bona fide purchaser for value shall be subject to forfeiture.

(b) If the trier of fact at the forfeiture hearing finds that the alleged property is forfeitable pursuant to Section 186.3 but does not find that a person holding a valid lien, mortgage, security interest, or interest under a conditional sales contract acquired that interest with actual knowledge that the property was to be used for a purpose for which forfeiture is permitted, and the amount due to that person is less than the appraised value of the property, that person may pay to the state or the local governmental entity which initiated the forfeiture proceeding, the amount of the registered owner's equity, which shall be deemed to be the difference between the appraised value and the amount of the lien, mortgage, security interest, or interest under a conditional sales contract. Upon that payment, the state or local governmental entity shall relinquish all claims to the property. If the holder of the interest elects not to make that payment to the state or local governmental entity, the property shall be deemed forfeited to the state or local governmental entity and the ownership certificate shall be forwarded. The appraised value shall be determined as of the date judgment is entered either by agreement between the legal owner and the governmental entity involved, or if they cannot agree, then by a court-appointed appraiser for the county in which the action is brought. A person holding a valid lien, mortgage, security interest, or interest under a conditional sales contract shall be paid the appraised value of his or her interest.

(c) If the amount due to a person holding a valid lien, mortgage, security interest, or interest under a conditional sales contract is less than the value of the property and the person elects not to make payment to the governmental entity, the property shall be sold at public auction by the Department of General Services or by the local governmental entity which shall provide notice of that sale by one publication in a newspaper published and circulated in the city, community, or locality where the sale is to take place.

(d) Notwithstanding subdivision (c), a county may dispose of any real property forfeited to the county pursuant to this chapter pursuant to Section 25538.5 of the Government Code.

(Amended by Stats. 1992, Ch. 1020, Sec. 3.7. Effective January 1, 1993.)

186.8.

Notwithstanding that no response or claim has been filed pursuant to Section 186.5, in all cases where property is forfeited pursuant to this chapter and, if necessary, sold by the Department of General Services or local governmental entity, the money forfeited or the proceeds of sale shall be distributed by the state or local governmental entity as follows:

(a) To the bona fide or innocent purchaser, conditional sales vendor, or holder of a valid lien, mortgage, or security interest, if any, up to the amount of his or her interest in the property or proceeds, when the court declaring the forfeiture orders a distribution to that person. The court shall endeavor to discover all those lienholders and protect their interests and may, at its discretion, order the proceeds placed in escrow for up to an additional 60 days to ensure that all valid claims are received and processed.

(b) To the Department of General Services or local governmental entity for all expenditures made or incurred by it in connection with the sale of the property, including expenditures for any necessary repairs, storage, or transportation of any property seized under this chapter.

(c) To the General Fund of the state or a general fund of a local governmental entity, whichever prosecutes.

(d) In any case involving a violation of subdivision (b) of Section 311.2, or Section 311.3 or 311.4, in lieu of the distribution of the proceeds provided for by subdivisions (b) and (c), the proceeds shall be deposited in the county children's trust fund, established pursuant to Section 18966 of the Welfare and Institutions Code, of the county that filed the petition of forfeiture. If the county does not have a children's trust fund, the funds shall be deposited in the State Children's Trust Fund, established pursuant to Section 18969 of the Welfare and Institutions Code.

(e) In any case involving crimes against the state beverage container recycling program, in lieu of the distribution of proceeds provided in subdivision (c), the proceeds shall be deposited in the penalty account established pursuant to subdivision (d) of Section 14580 of the Public Resources Code, except that a portion of the proceeds equivalent to the cost of prosecution in the case shall be distributed to the local prosecuting entity that filed the petition of forfeiture.

(f) (1) In any case described in paragraph (29) or (30) of subdivision (a) of Section 186.2, or paragraph (33) of subdivision (a) of Section 186.2 where the victim is a minor, in lieu of the distribution provided for in subdivision (c), the proceeds shall be deposited in the Victim-Witness Assistance Fund to be available for appropriation to fund child sexual exploitation and child sexual abuse victim counseling centers and prevention programs under Section 13837. Fifty percent of the funds deposited in the Victim-Witness Assistance Fund pursuant to this subdivision shall be granted to community-based organizations that serve minor victims of human trafficking.

(2) Notwithstanding paragraph (1), any proceeds specified in paragraph (1) that would otherwise be distributed to the General Fund of the state under subdivision (c) pursuant to a paragraph in subdivision (a) of Section 186.2 other than paragraph (29) or (30) of subdivision (a) of Section 186.2, or paragraph (33) of subdivision (a) of Section 186.2 where the victim is a minor, shall, except as otherwise required by law, continue to be distributed to the General Fund of the state as specified in subdivision (c).

(Amended by Stats. 2012, Ch. 514, Sec. 1. (SB 1133) Effective January 1, 2013.)

CHAPTER 10. Money Laundering [186.9 - 186.10]

(Chapter 10 added by Stats. 1986, Ch. 1039, Sec. 2.)

186.9.

As used in this chapter:

(a) "Conducts" includes, but is not limited to, initiating, concluding, or participating in conducting, initiating, or concluding a transaction.

(b) "Financial institution" means, when located or doing business in this state, any national bank or banking association, state bank or banking association, commercial bank or trust company organized under the laws of the United States or any state, any private bank, industrial savings bank, savings bank or thrift institution, savings and loan association, or building and loan association organized under the laws of the United States or any state, any insured institution as defined in Section 401 of the National Housing Act (12 U.S.C. Sec. 1724(a)), any credit union organized under the laws of the United States or any state, any national banking association or corporation acting under Chapter 6 (commencing with Section 601) of Title 12 of the United States Code, any agency, agent or branch of a foreign bank, any currency dealer or exchange, any person or business engaged primarily in the cashing of checks, any person or business who regularly engages in the issuing, selling, or redeeming of traveler's checks, money orders, or similar instruments, any broker or dealer in securities registered or required to be registered with the Securities and Exchange Commission under the Securities Exchange Act of 1934 or with the Commissioner of Corporations under Part 3 (commencing with Section 25200) of Division 1 of Title 4 of the Corporations Code, any licensed transmitter of funds or other person or business regularly engaged in transmitting funds to a foreign nation for others, any investment banker or investment company, any insurer, any dealer in gold, silver, or platinum bullion or coins, diamonds, emeralds, rubies, or sapphires, any pawnbroker, any telegraph company, any person or business regularly engaged in the delivery, transmittal, or holding of mail or packages, any person or business that conducts a transaction involving the transfer of title to any real property, vehicle, vessel, or aircraft, any personal property broker, any person or business acting as a real property securities dealer within the meaning of Section 10237 of the Business and Professions Code, whether licensed to do so or not, any person or business acting within the meaning and scope of subdivisions (d) and (e) of Section 10131 and Section 10131.1 of the Business and Professions Code, whether licensed to do so or not, any person or business regularly engaged in gaming within the meaning and scope of Section 330, any person or business regularly engaged in pool selling or bookmaking within the meaning and scope of Section 337a, any person or business regularly engaged in horse racing whether licensed to do so or not under the Business and Professions Code, any person or business engaged in the operation of a gambling ship within the meaning and scope of Section 11317, any person or business engaged in controlled gambling within the meaning and scope of subdivision (e) of Section 19805 of the Business and Professions Code, whether registered to do so or not, and any person or business defined as a "bank," "financial agency," or "financial institution" by Section 5312 of Title 31 of the United States Code or Section 103.11 of Title 31 of the Code of Federal Regulations and any successor provisions thereto.

(c) "Transaction" includes the deposit, withdrawal, transfer, bailment, loan, pledge, payment, or exchange of currency, or a monetary instrument, as defined by subdivision (d), or the electronic, wire, magnetic, or manual transfer of funds between accounts by, through, or to, a financial institution as defined by subdivision (b).

(d) "Monetary instrument" means United States currency and coin; the currency, coin, and foreign bank drafts of any foreign country; payment warrants issued by the United States, this state, or any city, county, or city and county of this state or any other political subdivision thereof; any bank check, cashier's check, traveler's check, or money order; any personal check, stock, investment security, or negotiable instrument in bearer form or otherwise in a form in which title thereto passes upon delivery; gold, silver, or platinum bullion or coins; and diamonds, emeralds, rubies, or sapphires. Except for foreign bank drafts and federal, state, county, or city warrants, "monetary instrument" does not include personal checks made payable to the order of a named party which have not been endorsed or which bear restrictive endorsements, and also does not include personal checks which have been endorsed by the named party and deposited by the named party into the named party's account with a financial institution.

(e) "Criminal activity" means a criminal offense punishable under the laws of this state by death, imprisonment in the state prison, or imprisonment pursuant to subdivision (h) of Section 1170 or from a criminal offense committed in another jurisdiction punishable under the laws of that jurisdiction by death or imprisonment for a term exceeding one year.

(f) "Foreign bank draft" means a bank draft or check issued or made out by a foreign bank, savings and loan, casa de cambio, credit union, currency dealer or exchanger, check cashing business, money transmitter, insurance company, investment or private bank, or any other foreign financial institution that provides similar financial services, on an account in the name of the foreign bank or foreign financial institution held at a bank or other financial institution located in the United States or a territory of the United States.

(Amended by Stats. 2012, Ch. 43, Sec. 15. (SB 1023) Effective June 27, 2012.)

186.10.

(a) Any person who conducts or attempts to conduct a transaction or more than one transaction within a seven-day period involving a monetary instrument or instruments of a total value exceeding five thousand dollars ($5,000), or a total value exceeding twenty-five thousand dollars ($25,000) within a 30-day period, through one or more financial institutions (1) with the specific intent to promote, manage, establish, carry on, or facilitate the promotion, management, establishment, or carrying on of any criminal activity, or (2) knowing that the monetary instrument represents the proceeds of, or is derived directly or indirectly from the proceeds of, criminal activity, is guilty of the crime of money laundering. The aggregation periods do not create an obligation for financial institutions to record, report, create, or implement tracking systems or otherwise monitor transactions involving monetary instruments in any time period. In consideration of the constitutional right to counsel afforded by the Sixth Amendment to the United States Constitution and Section 15 of Article I of the California Constitution, when a case involves an attorney who accepts a fee for representing a client in a criminal investigation or proceeding, the prosecution shall additionally be required to prove that the monetary instrument was accepted by the attorney with the intent to disguise or aid in disguising the source of the funds or the nature of the criminal activity.

A violation of this section shall be punished by imprisonment in a county jail for not more than one year or pursuant to subdivision (h) of Section 1170, by a fine of not more than two hundred fifty thousand dollars ($250,000) or twice the value of the property transacted, whichever is greater, or by both that imprisonment and fine. However, for a second or subsequent conviction for a violation of this section, the maximum fine that may be imposed is five hundred thousand dollars ($500,000) or five times the value of the property transacted, whichever is greater.

(b) Notwithstanding any other law, for purposes of this section, each individual transaction conducted in excess of five thousand dollars ($5,000), each series of transactions conducted within a seven-day period that total in excess of five thousand dollars ($5,000), or each series of transactions conducted within a 30-day period that total in excess of twenty-five thousand dollars ($25,000), shall constitute a separate, punishable offense.

(c) (1) Any person who is punished under subdivision (a) by imprisonment pursuant to subdivision (h) of Section 1170 shall also be subject to an additional term of imprisonment pursuant to subdivision (h) of Section 1170 as follows:

(A) If the value of the transaction or transactions exceeds fifty thousand dollars ($50,000) but is less than one hundred fifty thousand dollars ($150,000), the court, in addition to and consecutive to the felony punishment otherwise imposed pursuant to this section, shall impose an additional term of imprisonment of one year.

(B) If the value of the transaction or transactions exceeds one hundred fifty thousand dollars ($150,000) but is less than one million dollars ($1,000,000), the court, in addition to and consecutive to the felony punishment otherwise imposed pursuant to this section, shall impose an additional term of imprisonment of two years.

(C) If the value of the transaction or transactions exceeds one million dollars ($1,000,000), but is less than two million five hundred thousand dollars ($2,500,000), the court, in addition to and consecutive to the felony punishment otherwise imposed pursuant to this section, shall impose an additional term of imprisonment of three years.

(D) If the value of the transaction or transactions exceeds two million five hundred thousand dollars ($2,500,000), the court, in addition to and consecutive to the felony punishment otherwise prescribed by this section, shall impose an additional term of imprisonment of four years.

(2) (A) An additional term of imprisonment as provided for in this subdivision shall not be imposed unless the facts of a transaction or transactions, or attempted transaction or transactions, of a value described in paragraph (1), are charged in the accusatory pleading, and are either admitted to by the defendant or are found to be true by the trier of fact.

(B) An additional term of imprisonment as provided for in this subdivision may be imposed with respect to an accusatory pleading charging multiple violations of this section, regardless of whether any single violation charged in that pleading involves a transaction or attempted transaction of a value covered by paragraph (1), if the violations charged in that pleading arise from a common scheme or plan and the aggregate value of the alleged transactions or attempted transactions is of a value covered by paragraph (1).

(d) All pleadings under this section shall remain subject to the rules of joinder and severance stated in Section 954.

(Amended by Stats. 2011, Ch. 15, Sec. 273. (AB 109) Effective April 4, 2011. Operative October 1, 2011, by Sec. 636 of Ch. 15, as amended by Stats. 2011, Ch. 39, Sec. 68.)

CHAPTER 10.5. Fraud and Embezzlement: Victim Restitution [186.11 - 186.12]

(Chapter 10.5 added by Stats. 1996, Ch. 431, Sec. 2.)

186.11.

(a) (1) Any person who commits two or more related felonies, a material element of which is fraud or embezzlement, which involve a pattern of related felony conduct, and the pattern of related felony conduct involves the taking of, or results in the loss by another person or entity of, more than one hundred thousand dollars ($100,000), shall be punished, upon conviction of two or more felonies in a single criminal proceeding, in addition and consecutive to the punishment prescribed for the felony offenses of which he or she has been convicted, by an additional term of imprisonment in the state prison as specified in paragraph (2) or (3). This enhancement shall be known as the aggravated white collar crime enhancement. The aggravated white collar crime enhancement shall only be imposed once in a single criminal proceeding. For purposes of this section, "pattern of related felony conduct" means engaging in at least two felonies that have the same or similar purpose, result, principals, victims, or methods of commission, or are otherwise interrelated by distinguishing characteristics, and that are not isolated events. For purposes of this section, "two or more related felonies" means felonies committed against two or more separate victims, or against the same victim on two or more separate occasions.

(2) If the pattern of related felony conduct involves the taking of, or results in the loss by another person or entity of, more than five hundred thousand dollars ($500,000), the additional term of punishment shall be two, three, or five years in the state prison.

(3) If the pattern of related felony conduct involves the taking of, or results in the loss by another person or entity of, more than one hundred thousand dollars ($100,000), but not more than five hundred thousand dollars ($500,000), the additional term of punishment shall be the term specified in paragraph (1) or (2) of subdivision (a) of Section 12022.6.

(b) (1) The additional prison term and penalties provided for in subdivisions (a), (c), and (d) shall not be imposed unless the facts set forth in subdivision (a) are charged in the accusatory pleading and admitted or found to be true by the trier of fact.

(2) The additional prison term provided in paragraph (2) of subdivision (a) shall be in addition to any other punishment provided by law, including Section 12022.6, and shall not be limited by any other provision of law.

(c) Any person convicted of two or more felonies, as specified in subdivision (a), shall also be liable for a fine not to exceed five hundred thousand dollars ($500,000) or double the value of the taking, whichever is greater, if the existence of facts that would make the person subject to the aggravated white collar crime enhancement have been admitted or found to be true by the trier of fact. However, if the pattern of related felony conduct involves the taking of more than one hundred thousand dollars ($100,000), but not more than five hundred thousand dollars ($500,000), the fine shall not exceed one hundred thousand dollars ($100,000) or double the value of the taking, whichever is greater.

(d) (1) If a person is alleged to have committed two or more felonies, as specified in subdivision (a), and the aggravated white collar crime enhancement is also charged, or a person is charged in an accusatory pleading with a felony, a material element of which

is fraud or embezzlement, that involves the taking or loss of more than one hundred thousand dollars ($100,000), and an allegation as to the existence of those facts, any asset or property that is in the control of that person, and any asset or property that has been transferred by that person to a third party, subsequent to the commission of any criminal act alleged pursuant to subdivision (a), other than in a bona fide purchase, whether found within or outside the state, may be preserved by the superior court in order to pay restitution and fines. Upon conviction of two or more felonies, as specified in subdivision (a), or a felony, a material element of which is fraud or embezzlement, that involves the taking or loss of more than one hundred thousand dollars ($100,000), this property may be levied upon by the superior court to pay restitution and fines if the existence of facts that would make the person subject to the aggravated white collar crime enhancement or that demonstrate the taking or loss of more than one hundred thousand dollars ($100,000) in the commission of a felony, a material element of which is fraud or embezzlement, have been charged in the accusatory pleading and admitted or found to be true by the trier of fact.

(2) To prevent dissipation or secreting of assets or property, the prosecuting agency may, at the same time as or subsequent to the filing of a complaint or indictment charging two or more felonies, as specified in subdivision (a), and the enhancement specified in subdivision (a), or a felony, a material element of which is fraud or embezzlement, that involves the taking or loss of more than one hundred thousand dollars ($100,000), and an allegation as to the existence of those facts, file a petition with the criminal division of the superior court of the county in which the accusatory pleading was filed, seeking a temporary restraining order, preliminary injunction, the appointment of a receiver, or any other protective relief necessary to preserve the property or assets. This petition shall commence a proceeding that shall be pendent to the criminal proceeding and maintained solely to affect the criminal remedies provided for in this section. The proceeding shall not be subject to or governed by the provisions of the Civil Discovery Act as set forth in Title 4 (commencing with Section 2016.010) of Part 4 of the Code of Civil Procedure. The petition shall allege that the defendant has been charged with two or more felonies, as specified in subdivision (a), and is subject to the aggravated white collar crime enhancement specified in subdivision (a) or that the defendant has been charged with a felony, a material element of which is fraud or embezzlement, that involves the taking or loss of more than one hundred thousand dollars ($100,000), and an allegation as to the existence of those facts. The petition shall identify that criminal proceeding and the assets and property to be affected by an order issued pursuant to this section.

(3) A notice regarding the petition shall be provided, by personal service or registered mail, to every person who may have an interest in the property specified in the petition. Additionally, the notice shall be published for at least three successive weeks in a newspaper of general circulation in the county where the property affected by an order issued pursuant to this section is located. The notice shall state that any interested person may file a verified claim with the superior court stating the nature and amount of their claimed interest. The notice shall set forth the time within which a claim of interest in the protected property is required to be filed.

(4) If the property to be preserved is real property, the prosecuting agency shall record, at the time of filing the petition, a lis pendens in each county in which the real property is situated which specifically identifies the property by legal description, the name of the owner of record as shown on the latest equalized assessment roll, and the assessor's parcel number.

(5) If the property to be preserved are assets under the control of a banking or financial institution, the prosecuting agency, at the time of the filing of the petition, may obtain an order from the court directing the banking or financial institution to immediately disclose the account numbers and value of the assets of the accused held by the banking or financial institution. The prosecuting agency shall file a supplemental petition, specifically identifying which banking or financial institution accounts shall be subject to a temporary restraining order, preliminary injunction, or other protective remedy.

(6) Any person claiming an interest in the protected property may, at any time within 30 days from the date of the first publication of the notice of the petition, or within 30 days after receipt of actual notice, file with the superior court of the county in which the action is pending a verified claim stating the nature and amount of his or her interest in the property or assets. A verified copy of the claim shall be served by the claimant on the Attorney General or district attorney, as appropriate.

(7) The imposition of fines and restitution pursuant to this section shall be determined by the superior court in which the underlying criminal offense is sentenced. Any judge who is assigned to the criminal division of the superior court in the county where the petition is filed may issue a temporary restraining order in conjunction with, or subsequent to, the filing of an allegation pursuant to this section. Any subsequent hearing on the petition shall also be heard by a judge assigned to the criminal division of the superior court in the county in which the petition is filed. At the time of the filing of an information or indictment in the underlying criminal case, any subsequent hearing on the petition shall be heard by the superior court judge assigned to the underlying criminal case.

(e) Concurrent with or subsequent to the filing of the petition, the prosecuting agency may move the superior court for, and the superior court may issue, the following pendente lite orders to preserve the status quo of the property alleged in the petition:

(1) An injunction to restrain any person from transferring, encumbering, hypothecating, or otherwise disposing of that property.

(2) Appointment of a receiver to take possession of, care for, manage, and operate the assets and properties so that the property may be maintained and preserved. The court may order that a receiver appointed pursuant to this section shall be compensated for all reasonable expenditures made or incurred by him or her in connection with the possession, care, management, and operation of any property or assets that are subject to the provisions of this section.

(3) A bond or other undertaking, in lieu of other orders, of a value sufficient to ensure the satisfaction of restitution and fines imposed pursuant to this section.

(f) (1) No preliminary injunction may be granted or receiver appointed by the court without notice that meets the requirements of paragraph (3) of subdivision (d) to all known and reasonably ascertainable interested parties and upon a hearing to determine that an order is necessary to preserve the property pending the outcome of the criminal proceedings. A temporary restraining order may be issued by the court, ex parte, pending that hearing in conjunction with or subsequent to the filing of the petition upon the application of the prosecuting attorney. The temporary restraining order may be based upon the sworn declaration of a peace officer with personal knowledge of the criminal investigation that establishes probable cause to believe that aggravated white collar crime or a felony, a material element of which is fraud or embezzlement, that involves the taking or loss of more than one hundred thousand dollars ($100,000) has taken place and that the amount of restitution and fines exceeds or equals the worth of the assets subject to the temporary restraining order. The declaration may include the hearsay statements of witnesses to establish the necessary facts. The temporary restraining order may be issued without notice upon a showing of good cause to the court.

(2) The defendant, or a person who has filed a verified claim as provided in paragraph (6) of subdivision (d), shall have the right to have the court conduct an order to show cause hearing within 10 days of the service of the request for hearing upon the prosecuting agency, in order to determine whether the temporary restraining order should remain in effect, whether relief should be granted from any lis pendens recorded pursuant to paragraph (4) of subdivision (d), or whether any existing order should be modified in the interests of justice. Upon a showing of good cause, the hearing shall be

held within two days of the service of the request for hearing upon the prosecuting agency.

(3) In determining whether to issue a preliminary injunction or temporary restraining order in a proceeding brought by a prosecuting agency in conjunction with or subsequent to the filing of an allegation pursuant to this section, the court has the discretion to consider any matter that it deems reliable and appropriate, including hearsay statements, in order to reach a just and equitable decision. The court shall weigh the relative degree of certainty of the outcome on the merits and the consequences to each of the parties of granting the interim relief. If the prosecution is likely to prevail on the merits and the risk of the dissipation of assets outweighs the potential harm to the defendants and the interested parties, the court shall grant injunctive relief. The court shall give significant weight to the following factors:

(A) The public interest in preserving the property or assets pendente lite.

(B) The difficulty of preserving the property or assets pendente lite where the underlying alleged crimes involve issues of fraud and moral turpitude.

(C) The fact that the requested relief is being sought by a public prosecutor on behalf of alleged victims of white collar crimes.

(D) The likelihood that substantial public harm has occurred where aggravated white collar crime is alleged to have been committed.

(E) The significant public interest involved in compensating the victims of white collar crime and paying court-imposed restitution and fines.

(4) The court, in making its orders, may consider a defendant's request for the release of a portion of the property affected by this section in order to pay reasonable legal fees in connection with the criminal proceeding, any necessary and appropriate living expenses pending trial and sentencing, and for the purpose of posting bail. The court shall weigh the needs of the public to retain the property against the needs of the defendant to a portion of the property. The court shall consider the factors listed in paragraph (3) prior to making any order releasing property for these purposes.

(5) The court, in making its orders, shall seek to protect the interests of any innocent third persons, including an innocent spouse, who were not involved in the commission of any criminal activity.

(6) Any petition filed pursuant to this section is part of the criminal proceedings for purposes of appointment of counsel and shall be assigned to the criminal division of the superior court of the county in which the accusatory pleading was filed.

(7) Based upon a noticed motion brought by the receiver appointed pursuant to paragraph (2) of subdivision (e), the court may order an interlocutory sale of property named in the petition when the property is liable to perish, to waste, or to be significantly reduced in value, or when the expenses of maintaining the property are disproportionate to the value thereof. The proceeds of the interlocutory sale shall be deposited with the court or as directed by the court pending determination of the proceeding pursuant to this section.

(8) The court may make any orders that are necessary to preserve the continuing viability of any lawful business enterprise that is affected by the issuance of a temporary restraining order or preliminary injunction issued pursuant to this action.

(9) In making its orders, the court shall seek to prevent any asset subject to a temporary restraining order or preliminary injunction from perishing, spoiling, going to waste, or otherwise being significantly reduced in value. Where the potential for diminution in value exists, the court shall appoint a receiver to dispose of or otherwise protect the value of the property or asset.

(10) A preservation order shall not be issued against any assets of a business that are not likely to be dissipated and that may be subject to levy or attachment to meet the purposes of this section.

(g) If the allegation that the defendant is subject to the aggravated white collar crime enhancement or has committed a felony, a material element of which is fraud or embezzlement, that involves the taking or loss of more than one hundred thousand dollars ($100,000) is dismissed or found by the trier of fact to be untrue, any preliminary injunction or temporary restraining order issued pursuant to this section shall be dissolved. If a jury is the trier of fact, and the jury is unable to reach a unanimous verdict, the court shall have the discretion to continue or dissolve all or a portion of the preliminary injunction or temporary restraining order based upon the interests of justice. However, if the prosecuting agency elects not to retry the case, any preliminary injunction or temporary restraining order issued pursuant to this section shall be dissolved.

(h) (1) (A) If the defendant is convicted of two or more felonies, as specified in subdivision (a), and the existence of facts that would make the person subject to the aggravated white collar crime enhancement have been admitted or found to be true by the trier of fact, or the defendant is convicted of a felony, a material element of which is fraud or embezzlement, that involves the taking or loss of more than one hundred thousand dollars ($100,000), and an allegation as to the existence of those facts has been admitted or found to be true by the trier of fact, the trial judge shall continue the preliminary injunction or temporary restraining order until the date of the criminal sentencing and shall make a finding at that time as to what portion, if any, of the property or assets subject to the preliminary injunction or temporary restraining order shall be levied upon to pay fines and restitution to victims of the crime. The order imposing fines and restitution may exceed the total worth of the property or assets subjected to the preliminary injunction or temporary restraining order. The court may order the immediate transfer of the property or assets to satisfy any judgment and sentence made pursuant to this section. Additionally, upon motion of the prosecution, the court may enter an order as part of the judgment and sentence making the order imposing fines and restitution pursuant to this section enforceable pursuant to Title 9 (commencing with Section 680.010) of Part 2 of the Code of Civil Procedure.

(B) Additionally, the court shall order the defendant to make full restitution to the victim. The payment of the restitution ordered by the court pursuant to this section shall be made a condition of any probation granted by the court if the existence of facts that would make the defendant subject to the aggravated white collar crime enhancement or of facts demonstrating the person committed a felony, a material element of which is fraud or embezzlement, that involves the taking or loss of more than one hundred thousand dollars ($100,000) have been admitted or found to be true by the trier of fact. Notwithstanding any other provision of law, the court may order that the period of probation continue for up to 10 years or until full restitution is made to the victim, whichever is earlier.

(C) The sentencing court shall retain jurisdiction to enforce the order to pay additional fines and restitution and, in appropriate cases, may initiate probation violation proceedings or contempt of court proceedings against a defendant who is found to have willfully failed to comply with any lawful order of the court.

(D) If the execution of judgment is stayed pending an appeal of an order of the superior court pursuant to this section, the preliminary injunction or temporary restraining order shall be maintained in full force and effect during the pendency of the appellate period.

(2) The order imposing fines and restitution shall not affect the interest in real property of any third party that was acquired prior to the recording of the lis pendens, unless the property was obtained from the defendant other than as a bona fide purchaser for value. If any assets or property affected by this section are subject to a valid lien, mortgage, security interest, or interest under a conditional sales contract and the amount due to the holder of the lien, mortgage, interest, or contract is less than the appraised value of the property, that person may pay to the state or the local government that initiated the proceeding the amount of the difference between the appraised value of the property and the amount of the lien, mortgage, security interest, or interest under a conditional sales contract. Upon that payment, the state or local entity shall relinquish all claims to the property. If the holder of the interest elects not to make that payment to the state or local governmental entity, the interest in the property shall be deemed transferred to the state or local governmental entity and any indicia of ownership of the property shall be confirmed in the state or local governmental entity. The appraised value shall be determined as of the date judgment is entered either by agreement between the holder of the lien, mortgage, security interest, or interest under a conditional sales contract and the governmental entity involved, or, if they cannot agree, then by a court-appointed appraiser for the county in which the action is brought. A person holding a valid lien, mortgage, security interest, or interest under a conditional sales contract shall be paid the appraised value of his or her interest.

(3) In making its final order, the court shall seek to protect the legitimately acquired interests of any innocent third persons, including an innocent spouse, who were not involved in the commission of any criminal activity.

(i) In all cases where property is to be levied upon pursuant to this section, a receiver appointed by the court shall be empowered to liquidate all property or assets which shall be distributed in the following order of priority:

(1) To the receiver, or court-appointed appraiser, for all reasonable expenditures made or incurred by him or her in connection with the sale of the property or liquidation of assets, including all reasonable expenditures for any necessary repairs, storage, or transportation of any property levied upon under this section.

(2) To any holder of a valid lien, mortgage, or security interest up to the amount of his or her interest in the property or proceeds.

(3) To any victim as restitution for any fraudulent or unlawful acts alleged in the accusatory pleading that were proven by the prosecuting agency as part of the pattern of fraudulent or unlawful acts.

(4) For payment of any fine imposed pursuant to this section. The proceeds obtained in payment of a fine shall be paid to the treasurer of the county in which the judgment was entered, or if the action was undertaken by the Attorney General, to the Treasurer. If the payment of any fine imposed pursuant to this section involved losses resulting from violation of Section 550 of this code or Section 1871.4 of the Insurance Code, one-half of the fine collected shall be paid to the treasurer of the county in which the judgment was entered, and one-half of the fine collected shall be paid to the Department of Insurance for deposit in the appropriate account in the Insurance Fund. The proceeds from the fine first shall be used by a county to reimburse local prosecutors and enforcement agencies for the reasonable costs of investigation and prosecution of cases brought pursuant to this section.

(5) To the Restitution Fund, or in cases involving convictions relating to insurance fraud, to the Insurance Fund as restitution for crimes not specifically pleaded and proven in the accusatory pleading.

(j) If, after distribution pursuant to paragraphs (1) and (2) of subdivision (i), the value of the property to be levied upon pursuant to this section is insufficient to pay for restitution and fines, the court shall order an equitable sharing of the proceeds of the liquidation of the property, and any other recoveries, which shall specify the percentage of recoveries to be devoted to each purpose. At least 70 percent of the proceeds remaining after distribution pursuant to paragraphs (1) and (2) of subdivision (i) shall be devoted to restitution.

(k) Unless otherwise expressly provided, the remedies or penalties provided by this section are cumulative to each other and to the remedies or penalties available under all other laws of this state, except that two separate actions against the same defendant and pertaining to the same fraudulent or unlawful acts may not be brought by a district attorney or the Attorney General pursuant to this section and Chapter 5 (commencing with Section 17200) of Part 2 of Division 7 of the Business and Professions Code. If a fine is imposed under this section, it shall be in lieu of all other fines that may be imposed pursuant to any other provision of law for the crimes for which the defendant has been convicted in the action.

(Amended by Stats. 2016, Ch. 37, Sec. 1. (AB 2295) Effective January 1, 2017.)

186.12.

(a) (1) A felony for purposes of this section means a felony violation of subdivision (d) or (e) of Section 368, or a felony violation of subdivision (c) of Section 15656 of the Welfare and Institutions Code, that involves the taking or loss of more than one hundred thousand dollars ($100,000).

(2) If a person is charged with a felony as described in paragraph (1) and an allegation as to the existence of those facts has been made, any property that is in the control of that person, and any property that has been transferred by that person to a third party, subsequent to the commission of any criminal act alleged pursuant to this subdivision, other than in a bona fide purchase, whether found within or outside the state, may be preserved by the superior court in order to pay restitution imposed pursuant to this section. Upon conviction of the felony, this property may be levied upon by the superior court to pay restitution imposed pursuant to this section.

(b) (1) To prevent dissipation or secreting of property, the prosecuting agency may, at the same time as or subsequent to the filing of a complaint or indictment charging a felony subject to this section, file a petition with the criminal division of the superior court of the county in which the accusatory pleading was filed, seeking a temporary restraining order, preliminary injunction, the appointment of a receiver, or any other protective relief necessary to preserve the property. The filing of the petition shall commence a proceeding that shall be pendent to the criminal proceeding and maintained solely to affect the criminal remedies provided for in this section. The proceeding shall not be subject to or governed by the provisions of the Civil Discovery Act as set forth in Title 4 (commencing with Section 2016.010) of Part 4 of the Code of Civil Procedure. The petition shall allege that the defendant has been charged with a felony as described in paragraph (1) of subdivision (a) and shall identify that criminal proceeding and the property to be affected by an order issued pursuant to this section.

(2) A notice regarding the petition shall be provided, by personal service or registered mail, to every person who may have an interest in the property specified in the petition. Additionally, the notice shall be published for at least three successive weeks in a newspaper of general circulation in the county where the property affected by an order issued pursuant to this section is located. The notice shall state that any interested person may file a verified claim with the superior court stating the nature and amount of their claimed interest. The notice shall set forth the time within which a claim of interest in the protected property is required to be filed.

(3) If the property to be preserved is real property, the prosecuting agency shall record, at the time of filing the petition, a lis pendens in each county in which the real property is situated which specifically identifies the property by legal description, the name of the owner of record as shown on the latest equalized assessment roll, and the assessor's parcel number.

(4) If the property to be preserved are assets under the control of a banking or financial institution, the prosecuting agency, at the time of the filing of the petition, may obtain an order from the court directing the banking or financial institution to immediately disclose the account numbers and value of the assets of the accused held by the banking or financial institution. The prosecuting agency shall file a supplemental petition, specifically identifying which banking or financial institution accounts shall be subject to a temporary restraining order, preliminary injunction, or other protective remedy.

(5) Any person claiming an interest in the protected property may, at any time within 30 days from the date of the first publication of the notice of the petition, or within 30 days after receipt of actual notice, file with the superior court of the county in which the action is pending a verified claim stating the nature and amount of his or her interest in the property. A verified copy of the claim shall be served by the claimant on the Attorney General or district attorney, as appropriate.

(6) The imposition of restitution pursuant to this section shall be determined by the superior court in which the underlying criminal offense is sentenced. Any judge who is

assigned to the criminal division of the superior court in the county where the petition is filed may issue a temporary restraining order in conjunction with, or subsequent to, the filing of an allegation pursuant to this section. Any subsequent hearing on the petition shall also be heard by a judge assigned to the criminal division of the superior court in the county in which the petition is filed. At the time of the filing of an information or indictment in the underlying criminal case, any subsequent hearing on the petition shall be heard by the superior court judge assigned to the underlying criminal case.

(c) Concurrent with or subsequent to the filing of the petition pursuant to this section, the prosecuting agency may move the superior court for, and the superior court may issue, the following pendente lite orders to preserve the status quo of the property identified in the petition:

(1) An injunction to restrain any person from transferring, encumbering, hypothecating, or otherwise disposing of that property.

(2) Appointment of a receiver to take possession of, care for, manage, and operate the properties so that the property may be maintained and preserved. The court may order that a receiver appointed pursuant to this section shall be compensated for all reasonable expenditures made or incurred by him or her in connection with the possession, care, management, and operation of any property that is subject to this section.

(3) A bond or other undertaking, in lieu of other orders, of a value sufficient to ensure the satisfaction of restitution imposed pursuant to this section.

(d) (1) No preliminary injunction may be granted or receiver appointed by the court without notice that meets the requirements of paragraph (2) of subdivision (b) to all known and reasonably ascertainable interested parties and upon a hearing to determine that an order is necessary to preserve the property pending the outcome of the criminal proceedings. A temporary restraining order may be issued by the court, ex parte, pending that hearing in conjunction with or subsequent to the filing of the petition upon the application of the prosecuting attorney. The temporary restraining order may be based upon the sworn declaration of a peace officer with personal knowledge of the criminal investigation that establishes probable cause to believe that a felony has taken place and that the amount of restitution established by this section exceeds or equals the worth of the property subject to the temporary restraining order. The declaration may include the hearsay statements of witnesses to establish the necessary facts. The temporary restraining order may be issued without notice upon a showing of good cause to the court.

(2) The defendant, or a person who has filed a verified claim as provided in paragraph (5) of subdivision (b), shall have the right to have the court conduct an order to show cause hearing within 10 days of the service of the request for hearing upon the prosecuting agency, in order to determine whether the temporary restraining order should remain in effect, whether relief should be granted from any lis pendens recorded pursuant to paragraph (3) of subdivision (b), or whether any existing order should be modified in the interests of justice. Upon a showing of good cause, the hearing shall be held within two days of the service of the request for hearing upon the prosecuting agency.

(3) In determining whether to issue a preliminary injunction or temporary restraining order in a proceeding brought by a prosecuting agency in conjunction with or subsequent to the filing of an allegation pursuant to this section, the court has the discretion to consider any matter that it deems reliable and appropriate, including hearsay statements, in order to reach a just and equitable decision. The court shall weigh the relative degree of certainty of the outcome on the merits and the consequences to each of the parties of granting the interim relief. If the prosecution is likely to prevail on the merits and the risk of dissipation of the property outweighs the potential harm to the defendants and the interested parties, the court shall grant injunctive relief. The court shall give significant weight to the following factors:

(A) The public interest in preserving the property pendente lite.

(B) The difficulty of preserving the property pendente lite where the underlying alleged crimes involve issues of fraud and moral turpitude.

(C) The fact that the requested relief is being sought by a public prosecutor on behalf of alleged victims of elder or dependent adult financial abuse.

(D) The likelihood that substantial public harm has occurred where a felony is alleged to have been committed.

(E) The significant public interest involved in compensating the elder or dependent adult victim of financial abuse and paying court-imposed restitution.

(4) The court, in making its orders, may consider a defendant's request for the release of a portion of the property affected by this section in order to pay reasonable legal fees in connection with the criminal proceeding, any necessary and appropriate living expenses pending trial and sentencing, and for the purpose of posting bail. The court shall weigh the needs of the public to retain the property against the needs of the defendant to a portion of the property. The court shall consider the factors listed in paragraph (3) prior to making any order releasing property for these purposes.

(5) The court, in making its orders, shall seek to protect the interests of any innocent third persons, including an innocent spouse, who were not involved in the commission of any criminal activity.

(6) Any petition filed pursuant to this section shall be part of the criminal proceedings for purposes of appointment of counsel and shall be assigned to the criminal division of the superior court of the county in which the accusatory pleading was filed.

(7) Based upon a noticed motion brought by the receiver appointed pursuant to paragraph (2) of subdivision (c), the court may order an interlocutory sale of property identified in the petition when the property is liable to perish, to waste, or to be significantly reduced in value, or when the expenses of maintaining the property are disproportionate to the value thereof. The proceeds of the interlocutory sale shall be deposited with the court or as directed by the court pending determination of the proceeding pursuant to this section.

(8) The court may make any orders that are necessary to preserve the continuing viability of any lawful business enterprise that is affected by the issuance of a temporary restraining order or preliminary injunction issued pursuant to this action.

(9) In making its orders, the court shall seek to prevent any property subject to a temporary restraining order or preliminary injunction from perishing, spoiling, going to waste, or otherwise being significantly reduced in value. Where the potential for diminution in value exists, the court shall appoint a receiver to dispose of or otherwise protect the value of the property.

(10) A preservation order shall not be issued against any assets of a business that are not likely to be dissipated and that may be subject to levy or attachment to meet the purposes of this section.

(e) If the allegation that the defendant committed a felony subject to this section is dismissed or found by the trier of fact to be untrue, any preliminary injunction or temporary restraining order issued pursuant to this section shall be dissolved. If a jury is the trier of fact, and the jury is unable to reach a unanimous verdict, the court shall have the discretion to continue or dissolve all or a portion of the preliminary injunction or temporary restraining order based upon the interests of justice. However, if the prosecuting agency elects not to retry the case, any preliminary injunction or temporary restraining order issued pursuant to this section shall be dissolved.

(f) (1) (A) If the defendant is convicted of a felony subject to this section, the trial judge shall continue the preliminary injunction or temporary restraining order until the date of the criminal sentencing and shall make a finding at that time as to what portion, if any, of the property subject to the preliminary injunction or temporary restraining order shall be levied upon to pay restitution to victims of the crime. The order imposing restitution may exceed the total worth of the property subjected to the preliminary injunction or temporary restraining order. The court may order the immediate transfer of the property

to satisfy any judgment and sentence made pursuant to this section. Additionally, upon motion of the prosecution, the court may enter an order as part of the judgment and sentence making the order imposing restitution pursuant to this section enforceable pursuant to Title 9 (commencing with Section 680.010) of Part 2 of the Code of Civil Procedure.

(B) Additionally, the court shall order the defendant to make full restitution to the victim. The payment of the restitution ordered by the court pursuant to this section shall be made a condition of any probation granted by the court. Notwithstanding any other provision of law, the court may order that the period of probation continue for up to 10 years or until full restitution is made to the victim, whichever is earlier.

(C) The sentencing court shall retain jurisdiction to enforce the order to pay additional restitution and, in appropriate cases, may initiate probation violation proceedings or contempt of court proceedings against a defendant who is found to have willfully failed to comply with any lawful order of the court.

(D) If the execution of judgment is stayed pending an appeal of an order of the superior court pursuant to this section, the preliminary injunction or temporary restraining order shall be maintained in full force and effect during the pendency of the appellate period.

(2) The order imposing restitution shall not affect the interest in real property of any third party that was acquired prior to the recording of the lis pendens, unless the property was obtained from the defendant other than as a bona fide purchaser for value. If any assets or property affected by this section are subject to a valid lien, mortgage, security interest, or interest under a conditional sales contract and the amount due to the holder of the lien, mortgage, interest, or contract is less than the appraised value of the property, that person may pay to the state or the local government that initiated the proceeding the amount of the difference between the appraised value of the property and the amount of the lien, mortgage, security interest, or interest under a conditional sales contract. Upon that payment, the state or local entity shall relinquish all claims to the property. If the holder of the interest elects not to make that payment to the state or local governmental entity, the interest in the property shall be deemed transferred to the state or local governmental entity and any indicia of ownership of the property shall be confirmed in the state or local governmental entity. The appraised value shall be determined as of the date judgment is entered either by agreement between the holder of the lien, mortgage, security interest, or interest under a conditional sales contract and the governmental entity involved, or if they cannot agree, then by a court-appointed appraiser for the county in which the action is brought. A person holding a valid lien, mortgage, security interest, or interest under a conditional sales contract shall be paid the appraised value of his or her interest.

(3) In making its final order, the court shall seek to protect the legitimately acquired interests of any innocent third persons, including an innocent spouse, who were not involved in the commission of any criminal activity.

(g) In all cases where property is to be levied upon pursuant to this section, a receiver appointed by the court shall be empowered to liquidate all property, the proceeds of which shall be distributed in the following order of priority:

(1) To the receiver, or court-appointed appraiser, for all reasonable expenditures made or incurred by him or her in connection with the sale or liquidation of the property, including all reasonable expenditures for any necessary repairs, storage, or transportation of any property levied upon under this section.

(2) To any holder of a valid lien, mortgage, or security interest up to the amount of his or her interest in the property or proceeds.

(3) To any victim as restitution for any fraudulent or unlawful acts alleged in the accusatory pleading that were proven by the prosecuting agency as part of the pattern of fraudulent or unlawful acts.

(h) Unless otherwise expressly provided, the remedies or penalties provided by this section are cumulative to each other and to the remedies or penalties available under all other laws of this state, except that two separate actions against the same defendant and pertaining to the same fraudulent or unlawful acts may not be brought by a district attorney or the Attorney General pursuant to this section and Chapter 5 (commencing with Section 17200) of Part 2 of Division 7 of the Business and Professions Code.
(Amended by Stats. 2016, Ch. 37, Sec. 2. (AB 2295) Effective January 1, 2017.)

CHAPTER 11. Street Terrorism Enforcement and Prevention Act [186.20 - 186.36]

(Chapter 11 added by Stats. 1988, Ch. 1256, Sec. 1.)
186.20.
This chapter shall be known and may be cited as the "California Street Terrorism Enforcement and Prevention Act."
(Added by Stats. 1988, Ch. 1256, Sec. 1. Effective September 26, 1988.)
186.21.
The Legislature hereby finds and declares that it is the right of every person, regardless of race, color, creed, religion, national origin, gender, gender identity, gender expression, age, sexual orientation, or handicap, to be secure and protected from fear, intimidation, and physical harm caused by the activities of violent groups and individuals. It is not the intent of this chapter to interfere with the exercise of the constitutionally protected rights of freedom of expression and association. The Legislature hereby recognizes the constitutional right of every citizen to harbor and express beliefs on any lawful subject whatsoever, to lawfully associate with others who share similar beliefs, to petition lawfully constituted authority for a redress of perceived grievances, and to participate in the electoral process.
The Legislature, however, further finds that the State of California is in a state of crisis which has been caused by violent street gangs whose members threaten, terrorize, and commit a multitude of crimes against the peaceful citizens of their neighborhoods. These activities, both individually and collectively, present a clear and present danger to public order and safety and are not constitutionally protected. The Legislature finds that there are nearly 600 criminal street gangs operating in California, and that the number of gang-related murders is increasing. The Legislature also finds that in Los Angeles County alone there were 328 gang-related murders in 1986, and that gang homicides in 1987 have increased 80 percent over 1986. It is the intent of the Legislature in enacting this chapter to seek the eradication of criminal activity by street gangs by focusing upon patterns of criminal gang activity and upon the organized nature of street gangs, which together, are the chief source of terror created by street gangs. The Legislature further finds that an effective means of punishing and deterring the criminal activities of street gangs is through forfeiture of the profits, proceeds, and instrumentalities acquired, accumulated, or used by street gangs.
(Amended by Stats. 2011, Ch. 719, Sec. 30. (AB 887) Effective January 1, 2012.)
186.22.
(a) Any person who actively participates in any criminal street gang with knowledge that its members engage in, or have engaged in, a pattern of criminal gang activity, and who willfully promotes, furthers, or assists in any felonious criminal conduct by members of that gang, shall be punished by imprisonment in a county jail for a period not to exceed one year, or by imprisonment in the state prison for 16 months, or two or three years.
(b) (1) Except as provided in paragraphs (4) and (5), any person who is convicted of a felony committed for the benefit of, at the direction of, or in association with any criminal street gang, with the specific intent to promote, further, or assist in any criminal conduct by gang members, shall, upon conviction of that felony, in addition and consecutive to

the punishment prescribed for the felony or attempted felony of which he or she has been convicted, be punished as follows:

(A) Except as provided in subparagraphs (B) and (C), the person shall be punished by an additional term of two, three, or four years at the court's discretion.

(B) If the felony is a serious felony, as defined in subdivision (c) of Section 1192.7, the person shall be punished by an additional term of five years.

(C) If the felony is a violent felony, as defined in subdivision (c) of Section 667.5, the person shall be punished by an additional term of 10 years.

(2) If the underlying felony described in paragraph (1) is committed on the grounds of, or within 1,000 feet of, a public or private elementary, vocational, junior high, or high school, during hours in which the facility is open for classes or school-related programs or when minors are using the facility, that fact shall be a circumstance in aggravation of the crime in imposing a term under paragraph (1).

(3) The court shall select the sentence enhancement that, in the court's discretion, best serves the interests of justice and shall state the reasons for its choice on the record at the time of the sentencing in accordance with the provisions of subdivision (d) of Section 1170.1.

(4) Any person who is convicted of a felony enumerated in this paragraph committed for the benefit of, at the direction of, or in association with any criminal street gang, with the specific intent to promote, further, or assist in any criminal conduct by gang members, shall, upon conviction of that felony, be sentenced to an indeterminate term of life imprisonment with a minimum term of the indeterminate sentence calculated as the greater of:

(A) The term determined by the court pursuant to Section 1170 for the underlying conviction, including any enhancement applicable under Chapter 4.5 (commencing with Section 1170) of Title 7 of Part 2, or any period prescribed by Section 3046, if the felony is any of the offenses enumerated in subparagraph (B) or (C) of this paragraph.

(B) Imprisonment in the state prison for 15 years, if the felony is a home invasion robbery, in violation of subparagraph (A) of paragraph (1) of subdivision (a) of Section 213; carjacking, as defined in Section 215; a felony violation of Section 246; or a violation of Section 12022.55.

(C) Imprisonment in the state prison for seven years, if the felony is extortion, as defined in Section 519; or threats to victims and witnesses, as defined in Section 136.1.

(5) Except as provided in paragraph (4), any person who violates this subdivision in the commission of a felony punishable by imprisonment in the state prison for life shall not be paroled until a minimum of 15 calendar years have been served.

(c) If the court grants probation or suspends the execution of sentence imposed upon the defendant for a violation of subdivision (a), or in cases involving a true finding of the enhancement enumerated in subdivision (b), the court shall require that the defendant serve a minimum of 180 days in a county jail as a condition thereof.

(d) Any person who is convicted of a public offense punishable as a felony or a misdemeanor, which is committed for the benefit of, at the direction of, or in association with any criminal street gang, with the specific intent to promote, further, or assist in any criminal conduct by gang members, shall be punished by imprisonment in a county jail not to exceed one year, or by imprisonment in a state prison for one, two, or three years, provided that any person sentenced to imprisonment in the county jail shall be imprisoned for a period not to exceed one year, but not less than 180 days, and shall not be eligible for release upon completion of sentence, parole, or any other basis, until he or she has served 180 days. If the court grants probation or suspends the execution of sentence imposed upon the defendant, it shall require as a condition thereof that the defendant serve 180 days in a county jail.

(e) As used in this chapter, "pattern of criminal gang activity" means the commission of, attempted commission of, conspiracy to commit, or solicitation of, sustained juvenile petition for, or conviction of two or more of the following offenses, provided at least one of these offenses occurred after the effective date of this chapter and the last of those offenses occurred within three years after a prior offense, and the offenses were committed on separate occasions, or by two or more persons:

(1) Assault with a deadly weapon or by means of force likely to produce great bodily injury, as defined in Section 245.

(2) Robbery, as defined in Chapter 4 (commencing with Section 211) of Title 8.

(3) Unlawful homicide or manslaughter, as defined in Chapter 1 (commencing with Section 187) of Title 8.

(4) The sale, possession for sale, transportation, manufacture, offer for sale, or offer to manufacture controlled substances as defined in Sections 11054, 11055, 11056, 11057, and 11058 of the Health and Safety Code.

(5) Shooting at an inhabited dwelling or occupied motor vehicle, as defined in Section 246.

(6) Discharging or permitting the discharge of a firearm from a motor vehicle, as defined in subdivisions (a) and (b) of Section 12034 until January 1, 2012, and, on or after that date, subdivisions (a) and (b) of Section 26100.

(7) Arson, as defined in Chapter 1 (commencing with Section 450) of Title 13.

(8) The intimidation of witnesses and victims, as defined in Section 136.1.

(9) Grand theft, as defined in subdivision (a) or (c) of Section 487.

(10) Grand theft of any firearm, vehicle, trailer, or vessel.

(11) Burglary, as defined in Section 459.

(12) Rape, as defined in Section 261.

(13) Looting, as defined in Section 463.

(14) Money laundering, as defined in Section 186.10.

(15) Kidnapping, as defined in Section 207.

(16) Mayhem, as defined in Section 203.

(17) Aggravated mayhem, as defined in Section 205.

(18) Torture, as defined in Section 206.

(19) Felony extortion, as defined in Sections 518 and 520.

(20) Felony vandalism, as defined in paragraph (1) of subdivision (b) of Section 594.

(21) Carjacking, as defined in Section 215.

(22) The sale, delivery, or transfer of a firearm, as defined in Section 12072 until January 1, 2012, and, on or after that date, Article 1 (commencing with Section 27500) of Chapter 4 of Division 6 of Title 4 of Part 6.

(23) Possession of a pistol, revolver, or other firearm capable of being concealed upon the person in violation of paragraph (1) of subdivision (a) of Section 12101 until January 1, 2012, and, on or after that date, Section 29610.

(24) Threats to commit crimes resulting in death or great bodily injury, as defined in Section 422.

(25) Theft and unlawful taking or driving of a vehicle, as defined in Section 10851 of the Vehicle Code.

(26) Felony theft of an access card or account information, as defined in Section 484e.

(27) Counterfeiting, designing, using, or attempting to use an access card, as defined in Section 484f.

(28) Felony fraudulent use of an access card or account information, as defined in Section 484g.

(29) Unlawful use of personal identifying information to obtain credit, goods, services, or medical information, as defined in Section 530.5.

(30) Wrongfully obtaining Department of Motor Vehicles documentation, as defined in Section 529.7.

(31) Prohibited possession of a firearm in violation of Section 12021 until January 1, 2012, and on or after that date, Chapter 2 (commencing with Section 29800) of Division 9 of Title 4 of Part 6.

(32) Carrying a concealed firearm in violation of Section 12025 until January 1, 2012, and, on or after that date, Section 25400.

(33) Carrying a loaded firearm in violation of Section 12031 until January 1, 2012, and, on or after that date, Section 25850.

(f) As used in this chapter, "criminal street gang" means any ongoing organization, association, or group of three or more persons, whether formal or informal, having as one of its primary activities the commission of one or more of the criminal acts enumerated in paragraphs (1) to (25), inclusive, or (31) to (33), inclusive, of subdivision (e), having a common name or common identifying sign or symbol, and whose members individually or collectively engage in, or have engaged in, a pattern of criminal gang activity.

(g) Notwithstanding any other law, the court may strike the additional punishment for the enhancements provided in this section or refuse to impose the minimum jail sentence for misdemeanors in an unusual case where the interests of justice would best be served, if the court specifies on the record and enters into the minutes the circumstances indicating that the interests of justice would best be served by that disposition.

(h) Notwithstanding any other law, for each person committed to the Department of Corrections and Rehabilitation, Division of Juvenile Facilities for a conviction pursuant to subdivision (a) or (b) of this section, the offense shall be deemed one for which the state shall pay the rate of 100 percent of the per capita institutional cost of the Department of Corrections and Rehabilitation, Division of Juvenile Facilities, pursuant to former Section 912.5 of the Welfare and Institutions Code.

(i) In order to secure a conviction or sustain a juvenile petition, pursuant to subdivision (a) it is not necessary for the prosecution to prove that the person devotes all, or a substantial part, of his or her time or efforts to the criminal street gang, nor is it necessary to prove that the person is a member of the criminal street gang. Active participation in the criminal street gang is all that is required.

(j) A pattern of gang activity may be shown by the commission of one or more of the offenses enumerated in paragraphs (26) to (30), inclusive, of subdivision (e), and the commission of one or more of the offenses enumerated in paragraphs (1) to (25), inclusive, or (31) to (33), inclusive, of subdivision (e). A pattern of gang activity cannot be established solely by proof of commission of offenses enumerated in paragraphs (26) to (30), inclusive, of subdivision (e), alone.

(k) This section shall remain in effect only until January 1, 2022, and as of that date is repealed, unless a later enacted statute, that is enacted before January 1, 2022, deletes or extends that date.

(Amended (as amended by Stats. 2016, Ch. 887, Sec. 1) by Stats. 2017, Ch. 561, Sec. 178. (AB 1516) Effective January 1, 2018. Repealed as of January 1, 2022, by its own provisions. See later operative version, as amended by Sec. 179 of Stats. 2017, Ch. 561. Note: This section was amended on March 7, 2000, by initiative Prop. 21.)

186.22.

(a) Any person who actively participates in any criminal street gang with knowledge that its members engage in, or have engaged in, a pattern of criminal gang activity, and who willfully promotes, furthers, or assists in any felonious criminal conduct by members of that gang, shall be punished by imprisonment in a county jail for a period not to exceed one year, or by imprisonment in the state prison for 16 months, or two or three years.

(b) (1) Except as provided in paragraphs (4) and (5), any person who is convicted of a felony committed for the benefit of, at the direction of, or in association with any criminal street gang, with the specific intent to promote, further, or assist in any criminal conduct by gang members, shall, upon conviction of that felony, in addition and consecutive to the punishment prescribed for the felony or attempted felony of which he or she has been convicted, be punished as follows:

(A) Except as provided in subparagraphs (B) and (C), the person shall be punished by an additional term of two, three, or four years at the court's discretion.

(B) If the felony is a serious felony, as defined in subdivision (c) of Section 1192.7, the person shall be punished by an additional term of five years.

(C) If the felony is a violent felony, as defined in subdivision (c) of Section 667.5, the person shall be punished by an additional term of 10 years.

(2) If the underlying felony described in paragraph (1) is committed on the grounds of, or within 1,000 feet of, a public or private elementary, vocational, junior high, or high school, during hours in which the facility is open for classes or school-related programs or when minors are using the facility, that fact shall be a circumstance in aggravation of the crime in imposing a term under paragraph (1).

(3) The court shall order the imposition of the middle term of the sentence enhancement, unless there are circumstances in aggravation or mitigation. The court shall state the reasons for its choice of sentencing enhancements on the record at the time of the sentencing.

(4) Any person who is convicted of a felony enumerated in this paragraph committed for the benefit of, at the direction of, or in association with any criminal street gang, with the specific intent to promote, further, or assist in any criminal conduct by gang members, shall, upon conviction of that felony, be sentenced to an indeterminate term of life imprisonment with a minimum term of the indeterminate sentence calculated as the greater of:

(A) The term determined by the court pursuant to Section 1170 for the underlying conviction, including any enhancement applicable under Chapter 4.5 (commencing with Section 1170) of Title 7 of Part 2, or any period prescribed by Section 3046, if the felony is any of the offenses enumerated in subparagraph (B) or (C) of this paragraph.

(B) Imprisonment in the state prison for 15 years, if the felony is a home invasion robbery, in violation of subparagraph (A) of paragraph (1) of subdivision (a) of Section 213; carjacking, as defined in Section 215; a felony violation of Section 246; or a violation of Section 12022.55.

(C) Imprisonment in the state prison for seven years, if the felony is extortion, as defined in Section 519; or threats to victims and witnesses, as defined in Section 136.1.

(5) Except as provided in paragraph (4), any person who violates this subdivision in the commission of a felony punishable by imprisonment in the state prison for life shall not be paroled until a minimum of 15 calendar years have been served.

(c) If the court grants probation or suspends the execution of sentence imposed upon the defendant for a violation of subdivision (a), or in cases involving a true finding of the enhancement enumerated in subdivision (b), the court shall require that the defendant serve a minimum of 180 days in a county jail as a condition thereof.

(d) Any person who is convicted of a public offense punishable as a felony or a misdemeanor, which is committed for the benefit of, at the direction of, or in association with any criminal street gang, with the specific intent to promote, further, or assist in any criminal conduct by gang members, shall be punished by imprisonment in a county jail not to exceed one year, or by imprisonment in a state prison for one, two, or three years, provided that any person sentenced to imprisonment in the county jail shall be imprisoned for a period not to exceed one year, but not less than 180 days, and shall not be eligible for release upon completion of sentence, parole, or any other basis, until he or she has served 180 days. If the court grants probation or suspends the execution of sentence imposed upon the defendant, it shall require as a condition thereof that the defendant serve 180 days in a county jail.

(e) As used in this chapter, "pattern of criminal gang activity" means the commission of, attempted commission of, conspiracy to commit, or solicitation of, sustained juvenile petition for, or conviction of two or more of the following offenses, provided at least one of these offenses occurred after the effective date of this chapter and the last of those offenses occurred within three years after a prior offense, and the offenses were committed on separate occasions, or by two or more persons:

(1) Assault with a deadly weapon or by means of force likely to produce great bodily injury, as defined in Section 245.

(2) Robbery, as defined in Chapter 4 (commencing with Section 211) of Title 8.

(3) Unlawful homicide or manslaughter, as defined in Chapter 1 (commencing with Section 187) of Title 8.

(4) The sale, possession for sale, transportation, manufacture, offer for sale, or offer to manufacture controlled substances as defined in Sections 11054, 11055, 11056, 11057, and 11058 of the Health and Safety Code.

(5) Shooting at an inhabited dwelling or occupied motor vehicle, as defined in Section 246.

(6) Discharging or permitting the discharge of a firearm from a motor vehicle, as defined in subdivisions (a) and (b) of Section 12034 until January 1, 2012, and, on or after that date, subdivisions (a) and (b) of Section 26100.

(7) Arson, as defined in Chapter 1 (commencing with Section 450) of Title 13.

(8) The intimidation of witnesses and victims, as defined in Section 136.1.

(9) Grand theft, as defined in subdivision (a) or (c) of Section 487.

(10) Grand theft of any firearm, vehicle, trailer, or vessel.

(11) Burglary, as defined in Section 459.

(12) Rape, as defined in Section 261.

(13) Looting, as defined in Section 463.

(14) Money laundering, as defined in Section 186.10.

(15) Kidnapping, as defined in Section 207.

(16) Mayhem, as defined in Section 203.

(17) Aggravated mayhem, as defined in Section 205.

(18) Torture, as defined in Section 206.

(19) Felony extortion, as defined in Sections 518 and 520.

(20) Felony vandalism, as defined in paragraph (1) of subdivision (b) of Section 594.

(21) Carjacking, as defined in Section 215.

(22) The sale, delivery, or transfer of a firearm, as defined in Section 12072 until January 1, 2012, and, on or after that date, Article 1 (commencing with Section 27500) of Chapter 4 of Division 6 of Title 4 of Part 6.

(23) Possession of a pistol, revolver, or other firearm capable of being concealed upon the person in violation of paragraph (1) of subdivision (a) of Section 12101 until January 1, 2012, and, on or after that date, Section 29610.

(24) Threats to commit crimes resulting in death or great bodily injury, as defined in Section 422.

(25) Theft and unlawful taking or driving of a vehicle, as defined in Section 10851 of the Vehicle Code.

(26) Felony theft of an access card or account information, as defined in Section 484e.

(27) Counterfeiting, designing, using, or attempting to use an access card, as defined in Section 484f.

(28) Felony fraudulent use of an access card or account information, as defined in Section 484g.

(29) Unlawful use of personal identifying information to obtain credit, goods, services, or medical information, as defined in Section 530.5.

(30) Wrongfully obtaining Department of Motor Vehicles documentation, as defined in Section 529.7.

(31) Prohibited possession of a firearm in violation of Section 12021 until January 1, 2012, and, on or after that date, Chapter 2 (commencing with Section 29800) of Division 9 of Title 4 of Part 6.

(32) Carrying a concealed firearm in violation of Section 12025 until January 1, 2012, and, on or after that date, Section 25400.

(33) Carrying a loaded firearm in violation of Section 12031 until January 1, 2012, and, on or after that date, Section 25850.

(f) As used in this chapter, "criminal street gang" means any ongoing organization, association, or group of three or more persons, whether formal or informal, having as one of its primary activities the commission of one or more of the criminal acts enumerated in paragraphs (1) to (25), inclusive, or (31) to (33), inclusive, of subdivision (e), having a common name or common identifying sign or symbol, and whose members individually or collectively engage in, or have engaged in, a pattern of criminal gang activity.

(g) Notwithstanding any other law, the court may strike the additional punishment for the enhancements provided in this section or refuse to impose the minimum jail sentence for misdemeanors in an unusual case where the interests of justice would best be served, if the court specifies on the record and enters into the minutes the circumstances indicating that the interests of justice would best be served by that disposition.

(h) Notwithstanding any other law, for each person committed to the Department of Corrections and Rehabilitation, Division of Juvenile Facilities for a conviction pursuant to subdivision (a) or (b) of this section, the offense shall be deemed one for which the state shall pay the rate of 100 percent of the per capita institutional cost of the Department of Corrections and Rehabilitation, Division of Juvenile Facilities, pursuant to former Section 912.5 of the Welfare and Institutions Code.

(i) In order to secure a conviction or sustain a juvenile petition, pursuant to subdivision (a) it is not necessary for the prosecution to prove that the person devotes all, or a substantial part, of his or her time or efforts to the criminal street gang, nor is it necessary to prove that the person is a member of the criminal street gang. Active participation in the criminal street gang is all that is required.

(j) A pattern of gang activity may be shown by the commission of one or more of the offenses enumerated in paragraphs (26) to (30), inclusive, of subdivision (e), and the commission of one or more of the offenses enumerated in paragraphs (1) to (25), inclusive, or (31) to (33), inclusive, of subdivision (e). A pattern of gang activity cannot be established solely by proof of commission of offenses enumerated in paragraphs (26) to (30), inclusive, of subdivision (e), alone.

(k) This section shall become operative on January 1, 2022.

(Amended (as amended by Stats. 2016, Ch. 887, Sec. 2) by Stats. 2017, Ch. 561, Sec. 179. (AB 1516) Effective January 1, 2018. Section operative January 1, 2022, by its own provisions. Note: Section 186.22 was amended on March 7, 2000, by initiative Prop. 21.)

186.22a.

(a) Every building or place used by members of a criminal street gang for the purpose of the commission of the offenses listed in subdivision (e) of Section 186.22 or any offense involving dangerous or deadly weapons, burglary, or rape, and every building or place wherein or upon which that criminal conduct by gang members takes place, is a nuisance which shall be enjoined, abated, and prevented, and for which damages may be recovered, whether it is a public or private nuisance.

(b) Any action for injunction or abatement filed pursuant to subdivision (a), including an action filed by the Attorney General, shall proceed according to the provisions of Article 3 (commencing with Section 11570) of Chapter 10 of Division 10 of the Health and Safety Code, except that all of the following shall apply:

(1) The court shall not assess a civil penalty against any person unless that person knew or should have known of the unlawful acts.

(2) No order of eviction or closure may be entered.

(3) All injunctions issued shall be limited to those necessary to protect the health and safety of the residents or the public or those necessary to prevent further criminal activity.

(4) Suit may not be filed until 30-day notice of the unlawful use or criminal conduct has been provided to the owner by mail, return receipt requested, postage prepaid, to the last known address.

(c) Whenever an injunction is issued pursuant to subdivision (a), or Section 3479 of the Civil Code, to abate gang activity constituting a nuisance, the Attorney General or any district attorney or any prosecuting city attorney may maintain an action for money

damages on behalf of the community or neighborhood injured by that nuisance. Any money damages awarded shall be paid by or collected from assets of the criminal street gang or its members. Only members of the criminal street gang who created, maintained, or contributed to the creation or maintenance of the nuisance shall be personally liable for the payment of the damages awarded. In a civil action for damages brought pursuant to this subdivision, the Attorney General, district attorney, or city attorney may use, but is not limited to the use of, the testimony of experts to establish damages suffered by the community or neighborhood injured by the nuisance. The damages recovered pursuant to this subdivision shall be deposited into a separate segregated fund for payment to the governing body of the city or county in whose political subdivision the community or neighborhood is located, and that governing body shall use those assets solely for the benefit of the community or neighborhood that has been injured by the nuisance.

(d) No nonprofit or charitable organization which is conducting its affairs with ordinary care or skill, and no governmental entity, shall be abated pursuant to subdivisions (a) and (b).

(e) Nothing in this chapter shall preclude any aggrieved person from seeking any other remedy provided by law.

(f) (1) Any firearm, ammunition which may be used with the firearm, or any deadly or dangerous weapon which is owned or possessed by a member of a criminal street gang for the purpose of the commission of any of the offenses listed in subdivision (e) of Section 186.22, or the commission of any burglary or rape, may be confiscated by any law enforcement agency or peace officer.

(2) In those cases where a law enforcement agency believes that the return of the firearm, ammunition, or deadly weapon confiscated pursuant to this subdivision, is or will be used in criminal street gang activity or that the return of the item would be likely to result in endangering the safety of others, the law enforcement agency shall initiate a petition in the superior court to determine if the item confiscated should be returned or declared a nuisance.

(3) No firearm, ammunition, or deadly weapon shall be sold or destroyed unless reasonable notice is given to its lawful owner if his or her identity and address can be reasonably ascertained. The law enforcement agency shall inform the lawful owner, at that person's last known address by registered mail, that he or she has 30 days from the date of receipt of the notice to respond to the court clerk to confirm his or her desire for a hearing and that the failure to respond shall result in a default order forfeiting the confiscated firearm, ammunition, or deadly weapon as a nuisance.

(4) If the person requests a hearing, the court clerk shall set a hearing no later than 30 days from receipt of that request. The court clerk shall notify the person, the law enforcement agency involved, and the district attorney of the date, time, and place of the hearing.

(5) At the hearing, the burden of proof is upon the law enforcement agency or peace officer to show by a preponderance of the evidence that the seized item is or will be used in criminal street gang activity or that return of the item would be likely to result in endangering the safety of others. All returns of firearms shall be subject to Chapter 2 (commencing with Section 33850) of Division 11 of Title 4 of Part 6.

(6) If the person does not request a hearing within 30 days of the notice or the lawful owner cannot be ascertained, the law enforcement agency may file a petition that the confiscated firearm, ammunition, or deadly weapon be declared a nuisance. If the items are declared to be a nuisance, the law enforcement agency shall dispose of the items as provided in Sections 18000 and 18005.

(Amended by Stats. 2010, Ch. 178, Sec. 50. (SB 1115) Effective January 1, 2011. Operative January 1, 2012, by Sec. 107 of Ch. 178.)

186.23.

This chapter does not apply to employees engaged in concerted activities for their mutual aid and protection, or the activities of labor organizations or their members or agents.

(Added by Stats. 1988, Ch. 1256, Sec. 1. Effective September 26, 1988.)

186.24.

If any part or provision of this chapter, or the application thereof to any person or circumstance, is held invalid, the remainder of the chapter, including the application of that part or provision to other persons or circumstances, shall not be affected thereby and shall continue in full force and effect. To this end, the provisions of this chapter are severable.

(Added by Stats. 1988, Ch. 1256, Sec. 1. Effective September 26, 1988.)

186.25.

Nothing in this chapter shall prevent a local governing body from adopting and enforcing laws consistent with this chapter relating to gangs and gang violence. Where local laws duplicate or supplement this chapter, this chapter shall be construed as providing alternative remedies and not as preempting the field.

(Added by Stats. 1988, Ch. 1256, Sec. 1. Effective September 26, 1988.)

186.26.

(a) Any person who solicits or recruits another to actively participate in a criminal street gang, as defined in subdivision (f) of Section 186.22, with the intent that the person solicited or recruited participate in a pattern of criminal street gang activity, as defined in subdivision (e) of Section 186.22, or with the intent that the person solicited or recruited promote, further, or assist in any felonious conduct by members of the criminal street gang, shall be punished by imprisonment in the state prison for 16 months, or two or three years.

(b) Any person who threatens another person with physical violence on two or more separate occasions within any 30-day period with the intent to coerce, induce, or solicit any person to actively participate in a criminal street gang, as defined in subdivision (f) of Section 186.22, shall be punished by imprisonment in the state prison for two, three, or four years.

(c) Any person who uses physical violence to coerce, induce, or solicit another person to actively participate in any criminal street gang, as defined in subdivision (f) of Section 186.22, or to prevent the person from leaving a criminal street gang, shall be punished by imprisonment in the state prison for three, four, or five years.

(d) If the person solicited, recruited, coerced, or threatened pursuant to subdivision (a), (b), or (c) is a minor, an additional term of three years shall be imposed in addition and consecutive to the penalty prescribed for a violation of any of these subdivisions.

(e) Nothing in this section shall be construed to limit prosecution under any other provision of law.

(Amended (as amended by Stats. 2011, Ch. 15) by Stats. 2011, Ch. 39, Sec. 8. (AB 117) Effective June 30, 2011. Operative October 1, 2011, pursuant to Secs. 68 and 69 of Ch. 39. Note: This section was repealed and added on March 7, 2000, by initiative Prop. 21.)

186.28.

(a) Any person, corporation, or firm who shall knowingly supply, sell, or give possession or control of any firearm to another shall be punished by imprisonment pursuant to subdivision (h) of Section 1170, or in a county jail for a term not exceeding one year, or by a fine not exceeding one thousand dollars ($1,000), or by both that fine and imprisonment if all of the following apply:

(1) The person, corporation, or firm has actual knowledge that the person will use the firearm to commit a felony described in subdivision (e) of Section 186.22, while actively participating in any criminal street gang, as defined in subdivision (f) of Section 186.22, the members of which engage in a pattern of criminal activity, as defined in subdivision (e) of Section 186.22.

(2) The firearm is used to commit the felony.

(3) A conviction for the felony violation under subdivision (e) of Section 186.22 has first been obtained of the person to whom the firearm was supplied, sold, or given possession or control pursuant to this section.

(b) This section shall only be applicable where the person is not convicted as a principal to the felony offense committed by the person to whom the firearm was supplied, sold, or given possession or control pursuant to this section.

(Amended by Stats. 2011, Ch. 15, Sec. 278. (AB 109) Effective April 4, 2011. Operative October 1, 2011, by Sec. 636 of Ch. 15, as amended by Stats. 2011, Ch. 39, Sec. 68.)

186.30.

(a) Any person described in subdivision (b) shall register with the chief of police of the city in which he or she resides, or the sheriff of the county if he or she resides in an unincorporated area, within 10 days of release from custody or within 10 days of his or her arrival in any city, county, or city and county to reside there, whichever occurs first.

(b) Subdivision (a) shall apply to any person convicted in a criminal court or who has had a petition sustained in a juvenile court in this state for any of the following offenses:

(1) Subdivision (a) of Section 186.22.

(2) Any crime where the enhancement specified in subdivision (b) of Section 186.22 is found to be true.

(3) Any crime that the court finds is gang related at the time of sentencing or disposition.

(Added March 7, 2000, by initiative Proposition 21, Sec. 7.)

186.31.

At the time of sentencing in adult court, or at the time of the dispositional hearing in the juvenile court, the court shall inform any person subject to Section 186.30 of his or her duty to register pursuant to that section. This advisement shall be noted in the court minute order. The court clerk shall send a copy of the minute order to the law enforcement agency with jurisdiction for the last known address of the person subject to registration under Section 186.30. The parole officer or the probation officer assigned to that person shall verify that he or she has complied with the registration requirements of Section 186.30.

(Added March 7, 2000, by initiative Proposition 21, Sec. 8.)

186.32.

(a) The registration required by Section 186.30 shall consist of the following:

(1) Juvenile registration shall include the following:

(A) The juvenile shall appear at the law enforcement agency with a parent or guardian.

(B) The law enforcement agency shall serve the juvenile and the parent with a California Street Terrorism Enforcement and Prevention Act notification which shall include, where applicable, that the juvenile belongs to a gang whose members engage in or have engaged in a pattern of criminal gang activity as described in subdivision (e) of Section 186.22.

(C) A written statement signed by the juvenile, giving any information that may be required by the law enforcement agency, shall be submitted to the law enforcement agency.

(D) The fingerprints and current photograph of the juvenile shall be submitted to the law enforcement agency.

(2) Adult registration shall include the following:

(A) The adult shall appear at the law enforcement agency.

(B) The law enforcement agency shall serve the adult with a California Street Terrorism Enforcement and Prevention Act notification which shall include, where applicable, that the adult belongs to a gang whose members engage in or have engaged in a pattern of criminal gang activity as described in subdivision (e) of Section 186.22.

(C) A written statement, signed by the adult, giving any information that may be required by the law enforcement agency, shall be submitted to the law enforcement agency.

(D) The fingerprints and current photograph of the adult shall be submitted to the law enforcement agency.

(b) Within 10 days of changing his or her residence address, any person subject to Section 186.30 shall inform, in writing, the law enforcement agency with whom he or she last registered of his or her new address. If his or her new residence address is located within the jurisdiction of a law enforcement agency other than the agency where he or she last registered, he or she shall register with the new law enforcement agency, in writing, within 10 days of the change of residence.

(c) All registration requirements set forth in this article shall terminate five years after the last imposition of a registration requirement pursuant to Section 186.30.

(d) The statements, photographs and fingerprints required under this section shall not be open to inspection by any person other than a regularly employed peace or other law enforcement officer.

(e) Nothing in this section or Section 186.30 or 186.31 shall preclude a court in its discretion from imposing the registration requirements as set forth in those sections in a gang-related crime.

(Added March 7, 2000, by initiative Proposition 21, Sec. 9.)

186.33.

(a) Any person required to register pursuant to Section 186.30 who knowingly violates any of its provisions is guilty of a misdemeanor.

(b) (1) Any person who knowingly fails to register pursuant to Section 186.30 and is subsequently convicted of, or any person for whom a petition is subsequently sustained for a violation of, any of the offenses specified in Section 186.30, shall be punished by an additional term of imprisonment in the state prison for 16 months, or two or three years. The court shall select the sentence enhancement which, in the court's discretion, best serves the interests of justice and shall state the reasons for its choice on the record at the time of sentencing in accordance with the provisions of subdivision (d) of Section 1170.1.

(2) The existence of any fact bringing a person under this subdivision shall be alleged in the information, indictment, or petition, and be either admitted by the defendant or minor in open court, or found to be true or not true by the trier of fact.

(c) This section shall remain in effect only until January 1, 2022, and as of that date is repealed, unless a later enacted statute, that is enacted before January 1, 2022, deletes or extends that date.

(Amended (as amended by Stats. 2013, Ch. 508, Sec. 3) by Stats. 2016, Ch. 887, Sec. 3. (SB 1016) Effective January 1, 2017. Repealed as of January 1, 2022, by its own provisions. See later operative version, as amended by Sec. 4 of Stats. 2016, Ch. 887. Note: This section was amended on March 7, 2000, by initiative Prop. 21.)

186.33.

(a) Any person required to register pursuant to Section 186.30 who knowingly violates any of its provisions is guilty of a misdemeanor.

(b) (1) Any person who knowingly fails to register pursuant to Section 186.30 and is subsequently convicted of, or any person for whom a petition is subsequently sustained for a violation of, any of the offenses specified in Section 186.30, shall be punished by an additional term of imprisonment in the state prison for 16 months, or two or three years. The court shall order imposition of the middle term unless there are circumstances in aggravation or mitigation. The court shall state its reasons for the enhancement choice on the record at the time of sentencing.

(2) The existence of any fact bringing a person under this subdivision shall be alleged in the information, indictment, or petition, and be either admitted by the defendant or minor in open court, or found to be true or not true by the trier of fact.

(c) This section shall become operative on January 1, 2022.

(Amended (as amended by Stats. 2013, Ch. 508, Sec. 4) by Stats. 2016, Ch. 887, Sec. 4. (SB 1016) Effective January 1, 2017. Section operative January 1, 2022, by its own provisions. Note: Section 186.33 was amended on March 7, 2000, by initiative Prop. 21.)

186.34.

(a) For purposes of this section and Sections 186.35 and 186.36, the following definitions apply:

(1) "Criminal street gang" means an ongoing organization, association, or group of three or more persons, whether formal or informal, having as one of its primary activities the commission of crimes enumerated in paragraphs (1) to (25), inclusive, and paragraphs (31) to (33), inclusive, of subdivision (e) of Section 186.22 who have a common identifying sign, symbol, or name, and whose members individually or collectively engage in or have engaged in a pattern of definable criminal activity.

(2) "Gang database" means any database accessed by a law enforcement agency that designates a person as a gang member or associate, or includes or points to information, including, but not limited to, fact-based or uncorroborated information, that reflects a designation of that person as a gang member or associate.

(3) "Law enforcement agency" means a governmental agency or a subunit of a governmental agency, and its authorized support staff and contractors, whose primary function is detection, investigation, or apprehension of criminal offenders, or whose primary duties include detention, pretrial release, posttrial release, correctional supervision, or the collection, storage, or dissemination of criminal history record information.

(4) "Shared gang database" means a gang database that is accessed by an agency or person outside of the agency that created the records that populate the database.

(b) Notwithstanding subdivision (a), the following are not subject to this section, or Sections 186.35 and 186.36:

(1) Databases that designate persons as gang members or associates using only criminal offender record information, as defined in Section 13102, or information collected pursuant to Section 186.30.

(2) Databases accessed solely by jail or custodial facility staff for classification or operational decisions in the administration of the facility.

(c) (1) To the extent a local law enforcement agency elects to utilize a shared gang database prior to a local law enforcement agency designating a person as a suspected gang member, associate, or affiliate in a shared gang database, or submitting a document to the Attorney General's office for the purpose of designating a person in a shared gang database, or otherwise identifying the person in a shared gang database, the local law enforcement agency shall provide written notice to the person, and shall, if the person is under 18 years of age, provide written notice to the person and his or her parent or guardian, of the designation and the basis for the designation, unless providing that notification would compromise an active criminal investigation or compromise the health or safety of the minor.

(2) The notice described in paragraph (1) shall describe the process for the person, or, if the person is under 18 years of age, for his or her parent or guardian, or an attorney working on behalf of the person, to contest the designation of the person in the database. The notice shall also inform the person of the reason for his or her designation in the database.

(d) (1) (A) A person, or, if the person is under 18 years of age, his or her parent or guardian, or an attorney working on behalf of the person, may request information of any law enforcement agency as to whether the person is designated as a suspected gang member, associate, or affiliate in a shared gang database accessible by that law enforcement agency and the name of the law enforcement agency that made the designation. A request pursuant to this paragraph shall be in writing.

(B) If a person about whom information is requested pursuant to subparagraph (A) is designated as a suspected gang member, associate, or affiliate in a shared gang database by that law enforcement agency, the person making the request may also request information as to the basis for the designation for the purpose of contesting the designation as described in subdivision (e).

(2) The law enforcement agency shall provide information requested under paragraph (1), unless doing so would compromise an active criminal investigation or compromise the health or safety of the person if the person is under 18 years of age.

(3) The law enforcement agency shall respond to a valid request pursuant to paragraph (1) in writing to the person making the request within 30 calendar days of receipt of the request.

(e) Subsequent to the notice described in subdivision (c) or the law enforcement agency's response to an information request described in subdivision (d), the person designated or to be designated as a suspected gang member, associate, or affiliate, or his or her parent or guardian if the person is under 18 years of age, may submit written documentation to the local law enforcement agency contesting the designation. The local law enforcement agency shall review the documentation, and if the agency determines that the person is not a suspected gang member, associate, or affiliate, the agency shall remove the person from the shared gang database. The local law enforcement agency shall provide the person and, if the person is under 18 years of age, his or her parent or guardian, with written verification of the agency's decision within 30 days of submission of the written documentation contesting the designation. If the law enforcement agency denies the request for removal, the notice of its determination shall state the reason for the denial. If the law enforcement agency does not provide a verification of the agency's decision within the required 30-day period, the request to remove the person from the gang database shall be deemed denied. The person or, if the person is under 18 years of age, his or her parent or guardian may petition the court to review the law enforcement agency's denial of the request for removal and order the law enforcement agency to remove the person from the shared gang database pursuant to Section 186.35.

(f) Nothing in this section shall require a local law enforcement agency to disclose any information protected under Section 1040 or 1041 of the Evidence Code or Section 6254 of the Government Code.

(Repealed and added by Stats. 2017, Ch. 695, Sec. 4. (AB 90) Effective January 1, 2018.)

186.35.

(a) A person who is listed by a law enforcement agency in a shared gang database as a gang member, suspected gang member, associate, or affiliate and who has contested his or her designation pursuant to subdivision (e) of Section 186.34, may petition the court to review the law enforcement agency's denial of the request for removal and to order the law enforcement agency to remove the person from the shared gang database. The petition may be brought by the person or the person's attorney, or if the person is under 18 years of age, by his or her parent or guardian or an attorney on behalf of the parent or guardian.

(b) The petition shall be filed and served within 90 calendar days of the agency's mailing or personal service of the verification of the decision to deny the request for removal from the shared gang database or the date that the request is deemed denied under subdivision (e) of Section 186.34. A proceeding under this subdivision is not a criminal case. The petition shall be filed in either the superior court of the county in which the local law enforcement agency is located or, if the person resides in California, in the county in which the person resides. A copy of the petition shall be served on the agency in person or by first-class mail. Proof of service of the petition on the agency shall be filed in the superior court. For purposes of computing the 90-calendar-day period, Section 1013 of the Code of Civil Procedure shall be applicable.

(c) The evidentiary record for the court's determination of the petition shall be limited to the agency's statement of the basis of its designation made pursuant to subdivision (c) or (d) of Section 186.34, and the documentation provided to the agency by the person contesting the designation pursuant to subdivision (e) of Section 186.34.

(d) If, upon de novo review of the record and any arguments presented to the court, the court finds that the law enforcement agency has failed to establish the person's active gang membership, associate status, or affiliate status by clear and convincing evidence, the court shall order the law enforcement agency to remove the name of the person from the shared gang database.

(e) The fee for filing the petition is as provided in Section 70615 of the Government Code. The court shall notify the person of the appearance date by mail or personal delivery. The court shall retain the fee under Section 70615 of the Government Code regardless of the outcome of the petition. If the court finds in favor of the person, the amount of the fee shall be reimbursed to the person by the agency.

(Repealed and added by Stats. 2017, Ch. 695, Sec. 6. (AB 90) Effective January 1, 2018.)

186.36.

(a) The Department of Justice is responsible for establishing regulations for shared gang databases. All shared gang databases shall comply with those regulations.

(b) The department shall administer and oversee the CalGang database. Commencing January 1, 2018, the CalGang Executive Board shall not administer or oversee the CalGang database.

(c) The department shall establish the Gang Database Technical Advisory Committee.

(d) Each appointee to the committee, regardless of the appointing authority, shall have the following characteristics:

(1) Substantial prior knowledge of issues related to gang intervention, suppression, or prevention efforts.

(2) Decisionmaking authority for, or direct access to those who have decisionmaking authority for, the agency or organization he or she represents.

(3) A willingness to serve on the committee and a commitment to contribute to the committee's work.

(e) The membership of the committee shall be as follows:

(1) The Attorney General, or his or her designee.

(2) The President of the California District Attorneys Association, or his or her designee.

(3) The President of the California Public Defenders Association, or his or her designee.

(4) A representative of organizations that specialize in gang violence intervention, appointed by the Senate Committee on Rules.

(5) A representative of organizations that provide immigration services, appointed by the Senate Committee on Rules.

(6) The President of the California Gang Investigators Association, or his or her designee.

(7) A representative of community organizations that specialize in civil or human rights, appointed by the Speaker of the Assembly.

(8) A person who has personal experience with a shared gang database as someone who is or was impacted by gang labeling, appointed by the Speaker of the Assembly.

(9) The chairperson of the California Gang Node Advisory Committee, or his or her designee.

(10) The President of the California Police Chiefs Association, or his or her designee.

(11) The President of the California State Sheriffs' Association, or his or her designee.

(f) The committee shall appoint a chairperson from among the members appointed pursuant to subdivision (e). The chairperson shall serve in that capacity at the pleasure of the committee.

(g) Each member of the committee who is appointed pursuant to this section shall serve without compensation.

(h) If a committee member is unable to adequately perform his or her duties, he or she is subject to removal from the board by a majority vote of the full committee.

(i) A vacancy on the committee as a result of the removal of a member shall be filled by the appointing authority of the removed member within 30 days of the vacancy.

(j) Committee meetings are subject to the Bagley-Keene Open Meeting Act (Article 9 (commencing with Section 11120) of Chapter 1 of Part 1 of Division 3 of Title 2 of the Government Code).

(k) The department, with the advice of the committee, shall promulgate regulations governing the use, operation, and oversight of shared gang databases. The regulations issued by the department shall, at minimum, ensure the following:

(1) The system integrity of a shared gang database.

(2) All law enforcement agency and criminal justice agency personnel who access a shared gang database undergo comprehensive and standardized training on the use of shared gang databases and related policies and procedures.

(3) Proper criteria are established for supervisory reviews of all database entries and regular reviews of records entered into a shared gang database.

(4) Reasonable measures are taken to locate equipment related to the operation of a shared gang database in a secure area in order to preclude access by unauthorized personnel.

(5) Law enforcement agencies and criminal justice agencies notify the department of any missing equipment that could potentially compromise a shared gang database.

(6) Personnel authorized to access a shared gang database are limited to sworn law enforcement personnel, nonsworn law enforcement support personnel, or noncriminal justice technical or maintenance personnel, including information technology and information security staff and contract employees, who have been subject to character or security clearance and who have received approved training.

(7) Any records contained in a shared gang database are not disclosed for employment or military screening purposes.

(8) Any records contained in a shared gang database are not disclosed for purposes of enforcing federal immigration law, unless required by state or federal statute or regulation.

(9) The committee does not discuss or access individual records contained in a shared gang database.

(l) The regulations issued by the department shall include, but not be limited to, establishing the following:

(1) Policies and procedures for entering, reviewing, and purging documentation.

(2) Criteria for designating a person as a gang member or associate that are unambiguous, not overbroad, and consistent with empirical research on gangs and gang membership.

(3) Retention periods for information about a person in a shared gang database that is consistent with empirical research on the duration of gang membership.

(4) Criteria for designating an organization as a criminal street gang and retention periods for information about criminal street gangs.

(5) Policies and procedures for notice to a person in a shared gang database. This includes policies and procedures for when notification would compromise an active criminal investigation or the health or safety of a minor.

(6) Policies and procedures for responding to an information request, a request for removal, or a petition for removal under Sections 186.34 and 186.35, respectively. This includes policies and procedures for a request or petition that could compromise an active criminal investigation or the health or safety of a minor.

(7) Policies and procedures for sharing information from a shared gang database with a federal agency, multistate agency, or agency of another state that is otherwise denied access. This includes sharing of information with a partner in a joint task force.

(8) Implementation of supervisory review procedures and periodic record reviews by law enforcement agencies and criminal justice agencies, and reporting of the results of those reviews to the department.

(m) Shared gang databases shall be used and operated in compliance with all applicable state and federal regulations, statutes, and guidelines. These include Part 23 of Title 28 of the Code of Federal Regulations and the department's Model Standards and Procedures for Maintaining Criminal Intelligence Files and Criminal Intelligence Operational Activities.

(n) The department, with the advice of the committee, no later than January 1, 2020, shall promulgate regulations to provide for periodic audits of each CalGang node and user agency to ensure the accuracy, reliability, and proper use of the CalGang database. The department shall mandate the purge of any information for which a user agency cannot establish adequate support.

(o) The department, with the advice of the committee, shall develop and implement standardized periodic training for everyone with access to the CalGang database.

(p) Commencing February 15, 2018, and annually on February 15 thereafter, the department shall publish an annual report on the CalGang database.

(1) The report shall include, in a format developed by the department, that contains, by ZIP Code, referring agency, race, gender, and age, the following information for each user agency:

(A) The number of persons included in the CalGang database on the day of reporting.

(B) The number of persons added to the CalGang database during the immediately preceding 12 months.

(C) The number of requests for removal of information about a person from the CalGang database pursuant to Section 186.34 received during the immediately preceding 12 months.

(D) The number of requests for removal of information about a person from the CalGang database pursuant to Section 186.34 that were granted during the immediately preceding 12 months.

(E) The number of petitions for removal of information about a person from the CalGang database pursuant to Section 186.35 adjudicated in the immediately preceding 12 months, including their dispositions.

(F) The number of persons whose information was removed from the CalGang database due to the expiration of a retention period during the immediately preceding 12 months.

(G) The number of times an agency did not provide notice or documentation described in Section 186.34 because providing that notice or documentation would compromise an active criminal investigation, in the immediately preceding 12 months.

(H) The number of times an agency did not provide notice or documentation described in Section 186.34 because providing that notice or documentation would compromise the health or safety of the designated minor, in the immediately preceding 12 months.

(2) The report shall include the results from each user agency's periodic audit conducted pursuant to subdivision (n).

(3) The department shall post the report on the department's Internet Web site.

(4) The department shall invite and assess public comments following the report's release, and each report shall summarize public comments received on prior reports and the actions taken in response to comments.

(q) The department shall instruct all user agencies to review the records of criminal street gang members entered into a shared gang database to ensure the existence of proper support for each criterion for entry in the shared gang database.

(r) (1) The department shall instruct each CalGang node agency to purge from a shared gang database any record of a person entered into the database designated as a suspected gang member, associate, or affiliate that does not meet criteria for entry or whose entry was based upon the following criteria: jail classification, frequenting gang neighborhoods, or on the basis of an untested informant. Unsupported criteria shall be purged and the records of a person shall be purged if the remaining criteria are not sufficient to support the person's designation.

(2) After the purge is completed, the shared gang database shall be examined using a statistically valid sample, pursuant to professional auditing standards to ensure that all fields in the database are accurate.

(s) (1) Commencing January 1, 2018, any shared gang database operated by law enforcement in California including, but not limited to, the CalGang database, shall be under a moratorium. During the moratorium, data shall not be added to the database. Data in the database shall not be accessed by participating agencies or shared with other entities. The moratorium on a shared gang database shall not be lifted until the Attorney General certifies that the purge required in subdivision (r) has been completed. After the purge has been completed and before the department adopts the regulations required by this section, new data may be entered, provided the new data meets the criteria established by the conditions of the purge.

(2) The department shall not use regulations developed pursuant to this section to invalidate data entries entered prior to the adoption of those regulations.

(t) The department shall be responsible for overseeing shared gang database system discipline and conformity with all applicable state and federal regulations, statutes, and guidelines.

(u) The department may enforce a violation of a state or federal law or regulation with respect to a shared gang database, or a violation of regulation, policy, or procedure established by the department pursuant to this title by any of the following methods:

(1) Letter of censure.

(2) Temporary suspension of access privileges to the shared gang database system.

(3) Revocation of access privileges to the shared gang database system.

(v) The department shall temporarily suspend access to a shared gang database system or revoke access to a shared gang database system for any individual who shares information from a shared gang database for employment or military screening purposes.

(w) The department shall temporarily suspend access to a shared gang database system or revoke access to a shared gang database system for an individual who shares information from a shared gang database for federal immigration law purposes, unless required by state or federal statute or regulation.

(x) The department shall ensure that the shared gang database user account of an individual is disabled if the individual no longer has a need or right to access a shared gang database because he or she has separated from his or her employment with a user agency or for another reason.

(Added by Stats. 2017, Ch. 695, Sec. 7. (AB 90) Effective January 1, 2018.)

TITLE 8. OF CRIMES AGAINST THE PERSON [187 - 248]

(Title 8 enacted 1872.)

CHAPTER 1. Homicide [187 - 199]

(Chapter 1 enacted 1872.)

187.

(a) Murder is the unlawful killing of a human being, or a fetus, with malice aforethought.

(b) This section shall not apply to any person who commits an act that results in the death of a fetus if any of the following apply:

(1) The act complied with the Therapeutic Abortion Act, Article 2 (commencing with Section 123400) of Chapter 2 of Part 2 of Division 106 of the Health and Safety Code.

(2) The act was committed by a holder of a physician's and surgeon's certificate, as defined in the Business and Professions Code, in a case where, to a medical certainty, the result of childbirth would be death of the mother of the fetus or where her death from childbirth, although not medically certain, would be substantially certain or more likely than not.

(3) The act was solicited, aided, abetted, or consented to by the mother of the fetus.
(c) Subdivision (b) shall not be construed to prohibit the prosecution of any person under any other provision of law.
(Amended by Stats. 1996, Ch. 1023, Sec. 385. Effective September 29, 1996.)
188.
(a) For purposes of Section 187, malice may be express or implied.
(1) Malice is express when there is manifested a deliberate intention to unlawfully take away the life of a fellow creature.
(2) Malice is implied when no considerable provocation appears, or when the circumstances attending the killing show an abandoned and malignant heart.
(3) Except as stated in subdivision (e) of Section 189, in order to be convicted of murder, a principal in a crime shall act with malice aforethought. Malice shall not be imputed to a person based solely on his or her participation in a crime.
(b) If it is shown that the killing resulted from an intentional act with express or implied malice, as defined in subdivision (a), no other mental state need be shown to establish the mental state of malice aforethought. Neither an awareness of the obligation to act within the general body of laws regulating society nor acting despite that awareness is included within the definition of malice.
(Amended by Stats. 2018, Ch. 1015, Sec. 2. (SB 1437) Effective January 1, 2019.)
189.
(a) All murder that is perpetrated by means of a destructive device or explosive, a weapon of mass destruction, knowing use of ammunition designed primarily to penetrate metal or armor, poison, lying in wait, torture, or by any other kind of willful, deliberate, and premeditated killing, or that is committed in the perpetration of, or attempt to perpetrate, arson, rape, carjacking, robbery, burglary, mayhem, kidnapping, train wrecking, or any act punishable under Section 206, 286, 288, 288a, or 289, or murder that is perpetrated by means of discharging a firearm from a motor vehicle, intentionally at another person outside of the vehicle with the intent to inflict death, is murder of the first degree.
(b) All other kinds of murders are of the second degree.
(c) As used in this section, the following definitions apply:
(1) "Destructive device" has the same meaning as in Section 16460.
(2) "Explosive" has the same meaning as in Section 12000 of the Health and Safety Code.
(3) "Weapon of mass destruction" means any item defined in Section 11417.
(d) To prove the killing was "deliberate and premeditated," it is not necessary to prove the defendant maturely and meaningfully reflected upon the gravity of his or her act.
(e) A participant in the perpetration or attempted perpetration of a felony listed in subdivision (a) in which a death occurs is liable for murder only if one of the following is proven:
(1) The person was the actual killer.
(2) The person was not the actual killer, but, with the intent to kill, aided, abetted, counseled, commanded, induced, solicited, requested, or assisted the actual killer in the commission of murder in the first degree.
(3) The person was a major participant in the underlying felony and acted with reckless indifference to human life, as described in subdivision (d) of Section 190.2.
(f) Subdivision (e) does not apply to a defendant when the victim is a peace officer who was killed while in the course of his or her duties, where the defendant knew or reasonably should have known that the victim was a peace officer engaged in the performance of his or her duties.
(Amended by Stats. 2018, Ch. 1015, Sec. 3. (SB 1437) Effective January 1, 2019. Note: This section was amended on June 5, 1990, by initiative Prop. 115.)
189.1.
(a) The Legislature finds and declares that all unlawful killings that are willful, deliberate, and premeditated and in which the victim was a peace officer, as defined in Section 830, who was killed while engaged in the performance of his or her duties, where the defendant knew, or reasonably should have known, that the victim was a peace officer engaged in the performance of his or her duties, are considered murder of the first degree for all purposes, including the gravity of the offense and the support of the survivors.
(b) This section is declarative of existing law.
(Added by Stats. 2017, Ch. 214, Sec. 2. (AB 1459) Effective January 1, 2018.)
189.5.
(a) Upon a trial for murder, the commission of the homicide by the defendant being proved, the burden of proving circumstances of mitigation, or that justify or excuse it, devolves upon the defendant, unless the proof on the part of the prosecution tends to show that the crime committed only amounts to manslaughter, or that the defendant was justifiable or excusable.
(b) Nothing in this section shall apply to or affect any proceeding under Section 190.3 or 190.4.
(Added by Stats. 1989, Ch. 897, Sec. 16.)
190.
(a) Every person guilty of murder in the first degree shall be punished by death, imprisonment in the state prison for life without the possibility of parole, or imprisonment in the state prison for a term of 25 years to life. The penalty to be applied shall be determined as provided in Sections 190.1, 190.2, 190.3, 190.4, and 190.5.
Except as provided in subdivision (b), (c), or (d), every person guilty of murder in the second degree shall be punished by imprisonment in the state prison for a term of 15 years to life.
(b) Except as provided in subdivision (c), every person guilty of murder in the second degree shall be punished by imprisonment in the state prison for a term of 25 years to life if the victim was a peace officer, as defined in subdivision (a) of Section 830.1, subdivision (a), (b), or (c) of Section 830.2, subdivision (a) of Section 830.33, or Section 830.5, who was killed while engaged in the performance of his or her duties, and the defendant knew, or reasonably should have known, that the victim was a peace officer engaged in the performance of his or her duties.
(c) Every person guilty of murder in the second degree shall be punished by imprisonment in the state prison for a term of life without the possibility of parole if the victim was a peace officer, as defined in subdivision (a) of Section 830.1, subdivision (a), (b), or (c) of Section 830.2, subdivision (a) of Section 830.33, or Section 830.5, who was killed while engaged in the performance of his or her duties, and the defendant knew, or reasonably should have known, that the victim was a peace officer engaged in the performance of his or her duties, and any of the following facts has been charged and found true:
(1) The defendant specifically intended to kill the peace officer.
(2) The defendant specifically intended to inflict great bodily injury, as defined in Section 12022.7, on a peace officer.
(3) The defendant personally used a dangerous or deadly weapon in the commission of the offense, in violation of subdivision (b) of Section 12022.
(4) The defendant personally used a firearm in the commission of the offense, in violation of Section 12022.5.
(d) Every person guilty of murder in the second degree shall be punished by imprisonment in the state prison for a term of 20 years to life if the killing was perpetrated by means of shooting a firearm from a motor vehicle, intentionally at another person outside of the vehicle with the intent to inflict great bodily injury.
(e) Article 2.5 (commencing with Section 2930) of Chapter 7 of Title 1 of Part 3 shall not apply to reduce any minimum term of a sentence imposed pursuant to this section. A person sentenced pursuant to this section shall not be released on parole prior to serving the minimum term of confinement prescribed by this section.
(Amended by Stats. 1998, Ch. 760, Sec. 6. Approved in Proposition 19 at the March 7, 2000, election. Prior History: Added Nov. 7, 1978, by initiative Prop. 7; amended June 7, 1988, by Prop. 67 (from Stats. 1987, Ch. 1006); amended June 7, 1994, by Prop. 179 (from Stats. 1993, Ch. 609); amended June 2, 1998, by Prop. 222 (from Stats. 1997, Ch. 413, Sec. 1, which incorporated Stats. 1996, Ch. 598).)
190.03.
(a) A person who commits first-degree murder that is a hate crime shall be punished by imprisonment in the state prison for life without the possibility of parole.
(b) The term authorized by subdivision (a) shall not apply unless the allegation is charged in the accusatory pleading and admitted by the defendant or found true by the trier of fact. The court shall not strike the allegation, except in the interest of justice, in which case the court shall state its reasons in writing for striking the allegation.
(c) For the purpose of this section, "hate crime" has the same meaning as in Section 422.55.
(d) Nothing in this section shall be construed to prevent punishment instead pursuant to any other provision of law that imposes a greater or more severe punishment.
(Amended by Stats. 2004, Ch. 700, Sec. 5. Effective January 1, 2005.)
190.05.
(a) The penalty for a defendant found guilty of murder in the second degree, who has served a prior prison term for murder in the first or second degree, shall be confinement in the state prison for a term of life without the possibility of parole or confinement in the state prison for a term of 15 years to life. For purposes of this section, a prior prison term for murder of the first or second degree is that time period in which a defendant has spent actually incarcerated for his or her offense prior to release on parole.
(b) A prior prison term for murder for purposes of this section includes either of the following:
(1) A prison term served in any state prison or federal penal institution, including confinement in a hospital or other institution or facility credited as service of prison time in the jurisdiction of confinement, as punishment for the commission of an offense which includes all of the elements of murder in the first or second degree as defined under California law.
(2) Incarceration at a facility operated by the Youth Authority for murder of the first or second degree when the person was subject to the custody, control, and discipline of the Director of Corrections.
(c) The fact of a prior prison term for murder in the first or second degree shall be alleged in the accusatory pleading, and either admitted by the defendant in open court, or found to be true by the jury trying the issue of guilt or by the court where guilt is established by a plea of guilty or nolo contendere or by trial by the court sitting without a jury.
(d) In case of a reasonable doubt as to whether the defendant served a prior prison term for murder in the first or second degree, the defendant is entitled to a finding that the allegation is not true.
(e) If the trier of fact finds that the defendant has served a prior prison term for murder in the first or second degree, there shall be a separate penalty hearing before the same trier of fact, except as provided in subdivision (f).
(f) If the defendant was convicted by the court sitting without a jury, the trier of fact at the penalty hearing shall be a jury unless a jury is waived by the defendant and the people, in which case the trier of fact shall be the court. If the defendant was convicted by a plea of guilty or nolo contendere, the trier of fact shall be a jury unless a jury is waived by the defendant and the people.
If the trier of fact is a jury and has been unable to reach a unanimous verdict as to what the penalty shall be, the court shall dismiss the jury and shall order a new jury impaneled to try the issue as to what the penalty shall be. If the new jury is unable to reach a unanimous verdict as to what the penalty shall be, the court in its discretion shall either order a new jury or impose a punishment of confinement in the state prison for a term of 15 years to life.
(g) Evidence presented at any prior phase of the trial, including any proceeding under a plea of not guilty by reason of insanity pursuant to Section 1026, shall be considered at any subsequent phase of the trial, if the trier of fact of the prior phase is the same trier of fact at the subsequent phase.
(h) In the proceeding on the question of penalty, evidence may be presented by both the people and the defendant as to any matter relevant to aggravation, mitigation, and sentence, including, but not limited to, the nature and circumstances of the present offense, any prior felony conviction or convictions whether or not such conviction or convictions involved a crime of violence, the presence or absence of other criminal activity by the defendant which involved the use or attempted use of force or violence or which involved the express or implied threat to use force or violence, and the defendant's character, background, history, mental condition, and physical condition.
However, no evidence shall be admitted regarding other criminal activity by the defendant which did not involve the use or attempted use of force or violence or which did not involve the express or implied threat to use force or violence. As used in this section, criminal activity does not require a conviction.
However, in no event shall evidence of prior criminal activity be admitted for an offense for which the defendant was prosecuted and acquitted. The restriction on the use of this evidence is intended to apply only to proceedings pursuant to this section and is not intended to affect statutory or decisional law allowing such evidence to be used in any other proceedings.
Except for evidence in proof of the offense or the prior prison term for murder of the first or second degree which subjects a defendant to the punishment of life without the possibility of parole, no evidence may be presented by the prosecution in aggravation unless notice of the evidence to be introduced has been given to the defendant within a reasonable period of time as determined by the court, prior to trial. Evidence may be introduced without such notice in rebuttal to evidence introduced by the defendant in mitigation.
In determining the penalty, the trier of fact shall take into account any of the following factors if relevant:
(1) The circumstances of the crime of which the defendant was convicted in the present proceeding and the existence of the prior prison term for murder.
(2) The presence or absence of criminal activity by the defendant which involved the use or attempted use of force or violence or the express or implied threat to use force or violence.
(3) The presence or absence of any prior felony conviction.
(4) Whether or not the offense was committed while the defendant was under the influence of extreme mental or emotional disturbance.
(5) Whether or not the victim was a participant in the defendant's homicidal conduct or consented to the homicidal act.
(6) Whether or not the offense was committed under circumstances which the defendant reasonably believed to be a moral justification or extenuation for his or her conduct.
(7) Whether or not the defendant acted under extreme duress or under the substantial domination of another person.
(8) Whether or not at the time of the offense the ability of the defendant to appreciate the criminality of his or her conduct or to conform his or her conduct to the requirements of law was impaired as a result of mental disease or defect, or the effects of intoxication.
(9) The age of the defendant at the time of the crime.
(10) Whether or not the defendant was an accomplice to the offense and his or her participation in the commission of the offense was relatively minor.
(11) Any other circumstance which extenuates the gravity of the crime even though it is not a legal excuse for the crime.

After having heard and received all of the evidence, and after having heard and considered the arguments of counsel, the trier of fact shall consider, take into account, and be guided by the aggravating and mitigating circumstances referred to in this section, and shall impose a sentence of life without the possibility of parole if the trier of fact concludes that the aggravating circumstances outweigh the mitigating circumstances. If the trier of fact determines that the mitigating circumstances outweigh the aggravating circumstances, the trier of fact shall impose a sentence of confinement in the state prison for 15 years to life.

(i) Nothing in this section shall be construed to prohibit the charging of finding of any special circumstance pursuant to Sections 190.1, 190.2, 190.3, 190.4, and 190.5.
(Added by Stats. 1985, Ch. 1510, Sec. 1.)

190.1.
A case in which the death penalty may be imposed pursuant to this chapter shall be tried in separate phases as follows:

(a) The question of the defendant's guilt shall be first determined. If the trier of fact finds the defendant guilty of first degree murder, it shall at the same time determine the truth of all special circumstances charged as enumerated in Section 190.2 except for a special circumstance charged pursuant to paragraph (2) of subdivision (a) of Section 190.2 where it is alleged that the defendant had been convicted in a prior proceeding of the offense of murder in the first or second degree.

(b) If the defendant is found guilty of first degree murder and one of the special circumstances is charged pursuant to paragraph (2) of subdivision (a) of Section 190.2 which charges that the defendant had been convicted in a prior proceeding of the offense of murder of the first or second degree, there shall thereupon be further proceedings on the question of the truth of such special circumstance.

(c) If the defendant is found guilty of first degree murder and one or more special circumstances as enumerated in Section 190.2 has been charged and found to be true, his sanity on any plea of not guilty by reason of insanity under Section 1026 shall be determined as provided in Section 190.4. If he is found to be sane, there shall thereupon be further proceedings on the question of the penalty to be imposed. Such proceedings shall be conducted in accordance with the provisions of Section 190.3 and 190.4.
(Repealed and added November 7, 1978, by initiative Proposition 7, Sec. 4.)

190.2.
(a) The penalty for a defendant who is found guilty of murder in the first degree is death or imprisonment in the state prison for life without the possibility of parole if one or more of the following special circumstances has been found under Section 190.4 to be true:

(1) The murder was intentional and carried out for financial gain.

(2) The defendant was convicted previously of murder in the first or second degree. For the purpose of this paragraph, an offense committed in another jurisdiction, which if committed in California would be punishable as first or second degree murder, shall be deemed murder in the first or second degree.

(3) The defendant, in this proceeding, has been convicted of more than one offense of murder in the first or second degree.

(4) The murder was committed by means of a destructive device, bomb, or explosive planted, hidden, or concealed in any place, area, dwelling, building, or structure, and the defendant knew, or reasonably should have known, that his or her act or acts would create a great risk of death to one or more human beings.

(5) The murder was committed for the purpose of avoiding or preventing a lawful arrest, or perfecting or attempting to perfect, an escape from lawful custody.

(6) The murder was committed by means of a destructive device, bomb, or explosive that the defendant mailed or delivered, attempted to mail or deliver, or caused to be mailed or delivered, and the defendant knew, or reasonably should have known, that his or her act or acts would create a great risk of death to one or more human beings.

(7) The victim was a peace officer, as defined in Section 830.1, 830.2, 830.3, 830.31, 830.32, 830.33, 830.34, 830.35, 830.36, 830.37, 830.4, 830.5, 830.6, 830.10, 830.11, or 830.12, who, while engaged in the course of the performance of his or her duties, was intentionally killed, and the defendant knew, or reasonably should have known, that the victim was a peace officer engaged in the performance of his or her duties; or the victim was a peace officer, as defined in the above-enumerated sections, or a former peace officer under any of those sections, and was intentionally killed in retaliation for the performance of his or her official duties.

(8) The victim was a federal law enforcement officer or agent who, while engaged in the course of the performance of his or her duties, was intentionally killed, and the defendant knew, or reasonably should have known, that the victim was a federal law enforcement officer or agent engaged in the performance of his or her duties; or the victim was a federal law enforcement officer or agent, and was intentionally killed in retaliation for the performance of his or her official duties.

(9) The victim was a firefighter, as defined in Section 245.1, who, while engaged in the course of the performance of his or her duties, was intentionally killed, and the defendant knew, or reasonably should have known, that the victim was a firefighter engaged in the performance of his or her duties.

(10) The victim was a witness to a crime who was intentionally killed for the purpose of preventing his or her testimony in any criminal or juvenile proceeding, and the killing was not committed during the commission or attempted commission, of the crime to which he or she was a witness; or the victim was a witness to a crime and was intentionally killed in retaliation for his or her testimony in any criminal or juvenile proceeding. As used in this paragraph, "juvenile proceeding" means a proceeding brought pursuant to Section 602 or 707 of the Welfare and Institutions Code.

(11) The victim was a prosecutor or assistant prosecutor or a former prosecutor or assistant prosecutor of any local or state prosecutor's office in this or any other state, or of a federal prosecutor's office, and the murder was intentionally carried out in retaliation for, or to prevent the performance of, the victim's official duties.

(12) The victim was a judge or former judge of any court of record in the local, state, or federal system in this or any other state, and the murder was intentionally carried out in retaliation for, or to prevent the performance of, the victim's official duties.

(13) The victim was an elected or appointed official or former official of the federal government, or of any local or state government of this or any other state, and the killing was intentionally carried out in retaliation for, or to prevent the performance of, the victim's official duties.

(14) The murder was especially heinous, atrocious, or cruel, manifesting exceptional depravity. As used in this section, the phrase "especially heinous, atrocious, or cruel, manifesting exceptional depravity" means a conscienceless or pitiless crime that is unnecessarily torturous to the victim.

(15) The defendant intentionally killed the victim by means of lying in wait.

(16) The victim was intentionally killed because of his or her race, color, religion, nationality, or country of origin.

(17) The murder was committed while the defendant was engaged in, or was an accomplice in, the commission of, attempted commission of, or the immediate flight after committing, or attempting to commit, the following felonies:

(A) Robbery in violation of Section 211 or 212.5.

(B) Kidnapping in violation of Section 207, 209, or 209.5.

(C) Rape in violation of Section 261.

(D) Sodomy in violation of Section 286.

(E) The performance of a lewd or lascivious act upon the person of a child under the age of 14 years in violation of Section 288.

(F) Oral copulation in violation of Section 287 or former Section 288a.

(G) Burglary in the first or second degree in violation of Section 460.

(H) Arson in violation of subdivision (b) of Section 451.

(I) Train wrecking in violation of Section 219.

(J) Mayhem in violation of Section 203.

(K) Rape by instrument in violation of Section 289.

(L) Carjacking, as defined in Section 215.

(M) To prove the special circumstances of kidnapping in subparagraph (B), or arson in subparagraph (H), if there is specific intent to kill, it is only required that there be proof of the elements of those felonies. If so established, those two special circumstances are proven even if the felony of kidnapping or arson is committed primarily or solely for the purpose of facilitating the murder.

(18) The murder was intentional and involved the infliction of torture.

(19) The defendant intentionally killed the victim by the administration of poison.

(20) The victim was a juror in any court of record in the local, state, or federal system in this or any other state, and the murder was intentionally carried out in retaliation for, or to prevent the performance of, the victim's official duties.

(21) The murder was intentional and perpetrated by means of discharging a firearm from a motor vehicle, intentionally at another person or persons outside the vehicle with the intent to inflict death. For purposes of this paragraph, "motor vehicle" means any vehicle as defined in Section 415 of the Vehicle Code.

(22) The defendant intentionally killed the victim while the defendant was an active participant in a criminal street gang, as defined in subdivision (f) of Section 186.22, and the murder was carried out to further the activities of the criminal street gang.

(b) Unless an intent to kill is specifically required under subdivision (a) for a special circumstance enumerated therein, an actual killer, as to whom the special circumstance has been found to be true under Section 190.4, need not have had any intent to kill at the time of the commission of the offense which is the basis of the special circumstance in order to suffer death or confinement in the state prison for life without the possibility of parole.

(c) Every person, not the actual killer, who, with the intent to kill, aids, abets, counsels, commands, induces, solicits, requests, or assists any actor in the commission of murder in the first degree shall be punished by death or imprisonment in the state prison for life without the possibility of parole if one or more of the special circumstances enumerated in subdivision (a) has been found to be true under Section 190.4.

(d) Notwithstanding subdivision (c), every person, not the actual killer, who, with reckless indifference to human life and as a major participant, aids, abets, counsels, commands, induces, solicits, requests, or assists in the commission of a felony enumerated in paragraph (17) of subdivision (a) which results in the death of some person or persons, and who is found guilty of murder in the first degree therefor, shall be punished by death or imprisonment in the state prison for life without the possibility of parole if a special circumstance enumerated in paragraph (17) of subdivision (a) has been found to be true under Section 190.4.

The penalty shall be determined as provided in this section and Sections 190.1, 190.3, 190.4, and 190.5.
(Amended by Stats. 2018, Ch. 423, Sec. 43. (SB 1494) Effective January 1, 2019. Prior History: Added Nov. 7, 1978, by initiative Prop. 7; amended June 5, 1990, by Prop. 114 (from Stats. 1989, Ch. 1165) and by initiative Prop. 115; amended March 26, 1996, by Prop. 196 (from Stats. 1995, Ch. 478, Sec. 2).)

190.25.
(a) The penalty for a defendant found guilty of murder in the first degree shall be confinement in state prison for a term of life without the possibility of parole in any case in which any of the following special circumstances has been charged and specially found under Section 190.4, to be true: the victim was the operator or driver of a bus, taxicab, streetcar, cable car, trackless trolley, or other motor vehicle operated on land, including a vehicle operated on stationary rails or on a track or rail suspended in the air, used for the transportation of persons for hire, or the victim was a station agent or ticket agent for the entity providing such transportation, who, while engaged in the course of the performance of his or her duties was intentionally killed, and such defendant knew or reasonably should have known that such victim was the operator or driver of a bus, taxicab, streetcar, cable car, trackless trolley, or other motor vehicle operated on land, including a vehicle operated on stationary rails or on a track or rail suspended in the air, used for the transportation of persons for hire, or was a station agent or ticket agent for the entity providing such transportation, engaged in the performance of his or her duties.

(b) Every person whether or not the actual killer found guilty of intentionally aiding, abetting, counseling, commanding, inducing, soliciting, requesting, or assisting any actor in the commission of murder in the first degree shall suffer confinement in state prison for a term of life without the possibility of parole, in any case in which one or more of the special circumstances enumerated in subdivision (a) of this section has been charged and specially found under Section 190.4 to be true.

(c) Nothing in this section shall be construed to prohibit the charging or finding of any special circumstance pursuant to Sections 190.1, 190.2, 190.3, 190.4, and 190.5.
(Added by Stats. 1982, Ch. 172, Sec. 1. Effective April 27, 1982.)

190.3.
If the defendant has been found guilty of murder in the first degree, and a special circumstance has been charged and found to be true, or if the defendant may be subject to the death penalty after having been found guilty of violating subdivision (a) of Section 1672 of the Military and Veterans Code or Sections 37, 128, 219, or 4500 of this code, the trier of fact shall determine whether the penalty shall be death or confinement in state prison for a term of life without the possibility of parole. In the proceedings on the question of penalty, evidence may be presented by both the people and the defendant as to any matter relevant to aggravation, mitigation, and sentence including, but not limited to, the nature and circumstances of the present offense, any prior felony conviction or convictions whether or not such conviction or convictions involved a crime of violence, the presence or absence of other criminal activity by the defendant which involved the use or attempted use of force or violence or which involved the express or implied threat to use force or violence, and the defendant's character, background, history, mental condition and physical condition.

However, no evidence shall be admitted regarding other criminal activity by the defendant which did not involve the use or attempted use of force or violence or which did not involve the express or implied threat to use force or violence. As used in this section, criminal activity does not require a conviction.

However, in no event shall evidence of prior criminal activity be admitted for an offense for which the defendant was prosecuted and acquitted. The restriction on the use of this evidence is intended to apply only to proceedings pursuant to this section and is not intended to affect statutory or decisional law allowing such evidence to be used in any other proceedings.

Except for evidence in proof of the offense or special circumstances which subject a defendant to the death penalty, no evidence may be presented by the prosecution in aggravation unless notice of the evidence to be introduced has been given to the defendant within a reasonable period of time as determined by the court, prior to trial. Evidence may be introduced without such notice in rebuttal to evidence introduced by the defendant in mitigation.

The trier of fact shall be instructed that a sentence of confinement to state prison for a term of life without the possibility of parole may in future after sentence is imposed, be commuted or modified to a sentence that includes the possibility of parole by the Governor of the State of California.

In determining the penalty, the trier of fact shall take into account any of the following factors if relevant:

(a) The circumstances of the crime of which the defendant was convicted in the present proceeding and the existence of any special circumstances found to be true pursuant to Section 190.1.
(b) The presence or absence of criminal activity by the defendant which involved the use or attempted use of force or violence or the express or implied threat to use force or violence.
(c) The presence or absence of any prior felony conviction.
(d) Whether or not the offense was committed while the defendant was under the influence of extreme mental or emotional disturbance.
(e) Whether or not the victim was a participant in the defendant's homicidal conduct or consented to the homicidal act.
(f) Whether or not the offense was committed under circumstances which the defendant reasonably believed to be a moral justification or extenuation for his conduct.
(g) Whether or not defendant acted under extreme duress or under the substantial domination of another person.
(h) Whether or not at the time of the offense the capacity of the defendant to appreciate the criminality of his conduct or to conform his conduct to the requirements of law was impaired as a result of mental disease or defect, or the affects of intoxication.
(i) The age of the defendant at the time of the crime.
(j) Whether or not the defendant was an accomplice to the offense and his participation in the commission of the offense was relatively minor.
(k) Any other circumstance which extenuates the gravity of the crime even though it is not a legal excuse for the crime.
After having heard and received all of the evidence, and after having heard and considered the arguments of counsel, the trier of fact shall consider, take into account and be guided by the aggravating and mitigating circumstances referred to in this section, and shall impose a sentence of death if the trier of fact concludes that the aggravating circumstances outweigh the mitigating circumstances. If the trier of fact determines that the mitigating circumstances outweigh the aggravating circumstances the trier of fact shall impose a sentence of confinement in state prison for a term of life without the possibility of parole.
(Repealed and added November 7, 1978, by initiative Proposition 7, Sec. 8.)
190.4.
(a) Whenever special circumstances as enumerated in Section 190.2 are alleged and the trier of fact finds the defendant guilty of first degree murder, the trier of fact shall also make a special finding on the truth of each alleged special circumstance. The determination of the truth of any or all of the special circumstances shall be made by the trier of fact on the evidence presented at the trial or at the hearing held pursuant to Subdivision (b) of Section 190.1.
In case of a reasonable doubt as to whether a special circumstance is true, the defendant is entitled to a finding that is not true. The trier of fact shall make a special finding that each special circumstance charged is either true or not true. Whenever a special circumstance requires proof of the commission or attempted commission of a crime, such crime shall be charged and proved pursuant to the general law applying to the trial and conviction of the crime.
If the defendant was convicted by the court sitting without a jury, the trier of fact shall be a jury unless a jury is waived by the defendant and by the people, in which case the trier of fact shall be the court. If the defendant was convicted by a plea of guilty, the trier of fact shall be a jury unless a jury is waived by the defendant and by the people.
If the trier of fact finds that any one or more of the special circumstances enumerated in Section 190.2 as charged is true, there shall be a separate penalty hearing, and neither the finding that any of the remaining special circumstances charged is not true, nor if the trier of fact is a jury, the inability of the jury to agree on the issue of the truth or untruth of any of the remaining special circumstances charged, shall prevent the holding of a separate penalty hearing.
In any case in which the defendant has been found guilty by a jury, and the jury has been unable to reach an unanimous verdict that one or more of the special circumstances charged are true, and does not reach a unanimous verdict that all the special circumstances charged are not true, the court shall dismiss the jury and shall order a new jury impaneled to try the issues, but the issue of guilt shall not be tried by such jury, nor shall such jury retry the issue of the truth of any of the special circumstances which were found by an unanimous verdict of the previous jury to be untrue. If such new jury is unable to reach the unanimous verdict that one or more of the special circumstances it is trying are true, the court shall dismiss the jury and in the court's discretion shall either order a new jury impaneled to try the issues the previous jury was unable to reach the unanimous verdict on, or impose a punishment of confinement in state prison for a term of 25 years.
(b) If defendant was convicted by the court sitting without a jury the trier of fact at the penalty hearing shall be a jury unless a jury is waived by the defendant and the people, in which case the trier of fact shall be the court. If the defendant was convicted by a plea of guilty, the trier of fact shall be a jury unless a jury is waived by the defendant and the people.
If the trier of fact is a jury and has been unable to reach a unanimous verdict as to what the penalty shall be, the court shall dismiss the jury and shall order a new jury impaneled to try the issue as to what the penalty shall be. If such new jury is unable to reach a unanimous verdict as to what the penalty shall be, the court in its discretion shall either order a new jury or impose a punishment of confinement in state prison for a term of life without the possibility of parole.
(c) If the trier of fact which convicted the defendant of a crime for which he may be subject to the death penalty was a jury, the same jury shall consider any plea of not guilty by reason of insanity pursuant to Section 1026, the truth of any special circumstances which may be alleged, and the penalty to be applied, unless for good cause shown the court discharges that jury in which case a new jury shall be drawn. The court shall state facts in support of the finding of good cause upon the record and cause them to be entered into the minutes.
(d) In any case in which the defendant may be subject to the death penalty, evidence presented at any prior phase of the trial, including any proceeding under a plea of not guilty by reason of insanity pursuant to Section 1026 shall be considered an any subsequent phase of the trial, if the trier of fact of the prior phase is the same trier of fact at the subsequent phase.
(e) In every case in which the trier of fact has returned a verdict or finding imposing the death penalty, the defendant shall be deemed to have made an application for modification of such verdict or finding pursuant to Subdivision 7 of Section 11. In ruling on the application, the judge shall review the evidence, consider, take into account, and be guided by the aggravating and mitigating circumstances referred to in Section 190.3, and shall make a determination as to whether the jury's findings and verdicts that the aggravating circumstances outweigh the mitigating circumstances are contrary to law or the evidence presented. The judge shall state on the record the reasons for his findings. The judge shall set forth the reasons for his ruling on the application and direct that they be entered on the Clerk's minutes. The denial of the modification of the death penalty verdict pursuant to subdivision (7) of Section 1181 shall be reviewed on the defendant's automatic appeal pursuant to subdivision (b) of Section 1239. The granting of the application shall be reviewed on the People's appeal pursuant to paragraph (6).
(Repealed and added November 7, 1978, by initiative Proposition 7, Sec. 10.)
190.41.
Notwithstanding Section 190.4 or any other provision of law, the corpus delicti of a felony-based special circumstance enumerated in paragraph (17) of subdivision (a) of Section 190.2 need not be proved independently of a defendant's extrajudicial statement.
(Added June 5, 1990, by initiative Proposition 115, Sec. 11.)
190.5.
(a) Notwithstanding any other provision of law, the death penalty shall not be imposed upon any person who is under the age of 18 at the time of the commission of the crime. The burden of proof as to the age of such person shall be upon the defendant.
(b) The penalty for a defendant found guilty of murder in the first degree, in any case in which one or more special circumstances enumerated in Section 190.2 or 190.25 has been found to be true under Section 190.4, who was 16 years of age or older and under the age of 18 years at the time of the commission of the crime, shall be confinement in the state prison for life without the possibility of parole or, at the discretion of the court, 25 years to life.
(c) The trier of fact shall determine the existence of any special circumstance pursuant to the procedure set forth in Section 190.4.
(Amended June 5, 1990, by initiative Proposition 115, Sec. 12.)
190.6.
(a) The Legislature finds that the sentence in all capital cases should be imposed expeditiously.
(b) Therefore, in all cases in which a sentence of death has been imposed on or after January 1, 1997, the opening appellate brief in the appeal to the State Supreme Court shall be filed no later than seven months after the certification of the record for completeness under subdivision (d) of Section 190.8 or receipt by the appellant's counsel of the completed record, whichever is later, except for good cause. However, in those cases where the trial transcript exceeds 10,000 pages, the briefing shall be completed within the time limits and pursuant to the procedures set by the rules of court adopted by the Judicial Council.
(c) In all cases in which a sentence of death has been imposed on or after January 1, 1997, it is the Legislature's goal that the appeal be decided and an opinion reaching the merits be filed within 210 days of the completion of the briefing. However, where the appeal and a petition for writ of habeas corpus is heard at the same time, the petition should be decided and an opinion reaching the merits should be filed within 210 days of the completion of the briefing for the petition.
(d) The right of victims of crime to a prompt and final conclusion, as provided in paragraph (9) of subdivision (b) of Section 28 of Article I of the California Constitution, includes the right to have judgments of death carried out within a reasonable time. Within 18 months of the effective date of this initiative, the Judicial Council shall adopt initial rules and standards of administration designed to expedite the processing of capital appeals and state habeas corpus review. Within five years of the adoption of the initial rules or the entry of judgment, whichever is later, the state courts shall complete the state appeal and the initial state habeas corpus review in capital cases. The Judicial Council shall continuously monitor the timeliness of review of capital cases and shall amend the rules and standards as necessary to complete the state appeal and initial state habeas corpus proceedings within the five-year period provided in this subdivision.
(e) The failure of the parties or of a court to comply with the time limit in subdivision (b) shall not affect the validity of the judgment or require dismissal of an appeal or habeas corpus petition. If a court fails to comply without extraordinary and compelling reasons justifying the delay, either party or any victim of the offense may seek relief by petition for writ of mandate. The court in which the petition is filed shall act on it within 60 days of filing. Paragraph (1) of subdivision (c) of Section 28 of Article I of the California Constitution, regarding standing to enforce victims' rights, applies to this subdivision and subdivision (d).
(Amended November 8, 2016, by initiative Proposition 66, Sec. 3.)
190.7.
(a) The "entire record" referred to in Section 190.6 includes, but is not limited to, the following:
(1) The normal and additional record prescribed in the rules adopted by the Judicial Council pertaining to an appeal taken by the defendant from a judgment of conviction.
(2) A copy of any other paper or record on file or lodged with the superior or municipal court and a transcript of any other oral proceeding reported in the superior or municipal court pertaining to the trial of the cause.
(b) Notwithstanding this section, the Judicial Council may adopt rules, not inconsistent with the purpose of Section 190.6, specifically pertaining to the content, preparation and certification of the record on appeal when a judgment of death has been pronounced.
(Amended by Stats. 1996, Ch. 1086, Sec. 2. Effective January 1, 1997.)
190.8.
(a) In any case in which a death sentence has been imposed, the record on appeal shall be expeditiously certified in two stages, the first for completeness and the second for accuracy, as provided by this section. The trial court may use all reasonable means to ensure compliance with all applicable statutes and rules of court pertaining to record certification in capital appeals, including, but not limited to, the imposition of sanctions.
(b) Within 30 days of the imposition of the death sentence, the clerk of the superior court shall provide to trial counsel copies of the clerk's transcript and shall deliver the transcript as provided by the court reporter. Trial counsel shall promptly notify the court if he or she has not received the transcript within 30 days.
(c) During the course of a trial in which the death penalty is being sought, trial counsel shall alert the court's attention to any errors in the transcripts incidentally discovered by counsel while reviewing them in the ordinary course of trial preparation. The court shall periodically request that trial counsel provide a list of errors in the trial transcript during the course of trial and may hold hearings in connection therewith.
Corrections to the record shall not be required to include immaterial typographical errors that cannot conceivably cause confusion.
(d) The trial court shall certify the record for completeness and for incorporation of all corrections, as provided by subdivision (c), no later than 90 days after entry of the imposition of the death sentence unless good cause is shown. However, this time period may be extended for proceedings in which the trial transcript exceeds 10,000 pages in accordance with the timetable set forth in, or for good cause pursuant to the procedures set forth in, the rules of court adopted by the Judicial Council.
(e) Following the imposition of the death sentence and prior to the deadline set forth in subdivision (d), the trial court shall hold one or more hearings for trial counsel to address the completeness of the record and any outstanding errors that have come to their attention and to certify that they have reviewed all docket sheets to ensure that the record contains transcripts for any proceedings, hearings, or discussions that are required to be reported and that have occurred in the course of the case in any court, as well as all documents required by this code and the rules adopted by the Judicial Council.
(f) The clerk of the trial court shall deliver a copy of the record on appeal to appellate counsel when the clerk receives notice of counsel's appointment or retention, or when the record is certified for completeness under subdivision (d), whichever is later.
(g) The trial court shall certify the record for accuracy no later than 120 days after the record has been delivered to appellate counsel. However, this time may be extended pursuant to the timetable and procedures set forth in the rules of court adopted by the Judicial Council. The trial court may hold one or more status conferences for purposes of timely certification of the record for accuracy, as set forth in the rules of court adopted by the Judicial Council.
(h) The Supreme Court shall identify in writing to the Judicial Council any case that has not met the time limit for certification of the record for completeness under subdivision (d) or for accuracy under subdivision (g), and shall identify those cases, and its reasons, for which it has granted an extension of time. The Judicial Council shall include this information in its annual report to the Legislature.

(i) As used in this section, "trial counsel" means both the prosecution and the defense counsel in the trial in which the sentence of death has been imposed.

(j) This section shall be implemented pursuant to rules of court adopted by the Judicial Council.

(k) This section shall only apply to those proceedings in which a sentence of death has been imposed following a trial that was commenced on or after January 1, 1997.

(Amended by Stats. 1996, Ch. 1086, Sec. 3. Effective January 1, 1997.)

190.9.

(a) (1) In any case in which a death sentence may be imposed, all proceedings conducted in the superior court, including all conferences and proceedings, whether in open court, in conference in the courtroom, or in chambers, shall be conducted on the record with a court reporter present. The court reporter shall prepare and certify a daily transcript of all proceedings commencing with the preliminary hearing. Proceedings prior to the preliminary hearing shall be reported but need not be transcribed until the court receives notice as prescribed in paragraph (2).

(2) Upon receiving notification from the prosecution that the death penalty is being sought, the clerk shall order the transcription and preparation of the record of all proceedings prior to and including the preliminary hearing in the manner prescribed by the Judicial Council in the rules of court. The record of all proceedings prior to and including the preliminary hearing shall be certified by the court no later than 120 days following notification unless the time is extended pursuant to rules of court adopted by the Judicial Council. Upon certification, the record of all proceedings is incorporated into the superior court record.

(b) (1) The court shall assign a court reporter who uses computer-aided transcription equipment to report all proceedings under this section.

(2) Failure to comply with the requirements of this section relating to the assignment of court reporters who use computer-aided transcription equipment is not a ground for reversal.

(c) Any computer-readable transcript produced by court reporters pursuant to this section shall conform to the requirements of Section 271 of the Code of Civil Procedure.

(Amended by Stats. 2002, Ch. 71, Sec. 6. Effective January 1, 2003.)

191.

The rules of the common law, distinguishing the killing of a master by his servant, and of a husband by his wife, as petit treason, are abolished, and these offenses are homicides, punishable in the manner prescribed by this Chapter.

(Enacted 1872.)

191.5.

(a) Gross vehicular manslaughter while intoxicated is the unlawful killing of a human being without malice aforethought, in the driving of a vehicle, where the driving was in violation of Section 23140, 23152, or 23153 of the Vehicle Code, and the killing was either the proximate result of the commission of an unlawful act, not amounting to a felony, and with gross negligence, or the proximate result of the commission of a lawful act that might produce death, in an unlawful manner, and with gross negligence.

(b) Vehicular manslaughter while intoxicated is the unlawful killing of a human being without malice aforethought, in the driving of a vehicle, where the driving was in violation of Section 23140, 23152, or 23153 of the Vehicle Code, and the killing was either the proximate result of the commission of an unlawful act, not amounting to a felony, but without gross negligence, or the proximate result of the commission of a lawful act that might produce death, in an unlawful manner, but without gross negligence.

(c) (1) Except as provided in subdivision (d), gross vehicular manslaughter while intoxicated in violation of subdivision (a) is punishable by imprisonment in the state prison for 4, 6, or 10 years.

(2) Vehicular manslaughter while intoxicated in violation of subdivision (b) is punishable by imprisonment in a county jail for not more than one year or by imprisonment pursuant to subdivision (h) of Section 1170 for 16 months or two or four years.

(d) A person convicted of violating subdivision (a) who has one or more prior convictions of this section or of paragraph (1) of subdivision (c) of Section 192, subdivision (a) or (b) of Section 192.5 of this code, or of violating Section 23152 punishable under Sections 23540, 23542, 23546, 23548, 23550, or 23552 of, or convicted of Section 23153 of, the Vehicle Code, shall be punished by imprisonment in the state prison for a term of 15 years to life. Article 2.5 (commencing with Section 2930) of Chapter 7 of Title 1 of Part 3 shall apply to reduce the term imposed pursuant to this subdivision.

(e) This section shall not be construed as prohibiting or precluding a charge of murder under Section 188 upon facts exhibiting wantonness and a conscious disregard for life to support a finding of implied malice, or upon facts showing malice consistent with the holding of the California Supreme Court in People v. Watson, 30 Cal. 3d 290.

(f) This section shall not be construed as making any homicide in the driving of a vehicle or the operation of a vessel punishable which is not a proximate result of the commission of an unlawful act, not amounting to felony, or of the commission of a lawful act which might produce death, in an unlawful manner.

(g) For the penalties in subdivision (d) to apply, the existence of any fact required under subdivision (d) shall be alleged in the information or indictment and either admitted by the defendant in open court or found to be true by the trier of fact.

(Amended by Stats. 2011, Ch. 15, Sec. 281. (AB 109) Effective April 4, 2011. Operative October 1, 2011, by Sec. 636 of Ch. 15, as amended by Stats. 2011, Ch. 39, Sec. 68.)

192.

Manslaughter is the unlawful killing of a human being without malice. It is of three kinds:

(a) Voluntary—upon a sudden quarrel or heat of passion.

(b) Involuntary—in the commission of an unlawful act, not amounting to a felony; or in the commission of a lawful act which might produce death, in an unlawful manner, or without due caution and circumspection. This subdivision shall not apply to acts committed in the driving of a vehicle.

(c) Vehicular—

(1) Except as provided in subdivision (a) of Section 191.5, driving a vehicle in the commission of an unlawful act, not amounting to a felony, and with gross negligence; or driving a vehicle in the commission of a lawful act which might produce death, in an unlawful manner, and with gross negligence.

(2) Driving a vehicle in the commission of an unlawful act, not amounting to a felony, but without gross negligence; or driving a vehicle in the commission of a lawful act which might produce death, in an unlawful manner, but without gross negligence.

(3) Driving a vehicle in connection with a violation of paragraph (3) of subdivision (a) of Section 550, where the vehicular collision or vehicular accident was knowingly caused for financial gain and proximately resulted in the death of any person. This paragraph does not prevent prosecution of a defendant for the crime of murder.

(d) This section shall not be construed as making any homicide in the driving of a vehicle punishable that is not a proximate result of the commission of an unlawful act, not amounting to a felony, or of the commission of a lawful act which might produce death, in an unlawful manner.

(e) "Gross negligence," as used in this section, does not prohibit or preclude a charge of murder under Section 188 upon facts exhibiting wantonness and a conscious disregard for life to support a finding of implied malice, or upon facts showing malice, consistent with the holding of the California Supreme Court in People v. Watson (1981) 30 Cal.3d 290.

(f) (1) For purposes of determining sudden quarrel or heat of passion pursuant to subdivision (a), the provocation was not objectively reasonable if it resulted from the discovery of, knowledge about, or potential disclosure of the victim's actual or perceived gender, gender identity, gender expression, or sexual orientation, including under circumstances in which the victim made an unwanted nonforcible romantic or sexual

advance towards the defendant, or if the defendant and victim dated or had a romantic or sexual relationship. Nothing in this section shall preclude the jury from considering all relevant facts to determine whether the defendant was in fact provoked for purposes of establishing subjective provocation.

(2) For purposes of this subdivision, "gender" includes a person's gender identity and gender-related appearance and behavior regardless of whether that appearance or behavior is associated with the person's gender as determined at birth.

(Amended by Stats. 2014, Ch. 684, Sec. 1. (AB 2501) Effective January 1, 2015.)

192.5.

Vehicular manslaughter pursuant to subdivision (b) of Section 191.5 and subdivision (c) of Section 192 is the unlawful killing of a human being without malice aforethought, and includes:

(a) Operating a vessel in violation of subdivision (b), (c), (d), (e), or (f) of Section 655 of the Harbors and Navigation Code, and in the commission of an unlawful act, not amounting to felony, and with gross negligence; or operating a vessel in violation of subdivision (b), (c), (d), (e), or (f) of Section 655 of the Harbors and Navigation Code, and in the commission of a lawful act that might produce death, in an unlawful manner, and with gross negligence.

(b) Operating a vessel in violation of subdivision (b), (c), (d), (e), or (f) of Section 655 of the Harbors and Navigation Code, and in the commission of an unlawful act, not amounting to felony, but without gross negligence; or operating a vessel in violation of subdivision (b), (c), (d), (e), or (f) of Section 655 of the Harbors and Navigation Code, and in the commission of a lawful act that might produce death, in an unlawful manner, but without gross negligence.

(c) Operating a vessel in the commission of an unlawful act, not amounting to a felony, and with gross negligence; or operating a vessel in the commission of a lawful act that might produce death, in an unlawful manner, and with gross negligence.

(d) Operating a vessel in the commission of an unlawful act, not amounting to a felony, but without gross negligence; or operating a vessel in the commission of a lawful act that might produce death, in an unlawful manner, but without gross negligence.

(e) A person who flees the scene of the crime after committing a violation of subdivision (a), (b), or (c), upon conviction, in addition and consecutive to the punishment prescribed, shall be punished by an additional term of imprisonment of five years in the state prison. This additional term shall not be imposed unless the allegation is charged in the accusatory pleading and admitted by the defendant or found to be true by the trier of fact. The court shall not strike a finding that brings a person within the provisions of this subdivision or an allegation made pursuant to this subdivision.

(Amended by Stats. 2007, Ch. 747, Sec. 5. Effective January 1, 2008.)

193.

(a) Voluntary manslaughter is punishable by imprisonment in the state prison for 3, 6, or 11 years.

(b) Involuntary manslaughter is punishable by imprisonment pursuant to subdivision (h) of Section 1170 for two, three, or four years.

(c) Vehicular manslaughter is punishable as follows:

(1) A violation of paragraph (1) of subdivision (c) of Section 192 is punishable either by imprisonment in the county jail for not more than one year or by imprisonment in the state prison for two, four, or six years.

(2) A violation of paragraph (2) of subdivision (c) of Section 192 is punishable by imprisonment in the county jail for not more than one year.

(3) A violation of paragraph (3) of subdivision (c) of Section 192 is punishable by imprisonment in the state prison for 4, 6, or 10 years.

(Amended by Stats. 2011, Ch. 15, Sec. 282. (AB 109) Effective April 4, 2011. Operative October 1, 2011, by Sec. 636 of Ch. 15, as amended by Stats. 2011, Ch. 39, Sec. 68.)

193.5.

Manslaughter committed during the operation of a vessel is punishable as follows:

(a) A violation of subdivision (a) of Section 192.5 is punishable by imprisonment in the state prison for 4, 6, or 10 years.

(b) A violation of subdivision (b) of Section 192.5 is punishable by imprisonment in a county jail for not more than one year or by imprisonment pursuant to subdivision (h) of Section 1170 for 16 months or two or four years.

(c) A violation of subdivision (c) of Section 192.5 is punishable either by imprisonment in the county jail for not more than one year or by imprisonment in the state prison for two, four, or six years.

(d) A violation of subdivision (d) of Section 192.5 is punishable by imprisonment in the county jail for not more than one year.

(Amended by Stats. 2011, Ch. 15, Sec. 283. (AB 109) Effective April 4, 2011. Operative October 1, 2011, by Sec. 636 of Ch. 15, as amended by Stats. 2011, Ch. 39, Sec. 68.)

193.7.

A person convicted of a violation of subdivision (b) of Section 191.5 that occurred within seven years of two or more separate violations of Section 23103, as specified in Section 23103.5, of, or Section 23152 or 23153 of, the Vehicle Code, or any combination thereof, that resulted in convictions, shall be designated as an habitual traffic offender subject to paragraph (3) of subdivision (e) of Section 14601.3 of the Vehicle Code, for a period of three years, subsequent to the conviction. The person shall be advised of this designation pursuant to subdivision (b) of Section 13350 of the Vehicle Code.

(Amended by Stats. 2007, Ch. 747, Sec. 6. Effective January 1, 2008.)

193.8.

(a) An adult, who is the registered owner of a motor vehicle or in possession of a motor vehicle, shall not relinquish possession of the vehicle to a minor for the purpose of driving if the following conditions exist:

(1) The adult owner or person in possession of the vehicle knew or reasonably should have known that the minor was intoxicated at the time possession was relinquished.

(2) A petition was sustained or the minor was convicted of a violation of Section 23103 as specified in Section 23103.5, 23140, 23152, or 23153 of the Vehicle Code or a violation of Section 191.5 or subdivision (a) of Section 192.5.

(3) The minor does not otherwise have a lawful right to possession of the vehicle.

(b) The offense described in subdivision (a) shall not apply to commercial bailments, motor vehicle leases, or parking arrangements, whether or not for compensation, provided by hotels, motels, or food facilities for customers, guests, or other invitees thereof. For purposes of this subdivision, hotel and motel shall have the same meaning as in subdivision (b) of Section 25503.16 of the Business and Professions Code and food facility shall have the same meaning as in Section 113785 of the Health and Safety Code.

(c) If an adult is convicted of the offense described in subdivision (a), that person shall be punished by a fine not exceeding one thousand dollars ($1,000), or by imprisonment in a county jail not exceeding six months, or by both the fine and imprisonment. An adult convicted of the offense described in subdivision (a) shall not be subject to driver's license suspension or revocation or attendance at a licensed alcohol or drug education and counseling program for persons who drive under the influence.

(Amended by Stats. 2007, Ch. 747, Sec. 7. Effective January 1, 2008.)

194.

To make the killing either murder or manslaughter, it is not requisite that the party die within three years and a day after the stroke received or the cause of death administered. If death occurs beyond the time of three years and a day, there shall be a rebuttable presumption that the killing was not criminal. The prosecution shall bear the burden of overcoming this presumption. In the computation of time, the whole of the day on which the act was done shall be reckoned the first.

(Amended by Stats. 1996, Ch. 580, Sec. 1. Effective January 1, 1997.)

195.

Homicide is excusable in the following cases:
1. When committed by accident and misfortune, or in doing any other lawful act by lawful means, with usual and ordinary caution, and without any unlawful intent.
2. When committed by accident and misfortune, in the heat of passion, upon any sudden and sufficient provocation, or upon a sudden combat, when no undue advantage is taken, nor any dangerous weapon used, and when the killing is not done in a cruel or unusual manner.
(Amended by Stats. 1984, Ch. 438, Sec. 1.)
196.
Homicide is justifiable when committed by public officers and those acting by their command in their aid and assistance, either—
1. In obedience to any judgment of a competent Court; or,
2. When necessarily committed in overcoming actual resistance to the execution of some legal process, or in the discharge of any other legal duty; or,
3. When necessarily committed in retaking felons who have been rescued or have escaped, or when necessarily committed in arresting persons charged with felony, and who are fleeing from justice or resisting such arrest.
(Enacted 1872.)
197.
Homicide is also justifiable when committed by any person in any of the following cases:
(1) When resisting any attempt to murder any person, or to commit a felony, or to do some great bodily injury upon any person.
(2) When committed in defense of habitation, property, or person, against one who manifestly intends or endeavors, by violence or surprise, to commit a felony, or against one who manifestly intends and endeavors, in a violent, riotous, or tumultuous manner, to enter the habitation of another for the purpose of offering violence to any person therein.
(3) When committed in the lawful defense of such person, or of a spouse, parent, child, master, mistress, or servant of such person, when there is reasonable ground to apprehend a design to commit a felony or to do some great bodily injury, and imminent danger of such design being accomplished; but such person, or the person in whose behalf the defense was made, if he or she was the assailant or engaged in mutual combat, must really and in good faith have endeavored to decline any further struggle before the homicide was committed.
(4) When necessarily committed in attempting, by lawful ways and means, to apprehend any person for any felony committed, or in lawfully suppressing any riot, or in lawfully keeping and preserving the peace.
(Amended by Stats. 2016, Ch. 50, Sec. 67. (SB 1005) Effective January 1, 2017.)
198.
A bare fear of the commission of any of the offenses mentioned in subdivisions 2 and 3 of Section 197, to prevent which homicide may be lawfully committed, is not sufficient to justify it. But the circumstances must be sufficient to excite the fears of a reasonable person, and the party killing must have acted under the influence of such fears alone.
(Amended by Stats. 1987, Ch. 828, Sec. 8.)
198.5.
Any person using force intended or likely to cause death or great bodily injury within his or her residence shall be presumed to have held a reasonable fear of imminent peril of death or great bodily injury to self, family, or a member of the household when that force is used against another person, not a member of the family or household, who unlawfully and forcibly enters or has unlawfully and forcibly entered the residence and the person using the force knew or had reason to believe that an unlawful and forcible entry occurred.
As used in this section, great bodily injury means a significant or substantial physical injury.
(Added by Stats. 1984, Ch. 1666, Sec. 1.)
199.
The homicide appearing to be justifiable or excusable, the person indicted must, upon his trial, be fully acquitted and discharged.
(Enacted 1872.)

CHAPTER 2. Mayhem [203 - 206.1]

(Chapter 2 enacted 1872.)
203.
Every person who unlawfully and maliciously deprives a human being of a member of his body, or disables, disfigures, or renders it useless, or cuts or disables the tongue, or puts out an eye, or slits the nose, ear, or lip, is guilty of mayhem.
(Amended by Stats. 1989, Ch. 1360, Sec. 106.)
204.
Mayhem is punishable by imprisonment in the state prison for two, four, or eight years.
(Amended by Stats. 1986, Ch. 1424, Sec. 1.)
205.
A person is guilty of aggravated mayhem when he or she unlawfully, under circumstances manifesting extreme indifference to the physical or psychological well-being of another person, intentionally causes permanent disability or disfigurement of another human being or deprives a human being of a limb, organ, or member of his or her body. For purposes of this section, it is not necessary to prove an intent to kill. Aggravated mayhem is a felony punishable by imprisonment in the state prison for life with the possibility of parole.
(Added by Stats. 1987, Ch. 785, Sec. 1.)
206.
Every person who, with the intent to cause cruel or extreme pain and suffering for the purpose of revenge, extortion, persuasion, or for any sadistic purpose, inflicts great bodily injury as defined in Section 12022.7 upon the person of another, is guilty of torture.
The crime of torture does not require any proof that the victim suffered pain.
(Added June 5, 1990, by initiative Proposition 115, Sec. 13.)
206.1.
Torture is punishable by imprisonment in the state prison for a term of life.
(Added June 5, 1990, by initiative Proposition 115, Sec. 14.)

CHAPTER 3. Kidnapping [207 - 210]

(Chapter 3 enacted 1872.)
207.
(a) Every person who forcibly, or by any other means of instilling fear, steals or takes, or holds, detains, or arrests any person in this state, and carries the person into another country, state, or county, or into another part of the same county, is guilty of kidnapping.
(b) Every person, who for the purpose of committing any act defined in Section 288, hires, persuades, entices, decoys, or seduces by false promises, misrepresentations, or the like, any child under the age of 14 years to go out of this country, state, or county, or into another part of the same county, is guilty of kidnapping.
(c) Every person who forcibly, or by any other means of instilling fear, takes or holds, detains, or arrests any person, with a design to take the person out of this state, without having established a claim, according to the laws of the United States, or of this state, or who hires, persuades, entices, decoys, or seduces by false promises, misrepresentations, or the like, any person to go out of this state, or to be taken or removed therefrom, for the purpose and with the intent to sell that person into slavery or involuntary servitude, or otherwise to employ that person for his or her own use, or to the use of another, without the free will and consent of that persuaded person, is guilty of kidnapping.
(d) Every person who, being out of this state, abducts or takes by force or fraud any person contrary to the law of the place where that act is committed, and brings, sends, or conveys that person within the limits of this state, and is afterwards found within the limits thereof, is guilty of kidnapping.
(e) For purposes of those types of kidnapping requiring force, the amount of force required to kidnap an unresisting infant or child is the amount of physical force required to take and carry the child away a substantial distance for an illegal purpose or with an illegal intent.
(f) Subdivisions (a) to (d), inclusive, do not apply to any of the following:
(1) To any person who steals, takes, entices away, detains, conceals, or harbors any child under the age of 14 years, if that act is taken to protect the child from danger of imminent harm.
(2) To any person acting under Section 834 or 837.
(Amended by Stats. 2003, Ch. 23, Sec. 1. Effective January 1, 2004.)
208.
(a) Kidnapping is punishable by imprisonment in the state prison for three, five, or eight years.
(b) If the person kidnapped is under 14 years of age at the time of the commission of the crime, the kidnapping is punishable by imprisonment in the state prison for 5, 8, or 11 years. This subdivision is not applicable to the taking, detaining, or concealing, of a minor child by a biological parent, a natural father, as specified in Section 7611 of the Family Code, an adoptive parent, or a person who has been granted access to the minor child by a court order.
(c) In all cases in which probation is granted, the court shall, except in unusual cases where the interests of justice would best be served by a lesser penalty, require as a condition of the probation that the person be confined in the county jail for 12 months. If the court grants probation without requiring the defendant to be confined in the county jail for 12 months, it shall specify its reason or reasons for imposing a lesser penalty.
(Amended by Stats. 1997, Ch. 817, Sec. 1. Effective January 1, 1998.)
209.
(a) Any person who seizes, confines, inveigles, entices, decoys, abducts, conceals, kidnaps or carries away another person by any means whatsoever with intent to hold or detain, or who holds or detains, that person for ransom, reward or to commit extortion or to exact from another person any money or valuable thing, or any person who aids or abets any such act, is guilty of a felony, and upon conviction thereof, shall be punished by imprisonment in the state prison for life without possibility of parole in cases in which any person subjected to any such act suffers death or bodily harm, or is intentionally confined in a manner which exposes that person to a substantial likelihood of death, or shall be punished by imprisonment in the state prison for life with the possibility of parole in cases where no such person suffers death or bodily harm.
(b) (1) Any person who kidnaps or carries away any individual to commit robbery, rape, spousal rape, oral copulation, sodomy, or any violation of Section 264.1, 288, or 289, shall be punished by imprisonment in the state prison for life with the possibility of parole.
(2) This subdivision shall only apply if the movement of the victim is beyond that merely incidental to the commission of, and increases the risk of harm to the victim over and above that necessarily present in, the intended underlying offense.
(c) In all cases in which probation is granted, the court shall, except in unusual cases where the interests of justice would best be served by a lesser penalty, require as a condition of the probation that the person be confined in the county jail for 12 months. If the court grants probation without requiring the defendant to be confined in the county jail for 12 months, it shall specify its reason or reasons for imposing a lesser penalty.
(d) Subdivision (b) shall not be construed to supersede or affect Section 667.61. A person may be charged with a violation of subdivision (b) and Section 667.61. However, a person may not be punished under subdivision (b) and Section 667.61 for the same act that constitutes a violation of both subdivision (b) and Section 667.61.
(Amended November 7, 2006, by initiative Proposition 83, Sec. 3.)
209.5.
(a) Any person who, during the commission of a carjacking and in order to facilitate the commission of the carjacking, kidnaps another person who is not a principal in the commission of the carjacking shall be punished by imprisonment in the state prison for life with the possibility of parole.
(b) This section shall only apply if the movement of the victim is beyond that merely incidental to the commission of the carjacking, the victim is moved a substantial distance from the vicinity of the carjacking, and the movement of the victim increases the risk of harm to the victim over and above that necessarily present in the crime of carjacking itself.
(c) In all cases in which probation is granted, the court shall, except in unusual cases where the interests of justice would best be served by a lesser penalty, require as a condition of the probation that the person be confined in the county jail for 12 months. If the court grants probation without requiring the defendant to be confined in the county jail for 12 months, it shall specify its reason or reasons for imposing a lesser penalty.
(Added by Stats. 1993, Ch. 611, Sec. 5. Effective October 1, 1993.)
210.
Every person who for the purpose of obtaining any ransom or reward, or to extort or exact from any person any money or thing of value, poses as, or in any manner represents himself to be a person who has seized, confined, inveigled, enticed, decoyed, abducted, concealed, kidnapped or carried away any person, or who poses as, or in any manner represents himself to be a person who holds or detains such person, or who poses as, or in any manner represents himself to be a person who has aided or abetted any such act, or who poses as or in any manner represents himself to be a person who has the influence, power, or ability, to obtain the release of such person so seized, confined, inveigled, enticed, decoyed, abducted, concealed, kidnapped or carried away, is guilty of a felony and upon conviction thereof shall be punished by imprisonment for two, three or four years.
Nothing in this section prohibits any person who, in good faith believes that he can rescue any person who has been seized, confined, inveigled, enticed, decoyed, abducted, concealed, kidnapped or carried away, and who has had no part in, or connection with, such confinement, inveigling, decoying, abducting, concealing, kidnapping, or carrying away, from offering to rescue or obtain the release of such person for a monetary consideration or other thing of value.
(Amended by Stats. 1976, Ch. 1139.)

CHAPTER 3.5. Hostages [210.5- 210.5.]

(Chapter 3.5 added by Stats. 1987, Ch. 580, Sec. 1.)
210.5.
Every person who commits the offense of false imprisonment, as defined in Section 236, against a person for purposes of protection from arrest, which substantially increases the risk of harm to the victim, or for purposes of using the person as a shield is punishable by imprisonment pursuant to subdivision (h) of Section 1170 for three, five, or eight years.
(Amended by Stats. 2011, Ch. 15, Sec. 284. (AB 109) Effective April 4, 2011. Operative October 1, 2011, by Sec. 636 of Ch. 15, as amended by Stats. 2011, Ch. 39, Sec. 68.)

CHAPTER 4. Robbery [211 - 215]

(Chapter 4 enacted 1872.)
211.
Robbery is the felonious taking of personal property in the possession of another, from his person or immediate presence, and against his will, accomplished by means of force or fear.
(Enacted 1872.)
212.
The fear mentioned in Section 211 may be either:
1. The fear of an unlawful injury to the person or property of the person robbed, or of any relative of his or member of his family; or,
2. The fear of an immediate and unlawful injury to the person or property of anyone in the company of the person robbed at the time of the robbery.
(Amended by Stats. 1963, Ch. 372.)
212.5.
(a) Every robbery of any person who is performing his or her duties as an operator of any bus, taxicab, cable car, streetcar, trackless trolley, or other vehicle, including a vehicle operated on stationary rails or on a track or rail suspended in the air, and used for the transportation of persons for hire, every robbery of any passenger which is perpetrated on any of these vehicles, and every robbery which is perpetrated in an inhabited dwelling house, a vessel as defined in Section 21 of the Harbors and Navigation Code which is inhabited and designed for habitation, an inhabited floating home as defined in subdivision (d) of Section 18075.55 of the Health and Safety Code, a trailer coach as defined in the Vehicle Code which is inhabited, or the inhabited portion of any other building is robbery of the first degree.
(b) Every robbery of any person while using an automated teller machine or immediately after the person has used an automated teller machine and is in the vicinity of the automated teller machine is robbery of the first degree.
(c) All kinds of robbery other than those listed in subdivisions (a) and (b) are of the second degree.
(Amended by Stats. 1994, Ch. 919, Sec. 1. Effective January 1, 1995.)
213.
(a) Robbery is punishable as follows:
(1) Robbery of the first degree is punishable as follows:
(A) If the defendant, voluntarily acting in concert with two or more other persons, commits the robbery within an inhabited dwelling house, a vessel as defined in Section 21 of the Harbors and Navigation Code, which is inhabited and designed for habitation, an inhabited floating home as defined in subdivision (d) of Section 18075.55 of the Health and Safety Code, a trailer coach as defined in the Vehicle Code, which is inhabited, or the inhabited portion of any other building, by imprisonment in the state prison for three, six, or nine years.
(B) In all cases other than that specified in subparagraph (A), by imprisonment in the state prison for three, four, or six years.
(2) Robbery of the second degree is punishable by imprisonment in the state prison for two, three, or five years.
(b) Notwithstanding Section 664, attempted robbery in violation of paragraph (2) of subdivision (a) is punishable by imprisonment in the state prison.
(Amended by Stats. 1994, Ch. 789, Sec. 1. Effective January 1, 1995.)
214.
Every person who goes upon or boards any railroad train, car or engine, with the intention of robbing any passenger or other person on such train, car or engine, of any personal property thereon in the possession or care or under the control of any such passenger or other person, or who interferes in any manner with any switch, rail, sleeper, viaduct, culvert, embankment, structure or appliance pertaining to or connected with any railroad, or places any dynamite or other explosive substance or material upon or near the track of any railroad, or who sets fire to any railroad bridge or trestle, or who shows, masks, extinguishes or alters any light or other signal, or exhibits or compels any other person to exhibit any false light or signal, or who stops any such train, car or engine, or slackens the speed thereof, or who compels or attempts to compel any person in charge or control thereof to stop any such train, car or engine, or slacken the speed thereof, with the intention of robbing any passenger or other person on such train, car or engine, of any personal property thereon in the possession or charge or under the control of any such passenger or other person, is guilty of a felony.
(Added by Stats. 1905, Ch. 494.)
215.
(a) "Carjacking" is the felonious taking of a motor vehicle in the possession of another, from his or her person or immediate presence, or from the person or immediate presence of a passenger of the motor vehicle, against his or her will and with the intent to either permanently or temporarily deprive the person in possession of the motor vehicle of his or her possession, accomplished by means of force or fear.
(b) Carjacking is punishable by imprisonment in the state prison for a term of three, five, or nine years.
(c) This section shall not be construed to supersede or affect Section 211. A person may be charged with a violation of this section and Section 211. However, no defendant may be punished under this section and Section 211 for the same act which constitutes a violation of both this section and Section 211.
(Added by Stats. 1993, Ch. 611, Sec. 6. Effective October 1, 1993.)

CHAPTER 5. Attempts to Kill [217.1 - 219.3]

(Chapter 5 enacted 1872.)
217.1.
(a) Except as provided in subdivision (b), every person who commits any assault upon the President or Vice President of the United States, the Governor of any state or territory, any justice, judge, or former judge of any local, state, or federal court of record, any commissioner, referee, or other subordinate judicial officer of any court of record, the secretary or director of any executive agency or department of the United States or any state or territory, or any other official of the United States or any state or territory holding elective office, any mayor, city council member, county supervisor, sheriff, district attorney, prosecutor or assistant prosecutor of any local, state, or federal prosecutor's office, a former prosecutor or assistant prosecutor of any local, state, or federal prosecutor's office, public defender or assistant public defender of any local, state, or federal public defender's office, a former public defender or assistant public

defender of any local, state, or federal public defender's office, the chief of police of any municipal police department, any peace officer, any juror in any local, state, or federal court of record, or the immediate family of any of these officials, in retaliation for or to prevent the performance of the victim's official duties, shall be punished by imprisonment in the county jail not exceeding one year or by imprisonment pursuant to subdivision (h) of Section 1170.
(b) Notwithstanding subdivision (a), every person who attempts to commit murder against any person listed in subdivision (a) in retaliation for or to prevent the performance of the victim's official duties, shall be confined in the state prison for a term of 15 years to life. The provisions of Article 2.5 (commencing with Section 2930) of Chapter 7 of Title 1 of Part 3 shall apply to reduce any minimum term of 15 years in a state prison imposed pursuant to this section, but that person shall not otherwise be released on parole prior to that time.
(c) For the purposes of this section, the following words have the following meanings:
(1) "Immediate family" means spouse, child, stepchild, brother, stepbrother, sister, stepsister, mother, stepmother, father, or stepfather.
(2) "Peace officer" means any person specified in subdivision (a) of Section 830.1 or Section 830.5.
(Amended by Stats. 2011, Ch. 15, Sec. 285. (AB 109) Effective April 4, 2011. Operative October 1, 2011, by Sec. 636 of Ch. 15, as amended by Stats. 2011, Ch. 39, Sec. 68.)
218.
Every person who unlawfully throws out a switch, removes a rail, or places any obstruction on any railroad with the intention of derailing any passenger, freight or other train, car or engine, or who unlawfully places any dynamite or other explosive material or any other obstruction upon or near the track of any railroad with the intention of blowing up or derailing any such train, car or engine, or who unlawfully sets fire to any railroad bridge or trestle, over which any such train, car or engine must pass with the intention of wrecking such train, car or engine, is guilty of a felony, and shall be punished by imprisonment in the state prison for life without possibility of parole.
(Amended by Stats. 1976, Ch. 1139.)
218.1.
Any person who unlawfully and with gross negligence places or causes to be placed any obstruction upon or near the track of any railroad that proximately results in either the damaging or derailing of any passenger, freight, or other train, or injures a rail passenger or employee, shall be punished by imprisonment pursuant to subdivision (h) of Section 1170 for two, three, or four years, or by imprisonment in a county jail for not more than one year, or by a fine not to exceed two thousand five hundred dollars ($2,500), or by both that imprisonment and fine.
(Amended by Stats. 2011, Ch. 15, Sec. 286. (AB 109) Effective April 4, 2011. Operative October 1, 2011, by Sec. 636 of Ch. 15, as amended by Stats. 2011, Ch. 39, Sec. 68.)
219.
Every person who unlawfully throws out a switch, removes a rail, or places any obstruction on any railroad with the intention of derailing any passenger, freight or other train, car or engine and thus derails the same, or who unlawfully places any dynamite or other explosive material or any other obstruction upon or near the track of any railroad with the intention of blowing up or derailing any such train, car or engine and thus blows up or derails the same, or who unlawfully sets fire to any railroad bridge or trestle over which any such train, car or engine must pass with the intention of wrecking such train, car or engine, and thus wrecks the same, is guilty of a felony and punishable with death or imprisonment in the state prison for life without possibility of parole in cases where any person suffers death as a proximate result thereof, or imprisonment in the state prison for life with the possibility of parole, in cases where no person suffers death as a proximate result thereof. The penalty shall be determined pursuant to Sections 190.3 and 190.4.
(Amended by Stats. 1977, Ch. 316.)
219.1.
Every person who unlawfully throws, hurls or projects at a vehicle operated by a common carrier, while such vehicle is either in motion or stationary, any rock, stone, brick, bottle, piece of wood or metal or any other missile of any kind or character, or does any unlawful act, with the intention of wrecking such vehicle and doing bodily harm, and thus wrecks the same and causes bodily harm, is guilty of a felony and punishable by imprisonment pursuant to subdivision (h) of Section 1170 for two, four, or six years.
(Amended by Stats. 2011, Ch. 15, Sec. 287. (AB 109) Effective April 4, 2011. Operative October 1, 2011, by Sec. 636 of Ch. 15, as amended by Stats. 2011, Ch. 39, Sec. 68.)
219.2.
Every person who willfully throws, hurls, or projects a stone or other hard substance, or shoots a missile, at a train, locomotive, railway car, caboose, cable railway car, street railway car, or bus or at a steam vessel or watercraft used for carrying passengers or freight on any of the waters within or bordering on this state, is punishable by imprisonment in the county jail not exceeding one year, or in a state prison, or by fine not exceeding two thousand dollars ($2,000), or by both such fine and imprisonment.
(Amended by Stats. 1983, Ch. 1092, Sec. 248. Effective September 27, 1983. Operative January 1, 1984, by Sec. 427 of Ch. 1092.)
219.3.
Any person who wilfully drops or throws any object or missile from any toll bridge is guilty of a misdemeanor.
(Added by Stats. 1957, Ch. 1053.)

CHAPTER 6. Assaults With Intent to Commit Felony, Other Than Assaults With Intent to Murder [220 - 222]

(Chapter 6 enacted 1872.)
220.
(a) (1) Except as provided in subdivision (b), any person who assaults another with intent to commit mayhem, rape, sodomy, oral copulation, or any violation of Section 264.1, 288, or 289 shall be punished by imprisonment in the state prison for two, four, or six years.
(2) Except as provided in subdivision (b), any person who assaults another person under 18 years of age with the intent to commit rape, sodomy, oral copulation, or any violation of Section 264.1, 288, or 289 shall be punished by imprisonment in the state prison for five, seven, or nine years.
(b) Any person who, in the commission of a burglary of the first degree, as defined in subdivision (a) of Section 460, assaults another with intent to commit rape, sodomy, oral copulation, or any violation of Section 264.1, 288, or 289 shall be punished by imprisonment in the state prison for life with the possibility of parole.
(Amended by Stats. 2010, Ch. 219, Sec. 2. (AB 1844) Effective September 9, 2010. Note: This section was amended on Nov. 7, 2006, by initiative Prop. 83.)
222.
Every person guilty of administering to another any chloroform, ether, laudanum, or any controlled substance, anaesthetic, or intoxicating agent, with intent thereby to enable or assist himself or herself or any other person to commit a felony, is guilty of a felony punishable by imprisonment in the state prison for 16 months, or two or three years.

(Amended by Stats. 2011, Ch. 15, Sec. 287.5. (AB 109) Effective April 4, 2011. Operative October 1, 2011, by Sec. 636 of Ch. 15, as amended by Stats. 2011, Ch. 39, Sec. 68.)

CHAPTER 8. False Imprisonment and Human Trafficking [236 - 237]

(Heading of Chapter 8 amended November 6, 2012, by initiative Proposition 35, Sec. 5.)

236.
False imprisonment is the unlawful violation of the personal liberty of another.
(Enacted 1872.)

236.1.
(a) A person who deprives or violates the personal liberty of another with the intent to obtain forced labor or services, is guilty of human trafficking and shall be punished by imprisonment in the state prison for 5, 8, or 12 years and a fine of not more than five hundred thousand dollars ($500,000).
(b) A person who deprives or violates the personal liberty of another with the intent to effect or maintain a violation of Section 266, 266h, 266i, 266j, 267, 311.1, 311.2, 311.3, 311.4, 311.5, 311.6, or 518 is guilty of human trafficking and shall be punished by imprisonment in the state prison for 8, 14, or 20 years and a fine of not more than five hundred thousand dollars ($500,000).
(c) A person who causes, induces, or persuades, or attempts to cause, induce, or persuade, a person who is a minor at the time of commission of the offense to engage in a commercial sex act, with the intent to effect or maintain a violation of Section 266, 266h, 266i, 266j, 267, 311.1, 311.2, 311.3, 311.4, 311.5, 311.6, or 518 is guilty of human trafficking. A violation of this subdivision is punishable by imprisonment in the state prison as follows:
(1) Five, 8, or 12 years and a fine of not more than five hundred thousand dollars ($500,000).
(2) Fifteen years to life and a fine of not more than five hundred thousand dollars ($500,000) when the offense involves force, fear, fraud, deceit, coercion, violence, duress, menace, or threat of unlawful injury to the victim or to another person.
(d) In determining whether a minor was caused, induced, or persuaded to engage in a commercial sex act, the totality of the circumstances, including the age of the victim, his or her relationship to the trafficker or agents of the trafficker, and any handicap or disability of the victim, shall be considered.
(e) Consent by a victim of human trafficking who is a minor at the time of the commission of the offense is not a defense to a criminal prosecution under this section.
(f) Mistake of fact as to the age of a victim of human trafficking who is a minor at the time of the commission of the offense is not a defense to a criminal prosecution under this section.
(g) The Legislature finds that the definition of human trafficking in this section is equivalent to the federal definition of a severe form of trafficking found in Section 7102(9) of Title 22 of the United States Code.
(h) For purposes of this chapter, the following definitions apply:
(1) "Coercion" includes a scheme, plan, or pattern intended to cause a person to believe that failure to perform an act would result in serious harm to or physical restraint against any person; the abuse or threatened abuse of the legal process; debt bondage; or providing and facilitating the possession of a controlled substance to a person with the intent to impair the person's judgment.
(2) "Commercial sex act" means sexual conduct on account of which anything of value is given or received by a person.
(3) "Deprivation or violation of the personal liberty of another" includes substantial and sustained restriction of another's liberty accomplished through force, fear, fraud, deceit, coercion, violence, duress, menace, or threat of unlawful injury to the victim or to another person, under circumstances where the person receiving or apprehending the threat reasonably believes that it is likely that the person making the threat would carry it out.
(4) "Duress" includes a direct or implied threat of force, violence, danger, hardship, or retribution sufficient to cause a reasonable person to acquiesce in or perform an act which he or she would otherwise not have submitted to or performed; a direct or implied threat to destroy, conceal, remove, confiscate, or possess an actual or purported passport or immigration document of the victim; or knowingly destroying, concealing, removing, confiscating, or possessing an actual or purported passport or immigration document of the victim.
(5) "Forced labor or services" means labor or services that are performed or provided by a person and are obtained or maintained through force, fraud, duress, or coercion, or equivalent conduct that would reasonably overbear the will of the person.
(6) "Great bodily injury" means a significant or substantial physical injury.
(7) "Minor" means a person less than 18 years of age.
(8) "Serious harm" includes any harm, whether physical or nonphysical, including psychological, financial, or reputational harm, that is sufficiently serious, under all the surrounding circumstances, to compel a reasonable person of the same background and in the same circumstances to perform or to continue performing labor, services, or commercial sexual acts in order to avoid incurring that harm.
(i) The total circumstances, including the age of the victim, the relationship between the victim and the trafficker or agents of the trafficker, and any handicap or disability of the victim, shall be factors to consider in determining the presence of "deprivation or violation of the personal liberty of another," "duress," and "coercion" as described in this section.
(Amended by Stats. 2016, Ch. 86, Sec. 223.5. (SB 1171) Effective January 1, 2017. Note: Prop. 35 is titled the Californians Against Sexual Exploitation (CASE) Act.)

236.2.
Law enforcement agencies shall use due diligence to identify all victims of human trafficking, regardless of the citizenship of the person. When a peace officer comes into contact with a person who has been deprived of his or her personal liberty, a minor who has engaged in a commercial sex act, a person suspected of violating subdivision (a) or (b) of Section 647, or a victim of a crime of domestic violence or sexual assault, the peace officer shall consider whether the following indicators of human trafficking are present:
(a) Signs of trauma, fatigue, injury, or other evidence of poor care.
(b) The person is withdrawn, afraid to talk, or his or her communication is censored by another person.
(c) The person does not have freedom of movement.
(d) The person lives and works in one place.
(e) The person owes a debt to his or her employer.
(f) Security measures are used to control who has contact with the person.
(g) The person does not have control over his or her own government-issued identification or over his or her worker immigration documents.
(Amended November 6, 2012, by initiative Proposition 35, Sec. 7.)

236.23.
(a) In addition to any other affirmative defense, it is a defense to a charge of a crime that the person was coerced to commit the offense as a direct result of being a human trafficking victim at the time of the offense and had a reasonable fear of harm. This defense does not apply to a serious felony, as defined in subdivision (c) of Section

1192.7, or a violent felony, as defined in subdivision (c) of Section 667.5, or a violation of Section 236.1.
(b) A defendant asserting the affirmative defense specified in subdivision (a) has the burden of establishing the affirmative defense by a preponderance of the evidence.
(c) Certified records of a federal, state, tribal, or local court or governmental agency documenting the person's status as a victim of human trafficking at the time of the offense, including identification of a victim of human trafficking by a peace officer pursuant to Section 236.2 and certified records of approval notices or enforcement certifications generated from federal immigration proceedings, may be presented to establish an affirmative defense pursuant to this section.
(d) The affirmative defense may be asserted at any time before the entry of a plea of guilty or nolo contendere or admission to the truth of the charges and before the conclusion of any trial for the offense. If asserted before the preliminary hearing held in a case, the affirmative defense shall, upon request by the defendant, be determined at the preliminary hearing.
(e) If the defendant prevails on the affirmative defense provided under subdivision (a), the defendant is entitled to all of the following relief:
(1) (A) The court shall order that all records in the case be sealed pursuant to Section 851.86.
(B) Records that have been sealed pursuant to this paragraph may be accessed, inspected, or utilized by law enforcement for subsequent investigatory purposes involving persons other than the defendant.
(2) The person shall be released from all penalties and disabilities resulting from the charge, and all actions and proceedings by law enforcement personnel, courts, or other government employees that led to the charge shall be deemed not to have occurred.
(3) (A) The person may in all circumstances state that he or she has never been arrested for, or charged with, the crime that is the subject of the charge or conviction, including without limitation in response to questions on employment, housing, financial aid, or loan applications.
(B) The person may not be denied rights or benefits, including, without limitation, employment, housing, financial aid, welfare, or a loan or other financial accommodation, based on the arrest or charge or his or her failure or refusal to disclose the existence of or information concerning those events.
(C) The person may not be thereafter charged or convicted of perjury or otherwise of giving a false statement by reason of having failed to disclose or acknowledge the existence of the charge, or any arrest, indictment, trial, or other proceedings related thereto.
(f) If, in a proceeding pursuant to Section 602 of the Welfare and Institutions Code, the juvenile court finds that the offense on which the proceeding is based was committed as a direct result of the minor being a human trafficking victim, and the affirmative defense established in subdivision (a) is established by a preponderance of the evidence, the court shall dismiss the proceeding and order the relief prescribed in Section 786 of the Welfare and Institutions Code.
(Added by Stats. 2016, Ch. 636, Sec. 2. (AB 1761) Effective January 1, 2017.)

236.3.
Upon conviction of a violation of Section 236.1, if real property is used to facilitate the commission of the offense, the procedures for determining whether the property constitutes a nuisance and the remedies imposed therefor as provided in Article 2 (commencing with Section 11225) of Chapter 3 of Title 1 of Part 4 shall apply.
(Added by Stats. 2010, Ch. 625, Sec. 1. (SB 677) Effective January 1, 2011.)

236.4.
(a) Upon the conviction of a person of a violation of Section 236.1, the court may, in addition to any other penalty, fine, or restitution imposed, order the defendant to pay an additional fine not to exceed one million dollars ($1,000,000). In setting the amount of the fine, the court shall consider any relevant factors, including, but not limited to, the seriousness and gravity of the offense, the circumstances and duration of its commission, the amount of economic gain the defendant derived as a result of the crime, and the extent to which the victim suffered losses as a result of the crime.
(b) Any person who inflicts great bodily injury on a victim in the commission or attempted commission of a violation of Section 236.1 shall be punished by an additional and consecutive term of imprisonment in the state prison for 5, 7, or 10 years.
(c) Any person who has previously been convicted of a violation of any crime specified in Section 236.1 shall receive an additional and consecutive term of imprisonment in the state prison for 5 years for each additional conviction on charges separately brought and tried.
(d) Every fine imposed and collected pursuant to Section 236.1 and this section shall be deposited in the Victim-Witness Assistance Fund, to be administered by the California Emergency Management Agency (Cal EMA), to fund grants for services for victims of human trafficking. Seventy percent of the fines collected and deposited shall be granted to public agencies and nonprofit corporations that provide shelter, counseling, or other direct services for trafficked victims. Thirty percent of the fines collected and deposited shall be granted to law enforcement and prosecution agencies in the jurisdiction in which the charges were filed to fund human trafficking prevention, witness protection, and rescue operations.
(Added November 6, 2012, by initiative Proposition 35, Sec. 8.)

236.5.
(a) Within 15 business days of the first encounter with a victim of human trafficking, as defined by Section 236.1, law enforcement agencies shall provide brief letters that satisfy the following Law Enforcement Agency (LEA) endorsement regulations as found in paragraph (1) of subdivision (f) of Section 214.11 of Title 8 of the Code of Federal Regulations.
(b) The LEA must be submitted on Supplement B, Declaration of Law Enforcement Officer for Victim of Trafficking in Persons, of Form I-914. The LEA endorsement must be filled out completely in accordance with the instructions contained on the form and must attach the results of any name or database inquiry performed. In order to provide persuasive evidence, the LEA endorsement must contain a description of the victimization upon which the application is based, including the dates the trafficking in persons and victimization occurred, and be signed by a supervising official responsible for the investigation or prosecution of trafficking in persons. The LEA endorsement must address whether the victim had been recruited, harbored, transported, provided, or obtained specifically for either labor or services, or for the purposes of a commercial sex act.
(c) Where state law enforcement agencies find the grant of a LEA endorsement to be inappropriate for a victim of trafficking in persons, the agency shall within 15 days provide the victim with a letter explaining the grounds of the denial of the LEA. The victim may submit additional evidence to the law enforcement agency, which must reconsider the denial of the LEA within one week of the receipt of additional evidence.
(Added by renumbering Section 236.2 by Stats. 2008, Ch. 358, Sec. 3. Effective January 1, 2009.)

236.6.
(a) To prevent dissipation or secreting of assets or property, the prosecuting agency may, at the same time as or subsequent to the filing of a complaint or indictment charging human trafficking under Section 236.1, file a petition with the criminal division of the superior court of the county in which the accusatory pleading was filed, seeking a temporary restraining order, preliminary injunction, the appointment of a receiver, or any other protective relief necessary to preserve the property or assets. The filing of the petition shall start a proceeding that shall be pendent to the criminal proceeding and maintained solely to effect the remedies available for this crime, including, but not limited to, payment of restitution and payment of fines. The proceeding shall not be

subject to or governed by the provisions of the Civil Discovery Act as set forth in Title 4 (commencing with Section 2016.010) of Part 4 of the Code of Civil Procedure. The petition shall allege that the defendant has been charged with human trafficking under Section 236.1 and shall identify that criminal proceeding and the assets and property to be affected by an order issued pursuant to this section.

(b) The prosecuting agency shall, by personal service or registered mail, provide notice of the petition to every person who may have an interest in the property specified in the petition. Additionally, the notice shall be published for at least three successive weeks in a newspaper of general circulation in the county where the property affected by the order is located. The notice shall state that any interested person may file a verified claim with the superior court stating the nature and amount of his or her claimed interest. The notice shall set forth the time within which a claim of interest in the protected property shall be filed.

(c) If the property to be preserved is real property, the prosecuting agency shall record, at the time of filing the petition, a lis pendens in each county in which the real property is situated that specifically identifies the property by legal description, the name of the owner of record, as shown on the latest equalized assessment roll, and the assessor's parcel number.

(d) If the property to be preserved consists of assets under the control of a banking or financial institution, the prosecuting agency, at the time of filing the petition, may obtain an order from the court directing the banking or financial institution to immediately disclose the account numbers and value of the assets of the accused held by the banking or financial institution. The prosecuting agency shall file a supplemental petition, specifically identifying which banking or financial institution accounts shall be subject to a temporary restraining order, preliminary injunction, or other protective remedy.

(e) A person claiming an interest in the protected property or assets may, at any time within 30 days from the date of the first publication of the notice of the petition, or within 30 days after receipt of actual notice, whichever is later, file with the superior court of the county in which the action is pending a verified claim stating the nature and amount of his or her interest in the property or assets. A verified copy of the claim shall be served by the claimant on the Attorney General or district attorney, as appropriate.

(f) Concurrent with or subsequent to the filing of the petition, the prosecuting agency may move the superior court for, and the superior court may issue, any of the following pendente lite orders to preserve the status quo of the property or assets alleged in the petition:

(1) An injunction to restrain any person from transferring, encumbering, hypothecating, or otherwise disposing of the property or assets.

(2) Appointment of a receiver to take possession of, care for, manage, and operate the assets and properties so that they may be maintained and preserved. The court may order that a receiver appointed pursuant to this section shall be compensated for all reasonable expenditures made or incurred by him or her in connection with the possession, care, management, and operation of property or assets that are subject to the provisions of this section.

(3) Requiring a bond or other undertaking, in lieu of other orders, of a value sufficient to ensure the satisfaction of restitution and fines imposed pursuant to Section 236.1.

(g) The following procedures shall be followed in processing the petition:

(1) No preliminary injunction shall be granted or receiver appointed without notice to the interested parties and a hearing to determine that the order is necessary to preserve the property or assets, pending the outcome of the criminal proceedings. However, a temporary restraining order may be issued pending that hearing pursuant to the provisions of Section 527 of the Code of Civil Procedure. The temporary restraining order may be based upon the sworn declaration of a peace officer with personal knowledge of the criminal investigation that establishes probable cause to believe that human trafficking has taken place and that the amount of restitution and fines established pursuant to subdivision (f) exceeds or equals the worth of the property or assets subject to the temporary restraining order. The declaration may include the hearsay statements of witnesses to establish the necessary facts. The temporary restraining order may be issued without notice upon a showing of good cause to the court.

(2) The defendant, or a person who has filed a verified claim, shall have the right to have the court conduct an order to show cause hearing within 10 days of the service of the request for a hearing upon the prosecuting agency, in order to determine whether the temporary restraining order should remain in effect, whether relief should be granted from a lis pendens recorded pursuant to subdivision (c), or whether an existing order should be modified in the interests of justice. Upon a showing of good cause, the hearing shall be held within two days of the service of the request for a hearing upon the prosecuting agency.

(3) In determining whether to issue a preliminary injunction or temporary restraining order in a proceeding brought by a prosecuting agency in conjunction with or subsequent to the filing of an allegation pursuant to this section, the court has the discretion to consider any matter that it deems reliable and appropriate, including hearsay statements, in order to reach a just and equitable decision. The court shall weigh the relative degree of certainty of the outcome on the merits and the consequences to each of the parties of granting the interim relief. If the prosecution is likely to prevail on the merits and the risk of the dissipation of assets outweighs the potential harm to the defendants and the interested parties, the court shall grant injunctive relief. The court shall give significant weight to the following factors:

(A) The public interest in preserving the property or assets pendente lite.

(B) The difficulty of preserving the property or assets pendente lite where the underlying alleged crimes involve human trafficking.

(C) The fact that the requested relief is being sought by a public prosecutor on behalf of alleged victims of human trafficking.

(D) The likelihood that substantial public harm has occurred where the human trafficking is alleged to have been committed.

(E) The significant public interest involved in compensating victims of human trafficking and paying court-imposed restitution and fines.

(4) The court, in making its orders, may consider a defendant's request for the release of a portion of the property affected by this section in order to pay reasonable legal fees in connection with the criminal proceeding, necessary and appropriate living expenses pending trial and sentencing, and for the purpose of posting bail. The court shall weigh the needs of the public to retain the property against the needs of the defendant to a portion of the property. The court shall consider the factors listed in paragraph (3) prior to making an order releasing property for these purposes.

(5) The court, in making its orders, shall seek to protect the interests of innocent third parties, including an innocent spouse, who were not involved in the commission of criminal activity.

(6) The orders shall be no more extensive than necessary to effect the remedies available for the crime. In determining the amount of property to be held, the court shall ascertain the amount of fines that are assessed for a violation of this chapter and the amount of possible restitution.

(7) A petition filed pursuant to this section is part of the criminal proceedings for purposes of appointment of counsel and shall be assigned to the criminal division of the superior court of the county in which the accusatory pleading was filed.

(8) Based upon a noticed motion brought by the receiver appointed pursuant to paragraph (2) of subdivision (f), the court may order an interlocutory sale of property named in the petition when the property is liable to perish, to waste, or to be significantly reduced in value, or when the expenses of maintaining the property are disproportionate to the value of the property. The proceeds of the interlocutory sale

shall be deposited with the court or as directed by the court pending determination of the proceeding pursuant to this section.

(9) The court may make any orders that are necessary to preserve the continuing viability of a lawful business enterprise that is affected by the issuance of a temporary restraining order or preliminary injunction issued pursuant to this section.

(10) In making its orders, the court shall seek to prevent the property or asset subject to a temporary restraining order or preliminary injunction from perishing, spoiling, going to waste, or otherwise being significantly reduced in value. Where the potential for diminution in value exists, the court shall appoint a receiver to dispose of or otherwise protect the value of the property or asset.

(11) A preservation order shall not be issued against an asset of a business that is not likely to be dissipated and that may be subject to levy or attachment to meet the purposes of this section.

(h) If the allegation of human trafficking is dismissed or found by the trier of fact to be untrue, a preliminary injunction or temporary restraining order issued pursuant to this section shall be dissolved. If a jury is the trier of fact, and the jury is unable to reach a unanimous verdict, the court shall have the discretion to continue or dissolve all or a portion of the preliminary injunction or temporary restraining order based upon the interests of justice. However, if the prosecuting agency elects not to retry the case, a preliminary injunction or temporary restraining order issued pursuant to this section shall be dissolved.

(i) (1) (A) If the defendant is convicted of human trafficking, the trial judge shall continue the preliminary injunction or temporary restraining order until the date of the criminal sentencing and shall make a finding at that time as to what portion, if any, of the property or assets subject to the preliminary injunction or temporary restraining order shall be levied upon to pay fines and restitution to victims of the crime. The order imposing fines and restitution may exceed the total worth of the property or assets subjected to the preliminary injunction or temporary restraining order. The court may order the immediate transfer of the property or assets to satisfy a restitution order issued pursuant to Section 1202.4 and a fine imposed pursuant to this chapter.

(B) If the execution of judgment is stayed pending an appeal of an order of the superior court pursuant to this section, the preliminary injunction or temporary restraining order shall be maintained in full force and effect during the pendency of the appellate period.

(2) The order imposing fines and restitution shall not affect the interest in real property of a third party that was acquired prior to the recording of the lis pendens, unless the property was obtained from the defendant other than as a bona fide purchaser for value. If any assets or property affected by this section are subject to a valid lien, mortgage, security interest, or interest under a conditional sales contract and the amount due to the holder of the lien, mortgage, interest, or contract is less than the appraised value of the property, that person may pay to the state or the local government that initiated the proceeding the amount of the difference between the appraised value of the property and the amount of the lien, mortgage, security interest, or interest under a conditional sales contract. Upon that payment, the state or local entity shall relinquish all claims to the property. If the holder of the interest elects not to make that payment to the state or local governmental entity, the interest in the property shall be deemed transferred to the state or local governmental entity and any indicia of ownership of the property shall be confirmed in the state or local governmental entity. The appraised value shall be determined as of the date judgment is entered either by agreement between the holder of the lien, mortgage, security interest, or interest under a conditional sales contract and the governmental entity involved or, if they cannot agree, then by a court-appointed appraiser for the county in which the action is brought. A person holding a valid lien, mortgage, security interest, or interest under a conditional sales contract shall be paid the appraised value of his or her interest.

(3) In making its final order, the court shall seek to protect the legitimately acquired interests of innocent third parties, including an innocent spouse, who were not involved in the commission of criminal activity.

(j) In all cases where property is to be levied upon pursuant to this section, a receiver appointed by the court shall be empowered to liquidate all property or assets, which shall be distributed in the following order of priority:

(1) To the receiver, or court-appointed appraiser, for all reasonable expenditures made or incurred by him or her in connection with the sale of the property or liquidation of assets, including all reasonable expenditures for necessary repairs, storage, or transportation of property levied upon under this section.

(2) To a holder of a valid lien, mortgage, or security interest, up to the amount of his or her interest in the property or proceeds.

(3) To a victim as restitution for human trafficking that was alleged in the accusatory pleading and that was proven by the prosecution.

(4) For payment of a fine imposed. The proceeds obtained in payment of a fine shall be paid in the manner set forth in subdivision (h) of Section 236.1.

(Added by Stats. 2012, Ch. 512, Sec. 1. (AB 2466) Effective January 1, 2013.)
236.7.

(a) Any interest in a vehicle, boat, airplane, money, negotiable instruments, securities, real property, or other thing of value that was put to substantial use for the purpose of facilitating the crime of human trafficking that involves a commercial sex act, as defined in paragraph (2) of subdivision (g) of Section 236.1, where the victim was less than 18 years of age at the time of the commission of the crime, may be seized and ordered forfeited by the court upon the conviction of a person guilty of human trafficking that involves a commercial sex act where the victim is an individual under 18 years of age, pursuant to Section 236.1.

(b) In any case in which a defendant is convicted of human trafficking pursuant to Section 236.1 and an allegation is found to be true that the victim was a person under 18 years of age and the crime involved a commercial sex act, as defined in paragraph (2) of subdivision (g) of Section 236.1, the following assets shall be subject to forfeiture upon proof of the provisions of subdivision (d) of Section 236.9:

(1) Any property interest, whether tangible or intangible, acquired through human trafficking that involves a commercial sex act where the victim was less than 18 years of age at the time of the commission of the crime.

(2) All proceeds from human trafficking that involves a commercial sex act where the victim was less than 18 years of age at the time of the commission of the crime, which property shall include all things of value that may have been received in exchange for the proceeds immediately derived from the act.

(c) If a prosecuting agency petitions for forfeiture of an interest under subdivision (a) or (b), the process prescribed in Sections 236.8 to 236.12, inclusive, shall apply, but no local or state prosecuting agency shall be required to petition for forfeiture in any case.

(d) Real property that is used as a family residence or for other lawful purposes, or that is owned by two or more persons, one of whom had no knowledge of its unlawful use, shall not be subject to forfeiture.

(e) An interest in a vehicle that may be lawfully driven with a class C, class M1, or class M2 license, as prescribed in Section 12804.9 of the Vehicle Code, may not be forfeited under this section if there is a community property interest in the vehicle by a person other than the defendant and the vehicle is the sole vehicle of this type available to the defendant's immediate family.

(f) Real property subject to forfeiture may not be seized, absent exigent circumstances, without notice to the interested parties and a hearing to determine that seizure is necessary to preserve the property pending the outcome of the proceedings. At the hearing, the prosecution shall bear the burden of establishing that probable cause exists for the forfeiture of the property and that seizure is necessary to preserve the property pending the outcome of the forfeiture proceedings. The court may issue a seizure order pursuant to this section if it finds that seizure is warranted or a pendente

lite order pursuant to Section 236.10 if it finds that the status quo or value of the property can be preserved without seizure.
(g) For purposes of this section, no allegation or proof of a pattern of criminal profiteering activity is required.
(Added by Stats. 2012, Ch. 514, Sec. 2. (SB 1133) Effective January 1, 2013.)
236.8.
(a) If the prosecuting agency, in conjunction with the criminal proceeding, files a petition of forfeiture with the superior court of the county in which the defendant has been charged with human trafficking that involves a commercial sex act, as defined in paragraph (2) of subdivision (g) of Section 236.1, where the victim was less than 18 years of age at the time of the commission of the crime, the prosecuting agency shall make service of process of a notice regarding that petition upon every individual who may have a property interest in the alleged proceeds or instruments. The notice shall state that any interested party may file a verified claim with the superior court stating the amount of their claimed interest and an affirmation or denial of the prosecuting agency's allegation. If the notice cannot be given by registered mail or personal delivery, the notice shall be published for at least three successive weeks in a newspaper of general circulation in the county where the property is located. If the property alleged to be subject to forfeiture is real property, the prosecuting agency shall, at the time of filing the petition of forfeiture, record a lis pendens with the county recorder in each county in which the real property is situated that specifically identifies the real property alleged to be subject to forfeiture. The judgment of forfeiture shall not affect the interest in real property of a third party that was acquired prior to the recording of the lis pendens.
(b) All notices shall set forth the time within which a claim of interest in the property seized is required to be filed pursuant to Section 236.9.
(Added by Stats. 2012, Ch. 514, Sec. 3. (SB 1133) Effective January 1, 2013.)
236.9.
(a) A person claiming an interest in the property, proceeds, or instruments may, at any time within 30 days from the date of the first publication of the notice of seizure or within 30 days after receipt of actual notice, file with the superior court of the county in which the action is pending a verified claim stating his or her interest in the property, proceeds, or instruments. A verified copy of the claim shall be given by the claimant to the Attorney General or district attorney, as appropriate.
(b) (1) If, at the end of the time set forth in subdivision (a), an interested person, other than the defendant, has not filed a claim, the court, upon motion, shall declare that the person has defaulted upon his or her alleged interest and the interest shall be subject to forfeiture upon proof of the provisions of subdivision (d).
(2) The defendant may admit or deny that the property is subject to forfeiture pursuant to the provisions of this chapter. If the defendant fails to admit or deny or to file a claim of interest in the property, proceeds, or instruments, the court shall enter a response of denial on behalf of the defendant.
(c) (1) The forfeiture proceeding shall be set for hearing in the superior court in which the underlying criminal offense will be tried.
(2) If the defendant is found guilty of the underlying offense, the issue of forfeiture shall be promptly tried, either before the same jury or before a new jury in the discretion of the court, unless waived by the consent of all parties.
(d) At the forfeiture hearing, the prosecuting agency shall have the burden of establishing beyond a reasonable doubt that the property alleged in the petition comes within the provisions of Section 236.7.
(e) Unless the trier of fact finds that the seized property was used for a purpose for which forfeiture is permitted, the court shall order the seized property released to the person that the court determines is entitled to possession of that property. If the trier of fact finds that the seized property was used for a purpose for which forfeiture is permitted, but does not find that a person who has a valid interest in the property had actual knowledge that the property would be or was used for a purpose for which forfeiture is permitted and consented to that use, the court shall order the property released to the claimant.
(Added by Stats. 2012, Ch. 514, Sec. 4. (SB 1133) Effective January 1, 2013.)
236.10.
(a) Concurrent with or subsequent to the filing of the petition, the prosecuting agency may move the superior court for, and the superior court may issue, the following pendente lite orders to preserve the status quo of the property alleged in the petition:
(1) An injunction to restrain anyone from transferring, encumbering, hypothecating, or otherwise disposing of the property.
(2) Appointment of a receiver to take possession of, care for, manage, and operate the assets and properties so that the property may be maintained and preserved. The court may order that a receiver appointed pursuant to this section be compensated for all reasonable expenditures made or incurred by him or her in connection with the possession, care, management, and operation of property or assets that are subject to the provisions of this section.
(b) No preliminary injunction may be granted or receiver appointed without notice to the interested parties and a hearing to determine that an order is necessary to preserve the property, pending the outcome of the criminal proceedings, and that there is probable cause to believe that the property alleged in the forfeiture proceedings are proceeds, instruments, or property interests forfeitable under the provisions of Section 236.7. However, a temporary restraining order may issue pending that hearing pursuant to the provisions of Section 527 of the Code of Civil Procedure.
(c) Notwithstanding any other provision of law, the court in granting these motions may order a surety bond or undertaking to preserve the property interests of the interested parties.
(d) The court shall, in making its orders, seek to protect the interests of those who may be involved in the same enterprise as the defendant, but who were not involved in human trafficking that involves a commercial sex act, as defined in paragraph (2) of subdivision (g) of Section 236.1, where the victim was less than 18 years of age at the time of the commission of the crime.
(Added by Stats. 2012, Ch. 514, Sec. 5. (SB 1133) Effective January 1, 2013.)
236.11.
(a) If the trier of fact at the forfeiture hearing finds that the alleged property, instruments, or proceeds are forfeitable pursuant to Section 236.7 and the defendant was engaged in human trafficking that involves a commercial sex act, as defined in paragraph (2) of subdivision (g) of Section 236.1, where the victim was less than 18 years of age at the time of the commission of the crime, the court shall declare that property or proceeds forfeited to the state or local governmental entity, subject to distribution as provided in Section 236.12. No property solely owned by a bona fide purchaser for value shall be subject to forfeiture.
(b) If the trier of fact at the forfeiture hearing finds that the alleged property is forfeitable pursuant to Section 236.7 but does not find that a person holding a valid lien, mortgage, security interest, or interest under a conditional sales contract acquired that interest with actual knowledge that the property was to be used for a purpose for which forfeiture is permitted, and the amount due to that person is less than the appraised value of the property, that person may pay to the state or the local governmental entity that initiated the forfeiture proceeding the amount of the registered owner's equity, which shall be deemed to be the difference between the appraised value and the amount of the lien, mortgage, security interest, or interest under a conditional sales contract. Upon payment, the state or local governmental entity shall relinquish all claims to the property. If the holder of the interest elects not to pay the state or local governmental entity, the property shall be deemed forfeited to the state or local governmental entity and the ownership certificate shall be forwarded. The appraised value shall be determined as of the date judgment is entered either by agreement between the legal owner and the governmental entity involved, or, if they cannot agree, by a court-appointed appraiser for the county in which the action is brought. A person holding a valid lien, mortgage, security interest, or interest under a conditional sales contract shall be paid the appraised value of his or her interest.
(c) If the amount due to a person holding a valid lien, mortgage, security interest, or interest under a conditional sales contract is less than the value of the property and the person elects not to make payment to the governmental entity, the property shall be sold at public auction by the Department of General Services or by the local governmental entity. The seller shall provide notice of the sale by one publication in a newspaper published and circulated in the city, community, or locality where the sale is to take place.
(d) Notwithstanding subdivision (c), a county may dispose of real property forfeited to the county pursuant to this chapter by the process prescribed in Section 25538.5 of the Government Code.
(Added by Stats. 2012, Ch. 514, Sec. 6. (SB 1133) Effective January 1, 2013.)
236.12.
Notwithstanding that no response or claim has been filed pursuant to Section 236.9, in all cases where property is forfeited pursuant to this chapter and, if necessary, sold by the Department of General Services or local governmental entity, the money forfeited or the proceeds of sale shall be distributed by the state or local governmental entity as follows:
(a) To the bona fide or innocent purchaser, conditional sales vendor, or holder of a valid lien, mortgage, or security interest, if any, up to the amount of his or her interest in the property or proceeds, when the court declaring the forfeiture orders a distribution to that person. The court shall endeavor to discover all those lienholders and protect their interests and may, at its discretion, order the proceeds placed in escrow for up to an additional 60 days to ensure that all valid claims are received and processed.
(b) To the Department of General Services or local governmental entity for all expenditures made or incurred by it in connection with the sale of the property, including expenditures for necessary repairs, storage, or transportation of property seized under this chapter.
(c) (1) Fifty percent to the General Fund of the state or local governmental entity, whichever prosecutes or handles the forfeiture hearing.
(2) Fifty percent to the Victim-Witness Assistance Fund to be used upon appropriation for grants to community-based organizations that serve victims of human trafficking.
(Added by Stats. 2012, Ch. 514, Sec. 7. (SB 1133) Effective January 1, 2013.)
236.13.
(a) In a case involving a charge of human trafficking under Section 236.1, a minor who is a victim of the human trafficking shall be provided with assistance from the local county Victim Witness Assistance Center if the minor so desires.
(b) This section does not require a local agency to operate a Victim Witness Assistance Center.
(Added by Stats. 2016, Ch. 641, Sec. 1. (AB 2221) Effective January 1, 2017.)
236.14.
(a) If a person was arrested for or convicted of any nonviolent offense committed while he or she was a victim of human trafficking, including, but not limited to, prostitution as described in subdivision (b) of Section 647, the person may petition the court for vacatur relief of his or her convictions and arrests under this section. The petitioner shall establish, by clear and convincing evidence, that the arrest or conviction was the direct result of being a victim of human trafficking.
(b) The petition for relief shall be submitted under penalty of perjury and shall describe all of the available grounds and evidence that the petitioner was a victim of human trafficking and the arrest or conviction of a nonviolent offense was the direct result of being a victim of human trafficking.
(c) The petition for relief and supporting documentation shall be served on the state or local prosecutorial agency that obtained the conviction for which vacatur is sought or with jurisdiction over charging decisions with regard to the arrest. The state or local prosecutorial agency shall have 45 days from the date of receipt of service to respond to the petition for relief.
(d) If opposition to the petition is not filed by the applicable state or local prosecutorial agency, the court shall deem the petition unopposed and may grant the petition.
(e) The court may, with the agreement of the petitioner and all of the involved state or local prosecutorial agencies, consolidate into one hearing a petition with multiple convictions from different jurisdictions.
(f) If the petition is opposed or if the court otherwise deems it necessary, the court shall schedule a hearing on the petition. The hearing may consist of the following:
(1) Testimony by the petitioner, which may be required in support of the petition.
(2) Evidence and supporting documentation in support of the petition.
(3) Opposition evidence presented by any of the involved state or local prosecutorial agencies that obtained the conviction.
(g) After considering the totality of the evidence presented, the court may vacate the conviction and expunge the arrests and issue an order if it finds all of the following:
(1) That the petitioner was a victim of human trafficking at the time the nonviolent crime was committed.
(2) The commission of the crime was a direct result of being a victim of human trafficking.
(3) The victim is engaged in a good faith effort to distance himself or herself from the human trafficking scheme.
(4) It is in the best interest of the petitioner and in the interests of justice.
(h) In issuing an order of vacatur for the convictions, an order shall do the following:
(1) Set forth a finding that the petitioner was a victim of human trafficking when he or she committed the offense.
(2) Set aside the verdict of guilty or the adjudication and dismiss the accusation or information against the petitioner.
(3) Notify the Department of Justice that the petitioner was a victim of human trafficking when he or she committed the crime and of the relief that has been ordered.
(i) Notwithstanding this section, a petitioner shall not be relieved of any financial restitution order that directly benefits the victim of a nonviolent crime, unless it has already been paid.
(j) A person who was arrested as, or found to be, a person described in Section 602 of the Welfare and Institutions Code because he or she committed a nonviolent offense while he or she was a victim of human trafficking, including, but not limited to, prostitution, as described in subdivision (b) of Section 647, may petition the court for relief under this section. If the petitioner establishes that the arrest or adjudication was the direct result of being a victim of human trafficking the petitioner is entitled to a rebuttable presumption that the requirements for relief have been met.
(k) If the court issues an order as described in subdivision (a) or (j), the court shall also order the law enforcement agency having jurisdiction over the offense, the Department of Justice, and any law enforcement agency that arrested the petitioner or participated in the arrest of the petitioner to seal their records of the arrest and the court order to seal and destroy the records for three years from the date of the arrest, or within one year after the court order is granted, whichever occurs later, and thereafter to destroy their records of the arrest and the court order to seal and destroy those records. The court shall provide the petitioner a copy of any court order concerning the destruction of the arrest records.
(l) A petition pursuant to this section shall be made and heard within a reasonable time after the person has ceased to be a victim of human trafficking, or within a reasonable time after the petitioner has sought services for being a victim of human trafficking, whichever occurs later, subject to reasonable concerns for the safety of the petitioner,

family members of the petitioner, or other victims of human trafficking who may be jeopardized by the bringing of the application or for other reasons consistent with the purposes of this section.

(m) For the purposes of this section, official documentation of a petitioner's status as a victim of human trafficking may be introduced as evidence that his or her participation in the offense was the result of his or her status as a victim of human trafficking. For the purposes of this subdivision, "official documentation" means any documentation issued by a federal, state, or local agency that tends to show the petitioner's status as a victim of human trafficking. Official documentation shall not be required for the issuance of an order described in subdivision (a).

(n) A petitioner, or his or her attorney, may be excused from appearing in person at a hearing for relief pursuant to this section only if the court finds a compelling reason why the petitioner cannot attend the hearing, in which case the petitioner may appear telephonically, via videoconference, or by other electronic means established by the court.

(o) Notwithstanding any other law, a petitioner who has obtained an order pursuant to this section may lawfully deny or refuse to acknowledge an arrest, conviction, or adjudication that is set aside pursuant to the order.

(p) Notwithstanding any other law, the records of the arrest, conviction, or adjudication shall not be distributed to any state licensing board.

(q) The record of a proceeding related to a petition pursuant to this section that is accessible by the public shall not disclose the petitioner's full name.

(r) A court that grants relief pursuant to this section may take additional action as appropriate under the circumstances to carry out the purposes of this section.

(s) If the court denies the application because the evidence is insufficient to establish grounds for vacatur, the denial may be without prejudice. The court may state the reasons for its denial in writing or on the record that is memorialized by transcription, audio tape, or video tape, and if those reasons are based on curable deficiencies in the application, allow the applicant a reasonable time period to cure the deficiencies upon which the court based the denial.

(t) For the purposes of this section, the following terms apply:

(1) "Nonviolent offense" means any offense not listed in subdivision (c) of Section 667.5.

(2) "Vacate" means that the arrest and any adjudications or convictions suffered by the petitioner are deemed not to have occurred and that all records in the case are sealed and destroyed pursuant to this section. The court shall provide the petitioner with a copy of the orders described in subdivisions (a), (j), and (k), as applicable, and inform the petitioner that he or she may thereafter state that he or she was not arrested for the charge, or adjudicated or convicted of the charge, that was vacated.

(3) "Victim of human trafficking" means the victim of a crime described in subdivisions (a), (b), and (c) of Section 236.1.

(Added by Stats. 2016, Ch. 650, Sec. 1. (SB 823) Effective January 1, 2017.)

237.

(a) False imprisonment is punishable by a fine not exceeding one thousand dollars ($1,000), or by imprisonment in the county jail for not more than one year, or by both that fine and imprisonment. If the false imprisonment be effected by violence, menace, fraud, or deceit, it shall be punishable by imprisonment pursuant to subdivision (h) of Section 1170.

(b) False imprisonment of an elder or dependent adult by use of violence, menace, fraud, or deceit shall be punishable as described in subdivision (f) of Section 368.

(Amended by Stats. 2011, Ch. 15, Sec. 288. (AB 109) Effective April 4, 2011. Operative October 1, 2011, by Sec. 636 of Ch. 15, as amended by Stats. 2011, Ch. 39, Sec. 68.)

CHAPTER 9. Assault and Battery [240 - 248]

(Chapter 9 enacted 1872.)

240.

An assault is an unlawful attempt, coupled with a present ability, to commit a violent injury on the person of another.

(Enacted 1872.)

241.

(a) An assault is punishable by a fine not exceeding one thousand dollars ($1,000), or by imprisonment in the county jail not exceeding six months, or by both the fine and imprisonment.

(b) When an assault is committed against the person of a parking control officer engaged in the performance of his or her duties, and the person committing the offense knows or reasonably should know that the victim is a parking control officer, the assault is punishable by a fine not exceeding two thousand dollars ($2,000), or by imprisonment in the county jail not exceeding six months, or by both the fine and imprisonment.

(c) When an assault is committed against the person of a peace officer, firefighter, emergency medical technician, mobile intensive care paramedic, lifeguard, process server, traffic officer, code enforcement officer, animal control officer, or search and rescue member engaged in the performance of his or her duties, or a physician or nurse engaged in rendering emergency medical care outside a hospital, clinic, or other health care facility, and the person committing the offense knows or reasonably should know that the victim is a peace officer, firefighter, emergency medical technician, mobile intensive care paramedic, lifeguard, process server, traffic officer, code enforcement officer, animal control officer, or search and rescue member engaged in the performance of his or her duties, or a physician or nurse engaged in rendering emergency medical care, the assault is punishable by a fine not exceeding two thousand dollars ($2,000), or by imprisonment in a county jail not exceeding one year, or by both the fine and imprisonment.

(d) As used in this section, the following definitions apply:

(1) Peace officer means any person defined in Chapter 4.5 (commencing with Section 830) of Title 3 of Part 2.

(2) "Emergency medical technician" means a person possessing a valid course completion certificate from a program approved by the State Department of Health Care Services for the medical training and education of ambulance personnel, and who meets the standards of Division 2.5 (commencing with Section 1797) of the Health and Safety Code.

(3) "Mobile intensive care paramedic" refers to a person who meets the standards set forth in Division 2.5 (commencing with Section 1797) of the Health and Safety Code.

(4) "Nurse" means a person who meets the standards of Division 2.5 (commencing with Section 1797) of the Health and Safety Code.

(5) "Lifeguard" means a person who is:

(A) Employed as a lifeguard by the state, a county, or a city, and is designated by local ordinance as a public officer who has a duty and responsibility to enforce local ordinances and misdemeanors through the issuance of citations.

(B) Wearing distinctive clothing which includes written identification of the person's status as a lifeguard and which clearly identifies the employing organization.

(6) "Process server" means any person who meets the standards or is expressly exempt from the standards set forth in Section 22350 of the Business and Professions Code.

(7) "Traffic officer" means any person employed by a county or city to monitor and enforce state laws and local ordinances relating to parking and the operation of vehicles.

(8) "Animal control officer" means any person employed by a county or city for purposes of enforcing animal control laws or regulations.

(9) (A) "Code enforcement officer" means any person who is not described in Chapter 4.5 (commencing with Section 830) of Title 3 of Part 2 and who is employed by any governmental subdivision, public or quasi-public corporation, public agency, public service corporation, any town, city, county, or municipal corporation, whether incorporated or chartered, that has enforcement authority for health, safety, and welfare requirements, and whose duties include enforcement of any statute, rules, regulations, or standards, and who is authorized to issue citations, or file formal complaints.

(B) "Code enforcement officer" also includes any person who is employed by the Department of Housing and Community Development who has enforcement authority for health, safety, and welfare requirements pursuant to the Employee Housing Act (Part 1 (commencing with Section 17000) of Division 13 of the Health and Safety Code); the State Housing Law (Part 1.5 (commencing with Section 17910) of Division 13 of the Health and Safety Code); the Manufactured Housing Act of 1980 (Part 2 (commencing with Section 18000) of Division 13 of the Health and Safety Code); the Mobilehome Parks Act (Part 2.1 (commencing with Section 18200) of Division 13 of the Health and Safety Code); and the Special Occupancy Parks Act (Part 2.3 (commencing with Section 18860) of Division 13 of the Health and Safety Code).

(10) "Parking control officer" means any person employed by a city, county, or city and county, to monitor and enforce state laws and local ordinances relating to parking.

(11) "Search and rescue member" means any person who is part of an organized search and rescue team managed by a governmental agency.

(Amended by Stats. 2016, Ch. 86, Sec. 224. (SB 1171) Effective January 1, 2017.)

241.1.

When an assault is committed against the person of a custodial officer as defined in Section 831 or 831.5, and the person committing the offense knows or reasonably should know that the victim is a custodial officer engaged in the performance of his or her duties, the offense shall be punished by imprisonment in the county jail not exceeding one year or by imprisonment pursuant to subdivision (h) of Section 1170.

(Amended by Stats. 2011, Ch. 15, Sec. 289. (AB 109) Effective April 4, 2011. Operative October 1, 2011, by Sec. 636 of Ch. 15, as amended by Stats. 2011, Ch. 39, Sec. 68.)

241.2.

(a) (1) When an assault is committed on school or park property against any person, the assault is punishable by a fine not exceeding two thousand dollars ($2,000), or by imprisonment in the county jail not exceeding one year, or by both that fine and imprisonment.

(2) When a violation of this section is committed by a minor on school property, the court may, in addition to any other fine, sentence, or as a condition of probation, order the minor to attend counseling as deemed appropriate by the court at the expense of the minor's parents. The court shall take into consideration the ability of the minor's parents to pay, however, no minor shall be relieved of attending counseling because of the minor's parents' inability to pay for the counseling imposed by this section.

(b) "School," as used in this section, means any elementary school, junior high school, four-year high school, senior high school, adult school or any branch thereof, opportunity school, continuation high school, regional occupational center, evening high school, technical school, or community college.

(c) "Park," as used in this section, means any publicly maintained or operated park. It does not include any facility when used for professional sports or commercial events.

(Amended by Stats. 2001, Ch. 484, Sec. 2. Effective January 1, 2002.)

241.3.

(a) When an assault is committed against any person on the property of, or on a motor vehicle of, a public transportation provider, the offense shall be punished by a fine not to exceed two thousand dollars ($2,000), or by imprisonment in a county jail not to exceed one year, or by both the fine and imprisonment.

(b) As used in this section, "public transportation provider" means a publicly or privately owned entity that operates, for the transportation of persons for hire, a bus, taxicab, streetcar, cable car, trackless trolley, or other motor vehicle, including a vehicle operated on stationary rails or on a track or rail suspended in air, or that operates a schoolbus.

(c) As used in this section, "on the property of" means the entire station where public transportation is available, including the parking lot reserved for the public who utilize the transportation system.

(Repealed and added by Stats. 1996, Ch. 423, Sec. 2. Effective January 1, 1997.)

241.4.

An assault is punishable by fine not exceeding one thousand dollars ($1,000), or by imprisonment in the county jail not exceeding six months, or by both. When the assault is committed against the person of a peace officer engaged in the performance of his or her duties as a member of a police department of a school district pursuant to Section 38000 of the Education Code, and the person committing the offense knows or reasonably should know that the victim is a peace officer engaged in the performance of his or her duties, the offense shall be punished by imprisonment in the county jail not exceeding one year or by imprisonment pursuant to subdivision (h) of Section 1170.

(Amended by Stats. 2011, Ch. 15, Sec. 290. (AB 109) Effective April 4, 2011. Operative October 1, 2011, by Sec. 636 of Ch. 15, as amended by Stats. 2011, Ch. 39, Sec. 68.)

241.5.

(a) When an assault is committed against a highway worker engaged in the performance of his or her duties and the person committing the offense knows or reasonably should know that the victim is a highway worker engaged in the performance of his or her duties, the offense shall be punishable by a fine not to exceed two thousand dollars ($2,000) or by imprisonment in a county jail up to one year or by both that fine and imprisonment.

(b) As used in this section, "highway worker" means an employee of the Department of Transportation, a contractor or employee of a contractor while working under contract with the Department of Transportation, an employee of a city, county, or city and county, a contractor or employee of a contractor while working under contract with a city, county, or city and county, or a volunteer as defined in Section 1720.4 of the Labor Code who does one or more of the following:

(1) Performs maintenance, repair, or construction of state highway or local street or road infrastructures and associated rights-of-way in highway or local street or road work zones.

(2) Operates equipment on state highway or local street or road infrastructures and associated rights-of-way in highway or local street or road work zones.

(3) Performs any related maintenance work, as required, on state highway or local street or road infrastructures in highway or local street or road work zones.

(Amended by Stats. 2009, Ch. 116, Sec. 1. (AB 561) Effective January 1, 2010.)

241.6.

When an assault is committed against a school employee engaged in the performance of his or her duties, or in retaliation for an act performed in the course of his or her duties, whether on or off campus, during the schoolday or at any other time, and the person committing the offense knows or reasonably should know the victim is a school employee, the assault is punishable by imprisonment in a county jail not exceeding one year, or by a fine not exceeding two thousand dollars ($2,000), or by both the fine and imprisonment.

For purposes of this section, "school employee" has the same meaning as defined in subdivision (d) of Section 245.5.

This section shall not apply to conduct arising during the course of an otherwise lawful labor dispute.
(Amended by Stats. 1993, Ch. 1257, Sec. 5. Effective January 1, 1994.)
241.7.
Any person who is a party to a civil or criminal action in which a jury has been selected to try the case and who, while the legal action is pending or after the conclusion of the trial, commits an assault against any juror or alternate juror who was selected and sworn in that legal action, shall be punished by a fine not to exceed two thousand dollars ($2,000), or by imprisonment in the county jail not exceeding one year, or by both such fine and imprisonment, or by imprisonment pursuant to subdivision (h) of Section 1170.
(Amended by Stats. 2011, Ch. 15, Sec. 291. (AB 109) Effective April 4, 2011. Operative October 1, 2011, by Sec. 636 of Ch. 15, as amended by Stats. 2011, Ch. 39, Sec. 68.)
241.8.
(a) Any person who commits an assault against a member of the United States Armed Forces because of the victim's service in the United States Armed Forces shall be punished by a fine not exceeding two thousand dollars ($2,000), by imprisonment in a county jail for a period not exceeding one year, or by both that fine and imprisonment.
(b) "Because of" means that the bias motivation must be a cause in fact of the assault, whether or not other causes exist. When multiple concurrent motives exist, the prohibited bias must be a substantial factor in bringing about the assault.
(Added by Stats. 2003, Ch. 138, Sec. 1. Effective January 1, 2004.)
242.
A battery is any willful and unlawful use of force or violence upon the person of another.
(Enacted 1872.)
243.
(a) A battery is punishable by a fine not exceeding two thousand dollars ($2,000), or by imprisonment in a county jail not exceeding six months, or by both that fine and imprisonment.
(b) When a battery is committed against the person of a peace officer, custodial officer, firefighter, emergency medical technician, lifeguard, security officer, custody assistant, process server, traffic officer, code enforcement officer, animal control officer, or search and rescue member engaged in the performance of his or her duties, whether on or off duty, including when the peace officer is in a police uniform and is concurrently performing the duties required of him or her as a peace officer while also employed in a private capacity as a part-time or casual private security guard or patrolman, or a nonsworn employee of a probation department engaged in the performance of his or her duties, whether on or off duty, or a physician or nurse engaged in rendering emergency medical care outside a hospital, clinic, or other health care facility, and the person committing the offense knows or reasonably should know that the victim is a peace officer, custodial officer, firefighter, emergency medical technician, lifeguard, security officer, custody assistant, process server, traffic officer, code enforcement officer, animal control officer, or search and rescue member engaged in the performance of his or her duties, nonsworn employee of a probation department, or a physician or nurse engaged in rendering emergency medical care, the battery is punishable by a fine not exceeding two thousand dollars ($2,000), or by imprisonment in a county jail not exceeding one year, or by both that fine and imprisonment.
(c) (1) When a battery is committed against a custodial officer, firefighter, emergency medical technician, lifeguard, process server, traffic officer, or animal control officer engaged in the performance of his or her duties, whether on or off duty, or a nonsworn employee of a probation department engaged in the performance of his or her duties, whether on or off duty, or a physician or nurse engaged in rendering emergency medical care outside a hospital, clinic, or other health care facility, and the person committing the offense knows or reasonably should know that the victim is a nonsworn employee of a probation department, custodial officer, firefighter, emergency medical technician, lifeguard, process server, traffic officer, or animal control officer engaged in the performance of his or her duties, or a physician or nurse engaged in rendering emergency medical care, and an injury is inflicted on that victim, the battery is punishable by a fine of not more than two thousand dollars ($2,000), by imprisonment in a county jail not exceeding one year, or by both that fine and imprisonment, or by imprisonment pursuant to subdivision (h) of Section 1170 for 16 months, or two or three years.
(2) When the battery specified in paragraph (1) is committed against a peace officer engaged in the performance of his or her duties, whether on or off duty, including when the peace officer is in a police uniform and is concurrently performing the duties required of him or her as a peace officer while also employed in a private capacity as a part-time or casual private security guard or patrolman and the person committing the offense knows or reasonably should know that the victim is a peace officer engaged in the performance of his or her duties, the battery is punishable by a fine of not more than ten thousand dollars ($10,000), or by imprisonment in a county jail not exceeding one year or pursuant to subdivision (h) of Section 1170 for 16 months, or two or three years, or by both that fine and imprisonment.
(d) When a battery is committed against any person and serious bodily injury is inflicted on the person, the battery is punishable by imprisonment in a county jail not exceeding one year or imprisonment pursuant to subdivision (h) of Section 1170 for two, three, or four years.
(e) (1) When a battery is committed against a spouse, a person with whom the defendant is cohabiting, a person who is the parent of the defendant's child, former spouse, fiancé, or fiancée, or a person with whom the defendant currently has, or has previously had, a dating or engagement relationship, the battery is punishable by a fine not exceeding two thousand dollars ($2,000), or by imprisonment in a county jail for a period of not more than one year, or by both that fine and imprisonment. If probation is granted, or the execution or imposition of the sentence is suspended, it shall be a condition thereof that the defendant participate in, for no less than one year, and successfully complete, a batterer's treatment program, as described in Section 1203.097, or if none is available, another appropriate counseling program designated by the court. However, this provision shall not be construed as requiring a city, a county, or a city and county to provide a new program or higher level of service as contemplated by Section 6 of Article XIII B of the California Constitution.
(2) Upon conviction of a violation of this subdivision, if probation is granted, the conditions of probation may include, in lieu of a fine, one or both of the following requirements:
(A) That the defendant make payments to a battered women's shelter, up to a maximum of five thousand dollars ($5,000).
(B) That the defendant reimburse the victim for reasonable costs of counseling and other reasonable expenses that the court finds are the direct result of the defendant's offense.
For any order to pay a fine, make payments to a battered women's shelter, or pay restitution as a condition of probation under this subdivision, the court shall make a determination of the defendant's ability to pay. In no event shall any order to make payments to a battered women's shelter be made if it would impair the ability of the defendant to pay direct restitution to the victim or court-ordered child support. If the injury to a married person is caused in whole or in part by the criminal acts of his or her spouse in violation of this section, the community property shall not be used to discharge the liability of the offending spouse for restitution to the injured spouse, required by Section 1203.04, as operative on or before August 2, 1995, or Section 1202.4, or to a shelter for costs with regard to the injured spouse and dependents, required by this section, until all separate property of the offending spouse is exhausted.

(3) Upon conviction of a violation of this subdivision, if probation is granted or the execution or imposition of the sentence is suspended and the person has been previously convicted of a violation of this subdivision or Section 273.5, the person shall be imprisoned for not less than 48 hours in addition to the conditions in paragraph (1). However, the court, upon a showing of good cause, may elect not to impose the mandatory minimum imprisonment as required by this subdivision and may, under these circumstances, grant probation or order the suspension of the execution or imposition of the sentence.
(4) The Legislature finds and declares that these specified crimes merit special consideration when imposing a sentence so as to display society's condemnation for these crimes of violence upon victims with whom a close relationship has been formed.
(5) If a peace officer makes an arrest for a violation of paragraph (1) of subdivision (e) of this section, the peace officer is not required to inform the victim of his or her right to make a citizen's arrest pursuant to subdivision (b) of Section 836.
(f) As used in this section:
(1) "Peace officer" means any person defined in Chapter 4.5 (commencing with Section 830) of Title 3 of Part 2.
(2) "Emergency medical technician" means a person who is either an EMT-I, EMT-II, or EMT-P (paramedic), and possesses a valid certificate or license in accordance with the standards of Division 2.5 (commencing with Section 1797) of the Health and Safety Code.
(3) "Nurse" means a person who meets the standards of Division 2.5 (commencing with Section 1797) of the Health and Safety Code.
(4) "Serious bodily injury" means a serious impairment of physical condition, including, but not limited to, the following: loss of consciousness; concussion; bone fracture; protracted loss or impairment of function of any bodily member or organ; a wound requiring extensive suturing; and serious disfigurement.
(5) "Injury" means any physical injury which requires professional medical treatment.
(6) "Custodial officer" means any person who has the responsibilities and duties described in Section 831 and who is employed by a law enforcement agency of any city or county or who performs those duties as a volunteer.
(7) "Lifeguard" means a person defined in paragraph (5) of subdivision (d) of Section 241.
(8) "Traffic officer" means any person employed by a city, county, or city and county to monitor and enforce state laws and local ordinances relating to parking and the operation of vehicles.
(9) "Animal control officer" means any person employed by a city, county, or city and county for purposes of enforcing animal control laws or regulations.
(10) "Dating relationship" means frequent, intimate associations primarily characterized by the expectation of affectional or sexual involvement independent of financial considerations.
(11) (A) "Code enforcement officer" means any person who is not described in Chapter 4.5 (commencing with Section 830) of Title 3 of Part 2 and who is employed by any governmental subdivision, public or quasi-public corporation, public agency, public service corporation, any town, city, county, or municipal corporation, whether incorporated or chartered, who has enforcement authority for health, safety, and welfare requirements, and whose duties include enforcement of any statute, rules, regulations, or standards, and who is authorized to issue citations, or file formal complaints.
(B) "Code enforcement officer" also includes any person who is employed by the Department of Housing and Community Development who has enforcement authority for health, safety, and welfare requirements pursuant to the Employee Housing Act (Part 1 (commencing with Section 17000) of Division 13 of the Health and Safety Code); the State Housing Law (Part 1.5 (commencing with Section 17910) of Division 13 of the Health and Safety Code); the Manufactured Housing Act of 1980 (Part 2 (commencing with Section 18000) of Division 13 of the Health and Safety Code); the Mobilehome Parks Act (Part 2.1 (commencing with Section 18200) of Division 13 of the Health and Safety Code); and the Special Occupancy Parks Act (Part 2.3 (commencing with Section 18860) of Division 13 of the Health and Safety Code).
(12) "Custody assistant" means any person who has the responsibilities and duties described in Section 831.7 and who is employed by a law enforcement agency of any city, county, or city and county.
(13) "Search and rescue member" means any person who is part of an organized search and rescue team managed by a government agency.
(14) "Security officer" means any person who has the responsibilities and duties described in Section 831.4 and who is employed by a law enforcement agency of any city, county, or city and county.
(g) It is the intent of the Legislature by amendments to this section at the 1981–82 and 1983–84 Regular Sessions to abrogate the holdings in cases such as People v. Corey, 21 Cal. 3d 738, and Cervantez v. J.C. Penney Co., 24 Cal. 3d 579, and to reinstate prior judicial interpretations of this section as they relate to criminal sanctions for battery on peace officers who are employed, on a part-time or casual basis, while wearing a police uniform as private security guards or patrolmen and to allow the exercise of peace officer powers concurrently with that employment.
(Amended by Stats. 2015, Ch. 626, Sec. 1. (AB 545) Effective January 1, 2016.)
243.1.
When a battery is committed against the person of a custodial officer as defined in Section 831 of the Penal Code, and the person committing the offense knows or reasonably should know that the victim is a custodial officer engaged in the performance of his or her duties, and the custodial officer is engaged in the performance of his or her duties, the offense shall be punished by imprisonment pursuant to subdivision (h) of Section 1170.
(Amended by Stats. 2011, Ch. 15, Sec. 293. (AB 109) Effective April 4, 2011. Operative October 1, 2011, by Sec. 636 of Ch. 15, as amended by Stats. 2011, Ch. 39, Sec. 68.)
243.2.
(a) (1) Except as otherwise provided in Section 243.6, when a battery is committed on school property, park property, or the grounds of a public or private hospital, against any person, the battery is punishable by a fine not exceeding two thousand dollars ($2,000), or by imprisonment in the county jail not exceeding one year, or by both the fine and imprisonment.
(2) When a violation of this section is committed by a minor on school property, the court may, in addition to any other fine, sentence, or as a condition of probation, order the minor to attend counseling as deemed appropriate by the court at the expense of the minor's parents. The court shall take into consideration the ability of the minor's parents to pay, however, no minor shall be relieved of attending counseling because of the minor's parents' inability to pay for the counseling imposed by this section.
(b) For the purposes of this section, the following terms have the following meanings:
(1) "Hospital" means a facility for the diagnosis, care, and treatment of human illness that is subject to, or specifically exempted from, the licensure requirements of Chapter 2 (commencing with Section 1250) of Division 2 of the Health and Safety Code.
(2) "Park" means any publicly maintained or operated park. It does not include any facility when used for professional sports or commercial events.
(3) "School" means any elementary school, junior high school, four-year high school, senior high school, adult school or any branch thereof, opportunity school, continuation high school, regional occupational center, evening high school, technical school, or community college.
(c) This section shall not apply to conduct arising during the course of an otherwise lawful labor dispute.
(Amended by Stats. 2001, Ch. 484, Sec. 3. Effective January 1, 2002.)
243.25.

When a battery is committed against the person of an elder or a dependent adult as defined in Section 368, with knowledge that he or she is an elder or a dependent adult, the offense shall be punishable by a fine not to exceed two thousand dollars ($2,000), or by imprisonment in a county jail not to exceed one year, or by both that fine and imprisonment.

(Added by Stats. 2002, Ch. 369, Sec. 1. Effective January 1, 2003.)

243.3.

When a battery is committed against the person of an operator, driver, or passenger on a bus, taxicab, streetcar, cable car, trackless trolley, or other motor vehicle, including a vehicle operated on stationary rails or on a track or rail suspended in the air, used for the transportation of persons for hire, or against a schoolbus driver, or against the person of a station agent or ticket agent for the entity providing the transportation, and the person who commits the offense knows or reasonably should know that the victim, in the case of an operator, driver, or agent, is engaged in the performance of his or her duties, or is a passenger the offense shall be punished by a fine not exceeding ten thousand dollars ($10,000), or by imprisonment in a county jail not exceeding one year, or by both that fine and imprisonment. If an injury is inflicted on that victim, the offense shall be punished by a fine not exceeding ten thousand dollars ($10,000), or by imprisonment in a county jail not exceeding one year or in the state prison for 16 months, or two or three years, or by both that fine and imprisonment.

(Amended by Stats. 1997, Ch. 305, Sec. 1. Effective January 1, 1998.)

243.35.

(a) Except as provided in Section 243.3, when a battery is committed against any person on the property of, or in a motor vehicle of, a public transportation provider, the offense shall be punished by a fine not to exceed two thousand dollars ($2,000), or by imprisonment in a county jail not to exceed one year, or by both the fine and imprisonment.

(b) As used in this section, "public transportation provider" means a publicly or privately owned entity that operates, for the transportation of persons for hire, a bus, taxicab, streetcar, cable car, trackless trolley, or other motor vehicle, including a vehicle operated on stationary rails or on a track or rail suspended in air, or that operates a schoolbus.

(c) As used in this section, "on the property of" means the entire station where public transportation is available, including the parking lot reserved for the public who utilize the transportation system.

(Added by Stats. 1996, Ch. 423, Sec. 3. Effective January 1, 1997.)

243.4.

(a) Any person who touches an intimate part of another person while that person is unlawfully restrained by the accused or an accomplice, and if the touching is against the will of the person touched and is for the purpose of sexual arousal, sexual gratification, or sexual abuse, is guilty of sexual battery. A violation of this subdivision is punishable by imprisonment in a county jail for not more than one year, and by a fine not exceeding two thousand dollars ($2,000); or by imprisonment in the state prison for two, three, or four years, and by a fine not exceeding ten thousand dollars ($10,000).

(b) Any person who touches an intimate part of another person who is institutionalized for medical treatment and who is seriously disabled or medically incapacitated, if the touching is against the will of the person touched, and if the touching is for the purpose of sexual arousal, sexual gratification, or sexual abuse, is guilty of sexual battery. A violation of this subdivision is punishable by imprisonment in a county jail for not more than one year, and by a fine not exceeding two thousand dollars ($2,000); or by imprisonment in the state prison for two, three, or four years, and by a fine not exceeding ten thousand dollars ($10,000).

(c) Any person who touches an intimate part of another person for the purpose of sexual arousal, sexual gratification, or sexual abuse, and the victim is at the time unconscious of the nature of the act because the perpetrator fraudulently represented that the touching served a professional purpose, is guilty of sexual battery. A violation of this subdivision is punishable by imprisonment in a county jail for not more than one year, and by a fine not exceeding two thousand dollars ($2,000); or by imprisonment in the state prison for two, three, or four years, and by a fine not exceeding ten thousand dollars ($10,000).

(d) Any person who, for the purpose of sexual arousal, sexual gratification, or sexual abuse, causes another, against that person's will while that person is unlawfully restrained either by the accused or an accomplice, or is institutionalized for medical treatment and is seriously disabled or medically incapacitated, to masturbate or touch an intimate part of either of those persons or a third person, is guilty of sexual battery. A violation of this subdivision is punishable by imprisonment in a county jail for not more than one year, and by a fine not exceeding two thousand dollars ($2,000); or by imprisonment in the state prison for two, three, or four years, and by a fine not exceeding ten thousand dollars ($10,000).

(e) (1) Any person who touches an intimate part of another person, if the touching is against the will of the person touched, and is for the specific purpose of sexual arousal, sexual gratification, or sexual abuse, is guilty of misdemeanor sexual battery, punishable by a fine not exceeding two thousand dollars ($2,000), or by imprisonment in a county jail not exceeding six months, or by both that fine and imprisonment. However, if the defendant was an employer and the victim was an employee of the defendant, the misdemeanor sexual battery shall be punishable by a fine not exceeding three thousand dollars ($3,000), by imprisonment in a county jail not exceeding six months, or by both that fine and imprisonment. Notwithstanding any other provision of law, any amount of a fine above two thousand dollars ($2,000) which is collected from a defendant for a violation of this subdivision shall be transmitted to the State Treasury and, upon appropriation by the Legislature, distributed to the Department of Fair Employment and Housing for the purpose of enforcement of the California Fair Employment and Housing Act (Part 2.8 (commencing with Section 12900) of Division 3 of Title 2 of the Government Code), including, but not limited to, laws that proscribe sexual harassment in places of employment. However, in no event shall an amount over two thousand dollars ($2,000) be transmitted to the State Treasury until all fines, including any restitution fines that may have been imposed upon the defendant, have been paid in full.

(2) As used in this subdivision, "touches" means physical contact with another person, whether accomplished directly, through the clothing of the person committing the offense, or through the clothing of the victim.

(f) As used in subdivisions (a), (b), (c), and (d), "touches" means physical contact with the skin of another person whether accomplished directly or through the clothing of the person committing the offense.

(g) As used in this section, the following terms have the following meanings:

(1) "Intimate part" means the sexual organ, anus, groin, or buttocks of any person, and the breast of a female.

(2) "Sexual battery" does not include the crimes defined in Section 261 or 289.

(3) "Seriously disabled" means a person with severe physical or sensory disabilities.

(4) "Medically incapacitated" means a person who is incapacitated as a result of prescribed sedatives, anesthesia, or other medication.

(5) "Institutionalized" means a person who is located voluntarily or involuntarily in a hospital, medical treatment facility, nursing home, acute care facility, or mental hospital.

(6) "Minor" means a person under 18 years of age.

(h) This section shall not be construed to limit or prevent prosecution under any other law which also proscribes a course of conduct that also is proscribed by this section.

(i) In the case of a felony conviction for a violation of this section, the fact that the defendant was an employer and the victim was an employee of the defendant shall be a factor in aggravation in sentencing.

(j) A person who commits a violation of subdivision (a), (b), (c), or (d) against a minor when the person has a prior felony conviction for a violation of this section shall be guilty of a felony, punishable by imprisonment in the state prison for two, three, or four years and a fine not exceeding ten thousand dollars ($10,000).

(Amended by Stats. 2002, Ch. 302, Sec. 1. Effective January 1, 2003.)

243.5.

(a) When a person commits an assault or battery on school property during hours when school activities are being conducted, a peace officer may, without a warrant, notwithstanding paragraph (2) or (3) of subdivision (a) of Section 836, arrest the person who commits the assault or battery:

(1) Whenever the person has committed the assault or battery, although not in the peace officer's presence.

(2) Whenever the peace officer has reasonable cause to believe that the person to be arrested has committed the assault or battery, whether or not it has in fact been committed.

(b) "School," as used in this section, means any elementary school, junior high school, four-year high school, senior high school, adult school or any branch thereof, opportunity school, continuation high school, regional occupational center, evening high school, technical school, or community college.

(Amended by Stats. 1997, Ch. 324, Sec. 2. Effective January 1, 1998.)

243.6.

When a battery is committed against a school employee engaged in the performance of his or her duties, or in retaliation for an act performed in the course of his or her duties, whether on or off campus, during the schoolday or at any other time, and the person committing the offense knows or reasonably should know that the victim is a school employee, the battery is punishable by imprisonment in a county jail not exceeding one year, or by a fine not exceeding two thousand dollars ($2,000), or by both the fine and imprisonment. However, if an injury is inflicted on the victim, the battery shall be punishable by imprisonment in a county jail for not more than one year, or by a fine of not more than two thousand dollars ($2,000), or by imprisonment pursuant to subdivision (h) of Section 1170 for 16 months, or two or three years.

For purposes of this section, "school employee" has the same meaning as defined in subdivision (d) of Section 245.5.

This section shall not apply to conduct arising during the course of an otherwise lawful labor dispute.

(Amended by Stats. 2011, Ch. 15, Sec. 294. (AB 109) Effective April 4, 2011. Operative October 1, 2011, by Sec. 636 of Ch. 15, as amended by Stats. 2011, Ch. 39, Sec. 68.)

243.65.

(a) When a battery is committed against the person of a highway worker engaged in the performance of his or her duties and the person committing the offense knows or reasonably should know that the victim is a highway worker engaged in the performance of his or her duties, the offense shall be punished by a fine not exceeding two thousand dollars ($2,000), or by imprisonment in a county jail not exceeding one year, or by both that fine and imprisonment.

(b) As used in this section, "highway worker" means an employee of the Department of Transportation, a contractor or employee of a contractor while working under contract with the Department of Transportation, an employee of a city, county, or city and county, a contractor or employee of a contractor while working under contract with a city, county, or city and county, or a volunteer as defined in Section 1720.4 of the Labor Code who does one or more of the following:

(1) Performs maintenance, repair, or construction of state highway or local street or road infrastructures and associated rights-of-way in highway or local street or road work zones.

(2) Operates equipment on state highway or local street or road infrastructures and associated rights-of-way in highway or local street or road work zones.

(3) Performs any related maintenance work, as required, on state highway or local street or road infrastructures in highway or local street or road work zones.

(Amended by Stats. 2009, Ch. 116, Sec. 2. (AB 561) Effective January 1, 2010.)

243.7.

Any person who is a party to a civil or criminal action in which a jury has been selected to try the case and who, while the legal action is pending or after the conclusion of the trial commits a battery against any juror or alternate juror who was selected and sworn in that legal action shall be punished by a fine not to exceed five thousand dollars ($5,000), or by imprisonment in the county jail not exceeding one year, or by both such fine and imprisonment, or by the imprisonment in the state prison for 16 months, or for two or three years.

(Added by Stats. 1986, Ch. 616, Sec. 3.)

243.8.

(a) When a battery is committed against a sports official immediately prior to, during, or immediately following an interscholastic, intercollegiate, or any other organized amateur or professional athletic contest in which the sports official is participating, and the person who commits the offense knows or reasonably should know that the victim is engaged in the performance of his or her duties, the offense shall be punishable by a fine not exceeding two thousand dollars ($2,000), or by imprisonment in the county jail not exceeding one year, or by both that fine and imprisonment.

(b) For purposes of this section, "sports official" means any individual who serves as a referee, umpire, linesman, or who serves in a similar capacity but may be known by a different title or name and is duly registered by, or a member of, a local, state, regional, or national organization engaged in part in providing education and training to sports officials.

(Added by Stats. 1991, Ch. 575, Sec. 1.)

243.83.

(a) It is unlawful for any person attending a professional sporting event to do any of the following:

(1) Throw any object on or across the court or field of play with the intent to interfere with play or distract a player.

(2) Enter upon the court or field of play without permission from an authorized person any time after the authorized participants of play have entered the court or field to begin the sporting event and until the participants of play have completed the playing time of the sporting event.

(b) (1) The owner of the facility in which a professional sporting event is to be held shall provide a notice specifying the unlawful activity prohibited by this section and the punishment for engaging in that prohibited activity.

(2) The notice shall be prominently displayed throughout the facility or may be provided by some other manner, such as on a big screen or by a general public announcement. In addition, notice shall be posted at all controlled entry areas of the sporting facility.

(3) Failure to provide the notice shall not be a defense to a violation of this section.

(c) For the purposes of this section, the following terms have the following meanings:

(1) "Player" includes any authorized participant of play, including, but not limited to, team members, referees however designated, and support staff, whether or not any of those persons receive compensation.

(2) "Professional sporting event" means a scheduled sporting event involving a professional sports team or organization or a professional athlete for which an admission fee is charged to the public.

(d) A violation of subdivision (a) is an infraction punishable by a fine not exceeding two hundred fifty dollars ($250). The fine shall not be subject to penalty assessments as provided in Section 1464 or 1465.7 of this code or Section 76000 of the Government Code.

(e) This section shall apply to attendees at professional sporting events; this section shall not apply to players or to sports officials, as defined in Section 243.8.
(f) Nothing in this section shall be construed to limit or prevent prosecution under any applicable provision of law.
(Added by Stats. 2003, Ch. 818, Sec. 1. Effective January 1, 2004.)
243.85.
The owner of any professional sports facility shall post, visible from a majority of the seating in the stands at all times, at controlled entry areas, and at parking facilities that are part of the professional sports facility, written notices displaying the text message number and telephone number to contact security in order to report a violent act.
(Added by Stats. 2012, Ch. 261, Sec. 1. (AB 2464) Effective January 1, 2013.)
243.9.
(a) Every person confined in any local detention facility who commits a battery by gassing upon the person of any peace officer, as defined in Chapter 4.5 (commencing with Section 830) of Title 3 of Part 2, or employee of the local detention facility is guilty of aggravated battery and shall be punished by imprisonment in a county jail or by imprisonment in the state prison for two, three, or four years.
(b) For purposes of this section, "gassing" means intentionally placing or throwing, or causing to be placed or thrown, upon the person of another, any human excrement or other bodily fluids or bodily substances or any mixture containing human excrement or other bodily fluids or bodily substances that results in actual contact with the person's skin or membranes.
(c) The person in charge of the local detention facility shall use every available means to immediately investigate all reported or suspected violations of subdivision (a), including, but not limited to, the use of forensically acceptable means of preserving and testing the suspected gassing substance to confirm the presence of human excrement or other bodily fluids or bodily substances. If there is probable cause to believe that the inmate has violated subdivision (a), the chief medical officer of the local detention facility, or his or her designee, may, when he or she deems it medically necessary to protect the health of an officer or employee who may have been subject to a violation of this section, order the inmate to receive an examination or test for hepatitis or tuberculosis or both hepatitis and tuberculosis on either a voluntary or involuntary basis immediately after the event, and periodically thereafter as determined to be necessary by the medical officer in order to ensure that further hepatitis or tuberculosis transmission does not occur. These decisions shall be consistent with an occupational exposure as defined by the Center for Disease Control and Prevention. The results of any examination or test shall be provided to the officer or employee who has been subject to a reported or suspected violation of this section. Nothing in this subdivision shall be construed to otherwise supersede the operation of Title 8 (commencing with Section 7500). Any person performing tests, transmitting test results, or disclosing information pursuant to this section shall be immune from civil liability for any action taken in accordance with this section.
(d) The person in charge of the local detention facility shall refer all reports for which there is probable cause to believe that the inmate has violated subdivision (a) to the local district attorney for prosecution.
(e) Nothing in this section shall preclude prosecution under both this section and any other provision of law.
(Added by Stats. 2000, Ch. 627, Sec. 1. Effective January 1, 2001.)
243.10.
(a) Any person who commits a battery against a member of the United States Armed Forces because of the victim's service in the United States Armed Forces shall be punished by a fine not exceeding two thousand dollars ($2,000), by imprisonment in a county jail for a period not exceeding one year, or by both that fine and imprisonment.
(b) "Because of" means that the bias motivation must be a cause in fact of the battery, whether or not other causes exist. When multiple concurrent motives exist, the prohibited bias must be a substantial factor in bringing about the battery.
(Added by Stats. 2003, Ch. 138, Sec. 2. Effective January 1, 2004.)
243.15.
Every person confined in, sentenced to, or serving a sentence in, a city or county jail, industrial farm, or industrial road camp in this state, who commits a battery upon the person of any individual who is not himself or herself a person confined or sentenced therein, is guilty of a public offense and is subject to punishment by imprisonment pursuant to subdivision (h) of Section 1170, or in a county jail for not more than one year.
(Added by renumbering Section 4131.5 by Stats. 2015, Ch. 499, Sec. 4. (SB 795) Effective January 1, 2016.)
244.
Any person who willfully and maliciously places or throws, or causes to be placed or thrown, upon the person of another, any vitriol, corrosive acid, flammable substance, or caustic chemical of any nature, with the intent to injure the flesh or disfigure the body of that person, is punishable by imprisonment in the state prison for two, three or four years.
As used in this section, "flammable substance" means gasoline, petroleum products, or flammable liquids with a flashpoint of 150 degrees Fahrenheit or less.
(Amended by Stats. 1995, Ch. 468, Sec. 1. Effective January 1, 1996.)
244.5.
(a) As used in this section, "stun gun" means any item, except a less lethal weapon, as defined in Section 16780, used or intended to be used as either an offensive or defensive weapon that is capable of temporarily immobilizing a person by the infliction of an electrical charge.
(b) Every person who commits an assault upon the person of another with a stun gun or less lethal weapon, as defined in Section 16780, shall be punished by imprisonment in a county jail for a term not exceeding one year, or by imprisonment pursuant to subdivision (h) of Section 1170 for 16 months, two, or three years.
(c) Every person who commits an assault upon the person of a peace officer or firefighter with a stun gun or less lethal weapon, as defined in Section 16780, who knows or reasonably should know that the person is a peace officer or firefighter engaged in the performance of his or her duties, when the peace officer or firefighter is engaged in the performance of his or her duties, shall be punished by imprisonment in the county jail for a term not exceeding one year, or by imprisonment pursuant to subdivision (h) of Section 1170 for two, three, or four years.
(d) This section shall not be construed to preclude or in any way limit the applicability of Section 245 in any criminal prosecution.
(Amended (as amended by Stats. 2010, Ch. 178) by Stats. 2011, Ch. 15, Sec. 297. (AB 109) Effective April 4, 2011. Amending action operative October 1, 2011, by Sec. 636 of Ch. 15, as amended by Stats. 2011, Ch. 39, Sec. 68. Amended version operative January 1, 2012, pursuant to Stats. 2010, Ch. 178, Sec. 107.)
245.
(a) (1) Any person who commits an assault upon the person of another with a deadly weapon or instrument other than a firearm shall be punished by imprisonment in the state prison for two, three, or four years, or in a county jail for not exceeding one year, or by a fine not exceeding ten thousand dollars ($10,000), or by both the fine and imprisonment.
(2) Any person who commits an assault upon the person of another with a firearm shall be punished by imprisonment in the state prison for two, three, or four years, or in a county jail for not less than six months and not exceeding one year, or by both a fine not exceeding ten thousand dollars ($10,000) and imprisonment.
(3) Any person who commits an assault upon the person of another with a machinegun, as defined in Section 16880, or an assault weapon, as defined in Section 30510 or

30515, or a .50 BMG rifle, as defined in Section 30530, shall be punished by imprisonment in the state prison for 4, 8, or 12 years.
(4) Any person who commits an assault upon the person of another by any means of force likely to produce great bodily injury shall be punished by imprisonment in the state prison for two, three, or four years, or in a county jail for not exceeding one year, or by a fine not exceeding ten thousand dollars ($10,000), or by both the fine and imprisonment.
(b) Any person who commits an assault upon the person of another with a semiautomatic firearm shall be punished by imprisonment in the state prison for three, six, or nine years.
(c) Any person who commits an assault with a deadly weapon or instrument, other than a firearm, or by any means likely to produce great bodily injury upon the person of a peace officer or firefighter, and who knows or reasonably should know that the victim is a peace officer or firefighter engaged in the performance of his or her duties, when the peace officer or firefighter is engaged in the performance of his or her duties, shall be punished by imprisonment in the state prison for three, four, or five years.
(d) (1) Any person who commits an assault with a firearm upon the person of a peace officer or firefighter, and who knows or reasonably should know that the victim is a peace officer or firefighter engaged in the performance of his or her duties, when the peace officer or firefighter is engaged in the performance of his or her duties, shall be punished by imprisonment in the state prison for four, six, or eight years.
(2) Any person who commits an assault upon the person of a peace officer or firefighter with a semiautomatic firearm and who knows or reasonably should know that the victim is a peace officer or firefighter engaged in the performance of his or her duties, when the peace officer or firefighter is engaged in the performance of his or her duties, shall be punished by imprisonment in the state prison for five, seven, or nine years.
(3) Any person who commits an assault with a machinegun, as defined in Section 16880, or an assault weapon, as defined in Section 30510 or 30515, or a .50 BMG rifle, as defined in Section 30530, upon the person of a peace officer or firefighter, and who knows or reasonably should know that the victim is a peace officer or firefighter engaged in the performance of his or her duties, shall be punished by imprisonment in the state prison for 6, 9, or 12 years.
(e) When a person is convicted of a violation of this section in a case involving use of a deadly weapon or instrument or firearm, and the weapon or instrument or firearm is owned by that person, the court shall order that the weapon or instrument or firearm be deemed a nuisance, and it shall be confiscated and disposed of in the manner provided by Sections 18000 and 18005.
(f) As used in this section, "peace officer" refers to any person designated as a peace officer in Chapter 4.5 (commencing with Section 830) of Title 3 of Part 2.
(Amended (as amended by Stats. 2010, Ch. 178) by Stats. 2011, Ch. 183, Sec. 1. (AB 1026) Effective January 1, 2012. Amended version operative January 1, 2012, pursuant to Stats. 2010, Ch. 178, Sec. 107.)
245.1.
As used in Sections 148.2, 241, 243, 244.5, and 245, "fireman" or "firefighter" includes any person who is an officer, employee or member of a fire department or fire protection or firefighting agency of the federal government, the State of California, a city, county, city and county, district, or other public or municipal corporation or political subdivision of this state, whether this person is a volunteer or partly paid or fully paid. As used in Section 148.2, "emergency rescue personnel" means any person who is an officer, employee or member of a fire department or fire protection or firefighting agency of the federal government, the State of California, a city, county, city and county, district, or other public or municipal corporation or political subdivision of this state, whether this person is a volunteer or partly paid or fully paid, while he or she is actually engaged in the on-the-site rescue of persons or property during an emergency as defined by subdivision (c) of Section 148.3.
(Amended by Stats. 1998, Ch. 936, Sec. 3. Effective September 28, 1998.)
245.2.
Every person who commits an assault with a deadly weapon or instrument or by any means of force likely to produce great bodily injury upon the person of an operator, driver, or passenger on a bus, taxicab, streetcar, cable car, trackless trolley, or other motor vehicle, including a vehicle operated on stationary rails or on a track or rail suspended in the air, used for the transportation of persons for hire, or upon the person of a station agent or ticket agent for the entity providing such transportation, when the driver, operator, or agent is engaged in the performance of his or her duties, and where the person who commits the assault knows or reasonably should know that the victim is engaged in the performance of his or her duties, or is a passenger, shall be punished by imprisonment in the state prison for three, four, or five years.
(Amended by Stats. 1987, Ch. 801, Sec. 4.)
245.3.
Every person who commits an assault with a deadly weapon or instrument or by any means likely to produce great bodily injury upon the person of a custodial officer as defined in Section 831 or 831.5, and who knows or reasonably should know that the victim is a custodial officer engaged in the performance of that person's duties, shall be punished by imprisonment in the state prison for three, four, or five years.
When a person is convicted of a violation of this section in a case involving use of a deadly weapon or instrument, and such weapon or instrument is owned by that person, the court may, in its discretion, order that the weapon or instrument be deemed a nuisance and shall be confiscated and destroyed in the manner provided by Sections 18000 and 18005.
(Amended by Stats. 2010, Ch. 178, Sec. 54. (SB 1115) Effective January 1, 2011. Operative January 1, 2012, by Sec. 107 of Ch. 178.)
245.5.
(a) Every person who commits an assault with a deadly weapon or instrument, other than a firearm, or by any means likely to produce great bodily injury upon the person of a school employee, and who knows or reasonably should know that the victim is a school employee engaged in the performance of his or her duties, when that school employee is engaged in the performance of his or her duties, shall be punished by imprisonment in the state prison for three, four, or five years, or in a county jail not exceeding one year.
(b) Every person who commits an assault with a firearm upon the person of a school employee, and who knows or reasonably should know that the victim is a school employee engaged in the performance of his or her duties, when the school employee is engaged in the performance of his or her duties, shall be punished by imprisonment in the state prison for four, six, or eight years, or in a county jail for not less than six months and not exceeding one year.
(c) Every person who commits an assault upon the person of a school employee with a stun gun or taser, and who knows or reasonably should know that the person is a school employee engaged in the performance of his or her duties, when the school employee is engaged in the performance of his or her duties, shall be punished by imprisonment in a county jail for a term not exceeding one year or by imprisonment in the state prison for two, three, or four years.
This subdivision shall not be construed to preclude or in any way limit the applicability of Section 245 in any criminal prosecution.
(d) As used in the section, "school employee" means any person employed as a permanent or probationary certificated or classified employee of a school district on a part-time or full-time basis, including a substitute teacher. "School employee," as used in this section, also includes a student teacher, or a school board member. "School," as used in this section, has the same meaning as that term is defined in Section 626.
(Amended by Stats. 1992, Ch. 334, Sec. 1. Effective January 1, 1993.)

245.6.
(a) It shall be unlawful to engage in hazing, as defined in this section.
(b) "Hazing" means any method of initiation or preinitiation into a student organization or student body, whether or not the organization or body is officially recognized by an educational institution, which is likely to cause serious bodily injury to any former, current, or prospective student of any school, community college, college, university, or other educational institution in this state. The term "hazing" does not include customary athletic events or school-sanctioned events.
(c) A violation of this section that does not result in serious bodily injury is a misdemeanor, punishable by a fine of not less than one hundred dollars ($100), nor more than five thousand dollars ($5,000), or imprisonment in the county jail for not more than one year, or both.
(d) Any person who personally engages in hazing that results in death or serious bodily injury as defined in paragraph (4) of subdivision (f) of Section 243 of the Penal Code, is guilty of either a misdemeanor or a felony, and shall be punished by imprisonment in county jail not exceeding one year, or by imprisonment pursuant to subdivision (h) of Section 1170.
(e) The person against whom the hazing is directed may commence a civil action for injury or damages. The action may be brought against any participants in the hazing, or any organization to which the student is seeking membership whose agents, directors, trustees, managers, or officers authorized, requested, commanded, participated in, or ratified the hazing.
(f) Prosecution under this section shall not prohibit prosecution under any other provision of law.
(Amended by Stats. 2011, Ch. 15, Sec. 299. (AB 109) Effective April 4, 2011. Operative October 1, 2011, by Sec. 636 of Ch. 15, as amended by Stats. 2011, Ch. 39, Sec. 68.)
246.
Any person who shall maliciously and willfully discharge a firearm at an inhabited dwelling house, occupied building, occupied motor vehicle, occupied aircraft, inhabited housecar, as defined in Section 362 of the Vehicle Code, or inhabited camper, as defined in Section 243 of the Vehicle Code, is guilty of a felony, and upon conviction shall be punished by imprisonment in the state prison for three, five, or seven years, or by imprisonment in the county jail for a term of not less than six months and not exceeding one year.
As used in this section, "inhabited" means currently being used for dwelling purposes, whether occupied or not.
(Amended by Stats. 1988, Ch. 911, Sec. 1. Effective September 15, 1988.)
246.1.
(a) Except as provided in subdivision (f), upon the conviction of any person found guilty of murder in the first or second degree, manslaughter, attempted murder, assault with a deadly weapon, the unlawful discharge or brandishing of a firearm from or at an occupied vehicle where the victim was killed, attacked, or assaulted from or in a motor vehicle by the use of a firearm on a public street or highway, or the unlawful possession of a firearm by a member of a criminal street gang, as defined in subdivision (f) of Section 186.22, while present in a vehicle the court shall order a vehicle used in the commission of that offense sold.
Any vehicle ordered to be sold pursuant to this subdivision shall be surrendered to the sheriff of the county or the chief of police of the city in which the violation occurred. The officer to whom the vehicle is surrendered shall promptly ascertain from the Department of Motor Vehicles the names and addresses of all legal and registered owners of the vehicle and within five days of receiving that information, shall send by certified mail a notice to all legal and registered owners of the vehicle other than the defendant, at the addresses obtained from the department, informing them that the vehicle has been declared a nuisance and will be sold or otherwise disposed of pursuant to this section, and of the approximate date and location of the sale or other disposition. The notice shall also inform any legal owner of its right to conduct the sale pursuant to subdivision (b).
(b) Any legal owner which in the regular course of its business conducts sales of repossessed or surrendered motor vehicles may take possession and conduct the sale of the vehicle if it notifies the officer to whom the vehicle is surrendered of its intent to conduct the sale within 15 days of the mailing of the notice pursuant to subdivision (a). Sale of the vehicle pursuant to this subdivision may be conducted at the time, in the manner, and on the notice usually given by the legal owner for the sale of repossessed or surrendered vehicles. The proceeds of any sale conducted by the legal owner shall be disposed of as provided in subdivision (d).
(c) If the legal owner does not notify the officer to whom the vehicle is surrendered of its intent to conduct the sale as provided in subdivision (b), the officer shall offer the vehicle for sale at public auction within 60 days of receiving the vehicle. At least 10 days but not more than 20 days prior to the sale, not counting the day of sale, the officer shall give notice of the sale by advertising once in a newspaper of general circulation published in the city or county, as the case may be, in which the vehicle is located, which notice shall contain a description of the make, year, model, identification number, and license number of the vehicle, and the date, time, and location of the sale. For motorcycles, the engine number shall also be included. If there is no newspaper of general circulation published in the county, notice shall be given by posting a notice of sale containing the information required by this subdivision in three of the most public places in the city or county in which the vehicle is located and at the place where the vehicle is to be sold for 10 consecutive days prior to and including the day of the sale.
(d) The proceeds of a sale conducted pursuant to this section shall be disposed of in the following priority:
(1) To satisfy the costs of the sale, including costs incurred with respect to the taking and keeping of the vehicle pending sale.
(2) To the legal owner in an amount to satisfy the indebtedness owed to the legal owner remaining as of the date of sale, including accrued interest or finance charges and delinquency charges.
(3) To the holder of any subordinate lien or encumbrance on the vehicle to satisfy any indebtedness so secured if written notification of demand is received before distribution of the proceeds is completed. The holder of a subordinate lien or encumbrance, if requested, shall reasonably furnish reasonable proof of its interest, and unless it does so on request is not entitled to distribution pursuant to this paragraph.
(4) To any other person who can establish an interest in the vehicle, including a community property interest, to the extent of his or her provable interest.
(5) The balance, if any, to the city or county in which the violation occurred, to be deposited in a special account in its general fund to be used exclusively to pay the costs or a part of the costs of providing services or education to prevent juvenile violence.
The person conducting the sale shall disburse the proceeds of the sale as provided in this subdivision, and provide a written accounting regarding the disposition to all persons entitled to or claiming a share of the proceeds, within 15 days after the sale is conducted.
(e) If the vehicle to be sold under this section is not of the type that can readily be sold to the public generally, the vehicle shall be destroyed or donated to an eleemosynary institution.
(f) No vehicle may be sold pursuant to this section in either of the following circumstances:
(1) The vehicle is stolen, unless the identity of the legal and registered owners of the vehicle cannot be reasonably ascertained.
(2) The vehicle is owned by another, or there is a community property interest in the vehicle owned by a person other than the defendant and the vehicle is the only vehicle available to the defendant's immediate family which may be operated on the highway with a class 3 or class 4 driver's license.
(g) A vehicle is used in the commission of a violation of the offenses enumerated in subdivision (a) if a firearm is discharged either from the vehicle at another person or by an occupant of a vehicle other than the vehicle in which the victim is an occupant.
(Amended by Stats. 1994, 1st Ex. Sess., Ch. 33, Sec. 1. Effective November 30, 1994.)
246.3.
(a) Except as otherwise authorized by law, any person who willfully discharges a firearm in a grossly negligent manner which could result in injury or death to a person is guilty of a public offense and shall be punished by imprisonment in a county jail not exceeding one year, or by imprisonment pursuant to subdivision (h) of Section 1170.
(b) Except as otherwise authorized by law, any person who willfully discharges a BB device in a grossly negligent manner which could result in injury or death to a person is guilty of a public offense and shall be punished by imprisonment in a county jail not exceeding one year.
(c) As used in this section, "BB device" means any instrument that expels a projectile, such as a BB or a pellet, through the force of air pressure, gas pressure, or spring action.
(Amended by Stats. 2011, Ch. 15, Sec. 300. (AB 109) Effective April 4, 2011. Operative October 1, 2011, by Sec. 636 of Ch. 15, as amended by Stats. 2011, Ch. 39, Sec. 68.)
247.
(a) Any person who willfully and maliciously discharges a firearm at an unoccupied aircraft is guilty of a felony.
(b) Any person who discharges a firearm at an unoccupied motor vehicle or an uninhabited building or dwelling house is guilty of a public offense punishable by imprisonment in the county jail for not more than one year or in the state prison. This subdivision does not apply to shooting at an abandoned vehicle, unoccupied vehicle, uninhabited building, or dwelling house with the permission of the owner.
As used in this section and Section 246 "aircraft" means any contrivance intended for and capable of transporting persons through the airspace.
(Amended by Stats. 1988, Ch. 911, Sec. 2. Effective September 15, 1988.)
247.5.
Any person who willfully and maliciously discharges a laser at an aircraft, whether in motion or in flight, while occupied, is guilty of a violation of this section, which shall be punishable as either a misdemeanor by imprisonment in the county jail for not more than one year or by a fine of one thousand dollars ($1,000), or a felony by imprisonment pursuant to subdivision (h) of Section 1170 for 16 months, two years, or three years, or by a fine of two thousand dollars ($2,000). This section does not apply to the conduct of laser development activity by or on behalf of the United States Armed Forces.
As used in this section, "aircraft" means any contrivance intended for and capable of transporting persons through the airspace.
As used in this section, "laser" means a device that utilizes the natural oscillations of atoms or molecules between energy levels for generating coherent electromagnetic radiation in the ultraviolet, visible, or infrared region of the spectrum, and when discharged exceeds one milliwatt continuous wave.
(Amended by Stats. 2011, Ch. 15, Sec. 301. (AB 109) Effective April 4, 2011. Operative October 1, 2011, by Sec. 636 of Ch. 15, as amended by Stats. 2011, Ch. 39, Sec. 68.)
248.
Any person who, with the intent to interfere with the operation of an aircraft, willfully shines a light or other bright device, of an intensity capable of impairing the operation of an aircraft, at an aircraft, shall be punished by a fine not exceeding one thousand dollars ($1,000), or by imprisonment in a county jail not exceeding one year, or by both that fine and imprisonment.
(Amended by Stats. 1998, Ch. 218, Sec. 1. Effective January 1, 1999.)

TITLE 9. OF CRIMES AGAINST THE PERSON INVOLVING SEXUAL ASSAULT, AND CRIMES AGAINST PUBLIC DECENCY AND GOOD MORALS [261 - 368.5]

(Heading of Title 9 amended by Stats. 1982, Ch. 1111, Sec. 2.)

CHAPTER 1. Rape, Abduction, Carnal Abuse of Children, and Seduction [261 - 269]

(Chapter 1 enacted 1872.)
261.
(a) Rape is an act of sexual intercourse accomplished with a person not the spouse of the perpetrator, under any of the following circumstances:
(1) Where a person is incapable, because of a mental disorder or developmental or physical disability, of giving legal consent, and this is known or reasonably should be known to the person committing the act. Notwithstanding the existence of a conservatorship pursuant to the provisions of the Lanterman-Petris-Short Act (Part 1 (commencing with Section 5000) of Division 5 of the Welfare and Institutions Code), the prosecuting attorney shall prove, as an element of the crime, that a mental disorder or developmental or physical disability rendered the alleged victim incapable of giving consent.
(2) Where it is accomplished against a person's will by means of force, violence, duress, menace, or fear of immediate and unlawful bodily injury on the person or another.
(3) Where a person is prevented from resisting by any intoxicating or anesthetic substance, or any controlled substance, and this condition was known, or reasonably should have been known by the accused.
(4) Where a person is at the time unconscious of the nature of the act, and this is known to the accused. As used in this paragraph, "unconscious of the nature of the act" means incapable of resisting because the victim meets any one of the following conditions:
(A) Was unconscious or asleep.
(B) Was not aware, knowing, perceiving, or cognizant that the act occurred.
(C) Was not aware, knowing, perceiving, or cognizant of the essential characteristics of the act due to the perpetrator's fraud in fact.
(D) Was not aware, knowing, perceiving, or cognizant of the essential characteristics of the act due to the perpetrator's fraudulent representation that the sexual penetration served a professional purpose when it served no professional purpose.
(5) Where a person submits under the belief that the person committing the act is someone known to the victim other than the accused, and this belief is induced by any artifice, pretense, or concealment practiced by the accused, with intent to induce the belief.
(6) Where the act is accomplished against the victim's will by threatening to retaliate in the future against the victim or any other person, and there is a reasonable possibility that the perpetrator will execute the threat. As used in this paragraph, "threatening to retaliate" means a threat to kidnap or falsely imprison, or to inflict extreme pain, serious bodily injury, or death.

(7) Where the act is accomplished against the victim's will by threatening to use the authority of a public official to incarcerate, arrest, or deport the victim or another, and the victim has a reasonable belief that the perpetrator is a public official. As used in this paragraph, "public official" means a person employed by a governmental agency who has the authority, as part of that position, to incarcerate, arrest, or deport another. The perpetrator does not actually have to be a public official.

(b) As used in this section, "duress" means a direct or implied threat of force, violence, danger, or retribution sufficient to coerce a reasonable person of ordinary susceptibilities to perform an act which otherwise would not have been performed, or acquiesce in an act to which one otherwise would not have submitted. The total circumstances, including the age of the victim, and his or her relationship to the defendant, are factors to consider in appraising the existence of duress.

(c) As used in this section, "menace" means any threat, declaration, or act which shows an intention to inflict an injury upon another.

(Amended by Stats. 2013, Ch. 259, Sec. 1. (AB 65) Effective September 9, 2013.)

261.5.

(a) Unlawful sexual intercourse is an act of sexual intercourse accomplished with a person who is not the spouse of the perpetrator, if the person is a minor. For the purposes of this section, a "minor" is a person under the age of 18 years and an "adult" is a person who is at least 18 years of age.

(b) Any person who engages in an act of unlawful sexual intercourse with a minor who is not more than three years older or three years younger than the perpetrator, is guilty of a misdemeanor.

(c) Any person who engages in an act of unlawful sexual intercourse with a minor who is more than three years younger than the perpetrator is guilty of either a misdemeanor or a felony, and shall be punished by imprisonment in a county jail not exceeding one year, or by imprisonment pursuant to subdivision (h) of Section 1170.

(d) Any person 21 years of age or older who engages in an act of unlawful sexual intercourse with a minor who is under 16 years of age is guilty of either a misdemeanor or a felony, and shall be punished by imprisonment in a county jail not exceeding one year, or by imprisonment pursuant to subdivision (h) of Section 1170 for two, three, or four years.

(e) (1) Notwithstanding any other provision of this section, an adult who engages in an act of sexual intercourse with a minor in violation of this section may be liable for civil penalties in the following amounts:

(A) An adult who engages in an act of unlawful sexual intercourse with a minor less than two years younger than the adult is liable for a civil penalty not to exceed two thousand dollars ($2,000).

(B) An adult who engages in an act of unlawful sexual intercourse with a minor at least two years younger than the adult is liable for a civil penalty not to exceed five thousand dollars ($5,000).

(C) An adult who engages in an act of unlawful sexual intercourse with a minor at least three years younger than the adult is liable for a civil penalty not to exceed ten thousand dollars ($10,000).

(D) An adult over the age of 21 years who engages in an act of unlawful sexual intercourse with a minor under 16 years of age is liable for a civil penalty not to exceed twenty-five thousand dollars ($25,000).

(2) The district attorney may bring actions to recover civil penalties pursuant to this subdivision. From the amounts collected for each case, an amount equal to the costs of pursuing the action shall be deposited with the treasurer of the county in which the judgment was entered, and the remainder shall be deposited in the Underage Pregnancy Prevention Fund, which is hereby created in the State Treasury. Amounts deposited in the Underage Pregnancy Prevention Fund may be used only for the purpose of preventing underage pregnancy upon appropriation by the Legislature.

(3) In addition to any punishment imposed under this section, the judge may assess a fine not to exceed seventy dollars ($70) against any person who violates this section with the proceeds of this fine to be used in accordance with Section 1463.23. The court shall, however, take into consideration the defendant's ability to pay, and no defendant shall be denied probation because of his or her inability to pay the fine permitted under this subdivision.

(Amended by Stats. 2011, Ch. 15, Sec. 302. (AB 109) Effective April 4, 2011. Operative October 1, 2011, by Sec. 636 of Ch. 15, as amended by Stats. 2011, Ch. 39, Sec. 68.)

261.6.

In prosecutions under Section 261, 262, 286, 287, or 289, or former Section 288a, in which consent is at issue, "consent" shall be defined to mean positive cooperation in act or attitude pursuant to an exercise of free will. The person must act freely and voluntarily and have knowledge of the nature of the act or transaction involved.

A current or previous dating or marital relationship shall not be sufficient to constitute consent where consent is at issue in a prosecution under Section 261, 262, 286, 287, or 289, or former Section 288a.

Nothing in this section shall affect the admissibility of evidence or the burden of proof on the issue of consent.

(Amended by Stats. 2018, Ch. 423, Sec. 44. (SB 1494) Effective January 1, 2019.)

261.7.

In prosecutions under Section 261, 262, 286, 287, or 289, or former Section 288a, in which consent is at issue, evidence that the victim suggested, requested, or otherwise communicated to the defendant that the defendant use a condom or other birth control device, without additional evidence of consent, is not sufficient to constitute consent.

(Amended by Stats. 2018, Ch. 423, Sec. 45. (SB 1494) Effective January 1, 2019.)

261.9.

(a) Any person convicted of seeking to procure or procuring the sexual services of a prostitute in violation of subdivision (b) of Section 647, if the prostitute is under 18 years of age, shall be ordered by the court, in addition to any other penalty or fine imposed, to pay an additional fine in an amount not to exceed twenty-five thousand dollars ($25,000).

(b) Every fine imposed and collected pursuant to this section shall, upon appropriation by the Legislature, be available to fund programs and services for commercially sexually exploited minors in the counties where the underlying offenses are committed.

(Added by Stats. 2011, Ch. 75, Sec. 3. (AB 12) Effective January 1, 2012.)

262.

(a) Rape of a person who is the spouse of the perpetrator is an act of sexual intercourse accomplished under any of the following circumstances:

(1) Where it is accomplished against a person's will by means of force, violence, duress, menace, or fear of immediate and unlawful bodily injury on the person or another.

(2) Where a person is prevented from resisting by any intoxicating or anesthetic substance, or any controlled substance, and this condition was known, or reasonably should have been known, by the accused.

(3) Where a person is at the time unconscious of the nature of the act, and this is known to the accused. As used in this paragraph, "unconscious of the nature of the act" means incapable of resisting because the victim meets one of the following conditions:

(A) Was unconscious or asleep.

(B) Was not aware, knowing, perceiving, or cognizant that the act occurred.

(C) Was not aware, knowing, perceiving, or cognizant of the essential characteristics of the act due to the perpetrator's fraud in fact.

(4) Where the act is accomplished against the victim's will by threatening to retaliate in the future against the victim or any other person, and there is a reasonable possibility that the perpetrator will execute the threat. As used in this paragraph, "threatening to retaliate" means a threat to kidnap or falsely imprison, or to inflict extreme pain, serious bodily injury, or death.

(5) Where the act is accomplished against the victim's will by threatening to use the authority of a public official to incarcerate, arrest, or deport the victim or another, and the victim has a reasonable belief that the perpetrator is a public official. As used in this paragraph, "public official" means a person employed by a governmental agency who has the authority, as part of that position, to incarcerate, arrest, or deport another. The perpetrator does not actually have to be a public official.

(b) As used in this section, "duress" means a direct or implied threat of force, violence, danger, or retribution sufficient to coerce a reasonable person of ordinary susceptibilities to perform an act which otherwise would not have been performed, or acquiesce in an act to which one otherwise would not have submitted. The total circumstances, including the age of the victim, and his or her relationship to the defendant, are factors to consider in apprising the existence of duress.

(c) As used in this section, "menace" means any threat, declaration, or act that shows an intention to inflict an injury upon another.

(d) If probation is granted upon conviction of a violation of this section, the conditions of probation may include, in lieu of a fine, one or both of the following requirements:

(1) That the defendant make payments to a battered women's shelter, up to a maximum of one thousand dollars ($1,000).

(2) That the defendant reimburse the victim for reasonable costs of counseling and other reasonable expenses that the court finds are the direct result of the defendant's offense.

For any order to pay a fine, make payments to a battered women's shelter, or pay restitution as a condition of probation under this subdivision, the court shall make a determination of the defendant's ability to pay. In no event shall any order to make payments to a battered women's shelter be made if it would impair the ability of the defendant to pay direct restitution to the victim or court-ordered child support. Where the injury to a married person is caused in whole or in part by the criminal acts of his or her spouse in violation of this section, the community property may not be used to discharge the liability of the offending spouse for restitution to the injured spouse, required by Section 1203.04, as operative on or before August 2, 1995, or Section 1202.4, or to a shelter for costs with regard to the injured spouse and dependents, required by this section, until all separate property of the offending spouse is exhausted.

(Amended by Stats. 2006, Ch. 45, Sec. 1. Effective January 1, 2007.)

263.

The essential guilt of rape consists in the outrage to the person and feelings of the victim of the rape. Any sexual penetration, however slight, is sufficient to complete the crime.

(Amended by Stats. 1979, Ch. 994.)

263.1.

(a) The Legislature finds and declares that all forms of nonconsensual sexual assault may be considered rape for purposes of the gravity of the offense and the support of survivors.

(b) This section is declarative of existing law.

(Added by Stats. 2016, Ch. 848, Sec. 1. (AB 701) Effective January 1, 2017.)

264.

(a) Except as provided in subdivision (c), rape, as defined in Section 261 or 262, is punishable by imprisonment in the state prison for three, six, or eight years.

(b) In addition to any punishment imposed under this section the judge may assess a fine not to exceed seventy dollars ($70) against any person who violates Section 261 or 262 with the proceeds of this fine to be used in accordance with Section 1463.23. The court shall, however, take into consideration the defendant's ability to pay, and no defendant shall be denied probation because of his or her inability to pay the fine permitted under this subdivision.

(c) (1) Any person who commits rape in violation of paragraph (2) of subdivision (a) of Section 261 upon a child who is under 14 years of age shall be punished by imprisonment in the state prison for 9, 11, or 13 years.

(2) Any person who commits rape in violation of paragraph (2) of subdivision (a) of Section 261 upon a minor who is 14 years of age or older shall be punished by imprisonment in the state prison for 7, 9, or 11 years.

(3) This subdivision does not preclude prosecution under Section 269, Section 288.7, or any other provision of law.

(Amended by Stats. 2010, Ch. 219, Sec. 4. (AB 1844) Effective September 9, 2010.)

264.1.

(a) The provisions of Section 264 notwithstanding, in any case in which the defendant, voluntarily acting in concert with another person, by force or violence and against the will of the victim, committed an act described in Section 261, 262, or 289, either personally or by aiding and abetting the other person, that fact shall be charged in the indictment or information and if found to be true by the jury, upon a jury trial, or if found to be true by the court, upon a court trial, or if admitted by the defendant, the defendant shall suffer confinement in the state prison for five, seven, or nine years.

(b) (1) If the victim of an offense described in subdivision (a) is a child who is under 14 years of age, the defendant shall be punished by imprisonment in the state prison for 10, 12, or 14 years.

(2) If the victim of an offense described in subdivision (a) is a minor who is 14 years of age or older, the defendant shall be punished by imprisonment in the state prison for 7, 9, or 11 years.

(3) This subdivision does not preclude prosecution under Section 269, Section 288.7, or any other provision of law.

(Amended by Stats. 2010, Ch. 219, Sec. 5. (AB 1844) Effective September 9, 2010.)

264.2.

(a) Whenever there is an alleged violation or violations of subdivision (e) of Section 243, or Section 261, 261.5, 262, 273.5, 286, 287, or 289, the law enforcement officer assigned to the case shall immediately provide the victim of the crime with the "Victims of Domestic Violence" card, as specified in subparagraph (H) of paragraph (9) of subdivision (c) of Section 13701, or with the card described in subdivision (a) of Section 680.2, whichever is more applicable.

(b) (1) The law enforcement officer, or his or her agency, shall immediately notify the local rape victim counseling center, whenever a victim of an alleged violation of Section 261, 261.5, 262, 286, 287, or 289 is transported to a hospital for any medical evidentiary or physical examination. The hospital may notify the local rape victim counseling center, when the victim of the alleged violation of Section 261, 261.5, 262, 286, 287, or 289 is presented to the hospital for the medical or evidentiary physical examination, upon approval of the victim. The victim has the right to have a sexual assault counselor, as defined in Section 1035.2 of the Evidence Code, and a support person of the victim's choosing present at any medical evidentiary or physical examination.

(2) Prior to the commencement of any initial medical evidentiary or physical examination arising out of a sexual assault, the medical provider shall give the victim the card described in subdivision (a) of Section 680.2. This requirement shall apply only if the law enforcement agency has provided the card to the medical provider in a language understood by the victim.

(3) The hospital may verify with the law enforcement officer, or his or her agency, whether the local rape victim counseling center has been notified, upon the approval of the victim.

(4) A support person may be excluded from a medical evidentiary or physical examination if the law enforcement officer or medical provider determines that the presence of that individual would be detrimental to the purpose of the examination.

(5) After conducting the medical evidentiary or physical examination, the medical provider shall give the victim the opportunity to shower or bathe at no cost to the victim, unless a showering or bathing facility is not available.

(6) A medical provider shall, within 24 hours of obtaining sexual assault forensic evidence from the victim, notify the law enforcement agency having jurisdiction over the alleged violation if the medical provider knows the appropriate jurisdiction. If the medical provider does not know the appropriate jurisdiction, the medical provider shall notify the local law enforcement agency.

(Amended by Stats. 2018, Ch. 423, Sec. 46.) (SB 1494) Effective January 1, 2019.)

265.

Every person who takes any woman unlawfully, against her will, and by force, menace or duress, compels her to marry him, or to marry any other person, or to be defiled, is punishable by imprisonment pursuant to subdivision (h) of Section 1170.

(Amended by Stats. 2011, Ch. 15, Sec. 303. (AB 109) Effective April 4, 2011. Operative October 1, 2011, by Sec. 636 of Ch. 15, as amended by Stats. 2011, Ch. 39, Sec. 68.)

266.

Every person who inveigles or entices any unmarried female, of previous chaste character, under the age of 18 years, into any house of ill fame, or of assignation, or elsewhere, for the purpose of prostitution, or to have illicit carnal connection with any man; and every person who aids or assists in such inveiglement or enticement; and every person who, by any false pretenses, false representation, or other fraudulent means, procures any female to have illicit carnal connection with any man, is punishable by imprisonment in the state prison, or by imprisonment in a county jail not exceeding one year, or by a fine not exceeding two thousand dollars ($2,000), or by both such fine and imprisonment.

(Amended by Stats. 1983, Ch. 1092, Sec. 256. Effective September 27, 1983. Operative January 1, 1984, by Sec. 427 of Ch. 1092.)

266a.

Each person who, within this state, takes any person against his or her will and without his or her consent, or with his or her consent procured by fraudulent inducement or misrepresentation, for the purpose of prostitution, as defined in subdivision (b) of Section 647, is punishable by imprisonment in the state prison, and a fine not exceeding ten thousand dollars ($10,000).

(Amended by Stats. 2014, Ch. 109, Sec. 1. (AB 2424) Effective January 1, 2015.)

266b.

Every person who takes any other person unlawfully, and against his or her will, and by force, menace, or duress, compels him or her to live with such person in an illicit relation, against his or her consent, or to so live with any other person, is punishable by imprisonment pursuant to subdivision (h) of Section 1170.

(Amended by Stats. 2011, Ch. 15, Sec. 304. (AB 109) Effective April 4, 2011. Operative October 1, 2011, by Sec. 636 of Ch. 15, as amended by Stats. 2011, Ch. 39, Sec. 68.)

266c.

Every person who induces any other person to engage in sexual intercourse, sexual penetration, oral copulation, or sodomy when his or her consent is procured by false or fraudulent representation or pretense that is made with the intent to create fear, and which does induce fear, and that would cause a reasonable person in like circumstances to act contrary to the person's free will, and does cause the victim to so act, is punishable by imprisonment in a county jail for not more than one year or in the state prison for two, three, or four years.

As used in this section, "fear" means the fear of physical injury or death to the person or to any relative of the person or member of the person's family.

(Amended by Stats. 2000, Ch. 287, Sec. 4. Effective January 1, 2001.)

266d.

Any person who receives any money or other valuable thing for or on account of placing in custody any other person for the purpose of causing the other person to cohabit with any person to whom the other person is not married, is guilty of a felony.

(Amended by Stats. 1975, Ch. 996.)

266e.

Every person who purchases, or pays any money or other valuable thing for, any person for the purpose of prostitution as defined in subdivision (b) of Section 647, or for the purpose of placing such person, for immoral purposes, in any house or place against his or her will, is guilty of a felony punishable by imprisonment in the state prison for 16 months, or two or three years.

(Amended by Stats. 2011, Ch. 15, Sec. 304.5. (AB 109) Effective April 4, 2011. Operative October 1, 2011, by Sec. 636 of Ch. 15, as amended by Stats. 2011, Ch. 39, Sec. 68.)

266f.

Every person who sells any person or receives any money or other valuable thing for or on account of his or her placing in custody, for immoral purposes, any person, whether with or without his or her consent, is guilty of a felony punishable by imprisonment in the state prison for 16 months, or two or three years.

(Amended by Stats. 2011, Ch. 15, Sec. 304.7. (AB 109) Effective April 4, 2011. Operative October 1, 2011, by Sec. 636 of Ch. 15, as amended by Stats. 2011, Ch. 39, Sec. 68.)

266g.

Every man who, by force, intimidation, threats, persuasion, promises, or any other means, places or leaves, or procures any other person or persons to place or leave, his wife in a house of prostitution, or connives at or consents to, or permits, the placing or leaving of his wife in a house of prostitution, or allows or permits her to remain therein, is guilty of a felony and punishable by imprisonment pursuant to subdivision (h) of Section 1170 for two, three or four years; and in all prosecutions under this section a wife is a competent witness against her husband.

(Amended by Stats. 2011, Ch. 15, Sec. 305. (AB 109) Effective April 4, 2011. Operative October 1, 2011, by Sec. 636 of Ch. 15, as amended by Stats. 2011, Ch. 39, Sec. 68.)

266h.

(a) Except as provided in subdivision (b), any person who, knowing another person is a prostitute, lives or derives support or maintenance in whole or in part from the earnings or proceeds of the person's prostitution, or from money loaned or advanced to or charged against that person by any keeper or manager or inmate of a house or other place where prostitution is practiced or allowed, or who solicits or receives compensation for soliciting for the person, is guilty of pimping, a felony, and shall be punishable by imprisonment in the state prison for three, four, or six years.

(b) Any person who, knowing another person is a prostitute, lives or derives support or maintenance in whole or in part from the earnings or proceeds of the person's prostitution, or from money loaned or advanced to or charged against that person by any keeper or manager or inmate of a house or other place where prostitution is practiced or allowed, or who solicits or receives compensation for soliciting for the person, when the prostitute is a minor, is guilty of pimping a minor, a felony, and shall be punishable as follows:

(1) If the person engaged in prostitution is a minor 16 years of age or older, the offense is punishable by imprisonment in the state prison for three, four, or six years.

(2) If the person engaged in prostitution is under 16 years of age, the offense is punishable by imprisonment in the state prison for three, six, or eight years.

(Amended by Stats. 2010, Ch. 709, Sec. 8. (SB 1062) Effective January 1, 2011.)

266i.

(a) Except as provided in subdivision (b), any person who does any of the following is guilty of pandering, a felony, and shall be punishable by imprisonment in the state prison for three, four, or six years:

(1) Procures another person for the purpose of prostitution.

(2) By promises, threats, violence, or by any device or scheme, causes, induces, persuades, or encourages another person to become a prostitute.

(3) Procures for another person a place as an inmate in a house of prostitution or as an inmate of any place in which prostitution is encouraged or allowed within this state.

(4) By promises, threats, violence, or by any device or scheme, causes, induces, persuades, or encourages an inmate of a house of prostitution, or any other place in which prostitution is encouraged or allowed, to remain therein as an inmate.

(5) By fraud or artifice, or by duress of person or goods, or by abuse of any position of confidence or authority, procures another person for the purpose of prostitution, or to enter any place in which prostitution is encouraged or allowed within this state, or to come into this state or leave this state for the purpose of prostitution.

(6) Receives or gives, or agrees to receive or give, any money or thing of value for procuring, or attempting to procure, another person for the purpose of prostitution, or to come into this state or leave this state for the purpose of prostitution.

(b) Any person who does any of the acts described in subdivision (a) with another person who is a minor is guilty of pandering, a felony, and shall be punishable as follows:

(1) If the other person is a minor 16 years of age or older, the offense is punishable by imprisonment in the state prison for three, four, or six years.

(2) If the other person is under 16 years of age, the offense is punishable by imprisonment in the state prison for three, six, or eight years.

(Amended by Stats. 2010, Ch. 709, Sec. 9. (SB 1062) Effective January 1, 2011.)

266j.

Any person who intentionally gives, transports, provides, or makes available, or who offers to give, transport, provide, or make available to another person, a child under the age of 16 for the purpose of any lewd or lascivious act as defined in Section 288, or who causes, induces, or persuades a child under the age of 16 to engage in such an act with another person, is guilty of a felony and shall be imprisoned in the state prison for a term of three, six, or eight years, and by a fine not to exceed fifteen thousand dollars ($15,000).

(Amended by Stats. 1987, Ch. 1068, Sec. 1.)

266k.

(a) Upon the conviction of any person for a violation of Section 266h or 266i, the court may, in addition to any other penalty or fine imposed, order the defendant to pay an additional fine not to exceed five thousand dollars ($5,000). In setting the amount of the fine, the court shall consider any relevant factors including, but not limited to, the seriousness and gravity of the offense and the circumstances of its commission, whether the defendant derived any economic gain as the result of the crime, and the extent to which the victim suffered losses as a result of the crime. Every fine imposed and collected under this section shall be deposited in the Victim-Witness Assistance Fund to be available for appropriation to fund child sexual exploitation and child sexual abuse victim counseling centers and prevention programs under Section 13837.

(b) Upon the conviction of any person for a violation of Section 266j or 267, the court may, in addition to any other penalty or fine imposed, order the defendant to pay an additional fine not to exceed twenty-five thousand dollars ($25,000).

(c) Fifty percent of the fines collected pursuant to subdivision (b) and deposited in the Victim-Witness Assistance Fund pursuant to subdivision (a) shall be granted to community-based organizations that serve minor victims of human trafficking.

(d) If the court orders a fine to be imposed pursuant to this section, the actual administrative cost of collecting that fine, not to exceed 2 percent of the total amount paid, may be paid into the general fund of the county treasury for the use and benefit of the county.

(Amended by Stats. 2014, Ch. 714, Sec. 1. (SB 1388) Effective January 1, 2015.)

267.

Every person who takes away any other person under the age of 18 years from the father, mother, guardian, or other person having the legal charge of the other person, without their consent, for the purpose of prostitution, is punishable by imprisonment in the state prison, and a fine not exceeding two thousand dollars ($2,000).

(Amended by Stats. 1983, Ch. 1092, Sec. 258. Effective September 27, 1983. Operative January 1, 1984, by Sec. 427 of Ch. 1092.)

269.

(a) Any person who commits any of the following acts upon a child who is under 14 years of age and seven or more years younger than the person is guilty of aggravated sexual assault of a child:

(1) Rape, in violation of paragraph (2) or (6) of subdivision (a) of Section 261.

(2) Rape or sexual penetration, in concert, in violation of Section 264.1.

(3) Sodomy, in violation of paragraph (2) or (3) of subdivision (c), or subdivision (d), of Section 286.

(4) Oral copulation, in violation of paragraph (2) or (3) of subdivision (c), or subdivision (d), of Section 287 or former Section 288a.

(5) Sexual penetration, in violation of subdivision (a) of Section 289.

(b) Any person who violates this section is guilty of a felony and shall be punished by imprisonment in the state prison for 15 years to life.

(c) The court shall impose a consecutive sentence for each offense that results in a conviction under this section if the crimes involve separate victims or involve the same victim on separate occasions as defined in subdivision (d) of Section 667.6.

(Amended by Stats. 2018, Ch. 423, Sec. 47. (SB 1494) Effective January 1, 2019. Note: This section was amended November 7, 2006, by initiative Proposition 83.)

CHAPTER 2. Abandonment and Neglect of Children [270 - 273.75]

(Chapter 2 enacted 1872.)

270.

If a parent of a minor child willfully omits, without lawful excuse, to furnish necessary clothing, food, shelter or medical attendance, or other remedial care for his or her child, he or she is guilty of a misdemeanor punishable by a fine not exceeding two thousand dollars ($2,000), or by imprisonment in the county jail not exceeding one year, or by both such fine and imprisonment. If a court of competent jurisdiction has made a final adjudication in either a civil or a criminal action that a person is the parent of a minor child and the person has notice of such adjudication and he or she then willfully omits, without lawful excuse, to furnish necessary clothing, food, shelter, medical attendance or other remedial care for his or her child, this conduct is punishable by imprisonment in the county jail not exceeding one year or in a state prison for a determinate term of one year and one day, or by a fine not exceeding two thousand dollars ($2,000), or by both such fine and imprisonment. This statute shall not be construed so as to relieve such parent from the criminal liability defined herein for such omission merely because the other parent of such child is legally entitled to the custody of such child nor because the other parent of such child or any other person or organization voluntarily or involuntarily furnishes such necessary food, clothing, shelter or medical attendance or other remedial care for such child or undertakes to do so.

Proof of abandonment or desertion of a child by such parent, or the omission by such parent to furnish necessary food, clothing, shelter or medical attendance or other remedial care for his or her child is prima facie evidence that such abandonment or desertion or omission to furnish necessary food, clothing, shelter or medical attendance or other remedial care is willful and without lawful excuse.

The court, in determining the ability of the parent to support his or her child, shall consider all income, including social insurance benefits and gifts.

The provisions of this section are applicable whether the parents of such child are or were ever married or divorced, and regardless of any decree made in any divorce action relative to alimony or to the support of the child. A child conceived but not yet born is to be deemed an existing person insofar as this section is concerned.

The husband of a woman who bears a child as a result of artificial insemination shall be considered the father of that child for the purpose of this section, if he consented in writing to the artificial insemination.

If a parent provides a minor with treatment by spiritual means through prayer alone in accordance with the tenets and practices of a recognized church or religious denomination, by a duly accredited practitioner thereof, such treatment shall constitute "other remedial care", as used in this section.

(Amended by Stats. 1984, Ch. 1432, Sec. 1.)

270.1.

(a) A parent or guardian of a pupil of six years of age or more who is in kindergarten or any of grades 1 to 8, inclusive, and who is subject to compulsory full-time education or compulsory continuation education, whose child is a chronic truant as defined in Section 48263.6 of the Education Code, who has failed to reasonably supervise and encourage the pupil's school attendance, and who has been offered language accessible support services to address the pupil's truancy, is guilty of a misdemeanor punishable by a fine not exceeding two thousand dollars ($2,000), or by imprisonment in a county jail not exceeding one year, or by both that fine and imprisonment. A parent or guardian guilty of a misdemeanor under this subdivision may participate in the deferred entry of judgment program defined in subdivision (b).

(b) A superior court may establish a deferred entry of judgment program that includes the components listed in paragraphs (1) to (7), inclusive, to adjudicate cases involving parents or guardians of elementary school pupils who are chronic truants as defined in Section 48263.6 of the Education Code:

(1) A dedicated court calendar.

(2) Leadership by a judge of the superior court in that county.

(3) Meetings, scheduled and held periodically, with school district representatives designated by the chronic truant's school district of enrollment. Those representatives may include school psychologists, school counselors, teachers, school administrators, or other educational service providers deemed appropriate by the school district.

(4) Service referrals for parents or guardians, as appropriate to each case that may include, but are not limited to, all of the following:

(A) Case management.

(B) Mental and physical health services.

(C) Parenting classes and support.

(D) Substance abuse treatment.

(E) Child care and housing.

(5) A clear statement that, in lieu of trial, the court may grant deferred entry of judgment with respect to the current crime or crimes charged if the defendant pleads guilty to each charge and waives time for the pronouncement of judgment and that, upon the defendant's compliance with the terms and conditions set forth by the court and agreed to by the defendant upon the entry of his or her plea, and upon the motion of the prosecuting attorney, the court will dismiss the charge or charges against the defendant and the same procedures specified for successful completion of a drug diversion program or a deferred entry of judgment program pursuant to Section 851.90 and the provisions of Section 1203.4 shall apply.

(6) A clear statement that failure to comply with any condition under the program may result in the prosecuting attorney or the court making a motion for entry of judgment, whereupon the court will render a finding of guilty to the charge or charges pled, enter judgment, and schedule a sentencing hearing as otherwise provided in this code.

(7) An explanation of criminal record retention and disposition resulting from participation in the deferred entry of judgment program and the defendant's rights relative to answering questions about his or her arrest and deferred entry of judgment following successful completion of the program.

(c) Funding for the deferred entry of judgment program pursuant to this section shall be derived solely from nonstate sources.

(d) A parent or guardian of an elementary school pupil who is a chronic truant, as defined in Section 48263.6 of the Education Code, may not be punished for a violation of both this section and the provisions of Section 272 that involve criminal liability for parents and guardians of truant children.

(e) If any district attorney chooses to charge a defendant with a violation of subdivision (a) and the defendant is found by the prosecuting attorney to be eligible or ineligible for deferred entry of judgment, the prosecuting attorney shall file with the court a declaration in writing, or state for the record, the grounds upon which that determination is based.

(Added by Stats. 2010, Ch. 647, Sec. 2. (SB 1317) Effective January 1, 2011.)

270.5.

(a) Every parent who refuses, without lawful excuse, to accept his or her minor child into the parent's home, or, failing to do so, to provide alternative shelter, upon being requested to do so by a child protective agency and after being informed of the duty imposed by this statute to do so, is guilty of a misdemeanor and shall be punished by a fine of not more than five hundred dollars ($500).

(b) For purposes of this section, "child protective agency" means a police or sheriff's department, a county probation department, or a county welfare department.

(c) For purposes of this section, "lawful excuse" shall include, but not be limited to, a reasonable fear that the minor child's presence in the home will endanger the safety of the parent or other persons residing in the home.

(Added by Stats. 1984, Ch. 1616, Sec. 1.)

270.6.

If a court of competent jurisdiction has made a temporary or permanent order awarding spousal support that a person must pay, the person has notice of that order, and he or she then leaves the state with the intent to willfully omit, without lawful excuse, to furnish the spousal support, he or she is punishable by imprisonment in a county jail for a period not exceeding one year, a fine not exceeding two thousand dollars ($2,000), or both that imprisonment and fine.

(Added by Stats. 2002, Ch. 410, Sec. 1. Effective January 1, 2003.)

270a.

Every individual who has sufficient ability to provide for his or her spouse's support, or who is able to earn the means of such spouse's support, who willfully abandons and leaves his or her spouse in a destitute condition, or who refuses or neglects to provide such spouse with necessary food, clothing, shelter, or medical attendance, unless by such spouse's conduct the individual was justified in abandoning such spouse, is guilty of a misdemeanor.

(Amended by Stats. 1976, Ch. 1170.)

270b.

After arrest and before plea or trial, or after conviction or plea of guilty and before sentence under either Section 270 or 270a, if the defendant shall appear before the court and enter into an undertaking with sufficient sureties to the people of the State of California in such penal sum as the court may fix, to be approved by the court, and conditioned that the defendant will pay to the person having custody of such child or to such spouse, such sum per month as may be fixed by the court in order to thereby provide such minor child or such spouse as the case may be, with necessary food, shelter, clothing, medical attendance, or other remedial care, then the court may suspend proceedings or sentence therein; and such undertaking is valid and binding for two years, or such lesser time which the court shall fix; and upon the failure of defendant to comply with such undertaking, the defendant may be ordered to appear before the court and show cause why further proceedings should not be had in such action or why sentence should not be imposed, whereupon the court may proceed with such action, or

pass sentence, or for good cause shown may modify the order and take a new undertaking and further suspend proceedings or sentence for a like period.

(Amended by Stats. 1976, Ch. 1170.)

270c.

Except as provided in Chapter 2 (commencing with Section 4410) of Part 4 of Division 9 of the Family Code, every adult child who, having the ability so to do, fails to provide necessary food, clothing, shelter, or medical attendance for an indigent parent, is guilty of a misdemeanor.

(Amended by Stats. 1992, Ch. 163, Sec. 102. Effective January 1, 1993. Operative January 1, 1994, by Sec. 161 of Ch. 163.)

270d.

In any case where there is a conviction and sentence under the provisions of either Section 270 or Section 270a, should a fine be imposed, such fine shall be directed by the court to be paid in whole or in part to the spouse of the defendant or guardian or custodian of the child or children of such defendant, except as follows:

If the children are receiving public assistance, all fines, penalties or forfeitures imposed and all funds collected from the defendant shall be paid to the county department. Money so paid shall be applied first to support for the calendar month following its receipt by the county department and any balance remaining shall be applied to future needs, or be treated as reimbursement for past support furnished from public assistance funds.

(Amended by Stats. 1974, Ch. 893.)

270e.

No other evidence shall be required to prove marriage or registered domestic partnership of spouses, or that a person is the lawful father or mother of a child or children, than is or shall be required to prove such facts in a civil action. In all prosecutions under either Section 270a or 270 of this code, Sections 970, 971, and 980 of the Evidence Code do not apply, and both spouses or domestic partners shall be competent to testify to any and all relevant matters, including the fact of marriage or registered domestic partnership and the parentage of a child or children. Proof of the abandonment and nonsupport of a spouse, or of the omission to furnish necessary food, clothing, shelter, or of medical attendance for a child or children is prima facie evidence that such abandonment and nonsupport or omission to furnish necessary food, clothing, shelter, or medical attendance is willful. In any prosecution under Section 270, it shall be competent for the people to prove nonaccess of husband to wife or any other fact establishing nonpaternity of a husband. In any prosecution pursuant to Section 270, the final establishment of paternity or nonpaternity in another proceeding shall be admissible as evidence of paternity or nonpaternity.

(Amended by Stats. 2016, Ch. 50, Sec. 68. (SB 1005) Effective January 1, 2017.)

270f.

Where, under the provisions of this chapter, a report is filed by a parent of a child with the district attorney averring:

(1) That the other parent has failed to provide necessary support and

(2) That neither the child in need of assistance nor another on his behalf is receiving public assistance, the district attorney shall immediately investigate the verity of such report and determine the defaulting parent's location and financial ability to provide the needed support, and upon a finding that the report is true shall immediately take all steps necessary to obtain support for the child in need of assistance.

(Amended by Stats. 1974, Ch. 893.)

270g.

A review of each report filed with the district attorney under Section 270f shall be made at 90-day intervals unless the support payments have been legally terminated, the parties involved are permanently located beyond county jurisdiction, or the defaulting parent is complying with the provisions of this chapter.

(Amended by Stats. 1974, Ch. 893.)

270h.

In any case where there is a conviction under either Section 270 or 270a and there is an order granting probation which includes an order for support, the court may:

(a) Issue an execution on the order for the support payments that accrue during the time the probation order is in effect, in the same manner as on a judgment in a civil action for support payments. This remedy shall apply only when there is no existing civil order of this state or a foreign court order that has been reduced to a judgment of this state for support of the same person or persons included in the probation support order.

(b) Issue an earnings assignment order for support pursuant to Chapter 8 (commencing with Section 5200) of Part 5 of Division 9 of the Family Code as a condition of probation. This remedy shall apply only when there is no existing civil order for support of the same person or persons included in the probation support order upon which an assignment order has been entered pursuant to Chapter 8 (commencing with Section 5200) of Part 5 of Division 9 of the Family Code or pursuant to former Chapter 5 (commencing with Section 4390) of Title 1.5 of Part 5 of Division 4 of the Civil Code. These remedies are in addition to any other remedies available to the court.

(Amended by Stats. 1992, Ch. 163, Sec. 103. Effective January 1, 1993. Operative January 1, 1994, by Sec. 161 of Ch. 163.)

271.

Every parent of any child under the age of 14 years, and every person to whom any such child has been confided for nurture, or education, who deserts such child in any place whatever with intent to abandon it, is punishable by imprisonment pursuant to subdivision (h) of Section 1170 or in the county jail not exceeding one year or by fine not exceeding one thousand dollars ($1,000) or by both.

(Amended by Stats. 2011, Ch. 15, Sec. 306. (AB 109) Effective April 4, 2011. Operative October 1, 2011, by Sec. 636 of Ch. 15, as amended by Stats. 2011, Ch. 39, Sec. 68.)

271a.

Every person who knowingly and willfully abandons, or who, having ability so to do, fails or refuses to maintain his or her minor child under the age of 14 years, or who falsely, knowing the same to be false, represents to any manager, officer or agent of any orphan asylum or charitable institution for the care of orphans, that any child for whose admission into that asylum or institution application has been made is an orphan, is punishable by imprisonment pursuant to subdivision (h) of Section 1170, or in the county jail not exceeding one year, or by fine not exceeding one thousand dollars ($1,000), or by both.

(Amended by Stats. 2011, Ch. 15, Sec. 307. (AB 109) Effective April 4, 2011. Operative October 1, 2011, by Sec. 636 of Ch. 15, as amended by Stats. 2011, Ch. 39, Sec. 68.)

271.5.

(a) No parent or other individual having lawful custody of a minor child 72 hours old or younger may be prosecuted for a violation of Section 270, 270.5, 271, or 271a if he or she voluntarily surrenders physical custody of the child to personnel on duty at a safe-surrender site.

(b) For purposes of this section, "safe-surrender site" has the same meaning as defined in paragraph (1) of subdivision (a) of Section 1255.7 of the Health and Safety Code.

(c) (1) For purposes of this section, "lawful custody" has the same meaning as defined in subdivision (j) of Section 1255.7 of the Health and Safety Code.

(2) For purposes of this section, "personnel" has the same meaning as defined in paragraph (3) of subdivision (a) of Section 1255.7 of the Health and Safety Code.

(Amended by Stats. 2007, Ch. 130, Sec. 186. Effective January 1, 2008.)

272.

(a) (1) Every person who commits any act or omits the performance of any duty, which act or omission causes or tends to cause or encourage any person under the age of 18 years to come within the provisions of Section 300, 601, or 602 of the Welfare and

Institutions Code or which act or omission contributes thereto, or any person who, by any act or omission, or by threats, commands, or persuasion, induces or endeavors to induce any person under the age of 18 years or any ward or dependent child of the juvenile court to fail or refuse to conform to a lawful order of the juvenile court, or to do or to perform any act or to follow any course of conduct or to so live as would cause or manifestly tend to cause that person to become or to remain a person within the provisions of Section 300, 601, or 602 of the Welfare and Institutions Code, is guilty of a misdemeanor and upon conviction thereof shall be punished by a fine not exceeding two thousand five hundred dollars ($2,500), or by imprisonment in the county jail for not more than one year, or by both fine and imprisonment in a county jail, or may be released on probation for a period not exceeding five years.

(2) For purposes of this subdivision, a parent or legal guardian to any person under the age of 18 years shall have the duty to exercise reasonable care, supervision, protection, and control over their minor child.

(b) (1) An adult stranger who is 21 years of age or older, who knowingly contacts or communicates with a minor who is under 14 years of age, who knew or reasonably should have known that the minor is under 14 years of age, for the purpose of persuading and luring, or transporting, or attempting to persuade and lure, or transport, that minor away from the minor's home or from any location known by the minor's parent, legal guardian, or custodian, to be a place where the minor is located, for any purpose, without the express consent of the minor's parent or legal guardian, and with the intent to avoid the consent of the minor's parent or legal guardian, is guilty of an infraction or a misdemeanor, subject to subdivision (d) of Section 17.

(2) This subdivision shall not apply in an emergency situation.

(3) As used in this subdivision, the following terms are defined to mean:
(A) "Emergency situation" means a situation where the minor is threatened with imminent bodily harm, emotional harm, or psychological harm.
(B) "Contact" or "communication" includes, but is not limited to, the use of a telephone or the Internet, as defined in Section 17538 of the Business and Professions Code.
(C) "Stranger" means a person of casual acquaintance with whom no substantial relationship exists, or an individual with whom a relationship has been established or promoted for the primary purpose of victimization, as defined in subdivision (e) of Section 6600 of the Welfare and Institutions Code.
(D) "Express consent" means oral or written permission that is positive, direct, and unequivocal, requiring no inference or implication to supply its meaning.

(4) This section shall not be interpreted to criminalize acts of persons contacting minors within the scope and course of their employment, or status as a volunteer of a recognized civic or charitable organization.

(5) This section is intended to protect minors and to help parents and legal guardians exercise reasonable care, supervision, protection, and control over minor children.
(Amended by Stats. 2005, Ch. 461, Sec. 1. Effective January 1, 2006.)

273.
(a) It is a misdemeanor for any person or agency to pay, offer to pay, or to receive money or anything of value for the placement for adoption or for the consent to an adoption of a child. This subdivision shall not apply to any fee paid for adoption services provided by the State Department of Social Services, a licensed adoption agency, adoption services providers, as defined in Section 8502 of the Family Code, or an attorney providing adoption legal services.

(b) This section shall not make it unlawful to pay or receive the maternity-connected medical or hospital and necessary living expenses of the mother preceding and during confinement as an act of charity, as long as the payment is not contingent upon placement of the child for adoption, consent to the adoption, or cooperation in the completion of the adoption.

(c) It is a misdemeanor punishable by imprisonment in a county jail not exceeding one year or by a fine not exceeding two thousand five hundred dollars ($2,500) for any parent to obtain the financial benefits set forth in subdivision (b) with the intent to receive those financial benefits where there is an intent to do either of the following:
(1) Not complete the adoption.
(2) Not consent to the adoption.

(d) It is a misdemeanor punishable by imprisonment in a county jail not exceeding one year or by a fine not exceeding two thousand five hundred dollars ($2,500) for any parent to obtain the financial benefits set forth in subdivision (b) from two or more prospective adopting families or persons, if either parent does both of the following:
(1) Knowingly fails to disclose to those families or persons that there are other prospective adopting families or persons interested in adopting the child, with knowledge that there is an obligation to disclose that information.
(2) Knowingly accepts the financial benefits set forth in subdivision (b) if the aggregate amount exceeds the reasonable maternity-connected medical or hospital and necessary living expenses of the mother preceding and during the pregnancy.

(e) Any person who has been convicted previously of an offense described in subdivision (c) or (d), who is separately tried and convicted of a subsequent violation of subdivision (c) or (d), is guilty of a public offense punishable by imprisonment in a county jail or in the state prison.

(f) Nothing in this section shall be construed to prohibit the prosecution of any person for a misdemeanor or felony pursuant to Section 487 or any other provision of law in lieu of prosecution pursuant to this section.
(Amended by Stats. 1997, Ch. 185, Sec. 1. Effective January 1, 1998.)

273a.
(a) Any person who, under circumstances or conditions likely to produce great bodily harm or death, willfully causes or permits any child to suffer, or inflicts thereon unjustifiable physical pain or mental suffering, or having the care or custody of any child, willfully causes or permits the person or health of that child to be injured, or willfully causes or permits that child to be placed in a situation where his or her person or health is endangered, shall be punished by imprisonment in a county jail not exceeding one year, or in the state prison for two, four, or six years.

(b) Any person who, under circumstances or conditions other than those likely to produce great bodily harm or death, willfully causes or permits any child to suffer, or inflicts thereon unjustifiable physical pain or mental suffering, or having the care or custody of any child, willfully causes or permits the person or health of that child to be injured, or willfully causes or permits that child to be placed in a situation where his or her person or health may be endangered, is guilty of a misdemeanor.

(c) If a person is convicted of violating this section and probation is granted, the court shall require the following minimum conditions of probation:
(1) A mandatory minimum period of probation of 48 months.
(2) A criminal court protective order protecting the victim from further acts of violence or threats, and, if appropriate, residence exclusion or stay-away conditions.
(3) (A) Successful completion of no less than one year of a child abuser's treatment counseling program approved by the probation department. The defendant shall be ordered to begin participation in the program immediately upon the grant of probation. The counseling program shall meet the criteria specified in Section 273.1. The defendant shall produce documentation of program enrollment to the court within 30 days of enrollment, along with quarterly progress reports.
(B) The terms of probation for offenders shall not be lifted until all reasonable fees due to the counseling program have been paid in full, but in no case shall probation be extended beyond the term provided in subdivision (a) of Section 1203.1. If the court finds that the defendant does not have the ability to pay the fees based on the defendant's changed circumstances, the court may reduce or waive the fees.
(4) If the offense was committed while the defendant was under the influence of drugs or alcohol, the defendant shall abstain from the use of drugs or alcohol during the

period of probation and shall be subject to random drug testing by his or her probation officer.
(5) The court may waive any of the above minimum conditions of probation upon a finding that the condition would not be in the best interests of justice. The court shall state on the record its reasons for any waiver.
(Amended by Stats. 1997, Ch. 134, Sec. 1. Effective January 1, 1998.)

273ab.
(a) Any person, having the care or custody of a child who is under eight years of age, who assaults the child by means of force that to a reasonable person would be likely to produce great bodily injury, resulting in the child's death, shall be punished by imprisonment in the state prison for 25 years to life. Nothing in this section shall be construed as affecting the applicability of subdivision (a) of Section 187 or Section 189.

(b) Any person, having the care or custody of a child who is under eight years of age, who assaults the child by means of force that to a reasonable person would be likely to produce great bodily injury, resulting in the child becoming comatose due to brain injury or suffering paralysis of a permanent nature, shall be punished by imprisonment in the state prison for life with the possibility of parole. As used in this subdivision, "paralysis" means a major or complete loss of motor function resulting from injury to the nervous system or to a muscular mechanism.
(Amended by Stats. 2010, Ch. 300, Sec. 1. (AB 1280) Effective January 1, 2011.)

273b.
No child under the age of 16 years shall be placed in any courtroom, or in any vehicle for transportation to any place, in company with adults charged with or convicted of crime, except in the presence of a proper official.
(Amended by Stats. 1987, Ch. 828, Sec. 13.5.)

273c.
All fines, penalties, and forfeitures imposed and collected under the provisions of Sections 270, 271, 271a, 273a, and 273b, or under the provisions of any law relating to, or affecting, children, in every case where the prosecution is instituted or conducted by a society incorporated under the laws of this state for the prevention of cruelty to children, inure to such society in aid of the purposes for which it is incorporated.
(Amended by Stats. 1987, Ch. 828, Sec. 14.)

273d.
(a) Any person who willfully inflicts upon a child any cruel or inhuman corporal punishment or an injury resulting in a traumatic condition is guilty of a felony and shall be punished by imprisonment pursuant to subdivision (h) of Section 1170 for two, four, or six years, or in a county jail for not more than one year, by a fine of up to six thousand dollars ($6,000), or by both that imprisonment and fine.

(b) Any person who is found guilty of violating subdivision (a) shall receive a four-year enhancement for a prior conviction of that offense provided that no additional term shall be imposed under this subdivision for any prison term or term imposed under the provisions of subdivision (h) of Section 1170 served prior to a period of 10 years in which the defendant remained free of both the commission of an offense that results in a felony conviction and prison custody or custody in a county jail under the provisions of subdivision (h) of Section 1170.

(c) If a person is convicted of violating this section and probation is granted, the court shall require the following minimum conditions of probation:
(1) A mandatory minimum period of probation of 36 months.
(2) A criminal court protective order protecting the victim from further acts of violence or threats, and, if appropriate, residence exclusion or stay-away conditions.
(3) (A) Successful completion of no less than one year of a child abuser's treatment counseling program. The defendant shall be ordered to begin participation in the program immediately upon the grant of probation. The counseling program shall meet the criteria specified in Section 273.1. The defendant shall produce documentation of program enrollment to the court within 30 days of enrollment, along with quarterly progress reports.
(B) The terms of probation for offenders shall not be lifted until all reasonable fees due to the counseling program have been paid in full, but in no case shall probation be extended beyond the term provided in subdivision (a) of Section 1203.1. If the court finds that the defendant does not have the ability to pay the fees based on the defendant's changed circumstances, the court may reduce or waive the fees.
(4) If the offense was committed while the defendant was under the influence of drugs or alcohol, the defendant shall abstain from the use of drugs or alcohol during the period of probation and shall be subject to random drug testing by his or her probation officer.
(5) The court may waive any of the above minimum conditions of probation upon a finding that the condition would not be in the best interests of justice. The court shall state on the record its reasons for any waiver.
(Amended (as amended by Stats. 2011, Ch. 15, Sec. 312) by Stats. 2011, 1st Ex. Sess., Ch. 12, Sec. 8. (AB 17 1x) Effective September 21, 2011. Operative October 1, 2011, by Sec. 46 of Ch. 12.)

273e.
Every telephone, special delivery company or association, and every other corporation or person engaged in the delivery of packages, letters, notes, messages, or other matter, and every manager, superintendent, or other agent of such person, corporation, or association, who sends any minor in the employ or under the control of any such person, corporation, association, or agent, to the keeper of any house of prostitution, variety theater, or other place of questionable repute, or to any person connected with, or any inmate of, such house, theater, or other place, or who permits such minor to enter such house, theater, or other place, is guilty of a misdemeanor.
(Added by Stats. 1905, Ch. 568.)

273f.
Any person, whether as parent, guardian, employer, or otherwise, and any firm or corporation, who as employer or otherwise, shall send, direct, or cause to be sent or directed to any saloon, gambling house, house of prostitution, or other immoral place, any minor, is guilty of a misdemeanor.
(Amended by Stats. 1972, Ch. 579.)

273g.
Any person who in the presence of any child indulges in any degrading, lewd, immoral or vicious habits or practices, or who is habitually drunk in the presence of any child in his care, custody or control, is guilty of a misdemeanor.
(Added by Stats. 1907, Ch. 413.)

273h.
In all prosecutions under the provisions of either section 270, section 270a, section 270b, section 271 or section 271a, of this code, where a conviction is had and sentence of imprisonment in the county jail or in the city jail is imposed, the court may direct that the person so convicted shall be compelled to work upon the public roads or highways, or any other public work, in the county or in the city where such conviction is had, during the term of such sentence. And it shall be the duty of the board of supervisors of the county where such person is imprisoned in the county jail, and of the city council of the city where such person is imprisoned in the city jail, where such conviction and sentence are had and where such work is performed by a person under sentence to the county jail or to the city jail, to allow and order the payment out of any funds available, to the wife or to the guardian, or to the custodian of a child or children, or to an organization, or to an individual, appointed by the court as trustee, at the end of each calendar month, for the support of such wife or children, a sum not to exceed two dollars for each day's work of such person so imprisoned.
(Amended by Stats. 1927, Ch. 243.)

273i.

(a) Any person who publishes information describing or depicting a child, the physical appearance of a child, the location of a child, or locations where children may be found with the intent that another person imminently use the information to commit a crime against a child and the information is likely to aid in the imminent commission of a crime against a child, is guilty of a misdemeanor, punishable by imprisonment in a county jail for not more than one year, a fine of not more than one thousand dollars ($1,000), or by both a fine and imprisonment.

(b) For purposes of this section, "publishes" means making the information available to another person through any medium, including, but not limited to, the Internet, the World Wide Web, or e-mail.

(c) For purposes of this section, "child" means a person who is 14 years of age or younger.

(d) For purposes of this section, "information" includes, but is not limited to, an image, film, filmstrip, photograph, negative, slide, photocopy, videotape, video laser disc, or any other computer-generated image.

(e) Any parent or legal guardian of a child about whom information is published in violation of subdivision (a) may seek a preliminary injunction enjoining any further publication of that information.

(Added by Stats. 2008, Ch. 423, Sec. 1. Effective January 1, 2009.)
273j.

(a) (1) Any parent or guardian having the care, custody, or control of a child under 14 years of age who knows or should have known that the child has died shall notify a public safety agency, as defined in Section 53102 of the Government Code, within 24 hours of the time that the parent or guardian knew or should have known that the child has died.

(2) This subdivision shall not apply when a child is otherwise under the immediate care of a physician at the time of death, or if a public safety agency, a coroner, or a medical examiner is otherwise aware of the death.

(b) (1) Any parent or guardian having the care, custody, or control of a child under 14 years of age shall notify law enforcement within 24 hours of the time that the parent or guardian knows or should have known that the child is a missing person and there is evidence that the child is a person at risk, as those terms are defined in Section 14215.

(2) This subdivision shall not apply if law enforcement is otherwise aware that the child is a missing person.

(c) A violation of this section is a misdemeanor punishable by imprisonment in a county jail for not more than one year, or by a fine not exceeding one thousand dollars ($1,000), or by both that fine and imprisonment.

(d) Nothing in this section shall preclude prosecution under any other provision of law.

(Amended by Stats. 2014, Ch. 437, Sec. 8. (SB 1066) Effective January 1, 2015.)
273.1.

(a) Any treatment program to which a child abuser convicted of a violation of Section 273a or 273d is referred as a condition of probation shall meet the following criteria:

(1) Substantial expertise and experience in the treatment of victims of child abuse and the families in which abuse and violence have occurred.

(2) Staff providing direct service are therapists licensed to practice in this state or are under the direct supervision of a therapist licensed to practice in this state.

(3) Utilization of a treatment regimen designed to specifically address the offense, including methods of preventing and breaking the cycle of family violence, anger management, and parenting education that focuses, among other things, on means of identifying the developmental and emotional needs of the child.

(4) Utilization of group and individual therapy and counseling, with groups no larger than 12 persons.

(5) Capability of identifying substance abuse and either treating the abuse or referring the offender to a substance abuse program, to the extent that the court has not already done so.

(6) Entry into a written agreement with the defendant that includes an outline of the components of the program, the attendance requirements, a requirement to attend group session free of chemical influence, and a statement that the defendant may be removed from the program if it is determined that the defendant is not benefiting from the program or is disruptive to the program.

(7) The program may include, on the recommendation of the treatment counselor, family counseling. However, no child victim shall be compelled or required to participate in the program, including family counseling, and no program may condition a defendant's enrollment on participation by the child victim. The treatment counselor shall privately advise the child victim that his or her participation is voluntary.

(b) If the program finds that the defendant is unsuitable, the program shall immediately contact the probation department or the court. The probation department or court shall either recalendar the case for hearing or refer the defendant to an appropriate alternative child abuser's treatment counseling program.

(c) Upon request by the child abuser's treatment counseling program, the court shall provide the defendant's arrest report, prior incidents of violence, and treatment history to the program.

(d) The child abuser's treatment counseling program shall provide the probation department and the court with periodic progress reports at least every three months that include attendance, fee payment history, and program compliance. The program shall submit a final evaluation that includes the program's evaluation of the defendant's progress, and recommendation for either successful or unsuccessful termination of the program.

(e) The defendant shall pay for the full costs of the treatment program, including any drug testing. However, the court may waive any portion or all of that financial responsibility upon a finding of an inability to pay. Upon the request of the defendant, the court shall hold a hearing to determine the defendant's ability to pay for the treatment program. At the hearing the court may consider all relevant information, but shall consider the impact of the costs of the treatment program on the defendant's ability to provide food, clothing, and shelter for the child injured by a violation of Section 273a or 273d. If the court finds that the defendant is unable to pay for any portion of the costs of the treatment program, its reasons for that finding shall be stated on the record. In the event of this finding, the program fees or a portion thereof shall be waived.

(f) All programs accepting referrals of child abusers pursuant to this section shall accept offenders for whom fees have been partially or fully waived. However, the court shall require each qualifying program to serve no more than its proportionate share of those offenders who have been granted fee waivers, and require all qualifying programs to share equally in the cost of serving those offenders with fee waivers.

(Amended by Stats. 1997, Ch. 17, Sec. 95. Effective January 1, 1998.)
273.4.

(a) If the act constituting a felony violation of subdivision (a) of Section 273a was female genital mutilation, as defined in subdivision (b), the defendant shall be punished by an additional term of imprisonment in the state prison for one year, in addition and consecutive to the punishment prescribed by Section 273a.

(b) "Female genital mutilation" means the excision or infibulation of the labia majora, labia minora, clitoris, or vulva, performed for nonmedical purposes.

(c) Nothing in this section shall preclude prosecution under Section 203, 205, or 206 or any other provision of law.

(Amended (as amended by Stats. 2011, Ch. 15) by Stats. 2011, Ch. 39, Sec. 12. (AB 117) Effective June 30, 2011. Operative October 1, 2011, pursuant to Secs. 68 and 69 of Ch. 39.)
273.5.

(a) Any person who willfully inflicts corporal injury resulting in a traumatic condition upon a victim described in subdivision (b) is guilty of a felony, and upon conviction thereof shall be punished by imprisonment in the state prison for two, three, or four years, or in a county jail for not more than one year, or by a fine of up to six thousand dollars ($6,000), or by both that fine and imprisonment.

(b) Subdivision (a) shall apply if the victim is or was one or more of the following:

(1) The offender's spouse or former spouse.

(2) The offender's cohabitant or former cohabitant.

(3) The offender's fiancé or fiancée, or someone with whom the offender has, or previously had, an engagement or dating relationship, as defined in paragraph (10) of subdivision (f) of Section 243.

(4) The mother or father of the offender's child.

(c) Holding oneself out to be the spouse of the person with whom one is cohabiting is not necessary to constitute cohabitation as the term is used in this section.

(d) As used in this section, "traumatic condition" means a condition of the body, such as a wound, or external or internal injury, including, but not limited to, injury as a result of strangulation or suffocation, whether of a minor or serious nature, caused by a physical force. For purposes of this section, "strangulation" and "suffocation" include impeding the normal breathing or circulation of the blood of a person by applying pressure on the throat or neck.

(e) For the purpose of this section, a person shall be considered the father or mother of another person's child if the alleged male parent is presumed the natural father under Sections 7611 and 7612 of the Family Code.

(f) (1) Any person convicted of violating this section for acts occurring within seven years of a previous conviction under subdivision (a), or subdivision (d) of Section 243, or Section 243.4, 244, 244.5, or 245, shall be punished by imprisonment in a county jail for not more than one year, or by imprisonment in the state prison for two, four, or five years, or by both imprisonment and a fine of up to ten thousand dollars ($10,000).

(2) Any person convicted of a violation of this section for acts occurring within seven years of a previous conviction under subdivision (e) of Section 243 shall be punished by imprisonment in the state prison for two, three, or four years, or in a county jail for not more than one year, or by a fine of up to ten thousand dollars ($10,000), or by both that imprisonment and fine.

(g) If probation is granted to any person convicted under subdivision (a), the court shall impose probation consistent with the provisions of Section 1203.097.

(h) If probation is granted, or the execution or imposition of a sentence is suspended, for any defendant convicted under subdivision (a) who has been convicted of any prior offense specified in subdivision (f), the court shall impose one of the following conditions of probation:

(1) If the defendant has suffered one prior conviction within the previous seven years for a violation of any offense specified in subdivision (f), it shall be a condition of probation, in addition to the provisions contained in Section 1203.097, that he or she be imprisoned in a county jail for not less than 15 days.

(2) If the defendant has suffered two or more prior convictions within the previous seven years for a violation of any offense specified in subdivision (f), it shall be a condition of probation, in addition to the provisions contained in Section 1203.097, that he or she be imprisoned in a county jail for not less than 60 days.

(3) The court, upon a showing of good cause, may find that the mandatory imprisonment required by this subdivision shall not be imposed and shall state on the record its reasons for finding good cause.

(i) If probation is granted upon conviction of a violation of subdivision (a), the conditions of probation may include, consistent with the terms of probation imposed pursuant to Section 1203.097, in lieu of a fine, one or both of the following requirements:

(1) That the defendant make payments to a battered women's shelter, up to a maximum of five thousand dollars ($5,000), pursuant to Section 1203.097.

(2) (A) That the defendant reimburse the victim for reasonable costs of counseling and other reasonable expenses that the court finds are the direct result of the defendant's offense.

(B) For any order to pay a fine, make payments to a battered women's shelter, or pay restitution as a condition of probation under this subdivision, the court shall make a determination of the defendant's ability to pay. An order to make payments to a battered women's shelter shall not be made if it would impair the ability of the defendant to pay direct restitution to the victim or court-ordered child support. If the injury to a person who is married or in a registered domestic partnership is caused in whole or in part by the criminal acts of his or her spouse or domestic partner in violation of this section, the community property may not be used to discharge the liability of the offending spouse or domestic partner for restitution to the injured spouse or domestic partner, required by Section 1203.04, as operative on or before August 2, 1995, or Section 1202.4, or to a shelter for costs with regard to the injured spouse or domestic partner and dependents, required by this section, until all separate property of the offending spouse or domestic partner is exhausted.

(j) Upon conviction under subdivision (a), the sentencing court shall also consider issuing an order restraining the defendant from any contact with the victim, which may be valid for up to 10 years, as determined by the court. It is the intent of the Legislature that the length of any restraining order be based upon the seriousness of the facts before the court, the probability of future violations, and the safety of the victim and his or her immediate family. This protective order may be issued by the court whether the defendant is sentenced to state prison or county jail, or if imposition of sentence is suspended and the defendant is placed on probation.

(k) If a peace officer makes an arrest for a violation of this section, the peace officer is not required to inform the victim of his or her right to make a citizen's arrest pursuant to subdivision (b) of Section 836.

(Amended by Stats. 2016, Ch. 50, Sec. 69. (SB 1005) Effective January 1, 2017.)
273.6.

(a) Any intentional and knowing violation of a protective order, as defined in Section 6218 of the Family Code, or of an order issued pursuant to Section 527.6, 527.8, or 527.85 of the Code of Civil Procedure, or Section 15657.03 of the Welfare and Institutions Code, is a misdemeanor punishable by a fine of not more than one thousand dollars ($1,000), or by imprisonment in a county jail for not more than one year, or by both that fine and imprisonment.

(b) In the event of a violation of subdivision (a) that results in physical injury, the person shall be punished by a fine of not more than two thousand dollars ($2,000), or by imprisonment in a county jail for not less than 30 days nor more than one year, or by both that fine and imprisonment. However, if the person is imprisoned in a county jail for at least 48 hours, the court may, in the interest of justice and for reasons stated on the record, reduce or eliminate the 30-day minimum imprisonment required by this subdivision. In determining whether to reduce or eliminate the minimum imprisonment pursuant to this subdivision, the court shall consider the seriousness of the facts before the court, whether there are additional allegations of a violation of the order during the pendency of the case before the court, the probability of future violations, the safety of the victim, and whether the defendant has successfully completed or is making progress with counseling.

(c) Subdivisions (a) and (b) shall apply to the following court orders:

(1) Any order issued pursuant to Section 6320 or 6389 of the Family Code.

(2) An order excluding one party from the family dwelling or from the dwelling of the other.

(3) An order enjoining a party from specified behavior that the court determined was necessary to effectuate the order described in subdivision (a).

(4) Any order issued by another state that is recognized under Part 5 (commencing with Section 6400) of Division 10 of the Family Code.
(d) A subsequent conviction for a violation of an order described in subdivision (a), occurring within seven years of a prior conviction for a violation of an order described in subdivision (a) and involving an act of violence or "a credible threat" of violence, as defined in subdivision (c) of Section 139, is punishable by imprisonment in a county jail not to exceed one year, or pursuant to subdivision (h) of Section 1170.
(e) In the event of a subsequent conviction for a violation of an order described in subdivision (a) for an act occurring within one year of a prior conviction for a violation of an order described in subdivision (a) that results in physical injury to a victim, the person shall be punished by a fine of not more than two thousand dollars ($2,000), or by imprisonment in a county jail for not less than six months nor more than one year, by both that fine and imprisonment, or by imprisonment pursuant to subdivision (h) of Section 1170. However, if the person is imprisoned in a county jail for at least 30 days, the court may, in the interest of justice and for reasons stated in the record, reduce or eliminate the six-month minimum imprisonment required by this subdivision. In determining whether to reduce or eliminate the minimum imprisonment pursuant to this subdivision, the court shall consider the seriousness of the facts before the court, whether there are additional allegations of a violation of the order during the pendency of the case before the court, the probability of future violations, the safety of the victim, and whether the defendant has successfully completed or is making progress with counseling.
(f) The prosecuting agency of each county shall have the primary responsibility for the enforcement of orders described in subdivisions (a), (b), (d), and (e).
(g) (1) Every person who owns, possesses, purchases, or receives a firearm knowing he or she is prohibited from doing so by the provisions of a protective order as defined in Section 136.2 of this code, Section 6218 of the Family Code, or Section 527.6, 527.8, or 527.85 of the Code of Civil Procedure, or Section 15657.03 of the Welfare and Institutions Code, shall be punished under Section 29825.
(2) Every person subject to a protective order described in paragraph (1) shall not be prosecuted under this section for owning, possessing, purchasing, or receiving a firearm to the extent that firearm is granted an exemption pursuant to subdivision (f) of Section 527.9 of the Code of Civil Procedure, or subdivision (h) of Section 6389 of the Family Code.
(h) If probation is granted upon conviction of a violation of subdivision (a), (b), (c), (d), or (e), the court shall impose probation consistent with Section 1203.097, and the conditions of probation may include, in lieu of a fine, one or both of the following requirements:
(1) That the defendant make payments to a battered women's shelter or to a shelter for abused elder persons or dependent adults, up to a maximum of five thousand dollars ($5,000), pursuant to Section 1203.097.
(2) That the defendant reimburse the victim for reasonable costs of counseling and other reasonable expenses that the court finds are the direct result of the defendant's offense.
(i) For any order to pay a fine, make payments to a battered women's shelter, or pay restitution as a condition of probation under subdivision (e), the court shall make a determination of the defendant's ability to pay. In no event shall any order to make payments to a battered women's shelter be made if it would impair the ability of the defendant to pay direct restitution to the victim or court-ordered child support. Where the injury to a married person is caused in whole or in part by the criminal acts of his or her spouse in violation of this section, the community property may not be used to discharge the liability of the offending spouse for restitution to the injured spouse, required by Section 1203.04, as operative on or before August 2, 1995, or Section 1202.4, or to a shelter for costs with regard to the injured spouse and dependents, required by this section, until all separate property of the offending spouse is exhausted.
(Amended by Stats. 2013, Ch. 76, Sec. 145.7. (AB 383) Effective January 1, 2014.)
273.65.
(a) Any intentional and knowing violation of a protective order issued pursuant to Section 213.5, 304, or 362.4 of the Welfare and Institutions Code is a misdemeanor punishable by a fine of not more than one thousand dollars ($1,000), or by imprisonment in a county jail for not more than one year, or by both the fine and imprisonment.
(b) In the event of a violation of subdivision (a) which results in physical injury, the person shall be punished by a fine of not more than two thousand dollars ($2,000), or by imprisonment in a county jail for not less than 30 days nor more than one year, or by both the fine and imprisonment. However, if the person is imprisoned in a county jail for at least 48 hours, the court may, in the interests of justice and for reasons stated on the record, reduce or eliminate the 30-day minimum imprisonment required by this subdivision. In determining whether to reduce or eliminate the minimum imprisonment pursuant to this subdivision, the court shall consider the seriousness of the facts before the court, whether there are additional allegations of a violation of the order during the pendency of the case before the court, the probability of future violations, the safety of the victim, and whether the defendant has successfully completed or is making progress with counseling.
(c) Subdivisions (a) and (b) shall apply to the following court orders:
(1) An order enjoining any party from molesting, attacking, striking, threatening, sexually assaulting, battering, harassing, contacting repeatedly by mail with the intent to harass, or disturbing the peace of the other party, or other named family and household members.
(2) An order excluding one party from the family dwelling or from the dwelling of the other.
(3) An order enjoining a party from specified behavior which the court determined was necessary to effectuate the order under subdivision (a).
(d) A subsequent conviction for a violation of an order described in subdivision (a), occurring within seven years of a prior conviction for a violation of an order described in subdivision (a) and involving an act of violence or "a credible threat" of violence, as defined in subdivision (c) of Section 139, is punishable by imprisonment in a county jail not to exceed one year, or pursuant to subdivision (h) of Section 1170.
(e) In the event of a subsequent conviction for a violation of an order described in subdivision (a) for an act occurring within one year of a prior conviction for a violation of an order described in subdivision (a) which results in physical injury to the same victim, the person shall be punished by a fine of not more than two thousand dollars ($2,000), or by imprisonment in a county jail for not less than six months nor more than one year, by both that fine and imprisonment, or by imprisonment pursuant to subdivision (h) of Section 1170. However, if the person is imprisoned in a county jail for at least 30 days, the court may, in the interests of justice and for reasons stated in the record, reduce or eliminate the six-month minimum imprisonment required by this subdivision. In determining whether to reduce or eliminate the minimum imprisonment pursuant to this subdivision, the court shall consider the seriousness of the facts before the court, whether there are additional allegations of a violation of the order during the pendency of the case before the court, the probability of future violations, the safety of the victim, and whether the defendant has successfully completed or is making progress with counseling.
(f) The prosecuting agency of each county shall have the primary responsibility for the enforcement of orders issued pursuant to subdivisions (a), (b), (d), and (e).
(g) The court may order a person convicted under this section to undergo counseling, and, if appropriate, to complete a batterer's treatment program.
(h) If probation is granted upon conviction of a violation of subdivision (a), (b), or (c), the conditions of probation may include, in lieu of a fine, one or both of the following requirements:
(1) That the defendant make payments to a battered women's shelter, up to a maximum of five thousand dollars ($5,000), pursuant to Section 1203.097.
(2) That the defendant reimburse the victim for reasonable costs of counseling and other reasonable expenses that the court finds are the direct result of the defendant's offense.
(i) For any order to pay a fine, make payments to a battered women's shelter, or pay restitution as a condition of probation under subdivision (e), the court shall make a determination of the defendant's ability to pay. In no event shall any order to make payments to a battered women's shelter be made if it would impair the ability of the defendant to pay direct restitution to the victim or court-ordered child support.
(Amended by Stats. 2011, Ch. 15, Sec. 311. (AB 109) Effective April 4, 2011. Operative October 1, 2011, by Sec. 636 of Ch. 15, as amended by Stats. 2011, Ch. 39, Sec. 68.)
273.7.
(a) Any person who maliciously publishes, disseminates, or otherwise discloses the location of any trafficking shelter or domestic violence shelter or any place designated as a trafficking shelter or domestic violence shelter, without the authorization of that trafficking shelter or domestic violence shelter, is guilty of a misdemeanor.
(b) (1) For purposes of this section, "domestic violence shelter" means a confidential location that provides emergency housing on a 24-hour basis for victims of sexual assault, spousal abuse, or both, and their families.
(2) For purposes of this section, "trafficking shelter" means a confidential location that provides emergency housing on a 24-hour basis for victims of human trafficking, including any person who is a victim under Section 236.1.
(3) Sexual assault, spousal abuse, or both, include, but are not limited to, those crimes described in Sections 240, 242, 243.4, 261, 261.5, 262, 264.1, 266, 266a, 266b, 266c, 266f, 273.5, 273.6, 285, 288, and 289.
(c) Nothing in this section shall apply to confidential communications between an attorney and his or her client.
(Amended by Stats. 2006, Ch. 538, Sec. 499. Effective January 1, 2007.)
273.75.
(a) On any charge involving acts of domestic violence as defined in subdivisions (a) and (b) of Section 13700 of the Penal Code or Sections 6203 and 6211 of the Family Code, the district attorney or prosecuting city attorney shall perform or cause to be performed, by accessing the electronic databases enumerated in subdivision (b), a thorough investigation of the defendant's history, including, but not limited to, prior convictions for domestic violence, other forms of violence or weapons offenses and any current protective or restraining order issued by any civil or criminal court. This information shall be presented for consideration by the court (1) when setting bond or when releasing a defendant on his or her own recognizance at the arraignment, if the defendant is in custody, (2) upon consideration of any plea agreement, and (3) when issuing a protective order pursuant to Section 136.2 of the Penal Code, in accordance with subdivision (h) of that section. In determining bail or release upon a plea agreement, the court shall consider the safety of the victim, the victim's children, and any other person who may be in danger if the defendant is released.
(b) For purposes of this section, the district attorney or prosecuting city attorney shall search or cause to be searched the following databases, when readily available and reasonably accessible:
(1) The California Sex and Arson Registry (CSAR).
(2) The Supervised Release File.
(3) State summary criminal history information maintained by the Department of Justice pursuant to Section 11105 of the Penal Code.
(4) The Federal Bureau of Investigation's nationwide database.
(5) Locally maintained criminal history records or databases.
However, a record or database need not be searched if the information available in that record or database can be obtained as a result of a search conducted in another record or database.
(c) If the investigation required by this section reveals a current civil protective or restraining order or a protective or restraining order issued by another criminal court and involving the same or related parties, and if a protective or restraining order is issued in the current criminal proceeding, the district attorney or prosecuting city attorney shall send relevant information regarding the contents of the order issued in the current criminal proceeding, and any information regarding a conviction of the defendant, to the other court immediately after the order has been issued. When requested, the information described in this subdivision may be sent to the appropriate family, juvenile, or civil court. When requested, and upon a showing of a compelling need, the information described in this section may be sent to a court in another state.
(Amended by Stats. 2014, Ch. 54, Sec. 10. (SB 1461) Effective January 1, 2015.)

CHAPTER 2.5. Spousal Abusers [273.8 - 273.88]

(Chapter 2.5 added by Stats. 1985, Ch. 1122, Sec. 1.)
273.8.
The Legislature hereby finds that spousal abusers present a clear and present danger to the mental and physical well-being of the citizens of the State of California. The Legislature further finds that the concept of vertical prosecution, in which a specially trained deputy district attorney, deputy city attorney, or prosecution unit is assigned to a case after arraignment and continuing to its completion, is a proven way of demonstrably increasing the likelihood of convicting spousal abusers and ensuring appropriate sentences for those offenders. In enacting this chapter, the Legislature intends to support increased efforts by district attorneys' and city attorneys' offices to prosecute spousal abusers through organizational and operational techniques that have already proven their effectiveness in selected cities and counties in this and other states.
(Amended by Stats. 1994, Ch. 599, Sec. 2. Effective September 16, 1994.)
273.81.
(a) There is hereby established in the Department of Justice a program of financial and technical assistance for district attorneys' or city attorneys' offices, designated the Spousal Abuser Prosecution Program. All funds appropriated to the Department of Justice for the purposes of this chapter shall be administered and disbursed by the Attorney General, and shall to the greatest extent feasible, be coordinated or consolidated with any federal or local funds that may be made available for these purposes.
The Department of Justice shall establish guidelines for the provision of grant awards to proposed and existing programs prior to the allocation of funds under this chapter. These guidelines shall contain the criteria for the selection of agencies to receive funding and the terms and conditions upon which the Department of Justice is prepared to offer grants pursuant to statutory authority. The guidelines shall not constitute rules, regulations, orders, or standards of general application.
(b) The Attorney General may allocate and award funds to cities or counties, or both, in which spousal abuser prosecution units are established or are proposed to be established in substantial compliance with the policies and criteria set forth in this chapter.

(c) The allocation and award of funds shall be made upon application executed by the county's district attorney or by the city's attorney and approved by the county board of supervisors or by the city council. Funds disbursed under this chapter shall not supplant local funds that would, in the absence of the California Spousal Abuser Prosecution Program, be made available to support the prosecution of spousal abuser cases. Local grant awards made under this program shall not be subject to review as specified in Section 10295 of the Public Contract Code.
(d) Local government recipients shall provide 20 percent matching funds for every grant awarded under this program.
(Amended by Stats. 1994, Ch. 599, Sec. 3. Effective September 16, 1994.)
273.82.
Spousal abuser prosecution units receiving funds under this chapter shall concentrate enhanced prosecution efforts and resources upon individuals identified under selection criteria set forth in Section 273.83. Enhanced prosecution efforts and resources shall include, but not be limited to, all of the following:
(a) (1) Vertical prosecutorial representation, whereby the prosecutor who, or prosecution unit that, makes all major court appearances on that particular case through its conclusion, including bail evaluation, preliminary hearing, significant law and motion litigation, trial, and sentencing.
(2) Vertical counselor representation, whereby a trained domestic violence counselor maintains liaison from initial court appearances through the case's conclusion, including the sentencing phase.
(b) The assignment of highly qualified investigators and prosecutors to spousal abuser cases. "Highly qualified" for the purposes of this chapter means any of the following:
(1) Individuals with one year of experience in the investigation and prosecution of felonies.
(2) Individuals with at least two years of experience in the investigation and prosecution of misdemeanors.
(3) Individuals who have attended a program providing domestic violence training as approved by the Office of Emergency Services or the Department of Justice.
(c) A significant reduction of caseloads for investigators and prosecutors assigned to spousal abuser cases.
(d) Coordination with local rape victim counseling centers, spousal abuse services programs, and victim-witness assistance programs. That coordination shall include, but not be limited to: referrals of individuals to receive client services; participation in local training programs; membership and participation in local task forces established to improve communication between criminal justice system agencies and community service agencies; and cooperating with individuals serving as liaison representatives of local rape victim counseling centers, spousal abuse victim programs, and victim-witness assistance programs.
(Amended by Stats. 2013, Ch. 352, Sec. 403. (AB 1317) Effective September 26, 2013. Operative July 1, 2013, by Sec. 543 of Ch. 352.)
273.83.
(a) An individual shall be the subject of a spousal abuser prosecution effort who is under arrest for any act or omission described in subdivisions (a) and (b) of Section 13700.
(b) In applying the spousal abuser selection criteria set forth in subdivision (a), a district attorney or city attorney shall not reject cases for filing exclusively on the basis that there is a family or personal relationship between the victim and the alleged offender.
(c) In exercising the prosecutorial discretion granted by Section 273.85, the district attorney or city attorney shall consider the number and seriousness of the offenses currently charged against the defendant.
(Amended by Stats. 1994, Ch. 599, Sec. 5. Effective September 16, 1994.)
273.84.
Each district attorney's or city attorney's office establishing a spousal abuser prosecution unit and receiving state support under this chapter shall adopt and pursue the following policies for spousal abuser cases:
(a) All reasonable prosecutorial efforts shall be made to resist the pretrial release of a charged defendant meeting spousal abuser selection criteria.
(b) All reasonable prosecutorial efforts shall be made to persuade the court to impose the most severe authorized sentence upon a person convicted after prosecution as a spousal abuser. In the prosecution of an intrafamily sexual abuse case, discretion may be exercised as to the type and nature of sentence recommended to the court.
(c) All reasonable prosecutorial efforts shall be made to reduce the time between arrest and disposition of charge against an individual meeting spousal abuser criteria.
(Amended by Stats. 2000, Ch. 135, Sec. 131. Effective January 1, 2001.)
273.85.
(a) The selection criteria set forth in Section 273.84 shall be adhered to for each spousal abuser case unless, in the reasonable exercise of prosecutor's discretion, extraordinary circumstances require departure from those policies in order to promote the general purposes and intent of this chapter.
(b) Each district attorney's and city attorney's office establishing a spousal abuser prosecution unit and receiving state support under this chapter shall submit the following information, on a quarterly basis, to the Department of Justice:
(1) The number of spousal abuser cases referred to the district attorney's or city attorney's office for possible filing.
(2) The number of spousal abuser cases filed for prosecution.
(3) The number of spousal abuser cases taken to trial.
(4) The number of spousal abuser cases tried that resulted in conviction.
(Amended by Stats. 1994, Ch. 599, Sec. 7. Effective September 16, 1994.)
273.86.
The characterization of a defendant as a "spousal abuser" as defined by this chapter shall not be communicated to the trier of fact.
(Added by Stats. 1985, Ch. 1122, Sec. 1.)
273.87.
The Department of Justice is encouraged to utilize Federal Victims of Crimes Act (VOCA) funds or any other federal funds that may become available in order to implement this chapter.
(Amended by Stats. 1994, Ch. 599, Sec. 8. Effective September 16, 1994.)
273.88.
Administrative costs incurred by the Department of Justice pursuant to the Spousal Abuser Prosecution Program shall not exceed 5 percent of the total funds allocated for the program.
(Added by Stats. 1994, Ch. 599, Sec. 9. Effective September 16, 1994.)

CHAPTER 4. Child Abduction [277 - 280]

(Chapter 4 repealed and added by Stats. 1996, Ch. 988, Sec. 9.)
277.
The following definitions apply for the purposes of this chapter:
(a) "Child" means a person under the age of 18 years.
(b) "Court order" or "custody order" means a custody determination decree, judgment, or order issued by a court of competent jurisdiction, whether permanent or temporary, initial or modified, that affects the custody or visitation of a child, issued in the context of a custody proceeding. An order, once made, shall continue in effect until it expires, is modified, is rescinded, or terminates by operation of law.

(c) "Custody proceeding" means a proceeding in which a custody determination is an issue, including, but not limited to, an action for dissolution or separation, dependency, guardianship, termination of parental rights, adoption, paternity, except actions under Section 11350 or 11350.1 of the Welfare and Institutions Code, or protection from domestic violence proceedings, including an emergency protective order pursuant to Part 3 (commencing with Section 6240) of Division 10 of the Family Code.
(d) "Lawful custodian" means a person, guardian, or public agency having a right to custody of a child.
(e) A "right to custody" means the right to the physical care, custody, and control of a child pursuant to a custody order as defined in subdivision (b) or, in the absence of a court order, by operation of law, or pursuant to the Uniform Parentage Act contained in Part 3 (commencing with Section 7600) of Division 12 of the Family Code. Whenever a public agency takes protective custody or jurisdiction of the care, custody, control, or conduct of a child by statutory authority or court order, that agency is a lawful custodian of the child and has a right to physical custody of the child. In any subsequent placement of the child, the public agency continues to be a lawful custodian with a right to physical custody of the child until the public agency's right of custody is terminated by an order of a court of competent jurisdiction or by operation of law.
(f) In the absence of a court order to the contrary, a parent loses his or her right to custody of the child to the other parent if the parent having the right to custody is dead, is unable or refuses to take the custody, or has abandoned his or her family. A natural parent whose parental rights have been terminated by court order is no longer a lawful custodian and no longer has a right to physical custody.
(g) "Keeps" or "withholds" means retains physical possession of a child whether or not the child resists or objects.
(h) "Visitation" means the time for access to the child allotted to any person by court order.
(i) "Person" includes, but is not limited to, a parent or an agent of a parent.
(j) "Domestic violence" means domestic violence as defined in Section 6211 of the Family Code.
(k) "Abduct" means take, entice away, keep, withhold, or conceal.
(Repealed and added by Stats. 1996, Ch. 988, Sec. 9. Effective January 1, 1997.)
278.
Every person, not having a right to custody, who maliciously takes, entices away, keeps, withholds, or conceals any child with the intent to detain or conceal that child from a lawful custodian shall be punished by imprisonment in a county jail not exceeding one year, a fine not exceeding one thousand dollars ($1,000), or both that fine and imprisonment, or by imprisonment pursuant to subdivision (h) of Section 1170 for two, three, or four years, a fine not exceeding ten thousand dollars ($10,000), or both that fine and imprisonment.
(Amended by Stats. 2011, Ch. 15, Sec. 313. (AB 109) Effective April 4, 2011. Operative October 1, 2011, by Sec. 636 of Ch. 15, as amended by Stats. 2011, Ch. 39, Sec. 68.)
278.5.
(a) Every person who takes, entices away, keeps, withholds, or conceals a child and maliciously deprives a lawful custodian of a right to custody, or a person of a right to visitation, shall be punished by imprisonment in a county jail not exceeding one year, a fine not exceeding one thousand dollars ($1,000), or both that fine and imprisonment, or by imprisonment pursuant to subdivision (h) of Section 1170 for 16 months, or two or three years, a fine not exceeding ten thousand dollars ($10,000), or both that fine and imprisonment.
(b) Nothing contained in this section limits the court's contempt power.
(c) A custody order obtained after the taking, enticing away, keeping, withholding, or concealing of a child does not constitute a defense to a crime charged under this section.
(Amended by Stats. 2011, Ch. 15, Sec. 314. (AB 109) Effective April 4, 2011. Operative October 1, 2011, by Sec. 636 of Ch. 15, as amended by Stats. 2011, Ch. 39, Sec. 68.)
278.6.
(a) At the sentencing hearing following a conviction for a violation of Section 278 or 278.5, or both, the court shall consider any relevant factors and circumstances in aggravation, including, but not limited to, all of the following:
(1) The child was exposed to a substantial risk of physical injury or illness.
(2) The defendant inflicted or threatened to inflict physical harm on a parent or lawful custodian of the child or on the child at the time of or during the abduction.
(3) The defendant harmed or abandoned the child during the abduction.
(4) The child was taken, enticed away, kept, withheld, or concealed outside the United States.
(5) The child has not been returned to the lawful custodian.
(6) The defendant previously abducted or threatened to abduct the child.
(7) The defendant substantially altered the appearance or the name of the child.
(8) The defendant denied the child appropriate education during the abduction.
(9) The length of the abduction.
(10) The age of the child.
(b) At the sentencing hearing following a conviction for a violation of Section 278 or 278.5, or both, the court shall consider any relevant factors and circumstances in mitigation, including, but not limited to, both of the following:
(1) The defendant returned the child unharmed and prior to arrest or issuance of a warrant for arrest, whichever is first.
(2) The defendant provided information and assistance leading to the child's safe return.
(c) In addition to any other penalties provided for a violation of Section 278 or 278.5, a court shall order the defendant to pay restitution to the district attorney for any costs incurred in locating and returning the child as provided in Section 3134 of the Family Code, and to the victim for those expenses and costs reasonably incurred by, or on behalf of, the victim in locating and recovering the child. An award made pursuant to this section shall constitute a final judgment and shall be enforceable as such.
(Added by Stats. 1996, Ch. 988, Sec. 9. Effective January 1, 1997.)
278.7.
(a) Section 278.5 does not apply to a person with a right to custody of a child who, with a good faith and reasonable belief that the child, if left with the other person, will suffer immediate bodily injury or emotional harm, takes, entices away, keeps, withholds, or conceals that child.
(b) Section 278.5 does not apply to a person with a right to custody of a child who has been a victim of domestic violence who, with a good faith and reasonable belief that the child, if left with the other person, will suffer immediate bodily injury or emotional harm, takes, entices away, keeps, withholds, or conceals that child. "Emotional harm" includes having a parent who has committed domestic violence against the parent who is taking, enticing away, keeping, withholding, or concealing the child.
(c) The person who takes, entices away, keeps, withholds, or conceals a child shall do all of the following:
(1) Within a reasonable time from the taking, enticing away, keeping, withholding, or concealing, make a report to the office of the district attorney of the county where the child resided before the action. The report shall include the name of the person, the current address and telephone number of the child and the person, and the reasons the child was taken, enticed away, kept, withheld, or concealed.
(2) Within a reasonable time from the taking, enticing away, keeping, withholding, or concealing, commence a custody proceeding in a court of competent jurisdiction consistent with the federal Parental Kidnapping Prevention Act (Section 1738A, Title 28, United States Code) or the Uniform Child Custody Jurisdiction Act (Part 3 (commencing with Section 3400) of Division 8 of the Family Code).

(3) Inform the district attorney's office of any change of address or telephone number of the person and the child.
(d) For the purposes of this article, a reasonable time within which to make a report to the district attorney's office is at least 10 days and a reasonable time to commence a custody proceeding is at least 30 days. This section shall not preclude a person from making a report to the district attorney's office or commencing a custody proceeding earlier than those specified times.
(e) The address and telephone number of the person and the child provided pursuant to this section shall remain confidential unless released pursuant to state law or by a court order that contains appropriate safeguards to ensure the safety of the person and the child.
(Added by Stats. 1996, Ch. 988, Sec. 9. Effective January 1, 1997.)

279.

A violation of Section 278 or 278.5 by a person who was not a resident of, or present in, this state at the time of the alleged offense is punishable in this state, whether the intent to commit the offense is formed within or outside of this state, if any of the following apply:
(a) The child was a resident of, or present in, this state at the time the child was taken, enticed away, kept, withheld, or concealed.
(b) The child thereafter is found in this state.
(c) A lawful custodian or a person with a right to visitation is a resident of this state at the time the child was taken, enticed away, kept, withheld, or concealed.
(Repealed and added by Stats. 1996, Ch. 988, Sec. 9. Effective January 1, 1997.)

279.1.

The offenses enumerated in Sections 278 and 278.5 are continuous in nature, and continue for as long as the minor child is concealed or detained.
(Added by Stats. 1996, Ch. 988, Sec. 9. Effective January 1, 1997.)

279.5.

When a person is arrested for an alleged violation of Section 278 or 278.5, the court, in setting bail, shall take into consideration whether the child has been returned to the lawful custodian, and if not, shall consider whether there is an increased risk that the child may not be returned, or the defendant may flee the jurisdiction, or, by flight or concealment, evade the authority of the court.
(Added by Stats. 1996, Ch. 988, Sec. 9. Effective January 1, 1997.)

279.6.

(a) A law enforcement officer may take a child into protective custody under any of the following circumstances:
(1) It reasonably appears to the officer that a person is likely to conceal the child, flee the jurisdiction with the child, or, by flight or concealment, evade the authority of the court.
(2) There is no lawful custodian available to take custody of the child.
(3) There are conflicting custody orders or conflicting claims to custody and the parties cannot agree which party should take custody of the child.
(4) The child is an abducted child.
(b) When a law enforcement officer takes a child into protective custody pursuant to this section, the officer shall do one of the following:
(1) Release the child to the lawful custodian of the child, unless it reasonably appears that the release would cause the child to be endangered, abducted, or removed from the jurisdiction.
(2) Obtain an emergency protective order pursuant to Part 3 (commencing with Section 6240) of Division 10 of the Family Code ordering placement of the child with an interim custodian who agrees in writing to accept interim custody.
(3) Release the child to the social services agency responsible for arranging shelter or foster care.
(4) Return the child as ordered by a court of competent jurisdiction.
(c) Upon the arrest of a person for a violation of Section 278 or 278.5, a law enforcement officer shall take possession of an abducted child who is found in the company of, or under the control of, the arrested person and deliver the child as directed in subdivision (b).
(d) Notwithstanding any other law, when a person is arrested for an alleged violation of Section 278 or 278.5, the court shall, at the time of the arraignment or thereafter, order that the child shall be returned to the lawful custodian by or on a specific date, or that the person show cause on that date why the child has not been returned as ordered. If conflicting custodial orders exist within this state, or between this state and a foreign state, the court shall set a hearing within five court days to determine which court has jurisdiction under the laws of this state and determine which state has subject matter jurisdiction to issue a custodial order under the laws of this state, the Uniform Child Custody Jurisdiction Act (Part 3 (commencing with Section 3400) of Division 8 of the Family Code), or federal law, if applicable. At the conclusion of the hearing, or if the child has not been returned as ordered by the court at the time of arraignment, the court shall enter an order as to which custody order is valid and is to be enforced. If the child has not been returned at the conclusion of the hearing, the court shall set a date within a reasonable time by which the child shall be returned to the lawful custodian, and order the defendant to comply by this date, or to show cause on that date why he or she has not returned the child as directed. The court shall only enforce its order, or any subsequent orders for the return of the child, under subdivision (a) of Section 1219 of the Code of Civil Procedure, to ensure that the child is promptly placed with the lawful custodian. An order adverse to either the prosecution or defense is reviewable by a writ of mandate or prohibition addressed to the appropriate court.
(Added by Stats. 1996, Ch. 988, Sec. 9. Effective January 1, 1997.)

280.

Every person who willfully causes or permits the removal or concealment of any child in violation of Section 8713, 8803, or 8910 of the Family Code shall be punished as follows:
(a) By imprisonment in a county jail for not more than one year if the child is concealed within the county in which the adoption proceeding is pending or in which the child has been placed for adoption, or is removed from that county to a place within this state.
(b) By imprisonment pursuant to subdivision (h) of Section 1170, or by imprisonment in a county jail for not more than one year, if the child is removed from that county to a place outside of this state.
(Amended by Stats. 2011, Ch. 15, Sec. 315. (AB 109) Effective April 4, 2011. Operative October 1, 2011, by Sec. 636 of Ch. 15, as amended by Stats. 2011, Ch. 39, Sec. 68.)

CHAPTER 5. Bigamy, Incest, and the Crime Against Nature [281 - 289.6]

(Chapter 5 enacted 1872.)

281.

(a) Every person having a spouse living, who marries or enters into a registered domestic partnership with any other person, except in the cases specified in Section 282, is guilty of bigamy.
(b) Upon a trial for bigamy, it is not necessary to prove either of the marriages or registered domestic partnerships by the register, certificate, or other record evidence thereof, but the marriages or registered domestic partnerships may be proved by evidence which is admissible to prove a marriage or registered domestic partnership in other cases; and when the second marriage or registered domestic partnership took place out of this state, proof of that fact, accompanied with proof of cohabitation thereafter in this state, is sufficient to sustain the charge.
(Amended by Stats. 2016, Ch. 50, Sec. 70. (SB 1005) Effective January 1, 2017.)

282.

Section 281 does not extend to any of the following:
(a) To any person by reason of any former marriage or former registered domestic partnership whose spouse by such marriage or registered domestic partnership has been absent for five successive years without being known to such person within that time to be living.
(b) To any person by reason of any former marriage, or any former registered domestic partnership, which has been pronounced void, annulled, or dissolved by the judgment of a competent court.
(Amended by Stats. 2016, Ch. 50, Sec. 71. (SB 1005) Effective January 1, 2017.)

283.

Bigamy is punishable by a fine not exceeding ten thousand dollars ($10,000) or by imprisonment in a county jail not exceeding one year or in the state prison.
(Amended by Stats. 1983, Ch. 1092, Sec. 264. Effective September 27, 1983. Operative January 1, 1984, by Sec. 427 of Ch. 1092.)

284.

Every person who knowingly and willfully marries or enters into a registered domestic partnership with the spouse of another, in any case in which such spouse would be punishable under the provisions of this chapter, is punishable by a fine not less than five thousand dollars ($5,000), or by imprisonment pursuant to subdivision (h) of Section 1170.
(Amended by Stats. 2016, Ch. 50, Sec. 72. (SB 1005) Effective January 1, 2017.)

285.

Persons being within the degrees of consanguinity within which marriages are declared by law to be incestuous and void, who intermarry with each other, or who being 14 years of age or older, commit fornication or adultery with each other, are punishable by imprisonment in the state prison.
(Amended by Stats. 2005, Ch. 477, Sec. 1. Effective January 1, 2006.)

286.

(a) Sodomy is sexual conduct consisting of contact between the penis of one person and the anus of another person. Any sexual penetration, however slight, is sufficient to complete the crime of sodomy.
(b) (1) Except as provided in Section 288, any person who participates in an act of sodomy with another person who is under 18 years of age shall be punished by imprisonment in the state prison, or in a county jail for not more than one year.
(2) Except as provided in Section 288, any person over 21 years of age who participates in an act of sodomy with another person who is under 16 years of age shall be guilty of a felony.
(c) (1) Any person who participates in an act of sodomy with another person who is under 14 years of age and more than 10 years younger than he or she shall be punished by imprisonment in the state prison for three, six, or eight years.
(2) (A) Any person who commits an act of sodomy when the act is accomplished against the victim's will by means of force, violence, duress, menace, or fear of immediate and unlawful bodily injury on the victim or another person shall be punished by imprisonment in the state prison for three, six, or eight years.
(B) Any person who commits an act of sodomy with another person who is under 14 years of age when the act is accomplished against the victim's will by means of force, violence, duress, menace, or fear of immediate and unlawful bodily injury on the victim or another person shall be punished by imprisonment in the state prison for 9, 11, or 13 years.
(C) Any person who commits an act of sodomy with another person who is a minor 14 years of age or older when the act is accomplished against the victim's will by means of force, violence, duress, menace, or fear of immediate and unlawful bodily injury on the victim or another person shall be punished by imprisonment in the state prison for 7, 9, or 11 years.
(D) This paragraph does not preclude prosecution under Section 269, Section 288.7, or any other provision of law.
(3) Any person who commits an act of sodomy where the act is accomplished against the victim's will by threatening to retaliate in the future against the victim or any other person, and there is a reasonable possibility that the perpetrator will execute the threat, shall be punished by imprisonment in the state prison for three, six, or eight years.
(d) (1) Any person who, while voluntarily acting in concert with another person, either personally or aiding and abetting that other person, commits an act of sodomy when the act is accomplished against the victim's will by means of force or fear of immediate and unlawful bodily injury on the victim or another person or where the act is accomplished against the victim's will by threatening to retaliate in the future against the victim or any other person, and there is a reasonable possibility that the perpetrator will execute the threat, shall be punished by imprisonment in the state prison for five, seven, or nine years.
(2) Any person who, while voluntarily acting in concert with another person, either personally or aiding and abetting that other person, commits an act of sodomy upon a victim who is under 14 years of age, when the act is accomplished against the victim's will by means of force or fear of immediate and unlawful bodily injury on the victim or another person, shall be punished by imprisonment in the state prison for 10, 12, or 14 years.
(3) Any person who, while voluntarily acting in concert with another person, either personally or aiding and abetting that other person, commits an act of sodomy upon a victim who is a minor 14 years of age or older, when the act is accomplished against the victim's will by means of force or fear of immediate and unlawful bodily injury on the victim or another person, shall be punished by imprisonment in the state prison for 7, 9, or 11 years.
(4) This subdivision does not preclude prosecution under Section 269, Section 288.7, or any other provision of law.
(e) Any person who participates in an act of sodomy with any person of any age while confined in any state prison, as defined in Section 4504, or in any local detention facility, as defined in Section 6031.4, shall be punished by imprisonment in the state prison, or in a county jail for not more than one year.
(f) Any person who commits an act of sodomy, and the victim is at the time unconscious of the nature of the act and this is known to the person committing the act, shall be punished by imprisonment in the state prison for three, six, or eight years. As used in this subdivision, "unconscious of the nature of the act" means incapable of resisting because the victim meets one of the following conditions:
(1) Was unconscious or asleep.
(2) Was not aware, knowing, perceiving, or cognizant that the act occurred.
(3) Was not aware, knowing, perceiving, or cognizant of the essential characteristics of the act due to the perpetrator's fraud in fact.
(4) Was not aware, knowing, perceiving, or cognizant of the essential characteristics of the act due to the perpetrator's fraudulent representation that the sexual penetration served a professional purpose when it served no professional purpose.
(g) Except as provided in subdivision (h), a person who commits an act of sodomy, and the victim is at the time incapable, because of a mental disorder or developmental or physical disability, of giving legal consent, and this is known or reasonably should be known to the person committing the act, shall be punished by imprisonment in the state prison for three, six, or eight years. Notwithstanding the existence of a conservatorship pursuant to the Lanterman-Petris-Short Act (Part 1 (commencing with Section 5000) of Division 5 of the Welfare and Institutions Code), the prosecuting attorney shall prove, as

an element of the crime, that a mental disorder or developmental or physical disability rendered the alleged victim incapable of giving consent.
(h) Any person who commits an act of sodomy, and the victim is at the time incapable, because of a mental disorder or developmental or physical disability, of giving legal consent, and this is known or reasonably should be known to the person committing the act, and both the defendant and the victim are at the time confined in a state hospital for the care and treatment of the mentally disordered or in any other public or private facility for the care and treatment of the mentally disordered approved by a county mental health director, shall be punished by imprisonment in the state prison, or in a county jail for not more than one year. Notwithstanding the existence of a conservatorship pursuant to the Lanterman-Petris-Short Act (Part 1 (commencing with Section 5000) of Division 5 of the Welfare and Institutions Code), the prosecuting attorney shall prove, as an element of the crime, that a mental disorder or developmental or physical disability rendered the alleged victim incapable of giving legal consent.
(i) Any person who commits an act of sodomy, where the victim is prevented from resisting by an intoxicating or anesthetic substance, or any controlled substance, and this condition was known, or reasonably should have been known by the accused, shall be punished by imprisonment in the state prison for three, six, or eight years.
(j) Any person who commits an act of sodomy, where the victim submits under the belief that the person committing the act is someone known to the victim other than the accused, and this belief is induced by any artifice, pretense, or concealment practiced by the accused, with intent to induce the belief, shall be punished by imprisonment in the state prison for three, six, or eight years.
(k) Any person who commits an act of sodomy, where the act is accomplished against the victim's will by threatening to use the authority of a public official to incarcerate, arrest, or deport the victim or another, and the victim has a reasonable belief that the perpetrator is a public official, shall be punished by imprisonment in the state prison for three, six, or eight years.
As used in this subdivision, "public official" means a person employed by a governmental agency who has the authority, as part of that position, to incarcerate, arrest, or deport another. The perpetrator does not actually have to be a public official.
(l) As used in subdivisions (c) and (d), "threatening to retaliate" means a threat to kidnap or falsely imprison, or inflict extreme pain, serious bodily injury, or death.
(m) In addition to any punishment imposed under this section, the judge may assess a fine not to exceed seventy dollars ($70) against any person who violates this section, with the proceeds of this fine to be used in accordance with Section 1463.23. The court, however, shall take into consideration the defendant's ability to pay, and no defendant shall be denied probation because of his or her inability to pay the fine permitted under this subdivision.
(Amended by Stats. 2013, Ch. 259, Sec. 2. (AB 65) Effective September 9, 2013.)

286.5.
Any person who sexually assaults any animal protected by Section 597f for the purpose of arousing or gratifying the sexual desire of the person is guilty of a misdemeanor.
(Added by Stats. 1975, Ch. 71.)

287.
(a) Oral copulation is the act of copulating the mouth of one person with the sexual organ or anus of another person.
(b) (1) Except as provided in Section 288, any person who participates in an act of oral copulation with another person who is under 18 years of age shall be punished by imprisonment in the state prison, or in a county jail for a period of not more than one year.
(2) Except as provided in Section 288, any person over 21 years of age who participates in an act of oral copulation with another person who is under 16 years of age is guilty of a felony.
(c) (1) Any person who participates in an act of oral copulation with another person who is under 14 years of age and more than 10 years younger than he or she shall be punished by imprisonment in the state prison for three, six, or eight years.
(2) (A) Any person who commits an act of oral copulation when the act is accomplished against the victim's will by means of force, violence, duress, menace, or fear of immediate and unlawful bodily injury on the victim or another person shall be punished by imprisonment in the state prison for three, six, or eight years.
(B) Any person who commits an act of oral copulation upon a person who is under 14 years of age, when the act is accomplished against the victim's will by means of force, violence, duress, menace, or fear of immediate and unlawful bodily injury on the victim or another person, shall be punished by imprisonment in the state prison for 8, 10, or 12 years.
(C) Any person who commits an act of oral copulation upon a minor who is 14 years of age or older, when the act is accomplished against the victim's will by means of force, violence, duress, menace, or fear of immediate and unlawful bodily injury on the victim or another person, shall be punished by imprisonment in the state prison for 6, 8, or 10 years.
(D) This paragraph does not preclude prosecution under Section 269, Section 288.7, or any other provision of law.
(3) Any person who commits an act of oral copulation where the act is accomplished against the victim's will by threatening to retaliate in the future against the victim or any other person, and there is a reasonable possibility that the perpetrator will execute the threat, shall be punished by imprisonment in the state prison for three, six, or eight years.
(d) (1) Any person who, while voluntarily acting in concert with another person, either personally or by aiding and abetting that other person, commits an act of oral copulation (A) when the act is accomplished against the victim's will by means of force or fear of immediate and unlawful bodily injury on the victim or another person, or (B) where the act is accomplished against the victim's will by threatening to retaliate in the future against the victim or any other person, and there is a reasonable possibility that the perpetrator will execute the threat, or (C) where the victim is at the time incapable, because of a mental disorder or developmental or physical disability, of giving legal consent, and this is known or reasonably should be known to the person committing the act, shall be punished by imprisonment in the state prison for five, seven, or nine years. Notwithstanding the appointment of a conservator with respect to the victim pursuant to the provisions of the Lanterman-Petris-Short Act (Part 1 (commencing with Section 5000) of Division 5 of the Welfare and Institutions Code), the prosecuting attorney shall prove, as an element of the crime described under paragraph (3), that a mental disorder or developmental or physical disability rendered the alleged victim incapable of giving legal consent.
(2) Any person who, while voluntarily acting in concert with another person, either personally or aiding and abetting that other person, commits an act of oral copulation upon a victim who is under 14 years of age, when the act is accomplished against the victim's will by means of force or fear of immediate and unlawful bodily injury on the victim or another person, shall be punished by imprisonment in the state prison for 10, 12, or 14 years.
(3) Any person who, while voluntarily acting in concert with another person, either personally or aiding and abetting that other person, commits an act of oral copulation upon a victim who is a minor 14 years of age or older, when the act is accomplished against the victim's will by means of force or fear of immediate and unlawful bodily injury on the victim or another person, shall be punished by imprisonment in the state prison for 8, 10, or 12 years.
(4) This paragraph does not preclude prosecution under Section 269, Section 288.7, or any other provision of law.
(e) Any person who participates in an act of oral copulation while confined in any state prison, as defined in Section 4504 or in any local detention facility as defined in Section 6031.4, shall be punished by imprisonment in the state prison, or in a county jail for a period of not more than one year.
(f) Any person who commits an act of oral copulation, and the victim is at the time unconscious of the nature of the act and this is known to the person committing the act, shall be punished by imprisonment in the state prison for a period of three, six, or eight years. As used in this subdivision, "unconscious of the nature of the act" means incapable of resisting because the victim meets one of the following conditions:
(1) Was unconscious or asleep.
(2) Was not aware, knowing, perceiving, or cognizant that the act occurred.
(3) Was not aware, knowing, perceiving, or cognizant of the essential characteristics of the act due to the perpetrator's fraud in fact.
(4) Was not aware, knowing, perceiving, or cognizant of the essential characteristics of the act due to the perpetrator's fraudulent representation that the oral copulation served a professional purpose when it served no professional purpose.
(g) Except as provided in subdivision (h), any person who commits an act of oral copulation, and the victim is at the time incapable, because of a mental disorder or developmental or physical disability, of giving legal consent, and this is known or reasonably should be known to the person committing the act, shall be punished by imprisonment in the state prison, for three, six, or eight years. Notwithstanding the existence of a conservatorship pursuant to the provisions of the Lanterman-Petris-Short Act (Part 1 (commencing with Section 5000) of Division 5 of the Welfare and Institutions Code), the prosecuting attorney shall prove, as an element of the crime, that a mental disorder or developmental or physical disability rendered the alleged victim incapable of giving consent.
(h) Any person who commits an act of oral copulation, and the victim is at the time incapable, because of a mental disorder or developmental or physical disability, of giving legal consent, and this is known or reasonably should be known to the person committing the act, and both the defendant and the victim are at the time confined in a state hospital for the care and treatment of the mentally disordered or in any other public or private facility for the care and treatment of the mentally disordered approved by a county mental health director, shall be punished by imprisonment in the state prison, or in a county jail for a period of not more than one year. Notwithstanding the existence of a conservatorship pursuant to the provisions of the Lanterman-Petris-Short Act (Part 1 (commencing with Section 5000) of Division 5 of the Welfare and Institutions Code), the prosecuting attorney shall prove, as an element of the crime, that a mental disorder or developmental or physical disability rendered the alleged victim incapable of giving legal consent.
(i) Any person who commits an act of oral copulation, where the victim is prevented from resisting by any intoxicating or anesthetic substance, or any controlled substance, and this condition was known, or reasonably should have been known by the accused, shall be punished by imprisonment in the state prison for a period of three, six, or eight years.
(j) Any person who commits an act of oral copulation, where the victim submits under the belief that the person committing the act is someone known to the victim other than the accused, and this belief is induced by any artifice, pretense, or concealment practiced by the accused, with intent to induce the belief, shall be punished by imprisonment in the state prison for a period of three, six, or eight years.
(k) Any person who commits an act of oral copulation, where the act is accomplished against the victim's will by threatening to use the authority of a public official to incarcerate, arrest, or deport the victim or another, and the victim has a reasonable belief that the perpetrator is a public official, shall be punished by imprisonment in the state prison for a period of three, six, or eight years.
As used in this subdivision, "public official" means a person employed by a governmental agency who has the authority, as part of that position, to incarcerate, arrest, or deport another. The perpetrator does not actually have to be a public official.
(l) As used in subdivisions (c) and (d), "threatening to retaliate" means a threat to kidnap or falsely imprison, or to inflict extreme pain, serious bodily injury, or death.
(m) In addition to any punishment imposed under this section, the judge may assess a fine not to exceed seventy dollars ($70) against any person who violates this section, with the proceeds of this fine to be used in accordance with Section 1463.23. The court shall, however, take into consideration the defendant's ability to pay, and no defendant shall be denied probation because of his or her inability to pay the fine permitted under this subdivision.
(Added by renumbering Section 288a by Stats. 2018, Ch. 423, Sec. 49. (SB 1494) Effective January 1, 2019.)

288.
(a) Except as provided in subdivision (i), a person who willfully and lewdly commits any lewd or lascivious act, including any of the acts constituting other crimes provided for in Part 1, upon or with the body, or any part or member thereof, of a child who is under the age of 14 years, with the intent of arousing, appealing to, or gratifying the lust, passions, or sexual desires of that person or the child, is guilty of a felony and shall be punished by imprisonment in the state prison for three, six, or eight years.
(b) (1) A person who commits an act described in subdivision (a) by use of force, violence, duress, menace, or fear of immediate and unlawful bodily injury on the victim or another person, is guilty of a felony and shall be punished by imprisonment in the state prison for 5, 8, or 10 years.
(2) A person who is a caretaker and commits an act described in subdivision (a) upon a dependent person by use of force, violence, duress, menace, or fear of immediate and unlawful bodily injury on the victim or another person, with the intent described in subdivision (a), is guilty of a felony and shall be punished by imprisonment in the state prison for 5, 8, or 10 years.
(c) (1) A person who commits an act described in subdivision (a) with the intent described in that subdivision, and the victim is a child of 14 or 15 years, and that person is at least 10 years older than the child, is guilty of a public offense and shall be punished by imprisonment in the state prison for one, two, or three years, or by imprisonment in a county jail for not more than one year. In determining whether the person is at least 10 years older than the child, the difference in age shall be measured from the birth date of the person to the birth date of the child.
(2) A person who is a caretaker and commits an act described in subdivision (a) upon a dependent person, with the intent described in subdivision (a), is guilty of a public offense and shall be punished by imprisonment in the state prison for one, two, or three years, or by imprisonment in a county jail for not more than one year.
(d) In any arrest or prosecution under this section or Section 288.5, the peace officer, district attorney, and the court shall consider the needs of the child victim or dependent person and shall do whatever is necessary, within existing budgetary resources, and constitutionally permissible to prevent psychological harm to the child victim or to prevent psychological harm to the dependent person victim resulting from participation in the court process.
(e) (1) Upon the conviction of a person for a violation of subdivision (a) or (b), the court may, in addition to any other penalty or fine imposed, order the defendant to pay an additional fine not to exceed ten thousand dollars ($10,000). In setting the amount of the fine, the court shall consider any relevant factors, including, but not limited to, the seriousness and gravity of the offense, the circumstances of its commission, whether the defendant derived any economic gain as a result of the crime, and the extent to which the victim suffered economic losses as a result of the crime. Every fine imposed and collected under this section shall be deposited in the Victim-Witness Assistance Fund to

be available for appropriation to fund child sexual exploitation and child sexual abuse victim counseling centers and prevention programs pursuant to Section 13837.

(2) If the court orders a fine imposed pursuant to this subdivision, the actual administrative cost of collecting that fine, not to exceed 2 percent of the total amount paid, may be paid into the general fund of the county treasury for the use and benefit of the county.

(f) For purposes of paragraph (2) of subdivision (b) and paragraph (2) of subdivision (c), the following definitions apply:

(1) "Caretaker" means an owner, operator, administrator, employee, independent contractor, agent, or volunteer of any of the following public or private facilities when the facilities provide care for elder or dependent persons:

(A) Twenty-four hour health facilities, as defined in Sections 1250, 1250.2, and 1250.3 of the Health and Safety Code.

(B) Clinics.

(C) Home health agencies.

(D) Adult day health care centers.

(E) Secondary schools that serve dependent persons and postsecondary educational institutions that serve dependent persons or elders.

(F) Sheltered workshops.

(G) Camps.

(H) Community care facilities, as defined by Section 1402 of the Health and Safety Code, and residential care facilities for the elderly, as defined in Section 1569.2 of the Health and Safety Code.

(I) Respite care facilities.

(J) Foster homes.

(K) Regional centers for persons with developmental disabilities.

(L) A home health agency licensed in accordance with Chapter 8 (commencing with Section 1725) of Division 2 of the Health and Safety Code.

(M) An agency that supplies in-home supportive services.

(N) Board and care facilities.

(O) Any other protective or public assistance agency that provides health services or social services to elder or dependent persons, including, but not limited to, in-home supportive services, as defined in Section 14005.14 of the Welfare and Institutions Code.

(P) Private residences.

(2) "Board and care facilities" means licensed or unlicensed facilities that provide assistance with one or more of the following activities:

(A) Bathing.

(B) Dressing.

(C) Grooming.

(D) Medication storage.

(E) Medical dispensation.

(F) Money management.

(3) "Dependent person" means a person, regardless of whether the person lives independently, who has a physical or mental impairment that substantially restricts his or her ability to carry out normal activities or to protect his or her rights, including, but not limited to, persons who have physical or developmental disabilities or whose physical or mental abilities have significantly diminished because of age. "Dependent person" includes a person who is admitted as an inpatient to a 24-hour health facility, as defined in Sections 1250, 1250.2, and 1250.3 of the Health and Safety Code.

(g) Paragraph (2) of subdivision (b) and paragraph (2) of subdivision (c) apply to the owners, operators, administrators, employees, independent contractors, agents, or volunteers working at these public or private facilities and only to the extent that the individuals personally commit, conspire, aid, abet, or facilitate any act prohibited by paragraph (2) of subdivision (b) and paragraph (2) of subdivision (c).

(h) Paragraph (2) of subdivision (b) and paragraph (2) of subdivision (c) do not apply to a caretaker who is a spouse of, or who is in an equivalent domestic relationship with, the dependent person under care.

(i) (1) A person convicted of a violation of subdivision (a) shall be imprisoned in the state prison for life with the possibility of parole if the defendant personally inflicted bodily harm upon the victim.

(2) The penalty provided in this subdivision shall only apply if the fact that the defendant personally inflicted bodily harm upon the victim is pled and proved.

(3) As used in this subdivision, "bodily harm" means any substantial physical injury resulting from the use of force that is more than the force necessary to commit the offense.

(Amended by Stats. 2018, Ch. 70, Sec. 2. (AB 1934) Effective January 1, 2019.)

288.1.

Any person convicted of committing any lewd or lascivious act including any of the acts constituting other crimes provided for in Part 1 of this code upon or with the body, or any part or member thereof, of a child under the age of 14 years shall not have his or her sentence suspended until the court obtains a report from a reputable psychiatrist, from a reputable psychologist who meets the standards set forth in Section 1027, as to the mental condition of that person.

(Amended by Stats. 2005, Ch. 477, Sec. 2. Effective January 1, 2006.)

288.2.

(a) (1) Every person who knows, should have known, or believes that another person is a minor, and who knowingly distributes, sends, causes to be sent, exhibits, or offers to distribute or exhibit by any means, including by physical delivery, telephone, electronic communication, or in person, any harmful matter that depicts a minor or minors engaging in sexual conduct, to the other person with the intent of arousing, appealing to, or gratifying the lust or passions or sexual desires of that person or of the minor, and with the intent or for the purposes of engaging in sexual intercourse, sodomy, or oral copulation with the other person, or with the intent that either person touch an intimate body part of the other, is guilty of a misdemeanor, punishable by imprisonment in a county jail not exceeding one year, or is guilty of a felony, punishable by imprisonment in the state prison for two, three, or five years.

(2) If the matter used by the person is harmful matter but does not include a depiction or depictions of a minor or minors engaged in sexual conduct, the offense is punishable by imprisonment in a county jail not exceeding one year, or by imprisonment in the state prison for 16 months, or two or three years.

(3) For purposes of this subdivision, the offense described in paragraph (2) shall include all of the elements described in paragraph (1), except as to the element modified in paragraph (2).

(b) For purposes of this section, "sexual conduct" has the same meaning as defined in subdivision (d) of Section 311.4.

(c) For purposes of this section, "harmful matter" has the same meaning as defined in Section 313.

(d) For purposes of this section, an intimate body part includes the sexual organ, anus, groin, or buttocks of any person, or the breasts of a female.

(e) Prosecution under this section shall not preclude prosecution under any other provision of law.

(f) It shall be a defense to any prosecution under this section that a parent or guardian committed the act charged in aid of legitimate sex education.

(g) It shall be a defense in any prosecution under this section that the act charged was committed in aid of legitimate scientific or educational purposes.

(h) It does not constitute a violation of this section for a telephone corporation, as defined in Section 234 of the Public Utilities Code, a cable television company franchised pursuant to Section 53066 of the Government Code, or any of its affiliates, an Internet service provider, or commercial online service provider, to carry, broadcast, or transmit messages described in this section or perform related activities in providing telephone, cable television, Internet, or commercial online services.

(Repealed and added by Stats. 2013, Ch. 777, Sec. 2. (SB 145) Effective January 1, 2014.)

288.3.

(a) Every person who contacts or communicates with a minor, or attempts to contact or communicate with a minor, who knows or reasonably should know that the person is a minor, with intent to commit an offense specified in Section 207, 209, 261, 264.1, 273a, 286, 287, 288, 288.2, 289, 311.1, 311.2, 311.4 or 311.11, or former Section 288a, involving the minor shall be punished by imprisonment in the state prison for the term prescribed for an attempt to commit the intended offense.

(b) As used in this section, "contacts or communicates with" shall include direct and indirect contact or communication that may be achieved personally or by use of an agent or agency, any print medium, any postal service, a common carrier or communication common carrier, any electronic communications system, or any telecommunications, wire, computer, or radio communications device or system.

(c) A person convicted of a violation of subdivision (a) who has previously been convicted of a violation of subdivision (a) shall be punished by an additional and consecutive term of imprisonment in the state prison for five years.

(Amended by Stats. 2018, Ch. 423, Sec. 48. (SB 1494) Effective January 1, 2019. Note: This section was added November 7, 2006, by initiative Proposition 83.)

288.4.

(a) (1) Every person who, motivated by an unnatural or abnormal sexual interest in children, arranges a meeting with a minor or a person he or she believes to be a minor for the purpose of exposing his or her genitals or pubic or rectal area, having the child expose his or her genitals or pubic or rectal area, or engaging in lewd or lascivious behavior, shall be punished by a fine not exceeding five thousand dollars ($5,000), by imprisonment in a county jail not exceeding one year, or by both the fine and imprisonment.

(2) Every person who violates this subdivision after a prior conviction for an offense listed in subdivision (c) of Section 290 shall be punished by imprisonment in the state prison.

(b) Every person described in paragraph (1) of subdivision (a) who goes to the arranged meeting place at or about the arranged time, shall be punished by imprisonment in the state prison for two, three, or four years.

(c) Nothing in this section shall preclude or prohibit prosecution under any other provision of law.

(Added by renumbering Section 288.3 (as added by Stats. 2006, Ch. 337) by Stats. 2007, Ch. 579, Sec. 5. Effective October 13, 2007.)

288.5.

(a) Any person who either resides in the same home with the minor child or has recurring access to the child, who over a period of time, not less than three months in duration, engages in three or more acts of substantial sexual conduct with a child under the age of 14 years at the time of the commission of the offense, as defined in subdivision (b) of Section 1203.066, or three or more acts of lewd or lascivious conduct, as defined in Section 288, with a child under the age of 14 years at the time of the commission of the offense is guilty of the offense of continuous sexual abuse of a child and shall be punished by imprisonment in the state prison for a term of 6, 12, or 16 years.

(b) To convict under this section the trier of fact, if a jury, need unanimously agree only that the requisite number of acts occurred not on which acts constitute the requisite number.

(c) No other act of substantial sexual conduct, as defined in subdivision (b) of Section 1203.066, with a child under 14 years of age at the time of the commission of the offenses, or lewd and lascivious acts, as defined in Section 288, involving the same victim may be charged in the same proceeding with a charge under this section unless the other charged offense occurred outside the time period charged under this section or the other offense is charged in the alternative. A defendant may be charged with only one count under this section unless more than one victim is involved in which case a separate count may be charged for each victim.

(Amended by Stats. 2006, Ch. 337, Sec. 8. Effective September 20, 2006.)

288.7.

(a) Any person 18 years of age or older who engages in sexual intercourse or sodomy with a child who is 10 years of age or younger is guilty of a felony and shall be punished by imprisonment in the state prison for a term of 25 years to life.

(b) Any person 18 years of age or older who engages in oral copulation or sexual penetration, as defined in Section 289, with a child who is 10 years of age or younger is guilty of a felony and shall be punished by imprisonment in the state prison for a term of 15 years to life.

(Added by Stats. 2006, Ch. 337, Sec. 9. Effective September 20, 2006.)

289.

(a) (1) (A) Any person who commits an act of sexual penetration when the act is accomplished against the victim's will by means of force, violence, duress, menace, or fear of immediate and unlawful bodily injury on the victim or another person shall be punished by imprisonment in the state prison for three, six, or eight years.

(B) Any person who commits an act of sexual penetration upon a child who is under 14 years of age, when the act is accomplished against the victim's will by means of force, violence, duress, menace, or fear of immediate and unlawful bodily injury on the victim or another person, shall be punished by imprisonment in the state prison for 8, 10, or 12 years.

(C) Any person who commits an act of sexual penetration upon a minor who is 14 years of age or older, when the act is accomplished against the victim's will by means of force, violence, duress, menace, or fear of immediate and unlawful bodily injury on the victim or another person, shall be punished by imprisonment in the state prison for 6, 8, or 10 years.

(D) This paragraph does not preclude prosecution under Section 269, Section 288.7, or any other provision of law.

(2) Any person who commits an act of sexual penetration when the act is accomplished against the victim's will by threatening to retaliate in the future against the victim or any other person, and there is a reasonable possibility that the perpetrator will execute the threat, shall be punished by imprisonment in the state prison for three, six, or eight years.

(b) Except as provided in subdivision (c), any person who commits an act of sexual penetration, and the victim is at the time incapable, because of a mental disorder or developmental or physical disability, of giving legal consent, and this is known or reasonably should be known to the person committing the act or causing the act to be committed, shall be punished by imprisonment in the state prison for three, six, or eight years. Notwithstanding the appointment of a conservator with respect to the victim pursuant to the provisions of the Lanterman-Petris-Short Act (Part 1 (commencing with Section 5000) of Division 5 of the Welfare and Institutions Code), the prosecuting attorney shall prove, as an element of the crime, that a mental disorder or developmental or physical disability rendered the alleged victim incapable of giving legal consent.

(c) Any person who commits an act of sexual penetration, and the victim is at the time incapable, because of a mental disorder or developmental or physical disability, of giving legal consent, and this is known or reasonably should be known to the person committing the act or causing the act to be committed and both the defendant and the victim are at the time confined in a state hospital for the care and treatment of the mentally disordered or in any other public or private facility for the care and treatment of the mentally disordered approved by a county mental health director, shall be punished by imprisonment in the state prison, or in a county jail for a period of not more than one year. Notwithstanding the existence of a conservatorship pursuant to the provisions of the Lanterman-Petris-Short Act (Part 1 (commencing with Section 5000) of Division 5 of the Welfare and Institutions Code), the prosecuting attorney shall prove, as an element of the crime, that a mental disorder or developmental or physical disability rendered the alleged victim incapable of giving legal consent.

(d) Any person who commits an act of sexual penetration, and the victim is at the time unconscious of the nature of the act and this is known to the person committing the act or causing the act to be committed, shall be punished by imprisonment in the state prison for three, six, or eight years. As used in this subdivision, "unconscious of the nature of the act" means incapable of resisting because the victim meets one of the following conditions:

(1) Was unconscious or asleep.

(2) Was not aware, knowing, perceiving, or cognizant that the act occurred.

(3) Was not aware, knowing, perceiving, or cognizant of the essential characteristics of the act due to the perpetrator's fraud in fact.

(4) Was not aware, knowing, perceiving, or cognizant of the essential characteristics of the act due to the perpetrator's fraudulent representation that the sexual penetration served a professional purpose when it served no professional purpose.

(e) Any person who commits an act of sexual penetration when the victim is prevented from resisting by any intoxicating or anesthetic substance, or any controlled substance, and this condition was known, or reasonably should have been known by the accused, shall be punished by imprisonment in the state prison for a period of three, six, or eight years.

(f) Any person who commits an act of sexual penetration when the victim submits under the belief that the person committing the act or causing the act to be committed is someone known to the victim other than the accused, and this belief is induced by any artifice, pretense, or concealment practiced by the accused, with intent to induce the belief, shall be punished by imprisonment in the state prison for a period of three, six, or eight years.

(g) Any person who commits an act of sexual penetration when the act is accomplished against the victim's will by threatening to use the authority of a public official to incarcerate, arrest, or deport the victim or another, and the victim has a reasonable belief that the perpetrator is a public official, shall be punished by imprisonment in the state prison for a period of three, six, or eight years.

As used in this subdivision, "public official" means a person employed by a governmental agency who has the authority, as part of that position, to incarcerate, arrest, or deport another. The perpetrator does not actually have to be a public official.

(h) Except as provided in Section 288, any person who participates in an act of sexual penetration with another person who is under 18 years of age shall be punished by imprisonment in the state prison or in a county jail for a period of not more than one year.

(i) Except as provided in Section 288, any person over 21 years of age who participates in an act of sexual penetration with another person who is under 16 years of age shall be guilty of a felony.

(j) Any person who participates in an act of sexual penetration with another person who is under 14 years of age and who is more than 10 years younger than he or she shall be punished by imprisonment in the state prison for three, six, or eight years.

(k) As used in this section:

(1) "Sexual penetration" is the act of causing the penetration, however slight, of the genital or anal opening of any person or causing another person to so penetrate the defendant's or another person's genital or anal opening for the purpose of sexual arousal, gratification, or abuse by any foreign object, substance, instrument, or device, or by any unknown object.

(2) "Foreign object, substance, instrument, or device" shall include any part of the body, except a sexual organ.

(3) "Unknown object" shall include any foreign object, substance, instrument, or device, or any part of the body, including a penis, when it is not known whether penetration was by a penis or by a foreign object, substance, instrument, or device, or by any other part of the body.

(l) As used in subdivision (a), "threatening to retaliate" means a threat to kidnap or falsely imprison, or inflict extreme pain, serious bodily injury or death.

(m) As used in this section, "victim" includes any person who the defendant causes to penetrate the genital or anal opening of the defendant or another person or whose genital or anal opening is caused to be penetrated by the defendant or another person and who otherwise qualifies as a victim under the requirements of this section.

(Amended by Stats. 2013, Ch. 282, Sec. 2. (SB 59) Effective September 9, 2013.)

289.5.

(a) Every person who flees to this state with the intent to avoid prosecution for an offense which, if committed or attempted in this state, would have been punishable as one or more of the offenses described in subdivision (c) of Section 290, and who has been charged with that offense under the laws of the jurisdiction from which the person fled, is guilty of a misdemeanor.

(b) Every person who flees to this state with the intent to avoid custody or confinement imposed for conviction of an offense under the laws of the jurisdiction from which the person fled, which offense, if committed or attempted in this state, would have been punishable as one or more of the offenses described in subdivision (c) of Section 290, is guilty of a misdemeanor.

(c) No person shall be charged and prosecuted for an offense under this section unless the prosecutor has requested the other jurisdiction to extradite the person and the other jurisdiction has refused to do so.

(d) Any person who is convicted of any felony sex offense described in subdivision (c) of Section 290, that is committed after fleeing to this state under the circumstances described in subdivision (a) or (b) of this section, shall, in addition and consecutive to the punishment for that conviction, receive an additional term of two years' imprisonment.

(Amended by Stats. 2007, Ch. 579, Sec. 6. Effective October 13, 2007.)

289.6.

(a) (1) An employee or officer of a public entity health facility, or an employee, officer, or agent of a private person or entity that provides a health facility or staff for a health facility under contract with a public entity, who engages in sexual activity with a consenting adult who is confined in a health facility is guilty of a public offense. As used in this paragraph, "health facility" means a health facility as defined in subdivisions (b), (e), (g), (h), and (j) of, and subparagraph (C) of paragraph (2) of subdivision (i) of, Section 1250 of the Health and Safety Code, in which the victim has been confined involuntarily.

(2) An employee or officer of a public entity detention facility, or an employee, officer, agent of a private person or entity that provides a detention facility or staff for a detention facility, a person or agent of a public or private entity under contract with a detention facility, a volunteer of a private or public entity detention facility, or a peace officer who engages in sexual activity with a consenting adult who is confined in a detention facility is guilty of a public offense.

(3) An employee with a department, board, or authority under the Department of Corrections and Rehabilitation or a facility under contract with a department, board, or authority under the Department of Corrections and Rehabilitation, who, during the course of his or her employment directly provides treatment, care, control, or

supervision of inmates, wards, or parolees, and who engages in sexual activity with a consenting adult who is an inmate, ward, or parolee, is guilty of a public offense.

(b) As used in this section, the term "public entity" means the state, federal government, a city, a county, a city and county, a joint county jail district, or any entity created as a result of a joint powers agreement between two or more public entities.

(c) As used in this section, the term "detention facility" means:

(1) A prison, jail, camp, or other correctional facility used for the confinement of adults or both adults and minors.

(2) A building or facility used for the confinement of adults or adults and minors pursuant to a contract with a public entity.

(3) A room that is used for holding persons for interviews, interrogations, or investigations and that is separate from a jail or located in the administrative area of a law enforcement facility.

(4) A vehicle used to transport confined persons during their period of confinement, including transporting a person after he or she has been arrested but has not been booked.

(5) A court holding facility located within or adjacent to a court building that is used for the confinement of persons for the purpose of court appearances.

(d) As used in this section, "sexual activity" means:

(1) Sexual intercourse.

(2) Sodomy, as defined in subdivision (a) of Section 286.

(3) Oral copulation, as defined in subdivision (a) of Section 287 or former Section 288a.

(4) Sexual penetration, as defined in subdivision (k) of Section 289.

(5) The rubbing or touching of the breasts or sexual organs of another, or of oneself in the presence of and with knowledge of another, with the intent of arousing, appealing to, or gratifying the lust, passions, or sexual desires of oneself or another.

(e) Consent by a confined person or parolee to sexual activity proscribed by this section is not a defense to a criminal prosecution for violation of this section.

(f) This section does not apply to sexual activity between consenting adults that occurs during an overnight conjugal visit that takes place pursuant to a court order or with the written approval of an authorized representative of the public entity that operates or contracts for the operation of the detention facility where the conjugal visit takes place, to physical contact or penetration made pursuant to a lawful search, or bona fide medical examinations or treatments, including clinical treatments.

(g) Any violation of paragraph (1) of subdivision (a), or a violation of paragraph (2) or (3) of subdivision (a) as described in paragraph (5) of subdivision (d), is a misdemeanor.

(h) Any violation of paragraph (2) or (3) of subdivision (a), as described in paragraph (1), (2), (3), or (4) of subdivision (d), shall be punished by imprisonment in a county jail not exceeding one year, or in the state prison, or by a fine of not more than ten thousand dollars ($10,000) or by both that fine and imprisonment.

(i) Any person previously convicted of a violation of this section shall, upon a subsequent violation, be guilty of a felony.

(j) Anyone who is convicted of a felony violation of this section who is employed by a department, board, or authority within the Department of Corrections and Rehabilitation shall be terminated in accordance with the State Civil Service Act (Part 2 (commencing with Section 18500) of Division 5 of Title 2 of the Government Code). Anyone who has been convicted of a felony violation of this section shall not be eligible to be hired or reinstated by a department, board, or authority within the Department of Corrections and Rehabilitation.

(Amended by Stats. 2018, Ch. 423, Sec. 50. (SB 1494) Effective January 1, 2019.)

CHAPTER 5.5. Sex Offenders [290 - 294]

(Chapter 5.5 heading added by Stats. 2006, Ch. 337, Sec. 10.)

290.

(a) Sections 290 to 290.024, inclusive, shall be known and may be cited as the Sex Offender Registration Act. All references to "the Act" in those sections are to the Sex Offender Registration Act.

(b) Every person described in subdivision (c), for the rest of his or her life while residing in California, or while attending school or working in California, as described in Sections 290.002 and 290.01, shall register with the chief of police of the city in which he or she is residing, or the sheriff of the county if he or she is residing in an unincorporated area or city that has no police department, and, additionally, with the chief of police of a campus of the University of California, the California State University, or community college if he or she is residing upon the campus or in any of its facilities, within five working days of coming into, or changing his or her residence within, any city, county, or city and county, or campus in which he or she temporarily resides, and shall be required to register thereafter in accordance with the Act.

(c) The following persons shall register:

Any person who, since July 1, 1944, has been or is hereafter convicted in any court in this state or in any federal or military court of a violation of Section 187 committed in the perpetration, or an attempt to perpetrate, rape or any act punishable under Section 286, 287, 288, or 289 or former Section 288a, Section 207 or 209 committed with intent to violate Section 261, 286, 287, 288, or 289 or former Section 288a, Section 220, except assault to commit mayhem, subdivision (b) and (c) of Section 236.1, Section 243.4, Section 261, paragraph (1) of subdivision (a) of Section 262 involving the use of force or violence for which the person is sentenced to the state prison, Section 264.1, 266, or 266c, subdivision (b) of Section 266h, subdivision (b) of Section 266i, Section 266j, 267, 269, 285, 286, 287, 288, 288.3, 288.4, 288.5, 288.7, 289, or 311.1, or former Section 288a, subdivision (b), (c), or (d) of Section 311.2, Section 311.3, 311.4, 311.10, 311.11, or 647.6, former Section 647a, subdivision (c) of Section 653f, subdivision 1 or 2 of Section 314, any offense involving lewd or lascivious conduct under Section 272, or any felony violation of Section 288.2; any statutory predecessor that includes all elements of one of the above-mentioned offenses; or any person who since that date has been or is hereafter convicted of the attempt or conspiracy to commit any of the above-mentioned offenses.

(d) This section shall remain in effect only until January 1, 2021, and as of that date is repealed.

(Amended (as amended by Stats. 2017, Ch. 541, Sec. 1.5) by Stats. 2018, Ch. 423, Sec. 51. (SB 1494) Effective January 1, 2019. Repealed as of January 1, 2021, by its own provisions. See later operative version amended by Sec. 52 of Stats. 2018, Ch. 290. Note: This section was amended on November 6, 2012, by initiative Prop. 35.)

290.

(a) Sections 290 to 290.024, inclusive, shall be known, and may be cited, as the Sex Offender Registration Act. All references to "the Act" in those sections are to the Sex Offender Registration Act.

(b) Every person described in subdivision (c), for the period specified in subdivision (d) while residing in California, or while attending school or working in California, as described in Sections 290.002 and 290.01, shall register with the chief of police of the city in which he or she is residing, or the sheriff of the county if he or she is residing in an unincorporated area or city that has no police department, and, additionally, with the chief of police of a campus of the University of California, the California State University, or community college if he or she is residing upon the campus or in any of its facilities, within five working days of coming into, or changing his or her residence within, any city, county, or city and county, or campus in which he or she temporarily resides, and shall register thereafter in accordance with the Act, unless the duty to register is terminated pursuant to Section 290.5 or as otherwise provided by law.

(c) The following persons shall register:

Every person who, since July 1, 1944, has been or is hereafter convicted in any court in this state or in any federal or military court of a violation of Section 187 committed in the perpetration, or an attempt to perpetrate, rape or any act punishable under Section 286, 287, 288, or 289 or former Section 288a, Section 207 or 209 committed with intent to violate Section 261, 286, 287, 288, or 289 or former Section 288a, Section 220, except assault to commit mayhem, subdivision (b) or (c) of Section 236.1, Section 243.4, Section 261, paragraph (1) of subdivision (a) of Section 262 involving the use of force or violence for which the person is sentenced to the state prison, Section 264.1, 266, or 266c, subdivision (b) of Section 266h, subdivision (b) of Section 266i, Section 266j, 267, 269, 285, 286, 287, 288, 288.3, 288.4, 288.5, 288.7, 289, or 311.1, or former Section 288a, subdivision (b), (c), or (d) of Section 311.2, Section 311.3, 311.4, 311.10, 311.11, or 647.6, former Section 647a, subdivision (c) of Section 653f, subdivision 1 or 2 of Section 314, any offense involving lewd or lascivious conduct under Section 272, or any felony violation of Section 288.2; any statutory predecessor that includes all elements of one of the offenses described in this subdivision; or any person who since that date has been or is hereafter convicted of the attempt or conspiracy to commit any of the offenses described in this subdivision.

(d) A person described in subdivision (c), or who is otherwise required to register pursuant to the Act shall register for 10 years, 20 years, or life, following a conviction and release from incarceration, placement, commitment, or release on probation or other supervision, as follows:

(1) (A) A tier one offender is subject to registration for a minimum of 10 years. A person is a tier one offender if the person is required to register for conviction of a misdemeanor described in subdivision (c), or for conviction of a felony described in subdivision (c) that was not a serious or violent felony as described in subdivision (c) of Section 667.5 or subdivision (c) of Section 1192.7.

(B) This paragraph does not apply to a person who is subject to registration pursuant to paragraph (2) or (3).

(2) (A) A tier two offender is subject to registration for a minimum of 20 years. A person is a tier two offender if the person was convicted of an offense described in subdivision (c) that is also described in subdivision (c) of Section 667.5 or subdivision (c) of Section 1192.7, Section 285, subdivision (g) or (h) of Section 286, subdivision (g) or (h) of Section 287 or former Section 288a, subdivision (b) of Section 289, or Section 647.6 if it is a second or subsequent conviction for that offense that was brought and tried separately.

(B) This paragraph does not apply if the person is subject to lifetime registration as required in paragraph (3).

(3) A tier three offender is subject to registration for life. A person is a tier three offender if any one of the following applies:

(A) Following conviction of a registerable offense, the person was subsequently convicted in a separate proceeding of committing an offense described in subdivision (c) and the conviction is for commission of a violent felony described in subdivision (c) of Section 667.5, or the person was subsequently convicted of committing an offense for which the person was ordered to register pursuant to Section 290.006, and the conviction is for the commission of a violent felony described in subdivision (c) of Section 667.5.

(B) The person was committed to a state mental hospital as a sexually violent predator pursuant to Article 4 (commencing with Section 6600) of Chapter 2 of Part 2 of Division 6 of the Welfare and Institutions Code.

(C) The person was convicted of violating any of the following:

(i) Section 187 while attempting to commit or committing an act punishable under Section 261, 286, 287, 288, or 289 or former Section 288a.

(ii) Section 207 or 209 with intent to violate Section 261, 286, 287, 288, or 289 or former Section 288a.

(iii) Section 220.

(iv) Subdivision (b) of Section 266h.

(v) Subdivision (b) of Section 266i.

(vi) Section 266j.

(vii) Section 267.

(viii) Section 269.

(ix) Subdivision (b) or (c) of Section 288.

(x) Section 288.2.

(xi) Section 288.3, unless committed with the intent to commit a violation of subdivision (b) of Section 286, subdivision (b) of Section 287 or former Section 288a, or subdivision (h) or (i) of Section 289.

(xii) Section 288.4.

(xiii) Section 288.5.

(xiv) Section 288.7.

(xv) Subdivision (c) of Section 653f.

(xvi) Any offense for which the person is sentenced to a life term pursuant to Section 667.61.

(D) The person's risk level on the static risk assessment instrument for sex offenders (SARATSO), pursuant to Section 290.04, is well above average risk at the time of release on the index sex offense into the community, as defined in the Coding Rules for that instrument.

(E) The person is a habitual sex offender pursuant to Section 667.71.

(F) The person was convicted of violating subdivision (a) of Section 288 in two proceedings brought and tried separately.

(G) The person was sentenced to 15 to 25 years to life for an offense listed in Section 667.61.

(H) The person is required to register pursuant to Section 290.004.

(I) The person was convicted of a felony offense described in subdivision (b) or (c) of Section 236.1.

(J) The person was convicted of a felony offense described in subdivision (a), (c), or (d) of Section 243.4.

(K) The person was convicted of violating paragraph (2), (3), or (4) of subdivision (a) of Section 261 or was convicted of violating Section 261 and punished pursuant to paragraph (1) or (2) of subdivision (c) of Section 264.

(L) The person was convicted of violating paragraph (1) of subdivision (a) of Section 262.

(M) The person was convicted of violating Section 264.1.

(N) The person was convicted of any offense involving lewd or lascivious conduct under Section 272.

(O) The person was convicted of violating paragraph (2) of subdivision (c) or subdivision (d), (f), or (i) of Section 286.

(P) The person was convicted of violating paragraph (2) of subdivision (c) or subdivision (d), (f), or (i) of Section 287 or former Section 288a.

(Q) The person was convicted of violating paragraph (1) of subdivision (a) or subdivision (d), (e), or (j) of Section 289.

(R) The person was convicted of a felony violation of Section 311.1 or 311.11 or of violating subdivision (b), (c), or (d) of Section 311.2, Section 311.3, 311.4, or 311.10.

(4) (A) A person who is required to register pursuant to Section 290.005 shall be placed in the appropriate tier if the offense is assessed as equivalent to a California registerable offense described in subdivision (c).

(B) If the person's duty to register pursuant to Section 290.005 is based solely on the requirement of registration in another jurisdiction, and there is no equivalent California

registerable offense, the person shall be subject to registration as a tier two offender, except that the person is subject to registration as a tier three offender if one of the following applies:

(i) The person's risk level on the static risk assessment instrument (SARATSO), pursuant to Section 290.06, is well above average risk at the time of release on the index sex offense into the community, as defined in the Coding Rules for that instrument.

(ii) The person was subsequently convicted in a separate proceeding of an offense substantially similar to an offense listed in subdivision (c) which is also substantially similar to an offense described in subdivision (c) of Section 667.5, or is substantially similar to Section 269 or 288.7.

(iii) The person has ever been committed to a state mental hospital or mental health facility in a proceeding substantially similar to civil commitment as a sexually violent predator pursuant to Article 4 (commencing with Section 6600) of Chapter 2 of Part 2 of Division 6 of the Welfare and Institutions Code.

(5) (A) The Department of Justice may place a person described in subdivision (c), or who is otherwise required to register pursuant to the Act, in a tier-to-be-determined category if his or her appropriate tier designation described in this subdivision cannot be immediately ascertained. An individual placed in this tier-to-be-determined category shall continue to register in accordance with the Act. The individual shall be given credit for any period for which he or she registers towards his or her mandated minimum registration period.

(B) The Department of Justice shall ascertain an individual's appropriate tier designation as described in this subdivision within 24 months of his or her placement in the tier-to-be-determined category.

(e) The minimum time period for the completion of the required registration period in tier one or two commences on the date of release from incarceration, placement, or commitment, including any related civil commitment on the registerable offense. The minimum time for the completion of the required registration period for a designated tier is tolled during any period of subsequent incarceration, placement, or commitment, including any subsequent civil commitment, except that arrests not resulting in conviction, adjudication, or revocation of probation or parole shall not toll the required registration period. The minimum time period shall be extended by one year for each misdemeanor conviction of failing to register under this act, and by three years for each felony conviction of failing to register under this act, without regard to the actual time served in custody for the conviction. If a registrant is subsequently convicted of another offense requiring registration pursuant to the Act, a new minimum time period for the completion of the registration requirement for the applicable tier shall commence upon that person's release from incarceration, placement, or commitment, including any related civil commitment. If the subsequent conviction requiring registration pursuant to the Act occurs prior to an order to terminate the registrant from the registry after completion of a tier associated with the first conviction for a registerable offense, the applicable tier shall be the highest tier associated with the convictions.

(f) Nothing in this section shall be construed to require a ward of the juvenile court to register under the Act, except as provided in Section 290.008.

(g) This section shall become operative on January 1, 2021.

(Amended (as added by Stats. 2017, Ch. 541, Sec. 2.5) by Stats. 2018, Ch. 423, Sec. 52. (SB 1494) Effective January 1, 2019. Section operative January 1, 2021, by its own provisions. Note: This section was amended on November 6, 2012, by initiative Prop. 35.)

290.001.

Every person who has ever been adjudicated a sexually violent predator, as defined in Section 6600 of the Welfare and Institutions Code, shall register in accordance with the Act.

(Added by Stats. 2007, Ch. 579, Sec. 9. Effective October 13, 2007.)

290.002.

Persons required to register in their state of residence who are out-of-state residents employed, or carrying on a vocation in California on a full-time or part-time basis, with or without compensation, for more than 14 days, or for an aggregate period exceeding 30 days in a calendar year, shall register in accordance with the Act. Persons described in the Act who are out-of-state residents enrolled in any educational institution in California, as defined in Section 22129 of the Education Code, on a full-time or part-time basis, shall register in accordance with the Act. The place where the out-of-state resident is located, for purposes of registration, shall be the place where the person is employed, carrying on a vocation, or attending school. The out-of-state resident subject to this section shall, in addition to the information required pursuant to Section 290.015, provide the registering authority with the name of his or her place of employment or the name of the school attended in California, and his or her address or location in his or her state of residence. The registration requirement for persons subject to this section shall become operative on November 25, 2000. The terms "employed or carries on a vocation" include employment whether or not financially compensated, volunteered, or performed for government or educational benefit.

(Added by Stats. 2007, Ch. 579, Sec. 10. Effective October 13, 2007.)

290.003.

Any person who, since July 1, 1944, has been or hereafter is released, discharged, or paroled from a penal institution where he or she was confined because of the commission or attempted commission of one of the offenses described in subdivision (c) of Section 290, shall register in accordance with the Act.

(Added by Stats. 2007, Ch. 579, Sec. 11. Effective October 13, 2007.)

290.004.

Any person who, since July 1, 1944, has been or hereafter is determined to be a mentally disordered sex offender under Article 1 (commencing with Section 6300) of Chapter 2 of Part 2 of Division 6 of the Welfare and Institutions Code, or any person who has been found guilty in the guilt phase of a trial for an offense for which registration is required by this act but who has been found not guilty by reason of insanity in the sanity phase of the trial shall register in accordance with the act.

(Amended by Stats. 2017, Ch. 269, Sec. 8. (SB 811) Effective January 1, 2018.)

290.005.

The following persons shall register in accordance with the Act:

(a) Except as provided in subdivision (c) or (d), any person who, since July 1, 1944, has been, or is hereafter convicted in any other court, including any state, federal, or military court, of any offense that, if committed or attempted in this state, based on the elements of the convicted offense or facts admitted by the person or found true by the trier of fact or stipulated facts in the record of military proceedings, would have been punishable as one or more of the offenses described in subdivision (c) of Section 290, including offenses in which the person was a principal, as defined in Section 31.

(b) Any person ordered by any other court, including any state, federal, or military court, to register as a sex offender for any offense, if the court found at the time of conviction or sentencing that the person committed the offense as a result of sexual compulsion or for purposes of sexual gratification.

(c) Except as provided in subdivision (d), any person who would be required to register while residing in the state of conviction for a sex offense committed in that state.

(d) Notwithstanding any other law, a person convicted in another state of an offense similar to one of the following offenses who is required to register in the state of conviction shall not be required to register in California unless the out-of-state offense, based on the elements of the conviction offense or proven or stipulated facts in the record of conviction, contains all of the elements of a registerable California offense described in subdivision (c) of Section 290:

(1) Indecent exposure, pursuant to Section 314.

(2) Unlawful sexual intercourse, pursuant to Section 261.5.

(3) Incest, pursuant to Section 285.
(4) Sodomy, pursuant to Section 286, or oral copulation, pursuant to Section 287 or former Section 288a, provided that the offender notifies the Department of Justice that the sodomy or oral copulation conviction was for conduct between consenting adults, as described in Section 290.019, and the department is able, upon the exercise of reasonable diligence, to verify that fact.
(5) Pimping, pursuant to Section 266h, or pandering, pursuant to Section 266i.
(Amended by Stats. 2018, Ch. 423, Sec. 53. (SB 1494) Effective January 1, 2019.)
290.006.
(a) Any person ordered by any court to register pursuant to the Act for any offense not included specifically in subdivision (c) of Section 290, shall so register, if the court finds at the time of conviction or sentencing that the person committed the offense as a result of sexual compulsion or for purposes of sexual gratification. The court shall state on the record the reasons for its findings and the reasons for requiring registration.
(b) This section shall remain in effect only until January 1, 2021, and as of that date is repealed.
(Amended by Stats. 2017, Ch. 541, Sec. 3. (SB 384) Effective January 1, 2018. Repealed as of January 1, 2021, by its own provisions. See later operative version added by Sec. 4 of Stats. 2017, Ch.541.)
290.006.
(a) Any person ordered by any court to register pursuant to the Act for any offense not included specifically in subdivision (c) of Section 290, shall so register, if the court finds at the time of conviction or sentencing that the person committed the offense as a result of sexual compulsion or for purposes of sexual gratification. The court shall state on the record the reasons for its findings and the reasons for requiring registration.
(b) The person shall register as a tier one offender in accordance with paragraph (1) of subdivision (d) of Section 290, unless the court finds the person should register as a tier two or tier three offender and states on the record the reasons for its finding.
(c) In determining whether to require the person to register as a tier two or tier three offender, the court shall consider all of the following:
(1) The nature of the registerable offense.
(2) The age and number of victims, and whether any victim was personally unknown to the person at the time of the offense. A victim is personally unknown to the person for purposes of this paragraph if the victim was known to the offender for less than 24 hours.
(3) The criminal and relevant noncriminal behavior of the person before and after conviction for the registerable offense.
(4) Whether the person has previously been arrested for, or convicted of, a sexually motivated offense.
(5) The person's current risk of sexual or violent reoffense, including the person's risk level on the SARATSO static risk assessment instrument, and, if available from past supervision for a sexual offense, the person's risk level on the SARATSO dynamic and violence risk assessment instruments.
(d) This section shall become operative on January 1, 2021.
(Repealed (in Sec. 3) and added by Stats. 2017, Ch. 541, Sec. 4. (SB 384) Effective January 1, 2018. Section operative January 1, 2021, by its own provisions.)
290.007.
A person required to register pursuant to any provision of the Act shall register in accordance with the Act, regardless of whether the person's conviction has been dismissed pursuant to Section 1203.4, unless the person obtains a certificate of rehabilitation and is entitled to relief from registration pursuant to Section 290.5, or is exonerated pursuant to subdivision (e) of Section 3007.05 of the conviction requiring registration and the person is not otherwise required to register.
(Amended by Stats. 2018, Ch. 979, Sec. 1. (SB 1050) Effective January 1, 2019.)
290.008.
(a) Any person who, on or after January 1, 1986, is discharged or paroled from the Department of Corrections and Rehabilitation to the custody of which he or she was committed after having been adjudicated a ward of the juvenile court pursuant to Section 602 of the Welfare and Institutions Code because of the commission or attempted commission of any offense described in subdivision (c) shall register in accordance with the Act.
(b) Any person who is discharged or paroled from a facility in another state that is equivalent to the Division of Juvenile Justice, to the custody of which he or she was committed because of an offense which, if committed or attempted in this state, would have been punishable as one or more of the offenses described in subdivision (c) shall register in accordance with the Act.
(c) Any person described in this section who committed an offense in violation of any of the following provisions shall be required to register pursuant to the Act:
(1) Assault with intent to commit rape, sodomy, oral copulation, or any violation of Section 264.1, 288, or 289 under Section 220.
(2) Any offense defined in paragraph (1), (2), (3), (4), or (6) of subdivision (a) of Section 261, Section 264.1, 266c, or 267, paragraph (1) of subdivision (b) of, or subdivision (c) or (d) of, Section 286, paragraph (1) of subdivision (b) of, or subdivision (c) or (d) of, Section 287, Section 288 or 288.5, paragraph (1) of subdivision (b) of, or subdivision (c) or (d) of, former Section 288a, subdivision (a) of Section 289, or Section 647.6.
(3) A violation of Section 207 or 209 committed with the intent to violate Section 261, 286, 287, 288, or 289, or former Section 288a.
(d) Prior to discharge or parole from the Department of Corrections and Rehabilitation, any person who is subject to registration under this section shall be informed of the duty to register under the procedures set forth in the Act. Department officials shall transmit the required forms and information to the Department of Justice.
(e) All records specifically relating to the registration in the custody of the Department of Justice, law enforcement agencies, and other agencies or public officials shall be destroyed when the person who is required to register has his or her records sealed under the procedures set forth in Section 781 of the Welfare and Institutions Code. This section shall not be construed as requiring the destruction of other criminal offender or juvenile records relating to the case that are maintained by the Department of Justice, law enforcement agencies, the juvenile court, or other agencies and public officials unless ordered by a court under Section 781 of the Welfare and Institutions Code.
(f) This section shall remain in effect only until January 1, 2021, and as of that date is repealed.
(Amended (as amended by Stats. 2017, Ch. 541, Sec. 5) by Stats. 2018, Ch. 423, Sec. 54. (SB 1494) Effective January 1, 2019. Repealed as of January 1, 2021, by its own provisions. See later operative version amended by Sec. 55 of Stats. 2018, Ch. 423.)
290.008.
(a) Any person who, on or after January 1, 1986, is discharged or paroled from the Department of Corrections and Rehabilitation to the custody of which he or she was committed after having been adjudicated a ward of the juvenile court pursuant to Section 602 of the Welfare and Institutions Code because of the commission or attempted commission of any offense described in subdivision (c) shall register in accordance with the Act unless the duty to register is terminated pursuant to Section 290.5 or as otherwise provided by law.
(b) Any person who is discharged or paroled from a facility in another state that is equivalent to the Division of Juvenile Justice, to the custody of which he or she was committed because of an offense which, if committed or attempted in this state, would have been punishable as one or more of the offenses described in subdivision (c) shall register in accordance with the Act.

(c) Any person described in this section who committed an offense in violation of any of the following provisions shall be required to register pursuant to the Act:
(1) Assault with intent to commit rape, sodomy, oral copulation, or any violation of Section 264.1, 288, or 289 under Section 220.
(2) Any offense defined in paragraph (1), (2), (3), (4), or (6) of subdivision (a) of Section 261, Section 264.1, 266c, or 267, paragraph (1) of subdivision (b) of, or subdivision (c) or (d) of, Section 286, paragraph (1) of subdivision (b) of, or subdivision (c) or (d) of, Section 287, Section 288 or 288.5, paragraph (1) of subdivision (b) of, or subdivision (c) or (d) of, former Section 288a, subdivision (a) of Section 289, or Section 647.6.
(3) A violation of Section 207 or 209 committed with the intent to violate Section 261, 286, 287, 288, or 289, or former Section 288a.
(d) (1) A tier one juvenile offender is subject to registration for a minimum of five years. A person is a tier one juvenile offender if the person is required to register after being adjudicated as a ward of the court and discharged or paroled from the Department of Corrections and Rehabilitation for an offense listed in subdivision (c) that is not a serious or violent felony as described in subdivision (c) of Section 667.5 or subdivision (c) of Section 1192.7.
(2) A tier two juvenile offender is subject to registration for a minimum of 10 years. A person is a tier two juvenile offender if the person is required to register after being adjudicated as a ward of the court and discharged or paroled from the Department of Corrections and Rehabilitation for an offense listed in subdivision (c) that is a serious or violent felony as described in subdivision (c) of Section 667.5 or subdivision (c) of Section 1192.7.
(3) A person who is required to register as a sex offender pursuant to this section may file a petition for termination from the sex offender registry in the juvenile court in the county in which he or she is registered at the expiration of his or her mandated minimum registration period, pursuant to Section 290.5.
(e) Prior to discharge or parole from the Department of Corrections and Rehabilitation, any person who is subject to registration under this section shall be informed of the duty to register under the procedures set forth in the Act. Department officials shall transmit the required forms and information to the Department of Justice.
(f) All records specifically relating to the registration in the custody of the Department of Justice, law enforcement agencies, and other agencies or public officials shall be destroyed when the person who is required to register has his or her records sealed under the procedures set forth in Section 781 of the Welfare and Institutions Code. This section shall not be construed as requiring the destruction of other criminal offender or juvenile records relating to the case that are maintained by the Department of Justice, law enforcement agencies, the juvenile court, or other agencies and public officials unless ordered by a court under Section 781 of the Welfare and Institutions Code.
(g) This section shall become operative on January 1, 2021.
(Amended (as added by Stats. 2017, Ch. 541, Sec. 6) by Stats. 2018, Ch. 423, Sec. 55. (SB 1494) Effective January 1, 2019. Section operative January 1, 2021, by its own provisions.)
290.009.
Any person required to register under the Act who is enrolled as a student or is an employee or carries on a vocation, with or without compensation, at an institution of higher learning in this state, shall register pursuant to the provisions of the Act.
(Added by Stats. 2007, Ch. 579, Sec. 17. Effective October 13, 2007.)
290.010.
If the person who is registering has more than one residence address at which he or she regularly resides, he or she shall register in accordance with the Act in each of the jurisdictions in which he or she regularly resides, regardless of the number of days or nights spent there. If all of the addresses are within the same jurisdiction, the person shall provide the registering authority with all of the addresses where he or she regularly resides.
(Added by Stats. 2007, Ch. 579, Sec. 18. Effective October 13, 2007.)
290.011.
Every person who is required to register pursuant to the act who is living as a transient shall be required to register for the rest of his or her life as follows:
(a) He or she shall register, or reregister if the person has previously registered, within five working days from release from incarceration, placement or commitment, or release on probation, pursuant to subdivision (b) of Section 290, except that if the person previously registered as a transient less than 30 days from the date of his or her release from incarceration, he or she does not need to reregister as a transient until his or her next required 30-day update of registration. If a transient convicted in another jurisdiction enters the state, he or she shall register within five working days of coming into California with the chief of police of the city in which he or she is present or the sheriff of the county if he or she is present in an unincorporated area or city that has no police department. If a transient is not physically present in any one jurisdiction for five consecutive working days, he or she shall register in the jurisdiction in which he or she is physically present on the fifth working day following release, pursuant to subdivision (b) of Section 290. Beginning on or before the 30th day following initial registration upon release, a transient shall reregister no less than once every 30 days thereafter. A transient shall register with the chief of police of the city in which he or she is physically present within that 30-day period, or the sheriff of the county if he or she is physically present in an unincorporated area or city that has no police department, and additionally, with the chief of police of a campus of the University of California, the California State University, or community college if he or she is physically present upon the campus or in any of its facilities. A transient shall reregister no less than once every 30 days regardless of the length of time he or she has been physically present in the particular jurisdiction in which he or she reregisters. If a transient fails to reregister within any 30-day period, he or she may be prosecuted in any jurisdiction in which he or she is physically present.
(b) A transient who moves to a residence shall have five working days within which to register at that address, in accordance with subdivision (b) of Section 290. A person registered at a residence address in accordance with that provision who becomes transient shall have five working days within which to reregister as a transient in accordance with subdivision (a).
(c) Beginning on his or her first birthday following registration, a transient shall register annually, within five working days of his or her birthday, to update his or her registration with the entities described in subdivision (a). A transient shall register in whichever jurisdiction he or she is physically present on that date. At the 30-day updates and the annual update, a transient shall provide current information as required on the Department of Justice annual update form, including the information described in paragraphs (1) to (3), inclusive, of subdivision (a) of Section 290.015, and the information specified in subdivision (d).
(d) A transient shall, upon registration and reregistration, provide current information as required on the Department of Justice registration forms, and shall also list the places where he or she sleeps, eats, works, frequents, and engages in leisure activities. If a transient changes or adds to the places listed on the form during the 30-day period, he or she does not need to report the new place or places until the next required reregistration.
(e) Failure to comply with the requirement of reregistering every 30 days following initial registration pursuant to subdivision (a) shall be punished in accordance with subdivision (g) of Section 290.018. Failure to comply with any other requirement of this section shall be punished in accordance with either subdivision (a) or (b) of Section 290.018.
(f) A transient who moves out of state shall inform, in person, the chief of police in the city in which he or she is physically present, or the sheriff of the county if he or she is

physically present in an unincorporated area or city that has no police department, within five working days, of his or her move out of state. The transient shall inform that registering agency of his or her planned destination, residence or transient location out of state, and any plans he or she has to return to California, if known. The law enforcement agency shall, within three days after receipt of this information, forward a copy of the change of location information to the Department of Justice. The department shall forward appropriate registration data to the law enforcement agency having local jurisdiction of the new place of residence or location.

(g) For purposes of the act, "transient" means a person who has no residence. "Residence" means one or more addresses at which a person regularly resides, regardless of the number of days or nights spent there, such as a shelter or structure that can be located by a street address, including, but not limited to, houses, apartment buildings, motels, hotels, homeless shelters, and recreational and other vehicles.

(h) The transient registrant's duty to update his or her registration no less than every 30 days shall begin with his or her second transient update following the date this section became effective.

(Amended by Stats. 2010, Ch. 328, Sec. 153. (SB 1330) Effective January 1, 2011.)
290.012.
(a) Beginning on his or her first birthday following registration or change of address, the person shall be required to register annually, within five working days of his or her birthday, to update his or her registration with the entities described in subdivision (b) of Section 290. At the annual update, the person shall provide current information as required on the Department of Justice annual update form, including the information described in paragraphs (1) to (4), inclusive, of subdivision (a) of Section 290.015. The registering agency shall give the registrant a copy of the registration requirements from the Department of Justice form.

(b) In addition, every person who has ever been adjudicated a sexually violent predator, as defined in Section 6600 of the Welfare and Institutions Code, shall, after his or her release from custody, verify his or her address no less than once every 90 days and place of employment, including the name and address of the employer, in a manner established by the Department of Justice. Every person who, as a sexually violent predator, is required to verify his or her registration every 90 days, shall be notified wherever he or she next registers of his or her increased registration obligations. This notice shall be provided in writing by the registering agency or agencies. Failure to receive this notice shall be a defense to the penalties prescribed in subdivision (f) of Section 290.018.

(c) In addition, every person subject to the Act, while living as a transient in California, shall update his or her registration at least every 30 days, in accordance with Section 290.011.

(d) No entity shall require a person to pay a fee to register or update his or her registration pursuant to this section. The registering agency shall submit registrations, including annual updates or changes of address, directly into the Department of Justice California Sex and Arson Registry (CSAR).

(Amended by Stats. 2016, Ch. 772, Sec. 2. (SB 448) Effective January 1, 2017. Note: This section was amended on Nov. 6, 2012, by initiative Prop. 35.)
290.013.
(a) A person who was last registered at a residence address pursuant to the Act who changes his or her residence address, whether within the jurisdiction in which he or she is currently registered or to a new jurisdiction inside or outside the state, shall, in person, within five working days of the move, inform the law enforcement agency or agencies with which he or she last registered of the move, the new address or transient location, if known, and any plans he or she has to return to California.

(b) If the person does not know the new residence address or location at the time of the move, the registrant shall, in person, within five working days of the move, inform the last registering agency or agencies that he or she is moving. The person shall later notify the last registering agency or agencies, in writing, sent by certified or registered mail, of the new address or location within five working days of moving into the new residence address or location, whether temporary or permanent.

(c) The law enforcement agency or agencies shall, within three working days after receipt of this information, forward a copy of the change of address information to the Department of Justice. The Department of Justice shall forward appropriate registration data to the law enforcement agency or agencies having local jurisdiction of the new place of residence.

(d) If the person is being admitted to or released from a Department of Corrections and Rehabilitation facility, a county or local custodial facility, or state mental institution, an official of the place of incarceration, placement, or commitment shall, within 15 working days of both receipt and release of the person, forward the registrant's change of address information to the Department of Justice in a manner prescribed by the department. If the person is being admitted to the facility, the agency need not provide a physical address for the registrant but shall indicate that he or she is serving a period of incarceration or commitment in a facility under the agency's jurisdiction. This subdivision shall apply to persons received in a department facility, county or local custodial facility, or state mental institution on or after January 1, 1999. The Department of Justice shall forward the change of address information to the agency with which the person last registered.

(Amended by Stats. 2018, Ch. 811, Sec. 1. (AB 1994) Effective January 1, 2019.)
290.014.
(a) If any person who is required to register pursuant to the Act changes his or her name, the person shall inform, in person, the law enforcement agency or agencies with which he or she is currently registered within five working days. The law enforcement agency or agencies shall forward a copy of this information to the Department of Justice within three working days of its receipt.

(b) If any person who is required to register Internet identifiers pursuant to Section 290.024 adds or changes an Internet identifier, as defined in Section 290.024, the person shall send written notice by mail of the addition or change to the law enforcement agency or agencies with which he or she is currently registered within 30 working days of the addition or change. The law enforcement agency or agencies shall make the information available to the Department of Justice.

(Amended by Stats. 2016, Ch. 772, Sec. 3. (SB 448) Effective January 1, 2017. Note: This section was amended on Nov. 6, 2012, by initiative Prop. 35.)
290.015.
(a) A person who is subject to the Act shall register, or reregister if he or she has previously registered, upon release from incarceration, placement, commitment, or release on probation pursuant to subdivision (b) of Section 290. This section shall not apply to a person who is incarcerated for less than 30 days if he or she has registered as required by the Act, he or she returns after incarceration to the last registered address, and the annual update of registration that is required to occur within five working days of his or her birthday, pursuant to subdivision (a) of Section 290.012, did not fall within that incarceration period. The registration shall consist of all of the following:

(1) A statement in writing signed by the person, giving information as shall be required by the Department of Justice and giving the name and address of the person's employer, and the address of the person's place of employment if that is different from the employer's main address.

(2) The fingerprints and a current photograph of the person taken by the registering official.

(3) The license plate number of any vehicle owned by, regularly driven by, or registered in the name of the person.

(4) A list of all Internet identifiers actually used by the person, as required by Section 290.024.

(5) A statement in writing, signed by the person, acknowledging that the person is required to register and update the information in paragraph (4), as required by this chapter.

(6) Notice to the person that, in addition to the requirements of the Act, he or she may have a duty to register in any other state where he or she may relocate.

(7) Copies of adequate proof of residence, which shall be limited to a California driver's license, California identification card, recent rent or utility receipt, printed personalized checks or other recent banking documents showing that person's name and address, or any other information that the registering official believes is reliable. If the person has no residence and no reasonable expectation of obtaining a residence in the foreseeable future, the person shall so advise the registering official and shall sign a statement provided by the registering official stating that fact. Upon presentation of proof of residence to the registering official or a signed statement that the person has no residence, the person shall be allowed to register. If the person claims that he or she has a residence but does not have any proof of residence, he or she shall be allowed to register but shall furnish proof of residence within 30 days of the date he or she is allowed to register.

(b) Within three days thereafter, the registering law enforcement agency or agencies shall forward the statement, fingerprints, photograph, and vehicle license plate number, if any, to the Department of Justice.

(c) (1) If a person fails to register in accordance with subdivision (a) after release, the district attorney in the jurisdiction where the person was to be paroled or to be on probation may request that a warrant be issued for the person's arrest and shall have the authority to prosecute that person pursuant to Section 290.018.

(2) If the person was not on parole or probation or on postrelease community supervision or mandatory supervision at the time of release, the district attorney in the following applicable jurisdiction shall have the authority to prosecute that person pursuant to Section 290.018:

(A) If the person was previously registered, in the jurisdiction in which the person last registered.

(B) If there is no prior registration, but the person indicated on the Department of Justice notice of sex offender registration requirement form where he or she expected to reside, in the jurisdiction where he or she expected to reside.

(C) If neither subparagraph (A) nor (B) applies, in the jurisdiction where the offense subjecting the person to registration pursuant to this Act was committed.

(Amended (as amended Nov. 6, 2012, by Prop. 35) by Stats. 2016, Ch. 772, Sec. 4. (SB 448) Effective January 1, 2017. Note: This section was amended on Nov. 6, 2012, by initiative Prop. 35.)
290.016.
(a) On or after January 1, 1998, upon incarceration, placement, or commitment, or prior to release on probation, any person who is required to register under the Act shall preregister. The preregistering official shall be the admitting officer at the place of incarceration, placement, or commitment, or the probation officer if the person is to be released on probation. The preregistration shall consist of all of the following:

(1) A preregistration statement in writing, signed by the person, giving information that shall be required by the Department of Justice.

(2) The fingerprints and a current photograph of the person.

(3) Any person who is preregistered pursuant to this subdivision is required to be preregistered only once.

(b) Within three days thereafter, the preregistering official shall forward the statement, fingerprints, photograph, and vehicle license plate number, if any, to the Department of Justice.

(Added by Stats. 2007, Ch. 579, Sec. 24. Effective October 13, 2007.)
290.017.
(a) Any person who is released, discharged, or paroled from a jail, state or federal prison, school, road camp, or other institution where he or she was confined, who is required to register pursuant to the Act, shall, prior to discharge, parole, or release, be informed of his or her duty to register under the Act by the official in charge of the place of confinement or hospital, and the official shall require the person to read and sign any form that may be required by the Department of Justice, stating that the duty of the person to register under the Act has been explained to the person. The official in charge of the place of confinement or hospital shall obtain the address where the person expects to reside upon his or her discharge, parole, or release and shall report the address to the Department of Justice. The official shall at the same time forward a current photograph of the person to the Department of Justice.

(b) The official in charge of the place of confinement or hospital shall give one copy of the form to the person and shall send one copy to the Department of Justice and one copy to the appropriate law enforcement agency or agencies having jurisdiction over the place the person expects to reside upon discharge, parole, or release. If the conviction that makes the person subject to the Act is a felony conviction, the official in charge shall, not later than 45 days prior to the scheduled release of the person, send one copy to the appropriate law enforcement agency or agencies having local jurisdiction where the person expects to reside upon discharge, parole, or release; one copy to the prosecuting agency that prosecuted the person; and one copy to the Department of Justice. The official in charge of the place of confinement or hospital shall retain one copy.

(c) Any person who is required to register pursuant to the Act and who is released on probation, shall, prior to release or discharge, be informed of the duty to register under the Act by the probation department, and a probation officer shall require the person to read and sign any form that may be required by the Department of Justice, stating that the duty of the person to register has been explained to him or her. The probation officer shall obtain the address where the person expects to reside upon release or discharge and shall report within three days the address to the Department of Justice. The probation officer shall give one copy of the form to the person, send one copy to the Department of Justice, and forward one copy to the appropriate law enforcement agency or agencies having local jurisdiction where the person expects to reside upon his or her discharge, parole, or release.

(d) Any person who is required to register pursuant to the Act and who is granted conditional release without supervised probation, or discharged upon payment of a fine, shall, prior to release or discharge, be informed of the duty to register under the Act in open court by the court in which the person has been convicted, and the court shall require the person to read and sign any form that may be required by the Department of Justice, stating that the duty of the person to register has been explained to him or her. If the court finds that it is in the interest of the efficiency of the court, the court may assign the bailiff to require the person to read and sign forms under the Act. The court shall obtain the address where the person expects to reside upon release or discharge and shall report within three days the address to the Department of Justice. The court shall give one copy of the form to the person, send one copy to the Department of Justice, and forward one copy to the appropriate law enforcement agency or agencies having local jurisdiction where the person expects to reside upon his or her discharge, parole, or release.

(Added by Stats. 2007, Ch. 579, Sec. 25. Effective October 13, 2007.)
290.018.
(a) A person who is required to register under the Act based on a misdemeanor conviction or juvenile adjudication who willfully violates any requirement of the act is guilty of a misdemeanor punishable by imprisonment in a county jail not exceeding one year.

(b) Except as provided in subdivisions (f), (h), (i), and (k), a person who is required to register under the act based on a felony conviction or juvenile adjudication who willfully violates any requirement of the act or who has a prior conviction or juvenile adjudication for the offense of failing to register under the act and who subsequently and willfully violates any requirement of the act is guilty of a felony and shall be punished by imprisonment in the state prison for 16 months, or two or three years.
(c) If probation is granted or if the imposition or execution of sentence is suspended, it shall be a condition of the probation or suspension that the person serve at least 90 days in a county jail. The penalty described in subdivision (b) or this subdivision shall apply whether or not the person has been released on parole or has been discharged from parole.
(d) A person determined to be a mentally disordered sex offender or who has been found guilty in the guilt phase of trial for an offense for which registration is required under the act, but who has been found not guilty by reason of insanity in the sanity phase of the trial, or who has had a petition sustained in a juvenile adjudication for an offense for which registration is required pursuant to Section 290.008, but who has been found not guilty by reason of insanity, who willfully violates any requirement of the act is guilty of a misdemeanor and shall be punished by imprisonment in a county jail not exceeding one year. For any second or subsequent willful violation of any requirement of the act, the person is guilty of a felony and shall be punished by imprisonment in the state prison for 16 months, or two or three years.
(e) If, after discharge from parole, the person is convicted of a felony or suffers a juvenile adjudication as specified in this act, he or she shall be required to complete parole of at least one year, in addition to any other punishment imposed under this section. A person convicted of a felony as specified in this section may be granted probation only in the unusual case where the interests of justice would best be served. When probation is granted under this act, the court shall specify on the record and shall enter into the minutes the circumstances indicating that the interests of justice would best be served by the disposition.
(f) A person who has ever been adjudicated a sexually violent predator, as defined in Section 6600 of the Welfare and Institutions Code, and who fails to verify his or her registration every 90 days as required pursuant to subdivision (b) of Section 290.012, shall be punished by imprisonment in the state prison or in a county jail not exceeding one year.
(g) Except as otherwise provided in subdivision (f), a person who is required to register or reregister pursuant to Section 290.011 and willfully fails to comply with the requirement that he or she reregister no less than every 30 days is guilty of a misdemeanor and shall be punished by imprisonment in a county jail for at least 30 days, but not exceeding six months. A person who willfully fails to comply with the requirement that he or she reregister no less than every 30 days shall not be charged with this violation more often than once for a failure to register in any period of 90 days. A person who willfully commits a third or subsequent violation of the requirements of Section 290.011 that he or she reregister no less than every 30 days shall be punished in accordance with either subdivision (a) or (b).
(h) A person who fails to provide proof of residence as required by paragraph (7) of subdivision (a) of Section 290.015, regardless of the offense upon which the duty to register is based, is guilty of a misdemeanor punishable by imprisonment in a county jail not exceeding six months.
(i) A person who fails to provide his or her Internet identifiers, as required by paragraph (4) of subdivision (a) of Section 290.015, regardless of the offense upon which the duty to register is based, is guilty of a misdemeanor punishable in a county jail not exceeding six months.
(j) A person who is required to register under the act who willfully violates any requirement of the act is guilty of a continuing offense as to each requirement he or she violated.
(k) In addition to any other penalty imposed under this section, the failure to provide information required on registration and reregistration forms of the Department of Justice, or the provision of false information, is a crime punishable by imprisonment in a county jail for a period not exceeding one year. This subdivision shall not be construed to limit or prevent prosecution under any applicable law.
(l) Whenever a person is released on parole or probation and is required to register under the act but fails to do so within the time prescribed, the parole authority or the court, as the case may be, shall order the parole or probation of the person revoked. For purposes of this subdivision, "parole authority" has the same meaning as described in Section 3000.
(Amended by Stats. 2016, Ch. 772, Sec. 6. (SB 448) Effective January 1, 2017.)
290.019.
(a) Notwithstanding any other section in the Act, a person who was convicted before January 1, 1976, under subdivision (a) of Section 286, or former Section 288a, shall not be required to register pursuant to the Act for that conviction if the conviction was for conduct between consenting adults that was decriminalized by Chapter 71 of the Statutes of 1975 or Chapter 1139 of the Statutes of 1976. The Department of Justice shall remove that person from the Sex Offender Registry, and the person is discharged from his or her duty to register pursuant to either of the following procedures:
(1) The person submits to the Department of Justice official documentary evidence, including court records or police reports, that demonstrate that the person's conviction pursuant to either of those sections was for conduct between consenting adults that was decriminalized.
(2) The person submits to the department a declaration stating that the person's conviction pursuant to either of those sections was for consensual conduct between adults that has been decriminalized. The declaration shall be confidential and not a public record, and shall include the person's name, address, telephone number, date of birth, and a summary of the circumstances leading to the conviction, including the date of the conviction and county of the occurrence.
(b) The department shall determine whether the person's conviction was for conduct between consensual adults that has been decriminalized. If the conviction was for consensual conduct between adults that has been decriminalized, and the person has no other offenses for which he or she is required to register pursuant to the Act, the department shall, within 60 days of receipt of those documents, notify the person that he or she is relieved of the duty to register, and shall notify the local law enforcement agency with which the person is registered that he or she has been relieved of the duty to register. The local law enforcement agency shall remove the person's registration from its files within 30 days of receipt of notification. If the documentary or other evidence submitted is insufficient to establish the person's claim, the department shall, within 60 days of receipt of those documents, notify the person that his or her claim cannot be established, and that the person shall continue to register pursuant to the Act. The department shall provide, upon the person's request, any information relied upon by the department in making its determination that the person shall continue to register pursuant to the Act. Any person whose claim has been denied by the department pursuant to this subdivision may petition the court to appeal the department's denial of the person's claim.
(Amended by Stats. 2018, Ch. 423, Sec. 56. (SB 1494) Effective January 1, 2019.)
290.020.
In any case in which a person who would be required to register pursuant to the Act for a felony conviction is to be temporarily sent outside the institution where he or she is confined on any assignment within a city or county including firefighting, disaster control, or of whatever nature the assignment may be, the local law enforcement agency having jurisdiction over the place or places where the assignment shall occur shall be notified within a reasonable time prior to removal from the institution. This section shall not apply to any person who is temporarily released under guard from the institution where he or she is confined.
(Added by Stats. 2007, Ch. 579, Sec. 28. Effective October 13, 2007.)
290.021.
Except as otherwise provided by law, the statements, photographs, and fingerprints required by the Act shall not be open to inspection by the public or by any person other than a regularly employed peace officer or other law enforcement officer.
(Added by Stats. 2007, Ch. 579, Sec. 29. Effective October 13, 2007.)
290.022.
On or before July 1, 2010, the Department of Justice shall renovate the VCIN to do the following:
(1) Correct all software deficiencies affecting data integrity and include designated data fields for all mandated sex offender data.
(2) Consolidate and simplify program logic, thereby increasing system performance and reducing system maintenance costs.
(3) Provide all necessary data storage, processing, and search capabilities.
(4) Provide law enforcement agencies with full Internet access to all sex offender data and photos.
(5) Incorporate a flexible design structure to readily meet future demands for enhanced system functionality, including public Internet access to sex offender information pursuant to Section 290.46.
(Added by Stats. 2007, Ch. 579, Sec. 30. Effective October 13, 2007.)
290.023.
The registration provisions of the Act are applicable to every person described in the Act, without regard to when his or her crime or crimes were committed or his or her duty to register pursuant to the Act arose, and to every offense described in the Act, regardless of when it was committed.
(Added by Stats. 2007, Ch. 579, Sec. 31. Effective October 13, 2007.)
290.024.
For purposes of this chapter:
(a) A person who is convicted of a felony on or after January 1, 2017, requiring registration pursuant to the Act, shall register his or her Internet identifiers if a court determines at the time of sentencing that any of the following apply:
(1) The person used the Internet to collect any private information to identify the victim of the crime to further the commission of the crime.
(2) The person was convicted of a felony pursuant to subdivision (b) or (c) of Section 236.1 and used the Internet to traffic the victim of the crime.
(3) The person was convicted of a felony pursuant to Chapter 7.5 (commencing with Section 311) and used the Internet to prepare, publish, distribute, send, exchange, or download the obscene matter or matter depicting a minor engaging in sexual conduct, as defined in subdivision (d) of Section 311.4.
(b) For purposes of this chapter:
(1) "Internet identifier" means any electronic mail address or user name used for instant messaging or social networking that is actually used for direct communication between users on the Internet in a manner that makes the communication not accessible to the general public. "Internet identifier" does not include Internet passwords, date of birth, social security number, or PIN number.
(2) "Private information" means any information that identifies or describes an individual, including, but not limited to, his or her name; electronic mail, chat, instant messenger, social networking, or similar name used for Internet communication; social security number; account numbers; passwords; personal identification numbers; physical description; physical location; home address; home telephone number; education; financial matters; medical or employment history; and statements made by, or attributed to, the individual.
(Amended by Stats. 2016, Ch. 772, Sec. 7. (SB 448) Effective January 1, 2017. Note: This section was amended on Nov. 6, 2012, by initiative Prop. 35.)
290.01.
(a) (1) Commencing October 28, 2002, every person required to register pursuant to Sections 290 to 290.009, inclusive, of the Sex Offender Registration Act who is enrolled as a student of any university, college, community college, or other institution of higher learning, or is, with or without compensation, a full-time or part-time employee of that university, college, community college, or other institution of higher learning, or is carrying on a vocation at the university, college, community college, or other institution of higher learning, for more than 14 days, or for an aggregate period exceeding 30 days in a calendar year, shall, in addition to the registration required by the Sex Offender Registration Act, register with the campus police department within five working days of commencing enrollment or employment at that university, college, community college, or other institution of higher learning, on a form as may be required by the Department of Justice. The terms "employed or carries on a vocation" include employment whether or not financially compensated, volunteered, or performed for government or educational benefit. The registrant shall also notify the campus police department within five working days of ceasing to be enrolled or employed, or ceasing to carry on a vocation, at the university, college, community college, or other institution of higher learning.
(2) For purposes of this section, a campus police department is a police department of the University of California, California State University, or California Community College, established pursuant to Section 72330, 89560, or 92600 of the Education Code, or is a police department staffed with deputized or appointed personnel with peace officer status as provided in Section 830.6 of the Penal Code and is the law enforcement agency with the primary responsibility for investigating crimes occurring on the college or university campus on which it is located.
(b) If the university, college, community college, or other institution of higher learning has no campus police department, the registrant shall instead register pursuant to subdivision (a) with the police of the city in which the campus is located or the sheriff of the county in which the campus is located if the campus is located in an unincorporated area or in a city that has no police department, on a form as may be required by the Department of Justice. The requirements of subdivisions (a) and (b) are in addition to the requirements of the Sex Offender Registration Act.
(c) A first violation of this section is a misdemeanor punishable by a fine not to exceed one thousand dollars ($1,000). A second violation of this section is a misdemeanor punishable by imprisonment in a county jail for not more than six months, by a fine not to exceed one thousand dollars ($1,000), or by both that imprisonment and fine. A third or subsequent violation of this section is a misdemeanor punishable by imprisonment in a county jail for not more than one year, by a fine not exceeding one thousand dollars ($1,000), or by both that imprisonment and fine.
(d) (1) (A) The following information regarding a registered sex offender on campus as to whom information shall not be made available to the public via the Internet Web site as provided in Section 290.46 may be released to members of the campus community by any campus police department or, if the university, college, community college, or other institution of higher learning has no police department, the police department or sheriff's department with jurisdiction over the campus, and any employees of those agencies, as required by Section 1092(f)(1)(I) of Title 20 of the United States Code:
(i) The offender's full name.
(ii) The offender's known aliases.
(iii) The offender's gender.
(iv) The offender's race.
(v) The offender's physical description.
(vi) The offender's photograph.
(vii) The offender's date of birth.

(viii) Crimes resulting in registration under Section 290.

(ix) The date of last registration or reregistration.

(B) The authority provided in this subdivision is in addition to the authority of a peace officer or law enforcement agency to provide information about a registered sex offender pursuant to Section 290.45, and exists notwithstanding Section 290.021 or any other provision of law.

(2) Any law enforcement entity and employees of any law enforcement entity listed in paragraph (1) shall be immune from civil or criminal liability for good faith conduct under this subdivision.

(3) Nothing in this subdivision shall be construed to authorize campus police departments or, if the university, college, community college, or other institution has no police department, the police department or sheriff's department with jurisdiction over the campus, to make disclosures about registrants intended to reach persons beyond the campus community.

(4) (A) Before being provided any information by an agency pursuant to this subdivision, a member of the campus community who requests that information shall sign a statement, on a form provided by the Department of Justice, stating that he or she is not a registered sex offender, that he or she understands the purpose of the release of information is to allow members of the campus community to protect themselves and their children from sex offenders, and that he or she understands it is unlawful to use information obtained pursuant to this subdivision to commit a crime against any registrant or to engage in illegal discrimination or harassment of any registrant. The signed statement shall be maintained in a file in the agency's office for a minimum of five years.

(B) An agency disseminating printed information pursuant to this subdivision shall maintain records of the means and dates of dissemination for a minimum of five years.

(5) For purposes of this subdivision, "campus community" means those persons present at, and those persons regularly frequenting, any place associated with an institution of higher education, including campuses; administrative and educational offices; laboratories; satellite facilities owned or utilized by the institution for educational instruction, business, or institutional events; and public areas contiguous to any campus or facility that are regularly frequented by students, employees, or volunteers of the campus.

(Amended by Stats. 2007, Ch. 579, Sec. 32. Effective October 13, 2007. Note: Sections 290.010 to 290.019 precede this section and follow Section 290.009.)

290.02.

(a) Notwithstanding any other law, the Department of Justice shall identify the names of persons required to register pursuant to Section 290 from a list of persons provided by the requesting agency, and provide those names and other information necessary to verify proper identification, to any state governmental entity responsible for authorizing or providing publicly funded prescription drugs or other therapies to treat erectile dysfunction of those persons. State governmental entities shall use information received pursuant to this section to protect public safety by preventing the use of prescription drugs or other therapies to treat erectile dysfunction by convicted sex offenders.

(b) Use or disclosure of the information disclosed pursuant to this section is prohibited for any purpose other than that authorized by this section or Section 14133.225 of the Welfare and Institutions Code. The Department of Justice may establish a fee for requests, including all actual and reasonable costs associated with the service.

(c) Notwithstanding any other provision of law, any state governmental entity that is responsible for authorizing or providing publicly funded prescription drugs or other therapies to treat erectile dysfunction may use the sex offender database authorized by Section 290.46 to protect public safety by preventing the use of those drugs or therapies for convicted sex offenders.

(Added by Stats. 2005, Ch. 469, Sec. 2. Effective October 4, 2005. Note: Sections 290.020 to 290.024 precede Section 290.01 and follow Section 290.019.)

290.03.

(a) The Legislature finds and declares that a comprehensive system of risk assessment, supervision, monitoring and containment for registered sex offenders residing in California communities is necessary to enhance public safety and reduce the risk of recidivism posed by these offenders. The Legislature further affirms and incorporates the following findings and declarations, previously reflected in its enactment of "Megan's Law":

(1) Sex offenders pose a potentially high risk of committing further sex offenses after release from incarceration or commitment, and the protection of the public from reoffending by these offenders is a paramount public interest.

(2) It is a compelling and necessary public interest that the public have information concerning persons convicted of offenses involving unlawful sexual behavior collected pursuant to Sections 290 and 290.4 to allow members of the public to adequately protect themselves and their children from these persons.

(3) Persons convicted of these offenses involving unlawful sexual behavior have a reduced expectation of privacy because of the public's interest in public safety.

(4) In balancing the offenders' due process and other rights against the interests of public security, the Legislature finds that releasing information about sex offenders under the circumstances specified in the Sex Offender Punishment, Control, and Containment Act of 2006 will further the primary government interest of protecting vulnerable populations from potential harm.

(5) The registration of sex offenders, the public release of specified information about certain sex offenders pursuant to Sections 290 and 290.4, and public notice of the presence of certain high risk sex offenders in communities will further the governmental interests of public safety and public scrutiny of the criminal and mental health systems that deal with these offenders.

(6) To protect the safety and general welfare of the people of this state, it is necessary to provide for continued registration of sex offenders, for the public release of specified information regarding certain more serious sex offenders, and for community notification regarding high risk sex offenders who are about to be released from custody or who already reside in communities in this state. This policy of authorizing the release of necessary and relevant information about serious and high risk sex offenders to members of the general public is a means of assuring public protection and shall not be construed as punitive.

(7) The Legislature also declares, however, that in making information available about certain sex offenders to the public, it does not intend that the information be used to inflict retribution or additional punishment on any person convicted of a sex offense. While the Legislature is aware of the possibility of misuse, it finds that the dangers to the public of nondisclosure far outweigh the risk of possible misuse of the information. The Legislature is further aware of studies in Oregon and Washington indicating that community notification laws and public release of similar information in those states have resulted in little criminal misuse of the information and that the enhancement to public safety has been significant.

(b) In enacting the Sex Offender Punishment, Control, and Containment Act of 2006, the Legislature hereby creates a standardized, statewide system to identify, assess, monitor and contain known sex offenders for the purpose of reducing the risk of recidivism posed by these offenders, thereby protecting victims and potential victims from future harm.

(Added by Stats. 2006, Ch. 337, Sec. 12. Effective September 20, 2006.)

290.04.

(a) (1) The sex offender risk assessment tools authorized by this section for use with selected populations shall be known, with respect to each population, as the State-Authorized Risk Assessment Tool for Sex Offenders (SARATSO). If a SARATSO has not been selected for a given population pursuant to this section, no duty to administer the

SARATSO elsewhere in this code shall apply with respect to that population. Every person required to register as a sex offender shall be subject to assessment with the SARATSO as set forth in this section and elsewhere in this code.

(2) A representative of the Department of Corrections and Rehabilitation, in consultation with a representative of the State Department of State Hospitals and a representative of the Attorney General's office, shall comprise the SARATSO Review Committee. The purpose of the committee, which shall be staffed by the Department of Corrections and Rehabilitation, shall be to ensure that the SARATSO reflects the most reliable, objective, and well-established protocols for predicting sex offender risk of recidivism, has been scientifically validated and cross validated, and is, or is reasonably likely to be, widely accepted by the courts. The committee shall consult with experts in the fields of risk assessment and the use of actuarial instruments in predicting sex offender risk, sex offending, sex offender treatment, mental health, and law, as it deems appropriate.

(b) (1) Commencing January 1, 2007, the SARATSO for adult males required to register as sex offenders shall be the STATIC-99 risk assessment scale, which shall be the SARATSO static tool for adult males.

(2) The SARATSO Review Committee shall determine whether the STATIC-99 should be supplemented with an empirically derived instrument that measures dynamic risk factors or whether the STATIC-99 should be replaced as the SARATSO with a different risk assessment tool. The SARATSO Review Committee shall select an empirically derived instrument that measures dynamic risk factors and an empirically derived instrument that measures risk of future violence. The selected instruments shall be the SARATSO dynamic tool for adult males and the SARATSO future violence tool for adult males. If the committee unanimously agrees on changes to be made to a designated SARATSO, it shall advise the Governor and the Legislature of the changes, and the Department of Corrections and Rehabilitation shall post the decision on its Internet Web site. Sixty days after the decision is posted, the selected tool shall become the SARATSO for adult males.

(c) On or before July 1, 2007, the SARATSO Review Committee shall research risk assessment tools for adult females required to register as sex offenders. If the committee unanimously agrees on an appropriate risk assessment tool to be used to assess this population, it shall advise the Governor and the Legislature of the selected tool, and the State Department of Mental Health shall post the decision on its Internet Web site. Sixty days after the decision is posted, the selected tool shall become the SARATSO for adult females.

(d) On or before July 1, 2007, the SARATSO Review Committee shall research risk assessment tools for male juveniles required to register as sex offenders. If the committee unanimously agrees on an appropriate risk assessment tool to be used to assess this population, it shall advise the Governor and the Legislature of the selected tool, and the State Department of Mental Health shall post the decision on its Internet Web site. Sixty days after the decision is posted, the selected tool shall become the SARATSO for male juveniles.

(e) On or before July 1, 2007, the SARATSO Review Committee shall research risk assessment tools for female juveniles required to register as sex offenders. If the committee unanimously agrees on an appropriate risk assessment tool to be used to assess this population, it shall advise the Governor and the Legislature of the selected tool, and the State Department of Mental Health shall post the decision on its Internet Web site. Sixty days after the decision is posted, the selected tool shall become the SARATSO for female juveniles.

(f) The committee shall periodically evaluate the SARATSO static, dynamic, and risk of future violence tools for each specified population. If the committee unanimously agrees on a change to the SARATSO for any population, it shall advise the Governor and the Legislature of the selected tool, and the Department of Corrections and Rehabilitation shall post the decision on its Internet Web site. Sixty days after the decision is posted, the selected tool shall become the SARATSO for that population.

(g) The committee shall perform other functions consistent with the provisions of this act or as may be otherwise required by law, including, but not limited to, defining tiers of risk based on the SARATSO. The committee shall be immune from liability for good faith conduct under this act.

(Amended by Stats. 2012, Ch. 24, Sec. 15. (AB 1470) Effective June 27, 2012.)

290.05.

(a) The SARATSO Training Committee shall be comprised of a representative of the State Department of State Hospitals, a representative of the Department of Corrections and Rehabilitation, a representative of the Attorney General's Office, and a representative of the Chief Probation Officers of California.

(b) On or before January 1, 2008, the SARATSO Training Committee, in consultation with the Corrections Standards Authority and the Commission on Peace Officer Standards and Training, shall develop a training program for persons authorized by this code to administer the static SARATSO, as set forth in Section 290.04.

(c) (1) The Department of Corrections and Rehabilitation shall be responsible for overseeing the training of persons who will administer the static SARATSO pursuant to paragraph (1) or (2) of subdivision (a) of Section 290.06.

(2) The State Department of State Hospitals shall be responsible for overseeing the training of persons who will administer the static SARATSO pursuant to paragraph (3) of subdivision (a) of Section 290.06.

(3) The Correction Standards Authority shall be responsible for developing standards for the training of persons who will administer the static SARATSO pursuant to paragraph (5) or (6) of subdivision (a) of Section 290.06.

(4) The Commission on Peace Officer Standards and Training shall be responsible for developing standards for the training of persons who will administer the static SARATSO pursuant to subdivision (b) of Section 290.06.

(d) The training shall be conducted by experts in the field of risk assessment and the use of actuarial instruments in predicting sex offender risk. Subject to requirements established by the committee, the Department of Corrections and Rehabilitation, the State Department of State Hospitals, probation departments, and authorized local law enforcement agencies shall designate key persons within their organizations to attend training and, as authorized by the department, to train others within their organizations designated to perform risk assessments as required or authorized by law. Any person who administers the static SARATSO shall receive training no less frequently than every two years.

(e) If the agency responsible for scoring the static SARATSO believes an individual score does not represent the person's true risk level, based on factors in the offender's record, the agency may submit the case to the experts retained by the SARATSO Review Committee to monitor the scoring of the SARATSO. Those experts shall be guided by empirical research in determining whether to raise or lower the risk level. Agencies that score the static SARATSO shall develop a protocol for submission of risk level override requests to the experts retained in accordance with this subdivision.

(f) The static SARATSO may be performed for purposes authorized by statute only by persons trained pursuant to this section. Persons who administer the dynamic SARATSO and the future violence SARATSO shall be trained to administer the dynamic and future violence SARATSO tools as required in Section 290.09. Probation officers or parole agents may be trained by SARATSO experts on the dynamic SARATSO tool and perform assessments on that tool only if authorized by the SARATSO Training Committee to do so after successful completion of training.

(Amended by Stats. 2012, Ch. 24, Sec. 16. (AB 1470) Effective June 27, 2012.)

290.06.

The static SARATSO, as set forth in Section 290.04, shall be administered as follows:

(a) (1) The Department of Corrections and Rehabilitation shall assess every eligible person who is incarcerated in state prison. Whenever possible, the assessment shall take place at least four months, but no sooner than 10 months, prior to release from incarceration.

(2) The department shall assess every eligible person who is on parole if the person was not assessed prior to release from state prison. Whenever possible, the assessment shall take place at least four months, but no sooner than 10 months, prior to termination of parole. The department shall record in a database the risk assessment scores of persons assessed pursuant to this paragraph and paragraph (1), and any risk assessment score that was submitted to the department by a probation officer pursuant to Section 1203.

(3) The department shall assess every person on parole transferred from any other state or by the federal government to this state who has been, or is hereafter convicted in any other court, including any state, federal, or military court, of any offense that, if committed or attempted in this state, would have been punishable as one or more of the offenses described in subdivision (c) of Section 290. The assessment required by this paragraph shall occur no later than 60 days after a determination by the Department of Justice that the person is required to register as a sex offender in California pursuant to Section 290.005.

(4) The State Department of State Hospitals shall assess every eligible person who is committed to that department. Whenever possible, the assessment shall take place at least four months, but no sooner than 10 months, prior to release from commitment. The State Department of State Hospitals shall record in a database the risk assessment scores of persons assessed pursuant to this paragraph and any risk assessment score that was submitted to the department by a probation officer pursuant to Section 1203.

(5) Commencing January 1, 2010, the Department of Corrections and Rehabilitation and the State Department of State Hospitals shall send the scores obtained in accordance with paragraphs (2), (3), and (4) to the Department of Justice not later than 30 days after the date of the assessment. The risk assessment score of an offender shall be made part of his or her file maintained by the Department of Justice as soon as possible without financial impact, but no later than January 1, 2012.

(6) Each probation department shall, prior to sentencing, assess every eligible person as defined in subdivision (c), whether or not a report is prepared pursuant to Section 1203.

(7) Each probation department shall assess every eligible person under its supervision who was not assessed pursuant to paragraph (6). The assessment shall take place prior to the termination of probation, but no later than January 1, 2010.

(b) Eligible persons not assessed pursuant to subdivision (a) may be assessed as follows:

(1) Upon request of the law enforcement agency in the jurisdiction in which the person is registered pursuant to Sections 290 to 290.023, inclusive, the person shall be assessed. The law enforcement agency may enter into a memorandum of understanding with a probation department to perform the assessment. In the alternative, the law enforcement agency may arrange to have personnel trained to perform the risk assessment in accordance with subdivision (d) of Section 290.05.

(2) Eligible persons not assessed pursuant to subdivision (a) may request that a risk assessment be performed. A request form shall be available at registering law enforcement agencies. The person requesting the assessment shall pay a fee for the assessment that shall be sufficient to cover the cost of the assessment. The risk assessment so requested shall be performed either by the probation department, if a memorandum of understanding is established between the law enforcement agency and the probation department, or by personnel who have been trained to perform risk assessment in accordance with subdivision (d) of Section 290.05.

(c) For purposes of this section, "eligible person" means a person who was convicted of an offense that requires him or her to register as a sex offender pursuant to the Sex Offender Registration Act and who is eligible for assessment, pursuant to the official Coding Rules designated for use with the risk assessment instrument by the author of any risk assessment instrument (SARATSO) selected by the SARATSO Review Committee.

(d) Persons authorized to perform risk assessments pursuant to this section, Section 1203, and Section 706 of the Welfare and Institutions Code shall be immune from liability for good faith conduct under this act.

(Amended by Stats. 2016, Ch. 59, Sec. 1. (SB 1474) Effective January 1, 2017.)
290.07.
Notwithstanding any other provision of law, a person authorized by statute to administer the State Authorized Risk Assessment Tool for Sex Offenders (SARATSO) and trained pursuant to Section 290.06 or 290.09, and a person acting under authority from the SARATSO Review Committee as an expert to train, monitor, or review scoring by persons who administer the SARATSO pursuant to Section 290.05 or 1203 of this code or Section 706 of the Welfare and Institutions Code, shall be granted access to all relevant records pertaining to a registered sex offender, including, but not limited to, criminal histories, sex offender registration records, police reports, probation and presentencing reports, judicial records and case files, juvenile records, psychological evaluations and psychiatric hospital reports, sexually violent predator treatment program reports, and records that have been sealed by the courts or the Department of Justice. Records and information obtained under this section shall not be subject to the California Public Records Act, Chapter 3.5 (commencing with Section 6250) of Division 7 of Title 1 of the Government Code.

(Amended by Stats. 2012, Ch. 174, Sec. 1. (AB 1835) Effective January 1, 2013.)
290.08.
Every district attorney's office and the Department of Justice shall retain records relating to a person convicted of an offense for which registration is required pursuant to Section 290 for a period of 75 years after disposition of the case.

(Added by Stats. 2006, Ch. 337, Sec. 17. Effective September 20, 2006.)
290.09.
On or before July 2012, the SARATSO dynamic tool and the SARATSO future violence tool, as set forth in Section 290.04, shall be administered as follows:

(a) (1) Every sex offender required to register pursuant to Sections 290 to 290.023, inclusive, shall, while on parole or formal probation, participate in an approved sex offender management program, pursuant to Sections 1203.067 and 3008.

(2) The sex offender management program shall meet the certification requirements developed by the California Sex Offender Management Board pursuant to Section 9003. Probation departments and the Department of Corrections and Rehabilitation shall not employ or contract with, and shall not allow a sex offender to employ or contract with, any individual or entity to provide sex offender evaluation or treatment services pursuant to this section unless the sex offender evaluation or treatment services to be provided by the individual or entity conforms with the standards developed pursuant to Section 9003.

(b) (1) The sex offender management professionals certified by the California Sex Offender Management Board in accordance with Section 9003 who provide sex offender management programs for any probation department or the Department of Corrections and Rehabilitation shall assess each registered sex offender on formal probation or parole using the SARATSO dynamic tool, when a dynamic risk factor changes, and shall do a final dynamic assessment within six months of the offender's release from supervision. The management professional shall also assess the sex offenders in the program with the SARATSO future violence tool.

(2) The certified sex offender management professional shall, as soon as possible but not later than 30 days after the assessment, provide the person's score on the SARATSO dynamic tool and the future violence tool to the person's parole agent or probation officer. Within five working days of receipt of the score, the parole or probation officer shall send the score to the Department of Justice, and the score shall

be accessible to law enforcement through the Department of Justice's Internet Web site for the California Sex and Arson Registry (CSAR).

(c) The certified sex offender management professional shall communicate with the offender's probation officer or parole agent on a regular basis, but at least once a month, about the offender's progress in the program and dynamic risk assessment issues, and shall share pertinent information with the certified polygraph examiner as required.

(d) The SARATSO Training Committee shall provide annual training on the SARATSO dynamic tool and the SARATSO future violence tool. Certified sex offender management professionals shall attend this training once to obtain authorization to perform the assessments, and thereafter attend training updates as required by the SARATSO Training Committee. If a sex offender management professional is certified pursuant to Section 9003 to conduct an approved sex offender management program prior to attending SARATSO training on the dynamic and violent risk assessment tools, he or she shall present to the SARATSO Training Committee proof of training on these tools from a risk assessment expert approved by the SARATSO Training Committee.

(Amended by Stats. 2011, Ch. 357, Sec. 3. (AB 813) Effective January 1, 2012.)
290.3.
(a) Every person who is convicted of any offense specified in subdivision (c) of Section 290 shall, in addition to any imprisonment or fine, or both, imposed for commission of the underlying offense, be punished by a fine of three hundred dollars ($300) upon the first conviction or a fine of five hundred dollars ($500) upon the second and each subsequent conviction, unless the court determines that the defendant does not have the ability to pay the fine.

An amount equal to all fines collected pursuant to this subdivision during the preceding month upon conviction of, or upon the forfeiture of bail by, any person arrested for, or convicted of, committing an offense specified in subdivision (c) of Section 290, shall be transferred once a month by the county treasurer to the Controller for deposit in the General Fund. Moneys deposited in the General Fund pursuant to this subdivision shall be transferred by the Controller as provided in subdivision (b).

(b) Except as provided in subdivision (d), out of the moneys deposited pursuant to subdivision (a) as a result of second and subsequent convictions of Section 290, one-third shall first be transferred to the Department of Justice Sexual Habitual Offender Fund, as provided in paragraph (1) of this subdivision. Out of the remainder of all moneys deposited pursuant to subdivision (a), 50 percent shall be transferred to the Department of Justice Sexual Habitual Offender Fund, as provided in paragraph (1), 25 percent shall be transferred to the DNA Identification Fund, as established by Section 76104.6 of the Government Code, and 25 percent shall be allocated equally to counties that maintain a local DNA testing laboratory, as provided in paragraph (2).

(1) Those moneys so designated shall be transferred to the Department of Justice Sexual Habitual Offender Fund created pursuant to paragraph (5) of subdivision (b) of Section 11170 and, when appropriated by the Legislature, shall be used for the purposes of Chapter 9.5 (commencing with Section 13885) and Chapter 10 (commencing with Section 13890) of Title 6 of Part 4 for the purpose of monitoring, apprehending, and prosecuting sexual habitual offenders.

(2) Those moneys so designated shall be allocated equally and distributed quarterly to counties that maintain a local DNA testing laboratory. Before making any allocations under this paragraph, the Controller shall deduct the estimated costs that will be incurred to set up and administer the payment of these funds to the counties. Any funds allocated to a county pursuant to this paragraph shall be used by that county for the exclusive purpose of testing DNA samples for law enforcement purposes.

(c) Notwithstanding any other provision of this section, the Department of Corrections and Rehabilitation may collect a fine imposed pursuant to this section from a person convicted of a violation of any offense listed in subdivision (c) of Section 290, that results in incarceration in a facility under the jurisdiction of the Department of Corrections and Rehabilitation. All moneys collected by the Department of Corrections and Rehabilitation under this subdivision shall be transferred, once a month, to the Controller for deposit in the General Fund, as provided in subdivision (a), for transfer by the Controller, as provided in subdivision (b).

(d) An amount equal to one-third of every first conviction fine collected and one-fifth of every second conviction fine collected pursuant to subdivision (a) shall be transferred to the Department of Corrections and Rehabilitation to help defray the cost of the global positioning system used to monitor sex offender parolees.

(Amended by Stats. 2008, Ch. 699, Sec. 9. Effective January 1, 2009. Note: This section was amended on Nov. 7, 2006, by initiative Prop. 83.)
290.4.
(a) The department shall operate a service through which members of the public may provide a list of at least six persons on a form approved by the Department of Justice and inquire whether any of those persons is required to register as a sex offender and is subject to public notification. The Department of Justice shall respond with information on any person as to whom information may be available to the public via the Internet Web site as provided in Section 290.46, to the extent that information may be disclosed pursuant to Section 290.46. The Department of Justice may establish a fee for requests, including all actual and reasonable costs associated with the service.

(b) The income from the operation of the service specified in subdivision (a) shall be deposited in the Sexual Predator Public Information Account within the Department of Justice for the purpose of the implementation of this section by the Department of Justice.

The moneys in the account shall consist of income from the operation of the service authorized by subdivision (a), and any other funds made available to the account by the Legislature. Moneys in the account shall be available to the Department of Justice upon appropriation by the Legislature for the purpose specified in subdivision (a).

(c) (1) Any person who uses information disclosed pursuant to this section to commit a felony shall be punished, in addition and consecutive to, any other punishment, by a five-year term of imprisonment pursuant to subdivision (h) of Section 1170.

(2) Any person who, without authorization, uses information disclosed pursuant to this section to commit a misdemeanor shall be subject to, in addition to any other penalty or fine imposed, a fine of not less than five hundred dollars ($500) and not more than one thousand dollars ($1,000).

(d) (1) A person is authorized to use information disclosed pursuant to this section only to protect a person at risk.

(2) Except as authorized under paragraph (1) or any other provision of law, use of any information that is disclosed pursuant to this section for purposes relating to any of the following is prohibited:

(A) Health insurance.
(B) Insurance.
(C) Loans.
(D) Credit.
(E) Employment.
(F) Education, scholarships, or fellowships.
(G) Housing or accommodations.
(H) Benefits, privileges, or services provided by any business establishment.

(3) This section shall not affect authorized access to, or use of, information pursuant to, among other provisions, Sections 11105 and 11105.3 of this code, Section 226.55 of the Civil Code, Sections 777.5 and 14409.2 of the Financial Code, Sections 1522.01 and 1596.871 of the Health and Safety Code, and Section 432.7 of the Labor Code.

(4) (A) Any use of information disclosed pursuant to this section for purposes other than those provided by paragraph (1) or in violation of paragraph (2) shall make the user liable for the actual damages, and any amount that may be determined by a jury or

a court sitting without a jury, not exceeding three times the amount of actual damage, and not less than two hundred fifty dollars ($250), and attorney's fees, exemplary damages, or a civil penalty not exceeding twenty-five thousand dollars ($25,000).

(B) Whenever there is reasonable cause to believe that any person or group of persons is engaged in a pattern or practice of misuse of the service specified in subdivision (a), in violation of paragraph (2), the Attorney General, any district attorney, or city attorney, or any person aggrieved by the misuse of the service is authorized to bring a civil action in the appropriate court requesting preventive relief, including an application for a permanent or temporary injunction, restraining order, or other order against the person or group of persons responsible for the pattern or practice of misuse. The foregoing remedies shall be independent of any other remedies or procedures that may be available to an aggrieved party under other provisions of law, including Part 2 (commencing with Section 43) of Division 1 of the Civil Code.

(e) The Department of Justice and its employees shall be immune from liability for good faith conduct under this section.

(f) The public notification provisions of this section are applicable to every person described in subdivision (a), without regard to when his or her crimes were committed or his or her duty to register pursuant to Section 290 arose, and to every offense subject to public notification pursuant to Section 290.46, regardless of when it was committed.

(Amended by Stats. 2011, Ch. 15, Sec. 319. (AB 109) Effective April 4, 2011. Operative October 1, 2011, by Sec. 636 of Ch. 15, as amended by Stats. 2011, Ch. 39, Sec. 68.)

290.45.
(a) (1) Notwithstanding any other law, and except as provided in paragraph (2), any designated law enforcement entity may provide information to the public about a person required to register as a sex offender pursuant to Section 290, by whatever means the entity deems appropriate, when necessary to ensure the public safety based upon information available to the entity concerning that specific person.

(2) The law enforcement entity shall include, with the disclosure, a statement that the purpose of the release of information is to allow members of the public to protect themselves and their children from sex offenders.

(3) Community notification by way of an Internet Web site shall be governed by Section 290.46, and a designated law enforcement entity may not post on an Internet Web site any information identifying an individual as a person required to register as a sex offender except as provided in that section unless there is a warrant outstanding for that person's arrest.

(b) Information that may be provided pursuant to subdivision (a) may include, but is not limited to, the offender's name, known aliases, gender, race, physical description, photograph, date of birth, address, which shall be verified prior to publication, description and license plate number of the offender's vehicles or vehicles the offender is known to drive, type of victim targeted by the offender, relevant parole or probation conditions, crimes resulting in classification under this section, and date of release from confinement, but excluding information that would identify the victim. It shall not include any Internet identifier submitted pursuant to this chapter.

(c) (1) The designated law enforcement entity may authorize persons and entities who receive the information pursuant to this section to disclose information to additional persons only if the entity determines that disclosure to the additional persons will enhance the public safety and identifies the appropriate scope of further disclosure. A law enforcement entity may not authorize any disclosure of this information by placing that information on an Internet Web site, and shall not authorize disclosure of Internet identifiers submitted pursuant to this chapter, except as provided in subdivision (h).

(2) A person who receives information from a law enforcement entity pursuant to paragraph (1) may disclose that information only in the manner and to the extent authorized by the law enforcement entity.

(d) (1) A designated law enforcement entity and its employees shall be immune from liability for good faith conduct under this section.

(2) A public or private educational institution, a day care facility, or a child care custodian described in Section 11165.7, or an employee of a public or private educational institution or day care facility which in good faith disseminates information as authorized pursuant to subdivision (c) shall be immune from civil liability.

(e) (1) A person who uses information disclosed pursuant to this section to commit a felony shall be punished, in addition and consecutive to any other punishment, by a five-year term of imprisonment pursuant to subdivision (h) of Section 1170.

(2) A person who uses information disclosed pursuant to this section to commit a misdemeanor shall be subject to, in addition to any other penalty or fine imposed, a fine of not less than five hundred dollars ($500) and not more than one thousand dollars ($1,000).

(f) For purposes of this section, "designated law enforcement entity" means the Department of Justice, every district attorney, the Department of Corrections, the Department of the Youth Authority, and every state or local agency expressly authorized by statute to investigate or prosecute law violators.

(g) The public notification provisions of this section are applicable to every person required to register pursuant to Section 290, without regard to when his or her crimes were committed or his or her duty to register pursuant to Section 290 arose, and to every offense described in Section 290, regardless of when it was committed.

(h) (1) Notwithstanding any other law, a designated law enforcement entity shall only use an Internet identifier submitted pursuant to this chapter, or release that Internet identifier to another law enforcement entity, for the purpose of investigating a sex-related crime, a kidnapping, or human trafficking.

(2) A designated law enforcement entity shall not disclose or authorize persons or entities to disclose an Internet identifier submitted pursuant to this chapter to the public or other persons, except as required by court order.

(i) This section shall remain in effect only until January 1, 2021, and as of that date is repealed.

(Amended by Stats. 2017, Ch. 541, Sec. 7. (SB 384) Effective January 1, 2018. Repealed as of January 1, 2021, by its own provisions. See later operative version added by Sec. of Stats. 2017, Ch.541.)

290.45.
(a) (1) Notwithstanding any other law, and except as provided in paragraph (2), any designated law enforcement entity may provide information to the public about a person required to register as a sex offender pursuant to Section 290, by whatever means the entity deems appropriate, when necessary to ensure the public safety based upon information available to the entity concerning that specific person's current risk of sexual or violent reoffense, including, but not limited to, the person's static, dynamic, and violence risk levels on the SARATSO risk tools described in subdivision (f) of Section 290.04.

(2) The law enforcement entity shall include, with the disclosure, a statement that the purpose of the release of information is to allow members of the public to protect themselves and their children from sex offenders.

(3) Community notification by way of an Internet Web site shall be governed by Section 290.46, and a designated law enforcement entity may not post on an Internet Web site any information identifying an individual as a person required to register as a sex offender except as provided in that section unless there is a warrant outstanding for that person's arrest.

(b) Information that may be provided pursuant to subdivision (a) may include, but is not limited to, the offender's name, known aliases, gender, race, physical description, photograph, date of birth, address, which shall be verified prior to publication, description and license plate number of the offender's vehicles or vehicles the offender is known to drive, type of victim targeted by the offender, relevant parole or probation

conditions, crimes resulting in classification under this section, and date of release from confinement, but excluding information that would identify the victim. It shall not include any Internet identifier submitted pursuant to this chapter.

(c) (1) The designated law enforcement entity may authorize persons and entities who receive the information pursuant to this section to disclose information to additional persons only if the entity determines that disclosure to the additional persons will enhance the public safety and identifies the appropriate scope of further disclosure. A law enforcement entity may not authorize any disclosure of this information by placing that information on an Internet Web site, and shall not authorize disclosure of Internet identifiers submitted pursuant to this chapter, except as provided in subdivision (h).

(2) A person who receives information from a law enforcement entity pursuant to paragraph (1) may disclose that information only in the manner and to the extent authorized by the law enforcement entity.

(d) (1) A designated law enforcement entity and its employees shall be immune from liability for good faith conduct under this section.

(2) A public or private educational institution, a day care facility, or a child care custodian described in Section 11165.7, or an employee of a public or private educational institution or day care facility which in good faith disseminates information as authorized pursuant to subdivision (c) shall be immune from civil liability.

(e) (1) A person who uses information disclosed pursuant to this section to commit a felony shall be punished, in addition and consecutive to any other punishment, by a five-year term of imprisonment pursuant to subdivision (h) of Section 1170.

(2) A person who uses information disclosed pursuant to this section to commit a misdemeanor shall be subject to, in addition to any other penalty or fine imposed, a fine of not less than five hundred dollars ($500) and not more than one thousand dollars ($1,000).

(f) For purposes of this section, "designated law enforcement entity" means the Department of Justice, a district attorney, the Department of Corrections and Rehabilitation, the Division of Juvenile Justice, and every state or local agency expressly authorized by statute to investigate or prosecute law violators.

(g) The public notification provisions of this section are applicable to every person required to register pursuant to Section 290, without regard to when his or her crimes were committed or his or her duty to register pursuant to Section 290 arose, and to each offense described in Section 290, regardless of when it was committed.

(h) (1) Notwithstanding any other law, a designated law enforcement entity shall only use an Internet identifier submitted pursuant to this chapter, or release that Internet identifier to another law enforcement entity, for the purpose of investigating a sex-related crime, a kidnapping, or human trafficking.

(2) A designated law enforcement entity shall not disclose or authorize persons or entities to disclose an Internet identifier submitted pursuant to this chapter to the public or other persons, except as required by court order.

(i) This section shall become operative on January 1, 2021.

(Repealed (in Sec. 7) and added by Stats. 2017, Ch. 541, Sec. 8. (SB 384) Effective January 1, 2018. Section operative January 1, 2021, by its own provisions.)

290.46.
(a) (1) On or before the dates specified in this section, the Department of Justice shall make available information concerning persons who are required to register pursuant to Section 290 to the public via an Internet Web site as specified in this section. The department shall update the Internet Web site on an ongoing basis. All information identifying the victim by name, birth date, address, or relationship to the registrant shall be excluded from the Internet Web site. The name or address of the person's employer and the listed person's criminal history other than the specific crimes for which the person is required to register shall not be included on the Internet Web site. The Internet Web site shall be translated into languages other than English as determined by the department.

(2) (A) On or before July 1, 2010, the Department of Justice shall make available to the public, via an Internet Web site as specified in this section, as to any person described in subdivision (b), (c), or (d), the following information:

(i) The year of conviction of his or her most recent offense requiring registration pursuant to Section 290.

(ii) The year he or she was released from incarceration for that offense.

(iii) Whether he or she was subsequently incarcerated for any other felony, if that fact is reported to the department. If the department has no information about a subsequent incarceration for any felony, that fact shall be noted on the Internet Web site. However, no year of conviction shall be made available to the public unless the department also is able to make available the corresponding year of release of incarceration for that offense, and the required notation regarding any subsequent felony.

(B) (i) Any state facility that releases from incarceration a person who was incarcerated because of a crime for which he or she is required to register as a sex offender pursuant to Section 290 shall, within 30 days of release, provide the year of release for his or her most recent offense requiring registration to the Department of Justice in a manner and format approved by the department.

(ii) Any state facility that releases a person who is required to register pursuant to Section 290 from incarceration whose incarceration was for a felony committed subsequently to the offense for which he or she is required to register shall, within 30 days of release, advise the Department of Justice of that fact.

(iii) Any state facility that, prior to January 1, 2007, released from incarceration a person who was incarcerated because of a crime for which he or she is required to register as a sex offender pursuant to Section 290 shall provide the year of release for his or her most recent offense requiring registration to the Department of Justice in a manner and format approved by the department. The information provided by the Department of Corrections and Rehabilitation shall be limited to information that is currently maintained in an electronic format.

(iv) Any state facility that, prior to January 1, 2007, released a person who is required to register pursuant to Section 290 from incarceration whose incarceration was for a felony committed subsequently to the offense for which he or she is required to register shall advise the Department of Justice of that fact in a manner and format approved by the department. The information provided by the Department of Corrections and Rehabilitation shall be limited to information that is currently maintained in an electronic format.

(3) The State Department of State Hospitals shall provide to the Department of Justice the names of all persons committed to its custody pursuant to Article 4 (commencing with Section 6600) of Chapter 2 of Part 2 of Division 6 of the Welfare and Institutions Code, within 30 days of commitment, and shall provide the names of all of those persons released from its custody within five working days of release.

(b) (1) On or before July 1, 2005, with respect to a person who has been convicted of the commission or the attempted commission of any of the offenses listed in, or who is described in, paragraph (2), the Department of Justice shall make available to the public via the Internet Web site his or her name and known aliases, a photograph, a physical description, including gender and race, date of birth, criminal history, prior adjudication as a sexually violent predator, the address at which the person resides, and any other information that the Department of Justice deems relevant, but not the information excluded pursuant to subdivision (a). On or before January 1, 2013, the department shall make available to the public via the Internet Web site his or her static SARATSO score and information on an elevated risk level based on the SARATSO future violence tool.

(2) This subdivision shall apply to the following offenses and offenders:

(A) Section 187 committed in the perpetration, or an attempt to perpetrate, rape or any act punishable under Section 286, 287, 288, or 289, or former Section 288a.

(B) Section 207 committed with intent to violate Section 261, 286, 287, 288, or 289, or former Section 288a.

(C) Section 209 committed with intent to violate Section 261, 286, 287, 288, or 289, or former Section 288a.

(D) Paragraph (2) or (6) of subdivision (a) of Section 261.

(E) Section 264.1.

(F) Section 269.

(G) Subdivision (c) or (d) of Section 286.

(H) Subdivision (a), (b), or (c) of Section 288, provided that the offense is a felony.

(I) Subdivision (c) or (d) of Section 287 or of former Section 288a.

(J) Section 288.3, provided that the offense is a felony.

(K) Section 288.4, provided that the offense is a felony.

(L) Section 288.5.

(M) Subdivision (a) or (j) of Section 289.

(N) Section 288.7.

(O) Any person who has ever been adjudicated a sexually violent predator, as defined in Section 6600 of the Welfare and Institutions Code.

(P) A felony violation of Section 311.1.

(Q) A felony violation of subdivision (b), (c), or (d) of Section 311.2.

(R) A felony violation of Section 311.3.

(S) A felony violation of subdivision (a), (b), or (c) of Section 311.4.

(T) Section 311.10.

(U) A felony violation of Section 311.11.

(c) (1) On or before July 1, 2005, with respect to a person who has been convicted of the commission or the attempted commission of any of the offenses listed in paragraph (2), the Department of Justice shall make available to the public via the Internet Web site his or her name and known aliases, a photograph, a physical description, including gender and race, date of birth, criminal history, the community of residence and ZIP Code in which the person resides or the county in which the person is registered as a transient, and any other information that the Department of Justice deems relevant, but not the information excluded pursuant to subdivision (a). On or before July 1, 2006, the Department of Justice shall determine whether any person convicted of an offense listed in paragraph (2) also has one or more prior or subsequent convictions of an offense listed in subdivision (c) of Section 290, and, for those persons, the Department of Justice shall make available to the public via the Internet Web site the address at which the person resides. However, the address at which the person resides shall not be disclosed until a determination is made that the person is, by virtue of his or her additional prior or subsequent conviction of an offense listed in subdivision (c) of Section 290, subject to this subdivision.

(2) This subdivision shall apply to the following offenses:

(A) Section 220, except assault to commit mayhem.

(B) Paragraph (1), (3), or (4) of subdivision (a) of Section 261.

(C) Paragraph (2) of subdivision (b), or subdivision (f), (g), or (i), of Section 286.

(D) Paragraph (2) of subdivision (b), or subdivision (f), (g), or (i), of Section 287 or of former Section 288a.

(E) Subdivision (b), (d), (e), or (i) of Section 289.

(d) (1) On or before July 1, 2005, with respect to a person who has been convicted of the commission or the attempted commission of any of the offenses listed in, or who is described in, this subdivision, the Department of Justice shall make available to the public via the Internet Web site his or her name and known aliases, a photograph, a physical description, including gender and race, date of birth, criminal history, the community of residence and ZIP Code in which the person resides or the county in which the person is registered as a transient, and any other information that the Department of Justice deems relevant, but not the information excluded pursuant to subdivision (a) or the address at which the person resides.

(2) This subdivision shall apply to the following offenses and offenders:

(A) Subdivision (a) of Section 243.4, provided that the offense is a felony.

(B) Section 266, provided that the offense is a felony.

(C) Section 266c, provided that the offense is a felony.

(D) Section 266j.

(E) Section 267.

(F) Subdivision (c) of Section 288, provided that the offense is a misdemeanor.

(G) Section 288.3, provided that the offense is a misdemeanor.

(H) Section 288.4, provided that the offense is a misdemeanor.

(I) Section 626.81.

(J) Section 647.6.

(K) Section 653c.

(L) Any person required to register pursuant to Section 290 based upon an out-of-state conviction, unless that person is excluded from the Internet Web site pursuant to subdivision (e). However, if the Department of Justice has determined that the out-of-state crime, if committed or attempted in this state, would have been punishable in this state as a crime described in subdivision (c) of Section 290, the person shall be placed on the Internet Web site as provided in subdivision (b) or (c), as applicable to the crime.

(e) (1) If a person has been convicted of the commission or the attempted commission of any of the offenses listed in this subdivision, and he or she has been convicted of no other offense listed in subdivision (b), (c), or (d) other than those listed in this subdivision, that person may file an application with the Department of Justice, on a form approved by the department, for exclusion from the Internet Web site. If the department determines that the person meets the requirements of this subdivision, the department shall grant the exclusion and no information concerning the person shall be made available via the Internet Web site described in this section. He or she bears the burden of proving the facts that make him or her eligible for exclusion from the Internet Web site. However, a person who has filed for or been granted an exclusion from the Internet Web site is not relieved of his or her duty to register as a sex offender pursuant to Section 290 nor from any otherwise applicable provision of law.

(2) This subdivision shall apply to the following offenses:

(A) A felony violation of subdivision (a) of Section 243.4.

(B) Section 647.6, if the offense is a misdemeanor.

(C) A felony violation of Section 311.1, subdivision (b), (c), or (d) of Section 311.2, or Section 311.3, 311.4, 311.10, or 311.11 if the person submits to the department a certified copy of a probation report filed in court that clearly states that all victims involved in the commission of the offense were at least 16 years of age or older at the time of the commission of the offense.

(D) (i) An offense for which the offender successfully completed probation, provided that the offender submits to the department a certified copy of a probation report, presentencing report, report prepared pursuant to Section 288.1, or other official court document that clearly demonstrates that the offender was the victim's parent, stepparent, sibling, or grandparent and that the crime did not involve either oral copulation or penetration of the vagina or rectum of either the victim or the offender by the penis of the other or by any foreign object.

(ii) An offense for which the offender is on probation at the time of his or her application, provided that the offender submits to the department a certified copy of a probation report, presentencing report, report prepared pursuant to Section 288.1, or other official court document that clearly demonstrates that the offender was the victim's parent, stepparent, sibling, or grandparent and that the crime did not involve either oral copulation or penetration of the vagina or rectum of either the victim or the offender by the penis of the other or by any foreign object.

(iii) If, subsequent to his or her application, the offender commits a violation of probation resulting in his or her incarceration in county jail or state prison, his or her exclusion, or application for exclusion, from the Internet Web site shall be terminated.

(iv) For the purposes of this subparagraph, "successfully completed probation" means that during the period of probation the offender neither received additional county jail or state prison time for a violation of probation nor was convicted of another offense resulting in a sentence to county jail or state prison.

(3) If the department determines that a person who was granted an exclusion under a former version of this subdivision would not qualify for an exclusion under the current version of this subdivision, the department shall rescind the exclusion, make a reasonable effort to provide notification to the person that the exclusion has been rescinded, and, no sooner than 30 days after notification is attempted, make information about the offender available to the public on the Internet Web site as provided in this section.

(4) Effective January 1, 2012, no person shall be excluded pursuant to this subdivision unless the offender has submitted to the department documentation sufficient for the department to determine that he or she has a SARATSO risk level of low or moderate-low.

(f) The Department of Justice shall make a reasonable effort to provide notification to persons who have been convicted of the commission or attempted commission of an offense specified in subdivision (b), (c), or (d), that on or before July 1, 2005, the department is required to make information about specified sex offenders available to the public via an Internet Web site as specified in this section. The Department of Justice shall also make a reasonable effort to provide notice that some offenders are eligible to apply for exclusion from the Internet Web site.

(g) (1) A designated law enforcement entity, as defined in subdivision (f) of Section 290.45, may make available information concerning persons who are required to register pursuant to Section 290 to the public via an Internet Web site as specified in paragraph (2).

(2) The law enforcement entity may make available by way of an Internet Web site the information described in subdivision (c) if it determines that the public disclosure of the information about a specific offender by way of the entity's Internet Web site is necessary to ensure the public safety based upon information available to the entity concerning that specific offender.

(3) The information that may be provided pursuant to this subdivision may include the information specified in subdivision (b) of Section 290.45. However, that offender's address may not be disclosed unless he or she is a person whose address is on the Department of Justice's Internet Web site pursuant to subdivision (b) or (c).

(h) For purposes of this section, "offense" includes the statutory predecessors of that offense, or any offense committed in another jurisdiction that, if committed or attempted to be committed in this state, would have been punishable in this state as an offense listed in subdivision (c) of Section 290.

(i) Notwithstanding Section 6254.5 of the Government Code, disclosure of information pursuant to this section is not a waiver of exemptions under Chapter 3.5 (commencing with Section 6250) of Title 1 of Division 7 of the Government Code and does not affect other statutory restrictions on disclosure in other situations.

(j) (1) Any person who uses information disclosed pursuant to this section to commit a misdemeanor shall be subject to, in addition to any other penalty or fine imposed, a fine of not less than ten thousand dollars ($10,000) and not more than fifty thousand dollars ($50,000).

(2) Any person who uses information disclosed pursuant to this section to commit a felony shall be punished, in addition and consecutive to any other punishment, by a five-year term of imprisonment pursuant to subdivision (h) of Section 1170.

(k) Any person who is required to register pursuant to Section 290 who enters an Internet Web site established pursuant to this section shall be punished by a fine not exceeding one thousand dollars ($1,000), imprisonment in a county jail for a period not to exceed six months, or by both that fine and imprisonment.

(l) (1) A person is authorized to use information disclosed pursuant to this section only to protect a person at risk.

(2) Except as authorized under paragraph (1) or any other provision of law, use of any information that is disclosed pursuant to this section for purposes relating to any of the following is prohibited:

(A) Health insurance.

(B) Insurance.

(C) Loans.

(D) Credit.

(E) Employment.

(F) Education, scholarships, or fellowships.

(G) Housing or accommodations.

(H) Benefits, privileges, or services provided by any business establishment.

(3) This section shall not affect authorized access to, or use of, information pursuant to, among other provisions, Sections 11105 and 11105.3, Section 8808 of the Family Code, Sections 777.5 and 14409.2 of the Financial Code, Sections 1522.01 and 1596.871 of the Health and Safety Code, and Section 432.7 of the Labor Code.

(4) (A) Any use of information disclosed pursuant to this section for purposes other than those provided by paragraph (1) or in violation of paragraph (2) shall make the user liable for the actual damages, and any amount that may be determined by a jury or a court sitting without a jury, not exceeding three times the amount of actual damage, and not less than two hundred fifty dollars ($250), and attorney's fees, exemplary damages, or a civil penalty not exceeding twenty-five thousand dollars ($25,000).

(B) Whenever there is reasonable cause to believe that any person or group of persons is engaged in a pattern or practice of misuse of the information available via an Internet Web site established pursuant to this section in violation of paragraph (2), the Attorney General, any district attorney, or city attorney, or any person aggrieved by the misuse is authorized to bring a civil action in the appropriate court requesting preventive relief, including an application for a permanent or temporary injunction, restraining order, or other order against the person or group of persons responsible for the pattern or practice of misuse. The foregoing remedies shall be independent of any other remedies or procedures that may be available to an aggrieved party under other provisions of law, including Part 2 (commencing with Section 43) of Division 1 of the Civil Code.

(m) The public notification provisions of this section are applicable to every person described in this section, without regard to when his or her crimes were committed or his or her duty to register pursuant to Section 290 arose, and to every offense described in this section, regardless of when it was committed.

(n) A designated law enforcement entity and its employees shall be immune from liability for good faith conduct under this section.

(o) The Attorney General, in collaboration with local law enforcement and others knowledgeable about sex offenders, shall develop strategies to assist members of the public in understanding and using publicly available information about registered sex offenders to further public safety. These strategies may include, but are not limited to, a hotline for community inquiries, neighborhood and business guidelines for how to respond to information posted on this Internet Web site, and any other resource that promotes public education about these offenders.

(p) This section shall remain in effect only until January 1, 2022, and as of that date is repealed.

(Amended (as amended by Stats. 2017, Ch. 541, Sec. 9) by Stats. 2018, Ch. 423, Sec. 57. (SB 1494) Effective January 1, 2019. Repealed as of January 1, 2022, by its own provisions. See later operative version amended by Sec. 58 of Stats. 2018, Ch. 423.)
290.46.

(a) (1) On or before the dates specified in this section, the Department of Justice shall make available information concerning persons who are required to register pursuant to Section 290 to the public via an Internet Web site as specified in this section. The department shall update the Internet Web site on an ongoing basis. All information identifying the victim by name, birth date, address, or relationship to the registrant shall be excluded from the Internet Web site. The name or address of the person's employer and the listed person's criminal history other than the specific crimes for which the person is required to register shall not be included on the Internet Web site. The Internet Web site shall be translated into languages other than English as determined by the department.

(2) (A) On or before July 1, 2010, the Department of Justice shall make available to the public, via an Internet Web site as specified in this section, as to any person described in subdivision (b), the following information:

(i) The year of conviction of his or her most recent offense requiring registration pursuant to Section 290.

(ii) The year he or she was released from incarceration for that offense.

However, no year of conviction shall be made available to the public unless the department also is able to make available the corresponding year of release of incarceration for that offense, and the required notation regarding any subsequent felony.

(B) (i) Any state facility that releases from incarceration a person who was incarcerated because of a crime for which he or she is required to register as a sex offender pursuant to Section 290 shall, within 30 days of release, provide the year of release for his or her most recent offense requiring registration to the Department of Justice in a manner and format approved by the department.

(ii) Any state facility that releases a person who is required to register pursuant to Section 290 from incarceration whose incarceration was for a felony committed subsequently to the offense for which he or she is required to register shall, within 30 days of release, advise the Department of Justice of that fact.

(iii) Any state facility that, prior to January 1, 2007, released from incarceration a person who was incarcerated because of a crime for which he or she is required to register as a sex offender pursuant to Section 290 shall provide the year of release for his or her most recent offense requiring registration to the Department of Justice in a manner and format approved by the department. The information provided by the Department of Corrections and Rehabilitation shall be limited to information that is currently maintained in an electronic format.

(iv) Any state facility that, prior to January 1, 2007, released a person who is required to register pursuant to Section 290 from incarceration whose incarceration was for a felony committed subsequently to the offense for which he or she is required to register shall advise the Department of Justice of that fact in a manner and format approved by the department. The information provided by the Department of Corrections and Rehabilitation shall be limited to information that is currently maintained in an electronic format.

(3) The State Department of State Hospitals shall provide to the Department of Justice the names of all persons committed to its custody pursuant to Article 4 (commencing with Section 6600) of Chapter 2 of Part 2 of Division 6 of the Welfare and Institutions Code, within 30 days of commitment, and shall provide the names of all of those persons released from its custody within five working days of release.

(b) (1) With respect to a person who has been convicted of the commission or the attempted commission of any of the offenses listed in, or who is otherwise described in, paragraph (2), or who is a tier three offender as described in paragraph (3) of subdivision (d) of Section 290, the Department of Justice shall make available to the public via the Internet Web site his or her name and known aliases, a photograph, a physical description, including gender and race, date of birth, criminal history, prior adjudication as a sexually violent predator, the address at which the person resides, and any other information that the Department of Justice deems relevant, but not the information excluded pursuant to subdivision (a), except that information about persons required to register as a result of an adjudication as a ward of the juvenile court pursuant to Section 290.008 shall not be made available on the Internet Web site. The department shall also make available to the public via the Internet Web site his or her static SARATSO risk level, if any, and information on an elevated risk level based on the SARATSO future violence tool. Any registrant whose information is listed on the public Internet Web site on January 1, 2022, by the Department of Justice pursuant to this subdivision, may continue to be included on the public Internet Web site while the registrant is placed in the tier-to-be-determined category described in paragraph (5) of subdivision (d) of Section 290.

(2) This subdivision shall apply to the following offenses and offenders:

(A) Section 187 committed in the perpetration, or an attempt to perpetrate, rape or any act punishable under Section 286, 287, 288, or 289, or former Section 288a.

(B) Section 207 committed with intent to violate Section 261, 286, 287, 288, or 289, or former Section 288a.

(C) Section 209 committed with intent to violate Section 261, 286, 287, 288, or 289, or former Section 288a.

(D) Paragraph (2) or (6) of subdivision (a) of Section 261.

(E) Section 264.1.

(F) Section 269.

(G) Subdivision (c) or (d) of Section 286.

(H) Subdivision (a), (b), or (c) of Section 288, provided that the offense is a felony.

(I) Subdivision (c) or (d) of Section 287 or of former Section 288a.

(J) Section 288.3, provided that the offense is a felony.

(K) Section 288.4, provided that the offense is a felony.

(L) Section 288.5.

(M) Subdivision (a) or (j) of Section 289.

(N) Section 288.7.

(O) Any person who has ever been adjudicated a sexually violent predator, as defined in Section 6600 of the Welfare and Institutions Code.

(P) A felony violation of Section 311.1.

(Q) A felony violation of subdivision (b), (c), or (d) of Section 311.2.

(R) A felony violation of Section 311.3.

(S) A felony violation of subdivision (a), (b), or (c) of Section 311.4.

(T) Section 311.10.

(U) A felony violation of Section 311.11.

(V) A tier three offender, as described in paragraph (3) of subdivision (d) of Section 290.

(c) (1) With respect to a person who has been convicted of the commission or the attempted commission of any of the offenses listed in, or who is otherwise described in, paragraph (2) of subdivision (d) of Section 290 and who is a tier two offender, and with respect to a person who has been convicted of the commission or the attempted commission of Section 647.6, the Department of Justice shall make available to the public via the Internet Web site his or her name and known aliases, a photograph, a physical description, including gender and race, date of birth, criminal history, the community of residence and ZIP Code in which the person resides or the county in which the person is registered as a transient, and any other information that the Department of Justice deems relevant, but not the information excluded pursuant to subdivision (a) or the address at which the person resides, except that information about persons required to register as a result of an adjudication as a ward of the juvenile court pursuant to Section 290.008 shall not be made available on the Internet Web site. Any registrant whose information is listed on the public Internet Web site on January 1, 2022, by the Department of Justice pursuant to this subdivision may continue to be

included on the public Internet Web site while the registrant is placed in the tier-to-be-determined category described in paragraph (5) of subdivision (d) of Section 290.

(2) Any registrant whose information was not included on the public Internet Web site on January 1, 2022, and who is placed in the tier-to-be-determined category described in paragraph (5) of subdivision (d) of Section 290 may have the information described in this subdivision made available to the public via the public Internet Web site.

(d) (1) (A) An offender who is required to register pursuant to the Sex Offender Registration Act may apply for exclusion from the Internet Web site if he or she demonstrates that the person's only registerable offense is either of the following:

(i) An offense for which the offender successfully completed probation, provided that the offender submits to the department a certified copy of a probation report, presentencing report, report prepared pursuant to Section 288.1, or other official court document that clearly demonstrates that the offender was the victim's parent, stepparent, sibling, or grandparent and that the crime did not involve either oral copulation or penetration of the vagina or rectum of either the victim or the offender by the penis of the other or by any foreign object.

(ii) An offense for which the offender is on probation at the time of his or her application, provided that the offender submits to the department a certified copy of a probation report, presentencing report, report prepared pursuant to Section 288.1, or other official court document that clearly demonstrates that the offender was the victim's parent, stepparent, sibling, or grandparent and that the crime did not involve either oral copulation or penetration of the vagina or rectum of either the victim or the offender by the penis of the other or by any foreign object.

(B) If, subsequent to his or her application, the offender commits a violation of probation resulting in his or her incarceration in county jail or state prison, his or her exclusion, or application for exclusion, from the Internet Web site shall be terminated.

(C) For the purposes of this paragraph, "successfully completed probation" means that during the period of probation the offender neither received additional county jail or state prison time for a violation of probation nor was convicted of another offense resulting in a sentence to county jail or state prison.

(2) If the department determines that a person who was granted an exclusion under a former version of this subdivision would not qualify for an exclusion under the current version of this subdivision, the department shall rescind the exclusion, make a reasonable effort to provide notification to the person that the exclusion has been rescinded, and, no sooner than 30 days after notification is attempted, make information about the offender available to the public on the Internet Web site as provided in this section.

(3) Effective January 1, 2012, no person shall be excluded pursuant to this subdivision unless the offender has submitted to the department documentation sufficient for the department to determine that he or she has a SARATSO risk level of average, below average, or very low as determined by the Coding Rules for the SARATSO static risk assessment instrument.

(e) (1) A designated law enforcement entity, as defined in subdivision (f) of Section 290.45, may make available information concerning persons who are required to register pursuant to Section 290 to the public via an Internet Web site as specified in paragraph (2), provided that the information about that person is also displayed on the Department of Justice's Megan's Law Internet Web site.

(2) The law enforcement entity may make available by way of an Internet Web site the information described in subdivision (c) if it determines that the public disclosure of the information about a specific offender by way of the entity's Internet Web site is necessary to ensure the public safety based upon information available to the entity concerning the current risk posed by a specific offender, including his or her risk of sexual or violent reoffense, as indicated by the person's SARATSO static, dynamic, and violence risk levels, as described in Section 290.04, if available.

(3) The information that may be provided pursuant to this subdivision may include the information specified in subdivision (b) of Section 290.45. However, that offender's address may not be disclosed unless he or she is a person whose address is on the Department of Justice's Internet Web site pursuant to subdivision (b).

(f) For purposes of this section, "offense" includes the statutory predecessors of that offense, or any offense committed in another jurisdiction that, if committed or attempted to be committed in this state, would have been punishable in this state as an offense listed in subdivision (c) of Section 290.

(g) Notwithstanding Section 6254.5 of the Government Code, disclosure of information pursuant to this section is not a waiver of exemptions under Chapter 3.5 (commencing with Section 6250) of Title 1 of Division 7 of the Government Code and does not affect other statutory restrictions on disclosure in other situations.

(h) (1) Any person who uses information disclosed pursuant to this section to commit a misdemeanor shall be subject to, in addition to any other penalty or fine imposed, a fine of not less than ten thousand dollars ($10,000) and not more than fifty thousand dollars ($50,000).

(2) Any person who uses information disclosed pursuant to this section to commit a felony shall be punished, in addition and consecutive to any other punishment, by a five-year term of imprisonment pursuant to subdivision (h) of Section 1170.

(i) Any person who is required to register pursuant to Section 290 who enters an Internet Web site established pursuant to this section shall be punished by a fine not exceeding one thousand dollars ($1,000), imprisonment in a county jail for a period not to exceed six months, or by both that fine and imprisonment.

(j) (1) A person is authorized to use information disclosed pursuant to this section only to protect a person at risk.

(2) Except as authorized under paragraph (1) or any other provision of law, use of any information that is disclosed pursuant to this section for purposes relating to any of the following is prohibited:

(A) Health insurance.

(B) Insurance.

(C) Loans.

(D) Credit.

(E) Employment.

(F) Education, scholarships, or fellowships.

(G) Housing or accommodations.

(H) Benefits, privileges, or services provided by any business establishment.

(3) This section shall not affect authorized access to, or use of, information pursuant to, among other provisions, Sections 11105 and 11105.3 of this code, Section 8808 of the Family Code, Sections 777.5 and 14409.2 of the Financial Code, Sections 1522.01 and 1596.871 of the Health and Safety Code, and Section 432.7 of the Labor Code.

(4) (A) Any use of information disclosed pursuant to this section for purposes other than those provided by paragraph (1) or in violation of paragraph (2) shall make the user liable for the actual damages, and any amount that may be determined by a jury or a court sitting without a jury, not exceeding three times the amount of actual damage, and not less than two hundred fifty dollars ($250), and attorney's fees, exemplary damages, or a civil penalty not exceeding twenty-five thousand dollars ($25,000).

(B) Whenever there is reasonable cause to believe that any person or group of persons is engaged in a pattern or practice of misuse of the information available via an Internet Web site established pursuant to this section in violation of paragraph (2), the Attorney General, any district attorney, or city attorney, or any person aggrieved by the misuse is authorized to bring a civil action in the appropriate court requesting preventive relief, including an application for a permanent or temporary injunction, restraining order, or other order against the person or group of persons responsible for the pattern or practice of misuse. The foregoing remedies shall be independent of any other remedies or procedures that may be available to an aggrieved party under other provisions of law, including Part 2 (commencing with Section 43) of Division 1 of the Civil Code.

(k) The public notification provisions of this section are applicable to every person described in this section, without regard to when his or her crimes were committed or his or her duty to register pursuant to Section 290 arose, and to every offense described in this section, regardless of when it was committed.

(l) A designated law enforcement entity and its employees shall be immune from liability for good faith conduct under this section.

(m) The Attorney General, in collaboration with local law enforcement and others knowledgeable about sex offenders, shall develop strategies to assist members of the public in understanding and using publicly available information about registered sex offenders to further public safety. These strategies may include, but are not limited to, a hotline for community inquiries, neighborhood and business guidelines for how to respond to information posted on this Internet Web site, and any other resource that promotes public education about these offenders.

(n) This section shall become operative on January 1, 2022.

(Amended (as added by Stats. 2017, Ch. 541, Sec. 10) by Stats. 2018, Ch. 423, Sec. 58. (SB 1494) Effective January 1, 2019. Section operative January 1, 2022, by its own provisions.)

290.47.

The Department of Justice shall record the address at which a registered sex offender resides with a unique identifier for the address. The information for this identifier shall be captured pursuant to Section 290.015 and the identifier shall consist of a description of the nature of the dwelling, with the choices of a single family residence, an apartment/condominium, a motel/hotel, or a licensed facility. Each address and its association with any specific registered sex offender shall be stored by the department in the same database as the registration data recorded pursuant to Section 290.015. The department shall make that information available to the State Department of Social Services or any other state agency when the agency needs the information for law enforcement purposes relating to investigative responsibilities relative to sex offenders. This section shall become operative on January 1, 2012.

(Added by Stats. 2009, Ch. 55, Sec. 1. (SB 583) Effective January 1, 2010. Section operative January 1, 2012, by its own provisions.)

290.5.

(a) (1) A person required to register under Section 290 for an offense not listed in paragraph (2), upon obtaining a certificate of rehabilitation under Chapter 3.5 (commencing with Section 4852.01) of Title 6 of Part 3, shall be relieved of any further duty to register under Section 290 if he or she is not in custody, on parole, or on probation.

(2) A person required to register under Section 290, upon obtaining a certificate of rehabilitation under Chapter 3.5 (commencing with Section 4852.01) of Title 6 of Part 3, shall not be relieved of the duty to register under Section 290, or of the duty to register under Section 290 for any offense subject to that section of which he or she is convicted in the future, if his or her conviction is for one of the following offenses:

(A) Section 207 or 209 committed with the intent to violate Section 261, 286, 287, 288, or 289 or former Section 288a.

(B) Section 220, except assault to commit mayhem.

(C) Section 243.4, provided that the offense is a felony.

(D) Paragraph (1), (2), (3), (4), or (6) of subdivision (a) of Section 261.

(E) Section 264.1.

(F) Section 266, provided that the offense is a felony.

(G) Section 266c, provided that the offense is a felony.

(H) Section 266j.

(I) Section 267.

(J) Section 269.

(K) Paragraph (1) of subdivision (b) of Section 286, provided that the offense is a felony.

(L) Paragraph (2) of subdivision (b) of, or subdivision (c), (d), (f), (g), (i), (j), or (k) of, Section 286.

(M) Section 288.

(N) Paragraph (1) of subdivision (b) of Section 287 or former Section 288a, provided that the offense is a felony.

(O) Paragraph (2) of subdivision (b) of, or subdivision (c), (d), (f), (g), (i), (j), or (k) of, Section 287 or former Section 288a.

(P) Section 288.5.

(Q) Section 288.7.

(R) Subdivision (a), (b), (d), (e), (f), (g), or (h) of Section 289, provided that the offense is a felony.

(S) Subdivision (i) or (j) of Section 289.

(T) Section 647.6.

(U) The attempted commission of any of the offenses specified in this paragraph.

(V) The statutory predecessor of any of the offenses specified in this paragraph.

(W) Any offense which, if committed or attempted in this state, would have been punishable as one or more of the offenses specified in this paragraph.

(b) (1) Except as provided in paragraphs (2) and (3), a person described in paragraph (2) of subdivision (a) shall not be relieved of the duty to register until that person has obtained a full pardon as provided in Chapter 1 (commencing with Section 4800) or Chapter 3 (commencing with Section 4850) of Title 6 of Part 3.

(2) This subdivision does not apply to misdemeanor violations of Section 647.6.

(3) The court, upon granting a petition for a certificate of rehabilitation pursuant to Chapter 3.5 (commencing with Section 4852.01) of Title 6 of Part 3, if the petition was granted prior to January 1, 1998, may relieve a person of the duty to register under Section 290 for a violation of Section 288 or 288.5, provided that the person was granted probation pursuant to subdivision (d) of Section 1203.066, has complied with the provisions of Section 290 for a continuous period of at least 10 years immediately preceding the filing of the petition, and has not been convicted of a felony during that period.

(c) This section shall remain in effect only until July 1, 2021, and as of that date is repealed.

(Amended (as amended by Stats. 2017, Ch. 541, Sec. 11) by Stats. 2018, Ch. 423, Sec. 59. (SB 1494) Effective January 1, 2019. Repealed as of July 1, 2021, by its own provisions. See later operative version added by Sec. 12 of Stats. 2017, Ch.541.)

290.5.

(a) (1) A person who is required to register pursuant to Section 290 and who is a tier one or tier two offender may file a petition in the superior court in the county in which he or she is registered for termination from the sex offender registry at the expiration of his or her mandated minimum registration period, or if the person is required to register pursuant to Section 290.008, he or she may file the petition in juvenile court on or after his or her birthday following the expiration of the mandated minimum registration period. The petition shall contain proof of the person's current registration as a sex offender.

(2) The petition shall be served on the registering law enforcement agency and the district attorney in the county where the petition is filed and on the law enforcement agency and the district attorney of the county of conviction of a registerable offense if different than the county where the petition is filed. The registering law enforcement agency and the law enforcement agency of the county of conviction of a registerable offense if different than the county where the petition is filed shall, within 60 days of receipt of the petition, report to the district attorney and the superior or juvenile court in which the petition is filed regarding whether the person has met the requirements for

termination pursuant to subdivision (e) of Section 290. If an offense which may require registration pursuant to Section 290.005 is identified by the registering law enforcement agency which has not previously been assessed by the Department of Justice, the registering law enforcement agency shall refer that conviction to the department for assessment and determination of whether the conviction changes the tier designation assigned by the department to the offender. If the newly discovered offense changes the tier designation for that person, the department shall change the tier designation pursuant to subdivision (d) of Section 290 within three months of receipt of the request by the registering law enforcement agency and notify the registering law enforcement agency. If more time is required to obtain the documents needed to make the assessment, the department shall notify the registering law enforcement agency of the reason that an extension of time is necessary to complete the tier designation. The registering law enforcement agency shall report to the district attorney and the court that the department has requested an extension of time to determine the person's tier designation based on the newly discovered offense, the reason for the request, and the estimated time needed to complete the tier designation. The district attorney in the county where the petition is filed may, within 60 days of receipt of the report from either the registering law enforcement agency, the law enforcement agency of the county of conviction of a registerable offense if different than the county where the petition is filed, or the district attorney of the county of conviction of a registerable offense, request a hearing on the petition if the petitioner has not fulfilled the requirement described in subdivision (e) of Section 290, or if community safety would be significantly enhanced by the person's continued registration. If no hearing is requested, the petition for termination shall be granted if the court finds the required proof of current registration is presented in the petition, provided that the registering agency reported that the person met the requirement for termination pursuant to subdivision (e) of Section 290, there are no pending charges against the person which could extend the time to complete the registration requirements of the tier or change the person's tier status, and the person is not in custody or on parole, probation, or supervised release.

(3) If the district attorney requests a hearing, he or she shall be entitled to present evidence regarding whether community safety would be significantly enhanced by requiring continued registration. In determining whether to order continued registration, the court shall consider: the nature and facts of the registerable offense; the age and number of victims; whether any victim was a stranger at the time of the offense (known to the offender for less than 24 hours); criminal and relevant noncriminal behavior before and after conviction for the registerable offense; the time period during which the person has not reoffended; successful completion, if any, of a Sex Offender Management Board-certified sex offender treatment program; and the person's current risk of sexual or violent reoffense, including the person's risk levels on SARATSO static, dynamic, and violence risk assessment instruments, if available. Any judicial determination made pursuant to this section may be heard and determined upon declarations, affidavits, police reports, or any other evidence submitted by the parties which is reliable, material, and relevant.

(4) If termination from the registry is denied, the court shall set the time period after which the person can repetition for termination, which shall be at least one year from the date of the denial, but not to exceed five years, based on facts presented at the hearing. The court shall state on the record the reason for its determination setting the time period after which the person may repetition.

(5) The court shall notify the Department of Justice, California Sex Offender Registry, when a petition for termination from the registry is granted or denied. If the petition is denied, the court shall also notify the Department of Justice, California Sex Offender Registry, of the time period after which the person can file a new petition for termination.

(b) (1) A person required to register as a tier two offender, pursuant to paragraph (2) of subdivision (d) of Section 290, may petition the superior court for termination from the registry after 10 years from release from custody on the registerable offense if all of the following apply: (A) the registerable offense involved no more than one victim 14 to 17 years of age, inclusive; (B) the offender was under 21 years of age at the time of the offense; (C) the registerable offense is not specified in subdivision (c) of Section 667.5, except subdivision (a) of Section 288; and (D) the registerable offense is not specified in Section 236.1.

(2) A tier two offender described in paragraph (1) of subdivision (b) may file a petition with the superior court for termination from the registry only if he or she has not been convicted of a new offense requiring sex offender registration or an offense described in subdivision (c) of Section 667.5 since the person was released from custody on the offense requiring registration pursuant to Section 290, and has registered for 10 years pursuant to subdivision (e) of Section 290. The court shall determine whether community safety would be significantly enhanced by requiring continued registration and may consider the following factors: whether the victim was a stranger (known less than 24 hours) at the time of the offense; the nature of the registerable offense, including whether the offender took advantage of a position of trust; criminal and relevant noncriminal behavior before and after the conviction for the registerable offense; whether the offender has successfully completed a Sex Offender Management Board-certified sex offender treatment program; whether the offender initiated a relationship for the purpose of facilitating the offense; and the person's current risk of sexual or violent reoffense, including the person's risk levels on SARATSO static, dynamic, and violence risk assessment instruments, if known. If the petition is denied, the person may not repetition for termination for at least one year.

(3) A person required to register as a tier three offender based solely on his or her risk level, pursuant to subparagraph (D) of paragraph (3) of subdivision (d) of Section 290, may petition the court for termination from the registry after 20 years from release from custody on the registerable offense, if the person (A) has not been convicted of a new offense requiring sex offender registration or an offense described in subdivision (c) of Section 667.5 since the person was released from custody on the offense requiring registration pursuant to Section 290, and (B) has registered for 20 years pursuant to subdivision (e) of Section 290; except that a person required to register for a conviction pursuant to Section 288 or an offense listed in subdivision (c) of Section 1192.7 who is a tier three offender based on his or her risk level, pursuant to subparagraph (D) of paragraph (3) of subdivision (d) of Section 290, shall not be permitted to petition for removal from the registry. The court shall determine whether community safety would be significantly enhanced by requiring continued registration and may consider the following factors: whether the victim was a stranger (known less than 24 hours) at the time of the offense; the nature of the registerable offense, including whether the offender took advantage of a position of trust; criminal and relevant noncriminal behavior before and after the conviction for the registerable offense; whether the offender has successfully completed a Sex Offender Management Board-certified sex offender treatment program; whether the offender initiated a relationship for the purpose of facilitating the offense; and the person's current risk of sexual or violent reoffense, including the person's risk levels on SARATSO static, dynamic, and violence risk assessment instruments, if known. If the petition is denied, the person may not re-petition for termination for at least three years.

(c) This section shall become operative on July 1, 2021.

(Repealed (in Sec. 11) and added by Stats. 2017, Ch. 541, Sec. 12. (SB 384) Effective January 1, 2018. Section operative July 1, 2021, by its own provisions.)

290.6.

(a) Fifteen days before the scheduled release date of a person described in subdivision (b), the Department of Corrections and Rehabilitation shall provide to local law enforcement all of the following information regarding the person:

(1) Name.

(2) Community residence and address, including ZIP Code.

(3) Physical description.
(4) Conviction information.
(b) This subdivision shall apply to any person sentenced to the state prison who is required to register pursuant to Section 290 for a conviction of an offense specified in subdivision (b), (c), or (d) of Section 290.46 and to any person described in those subdivisions.
(c) For the purpose of this section, "law enforcement" includes any agency with which the person will be required to register upon his or her release pursuant to Section 290 based upon the person's community of residence upon release.
(d) If it is not possible for the Department of Corrections and Rehabilitation to provide the information specified in subdivision (a) on a date that is 15 days before the scheduled release date, the information shall be provided on the next business day following that date.
(e) The Department of Corrections and Rehabilitation shall notify local law enforcement within 36 hours of learning of the change if the scheduled release date or any of the required information changes prior to the scheduled release date.
(Amended by Stats. 2006, Ch. 538, Sec. 501. Effective January 1, 2007.)

290.7.
The Department of Corrections shall provide samples of blood and saliva taken from a prison inmate pursuant to the DNA and Forensic Identification Data Base and Data Bank Act of 1998 (Chapter 6 (commencing with Section 295) of Title 9 of Part 1 of the Penal Code) to the county in which the inmate is to be released if the county maintains a local DNA testing laboratory.
(Amended by Stats. 1999, Ch. 475, Sec. 2. Effective January 1, 2000.)

290.8.
Effective January 1, 1999, any local law enforcement agency that does not register sex offenders during regular daytime business hours on a daily basis, excluding weekends and holidays, shall notify the regional parole office for the Department of Corrections and the regional parole office for the Department of the Youth Authority of the days, times, and locations the agency is available for registration of sex offenders pursuant to Section 290.
(Added by Stats. 1998, Ch. 960, Sec. 4. Effective January 1, 1999.)

290.85.
(a) Every person released on probation or parole who is required to register as a sex offender, pursuant to Section 290, shall provide proof of registration to his or her probation officer or parole agent within six working days of release on probation or parole. The six-day period for providing proof of registration may be extended only upon determination by the probation officer or parole agent that unusual circumstances exist relating to the availability of local law enforcement registration capabilities that preclude the person's ability to meet the deadline.
(b) Every person released on probation or parole who is required to register as a sex offender pursuant to Section 290 shall provide proof of any change or update to his or her registration information to his or her probation officer or parole agent within five working days for so long as he or she is required to be under the supervision of a probation officer or parole agent.
(c) A probation officer or parole agent who supervises an individual who is required to register as a sex offender pursuant to Section 290 shall inform that individual of his or her duties under this section not fewer than six days prior to the date on which proof of registration or proof of any change or update to registration information is to be provided to the probation officer or parole agent.
(d) For purposes of this section, "proof of registration" means a photocopy of the actual registration form. A law enforcement agency that registers an individual as a sex offender pursuant to Section 290 who is released on probation or parole and is therefore subject to this section shall provide that individual with proof of his or her registration free of charge when requested by the registrant to fulfill the requirements of this section or any other provision of law.
(Amended by Stats. 2003, Ch. 245, Sec. 1. Effective January 1, 2004.)

290.9.
Notwithstanding any other provision of law, any state or local governmental agency shall, upon written request, provide to the Department of Justice the address of any person represented by the department to be a person who is in violation of his or her duty to register under Section 290.
(Added by Stats. 2004, Ch. 127, Sec. 1. Effective January 1, 2005.)

290.95.
(a) Every person required to register under Section 290, who applies for or accepts a position as an employee or volunteer with any person, group, or organization where the registrant would be working directly and in an unaccompanied setting with minor children on more than an incidental and occasional basis or have supervision or disciplinary power over minor children, shall disclose his or her status as a registrant, upon application or acceptance of a position, to that person, group, or organization.
(b) Every person required to register under Section 290 who applies for or accepts a position as an employee or volunteer with any person, group, or organization where the applicant would be working directly and in an accompanied setting with minor children, and the applicant's work would require him or her to touch the minor children on more than an incidental basis, shall disclose his or her status as a registrant, upon application or acceptance of the position, to that person, group, or organization.
(c) No person who is required to register under Section 290 because of a conviction for a crime where the victim was a minor under 16 years of age shall be an employer, employee, or independent contractor, or act as a volunteer with any person, group, or organization in a capacity in which the registrant would be working directly and in an unaccompanied setting with minor children on more than an incidental and occasional basis or have supervision or disciplinary power over minor children. This subdivision shall not apply to a business owner or an independent contractor who does not work directly in an unaccompanied setting with minors.
(d) For purposes of this section, "working directly and in an unaccompanied setting" includes, but is not limited to, providing goods or services to minors.
(e) A violation of this section is a misdemeanor punishable by imprisonment in a county jail for not exceeding six months, by a fine not exceeding one thousand dollars ($1,000), or by both that imprisonment and fine, and a violation of this section shall not constitute a continuing offense.
(Amended by Stats. 2009, Ch. 430, Sec. 1. (AB 307) Effective October 11, 2009.)

291.
Every sheriff, chief of police, or the Commissioner of the California Highway Patrol, upon the arrest for any of the offenses enumerated in Section 290, subdivision (a) of Section 261, or Section 44010 of the Education Code, of any school employee, shall, provided that he or she knows that the arrestee is a school employee, do either of the following:
(a) If the school employee is a teacher in any of the public schools of this state, the sheriff, chief of police, or Commissioner of the California Highway Patrol shall immediately notify by telephone the superintendent of schools of the school district employing the teacher and shall immediately give written notice of the arrest to the Commission on Teacher Credentialing and to the superintendent of schools in the county where the person is employed. Upon receipt of the notice, the county superintendent of schools and the Commission on Teacher Credentialing shall immediately notify the governing board of the school district employing the person.
(b) If the school employee is a nonteacher in any of the public schools of this state, the sheriff, chief of police, or Commissioner of the California Highway Patrol shall immediately notify by telephone the superintendent of schools of the school district employing the nonteacher and shall immediately give written notice of the arrest to the governing board of the school district employing the person.
(Amended by Stats. 2003, Ch. 536, Sec. 2. Effective January 1, 2004.)

291.1.
Every sheriff or chief of police, or Commissioner of the California Highway Patrol, upon the arrest for any of the offenses enumerated in Section 290 or Section 44010 of the Education Code, of any person who is employed as a teacher in any private school of this state, shall, provided that he or she knows that the arrestee is a school employee, immediately give written notice of the arrest to the private school authorities employing the teacher. The sheriff, chief of police, or Commissioner of the California Highway Patrol, provided that he or she knows that the arrestee is a school employee, shall immediately notify by telephone the private school authorities employing the teacher of the arrest.
(Amended by Stats. 2003, Ch. 536, Sec. 3. Effective January 1, 2004.)

291.5.
Every sheriff or chief of police, upon the arrest for any of the offenses enumerated in Section 290 or in subdivision (1) of Section 261 of any teacher or instructor employed in any community college district shall immediately notify by telephone the superintendent of the community college district employing the teacher or instructor and shall immediately give written notice of the arrest to the Office of the Chancellor of the California Community Colleges. Upon receipt of such notice, the district superintendent shall immediately notify the governing board of the community college district employing the person.
(Added by Stats. 1983, Ch. 1032, Sec. 4.)

292.
It is the intention of the Legislature in enacting this section to clarify that for the purposes of subdivisions (b) and (c) of Section 12 of Article I of the California Constitution, a violation of paragraph (2) or (6) of subdivision (a) of Section 261, paragraph (1) or (4) of subdivision (a) of Section 262, Section 264.1, subdivision (c) or (d) of Section 286, subdivision (c) or (d) of Section 287 or former Section 288a, subdivision (b) of Section 288, or subdivision (a) of Section 289, shall be deemed to be a felony offense involving an act of violence and a felony offense involving great bodily harm.
(Amended by Stats. 2018, Ch. 423, Sec. 60. (SB 1494) Effective January 1, 2019.)

293.
(a) An employee of a law enforcement agency who personally receives a report from a person, alleging that the person making the report has been the victim of a sex offense, shall inform that person that his or her name will become a matter of public record unless he or she requests that it not become a matter of public record, pursuant to Section 6254 of the Government Code.
(b) A written report of an alleged sex offense shall indicate that the alleged victim has been properly informed pursuant to subdivision (a) and shall memorialize his or her response.
(c) A law enforcement agency shall not disclose to a person, except the prosecutor, parole officers of the Department of Corrections and Rehabilitation, hearing officers of the parole authority, probation officers of county probation departments, or other persons or public agencies where authorized or required by law, the address of a person who alleges to be the victim of a sex offense.
(d) A law enforcement agency shall not disclose to a person, except the prosecutor, parole officers of the Department of Corrections and Rehabilitation, hearing officers of the parole authority, probation officers of county probation departments, or other persons or public agencies where authorized or required by law, the name of a person who alleges to be the victim of a sex offense if that person has elected to exercise his or her right pursuant to this section and Section 6254 of the Government Code.
(e) A law enforcement agency shall not disclose to a person, except the prosecutor, parole officers of the Department of Corrections and Rehabilitation, hearing officers of the parole authority, probation officers of county probation departments, or other persons or public agencies if authorized or required by law, names, addresses, or images of a person who alleges to be the victim of human trafficking, as defined in Section 236.1, or of that alleged victim's immediate family, other than a family member who is charged with a criminal offense arising from the same incident, and that information and those images shall be withheld and remain confidential. The law enforcement agency shall orally inform the person who alleges to be the victim of human trafficking of his or her right to have his or her name, addresses, and images, and the names, addresses, and images of his or her immediate family members withheld and kept confidential pursuant to this section and Section 6254 of the Government Code. For purposes of this subdivision, "immediate family" shall have the same meaning as that provided in paragraph (3) of subdivision (b) of Section 422.4 of the Penal Code.
(f) For purposes of this section, sex offense means any crime listed in subparagraph (A) of paragraph (2) of subdivision (f) of Section 6254 of the Government Code.
(g) Parole officers of the Department of Corrections and Rehabilitation, hearing officers of the parole authority, and probation officers of county probation departments shall be entitled to receive information pursuant to subdivisions (c), (d), and (e) only if the person to whom the information pertains alleges that he or she is the victim of a sex offense or is the victim of human trafficking, as defined in Section 236.1, the alleged perpetrator of which is a parolee who is alleged to have committed the offense while on parole, or in the case of a county probation officer, the person who is alleged to have committed the offense is a probationer or is under investigation by a county probation department.
(Amended by Stats. 2016, Ch. 644, Sec. 2. (AB 2498) Effective January 1, 2017.)

293.5.
(a) Except as provided in Chapter 10 (commencing with Section 1054) of Part 2 of Title 7, or for cases in which the alleged victim of a sex offense, as specified in subdivision (f) of Section 293, has not elected to exercise his or her right pursuant to Section 6254 of the Government Code, the court, at the request of the alleged victim, may order the identity of the alleged victim in all records and during all proceedings to be either Jane Doe or John Doe, if the court finds that such an order is reasonably necessary to protect the privacy of the person and will not unduly prejudice the prosecution or the defense.
(b) If the court orders the alleged victim to be identified as Jane Doe or John Doe pursuant to subdivision (a) and if there is a jury trial, the court shall instruct the jury, at the beginning and at the end of the trial, that the alleged victim is being so identified only for the purpose of protecting his or her privacy pursuant to this section.
(Amended by Stats. 2016, Ch. 644, Sec. 3. (AB 2498) Effective January 1, 2017.)

294.
(a) Upon conviction of any person for a violation of Section 273a, 273d, 288.5, 311.2, 311.3, or 647.6, the court may, in addition to any other penalty or restitution fine imposed, order the defendant to pay a restitution fine based on the defendant's ability to pay not to exceed five thousand dollars ($5,000), upon a felony conviction, or one thousand dollars ($1,000), upon a misdemeanor conviction, to be deposited in the Restitution Fund to be transferred to the county children's trust fund for the purposes of child abuse prevention.
(b) Upon conviction of any person for a violation of Section 261, 264.1, 285, 286, 287, or 289 or former Section 288a, where the violation is with a minor under the age of 14 years, the court may, in addition to any other penalty or restitution fine imposed, order the defendant to pay a restitution fine based on the defendant's ability to pay not to exceed five thousand dollars ($5,000), upon a felony conviction, or one thousand dollars ($1,000), upon a misdemeanor conviction, to be deposited in the Restitution Fund to be transferred to the county children's trust fund for the purpose of child abuse prevention.

(c) If the perpetrator is a member of the immediate family of the victim, the court shall consider in its decision to impose a fine under this section any hardship that may impact the victim from the imposition of the fine.

(d) If the court orders a fine to be imposed pursuant to this section, the actual administrative cost of collecting that fine, not to exceed 2 percent of the total amount paid, may be paid into the general fund of the county treasury for the use and benefit of the county.

(Amended by Stats. 2018, Ch. 423, Sec. 61. (SB 1494) Effective January 1, 2019.)

CHAPTER 6.
DNA and Forensic Identification Data Base and Data Bank Act of 1998 [295 - 300.3]

(Chapter 6 added by Stats. 1998, Ch. 696, Sec. 2.)

ARTICLE 1. Purpose and Administration [295 - 295.2]
(Article 1 added by Stats. 1998, Ch. 696, Sec. 2.)

295.

(a) This chapter shall be known and may be cited as the DNA and Forensic Identification Database and Data Bank Act of 1998, as amended.

(b) The people of the State of California set forth all of the following:

(1) Deoxyribonucleic acid (DNA) and forensic identification analysis is a useful law enforcement tool for identifying and prosecuting criminal offenders and exonerating the innocent.

(2) It is the intent of the people of the State of California, in order to further the purposes of this chapter, to require DNA and forensic identification data bank samples from all persons, including juveniles, for the felony and misdemeanor offenses described in subdivision (a) of Section 296.

(3) It is necessary to enact this act defining and governing the state's DNA and forensic identification database and data bank in order to clarify existing law and to enable the state's DNA and Forensic Identification Database and Data Bank Program to become a more effective law enforcement tool.

(c) The purpose of the DNA and Forensic Identification Database and Data Bank Program is to assist federal, state, and local criminal justice and law enforcement agencies within and outside California in the expeditious and accurate detection and prosecution of individuals responsible for sex offenses and other crimes, the exclusion of suspects who are being investigated for these crimes, and the identification of missing and unidentified persons, particularly abducted children.

(d) Like the collection of fingerprints, the collection of DNA samples pursuant to this chapter is an administrative requirement to assist in the accurate identification of criminal offenders.

(e) Unless otherwise requested by the Department of Justice, collection of biological samples for DNA analysis from qualifying persons under this chapter is limited to collection of inner cheek cells of the mouth (buccal swab samples).

(f) The Department of Justice DNA Laboratory may obtain through federal, state, or local law enforcement agencies blood specimens from qualifying persons as defined in subdivision (a) of Section 296, and according to procedures set forth in Section 298, when it is determined in the discretion of the Department of Justice that such specimens are necessary in a particular case or would aid the department in obtaining an accurate forensic DNA profile for identification purposes.

(g) The Department of Justice, through its DNA Laboratory, shall be responsible for the management and administration of the state's DNA and Forensic Identification Database and Data Bank Program and for liaison with the Federal Bureau of Investigation (FBI) regarding the state's participation in a national or international DNA database and data bank program such as the FBI's Combined DNA Index System (CODIS) that allows the storage and exchange of DNA records submitted by state and local forensic DNA laboratories nationwide.

(h) The Department of Justice shall be responsible for implementing this chapter.

(1) The Department of Justice DNA Laboratory, and the Department of Corrections and Rehabilitation may adopt policies and enact regulations for the implementation of this chapter, as necessary, to give effect to the intent and purpose of this chapter, and to ensure that data bank blood specimens, buccal swab samples, and thumb and palm print impressions as required by this chapter are collected from qualifying persons in a timely manner, as soon as possible after arrest, conviction, or a plea or finding of guilty, no contest, or not guilty by reason of insanity, or upon any disposition rendered in the case of a juvenile who is adjudicated under Section 602 of the Welfare and Institutions Code for commission of any of this chapter's enumerated qualifying offenses, including attempts, or when it is determined that a qualifying person has not given the required specimens, samples or print impressions. Before adopting any policy or regulation implementing this chapter, the Department of Corrections and Rehabilitation shall seek advice from and consult with the Department of Justice DNA Laboratory Director.

(2) Given the specificity of this chapter, and except as provided in subdivision (c) of Section 298.1, any administrative bulletins, notices, regulations, policies, procedures, or guidelines adopted by the Department of Justice and its DNA Laboratory or the Department of Corrections and Rehabilitation for the purpose of the implementing this chapter are exempt from the provisions of the Administrative Procedure Act, Chapter 3.5 (commencing with Section 11340), Chapter 4 (commencing with Section 11370), Chapter 4.5 (commencing with Section 11400), and Chapter 5 (commencing with Section 11500) of Part 1 of Division 3 of Title 2 of the Government Code.

(3) The Department of Corrections and Rehabilitation shall submit copies of any of its policies and regulations with respect to this chapter to the Department of Justice DNA Laboratory Director, and quarterly shall submit to the director written reports updating the director as to the status of its compliance with this chapter.

(4) On or before April 1 in the year following adoption of the act that added this paragraph, and quarterly thereafter, the Department of Justice DNA Laboratory shall submit a quarterly report to be published electronically on a Department of Justice Internet Web site and made available for public review. The quarterly report shall state the total number of samples received, the number of samples received from the Department of Corrections and Rehabilitation, the number of samples fully analyzed for inclusion in the CODIS database, and the number of profiles uploaded into the CODIS database for the reporting period. Each quarterly report shall state the total, annual, and quarterly number of qualifying profiles in the Department of Justice DNA Laboratory data bank both from persons and case evidence, and the number of hits and investigations aided, as reported to the National DNA Index System. The quarterly report shall also confirm the laboratory's accreditation status and participation in CODIS and shall include an accounting of the funds collected, expended, and disbursed pursuant to subdivision (k).

(5) On or before April 1 in the year following adoption of the act that added this paragraph, and quarterly thereafter, the Department of Corrections and Rehabilitation shall submit a quarterly report to be published electronically on a Department of Corrections and Rehabilitation Internet Web site and made available for public review. The quarterly report shall state the total number of inmates housed in state correctional facilities, including a breakdown of those housed in state prisons, camps, community correctional facilities, and other facilities such as prisoner mother facilities. Each quarterly report shall also state the total, annual, and quarterly number of inmates who have yet to provide specimens, samples and print impressions pursuant to this chapter

and the number of specimens, samples and print impressions that have yet to be forwarded to the Department of Justice DNA Laboratory within 30 days of collection.

(i) (1) When the specimens, samples, and print impressions required by this chapter are collected at a county jail or other county facility, including a private community correctional facility, the county sheriff or chief administrative officer of the county jail or other facility shall be responsible for ensuring all of the following:

(A) The requisite specimens, samples, and print impressions are collected from qualifying persons immediately following arrest, conviction, or adjudication, or during the booking or intake or reception center process at that facility, or reasonably promptly thereafter.

(B) The requisite specimens, samples, and print impressions are collected as soon as administratively practicable after a qualifying person reports to the facility for the purpose of providing specimens, samples, and print impressions.

(C) The specimens, samples, and print impressions collected pursuant to this chapter are forwarded immediately to the Department of Justice, and in compliance with department policies.

(2) The specimens, samples, and print impressions required by this chapter shall be collected by a person using a collection kit approved by the Department of Justice and in accordance with the requirements and procedures set forth in subdivision (b) of Section 298.

(3) The counties shall be reimbursed for the costs of obtaining specimens, samples, and print impressions subject to the conditions and limitations set forth by the Department of Justice policies governing reimbursement for collecting specimens, samples, and print impressions pursuant to Section 76104.6 of the Government Code.

(j) The trial court may order that a portion of the costs assessed pursuant to Section 1203.1c, 1203.1e, or 1203.1m include a reasonable portion of the cost of obtaining specimens, samples, and print impressions in furtherance of this chapter and the funds collected pursuant to this subdivision shall be deposited in the DNA Identification Fund as created by Section 76104.6 of the Government Code.

(k) The Department of Justice DNA Laboratory shall be known as the Jan Bashinski DNA Laboratory.

(Amended by Stats. 2007, Ch. 130, Sec. 188. Effective January 1, 2008. Note: This section was amended on Nov. 2, 2004, by initiative Prop. 69.)

295.1.

(a) The Department of Justice shall perform DNA analysis and other forensic identification analysis pursuant to this chapter only for identification purposes.

(b) The Department of Justice Bureau of Criminal Identification and Information shall perform examinations of palm prints pursuant to this chapter only for identification purposes.

(c) The DNA Laboratory of the Department of Justice shall serve as a repository for blood specimens and buccal swab and other biological samples collected, and shall analyze specimens and samples, and store, compile, correlate, compare, maintain, and use DNA and forensic identification profiles and records related to the following:

(1) Forensic casework and forensic unknowns.

(2) Known and evidentiary specimens and samples from crime scenes or criminal investigations.

(3) Missing or unidentified persons.

(4) Persons required to provide specimens, samples, and print impressions under this chapter.

(5) Legally obtained samples.

(6) Anonymous DNA records used for training, research, statistical analysis of populations, quality assurance, or quality control.

(d) The computerized data bank and database of the DNA Laboratory of the Department of Justice shall include files as necessary to implement this chapter.

(e) Nothing in this section shall be construed as requiring the Department of Justice to provide specimens or samples for quality control or other purposes to those who request specimens or samples.

(f) Submission of samples, specimens, or profiles for the state DNA Database and Data Bank Program shall include information as required by the Department of Justice for ensuring search capabilities and compliance with National DNA Index System (NDIS) standards.

(Amended November 2, 2004, by initiative Proposition 69, Sec. 2.)

295.2.

The DNA and forensic identification database and databank and the Department of Justice DNA Laboratory shall not be used as a source of genetic material for testing, research, or experiments, by any person, agency, or entity seeking to find a causal link between genetics and behavior or health.

(Amended by Stats. 2015, Ch. 303, Sec. 386. (AB 731) Effective January 1, 2016.)

ARTICLE 2. Offenders Subject to Sample Collection [296 - 296.2]
(Article 2 added by Stats. 1998, Ch. 696, Sec. 2.)

296.

(a) The following persons shall provide buccal swab samples, right thumbprints, and a full palm print impression of each hand, and any blood specimens or other biological samples required pursuant to this chapter for law enforcement identification analysis:

(1) Any person, including any juvenile, who is convicted of or pleads guilty or no contest to any felony offense, or is found not guilty by reason of insanity of any felony offense, or any juvenile who is adjudicated under Section 602 of the Welfare and Institutions Code for committing any felony offense.

(2) Any adult person who is arrested for or charged with any of the following felony offenses:

(A) Any felony offense specified in Section 290 or attempt to commit any felony offense described in Section 290, or any felony offense that imposes upon a person the duty to register in California as a sex offender under Section 290.

(B) Murder or voluntary manslaughter or any attempt to commit murder or voluntary manslaughter.

(C) Commencing on January 1 of the fifth year following enactment of the act that added this subparagraph, as amended, any adult person arrested or charged with any felony offense.

(3) Any person, including any juvenile, who is required to register under Section 290 or 457.1 because of the commission of, or the attempt to commit, a felony or misdemeanor offense, or any person, including any juvenile, who is housed in a mental health facility or sex offender treatment program after referral to such facility or program by a court after being charged with any felony offense.

(4) The term "felony" as used in this subdivision includes an attempt to commit the offense.

(5) Nothing in this chapter shall be construed as prohibiting collection and analysis of specimens, samples, or print impressions as a condition of a plea for a non-qualifying offense.

(b) The provisions of this chapter and its requirements for submission of specimens, samples and print impressions as soon as administratively practicable shall apply to all qualifying persons regardless of sentence imposed, including any sentence of death, life without the possibility of parole, or any life or indeterminate term, or any other disposition rendered in the case of an adult or juvenile tried as an adult, or whether the person is diverted, fined, or referred for evaluation, and regardless of disposition rendered or placement made in the case of juvenile who is found to have committed any felony offense or is adjudicated under Section 602 of the Welfare and Institutions Code.

(c) The provisions of this chapter and its requirements for submission of specimens, samples, and print impressions as soon as administratively practicable by qualified persons as described in subdivision (a) shall apply regardless of placement or

confinement in any mental hospital or other public or private treatment facility, and shall include, but not be limited to, the following persons, including juveniles:
(1) Any person committed to a state hospital or other treatment facility as a mentally disordered sex offender under Article 1 (commencing with Section 6300) of Chapter 2 of Part 2 of Division 6 of the Welfare and Institutions Code.
(2) Any person who has a severe mental disorder as set forth within the provisions of Article 4 (commencing with Section 2960) of Chapter 7 of Title 1 of Part 3 of the Penal Code.
(3) Any person found to be a sexually violent predator pursuant to Article 4 (commencing with Section 6600) of Chapter 2 of Part 2 of Division 6 of the Welfare and Institutions Code.
(d) The provisions of this chapter are mandatory and apply whether or not the court advises a person, including any juvenile, that he or she must provide the data bank and database specimens, samples, and print impressions as a condition of probation, parole, or any plea of guilty, no contest, or not guilty by reason of insanity, or any admission to any of the offenses described in subdivision (a).
(e) If at any stage of court proceedings the prosecuting attorney determines that specimens, samples, and print impressions required by this chapter have not already been taken from any person, as defined under subdivision (a) of Section 296, the prosecuting attorney shall notify the court orally on the record, or in writing, and request that the court order collection of the specimens, samples, and print impressions required by law. However, a failure by the prosecuting attorney or any other law enforcement agency to notify the court shall not relieve a person of the obligation to provide specimens, samples, and print impressions pursuant to this chapter.
(f) Prior to final disposition or sentencing in the case the court shall inquire and verify that the specimens, samples, and print impressions required by this chapter have been obtained and that this fact is included in the abstract of judgment or dispositional order in the case of a juvenile. The abstract of judgment issued by the court shall indicate that the court has ordered the person to comply with the requirements of this chapter and that the person shall be included in the state's DNA and Forensic Identification Data Base and Data Bank program and be subject to this chapter.
However, failure by the court to verify specimen, sample, and print impression collection or enter these facts in the abstract of judgment or dispositional order in the case of a juvenile shall not invalidate an arrest, plea, conviction, or disposition, or otherwise relieve a person from the requirements of this chapter.
(Amended November 2, 2004, by initiative Proposition 69, Sec. 3.)

296.1.

(a) The specimens, samples, and print impressions required by this chapter shall be collected from persons described in subdivision (a) of Section 296 for present and past qualifying offenses of record as follows:
(1) Collection from any adult person following arrest for a felony offense as specified in subparagraphs (A), (B), and (C) of paragraph (2) of subdivision (a) of Section 296:
(A) Each adult person arrested for a felony offense as specified in subparagraphs (A), (B), and (C) of paragraph (2) of subdivision (a) of Section 296 shall provide the buccal swab samples and thumb and palm print impressions and any blood or other specimens required pursuant to this chapter immediately following arrest, or during the booking or intake or prison reception center process or as soon as administratively practicable after arrest, but, in any case, prior to release on bail or pending trial or any physical release from confinement or custody.
(B) If the person subject to this chapter did not have specimens, samples, and print impressions taken immediately following arrest or during booking or intake procedures or is released on bail or pending trial or is not confined or incarcerated at the time of sentencing or otherwise bypasses a prison inmate reception center maintained by the Department of Corrections and Rehabilitation, the court shall order the person to report within five calendar days to a county jail facility or to a city, state, local, private, or other designated facility to provide the required specimens, samples, and print impressions in accordance with subdivision (i) of Section 295.
(2) Collection from persons confined or in custody after conviction or adjudication:
(A) Any person, including any juvenile who is imprisoned or confined or placed in a state correctional institution, a county jail, a facility within the jurisdiction of the Department of Corrections and Rehabilitation, the Corrections Standards Authority, a residential treatment program, or any state, local, city, private, or other facility after a conviction of any felony or misdemeanor offense, or any adjudication or disposition rendered in the case of a juvenile, whether or not that crime or offense is one set forth in subdivision (a) of Section 296, shall provide buccal swab samples and thumb and palm print impressions and any blood or other specimens required pursuant to this chapter, immediately at intake, or during the prison reception center process, or as soon as administratively practicable at the appropriate custodial or receiving institution or the program in which the person is placed, if:
(i) The person has a record of any past or present conviction or adjudication as a ward of the court in California of a qualifying offense described in subdivision (a) of Section 296 or has a record of any past or present conviction or adjudication in any other court, including any state, federal, or military court, of any offense that, if committed or attempted in this state, would have been punishable as an offense described in subdivision (a) of Section 296; and
(ii) The person's blood specimens, buccal swab samples, and thumb and palm print impressions authorized by this chapter are not in the possession of the Department of Justice DNA Laboratory or have not been recorded as part of the department's DNA databank program.
(3) Collection from persons on probation, parole, or other release:
(A) Any person, including any juvenile, who has a record of any past or present conviction or adjudication for an offense set forth in subdivision (a) of Section 296, and who is on probation, parole, postrelease community supervision, or mandatory supervision pursuant to paragraph (5) of subdivision (h) of Section 1170 for any felony or misdemeanor offense, whether or not that crime or offense is one set forth in subdivision (a) of Section 296, shall provide buccal swab samples and thumb and palm print impressions and any blood specimens required pursuant to this chapter, if:
(i) The person has a record of any past or present conviction or adjudication as a ward of the court in California of a qualifying offense described in subdivision (a) of Section 296 or has a record of any past or present conviction or adjudication in any other court, including any state, federal, or military court, of any offense that, if committed or attempted in this state, would have been punishable as an offense described in subdivision (a) of Section 296; and
(ii) The person's blood specimens, buccal swab samples, and thumb and palm print impressions authorized by this chapter are not in the possession of the Department of Justice DNA Laboratory or have not been recorded as part of the department's DNA databank program.
(B) The person shall have any required specimens, samples, and print impressions collected within five calendar days of being notified by the court, or a law enforcement agency or other agency authorized by the Department of Justice. The specimens, samples, and print impressions shall be collected in accordance with subdivision (i) of Section 295 at a county jail facility or a city, state, local, private, or other facility designated for this collection.
(4) Collection from parole violators and others returned to custody:
(A) If a person, including any juvenile, who has been released on parole, furlough, or other release for any offense or crime, whether or not set forth in subdivision (a) of Section 296, is returned to a state correctional or other institution for a violation of a condition of his or her parole, furlough, or other release, or for any other reason, that person shall provide buccal swab samples and thumb and palm print impressions and any blood or other specimens required pursuant to this chapter, at a state correctional or other receiving institution, if:
(i) The person has a record of any past or present conviction or adjudication as a ward of the court in California of a qualifying offense described in subdivision (a) of Section 296 or has a record of any past or present conviction or adjudication in any other court, including any state, federal, or military court, of any offense that, if committed or attempted in this state, would have been punishable as an offense described in subdivision (a) of Section 296; and
(ii) The person's blood specimens, buccal swab samples, and thumb and palm print impressions authorized by this chapter are not in the possession of the Department of Justice DNA Laboratory or have not been recorded as part of the department's DNA databank program.
(5) Collection from persons accepted into California from other jurisdictions:
(A) When an offender from another state is accepted into this state under any of the interstate compacts described in Article 3 (commencing with Section 11175) or Article 4 (commencing with Section 11189) of Chapter 2 of Title 1 of Part 4 of this code, or Chapter 4 (commencing with Section 1400) of Part 1 of Division 2 of the Welfare and Institutions Code, or under any other reciprocal agreement with any county, state, or federal agency, or any other provision of law, whether or not the offender is confined or released, the acceptance is conditional on the offender providing blood specimens, buccal swab samples, and palm and thumb print impressions pursuant to this chapter, if the offender has a record of any past or present conviction or adjudication in California of a qualifying offense described in subdivision (a) of Section 296 or has a record of any past or present conviction or adjudication or had a disposition rendered in any other court, including any state, federal, or military court, of any offense that, if committed or attempted in this state, would have been punishable as an offense described in subdivision (a) of Section 296.
(B) If the person is not confined, the specimens, samples, and print impressions required by this chapter must be provided within five calendar days after the person reports to the supervising agent or within five calendar days of notice to the person, whichever occurs first. The person shall report to a county jail facility in the county where he or she resides or temporarily is located to have the specimens, samples, and print impressions collected pursuant to this chapter. The specimens, samples, and print impressions shall be collected in accordance with subdivision (i) of Section 295.
(C) If the person is confined, he or she shall provide the blood specimens, buccal swab samples, and thumb and palm print impressions required by this chapter as soon as practicable after his or her receipt in a state, county, city, local, private, or other designated facility.
(6) Collection from persons in federal institutions:
(A) Subject to the approval of the Director of the FBI, persons confined or incarcerated in a federal prison or federal institution who have a record of any past or present conviction or juvenile adjudication for a qualifying offense described in subdivision (a) of Section 296, or of a similar crime under the laws of the United States or any other state that would constitute an offense described in subdivision (a) of Section 296, are subject to this chapter and shall provide blood specimens, buccal swab samples, and thumb and palm print impressions pursuant to this chapter if any of the following apply:
(i) The person committed a qualifying offense in California.
(ii) The person was a resident of California at the time of the qualifying offense.
(iii) The person has any record of a California conviction for an offense described in subdivision (a) of Section 296, regardless of when the crime was committed.
(iv) The person will be released in California.
(B) The Department of Justice DNA Laboratory shall, upon the request of the United States Department of Justice, forward portions of the specimens or samples, taken pursuant to this chapter, to the United States Department of Justice DNA databank laboratory. The specimens and samples required by this chapter shall be taken in accordance with the procedures set forth in subdivision (i) of Section 295. The Department of Justice DNA Laboratory is authorized to analyze and upload specimens and samples collected pursuant to this section upon approval of the Director of the FBI.
(b) Paragraphs (2), (3), (4), (5), and (6) of subdivision (a) shall have retroactive application. Collection shall occur pursuant to paragraphs (2), (3), (4), (5), and (6) of subdivision (a) regardless of when the crime charged or committed became a qualifying offense pursuant to this chapter, and regardless of when the person was convicted of the qualifying offense described in subdivision (a) of Section 296 or a similar crime under the laws of the United States or any other state, or pursuant to the United States Code of Military Justice, 10 U.S.C., Sections 801 and following, or when a juvenile petition is sustained for commission of a qualifying offense described in subdivision (a) of Section 296 or a similar crime under the laws of the United States or any other state.
(Amended by Stats. 2012, Ch. 43, Sec. 17. (SB 1023) Effective June 27, 2012. Note: This section was amended on Nov. 2, 2004, by initiative Prop. 69.)

296.2.

(a) Whenever the DNA Laboratory of the Department of Justice notifies the Department of Corrections and Rehabilitation or any law enforcement agency that a biological specimen or sample, or print impression is not usable for any reason, the person who provided the original specimen, sample, or print impression shall submit to collection of additional specimens, samples, or print impressions. The Department of Corrections and Rehabilitation or other responsible law enforcement agency shall collect additional specimens, samples, and print impressions from these persons as necessary to fulfill the requirements of this chapter, and transmit these specimens, samples, and print impressions to the appropriate agencies of the Department of Justice.
(b) If a person, including any juvenile, is convicted of, pleads guilty or no contest to, is found not guilty by reason of insanity of, or is adjudged a ward of the court under Section 602 of the Welfare and Institutions Code for committing, any of the offenses described in subdivision (a) of Section 296, and has given a blood specimen or other biological sample or samples to law enforcement for any purpose, the DNA Laboratory of the Department of Justice is authorized to analyze the blood specimen and other biological sample or samples for forensic identification markers, including DNA markers, and to include the DNA and forensic identification profiles from these specimens and samples in the state's DNA and forensic identification databank and databases.
This subdivision applies whether or not the blood specimen or other biological sample originally was collected from the sexual or violent offender pursuant to the databank and database program, and whether or not the crime committed predated the enactment of the state's DNA and forensic identification databank program, or any amendments thereto. This subdivision does not relieve a person convicted of a crime described in subdivision (a) of Section 296, or otherwise subject to this chapter, from the requirement to give blood specimens, saliva samples, and thumb and palm print impressions for the DNA and forensic identification databank and database program as described in this chapter.
(c) Any person who is required to register under the Sex Offender Registration Act who has not provided the specimens, samples, and print impressions described in this chapter for any reason including the release of the person prior to the enactment of the state's DNA and forensic identification database and databank program, an oversight or error, or because of the transfer of the person from another state, the person, as an additional requirement of registration or of updating his or her annual registration pursuant to the Sex Offender Registration Act shall give specimens, samples, and print impressions as described in this chapter for inclusion in the state's DNA and forensic identification database and databank.
At the time the person registers or updates his or her registration, he or she shall receive an appointment designating a time and place for the collection of the specimens,

samples, and print impressions described in this chapter, if he or she has not already complied with the provisions of this chapter.

As specified in the appointment, the person shall report to a county jail facility in the county where he or she resides or is temporarily located to have specimens, samples, and print impressions collected pursuant to this chapter or other facility approved by the Department of Justice for this collection. The specimens, samples, and print impressions shall be collected in accordance with subdivision (f) of Section 295.

If, prior to the time of the annual registration update, a person is notified by the Department of Justice, a probation or parole officer, other law enforcement officer, or officer of the court, that he or she is subject to this chapter, then the person shall provide the specimens, samples, and print impressions required by this chapter within 10 calendar days of the notification at a county jail facility or other facility approved by the department for this collection.

(Amended by Stats. 2007, Ch. 579, Sec. 37. Effective October 13, 2007.)

ARTICLE 3. Data Base Applications [297- 297.]
(Article 3 added by Stats. 1998, Ch. 696, Sec. 2.)

297.
(a) Subject to the limitations in paragraph (3) of this subdivision, only the following laboratories are authorized to analyze crime scene samples and other forensic identification samples of known and unknown origin and to upload and compare those profiles against available state and national DNA and forensic identification databanks and databases in order to establish identity and origin of samples for forensic identification purposes pursuant to this chapter:
(1) The DNA laboratories of the Department of Justice that meet state and federal requirements, including the Federal Bureau of Investigation (FBI) Quality Assurance Standards, and that are accredited by an organization approved by the National DNA Index System (NDIS) Procedures Board.
(2) Public law enforcement crime laboratories designated by the Department of Justice that meet state and federal requirements, including the FBI Quality Assurance Standards, and that are accredited by an organization approved by the NDIS Procedures Board.
(3) Only the laboratories of the Department of Justice that meet the requirements of paragraph (1) of subdivision (a) are authorized to upload DNA profiles from arrestees and other qualifying offender samples collected pursuant to this section, Section 296, and Section 296.2.
(b) The laboratories of the Department of Justice and public law enforcement crime laboratories that meet the requirements of subdivision (a) may, subject to the laboratory's discretion, and the limitations of paragraph (3) of subdivision (a), upload to available state and national DNA and forensic identification databanks and databases qualifying DNA profiles from forensic identification samples of known and unknown origin that are generated by private forensic laboratories that meet state and federal requirements, including the FBI Quality Assurance Standards, and that are accredited by an organization approved by the NDIS Procedures Board. Prior to uploading DNA profiles generated by a private laboratory, the public laboratory shall conduct the quality assessment and review required by the FBI Quality Assurance Standards.
(c) (1) A biological sample obtained from a suspect in a criminal investigation for the commission of any crime may be analyzed for forensic identification profiles, including DNA profiles, by the DNA Laboratory of the Department of Justice or any law enforcement crime laboratory or private forensic laboratory that meets all of the FBI Quality Assurance Standards and accreditation requirements in paragraphs (1) and (2) of subdivision (a) and then compared by the Department of Justice in and between as many cases and investigations as necessary, and searched against the forensic identification profiles, including DNA profiles, stored in the files of the Department of Justice DNA databank or database or any available databanks or databases as part of the Department of Justice DNA Database and databank Program.
(2) The law enforcement investigating agency submitting a specimen, sample, or print impression to the DNA Laboratory of the Department of Justice or law enforcement crime laboratory pursuant to this section shall inform the Department of Justice DNA Laboratory within two years whether the person remains a suspect in a criminal investigation. Upon written notification from a law enforcement agency that a person is no longer a suspect in a criminal investigation, the Department of Justice DNA Laboratory shall remove the suspect sample from its databank files and databases. However, any identification, warrant, arrest, or prosecution based upon a databank or database match shall not be invalidated or dismissed due to a failure to purge or delay in purging records.
(d) All laboratories, including the Department of Justice DNA laboratories, contributing DNA profiles for inclusion in California's DNA databank shall meet state and federal requirements, including the FBI Quality Assurance Standards and accreditation requirements, and shall be accredited by an organization approved by the National DNA Index System (NDIS) Procedures Board. Additionally, each laboratory shall submit to the Department of Justice for review the annual report required by the submitting laboratory's accrediting organization that documents the laboratory's adherence to FBI Quality Assurance Standards and the standards of the accrediting organization. The requirements of this subdivision do not preclude DNA profiles developed in California from being searched in the NDIS.
(e) Nothing in this section precludes local law enforcement DNA laboratories from maintaining local forensic databases and databanks or performing forensic identification analyses, including DNA profiling, independently from the Department of Justice DNA laboratories and Forensic Identification Data Base and databank Program.
(f) The limitation on the types of offenses set forth in subdivision (a) of Section 296 as subject to the collection and testing procedures of this chapter is for the purpose of facilitating the administration of this chapter by the Department of Justice, and shall not be considered cause for dismissing an investigation or prosecution or reversing a verdict or disposition.
(g) The detention, arrest, wardship, adjudication, or conviction of a person based upon a databank match or database information is not invalidated if it is determined that the specimens, samples, or print impressions were obtained or placed or retained in a databank or database by mistake.

(Amended by Stats. 2006, Ch. 170, Sec. 2. Effective January 1, 2007. Note: This section was amended on Nov. 2, 2004, by initiative Prop. 69.)

ARTICLE 4. Collection and Forwarding of Samples [298 - 298.3]
(Article 4 added by Stats. 1998, Ch. 696, Sec. 2.)

298.
(a) The Secretary of the Department of Corrections and Rehabilitation, or the Chief Administrative Officer of the detention facility, jail, or other facility at which the blood specimens, buccal swab samples, and thumb and palm print impressions were collected shall cause these specimens, samples, and print impressions to be forwarded promptly to the Department of Justice. The specimens, samples, and print impressions shall be collected by a person using a Department of Justice approved collection kit and in accordance with the requirements and procedures set forth in subdivision (b).
(b) (1) The Department of Justice shall provide all blood specimen vials, buccal swab collectors, mailing tubes, labels, and instructions for the collection of the blood specimens, buccal swab samples, and thumbprints. The specimens, samples, and thumbprints shall thereafter be forwarded to the DNA Laboratory of the Department of Justice for analysis of DNA and other forensic identification markers.
Additionally, the Department of Justice shall provide all full palm print cards, mailing envelopes, and instructions for the collection of full palm prints. The full palm prints, on

a form prescribed by the Department of Justice, shall thereafter be forwarded to the Department of Justice for maintenance in a file for identification purposes.
(2) The withdrawal of blood shall be performed in a medically approved manner. Only health care providers trained and certified to draw blood may withdraw the blood specimens for purposes of this section.
(3) Buccal swab samples may be procured by law enforcement or corrections personnel or other individuals trained to assist in buccal swab collection.
(4) Right thumbprints and a full palm print impression of each hand shall be taken on forms prescribed by the Department of Justice. The palm print forms shall be forwarded to and maintained by the Bureau of Criminal Identification and Information of the Department of Justice. Right thumbprints also shall be taken at the time of the collection of samples and specimens and shall be placed on the sample and specimen containers and forms as directed by the Department of Justice. The samples, specimens, and forms shall be forwarded to and maintained by the DNA Laboratory of the Department of Justice.
(5) The law enforcement or custodial agency collecting specimens, samples, or print impressions is responsible for confirming that the person qualifies for entry into the Department of Justice DNA Database and Databank Program prior to collecting the specimens, samples, or print impressions pursuant to this chapter.
(6) The DNA Laboratory of the Department of Justice is responsible for establishing procedures for entering databank and database information.
(c) (1) Persons authorized to draw blood or obtain samples or print impressions under this chapter for the databank or database shall not be civilly or criminally liable either for withdrawing blood when done in accordance with medically accepted procedures, or for obtaining buccal swab samples by scraping inner cheek cells of the mouth, or thumb or palm print impressions when performed in accordance with standard professional practices.
(2) There is no civil or criminal cause of action against any law enforcement agency or the Department of Justice, or any employee thereof, for a mistake in confirming a person's or sample's qualifying status for inclusion within the database or databank or in placing an entry in a databank or a database.
(3) The failure of the Department of Justice or local law enforcement to comply with Article 4 or any other provision of this chapter shall not invalidate an arrest, plea, conviction, or disposition.
(d) This section shall become inoperative if the California Supreme Court rules to uphold the California Court of Appeal decision in People v. Buza (2014) 231 Cal.App.4th 1446 in regard to the provisions of Section 298 of the Penal Code, as amended by Section 6 of the DNA Fingerprint, Unsolved Crime and Innocence Protection Act, Proposition 69, approved by the voters at the November 2, 2004, statewide general election, in which case this section shall become inoperative immediately upon that ruling becoming final.
(Amended by Stats. 2015, Ch. 487, Sec. 2. (AB 1492) Effective January 1, 2016. Conditionally inoperative as prescribed by its own provisions. See later operative version, as amended by Sec. 3 of Stats. 2015, Ch. 487. This section was amended on Nov. 2, 2004, by initiative Prop. 69.)

298.
(a) (1) (A) The Secretary of the Department of Corrections and Rehabilitation, or the Chief Administrative Officer of the detention facility, jail, or other facility at which the blood specimens, buccal swab samples, and thumb and palm print impressions were collected shall cause these specimens, samples, and print impressions to be forwarded promptly to the Department of Justice, except that a blood specimen or buccal swab sample taken from a person arrested for the commission of a felony as specified in paragraph (2) of subdivision (a) of Section 296 shall be forwarded to the Department of Justice only after one of the following has occurred, which shall be deemed a finding of probable cause, whichever occurs first:
(i) A felony arrest warrant has been signed by a judicial officer pursuant to Section 813 or 817.
(ii) A grand jury indictment has been found and issued pursuant to Section 939.8, 940, or 944.
(iii) A judicial officer has determined that probable cause exists to believe the person has committed the offense for which he or she was arrested.
(B) The specimens, samples, and print impressions shall be collected by a person using a Department of Justice approved collection kit and in accordance with the requirements and procedures set forth in subdivision (b).
(2) A blood specimen or buccal swab sample taken from a person arrested for the commission of a felony as specified in paragraph (2) of subdivision (a) of Section 296 that has not been forwarded to the Department of Justice within six months following the arrest of that person because the agency that took the blood specimen or buccal swab sample has not received notice to forward the DNA specimen or sample to the Department of Justice for inclusion in the state's DNA and Forensic Identification Database and Databank Program pursuant to paragraph (1) following a determination of probable cause, shall be destroyed by the agency that collected the blood specimen or buccal swab sample.
(b) (1) The Department of Justice shall provide all blood specimen vials, buccal swab collectors, mailing tubes, labels, and instructions for the collection of the blood specimens, buccal swab samples, and thumbprints. The specimens, samples, and thumbprints shall thereafter be forwarded to the DNA Laboratory of the Department of Justice for analysis of DNA and other forensic identification markers.
Additionally, the Department of Justice shall provide all full palm print cards, mailing envelopes, and instructions for the collection of full palm prints. The full palm prints, on a form prescribed by the Department of Justice, shall thereafter be forwarded to the Department of Justice for maintenance in a file for identification purposes.
(2) The withdrawal of blood shall be performed in a medically approved manner. Only health care providers trained and certified to draw blood may withdraw the blood specimens for purposes of this section.
(3) Buccal swab samples may be procured by law enforcement or corrections personnel or other individuals trained to assist in buccal swab collection.
(4) Right thumbprints and a full palm print impression of each hand shall be taken on forms prescribed by the Department of Justice. The palm print forms shall be forwarded to and maintained by the Bureau of Criminal Identification and Information of the Department of Justice. Right thumbprints also shall be taken at the time of the collection of samples and specimens and shall be placed on the sample and specimen containers and forms as directed by the Department of Justice. The samples, specimens, and forms shall be forwarded to and maintained by the DNA Laboratory of the Department of Justice.
(5) The law enforcement or custodial agency collecting specimens, samples, or print impressions is responsible for confirming that the person qualifies for entry into the Department of Justice DNA and Forensic Identification Database and Databank Program prior to collecting the specimens, samples, or print impressions pursuant to this chapter.
(6) The DNA Laboratory of the Department of Justice is responsible for establishing procedures for entering databank and database information.
(c) (1) Persons authorized to draw blood or obtain samples or print impressions under this chapter for the databank or database shall not be civilly or criminally liable either for withdrawing blood when done in accordance with medically accepted procedures, or for obtaining buccal swab samples by scraping inner cheek cells of the mouth, or thumb or palm print impressions when performed in accordance with standard professional practices.
(2) There is no civil or criminal cause of action against any law enforcement agency or the Department of Justice, or any employee thereof, for a mistake in confirming a

person's or sample's qualifying status for inclusion within the database or databank or in placing an entry in a databank or a database.
(3) The failure of the Department of Justice or local law enforcement to comply with Article 4 or any other provision of this chapter shall not invalidate an arrest, plea, conviction, or disposition.
(d) This section shall only become operative if the California Supreme Court rules to uphold the California Court of Appeal decision in People v. Buza (2014) 231 Cal.App.4th 1446 in regard to the provisions of Section 298 of the Penal Code, as amended by Section 6 of the DNA Fingerprint, Unsolved Crime and Innocence Protection Act, Proposition 69, approved by the voters at the November 2, 2004, statewide general election, in which case this section shall become operative immediately upon that ruling becoming final.
(Added by Stats. 2015, Ch. 487, Sec. 3. (AB 1492) Effective January 1, 2016. Conditionally operative, as prescribed by its own provisions, coinciding with inoperation of the previous version, as amended by Sec. 2 of Stats. 2015, Ch. 487. Note: This section was amended on Nov. 2, 2004, by initiative Prop. 69.)
298.1.
(a) On and after January 1, 1999, any person who refuses to give any or all of the following, blood specimens, saliva samples, or thumb or palm print impressions as required by this chapter, once he or she has received written notice from the Department of Justice, the Department of Corrections and Rehabilitation, any law enforcement personnel, or officer of the court that he or she is required to provide specimens, samples, and print impressions pursuant to this chapter is guilty of a misdemeanor. The refusal or failure to give any or all of the following, a blood specimen, saliva sample, or thumb or palm print impression is punishable as a separate offense by both a fine of five hundred dollars ($500) and imprisonment of up to one year in a county jail, or if the person is already imprisoned in the state prison, by sanctions for misdemeanors according to a schedule determined by the Department of Corrections and Rehabilitation.
(b) (1) Notwithstanding subdivision (a), authorized law enforcement, custodial, or corrections personnel, including peace officers as defined in Sections 830, 830.1, subdivision (d) of Section 830.2, Sections 830.38, 830.5, or 830.55, may employ reasonable force to collect blood specimens, saliva samples, or thumb or palm print impressions pursuant to this chapter from individuals who, after written or oral request, refuse to provide those specimens, samples, or thumb or palm print impressions.
(2) The withdrawal of blood shall be performed in a medically approved manner in accordance with the requirements of paragraph (2) of subdivision (b) of Section 298.
(3) The use of reasonable force as provided in this subdivision shall be carried out in a manner consistent with regulations and guidelines adopted pursuant to subdivision (c).
(c) (1) The Department of Corrections and Rehabilitation and the Division of Juvenile Justice shall adopt regulations governing the use of reasonable force as provided in subdivision (b), which shall include the following:
(A) "Use of reasonable force" shall be defined as the force that an objective, trained, and competent correctional employee, faced with similar facts and circumstances, would consider necessary and reasonable to gain compliance with this chapter.
(B) The use of reasonable force shall not be authorized without the prior written authorization of the supervising officer on duty. The authorization shall include information that reflects the fact that the offender was asked to provide the requisite specimen, sample, or impression and refused.
(C) The use of reasonable force shall be preceded by efforts to secure voluntary compliance with this section.
(D) If the use of reasonable force includes a cell extraction, the regulations shall provide that the extraction be video recorded.
(2) The Corrections Standards Authority shall adopt guidelines governing the use of reasonable force as provided in subdivision (b) for local detention facilities, which shall include the following:
(A) "Use of reasonable force" shall be defined as the force that an objective, trained and competent correctional employee, faced with similar facts and circumstances, would consider necessary and reasonable to gain compliance with this chapter.
(B) The use of reasonable force shall not be authorized without the prior written authorization of the supervising officer on duty. The authorization shall include information that reflects the fact that the offender was asked to provide the requisite specimen, sample, or impression and refused.
(C) The use of reasonable force shall be preceded by efforts to secure voluntary compliance with this section.
(D) If the use of reasonable force includes a cell extraction, the extraction shall be video recorded.
(3) The Department of Corrections and Rehabilitation, the Division of Juvenile Justice, and the Corrections Standards Authority shall report to the Legislature not later than January 1, 2005, on the use of reasonable force pursuant to this section. The report shall include, but is not limited to, the number of refusals, the number of incidents of the use of reasonable force under this section, the type of force used, the efforts undertaken to obtain voluntary compliance, if any, and whether any medical attention was needed by the prisoner or personnel as a result of force being used.
(Amended by Stats. 2009, Ch. 88, Sec. 71. (AB 176) Effective January 1, 2010.)
298.2.
(a) Any person who is required to submit a specimen sample or print impression pursuant to this chapter who engages or attempts to engage in any of the following acts is guilty of a felony punishable by imprisonment in the state prison for two, three, or four years:
(1) Knowingly facilitates the collection of a wrongfully attributed blood specimen, buccal swab sample, or thumb or palm print impression, with the intent that a government agent or employee be deceived as to the origin of a DNA profile or as to any identification information associated with a specimen, sample, or print impression required for submission pursuant to this chapter.
(2) Knowingly tampers with any specimen, sample, print, or the collection container for any specimen or sample, with the intent that any government agent or employee be deceived as to the identity of the person to whom the specimen, sample, or print relates.
(Amended (as amended by Stats. 2011, Ch. 15) by Stats. 2011, Ch. 39, Sec. 14. (AB 117) Effective June 30, 2011. Operative October 1, 2011, pursuant to Secs. 68 and 69 of Ch. 39. Note: This section was amended on Nov. 2, 2004, by initiative Prop. 69.)
298.3.
(a) To ensure expeditious and economical processing of offender specimens and samples for inclusion in the FBI's CODIS System and the state's DNA Database and Data Bank Program, the Department of Justice DNA Laboratory is authorized to contract with other laboratories, whether public or private, including law enforcement laboratories, that have the capability of fully analyzing offender specimens or samples within 60 days of receipt, for the anonymous analysis of specimens and samples for forensic identification testing as provided in this chapter and in accordance with the quality assurance requirement established by CODIS and ASCLD/LAB.
(b) Contingent upon the availability of sufficient funds in the state's DNA Identification Fund established pursuant to Section 76104.6, the Department of Justice DNA Laboratory shall immediately contract with other laboratories, whether public or private, including law enforcement laboratories, for the anonymous analysis of offender reference specimens or samples and any arrestee reference specimens or samples collected pursuant to subdivision (a) of Section 296 for forensic identification testing as provided in subdivision (a) of this section and in accordance with the quality assurance requirements established by CODIS and ASCLD/LAB for any specimens or samples that are not fully analyzed and uploaded into the CODIS database within six months of the receipt of the reference specimens or samples by the Department of Justice DNA Laboratory.
(Added November 2, 2004, by initiative Proposition 69, Sec. 8. Note: Prop. 69 is titled the DNA Fingerprint, Unsolved Crime and Innocence Protection Act.)

ARTICLE 5. Expungement of Information [299- 299.]

(Article 5 added by Stats. 1998, Ch. 696, Sec. 2.)
299.
(a) A person whose DNA profile has been included in the databank pursuant to this chapter shall have his or her DNA specimen and sample destroyed and searchable database profile expunged from the databank program pursuant to the procedures set forth in subdivision (b) if the person has no past or present offense or pending charge which qualifies that person for inclusion within the state's DNA and Forensic Identification Database and Databank Program and there otherwise is no legal basis for retaining the specimen or sample or searchable profile.
(b) Pursuant to subdivision (a), a person who has no past or present qualifying offense, and for whom there otherwise is no legal basis for retaining the specimen or sample or searchable profile, may make a written request to have his or her specimen and sample destroyed and searchable database profile expunged from the databank program if any of the following apply:
(1) Following arrest, no accusatory pleading has been filed within the applicable period allowed by law, charging the person with a qualifying offense as set forth in subdivision (a) of Section 296 or if the charges which served as the basis for including the DNA profile in the state's DNA and Forensic Identification Database and Databank Program have been dismissed prior to adjudication by a trier of fact;
(2) The underlying conviction or disposition serving as the basis for including the DNA profile has been reversed and the case dismissed;
(3) The person has been found factually innocent of the underlying offense pursuant to Section 851.8, or Section 781.5 of the Welfare and Institutions Code; or
(4) The defendant has been found not guilty or the defendant has been acquitted of the underlying offense.
(c) (1) The person requesting the databank entry to be expunged must send a copy of his or her request to the trial court of the county where the arrest occurred, or that entered the conviction or rendered disposition in the case, to the DNA Laboratory of the Department of Justice, and to the prosecuting attorney of the county in which he or she was arrested or, convicted, or adjudicated, with proof of service on all parties. The court has the discretion to grant or deny the request for expungement. The denial of a request for expungement is a nonappealable order and shall not be reviewed by petition for writ.
(2) Except as provided in this section, the Department of Justice shall destroy a specimen and sample and expunge the searchable DNA database profile pertaining to the person who has no present or past qualifying offense of record upon receipt of a court order that verifies the applicant has made the necessary showing at a noticed hearing, and that includes all of the following:
(A) The written request for expungement pursuant to this section.
(B) A certified copy of the court order reversing and dismissing the conviction or case, or a letter from the district attorney certifying that no accusatory pleading has been filed or the charges which served as the basis for collecting a DNA specimen and sample have been dismissed prior to adjudication by a trier of fact, the defendant has been found factually innocent, the defendant has been found not guilty, the defendant has been acquitted of the underlying offense, or the underlying conviction has been reversed and the case dismissed.
(C) Proof of written notice to the prosecuting attorney and the Department of Justice that expungement has been requested.
(D) A court order verifying that no retrial or appeal of the case is pending, that it has been at least 180 days since the defendant or minor has notified the prosecuting attorney and the Department of Justice of the expungement request, and that the court has not received an objection from the Department of Justice or the prosecuting attorney.
(d) Upon order from the court, the Department of Justice shall destroy any specimen or sample collected from the person and any searchable DNA database profile pertaining to the person, unless the department determines that the person is subject to the provisions of this chapter because of a past qualifying offense of record or is or has otherwise become obligated to submit a blood specimen or buccal swab sample as a result of a separate arrest, conviction, juvenile adjudication, or finding of guilty or not guilty by reason of insanity for an offense described in subdivision (a) of Section 296, or as a condition of a plea.
The Department of Justice is not required to destroy analytical data or other items obtained from a blood specimen or saliva, or buccal swab sample, if evidence relating to another person subject to the provisions of this chapter would thereby be destroyed or otherwise compromised.
Any identification, warrant, probable cause to arrest, or arrest based upon a databank or database match is not invalidated due to a failure to expunge or a delay in expunging records.
(e) Notwithstanding any other law, the Department of Justice DNA Laboratory is not required to expunge DNA profile or forensic identification information or destroy or return specimens, samples, or print impressions taken pursuant to this section if the duty to register under Section 290 or 457.1 is terminated.
(f) Notwithstanding any other law, including Sections 17, 1170.18, 1203.4, and 1203.4a, a judge is not authorized to relieve a person of the separate administrative duty to provide specimens, samples, or print impressions required by this chapter if a person has been found guilty or was adjudicated a ward of the court by a trier of fact of a qualifying offense as defined in subdivision (a) of Section 296, or was found not guilty by reason of insanity or pleads no contest to a qualifying offense as defined in subdivision (a) of Section 296.
(g) This section shall become inoperative if the California Supreme Court rules to uphold the California Court of Appeal decision in People v. Buza (2014) 231 Cal.App.4th 1446 in regard to the provisions of Section 299 of the Penal Code, as amended by Section 9 of the DNA Fingerprint, Unsolved Crime and Innocence Protection Act, Proposition 69, approved by the voters at the November 2, 2004, statewide general election, in which case this section shall become inoperative immediately upon that ruling becoming final.
(Amended by Stats. 2015, Ch. 487, Sec. 4. (AB 1492) Effective January 1, 2016. Conditionally inoperative as prescribed by its own provisions. See later operative version, as amended by Sec. 5 of Stats. 2015, Ch. 487. This section was amended on Nov. 2, 2004, by initiative Prop. 69.)
299.
(a) A person whose DNA profile has been included in the databank pursuant to this chapter shall have his or her DNA specimen and sample destroyed and searchable database profile expunged from the databank program if the person has no past or present offense or pending charge which qualifies that person for inclusion within the state's DNA and Forensic Identification Database and Databank Program and there otherwise is no legal basis for retaining the specimen or sample or searchable profile.
(b) Pursuant to subdivision (a), a person who has no past or present qualifying offense, and for whom there otherwise is no legal basis for retaining the specimen or sample or searchable profile shall have his or her specimen and sample destroyed and searchable database profile expunged from the databank program if any of the following apply:
(1) Following arrest, and after the applicable law enforcement agency has provided notice to the prosecuting attorney that the criminal case will not be presented to the prosecuting attorney for review, or after the applicable law enforcement agency has

submitted a criminal case to the prosecuting attorney for review, no accusatory pleading has been filed within the applicable period allowed by law, charging the person with a qualifying offense as set forth in subdivision (a) of Section 296, in which case the prosecuting attorney shall immediately, or as soon as practically possible, submit a letter to the Department of Justice indicating that an accusatory pleading has not been filed.

(2) The charges which served as the basis for including the DNA profile in the state's DNA and Forensic Identification Database and Databank Program have been dismissed prior to adjudication by a trier of fact, in which case the court shall forward an order to the Department of Justice upon disposition of the case, indicating that the charges have been dismissed.

(3) The underlying conviction or disposition serving as the basis for including the DNA profile has been reversed and the case dismissed, in which case the court shall forward its order to the Department of Justice upon disposition of the case.

(4) The person has been found factually innocent of the underlying offense pursuant to Section 851.8, or Section 781.5 of the Welfare and Institutions Code, in which case the court shall forward its order to the Department of Justice upon disposition of the case.

(5) The defendant has been found not guilty or the defendant has been acquitted of the underlying offense, in which case the court shall forward its order to the Department of Justice upon disposition of the case.

(c) Except as provided in this section, the Department of Justice shall destroy a specimen and sample and expunge the searchable DNA database profile pertaining to the person who has no present or past qualifying offense of record upon receipt of the following:

(1) A certified copy of the court order reversing and dismissing the conviction or case, or a letter from the district attorney certifying that no accusatory pleading has been filed or the charges which served as the basis for collecting a DNA specimen and sample have been dismissed prior to adjudication by a trier of fact, the defendant has been found factually innocent, the defendant has been found not guilty, the defendant has been acquitted of the underlying offense, or the underlying conviction has been reversed and the case dismissed.

(2) A court order verifying that no retrial or appeal of the case is pending.

(d) Pursuant to this section, the Department of Justice shall destroy any specimen or sample collected from the person and any searchable DNA database profile pertaining to the person, unless the department determines that the person is subject to the provisions of this chapter because of a past qualifying offense of record or is or has otherwise become obligated to submit a blood specimen or buccal swab sample as a result of a separate arrest, conviction, juvenile adjudication, or finding of guilty or not guilty by reason of insanity for an offense described in subdivision (a) of Section 296, or as a condition of a plea.

The Department of Justice is not required to destroy analytical data or other items obtained from a blood specimen or saliva, or buccal swab sample, if evidence relating to another person subject to the provisions of this chapter would thereby be destroyed or otherwise compromised.

Any identification, warrant, probable cause to arrest, or arrest based upon a databank or database match is not invalidated due to a failure to expunge or a delay in expunging records.

(e) Notwithstanding any other law, the Department of Justice DNA Laboratory is not required to expunge DNA profile or forensic identification information or destroy or return specimens, samples, or print impressions taken pursuant to this section if the duty to register under Section 290 or 457.1 is terminated.

(f) Notwithstanding any other law, including Sections 17, 1170.18, 1203.4, and 1203.4a, a judge is not authorized to relieve a person of the separate administrative duty to provide specimens, samples, or print impressions required by this chapter if a person has been found guilty or was adjudicated a ward of the court by a trier of fact of a qualifying offense as defined in subdivision (a) of Section 296, or was found not guilty by reason of insanity or pleads no contest to a qualifying offense as defined in subdivision (a) of Section 296.

(g) This section shall only become operative if the California Supreme Court rules to uphold the California Court of Appeal decision in People v. Buza (2014) 231 Cal.App.4th 1446 in regard to the provisions of Section 299 of the Penal Code, as amended by Section 9 of the DNA Fingerprint, Unsolved Crime and Innocence Protection Act, Proposition 69, approved by the voters at the November 2, 2004, statewide general election, in which case this section shall become operative immediately upon that ruling becoming final.

(Added by Stats. 2015, Ch. 487, Sec. 5. (AB 1492) Effective January 1, 2016. Conditionally operative as prescribed by its own provisions. This section was amended on Nov. 2, 2004, by initiative Prop. 69.)

ARTICLE 6. Limitations on Disclosure [299.5 - 299.7]
(Article 6 added by Stats. 1998, Ch. 696, Sec. 2.)

299.5.
(a) All DNA and forensic identification profiles and other identification information retained by the Department of Justice pursuant to this chapter are exempt from any law requiring disclosure of information to the public and shall be confidential except as otherwise provided in this chapter.

(b) All evidence and forensic samples containing biological material retained by the Department of Justice DNA Laboratory or other state law enforcement agency are exempt from any law requiring disclosure of information to the public or the return of biological specimens, samples, or print impressions.

(c) Non-DNA forensic identification information may be filed with the offender's file maintained by the Sex Registration Unit of the Department of Justice or in other computerized data bank or database systems maintained by the Department of Justice.

(d) The DNA and other forensic identification information retained by the Department of Justice pursuant to this chapter shall not be included in the state summary criminal history information. However, nothing in this chapter precludes law enforcement personnel from entering into a person's criminal history information or offender file maintained by the Department of Justice, the fact that the specimens, samples, and print impressions required by this chapter have or have not been collected from that person.

(e) The fact that the blood specimens, saliva or buccal swab samples, and print impressions required by this chapter have been received by the DNA Laboratory of the Department of Justice shall be included in the state summary criminal history information as soon as administratively practicable.

The full palm prints of each hand shall be filed and maintained by the Automated Latent Print Section of the Bureau of Criminal Identification and Information of the Department of Justice, and may be included in the state summary criminal history information.

(f) DNA samples and DNA profiles and other forensic identification information shall be released only to law enforcement agencies, including, but not limited to, parole officers of the Department of Corrections, hearing officers of the parole authority, probation officers, the Attorney General's office, district attorneys' offices, and prosecuting city attorneys' offices, unless otherwise specifically authorized by this chapter. Dissemination of DNA specimens, samples, and DNA profiles and other forensic identification information to law enforcement agencies and district attorneys' offices outside this state shall be performed in conformity with the provisions of this chapter.

(g) A defendant's DNA and other forensic identification information developed pursuant to this chapter shall be available to his or her defense counsel upon court order made pursuant to Chapter 10 (commencing with Section 1054) of Title 6 of Part 2.

(h) Except as provided in subdivision (g) and in order to protect the confidentiality and privacy of database and data bank information, the Department of Justice and local public DNA laboratories shall not otherwise be compelled in a criminal or civil proceeding

to provide any DNA profile or forensic identification database or data bank information or its computer database program software or structures to any person or party seeking such records or information whether by subpoena or discovery, or other procedural device or inquiry.

(i) (1) (A) Any person who knowingly uses an offender specimen, sample, or DNA profile collected pursuant to this chapter for other than criminal identification or exclusion purposes, or for other than the identification of missing persons, or who knowingly discloses DNA or other forensic identification information developed pursuant to this section to an unauthorized individual or agency, for other than criminal identification or exclusion purposes, or for the identification of missing persons, in violation of this chapter, shall be punished by imprisonment in a county jail not exceeding one year or by imprisonment in the state prison for 16 months, or two or three years.

(B) Any person who, for the purpose of financial gain, knowingly uses a specimen, sample, or DNA profile collected pursuant to this chapter for other than criminal identification or exclusion purposes or for the identification of missing persons or who, for the purpose of financial gain, knowingly discloses DNA or other forensic identification information developed pursuant to this section to an unauthorized individual or agency, for other than criminal identification or exclusion purposes or for other than the identification of missing persons, in violation of this chapter, shall, in addition to the penalty provided in subparagraph (A), be punished by a criminal fine in an amount three times that of any financial gain received or ten thousand dollars ($10,000), whichever is greater.

(2) (A) If any employee of the Department of Justice knowingly uses a specimen, sample, or DNA profile collected pursuant to this chapter for other than criminal identification or exclusion purposes, or knowingly discloses DNA or other forensic identification information developed pursuant to this section to an unauthorized individual or agency, for other than criminal identification or exclusion purposes or for other than the identification of missing persons, in violation of this chapter, the department shall be liable in civil damages to the donor of the DNA identification information in the amount of five thousand dollars ($5,000) for each violation, plus attorney's fees and costs. In the event of multiple disclosures, the total damages available to the donor of the DNA is limited to fifty thousand dollars ($50,000) plus attorney's fees and costs.

(B) (i) Notwithstanding any other law, this shall be the sole and exclusive remedy against the Department of Justice and its employees available to the donor of the DNA.
(ii) The Department of Justice employee disclosing DNA identification information in violation of this chapter shall be absolutely immune from civil liability under this or any other law.

(3) It is not a violation of this section for a law enforcement agency in its discretion to publicly disclose the fact of a DNA profile match, or the name of the person identified by the DNA match when this match is the basis of law enforcement's investigation, arrest, or prosecution of a particular person, or the identification of a missing or abducted person.

(j) It is not a violation of this chapter to furnish DNA or other forensic identification information of the defendant to his or her defense counsel for criminal defense purposes in compliance with discovery.

(k) It is not a violation of this section for law enforcement to release DNA and other forensic identification information developed pursuant to this chapter to a jury or grand jury, or in a document filed with a court or administrative agency, or as part of a judicial or administrative proceeding, or for this information to become part of the public transcript or record of proceedings when, in the discretion of law enforcement, disclosure is necessary because the DNA information pertains to the basis for law enforcement's identification, arrest, investigation, prosecution, or exclusion of a particular person related to the case.

(l) It is not a violation of this section to include information obtained from a file in a transcript or record of a judicial proceeding, or in any other public record when the inclusion of the information in the public record is authorized by a court, statute, or decisional law.

(m) It is not a violation of this section for the DNA Laboratory of the Department of Justice, or an organization retained as an agent of the Department of Justice, or a local public laboratory to use anonymous records or criminal history information obtained pursuant to this chapter for training, research, statistical analysis of populations, or quality assurance or quality control.

(n) The Department of Justice shall make public the methodology and procedures to be used in its DNA program prior to the commencement of DNA testing in its laboratories. The Department of Justice shall review and consider on an ongoing basis the findings and results of any peer review and validation studies submitted to the department by members of the relevant scientific community experienced in the use of DNA technology. This material shall be available to criminal defense counsel upon court order made pursuant to Chapter 10 (commencing with Section 1054) of Title 6 of Part 2.

(o) In order to maintain the computer system security of the Department of Justice DNA and Forensic Identification Database and Data Bank Program, the computer software and database structures used by the DNA Laboratory of the Department of Justice to implement this chapter are confidential.

(Amended (as amended by Stats. 2011, Ch. 15) by Stats. 2011, Ch. 39, Sec. 15. (AB 117) Effective June 30, 2011. Operative October 1, 2011, pursuant to Secs. 68 and 69 of Ch. 39. Note: This section was amended on Nov. 2, 2004, by initiative Prop. 69.)

299.6.
(a) Nothing in this chapter shall prohibit the Department of Justice, in its sole discretion, from the sharing or disseminating of population database or data bank information, DNA profile or forensic identification database or data bank information, analytical data and results generated for forensic identification database and data bank purposes, or protocol and forensic DNA analysis methods and quality assurance or quality control procedures with any of the following:

(1) Federal, state, or local law enforcement agencies.
(2) Crime laboratories, whether public or private, that serve federal, state, and local law enforcement agencies that have been approved by the Department of Justice.
(3) The attorney general's office of any state.
(4) Any state or federally authorized auditing agent or board that inspects or reviews the work of the Department of Justice DNA Laboratory for the purpose of ensuring that the laboratory meets ASCLD/LAB and FBI standards for accreditation and quality assurance standards necessary under this chapter and for the state's participation in CODIS and other national or international crime-solving networks.
(5) Any third party that the Department of Justice deems necessary to assist the department's crime laboratory with statistical analyses of population databases, or the analyses of forensic protocol, research methods, or quality control procedures, or to assist in the recovery or identification of human remains for humanitarian purposes, including identification of missing persons.

(b) The population databases and data banks of the DNA Laboratory of the Department of Justice may be made available to and searched by the FBI and any other agency participating in the FBI's CODIS System or any other national or international law enforcement database or data bank system.

(c) The Department of Justice may provide portions of biological samples including blood specimens, saliva samples, and buccal swab samples collected pursuant to this chapter to local public law enforcement DNA laboratories for identification purposes provided that the privacy provisions of this section are followed by the local public law enforcement laboratory and if each of the following conditions is met:

(1) The procedures used by the local public DNA laboratory for the handling of specimens and samples and the disclosure of results are the same as those established by the Department of Justice pursuant to Sections 297, 298, and 299.5.

(2) The methodologies and procedures used by the local public DNA laboratory for DNA or forensic identification analysis are compatible with those used by the Department of Justice, or otherwise are determined by the Department of Justice to be valid and appropriate for identification purposes.

(3) Only tests of value to law enforcement for identification purposes are performed and a copy of the results of the analysis are sent to the Department of Justice.

(4) All provisions of this section concerning privacy and security are followed.

(5) The local public law enforcement DNA laboratory assumes all costs of securing the specimens and samples and provides appropriate tubes, labels, and materials necessary to secure the specimens and samples.

(d) Any local DNA laboratory that produces DNA profiles of known reference samples for inclusion within the permanent files of the state's DNA Data Bank program shall follow the policies of the DNA Laboratory of the Department of Justice.

(Amended November 2, 2004, by initiative Proposition 69, Sec. 11.)

299.7.

The Department of Justice is authorized to dispose of unused specimens and samples, unused portions of specimens and samples, and expired specimens and samples in the normal course of business and in a reasonable manner as long as the disposal method is designed to protect the identity and origin of specimens and samples from disclosure to third persons who are not a part of law enforcement.

(Added by Stats. 1998, Ch. 696, Sec. 2. Effective January 1, 1999.)

ARTICLE 7. Construction and Severability [300 - 300.4]

(Article 7 added by Stats. 1998, Ch. 696, Sec. 2.)

300.

Nothing in this chapter shall limit or abrogate any existing authority of law enforcement officers to take, maintain, store, and utilize DNA or forensic identification markers, blood specimens, buccal swab samples, saliva samples, or thumb or palm print impressions for identification purposes.

(Amended November 2, 2004, by initiative Proposition 69, Sec. 12.)

300.1.

(a) Nothing in this chapter shall be construed to restrict the authority of local law enforcement to maintain their own DNA-related databases or data banks, or to restrict the Department of Justice with respect to data banks and databases created by other statutory authority, including, but not limited to, databases related to fingerprints, firearms and other weapons, child abuse, domestic violence deaths, child deaths, driving offenses, missing persons, violent crime information as described in Title 12 (commencing with Section 14200) of Part 4, and criminal justice statistics permitted by Section 13305.

(b) Nothing in this chapter shall be construed to limit the authority of local or county coroners or their agents, in the course of their scientific investigation, to utilize genetic and DNA technology to inquire into and determine the circumstances, manner, and cause of death, or to employ or use outside laboratories, hospitals, or research institutions that utilize genetic and DNA technology.

(Amended November 2, 2004, by initiative Proposition 69, Sec. 13.)

300.2.

Any requirement to provide saliva samples pursuant to this chapter shall be construed as a requirement to provide buccal swab samples as of the effective date of the act that added this section. However, the Department of Justice may retain and use previously collected saliva and other biological samples as part of its database and databank program and for quality control purposes in conformity with the provisions of this chapter.

(Added November 2, 2004, by initiative Proposition 69, Sec. 14.)

300.3.

The duties and requirements of the Department of Corrections and the Department of the Youth Authority pursuant to this chapter shall commence on July 1, 1999.

(Added by Stats. 1998, Ch. 696, Sec. 2. Effective January 1, 1999.)

300.4.

The provisions of this chapter are severable. If any provision of this chapter or its application is held invalid, that invalidity shall not affect other provisions or applications that can be given effect without the invalid provision or application.

(Added by renumbering Section 300.2 (as added by Stats. 1998, Ch. 696, Sec. 2) by Stats. 2015, Ch. 303, Sec. 387. (AB 731) Effective January 1, 2016.)

CHAPTER 7. Of Crimes Against Religion and Conscience, and Other Offenses Against Good Morals [302 - 310.5]

(Chapter 7 enacted 1872.)

302.

(a) Every person who intentionally disturbs or disquiets any assemblage of people met for religious worship at a tax-exempt place of worship, by profane discourse, rude or indecent behavior, or by any unnecessary noise, either within the place where the meeting is held, or so near it as to disturb the order and solemnity of the meeting, is guilty of a misdemeanor punishable by a fine not exceeding one thousand dollars ($1,000), or by imprisonment in a county jail for a period not exceeding one year, or by both that fine and imprisonment.

(b) A court may require performance of community service of not less than 50 hours and not exceeding 80 hours as an alternative to imprisonment or a fine.

(c) In addition to the penalty set forth in subdivision (a), a person who has suffered a previous conviction of a violation of this section or Section 403, shall be required to perform community service of not less than 120 hours and not exceeding 160 hours.

(d) The existence of any fact which would bring a person under subdivision (c) or (d) shall be alleged in the complaint, information, or indictment and either:

(1) Admitted by the defendant in open court.

(2) Found to be true by a jury trying the issue of guilt.

(3) Found to be true by the court where guilt is established by a plea of guilty or nolo contendere.

(4) Found to be true by trial by the court sitting without a jury.

(e) Upon conviction of any person under this section for disturbances of religious worship, the court may, in accordance with the performance of community service imposed under this section, consistent with public safety interests and with the victim's consent, order the defendant to perform a portion of, or all of, the required community service at the place where the disturbance of religious worship occurred.

(f) The court may waive the mandatory minimum requirements for community service whenever it is in the interest of justice to do so. When a waiver is granted, the court shall state on the record all reasons supporting the waiver.

(Amended by Stats. 1994, Ch. 401, Sec. 1. Effective January 1, 1995.)

303.

It shall be unlawful for any person engaged in the sale of alcoholic beverages, other than in the original package, to employ upon the premises where the alcoholic beverages are sold any person for the purpose of procuring or encouraging the purchase or sale of such beverages, or to pay any person a percentage or commission on the sale of such beverages for procuring or encouraging such purchase or sale. Violation of this section shall be a misdemeanor.

(Added by Stats. 1935, Ch. 504.)

303a.

It shall be unlawful, in any place of business where alcoholic beverages are sold to be consumed upon the premises, for any person to loiter in or about said premises for the purpose of begging or soliciting any patron or customer of, or visitor in, such premises to purchase any alcoholic beverage for the one begging or soliciting. Violation of this section shall be a misdemeanor.

(Added by Stats. 1953, Ch. 1591.)

307.

Every person, firm, or corporation which sells or gives or in any way furnishes to another person, who is in fact under the age of 21 years, any candy, cake, cookie, or chewing gum which contains alcohol in excess of $1/2$ of 1 percent by weight, is guilty of a misdemeanor.

(Amended by Stats. 1985, Ch. 934, Sec. 4.)

308.

(a) (1) (A) (i) Every person, firm, or corporation that knowingly or under circumstances in which it has knowledge, or should otherwise have grounds for knowledge, sells, gives, or in any way furnishes to another person who is under 21 years of age any tobacco, cigarette, or cigarette papers, or blunt wraps, or any other preparation of tobacco, or any other instrument or paraphernalia that is designed for the smoking or ingestion of tobacco, tobacco products, or any controlled substance, is subject to either a criminal action for a misdemeanor or a civil action brought by a city attorney, a county counsel, or a district attorney, punishable by a fine of two hundred dollars ($200) for the first offense, five hundred dollars ($500) for the second offense, and one thousand dollars ($1,000) for the third offense.

(ii) This subparagraph does not apply to the sale, giving, or furnishing of any of the products specified in clause (i) to active duty military personnel who are 18 years of age or older. An identification card issued by the United States Armed Forces shall be used as proof of age for this purpose.

(B) Notwithstanding Section 1464 or any other law, 25 percent of each civil and criminal penalty collected pursuant to this subdivision shall be paid to the office of the city attorney, county counsel, or district attorney, whoever is responsible for bringing the successful action.

(C) Proof that a defendant, or his or her employee or agent, demanded, was shown, and reasonably relied upon evidence of majority shall be defense to any action brought pursuant to this subdivision. Evidence of majority of a person is a facsimile of, or a reasonable likeness of, a document issued by a federal, state, county, or municipal government, or subdivision or agency thereof, including, but not limited to, a motor vehicle operator's license, a registration certificate issued under the federal Military Selective Service Act (50 U.S.C. Sec. 3801 et seq.), or an identification card issued to a member of the Armed Forces.

(D) For purposes of this section, the person liable for selling or furnishing tobacco products to persons under 21 years of age by a tobacco vending machine shall be the person authorizing the installation or placement of the tobacco vending machine upon premises he or she manages or otherwise controls and under circumstances in which he or she has knowledge, or should otherwise have grounds for knowledge, that the tobacco vending machine will be utilized by persons under 21 years of age.

(2) For purposes of this section, "blunt wraps" means cigar papers or cigar wrappers of all types that are designed for smoking or ingestion of tobacco products and contain less than 50 percent tobacco.

(b) Every person, firm, or corporation that sells, or deals in tobacco or any preparation thereof, shall post conspicuously and keep so posted in his, her, or their place of business at each point of purchase the notice required pursuant to subdivision (b) of Section 22952 of the Business and Professions Code, and any person failing to do so shall, upon conviction, be punished by a fine of fifty dollars ($50) for the first offense, one hundred dollars ($100) for the second offense, two hundred fifty dollars ($250) for the third offense, and five hundred dollars ($500) for the fourth offense and each subsequent violation of this provision, or by imprisonment in a county jail not exceeding 30 days.

(c) For purposes of determining the liability of persons, firms, or corporations controlling franchises or business operations in multiple locations for the second and subsequent violations of this section, each individual franchise or business location shall be deemed a separate entity.

(d) It is the Legislature's intent to regulate the subject matter of this section. As a result, a city, county, or city and county shall not adopt any ordinance or regulation inconsistent with this section.

(e) For purposes of this section, "smoking" has the same meaning as in subdivision (c) of Section 22950.5 of the Business and Professions Code.

(f) For purposes of this section, "tobacco products" means a product or device as defined in subdivision (d) of Section 22950.5 of the Business and Professions Code.

(Amended by Stats. 2017, Ch. 561, Sec. 180. (AB 1516) Effective January 1, 2018.)

308.1.

(a) Notwithstanding any other law, no person shall sell, offer for sale, distribute, or import any tobacco product commonly referred to as "bidis" or "beedies," unless that tobacco product is sold, offered for sale, or intended to be sold in a business establishment that prohibits the presence of persons under 18 years of age on its premises.

(b) For purposes of this section, "bidis" or "beedies" means any of the following:

(1) A product containing tobacco that is wrapped in temburni leaf (diospyros melanoxylon) or tendu leaf (diospyros exculpra).

(2) A product that is marketed and sold as "bidis" or "beedies."

(c) Any person who violates this section is guilty of a misdemeanor and is also subject to a civil action brought by the Attorney General, a city attorney, county counsel, or district attorney for an injunction and a civil penalty of up to two thousand dollars ($2,000) per violation. This subdivision does not affect any other remedies available for a violation of this section.

(Amended by Stats. 2010, Ch. 265, Sec. 5. (AB 2496) Effective January 1, 2011.)

308.2.

(a) Every person who sells one or more cigarettes, other than in a sealed and properly labeled package, is guilty of an infraction.

(b) "A sealed and properly labeled package," as used in this section, means the original packaging or sanitary wrapping of the manufacturer or importer which conforms to federal labeling requirements, including the federal warning label.

(Added by Stats. 1991, Ch. 1231, Sec. 1.)

308.3.

(a) A person, firm, corporation, or business may not manufacture for sale, distribute, sell, or offer to sell any cigarette, except in a package containing at least 20 cigarettes. A person, firm, corporation, or business may not manufacture for sale, distribute, sell, or offer to sell any roll-your-own tobacco, except in a package containing at least 0.60 ounces of tobacco.

(b) As used in subdivision (a), "cigarette" means any product that contains nicotine, is intended to be burned or heated under ordinary conditions of use, and consists of, or contains any of, the following:

(1) Any roll of tobacco wrapped in paper or in any substance not containing tobacco.

(2) Tobacco, in any form, that is functional in the product, that, because of its appearance, the type of tobacco used in the filler, or its packaging and labeling, is likely to be offered to, or purchased by, consumers as a cigarette.

(3) Any roll of tobacco wrapped in any substance containing tobacco which, because of its appearance, the type of tobacco used in the filler, or its packaging and labeling, is likely to be offered to, or purchased by, consumers as a cigarette described in this subdivision.

(c) Any person, firm, corporation, or business that violates this section is liable for an infraction, or in an action brought by the Attorney General, a district attorney, a county counsel, or a city attorney for a civil penalty of two hundred dollars ($200) for the first violation, five hundred dollars ($500) for the second violation, and one thousand dollars ($1,000) for each subsequent act constituting a violation.

(Added by Stats. 2001, Ch. 376, Sec. 5. Effective January 1, 2002.)

308.5.

(a) No person or business shall sell, lease, rent, or provide, or offer to sell, lease, rent, or otherwise offer to the public or to public establishments in this state, any video game intended for either private use or for use in a public establishment and intended primarily for use by any person under the age of 18 years, which contains, in its design and in the on-screen presentation of the video game, any paid commercial advertisement of alcoholic beverage or tobacco product containers or other forms of consumer packaging, particular brand names, trademarks, or copyrighted slogans of alcoholic beverages or tobacco products.

(b) As used in this section, "video game" means any electronic amusement device that utilizes a computer, microprocessor, or similar electronic circuitry and its own cathode ray tube, or is designed to be used with a television set or a monitor, that interacts with the user of the device.

(c) A violation of this section is a misdemeanor.

(Added by Stats. 1990, Ch. 639, Sec. 2.)

308b.

(a) Except as provided in subdivision (b), every person who knowingly delivers or causes to be delivered to any residence in this state any tobacco products unsolicited by any person residing therein is guilty of a misdemeanor.

(b) It is a defense to a violation of this section that the recipient of the tobacco products is personally known to the defendant at the time of the delivery.

(c) The distribution of unsolicited tobacco products to residences in violation of this section is a nuisance within the meaning of Section 3479 of the Civil Code.

(d) Nothing in this section shall be construed to impose any liability on any employee of the United States Postal Service for actions performed in the scope of his employment by the United States Postal Service.

(Added by Stats. 1971, Ch. 1005.)

309.

Any proprietor, keeper, manager, conductor, or person having the control of any house of prostitution, or any house or room resorted to for the purpose of prostitution, who shall admit or keep any minor of either sex therein; or any parent or guardian of any such minor, who shall admit or keep such minor, or sanction, or connive at the admission or keeping thereof, into, or in any such house, or room, shall be guilty of a misdemeanor.

(Added by Code Amendments 1880, Ch. 58.)

310.

(a) Any minor under 16 years of age who visits or attends any prizefight or place where any prizefight is advertised to take place, and any owner, lessee, or proprietor, or the agent of any owner, lessee, or proprietor of any place where any prizefight is advertised or represented to take place who admits any minor to a place where any prizefight is advertised or represented to take place or who admits, sells, or gives to any minor a ticket or other paper by which that minor may be admitted to a place where a prizefight is advertised to take place, is guilty of a misdemeanor, and is punishable by a fine not exceeding one hundred dollars ($100) or by imprisonment in the county jail for not more than 25 days.

(b) Any minor under 16 years of age who visits or attends any cockfight or place where any cockfight is advertised to take place, and any owner, lessee, or proprietor, or the agent of any owner, lessee, or proprietor of any place where any cockfight is advertised or represented to take place who admits any minor to a place where any cockfight is advertised or represented to take place or who admits, sells, or gives to any minor a ticket or other paper by which that minor may be admitted to a place where a cockfight is advertised to take place, is guilty of a misdemeanor, and is punishable by a fine not exceeding five hundred dollars ($500) or by imprisonment in the county jail for not more than 25 days.

(Amended by Stats. 2011, Ch. 562, Sec. 1. (SB 425) Effective January 1, 2012.)

310.2.

(a) Any coach, trainer, or other person acting in an official or nonofficial capacity as an adult supervisor for an athletic team consisting of minors under the age of 18 who sells, gives, or otherwise furnishes to any member of that team a diuretic, diet pill, or laxative with the intent that it be consumed, injected, or administered for any nonmedical purpose such as loss of weight or altering the body in any way related to participation on the team or league, is guilty of a misdemeanor.

(b) Subdivision (a) does not apply to a minor's parent or guardian, or any person acting at the written direction of, or with the written consent of, the parent or guardian, if that person is in fact acting with that authority. Subdivision (a) does not apply to a physician.

(Added by Stats. 1987, Ch. 999, Sec. 1.)

310.5.

(a) Any parent or guardian of a child who enters into an agreement on behalf of that child which is in violation of Section 1669.5 of the Civil Code, and any alleged perpetrator of an unlawful sex act upon that child who enters into such an agreement, is guilty of a misdemeanor.

(b) Every person convicted of a violation of subdivision (a) shall be punished by a fine of not less than one hundred dollars ($100) nor more than one thousand dollars ($1,000), by imprisonment in the county jail for not less than 30 days nor more than six months, or by both such a fine and imprisonment, at the discretion of the court.

(c) For purposes of this section, "unlawful sex act," means a felony sex offense committed against a minor.

(Added by Stats. 1994, 1st Ex. Sess., Ch. 54, Sec. 2. Effective November 30, 1994.)

CHAPTER 7.5. Obscene Matter [311 - 312.7]

(Chapter 7.5 added by Stats. 1961, Ch. 2147.)

311.

As used in this chapter, the following definitions apply:

(a) "Obscene matter" means matter, taken as a whole, that to the average person, applying contemporary statewide standards, appeals to the prurient interest, that, taken as a whole, depicts or describes sexual conduct in a patently offensive way, and that, taken as a whole, lacks serious literary, artistic, political, or scientific value.

(1) If it appears from the nature of the matter or the circumstances of its dissemination, distribution, or exhibition that it is designed for clearly defined deviant sexual groups, the appeal of the matter shall be judged with reference to its intended recipient group.

(2) In prosecutions under this chapter, if circumstances of production, presentation, sale, dissemination, distribution, or publicity indicate that matter is being commercially exploited by the defendant for the sake of its prurient appeal, this evidence is probative with respect to the nature of the matter and may justify the conclusion that the matter lacks serious literary, artistic, political, or scientific value.

(3) In determining whether the matter taken as a whole lacks serious literary, artistic, political, or scientific value in description or representation of those matters, the fact that the defendant knew that the matter depicts persons under the age of 16 years engaged in sexual conduct, as defined in subdivision (c) of Section 311.4, is a factor that may be considered in making that determination.

(b) "Matter" means any book, magazine, newspaper, or other printed or written material, or any picture, drawing, photograph, motion picture, or other pictorial representation, or any statue or other figure, or any recording, transcription, or mechanical, chemical, or electrical reproduction, or any other article, equipment, machine, or material. "Matter" also means live or recorded telephone messages if transmitted, disseminated, or distributed as part of a commercial transaction.

(c) "Person" means any individual, partnership, firm, association, corporation, limited liability company, or other legal entity.

(d) "Distribute" means transfer possession of, whether with or without consideration.

(e) "Knowingly" means being aware of the character of the matter or live conduct.

(f) "Exhibit" means show.

(g) "Obscene live conduct" means any physical human body activity, whether performed or engaged in alone or with other persons, including but not limited to singing, speaking, dancing, acting, simulating, or pantomiming, taken as a whole, that to the average person, applying contemporary statewide standards, appeals to the prurient interest and is conduct that, taken as a whole, depicts or describes sexual conduct in a patently offensive way and that, taken as a whole, lacks serious literary, artistic, political, or scientific value.

(1) If it appears from the nature of the conduct or the circumstances of its production, presentation, or exhibition that it is designed for clearly defined deviant sexual groups, the appeal of the conduct shall be judged with reference to its intended recipient group.

(2) In prosecutions under this chapter, if circumstances of production, presentation, advertising, or exhibition indicate that live conduct is being commercially exploited by the defendant for the sake of its prurient appeal, that evidence is probative with respect to the nature of the conduct and may justify the conclusion that the conduct lacks serious literary, artistic, political, or scientific value.

(3) In determining whether the live conduct taken as a whole lacks serious literary, artistic, political, or scientific value in description or representation of those matters, the fact that the defendant knew that the live conduct depicts persons under the age of 16 years engaged in sexual conduct, as defined in subdivision (c) of Section 311.4, is a factor that may be considered in making that determination.

(h) The Legislature expresses its approval of the holding of People v. Cantrell, 7 Cal. App. 4th 523, that, for the purposes of this chapter, matter that "depicts a person under the age of 18 years personally engaging in or personally simulating sexual conduct" is limited to visual works that depict that conduct.

(Amended by Stats. 1997, Ch. 17, Sec. 98. Effective January 1, 1998.)

311.1.

(a) Every person who knowingly sends or causes to be sent, or brings or causes to be brought, into this state for sale or distribution, or in this state possesses, prepares, publishes, produces, develops, duplicates, or prints any representation of information, data, or image, including, but not limited to, any film, filmstrip, photograph, negative, slide, photocopy, videotape, video laser disc, computer hardware, computer software, computer floppy disc, data storage media, CD-ROM, or computer-generated equipment or any other computer-generated image that contains or incorporates in any manner, any film or filmstrip, with intent to distribute or to exhibit to, or to exchange with, others, or who offers to distribute, distributes, or exhibits to, or exchanges with, others, any obscene matter, knowing that the matter depicts a person under the age of 18 years personally engaging in or personally simulating sexual conduct, as defined in Section 311.4, shall be punished either by imprisonment in the county jail for up to one year, by a fine not to exceed one thousand dollars ($1,000), or by both the fine and imprisonment, or by imprisonment in the state prison, by a fine not to exceed ten thousand dollars ($10,000), or by the fine and imprisonment.

(b) This section does not apply to the activities of law enforcement and prosecuting agencies in the investigation and prosecution of criminal offenses or to legitimate medical, scientific, or educational activities, or to lawful conduct between spouses.

(c) This section does not apply to matter which depicts a child under the age of 18, which child is legally emancipated, including lawful conduct between spouses when one or both are under the age of 18.

(d) It does not constitute a violation of this section for a telephone corporation, as defined by Section 234 of the Public Utilities Code, to carry or transmit messages described in this chapter or perform related activities in providing telephone services.

(Amended by Stats. 1996, Ch. 1080, Sec. 2. Effective January 1, 1997.)

311.2.

(a) Every person who knowingly sends or causes to be sent, or brings or causes to be brought, into this state for sale or distribution, or in this state possesses, prepares, publishes, produces, or prints, with intent to distribute or to exhibit to others, or who offers to distribute, distributes, or exhibits to others, any obscene matter is for a first offense, guilty of a misdemeanor. If the person has previously been convicted of any violation of this section, the court may, in addition to the punishment authorized in Section 311.9, impose a fine not exceeding fifty thousand dollars ($50,000).

(b) Every person who knowingly sends or causes to be sent, or brings or causes to be brought, into this state for sale or distribution, or in this state possesses, prepares, publishes, produces, develops, duplicates, or prints any representation of information, data, or image, including, but not limited to, any film, filmstrip, photograph, negative, slide, photocopy, videotape, video laser disc, computer hardware, computer software, computer floppy disc, data storage media, CD-ROM, or computer-generated equipment or any other computer-generated image that contains or incorporates in any manner, any film or filmstrip, with intent to distribute or to exhibit to, or to exchange with, others for commercial consideration, or who offers to distribute, distributes, or exhibits to, or exchanges with, others for commercial consideration, any obscene matter, knowing that the matter depicts a person under the age of 18 years personally engaging in or personally simulating sexual conduct, as defined in Section 311.4, is guilty of a felony and shall be punished by imprisonment in the state prison for two, three, or six years, or by a fine not exceeding one hundred thousand dollars ($100,000), in the absence of a finding that the defendant would be incapable of paying that fine, or by both that fine and imprisonment.

(c) Every person who knowingly sends or causes to be sent, or brings or causes to be brought, into this state for sale or distribution, or in this state possesses, prepares, publishes, produces, develops, duplicates, or prints any representation of information, data, or image, including, but not limited to, any film, filmstrip, photograph, negative, slide, photocopy, videotape, video laser disc, computer hardware, computer software, computer floppy disc, data storage media, CD-ROM, or computer-generated equipment or any other computer-generated image that contains or incorporates in any manner, any film or filmstrip, with intent to distribute or exhibit to, or to exchange with, a person 18 years of age or older, or who offers to distribute, distributes, or exhibits to, or exchanges with, a person 18 years of age or older any matter, knowing that the matter depicts a person under the age of 18 years personally engaging in or personally simulating sexual conduct, as defined in Section 311.4, shall be punished by imprisonment in the county jail for up to one year, or by a fine not exceeding two thousand dollars ($2,000), or by both that fine and imprisonment, or by imprisonment in the state prison. It is not necessary to prove commercial consideration or that the matter is obscene in order to establish a violation of this subdivision. If a person has been previously convicted of a violation of this subdivision, he or she is guilty of a felony.

(d) Every person who knowingly sends or causes to be sent, or brings or causes to be brought, into this state for sale or distribution, or in this state possesses, prepares, publishes, produces, develops, duplicates, or prints any representation of information, data, or image, including, but not limited to, any film, filmstrip, photograph, negative, slide, photocopy, videotape, video laser disc, computer hardware, computer software, computer floppy disc, data storage media, CD-ROM, or computer-generated equipment or any other computer-generated image that contains or incorporates in any manner, any film or filmstrip, with intent to distribute or exhibit to, or to exchange with, a person under 18 years of age, or who offers to distribute, distributes, or exhibits to, or exchanges with, a person under 18 years of age any matter, knowing that the matter depicts a person under the age of 18 years personally engaging in or personally simulating sexual conduct, as defined in Section 311.4, is guilty of a felony. It is not necessary to prove commercial consideration or that the matter is obscene in order to establish a violation of this subdivision.

(e) Subdivisions (a) to (d), inclusive, do not apply to the activities of law enforcement and prosecuting agencies in the investigation and prosecution of criminal offenses, to legitimate medical, scientific, or educational activities, or to lawful conduct between spouses.

(f) This section does not apply to matter that depicts a legally emancipated child under the age of 18 years or to lawful conduct between spouses when one or both are under the age of 18 years.

(g) It does not constitute a violation of this section for a telephone corporation, as defined by Section 234 of the Public Utilities Code, to carry or transmit messages described in this chapter or to perform related activities in providing telephone services.

(Amended by Stats. 2006, Ch. 337, Sec. 20. Effective September 20, 2006.)
311.3.

(a) A person is guilty of sexual exploitation of a child if he or she knowingly develops, duplicates, prints, or exchanges any representation of information, data, or image, including, but not limited to, any film, filmstrip, photograph, negative, slide, photocopy, videotape, video laser disc, computer hardware, computer software, computer floppy disc, data storage media, CD-ROM, or computer-generated equipment or any other computer-generated image that contains or incorporates in any manner, any film or filmstrip that depicts a person under the age of 18 years engaged in an act of sexual conduct.

(b) As used in this section, "sexual conduct" means any of the following:
(1) Sexual intercourse, including genital-genital, oral-genital, anal-genital, or oral-anal, whether between persons of the same or opposite sex or between humans and animals.
(2) Penetration of the vagina or rectum by any object.
(3) Masturbation for the purpose of sexual stimulation of the viewer.
(4) Sadomasochistic abuse for the purpose of sexual stimulation of the viewer.
(5) Exhibition of the genitals or the pubic or rectal area of any person for the purpose of sexual stimulation of the viewer.
(6) Defecation or urination for the purpose of sexual stimulation of the viewer.

(c) Subdivision (a) does not apply to the activities of law enforcement and prosecution agencies in the investigation and prosecution of criminal offenses or to legitimate medical, scientific, or educational activities, or to lawful conduct between spouses.

(d) Every person who violates subdivision (a) shall be punished by a fine of not more than two thousand dollars ($2,000) or by imprisonment in a county jail for not more than one year, or by both that fine and imprisonment. If the person has been previously convicted of a violation of subdivision (a) or any section of this chapter, he or she shall be punished by imprisonment in the state prison.

(e) The provisions of this section do not apply to an employee of a commercial film developer who is acting within the scope of his or her employment and in accordance with the instructions of his or her employer, provided that the employee has no financial interest in the commercial developer by which he or she is employed.

(f) Subdivision (a) does not apply to matter that is unsolicited and is received without knowledge or consent through a facility, system, or network over which the person or entity has no control.

(Amended by Stats. 1996, Ch. 1080, Sec. 4.1. Effective January 1, 1997.)
311.4.

(a) Every person who, with knowledge that a person is a minor, or who, while in possession of any facts on the basis of which he or she should reasonably know that the person is a minor, hires, employs, or uses the minor to do or assist in doing any of the acts described in Section 311.2, shall be punished by imprisonment in the county jail for up to one year, or by a fine not exceeding two thousand dollars ($2,000), or by both that fine and imprisonment, or by imprisonment in the state prison. If the person has previously been convicted of any violation of this section, the court may, in addition to the punishment authorized in Section 311.9, impose a fine not exceeding fifty thousand dollars ($50,000).

(b) Every person who, with knowledge that a person is a minor under the age of 18 years, or who, while in possession of any facts on the basis of which he or she should reasonably know that the person is a minor under the age of 18 years, knowingly promotes, employs, uses, persuades, induces, or coerces a minor under the age of 18 years, or any parent or guardian of a minor under the age of 18 years under his or her control who knowingly permits the minor, to engage in or assist others to engage in either posing or modeling alone or with others for purposes of preparing any representation of information, data, or image, including, but not limited to, any film, filmstrip, photograph, negative, slide, photocopy, videotape, video laser disc, computer hardware, computer software, computer floppy disc, data storage media, CD-ROM, or computer-generated equipment or any other computer-generated image that contains or incorporates in any manner, any film, filmstrip, or a live performance involving, sexual conduct by a minor under the age of 18 years alone or with other persons or animals, for commercial purposes, is guilty of a felony and shall be punished by imprisonment in the state prison for three, six, or eight years.

(c) Every person who, with knowledge that a person is a minor under the age of 18 years, or who, while in possession of any facts on the basis of which he or she should reasonably know that the person is a minor under the age of 18 years, knowingly promotes, employs, uses, persuades, induces, or coerces a minor under the age of 18 years, or any parent or guardian of a minor under the age of 18 years under his or her control who knowingly permits the minor, to engage in or assist others to engage in either posing or modeling alone or with others for purposes of preparing any representation of information, data, or image, including, but not limited to, any film, filmstrip, photograph, negative, slide, photocopy, videotape, video laser disc, computer hardware, computer software, computer floppy disc, data storage media, CD-ROM, or computer-generated equipment or any other computer-generated image that contains or incorporates in any manner, any film, filmstrip, or a live performance involving, sexual conduct by a minor under the age of 18 years alone or with other persons or animals, is guilty of a felony. It is not necessary to prove commercial purposes in order to establish a violation of this subdivision.

(d) (1) As used in subdivisions (b) and (c), "sexual conduct" means any of the following, whether actual or simulated: sexual intercourse, oral copulation, anal intercourse, anal oral copulation, masturbation, bestiality, sexual sadism, sexual masochism, penetration of the vagina or rectum by any object in a lewd or lascivious manner, exhibition of the genitals or pubic or rectal area for the purpose of sexual stimulation of the viewer, any lewd or lascivious sexual act as defined in Section 288, or excretory functions performed in a lewd or lascivious manner, whether or not any of the above conduct is performed alone or between members of the same or opposite sex or between humans and animals. An act is simulated when it gives the appearance of being sexual conduct.

(2) As used in subdivisions (b) and (c), "matter" means any film, filmstrip, photograph, negative, slide, photocopy, videotape, video laser disc, computer hardware, computer software, computer floppy disc, or any other computer-related equipment or computer-generated image that contains or incorporates in any manner, any film, filmstrip, photograph, negative, slide, photocopy, videotape, or video laser disc.

(e) This section does not apply to a legally emancipated minor or to lawful conduct between spouses if one or both are under the age of 18.

(f) In every prosecution under this section involving a minor under the age of 14 years at the time of the offense, the age of the victim shall be pled and proven for the purpose of the enhanced penalty provided in Section 647.6. Failure to plead and prove that the victim was under the age of 14 years at the time of the offense is not a bar to prosecution under this section if it is proven that the victim was under the age of 18 years at the time of the offense.

(Amended by Stats. 2006, Ch. 337, Sec. 21. Effective September 20, 2006.)
311.5.

Every person who writes, creates, or solicits the publication or distribution of advertising or other promotional material, or who in any manner promotes, the sale, distribution, or exhibition of matter represented or held out by him to be obscene, is guilty of a misdemeanor.

(Amended by Stats. 1969, Ch. 249.)
311.6.

Every person who knowingly engages or participates in, manages, produces, sponsors, presents or exhibits obscene live conduct to or before an assembly or audience consisting of at least one person or spectator in any public place or in any place exposed to public view, or in any place open to the public or to a segment thereof, whether or not an admission fee is charged, or whether or not attendance is conditioned upon the presentation of a membership card or other token, is guilty of a misdemeanor.

(Amended by Stats. 1970, Ch. 1072.)
311.7.

Every person who, knowingly, as a condition to a sale, allocation, consignment, or delivery for resale of any paper, magazine, book, periodical, publication or other merchandise, requires that the purchaser or consignee receive any obscene matter or who denies or threatens to deny a franchise, revokes or threatens to revoke, or imposes any penalty, financial or otherwise, by reason of the failure of any person to accept obscene matter, or by reason of the return of such obscene matter, is guilty of a misdemeanor.

(Added by Stats. 1961, Ch. 2147.)
311.8.

(a) It shall be a defense in any prosecution for a violation of this chapter that the act charged was committed in aid of legitimate scientific or educational purposes.

(b) It shall be a defense in any prosecution for a violation of this chapter by a person who knowingly distributed any obscene matter by the use of telephones or telephone facilities to any person under the age of 18 years that the defendant has taken either of the following measures to restrict access to the obscene matter by persons under 18 years of age:
(1) Required the person receiving the obscene matter to use an authorized access or identification code, as provided by the information provider, before transmission of the obscene matter begins, where the defendant has previously issued the code by mailing it to the applicant therefor after taking reasonable measures to ascertain that the applicant was 18 years of age or older and has established a procedure to immediately cancel the code of any person after receiving notice, in writing or by telephone, that the code has been lost, stolen, or used by persons under the age of 18 years or that the code is no longer desired.
(2) Required payment by credit card before transmission of the matter.

(c) Any list of applicants or recipients compiled or maintained by an information-access service provider for purposes of compliance with subdivision (b) is confidential and shall not be sold or otherwise disseminated except upon order of the court.

(Amended by Stats. 1987, Ch. 1101, Sec. 1.)
311.9.

(a) Every person who violates subdivision (a) of Section 311.2 or Section 311.5 is punishable by fine of not more than one thousand dollars ($1,000) plus five dollars ($5) for each additional unit of material coming within the provisions of this chapter, which is involved in the offense, not to exceed ten thousand dollars ($10,000), or by imprisonment in the county jail for not more than six months plus one day for each additional unit of material coming within the provisions of this chapter, and which is involved in the offense, not to exceed a total of 360 days in the county jail, or by both that fine and imprisonment. If that person has previously been convicted of any offense in this chapter, or of a violation of Section 313.1, a violation of subdivision (a) of Section 311.2 or Section 311.5 is punishable as a felony by imprisonment pursuant to subdivision (h) of Section 1170.

(b) Every person who violates subdivision (a) of Section 311.4 is punishable by fine of not more than two thousand dollars ($2,000) or by imprisonment in the county jail for not more than one year, or by both that fine and imprisonment, or by imprisonment pursuant to subdivision (h) of Section 1170. If that person has been previously convicted of a violation of former Section 311.3 or Section 311.4 he or she is punishable by imprisonment pursuant to subdivision (h) of Section 1170.

(c) Every person who violates Section 311.7 is punishable by fine of not more than one thousand dollars ($1,000) or by imprisonment in the county jail for not more than six months, or by both that fine and imprisonment. For a second and subsequent offense he or she shall be punished by a fine of not more than two thousand dollars ($2,000), or by imprisonment in the county jail for not more than one year, or by both that fine and imprisonment. If the person has been twice convicted of a violation of this chapter, a violation of Section 311.7 is punishable as a felony by imprisonment pursuant to subdivision (h) of Section 1170.

(Amended by Stats. 2011, Ch. 15, Sec. 324. (AB 109) Effective April 4, 2011. Operative October 1, 2011, by Sec. 636 of Ch. 15, as amended by Stats. 2011, Ch. 39, Sec. 68.)
311.10.

(a) Any person who advertises for sale or distribution any obscene matter knowing that it depicts a person under the age of 18 years personally engaging in or personally simulating sexual conduct, as defined in Section 311.4, is guilty of a felony and is punishable by imprisonment in the state prison for two, three, or four years, or in a county jail not exceeding one year, or by a fine not exceeding fifty thousand dollars ($50,000), or by both such fine and imprisonment.

(b) Subdivision (a) shall not apply to the activities of law enforcement and prosecution agencies in the investigation and prosecution of criminal offenses.

(Added by Stats. 1985, Ch. 1550, Sec. 1.)
311.11.

(a) Every person who knowingly possesses or controls any matter, representation of information, data, or image, including, but not limited to, any film, filmstrip, photograph, negative, slide, photocopy, videotape, video laser disc, computer hardware, computer software, computer floppy disc, data storage media, CD-ROM, or computer-generated equipment or any other computer-generated image that contains or incorporates in any manner, any film or filmstrip, the production of which involves the use of a person under 18 years of age, knowing that the matter depicts a person under 18 years of age personally engaging in or simulating sexual conduct, as defined in subdivision (d) of Section 311.4, is guilty of a felony and shall be punished by imprisonment in the state prison, or a county jail for up to one year, or by a fine not exceeding two thousand five hundred dollars ($2,500), or by both the fine and imprisonment.

(b) Every person who commits a violation of subdivision (a), and who has been previously convicted of a violation of this section, an offense requiring registration under the Sex Offender Registration Act, or an attempt to commit any of the above-mentioned offenses, is guilty of a felony and shall be punished by imprisonment in the state prison for two, four, or six years.
(c) Each person who commits a violation of subdivision (a) shall be punished by imprisonment in the state prison for 16 months, or two or five years, or shall be punished by imprisonment in a county jail for up to one year, or by a fine not exceeding two thousand five hundred dollars ($2,500), or by both the fine and imprisonment, if one of the following factors exists:
(1) The matter contains more than 600 images that violate subdivision (a), and the matter contains 10 or more images involving a prepubescent minor or a minor who has not attained 12 years of age.
(2) The matter portrays sexual sadism or sexual masochism involving a person under 18 years of age. For purposes of this section, "sexual sadism" means the intentional infliction of pain for purposes of sexual gratification or stimulation. For purposes of this section, "sexual masochism" means intentionally experiencing pain for purposes of sexual gratification or stimulation.
(d) It is not necessary to prove that the matter is obscene in order to establish a violation of this section.
(e) This section does not apply to drawings, figurines, statues, or any film rated by the Motion Picture Association of America, nor does it apply to live or recorded telephone messages when transmitted, disseminated, or distributed as part of a commercial transaction.
(f) For purposes of determining the number of images under paragraph (1) of subdivision (c), the following shall apply:
(1) Each photograph, picture, computer or computer-generated image, or any similar visual depiction shall be considered to be one image.
(2) Each video, video-clip, movie, or similar visual depiction shall be considered to have 50 images.
(Amended by Stats. 2014, Ch. 54, Sec. 12. (SB 1461) Effective January 1, 2015. Note: This section was amended on Nov. 7, 2006, by initiative Prop. 83.)
311.12.
(a) (1) Every person who is convicted of a violation of Section 311.1, 311.2, 311.3, 311.10, or 311.11 in which the offense involves the production, use, possession, control, or advertising of matter or image that depicts a person under 18 years of age personally engaging in or simulating sexual conduct, as defined in subdivision (d) of Section 311.4, in which the violation is committed on, or via, a government-owned computer or via a government-owned computer network, shall, in addition to any imprisonment or fine imposed for the commission of the underlying offense, be punished by a fine not exceeding two thousand dollars ($2,000), unless the court determines that the defendant does not have the ability to pay.
(2) Every person who is convicted of a violation of Section 311.1, 311.2, 311.3, 311.10, or 311.11 in which the offense involves the production, use, possession, control, or advertising of matter or image that depicts a person under 18 years of age personally engaging in or simulating sexual conduct, as defined in subdivision (d) of Section 311.4, in which the production, transportation, or distribution of which involves the use, possession, or control of government-owned property shall, in addition to any imprisonment or fine imposed for the commission of the underlying offense, be punished by a fine not exceeding two thousand dollars ($2,000), unless the court determines that the defendant does not have the ability to pay.
(b) The fines in subdivision (a) shall not be subject to the provisions of Sections 70372, 76000, 76000.5, and 76104.6 of the Government Code, or Sections 1464 and 1465.7 of this code.
(c) Revenue from any fines collected pursuant to this section shall be deposited into a county fund established for that purpose and allocated as follows, and a county may transfer all or part of any of those allocations to another county for the allocated use:
(1) One-third for sexual assault investigator training.
(2) One-third for public agencies and nonprofit corporations that provide shelter, counseling, or other direct services for victims of human trafficking.
(3) One-third for multidisciplinary teams.
(d) As used in this section:
(1) "Computer" includes any computer hardware, computer software, computer floppy disk, data storage medium, or CD-ROM.
(2) "Government-owned" includes property and networks owned or operated by state government, city government, city and county government, county government, a public library, or a public college or university.
(3) "Multidisciplinary teams" means a child-focused, facility-based program in which representatives from many disciplines, including law enforcement, child protection, prosecution, medical and mental health, and victim and child advocacy work together to conduct interviews and make team decisions about the investigation, treatment, management, and prosecution of child abuse cases, including child sexual abuse cases. It is the intent of the Legislature that this multidisciplinary team approach will protect victims of child abuse from multiple interviews, result in a more complete understanding of case issues, and provide the most effective child- and family-focused system response possible.
(e) This section shall not be construed to require any government or government entity to retain data in violation of any provision of state or federal law.
(Amended by Stats. 2014, Ch. 71, Sec. 120. (SB 1304) Effective January 1, 2015.)
312.
Upon the conviction of the accused, the court may, when the conviction becomes final, order any matter or advertisement, in respect whereof the accused stands convicted, and which remains in the possession or under the control of the district attorney or any law enforcement agency, to be destroyed, and the court may cause to be destroyed any such material in its possession or under its control.
(Repealed and added by Stats. 1961, Ch. 2147.)
312.1.
In any prosecution for a violation of the provisions of this chapter or of Chapter 7.6 (commencing with Section 313), neither the prosecution nor the defense shall be required to introduce expert witness testimony concerning the obscene or harmful character of the matter or live conduct which is the subject of the prosecution. Any evidence which tends to establish contemporary community standards of appeal to prurient interest or of customary limits of candor in the description or representation of nudity, sex, or excretion, or which bears upon the question of significant literary, artistic, political, educational, or scientific value shall, subject to the provisions of the Evidence Code, be admissible when offered by either the prosecution or by the defense.
(Amended by Stats. 2001, Ch. 854, Sec. 25. Effective January 1, 2002.)
312.3.
(a) Matter that depicts a person under the age of 18 years personally engaging in or personally simulating sexual conduct as defined in Section 311.4 and that is in the possession of any city, county, city and county, or state official or agency is subject to forfeiture pursuant to this section.
(b) An action to forfeit matter described in subdivision (a) may be brought by the Attorney General, the district attorney, county counsel, or the city attorney. Proceedings shall be initiated by a petition of forfeiture filed in the superior court of the county in which the matter is located.
(c) The prosecuting agency shall make service of process of a notice regarding that petition upon every individual who may have a property interest in the alleged proceeds. The notice shall state that any interested party may file a verified claim with the superior court stating the amount of their claimed interest and an affirmation or denial of the prosecuting agency's allegation. If the notice cannot be given by registered mail or personal delivery, the notice shall be published for at least three successive weeks in a newspaper of general circulation in the county where the property is located. All notices shall set forth the time within which a claim of interest in the property seized is required to be filed.
(d) (1) Any person claiming an interest in the property or proceeds may, at any time within 30 days from the date of the first publication of the notice of seizure, or within 30 days after receipt of actual notice, file with the superior court of the county in which the action is pending a verified claim stating his or her interest in the property or proceeds. A verified copy of the claim shall be given by the claimant to the Attorney General or district attorney, county counsel, or city attorney, as appropriate.
(2) If, at the end of the time set forth in paragraph (1), an interested person has not filed a claim, the court, upon motion, shall declare that the person has defaulted upon his or her alleged interest, and it shall be subject to forfeiture upon proof of compliance with subdivision (c).
(e) The burden is on the petitioner to prove beyond a reasonable doubt that matter is subject to forfeiture pursuant to this section.
(f) It is not necessary to seek or obtain a criminal conviction prior to the entry of an order for the destruction of matter pursuant to this section. Any matter described in subdivision (a) that is in the possession of any city, county, city and county, or state official or agency, including found property, or property obtained as the result of a case in which no trial was had or that has been disposed of by way of dismissal or otherwise than by way of conviction may be ordered destroyed.
(g) A court order for destruction of matter described in subdivision (a) may be carried out by a police or sheriff's department or by the Department of Justice. The court order shall specify the agency responsible for the destruction.
(h) As used in this section, "matter" means any book, magazine, newspaper, or other printed or written material or any picture, drawing, photograph, motion picture, or other pictorial representation, or any statue or other figure, or any recording, transcription or mechanical, chemical or electrical reproduction, or any other articles, equipment, machines, or materials. "Matter" also means any representation of information, data, or image, including, but not limited to, any film, filmstrip, photograph, negative, slide, photocopy, videotape, video laser disc, computer hardware, computer software, computer floppy disc, data storage media, CD-ROM, or computer-generated equipment or any other computer-generated image that contains or incorporates in any manner any film or filmstrip.
(i) This section does not apply to a depiction of a legally emancipated minor or to lawful conduct between spouses if one or both are under the age of 18.
(j) It is a defense in any forfeiture proceeding that the matter seized was lawfully possessed in aid of legitimate scientific or educational purposes.
(Amended by Stats. 1996, Ch. 1080, Sec. 7. Effective January 1, 1997.)
312.5.
If any phrase, clause, sentence, section or provision of this chapter or application thereof to any person or circumstance is held invalid, such invalidity shall not affect any other phrase, clause, sentence, section, provision or application of this chapter, which can be given effect without the invalid phrase, clause, sentence, section, provision or application and to this end the provisions of this chapter are declared to be severable.
(Added by Stats. 1969, Ch. 249.)
312.6.
(a) It does not constitute a violation of this chapter for a person or entity solely to provide access or connection to or from a facility, system, or network over which that person or entity has no control, including related capabilities that are incidental to providing access or connection. This subdivision does not apply to an individual or entity that is owned or controlled by, or a conspirator with, an entity actively involved in the creation, editing, or knowing distribution of communications that violate this chapter.
(b) An employer is not liable under this chapter for the actions of an employee or agent unless the employee's or agent's conduct is within the scope of his or her employment or agency and the employer has knowledge of, authorizes, or ratifies the employee's or agent's conduct.
(c) It is a defense to prosecution under this chapter and in any civil action that may be instituted based on a violation of this chapter that a person has taken reasonable, effective, and appropriate actions in good faith to restrict or prevent the transmission of, or access to, a communication specified in this chapter.
(Added by Stats. 1996, Ch. 1080, Sec. 8. Effective January 1, 1997.)
312.7.
Nothing in this chapter shall be construed to apply to interstate services or to any other activities or actions for which states are prohibited from imposing liability pursuant to Paragraph (4) of subsection (g) of Section 223 of Title 47 of the United States Code.
(Added by Stats. 1996, Ch. 1080, Sec. 9. Effective January 1, 1997.)

CHAPTER 7.6. Harmful Matter [313 - 313.5]

(Chapter 7.6 added by Stats. 1969, Ch. 248.)
313.
As used in this chapter:
(a) "Harmful matter" means matter, taken as a whole, which to the average person, applying contemporary statewide standards, appeals to the prurient interest, and is matter which, taken as a whole, depicts or describes in a patently offensive way sexual conduct and which, taken as a whole, lacks serious literary, artistic, political, or scientific value for minors.
(1) When it appears from the nature of the matter or the circumstances of its dissemination, distribution or exhibition that it is designed for clearly defined deviant sexual groups, the appeal of the matter shall be judged with reference to its intended recipient group.
(2) In prosecutions under this chapter, where circumstances of production, presentation, sale, dissemination, distribution, or publicity indicate that matter is being commercially exploited by the defendant for the sake of its prurient appeal, that evidence is probative with respect to the nature of the matter and can justify the conclusion that the matter lacks serious literary, artistic, political, or scientific value for minors.
(b) "Matter" means any book, magazine, newspaper, video recording, or other printed or written material or any picture, drawing, photograph, motion picture, or other pictorial representation or any statue or other figure, or any recording, transcription, or mechanical, chemical, or electrical reproduction or any other articles, equipment, machines, or materials. "Matter" also includes live or recorded telephone messages when transmitted, disseminated, or distributed as part of a commercial transaction.
(c) "Person" means any individual, partnership, firm, association, corporation, limited liability company, or other legal entity.
(d) "Distribute" means to transfer possession of, whether with or without consideration.
(e) "Knowingly" means being aware of the character of the matter.
(f) "Exhibit" means to show.
(g) "Minor" means any natural person under 18 years of age.
(Amended by Stats. 1994, Ch. 1010, Sec. 190. Effective January 1, 1995.)
313.1.

(a) Every person who, with knowledge that a person is a minor, or who fails to exercise reasonable care in ascertaining the true age of a minor, knowingly sells, rents, distributes, sends, causes to be sent, exhibits, or offers to distribute or exhibit by any means, including, but not limited to, live or recorded telephone messages, any harmful matter to the minor shall be punished as specified in Section 313.4.
It does not constitute a violation of this section for a telephone corporation, as defined by Section 234 of the Public Utilities Code, to carry or transmit messages described in this chapter or to perform related activities in providing telephone services.
(b) Every person who misrepresents himself or herself to be the parent or guardian of a minor and thereby causes the minor to be admitted to an exhibition of any harmful matter shall be punished as specified in Section 313.4.
(c) (1) Any person who knowingly displays, sells, or offers to sell in any coin-operated or slug-operated vending machine or mechanically or electronically controlled vending machine that is located in a public place, other than a public place from which minors are excluded, any harmful matter displaying to the public view photographs or pictorial representations of the commission of any of the following acts shall be punished as specified in Section 313.4: sodomy, oral copulation, sexual intercourse, masturbation, bestiality, or a photograph of an exposed penis in an erect and turgid state.
(2) Any person who knowingly displays, sells, or offers to sell in any coin-operated vending machine that is not supervised by an adult and that is located in a public place, other than a public place from which minors are excluded, any harmful matter, as defined in subdivision (a) of Section 313, shall be punished as specified in Section 313.4.
(d) Nothing in this section invalidates or prohibits the adoption of an ordinance by a city, county, or city and county that restricts the display of material that is harmful to minors, as defined in this chapter, in a public place, other than a public place from which minors are excluded, by requiring the placement of devices commonly known as blinder racks in front of the material, so that the lower two-thirds of the material is not exposed to view.
(e) Any person who sells or rents video recordings of harmful matter shall create an area within his or her business establishment for the placement of video recordings of harmful matter and for any material that advertises the sale or rental of these video recordings. This area shall be labeled "adults only." The failure to create and label the area is an infraction, punishable by a fine not to exceed one hundred dollars ($100). The failure to place a video recording or advertisement, regardless of its content, in this area shall not constitute an infraction. Any person who sells or distributes video recordings of harmful matter to others for resale purposes shall inform the purchaser of the requirements of this section. This subdivision shall not apply to public libraries as defined in Section 18710 of the Education Code.
(f) Any person who rents a video recording and alters the video recording by adding harmful material, and who then returns the video recording to a video rental store, shall be guilty of a misdemeanor. It shall be a defense in any prosecution for a violation of this subdivision that the video rental store failed to post a sign, reasonably visible to all customers, delineating the provisions of this subdivision.
(g) It shall be a defense in any prosecution for a violation of subdivision (a) by a person who knowingly distributed any harmful matter by the use of telephones or telephone facilities to any person under the age of 18 years that the defendant has taken either of the following measures to restrict access to the harmful matter by persons under 18 years of age:
(1) Required the person receiving the harmful matter to use an authorized access or identification code, as provided by the information provider, before transmission of the harmful matter begins, where the defendant previously has issued the code by mailing it to the applicant after taking reasonable measures to ascertain that the applicant was 18 years of age or older and has established a procedure to immediately cancel the code of any person after receiving notice, in writing or by telephone, that the code has been lost, stolen, or used by persons under the age of 18 years or that the code is no longer desired.
(2) Required payment by credit card before transmission of the matter.
(h) It shall be a defense in any prosecution for a violation of paragraph (2) of subdivision (c) that the defendant has taken either of the following measures to restrict access to the harmful matter by persons under 18 years of age:
(1) Required the person receiving the harmful matter to use an authorized access or identification card to the vending machine after taking reasonable measures to ascertain that the applicant was 18 years of age or older and has established a procedure to immediately cancel the card of any person after receiving notice, in writing or by telephone, that the code has been lost, stolen, or used by persons under the age of 18 years or that the card is no longer desired.
(2) Required the person receiving the harmful matter to use a token in order to utilize the vending machine after taking reasonable measures to ascertain that the person was 18 years of age or older.
(i) Any list of applicants or recipients compiled or maintained by an information-access service provider for purposes of compliance with paragraph (1) of subdivision (g) is confidential and shall not be sold or otherwise disseminated except upon order of the court.
(Amended by Stats. 1994, Ch. 38, Sec. 1. Effective January 1, 1995.)
313.2.
(a) Nothing in this chapter shall prohibit any parent or guardian from distributing any harmful matter to his child or ward or permitting his child or ward to attend an exhibition of any harmful matter if the child or ward is accompanied by him.
(b) Nothing in this chapter shall prohibit any person from exhibiting any harmful matter to any of the following:
(1) A minor who is accompanied by his parent or guardian.
(2) A minor who is accompanied by an adult who represents himself to be the parent or guardian of the minor and whom the person, by the exercise of reasonable care, does not have reason to know is not the parent or guardian of the minor.
(Amended by Stats. 1970, Ch. 257.)
313.3.
It shall be a defense in any prosecution for a violation of this chapter that the act charged was committed in aid of legitimate scientific or educational purposes.
(Added by Stats. 1969, Ch. 248.)
313.4.
Every person who violates Section 313.1, other than subdivision (e), is punishable by fine of not more than two thousand dollars ($2,000), by imprisonment in the county jail for not more than one year, or by both that fine and imprisonment. However, if the person has been previously convicted of a violation of Section 313.1, other than subdivision (e), or of any section of Chapter 7.5 (commencing with Section 311) of Title 9 of Part 1 of this code, the person shall be punished by imprisonment pursuant to subdivision (h) of Section 1170.
(Amended by Stats. 2011, Ch. 15, Sec. 325. (AB 109) Effective April 4, 2011. Operative October 1, 2011, by Sec. 636 of Ch. 15, as amended by Stats. 2011, Ch. 39, Sec. 68.)
313.5.
If any phrase, clause, sentence, section or provision of this chapter or application thereof to any person or circumstance is held invalid, such invalidity shall not affect any other phrase, clause, sentence, section, provision or application of this chapter, which can be given effect without the invalid phrase, clause, sentence, section, provision or application and to this end the provisions of this chapter are declared to be severable.
(Added by Stats. 1969, Ch. 248.)

CHAPTER 8. Indecent Exposure, Obscene Exhibitions, and Bawdy and Other Disorderly Houses [314 - 318.6]

(Heading of Chapter 8 amended by Stats. 1961, Ch. 2147.)
314.
Every person who willfully and lewdly, either:
1. Exposes his person, or the private parts thereof, in any public place, or in any place where there are present other persons to be offended or annoyed thereby; or,
2. Procures, counsels, or assists any person so to expose himself or take part in any model artist exhibition, or to make any other exhibition of himself to public view, or the view of any number of persons, such as is offensive to decency, or is adapted to excite to vicious or lewd thoughts or acts,

is guilty of a misdemeanor.
Every person who violates subdivision 1 of this section after having entered, without consent, an inhabited dwelling house, or trailer coach as defined in Section 635 of the Vehicle Code, or the inhabited portion of any other building, is punishable by imprisonment in the state prison, or in the county jail not exceeding one year.
Upon the second and each subsequent conviction under subdivision 1 of this section, or upon a first conviction under subdivision 1 of this section after a previous conviction under Section 288, every person so convicted is guilty of a felony, and is punishable by imprisonment in state prison.
(Amended by Stats. 1982, Ch. 1113, Sec. 2.)
315.
Every person who keeps a house of ill-fame in this state, resorted to for the purposes of prostitution or lewdness, or who willfully resides in such house, is guilty of a misdemeanor; and in all prosecutions for keeping or resorting to such a house common repute may be received as competent evidence of the character of the house, the purpose for which it is kept or used, and the character of the women inhabiting or resorting to it.
(Amended by Stats. 1905, Ch. 507.)
316.
Every person who keeps any disorderly house, or any house for the purpose of assignation or prostitution, or any house of public resort, by which the peace, comfort, or decency of the immediate neighborhood is habitually disturbed, or who keeps any inn in a disorderly manner; and every person who lets any apartment or tenement, knowing that it is to be used for the purpose of assignation or prostitution, is guilty of a misdemeanor.
(Amended by Stats. 1989, Ch. 1360, Sec. 108.)
318.
Whoever, through invitation or device, prevails upon any person to visit any room, building, or other places kept for the purpose of illegal gambling or prostitution, is guilty of a misdemeanor, and, upon conviction thereof, shall be confined in the county jail not exceeding six months, or fined not exceeding five hundred dollars ($500), or be punished by both that fine and imprisonment.
(Amended by Stats. 1991, Ch. 684, Sec. 2.)
318.5.
(a) Nothing in this code shall invalidate an ordinance of, or be construed to prohibit the adoption of an ordinance by, a county or city, if that ordinance directly regulates the exposure of the genitals or buttocks of any person, or the breasts of any female person, who acts as a waiter, waitress, or entertainer, whether or not the owner of the establishment in which the activity is performed employs or pays any compensation to that person to perform the activity, in an adult or sexually oriented business. For purposes of this section, an "adult or sexually oriented business" includes any establishment that regularly features live performances which are distinguished or characterized by an emphasis on the exposure of the genitals or buttocks of any person, or the breasts of any female person, or specified sexual activities that involve the exposure of the genitals or buttocks of any person, or the breasts of any female person.
(b) The provisions of this section shall not be construed to apply to any adult or sexually oriented business, as defined herein, that has been adjudicated by a court of competent jurisdiction to be, or by action of a local body such as issuance of an adult entertainment establishment license or permit allowing the business to operate on or before July 1, 1998, as, a theater, concert hall, or similar establishment primarily devoted to theatrical performances for purposes of this section.
This section shall be known and may be cited as the "Quimby-Walsh Act."
(Amended by Stats. 1998, Ch. 294, Sec. 2. Effective January 1, 1999.)
318.6.
(a) Nothing in this code shall invalidate an ordinance of, or be construed to prohibit the adoption of an ordinance by, a city or county, if that ordinance relates to any live acts, demonstrations, or exhibitions occurring within adult or sexually oriented businesses and involve the exposure of the genitals or buttocks of any participant or the breasts of any female participant, and if that ordinance prohibits an act or acts which are not expressly authorized or prohibited by this code.
(b) For purposes of this section, an "adult or sexually oriented business" includes any establishment that regularly features live performances which are distinguished or characterized by an emphasis on the exposure of the genitals or buttocks of any person, or the breasts of any female person or sexual activities that involve the exposure of the genitals or buttocks of any person, or the breasts of any female person.
(c) The provisions of this section shall not be construed to apply to any adult or sexually oriented business, as defined herein, that has been adjudicated by a court of competent jurisdiction to be, or by action of a local body such as issuance of an adult entertainment establishment license or permit allowing the business to operate on or before July 1, 1998, as, a theater, concert hall, or similar establishment primarily devoted to theatrical performances for purposes of this section.
(d) This section shall not be construed to preempt the legislative body of any city or county from regulating an adult or sexually oriented business, or similar establishment, in the manner and to the extent permitted by the United States Constitution and the California Constitution.
(Amended by Stats. 1998, Ch. 294, Sec. 3. Effective January 1, 1999.)

CHAPTER 9. Lotteries [319 - 329]

(Chapter 9 enacted 1872.)
319.
A lottery is any scheme for the disposal or distribution of property by chance, among persons who have paid or promised to pay any valuable consideration for the chance of obtaining such property or a portion of it, or for any share or any interest in such property, upon any agreement, understanding, or expectation that it is to be distributed or disposed of by lot or chance, whether called a lottery, raffle, or gift enterprise, or by whatever name the same may be known.
(Enacted 1872.)

319.3.

(a) In addition to Section 319, a lottery also shall include a grab bag game which is a scheme whereby, for the disposal or distribution of sports trading cards by chance, a person pays valuable consideration to purchase a sports trading card grab bag with the understanding that the purchaser has a chance to win a designated prize or prizes listed by the seller as being contained in one or more, but not all, of the grab bags.

(b) For purposes of this section, the following definitions shall apply:

(1) "Sports trading card grab bag" means a sealed package which contains one or more sports trading cards that have been removed from the manufacturer's original packaging. A "sports trading card grab bag" does not include a sweepstakes, or procedure for the distribution of any sports trading card of value by lot or by chance, which is not unlawful under other provisions of law.

(2) "Sports trading card" means any card produced for use in commerce that contains a company name or logo, or both, and an image, representation, or facsimile of one or more players or other team member or members in any pose, and that is produced pursuant to an appropriate licensing agreement.

(Added by Stats. 1994, Ch. 1074, Sec. 3. Effective January 1, 1995.)

319.5.

Neither this chapter nor Chapter 10 (commencing with Section 330) applies to the possession or operation of a reverse vending machine. As used in this section a reverse vending machine is a machine in which empty beverage containers are deposited for recycling and which provides a payment of money, merchandise, vouchers, or other incentives at a frequency less than upon each deposit. The pay out of a reverse vending machine is made on a deposit selected at random within the designated number of required deposits.

The deposit of an empty beverage container in a reverse vending machine does not constitute consideration within the definition of lottery in Section 319.

(Added by Stats. 1982, Ch. 456, Sec. 1. Effective July 8, 1982.)

320.

Every person who contrives, prepares, sets up, proposes, or draws any lottery, is guilty of a misdemeanor.

(Enacted 1872.)

320.5.

(a) Nothing in this chapter applies to any raffle conducted by an eligible organization as defined in subdivision (c) for the purpose of directly supporting beneficial or charitable purposes or financially supporting another private, nonprofit, eligible organization that performs beneficial or charitable purposes if the raffle is conducted in accordance with this section.

(b) For purposes of this section, "raffle" means a scheme for the distribution of prizes by chance among persons who have paid money for paper tickets that provide the opportunity to win these prizes, where all of the following are true:

(1) Each ticket is sold with a detachable coupon or stub, and both the ticket and its associated coupon or stub are marked with a unique and matching identifier.

(2) Winners of the prizes are determined by draw from among the coupons or stubs described in paragraph (1) that have been detached from all tickets sold for entry in the draw.

(3) The draw is conducted in California under the supervision of a natural person who is 18 years of age or older.

(4) (A) At least 90 percent of the gross receipts generated from the sale of raffle tickets for any given draw are used by the eligible organization conducting the raffle to benefit or provide support for beneficial or charitable purposes, or it may use those revenues to benefit another private, nonprofit organization, provided that an organization receiving these funds is itself an eligible organization as defined in subdivision (c). As used in this section, "beneficial purposes" excludes purposes that are intended to benefit officers, directors, or members, as defined by Section 5056 of the Corporations Code, of the eligible organization. In no event shall funds raised by raffles conducted pursuant to this section be used to fund any beneficial, charitable, or other purpose outside of California. This section does not preclude an eligible organization from using funds from sources other than the sale of raffle tickets to pay for the administration or other costs of conducting a raffle.

(B) An employee of an eligible organization who is a direct seller of raffle tickets shall not be treated as an employee for purposes of workers' compensation under Section 3351 of the Labor Code if the following conditions are satisfied:

(i) Substantially all of the remuneration (whether or not paid in cash) for the performance of the service of selling raffle tickets is directly related to sales rather than to the number of hours worked.

(ii) The services performed by the person are performed pursuant to a written contract between the seller and the eligible organization and the contract provides that the person will not be treated as an employee with respect to the selling of raffle tickets for workers' compensation purposes.

(C) For purposes of this section, employees selling raffle tickets shall be deemed to be direct sellers as described in Section 650 of the Unemployment Insurance Code as long as they meet the requirements of that section.

(c) For purposes of this section, "eligible organization" means a private, nonprofit organization that has been qualified to conduct business in California for at least one year prior to conducting a raffle and is exempt from taxation pursuant to Sections 23701a, 23701b, 23701d, 23701e, 23701f, 23701g, 23701k, 23701l, 23701t, or 23701w of the Revenue and Taxation Code.

(d) Any person who receives compensation in connection with the operation of the raffle shall be an employee of the eligible organization that is conducting the raffle, and in no event may compensation be paid from revenues required to be dedicated to beneficial or charitable purposes.

(e) No raffle otherwise permitted under this section may be conducted by means of, or otherwise utilize, any gaming machine, apparatus, or device, whether or not that machine, apparatus, or device meets the definition of slot machine contained in Section 330a, 330b, or 330.1.

(f) (1) No raffle otherwise permitted under this section may be conducted, nor may tickets for a raffle be sold, within an operating satellite wagering facility or racetrack inclosure licensed pursuant to the Horse Racing Law (Chapter 4 (commencing with Section 19400) of Division 8 of the Business and Professions Code) or within a gambling establishment licensed pursuant to the Gambling Control Act (Chapter 5 (commencing with Section 19800) of Division 8 of the Business and Professions Code).

(2) A raffle may not be operated or conducted in any manner over the Internet, nor may raffle tickets be sold, traded, or redeemed over the Internet. For purposes of this paragraph, an eligible organization shall not be deemed to operate or conduct a raffle over the Internet, or sell raffle tickets over the Internet, if the eligible organization advertises its raffle on the Internet or permits others to do so. Information that may be conveyed on an Internet Web site pursuant to this paragraph includes, but is not limited to, all of the following:

(A) Lists, descriptions, photographs, or videos of the raffle prizes.

(B) Lists of the prize winners.

(C) The rules of the raffle.

(D) Frequently asked questions and their answers.

(E) Raffle entry forms, which may be downloaded from the Internet Web site for manual completion by raffle ticket purchasers, but shall not be submitted to the eligible organization through the Internet.

(F) Raffle contact information, including the eligible organization's name, address, telephone number, facsimile number, or e-mail address.

(g) No individual, corporation, partnership, or other legal entity shall hold a financial interest in the conduct of a raffle, except the eligible organization that is itself authorized to conduct that raffle, and any private, nonprofit, eligible organizations receiving financial support from that charitable organization pursuant to subdivisions (a) and (b).

(h) (1) An eligible organization may not conduct a raffle authorized under this section, unless it registers annually with the Department of Justice. The department shall furnish a registration form via the Internet or upon request to eligible nonprofit organizations. The department shall, by regulation, collect only the information necessary to carry out the provisions of this section on this form. This information shall include, but is not limited to, the following:

(A) The name and address of the eligible organization.

(B) The federal tax identification number, the corporate number issued by the Secretary of State, the organization number issued by the Franchise Tax Board, or the California charitable trust identification number of the eligible organization.

(C) The name and title of a responsible fiduciary of the organization.

(2) The department may require an eligible organization to pay an annual registration fee of ten dollars ($10) to cover the actual costs of the department to administer and enforce this section. The department may, by regulation, adjust the annual registration fee as needed to ensure that revenues willfully offset, but do not exceed, the actual costs incurred by the department pursuant to this section. The fee shall be deposited by the department into the General Fund.

(3) The department shall receive General Fund moneys for the costs incurred pursuant to this section subject to an appropriation by the Legislature.

(4) The department shall adopt regulations necessary to effectuate this section, including emergency regulations, pursuant to the Administrative Procedure Act (Chapter 3.5 (commencing with Section 11340) of Part 1 of Division 3 of Title 2 of the Government Code).

(5) The department shall maintain an automated database of all registrants. Each local law enforcement agency shall notify the department of any arrests or investigation that may result in an administrative or criminal action against a registrant. The department may audit the records and other documents of a registrant to ensure compliance with this section.

(6) Once registered, an eligible organization must file annually thereafter with the department a report that includes the following:

(A) The aggregate gross receipts from the operation of raffles.

(B) The aggregate direct costs incurred by the eligible organization from the operation of raffles.

(C) The charitable or beneficial purposes for which proceeds of the raffles were used, or identify the eligible recipient organization to which proceeds were directed, and the amount of those proceeds.

(7) The department shall annually furnish to registrants a form to collect this information.

(8) The registration and reporting provisions of this section do not apply to any religious corporation sole or other religious corporation or organization that holds property for religious purposes, to a cemetery corporation regulated under Chapter 19 of Division 3 of the Business and Professions Code, or to any committee as defined in Section 82013 that is required to and does file any statement pursuant to the provisions of Article 2 (commencing with Section 84200) of Chapter 4 of Title 9, or to a charitable corporation organized and operated primarily as a religious organization, educational institution, hospital, or a health care service plan licensed pursuant to Section 1349 of the Health and Safety Code.

(i) The department may take legal action against a registrant if it determines that the registrant has violated this section or any regulation adopted pursuant to this section, or that the registrant has engaged in any conduct that is not in the best interests of the public's health, safety, or general welfare. Any action taken pursuant to this subdivision does not prohibit the commencement of an administrative or criminal action by the Attorney General, a district attorney, city attorney, or county counsel.

(j) Each action and hearing conducted to deny, revoke, or suspend a registry, or other administrative action taken against a registrant shall be conducted pursuant to the Administrative Procedure Act (Chapters 4.5 (commencing with Section 11400) and 5 (commencing with Section 11500) of Part 1 of Division 3 of Title 2 of the Government Code). The department may seek recovery of the costs incurred in investigating or prosecuting an action against a registrant or applicant in accordance with those procedures specified in Section 125.3 of the Business and Professions Code. A proceeding conducted under this subdivision is subject to judicial review pursuant to Section 1094.5 of the Code of Civil Procedure.

(k) The Department of Justice shall conduct a study and report to the Legislature by December 31, 2003, on the impact of this section on raffle practices in California. Specifically, the study shall include, but not be limited to, information on whether the number of raffles has increased, the amount of money raised through raffles and whether this amount has increased, whether there are consumer complaints, and whether there is increased fraud in the operation of raffles.

(l) This section shall become operative on July 1, 2001.

(m) A raffle shall be exempt from this section if it satisfies all of the following requirements:

(1) It involves a general and indiscriminate distribution of the tickets.

(2) The tickets are offered on the same terms and conditions as the tickets for which a donation is given.

(3) The scheme does not require any of the participants to pay for a chance to win.

(Amended by Stats. 2009, Ch. 38, Sec. 1. (SB 200) Effective January 1, 2010.)

320.6.

(a) Notwithstanding Section 320.5, this section applies to an eligible organization.

(b) A raffle that is conducted by an eligible organization for the purpose of directly supporting beneficial or charitable purposes or financially supporting another private, nonprofit eligible organization, as defined in subdivision (c) of Section 320.5, that performs beneficial or charitable purposes may be conducted in accordance with this section.

(c) For purposes of this section, "eligible organization" means a private, nonprofit organization established by, or affiliated with, a team from the Major League Baseball, National Hockey League, National Basketball Association, National Football League, Women's National Basketball Association, or Major League Soccer, or a private, nonprofit organization established by the Professional Golfers' Association of America, Ladies Professional Golf Association, or National Association for Stock Car Auto Racing that has been qualified to conduct business in California for at least one year before conducting a raffle, is qualified for an exemption under Section 501(c)(3) of the Internal Revenue Code, and is exempt from taxation pursuant to Section 23701a, 23701b, 23701d, 23701e, 23701f, 23701g, 23701k, 23701l, 23701t, or 23701w of the Revenue and Taxation Code.

(d) For purposes of this section, "raffle" means a scheme for the distribution of prizes by chance among persons who have paid money for paper tickets that provide the opportunity to win these prizes, in which all of the following are true:

(1) Each ticket sold contains a unique and matching identifier.

(2) (A) Winners of the prizes are determined by a manual draw from tickets described in paragraph (1) that have been sold for entry in the manual draw.

(B) An electronic device may be used to sell tickets. The ticket receipt issued by the electronic device to the purchaser may include more than one unique and matching identifier, representative of and matched to the number of tickets purchased in a single transaction.

(C) A random number generator is not used for the manual draw or to sell tickets.

(D) The prize paid to the winner is comprised of one-half or 50 percent of the gross receipts generated from the sale of raffle tickets for a raffle.

(3) The manual draw is conducted in California under the supervision of a natural person who meets all of the following requirements:

(A) The person is 18 years of age or older.

(B) The person is affiliated with the eligible organization conducting the raffle.

(C) The person is registered with the Department of Justice pursuant to paragraph (4) of subdivision (o).

(4) (A) Fifty percent of the gross receipts generated from the sale of raffle tickets for any given manual draw are used by the eligible organization conducting the raffle solely for charitable purposes, or used to benefit another private, nonprofit organization, provided that an organization receiving these funds is itself an eligible organization as defined in subdivision (c) of Section 320.5. As used in this section, "charitable purposes" excludes purposes that are intended to benefit officers, directors, or members, as defined by Section 5056 of the Corporations Code, of the eligible organization. Funds raised by raffles conducted pursuant to this section shall not be used to fund any beneficial, charitable, or other purpose outside of California. This section does not preclude an eligible organization from using funds from sources other than the sale of raffle tickets to pay for the administration or other costs of conducting a raffle if these expenses comply with legal standard of care requirements described in Sections 5231, 7231, and 9241 of the Corporations Code.

(B) An employee of an eligible organization who is a direct seller of raffle tickets shall not be treated as an employee for purposes of workers' compensation under Section 3351 of the Labor Code if both of the following conditions are satisfied:

(i) Substantially all of the remuneration, whether or not paid in cash, for the performance of the service of selling raffle tickets is directly related to sales rather than to the number of hours worked.

(ii) The services performed by the person are performed pursuant to a written contract between the seller and the eligible organization and the contract provides that the person will not be treated as an employee with respect to the selling of raffle tickets for workers' compensation purposes.

(C) For purposes of this section, an employee selling raffle tickets shall be deemed to be a direct seller, as described in Section 650 of the Unemployment Insurance Code, as long as the employee meets the requirements of that section.

(e) A person who receives compensation in connection with the operation of the raffle shall be an employee of the eligible organization that is conducting the raffle, and in no event may compensation be paid from revenues required to be dedicated to beneficial or charitable purposes.

(f) A raffle ticket shall not be sold in exchange for Bitcoin or any other cryptocurrency.

(g) A raffle that is otherwise permitted under this section shall not be conducted by means of, or otherwise utilize, any gaming machine that meets the definition of slot machine contained in Section 330a, 330b, or 330.1.

(h) (1) A raffle otherwise permitted under this section shall not be conducted, nor may tickets for a raffle be sold, within an operating satellite wagering facility or racetrack inclosure licensed pursuant to the Horse Racing Law (Chapter 4 (commencing with Section 19400) of Division 8 of the Business and Professions Code) or within a gambling establishment licensed pursuant to the Gambling Control Act (Chapter 5 (commencing with Section 19800) of Division 8 of the Business and Professions Code).

(2) A raffle shall not be operated or conducted in any manner over the internet, nor may raffle tickets be sold, traded, or redeemed over the Internet. For purposes of this paragraph, an eligible organization shall not be deemed to operate or conduct a raffle over the internet, or sell raffle tickets over the internet, if the eligible organization advertises its raffle on the internet or permits others to do so. Information that may be conveyed on an internet website pursuant to this paragraph includes, but is not limited to, all of the following:

(A) Lists, descriptions, photographs, or videos of the raffle prizes.

(B) Lists of the prize winners.

(C) The rules of the raffle.

(D) Frequently asked questions and their answers.

(E) Raffle entry forms, which may be downloaded from the internet website for manual completion by raffle ticket purchasers, but shall not be submitted to the eligible organization through the Internet.

(F) Raffle contact information, including the eligible organization's name, address, telephone number, facsimile number, or email address.

(i) An individual, corporation, partnership, or other legal entity shall not hold a financial interest in the conduct of a raffle, except the eligible organization that is itself authorized to conduct that raffle, and any private, nonprofit, eligible organizations receiving financial support from that charitable organization pursuant to subdivisions (b) and (d).

(j) (1) An eligible organization may conduct a major league sports raffle only at a home game.

(2) An eligible organization shall not conduct more than one major league sports raffle per home game.

(k) An employee shall not sell raffle tickets in any seating area designated as a family section.

(l) An eligible organization shall disclose to all ticket purchasers the designated private, nonprofit, eligible organization for which the raffle is being conducted.

(m) An eligible organization that conducts a raffle to financially support another private, nonprofit eligible organization, as defined in subdivision (c) of Section 320.5, shall distribute all proceeds not paid out to the winners of the prizes to the private, nonprofit organization within 15 days of conducting the raffle, in accordance with this section.

(n) Any raffle prize remaining unclaimed by a winner at the end of the season for a team with an affiliated eligible organization that conducted a raffle to financially support another private, nonprofit eligible organization, as defined in subdivision (c) of Section 320.5, shall be donated within 30 days from the end of the season by the eligible organization to the designated private, nonprofit organization for which the raffle was conducted.

(o) (1) (A) An eligible organization shall not conduct a raffle authorized under this section, unless it has a valid registration issued by the Department of Justice. The department shall furnish a registration form via the Internet or upon request to eligible nonprofit organizations. The department shall, by regulation, collect only the information necessary to carry out the provisions of this section on this form. This information shall include, but is not limited to, all of the following:

(i) The name and address of the eligible organization.

(ii) The federal tax identification number, the corporate number issued by the Secretary of State, the organization number issued by the Franchise Tax Board, or the California charitable trust identification number of the eligible organization.

(iii) The name and title of a responsible fiduciary of the organization.

(B) (i) The department may require an eligible organization to pay a minimum annual registration fee of ten thousand dollars ($10,000) to cover the reasonable costs of the department to administer and enforce this section.

(ii) An eligible organization shall pay, in addition to the annual registration application fee, two hundred dollars ($200) for every individual raffle conducted at an eligible location to cover the reasonable costs of the department to administer and enforce this section. This fee shall be submitted in conjunction with the annual registration form.

(2) (A) A manufacturer or distributor of raffle-related products or services shall not conduct business with an eligible organization for purposes of conducting a raffle pursuant to this section unless the manufacturer or distributor has a valid annual registration issued by the department.

(B) The department may require a manufacturer or distributor of raffle-related products or services to pay a minimum annual registration fee of ten thousand dollars ($10,000) to cover the reasonable costs of the department to administer and enforce this section.

(3) An eligible organization shall register the equipment used in the sale and distribution of raffle tickets, and shall have the equipment tested by an independent gaming testing lab.

(4) (A) A person affiliated with an eligible organization who conducts the manual draw shall annually register with the department.

(B) The department may require a person affiliated with an eligible organization who conducts the manual draw to pay a minimum annual registration fee of twenty dollars ($20) to cover the reasonable costs of the department to administer and enforce this section.

(5) (A) The department may, by regulation, adjust the annual registration fees described in this section as needed to ensure that revenues will fully offset, but not exceed, the reasonable costs incurred by the department pursuant to this section. The fees shall be deposited by the department into the Major League Sporting Event Raffle Fund, which is hereby created in the State Treasury.

(B) A loan is hereby authorized from the General Fund to the Major League Sporting Event Raffle Fund on or after July 1, 2016, in an amount of up to one million five thousand dollars ($1,005,000) to address department workload related to the initial implementation activities relating to this section by the department's Indian and Gaming Law Section. The terms and conditions of the loan shall first be approved by the Department of Finance pursuant to appropriate fiscal standards. The loan shall be subject to all of the following conditions:

(i) Of the total amount loaned, no more than three hundred thirty-five thousand dollars ($335,000) shall be provided annually to the department.

(ii) The loan shall be repaid to the General Fund as soon as there is sufficient money in the Major League Sporting Event Raffle Fund to repay the loan, but no later than December 31, 2023.

(iii) Interest on the loan shall be paid from the Major League Sporting Event Raffle Fund at the rate accruing to moneys in the Pooled Money Investment Account.

(6) The department shall receive moneys for the costs incurred pursuant to this section subject to an appropriation by the Legislature.

(7) The department shall adopt regulations necessary to effectuate this section, including emergency regulations, pursuant to the Administrative Procedure Act (Chapter 3.5 (commencing with Section 11340) of Part 1 of Division 3 of Title 2 of the Government Code).

(8) The department shall maintain an automated database of all registrants.

(9) A local law enforcement agency shall notify the department of any arrests or investigation that may result in an administrative or criminal action against a registrant.

(10) The department may, to the extent the Legislature appropriates funds for this purpose, investigate all suspected violations of this section or any regulation adopted pursuant to this section, or any activity that the registrant has engaged in that is not in the best interests of the public's health, safety, or general welfare as it pertains to charitable raffles.

(11) The department may, to the extent the Legislature appropriates funds for this purpose, audit the records and other documents of a registrant to ensure compliance with this section.

(12) Once registered, an eligible organization shall post all of the following information on either its internet website or the affiliated sport team's internet website for each raffle:

(A) The gross receipts generated from the sale of raffle tickets.

(B) Each eligible recipient organization and the amount each eligible recipient organization received.

(C) The prize total.

(D) The winning ticket number and whether the prize was claimed.

(13) (A) Once registered, an eligible organization shall file with the department, each season or year thereafter, a report that includes all of the following information:

(i) For each raffle, all of the following information:

(I) The gross receipts generated from the sale of raffle tickets.

(II) Each eligible recipient organization and the amount each eligible recipient organization received.

(III) The prize total.

(IV) The winning ticket number and whether the prize was claimed.

(ii) The total number of raffles conducted for the season or year.

(iii) The gross receipts generated from the sale of raffle tickets for the season or year.

(iv) The average per raffle gross receipts generated from the sale of raffle tickets for the season or year.

(v) The prize total for the season or year, including any prize that was not claimed.

(vi) The average per raffle prize total for the season or year, including any prize that was not claimed.

(vii) The prize total that was not claimed, if any, during the season or year. For each raffle in which the prize was not claimed, the name of the eligible recipient organization who received the prize.

(viii) A schedule of all vendors used to operate the raffles and total payments made to each vendor.

(ix) An itemization of the direct costs of conducting the raffles, including labor, raffle equipment, software, marketing, and consulting costs.

(B) Failure to timely submit the seasonal or annual report to the department, as required in this paragraph, shall be grounds for denial of an annual registration and for the imposition of penalties under Section 12591.1 of the Government Code.

(C) Failure to submit a complete financial report shall be grounds for the denial of an annual registration and for the imposition of penalties under Section 12591.1 of the Government Code if the filer does not resubmit a complete form within 30 days of receiving a notice of incomplete filing.

(D) (i) An eligible organization shall file with the department and post on either its internet website or the affiliated sport team's internet website the report required by this paragraph no later than 60 days after the end of the league season or year.

(ii) The department shall post the reports required by this paragraph on its internet website, but shall not post the report on the online search portal of the Attorney General's Registry of Charitable Trusts maintained pursuant to Section 12584 of the Government Code.

(14) The department shall annually furnish to registrants a form to collect this information.

(p) The department may take legal action against a registrant if it determines that the registrant has violated this section or a regulation adopted pursuant to this section, or that the registrant has engaged in any conduct that is not in the best interests of the public's health, safety, or general welfare. An action taken pursuant to this subdivision does not prohibit the commencement of an administrative or criminal action by the Attorney General, a district attorney, city attorney, or county counsel.

(q) An action and hearing conducted to deny, revoke, or suspend a registry, or other administrative action taken against a registrant, shall be conducted pursuant to the Administrative Procedure Act (Chapters 4.5 (commencing with Section 11400) and 5 (commencing with Section 11500) of Part 1 of Division 3 of Title 2 of the Government Code). The department may seek civil remedies, including imposing fines, for violations of this section, and may seek recovery of the costs incurred in investigating or prosecuting an action against a registrant or applicant in accordance with those procedures specified in Section 125.3 of the Business and Professions Code. A proceeding conducted under this subdivision is subject to judicial review pursuant to

Section 1094.5 of the Code of Civil Procedure. A violation of this section shall not constitute a crime.

(r) This section shall remain in effect only until January 1, 2024, and as of that date is repealed.

(Amended by Stats. 2019, Ch. 29, Sec. 127. (SB 82) Effective June 27, 2019. Repealed as of January 1, 2024, by its own provisions.)

321.
Every person who sells, gives, or in any manner whatever, furnishes or transfers to or for any other person any ticket, chance, share, or interest, or any paper, certificate, or instrument purporting or understood to be or to represent any ticket, chance, share, or interest in, or depending upon the event of any lottery, is guilty of a misdemeanor.

(Enacted 1872.)

322.
Every person who aids or assists, either by printing, writing, advertising, publishing, or otherwise in setting up, managing, or drawing any lottery, or in selling or disposing of any ticket, chance, or share therein, is guilty of a misdemeanor.

(Enacted 1872.)

323.
Every person who opens, sets up, or keeps, by himself or by any other person, any office or other place for the sale of, or for registering the number of any ticket in any lottery, or who, by printing, writing, or otherwise, advertises or publishes the setting up, opening, or using of any such office, is guilty of a misdemeanor.

(Enacted 1872.)

324.
Every person who insures or receives any consideration for insuring for or against the drawing of any ticket in any lottery whatever, whether drawn or to be drawn within this State or not, or who receives any valuable consideration upon any agreement to repay any sum, or deliver the same, or any other property, if any lottery ticket or number of any ticket in any lottery shall prove fortunate or unfortunate, or shall be drawn or not be drawn, at any particular time or in any particular order, or who promises or agrees to pay any sum of money, or to deliver any goods, things in action, or property, or to forbear to do anything for the benefit of any person, with or without consideration, upon any event or contingency dependent on the drawing of any ticket in any lottery, or who publishes any notice or proposal of any of the purposes aforesaid, is guilty of a misdemeanor.

(Enacted 1872.)

325.
All moneys and property offered for sale or distribution in violation of any of the provisions of this chapter are forfeited to the state, and may be recovered by information filed, or by an action brought by the Attorney General, or by any district attorney, in the name of the state. Upon the filing of the information or complaint, the clerk of the court must issue an attachment against the property mentioned in the complaint or information, which attachment has the same force and effect against such property, and is issued in the same manner as attachments issued from the superior courts in civil cases.

(Amended by Stats. 1977, Ch. 1257.)

326.
Every person who lets, or permits to be used, any building or vessel, or any portion thereof, knowing that it is to be used for setting up, managing, or drawing any lottery, or for the purpose of selling or disposing of lottery tickets, is guilty of a misdemeanor.

(Enacted 1872.)

326.4.
(a) Consistent with the Legislature's finding that card-minding devices, as described in subdivision (p) of Section 326.5, are the only permissible electronic devices to be used by charity bingo players, and in an effort to ease the transition to remote caller bingo on the part of those nonprofit organizations that, as of July 1, 2008, used electronic devices other than card-minding devices to conduct games in reliance on an ordinance of a city, county, or city and county that, as of July 1, 2008, expressly recognized the operation of electronic devices other than card-minding devices by organizations purportedly authorized to conduct bingo in the city, county, or city and county, there is hereby created the Charity Bingo Mitigation Fund.

(b) The Charity Bingo Mitigation Fund shall be administered by the Department of Justice.

(c) Mitigation payments to be made by the Charity Bingo Mitigation Fund shall not exceed five million dollars ($5,000,000) in the aggregate.

(d) (1) To allow the Charity Bingo Mitigation Fund to become immediately operable, five million dollars ($5,000,000) shall be loaned from the accrued interest in the Indian Gaming Special Distribution Fund to the Charity Bingo Mitigation Fund on or after January 1, 2009, to make mitigation payments to eligible nonprofit organizations. Five million dollars ($5,000,000) of this loan amount is hereby appropriated to the California Gambling Control Commission for the purposes of providing mitigation payments to certain charitable organizations, as described in subdivision (e). Pursuant to Section 16304 of the Government Code, after three years the unexpended balance shall revert back to the Charity Bingo Mitigation Fund.

(2) To reimburse the Special Distribution Fund, those nonprofit organizations that conduct a remote caller bingo game pursuant to Section 326.3 shall pay to the Department of Justice an amount equal to 5 percent of the gross revenues of each remote caller bingo game played until that time as the full advanced amount plus interest on the loan at the rate accruing to moneys in the Pooled Money Investment Account is reimbursed.

(e) (1) An organization meeting the requirements in subdivision (a) shall be eligible to receive mitigation payments from the Charity Bingo Mitigation Fund only if the city, county, or city and county in which the organization is located maintained official records of the net revenues generated for the fiscal year ending June 30, 2008, by the organization from the use of electronic devices or the organization maintained audited financial records for the fiscal year ending June 30, 2008, which show the net revenues generated from the use of electronic devices.

(2) In addition, an organization applying for mitigation payments shall provide proof that its board of directors has adopted a resolution and its chief executive officer has signed a statement executed under penalty of perjury stating that, as of January 1, 2009, the organization has ceased using electronic devices other than card-minding devices, as described in subdivision (p) of Section 326.5, as a fundraising tool.

(3) Each eligible organization may apply to the California Gambling Control Commission no later than January 31, 2009, for the mitigation payments in the amount equal to net revenues from the fiscal year ending June 30, 2008, by filing an application, including therewith documents and other proof of eligibility, including any and all financial records documenting the organization's net revenues for the fiscal year ending June 30, 2008, as the California Gambling Control Commission may require. The California Gambling Control Commission is authorized to access and examine the financial records of charities requesting funding in order to confirm the legitimacy of the request for funding. In the event that the total of those requests exceeds five million dollars ($5,000,000), payments to all eligible applicants shall be reduced in proportion to each requesting organization's reported or audited net revenues from the operation of electronic devices.

(Amended by Stats. 2013, Ch. 353, Sec. 121. (SB 820) Effective September 26, 2013. Operative July 1, 2013, by Sec. 129 of Ch. 353.)

326.45.
Up to five hundred thousand dollars ($500,000), as determined by order of the Director of Finance, is hereby appropriated from the California Bingo Fund to the California

Gambling Control Commission for use in the 2008–09 fiscal year for the purposes described in subparagraph (C) of paragraph (3) of subdivision (q) of Section 326.3.

(Amended by Stats. 2009, Ch. 562, Sec. 3. (SB 126) Effective October 11, 2009.)

326.5.
(a) Neither the prohibition on gambling in this chapter nor in Chapter 10 (commencing with Section 330) applies to any bingo game that is conducted in a city, county, or city and county pursuant to an ordinance enacted under Section 19 of Article IV of the State Constitution, if the ordinance allows games to be conducted only in accordance with this section and only by organizations exempted from the payment of the bank and corporation tax by Sections 23701a, 23701b, 23701d, 23701e, 23701f, 23701g, 23701k, 23701w, and 23701l of the Revenue and Taxation Code and by mobilehome park associations, senior citizens organizations, and charitable organizations affiliated with a school district; and if the receipts of those games are used only for charitable purposes.

(b) It is a misdemeanor for any person to receive or pay a profit, wage, or salary from any bingo game authorized by Section 19 of Article IV of the State Constitution. Security personnel employed by the organization conducting the bingo game may be paid from the revenues of bingo games, as provided in subdivisions (j) and (k).

(c) A violation of subdivision (b) shall be punishable by a fine not to exceed ten thousand dollars ($10,000), which fine is deposited in the general fund of the city, county, or city and county that enacted the ordinance authorizing the bingo game. A violation of any provision of this section, other than subdivision (b), is a misdemeanor.

(d) The city, county, or city and county that enacted the ordinance authorizing the bingo game may bring an action to enjoin a violation of this section.

(e) Minors shall not be allowed to participate in any bingo game.

(f) An organization authorized to conduct bingo games pursuant to subdivision (a) shall conduct a bingo game only on property owned or leased by it, or property whose use is donated to the organization, and which property is used by that organization for an office or for performance of the purposes for which the organization is organized. Nothing in this subdivision shall be construed to require that the property owned or leased by, or whose use is donated to, the organization be used or leased exclusively by, or donated exclusively to, that organization.

(g) All bingo games shall be open to the public, not just to the members of the authorized organization.

(h) A bingo game shall be operated and staffed only by members of the authorized organization that organized it. Those members shall not receive a profit, wage, or salary from any bingo game. Only the organization authorized to conduct a bingo game shall operate such a game, or participate in the promotion, supervision, or any other phase of a bingo game. This subdivision does not preclude the employment of security personnel who are not members of the authorized organization at a bingo game by the organization conducting the game.

(i) Any individual, corporation, partnership, or other legal entity, except the organization authorized to conduct a bingo game, shall not hold a financial interest in the conduct of a bingo game.

(j) With respect to organizations exempt from payment of the bank and corporation tax by Section 23701d of the Revenue and Taxation Code, all profits derived from a bingo game shall be kept in a special fund or account and shall not be commingled with any other fund or account. Those profits shall be used only for charitable purposes.

(k) With respect to other organizations authorized to conduct bingo games pursuant to this section, all proceeds derived from a bingo game shall be kept in a special fund or account and shall not be commingled with any other fund or account. Proceeds are the receipts of bingo games conducted by organizations not within subdivision (j). Those proceeds shall be used only for charitable purposes, except as follows:

(1) The proceeds may be used for prizes.

(2) (A) Except as provided in subparagraph (B), a portion of the proceeds, not to exceed 20 percent of the proceeds before the deduction for prizes, or two thousand dollars ($2,000) per month, whichever is less, may be used for the rental of property and for overhead, including the purchase of bingo equipment, administrative expenses, security equipment, and security personnel.

(B) For the purposes of bingo games conducted by the Lake Elsinore Elks Lodge, a portion of the proceeds, not to exceed 20 percent of the proceeds before the deduction for prizes, or three thousand dollars ($3,000) per month, whichever is less, may be used for the rental of property and for overhead, including the purchase of bingo equipment, administrative expenses, security equipment, and security personnel. Any amount of the proceeds that is additional to that permitted under subparagraph (A), up to one thousand dollars ($1,000), shall be used for the purpose of financing the rebuilding of the facility and the replacement of equipment that was destroyed by fire in 2007. The exception to subparagraph (A) that is provided by this subparagraph shall remain in effect only until the cost of rebuilding the facility is repaid, or January 1, 2019, whichever occurs first.

(3) The proceeds may be used to pay license fees.

(4) A city, county, or city and county that enacts an ordinance permitting bingo games may specify in the ordinance that if the monthly gross receipts from bingo games of an organization within this subdivision exceed five thousand dollars ($5,000), a minimum percentage of the proceeds shall be used only for charitable purposes not relating to the conducting of bingo games and that the balance shall be used for prizes, rental of property, overhead, administrative expenses, and payment of license fees. The amount of proceeds used for rental of property, overhead, and administrative expenses is subject to the limitations specified in paragraph (2).

(l) (1) A city, county, or city and county may impose a license fee on each organization that it authorizes to conduct bingo games. The fee, whether for the initial license or renewal, shall not exceed fifty dollars ($50) annually, except as provided in paragraph (2). If an application for a license is denied, one-half of any license fee paid shall be refunded to the organization.

(2) In lieu of the license fee permitted under paragraph (1), a city, county, or city and county may impose a license fee of fifty dollars ($50) paid upon application. If an application for a license is denied, one-half of the application fee shall be refunded to the organization. An additional fee for law enforcement and public safety costs incurred by the city, county, or city and county that are directly related to bingo activities may be imposed and shall be collected monthly by the city, county, or city and county issuing the license; however, the fee shall not exceed the actual costs incurred in providing the service.

(m) A person shall not be allowed to participate in a bingo game, unless the person is physically present at the time and place where the bingo game is being conducted.

(n) The total value of prizes available to be awarded during the conduct of any bingo games shall not exceed five hundred dollars ($500) in cash or kind, or both, for each separate game which is held.

(o) As used in this section, "bingo" means a game of chance in which prizes are awarded on the basis of designated numbers or symbols that are marked or covered by the player on a tangible card in the player's possession and that conform to numbers or symbols, selected at random and announced by a live caller. Notwithstanding Section 330c, as used in this section, the game of bingo includes tangible cards having numbers or symbols that are concealed and preprinted in a manner providing for distribution of prizes. Electronics or video displays shall not be used in connection with the game of bingo, except in connection with the caller's drawing of numbers or symbols and the public display of that drawing, and except as provided in subdivision (p). The winning cards shall not be known prior to the game by any person participating in the playing or operation of the bingo game. All preprinted cards shall bear the legend, "for sale or use only in a bingo game authorized under California law and pursuant to local ordinance."

Only a covered or marked tangible card possessed by a player and presented to an attendant may be used to claim a prize. It is the intention of the Legislature that bingo as defined in this subdivision applies exclusively to this section and shall not be applied in the construction or enforcement of any other provision of law.

(p) (1) Players who are physically present at a bingo game may use hand-held, portable card-minding devices, as described in this subdivision, to assist in monitoring the numbers or symbols announced by a live caller as those numbers or symbols are called in a live game. Card-minding devices may not be used in connection with any game where a bingo card may be sold or distributed after the start of the ball draw for that game. A card-minding device shall do all of the following:

(A) Be capable of storing in the memory of the device bingo faces of tangible cards purchased by a player.

(B) Provide a means for bingo players to input manually each individual number or symbol announced by a live caller.

(C) Compare the numbers or symbols entered by the player to the bingo faces previously stored in the memory of the device.

(D) Identify winning bingo patterns that exist on the stored bingo faces.

(2) A card-minding device shall perform no functions involving the play of the game other than those described in paragraph (1). Card-minding devices shall not do any of the following:

(A) Be capable of accepting or dispensing any coins, currency, or other representative of value or on which value has been encoded.

(B) Be capable of monitoring any bingo card face other than the faces of the tangible bingo card or cards purchased by the player for that game.

(C) Display or represent the game result through any means, including, but not limited to, video or mechanical reels or other slot machine or casino game themes, other than highlighting the winning numbers or symbols marked or covered on the tangible bingo cards or giving an audio alert that the player's card has a prize-winning pattern.

(D) Determine the outcome of any game or be physically or electronically connected to any component that determines the outcome of a game or to any other bingo equipment, including, but not limited to, the ball call station, or to any other card-minding device. No other player-operated or player-activated electronic or electromechanical device or equipment is permitted to be used in connection with a bingo game.

(3) (A) A card-minding device shall be approved in advance by the department as meeting the requirements of this section and any additional requirements stated in regulations adopted by the department. Any proposed material change to the device, including any change to the software used by the device, shall be submitted to the department and approved by the department prior to implementation.

(B) In accordance with Chapter 5 (commencing with Section 19800) of Division 8 of the Business and Professions Code, the commission shall establish reasonable criteria for, and require the licensure of, any person that directly or indirectly manufactures, distributes, supplies, vends, leases, or otherwise provides card-minding devices or other supplies, equipment, or services related to card-minding devices designed for use in the playing of bingo games by any nonprofit organization.

(C) A person or entity that supplies or services any card-minding device shall meet all licensing requirements established by the commission in regulations.

(4) The costs of any testing, certification, license, or determination required by this subdivision shall be borne by the person or entity seeking it.

(5) On and after January 1, 2010, the Department of Justice may inspect all card-minding devices at any time without notice, and may immediately prohibit the use of any device that does not comply with the requirements established by the department in regulations. The Department of Justice may at any time, without notice, impound any device the use of which has been prohibited by the commission.

(6) The Department of Justice shall issue regulations to implement the requirements of this subdivision, and the California Gambling Control Commission may issue regulations regarding the means by which the operator of a bingo game, as required by applicable law, may offer assistance to a player with disabilities in order to enable that player to participate in a bingo game, provided that the means of providing that assistance shall not be through any electronic, electromechanical, or other device or equipment that accepts the insertion of any coin, currency, token, credit card, or other means of transmitting value, and does not constitute or is not a part of a system that constitutes a video lottery terminal, slot machine, or device prohibited by Chapter 10 (commencing with Section 330).

(7) The following definitions apply for purposes of this subdivision:

(A) "Commission" means the California Gambling Control Commission.

(B) "Department" means the Department of Justice.

(C) "Person" includes a natural person, corporation, limited liability company, partnership, trust, joint venture, association, or any other business organization.

(Amended by Stats. 2013, Ch. 353, Sec. 122. (SB 820) Effective September 26, 2013. Operative July 1, 2013, by Sec. 129 of Ch. 353.)

327.

Every person who contrives, prepares, sets up, proposes, or operates any endless chain is guilty of a public offense, and is punishable by imprisonment in the county jail not exceeding one year or in state prison for 16 months, two, or three years.

As used in this section, an "endless chain" means any scheme for the disposal or distribution of property whereby a participant pays a valuable consideration for the chance to receive compensation for introducing one or more additional persons into participation in the scheme or for the chance to receive compensation when a person introduced by the participant introduces a new participant. Compensation, as used in this section, does not mean or include payment based upon sales made to persons who are not participants in the scheme and who are not purchasing in order to participate in the scheme.

(Amended by Stats. 1989, Ch. 436, Sec. 2.)

328.

Nothing in this chapter shall make unlawful the printing or other production of any advertisements for, or any ticket, chance, or share in a lottery conducted in any other state or nation where such lottery is not prohibited by the laws of such state or nation; or the sale of such materials by the manufacturer thereof to any person or entity conducting or participating in the conduct of such a lottery in any such state or nation. This section does not authorize any advertisement within California relating to lotteries, or the sale or resale within California of lottery tickets, chances, or shares to individuals, or acts otherwise in violation of any laws of the state.

(Added by Stats. 1980, Ch. 216, Sec. 1. Effective June 23, 1980.)

329.

Upon a trial for the violation of any of the provisions of this chapter, it is not necessary to prove the existence of any lottery in which any lottery ticket purports to have been issued, or to prove the actual signing of any such ticket or share, or pretended ticket or share, of any pretended lottery, nor that any lottery ticket, share, or interest was signed or issued by the authority of any manager, or of any person assuming to have authority as manager; but in all cases proof of the sale, furnishing, bartering, or procuring of any ticket, share, or interest therein, or of any instrument purporting to be a ticket, or part or share of any such ticket, is evidence that such share or interest was signed and issued according to the purport thereof.

(Added by Stats. 1989, Ch. 897, Sec. 19.)

CHAPTER 10. Gaming [330 - 337z]

(Chapter 10 enacted 1872.)

330.

Every person who deals, plays, or carries on, opens, or causes to be opened, or who conducts, either as owner or employee, whether for hire or not, any game of faro, monte, roulette, lansquenet, rouge et noire, rondo, tan, fan-tan, seven-and-a-half, twenty-one, hokey-pokey, or any banking or percentage game played with cards, dice, or any device, for money, checks, credit, or other representative of value, and every person who plays or bets at or against any of those prohibited games, is guilty of a misdemeanor, and shall be punishable by a fine not less than one hundred dollars ($100) nor more than one thousand dollars ($1,000), or by imprisonment in the county jail not exceeding six months, or by both the fine and imprisonment.

(Amended by Stats. 1991, Ch. 71, Sec. 1.)

330a.

(a) Every person, who has in his or her possession or under his or her control, either as owner, lessee, agent, employee, mortgagee, or otherwise, or who permits to be placed, maintained, or kept in any room, space, inclosure, or building owned, leased, or occupied by him or her, or under his or her management or control, any slot or card machine, contrivance, appliance or mechanical device, upon the result of action of which money or other valuable thing is staked or hazarded, and which is operated, or played, by placing or depositing therein any coins, checks, slugs, balls, or other articles or device, or in any other manner and by means whereof, or as a result of the operation of which any merchandise, money, representative or articles of value, checks, or tokens, redeemable in or exchangeable for money or any other thing of value, is won or lost, or taken from or obtained from the machine, when the result of action or operation of the machine, contrivance, appliance, or mechanical device is dependent upon hazard or chance, and every person, who has in his or her possession or under his or her control, either as owner, lessee, agent, employee, mortgagee, or otherwise, or who permits to be placed, maintained, or kept in any room, space, inclosure, or building owned, leased, or occupied by him or her, or under his or her management or control, any card dice, or any dice having more than six faces or bases each, upon the result of action of which any money or other valuable thing is staked or hazarded, or as a result of the operation of which any merchandise, money, representative or article of value, check or token, redeemable in or exchangeable for money or any other thing of value, is won or lost or taken, when the result of action or operation of the dice is dependent upon hazard or chance, is guilty of a misdemeanor.

(b) A first violation of this section shall be punishable by a fine of not less than five hundred dollars ($500) nor more than one thousand dollars ($1,000), or by imprisonment in a county jail not exceeding six months, or by both that fine and imprisonment.

(c) A second offense shall be punishable by a fine of not less than one thousand dollars ($1,000) nor more than ten thousand dollars ($10,000), or by imprisonment in a county jail not exceeding six months, or by both that fine and imprisonment.

(d) A third or subsequent offense shall be punishable by a fine of not less than ten thousand dollars ($10,000) nor more than twenty-five thousand dollars ($25,000), or by imprisonment in a county jail not exceeding one year, or by both that fine and imprisonment.

(e) If the offense involved more than one machine or more than one location, an additional fine of not less than one thousand dollars ($1,000) nor more than five thousand dollars ($5,000) shall be imposed per machine and per location.

(Amended by Stats. 2010, Ch. 577, Sec. 1. (AB 1753) Effective January 1, 2011.)

330b.

(a) It is unlawful for any person to manufacture, repair, own, store, possess, sell, rent, lease, let on shares, lend or give away, transport, or expose for sale or lease, or to offer to repair, sell, rent, lease, let on shares, lend or give away, or permit the operation, placement, maintenance, or keeping of, in any place, room, space, or building owned, leased, or occupied, managed, or controlled by that person, any slot machine or device, as defined in this section.

It is unlawful for any person to make or to permit the making of an agreement with another person regarding any slot machine or device, by which the user of the slot machine or device, as a result of the element of hazard or chance or other unpredictable outcome, may become entitled to receive money, credit, allowance, or other thing of value or additional chance or right to use the slot machine or device, or to receive any check, slug, token, or memorandum entitling the holder to receive money, credit, allowance, or other thing of value.

(b) The limitations of subdivision (a), insofar as they relate to owning, storing, possessing, or transporting any slot machine or device, do not apply to any slot machine or device located upon or being transported by any vessel regularly operated and engaged in interstate or foreign commerce, so long as the slot machine or device is located in a locked compartment of the vessel, is not accessible for use, and is not used or operated within the territorial jurisdiction of this state.

(c) The limitations of subdivision (a) do not apply to a manufacturer's business activities that are conducted in accordance with the terms of a license issued by a tribal gaming agency pursuant to the tribal-state gaming compacts entered into in accordance with the Indian Gaming Regulatory Act (18 U.S.C. Sec. 1166 to 1168, inclusive, and 25 U.S.C. Sec. 2701 et seq.).

(d) For purposes of this section, "slot machine or device" means a machine, apparatus, or device that is adapted, or may readily be converted, for use in a way that, as a result of the insertion of any piece of money or coin or other object, or by any other means, the machine or device is caused to operate or may be operated, and by reason of any element of hazard or chance or of other outcome of operation unpredictable by him or her, the user may receive or become entitled to receive any piece of money, credit, allowance, or thing of value, or additional chance or right to use the slot machine or device, or any check, slug, token, or memorandum, whether of value or otherwise, which may be exchanged for any money, credit, allowance, or thing of value, or which may be given in trade, irrespective of whether it may, apart from any element of hazard or chance or unpredictable outcome of operation, also sell, deliver, or present some merchandise, indication of weight, entertainment, or other thing of value.

(e) Every person who violates this section is guilty of a misdemeanor.

(1) A first violation of this section shall be punishable by a fine of not less than five hundred dollars ($500) nor more than one thousand dollars ($1,000), or by imprisonment in a county jail not exceeding six months, or by both that fine and imprisonment.

(2) A second offense shall be punishable by a fine of not less than one thousand dollars ($1,000) nor more than ten thousand dollars ($10,000), or by imprisonment in a county jail not exceeding six months, or by both that fine and imprisonment.

(3) A third or subsequent offense shall be punishable by a fine of not less than ten thousand dollars ($10,000) nor more than twenty-five thousand dollars ($25,000), or by imprisonment in a county jail not exceeding one year, or by both that fine and imprisonment.

(4) If the offense involved more than one machine or more than one location, an additional fine of not less than one thousand dollars ($1,000) nor more than five thousand dollars ($5,000) shall be imposed per machine and per location.

(f) Pinball and other amusement machines or devices, which are predominantly games of skill, whether affording the opportunity of additional chances or free plays or not, are not included within the term slot machine or device, as defined in this section.

(Amended by Stats. 2010, Ch. 577, Sec. 2. (AB 1753) Effective January 1, 2011.)

330c.

A punchboard as hereinafter defined is hereby declared to be a slot machine or device within the meaning of Section 330b of this code and shall be subject to the provisions

thereof. For the purposes of this section, a punchboard is any card, board or other device which may be played or operated by pulling, pressing, punching out or otherwise removing any slip, tab, paper or other substance therefrom to disclose any concealed number, name or symbol.
(Added by Stats. 1953, Ch. 379.)
330.1.
(a) Every person who manufactures, owns, stores, keeps, possesses, sells, rents, leases, lets on shares, lends or gives away, transports, or exposes for sale or lease, or offers to sell, rent, lease, let on shares, lend or give away or who permits the operation of or permits to be placed, maintained, used, or kept in any room, space, or building owned, leased, or occupied by him or her or under his or her management or control, any slot machine or device as hereinafter defined, and every person who makes or permits to be made with any person any agreement with reference to any slot machine or device as hereinafter defined, pursuant to which agreement the user thereof, as a result of any element of hazard or chance, may become entitled to receive anything of value or additional chance or right to use that slot machine or device, or to receive any check, slug, token, or memorandum, whether of value or otherwise, entitling the holder to receive anything of value, is guilty of a misdemeanor.
(b) A first violation of this section shall be punishable by a fine of not more than one thousand dollars ($1,000), or by imprisonment in a county jail not exceeding six months, or by both that fine and imprisonment.
(c) A second offense shall be punishable by a fine of not less than one thousand dollars ($1,000) nor more than ten thousand dollars ($10,000), or by imprisonment in a county jail not exceeding six months, or by both that fine and imprisonment.
(d) A third or subsequent offense shall be punishable by a fine of not less than ten thousand dollars ($10,000) nor more than twenty-five thousand dollars ($25,000), or by imprisonment in a county jail not exceeding one year, or by both that fine and imprisonment.
(e) If the offense involved more than one machine or more than one location, an additional fine of not less than one thousand dollars ($1,000) nor more than five thousand dollars ($5,000) shall be imposed per machine and per location.
(f) A slot machine or device within the meaning of Sections 330.1 to 330.5, inclusive, of this code is one that is, or may be, used or operated in such a way that, as a result of the insertion of any piece of money or coin or other object the machine or device is caused to operate or may be operated or played, mechanically, electrically, automatically, or manually, and by reason of any element of hazard or chance, the user may receive or become entitled to receive anything of value or any check, slug, token, or memorandum, whether of value or otherwise, which may be given in trade, or the user may secure additional chances or rights to use such machine or device, irrespective of whether it may, apart from any element of hazard or chance, also sell, deliver, or present some merchandise, indication of weight, entertainment, or other thing of value.
(Amended by Stats. 2011, Ch. 296, Sec. 202. (AB 1023) Effective January 1, 2012.)
330.2.
As used in Sections 330.1 to 330.5, inclusive, of this code a "thing of value" is defined to be any money, coin, currency, check, chip, allowance, token, credit, merchandise, property, or any representative of value.
(Added by Stats. 1950, 1st Ex. Sess., Ch. 18.)
330.3.
In addition to any other remedy provided by law any slot machine or device may be seized by any of the officers designated by Sections 335 and 335a of the Penal Code, and in such cases shall be disposed of, together with any and all money seized in or in connection with such machine or device, as provided in Section 335a of the Penal Code.
(Added by Stats. 1950, 1st Ex. Sess., Ch. 18.)
330.4.
It is specifically declared that the mere possession or control, either as owner, lessee, agent, employee, mortgagor, or otherwise of any slot machine or device, as defined in Section 330.1 of this code, is prohibited and penalized by the provisions of Sections 330.1 to 330.5, inclusive, of this code.
It is specifically declared that every person who permits to be placed, maintained or kept in any room, space, enclosure, or building owned, leased or occupied by him, or under his management or control, whether for use or operation or for storage, bailment, safekeeping or deposit only, any slot machine or device, as defined in Section 330.1 of this code, is guilty of a misdemeanor and punishable as provided in Section 330.1 of this code.
It is further declared that the provisions of this section specifically render any slot machine or device as defined in Section 330.1 of this code subject to confiscation as provided in Section 335a of this code.
(Added by Stats. 1950, 1st Ex. Sess., Ch. 18.)
330.5.
It is further expressly provided that Sections 330.1 to 330.4, inclusive, of this code shall not apply to music machines, weighing machines and machines which vend cigarettes, candy, ice cream, food, confections or other merchandise, in which there is deposited an exact consideration and from which in every case the customer obtains that which he purchases; and it is further expressly provided that with respect to the provisions of Sections 330.1 to 330.4, inclusive, only, of this code, pin ball, and other amusement machines or devices which are predominantly games of skill, whether affording the opportunity of additional chances or free plays or not, are not intended to be and are not included within the term slot machine or device as defined within Sections 330.1 to 330.4, inclusive, of this code.
(Added by Stats. 1950, 1st Ex. Sess., Ch. 18.)
330.6.
The provisions of Sections 330.1 to 330.5, inclusive, of this code, with respect to owning, storing, keeping, possessing, or transporting any slot machine or device as therein defined, shall not apply to any slot machine or device as therein defined, located upon or being transported by any vessel regularly operated and engaged in interstate or foreign commerce, so long as such slot machine or device is located in a locked compartment of the vessel, is not accessible for use and is not used or operated within the territorial jurisdiction of this State.
(Added by Stats. 1950, 1st Ex. Sess., Ch. 18.)
330.7.
(a) It shall be a defense to any prosecution under this chapter relating to slot machines, as defined in subdivision (d) of Section 330b, if the defendant shows that the slot machine is an antique slot machine and was not operated for gambling purposes while in the defendant's possession. For the purposes of this section, the term "antique slot machine" means a slot machine that is over 25 years of age.
(b) Notwithstanding Section 335a, whenever the defense provided by subdivision (a) is offered, no slot machine seized from a defendant shall be destroyed or otherwise altered until after a final court determination that the defense is not applicable. If the defense is applicable, the machine shall be returned pursuant to provisions of law providing for the return of property.
(c) It is the purpose of this section to protect the collection and restoration of antique slot machines not presently utilized for gambling purposes because of their aesthetic interest and importance in California history.
(Amended by Stats. 2004, Ch. 183, Sec. 268. Effective January 1, 2005.)
330.8.
Notwithstanding Sections 330a, 330b, and 330.1 to 330.5, inclusive, the sale, transportation, storage, and manufacture of gambling devices, as defined in Section 330.1, including the acquisition of essential parts therefor and the assembly of such parts, is permitted, provided those devices are sold, transported, stored, and manufactured only for subsequent transportation in interstate or foreign commerce when that transportation is not prohibited by any applicable federal law. Those activities may be conducted only by persons who have registered with the United States government pursuant to Chapter 24 (commencing with Section 1171) of Title 15 of the United States Code, as amended. Those gambling devices shall not be displayed to the general public or sold for use in California regardless of where purchased, nor held nor manufactured in violation of any applicable federal law. A violation of this section is a misdemeanor.
(Amended by Stats. 1987, Ch. 828, Sec. 18.5.)
330.9.
(a) Notwithstanding Sections 330a, 330b, 330.1 to 330.5, inclusive, or any other provision of law, it shall be lawful for any person to transport and possess any slot machine or device for display at a trade show, conference, or convention being held within this state, or if used solely as a prop for a motion picture, television, or video production.
(b) Subdivision (a) shall apply only if the slot machine or device is adjusted to render the machine or device inoperable, or if the slot machine or device is set on demonstration mode.
(c) This section is intended to constitute a state exemption as provided in Section 1172 of Title 15 of the United States Code.
(d) For purposes of this section:
(1) "Demonstration mode" means that the programming or settings of a slot machine or device have been programmed, set, or selected to operate normally, but to not accept or pay out cash or any other consideration.
(2) "Slot machine or device" has the same meaning as "slot machine or device" as defined in Section 330.1, or "gambling device" as defined in paragraph (1) of subsection (a) of Section 1171 of Title 15 of the United States Code.
(Amended by Stats. 2005, Ch. 546, Sec. 2. Effective January 1, 2006.)
330.11.
"Banking game" or "banked game" does not include a controlled game if the published rules of the game feature a player-dealer position and provide that this position must be continuously and systematically rotated amongst each of the participants during the play of the game, ensure that the player-dealer is able to win or lose only a fixed and limited wager during the play of the game, and preclude the house, another entity, a player, or an observer from maintaining or operating as a bank during the course of the game. For purposes of this section it is not the intent of the Legislature to mandate acceptance of the deal by every player if the division finds that the rules of the game render the maintenance of or operation of a bank impossible by other means. The house shall not occupy the player-dealer position.
(Amended by Stats. 2001, Ch. 941, Sec. 2. Effective January 1, 2002.)
331.
Every person who knowingly permits any of the games mentioned in Sections 330 and 330a to be played, conducted, or dealt in any house owned or rented by such person, in whole or in part, is punishable as provided in Sections 330 and 330a.
(Amended by Stats. 1987, Ch. 828, Sec. 19.)
332.
(a) Every person who by the game of "three card monte," so-called, or any other game, device, sleight of hand, pretensions to fortune telling, trick, or other means whatever, by use of cards or other implements or instruments, or while betting on sides or hands of any play or game, fraudulently obtains from another person money or property of any description, shall be punished as in the case of larceny of property of like value for the first offense, except that the fine may not exceed more than five thousand dollars ($5,000). A second offense of this section is punishable, as in the case of larceny, except that the fine shall not exceed ten thousand dollars ($10,000), or both imprisonment and fine.
(b) For the purposes of this section, "fraudulently obtains" includes, but is not limited to, cheating, including, for example, gaining an unfair advantage for any player in any game through a technique or device not sanctioned by the rules of the game.
(c) For the purposes of establishing the value of property under this section, poker chips, tokens, or markers have the monetary value assigned to them by the players in any game.
(Amended by Stats. 2005, Ch. 546, Sec. 3. Effective January 1, 2006.)
333.
Every person duly summoned as a witness for the prosecution, on any proceedings had under this Chapter, who neglects or refuses to attend, as required, is guilty of a misdemeanor.
(Enacted 1872.)
334.
(a) Every person who owns or operates any concession, and who fraudulently obtains money from another by means of any hidden mechanical device or obstruction with intent to diminish the chance of any patron to win a prize, or by any other fraudulent means, shall be punished as in the case of theft of property of like value.
(b) Any person who manufactures or sells any mechanical device or obstruction for a concession which he knows or reasonably should know will be fraudulently used to diminish the chance of any patron to win a prize is guilty of a misdemeanor.
(c) Any person who owns or operates any game, at a fair or carnival of a type known as razzle-dazzle is guilty of a misdemeanor.
As used in this subdivision, "razzle-dazzle" means a series of games of skill or chance in which the player pays money or other valuable consideration in return for each opportunity to make successive attempts to obtain points by the use of dice, darts, marbles or other implements, and where such points are accumulated in successive games by the player toward a total number of points, determined by the operator, which is required for the player to win a prize or other valuable consideration.
(d) As used in this section, "concession" means any game or concession open to the public and operated for profit in which the patron pays a fee for participating and may receive a prize upon a later happening.
(e) Nothing in this section shall be construed to prohibit or preempt more restrictive regulation of any concession at a fair or carnival by any local governmental entity.
(Added by Stats. 1974, Ch. 626.)
335.
Every district attorney, sheriff, or police officer must inform against and diligently prosecute persons whom they have reasonable cause to believe offenders against the provisions of this chapter, and every officer refusing or neglecting so to do, is guilty of a misdemeanor.
(Amended by Stats. 1996, Ch. 872, Sec. 110. Effective January 1, 1997.)
335a.
In addition to any other remedy provided by law any machine or other device the possession or control of which is penalized by the laws of this State prohibiting lotteries or gambling may be seized by any peace officer, and a notice of intention summarily to destroy such machine or device as provided in this section must be posted in a conspicuous place upon the premises in or upon which such machine or device was seized. Such machine or device shall be held by such officer for 30 days after such posting, and if no action is commenced to recover possession of such machine or device, within such time, the same shall be summarily destroyed by such officer, or if such machine or device shall be held by the court, in any such action, to be in violation of such laws, or any of them, the same shall be summarily destroyed by such officer immediately after the decision of the court has become final.

The superior court shall have jurisdiction of any such actions or proceedings commenced to recover the possession of such machine or device or any money seized in connection therewith.

Any and all money seized in or in connection with such machine or device shall, immediately after such machine or device has been so destroyed, be paid into the treasury of the city or county, as the case may be, where seized, said money to be deposited in the general fund.

(Added by Stats. 1941, Ch. 192.)

336.

Every owner, lessee, or keeper of any house used in whole, or in part, as a saloon or drinking place, who knowingly permits any person under 18 years of age to play at any game of chance therein, is guilty of a misdemeanor.

(Amended by Stats. 1972, Ch. 579.)

336.5.

Gaming chips may be used on the gaming floor by a patron of a gambling establishment, as defined in subdivision (o) of Section 19805 of the Business and Professions Code, to pay for food and beverage items that are served at the table.

(Amended by Stats. 2012, Ch. 162, Sec. 123. (SB 1171) Effective January 1, 2013.)

336.9.

(a) Notwithstanding Section 337a, and except as provided in subdivision (b), any person who, not for gain, hire, or reward other than that at stake under conditions available to every participant, knowingly participates in any of the ways specified in paragraph (2), (3), (4), (5), or (6) of subdivision (a) of Section 337a in any bet, bets, wager, wagers, or betting pool or pools made between the person and any other person or group of persons who are not acting for gain, hire, or reward, other than that at stake under conditions available to every participant, upon the result of any lawful trial, or purported trial, or contest, or purported contest, of skill, speed, or power of endurance of person or animal, or between persons, animals, or mechanical apparatus, is guilty of an infraction, punishable by a fine not to exceed two hundred fifty dollars ($250).

(b) Subdivision (a) does not apply to either of the following situations:

(1) Any bet, bets, wager, wagers, or betting pool or pools made online.

(2) Betting pools with more than two thousand five hundred dollars ($2,500) at stake.

(Amended by Stats. 2010, Ch. 328, Sec. 155. (SB 1330) Effective January 1, 2011.)

337.

Every state, county, city, city and county, town, or judicial district officer, or other person who shall ask for, receive, or collect any money, or other valuable consideration, either for his own or the public use, for and with the understanding that he will aid, exempt, or otherwise assist any person from arrest or conviction for a violation of Section 330 of the Penal Code; or who shall issue, deliver, or cause to be given or delivered to any person or persons, any license, permit, or other privilege, giving, or pretending to give, any authority or right to any person or persons to carry on, conduct, open, or cause to be opened, any game or games which are forbidden or prohibited by Section 330 of said code; and any of such officer or officers who shall vote for the passage of any ordinance or by-law, giving, granting, or pretending to give or grant to any person or persons any authority or privilege to open, carry on, conduct, or cause to be opened, carried on, or conducted, any game or games prohibited by said Section 330 of the Penal Code, is guilty of a felony.

(Amended by Stats. 1951, Ch. 1608.)

337a.

(a) Except as provided in Section 336.9, every person who engages in one of the following offenses, shall be punished for a first offense by imprisonment in a county jail for a period of not more than one year or in the state prison, or by a fine not to exceed five thousand dollars ($5,000), or by both imprisonment and fine:

(1) Pool selling or bookmaking, with or without writing, at any time or place.

(2) Whether for gain, hire, reward, or gratuitously, or otherwise, keeps or occupies, for any period of time whatsoever, any room, shed, tenement, tent, booth, building, float, vessel, place, stand or enclosure, of any kind, or any part thereof, with a book or books, paper or papers, apparatus, device or paraphernalia, for the purpose of recording or registering any bet or bets, any purported bet or bets, wager or wagers, any purported wager or wagers, selling pools, or purported pools, upon the result, or purported result, of any trial, purported trial, contest, or purported contest of skill, speed or power of endurance of person or animal, or between persons, animals, or mechanical apparatus, or upon the result, or purported result, of any lot, chance, casualty, unknown or contingent event whatsoever.

(3) Whether for gain, hire, reward, or gratuitously, or otherwise, receives, holds, or forwards, or purports or pretends to receive, hold, or forward, in any manner whatsoever, any money, thing or consideration of value, or the equivalent or memorandum thereof, staked, pledged, bet or wagered, or to be staked, pledged, bet or wagered, or offered for the purpose of being staked, pledged, bet or wagered, upon the result, or purported result, of any trial, or purported trial, or contest, or purported contest, of skill, speed or power of endurance of person or animal, or between persons, animals, or mechanical apparatus, or upon the result, or purported result, of any lot, chance, casualty, unknown or contingent event whatsoever.

(4) Whether for gain, hire, reward, or gratuitously, or otherwise, at any time or place, records, or registers any bet or bets, wager or wagers, upon the result, or purported result, of any trial, or purported trial, or contest, or purported contest of skill, speed or power of endurance of person or animal, or between persons, animals, or mechanical apparatus, or upon the result, or purported result, of any lot, chance, casualty, unknown or contingent event whatsoever.

(5) Being the owner, lessee or occupant of any room, shed, tenement, tent, booth, building, float, vessel, place, stand, enclosure or grounds, or any part thereof, whether for gain, hire, reward, or gratuitously, or otherwise, permits that space to be used or occupied for any purpose, or in any manner prohibited by paragraph (1), (2), (3), or (4).

(6) Lays, makes, offers or accepts any bet or bets, or wager or wagers, upon the result, or purported result, of any trial, or purported trial, or contest, or purported contest, of skill, speed or power of endurance of person or animal, or between persons, animals, or mechanical apparatus.

(b) In any accusatory pleading charging a violation of this section, if the defendant has been once previously convicted of a violation of any subdivision of this section, the previous conviction shall be charged in the accusatory pleading, and, if the previous conviction is found to be true by the jury, upon a jury trial, or by the court, upon a court trial, or is admitted by the defendant, the defendant shall, if he or she is not imprisoned in the state prison, be imprisoned in the county jail for a period of not more than one year and pay a fine of not less than one thousand dollars ($1,000) and not to exceed ten thousand dollars ($10,000). Nothing in this paragraph shall prohibit a court from placing a person subject to this subdivision on probation. However, that person shall be required to pay a fine of not less than one thousand dollars ($1,000) nor more than ten thousand dollars ($10,000) or be imprisoned in the county jail for a period of not more than one year, as a condition thereof. In no event does the court have the power to absolve a person convicted pursuant to this subdivision from either being imprisoned or from paying a fine of not less than one thousand dollars ($1,000) and not more than ten thousand dollars ($10,000).

(c) In any accusatory pleading charging a violation of this section, if the defendant has been previously convicted two or more times of a violation of any subdivision of this section, each previous conviction shall be charged in the accusatory pleadings. If two or more of the previous convictions are found to be true by the jury, upon a jury trial, or by the court, upon a court trial, or are admitted by the defendant, the defendant shall, if he or she is not imprisoned in the state prison, be imprisoned in the county jail for a period

of not more than one year or pay a fine of not less than one thousand dollars ($1,000) nor more than fifteen thousand dollars ($15,000), or be punished by both imprisonment and fine. Nothing in this paragraph shall prohibit a court from placing a person subject to this subdivision on probation. However, that person shall be required to pay a fine of not less than one thousand dollars ($1,000) nor more than fifteen thousand dollars ($15,000), or be imprisoned in the county jail for a period of not more than one year as a condition thereof. In no event does the court have the power to absolve a person convicted and subject to this subdivision from either being imprisoned or from paying a fine of not more than fifteen thousand dollars ($15,000).

(d) Except where the existence of a previous conviction of any subdivision of this section was not admitted or not found to be true pursuant to this section, or the court finds that a prior conviction was invalid, the court shall not strike or dismiss any prior convictions alleged in the information or indictment.

(e) This section applies not only to persons who commit any of the acts designated in paragraphs (1) to (6), inclusive, of subdivision (a), as a business or occupation, but also applies to every person who in a single instance engages in any one of the acts specified in paragraphs (1) to (6), inclusive, of subdivision (a).

(Amended by Stats. 2009, Ch. 72, Sec. 2. (AB 58) Effective January 1, 2010.)

337b.

Any person who gives, or offers or promises to give, or attempts to give or offer, any money, bribe, or thing of value, to any participant or player, or to any prospective participant or player, in any sporting event, contest, or exhibition of any kind whatsoever, except a wrestling exhibition as defined in Section 18626 of the Business and Professions Code, and specifically including, but without being limited to, such sporting events, contests, and exhibitions as baseball, football, basketball, boxing, horse racing, and wrestling matches, with the intention or understanding or agreement that such participant or player or such prospective participant or player shall not use his or her best efforts to win such sporting event, contest, or exhibition, or shall so conduct himself or herself in such sporting event, contest, or exhibition that any other player, participant or team of players or participants shall thereby be assisted or enabled to win such sporting event, contest, or exhibition, or shall so conduct himself or herself in such sporting event, contest, or exhibition as to limit his or her or his or her team's margin of victory in such sporting event, contest, or exhibition, is guilty of a felony, and shall be punished by imprisonment pursuant to subdivision (h) of Section 1170, or by a fine not exceeding five thousand dollars ($5,000), or by both that fine and imprisonment.

(Amended by Stats. 2011, Ch. 15, Sec. 328. (AB 109) Effective April 4, 2011. Operative October 1, 2011, by Sec. 636 of Ch. 15, as amended by Stats. 2011, Ch. 39, Sec. 68.)

337c.

Any person who accepts, or attempts to accept, or offers to accept, or agrees to accept, any money, bribe or thing of value, with the intention or understanding or agreement that he or she will not use his or her best efforts to win any sporting event, contest, or exhibition of any kind whatsoever, except a wrestling exhibition as defined in Section 18626 of the Business and Professions Code, and specifically including, but without being limited to, such sporting events, contests, or exhibitions as baseball, football, basketball, boxing, horse racing, and wrestling matches, in which he or she is playing or participating or is about to play or participate in, or will so conduct himself or herself in such sporting event, contest, or exhibition that any other player or participant or team of players or participants shall thereby be assisted or enabled to win such sporting event, contest, or exhibition, or will so conduct himself or herself in such sporting event, contest, or exhibition as to limit his or her or his or her team's margin of victory in such sporting event, contest, or exhibition, is guilty of a felony, and shall be punished by imprisonment pursuant to subdivision (h) of Section 1170, or by a fine not exceeding five thousand dollars ($5,000), or by both that fine and imprisonment.

(Amended by Stats. 2011, Ch. 15, Sec. 329. (AB 109) Effective April 4, 2011. Operative October 1, 2011, by Sec. 636 of Ch. 15, as amended by Stats. 2011, Ch. 39, Sec. 68.)

337d.

Any person who gives, offers to give, promises to give, or attempts to give, any money, bribe, or thing of value to any person who is umpiring, managing, directing, refereeing, supervising, judging, presiding, or officiating at, or who is about to umpire, manage, direct, referee, supervise, judge, preside, or officiate at any sporting event, contest, or exhibition of any kind whatsoever, including, but not limited to, sporting events, contests, and exhibitions such as baseball, football, boxing, horse racing, and wrestling matches, with the intention or agreement or understanding that the person shall corruptly or dishonestly umpire, manage, direct, referee, supervise, judge, preside, or officiate at, any sporting event, contest, or exhibition, or the players or participants thereof, with the intention or purpose that the result of the sporting event, contest, or exhibition will be affected or influenced thereby, is guilty of a felony and shall be punished by imprisonment pursuant to subdivision (h) of Section 1170 or by a fine of not more than ten thousand dollars ($10,000), or by imprisonment and fine. A second offense of this section is a felony and shall be punished by imprisonment pursuant to subdivision (h) of Section 1170 or by a fine of not more than fifteen thousand dollars ($15,000), or by both that imprisonment and fine.

(Amended by Stats. 2011, Ch. 15, Sec. 330. (AB 109) Effective April 4, 2011. Operative October 1, 2011, by Sec. 636 of Ch. 15, as amended by Stats. 2011, Ch. 39, Sec. 68.)

337e.

Any person who as umpire, manager, director, referee, supervisor, judge, presiding officer or official receives or agrees to receive, or attempts to receive any money, bribe or thing of value, with the understanding or agreement that such umpire, manager, director, referee, supervisor, judge, presiding officer, or official shall corruptly conduct himself or shall corruptly umpire, manage, direct, referee, supervise, judge, preside, or officiate at, any sporting event, contest, or exhibition of any kind whatsoever, and specifically including, but without being limited to, such sporting events, contests, and exhibitions as baseball, football, boxing, horse racing, and wrestling matches, or any player or participant thereof, with the intention or purpose that the result of the sporting event, contest, or exhibition will be affected or influenced thereby, is guilty of a felony and shall be punished by imprisonment pursuant to subdivision (h) of Section 1170, or by a fine not exceeding five thousand dollars ($5,000), or by both that fine and imprisonment.

(Amended by Stats. 2011, Ch. 15, Sec. 331. (AB 109) Effective April 4, 2011. Operative October 1, 2011, by Sec. 636 of Ch. 15, as amended by Stats. 2011, Ch. 39, Sec. 68.)

337f.

(a) Any person who does any of the following is punishable by a fine not exceeding five thousand dollars ($5,000), or by imprisonment in a county jail not exceeding one year, or by imprisonment pursuant to subdivision (h) of Section 1170, or by both that fine and imprisonment:

(1) Influences, or induces, or conspires with, any owner, trainer, jockey, groom, or other person associated with or interested in any stable, horse, or race in which a horse participates, to affect the result of that race by stimulating or depressing a horse through the administration of any drug to that horse, or by the use of any electrical device or any electrical equipment or by any mechanical or other device not generally accepted as regulation racing equipment, or so stimulates or depresses a horse.

(2) Knowingly enters any horse in any race within a period of 24 hours after any drug has been administered to that horse for the purpose of increasing or retarding the speed of that horse.

(3) Willfully or unjustifiably enters or races any horse in any running or trotting race under any name or designation other than the name or designation assigned to that horse by and registered with the Jockey Club or the United States Trotting Association or willfully sets on foot, instigates, engages in or in any way furthers any act by which any horse is entered or raced in any running or trotting race under any name or designation

other than the name or designation duly assigned by and registered with the Jockey Club or the United States Trotting Association.
(b) For purposes of this section, the term "drug" includes all substances recognized as having the power of stimulating or depressing the central nervous system, respiration, or blood pressure of an animal, such as narcotics, hypnotics, benzedrine or its derivatives, but shall not include recognized vitamins or supplemental feeds approved by or in compliance with the rules and regulations or policies of the California Horse Racing Board.
(Amended by Stats. 2011, Ch. 15, Sec. 332. (AB 109) Effective April 4, 2011. Operative October 1, 2011, by Sec. 636 of Ch. 15, as amended by Stats. 2011, Ch. 39, Sec. 68.)

337g.
The possession, transport or use of any local anaesthetic of the cocaine group, including but not limited to natural or synthetic drugs of this group, such as allocaine, apothesine, alypine, benzyl carbinol, butyn, procaine, nupercaine, beta-eucaine, novol or anestubes, within the racing inclosure is prohibited, except upon a bona fide veterinarian's prescription with complete statement of uses and purposes of same on the container. A copy of such prescription shall be filed with the stewards, and such substances may be used only with approval of the stewards and under the supervision of the veterinarian representing the board.
(Added by Stats. 1943, Ch. 1001.)

337h.
Any person who, except for medicinal purposes, administers any poison, drug, medicine, or other noxious substance, to any horse, stud, mule, ass, mare, horned cattle, neat cattle, gelding, colt, filly, dog, animals, or other livestock, entered or about to be entered in any race or upon any race course, or entered or about to be entered at or with any agricultural park, or association, race course, or corporation, or other exhibition for competition for prize, reward, purse, premium, stake, sweepstakes, or other reward, or who exposes any poison, drug, medicine, or noxious substance, with intent that it shall be taken, inhaled, swallowed, or otherwise received by any of these animals or other livestock, with intent to impede or affect its speed, endurance, sense, health, physical condition, or other character or quality, or who causes to be taken by or placed upon or in the body of any of these animals or other livestock, entered or about to be entered in any race or competition described in this section any sponge, wood, or foreign substance of any kind, with intent to impede or affect its speed, endurance, sense, health, or physical condition, is guilty of a misdemeanor.
(Added by Stats. 1953, Ch. 32.)

337i.
Every person who knowingly transmits information as to the progress or results of a horserace, or information as to wagers, betting odds, changes in betting odds, post or off times, jockey or player changes in any contest or trial, or purported contest or trial, involving humans, beasts, or mechanical apparatus by any means whatsoever including, but not limited to telephone, telegraph, radio, and semaphore when such information is transmitted to or by a person or persons engaged in illegal gambling operations, is punishable by imprisonment in the county jail for a period of not more than one year or in the state prison.
This section shall not be construed as prohibiting a newspaper from printing such results or information as news, or any television or radio station from telecasting or broadcasting such results or information as news. This section shall not be so construed as to place in jeopardy any common carrier or its agents performing operations within the scope of a public franchise, or any gambling operation authorized by law.
(Amended by Stats. 1976, Ch. 1139.)

337j.
(a) It is unlawful for any person, as owner, lessee, or employee, whether for hire or not, either solely or in conjunction with others, to do any of the following without having first procured and thereafter maintained in effect all federal, state, and local licenses required by law:
(1) To deal, operate, carry on, conduct, maintain, or expose for play in this state any controlled game.
(2) To receive, directly or indirectly, any compensation or reward or any percentage or share of the revenue, for keeping, running, or carrying on any controlled game.
(3) To manufacture, distribute, or repair any gambling equipment within the boundaries of this state, or to receive, directly or indirectly, any compensation or reward for the manufacture, distribution, or repair of any gambling equipment within the boundaries of this state.
(b) It is unlawful for any person to knowingly permit any controlled game to be conducted, operated, dealt, or carried on in any house or building or other premises that he or she owns or leases, in whole or in part, if that activity is undertaken by a person who is not licensed as required by state law, or by an employee of that person.
(c) It is unlawful for any person to knowingly permit any gambling equipment to be manufactured, stored, or repaired in any house or building or other premises that the person owns or leases, in whole or in part, if that activity is undertaken by a person who is not licensed as required by state law, or by an employee of that person.
(d) Any person who violates, attempts to violate, or conspires to violate this section shall be punished by imprisonment in a county jail for not more than one year or by a fine of not more than ten thousand dollars ($10,000), or by both imprisonment and fine. A second offense of this section is punishable by imprisonment in a county jail for a period of not more than one year or in the state prison or by a fine of not more than ten thousand dollars ($10,000), or by both imprisonment and fine.
(e) (1) As used in this section, "controlled game" means any poker or Pai Gow game, and any other game played with cards or tiles, or both, and approved by the Department of Justice, and any game of chance, including any gambling device, played for currency, check, credit, or any other thing of value that is not prohibited and made unlawful by statute or local ordinance.
(2) As used in this section, "controlled game" does not include any of the following:
(A) The game of bingo conducted pursuant to Section 326.3 or 326.5.
(B) Parimutuel racing on horse races regulated by the California Horse Racing Board.
(C) Any lottery game conducted by the California State Lottery.
(D) Games played with cards in private homes or residences, in which no person makes money for operating the game, except as a player.
(f) This subdivision is intended to be dispositive of the law relating to the collection of player fees in gambling establishments. A fee may not be calculated as a fraction or percentage of wagers made or winnings earned. The amount of fees charged for all wagers shall be determined prior to the start of play of any hand or round. However, the gambling establishment may waive collection of the fee or portion of the fee in any hand or round of play after the hand or round has begun pursuant to the published rules of the game and the notice provided to the public. The actual collection of the fee may occur before or after the start of play. Ample notice shall be provided to the patrons of gambling establishments relating to the assessment of fees. Flat fees on each wager may be assessed at different collection rates, but no more than five collection rates may be established per table. However, if the gambling establishment waives its collection fee, this fee does not constitute one of the five collection rates.
(Amended by Stats. 2008, Ch. 748, Sec. 7. Effective January 1, 2009.)

337k.
(a) It is unlawful for any person to advertise, or to facilitate the advertisement of, nonparimutuel wagering on horse races.
(b) Violation of this section is an infraction punishable by a fine of five hundred dollars ($500). A second conviction for a violation of this section is a misdemeanor punishable by a fine of up to ten thousand dollars ($10,000).
(Added by Stats. 2006, Ch. 305, Sec. 1. Effective January 1, 2007.)

337s.
(a) This section applies only in counties with a population exceeding 4,000,000.
(b) Every person who deals, plays, or carries on, opens, or causes to be opened, or who conducts, either as owner or employee, whether for hire or not, any game of draw poker, including lowball poker, is guilty of a misdemeanor.
(c) Subdivision (b) shall become operative in a county only if the board of supervisors thereof by resolution directs that there be placed on the ballot at a designated county election the question whether draw poker, including lowball poker, shall be prohibited in the county and a majority of electors voting thereon vote affirmatively. The question shall appear on the ballot in substantially the following form:
"Shall draw poker, including lowball poker, be prohibited in ______ County? Yes ______ No ______"
If a majority of electors voting thereon vote affirmatively, draw poker shall be prohibited in the unincorporated territory in the county.
(d) Any county ordinance in any county prohibiting, restricting, or regulating the playing of draw poker and other acts relating to draw poker shall not be superseded until, pursuant to subdivision (c), the electorate of the county determines that subdivision (b) shall be operative in the county.
(e) The Legislature finds that in counties with a large, concentrated population, problems incident to the playing of draw poker are, in part, qualitatively, as well as quantitatively, different from the problems in smaller counties.
The Legislature finds that counties with a population exceeding 4,000,000 constitute a special problem, and it is reasonable classification to adopt prohibitory legislation applicable only to such counties.
(f) If any provision of this section is held invalid, the entire section shall be invalid. The provisions of this section are not severable.
(Amended by Stats. 1993, Ch. 98, Sec. 1. Effective January 1, 1994.)

337t.
The following definitions govern the construction of this section and Sections 337u, 337w, 337x, and 337y:
(a) "Associated equipment" means any equipment or mechanical, electromechanical, or electronic contrivance, component or machine used remotely or directly in connection with gaming or any game that would not otherwise be classified as a gaming device, including dice, playing cards, links which connect to progressive slot machines, equipment which affects the proper reporting of gross revenue, computerized systems for monitoring slot machines and devices for weighing or counting money.
(b) "Cashless wagering system" means a method of wagering and accounting in which the validity and value of a wagering instrument or wagering credits are determined, monitored, and retained by a computer that is operated and maintained by a licensee and that maintains a record of each transaction involving the wagering instrument or wagering credits, exclusive of the game or gaming device on which wagers are being made. The term includes computerized systems which facilitate electronic transfers of money directly to or from a game or gaming device.
(c) "Cheat" means to alter the normal elements of chance, method of selection, or criteria, excluding those alterations to the game generally done by the casino to provide variety to games and that are known, or should be known, by the wagering players, which determine any of the following:
(1) The result of a gambling game.
(2) The amount or frequency of payment in a gambling game.
(3) The value of a wagering instrument.
(4) The value of a wagering credit.
(d) "Drop box" means the box that serves as a repository for cash, chips, tokens, or other wagering instruments.
(e) "Gambling establishment" means any premises wherein or whereon any gaming is done.
(f) "Gambling game device" means any equipment or mechanical, electromechanical, or electronic contrivance, component or machine used remotely or directly in connection with gaming or any game which affects the result of a wager by determining win or loss. The term includes any of the following:
(1) A slot machine.
(2) A collection of two or more of the following components:
(A) An assembled electronic circuit which cannot be reasonably demonstrated to have any use other than in a slot machine.
(B) A cabinet with electrical wiring and provisions for mounting a coin, token, or currency acceptor and provisions for mounting a dispenser of coins, tokens, or anything of value.
(C) A storage medium containing the source language or executable code of a computer program that cannot be reasonably demonstrated to have any use other than in a slot machine.
(D) An assembled video display unit.
(E) An assembled mechanical or electromechanical display unit intended for use in gambling.
(F) An assembled mechanical or electromechanical unit which cannot be demonstrated to have any use other than in a slot machine.
(3) Any mechanical, electrical, or other device that may be connected to or used with a slot machine to alter the normal criteria of random selection or affect the outcome of a game.
(4) A system for the accounting or management of any game in which the result of the wager is determined electronically by using any combination of hardware or software for computers.
(5) Any combination of one of the components set forth in subparagraphs (A) to (F), inclusive, of paragraph (2) and any other component that the commission determines, by regulation, to be a machine used directly or remotely in connection with gaming or any game which affects the results of a wager by determining a win or loss.
(g) "Past-posting" means the placing of a wager by an individual at a game after having knowledge of the result or outcome of that game.
(h) "Pinching wagers" means to reduce the amount wagered or to cancel the wager after acquiring knowledge of the outcome of the game or other event that is the subject of the wager.
(i) "Pressing wagers" means to increase a wager after acquiring knowledge of the outcome of the game or other event that is the subject of the wager.
(j) "Tribal Gaming Agency" means the person, agency, board, committee, commission, or council designated under tribal law, including, but not limited to, an intertribal gaming regulatory agency approved to fulfill those functions by the National Indian Gaming Commission, as primarily responsible for carrying out the regulatory responsibilities of the tribe under the Indian Gaming and Regulatory Act (25 U.S.C. Sec. 2701) and a tribal gaming ordinance.
(k) "Wagering credit" means a representative of value, other than a chip, token, or wagering instrument, that is used for wagering at a game or gaming device and is obtained by the payment of cash or a cash equivalent, the use of a wagering instrument or the electronic transfer of money.
(l) "Wagering instrument" means a representative of value, other than a chip or token, that is issued by a licensee and approved by the California Gambling Control Commission or a tribal gaming agency, for use in a cashless wagering system.
(Added by Stats. 2002, Ch. 624, Sec. 1. Effective January 1, 2003.)

337u.
It is unlawful for any person to commit any of the following acts:

(a) To alter or misrepresent the outcome of a gambling game or other event on which wagers lawfully have been made after the outcome is determined, but before it is revealed to the players.

(b) To place, increase, or decrease a wager or to determine the course of play after acquiring knowledge, not available to all players, of the outcome of the gambling game or any event that affects the outcome of the gambling game or which is the subject of the wager or to aid anyone in acquiring that knowledge for the purpose of placing, increasing, or decreasing a wager or determining the course of play contingent upon that event or outcome.

(c) To claim, collect, or take, or attempt to claim, collect, or take, money or anything of value in or from a gambling game, with intent to defraud, without having made a wager contingent on the game, or to claim, collect, or take an amount greater than the amount actually won.

(d) Knowingly to entice or induce another to go to any place where a gambling game is being conducted or operated in violation of this section, or Section 337v, 337w, 337x, or 337y, with the intent that the other person play or participate in that gambling game.

(e) To place or increase a wager after acquiring knowledge of the outcome of the gambling game or other event which is the subject of the wager, including past-posting and pressing wagers.

(f) To reduce the amount wagered or cancel the wager after acquiring knowledge of the outcome of the gambling game or other event which is the subject of the bet, including pinching wagers.

(g) To manipulate, with the intent to cheat, any component of a gambling game device in a manner contrary to the designed and normal operational purpose for the component, including, but not limited to, varying the pull of the handle of a slot machine, with knowledge that the manipulation affects the outcome of the gambling game or with knowledge of any event that affects the outcome of the gambling game.

(Amended by Stats. 2003, Ch. 62, Sec. 225. Effective January 1, 2004.)

337v.

It is unlawful for any person at a gambling establishment to use, or to possess with the intent to use, any device to assist in any of the following:

(a) In projecting the outcome of the gambling game.

(b) In keeping track of the cards played.

(c) In analyzing the probability of the occurrence of an event relating to the gambling game.

(d) In analyzing the strategy for playing or wagering to be used in the gambling game, except as permitted by the California Gambling Control Commission or a tribal gaming agency.

(Added by Stats. 2002, Ch. 624, Sec. 3. Effective January 1, 2003.)

337w.

(a) It is unlawful for any person to use counterfeit chips, counterfeit debit instruments, or other counterfeit wagering instruments in a gambling game, the equipment associated with a gambling game, or a cashless wagering system.

(b) It is unlawful for any person, in playing or using any gambling game, the equipment associated with a gambling game, or a cashless wagering system designed to be played with, receive, or be operated by chips, tokens, wagering credits or other wagering instruments approved by the California Gambling Control Commission or a tribal gaming agency, or by lawful coin of the United States of America to either:

(1) Knowingly use chips, tokens, wagering credits, or other wagering instruments not approved by the California Gambling Control Commission or a tribal gaming agency, or lawful coin, legal tender of the United States of America, or use coins or tokens not of the same denomination as the coins or tokens intended to be used in that gambling game, associated equipment, or cashless wagering system.

(2) Use any device or means to violate this section or Section 337u, 337v, 337x, or 337y.

(c) It is unlawful for any person, not a duly authorized employee of a gambling establishment acting in furtherance of his or her employment within that establishment, to possess any device intended to be used to violate this section or Section 337u, 337v, 337x, or 337y.

(d) It is unlawful for any person, not a duly authorized employee of a gambling establishment acting in furtherance of his or her employment within that establishment, to possess any key or device known to have been designed for the purpose of, and suitable for, opening, entering, or affecting the operation of any gambling game, cashless wagering system, or dropbox, or for removing money or other contents from the game, system, or box.

(e) It is unlawful for any person to possess any paraphernalia for manufacturing slugs. As used in this subdivision, "paraphernalia for manufacturing slugs" means the equipment, products, and materials that are intended for use or designed for use in manufacturing, producing, fabricating, preparing, testing, analyzing, packaging, storing, or concealing a counterfeit facsimile of the chips, tokens, debit instruments, or other wagering instruments approved by the California Gambling Control Commission or a tribal gaming agency, or a lawful coin of the United States, the use of which is unlawful pursuant to subdivision (b). The term "paraphernalia for manufacturing slugs" includes, but is not limited to, any of the following:

(1) Lead or lead alloys.

(2) Molds, forms, or similar equipment capable of producing a likeness of a gaming token or lawful coin of the United States.

(3) Melting pots or other receptacles.

(4) Torches.

(5) Tongs, trimming tools, or other similar equipment.

(6) Equipment which can be reasonably demonstrated to manufacture facsimiles of debit instruments or wagering instruments approved by the California Gambling Control Commission or a tribal gaming agency.

(Added by Stats. 2002, Ch. 624, Sec. 4. Effective January 1, 2003.)

337x.

It is unlawful to cheat at any gambling game in a gambling establishment.

(Added by Stats. 2002, Ch. 624, Sec. 5. Effective January 1, 2003.)

337y.

It is unlawful to do either of the following:

(a) Manufacture, sell, or distribute any cards, chips, dice, game, or device which is intended to be used to violate Section 337u, 337v, 337w, or 337x.

(b) Mark, alter, or otherwise modify any gambling game device or associated equipment in a manner that either:

(1) Affects the result of a wager by determining win or loss.

(2) Alters the normal criteria of random selection, which affects the operation of a gambling game or which determines the outcome of a game.

(c) It is unlawful for any person to instruct another in cheating or in the use of any device for that purpose, with the knowledge or intent that the information or use conveyed may be employed to violate Section 337u, 337v, 337w, or 337x.

(Added by Stats. 2002, Ch. 624, Sec. 6. Effective January 1, 2003.)

337z.

(a) Any person who violates Section 337u, 337v, 337w, 337x, or 337y shall be punished as follows:

(1) For the first violation, by imprisonment in a county jail for a term not to exceed one year, or by a fine of not more than ten thousand dollars ($10,000), or by both imprisonment and fine.

(2) For a second or subsequent violation of any of those sections, by imprisonment in a county jail for a term not to exceed one year or by a fine of not more than fifteen thousand dollars ($15,000), or by both imprisonment and fine.

(b) A person who attempts to violate Section 337u, 337v, 337w, 337x, or 337y shall be punished in the same manner as the underlying crime.

(c) This section does not preclude prosecution under Section 332 or any other provision of law.

(Amended by Stats. 2005, Ch. 546, Sec. 7. Effective January 1, 2006.)

CHAPTER 10.5. Horse Racing [337.1 - 337.9]

(Chapter 10.5 added by Stats. 1945, Ch. 1524.)

337.1.

Any person, who knowingly and designedly by false representation attempts to, or does persuade, procure or cause another person to wager on a horse in a race to be run in this state or elsewhere, and upon which money is wagered in this state, and who asks or demands compensation as a reward for information or purported information given in such case is a tout, and is guilty of touting.

(Amended by Stats. 1987, Ch. 828, Sec. 22.)

337.2.

Any person who is a tout, or who attempts or conspires to commit touting, is guilty of a misdemeanor and is punishable by a fine of not more than five hundred dollars ($500) or by imprisonment in the county jail for not more than six months, or by both such fine and imprisonment. For a second offense in this State, he shall be imprisoned.

(Added by Stats. 1945, Ch. 1524.)

337.3.

Any person who in the commission of touting falsely uses the name of any official of the California Horse Racing Board, its inspectors or attachés, or of any official of any race track association, or the names of any owner, trainer, jockey or other person licensed by the California Horse Racing Board as the source of any information or purported information is guilty of a felony and is punishable by a fine of not more than five thousand dollars ($5,000) or by imprisonment pursuant to subdivision (h) of Section 1170, or by both that fine and imprisonment.

(Amended by Stats. 2011, Ch. 15, Sec. 326. (AB 109) Effective April 4, 2011. Operative October 1, 2011, by Sec. 636 of Ch. 15, as amended by Stats. 2011, Ch. 39, Sec. 68.)

337.4.

Any person who in the commission of touting obtains money in excess of nine hundred fifty dollars ($950) may, in addition to being prosecuted for the violation of any provision of this chapter, be prosecuted for the violation of Section 487 of this code.

(Amended by Stats. 2009, 3rd Ex. Sess., Ch. 28, Sec. 8. (SB 18 3x) Effective January 25, 2010.)

337.5.

Any person who has been convicted of touting, and the record of whose conviction on such charge is on file in the office of the California Horse Racing Board or in the State Bureau of Criminal Identification and Investigation or of the Federal Bureau of Investigation, or any person who has been ejected from any racetrack of this or any other state for touting or practices inimical to the public interest shall be excluded from all racetracks in this State. Any such person who refuses to leave such track when ordered to do so by inspectors of the California Horse Racing Board, or by any peace officer, or by an accredited attaché of a racetrack or association is guilty of a misdemeanor.

(Amended by Stats. 1963, Ch. 372.)

337.6.

Any credential or license issued by the California Horse Racing Board to licensees, if used by the holder thereof for a purpose other than identification and in the performance of legitimate duties on a race track, shall be automatically revoked whether so used on or off a race track.

(Added by Stats. 1945, Ch. 1524.)

337.7.

Any person other than the lawful holder thereof who has in his possession any credential or license issued by the California Horse Racing Board to licensees and any person who has a forged or simulated credential or license of said board in his possession, and who uses such credential or license for the purpose of misrepresentation, fraud or touting is guilty of a felony and shall be punished by a fine of five thousand dollars ($5,000) or by imprisonment pursuant to subdivision (h) of Section 1170, or by both that fine and imprisonment. If he or she has previously been convicted of any offense under this chapter, he or she shall be imprisoned pursuant to subdivision (h) of Section 1170.

(Amended by Stats. 2011, Ch. 15, Sec. 327. (AB 109) Effective April 4, 2011. Operative October 1, 2011, by Sec. 636 of Ch. 15, as amended by Stats. 2011, Ch. 39, Sec. 68.)

337.8.

Any person who uses any credential, other than a credential or license issued by the California Horse Racing Board, for the purpose of touting is guilty of touting, and if the credential has been forged shall be imprisoned as provided in this chapter, whether the offense was committed on or off a race track.

(Added by Stats. 1945, Ch. 1524.)

337.9.

The secretary and chief investigator of the California Horse Racing Board shall coordinate a policy for the enforcement of this chapter with all other enforcement bureaus in the State in order to insure prosecution of all persons who commit any offense against the horse racing laws of this State. For such purposes the secretary and chief investigator are peace officers and have all the powers thereof.

(Added by Stats. 1945, Ch. 1524.)

CHAPTER 11. Pawnbrokers [343- 343.]

(Chapter 11 enacted 1872.)

343.

Every person who purchases gold bullion, gold bars or gold quartz or mineral containing gold, who fails, refuses, or neglects to produce for inspection his register, or to exhibit all articles received by him in pledge, or his account of sales, to any officer holding a warrant authorizing him to search for personal property or to any person appointed by the sheriff or head of the police department of any city, city and county or town, or an order of a committing magistrate directing such officer to inspect such register, or examine such articles or account of sales, is guilty of a misdemeanor.

(Amended by Stats. 1959, Ch. 638.)

CHAPTER 12. Other Injuries to Persons [346 - 367g]

(Chapter 12 enacted 1872.)

346.

Any person who, without the written permission of the owner or operator of the property on which an entertainment event is to be held or is being held, sells a ticket of admission to the entertainment event, which was obtained for the purpose of resale, at any price which is in excess of the price that is printed or endorsed upon the ticket, while on the grounds of or in the stadium, arena, theater, or other place where an event for which admission tickets are sold is to be held or is being held, is guilty of a misdemeanor.
(Added by Stats. 1972, Ch. 529.)
347.
(a) (1) Every person who willfully mingles any poison or harmful substance with any food, drink, medicine, or pharmaceutical product or who willfully places any poison or harmful substance in any spring, well, reservoir, or public water supply, where the person knows or should have known that the same would be taken by any human being to his or her injury, is guilty of a felony punishable by imprisonment in the state prison for two, four, or five years.
(2) Any violation of paragraph (1) involving the use of a poison or harmful substance that may cause death if ingested or that causes the infliction of great bodily injury on any person shall be punished by an additional term of three years.
(b) Any person who maliciously informs any other person that a poison or other harmful substance has been or will be placed in any food, drink, medicine, pharmaceutical product, or public water supply, knowing that such report is false, is guilty of a crime punishable by imprisonment in the state prison, or by imprisonment in the county jail not to exceed one year.
(c) The court may impose the maximum fine for each item tampered with in violation of subdivision (a).
(Amended by Stats. 2000, Ch. 287, Sec. 8. Effective January 1, 2001.)
347b.
It shall be unlawful for any person, firm or corporation to manufacture, sell, furnish, or give away, or offer to manufacture, sell, furnish, or give away any alcoholic solution of a potable nature containing any deleterious or poisonous substance, and the burden of proof shall be upon the person, firm, or corporation manufacturing, selling, furnishing, or giving away, or offering to manufacture, sell, furnish, or give away, any such alcoholic solution of a potable nature containing any deleterious or poisonous substance, to show that such alcoholic solution of a potable nature did not contain any deleterious or poisonous substance. Every person who violates any of the provisions of this section is guilty of a misdemeanor, and shall be punished by a fine not exceeding two thousand five hundred dollars ($2,500), or by imprisonment in a county jail not exceeding one year, or by both such fine and imprisonment.
(Amended by Stats. 1976, Ch. 1125.)
350.
(a) Any person who willfully manufactures, intentionally sells, or knowingly possesses for sale any counterfeit mark registered with the Secretary of State or registered on the Principal Register of the United States Patent and Trademark Office, shall, upon conviction, be punishable as follows:
(1) When the offense involves less than 1,000 of the articles described in this subdivision, with a total retail or fair market value less than that required for grand theft as defined in Section 487, and if the person is an individual, he or she shall be punished by a fine of not more than ten thousand dollars ($10,000), or by imprisonment in a county jail for not more than one year, or by both that fine and imprisonment; or, if the person is a business entity, by a fine of not more than two hundred thousand dollars ($200,000).
(2) When the offense involves 1,000 or more of the articles described in this subdivision, or has a total retail or fair market value equal to or greater than that required for grand theft as defined in Section 487, and if the person is an individual, he or she shall be punished by imprisonment in a county jail not to exceed one year, or pursuant to subdivision (h) of Section 1170 for 16 months, or two or three years, or by a fine not to exceed five hundred thousand dollars ($500,000), or by both that imprisonment and fine; or, if the person is a business entity, by a fine not to exceed one million dollars ($1,000,000).
(b) Any person who has been convicted of a violation of either paragraph (1) or (2) of subdivision (a) shall, upon a subsequent conviction of paragraph (1) of subdivision (a), if the person is an individual, be punished by a fine of not more than one hundred thousand dollars ($100,000), or by imprisonment in a county jail for not more than one year, or pursuant to subdivision (h) of Section 1170 for 16 months, or two or three years, or by both that fine and imprisonment; or, if the person is a business entity, by a fine of not more than four hundred thousand dollars ($400,000).
(c) Any person who has been convicted of a violation of subdivision (a) and who, by virtue of the conduct that was the basis of the conviction, has directly and foreseeably caused death or great bodily injury to another through reliance on the counterfeited item for its intended purpose shall, if the person is an individual, be punished by a fine of not more than one hundred thousand dollars ($100,000), or by imprisonment pursuant to subdivision (h) of Section 1170 for two, three, or four years, or by both that fine and imprisonment; or, if the person is a business entity, by a fine of not more than four hundred thousand dollars ($400,000).
(d) (1) Except as provided in paragraph (2), in any action brought under this section resulting in a conviction or a plea of nolo contendere, the court shall order the forfeiture and destruction of all of those marks and of all goods, articles, or other matter bearing the marks, and the forfeiture and destruction or other disposition of all means of making the marks, and any and all electrical, mechanical, or other devices for manufacturing, reproducing, transporting, or assembling these marks, that were used in connection with, or were part of, any violation of this section.
(2) Upon request of any law enforcement agency and consent from the specific registrants, the court may consider a motion to have the items described in paragraph (1), not including recordings or audiovisual works as defined in Section 653w, donated to a nonprofit organization for the purpose of distributing the goods to persons living in poverty at no charge to the persons served by the organization.
(3) Forfeiture of the proceeds of the crime shall be subject to Chapter 9 (commencing with Section 186) of Title 7 of Part 1. However, no vehicle shall be forfeited under this section that may be lawfully driven on the highway with a class C, M1, or M2 license, as prescribed in Section 12804.9 of the Vehicle Code, and that is any of the following:
(A) A community property asset of a person other than the defendant.
(B) The sole class C, M1, or M2 vehicle available to the immediate family of that person or of the defendant.
(C) Reasonably necessary to be retained by the defendant for the purpose of lawfully earning a living, or for any other reasonable and lawful purpose.
(e) For the purposes of this section, the following definitions shall apply:
(1) When counterfeited but unassembled components of computer software packages are recovered, including, but not limited to, counterfeited computer diskettes, instruction manuals, or licensing envelopes, the number of "articles" shall be equivalent to the number of completed computer software packages that could have been made from those components.
(2) "Business entity" includes, but is not limited to, a corporation, limited liability company, or partnership. "Business entity" does not include a sole proprietorship.
(3) "Counterfeit mark" means a spurious mark that is identical with, or confusingly similar to, a registered mark and is used, or intended to be used, on or in connection with the same type of goods or services for which the genuine mark is registered. It is not necessary for the mark to be displayed on the outside of an article for there to be a violation. For articles containing digitally stored information, it shall be sufficient to constitute a violation if the counterfeit mark appears on a video display when the information is retrieved from the article. The term "spurious mark" includes genuine marks used on or in connection with spurious articles and includes identical articles containing identical marks, where the goods or marks were reproduced without authorization of, or in excess of any authorization granted by, the registrant. When counterfeited but unassembled components of any articles described under subdivision (a) are recovered, including, but not limited to, labels, patches, fabric, stickers, wrappers, badges, emblems, medallions, charms, boxes, containers, cans, cases, hangtags, documentation, or packaging, or any other components of any type or nature that are designed, marketed, or otherwise intended to be used on or in connection with any articles described under subdivision (a), the number of "articles" shall be equivalent to the number of completed articles that could have been made from those components.
(4) "Knowingly possess" means that the person possessing an article knew or had reason to believe that it was spurious, or that it was used on or in connection with spurious articles, or that it was reproduced without authorization of, or in excess of any authorization granted by, the registrant.
(5) Notwithstanding Section 7, "person" includes, but is not limited to, a business entity.
(6) "Registrant" means any person to whom the registration of a mark is issued and that person's legal representatives, successors, or assigns.
(7) "Sale" includes resale.
(8) "Value" has the following meanings:
(A) When counterfeit items of computer software are manufactured or possessed for sale, the "value" of those items shall be equivalent to the retail price or fair market price of the true items that are counterfeited.
(B) When counterfeited but unassembled components of computer software packages or any other articles described under subdivision (a) are recovered, including, but not limited to, counterfeited digital disks, instruction manuals, licensing envelopes, labels, patches, fabric, stickers, wrappers, badges, emblems, medallions, charms, boxes, containers, cans, cases, hangtags, documentation, or packaging, or any other components of any type or nature that are designed, marketed, or otherwise intended to be used on or in connection with any articles described under subdivision (a), the "value" of those components shall be equivalent to the retail price or fair market value of the number of completed computer software packages or other completed articles described under subdivision (a) that could have been made from those components.
(C) "Retail or fair market value" of a counterfeit article means a value equivalent to the retail price or fair market value, as of the last day of the charged crime, of a completed similar genuine article containing a genuine mark.
(f) This section shall not be enforced against any party who has adopted and lawfully used the same or confusingly similar mark in the rendition of like services or the manufacture or sale of like goods in this state from a date prior to the earliest effective date of registration of the service mark or trademark either with the Secretary of State or on the Principle Register of the United States Patent and Trademark Office.
(g) An owner, officer, employee, or agent who provides, rents, leases, licenses, or sells real property upon which a violation of subdivision (a) occurs shall not be subject to a criminal penalty pursuant to this section, unless he or she sells, or possesses for sale, articles bearing a counterfeit mark in violation of this section. This subdivision shall not be construed to abrogate or limit any civil rights or remedies for a trademark violation.
(h) This section shall not be enforced against any party who engages in fair uses of a mark, as specified in Section 14247 of the Business and Professions Code.
(i) When a person is convicted of an offense under this section, the court shall order the person to pay restitution to the trademark owner and any other victim of the offense pursuant to Section 1202.4.
(Amended by Stats. 2012, Ch. 867, Sec. 19. (SB 1144) Effective January 1, 2013.)
351a.
Any person who sells, attempts to sell, offers for sale or assists in the sale of any goods, product or output, and who willfully and falsely represents such goods, product or output to be the goods, product or output of any dealer, manufacturer or producer, other than the true dealer, manufacturer or producer, or any member of a firm or any officer of a corporation, who knowingly permits any employee of such firm or corporation to sell, offer for sale or assist in the sale of any goods, product or output or to falsely represent such goods, product or output to be the goods, product or output of any dealer, manufacturer or producer, other than the true dealer, manufacturer or producer, is guilty of a misdemeanor and punishable by a fine of not less than one hundred dollars ($100) or more than six hundred dollars ($600), or by imprisonment in the county jail for not less than 20 or more than 90 days, or both. This section shall not apply to any person who sells or offers for sale under his own name or brand the product or output of another manufacturer or producer with the written consent of such manufacturer or producer.
(Amended by Stats. 1983, Ch. 1092, Sec. 271. Effective September 27, 1983. Operative January 1, 1984, by Sec. 427 of Ch. 1092.)
355.
Every person who defaces or obliterates the marks upon wrecked property, or in any manner disguises the appearance thereof, with intent to prevent the owner from discovering its identity, or who destroys or suppresses any invoice, bill of lading, or other document tending to show the ownership, is guilty of a misdemeanor.
(Enacted 1872.)
356.
Every person who cuts out, alters, or defaces any mark made upon any log, lumber, or wood, or puts a false mark thereon with intent to prevent the owner from discovering its identity, is guilty of a misdemeanor.
(Enacted 1872.)
359.
Every person authorized to solemnize marriage, who willfully and knowingly solemnizes any incestuous or other marriage forbidden by law, is punishable by fine of not less than one hundred nor more than one thousand dollars, or by imprisonment in the County Jail not less than three months nor more than one year, or by both.
(Enacted 1872.)
360.
Every person authorized to solemnize any marriage, who solemnizes a marriage without first being presented with the marriage license, as required by Section 421 of the Family Code; or who solemnizes a marriage pursuant to Part 4 (commencing with Section 500) of Division 3 of the Family Code without the authorization required by that part; or who willfully makes a false return of any marriage or pretended marriage to the recorder or clerk and every person who willfully makes a false record of any marriage return, is guilty of a misdemeanor.
(Amended by Stats. 2001, Ch. 39, Sec. 11. Effective January 1, 2002.)
362.
Every officer or person to whom a writ of habeas corpus may be directed, who, after service thereof, neglects or refuses to obey the command thereof, is guilty of a misdemeanor.
(Enacted 1872.)
363.
Every person who, either solely or as member of a Court, knowingly and unlawfully recommits, imprisons, or restrains of his liberty, for the same cause, any person who has been discharged upon a writ of habeas corpus, is guilty of a misdemeanor.
(Enacted 1872.)
364.
Every person having in his custody, or under his restraint or power, any person for whose relief a writ of habeas corpus has been issued, who, with the intent to elude the service of such writ or to avoid the effect thereof, transfers such person to the custody

of another, or places him under the power or control of another, or conceals or changes the place of his confinement or restraint, or removes him without the jurisdiction of the Court or Judge issuing the writ, is guilty of a misdemeanor.

(Enacted 1872.)

365.

Every person, and every agent or officer of any corporation carrying on business as an innkeeper, or as a common carrier of passengers, who refuses, without just cause or excuse, to receive and entertain any guest, or to receive and carry any passenger, is guilty of a misdemeanor. However, an innkeeper who has proceeded as authorized by Section 1865 of the Civil Code shall be rebuttably presumed to have acted with just cause or excuse for purposes of this section.

(Amended by Stats. 1999, Ch. 354, Sec. 3. Effective January 1, 2000.)

365.5.

(a) Any blind person, deaf person, or disabled person, who is a passenger on any common carrier, airplane, motor vehicle, railway train, motorbus, streetcar, boat, or any other public conveyance or mode of transportation operating within this state, shall be entitled to have with him or her a specially trained guide dog, signal dog, or service dog.

(b) No blind person, deaf person, or disabled person and his or her specially trained guide dog, signal dog, or service dog shall be denied admittance to accommodations, advantages, facilities, medical facilities, including hospitals, clinics, and physicians' offices, telephone facilities, adoption agencies, private schools, hotels, lodging places, places of public accommodation, amusement, or resort, and other places to which the general public is invited within this state because of that guide dog, signal dog, or service dog.

(c) Any person, firm, association, or corporation, or the agent of any person, firm, association, or corporation, who prevents a disabled person from exercising, or interferes with a disabled person in the exercise of, the rights specified in this section is guilty of a misdemeanor, punishable by a fine not exceeding two thousand five hundred dollars ($2,500).

(d) As used in this section, "guide dog" means any guide dog or Seeing Eye dog that was trained by a person licensed under Chapter 9.5 (commencing with Section 7200) of Division 3 of the Business and Professions Code or that meets the definitional criteria under federal regulations adopted to implement Title III of the Americans with Disabilities Act of 1990 (Public Law 101-336).

(e) As used in this section, "signal dog" means any dog trained to alert a deaf person, or a person whose hearing is impaired, to intruders or sounds.

(f) As used in this section, "service dog" means any dog individually trained to do work or perform tasks for the benefit of an individual with a disability, including, but not limited to, minimal protection work, rescue work, pulling a wheelchair, or fetching dropped items.

(g) (1) Nothing in this section is intended to affect any civil remedies available for a violation of this section.

(2) This section is intended to provide equal accessibility for all owners or trainers of animals that are trained as guide dogs, signal dogs, or service dogs in a manner that is no less than that provided by the Americans with Disabilities Act of 1990 (Public Law 101-336) and the Air Carrier Access Act of 1986 (Public Law 99-435).

(h) The exercise of rights specified in subdivisions (a) and (b) by any person may not be conditioned upon payment of any extra charge, provided that the person shall be liable for any provable damage done to the premises or facilities by his or her dog.

(i) Any trainer or individual with a disability may take dogs in any of the places specified in subdivisions (a) and (b) for the purpose of training the dogs as guide dogs, signal dogs, or service dogs. The person shall ensure that the dog is on a leash and tagged as a guide dog, signal dog, or service dog by an identification tag issued by the county clerk or animal control department as authorized by Chapter 3.5 (commencing with Section 30850) of Division 14 of the Food and Agricultural Code. In addition, the person shall be liable for any provable damage done to the premises or facilities by his or her dog.

(Amended by Stats. 1996, Ch. 498, Sec. 6. Effective January 1, 1997.)

365.6.

(a) Any person who, with no legal justification, intentionally interferes with the use of a guide, signal, or service dog or mobility aid by harassing or obstructing the guide, signal, or service dog or mobility aid user or his or her guide, signal, or service dog, is guilty of a misdemeanor, punishable by imprisonment in a county jail not exceeding six months, or by a fine of not less than one thousand five hundred dollars ($1,500) nor more than two thousand five hundred dollars ($2,500), or both that fine and imprisonment.

(b) As used in this section, the following definitions shall apply:

(1) "Mobility aid" means any device enabling a person with a disability, as defined in subdivision (b) of Section 54 of the Civil Code, to travel independently, including, but not limited to, a guide, signal, or service dog, as defined in Section 54.1 of the Civil Code, a wheelchair, walker or white cane.

(2) "Guide, signal, or service dog" means any dog trained to do work or perform tasks for the benefit of an individual with a disability, including, but not limited to, guiding individuals with impaired vision, alerting individuals with impaired hearing to intruders or sounds, pulling a wheelchair, or fetching dropped items.

(c) Nothing in this section is intended to affect any civil remedies available for a violation of this section.

(Amended by Stats. 2004, Ch. 322, Sec. 1. Effective January 1, 2005.)

365.7.

(a) Any person who knowingly and fraudulently represents himself or herself, through verbal or written notice, to be the owner or trainer of any canine licensed as, to be qualified as, or identified as, a guide, signal, or service dog, as defined in subdivisions (d), (e), and (f) of Section 365.5 and paragraph (6) of subdivision (b) of Section 54.1 of the Civil Code, shall be guilty of a misdemeanor punishable by imprisonment in the county jail not exceeding six months, by a fine not exceeding one thousand dollars ($1,000), or by both that fine and imprisonment.

(b) As used in this section, "owner" means any person who owns a guide, signal, or service dog, or who is authorized by the owner to use the guide, signal, or service dog.

(Added by Stats. 1994, Ch. 1257, Sec. 12. Effective January 1, 1995.)

367f.

(a) Except as provided in subdivisions (d) and (e), it shall be unlawful for any person to knowingly acquire, receive, sell, promote the transfer of, or otherwise transfer any human organ, for purposes of transplantation, for valuable consideration.

(b) Except as provided in subdivisions (d), (e), and (f), it shall be unlawful to remove or transplant any human organ with the knowledge that the organ has been acquired or will be transferred or sold for valuable consideration in violation of subdivision (a).

(c) For purposes of this section, the following definitions apply:

(1) "Human organ" includes, but is not limited to, a human kidney, liver, heart, lung, pancreas, or any other human organ or nonrenewable or nonregenerative tissue except plasma and sperm.

(2) "Valuable consideration" means financial gain or advantage, but does not include the reasonable costs associated with the removal, storage, transportation, and transplantation of a human organ, or reimbursement for those services, or the expenses of travel, housing, and lost wages incurred by the donor of a human organ in connection with the donation of the organ.

(d) No act respecting the nonsale donation of organs or other nonsale conduct pursuant to or in the furtherance of the purposes of the Uniform Anatomical Gift Act, Chapter 3.5 (commencing with Section 7150) Part 1 of Division 7 of the Health and

Safety Code, including acts pursuant to anatomical gifts offered under Section 12811 of the Vehicle Code, shall be made unlawful by this section.

(e) This section shall not apply to the person from whom the organ is removed, nor to the person who receives the transplant, or those persons' next-of-kin who assisted in obtaining the organ for purposes of transplantations.

(f) A licensed physician and surgeon who transplants a human organ in violation of subdivision (b) shall not be criminally liable under that subdivision if the act is performed under emergency and life-threatening conditions.

(g) Any person who violates subdivision (a) or (b) shall be punished by a fine not to exceed fifty thousand dollars ($50,000), or by imprisonment pursuant to subdivision (h) of Section 1170 for three, four, or five years, or by both that fine and imprisonment.

(Amended by Stats. 2011, Ch. 15, Sec. 334. (AB 109) Effective April 4, 2011. Operative October 1, 2011, by Sec. 636 of Ch. 15, as amended by Stats. 2011, Ch. 39, Sec. 68.)

367g.

(a) It shall be unlawful for anyone to knowingly use sperm, ova, or embryos in assisted reproduction technology, for any purpose other than that indicated by the sperm, ova, or embryo provider's signature on a written consent form.

(b) It shall be unlawful for anyone to knowingly implant sperm, ova, or embryos, through the use of assisted reproduction technology, into a recipient who is not the sperm, ova, or embryo provider, without the signed written consent of the sperm, ova, or embryo provider and recipient.

(c) Any person who violates this section shall be punished by imprisonment pursuant to subdivision (h) of Section 1170 for three, four, or five years, by a fine not to exceed fifty thousand dollars ($50,000), or by both that fine and imprisonment.

(d) Written consent, for the purposes of this section, shall not be required of men who donate sperm to a licensed tissue bank.

(Amended by Stats. 2011, Ch. 15, Sec. 335. (AB 109) Effective April 4, 2011. Operative October 1, 2011, by Sec. 636 of Ch. 15, as amended by Stats. 2011, Ch. 39, Sec. 68.)

CHAPTER 13. Crimes Against Elders, Dependent Adults, and Persons with Disabilities [368 - 368.7]

(Chapter 13 heading added by Stats. 2010, Ch. 617, Sec. 2.)

368.

(a) The Legislature finds and declares that elders, adults whose physical or mental disabilities or other limitations restrict their ability to carry out normal activities or to protect their rights, and adults admitted as inpatients to a 24-hour health facility deserve special consideration and protection.

(b) (1) A person who knows or reasonably should know that a person is an elder or dependent adult and who, under circumstances or conditions likely to produce great bodily harm or death, willfully causes or permits any elder or dependent adult to suffer, or inflicts thereon unjustifiable physical pain or mental suffering, or having the care or custody of any elder or dependent adult, willfully causes or permits the person or health of the elder or dependent adult to be injured, or willfully causes or permits the elder or dependent adult to be placed in a situation in which his or her person or health is endangered, is punishable by imprisonment in a county jail not exceeding one year, or by a fine not to exceed six thousand dollars ($6,000), or by both that fine and imprisonment, or by imprisonment in the state prison for two, three, or four years.

(2) If, in the commission of an offense described in paragraph (1), the victim suffers great bodily injury, as defined in Section 12022.7, the defendant shall receive an additional term in the state prison as follows:

(A) Three years if the victim is under 70 years of age.

(B) Five years if the victim is 70 years of age or older.

(3) If, in the commission of an offense described in paragraph (1), the defendant proximately causes the death of the victim, the defendant shall receive an additional term in the state prison as follows:

(A) Five years if the victim is under 70 years of age.

(B) Seven years if the victim is 70 years of age or older.

(c) A person who knows or reasonably should know that a person is an elder or dependent adult and who, under circumstances or conditions other than those likely to produce great bodily harm or death, willfully causes or permits any elder or dependent adult to suffer, or inflicts thereon unjustifiable physical pain or mental suffering, or having the care or custody of any elder or dependent adult, willfully causes or permits the person or health of the elder or dependent adult to be injured or willfully causes or permits the elder or dependent adult to be placed in a situation in which his or her person or health may be endangered, is guilty of a misdemeanor. A second or subsequent violation of this subdivision is punishable by a fine not to exceed two thousand dollars ($2,000), or by imprisonment in a county jail not to exceed one year, or by both that fine and imprisonment.

(d) A person who is not a caretaker who violates any provision of law proscribing theft, embezzlement, forgery, or fraud, or who violates Section 530.5 proscribing identity theft, with respect to the property or personal identifying information of an elder or a dependent adult, and who knows or reasonably should know that the victim is an elder or a dependent adult, is punishable as follows:

(1) By a fine not exceeding two thousand five hundred dollars ($2,500), or by imprisonment in a county jail not exceeding one year, or by both that fine and imprisonment, or by a fine not exceeding ten thousand dollars ($10,000), or by imprisonment pursuant to subdivision (h) of Section 1170 for two, three, or four years, or by both that fine and imprisonment, when the moneys, labor, goods, services, or real or personal property taken or obtained is of a value exceeding nine hundred fifty dollars ($950).

(2) By a fine not exceeding one thousand dollars ($1,000), by imprisonment in a county jail not exceeding one year, or by both that fine and imprisonment, when the moneys, labor, goods, services, or real or personal property taken or obtained is of a value not exceeding nine hundred fifty dollars ($950).

(e) A caretaker of an elder or a dependent adult who violates any provision of law proscribing theft, embezzlement, forgery, or fraud, or who violates Section 530.5 proscribing identity theft, with respect to the property or personal identifying information of that elder or dependent adult, is punishable as follows:

(1) By a fine not exceeding two thousand five hundred dollars ($2,500), or by imprisonment in a county jail not exceeding one year, or by both that fine and imprisonment, or by a fine not exceeding ten thousand dollars ($10,000), or by imprisonment pursuant to subdivision (h) of Section 1170 for two, three, or four years, or by both that fine and imprisonment, when the moneys, labor, goods, services, or real or personal property taken or obtained is of a value exceeding nine hundred fifty dollars ($950).

(2) By a fine not exceeding one thousand dollars ($1,000), by imprisonment in a county jail not exceeding one year, or by both that fine and imprisonment, when the moneys, labor, goods, services, or real or personal property taken or obtained is of a value not exceeding nine hundred fifty dollars ($950).

(f) A person who commits the false imprisonment of an elder or a dependent adult by the use of violence, menace, fraud, or deceit is punishable by imprisonment pursuant to subdivision (h) of Section 1170 for two, three, or four years.

(g) As used in this section, "elder" means a person who is 65 years of age or older.

(h) As used in this section, "dependent adult" means a person, regardless of whether the person lives independently, who is between the ages of 18 and 64, who has physical or mental limitations which restrict his or her ability to carry out normal activities or to protect his or her rights, including, but not limited to, persons who have physical or developmental disabilities or whose physical or mental abilities have diminished because of age. "Dependent adult" includes a person between the ages of 18 and 64 who is admitted as an inpatient to a 24-hour health facility, as defined in Sections 1250, 1250.2, and 1250.3 of the Health and Safety Code.

(i) As used in this section, "caretaker" means a person who has the care, custody, or control of, or who stands in a position of trust with, an elder or a dependent adult.

(j) Nothing in this section shall preclude prosecution under both this section and Section 187 or 12022.7 or any other provision of law. However, a person shall not receive an additional term of imprisonment under both paragraphs (2) and (3) of subdivision (b) for a single offense, nor shall a person receive an additional term of imprisonment under both Section 12022.7 and paragraph (2) or (3) of subdivision (b) for a single offense.

(k) In any case in which a person is convicted of violating these provisions, the court may require him or her to receive appropriate counseling as a condition of probation. A defendant ordered to be placed in a counseling program shall be responsible for paying the expense of his or her participation in the counseling program as determined by the court. The court shall take into consideration the ability of the defendant to pay, and no defendant shall be denied probation because of his or her inability to pay.

(l) Upon conviction for a violation of subdivision (b), (c), (d), (e), or (f), the sentencing court shall also consider issuing an order restraining the defendant from any contact with the victim, which may be valid for up to 10 years, as determined by the court. It is the intent of the Legislature that the length of any restraining order be based upon the seriousness of the facts before the court, the probability of future violations, and the safety of the victim and his or her immediate family. This protective order may be issued by the court whether the defendant is sentenced to state prison or county jail, or if imposition of sentence is suspended and the defendant is placed on probation.

(Amended by Stats. 2018, Ch. 70, Sec. 3. (AB 1934) Effective January 1, 2019.)

368.5.

(a) Local law enforcement agencies and state law enforcement agencies with jurisdiction shall have concurrent jurisdiction to investigate elder and dependent adult abuse and all other crimes against elder victims and victims with disabilities.

(b) Adult protective services agencies and local long-term care ombudsman programs also have jurisdiction within their statutory authority to investigate elder and dependent adult abuse and criminal neglect, and may assist local law enforcement agencies in criminal investigations at the law enforcement agencies' request; however, law enforcement agencies retain exclusive responsibility for criminal investigations, notwithstanding any law to the contrary.

(c) (1) Every local law enforcement agency and long-term care ombudsman program shall, when the agency or program next undertakes the policy revision process, revise or include in the portion of its policy manual relating to elder and dependent adult abuse, if that policy manual exists, the following information:

(A) The elements of the offense specified in subdivision (c) of Section 368.

(B) The elements of the offense specified in subdivision (f) of Section 368.

(C) The requirement, pursuant to subdivisions (a) and (b), that law enforcement agencies have the responsibility for criminal investigations of elder and dependent adult abuse and criminal neglect, however, adult protective services agencies and long-term care ombudsman programs have authority to investigate incidents of elder and dependent adult abuse and neglect and may, if requested, assist law enforcement agencies with criminal investigations.

(D) As a guideline to investigators and first responders, the definition of elder and dependent adult abuse provided by the Department of Justice in its policy and procedures manual, dated March 2015, which defines elder and dependent adult abuse as physical "abuse, neglect, financial abuse, abandonment, isolation, abduction, or other treatment with resulting physical harm or pain or mental suffering; or the deprivation by a care custodian of goods or services that are necessary to avoid physical harm or mental suffering."

(2) This subdivision does not require a long-term care ombudsman program that does not have a policy manual to create or adopt a policy manual.

(3) As used in this subdivision, the following terms have the following meanings:

(A) "Local law enforcement agency" means every municipal police department and county sheriffs' department.

(B) "Policy manual" means any general orders, patrol manual, duty manual, or other written document or collection of documents that provides field or investigative personnel with policies, procedures, or guidelines for responding to or investigating crimes, complaints, or incidents.

(Amended by Stats. 2018, Ch. 513, Sec. 1. (SB 1191) Effective January 1, 2019.)

368.7.

The Department of Justice shall develop and distribute an informational notice that warns the public about elder and dependent adult fraud and directs them to information and resources necessary to determine whether they are victims of fraud. The notice shall provide information regarding how and where to file complaints. The notice shall also be made available on the Internet Web site of the Attorney General.

(Added by Stats. 2016, Ch. 80, Sec. 1. (AB 2721) Effective January 1, 2017.)

TITLE 10. OF CRIMES AGAINST THE PUBLIC HEALTH AND SAFETY [369a - 402c]

(Title 10 enacted 1872.)

369a.

(a) The Legislature hereby finds and declares the following:

(1) Rail transit traffic safety programs are necessary to educate the public about the potential for harm and injury arising from an individual's disregard for, and violation of, rail-related traffic safety laws, and to increase the consequences for those persons violating rail-related traffic safety laws.

(2) Currently, there does not exist a unified statewide system to deal with the ever increasing problem of rail-related traffic safety violators, and to provide a method of educating the public.

(b) In each county with a population greater than 500,000 in which a transportation commission or authority has been established and it owns or operates rail transit facilities, the commission or authority may provide and disseminate appropriate educational materials to traffic schools to aid in reducing the number of rail-related traffic accidents, including, but not limited to, a film developed or caused to be developed by the transportation commission or authority on rail transit safety.

(Added by Stats. 1993, Ch. 722, Sec. 2. Effective January 1, 1994.)

369b.

(a) This section shall only apply to counties with a population greater than 500,000.

(b) The court may order any person convicted of a rail transit related traffic violation, as listed in subdivision (c), to attend a traffic school that offers, as a part of its curriculum, a film developed or caused to be developed by a transportation commission or authority on rail transit safety.

(c) For a first offense, a court, at its discretion, may order any person cited for any of the following violations to attend a traffic school offering a rail safety presentation, Internet rail safety test, or rail transit safety film prepared by a county transportation commission or authority, pay an additional fine of one hundred dollars ($100), or both:

(1) Section 369g.

(2) Section 369i.

(3) Subdivision (c) of Section 21752, Section 22450, 22451, or 22452, or subdivision (c) of Section 22526, of the Vehicle Code, involving railroad grade crossings.

(d) For a second or subsequent violation as provided in subdivision (c), a court shall order a person to pay an additional fine of up to two hundred dollars ($200) and to attend a traffic school offering a rail safety presentation, Internet rail safety test, or rail safety film prepared by a county transportation commission or authority.

(e) All fines collected according to this section shall be distributed pursuant to Sections 1463 and 1463.12, as applicable.

(Amended by Stats. 2005, Ch. 716, Sec. 3. Effective January 1, 2006.)

369d.

Any person who enters upon or crosses any railroad, at any private passway, which is inclosed by bars or gates, and neglects to leave the same securely closed after him, is guilty of a misdemeanor.

(Added by Stats. 1905, Ch. 573.)

369g.

(a) Any person who rides, drives, or propels any vehicle upon and along the track of any railroad through or over its private right-of-way, without the authorization of its superintendent or other officer in charge thereof, is guilty of a misdemeanor.

(b) Any person who rides, drives, or propels any vehicle upon and along the track of any railline owned or operated by a county transportation commission or transportation authority without the authorization of the commission or authority is guilty of a misdemeanor.

(Amended by Stats. 1993, Ch. 722, Sec. 4. Effective January 1, 1994.)

369h.

Any person, partnership, firm or corporation installing, setting up, maintaining or operating upon public or private property, any sign or light in line of vision along any main line track of any railroad in this State of such type or in such form or manner that it may be mistaken for any fixed or standard railroad signal when viewed from an approaching locomotive cab, railway car, or train, by the operators or employees upon such locomotive cab, railway car or train, so as to hinder the safe and efficient operation of such locomotive, railway car or train, and endanger the safety of persons or property upon such locomotive, railway car, or train, shall be guilty of maintaining a public nuisance. No sign, signal, flare or light placed within the right of way of any street or highway by public authorities in charge thereof, considered necessary by them to direct or warn highway traffic, shall be deemed to violate this section.

(Added by Stats. 1941, Ch. 153.)

369i.

(a) Any person who enters or remains upon the property of any railroad without the permission of the owner of the land, the owner's agent, or the person in lawful possession and whose entry, presence, or conduct upon the property interferes with, interrupts, or hinders, or which, if allowed to continue, would interfere with, interrupt, or hinder the safe and efficient operation of any locomotive, railway car, or train is guilty of a misdemeanor.

As used in this subdivision, "property of any railroad" means any land owned, leased, or possessed by a railroad upon which is placed a railroad track and the land immediately adjacent thereto, to the distance of 20 feet on either side of the track, which is owned, leased, or possessed by a railroad.

(b) Any person who enters or remains upon any transit-related property without permission or whose entry, presence, or conduct upon the property interferes with, interrupts, or hinders the safe and efficient operation of the transit-related facility is guilty of a misdemeanor.

As used in this subdivision, "transit-related property" means any land, facilities, or vehicles owned, leased, or possessed by a county transportation commission, transportation authority, or transit district, as defined in Section 99170 of the Public Utilities Code, that are used to provide public transportation by rail or passenger bus or are directly related to that use.

(c) This section does not prohibit picketing in the immediately adjacent area of the property of any railroad or transit-related property or any lawful activity by which the public is informed of the existence of an alleged labor dispute.

(Amended by Stats. 2011, Ch. 534, Sec. 1. (AB 716) Effective January 1, 2012.)

[370.]

Section Three Hundred and Seventy. Anything which is injurious to health, or is indecent, or offensive to the senses, or an obstruction to the free use of property, so as to interfere with the comfortable enjoyment of life or property by an entire community or neighborhood, or by any considerable number of persons, or unlawfully obstructs the free passage or use, in the customary manner, of any navigable lake, or river, bay, stream, canal, or basin, or any public park, square, street, or highway, is a public nuisance.

(Amended by Code Amendments 1873-74, Ch. 614.)

371.

An act which affects an entire community or neighborhood, or any considerable number of persons, as specified in the last section, is not less a nuisance because the extent of the annoyance or damage inflicted upon individuals is unequal.

(Amended by Stats. 1989, Ch. 1360, Sec. 109.)

372.

Every person who maintains or commits any public nuisance, the punishment for which is not otherwise prescribed, or who willfully omits to perform any legal duty relating to the removal of a public nuisance, is guilty of a misdemeanor.

(Enacted 1872.)

373a.

Each person who maintains, permits, or allows a public nuisance to exist upon his or her property or premises, and each person occupying or leasing the property or premises of another who maintains, permits, or allows a public nuisance to exist on the property, after reasonable notice in writing from a health officer, district attorney, city attorney, or city prosecutor to remove, discontinue, or abate the public nuisance has been served upon the person, is guilty of a misdemeanor. The existence of the public nuisance for each and every day after the service of the notice is a separate and distinct offense, and it is the duty of the district attorney, or the city attorney or city prosecutor of any city the charter of which imposes the duty upon the city attorney or city prosecutor to prosecute state misdemeanors, to continuously prosecute all persons guilty of violating this section until the nuisance is abated and removed.

(Amended by Stats. 2017, Ch. 299, Sec. 1. (AB 1418) Effective January 1, 2018.)

374.

(a) Littering means the willful or negligent throwing, dropping, placing, depositing, or sweeping, or causing any such acts, of any waste matter on land or water in other than appropriate storage containers or areas designated for such purposes.

(b) Waste matter means discarded, used, or leftover substance including, but not limited to, a lighted or nonlighted cigarette, cigar, match, or any flaming or glowing material, or any garbage, trash, refuse, paper, container, packaging or construction material, carcass of a dead animal, any nauseous or offensive matter of any kind, or any object likely to injure any person or create a traffic hazard.

(Added by Stats. 1970, Ch. 1548.)

374.2.

(a) It is unlawful for any person to maliciously discharge, dump, release, place, drop, pour, or otherwise deposit, or to maliciously cause to be discharged, dumped, released, placed, dropped, poured, or otherwise deposited, any substance capable of causing substantial damage or harm to the operation of a public sewer sanitary facility, or to deposit in commercial quantities any other substance, into a manhole, cleanout, or other sanitary sewer facility, not intended for use as a point of deposit for sewage, which is connected to a public sanitary sewer system, without possessing a written authorization therefor granted by the public entity which is charged with the administration of the use of the affected public sanitary sewer system or the affected portion of the public sanitary sewer system.

As used in this section, "maliciously" means an intent to do a wrongful act.

(b) For the purposes of this section "person" means an individual, trust, firm, partnership, joint stock company, limited liability company, or corporation, and "deposited in commercial quantities" refers to any substance deposited or otherwise discharged in any amount greater than for normal domestic sewer use.

(c) Lack of specific knowledge that the facility into which the prohibited discharge or release occurred is connected to a public sanitary sewer system shall not constitute a defense to a violation charged under this section.

(d) Any person who violates this section shall be punished by imprisonment in the county jail for not more than one year, or by a fine of up to twenty-five thousand dollars ($25,000), or by both a fine and imprisonment. If the conviction is for a second or subsequent violation, the person shall be punished by imprisonment in the county jail for not more than one year, or imprisonment pursuant to subdivision (h) of Section 1170 for 16, 20, or 24 months, and by a fine of not less than five thousand dollars ($5,000) or more than twenty-five thousand dollars ($25,000).

(Amended by Stats. 2011, Ch. 15, Sec. 337. (AB 109) Effective April 4, 2011. Operative October 1, 2011, by Sec. 636 of Ch. 15, as amended by Stats. 2011, Ch. 39, Sec. 68.)

374.3.

(a) It is unlawful to dump or cause to be dumped waste matter in or upon a public or private highway or road, including any portion of the right-of-way thereof, or in or upon private property into or upon which the public is admitted by easement or license, or upon private property without the consent of the owner, or in or upon a public park or other public property other than property designated or set aside for that purpose by the governing board or body having charge of that property.

(b) It is unlawful to place, deposit, or dump, or cause to be placed, deposited, or dumped, rocks, concrete, asphalt, or dirt in or upon a private highway or road, including any portion of the right-of-way of the private highway or road, or private property, without the consent of the owner or a contractor under contract with the owner for the materials, or in or upon a public park or other public property, without the consent of the state or local agency having jurisdiction over the highway, road, or property.

(c) A person violating this section is guilty of an infraction. Each day that waste placed, deposited, or dumped in violation of subdivision (a) or (b) remains is a separate violation.

(d) This section does not restrict a private owner in the use of his or her own private property, unless the placing, depositing, or dumping of the waste matter on the property creates a public health and safety hazard, a public nuisance, or a fire hazard, as determined by a local health department, local fire department or district providing fire protection services, or the Department of Forestry and Fire Protection, in which case this section applies.

(e) A person convicted of a violation of this section shall be punished by a mandatory fine of not less than two hundred fifty dollars ($250) nor more than one thousand dollars ($1,000) upon a first conviction, by a mandatory fine of not less than five hundred dollars ($500) nor more than one thousand five hundred dollars ($1,500) upon a second conviction, and by a mandatory fine of not less than seven hundred fifty dollars ($750) nor more than three thousand dollars ($3,000) upon a third or subsequent conviction. If the court finds that the waste matter placed, deposited, or dumped was used tires, the fine prescribed in this subdivision shall be doubled.

(f) The court may require, in addition to any fine imposed upon a conviction, that, as a condition of probation and in addition to any other condition of probation, a person convicted under this section remove, or pay the cost of removing, any waste matter which the convicted person dumped or caused to be dumped upon public or private property.

(g) Except when the court requires the convicted person to remove waste matter which he or she is responsible for dumping as a condition of probation, the court may, in addition to the fine imposed upon a conviction, require as a condition of probation, in addition to any other condition of probation, that a person convicted of a violation of this section pick up waste matter at a time and place within the jurisdiction of the court for not less than 12 hours.

(h) (1) A person who places, deposits, or dumps, or causes to be placed, deposited, or dumped, waste matter in violation of this section in commercial quantities shall be guilty of a misdemeanor punishable by imprisonment in a county jail for not more than six months and by a fine. The fine is mandatory and shall amount to not less than one thousand dollars ($1,000) nor more than three thousand dollars ($3,000) upon a first conviction, not less than three thousand dollars ($3,000) nor more than six thousand dollars ($6,000) upon a second conviction, and not less than six thousand dollars ($6,000) nor more than ten thousand dollars ($10,000) upon a third or subsequent conviction.

(2) "Commercial quantities" means an amount of waste matter generated in the course of a trade, business, profession, or occupation, or an amount equal to or in excess of one cubic yard. This subdivision does not apply to the dumping of household waste at a person's residence.

(i) For purposes of this section, "person" means an individual, trust, firm, partnership, joint stock company, joint venture, or corporation.

(j) Except in unusual cases where the interests of justice would be best served by waiving or reducing a fine, the minimum fines provided by this section shall not be waived or reduced.

(Amended by Stats. 2006, Ch. 416, Sec. 7. Effective January 1, 2007.)

374.4.

(a) It is unlawful to litter or cause to be littered in or upon public or private property. A person, firm, or corporation violating this section is guilty of an infraction.

(b) This section does not restrict a private owner in the use of his or her own property, unless the littering of waste matter on the property creates a public health and safety hazard, a public nuisance, or a fire hazard, as determined by a local health department, local fire department or district providing fire protection services, or the Department of Forestry and Fire Protection, in which case this section applies.

(c) As used in this section, "litter" means the discarding, dropping, or scattering of small quantities of waste matter ordinarily carried on or about the person, including, but not limited to, beverage containers and closures, packaging, wrappers, wastepaper, newspapers, and magazines, in a place other than a place or container for the proper disposal thereof, and including waste matter that escapes or is allowed to escape from a container, receptacle, or package.

(d) A person, firm, or corporation convicted of a violation of this section shall be punished by a mandatory fine of not less than two hundred fifty dollars ($250) nor more than one thousand dollars ($1,000) upon a first conviction, by a mandatory fine of not less than five hundred dollars ($500) nor more than one thousand five hundred dollars ($1,500) upon a second conviction, and by a mandatory fine of not less than seven hundred fifty dollars ($750) nor more than three thousand dollars ($3,000) upon a third or subsequent conviction.

(e) The court may, in addition to the fine imposed upon a conviction, require as a condition of probation, in addition to any other condition of probation, that any person convicted of a violation of this section pick up litter at a time and place within the jurisdiction of the court for not less than eight hours.

(Amended by Stats. 2006, Ch. 416, Sec. 8. Effective January 1, 2007.)

374.5.

(a) It is unlawful for any grease waste hauler to do either of the following:

(1) Reinsert, deposit, dump, place, release, or discharge into a grease trap, grease interceptor, manhole, cleanout, or other sanitary sewer appurtenance any materials that the hauler has removed from the grease trap or grease interceptor, or to cause those materials to be so handled.

(2) Cause or permit to be discharged in or on any waters of the state, or discharged in or deposited where it is, or probably will be, discharged in or on any waters of the state, any materials that the hauler has removed from the grease trap or grease interceptor, or to cause those materials to be so handled.

(b) The prohibition in subdivision (a), as it pertains to reinsertion of material removed from a grease trap or grease interceptor, shall not apply to a grease waste hauler if all of the following conditions are met:

(1) The local sewer authority having jurisdiction over the pumping and disposal of the material specifically allows a registered grease waste hauler to obtain written approval for the reinsertion of decanted liquid.

(2) The local sewer authority has determined that, if reinsertion is allowed, it is feasible to enforce local discharge limits for fats, oil, and grease, if any, and other local requirements for best management or operating practices, if any.

(3) The grease waste hauler is registered pursuant to Section 19310 of the Food and Agricultural Code.

(4) The registered grease waste hauler demonstrates to the satisfaction of the local sewer authority all of the following:

(A) It will use equipment that will adequately separate the water from the grease waste and solids in the material so as to comply with applicable regulations.

(B) Its employees are adequately trained in the use of that equipment.

(5) The registered grease waste hauler demonstrates both of the following:

(A) It has informed the managerial personnel of the owner or operator of the grease trap or interceptor, in writing, that the grease waste hauler may reinsert the decanted materials, unless the owner or operator objects to the reinsertion.

(B) The owner or operator has not objected to the reinsertion of the decanted materials. If the owner or operator of the grease trap or interceptor objects to the reinsertion, no decanted material may be inserted in that grease trap or interceptor.

(c) A grease waste hauler shall not transport grease removed from a grease trap or grease interceptor in the same vehicle used for transporting other waste, including, but not limited to, yellow grease, cooking grease, recyclable cooking oil, septic waste, or fluids collected at car washes.

(d) For purposes of this section, a "grease waste hauler" is a transporter of inedible kitchen grease subject to registration requirements pursuant to Section 19310 of the Food and Agricultural Code.

(e) Any person who violates this section shall be guilty of a misdemeanor punishable by imprisonment in a county jail for not more than six months or a fine of not more than ten thousand dollars ($10,000), or both a fine and imprisonment.

A second and subsequent conviction, shall be punishable by imprisonment in a county jail for not more than one year, or a fine of not more than twenty-five thousand dollars ($25,000), or both a fine and imprisonment.

(f) Notwithstanding Section 1463, the fines paid pursuant to this section shall be apportioned as follows:

(1) Fifty percent shall be deposited in the Environmental Enforcement and Training Account established pursuant to Section 14303, and used for purposes of Title 13 (commencing with Section 14300) of Part 4.

(2) Twenty-five percent shall be distributed pursuant to Section 1463.001.

(3) Twenty-five percent to the local health officer or other local public officer or agency that investigated the matter which led to bringing the action.

(g) If the court finds that the violator has engaged in a practice or pattern of violation, consisting of two or more convictions, the court may bar the violating individual or business from engaging in the business of grease waste hauling for a period not to exceed five years.

(h) The court may require, in addition to any fine imposed upon conviction, that as a condition of probation and in addition to any other punishment or condition of probation, that a person convicted under this section remove, or pay the cost of removing, to the extent they are able, any materials which the convicted person dumped or caused to be dumped in violation of this section.

(i) This section does not prohibit the direct receipt of trucked grease by a publicly owned treatment works.

(Amended by Stats. 2007, Ch. 130, Sec. 190. Effective January 1, 2008.)

374.7.

(a) A person who litters or causes to be littered, or dumps or causes to be dumped, waste matter into a bay, lagoon, channel, river, creek, slough, canal, lake, or reservoir, or other stream or body of water, or upon a bank, beach, or shore within 150 feet of the high water mark of a stream or body of water, is guilty of a misdemeanor.

(b) A person convicted of a violation of subdivision (a) shall be punished by a mandatory fine of not less than two hundred fifty dollars ($250) nor more than one thousand dollars ($1,000) upon a first conviction, by a mandatory fine of not less than five hundred dollars ($500) nor more than one thousand five hundred dollars ($1,500) upon a second conviction, and by a mandatory fine of not less than seven hundred fifty dollars ($750) nor more than three thousand dollars ($3,000) upon a third or subsequent conviction.

(c) The court may, in addition to the fine imposed upon a conviction, require as a condition of probation, in addition to any other condition of probation, that any person convicted of a violation of subdivision (a), pick up litter at a time and place within the jurisdiction of the court for not less than eight hours.

(Amended by Stats. 2006, Ch. 416, Sec. 9. Effective January 1, 2007.)

374.8.

(a) In any prosecution under this section, proof of the elements of the offense shall not be dependent upon the requirements of Title 22 of the California Code of Regulations.

(b) Any person who knowingly causes any hazardous substance to be deposited into or upon any road, street, highway, alley, or railroad right-of-way, or upon the land of another, without the permission of the owner, or into the waters of this state is punishable by imprisonment in the county jail for not more than one year or by imprisonment pursuant to subdivision (h) of Section 1170 for a term of 16 months, two years, or three years, or by a fine of not less than fifty dollars ($50) nor more than ten thousand dollars ($10,000), or by both the fine and imprisonment, unless the deposit occurred as a result of an emergency that the person promptly reported to the appropriate regulatory authority.

(c) For purposes of this section, "hazardous substance" means either of the following:

(1) Any material that, because of its quantity, concentration, or physical or chemical characteristics, poses a significant present or potential hazard to human health and safety or to the environment if released into the environment, including, but not limited to, hazardous waste and any material that the administering agency or a handler, as defined in Chapter 6.91 (commencing with Section 25410) of Division 20 of the Health and Safety Code, has a reasonable basis for believing would be injurious to the health and safety of persons or harmful to the environment if released into the environment.

(2) Any substance or chemical product for which one of the following applies:

(A) The manufacturer or producer is required to prepare a MSDS, as defined in Section 6374 of the Labor Code, for the substance or product pursuant to the Hazardous Substances Information Training Act (Chapter 2.5 (commencing with Section 6360) of Part 1 of Division 5 of the Labor Code) or pursuant to any applicable federal law or regulation.

(B) The substance is described as a radioactive material in Chapter 1 of Title 10 of the Code of Federal Regulations maintained and updated by the Nuclear Regulatory Commission.

(C) The substance is designated by the Secretary of Transportation in Chapter 27 (commencing with Section 1801) of the appendix to Title 49 of the United States Code and taxed as a radioactive substance or material.

(D) The materials listed in subdivision (b) of Section 6382 of the Labor Code.

(Amended by Stats. 2011, Ch. 15, Sec. 338. (AB 109) Effective April 4, 2011. Operative October 1, 2011, by Sec. 636 of Ch. 15, as amended by Stats. 2011, Ch. 39, Sec. 68.)

374a.

A person giving information leading to the arrest and conviction of a person for a violation of Section 374c, 374.2, 374.3, 374.4, or 374.7 is entitled to a reward for providing the information.

The amount of the reward for each arrest and conviction shall be 50 percent of the fine levied against and collected from the person who violated Section 374c, 374.2, 374.3, 374.4, or 374.7 and shall be paid by the court. If the reward is payable to two or more persons, it shall be divided equally. The amount of collected fine to be paid under this section shall be paid prior to any distribution of the fine that may be prescribed by any other section, including Section 1463.9, with respect to the same fine.

(Amended by Stats. 2006, Ch. 416, Sec. 6. Effective January 1, 2007.)

374c.

Every person who shoots any firearm from or upon a public road or highway is guilty of a misdemeanor.

(Added by Stats. 1933, Ch. 203.)

374d.

Every person who knowingly allows the carcass of any dead animal which belonged to him at the time of its death to be put, or to remain, within 100 feet of any street, alley, public highway, or road in common use, and every person who puts the carcass of any dead animal within 100 feet of any street, alley, highway, or road in common use is guilty of a misdemeanor.

(Added by Stats. 1951, Ch. 657.)

375.

(a) It shall be unlawful to throw, drop, pour, deposit, release, discharge or expose, or to attempt to throw, drop, pour, deposit, release, discharge or expose in, upon or about any theater, restaurant, place of business, place of amusement or any place of public assemblage, any liquid, gaseous or solid substance or matter of any kind which is injurious to person or property, or is nauseous, sickening, irritating or offensive to any of the senses.

(b) It shall be unlawful to manufacture or prepare, or to possess any liquid, gaseous, or solid substance or matter of any kind which is injurious to person or property, or is nauseous, sickening, irritating or offensive, to any of the senses with intent to throw, drop, pour, deposit, release, discharge or expose the same in, upon or about any theater, restaurant, place of business, place of amusement, or any other place of public assemblage.

(c) Any person violating any of the provisions hereof shall be punished by imprisonment in the county jail for not less than three months and not more than one year, or by a fine of not less than five hundred dollars ($500) and not more than two thousand dollars ($2,000), or by both that fine and imprisonment.

(d) Any person who, in violating any of the provisions of subdivision (a), willfully employs or uses any liquid, gaseous or solid substance which may produce serious illness or permanent injury through being vaporized or otherwise dispersed in the air or who, in violating any of the provisions of subdivision (a), willfully employs or uses any tear gas, mustard gas or any of the combinations or compounds thereof, or willfully employs or uses acid or explosives, shall be guilty of a felony and shall be punished by imprisonment pursuant to subdivision (h) of Section 1170.

(Amended by Stats. 2011, Ch. 15, Sec. 339. (AB 109) Effective April 4, 2011. Operative October 1, 2011, by Sec. 636 of Ch. 15, as amended by Stats. 2011, Ch. 39, Sec. 68.)

377.

Every person who, in order to obtain for himself or another any drug that can be lawfully dispensed by a pharmacist only on prescription, falsely represents himself to be a physician or other person who can lawfully prescribe such drug, or falsely represents that he is acting on behalf of a person who can lawfully prescribe such drug, in a telephone communication with a pharmacist, is guilty of a misdemeanor.

(Added by Stats. 1963, Ch. 1272.)

379.

Every person who sells, dispenses, distributes, furnishes, administers, gives, or offers to sell, dispense, distribute, furnish, administer, or give Salvia divinorum or Salvinorin A, or any substance or material containing Salvia divinorum or Salvinorin A, to any person who is less than 18 years of age, is guilty of a misdemeanor punishable by imprisonment in a county jail not exceeding six months, or by a fine not exceeding one thousand dollars ($1,000), or by both that fine and imprisonment.

(Added by Stats. 2008, Ch. 184, Sec. 1. Effective January 1, 2009.)

380.

(a) Every person who sells, dispenses or distributes toluene, or any substance or material containing toluene, to any person who is less than 18 years of age shall be guilty of a misdemeanor, and upon conviction shall be fined in a sum of not less than one thousand dollars ($1,000), nor more than two thousand five hundred dollars ($2,500), or by imprisonment for not less than six months nor more than one year.

(b) The court shall order the suspension of the business license, for a period of one year, of a person who knowingly violates any of the provisions of this section after having been previously convicted of a violation of this section unless the owner of such business license can demonstrate a good faith attempt to prevent illegal sales or deliveries by employees. The provisions of this subdivision shall become operative on July 1, 1980.

(c) The provisions of this section shall apply to, but are not limited to, the sale or distribution of glue, cement, dope, paint thinners, paint, and any combination of hydrocarbons either alone or in combination with any substance or material including, but not limited to, paint, paint thinners, shellac thinners, and solvents which, when inhaled, ingested or breathed, can cause a person to be under the influence of, or intoxicated from, any such combination of hydrocarbons.

This section shall not prohibit the sale of gasoline or other motor vehicle fuels to persons less than 18 years of age.

(d) This section shall not apply to any glue or cement which has been certified by the State Department of Health Services as containing a substance which makes such glue or cement malodorous or causes such glue or cement to induce sneezing, nor shall this section apply where the glue or cement is sold, delivered, or given away simultaneously with or as part of a kit used for the construction of model airplanes, model boats, model automobiles, model trains, or other similar models or used for the assembly or creation of hobby craft items using such components as beads, tiles, tiffany glass, ceramics, clay, or other craft-related components.

(Amended by Stats. 1980, Ch. 1011, Sec. 1. Effective September 21, 1980.)

381.

(a) Any person who possesses toluene or any substance or material containing toluene, including, but not limited to, glue, cement, dope, paint thinner, paint and any combination of hydrocarbons, either alone or in combination with any substance or material including but not limited to paint, paint thinner, shellac thinner, and solvents, with the intent to breathe, inhale, or ingest for the purpose of causing a condition of intoxication, elation, euphoria, dizziness, stupefaction, or dulling of the senses or for the purpose of, in any manner, changing, distorting, or disturbing the audio, visual, or

mental processes, or who knowingly and with the intent to do so is under the influence of toluene or any material containing toluene, or any combination of hydrocarbons is guilty of a misdemeanor.

(b) Any person who possesses any substance or material, which the State Department of Public Health has determined by regulations adopted pursuant to the Administrative Procedure Act (Chapter 3.5 (commencing with Section 11340) of Part 1 of Division 3 of Title 2 of the Government Code) has toxic qualities similar to toluene, with the intent to breathe, inhale, or ingest for the purpose of causing a condition of intoxication, elation, euphoria, dizziness, excitement, irrational behavior, exhilaration, satisfaction, stupefaction, or dulling of the senses or for the purpose of, in any manner, changing, distorting, or disturbing the audio, visual, or mental processes, or who is under the influence of such substance or material is guilty of a misdemeanor.

(Amended by Stats. 2011, Ch. 296, Sec. 203. (AB 1023) Effective January 1, 2012.)

381a.

Any person, or persons, whether as principals, agents, managers, or otherwise, who buy or sell dairy products, or deal in milk, cream or butter, and who buy or sell the same upon the basis of their richness or weight or the percentage of cream, or butter-fat contained therein, who use any apparatus, test bottle or other appliance, or who use the "Babcock test" or machine of like character for testing such dairy products, cream or butter, which is not accurate and correct, or which gives wrong or false percentages, or which is calculated in any way to defraud or injure the person with whom he deals, is guilty of a misdemeanor, and upon conviction shall be fined not more than one thousand dollars ($1,000) or imprisoned in the county jail not more than six (6) months.

(Amended by Stats. 1983, Ch. 1092, Sec. 275. Effective September 27, 1983. Operative January 1, 1984, by Sec. 427 of Ch. 1092.)

381b.

Any person who possesses nitrous oxide or any substance containing nitrous oxide, with the intent to breathe, inhale, or ingest for the purpose of causing a condition of intoxication, elation, euphoria, dizziness, stupefaction, or dulling of the senses or for the purpose of, in any manner, changing, distorting, or disturbing the audio, visual, or mental processes, or who knowingly and with the intent to do so is under the influence of nitrous oxide or any material containing nitrous oxide is guilty of a misdemeanor. This section shall not apply to any person who is under the influence of nitrous oxide or any material containing nitrous oxide pursuant to an administration for the purpose of medical, surgical, or dental care by a person duly licensed to administer such an agent.

(Amended by Stats. 1984, Ch. 999, Sec. 1.)

381c.

(a) As used in this section, "nitrous oxide" refers to any of the following substances: N2O, dinitrogen monoxide, dinitrogen oxide, nitrogen oxide, or laughing gas.

(b) Every person who sells, furnishes, administers, distributes, gives away, or offers to sell, furnish, administer, distribute, or give away a device, canister, tank, or receptacle either exclusively containing nitrous oxide or exclusively containing a chemical compound mixed with nitrous oxide, to a person under 18 years of age is guilty of a misdemeanor. The court shall consider ordering the person to perform community service as a condition of probation.

(c) (1) It is a defense to this crime that the defendant honestly and reasonably believed that the minor involved in the offense was at least 18 years of age.

(2) The defendant shall bear the burden of establishing this defense by a preponderance of the evidence.

(d) For the purpose of preventing a violation of this section, any person may refuse to sell, furnish, administer, distribute, or give away a device, canister, tank, or receptacle either exclusively containing nitrous oxide or exclusively containing a chemical compound mixed with nitrous oxide to a person who is unable to produce adequate proof of age of majority.

(e) On and after July 1, 2010, the court shall order the suspension of the business license, for a period of up to one year, of a person who knowingly violates this section after having been previously convicted of a violation of this section, unless the owner of the business license can demonstrate a good faith attempt to prevent illegal sales or deliveries by the owner's employees.

(f) This section shall not apply to any person who administers nitrous oxide for the purpose of providing medical or dental care, if administered by a medical or dental practitioner licensed by this state or at the direction or under the supervision of a practitioner licensed by this state.

(g) This section does not apply to the sale of nitrous oxide contained in food products for use as a propellant.

(Added by Stats. 2009, Ch. 266, Sec. 1. (AB 1015) Effective January 1, 2010.)

381d.

(a) A person who dispenses or distributes nitrous oxide to a person, and knows or should know that the person is going to use the nitrous oxide in violation of Section 381b, and that person proximately causes great bodily injury or death to himself, herself, or another person, is guilty of a misdemeanor, and shall be punished by imprisonment in a county jail, not to exceed six months, or by a fine not to exceed one thousand dollars ($1,000), or by both that fine and imprisonment.

(b) This section shall not preclude prosecution under any other law.

(Added by Stats. 2014, Ch. 458, Sec. 1. (AB 1735) Effective January 1, 2015.)

381e.

(a) A person who dispenses or distributes nitrous oxide shall record each transaction involving the dispensing or distribution of nitrous oxide in a written or electronic document. The person dispensing or distributing the nitrous oxide shall require the purchaser to sign the document and provide a complete residential address and present a valid government-issued photo identification. The person dispensing or distributing the nitrous oxide shall sign and date the document and shall retain the document at the person's business address for one year from the date of the transaction. The person shall make the documents available during normal business hours for inspection and copying, upon presentation of a duly authorized search warrant, by officers or employees of the California State Board of Pharmacy or of other law enforcement agencies of this state or the United States.

(b) The document used to record each transaction shall inform the purchaser of all of the following:

(1) That inhalation of nitrous oxide outside of a clinical setting may have dangerous health effects.

(2) That it is a violation of state law to possess nitrous oxide or any substance containing nitrous oxide, with the intent to breathe, inhale, or ingest it for the purpose of intoxication.

(3) That it is a violation of state law to knowingly distribute or dispense nitrous oxide or any substance containing nitrous oxide, to a person who intends to breathe, inhale, or ingest it for the purpose of intoxication.

(c) This section shall not apply to any person who administers nitrous oxide for the purpose of providing medical or dental care, if administered by a medical or dental practitioner licensed by this state or at the direction or under the supervision of a practitioner licensed by this state.

(d) This section does not apply to the sale of nitrous oxide contained in food products for use as a propellant.

(e) This section shall not apply to the sale or distribution of nitrous oxide by a wholesaler licensed by the Board of Pharmacy or manufacturer classified under Code Number 325120 or 424690 of the North American Industry Classification System (NAICS).

(f) (1) Information obtained from a person to whom nitrous oxide was distributed or dispensed pursuant to this section shall be confidential and shall be used solely for the purposes provided in this section.

(2) Except as provided in this section, a person who dispenses or distributes nitrous oxide shall not use, review, or disclose any information obtained pursuant to this section.

(3) A person who violates this subdivision shall be guilty of a misdemeanor, punishable by imprisonment in a county jail not to exceed six months, or by a fine not to exceed one thousand dollars ($1,000), or by both that fine and imprisonment.

(Added by Stats. 2014, Ch. 458, Sec. 2. (AB 1735) Effective January 1, 2015.)

382.

Every person who adulterates or dilutes any article of food, drink, drug, medicine, spirituous or malt liquor, or wine, or any article useful in compounding them, with the fraudulent intent to offer the same, or cause or permit it to be offered for sale as unadulterated or undiluted; and every person who fraudulently sells, or keeps or offers for sale the same, as unadulterated or undiluted, or who, in response to an inquiry for any article of food, drink, drug, medicine, spirituous or malt liquor, or wine, sells or offers for sale, a different article, or an article of a different character or manufacture, without first informing such purchaser of such difference, is guilty of a misdemeanor; provided, that no retail dealer shall be convicted under the provisions of this section if he shall prove a written guaranty of purity obtained from the person from whom he purchased such adulterated or diluted goods.

(Amended by Stats. 1903, Ch. 254.)

382.4.

No person, other than a licensed veterinarian, shall administer succinylcholine, also known as sucostrin, to any dog or cat.

Violation of this section shall constitute a misdemeanor.

(Added by Stats. 1976, Ch. 1083.)

382.5.

Every person who sells, dispenses, administers or prescribes dinitrophenol for any purpose shall be guilty of a felony, punishable by a fine not less than one thousand dollars ($1,000) nor more than ten thousand dollars ($10,000), or by imprisonment pursuant to subdivision (h) of Section 1170, or by both that fine and imprisonment. This section shall not apply to dinitrophenol manufactured or sold as an economic poison registered under the provision of Section 12811 of the Food and Agricultural Code nor to sales for use in manufacturing or for scientific purposes, and not for human consumption.

(Amended by Stats. 2011, Ch. 15, Sec. 340. (AB 109) Effective April 4, 2011. Operative October 1, 2011, by Sec. 636 of Ch. 15, as amended by Stats. 2011, Ch. 39, Sec. 68.)

382.6.

Every person who sells, dispenses, administers or prescribes preparations containing diphenylamine, paraphenylenediamine, or paratoluylenediamine, or a derivative of any such chemicals, to be used as eyebrow and eyelash dye, shall be guilty of a felony, punishable by a fine not less than one thousand dollars ($1,000) nor more than ten thousand dollars ($10,000), or by imprisonment pursuant to subdivision (h) of Section 1170, or by both that fine and imprisonment.

(Amended by Stats. 2011, Ch. 15, Sec. 341. (AB 109) Effective April 4, 2011. Operative October 1, 2011, by Sec. 636 of Ch. 15, as amended by Stats. 2011, Ch. 39, Sec. 68.)

382.7.

Every person who knowingly prescribes, dispenses, administers, or furnishes any liquid silicone substance for the purpose of injection into a human breast or mammary is guilty of a misdemeanor.

(Added by Stats. 1976, Ch. 949.)

383.

Every person who knowingly sells, or keeps or offers for sale, or otherwise disposes of any article of food, drink, drug, or medicine, knowing that the same is adulterated or has become tainted, decayed, spoiled, or otherwise unwholesome or unfit to be eaten or drunk, with intent to permit the same to be eaten or drunk, is guilty of a misdemeanor, and must be fined not exceeding one thousand dollars ($1,000), or imprisoned in the county jail not exceeding six months, or both, and may, in the discretion of the court, be adjudged to pay, in addition, all the necessary expenses, not exceeding one thousand dollars ($1,000), incurred in inspecting and analyzing such articles. The term "drug," as used herein, includes all medicines for internal or external use, antiseptics, disinfectants, and cosmetics. The term "food," as used herein, includes all articles used for food or drink by man, whether simple, mixed, or compound. Any article is deemed to be adulterated within the meaning of this section:

(a) In case of drugs: (1) if, when sold under or by a name recognized in the United States Pharmacopoeia, it differs materially from the standard of strength, quality, or purity laid down therein; (2) if, when sold under or by a name not recognized in the United States Pharmacopoeia, but which is found in some other pharmacopoeia or other standard work on materia medica, it differs materially from the standard of strength, quality, or purity laid down in such work; (3) if its strength, quality, or purity falls below the professed standard under which it is sold.

(b) In the case of food: (1) if any substance or substances have been mixed with it, so as to lower or depreciate, or injuriously affect its quality, strength, or purity; (2) if any inferior or cheaper substance or substances have been substituted wholly or in part for it; (3) if any valuable or necessary constituent or ingredient has been wholly or in part abstracted from it; (4) if it is an imitation of, or is sold under the name of, another article; (5) if it consists wholly, or in part, of a diseased, decomposed, putrid, infected, tainted, or rotten animal or vegetable substance or article, whether manufactured or not; or in the case of milk, if it is the produce of a diseased animal; (6) if it is colored, coated, polished, or powdered, whereby damage or inferiority is concealed, or if by any means it is made to appear better or of greater value than it really is; (7) if it contains any added substance or ingredient which is poisonous or injurious to health.

(Amended by Stats. 1976, Ch. 1125.)

383a.

Any person, firm, or corporation, who sells or offers for sale, or has in his or its possession for sale, any butter manufactured by boiling, melting, deodorizing, or renovating, which is the product of stale, rancid, or decomposed butter, or by any other process whereby stale, rancid, or decomposed butter is manufactured to resemble or appear like creamery or dairy butter, unless the same is plainly stenciled or branded upon each and every package, barrel, firkin, tub, pail, square, or roll, in letters not less than one half inch in length, "process butter," or "renovated butter," in such a manner as to advise the purchaser of the real character of such "process" or "renovated" butter, is guilty of a misdemeanor.

(Added by Stats. 1905, Ch. 573.)

383b.

Every person who with intent to defraud, sells or exposes for sale any meat or meat preparations, and falsely represents the same to be kosher, whether such meat or meat preparations be raw or prepared for human consumption, or as having been prepared under and from a product or products sanctioned by the orthodox Hebrew religious requirements; or falsely represents any food product, or the contents of any package or container, to be so constituted and prepared, by having or permitting to be inscribed thereon the words "kosher" in any language; or sells or exposes for sale in the same place of business both kosher and nonkosher meat or meat preparations, either raw or prepared for human consumption, who fails to indicate on his window signs in all display advertising in block letters at least four inches in height "kosher and nonkosher meats sold here"; or who exposes for sale in any show window or place of business as both kosher and nonkosher meat preparations, either raw or prepared for human

consumption, who fails to display over each kind of meat or meat preparation so exposed a sign in block letters at least four inches in height, reading "kosher meat" or "nonkosher meat" as the case may be; or sells or exposes for sale in any restaurant or any other place where food products are sold for consumption on the premises, any article of food or food preparations and falsely represents the same to be kosher, or as having been prepared in accordance with the orthodox Hebrew religious requirements; or sells or exposes for sale in such restaurant, or such other place, both kosher and nonkosher food or food preparations for consumption on the premises, not prepared in accordance with the Jewish ritual, or not sanctioned by the Hebrew orthodox religious requirements, and who fails to display on his window signs in all display advertising, in block letters at least four inches in height "kosher and nonkosher food served here" is guilty of a misdemeanor and upon conviction thereof be punishable by a fine of not less than one hundred dollars ($100), nor more than six hundred dollars ($600), or imprisonment in the county jail of not less than 30 days, nor more than 90 days, or both such fine and imprisonment.

The word "kosher" is here defined to mean a strict compliance with every Jewish law and custom pertaining and relating to the killing of the animal or fowl from which the meat is taken or extracted, the dressing, treatment and preparation thereof for human consumption, and the manufacture, production, treatment and preparation of such other food or foods in connection wherewith Jewish laws and customs obtain and to the use of tools, implements, vessels, utensils, dishes and containers that are used in connection with the killing of such animals and fowls and the dressing, preparation, production, manufacture and treatment of such meats and other products, foods and food stuffs.

(Amended by Stats. 1983, Ch. 1092, Sec. 278. Effective September 27, 1983. Operative January 1, 1984, by Sec. 427 of Ch. 1092.)

383c.

Every person who with intent to defraud, sells or exposes for sale any meat or meat preparations, and falsely represents the same to be halal, whether the meat or meat preparations is raw or prepared for human consumption, or as having been prepared under and from a product or products sanctioned by the Islamic religious requirements; or falsely represents any food product, or the contents of any package or container, to be so constituted and prepared, by having or permitting to be inscribed thereon the word "halal" in any language; or sells or exposes for sale in the same place of business both halal and nonhalal meat or meat preparations, either raw or prepared for human consumption, who fails to indicate on his or her window signs in all display advertising in block letters at least four inches in height "halal and nonhalal meats sold here"; or who exposes for sale in any show window or place of business as both halal and nonhalal meat preparations, either raw or prepared for human consumption, who fails to display over each kind of meat or meat preparation so exposed a sign in block letters at least four inches in height, reading "halal meat" or "nonhalal meat" as the case may be; or sells or exposes for sale in any restaurant or any other place where food products are sold for consumption on the premises, any article of food or food preparations and falsely represents the same to be halal, or as having been prepared in accordance with the Islamic religious requirements; or sells or exposes for sale in a restaurant, or other place, both halal and nonhalal food or food preparations for consumption on the premises, not prepared in accordance with the Islamic ritual, or not sanctioned by Islamic religious requirements, and who fails to display on his or her window signs in all display advertising, in block letters at least four inches in height "halal and nonhalal food served here" is guilty of a misdemeanor and upon conviction thereof be punishable by a fine of not less than one hundred dollars ($100), nor more than six hundred dollars ($600), or imprisonment in a county jail of not less than 30 days, nor more than 90 days, or both that fine and imprisonment.

The word "halal" is here defined to mean a strict compliance with every Islamic law and custom pertaining and relating to the killing of the animal or fowl from which the meat is taken or extracted, the dressing, treatment, and preparation thereof for human consumption, and the manufacture, production, treatment, and preparation of other food or foods in connection wherewith Islamic laws and customs obtain and to the use of tools, implements, vessels, utensils, dishes, and containers that are used in connection with the killing of animals and fowls and the dressing, preparation, production, manufacture, and treatment of meats and other products, foods, and food stuffs.

(Amended by Stats. 2003, Ch. 62, Sec. 226. Effective January 1, 2004.)

384.

(a) Any person who shall wilfully refuse to immediately relinquish a party line when informed that such line is needed for an emergency call, and in fact such line is needed for an emergency call, to a fire department or police department or for medical aid or ambulance service, or any person who shall secure the use of a party line by falsely stating that such line is needed for an emergency call, shall be guilty of a misdemeanor.

(b) "Party line" as used in this section means a subscribers' line telephone circuit, consisting of two or more main telephone stations connected therewith, each station with a distinctive ring or telephone number. "Emergency" as used in this section means a situation in which property or human life is in jeopardy and the prompt summoning of aid is essential.

(c) Every telephone directory hereafter published and distributed to the members of the general public in this State or in any portion thereof which lists the calling numbers of telephones of any telephone exchange located in this State shall contain a notice which explains the offense provided for in this section, such notice to be printed in type which is not smaller than any other type on the same page and to be preceded by the word "warning" printed in type at least as large as the largest type on the same page; provided, that the provisions of this subdivision shall not apply to those directories distributed solely for business advertising purposes, commonly known as classified directories, nor to any telephone directory heretofore distributed to the general public.

Any person, firm or corporation providing telephone service which distributes or causes to be distributed in this State copies of a telephone directory which is subject to the provisions of this section and which do not contain the notice herein provided for shall be guilty of a misdemeanor.

(Added by Stats. 1957, Ch. 533.)

384.5.

(a) (1) Any person who removes any minor forest products from the property where the products were cut and transports the products upon any public road or highway shall have in the person's possession a valid bill of sale for the products or a written permit issued by the owner of the property from which the products were removed authorizing the removal and transport.

(2) Any such permit or bill of sale shall include, but is not limited to, all of the following:

(A) The name, address, and signature of the landowner, and phone number, if available.

(B) The name, address, and signature of the permittee or purchaser.

(C) The amount, species, and type of minor forest products to be removed and transported.

(D) A description sufficient to identify the property from which the minor forest products are to be removed.

(E) The date of issuance of the permit or bill of sale and the duration of the period of time within which the minor forest products may be removed.

(F) Any conditions or additional information which the landowner may impose or include.

(3) Any permit for the removal of minor forest products from public lands that is issued by the United States Forest Service or the Bureau of Land Management is sufficient for the purposes of this subdivision, regardless of whether the permit conforms to the specific requirements as to content set forth in paragraph (2).

(4) For the purposes of this subdivision, "minor forest products" means firewood, posts, shakeboards, shake and shingle bolts, or split products, in quantities exceeding 20 cubic feet in volume, and burlwood or stumps, in quantities of two or more.

(b) This section shall not apply to the transport of any minor forest products carried in a passenger vehicle, as defined in Section 465 of the Vehicle Code.
(c) Violation of subdivision (a) is a misdemeanor punishable by a fine of not more than one thousand dollars ($1,000) or by imprisonment in a county jail for not more than six months or by both that fine and imprisonment.
(Amended by Stats. 1988, Ch. 225, Sec. 1.)

384a.
(a) (1) A person shall not willfully or negligently cut, destroy, mutilate, or remove plant material that is growing upon state or county highway rights-of-way.
(2) A person shall not willfully or negligently cut, destroy, mutilate, or remove plant material that is growing upon public land or upon land that is not his or hers without a written permit from the owner of the land, signed by the owner of the land or the owner's authorized agent, as provided in subdivision (c).
(3) A person shall not knowingly sell, offer or expose for sale, or transport for sale plant material that is cut or removed in violation of this subdivision.
(b) For purposes of this section, "plant material" means a tree, shrub, fern, herb, bulb, cactus, flower, huckleberry, or redwood green, or a portion of any of those, or the leaf mold on those plants. "Plant material" does not include a tree, shrub, fern, herb, bulb, cactus, flower, or greens declared by law to be a public nuisance.
(c) (1) The written permit required by paragraph (2) of subdivision (a) shall be signed by the landowner, or the landowner's authorized agent, and acknowledged before a notary public, or other person authorized by law to take acknowledgments. The permit shall contain the number and species of trees and amount of plant material, and shall contain the legal description of the real property as usually found in deeds and conveyances of the land on which cutting or removal shall take place. One copy of the permit shall be filed in the office of the sheriff of the county in which the land described in the permit is located. The permit shall be filed prior to the commencement of cutting or removal of plant material authorized by the permit.
(2) The permit required by this section need not be notarized or filed with the sheriff when five or less pounds of shrubs or boughs are to be cut or removed.
(d) A county or state fire warden; personnel of the Department of Forestry and Fire Protection, as designated by the Director of Forestry and Fire Protection; personnel of the United States Forest Service, as designated by the Regional Forester, Region 5, of the United States Forest Service; or a peace officer of the State of California, may enforce the provisions of this section and may confiscate any and all plant material unlawfully cut or removed or knowingly sold, offered, or exposed or transported for sale as provided in this section.
(e) This section does not apply to any of the following:
(1) An employee of the state or of a political subdivision of the state who is engaged in work upon a state, county, or public road or highway while performing work under the supervision of the state or a political subdivision of the state.
(2) A person engaged in the necessary cutting or trimming of plant material for the purpose of protecting or maintaining an electric powerline, telephone line, or other property of a public utility.
(3) A person engaged in logging operations or fire suppression.
(f) A violation of this section shall be a misdemeanor, punishable by a fine of not more than one thousand dollars ($1,000), by imprisonment in a county jail for not more than six months, or by both that fine and imprisonment.
(Amended by Stats. 2015, Ch. 499, Sec. 2. (SB 795) Effective January 1, 2016.)

384b.
For the purposes of Sections 384c through 384f, inclusive, unless the context otherwise requires, the definitions contained in this section govern the construction of those sections.
(a) "Person" includes an employee with wages as his or her sole compensation.
(b) "Permit" means a permit as required by Section 384a.
(c) "Tree" means any evergreen tree or top thereof which is harvested without having the limbs and foliage removed.
(d) "Shrub" means any toyon or Christmas red-berry shrub or any of the following native desert plants: all species of the family Cactaceae (cactus family); and Agave deserti (desert agave), Agave utahensis (Utah agave), Nolina bigelovii, Nolina parryi (Parry nolina), Nolina wolfii, Yucca baccata, Yucca brevifolia (Joshua tree), Yucca schidigera (Mohave yucca), Yucca whipplei (Whipple yucca), Cercidium floridum (blue palo verde), Cercidium microphyllum (little leaf palo verde), Dalea spinosa (smoke tree), Olneya tesota (ironwood tree), and Fouquieria splendens (ocotillo), or any part thereof, except the fruit thereof, which is harvested without having the limbs and foliage removed.
(e) "Bough" means any limb or foliage removed from an evergreen tree.
(f) "Peace officer" means any county or state fire warden, personnel of the Department of Forestry and Fire Protection as designated by the Director of Forestry and Fire Protection, personnel of the United States Forest Service as designated by the Regional Forester, Region 5 of the United States Forest Service, personnel of the United States Department of the Interior as designated by them, or any peace officer of the State of California.
(g) "Harvest" means to remove or cut and remove from the place where grown.
(h) "Harvester" means a person who harvests a tree, shrub, or bough.
(Amended by Stats. 1992, Ch. 427, Sec. 126. Effective January 1, 1993.)

384c.
Persons purchasing trees, shrubs, or boughs from harvesters thereof shall not transport more than five trees or more than five pounds of shrubs or boughs on the public roads or highways without obtaining from the seller of the trees, shrubs, or boughs and having validated as provided in Section 384d a transportation tag for each load of the trees, shrubs, or boughs.
Unless a valid transportation tag issued in California for a tree, shrub, or bough has already been obtained, persons who harvest trees, shrubs, or boughs from their own land or the land of another or who are in possession of trees, shrubs, or boughs shall, before transporting on the public roads or highways or selling or consigning for removal and transportation over the public roads and highways more than five trees or more than five pounds of other shrubs or boughs, file with the sheriff of each county in which the trees, shrubs, or boughs are to be harvested an application for transportation tags and obtain a supply of these transportation tags sufficient to provide one tag for each load of trees, shrubs, or boughs to be so transported or sold.
No person shall knowingly make any false statement on any application for the transportation tags and the application shall contain, but is not limited to, the following information:
(a) The name and address of the applicant.
(b) The amount and species of trees, shrubs, or boughs to be transported.
(c) The name of the county from which the trees, shrubs, or boughs are to be removed.
(d) A legal description of the real property from which the trees, shrubs, or boughs are to be removed.
(e) The name or names of the owner of the real property from which the trees, shrubs, or boughs are to be removed.
(f) The applicant's timber operator permit number, if the harvesting of the trees, shrubs, or boughs is subject to the Z'berg-Nejedly Forest Practice Act of 1973 (Chapter 8 (commencing with Section 4511) of Part 2 of Division 4 of the Public Resources Code).
(g) The destination of the trees, shrubs, or boughs.
(h) The proposed date or dates of the transportation.
Every applicant shall, at the time of application, show to the sheriff his or her permit or proof of ownership of the trees, shrubs, or boughs. The application forms and transportation tags shall be printed and distributed by the sheriff of each county.

(Amended by Stats. 1982, Ch. 1318, Sec. 3.)

384d.
Upon the filing of an application containing the information required by Section 384c, and the presentation of a permit or proof of ownership as required by Section 384c, the county sheriff's office shall issue to persons who harvest or have in their possession, trees, shrubs or boughs within the county sufficient transportation tags stamped with the county seal and identified by the applicant's timber operator permit number, if any, to enable the person transporting any of the trees, shrubs or boughs harvested within the county by the applicant to have a tag accompany each and every load of such trees, shrubs or boughs. Harvesters of trees, shrubs or boughs, when selling from stockpile location, shall furnish to the purchaser of trees, shrubs or boughs a bill of sale and a transportation tag for each load or part thereof bearing the harvester's timber operator permit number, if any, and other information as hereinafter required.
The purchaser of harvested trees, shrubs or boughs or the harvester when transporting his own trees, shrubs or boughs shall have the transportation tag validated by a peace officer in the county of purchase or harvest or by the nearest peace officer in an adjacent county when the transportation route used does not pass an office of a peace officer in the county of purchase or harvest. The validated transportation tag or tags shall remain with the load to the marketing area.
The transportation tags shall be in two parts; one to be retained by the transporting party; one to be retained by the validating peace officer and forwarded to the county sheriff. The transportation tags shall be validated and in force only for the proposed date or dates of transportation as specified in the application for the transportation tags. The transportation tags will be validated without fee and each shall contain the following information: name and address of the person obtaining and using the tag; number or amount of each species of trees, shrubs and boughs in the load; make, model and license number of the transporting vehicle; the county of origin and county of destination; the specified period of time during which the transportation tag is in force; date and validating signature and title of a peace officer.
(Amended by Stats. 1977, Ch. 32.)

384e.
(a) The transportation tag described in Section 384d shall be presented to any peace officer upon demand.
(b) Failure to produce a transportation tag properly filled out and validated upon demand of any peace officer shall constitute sufficient grounds to hold in protective custody the entire load of trees, shrubs or boughs, until proof of legal right to transport is furnished.
(Added by Stats. 1963, Ch. 1830.)

384f.
Any person violating any of the provisions of Sections 384b through 384f shall be guilty of a misdemeanor and upon conviction thereof shall be punished by a fine of not more than one thousand dollars ($1,000) or by imprisonment in the county jail not exceeding six months or by both such fine and imprisonment.
(Amended by Stats. 1983, Ch. 1092, Sec. 281. Effective September 27, 1983. Operative January 1, 1984, by Sec. 427 of Ch. 1092.)

384h.
Every person who willfully or negligently, while hunting upon the inclosed lands of another, kills, maims, or wounds an animal, the property of another, is guilty of a misdemeanor.
(Added by renumbering Section 384c by Stats. 1963, Ch. 1830.)

384i.
(a) Sections 384a to 384f, inclusive, shall not apply to maintenance and construction activities of public agencies and their employees.
(b) Sections 384b to 384f, inclusive, shall not apply to native desert plants described in subdivision (b) of Section 384b, that have been propagated and cultivated by human beings and which are being transported under Section 6922 or 6923 of the Food and Agricultural Code, pursuant to a valid nursery stock certificate.
(c) Sections 384a to 384f, inclusive, shall not apply to any act regulated by the provisions of Division 23 (commencing with Section 80001) of the Food and Agricultural Code.
(Amended by Stats. 1987, Ch. 828, Sec. 25.)

385.
(a) The term "high voltage" as used in this section means a voltage in excess of 750 volts, measured between conductors or measured between the conductor and the ground.
The term "overhead conductor" as used in this section means any electrical conductor (either bare or insulated) installed above the ground except such conductors as are enclosed in iron pipe or other metal covering of equal strength.
(b) Any person who either personally or through an employee or agent, or as an employee or agent of another, operates, places, erects or moves any tools, machinery, equipment, material, building or structure within six feet of a high voltage overhead conductor is guilty of a misdemeanor.
(c) It shall be a misdemeanor to own, operate or to employ any person to operate, any crane, derrick, power shovel, drilling rig, hay loader, hay stacker, pile driver, or similar apparatus, any part of which is capable of vertical, lateral or swinging motion, unless there is posted and maintained in plain view of the operator thereof, a durable warning sign legible at 12 feet, reading: "Unlawful to operate this equipment within six feet of high voltage lines."
Each day's failure to post or maintain such sign shall constitute a separate violation.
(d) The provisions of this section shall not apply to (1) the construction, reconstruction, operation or maintenance of any high voltage overhead conductor, or its supporting structures or appurtenances by persons authorized by the owner, or (2) the operation of standard rail equipment which is normally used in the transportation of freight or passengers, or the operation of relief trains or other emergency railroad equipment by persons authorized by the owner, or (3) any construction, reconstruction, operation or maintenance of any overhead structures covered by the rules for overhead line construction prescribed by the Public Utilities Commission of the State of California.
(Added by Stats. 1947, Ch. 1229.)

386.
(a) Any person who willfully or maliciously constructs or maintains a fire-protection system in any structure with the intent to install a fire protection system which is known to be inoperable or to impair the effective operation of a system, so as to threaten the safety of any occupant or user of the structure in the event of a fire, shall be subject to imprisonment pursuant to subdivision (h) of Section 1170 for two, three, or four years.
(b) A violation of subdivision (a) which proximately results in great bodily injury or death is a felony punishable by imprisonment pursuant to subdivision (h) of Section 1170 for five, six, or seven years.
(c) As used in this section, "fire-protection system" includes, but is not limited to, an automatic fire sprinkler system, standpipe system, automatic fixed fire extinguishing system, and fire alarm system.
(d) For purposes of this section, the following definitions shall control:
(1) "Automatic fire sprinkler system" means an integrated system of underground and overhead piping designed in accordance with fire protection engineering standards. The portion of the sprinkler system above ground is a network of specially sized or hydraulically designed piping installed in a building, structure, or area, generally overhead, and to which sprinklers are attached in a systematic pattern. The valve controlling each system riser is located in the system riser or its supply piping. Each sprinkler system riser includes a device for activating an alarm when the system is in

operation. The system is normally activated by heat from a fire, and it discharges water over the fire area.
(2) "Standpipe system" means an arrangement of piping, valves, and hose connectors and allied equipment installed in a building or structure with the hose connectors located in a manner that water can be discharged in streams or spray patterns through attached hose and nozzles. The purpose of the system is to extinguish a fire, thereby protecting a building or structure and its contents and occupants. This system relies upon connections to water supply systems or pumps, tanks, and other equipment necessary to provide an adequate supply of water to the hose connectors.
(3) "Automatic fixed fire extinguishing system" means either of the following:
(A) An engineered fixed extinguishing system which is custom designed for a particular hazard, using components which are approved or listed only for their broad performance characteristics. Components may be arranged into a variety of configurations. These systems shall include, but not be limited to, dry chemical systems, carbon dioxide systems, halogenated agent systems, steam systems, high expansion foam systems, foam extinguishing systems, and liquid agent systems.
(B) A pre-engineered fixed extinguishing system is a system where the number of components and their configurations are included in the description of the system's approval and listing. These systems include, but are not limited to, dry chemical systems, carbon dioxide systems, halogenated agent systems, and liquid agent systems.
(4) "Fire alarm system" means a control unit and a combination of electrical interconnected devices designed and intended to cause an alarm or warning of fire in a building or structure by either manual or automatic activation, or by both, and includes the systems installed throughout any building or portion thereof.
(5) "Structure" means any building, whether private, commercial, or public, or any bridge, tunnel, or powerplant.
(Amended by Stats. 2011, Ch. 15, Sec. 342. (AB 109) Effective April 4, 2011. Operative October 1, 2011, by Sec. 636 of Ch. 15, as amended by Stats. 2011, Ch. 39, Sec. 68.)
387.
(a) Any corporation, limited liability company, or person who is a manager with respect to a product, facility, equipment, process, place of employment, or business practice, is guilty of a public offense punishable by imprisonment in the county jail for a term not exceeding one year, or by a fine not exceeding ten thousand dollars ($10,000), or by both that fine and imprisonment; or by imprisonment pursuant to subdivision (h) of Section 1170 for 16 months, two, or three years, or by a fine not exceeding twenty-five thousand dollars ($25,000); or by both that fine and imprisonment, but if the defendant is a corporation or a limited liability company the fine shall not exceed one million dollars ($1,000,000), if that corporation, limited liability company, or person does all of the following:
(1) Has actual knowledge of a serious concealed danger that is subject to the regulatory authority of an appropriate agency and is associated with that product or a component of that product or business practice.
(2) Knowingly fails during the period ending 15 days after the actual knowledge is acquired, or if there is imminent risk of great bodily harm or death, immediately, to do both of the following:
(A) Inform the Division of Occupational Safety and Health in the Department of Industrial Relations in writing, unless the corporation, limited liability company, or manager has actual knowledge that the division has been so informed.
Where the concealed danger reported pursuant to this paragraph is subject to the regulatory authority of an agency other than the Division of Occupational Safety and Health in the Department of Industrial Relations, it shall be the responsibility of the Division of Occupational Safety and Health in the Department of Industrial Relations, within 24 hours of receipt of the information, to telephonically notify the appropriate government agency of the hazard, and promptly forward any written notification received.
(B) Warn its affected employees in writing, unless the corporation, limited liability company, or manager has actual knowledge that the employees have been so warned.
The requirement for disclosure is not applicable if the hazard is abated within the time prescribed for reporting, unless the appropriate regulatory agency nonetheless requires disclosure by regulation.
Where the Division of Occupational Safety and Health in the Department of Industrial Relations was not notified, but the corporation, limited liability company, or manager reasonably and in good faith believed that they were complying with the notification requirements of this section by notifying another government agency, as listed in paragraph (8) of subdivision (d), no penalties shall apply.
(b) As used in this section:
(1) "Manager" means a person having both of the following:
(A) Management authority in or as a business entity.
(B) Significant responsibility for any aspect of a business that includes actual authority for the safety of a product or business practice or for the conduct of research or testing in connection with a product or business practice.
(2) "Product" means an article of trade or commerce or other item of merchandise that is a tangible or an intangible good, and includes services.
(3) "Actual knowledge," used with respect to a serious concealed danger, means has information that would convince a reasonable person in the circumstances in which the manager is situated that the serious concealed danger exists.
(4) "Serious concealed danger," used with respect to a product or business practice, means that the normal or reasonably foreseeable use of, or the exposure of an individual to, the product or business practice creates a substantial probability of death, great bodily harm, or serious exposure to an individual, and the danger is not readily apparent to an individual who is likely to be exposed.
(5) "Great bodily harm" means a significant or substantial physical injury.
(6) "Serious exposure" means any exposure to a hazardous substance, when the exposure occurs as a result of an incident or exposure over time and to a degree or in an amount sufficient to create a substantial probability that death or great bodily harm in the future would result from the exposure.
(7) "Warn its affected employees" means give sufficient description of the serious concealed danger to all individuals working for or in the business entity who are likely to be subject to the serious concealed danger in the course of that work to make those individuals aware of that danger.
(8) "Appropriate government agency" means an agency on the following list that has regulatory authority with respect to the product or business practice and serious concealed dangers of the sort discovered:
(A) The Division of Occupational Safety and Health in the Department of Industrial Relations.
(B) State Department of Health Services.
(C) Department of Agriculture.
(D) County departments of health.
(E) The United States Food and Drug Administration.
(F) The United States Environmental Protection Agency.
(G) The National Highway Traffic Safety Administration.
(H) The Federal Occupation Safety and Health Administration.
(I) The Nuclear Regulatory Commission.
(J) The Consumer Product Safety Commission.
(K) The Federal Aviation Administration.
(L) The Federal Mine Safety and Health Review Commission.
(c) Notification received pursuant to this section shall not be used against any manager in any criminal case, except a prosecution for perjury or for giving a false statement.
(d) No person who is a manager of a limited liability company shall be personally liable for acts or omissions for which the limited liability company is liable under subdivision (a) solely by reason of being a manager of the limited liability company. A person who is a manager of a limited liability company may be held liable under subdivision (a) if that person is also a "manager" within the meaning of paragraph (1) of subdivision (b).
(Amended by Stats. 2011, Ch. 15, Sec. 343. (AB 109) Effective April 4, 2011. Operative October 1, 2011, by Sec. 636 of Ch. 15, as amended by Stats. 2011, Ch. 39, Sec. 68.)
395.
Every person who willfully makes or publishes any false statement, spreads any false rumor, or employs any other false or fraudulent means or device, with intent to affect the market price of any kind of property, is guilty of a misdemeanor.
(Enacted 1872.)
396.
(a) The Legislature hereby finds that during a state of emergency or local emergency, including, but not limited to, an earthquake, flood, fire, riot, storm, drought, plant or animal infestation or disease, or other natural or manmade disaster, some merchants have taken unfair advantage of consumers by greatly increasing prices for essential consumer goods and services. While the pricing of consumer goods and services is generally best left to the marketplace under ordinary conditions, when a declared state of emergency or local emergency results in abnormal disruptions of the market, the public interest requires that excessive and unjustified increases in the prices of essential consumer goods and services be prohibited. It is the intent of the Legislature in enacting this act to protect citizens from excessive and unjustified increases in the prices charged during or shortly after a declared state of emergency or local emergency for goods and services that are vital and necessary for the health, safety, and welfare of consumers. Further, it is the intent of the Legislature that this section be liberally construed so that its beneficial purposes may be served.
(b) Upon the proclamation of a state of emergency declared by the President of the United States or the Governor, or upon the declaration of a local emergency by an official, board, or other governing body vested with authority to make that declaration in any county, city, or city and county, and for a period of 30 days following that proclamation or declaration, it is unlawful for a person, contractor, business, or other entity to sell or offer to sell any consumer food items or goods, goods or services used for emergency cleanup, emergency supplies, medical supplies, home heating oil, building materials, housing, transportation, freight, and storage services, or gasoline or other motor fuels for a price of more than 10 percent greater than the price charged by that person for those goods or services immediately prior to the proclamation or declaration of emergency. However, a greater price increase is not unlawful if that person can prove that the increase in price was directly attributable to additional costs imposed on it by the supplier of the goods, or directly attributable to additional costs for labor or materials used to provide the services, during the state of emergency or local emergency, and the price is no more than 10 percent greater than the total of the cost to the seller plus the markup customarily applied by the seller for that good or service in the usual course of business immediately prior to the onset of the state of emergency or local emergency.
(c) Upon the proclamation of a state of emergency declared by the President of the United States or the Governor, or upon the declaration of a local emergency by an official, board, or other governing body vested with authority to make that declaration in any county, city, or city and county, and for a period of 180 days following that proclamation or declaration, it is unlawful for a contractor to sell or offer to sell any repair or reconstruction services or any services used in emergency cleanup for a price of more than 10 percent above the price charged by that person for those services immediately prior to the proclamation or declaration of emergency. However, a greater price increase is not unlawful if that person can prove that the increase in price was directly attributable to additional costs imposed on it by the supplier of the goods, or directly attributable to additional costs for labor or materials used to provide the services, during the state of emergency or local emergency, and the price represents no more than 10 percent greater than the total of the cost to the contractor plus the markup customarily applied by the contractor for that good or service in the usual course of business immediately prior to the onset of the state of emergency or local emergency.
(d) Upon the proclamation of a state of emergency declared by the President of the United States or the Governor, or upon the declaration of a local emergency by an official, board, or other governing body vested with authority to make that declaration in any county, city, or city and county, and for a period of 30 days following that proclamation or declaration, it is unlawful for an owner or operator of a hotel or motel to increase the hotel or motel's regular rates, as advertised immediately prior to the proclamation or declaration of emergency, by more than 10 percent. However, a greater price increase is not unlawful if the owner or operator can prove that the increase in price is directly attributable to additional costs imposed on it for goods or labor used in its business, to seasonal adjustments in rates that are regularly scheduled, or to previously contracted rates.
(e) Upon the proclamation of a state of emergency declared by the President of the United States or the Governor, or upon the declaration of a local emergency by an official, board, or other governing body vested with authority to make that declaration in any city, county, or city and county, and for a period of 30 days following that proclamation or declaration, or any period the proclamation or declaration is extended by the applicable authority, it is unlawful for any person, business, or other entity, to increase the rental price, as defined in paragraph (11) of subdivision (j), advertised, offered, or charged for housing, to an existing or prospective tenant, by more than 10 percent. However, a greater rental price increase is not unlawful if that person can prove that the increase is directly attributable to additional costs for repairs or additions beyond normal maintenance that were amortized over the rental term that caused the rent to be increased greater than 10 percent or that an increase was contractually agreed to by the tenant prior to the proclamation or declaration. It shall not be a defense to a prosecution under this subdivision that an increase in rental price was based on the length of the rental term, the inclusion of additional goods or services, except as provided in paragraph (11) of subdivision (j) with respect to furniture, or that the rent was offered by, or paid by, an insurance company, or other third party, on behalf of a tenant. This subdivision does not authorize a landlord to charge a price greater than the amount authorized by a local rent control ordinance.
(f) It is unlawful for a person, business, or other entity to evict any residential tenant of residential housing after the proclamation of a state of emergency declared by the President of the United States or the Governor, or upon the declaration of a local emergency by an official, board, or other governing body vested with authority to make that declaration in any city, county, or city and county, and for a period of 30 days following that proclamation or declaration, or any period that the proclamation or declaration is extended by the applicable authority and rent or offer to rent to another person at a rental price greater than the evicted tenant could be charged under this section. It shall not be a violation of this subdivision for a person, business, or other entity to continue an eviction process that was lawfully begun prior to the proclamation or declaration of emergency.
(g) The prohibitions of this section may be extended for additional 30-day periods, as needed, by a local legislative body, local official, the Governor, or the Legislature, if deemed necessary to protect the lives, property, or welfare of the citizens.
(h) A violation of this section is a misdemeanor punishable by imprisonment in a county jail for a period not exceeding one year, or by a fine of not more than ten thousand dollars ($10,000), or by both that fine and imprisonment.

(i) A violation of this section shall constitute an unlawful business practice and an act of unfair competition within the meaning of Section 17200 of the Business and Professions Code. The remedies and penalties provided by this section are cumulative to each other, the remedies under Section 17200 of the Business and Professions Code, and the remedies or penalties available under all other laws of this state.

(j) For the purposes of this section, the following terms have the following meanings:

(1) "State of emergency" means a natural or manmade emergency resulting from an earthquake, flood, fire, riot, storm, drought, plant or animal infestation or disease, or other natural or manmade disaster for which a state of emergency has been declared by the President of the United States or the Governor.

(2) "Local emergency" means a natural or manmade emergency resulting from an earthquake, flood, fire, riot, storm, drought, plant or animal infestation or disease, or other natural or manmade disaster for which a local emergency has been declared by an official, board, or other governing body vested with authority to make that declaration in any county, city, or city and county in California.

(3) "Consumer food item" means any article that is used or intended for use for food, drink, confection, or condiment by a person or animal.

(4) "Repair or reconstruction services" means services performed by any person who is required to be licensed under the Contractors' State License Law (Chapter 9 (commencing with Section 7000) of Division 3 of the Business and Professions Code), for repairs to residential or commercial property of any type that is damaged as a result of a disaster.

(5) "Emergency supplies" includes, but is not limited to, water, flashlights, radios, batteries, candles, blankets, soaps, diapers, temporary shelters, tape, toiletries, plywood, nails, and hammers.

(6) "Medical supplies" includes, but is not limited to, prescription and nonprescription medications, bandages, gauze, isopropyl alcohol, and antibacterial products.

(7) "Building materials" means lumber, construction tools, windows, and anything else used in the building or rebuilding of property.

(8) "Gasoline" means any fuel used to power any motor vehicle or power tool.

(9) "Transportation, freight, and storage services" means any service that is performed by any company that contracts to move, store, or transport personal or business property or that rents equipment for those purposes, including towing services.

(10) "Housing" means any rental housing with an initial lease term of no longer than one year, including, but not limited to, a space rented in a mobilehome park or campground.

(11) "Rental price" for housing means any of the following:

(A) For housing rented within one year prior to the time of the proclamation or declaration of emergency, the actual rental price paid by the tenant. For housing not rented at the time of the declaration or proclamation, but rented, or offered for rent, within one year prior to the proclamation or declaration of emergency, the most recent rental price offered before the proclamation or declaration of emergency. For housing rented at the time of the proclamation or declaration of emergency but which becomes vacant while the proclamation or declaration of emergency remains in effect and which is subject to any ordinance, rule, regulation, or initiative measure adopted by any local governmental entity that establishes a maximum amount that a landlord may charge a tenant for rent, the actual rental price paid by the previous tenant or the amount specified in subparagraph (B), whichever is greater. This amount may be increased by 5 percent if the housing was previously rented or offered for rent unfurnished, and it is now being offered for rent fully furnished. This amount shall not be adjusted for any other good or service, including, but not limited to, gardening or utilities currently or formerly provided in connection with the lease.

(B) For housing not rented and not offered for rent within one year prior to the proclamation or declaration of emergency, 160 percent of the fair market rent established by the United States Department of Housing and Urban Development. This amount may be increased by 5 percent if the housing is offered for rent fully furnished. This amount shall not be adjusted for any other good or service, including, but not limited to, gardening or utilities currently or formerly provided in connection with the lease.

(C) Housing advertised, offered, or charged, at a daily rate at the time of the declaration or proclamation of emergency, shall be subject to the rental price described in subparagraph (A), if the housing continues to be advertised, offered, or charged, at a daily rate. Housing advertised, offered, or charged, on a daily basis at the time of the declaration or proclamation of emergency, shall be subject to the rental price in subparagraph (B), if the housing is advertised, offered, or charged, on a periodic lease agreement after the declaration or proclamation of emergency.

(D) For mobilehome spaces rented to existing tenants at the time of the proclamation or declaration of emergency and subject to a local rent control ordinance, the amount authorized under the local rent control ordinance. For new tenants who enter into a rental agreement for a mobilehome space that is subject to rent control but not rented at the time of the proclamation or declaration of emergency, the amount of rent last charged for a space in the same mobilehome park. For mobilehome spaces not subject to a local rent control ordinance and not rented at the time of the proclamation or declaration of emergency, the amount of rent last charged for the space.

(12) "Goods" has the same meaning as defined in subdivision (c) of Section 1689.5 of the Civil Code.

(k) This section does not preempt any local ordinance prohibiting the same or similar conduct or imposing a more severe penalty for the same conduct prohibited by this section.

(l) A business offering an item for sale at a reduced price immediately prior to the proclamation or declaration of the emergency may use the price at which it usually sells the item to calculate the price pursuant to subdivision (b) or (c).

(m) This section does not prohibit an owner from evicting a tenant for any lawful reason, including pursuant to Section 1161 of the Code of Civil Procedure.

(Amended by Stats. 2018, Ch. 631, Sec. 2. (AB 1919) Effective January 1, 2019.)

396.5.

It shall be unlawful for any retail food store or wholesale food concern, as defined in Section 3(k) of the federal Food and Nutrition Act of 2008 (Public Law 95-113) (7 U.S.C. Sec. 2012(k)), or any person, to sell, furnish or give away any goods or services, other than those items authorized by the Food Stamp Act of 1964, as amended (Public Law 88-525) (Chapter 51 (commencing with Section 2011) of Title 7 of the United States Code), in exchange for CalFresh benefits issued pursuant to Chapter 10 (commencing with Section 18900), Part 6, Division 9 of the Welfare and Institutions Code.

Any violator of this section is guilty of a misdemeanor and shall be punished by a fine of not more than five thousand dollars ($5,000) or by imprisonment in the county jail not exceeding 90 days, or by both that fine and imprisonment.

(Amended by Stats. 2011, Ch. 227, Sec. 15. (AB 1400) Effective January 1, 2012.)

397.

Every person who sells or furnishes, or causes to be sold or furnished, intoxicating liquors to any habitual or common drunkard, or to any person who has been adjudged legally incompetent or insane by any court of this State and has not been restored to legal capacity, knowing such person to have been so adjudged, is guilty of a misdemeanor.

(Amended by Stats. 1953, Ch. 146.)

398.

(a) If a person owning or having custody or control of an animal knows, or has reason to know, that the animal bit another person, he or she shall, as soon as is practicable, but no later than 48 hours thereafter, provide the other person with his or her name,

address, telephone number, and the name and license tag number of the animal who bit the other person. If the person with custody or control of the animal at the time the bite occurs is a minor, he or she shall instead provide identification or contact information of an adult owner or responsible party. If the animal is required by law to be vaccinated against rabies, the person owning or having custody or control of the animal shall, within 48 hours of the bite, provide the other person with information regarding the status of the animal's vaccinations. Violation of this section is an infraction punishable by a fine of not more than one hundred dollars ($100).

(b) For purposes of this section, it is necessary for the skin of the person to be broken or punctured by the animal for the contact to be classified as a bite.

(Amended by Stats. 2008, Ch. 179, Sec. 178. Effective January 1, 2009.)

399.

(a) If any person owning or having custody or control of a mischievous animal, knowing its propensities, willfully suffers it to go at large, or keeps it without ordinary care, and the animal, while so at large, or while not kept with ordinary care, kills any human being who has taken all the precautions that the circumstances permitted, or which a reasonable person would ordinarily take in the same situation, is guilty of a felony.

(b) If any person owning or having custody or control of a mischievous animal, knowing its propensities, willfully suffers it to go at large, or keeps it without ordinary care, and the animal, while so at large, or while not kept with ordinary care, causes serious bodily injury to any human being who has taken all the precautions that the circumstances permitted, or which a reasonable person would ordinarily take in the same situation, is guilty of a misdemeanor or a felony.

(Amended by Stats. 2001, Ch. 257, Sec. 1. Effective September 5, 2001.)

399.5.

(a) Any person owning or having custody or control of a dog trained to fight, attack, or kill is guilty of a felony or a misdemeanor, punishable by imprisonment in a county jail not to exceed one year, or imprisonment pursuant to subdivision (h) of Section 1170 for two, three, or four years, or by a fine not exceeding ten thousand dollars ($10,000), or by both the fine and imprisonment, if, as a result of that person's failure to exercise ordinary care, the dog bites a human being, on two separate occasions or on one occasion causing substantial physical injury. No person shall be criminally liable under this section, however, unless he or she knew or reasonably should have known of the vicious or dangerous nature of the dog, or if the victim failed to take all the precautions that a reasonable person would ordinarily take in the same situation.

(b) Following the conviction of an individual for a violation of this section, the court shall hold a hearing to determine whether conditions of the treatment or confinement of the dog or other circumstances existing at the time of the bite or bites have changed so as to remove the danger to other persons presented by the animal. The court, after hearing, may make any order it deems appropriate to prevent the recurrence of such an incident, including, but not limited to, the removal of the animal from the area or its destruction if necessary.

(c) Nothing in this section shall authorize the bringing of an action pursuant to subdivision (a) based on a bite or bites inflicted upon a trespasser, upon a person who has provoked the dog or contributed to his or her own injuries, or by a dog used in military or police work if the bite or bites occurred while the dog was actually performing in that capacity. As used in this subdivision, "provocation" includes, but is not limited to, situations where a dog held on a leash by its owner or custodian reacts in a protective manner to a person or persons who approach the owner or custodian in a threatening manner.

(d) Nothing in this section shall be construed to affect the liability of the owner of a dog under Section 399 or any other provision of law.

(e) This section shall not apply to a veterinarian or an on-duty animal control officer while in the performance of his or her duties, or to a peace officer, as defined in Chapter 4.5 (commencing with Section 830) of Title 3 of Part 2, if he or she is assigned to a canine unit.

(Amended by Stats. 2011, Ch. 15, Sec. 344. (AB 109) Effective April 4, 2011. Operative October 1, 2011, by Sec. 636 of Ch. 15, as amended by Stats. 2011, Ch. 39, Sec. 68.)

401.

(a) Any person who deliberately aids, advises, or encourages another to commit suicide is guilty of a felony.

(b) A person whose actions are compliant with the provisions of the End of Life Option Act (Part 1.85 (commencing with Section 443) of Division 1 of the Health and Safety Code) shall not be prosecuted under this section.

(Amended by Stats. 2018, Ch. 245, Sec. 1. (AB 282) Effective January 1, 2019.)

402.

(a) (1) Every person who goes to the scene of an emergency, or stops at the scene of an emergency, for the purpose of viewing the scene or the activities of police officers, firefighters, emergency medical, or other emergency personnel, or military personnel coping with the emergency in the course of their duties during the time it is necessary for emergency vehicles or those personnel to be at the scene of the emergency or to be moving to or from the scene of the emergency for the purpose of protecting lives or property, unless it is part of the duties of that person's employment to view that scene or those activities, and thereby impedes police officers, firefighters, emergency medical, or other emergency personnel or military personnel, in the performance of their duties in coping with the emergency, is guilty of a misdemeanor.

(2) For purposes of this subdivision, a person shall include a person, regardless of his or her location, who operates or uses an unmanned aerial vehicle, remote piloted aircraft, or drone that is at the scene of an emergency.

(b) Every person who knowingly resists or interferes with the lawful efforts of a lifeguard in the discharge or attempted discharge of an official duty in an emergency situation, when the person knows or reasonably should know that the lifeguard is engaged in the performance of his or her official duty, is guilty of a misdemeanor.

(c) For the purposes of this section, an emergency includes a condition or situation involving injury to persons, damage to property, or peril to the safety of persons or property, which results from a fire, an explosion, an airplane crash, flooding, windstorm damage, a railroad accident, a traffic accident, a powerplant accident, a toxic chemical or biological spill, or any other natural or human-caused event.

(Amended by Stats. 2016, Ch. 817, Sec. 1. (AB 1680) Effective January 1, 2017.)

402a.

Every person who adulterates candy by using in its manufacture terra alba or other deleterious substances, or who sells or keeps for sale any candy or candies adulterated with terra alba, or any other deleterious substance, knowing the same to be adulterated, is guilty of a misdemeanor.

(Added by renumbering Section 402¼ by Stats. 1905, Ch. 573.)

402b.

Any person who discards or abandons or leaves in any place accessible to children any refrigerator, icebox, deep-freeze locker, clothes dryer, washing machine, or other appliance, having a capacity of one and one-half cubic feet or more, which is no longer in use, and which has not had the door removed or the hinges and such portion of the latch mechanism removed to prevent latching or locking of the door, is guilty of a misdemeanor. Any owner, lessee, or manager who knowingly permits such a refrigerator, icebox, deep-freeze locker, clothes dryer, washing machine, or other appliance to remain on premises under his control without having the door removed or the hinges and such portion of the latch mechanism removed to prevent latching or locking of the door, is guilty of a misdemeanor. Guilt of a violation of this section shall not, in itself, render one guilty of manslaughter, battery or other crime against a person who may suffer death or injury from entrapment in such a refrigerator, icebox, deep-freeze locker, clothes dryer, washing machine, or other appliance.

The provisions of this section shall not apply to any vendor or seller of refrigerators, iceboxes, deep-freeze lockers, clothes dryers, washing machines, or other appliances, who keeps or stores them for sale purposes, if the vendor or seller takes reasonable precautions to effectively secure the door of any such refrigerator, icebox, deep-freeze locker, clothes dryer, washing machine, or other appliance so as to prevent entrance by children small enough to fit therein.
(Amended by Stats. 1976, Ch. 1122.)

402c.
On and after January 1, 1970, any person who sells a new refrigerator, icebox, or deep-freeze locker not equipped with an integral lock in this state, having a capacity of two cubic feet or more, which cannot be opened from the inside by the exertion of 15 pounds of force against the latch edge of the closed door is guilty of a misdemeanor.
(Added by Stats. 1968, Ch. 232.)

TITLE 11. OF CRIMES AGAINST THE PUBLIC PEACE [403 - 420.1]
(Title 11 enacted 1872.)

403.
Every person who, without authority of law, willfully disturbs or breaks up any assembly or meeting that is not unlawful in its character, other than an assembly or meeting referred to in Section 302 of the Penal Code or Section 18340 of the Elections Code, is guilty of a misdemeanor.
(Amended by Stats. 1994, Ch. 923, Sec. 159. Effective January 1, 1995.)

404.
(a) Any use of force or violence, disturbing the public peace, or any threat to use force or violence, if accompanied by immediate power of execution, by two or more persons acting together, and without authority of law, is a riot.
(b) As used in this section, disturbing the public peace may occur in any place of confinement. Place of confinement means any state prison, county jail, industrial farm, or road camp, or any city jail, industrial farm, or road camp, or any juvenile hall, juvenile camp, juvenile ranch, or juvenile forestry camp.
(Amended by Stats. 1995, Ch. 132, Sec. 1. Effective January 1, 1996.)

404.6.
(a) Every person who with the intent to cause a riot does an act or engages in conduct that urges a riot, or urges others to commit acts of force or violence, or the burning or destroying of property, and at a time and place and under circumstances that produce a clear and present and immediate danger of acts of force or violence or the burning or destroying of property, is guilty of incitement to riot.
(b) Incitement to riot is punishable by a fine not exceeding one thousand dollars ($1,000), or by imprisonment in a county jail not exceeding one year, or by both that fine and imprisonment.
(c) Every person who incites any riot in the state prison or a county jail that results in serious bodily injury, shall be punished by either imprisonment in a county jail for not more than one year, or imprisonment pursuant to subdivision (h) of Section 1170.
(d) The existence of any fact that would bring a person under subdivision (c) shall be alleged in the complaint, information, or indictment and either admitted by the defendant in open court, or found to be true by the jury trying the issue of guilt, by the court where guilt is established by a plea of guilty or nolo contendere, or by trial by the court sitting without a jury.
(Amended by Stats. 2011, Ch. 15, Sec. 345. (AB 109) Effective April 4, 2011. Operative October 1, 2011, by Sec. 636 of Ch. 15, as amended by Stats. 2011, Ch. 39, Sec. 68.)

405.
Every person who participates in any riot is punishable by a fine not exceeding one thousand dollars, or by imprisonment in a county jail not exceeding one year, or by both such fine and imprisonment.
(Amended by Stats. 1957, Ch. 139.)

405a.
A person who participates in the taking by means of a riot of another person from the lawful custody of a peace officer is guilty of a felony, punishable by imprisonment pursuant to subdivision (h) of Section 1170 for two, three, or four years.
(Amended by Stats. 2015, Ch. 47, Sec. 1. (SB 629) Effective January 1, 2016.)

406.
Whenever two or more persons, assembled and acting together, make any attempt or advance toward the commission of an act which would be a riot if actually committed, such assembly is a rout.
(Enacted 1872.)

407.
Whenever two or more persons assemble together to do an unlawful act, or do a lawful act in a violent, boisterous, or tumultuous manner, such assembly is an unlawful assembly.
(Amended by Stats. 1969, Ch. 365.)

408.
Every person who participates in any rout or unlawful assembly is guilty of a misdemeanor.
(Enacted 1872.)

409.
Every person remaining present at the place of any riot, rout, or unlawful assembly, after the same has been lawfully warned to disperse, except public officers and persons assisting them in attempting to disperse the same, is guilty of a misdemeanor.
(Enacted 1872.)

409.3.
Whenever law enforcement officers and emergency medical technicians are at the scene of an accident, management of the scene of the accident shall be vested in the appropriate law enforcement agency, whose representative shall consult with representatives of other response agencies at the scene to ensure that all appropriate resources are properly utilized. However, authority for patient care management at the scene of an accident shall be determined in accordance with Section 1798.6 of the Health and Safety Code.
For purposes of this section, "management of the scene of an accident" means the coordination of operations which occur at the location of an accident.
(Amended by Stats. 1987, Ch. 1058, Sec. 6.)

409.5.
(a) Whenever a menace to the public health or safety is created by a calamity including a flood, storm, fire, earthquake, explosion, accident, or other disaster, officers of the Department of the California Highway Patrol, police departments, marshal's office or sheriff's office, any officer or employee of the Department of Forestry and Fire Protection designated a peace officer by subdivision (g) of Section 830.2, any officer or employee of the Department of Parks and Recreation designated a peace officer by subdivision (f) of Section 830.2, any officer or employee of the Department of Fish and Game designated a peace officer under subdivision (e) of Section 830.2, and any publicly employed full-time lifeguard or publicly employed full-time marine safety officer while acting in a supervisory position in the performance of his or her official duties, may close the area where the menace exists for the duration thereof by means of ropes, markers, or guards to any and all persons not authorized by the lifeguard or officer to enter or remain within the enclosed area. If the calamity creates an immediate menace

to the public health, the local health officer may close the area where the menace exists pursuant to the conditions set forth in this section.
(b) Officers of the Department of the California Highway Patrol, police departments, marshal's office or sheriff's office, officers of the Department of Fish and Game designated as peace officers by subdivision (e) of Section 830.2, or officers of the Department of Forestry and Fire Protection designated as peace officers by subdivision (g) of Section 830.2 may close the immediate area surrounding any emergency field command post or any other command post activated for the purpose of abating any calamity enumerated in this section or any riot or other civil disturbance to any and all unauthorized persons pursuant to the conditions set forth in this section whether or not the field command post or other command post is located near to the actual calamity or riot or other civil disturbance.
(c) Any unauthorized person who willfully and knowingly enters an area closed pursuant to subdivision (a) or (b) and who willfully remains within the area after receiving notice to evacuate or leave shall be guilty of a misdemeanor.
(d) Nothing in this section shall prevent a duly authorized representative of any news service, newspaper, or radio or television station or network from entering the areas closed pursuant to this section.
(Amended by Stats. 1996, Ch. 305, Sec. 44. Effective January 1, 1997.)

409.6.
(a) Whenever a menace to the public health or safety is created by an avalanche, officers of the Department of the California Highway Patrol, police departments, or sheriff's offices, any officer or employee of the Department of Forestry and Fire Protection designated a peace officer by subdivision (g) of Section 830.2, and any officer or employee of the Department of Parks and Recreation designated a peace officer by subdivision (f) of Section 830.2, may close the area where the menace exists for the duration thereof by means of ropes, markers, or guards to any and all persons not authorized by that officer to enter or remain within the closed area. If an avalanche creates an immediate menace to the public health, the local health officer may close the area where the menace exists pursuant to the conditions which are set forth above in this section.
(b) Officers of the Department of the California Highway Patrol, police departments, or sheriff's offices, or officers of the Department of Forestry and Fire Protection designated as peace officers by subdivision (g) of Section 830.2, may close the immediate area surrounding any emergency field command post or any other command post activated for the purpose of abating hazardous conditions created by an avalanche to any and all unauthorized persons pursuant to the conditions which are set forth in this section whether or not that field command post or other command post is located near the avalanche.
(c) Any unauthorized person who willfully and knowingly enters an area closed pursuant to subdivision (a) or (b) and who willfully remains within that area, or any unauthorized person who willfully remains within an area closed pursuant to subdivision (a) or (b), after receiving notice to evacuate or leave from a peace officer named in subdivision (a) or (b), shall be guilty of a misdemeanor. If necessary, a peace officer named in subdivision (a) or (b) may use reasonable force to remove from the closed area any unauthorized person who willfully remains within that area after receiving notice to evacuate or leave.
(d) Nothing in this section shall prevent a duly authorized representative of any news service, newspaper, or radio or television station or network from entering the areas closed pursuant to this section.
(Amended by Stats. 1996, Ch. 305, Sec. 45. Effective January 1, 1997.)

410.
If a magistrate or officer, having notice of an unlawful or riotous assembly, mentioned in this Chapter, neglects to proceed to the place of assembly, or as near thereto as he can with safety, and to exercise the authority with which he is invested for suppressing the same and arresting the offenders, he is guilty of a misdemeanor.
(Enacted 1872.)

412.
Any person, who, within this state, engages in, or instigates, aids, encourages, or does any act to further, a pugilistic contest, or fight, or ring or prize fight, or sparring or boxing exhibition, taking or to take place either within or without this state, between two or more persons, with or without gloves, for any price, reward or compensation, directly or indirectly, or who goes into training preparatory to such pugilistic contest, or fight, or ring or prize fight, or sparring or boxing exhibition, or acts as aider, abettor, backer, umpire, referee, trainer, second, surgeon, or assistant, at such pugilistic contest, or fight, or ring or prize fight, or sparring or boxing exhibition, or who sends or publishes a challenge or acceptance of a challenge, or who knowingly carries or delivers such challenge or acceptance, or who gives or takes or receives any tickets, tokens, prize, money, or thing of value, from any person or persons, for the purpose of seeing or witnessing any such pugilistic contest, or fight, or ring or prize fight, or sparring or boxing exhibition, or who, being the owner, lessee, agent, or occupant of any vessel, building, hotel, room, enclosure or ground, or any part thereof, whether for gain, hire, reward or gratuitously or otherwise, permits the same to be used or occupied for such a pugilistic contest, or fight, or ring or prize fight, or sparring or boxing exhibition, or who lays, makes, offers or accepts, a bet or bets, or wager or wagers, upon the result or any feature of any pugilistic contest, or fight, or ring or prize fight, or sparring or boxing exhibition, or acts as stakeholder of any such bet or bets, or wager or wagers, shall be guilty of a misdemeanor, and upon conviction thereof, shall be fined not less than one hundred dollars nor more than one thousand dollars and be imprisoned in the county jail not less than thirty days nor exceeding one year; provided, however, that amateur boxing exhibitions may be held within this state, of a limited number of rounds, not exceeding four of the duration of three minutes each; the interval between each round shall be one minute, and the contestants weighing one hundred and forty-five pounds or over shall wear gloves of not less than eight ounces each in weight, and contestants weighing under one hundred and forty-five pounds may wear gloves of not less than six ounces each in weight. All gloves used by contestants in such amateur boxing exhibitions shall be so constructed, as that the soft padding between the outside coverings shall be evenly distributed over the back of said gloves and cover the knuckles and back of the hands. And no bandages of any kind shall be used on the hands or arms of the contestants. For the purpose of this statute an amateur boxing exhibition shall be and is hereby defined as one in which no contestant has received or shall receive in any form, directly or indirectly, any money, prize, reward or compensation either for the expenses of training for such contest or for taking part therein, except as herein expressly provided. Nor shall any person appear as contestant in such amateur exhibition who prior thereto has received any compensation or reward in any form for displaying, exercising or giving any example of his skill in or knowledge of athletic exercises, or for rendering services of any kind to any athletic organization or to any person or persons as trainer, coach, instructor or otherwise, or who shall have been employed in any manner professionally by reason of his athletic skill or knowledge; provided, however, that a medal or trophy may be awarded to each contestant in such amateur boxing exhibitions, not to exceed in value the sum of $35.00 each, which such medal or trophy must have engraved thereon the name of the winner and the date of the event; but no portion of any admission fee or fees charged or received for any amateur boxing exhibition shall be paid or given to any contestant in such amateur boxing exhibition, either directly or indirectly, nor shall any gift be given to or received by such contestants for participating in such boxing exhibition, except said medal or trophy. At every amateur boxing exhibition held in this state and permitted by this section of the Penal Code, any sheriff, constable, marshal, policeman or other peace officer of the city, county or other political subdivision, where such exhibition is being

held, shall have the right to, and it is hereby declared to be his duty to stop such exhibition, whenever it shall appear to him that the contestants are so unevenly matched or for any other reason, the said contestants have been, or either of them, has been seriously injured or there is danger that said contestants, or either of them, will be seriously injured if such contest continues, and he may call to his assistance in enforcing his order to stop said exhibition, as many peace officers or male citizens of the state as may be necessary for that purpose. Provided, further, that any contestant who shall continue to participate in such exhibition after an order to stop such exhibition shall have been given by such peace officer, or who shall violate any of the regulations herein prescribed, for governing amateur boxing exhibitions, shall be deemed guilty of violating this section of the Penal Code and subject to the punishment herein provided.

Nothing in this section contained shall be construed to prevent any county, city and county, or incorporated city or town from prohibiting, by ordinance, the holding or conducting of any boxing exhibition, or any person from engaging in any such boxing exhibition therein.

(Amended November 3, 1914, by initiative Proposition 20.)

413.

Every person wilfully present as spectator at any fight or contention prohibited in the preceding section, is guilty of a misdemeanor.

An information may be laid before any of the magistrates mentioned in section eight hundred and eight of this code, that a person has taken steps toward promoting or participating in a contemplated pugilistic contest, or fight, or ring or prize fight, or sparring or boxing exhibition, prohibited under the provision of section four hundred and twelve of this code, or is about to commit an offense under said section four hundred and twelve. When said information is laid before said magistrate, he must examine, on oath, the informer, and any witness or witnesses he may produce, and must take their depositions in writing and cause them to be subscribed by the parties making them. If it appears from the deposition that there is just reason to fear the commission of the offense contemplated by the person so informed against, the magistrate must issue a warrant directed generally to the sheriff of the county, or any constable, marshal, or policeman in the state, reciting the substance of the information and commanding the officer forthwith to arrest the person informed against and bring him before the magistrate. When the person informed against is brought before the magistrate, if the charge be controverted, the magistrate must take testimony in relation thereto. The evidence must be reduced to writing and subscribed by the witnesses. If it appears there is no just reason to fear the commission of the offense alleged to have been contemplated, the person complained against must be discharged. If, however, there is just reason to fear the commission of the offense, the person complained of must be required to enter into an undertaking in such sum, not less than three thousand dollars, as the magistrate may direct, with one or more sufficient sureties, conditioned that such person will not, for a period of one year thereafter, commit any such contemplated offense.

(Amended November 3, 1914, by initiative Proposition 20.)

414.

Every person who leaves this state with intent to evade any of the provisions of Section 412 or 413, and to commit any act out of this state such as is prohibited by them, and who does any act which would be punishable under these provisions if committed within this state, is punishable in the same manner as he or she would have been in case such act had been committed within this state.

(Amended by Stats. 1987, Ch. 828, Sec. 27.)

414a.

No person, otherwise competent as a witness, is disqualified from testifying as such, concerning any offense under this act, on the ground that such testimony may incriminate himself, but no prosecution can afterwards be had against him for any offense concerning which he testified. The provisions of section 1111 of the Penal Code of this state are not applicable to any prosecutions brought under the provisions of this act.

(Added November 3, 1914, by initiative Proposition 20.)

415.

Any of the following persons shall be punished by imprisonment in the county jail for a period of not more than 90 days, a fine of not more than four hundred dollars ($400), or both such imprisonment and fine:

(1) Any person who unlawfully fights in a public place or challenges another person in a public place to fight.

(2) Any person who maliciously and willfully disturbs another person by loud and unreasonable noise.

(3) Any person who uses offensive words in a public place which are inherently likely to provoke an immediate violent reaction.

(Amended by Stats. 1983, Ch. 1092, Sec. 283. Effective September 27, 1983. Operative January 1, 1984, by Sec. 427 of Ch. 1092.)

415.5.

(a) Any person who (1) unlawfully fights within any building or upon the grounds of any school, community college, university, or state university or challenges another person within any building or upon the grounds to fight, or (2) maliciously and willfully disturbs another person within any of these buildings or upon the grounds by loud and unreasonable noise, or (3) uses offensive words within any of these buildings or upon the grounds which are inherently likely to provoke an immediate violent reaction is guilty of a misdemeanor punishable by a fine not exceeding four hundred dollars ($400) or by imprisonment in the county jail for a period of not more than 90 days, or both.

(b) If the defendant has been previously convicted once of a violation of this section or of any offense defined in Chapter 1 (commencing with Section 626) of Title 15 of Part 1, the defendant shall be sentenced to imprisonment in the county jail for a period of not less than 10 days or more than six months, or by both that imprisonment and a fine of not exceeding one thousand dollars ($1,000), and shall not be released on probation, parole, or any other basis until not less than 10 days of imprisonment has been served.

(c) If the defendant has been previously convicted two or more times of a violation of this section or of any offense defined in Chapter 1 (commencing with Section 626) of Title 15 of Part 1, the defendant shall be sentenced to imprisonment in the county jail for a period of not less than 90 days or more than six months, or by both that imprisonment and a fine of not exceeding one thousand dollars ($1,000), and shall not be released on probation, parole, or any other basis until not less than 90 days of imprisonment has been served.

(d) For the purpose of determining the penalty to be imposed pursuant to this section, the court may consider a written report from the Department of Justice containing information from its records showing prior convictions; and the communication is prima facie evidence of such convictions, if the defendant admits them, regardless of whether or not the complaint commencing the proceedings has alleged prior convictions.

(e) As used in this section "state university," "university," "community college," and "school" have the same meaning as these terms are given in Section 626.

(f) This section shall not apply to any person who is a registered student of the school, or to any person who is engaged in any otherwise lawful employee concerted activity.

(Amended by Stats. 1988, Ch. 1113, Sec. 3.)

416.

(a) If two or more persons assemble for the purpose of disturbing the public peace, or committing any unlawful act, and do not disperse on being desired or commanded so to do by a public officer, the persons so offending are severally guilty of a misdemeanor.

(b) Any person who, as a result of violating subdivision (a), personally causes damage to real or personal property, which is either publicly or privately owned, shall make restitution for the damage he or she caused, including, but not limited to, the costs of

cleaning up, repairing, replacing, or restoring the property. Any restitution required to be paid pursuant to this subdivision shall be paid directly to the victim. If the court determines that the defendant is unable to pay restitution, the court shall order the defendant to perform community service, as the court deems appropriate, in lieu of the direct restitution payment.

(c) This section shall not preclude the court from imposing restitution in the form of a penalty assessment pursuant to Section 1464 if the court, in its discretion, deems that additional restitution appropriate.

(d) The burden of proof on the issue of whether any defendant or defendants personally caused any property damage shall rest with the prosecuting agency or claimant. In no event shall the burden of proof on this issue shift to the defendant or any of several defendants to prove that he or she was not responsible for the property damage.

(Amended by Stats. 1989, Ch. 572, Sec. 1.)

417.

(a) (1) Every person who, except in self-defense, in the presence of any other person, draws or exhibits any deadly weapon whatsoever, other than a firearm, in a rude, angry, or threatening manner, or who in any manner, unlawfully uses a deadly weapon other than a firearm in any fight or quarrel is guilty of a misdemeanor, punishable by imprisonment in a county jail for not less than 30 days.

(2) Every person who, except in self-defense, in the presence of any other person, draws or exhibits any firearm, whether loaded or unloaded, in a rude, angry, or threatening manner, or who in any manner, unlawfully uses a firearm in any fight or quarrel is punishable as follows:

(A) If the violation occurs in a public place and the firearm is a pistol, revolver, or other firearm capable of being concealed upon the person, by imprisonment in a county jail for not less than three months and not more than one year, by a fine not to exceed one thousand dollars ($1,000), or by both that fine and imprisonment.

(B) In all cases other than that set forth in subparagraph (A), a misdemeanor, punishable by imprisonment in a county jail for not less than three months.

(b) Every person who, except in self-defense, in the presence of any other person, draws or exhibits any loaded firearm in a rude, angry, or threatening manner, or who, in any manner, unlawfully uses any loaded firearm in any fight or quarrel upon the grounds of any day care center, as defined in Section 1596.76 of the Health and Safety Code, or any facility where programs, including day care programs or recreational programs, are being conducted for persons under 18 years of age, including programs conducted by a nonprofit organization, during the hours in which the center or facility is open for use, shall be punished by imprisonment in the state prison for 16 months, or two or three years, or by imprisonment in a county jail for not less than three months, nor more than one year.

(c) Every person who, in the immediate presence of a peace officer, draws or exhibits any firearm, whether loaded or unloaded, in a rude, angry, or threatening manner, and who knows, or reasonably should know, by the officer's uniformed appearance or other action of identification by the officer, that he or she is a peace officer engaged in the performance of his or her duties, and that peace officer is engaged in the performance of his or her duties, shall be punished by imprisonment in a county jail for not less than nine months and not to exceed one year, or in the state prison for 16 months, or two or three years.

(d) Except where a different penalty applies, every person who violates this section when the other person is in the process of cleaning up graffiti or vandalism is guilty of a misdemeanor, punishable by imprisonment in a county jail for not less than three months nor more than one year.

(e) As used in this section, "peace officer" means any person designated as a peace officer pursuant to Chapter 4.5 (commencing with Section 830) of Title 3 of Part 2.

(f) As used in this section, "public place" means any of the following:

(1) A public place in an incorporated city.

(2) A public street in an incorporated city.

(3) A public street in an unincorporated area.

(Amended by Stats. 2011, Ch. 15, Sec. 347. (AB 109) Effective April 4, 2011. Operative October 1, 2011, by Sec. 636 of Ch. 15, as amended by Stats. 2011, Ch. 39, Sec. 68.)

417.25.

(a) Every person who, except in self-defense, aims or points a laser scope, as defined in subdivision (b), or a laser pointer, as defined in subdivision (c), at another person in a threatening manner with the specific intent to cause a reasonable person fear of bodily harm is guilty of a misdemeanor, punishable by imprisonment in a county jail for up to 30 days. For purposes of this section, the laser scope need not be attached to a firearm.

(b) As used in this section, "laser scope" means a portable battery-powered device capable of being attached to a firearm and capable of projecting a laser light on objects at a distance.

(c) As used in this section, "laser pointer" means any hand held laser beam device or demonstration laser product that emits a single point of light amplified by the stimulated emission of radiation that is visible to the human eye.

(Amended by Stats. 1999, Ch. 621, Sec. 1. Effective January 1, 2000.)

417.26.

(a) Any person who aims or points a laser scope as defined in subdivision (b) of Section 417.25, or a laser pointer, as defined in subdivision (c) of that section, at a peace officer with the specific intent to cause the officer apprehension or fear of bodily harm and who knows or reasonably should know that the person at whom he or she is aiming or pointing is a peace officer, is guilty of a misdemeanor punishable by imprisonment in a county jail for a term not exceeding six months.

(b) Any person who commits a second or subsequent violation of subdivision (a) shall be punished by imprisonment in a county jail for not more than one year.

(Added by Stats. 1999, Ch. 438, Sec. 2. Effective January 1, 2000.)

417.27.

(a) No person, corporation, firm, or business entity of any kind shall knowingly sell a laser pointer to a person 17 years of age or younger, unless he or she is accompanied and supervised by a parent, legal guardian, or any other adult 18 years of age or older.

(b) No student shall possess a laser pointer on any elementary or secondary school premises unless possession of a laser pointer on the elementary or secondary school premises is for a valid instructional or other school-related purpose, including employment.

(c) No person shall direct the beam from a laser pointer directly or indirectly into the eye or eyes of another person or into a moving vehicle with the intent to harass or annoy the other person or the occupants of the moving vehicle.

(d) No person shall direct the beam from a laser pointer directly or indirectly into the eye or eyes of a guide dog, signal dog, service dog, or dog being used by a peace officer with the intent to harass or annoy the animal.

(e) A violation of subdivision (a), (b), (c), or (d) shall be an infraction that is punished by either a fine of fifty dollars ($50) or four hours of community service, and a second or subsequent violation of any of these subdivisions shall be an infraction that is punished by either a fine of one hundred dollars ($100) or eight hours of community service.

(f) As used in this section, "laser pointer" has the same meaning as set forth in subdivision (c) of Section 417.25.

(g) As used in this section, "guide dog," "signal dog," and "service dog," respectively, have the same meaning as set forth in subdivisions (d), (e), and (f) of Section 365.5.

(Added by Stats. 1999, Ch. 621, Sec. 2. Effective January 1, 2000.)

417.3.

Every person who, except in self-defense, in the presence of any other person who is an occupant of a motor vehicle proceeding on a public street or highway, draws or exhibits any firearm, whether loaded or unloaded, in a threatening manner against another person in such a way as to cause a reasonable person apprehension or fear of bodily harm is guilty of a felony punishable by imprisonment pursuant to subdivision (h) of Section 1170 for 16 months or two or three years or by imprisonment for 16 months or two or three years and a three thousand dollar ($3,000) fine.

Nothing in this section shall preclude or prohibit prosecution under any other statute.

(Amended by Stats. 2011, Ch. 15, Sec. 348. (AB 109) Effective April 4, 2011. Operative October 1, 2011, by Sec. 636 of Ch. 15, as amended by Stats. 2011, Ch. 39, Sec. 68.)

417.4.

Every person who, except in self-defense, draws or exhibits an imitation firearm, as defined in subdivision (a) of Section 16700, in a threatening manner against another in such a way as to cause a reasonable person apprehension or fear of bodily harm is guilty of a misdemeanor punishable by imprisonment in a county jail for a term of not less than 30 days.

(Amended by Stats. 2010, Ch. 178, Sec. 56. (SB 1115) Effective January 1, 2011. Operative January 1, 2012, by Sec. 107 of Ch. 178.)

417.6.

(a) If, in the commission of a violation of Section 417 or 417.8, serious bodily injury is intentionally inflicted by the person drawing or exhibiting the firearm or deadly weapon, the offense shall be punished by imprisonment in the county jail not exceeding one year or by imprisonment in state prison.

(b) As used in this section, "serious bodily injury" means a serious impairment of physical condition, including, but not limited to, the following: loss of consciousness; concussion; bone fracture; protracted loss or impairment of function of any bodily member or organ; a wound requiring extensive suturing; and serious disfigurement.

(c) When a person is convicted of a violation of Section 417 or 417.8 and the deadly weapon or firearm used by the person is owned by that person, the court shall order that the weapon or firearm be deemed a nuisance and disposed of in the manner provided by Sections 18000 and 18005.

(Amended by Stats. 2012, Ch. 43, Sec. 18. (SB 1023) Effective June 27, 2012.)

417.8.

Every person who draws or exhibits any firearm, whether loaded or unloaded, or other deadly weapon, with the intent to resist or prevent the arrest or detention of himself or another by a peace officer shall be imprisoned in the state prison for two, three, or four years.

(Added by Stats. 1982, Ch. 142, Sec. 2.5.)

418.

Every person using or procuring, encouraging or assisting another to use, any force or violence in entering upon or detaining any lands or other possessions of another, except in the cases and in the manner allowed by law, is guilty of a misdemeanor.

(Enacted 1872.)

419.

Every person who has been removed from any lands by process of law, or who has removed from any lands pursuant to the lawful adjudication or direction of any Court, tribunal, or officer, and who afterwards unlawfully returns to settle, reside upon, or take possession of such lands, is guilty of a misdemeanor.

(Enacted 1872.)

420.

Every person who unlawfully prevents, hinders, or obstructs any person from peaceably entering upon or establishing a settlement or residence on any tract of public land of the United States within the State of California, subject to settlement or entry under any of the public land laws of the United States; or who unlawfully hinders, prevents, or obstructs free passage over or through the public lands of the United States within the State of California, for the purpose of entry, settlement, or residence, as aforesaid, is guilty of a misdemeanor.

(Added by Stats. 1905, Ch. 516.)

420.1.

Anyone who willfully and knowingly prevents, hinders, or obstructs any person from entering, passing over, or leaving land in which that person enjoys, either personally or as an agent, guest, licensee, successor-in-interest, or contractor, a right to enter, use, cross, or inspect the property pursuant to an easement, covenant, license, profit, or other interest in the land, is guilty of an infraction punishable by a fine not to exceed five hundred dollars ($500), provided that the interest to be exercised has been duly recorded with the county recorder's office. This section shall not apply to the following persons: (1) any person engaged in lawful labor union activities that are permitted to be carried out by state or federal law; or (2) any person who is engaging in activities protected by the California Constitution or the United States Constitution.

(Added by Stats. 1998, Ch. 271, Sec. 1. Effective January 1, 1999.)

TITLE 11.5. CRIMINAL THREATS [422 - 422.4]

(Heading of Title 11.5 amended by Stats. 2000, Ch. 1001, Sec. 4.)

422.

(a) Any person who willfully threatens to commit a crime which will result in death or great bodily injury to another person, with the specific intent that the statement, made verbally, in writing, or by means of an electronic communication device, is to be taken as a threat, even if there is no intent of actually carrying it out, which, on its face and under the circumstances in which it is made, is so unequivocal, unconditional, immediate, and specific as to convey to the person threatened, a gravity of purpose and an immediate prospect of execution of the threat, and thereby causes that person reasonably to be in sustained fear for his or her own safety or for his or her immediate family's safety, shall be punished by imprisonment in the county jail not to exceed one year, or by imprisonment in the state prison.

(b) For purposes of this section, "immediate family" means any spouse, whether by marriage or not, parent, child, any person related by consanguinity or affinity within the second degree, or any other person who regularly resides in the household, or who, within the prior six months, regularly resided in the household.

(c) "Electronic communication device" includes, but is not limited to, telephones, cellular telephones, computers, video recorders, fax machines, or pagers. "Electronic communication" has the same meaning as the term defined in Subsection 12 of Section 2510 of Title 18 of the United States Code.

(Amended (as amended by Stats. 2011, Ch. 15) by Stats. 2011, Ch. 39, Sec. 16. (AB 117) Effective June 30, 2011. Operative October 1, 2011, pursuant to Secs. 68 and 69 of Ch. 39.)

422.1.

Every person who is convicted of a felony violation of Section 148.1 or 11418.1, under circumstances in which the defendant knew the underlying report was false, in addition to being ordered to comply with all other applicable restitution requirements and fine and fee provisions, shall also be ordered to pay full restitution to each of the following:

(a) Any person, corporation, business trust, estate, trust, partnership, association, joint venture, government, governmental subdivision, agency or instrumentality, or any other legal or commercial entity for any personnel, equipment, material, or clean up costs, and for any property damage, caused by the violation directly, or stemming from any emergency response to the violation or its aftermath.

(b) Any public or private entity incurring any costs for actual emergency response, for all costs of that response and for any clean up costs, including any overtime paid to uninvolved personnel made necessary by the allocation of resources to the emergency response and clean up.

(c) Restitution for the costs of response by a government entity under this section shall be determined in a hearing separate from the determination of guilt. The court shall order restitution in an amount no greater than the reasonable costs of the response. The burden shall be on the people to prove the reasonable costs of the response.

(d) In determining the restitution for the costs of response by a government entity, the court shall consider the amount of restitution to be paid to the direct victim, as defined in subdivision (k) of Section 1202.4.

(Added by Stats. 2002, Ch. 281, Sec. 1. Effective January 1, 2003.)

422.4.

(a) Any person who publishes information describing or depicting an academic researcher or his or her immediate family member, or the location or locations where an academic researcher or an immediate family member of an academic researcher may be found, with the intent that another person imminently use the information to commit a crime involving violence or a threat of violence against an academic researcher or his or her immediate family member, and the information is likely to produce the imminent commission of such a crime, is guilty of a misdemeanor, punishable by imprisonment in a county jail for not more than one year, a fine of not more than one thousand dollars ($1,000), or by both a fine and imprisonment.

(b) For the purposes of this section, all of the following apply:

(1) "Publishes" means making the information available to another person through any medium, including, but not limited to, the Internet, the World Wide Web, or e-mail.

(2) "Academic researcher" has the same meaning as in Section 602.12.

(3) "Immediate family" means any spouse, whether by marriage or not, domestic partner, parent, child, any person related by consanguinity or affinity within the second degree, or any other person who regularly resides in the household, or who, within the prior six months, regularly resided in the household.

(4) "Information" includes, but is not limited to, an image, film, filmstrip, photograph, negative, slide, photocopy, videotape, video laser disc, or any other computer-generated image.

(c) Any academic researcher about whom information is published in violation of subdivision (a) may seek a preliminary injunction enjoining any further publication of that information. This subdivision shall not apply to a person or entity protected pursuant to Section 1070 of the Evidence Code.

(d) This section shall not apply to any person who is lawfully engaged in labor union activities that are protected under state or federal law.

(e) This section shall not preclude prosecution under any other provision of law.

(Added by Stats. 2008, Ch. 492, Sec. 3. Effective September 28, 2008.)

TITLE 11.6. CIVIL RIGHTS [422.55 - 422.93]

(Title 11.6 added by Stats. 1987, Ch. 1277, Sec. 4.)

CHAPTER 1. Definitions [422.55 - 422.57]

(Chapter 1 added by Stats. 2004, Ch. 700, Sec. 6.)

422.55.

For purposes of this title, and for purposes of all other state law unless an explicit provision of law or the context clearly requires a different meaning, the following shall apply:

(a) "Hate crime" means a criminal act committed, in whole or in part, because of one or more of the following actual or perceived characteristics of the victim:

(1) Disability.
(2) Gender.
(3) Nationality.
(4) Race or ethnicity.
(5) Religion.
(6) Sexual orientation.
(7) Association with a person or group with one or more of these actual or perceived characteristics.

(b) "Hate crime" includes, but is not limited to, a violation of Section 422.6.

(Added by Stats. 2004, Ch. 700, Sec. 6. Effective January 1, 2005.)

422.56.

For purposes of this title, the following definitions shall apply:

(a) "Association with a person or group with these actual or perceived characteristics" includes advocacy for, identification with, or being on the ground owned or rented by, or adjacent to, any of the following: a community center, educational facility, family, individual, office, meeting hall, place of worship, private institution, public agency, library, or other entity, group, or person that has, or is identified with people who have, one or more of those characteristics listed in the definition of "hate crime" under paragraphs (1) to (6), inclusive, of subdivision (a) of Section 422.55.

(b) "Disability" includes mental disability and physical disability as defined in Section 12926 of the Government Code regardless of whether those disabilities are temporary, permanent, congenital, or acquired by heredity, accident, injury, advanced age, or illness. This definition is declaratory of existing law.

(c) "Gender" means sex, and includes a person's gender identity and gender expression. "Gender expression" means a person's gender-related appearance and behavior whether or not stereotypically associated with the person's assigned sex at birth.

(d) "In whole or in part because of" means that the bias motivation must be a cause in fact of the offense, whether or not other causes also exist. When multiple concurrent motives exist, the prohibited bias must be a substantial factor in bringing about the particular result. There is no requirement that the bias be a main factor, or that the crime would not have been committed but for the actual or perceived characteristic. This subdivision does not constitute a change in, but is declaratory of, existing law under In re M.S. (1995) 10 Cal.4th 698 and People v. Superior Court (Aishman) (1995) 10 Cal.4th 735.

(e) "Nationality" includes citizenship, country of origin, and national origin.

(f) "Race or ethnicity" includes ancestry, color, and ethnic background.

(g) "Religion" includes all aspects of religious belief, observance, and practice and includes agnosticism and atheism.

(h) "Sexual orientation" means heterosexuality, homosexuality, or bisexuality.

(i) "Victim" includes, but is not limited to, a community center, educational facility, entity, family, group, individual, office, meeting hall, person, place of worship, private institution, public agency, library, or other victim or intended victim of the offense.

(Amended by Stats. 2018, Ch. 26, Sec. 2. (AB 1985) Effective January 1, 2019.)

422.57.

For purposes this code, unless an explicit provision of law or the context clearly requires a different meaning, "gender" has the same meaning as in Section 422.56.

(Added by Stats. 2004, Ch. 700, Sec. 6. Effective January 1, 2005.)

CHAPTER 2. Crimes and Penalties [422.6 - 422.865]

(Chapter 2 heading added by Stats. 2004, Ch. 700, Sec. 7.)

422.6.

(a) No person, whether or not acting under color of law, shall by force or threat of force, willfully injure, intimidate, interfere with, oppress, or threaten any other person in the free exercise or enjoyment of any right or privilege secured to him or her by the Constitution or laws of this state or by the Constitution or laws of the United States in whole or in part because of one or more of the actual or perceived characteristics of the victim listed in subdivision (a) of Section 422.55.

(b) No person, whether or not acting under color of law, shall knowingly deface, damage, or destroy the real or personal property of any other person for the purpose of intimidating or interfering with the free exercise or enjoyment of any right or privilege secured to the other person by the Constitution or laws of this state or by the Constitution or laws of the United States, in whole or in part because of one or more of the actual or perceived characteristics of the victim listed in subdivision (a) of Section 422.55.

(c) Any person convicted of violating subdivision (a) or (b) shall be punished by imprisonment in a county jail not to exceed one year, or by a fine not to exceed five thousand dollars ($5,000), or by both the above imprisonment and fine, and the court shall order the defendant to perform a minimum of community service, not to exceed 400 hours, to be performed over a period not to exceed 350 days, during a time other than his or her hours of employment or school attendance. However, no person may be convicted of violating subdivision (a) based upon speech alone, except upon a showing that the speech itself threatened violence against a specific person or group of persons and that the defendant had the apparent ability to carry out the threat.

(d) Conduct that violates this and any other provision of law, including, but not limited to, an offense described in Article 4.5 (commencing with Section 11410) of Chapter 3 of Title 1 of Part 4, may be charged under all applicable provisions. However, an act or omission punishable in different ways by this section and other provisions of law shall not be punished under more than one provision, and the penalty to be imposed shall be determined as set forth in Section 654.

(Amended by Stats. 2004, Ch. 700, Sec. 8. Effective January 1, 2005.)

422.7.

Except in the case of a person punished under Section 422.6, any hate crime that is not made punishable by imprisonment in the state prison shall be punishable by imprisonment in a county jail not to exceed one year, or by imprisonment pursuant to subdivision (h) of Section 1170, or by a fine not to exceed ten thousand dollars ($10,000), or by both that imprisonment and fine, if the crime is committed against the person or property of another for the purpose of intimidating or interfering with that other person's free exercise or enjoyment of any right secured to him or her by the Constitution or laws of this state or by the Constitution or laws of the United States under any of the following circumstances, which shall be charged in the accusatory pleading:

(a) The crime against the person of another either includes the present ability to commit a violent injury or causes actual physical injury.

(b) The crime against property causes damage in excess of nine hundred fifty dollars ($950).

(c) The person charged with a crime under this section has been convicted previously of a violation of subdivision (a) or (b) of Section 422.6, or has been convicted previously of a conspiracy to commit a crime described in subdivision (a) or (b) of Section 422.6.

(Amended by Stats. 2011, Ch. 15, Sec. 352. (AB 109) Effective April 4, 2011. Operative October 1, 2011, by Sec. 636 of Ch. 15, as amended by Stats. 2011, Ch. 39, Sec. 68.)

422.75.

(a) Except in the case of a person punished under Section 422.7, a person who commits a felony that is a hate crime or attempts to commit a felony that is a hate crime, shall receive an additional term of one, two, or three years in the state prison, at the court's discretion.

(b) Except in the case of a person punished under Section 422.7 or subdivision (a) of this section, any person who commits a felony that is a hate crime, or attempts to commit a felony that is a hate crime, and who voluntarily acted in concert with another person, either personally or by aiding and abetting another person, shall receive an additional two, three, or four years in the state prison, at the court's discretion.

(c) For the purpose of imposing an additional term under subdivision (a) or (b), it shall be a factor in aggravation that the defendant personally used a firearm in the commission of the offense. Nothing in this subdivision shall preclude a court from also imposing a sentence enhancement pursuant to Section 12022.5, 12022.53, or 12022.55, or any other law.

(d) A person who is punished pursuant to this section also shall receive an additional term of one year in the state prison for each prior felony conviction on charges brought and tried separately in which it was found by the trier of fact or admitted by the defendant that the crime was a hate crime. This additional term shall only apply where a sentence enhancement is not imposed pursuant to Section 667 or 667.5.

(e) Any additional term authorized by this section shall not be imposed unless the allegation is charged in the accusatory pleading and admitted by the defendant or found to be true by the trier of fact.

(f) Any additional term imposed pursuant to this section shall be in addition to any other punishment provided by law.

(g) Notwithstanding any other provision of law, the court may strike any additional term imposed by this section if the court determines that there are mitigating circumstances and states on the record the reasons for striking the additional punishment.

(Amended by Stats. 2004, Ch. 700, Sec. 10. Effective January 1, 2005.)

422.76.

Except where the court imposes additional punishment under Section 422.75 or in a case in which the person has been convicted of an offense subject to Section 1170.8, the fact that a person committed a felony or attempted to commit a felony that is a hate crime shall be considered a circumstance in aggravation of the crime in imposing a term under subdivision (b) of Section 1170.

(Added by renumbering Section 1170.75 by Stats. 2004, Ch. 700, Sec. 23. Effective January 1, 2005.)

422.77.

(a) Any willful and knowing violation of any order issued pursuant to subdivision (a) or (b) of Section 52.1 of the Civil Code shall be a misdemeanor punishable by a fine of not more than one thousand dollars ($1,000), or by imprisonment in the county jail for not more than six months, or by both the fine and imprisonment.

(b) A person who has previously been convicted one or more times of violating an order issued pursuant to subdivision (a) or (b) of Section 52.1 of the Civil Code upon charges separately brought and tried shall be imprisoned in the county jail for not more than one year. Subject to the discretion of the court, the prosecution shall have the opportunity to present witnesses and relevant evidence at the time of the sentencing of a defendant pursuant to this subdivision.

(c) The prosecuting agency of each county shall have the primary responsibility for the enforcement of orders issued pursuant to Section 52.1 of the Civil Code.

(d) The court may order a defendant who is convicted of a hate crime to perform a minimum of community service, not to exceed 400 hours, to be performed over a period not to exceed 350 days, during a time other than his or her hours of employment or school attendance.

(Added by Stats. 2004, Ch. 700, Sec. 12. Effective January 1, 2005.)

422.78.

The prosecuting agency of each county shall have the primary responsibility for the enforcement of orders issued pursuant to this title or Section 52.1 of the Civil Code.

(Added by Stats. 2004, Ch. 700, Sec. 13. Effective January 1, 2005.)

422.8.

Except as otherwise required by law, nothing in this title shall be construed to prevent or limit the prosecution of any person pursuant to any provision of law.

(Amended by Stats. 1991, Ch. 839, Sec. 4.)

422.85.

(a) In the case of any person who is convicted of any offense against the person or property of another individual, private institution, or public agency, committed because of the victim's actual or perceived race, color, ethnicity, religion, nationality, country of origin, ancestry, disability, gender, gender identity, gender expression, or sexual orientation, including, but not limited to, offenses defined in Section 302, 423.2, 594.3, 11411, 11412, or 11413, or for any hate crime, the court, absent compelling circumstances stated on the record, shall make an order protecting the victim, or known immediate family or domestic partner of the victim, from further acts of violence, threats, stalking, or harassment by the defendant, including any stay-away conditions the court deems appropriate, and shall make obedience of that order a condition of the defendant's probation. In these cases the court may also order that the defendant be required to do one or more of the following as a condition of probation:

(1) Complete a class or program on racial or ethnic sensitivity, or other similar training in the area of civil rights, or a one-year counseling program intended to reduce the tendency toward violent and antisocial behavior if that class, program, or training is available and was developed or authorized by the court or local agencies in cooperation with organizations serving the affected community.

(2) Make payments or other compensation to a community-based program or local agency that provides services to victims of hate violence.

(3) Reimburse the victim for reasonable costs of counseling and other reasonable expenses that the court finds are the direct result of the defendant's acts.

(b) Any payments or other compensation ordered under this section shall be in addition to restitution payments required under Section 1203.04, and shall be made only after that restitution is paid in full.

(Amended by Stats. 2011, Ch. 719, Sec. 32. (AB 887) Effective January 1, 2012.)

422.86.

(a) It is the public policy of this state that the principal goals of sentencing for hate crimes, are the following:

(1) Punishment for the hate crimes committed.

(2) Crime and violence prevention, including prevention of recidivism and prevention of crimes and violence in prisons and jails.

(3) Restorative justice for the immediate victims of the hate crimes and for the classes of persons terrorized by the hate crimes.

(b) The Judicial Council shall develop a rule of court guiding hate crime sentencing to implement the policy in subdivision (a). In developing the rule of court, the council shall consult experts including organizations representing hate crime victims.

(Added by Stats. 2004, Ch. 700, Sec. 14. Effective January 1, 2005.)

422.865.

(a) In the case of any person who is committed to a state hospital or other treatment facility under the provisions of Section 1026 for any offense against the person or property of another individual, private institution, or public agency because of the victim's actual or perceived race, color, ethnicity, religion, nationality, country of origin, ancestry, disability, gender, or sexual orientation, including, but not limited to, offenses defined in Section 302, 423.2, 594.3, 11411, 11412, or 11413, or for any hate crime, and then is either placed on outpatient status or conditional release from the state hospital or other treatment facility, the court or community program director may order that the defendant be required as a condition of outpatient status or conditional release to complete a class or program on racial or ethnic sensitivity, or other similar training in the area of civil rights, or a one-year counseling program intended to reduce the tendency toward violent and antisocial behavior if that class, program, or training is available and was developed or authorized by the court or local agencies in cooperation with organizations serving the affected community.

(b) In the case of any person who is committed to a state hospital or other treatment facility under the provisions of Section 1026 for any offense against the person or property of another individual, private institution, or public agency committed because of the victim's actual or perceived race, color, ethnicity, religion, nationality, country of origin, ancestry, disability, gender, or sexual orientation, including, but not limited to, offenses defined in Section 302, 423.2, 594.3, 11411, 11412, or 11413, or for any hate crime, and then is either placed on outpatient status or conditional release from the state hospital or other treatment facility, the court, absent compelling circumstances stated on the record, shall make an order protecting the victim, or known immediate family or domestic partner of the victim, from further acts of violence, threats, stalking, or harassment by the defendant, including any stay-away conditions as the court deems appropriate, and shall make obedience of that order a condition of the defendant's outpatient status or conditional release.

(c) It is the intent of the Legislature to encourage state agencies and treatment facilities to establish education and training programs to prevent violations of civil rights and hate crimes.

(Added by Stats. 2004, Ch. 809, Sec. 1. Effective January 1, 2005.)

CHAPTER 2.5. Law Enforcement Agency Policies [422.87- 422.87.]

(Chapter 2.5 added by Stats. 2018, Ch. 26, Sec. 3.)

422.87.

(a) Each local law enforcement agency may adopt a hate crimes policy. Any local law enforcement agency that updates an existing hate crimes policy or adopts a new hate crimes policy shall include, but not be limited to, all of the following:

(1) The definitions in Sections 422.55 and 422.56.

(2) The content of the model policy framework that the Commission on Peace Officer Standards and Training developed pursuant to Section 13519.6, and any content that the commission may revise or add in the future, including any policy, definitions, response and reporting responsibilities, training resources, and planning and prevention methods.

(3) (A) Information regarding bias motivation.

(B) For the purposes of this paragraph, "bias motivation" is a preexisting negative attitude toward actual or perceived characteristics referenced in Section 422.55. Depending on the circumstances of each case, bias motivation may include, but is not limited to, hatred, animosity, resentment, revulsion, contempt, unreasonable fear, paranoia, callousness, thrill-seeking, desire for social dominance, desire for social bonding with those of one's "own kind," or a perception of the vulnerability of the victim due to the victim being perceived as being weak, worthless, or fair game because of a protected characteristic, including, but not limited to, disability or gender.

(C) (i) In recognizing suspected disability-bias hate crimes, the policy shall advise officers to consider whether there is any indication that the perpetrator was motivated by hostility or other bias, occasioned by factors such as, but not limited to, dislike of persons who arouse fear or guilt, a perception that persons with disabilities are inferior and therefore "deserving victims," a fear of persons whose visible traits are perceived as being disturbing to others, or resentment of those who need, demand, or receive alternative educational, physical, or social accommodations.
(ii) In recognizing suspected disability-bias hate crimes, the policy also shall advise officers to consider whether there is any indication that the perpetrator perceived the victim to be vulnerable and, if so, if this perception is grounded, in whole or in part, in antidisability bias. This includes, but is not limited to, if a perpetrator targets a person with a particular perceived disability while avoiding other vulnerable-appearing persons such as inebriated persons or persons with perceived disabilities different than those of the victim, those circumstances could be evidence that the perpetrator's motivations included bias against persons with the perceived disability of the victim and that the crime must be reported as a suspected hate crime and not a mere crime of opportunity.
(4) Information regarding the general underreporting of hate crimes and the more extreme underreporting of antidisability and antigender hate crimes and a plan for the agency to remedy this underreporting.
(5) A protocol for reporting suspected hate crimes to the Department of Justice pursuant to Section 13023.
(6) A checklist of first responder responsibilities, including, but not limited to, being sensitive to effects of the crime on the victim, determining whether any additional resources are needed on the scene to assist the victim or whether to refer the victim to appropriate community and legal services, and giving the victims and any interested persons the agency's hate crimes brochure, as required by Section 422.92.
(7) A specific procedure for transmitting and periodically retransmitting the policy and any related orders to all officers, including a simple and immediate way for officers to access the policy in the field when needed.
(8) The title or titles of the officer or officers responsible for assuring that the department has a hate crime brochure as required by Section 422.92 and ensuring that all officers are trained to distribute the brochure to all suspected hate crime victims and all other interested persons.
(9) A requirement that all officers be familiar with the policy and carry out the policy at all times unless directed by the chief, sheriff, director, or other chief executive of the law enforcement agency or other command-level officer to whom the chief executive officer formally delegates this responsibility.
(b) Any local law enforcement agency that updates an existing hate crimes policy or adopts a new hate crimes policy may include any of the provisions of a model hate crime policy and other relevant documents developed by the International Association of Chiefs of Police that are relevant to California and consistent with this chapter.
(Added by Stats. 2018, Ch. 26, Sec. 3. (AB 1985) Effective January 1, 2019.)

CHAPTER 3. General Provisions [422.88 - 422.93]

(Chapter 3 added by Stats. 2004, Ch. 700, Sec. 15.)
422.88.
(a) The court in which a criminal proceeding stemming from a hate crime or alleged hate crime is filed shall take all actions reasonably required, including granting restraining orders, to safeguard the health, safety, or privacy of the alleged victim, or of a person who is a victim of, or at risk of becoming a victim of, a hate crime.
(b) Restraining orders issued pursuant to subdivision (a) may include provisions prohibiting or restricting the photographing of a person who is a victim of, or at risk of becoming a victim of, a hate crime when reasonably required to safeguard the health, safety, or privacy of that person.
(Added by Stats. 2004, Ch. 700, Sec. 15. Effective January 1, 2005.)
422.89.
It is the intent of the Legislature to encourage counties, cities, law enforcement agencies, and school districts to establish education and training programs to prevent violations of civil rights and hate crimes and to assist victims.
(Added by Stats. 2004, Ch. 700, Sec. 16. Effective January 1, 2005.)
422.9.
All state and local agencies shall use the definition of "hate crime" set forth in subdivision (a) of Section 422.55 exclusively, except as other explicit provisions of state or federal law may require otherwise.
(Repealed and added by Stats. 2004, Ch. 700, Sec. 18. Effective January 1, 2005.)
422.91.
The Department of Corrections and the California Youth Authority, subject to available funding, shall do each of the following:
(a) Cooperate fully and participate actively with federal, state, and local law enforcement agencies and community hate crime prevention and response networks and other anti-hate groups concerning hate crimes and gangs.
(b) Strive to provide inmates with safe environments in which they are not pressured to join gangs or hate groups and do not feel a need to join them in self-defense.
(Added by Stats. 2004, Ch. 700, Sec. 19. Effective January 1, 2005.)
422.92.
(a) Every state and local law enforcement agency in this state shall make available a brochure on hate crimes to victims of these crimes and the public.
(b) The Department of Fair Employment and Housing shall provide existing brochures, making revisions as needed, to local law enforcement agencies upon request for reproduction and distribution to victims of hate crimes and other interested parties. In carrying out these responsibilities, the department shall consult the Fair Employment and Housing Council, the Department of Justice, and the California Victim Compensation Board.
(Amended by Stats. 2016, Ch. 31, Sec. 232. (SB 836) Effective June 27, 2016.)
422.93.
(a) It is the public policy of this state to protect the public from crime and violence by encouraging all persons who are victims of or witnesses to crimes, or who otherwise can give evidence in a criminal investigation, to cooperate with the criminal justice system and not to penalize these persons for being victims or for cooperating with the criminal justice system.
(b) Whenever an individual who is a victim of or witness to a hate crime, or who otherwise can give evidence in a hate crime investigation, is not charged with or convicted of committing any crime under state law, a peace officer may not detain the individual exclusively for any actual or suspected immigration violation or report or turn the individual over to federal immigration authorities.
(Added by Stats. 2004, Ch. 700, Sec. 20. Effective January 1, 2005.)

TITLE 11.7. CALIFORNIA FREEDOM OF ACCESS TO CLINIC AND CHURCH ENTRANCES ACT [423 - 423.6]

(Title 11.7 added by Stats. 2001, Ch. 899, Sec. 2.)
423.
This title shall be known and may be cited as the California Freedom of Access to Clinic and Church Entrances Act, or the California FACE Act.
(Added by Stats. 2001, Ch. 899, Sec. 2. Effective January 1, 2002.)
423.1.
The following definitions apply for the purposes of this title:
(a) "Crime of violence" means an offense that has as an element the use, attempted use, or threatened use of physical force against the person or property of another.
(b) "Interfere with" means to restrict a person's freedom of movement.
(c) "Intimidate" means to place a person in reasonable apprehension of bodily harm to herself or himself or to another.
(d) "Nonviolent" means conduct that would not constitute a crime of violence.
(e) "Physical obstruction" means rendering ingress to or egress from a reproductive health services facility or to or from a place of religious worship impassable to another person, or rendering passage to or from a reproductive health services facility or a place of religious worship unreasonably difficult or hazardous to another person.
(f) "Reproductive health services" means reproductive health services provided in a hospital, clinic, physician's office, or other facility and includes medical, surgical, counseling, or referral services relating to the human reproductive system, including services relating to pregnancy or the termination of a pregnancy.
(g) "Reproductive health services client, provider, or assistant" means a person or entity that is or was involved in obtaining, seeking to obtain, providing, seeking to provide, or assisting or seeking to assist another person, at that other person's request, to obtain or provide any services in a reproductive health services facility, or a person or entity that is or was involved in owning or operating or seeking to own or operate, a reproductive health services facility.
(h) "Reproductive health services facility" includes a hospital, clinic, physician's office, or other facility that provides or seeks to provide reproductive health services and includes the building or structure in which the facility is located.
(Added by Stats. 2001, Ch. 899, Sec. 2. Effective January 1, 2002.)
423.2.
Every person who, except a parent or guardian acting towards his or her minor child or ward, commits any of the following acts shall be subject to the punishment specified in Section 423.3.
(a) By force, threat of force, or physical obstruction that is a crime of violence, intentionally injures, intimidates, interferes with, or attempts to injure, intimidate, or interfere with, any person or entity because that person or entity is a reproductive health services client, provider, or assistant, or in order to intimidate any person or entity, or any class of persons or entities, from becoming or remaining a reproductive health services client, provider, or assistant.
(b) By force, threat of force, or physical obstruction that is a crime of violence, intentionally injures, intimidates, interferes with, or attempts to injure, intimidate, or interfere with any person lawfully exercising or seeking to exercise the First Amendment right of religious freedom at a place of religious worship.
(c) By nonviolent physical obstruction, intentionally injures, intimidates, or interferes with, or attempts to injure, intimidate, or interfere with, any person or entity because that person or entity is a reproductive health services client, provider, or assistant, or in order to intimidate any person or entity, or any class of persons or entities, from becoming or remaining a reproductive health services client, provider, or assistant.
(d) By nonviolent physical obstruction, intentionally injures, intimidates, or interferes with, or attempts to injure, intimidate, or interfere with, any person lawfully exercising or seeking to exercise the First Amendment right of religious freedom at a place of religious worship.
(e) Intentionally damages or destroys the property of a person, entity, or facility, or attempts to do so, because the person, entity, or facility is a reproductive health services client, provider, assistant, or facility.
(f) Intentionally damages or destroys the property of a place of religious worship.
(Added by Stats. 2001, Ch. 899, Sec. 2. Effective January 1, 2002.)
423.3.
(a) A first violation of subdivision (c) or (d) of Section 423.2 is a misdemeanor, punishable by imprisonment in a county jail for a period of not more than six months and a fine not to exceed two thousand dollars ($2,000).
(b) A second or subsequent violation of subdivision (c) or (d) of Section 423.2 is a misdemeanor, punishable by imprisonment in a county jail for a period of not more than six months and a fine not to exceed five thousand dollars ($5,000).
(c) A first violation of subdivision (a), (b), (e), or (f) of Section 423.2 is a misdemeanor, punishable by imprisonment in a county jail for a period of not more than one year and a fine not to exceed twenty-five thousand dollars ($25,000).
(d) A second or subsequent violation of subdivision (a), (b), (e), or (f) of Section 423.2 is a misdemeanor, punishable by imprisonment in a county jail for a period of not more than one year and a fine not to exceed fifty thousand dollars ($50,000).
(e) In imposing fines pursuant to this section, the court shall consider applicable factors in aggravation and mitigation set out in Rules 4.421 and 4.423 of the California Rules of Court, and shall consider a prior violation of the federal Freedom of Access to Clinic Entrances Act of 1994 (18 U.S.C. Sec. 248), or a prior violation of a statute of another jurisdiction that would constitute a violation of Section 423.2 or of the federal Freedom of Access to Clinic Entrances Act of 1994, to be a prior violation of Section 423.2.
(f) This title establishes concurrent state jurisdiction over conduct that is also prohibited by the federal Freedom of Access to Clinic Entrances Act of 1994 (18 U.S.C. Sec. 248), which provides for more severe misdemeanor penalties for first violations and felony-misdemeanor penalties for second and subsequent violations. State law enforcement agencies and prosecutors shall cooperate with federal authorities in the prevention, apprehension, and prosecution of these crimes, and shall seek federal prosecutions when appropriate.
(g) No person shall be convicted under this article for conduct in violation of Section 423.2 that was done on a particular occasion where the identical conduct on that occasion was the basis for a conviction of that person under the federal Freedom of Access to Clinic Entrances Act of 1994 (18 U.S.C. Sec. 248).
(Added by Stats. 2001, Ch. 899, Sec. 2. Effective January 1, 2002.)
423.4.
(a) A person aggrieved by a violation of Section 423.2 may bring a civil action to enjoin the violation, for compensatory and punitive damages, and for the costs of suit and reasonable fees for attorneys and expert witnesses, except that only a reproductive health services client, provider, or assistant may bring an action under subdivision (a), (c), or (e) of Section 423.2, and only a person lawfully exercising or seeking to exercise the First Amendment right of religious freedom in a place of religious worship, or the entity that owns or operates a place of religious worship, may bring an action under subdivision (b), (d), or (f) of Section 423.2. With respect to compensatory damages, the plaintiff may elect, at any time prior to the rendering of a final judgment, to recover, in lieu of actual damages, an award of statutory damages in the amount of one thousand dollars ($1,000) per exclusively nonviolent violation, and five thousand dollars ($5,000) per any other violation, for each violation committed.
(b) The Attorney General, a district attorney, or a city attorney may bring a civil action to enjoin a violation of Section 423.2, for compensatory damages to persons aggrieved as described in subdivision (a) and for the assessment of a civil penalty against each respondent. The civil penalty shall not exceed two thousand dollars ($2,000) for an exclusively nonviolent first violation, and fifteen thousand dollars ($15,000) for any other first violation, and shall not exceed five thousand dollars ($5,000) for an exclusively nonviolent subsequent violation, and twenty-five thousand dollars ($25,000)

for any other subsequent violation. In imposing civil penalties pursuant to this subdivision, the court shall consider a prior violation of the federal Freedom of Access to Clinic Entrances Act of 1994 (18 U.S.C. Sec. 248), or a prior violation of a statute of another jurisdiction that would constitute a violation of Section 423.2 or the federal Freedom of Access to Clinic Entrances Act of 1994, to be a prior violation of Section 423.2.

(c) No person shall be found liable under this section for conduct in violation of Section 423.2 done on a particular occasion where the identical conduct on that occasion was the basis for a finding of liability by that person under the federal Freedom of Access to Clinic Entrances Act of 1994 (18 U.S.C. Sec. 248).

(Added by Stats. 2001, Ch. 899, Sec. 2. Effective January 1, 2002.)

423.5.

(a) (1) The court in which a criminal or civil proceeding is filed for a violation of subdivision (a), (c), or (e) of Section 423.2 shall take all action reasonably required, including granting restraining orders, to safeguard the health, safety, or privacy of either of the following:

(A) A reproductive health services client, provider, or assistant who is a party or witness in the proceeding.

(B) A person who is a victim of, or at risk of becoming a victim of, conduct prohibited by subdivision (a), (c), or (e) of Section 423.2.

(2) The court in which a criminal or civil proceeding is filed for a violation of subdivision (b), (d), or (f) of Section 423.2 shall take all action reasonably required, including granting restraining orders, to safeguard the health, safety, or privacy of either of the following:

(A) A person lawfully exercising or seeking to exercise the First Amendment right of religious freedom at a place of religious worship.

(B) An entity that owns or operates a place of religious worship.

(b) Restraining orders issued pursuant to paragraph (1) of subdivision (a) may include provisions prohibiting or restricting the photographing of persons described in subparagraphs (A) and (B) of paragraph (1) of subdivision (a) when reasonably required to safeguard the health, safety, or privacy of those persons. Restraining orders issued pursuant to paragraph (2) of subdivision (a) may include provisions prohibiting or restricting the photographing of persons described in subparagraphs (A) and (B) of paragraph (2) of subdivision (a) when reasonably required to safeguard the health, safety, or privacy of those persons.

(c) A court may, in its discretion, permit an individual described in subparagraph (A) or (B) of paragraph (1) of subdivision (a) to use a pseudonym in a civil proceeding described in paragraph (1) of subdivision (a) when reasonably required to safeguard the health, safety, or privacy of those persons. A court may, in its discretion, permit an individual described in subparagraph (A) or (B) of paragraph (2) of subdivision (a) to use a pseudonym in a civil proceeding described in paragraph (2) of subdivision (a) when reasonably required to safeguard the health, safety, or privacy of those persons.

(Added by Stats. 2001, Ch. 899, Sec. 2. Effective January 1, 2002.)

423.6.

This title shall not be construed for any of the following purposes:

(a) To impair any constitutionally protected activity, or any activity protected by the laws of California or of the United States of America.

(b) To provide exclusive civil or criminal remedies or to preempt or to preclude any county, city, or city and county from passing any law to provide a remedy for the commission of any of the acts prohibited by this title or to make any of those acts a crime.

(c) To interfere with the enforcement of any federal, state, or local laws regulating the performance of abortions or the provision of other reproductive health services.

(d) To negate, supercede, or otherwise interfere with the operation of any provision of Chapter 10 (commencing with Section 1138) of Part 3 of Division 2 of the Labor Code.

(e) To create additional civil or criminal remedies or to limit any existing civil or criminal remedies to redress an activity that interferes with the exercise of any other rights protected by the First Amendment to the United States Constitution or of Article I of the California Constitution.

(f) To preclude prosecution under both this title and any other provision of law, except as provided in subdivision (g) of Section 423.3.

(Added by Stats. 2001, Ch. 899, Sec. 2. Effective January 1, 2002.)

TITLE 12. OF CRIMES AGAINST THE REVENUE AND PROPERTY OF THIS STATE [424 - 440]

(Title 12 enacted 1872.)

424.

(a) Each officer of this state, or of any county, city, town, or district of this state, and every other person charged with the receipt, safekeeping, transfer, or disbursement of public moneys, who either:

1. Without authority of law, appropriates the same, or any portion thereof, to his or her own use, or to the use of another; or,

2. Loans the same or any portion thereof; makes any profit out of, or uses the same for any purpose not authorized by law; or,

3. Knowingly keeps any false account, or makes any false entry or erasure in any account of or relating to the same; or,

4. Fraudulently alters, falsifies, conceals, destroys, or obliterates any account; or,

5. Willfully refuses or omits to pay over, on demand, any public moneys in his or her hands, upon the presentation of a draft, order, or warrant drawn upon these moneys by competent authority; or,

6. Willfully omits to transfer the same, when transfer is required by law; or,

7. Willfully omits or refuses to pay over to any officer or person authorized by law to receive the same, any money received by him or her under any duty imposed by law so to pay over the same;—

Is punishable by imprisonment in the state prison for two, three, or four years, and is disqualified from holding any office in this state.

(b) As used in this section, "public moneys" includes the proceeds derived from the sale of bonds or other evidence or indebtedness authorized by the legislative body of any city, county, district, or public agency.

(c) This section does not apply to the incidental and minimal use of public resources authorized by Section 8314 of the Government Code.

(Amended by Stats. 2003, Ch. 62, Sec. 227. Effective January 1, 2004.)

425.

Every officer charged with the receipt, safe keeping, or disbursement of public moneys, who neglects or fails to keep and pay over the same in the manner prescribed by law, is guilty of felony.

(Enacted 1872.)

426.

The phrase "public moneys," as used in Sections 424 and 425, includes all bonds and evidence of indebtedness, and all moneys belonging to the state, or any city, county, town, district, or public agency therein, and all moneys, bonds, and evidences of indebtedness received or held by state, county, district, city, town, or public agency officers in their official capacity.

(Amended by Stats. 1987, Ch. 828, Sec. 29.)

428.

Every person who willfully obstructs or hinders any public officer from collecting any revenue, taxes, or other sums of money in which the people of this State are interested, and which such officer is by law empowered to collect, is guilty of a misdemeanor.

(Enacted 1872.)

429.

Any provider of telecommunications services in this state that intentionally fails to collect or remit, as may be required, the annual fee imposed pursuant to Section 431 of the Public Utilities Code, the universal telephone service surcharge imposed pursuant to Section 879 or 879.5 of the Public Utilities Code, the fee for filing an application for a certificate of public convenience and necessity as provided in Section 1904 of the Public Utilities Code, or the surcharge imposed pursuant to subdivision (g) of Section 2881 of the Public Utilities Code, whether imposed on the provider or measured by the provider's service charges, is guilty of a misdemeanor.

(Amended by Stats. 2012, Ch. 162, Sec. 124. (SB 1171) Effective January 1, 2013.)

431.

Every person who uses or gives any receipt, except that prescribed by law, as evidence of the payment of any poll tax, road tax, or license of any kind, or who receives payment of such tax or license without delivering the receipt prescribed by law, or who inserts the name of more than one person therein, is guilty of a misdemeanor.

(Enacted 1872.)

432.

Every person who has in his possession, with intent to circulate or sell, any blank licenses or poll tax receipts other than those furnished by the Controller of State or County Auditor, is guilty of felony.

(Enacted 1872.)

436.

Every person who acts as an auctioneer in violation of the laws of this State relating to auctions and auctioneers, is guilty of a misdemeanor.

(Enacted 1872.)

439.

Every person who in this State procures, or agrees to procure, any insurance for a resident of this State, from any insurance company not incorporated under the laws of this State, unless such company or its agent has filed the bond required by the laws of this State relating to insurance, is guilty of a misdemeanor.

(Enacted 1872.)

440.

Every officer charged with the collection, receipt, or disbursement of any portion of the revenue of this State, who, upon demand, fails or refuses to permit the Controller or Attorney General to inspect his books, papers, receipts, and records pertaining to his office, is guilty of a misdemeanor.

(Enacted 1872.)

TITLE 13. OF CRIMES AGAINST PROPERTY [450 - 593g]

(Title 13 enacted 1872.)

CHAPTER 1. Arson [450 - 457.1]

(Chapter 1 enacted 1872.)

450.

In this chapter, the following terms have the following meanings:

(a) "Structure" means any building, or commercial or public tent, bridge, tunnel, or powerplant.

(b) "Forest land" means any brush covered land, cut-over land, forest, grasslands, or woods.

(c) "Property" means real property or personal property, other than a structure or forest land.

(d) "Inhabited" means currently being used for dwelling purposes whether occupied or not. "Inhabited structure" and "inhabited property" do not include the real property on which an inhabited structure or an inhabited property is located.

(e) "Maliciously" imports a wish to vex, defraud, annoy, or injure another person, or an intent to do a wrongful act, established either by proof or presumption of law.

(f) "Recklessly" means a person is aware of and consciously disregards a substantial and unjustifiable risk that his or her act will set fire to, burn, or cause to burn a structure, forest land, or property. The risk shall be of such nature and degree that disregard thereof constitutes a gross deviation from the standard of conduct that a reasonable person would observe in the situation. A person who creates such a risk but is unaware thereof solely by reason of voluntary intoxication also acts recklessly with respect thereto.

(Added by Stats. 1979, Ch. 145.)

451.

A person is guilty of arson when he or she willfully and maliciously sets fire to or burns or causes to be burned or who aids, counsels, or procures the burning of, any structure, forest land, or property.

(a) Arson that causes great bodily injury is a felony punishable by imprisonment in the state prison for five, seven, or nine years.

(b) Arson that causes an inhabited structure or inhabited property to burn is a felony punishable by imprisonment in the state prison for three, five, or eight years.

(c) Arson of a structure or forest land is a felony punishable by imprisonment in the state prison for two, four, or six years.

(d) Arson of property is a felony punishable by imprisonment in the state prison for 16 months, two, or three years. For purposes of this paragraph, arson of property does not include one burning or causing to be burned his or her own personal property unless there is an intent to defraud or there is injury to another person or another person's structure, forest land, or property.

(e) In the case of any person convicted of violating this section while confined in a state prison, prison road camp, prison forestry camp, or other prison camp or prison farm, or while confined in a county jail while serving a term of imprisonment for a felony or misdemeanor conviction, any sentence imposed shall be consecutive to the sentence for which the person was then confined.

(Amended by Stats. 1994, Ch. 421, Sec. 1. Effective September 7, 1994.)

451.1.

(a) Notwithstanding any other law, any person who is convicted of a felony violation of Section 451 shall be punished by a three-, four-, or five-year enhancement if one or more of the following circumstances is found to be true:

(1) The defendant has been previously convicted of a felony violation of Section 451 or 452.

(2) A firefighter, peace officer, or other emergency personnel suffered great bodily injury as a result of the offense. The additional term provided by this subdivision shall be imposed whenever applicable, including any instance in which there is a violation of subdivision (a) of Section 451.

(3) The defendant proximately caused great bodily injury to more than one victim in any single violation of Section 451. The additional term provided by this subdivision shall be imposed whenever applicable, including any instance in which there is a violation of subdivision (a) of Section 451.
(4) The defendant proximately caused multiple structures to burn in any single violation of Section 451.
(5) The defendant committed arson as described in subdivision (a), (b), or (c) of Section 451 and the arson was caused by use of a device designed to accelerate the fire or delay ignition.
(b) The additional term specified in subdivision (a) shall not be imposed unless the existence of any fact required under this section shall be alleged in the accusatory pleading and either admitted by the defendant in open court or found to be true by the trier of fact.
(Added by Stats. 1994, Ch. 421, Sec. 2. Effective September 7, 1994.)
451.5.
(a) A person who willfully, maliciously, deliberately, with premeditation, and with intent to cause injury to one or more persons, or to cause damage to property under circumstances likely to produce injury to one or more persons, or to cause damage to one or more structures or inhabited dwellings, sets fire to, burns, or causes to be burned, or aids, counsels, or procures the burning of any residence, structure, forest land, or property, is guilty of aggravated arson if one or more of the following aggravating factors exists:
(1) The defendant has been previously convicted of arson on one or more occasions within the past 10 years.
(2) (A) The fire caused property damage and other losses in excess of eight million three hundred thousand dollars ($8,300,000).
(B) In calculating the total amount of property damage and other losses under subparagraph (A), the court shall consider the cost of fire suppression. It is the intent of the Legislature that this paragraph be reviewed within five years to consider the effects of inflation on the dollar amount stated herein.
(3) The fire caused damage to, or the destruction of, five or more inhabited structures.
(b) A person who is convicted under subdivision (a) shall be punished by imprisonment in the state prison for 10 years to life.
(c) A person who is sentenced under subdivision (b) shall not be eligible for release on parole until 10 calendar years have elapsed.
(d) This section shall remain in effect only until January 1, 2024, and as of that date is repealed.
(Amended (as amended by Stats. 2014, Ch. 481, Sec. 1) by Stats. 2018, Ch. 619, Sec. 1. (SB 896) Effective January 1, 2019. Repealed as of January 1, 2024, by its own provisions. See later operative version amended by Sec. 2 of Stats. 2018, Ch. 619)
451.5.
(a) A person who willfully, maliciously, deliberately, with premeditation, and with intent to cause injury to one or more persons, or to cause damage to property under circumstances likely to produce injury to one or more persons, or to cause damage to one or more structures or inhabited dwellings, sets fire to, burns, or causes to be burned, or aids, counsels, or procures the burning of any residence, structure, forest land, or property, is guilty of aggravated arson if either of the following aggravating factors exists:
(1) The defendant has been previously convicted of arson on one or more occasions within the past 10 years.
(2) The fire caused damage to, or the destruction of, five or more inhabited structures.
(b) A person who is convicted under subdivision (a) shall be punished by imprisonment in the state prison for 10 years to life.
(c) A person who is sentenced under subdivision (b) shall not be eligible for release on parole until 10 calendar years have elapsed.
(d) This section shall become operative on January 1, 2024.
(Amended (as added by Stats. 2014, Ch. 481, Sec. 2) by Stats. 2018, Ch. 619, Sec. 2. (SB 896) Effective January 1, 2019. Section operative January 1, 2024, by its own provisions.)
452.
A person is guilty of unlawfully causing a fire when he recklessly sets fire to or burns or causes to be burned, any structure, forest land or property.
(a) Unlawfully causing a fire that causes great bodily injury is a felony punishable by imprisonment in the state prison for two, four or six years, or by imprisonment in the county jail for not more than one year, or by a fine, or by both such imprisonment and fine.
(b) Unlawfully causing a fire that causes an inhabited structure or inhabited property to burn is a felony punishable by imprisonment in the state prison for two, three or four years, or by imprisonment in the county jail for not more than one year, or by a fine, or by both such imprisonment and fine.
(c) Unlawfully causing a fire of a structure or forest land is a felony punishable by imprisonment in the state prison for 16 months, two or three years, or by imprisonment in the county jail for not more than six months, or by a fine, or by both such imprisonment and fine.
(d) Unlawfully causing a fire of property is a misdemeanor. For purposes of this paragraph, unlawfully causing a fire of property does not include one burning or causing to be burned his own personal property unless there is injury to another person or to another person's structure, forest land or property.
(e) In the case of any person convicted of violating this section while confined in a state prison, prison road camp, prison forestry camp, or other prison camp or prison farm, or while confined in a county jail while serving a term of imprisonment for a felony or misdemeanor conviction, any sentence imposed shall be consecutive to the sentence for which the person was then confined.
(Amended by Stats. 1982, Ch. 1133, Sec. 2. Effective September 17, 1982.)
452.1.
(a) Notwithstanding any other law, any person who is convicted of a felony violation of Section 452 shall be punished by a one-, two-, or three-year enhancement for each of the following circumstances that is found to be true:
(1) The defendant has been previously convicted of a felony violation of Section 451 or 452.
(2) A firefighter, peace officer, or other emergency personnel suffered great bodily injury as a result of the offense. The additional term provided by this subdivision shall be imposed whenever applicable, including any instance in which there is a violation of subdivision (a) of Section 452.
(3) The defendant proximately caused great bodily injury to more than one victim in any single violation of Section 452. The additional term provided by this subdivision shall be imposed whenever applicable, including any instance in which there is a violation of subdivision (a) of Section 452.
(4) The defendant proximately caused multiple structures to burn in any single violation of Section 452.
(b) The additional term specified in subdivision (a) of Section 452.1 shall not be imposed unless the existence of any fact required under this section shall be alleged in the accusatory pleading and either admitted by the defendant in open court or found to be true by the trier of fact.
(Added by Stats. 1994, Ch. 421, Sec. 4. Effective September 7, 1994.)
453.
(a) Every person who possesses, manufactures, or disposes of any flammable, or combustible material or substance, or any incendiary device in an arrangement or preparation, with intent to willfully and maliciously use this material, substance, or device

to set fire to or burn any structure, forest land, or property, shall be punished by imprisonment pursuant to subdivision (h) of Section 1170, or in a county jail, not exceeding one year.
(b) For the purposes of this section:
(1) "Disposes of" means to give, give away, loan, offer, offer for sale, sell, or transfer.
(2) "Incendiary device" means a device that is constructed or designed to start an incendiary fire by remote, delayed, or instant means, but no device commercially manufactured primarily for the purpose of illumination shall be deemed to be an incendiary device for the purposes of this section.
(3) "Incendiary fire" means a fire that is deliberately ignited under circumstances in which a person knows that the fire should not be ignited.
(c) Subdivision (a) does not prohibit the authorized use or possession of any material, substance or device described therein by a member of the armed forces of the United States or by firemen, police officers, peace officers, or law enforcement officers authorized by the properly constituted authorities; nor does that subdivision prohibit the use or possession of any material, substance or device described therein when used solely for scientific research or educational purposes, or for disposal of brush under permit as provided for in Section 4494 of the Public Resources Code, or for any other lawful burning. Subdivision (a) does not prohibit the manufacture or disposal of an incendiary device for the parties or purposes described in this subdivision.
(Amended by Stats. 2011, Ch. 15, Sec. 353. (AB 109) Effective April 4, 2011. Operative October 1, 2011, by Sec. 636 of Ch. 15, as amended by Stats. 2011, Ch. 39, Sec. 68.)
454.
(a) Every person who violates Section 451 or 452 during and within an area of any of the following, when proclaimed by the Governor, shall be punished by imprisonment in the state prison, as specified in subdivision (b):
(1) A state of insurrection pursuant to Section 143 of the Military and Veterans Code.
(2) A state of emergency pursuant to Section 8625 of the Government Code.
(b) Any person who is described in subdivision (a) and who violates subdivision (a), (b), or (c) of Section 451 shall be punished by imprisonment in the state prison for five, seven, or nine years. All other persons who are described in subdivision (a) shall be punished by imprisonment in the state prison for three, five, or seven years.
(c) Probation shall not be granted to any person who is convicted of violating this section, except in unusual cases where the interest of justice would best be served.
(Amended by Stats. 1997, Ch. 260, Sec. 3. Effective January 1, 1998.)
455.
(a) Any person who willfully and maliciously attempts to set fire to or attempts to burn or to aid, counsel or procure the burning of any structure, forest land or property, or who commits any act preliminary thereto, or in furtherance thereof, is punishable by imprisonment in the state prison for 16 months, two or three years.
(b) The placing or distributing of any flammable, explosive or combustible material or substance, or any device in or about any structure, forest land or property in an arrangement or preparation with intent to eventually willfully and maliciously set fire to or burn same, or to procure the setting fire to or burning of the same shall, for the purposes of this act constitute an attempt to burn such structure, forest land or property.
(Amended (as amended by Stats. 2011, Ch. 15) by Stats. 2011, Ch. 39, Sec. 17. (AB 117) Effective June 30, 2011. Operative October 1, 2011, pursuant to Secs. 68 and 69 of Ch. 39.)
456.
(a) Upon conviction for any felony violation of this chapter, in addition to the penalty prescribed, the court may impose a fine not to exceed fifty thousand dollars ($50,000) unless a greater amount is provided by law.
(b) When any person is convicted of a violation of any provision of this chapter and the reason he committed the violation was for pecuniary gain, in addition to the penalty prescribed and instead of the fine provided in subdivision (a), the court may impose a fine of twice the anticipated or actual gross gain.
(Amended by Stats. 1979, Ch. 145.)
457.
Upon conviction of any person for a violation of any provision of this chapter, the court may order that such person, for the purpose of sentencing, submit to a psychiatric or psychological examination.
(Added by renumbering Section 455 by Stats. 1979, Ch. 145.)
457.1.
(a) As used in this section, "arson" means a violation of Section 451, 451.5, or 453, and attempted arson, which includes, but is not limited to, a violation of Section 455.
(b) (1) Every person described in paragraph (2), (3), and (4), for the periods specified therein, shall, while residing in, or if the person has no residence, while located in California, be required to, within 14 days of coming into, or changing the person's residence or location within any city, county, city and county, or campus wherein the person temporarily resides, or if the person has no residence, is located:
(A) Register with the chief of police of the city where the person is residing, or if the person has no residence, where the person is located.
(B) Register with the sheriff of the county where the person is residing, or if the person has no residence, where the person is located in an unincorporated area or city that has no police department.
(C) In addition to (A) or (B) above, register with the chief of police of a campus of the University of California, the California State University, or community college where the person is residing, or if the person has no residence, where the person is located upon the campus or any of its facilities.
(2) Any person who, on or after November 30, 1994, is convicted in any court in this state of arson or attempted arson shall be required to register, in accordance with the provisions of this section, for the rest of his or her life.
(3) Any person who, having committed the offense of arson or attempted arson, and after having been adjudicated a ward of the juvenile court on or after January 1, 1993, is discharged or paroled from the Department of the Youth Authority shall be required to register, in accordance with the provisions of this section, until that person attains the age of 25 years, or until the person has his or her records sealed pursuant to Section 781 of the Welfare and Institutions Code, whichever comes first.
(4) Any person convicted of the offense of arson or attempted arson on or after January 1, 1985, through November 29, 1994, inclusive, in any court of this state, shall be required to register, in accordance with the provisions of this section, for a period of five years commencing, in the case where the person was confined for the offense, from the date of their release from confinement, or in the case where the person was not confined for the offense, from the date of sentencing or discharge, if that person was ordered by the court at the time that person was sentenced to register as an arson offender. The law enforcement agencies shall make registration information available to the chief fire official of a legally organized fire department or fire protection district having local jurisdiction where the person resides.
(c) Any person required to register pursuant to this section who is discharged or paroled from a jail, prison, school, road camp, or other penal institution, or from the Department of the Youth Authority where he or she was confined because of the commission or attempted commission of arson, shall, prior to the discharge, parole, or release, be informed of his or her duty to register under this section by the official in charge of the place of confinement. The official shall require the person to read and sign the form as may be required by the Department of Justice, stating that the duty of the person to register under this section has been explained to him or her. The official in charge of the place of confinement shall obtain the address where the person expects to reside upon his or her discharge, parole, or release and shall report the address to the

Department of Justice. The official in charge of the place of confinement shall give one copy of the form to the person, and shall, not later than 45 days prior to the scheduled release of the person, send one copy to the appropriate law enforcement agency having local jurisdiction where the person expects to reside upon his or her discharge, parole, or release; one copy to the prosecuting agency that prosecuted the person; one copy to the chief fire official of a legally organized fire department or fire protection district having local jurisdiction where the person expects to reside upon his or her discharge, parole, or release; and one copy to the Department of Justice. The official in charge of the place of confinement shall retain one copy. All forms shall be transmitted in time so as to be received by the local law enforcement agency and prosecuting agency 30 days prior to the discharge, parole, or release of the person.

(d) All records relating specifically to the registration in the custody of the Department of Justice, law enforcement agencies, and other agencies or public officials shall be destroyed when the person required to register under this subdivision for offenses adjudicated by a juvenile court attains the age of 25 years or has his or her records sealed under the procedures set forth in Section 781 of the Welfare and Institutions Code, whichever event occurs first. This subdivision shall not be construed to require the destruction of other criminal offender or juvenile records relating to the case that are maintained by the Department of Justice, law enforcement agencies, the juvenile court, or other agencies and public officials unless ordered by the court under Section 781 of the Welfare and Institutions Code.

(e) Any person who is required to register pursuant to this section who is released on probation or discharged upon payment of a fine shall, prior to the release or discharge, be informed of his or her duty to register under this section by the probation department of the county in which he or she has been convicted, and the probation officer shall require the person to read and sign the form as may be required by the Department of Justice, stating that the duty of the person to register under this section has been explained to him or her. The probation officer shall obtain the address where the person expects to reside upon his or her release or discharge and shall report within three days the address to the Department of Justice. The probation officer shall give one copy of the form to the person, and shall send one copy to the appropriate law enforcement agency having local jurisdiction where the person expects to reside upon his or her discharge or release, one copy to the prosecuting agency that prosecuted the person, one copy to the chief fire official of a legally organized fire department or fire protection district having local jurisdiction where the person expects to reside upon his or her discharge or release, and one copy to the Department of Justice. The probation officer shall also retain one copy.

(f) The registration shall consist of (1) a statement in writing signed by the person, giving the information as may be required by the Department of Justice, and (2) the fingerprints and photograph of the person. Within three days thereafter, the registering law enforcement agency shall electronically forward the statement, fingerprints, and photograph to the Department of Justice.

(g) If any person required to register by this section changes his or her residence address, he or she shall inform, in writing within 10 days, the law enforcement agency with whom he or she last registered of his or her new address. The law enforcement agency shall, within three days after receipt of the information, electronically forward it to the Department of Justice. The Department of Justice shall forward appropriate registration data to the law enforcement agency having local jurisdiction of the new place of residence.

(h) Any person required to register under this section who violates any of the provisions thereof is guilty of a misdemeanor. Any person who has been convicted of arson or attempted arson and who is required to register under this section who willfully violates any of the provisions thereof is guilty of a misdemeanor and shall be sentenced to serve a term of not less than 90 days nor more than one year in a county jail. In no event does the court have the power to absolve a person who willfully violates this section from the obligation of spending at least 90 days of confinement in a county jail and of completing probation of at least one year.

(i) Whenever any person is released on parole or probation and is required to register under this section but fails to do so within the time prescribed, the Board of Prison Terms, the Department of the Youth Authority, or the court, as the case may be, shall order the parole or probation of that person revoked.

(j) The statements, photographs, and fingerprints required by this section shall not be open to inspection by the public or by any person other than a regularly employed peace officer or other law enforcement officer.

(k) In any case in which a person who would be required to register pursuant to this section is to be temporarily sent outside the institution where he or she is confined on any assignment within a city or county, including, but not limited to, firefighting or disaster control, the local law enforcement agency having jurisdiction over the place or places where that assignment shall occur shall be notified within a reasonable time prior to removal from the institution. This subdivision shall not apply to any person temporarily released under guard from the institution where he or she is confined.

(l) Nothing in this section shall be construed to conflict with Section 1203.4 concerning termination of probation and release from penalties and disabilities of probation.

A person required to register under this section may initiate a proceeding under Chapter 3.5 (commencing with Section 4852.01) of Title 6 of Part 3 and, upon obtaining a certificate of rehabilitation, shall be relieved of any further duty to register under this section. This certificate shall not relieve the petitioner of the duty to register under this section for any offense subject to this section of which he or she is convicted in the future.

Any person who is required to register under this section due to a misdemeanor conviction shall be relieved of the requirement to register if that person is granted relief pursuant to Section 1203.4.

(Amended by Stats. 1999, Ch. 518, Sec. 2. Effective January 1, 2000.)

CHAPTER 2. Burglary [458 - 464]

(Heading of Chapter 2 amended by Stats. 1984, Ch. 193, Sec. 99.)

458.
As used in this chapter, the term "cargo container" means a receptacle with all of the following characteristics:
(a) Of a permanent character and accordingly strong enough to be suitable for repeated use.
(b) Specially designed to facilitate the carriage of goods, by one or more modes of transport, one of which shall be by vessels, without intermediate reloading.
(c) Fitted with devices permitting its ready handling, particularly its transfer from one mode of transport to another.
(d) So designed to be easy to fill and empty.
(e) Having a cubic displacement of 1,000 cubic feet or more.
(Added by Stats. 1984, Ch. 854, Sec. 1.)

459.
Every person who enters any house, room, apartment, tenement, shop, warehouse, store, mill, barn, stable, outhouse or other building, tent, vessel, as defined in Section 21 of the Harbors and Navigation Code, floating home, as defined in subdivision (d) of Section 18075.55 of the Health and Safety Code, railroad car, locked or sealed cargo container, whether or not mounted on a vehicle, trailer coach, as defined in Section 635 of the Vehicle Code, any house car, as defined in Section 362 of the Vehicle Code,

inhabited camper, as defined in Section 243 of the Vehicle Code, vehicle as defined by the Vehicle Code, when the doors are locked, aircraft as defined by Section 21012 of the Public Utilities Code, or mine or any underground portion thereof, with intent to commit grand or petit larceny or any felony is guilty of burglary. As used in this chapter, "inhabited" means currently being used for dwelling purposes, whether occupied or not. A house, trailer, vessel designed for habitation, or portion of a building is currently being used for dwelling purposes if, at the time of the burglary, it was not occupied solely because a natural or other disaster caused the occupants to leave the premises.
(Amended by Stats. 1991, Ch. 942, Sec. 14.)

459.5.
(a) Notwithstanding Section 459, shoplifting is defined as entering a commercial establishment with intent to commit larceny while that establishment is open during regular business hours, where the value of the property that is taken or intended to be taken does not exceed nine hundred fifty dollars ($950). Any other entry into a commercial establishment with intent to commit larceny is burglary. Shoplifting shall be punished as a misdemeanor, except that a person with one or more prior convictions for an offense specified in clause (iv) of subparagraph (C) of paragraph (2) of subdivision (e) of Section 667 or for an offense requiring registration pursuant to subdivision (c) of Section 290 may be punished pursuant to subdivision (h) of Section 1170.
(b) Any act of shoplifting as defined in subdivision (a) shall be charged as shoplifting. No person who is charged with shoplifting may also be charged with burglary or theft of the same property.
(Added November 4, 2014, by initiative Proposition 47, Sec. 5.)

460.
(a) Every burglary of an inhabited dwelling house, vessel, as defined in the Harbors and Navigation Code, which is inhabited and designed for habitation, floating home, as defined in subdivision (d) of Section 18075.55 of the Health and Safety Code, or trailer coach, as defined by the Vehicle Code, or the inhabited portion of any other building, is burglary of the first degree.
(b) All other kinds of burglary are of the second degree.
(c) This section shall not be construed to supersede or affect Section 464 of the Penal Code.
(Amended by Stats. 1991, Ch. 942, Sec. 15.)

461.
Burglary is punishable as follows:
(a) Burglary in the first degree: by imprisonment in the state prison for two, four, or six years.
(b) Burglary in the second degree: by imprisonment in the county jail not exceeding one year or imprisonment pursuant to subdivision (h) of Section 1170.
(Amended by Stats. 2011, Ch. 15, Sec. 355. (AB 109) Effective April 4, 2011. Operative October 1, 2011, by Sec. 636 of Ch. 15, as amended by Stats. 2011, Ch. 39, Sec. 68.)

462.
(a) Except in unusual cases where the interests of justice would best be served if the person is granted probation, probation shall not be granted to any person who is convicted of a burglary of an inhabited dwelling house or trailer coach as defined in Section 635 of the Vehicle Code, an inhabited floating home as defined in subdivision (d) of Section 18075.55 of the Health and Safety Code, or the inhabited portion of any other building.
(b) If the court grants probation under subdivision (a), it shall specify the reason or reasons for that order on the court record.
(Amended by Stats. 1993, Ch. 162, Sec. 2. Effective January 1, 1994.)

462.5.
(a) Except in unusual cases where the interests of justice would best be served if the person is granted probation, probation shall not be granted to any person who is convicted of a felony custodial institution burglary. In any case in which a person is convicted of a misdemeanor custodial institution burglary, such person shall be confined in the county jail for not less than 90 days nor more than one year except in unusual cases where the interests of justice would best be served by the granting of probation.
(b) As used in this section, "custodial institution burglary" shall mean a violation of Section 459 on the grounds of any jail or correctional institution with the intent to steal items to use or convert for use as weapons, escape tools, or intoxicating drugs.
(c) If the court grants probation under subdivision (a), it shall specify the reason or reasons for such order on the court record.
(d) Any person convicted of custodial institution burglary shall serve his or her sentence, including enhancements, consecutive to any other sentence in effect or pending. The felony sentence shall be calculated under Section 1170.1.
(Added by Stats. 1982, Ch. 1132, Sec. 1.)

463.
(a) Every person who violates Section 459, punishable as a second-degree burglary pursuant to subdivision (b) of Section 461, during and within an affected county in a "state of emergency" or a "local emergency," or under an "evacuation order," resulting from an earthquake, fire, flood, riot, or other natural or manmade disaster shall be guilty of the crime of looting, punishable by imprisonment in a county jail for one year or pursuant to subdivision (h) of Section 1170. Any person convicted under this subdivision who is eligible for probation and who is granted probation shall, as a condition thereof, be confined in a county jail for at least 180 days, except that the court may, in the case where the interest of justice would best be served, reduce or eliminate that mandatory jail sentence, if the court specifies on the record and enters into the minutes the circumstances indicating that the interest of justice would best be served by that disposition. In addition to whatever custody is ordered, the court, in its discretion, may require any person granted probation following conviction under this subdivision to serve up to 240 hours of community service in any program deemed appropriate by the court, including any program created to rebuild the community.
For purposes of this subdivision, the fact that the structure entered has been damaged by the earthquake, fire, flood, or other natural or manmade disaster shall not, in and of itself, preclude conviction.
(b) Every person who commits the crime of grand theft, as defined in Section 487 or subdivision (a) of Section 487a, except grand theft of a firearm, during and within an affected county in a "state of emergency" or a "local emergency," or under an "evacuation order," resulting from an earthquake, fire, flood, riot, or other natural or unnatural disaster shall be guilty of the crime of looting, punishable by imprisonment in a county jail for one year or pursuant to subdivision (h) of Section 1170. Every person who commits the crime of grand theft of a firearm, as defined in Section 487, during and within an affected county in a "state of emergency" or a "local emergency" resulting from an earthquake, fire, flood, riot, or other natural or unnatural disaster shall be guilty of the crime of looting, punishable by imprisonment in the state prison, as set forth in subdivision (a) of Section 489. Any person convicted under this subdivision who is eligible for probation and who is granted probation shall, as a condition thereof, be confined in a county jail for at least 180 days, except that the court may, in the case where the interest of justice would best be served, reduce or eliminate that mandatory jail sentence, if the court specifies on the record and enters into the minutes the circumstances indicating that the interest of justice would best be served by that disposition. In addition to whatever custody is ordered, the court, in its discretion, may require any person granted probation following conviction under this subdivision to serve up to 160 hours of community service in any program deemed appropriate by the court, including any program created to rebuild the community.
(c) Every person who commits the crime of petty theft, as defined in Section 488, during and within an affected county in a "state of emergency" or a "local emergency," or under an "evacuation order," resulting from an earthquake, fire, flood, riot, or other

natural or manmade disaster shall be guilty of a misdemeanor, punishable by imprisonment in a county jail for six months. Any person convicted under this subdivision who is eligible for probation and who is granted probation shall, as a condition thereof, be confined in a county jail for at least 90 days, except that the court may, in the case where the interest of justice would best be served, reduce or eliminate that mandatory minimum jail sentence, if the court specifies on the record and enters into the minutes the circumstances indicating that the interest of justice would best be served by that disposition. In addition to whatever custody is ordered, the court, in its discretion, may require any person granted probation following conviction under this subdivision to serve up to 80 hours of community service in any program deemed appropriate by the court, including any program created to rebuild the community.

(d) (1) For purposes of this section, "state of emergency" means conditions that, by reason of their magnitude, are, or are likely to be, beyond the control of the services, personnel, equipment, and facilities of any single county, city and county, or city and require the combined forces of a mutual aid region or regions to combat.

(2) For purposes of this section, "local emergency" means conditions that, by reason of their magnitude, are, or are likely to be, beyond the control of the services, personnel, equipment, and facilities of any single county, city and county, or city and require the combined forces of a mutual aid region or regions to combat.

(3) For purposes of this section, a "state of emergency" shall exist from the time of the proclamation of the condition of the emergency until terminated pursuant to Section 8629 of the Government Code. For purposes of this section only, a "local emergency" shall exist from the time of the proclamation of the condition of the emergency by the local governing body until terminated pursuant to Section 8630 of the Government Code.

(4) For purposes of this section, "evacuation order" means an order from the Governor, or a county sheriff, chief of police, or fire marshal, under which persons subject to the order are required to relocate outside of the geographic area covered by the order due to an imminent danger resulting from an earthquake, fire, flood, riot, or other natural or manmade disaster.

(5) Consensual entry into a commercial structure with the intent to commit a violation of Section 470, 476, 476a, 484f, or 484g shall not be charged as a violation under this section.

(Amended by Stats. 2018, Ch. 132, Sec. 1. (AB 3078) Effective January 1, 2019.)

464.
Any person who, with intent to commit crime, enters, either by day or by night, any building, whether inhabited or not, and opens or attempts to open any vault, safe, or other secure place by use of acetylene torch or electric arc, burning bar, thermal lance, oxygen lance, or any other similar device capable of burning through steel, concrete, or any other solid substance, or by use of nitroglycerine, dynamite, gunpowder, or any other explosive, is guilty of a felony and, upon conviction, shall be punished by imprisonment pursuant to subdivision (h) of Section 1170 for a term of three, five, or seven years.

(Amended by Stats. 2011, Ch. 15, Sec. 357. (AB 109) Effective April 4, 2011. Operative October 1, 2011, by Sec. 636 of Ch. 15, as amended by Stats. 2011, Ch. 39, Sec. 68.)

CHAPTER 3. Burglarious and Larcenous Instruments and Deadly Weapons [466 - 469]

(Heading of Chapter 3 amended by Stats. 1977, Ch. 1147.)

466.
Every person having upon him or her in his or her possession a picklock, crow, keybit, crowbar, screwdriver, vise grip pliers, water-pump pliers, slidehammer, slim jim, tension bar, lock pick gun, tubular lock pick, bump key, floor-safe door puller, master key, ceramic or porcelain spark plug chips or pieces, or other instrument or tool with intent feloniously to break or enter into any building, railroad car, aircraft, or vessel, trailer coach, or vehicle as defined in the Vehicle Code, or who shall knowingly make or alter, or shall attempt to make or alter, any key or other instrument named above so that the same will fit or open the lock of a building, railroad car, aircraft, vessel, trailer coach, or vehicle as defined in the Vehicle Code, without being requested to do so by some person having the right to open the same, or who shall make, alter, or repair any instrument or thing, knowing or having reason to believe that it is intended to be used in committing a misdemeanor or felony, is guilty of a misdemeanor. Any of the structures mentioned in Section 459 shall be deemed to be a building within the meaning of this section.

(Amended by Stats. 2008, Ch. 119, Sec. 1. Effective January 1, 2009.)

466.1.
Any person who knowingly and willfully sells or provides a lock pick, a tension bar, a lock pick gun, a tubular lock pick, or a floor-safe door puller, to another, whether or not for compensation, shall obtain the name, address, telephone number, if any, date of birth, and driver's license number or identification number, if any, of the person to whom the device is sold or provided. This information, together with the date the device was sold or provided and the signature of the person to whom the device was sold or provided, shall be set forth on a bill of sale or receipt. A copy of each bill of sale or receipt shall be retained for one year and shall be open to inspection by any peace officer during business hours.

Any person who violates any provision of this section is guilty of a misdemeanor.

(Added by Stats. 1984, Ch. 82, Sec. 2.)

466.3.
(a) Whoever possesses a key, tool, instrument, explosive, or device, or a drawing, print, or mold of a key, tool, instrument, explosive, or device, designed to open, break into, tamper with, or damage a coin-operated machine as defined in subdivision (b), with intent to commit a theft from such machine, is punishable by imprisonment in the county jail for not more than one year, or by fine of not more than one thousand dollars ($1,000), or by both.

(b) As used in this section, the term "coin-operated machine" shall include any automatic vending machine or any part thereof, parking meter, coin telephone, coin laundry machine, coin dry cleaning machine, amusement machine, music machine, vending machine dispensing goods or services, or moneychanger.

(Added by Stats. 1972, Ch. 1088.)

466.5.
(a) Every person who, with the intent to use it in the commission of an unlawful act, possesses a motor vehicle master key or a motor vehicle wheel lock master key is guilty of a misdemeanor.

(b) Every person who, with the intent to use it in the commission of an unlawful act, uses a motor vehicle master key to open a lock or operate the ignition switch of any motor vehicle or uses a motor vehicle wheel lock master key to open a wheel lock on any motor vehicle is guilty of a misdemeanor.

(c) Every person who knowingly manufactures for sale, advertises for sale, offers for sale, or sells a motor vehicle master key or a motor vehicle wheel lock master key, except to persons who use such keys in their lawful occupations or businesses, is guilty of a misdemeanor.

(d) As used in this section:
(1) "Motor vehicle master key" means a key which will operate all the locks or ignition switches, or both the locks and ignition switches, in a given group of motor vehicle locks or motor vehicle ignition switches, or both motor vehicle locks and motor vehicle ignition

switches, each of which can be operated by a key which will not operate one or more of the other locks or ignition switches in such group.

(2) "Motor vehicle wheel lock" means a device attached to a motor vehicle wheel for theft protection purposes which can be removed only by a key unit unique to the wheel lock attached to a particular motor vehicle.

(3) "Motor vehicle wheel lock master key" means a key unit which will operate all the wheel locks in a given group of motor vehicle wheel locks, each of which can be operated by a key unit which will not operate any of the other wheel locks in the group.

(Amended by Stats. 1976, Ch. 138.)

466.6.
(a) Any person who makes a key capable of operating the ignition of a motor vehicle or personal property registered under the Vehicle Code for another by any method other than by the duplication of an existing key, whether or not for compensation, shall obtain the name, address, telephone number, if any, date of birth, and driver's license number or identification number of the person requesting or purchasing the key; and the registration or identification number, license number, year, make, model, color, and vehicle identification number of the vehicle or personal property registered under the Vehicle Code for which the key is to be made. Such information, together with the date the key was made and the signature of the person for whom the key was made, shall be set forth on a work order. A copy of each such work order shall be retained for two years, shall include the name and permit number of the locksmith performing the service, and shall be open to inspection by any peace officer or by the Bureau of Collection and Investigative Services during business hours or submitted to the bureau upon request.

Any person who violates any provision of this subdivision is guilty of a misdemeanor.
(b) The provisions of this section shall include, but are not limited to, the making of a key from key codes or impressions.
(c) Nothing contained in this section shall be construed to prohibit the duplication of any key for a motor vehicle from another key.

(Amended by Stats. 1992, Ch. 1135, Sec. 27. Effective January 1, 1993.)

466.65.
(a) Every person who possesses, gives, or lends any device designed to bypass the factory-installed ignition of a motorcycle in order to start the engine of a motorcycle without a manufacturer's key, or who possesses, gives, or lends any motorcycle ignition, or part thereof, with the intent to unlawfully take or drive, or to facilitate the unlawful taking or driving of, a motorcycle without the consent of the owner, is guilty of a misdemeanor.

(b) Every person who possesses, gives, or lends any item of hardware, including, but not limited to, boltcutters, electrical tape, wirecutters, wire strippers, or allen wrenches, with the intent to unlawfully take or drive, or to facilitate the unlawful taking or driving of, a motorcycle without the consent of the owner, is guilty of a misdemeanor.

(Added by Stats. 2010, Ch. 120, Sec. 1. (AB 1848) Effective January 1, 2011.)

466.7.
Every person who, with the intent to use it in the commission of an unlawful act, possesses a motor vehicle key with knowledge that such key was made without the consent of either the registered or legal owner of the motor vehicle or of a person who is in lawful possession of the motor vehicle, is guilty of a misdemeanor.

(Added by Stats. 1977, Ch. 1147.)

466.8.
(a) Any person who knowingly and willfully makes a key capable of opening any door or other means of entrance to any residence or commercial establishment for another by any method involving an onsite inspection of such door or entrance, whether or not for compensation, shall obtain, together with the date the key was made, the street address of the residence or commercial establishment, and the signature of the person for whom the key was made, on a work order form, the following information regarding the person requesting or purchasing the key:
(1) Name.
(2) Address.
(3) Telephone number, if any.
(4) Date of birth.
(5) Driver's license number or identification number, if any.
A copy of each such work order shall be retained for two years and shall be open to inspection by any peace officer or by the Bureau of Collection and Investigative Services during business hours or submitted to the bureau upon request.
Any person who violates any provision of this subdivision is guilty of a misdemeanor.
(b) Nothing contained in this section shall be construed to prohibit the duplication of any key for a residence or commercial establishment from another such key.
(c) Locksmiths licensed by the Bureau of Collection and Investigative Services are subject to the provisions set forth in Chapter 8.5 (commencing with Section 6980) of Division 3 of the Business and Professions Code.
(d) The provisions of this section shall include, but are not limited to, the making of a key from key codes or impressions.

(Amended by Stats. 1992, Ch. 1135, Sec. 28. Effective January 1, 1993.)

466.9.
(a) Every person who possesses a code grabbing device, with the intent to use it in the commission of an unlawful act, is guilty of a misdemeanor.
(b) Every person who uses a code grabbing device to disarm the security alarm system of a motor vehicle, with the intent to use the device in the commission of an unlawful act, is guilty of a misdemeanor.
(c) As used in this section, "code grabbing device" means a device that can receive and record the coded signal sent by the transmitter of a motor vehicle security alarm system and can play back the signal to disarm that system.

(Added by renumbering Section 446.9 by Stats. 1995, Ch. 91, Sec. 124. Effective January 1, 1996.)

468.
Any person who knowingly buys, sells, receives, disposes of, conceals, or has in his possession a sniperscope shall be guilty of a misdemeanor, punishable by a fine not to exceed one thousand dollars ($1,000) or by imprisonment in the county jail for not more than one year, or by both such fine and imprisonment.

As used in this section, sniperscope means any attachment, device or similar contrivance designed for or adaptable to use on a firearm which, through the use of a projected infrared light source and electronic telescope, enables the operator thereof to visually determine and locate the presence of objects during the nighttime.

This section shall not prohibit the authorized use or possession of such sniperscope by a member of the armed forces of the United States or by police officers, peace officers, or law enforcement officers authorized by the properly constituted authorities for the enforcement of law or ordinances; nor shall this section prohibit the use or possession of such sniperscope when used solely for scientific research or educational purposes.

(Added by Stats. 1958, 1st Ex. Sess., Ch. 76.)

469.
Any person who knowingly makes, duplicates, causes to be duplicated, or uses, or attempts to make, duplicate, cause to be duplicated, or use, or has in his possession any key to a building or other area owned, operated, or controlled by the State of California, any state agency, board, or commission, a county, city, or any public school or community college district without authorization from the person in charge of such building or area or his designated representative and with knowledge of the lack of such authorization is guilty of a misdemeanor.

(Added by Stats. 1970, Ch. 1090.)

CHAPTER 4. Forgery and Counterfeiting [470 - 483.5]

(Chapter 4 enacted 1872.)
470.
(a) Every person who, with the intent to defraud, knowing that he or she has no authority to do so, signs the name of another person or of a fictitious person to any of the items listed in subdivision (d) is guilty of forgery.
(b) Every person who, with the intent to defraud, counterfeits or forges the seal or handwriting of another is guilty of forgery.
(c) Every person who, with the intent to defraud, alters, corrupts, or falsifies any record of any will, codicil, conveyance, or other instrument, the record of which is by law evidence, or any record of any judgment of a court or the return of any officer to any process of any court, is guilty of forgery.
(d) Every person who, with the intent to defraud, falsely makes, alters, forges, or counterfeits, utters, publishes, passes or attempts or offers to pass, as true and genuine, any of the following items, knowing the same to be false, altered, forged, or counterfeited, is guilty of forgery: any check, bond, bank bill, or note, cashier's check, traveler's check, money order, post note, draft, any controller's warrant for the payment of money at the treasury, county order or warrant, or request for the payment of money, receipt for money or goods, bill of exchange, promissory note, order, or any assignment of any bond, writing obligatory, or other contract for money or other property, contract, due bill for payment of money or property, receipt for money or property, passage ticket, lottery ticket or share purporting to be issued under the California State Lottery Act of 1984, trading stamp, power of attorney, certificate of ownership or other document evidencing ownership of a vehicle or undocumented vessel, or any certificate of any share, right, or interest in the stock of any corporation or association, or the delivery of goods or chattels of any kind, or for the delivery of any instrument of writing, or acquittance, release or discharge of any debt, account, suit, action, demand, or any other thing, real or personal, or any transfer or assurance of money, certificate of shares of stock, goods, chattels, or other property whatever, or any letter of attorney, or other power to receive money, or to receive or transfer certificates of shares of stock or annuities, or to let, lease, dispose of, alien, or convey any goods, chattels, lands, or tenements, or other estate, real or personal, or falsifies the acknowledgment of any notary public, or any notary public who issues an acknowledgment knowing it to be false; or any matter described in subdivision (b).
(e) Upon a trial for forging any bill or note purporting to be the bill or note of an incorporated company or bank, or for passing, or attempting to pass, or having in possession with intent to pass, any forged bill or note, it is not necessary to prove the incorporation of the bank or company by the charter or act of incorporation, but it may be proved by general reputation; and persons of skill are competent witnesses to prove that the bill or note is forged or counterfeited.
(Amended by Stats. 2005, Ch. 295, Sec. 5. Effective January 1, 2006.)
470a.
Every person who alters, falsifies, forges, duplicates or in any manner reproduces or counterfeits any driver's license or identification card issued by a governmental agency with the intent that such driver's license or identification card be used to facilitate the commission of any forgery, is punishable by imprisonment in a county jail for not more than one year, or by imprisonment pursuant to subdivision (h) of Section 1170.
(Amended by Stats. 2011, Ch. 15, Sec. 358. (AB 109) Effective April 4, 2011. Operative October 1, 2011, by Sec. 636 of Ch. 15, as amended by Stats. 2011, Ch. 39, Sec. 68.)
470b.
Every person who displays or causes or permits to be displayed or has in his or her possession any driver's license or identification card of the type enumerated in Section 470a with the intent that the driver's license or identification card be used to facilitate the commission of any forgery, is punishable by imprisonment in a county jail for not more than one year, or by imprisonment pursuant to subdivision (h) of Section 1170.
(Amended by Stats. 2011, Ch. 15, Sec. 359. (AB 109) Effective April 4, 2011. Operative October 1, 2011, by Sec. 636 of Ch. 15, as amended by Stats. 2011, Ch. 39, Sec. 68.)
471.
Every person who, with intent to defraud another, makes, forges, or alters any entry in any book of records, or any instrument purporting to be any record or return specified in Section 470, is guilty of forgery.
(Amended by Stats. 2002, Ch. 787, Sec. 11. Effective January 1, 2003.)
471.5.
Any person who alters or modifies the medical record of any person, with fraudulent intent, or who, with fraudulent intent, creates any false medical record, is guilty of a misdemeanor.
(Amended by Stats. 1979, Ch. 644.)
472.
Every person who, with intent to defraud another, forges, or counterfeits the seal of this State, the seal of any public officer authorized by law, the seal of any Court of record, or the seal of any corporation, or any other public seal authorized or recognized by the laws of this State, or of any other State, Government, or country, or who falsely makes, forges, or counterfeits any impression purporting to be an impression of any such seal, or who has in his possession any such counterfeited seal or impression thereof, knowing it to be counterfeited, and willfully conceals the same, is guilty of forgery.
(Enacted 1872.)
473.
(a) Forgery is punishable by imprisonment in a county jail for not more than one year, or by imprisonment pursuant to subdivision (h) of Section 1170.
(b) Notwithstanding subdivision (a), any person who is guilty of forgery relating to a check, bond, bank bill, note, cashier's check, traveler's check, or money order, where the value of the check, bond, bank bill, note, cashier's check, traveler's check, or money order does not exceed nine hundred fifty dollars ($950), shall be punishable by imprisonment in a county jail for not more than one year, except that such person may instead be punished pursuant to subdivision (h) of Section 1170 if that person has one or more prior convictions for an offense specified in clause (iv) of subparagraph (C) of paragraph (2) of subdivision (e) of Section 667 or for an offense requiring registration pursuant to subdivision (c) of Section 290. This subdivision shall not be applicable to any person who is convicted both of forgery and of identity theft, as defined in Section 530.5.
(Amended November 4, 2014, by initiative Proposition 47, Sec. 6.)
474.
Every person who knowingly and willfully sends by telegraph or telephone to any person a false or forged message, purporting to be from a telegraph or telephone office, or from any other person, or who willfully delivers or causes to be delivered to any person any such message falsely purporting to have been received by telegraph or telephone, or who furnishes, or conspires to furnish, or causes to be furnished to any agent, operator, or employee, to be sent by telegraph or telephone, or to be delivered, any such message, knowing the same to be false or forged, with the intent to deceive, injure, or defraud another, is punishable by imprisonment in a county jail not exceeding one year, or by imprisonment pursuant to subdivision (h) of Section 1170, or by a fine not exceeding ten thousand dollars ($10,000), or by both that fine and imprisonment.
(Amended by Stats. 2011, Ch. 15, Sec. 361. (AB 109) Effective April 4, 2011. Operative October 1, 2011, by Sec. 636 of Ch. 15, as amended by Stats. 2011, Ch. 39, Sec. 68.)
475.
(a) Every person who possesses or receives, with the intent to pass or facilitate the passage or utterance of any forged, altered, or counterfeit items, or completed items contained in subdivision (d) of Section 470 with intent to defraud, knowing the same to be forged, altered, or counterfeit, is guilty of forgery.
(b) Every person who possesses any blank or unfinished check, note, bank bill, money order, or traveler's check, whether real or fictitious, with the intention of completing the same or the intention of facilitating the completion of the same, in order to defraud any person, is guilty of forgery.
(c) Every person who possesses any completed check, money order, traveler's check, warrant or county order, whether real or fictitious, with the intent to utter or pass or facilitate the utterance or passage of the same, in order to defraud any person, is guilty of forgery.
(Repealed and added by Stats. 1998, Ch. 468, Sec. 4. Effective January 1, 1999.)
476.
Every person who makes, passes, utters, or publishes, with intent to defraud any other person, or who, with the like intent, attempts to pass, utter, or publish, or who has in his or her possession, with like intent to utter, pass, or publish, any fictitious or altered bill, note, or check, purporting to be the bill, note, or check, or other instrument in writing for the payment of money or property of any real or fictitious financial institution as defined in Section 186.9 is guilty of forgery.
(Repealed and added by Stats. 1998, Ch. 468, Sec. 7. Effective January 1, 1999.)
476a.
(a) Any person who, for himself or herself, as the agent or representative of another, or as an officer of a corporation, willfully, with intent to defraud, makes or draws or utters or delivers a check, draft, or order upon a bank or depositary, a person, a firm, or a corporation, for the payment of money, knowing at the time of that making, drawing, uttering, or delivering that the maker or drawer or the corporation has not sufficient funds in, or credit with the bank or depositary, person, firm, or corporation, for the payment of that check, draft, or order and all other checks, drafts, or orders upon funds then outstanding, in full upon its presentation, although no express representation is made with reference thereto, is punishable by imprisonment in a county jail for not more than one year, or pursuant to subdivision (h) of Section 1170.
(b) However, if the total amount of all checks, drafts, or orders that the defendant is charged with and convicted of making, drawing, or uttering does not exceed nine hundred fifty dollars ($950), the offense is punishable only by imprisonment in the county jail for not more than one year, except that such person may instead be punished pursuant to subdivision (h) of Section 1170 if that person has one or more prior convictions for an offense specified in clause (iv) of subparagraph (C) of paragraph (2) of subdivision (e) of Section 667 or for an offense requiring registration pursuant to subdivision (c) of Section 290. This subdivision shall not be applicable if the defendant has previously been convicted of three or more violations of Section 470, 475, or 476, or of this section, or of the crime of petty theft in a case in which defendant's offense was a violation also of Section 470, 475, or 476 or of this section or if the defendant has previously been convicted of any offense under the laws of any other state or of the United States which, if committed in this state, would have been punishable as a violation of Section 470, 475 or 476 or of this section or if he has been so convicted of the crime of petty theft in a case in which, if defendant's offense had been committed in this state, it would have been a violation also of Section 470, 475, or 476, or of this section.
(c) Where the check, draft, or order is protested on the ground of insufficiency of funds or credit, the notice of protest shall be admissible as proof of presentation, nonpayment, and protest and shall be presumptive evidence of knowledge of insufficiency of funds or credit with the bank or depositary, person, firm, or corporation.
(d) In any prosecution under this section involving two or more checks, drafts, or orders, it shall constitute prima facie evidence of the identity of the drawer of a check, draft, or order if both of the following occur:
(1) When the payee accepts the check, draft, or order from the drawer, he or she obtains from the drawer the following information: name and residence of the drawer, business or mailing address, either a valid driver's license number or Department of Motor Vehicles identification card number, and the drawer's home or work phone number or place of employment. That information may be recorded on the check, draft, or order itself or may be retained on file by the payee and referred to on the check, draft, or order by identifying number or other similar means.
(2) The person receiving the check, draft, or order witnesses the drawer's signature or endorsement, and, as evidence of that, initials the check, draft, or order at the time of receipt.
(e) The word "credit" as used herein shall be construed to mean an arrangement or understanding with the bank or depositary, person, firm, or corporation for the payment of a check, draft, or order.
(f) If any of the preceding paragraphs, or parts thereof, shall be found unconstitutional or invalid, the remainder of this section shall not thereby be invalidated, but shall remain in full force and effect.
(g) A sheriff's department, police department, or other law enforcement agency may collect a fee from the defendant for investigation, collection, and processing of checks referred to their agency for investigation of alleged violations of this section or Section 476.
(h) The amount of the fee shall not exceed twenty-five dollars ($25) for each bad check, in addition to the amount of any bank charges incurred by the victim as a result of the alleged offense. If the sheriff's department, police department, or other law enforcement agency collects a fee for bank charges incurred by the victim pursuant to this section, that fee shall be paid to the victim for any bank fees the victim may have been assessed. In no event shall reimbursement of the bank charge to the victim pursuant to this section exceed ten dollars ($10) per check.
(Amended November 4, 2014, by initiative Proposition 47, Sec. 7.)
477.
Every person who counterfeits any of the species of gold or silver coin current in this State, or any kind or species of gold dust, gold or silver bullion, or bars, lumps, pieces, or nuggets, or who sells, passes, or gives in payment such counterfeit coin, dust, bullion, bars, lumps, pieces, or nuggets, or permits, causes, or procures the same to be sold, uttered, or passed, with intention to defraud any person, knowing the same to be counterfeited, is guilty of counterfeiting.
(Enacted 1872.)
478.
Counterfeiting is punishable by imprisonment pursuant to subdivision (h) of Section 1170 for two, three or four years.
(Amended by Stats. 2011, Ch. 15, Sec. 362. (AB 109) Effective April 4, 2011. Operative October 1, 2011, by Sec. 636 of Ch. 15, as amended by Stats. 2011, Ch. 39, Sec. 68.)
479.
Every person who has in his possession, or receives for any other person, any counterfeit gold or silver coin of the species current in this state, or any counterfeit gold dust, gold or silver bullion or bars, lumps, pieces or nuggets, with the intention to sell, utter, put off or pass the same, or permits, causes or procures the same to be sold, uttered or passed, with intention to defraud any person, knowing the same to be counterfeit, is punishable by imprisonment pursuant to subdivision (h) of Section 1170 for two, three or four years.
(Amended by Stats. 2011, Ch. 15, Sec. 363. (AB 109) Effective April 4, 2011. Operative October 1, 2011, by Sec. 636 of Ch. 15, as amended by Stats. 2011, Ch. 39, Sec. 68.)
480.

(a) Every person who makes, or knowingly has in his or her possession any die, plate, or any apparatus, paper, metal, machine, or other thing whatever, made use of in counterfeiting coin current in this state, or in counterfeiting gold dust, gold or silver bars, bullion, lumps, pieces, or nuggets, or in counterfeiting bank notes or bills, is punishable by imprisonment pursuant to subdivision (h) of Section 1170 for two, three, or four years; and all dies, plates, apparatus, papers, metals, or machines intended for the purpose aforesaid, must be destroyed.
(b) (1) If the counterfeiting apparatus or machine used to violate this section is a computer, computer system, or computer network, the apparatus or machine shall be disposed of pursuant to Section 502.01.
(2) For the purposes of this section, "computer system" and "computer network" have the same meaning as that specified in Section 502. The terms "computer, computer system, or computer network" include any software or data residing on the computer, computer system, or computer network used in a violation of this section.
(Amended by Stats. 2011, Ch. 15, Sec. 364. (AB 109) Effective April 4, 2011. Operative October 1, 2011, by Sec. 636 of Ch. 15, as amended by Stats. 2011, Ch. 39, Sec. 68.)
481.
Every person who counterfeits, forges, or alters any ticket, check, order, coupon, receipt for fare, or pass, issued by any railroad or steamship company, or by any lessee or manager thereof, designed to entitle the holder to ride in the cars or vessels of such company, or who utters, publishes, or puts into circulation, any such counterfeit or altered ticket, check, or order, coupon, receipt for fare, or pass, with intent to defraud any such railroad or steamship company, or any lessee thereof, or any other person, is punishable by imprisonment in a county jail, not exceeding one year, or by imprisonment pursuant to subdivision (h) of Section 1170, or by fine not exceeding one thousand dollars, or by both that imprisonment and fine.
(Amended by Stats. 2011, Ch. 15, Sec. 365. (AB 109) Effective April 4, 2011. Operative October 1, 2011, by Sec. 636 of Ch. 15, as amended by Stats. 2011, Ch. 39, Sec. 68.)
481.1.
(a) Every person who counterfeits, forges, or alters any fare media designed to entitle the holder to a ride on vehicles of a public transportation system, as defined by Section 99211 of the Public Utilities Code, or on vehicles operated by entities subsidized by the Department of Transportation is punishable by imprisonment in a county jail, not exceeding one year, or in the state prison.
(b) Every person who knowingly possesses any counterfeit, forged, or altered fare media designed to entitle the holder to a ride on vehicles of a public transportation system, as defined by Section 99211 of the Public Utilities Code, or on vehicles operated by entities subsidized by the Department of Transportation, or who utters, publishes, or puts into circulation any fare media with intent to defraud is punishable by imprisonment in a county jail not exceeding one year, or by a fine not exceeding one thousand dollars ($1,000), or by both that imprisonment and fine.
(Amended by Stats. 2001, Ch. 854, Sec. 29. Effective January 1, 2002.)
482.
Every person who, for the purpose of restoring to its original appearance and nominal value in whole or in part, removes, conceals, fills up, or obliterates, the cuts, marks, punch-holes, or other evidence of cancellation, from any ticket, check, order, coupon, receipt for fare, or pass, issued by any railroad or steamship company, or any lessee or manager thereof, canceled in whole or in part, with intent to dispose of by sale or gift, or to circulate the same, or with intent to defraud the railroad or steamship company, or lessee thereof, or any other person, or who, with like intent to defraud, offers for sale, or in payment of fare on the railroad or vessel of the company, such ticket, check, order, coupon, or pass, knowing the same to have been so restored, in whole or in part, is punishable by imprisonment in the county jail not exceeding six months, or by a fine not exceeding one thousand dollars, or by both such imprisonment and fine.
(Amended by Stats. 1905, Ch. 515.)
483.
Except as otherwise provided in Section 26002.5 of the Government Code and Sections 40180.5 and 99151 of the Public Utilities Code, any person, firm, corporation, partnership, or association that shall sell to another any ticket, pass, scrip, mileage or commutation book, coupon, or other instrument for passage on a common carrier, for the use of any person not entitled to use the same according to the terms thereof, or of the book or portion thereof from which it was detached, shall be guilty of a misdemeanor.
(Amended by Stats. 1979, Ch. 161.)
483.5.
(a) No deceptive identification document shall be manufactured, sold, offered for sale, furnished, offered to be furnished, transported, offered to be transported, or imported or offered to be imported into this state unless there is diagonally across the face of the document, in not less than 14-point type and printed conspicuously on the document in permanent ink, the following statement:
NOT A GOVERNMENT DOCUMENT
and, also printed conspicuously on the document, the name of the manufacturer.
(b) No document-making device may be possessed with the intent that the device will be used to manufacture, alter, or authenticate a deceptive identification document.
(c) As used in this section, "deceptive identification document" means any document not issued by a governmental agency of this state, another state, the federal government, a foreign government, a political subdivision of a foreign government, an international government, or an international quasi-governmental organization, which purports to be, or which might deceive an ordinary reasonable person into believing that it is, a document issued by such an agency, including, but not limited to, a driver's license, identification card, birth certificate, passport, or social security card.
(d) As used in this section, "document-making device" includes, but is not limited to, an implement, tool, equipment, impression, laminate, card, template, computer file, computer disk, electronic device, hologram, laminate machine or computer hardware or software.
(e) Any person who violates or proposes to violate this section may be enjoined by any court of competent jurisdiction. Actions for injunction under this section may be prosecuted by the Attorney General, any district attorney, or any city attorney prosecuting on behalf of the people of the State of California under Section 41803.5 of the Government Code in this state in the name of the people of the State of California upon their own complaint or upon the complaint of any person.
(f) Any person who violates the provisions of subdivision (a) who knows or reasonably should know that the deceptive identification document will be used for fraudulent purposes is guilty of a crime, and upon conviction therefor, shall be punished by imprisonment in a county jail not to exceed one year, or by imprisonment pursuant to subdivision (h) of Section 1170. Any person who violates the provisions of subdivision (b) is guilty of a misdemeanor punishable by imprisonment in a county jail not exceeding one year, or by a fine not exceeding one thousand dollars ($1,000), or by both imprisonment and a fine. Any document-making device may be seized by law enforcement and shall be forfeited to law enforcement or destroyed by order of the court upon a finding that the device was intended to be used to manufacture, alter, or authenticate a deceptive identification document. The court may make such a finding in the absence of a defendant for whom a bench warrant has been issued by the court.
(Amended by Stats. 2011, Ch. 15, Sec. 366. (AB 109) Effective April 4, 2011. Operative October 1, 2011, by Sec. 636 of Ch. 15, as amended by Stats. 2011, Ch. 39, Sec. 68.)

CHAPTER 5. Larceny [484 - 502.9]

(Chapter 5 enacted 1872.)
484.
(a) Every person who shall feloniously steal, take, carry, lead, or drive away the personal property of another, or who shall fraudulently appropriate property which has been entrusted to him or her, or who shall knowingly and designedly, by any false or fraudulent representation or pretense, defraud any other person of money, labor or real or personal property, or who causes or procures others to report falsely of his or her wealth or mercantile character and by thus imposing upon any person, obtains credit and thereby fraudulently gets or obtains possession of money, or property or obtains the labor or service of another, is guilty of theft. In determining the value of the property obtained, for the purposes of this section, the reasonable and fair market value shall be the test, and in determining the value of services received the contract price shall be the test. If there be no contract price, the reasonable and going wage for the service rendered shall govern. For the purposes of this section, any false or fraudulent representation or pretense made shall be treated as continuing, so as to cover any money, property or service received as a result thereof, and the complaint, information or indictment may charge that the crime was committed on any date during the particular period in question. The hiring of any additional employee or employees without advising each of them of every labor claim due and unpaid and every judgment that the employer has been unable to meet shall be prima facie evidence of intent to defraud.
(b) (1) Except as provided in Section 10855 of the Vehicle Code, where a person has leased or rented the personal property of another person pursuant to a written contract, and that property has a value greater than one thousand dollars ($1,000) and is not a commonly used household item, intent to commit theft by fraud shall be rebuttably presumed if the person fails to return the personal property to its owner within 10 days after the owner has made written demand by certified or registered mail following the expiration of the lease or rental agreement for return of the property so leased or rented.
(2) Except as provided in Section 10855 of the Vehicle Code, where a person has leased or rented the personal property of another person pursuant to a written contract, and where the property has a value no greater than one thousand dollars ($1,000), or where the property is a commonly used household item, intent to commit theft by fraud shall be rebuttably presumed if the person fails to return the personal property to its owner within 20 days after the owner has made written demand by certified or registered mail following the expiration of the lease or rental agreement for return of the property so leased or rented.
(c) Notwithstanding the provisions of subdivision (b), if one presents with criminal intent identification which bears a false or fictitious name or address for the purpose of obtaining the lease or rental of the personal property of another, the presumption created herein shall apply upon the failure of the lessee to return the rental property at the expiration of the lease or rental agreement, and no written demand for the return of the leased or rented property shall be required.
(d) The presumptions created by subdivisions (b) and (c) are presumptions affecting the burden of producing evidence.
(e) Within 30 days after the lease or rental agreement has expired, the owner shall make written demand for return of the property so leased or rented. Notice addressed and mailed to the lessee or renter at the address given at the time of the making of the lease or rental agreement and to any other known address shall constitute proper demand. Where the owner fails to make such written demand the presumption created by subdivision (b) shall not apply.
(Amended by Stats. 2000, Ch. 176, Sec. 1. Effective January 1, 2001.)
484.1.
(a) Any person who knowingly gives false information or provides false verification as to the person's true identity or as to the person's ownership interest in property or the person's authority to sell property in order to receive money or other valuable consideration from a pawnbroker or secondhand dealer and who receives money or other valuable consideration from the pawnbroker or secondhand dealer is guilty of theft.
(b) Upon conviction of the offense described in subdivision (a), the court may require, in addition to any sentence or fine imposed, that the defendant make restitution to the pawnbroker or secondhand dealer in an amount not exceeding the actual losses sustained pursuant to the provisions of subdivision (c) of Section 13967 of the Government Code, as operative on or before September 28, 1994, if the defendant is denied probation, or Section 1203.04, as operative on or before August 2, 1995, if the defendant is granted probation or Section 1202.4.
(c) Upon the setting of a court hearing date for sentencing of any person convicted under this section, the probation officer, if one is assigned, shall notify the pawnbroker or secondhand dealer or coin dealer of the time and place of the hearing.
(Amended by Stats. 1996, Ch. 1077, Sec. 18.5. Effective January 1, 1997.)
484b.
Any person who receives money for the purpose of obtaining or paying for services, labor, materials or equipment and willfully fails to apply such money for such purpose by either willfully failing to complete the improvements for which funds were provided or willfully failing to pay for services, labor, materials or equipment provided incident to such construction, and wrongfully diverts the funds to a use other than that for which the funds were received, shall be guilty of a public offense and shall be punishable by a fine not exceeding ten thousand dollars ($10,000), or by imprisonment in a county jail not exceeding one year, or by imprisonment pursuant to subdivision (h) of Section 1170, or by both that fine and that imprisonment if the amount diverted is in excess of two thousand three hundred fifty dollars ($2,350). If the amount diverted is less than or equal to two thousand three hundred fifty dollars ($2,350), the person shall be guilty of a misdemeanor.
(Amended by Stats. 2011, Ch. 15, Sec. 367. (AB 109) Effective April 4, 2011. Operative October 1, 2011, by Sec. 636 of Ch. 15, as amended by Stats. 2011, Ch. 39, Sec. 68.)
484c.
Any person who submits a false voucher to obtain construction loan funds and does not use the funds for the purpose for which the claim was submitted is guilty of embezzlement.
(Added by Stats. 1965, Ch. 1145.)
484d.
As used in this section and Sections 484e to 484j, inclusive:
(1) "Cardholder" means any person to whom an access card is issued or any person who has agreed with the card issuer to pay obligations arising from the issuance of an access card to another person.
(2) "Access card" means any card, plate, code, account number, or other means of account access that can be used, alone or in conjunction with another access card, to obtain money, goods, services, or any other thing of value, or that can be used to initiate a transfer of funds, other than a transfer originated solely by a paper instrument.
(3) "Expired access card" means an access card which shows on its face it has elapsed.
(4) "Card issuer" means any person who issues an access card or the agent of that person with respect to that card.
(5) "Retailer" means every person who is authorized by an issuer to furnish money, goods, services, or anything else of value upon presentation of an access card by a cardholder.
(6) An access card is "incomplete" if part of the matter other than the signature of the cardholder which an issuer requires to appear on the access card before it can be used by a cardholder has not been stamped, embossed, imprinted, or written on it.

(7) "Revoked access card" means an access card which is no longer authorized for use by the issuer, that authorization having been suspended or terminated and written notice thereof having been given to the cardholder.

(8) "Counterfeit access card" means any access card that is counterfeit, fictitious, altered, or forged, or any false representation or depiction of an access card or a component thereof.

(9) "Traffic" means to transfer or otherwise dispose of property to another, or to obtain control of property with intent to transfer or dispose of it to another.

(10) "Card making equipment" means any equipment, machine, plate, mechanism, impression, or other device designed, used, or intended to be used to produce an access card.

(Amended by Stats. 1986, Ch. 1436, Sec. 1.)

484e.

(a) Every person who, with intent to defraud, sells, transfers, or conveys, an access card, without the cardholder's or issuer's consent, is guilty of grand theft.

(b) Every person, other than the issuer, who within any consecutive 12-month period, acquires access cards issued in the names of four or more persons which he or she has reason to know were taken or retained under circumstances which constitute a violation of subdivision (a), (c), or (d) is guilty of grand theft.

(c) Every person who, with the intent to defraud, acquires or retains possession of an access card without the cardholder's or issuer's consent, with intent to use, sell, or transfer it to a person other than the cardholder or issuer is guilty of petty theft.

(d) Every person who acquires or retains possession of access card account information with respect to an access card validly issued to another person, without the cardholder's or issuer's consent, with the intent to use it fraudulently, is guilty of grand theft.

(Repealed and added by Stats. 1998, Ch. 468, Sec. 9. Effective January 1, 1999.)

484f.

(a) Every person who, with the intent to defraud, designs, makes, alters, or embosses a counterfeit access card or utters or otherwise attempts to use a counterfeit access card is guilty of forgery.

(b) A person other than the cardholder or a person authorized by him or her who, with the intent to defraud, signs the name of another or of a fictitious person to an access card, sales slip, sales draft, or instrument for the payment of money which evidences an access card transaction, is guilty of forgery.

(Repealed and added by Stats. 1998, Ch. 468, Sec. 11. Effective January 1, 1999.)

484g.

Every person who, with the intent to defraud, (a) uses, for the purpose of obtaining money, goods, services, or anything else of value, an access card or access card account information that has been altered, obtained, or retained in violation of Section 484e or 484f, or an access card which he or she knows is forged, expired, or revoked, or (b) obtains money, goods, services, or anything else of value by representing without the consent of the cardholder that he or she is the holder of an access card and the card has not in fact been issued, is guilty of theft. If the value of all money, goods, services, and other things of value obtained in violation of this section exceeds nine hundred fifty dollars ($950) in any consecutive six-month period, then the same shall constitute grand theft.

(Amended by Stats. 2009, 3rd Ex. Sess., Ch. 28, Sec. 15. (SB 18 3x) Effective January 25, 2010.)

484h.

Every retailer or other person who, with intent to defraud:

(a) Furnishes money, goods, services or anything else of value upon presentation of an access card obtained or retained in violation of Section 484e or an access card which he or she knows is a counterfeit access card or is forged, expired, or revoked, and who receives any payment therefor, is guilty of theft. If the payment received by the retailer or other person for all money, goods, services, and other things of value furnished in violation of this section exceeds nine hundred fifty dollars ($950) in any consecutive six-month period, then the same shall constitute grand theft.

(b) Presents for payment a sales slip or other evidence of an access card transaction, and receives payment therefor, without furnishing in the transaction money, goods, services, or anything else of value that is equal in value to the amount of the sales slip or other evidence of an access card transaction, is guilty of theft. If the difference between the value of all money, goods, services, and anything else of value actually furnished and the payment or payments received by the retailer or other person therefor upon presentation of a sales slip or other evidence of an access card transaction exceeds nine hundred fifty dollars ($950) in any consecutive six-month period, then the same shall constitute grand theft.

(Amended by Stats. 2009, 3rd Ex. Sess., Ch. 28, Sec. 16. (SB 18 3x) Effective January 25, 2010.)

484i.

(a) Every person who possesses an incomplete access card, with intent to complete it without the consent of the issuer, is guilty of a misdemeanor.

(b) Every person who, with the intent to defraud, makes, alters, varies, changes, or modifies access card account information on any part of an access card, including information encoded in a magnetic stripe or other medium on the access card not directly readable by the human eye, or who authorizes or consents to alteration, variance, change, or modification of access card account information by another, in a manner that causes transactions initiated by that access card to be charged or billed to a person other than the cardholder to whom the access card was issued, is guilty of forgery.

(c) Every person who designs, makes, possesses, or traffics in card making equipment or incomplete access cards with the intent that the equipment or cards be used to make counterfeit access cards, is punishable by imprisonment in a county jail for not more than one year, or by imprisonment pursuant to subdivision (h) of Section 1170.

(Amended by Stats. 2011, Ch. 15, Sec. 368. (AB 109) Effective April 4, 2011. Operative October 1, 2011, by Sec. 636 of Ch. 15, as amended by Stats. 2011, Ch. 39, Sec. 68.)

484j.

Any person who publishes the number or code of an existing, canceled, revoked, expired or nonexistent access card, personal identification number, computer password, access code, debit card number, bank account number, or the numbering or coding which is employed in the issuance of access cards, with the intent that it be used or with knowledge or reason to believe that it will be used to avoid the payment of any lawful charge, or with intent to defraud or aid another in defrauding, is guilty of a misdemeanor. As used in this section, "publishes" means the communication of information to any one or more persons, either orally, in person or by telephone, radio or television, or on a computer network or computer bulletin board, or in a writing of any kind, including without limitation a letter or memorandum, circular or handbill, newspaper or magazine article, or book.

(Amended by Stats. 1986, Ch. 1437, Sec. 2.)

485.

One who finds lost property under circumstances which give him knowledge of or means of inquiry as to the true owner, and who appropriates such property to his own use, or to the use of another person not entitled thereto, without first making reasonable and just efforts to find the owner and to restore the property to him, is guilty of theft.

(Amended by Stats. 1927, Ch. 619.)

486.

Theft is divided into two degrees, the first of which is termed grand theft; the second, petty theft.

(Amended by Stats. 1927, Ch. 619.)

487.

Grand theft is theft committed in any of the following cases:

(a) When the money, labor, or real or personal property taken is of a value exceeding nine hundred fifty dollars ($950), except as provided in subdivision (b).

(b) Notwithstanding subdivision (a), grand theft is committed in any of the following cases:

(1) (A) When domestic fowls, avocados, olives, citrus or deciduous fruits, other fruits, vegetables, nuts, artichokes, or other farm crops are taken of a value exceeding two hundred fifty dollars ($250).

(B) For the purposes of establishing that the value of domestic fowls, avocados, olives, citrus or deciduous fruits, other fruits, vegetables, nuts, artichokes, or other farm crops under this paragraph exceeds two hundred fifty dollars ($250), that value may be shown by the presentation of credible evidence which establishes that on the day of the theft domestic fowls, avocados, olives, citrus or deciduous fruits, other fruits, vegetables, nuts, artichokes, or other farm crops of the same variety and weight exceeded two hundred fifty dollars ($250) in wholesale value.

(2) When fish, shellfish, mollusks, crustaceans, kelp, algae, or other aquacultural products are taken from a commercial or research operation which is producing that product, of a value exceeding two hundred fifty dollars ($250).

(3) Where the money, labor, or real or personal property is taken by a servant, agent, or employee from his or her principal or employer and aggregates nine hundred fifty dollars ($950) or more in any 12 consecutive month period.

(c) When the property is taken from the person of another.

(d) When the property taken is any of the following:

(1) An automobile.

(2) A firearm.

(Amended by Stats. 2013, Ch. 618, Sec. 7. (AB 924) Effective January 1, 2014.)

487a.

(a) Every person who feloniously steals, takes, carries, leads, or drives away any horse, mare, gelding, any bovine animal, any caprine animal, mule, jack, jenny, sheep, lamb, hog, sow, boar, gilt, barrow, or pig, which is the personal property of another, or who fraudulently appropriates that same property which has been entrusted to him or her, or who knowingly and designedly, by any false or fraudulent representation or pretense, defrauds any other person of that same property, or who causes or procures others to report falsely of his or her wealth or mercantile character and by thus imposing upon any person, obtains credit and thereby fraudulently gets or obtains possession of that same property, is guilty of grand theft.

(b) Every person who shall feloniously steal, take, transport or carry the carcass of any bovine, caprine, equine, ovine, or suine animal or of any mule, jack or jenny, which is the personal property of another, or who shall fraudulently appropriate such property which has been entrusted to him or her, is guilty of grand theft.

(c) Every person who shall feloniously steal, take, transport, or carry any portion of the carcass of any bovine, caprine, equine, ovine, or suine animal or of any mule, jack, or jenny, which has been killed without the consent of the owner thereof, is guilty of grand theft.

(Amended by Stats. 2014, Ch. 71, Sec. 122. (SB 1304) Effective January 1, 2015.)

487b.

Every person who converts real estate of the value of two hundred fifty dollars ($250) or more into personal property by severance from the realty of another, and with felonious intent to do so, steals, takes, and carries away that property is guilty of grand theft and is punishable by imprisonment pursuant to subdivision (h) of Section 1170.

(Amended by Stats. 2011, Ch. 15, Sec. 369. (AB 109) Effective April 4, 2011. Operative October 1, 2011, by Sec. 636 of Ch. 15, as amended by Stats. 2011, Ch. 39, Sec. 68.)

487c.

Every person who converts real estate of the value of less than two hundred fifty dollars ($250) into personal property by severance from the realty of another, and with felonious intent to do so steals, takes, and carries away that property is guilty of petty theft and is punishable by imprisonment in the county jail for not more than one year, or by a fine not exceeding one thousand dollars ($1,000), or by both that fine and imprisonment.

(Amended by Stats. 2009, 3rd Ex. Sess., Ch. 28, Sec. 19. (SB 18 3x) Effective January 25, 2010.)

487d.

Every person who feloniously steals, takes, and carries away, or attempts to take, steal, and carry from any mining claim, tunnel, sluice, undercurrent, riffle box, or sulfurate machine, another's gold dust, amalgam, or quicksilver is guilty of grand theft and is punishable by imprisonment pursuant to subdivision (h) of Section 1170.

(Amended by Stats. 2011, Ch. 15, Sec. 370. (AB 109) Effective April 4, 2011. Operative October 1, 2011, by Sec. 636 of Ch. 15, as amended by Stats. 2011, Ch. 39, Sec. 68.)

487e.

Every person who feloniously steals, takes, or carries away a dog of another which is of a value exceeding nine hundred fifty dollars ($950) is guilty of grand theft.

(Amended by Stats. 2009, 3rd Ex. Sess., Ch. 28, Sec. 20. (SB 18 3x) Effective January 25, 2010.)

487f.

Every person who feloniously steals, takes, or carries away a dog of another which is of a value not exceeding nine hundred fifty dollars ($950) is guilty of petty theft.

(Amended by Stats. 2009, 3rd Ex. Sess., Ch. 28, Sec. 21. (SB 18 3x) Effective January 25, 2010.)

487g.

Every person who steals or maliciously takes or carries away any animal of another for purposes of sale, medical research, slaughter, or other commercial use, or who knowingly, by any false representation or pretense, defrauds another person of any animal for purposes of sale, medical research, slaughter, or other commercial use is guilty of a public offense punishable by imprisonment in a county jail not exceeding one year or in the state prison.

(Amended by Stats. 1995, Ch. 151, Sec. 1. Effective January 1, 1996.)

487h.

(a) Every person who steals, takes, or carries away cargo of another, if the cargo taken is of a value exceeding nine hundred fifty dollars ($950), except as provided in Sections 487, 487a, and 487d, is guilty of grand theft.

(b) For the purposes of this section, "cargo" means any goods, wares, products, or manufactured merchandise that has been loaded into a trailer, railcar, or cargo container, awaiting or in transit.

(Amended by Stats. 2009, Ch. 607, Sec. 1. (SB 24) Effective January 1, 2010.)

487i.

Any person who defrauds a housing program of a public housing authority of more than four hundred dollars ($400) is guilty of grand theft.

(Added by Stats. 2008, Ch. 105, Sec. 1. Effective January 1, 2009.)

487j.

Every person who steals, takes, or carries away copper materials of another, including, but not limited to, copper wire, copper cable, copper tubing, and copper piping, which are of a value exceeding nine hundred fifty dollars ($950) is guilty of grand theft. Grand theft of copper shall be punishable by a fine not exceeding two thousand five hundred dollars ($2,500), by imprisonment in a county jail not exceeding one year, or by both that fine and imprisonment, or by imprisonment pursuant to subdivision (h) of Section 1170 and a fine not exceeding ten thousand dollars ($10,000).

(Added by Stats. 2011, Ch. 317, Sec. 2. (AB 316) Effective January 1, 2012.)

488.

Theft in other cases is petty theft.

(Amended by Stats. 1927, Ch. 619.)
489.
Grand theft is punishable as follows:
(a) If the grand theft involves the theft of a firearm, by imprisonment in the state prison for 16 months, or two or three years.
(b) If the grand theft involves a violation of Section 487a, by imprisonment in a county jail not exceeding one year or pursuant to subdivision (h) of Section 1170, or by a fine not exceeding five thousand dollars ($5,000), or by both that fine and imprisonment. The proceeds of this fine shall be allocated to the Bureau of Livestock Identification to be used, upon appropriation by the Legislature, for purposes relating to the investigation of cases involving grand theft of any animal or animals, or of the carcass or carcasses of, or any portion of the carcass or carcasses of, any animal specified in Section 487a.
(c) In all other cases, by imprisonment in a county jail not exceeding one year or pursuant to subdivision (h) of Section 1170.
(Amended by Stats. 2013, Ch. 618, Sec. 9. (AB 924) Effective January 1, 2014.)
490.
Petty theft is punishable by fine not exceeding one thousand dollars ($1,000), or by imprisonment in the county jail not exceeding six months, or both.
(Amended by Stats. 1976, Ch. 1125.)
490a.
Wherever any law or statute of this state refers to or mentions larceny, embezzlement, or stealing, said law or statute shall hereafter be read and interpreted as if the word "theft" were substituted therefor.
(Added by Stats. 1927, Ch. 619.)
490.1.
(a) Petty theft, where the value of the money, labor, real or personal property taken is of a value which does not exceed fifty dollars ($50), may be charged as a misdemeanor or an infraction, at the discretion of the prosecutor, provided that the person charged with the offense has no other theft or theft-related conviction.
(b) Any offense charged as an infraction under this section shall be subject to the provisions of subdivision (d) of Section 17 and Sections 19.6 and 19.7.
A violation which is an infraction under this section is punishable by a fine not exceeding two hundred fifty dollars ($250).
(Added by Stats. 1991, Ch. 638, Sec. 2.)
490.2.
(a) Notwithstanding Section 487 or any other provision of law defining grand theft, obtaining any property by theft where the value of the money, labor, real or personal property taken does not exceed nine hundred fifty dollars ($950) shall be considered petty theft and shall be punished as a misdemeanor, except that such person may instead be punished pursuant to subdivision (h) of Section 1170 if that person has one or more prior convictions for an offense specified in clause (iv) of subparagraph (C) of paragraph (2) of subdivision (e) of Section 667 or for an offense requiring registration pursuant to subdivision (c) of Section 290.
(b) This section shall not be applicable to any theft that may be charged as an infraction pursuant to any other provision of law.
(c) This section shall not apply to theft of a firearm.
(Amended November 8, 2016, by initiative Proposition 63, Sec. 11.1. Note: This section was added on Nov. 4, 2014, by initiative Prop. 47.)
490.4.
(a) A person who commits any of the following acts is guilty of organized retail theft, and shall be punished pursuant to subdivision (b):
(1) Acts in concert with one or more persons to steal merchandise from one or more merchant's premises or online marketplace with the intent to sell, exchange, or return the merchandise for value.
(2) Acts in concert with two or more persons to receive, purchase, or possess merchandise described in paragraph (1), knowing or believing it to have been stolen.
(3) Acts as an agent of another individual or group of individuals to steal merchandise from one or more merchant's premises or online marketplaces as part of an organized plan to commit theft.
(4) Recruits, coordinates, organizes, supervises, directs, manages, or finances another to undertake any of the acts described in paragraph (1) or (2) or any other statute defining theft of merchandise.
(b) Organized retail theft is punishable as follows:
(1) If violations of paragraph (1), (2), or (3) of subdivision (a) are committed on two or more separate occasions within a 12-month period, and if the aggregated value of the merchandise stolen, received, purchased, or possessed within that 12-month period exceeds nine hundred fifty dollars ($950), the offense is punishable by imprisonment in a county jail not exceeding one year or pursuant to subdivision (h) of Section 1170.
(2) Any other violation of paragraph (1), (2), or (3) of subdivision (a) that is not described in paragraph (1) of this subdivision is punishable by imprisonment in a county jail not exceeding one year.
(3) A violation of paragraph (4) of subdivision (a) is punishable by imprisonment in a county jail not exceeding one year or pursuant to subdivision (h) of Section 1170.
(c) For the purpose of determining whether the defendant acted in concert with another person or persons in any proceeding, the trier of fact may consider any competent evidence, including, but not limited to, all of the following:
(1) The defendant has previously acted in concert with another person or persons in committing acts constituting theft, or any related offense, including any conduct that occurred in counties other than the county of the current offense, if relevant to demonstrate a fact other than the defendant's disposition to commit the act.
(2) That the defendant used or possessed an artifice, instrument, container, device, or other article capable of facilitating the removal of merchandise from a retail establishment without paying the purchase price and use of the artifice, instrument, container, or device or other article is part of an organized plan to commit theft.
(3) The property involved in the offense is of a type or quantity that would not normally be purchased for personal use or consumption and the property is intended for resale.
(d) In a prosecution under this section, the prosecutor shall not be required to charge any other coparticipant of the organized retail theft.
(e) Upon conviction of an offense under this section, the court shall consider ordering, as a condition of probation, that the defendant stay away from retail establishments with a reasonable nexus to the crime committed.
(f) This section shall remain in effect only until July 1, 2021, and as of that date is repealed.
(Amended by Stats. 2019, Ch. 25, Sec. 28. (SB 94) Effective June 27, 2019. Repealed as of July 1, 2021, by its own provisions.)
490.5.
(a) Upon a first conviction for petty theft involving merchandise taken from a merchant's premises or a book or other library materials taken from a library facility, a person shall be punished by a mandatory fine of not less than fifty dollars ($50) and not more than one thousand dollars ($1,000) for each such violation; and may also be punished by imprisonment in the county jail, not exceeding six months, or both such fine and imprisonment.
(b) When an unemancipated minor's willful conduct would constitute petty theft involving merchandise taken from a merchant's premises or a book or other library materials taken from a library facility, any merchant or library facility who has been injured by that conduct may bring a civil action against the parent or legal guardian having control and custody of the minor. For the purposes of those actions the misconduct of the unemancipated minor shall be imputed to the parent or legal guardian having control

and custody of the minor. The parent or legal guardian having control or custody of an unemancipated minor whose conduct violates this subdivision shall be jointly and severally liable with the minor to a merchant or to a library facility for damages of not less than fifty dollars ($50) nor more than five hundred dollars ($500), plus costs. In addition to the foregoing damages, the parent or legal guardian shall be jointly and severally liable with the minor to the merchant for the retail value of the merchandise if it is not recovered in a merchantable condition, or to a library facility for the fair market value of its book or other library materials. Recovery of these damages may be had in addition to, and is not limited by, any other provision of law which limits the liability of a parent or legal guardian for the tortious conduct of a minor. An action for recovery of damages, pursuant to this subdivision, may be brought in small claims court if the total damages do not exceed the jurisdictional limit of that court, or in any other appropriate court; however, total damages, including the value of the merchandise or book or other library materials, shall not exceed five hundred dollars ($500) for each action brought under this section.
The provisions of this subdivision are in addition to other civil remedies and do not limit merchants or other persons to elect to pursue other civil remedies, except that the provisions of Section 1714.1 of the Civil Code shall not apply herein.
(c) When an adult or emancipated minor has unlawfully taken merchandise from a merchant's premises, or a book or other library materials from a library facility, the adult or emancipated minor shall be liable to the merchant or library facility for damages of not less than fifty dollars ($50) nor more than five hundred dollars ($500), plus costs. In addition to the foregoing damages, the adult or emancipated minor shall be liable to the merchant for the retail value of the merchandise if it is not recovered in merchantable condition, or to a library facility for the fair market value of its book or other library materials. An action for recovery of damages, pursuant to this subdivision, may be brought in small claims court if the total damages do not exceed the jurisdictional limit of such court, or in any other appropriate court. The provisions of this subdivision are in addition to other civil remedies and do not limit merchants or other persons to elect to pursue other civil remedies.
(d) In lieu of the fines prescribed by subdivision (a), any person may be required to perform public services designated by the court, provided that in no event shall any such person be required to perform less than the number of hours of such public service necessary to satisfy the fine assessed by the court as provided by subdivision (a) at the minimum wage prevailing in the state at the time of sentencing.
(e) All fines collected under this section shall be collected and distributed in accordance with Sections 1463 and 1463.1 of the Penal Code; provided, however, that a county may, by a majority vote of the members of its board of supervisors, allocate any amount up to, but not exceeding 50 percent of such fines to the county superintendent of schools for allocation to local school districts. The fines allocated shall be administered by the county superintendent of schools to finance public school programs, which provide counseling or other educational services designed to discourage shoplifting, theft, and burglary. Subject to rules and regulations as may be adopted by the Superintendent of Public Instruction, each county superintendent of schools shall allocate such funds to school districts within the county which submit project applications designed to further the educational purposes of this section. The costs of administration of this section by each county superintendent of schools shall be paid from the funds allocated to the county superintendent of schools.
(f) (1) A merchant may detain a person for a reasonable time for the purpose of conducting an investigation in a reasonable manner whenever the merchant has probable cause to believe the person to be detained is attempting to unlawfully take or has unlawfully taken merchandise from the merchant's premises.
A theater owner may detain a person for a reasonable time for the purpose of conducting an investigation in a reasonable manner whenever the theater owner has probable cause to believe the person to be detained is attempting to operate a video recording device within the premises of a motion picture theater without the authority of the owner of the theater.
A person employed by a library facility may detain a person for a reasonable time for the purpose of conducting an investigation in a reasonable manner whenever the person employed by a library facility has probable cause to believe the person to be detained is attempting to unlawfully remove or has unlawfully removed books or library materials from the premises of the library facility.
(2) In making the detention a merchant, theater owner, or a person employed by a library facility may use a reasonable amount of nondeadly force necessary to protect himself or herself and to prevent escape of the person detained or the loss of tangible or intangible property.
(3) During the period of detention any items which a merchant or theater owner, or any items which a person employed by a library facility has probable cause to believe are unlawfully taken from the premises of the merchant or library facility, or recorded on theater premises, and which are in plain view may be examined by the merchant, theater owner, or person employed by a library facility for the purposes of ascertaining the ownership thereof.
(4) A merchant, theater owner, a person employed by a library facility, or an agent thereof, having probable cause to believe the person detained was attempting to unlawfully take or has taken any item from the premises, or was attempting to operate a video recording device within the premises of a motion picture theater without the authority of the owner of the theater, may request the person detained to voluntarily surrender the item or recording. Should the person detained refuse to surrender the recording or item of which there is probable cause to believe has been recorded on or unlawfully taken from the premises, or attempted to be recorded or unlawfully taken from the premises, a limited and reasonable search may be conducted by those authorized to make the detention in order to recover the item. Only packages, shopping bags, handbags or other property in the immediate possession of the person detained, but not including any clothing worn by the person, may be searched pursuant to this subdivision. Upon surrender or discovery of the item, the person detained may also be requested, but may not be required, to provide adequate proof of his or her true identity.
(5) If any person admitted to a theater in which a motion picture is to be or is being exhibited, refuses or fails to give or surrender possession or to cease operation of any video recording device that the person has brought into or attempts to bring into that theater, then a theater owner shall have the right to refuse admission to that person or request that the person leave the premises and shall thereupon offer to refund and, unless that offer is refused, refund to that person the price paid by that person for admission to that theater. If the person thereafter refuses to leave the theater or cease operation of the video recording device, then the person shall be deemed to be intentionally interfering with and obstructing those attempting to carry on a lawful business within the meaning of Section 602.1.
(6) A peace officer who accepts custody of a person arrested for an offense contained in this section may, subsequent to the arrest, search the person arrested and his or her immediate possessions for any item or items alleged to have been taken.
(7) In any civil action brought by any person resulting from a detention or arrest by a merchant, it shall be a defense to such action that the merchant detaining or arresting such person had probable cause to believe that the person had stolen or attempted to steal merchandise and that the merchant acted reasonably under all the circumstances. In any civil action brought by any person resulting from a detention or arrest by a theater owner or person employed by a library facility, it shall be a defense to that action that the theater owner or person employed by a library facility detaining or arresting that person had probable cause to believe that the person was attempting to operate a video recording device within the premises of a motion picture theater without

the authority of the owner of the theater or had stolen or attempted to steal books or library materials and that the person employed by a library facility acted reasonably under all the circumstances.
(g) As used in this section:
(1) "Merchandise" means any personal property, capable of manual delivery, displayed, held or offered for retail sale by a merchant.
(2) "Merchant" means an owner or operator, and the agent, consignee, employee, lessee, or officer of an owner or operator, of any premises used for the retail purchase or sale of any personal property capable of manual delivery.
(3) "Theater owner" means an owner or operator, and the agent, employee, consignee, lessee, or officer of an owner or operator, of any premises used for the exhibition or performance of motion pictures to the general public.
(4) The terms "book or other library materials" include any book, plate, picture, photograph, engraving, painting, drawing, map, newspaper, magazine, pamphlet, broadside, manuscript, document, letter, public record, microform, sound recording, audiovisual material in any format, magnetic or other tape, electronic data-processing record, artifact, or other documentary, written or printed material regardless of physical form or characteristics, or any part thereof, belonging to, on loan to, or otherwise in the custody of a library facility.
(5) The term "library facility" includes any public library; any library of an educational, historical or eleemosynary institution, organization or society; any museum; any repository of public records.
(h) Any library facility shall post at its entrance and exit a conspicuous sign to read as follows:
"IN ORDER TO PREVENT THE THEFT OF BOOKS AND LIBRARY MATERIALS, STATE LAW AUTHORIZES THE DETENTION FOR A REASONABLE PERIOD OF ANY PERSON USING THESE FACILITIES SUSPECTED OF COMMITTING "LIBRARY THEFT" (PENAL CODE SECTION 490.5)."
(Amended by Stats. 1994, 1st Ex. Sess., Ch. 34, Sec. 1. Effective November 30, 1994.)

490.6.

(a) A person employed by an amusement park may detain a person for a reasonable time for the purpose of conducting an investigation in a reasonable manner whenever the person employed by the amusement park has probable cause to believe the person to be detained is violating lawful amusement park rules.
(b) If any person admitted to an amusement park refuses or fails to follow lawful amusement park rules, after being so informed, then an amusement park employee may request that the person either comply or leave the premises. If the person refuses to leave the premises or comply with lawful park rules, then the person shall be deemed to be intentionally interfering with and obstructing those attempting to carry on a lawful business within the meaning of Section 602.1.
(c) In any civil action brought by any person resulting from a detention or an arrest by a person employed by an amusement park, it shall be a defense to that action that the amusement park employee detaining or arresting the person had probable cause to believe that the person was not following lawful amusement park rules and that the amusement park employee acted reasonably under all the circumstances.
(Added by Stats. 1996, Ch. 731, Sec. 1. Effective January 1, 1997.)

490.7.

(a) The Legislature finds that free newspapers provide a key source of information to the public, in many cases providing an important alternative to the news and ideas expressed in other local media sources. The Legislature further finds that the unauthorized taking of multiple copies of free newspapers, whether done to sell them to recycling centers, to injure a business competitor, to deprive others of the opportunity to read them, or for any other reason, injures the rights of readers, writers, publishers, and advertisers, and impoverishes the marketplace of ideas in California.
(b) No person shall take more than twenty-five (25) copies of the current issue of a free or complimentary newspaper if done with the intent to do one or more of the following:
(1) Recycle the newspapers for cash or other payment.
(2) Sell or barter the newspaper.
(3) Deprive others of the opportunity to read or enjoy the newspaper.
(4) Harm a business competitor.
(c) This section does not apply to the owner or operator of the newsrack in which the copies are placed, the owner or operator of the property on which the newsrack is placed, the publisher, the printer, the distributor, the deliverer of the newspaper, or to any advertiser in that issue, or to any other person who has the express permission to do so from any of these entities.
(d) Any newspaper publisher may provide express permission to take more than twenty-five (25) copies of the current issue of a free or complimentary newspaper by indicating on the newsrack or in the newspaper itself, that people may take a greater number of copies if they wish.
(e) A first violation of subdivision (b) shall be an infraction punishable by a fine not exceeding two hundred fifty dollars ($250). A second or subsequent violation shall be punishable as an infraction or a misdemeanor. A misdemeanor conviction under this section is punishable by a fine not exceeding five hundred dollars ($500), imprisonment of up to 10 days in a county jail, or by both that fine and imprisonment. The court may order community service in lieu of the punishment otherwise provided for an infraction or misdemeanor in the amount of 20 hours for an infraction, and 40 hours for a misdemeanor. A misdemeanor conviction under this section shall not constitute a conviction for petty theft.
(f) This section shall not be construed to repeal, modify, or weaken any existing legal prohibitions against the taking of private property.
(g) For purposes of this section, an issue is current if no more than half of the period of time until the distribution of the next issue has passed.
(Added by Stats. 2006, Ch. 228, Sec. 2. Effective January 1, 2007.)

491.

Dogs are personal property, and their value is to be ascertained in the same manner as the value of other property.
(Amended by Stats. 1887, Ch. 109.)

492.

If the thing stolen consists of any evidence of debt, or other written instrument, the amount of money due thereupon, or secured to be paid thereby, and remaining unsatisfied, or which in any contingency might be collected thereon, or the value of the property the title to which is shown thereby, or the sum which might be recovered in the absence thereof, is the value of the thing stolen.
(Enacted 1872.)

493.

If the thing stolen is any ticket or other paper or writing entitling or purporting to entitle the holder or proprietor thereof to a passage upon any railroad or vessel or other public conveyance, the price at which tickets entitling a person to a like passage are usually sold by the proprietors of such conveyance is the value of such ticket, paper, or writing.
(Enacted 1872.)

494.

All the provisions of this Chapter apply where the property taken is an instrument for the payment of money, evidence of debt, public security, or passage ticket, completed and ready to be issued or delivered, although the same has never been issued or delivered by the makers thereof to any person as a purchaser or owner.
(Enacted 1872.)

495.

The provisions of this Chapter apply where the thing taken is any fixture or part of the realty, and is severed at the time of the taking, in the same manner as if the thing had been severed by another person at some previous time.
(Enacted 1872.)

496.

(a) Every person who buys or receives any property that has been stolen or that has been obtained in any manner constituting theft or extortion, knowing the property to be so stolen or obtained, or who conceals, sells, withholds, or aids in concealing, selling, or withholding any property from the owner, knowing the property to be so stolen or obtained, shall be punished by imprisonment in a county jail for not more than one year, or imprisonment pursuant to subdivision (h) of Section 1170. However, if the value of the property does not exceed nine hundred fifty dollars ($950), the offense shall be a misdemeanor, punishable only by imprisonment in a county jail not exceeding one year, if such person has no prior convictions for an offense specified in clause (iv) of subparagraph (C) of paragraph (2) of subdivision (e) of Section 667 or for an offense requiring registration pursuant to subdivision (c) of Section 290.
A principal in the actual theft of the property may be convicted pursuant to this section. However, no person may be convicted both pursuant to this section and of the theft of the same property.
(b) Every swap meet vendor, as defined in Section 21661 of the Business and Professions Code, and every person whose principal business is dealing in, or collecting, merchandise or personal property, and every agent, employee, or representative of that person, who buys or receives any property of a value in excess of nine hundred fifty dollars ($950) that has been stolen or obtained in any manner constituting theft or extortion, under circumstances that should cause the person, agent, employee, or representative to make reasonable inquiry to ascertain that the person from whom the property was bought or received had the legal right to sell or deliver it, without making a reasonable inquiry, shall be punished by imprisonment in a county jail for not more than one year, or imprisonment pursuant to subdivision (h) of Section 1170.
Every swap meet vendor, as defined in Section 21661 of the Business and Professions Code, and every person whose principal business is dealing in, or collecting, merchandise or personal property, and every agent, employee, or representative of that person, who buys or receives any property of a value of nine hundred fifty dollars ($950) or less that has been stolen or obtained in any manner constituting theft or extortion, under circumstances that should cause the person, agent, employee, or representative to make reasonable inquiry to ascertain that the person from whom the property was bought or received had the legal right to sell or deliver it, without making a reasonable inquiry, shall be guilty of a misdemeanor.
(c) Any person who has been injured by a violation of subdivision (a) or (b) may bring an action for three times the amount of actual damages, if any, sustained by the plaintiff, costs of suit, and reasonable attorney's fees.
(d) Notwithstanding Section 664, any attempt to commit any act prohibited by this section, except an offense specified in the accusatory pleading as a misdemeanor, is punishable by imprisonment in a county jail for not more than one year, or by imprisonment pursuant to subdivision (h) of Section 1170.
(Amended November 4, 2014, by initiative Proposition 47, Sec. 9.)

496a.

(a) Every person who is a dealer in or collector of junk, metals, or secondhand materials, or the agent, employee, or representative of such dealer or collector, and who buys or receives any wire, cable, copper, lead, solder, mercury, iron, or brass which he or she knows or reasonably should know is ordinarily used by or ordinarily belongs to a railroad or other transportation, telephone, telegraph, gas, water, or electric light company, or a county, city, city and county, or other political subdivision of this state engaged in furnishing public utility service, without using due diligence to ascertain that the person selling or delivering the same has a legal right to do so, is guilty of criminally receiving that property, and shall be punished by imprisonment in a county jail for not more than one year, or by imprisonment pursuant to subdivision (h) of Section 1170, or by a fine of not more than one thousand dollars ($1,000), or by both that fine and imprisonment.
(b) Any person who buys or receives material pursuant to subdivision (a) shall obtain evidence of his or her identity from the seller, including, but not limited to, that person's full name, signature, address, driver's license number, and vehicle license number, and the license number of the vehicle delivering the material.
(c) The record of the transaction shall include an appropriate description of the material purchased and the record shall be maintained pursuant to Section 21607 of the Business and Professions Code.
(Amended by Stats. 2013, Ch. 76, Sec. 147. (AB 383) Effective January 1, 2014.)

496b.

Every person who, being a dealer in or collector of second-hand books or other literary material, or the agent, employee or representative of such dealer, or collector, buys or receives any book, manuscript, map, chart, or other work of literature, belonging to, and bearing any mark or indicia of ownership by a public or incorporated library, college or university, without ascertaining by diligent inquiry that the person selling or delivering the same has a legal right to do so, is guilty of criminally receiving such property in the first degree if such property be of the value of more than fifty dollars, and is punishable by imprisonment in the county jail for not more than one year, or by a fine of not more than twice the value of the property received, or by both such fine and imprisonment; and is guilty of criminally receiving such property in the second degree if such property be of the value of fifty dollars or under, and is punishable by imprisonment in the county jail for not more than one month, or by a fine of not more than twice the value of the property received, or by both such fine and imprisonment.
(Added by Stats. 1923, Ch. 192.)

496c.

Any person who shall copy, transcribe, photograph or otherwise make a record or memorandum of the contents of any private and unpublished paper, book, record, map or file, containing information relating to the title to real property or containing information used in the business of examining, certifying or insuring titles to real property and belonging to any person, firm or corporation engaged in the business of examining, certifying, or insuring titles to real property, without the consent of the owner of such paper, book, record, map or file, and with the intent to use the same or the contents thereof, or to dispose of the same or the contents thereof to others for use, in the business of examining, certifying, or insuring titles to real property, shall be guilty of theft, and any person who shall induce another to violate the provisions of this section by giving, offering, or promising to such another any gift, gratuity, or thing of value or by doing or promising to do any act beneficial to such another, shall be guilty of theft; and any person who shall receive or acquire from another any copy, transcription, photograph or other record or memorandum of the contents of any private and unpublished paper, book, record, map or file containing information relating to the title to real property or containing information used in the business of examining, certifying or insuring titles to real property, with the knowledge that the same or the contents thereof has or have been acquired, prepared or compiled in violation of this section shall be guilty of theft. The contents of any such private and unpublished paper, book, record, map or file is hereby defined to be personal property, and in determining the value thereof for the purposes of this section the cost of acquiring and compiling the same shall be the test.
(Added by Stats. 1931, Ch. 732.)

496d.

(a) Every person who buys or receives any motor vehicle, as defined in Section 415 of the Vehicle Code, any trailer, as defined in Section 630 of the Vehicle Code, any special construction equipment, as defined in Section 565 of the Vehicle Code, or any vessel, as defined in Section 21 of the Harbors and Navigation Code, that has been stolen or that has been obtained in any manner constituting theft or extortion, knowing the property to be stolen or obtained, or who conceals, sells, withholds, or aids in concealing, selling, or withholding any motor vehicle, trailer, special construction equipment, or vessel from the owner, knowing the property to be so stolen or obtained, shall be punished by imprisonment pursuant to subdivision (h) of Section 1170 for 16 months or two or three years or a fine of not more than ten thousand dollars ($10,000), or both, or by imprisonment in a county jail not to exceed one year or a fine of not more than one thousand dollars ($1,000), or both.

(b) For the purposes of this section, the terms "special construction equipment" and "vessel" are limited to motorized vehicles and vessels.

(Amended by Stats. 2011, Ch. 15, Sec. 374. (AB 109) Effective April 4, 2011. Operative October 1, 2011, by Sec. 636 of Ch. 15, as amended by Stats. 2011, Ch. 39, Sec. 68.)

496e.

(a) Any person who is engaged in the salvage, recycling, purchase, or sale of scrap metal and who possesses any of the following items that were owned or previously owned by any public agency, city, county, city and county, special district, or private utility that have been stolen or obtained in any manner constituting theft or extortion, knowing the property to be so stolen or obtained, or fails to report possession of the items pursuant to Section 21609.1 of the Business and Professions Code, is guilty of a crime:

(1) A fire hydrant or any reasonably recognizable part of that hydrant.

(2) Any fire department connection, including, but not limited to, reasonably recognizable bronze or brass fittings and parts.

(3) Manhole covers or lids, or any reasonably recognizable part of those manhole covers and lids.

(4) Backflow devices and connections to that device, or any part of that device.

(b) A person who violates subdivision (a) shall, in addition to any other penalty provided by law, be subject to a criminal fine of not more than three thousand dollars ($3,000).

(Amended by Stats. 2012, Ch. 656, Sec. 4. (SB 1387) Effective January 1, 2013.)

497.

Every person who, in another state or country steals or embezzles the property of another, or receives such property knowing it to have been stolen or embezzled, and brings the same into this state, may be convicted and punished in the same manner as if such larceny, or embezzlement, or receiving, had been committed in this state.

(Amended by Stats. 1905, Ch. 554.)

498.

(a) The following definitions govern the construction of this section:

(1) "Person" means any individual, or any partnership, firm, association, corporation, limited liability company, or other legal entity.

(2) "Utility" means any electrical, gas, or water corporation as those terms are defined in the Public Utilities Code, and electrical, gas, or water systems operated by any political subdivision.

(3) "Customer" means the person in whose name utility service is provided.

(4) "Utility service" means the provision of electricity, gas, water, or any other service provided by the utility for compensation.

(5) "Divert" means to change the intended course or path of electricity, gas, or water without the authorization or consent of the utility.

(6) "Tamper" means to rearrange, injure, alter, interfere with, or otherwise prevent from performing a normal or customary function.

(7) "Reconnection" means the reconnection of utility service by a customer or other person after service has been lawfully disconnected by the utility.

(b) Any person who, with intent to obtain for himself or herself utility services without paying the full lawful charge therefor, or with intent to enable another person to do so, or with intent to deprive any utility of any part of the full lawful charge for utility services it provides, commits, authorizes, solicits, aids, or abets any of the following shall be guilty of a misdemeanor:

(1) Diverts or causes to be diverted utility services, by any means.

(2) Prevents any utility meter, or other device used in determining the charge for utility services, from accurately performing its measuring function by tampering or by any other means.

(3) Tampers with any property owned by or used by the utility to provide utility services.

(4) Makes or causes to be made any connection with or reconnection with property owned or used by the utility to provide utility services without the authorization or consent of the utility.

(5) Uses or receives the direct benefit of all or a portion of utility services with knowledge or reason to believe that the diversion, tampering, or unauthorized connection existed at the time of that use, or that the use or receipt was otherwise without the authorization or consent of the utility.

(c) In any prosecution under this section, the presence of any of the following objects, circumstances, or conditions on premises controlled by the customer or by the person using or receiving the direct benefit of all or a portion of utility services obtained in violation of this section shall permit an inference that the customer or person intended to and did violate this section:

(1) Any instrument, apparatus, or device primarily designed to be used to obtain utility services without paying the full lawful charge therefor.

(2) Any meter that has been altered, tampered with, or bypassed so as to cause no measurement or inaccurate measurement of utility services.

(d) If the value of all utility services obtained in violation of this section totals more than nine hundred fifty dollars ($950) or if the defendant has previously been convicted of an offense under this section or any former section which would be an offense under this section, or of an offense under the laws of another state or of the United States which would have been an offense under this section if committed in this state, then the violation is punishable by imprisonment in a county jail for not more than one year, or in the state prison.

(e) This section shall not be construed to preclude the applicability of any other provision of the criminal law of this state.

(Amended by Stats. 2009, 3rd Ex. Sess., Ch. 28, Sec. 24. (SB 18 3x) Effective January 25, 2010.)

499.

(a) Any person who, having been convicted of a previous violation of Section 10851 of the Vehicle Code, or of subdivision (d) of Section 487, involving a vehicle or vessel, and having served a term therefor in any penal institution or having been imprisoned therein as a condition of probation for the offense, is subsequently convicted of a violation of Section 499b, involving a vehicle or vessel, is punishable for the subsequent offense by imprisonment in the county jail not exceeding one year or the state prison for 16 months, two, or three years.

(b) Any person convicted of a violation of Section 499b, who has been previously convicted under charges separately brought and tried two or more times of a violation of Section 499b, all such violations involving a vehicle or vessel, and who has been imprisoned therefore as a condition of probation or otherwise at least once, is punishable by imprisonment in the county jail for not more than one year or in the state prison for 16 months, two, or three years.

(c) This section shall become operative on January 1, 1997.

(Repealed (in Sec. 7) and added by Stats. 1993, Ch. 1125, Sec. 8. Effective October 11, 1993. Section operative January 1, 1997, by its own provisions.)

499b.

(a) Any person who shall, without the permission of the owner thereof, take any bicycle for the purpose of temporarily using or operating the same, is guilty of a misdemeanor, and shall be punishable by a fine not exceeding four hundred dollars ($400), or by imprisonment in a county jail not exceeding three months, or by both that fine and imprisonment.

(b) Any person who shall, without the permission of the owner thereof, take any vessel for the purpose of temporarily using or operating the same, is guilty of a misdemeanor, and shall be punishable by a fine not exceeding one thousand dollars ($1,000), or by imprisonment in a county jail not exceeding one year, or by both that fine and imprisonment.

(Amended by Stats. 2003, Ch. 391, Sec. 1. Effective January 1, 2004.)

499c.

(a) As used in this section:

(1) "Access" means to approach, a way or means of approaching, nearing, admittance to, including to instruct, communicate with, store information in, or retrieve information from a computer system or computer network.

(2) "Article" means any object, material, device, or substance or copy thereof, including any writing, record, recording, drawing, sample, specimen, prototype, model, photograph, micro-organism, blueprint, map, or tangible representation of a computer program or information, including both human and computer readable information and information while in transit.

(3) "Benefit" means gain or advantage, or anything regarded by the beneficiary as gain or advantage, including benefit to any other person or entity in whose welfare he or she is interested.

(4) "Computer system" means a machine or collection of machines, one or more of which contain computer programs and information, that performs functions, including, but not limited to, logic, arithmetic, information storage and retrieval, communications, and control.

(5) "Computer network" means an interconnection of two or more computer systems.

(6) "Computer program" means an ordered set of instructions or statements, and related information that, when automatically executed in actual or modified form in a computer system, causes it to perform specified functions.

(7) "Copy" means any facsimile, replica, photograph or other reproduction of an article, and any note, drawing or sketch made of or from an article.

(8) "Representing" means describing, depicting, containing, constituting, reflecting or recording.

(9) "Trade secret" means information, including a formula, pattern, compilation, program, device, method, technique, or process, that:

(A) Derives independent economic value, actual or potential, from not being generally known to the public or to other persons who can obtain economic value from its disclosure or use; and

(B) Is the subject of efforts that are reasonable under the circumstances to maintain its secrecy.

(b) Every person is guilty of theft who, with intent to deprive or withhold the control of a trade secret from its owner, or with an intent to appropriate a trade secret to his or her own use or to the use of another, does any of the following:

(1) Steals, takes, carries away, or uses without authorization, a trade secret.

(2) Fraudulently appropriates any article representing a trade secret entrusted to him or her.

(3) Having unlawfully obtained access to the article, without authority makes or causes to be made a copy of any article representing a trade secret.

(4) Having obtained access to the article through a relationship of trust and confidence, without authority and in breach of the obligations created by that relationship, makes or causes to be made, directly from and in the presence of the article, a copy of any article representing a trade secret.

(c) Every person who promises, offers or gives, or conspires to promise or offer to give, to any present or former agent, employee or servant of another, a benefit as an inducement, bribe or reward for conveying, delivering or otherwise making available an article representing a trade secret owned by his or her present or former principal, employer or master, to any person not authorized by the owner to receive or acquire the trade secret and every present or former agent, employee, or servant, who solicits, accepts, receives or takes a benefit as an inducement, bribe or reward for conveying, delivering or otherwise making available an article representing a trade secret owned by his or her present or former principal, employer or master, to any person not authorized by the owner to receive or acquire the trade secret, shall be punished by imprisonment in a county jail not exceeding one year, or by imprisonment pursuant to subdivision (h) of Section 1170, or by a fine not exceeding five thousand dollars ($5,000), or by both that fine and imprisonment.

(d) In a prosecution for a violation of this section, it shall be no defense that the person returned or intended to return the article.

(Amended by Stats. 2011, Ch. 15, Sec. 375. (AB 109) Effective April 4, 2011. Operative October 1, 2011, by Sec. 636 of Ch. 15, as amended by Stats. 2011, Ch. 39, Sec. 68.)

499d.

Any person who operates or takes an aircraft not his own, without the consent of the owner thereof, and with intent to either permanently or temporarily deprive the owner thereof of his title to or possession of such vehicle, whether with or without intent to steal the same, or any person who is a party or accessory to or an accomplice in any operation or unauthorized taking or stealing is guilty of a felony, and upon conviction thereof shall be punished by imprisonment in a county jail for not more than one year or by imprisonment pursuant to subdivision (h) of Section 1170, or by a fine of not more than ten thousand dollars ($10,000) or by both that fine and imprisonment.

(Amended by Stats. 2011, Ch. 15, Sec. 376. (AB 109) Effective April 4, 2011. Operative October 1, 2011, by Sec. 636 of Ch. 15, as amended by Stats. 2011, Ch. 39, Sec. 68.)

500.

(a) Any person who receives money for the actual or purported purpose of transmitting the same or its equivalent to foreign countries as specified in Section 1800.5 of the Financial Code who fails to do at least one of the following acts unless otherwise instructed by the customer is guilty of a misdemeanor or felony as set forth in subdivision (b):

(1) Forward the money as represented to the customer within 10 days of receipt of the funds.

(2) Give instructions within 10 days of receipt of the customer's funds, committing equivalent funds to the person designated by the customer.

(3) Refund to the customer any money not forwarded as represented within 10 days of the customer's written request for a refund pursuant to subdivision (a) of Section 1810.5 of the Financial Code.

(b) (1) If the total value of the funds received from the customer is less than nine hundred fifty dollars ($950), the offense set forth in subdivision (a) is punishable by imprisonment in a county jail not exceeding one year or by a fine not exceeding one thousand dollars ($1,000), or by both that imprisonment and fine.

(2) If the total value of the money received from the customer is nine hundred fifty dollars ($950) or more, or if the total value of all moneys received by the person from different customers is nine hundred fifty dollars ($950) or more, and the receipts were part of a common scheme or plan, the offense set forth in subdivision (a) is punishable by imprisonment pursuant to subdivision (h) of Section 1170 for 16 months, two, or three years, by a fine not exceeding ten thousand dollars ($10,000), or by both that imprisonment and fine.

(Amended by Stats. 2011, Ch. 15, Sec. 377. (AB 109) Effective April 4, 2011. Operative October 1, 2011, by Sec. 636 of Ch. 15, as amended by Stats. 2011, Ch. 39, Sec. 68.)

501.

Upon a trial for larceny or embezzlement of money, bank notes, certificates of stock, or valuable securities, the allegation of the indictment or information, so far as regards the description of the property, is sustained, if the offender be proved to have embezzled or stolen any money, bank notes, certificates of stock, or valuable security, although the particular species of coin or other money, or the number, denomination, or kind of bank notes, certificates of stock, or valuable security, is not proved; and upon a trial for embezzlement, if the offender is proved to have embezzled any piece of coin or other money, any bank note, certificate of stock, or valuable security, although the piece of coin or other money, or bank note, certificate of stock, or valuable security, may have been delivered to him or her in order that some part of the value thereof should be returned to the party delivering the same, and such part shall have been returned accordingly.

(Added by Stats. 1989, Ch. 897, Sec. 21.)

502.

(a) It is the intent of the Legislature in enacting this section to expand the degree of protection afforded to individuals, businesses, and governmental agencies from tampering, interference, damage, and unauthorized access to lawfully created computer data and computer systems. The Legislature finds and declares that the proliferation of computer technology has resulted in a concomitant proliferation of computer crime and other forms of unauthorized access to computers, computer systems, and computer data.

The Legislature further finds and declares that protection of the integrity of all types and forms of lawfully created computers, computer systems, and computer data is vital to the protection of the privacy of individuals as well as to the well-being of financial institutions, business concerns, governmental agencies, and others within this state that lawfully utilize those computers, computer systems, and data.

(b) For the purposes of this section, the following terms have the following meanings:

(1) "Access" means to gain entry to, instruct, cause input to, cause output from, cause data processing with, or communicate with, the logical, arithmetical, or memory function resources of a computer, computer system, or computer network.

(2) "Computer network" means any system that provides communications between one or more computer systems and input/output devices, including, but not limited to, display terminals, remote systems, mobile devices, and printers connected by telecommunication facilities.

(3) "Computer program or software" means a set of instructions or statements, and related data, that when executed in actual or modified form, cause a computer, computer system, or computer network to perform specified functions.

(4) "Computer services" includes, but is not limited to, computer time, data processing, or storage functions, Internet services, electronic mail services, electronic message services, or other uses of a computer, computer system, or computer network.

(5) "Computer system" means a device or collection of devices, including support devices and excluding calculators that are not programmable and capable of being used in conjunction with external files, one or more of which contain computer programs, electronic instructions, input data, and output data, that performs functions, including, but not limited to, logic, arithmetic, data storage and retrieval, communication, and control.

(6) "Government computer system" means any computer system, or part thereof, that is owned, operated, or used by any federal, state, or local governmental entity.

(7) "Public safety infrastructure computer system" means any computer system, or part thereof, that is necessary for the health and safety of the public including computer systems owned, operated, or used by drinking water and wastewater treatment facilities, hospitals, emergency service providers, telecommunication companies, and gas and electric utility companies.

(8) "Data" means a representation of information, knowledge, facts, concepts, computer software, or computer programs or instructions. Data may be in any form, in storage media, or as stored in the memory of the computer or in transit or presented on a display device.

(9) "Supporting documentation" includes, but is not limited to, all information, in any form, pertaining to the design, construction, classification, implementation, use, or modification of a computer, computer system, computer network, computer program, or computer software, which information is not generally available to the public and is necessary for the operation of a computer, computer system, computer network, computer program, or computer software.

(10) "Injury" means any alteration, deletion, damage, or destruction of a computer system, computer network, computer program, or data caused by the access, or the denial of access to legitimate users of a computer system, network, or program.

(11) "Victim expenditure" means any expenditure reasonably and necessarily incurred by the owner or lessee to verify that a computer system, computer network, computer program, or data was or was not altered, deleted, damaged, or destroyed by the access.

(12) "Computer contaminant" means any set of computer instructions that are designed to modify, damage, destroy, record, or transmit information within a computer, computer system, or computer network without the intent or permission of the owner of the information. They include, but are not limited to, a group of computer instructions commonly called viruses or worms, that are self-replicating or self-propagating and are designed to contaminate other computer programs or computer data, consume computer resources, modify, destroy, record, or transmit data, or in some other fashion usurp the normal operation of the computer, computer system, or computer network.

(13) "Internet domain name" means a globally unique, hierarchical reference to an Internet host or service, assigned through centralized Internet naming authorities, comprising a series of character strings separated by periods, with the rightmost character string specifying the top of the hierarchy.

(14) "Electronic mail" means an electronic message or computer file that is transmitted between two or more telecommunications devices; computers; computer networks, regardless of whether the network is a local, regional, or global network; or electronic devices capable of receiving electronic messages, regardless of whether the message is converted to hard copy format after receipt, viewed upon transmission, or stored for later retrieval.

(15) "Profile" means either of the following:

(A) A configuration of user data required by a computer so that the user may access programs or services and have the desired functionality on that computer.

(B) An Internet Web site user's personal page or section of a page that is made up of data, in text or graphical form, that displays significant, unique, or identifying information, including, but not limited to, listing acquaintances, interests, associations, activities, or personal statements.

(c) Except as provided in subdivision (h), any person who commits any of the following acts is guilty of a public offense:

(1) Knowingly accesses and without permission alters, damages, deletes, destroys, or otherwise uses any data, computer, computer system, or computer network in order to either (A) devise or execute any scheme or artifice to defraud, deceive, or extort, or (B) wrongfully control or obtain money, property, or data.

(2) Knowingly accesses and without permission takes, copies, or makes use of any data from a computer, computer system, or computer network, or takes or copies any supporting documentation, whether existing or residing internal or external to a computer, computer system, or computer network.

(3) Knowingly and without permission uses or causes to be used computer services.

(4) Knowingly accesses and without permission adds, alters, damages, deletes, or destroys any data, computer software, or computer programs which reside or exist internal or external to a computer, computer system, or computer network.

(5) Knowingly and without permission disrupts or causes the disruption of computer services or denies or causes the denial of computer services to an authorized user of a computer, computer system, or computer network.

(6) Knowingly and without permission provides or assists in providing a means of accessing a computer, computer system, or computer network in violation of this section.

(7) Knowingly and without permission accesses or causes to be accessed any computer, computer system, or computer network.

(8) Knowingly introduces any computer contaminant into any computer, computer system, or computer network.

(9) Knowingly and without permission uses the Internet domain name or profile of another individual, corporation, or entity in connection with the sending of one or more electronic mail messages or posts and thereby damages or causes damage to a computer, computer data, computer system, or computer network.

(10) Knowingly and without permission disrupts or causes the disruption of government computer services or denies or causes the denial of government computer services to an authorized user of a government computer, computer system, or computer network.

(11) Knowingly accesses and without permission adds, alters, damages, deletes, or destroys any data, computer software, or computer programs which reside or exist internal or external to a public safety infrastructure computer system computer, computer system, or computer network.

(12) Knowingly and without permission disrupts or causes the disruption of public safety infrastructure computer system computer services or denies or causes the denial of computer services to an authorized user of a public safety infrastructure computer system computer, computer system, or computer network.

(13) Knowingly and without permission provides or assists in providing a means of accessing a computer, computer system, or public safety infrastructure computer system computer, computer system, or computer network in violation of this section.

(14) Knowingly introduces any computer contaminant into any public safety infrastructure computer system computer, computer system, or computer network.

(d) (1) Any person who violates any of the provisions of paragraph (1), (2), (4), (5), (10), (11), or (12) of subdivision (c) is guilty of a felony, punishable by imprisonment pursuant to subdivision (h) of Section 1170 for 16 months, or two or three years and a fine not exceeding ten thousand dollars ($10,000), or a misdemeanor, punishable by imprisonment in a county jail not exceeding one year, by a fine not exceeding five thousand dollars ($5,000), or by both that fine and imprisonment.

(2) Any person who violates paragraph (3) of subdivision (c) is punishable as follows:

(A) For the first violation that does not result in injury, and where the value of the computer services used does not exceed nine hundred fifty dollars ($950), by a fine not exceeding five thousand dollars ($5,000), or by imprisonment in a county jail not exceeding one year, or by both that fine and imprisonment.

(B) For any violation that results in a victim expenditure in an amount greater than five thousand dollars ($5,000) or in an injury, or if the value of the computer services used exceeds nine hundred fifty dollars ($950), or for any second or subsequent violation, by a fine not exceeding ten thousand dollars ($10,000), or by imprisonment pursuant to subdivision (h) of Section 1170 for 16 months, or two or three years, or by both that fine and imprisonment, or by a fine not exceeding five thousand dollars ($5,000), or by imprisonment in a county jail not exceeding one year, or by both that fine and imprisonment.

(3) Any person who violates paragraph (6), (7), or (13) of subdivision (c) is punishable as follows:

(A) For a first violation that does not result in injury, an infraction punishable by a fine not exceeding one thousand dollars ($1,000).

(B) For any violation that results in a victim expenditure in an amount not greater than five thousand dollars ($5,000), or for a second or subsequent violation, by a fine not exceeding five thousand dollars ($5,000), or by imprisonment in a county jail not exceeding one year, or by both that fine and imprisonment.

(C) For any violation that results in a victim expenditure in an amount greater than five thousand dollars ($5,000), by a fine not exceeding ten thousand dollars ($10,000), or by imprisonment pursuant to subdivision (h) of Section 1170 for 16 months, or two or three years, or by both that fine and imprisonment, or by a fine not exceeding five thousand dollars ($5,000), or by imprisonment in a county jail not exceeding one year, or by both that fine and imprisonment.

(4) Any person who violates paragraph (8) or (14) of subdivision (c) is punishable as follows:

(A) For a first violation that does not result in injury, a misdemeanor punishable by a fine not exceeding five thousand dollars ($5,000), or by imprisonment in a county jail not exceeding one year, or by both that fine and imprisonment.

(B) For any violation that results in injury, or for a second or subsequent violation, by a fine not exceeding ten thousand dollars ($10,000), or by imprisonment in a county jail not exceeding one year, or by imprisonment pursuant to subdivision (h) of Section 1170, or by both that fine and imprisonment.

(5) Any person who violates paragraph (9) of subdivision (c) is punishable as follows:

(A) For a first violation that does not result in injury, an infraction punishable by a fine not exceeding one thousand dollars ($1,000).

(B) For any violation that results in injury, or for a second or subsequent violation, by a fine not exceeding five thousand dollars ($5,000), or by imprisonment in a county jail not exceeding one year, or by both that fine and imprisonment.

(e) (1) In addition to any other civil remedy available, the owner or lessee of the computer, computer system, computer network, computer program, or data who suffers damage or loss by reason of a violation of any of the provisions of subdivision (c) may bring a civil action against the violator for compensatory damages and injunctive relief or other equitable relief. Compensatory damages shall include any expenditure reasonably and necessarily incurred by the owner or lessee to verify that a computer system, computer network, computer program, or data was or was not altered, damaged, or deleted by the access. For the purposes of actions authorized by this subdivision, the conduct of an unemancipated minor shall be imputed to the parent or legal guardian having control or custody of the minor, pursuant to the provisions of Section 1714.1 of the Civil Code.

(2) In any action brought pursuant to this subdivision the court may award reasonable attorney's fees.

(3) A community college, state university, or academic institution accredited in this state is required to include computer-related crimes as a specific violation of college or university student conduct policies and regulations that may subject a student to disciplinary sanctions up to and including dismissal from the academic institution. This paragraph shall not apply to the University of California unless the Board of Regents adopts a resolution to that effect.

(4) In any action brought pursuant to this subdivision for a willful violation of the provisions of subdivision (c), where it is proved by clear and convincing evidence that a defendant has been guilty of oppression, fraud, or malice as defined in subdivision (c) of Section 3294 of the Civil Code, the court may additionally award punitive or exemplary damages.

(5) No action may be brought pursuant to this subdivision unless it is initiated within three years of the date of the act complained of, or the date of the discovery of the damage, whichever is later.

(f) This section shall not be construed to preclude the applicability of any other provision of the criminal law of this state which applies or may apply to any transaction, nor shall it make illegal any employee labor relations activities that are within the scope and protection of state or federal labor laws.
(g) Any computer, computer system, computer network, or any software or data, owned by the defendant, that is used during the commission of any public offense described in subdivision (c) or any computer, owned by the defendant, which is used as a repository for the storage of software or data illegally obtained in violation of subdivision (c) shall be subject to forfeiture, as specified in Section 502.01.
(h) (1) Subdivision (c) does not apply to punish any acts which are committed by a person within the scope of his or her lawful employment. For purposes of this section, a person acts within the scope of his or her employment when he or she performs acts which are reasonably necessary to the performance of his or her work assignment.
(2) Paragraph (3) of subdivision (c) does not apply to penalize any acts committed by a person acting outside of his or her lawful employment, provided that the employee's activities do not cause an injury, to the employer or another, or provided that the value of supplies or computer services which are used does not exceed an accumulated total of two hundred fifty dollars ($250).
(i) No activity exempted from prosecution under paragraph (2) of subdivision (h) which incidentally violates paragraph (2), (4), or (7) of subdivision (c) shall be prosecuted under those paragraphs.
(j) For purposes of bringing a civil or a criminal action under this section, a person who causes, by any means, the access of a computer, computer system, or computer network in one jurisdiction from another jurisdiction is deemed to have personally accessed the computer, computer system, or computer network in each jurisdiction.
(k) In determining the terms and conditions applicable to a person convicted of a violation of this section the court shall consider the following:
(1) The court shall consider prohibitions on access to and use of computers.
(2) Except as otherwise required by law, the court shall consider alternate sentencing, including community service, if the defendant shows remorse and recognition of the wrongdoing, and an inclination not to repeat the offense.
(Amended by Stats. 2015, Ch. 614, Sec. 1. (AB 32) Effective January 1, 2016.)

502.01.

(a) As used in this section:
(1) "Property subject to forfeiture" means any property of the defendant that is illegal telecommunications equipment as defined in subdivision (g) of Section 502.8, or a computer, computer system, or computer network, and any software or data residing thereon, if the telecommunications device, computer, computer system, or computer network was used in committing a violation of, or conspiracy to commit a violation of, subdivision (b) of Section 272, Section 288, 288.2, 311.1, 311.2, 311.3, 311.4, 311.5, 311.10, 311.11, 422, 470, 470a, 472, 475, 476, 480, 483.5, 484g, or subdivision (a), (b), or (d) of Section 484e, subdivision (a) of Section 484f, subdivision (b) or (c) of Section 484i, subdivision (c) of Section 502, or Section 502.7, 502.8, 529, 529a, or 530.5, 537e, 593d, 593e, 646.9, or subdivision (j) of Section 647, or was used as a repository for the storage of software or data obtained in violation of those provisions. Forfeiture shall not be available for any property used solely in the commission of an infraction. If the defendant is a minor, it also includes property of the parent or guardian of the defendant.
(2) "Sentencing court" means the court sentencing a person found guilty of violating or conspiring to commit a violation of subdivision (b) of Section 272, Section 288, 288.2, 311.1, 311.2, 311.3, 311.4, 311.5, 311.10, 311.11, 422, 470, 470a, 472, 475, 476, 480, 483.5, 484g, or subdivision (a), (b), or (d) of Section 484e, subdivision (d) of Section 484e, subdivision (a) of Section 484f, subdivision (b) or (c) of Section 484i, subdivision (c) of Section 502, or Section 502.7, 502.8, 529, 529a, 530.5, 537e, 593d, 593e, 646.9, or subdivision (j) of Section 647, or, in the case of a minor, found to be a person described in Section 602 of the Welfare and Institutions Code because of a violation of those provisions, the juvenile court.
(3) "Interest" means any property interest in the property subject to forfeiture.
(4) "Security interest" means an interest that is a lien, mortgage, security interest, or interest under a conditional sales contract.
(5) "Value" has the following meanings:
(A) When counterfeit items of computer software are manufactured or possessed for sale, the "value" of those items shall be equivalent to the retail price or fair market price of the true items that are counterfeited.
(B) When counterfeited but unassembled components of computer software packages are recovered, including, but not limited to, counterfeited computer diskettes, instruction manuals, or licensing envelopes, the "value" of those components of computer software packages shall be equivalent to the retail price or fair market price of the number of completed computer software packages that could have been made from those components.
(b) The sentencing court shall, upon petition by the prosecuting attorney, at any time following sentencing, or by agreement of all parties, at the time of sentencing, conduct a hearing to determine whether any property or property interest is subject to forfeiture under this section. At the forfeiture hearing, the prosecuting attorney shall have the burden of establishing, by a preponderance of the evidence, that the property or property interests are subject to forfeiture. The prosecuting attorney may retain seized property that may be subject to forfeiture until the sentencing hearing.
(c) (1) Prior to the commencement of a forfeiture proceeding, the law enforcement agency seizing the property subject to forfeiture shall make an investigation as to any person other than the defendant who may have an interest in it. At least 30 days before the hearing to determine whether the property should be forfeited, the prosecuting agency shall send notice of the hearing to any person who may have an interest in the property that arose before the seizure.
(2) A person claiming an interest in the property shall file a motion for the redemption of that interest at least 10 days before the hearing on forfeiture, and shall send a copy of the motion to the prosecuting agency and to the probation department.
(3) If a motion to redeem an interest has been filed, the sentencing court shall hold a hearing to identify all persons who possess valid interests in the property. No person shall hold a valid interest in the property if, by a preponderance of the evidence, the prosecuting agency shows that the person knew or should have known that the property was being used in violation of, or conspiracy to commit a violation of, subdivision (b) of Section 272, Section 288, 288.2, 311.1, 311.2, 311.3, 311.4, 311.5, 311.10, 311.11, 470, 470a, 472, 475, 476, 480, 483.5, 484g, or subdivision (a), (b), or (d) of Section 484e, subdivision (a) of Section 484f, subdivision (b) or (c) of Section 484i, subdivision (c) of Section 502, or Section 502.7, 502.8, 529, 529a, 530.5, 537e, 593d, 593e, 646.9, or subdivision (j) of Section 647, and that the person did not take reasonable steps to prevent that use, or if the interest is a security interest, the person knew or should have known at the time that the security interest was created that the property would be used for a violation.
(d) If the sentencing court finds that a person holds a valid interest in the property, the following provisions shall apply:
(1) The court shall determine the value of the property.
(2) The court shall determine the value of each valid interest in the property.
(3) If the value of the property is greater than the value of the interest, the holder of the interest shall be entitled to ownership of the property upon paying the court the difference between the value of the property and the value of the valid interest.
If the holder of the interest declines to pay the amount determined under paragraph (2), the court may order the property sold and designate the prosecutor or any other agency to sell the property. The designated agency shall be entitled to seize the property and the holder of the interest shall forward any documentation underlying the interest, including any ownership certificates for that property, to the designated agency. The designated agency shall sell the property and pay the owner of the interest the proceeds, up to the value of that interest.
(4) If the value of the property is less than the value of the interest, the designated agency shall sell the property and pay the owner of the interest the proceeds, up to the value of that interest.
(e) If the defendant was a minor at the time of the offense, this subdivision shall apply to property subject to forfeiture that is the property of the parent or guardian of the minor.
(1) The prosecuting agency shall notify the parent or guardian of the forfeiture hearing at least 30 days before the date set for the hearing.
(2) The computer or telecommunications device shall not be subject to forfeiture if the parent or guardian files a signed statement with the court at least 10 days before the date set for the hearing that the minor shall not have access to any computer or telecommunications device owned by the parent or guardian for two years after the date on which the minor is sentenced.
(3) If the minor is convicted of a violation of Section 288, 288.2, 311.1, 311.2, 311.3, 311.4, 311.5, 311.10, 311.11, 470, 470a, 472, 476, 480, or subdivision (b) of Section 484e, subdivision (d) of Section 484e, subdivision (a) of Section 484f, subdivision (b) of Section 484i, subdivision (c) of Section 502, or Section 502.7, 502.8, 529, 529a, 530.5, or subdivision (j) of Section 647, within two years after the date on which the minor is sentenced, and the violation involves a computer or telecommunications device owned by the parent or guardian, the original property subject to forfeiture, and the property involved in the new offense, shall be subject to forfeiture notwithstanding paragraph (2).
(4) Notwithstanding paragraph (1), (2), or (3), or any other provision of this chapter, if a minor's parent or guardian makes full restitution to the victim of a crime enumerated in this chapter in an amount or manner determined by the court, the forfeiture provisions of this chapter do not apply to the property of that parent or guardian if the property was located in the family's primary residence during the commission of the crime.
(f) Notwithstanding any other provision of this chapter, the court may exercise its discretion to deny forfeiture where the court finds that the convicted defendant, or minor adjudicated to come within the jurisdiction of the juvenile court, is not likely to use the property otherwise subject to forfeiture for future illegal acts.
(g) If the defendant is found to have the only valid interest in the property subject to forfeiture, it shall be distributed as follows:
(1) First, to the victim, if the victim elects to take the property as full or partial restitution for injury, victim expenditures, or compensatory damages, as defined in paragraph (1) of subdivision (e) of Section 502. If the victim elects to receive the property under this paragraph, the value of the property shall be determined by the court and that amount shall be credited against the restitution owed by the defendant. The victim shall not be penalized for electing not to accept the forfeited property in lieu of full or partial restitution.
(2) Second, at the discretion of the court, to one or more of the following agencies or entities:
(A) The prosecuting agency.
(B) The public entity of which the prosecuting agency is a part.
(C) The public entity whose officers or employees conducted the investigation resulting in forfeiture.
(D) Other state and local public entities, including school districts.
(E) Nonprofit charitable organizations.
(h) If the property is to be sold, the court may designate the prosecuting agency or any other agency to sell the property at auction. The proceeds of the sale shall be distributed by the court as follows:
(1) To the bona fide or innocent purchaser or encumbrancer, conditional sales vendor, or mortgagee of the property up to the amount of his or her interest in the property, if the court orders a distribution to that person.
(2) The balance, if any, to be retained by the court, subject to the provisions for distribution under subdivision (g).
(Amended by Stats. 2015, Ch. 291, Sec. 1. (SB 676) Effective January 1, 2016.)

502.5.

Every person who, after mortgaging or encumbering by deed of trust any real property, and during the existence of such mortgage or deed of trust, or after such mortgaged or encumbered property shall have been sold under an order and decree of foreclosure or at trustee's sale, and with intent to defraud or injure the mortgagee or the beneficiary or trustee, under such deed of trust, his representatives, successors or assigns, or the purchaser of such mortgaged or encumbered premises at such foreclosure or trustee's sale, his representatives, successors or assigns, takes, removes or carries away from such mortgaged or encumbered premises, or otherwise disposes of or permits the taking, removal or carrying away or otherwise disposing of any house, barn, windmill, water tank, pump, engine or other part of the freehold that is attached or affixed to such premises as an improvement thereon, without the written consent of the mortgagee or beneficiary, under deed of trust, his representatives, successors or assigns, or the purchaser at such foreclosure or trustee's sale, his representatives, successors or assigns, is guilty of larceny and shall be punished accordingly.
(Added by renumbering Section 502½ by Stats. 1979, Ch. 373.)

502.6.

(a) Any person who knowingly, willfully, and with the intent to defraud, possesses a scanning device, or who knowingly, willfully, and with intent to defraud, uses a scanning device to access, read, obtain, memorize or store, temporarily or permanently, information encoded on the magnetic strip or stripe of a payment card without the permission of the authorized user of the payment card is guilty of a misdemeanor, punishable by a term in a county jail not to exceed one year, or a fine of one thousand dollars ($1,000), or both the imprisonment and fine.
(b) Any person who knowingly, willfully, and with the intent to defraud, possesses a reencoder, or who knowingly, willfully, and with intent to defraud, uses a reencoder to place encoded information on the magnetic strip or stripe of a payment card or any electronic medium that allows an authorized transaction to occur, without the permission of the authorized user of the payment card from which the information is being reencoded is guilty of a misdemeanor, punishable by a term in a county jail not to exceed one year, or a fine of one thousand dollars ($1,000), or both the imprisonment and fine.
(c) Any scanning device or reencoder described in subdivision (e) owned by the defendant and possessed or used in violation of subdivision (a) or (b) may be seized and be destroyed as contraband by the sheriff of the county in which the scanning device or reencoder was seized.
(d) Any computer, computer system, computer network, or any software or data, owned by the defendant, which is used during the commission of any public offense described in this section or any computer, owned by the defendant, which is used as a repository for the storage of software or data illegally obtained in violation of this section shall be subject to forfeiture.
(e) As used in this section, the following definitions apply:
(1) "Scanning device" means a scanner, reader, or any other electronic device that is used to access, read, scan, obtain, memorize, or store, temporarily or permanently, information encoded on the magnetic strip or stripe of a payment card.
(2) "Reencoder" means an electronic device that places encoded information from the magnetic strip or stripe of a payment card on to the magnetic strip or stripe of a different payment card.

(3) "Payment card" means a credit card, debit card, or any other card that is issued to an authorized user and that allows the user to obtain, purchase, or receive goods, services, money, or anything else of value.
(f) Nothing in this section shall preclude prosecution under any other provision of law.
(Added by Stats. 2002, Ch. 861, Sec. 1. Effective January 1, 2003.)
502.7.
(a) Any person who, knowingly, willfully, and with intent to defraud a person providing telephone or telegraph service, avoids or attempts to avoid, or aids, abets or causes another to avoid the lawful charge, in whole or in part, for telephone or telegraph service by any of the following means is guilty of a misdemeanor or a felony, except as provided in subdivision (g):
(1) By charging the service to an existing telephone number or credit card number without the authority of the subscriber thereto or the lawful holder thereof.
(2) By charging the service to a nonexistent telephone number or credit card number, or to a number associated with telephone service which is suspended or terminated, or to a revoked or canceled (as distinguished from expired) credit card number, notice of the suspension, termination, revocation, or cancellation of the telephone service or credit card having been given to the subscriber thereto or the holder thereof.
(3) By use of a code, prearranged scheme, or other similar stratagem or device whereby the person, in effect, sends or receives information.
(4) By rearranging, tampering with, or making connection with telephone or telegraph facilities or equipment, whether physically, electrically, acoustically, inductively, or otherwise, or by using telephone or telegraph service with knowledge or reason to believe that the rearrangement, tampering, or connection existed at the time of the use.
(5) By using any other deception, false pretense, trick, scheme, device, conspiracy, or means, including the fraudulent use of false, altered, or stolen identification.
(b) Any person who does either of the following is guilty of a misdemeanor or a felony, except as provided in subdivision (g):
(1) Makes, possesses, sells, gives, or otherwise transfers to another, or offers or advertises any instrument, apparatus, or device with intent to use it or with knowledge or reason to believe it is intended to be used to avoid any lawful telephone or telegraph toll charge or to conceal the existence or place of origin or destination of any telephone or telegraph message.
(2) Sells, gives, or otherwise transfers to another or offers, or advertises plans or instructions for making or assembling an instrument, apparatus, or device described in paragraph (1) of this subdivision with knowledge or reason to believe that they may be used to make or assemble the instrument, apparatus, or device.
(c) Any person who publishes the number or code of an existing, canceled, revoked, expired, or nonexistent credit card, or the numbering or coding which is employed in the issuance of credit cards, with the intent that it be used or with knowledge or reason to believe that it will be used to avoid the payment of any lawful telephone or telegraph toll charge is guilty of a misdemeanor. Subdivision (g) shall not apply to this subdivision. As used in this section, "publishes" means the communication of information to any one or more persons, either orally, in person or by telephone, radio, or television, or electronic means, including, but not limited to, a bulletin board system, or in a writing of any kind, including without limitation a letter or memorandum, circular or handbill, newspaper, or magazine article, or book.
(d) Any person who is the issuee of a calling card, credit card, calling code, or any other means or device for the legal use of telecommunications services and who receives anything of value for knowingly allowing another person to use the means or device in order to fraudulently obtain telecommunications services is guilty of a misdemeanor or a felony, except as provided in subdivision (g).
(e) Subdivision (a) applies when the telephone or telegraph communication involved either originates or terminates, or both originates and terminates, in this state, or when the charges for service would have been billable, in normal course, by a person providing telephone or telegraph service in this state, but for the fact that the charge for service was avoided, or attempted to be avoided, by one or more of the means set forth in subdivision (a).
(f) Jurisdiction of an offense under this section is in the jurisdictional territory where the telephone call or telegram involved in the offense originates or where it terminates, or the jurisdictional territory to which the bill for the service is sent or would have been sent but for the fact that the service was obtained or attempted to be obtained by one or more of the means set forth in subdivision (a).
(g) Theft of any telephone or telegraph services under this section by a person who has a prior misdemeanor or felony conviction for theft of services under this section within the past five years, is a felony.
(h) Any person or telephone company defrauded by any acts prohibited under this section shall be entitled to restitution for the entire amount of the charges avoided from any person or persons convicted under this section.
(i) Any instrument, apparatus, device, plans, instructions, or written publication described in subdivision (b) or (c) may be seized under warrant or incident to a lawful arrest, and, upon the conviction of a person for a violation of subdivision (a), (b), or (c), the instrument, apparatus, device, plans, instructions, or written publication may be destroyed as contraband by the sheriff of the county in which the person was convicted or turned over to the person providing telephone or telegraph service in the territory in which it was seized.
(j) Any computer, computer system, computer network, or any software or data, owned by the defendant, which is used during the commission of any public offense described in this section or any computer, owned by the defendant, which is used as a repository for the storage of software or data illegally obtained in violation of this section shall be subject to forfeiture.
(Amended by Stats. 1993, Ch. 1014, Sec. 1. Effective January 1, 1994.)
502.8.
(a) Any person who knowingly advertises illegal telecommunications equipment is guilty of a misdemeanor.
(b) Any person who possesses or uses illegal telecommunications equipment intending to avoid the payment of any lawful charge for telecommunications service or to facilitate other criminal conduct is guilty of a misdemeanor.
(c) Any person found guilty of violating subdivision (b), who has previously been convicted of the same offense, shall be guilty of a felony, punishable by imprisonment in state prison, a fine of up to fifty thousand dollars ($50,000), or both.
(d) Any person who possesses illegal telecommunications equipment with intent to sell, transfer, or furnish or offer to sell, transfer, or furnish the equipment to another, intending to avoid the payment of any lawful charge for telecommunications service or to facilitate other criminal conduct is guilty of a misdemeanor punishable by one year in a county jail or imprisonment in state prison or a fine of up to ten thousand dollars ($10,000), or both.
(e) Any person who possesses 10 or more items of illegal telecommunications equipment with intent to sell or offer to sell the equipment to another, intending to avoid payment of any lawful charge for telecommunications service or to facilitate other criminal conduct, is guilty of a felony, punishable by imprisonment in state prison, a fine of up to fifty thousand dollars ($50,000), or both.
(f) Any person who manufactures 10 or more items of illegal telecommunications equipment with intent to sell or offer to sell the equipment to another, intending to avoid the payment of any lawful charge for telecommunications service or to facilitate other criminal conduct is guilty of a felony punishable by imprisonment in state prison or a fine of up to fifty thousand dollars ($50,000), or both.
(g) For purposes of this section, "illegal telecommunications equipment" means equipment that operates to evade the lawful charges for any telecommunications service; surreptitiously intercept electronic serial numbers or mobile identification numbers; alter electronic serial numbers; circumvent efforts to confirm legitimate access to a telecommunications account; conceal from any telecommunications service provider or lawful authority the existence, place of origin, or destination of any telecommunication; or otherwise facilitate any other criminal conduct. "Illegal telecommunications equipment" includes, but is not limited to, any unauthorized electronic serial number or mobile identification number, whether incorporated into a wireless telephone or other device or otherwise. Items specified in this subdivision shall be considered illegal telecommunications equipment notwithstanding any statement or disclaimer that the items are intended for educational, instructional, or similar purposes.
(h) (1) In the event that a person violates the provisions of this section with the intent to avoid the payment of any lawful charge for telecommunications service to a telecommunications service provider, the court shall order the person to pay restitution to the telecommunications service provider in an amount that is the greater of the following:
(A) Five thousand dollars ($5,000).
(B) Three times the amount of actual damages, if any, sustained by the telecommunications service provider, plus reasonable attorney fees.
(2) It is not a necessary prerequisite to an order of restitution under this section that the telecommunications service provider has suffered, or be threatened with, actual damages.
(Amended by Stats. 2016, Ch. 86, Sec. 225. (SB 1171) Effective January 1, 2017.)
502.9.
Upon conviction of a felony violation under this chapter, the fact that the victim was an elder or dependent person, as defined in Section 288, shall be considered a circumstance in aggravation when imposing a term under subdivision (b) of Section 1170.
(Amended by Stats. 2004, Ch. 823, Sec. 8. Effective January 1, 2005.)

CHAPTER 6. Embezzlement [503 - 515]

(Chapter 6 enacted 1872.)
503.
Embezzlement is the fraudulent appropriation of property by a person to whom it has been intrusted.
(Enacted 1872.)
504.
Every officer of this state, or of any county, city, city and county, or other municipal corporation or subdivision thereof, and every deputy, clerk, or servant of that officer, and every officer, director, trustee, clerk, servant, or agent of any association, society, or corporation (public or private), who fraudulently appropriates to any use or purpose not in the due and lawful execution of that person's trust, any property in his or her possession or under his or her control by virtue of that trust, or secretes it with a fraudulent intent to appropriate it to that use or purpose, is guilty of embezzlement.
(Amended by Stats. 2002, Ch. 787, Sec. 13. Effective January 1, 2003.)
504a.
Every person who shall fraudulently remove, conceal or dispose of any goods, chattels or effects, leased or let to him by any instrument in writing, or any personal property or effects of another in his possession, under a contract of purchase not yet fulfilled, and any person in possession of such goods, chattels, or effects knowing them to be subject to such lease or contract of purchase who shall so remove, conceal or dispose of the same with intent to injure or defraud the lessor or owner thereof, is guilty of embezzlement.
(Added by Stats. 1917, Ch. 180.)
504b.
Where under the terms of a security agreement, as defined in paragraph (74) of subdivision (a) of Section 9102 of the Commercial Code, the debtor has the right to sell the property covered thereby and is to account to the secured party for, and pay to the secured party the indebtedness secured by the security agreement from, the proceeds of the sale of any of the property, and where the debtor, having sold the property covered by the security agreement and having received the proceeds of the sale, willfully and wrongfully, and with the intent to defraud, fails to pay to the secured party the amounts due under the security agreement, or the proceeds of the sale, whichever is the lesser amount, and appropriates the money to his or her own use, the debtor shall be guilty of embezzlement and shall be punishable as provided in Section 514.
(Amended by Stats. 2013, Ch. 531, Sec. 26. (AB 502) Effective January 1, 2014. Operative July 1, 2014, by Sec. 28 of Ch. 531.)
505.
Every carrier or other person having under his control personal property for the purpose of transportation for hire, who fraudulently appropriates it to any use or purpose inconsistent with the safe keeping of such property and its transportation according to his trust, is guilty of embezzlement, whether he has broken the package in which such property is contained, or has otherwise separated the items thereof, or not.
(Enacted 1872.)
506.
Every trustee, banker, merchant, broker, attorney, agent, assignee in trust, executor, administrator, or collector, or person otherwise intrusted with or having in his control property for the use of any other person, who fraudulently appropriates it to any use or purpose not in the due and lawful execution of his trust, or secretes it with a fraudulent intent to appropriate it to such use or purpose, and any contractor who appropriates money paid to him for any use or purpose, other than for that which he received it, is guilty of embezzlement, and the payment of laborers and materialmen for work performed or material furnished in the performance of any contract is hereby declared to be the use and purpose to which the contract price of such contract, or any part thereof, received by the contractor shall be applied.
(Amended by Stats. 1919, Ch. 518.)
506a.
Any person who, acting as collector, or acting in any capacity in or about a business conducted for the collection of accounts or debts owing by another person, and who violates Section 506 of the Penal Code, shall be deemed to be an agent or person as defined in Section 506, and subject for a violation of Section 506, to be prosecuted, tried, and punished in accordance therewith and with law; and "collector" means every such person who collects, or who has in his or her possession or under his or her control property or money for the use of any other person, whether in his or her own name and mixed with his or her own property or money, or otherwise, or whether he or she has any interest, direct or indirect, in or to such property or money, or any portion thereof, and who fraudulently appropriates to his or her own use, or the use of any person other than the true owner, or person entitled thereto, or secretes that property or money, or any portion thereof, or interest therein not his or her own, with a fraudulent intent to appropriate it to any use or purpose not in the due and lawful execution of his or her trust.
(Amended by Stats. 1987, Ch. 828, Sec. 30.)
506b.
Any person who violates Section 2985.3 or 2985.4 of the Civil Code, relating to real property sales contracts, is guilty of a public offense punishable by a fine not exceeding ten thousand dollars ($10,000), or by imprisonment in a the county jail not exceeding

one year, or by imprisonment pursuant to subdivision (h) of Section 1170, or by both that fine and imprisonment.
(Amended by Stats. 2011, Ch. 15, Sec. 379. (AB 109) Effective April 4, 2011. Operative October 1, 2011, by Sec. 636 of Ch. 15, as amended by Stats. 2011, Ch. 39, Sec. 68.)

507.
Every person intrusted with any property as bailee, tenant, or lodger, or with any power of attorney for the sale or transfer thereof, who fraudulently converts the same or the proceeds thereof to his own use, or secretes it or them with a fraudulent intent to convert to his own use, is guilty of embezzlement.
(Enacted 1872.)

508.
Every clerk, agent, or servant of any person who fraudulently appropriates to his own use, or secretes with a fraudulent intent to appropriate to his own use, any property of another which has come into his control or care by virtue of his employment as such clerk, agent, or servant, is guilty of embezzlement.
(Enacted 1872.)

509.
A distinct act of taking is not necessary to constitute embezzlement.
(Enacted 1872.)

510.
Any evidence of debt, negotiable by delivery only, and actually executed, is the subject of embezzlement, whether it has been delivered or issued as a valid instrument or not.
(Enacted 1872.)

511.
Upon any indictment for embezzlement, it is a sufficient defense that the property was appropriated openly and avowedly, and under a claim of title preferred in good faith, even though such claim is untenable. But this provision does not excuse the unlawful retention of the property of another to offset or pay demands held against him.
(Enacted 1872.)

512.
The fact that the accused intended to restore the property embezzled, is no ground of defense or mitigation of punishment, if it has not been restored before an information has been laid before a magistrate, or an indictment found by a grand jury, charging the commission of the offense.
(Amended by Stats. 1905, Ch. 520.)

513.
Whenever, prior to an information laid before a magistrate, or an indictment found by a grand jury, charging the commission of embezzlement, the person accused voluntarily and actually restores or tenders restoration of the property alleged to have been embezzled, or any part thereof, such fact is not a ground of defense, but it authorizes the court to mitigate punishment, in its discretion.
(Amended by Stats. 1905, Ch. 520.)

514.
Every person guilty of embezzlement is punishable in the manner prescribed for theft of property of the value or kind embezzled; and where the property embezzled is an evidence of debt or right of action, the sum due upon it or secured to be paid by it must be taken as its value; if the embezzlement or defalcation is of the public funds of the United States, or of this state, or of any county or municipality within this state, the offense is a felony, and is punishable by imprisonment in the state prison; and the person so convicted is ineligible thereafter to any office of honor, trust, or profit in this state.
(Amended by Stats. 1976, Ch. 1139.)

515.
Upon conviction of a felony violation under this chapter, the fact that the victim was an elder or dependent person, as defined in Section 288, shall be considered a circumstance in aggravation when imposing a term under subdivision (b) of Section 1170.
(Amended by Stats. 2004, Ch. 823, Sec. 9. Effective January 1, 2005.)

CHAPTER 7. Extortion [518 - 527]

(Chapter 7 enacted 1872.)

518.
(a) Extortion is the obtaining of property or other consideration from another, with his or her consent, or the obtaining of an official act of a public officer, induced by a wrongful use of force or fear, or under color of official right.
(b) For purposes of this chapter, "consideration" means anything of value, including sexual conduct as defined in subdivision (b) of Section 311.3, or an image of an intimate body part as defined in subparagraph (C) of paragraph (4) of subdivision (j) of Section 647.
(c) Notwithstanding subdivision (a), this section does not apply to a person under 18 years of age who has obtained consideration consisting of sexual conduct or an image of an intimate body part.
(Amended by Stats. 2017, Ch. 518, Sec. 1. (SB 500) Effective January 1, 2018.)

519.
Fear, such as will constitute extortion, may be induced by a threat of any of the following:
1. To do an unlawful injury to the person or property of the individual threatened or of a third person.
2. To accuse the individual threatened, or a relative of his or her, or a member of his or her family, of a crime.
3. To expose, or to impute to him, her, or them a deformity, disgrace, or crime.
4. To expose a secret affecting him, her, or them.
5. To report his, her, or their immigration status or suspected immigration status.
(Amended by Stats. 2014, Ch. 71, Sec. 123. (SB 1304) Effective January 1, 2015.)

520.
Every person who extorts property or other consideration from another, under circumstances not amounting to robbery or carjacking, by means of force, or any threat, such as is mentioned in Section 519, shall be punished by imprisonment pursuant to subdivision (h) of Section 1170 for two, three or four years.
(Amended by Stats. 2017, Ch. 518, Sec. 2. (SB 500) Effective January 1, 2018.)

521.
Every person who commits any extortion under color of official right, in cases for which a different punishment is not prescribed in this Code, is guilty of a misdemeanor.
(Enacted 1872.)

522.
Every person who, by any extortionate means, obtains from another his signature to any paper or instrument, whereby, if such signature were freely given, any property would be transferred, or any debt, demand, charge, or right of action created, is punishable in the same manner as if the actual delivery of such debt, demand, charge, or right of action were obtained.
(Enacted 1872.)

523.
(a) Every person who, with intent to extort property or other consideration from another, sends or delivers to any person any letter or other writing, whether subscribed or not, expressing or implying, or adapted to imply, any threat such as is specified in

Section 519 is punishable in the same manner as if such property or other consideration were actually obtained by means of such threat.
(b) (1) Every person who, with intent to extort property or other consideration from another, introduces ransomware into any computer, computer system, or computer network is punishable pursuant to Section 520 in the same manner as if such property or other consideration were actually obtained by means of the ransomware.
(2) Prosecution pursuant to this subdivision does not prohibit or limit prosecution under any other law.
(c) (1) "Ransomware" means a computer contaminant, as defined in Section 502, or lock placed or introduced without authorization into a computer, computer system, or computer network that restricts access by an authorized person to the computer, computer system, computer network, or any data therein under circumstances in which the person responsible for the placement or introduction of the ransomware demands payment of money or other consideration to remove the computer contaminant, restore access to the computer, computer system, computer network, or data, or otherwise remediate the impact of the computer contaminant or lock.
(2) A person is responsible for placing or introducing ransomware into a computer, computer system, or computer network if the person directly places or introduces the ransomware or directs or induces another person to do so, with the intent of demanding payment or other consideration to remove the ransomware, restore access, or otherwise remediate the impact of the ransomware.
(Amended by Stats. 2017, Ch. 518, Sec. 3. (SB 500) Effective January 1, 2018.)

524.
Every person who attempts, by means of any threat, such as is specified in Section 519 of this code, to extort property or other consideration from another is punishable by imprisonment in the county jail not longer than one year or in the state prison or by fine not exceeding ten thousand dollars ($10,000), or by both such fine and imprisonment.
(Amended by Stats. 2017, Ch. 518, Sec. 4. (SB 500) Effective January 1, 2018.)

525.
Upon conviction of a felony violation under this chapter, the fact that the victim was an elder or dependent person, as defined in Section 288, shall be considered a circumstance in aggravation when imposing a term under subdivision (b) of Section 1170.
(Amended by Stats. 2004, Ch. 823, Sec. 10. Effective January 1, 2005.)

526.
Any person, who, with intent to obtain from another person any property or other consideration, delivers or causes to be delivered to the other person any paper, document or written, typed or printed form purporting to be an order or other process of a court, or designed or calculated by its writing, typing or printing, or the arrangement thereof, to cause or lead the other person to believe it to be an order or other process of a court, when in fact such paper, document or written, typed or printed form is not an order or process of a court, is guilty of a misdemeanor, and each separate delivery of any paper, document or written, typed or printed form shall constitute a separate offense.
(Amended by Stats. 2017, Ch. 518, Sec. 5. (SB 500) Effective January 1, 2018.)

527.
Any person who shall sell or offer for sale, print, publish, or distribute any paper, document or written, typed or printed form, designed or calculated by its writing, typing or printing, or the arrangement thereof, to cause or lead any person to believe it to be, or that it will be used as an order or other process of a court when in fact such paper, document or written, typed or printed form is not to be used as the order or process of a court, is guilty of a misdemeanor, and each separate publication, printing, distribution, sale or offer to sell any such paper, document or written, typed or printed form shall constitute a separate offense, and upon conviction thereof in addition to any other sentence imposed the court may order that all such papers or documents or written, typed or printed forms in the possession or under the control of the person found guilty of such misdemeanor shall be delivered to such court or the clerk thereof for destruction.
(Added by Stats. 1929, Ch. 593.)

CHAPTER 8. False Personation and Cheats [528 - 539]

(Chapter 8 enacted 1872.)

528.
Every person who falsely personates another, and in such assumed character marries or pretends to marry, or to sustain the marriage relation towards another, with or without the connivance of such other, is guilty of a felony.
(Enacted 1872.)

528.5.
(a) Notwithstanding any other provision of law, any person who knowingly and without consent credibly impersonates another actual person through or on an Internet Web site or by other electronic means for purposes of harming, intimidating, threatening, or defrauding another person is guilty of a public offense punishable pursuant to subdivision (d).
(b) For purposes of this section, an impersonation is credible if another person would reasonably believe, or did reasonably believe, that the defendant was or is the person who was impersonated.
(c) For purposes of this section, "electronic means" shall include opening an e-mail account or an account or profile on a social networking Internet Web site in another person's name.
(d) A violation of subdivision (a) is punishable by a fine not exceeding one thousand dollars ($1,000), or by imprisonment in a county jail not exceeding one year, or by both that fine and imprisonment.
(e) In addition to any other civil remedy available, a person who suffers damage or loss by reason of a violation of subdivision (a) may bring a civil action against the violator for compensatory damages and injunctive relief or other equitable relief pursuant to paragraphs (1), (2), (4), and (5) of subdivision (e) and subdivision (g) of Section 502.
(f) This section shall not preclude prosecution under any other law.
(Added by Stats. 2010, Ch. 335, Sec. 1. (SB 1411) Effective January 1, 2011.)

529.
(a) Every person who falsely personates another in either his or her private or official capacity, and in that assumed character does any of the following, is punishable pursuant to subdivision (b):
(1) Becomes bail or surety for any party in any proceeding whatever, before any court or officer authorized to take that bail or surety.
(2) Verifies, publishes, acknowledges, or proves, in the name of another person, any written instrument, with intent that the same may be recorded, delivered, or used as true.
(3) Does any other act whereby, if done by the person falsely personated, he might, in any event, become liable to any suit or prosecution, or to pay any sum of money, or to incur any charge, forfeiture, or penalty, or whereby any benefit might accrue to the party personating, or to any other person.
(b) By a fine not exceeding ten thousand dollars ($10,000), or by imprisonment in a county jail not exceeding one year, or imprisonment pursuant to subdivision (h) of Section 1170, or by both that fine and imprisonment.

(Amended by Stats. 2011, Ch. 15, Sec. 381. (AB 109) Effective April 4, 2011. Operative October 1, 2011, by Sec. 636 of Ch. 15, as amended by Stats. 2011, Ch. 39, Sec. 68.)

529a.

Every person who manufactures, produces, sells, offers, or transfers to another any document purporting to be either a certificate of birth or certificate of baptism, knowing such document to be false or counterfeit and with the intent to deceive, is guilty of a crime, and upon conviction therefor, shall be punished by imprisonment in a county jail not to exceed one year, or by imprisonment pursuant to subdivision (h) of Section 1170. Every person who offers, displays, or has in his or her possession any false or counterfeit certificate of birth or certificate of baptism, or any genuine certificate of birth which describes a person then living or deceased, with intent to represent himself or herself as another or to conceal his or her true identity, is guilty of a crime, and upon conviction therefor, shall be punished by imprisonment in the county jail not to exceed one year.

(Amended by Stats. 2011, Ch. 15, Sec. 382. (AB 109) Effective April 4, 2011. Operative October 1, 2011, by Sec. 636 of Ch. 15, as amended by Stats. 2011, Ch. 39, Sec. 68.)

529.5.

(a) Every person who manufactures, sells, offers for sale, or transfers any document, not amounting to counterfeit, purporting to be a government-issued identification card or driver's license, which by virtue of the wording or appearance thereon could reasonably deceive an ordinary person into believing that it is issued by a government agency, and who knows that the document is not a government-issued document, is guilty of a misdemeanor, punishable by imprisonment in a county jail not exceeding one year, or by a fine not exceeding one thousand dollars ($1,000), or by both the fine and imprisonment.

(b) Any person who, having been convicted of a violation of subdivision (a), is subsequently convicted of a violation of subdivision (a), is punishable for the subsequent conviction by imprisonment in a county jail not exceeding one year, or by a fine not exceeding five thousand dollars ($5,000), or by both the fine and imprisonment.

(c) Any person who possesses a document described in subdivision (a) and who knows that the document is not a government-issued document is guilty of a misdemeanor punishable by a fine of not less than one thousand dollars ($1,000) and not more than two thousand five hundred dollars ($2,500). The misdemeanor fine shall be imposed except in unusual cases where the interests of justice would be served. The court may allow an offender to work off the fine by doing community service. If community service work is not available, the misdemeanor shall be punishable by a fine of up to one thousand dollars ($1,000), based on the person's ability to pay.

(d) If an offense specified in this section is committed by a person when he or she is under 21 years of age, but is 13 years of age or older, the court also may suspend the person's driving privilege for one year, pursuant to Section 13202.5 of the Vehicle Code.

(Amended by Stats. 1990, Ch. 960, Sec. 1.)

529.7.

Any person who obtains, or assists another person in obtaining, a driver's license, identification card, vehicle registration certificate, or any other official document issued by the Department of Motor Vehicles, with knowledge that the person obtaining the document is not entitled to the document, is guilty of a misdemeanor, and is punishable by imprisonment in a county jail for up to one year, or a fine of up to one thousand dollars ($1,000), or both.

(Added by Stats. 2002, Ch. 907, Sec. 2. Effective January 1, 2003.)

530.

Every person who falsely personates another, in either his private or official capacity, and in such assumed character receives any money or property, knowing that it is intended to be delivered to the individual so personated, with intent to convert the same to his own use, or to that of another person, or to deprive the true owner thereof, is punishable in the same manner and to the same extent as for larceny of the money or property so received.

(Amended by Stats. 1905, Ch. 523.)

530.5.

(a) Every person who willfully obtains personal identifying information, as defined in subdivision (b) of Section 530.55, of another person, and uses that information for any unlawful purpose, including to obtain, or attempt to obtain, credit, goods, services, real property, or medical information without the consent of that person, is guilty of a public offense, and upon conviction therefor, shall be punished by a fine, by imprisonment in a county jail not to exceed one year, or by both a fine and imprisonment, or by imprisonment pursuant to subdivision (h) of Section 1170.

(b) In any case in which a person willfully obtains personal identifying information of another person, uses that information to commit a crime in addition to a violation of subdivision (a), and is convicted of that crime, the court records shall reflect that the person whose identity was falsely used to commit the crime did not commit the crime.

(c) (1) Every person who, with the intent to defraud, acquires or retains possession of the personal identifying information, as defined in subdivision (b) of Section 530.55, of another person is guilty of a public offense, and upon conviction therefor, shall be punished by a fine, by imprisonment in a county jail not to exceed one year, or by both a fine and imprisonment.

(2) Every person who, with the intent to defraud, acquires or retains possession of the personal identifying information, as defined in subdivision (b) of Section 530.55, of another person, and who has previously been convicted of a violation of this section, upon conviction therefor shall be punished by a fine, by imprisonment in a county jail not to exceed one year, or by both a fine and imprisonment, or by imprisonment pursuant to subdivision (h) of Section 1170.

(3) Every person who, with the intent to defraud, acquires or retains possession of the personal identifying information, as defined in subdivision (b) of Section 530.55, of 10 or more other persons is guilty of a public offense, and upon conviction therefor, shall be punished by a fine, by imprisonment in a county jail not to exceed one year, or by both a fine and imprisonment, or by imprisonment pursuant to subdivision (h) of Section 1170.

(d) (1) Every person who, with the intent to defraud, sells, transfers, or conveys the personal identifying information, as defined in subdivision (b) of Section 530.55, of another person is guilty of a public offense, and upon conviction therefor, shall be punished by a fine, by imprisonment in a county jail not to exceed one year, or by both a fine and imprisonment, or by imprisonment pursuant to subdivision (h) of Section 1170.

(2) Every person who, with actual knowledge that the personal identifying information, as defined in subdivision (b) of Section 530.55, of a specific person will be used to commit a violation of subdivision (a), sells, transfers, or conveys that same personal identifying information is guilty of a public offense, and upon conviction therefor, shall be punished by a fine, by imprisonment pursuant to subdivision (h) of Section 1170, or by both a fine and imprisonment.

(e) Every person who commits mail theft, as defined in Section 1708 of Title 18 of the United States Code, is guilty of a public offense, and upon conviction therefor shall be punished by a fine, by imprisonment in a county jail not to exceed one year, or by both a fine and imprisonment. Prosecution under this subdivision shall not limit or preclude prosecution under any other provision of law, including, but not limited to, subdivisions (a) to (c), inclusive, of this section.

(f) An interactive computer service or access software provider, as defined in subsection (f) of Section 230 of Title 47 of the United States Code, shall not be liable under this section unless the service or provider acquires, transfers, sells, conveys, or retains possession of personal information with the intent to defraud.

(Amended by Stats. 2011, Ch. 15, Sec. 383. (AB 109) Effective April 4, 2011. Operative October 1, 2011, by Sec. 636 of Ch. 15, as amended by Stats. 2011, Ch. 39, Sec. 68.)

530.55.

(a) For purposes of this chapter, "person" means a natural person, living or deceased, firm, association, organization, partnership, business trust, company, corporation, limited liability company, or public entity, or any other legal entity.

(b) For purposes of this chapter, "personal identifying information" means any name, address, telephone number, health insurance number, taxpayer identification number, school identification number, state or federal driver's license, or identification number, social security number, place of employment, employee identification number, professional or occupational number, mother's maiden name, demand deposit account number, savings account number, checking account number, PIN (personal identification number) or password, alien registration number, government passport number, date of birth, unique biometric data including fingerprint, facial scan identifiers, voiceprint, retina or iris image, or other unique physical representation, unique electronic data including information identification number assigned to the person, address or routing code, telecommunication identifying information or access device, information contained in a birth or death certificate, or credit card number of an individual person, or an equivalent form of identification.

(Added by Stats. 2006, Ch. 522, Sec. 3. Effective January 1, 2007.)

530.6.

(a) A person who has learned or reasonably suspects that his or her personal identifying information has been unlawfully used by another, as described in subdivision (a) of Section 530.5, may initiate a law enforcement investigation by contacting the local law enforcement agency that has jurisdiction over his or her actual residence or place of business, which shall take a police report of the matter, provide the complainant with a copy of that report, and begin an investigation of the facts. If the suspected crime was committed in a different jurisdiction, the local law enforcement agency may refer the matter to the law enforcement agency where the suspected crime was committed for further investigation of the facts.

(b) A person who reasonably believes that he or she is the victim of identity theft may petition a court, or the court, on its own motion or upon application of the prosecuting attorney, may move, for an expedited judicial determination of his or her factual innocence, where the perpetrator of the identity theft was arrested for, cited for, or convicted of a crime under the victim's identity, or where a criminal complaint has been filed against the perpetrator in the victim's name, or where the victim's identity has been mistakenly associated with a record of criminal conviction. Any judicial determination of factual innocence made pursuant to this section may be heard and determined upon declarations, affidavits, police reports, or other material, relevant, and reliable information submitted by the parties or ordered to be part of the record by the court. Where the court determines that the petition or motion is meritorious and that there is no reasonable cause to believe that the victim committed the offense for which the perpetrator of the identity theft was arrested, cited, convicted, or subject to a criminal complaint in the victim's name, or that the victim's identity has been mistakenly associated with a record of criminal conviction, the court shall find the victim factually innocent of that offense. If the victim is found factually innocent, the court shall issue an order certifying this determination.

(c) After a court has issued a determination of factual innocence pursuant to this section, the court may order the name and associated personal identifying information contained in court records, files, and indexes accessible by the public deleted, sealed, or labeled to show that the data is impersonated and does not reflect the defendant's identity.

(d) A court that has issued a determination of factual innocence pursuant to this section may at any time vacate that determination if the petition, or any information submitted in support of the petition, is found to contain any material misrepresentation or fraud.

(e) The Judicial Council of California shall develop a form for use in issuing an order pursuant to this section.

(f) For purposes of this section, "person" means a natural person, firm, association, organization, partnership, business trust, company, corporation, limited liability company, or public entity.

(Amended by Stats. 2006, Ch. 10, Sec. 2. Effective February 25, 2006.)

530.7.

(a) In order for a victim of identity theft to be included in the data base established pursuant to subdivision (c), he or she shall submit to the Department of Justice a court order obtained pursuant to any provision of law, a full set of fingerprints, and any other information prescribed by the department.

(b) Upon receiving information pursuant to subdivision (a), the Department of Justice shall verify the identity of the victim against any driver's license or other identification record maintained by the Department of Motor Vehicles.

(c) The Department of Justice shall establish and maintain a data base of individuals who have been victims of identity theft. The department shall provide a victim of identity theft or his or her authorized representative access to the data base in order to establish that the individual has been a victim of identity theft. Access to the data base shall be limited to criminal justice agencies, victims of identity theft, and individuals and agencies authorized by the victims.

(d) The Department of Justice shall establish and maintain a toll-free telephone number to provide access to information under subdivision (c).

(e) This section shall be operative September 1, 2001.

(Amended by Stats. 2001, Ch. 854, Sec. 30. Effective January 1, 2002.)

530.8.

(a) If a person discovers that an application in his or her name for a loan, credit line or account, credit card, charge card, public utility service, mail receiving or forwarding service, office or desk space rental service, or commercial mobile radio service has been filed with any person or entity by an unauthorized person, or that an account in his or her name has been opened with a bank, trust company, savings association, credit union, public utility, mail receiving or forwarding service, office or desk space rental service, or commercial mobile radio service provider by an unauthorized person, then, upon presenting to the person or entity with which the application was filed or the account was opened a copy of a police report prepared pursuant to Section 530.6 and identifying information in the categories of information that the unauthorized person used to complete the application or to open the account, the person, or a law enforcement officer specified by the person, shall be entitled to receive information related to the application or account, including a copy of the unauthorized person's application or application information and a record of transactions or charges associated with the application or account. Upon request by the person in whose name the application was filed or in whose name the account was opened, the person or entity with which the application was filed shall inform him or her of the categories of identifying information that the unauthorized person used to complete the application or to open the account. The person or entity with which the application was filed or the account was opened shall provide copies of all paper records, records of telephone applications or authorizations, or records of electronic applications or authorizations required by this section, without charge, within 10 business days of receipt of the person's request and submission of the required copy of the police report and identifying information.

(b) Any request made pursuant to subdivision (a) to a person or entity subject to the provisions of Section 2891 of the Public Utilities Code shall be in writing and the requesting person shall be deemed to be the subscriber for purposes of that section.

(c) (1) Before a person or entity provides copies to a law enforcement officer pursuant to subdivision (a), the person or entity may require the requesting person to submit a signed and dated statement by which the requesting person does all of the following:
(A) Authorizes disclosure for a stated period.
(B) Specifies the name of the agency or department to which the disclosure is authorized.
(C) Identifies the types of records that the requesting person authorizes to be disclosed.
(2) The person or entity shall include in the statement to be signed by the requesting person a notice that the requesting person has the right at any time to revoke the authorization.
(d) (1) A failure to produce records pursuant to subdivision (a) shall be addressed by the court in the jurisdiction in which the victim resides or in which the request for information was issued. At the victim's request, the Attorney General, the district attorney, or the prosecuting city attorney may file a petition to compel the attendance of the person or entity in possession of the records, as described in subdivision (a), and order the production of the requested records to the court. The petition shall contain a declaration from the victim stating when the request for information was made, that the information requested was not provided, and what response, if any, was made by the person or entity. The petition shall also contain copies of the police report prepared pursuant to Section 530.6 and the request for information made pursuant to this section upon the person or entity in possession of the records, as described in subdivision (a), and these two documents shall be kept confidential by the court. The petition and copies of the police report and the application shall be served upon the person or entity in possession of the records, as described in subdivision (a). The court shall hold a hearing on the petition no later than 10 court days after the petition is served and filed. The court shall order the release of records to the victim as required pursuant to this section.
(2) In addition to any other civil remedy available, the victim may bring a civil action against the entity for damages, injunctive relief or other equitable relief, and a penalty of one hundred dollars ($100) per day of noncompliance, plus reasonable attorneys' fees.
(e) For the purposes of this section, the following terms have the following meanings:
(1) "Application" means a new application for credit or service, the addition of authorized users to an existing account, the renewal of an existing account, or any other changes made to an existing account.
(2) "Commercial mobile radio service" means "commercial mobile radio service" as defined in Section 20.3 of Title 47 of the Code of Federal Regulations.
(3) "Law enforcement officer" means a peace officer as defined by Section 830.1.
(4) "Person" means a natural person, firm, association, organization, partnership, business trust, company, corporation, limited liability company, or public entity.
(Amended by Stats. 2006, Ch. 10, Sec. 3. Effective February 25, 2006.)

531.
Every person who is a party to any fraudulent conveyance of any lands, tenements, or hereditaments, goods or chattels, or any right or interest issuing out of the same, or to any bond, suit, judgment, or execution, contract or conveyance, had, made, or contrived with intent to deceive and defraud others, or to defeat, hinder, or delay creditors or others of their just debts, damages, or demands; or who, being a party as aforesaid, at any time wittingly and willingly puts in, uses, avows, maintains, justifies, or defends the same, or any of them, as true, and done, had, or made in good faith, or upon good consideration, or aliens, assigns, or sells any of the lands, tenements, hereditaments, goods, chattels, or other things before mentioned, to him or them conveyed as aforesaid, or any part thereof, is guilty of a misdemeanor.
(Enacted 1872.)

531a.
Every person who, with intent to defraud, knowingly executes or procures another to execute any instrument purporting to convey any real property, or any right or interest therein, knowing that such person so executing has no right to or interest in such property, or who files or procures the filing of any such instrument, knowing that the person executing the same had no right, title or interest in the property so purported to be conveyed, is guilty of a misdemeanor and is punishable by imprisonment for not more than one year or by fine of five thousand dollars or both.
(Added by Stats. 1929, Ch. 337.)

532.
(a) Every person who knowingly and designedly, by any false or fraudulent representation or pretense, defrauds any other person of money, labor, or property, whether real or personal, or who causes or procures others to report falsely of his or her wealth or mercantile character, and by thus imposing upon any person obtains credit, and thereby fraudulently gets possession of money or property, or obtains the labor or service of another, is punishable in the same manner and to the same extent as for larceny of the money or property so obtained.
(b) Upon a trial for having, with an intent to cheat or defraud another designedly, by any false pretense, obtained the signature of any person to a written instrument, or having obtained from any person any labor, money, or property, whether real or personal, or valuable thing, the defendant cannot be convicted if the false pretense was expressed in language unaccompanied by a false token or writing, unless the pretense, or some note or memorandum thereof is in writing, subscribed by or in the handwriting of the defendant, or unless the pretense is proven by the testimony of two witnesses, or that of one witness and corroborating circumstances. This section does not apply to a prosecution for falsely representing or personating another, and, in that assumed character, marrying, or receiving any money or property.
(Amended by Stats. 1989, Ch. 897, Sec. 22.)

532a.
(1) Any person who shall knowingly make or cause to be made, either directly or indirectly or through any agency whatsoever, any false statement in writing, with intent that it shall be relied upon, respecting the financial condition, or means or ability to pay, of himself or herself, or any other person, firm or corporation, in whom he or she is interested, or for whom he or she is acting, for the purpose of procuring in any form whatsoever, either the delivery of personal property, the payment of cash, the making of a loan or credit, the extension of a credit, the execution of a contract of guaranty or suretyship, the discount of an account receivable, or the making, acceptance, discount, sale or endorsement of a bill of exchange, or promissory note, for the benefit of either himself or herself or of that person, firm or corporation shall be guilty of a public offense.
(2) Any person who knowing that a false statement in writing has been made, respecting the financial condition or means or ability to pay, of himself or herself, or a person, firm or corporation in which he or she is interested, or for whom he or she is acting, procures, upon the faith thereof, for the benefit either of himself or herself, or of that person, firm or corporation, either or any of the things of benefit mentioned in the first subdivision of this section shall be guilty of a public offense.
(3) Any person who knowing that a statement in writing has been made, respecting the financial condition or means or ability to pay of himself or herself or a person, firm or corporation, in which he or she is interested, or for whom he or she is acting, represents on a later day in writing that the statement theretofore made, if then again made on said day, would be then true, when in fact, said statement if then made would be false, and procures upon the faith thereof, for the benefit either of himself or herself or of that person, firm or corporation either or any of the things of benefit mentioned in the first subdivision of this section shall be guilty of a public offense.
(4) Any person committing a public offense under subdivision (1), (2), or (3) shall be guilty of a misdemeanor, punishable by a fine of not more than one thousand dollars ($1,000), or by imprisonment in the county jail for not more than six months, or by both that fine and imprisonment. Any person who violates the provisions of subdivision (1), (2), or (3), by using a fictitious name, social security number, business name, or business address, or by falsely representing himself or herself to be another person or another business, is guilty of a felony and is punishable by a fine not exceeding five thousand dollars ($5,000) or by imprisonment pursuant to subdivision (h) of Section 1170, or by both that fine and imprisonment, or by a fine not exceeding two thousand five hundred dollars ($2,500) or by imprisonment in the county jail not exceeding one year, or by both such fine and imprisonment.
(5) This section shall not be construed to preclude the applicability of any other provision of the criminal law of this state which applies or may apply to any transaction.
(Amended by Stats. 2011, Ch. 15, Sec. 384. (AB 109) Effective April 4, 2011. Operative October 1, 2011, by Sec. 636 of Ch. 15, as amended by Stats. 2011, Ch. 39, Sec. 68.)

532b.
(a) A person who fraudulently represents himself or herself as a veteran or ex-serviceman of a war in which the United States was engaged, in connection with the soliciting of aid or the sale or attempted sale of any property, is guilty of a misdemeanor.
(b) A person who fraudulently claims, or presents himself or herself, to be a veteran or member of the Armed Forces of the United States, the California National Guard, the State Military Reserve, the Naval Militia, the national guard of any other state, or any other reserve component of the Armed Forces of the United States, with the intent to obtain money, property, or other tangible benefit, is guilty of a misdemeanor.
(c) (1) Except as provided in paragraph (2), a person who, orally, in writing, or by wearing any military decoration, fraudulently represents himself or herself to have been awarded a military decoration, with the intent to obtain money, property, or other tangible benefit, is guilty of a misdemeanor.
(2) This offense is an infraction or a misdemeanor, subject to Sections 19.6, 19.7, and 19.8, if the person committing the offense is a veteran of the Armed Forces of the United States.
(d) A person who forges documentation reflecting the awarding of a military decoration that he or she has not received for the purposes of obtaining money, property, or receiving a tangible benefit is guilty of a misdemeanor.
(e) A person who knowingly, with the intent to impersonate and to deceive, for the purposes of obtaining money, property, or receiving a tangible benefit, misrepresents himself or herself as a member or veteran of the Armed Forces of the United States, the California National Guard, the State Military Reserve, or the Naval Militia by wearing the uniform or military decoration authorized for use by the members or veterans of those forces, is guilty of a misdemeanor.
(f) A person who knowingly utilizes falsified military identification for the purposes of obtaining money, property, or receiving a tangible benefit, is guilty of a misdemeanor.
(g) A person who knowingly, with the intent to impersonate, for the purposes of promoting a business, charity, or endeavor, misrepresents himself or herself as a member or veteran of the Armed Forces of the United States, the California National Guard, the State Military Reserve, or the Naval Militia by wearing the uniform or military decoration authorized for use by the members or veterans of those forces, is guilty of a misdemeanor.
(h) A person who knowingly, with the intent to gain an advantage for employment purposes, misrepresents himself or herself as a member or veteran of the Armed Forces of the United States, the California National Guard, the State Military Reserve, or the Naval Militia by wearing the uniform or military decoration authorized for use by the members or veterans of those forces, is guilty of a misdemeanor.
(i) This section does not apply to face-to-face solicitations involving less than ten dollars ($10).
(j) This section, Section 3003 of the Government Code, and Section 1821 of the Military and Veterans Code shall be known, and may be cited as, the California Stolen Valor Act.
(k) For purposes of this section, the following terms shall have the following meanings:
(1) "Military decoration" means any decoration or medal from the Armed Forces of the United States, the California National Guard, the State Military Reserve, or the Naval Militia, or any service medals or badges awarded to the members of those forces, or the ribbon, button, or rosette of that badge, decoration, or medal, or any colorable imitation of that item.
(2) "Tangible benefit" means financial remuneration, an effect on the outcome of a criminal or civil court proceeding, or any benefit relating to service in the military that is provided by a federal, state, or local governmental entity.
(Amended by Stats. 2017, Ch. 576, Sec. 2. (AB 153) Effective January 1, 2018.)

532c.
Any person, firm, corporation or copartnership who knowingly and designedly offers or gives with winning numbers at any drawing of numbers or with tickets of admission to places of public assemblage, any lot or parcel of real property and charges or collects fees in connection with the transfer thereof, is guilty of a misdemeanor.
(Added by renumbering Section 532a (as added by Stats. 1913, Ch. 70) by Stats. 1935, Ch. 338.)

532d.
(a) Any person who solicits or attempts to solicit or receives money or property of any kind for a charitable, religious or eleemosynary purpose and who, directly or indirectly, makes, utters, or delivers, either orally or in writing, an unqualified statement of fact concerning the purpose or organization for which the money or property is solicited or received, or concerning the cost and expense of solicitation or the manner in which the money or property or any part thereof is to be used, which statement is in fact false and was made, uttered, or delivered by that person either willfully and with knowledge of its falsity or negligently without due consideration of those facts which by the use of ordinary care he or she should have known, is guilty of a misdemeanor, and is punishable by imprisonment in the county jail for not more than one year, by a fine not exceeding five thousand dollars ($5,000), or by both that imprisonment and fine.
(b) An offense charged in violation of this section shall be proven by the testimony of one witness and corroborating circumstances.
(c) Nothing contained in this section shall be construed to limit the right of any city, county, or city and county to adopt regulations for charitable solicitations which are not in conflict with this section.
(Amended by Stats. 1998, Ch. 166, Sec. 1. Effective January 1, 1999.)

532e.
Any person who receives money for the purpose of obtaining or paying for services, labor, materials or equipment incident to constructing improvements on real property and willfully rebates any part of the money to or on behalf of anyone contracting with such person, for provision of the services, labor, materials or equipment for which the money was given, shall be guilty of a misdemeanor; provided, however, that normal trade discount for prompt payment shall not be considered a violation of this section.
(Added by Stats. 1965, Ch. 1145.)

532f.
(a) A person commits mortgage fraud if, with the intent to defraud, the person does any of the following:
(1) Deliberately makes any misstatement, misrepresentation, or omission during the mortgage lending process with the intention that it be relied on by a mortgage lender, borrower, or any other party to the mortgage lending process.
(2) Deliberately uses or facilitates the use of any misstatement, misrepresentation, or omission, knowing the same to contain a misstatement, misrepresentation, or omission, during the mortgage lending process with the intention that it be relied on by a mortgage lender, borrower, or any other party to the mortgage lending process.

(3) Receives any proceeds or any other funds in connection with a mortgage loan closing that the person knew resulted from a violation of paragraph (1) or (2) of this subdivision.

(4) Files or causes to be filed with the recorder of any county in connection with a mortgage loan transaction any document the person knows to contain a deliberate misstatement, misrepresentation, or omission.

(b) An offense involving mortgage fraud shall not be based solely on information lawfully disclosed pursuant to federal disclosure laws, regulations, or interpretations related to the mortgage lending process.

(c) (1) Notwithstanding any other provision of law, an order for the production of any or all relevant records possessed by a real estate recordholder in whatever form and however stored may be issued by a judge upon a written ex parte application made under penalty of perjury by a peace officer stating that there are reasonable grounds to believe that the records sought are relevant and material to an ongoing investigation of a felony fraud violation.

(2) The ex parte application shall specify with particularity the records to be produced, which shall relate to a party or parties in the criminal investigation.

(3) Relevant records may include, but are not limited to, purchase contracts, loan applications, settlement statements, closing statements, escrow instructions, payoff demands, disbursement reports, or checks.

(4) The ex parte application and any subsequent judicial order may be ordered sealed by the court upon a sufficient showing that it is necessary for the effective continuation of the investigation.

(5) The records ordered to be produced shall be provided to the peace officer applicant or his or her designee within a reasonable time period after service of the order upon the real estate recordholder.

(d) (1) Nothing in this section shall preclude the real estate recordholder from notifying a customer of the receipt of the order for production of records, unless a court orders the real estate recordholder to withhold notification to the customer upon a finding that this notice would impede the investigation.

(2) If a court has made an order to withhold notification to the customer under this subdivision, the peace officer who or law enforcement agency that obtained the records shall notify the customer by delivering a copy of the ex parte order to the customer within 10 days of the termination of the investigation.

(e) (1) Nothing in this section shall preclude the real estate recordholder from voluntarily disclosing information or providing records to law enforcement upon request.

(2) This section shall not preclude a real estate recordholder, in its discretion, from initiating contact with, and thereafter communicating with and disclosing records to, appropriate state or local agencies concerning a suspected violation of any law.

(f) No real estate recordholder, or any officer, employee, or agent of the real estate recordholder, shall be liable to any person for either of the following:

(1) Disclosing information in response to an order pursuant to this section.

(2) Complying with an order under this section not to disclose to the customer the order, or the dissemination of information pursuant to the order.

(g) Any records required to be produced pursuant to this section shall be accompanied by an affidavit of a custodian of records of the real estate recordholder or other qualified witness which states, or includes in substance, all of the following:

(1) The affiant is the duly authorized custodian of the records or other qualified witness and has authority to certify the records.

(2) The identity of the records.

(3) A description of the mode of preparation of the records.

(4) The records were prepared by the personnel of the business in the regular course of business at or near the time of an act, condition, or event.

(5) Any copies of records described in the order are true copies.

(h) A person who violates this section is guilty of a public offense punishable by imprisonment in a county jail for not more than one year or by imprisonment pursuant to subdivision (h) of Section 1170.

(i) For the purposes of this section, the following terms shall have the following meanings:

(1) "Person" means any individual, partnership, firm, association, corporation, limited liability company, or other legal entity.

(2) "Mortgage lending process" means the process through which a person seeks or obtains a mortgage loan, including, but not limited to, solicitation, application, origination, negotiation of terms, third-party provider services, underwriting, signing and closing, and funding of the loan.

(3) "Mortgage loan" means a loan or agreement to extend credit to a person that is secured by a deed of trust or other document representing a security interest or lien upon any interest in real property, including the renewal or refinancing of the loan.

(4) "Real estate recordholder" means any person, licensed or unlicensed, that meets any of the following conditions:

(A) Is a title insurer that engages in the "business of title insurance" as defined by Section 12340.3 of the Insurance Code, an underwritten title company, or an escrow company.

(B) Functions as a broker or salesperson by engaging in any of the type of acts set forth in Sections 10131, 10131.1, 10131.2, 10131.3, 10131.4, and 10131.6 of the Business and Professions Code.

(C) Engages in the making or servicing of loans secured by real property.

(j) Fraud involving a mortgage loan may only be prosecuted under this section when the value of the alleged fraud meets the threshold for grand theft as set out in subdivision (a) of Section 487.

(Amended by Stats. 2011, Ch. 15, Sec. 385. (AB 109) Effective April 4, 2011. Operative October 1, 2011, by Sec. 636 of Ch. 15, as amended by Stats. 2011, Ch. 39, Sec. 68.)

533.

Every person who, after once selling, bartering, or disposing of any tract of land or town lot, or after executing any bond or agreement for the sale of any land or town lot, again willfully and with intent to defraud previous or subsequent purchasers, sells, barters, or disposes of the same tract of land or town lot, or any part thereof, or willfully and with intent to defraud previous or subsequent purchasers, executes any bond or agreement to sell, barter, or dispose of the same land or lot, or any part thereof, to any other person for a valuable consideration, is punishable by imprisonment pursuant to subdivision (h) of Section 1170.

(Amended by Stats. 2011, Ch. 15, Sec. 386. (AB 109) Effective April 4, 2011. Operative October 1, 2011, by Sec. 636 of Ch. 15, as amended by Stats. 2011, Ch. 39, Sec. 68.)

534.

Every person who is married or in a registered domestic partnership, who falsely and fraudulently represents himself or herself as competent to sell or mortgage any real estate, to the validity of which sale or mortgage the assent or concurrence of his or her spouse is necessary, and under such representations willfully conveys or mortgages the same, is guilty of a felony.

(Amended by Stats. 2016, Ch. 50, Sec. 73. (SB 1005) Effective January 1, 2017.)

535.

Every person who obtains any money or property from another, or obtains the signature of another to any written instrument, the false making of which would be forgery, by means of any false or fraudulent sale of property or pretended property, by auction, or by any of the practices known as mock auctions, is punishable by imprisonment in a county jail not exceeding one year, or by imprisonment pursuant to subdivision (h) of Section 1170, or by a fine not exceeding two thousand dollars ($2,000), or by both that fine and imprisonment, and, in addition, is disqualified for a period of three years from acting as an auctioneer in this state.

(Amended by Stats. 2011, Ch. 15, Sec. 387. (AB 109) Effective April 4, 2011. Operative October 1, 2011, by Sec. 636 of Ch. 15, as amended by Stats. 2011, Ch. 39, Sec. 68.)

536.

Every commission merchant, broker, agent, factor, or consignee, who shall willfully and corruptly make, or cause to be made, to the principal or consignor of such commission merchant, agent, broker, factor, or consignee, a false statement as to the price obtained for any property consigned or entrusted for sale, or as to the quality or quantity of any property so consigned or entrusted, or as to any expenditures made in connection therewith, shall be deemed guilty of a misdemeanor, and on conviction thereof, shall be punished by fine not exceeding one thousand dollars ($1,000) and not less than two hundred dollars ($200), or by imprisonment in the county jail not exceeding six months and not less than 10 days, or by both such fine and imprisonment.

(Amended by Stats. 1983, Ch. 1092, Sec. 299. Effective September 27, 1983. Operative January 1, 1984, by Sec. 427 of Ch. 1092.)

536a.

It is hereby made the duty of every commission merchant, broker, factor, or consignee, to whom any property is consigned or entrusted for sale, to make, when accounting therefor or subsequently, upon the written demand of his principal or consignor, a true written statement setting forth the name and address of the person or persons to whom a sale of the said property, or any portion thereof, was made, the quantity so sold to each purchaser, and the respective prices obtained therefor; provided, however, that unless separate written demand shall be made as to each consignment or shipment regarding which said statement is desired, prior to sale, it shall be sufficient to set forth in said statement only so many of said matters above enumerated as said commission merchant, broker, factor, or consignee may be able to obtain from the books of account kept by him; and that said statement shall not be required in case of cash sales where the amount of the transaction is less than fifty dollars. Any person violating the provisions of this section is guilty of a misdemeanor.

(Added by Stats. 1909, Ch. 706.)

537.

(a) Any person who obtains any food, fuel, services, or accommodations at a hotel, inn, restaurant, boardinghouse, lodginghouse, apartment house, bungalow court, motel, marina, marine facility, autocamp, ski area, or public or private campground, without paying therefor, with intent to defraud the proprietor or manager thereof, or who obtains credit at an hotel, inn, restaurant, boardinghouse, lodginghouse, apartment house, bungalow court, motel, marina, marine facility, autocamp, or public or private campground by the use of any false pretense, or who, after obtaining credit, food, fuel, services, or accommodations, at an hotel, inn, restaurant, boardinghouse, lodginghouse, apartment house, bungalow court, motel, marina, marine facility, autocamp, or public or private campground, absconds, or surreptitiously, or by force, menace, or threats, removes any part of his or her baggage therefrom with the intent not to pay for his or her food or accommodations is guilty of a public offense punishable as follows:

(1) If the value of the credit, food, fuel, services, or accommodations is nine hundred fifty dollars ($950) or less, by a fine not exceeding one thousand dollars ($1,000) or by imprisonment in the county jail for a term not exceeding six months, or both.

(2) If the value of the credit, food, fuel, services, or accommodations is greater than nine hundred fifty dollars ($950), by imprisonment in a county jail for a term of not more than one year, or in the state prison.

(b) Any person who uses or attempts to use ski area facilities for which payment is required without paying as required, or who resells a ski lift ticket to another when the resale is not authorized by the proprietor, is guilty of an infraction.

(c) Evidence that a person left the premises of such an hotel, inn, restaurant, boardinghouse, lodginghouse, apartment house, bungalow court, motel, marina, marine facility, autocamp, ski area, or public or private campground, without paying or offering to pay for such food, fuel, services, use of facilities, or accommodation, or that the person, without authorization from the proprietor, resold his or her ski lift ticket to another person after making use of such facilities, shall be prima facie evidence of the following:

(1) That the person obtained such food, fuel, services, use of facilities or accommodations with intent to defraud the proprietor or manager.

(2) That, if, after obtaining the credit, food, fuel, services, or accommodations, the person absconded, or surreptitiously, or by force, menace, or threats, removed part of his or her baggage therefrom, the person did so with the intent not to pay for the credit, food, fuel, services, or accommodations.

(Amended by Stats. 2009, 3rd Ex. Sess., Ch. 28, Sec. 27. (SB 18 3x) Effective January 25, 2010.)

537b.

Any person who obtains any livery hire or other accommodation at any livery or feed stable, kept for profit, in this state, without paying therefor, with intent to defraud the proprietor or manager thereof; or who obtains credit at any such livery or feed stable by the use of any false pretense; or who after obtaining a horse, vehicle, or other property at such livery or feed stable, willfully or maliciously abuses the same by beating, goading, overdriving or other willful or malicious conduct, or who after obtaining such horse, vehicle, or other property, shall, with intent to defraud the owner, manager or proprietor of such livery or feed stable, keep the same for a longer period, or take the same to a greater distance than contracted for; or allow a feed bill or other charges to accumulate against such property, without paying therefor; or abandon or leave the same, is guilty of a misdemeanor.

(Added by renumbering Section 537¾ by Stats. 1905, Ch. 523.)

537c.

Every owner, manager, proprietor, or other person, having the management, charge or control of any livery stable, feed or boarding stable, and every person pasturing stock, who shall receive and take into his possession, charge, care or control, any horse, mare, or other animal, or any buggy, or other vehicle, belonging to any other person, to be by him kept, fed, or cared for, and who, while said horse, mare or other animal or buggy or other vehicle, is thus in his possession, charge, care or under his control, as aforesaid, shall drive, ride or use, or knowingly permit or allow any person other than the owner or other person entitled so to do, to drive, ride, or otherwise use the same, without the consent or permission of the owner thereof, or other person charged with the care, control or possession of such property, shall be guilty of a misdemeanor.

(Added by Stats. 1909, Ch. 178.)

537e.

(a) Any person who knowingly buys, sells, receives, disposes of, conceals, or has in his or her possession any personal property from which the manufacturer's serial number, identification number, electronic serial number, or any other distinguishing number or identification mark has been removed, defaced, covered, altered, or destroyed, is guilty of a public offense, punishable as follows:

(1) If the value of the property does not exceed nine hundred fifty dollars ($950), by imprisonment in a county jail not exceeding six months.

(2) If the value of the property exceeds nine hundred fifty dollars ($950), by imprisonment in a county jail not exceeding one year.

(3) If the property is an integrated computer chip or panel of a value of nine hundred fifty dollars ($950) or more, by imprisonment pursuant to subdivision (h) of Section 1170 for 16 months, or two or three years or by imprisonment in a county jail not exceeding one year.

(b) For purposes of this subdivision, "personal property" includes, but is not limited to, the following:

(1) Any television, radio, recorder, phonograph, telephone, piano, or any other musical instrument or sound equipment.

(2) Any washing machine, sewing machine, vacuum cleaner, or other household appliance or furnishings.
(3) Any typewriter, adding machine, dictaphone, or any other office equipment or furnishings.
(4) Any computer, printed circuit, integrated chip or panel, or other part of a computer.
(5) Any tool or similar device, including any technical or scientific equipment.
(6) Any bicycle, exercise equipment, or any other entertainment or recreational equipment.
(7) Any electrical or mechanical equipment, contrivance, material, or piece of apparatus or equipment.
(8) Any clock, watch, watch case, or watch movement.
(9) Any vehicle or vessel, or any component part thereof.
(c) When property described in subdivision (a) comes into the custody of a peace officer it shall become subject to the provision of Chapter 12 (commencing with Section 1407) of Title 10 of Part 2, relating to the disposal of stolen or embezzled property. Property subject to this section shall be considered stolen or embezzled property for the purposes of that chapter, and prior to being disposed of, shall have an identification mark imbedded or engraved in, or permanently affixed to it.
(d) This section does not apply to those cases or instances where any of the changes or alterations enumerated in subdivision (a) have been customarily made or done as an established practice in the ordinary and regular conduct of business, by the original manufacturer, or by his or her duly appointed direct representative, or under specific authorization from the original manufacturer.
(Amended by Stats. 2011, Ch. 15, Sec. 388. (AB 109) Effective April 4, 2011. Operative October 1, 2011, by Sec. 636 of Ch. 15, as amended by Stats. 2011, Ch. 39, Sec. 68.)

537f.

No storage battery composed in whole or in part of a used container, or used plate or plates and intended for use in the starting, lighting or ignition of automobiles, shall be sold or offered for sale in this State unless: the word "Rebuilt" together with the rebuilder's name and address is labeled on one side of the battery in letters not less than one-half inch in height with a one-eighth inch stroke.
Any person selling or offering for sale such a battery in violation of this section shall be guilty of a misdemeanor, punishable by a fine not exceeding two hundred fifty dollars, or by imprisonment in the county jail for not more than six months, or by both such fine and imprisonment.
(Added by Stats. 1933, Ch. 925.)

537g.

(a) Unless otherwise provided by law, any person who knowingly removes, defaces, covers, alters or destroys a National Crime Information Center owner identification number from the personal property of another without permission is guilty of a misdemeanor punishable by a fine not to exceed four hundred dollars ($400), imprisonment in the county jail not to exceed one year, or both.
(b) This section shall not apply to any action taken by an authorized person to dispose of property pursuant to Article 1 (commencing with Section 2080) of Chapter 4 of Title 6 of Part 4 of Division 3 of the Civil Code or pursuant to Chapter 12 (commencing with Section 1407) of Title 10 of Part 2 of this code.
(Added by Stats. 1983, Ch. 878, Sec. 2.)

538.

Every person, who, after mortgaging any of the property permitted to be mortgaged by the provisions of Sections 9102 and 9109 of the Commercial Code, excepting locomotives, engines, rolling stock of a railroad, steamboat machinery in actual use, and vessels, during the existence of the mortgage, with intent to defraud the mortgagee, his or her representative or assigns, takes, drives, carries away, or otherwise removes or permits the taking, driving, or carrying away, or other removal of the mortgaged property, or any part thereof, from the county where it was situated when mortgaged, without the written consent of the mortgagee, or who sells, transfers, slaughters, destroys, or in any manner further encumbers the mortgaged property, or any part thereof, or causes it to be sold, transferred, slaughtered, destroyed, or further encumbered, is guilty of theft, and is punishable accordingly. In the case of a sale, transfer, or further encumbrance at or before the time of making the sale, transfer, or encumbrance, the mortgagor informs the person to whom the sale, transfer, or encumbrance is made, of the existence of the prior mortgage, and also informs the prior mortgagee of the intended sale, transfer, or encumbrance, in writing, by giving the name and place of residence of the party to whom the sale, transfer, or encumbrance is to be made.
(Amended by Stats. 1999, Ch. 991, Sec. 54. Effective January 1, 2000. Operative July 1, 2001, by Sec. 75 of Ch. 991.)

538a.

Every person who signs any letter addressed to a newspaper with the name of a person other than himself and sends such letter to the newspaper, or causes it to be sent to such newspaper, with intent to lead the newspaper to believe that such letter was written by the person whose name is signed thereto, is guilty of a misdemeanor.
(Added by renumbering Section 480 (as added by Stats. 1963, Ch. 1256) by Stats. 1972, Ch. 449.)

538b.

Any person who wilfully wears the badge, lapel button, rosette, or any part of the garb, robe, habit, or any other recognized and established insignia or apparel of any secret society, or fraternal or religious order or organization, or of any sect, church or religious denomination, or uses the same to obtain aid or assistance within this State, with intent to deceive, unless entitled to wear and use the same under the constitution, by-laws or rules and regulations, or other laws or enactments of such society, order, organization, sect, church or religious denomination is guilty of a misdemeanor.
(Amended by Stats. 1937, Ch. 255.)

538c.

(a) Except as provided in subdivision (c), any person who attaches or inserts an unauthorized advertisement in a newspaper, whether alone or in concert with another, and who redistributes it to the public or who has the intent to redistribute it to the public, is guilty of the crime of theft of advertising services which shall be punishable as a misdemeanor.
(b) As used in this section:
(1) "Unauthorized advertisement" means any form of representation or communication, including any handbill, newsletter, pamphlet, or notice that contains any letters, words, or pictorial representation that is attached to or inserted in a newspaper without a contractual agreement between the publisher and an advertiser.
(2) "Newspaper" includes any newspaper, magazine, periodical, or other tangible publication, whether offered for retail sale or distributed without charge.
(c) This section does not apply if the publisher or authorized distributor of the newspaper consents to the attachment or insertion of the advertisement.
(d) This section does not apply to a newspaper distributor who is directed to insert an unauthorized advertisement by a person or company supplying the newspapers, and who is not aware that the advertisement is unauthorized.
(e) A conviction under this section shall not constitute a conviction for petty theft.
(Amended by Stats. 2002, Ch. 1134, Sec. 1. Effective January 1, 2003.)

538d.

(a) Any person other than one who by law is given the authority of a peace officer, who willfully wears, exhibits, or uses the authorized uniform, insignia, emblem, device, label, certificate, card, or writing, of a peace officer, with the intent of fraudulently impersonating a peace officer, or of fraudulently inducing the belief that he or she is a peace officer, is guilty of a misdemeanor.
(b) (1) Any person, other than the one who by law is given the authority of a peace officer, who willfully wears, exhibits, or uses the badge of a peace officer with the intent of fraudulently impersonating a peace officer, or of fraudulently inducing the belief that he or she is a peace officer, is guilty of a misdemeanor punishable by imprisonment in a county jail not to exceed one year, by a fine not to exceed two thousand dollars ($2,000), or by both that imprisonment and fine.
(2) Any person who willfully wears or uses any badge that falsely purports to be authorized for the use of one who by law is given the authority of a peace officer, or which so resembles the authorized badge of a peace officer as would deceive any ordinary reasonable person into believing that it is authorized for the use of one who by law is given the authority of a peace officer, for the purpose of fraudulently impersonating a peace officer, or of fraudulently inducing the belief that he or she is a peace officer, is guilty of a misdemeanor punishable by imprisonment in a county jail not to exceed one year, by a fine not to exceed two thousand dollars ($2,000), or by both that imprisonment and fine.
(c) (1) Except as provided in subdivision (d), any person who willfully wears, exhibits, or uses, or who willfully makes, sells, loans, gives, or transfers to another, any badge, insignia, emblem, device, or any label, certificate, card, or writing, which falsely purports to be authorized for the use of one who by law is given the authority of a peace officer, or which so resembles the authorized badge, insignia, emblem, device, label, certificate, card, or writing of a peace officer as would deceive an ordinary reasonable person into believing that it is authorized for the use of one who by law is given the authority of a peace officer, is guilty of a misdemeanor punishable by imprisonment in a county jail not to exceed six months, by a fine not to exceed two thousand dollars ($2,000), or by both that imprisonment and fine, except that any person who makes or sells any badge under the circumstances described in this subdivision is subject to a fine not to exceed fifteen thousand dollars ($15,000).
(2) A local law enforcement agency in the jurisdiction that files charges against a person for a violation of paragraph (1) shall seize the badge, insignia, emblem, device, label, certificate, card, or writing described in paragraph (1).
(d) (1) The head of an agency that employs peace officers, as defined in Sections 830.1 and 830.2, is authorized to issue identification in the form of a badge, insignia, emblem, device, label, certificate, card, or writing that clearly states that the person has honorably retired following service as a peace officer from that agency. The identification authorized pursuant to this subdivision is separate and distinct from the identification authorized by Article 2 (commencing with Section 25450) of Chapter 2 of Division 5 of Title 4 of Part 6.
(2) If the head of an agency issues a badge to an honorably retired peace officer that is not affixed to a plaque or other memento commemorating the retiree's service for the agency, the words "Honorably Retired" shall be clearly visible above, underneath, or on the badge itself.
(3) The head of an agency that employs peace officers as defined in Sections 830.1 and 830.2 is authorized to revoke identification granted pursuant to this subdivision in the event of misuse or abuse.
(4) For the purposes of this subdivision, the term "honorably retired" does not include an officer who has agreed to a service retirement in lieu of termination.
(e) (1) Vendors of law enforcement uniforms shall verify that a person purchasing a uniform identifying a law enforcement agency is an employee of the agency identified on the uniform. Presentation and examination of a valid identification card with a picture of the person purchasing the uniform and identification, on the letterhead of the law enforcement agency, of the person buying the uniform as an employee of the agency identified on the uniform shall be sufficient verification.
(2) Any uniform vendor who sells a uniform identifying a law enforcement agency, without verifying that the purchaser is an employee of the agency, is guilty of a misdemeanor, punishable by a fine of not more than one thousand dollars ($1,000).
(3) This subdivision shall not apply if the uniform is to be used solely as a prop for a motion picture, television, video production, or a theatrical event, and prior written permission has been obtained from the identified law enforcement agency.
(Amended by Stats. 2014, Ch. 514, Sec. 1. (SB 702) Effective January 1, 2015.)

538e.

(a) Any person, other than an officer or member of a fire department, who willfully wears, exhibits, or uses the authorized uniform, insignia, emblem, device, label, certificate, card, or writing of an officer or member of a fire department or a deputy state fire marshal, with the intent of fraudulently impersonating an officer or member of a fire department or the Office of the State Fire Marshal, or of fraudulently inducing the belief that he or she is an officer or member of a fire department or the Office of the State Fire Marshal, is guilty of a misdemeanor.
(b) (1) Any person, other than the one who by law is given the authority of an officer or member of a fire department, or a deputy state fire marshal, who willfully wears, exhibits, or uses the badge of a fire department or the Office of the State Fire Marshal with the intent of fraudulently impersonating an officer, or member of a fire department, or a deputy state fire marshal, or of fraudulently inducing the belief that he or she is an officer or member of a fire department, or a deputy state fire marshal, is guilty of a misdemeanor punishable by imprisonment in a county jail not to exceed one year, by a fine not to exceed two thousand dollars ($2,000), or by both that imprisonment and fine.
(2) Any person who willfully wears or uses any badge that falsely purports to be authorized for the use of one who by law is given the authority of an officer or member of a fire department, or a deputy state fire marshal, or which so resembles the authorized badge of an officer or member of a fire department, or a deputy state fire marshal as would deceive any ordinary reasonable person into believing that it is authorized for the use of one who by law is given the authority of an officer or member of a fire department or a deputy state fire marshal, for the purpose of fraudulently impersonating an officer or member of a fire department, or a deputy state fire marshal, or of fraudulently inducing the belief that he or she is an officer or member of a fire department, or a deputy state fire marshal, is guilty of a misdemeanor punishable by imprisonment in a county jail not to exceed one year, by a fine not to exceed two thousand dollars ($2,000), or by both that imprisonment and fine.
(c) Any person who willfully wears, exhibits, or uses, or who willfully makes, sells, loans, gives, or transfers to another, any badge, insignia, emblem, device, or any label, certificate, card, or writing, which falsely purports to be authorized for the use of one who by law is given the authority of an officer, or member of a fire department or a deputy state fire marshal, or which so resembles the authorized badge, insignia, emblem, device, label, certificate, card, or writing of an officer or member of a fire department or a deputy state fire marshal as would deceive an ordinary reasonable person into believing that it is authorized for use by an officer or member of a fire department or a deputy state fire marshal, is guilty of a misdemeanor, except that any person who makes or sells any badge under the circumstances described in this subdivision is guilty of a misdemeanor punishable by a fine not to exceed fifteen thousand dollars ($15,000).
(d) Any person who, for the purpose of selling, leasing or otherwise disposing of merchandise, supplies or equipment used in fire prevention or suppression, falsely represents, in any manner whatsoever, to any other person that he or she is a fire marshal, fire inspector or member of a fire department, or that he or she has the approval, endorsement or authorization of any fire marshal, fire inspector or fire department, or member thereof, is guilty of a misdemeanor.
(e) (1) Vendors of uniforms shall verify that a person purchasing a uniform identifying a firefighting agency or department is an employee or authorized member of the agency or department identified on the uniform. Examination of a valid photo identification card

issued by a firefighting agency or department that designates the person as an employee or authorized member of the agency or department identified on the uniform shall be sufficient verification.
(2) If a person purchasing a uniform does not have a valid photo identification card issued by a firefighting agency or department, the person shall present an official letter of authorization from the firefighting agency or department designating that person as an employee or authorized member of the agency or department. The person shall also present a government issued photo identification card bearing the same name as listed in the letter of authorization issued by the agency or department.
(3) Any uniform vendor who sells a uniform identifying a firefighting agency or department without verifying that the purchaser is an employee or authorized member of the agency or department is guilty of a misdemeanor, punishable by a fine of not more than one thousand dollars ($1,000).
(4) This subdivision shall not apply if the uniform is to be used solely as a prop for a motion picture, television, video production, or a theatrical event, and prior written permission has been obtained from the identified firefighting agency or department.
(f) This section shall not apply to either of the following:
(1) Use of a badge solely as a prop for a motion picture, television, or video production, or an entertainment or theatrical event.
(2) A badge supplied by a recognized employee organization as defined in Section 3501 of the Government Code representing firefighters or a state or international organization to which it is affiliated.
(Amended by Stats. 2009, Ch. 100, Sec. 1. (AB 388) Effective January 1, 2010.)
538f.
Any person, other than an employee of a public utility or district as defined in Sections 216 and 11503 of the Public Utilities Code, respectively, who willfully presents himself or herself to a utility or district customer with the intent of fraudulently personating an employee of a public utility or district, or of fraudulently inducing the belief that he or she is an employee of a public utility or district, is guilty of a misdemeanor and shall be punished by imprisonment in a county jail not to exceed six months, or by a fine not to exceed one thousand dollars ($1,000), or by both that fine and imprisonment. Nothing in this section shall be construed to prohibit conduct that arguably constitutes protected activity under state labor law or the National Labor Relations Act (Title 29, United States Code, Section 151 and following).
(Added by Stats. 1995, Ch. 460, Sec. 1. Effective January 1, 1996.)
538g.
(a) Any person, other than a state, county, city, special district, or city and county officer or employee, who willfully wears, exhibits, or uses the authorized badge, photographic identification card, or insignia of a state, county, city, special district, or city and county officer or employee, with the intent of fraudulently personating a state, county, city, special district, or city and county officer or employee, or of fraudulently inducing the belief that he or she is a state, county, city, special district, or city and county officer or employee, is guilty of a misdemeanor.
(b) Any person who willfully wears, exhibits, or uses, or willfully makes, sells, loans, gives, or transfers to another, any badge, photographic identification card, or insignia, which falsely purports to be for the use of a state, county, city, special district, or city and county officer or employee, or which so resembles the authorized badge, photographic identification card, or insignia of a state, county, city, special district, or city and county officer or employee as would deceive an ordinary reasonable person into believing that it is authorized for use by a state, county, city, special district, or city and county officer or employee, is guilty of a misdemeanor, except that any person who makes or sells any badge under the circumstances described in this subdivision is subject to a fine not to exceed fifteen thousand dollars ($15,000).
(c) This section shall not apply to either of the following:
(1) Use of a badge solely as a prop for a motion picture, television, or video production, or an entertainment or theatrical event.
(2) A badge supplied by a recognized employee organization as defined in Section 3501 of the Government Code or a state or international organization to which it is affiliated.
(Added by Stats. 2004, Ch. 22, Sec. 2. Effective March 5, 2004.)
538h.
(a) Any person, other than an officer or member of a government agency managed or affiliated search and rescue unit or team, who willfully wears, exhibits, or uses the authorized uniform, insignia, emblem, device, label, certificate, card, or writing of an officer or member of a government agency managed or affiliated search and rescue unit or team, with the intent of fraudulently impersonating an officer or member of a government agency managed or affiliated search and rescue unit or team, or of fraudulently inducing the belief that he or she is an officer or member of a government agency managed or affiliated search and rescue unit or team, or uses the same to obtain aid, money, or assistance within this state, is guilty of a misdemeanor.
(b) (1) Any person, other than the one who by law is given the authority of an officer or member of a government agency managed or affiliated search and rescue unit or team, who willfully wears, exhibits, or uses the badge of a government agency managed or affiliated search and rescue unit or team with the intent of fraudulently impersonating an officer or member of a government agency managed or affiliated search and rescue unit or team, or fraudulently inducing the belief that he or she is an officer or member of a government agency managed or affiliated search and rescue unit or team, is guilty of a misdemeanor punishable by imprisonment in a county jail not to exceed one year, by a fine not to exceed two thousand dollars ($2,000), or by both that imprisonment and fine.
(2) Any person who willfully wears or uses any badge that falsely purports to be authorized for the use of one who by law is given the authority of an officer or member of a government agency managed or affiliated search and rescue unit or team, or that resembles the authorized badge of an officer or member of a government agency managed or affiliated search and rescue unit or team as would deceive any ordinary reasonable person into believing that it is authorized for the use of one who by law is given the authority of an officer or member of a government agency managed or affiliated search and rescue unit or team, for the purpose of fraudulently impersonating an officer or member of a government agency managed or affiliated search and rescue unit or team, or of fraudulently inducing the belief that he or she is an officer or member of a government agency managed or affiliated search and rescue unit or team, is guilty of a misdemeanor punishable by imprisonment in a county jail not to exceed one year, by a fine not to exceed two thousand dollars ($2,000), or by both that fine and imprisonment.
(c) As used in this section, the following terms have the following meanings:
(1) "Member" means any natural person who is registered with an accredited disaster council for the purpose of engaging in disaster service without pay or other consideration. Food and lodging provided, or expenses reimbursed for these items, during a member's activation do not constitute other consideration.
(2) "Search and rescue unit or team" means an entity engaged in the acts of searching for, rescuing, or recovering by means of ground, marine, or air activity, any person that becomes lost, injured, or is killed while outdoors or as a result of a natural or manmade disaster, including instances involving searches for downed or missing aircraft.
(Added by Stats. 2018, Ch. 252, Sec. 1. (AB 1920) Effective January 1, 2019.)
538.5.
Every person who transmits or causes to be transmitted by means of wire, radio or television communication any words, sounds, writings, signs, signals, or pictures for the purpose of furthering or executing a scheme or artifice to obtain, from a public utility, confidential, privileged, or proprietary information, trade secrets, trade lists, customer records, billing records, customer credit data, or accounting data by means of false or fraudulent pretenses, representations, personations, or promises is guilty of an offense punishable by imprisonment pursuant to subdivision (h) of Section 1170, or by imprisonment in the county jail not exceeding one year.
(Amended by Stats. 2011, Ch. 15, Sec. 389. (AB 109) Effective April 4, 2011. Operative October 1, 2011, by Sec. 636 of Ch. 15, as amended by Stats. 2011, Ch. 39, Sec. 68.)
539.
Every person who, with the intent to defraud, certifies that a person ordered by the court to participate in community service as a condition of probation has completed the number of hours of community service prescribed in the court order and the participant has not completed the prescribed number of hours, is guilty of a misdemeanor.
(Added by Stats. 1993, Ch. 371, Sec. 1. Effective January 1, 1994.)

CHAPTER 10. Crimes Against Insured Property and Insurers [548 - 551]

(Heading of Chapter 10 renumbered from Chapter 11 by Stats. 1979, Ch. 373.)
548.
(a) Every person who willfully injures, destroys, secretes, abandons, or disposes of any property which at the time is insured against loss or damage by theft, or embezzlement, or any casualty with intent to defraud or prejudice the insurer, whether the property is the property or in the possession of that person or any other person, is punishable by imprisonment pursuant to subdivision (h) of Section 1170 for two, three, or five years and by a fine not exceeding fifty thousand dollars ($50,000).
For purposes of this section, "casualty" does not include fire.
(b) Any person who violates subdivision (a) and who has a prior conviction of the offense set forth in that subdivision, in Section 550 of this code, or in former Section 556 or former Section 1871.1 of the Insurance Code, shall receive a two-year enhancement for each prior conviction in addition to the sentence provided under subdivision (a). The existence of any fact which would subject a person to a penalty enhancement shall be alleged in the information or indictment and either admitted by the defendant in open court, or found to be true by the jury trying the issue of guilt or by the court where guilt is established by plea of guilty or nolo contendere or by trial by the court sitting without a jury.
(Amended by Stats. 2011, Ch. 15, Sec. 390. (AB 109) Effective April 4, 2011. Operative October 1, 2011, by Sec. 636 of Ch. 15, as amended by Stats. 2011, Ch. 39, Sec. 68.)
549.
Any firm, corporation, partnership, or association, or any person acting in his or her individual capacity, or in his or her capacity as a public or private employee, who solicits, accepts, or refers any business to or from any individual or entity with the knowledge that, or with reckless disregard for whether, the individual or entity for or from whom the solicitation or referral is made, or the individual or entity who is solicited or referred, intends to violate Section 550 of this code or Section 1871.4 of the Insurance Code is guilty of a crime, punishable upon a first conviction by imprisonment in the county jail for not more than one year or by imprisonment pursuant to subdivision (h) of Section 1170 for 16 months, two years, or three years, or by a fine not exceeding fifty thousand dollars ($50,000) or double the amount of the fraud, whichever is greater, or by both that imprisonment and fine. A second or subsequent conviction is punishable by imprisonment pursuant to subdivision (h) of Section 1170 or by that imprisonment and a fine of fifty thousand dollars ($50,000). Restitution shall be ordered, including restitution for any medical evaluation or treatment services obtained or provided. The court shall determine the amount of restitution and the person or persons to whom the restitution shall be paid.
(Amended by Stats. 2011, Ch. 15, Sec. 391. (AB 109) Effective April 4, 2011. Operative October 1, 2011, by Sec. 636 of Ch. 15, as amended by Stats. 2011, Ch. 39, Sec. 68.)
550.
(a) It is unlawful to do any of the following, or to aid, abet, solicit, or conspire with any person to do any of the following:
(1) Knowingly present or cause to be presented any false or fraudulent claim for the payment of a loss or injury, including payment of a loss or injury under a contract of insurance.
(2) Knowingly present multiple claims for the same loss or injury, including presentation of multiple claims to more than one insurer, with an intent to defraud.
(3) Knowingly cause or participate in a vehicular collision, or any other vehicular accident, for the purpose of presenting any false or fraudulent claim.
(4) Knowingly present a false or fraudulent claim for the payments of a loss for theft, destruction, damage, or conversion of a motor vehicle, a motor vehicle part, or contents of a motor vehicle.
(5) Knowingly prepare, make, or subscribe any writing, with the intent to present or use it, or to allow it to be presented, in support of any false or fraudulent claim.
(6) Knowingly make or cause to be made any false or fraudulent claim for payment of a health care benefit.
(7) Knowingly submit a claim for a health care benefit that was not used by, or on behalf of, the claimant.
(8) Knowingly present multiple claims for payment of the same health care benefit with an intent to defraud.
(9) Knowingly present for payment any undercharges for health care benefits on behalf of a specific claimant unless any known overcharges for health care benefits for that claimant are presented for reconciliation at that same time.
(10) For purposes of paragraphs (6) to (9), inclusive, a claim or a claim for payment of a health care benefit also means a claim or claim for payment submitted by or on the behalf of a provider of any workers' compensation health benefits under the Labor Code.
(b) It is unlawful to do, or to knowingly assist or conspire with any person to do, any of the following:
(1) Present or cause to be presented any written or oral statement as part of, or in support of or opposition to, a claim for payment or other benefit pursuant to an insurance policy, knowing that the statement contains any false or misleading information concerning any material fact.
(2) Prepare or make any written or oral statement that is intended to be presented to any insurer or any insurance claimant in connection with, or in support of or opposition to, any claim or payment or other benefit pursuant to an insurance policy, knowing that the statement contains any false or misleading information concerning any material fact.
(3) Conceal, or knowingly fail to disclose the occurrence of, an event that affects any person's initial or continued right or entitlement to any insurance benefit or payment, or the amount of any benefit or payment to which the person is entitled.
(4) Prepare or make any written or oral statement, intended to be presented to any insurer or producer for the purpose of obtaining a motor vehicle insurance policy, that the person to be the insured resides or is domiciled in this state when, in fact, that person resides or is domiciled in a state other than this state.
(c) (1) Every person who violates paragraph (1), (2), (3), (4), or (5) of subdivision (a) is guilty of a felony punishable by imprisonment pursuant to subdivision (h) of Section 1170 for two, three, or five years, and by a fine not exceeding fifty thousand dollars ($50,000), or double the amount of the fraud, whichever is greater.
(2) Every person who violates paragraph (6), (7), (8), or (9) of subdivision (a) is guilty of a public offense.

(A) When the claim or amount at issue exceeds nine hundred fifty dollars ($950), the offense is punishable by imprisonment pursuant to subdivision (h) of Section 1170 for two, three, or five years, or by a fine not exceeding fifty thousand dollars ($50,000) or double the amount of the fraud, whichever is greater, or by both that imprisonment and fine, or by imprisonment in a county jail not to exceed one year, by a fine of not more than ten thousand dollars ($10,000), or by both that imprisonment and fine.

(B) When the claim or amount at issue is nine hundred fifty dollars ($950) or less, the offense is punishable by imprisonment in a county jail not to exceed six months, or by a fine of not more than one thousand dollars ($1,000), or by both that imprisonment and fine, unless the aggregate amount of the claims or amount at issue exceeds nine hundred fifty dollars ($950) in any 12-consecutive-month period, in which case the claims or amounts may be charged as in subparagraph (A).

(3) Every person who violates paragraph (1), (2), (3), or (4) of subdivision (b) shall be punished by imprisonment pursuant to subdivision (h) of Section 1170 for two, three, or five years, or by a fine not exceeding fifty thousand dollars ($50,000) or double the amount of the fraud, whichever is greater, or by both that imprisonment and fine, or by imprisonment in a county jail not to exceed one year, or by a fine of not more than ten thousand dollars ($10,000), or by both that imprisonment and fine.

(4) Restitution shall be ordered for a person convicted of violating this section, including restitution for any medical evaluation or treatment services obtained or provided. The court shall determine the amount of restitution and the person or persons to whom the restitution shall be paid.

(d) Notwithstanding any other provision of law, probation shall not be granted to, nor shall the execution or imposition of a sentence be suspended for, any adult person convicted of felony violations of this section who previously has been convicted of felony violations of this section or Section 548, or of Section 1871.4 of the Insurance Code, or former Section 556 of the Insurance Code, or former Section 1871.1 of the Insurance Code as an adult under charges separately brought and tried two or more times. The existence of any fact that would make a person ineligible for probation under this subdivision shall be alleged in the information or indictment, and either admitted by the defendant in an open court, or found to be true by the jury trying the issue of guilt or by the court where guilt is established by plea of guilty or nolo contendere or by trial by the court sitting without a jury.

Except when the existence of the fact was not admitted or found to be true or the court finds that a prior felony conviction was invalid, the court shall not strike or dismiss any prior felony convictions alleged in the information or indictment.

This subdivision does not prohibit the adjournment of criminal proceedings pursuant to Division 3 (commencing with Section 3000) or Division 6 (commencing with Section 6000) of the Welfare and Institutions Code.

(e) Except as otherwise provided in subdivision (f), any person who violates subdivision (a) or (b) and who has a prior felony conviction of an offense set forth in either subdivision (a) or (b), in Section 548, in Section 1871.4 of the Insurance Code, in former Section 556 of the Insurance Code, or in former Section 1871.1 of the Insurance Code shall receive a two-year enhancement for each prior felony conviction in addition to the sentence provided in subdivision (c). The existence of any fact that would subject a person to a penalty enhancement shall be alleged in the information or indictment and either admitted by the defendant in open court, or found to be true by the jury trying the issue of guilt or by the court where guilt is established by plea of guilty or nolo contendere or by trial by the court sitting without a jury. Any person who violates this section shall be subject to appropriate orders of restitution pursuant to Section 13967 of the Government Code.

(f) Any person who violates paragraph (3) of subdivision (a) and who has two prior felony convictions for a violation of paragraph (3) of subdivision (a) shall receive a five-year enhancement in addition to the sentence provided in subdivision (c). The existence of any fact that would subject a person to a penalty enhancement shall be alleged in the information or indictment and either admitted by the defendant in open court, or found to be true by the jury trying the issue of guilt or by the court where guilt is established by plea of guilty or nolo contendere or by trial by the court sitting without a jury.

(g) Except as otherwise provided in Section 12022.7, any person who violates paragraph (3) of subdivision (a) shall receive a two-year enhancement for each person other than an accomplice who suffers serious bodily injury resulting from the vehicular collision or accident in a violation of paragraph (3) of subdivision (a).

(h) This section shall not be construed to preclude the applicability of any other provision of criminal law or equitable remedy that applies or may apply to any act committed or alleged to have been committed by a person.

(i) Any fine imposed pursuant to this section shall be doubled if the offense was committed in connection with any claim pursuant to any automobile insurance policy in an auto insurance fraud crisis area designated by the Insurance Commissioner pursuant to Article 4.6 (commencing with Section 1874.90) of Chapter 12 of Part 2 of Division 1 of the Insurance Code.

(Amended by Stats. 2011, Ch. 15, Sec. 392. (AB 109) Effective April 4, 2011. Operative October 1, 2011, by Sec. 636 of Ch. 15, as amended by Stats. 2011, Ch. 39, Sec. 68.)

551.
(a) It is unlawful for any automotive repair dealer, contractor, or employees or agents thereof to offer to any insurance agent, broker, or adjuster any fee, commission, profit sharing, or other form of direct or indirect consideration for referring an insured to an automotive repair dealer or its employees or agents for vehicle repairs covered under a policyholder's automobile physical damage or automobile collision coverage, or to a contractor or its employees or agents for repairs to or replacement of a structure covered by a residential or commercial insurance policy.

(b) Except in cases in which the amount of the repair or replacement claim has been determined by the insurer and the repair or replacement services are performed in accordance with that determination or in accordance with provided estimates that are accepted by the insurer, it is unlawful for any automotive repair dealer, contractor, or employees or agents thereof to knowingly offer or give any discount intended to offset a deductible required by a policy of insurance covering repairs to or replacement of a motor vehicle or residential or commercial structure. This subdivision does not prohibit an advertisement for repair or replacement services at a discount as long as the amount of the repair or replacement claim has been determined by the insurer and the repair or replacement services are performed in accordance with that determination or in accordance with provided estimates that are accepted by the insurer.

(c) A violation of this section is a public offense. Where the amount at issue exceeds nine hundred fifty dollars ($950), the offense is punishable by imprisonment pursuant to subdivision (h) of Section 1170 for 16 months, or two or three years, by a fine of not more than ten thousand dollars ($10,000), or by both that imprisonment and fine; or by imprisonment in a county jail not to exceed one year, by a fine of not more than one thousand dollars ($1,000), or by both that imprisonment and fine. In all other cases, the offense is punishable by imprisonment in a county jail not to exceed six months, by a fine of not more than one thousand dollars ($1,000), or by both that imprisonment and fine.

(d) Every person who, having been convicted of subdivision (a) or (b), or Section 7027.3 or former Section 9884.75 of the Business and Professions Code and having served a term therefor in any penal institution or having been imprisoned therein as a condition of probation for that offense, is subsequently convicted of subdivision (a) or (b), upon a subsequent conviction of one of those offenses, shall be punished by imprisonment pursuant to subdivision (h) of Section 1170 for 16 months, or two or three years, by a fine of not more than ten thousand dollars ($10,000), or by both that imprisonment and fine; or by imprisonment in a county jail not to exceed one year, by a

fine of not more than one thousand dollars ($1,000), or by both that imprisonment and fine.

(e) For purposes of this section:
(1) "Automotive repair dealer" means a person who, for compensation, engages in the business of repairing or diagnosing malfunctions of motor vehicles.
(2) "Contractor" has the same meaning as set forth in Section 7026 of the Business and Professions Code.

(Amended by Stats. 2011, Ch. 15, Sec. 393. (AB 109) Effective April 4, 2011. Operative October 1, 2011, by Sec. 636 of Ch. 15, as amended by Stats. 2011, Ch. 39, Sec. 68.)

CHAPTER 12. Unlawful Interference With Property [552 - 558.1]

(Chapter 12 added by Stats. 1953, Ch. 32.)

ARTICLE 1. Trespassing or Loitering Near Posted Industrial Property [552 - 555.5]

(Article 1 added by Stats. 1953, Ch. 32.)

552.
This article does not apply to any entry in the course of duty of any peace or police officer or other duly authorized public officer, nor does it apply to the lawful use of an established and existing right of way for public road purposes.
(Added by Stats. 1953, Ch. 32.)

552.1.
This article does not prohibit:
(a) Any lawful activity for the purpose of engaging in any organizational effort on behalf of any labor union, agent, or member thereof, or of any employee group, or any member thereof, employed or formerly employed in any place of business or manufacturing establishment described in this article, or for the purpose of carrying on the lawful activities of labor unions, or members thereof.
(b) Any lawful activity for the purpose of investigation of the safety of working conditions on posted property by a representative of a labor union or other employee group who has upon his person written evidence of due authorization by his labor union or employee group to make such investigation.
(Added by Stats. 1953, Ch. 32.)

553.
The following definitions apply to this article only:
(a) "Sign" means a sign not less than one (1) square foot in area and upon which in letters not less than two inches in height appear the words "trespassing-loitering forbidden by law," or words describing the use of the property followed by the words "no trespassing."
(b) "Posted property" means any property specified in Section 554 which is posted in a manner provided in Section 554.1.
(c) "Posted boundary" means a line running from sign to sign and such line need not conform to the legal boundary or legal description of any lot, parcel, or acreage of land, but only the area within the posted boundary shall constitute posted property, except as otherwise provided in subdivision (e) of Section 554. 1.
(Amended by Stats. 1988, Ch. 273, Sec. 1.)

554.
Any property, except that portion of such property to which the general public is accorded access, may be posted against trespassing and loitering in the manner provided in Section 554.1, and thereby become posted property subject to the provisions of this article applicable to posted property, if such property consists of, or is used, or is designed to be used, for any one or more of the following:
(a) An oil well, oilfield, tank farm, refinery, compressor plant, absorption plant, bulk plant, marine terminal, pipeline, pipeline pumping station, or reservoir, or any other plant, structure, or works, used for the production, extraction, treatment, handling, storage, or transportation, of oil, gas, gasoline, petroleum, or any product or products thereof.
(b) A gas plant, gas storage station, gas meter, gas valve, or regulator station, gas odorant station, gas pipeline, or appurtenances, or any other property used in the transmission or distribution of gas.
(c) A reservoir, dam, generating plant, receiving station, distributing station, transformer, transmission line, or any appurtenances, used for the storage of water for the generation of hydroelectric power, or for the generation of electricity by water or steam or by any other apparatus or method suitable for the generation of electricity, or for the handling, transmission, reception, or distribution of electric energy.
(d) Plant, structures or facilities used for or in connection with the rendering of telephone or telegraph service or for radio or television broadcasting.
(e) A water well, dam, reservoir, pumping plant, aqueduct, canal, tunnel, siphon, conduit, or any other structure, facility, or conductor for producing, storing, diverting, conserving, treating, or conveying water.
(f) The production, storage, or manufacture of munitions, dynamite, black blasting powder, gunpowder, or other explosives.
(g) A railroad right-of-way, railroad bridge, railroad tunnel, railroad shop, railroad yard, or other railroad facility.
(h) A plant and facility for the collection, pumping, transmission, treatment, outfall, and disposal of sanitary sewerage or storm and waste water, including a water pollution or quality control facility.
(i) A quarry used for the purpose of extracting surface or subsurface material or where explosives are stored or used for that purpose.
(Amended by Stats. 1982, Ch. 965, Sec. 1.)

554.1.
Any property described in Section 554 may be posted against trespassing and loitering in the following manner:
(a) If it is not enclosed within a fence and if it is of an area not exceeding one (1) acre and has no lineal dimension exceeding one (1) mile, by posting signs at each corner of the area and at each entrance.
(b) If it is not enclosed within a fence, and if it is of an area exceeding one (1) acre, or contains any lineal dimension exceeding one (1) mile, by posting signs along or near the exterior boundaries of the area at intervals of not more than 600 feet, and also at each corner, and, if such property has a definite entrance or entrances, at each such entrance.
(c) If it is enclosed within a fence and if it is of an area not exceeding one (1) acre, and has no lineal dimension exceeding one (1) mile, by posting signs at each corner of such fence and at each entrance.
(d) If it is enclosed within a fence and if it is of an area exceeding one (1) acre, or has any lineal dimension exceeding one (1) mile, by posting signs on, or along the line of, such fence at intervals of not more than 600 feet, and also at each corner and at each entrance.
(e) If it consists of poles or towers or appurtenant structures for the suspension of wires or other conductors for conveying electricity or telegraphic or telephonic messages or of towers or derricks for the production of oil or gas, by affixing a sign upon one or more sides of such poles, towers, or derricks, but such posting shall render only the pole, tower, derrick, or appurtenant structure posted property.
(Added by Stats. 1953, Ch. 32.)

555.

It is unlawful to enter or remain upon any posted property without the written permission of the owner, tenant, or occupant in legal possession or control thereof. Every person who enters or remains upon posted property without such written permission is guilty of a separate offense for each day during any portion of which he enters or remains upon such posted property.

(Added by Stats. 1953, Ch. 32.)

555.1.

It is unlawful, without authority, to tear down, deface or destroy any sign posted pursuant to this article.

(Added by Stats. 1953, Ch. 32.)

555.2.

It is unlawful to loiter in the immediate vicinity of any posted property. This section does not prohibit picketing in such immediate vicinity or any lawful activity by which the public is informed of the existence of an alleged labor dispute.

(Added by Stats. 1953, Ch. 32.)

555.3.

Violation of any of the provisions of this article is a misdemeanor.

(Added by Stats. 1953, Ch. 32.)

555.4.

The provisions of this article are applicable throughout the State in all counties and municipalities and no local authority shall enact or enforce any ordinance in conflict with such provisions.

(Added by Stats. 1953, Ch. 32.)

555.5.

If any provision of this article, or the application thereof to any person or circumstance, is held to be invalid, the remainder of the article, and the application of such provision to other persons or circumstances, shall not be affected thereby.

If any section, subsection, sentence, clause, or phrase of this article is for any reason held to be unconstitutional or invalid, such decision shall not affect the validity or constitutionality of the remaining portions of this article. The Legislature hereby declares that it would have passed this article and each section, subsection, sentence, clause, or phrase thereof, irrespective of the fact that one or more of the sections, subsections, sentences, clauses, or phrases thereof be declared unconstitutional or invalid.

(Added by Stats. 1953, Ch. 32.)

ARTICLE 2. Unlawfully Placing Signs on Public and Private Property [556 - 556.4]

(Article 2 added by Stats. 1953, Ch. 32.)

556.

It is a misdemeanor for any person to place or maintain, or cause to be placed or maintained without lawful permission upon any property of the State, or of a city or of a county, any sign, picture, transparency, advertisement, or mechanical device which is used for the purpose of advertising or which advertises or brings to notice any person, article of merchandise, business or profession, or anything that is to be or has been sold, bartered, or given away.

(Added by Stats. 1953, Ch. 32.)

556.1.

It is a misdemeanor for any person to place or maintain or cause to be placed or maintained upon any property in which he has no estate or right of possession any sign, picture, transparency, advertisement, or mechanical device which is used for the purpose of advertising, or which advertises or brings to notice any person, article of merchandise, business or profession, or anything that is to be or has been sold, bartered, or given away, without the consent of the owner, lessee, or person in lawful possession of such property before such sign, picture, transparency, advertisement, or mechanical device is placed upon the property.

(Added by Stats. 1953, Ch. 32.)

556.2.

Sections 556 and 556.1 do not prevent the posting of any notice required by law or order of any court, to be posted, nor the posting or placing of any notice, particularly pertaining to the grounds or premises upon which the notice is so posted or placed, nor the posting or placing of any notice, sign, or device used exclusively for giving public notice of the name, direction or condition of any highway, street, lane, road or alley.

(Added by Stats. 1953, Ch. 32.)

556.3.

Any sign, picture, transparency, advertisement, or mechanical device placed on any property contrary to the provisions of Sections 556 and 556.1, is a public nuisance.

(Added by Stats. 1953, Ch. 32.)

556.4.

For purposes of this article, information that appears on any sign, picture, transparency, advertisement, or mechanical device such as, but not limited to, the following, may be used as evidence to establish the fact, and may create an inference, that a person or entity is responsible for the posting of the sign, picture, transparency, advertisement, or mechanical device:

(a) The name, telephone number, address, or other identifying information regarding the real estate broker, real estate brokerage firm, real estate agent, or other person associated with the firm.

(b) The name, telephone number, address, or other identifying information of the owner or lessee of property used for a commercial activity or event.

(c) The name, telephone number, address, or other identifying information of the sponsor or promoter of a sporting event, concert, theatrical performance, or similar activity or event.

(Added by Stats. 1998, Ch. 192, Sec. 1. Effective January 1, 1999.)

ARTICLE 3. Trespass on Property Belonging to the University of California [558 - 558.1]

(Article 3 added by Stats. 1955, Ch. 41.)

558.

Every person other than an officer, employee or student of the University of California, or licensee of the Regents of the University of California, is forbidden to enter upon those lands bordering on the Pacific Ocean in San Diego County, which were granted by Section 1 of Chapter 514 of the Statutes of 1929 to the Regents of the University of California for the uses and purposes of the University of California in connection with scientific research and investigation at the Scripps Institution of Oceanography, or upon state waters adjacent thereto, or to trespass upon the same, or to interfere with the exclusive possession, occupation, and use thereof by the Regents of the University of California.

Nothing herein contained shall be deemed or construed to affect in any manner the rights of navigation and fishery reserved to the people by the Constitution.

(Added by Stats. 1955, Ch. 41.)

558.1.

Every person who violates any of the provisions of Section 558 is guilty of a misdemeanor and upon conviction thereof shall be punished by a fine of not more than six hundred dollars ($600) or by imprisonment for not more than 30 days, or by both such fine and imprisonment.

(Amended by Stats. 1983, Ch. 1092, Sec. 304. Effective September 27, 1983. Operative January 1, 1984, by Sec. 427 of Ch. 1092.)

CHAPTER 12.5. Crimes Involving Bailments [560 - 560.6]

(Chapter 12.5 added by Stats. 1963, Ch. 819.)

560.

Any bailee, as defined in Section 7102 of the Uniform Commercial Code, who issues or aids in issuing a document of title, or any person who secures the issue by a bailee of a document of title, or any person who negotiates or transfers for value a document of title knowing that the goods for which that document is issued have not been actually received by that bailee or are not under his or her control at the time of issuing that receipt shall be guilty of a crime and upon conviction shall be punished for each offense by imprisonment pursuant to subdivision (h) of Section 1170 or by a fine not exceeding ten thousand dollars ($10,000) or by both that fine and imprisonment.

(Amended by Stats. 2011, Ch. 15, Sec. 394. (AB 109) Effective April 4, 2011. Operative October 1, 2011, by Sec. 636 of Ch. 15, as amended by Stats. 2011, Ch. 39, Sec. 68.)

560.1.

Any bailee, as defined in Section 7102 of the Uniform Commercial Code, who fraudulently issues or aids in fraudulently issuing a receipt for goods knowing that it contains any false statement shall be guilty of a crime and upon conviction shall be punished for each offense by imprisonment not exceeding one year or by a fine not exceeding one thousand dollars ($1,000) or by both.

(Added by Stats. 1963, Ch. 819.)

560.2.

Any bailee, as defined in Section 7102 of the Uniform Commercial Code, who delivers goods out of the possession of such bailee knowing that a negotiable document of title the negotiation of which would transfer the right to the possession of such goods is outstanding and uncanceled without obtaining possession of such document at or before the time for such delivery shall, except for the cases in Sections 7210, 7308, 7601 and 7602 of the Uniform Commercial Code, be guilty of a crime and upon conviction shall be punished for each offense by imprisonment not exceeding one year or by a fine not exceeding one thousand dollars ($1,000) or by both.

(Added by Stats. 1963, Ch. 819.)

560.3.

Any person who deposits goods with a bailee, as defined in Section 7102 of the Uniform Commercial Code, to which he has not title or upon which there is a security interest and who takes for such goods a negotiable document of title which he afterwards negotiates for value with intent to deceive and without disclosing his want of title or the existence of the security interest shall be guilty of a crime, and upon conviction shall be punished for such offense by imprisonment not exceeding one year or by a fine not exceeding one thousand dollars ($1,000) or by both.

(Added by Stats. 1963, Ch. 819.)

560.4.

Any bailee, as defined in Section 7102 of the Uniform Commercial Code, who issues or aids in issuing a duplicate or additional negotiable document of title for goods knowing that a former negotiable document of title for the same goods or any part of them is outstanding and uncanceled without plainly placing upon the face thereof the word "duplicate," except in cases of bills in a set and documents issued as substitutes for lost, stolen or destroyed documents, shall be guilty of a crime and upon conviction shall be punished for each offense by imprisonment pursuant to subdivision (h) of Section 1170 or by a fine not exceeding ten thousand dollars ($10,000) or by both that fine and imprisonment.

(Amended by Stats. 2011, Ch. 15, Sec. 395. (AB 109) Effective April 4, 2011. Operative October 1, 2011, by Sec. 636 of Ch. 15, as amended by Stats. 2011, Ch. 39, Sec. 68.)

560.5.

Where there are deposited with or held by a warehouseman goods of which he is owner either solely or jointly or in common with others such warehouseman or any of his officers, agents, or servants who knowing of this ownership issues or aids in issuing a negotiable document of title for such goods which does not state such ownership, shall be guilty of a crime and upon conviction shall be punished for each offense by imprisonment not exceeding one year or by a fine not exceeding one thousand dollars ($1,000) or by both.

(Added by Stats. 1963, Ch. 819.)

560.6.

(1) A corporation, firm, or person, and its or his agents or employees shall not issue, sell, pledge, assign, or transfer in this State any receipt, certificate, or other written instrument purporting to be a warehouse receipt, or in the similitude of a warehouse receipt, or designed to be understood as a warehouse receipt, for goods, wares, or merchandise stored or deposited, or claimed to be stored or deposited, in any warehouse, public or private, in any other state, unless such receipt, certificate, or other written instrument has been issued by the warehouseman operating such warehouse.

(2) A corporation, firm, or person, and its or his agents or employees shall not issue, sell, pledge, assign, or transfer in this State any receipt, certificate, or other written instrument for goods, wares, or merchandise claimed to be stored or deposited, in any warehouse, public or private, in any other state, knowing that there is no such warehouse located at the place named in such receipt, certificate, or other written instrument, or if there is a warehouse at such place knowing that there are no goods, wares, or merchandise stored or deposited therein as specified in such receipt, certificate, or other written instrument.

(3) A corporation, firm, or person, and its or his agents or employees shall not issue, sign, sell, pledge, assign, or transfer in this State any receipt, certificate, or other written instrument evidencing, or purporting to evidence, the creation of a security interest in, or sale, or bailment, of any goods, wares, or merchandise stored or deposited, or claimed to be stored or deposited, in any warehouse, public or private, in any other state, unless such receipt, certificate, or other written instrument plainly designates the number and location of such warehouse and contains a full, true, and complete copy of the receipt issued by the warehouseman operating the warehouse in which such goods, wares, or merchandise is stored or deposited, or is claimed to be stored or deposited. This section shall not apply to the issue, signing, sale, pledge, assignment, or transfer of bona fide warehouse receipts issued by the warehouseman operating public or bonded warehouses in other states according to the laws of the state in which such warehouses are located.

(4) Every corporation, firm, person, agent, or employee, who knowingly violates any of the provisions of this section is guilty of a misdemeanor, and shall be fined not less than fifty dollars ($50) nor more than one thousand dollars ($1,000), and may in addition be imprisoned in the county jail for not exceeding six months.

(Added by Stats. 1963, Ch. 819.)

CHAPTER 12.6. Crimes Involving Branded Containers, Cabinets, or Other Dairy Equipment [565 - 566]

(Chapter 12.6 added by Stats. 1982, Ch. 1063, Sec. 6.)

565.

It is a misdemeanor, punishable by a fine not exceeding one thousand dollars ($1,000), or by imprisonment in the county jail not exceeding six months, or both, for an unauthorized person to possess or use, or to obliterate or destroy the brand registration upon, containers (including milk cases), cabinets, or other dairy equipment, which have a value of nine hundred fifty dollars ($950) or less, when the containers, cabinets, or other dairy equipment are marked with a brand that is registered pursuant to Chapter 10 (commencing with Section 34501) of Part 1 of Division 15 of the Food and Agricultural Code. "Unauthorized person" shall have the meaning of that term as defined in Section 34564 of the Food and Agricultural Code.
(Amended by Stats. 2009, 3rd Ex. Sess., Ch. 28, Sec. 31. (SB 18 3x) Effective January 25, 2010.)

566.
It is a felony, punishable by a fine not exceeding one thousand five hundred dollars ($1,500), or by imprisonment pursuant to subdivision (h) of Section 1170, or both, for an unauthorized person to possess or use, or to obliterate or destroy the brand registration upon, containers (including milk cases), cabinets, or other dairy equipment, which have a value in excess of nine hundred fifty dollars ($950), when the containers, cabinets, or other dairy equipment are marked with a brand that is registered pursuant to Chapter 10 (commencing with Section 34501) of Part 1 of Division 15 of the Food and Agricultural Code. "Unauthorized person" shall have the meaning of that term as defined in Section 34564 of the Food and Agricultural Code.
(Amended by Stats. 2011, Ch. 15, Sec. 396. (AB 109) Effective April 4, 2011. Operative October 1, 2011, by Sec. 636 of Ch. 15, as amended by Stats. 2011, Ch. 39, Sec. 68.)

CHAPTER 12.7. Unlawful Subleasing of Motor Vehicles [570 - 574]

(Chapter 12.7 added by Stats. 1987, Ch. 1072, Sec. 2.)

570.
An act of unlawful subleasing of a motor vehicle, as defined in Section 571, shall be punishable by imprisonment in a county jail for not more than one year, or by imprisonment pursuant to subdivision (h) of Section 1170, or by a fine of not more than ten thousand dollars ($10,000), or by both that fine and imprisonment.
(Amended by Stats. 2011, Ch. 15, Sec. 397. (AB 109) Effective April 4, 2011. Operative October 1, 2011, by Sec. 636 of Ch. 15, as amended by Stats. 2011, Ch. 39, Sec. 68.)

571.
(a) A person engages in an act of unlawful subleasing of a motor vehicle if all of the following conditions are met:
(1) The motor vehicle is subject to a lease contract, conditional sale contract, or security agreement the terms of which prohibit the transfer or assignment of any right or interest in the motor vehicle or under the lease contract, conditional sale contract, or security agreement.
(2) The person is not a party to the lease contract, conditional sale contract, or security agreement.
(3) The person transfers or assigns, or purports to transfer or assign, any right or interest in the motor vehicle or under the lease contract, conditional sale contract, or security agreement, to any person who is not a party to the lease contract, conditional sale contract, or security agreement.
(4) The person does not obtain, prior to the transfer or assignment described in paragraph (3), written consent to the transfer or assignment from the motor vehicle's lessor, seller, or secured party.
(5) The person receives compensation or some other consideration for the transfer or assignment described in paragraph (3).
(b) A person engages in an act of unlawful subleasing of a motor vehicle when the person is not a party to the lease contract, conditional sale contract, or security agreement, and assists, causes, or arranges an actual or purported transfer or assignment, as described in subdivision (a).
(Added by Stats. 1987, Ch. 1072, Sec. 2.)

572.
(a) The actual or purported transfer or assignment, or the assisting, causing, or arranging of an actual or purported transfer or assignment, of any right or interest in a motor vehicle or under a lease contract, conditional sale contract, or security agreement, by an individual who is a party to the lease contract, conditional sale contract, or security agreement is not an act of unlawful subleasing of a motor vehicle and is not subject to prosecution.
(b) This chapter shall not affect the enforceability of any provision of any lease contract, conditional sale contract, security agreement, or direct loan agreement by any party thereto.
(Added by Stats. 1987, Ch. 1072, Sec. 2.)

573.
(a) The penalties under this chapter are in addition to any other remedies or penalties provided by law for the conduct proscribed by this chapter.
(b) If any provision of this chapter or the application thereof to any person or circumstance is held to be unconstitutional, the remainder of the chapter and the application of its provisions to other persons and circumstances shall not be affected thereby.
(Added by Stats. 1987, Ch. 1072, Sec. 2.)

574.
As used in this chapter, the following terms have the following meanings:
(a) "Buyer" has the meaning set forth in subdivision (c) of Section 2981 of the Civil Code.
(b) "Conditional sale contract" has the meaning set forth in subdivision (a) of Section 2981 of the Civil Code. Notwithstanding subdivision (k) of Section 2981 of the Civil Code, "conditional sale contract" includes any contract for the sale or bailment of a motor vehicle between a buyer and a seller primarily for business or commercial purposes.
(c) "Direct loan agreement" means an agreement between a lender and a purchaser whereby the lender has advanced funds pursuant to a loan secured by the motor vehicle which the purchaser has purchased.
(d) "Lease contract" means a lease contract between a lessor and lessee as this term and these parties are defined in Section 2985.7 of the Civil Code. Notwithstanding subdivision (d) of Section 2985.7 of the Civil Code, "lease contract" includes a lease for business or commercial purposes.
(e) "Motor vehicle" means any vehicle required to be registered under the Vehicle Code.
(f) "Person" means an individual, company, firm, association, partnership, trust, corporation, limited liability company, or other legal entity.
(g) "Purchaser" has the meaning set forth in paragraph (30) of subdivision (b) of Section 1201 of the Commercial Code.
(h) "Security agreement" and "secured party" have the meanings set forth, respectively, in paragraphs (74) and (73) of subdivision (a) of Section 9102 of the Commercial Code. "Security interest" has the meaning set forth in paragraph (35) of subdivision (b) of Section 1201 of the Commercial Code.
(i) "Seller" has the meaning set forth in subdivision (b) of Section 2981 of the Civil Code, and includes the present holder of the conditional sale contract.
(Amended by Stats. 2013, Ch. 531, Sec. 27. (AB 502) Effective January 1, 2014. Operative July 1, 2014, by Sec. 28 of Ch. 531.)

CHAPTER 14. Fraudulent Issue of Documents of Title to Merchandise [577 - 583]

(Chapter 14 enacted 1872.)

577.
Every person, being the master, owner or agent of any vessel, or officer or agent of any railroad, express or transportation company, or otherwise being or representing any carrier, who delivers any bill of lading, receipt or other voucher, by which it appears that any merchandise of any description has been shipped on board any vessel, or delivered to any railroad, express or transportation company or other carrier, unless the same has been so shipped or delivered, and is at the time actually under the control of such carrier or the master, owner or agent of such vessel, or of some officer or agent of that company, to be forwarded as expressed in that bill of lading, receipt or voucher, is punishable by imprisonment pursuant to subdivision (h) of Section 1170, or by a fine not exceeding one thousand dollars ($1,000), or both.
(Amended by Stats. 2011, Ch. 15, Sec. 398. (AB 109) Effective April 4, 2011. Operative October 1, 2011, by Sec. 636 of Ch. 15, as amended by Stats. 2011, Ch. 39, Sec. 68.)

578.
Every person carrying on the business of a warehouseman, wharfinger, or other depositary of property, who issues any receipt, bill of lading, or other voucher for any merchandise of any description, which has not been actually received upon the premises of that person, and is not under his or her actual control at the time of issuing such instrument, whether that instrument is issued to a person as being the owner of that merchandise or as security for any indebtedness, is punishable by imprisonment pursuant to subdivision (h) of Section 1170, or by a fine not exceeding one thousand dollars ($1,000), or both.
(Amended by Stats. 2011, Ch. 15, Sec. 399. (AB 109) Effective April 4, 2011. Operative October 1, 2011, by Sec. 636 of Ch. 15, as amended by Stats. 2011, Ch. 39, Sec. 68.)

579.
No person shall be convicted of an offense under Section 577 or 578 by reason that the contents of any barrel, box, case, cask, or other vessel or package mentioned in the bill of lading, receipt, or other voucher did not correspond with the description given in the instrument of the merchandise received, if the description corresponded substantially with the marks, labels, or brands upon the outside of the vessel or package, unless it appears that the accused knew that the marks, labels, or brands were untrue.
(Amended by Stats. 1987, Ch. 828, Sec. 33.)

580.
Every person mentioned in this chapter, who issues any second or duplicate receipt or voucher, of a kind specified therein, at a time while any former receipt or voucher for the merchandise specified in that second receipt is outstanding and uncanceled, without writing across the face of the same the word "Duplicate," in a plain and legible manner, is punishable by imprisonment pursuant to subdivision (h) of Section 1170, or by a fine not exceeding one thousand dollars ($1,000), or both.
(Amended by Stats. 2011, Ch. 15, Sec. 400. (AB 109) Effective April 4, 2011. Operative October 1, 2011, by Sec. 636 of Ch. 15, as amended by Stats. 2011, Ch. 39, Sec. 68.)

581.
Every person mentioned in this chapter, who sells, hypothecates, or pledges any merchandise for which any bill of lading, receipt, or voucher has been issued by him or her, without the consent in writing thereto of the person holding that bill, receipt, or voucher, is punishable by imprisonment pursuant to subdivision (h) of Section 1170, or by a fine not exceeding one thousand dollars ($1,000), or both.
(Amended by Stats. 2011, Ch. 15, Sec. 401. (AB 109) Effective April 4, 2011. Operative October 1, 2011, by Sec. 636 of Ch. 15, as amended by Stats. 2011, Ch. 39, Sec. 68.)

583.
Section 581 does not apply where property is demanded or sold by virtue of process of law.
(Amended by Stats. 1987, Ch. 828, Sec. 34.)

CHAPTER 15. Malicious Injuries to Railroad Bridges, Highways, Bridges, and Telegraphs [587 - 593g]

(Chapter 15 enacted 1872.)

587.
Every person who maliciously does either of the following is punishable by imprisonment pursuant to subdivision (h) of Section 1170, or imprisonment in a county jail not exceeding one year:
(a) Removes, displaces, injures, or destroys any part of any railroad, whether for steam or horse cars, or any track of any railroad, or any branch or branchway, switch, turnout, bridge, viaduct, culvert, embankment, station house, or other structure or fixture, or any part thereof, attached to or connected with any railroad.
(b) Places any obstruction upon the rails or track of any railroad, or of any switch, branch, branchway, or turnout connected with any railroad.
(Amended by Stats. 2011, Ch. 15, Sec. 402. (AB 109) Effective April 4, 2011. Operative October 1, 2011, by Sec. 636 of Ch. 15, as amended by Stats. 2011, Ch. 39, Sec. 68.)

587.1.
(a) Every person who maliciously moves or causes to be moved, without authorization, any locomotive, is guilty of a misdemeanor punishable by imprisonment in the county jail not exceeding one year.
(b) Every person who maliciously moves or causes to be moved, without authorization, any locomotive, when the moving creates a substantial likelihood of causing personal injury or death to another, is guilty of a public offense punishable by imprisonment in a county jail not exceeding one year or by imprisonment pursuant to subdivision (h) of Section 1170.
(Amended by Stats. 2011, Ch. 15, Sec. 403. (AB 109) Effective April 4, 2011. Operative October 1, 2011, by Sec. 636 of Ch. 15, as amended by Stats. 2011, Ch. 39, Sec. 68.)

587a.
Every person, who, without being thereunto duly authorized by the owner, lessee, or person or corporation engaged in the operation of any railroad, shall manipulate or in anywise tamper or interfere with any air brake or other device, appliance or apparatus in or upon any car or locomotive upon such railroad, and used or provided for use in the operation of such car or locomotive, or of any train upon such railroad, or with any switch, signal or other appliance or apparatus used or provided for use in the operation of such railroad, shall be deemed guilty of a misdemeanor.
(Added by Stats. 1909, Ch. 372.)

587b.
Every person, who shall, without being thereunto authorized by the owner, lessee, person or corporation operating any railroad, enter into, climb upon, hold to, or in any manner attach himself to any locomotive, locomotive-engine tender, freight or passenger car upon such railroad, or any portion of any train thereon, shall be deemed guilty of a misdemeanor, and, upon conviction thereof shall be punished by a fine not exceeding fifty dollars ($50), or by imprisonment not exceeding 30 days, or by both such fine and imprisonment.

(Amended by Stats. 1949, Ch. 137.)
587c.
Every person who fraudulently evades, or attempts to evade the payment of his fare, while traveling upon any railroad, shall be deemed guilty of a misdemeanor, and upon conviction thereof, shall be punished by a fine of not more than five hundred dollars, or imprisonment not exceeding six months, or by both such fine and imprisonment.
(Added by Stats. 1909, Ch. 345.)
588.
Every person who negligently, willfully or maliciously digs up, removes, displaces, breaks down or otherwise injures or destroys any state or other public highway or bridge, or any private way, laid out by authority of law, or bridge upon any such highway or private way, or who negligently, willfully or maliciously sprinkles, drains, diverts or in any manner permits water from any sprinkler, ditch, canal, flume, or reservoir to flow upon or saturate by seepage any public highway, which act tends to damage such highway or tends to be a hazard to traffic thereon, shall be guilty of a misdemeanor. This section shall not apply to the natural flow of surface or flood waters that are not diverted, accelerated or concentrated by such person.
(Amended by Stats. 1963, Ch. 1625.)
588a.
Any person who throws or deposits any oil, glass bottle, glass, nails, tacks, hoops, wire, cans, or any other substance likely to injure any person, animal or vehicle upon any public highway in the State of California shall be guilty of a misdemeanor; provided, however, that any person who willfully deposits any such substance upon any public highway in the State of California with the intent to cause great bodily injury to other persons using the highway shall be guilty of a felony.
(Amended by Stats. 1963, Ch. 250.)
588b.
Any person who wilfully breaks down, removes, injures, or destroys any barrier or obstruction erected or placed in or upon any road or highway by the authorities in charge thereof, or by any authorized contractor engaged in the construction or maintenance thereof, or who tears down, defaces, removes, or destroys any warnings, notices, or directional signs erected, placed or posted in, upon, or adjacent to any road or highway, or who extinguishes, removes, injures, or destroys any warning light or lantern, or reflectorized warning or directional sign, erected, placed or maintained by any such authority in, upon or adjacent to any such road or highway, shall be guilty of a misdemeanor.
(Amended by Stats. 1933, Ch. 403.)
590.
Every person who maliciously removes, destroys, injures, breaks or defaces any mile post, board or stone, or guide post erected on or near any highway, or any inscription thereon, is guilty of a misdemeanor.
(Amended by Stats. 1907, Ch. 489.)
590a.
One-half of all fines imposed and collected under Section 590 shall be paid to the informer who first causes a complaint to be filed charging the defendant with the violation of Section 590.
(Amended by Stats. 1987, Ch. 828, Sec. 35.)
591.
A person who unlawfully and maliciously takes down, removes, injures, disconnects, cuts, or obstructs a line of telegraph, telephone, or cable television, or any line used to conduct electricity, or any part thereof, or appurtenances or apparatus connected therewith, including, but not limited to, a backup deep cycle battery or other power supply, or severs any wire thereof, or makes an unauthorized connection with any line, other than a telegraph, telephone, or cable television line, used to conduct electricity, or any part thereof, or appurtenances or apparatus connected therewith, is subject to punishment by imprisonment in a county jail not exceeding one year, by a fine not exceeding one thousand dollars ($1,000), or by both that imprisonment and fine, or by imprisonment in a county jail for 16 months, two or three years pursuant to subdivision (h) of Section 1170 and a fine of up to ten thousand dollars ($10,000).
(Amended by Stats. 2014, Ch. 332, Sec. 1. (AB 1782) Effective January 1, 2015.)
591.5.
A person who unlawfully and maliciously removes, injures, destroys, damages, or obstructs the use of any wireless communication device with the intent to prevent the use of the device to summon assistance or notify law enforcement or any public safety agency of a crime is guilty of a misdemeanor.
(Amended by Stats. 2006, Ch. 695, Sec. 1. Effective January 1, 2007.)
592.
(a) Every person who shall, without authority of the owner or managing agent, and with intent to defraud, take water from any canal, ditch, flume, or reservoir used for the purpose of holding or conveying water for manufacturing, agricultural, mining, irrigating, generation of power, or domestic uses is guilty of a misdemeanor.
(b) If the total retail value of all the water taken is more than nine hundred fifty dollars ($950), or if the defendant has previously been convicted of an offense under this section or any former section that would be an offense under this section, or of an offense under the laws of another state or of the United States that would have been an offense under this section if committed in this state, then the violation is punishable by imprisonment in a county jail for not more than one year, or in the state prison.
(Amended by Stats. 2009, 3rd Ex. Sess., Ch. 28, Sec. 33. (SB 18 3x) Effective January 25, 2010.)
593.
Every person who unlawfully and maliciously takes down, removes, injures, interferes with, or obstructs any line erected or maintained by proper authority for the purpose of transmitting electricity for light, heat, or power, or any part thereof, or any insulator or crossarm, appurtenance or apparatus connected therewith, or severs or in any way interferes with any wire, cable, or current thereof, is punishable by imprisonment pursuant to subdivision (h) of Section 1170, or by fine not exceeding one thousand dollars ($1,000), or imprisonment in the county jail not exceeding one year.
(Amended by Stats. 2011, Ch. 15, Sec. 405. (AB 109) Effective April 4, 2011. Operative October 1, 2011, by Sec. 636 of Ch. 15, as amended by Stats. 2011, Ch. 39, Sec. 68.)
593a.
(a) Every person who maliciously drives or places, in any tree, saw-log, shingle-bolt, or other wood, any iron, steel, ceramic, or other substance sufficiently hard to injure saws, knowing that the tree is intended to be harvested or that the saw-log, shingle-bolt, or other wood is intended to be manufactured into any kind of lumber or other wood product, is guilty of a felony.
(b) Any person who violates subdivision (a) and causes bodily injury to another person other than an accomplice shall, in addition and consecutive to the punishment prescribed for that felony, be punished by an additional prison term of three years.
(Amended by Stats. 1987, Ch. 1132, Sec. 1. Effective September 25, 1987. Operative September 30, 1987, by Sec. 4 of Ch. 1132.)
593b.
Every person who shall, without the written permission of the owner, lessee, or person or corporation operating any electrical transmission line, distributing line or system, climb upon any pole, tower or other structure which is a part of such line or system and is supporting or is designed to support a wire or wires, cable or cables, for the transmission or distribution of electric energy, shall be deemed guilty of a misdemeanor; provided, that nothing herein shall apply to employees of either privately or publicly owned public utilities engaged in the performance of their duties.
(Added by Stats. 1935, Ch. 106.)

593c.
Every person who willfully and maliciously breaks, digs up, obstructs, interferes with, removes or injures any pipe or main or hazardous liquid pipeline erected, operated, or maintained for the purpose of transporting, conveying or distributing gas or other hazardous liquids for light, heat, power or any other purpose, or any part thereof, or any valve, meter, holder, compressor, machinery, appurtenance, equipment or apparatus connected with any such main or pipeline, or used in connection with or affecting the operation thereof or the conveying of gas or hazardous liquid therethrough, or shuts off, removes, obstructs, injures, or in any way interferes with any valve or fitting installed on, connected to, or operated in connection with any such main or pipeline, or controlling or affecting the flow of gas or hazardous liquid through any such main or pipeline, is guilty of a felony.
(Amended by Stats. 1988, Ch. 844, Sec. 1.)
593d.
(a) Except as provided in subdivision (e), any person who, for the purpose of intercepting, receiving, or using any program or other service carried by a multichannel video or information services provider that the person is not authorized by that provider to receive or use, commits any of the following acts is guilty of a public offense:
(1) Knowingly and willfully makes or maintains an unauthorized connection or connections, whether physically, electrically, electronically, or inductively, to any cable, wire, or other component of a multichannel video or information services provider's system or to a cable, wire or other media, or receiver that is attached to a multichannel video or information services provider's system.
(2) Knowingly and willfully purchases, possesses, attaches, causes to be attached, assists others in attaching, or maintains the attachment of any unauthorized device or devices to any cable, wire, or other component of a multichannel video or information services provider's system or to a cable, wire or other media, or receiver that is attached to a multichannel video or information services provider's system.
(3) Knowingly and willfully makes or maintains any modification or alteration to any device installed with the authorization of a multichannel video or information services provider.
(4) Knowingly and willfully makes or maintains any modifications or alterations to an access device that authorizes services or knowingly and willfully obtains an unauthorized access device and uses the modified, altered, or unauthorized access device to obtain services from a multichannel video or information services provider.
For purposes of this section, each purchase, possession, connection, attachment, or modification shall constitute a separate violation of this section.
(b) Except as provided in subdivision (e), any person who knowingly and willfully manufactures, assembles, modifies, imports into this state, distributes, sells, offers to sell, advertises for sale, or possesses for any of these purposes, any device or kit for a device, designed, in whole or in part, to decrypt, decode, descramble, or otherwise make intelligible any encrypted, encoded, scrambled, or other nonstandard signal carried by a multichannel video or information services provider, unless the device has been granted an equipment authorization by the Federal Communications Commission (FCC), is guilty of a public offense.
For purposes of this subdivision, "encrypted, encoded, scrambled, or other nonstandard signal" means any type of signal or transmission that is not intended to produce an intelligible program or service without the use of a special device, signal, or information provided by the multichannel video or information services provider or its agents to authorized subscribers.
(c) Every person who knowingly and willfully makes or maintains an unauthorized connection or connections with, whether physically, electrically, electronically, or inductively, or who attaches, causes to be attached, assists others in attaching, or maintains any attachment to, any cable, wire, or other component of a multichannel video or information services provider's system, for the purpose of interfering with, altering, or degrading any multichannel video or information service being transmitted to others, or for the purpose of transmitting or broadcasting any program or other service not intended to be transmitted or broadcast by the multichannel video or information services provider, is guilty of a public offense.
For purposes of this section, each transmission or broadcast shall constitute a separate violation of this section.
(d) (1) Any person who violates subdivision (a) shall be punished by a fine not exceeding one thousand dollars ($1,000), by imprisonment in a county jail not exceeding 90 days, or by both that fine and imprisonment.
(2) Any person who violates subdivision (b) shall be punished as follows:
(A) If the violation involves the manufacture, assembly, modification, importation into this state, distribution, advertisement for sale, or possession for sale or for any of these purposes, of 10 or more of the items described in subdivision (b), or the sale or offering for sale of five or more items for financial gain, the person shall be punished by imprisonment in a county jail not exceeding one year, or in the state prison, by a fine not exceeding two hundred fifty thousand dollars ($250,000), or by both that imprisonment and fine.
(B) If the violation involves the manufacture, assembly, modification, importation into this state, distribution, advertisement for sale, or possession for sale or for any of these purposes, of nine or less of the items described in subdivision (b), or the sale or offering for sale of four or less items for financial gain, shall upon a conviction of a first offense, be punished by imprisonment in a county jail not exceeding one year, by a fine not exceeding twenty-five thousand dollars ($25,000), or by both that imprisonment and fine. A second or subsequent conviction shall be punished by imprisonment in a county jail not exceeding one year, or in the state prison, by a fine not exceeding one hundred thousand dollars ($100,000), or by both that imprisonment and fine.
(3) Any person who violates subdivision (c) shall be punished by a fine not exceeding ten thousand dollars ($10,000), by imprisonment in a county jail, or by both that fine and imprisonment.
(e) Any device or kit described in subdivision (a) or (b) seized under warrant or incident to a lawful arrest, upon the conviction of a person for a violation of subdivision (a) or (b), may be destroyed as contraband by the sheriff.
(f) Any person who violates this section shall be liable in a civil action to the multichannel video or information services provider for the greater of the following amounts:
(1) Five thousand dollars ($5,000).
(2) Three times the amount of actual damages, if any, sustained by the plaintiff plus reasonable attorney's fees.
A defendant who prevails in the action shall be awarded his or her reasonable attorney's fees.
(g) Any multichannel video or information services provider may, in accordance with the provisions of Chapter 3 (commencing with Section 525) of Title 7 of Part 2 of the Code of Civil Procedure, bring an action to enjoin and restrain any violation of this section, and may in the same action seek damages as provided in subdivision (f).
(h) It is not a necessary prerequisite to an action pursuant to this section that the plaintiff has suffered, or be threatened with, actual damages.
(i) For the purposes of this section, a "multichannel video or information services provider" means a franchised or otherwise duly licensed cable television system, video dialtone system, Multichannel Multipoint Distribution Service system, Direct Broadcast Satellite system, or other system providing video or information services that are distributed via cable, wire, radio frequency, or other media. A video dialtone system is a platform operated by a public utility telephone corporation for the transport of video programming as authorized by the Federal Communications Commission pursuant to

FCC Docket No. 87-266, and any subsequent decisions related to that docket, subject to any rules promulgated by the FCC pursuant to those decisions.
(Amended by Stats. 2001, Ch. 854, Sec. 31. Effective January 1, 2002.)
593e.
(a) Every person who knowingly and willfully makes or maintains an unauthorized connection or connections, whether physically, electrically, or inductively, or purchases, possesses, attaches, causes to be attached, assists others in or maintains the attachment of any unauthorized device or devices to a television set or to other equipment designed to receive a television broadcast or transmission, or makes or maintains any modification or alteration to any device installed with the authorization of a subscription television system, for the purpose of intercepting, receiving, or using any program or other service carried by the subscription television system which the person is not authorized by that subscription television system to receive or use, is guilty of a misdemeanor punishable by a fine not exceeding one thousand dollars ($1,000), or by imprisonment in a county jail not exceeding 90 days, or by both that fine and imprisonment. For the purposes of this section, each purchase, possession, connection, attachment or modification shall constitute a separate violation of this section.
(b) Every person who, without the express authorization of a subscription television system, knowingly and willfully manufactures, imports into this state, assembles, distributes, sells, offers to sell, possesses, advertises for sale, or otherwise provides any device, any plan, or any kit for a device or for a printed circuit, designed in whole or in part to decode, descramble, intercept, or otherwise make intelligible any encoded, scrambled, or other nonstandard signal carried by that subscription television system, is guilty of a misdemeanor punishable by a fine not exceeding ten thousand dollars ($10,000), or by imprisonment in a county jail, or by both that fine and imprisonment. A second or subsequent conviction is punishable by a fine not exceeding twenty thousand dollars ($20,000), or by imprisonment in a county jail for up to one year, or by both that fine and imprisonment.
(c) Any person who violates the provisions of subdivision (a) shall be liable to the subscription television system for civil damages in the amount of the value of the connection and subscription fees service actually charged by the subscription television system for the period of unauthorized use according to proof.
Any person who violates the provisions of subdivision (b) shall be liable to the subscription television system at the election of the subscription television system for either of the following amounts:
(1) An award of statutory damages in an aggregate amount of not less than five hundred dollars ($500) or more than ten thousand dollars ($10,000), as the court deems just, for each device, plan, or kit for a device, or for a printed circuit manufactured, imported, assembled, sold, offered for sale, possessed, advertised for sale, or otherwise provided in violation of subdivision (b), to be awarded instead of actual damages and profits.
(2) Three times the amount of actual damages sustained by the plaintiff as a result of the violation or violations of this section and any revenues which have been obtained by the defendant as a result of the violation or violations, or an amount equal to three times the value of the services unlawfully obtained, or the sum of five hundred dollars ($500) for each unauthorized device manufactured, sold, used, or distributed, whichever is greater, and, when appropriate, punitive damages. For the purposes of this subdivision, revenues which have been obtained by the defendant as a result of a violation or violations of this section shall not be included in computing actual damages. In a case where the court finds that any activity set forth in subdivision (b) was committed knowingly and willfully and for purposes of commercial advantage or private financial gain, the court in its discretion may increase the award of damages, whether actual or statutory, by an amount of not more than fifty thousand dollars ($50,000). It shall not constitute a use for "commercial advantage or private financial gain" for any person to receive a subscription television signal within a residential unit as defined herein.
(d) In any civil action filed pursuant to this section, the court shall allow the recovery of full costs plus an award of reasonable attorney's fees to the prevailing party.
(e) Any subscription television system may, in accordance with the provisions of Chapter 3 (commencing with Section 525) of Title 7 of Part 2 of the Code of Civil Procedure, bring an action to enjoin and restrain any violation of this section without having to make a showing of special or irreparable damage, and may in the same action seek damages as provided in subdivision (c). Upon the execution of a proper bond against damages for an injunction improvidently granted, a temporary restraining order or a preliminary injunction may be issued in any action before a final determination on the merits.
(f) It is not necessary that the plaintiff have incurred actual damages, or be threatened with incurring actual damages, as a prerequisite to bringing an action pursuant to this section.
(g) For the purposes of this section, an encoded, scrambled, or other nonstandard signal shall include, without limitation, any type of distorted signal or transmission that is not intended to produce an intelligible program or service without the use of special devices or information provided by the sender for the receipt of this type of signal or transmission.
(h) (1) For the purposes of this section, a "subscription television system" means a television system which sends an encoded, scrambled, or other nonstandard signal over the air which is not intended to be received in an intelligible form without special equipment provided by or authorized by the sender.
(2) For purposes of this section, "residential unit" is defined as any single-family residence, mobilehome within a mobilehome park, condominium, unit or an apartment or multiple-housing unit leased or rented for residential purposes.
(Amended by Stats. 2001, Ch. 854, Sec. 32. Effective January 1, 2002.)
593f.
Every person who for profit knowingly and willfully manufactures, distributes, or sells any device or plan or kit for a device, or printed circuit containing circuitry for decoding or addressing with the purpose or intention of facilitating decoding or addressing of any over-the-air transmission by a Multi-point Distribution Service or Instructional Television Fixed Service made pursuant to authority granted by the Federal Communications Commission which is not authorized by the Multi-point Distribution Service or the Instructional Television Fixed Service is guilty of a misdemeanor punishable by a fine not exceeding two thousand five hundred dollars ($2,500) or by imprisonment in the county jail not exceeding 90 days, or both.
(Added by Stats. 1984, Ch. 833, Sec. 1. Effective August 31, 1984.)
593g.
Every person who, with the intent to use it in a violation of Section 593a, possesses any iron, steel, ceramic, or other substance sufficiently hard to injure saws or wood manufacturing or processing equipment, shall be punished by imprisonment in the county jail not to exceed one year.
This section shall only become operative if Senate Bill 1176 of the 1987–88 Regular Session of the Legislature is enacted and becomes effective on or before January 1, 1988.
(Added by Stats. 1987, Ch. 1414, Sec. 1. Note: SB 1176 was enacted as Stats. 1987, Ch. 1132.)

TITLE 14. MALICIOUS MISCHIEF [594 – 625c]
(Title 14 enacted 1872.)

594.
(a) Every person who maliciously commits any of the following acts with respect to any real or personal property not his or her own, in cases other than those specified by state law, is guilty of vandalism:
(1) Defaces with graffiti or other inscribed material.
(2) Damages.
(3) Destroys.
Whenever a person violates this subdivision with respect to real property, vehicles, signs, fixtures, furnishings, or property belonging to any public entity, as defined by Section 811.2 of the Government Code, or the federal government, it shall be a permissive inference that the person neither owned the property nor had the permission of the owner to deface, damage, or destroy the property.
(b) (1) If the amount of defacement, damage, or destruction is four hundred dollars ($400) or more, vandalism is punishable by imprisonment pursuant to subdivision (h) of Section 1170 or in a county jail not exceeding one year, or by a fine of not more than ten thousand dollars ($10,000), or if the amount of defacement, damage, or destruction is ten thousand dollars ($10,000) or more, by a fine of not more than fifty thousand dollars ($50,000), or by both that fine and imprisonment.
(2) (A) If the amount of defacement, damage, or destruction is less than four hundred dollars ($400), vandalism is punishable by imprisonment in a county jail not exceeding one year, or by a fine of not more than one thousand dollars ($1,000), or by both that fine and imprisonment.
(B) If the amount of defacement, damage, or destruction is less than four hundred dollars ($400), and the defendant has been previously convicted of vandalism or affixing graffiti or other inscribed material under Section 594, 594.3, 594.4, 640.5, 640.6, or 640.7, vandalism is punishable by imprisonment in a county jail for not more than one year, or by a fine of not more than five thousand dollars ($5,000), or by both that fine and imprisonment.
(c) Upon conviction of any person under this section for acts of vandalism consisting of defacing property with graffiti or other inscribed materials, the court shall, when appropriate and feasible, in addition to any punishment imposed under subdivision (b), order the defendant to clean up, repair, or replace the damaged property himself or herself, or order the defendant, and his or her parents or guardians if the defendant is a minor, to keep the damaged property or another specified property in the community free of graffiti for up to one year. Participation of a parent or guardian is not required under this subdivision if the court deems this participation to be detrimental to the defendant, or if the parent or guardian is a single parent who must care for young children. If the court finds that graffiti cleanup is inappropriate, the court shall consider other types of community service, where feasible.
(d) If a minor is personally unable to pay a fine levied for acts prohibited by this section, the parent of that minor shall be liable for payment of the fine. A court may waive payment of the fine, or any part thereof, by the parent upon a finding of good cause.
(e) As used in this section, the term "graffiti or other inscribed material" includes any unauthorized inscription, word, figure, mark, or design, that is written, marked, etched, scratched, drawn, or painted on real or personal property.
(f) The court may order any person ordered to perform community service or graffiti removal pursuant to paragraph (1) of subdivision (c) to undergo counseling.
(g) This section shall become operative on January 1, 2002.
(Amended by Stats. 2011, Ch. 15, Sec. 406. (AB 109) Effective April 4, 2011. Operative October 1, 2011, by Sec. 636 of Ch. 15, as amended by Stats. 2011, Ch. 39, Sec. 68. Note: This section was amended on March 7, 2000, by initiative Prop. 21.)
594.05.
(a) For purposes of Section 594, "damages" includes damage caused to public transit property and facilities, public parks property and facilities, and public utilities and water property and facilities, in the course of stealing or attempting to steal nonferrous material, as defined in Section 21608.5 of the Business and Professions Code.
(b) This section is declaratory of existing law.
(Added by Stats. 2012, Ch. 82, Sec. 3. (AB 1971) Effective January 1, 2013.)
594.1.
(a) (1) It shall be unlawful for any person, firm, or corporation, except a parent or legal guardian, to sell or give or in any way furnish to another person, who is in fact under the age of 18 years, any etching cream or aerosol container of paint that is capable of defacing property without first obtaining bona fide evidence of majority and identity.
(2) For purposes of this section, "etching cream" means any caustic cream, gel, liquid, or solution capable, by means of a chemical action, of defacing, damaging, or destroying hard surfaces in a manner similar to acid.
(3) For purposes of this subdivision, "bona fide evidence of majority and identity" is any document evidencing the age and identity of an individual which has been issued by a federal, state, or local governmental entity, and includes, but is not limited to, a motor vehicle operator's license, a registration certificate issued under the federal Selective Service Act, or an identification card issued to a member of the armed forces.
(4) This subdivision shall not apply to the furnishing of six ounces or less of etching cream or an aerosol container of paint to a minor for the minor's use or possession under the supervision of the minor's parent, guardian, instructor, or employer.
(5) Etching cream, aerosol containers of paint, or related substances may be furnished for use in school-related activities that are part of the instructional program when used under controlled and supervised situations within the classroom or on the site of a supervised project. These containers may not leave the supervised site and shall be inventoried by the instructor. This use shall comply with Section 32060 of the Education Code regarding the safe use of toxic art supplies in schools.
(b) It shall be unlawful for any person under the age of 18 years to purchase etching cream or an aerosol container of paint that is capable of defacing property.
(c) Every retailer selling or offering for sale in this state etching cream or aerosol containers of paint capable of defacing property shall post in a conspicuous place a sign in letters at least three-eighths of an inch high stating: "Any person who maliciously defaces real or personal property with etching cream or paint is guilty of vandalism which is punishable by a fine, imprisonment, or both."
(d) It is unlawful for any person to carry on his or her person and in plain view to the public etching cream or an aerosol container of paint while in any posted public facility, park, playground, swimming pool, beach, or recreational area, other than a highway, street, alley, or way, unless he or she has first received valid authorization from the governmental entity which has jurisdiction over the public area.
As used in this subdivision, "posted" means a sign placed in a reasonable location or locations stating it is a misdemeanor to possess etching cream or a spray can of paint in that public facility, park, playground, swimming pool, beach, or recreational area without valid authorization.
(e) (1) It is unlawful for any person under the age of 18 years to possess etching cream or an aerosol container of paint for the purpose of defacing property while on any public highway, street, alley, or way, or other public place, regardless of whether that person is or is not in any automobile, vehicle, or other conveyance.
(2) As a condition of probation for any violation of this subdivision, the court may order a defendant convicted of a violation of this subdivision to perform community service as follows:
(A) For a first conviction under this subdivision, community service not to exceed 100 hours over a period not to exceed 90 days during a time other than his or her hours of school attendance or employment.
(B) If the person has a prior conviction under this subdivision, community service not to exceed 200 hours over a period of 180 days during a time other than his or her hours of school attendance or employment.

(C) If the person has two prior convictions under this subdivision, community service not to exceed 300 hours over a period not to exceed 240 days during a time other than his or her hours of school attendance or employment.

(f) Violation of any provision of this section is a misdemeanor. Upon conviction of any person under this section, the court may, in addition to any other punishment imposed, if the jurisdiction has adopted a graffiti abatement program as defined in subdivision (f) of Section 594, order the defendant, and his or her parents or guardians if the defendant is a minor, to keep the damaged property or another specified property in the community free of graffiti, as follows:

(1) For a first conviction under this section, for 90 days.

(2) If the defendant has a prior conviction under this section, for 180 days.

(3) If the defendant has two or more prior convictions under this section, for 240 days. Participation of a parent or guardian is not required under this subdivision if the court deems this participation to be detrimental to the defendant, or if the parent or guardian is a single parent who must care for young children.

(g) The court may order any person ordered to perform community service or graffiti removal pursuant to subdivision (e) or (f) to undergo counseling.

(Amended by Stats. 2002, Ch. 523, Sec. 1. Effective January 1, 2003.)

594.2.

(a) Every person who possesses a masonry or glass drill bit, a carbide drill bit, a glass cutter, a grinding stone, an awl, a chisel, a carbide scribe, an aerosol paint container, a felt tip marker, or any other marking substance with the intent to commit vandalism or graffiti, is guilty of a misdemeanor.

(b) As a condition of probation for any violation of this section, the court may order the defendant to perform community service not to exceed 90 hours during a time other than his or her hours of school attendance or employment.

(c) For the purposes of this section:

(1) "Felt tip marker" means any broad-tipped marker pen with a tip exceeding three-eighths of one inch in width, or any similar implement containing an ink that is not water soluble.

(2) "Marking substance" means any substance or implement, other than aerosol paint containers and felt tip markers, that could be used to draw, spray, paint, etch, or mark.

(Amended by Stats. 1994, Ch. 911, Sec. 1. Effective January 1, 1995.)

594.3.

(a) Any person who knowingly commits any act of vandalism to a church, synagogue, mosque, temple, building owned and occupied by a religious educational institution, or other place primarily used as a place of worship where religious services are regularly conducted or a cemetery is guilty of a crime punishable by imprisonment in a county jail for not exceeding one year or imprisonment pursuant to subdivision (h) of Section 1170.

(b) Any person who knowingly commits any act of vandalism to a church, synagogue, mosque, temple, building owned and occupied by a religious educational institution, or other place primarily used as a place of worship where religious services are regularly conducted or a cemetery, which is shown to have been a hate crime and to have been committed for the purpose of intimidating and deterring persons from freely exercising their religious beliefs, is guilty of a felony punishable by imprisonment pursuant to subdivision (h) of Section 1170.

(c) For purposes of this section, "hate crime" has the same meaning as Section 422.55.

(Amended by Stats. 2011, Ch. 15, Sec. 407. (AB 109) Effective April 4, 2011. Operative October 1, 2011, by Sec. 636 of Ch. 15, as amended by Stats. 2011, Ch. 39, Sec. 68.)

594.35.

Every person is guilty of a crime and punishable by imprisonment pursuant to subdivision (h) of Section 1170 or by imprisonment in a county jail for not exceeding one year, who maliciously does any of the following:

(a) Destroys, cuts, mutilates, effaces, or otherwise injures, tears down, or removes any tomb, monument, memorial, or marker in a cemetery, or any gate, door, fence, wall, post or railing, or any enclosure for the protection of a cemetery or mortuary or any property in a cemetery or mortuary.

(b) Obliterates any grave, vault, niche, or crypt.

(c) Destroys, cuts, breaks or injures any mortuary building or any building, statuary, or ornamentation within the limits of a cemetery.

(d) Disturbs, obstructs, detains or interferes with any person carrying or accompanying human remains to a cemetery or funeral establishment, or engaged in a funeral service, or an interment.

(Amended by Stats. 2011, Ch. 15, Sec. 408. (AB 109) Effective April 4, 2011. Operative October 1, 2011, by Sec. 636 of Ch. 15, as amended by Stats. 2011, Ch. 39, Sec. 68.)

594.37.

(a) It is unlawful, except upon private property, for a person to engage in picketing targeted at a funeral during the time period beginning one hour prior to the funeral and ending one hour after the conclusion of the funeral.

(b) Any violation of subdivision (a) is punishable by a fine not exceeding one thousand dollars ($1,000), imprisonment in a county jail not exceeding six months, or by both that fine and imprisonment.

(c) For purposes of this section:

(1) "Funeral" means the ceremony or memorial service held in connection with the burial or cremation of a deceased person. "Funeral" does not mean any nonburial or noncremation activities, businesses, or services.

(2) "Picketing," for purposes of this section only, means protest activities engaged in by any person within 300 feet of a burial site, mortuary, or place of worship.

(3) "Protest activities" includes oration, speech, use of sound amplification equipment in a manner that is intended to make or makes speech, including, but not limited to, oration audible to participants in a funeral, or similar conduct that is not part of the funeral, before an assembled group of people.

(4) "Targeted at" means directed at or toward the deceased person or the attendees of a funeral.

(d) The provisions of this section are severable. If any provision of this section or its application is held invalid, that invalidity shall not affect other provisions or applications that can be given effect without the invalid provision or application.

(Added by Stats. 2012, Ch. 354, Sec. 2. (SB 661) Effective January 1, 2013.)

594.4.

(a) Any person who willfully and maliciously injects into or throws upon, or otherwise defaces, damages, destroys, or contaminates, any structure with butyric acid, or any other similar noxious or caustic chemical or substance, is guilty of a public offense, punishable by imprisonment pursuant to subdivision (h) of Section 1170 or in a county jail not exceeding 6 months, by a fine as specified in subdivision (b), or by both that imprisonment and fine.

(b) (1) If the amount of the defacement, damage, destruction, or contamination is fifty thousand dollars ($50,000) or more, by a fine of not more than fifty thousand dollars ($50,000).

(2) If the amount of the defacement, damage, destruction, or contamination is five thousand dollars ($5,000) or more, but less than fifty thousand dollars ($50,000), by a fine of not more than ten thousand dollars ($10,000).

(3) If the amount of defacement, damage, destruction, or contamination is nine hundred fifty dollars ($950) or more, but less than five thousand dollars ($5,000), by a fine of not more than five thousand dollars ($5,000).

(4) If the amount of the defacement, damage, destruction, or contamination is less than nine hundred fifty dollars ($950), by a fine of not more than one thousand dollars ($1,000).

(c) For purposes of this section, "structure" includes any house or other building being used at the time of the offense for a dwelling or for commercial purposes.

(Amended by Stats. 2011, Ch. 15, Sec. 409. (AB 109) Effective April 4, 2011. Operative October 1, 2011, by Sec. 636 of Ch. 15, as amended by Stats. 2011, Ch. 39, Sec. 68.)

594.5.

Nothing in this code shall invalidate an ordinance of, nor be construed to prohibit the adoption of an ordinance by, a city, city and county, or county, if the ordinance regulates the sale of aerosol containers of paint or other liquid substances capable of defacing property or sets forth civil administrative regulations, procedures, or civil penalties governing the placement of graffiti or other inscribed material on public or private, real or personal property.

(Amended by Stats. 1995, Ch. 42, Sec. 1. Effective January 1, 1996.)

594.6.

(a) Every person who, having been convicted of vandalism or affixing graffiti or other inscribed material under Section 594, 594.3, 594.4, or 640.7, or any combination of these offenses, may be ordered by the court as a condition of probation to perform community service not to exceed 300 hours over a period not to exceed one year during a time other than his or her hours of school attendance or employment. Nothing in this subdivision shall limit the court from ordering the defendant to perform a longer period of community service if a longer period of community service is authorized under other provisions of law.

(b) In lieu of the community service that may be ordered pursuant to subdivision (a), the court may, if a jurisdiction has adopted a graffiti abatement program as defined in subdivision (f) of Section 594, order the defendant, and his or her parents or guardians if the defendant is a minor, as a condition of probation, to keep a specified property in the community free of graffiti for up to one year. Participation of a parent or guardian is not required under this subdivision if the court deems this participation to be detrimental to the defendant, or if the parent or guardian is a single parent who must care for young children.

(c) The court may order any person ordered to perform community service or graffiti removal pursuant to subdivision (a) or (b) to undergo counseling.

(Amended by Stats. 2013, Ch. 791, Sec. 1. (AB 1325) Effective January 1, 2014.)

594.7.

Notwithstanding subdivision (b) of Section 594, every person who, having been convicted previously of vandalism under Section 594 for maliciously defacing with graffiti or other inscribed material any real or personal property not his or her own on two separate occasions and having been incarcerated pursuant to a sentence, a conditional sentence, or a grant of probation for at least one of the convictions, is subsequently convicted of vandalism under Section 594, shall be punished by imprisonment in a county jail not exceeding one year, or in the state prison.

(Amended by Stats. 1994, Ch. 909, Sec. 6. Effective January 1, 1995.)

594.8.

(a) Any person convicted of possession of a destructive implement with intent to commit graffiti or willfully affixing graffiti under Section 594.2, 640.5, 640.6, or 640.7, where the offense was committed when he or she was under the age of 18 years, shall perform not less than 24 hours of community service during a time other than his or her hours of school attendance or employment. One parent or guardian shall be present at the community service site for at least one-half of the hours of community service required under this section unless participation by the parent, guardian, or foster parent is deemed by the court to be inappropriate or potentially detrimental to the child.

(b) In lieu of the community service required pursuant to subdivision (a), the court may, if a jurisdiction has adopted a graffiti abatement program as defined in subdivision (f) of Section 594, order the defendant, and his or her parents or guardians if the defendant is a minor, to keep a specified property in the community free of graffiti for at least 60 days. Participation of a parent or guardian is not required under this subdivision if the court deems this participation to be detrimental to the defendant, or if the parent or guardian is a single parent who must care for young children.

(c) The court may order any person ordered to perform community service or graffiti removal pursuant to subdivision (a) or (b) to undergo counseling.

(Amended by Stats. 1996, Ch. 600, Sec. 5. Effective January 1, 1997.)

595.

The specification of the Acts enumerated in the following sections of this Chapter is not intended to restrict or qualify the interpretation of the preceding section.

(Enacted 1872.)

596.

Every person who, without the consent of the owner, wilfully administers poison to any animal, the property of another, or exposes any poisonous substance, with the intent that the same shall be taken or swallowed by any such animal, is guilty of a misdemeanor.

However, the provisions of this section shall not apply in the case of a person who exposes poisonous substances upon premises or property owned or controlled by him for the purpose of controlling or destroying predatory animals or livestock-killing dogs and if, prior to or during the placing out of such poisonous substances, he shall have posted upon the property conspicuous signs located at intervals of distance not greater than one-third of a mile apart, and in any case not less than three such signs having words with letters at least one inch high reading "Warning—Poisoned bait placed out on these premises," which signs shall be kept in place until the poisonous substances have been removed. Whenever such signs have been conspicuously located upon the property or premises owned or controlled by him as hereinabove provided, such person shall not be charged with any civil liability to another party in the event that any domestic animal belonging to such party becomes injured or killed by trespassing or partaking of the poisonous substance or substances so placed.

(Amended by Stats. 1941, Ch. 494.)

596.5.

It shall be a misdemeanor for any owner or manager of an elephant to engage in abusive behavior towards the elephant, which behavior shall include the discipline of the elephant by any of the following methods:

(a) Deprivation of food, water, or rest.

(b) Use of electricity.

(c) Physical punishment resulting in damage, scarring, or breakage of skin.

(d) Insertion of any instrument into any bodily orifice.

(e) Use of martingales.

(f) Use of block and tackle.

(Added by Stats. 1989, Ch. 1423, Sec. 1.)

596.7.

(a) (1) For purposes of this section, "rodeo" means a performance featuring competition between persons that includes three or more of the following events: bareback bronc riding, saddle bronc riding, bull riding, calf roping, steer wrestling, or team roping.

(2) A rodeo performed on private property for which admission is charged, or that sells or accepts sponsorships, or is open to the public constitutes a performance for the purpose of this subdivision.

(b) The management of any professionally sanctioned or amateur rodeo that intends to perform in any city, county, or city and county, shall ensure that there is a veterinarian licensed to practice in this state present at all times during the performances of the rodeo, or a veterinarian licensed to practice in the state who is on-call and able to arrive at the rodeo within one hour after a determination has been made that there is an injury which requires treatment to be provided by a veterinarian.

(c) (1) The attending or on-call veterinarian shall have complete access to the site of any event in the rodeo that uses animals.

(2) The attending or on-call veterinarian may, for good cause, declare any animal unfit for use in any rodeo event.

(d) (1) Any animal that is injured during the course of, or as a result of, any rodeo event shall receive immediate examination and appropriate treatment by the attending veterinarian or shall begin receiving examination and appropriate treatment by a veterinarian licensed to practice in this state within one hour of the determination of the injury requiring veterinary treatment.

(2) The attending or on-call veterinarian shall submit a brief written listing of any animal injury requiring veterinary treatment to the Veterinary Medical Board within 48 hours of the conclusion of the rodeo.

(3) The rodeo management shall ensure that there is a conveyance available at all times for the immediate and humane removal of any injured animal.

(e) The rodeo management shall ensure that no electric prod or similar device is used on any animal once the animal is in the holding chute, unless necessary to protect the participants and spectators of the rodeo.

(f) A violation of this section is an infraction and shall be punishable as follows:

(1) A fine of not less than five hundred dollars ($500) and not more than two thousand dollars ($2,000) for a first violation.

(2) A fine of not less than one thousand five hundred dollars ($1,500) and not more than five thousand dollars ($5,000) for a second or subsequent violation.

(Amended by Stats. 2007, Ch. 714, Sec. 1. Effective January 1, 2008.)

597.

(a) Except as provided in subdivision (c) of this section or Section 599c, every person who maliciously and intentionally maims, mutilates, tortures, or wounds a living animal, or maliciously and intentionally kills an animal, is guilty of a crime punishable pursuant to subdivision (d).

(b) Except as otherwise provided in subdivision (a) or (c), every person who overdrives, overloads, drives when overloaded, overworks, tortures, torments, deprives of necessary sustenance, drink, or shelter, cruelly beats, mutilates, or cruelly kills any animal, or causes or procures any animal to be so overdriven, overloaded, driven when overloaded, overworked, tortured, tormented, deprived of necessary sustenance, drink, shelter, or to be cruelly beaten, mutilated, or cruelly killed; and whoever, having the charge or custody of any animal, either as owner or otherwise, subjects any animal to needless suffering, or inflicts unnecessary cruelty upon the animal, or in any manner abuses any animal, or fails to provide the animal with proper food, drink, or shelter or protection from the weather, or who drives, rides, or otherwise uses the animal when unfit for labor, is, for each offense, guilty of a crime punishable pursuant to subdivision (d).

(c) Every person who maliciously and intentionally maims, mutilates, or tortures any mammal, bird, reptile, amphibian, or fish, as described in subdivision (e), is guilty of a crime punishable pursuant to subdivision (d).

(d) A violation of subdivision (a), (b), or (c) is punishable as a felony by imprisonment pursuant to subdivision (h) of Section 1170, or by a fine of not more than twenty thousand dollars ($20,000), or by both that fine and imprisonment, or alternatively, as a misdemeanor by imprisonment in a county jail for not more than one year, or by a fine of not more than twenty thousand dollars ($20,000), or by both that fine and imprisonment.

(e) Subdivision (c) applies to any mammal, bird, reptile, amphibian, or fish which is a creature described as follows:

(1) Endangered species or threatened species as described in Chapter 1.5 (commencing with Section 2050) of Division 3 of the Fish and Game Code.

(2) Fully protected birds described in Section 3511 of the Fish and Game Code.

(3) Fully protected mammals described in Chapter 8 (commencing with Section 4700) of Part 3 of Division 4 of the Fish and Game Code.

(4) Fully protected reptiles and amphibians described in Chapter 2 (commencing with Section 5050) of Division 5 of the Fish and Game Code.

(5) Fully protected fish as described in Section 5515 of the Fish and Game Code. This subdivision does not supersede or affect any provisions of law relating to taking of the described species, including, but not limited to, Section 12008 of the Fish and Game Code.

(f) For the purposes of subdivision (c), each act of malicious and intentional maiming, mutilating, or torturing a separate specimen of a creature described in subdivision (e) is a separate offense. If any person is charged with a violation of subdivision (c), the proceedings shall be subject to Section 12157 of the Fish and Game Code.

(g) (1) Upon the conviction of a person charged with a violation of this section by causing or permitting an act of cruelty, as defined in Section 599b, all animals lawfully seized and impounded with respect to the violation by a peace officer, officer of a humane society, or officer of a pound or animal regulation department of a public agency shall be adjudged by the court to be forfeited and shall thereupon be awarded to the impounding officer for proper disposition. A person convicted of a violation of this section by causing or permitting an act of cruelty, as defined in Section 599b, shall be liable to the impounding officer for all costs of impoundment from the time of seizure to the time of proper disposition.

(2) Mandatory seizure or impoundment shall not apply to animals in properly conducted scientific experiments or investigations performed under the authority of the faculty of a regularly incorporated medical college or university of this state.

(h) Notwithstanding any other provision of law, if a defendant is granted probation for a conviction under this section, the court shall order the defendant to pay for, and successfully complete, counseling, as determined by the court, designed to evaluate and treat behavior or conduct disorders. If the court finds that the defendant is financially unable to pay for that counseling, the court may develop a sliding fee schedule based upon the defendant's ability to pay. An indigent defendant may negotiate a deferred payment schedule, but shall pay a nominal fee if the defendant has the ability to pay the nominal fee. County mental health departments or Medi-Cal shall be responsible for the costs of counseling required by this section only for those persons who meet the medical necessity criteria for mental health managed care pursuant to Section 1830.205 of Title 9 of the California Code of Regulations or the targeted population criteria specified in Section 5600.3 of the Welfare and Institutions Code. The counseling specified in this subdivision shall be in addition to any other terms and conditions of probation, including any term of imprisonment and any fine. This provision specifies a mandatory additional term of probation and is not to be utilized as an alternative in lieu of imprisonment pursuant to subdivision (h) of Section 1170 or county jail when that sentence is otherwise appropriate. If the court does not order custody as a condition of probation for a conviction under this section, the court shall specify on the court record the reason or reasons for not ordering custody. This subdivision shall not apply to cases involving police dogs or horses as described in Section 600.

(Amended (as amended by Stats. 2011, Ch. 15, Sec. 410) by Stats. 2011, Ch. 131, Sec. 1.5. (SB 917) Effective January 1, 2012.)

597.1.

(a) (1) Every owner, driver, or keeper of any animal who permits the animal to be in any building, enclosure, lane, street, square, or lot of any city, county, city and county, or judicial district without proper care and attention is guilty of a misdemeanor. Any peace officer, humane society officer, or animal control officer shall take possession of the stray or abandoned animal and shall provide care and treatment for the animal until the animal is deemed to be in suitable condition to be returned to the owner. When the officer has reasonable grounds to believe that very prompt action is required to protect the health or safety of the animal or the health or safety of others, the officer shall

immediately seize the animal and comply with subdivision (f). In all other cases, the officer shall comply with the provisions of subdivision (g). The full cost of caring for and treating any animal properly seized under this subdivision or pursuant to a search warrant shall constitute a lien on the animal and the animal shall not be returned to its owner until the charges are paid, if the seizure is upheld pursuant to this section.

(2) Notwithstanding any other law, if an animal control officer or humane officer, when necessary to protect the health and safety of a wild, stray, or abandoned animal or the health and safety of others, seeks to administer a tranquilizer that contains a controlled substance, as defined in Division 10 (commencing with Section 11000) of the Health and Safety Code, to gain control of that animal, he or she may possess and administer that tranquilizer with direct or indirect supervision as determined by a licensed veterinarian, provided that the officer has met each of the following requirements:

(A) Has received training in the administration of tranquilizers from a licensed veterinarian. The training shall be approved by the California Veterinary Medical Board.

(B) Has successfully completed the firearms component of a course relating to the exercise of police powers, as set forth in Section 832.

(C) Is authorized by his or her agency or organization to possess and administer the tranquilizer in accordance with a policy established by the agency or organization and approved by the veterinarian who obtained the controlled substance.

(D) Has successfully completed the euthanasia training set forth in Section 2039 of Title 16 of the California Code of Regulations.

(E) Has completed a state and federal fingerprinting background check and does not have any drug- or alcohol-related convictions.

(b) Every sick, disabled, infirm, or crippled animal, except a dog or cat, that is abandoned in any city, county, city and county, or judicial district may be killed by the officer if, after a reasonable search, no owner of the animal can be found. It shall be the duty of all peace officers, humane society officers, and animal control officers to cause the animal to be killed or rehabilitated and placed in a suitable home on information that the animal is stray or abandoned. The officer may likewise take charge of any animal, including a dog or cat, that by reason of lameness, sickness, feebleness, or neglect, is unfit for the labor it is performing, or that in any other manner is being cruelly treated, and provide care and treatment for the animal until it is deemed to be in a suitable condition to be returned to the owner. When the officer has reasonable grounds to believe that very prompt action is required to protect the health or safety of an animal or the health or safety of others, the officer shall immediately seize the animal and comply with subdivision (f). In all other cases, the officer shall comply with subdivision (g). The full cost of caring for and treating any animal properly seized under this subdivision or pursuant to a search warrant shall constitute a lien on the animal and the animal shall not be returned to its owner until the charges are paid.

(c) (1) Any peace officer, humane society officer, or animal control officer shall convey all injured cats and dogs found without their owners in a public place directly to a veterinarian known by the officer to be a veterinarian who ordinarily treats dogs and cats for a determination of whether the animal shall be immediately and humanely destroyed or shall be hospitalized under proper care and given emergency treatment.

(2) If the owner does not redeem the animal within the locally prescribed waiting period, the veterinarian may personally perform euthanasia on the animal. If the animal is treated and recovers from its injuries, the veterinarian may keep the animal for purposes of adoption, provided the responsible animal control agency has first been contacted and has refused to take possession of the animal.

(3) Whenever any animal is transferred to a veterinarian in a clinic, such as an emergency clinic that is not in continuous operation, the veterinarian may, in turn, transfer the animal to an appropriate facility.

(4) If the veterinarian determines that the animal shall be hospitalized under proper care and given emergency treatment, the costs of any services that are provided pending the owner's inquiry to the responsible agency, department, or society shall be paid from the dog license fees, fines, and fees for impounding dogs in the city, county, or city and county in which the animal was licensed or, if the animal is unlicensed, shall be paid by the jurisdiction in which the animal was found, subject to the provision that this cost be repaid by the animal's owner. The full cost of caring for and treating any animal seized under this subdivision shall constitute a lien on the animal and the animal shall not be returned to the owner until the charges are paid. No veterinarian shall be criminally or civilly liable for any decision that he or she makes or for services that he or she provides pursuant to this subdivision.

(d) An animal control agency that takes possession of an animal pursuant to subdivision (c) shall keep records of the whereabouts of the animal from the time of possession to the end of the animal's impoundment, and those records shall be available for inspection by the public upon request for three years after the date the animal's impoundment ended.

(e) Notwithstanding any other provision of this section, any peace officer, humane society officer, or any animal control officer may, with the approval of his or her immediate superior, humanely destroy any stray or abandoned animal in the field in any case where the animal is too severely injured to move or where a veterinarian is not available and it would be more humane to euthanize the animal.

(f) Whenever an officer authorized under this section seizes or impounds an animal based on a reasonable belief that prompt action is required to protect the health or safety of the animal or the health or safety of others, the officer shall, prior to the commencement of any criminal proceedings authorized by this section, provide the owner or keeper of the animal, if known or ascertainable after reasonable investigation, with the opportunity for a postseizure hearing to determine the validity of the seizure or impoundment, or both.

(1) The agency shall cause a notice to be affixed to a conspicuous place where the animal was situated or personally deliver a notice of the seizure or impoundment, or both, to the owner or keeper within 48 hours, excluding weekends and holidays. The notice shall include all of the following:

(A) The name, business address, and telephone number of the officer providing the notice.

(B) A description of the animal seized, including any identification upon the animal.

(C) The authority and purpose for the seizure or impoundment, including the time, place, and circumstances under which the animal was seized.

(D) A statement that, in order to receive a postseizure hearing, the owner or person authorized to keep the animal, or his or her agent, shall request the hearing by signing and returning an enclosed declaration of ownership or right to keep the animal to the agency providing the notice within 10 days, including weekends and holidays, of the date of the notice. The declaration may be returned by personal delivery or mail.

(E) A statement that the full cost of caring for and treating any animal properly seized under this section is a lien on the animal and that the animal shall not be returned to the owner until the charges are paid, and that failure to request or to attend a scheduled hearing shall result in liability for this cost.

(2) The postseizure hearing shall be conducted within 48 hours of the request, excluding weekends and holidays. The seizing agency may authorize its own officer or employee to conduct the hearing if the hearing officer is not the same person who directed the seizure or impoundment of the animal and is not junior in rank to that person. The agency may utilize the services of a hearing officer from outside the agency for the purposes of complying with this section.

(3) Failure of the owner or keeper, or of his or her agent, to request or to attend a scheduled hearing shall result in a forfeiture of any right to a postseizure hearing or right to challenge his or her liability for costs incurred.

(4) The agency, department, or society employing the person who directed the seizure shall be responsible for the costs incurred for caring and treating the animal, if it is

determined in the postseizure hearing that the seizing officer did not have reasonable grounds to believe very prompt action, including seizure of the animal, was required to protect the health or safety of the animal or the health or safety of others. If it is determined the seizure was justified, the owner or keeper shall be personally liable to the seizing agency for the full cost of the seizure and care of the animal. The charges for the seizure and care of the animal shall be a lien on the animal. The animal shall not be returned to its owner until the charges are paid and the owner demonstrates to the satisfaction of the seizing agency or the hearing officer that the owner can and will provide the necessary care for the animal.
(g) Where the need for immediate seizure is not present and prior to the commencement of any criminal proceedings authorized by this section, the agency shall provide the owner or keeper of the animal, if known or ascertainable after reasonable investigation, with the opportunity for a hearing prior to any seizure or impoundment of the animal. The owner shall produce the animal at the time of the hearing unless, prior to the hearing, the owner has made arrangements with the agency to view the animal upon request of the agency, or unless the owner can provide verification that the animal was humanely destroyed. Any person who willfully fails to produce the animal or provide the verification is guilty of an infraction, punishable by a fine of not less than two hundred fifty dollars ($250) nor more than one thousand dollars ($1,000).
(1) The agency shall cause a notice to be affixed to a conspicuous place where the animal was situated or personally deliver a notice stating the grounds for believing the animal should be seized under subdivision (a) or (b). The notice shall include all of the following:
(A) The name, business address, and telephone number of the officer providing the notice.
(B) A description of the animal to be seized, including any identification upon the animal.
(C) The authority and purpose for the possible seizure or impoundment.
(D) A statement that, in order to receive a hearing prior to any seizure, the owner or person authorized to keep the animal, or his or her agent, shall request the hearing by signing and returning the enclosed declaration of ownership or right to keep the animal to the officer providing the notice within two days, excluding weekends and holidays, of the date of the notice.
(E) A statement that the cost of caring for and treating any animal properly seized under this section is a lien on the animal, that any animal seized shall not be returned to the owner until the charges are paid, and that failure to request or to attend a scheduled hearing shall result in a conclusive determination that the animal may properly be seized and that the owner shall be liable for the charges.
(2) The preseizure hearing shall be conducted within 48 hours, excluding weekends and holidays, after receipt of the request. The seizing agency may authorize its own officer or employee to conduct the hearing if the hearing officer is not the same person who requests the seizure or impoundment of the animal and is not junior in rank to that person. The agency may utilize the services of a hearing officer from outside the agency for the purposes of complying with this section.
(3) Failure of the owner or keeper, or his or her agent, to request or to attend a scheduled hearing shall result in a forfeiture of any right to a preseizure hearing or right to challenge his or her liability for costs incurred pursuant to this section.
(4) The hearing officer, after the hearing, may affirm or deny the owner's or keeper's right to custody of the animal and, if reasonable grounds are established, may order the seizure or impoundment of the animal for care and treatment.
(h) If any animal is properly seized under this section or pursuant to a search warrant, the owner or keeper shall be personally liable to the seizing agency for the cost of the seizure and care of the animal. Further, if the charges for the seizure or impoundment and any other charges permitted under this section are not paid within 14 days of the seizure, or if the owner, within 14 days of notice of availability of the animal to be returned, fails to pay charges permitted under this section and take possession of the animal, the animal shall be deemed to have been abandoned and may be disposed of by the seizing agency.
(i) If the animal requires veterinary care and the humane society or public agency is not assured, within 14 days of the seizure of the animal, that the owner will provide the necessary care, the animal shall not be returned to its owner and shall be deemed to have been abandoned and may be disposed of by the seizing agency. A veterinarian may humanely destroy an impounded animal without regard to the prescribed holding period when it has been determined that the animal has incurred severe injuries or is incurably crippled. A veterinarian also may immediately humanely destroy an impounded animal afflicted with a serious contagious disease unless the owner or his or her agent immediately authorizes treatment of the animal by a veterinarian at the expense of the owner or agent.
(j) No animal properly seized under this section or pursuant to a search warrant shall be returned to its owner until the owner can demonstrate to the satisfaction of the seizing agency or hearing officer that the owner can and will provide the necessary care for the animal.
(k) (1) In the case of cats and dogs, prior to the final disposition of any criminal charges, the seizing agency or prosecuting attorney may file a petition in a criminal action requesting that, prior to that final disposition, the court issue an order forfeiting the animal to the city, county, or seizing agency. The petitioner shall serve a true copy of the petition upon the defendant and the prosecuting attorney.
(2) Upon receipt of the petition, the court shall set a hearing on the petition. The hearing shall be conducted within 14 days after the filing of the petition, or as soon as practicable.
(3) The petitioner shall have the burden of establishing beyond a reasonable doubt that, even in the event of an acquittal of the criminal charges, the owner will not legally be permitted to retain the animal in question. If the court finds that the petitioner has met its burden, the court shall order the immediate forfeiture of the animal as sought by the petition.
(4) Nothing in this subdivision is intended to authorize a seizing agency or prosecuting attorney to file a petition to determine an owner's ability to legally retain an animal pursuant to paragraph (3) of subdivision (l) if a petition has previously been filed pursuant to this subdivision.
(l) (1) Upon the conviction of a person charged with a violation of this section, or Section 597 or 597a, all animals lawfully seized and impounded with respect to the violation shall be adjudged by the court to be forfeited and shall thereupon be transferred to the impounding officer or appropriate public entity for proper adoption or other disposition. A person convicted of a violation of this section shall be personally liable to the seizing agency for all costs of impoundment from the time of seizure to the time of proper disposition. Upon conviction, the court shall order the convicted person to make payment to the appropriate public entity for the costs incurred in the housing, care, feeding, and treatment of the seized or impounded animals. Each person convicted in connection with a particular animal may be held jointly and severally liable for restitution for that particular animal. The payment shall be in addition to any other fine or sentence ordered by the court.
(2) The court may also order, as a condition of probation, that the convicted person be prohibited from owning, possessing, caring for, or residing with, animals of any kind, and require the convicted person to immediately deliver all animals in his or her possession to a designated public entity for adoption or other lawful disposition or provide proof to the court that the person no longer has possession, care, or control of any animals. In the event of the acquittal or final discharge without conviction of the person charged, if the animal is still impounded, the animal has not been previously deemed abandoned pursuant to subdivision (h), the court has not ordered that the animal be forfeited pursuant to subdivision (k), the court shall, on demand, direct the release of seized or impounded animals to the defendant upon a showing of proof of ownership.
(3) Any questions regarding ownership shall be determined in a separate hearing by the court where the criminal case was finally adjudicated and the court shall hear testimony from any persons who may assist the court in determining ownership of the animal. If the owner is determined to be unknown or the owner is prohibited or unable to retain possession of the animals for any reason, the court shall order the animals to be released to the appropriate public entity for adoption or other lawful disposition. This section is not intended to cause the release of any animal, bird, reptile, amphibian, or fish seized or impounded pursuant to any other statute, ordinance, or municipal regulation. This section shall not prohibit the seizure or impoundment of animals as evidence as provided for under any other provision of law.
(m) It shall be the duty of all peace officers, humane society officers, and animal control officers to use all currently acceptable methods of identification, both electronic and otherwise, to determine the lawful owner or caretaker of any seized or impounded animal. It shall also be their duty to make reasonable efforts to notify the owner or caretaker of the whereabouts of the animal and any procedures available for the lawful recovery of the animal and, upon the owner's and caretaker's initiation of recovery procedures, retain custody of the animal for a reasonable period of time to allow for completion of the recovery process. Efforts to locate or contact the owner or caretaker and communications with persons claiming to be the owner or caretaker shall be recorded and maintained and be made available for public inspection.
(Amended by Stats. 2012, Ch. 598, Sec. 1.5. (SB 1500) Effective January 1, 2013.)
597.2.
(a) It shall be the duty of an officer of a pound, humane society, or animal regulation department of a public agency to assist in a case involving the abandonment or voluntary relinquishment of an equine by the equine's owner. This section does not require a pound, humane society, or animal regulation department of a public agency to take actual possession of the equine.
(b) If a pound, humane society, or animal regulation department of a public agency sells an equine at a private or public auction or sale, it shall set the minimum bid for the sale of the equine at a price above the current slaughter price of the equine.
(c) (1) This section does not prohibit a pound, humane society, or animal regulation department of a public agency from placing an equine through an adoption program at an adoption fee that may be set below current slaughter price.
(2) A person adopting an equine under paragraph (1) shall submit a written statement declaring that the person is adopting the equine for personal use and not for purposes of resale, resale for slaughter, or holding or transporting the equine for slaughter.
(Added by Stats. 1996, Ch. 804, Sec. 1. Effective January 1, 1997.)
597.3.
(a) Every person who operates a live animal market shall do all of the following:
(1) Provide that no animal will be dismembered, flayed, cut open, or have its skin, scales, feathers, or shell removed while the animal is still alive.
(2) Provide that no live animals will be confined, held, or displayed in a manner that results, or is likely to result, in injury, starvation, dehydration, or suffocation.
(b) As used in this section:
(1) "Animal" means frogs, turtles, and birds sold for the purpose of human consumption, with the exception of poultry.
(2) "Live animal market" means a retail food market where, in the regular course of business, animals are stored alive and sold to consumers for the purpose of human consumption.
(c) Any person who fails to comply with any requirement of subdivision (a) shall for the first violation, be given a written warning in a written language that is understood by the person receiving the warning. A second or subsequent violation of subdivision (a) shall be an infraction, punishable by a fine of not less than two hundred fifty dollars ($250), nor more than one thousand dollars ($1,000). However, a fine paid for a second violation of subdivision (a) shall be deferred for six months if a course is available that is administered by a state or local agency on state law and local ordinances relating to live animal markets. If the defendant successfully completes that course within six months of entry of judgment, the fine shall be waived. The state or local agency may charge the participant a fee to take the course, not to exceed one hundred dollars ($100).
(Added by renumbering Section 597.2 (as added by Stats. 2000, Ch. 1061) by Stats. 2001, Ch. 854, Sec. 33. Effective January 1, 2002.)
597.4.
(a) It shall be unlawful for any person to willfully do either of the following:
(1) Sell or give away as part of a commercial transaction a live animal on any street, highway, public right-of-way, parking lot, carnival, or boardwalk.
(2) Display or offer for sale, or display or offer to give away as part of a commercial transaction, a live animal, if the act of selling or giving away the live animal is to occur on any street, highway, public right-of-way, parking lot, carnival, or boardwalk.
(b) (1) A person who violates this section for the first time shall be guilty of an infraction punishable by a fine not to exceed two hundred fifty dollars ($250).
(2) A person who violates this section for the first time and by that violation either causes or permits any animal to suffer or be injured, or causes or permits any animal to be placed in a situation in which its life or health may be endangered, shall be guilty of a misdemeanor.
(3) A person who violates this section for a second or subsequent time shall be guilty of a misdemeanor.
(c) A person who is guilty of a misdemeanor violation of this section shall be punishable by a fine not to exceed one thousand dollars ($1,000) per violation. The court shall weigh the gravity of the violation in setting the fine.
(d) A notice describing the charge and the penalty for a violation of this section may be issued by any peace officer, animal control officer, as defined in Section 830.9, or humane officer qualified pursuant to Section 14502 or 14503 of the Corporations Code.
(e) This section shall not apply to the following:
(1) Events held by 4-H Clubs, Junior Farmers Clubs, or Future Farmers Clubs.
(2) The California Exposition and State Fair, district agricultural association fairs, or county fairs.
(3) Stockyards with respect to which the Secretary of the United States Department of Agriculture has posted notice that the stockyards are regulated by the federal Packers and Stockyards Act, 1921 (7 U.S.C. Sec. 181 et seq.).
(4) The sale of cattle on consignment at any public cattle sales market, the sale of sheep on consignment at any public sheep sales market, the sale of swine on consignment at any public swine sales market, the sale of goats on consignment at any public goat sales market, and the sale of equines on consignment at any public equine sales market.
(5) Live animal markets regulated under Section 597.3.
(6) A public animal control agency or shelter, society for the prevention of cruelty to animals shelter, humane society shelter, or rescue group regulated under Division 14 (commencing with Section 30501) of the Food and Agricultural Code. For purposes of this section, "rescue group" is a not-for-profit entity whose primary purpose is the placement of dogs, cats, or other animals that have been removed from a public animal control agency or shelter, society for the prevention of cruelty to animals shelter, or humane society shelter, or that have been surrendered or relinquished to the entity by the previous owner.
(7) The sale of fish or shellfish, live or dead, from a fishing vessel or registered aquaculture facility, at a pier or wharf, or at a farmer's market by any licensed commercial fisherman or an owner or employee of a registered aquaculture facility to the public for human consumption.

(8) A cat show, dog show, or bird show, provided that all of the following circumstances exist:
(A) The show is validly permitted by the city or county in which the show is held.
(B) The show's sponsor or permittee ensures compliance with all federal, state, and local animal welfare and animal control laws.
(C) The participant has written documentation of the payment of a fee for the entry of his or her cat, dog, or bird in the show.
(D) The sale of a cat, dog, or bird occurs only on the premises and within the confines of the show.
(E) The show is a competitive event where the cats, dogs, or birds are exhibited and judged by an established standard or set of ideals established for each breed or species.
(9) A pet store as defined in subdivision (i) of Section 122350 of the Health and Safety Code.
(f) Nothing in this section shall be construed to in any way limit or affect the application or enforcement of any other law that protects animals or the rights of consumers, including, but not limited to, the Lockyer-Polanco-Farr Pet Protection Act contained in Article 2 (commencing with Section 122125) of Chapter 5 of Part 6 of Division 105 of the Health and Safety Code, or Sections 597 and 597l of this code.
(g) Nothing in this section limits or authorizes any act or omission that violates Section 597 or 597l, or any other local, state, or federal law. The procedures set forth in this section shall not apply to any civil violation of any other local, state, or federal law that protects animals or the rights of consumers, or to a violation of Section 597 or 597l, which is cited or prosecuted pursuant to one or both of those sections, or to a violation of any other local, state, or federal law that is cited or prosecuted pursuant to that law.
(Amended by Stats. 2012, Ch. 162, Sec. 125. (SB 1171) Effective January 1, 2013.)

597.5.
(a) Any person who does any of the following is guilty of a felony and is punishable by imprisonment pursuant to subdivision (h) of Section 1170 for 16 months, or two or three years, or by a fine not to exceed fifty thousand dollars ($50,000), or by both that fine and imprisonment:
(1) Owns, possesses, keeps, or trains any dog, with the intent that the dog shall be engaged in an exhibition of fighting with another dog.
(2) For amusement or gain, causes any dog to fight with another dog, or causes any dogs to injure each other.
(3) Permits any act in violation of paragraph (1) or (2) to be done on any premises under his or her charge or control, or aids or abets that act.
(b) Any person who is knowingly present, as a spectator, at any place, building, or tenement where preparations are being made for an exhibition of the fighting of dogs, with the intent to be present at those preparations, or is knowingly present at that exhibition or at any other fighting or injuring as described in paragraph (2) of subdivision (a), with the intent to be present at that exhibition, fighting, or injuring, is guilty of an offense punishable by imprisonment in a county jail not to exceed one year, or by a fine not to exceed five thousand dollars ($5,000), or by both that imprisonment and fine.
(c) Nothing in this section shall prohibit any of the following:
(1) The use of dogs in the management of livestock, as defined by Section 14205 of the Food and Agricultural Code, by the owner of the livestock or his or her employees or agents or other persons in lawful custody thereof.
(2) The use of dogs in hunting as permitted by the Fish and Game Code, including, but not limited to, Sections 4002 and 4756, and by the rules and regulations of the Fish and Game Commission.
(3) The training of dogs or the use of equipment in the training of dogs for any purpose not prohibited by law.
(Amended by Stats. 2011, Ch. 15, Sec. 411. (AB 109) Effective April 4, 2011. Operative October 1, 2011, by Sec. 636 of Ch. 15, as amended by Stats. 2011, Ch. 39, Sec. 68.)

597.6.
(a) (1) No person may perform, or otherwise procure or arrange for the performance of, surgical claw removal, declawing, onychectomy, or tendonectomy on any cat that is a member of an exotic or native wild cat species, and shall not otherwise alter such a cat's toes, claws, or paws to prevent the normal function of the cat's toes, claws, or paws.
(2) This subdivision does not apply to a procedure performed solely for a therapeutic purpose.
(b) Any person who violates this section is guilty of a misdemeanor punishable by imprisonment in a county jail for a period not to exceed one year, by a fine of ten thousand dollars ($10,000), or by both that imprisonment and fine.
(c) For purposes of this section, the following terms have the following meanings:
(1) "Declawing" and "onychectomy" mean any surgical procedure in which a portion of the animal's paw is amputated in order to remove the animal's claws.
(2) "Tendonectomy" means a procedure in which the tendons to an animal's limbs, paws, or toes are cut or modified so that the claws cannot be extended.
(3) "Exotic or native wild cat species" include all members of the taxonomic family Felidae, except domestic cats (Felis catus or Felis domesticus) or hybrids of wild and domestic cats that are greater than three generations removed from an exotic or native cat. "Exotic or native wild cat species" include, but are not limited to, lions, tigers, cougars, leopards, lynxes, bobcats, caracals, ocelots, margays, servals, cheetahs, snow leopards, clouded leopards, jungle cats, leopard cats, and jaguars, or any hybrid thereof.
(4) "Therapeutic purpose" means for the purpose of addressing an existing or recurring infection, disease, injury, or abnormal condition in the claw that jeopardizes the cat's health, where addressing the infection, disease, injury, or abnormal condition is a medical necessity.
(Added by Stats. 2004, Ch. 876, Sec. 1. Effective January 1, 2005.)

597.7.
(a) A person shall not leave or confine an animal in any unattended motor vehicle under conditions that endanger the health or well-being of an animal due to heat, cold, lack of adequate ventilation, or lack of food or water, or other circumstances that could reasonably be expected to cause suffering, disability, or death to the animal.
(b) (1) This section does not prevent a person from taking reasonable steps that are necessary to remove an animal from a motor vehicle if the person holds a reasonable belief that the animal's safety is in immediate danger from heat, cold, lack of adequate ventilation, lack of food or water, or other circumstances that could reasonably be expected to cause suffering, disability, or death to the animal.
(2) A person who removes an animal from a vehicle in accordance with paragraph (1) is not criminally liable for actions taken reasonably and in good faith if the person does all of the following:
(A) Determines the vehicle is locked or there is otherwise no reasonable manner for the animal to be removed from the vehicle.
(B) Has a good faith belief that forcible entry into the vehicle is necessary because the animal is in imminent danger of suffering harm if it is not immediately removed from the vehicle, and, based upon the circumstances known to the person at the time, the belief is a reasonable one.
(C) Has contacted a local law enforcement agency, the fire department, animal control, or the "911" emergency service prior to forcibly entering the vehicle.
(D) Remains with the animal in a safe location, out of the elements but reasonably close to the vehicle, until a peace officer, humane officer, animal control officer, or another emergency responder arrives.
(E) Used no more force to enter the vehicle and remove the animal from the vehicle than was necessary under the circumstances.
(F) Immediately turns the animal over to a representative from law enforcement, animal control, or another emergency responder who responds to the scene.
(c) Unless the animal suffers great bodily injury, a first conviction for violation of this section is punishable by a fine not exceeding one hundred dollars ($100) per animal. If the animal suffers great bodily injury, a violation of this section is punishable by a fine not exceeding five hundred dollars ($500), imprisonment in a county jail not exceeding six months, or by both a fine and imprisonment. Any subsequent violation of this section, regardless of injury to the animal, is also punishable by a fine not exceeding five hundred dollars ($500), imprisonment in a county jail not exceeding six months, or by both a fine and imprisonment.
(d) (1) This section does not prevent a peace officer, firefighter, humane officer, animal control officer, or other emergency responder from removing an animal from a motor vehicle if the animal's safety appears to be in immediate danger from heat, cold, lack of adequate ventilation, lack of food or water, or other circumstances that could reasonably be expected to cause suffering, disability, or death to the animal.
(2) A peace officer, firefighter, humane officer, animal control officer, or other emergency responder who removes an animal from a motor vehicle, or who takes possession of an animal that has been removed from a motor vehicle, shall take it to an animal shelter or other place of safekeeping or, if the officer deems necessary, to a veterinary hospital for treatment. The owner of the animal removed from the vehicle may be required to pay for charges that have accrued for the maintenance, care, medical treatment, or impoundment of the animal.
(3) A peace officer, firefighter, humane officer, animal control officer, or other emergency responder is authorized to take all steps that are reasonably necessary for the removal of an animal from a motor vehicle, including, but not limited to, breaking into the motor vehicle, after a reasonable effort to locate the owner or other person responsible.
(4) A peace officer, firefighter, humane officer, animal control officer, or other emergency responder who removes an animal from a motor vehicle or who receives an animal rescued from a vehicle from another person shall, in a secure and conspicuous location on or within the motor vehicle, leave written notice bearing his or her name and office, and the address of the location where the animal can be claimed. The animal may be claimed by the owner only after payment of all charges that have accrued for the maintenance, care, medical treatment, or impoundment of the animal.
(5) Except as provided in subdivision (b), this section does not affect in any way existing liabilities or immunities in current law, or create any new immunities or liabilities.
(e) Nothing in this section shall preclude prosecution under both this section and Section 597 or any other provision of law, including city or county ordinances.
(f) Nothing in this section shall be deemed to prohibit the transportation of horses, cattle, pigs, sheep, poultry, or other agricultural animals in motor vehicles designed to transport such animals for agricultural purposes.
(Amended by Stats. 2016, Ch. 554, Sec. 2. (AB 797) Effective January 1, 2017.)

597.9.
(a) Except as provided in subdivision (c) or (d), a person who has been convicted of a misdemeanor violation of subdivision (a) or (b) of Section 597, or Section 597a, 597b, 597h, 597j, 597s, or 597.1, and who, within five years after the conviction, owns, possesses, maintains, has custody of, resides with, or cares for any animal is guilty of a public offense, punishable by a fine of one thousand dollars ($1,000).
(b) Except as provided in subdivision (c) or (d), a person who has been convicted of a felony violation of subdivision (a) or (b) of Section 597, or Section 597b or 597.5, and who, within 10 years after the conviction, owns, possesses, maintains, has custody of, resides with, or cares for any animal is guilty of a public offense, punishable by a fine of one thousand dollars ($1,000).
(c) (1) In cases of owners of livestock, as defined in Section 14205 of the Food and Agricultural Code, a court may, in the interest of justice, exempt a defendant from the injunction required under subdivision (a) or (b), as it would apply to livestock, if the defendant files a petition with the court to establish, and does establish by a preponderance of the evidence, that the imposition of the provisions of this section would result in substantial or undue economic hardship to the defendant's livelihood and that the defendant has the ability to properly care for all livestock in his or her possession.
(2) Upon receipt of a petition from the defendant, the court shall set a hearing to be conducted within 30 days after the filing of the petition. The petitioner shall serve a copy of the petition upon the prosecuting attorney 10 calendar days prior to the requested hearing. The court shall grant the petition for exemption from subdivision (a) or (b) unless the prosecuting attorney shows by a preponderance of the evidence that either or both of the criteria for exemption under this subdivision are untrue.
(d) (1) A defendant may petition the court to reduce the duration of the mandatory ownership prohibition. Upon receipt of a petition from the defendant, the court shall set a hearing to be conducted within 30 days after the filing of the petition. The petitioner shall serve a copy of the petition upon the prosecuting attorney 10 calendar days prior to the requested hearing. At the hearing, the petitioner shall have the burden of establishing by a preponderance of the evidence all of the following:
(A) He or she does not present a danger to animals.
(B) He or she has the ability to properly care for all animals in his or her possession.
(C) He or she has successfully completed all classes or counseling ordered by the court.
(2) If the petitioner has met his or her burden, the court may reduce the mandatory ownership prohibition and may order that the defendant comply with reasonable and unannounced inspections by animal control agencies or law enforcement.
(e) An animal shelter administered by a public animal control agency, a humane society, or any society for the prevention of cruelty to animals, and an animal rescue or animal adoption organization may ask an individual who is attempting to adopt an animal from that entity whether he or she is prohibited from owning, possessing, maintaining, having custody of, or residing with an animal pursuant to this section.
(Amended by Stats. 2018, Ch. 877, Sec. 1. (AB 2774) Effective January 1, 2019.)

597a.
Whoever carries or causes to be carried in or upon any vehicle or otherwise any domestic animal in a cruel or inhuman manner, or knowingly and willfully authorizes or permits it to be subjected to unnecessary torture, suffering, or cruelty of any kind, is guilty of a misdemeanor; and whenever any such person is taken into custody therefor by any officer, such officer must take charge of such vehicle and its contents, together with the horse or team attached to such vehicle, and deposit the same in some place of custody; and any necessary expense incurred for taking care of and keeping the same, is a lien thereon, to be paid before the same can be lawfully recovered; and if such expense, or any part thereof, remains unpaid, it may be recovered, by the person incurring the same, of the owner of such domestic animal, in an action therefor.
(Added by Stats. 1905, Ch. 519.)

597b.
(a) Except as provided in subdivisions (b) and (c), any person who, for amusement or gain, causes any bull, bear, or other animal, not including any dog, to fight with like kind of animal or creature, or causes any animal, including any dog, to fight with a different kind of animal or creature, or with any human being, or who, for amusement or gain, worries or injures any bull, bear, dog, or other animal, or causes any bull, bear, or other animal, not including any dog, to worry or injure each other, or any person who permits the same to be done on any premises under his or her charge or control, or any person who aids or abets the fighting or worrying of an animal or creature, is guilty of a misdemeanor punishable by imprisonment in a county jail for a period not to exceed one year, by a fine not to exceed ten thousand dollars ($10,000), or by both that imprisonment and fine.

(b) Any person who, for amusement or gain, causes any cock to fight with another cock or with a different kind of animal or creature or with any human being; or who, for amusement or gain, worries or injures any cock, or causes any cock to worry or injure another animal; and any person who permits the same to be done on any premises under his or her charge or control, and any person who aids or abets the fighting or worrying of any cock is guilty of a misdemeanor punishable by imprisonment in a county jail for a period not to exceed one year, or by a fine not to exceed ten thousand dollars ($10,000), or by both that imprisonment and fine.
(c) A second or subsequent conviction of this section is a misdemeanor or a felony punishable by imprisonment in a county jail for a period not to exceed one year or the state prison for 16 months, two, or three years, by a fine not to exceed twenty-five thousand dollars ($25,000), or by both that imprisonment and fine, except in unusual circumstances in which the interests of justice would be better served by the imposition of a lesser sentence.
(d) For the purposes of this section, aiding and abetting a violation of this section shall consist of something more than merely being present or a spectator at a place where a violation is occurring.
(Amended by Stats. 2012, Ch. 133, Sec. 1. (SB 1145) Effective January 1, 2013.)

597c.
Any person who is knowingly present as a spectator at any place, building, or tenement for an exhibition of animal fighting, or who is knowingly present at that exhibition or is knowingly present where preparations are being made for the acts described in subdivision (a) or (b) of Section 597b, is guilty of a misdemeanor punishable by imprisonment in a county jail for a period not to exceed six months, or by a fine of five thousand dollars ($5,000), or by both that imprisonment and fine.
(Amended by Stats. 2012, Ch. 133, Sec. 2. (SB 1145) Effective January 1, 2013.)

597d.
Any sheriff, police, or peace officer, or officer qualified as provided in Section 14502 of the Corporations Code, may enter any place, building, or tenement, where there is an exhibition of the fighting of birds or animals, or where preparations are being made for such an exhibition, and, without a warrant, arrest all persons present.
(Amended by Stats. 1997, Ch. 598, Sec. 11. Effective January 1, 1998.)

597e.
Any person who impounds, or causes to be impounded in any pound, any domestic animal, shall supply it during such confinement with a sufficient quantity of good and wholesome food and water, and in default thereof, is guilty of a misdemeanor. In case any domestic animal is at any time so impounded and continues to be without necessary food and water for more than 12 consecutive hours, it is lawful for any person, from time to time, as may be deemed necessary, to enter into and upon any pound in which the animal is confined, and supply it with necessary food and water so long as it remains so confined. Such person is not liable for the entry and may collect the reasonable cost of the food and water from the owner of the animal, and the animal is subject to enforcement of a money judgment for the reasonable cost of such food and water.
(Amended by Stats. 1982, Ch. 497, Sec. 135. Operative July 1, 1983, by Sec. 185 of Ch. 497.)

597f.
(a) Every owner, driver, or possessor of any animal, who permits the animal to be in any building, enclosure, lane, street, square, or lot, of any city, city and county, or judicial district, without proper care and attention, shall, on conviction, be deemed guilty of a misdemeanor. And it shall be the duty of any peace officer, officer of the humane society, or officer of a pound or animal regulation department of a public agency, to take possession of the animal so abandoned or neglected and care for the animal until it is redeemed by the owner or claimant, and the cost of caring for the animal shall be a lien on the animal until the charges are paid. Every sick, disabled, infirm, or crippled animal, except a dog or cat, which shall be abandoned in any city, city and county, or judicial district, may, if after due search no owner can be found therefor, be killed by the officer; and it shall be the duty of all peace officers, an officer of such society, or officer of a pound or animal regulation department of a public agency to cause the animal to be killed on information of such abandonment. The officer may likewise take charge of any animal, including a dog or cat, that by reason of lameness, sickness, feebleness, or neglect, is unfit for the labor it is performing, or that in any other manner is being cruelly treated; and, if the animal is not then in the custody of its owner, the officer shall give notice thereof to the owner, if known, and may provide suitable care for the animal until it is deemed to be in a suitable condition to be delivered to the owner, and any necessary expenses which may be incurred for taking care of and keeping the animal shall be a lien thereon, to be paid before the animal can be lawfully recovered.
(b) It shall be the duty of all officers of pounds or humane societies, and animal regulation departments of public agencies to convey, and for police and sheriff departments, to cause to be conveyed all injured cats and dogs found without their owners in a public place directly to a veterinarian known by the officer or agency to be a veterinarian that ordinarily treats dogs and cats for a determination of whether the animal shall be immediately and humanely destroyed or shall be hospitalized under proper care and given emergency treatment.
If the owner does not redeem the animal within the locally prescribed waiting period, the veterinarian may personally perform euthanasia on the animal; or, if the animal is treated and recovers from its injuries, the veterinarian may keep the animal for purposes of adoption, provided the responsible animal control agency has first been contacted and has refused to take possession of the animal.
Whenever any animal is transferred pursuant to this subdivision to a veterinarian in a clinic, such as an emergency clinic which is not in continuous operation, the veterinarian may, in turn, transfer the animal to an appropriate facility.
If the veterinarian determines that the animal shall be hospitalized under proper care and given emergency treatment, the costs of any services which are provided pending the owner's inquiry to the agency, department, or society shall be paid from the dog license fees, fines, and fees for impounding dogs in the city, county, or city and county in which the animal was licensed or if the animal is unlicensed the jurisdiction in which the animal was found, subject to the provision that this cost be repaid by the animal's owner. No veterinarian shall be criminally or civilly liable for any decision which he or she makes or services which he or she provides pursuant to this section.
(c) An animal control agency which takes possession of an animal pursuant to subdivision (b), shall keep records of the whereabouts of the animal for a 72-hour period from the time of possession and those records shall be available to inspection by the public upon request.
(d) Notwithstanding any other provisions of this section, any officer of a pound or animal regulation department or humane society, or any officer of a police or sheriff's department may, with the approval of his or her immediate superior, humanely destroy any abandoned animal in the field in any case where the animal is too severely injured to move or where a veterinarian is not available and it would be more humane to dispose of the animal.
(Amended by Stats. 1989, Ch. 490, Sec. 1.)

597g.
(a) Poling a horse is a method of training horses to jump which consists of (1) forcing, persuading, or enticing a horse to jump in such manner that one or more of its legs will come in contact with an obstruction consisting of any kind of wire, or a pole, stick, rope or other object with brads, nails, tacks or other sharp points imbedded therein or attached thereto or (2) raising, throwing or moving a pole, stick, wire, rope or other object, against one or more of the legs of a horse while it is jumping an obstruction so that the horse, in either case, is induced to raise such leg or legs higher in order to clear the obstruction. Tripping a horse is an act that consists of the use of any wire, pole, stick, rope, or other object or apparatus whatsoever to cause a horse to fall or lose its balance. The poling or tripping of any horse is unlawful and any person violating the provisions of this section is guilty of a misdemeanor.
(b) It is a misdemeanor for any person to intentionally trip or fell an equine by the legs by any means whatsoever for the purposes of entertainment or sport.
(c) This section does not apply to the lawful laying down of a horse for medical or identification purposes, nor shall the section be construed as condemning or limiting any cultural or historical activities, except those prohibited herein.
(Amended by Stats. 1994, 1st Ex. Sess., Ch. 8, Sec. 1. Effective November 30, 1994.)

597h.
(a) It shall be unlawful for any person to tie or attach or fasten any live animal to any machine or device propelled by any power for the purpose of causing that animal to be pursued by a dog or dogs.
(b) Any person violating any of the provisions of this section shall be guilty of a misdemeanor punishable by a fine of two thousand five hundred dollars ($2,500) or by imprisonment in a county jail not exceeding six months, or by both that imprisonment and fine.
(Amended by Stats. 2011, Ch. 562, Sec. 2. (SB 425) Effective January 1, 2012.)

597i.
(a) It shall be unlawful for anyone to manufacture, buy, sell, barter, exchange, or have in his or her possession any of the implements commonly known as gaffs or slashers, or any other sharp implement designed to be attached in place of the natural spur of a gamecock or other fighting bird.
(b) Any person who violates any of the provisions of this section is guilty of a misdemeanor punishable by imprisonment in a county jail for a period not to exceed one year, by a fine not to exceed ten thousand dollars ($10,000), or by both that imprisonment and fine and upon conviction thereof shall, in addition to any judgment or sentence imposed by the court, forfeit possession or ownership of those implements.
(Amended by Stats. 2012, Ch. 133, Sec. 3. (SB 1145) Effective January 1, 2013.)

597j.
(a) Any person who owns, possesses, keeps, or trains any bird or other animal with the intent that it be used or engaged by himself or herself, by his or her vendee, or by any other person in an exhibition of fighting as described in Section 597b is guilty of a misdemeanor punishable by imprisonment in a county jail for a period not to exceed one year, by a fine not to exceed ten thousand dollars ($10,000), or by both that imprisonment and fine.
(b) This section shall not apply to an exhibition of fighting of a dog with another dog.
(c) A second or subsequent conviction of this section is a misdemeanor punishable by imprisonment in a county jail for a period not to exceed one year or by a fine not to exceed twenty-five thousand dollars ($25,000), or by both that imprisonment and fine, except in unusual circumstances in which the interests of justice would be better served by the imposition of a lesser sentence.
(Amended by Stats. 2012, Ch. 133, Sec. 4. (SB 1145) Effective January 1, 2013.)

597k.
Anyone who, having care, custody or control of any horse or other animal, uses what is known as the bristle bur, tack bur, or other like device, by whatsoever name known or designated, on such horse or other animal for any purpose whatsoever, is guilty of a misdemeanor and is punishable by a fine of not less than fifty dollars ($50) nor more than five hundred dollars ($500), or by imprisonment in the county jail for not less than 10 days nor more than 175 days, or by both such fine and imprisonment.
(Amended by Stats. 1983, Ch. 1092, Sec. 308. Effective September 27, 1983. Operative January 1, 1984, by Sec. 427 of Ch. 1092.)

597l.
(a) It shall be unlawful for any person who operates a pet shop to fail to do all of the following:
(1) Maintain the facilities used for the keeping of pet animals in a sanitary condition.
(2) Provide proper heating and ventilation for the facilities used for the keeping of pet animals.
(3) Provide adequate nutrition for, and humane care and treatment of, all pet animals under his or her care and control.
(4) Take reasonable care to release for sale, trade, or adoption only those pet animals that are free of disease or injuries.
(5) Provide adequate space appropriate to the size, weight, and specie of pet animals.
(b) (1) Sellers of pet animals shall provide buyers of a pet animal with general written recommendations for the generally accepted care of the class of pet animal sold, including recommendations as to the housing, equipment, cleaning, environment, and feeding of the animal. This written information shall be in a form determined by the sellers of pet animals and may include references to Web sites, books, pamphlets, videos, and compact discs.
(2) If a seller of pet animals distributes material prepared by a third party, the seller shall not be liable for damages caused by any erroneous information in that material unless a reasonable person exercising ordinary care should have known of the error causing the damage.
(3) This subdivision shall apply to any private or public retail business that sells pet animals to the public and is required to possess a permit pursuant to Section 6066 of the Revenue and Taxation Code.
(4) Charges brought against a seller of pet animals for a first violation of the provisions of this subdivision shall be dismissed if the person charged produces in court satisfactory proof of compliance. A second or subsequent violation is an infraction punishable by a fine not to exceed two hundred fifty dollars ($250).
(c) As used in this section, the following terms have the following meanings:
(1) "Pet animals" means dogs, cats, monkeys and other primates, rabbits, birds, guinea pigs, hamsters, mice, snakes, iguanas, turtles, and any other species of animal sold or retained for the purpose of being kept as a household pet.
(2) "Pet shop" means every place or premises where pet animals are kept for the purpose of either wholesale or retail sale. "Pet shop" does not include any place or premises where pet animals are occasionally sold.
(d) Any person who violates any provision of subdivision (a) is guilty of a misdemeanor and is punishable by a fine not exceeding one thousand dollars ($1,000), or by imprisonment in the county jail not exceeding 90 days, or by both that fine and imprisonment.
(Amended by Stats. 2003, Ch. 62, Sec. 228. Effective January 1, 2004.)

597m.
It shall be unlawful for any person to promote, advertise, stage, hold, manage, conduct, participate in, engage in, or carry on any bullfight exhibition, any bloodless bullfight contest or exhibition, or any similar contest or exhibition, whether for amusement or gain or otherwise; provided, that nothing herein shall be construed to prohibit rodeos or to prohibit measures necessary to the safety of participants at rodeos.
This section shall not, however, be construed as prohibiting bloodless bullfights, contests, or exhibitions held in connection with religious celebrations or religious festivals.
Any person violating the provisions of this section is guilty of a misdemeanor.
(Added by Stats. 1957, Ch. 2243.)

597n.
(a) Any person who cuts the solid part of the tail of any horse or cattle in the operation known as "docking," or in any other operation performed for the purpose of shortening the tail of any horse or cattle, within the State of California, or procures the same to be done, or imports or brings into this state any docked horse, or horses, or drives, works,

uses, races, or deals in any unregistered docked horse, or horses, within the State of California except as provided in Section 597r, is guilty of a misdemeanor.

(b) Subdivision (a) shall not apply to "docking" when the solid part of any cattle's tail must be removed in an emergency for the purpose of saving the cattle's life or relieving the cattle's pain, provided that the emergency treatment is performed consistent with the Veterinary Medicine Practice Act (commencing with Section 4811) of Article 1 of Chapter 11 of Division 2 of the Business and Professions Code.

(c) For the purposes of this section, "cattle" means any animal of the bovine species.

(Amended by Stats. 2009, Ch. 344, Sec. 1. (SB 135) Effective January 1, 2010.)

597o.

(a) Any person who transports an equine in a vehicle to slaughter shall meet the following requirements:

(1) The vehicle shall have sufficient clearance to allow the equine to be transported in a standing position with its head in a normal upright position above its withers.

(2) Any ramps and floors in the vehicle shall be covered with a nonskid surface to prevent the equine from slipping.

(3) The vehicle shall provide adequate ventilation to the equine while the equine is being transported.

(4) The sides and overhead of the vehicle shall be constructed to withstand the weight of any equine which may put pressure against the sides or overhead.

(5) Any compartments in the interior of the vehicle shall be constructed of smooth materials and shall contain no protrusions or sharp objects.

(6) The size of the vehicle shall be appropriate for the number of equine being transported and the welfare of the equine shall not be jeopardized by overcrowding.

(7) Stallions shall be segregated during transportation to slaughter.

(8) Diseased, sick, blind, dying, or otherwise disabled equine shall not be transported out of this state.

(9) Any equine being transported shall be able to bear weight on all four feet.

(10) Unweaned foals shall not be transported.

(11) Mares in their last trimester of pregnancy shall not be transported.

(12) The person shall notify a humane officer having jurisdiction 72 hours before loading the equine in order that the humane officer may perform a thorough inspection of the vehicle to determine if all requirements of this section have been satisfied.

(b) (1) Any person who violates this section is guilty of a misdemeanor and is subject to a fine of one hundred dollars ($100) per equine being transported.

(2) Any person who violates this section for a second or subsequent time is guilty of a misdemeanor and shall be fined five hundred dollars ($500) per equine being transported.

(c) Whenever a person is taken into custody by an officer for a violation of this section, the officer shall take charge of the vehicle and its contents and deposit the property in some place of custody.

(d) (1) Any necessary expense incurred for taking care of and keeping the property described in subdivision (c) is a lien thereon, to be paid before the property can be lawfully recovered.

(2) If the expense, or any part thereof, remains unpaid, it may be recovered by the person incurring the expense from the owner of the equine in an action therefor.

(e) For the purposes of this section, "equine" means any horse, pony, burro, or mule.

(Added by Stats. 1993, Ch. 1183, Sec. 1. Effective January 1, 1994.)

597p.

Within 30 days after the passage of this act, every owner, or user of any docked horse, within the State of California, shall register his or her docked horse, or horses by filing in the office of the county clerk of the county in which such docked horse, or horses, may then be kept, a certificate, which certificate shall contain the name, or names of the owner, together with his or her post office address, a full description of the color, age, size and the use made of such docked horse, or horses; which certificate shall be signed by the owner, or his, or her agent. The county clerk shall number such certificate consecutively and record the name in a book, or register to be kept for that purpose only; and shall receive as a fee for recording of such certificate, the sum of fifty cents ($0.50), and the clerk shall thereupon issue to such person so registering such horse or horses a certificate containing the facts recited in this section which upon demand shall be exhibited to any peace officer, and the same shall be conclusive evidence of a compliance with the provisions of Section 597n of this code.

(Added by renumbering Section 597b (as added by Stats. 1907, Ch. 220) by Stats. 1963, Ch. 372.)

597q.

The driving, working, keeping, racing or using of any unregistered docked horse, or horses, after 60 days after the passage of this act, shall be deemed prima facie evidence of the fact that the party driving, working, keeping, racing or using such unregistered docked horse, or horses, docked the tail of such horse or horses.

(Added by renumbering Section 597c (as added by Stats. 1907, Ch. 220) by Stats. 1963, Ch. 372.)

597r.

Any person or persons violating any of the provisions of this act, shall be deemed guilty of a misdemeanor; provided, however, that the provisions of Sections 597n, 597p, and 597q, shall not be applied to persons owning or possessing any docked purebred stallions and mares imported from foreign countries for breeding or exhibition purposes only, as provided by an act of Congress entitled "An act regulating the importation of breeding animals" and approved March 3, 1903, and to docked native-bred stallions and mares brought into this State and used for breeding or exhibition purposes only; and provided further, that a description of each such animal so brought into the State, together with the date of importation and name and address of importer, be filed with the county clerk of the county where such animal is kept, within 30 days after the importation of such animal.

(Added by renumbering Section 597d (as added by Stats. 1907, Ch. 220) by Stats. 1963, Ch. 372.)

597s.

(a) Every person who willfully abandons any animal is guilty of a misdemeanor.

(b) This section shall not apply to the release or rehabilitation and release of native California wildlife pursuant to statute or regulations of the California Department of Fish and Game.

(Amended by Stats. 1999, Ch. 303, Sec. 1. Effective January 1, 2000.)

597t.

Every person who keeps an animal confined in an enclosed area shall provide it with an adequate exercise area. If the animal is restricted by a leash, rope, or chain, the leash, rope, or chain shall be affixed in such a manner that it will prevent the animal from becoming entangled or injured and permit the animal's access to adequate shelter, food, and water. Violation of this section constitutes a misdemeanor.

This section shall not apply to an animal which is in transit, in a vehicle, or in the immediate control of a person.

(Amended by Stats. 1971, Ch. 243.)

597u.

(a) A person, peace officer, officer of a humane society, or officer of a pound or animal regulation department of a public agency shall not kill an animal by using either of the following methods:

(1) Carbon monoxide gas.

(2) Intracardiac injection of a euthanasia agent on a conscious animal, unless the animal is heavily sedated or anesthetized in a humane manner, or comatose, or unless, in light of all the relevant circumstances, the procedure is justifiable.

(b) With respect to the killing of a dog or cat, a person, peace officer, officer of a humane society, or officer of a pound or animal regulation department of a public agency shall not use any of the methods specified in subdivision (a) or any of the following methods:

(1) High-altitude decompression chamber.

(2) Nitrogen gas.

(3) Carbon dioxide gas.

(Amended by Stats. 2016, Ch. 105, Sec. 1. (AB 2505) Effective January 1, 2017.)

597v.

No person, peace officer, officer of a humane society, or officer of a pound or animal regulation department of a public agency shall kill any newborn dog or cat whose eyes have not yet opened by any other method than by the use of chloroform vapor or by inoculation of barbiturates.

(Amended by Stats. 1998, Ch. 751, Sec. 5. Effective January 1, 1999.)

597x.

(a) Notwithstanding Section 18734 of the Food and Agricultural Code or any other provision of law, it is unlawful for any person to sell, attempt to sell, load, cause to be loaded, transport, or attempt to transport any live horse, mule, burro, or pony that is disabled, if the animal is intended to be sold, loaded, or transported for commercial slaughter out of the state.

(b) For the purposes of this section, "disabled animal" includes, but is not limited to, any animal that has broken limbs, is unable to stand and balance itself without assistance, cannot walk, or is severely injured.

(c) A person who violates this section is guilty of a misdemeanor and subject to the same penalties imposed upon a person convicted of a misdemeanor under Section 597a.

(Added by Stats. 1993, Ch. 1213, Sec. 1. Effective January 1, 1994.)

597y.

A violation of Section 597u or 597v is a misdemeanor.

(Amended by Stats. 2011, Ch. 296, Sec. 206. (AB 1023) Effective January 1, 2012.)

597z.

(a) (1) Except as otherwise authorized under any other provision of law, it shall be a crime, punishable as specified in subdivision (b), for any person to sell one or more dogs under eight weeks of age, unless, prior to any physical transfer of the dog or dogs from the seller to the purchaser, the dog or dogs are approved for sale, as evidenced by written documentation from a veterinarian licensed to practice in California.

(2) For the purposes of this section, the sale of a dog or dogs shall not be considered complete, and thereby subject to the requirements and penalties of this section, unless and until the seller physically transfers the dog or dogs to the purchaser.

(b) (1) Any person who violates this section shall be guilty of an infraction or a misdemeanor.

(2) An infraction under this section shall be punishable by a fine not to exceed two hundred fifty dollars ($250).

(3) With respect to the sale of two or more dogs in violation of this section, each dog unlawfully sold shall represent a separate offense under this section.

(c) This section shall not apply to any of the following:

(1) An organization, as defined in Section 501(c)(3) of the Internal Revenue Code, or any other organization that provides, or contracts to provide, services as a public animal sheltering agency.

(2) A pet dealer as defined under Article 2 (commencing with Section 122125) of Chapter 5 of Part 6 of Division 105 of the Health and Safety Code.

(3) A public animal control agency or shelter, society for the prevention of cruelty to animals shelter, humane society shelter, or rescue group regulated under Division 14 (commencing with Section 30501) of the Food and Agricultural Code.

(Added by Stats. 2005, Ch. 669, Sec. 1. Effective January 1, 2006.)

598.

Every person who, within any public cemetery or burying ground, kills, wounds, or traps any bird, or destroys any bird's nest other than swallows' nests, or removes any eggs or young birds from any nest, is guilty of a misdemeanor.

(Enacted 1872.)

598.1.

(a) The prosecuting agency in a criminal proceeding in which the defendant has been charged with the commission of any of the crimes listed in subdivision (a) of Section 597.5 or subdivision (b) of Section 597b may, in conjunction with the criminal proceeding, file a petition for forfeiture as provided in subdivision (c). If the prosecuting agency has filed a petition for forfeiture pursuant to subdivision (c) and the defendant is convicted of any of the crimes described in subdivision (a) of Section 597.5 or subdivision (b) of Section 597b, the assets listed in subdivision (b) shall be subject to forfeiture upon proof of the elements of subdivision (b) and in accordance with this section.

(b) (1) Any property interest, whether tangible or intangible, that was acquired through the commission of any of the crimes listed in subdivision (a) of Section 597.5 or subdivision (b) of Section 597b shall be subject to forfeiture, including both personal and real property, profits, proceeds, and the instrumentalities acquired, accumulated, or used by cockfighting or dogfighting participants, organizers, transporters of animals and equipment, breeders and trainers of fighting birds or fighting dogs, and persons who steal or illegally obtain dogs or other animals for fighting, including bait and sparring animals.

(2) Notwithstanding paragraph (1), the following property shall not be subject to forfeiture under this section:

(A) Property solely owned by a bona fide purchaser for value, who was without knowledge that the property was intended to be used for a purpose which would subject it to forfeiture under this section, or is subject to forfeiture under this section.

(B) Property used as a family residence and owned by two or more inhabitants, one of whom had no knowledge of its unlawful use.

(c) (1) If the prosecuting agency proceeds under subdivision (a), that agency shall, in conjunction with the criminal proceeding, file a petition for forfeiture with the superior court of the county in which the defendant has been charged with the commission of any of the crimes listed in subdivision (a) of Section 597.5 or subdivision (b) of Section 597b, that shall allege that the defendant has committed those crimes and the property is forfeitable pursuant to subdivision (a).

(2) The prosecuting agency shall make service of process of a notice regarding that petition upon every individual who may have a property interest in the alleged proceeds, and that notice shall state that any interested party may file a verified claim with the superior court stating the amount of the party's claimed interest and an affirmation or denial of the prosecuting agency's allegation.

(3) If the notices cannot be served by registered mail or personal delivery, the notices shall be published for at least three consecutive weeks in a newspaper of general circulation in the county where the property is located.

(4) If the property alleged to be subject to forfeiture is real property, the prosecuting agency shall, at the time of filing the petition for forfeiture, record a lis pendens in each county in which real property alleged to be subject to forfeiture is located.

(5) The judgment of forfeiture shall not affect the interest of any third party in real property that was acquired prior to the recording of the lis pendens.

(6) All notices shall set forth the time within which a claim of interest in the property seized is required to be filed pursuant to this section.

(d) Any person claiming an interest in the property or proceeds seized may, at any time within 30 days from the date of the first publication of the notice of seizure, or within 30 days after receipt of the actual notice, file with the superior court of the county in which the action is pending a verified claim stating his or her interest in the property or proceeds. A verified copy of the claim shall be given by the claimant to the Attorney General, or the district or city attorney, whichever is the prosecuting agency of the underlying crime.

(e) (1) If, at the end of the time set forth in subdivision (d), an interested person, other than the defendant, has not filed a claim, the court, upon a motion, shall declare that the person has defaulted upon his or her alleged interest, and that interest shall be subject to forfeiture upon proof of the elements of subdivision (b).

(2) The defendant may admit or deny that the property is subject to forfeiture pursuant to this section. If the defendant fails to admit or deny, or fails to file a claim of interest in the property or proceeds, the court shall enter a response of denial on behalf of the defendant.

(f) (1) The forfeiture proceeding shall be set for hearing in the superior court in which the underlying criminal offense will be tried.

(2) If the defendant is found guilty of the underlying offense, the issue of forfeiture shall be promptly tried, either before the same jury or before a new jury in the discretion of the court, unless waived by the consent of all parties.

(g) At the forfeiture hearing, the prosecuting agency shall have the burden of establishing beyond a reasonable doubt that the defendant was engaged in any of the crimes described in subdivision (a) of Section 597.5 or subdivision (b) of Section 597b and that the property comes within the provisions of subdivision (b).

(h) Concurrent with, or subsequent to, the filing of the petition, the prosecuting agency may move the superior court for the following pendente lite orders to preserve the status quo of the property alleged in the petition of forfeiture:

(1) An injunction to restrain all interested parties and enjoin them from transferring, encumbering, hypothecating, or otherwise disposing of that property.

(2) Appointment of a receiver to take possession of, care for, manage, and operate the assets and properties so that the property may be maintained and preserved.

(i) (1) No preliminary injunction may be granted or receiver appointed without notice to the interested parties and a hearing to determine that the order is necessary to preserve the property, pending the outcome of the criminal proceedings, and that there is probable cause to believe that the property alleged in the forfeiture proceedings are proceeds or property interests forfeitable under subdivision (a). However, a temporary restraining order may issue pending that hearing pursuant to the provisions of Section 527 of the Code of Civil Procedure.

(2) Notwithstanding any other provision of law, the court, when granting or issuing these orders may order a surety bond or undertaking to preserve the property interests of the interested parties. The court shall, in making its orders, seek to protect the interest of those who may be involved in the same enterprise as the defendant, but who are not involved in any of the crimes described in subdivision (a) of Section 597.5 or subdivision (b) of Section 597b.

(j) If the trier of fact at the forfeiture hearing finds that the alleged property or proceeds are forfeitable pursuant to subdivision (a), and that the defendant was convicted of a crime listed in subdivision (a) of Section 597.5 or subdivision (b) of Section 597b, the court shall declare that property or proceeds forfeited to the state or local governmental entity, subject to distribution as provided in subdivision (l).

(k) (1) If the trier of fact at the forfeiture hearing finds that the alleged property is forfeitable pursuant to subdivision (a) but does not find that a person holding a valid lien, mortgage, security interest, or interest under a conditional sales contract acquired that interest with actual knowledge that the property was to be used for a purpose for which forfeiture is permitted, and the amount due to that person is less than the appraised value of the property, that person may pay to the state or the local governmental entity that initiated the forfeiture proceeding the amount of the registered owner's equity, which shall be deemed to be the difference between the appraised value and the amount of the lien, mortgage, security interest, or interest under a conditional sales contract. Upon that payment, the state or local governmental entity shall relinquish all claims to the property.

(2) If the holder of the interest elects not to make that payment to the state or local governmental entity, the property shall be deemed forfeited to the state or local governmental entity.

(3) The appraised value shall be determined as of the date judgment is entered either by agreement between the legal owner and the governmental entity involved, or if they cannot agree, then by a court-appointed appraiser for the county in which the action is brought.

(4) If the amount due to a person holding a valid lien, mortgage, security interest, or interest under a conditional sales contract is less than the value of the property and the person elects not to make payment to the governmental entity, the property shall be sold at public auction by the Department of General Services or by the local governmental entity which shall provide notice of that sale by one publication in a newspaper published and circulated in the city, community, or locality where the sale is to take place. Proceeds of the sale shall be distributed pursuant to subdivision (l).

(l) Notwithstanding that no response or claim has been filed pursuant to subdivision (d), in all cases where property is forfeited pursuant to this section and is sold by the Department of General Services or a local governmental entity, the property forfeited or the proceeds of the sale shall be distributed by the state or local governmental entity, as follows:

(1) To the bona fide or innocent purchaser, conditional sales vendor, or holder of a valid lien, mortgage, or security interest, if any, up to the amount of his or her interest in the property or proceeds, when the court declaring the forfeiture orders a distribution to that person. The court shall endeavor to discover all those lienholders and protect their interests and may, at its discretion, order the proceeds placed in escrow for a period not to exceed 60 additional days to ensure that all valid claims are received and processed.

(2) To the Department of General Services or local governmental entity for all expenditures made or incurred by it in connection with the sale of the property, including expenditures for any necessary repairs, storage, or transportation of any property seized under this section.

(3) To local nonprofit organizations exempt under Section 501(c)(3) of the Internal Revenue Code, the primary activities of which include ongoing rescue, foster, or other care of animals that are the victims of cockfighting or dogfighting, and to law enforcement entities, including multiagency task forces, that actively investigate and prosecute animal fighting crimes.

(4) Any remaining funds not fully distributed to organizations or entities pursuant to paragraph (3) shall be deposited in an escrow account or restricted fund to be distributed as soon as possible in accordance with paragraph (3).

(Amended by Stats. 2011, Ch. 562, Sec. 3. (SB 425) Effective January 1, 2012.)
598a.

(a) Every person is guilty of a misdemeanor who kills any dog or cat with the sole intent of selling or giving away the pelt of such animal.

(b) Every person is guilty of a misdemeanor who possesses, imports into this state, sells, buys, gives away, or accepts any pelt of a dog or cat with the sole intent of selling or giving away the pelt of the dog or cat, or who possesses, imports into this state, sells, buys, gives away, or accepts any dog or cat, with the sole intent of killing or having killed such dog or cat for the purpose of selling or giving away the pelt of such animal.

(Added by Stats. 1973, Ch. 778.)
598b.

(a) Every person is guilty of a misdemeanor who possesses, imports into, or exports from, this state, sells, buys, gives away, or accepts any carcass or part of any carcass of any animal traditionally or commonly kept as a pet or companion with the intent of using or having another person use any part of that carcass for food.

(b) Every person is guilty of a misdemeanor who possesses, imports into, or exports from, this state, sells, buys, gives away, or accepts any animal traditionally or commonly kept as a pet or companion with the intent of killing or having another person kill that animal for the purpose of using or having another person use any part of the animal for food.

(c) This section shall not be construed to interfere with the production, marketing, or disposal of any livestock, poultry, fish, shellfish, or any other agricultural commodity produced in this state. Nor shall this section be construed to interfere with the lawful killing of wildlife, or the lawful killing of any other animal under the laws of this state pertaining to game animals.

(Amended by Stats. 1996, Ch. 381, Sec. 1. Effective January 1, 1997.)
598c.

(a) Notwithstanding any other provision of law, it is unlawful for any person to possess, to import into or export from the state, or to sell, buy, give away, hold, or accept any horse with the intent of killing, or having another kill, that horse, if that person knows or should have known that any part of that horse will be used for human consumption.

(b) For purposes of this section, "horse" means any equine, including any horse, pony, burro, or mule.

(c) Violation of this section is a felony punishable by imprisonment in the state prison for 16 months, or two or three years.

(d) It is not the intent of this section to affect any commonly accepted commercial, noncommercial, recreational, or sporting activity that relates to horses.

(e) It is not the intent of this section to affect any existing law that relates to horse taxation or zoning.

(Amended (as amended by Stats. 2011, Ch. 15) by Stats. 2011, Ch. 39, Sec. 18. (AB 117) Effective June 30, 2011. Operative October 1, 2011, pursuant to Secs. 68 and 69 of Ch. 39. Note: This section was added on Nov. 3, 1998, by initiative Prop. 6.)
598d.

(a) Notwithstanding any other provision of law, horsemeat may not be offered for sale for human consumption. No restaurant, cafe, or other public eating place may offer horsemeat for human consumption.

(b) Violation of this section is a misdemeanor punishable by a fine of not more than one thousand dollars ($1,000), or by confinement in jail for not less than 30 days nor more than two years, or by both that fine and confinement.

(c) A second or subsequent offense under this section is punishable by imprisonment in the state prison for not less than two years nor more than five years.

(Amended (as amended by Stats. 2011, Ch. 15) by Stats. 2011, Ch. 39, Sec. 19. (AB 117) Effective June 30, 2011. Operative October 1, 2011, pursuant to Secs. 68 and 69 of Ch. 39. Note: This section was added on Nov. 3, 1998, by initiative Prop. 6.)
599.

Every person is guilty of a misdemeanor who:

(a) Sells or gives away, any live chicks, rabbits, ducklings, or other fowl as a prize for, or as an inducement to enter, any contest, game or other competition or as an inducement to enter a place of amusement or place of business; or

(b) Dyes or otherwise artificially colors any live chicks, rabbits, ducklings or other fowl, or sells, offers for sale, or gives away any live chicks, rabbits, ducklings, or other fowl which has been dyed or artificially colored; or

(c) Maintains or possesses any live chicks, rabbits, ducklings, or other fowl for the purpose of sale or display without adequate facilities for supplying food, water and temperature control needed to maintain the health of such fowl or rabbit; or

(d) Sells, offers for sale, barters, or for commercial purposes gives away, any live chicks, rabbits, ducklings, or other fowl on any street or highway. This section shall not be construed to prohibit established hatchery management procedures or the display, or sale of natural chicks, rabbits, ducklings, or other fowl in proper facilities by dealers, hatcheries, poultrymen, or stores regularly engaged in the business of selling the same.

(Amended by Stats. 1967, Ch. 708.)
599a.

When complaint is made, on oath, to any magistrate authorized to issue warrants in criminal cases, that the complainant believes that any provision of law relating to, or in any way affecting, dumb animals or birds, is being, or is about to be violated in any particular building or place, the magistrate must issue and deliver immediately a warrant directed to any sheriff, police or peace officer or officer of any incorporated association qualified as provided by law, authorizing him to enter and search that building or place, and to arrest any person there present violating, or attempting to violate, any law relating to, or in any way affecting, dumb animals or birds, and to bring that person before some court or magistrate of competent jurisdiction, within the city, city and county, or judicial district within which the offense has been committed or attempted, to be dealt with according to law, and the attempt must be held to be a violation of Section 597.

(Amended by Stats. 1996, Ch. 872, Sec. 112. Effective January 1, 1997.)
599aa.

(a) Any authorized officer making an arrest under Section 597.5 shall, and any authorized officer making an arrest under Section 597b, 597c, 597j, or 599a may, lawfully take possession of all birds or animals and all paraphernalia, implements, or other property or things used or employed, or about to be employed, in the violation of any of the provisions of this code relating to the fighting of birds or animals that can be used in animal or bird fighting, in training animals or birds to fight, or to inflict pain or cruelty upon animals or birds with respect to animal or bird fighting.

(b) Upon taking possession, the officer shall inventory the items seized and question the persons present as to the identity of the owner or owners of the items. The inventory list shall identify the location where the items were seized, the names of the persons from whom the property was seized, and the names of any known owners of the property. Any person claiming ownership or possession of any item shall be provided with a signed copy of the inventory list, which shall identify the seizing officer and his or her employing agency. If no person claims ownership or possession of the items, a copy of the inventory list shall be left at the location from which the items were seized.

(c) The officer shall file with the magistrate before whom the complaint against the arrested person is made, a copy of the inventory list and an affidavit stating the affiant's basis for his or her belief that the property and items taken were in violation of this code. On receipt of the affidavit, the magistrate shall order the items seized to be held until the final disposition of any charges filed in the case subject to subdivision (e).

(d) All animals and birds seized shall, at the discretion of the seizing officer, be taken promptly to an appropriate animal storage facility. For purposes of this subdivision, an appropriate animal storage facility is one in which the animals or birds may be stored humanely. However, if an appropriate animal storage facility is not available, the officer may cause the animals or birds used in committing or possessed for the purpose of the alleged offenses to remain at the location at which they were found. In determining whether it is more humane to leave the animals or birds at the location at which they were found than to take the animals or birds to an animal storage facility, the officer shall, at a minimum, consider the difficulty of transporting the animals or birds and the adequacy of the available animal storage facility. When the officer does not seize and transport all animals or birds to a storage facility, he or she shall do both of the following:

(1) Seize a representative sample of animals or birds for evidentiary purposes from the animals or birds found at the site of the alleged offenses. The animals or birds seized as a representative sample shall be transported to an appropriate animal storage facility.

(2) Cause all animals or birds used in committing or possessed for the purpose of the alleged offenses to be banded, tagged, or marked by microchip, and photographed or video recorded for evidentiary purposes.

(e) (1) If ownership of the seized animals or birds cannot be determined after reasonable efforts, the officer or other person named and designated in the order as custodian of the animals or birds may, after holding the animals and birds for a period of not less than 10 days, petition the magistrate for permission to humanely destroy or otherwise dispose of the animals or birds. The petition shall be published for three successive days in a newspaper of general circulation. The magistrate shall hold a hearing on the petition not less than 10 days after seizure of the animals or birds, after which he or she may order the animals or birds to be humanely destroyed or otherwise disposed of, or to be retained by the officer or person with custody until the conviction or final discharge of the arrested person. No animal or bird may be destroyed or otherwise disposed of until four days after the order.

(2) Paragraph (1) shall apply only to those animals and birds seized under any of the following circumstances:

(A) After having been used in violation of any of the provisions of this code relating to the fighting of birds or animals.

(B) At the scene or site of a violation of any of the provisions of this code relating to the fighting of birds or animals.

(f) Upon the conviction of the arrested person, all property seized shall be adjudged by the court to be forfeited and shall then be destroyed or otherwise disposed of as the court may order. Upon the conviction of the arrested person, the court may order the person to make payment to the appropriate public entity for the costs incurred in the housing, care, feeding, and treatment of the animals or birds. Each person convicted in connection with a particular animal or bird, excluding any person convicted as a spectator pursuant to Section 597b or 597c, or subdivision (b) of Section 597.5, may be held jointly and severally liable for restitution pursuant to this subdivision. This payment shall be in addition to any other fine or other sentence ordered by the court. The court shall specify in the order that the public entity shall not enforce the order until the defendant satisfies all other outstanding fines, penalties, assessments, restitution fines, and restitution orders. The court may relieve any convicted person of the obligation to make payment pursuant to this subdivision for good cause but shall state the reasons for that decision in the record. In the event of the acquittal or final discharge without conviction of the arrested person, the court shall, on demand, direct the delivery of the property held in custody to the owner. If the owner is unknown, the court shall order the animals or birds to be humanely destroyed or otherwise disposed of.

(Amended by Stats. 2009, Ch. 88, Sec. 72. (AB 176) Effective January 1, 2010.)
599b.
In this title, the word "animal" includes every dumb creature; the words "torment," "torture," and "cruelty" include every act, omission, or neglect whereby unnecessary or unjustifiable physical pain or suffering is caused or permitted; and the words "owner" and "person" include corporations as well as individuals; and the knowledge and acts of any agent of, or person employed by, a corporation in regard to animals transported, owned, or employed by, or in the custody of, the corporation, must be held to be the act and knowledge of the corporation as well as the agent or employee.
(Amended by Stats. 2002, Ch. 787, Sec. 14. Effective January 1, 2003.)
599c.
No part of this title shall be construed as interfering with any of the laws of this state known as the "game laws," or any laws for or against the destruction of certain birds, nor must this title be construed as interfering with the right to destroy any venomous reptile, or any animal known as dangerous to life, limb, or property, or to interfere with the right to kill all animals used for food, or with properly conducted scientific experiments or investigations performed under the authority of the faculty of a regularly incorporated medical college or university of this state.
(Added by Stats. 1905, Ch. 519.)
599d.
(a) It is the policy of the state that no adoptable animal should be euthanized if it can be adopted into a suitable home. Adoptable animals include only those animals eight weeks of age or older that, at or subsequent to the time the animal is impounded or otherwise taken into possession, have manifested no sign of a behavioral or temperamental defect that could pose a health or safety risk or otherwise make the animal unsuitable for placement as a pet, and have manifested no sign of disease, injury, or congenital or hereditary condition that adversely affects the health of the animal or that is likely to adversely affect the animal's health in the future.
(b) It is the policy of the state that no treatable animal should be euthanized. A treatable animal shall include any animal that is not adoptable but that could become adoptable with reasonable efforts. This subdivision, by itself, shall not be the basis of liability for damages regarding euthanasia.
(Added by Stats. 1998, Ch. 752, Sec. 20. Effective January 1, 1999.)
599e.
Every animal which is unfit, by reason of its physical condition, for the purpose for which such animals are usually employed, and when there is no reasonable probability of such animal ever becoming fit for the purpose for which it is usually employed, shall be by the owner or lawful possessor of the same, deprived of life within 12 hours after being notified by any peace officer, officer of said society, or employee of a pound or animal regulation department of a public agency who is a veterinarian, to kill the same, and such owner, possessor, or person omitting or refusing to comply with the provisions of this section shall, upon conviction, be deemed guilty of a misdemeanor, and after such conviction the court or magistrate having jurisdiction of such offense shall order any peace officer, officer of said society, or officer of a pound or animal regulation department of a public agency, to immediately kill such animal; provided, that this shall not apply to such owner keeping any old or diseased animal belonging to him on his own premises with proper care.
(Amended by Stats. 1963, Ch. 1583.)
599f.
(a) No slaughterhouse, stockyard, auction, market agency, or dealer shall buy, sell, or receive a nonambulatory animal.
(b) No slaughterhouse shall process, butcher, or sell meat or products of nonambulatory animals for human consumption.
(c) No slaughterhouse shall hold a nonambulatory animal without taking immediate action to humanely euthanize the animal.
(d) No stockyard, auction, market agency, or dealer shall hold a nonambulatory animal without taking immediate action to humanely euthanize the animal or to provide immediate veterinary treatment.
(e) While in transit or on the premises of a stockyard, auction, market agency, dealer, or slaughterhouse, a nonambulatory animal may not be dragged at any time, or pushed with equipment at any time, but shall be moved with a sling or on a stoneboat or other sled-like or wheeled conveyance.
(f) No person shall sell, consign, or ship any nonambulatory animal for the purpose of delivering a nonambulatory animal to a slaughterhouse, stockyard, auction, market agency, or dealer.
(g) No person shall accept a nonambulatory animal for transport or delivery to a slaughterhouse, stockyard, auction, market agency, or dealer.
(h) A violation of this section is subject to imprisonment in a county jail for a period not to exceed one year, or by a fine of not more than twenty thousand dollars ($20,000), or by both that fine and imprisonment.
(i) As used in this section, "nonambulatory" means unable to stand and walk without assistance.
(j) As used in this section, "animal" means live cattle, swine, sheep, or goats.

(k) As used in this section, "humanely euthanize" means to kill by a mechanical, chemical, or electrical method that rapidly and effectively renders the animal insensitive to pain.
(Amended by Stats. 2009, Ch. 140, Sec. 141. (AB 1164) Effective January 1, 2010.)
600.
(a) Any person who willfully and maliciously and with no legal justification strikes, beats, kicks, cuts, stabs, shoots with a firearm, administers any poison or other harmful or stupefying substance to, or throws, hurls, or projects at, or places any rock, object, or other substance which is used in such a manner as to be capable of producing injury and likely to produce injury, on or in the path of, a horse being used by, or a dog under the supervision of, a peace officer in the discharge or attempted discharge of his or her duties, or a volunteer who is acting under the direct supervision of a peace officer in the discharge or attempted discharge of his or her assigned volunteer duties, is guilty of a public offense. If the injury inflicted is a serious injury, as described in subdivision (c), the person shall be punished by imprisonment pursuant to subdivision (h) of Section 1170 for 16 months, two or three years, or in a county jail for not exceeding one year, or by a fine not exceeding two thousand dollars ($2,000), or by both a fine and imprisonment. If the injury inflicted is not a serious injury, the person shall be punished by imprisonment in the county jail for not exceeding one year, or by a fine not exceeding one thousand dollars ($1,000), or by both a fine and imprisonment.
(b) Any person who willfully and maliciously and with no legal justification interferes with or obstructs a horse or dog being used by a peace officer in the discharge or attempted discharge of his or her duties, or a volunteer who is acting under the direct supervision of a peace officer in the discharge or attempted discharge of his or her assigned volunteer duties, by frightening, teasing, agitating, harassing, or hindering the horse or dog shall be punished by imprisonment in a county jail for not exceeding one year, or by a fine not exceeding one thousand dollars ($1,000), or by both a fine and imprisonment.
(c) Any person who, in violation of this section, and with intent to inflict that injury or death, personally causes the death, destruction, or serious physical injury including bone fracture, loss or impairment of function of any bodily member, wounds requiring extensive suturing, or serious crippling, of a horse or dog, shall, upon conviction of a felony under this section, in addition and consecutive to the punishment prescribed for the felony, be punished by an additional term of imprisonment pursuant to subdivision (h) of Section 1170 for one year.
(d) Any person who, in violation of this section, and with the intent to inflict that injury, personally causes great bodily injury, as defined in Section 12022.7, to any person not an accomplice, shall, upon conviction of a felony under this section, in addition and consecutive to the punishment prescribed for the felony, be punished by an additional term of imprisonment in the state prison for two years unless the conduct described in this subdivision is an element of any other offense of which the person is convicted or receives an enhancement under Section 12022.7.
(e) A defendant convicted of a violation of this section shall be ordered to make restitution to the agency owning the animal and employing the peace officer, to a volunteer who is acting under the direct supervision of a peace officer who is using his or her horse or supervising his or her dog in the performance of his or her assigned duties, or to the agency that provides, or the individual who provides, veterinary health care coverage or veterinary care for a horse or dog being used by, or under the supervision of, a volunteer who is acting under the direct supervision of a peace officer for any veterinary bills, replacement costs of the animal if it is disabled or killed, and, if applicable, the salary of the peace officer for the period of time his or her services are lost to the agency.
(Amended by Stats. 2015, Ch. 201, Sec. 1. (AB 794) Effective January 1, 2016.)
600.2.
(a) It is a crime for any person to permit any dog which is owned, harbored, or controlled by him or her to cause injury to or the death of any guide, signal, or service dog, as defined by Section 54.1 of the Civil Code, while the guide, signal, or service dog is in discharge of its duties.
(b) A violation of this section is an infraction punishable by a fine not to exceed two hundred fifty dollars ($250) if the injury or death to any guide, signal, or service dog is caused by the person's failure to exercise ordinary care in the control of his or her dog.
(c) A violation of this section is a misdemeanor if the injury or death to any guide, signal, or service dog is caused by the person's reckless disregard in the exercise of control over his or her dog, under circumstances that constitute such a departure from the conduct of a reasonable person as to be incompatible with a proper regard for the safety and life of any guide, signal, or service dog. A violation of this subdivision shall be punishable by imprisonment in a county jail not exceeding one year, or by a fine of not less than two thousand five hundred dollars ($2,500) nor more than five thousand dollars ($5,000), or both. The court shall consider the costs ordered pursuant to subdivision (d) when determining the amount of any fines.
(d) In any case in which a defendant is convicted of a violation of this section, the defendant shall be ordered to make restitution to the person with a disability who has custody or ownership of the guide, signal, or service dog for any veterinary bills and replacement costs of the dog if it is disabled or killed, or other reasonable costs deemed appropriate by the court. The costs ordered pursuant to this subdivision shall be paid prior to any fines. The person with the disability may apply for compensation by the California Victim Compensation Board pursuant to Chapter 5 (commencing with Section 13950) of Part 4 of Division 3 of Title 2 of the Government Code, in an amount not to exceed ten thousand dollars ($10,000).
(Amended by Stats. 2016, Ch. 31, Sec. 233. (SB 836) Effective June 27, 2016.)
600.5.
(a) Any person who intentionally causes injury to or the death of any guide, signal, or service dog, as defined by Section 54.1 of the Civil Code, while the dog is in discharge of its duties, is guilty of a misdemeanor, punishable by imprisonment in a county jail not exceeding one year, or by a fine not exceeding ten thousand dollars ($10,000), or by both a fine and imprisonment. The court shall consider the costs ordered pursuant to subdivision (b) when determining the amount of any fines.
(b) In any case in which a defendant is convicted of a violation of this section, the defendant shall be ordered to make restitution to the person with a disability who has custody or ownership of the dog for any veterinary bills and replacement costs of the dog if it is disabled or killed, or other reasonable costs deemed appropriate by the court. The costs ordered pursuant to this subdivision shall be paid prior to any fines. The person with the disability may apply for compensation by the California Victim Compensation Board pursuant to Chapter 5 (commencing with Section 13950) of Part 4 of Division 3 of Title 2 of the Government Code, in an amount not to exceed ten thousand dollars ($10,000).
(Amended by Stats. 2016, Ch. 31, Sec. 234. (SB 836) Effective June 27, 2016.)
601.
(a) Any person is guilty of trespass who makes a credible threat to cause serious bodily injury, as defined in subdivision (a) of Section 417.6, to another person with the intent to place that other person in reasonable fear for his or her safety, or the safety of his or her immediate family, as defined in subdivision (l) of Section 646.9, and who does any of the following:
(1) Within 30 days of the threat, unlawfully enters into the residence or real property contiguous to the residence of the person threatened without lawful purpose, and with the intent to execute the threat against the target of the threat.
(2) Within 30 days of the threat, knowing that the place is the threatened person's workplace, unlawfully enters into the workplace of the person threatened and carries out

an act or acts to locate the threatened person within the workplace premises without lawful purpose, and with the intent to execute the threat against the target of the threat.

(b) Subdivision (a) shall not apply if the residence, real property, or workplace described in paragraph (1) or (2) that is entered is the residence, real property, or workplace of the person making the threat.

(c) This section shall not apply to any person who is engaged in labor union activities which are permitted to be carried out on the property by the California Agricultural Labor Relations Act, Part 3.5 (commencing with Section 1140) of Division 2 of the Labor Code, or by the National Labor Relations Act.

(d) A violation of this section shall be punishable by imprisonment pursuant to subdivision (h) of Section 1170, or by imprisonment in a county jail not exceeding one year, or by a fine not exceeding two thousand dollars ($2,000), or by both that fine and imprisonment.

(Amended by Stats. 2011, Ch. 15, Sec. 415. (AB 109) Effective April 4, 2011. Operative October 1, 2011, by Sec. 636 of Ch. 15, as amended by Stats. 2011, Ch. 39, Sec. 68.)

602.

Except as provided in subdivisions (u), (v), and (x), and Section 602.8, every person who willfully commits a trespass by any of the following acts is guilty of a misdemeanor:

(a) Cutting down, destroying, or injuring any kind of wood or timber standing or growing upon the lands of another.

(b) Carrying away any kind of wood or timber lying on those lands.

(c) Maliciously injuring or severing from the freehold of another anything attached to it, or its produce.

(d) Digging, taking, or carrying away from any lot situated within the limits of any incorporated city, without the license of the owner or legal occupant, any earth, soil, or stone.

(e) Digging, taking, or carrying away from land in any city or town laid down on the map or plan of the city, or otherwise recognized or established as a street, alley, avenue, or park, without the license of the proper authorities, any earth, soil, or stone.

(f) Maliciously tearing down, damaging, mutilating, or destroying any sign, signboard, or notice placed upon, or affixed to, any property belonging to the state, or to any city, county, city and county, town, or village, or upon any property of any person, by the state or by an automobile association, which sign, signboard, or notice is intended to indicate or designate a road or a highway, or is intended to direct travelers from one point to another, or relates to fires, fire control, or any other matter involving the protection of the property, or putting up, affixing, fastening, printing, or painting upon any property belonging to the state, or to any city, county, town, or village, or dedicated to the public, or upon any property of any person, without license from the owner, any notice, advertisement, or designation of, or any name for any commodity, whether for sale or otherwise, or any picture, sign, or device intended to call attention to it.

(g) Entering upon any lands owned by any other person whereon oysters or other shellfish are planted or growing; or injuring, gathering, or carrying away any oysters or other shellfish planted, growing, or on any of those lands, whether covered by water or not, without the license of the owner or legal occupant; or damaging, destroying, or removing, or causing to be removed, damaged, or destroyed, any stakes, marks, fences, or signs intended to designate the boundaries and limits of any of those lands.

(h) (1) Entering upon lands or buildings owned by any other person without the license of the owner or legal occupant, where signs forbidding trespass are displayed, and whereon cattle, goats, pigs, sheep, fowl, or any other animal is being raised, bred, fed, or held for the purpose of food for human consumption; or injuring, gathering, or carrying away any animal being housed on any of those lands, without the license of the owner or legal occupant; or damaging, destroying, or removing, or causing to be removed, damaged, or destroyed, any stakes, marks, fences, or signs intended to designate the boundaries and limits of any of those lands.

(2) In order for there to be a violation of this subdivision, the trespass signs under paragraph (1) shall be displayed at intervals not less than three per mile along all exterior boundaries and at all roads and trails entering the land.

(3) This subdivision shall not be construed to preclude prosecution or punishment under any other law, including, but not limited to, grand theft or any provision that provides for a greater penalty or longer term of imprisonment.

(i) Willfully opening, tearing down, or otherwise destroying any fence on the enclosed land of another, or opening any gate, bar, or fence of another and willfully leaving it open without the written permission of the owner, or maliciously tearing down, mutilating, or destroying any sign, signboard, or other notice forbidding shooting on private property.

(j) Building fires upon any lands owned by another where signs forbidding trespass are displayed at intervals not greater than one mile along the exterior boundaries and at all roads and trails entering the lands, without first having obtained written permission from the owner of the lands or the owner's agent, or the person in lawful possession.

(k) Entering any lands, whether unenclosed or enclosed by fence, for the purpose of injuring any property or property rights or with the intention of interfering with, obstructing, or injuring any lawful business or occupation carried on by the owner of the land, the owner's agent, or the person in lawful possession.

(l) Entering any lands under cultivation or enclosed by fence, belonging to, or occupied by, another, or entering upon uncultivated or unenclosed lands where signs forbidding trespass are displayed at intervals not less than three to the mile along all exterior boundaries and at all roads and trails entering the lands without the written permission of the owner of the land, the owner's agent, or the person in lawful possession, and any of the following:

(1) Refusing or failing to leave the lands immediately upon being requested by the owner of the land, the owner's agent, or by the person in lawful possession to leave the lands.

(2) Tearing down, mutilating, or destroying any sign, signboard, or notice forbidding trespass or hunting on the lands.

(3) Removing, injuring, unlocking, or tampering with any lock on any gate on or leading into the lands.

(4) Discharging any firearm.

(m) Entering and occupying real property or structures of any kind without the consent of the owner, the owner's agent, or the person in lawful possession.

(n) Driving any vehicle, as defined in Section 670 of the Vehicle Code, upon real property belonging to, or lawfully occupied by, another and known not to be open to the general public, without the consent of the owner, the owner's agent, or the person in lawful possession. This subdivision does not apply to any person described in Section 22350 of the Business and Professions Code who is making a lawful service of process, provided that upon exiting the vehicle, the person proceeds immediately to attempt the service of process, and leaves immediately upon completing the service of process or upon the request of the owner, the owner's agent, or the person in lawful possession.

(o) Refusing or failing to leave land, real property, or structures belonging to or lawfully occupied by another and not open to the general public, upon being requested to leave by (1) a peace officer at the request of the owner, the owner's agent, or the person in lawful possession, and upon being informed by the peace officer that he or she is acting at the request of the owner, the owner's agent, or the person in lawful possession, or (2) the owner, the owner's agent, or the person in lawful possession. The owner, the owner's agent, or the person in lawful possession shall make a separate request to the peace officer on each occasion when the peace officer's assistance in dealing with a trespass is requested. However, a single request for a peace officer's assistance may be made to cover a limited period of time not to exceed 30 days and identified by specific dates, during which there is a fire hazard or the owner, owner's agent, or person in lawful possession is absent from the premises or property. In addition, a single request

for a peace officer's assistance may be made for a period not to exceed 12 months when the premises or property is closed to the public and posted as being closed. The requestor shall inform the law enforcement agency to which the request was made when the assistance is no longer desired, before the period not exceeding 12 months expires. The request for assistance shall expire upon transfer of ownership of the property or upon a change in the person in lawful possession. However, this subdivision does not apply to persons engaged in lawful labor union activities which are permitted to be carried out on the property by the Alatorre-Zenovich-Dunlap-Berman Agricultural Labor Relations Act of 1975 (Part 3.5 (commencing with Section 1140) of Division 2 of the Labor Code) or by the federal National Labor Relations Act. For purposes of this section, land, real property, or structures owned or operated by any housing authority for tenants, as defined in Section 34213.5 of the Health and Safety Code, constitutes property not open to the general public; however, this subdivision shall not apply to persons on the premises who are engaging in activities protected by the California or United States Constitution, or to persons who are on the premises at the request of a resident or management and who are not loitering or otherwise suspected of violating or actually violating any law or ordinance.

(p) Entering upon any lands declared closed to entry as provided in Section 4256 of the Public Resources Code, if the closed areas have been posted with notices declaring the closure, at intervals not greater than one mile along the exterior boundaries or along roads and trails passing through the lands.

(q) Refusing or failing to leave a public building of a public agency during those hours of the day or night when the building is regularly closed to the public upon being requested to do so by a regularly employed guard, watchperson, or custodian of the public agency owning or maintaining the building or property, if the surrounding circumstances would indicate to a reasonable person that the person has no apparent lawful business to pursue.

(r) Knowingly skiing in an area or on a ski trail that is closed to the public and that has signs posted indicating the closure.

(s) Refusing or failing to leave a hotel or motel, where he or she has obtained accommodations and has refused to pay for those accommodations, upon request of the proprietor or manager, and the occupancy is exempt, pursuant to subdivision (b) of Section 1940 of the Civil Code, from Chapter 2 (commencing with Section 1940) of Title 5 of Part 4 of Division 3 of the Civil Code. For purposes of this subdivision, occupancy at a hotel or motel for a continuous period of 30 days or less shall, in the absence of a written agreement to the contrary, or other written evidence of a periodic tenancy of indefinite duration, be exempt from Chapter 2 (commencing with Section 1940) of Title 5 of Part 4 of Division 3 of the Civil Code.

(t) (1) Entering upon private property, including contiguous land, real property, or structures thereon belonging to the same owner, whether or not generally open to the public, after having been informed by a peace officer at the request of the owner, the owner's agent, or the person in lawful possession, and upon being informed by the peace officer that he or she is acting at the request of the owner, the owner's agent, or the person in lawful possession, that the property is not open to the particular person; or refusing or failing to leave the property upon being asked to leave the property in the manner provided in this subdivision.

(2) This subdivision applies only to a person who has been convicted of a crime committed upon the particular private property.

(3) A single notification or request to the person as set forth above shall be valid and enforceable under this subdivision unless and until rescinded by the owner, the owner's agent, or the person in lawful possession of the property.

(4) Where the person has been convicted of a violent felony, as described in subdivision (c) of Section 667.5, this subdivision applies without time limitation. Where the person has been convicted of any other felony, this subdivision applies for no more than five years from the date of conviction. Where the person has been convicted of a misdemeanor, this subdivision applies for no more than two years from the date of conviction. Where the person was convicted for an infraction pursuant to Section 490.1, this subdivision applies for no more than one year from the date of conviction. This subdivision does not apply to convictions for any other infraction.

(u) (1) Knowingly entering, by an unauthorized person, upon any airport operations area, passenger vessel terminal, or public transit facility if the area has been posted with notices restricting access to authorized personnel only and the postings occur not greater than every 150 feet along the exterior boundary, to the extent, in the case of a passenger vessel terminal, as defined in subparagraph (B) of paragraph (3), that the exterior boundary extends shoreside. To the extent that the exterior boundary of a passenger vessel terminal operations area extends waterside, this prohibition applies if notices have been posted in a manner consistent with the requirements for the shoreside exterior boundary, or in any other manner approved by the captain of the port.

(2) A person convicted of a violation of paragraph (1) shall be punished as follows:

(A) By a fine not exceeding one hundred dollars ($100).

(B) By imprisonment in a county jail not exceeding six months, or by a fine not exceeding one thousand dollars ($1,000), or by both that fine and imprisonment, if the person refuses to leave the airport or passenger vessel terminal after being requested to leave by a peace officer or authorized personnel.

(C) By imprisonment in a county jail not exceeding six months, or by a fine not exceeding one thousand dollars ($1,000), or by both that fine and imprisonment, for a second or subsequent offense.

(3) As used in this subdivision, the following definitions shall control:

(A) "Airport operations area" means that part of the airport used by aircraft for landing, taking off, surface maneuvering, loading and unloading, refueling, parking, or maintenance, where aircraft support vehicles and facilities exist, and which is not for public use or public vehicular traffic.

(B) "Passenger vessel terminal" means only that portion of a harbor or port facility, as described in Section 105.105(a)(2) of Title 33 of the Code of Federal Regulations, with a secured area that regularly serves scheduled commuter or passenger operations. For the purposes of this section, "passenger vessel terminal" does not include any area designated a public access area pursuant to Section 105.106 of Title 33 of the Code of Federal Regulations.

(C) "Public transit facility" has the same meaning as specified in Section 171.7.

(D) "Authorized personnel" means any person who has a valid airport identification card issued by the airport operator or has a valid airline identification card recognized by the airport operator, or any person not in possession of an airport or airline identification card who is being escorted for legitimate purposes by a person with an airport or airline identification card. "Authorized personnel" also means any person who has a valid port identification card issued by the harbor operator, or who has a valid company identification card issued by a commercial maritime enterprise recognized by the harbor operator, or any other person who is being escorted for legitimate purposes by a person with a valid port or qualifying company identification card. "Authorized personnel" also means any person who has a valid public transit employee identification.

(E) "Airport" means any facility whose function is to support commercial aviation.

(v) (1) Except as permitted by federal law, intentionally avoiding submission to the screening and inspection of one's person and accessible property in accordance with the procedures being applied to control access when entering or reentering a sterile area of an airport, passenger vessel terminal, as defined in subdivision (u), or public transit facility, as defined in Section 171.7, if the sterile area is posted with a statement providing reasonable notice that prosecution may result from a trespass described in this subdivision, is a violation of this subdivision, punishable by a fine of not more than five hundred dollars ($500) for the first offense. A second and subsequent violation is a misdemeanor, punishable by imprisonment in a county jail for a period of not more than one year, or by a fine not to exceed one thousand dollars ($1,000), or by both that fine and imprisonment.

(2) Notwithstanding paragraph (1), if a first violation of this subdivision is responsible for the evacuation of an airport terminal, passenger vessel terminal, or public transit facility and is responsible in any part for delays or cancellations of scheduled flights or departures, it is punishable by imprisonment of not more than one year in a county jail.

(w) Refusing or failing to leave a battered women's shelter at any time after being requested to leave by a managing authority of the shelter.

(1) A person who is convicted of violating this subdivision shall be punished by imprisonment in a county jail for not more than one year.

(2) The court may order a defendant who is convicted of violating this subdivision to make restitution to a battered woman in an amount equal to the relocation expenses of the battered woman and her children if those expenses are incurred as a result of trespass by the defendant at a battered women's shelter.

(x) (1) Knowingly entering or remaining in a neonatal unit, maternity ward, or birthing center located in a hospital or clinic without lawful business to pursue therein, if the area has been posted so as to give reasonable notice restricting access to those with lawful business to pursue therein and the surrounding circumstances would indicate to a reasonable person that he or she has no lawful business to pursue therein. Reasonable notice is that which would give actual notice to a reasonable person, and is posted, at a minimum, at each entrance into the area.

(2) A person convicted of a violation of paragraph (1) shall be punished as follows:

(A) As an infraction, by a fine not exceeding one hundred dollars ($100).

(B) By imprisonment in a county jail not exceeding one year, or by a fine not exceeding one thousand dollars ($1,000), or by both that fine and imprisonment, if the person refuses to leave the posted area after being requested to leave by a peace officer or other authorized person.

(C) By imprisonment in a county jail not exceeding one year, or by a fine not exceeding two thousand dollars ($2,000), or by both that fine and imprisonment, for a second or subsequent offense.

(D) If probation is granted or the execution or imposition of sentencing is suspended for any person convicted under this subdivision, it shall be a condition of probation that the person participate in counseling, as designated by the court, unless the court finds good cause not to impose this requirement. The court shall require the person to pay for this counseling, if ordered, unless good cause not to pay is shown.

(y) Except as permitted by federal law, intentionally avoiding submission to the screening and inspection of one's person and accessible property in accordance with the procedures being applied to control access when entering or reentering a courthouse or a city, county, city and county, or state building if entrances to the courthouse or the city, county, city and county, or state building have been posted with a statement providing reasonable notice that prosecution may result from a trespass described in this subdivision.

(Amended by Stats. 2015, Ch. 303, Sec. 389. (AB 731) Effective January 1, 2016.)

602.1.

(a) Any person who intentionally interferes with any lawful business or occupation carried on by the owner or agent of a business establishment open to the public, by obstructing or intimidating those attempting to carry on business, or their customers, and who refuses to leave the premises of the business establishment after being requested to leave by the owner or the owner's agent, or by a peace officer acting at the request of the owner or owner's agent, is guilty of a misdemeanor, punishable by imprisonment in a county jail for up to 90 days, or by a fine of up to four hundred dollars ($400), or by both that imprisonment and fine.

(b) Any person who intentionally interferes with any lawful business carried on by the employees of a public agency open to the public, by obstructing or intimidating those attempting to carry on business, or those persons there to transact business with the public agency, and who refuses to leave the premises of the public agency after being requested to leave by the office manager or a supervisor of the public agency, or by a peace officer acting at the request of the office manager or a supervisor of the public agency, is guilty of a misdemeanor, punishable by imprisonment in a county jail for up to 90 days, or by a fine of up to four hundred dollars ($400), or by both that imprisonment and fine.

(c) Any person who intentionally interferes with any lawful business carried on by the employees of a public agency open to the public, by knowingly making a material misrepresentation of the law to those persons there to transact business with the public agency, and who refuses to leave the premises of the public agency after being requested to leave by the office manager or a supervisor of the public agency, or by a peace officer acting at the request of the office manager or a supervisor of the public agency, is guilty of an infraction, punishable by a fine of up to four hundred dollars ($400).

(d) This section shall not apply to any of the following persons:

(1) Any person engaged in lawful labor union activities that are permitted to be carried out on the property by state or federal law.

(2) Any person on the premises who is engaging in activities protected by the California Constitution or the United States Constitution.

(e) Nothing in this section shall be deemed to supersede the application of any other law.

(Amended by Stats. 2017, Ch. 381, Sec. 1. (AB 660) Effective January 1, 2018.)

602.2.

Any ordinance or resolution adopted by a county which requires written permission to enter vacant or unimproved private land from either the owner, the owner's agent, or the person in lawful possession of private land, shall not apply unless the land is immediately adjacent and contiguous to residential property, or enclosed by fence, or under cultivation, or posted with signs forbidding trespass, displayed at intervals of not less than three to a mile, along all exterior boundaries and at all roads and trails entering the private land.

(Added by Stats. 1986, Ch. 34, Sec. 1.)

602.3.

(a) A lodger who is subject to Section 1946.5 of the Civil Code and who remains on the premises of an owner-occupied dwelling unit after receipt of a notice terminating the hiring, and expiration of the notice period, provided in Section 1946.5 of the Civil Code is guilty of an infraction and may, pursuant to Section 837, be arrested for the offense by the owner, or in the event the owner is represented by a court-appointed conservator, executor, or administrator, by the owner's representative. Notwithstanding Section 853.5, the requirement of that section for release upon a written promise to appear shall not preclude an assisting peace officer from removing the person from the owner-occupied dwelling unit.

(b) The removal of a lodger from a dwelling unit by the owner pursuant to subdivision (a) is not a forcible entry under the provisions of Section 1159 of the Code of Civil Procedure and shall not be a basis for civil liability under that section.

(c) Chapter 5 (commencing with Section 1980) of Title 5 of Part 4 of Division 3 of the Civil Code applies to any personal property of the lodger which remains on the premises following the lodger's removal from the premises pursuant to this section.

(d) Nothing in this section shall be construed to limit the owner's right to have a lodger removed under other provisions of law.

(e) Except as provided in subdivision (b), nothing in this section shall be construed to limit or affect in any way any cause of action an owner or lodger may have for damages for any breach of the contract of the parties respecting the lodging.

(f) This section applies only to owner-occupied dwellings where a single lodger resides. Nothing in this section shall be construed to determine or affect in any way the rights of persons residing as lodgers in an owner-occupied dwelling where more than one lodger resides.

(Amended by Stats. 1991, Ch. 930, Sec. 1.)

602.4.

(a) A person who enters or remains on airport property owned by a city, county, or city and county, but located in another county, and sells, peddles, or offers for sale any goods, merchandise, property, or services of any kind whatsoever, including transportation services to, on, or from the airport property, to members of the public without the express written consent of the governing board of the airport property, or its duly authorized representative, is guilty of a misdemeanor.

(b) Nothing in this section affects the power of a county, city, or city and county to regulate the sale, peddling, or offering for sale of goods, merchandise, property, or services.

(c) For purposes of this section, when a charter-party carrier licensed by the Public Utilities Commission operates at an airport on a prearranged basis, as defined in Section 5360.5 of the Public Utilities Code, that operation shall not constitute the sale, peddling, or offering of goods, merchandise, property, or services.

(Amended by Stats. 2014, Ch. 323, Sec. 1. (SB 1430) Effective September 15, 2014.)

602.5.

(a) Every person other than a public officer or employee acting within the course and scope of his or her employment in performance of a duty imposed by law, who enters or remains in any noncommercial dwelling house, apartment, or other residential place without consent of the owner, his or her agent, or the person in lawful possession thereof, is guilty of a misdemeanor.

(b) Every person other than a public officer or an employee acting within the course and scope of his employment in performance of a duty imposed by law, who, without the consent of the owner, his or her agent, or the person in lawful possession thereof, enters or remains in any noncommercial dwelling house, apartment, or other residential place while a resident, or another person authorized to be in the dwelling, is present at any time during the course of the incident is guilty of aggravated trespass punishable by imprisonment in a county jail for not more than one year or by a fine of not more than one thousand dollars ($1,000), or by both that fine and imprisonment.

(c) If the court grants probation, it may order a person convicted of a misdemeanor under subdivision (b) to up to three years of supervised probation. It shall be a condition of probation that the person participate in counseling, as designated by the court.

(d) If a person is convicted of a misdemeanor under subdivision (b), the sentencing court shall also consider issuing an order restraining the defendant from any contact with the victim, that may be valid for up to three years, as determined by the court. In determining the length of the restraining order, the court shall consider, among other factors, the seriousness of the facts before the court, the probability of future violations, and the safety of the victim and his or her immediate family.

(e) Nothing in this section shall preclude prosecution under Section 459 or any other provision of law.

(Amended by Stats. 2000, Ch. 563, Sec. 1. Effective January 1, 2001.)

602.6.

Every person who enters or remains in, or upon, any state, county, district, or citrus fruit fair buildings or grounds, when the buildings or grounds are not open to the general public, after having been ordered or directed by a peace officer or a fair manager to leave the building or grounds and when the order or direction to leave is issued after determination that the person has no apparent lawful business or other legitimate reason for remaining on the property, and fails to identify himself or herself and account for his or her presence, is guilty of a misdemeanor.

(Added by Stats. 1990, Ch. 631, Sec. 1.)

602.7.

Every person who enters or remains on any property, facility, or vehicle owned by the San Francisco Bay Area Rapid Transit District or the Southern California Rapid Transit District, and sells or peddles any goods, merchandise, property, or services of any kind whatsoever on the property, facilities, or vehicles, without the express written consent of the governing board of the San Francisco Bay Area Rapid Transit District or the governing board of the Southern California Rapid Transit District, or its duly authorized representatives, is guilty of an infraction.

Nothing in this section affects the power of a county, city, transit district, or city and county to regulate the sale or peddling of goods, merchandise, property, or services.

(Added by Stats. 1986, Ch. 1232, Sec. 1.)

602.8.

(a) Any person who without the written permission of the landowner, the owner's agent, or the person in lawful possession of the land, willfully enters any lands under cultivation or enclosed by fence, belonging to, or occupied by, another, or who willfully enters upon uncultivated or unenclosed lands where signs forbidding trespass are displayed at intervals not less than three to the mile along all exterior boundaries and at all roads and trails entering the lands, is guilty of a public offense.

(b) Any person convicted of a violation of subdivision (a) shall be punished as follows:

(1) A first offense is an infraction punishable by a fine of seventy-five dollars ($75).

(2) A second offense on the same land or any contiguous land of the same landowner, without the permission of the landowner, the landowner's agent, or the person in lawful possession of the land, is an infraction punishable by a fine of two hundred fifty dollars ($250).

(3) A third or subsequent offense on the same land or any contiguous land of the same landowner, without the permission of the landowner, the landowner's agent, or the person in lawful possession of the land, is a misdemeanor.

(c) Subdivision (a) shall not apply to any of the following:

(1) Any person engaged in lawful labor union activities which are permitted to be carried out on property by the California Agricultural Labor Relations Act, Part 3.5 (commencing with Section 1140) of Division 2 of the Labor Code, or by the National Labor Relations Act.

(2) Any person on the premises who is engaging in activities protected by the California or United States Constitution.

(3) Any person described in Section 22350 of the Business and Professions Code who is making a lawful service of process.

(4) Any person licensed pursuant to Chapter 15 (commencing with Section 8700) of Division 3 of the Business and Professions Code who is engaged in the lawful practice of land surveying as authorized by Section 846.5 of the Civil Code.

(d) For any infraction charged pursuant to this section, the defendant shall have the option to forfeit bail in lieu of making a court appearance. Notwithstanding subdivision (e) of Section 853.6, if the offender elects to forfeit bail pursuant to this subdivision, no further proceedings shall be had in the case.

(Amended by Stats. 2003, Ch. 101, Sec. 1. Effective January 1, 2004.)

602.9.

(a) Except as provided in subdivision (c), any person who, without the owner's or owner's agent's consent, claims ownership or claims or takes possession of a residential dwelling for the purpose of renting that dwelling to another is guilty of a misdemeanor punishable by imprisonment in a county jail not exceeding one year, or by a fine not exceeding two thousand five hundred dollars ($2,500), or by both that imprisonment and fine. Each violation is a separate offense.

(b) Except as provided in subdivision (c), any person who, without the owner's or owner's agent's consent, causes another person to enter or remain in any residential

dwelling for the purpose of renting that dwelling to another, is guilty of a misdemeanor punishable by imprisonment in a county jail not exceeding one year, or by a fine not exceeding two thousand five hundred dollars ($2,500), or by both that imprisonment and fine. Each violation is a separate offense.
(c) This section does not apply to any tenant, subtenant, lessee, sublessee, or assignee, nor to any other hirer having a lawful occupancy interest in the residential dwelling.
(d) Nothing in this section shall preclude the prosecution of a person under any other applicable provision of law.
(e) It is the intent of the Legislature that this section shall not preclude the prosecution of a person on grand theft or fraud charges. The Legislature finds that this section has never precluded prosecution of a person on grand theft or fraud charges.
(Amended by Stats. 2010, Ch. 580, Sec. 1. (AB 1800) Effective January 1, 2011.)

602.10.
Every person who, by physical force and with the intent to prevent attendance or instruction, willfully obstructs or attempts to obstruct any student or teacher seeking to attend or instruct classes at any of the campuses or facilities owned, controlled, or administered by the Regents of the University of California, the Trustees of the California State University, or the governing board of a community college district shall be punished by a fine not exceeding five hundred dollars ($500), by imprisonment in a county jail for a period of not exceeding one year, or by both such fine and imprisonment.
As used in this section, "physical force" includes, but is not limited to, use of one's person, individually or in concert with others, to impede access to, or movement within, or otherwise to obstruct the students and teachers of the classes to which the premises are devoted.
(Amended by Stats. 1983, Ch. 143, Sec. 202.)

602.11.
(a) Any person, alone or in concert with others, who intentionally prevents an individual from entering or exiting a health care facility, place of worship, or school by physically detaining the individual or physically obstructing the individual's passage shall be guilty of a misdemeanor punishable by imprisonment in the county jail, or a fine of not more than two hundred fifty dollars ($250), or both, for the first offense; imprisonment in the county jail for not less than five days and a fine of not more than five hundred dollars ($500) for the second offense; and imprisonment in the county jail for not less than 30 days and a fine of not more than two thousand dollars ($2,000) for a third or subsequent offense. However, the court may order the defendant to perform community service, in lieu of any fine or any imprisonment imposed under this section, if it determines that paying the fine would result in undue hardship to the defendant or his or her dependents.
(b) As used in subdivision (a), the following terms have the following meanings:
(1) "Physically" does not include speech.
(2) "Health care facility" means a facility licensed pursuant to Chapter 1 (commencing with Section 1200) of Division 2 of the Health and Safety Code, a health facility licensed pursuant to Chapter 2 (commencing with Section 1250) of Division 2 of the Health and Safety Code, or any facility where medical care is regularly provided to individuals by persons licensed under Division 2 (commencing with Section 500) of the Business and Professions Code, the Osteopathic Initiative Act, or the Chiropractic Initiative Act.
(3) "Person" does not include an officer, employee, or agent of the health care facility, or a law enforcement officer, acting in the course of his or her employment.
(c) This section shall not be interpreted to prohibit any lawful activities permitted under the laws of the State of California or by the National Labor Relations Act in connection with a labor dispute.
(Added by Stats. 1992, Ch. 935, Sec. 2. Effective January 1, 1993.)

602.12.
(a) Any person who enters the residential real property of an academic researcher for the purpose of chilling, preventing the exercise of, or interfering with the researcher's academic freedom is guilty of trespass, a misdemeanor.
(b) For the purposes of this section, the following definitions apply:
(1) "Academic researcher" means any person lawfully engaged in academic research who is a student, trainee, employee, or affiliated physician of an accredited California community college, a campus of the California State University or the University of California, or a Western Association of Schools and Colleges accredited, degree granting, nonprofit institution. Academic research does not include routine, nonlaboratory coursework or assignments.
(2) "Academic freedom" means the lawful performance, dissemination, or publication of academic research or instruction.
(c) This section shall not apply to any person who is lawfully engaged in labor union activities that are protected under state or federal law.
(d) This section shall not preclude prosecution under any other provision of law.
(Added by Stats. 2008, Ch. 492, Sec. 4. Effective September 28, 2008.)

602.13.
(a) Every person who enters into an animal enclosure at a zoo, circus, or traveling animal exhibit, if the zoo, circus, or exhibit is licensed or permitted to display living animals to the public, and if signs prohibiting entrance into the animal enclosures have been posted either at the entrance to the zoo, circus, or traveling animal exhibit, or on the animal enclosure itself, without the consent of the governing authority of the zoo, circus, or traveling animal exhibit, or a representative authorized by the governing authority, is guilty of an infraction or a misdemeanor, subject to Section 19.8. This subdivision shall not apply to an employee of the zoo, circus, or traveling animal exhibit, or to a public officer acting within the course and scope of his or her employment.
(b) For purposes of this section, "zoo" means a permanent or semipermanent collection of living animals kept in enclosures for the purpose of displaying the animals to the public. The term "zoo" includes a public aquarium displaying aquatic animals.
(c) For purposes of this section, an "animal enclosure" means the interior of any cage, stall, container, pen, aquarium or tank, or other discrete containment area that is used to house or display an animal and that is not generally accessible to the public.
(d) Prosecution under this section does not preclude prosecution under any other provision of law.
(Added by Stats. 2010, Ch. 536, Sec. 2. (AB 1675) Effective January 1, 2011.)

603.
Every person other than a peace officer engaged in the performance of his duties as such who forcibly and without the consent of the owner, representative of the owner, lessee or representative of the lessee thereof, enters a dwelling house, cabin, or other building occupied or constructed for occupation by humans, and who damages, injures or destroys any property of value in, around or appertaining to such dwelling house, cabin or other building, is guilty of a misdemeanor.
(Added by Stats. 1941, Ch. 635.)

604.
Every person who maliciously injures or destroys any standing crops, grain, cultivated fruits or vegetables, the property of another, in any case for which a punishment is not otherwise prescribed by this Code, is guilty of a misdemeanor.
(Enacted 1872.)

605.
Every person who either:
1. Maliciously removes any monument erected for the purpose of designating any point in the boundary of any lot or tract of land, or a place where a subaqueous telegraph cable lies; or,
2. Maliciously defaces or alters the marks upon any such monument; or,
3. Maliciously cuts down or removes any tree upon which any such marks have been made for such purpose, with intent to destroy such marks;
—Is guilty of a misdemeanor.
(Enacted 1872.)

607.
Every person who willfully and maliciously cuts, breaks, injures, or destroys, or who, without the authority of the owner or managing agent, operates any gate or control of, any bridge, dam, canal, flume, aqueduct, levee, embankment, reservoir, or other structure erected to create hydraulic power, or to drain or reclaim any swamp, overflow, tide, or marsh land, or to store or conduct water for mining, manufacturing, reclamation, or agricultural purposes, or for the supply of the inhabitants of any city or town, or any embankment necessary to the same, or either of them, or willfully or maliciously makes, or causes to be made, any aperture or plows up the bottom or sides in the dam, canal, flume, aqueduct, reservoir, embankment, levee, or structure, with intent to injure or destroy the same; or draws up, cuts, or injures any piles fixed in the ground for the purpose of securing any sea bank, sea wall, dock, quay, jetty, or lock; or who, between the first day of October and the fifteenth day of April of each year, plows up or loosens the soil in the bed on the side of any natural water course, reclamation ditch, or drainage ditch, with an intent to destroy the same without removing the soil within 24 hours from the water course, reclamation ditch, or drainage ditch, or who, between the fifteenth day of April and the first day of October of each year, plows up or loosens the soil in the bed or on the sides of the natural water course, reclamation ditch, or drainage ditch, with an intent to destroy the same and does not remove therefrom the soil so plowed up or loosened before the first day of October next thereafter, is guilty of vandalism under Section 594. Nothing in this section shall be construed so as to in any manner prohibit any person from digging or removing soil from any water course, reclamation ditch, or drainage ditch for the purpose of mining.
(Amended by Stats. 1992, Ch. 402, Sec. 2. Effective January 1, 1993.)

610.
Every person who unlawfully masks, alters, or removes any light or signal, or willfully exhibits any light or signal, with intent to bring any vessel into danger, is punishable by imprisonment pursuant to subdivision (h) of Section 1170.
(Amended by Stats. 2011, Ch. 15, Sec. 416. (AB 109) Effective April 4, 2011. Operative October 1, 2011, by Sec. 636 of Ch. 15, as amended by Stats. 2011, Ch. 39, Sec. 68.)

615.
Every person who willfully injures, defaces, or removes any signal, monument, building, or appurtenance thereto, placed, erected, or used by persons engaged in the United States Coast Survey, is guilty of a misdemeanor.
(Enacted 1872.)

616.
Every person who intentionally defaces, obliterates, tears down, or destroys any copy or transcript, or extract from or of any law of the United States or of this State, or any proclamation, advertisement, or notification set up at any place in this State, by authority of any law of the United States or of this State, or by order of any Court, before the expiration of the time for which the same was to remain set up, is punishable by fine not less than twenty nor more than one hundred dollars, or by imprisonment in the County Jail not more than one month.
(Enacted 1872.)

617.
Every person who maliciously mutilates, tears, defaces, obliterates, or destroys any written instrument, the property of another, the false making of which would be forgery, is punishable by imprisonment pursuant to subdivision (h) of Section 1170.
(Amended by Stats. 2011, Ch. 15, Sec. 417. (AB 109) Effective April 4, 2011. Operative October 1, 2011, by Sec. 636 of Ch. 15, as amended by Stats. 2011, Ch. 39, Sec. 68.)

618.
Every person who willfully opens or reads, or causes to be read, any sealed letter not addressed to himself, without being authorized so to do, either by the writer of such letter or by the person to whom it is addressed, and every person who, without the like authority, publishes any of the contents of such letter, knowing the same to have been unlawfully opened, is guilty of a misdemeanor.
(Enacted 1872.)

620.
Every person who willfully alters the purport, effect, or meaning of a telegraphic or telephonic message to the injury of another, is punishable by imprisonment pursuant to subdivision (h) of Section 1170, or in a county jail not exceeding one year, or by fine not exceeding ten thousand dollars ($10,000), or by both that fine and imprisonment.
(Amended by Stats. 2011, Ch. 15, Sec. 418. (AB 109) Effective April 4, 2011. Operative October 1, 2011, by Sec. 636 of Ch. 15, as amended by Stats. 2011, Ch. 39, Sec. 68.)

621.
(a) Every person who maliciously destroys, cuts, breaks, mutilates, effaces, or otherwise injures, tears down, or removes any law enforcement memorial or firefighter's memorial is guilty of a crime punishable by imprisonment pursuant to subdivision (h) of Section 1170 or by imprisonment in a county jail for less than one year.
(b) This section does not preclude prosecution under any other provision of law, including Section 1318 of the Military and Veterans Code.
(Amended by Stats. 2018, Ch. 549, Sec. 1. (AB 2801) Effective January 1, 2019.)

622.
Every person, not the owner thereof, who willfully injures, disfigures, or destroys any monument, work of art, or useful or ornamental improvement within the limits of any village, town, or city, or any shade tree or ornamental plant growing therein, whether situated upon private ground or on any street, sidewalk, or public park or place, is guilty of a misdemeanor.
(Enacted 1872.)

622½.
Every person, not the owner thereof, who wilfully injures, disfigures, defaces, or destroys any object or thing of archeological or historical interest or value, whether situated on private lands or within any public park or place, is guilty of a misdemeanor.
(Added by Stats. 1939, Ch. 90.)

623.
(a) Except as otherwise provided in Section 599c, any person who, without the prior written permission of the owner of a cave, intentionally and knowingly does any of the following acts is guilty of a misdemeanor punishable by imprisonment in the county jail not exceeding one year, or by a fine not exceeding one thousand dollars ($1,000), or by both such fine and imprisonment:
(1) Breaks, breaks off, cracks, carves upon, paints, writes or otherwise marks upon or in any manner destroys, mutilates, injures, defaces, mars, or harms any natural material found in any cave.
(2) Disturbs or alters any archaeological evidence of prior occupation in any cave.
(3) Kills, harms, or removes any animal or plant life found in any cave.
(4) Burns any material which produces any smoke or gas which is harmful to any plant or animal found in any cave.
(5) Removes any material found in any cave.
(6) Breaks, forces, tampers with, removes or otherwise disturbs any lock, gate, door, or any other structure or obstruction designed to prevent entrance to any cave, whether or not entrance is gained.
(b) For purposes of this section:
(1) "Cave" means any natural geologically formed void or cavity beneath the surface of the earth, not including any mine, tunnel, aqueduct, or other manmade excavation, which is large enough to permit a person to enter.

(2) "Owner" means the person or private or public agency which has the right of possession to the cave.

(3) "Natural material" means any stalactite, stalagmite, helictite, anthodite, gypsum flower or needle, flowstone, drapery, column, tufa dam, clay or mud formation or concretion, crystalline mineral formation, and any wall, ceiling, or mineral protuberance therefrom, whether attached or broken, found in any cave.

(4) "Material" means all or any part of any archaeological, paleontological, biological, or historical item including, but not limited to, any petroglyph, pictograph, basketry, human remains, tool, beads, pottery, projectile point, remains of historical mining activity or any other occupation found in any cave.

(c) The entering or remaining in a cave by itself shall not constitute a violation of this section.

(Amended by Stats. 1983, Ch. 1092, Sec. 312. Effective September 27, 1983. Operative January 1, 1984, by Sec. 427 of Ch. 1092.)

624.

Every person who wilfully breaks, digs up, obstructs, or injures any pipe or main for conducting water, or any works erected for supplying buildings with water, or any appurtenances or appendages connected thereto, is guilty of a misdemeanor.

(Amended by Stats. 1939, Ch. 369.)

625.

Every person who, with intent to defraud or injure, opens or causes to be opened, or draws water from any stopcock or faucet by which the flow of water is controlled, after having been notified that the same has been closed or shut for specific cause, by order of competent authority, is guilty of a misdemeanor.

(Enacted 1872.)

625b.

(a) Every person who willfully injures or tampers with any aircraft or the contents or parts thereof, or removes any part of or from an aircraft without the consent of the owner, and every person who, with intent to commit any malicious mischief, injury or other crime, climbs into or upon an aircraft or attempts to manipulate any of the controls, starting mechanism, brakes or other mechanism or device of an aircraft while it is at rest and unattended or who sets in motion any aircraft while it is at rest and unattended, is guilty of a misdemeanor and upon conviction shall be punished by imprisonment for not more than six months or by a fine of not more than one thousand dollars ($1,000), or by both that fine and imprisonment.

(b) Every person who willfully and maliciously damages, injures, or destroys any aircraft, or the contents or any part thereof, in such a manner as to render the aircraft unsafe for those flight operations for which it is designed and equipped is punishable by imprisonment pursuant to subdivision (h) of Section 1170, or by imprisonment in a county jail not exceeding one year, or by a fine not exceeding ten thousand dollars ($10,000), or by both such fine and imprisonment.

(Amended by Stats. 2011, Ch. 15, Sec. 420. (AB 109) Effective April 4, 2011. Operative October 1, 2011, by Sec. 636 of Ch. 15, as amended by Stats. 2011, Ch. 39, Sec. 68.)

625c.

Any person who, with the intent to cause great bodily injury to another person, willfully removes, tampers with, injures or destroys any passenger transit vehicle or the contents or parts thereof, or who willfully removes, tampers with or destroys, or places an obstruction upon any part of the transit system, including its right-of-way, structures, fixtures, tracks, switches or controls, or who willfully sets a vehicle in motion while it is at rest and unattended is guilty of a felony.

(Added by Stats. 1980, Ch. 993, Sec. 1.)

TITLE 15. MISCELLANEOUS CRIMES [626 - 653.75]

(Title 15 enacted 1872.)

CHAPTER 1. Schools [626 - 626.11]

(Chapter 1 added by Stats. 1969, Ch. 1424.)

626.

(a) As used in this chapter, the following definitions apply:

(1) "University" means the University of California, and includes any affiliated institution thereof and any campus or facility owned, operated, or controlled by the Regents of the University of California.

(2) "State university" means any California state university, and includes any campus or facility owned, operated, or controlled by the Trustees of the California State University.

(3) "Community college" means any public community college established pursuant to the Education Code.

(4) "School" means any public or private elementary school, junior high school, four-year high school, senior high school, adult school or any branch thereof, opportunity school, continuation high school, regional occupational center, evening high school, or technical school or any public right-of-way situated immediately adjacent to school property or any other place if a teacher and one or more pupils are required to be at that place in connection with assigned school activities.

(5) "Chief administrative officer" means either of the following:

(A) The president of the university or a state university, the Chancellor of the California State University, or the officer designated by the Regents of the University of California or pursuant to authority granted by the Regents of the University of California to administer and be the officer in charge of a campus or other facility owned, operated, or controlled by the Regents of the University of California, or the superintendent of a community college district.

(B) For a school, the principal of the school, a person who possesses a standard supervision credential or a standard administrative credential and who is designated by the principal, or a person who carries out the same functions as a person who possesses a credential and who is designated by the principal.

(b) For the purpose of determining the penalty to be imposed pursuant to this chapter, the court may consider a written report from the Department of Justice containing information from its records showing prior convictions; and that communication is prima facie evidence of the convictions, if the defendant admits them, regardless of whether or not the complaint commencing the proceedings has alleged prior convictions.

(c) As used in this code, the following definitions apply:

(1) "Pupil currently attending school" means a pupil enrolled in a public or private school who has been in attendance or has had an excused absence, for purposes of attendance accounting, for a majority of the days for which the pupil has been enrolled in that school during the school year.

(2) "Safe school zone" means an area that encompasses any of the following places during regular school hours or within 60 minutes before or after the schoolday or 60 minutes before or after a school-sponsored activity at the schoolsite:

(A) Within 100 feet of a bus stop, whether or not a public transit bus stop, that has been publicly designated by the school district as a schoolbus stop. This definition applies only if the school district has chosen to mark the bus stop as a schoolbus stop.

(B) Within 1,500 feet of a school, as designated by the school district.

(Amended by Stats. 2008, Ch. 726, Sec. 1. Effective January 1, 2009.)

626.2.

Every student or employee who, after a hearing, has been suspended or dismissed from a community college, a state university, the university, or a public or private school for disrupting the orderly operation of the campus or facility of the institution, and as a condition of the suspension or dismissal has been denied access to the campus or facility, or both, of the institution for the period of the suspension or in the case of dismissal for a period not to exceed one year; who has been served by registered or certified mail, at the last address given by that person, with a written notice of the suspension or dismissal and condition; and who willfully and knowingly enters upon the campus or facility of the institution to which he or she has been denied access, without the express written permission of the chief administrative officer of the campus or facility, is guilty of a misdemeanor and shall be punished as follows:

(a) Upon a first conviction, by a fine not exceeding five hundred dollars ($500), by imprisonment in a county jail for a period of not more than six months, or by both that fine and imprisonment.

(b) If the defendant has been previously convicted once of a violation of any offense defined in this chapter or Section 415.5, by imprisonment in a county jail for a period of not less than 10 days or more than six months, or by both that imprisonment and a fine not exceeding five hundred dollars ($500), and shall not be released on probation, parole, or any other basis until he or she has served not less than 10 days.

(c) If the defendant has been previously convicted two or more times of a violation of any offense defined in this chapter or Section 415.5, by imprisonment in a county jail for a period of not less than 90 days or more than six months, or by both that imprisonment and a fine not exceeding five hundred dollars ($500), and shall not be released on probation, parole, or any other basis until he or she has served not less than 90 days.

Knowledge shall be presumed if notice has been given as prescribed in this section. The presumption established by this section is a presumption affecting the burden of proof.

(Amended by Stats. 2009, Ch. 140, Sec. 142. (AB 1164) Effective January 1, 2010.)

626.4.

(a) The chief administrative officer of a campus or other facility of a community college, a state university, the university, or a school, or an officer or employee designated by the chief administrative officer to maintain order on such campus or facility, may notify a person that consent to remain on the campus or other facility under the control of the chief administrative officer has been withdrawn whenever there is reasonable cause to believe that such person has willfully disrupted the orderly operation of such campus or facility.

(b) Whenever consent is withdrawn by any authorized officer or employee, other than the chief administrative officer, such officer or employee shall as soon as is reasonably possible submit a written report to the chief administrative officer. The report shall contain all of the following:

(1) The description of the person from whom consent was withdrawn, including, if available, the person's name, address, and phone number.

(2) A statement of the facts giving rise to the withdrawal of consent.

If the chief administrative officer or, in the chief administrative officer's absence, a person designated by him or her for this purpose, upon reviewing the report, finds that there was reasonable cause to believe that such person has willfully disrupted the orderly operation of the campus or facility, he or she may enter written confirmation upon the report of the action taken by the officer or employee. If the chief administrative officer or, in the chief administrative officer's absence, the person designated by him or her, does not confirm the action of the officer or employee within 24 hours after the time that consent was withdrawn, the action of the officer or employee shall be deemed void and of no force or effect, except that any arrest made during such period shall not for this reason be deemed not to have been made for probable cause.

(c) Consent shall be reinstated by the chief administrative officer whenever he or she has reason to believe that the presence of the person from whom consent was withdrawn will not constitute a substantial and material threat to the orderly operation of the campus or facility. In no case shall consent be withdrawn for longer than 14 days from the date upon which consent was initially withdrawn. The person from whom consent has been withdrawn may submit a written request for a hearing on the withdrawal within the two-week period. The written request shall state the address to which notice of hearing is to be sent. The chief administrative officer shall grant such a hearing not later than seven days from the date of receipt of the request and shall immediately mail a written notice of the time, place, and date of such hearing to such person.

(d) Any person who has been notified by the chief administrative officer of a campus or other facility of a community college, a state university, the university, or a school, or by an officer or employee designated by the chief administrative officer to maintain order on such campus or facility, that consent to remain on the campus or facility has been withdrawn pursuant to subdivision (a); who has not had such consent reinstated; and who willfully and knowingly enters or remains upon such campus or facility during the period for which consent has been withdrawn is guilty of a misdemeanor. This subdivision does not apply to any person who enters or remains on such campus or facility for the sole purpose of applying to the chief administrative officer for the reinstatement of consent or for the sole purpose of attending a hearing on the withdrawal.

(e) This section shall not affect the power of the duly constituted authorities of a community college, a state university, the university, or a school, to suspend, dismiss, or expel any student or employee at the college, state university, university, or school.

(f) Any person convicted under this section shall be punished as follows:

(1) Upon a first conviction, by a fine of not exceeding five hundred dollars ($500), by imprisonment in the county jail for a period of not more than six months, or by both such fine and imprisonment.

(2) If the defendant has been previously convicted once of a violation of any offense defined in this chapter or Section 415.5, by imprisonment in the county jail for a period of not less than 10 days or more than six months, or by both such imprisonment and a fine of not exceeding five hundred dollars ($500), and shall not be released on probation, parole, or any other basis until he or she has served not less than 10 days.

(3) If the defendant has been previously convicted two or more times of a violation of any offense defined in this chapter or Section 415.5, by imprisonment in the county jail for a period of not less than 90 days or more than six months, or by both such imprisonment and a fine of not exceeding five hundred dollars ($500), and shall not be released on probation, parole, or any other basis until he or she has served not less than 90 days.

(g) This section shall not affect the rights of representatives of employee organizations to enter, or remain upon, school grounds while actually engaged in activities related to representation, as provided for in Chapter 10.7 (commencing with Section 3540) of Division 4 of Title 1 of the Government Code.

(Amended by Stats. 1983, Ch. 143, Sec. 205.)

626.6.

(a) If a person who is not a student, officer or employee of a college or university and who is not required by his or her employment to be on the campus or any other facility owned, operated, or controlled by the governing board of that college or university, enters a campus or facility, and it reasonably appears to the chief administrative officer of the campus or facility, or to an officer or employee designated by the chief administrative officer to maintain order on the campus or facility, that the person is committing any act likely to interfere with the peaceful conduct of the activities of the campus or facility, or has entered the campus or facility for the purpose of committing any such act, the chief administrative officer or his or her designee may direct the person to leave the campus or facility. If that person fails to do so or if the person willfully and knowingly reenters upon the campus or facility within seven days after being directed to leave, he or she is guilty of a misdemeanor and shall be punished as follows:

(1) Upon a first conviction, by a fine of not more than five hundred dollars ($500), by imprisonment in the county jail for a period of not more than six months, or by both that fine and imprisonment.

(2) If the defendant has been previously convicted once of a violation of any offense defined in this chapter or Section 415.5, by imprisonment in the county jail for a period of not less than 10 days or more than six months, or by both that imprisonment and a fine of not more than five hundred dollars ($500), and shall not be released on probation, parole, or any other basis until he or she has served not less than 10 days.

(3) If the defendant has been previously convicted two or more times of a violation of any offense defined in this chapter or Section 415.5, by imprisonment in the county jail for a period of not less than 90 days or more than six months, or by both that imprisonment and a fine of not more than five hundred dollars ($500), and shall not be released on probation, parole, or any other basis until he or she has served not less than 90 days.

(b) The provisions of this section shall not be utilized to impinge upon the lawful exercise of constitutionally protected rights of freedom of speech or assembly.

(c) When a person is directed to leave pursuant to subdivision (a), the person directing him or her to leave shall inform the person that if he or she reenters the campus or facility within seven days he or she will be guilty of a crime.

(Amended by Stats. 1995, Ch. 163, Sec. 1. Effective January 1, 1996.)

626.7.

(a) If a person who is not a student, officer, or employee of a public school, and who is not required by his or her employment to be on the campus or any other facility owned, operated, or controlled by the governing board of that school, enters a campus or facility outside of the common areas where public business is conducted, and it reasonably appears to the chief administrative officer of the campus or facility, or to an officer or employee designated by the chief administrative officer to maintain order on the campus or facility, that the person is committing any act likely to interfere with the peaceful conduct of the activities of the campus or facility, or has entered the campus or facility for the purpose of committing any such act, the chief administrative officer or his or her designee may direct the person to leave the campus or facility. If that person fails to do so or if the person returns without following the posted requirements to contact the administrative offices of the campus, he or she is guilty of a misdemeanor and shall be punished as follows:

(1) Upon a first conviction, by a fine of not more than five hundred dollars ($500), by imprisonment in a county jail for a period of not more than six months, or by both that fine and imprisonment.

(2) If the defendant has been previously convicted once of a violation of any offense defined in this chapter or Section 415.5, by imprisonment in a county jail for a period of not less than 10 days or more than six months, or by both that imprisonment and a fine of not more than five hundred dollars ($500), and the defendant shall not be released on probation, parole, or any other basis until he or she has served not less than 10 days.

(3) If the defendant has been previously convicted two or more times of a violation of any offense defined in this chapter or Section 415.5, by imprisonment in a county jail for a period of not less than 90 days or more than six months, or by both that imprisonment and a fine of not more than five hundred dollars ($500), and the defendant shall not be released on probation, parole, or any other basis until he or she has served not less than 90 days.

For purposes of this section, a representative of a school employee organization engaged in activities related to representation, as provided for in Chapter 10.7 (commencing with Section 3540) of Division 4 of Title 1 of the Government Code, shall be deemed a person required by his or her employment to be in a school building or on the grounds of a school.

(b) The provisions of this section shall not be utilized to impinge upon the lawful exercise of constitutionally protected rights of freedom of speech or assembly.

(c) When a person is directed to leave pursuant to subdivision (a), the person directing him or her to leave shall inform the person that if he or she reenters the campus or facility without following the posted requirements to contact the administrative offices of the campus, he or she will be guilty of a crime.

(d) Notwithstanding any other subdivision of this section, the chief administrative officer, or his or her designee, shall allow a person previously directed to leave the campus or facility pursuant to this section to reenter the campus if the person is a parent or guardian of a pupil enrolled at the campus or facility who has to retrieve the pupil for disciplinary reasons, for medical attention, or for a family emergency.

(Amended by Stats. 2002, Ch. 343, Sec. 1. Effective January 1, 2003.)

626.8.

(a) Any person who comes into any school building or upon any school ground, or street, sidewalk, or public way adjacent thereto, without lawful business thereon, and whose presence or acts interfere with the peaceful conduct of the activities of the school or disrupt the school or its pupils or school activities, is guilty of a misdemeanor if he or she does any of the following:

(1) Remains there after being asked to leave by the chief administrative official of that school or his or her designated representative, or by a person employed as a member of a security or police department of a school district pursuant to Chapter 1 (commencing with Section 38000) of Part 23 of Division 3 of Title 2 of the Education Code, or a city police officer, or sheriff or deputy sheriff, or a Department of the California Highway Patrol peace officer.

(2) Reenters or comes upon that place within seven days of being asked to leave by a person specified in paragraph (1).

(3) Has otherwise established a continued pattern of unauthorized entry.

(4) Willfully or knowingly creates a disruption with the intent to threaten the immediate physical safety of any pupil in preschool, kindergarten, or any of grades 1 to 8, inclusive, arriving at, attending, or leaving from school.

(b) Punishment for violation of this section shall be as follows:

(1) Upon a first conviction by a fine not exceeding five hundred dollars ($500), by imprisonment in a county jail for a period of not more than six months, or by both that fine and imprisonment.

(2) If the defendant has been previously convicted once of a violation of any offense defined in this chapter or Section 415.5, by imprisonment in a county jail for a period of not less than 10 days or more than six months, or by both imprisonment and a fine not exceeding five hundred dollars ($500), and shall not be released on probation, parole, or any other basis until he or she has served not less than 10 days.

(3) If the defendant has been previously convicted two or more times of a violation of any offense defined in this chapter or Section 415.5, by imprisonment in a county jail for a period of not less than 90 days or more than six months, or by both imprisonment and a fine not exceeding five hundred dollars ($500), and shall not be released on probation, parole, or any other basis until he or she has served not less than 90 days.

(c) As used in this section, the following definitions apply:

(1) "Lawful business" means a reason for being present upon school property which is not otherwise prohibited by statute, by ordinance, or by any regulation adopted pursuant to statute or ordinance.

(2) "Continued pattern of unauthorized entry" means that on at least two prior occasions in the same school year the defendant came into any school building or upon any school ground, or street, sidewalk, or public way adjacent thereto, without lawful business thereon, and his or her presence or acts interfered with the peaceful conduct

of the activities of the school or disrupted the school or its pupils or school activities, and the defendant was asked to leave by a person specified in paragraph (1) of subdivision (a).

(3) "School" means any preschool or public or private school having kindergarten or any of grades 1 to 12, inclusive.

(d) When a person is directed to leave pursuant to paragraph (1) of subdivision (a), the person directing him or her to leave shall inform the person that if he or she reenters the place within seven days he or she will be guilty of a crime.

(e) This section shall not be utilized to impinge upon the lawful exercise of constitutionally protected rights of speech or assembly.

(Amended by Stats. 2011, Ch. 161, Sec. 1. (AB 123) Effective January 1, 2012.)

626.81.

(a) A person who is required to register as a sex offender pursuant to Section 290, who comes into any school building or upon any school ground without lawful business thereon and written permission indicating the date or dates and times for which permission has been granted from the chief administrative official of that school, is guilty of a misdemeanor.

(b) (1) The chief administrative official of a school may grant a person who is subject to this section and not a family member of a pupil who attends that school, permission to come into a school building or upon the school grounds to volunteer at the school, provided that, notwithstanding subdivisions (a) and (c) of Section 290.45, at least 14 days prior to the first date for which permission has been granted, the chief administrative official notifies or causes to be notified the parent or guardian of each child attending the school that a person who is required to register as a sex offender pursuant to Section 290 has been granted permission to come into a school building or upon school grounds, the date or dates and times for which permission has been granted, and his or her right to obtain information regarding the person from a designated law enforcement entity pursuant to Section 290.45. The notice required by this paragraph shall be provided by one of the methods identified in Section 48981 of the Education Code.

(2) Any chief administrative official or school employee who in good faith disseminates the notification and information as required by paragraph (1) shall be immune from civil liability for action taken in accordance with that paragraph.

(c) Punishment for a violation of this section shall be as follows:

(1) Upon a first conviction by a fine of not exceeding five hundred dollars ($500), by imprisonment in a county jail for a period of not more than six months, or by both the fine and imprisonment.

(2) If the defendant has been previously convicted once of a violation of this section, by imprisonment in a county jail for a period of not less than 10 days or more than six months, or by both imprisonment and a fine of not exceeding five hundred dollars ($500), and shall not be released on probation, parole, or any other basis until he or she has served not less than 10 days.

(3) If the defendant has been previously convicted two or more times of a violation of this section, by imprisonment in a county jail for a period of not less than 90 days or more than six months, or by both imprisonment and a fine of not exceeding five hundred dollars ($500), and shall not be released on probation, parole, or any other basis until he or she has served not less than 90 days.

(d) Nothing in this section shall preclude or prohibit prosecution under any other provision of law.

(Amended by Stats. 2013, Ch. 279, Sec. 1. (SB 326) Effective January 1, 2014.)

626.85.

(a) Any specified drug offender who, at any time, comes into any school building or upon any school ground, or adjacent street, sidewalk, or public way, unless the person is a parent or guardian of a child attending that school and his or her presence is during any school activity, or is a student at the school and his or her presence is during any school activity, or has prior written permission for the entry from the chief administrative officer of that school, is guilty of a misdemeanor if he or she does any of the following:

(1) Remains there after being asked to leave by the chief administrative officer of that school or his or her designated representative, or by a person employed as a member of a security or police department of a school district pursuant to Section 39670 of the Education Code, or a city police officer, sheriff, or a Department of the California Highway Patrol peace officer.

(2) Reenters or comes upon that place within seven days of being asked to leave by a person specified in paragraph (1) of subdivision (a).

(3) Has otherwise established a continued pattern of unauthorized entry.

This section shall not be utilized to impinge upon the lawful exercise of constitutionally protected rights of freedom of speech or assembly, or to prohibit any lawful act, including picketing, strikes, or collective bargaining.

(b) Punishment for violation of this section shall be as follows:

(1) Upon a first conviction, by a fine not exceeding one thousand dollars ($1,000), by imprisonment in the county jail for a period of not more than six months, or by both that fine and imprisonment.

(2) If the defendant has been previously convicted once of a violation of any offense defined in this chapter or Section 415.5, by imprisonment in the county jail for a period of not less than 10 days or more than six months, or by both imprisonment and a fine not exceeding one thousand dollars ($1,000), and the defendant shall not be released on probation, parole, or any other basis until he or she has served not less than 10 days.

(3) If the defendant has been previously convicted two or more times of a violation of any offense defined in this chapter or Section 415.5, by imprisonment in the county jail for a period of not less than 90 days or more than six months, or by both imprisonment and a fine not exceeding one thousand dollars ($1,000), and the defendant shall not be released on probation, parole, or any other basis until he or she has served not less than 90 days.

(c) As used in this section:

(1) "Specified drug offender" means any person who, within the immediately preceding three years, has a felony or misdemeanor conviction of either:

(A) Unlawful sale, or possession for sale, of any controlled substance, as defined in Section 11007 of the Health and Safety Code.

(B) Unlawful use, possession, or being under the influence of any controlled substance, as defined in Section 11007 of the Health and Safety Code, where that conviction was based on conduct which occurred, wholly or partly, in any school building or upon any school ground, or adjacent street, sidewalk, or public way.

(2) "Continued pattern of unauthorized entry" means that on at least two prior occasions in the same calendar year the defendant came into any school building or upon any school ground, or adjacent street, sidewalk, or public way, and the defendant was asked to leave by a person specified in paragraph (1) of subdivision (a).

(3) "School" means any preschool or public or private school having any of grades kindergarten to 12, inclusive.

(4) "School activity" means and includes any school session, any extracurricular activity or event sponsored by or participated in by the school, and the 30-minute periods immediately preceding and following any session, activity, or event.

(d) When a person is directed to leave pursuant to paragraph (1) of subdivision (a), the person directing him or her to leave shall inform the person that if he or she reenters the place he or she will be guilty of a crime.

(Amended by Stats. 2008, Ch. 726, Sec. 4. Effective January 1, 2009.)

626.9.

(a) This section shall be known, and may be cited, as the Gun-Free School Zone Act of 1995.

(b) Any person who possesses a firearm in a place that the person knows, or reasonably should know, is a school zone, as defined in paragraph (4) of subdivision (e), shall be punished as specified in subdivision (f).

(c) Subdivision (b) does not apply to the possession of a firearm under any of the following circumstances:

(1) Within a place of residence or place of business or on private property, if the place of residence, place of business, or private property is not part of the school grounds and the possession of the firearm is otherwise lawful.

(2) When the firearm is an unloaded pistol, revolver, or other firearm capable of being concealed on the person and is in a locked container or within the locked trunk of a motor vehicle.

This section does not prohibit or limit the otherwise lawful transportation of any other firearm, other than a pistol, revolver, or other firearm capable of being concealed on the person, in accordance with state law.

(3) When the person possessing the firearm reasonably believes that he or she is in grave danger because of circumstances forming the basis of a current restraining order issued by a court against another person or persons who has or have been found to pose a threat to his or her life or safety. This subdivision does not apply when the circumstances involve a mutual restraining order issued pursuant to Division 10 (commencing with Section 6200) of the Family Code absent a factual finding of a specific threat to the person's life or safety. Upon a trial for violating subdivision (b), the trier of a fact shall determine whether the defendant was acting out of a reasonable belief that he or she was in grave danger.

(4) When the person is exempt from the prohibition against carrying a concealed firearm pursuant to Section 25615, 25625, 25630, or 25645.

(5) When the person holds a valid license to carry the firearm pursuant to Chapter 4 (commencing with Section 26150) of Division 5 of Title 4 of Part 6, who is carrying that firearm in an area that is not in, or on the grounds of, a public or private school providing instruction in kindergarten or grades 1 to 12, inclusive, but within a distance of 1,000 feet from the grounds of the public or private school.

(d) Except as provided in subdivision (b), it shall be unlawful for any person, with reckless disregard for the safety of another, to discharge, or attempt to discharge, a firearm in a school zone, as defined in paragraph (4) of subdivision (e).

The prohibition contained in this subdivision does not apply to the discharge of a firearm to the extent that the conditions of paragraph (1) of subdivision (c) are satisfied.

(e) As used in this section, the following definitions shall apply:

(1) "Concealed firearm" has the same meaning as that term is given in Sections 25400 and 25610.

(2) "Firearm" has the same meaning as that term is given in subdivisions (a) to (d), inclusive, of Section 16520.

(3) "Locked container" has the same meaning as that term is given in Section 16850.

(4) "School zone" means an area in, or on the grounds of, a public or private school providing instruction in kindergarten or grades 1 to 12, inclusive, or within a distance of 1,000 feet from the grounds of the public or private school.

(f) (1) A person who violates subdivision (b) by possessing a firearm in, or on the grounds of, a public or private school providing instruction in kindergarten or grades 1 to 12, inclusive, shall be punished by imprisonment pursuant to subdivision (h) of Section 1170 for two, three, or five years.

(2) A person who violates subdivision (b) by possessing a firearm within a distance of 1,000 feet from the grounds of a public or private school providing instruction in kindergarten or grades 1 to 12, inclusive, shall be punished as follows:

(A) By imprisonment pursuant to subdivision (h) of Section 1170 for two, three, or five years, if any of the following circumstances apply:

(i) If the person previously has been convicted of any felony, or of any crime made punishable by any provision listed in Section 16580.

(ii) If the person is within a class of persons prohibited from possessing or acquiring a firearm pursuant to Chapter 2 (commencing with Section 29800) or Chapter 3 (commencing with Section 29900) of Division 9 of Title 4 of Part 6 of this code or Section 8100 or 8103 of the Welfare and Institutions Code.

(iii) If the firearm is any pistol, revolver, or other firearm capable of being concealed upon the person and the offense is punished as a felony pursuant to Section 25400.

(B) By imprisonment in a county jail for not more than one year or by imprisonment pursuant to subdivision (h) of Section 1170 for two, three, or five years, in all cases other than those specified in subparagraph (A).

(3) A person who violates subdivision (d) shall be punished by imprisonment pursuant to subdivision (h) of Section 1170 for three, five, or seven years.

(g) (1) A person convicted under this section for a misdemeanor violation of subdivision (b) who has been convicted previously of a misdemeanor offense enumerated in Section 23515 shall be punished by imprisonment in a county jail for not less than three months, or if probation is granted or if the execution or imposition of sentence is suspended, it shall be a condition thereof that he or she be imprisoned in a county jail for not less than three months.

(2) A person convicted under this section of a felony violation of subdivision (b) or (d) who has been convicted previously of a misdemeanor offense enumerated in Section 23515, if probation is granted or if the execution of sentence is suspended, it shall be a condition thereof that he or she be imprisoned in a county jail for not less than three months.

(3) A person convicted under this section for a felony violation of subdivision (b) or (d) who has been convicted previously of any felony, or of any crime made punishable by any provision listed in Section 16580, if probation is granted or if the execution or imposition of sentence is suspended, it shall be a condition thereof that he or she be imprisoned in a county jail for not less than three months.

(4) The court shall apply the three-month minimum sentence specified in this subdivision, except in unusual cases where the interests of justice would best be served by granting probation or suspending the execution or imposition of sentence without the minimum imprisonment required in this subdivision or by granting probation or suspending the execution or imposition of sentence with conditions other than those set forth in this subdivision, in which case the court shall specify on the record and shall enter on the minutes the circumstances indicating that the interests of justice would best be served by this disposition.

(h) Notwithstanding Section 25605, any person who brings or possesses a loaded firearm upon the grounds of a campus of, or buildings owned or operated for student housing, teaching, research, or administration by, a public or private university or college, that are contiguous or are clearly marked university property, unless it is with the written permission of the university or college president, his or her designee, or equivalent university or college authority, shall be punished by imprisonment pursuant to subdivision (h) of Section 1170 for two, three, or four years. Notwithstanding subdivision (k), a university or college shall post a prominent notice at primary entrances on noncontiguous property stating that firearms are prohibited on that property pursuant to this subdivision.

(i) Notwithstanding Section 25605, any person who brings or possesses a firearm upon the grounds of a campus of, or buildings owned or operated for student housing, teaching, research, or administration by, a public or private university or college, that are contiguous or are clearly marked university property, unless it is with the written permission of the university or college president, his or her designee, or equivalent university or college authority, shall be punished by imprisonment pursuant to subdivision (h) of Section 1170 for one, two, or three years. Notwithstanding subdivision (k), a university or college shall post a prominent notice at primary entrances on noncontiguous property stating that firearms are prohibited on that property pursuant to this subdivision.

(j) For purposes of this section, a firearm shall be deemed to be loaded when there is an unexpended cartridge or shell, consisting of a case that holds a charge of powder and a bullet or shot, in, or attached in any manner to, the firearm, including, but not limited to, in the firing chamber, magazine, or clip thereof attached to the firearm. A muzzle-loader firearm shall be deemed to be loaded when it is capped or primed and has a powder charge and ball or shot in the barrel or cylinder.

(k) This section does not require that notice be posted regarding the proscribed conduct.

(l) This section does not apply to a duly appointed peace officer as defined in Chapter 4.5 (commencing with Section 830) of Title 3 of Part 2, a full-time paid peace officer of another state or the federal government who is carrying out official duties while in California, any person summoned by any of these officers to assist in making arrests or preserving the peace while he or she is actually engaged in assisting the officer, a member of the military forces of this state or of the United States who is engaged in the performance of his or her duties, or an armored vehicle guard, engaged in the performance of his or her duties, as defined in subdivision (d) of Section 7582.1 of the Business and Professions Code.

(m) This section does not apply to a security guard authorized to carry a loaded firearm pursuant to Article 4 (commencing with Section 26000) of Chapter 3 of Division 5 of Title 4 of Part 6.

(n) This section does not apply to an existing shooting range at a public or private school or university or college campus.

(o) This section does not apply to an honorably retired peace officer authorized to carry a concealed or loaded firearm pursuant to any of the following:

(1) Article 2 (commencing with Section 25450) of Chapter 2 of Division 5 of Title 4 of Part 6.

(2) Section 25650.

(3) Sections 25900 to 25910, inclusive.

(4) Section 26020.

(5) Paragraph (2) of subdivision (c) of Section 26300.

(p) This section does not apply to a peace officer appointed pursuant to Section 830.6 who is authorized to carry a firearm by the appointing agency.

(q) (1) This section does not apply to the activities of a program involving shooting sports or activities, including, but not limited to, trap shooting, skeet shooting, sporting clays, and pistol shooting, that are sanctioned by a school, school district, college, university, or other governing body of the institution, that occur on the grounds of a public or private school or university or college campus.

(2) This section does not apply to the activities of a state-certified hunter education program pursuant to Section 3051 of the Fish and Game Code if all firearms are unloaded and participants do not possess live ammunition in a school building.

(Amended by Stats. 2017, Ch. 779, Sec. 1. (AB 424) Effective January 1, 2018.)

626.91.

Possession of ammunition on school grounds is governed by Section 30310.

(Added by Stats. 2010, Ch. 711, Sec. 1. (SB 1080) Effective January 1, 2011. Operative January 1, 2012, by Sec. 10 of Ch. 711.)

626.92.

Section 626.9 does not apply to or affect any of the following:

(a) A security guard authorized to openly carry an unloaded handgun pursuant to Chapter 6 (commencing with Section 26350) of Division 5 of Title 4 of Part 6.

(b) An honorably retired peace officer authorized to openly carry an unloaded handgun pursuant to Section 26361.

(c) A security guard authorized to openly carry an unloaded firearm that is not a handgun pursuant to Chapter 7 (commencing with Section 26400) of Division 5 of Title 4 of Part 6.

(d) An honorably retired peace officer authorized to openly carry an unloaded firearm that is not a handgun pursuant to Section 26405.

(Amended by Stats. 2012, Ch. 700, Sec. 3. (AB 1527) Effective January 1, 2013.)

626.95.

(a) Any person who is in violation of paragraph (2) of subdivision (a), or subdivision (b), of Section 417, or Section 25400 or 25850, upon the grounds of or within a playground, or a public or private youth center during hours in which the facility is open for business, classes, or school-related programs, or at any time when minors are using the facility, knowing that he or she is on or within those grounds, shall be punished by imprisonment pursuant to subdivision (h) of Section 1170 for one, two, or three years, or in a county jail not exceeding one year.

(b) State and local authorities are encouraged to cause signs to be posted around playgrounds and youth centers giving warning of prohibition of the possession of firearms upon the grounds of or within playgrounds or youth centers.

(c) For purposes of this section, the following definitions shall apply:

(1) "Playground" means any park or recreational area specifically designed to be used by children that has play equipment installed, including public grounds designed for athletic activities such as baseball, football, soccer, or basketball, or any similar facility located on public or private school grounds, or on city or county parks.

(2) "Youth center" means any public or private facility that is used to host recreational or social activities for minors while minors are present.

(d) It is the Legislature's intent that only an actual conviction of a felony of one of the offenses specified in this section would subject the person to firearms disabilities under the federal Gun Control Act of 1968 (P.L. 90-618; 18 U.S.C. Sec. 921 et seq.).

(Amended by Stats. 2013, Ch. 76, Sec. 147.3. (AB 383) Effective January 1, 2014.)

626.10.

(a) (1) Any person, except a duly appointed peace officer as defined in Chapter 4.5 (commencing with Section 830) of Title 3 of Part 2, a full-time paid peace officer of another state or the federal government who is carrying out official duties while in this state, a person summoned by any officer to assist in making arrests or preserving the peace while the person is actually engaged in assisting any officer, or a member of the military forces of this state or the United States who is engaged in the performance of his or her duties, who brings or possesses any dirk, dagger, ice pick, knife having a blade longer than 2 1/2 inches, folding knife with a blade that locks into place, razor with an unguarded blade, taser, or stun gun, as defined in subdivision (a) of Section 244.5, any instrument that expels a metallic projectile, such as a BB or a pellet, through the force of air pressure, CO2 pressure, or spring action, or any spot marker gun, upon the grounds of, or within, any public or private school providing instruction in kindergarten or any of grades 1 to 12, inclusive, is guilty of a public offense, punishable by imprisonment in a county jail not exceeding one year, or by imprisonment pursuant to subdivision (h) of Section 1170.

(2) Any person, except a duly appointed peace officer as defined in Chapter 4.5 (commencing with Section 830) of Title 3 of Part 2, a full-time paid peace officer of another state or the federal government who is carrying out official duties while in this state, a person summoned by any officer to assist in making arrests or preserving the peace while the person is actually engaged in assisting any officer, or a member of the military forces of this state or the United States who is engaged in the performance of his or her duties, who brings or possesses a razor blade or a box cutter upon the grounds of, or within, any public or private school providing instruction in kindergarten or any of grades 1 to 12, inclusive, is guilty of a public offense, punishable by imprisonment in a county jail not exceeding one year.

(b) Any person, except a duly appointed peace officer as defined in Chapter 4.5 (commencing with Section 830) of Title 3 of Part 2, a full-time paid peace officer of another state or the federal government who is carrying out official duties while in this state, a person summoned by any officer to assist in making arrests or preserving the peace while the person is actually engaged in assisting any officer, or a member of the military forces of this state or the United States who is engaged in the performance of his or her duties, who brings or possesses any dirk, dagger, ice pick, or knife having a fixed blade longer than 2½ inches upon the grounds of, or within, any private university, the University of California, the California State University, or the California Community Colleges is guilty of a public offense, punishable by imprisonment in a county jail not exceeding one year, or by imprisonment pursuant to subdivision (h) of Section 1170.

(c) Subdivisions (a) and (b) do not apply to any person who brings or possesses a knife having a blade longer than 2½ inches, a razor with an unguarded blade, a razor blade, or a box cutter upon the grounds of, or within, a public or private school providing instruction in kindergarten or any of grades 1 to 12, inclusive, or any private university, state university, or community college at the direction of a faculty member of the private university, state university, or community college, or a certificated or classified employee of the school for use in a private university, state university, community college, or school-sponsored activity or class.

(d) Subdivisions (a) and (b) do not apply to any person who brings or possesses an ice pick, a knife having a blade longer than 2½ inches, a razor with an unguarded blade, a razor blade, or a box cutter upon the grounds of, or within, a public or private school providing instruction in kindergarten or any of grades 1 to 12, inclusive, or any private university, state university, or community college for a lawful purpose within the scope of the person's employment.

(e) Subdivision (b) does not apply to any person who brings or possesses an ice pick or a knife having a fixed blade longer than 2½ inches upon the grounds of, or within, any private university, state university, or community college for lawful use in or around a residence or residential facility located upon those grounds or for lawful use in food preparation or consumption.

(f) Subdivision (a) does not apply to any person who brings an instrument that expels a metallic projectile, such as a BB or a pellet, through the force of air pressure, CO2 pressure, or spring action, or any spot marker gun, or any razor blade or box cutter upon the grounds of, or within, a public or private school providing instruction in kindergarten or any of grades 1 to 12, inclusive, if the person has the written permission of the school principal or his or her designee.

(g) Any certificated or classified employee or school peace officer of a public or private school providing instruction in kindergarten or any of grades 1 to 12, inclusive, may seize any of the weapons described in subdivision (a), and any certificated or classified employee or school peace officer of any private university, state university, or community college may seize any of the weapons described in subdivision (b), from the possession of any person upon the grounds of, or within, the school if he or she knows, or has reasonable cause to know, the person is prohibited from bringing or possessing the weapon upon the grounds of, or within, the school.

(h) As used in this section, "dirk" or "dagger" means a knife or other instrument with or without a handguard that is capable of ready use as a stabbing weapon that may inflict great bodily injury or death.

(i) Any person who, without the written permission of the college or university president or chancellor or his or her designee, brings or possesses a less lethal weapon, as defined in Section 16780, or a stun gun, as defined in Section 17230, upon the grounds of, or within, a public or private college or university campus is guilty of a misdemeanor.

(Amended by Stats. 2013, Ch. 76, Sec. 147.5. (AB 383) Effective January 1, 2014.)

626.11.

(a) Any evidence seized by a teacher, official, employee, or governing board member of any university, state university, or community college, or by any person acting under his or her direction or with his or her consent in violation of standards relating to rights under the Fourth Amendment to the United States Constitution or under Section 13 of Article I of the State Constitution to be free from unreasonable searches and seizures, or in violation of state or federal constitutional rights to privacy, or any of them, is inadmissible in administrative disciplinary proceedings.

(b) Any provision in an agreement between a student and an educational institution specified in subdivision (a) relating to the leasing, renting, or use of a room of any student dormitory owned or operated by the institution by which the student waives a constitutional right under the Fourth Amendment to the United States Constitution or under Section 13 of Article I of the State Constitution, or under state or federal constitutional provision guaranteeing a right to privacy, or any of them, is contrary to public policy and void.

(c) Any evidence seized by a person specified in subdivision (a) after a nonconsensual entry not in violation of subdivision (a) into a dormitory room, which evidence is not directly related to the purpose for which the entry was initially made, is not admissible in administrative disciplinary proceedings.

(Amended by Stats. 1983, Ch. 143, Sec. 208.)

CHAPTER 1.1. Access to School Premises [627 - 627.10]

(Chapter 1.1 added by Stats. 1982, Ch. 76, Sec. 1.)

627.

(a) The Legislature finds the following:

(1) Violent crimes perpetrated on public school grounds interfere with the education of students and threaten the health and safety of teachers, other employees, and students.

(2) Many serious crimes of violence are committed on school grounds by persons who are neither students nor school employees and who are not otherwise authorized to be present on school grounds.

(3) School officials and law enforcement officers, in seeking to control these persons, have been hindered by the lack of effective legislation restricting the access of unauthorized persons to school grounds and providing appropriate criminal sanctions for unauthorized entry.

(b) The Legislature declares that the purpose of this chapter is to safeguard the teachers, other employees, students, and property of public schools. The Legislature recognizes the right to visit school grounds for legitimate nonviolent purposes and does not intend by this enactment to interfere with the exercise of that right.

(c) The Legislature finds and declares that a disproportionate share of crimes committed on school campuses are committed by persons who are neither students, school officials, or staff, and who have no lawful business on the school grounds. It is the intent of the Legislature in enacting this chapter to promote the safety and security of the public schools by restricting and conditioning the access of unauthorized persons to school campuses and to thereby implement the provisions of Section 28 of Article 1 of the California Constitution which guarantee all students and staff the inalienable constitutional right to attend safe, secure, and peaceful public schools. It is also the intent of the Legislature that the provisions of this chapter shall not be construed to infringe upon the legitimate exercise of constitutionally protected rights of freedom of speech and expression which may be expressed through rallies, demonstrations, and other forms of expression which may be appropriately engaged in by students and nonstudents in a campus setting.

(Amended by Stats. 1984, Ch. 395, Sec. 1.)

627.1.

As used in this chapter, with regard to a public school:

(a) An "outsider" is any person other than:

(1) A student of the school; except that a student who is currently suspended from the school shall be deemed an outsider for purposes of this chapter.

(2) A parent or guardian of a student of the school.

(3) An officer or employee of the school district that maintains the school.

(4) A public employee whose employment requires him or her to be on school grounds, or any person who is on school grounds at the request of the school.

(5) A representative of a school employee organization who is engaged in activities related to the representation of school employees.

(6) An elected public official.

(7) A person who comes within the provisions of Section 1070 of the Evidence Code by virtue of his or her current employment or occupation.

(b) "School grounds" are the buildings and grounds of the public school.

(c) "School hours" extend from one hour before classes begin until one hour after classes end.

(d) "Principal" is the chief administrative officer of the public school.

(e) "Designee" is a person whom the principal has authorized to register outsiders pursuant to this chapter.

(f) "Superintendent" is the superintendent of the school district that maintains the school or a person (other than the principal or someone employed under the principal's supervision) who the superintendent has authorized to conduct hearings pursuant to Section 627.5.

(Added by Stats. 1982, Ch. 76, Sec. 1. Effective March 1, 1982.)

627.2.

No outsider shall enter or remain on school grounds during school hours without having registered with the principal or designee, except to proceed expeditiously to the office of the principal or designee for the purpose of registering. If signs posted in accordance with Section 627.6 restrict the entrance or route that outsiders may use to reach the office of the principal or designee, an outsider shall comply with such signs.

(Added by Stats. 1982, Ch. 76, Sec. 1. Effective March 1, 1982.)

627.3.

In order to register, an outsider shall upon request furnish the principal or designee with the following:

(1) His or her name, address, and occupation.

(2) His or her age, if less than 21.

(3) His or her purpose in entering school grounds.

(4) Proof of identity.

(5) Other information consistent with the purposes of this chapter and with other provisions of law.

No person who furnishes the information and the proof of identity required by this section shall be refused registration except as provided by Section 627.4.

(Added by Stats. 1982, Ch. 76, Sec. 1. Effective March 1, 1982.)

627.4.

(a) The principal or his or her designee may refuse to register an outsider if he or she has a reasonable basis for concluding that the outsider's presence or acts would disrupt the school, its students, its teachers, or its other employees; would result in damage to property; or would result in the distribution or use of unlawful or controlled substances.

(b) The principal, his or her designee, or school security officer may revoke an outsider's registration if he or she has a reasonable basis for concluding that the outsider's presence on school grounds would interfere or is interfering with the peaceful conduct of the activities of the school, or would disrupt or is disrupting the school, its students, its teachers, or its other employees.

(Repealed and added by Stats. 1984, Ch. 395, Sec. 3.)

627.5.

Any person who is denied registration or whose registration is revoked may request a hearing before the principal or superintendent on the propriety of the denial or revocation. The request shall be in writing, shall state why the denial or revocation was improper, shall give the address to which notice of hearing is to be sent, and shall be delivered to either the principal or the superintendent within five days after the denial or revocation. The principal or superintendent shall promptly mail a written notice of the date, time, and place of the hearing to the person who requested the hearing. A hearing before the principal shall be held within seven days after the principal receives the request. A hearing before the superintendent shall be held within seven days after the superintendent receives the request.

(Added by Stats. 1982, Ch. 76, Sec. 1. Effective March 1, 1982.)

627.6.

At each entrance to the school grounds of every public school at which this chapter is in force, signs shall be posted specifying the hours during which registration is required pursuant to Section 627.2, stating where the office of the principal or designee is located and what route to take to that office, and setting forth the applicable requirements of Section 627.2 and the penalties for violation of this chapter.

(Added by Stats. 1982, Ch. 76, Sec. 1. Effective March 1, 1982.)

627.7.

(a) It is a misdemeanor punishable by imprisonment in the county jail not to exceed six months, or by a fine not to exceed five hundred dollars ($500), or by both, for an outsider to fail or refuse to leave the school grounds promptly after the principal, designee, or school security officer has requested the outsider to leave or to fail to remain off the school grounds for 7 days after being requested to leave, if the outsider does any of the following:

(1) Enters or remains on school grounds without having registered as required by Section 627.2.

(2) Enters or remains on school grounds after having been denied registration pursuant to subdivision (a) of Section 627.4.

(3) Enters or remains on school grounds after having registration revoked pursuant to subdivision (b) of Section 627.4.

(b) The provisions of this section shall not be utilized to impinge upon the lawful exercise of constitutionally protected rights of freedom of speech or assembly.

(c) When a person is directed to leave pursuant to subdivision (a), the person directing him or her to leave shall inform the person that if he or she reenters the place within 7 days he or she will be guilty of a crime.

(Amended by Stats. 1989, Ch. 1054, Sec. 3.)

627.8.

Every outsider who willfully and knowingly violates this chapter after having been previously convicted of a violation of this chapter committed within seven years of the date of two or more prior violations that resulted in conviction, shall be punished by imprisonment in the county jail for not less than 10 days nor more than six months, or by both such imprisonment and a fine not exceeding five hundred dollars ($500).

(Amended by Stats. 1984, Ch. 395, Sec. 6.)

627.8a.

The penalties imposed by the provisions of this chapter shall be utilized to prevent, deter, and punish those committing crimes on school campuses. The penalties imposed by the provisions of this chapter shall not be utilized to infringe upon the legitimate exercise of constitutionally protected rights of free speech or assembly.

(Added by Stats. 1984, Ch. 395, Sec. 7.)

627.9.

The governing board of any school district may:

(a) Exempt the district or any school or class of schools in the district from the operation of this chapter.
(b) Make exceptions to Section 627.2 for particular classes of outsiders.
(c) Authorize principals to exempt individual outsiders from the operation of Section 627.2; but any such exemption shall be in a writing which is signed and dated by the principal and which specifies the person or persons exempted and the date on which the exemption will expire.
(d) Exempt, or authorize principals to exempt, designated portions of school grounds from the operation of this chapter during some or all school hours.
(Added by Stats. 1982, Ch. 76, Sec. 1. Effective March 1, 1982.)
627.10.
A person whose presence or conduct on school grounds violates another provision of law may be punished for that violation, regardless of whether he or she was registered pursuant to this chapter at the time of the violation; but no punishment shall be imposed contrary to Section 654.
(Added by Stats. 1982, Ch. 76, Sec. 1. Effective March 1, 1982.)

CHAPTER 1.3. Massage Therapy [628 - 628.5]

(Chapter 1.3 added by Stats. 2011, Ch. 149, Sec. 1.)
628.
A person who provides a certificate, transcript, diploma, or other document, or otherwise affirms that a person has received instruction in massage therapy knowing that the person has not received instruction in massage therapy or knowing that the person has not received massage therapy instruction consistent with that document or affirmation is guilty of a misdemeanor and is punishable by a fine of not more than two thousand five hundred dollars ($2,500) per violation, or imprisonment in a county jail for not more than one year, or by both that fine and imprisonment.
(Added by Stats. 2011, Ch. 149, Sec. 1. (SB 285) Effective January 1, 2012.)
628.5.
For any person that is criminally prosecuted for a violation of law in connection with massage therapy, including for crimes relating to prostitution, the arresting law enforcement agency may provide to the California Massage Therapy Council, created pursuant to Section 4600.5 of the Business and Professions Code, information concerning the massage therapy instruction received by the person prosecuted, including the name of the school attended, if any.
(Added by Stats. 2011, Ch. 149, Sec. 1. (SB 285) Effective January 1, 2012.)

CHAPTER 1.4. Interception of Wire, Electronic Digital Pager, or Electronic Cellular Telephone Communications [629.50 - 629.98]

(Chapter 1.4 added by Stats. 1995, Ch. 971, Sec. 10.)
629.50.
(a) Each application for an order authorizing the interception of a wire or electronic communication shall be made in writing upon the personal oath or affirmation of the Attorney General, Chief Deputy Attorney General, or Chief Assistant Attorney General, Criminal Law Division, or of a district attorney, or the person designated to act as district attorney in the district attorney's absence, to the presiding judge of the superior court or one other judge designated by the presiding judge. An ordered list of additional judges may be authorized by the presiding judge to sign an order authorizing an interception. One of these judges may hear an application and sign an order only if that judge makes a determination that the presiding judge, the first designated judge, and those judges higher on the list are unavailable. Each application shall include all of the following information:
(1) The identity of the investigative or law enforcement officer making the application, and the officer authorizing the application.
(2) The identity of the law enforcement agency that is to execute the order.
(3) A statement attesting to a review of the application and the circumstances in support thereof by the chief executive officer, or his or her designee, of the law enforcement agency making the application. This statement shall name the chief executive officer or the designee who effected this review.
(4) A full and complete statement of the facts and circumstances relied upon by the applicant to justify his or her belief that an order should be issued, including (A) details as to the particular offense that has been, is being, or is about to be committed, (B) the fact that conventional investigative techniques had been tried and were unsuccessful, or why they reasonably appear to be unlikely to succeed or to be too dangerous, (C) a particular description of the nature and location of the facilities from which or the place where the communication is to be intercepted, (D) a particular description of the type of communication sought to be intercepted, and (E) the identity, if known, of the person committing the offense and whose communications are to be intercepted, or if that person's identity is not known, then the information relating to the person's identity that is known to the applicant.
(5) A statement of the period of time for which the interception is required to be maintained, and if the nature of the investigation is such that the authorization for interception should not automatically terminate when the described type of communication has been first obtained, a particular description of the facts establishing probable cause to believe that additional communications of the same type will occur thereafter.
(6) A full and complete statement of the facts concerning all previous applications known, to the individual authorizing and to the individual making the application, to have been made to any judge of a state or federal court for authorization to intercept wire or electronic communications involving any of the same persons, facilities, or places specified in the application, and the action taken by the judge on each of those applications. This requirement may be satisfied by making inquiry of the California Attorney General and the United States Department of Justice and reporting the results of these inquiries in the application.
(7) If the application is for the extension of an order, a statement setting forth the number of communications intercepted pursuant to the original order, and the results thus far obtained from the interception, or a reasonable explanation of the failure to obtain results.
(8) An application for modification of an order may be made when there is probable cause to believe that the person or persons identified in the original order have commenced to use a facility or device that is not subject to the original order. Any modification under this subdivision shall only be valid for the period authorized under the order being modified. The application for modification shall meet all of the requirements in paragraphs (1) to (6), inclusive, and shall include a statement of the results thus far obtained from the interception, or a reasonable explanation for the failure to obtain results.
(b) The judge may require the applicant to furnish additional testimony or documentary evidence in support of an application for an order under this section.
(c) The judge shall accept a facsimile copy of the signature of any person required to give a personal oath or affirmation pursuant to subdivision (a) as an original signature to the application. The original signed document shall be sealed and kept with the application pursuant to the provisions of Section 629.66 and custody of the original signed document shall be in the same manner as the judge orders for the application.
(Amended by Stats. 2010, Ch. 707, Sec. 1. (SB 1428) Effective January 1, 2011. Repealed as of January 1, 2020, pursuant to Section 629.98.)
629.51.
(a) For the purposes of this chapter, the following terms have the following meanings:
(1) "Wire communication" means any aural transfer made in whole or in part through the use of facilities for the transmission of communications by the aid of wire, cable, or other like connection between the point of origin and the point of reception (including the use of a like connection in a switching station), furnished or operated by any person engaged in providing or operating these facilities for the transmission of communications.
(2) "Electronic communication" means any transfer of signs, signals, writings, images, sounds, data, or intelligence of any nature in whole or in part by a wire, radio, electromagnetic, photoelectric, or photo-optical system, but does not include any of the following:
(A) Any wire communication defined in paragraph (1).
(B) Any communication made through a tone-only paging device.
(C) Any communication from a tracking device.
(D) Electronic funds transfer information stored by a financial institution in a communications system used for the electronic storage and transfer of funds.
(3) "Tracking device" means an electronic or mechanical device that permits the tracking of the movement of a person or object.
(4) "Aural transfer" means a transfer containing the human voice at any point between and including the point of origin and the point of reception.
(b) This chapter applies to the interceptions of wire and electronic communications. It does not apply to stored communications or stored content.
(c) The act that added this subdivision is not intended to change the law as to stored communications or stored content.
(Amended by Stats. 2010, Ch. 707, Sec. 2. (SB 1428) Effective January 1, 2011. Repealed as of January 1, 2020, pursuant to Section 629.98.)
629.52.
Upon application made under Section 629.50, the judge may enter an ex parte order, as requested or modified, authorizing interception of wire or electronic communications initially intercepted within the territorial jurisdiction of the court in which the judge is sitting, if the judge determines, on the basis of the facts submitted by the applicant, all of the following:
(a) There is probable cause to believe that an individual is committing, has committed, or is about to commit, one of the following offenses:
(1) Importation, possession for sale, transportation, manufacture, or sale of controlled substances in violation of Section 11351, 11351.5, 11352, 11370.6, 11378, 11378.5, 11379, 11379.5, or 11379.6 of the Health and Safety Code with respect to a substance containing heroin, cocaine, PCP, methamphetamine, fentanyl, or their precursors or analogs where the substance exceeds 10 gallons by liquid volume or three pounds of solid substance by weight.
(2) Murder, solicitation to commit murder, a violation of Section 209, or the commission of a felony involving a destructive device in violation of Section 18710, 18715, 18720, 18725, 18730, 18740, 18745, 18750, or 18755.
(3) A felony violation of Section 186.22.
(4) A felony violation of Section 11418, relating to weapons of mass destruction, Section 11418.5, relating to threats to use weapons of mass destruction, or Section 11419, relating to restricted biological agents.
(5) A violation of Section 236.1.
(6) An attempt or conspiracy to commit any of the above-mentioned crimes.
(b) There is probable cause to believe that particular communications concerning the illegal activities will be obtained through that interception, including, but not limited to, communications that may be utilized for locating or rescuing a kidnap victim.
(c) There is probable cause to believe that the facilities from which, or the place where, the wire or electronic communications are to be intercepted are being used, or are about to be used, in connection with the commission of the offense, or are leased to, listed in the name of, or commonly used by the person whose communications are to be intercepted.
(d) Normal investigative procedures have been tried and have failed or reasonably appear either unlikely to succeed if tried or too dangerous.
(Amended by Stats. 2018, Ch. 294, Sec. 1. (AB 1948) Effective January 1, 2019. Repealed as of January 1, 2020, pursuant to Section 629.98. Note: This section was amended on March 7, 2000, by initiative Prop. 21.)
629.53.
The Judicial Council may establish guidelines for judges to follow in granting an order authorizing the interception of any wire or electronic communications.
(Amended by Stats. 2010, Ch. 707, Sec. 4. (SB 1428) Effective January 1, 2011. Repealed as of January 1, 2020, pursuant to Section 629.98.)
629.54.
Each order authorizing the interception of any wire or electronic communication shall specify all of the following:
(a) The identity, if known, of the person whose communications are to be intercepted, or if the identity is not known, then that information relating to the person's identity known to the applicant.
(b) The nature and location of the communication facilities as to which, or the place where, authority to intercept is granted.
(c) A particular description of the type of communication sought to be intercepted, and a statement of the illegal activities to which it relates.
(d) The identity of the agency authorized to intercept the communications and of the person making the application.
(e) The period of time during which the interception is authorized including a statement as to whether or not the interception shall automatically terminate when the described communication has been first obtained.
(Amended by Stats. 2010, Ch. 707, Sec. 5. (SB 1428) Effective January 1, 2011. Repealed as of January 1, 2020, pursuant to Section 629.98.)
629.56.
(a) Upon informal application by the Attorney General, Chief Deputy Attorney General, or Chief Assistant Attorney General, Criminal Law Division, or a district attorney, or the person designated to act as district attorney in the district attorney's absence, the presiding judge of the superior court or the first available judge designated as provided in Section 629.50 may grant oral approval for an interception, without an order, if he or she determines all of the following:
(1) There are grounds upon which an order could be issued under this chapter.
(2) There is probable cause to believe that an emergency situation exists with respect to the investigation of an offense enumerated in this chapter.
(3) There is probable cause to believe that a substantial danger to life or limb exists justifying the authorization for immediate interception of a private wire or electronic communication before an application for an order could with due diligence be submitted and acted upon.
(b) Approval for an interception under this section shall be conditioned upon filing with the judge, by midnight of the second full court day after the oral approval, a written application for an order which, if granted consistent with this chapter, shall also recite

the oral approval under this subdivision and be retroactive to the time of the oral approval.
(Amended by Stats. 2010, Ch. 707, Sec. 6. (SB 1428) Effective January 1, 2011. Repealed as of January 1, 2020, pursuant to Section 629.98.)
629.58.
No order entered under this chapter shall authorize the interception of any wire or electronic communication for any period longer than is necessary to achieve the objective of the authorization, nor in any event longer than 30 days, commencing on the day of the initial interception, or 10 days after the issuance of the order, whichever comes first. Extensions of an order may be granted, but only upon application for an extension made in accordance with Section 629.50 and upon the court making findings required by Section 629.52. The period of extension shall be no longer than the authorizing judge deems necessary to achieve the purposes for which it was granted and in no event any longer than 30 days. Every order and extension thereof shall contain a provision that the authorization to intercept shall be executed as soon as practicable, shall be conducted so as to minimize the interception of communications not otherwise subject to interception under this chapter, and shall terminate upon attainment of the authorized objective, or in any event at the time expiration of the term designated in the order or any extensions. In the event the intercepted communication is in a foreign language, an interpreter of that foreign language may assist peace officers in executing the authorization provided in this chapter, provided that the interpreter has the same training as any other intercepter authorized under this chapter and provided that the interception shall be conducted so as to minimize the interception of communications not otherwise subject to interception under this chapter.
(Amended by Stats. 2010, Ch. 707, Sec. 7. (SB 1428) Effective January 1, 2011. Repealed as of January 1, 2020, pursuant to Section 629.98.)
629.60.
Whenever an order authorizing an interception is entered, the order shall require reports in writing or otherwise to be made to the judge who issued the order showing the number of communications intercepted pursuant to the original order, and a statement setting forth what progress has been made toward achievement of the authorized objective, or a satisfactory explanation for its lack, and the need for continued interception. If the judge finds that progress has not been made, that the explanation for its lack is not satisfactory, or that no need exists for continued interception, he or she shall order that the interception immediately terminate. The reports shall be filed with the court at the intervals that the judge may require, but not less than one for each period of 10 days, commencing with the date of the signing of the order, and shall be made by any reasonable and reliable means, as determined by the judge.
(Amended by Stats. 2010, Ch. 707, Sec. 8. (SB 1428) Effective January 1, 2011. Repealed as of January 1, 2020, pursuant to Section 629.98.)
629.61.
(a) Whenever an order authorizing an interception is entered, the order shall require a report in writing or otherwise to be made to the Attorney General showing what persons, facilities, places, or any combination of these are to be intercepted pursuant to the application, and the action taken by the judge on each of those applications. The report shall be made at the interval that the order may require, but not more than 10 days after the order was issued, and shall be made by any reasonable and reliable means, as determined by the Attorney General.
(b) The Attorney General may issue regulations prescribing the collection and dissemination of information collected pursuant to this chapter.
(c) The Attorney General shall, upon the request of an individual making an application for an interception order pursuant to this chapter, provide any information known as a result of these reporting requirements and in compliance with paragraph (6) of subdivision (a) of Section 629.50.
(Amended by Stats. 2004, Ch. 405, Sec. 9. Effective January 1, 2005. Repealed as of January 1, 2020, pursuant to Section 629.98.)
629.62.
(a) The Attorney General shall prepare and submit an annual report to the Legislature, the Judicial Council, and the Director of the Administrative Office of the United States Courts on interceptions conducted under the authority of this chapter during the preceding year. Information for this report shall be provided to the Attorney General by any prosecutorial agency seeking an order pursuant to this chapter.
(b) The report shall include all of the following data:
(1) The number of orders or extensions applied for.
(2) The kinds of orders or extensions applied for.
(3) The fact that the order or extension was granted as applied for, was modified, or was denied.
(4) The number of wire or electronic communication devices that are the subject of each order granted.
(5) The period of interceptions authorized by the order, and the number and duration of any extensions of the order.
(6) The offense specified in the order or application, or extension of an order.
(7) The identity of the applying law enforcement officer and agency making the application and the person authorizing the application.
(8) The nature of the facilities from which or the place where communications were to be intercepted.
(9) A general description of the interceptions made under the order or extension, including (A) the number of persons whose communications were intercepted, (B) the number of communications intercepted, (C) the percentage of incriminating communications intercepted and the percentage of other communications intercepted, and (D) the approximate nature, amount, and cost of the manpower and other resources used in the interceptions.
(10) The number of arrests resulting from interceptions made under the order or extension, and the offenses for which arrests were made.
(11) The number of trials resulting from the interceptions.
(12) The number of motions to suppress made with respect to the interceptions, and the number granted or denied.
(13) The number of convictions resulting from the interceptions and the offenses for which the convictions were obtained and a general assessment of the importance of the interceptions.
(14) Except with regard to the initial report required by this section, the information required by paragraphs (9) to (13), inclusive, with respect to orders or extensions obtained in a preceding calendar year.
(15) The date of the order for service of inventory made pursuant to Section 629.68, confirmation of compliance with the order, and the number of notices sent.
(16) Other data that the Legislature, the Judicial Council, or the Director of the Administrative Office of the United States Courts shall require.
(c) The annual report shall be filed no later than April of each year, and shall also include a summary analysis of the data reported pursuant to subdivision (b). The Attorney General may issue regulations prescribing the content and form of the reports required to be filed pursuant to this section by any prosecutorial agency seeking an order to intercept wire or electronic communications.
(d) The Attorney General shall, upon the request of an individual making an application, provide any information known to him or her as a result of these reporting requirements that would enable the individual making an application to comply with paragraph (6) of subdivision (a) of Section 629.50.
(Amended by Stats. 2012, Ch. 162, Sec. 126. (SB 1171) Effective January 1, 2013. Repealed as of January 1, 2020, pursuant to Section 629.98.)

629.64.
The contents of any wire or electronic communication intercepted by any means authorized by this chapter shall, if possible, be recorded on any recording media. The recording of the contents of any wire or electronic communication pursuant to this chapter shall be done in a way that will protect the recording from editing or other alterations and ensure that the recording can be immediately verified as to its authenticity and originality and that any alteration can be immediately detected. In addition, the monitoring or recording device shall be of a type and shall be installed to preclude any interruption or monitoring of the interception by any unauthorized means. Immediately upon the expiration of the period of the order, or extensions thereof, the recordings shall be made available to the judge issuing the order and sealed under his or her directions. Custody of the recordings shall be where the judge orders. They shall not be destroyed except upon an order of the issuing or denying judge and in any event shall be kept for 10 years. Duplicate recordings may be made for use or disclosure pursuant to the provisions of Sections 629.74 and 629.76 for investigations. The presence of the seal provided for by this section, or a satisfactory explanation for the absence thereof, shall be a prerequisite for the use or disclosure of the contents of any wire or electronic communication or evidence derived therefrom under Section 629.78.
(Amended by Stats. 2010, Ch. 707, Sec. 10. (SB 1428) Effective January 1, 2011. Repealed as of January 1, 2020, pursuant to Section 629.98.)
629.66.
Applications made and orders granted pursuant to this chapter shall be sealed by the judge. Custody of the applications and orders shall be where the judge orders. The applications and orders shall be disclosed only upon a showing of good cause before a judge or for compliance with the provisions of subdivisions (b) and (c) of Section 629.70 and shall not be destroyed except on order of the issuing or denying judge, and in any event shall be kept for 10 years.
(Amended by Stats. 2010, Ch. 707, Sec. 11. (SB 1428) Effective January 1, 2011. Repealed as of January 1, 2020, pursuant to Section 629.98.)
629.68.
Within a reasonable time, but no later than 90 days, after the termination of the period of an order or extensions thereof, or after the filing of an application for an order of approval under Section 629.56 which has been denied, the issuing judge shall issue an order that shall require the requesting agency to serve upon persons named in the order or the application, and other known parties to intercepted communications, an inventory which shall include notice of all of the following:
(a) The fact of the entry of the order.
(b) The date of the entry and the period of authorized interception.
(c) The fact that during the period wire or electronic communications were or were not intercepted.
The judge, upon filing of a motion, may, in his or her discretion, make available to the person or his or her counsel for inspection the portions of the intercepted communications, applications, and orders that the judge determines to be in the interest of justice. On an ex parte showing of good cause to a judge, the serving of the inventory required by this section may be postponed. The period of postponement shall be no longer than the authorizing judge deems necessary to achieve the purposes for which it was granted.
(Amended by Stats. 2010, Ch. 707, Sec. 12. (SB 1428) Effective January 1, 2011. Repealed as of January 1, 2020, pursuant to Section 629.98.)
629.70.
(a) A defendant shall be notified that he or she was identified as the result of an interception that was obtained pursuant to this chapter. The notice shall be provided prior to the entry of a plea of guilty or nolo contendere, or at least 10 days prior to any trial, hearing, or proceeding in the case other than an arraignment or grand jury proceeding.
(b) Within the time period specified in subdivision (c), the prosecution shall provide to the defendant a copy of all recorded interceptions from which evidence against the defendant was derived, including a copy of the court order, accompanying application, and monitoring logs.
(c) Neither the contents of any intercepted wire or electronic communication nor evidence derived from those contents shall be received in evidence or otherwise disclosed in any trial, hearing, or other proceeding, except a grand jury proceeding, unless each party, not less than 10 days before the trial, hearing, or proceeding, has been furnished with a transcript of the contents of the interception and with the materials specified in subdivision (b). This 10-day period may be waived by the judge with regard to the transcript if he or she finds that it was not possible to furnish the party with the transcript 10 days before the trial, hearing, or proceeding, and that the party will not be prejudiced by the delay in receiving that transcript.
(d) A court may issue an order limiting disclosures pursuant to subdivisions (a) and (b) upon a showing of good cause.
(Amended by Stats. 2010, Ch. 707, Sec. 13. (SB 1428) Effective January 1, 2011. Repealed as of January 1, 2020, pursuant to Section 629.98.)
629.72.
Any person in any trial, hearing, or proceeding, may move to suppress some or all of the contents of any intercepted wire or electronic communications, or evidence derived therefrom, only on the basis that the contents or evidence were obtained in violation of the Fourth Amendment of the United States Constitution or of this chapter. The motion shall be made, determined, and be subject to review in accordance with the procedures set forth in Section 1538.5.
(Amended by Stats. 2010, Ch. 707, Sec. 14. (SB 1428) Effective January 1, 2011. Repealed as of January 1, 2020, pursuant to Section 629.98.)
629.74.
The Attorney General, any deputy attorney general, district attorney, or deputy district attorney, or any peace officer who, by any means authorized by this chapter, has obtained knowledge of the contents of any wire or electronic communication, or evidence derived therefrom, may disclose the contents to one of the individuals referred to in this section, to any judge or magistrate in the state, and to any investigative or law enforcement officer as defined in subdivision (7) of Section 2510 of Title 18 of the United States Code to the extent that the disclosure is permitted pursuant to Section 629.82 and is appropriate to the proper performance of the official duties of the individual making or receiving the disclosure. No other disclosure, except to a grand jury, of intercepted information is permitted prior to a public court hearing by any person regardless of how the person may have come into possession thereof.
(Amended by Stats. 2010, Ch. 707, Sec. 15. (SB 1428) Effective January 1, 2011. Repealed as of January 1, 2020, pursuant to Section 629.98.)
629.76.
The Attorney General, any deputy attorney general, district attorney, or deputy district attorney, or any peace officer or federal law enforcement officer who, by any means authorized by this chapter, has obtained knowledge of the contents of any wire or electronic communication, or evidence derived therefrom, may use the contents or evidence to the extent the use is appropriate to the proper performance of his or her official duties and is permitted pursuant to Section 629.82.
(Amended by Stats. 2010, Ch. 707, Sec. 16. (SB 1428) Effective January 1, 2011. Repealed as of January 1, 2020, pursuant to Section 629.98.)
629.78.
Any person who has received, by any means authorized by this chapter, any information concerning a wire or electronic communication, or evidence derived therefrom, intercepted in accordance with the provisions of this chapter, may, pursuant to Section 629.82, disclose the contents of that communication or derivative evidence while giving

testimony under oath or affirmation in any criminal court proceeding or in any grand jury proceeding.
(Amended by Stats. 2010, Ch. 707, Sec. 17. (SB 1428) Effective January 1, 2011. Repealed as of January 1, 2020, pursuant to Section 629.98.)
629.80.
No otherwise privileged communication intercepted in accordance with, or in violation of, the provisions of this chapter shall lose its privileged character. When a peace officer or federal law enforcement officer, while engaged in intercepting wire or electronic communications in the manner authorized by this chapter, intercepts wire or electronic communications that are of a privileged nature he or she shall immediately cease the interception for at least two minutes. After a period of at least two minutes, interception may be resumed for up to 30 seconds during which time the officer shall determine if the nature of the communication is still privileged. If still of a privileged nature, the officer shall again cease interception for at least two minutes, after which the officer may again resume interception for up to 30 seconds to redetermine the nature of the communication. The officer shall continue to go online and offline in this manner until the time that the communication is no longer privileged or the communication ends. The recording device shall be metered so as to authenticate upon review that interruptions occurred as set forth in this chapter.
(Amended by Stats. 2010, Ch. 707, Sec. 18. (SB 1428) Effective January 1, 2011. Repealed as of January 1, 2020, pursuant to Section 629.98.)
629.82.
(a) If a peace officer or federal law enforcement officer, while engaged in intercepting wire or electronic communications in the manner authorized by this chapter, intercepts wire or electronic communications relating to crimes other than those specified in the order of authorization, but which are enumerated in subdivision (a) of Section 629.52, or any violent felony as defined in subdivision (c) of Section 667.5, (1) the contents thereof, and evidence derived therefrom, may be disclosed or used as provided in Sections 629.74 and 629.76 and (2) the contents and any evidence derived therefrom may be used under Section 629.78 when authorized by a judge if the judge finds, upon subsequent application, that the contents were otherwise intercepted in accordance with the provisions of this chapter. The application shall be made as soon as practicable.
(b) If a peace officer or federal law enforcement officer, while engaged in intercepting wire or electronic communications in the manner authorized by this chapter, intercepts wire or electronic communications relating to crimes other than those specified in subdivision (a), the contents thereof, and evidence derived therefrom, may not be disclosed or used as provided in Sections 629.74 and 629.76, except to prevent the commission of a public offense. The contents and any evidence derived therefrom may not be used under Section 629.78, except where the evidence was obtained through an independent source or inevitably would have been discovered, and the use is authorized by a judge who finds that the contents were intercepted in accordance with this chapter.
(c) The use of the contents of an intercepted wire or electronic communication relating to crimes other than those specified in the order of authorization to obtain a search or arrest warrant entitles the person named in the warrant to notice of the intercepted wire or electronic communication and a copy of the contents thereof that were used to obtain the warrant.
(Amended by Stats. 2010, Ch. 707, Sec. 19. (SB 1428) Effective January 1, 2011. Repealed as of January 1, 2020, pursuant to Section 629.98.)
629.84.
Any violation of this chapter is punishable by a fine not exceeding two thousand five hundred dollars ($2,500), or by imprisonment in the county jail not exceeding one year, or by imprisonment pursuant to subdivision (h) of Section 1170, or by both that fine and imprisonment.
(Amended by Stats. 2011, Ch. 15, Sec. 427. (AB 109) Effective April 4, 2011. Operative October 1, 2011, by Sec. 636 of Ch. 15, as amended by Stats. 2011, Ch. 39, Sec. 68. Repealed as of January 1, 2020, pursuant to Section 629.98.)
629.86.
Any person whose wire or electronic communication is intercepted, disclosed, or used in violation of this chapter shall have the following remedies:
(a) Have a civil cause of action against any person who intercepts, discloses, or uses, or procures any other person to intercept, disclose, or use, the communications.
(b) Be entitled to recover, in that action, all of the following:
(1) Actual damages but not less than liquidated damages computed at the rate of one hundred dollars ($100) a day for each day of violation or one thousand dollars ($1,000), whichever is greater.
(2) Punitive damages.
(3) Reasonable attorney's fees and other litigation costs reasonably incurred.
A good faith reliance on a court order is a complete defense to any civil or criminal action brought under this chapter, or under Chapter 1.5 (commencing with Section 630) or any other law.
(Amended by Stats. 2010, Ch. 707, Sec. 20. (SB 1428) Effective January 1, 2011. Repealed as of January 1, 2020, pursuant to Section 629.98.)
629.88.
Nothing in Section 631, 632.5, 632.6, or 632.7 shall be construed as prohibiting any peace officer or federal law enforcement officer from intercepting any wire or electronic communication pursuant to an order issued in accordance with the provisions of this chapter. Nothing in Section 631, 632.5, 632.6, or 632.7 shall be construed as rendering inadmissible in any criminal proceeding in any court or before any grand jury any evidence obtained by means of an order issued in accordance with the provisions of this chapter. Nothing in Section 637 shall be construed as prohibiting the disclosure of the contents of any wire or electronic communication obtained by any means authorized by this chapter, if the disclosure is authorized by this chapter. Nothing in this chapter shall apply to any conduct authorized by Section 633.
(Amended by Stats. 2010, Ch. 707, Sec. 21. (SB 1428) Effective January 1, 2011. Repealed as of January 1, 2020, pursuant to Section 629.98.)
629.89.
No order issued pursuant to this chapter shall either directly or indirectly authorize covert entry into or upon the premises of a residential dwelling, hotel room, or motel room for installation or removal of any interception device or for any other purpose. Notwithstanding that this entry is otherwise prohibited by any other section or code, this chapter expressly prohibits covert entry of a residential dwelling, hotel room, or motel room to facilitate an order to intercept wire or electronic communications.
(Amended by Stats. 2010, Ch. 707, Sec. 22. (SB 1428) Effective January 1, 2011. Repealed as of January 1, 2020, pursuant to Section 629.98.)
629.90.
An order authorizing the interception of a wire or electronic communication shall direct, upon request of the applicant, that a public utility engaged in the business of providing communications services and facilities, a landlord, custodian, or any other person furnish the applicant forthwith all information, facilities, and technical assistance necessary to accomplish the interception unobtrusively and with a minimum of interference with the services which the public utility, landlord, custodian, or other person is providing the person whose communications are to be intercepted. Any such public utility, landlord, custodian, or other person furnishing facilities or technical assistance shall be fully compensated by the applicant for the reasonable costs of furnishing the facilities and technical assistance.
(Amended by Stats. 2010, Ch. 707, Sec. 23. (SB 1428) Effective January 1, 2011. Repealed as of January 1, 2020, pursuant to Section 629.98.)
629.91.

A good faith reliance on a court order issued in accordance with this chapter by any public utility, landlord, custodian, or any other person furnishing information, facilities, and technical assistance as directed by the order is a complete defense to any civil or criminal action brought under this chapter, Chapter 1.5 (commencing with Section 630), or any other law.
(Added by Stats. 1995, Ch. 971, Sec. 10. Effective January 1, 1996. Repealed as of January 1, 2020, pursuant to Section 629.98.)
629.92.
Notwithstanding any other provision of law, any court to which an application is made in accordance with this chapter may take any evidence, make any finding, or issue any order required to conform the proceedings or the issuance of any order of authorization or approval to the provisions of the Constitution of the United States, any law of the United States, or this chapter.
(Added by Stats. 1995, Ch. 971, Sec. 10. Effective January 1, 1996. Repealed as of January 1, 2020, pursuant to Section 629.98.)
629.94.
(a) The Commission on Peace Officer Standards and Training, in consultation with the Attorney General, shall establish a course of training in the legal, practical, and technical aspects of the interception of private wire or electronic communications and related investigative techniques.
(b) The Attorney General shall set minimum standards for certification and periodic recertification of the following persons as eligible to apply for orders authorizing the interception of private wire or electronic communications, to conduct the interceptions, and to use the communications or evidence derived from them in official proceedings:
(1) Investigative or law enforcement officers.
(2) Other persons, when necessary, to provide linguistic interpretation who are designated by the Attorney General, Chief Deputy Attorney General, or Chief Assistant Attorney General, Criminal Law Division, or the district attorney, or the district attorney's designee and are supervised by an investigative or law enforcement officer.
(c) The Commission on Peace Officer Standards and Training may charge a reasonable enrollment fee for those students who are employed by an agency not eligible for reimbursement by the commission to offset the costs of the training. The Attorney General may charge a reasonable fee to offset the cost of certification.
(Amended by Stats. 2010, Ch. 707, Sec. 24. (SB 1428) Effective January 1, 2011. Repealed as of January 1, 2020, pursuant to Section 629.98.)
629.96.
If any provision of this chapter, or the application thereof to any person or circumstances, is held invalid, the remainder of the chapter, and the application of its provisions to other persons or circumstances, shall not be affected thereby.
(Added by Stats. 1995, Ch. 971, Sec. 10. Effective January 1, 1996. Repealed as of January 1, 2020, pursuant to Section 629.98.)
629.98.
This chapter shall only remain in effect until January 1, 2020, and as of that date is repealed.
(Amended by Stats. 2014, Ch. 745, Sec. 1. (SB 35) Effective January 1, 2015. Repealed as of January 1, 2020, by its own provisions. Note: Repeal affects Chapter 1.4, commencing with Section 629.50.)

CHAPTER 1.4. Interception of Wire, Electronic Digital Pager, or Electronic Cellular Telephone Communications [629.50 - 629.98]

(Chapter 1.4 added by Stats. 1995, Ch. 971, Sec. 10.)
629.50.
(a) Each application for an order authorizing the interception of a wire or electronic communication shall be made in writing upon the personal oath or affirmation of the Attorney General, Chief Deputy Attorney General, or Chief Assistant Attorney General, Criminal Law Division, or of a district attorney, or the person designated to act as district attorney in the district attorney's absence, to the presiding judge of the superior court or one other judge designated by the presiding judge. An ordered list of additional judges may be authorized by the presiding judge to sign an order authorizing an interception. One of these judges may hear an application and sign an order only if that judge makes a determination that the presiding judge, the first designated judge, and those judges higher on the list are unavailable. Each application shall include all of the following information:
(1) The identity of the investigative or law enforcement officer making the application, and the officer authorizing the application.
(2) The identity of the law enforcement agency that is to execute the order.
(3) A statement attesting to a review of the application and the circumstances in support thereof by the chief executive officer, or his or her designee, of the law enforcement agency making the application. This statement shall name the chief executive officer or the designee who effected this review.
(4) A full and complete statement of the facts and circumstances relied upon by the applicant to justify his or her belief that an order should be issued, including (A) details as to the particular offense that has been, is being, or is about to be committed, (B) the fact that conventional investigative techniques had been tried and were unsuccessful, or why they reasonably appear to be unlikely to succeed or to be too dangerous, (C) a particular description of the nature and location of the facilities from which or the place where the communication is to be intercepted, (D) a particular description of the type of communication sought to be intercepted, and (E) the identity, if known, of the person committing the offense and whose communications are to be intercepted, or if that person's identity is not known, then the information relating to the person's identity that is known to the applicant.
(5) A statement of the period of time for which the interception is required to be maintained, and if the nature of the investigation is such that the authorization for interception should not automatically terminate when the described type of communication has been first obtained, a particular description of the facts establishing probable cause to believe that additional communications of the same type will occur thereafter.
(6) A full and complete statement of the facts concerning all previous applications known, to the individual authorizing and to the individual making the application, to have been made to any judge of a state or federal court for authorization to intercept wire or electronic communications involving any of the same persons, facilities, or places specified in the application, and the action taken by the judge on each of those applications. This requirement may be satisfied by making inquiry of the California Attorney General and the United States Department of Justice and reporting the results of these inquiries in the application.
(7) If the application is for the extension of an order, a statement setting forth the number of communications intercepted pursuant to the original order, and the results thus far obtained from the interception, or a reasonable explanation of the failure to obtain results.
(8) An application for modification of an order may be made when there is probable cause to believe that the person or persons identified in the original order have

commenced to use a facility or device that is not subject to the original order. Any modification under this subdivision shall only be valid for the period authorized under the order being modified. The application for modification shall meet all of the requirements in paragraphs (1) to (6), inclusive, and shall include a statement of the results thus far obtained from the interception, or a reasonable explanation for the failure to obtain results.

(b) The judge may require the applicant to furnish additional testimony or documentary evidence in support of an application for an order under this section.

(c) The judge shall accept a facsimile copy of the signature of any person required to give a personal oath or affirmation pursuant to subdivision (a) as an original signature to the application. The original signed document shall be sealed and kept with the application pursuant to the provisions of Section 629.66 and custody of the original signed document shall be in the same manner as the judge orders for the application.

(Amended by Stats. 2010, Ch. 707, Sec. 1. (SB 1428) Effective January 1, 2011. Repealed as of January 1, 2020, pursuant to Section 629.98.)

629.51.

(a) For the purposes of this chapter, the following terms have the following meanings:

(1) "Wire communication" means any aural transfer made in whole or in part through the use of facilities for the transmission of communications by the aid of wire, cable, or other like connection between the point of origin and the point of reception (including the use of a like connection in a switching station), furnished or operated by any person engaged in providing or operating these facilities for the transmission of communications.

(2) "Electronic communication" means any transfer of signs, signals, writings, images, sounds, data, or intelligence of any nature in whole or in part by a wire, radio, electromagnetic, photoelectric, or photo-optical system, but does not include any of the following:

(A) Any wire communication defined in paragraph (1).

(B) Any communication made through a tone-only paging device.

(C) Any communication from a tracking device.

(D) Electronic funds transfer information stored by a financial institution in a communications system used for the electronic storage and transfer of funds.

(3) "Tracking device" means an electronic or mechanical device that permits the tracking of the movement of a person or object.

(4) "Aural transfer" means a transfer containing the human voice at any point between and including the point of origin and the point of reception.

(b) This chapter applies to the interceptions of wire and electronic communications. It does not apply to stored communications or stored content.

(c) The act that added this subdivision is not intended to change the law as to stored communications or stored content.

(Amended by Stats. 2010, Ch. 707, Sec. 2. (SB 1428) Effective January 1, 2011. Repealed as of January 1, 2020, pursuant to Section 629.98.)

629.52.

Upon application made under Section 629.50, the judge may enter an ex parte order, as requested or modified, authorizing interception of wire or electronic communications initially intercepted within the territorial jurisdiction of the court in which the judge is sitting, if the judge determines, on the basis of the facts submitted by the applicant, all of the following:

(a) There is probable cause to believe that an individual is committing, has committed, or is about to commit, one of the following offenses:

(1) Importation, possession for sale, transportation, manufacture, or sale of controlled substances in violation of Section 11351, 11351.5, 11352, 11370.6, 11378, 11378.5, 11379, 11379.5, or 11379.6 of the Health and Safety Code with respect to a substance containing heroin, cocaine, PCP, methamphetamine, fentanyl, or their precursors or analogs where the substance exceeds 10 gallons by liquid volume or three pounds of solid substance by weight.

(2) Murder, solicitation to commit murder, a violation of Section 209, or the commission of a felony involving a destructive device in violation of Section 18710, 18715, 18720, 18725, 18730, 18740, 18745, 18750, or 18755.

(3) A felony violation of Section 186.22.

(4) A felony violation of Section 11418, relating to weapons of mass destruction, Section 11418.5, relating to threats to use weapons of mass destruction, or Section 11419, relating to restricted biological agents.

(5) A violation of Section 236.1.

(6) An attempt or conspiracy to commit any of the above-mentioned crimes.

(b) There is probable cause to believe that particular communications concerning the illegal activities will be obtained through that interception, including, but not limited to, communications that may be utilized for locating or rescuing a kidnap victim.

(c) There is probable cause to believe that the facilities from which, or the place where, the wire or electronic communications are to be intercepted are being used, or are about to be used, in connection with the commission of the offense, or are leased to, listed in the name of, or commonly used by the person whose communications are to be intercepted.

(d) Normal investigative procedures have been tried and have failed or reasonably appear either unlikely to succeed if tried or too dangerous.

(Amended by Stats. 2018, Ch. 294, Sec. 1. (AB 1948) Effective January 1, 2019. Repealed as of January 1, 2020, pursuant to Section 629.98. Note: This section was amended on March 7, 2000, by initiative Prop. 21.)

629.53.

The Judicial Council may establish guidelines for judges to follow in granting an order authorizing the interception of any wire or electronic communications.

(Amended by Stats. 2010, Ch. 707, Sec. 4. (SB 1428) Effective January 1, 2011. Repealed as of January 1, 2020, pursuant to Section 629.98.)

629.54.

Each order authorizing the interception of any wire or electronic communication shall specify all of the following:

(a) The identity, if known, of the person whose communications are to be intercepted, or if the identity is not known, then that information relating to the person's identity known to the applicant.

(b) The nature and location of the communication facilities as to which, or the place where, authority to intercept is granted.

(c) A particular description of the type of communication sought to be intercepted, and a statement of the illegal activities to which it relates.

(d) The identity of the agency authorized to intercept the communications and of the person making the application.

(e) The period of time during which the interception is authorized including a statement as to whether or not the interception shall automatically terminate when the described communication has been first obtained.

(Amended by Stats. 2010, Ch. 707, Sec. 5. (SB 1428) Effective January 1, 2011. Repealed as of January 1, 2020, pursuant to Section 629.98.)

629.56.

(a) Upon informal application by the Attorney General, Chief Deputy Attorney General, or Chief Assistant Attorney General, Criminal Law Division, or a district attorney, or the person designated to act as district attorney in the district attorney's absence, the presiding judge of the superior court or the first available judge designated as provided in Section 629.50 may grant oral approval for an interception, without an order, if he or she determines all of the following:

(1) There are grounds upon which an order could be issued under this chapter.

(2) There is probable cause to believe that an emergency situation exists with respect to the investigation of an offense enumerated in this chapter.

(3) There is probable cause to believe that a substantial danger to life or limb exists justifying the authorization for immediate interception of a private wire or electronic communication before an application for an order could with due diligence be submitted and acted upon.

(b) Approval for an interception under this section shall be conditioned upon filing with the judge, by midnight of the second full court day after the oral approval, a written application for an order which, if granted consistent with this chapter, shall also recite the oral approval under this subdivision and be retroactive to the time of the oral approval.

(Amended by Stats. 2010, Ch. 707, Sec. 6. (SB 1428) Effective January 1, 2011. Repealed as of January 1, 2020, pursuant to Section 629.98.)

629.58.

No order entered under this chapter shall authorize the interception of any wire or electronic communication for any period longer than is necessary to achieve the objective of the authorization, nor in any event longer than 30 days, commencing on the day of the initial interception, or 10 days after the issuance of the order, whichever comes first. Extensions of an order may be granted, but only upon application for an extension made in accordance with Section 629.50 and upon the court making findings required by Section 629.52. The period of extension shall be no longer than the authorizing judge deems necessary to achieve the purposes for which it was granted and in no event any longer than 30 days. Every order and extension thereof shall contain a provision that the authorization to intercept shall be executed as soon as practicable, shall be conducted so as to minimize the interception of communications not otherwise subject to interception under this chapter, and shall terminate upon attainment of the authorized objective, or in any event at the time expiration of the term designated in the order or any extensions. In the event the intercepted communication is in a foreign language, an interpreter of that foreign language may assist peace officers in executing the authorization provided in this chapter, provided that the interpreter has the same training as any other intercepter authorized under this chapter and provided that the interception shall be conducted so as to minimize the interception of communications not otherwise subject to interception under this chapter.

(Amended by Stats. 2010, Ch. 707, Sec. 7. (SB 1428) Effective January 1, 2011. Repealed as of January 1, 2020, pursuant to Section 629.98.)

629.60.

Whenever an order authorizing an interception is entered, the order shall require reports in writing or otherwise to be made to the judge who issued the order showing the number of communications intercepted pursuant to the original order, and a statement setting forth what progress has been made toward achievement of the authorized objective, or a satisfactory explanation for its lack, and the need for continued interception. If the judge finds that progress has not been made, that the explanation for its lack is not satisfactory, or that no need exists for continued interception, he or she shall order that the interception immediately terminate. The reports shall be filed with the court at the intervals that the judge may require, but not less than one for each period of 10 days, commencing with the date of the signing of the order, and shall be made by any reasonable and reliable means, as determined by the judge.

(Amended by Stats. 2010, Ch. 707, Sec. 8. (SB 1428) Effective January 1, 2011. Repealed as of January 1, 2020, pursuant to Section 629.98.)

629.61.

(a) Whenever an order authorizing an interception is entered, the order shall require a report in writing or otherwise to be made to the Attorney General showing what persons, facilities, places, or any combination of these are to be intercepted pursuant to the application, and the action taken by the judge on each of those applications. The report shall be made at the interval that the order may require, but not more than 10 days after the order was issued, and shall be made by any reasonable and reliable means, as determined by the Attorney General.

(b) The Attorney General may issue regulations prescribing the collection and dissemination of information collected pursuant to this chapter.

(c) The Attorney General shall, upon the request of an individual making an application for an interception order pursuant to this chapter, provide any information known as a result of these reporting requirements and in compliance with paragraph (6) of subdivision (a) of Section 629.50.

(Amended by Stats. 2004, Ch. 405, Sec. 9. Effective January 1, 2005. Repealed as of January 1, 2020, pursuant to Section 629.98.)

629.62.

(a) The Attorney General shall prepare and submit an annual report to the Legislature, the Judicial Council, and the Director of the Administrative Office of the United States Courts on interceptions conducted under the authority of this chapter during the preceding year. Information for this report shall be provided to the Attorney General by any prosecutorial agency seeking an order pursuant to this chapter.

(b) The report shall include all of the following data:

(1) The number of orders or extensions applied for.

(2) The kinds of orders or extensions applied for.

(3) The fact that the order or extension was granted as applied for, was modified, or was denied.

(4) The number of wire or electronic communication devices that are the subject of each order granted.

(5) The period of interceptions authorized by the order, and the number and duration of any extensions of the order.

(6) The offense specified in the order or application, or extension of an order.

(7) The identity of the applying law enforcement officer and agency making the application and the person authorizing the application.

(8) The nature of the facilities from which or the place where communications were to be intercepted.

(9) A general description of the interceptions made under the order or extension, including (A) the number of persons whose communications were intercepted, (B) the number of communications intercepted, (C) the percentage of incriminating communications intercepted and the percentage of other communications intercepted, and (D) the approximate nature, amount, and cost of the manpower and other resources used in the interceptions.

(10) The number of arrests resulting from interceptions made under the order or extension, and the offenses for which arrests were made.

(11) The number of trials resulting from the interceptions.

(12) The number of motions to suppress made with respect to the interceptions, and the number granted or denied.

(13) The number of convictions resulting from the interceptions and the offenses for which the convictions were obtained and a general assessment of the importance of the interceptions.

(14) Except with regard to the initial report required by this section, the information required by paragraphs (9) to (13), inclusive, with respect to orders or extensions obtained in a preceding calendar year.

(15) The date of the order for service of inventory made pursuant to Section 629.68, confirmation of compliance with the order, and the number of notices sent.

(16) Other data that the Legislature, the Judicial Council, or the Director of the Administrative Office of the United States Courts shall require.

(c) The annual report shall be filed no later than April of each year, and shall also include a summary analysis of the data reported pursuant to subdivision (b). The

Attorney General may issue regulations prescribing the content and form of the reports required to be filed pursuant to this section by any prosecutorial agency seeking an order to intercept wire or electronic communications.

(d) The Attorney General shall, upon the request of an individual making an application, provide any information known to him or her as a result of these reporting requirements that would enable the individual making an application to comply with paragraph (6) of subdivision (a) of Section 629.50.

(Amended by Stats. 2012, Ch. 162, Sec. 126. (SB 1171) Effective January 1, 2013. Repealed as of January 1, 2020, pursuant to Section 629.98.)

629.64.

The contents of any wire or electronic communication intercepted by any means authorized by this chapter shall, if possible, be recorded on any recording media. The recording of the contents of any wire or electronic communication pursuant to this chapter shall be done in a way that will protect the recording from editing or other alterations and ensure that the recording can be immediately verified as to its authenticity and originality and that any alteration can be immediately detected. In addition, the monitoring or recording device shall be of a type and shall be installed to preclude any interruption or monitoring of the interception by any unauthorized means. Immediately upon the expiration of the period of the order, or extensions thereof, the recordings shall be made available to the judge issuing the order and sealed under his or her directions. Custody of the recordings shall be where the judge orders. They shall not be destroyed except upon an order of the issuing or denying judge and in any event shall be kept for 10 years. Duplicate recordings may be made for use or disclosure pursuant to the provisions of Sections 629.74 and 629.76 for investigations. The presence of the seal provided for by this section, or a satisfactory explanation for the absence thereof, shall be a prerequisite for the use or disclosure of the contents of any wire or electronic communication or evidence derived therefrom under Section 629.78.

(Amended by Stats. 2010, Ch. 707, Sec. 10. (SB 1428) Effective January 1, 2011. Repealed as of January 1, 2020, pursuant to Section 629.98.)

629.66.

Applications made and orders granted pursuant to this chapter shall be sealed by the judge. Custody of the applications and orders shall be where the judge orders. The applications and orders shall be disclosed only upon a showing of good cause before a judge or for compliance with the provisions of subdivisions (b) and (c) of Section 629.70 and shall not be destroyed except on order of the issuing or denying judge, and in any event shall be kept for 10 years.

(Amended by Stats. 2010, Ch. 707, Sec. 11. (SB 1428) Effective January 1, 2011. Repealed as of January 1, 2020, pursuant to Section 629.98.)

629.68.

Within a reasonable time, but no later than 90 days, after the termination of the period of an order or extensions thereof, or after the filing of an application for an order of approval under Section 629.56 which has been denied, the issuing judge shall issue an order that shall require the requesting agency to serve upon persons named in the order or the application, and other known parties to intercepted communications, an inventory which shall include notice of all of the following:

(a) The fact of the entry of the order.

(b) The date of the entry and the period of authorized interception.

(c) The fact that during the period wire or electronic communications were or were not intercepted.

The judge, upon filing of a motion, may, in his or her discretion, make available to the person or his or her counsel for inspection the portions of the intercepted communications, applications, and orders that the judge determines to be in the interest of justice. On an ex parte showing of good cause to a judge, the serving of the inventory required by this section may be postponed. The period of postponement shall be no longer than the authorizing judge deems necessary to achieve the purposes for which it was granted.

(Amended by Stats. 2010, Ch. 707, Sec. 12. (SB 1428) Effective January 1, 2011. Repealed as of January 1, 2020, pursuant to Section 629.98.)

629.70.

(a) A defendant shall be notified that he or she was identified as the result of an interception that was obtained pursuant to this chapter. The notice shall be provided prior to the entry of a plea of guilty or nolo contendere, or at least 10 days prior to any trial, hearing, or proceeding in the case other than an arraignment or grand jury proceeding.

(b) Within the time period specified in subdivision (c), the prosecution shall provide to the defendant a copy of all recorded interceptions from which evidence against the defendant was derived, including a copy of the court order, accompanying application, and monitoring logs.

(c) Neither the contents of any intercepted wire or electronic communication nor evidence derived from those contents shall be received in evidence or otherwise disclosed in any trial, hearing, or other proceeding, except a grand jury proceeding, unless each party, not less than 10 days before the trial, hearing, or proceeding, has been furnished with a transcript of the contents of the interception and with the materials specified in subdivision (b). This 10-day period may be waived by the judge with regard to the transcript if he or she finds that it was not possible to furnish the party with the transcript 10 days before the trial, hearing, or proceeding, and that the party will not be prejudiced by the delay in receiving that transcript.

(d) A court may issue an order limiting disclosures pursuant to subdivisions (a) and (b) upon a showing of good cause.

(Amended by Stats. 2010, Ch. 707, Sec. 13. (SB 1428) Effective January 1, 2011. Repealed as of January 1, 2020, pursuant to Section 629.98.)

629.72.

Any person in any trial, hearing, or proceeding, may move to suppress some or all of the contents of any intercepted wire or electronic communications, or evidence derived therefrom, only on the basis that the contents or evidence were obtained in violation of the Fourth Amendment of the United States Constitution or of this chapter. The motion shall be made, determined, and be subject to review in accordance with the procedures set forth in Section 1538.5.

(Amended by Stats. 2010, Ch. 707, Sec. 14. (SB 1428) Effective January 1, 2011. Repealed as of January 1, 2020, pursuant to Section 629.98.)

629.74.

The Attorney General, any deputy attorney general, district attorney, or deputy district attorney, or any peace officer who, by any means authorized by this chapter, has obtained knowledge of the contents of any wire or electronic communication, or evidence derived therefrom, may disclose the contents to one of the individuals referred to in this section, to any judge or magistrate in the state, and to any investigative or law enforcement officer as defined in subdivision (7) of Section 2510 of Title 18 of the United States Code to the extent that the disclosure is permitted pursuant to Section 629.82 and is appropriate to the proper performance of the official duties of the individual making or receiving the disclosure. No other disclosure, except to a grand jury, of intercepted information is permitted prior to a public court hearing by any person regardless of how the person may have come into possession thereof.

(Amended by Stats. 2010, Ch. 707, Sec. 15. (SB 1428) Effective January 1, 2011. Repealed as of January 1, 2020, pursuant to Section 629.98.)

629.76.

The Attorney General, any deputy attorney general, district attorney, or deputy district attorney, or any peace officer or federal law enforcement officer who, by any means authorized by this chapter, has obtained knowledge of the contents of any wire or electronic communication, or evidence derived therefrom, may use the contents or

evidence to the extent the use is appropriate to the proper performance of his or her official duties and is permitted pursuant to Section 629.82.

(Amended by Stats. 2010, Ch. 707, Sec. 16. (SB 1428) Effective January 1, 2011. Repealed as of January 1, 2020, pursuant to Section 629.98.)

629.78.

Any person who has received, by any means authorized by this chapter, any information concerning a wire or electronic communication, or evidence derived therefrom, intercepted in accordance with the provisions of this chapter, may, pursuant to Section 629.82, disclose the contents of that communication or derivative evidence while giving testimony under oath or affirmation in any criminal court proceeding or in any grand jury proceeding.

(Amended by Stats. 2010, Ch. 707, Sec. 17. (SB 1428) Effective January 1, 2011. Repealed as of January 1, 2020, pursuant to Section 629.98.)

629.80.

No otherwise privileged communication intercepted in accordance with, or in violation of, the provisions of this chapter shall lose its privileged character. When a peace officer or federal law enforcement officer, while engaged in intercepting wire or electronic communications in the manner authorized by this chapter, intercepts wire or electronic communications that are of a privileged nature he or she shall immediately cease the interception for at least two minutes. After a period of at least two minutes, interception may be resumed for up to 30 seconds during which time the officer shall determine if the nature of the communication is still privileged. If still of a privileged nature, the officer shall again cease interception for at least two minutes, after which the officer may again resume interception for up to 30 seconds to redetermine the nature of the communication. The officer shall continue to go online and offline in this manner until the time that the communication is no longer privileged or the communication ends. The recording device shall be metered so as to authenticate upon review that interruptions occurred as set forth in this chapter.

(Amended by Stats. 2010, Ch. 707, Sec. 18. (SB 1428) Effective January 1, 2011. Repealed as of January 1, 2020, pursuant to Section 629.98.)

629.82.

(a) If a peace officer or federal law enforcement officer, while engaged in intercepting wire or electronic communications in the manner authorized by this chapter, intercepts wire or electronic communications relating to crimes other than those specified in the order of authorization, but which are enumerated in subdivision (a) of Section 629.52, or any violent felony as defined in subdivision (c) of Section 667.5, (1) the contents thereof, and evidence derived therefrom, may be disclosed or used as provided in Sections 629.74 and 629.76 and (2) the contents and any evidence derived therefrom may be used under Section 629.78 when authorized by a judge if the judge finds, upon subsequent application, that the contents were otherwise intercepted in accordance with the provisions of this chapter. The application shall be made as soon as practicable.

(b) If a peace officer or federal law enforcement officer, while engaged in intercepting wire or electronic communications in the manner authorized by this chapter, intercepts wire or electronic communications relating to crimes other than those specified in subdivision (a), the contents thereof, and evidence derived therefrom, may not be disclosed or used as provided in Sections 629.74 and 629.76, except to prevent the commission of a public offense. The contents and any evidence derived therefrom may not be used under Section 629.78, except where the evidence was obtained through an independent source or inevitably would have been discovered, and the use is authorized by a judge who finds that the contents were intercepted in accordance with this chapter.

(c) The use of the contents of an intercepted wire or electronic communication relating to crimes other than those specified in the order of authorization to obtain a search or arrest warrant entitles the person named in the warrant to notice of the intercepted wire or electronic communication and a copy of the contents thereof that were used to obtain the warrant.

(Amended by Stats. 2010, Ch. 707, Sec. 19. (SB 1428) Effective January 1, 2011. Repealed as of January 1, 2020, pursuant to Section 629.98.)

629.84.

Any violation of this chapter is punishable by a fine not exceeding two thousand five hundred dollars ($2,500), or by imprisonment in the county jail not exceeding one year, or by imprisonment pursuant to subdivision (h) of Section 1170, or by both that fine and imprisonment.

(Amended by Stats. 2011, Ch. 15, Sec. 427. (AB 109) Effective April 4, 2011. Operative October 1, 2011, by Sec. 636 of Ch. 15, as amended by Stats. 2011, Ch. 39, Sec. 68. Repealed as of January 1, 2020, pursuant to Section 629.98.)

629.86.

Any person whose wire or electronic communication is intercepted, disclosed, or used in violation of this chapter shall have the following remedies:

(a) Have a civil cause of action against any person who intercepts, discloses, or uses, or procures any other person to intercept, disclose, or use, the communications.

(b) Be entitled to recover, in that action, all of the following:

(1) Actual damages but not less than liquidated damages computed at the rate of one hundred dollars ($100) a day for each day of violation or one thousand dollars ($1,000), whichever is greater.

(2) Punitive damages.

(3) Reasonable attorney's fees and other litigation costs reasonably incurred.

A good faith reliance on a court order is a complete defense to any civil or criminal action brought under this chapter, or under Chapter 1.5 (commencing with Section 630) or any other law.

(Amended by Stats. 2010, Ch. 707, Sec. 20. (SB 1428) Effective January 1, 2011. Repealed as of January 1, 2020, pursuant to Section 629.98.)

629.88.

Nothing in Section 631, 632.5, 632.6, or 632.7 shall be construed as prohibiting any peace officer or federal law enforcement officer from intercepting any wire or electronic communication pursuant to an order issued in accordance with the provisions of this chapter. Nothing in Section 631, 632.5, 632.6, or 632.7 shall be construed as rendering inadmissible in any criminal proceeding in any court or before any grand jury any evidence obtained by means of an order issued in accordance with the provisions of this chapter. Nothing in Section 637 shall be construed as prohibiting the disclosure of the contents of any wire or electronic communication obtained by any means authorized by this chapter, if the disclosure is authorized by this chapter. Nothing in this chapter shall apply to any conduct authorized by Section 633.

(Amended by Stats. 2010, Ch. 707, Sec. 21. (SB 1428) Effective January 1, 2011. Repealed as of January 1, 2020, pursuant to Section 629.98.)

629.89.

No order issued pursuant to this chapter shall either directly or indirectly authorize covert entry into or upon the premises of a residential dwelling, hotel room, or motel room for installation or removal of any interception device or for any other purpose. Notwithstanding that this entry is otherwise prohibited by any other section or code, this chapter expressly prohibits covert entry of a residential dwelling, hotel room, or motel room to facilitate an order to intercept wire or electronic communications.

(Amended by Stats. 2010, Ch. 707, Sec. 22. (SB 1428) Effective January 1, 2011. Repealed as of January 1, 2020, pursuant to Section 629.98.)

629.90.

An order authorizing the interception of a wire or electronic communication shall direct, upon request of the applicant, that a public utility engaged in the business of providing communications services and facilities, a landlord, custodian, or any other person furnish the applicant forthwith all information, facilities, and technical assistance necessary to accomplish the interception unobtrusively and with a minimum of

interference with the services which the public utility, landlord, custodian, or other person is providing the person whose communications are to be intercepted. Any such public utility, landlord, custodian, or other person furnishing facilities or technical assistance shall be fully compensated by the applicant for the reasonable costs of furnishing the facilities and technical assistance.
(Amended by Stats. 2010, Ch. 707, Sec. 23. (SB 1428) Effective January 1, 2011. Repealed as of January 1, 2020, pursuant to Section 629.98.)
629.91.
A good faith reliance on a court order issued in accordance with this chapter by any public utility, landlord, custodian, or any other person furnishing information, facilities, and technical assistance as directed by the order is a complete defense to any civil or criminal action brought under this chapter, Chapter 1.5 (commencing with Section 630), or any other law.
(Added by Stats. 1995, Ch. 971, Sec. 10. Effective January 1, 1996. Repealed as of January 1, 2020, pursuant to Section 629.98.)
629.92.
Notwithstanding any other provision of law, any court to which an application is made in accordance with this chapter may take any evidence, make any finding, or issue any order required to conform the proceedings or the issuance of any order of authorization or approval to the provisions of the Constitution of the United States, any law of the United States, or this chapter.
(Added by Stats. 1995, Ch. 971, Sec. 10. Effective January 1, 1996. Repealed as of January 1, 2020, pursuant to Section 629.98.)
629.94.
(a) The Commission on Peace Officer Standards and Training, in consultation with the Attorney General, shall establish a course of training in the legal, practical, and technical aspects of the interception of private wire or electronic communications and related investigative techniques.
(b) The Attorney General shall set minimum standards for certification and periodic recertification of the following persons as eligible to apply for orders authorizing the interception of private wire or electronic communications, to conduct the interceptions, and to use the communications or evidence derived from them in official proceedings:
(1) Investigative or law enforcement officers.
(2) Other persons, when necessary, to provide linguistic interpretation who are designated by the Attorney General, Chief Deputy Attorney General, or Chief Assistant Attorney General, Criminal Law Division, or the district attorney, or the district attorney's designee and are supervised by an investigative or law enforcement officer.
(c) The Commission on Peace Officer Standards and Training may charge a reasonable enrollment fee for those students who are employed by an agency not eligible for reimbursement by the commission to offset the costs of the training. The Attorney General may charge a reasonable fee to offset the cost of certification.
(Amended by Stats. 2010, Ch. 707, Sec. 24. (SB 1428) Effective January 1, 2011. Repealed as of January 1, 2020, pursuant to Section 629.98.)
629.96.
If any provision of this chapter, or the application thereof to any person or circumstances, is held invalid, the remainder of the chapter, and the application of its provisions to other persons or circumstances, shall not be affected thereby.
(Added by Stats. 1995, Ch. 971, Sec. 10. Effective January 1, 1996. Repealed as of January 1, 2020, pursuant to Section 629.98.)
629.98.
This chapter shall only remain in effect until January 1, 2020, and as of that date is repealed.
(Amended by Stats. 2014, Ch. 745, Sec. 1. (SB 35) Effective January 1, 2015. Repealed as of January 1, 2020, by its own provisions. Note: Repeal affects Chapter 1.4, commencing with Section 629.50.)

CHAPTER 1.5. Invasion of Privacy [630 - 638.55]

(Chapter 1.5 added by Stats. 1967, Ch. 1509.)
630.
The Legislature hereby declares that advances in science and technology have led to the development of new devices and techniques for the purpose of eavesdropping upon private communications and that the invasion of privacy resulting from the continual and increasing use of such devices and techniques has created a serious threat to the free exercise of personal liberties and cannot be tolerated in a free and civilized society.
The Legislature by this chapter intends to protect the right of privacy of the people of this state.
The Legislature recognizes that law enforcement agencies have a legitimate need to employ modern listening devices and techniques in the investigation of criminal conduct and the apprehension of lawbreakers. Therefore, it is not the intent of the Legislature to place greater restraints on the use of listening devices and techniques by law enforcement agencies than existed prior to the effective date of this chapter.
(Added by Stats. 1967, Ch. 1509.)
631.
(a) Any person who, by means of any machine, instrument, or contrivance, or in any other manner, intentionally taps, or makes any unauthorized connection, whether physically, electrically, acoustically, inductively, or otherwise, with any telegraph or telephone wire, line, cable, or instrument, including the wire, line, cable, or instrument of any internal telephonic communication system, or who willfully and without the consent of all parties to the communication, or in any unauthorized manner, reads, or attempts to read, or to learn the contents or meaning of any message, report, or communication while the same is in transit or passing over any wire, line, or cable, or is being sent from, or received at any place within this state; or who uses, or attempts to use, in any manner, or for any purpose, or to communicate in any way, any information so obtained, or who aids, agrees with, employs, or conspires with any person or persons to unlawfully do, or permit, or cause to be done any of the acts or things mentioned above in this section, is punishable by a fine not exceeding two thousand five hundred dollars ($2,500), or by imprisonment in the county jail not exceeding one year, or by imprisonment pursuant to subdivision (h) of Section 1170, or by both a fine and imprisonment in the county jail or pursuant to subdivision (h) of Section 1170. If the person has previously been convicted of a violation of this section or Section 632, 632.5, 632.6, 632.7, or 636, he or she is punishable by a fine not exceeding ten thousand dollars ($10,000), or by imprisonment in the county jail not exceeding one year, or by imprisonment pursuant to subdivision (h) of Section 1170, or by both that fine and imprisonment.
(b) This section shall not apply (1) to any public utility engaged in the business of providing communications services and facilities, or to the officers, employees or agents thereof, where the acts otherwise prohibited herein are for the purpose of construction, maintenance, conduct or operation of the services and facilities of the public utility, or (2) to the use of any instrument, equipment, facility, or service furnished and used pursuant to the tariffs of a public utility, or (3) to any telephonic communication system used for communication exclusively within a state, county, city and county, or city correctional facility.
(c) Except as proof in an action or prosecution for violation of this section, no evidence obtained in violation of this section shall be admissible in any judicial, administrative, legislative, or other proceeding.
(d) This section shall become operative on January 1, 1994.
(Amended by Stats. 2011, Ch. 15, Sec. 428. (AB 109) Effective April 4, 2011. Operative October 1, 2011, by Sec. 636 of Ch. 15, as amended by Stats. 2011, Ch. 39, Sec. 68.)
632.
(a) A person who, intentionally and without the consent of all parties to a confidential communication, uses an electronic amplifying or recording device to eavesdrop upon or record the confidential communication, whether the communication is carried on among the parties in the presence of one another or by means of a telegraph, telephone, or other device, except a radio, shall be punished by a fine not exceeding two thousand five hundred dollars ($2,500) per violation, or imprisonment in a county jail not exceeding one year, or in the state prison, or by both that fine and imprisonment. If the person has previously been convicted of a violation of this section or Section 631, 632.5, 632.6, 632.7, or 636, the person shall be punished by a fine not exceeding ten thousand dollars ($10,000) per violation, by imprisonment in a county jail not exceeding one year, or in the state prison, or by both that fine and imprisonment.
(b) For the purposes of this section, "person" means an individual, business association, partnership, corporation, limited liability company, or other legal entity, and an individual acting or purporting to act for or on behalf of any government or subdivision thereof, whether federal, state, or local, but excludes an individual known by all parties to a confidential communication to be overhearing or recording the communication.
(c) For the purposes of this section, "confidential communication" means any communication carried on in circumstances as may reasonably indicate that any party to the communication desires it to be confined to the parties thereto, but excludes a communication made in a public gathering or in any legislative, judicial, executive, or administrative proceeding open to the public, or in any other circumstance in which the parties to the communication may reasonably expect that the communication may be overheard or recorded.
(d) Except as proof in an action or prosecution for violation of this section, evidence obtained as a result of eavesdropping upon or recording a confidential communication in violation of this section is not admissible in any judicial, administrative, legislative, or other proceeding.
(e) This section does not apply (1) to any public utility engaged in the business of providing communications services and facilities, or to the officers, employees, or agents thereof, if the acts otherwise prohibited by this section are for the purpose of construction, maintenance, conduct, or operation of the services and facilities of the public utility, (2) to the use of any instrument, equipment, facility, or service furnished and used pursuant to the tariffs of a public utility, or (3) to any telephonic communication system used for communication exclusively within a state, county, city and county, or city correctional facility.
(f) This section does not apply to the use of hearing aids and similar devices, by persons afflicted with impaired hearing, for the purpose of overcoming the impairment to permit the hearing of sounds ordinarily audible to the human ear.
(Amended by Stats. 2016, Ch. 855, Sec. 1. (AB 1671) Effective January 1, 2017.)
632.01.
(a) (1) A person who violates subdivision (a) of Section 632 shall be punished pursuant to subdivision (b) if the person intentionally discloses or distributes, in any manner, in any forum, including, but not limited to, Internet Web sites and social media, or for any purpose, the contents of a confidential communication with a health care provider that is obtained by that person in violation of subdivision (a) of Section 632. For purposes of this subdivision, "social media" means an electronic service or account, or electronic content, including, but not limited to, videos or still photographs, blogs, video blogs, podcasts, instant and text messages, email, online services or accounts, or Internet Web site profiles or locations.
(2) Notwithstanding any other provision of law, to aid and abet a violation of paragraph (1), for the purposes of Section 31, the person shall either violate, or aid and abet in a violation of, both Section 632 and paragraph (1).
(b) A violation of subdivision (a) shall be punished by a fine not exceeding two thousand five hundred dollars ($2,500) per violation, or imprisonment in a county jail not exceeding one year, or in the state prison, or by both that fine and imprisonment. If the person has previously been convicted of a violation of this section, the person shall be punished by a fine not exceeding ten thousand dollars ($10,000) per violation, by imprisonment in a county jail not exceeding one year, or in the state prison, or by both that fine and imprisonment.
(c) For purposes of this section, "health care provider" means any of the following:
(1) A person licensed or certified pursuant to Division 2 (commencing with Section 500) of the Business and Professions Code.
(2) A person licensed pursuant to the Osteopathic Initiative Act or the Chiropractic Initiative Act.
(3) A person certified pursuant to Division 2.5 (commencing with Section 1797) of the Health and Safety Code.
(4) A clinic, health dispensary, or health facility licensed or exempt from licensure pursuant to Division 2 (commencing with Section 1200) of the Health and Safety Code.
(5) An employee, volunteer, or contracted agent of any group practice prepayment health care service plan regulated pursuant to the Knox-Keene Health Care Service Plan Act of 1975 (Chapter 2.2 (commencing with Section 1340) of Division 2 of the Health and Safety Code).
(6) An employee, volunteer, independent contractor, or professional student of a clinic, health dispensary, or health care facility or health care provider described in this subdivision.
(7) A professional organization that represents any of the other health care providers described in this subdivision.
(d) (1) Subdivision (a) does not apply to the disclosure or distribution of a confidential communication pursuant to any of the following:
(A) Any party as described in Section 633 acting within the scope of his or her authority overhearing or recording a confidential communication that he or she may lawfully overhear or record pursuant to that section.
(B) Any party as described in Section 633.02 overhearing or recording a confidential communication related to sexual assault or other sexual offense that he or she may lawfully overhear or record pursuant to that section, or using or operating a body-worn camera as authorized pursuant to that section.
(C) A city attorney as described in Section 633.05 overhearing or recording any communication that he or she may lawfully overhear or record pursuant to that section.
(D) An airport law enforcement officer recording a communication received on an incoming telephone line pursuant to Section 633.1.
(E) A party to a confidential communication recording the communication for the purpose of obtaining evidence reasonably believed to relate to the commission by another party to the communication of a crime as specified in Section 633.5.
(F) A victim of domestic violence recording a prohibited communication made to him or her by the perpetrator pursuant to Section 633.6.
(G) A peace officer using electronic amplifying or recording devices to eavesdrop on and record the otherwise confidential oral communications of individuals within a location when responding to an emergency situation that involves the taking of a hostage or the barricading of a location pursuant to Section 633.8.
(2) This section does not affect the admissibility of any evidence that would otherwise be admissible pursuant to the authority of any section specified in paragraph (1).
(Added by Stats. 2016, Ch. 855, Sec. 2. (AB 1671) Effective January 1, 2017.)
632.5.

(a) Every person who, maliciously and without the consent of all parties to the communication, intercepts, receives, or assists in intercepting or receiving a communication transmitted between cellular radio telephones or between any cellular radio telephone and a landline telephone shall be punished by a fine not exceeding two thousand five hundred dollars ($2,500), by imprisonment in the county jail not exceeding one year or in the state prison, or by both that fine and imprisonment. If the person has been previously convicted of a violation of this section or Section 631, 632, 632.6, 632.7, or 636, the person shall be punished by a fine not exceeding ten thousand dollars ($10,000), by imprisonment in the county jail not exceeding one year or in the state prison, or by both that fine and imprisonment.
(b) In the following instances, this section shall not apply:
(1) To any public utility engaged in the business of providing communications services and facilities, or to the officers, employees, or agents thereof, where the acts otherwise prohibited are for the purpose of construction, maintenance, conduct, or operation of the services and facilities of the public utility.
(2) To the use of any instrument, equipment, facility, or service furnished and used pursuant to the tariffs of the public utility.
(3) To any telephonic communication system used for communication exclusively within a state, county, city and county, or city correctional facility.
(c) As used in this section and Section 635, "cellular radio telephone" means a wireless telephone authorized by the Federal Communications Commission to operate in the frequency bandwidth reserved for cellular radio telephones.
(Amended by Stats. 1992, Ch. 298, Sec. 4. Effective January 1, 1993.)
632.6.
(a) Every person who, maliciously and without the consent of all parties to the communication, intercepts, receives, or assists in intercepting or receiving a communication transmitted between cordless telephones as defined in subdivision (c), between any cordless telephone and a landline telephone, or between a cordless telephone and a cellular telephone shall be punished by a fine not exceeding two thousand five hundred dollars ($2,500), by imprisonment in the county jail not exceeding one year, or in the state prison, or by both that fine and imprisonment. If the person has been convicted previously of a violation of Section 631, 632, 632.5, 632.7, or 636, the person shall be punished by a fine not exceeding ten thousand dollars ($10,000), or by imprisonment in the county jail not exceeding one year, or in the state prison, or by both that fine and imprisonment.
(b) This section shall not apply in any of the following instances:
(1) To any public utility engaged in the business of providing communications services and facilities, or to the officers, employees, or agents thereof, where the acts otherwise prohibited are for the purpose of construction, maintenance, conduct, or operation of the services and facilities of the public utility.
(2) To the use of any instrument, equipment, facility, or service furnished and used pursuant to the tariffs of the public utility.
(3) To any telephonic communications system used for communication exclusively within a state, county, city and county, or city correctional facility.
(c) As used in this section and in Section 635, "cordless telephone" means a two-way low power communication system consisting of two parts—a "base" unit which connects to the public switched telephone network and a handset or "remote" unit—which are connected by a radio link and authorized by the Federal Communications Commission to operate in the frequency bandwidths reserved for cordless telephones.
(Amended by Stats. 1992, Ch. 298, Sec. 5. Effective January 1, 1993.)
632.7.
(a) Every person who, without the consent of all parties to a communication, intercepts or receives and intentionally records, or assists in the interception or reception and intentional recordation of, a communication transmitted between two cellular radio telephones, a cellular radio telephone and a landline telephone, two cordless telephones, a cordless telephone and a landline telephone, or a cordless telephone and a cellular radio telephone, shall be punished by a fine not exceeding two thousand five hundred dollars ($2,500), or by imprisonment in a county jail not exceeding one year, or in the state prison, or by both that fine and imprisonment. If the person has been convicted previously of a violation of this section or of Section 631, 632, 632.5, 632.6, or 636, the person shall be punished by a fine not exceeding ten thousand dollars ($10,000), by imprisonment in a county jail not exceeding one year, or in the state prison, or by both that fine and imprisonment.
(b) This section shall not apply to any of the following:
(1) Any public utility engaged in the business of providing communications services and facilities, or to the officers, employees, or agents thereof, where the acts otherwise prohibited are for the purpose of construction, maintenance, conduct, or operation of the services and facilities of the public utility.
(2) The use of any instrument, equipment, facility, or service furnished and used pursuant to the tariffs of the public utility.
(3) Any telephonic communication system used for communication exclusively within a state, county, city and county, or city correctional facility.
(c) As used in this section, each of the following terms have the following meaning:
(1) "Cellular radio telephone" means a wireless telephone authorized by the Federal Communications Commission to operate in the frequency bandwidth reserved for cellular radio telephones.
(2) "Cordless telephone" means a two-way, low power communication system consisting of two parts, a "base" unit which connects to the public switched telephone network and a handset or "remote" unit, that are connected by a radio link and authorized by the Federal Communications Commission to operate in the frequency bandwidths reserved for cordless telephones.
(3) "Communication" includes, but is not limited to, communications transmitted by voice, data, or image, including facsimile.
(Amended by Stats. 1993, Ch. 536, Sec. 1. Effective September 27, 1993.)
633.
(a) Nothing in Section 631, 632, 632.5, 632.6, or 632.7 prohibits the Attorney General, any district attorney, or any assistant, deputy, or investigator of the Attorney General or any district attorney, any officer of the California Highway Patrol, any peace officer of the Office of Internal Affairs of the Department of Corrections and Rehabilitation, any chief of police, assistant chief of police, or police officer of a city or city and county, any sheriff, undersheriff, or deputy sheriff regularly employed and paid in that capacity by a county, police officer of the County of Los Angeles, or any person acting pursuant to the direction of one of these law enforcement officers acting within the scope of his or her authority, from overhearing or recording any communication that they could lawfully overhear or record prior to January 1, 1968.
(b) Nothing in Section 631, 632, 632.5, 632.6, or 632.7 renders inadmissible any evidence obtained by the above-named persons by means of overhearing or recording any communication that they could lawfully overhear or record prior to January 1, 1968.
(Amended by Stats. 2018, Ch. 175, Sec. 1. (AB 2669) Effective January 1, 2019.)
633.02.
(a) Nothing in Section 631, 632, 632.5, 632.6, or 632.7 prohibits any POST-certified chief of police, assistant chief of police, or police officer of a university or college campus acting within the scope of his or her authority, from overhearing or recording any communication that he or she could lawfully overhear or record prior to January 1, 1968, in any criminal investigation related to sexual assault or other sexual offense.
(b) Nothing in Section 631, 632, 632.5, 632.6, or 632.7 shall prohibit any POST-certified chief of police, assistant chief of police, or police officer of a university or college campus from using or operating body-worn cameras.
(c) This section shall not be construed to affect Section 633.

(d) This section shall not be used to impinge upon the lawful exercise of constitutionally protected rights of freedom of speech or assembly, or the constitutionally protected right of personal privacy.
(Added by Stats. 2015, Ch. 159, Sec. 1. (SB 424) Effective January 1, 2016.)
633.05.
(a) Nothing in Section 632, 632.5, 632.6, or 632.7 prohibits a city attorney acting under authority of Section 41803.5 of the Government Code, provided that authority is granted prior to January 1, 2012, or any person acting pursuant to the direction of one of those city attorneys acting within the scope of his or her authority, from overhearing or recording any communication that they could lawfully overhear or record.
(b) Nothing in Section 632, 632.5, 632.6, or 632.7 renders inadmissible any evidence obtained by the above-named persons by means of overhearing or recording any communication that they could lawfully overhear or record.
(Added by Stats. 2011, Ch. 659, Sec. 1. (AB 1010) Effective January 1, 2012.)
633.1.
(a) Nothing in Section 631, 632, 632.5, 632.6, or 632.7 prohibits any person regularly employed as an airport law enforcement officer, as described in subdivision (d) of Section 830.33, acting within the scope of his or her authority, from recording any communication which is received on an incoming telephone line, for which the person initiating the call utilized a telephone number known to the public to be a means of contacting airport law enforcement officers. In order for a telephone call to be recorded under this subdivision, a series of electronic tones shall be used, placing the caller on notice that his or her telephone call is being recorded.
(b) Nothing in Section 631, 632, 632.5, 632.6, or 632.7 renders inadmissible any evidence obtained by an officer described in subdivision (a) if the evidence was received by means of recording any communication which is received on an incoming public telephone line, for which the person initiating the call utilized a telephone number known to the public to be a means of contacting airport law enforcement officers.
(c) This section shall only apply to airport law enforcement officers who are employed at an airport which maintains regularly scheduled international airport service and which maintains permanent facilities of the United States Customs Service.
(Amended by Stats. 1995, Ch. 62, Sec. 1. Effective January 1, 1996.)
633.5.
Sections 631, 632, 632.5, 632.6, and 632.7 do not prohibit one party to a confidential communication from recording the communication for the purpose of obtaining evidence reasonably believed to relate to the commission by another party to the communication of the crime of extortion, kidnapping, bribery, any felony involving violence against the person, including, but not limited to, human trafficking, as defined in Section 236.1, or a violation of Section 653m, or domestic violence as defined in Section 13700. Sections 631, 632, 632.5, 632.6, and 632.7 do not render any evidence so obtained inadmissible in a prosecution for extortion, kidnapping, bribery, any felony involving violence against the person, including, but not limited to, human trafficking, as defined in Section 236.1, a violation of Section 653m, or domestic violence as defined in Section 13700, or any crime in connection therewith.
(Amended by Stats. 2017, Ch. 191, Sec. 1. (AB 413) Effective January 1, 2018.)
633.6.
(a) Notwithstanding the provisions of this chapter, and in accordance with federal law, upon the request of a victim of domestic violence who is seeking a domestic violence restraining order, a judge issuing the order may include a provision in the order that permits the victim to record any prohibited communication made to him or her by the perpetrator.
(b) Notwithstanding the provisions of this chapter, and in accordance with federal law, a victim of domestic violence who is seeking a domestic violence restraining order from a court, and who reasonably believes that a confidential communication made to him or her by the perpetrator may contain evidence germane to that restraining order, may record that communication for the exclusive purpose and use of providing that evidence to the court.
(c) The Judicial Council shall amend its domestic violence prevention application and order forms to incorporate the provisions of this section.
(Amended by Stats. 2017, Ch. 191, Sec. 2. (AB 413) Effective January 1, 2018.)
633.8.
(a) It is the intent of the Legislature in enacting this section to provide law enforcement with the ability to use electronic amplifying or recording devices to eavesdrop on and record the otherwise confidential oral communications of individuals within a location when responding to an emergency situation that involves the taking of a hostage or the barricading of a location. It is the intent of the Legislature that eavesdropping on oral communications pursuant to this section comply with paragraph (7) of Section 2518 of Title 18 of the United States Code.
(b) Notwithstanding the provisions of this chapter, and in accordance with federal law, a designated peace officer described in subdivision (c) may use, or authorize the use of, an electronic amplifying or recording device to eavesdrop on or record, or both, any oral communication within a particular location in response to an emergency situation involving the taking of a hostage or hostages or the barricading of a location if all of the following conditions are satisfied:
(1) The officer reasonably determines that an emergency situation exists involving the immediate danger of death or serious physical injury to any person, within the meaning of Section 2518(7)(a)(i) of Title 18 of the United States Code.
(2) The officer reasonably determines that the emergency situation requires that the eavesdropping on oral communication occur immediately.
(3) There are grounds upon which an order could be obtained pursuant to Section 2516(2) of Title 18 of the United States Code in regard to the offenses enumerated therein.
(c) Only a peace officer who has been designated by either a district attorney in the county where the emergency exists, or by the Attorney General to make the necessary determinations pursuant to paragraphs (1), (2), and (3) of subdivision (b) may make those determinations for purposes of this section.
(d) If the determination is made by a designated peace officer described in subdivision (c) that an emergency situation exists, a peace officer shall not be required to knock and announce his or her presence before entering, installing, and using any electronic amplifying or recording devices.
(e) If the determination is made by a designated peace officer described in subdivision (c) that an emergency situation exists and an eavesdropping device has been deployed, an application for an order approving the eavesdropping shall be made within 48 hours of the beginning of the eavesdropping and shall comply with the requirements of Section 629.50. A court may grant an application authorizing the use of electronic amplifying or recording devices to eavesdrop on and record otherwise confidential oral communications in barricade or hostage situations where there is probable cause to believe that an individual is committing, has committed, or is about to commit an offense listed in Section 2516(2) of Title 18 of the United States Code.
(f) The contents of any oral communications overheard pursuant to this section shall be recorded on tape or other comparable device. The recording of the contents shall be done so as to protect the recording from editing or other alterations.
(g) For purposes of this section, a "barricading" occurs when a person refuses to come out from a covered or enclosed position. Barricading also occurs when a person is held against his or her will and the captor has not made a demand.
(h) For purposes of this section, a "hostage situation" occurs when a person is held against his or her will and the captor has made a demand.
(i) A judge shall not grant an application made pursuant to this section in anticipation that an emergency situation will arise. A judge shall grant an application authorizing the

use of electronic amplifying or recording devices to eavesdrop on and record otherwise confidential oral communications in barricade or hostage situations where there is probable cause to believe that an individual is committing, has committed, or is about to commit an offense listed in Section 2516(2) of Title 18 of the United States Code, and only if the peace officer has fully complied with the requirements of this section. If an application is granted pursuant to this section, an inventory shall be served pursuant to Section 629.68.
(j) This section does not require that a peace officer designated pursuant to subdivision (c) undergo training pursuant to Section 629.94.
(k) A peace officer who has been designated pursuant to subdivision (c) to use an eavesdropping device shall cease use of the device upon the termination of the barricade or hostage situation, or upon the denial by a judge of an application for an order to approve the eavesdropping, whichever is earlier.
(l) Nothing in this section shall be deemed to affect the admissibility or inadmissibility of evidence.
(Amended by Stats. 2011, Ch. 304, Sec. 6. (SB 428) Effective January 1, 2012.)
634.
Any person who trespasses on property for the purpose of committing any act, or attempting to commit any act, in violation of Section 631, 632, 632.5, 632.6, 632.7, or 636 shall be punished by a fine not exceeding two thousand five hundred dollars ($2,500), by imprisonment in the county jail not exceeding one year or in the state prison, or by both that fine and imprisonment. If the person has previously been convicted of a violation of this section or Section 631, 632, 632.5, 632.6, 632.7, or 636, the person shall be punished by a fine not exceeding ten thousand dollars ($10,000), by imprisonment in the county jail not exceeding one year or in the state prison, or by both that fine and imprisonment.
(Amended by Stats. 1992, Ch. 298, Sec. 10. Effective January 1, 1993.)
635.
(a) Every person who manufactures, assembles, sells, offers for sale, advertises for sale, possesses, transports, imports, or furnishes to another any device which is primarily or exclusively designed or intended for eavesdropping upon the communication of another, or any device which is primarily or exclusively designed or intended for the unauthorized interception or reception of communications between cellular radio telephones or between a cellular radio telephone and a landline telephone in violation of Section 632.5, or communications between cordless telephones or between a cordless telephone and a landline telephone in violation of Section 632.6, shall be punished by a fine not exceeding two thousand five hundred dollars ($2,500), by imprisonment in the county jail not exceeding one year, or in the state prison, or by both that fine and imprisonment. If the person has previously been convicted of a violation of this section, the person shall be punished by a fine not exceeding ten thousand dollars ($10,000), by imprisonment in the county jail not exceeding one year, or in the state prison, or by both that fine and imprisonment.
(b) This section does not apply to either of the following:
(1) An act otherwise prohibited by this section when performed by any of the following:
(A) A communication utility or an officer, employee or agent thereof for the purpose of construction, maintenance, conduct, or operation of, or otherwise incident to the use of, the services or facilities of the utility.
(B) A state, county, or municipal law enforcement agency or an agency of the federal government.
(C) A person engaged in selling devices specified in subdivision (a) for use by, or resale to, agencies of a foreign government under terms approved by the federal government, communication utilities, state, county, or municipal law enforcement agencies, or agencies of the federal government.
(2) Possession by a subscriber to communication utility service of a device specified in subdivision (a) furnished by the utility pursuant to its tariffs.
(Amended by Stats. 1990, Ch. 696, Sec. 8.)
636.
(a) Every person who, without permission from all parties to the conversation, eavesdrops on or records, by means of an electronic device, a conversation, or any portion thereof, between a person who is in the physical custody of a law enforcement officer or other public officer, or who is on the property of a law enforcement agency or other public agency, and that person's attorney, religious adviser, or licensed physician, is guilty of a felony punishable by imprisonment pursuant to subdivision (h) of Section 1170.
(b) Every person who, intentionally and without permission from all parties to the conversation, nonelectronically eavesdrops upon a conversation, or any portion thereof, that occurs between a person who is in the physical custody of a law enforcement officer or other public officer and that person's attorney, religious adviser, or licensed physician, is guilty of a public offense. This subdivision applies to conversations that occur in a place, and under circumstances, where there exists a reasonable expectation of privacy, including a custody holding area, holding area, or anteroom. This subdivision does not apply to conversations that are inadvertently overheard or that take place in a courtroom or other room used for adjudicatory proceedings. A person who is convicted of violating this subdivision shall be punished by imprisonment pursuant to subdivision (h) of Section 1170, or in a county jail for a term not to exceed one year, or by a fine not to exceed two thousand five hundred dollars ($2,500), or by both that fine and imprisonment.
(c) This section shall not apply to any employee of a public utility engaged in the business of providing service and facilities for telephone or telegraph communications while engaged in the construction, maintenance, conduct, or operation of the service or facilities of that public utility who listens in to conversations for the limited purpose of testing or servicing equipment.
(Amended by Stats. 2011, Ch. 15, Sec. 429. (AB 109) Effective April 4, 2011. Operative October 1, 2011, by Sec. 636 of Ch. 15, as amended by Stats. 2011, Ch. 39, Sec. 68.)
636.5.
Any person not authorized by the sender, who intercepts any public safety radio service communication, by use of a scanner or any other means, for the purpose of using that communication to assist in the commission of a criminal offense or to avoid or escape arrest, trial, conviction, or punishment or who divulges to any person he or she knows to be a suspect in the commission of any criminal offense, the existence, contents, substance, purport, effect or meaning of that communication concerning the offense with the intent that the suspect may avoid or escape from arrest, trial, conviction, or punishment is guilty of a misdemeanor.
Nothing in this section shall preclude prosecution of any person under Section 31 or 32.
As used in this section, "public safety radio service communication" means a communication authorized by the Federal Communications Commission to be transmitted by a station in the public safety radio service.
(Amended by Stats. 1999, Ch. 853, Sec. 13. Effective January 1, 2000.)
637.
Every person not a party to a telegraphic or telephonic communication who willfully discloses the contents of a telegraphic or telephonic message, or any part thereof, addressed to another person, without the permission of that person, unless directed so to do by the lawful order of a court, is punishable by imprisonment pursuant to subdivision (h) of Section 1170, or in a county jail not exceeding one year, or by fine not exceeding five thousand dollars ($5,000), or by both that fine and imprisonment.
(Amended by Stats. 2011, Ch. 15, Sec. 430. (AB 109) Effective April 4, 2011. Operative October 1, 2011, by Sec. 636 of Ch. 15, as amended by Stats. 2011, Ch. 39, Sec. 68.)
637.1.
Every person not connected with any telegraph or telephone office who, without the authority or consent of the person to whom the same may be directed, willfully opens any sealed envelope enclosing a telegraphic or telephonic message, addressed to another person, with the purpose of learning the contents of such message, or who fraudulently represents another person and thereby procures to be delivered to himself any telegraphic or telephonic message addressed to such other person, with the intent to use, destroy, or detain the same from the person entitled to receive such message, is punishable as provided in Section 637.
(Added by Stats. 1967, Ch. 1509.)
637.2.
(a) Any person who has been injured by a violation of this chapter may bring an action against the person who committed the violation for the greater of the following amounts:
(1) Five thousand dollars ($5,000) per violation.
(2) Three times the amount of actual damages, if any, sustained by the plaintiff.
(b) Any person may, in accordance with Chapter 3 (commencing with Section 525) of Title 7 of Part 2 of the Code of Civil Procedure, bring an action to enjoin and restrain any violation of this chapter, and may in the same action seek damages as provided by subdivision (a).
(c) It is not a necessary prerequisite to an action pursuant to this section that the plaintiff has suffered, or be threatened with, actual damages.
(d) This section shall not be construed to affect Title 4 (commencing with Section 3425.1) of Part 1 of Division 4 of the Civil Code.
(Amended by Stats. 2016, Ch. 855, Sec. 4. (AB 1671) Effective January 1, 2017.)
637.3.
(a) No person or entity in this state shall use any system which examines or records in any manner voice prints or other voice stress patterns of another person to determine the truth or falsity of statements made by such other person without his or her express written consent given in advance of the examination or recordation.
(b) This section shall not apply to any peace officer, as defined in Section 830, while he is carrying out his official duties.
(c) Any person who has been injured by a violator of this section may bring an action against the violator for his actual damages or one thousand dollars ($1,000), whichever is greater.
(Added by Stats. 1978, Ch. 1251.)
637.4.
(a) No state or local governmental agency involved in the investigation or prosecution of crimes, or any employee thereof, shall require or request any complaining witness, in a case involving the use of force, violence, duress, menace, or threat of great bodily harm in the commission of any sex offense, to submit to a polygraph examination as a prerequisite to filing an accusatory pleading.
(b) Any person who has been injured by a violator of this section may bring an action against the violator for his actual damages or one thousand dollars ($1,000), whichever is greater.
(Added by Stats. 1980, Ch. 880, Sec. 1.)
637.5.
(a) No person who owns, controls, operates, or manages a satellite or cable television corporation, or who leases channels on a satellite or cable system shall:
(1) Use any electronic device to record, transmit, or observe any events or listen to, record, or monitor any conversations that take place inside a subscriber's residence, workplace, or place of business, without obtaining the express written consent of the subscriber. A satellite or cable television corporation may conduct electronic sweeps of subscriber households to monitor for signal quality.
(2) Provide any person with any individually identifiable information regarding any of its subscribers, including, but not limited to, the subscriber's television viewing habits, shopping choices, interests, opinions, energy uses, medical information, banking data or information, or any other personal or private information, without the subscriber's express written consent.
(b) Individual subscriber viewing responses or other individually identifiable information derived from subscribers may be retained and used by a satellite or cable television corporation only to the extent reasonably necessary for billing purposes and internal business practices, and to monitor for unauthorized reception of services. A satellite or cable television corporation may compile, maintain, and distribute a list containing the names and addresses of its subscribers if the list contains no other individually identifiable information and if subscribers are afforded the right to elect not to be included on the list. However, a satellite or cable television corporation shall maintain adequate safeguards to ensure the physical security and confidentiality of the subscriber information.
(c) A satellite or cable television corporation shall not make individual subscriber information available to government agencies in the absence of legal compulsion, including, but not limited to, a court order or subpoena. If requests for information are made, a satellite or cable television corporation shall promptly notify the subscriber of the nature of the request and what government agency has requested the information prior to responding unless otherwise prohibited from doing so by law.
Nothing in this section shall be construed to prevent local franchising authorities from obtaining information necessary to monitor franchise compliance pursuant to franchise or license agreements. This information shall be provided so as to omit individually identifiable subscriber information whenever possible. Information obtained by local franchising authorities shall be used solely for monitoring franchise compliance and shall not be subject to the California Public Records Act (Chapter 3.5 (commencing with Section 6250) of Division 7 of Title 1 of the Government Code).
(d) Any individually identifiable subscriber information gathered by a satellite or cable television corporation shall be made available for subscriber examination within 30 days of receiving a request by a subscriber to examine the information on the premises of the corporation. Upon a reasonable showing by the subscriber that the information is inaccurate, a satellite or cable television corporation shall correct the information.
(e) Upon a subscriber's application for satellite or cable television service, including, but not limited to, interactive service, a satellite or cable television corporation shall provide the applicant with a separate notice in an appropriate form explaining the subscriber's right to privacy protection afforded by this section.
(f) As used in this section:
(1) "Cable television corporation" shall have the same meaning as that term is given by Section 216.4 of the Public Utilities Code.
(2) "Individually identifiable information" means any information identifying an individual or his or her use of any service provided by a satellite or cable system other than the mere fact that the individual is a satellite or cable television subscriber. "Individually identifiable information" shall not include anonymous, aggregate, or any other information that does not identify an individual subscriber of a video provider service.
(3) "Person" includes an individual, business association, partnership, corporation, limited liability company, or other legal entity, and an individual acting or purporting to act for or on behalf of any government, or subdivision thereof, whether federal, state, or local.
(4) "Interactive service" means any service offered by a satellite or cable television corporation involving the collection, reception, aggregation, storage, or use of electronic information transmitted from a subscriber to any other receiving point under the control of the satellite or cable television corporation, or vice versa.
(g) Nothing in this section shall be construed to limit the ability of a satellite or cable television corporation to market satellite or cable television or ancillary services to its subscribers.

(h) Any person receiving subscriber information from a satellite or cable television corporation shall be subject to the provisions of this section.

(i) Any aggrieved person may commence a civil action for damages for invasion of privacy against any satellite or cable television corporation, service provider, or person that leases a channel or channels on a satellite or cable television system that violates the provisions of this section.

(j) Any person who violates the provisions of this section is guilty of a misdemeanor punishable by a fine not exceeding three thousand dollars ($3,000), or by imprisonment in the county jail not exceeding one year, or by both that fine and imprisonment.

(k) The penalties and remedies provided by subdivisions (i) and (j) are cumulative, and shall not be construed as restricting any penalty or remedy, provisional or otherwise, provided by law for the benefit of any person, and no judgment under this section shall preclude any person from obtaining additional relief based upon the same facts.

(l) The provisions of this section are intended to set forth minimum state standards for protecting the privacy of subscribers to cable television services and are not intended to preempt more restrictive local standards.

(Amended by Stats. 2006, Ch. 198, Sec. 5. Effective January 1, 2007.)
637.6.
(a) No person who, in the course of business, acquires or has access to personal information concerning an individual, including, but not limited to, the individual's residence address, employment address, or hours of employment, for the purpose of assisting private entities in the establishment or implementation of carpooling or ridesharing programs, shall disclose that information to any other person or use that information for any other purpose without the prior written consent of the individual.

(b) As used in this section, "carpooling or ridesharing programs" include, but shall not be limited to, the formation of carpools, vanpools, buspools, the provision of transit routes, rideshare research, and the development of other demand management strategies such as variable working hours and telecommuting.

(c) Any person who violates this section is guilty of a misdemeanor, punishable by imprisonment in the county jail for not exceeding one year, or by a fine of not exceeding one thousand dollars ($1,000), or by both that imprisonment and fine.

(Added by Stats. 1990, Ch. 304, Sec. 1.)
637.7.
(a) No person or entity in this state shall use an electronic tracking device to determine the location or movement of a person.

(b) This section shall not apply when the registered owner, lessor, or lessee of a vehicle has consented to the use of the electronic tracking device with respect to that vehicle.

(c) This section shall not apply to the lawful use of an electronic tracking device by a law enforcement agency.

(d) As used in this section, "electronic tracking device" means any device attached to a vehicle or other movable thing that reveals its location or movement by the transmission of electronic signals.

(e) A violation of this section is a misdemeanor.

(f) A violation of this section by a person, business, firm, company, association, partnership, or corporation licensed under Division 3 (commencing with Section 5000) of the Business and Professions Code shall constitute grounds for revocation of the license issued to that person, business, firm, company, association, partnership, or corporation, pursuant to the provisions that provide for the revocation of the license as set forth in Division 3 (commencing with Section 5000) of the Business and Professions Code.

(Added by Stats. 1998, Ch. 449, Sec. 2. Effective January 1, 1999.)
637.9.
(a) Any person who, in the course of business, provides mailing lists, computerized or telephone-based reference services, or similar products or services utilizing lists, as defined, knowingly does any of the following is guilty of a misdemeanor:

(1) Fails, prior to selling or distributing a list to a first-time buyer, to obtain the buyer's name, address, telephone number, tax identification number if the buyer is a forprofit entity, a sample of the type of material to be distributed using the list, or to make a good-faith effort to verify the nature and legitimacy of the business or organization to which the list is being sold or distributed.

(2) Knowingly provides access to personal information about children to any person who he or she knows is registered or required to register as a sex offender.

(b) Any person who uses personal information about a child that was obtained for commercial purposes to directly contact the child or the child's parent to offer a commercial product or service to the child and who knowingly fails to comply with the parent's request to take steps to limit access to personal information about a child only to authorized persons is guilty of a misdemeanor.

(c) Any person who knowingly distributes or receives any personal information about a child with knowledge that the information will be used to abuse or physically harm the child is guilty of a misdemeanor.

(d) (1) List brokers shall, upon a written request from a parent that specifically identifies the child, provide the parent with procedures that the parent must follow in order to withdraw consent to use personal information relating to his or her child. Any list broker who fails to discontinue disclosing personal information about a child within 20 days after being so requested in writing by the child's parent, is guilty of a misdemeanor.

(2) Any person who, through the mail, markets or sells products or services directed to children, shall maintain a list of all individuals, and their addresses, who have requested in writing that the person discontinue sending any marketing or sales materials to the individual or the individual's child or children. No person who is obligated to maintain that list shall cause any marketing or sales materials, other than those that are already in the process of dissemination, to be sent to any individual's child or children, after that individual has made that written request. Any person who is subject to the provisions of this paragraph, who fails to comply with the requirements of this paragraph or who violates the provisions of this paragraph is guilty of a misdemeanor.

(e) The following shall be exempt from subdivisions (a) and (b):

(1) Any federal, state, or local government agency or law enforcement agency.

(2) The National Center for Missing and Exploited Children.

(3) Any educational institution, consortia, organization, or professional association, which shall include, but not be limited to, the California community colleges; the California State University, and each campus, branch, and function thereof; each campus, branch, and function of the University of California; the California Maritime Academy; or any independent institution of higher education accredited by an agency recognized by the federal Department of Education. For the purposes of this paragraph, "independent institution of higher education" means any nonpublic higher education institution that grants undergraduate degrees, graduate degrees, or both undergraduate and graduate degrees, is formed as a nonprofit corporation in this state, and is accredited by an agency recognized by the federal Department of Education; or any private postsecondary vocational institution registered, approved, or exempted by the Bureau of Private Postsecondary Vocational Education.

(4) Any nonprofit organization that is exempt from taxation under Section 23701d of the Revenue and Taxation Code.

(f) As used in this section:

(1) "Child" means a person who is under 16 years of age.

(2) "Parent" shall include a legal guardian.

(3) "Personal information" means any information that identifies a child and that would suffice to locate and contact the child, including, but not limited to, the name, postal or electronic mail address, telephone number, social security number, date of birth, physical description of the child, or family income.

(4) "List" may include, but is not limited to, a collection of name and address records of individuals sharing a common interest, purchase history, demographic profile, membership, or affiliation.

(Added by Stats. 1998, Ch. 763, Sec. 1. Effective January 1, 1999.)
638.
(a) Any person who purchases, sells, offers to purchase or sell, or conspires to purchase or sell any telephone calling pattern record or list, without the written consent of the subscriber, or any person who procures or obtains through fraud or deceit, or attempts to procure or obtain through fraud or deceit any telephone calling pattern record or list shall be punished by a fine not exceeding two thousand five hundred dollars ($2,500), or by imprisonment in a county jail not exceeding one year, or by both a fine and imprisonment. If the person has previously been convicted of a violation of this section, he or she is punishable by a fine not exceeding ten thousand dollars ($10,000), or by imprisonment in a county jail not exceeding one year, or by both a fine and imprisonment.

(b) Any personal information contained in a telephone calling pattern record or list that is obtained in violation of this section shall be inadmissible as evidence in any judicial, administrative, legislative, or other proceeding except when that information is offered as proof in an action or prosecution for a violation of this section, or when otherwise authorized by law, in any criminal prosecution.

(c) For purposes of this section:

(1) "Person" includes an individual, business association, partnership, limited partnership, corporation, limited liability company, or other legal entity.

(2) "Telephone calling pattern record or list" means information retained by a telephone company that relates to the telephone number dialed by the subscriber, or other person using the subscriber's telephone with permission, or the incoming number of a call directed to the subscriber, or other data related to such calls typically contained on a subscriber telephone bill such as the time the call started and ended, the duration of the call, any charges applied, and any information described in subdivision (a) of Section 2891 of the Public Utilities Code whether the call was made from or to a telephone connected to the public switched telephone network, a cordless telephone, as defined in Section 632.6, a telephony device operating over the Internet utilizing voice over Internet protocol, a satellite telephone, or commercially available interconnected mobile phone service that provides access to the public switched telephone network via a mobile communication device employing radiowave technology to transmit calls, including cellular radiotelephone, broadband Personal Communications Services, and digital Specialized Mobile Radio.

(3) "Telephone company" means a telephone corporation as defined in Section 234 of the Public Utilities Code or any other person that provides residential or commercial telephone service to a subscriber utilizing any of the technologies or methods enumerated in paragraph (2).

(4) For purposes of this section, "purchase" and "sell" shall not include information provided to a collection agency or assignee of the debt by the telephone corporation, and used exclusively for the collection of the unpaid debt assigned by the telephone corporation, provided that the collection agency or assignee of the debt shall be liable for any disclosure of the information that is in violation of this section.

(d) An employer of, or entity contracting with, a person who violates subdivision (a) shall only be subject to prosecution pursuant to that provision if the employer or contracting entity knowingly allowed the employee or contractor to engage in conduct that violated subdivision (a).

(e) It is the intent of the Legislature to ensure that telephone companies maintain telephone calling pattern records or lists in the strictest confidence, and protect the privacy of their subscribers with all due care. While it is not the intent of the Legislature in this act to preclude the sharing of information that is currently allowed by both state and federal laws and rules governing those records, it is the Legislature's intent in this act to preclude any unauthorized purchase or sale of that information.

(f) This section shall not be construed to prevent a law enforcement or prosecutorial agency, or any officer, employee, or agent thereof from obtaining telephone records in connection with the performance of the official duties of the agency consistent with any other applicable state and federal law.

(g) Nothing in this section shall preclude prosecution under any other provision of law.

(h) The Legislature hereby finds and declares that, notwithstanding the prohibition on specific means of making available or obtaining personal calling records pursuant to this section, the disclosure of personal calling records through any other means is no less harmful to the privacy and security interests of Californians. This section is not intended to limit the scope or force of Section 2891 of the Public Utilities Code in any way.

(Added by Stats. 2006, Ch. 626, Sec. 1. Effective January 1, 2007.)
638.50.
For purposes of this chapter, the following terms have the following meanings:

(a) "Wire communication" and "electronic communication" have the meanings set forth in subdivision (a) of Section 629.51.

(b) "Pen register" means a device or process that records or decodes dialing, routing, addressing, or signaling information transmitted by an instrument or facility from which a wire or electronic communication is transmitted, but not the contents of a communication. "Pen register" does not include a device or process used by a provider or customer of a wire or electronic communication service for billing, or recording as an incident to billing, for communications services provided by such provider, or a device or process used by a provider or customer of a wire communication service for cost accounting or other similar purposes in the ordinary course of its business.

(c) "Trap and trace device" means a device or process that captures the incoming electronic or other impulses that identify the originating number or other dialing, routing, addressing, or signaling information reasonably likely to identify the source of a wire or electronic communication, but not the contents of a communication.

(Added by Stats. 2015, Ch. 204, Sec. 1. (AB 929) Effective January 1, 2016.)
638.51.
(a) Except as provided in subdivision (b), a person may not install or use a pen register or a trap and trace device without first obtaining a court order pursuant to Section 638.52 or 638.53.

(b) A provider of electronic or wire communication service may use a pen register or a trap and trace device for any of the following purposes:

(1) To operate, maintain, and test a wire or electronic communication service.

(2) To protect the rights or property of the provider.

(3) To protect users of the service from abuse of service or unlawful use of service.

(4) To record the fact that a wire or electronic communication was initiated or completed to protect the provider, another provider furnishing service toward the completion of the wire communication, or a user of that service, from fraudulent, unlawful, or abusive use of service.

(5) If the consent of the user of that service has been obtained.

(c) A violation of this section is punishable by a fine not exceeding two thousand five hundred dollars ($2,500), or by imprisonment in the county jail not exceeding one year, or by imprisonment pursuant to subdivision (h) of Section 1170, or by both that fine and imprisonment.

(d) A good faith reliance on an order issued pursuant to Section 638.52, or an authorization made pursuant to Section 638.53, is a complete defense to a civil or criminal action brought under this section or under this chapter.

(Added by Stats. 2015, Ch. 204, Sec. 2. (AB 929) Effective January 1, 2016.)
638.52.
(a) A peace officer may make an application to a magistrate for an order or an extension of an order authorizing or approving the installation and use of a pen register

or a trap and trace device. The application shall be in writing under oath or equivalent affirmation, and shall include the identity of the peace officer making the application and the identity of the law enforcement agency conducting the investigation. The applicant shall certify that the information likely to be obtained is relevant to an ongoing criminal investigation and shall include a statement of the offense to which the information likely to be obtained by the pen register or trap and trace device relates.

(b) The magistrate shall enter an ex parte order authorizing the installation and use of a pen register or a trap and trace device if he or she finds that the information likely to be obtained by the installation and use of a pen register or a trap and trace device is relevant to an ongoing investigation and that there is probable cause to believe that the pen register or trap and trace device will lead to any of the following:

(1) Recovery of stolen or embezzled property.

(2) Property or things used as the means of committing a felony.

(3) Property or things in the possession of a person with the intent to use them as a means of committing a public offense, or in the possession of another to whom he or she may have delivered them for the purpose of concealing them or preventing them from being discovered.

(4) Evidence that tends to show a felony has been committed, or tends to show that a particular person has committed or is committing a felony.

(5) Evidence that tends to show that sexual exploitation of a child, in violation of Section 311.3, or possession of matter depicting sexual conduct of a person under 18 years of age, in violation of Section 311.11, has occurred or is occurring.

(6) The location of a person who is unlawfully restrained or reasonably believed to be a witness in a criminal investigation or for whose arrest there is probable cause.

(7) Evidence that tends to show a violation of Section 3700.5 of the Labor Code, or tends to show that a particular person has violated Section 3700.5 of the Labor Code.

(8) Evidence that does any of the following:

(A) Tends to show that a felony, a misdemeanor violation of the Fish and Game Code, or a misdemeanor violation of the Public Resources Code, has been committed or is being committed.

(B) Tends to show that a particular person has committed or is committing a felony, a misdemeanor violation of the Fish and Game Code, or a misdemeanor violation of the Public Resources Code.

(C) Will assist in locating an individual who has committed or is committing a felony, a misdemeanor violation of the Fish and Game Code, or a misdemeanor violation of the Public Resources Code.

(c) Information acquired solely pursuant to the authority for a pen register or a trap and trace device shall not include any information that may disclose the physical location of the subscriber, except to the extent that the location may be determined from the telephone number. Upon the request of the person seeking the pen register or trap and trace device, the magistrate may seal portions of the application pursuant to People v. Hobbs (1994) 7 Cal.4th 948, and Sections 1040, 1041, and 1042 of the Evidence Code.

(d) An order issued pursuant to subdivision (b) shall specify all of the following:

(1) The identity, if known, of the person to whom is leased or in whose name is listed the telephone line to which the pen register or trap and trace device is to be attached.

(2) The identity, if known, of the person who is the subject of the criminal investigation.

(3) The number and, if known, physical location of the telephone line to which the pen register or trap and trace device is to be attached and, in the case of a trap and trace device, the geographic limits of the trap and trace order.

(4) A statement of the offense to which the information likely to be obtained by the pen register or trap and trace device relates.

(5) The order shall direct, if the applicant has requested, the furnishing of information, facilities, and technical assistance necessary to accomplish the installation of the pen register or trap and trace device.

(e) An order issued under this section shall authorize the installation and use of a pen register or a trap and trace device for a period not to exceed 60 days.

(f) Extensions of the original order may be granted upon a new application for an order under subdivisions (a) and (b) if the officer shows that there is a continued probable cause that the information or items sought under this subdivision are likely to be obtained under the extension. The period of an extension shall not exceed 60 days.

(g) An order or extension order authorizing or approving the installation and use of a pen register or a trap and trace device shall direct that the order be sealed until the order, including any extensions, expires, and that the person owning or leasing the line to which the pen register or trap and trace device is attached not disclose the existence of the pen register or trap and trace device or the existence of the investigation to the listed subscriber or to any other person.

(h) Upon the presentation of an order, entered under subdivisions (b) or (f), by a peace officer authorized to install and use a pen register, a provider of wire or electronic communication service, landlord, custodian, or other person shall immediately provide the peace officer all information, facilities, and technical assistance necessary to accomplish the installation of the pen register unobtrusively and with a minimum of interference with the services provided to the party with respect to whom the installation and use is to take place, if the assistance is directed by the order.

(i) Upon the request of a peace officer authorized to receive the results of a trap and trace device, a provider of a wire or electronic communication service, landlord, custodian, or other person shall immediately install the device on the appropriate line and provide the peace officer all information, facilities, and technical assistance, including installation and operation of the device unobtrusively and with a minimum of interference with the services provided to the party with respect to whom the installation and use is to take place, if the installation and assistance is directed by the order.

(j) A provider of a wire or electronic communication service, landlord, custodian, or other person who provides facilities or technical assistance pursuant to this section shall be reasonably compensated by the requesting peace officer's law enforcement agency for the reasonable expenses incurred in providing the facilities and assistance.

(k) Unless otherwise ordered by the magistrate, the results of the pen register or trap and trace device shall be provided to the peace officer at reasonable intervals during regular business hours for the duration of the order.

(l) The magistrate, before issuing the order pursuant to subdivision (b), may examine on oath the person seeking the pen register or the trap and trace device, and any witnesses the person may produce, and shall take his or her affidavit or their affidavits in writing, and cause the affidavit or affidavits to be subscribed by the parties making them.

(Amended by Stats. 2016, Ch. 511, Sec. 1. (AB 1924) Effective September 23, 2016.)

638.53.

(a) Except as otherwise provided in this chapter, upon an oral application by a peace officer, a magistrate may grant oral approval for the installation and use of a pen register or a trap and trace device, without an order, if he or she determines all of the following:

(1) There are grounds upon which an order could be issued under Section 638.52.

(2) There is probable cause to believe that an emergency situation exists with respect to the investigation of a crime.

(3) There is probable cause to believe that a substantial danger to life or limb exists justifying the authorization for immediate installation and use of a pen register or a trap and trace device before an order authorizing the installation and use can, with due diligence, be submitted and acted upon.

(b) (1) By midnight of the second full court day after the pen register or trap and trace device is installed, a written application pursuant to Section 638.52 shall be submitted by the peace officer who made the oral application to the magistrate who orally approved the installation and use of a pen register or trap and trace device. If an order

is issued pursuant to Section 638.52, the order shall also recite the time of the oral approval under subdivision (a) and shall be retroactive to the time of the original oral approval.

(2) In the absence of an authorizing order pursuant to paragraph (1), the use shall immediately terminate when the information sought is obtained, when the application for the order is denied, or by midnight of the second full court day after the pen register or trap and trace device is installed, whichever is earlier.

(c) A provider of a wire or electronic communication service, landlord, custodian, or other person who provides facilities or technical assistance pursuant to this section shall be reasonably compensated by the requesting peace officer's law enforcement agency for the reasonable expenses incurred in providing the facilities and assistance.

(Added by Stats. 2015, Ch. 204, Sec. 4. (AB 929) Effective January 1, 2016.)

638.54.

(a) Except as otherwise provided in this section, a government entity that obtains information pursuant to Section 638.52, or obtains information pursuant to oral authorization pursuant to Section 638.53, shall serve upon, or deliver to by registered or first-class mail, electronic mail, or other means reasonably calculated to be effective, the identified targets of the order a notice that informs the recipient that information about the recipient has been compelled or requested and states with reasonable specificity the nature of the government investigation under which the information is sought. The notice shall include a copy of the order or a written statement setting forth facts giving rise to the emergency. The notice shall be provided no later than 30 days after the termination of the period of the order, any extensions, or an emergency request.

(b) (1) Prior to the expiration of the 30-day period specified in subdivision (a), the government entity may submit a request, supported by a sworn affidavit, for an order delaying unsealing of the order and notification and prohibiting the person owning or leasing the line to which the pen register or trap and trace device is attached from disclosing the existence of the pen register or trap and trace device or the existence of the investigation to the listed subscriber or any other person. The court shall issue the order if the court determines that there is reason to believe that notification may have an adverse result, but only for the period of time that the court finds there is reason to believe that the notification may have that adverse result, and not to exceed 90 days.

(2) The court may grant extensions of the delay of up to 90 days each on the same grounds as provided in paragraph (1).

(3) Upon expiration of the period of delay of the notification, the government entity shall serve upon, or deliver to by registered or first-class mail, electronic mail, or other means reasonably calculated to be effective as specified by the court issuing the order authorizing delayed notification, the identified targets of the order or emergency authorization a document that includes the information described in subdivision (a) and a copy of all electronic information obtained or a summary of that information, including, at a minimum, the number and types of records disclosed, the date and time when the earliest and latest records were created, and a statement of the grounds for the court's determination to grant a delay in notifying the individual. The notice shall be provided no later than three days after the expiration of the period of delay of the notification.

(c) If there is no identified target of an order or emergency request at the time of its issuance, the government entity shall submit to the Department of Justice, no later than three days after the termination of the period of the order, any extensions, or an emergency request, all of the information required in subdivision (a). If an order delaying notice is obtained pursuant to subdivision (b), the government entity shall submit to the department, no later than three days after the expiration of the period of delay of the notification, all of the information required in paragraph (3) of subdivision (b). The department shall publish all those reports on its Internet Web site within 90 days of receipt. The department may redact names or other personal identifying information from the reports.

(d) For the purposes of this section, "adverse result" has the meaning set forth in subdivision (a) of Section 1546.

(Added by Stats. 2016, Ch. 511, Sec. 2. (AB 1924) Effective September 23, 2016.)

638.55.

(a) Any person in a trial, hearing, or proceeding may move to suppress wire or electronic information obtained or retained in violation of the Fourth Amendment to the United States Constitution or of this chapter. The motion shall be made, determined, and be subject to review in accordance with the procedures set forth in subdivisions (b) to (q), inclusive, of Section 1538.5.

(b) The Attorney General may commence a civil action to compel any government entity to comply with the provisions of this chapter.

(c) An individual whose information is targeted by a warrant, order, or other legal process that is not in compliance with this chapter, the California Constitution, or the United States Constitution, or a service provider or any other recipient of the warrant, order, or other legal process may petition the issuing court to void or modify the warrant, order, or process, or to order the destruction of any information obtained in violation of this chapter, the California Constitution, or the United States Constitution.

(Added by Stats. 2016, Ch. 511, Sec. 3. (AB 1924) Effective September 23, 2016.)

CHAPTER 1.5. Invasion of Privacy [630 - 638.55]

(Chapter 1.5 added by Stats. 1967, Ch. 1509.)

630.

The Legislature hereby declares that advances in science and technology have led to the development of new devices and techniques for the purpose of eavesdropping upon private communications and that the invasion of privacy resulting from the continual and increasing use of such devices and techniques has created a serious threat to the free exercise of personal liberties and cannot be tolerated in a free and civilized society. The Legislature by this chapter intends to protect the right of privacy of the people of this state.

The Legislature recognizes that law enforcement agencies have a legitimate need to employ modern listening devices and techniques in the investigation of criminal conduct and the apprehension of lawbreakers. Therefore, it is not the intent of the Legislature to place greater restraints on the use of listening devices and techniques by law enforcement agencies than existed prior to the effective date of this chapter.

(Added by Stats. 1967, Ch. 1509.)

631.

(a) Any person who, by means of any machine, instrument, or contrivance, or in any other manner, intentionally taps, or makes any unauthorized connection, whether physically, electrically, acoustically, inductively, or otherwise, with any telegraph or telephone wire, line, cable, or instrument, including the wire, line, cable, or instrument of any internal telephonic communication system, or who willfully and without the consent of all parties to the communication, or in any unauthorized manner, reads, or attempts to read, or to learn the contents or meaning of any message, report, or communication while the same is in transit or passing over any wire, line, or cable, or is being sent from, or received at any place within this state; or who uses, or attempts to use, in any manner, or for any purpose, or to communicate in any way, any information so obtained, or who aids, agrees with, employs, or conspires with any person or persons to unlawfully do, or permit, or cause to be done any of the acts or things mentioned above in this section, is punishable by a fine not exceeding two thousand five hundred dollars ($2,500), or by imprisonment in the county jail not exceeding one year, or by imprisonment pursuant to subdivision (h) of Section 1170, or by both a fine and imprisonment in the county jail or pursuant to subdivision (h) of Section 1170. If the person has previously been convicted of a violation of this section or Section 632, 632.5, 632.6, 632.7, or 636, he or she is punishable by a fine not exceeding ten thousand dollars ($10,000), or by imprisonment in the county jail not exceeding one year, or by imprisonment pursuant to subdivision (h) of Section 1170, or by both that fine and imprisonment.

(b) This section shall not apply (1) to any public utility engaged in the business of providing communications services and facilities, or to the officers, employees or agents thereof, where the acts otherwise prohibited herein are for the purpose of construction, maintenance, conduct or operation of the services and facilities of the public utility, or (2) to the use of any instrument, equipment, facility, or service furnished and used pursuant to the tariffs of a public utility, or (3) to any telephonic communication system used for communication exclusively within a state, county, city and county, or city correctional facility.

(c) Except as proof in an action or prosecution for violation of this section, no evidence obtained in violation of this section shall be admissible in any judicial, administrative, legislative, or other proceeding.

(d) This section shall become operative on January 1, 1994.

(Amended by Stats. 2011, Ch. 15, Sec. 428. (AB 109) Effective April 4, 2011. Operative October 1, 2011, by Sec. 636 of Ch. 15, as amended by Stats. 2011, Ch. 39, Sec. 68.)

632.

(a) A person who, intentionally and without the consent of all parties to a confidential communication, uses an electronic amplifying or recording device to eavesdrop upon or record the confidential communication, whether the communication is carried on among the parties in the presence of one another or by means of a telegraph, telephone, or other device, except a radio, shall be punished by a fine not exceeding two thousand five hundred dollars ($2,500) per violation, or imprisonment in a county jail not exceeding one year, or in the state prison, or by both that fine and imprisonment. If the person has previously been convicted of a violation of this section or Section 631, 632.5, 632.6, 632.7, or 636, the person shall be punished by a fine not exceeding ten thousand dollars ($10,000) per violation, by imprisonment in a county jail not exceeding one year, or in the state prison, or by both that fine and imprisonment.

(b) For the purposes of this section, "person" means an individual, business association, partnership, corporation, limited liability company, or other legal entity, and an individual acting or purporting to act for or on behalf of any government or subdivision thereof, whether federal, state, or local, but excludes an individual known by all parties to a confidential communication to be overhearing or recording the communication.

(c) For the purposes of this section, "confidential communication" means any communication carried on in circumstances as may reasonably indicate that any party to the communication desires it to be confined to the parties thereto, but excludes a communication made in a public gathering or in any legislative, judicial, executive, or administrative proceeding open to the public, or in any other circumstance in which the parties to the communication may reasonably expect that the communication may be overheard or recorded.

(d) Except as proof in an action or prosecution for violation of this section, evidence obtained as a result of eavesdropping upon or recording a confidential communication in violation of this section is not admissible in any judicial, administrative, legislative, or other proceeding.

(e) This section does not apply (1) to any public utility engaged in the business of providing communications services and facilities, or to the officers, employees, or agents thereof, if the acts otherwise prohibited by this section are for the purpose of construction, maintenance, conduct, or operation of the services and facilities of the public utility, (2) to the use of any instrument, equipment, facility, or service furnished and used pursuant to the tariffs of a public utility, or (3) to any telephonic communication system used for communication exclusively within a state, county, city and county, or city correctional facility.

(f) This section does not apply to the use of hearing aids and similar devices, by persons afflicted with impaired hearing, for the purpose of overcoming the impairment to permit the hearing of sounds ordinarily audible to the human ear.

(Amended by Stats. 2016, Ch. 855, Sec. 1. (AB 1671) Effective January 1, 2017.)

632.01.

(a) (1) A person who violates subdivision (a) of Section 632 shall be punished pursuant to subdivision (b) if the person intentionally discloses or distributes, in any manner, in any forum, including, but not limited to, Internet Web sites and social media, or for any purpose, the contents of a confidential communication with a health care provider that is obtained by that person in violation of subdivision (a) of Section 632. For purposes of this subdivision, "social media" means an electronic service or account, or electronic content, including, but not limited to, videos or still photographs, blogs, video blogs, podcasts, instant and text messages, email, online services or accounts, or Internet Web site profiles or locations.

(2) Notwithstanding any other provision of law, to aid and abet a violation of paragraph (1), for the purposes of Section 31, the person shall either violate, or aid and abet in a violation of, both Section 632 and paragraph (1).

(b) A violation of subdivision (a) shall be punished by a fine not exceeding two thousand five hundred dollars ($2,500) per violation, or imprisonment in a county jail not exceeding one year, or in the state prison, or by both that fine and imprisonment. If the person has previously been convicted of a violation of this section, the person shall be punished by a fine not exceeding ten thousand dollars ($10,000) per violation, by imprisonment in a county jail not exceeding one year, or in the state prison, or by both that fine and imprisonment.

(c) For purposes of this section, "health care provider" means any of the following:

(1) A person licensed or certified pursuant to Division 2 (commencing with Section 500) of the Business and Professions Code.

(2) A person licensed pursuant to the Osteopathic Initiative Act or the Chiropractic Initiative Act.

(3) A person certified pursuant to Division 2.5 (commencing with Section 1797) of the Health and Safety Code.

(4) A clinic, health dispensary, or health facility licensed or exempt from licensure pursuant to Division 2 (commencing with Section 1200) of the Health and Safety Code.

(5) An employee, volunteer, or contracted agent of any group practice prepayment health care service plan regulated pursuant to the Knox-Keene Health Care Service Plan Act of 1975 (Chapter 2.2 (commencing with Section 1340) of Division 2 of the Health and Safety Code).

(6) An employee, volunteer, independent contractor, or professional student of a clinic, health dispensary, or health care facility or health care provider described in this subdivision.

(7) A professional organization that represents any of the other health care providers described in this subdivision.

(d) (1) Subdivision (a) does not apply to the disclosure or distribution of a confidential communication pursuant to any of the following:

(A) Any party as described in Section 633 acting within the scope of his or her authority overhearing or recording a confidential communication that he or she may lawfully overhear or record pursuant to that section.

(B) Any party as described in Section 633.02 overhearing or recording a confidential communication related to sexual assault or other sexual offense that he or she may lawfully overhear or record pursuant to that section, or using or operating a body-worn camera as authorized pursuant to that section.

(C) A city attorney as described in Section 633.05 overhearing or recording any communication that he or she may lawfully overhear or record pursuant to that section.

(D) An airport law enforcement officer recording a communication received on an incoming telephone line pursuant to Section 633.1.

(E) A party to a confidential communication recording the communication for the purpose of obtaining evidence reasonably believed to relate to the commission by another party to the communication of a crime as specified in Section 633.5.

(F) A victim of domestic violence recording a prohibited communication made to him or her by the perpetrator pursuant to Section 633.6.

(G) A peace officer using electronic amplifying or recording devices to eavesdrop on and record the otherwise confidential oral communications of individuals within a location when responding to an emergency situation that involves the taking of a hostage or the barricading of a location pursuant to Section 633.8.

(2) This section does not affect the admissibility of any evidence that would otherwise be admissible pursuant to the authority of any section specified in paragraph (1).

(Added by Stats. 2016, Ch. 855, Sec. 2. (AB 1671) Effective January 1, 2017.)

632.5.

(a) Every person who, maliciously and without the consent of all parties to the communication, intercepts, receives, or assists in intercepting or receiving a communication transmitted between cellular radio telephones or between any cellular radio telephone and a landline telephone shall be punished by a fine not exceeding two thousand five hundred dollars ($2,500), by imprisonment in the county jail not exceeding one year or in the state prison, or by both that fine and imprisonment. If the person has been previously convicted of a violation of this section or Section 631, 632, 632.6, 632.7, or 636, the person shall be punished by a fine not exceeding ten thousand dollars ($10,000), by imprisonment in the county jail not exceeding one year or in the state prison, or by both that fine and imprisonment.

(b) In the following instances, this section shall not apply:

(1) To any public utility engaged in the business of providing communications services and facilities, or to the officers, employees, or agents thereof, where the acts otherwise prohibited are for the purpose of construction, maintenance, conduct, or operation of the services and facilities of the public utility.

(2) To the use of any instrument, equipment, facility, or service furnished and used pursuant to the tariffs of the public utility.

(3) To any telephonic communication system used for communication exclusively within a state, county, city and county, or city correctional facility.

(c) As used in this section and Section 635, "cellular radio telephone" means a wireless telephone authorized by the Federal Communications Commission to operate in the frequency bandwidth reserved for cellular radio telephones.

(Amended by Stats. 1992, Ch. 298, Sec. 4. Effective January 1, 1993.)

632.6.

(a) Every person who, maliciously and without the consent of all parties to the communication, intercepts, receives, or assists in intercepting or receiving a communication transmitted between cordless telephones as defined in subdivision (c), between any cordless telephone and a landline telephone, or between a cordless telephone and a cellular telephone shall be punished by a fine not exceeding two thousand five hundred dollars ($2,500), by imprisonment in the county jail not exceeding one year, or in the state prison, or by both that fine and imprisonment. If the person has been convicted previously of a violation of Section 631, 632, 632.5, 632.7, or 636, the person shall be punished by a fine not exceeding ten thousand dollars ($10,000), or by imprisonment in the county jail not exceeding one year, or in the state prison, or by both that fine and imprisonment.

(b) This section shall not apply in any of the following instances:

(1) To any public utility engaged in the business of providing communications services and facilities, or to the officers, employees, or agents thereof, where the acts otherwise prohibited are for the purpose of construction, maintenance, conduct, or operation of the services and facilities of the public utility.

(2) To the use of any instrument, equipment, facility, or service furnished and used pursuant to the tariffs of the public utility.

(3) To any telephonic communications system used for communication exclusively within a state, county, city and county, or city correctional facility.

(c) As used in this section and in Section 635, "cordless telephone" means a two-way low power communication system consisting of two parts—a "base" unit which connects to the public switched telephone network and a handset or "remote" unit—which are connected by a radio link and authorized by the Federal Communications Commission to operate in the frequency bandwidths reserved for cordless telephones.

(Amended by Stats. 1992, Ch. 298, Sec. 5. Effective January 1, 1993.)

632.7.

(a) Every person who, without the consent of all parties to a communication, intercepts or receives and intentionally records, or assists in the interception or reception and intentional recordation of, a communication transmitted between two cellular radio telephones, a cellular radio telephone and a landline telephone, two cordless telephones, a cordless telephone and a landline telephone, or a cordless telephone and a cellular radio telephone, shall be punished by a fine not exceeding two thousand five hundred dollars ($2,500), or by imprisonment in a county jail not exceeding one year, or in the state prison, or by both that fine and imprisonment. If the person has been convicted previously of a violation of this section or of Section 631, 632, 632.5, 632.6, or 636, the person shall be punished by a fine not exceeding ten thousand dollars ($10,000), by imprisonment in a county jail not exceeding one year, or in the state prison, or by both that fine and imprisonment.

(b) This section shall not apply to any of the following:

(1) Any public utility engaged in the business of providing communications services and facilities, or to the officers, employees, or agents thereof, where the acts otherwise prohibited are for the purpose of construction, maintenance, conduct, or operation of the services and facilities of the public utility.

(2) The use of any instrument, equipment, facility, or service furnished and used pursuant to the tariffs of the public utility.

(3) Any telephonic communication system used for communication exclusively within a state, county, city and county, or city correctional facility.

(c) As used in this section, each of the following terms have the following meaning:

(1) "Cellular radio telephone" means a wireless telephone authorized by the Federal Communications Commission to operate in the frequency bandwidth reserved for cellular radio telephones.

(2) "Cordless telephone" means a two-way, low power communication system consisting of two parts, a "base" unit which connects to the public switched telephone network and a handset or "remote" unit, that are connected by a radio link and authorized by the Federal Communications Commission to operate in the frequency bandwidths reserved for cordless telephones.

(3) "Communication" includes, but is not limited to, communications transmitted by voice, data, or image, including facsimile.

(Amended by Stats. 1993, Ch. 536, Sec. 1. Effective September 27, 1993.)

633.

(a) Nothing in Section 631, 632, 632.5, 632.6, or 632.7 prohibits the Attorney General, any district attorney, or any assistant, deputy, or investigator of the Attorney General or any district attorney, any officer of the California Highway Patrol, any peace officer of the Office of Internal Affairs of the Department of Corrections and Rehabilitation, any chief of police, assistant chief of police, or police officer of a city or city and county, any sheriff, undersheriff, or deputy sheriff regularly employed and paid in that capacity by a county, police officer of the County of Los Angeles, or any person acting pursuant to the

direction of one of these law enforcement officers acting within the scope of his or her authority, from overhearing or recording any communication that they could lawfully overhear or record prior to January 1, 1968.
(b) Nothing in Section 631, 632, 632.5, 632.6, or 632.7 renders inadmissible any evidence obtained by the above-named persons by means of overhearing or recording any communication that they could lawfully overhear or record prior to January 1, 1968.
(Amended by Stats. 2018, Ch. 175, Sec. 1. (AB 2669) Effective January 1, 2019.)
633.02.
(a) Nothing in Section 631, 632, 632.5, 632.6, or 632.7 prohibits any POST-certified chief of police, assistant chief of police, or police officer of a university or college campus acting within the scope of his or her authority, from overhearing or recording any communication that he or she could lawfully overhear or record prior to January 1, 1968, in any criminal investigation related to sexual assault or other sexual offense.
(b) Nothing in Section 631, 632, 632.5, 632.6, or 632.7 shall prohibit any POST-certified chief of police, assistant chief of police, or police officer of a university or college campus from using or operating body-worn cameras.
(c) This section shall not be construed to affect Section 633.
(d) This section shall not be used to impinge upon the lawful exercise of constitutionally protected rights of freedom of speech or assembly, or the constitutionally protected right of personal privacy.
(Added by Stats. 2015, Ch. 159, Sec. 1. (SB 424) Effective January 1, 2016.)
633.05.
(a) Nothing in Section 632, 632.5, 632.6, or 632.7 prohibits a city attorney acting under authority of Section 41803.5 of the Government Code, provided that authority is granted prior to January 1, 2012, or any person acting pursuant to the direction of one of those city attorneys acting within the scope of his or her authority, from overhearing or recording any communication that they could lawfully overhear or record.
(b) Nothing in Section 632, 632.5, 632.6, or 632.7 renders inadmissible any evidence obtained by the above-named persons by means of overhearing or recording any communication that they could lawfully overhear or record.
(Added by Stats. 2011, Ch. 659, Sec. 1. (AB 1010) Effective January 1, 2012.)
633.1.
(a) Nothing in Section 631, 632, 632.5, 632.6, or 632.7 prohibits any person regularly employed as an airport law enforcement officer, as described in subdivision (d) of Section 830.33, acting within the scope of his or her authority, from recording any communication which is received on an incoming telephone line, for which the person initiating the call utilized a telephone number known to the public to be a means of contacting airport law enforcement officers. In order for a telephone call to be recorded under this subdivision, a series of electronic tones shall be used, placing the caller on notice that his or her telephone call is being recorded.
(b) Nothing in Section 631, 632, 632.5, 632.6, or 632.7 renders inadmissible any evidence obtained by an officer described in subdivision (a) if the evidence was received by means of recording any communication which is received on an incoming public telephone line, for which the person initiating the call utilized a telephone number known to the public to be a means of contacting airport law enforcement officers.
(c) This section shall only apply to airport law enforcement officers who are employed at an airport which maintains regularly scheduled international airport service and which maintains permanent facilities of the United States Customs Service.
(Amended by Stats. 1995, Ch. 62, Sec. 1. Effective January 1, 1996.)
633.5.
Sections 631, 632, 632.5, 632.6, and 632.7 do not prohibit one party to a confidential communication from recording the communication for the purpose of obtaining evidence reasonably believed to relate to the commission by another party to the communication of the crime of extortion, kidnapping, bribery, any felony involving violence against the person, including, but not limited to, human trafficking, as defined in Section 236.1, or a violation of Section 653m, or domestic violence as defined in Section 13700. Sections 631, 632, 632.5, 632.6, and 632.7 do not render any evidence so obtained inadmissible in a prosecution for extortion, kidnapping, bribery, any felony involving violence against the person, including, but not limited to, human trafficking, as defined in Section 236.1, a violation of Section 653m, or domestic violence as defined in Section 13700, or any crime in connection therewith.
(Amended by Stats. 2017, Ch. 191, Sec. 1. (AB 413) Effective January 1, 2018.)
633.6.
(a) Notwithstanding the provisions of this chapter, and in accordance with federal law, upon the request of a victim of domestic violence who is seeking a domestic violence restraining order, a judge issuing the order may include a provision in the order that permits the victim to record any prohibited communication made to him or her by the perpetrator.
(b) Notwithstanding the provisions of this chapter, and in accordance with federal law, a victim of domestic violence who is seeking a domestic violence restraining order from a court, and who reasonably believes that a confidential communication made to him or her by the perpetrator may contain evidence germane to that restraining order, may record that communication for the exclusive purpose and use of providing that evidence to the court.
(c) The Judicial Council shall amend its domestic violence prevention application and order forms to incorporate the provisions of this section.
(Amended by Stats. 2017, Ch. 191, Sec. 2. (AB 413) Effective January 1, 2018.)
633.8.
(a) It is the intent of the Legislature in enacting this section to provide law enforcement with the ability to use electronic amplifying or recording devices to eavesdrop on and record the otherwise confidential oral communications of individuals within a location when responding to an emergency situation that involves the taking of a hostage or the barricading of a location. It is the intent of the Legislature that eavesdropping on oral communications pursuant to this section comply with paragraph (7) of Section 2518 of Title 18 of the United States Code.
(b) Notwithstanding the provisions of this chapter, and in accordance with federal law, a designated peace officer described in subdivision (c) may use, or authorize the use of, an electronic amplifying or recording device to eavesdrop on or record, or both, any oral communication within a particular location in response to an emergency situation involving the taking of a hostage or hostages or the barricading of a location if all of the following conditions are satisfied:
(1) The officer reasonably determines that an emergency situation exists involving the immediate danger of death or serious physical injury to any person, within the meaning of Section 2518(7)(a)(i) of Title 18 of the United States Code.
(2) The officer reasonably determines that the emergency situation requires that the eavesdropping on oral communication occur immediately.
(3) There are grounds upon which an order could be obtained pursuant to Section 2516(2) of Title 18 of the United States Code in regard to the offenses enumerated therein.
(c) Only a peace officer who has been designated by either a district attorney in the county where the emergency exists, or by the Attorney General to make the necessary determinations pursuant to paragraphs (1), (2), and (3) of subdivision (b) may make those determinations for purposes of this section.
(d) If the determination is made by a designated peace officer described in subdivision (c) that an emergency situation exists, a peace officer shall not be required to knock and announce his or her presence before entering, installing, and using any electronic amplifying or recording devices.
(e) If the determination is made by a designated peace officer described in subdivision (c) that an emergency situation exists and an eavesdropping device has been deployed, an application for an order approving the eavesdropping shall be made within 48 hours of the beginning of the eavesdropping and shall comply with the requirements of Section 629.50. A court may grant an application authorizing the use of electronic amplifying or recording devices to eavesdrop on and record otherwise confidential oral communications in barricade or hostage situations where there is probable cause to believe that an individual is committing, has committed, or is about to commit an offense listed in Section 2516(2) of Title 18 of the United States Code.
(f) The contents of any oral communications overheard pursuant to this section shall be recorded on tape or other comparable device. The recording of the contents shall be done so as to protect the recording from editing or other alterations.
(g) For purposes of this section, a "barricading" occurs when a person refuses to come out from a covered or enclosed position. Barricading also occurs when a person is held against his or her will and the captor has not made a demand.
(h) For purposes of this section, a "hostage situation" occurs when a person is held against his or her will and the captor has made a demand.
(i) A judge shall not grant an application made pursuant to this section in anticipation that an emergency situation will arise. A judge shall grant an application authorizing the use of electronic amplifying or recording devices to eavesdrop on and record otherwise confidential oral communications in barricade or hostage situations where there is probable cause to believe that an individual is committing, has committed, or is about to commit an offense listed in Section 2516(2) of Title 18 of the United States Code, and only if the peace officer has fully complied with the requirements of this section. If an application is granted pursuant to this section, an inventory shall be served pursuant to Section 629.68.
(j) This section does not require that a peace officer designated pursuant to subdivision (c) undergo training pursuant to Section 629.94.
(k) A peace officer who has been designated pursuant to subdivision (c) to use an eavesdropping device shall cease use of the device upon the termination of the barricade or hostage situation, or upon the denial by a judge of an application for an order to approve the eavesdropping, whichever is earlier.
(l) Nothing in this section shall be deemed to affect the admissibility or inadmissibility of evidence.
(Amended by Stats. 2011, Ch. 304, Sec. 6. (SB 428) Effective January 1, 2012.)
634.
Any person who trespasses on property for the purpose of committing any act, or attempting to commit any act, in violation of Section 631, 632, 632.5, 632.6, 632.7, or 636 shall be punished by a fine not exceeding two thousand five hundred dollars ($2,500), by imprisonment in the county jail not exceeding one year or in the state prison, or by both that fine and imprisonment. If the person has previously been convicted of a violation of this section or Section 631, 632, 632.5, 632.6, 632.7, or 636, the person shall be punished by a fine not exceeding ten thousand dollars ($10,000), by imprisonment in the county jail not exceeding one year or in the state prison, or by both that fine and imprisonment.
(Amended by Stats. 1992, Ch. 298, Sec. 10. Effective January 1, 1993.)
635.
(a) Every person who manufactures, assembles, sells, offers for sale, advertises for sale, possesses, transports, imports, or furnishes to another any device which is primarily or exclusively designed or intended for eavesdropping upon the communication of another, or any device which is primarily or exclusively designed or intended for the unauthorized interception or reception of communications between cellular radio telephones or between a cellular radio telephone and a landline telephone in violation of Section 632.5, or communications between cordless telephones or between a cordless telephone and a landline telephone in violation of Section 632.6, shall be punished by a fine not exceeding two thousand five hundred dollars ($2,500), by imprisonment in the county jail not exceeding one year, or in the state prison, or by both that fine and imprisonment. If the person has previously been convicted of a violation of this section, the person shall be punished by a fine not exceeding ten thousand dollars ($10,000), by imprisonment in the county jail not exceeding one year, or in the state prison, or by both that fine and imprisonment.
(b) This section does not apply to either of the following:
(1) An act otherwise prohibited by this section when performed by any of the following:
(A) A communication utility or an officer, employee or agent thereof for the purpose of construction, maintenance, conduct, or operation of, or otherwise incident to the use of, the services or facilities of the utility.
(B) A state, county, or municipal law enforcement agency or an agency of the federal government.
(C) A person engaged in selling devices specified in subdivision (a) for use by, or resale to, agencies of a foreign government under terms approved by the federal government, communication utilities, state, county, or municipal law enforcement agencies, or agencies of the federal government.
(2) Possession by a subscriber to communication utility service of a device specified in subdivision (a) furnished by the utility pursuant to its tariffs.
(Amended by Stats. 1990, Ch. 696, Sec. 8.)
636.
(a) Every person who, without permission from all parties to the conversation, eavesdrops on or records, by means of an electronic device, a conversation, or any portion thereof, between a person who is in the physical custody of a law enforcement officer or other public officer, or who is on the property of a law enforcement agency or other public agency, and that person's attorney, religious adviser, or licensed physician, is guilty of a felony punishable by imprisonment pursuant to subdivision (h) of Section 1170.
(b) Every person who, intentionally and without permission from all parties to the conversation, nonelectronically eavesdrops upon a conversation, or any portion thereof, that occurs between a person who is in the physical custody of a law enforcement officer or other public officer and that person's attorney, religious adviser, or licensed physician, is guilty of a public offense. This subdivision applies to conversations that occur in a place, and under circumstances, where there exists a reasonable expectation of privacy, including a custody holding area, holding area, or anteroom. This subdivision does not apply to conversations that are inadvertently overheard or that take place in a courtroom or other room used for adjudicatory proceedings. A person who is convicted of violating this subdivision shall be punished by imprisonment pursuant to subdivision (h) of Section 1170, or in a county jail for a term not to exceed one year, or by a fine not to exceed two thousand five hundred dollars ($2,500), or by both that fine and imprisonment.
(c) This section shall not apply to any employee of a public utility engaged in the business of providing service and facilities for telephone or telegraph communications while engaged in the construction, maintenance, conduct, or operation of the service or facilities of that public utility who listens in to conversations for the limited purpose of testing or servicing equipment.
(Amended by Stats. 2011, Ch. 15, Sec. 429. (AB 109) Effective April 4, 2011. Operative October 1, 2011, by Sec. 636 of Ch. 15, as amended by Stats. 2011, Ch. 39, Sec. 68.)
636.5.
Any person not authorized by the sender, who intercepts any public safety radio service communication, by use of a scanner or any other means, for the purpose of using that communication to assist in the commission of a criminal offense or to avoid or escape arrest, trial, conviction, or punishment or who divulges to any person he or she knows to be a suspect in the commission of any criminal offense, the existence, contents, substance, purport, effect or meaning of that communication concerning the offense with

the intent that the suspect may avoid or escape from arrest, trial, conviction, or punishment is guilty of a misdemeanor.
Nothing in this section shall preclude prosecution of any person under Section 31 or 32.
As used in this section, "public safety radio service communication" means a communication authorized by the Federal Communications Commission to be transmitted by a station in the public safety radio service.
(Amended by Stats. 1999, Ch. 853, Sec. 13. Effective January 1, 2000.)

637.

Every person not a party to a telegraphic or telephonic communication who willfully discloses the contents of a telegraphic or telephonic message, or any part thereof, addressed to another person, without the permission of that person, unless directed so to do by the lawful order of a court, is punishable by imprisonment pursuant to subdivision (h) of Section 1170, or in a county jail not exceeding one year, or by fine not exceeding five thousand dollars ($5,000), or by both that fine and imprisonment.
(Amended by Stats. 2011, Ch. 15, Sec. 430. (AB 109) Effective April 4, 2011. Operative October 1, 2011, by Sec. 636 of Ch. 15, as amended by Stats. 2011, Ch. 39, Sec. 68.)

637.1.

Every person not connected with any telegraph or telephone office who, without the authority or consent of the person to whom the same may be directed, willfully opens any sealed envelope enclosing a telegraphic or telephonic message, addressed to another person, with the purpose of learning the contents of such message, or who fraudulently represents another person and thereby procures to be delivered to himself any telegraphic or telephonic message addressed to such other person, with the intent to use, destroy, or detain the same from the person entitled to receive such message, is punishable as provided in Section 637.
(Added by Stats. 1967, Ch. 1509.)

637.2.

(a) Any person who has been injured by a violation of this chapter may bring an action against the person who committed the violation for the greater of the following amounts:
(1) Five thousand dollars ($5,000) per violation.
(2) Three times the amount of actual damages, if any, sustained by the plaintiff.
(b) Any person may, in accordance with Chapter 3 (commencing with Section 525) of Title 7 of Part 2 of the Code of Civil Procedure, bring an action to enjoin and restrain any violation of this chapter, and may in the same action seek damages as provided by subdivision (a).
(c) It is not a necessary prerequisite to an action pursuant to this section that the plaintiff has suffered, or be threatened with, actual damages.
(d) This section shall not be construed to affect Title 4 (commencing with Section 3425.1) of Part 1 of Division 4 of the Civil Code.
(Amended by Stats. 2016, Ch. 855, Sec. 4. (AB 1671) Effective January 1, 2017.)

637.3.

(a) No person or entity in this state shall use any system which examines or records in any manner voice prints or other voice stress patterns of another person to determine the truth or falsity of statements made by such other person without his or her express written consent given in advance of the examination or recordation.
(b) This section shall not apply to any peace officer, as defined in Section 830, while he is carrying out his official duties.
(c) Any person who has been injured by a violator of this section may bring an action against the violator for his actual damages or one thousand dollars ($1,000), whichever is greater.
(Added by Stats. 1978, Ch. 1251.)

637.4.

(a) No state or local governmental agency involved in the investigation or prosecution of crimes, or any employee thereof, shall require or request any complaining witness, in a case involving the use of force, violence, duress, menace, or threat of great bodily harm in the commission of any sex offense, to submit to a polygraph examination as a prerequisite to filing an accusatory pleading.
(b) Any person who has been injured by a violator of this section may bring an action against the violator for his actual damages or one thousand dollars ($1,000), whichever is greater.
(Added by Stats. 1980, Ch. 880, Sec. 1.)

637.5.

(a) No person who owns, controls, operates, or manages a satellite or cable television corporation, or who leases channels on a satellite or cable system shall:
(1) Use any electronic device to record, transmit, or observe any events or listen to, record, or monitor any conversations that take place inside a subscriber's residence, workplace, or place of business, without obtaining the express written consent of the subscriber. A satellite or cable television corporation may conduct electronic sweeps of subscriber households to monitor for signal quality.
(2) Provide any person with any individually identifiable information regarding any of its subscribers, including, but not limited to, the subscriber's television viewing habits, shopping choices, interests, opinions, energy uses, medical information, banking data or information, or any other personal or private information, without the subscriber's express written consent.
(b) Individual subscriber viewing responses or other individually identifiable information derived from subscribers may be retained and used by a satellite or cable television corporation only to the extent reasonably necessary for billing purposes and internal business practices, and to monitor for unauthorized reception of services. A satellite or cable television corporation may compile, maintain, and distribute a list containing the names and addresses of its subscribers if the list contains no other individually identifiable information and if subscribers are afforded the right to elect not to be included on the list. However, a satellite or cable television corporation shall maintain adequate safeguards to ensure the physical security and confidentiality of the subscriber information.
(c) A satellite or cable television corporation shall not make individual subscriber information available to government agencies in the absence of legal compulsion, including, but not limited to, a court order or subpoena. If requests for information are made, a satellite or cable television corporation shall promptly notify the subscriber of the nature of the request and what government agency has requested the information prior to responding unless otherwise prohibited from doing so by law.
Nothing in this section shall be construed to prevent local franchising authorities from obtaining information necessary to monitor franchise compliance pursuant to franchise or license agreements. This information shall be provided so as to omit individually identifiable subscriber information whenever possible. Information obtained by local franchising authorities shall be used solely for monitoring franchise compliance and shall not be subject to the California Public Records Act (Chapter 3.5 (commencing with Section 6250) of Division 7 of Title 1 of the Government Code).
(d) Any individually identifiable subscriber information gathered by a satellite or cable television corporation shall be made available for subscriber examination within 30 days of receiving a request by a subscriber to examine the information on the premises of the corporation. Upon a reasonable showing by the subscriber that the information is inaccurate, a satellite or cable television corporation shall correct the information.
(e) Upon a subscriber's application for satellite or cable television service, including, but not limited to, interactive service, a satellite or cable television corporation shall provide the applicant with a separate notice in an appropriate form explaining the subscriber's right to privacy protection afforded by this section.
(f) As used in this section:
(1) "Cable television corporation" shall have the same meaning as that term is given by Section 216.4 of the Public Utilities Code.
(2) "Individually identifiable information" means any information identifying an individual or his or her use of any service provided by a satellite or cable system other than the mere fact that the individual is a satellite or cable television subscriber. "Individually identifiable information" shall not include anonymous, aggregate, or any other information that does not identify an individual subscriber of a video provider service.
(3) "Person" includes an individual, business association, partnership, corporation, limited liability company, or other legal entity, and an individual acting or purporting to act for or on behalf of any government, or subdivision thereof, whether federal, state, or local.
(4) "Interactive service" means any service offered by a satellite or cable television corporation involving the collection, reception, aggregation, storage, or use of electronic information transmitted from a subscriber to any other receiving point under the control of the satellite or cable television corporation, or vice versa.
(g) Nothing in this section shall be construed to limit the ability of a satellite or cable television corporation to market satellite or cable television or ancillary services to its subscribers.
(h) Any person receiving subscriber information from a satellite or cable television corporation shall be subject to the provisions of this section.
(i) Any aggrieved person may commence a civil action for damages for invasion of privacy against any satellite or cable television corporation, service provider, or person that leases a channel or channels on a satellite or cable television system that violates the provisions of this section.
(j) Any person who violates the provisions of this section is guilty of a misdemeanor punishable by a fine not exceeding three thousand dollars ($3,000), or by imprisonment in the county jail not exceeding one year, or by both that fine and imprisonment.
(k) The penalties and remedies provided by subdivisions (i) and (j) are cumulative, and shall not be construed as restricting any penalty or remedy, provisional or otherwise, provided by law for the benefit of any person, and no judgment under this section shall preclude any person from obtaining additional relief based upon the same facts.
(l) The provisions of this section are intended to set forth minimum state standards for protecting the privacy of subscribers to cable television services and are not intended to preempt more restrictive local standards.
(Amended by Stats. 2006, Ch. 198, Sec. 5. Effective January 1, 2007.)

637.6.

(a) No person who, in the course of business, acquires or has access to personal information concerning an individual, including, but not limited to, the individual's residence address, employment address, or hours of employment, for the purpose of assisting private entities in the establishment or implementation of carpooling or ridesharing programs, shall disclose that information to any other person or use that information for any other purpose without the prior written consent of the individual.
(b) As used in this section, "carpooling or ridesharing programs" include, but shall not be limited to, the formation of carpools, vanpools, buspools, the provision of transit routes, rideshare research, and the development of other demand management strategies such as variable working hours and telecommuting.
(c) Any person who violates this section is guilty of a misdemeanor, punishable by imprisonment in the county jail for not exceeding one year, or by a fine of not exceeding one thousand dollars ($1,000), or by both that imprisonment and fine.
(Added by Stats. 1990, Ch. 304, Sec. 1.)

637.7.

(a) No person or entity in this state shall use an electronic tracking device to determine the location or movement of a person.
(b) This section shall not apply when the registered owner, lessor, or lessee of a vehicle has consented to the use of the electronic tracking device with respect to that vehicle.
(c) This section shall not apply to the lawful use of an electronic tracking device by a law enforcement agency.
(d) As used in this section, "electronic tracking device" means any device attached to a vehicle or other movable thing that reveals its location or movement by the transmission of electronic signals.
(e) A violation of this section is a misdemeanor.
(f) A violation of this section by a person, business, firm, company, association, partnership, or corporation licensed under Division 3 (commencing with Section 5000) of the Business and Professions Code shall constitute grounds for revocation of the license issued to that person, business, firm, company, association, partnership, or corporation, pursuant to the provisions that provide for the revocation of the license as set forth in Division 3 (commencing with Section 5000) of the Business and Professions Code.
(Added by Stats. 1998, Ch. 449, Sec. 2. Effective January 1, 1999.)

637.9.

(a) Any person who, in the course of business, provides mailing lists, computerized or telephone-based reference services, or similar products or services utilizing lists, as defined, knowingly does any of the following is guilty of a misdemeanor:
(1) Fails, prior to selling or distributing a list to a first-time buyer, to obtain the buyer's name, address, telephone number, tax identification number if the buyer is a forprofit entity, a sample of the type of material to be distributed using the list, or to make a good-faith effort to verify the nature and legitimacy of the business or organization to which the list is being sold or distributed.
(2) Knowingly provides access to personal information about children to any person who he or she knows is registered or required to register as a sex offender.
(b) Any person who uses personal information about a child that was obtained for commercial purposes to directly contact the child or the child's parent to offer a commercial product or service to the child and who knowingly fails to comply with the parent's request to take steps to limit access to personal information about a child only to authorized persons is guilty of a misdemeanor.
(c) Any person who knowingly distributes or receives any personal information about a child with knowledge that the information will be used to abuse or physically harm the child is guilty of a misdemeanor.
(d) (1) List brokers shall, upon a written request from a parent that specifically identifies the child, provide the parent with procedures that the parent must follow in order to withdraw consent to use personal information relating to his or her child. Any list broker who fails to discontinue disclosing personal information about a child within 20 days after being so requested in writing by the child's parent, is guilty of a misdemeanor.
(2) Any person who, through the mail, markets or sells products or services directed to children, shall maintain a list of all individuals, and their addresses, who have requested in writing that the person discontinue sending any marketing or sales materials to the individual or the individual's child or children. No person who is obligated to maintain that list shall cause any marketing or sales materials, other than those that are already in the process of dissemination, to be sent to any individual's child or children, after that individual has made that written request. Any person who is subject to the provisions of this paragraph, who fails to comply with the requirements of this paragraph or who violates the provisions of this paragraph is guilty of a misdemeanor.
(e) The following shall be exempt from subdivisions (a) and (b):
(1) Any federal, state, or local government agency or law enforcement agency.
(2) The National Center for Missing and Exploited Children.
(3) Any educational institution, consortia, organization, or professional association, which shall include, but not be limited to, the California community colleges; the California State University, and each campus, branch, and function thereof; each campus, branch, and function of the University of California; the California Maritime Academy; or any independent institution of higher education accredited by an agency recognized by the federal Department of Education. For the purposes of this paragraph,

"independent institution of higher education" means any nonpublic higher education institution that grants undergraduate degrees, graduate degrees, or both undergraduate and graduate degrees, is formed as a nonprofit corporation in this state, and is accredited by an agency recognized by the federal Department of Education; or any private postsecondary vocational institution registered, approved, or exempted by the Bureau of Private Postsecondary Vocational Education.

(4) Any nonprofit organization that is exempt from taxation under Section 23701d of the Revenue and Taxation Code.

(f) As used in this section:

(1) "Child" means a person who is under 16 years of age.

(2) "Parent" shall include a legal guardian.

(3) "Personal information" means any information that identifies a child and that would suffice to locate and contact the child, including, but not limited to, the name, postal or electronic mail address, telephone number, social security number, date of birth, physical description of the child, or family income.

(4) "List" may include, but is not limited to, a collection of name and address records of individuals sharing a common interest, purchase history, demographic profile, membership, or affiliation.

(Added by Stats. 1998, Ch. 763, Sec. 1. Effective January 1, 1999.)

638.

(a) Any person who purchases, sells, offers to purchase or sell, or conspires to purchase or sell any telephone calling pattern record or list, without the written consent of the subscriber, or any person who procures or obtains through fraud or deceit, or attempts to procure or obtain through fraud or deceit any telephone calling pattern record or list shall be punished by a fine not exceeding two thousand five hundred dollars ($2,500), or by imprisonment in a county jail not exceeding one year, or by both a fine and imprisonment. If the person has previously been convicted of a violation of this section, he or she is punishable by a fine not exceeding ten thousand dollars ($10,000), or by imprisonment in a county jail not exceeding one year, or by both a fine and imprisonment.

(b) Any personal information contained in a telephone calling pattern record or list that is obtained in violation of this section shall be inadmissible as evidence in any judicial, administrative, legislative, or other proceeding except when that information is offered as proof in an action or prosecution for a violation of this section, or when otherwise authorized by law, in any criminal prosecution.

(c) For purposes of this section:

(1) "Person" includes an individual, business association, partnership, limited partnership, corporation, limited liability company, or other legal entity.

(2) "Telephone calling pattern record or list" means information retained by a telephone company that relates to the telephone number dialed by the subscriber, or other person using the subscriber's telephone with permission, or the incoming number of a call directed to the subscriber, or other data related to such calls typically contained on a subscriber telephone bill such as the time the call started and ended, the duration of the call, any charges applied, and any information described in subdivision (a) of Section 2891 of the Public Utilities Code whether the call was made from or to a telephone connected to the public switched telephone network, a cordless telephone, as defined in Section 632.6, a telephony device operating over the Internet utilizing voice over Internet protocol, a satellite telephone, or commercially available interconnected mobile phone service that provides access to the public switched telephone network via a mobile communication device employing radiowave technology to transmit calls, including cellular radiotelephone, broadband Personal Communications Services, and digital Specialized Mobile Radio.

(3) "Telephone company" means a telephone corporation as defined in Section 234 of the Public Utilities Code or any other person that provides residential or commercial telephone service to a subscriber utilizing any of the technologies or methods enumerated in paragraph (2).

(4) For purposes of this section, "purchase" and "sell" shall not include information provided to a collection agency or assignee of the debt by the telephone corporation, and used exclusively for the collection of the unpaid debt assigned by the telephone corporation, provided that the collection agency or assignee of the debt shall be liable for any disclosure of the information that is in violation of this section.

(d) An employer of, or entity contracting with, a person who violates subdivision (a) shall only be subject to prosecution pursuant to that provision if the employer or contracting entity knowingly allowed the employee or contractor to engage in conduct that violated subdivision (a).

(e) It is the intent of the Legislature to ensure that telephone companies maintain telephone calling pattern records or lists in the strictest confidence, and protect the privacy of their subscribers with all due care. While it is not the intent of the Legislature in this act to preclude the sharing of information that is currently allowed by both state and federal laws and rules governing those records, it is the Legislature's intent in this act to preclude any unauthorized purchase or sale of that information.

(f) This section shall not be construed to prevent a law enforcement or prosecutorial agency, or any officer, employee, or agent thereof from obtaining telephone records in connection with the performance of the official duties of the agency consistent with any other applicable state and federal law.

(g) Nothing in this section shall preclude prosecution under any other provision of law.

(h) The Legislature hereby finds and declares that, notwithstanding the prohibition on specific means of making available or obtaining personal calling records pursuant to this section, the disclosure of personal calling records through any other means is no less harmful to the privacy and security interests of Californians. This section is not intended to limit the scope or force of Section 2891 of the Public Utilities Code in any way.

(Added by Stats. 2006, Ch. 626, Sec. 1. Effective January 1, 2007.)

638.50.

For purposes of this chapter, the following terms have the following meanings:

(a) "Wire communication" and "electronic communication" have the meanings set forth in subdivision (a) of Section 629.51.

(b) "Pen register" means a device or process that records or decodes dialing, routing, addressing, or signaling information transmitted by an instrument or facility from which a wire or electronic communication is transmitted, but not the contents of a communication. "Pen register" does not include a device or process used by a provider or customer of a wire or electronic communication service for billing, or recording as an incident to billing, for communications services provided by such provider, or a device or process used by a provider or customer of a wire communication service for cost accounting or other similar purposes in the ordinary course of its business.

(c) "Trap and trace device" means a device or process that captures the incoming electronic or other impulses that identify the originating number or other dialing, routing, addressing, or signaling information reasonably likely to identify the source of a wire or electronic communication, but not the contents of a communication.

(Added by Stats. 2015, Ch. 204, Sec. 1. (AB 929) Effective January 1, 2016.)

638.51.

(a) Except as provided in subdivision (b), a person may not install or use a pen register or a trap and trace device without first obtaining a court order pursuant to Section 638.52 or 638.53.

(b) A provider of electronic or wire communication service may use a pen register or a trap and trace device for any of the following purposes:

(1) To operate, maintain, and test a wire or electronic communication service.

(2) To protect the rights or property of the provider.

(3) To protect users of the service from abuse of service or unlawful use of service.

(4) To record the fact that a wire or electronic communication was initiated or completed to protect the provider, another provider furnishing service toward the completion of the wire communication, or a user of that service, from fraudulent, unlawful, or abusive use of service.

(5) If the consent of the user of that service has been obtained.

(c) A violation of this section is punishable by a fine not exceeding two thousand five hundred dollars ($2,500), or by imprisonment in the county jail not exceeding one year, or by imprisonment pursuant to subdivision (h) of Section 1170, or by both that fine and imprisonment.

(d) A good faith reliance on an order issued pursuant to Section 638.52, or an authorization made pursuant to Section 638.53, is a complete defense to a civil or criminal action brought under this section or under this chapter.

(Added by Stats. 2015, Ch. 204, Sec. 2. (AB 929) Effective January 1, 2016.)

638.52.

(a) A peace officer may make an application to a magistrate for an order or an extension of an order authorizing or approving the installation and use of a pen register or a trap and trace device. The application shall be in writing under oath or equivalent affirmation, and shall include the identity of the peace officer making the application and the identity of the law enforcement agency conducting the investigation. The applicant shall certify that the information likely to be obtained is relevant to an ongoing criminal investigation and shall include a statement of the offense to which the information likely to be obtained by the pen register or trap and trace device relates.

(b) The magistrate shall enter an ex parte order authorizing the installation and use of a pen register or a trap and trace device if he or she finds that the information likely to be obtained by the installation and use of a pen register or a trap and trace device is relevant to an ongoing investigation and that there is probable cause to believe that the pen register or trap and trace device will lead to any of the following:

(1) Recovery of stolen or embezzled property.

(2) Property or things used as the means of committing a felony.

(3) Property or things in the possession of a person with the intent to use them as a means of committing a public offense, or in the possession of another to whom he or she may have delivered them for the purpose of concealing them or preventing them from being discovered.

(4) Evidence that tends to show a felony has been committed, or tends to show that a particular person has committed or is committing a felony.

(5) Evidence that tends to show that sexual exploitation of a child, in violation of Section 311.3, or possession of matter depicting sexual conduct of a person under 18 years of age, in violation of Section 311.11, has occurred or is occurring.

(6) The location of a person who is unlawfully restrained or reasonably believed to be a witness in a criminal investigation or for whose arrest there is probable cause.

(7) Evidence that tends to show a violation of Section 3700.5 of the Labor Code, or tends to show that a particular person has violated Section 3700.5 of the Labor Code.

(8) Evidence that does any of the following:

(A) Tends to show that a felony, a misdemeanor violation of the Fish and Game Code, or a misdemeanor violation of the Public Resources Code, has been committed or is being committed.

(B) Tends to show that a particular person has committed or is committing a felony, a misdemeanor violation of the Fish and Game Code, or a misdemeanor violation of the Public Resources Code.

(C) Will assist in locating an individual who has committed or is committing a felony, a misdemeanor violation of the Fish and Game Code, or a misdemeanor violation of the Public Resources Code.

(c) Information acquired solely pursuant to the authority for a pen register or a trap and trace device shall not include any information that may disclose the physical location of the subscriber, except to the extent that the location may be determined from the telephone number. Upon the request of the person seeking the pen register or trap and trace device, the magistrate may seal portions of the application pursuant to People v. Hobbs (1994) 7 Cal.4th 948, and Sections 1040, 1041, and 1042 of the Evidence Code.

(d) An order issued pursuant to subdivision (b) shall specify all of the following:

(1) The identity, if known, of the person to whom is leased or in whose name is listed the telephone line to which the pen register or trap and trace device is to be attached.

(2) The identity, if known, of the person who is the subject of the criminal investigation.

(3) The number and, if known, physical location of the telephone line to which the pen register or trap and trace device is to be attached and, in the case of a trap and trace device, the geographic limits of the trap and trace order.

(4) A statement of the offense to which the information likely to be obtained by the pen register or trap and trace device relates.

(5) The order shall direct, if the applicant has requested, the furnishing of information, facilities, and technical assistance necessary to accomplish the installation of the pen register or trap and trace device.

(e) An order issued under this section shall authorize the installation and use of a pen register or a trap and trace device for a period not to exceed 60 days.

(f) Extensions of the original order may be granted upon a new application for an order under subdivisions (a) and (b) if the officer shows that there is a continued probable cause that the information or items sought under this subdivision are likely to be obtained under the extension. The period of an extension shall not exceed 60 days.

(g) An order or extension order authorizing or approving the installation and use of a pen register or a trap and trace device shall direct that the order be sealed until the order, including any extensions, expires, and that the person owning or leasing the line to which the pen register or trap and trace device is attached not disclose the existence of the pen register or trap and trace device or the existence of the investigation to the listed subscriber or to any other person.

(h) Upon the presentation of an order, entered under subdivisions (b) or (f), by a peace officer authorized to install and use a pen register, a provider of wire or electronic communication service, landlord, custodian, or other person shall immediately provide the peace officer all information, facilities, and technical assistance necessary to accomplish the installation of the pen register unobtrusively and with a minimum of interference with the services provided to the party with respect to whom the installation and use is to take place, if the assistance is directed by the order.

(i) Upon the request of a peace officer authorized to receive the results of a trap and trace device, a provider of a wire or electronic communication service, landlord, custodian, or other person shall immediately install the device on the appropriate line and provide the peace officer all information, facilities, and technical assistance, including installation and operation of the device unobtrusively and with a minimum of interference with the services provided to the party with respect to whom the installation and use is to take place, if the installation and assistance is directed by the order.

(j) A provider of a wire or electronic communication service, landlord, custodian, or other person who provides facilities or technical assistance pursuant to this section shall be reasonably compensated by the requesting peace officer's law enforcement agency for the reasonable expenses incurred in providing the facilities and assistance.

(k) Unless otherwise ordered by the magistrate, the results of the pen register or trap and trace device shall be provided to the peace officer at reasonable intervals during regular business hours for the duration of the order.

(l) The magistrate, before issuing the order pursuant to subdivision (b), may examine on oath the person seeking the pen register or the trap and trace device, and any witnesses the person may produce, and shall take his or her affidavit or their affidavits in writing, and cause the affidavit or affidavits to be subscribed by the parties making them.

(Amended by Stats. 2016, Ch. 511, Sec. 1. (AB 1924) Effective September 23, 2016.)

638.53.
(a) Except as otherwise provided in this chapter, upon an oral application by a peace officer, a magistrate may grant oral approval for the installation and use of a pen register or a trap and trace device, without an order, if he or she determines all of the following:
(1) There are grounds upon which an order could be issued under Section 638.52.
(2) There is probable cause to believe that an emergency situation exists with respect to the investigation of a crime.
(3) There is probable cause to believe that a substantial danger to life or limb exists justifying the authorization for immediate installation and use of a pen register or a trap and trace device before an order authorizing the installation and use can, with due diligence, be submitted and acted upon.
(b) (1) By midnight of the second full court day after the pen register or trap and trace device is installed, a written application pursuant to Section 638.52 shall be submitted by the peace officer who made the oral application to the magistrate who orally approved the installation and use of a pen register or trap and trace device. If an order is issued pursuant to Section 638.52, the order shall also recite the time of the oral approval under subdivision (a) and shall be retroactive to the time of the original oral approval.
(2) In the absence of an authorizing order pursuant to paragraph (1), the use shall immediately terminate when the information sought is obtained, when the application for the order is denied, or by midnight of the second full court day after the pen register or trap and trace device is installed, whichever is earlier.
(c) A provider of a wire or electronic communication service, landlord, custodian, or other person who provides facilities or technical assistance pursuant to this section shall be reasonably compensated by the requesting peace officer's law enforcement agency for the reasonable expenses incurred in providing the facilities and assistance.
(Added by Stats. 2015, Ch. 204, Sec. 4. (AB 929) Effective January 1, 2016.)
638.54.
(a) Except as otherwise provided in this section, a government entity that obtains information pursuant to Section 638.52, or obtains information pursuant to oral authorization pursuant to Section 638.53, shall serve upon, or deliver to by registered or first-class mail, electronic mail, or other means reasonably calculated to be effective, the identified targets of the order a notice that informs the recipient that information about the recipient has been compelled or requested and states with reasonable specificity the nature of the government investigation under which the information is sought. The notice shall include a copy of the order or a written statement setting forth facts giving rise to the emergency. The notice shall be provided no later than 30 days after the termination of the period of the order, any extensions, or an emergency request.
(b) (1) Prior to the expiration of the 30-day period specified in subdivision (a), the government entity may submit a request, supported by a sworn affidavit, for an order delaying unsealing of the order and notification and prohibiting the person owning or leasing the line to which the pen register or trap and trace device is attached from disclosing the existence of the pen register or trap and trace device or the existence of the investigation to the listed subscriber or any other person. The court shall issue the order if the court determines that there is reason to believe that notification may have an adverse result, but only for the period of time that the court finds there is reason to believe that the notification may have that adverse result, and not to exceed 90 days.
(2) The court may grant extensions of the delay of up to 90 days each on the same grounds as provided in paragraph (1).
(3) Upon expiration of the period of delay of the notification, the government entity shall serve upon, or deliver to by registered or first-class mail, electronic mail, or other means reasonably calculated to be effective as specified by the court issuing the order authorizing delayed notification, the identified targets of the order or emergency authorization a document that includes the information described in subdivision (a) and a copy of all electronic information obtained or a summary of that information, including, at a minimum, the number and types of records disclosed, the date and time when the earliest and latest records were created, and a statement of the grounds for the court's determination to grant a delay in notifying the individual. The notice shall be provided no later than three days after the expiration of the period of delay of the notification.
(c) If there is no identified target of an order or emergency request at the time of its issuance, the government entity shall submit to the Department of Justice, no later than three days after the termination of the period of the order, any extensions, or an emergency request, all of the information required in subdivision (a). If an order delaying notice is obtained pursuant to subdivision (b), the government entity shall submit to the department, no later than three days after the expiration of the period of delay of the notification, all of the information required in paragraph (3) of subdivision (b). The department shall publish all those reports on its Internet Web site within 90 days of receipt. The department may redact names or other personal identifying information from the reports.
(d) For the purposes of this section, "adverse result" has the meaning set forth in subdivision (a) of Section 1546.
(Added by Stats. 2016, Ch. 511, Sec. 2. (AB 1924) Effective September 23, 2016.)
638.55.
(a) Any person in a trial, hearing, or proceeding may move to suppress wire or electronic information obtained or retained in violation of the Fourth Amendment to the United States Constitution or of this chapter. The motion shall be made, determined, and be subject to review in accordance with the procedures set forth in subdivisions (b) to (q), inclusive, of Section 1538.5.
(b) The Attorney General may commence a civil action to compel any government entity to comply with the provisions of this chapter.
(c) An individual whose information is targeted by a warrant, order, or other legal process that is not in compliance with this chapter, the California Constitution, or the United States Constitution, or a service provider or any other recipient of the warrant, order, or other legal process may petition the issuing court to void or modify the warrant, order, or process, or to order the destruction of any information obtained in violation of this chapter, the California Constitution, or the United States Constitution.
(Added by Stats. 2016, Ch. 511, Sec. 3. (AB 1924) Effective September 23, 2016.)

CHAPTER 2. Of Other and Miscellaneous Offenses [639 - 653.2]

(Chapter 2 enacted 1872.)
639.
Every person who gives, offers, or agrees to give to any director, officer, or employee of a financial institution any emolument, gratuity, or reward, or any money, property, or thing of value for his own personal benefit or of personal advantage, for procuring or endeavoring to procure for any person a loan or extension of credit from such financial institution is guilty of a felony.
As used in this section and Section 639a, "financial institution" means any person or persons engaged in the business of making loans or extending credit or procuring the making of loans or extension of credit, including, but not limited to, state and federal banks, savings and loan associations, trust companies, industrial loan companies, personal property brokers, consumer finance lenders, commercial finance lenders, credit unions, escrow companies, title insurance companies, insurance companies, small business investment companies, pawnbrokers, and retirement funds.
As used in this section and Section 639a the word "person" includes any person, firm, partnership, association, corporation, limited liability company, company, syndicate, estate, trust, business trust, or organization of any kind.
(Amended by Stats. 1994, Ch. 1010, Sec. 196. Effective January 1, 1995.)
639a.
Any officer, director or employee of a financial institution who asks, receives, consents, or agrees to receive any commission, emolument, gratuity, or reward or any money, property, or thing of value for his own personal benefit or of personal advantage for procuring or endeavoring to procure for any person a loan from such financial institution is guilty of a felony.
(Added by Stats. 1967, Ch. 1023.)
640.
(a) (1) Any of the acts described in paragraphs (1) to (6), inclusive, of subdivision (b) is an infraction punishable by a fine not to exceed two hundred fifty dollars ($250) and by community service for a total time not to exceed 48 hours over a period not to exceed 30 days, during a time other than during the violator's hours of school attendance or employment. Except as provided in subdivision (g), any of the acts described in paragraphs (1) to (3), inclusive, of subdivision (c), upon a first or second violation, is an infraction punishable by a fine not to exceed two hundred fifty dollars ($250) and by community service for a total time not to exceed 48 hours over a period not to exceed 30 days, during a time other than during the violator's hours of school attendance or employment. Except as provided in subdivision (g), a third or subsequent violation of any of the acts described in paragraphs (1) to (3), inclusive, of subdivision (c) is a misdemeanor punishable by a fine of not more than four hundred dollars ($400) or by imprisonment in a county jail for a period of not more than 90 days, or by both that fine and imprisonment. Any of the acts described in subdivision (d) shall be punishable by a fine of not more than four hundred dollars ($400), by imprisonment in a county jail for a period of not more than 90 days, or by both that fine and imprisonment.
(2) This section shall apply only to acts committed on or in a facility or vehicle of a public transportation system.
(b) (1) Eating or drinking in or on a system facility or vehicle in areas where those activities are prohibited by that system.
(2) Playing unreasonably loud sound equipment on or in a system facility or vehicle, or failing to comply with the warning of a transit official related to disturbing another person by loud or unreasonable noise.
(3) Smoking in or on a system facility or vehicle in areas where those activities are prohibited by that system.
(4) Expectorating upon a system facility or vehicle.
(5) Skateboarding, roller skating, bicycle riding, roller blading, or operating a motorized scooter or similar device, as defined in Section 407.5 of the Vehicle Code, in a system facility, vehicle, or parking structure. This paragraph does not apply to an activity that is necessary for utilization of the transit facility by a bicyclist, including, but not limited to, an activity that is necessary for parking a bicycle or transporting a bicycle aboard a transit vehicle, if that activity is conducted with the permission of the transit agency in a manner that does not interfere with the safety of the bicyclist or other patrons of the transit facility.
(6) Selling or peddling any goods, merchandise, property, or services of any kind whatsoever on the facilities, vehicles, or property of the public transportation system if the public transportation system has prohibited those acts and neither the public transportation system nor its duly authorized representatives have granted written consent to engage in those acts.
(c) (1) Evasion of the payment of a fare of the system. For purposes of this section, fare evasion includes entering an enclosed area of a public transit facility beyond posted signs prohibiting entrance without obtaining valid fare, in addition to entering a transit vehicle without valid fare.
(2) Misuse of a transfer, pass, ticket, or token with the intent to evade the payment of a fare.
(3) (A) Unauthorized use of a discount ticket or failure to present, upon request from a transit system representative, acceptable proof of eligibility to use a discount ticket, in accordance with Section 99155 of the Public Utilities Code and posted system identification policies when entering or exiting a transit station or vehicle. Acceptable proof of eligibility must be clearly defined in the posting.
(B) If an eligible discount ticket user is not in possession of acceptable proof at the time of request, a citation issued shall be held for a period of 72 hours to allow the user to produce acceptable proof. If the proof is provided, the citation shall be voided. If the proof is not produced within that time period, the citation shall be processed.
(d) (1) Willfully disturbing others on or in a system facility or vehicle by engaging in boisterous or unruly behavior.
(2) Carrying an explosive, acid, or flammable liquid in a public transit facility or vehicle.
(3) Urinating or defecating in a system facility or vehicle, except in a lavatory. However, this paragraph shall not apply to a person who cannot comply with this paragraph as a result of a disability, age, or a medical condition.
(4) Willfully blocking the free movement of another person in a system facility or vehicle. This paragraph shall not be interpreted to affect any lawful activities permitted or First Amendment rights protected under the laws of this state or applicable federal law, including, but not limited to, laws related to collective bargaining, labor relations, or labor disputes.
(5) Willfully tampering with, removing, displacing, injuring, or destroying any part of a facility or vehicle of a public transportation system.
(e) Notwithstanding subdivision (a) or (g), a public transportation agency, as defined in paragraph (4) of subdivision (c) of Section 99580 of the Public Utilities Code, may do either of the following:
(1) Enact and enforce an ordinance providing that a person who is the subject of a citation for any of the acts described in subdivision (b) of Section 99580 of the Public Utilities Code on or in a facility or vehicle described in subdivision (a) for which the public transportation agency has jurisdiction shall, under the circumstances set forth by the ordinance, be afforded an opportunity to complete an administrative process that imposes only an administrative penalty enforced in a civil proceeding. The ordinance for imposing and enforcing the administrative penalty shall be governed by Chapter 8 (commencing with Section 99580) of Part 11 of Division 10 of the Public Utilities Code.
(2) Enforce as an infraction pursuant to subdivision (b) the act of failing to yield seating reserved for an elderly or disabled person in a facility or vehicle for which the public transportation agency has jurisdiction, provided that the governing board of the public transportation agency enacts an ordinance to that effect after a public hearing on the issue.
(f) For purposes of this section, "facility or vehicle of a public transportation system" means any of the following:
(1) A facility or vehicle of a public transportation system as defined by Section 99211 of the Public Utilities Code.
(2) A facility of, or vehicle operated by, an entity subsidized by, the Department of Transportation.
(3) A facility or vehicle of a rail authority, whether owned or leased, including, but not limited to, any part of a railroad, or track of a railroad, or any branch or branchway, switch, turnout, bridge, viaduct, culvert, embankment, station house, or other structure or fixture, or any part thereof, attached or connected to a railroad.

(4) A leased or rented facility or vehicle for which any of the entities described in paragraph (1), (2), or (3) incurs costs of cleanup, repair, or replacement as a result of any of those acts.
(g) A minor shall not be charged with an infraction or a misdemeanor for violation of paragraphs (1) to (3), inclusive, of subdivision (c). Nothing in this subdivision shall limit the ability of a public transportation agency to assess an administrative penalty as established in paragraph (1) of subdivision (e) and in Section 99580 of the Public Utilities Code, not to exceed one hundred twenty-five dollars ($125) upon a first or second violation and not to exceed two hundred dollars ($200) upon a third or subsequent violation, to permit the performance of community service in lieu of payment of the fare evasion or passenger conduct penalty pursuant to Section 99580 of the Public Utilities Code, or to allow payment of the fare evasion or passenger conduct penalty in installments or deferred payment pursuant to Section 99580 of the Public Utilities Code.
(Amended by Stats. 2017, Ch. 219, Sec. 1. (SB 614) Effective January 1, 2018.)

640.2.

(a) Any person who stamps, prints, places, or inserts any writing in or on any product or box, package, or other container containing a consumer product offered for sale is guilty of a misdemeanor.
(b) This section does not apply if the owner or manager of the premises where the product is stored or sold, or his or her designee, or the product manufacturer or authorized distributor or retailer of the product consents to the placing or inserting of the writing.
(c) As used in this section, "writing" means any form of representation or communication, including handbills, notices, or advertising, that contains letters, words, or pictorial representations.
(Added by Stats. 1996, Ch. 140, Sec. 1. Effective July 12, 1996.)

640.5.

(a) (1) Any person who defaces with graffiti or other inscribed material the interior or exterior of the facilities or vehicles of a governmental entity, as defined by Section 811.2 of the Government Code, or the interior or exterior of the facilities or vehicles of a public transportation system as defined by Section 99211 of the Public Utilities Code, or the interior or exterior of the facilities of or vehicles operated by entities subsidized by the Department of Transportation or the interior or exterior of any leased or rented facilities or vehicles for which any of the above entities incur costs of less than two hundred fifty dollars ($250) for cleanup, repair, or replacement is guilty of an infraction, punishable by a fine not to exceed one thousand dollars ($1,000) and by a minimum of 48 hours of community service for a total time not to exceed 200 hours over a period not to exceed 180 days, during a time other than his or her hours of school attendance or employment. This subdivision does not preclude application of Section 594.
(2) In lieu of the community service required pursuant to paragraph (1), the court may, if a jurisdiction has adopted a graffiti abatement program as defined in subdivision (f) of Section 594, order the defendant, and his or her parents or guardians if the defendant is a minor, to keep a specified property in the community free of graffiti for 90 days. Participation of a parent or guardian is not required under this paragraph if the court deems this participation to be detrimental to the defendant, or if the parent or guardian is a single parent who must care for young children.
(b) (1) If the person has been convicted previously of an infraction under subdivision (a) or has a prior conviction of Section 594, 594.3, 594.4, 640.6, or 640.7, the offense is a misdemeanor, punishable by imprisonment in a county jail not to exceed six months, by a fine not to exceed two thousand dollars ($2,000), or by both that imprisonment and fine. As a condition of probation, the court shall order the defendant to perform a minimum of 96 hours of community service not to exceed 400 hours over a period not to exceed 350 days during a time other than his or her hours of school attendance or employment.
(2) In lieu of the community service required pursuant to paragraph (1), the court may, if a jurisdiction has adopted a graffiti abatement program as defined in subdivision (f) of Section 594, order the defendant, and his or her parents or guardians if the defendant is a minor, as a condition of probation, to keep a specified property in the community free of graffiti for 180 days. Participation of a parent or guardian is not required under this paragraph if the court deems this participation to be detrimental to the defendant, or if the parent or guardian is a single parent who must care for young children.
(c) (1) Every person who, having been convicted previously under this section or Section 594, 594.3, 594.4, 640.6, or 640.7, or any combination of these offenses, on two separate occasions, and having been incarcerated pursuant to a sentence, a conditional sentence, or a grant of probation for at least one of the convictions, is subsequently convicted under this section, shall be punished by imprisonment in a county jail not to exceed one year, by a fine not to exceed three thousand dollars ($3,000), or by both that imprisonment and fine. As a condition of probation, the court may order the defendant to perform community service not to exceed 600 hours over a period not to exceed 480 days during a time other than his or her hours of school attendance or employment.
(2) In lieu of the community service that may be ordered pursuant to paragraph (1), the court may, if a jurisdiction has adopted a graffiti abatement program as defined in subdivision (f) of Section 594, order the defendant, and his or her parents or guardians if the defendant is a minor, as a condition of probation, to keep a specified property in the community free of graffiti for 240 days. Participation of a parent or guardian is not required under this paragraph if the court deems this participation to be detrimental to the defendant, or if the parent or guardian is a single parent who must care for young children.
(d) (1) Upon conviction of any person under subdivision (a), the court, in addition to any punishment imposed pursuant to subdivision (a), (b), or (c), at the victim's option, may order the defendant to perform the necessary labor to clean up, repair, or replace the property damaged by that person.
(2) If a minor is personally unable to pay any fine levied for violating subdivision (a), (b), or (c), the parent or legal guardian of the minor shall be liable for payment of the fine. A court may waive payment of the fine or any part thereof by the parent or legal guardian upon a finding of good cause.
(e) Any fine levied for a violation of subdivision (a), (b), or (c) shall be credited by the county treasurer pursuant to Section 1463.29 to the governmental entity having jurisdiction over, or responsibility for, the facility or vehicle involved, to be used for removal of the graffiti or other inscribed material or replacement or repair of the property defaced by the graffiti or other inscribed material. Before crediting these fines to the appropriate governmental entity, the county may determine the administrative costs it has incurred pursuant to this section, and retain an amount equal to those costs.
Any community service which is required pursuant to subdivision (a), (b), or (c) of a person under the age of 18 years may be performed in the presence, and under the direct supervision, of the person's parent or legal guardian.
(f) As used in this section, the term "graffiti or other inscribed material" includes any unauthorized inscription, word, figure, mark, or design that is written, marked, etched, scratched, drawn, or painted on real or personal property.
(g) The court may order any person ordered to perform community service or graffiti removal pursuant to subdivision (a), (b), (c), or (d) to undergo counseling.
(Amended by Stats. 1996, Ch. 847, Sec. 1.5. Effective January 1, 1997.)

640.6.

(a) (1) Except as provided in Section 640.5, any person who defaces with graffiti or other inscribed material any real or personal property not his or her own, when the amount of the defacement, damage, or destruction is less than two hundred fifty dollars ($250), is guilty of an infraction, punishable by a fine not to exceed one thousand dollars ($1,000). This subdivision does not preclude application of Section 594.
In addition to the penalty set forth in this section, the court shall order the defendant to perform a minimum of 48 hours of community service not to exceed 200 hours over a period not to exceed 180 days during a time other than his or her hours of school attendance or employment.
(2) In lieu of the community service required pursuant to paragraph (1), the court may, if a jurisdiction has adopted a graffiti abatement program as defined in subdivision (f) of Section 594, order the defendant, and his or her parents or guardians if the defendant is a minor, to keep a specified property in the community free of graffiti for 90 days. Participation of a parent or guardian is not required under this paragraph if the court deems this participation to be detrimental to the defendant, or if the parent or guardian is a single parent who must care for young children.
(b) (1) If the person has been convicted previously of an infraction under subdivision (a) or has a prior conviction of Section 594, 594.3, 594.4, 640.5, or 640.7, the offense is a misdemeanor, punishable by not to exceed six months in a county jail, by a fine not to exceed two thousand dollars ($2,000), or by both that imprisonment and fine. As a condition of probation, the court shall order the defendant to perform a minimum of 96 hours of community service not to exceed 400 hours over a period not to exceed 350 days during a time other than his or her hours of school attendance or employment.
(2) In lieu of the community service required pursuant to paragraph (1), the court may, if a jurisdiction has adopted a graffiti abatement program as defined in subdivision (f) of Section 594, order the defendant, and his or her parents or guardians if the defendant is a minor, as a condition of probation, to keep a specified property in the community free of graffiti for 180 days. Participation of a parent or guardian is not required under this paragraph if the court deems this participation to be detrimental to the defendant, or if the parent or guardian is a single parent who must care for young children.
(c) (1) Every person who, having been convicted previously under this section or Section 594, 594.3, 594.4, 640.5, or 640.7, or any combination of these offenses, on two separate occasions, and having been incarcerated pursuant to a sentence, a conditional sentence, or a grant of probation for at least one of the convictions, is subsequently convicted under this section, shall be punished by imprisonment in a county jail not to exceed one year, by a fine not to exceed three thousand dollars ($3,000), or by both that imprisonment and fine. As a condition of probation, the court may order the defendant to perform community service not to exceed 600 hours over a period not to exceed 480 days during a time other than his or her hours of school attendance or employment.
(2) In lieu of the community service that may be ordered pursuant to paragraph (1), the court may, if a jurisdiction has adopted a graffiti abatement program as defined in subdivision (f) of Section 594, order the defendant, and his or her parents or guardians if the defendant is a minor, as a condition of probation, to keep a specified property in the community free of graffiti for 240 days. Participation of a parent or guardian is not required under this paragraph if the court deems this participation to be detrimental to the defendant, or if the parent or guardian is a single parent who must care for young children.
(d) Upon conviction of any person under subdivision (a), the court, in addition to any punishment imposed pursuant to subdivision (a), (b), or (c), at the victim's option, may order the defendant to perform the necessary labor to clean up, repair, or replace the property damaged by that person.
(e) If a minor is personally unable to pay any fine levied for violating subdivision (a), (b), or (c), the parent or legal guardian of the minor shall be liable for payment of the fine. A court may waive payment of the fine or any part thereof by the parent or legal guardian upon a finding of good cause.
Any community service which is required pursuant to subdivision (a), (b), or (c) of a person under the age of 18 years may be performed in the presence, and under the direct supervision, of the person's parent or legal guardian.
(f) As used in this section, the term "graffiti or other inscribed material" includes any unauthorized inscription, word, figure, mark, or design that is written, marked, etched, scratched, drawn, or painted on real or personal property.
(g) The court may order any person ordered to perform community service or graffiti removal pursuant to subdivision (a), (b), (c), or (d) to undergo counseling.
(Amended by Stats. 1996, Ch. 847, Sec. 2.5. Effective January 1, 1997.)

640.7.

Any person who violates Section 594, 640.5, or 640.6 on or within 100 feet of a highway, or its appurtenances, including, but not limited to, guardrails, signs, traffic signals, snow poles, and similar facilities, excluding signs naming streets, is guilty of a misdemeanor, punishable by imprisonment in a county jail not exceeding six months, or by a fine not exceeding one thousand dollars ($1,000), or by both that imprisonment and fine. A second conviction is punishable by imprisonment in a county jail not exceeding one year, or by a fine not exceeding one thousand dollars ($1,000), or by both that imprisonment and fine.
(Amended by Stats. 1998, Ch. 853, Sec. 3. Effective January 1, 1999.)

640.8.

Any person who violates Section 594, 640.5, or 640.6, on a freeway, or its appurtenances, including sound walls, overpasses, overpass supports, guardrails, signs, signals, and other traffic control devices, is guilty of a misdemeanor, punishable by imprisonment in a county jail not to exceed one year, by a fine not to exceed five thousand dollars ($5,000), or by both that imprisonment and fine. As a condition of probation, the court may order the defendant to perform community service not to exceed 480 hours over a period not to exceed 420 days during a time other than his or her hours of school attendance or employment.
(Added by Stats. 1996, Ch. 847, Sec. 3. Effective January 1, 1997.)

640a.

1. Any person who shall knowingly and wilfully operate, or cause to be operated, or who shall attempt to operate, or attempt to cause to be operated, any automatic vending machine, slot machine or other receptacle designed to receive lawful coin of the United States of America in connection with the sale, use or enjoyment of property or service, by means of a slug or any false, counterfeited, mutilated, sweated or foreign coin, or by any means, method, trick or device whatsoever not lawfully authorized by the owner, lessee or licensee of such machine or receptacle, or who shall take, obtain or receive from or in connection with any automatic vending machine, slot machine or other receptacle designed to receive lawful coin of the United States of America in connection with the sale, use or enjoyment of property or service, any goods, wares, merchandise, gas, electric current, article of value, or the use or enjoyment of any musical instrument, phonograph or other property, without depositing in and surrendering to such machine or receptacle lawful coin of the United States of America to the amount required therefor by the owner, lessee or licensee of such machine or receptacle shall be guilty of a misdemeanor.
2. Any person who, with intent to cheat or defraud the owner, lessee, licensee or other person entitled to the contents of any automatic vending machine, slot machine or other receptacle, depository or contrivance designed to receive lawful coin of the United States of America in connection with the sale, use or enjoyment of property or service, or who, knowing or having cause to believe that the same is intended for unlawful use, shall manufacture for sale, or sell or give away any slug, device or substance whatsoever intended or calculated to be placed or deposited in any such automatic vending machine, slot machine or other such receptacle, depository or contrivance, shall be guilty of a misdemeanor.
(Amended by Stats. 1957, Ch. 2096.)

640b.

1. Any person who knowingly, wilfully and with intent to defraud the owner, lessee or licensee of any coin-box telephone, shall operate or cause to be operated, attempt to operate, or attempt to cause to be operated, any coin-box telephone by means of any slug or any false, counterfeited, mutilated, sweated or foreign coin, or by any means, method, trick or device whatsoever not lawfully authorized by such owner, lessee or licensee, or any person who, knowingly, wilfully and with intent to defraud the owner, lessee or licensee of any coin-box telephone, shall take, obtain or receive from or in connection with any such coin-box telephone, the use or enjoyment of any telephone or telegraph facilities or service, without depositing in or surrendering to such coin-box telephone lawful coin of the United States of America to the amount required therefor by such owner, lessee or licensee, shall be guilty of a misdemeanor.

2. Any person who, with the intent to cheat or defraud the owner, lessee or licensee or other person entitled to the contents of any coin-box telephone, or who, knowing or having cause to believe that the same is intended for unlawful use, shall manufacture for sale, or sell or give away any slug, device or substance whatsoever intended or calculated to be placed or deposited in any such coin-box telephone, shall be guilty of a misdemeanor.

(Added by Stats. 1957, Ch. 2096.)

641.

Every person who, by the payment or promise of any bribe, inducement, or reward, procures or attempts to procure any telegraph or telephone agent, operator, or employee to disclose any private message, or the contents, purport, substance, or meaning thereof, or offers to any agent, operator, or employee any bribe, compensation, or reward for the disclosure of any private information received by him or her by reason of his or her trust as agent, operator, or employee, or uses or attempts to use any information so obtained, is punishable as provided in Section 639.

(Amended by Stats. 1987, Ch. 828, Sec. 40.)

641.3.

(a) Any employee who solicits, accepts, or agrees to accept money or any thing of value from a person other than his or her employer, other than in trust for the employer, corruptly and without the knowledge or consent of the employer, in return for using or agreeing to use his or her position for the benefit of that other person, and any person who offers or gives an employee money or any thing of value under those circumstances, is guilty of commercial bribery.

(b) This section does not apply where the amount of money or monetary worth of the thing of value is two hundred fifty dollars ($250) or less.

(c) Commercial bribery is punishable by imprisonment in the county jail for not more than one year if the amount of the bribe is one thousand dollars ($1,000) or less, or by imprisonment in the county jail, or in the state prison for 16 months, or two or three years if the amount of the bribe exceeds one thousand dollars ($1,000).

(d) For purposes of this section:

(1) "Employee" means an officer, director, agent, trustee, partner, or employee.

(2) "Employer" means a corporation, association, organization, trust, partnership, or sole proprietorship.

(3) "Corruptly" means that the person specifically intends to injure or defraud (A) his or her employer, (B) the employer of the person to whom he or she offers, gives, or agrees to give the money or a thing of value, (C) the employer of the person from whom he or she requests, receives, or agrees to receive the money or a thing of value, or (D) a competitor of any such employer.

(Amended by Stats. 2009, 3rd Ex. Sess., Ch. 28, Sec. 35. (SB 18 3x) Effective January 25, 2010.)

641.4.

(a) An employee of a title insurer, underwritten title company, or controlled escrow company who corruptly violates Section 12404 of the Insurance Code by paying, directly or indirectly, a commission, compensation, or other consideration to a licensee, as defined in Section 10011 of the Business and Professions Code, or a licensee who corruptly violates Section 10177.4 of the Business and Professions Code by receiving from an employee of a title insurer, underwritten title company, or controlled escrow company a commission, compensation, or other consideration, as an inducement for the placement or referral of title business, is guilty of commercial bribery.

(b) For purposes of this section, commercial bribery is punishable by imprisonment in a county jail for not more than one year, or by a fine of ten thousand dollars ($10,000) for each unlawful transaction, or by both a fine and imprisonment.

(c) For purposes of this section, "title business" has the same meaning as that used in Section 12404 of the Insurance Code.

(d) This section shall not preclude prosecution under any other law.

(e) This section shall not be construed to supersede or affect Section 641.3. A person may be charged with a violation of this section and Section 641.3. However, a defendant may not be punished under this section and Section 641.3 for the same act that constitutes a violation of both this section and Section 641.3.

(Added by Stats. 1997, Ch. 718, Sec. 3. Effective January 1, 1998.)

641.5.

(a) In any clothes cleaning establishment in which more than one gallon of a volatile, commercially moisture-free solvent of the chlorinated hydrocarbon type is used for dry cleaning, the performance of all the dry cleaning, drying, and deodorizing processes shall be completed entirely within fluid-tight machines or apparatus vented to the open air at a point not less than eight feet from any window or other opening and so used and operated as to prevent the escape of fumes, gases, or vapors into workrooms or workplaces.

(b) Except when operations are performed as provided in subdivision (a), no person shall operate a clothes cleaning establishment in which more than one gallon of a volatile, commercially moisture-free solvent of the chlorinated hydrocarbon type is used for dry cleaning except under either of the following conditions:

(1) All of the dry cleaning, drying, and deodorizing processes are performed in a single room or compartment designed and ventilated in such a manner that dangerous toxic concentrations of vapors will not accumulate in working areas.

(2) The dry cleaning processes are performed in fluid-tight machines or apparatus designed, installed, and operated in a manner that will prevent the escape of dangerous toxic concentrations of vapors to the working areas.

(c) "Volatile, commercially moisture-free solvent" means either of the following:

(1) Any commercially moisture-free liquid, volatile product or substance having the capacity to evaporate and, during evaporation, to generate and emit a gas or vapor.

(2) Any solvent commonly known to the clothes cleaning industry as a "chlorinated hydrocarbon solvent."

(d) Any violation of this section is a misdemeanor.

(Added by Stats. 1986, Ch. 478, Sec. 2.)

641.6.

Notwithstanding any other provision of law, no person engaged in the business of dry cleaning shall use carbon tetrachloride or trichlorethylene as a cleaning agent when engaged in onsite dry cleaning. For purposes of this section, "onsite dry cleaning" means dry cleaning which is performed in a residence or any commercial or public building other than a clothes cleaning establishment or plant. A violation of this section is a misdemeanor.

(Added by Stats. 1986, Ch. 478, Sec. 3.)

642.

Every person who wilfully and maliciously removes and keeps possession of and appropriates for his own use articles of value from a dead human body, the theft of which articles would be petty theft is guilty of a misdemeanor, or if the theft of the articles would be grand theft, a felony. This section shall not apply to articles removed at

the request or direction of one of the persons enumerated in section 7111 of the Health and Safety Code.

(Added by Stats. 1939, Ch. 691.)

643.

No person knowingly shall dispose of fetal remains in a public or private dump, refuse, or disposal site or place open to public view. For the purposes of this section, "fetal remains" means the lifeless product of conception regardless of the duration of the pregnancy.

Any violation of this section is a misdemeanor.

(Added by Stats. 1971, Ch. 377.)

645.

(a) Any person guilty of a first conviction of any offense specified in subdivision (c), where the victim has not attained 13 years of age, may, upon parole, undergo medroxyprogesterone acetate treatment or its chemical equivalent, in addition to any other punishment prescribed for that offense or any other provision of law, at the discretion of the court.

(b) Any person guilty of a second conviction of any offense specified in subdivision (c), where the victim has not attained 13 years of age, shall, upon parole, undergo medroxyprogesterone acetate treatment or its chemical equivalent, in addition to any other punishment prescribed for that offense or any other provision of law.

(c) This section shall apply to the following offenses:

(1) Subdivision (c) or (d) of Section 286.

(2) Paragraph (1) of subdivision (b) of Section 288.

(3) Subdivision (c) or (d) of Section 287 or of former Section 288a.

(4) Subdivision (a) or (j) of Section 289.

(d) The parolee shall begin medroxyprogesterone acetate treatment one week prior to his or her release from confinement in the state prison or other institution and shall continue treatments until the Department of Corrections demonstrates to the Board of Prison Terms that this treatment is no longer necessary.

(e) If a person voluntarily undergoes a permanent, surgical alternative to hormonal chemical treatment for sex offenders, he or she shall not be subject to this section.

(f) The Department of Corrections shall administer this section and implement the protocols required by this section. Nothing in the protocols shall require an employee of the Department of Corrections who is a physician and surgeon licensed pursuant to Chapter 5 (commencing with Section 2000) of Division 2 of the Business and Professions Code or the Osteopathic Initiative Act to participate against his or her will in the administration of the provisions of this section. These protocols shall include, but not be limited to, a requirement to inform the person about the effect of hormonal chemical treatment and any side effects that may result from it. A person subject to this section shall acknowledge the receipt of this information.

(Amended by Stats. 2018, Ch. 423, Sec. 62. (SB 1494) Effective January 1, 2019.)

646.

It is unlawful for any person with the intent, or for the purpose of instituting a suit thereon outside of this state, to seek or solicit the business of collecting any claim for damages for personal injury sustained within this state, or for death resulting therefrom, with the intention of instituting suit thereon outside of this state, in cases where such right of action rests in a resident of this state, or his legal representative, and is against a person, copartnership, or corporation subject to personal service within this state.

Any person violating any of the provisions of this section is guilty of a misdemeanor, and is punishable by a fine of not less than one hundred dollars ($100) nor more than one thousand dollars ($1,000), by imprisonment in the county jail not less than 30 days nor more than six months, or by both fine and imprisonment at the discretion of the court but within said limits.

(Amended by Stats. 1983, Ch. 1092, Sec. 314. Effective September 27, 1983. Operative January 1, 1984, by Sec. 427 of Ch. 1092.)

646.5.

No person shall knowingly and directly solicit employment from any injured person or from any other person to obtain authorization on behalf of the injured person, as an investigator to investigate the accident or act which resulted in injury or death to such person or damage to the property of such person. Nothing in this section shall prohibit the soliciting of employment as an investigator from such injured person's attorney.

Any person violating any provision of this section is guilty of a misdemeanor.

This section shall not apply to any business agent or attorney employed by a labor organization.

(Added by Stats. 1971, Ch. 694.)

646.6.

No person shall knowingly and directly solicit any injured person, or anyone acting on behalf of any injured person, for the sale or use of photographs relating to the accident which resulted in the injury or death of such injured person.

Any person violating any provision of this section is guilty of a misdemeanor. Nothing in this section shall prohibit a person, other than a public employee acting within the scope of his or her employment, from soliciting the injured person's attorney for the sale or use of such photographs.

(Amended by Stats. 1976, Ch. 495.)

646.9.

(a) Any person who willfully, maliciously, and repeatedly follows or willfully and maliciously harasses another person and who makes a credible threat with the intent to place that person in reasonable fear for his or her safety, or the safety of his or her immediate family is guilty of the crime of stalking, punishable by imprisonment in a county jail for not more than one year, or by a fine of not more than one thousand dollars ($1,000), or by both that fine and imprisonment, or by imprisonment in the state prison.

(b) Any person who violates subdivision (a) when there is a temporary restraining order, injunction, or any other court order in effect prohibiting the behavior described in subdivision (a) against the same party, shall be punished by imprisonment in the state prison for two, three, or four years.

(c) (1) Every person who, after having been convicted of a felony under Section 273.5, 273.6, or 422, commits a violation of subdivision (a) shall be punished by imprisonment in a county jail for not more than one year, or by a fine of not more than one thousand dollars ($1,000), or by both that fine and imprisonment, or by imprisonment in the state prison for two, three, or five years.

(2) Every person who, after having been convicted of a felony under subdivision (a), commits a violation of this section shall be punished by imprisonment in the state prison for two, three, or five years.

(d) In addition to the penalties provided in this section, the sentencing court may order a person convicted of a felony under this section to register as a sex offender pursuant to Section 290.006.

(e) For the purposes of this section, "harasses" means engages in a knowing and willful course of conduct directed at a specific person that seriously alarms, annoys, torments, or terrorizes the person, and that serves no legitimate purpose.

(f) For the purposes of this section, "course of conduct" means two or more acts occurring over a period of time, however short, evidencing a continuity of purpose. Constitutionally protected activity is not included within the meaning of "course of conduct."

(g) For the purposes of this section, "credible threat" means a verbal or written threat, including that performed through the use of an electronic communication device, or a threat implied by a pattern of conduct or a combination of verbal, written, or electronically communicated statements and conduct, made with the intent to place the person that is the target of the threat in reasonable fear for his or her safety or the safety of his or her family, and made with the apparent ability to carry out the threat so as to cause the person who is the target of the threat to reasonably fear for his or her safety or the safety of his or her family. It is not necessary to prove that the defendant had the intent to actually carry out the threat. The present incarceration of a person making the threat shall not be a bar to prosecution under this section. Constitutionally protected activity is not included within the meaning of "credible threat."

(h) For purposes of this section, the term "electronic communication device" includes, but is not limited to, telephones, cellular phones, computers, video recorders, fax machines, or pagers. "Electronic communication" has the same meaning as the term defined in Subsection 12 of Section 2510 of Title 18 of the United States Code.

(i) This section shall not apply to conduct that occurs during labor picketing.

(j) If probation is granted, or the execution or imposition of a sentence is suspended, for any person convicted under this section, it shall be a condition of probation that the person participate in counseling, as designated by the court. However, the court, upon a showing of good cause, may find that the counseling requirement shall not be imposed.

(k) (1) The sentencing court also shall consider issuing an order restraining the defendant from any contact with the victim, that may be valid for up to 10 years, as determined by the court. It is the intent of the Legislature that the length of any restraining order be based upon the seriousness of the facts before the court, the probability of future violations, and the safety of the victim and his or her immediate family.

(2) This protective order may be issued by the court whether the defendant is sentenced to state prison, county jail, or if imposition of sentence is suspended and the defendant is placed on probation.

(l) For purposes of this section, "immediate family" means any spouse, parent, child, any person related by consanguinity or affinity within the second degree, or any other person who regularly resides in the household, or who, within the prior six months, regularly resided in the household.

(m) The court shall consider whether the defendant would benefit from treatment pursuant to Section 2684. If it is determined to be appropriate, the court shall recommend that the Department of Corrections and Rehabilitation make a certification as provided in Section 2684. Upon the certification, the defendant shall be evaluated and transferred to the appropriate hospital for treatment pursuant to Section 2684.
(Amended by Stats. 2007, Ch. 582, Sec. 2.5. Effective January 1, 2008.)
646.91.
(a) Notwithstanding any other law, a judicial officer may issue an ex parte emergency protective order if a peace officer, as defined in Section 830.1, 830.2, 830.32, or subdivision (a) of Section 830.33, asserts reasonable grounds to believe that a person is in immediate and present danger of stalking based upon the person's allegation that he or she has been willfully, maliciously, and repeatedly followed or harassed by another person who has made a credible threat with the intent of placing the person who is the target of the threat in reasonable fear for his or her safety, or the safety of his or her immediate family, within the meaning of Section 646.9.

(b) A peace officer who requests an emergency protective order shall reduce the order to writing and sign it.

(c) An emergency protective order shall include all of the following:

(1) A statement of the grounds asserted for the order.

(2) The date and time the order expires.

(3) The address of the superior court for the district or county in which the protected party resides.

(4) The following statements, which shall be printed in English and Spanish:

(A) "To the protected person: This order will last until the date and time noted above. If you wish to seek continuing protection, you will have to apply for an order from the court at the address noted above. You may seek the advice of an attorney as to any matter connected with your application for any future court orders. The attorney should be consulted promptly so that the attorney may assist you in making your application."

(B) "To the restrained person: This order will last until the date and time noted above. The protected party may, however, obtain a more permanent restraining order from the court. You may seek the advice of an attorney as to any matter connected with the application. The attorney should be consulted promptly so that the attorney may assist you in responding to the application. You may not own, possess, purchase, or receive, or attempt to purchase or receive, a firearm while this order is in effect."

(d) An emergency protective order may be issued under this section only if the judicial officer finds both of the following:

(1) That reasonable grounds have been asserted to believe that an immediate and present danger of stalking, as defined in Section 646.9, exists.

(2) That an emergency protective order is necessary to prevent the occurrence or reoccurrence of the stalking activity.

(e) An emergency protective order may include either of the following specific orders as appropriate:

(1) A harassment protective order as described in Section 527.6 of the Code of Civil Procedure.

(2) A workplace violence protective order as described in Section 527.8 of the Code of Civil Procedure.

(f) An emergency protective order shall be issued without prejudice to any person.

(g) An emergency protective order expires at the earlier of the following times:

(1) The close of judicial business on the fifth court day following the day of its issuance.

(2) The seventh calendar day following the day of its issuance.

(h) A peace officer who requests an emergency protective order shall do all of the following:

(1) Serve the order on the restrained person, if the restrained person can reasonably be located.

(2) Give a copy of the order to the protected person, or, if the protected person is a minor child, to a parent or guardian of the protected child if the parent or guardian can reasonably be located, or to a person having temporary custody of the child.

(3) File a copy of the order with the court as soon as practicable after issuance.

(4) Have the order entered into the computer database system for protective and restraining orders maintained by the Department of Justice.

(i) A peace officer shall use every reasonable means to enforce an emergency protective order.

(j) A peace officer who acts in good faith to enforce an emergency protective order is not civilly or criminally liable.

(k) A peace officer described in subdivision (a) or (b) of Section 830.32 who requests an emergency protective order pursuant to this section shall also notify the sheriff or police chief of the city in whose jurisdiction the peace officer's college or school is located after issuance of the order.

(l) "Judicial officer," as used in this section, means a judge, commissioner, or referee.

(m) A person subject to an emergency protective order under this section shall not own, possess, purchase, or receive a firearm while the order is in effect.

(n) Nothing in this section shall be construed to permit a court to issue an emergency protective order prohibiting speech or other activities that are constitutionally protected or protected by the laws of this state or by the United States or activities occurring during a labor dispute, as defined by Section 527.3 of the Code of Civil Procedure, including, but not limited to, picketing and hand billing.

(o) The Judicial Council shall develop forms, instructions, and rules for the scheduling of hearings and other procedures established pursuant to this section.

(p) Any intentional disobedience of any emergency protective order granted under this section is punishable pursuant to Section 166. Nothing in this subdivision shall be construed to prevent punishment under Section 646.9, in lieu of punishment under this section, if a violation of Section 646.9 is also pled and proven.
(Amended by Stats. 2014, Ch. 559, Sec. 1. (SB 1154) Effective January 1, 2015.)
646.91a.
(a) The court shall order that any party enjoined pursuant to Section 646.91 be prohibited from taking any action to obtain the address or location of a protected party or a protected party's family members, caretakers, or guardian, unless there is good cause not to make that order.

(b) The Judicial Council shall promulgate forms necessary to effectuate this section.
(Added by renumbering Section 646.91A by Stats. 2006, Ch. 901, Sec. 6.1. Effective January 1, 2007.)
646.92.
(a) (1) The Department of Corrections and Rehabilitation, county sheriff, or director of the local department of corrections shall give notice not less than 15 days prior to the release from the state prison or a county jail of any person who is convicted of violating Section 646.9 or convicted of a felony offense involving domestic violence, as defined in Section 6211 of the Family Code, or any change in the parole status or relevant change in the parole location of the convicted person, or if the convicted person absconds from supervision while on parole, to any person the court identifies as a victim of the offense, a family member of the victim, or a witness to the offense by telephone, electronic mail, or certified mail at his or her last known address, upon request and using the method of communication selected by the requesting party, if that method is available. A victim, family member, or witness shall keep the department or county sheriff informed of his or her current contact information to be entitled to receive notice. A victim may designate another person for the purpose of receiving notification. The department, county sheriff, or director of the local department of corrections, shall make reasonable attempts to locate a person who has requested notification but whose contact information is incorrect or not current. However, the duty to keep the department or county sheriff informed of current contact information shall remain with the victim.

(2) Following notification by the department pursuant to Section 3058.61, in the event the victim had not originally requested notification under this section, the sheriff or the chief of police, as appropriate, shall make an attempt to advise the victim or, if the victim is a minor, the parent or guardian of the victim, of the victim's right to notification under this section.

(b) All information relating to any person who receives notice under this section shall remain confidential and shall not be made available to the person convicted of violating this section.

(c) For purposes of this section, "release" includes a release from the state prison or a county jail because time has been served, a release from the state prison or a county jail to parole or probation supervision, or an escape from an institution or reentry facility.

(d) The department or county sheriff shall give notice of an escape from an institution or reentry facility of any person convicted of violating Section 646.9 or convicted of a felony offense involving domestic violence, as defined in Section 6211 of the Family Code, to the notice recipients described in subdivision (a).

(e) Substantial compliance satisfies the notification requirements of subdivision (a).
(Amended by Stats. 2011, Ch. 364, Sec. 1. (SB 852) Effective September 29, 2011.)
646.93.
(a) (1) In those counties where the arrestee is initially incarcerated in a jail operated by the county sheriff, the sheriff shall designate a telephone number that shall be available to the public to inquire about bail status or to determine if the person arrested has been released and if not yet released, the scheduled release date, if known. This subdivision does not require a county sheriff or jail administrator to establish a new telephone number but shall require that the information contained on the victim resource card, as defined in Section 264.2, specify the phone number that a victim should call to obtain this information. This subdivision shall not require the county sheriff or municipal police departments to produce new victim resource cards containing a designated phone number for the public to inquire about the bail or custody status of a person who has been arrested until their existing supply of victim resource cards has been exhausted.

(2) In those counties where the arrestee is initially incarcerated in an incarceration facility other than a jail operated by the county sheriff and in those counties that do not operate a Victim Notification (VNE) system, a telephone number shall be available to the public to inquire about bail status or to determine if the person arrested has been released and if not yet released, the scheduled release date, if known. This subdivision does not require a municipal police agency or jail administrator to establish a new telephone number but shall require that the information contained on the victim resource card, as defined in Section 264.2, specify the phone number that a victim should call to obtain this information. This subdivision shall not require the county sheriff or municipal police departments to produce new victim resource cards containing a designated phone number for the public to inquire about the bail or custody status of a person who has been arrested until their existing supply of victim resource cards has been exhausted.

(3) If an arrestee is transferred to another incarceration facility and is no longer in the custody of the initial arresting agency, the transfer date and new incarceration location shall be made available through the telephone number designated by the arresting agency.

(4) The resource card provided to victims pursuant to Section 264.2 shall list the designated telephone numbers to which this section refers.

(b) Any request to lower bail shall be heard in open court in accordance with Section 1270.1. In addition, the prosecutor shall make all reasonable efforts to notify the victim or victims of the bail hearing. The victims may be present at the hearing and shall be permitted to address the court on the issue of bail.

(c) Unless good cause is shown not to impose the following conditions, the judge shall impose as additional conditions of release on bail that:

(1) The defendant shall not initiate contact in person, by telephone, or any other means with the alleged victims.

(2) The defendant shall not knowingly go within 100 yards of the alleged victims, their residence, or place of employment.

(3) The defendant shall not possess any firearms or other deadly or dangerous weapons.

(4) The defendant shall obey all laws.

(5) The defendant, upon request at the time of his or her appearance in court, shall provide the court with an address where he or she is residing or will reside, a business address and telephone number if employed, and a residence telephone number if the defendant's residence has a telephone.

A showing by declaration that any of these conditions are violated shall, unless good cause is shown, result in the issuance of a no-bail warrant.
(Amended by Stats. 2001, Ch. 854, Sec. 35. Effective January 1, 2002.)
646.94.
(a) Contingent upon a Budget Act appropriation, the Department of Corrections shall ensure that any parolee convicted of violating Section 646.9 on or after January 1, 2002, who is deemed to pose a high risk of committing a repeat stalking offense be placed on an intensive and specialized parole supervision program for a period not to exceed the period of parole.

(b) (1) The program shall include referral to specialized services, for example substance abuse treatment, for offenders needing those specialized services.

(2) Parolees participating in this program shall be required to participate in relapse prevention classes as a condition of parole.

(3) Parole agents may conduct group counseling sessions as part of the program.

(4) The department may include other appropriate offenders in the treatment program if doing so facilitates the effectiveness of the treatment program.

(c) The program shall be established with the assistance and supervision of the staff of the department primarily by obtaining the services of mental health providers specializing in the treatment of stalking patients. Each parolee placed into this program shall be required to participate in clinical counseling programs aimed at reducing the likelihood that the parolee will commit or attempt to commit acts of violence or stalk their victim.

(d) The department may require persons subject to this section to pay some or all of the costs associated with this treatment, subject to the person's ability to pay. "Ability to pay" means the overall capability of the person to reimburse the costs, or a portion of the costs, of providing mental health treatment, and shall include, but shall not be limited to, consideration of all of the following factors:

(1) Present financial position.

(2) Reasonably discernible future financial position.

(3) Likelihood that the person shall be able to obtain employment after the date of parole.

(4) Any other factor or factors that may bear upon the person's financial capability to reimburse the department for the costs.

(e) For purposes of this section, a mental health provider specializing in the treatment of stalking patients shall meet all of the following requirements:

(1) Be a licensed clinical social worker, as defined in Article 4 (commencing with Section 4996) of Chapter 14 of Division 2 of the Business and Professions Code, a clinical psychologist, as defined in Section 1316.5 of the Health and Safety Code, or a physician and surgeon engaged in the practice of psychiatry.

(2) Have clinical experience in the area of assessment and treatment of stalking patients.

(3) Have two letters of reference from professionals who can attest to the applicant's experience in counseling stalking patients.

(f) The program shall target parolees convicted of violating Section 646.9 who meet the following conditions:

(1) The offender has been subject to a clinical assessment.

(2) A review of the offender's criminal history indicates that the offender poses a high risk of committing further acts of stalking or acts of violence against his or her victim or other persons upon his or her release on parole.

(3) The parolee, based on his or her clinical assessment, may be amenable to treatment.

(g) On or before January 1, 2006, the Department of Corrections shall evaluate the intensive and specialized parole supervision program and make a report to the Legislature regarding the results of the program, including, but not limited to, the recidivism rate for repeat stalking related offenses committed by persons placed into the program and a cost-benefit analysis of the program.

(h) This section shall become operative upon the appropriation of sufficient funds in the Budget Act to implement this section.

(Amended by Stats. 2001, Ch. 159, Sec. 163. Effective January 1, 2002. Operation of section is contingent upon funding, as provided in subd. (h).)

647.

Except as provided in paragraph (5) of subdivision (b) and subdivision (l), every person who commits any of the following acts is guilty of disorderly conduct, a misdemeanor:

(a) An individual who solicits anyone to engage in or who engages in lewd or dissolute conduct in any public place or in any place open to the public or exposed to public view.

(b) (1) An individual who solicits, or who agrees to engage in, or who engages in, any act of prostitution with the intent to receive compensation, money, or anything of value from another person. An individual agrees to engage in an act of prostitution when, with specific intent to so engage, he or she manifests an acceptance of an offer or solicitation by another person to so engage, regardless of whether the offer or solicitation was made by a person who also possessed the specific intent to engage in an act of prostitution.

(2) An individual who solicits, or who agrees to engage in, or who engages in, any act of prostitution with another person who is 18 years of age or older in exchange for the individual providing compensation, money, or anything of value to the other person. An individual agrees to engage in an act of prostitution when, with specific intent to so engage, he or she manifests an acceptance of an offer or solicitation by another person who is 18 years of age or older to so engage, regardless of whether the offer or solicitation was made by a person who also possessed the specific intent to engage in an act of prostitution.

(3) An individual who solicits, or who agrees to engage in, or who engages in, any act of prostitution with another person who is a minor in exchange for the individual providing compensation, money, or anything of value to the minor. An individual agrees to engage in an act of prostitution when, with specific intent to so engage, he or she manifests an acceptance of an offer or solicitation by someone who is a minor to so engage, regardless of whether the offer or solicitation was made by a minor who also possessed the specific intent to engage in an act of prostitution.

(4) A manifestation of acceptance of an offer or solicitation to engage in an act of prostitution does not constitute a violation of this subdivision unless some act, in addition to the manifestation of acceptance, is done within this state in furtherance of the commission of the act of prostitution by the person manifesting an acceptance of an offer or solicitation to engage in that act. As used in this subdivision, "prostitution" includes any lewd act between persons for money or other consideration.

(5) Notwithstanding paragraphs (1) to (3), inclusive, this subdivision does not apply to a child under 18 years of age who is alleged to have engaged in conduct to receive money or other consideration that would, if committed by an adult, violate this subdivision. A commercially exploited child under this paragraph may be adjudged a dependent child of the court pursuant to paragraph (2) of subdivision (b) of Section 300 of the Welfare and Institutions Code and may be taken into temporary custody pursuant to subdivision (a) of Section 305 of the Welfare and Institutions Code, if the conditions allowing temporary custody without warrant are met.

(c) Who accosts other persons in any public place or in any place open to the public for the purpose of begging or soliciting alms.

(d) Who loiters in or about any toilet open to the public for the purpose of engaging in or soliciting any lewd or lascivious or any unlawful act.

(e) Who lodges in any building, structure, vehicle, or place, whether public or private, without the permission of the owner or person entitled to the possession or in control of it.

(f) Who is found in any public place under the influence of intoxicating liquor, any drug, controlled substance, toluene, or any combination of any intoxicating liquor, drug, controlled substance, or toluene, in a condition that he or she is unable to exercise care for his or her own safety or the safety of others, or by reason of his or her being under the influence of intoxicating liquor, any drug, controlled substance, toluene, or any combination of any intoxicating liquor, drug, or toluene, interferes with or obstructs or prevents the free use of any street, sidewalk, or other public way.

(g) If a person has violated subdivision (f), a peace officer, if he or she is reasonably able to do so, shall place the person, or cause him or her to be placed, in civil protective custody. The person shall be taken to a facility, designated pursuant to Section 5170 of the Welfare and Institutions Code, for the 72-hour treatment and evaluation of inebriates. A peace officer may place a person in civil protective custody with that kind and degree of force that would be lawful were he or she effecting an arrest for a misdemeanor without a warrant. A person who has been placed in civil protective custody shall not thereafter be subject to any criminal prosecution or juvenile court

proceeding based on the facts giving rise to this placement. This subdivision does not apply to the following persons:

(1) A person who is under the influence of any drug, or under the combined influence of intoxicating liquor and any drug.

(2) A person who a peace officer has probable cause to believe has committed any felony, or who has committed any misdemeanor in addition to subdivision (f).

(3) A person who a peace officer in good faith believes will attempt escape or will be unreasonably difficult for medical personnel to control.

(h) Who loiters, prowls, or wanders upon the private property of another, at any time, without visible or lawful business with the owner or occupant. As used in this subdivision, "loiter" means to delay or linger without a lawful purpose for being on the property and for the purpose of committing a crime as opportunity may be discovered.

(i) Who, while loitering, prowling, or wandering upon the private property of another, at any time, peeks in the door or window of any inhabited building or structure, without visible or lawful business with the owner or occupant.

(j) (1) A person who looks through a hole or opening, into, or otherwise views, by means of any instrumentality, including, but not limited to, a periscope, telescope, binoculars, camera, motion picture camera, camcorder, or mobile phone, the interior of a bedroom, bathroom, changing room, fitting room, dressing room, or tanning booth, or the interior of any other area in which the occupant has a reasonable expectation of privacy, with the intent to invade the privacy of a person or persons inside. This subdivision does not apply to those areas of a private business used to count currency or other negotiable instruments.

(2) A person who uses a concealed camcorder, motion picture camera, or photographic camera of any type, to secretly videotape, film, photograph, or record by electronic means, another identifiable person under or through the clothing being worn by that other person, for the purpose of viewing the body of, or the undergarments worn by, that other person, without the consent or knowledge of that other person, with the intent to arouse, appeal to, or gratify the lust, passions, or sexual desires of that person and invade the privacy of that other person, under circumstances in which the other person has a reasonable expectation of privacy. For the purposes of this paragraph, "identifiable" means capable of identification, or capable of being recognized, meaning that someone could identify or recognize the victim, including the victim herself or himself. It does not require the victim's identity to actually be established.

(3) (A) A person who uses a concealed camcorder, motion picture camera, or photographic camera of any type, to secretly videotape, film, photograph, or record by electronic means, another identifiable person who may be in a state of full or partial undress, for the purpose of viewing the body of, or the undergarments worn by, that other person, without the consent or knowledge of that other person, in the interior of a bedroom, bathroom, changing room, fitting room, dressing room, or tanning booth, or the interior of any other area in which that other person has a reasonable expectation of privacy, with the intent to invade the privacy of that other person. For the purposes of this paragraph, "identifiable" means capable of identification, or capable of being recognized, meaning that someone could identify or recognize the victim, including the victim herself or himself. It does not require the victim's identity to actually be established.

(B) Neither of the following is a defense to the crime specified in this paragraph:

(i) The defendant was a cohabitant, landlord, tenant, cotenant, employer, employee, or business partner or associate of the victim, or an agent of any of these.

(ii) The victim was not in a state of full or partial undress.

(4) (A) A person who intentionally distributes the image of the intimate body part or parts of another identifiable person, or an image of the person depicted engaged in an act of sexual intercourse, sodomy, oral copulation, sexual penetration, or an image of masturbation by the person depicted or in which the person depicted participates, under circumstances in which the persons agree or understand that the image shall remain private, the person distributing the image knows or should know that distribution of the image will cause serious emotional distress, and the person depicted suffers that distress.

(B) A person intentionally distributes an image described in subparagraph (A) when he or she personally distributes the image, or arranges, specifically requests, or intentionally causes another person to distribute that image.

(C) As used in this paragraph, "intimate body part" means any portion of the genitals, the anus and in the case of a female, also includes any portion of the breasts below the top of the areola, that is either uncovered or clearly visible through clothing.

(D) It shall not be a violation of this paragraph to distribute an image described in subparagraph (A) if any of the following applies:

(i) The distribution is made in the course of reporting an unlawful activity.

(ii) The distribution is made in compliance with a subpoena or other court order for use in a legal proceeding.

(iii) The distribution is made in the course of a lawful public proceeding.

(5) This subdivision does not preclude punishment under any section of law providing for greater punishment.

(k) In addition to any punishment prescribed by this section, a court may suspend, for not more than 30 days, the privilege of the person to operate a motor vehicle pursuant to Section 13201.5 of the Vehicle Code for any violation of subdivision (b) that was committed within 1,000 feet of a private residence and with the use of a vehicle. In lieu of the suspension, the court may order a person's privilege to operate a motor vehicle restricted, for not more than six months, to necessary travel to and from the person's place of employment or education. If driving a motor vehicle is necessary to perform the duties of the person's employment, the court may also allow the person to drive in that person's scope of employment.

(l) (1) A second or subsequent violation of subdivision (j) is punishable by imprisonment in a county jail not exceeding one year, or by a fine not exceeding two thousand dollars ($2,000), or by both that fine and imprisonment.

(2) If the victim of a violation of subdivision (j) was a minor at the time of the offense, the violation is punishable by imprisonment in a county jail not exceeding one year, or by a fine not exceeding two thousand dollars ($2,000), or by both that fine and imprisonment.

(m) (1) If a crime is committed in violation of subdivision (b) and the person who was solicited was a minor at the time of the offense, and if the defendant knew or should have known that the person who was solicited was a minor at the time of the offense, the violation is punishable by imprisonment in a county jail for not less than two days and not more than one year, or by a fine not exceeding ten thousand dollars ($10,000), or by both that fine and imprisonment.

(2) The court may, in unusual cases, when the interests of justice are best served, reduce or eliminate the mandatory two days of imprisonment in a county jail required by this subdivision. If the court reduces or eliminates the mandatory two days' imprisonment, the court shall specify the reason on the record.

(Amended by Stats. 2018, Ch. 246, Sec. 2. (AB 324) Effective January 1, 2019.)

647.1.

In addition to any fine assessed under Section 647, the judge may assess a fine not to exceed seventy dollars ($70) against any person who violates subdivision (a) or (b) of Section 647, or, if the offense involves intravenous use of a controlled substance, subdivision (f) of Section 647, with the proceeds of this fine to be used in accordance with Section 1463.23.

The court shall, however, take into consideration the defendant's ability to pay and no defendant shall be denied probation because of his or her inability to pay the fine permitted under this section.

(Added by Stats. 1988, Ch. 1243, Sec. 8.)

647.2.

If a person is convicted of a violation of subdivision (f) of Section 647 and is granted probation, the court may order, with the consent of the defendant, as a term and condition of probation, in addition to any other term and condition required or authorized by law, that the defendant participate in the program prescribed in Section 23509 of the Vehicle Code.

(Amended by Stats. 1998, Ch. 118, Sec. 1.21. Effective January 1, 1999. Operative July 1, 1999, by Sec. 85 of Ch. 118.)

647.6.

(a) (1) Every person who annoys or molests any child under 18 years of age shall be punished by a fine not exceeding five thousand dollars ($5,000), by imprisonment in a county jail not exceeding one year, or by both the fine and imprisonment.

(2) Every person who, motivated by an unnatural or abnormal sexual interest in children, engages in conduct with an adult whom he or she believes to be a child under 18 years of age, which conduct, if directed toward a child under 18 years of age, would be a violation of this section, shall be punished by a fine not exceeding five thousand dollars ($5,000), by imprisonment in a county jail for up to one year, or by both that fine and imprisonment.

(b) Every person who violates this section after having entered, without consent, an inhabited dwelling house, or trailer coach as defined in Section 635 of the Vehicle Code, or the inhabited portion of any other building, shall be punished by imprisonment in the state prison, or in a county jail not exceeding one year, and by a fine not exceeding five thousand dollars ($5,000).

(c) (1) Every person who violates this section shall be punished upon the second and each subsequent conviction by imprisonment in the state prison.

(2) Every person who violates this section after a previous felony conviction under Section 261, 264.1, 269, 285, 286, 287, 288.5, or 289, or former Section 288a, any of which involved a minor under 16 years of age, or a previous felony conviction under this section, a conviction under Section 288, or a felony conviction under Section 311.4 involving a minor under 14 years of age shall be punished by imprisonment in the state prison for two, four, or six years.

(d) (1) In any case in which a person is convicted of violating this section and probation is granted, the court shall require counseling as a condition of probation, unless the court makes a written statement in the court record, that counseling would be inappropriate or ineffective.

(2) In any case in which a person is convicted of violating this section, and as a condition of probation, the court prohibits the defendant from having contact with the victim, the court order prohibiting contact shall not be modified except upon the request of the victim and a finding by the court that the modification is in the best interest of the victim. As used in this paragraph, "contact with the victim" includes all physical contact, being in the presence of the victim, communication by any means, any communication by a third party acting on behalf of the defendant, and any gifts.

(e) Nothing in this section prohibits prosecution under any other provision of law.

(Amended by Stats. 2018, Ch. 423, Sec. 63. (SB 1494) Effective January 1, 2019.)

647.7.

(a) In any case in which a person is convicted of violating subdivision (i) or (j) of Section 647, the court may require counseling as a condition of probation. Any defendant so ordered to be placed in a counseling program shall be responsible for paying the expense of his or her participation in the counseling program as determined by the court. The court shall take into consideration the ability of the defendant to pay, and no defendant shall be denied probation because of his or her inability to pay.

(b) Every person who, having been convicted of violating subdivision (i) or (j) of Section 647, commits a second or subsequent violation of subdivision (i) or (j) of Section 647, shall be punished by imprisonment in a county jail not exceeding one year, by a fine not exceeding one thousand dollars ($1,000), or by both that fine and imprisonment, except as provided in subdivision (c).

(c) Every person who, having been previously convicted of violating subdivision (i) or (j) of Section 647, commits a violation of paragraph (3) of subdivision (j) of Section 647 regardless of whether it is a first, second, or subsequent violation of that paragraph, shall be punished by imprisonment in a county jail not exceeding one year, by a fine not exceeding five thousand dollars ($5,000), or by both that fine and imprisonment.

(Amended by Stats. 2011, Ch. 296, Sec. 209. (AB 1023) Effective January 1, 2012.)

647.8.

(a) Matter that is obtained or distributed in violation of subdivision (j) of Section 647 and that is in the possession of any city, county, city and county, or state official or agency is subject to forfeiture pursuant to this section.

(b) An action to forfeit matter described in subdivision (a) may be brought by the Attorney General, the district attorney, county counsel, or the city attorney. Proceedings shall be initiated by a petition of forfeiture filed in the superior court of the county in which the matter is located.

(c) The prosecuting agency shall make service of process of a notice regarding that petition upon every individual who may have a property interest in the alleged proceeds. The notice shall state that any interested party may file a verified claim with the superior court stating the amount of his or her claimed interest and an affirmation or denial of the prosecuting agency's allegation. If the notice cannot be given by registered mail or personal delivery, the notice shall be published for at least three successive weeks in a newspaper of general circulation in the county where the property is located. All notices shall set forth the time within which a claim of interest in the property seized is required to be filed.

(d) (1) Any person claiming an interest in the property or proceeds may, at any time within 30 days from the date of the first publication of the notice of seizure, or within 30 days after receipt of actual notice, file with the superior court of the county in which the action is pending a verified claim stating his or her interest in the property or proceeds. A verified copy of the claim shall be given by the claimant to the Attorney General or district attorney, county counsel, or city attorney, as appropriate.

(2) If, at the end of the time set forth in paragraph (1), an interested person has not filed a claim, the court, upon motion, shall declare that the person has defaulted upon his or her alleged interest, and it shall be subject to forfeiture upon proof of compliance with subdivision (c).

(e) The burden is on the petitioner to prove beyond a reasonable doubt that matter is subject to forfeiture pursuant to this section.

(f) It is not necessary to seek or obtain a criminal conviction prior to the entry of an order for the destruction of matter pursuant to this section. Any matter described in subdivision (a) that is in the possession of any city, county, city and county, or state official or agency, including found property, or property obtained as the result of a case in which no trial was had or that has been disposed of by way of dismissal or otherwise than by way of conviction may be ordered destroyed.

(g) A court order for destruction of matter described in subdivision (a) may be carried out by a police or sheriff's department or by the Department of Justice. The court order shall specify the agency responsible for the destruction.

(h) As used in this section, "matter" means any picture, photograph, image, motion picture, video tape, film, filmstrip, negative, slide, photocopy, or other pictorial representation, recording, or electrical reproduction. "Matter" also means any data storage media that contains the image at issue, but does not include the computer, camera, telecommunication or electronic device, unless the matter consists solely of electronic information stored on a device that cannot be altered or erased.

(i) Prior for granting an order for destruction of matter pursuant to this section, the court may require the petitioner to demonstrate that the petition covers no more property than necessary to remove possession of the offending matter.

(j) It is a defense in any forfeiture proceeding that the matter seized was lawfully possessed in aid of legitimate scientific or educational purposes.

(Added by Stats. 2015, Ch. 291, Sec. 2. (SB 676) Effective January 1, 2016.)

647a.

(a) Any peace officer, as defined in subdivision (a) of Section 830.1 or Section 830.31, 830.32, or 830.33, may transport any person, as quickly as is feasible, to the nearest homeless shelter, or any runaway youth or youth in crisis to the nearest runaway shelter, if the officer inquires whether the person desires the transportation, and the person does not object to the transportation. Any officer exercising due care and precaution shall not be liable for any damages or injury incurred during transportation.

(b) Notwithstanding any other provision of law, this section shall become operative in a county only if the board of supervisors adopts the provisions of this section by ordinance. The ordinance shall include a provision requiring peace officers to determine the availability of space at the nearest homeless or runaway shelter prior to transporting any person.

(Amended by Stats. 1998, Ch. 1065, Sec. 1. Effective January 1, 1999.)

647b.

Every person who loiters about any school in which adults are in attendance at courses established pursuant to Chapter 10 (commencing with Section 52500) of Part 28 of the Education Code, and who annoys or molests any person in attendance therein shall be punished by a fine of not exceeding one thousand dollars ($1,000) or by imprisonment in the county jail for not exceeding six months, or by both such fine and imprisonment.

(Amended by Stats. 1987, Ch. 828, Sec. 42.)

647c.

Every person who willfully and maliciously obstructs the free movement of any person on any street, sidewalk, or other public place or on or in any place open to the public is guilty of a misdemeanor.

Nothing in this section affects the power of a county or a city to regulate conduct upon a street, sidewalk, or other public place or on or in a place open to the public.

(Amended by Stats. 1968, Ch. 122.)

647d.

(a) Notwithstanding any other provision of law, subdivision (b) shall become operative in a county only if the board of supervisors adopts the provisions of subdivision (b) by ordinance after a finding that sufficient alcohol treatment and recovery facilities exist or will exist to accommodate the persons described in that subdivision.

(b) In any accusatory pleading charging a violation of subdivision (f) of Section 647, if the defendant has been previously convicted two or more times of a violation of subdivision (f) of Section 647 within the previous 12 months, each such previous conviction shall be charged in the accusatory pleading. If two or more of the previous convictions are found to be true by the jury, upon a jury trial, or by the court, upon a court trial, or are admitted by the defendant, the defendant shall be imprisoned in the county jail for a period of not less than 90 days. The trial court may grant probation or suspend the execution of sentence imposed upon the defendant if the court, as a condition of the probation or suspension, orders the defendant to spend 60 days in an alcohol treatment and recovery program in a facility which, as a minimum, meets the standards described in the guidelines for alcoholic recovery home programs issued by the Division of Alcohol Programs of the Department of Alcohol and Drug Abuse.

(c) The provisions of Section 4019 shall apply to the conditional attendance of an alcohol treatment and recovery program described in subdivision (b).

(Added by Stats. 1981, Ch. 1009, Sec. 1.)

647e.

(a) A city, county, or city and county may by local ordinance provide that no person who has in his or her possession any bottle, can or other receptacle containing any alcoholic beverage which has been opened, or a seal broken, or the contents of which have been partially removed, shall enter, be, or remain on the posted premises of, including the posted parking lot immediately adjacent to, any retail package off-sale alcoholic beverage licensee licensed pursuant to Division 9 (commencing with Section 23000) of the Business and Professions Code, or on any public sidewalk immediately adjacent to the licensed and posted premises. Any person violating any provision of such an ordinance shall be guilty of an infraction.

(b) As used in subdivision (a), "posted premises" means those premises which are subject to licensure under any retail package off-sale alcoholic beverage license, the parking lot immediately adjacent to the licensed premises and any public sidewalk immediately adjacent to the licensed premises on which clearly visible notices indicate to the patrons of the licensee and parking lot and to persons on the public sidewalk, that the provisions of subdivision (a) are applicable. Any local ordinance adopted pursuant to this section shall require posting of the premises.

(c) The provisions of this section shall not apply to a private residential parking lot which is immediately adjacent to the posted premises.

Nothing in this section shall affect the power of a county or a city, or city and county, to regulate the possession of an opened alcoholic beverage in any public place or in a place open to the public.

(Added by Stats. 1983, Ch. 514, Sec. 1. Effective July 28, 1983.)

648.

Every person who makes, issues, or puts in circulation any bill, check, ticket, certificate, promissory note, or the paper of any bank, to circulate as money, except as authorized by the laws of the United States, for the first offense, is guilty of a misdemeanor, and for each and every subsequent offense, is guilty of felony.

(Enacted 1872.)

648a.

(a) Every person who has in his or her possession for any illegal purpose or who makes, sells, issues, or puts in circulation any slug or token that does not conform to the limitations on size, shape, weight, construction, and use specified in subdivision (b) is guilty of a misdemeanor. The term "slug" and the term "token," as used in this section, mean any piece of metal or other material not a coin of the United States or a foreign country. However, tokens sold by and accepted as fares by electric railways and lettered checks having a returnable trade value shall not be subject to the provisions of this section.

(b) (1) The slug or token shall either be clearly identified with the name and location of the establishment from which it originates on at least one side or shall contain an identifying mark or logo that clearly indicates the identity of the manufacturer.

(2) The slug or token shall not be within any of the following diameter ranges in inches:

(A) 0.680-0.775.

(B) 0.810-0.860.

(C) 0.910-0.980.

(D) 1.018-1.068.

(E) 1.180-1.230.

(F) 1.475-1.525.

(3) The slug or token shall not be manufactured from a three-layered material consisting of a copper-nickel alloy clad on both sides of a pure core, nor from a copper-based material except if the total of zinc, nickel, aluminum, magnesium, and other alloying materials is at least 20 percent of the token's weight.

(4) The slug or token shall not possess sufficient magnetic properties so as to be accepted by a coin mechanism.

(5) The design on the slug or token shall not resemble any current or past foreign or United States coinage.

(6) Establishments using these slugs or tokens shall prominently and conspicuously post signs on their premises notifying patrons that federal law prohibits the use of the slugs or tokens outside the premises for any monetary purpose.

(7) The issuing establishment shall not accept slugs or tokens as payment for any goods or services offered by the establishment with the exception of the specific use for which the slugs or tokens were designed.
(Amended by Stats. 1997, Ch. 354, Sec. 1. Effective January 1, 1998.)
649.
Any person engaged in the transportation of persons by taxicab or other means of conveyance who knowingly misdirects a prospective guest of any hotel, inn, boardinghouse or lodginghouse or knowingly takes such a prospective guest to a hotel, inn, boardinghouse or lodginghouse different from that of his instructions from such prospective guest is guilty of a misdemeanor.
(Added by Stats. 1953, Ch. 32.)
649a.
Any person engaged in the operation of any hotel, inn, boardinghouse or lodginghouse who pays another any compensation for inducing or attempting to induce, by false statement or misrepresentation, prospective guests of a given hotel, inn, boardinghouse or lodginghouse to enter, lodge at or become a guest of any other hotel, inn, boardinghouse or lodginghouse is guilty of a misdemeanor.
(Added by Stats. 1953, Ch. 32.)
651.
It is a misdemeanor for any person to buy, receive, sell, give away, dispose of, exchange or barter any Federal order stamps except for the foods or cotton goods for which they are issued.
This section does not apply to any person buying, receiving, selling, giving away, disposing of, exchanging or bartering any Federal order stamps subsequent to the redemption of such stamps in the manner provided by State or Federal law for the foods or cotton goods for which they are issued.
As used in this section, Federal order stamps refers to stamps issued by the United States Department of Agriculture or its duly authorized agent for food and surplus food or cotton and surplus cotton.
(Added by Stats. 1941, Ch. 682.)
652.
(a) It shall be an infraction for any person to perform or offer to perform body piercing upon a person under the age of 18 years, unless the body piercing is performed in the presence of, or as directed by a notarized writing by, the person's parent or guardian.
(b) This section does not apply to the body piercing of an emancipated minor.
(c) As used in this section, "body piercing" means the creation of an opening in the body of a human being for the purpose of inserting jewelry or other decoration, including, but not limited to, the piercing of a lip, tongue, nose, or eyebrow. "Body piercing" does not include the piercing of an ear.
(d) Neither the minor upon whom the body piercing was performed, nor the parent or guardian of that minor, nor any other minor is liable for punishment under this section.
(Amended by Stats. 2006, Ch. 538, Sec. 502. Effective January 1, 2007.)
653.
Every person who tattoos or offers to tattoo a person under the age of 18 years is guilty of a misdemeanor.
As used in this section, to "tattoo" means to insert pigment under the surface of the skin of a human being, by pricking with a needle or otherwise, so as to produce an indelible mark or figure visible through the skin.
This section is not intended to apply to any act of a licensed practitioner of the healing arts performed in the course of his practice.
(Added by Stats. 1955, Ch. 1422.)
653b.
(a) Except as provided in subdivision (b) or (c), every person who loiters about any school or public place at or near which children attend or normally congregate and who remains at any school or public place at or near which children attend or normally congregate, or who reenters or comes upon a school or place within 72 hours, after being asked to leave by the chief administrative official of that school or, in the absence of the chief administrative official, the person acting as the chief administrative official, or by a member of the security patrol of the school district who has been given authorization, in writing, by the chief administrative official of that school to act as his or her agent in performing this duty, or a city police officer, or sheriff or deputy sheriff, or Department of the California Highway Patrol peace officer is a vagrant, and is punishable by a fine of not exceeding one thousand dollars ($1,000) or by imprisonment in a county jail for a period not exceeding six months, or by both that fine and imprisonment.
(b) Every person required to register as a sex offender who violates subdivision (a) shall be punished as follows:
(1) Upon a first conviction, by a fine not exceeding two thousand dollars ($2,000), by imprisonment in a county jail for a period of not more than six months, or by both that fine and imprisonment.
(2) If the defendant has been previously convicted once of a violation of this section or former Section 653g, by imprisonment in a county jail for a period of not less than 10 days or more than six months, or by both imprisonment and a fine of not exceeding two thousand dollars ($2,000), and shall not be released on probation, parole, or any other basis until he or she has served at least 10 days.
(3) If the defendant has been previously convicted two or more times of a violation of this section or former Section 653g, by imprisonment in a county jail for a period of not less than 90 days or more than six months, or by both imprisonment and a fine of not exceeding two thousand dollars ($2,000), and shall not be released on probation, parole, or any other basis until he or she has served at least 90 days.
(c) Any person required to register with the chief of police or sheriff pursuant to Section 186.30 who violates subdivision (a) shall be punished as follows:
(1) Upon first conviction, by a fine not exceeding one thousand dollars ($1,000), by imprisonment in a county jail for a period of not more than one year, or by both that fine and imprisonment.
(2) Upon a second conviction, by a fine not exceeding two thousand dollars ($2,000), by imprisonment in a county jail for a period of not more than one year, or by both that fine and imprisonment. The court shall consider a period of imprisonment of at least 10 days.
(3) If the defendant has been previously convicted two or more times, by a fine not exceeding two thousand dollars ($2,000), by imprisonment in a county jail for a period of not more than one year, or by both that fine and imprisonment. The court shall consider a period of imprisonment of at least 90 days.
(d) As used in this section, "loiter" means to delay, to linger, or to idle about a school or public place without lawful business for being present.
(e) Nothing in this section shall preclude or prohibit prosecution under any other provision of law.
(Amended by Stats. 2009, Ch. 592, Sec. 1. (SB 492) Effective January 1, 2010.)
653c.
(a) No person required to register as a sex offender pursuant to Section 290 for an offense committed against an elder or dependent adult, as defined in Section 368, other than a resident of the facility, shall enter or remain on the grounds of a day care or residential facility where elders or dependent adults are regularly present or living, without having registered with the facility administrator or his or her designees, except to proceed expeditiously to the office of the facility administrator or designee for the purpose of registering.
(b) In order to register pursuant to subdivision (a), a sex offender shall advise the facility administrator or designee that he or she is a sex offender; provide his or her name, address, and purpose for entering the facility; and provide proof of identity.
(c) The facility administrator may refuse to register, impose restrictions on registration, or revoke the registration of a sex offender if he or she has a reasonable basis for concluding that the offender's presence or acts would disrupt, or have disrupted, the facility, any resident, employee, volunteer, or visitor; would result, or has resulted, in damage to property; the offender's presence at the facility would interfere, or has interfered, with the peaceful conduct of the activities of the facility; or would otherwise place at risk the facility, or any employee, volunteer or visitor.
(d) Punishment for any violation of this section shall be as follows:
(1) Upon a first conviction by a fine of not exceeding two thousand dollars ($2,000), by imprisonment in a county jail for a period of not more than six months, or by both that fine and imprisonment.
(2) If the defendant has been previously convicted once of a violation of this section, by imprisonment in a county jail for a period of not less than 10 days or more than six months, or by both imprisonment and a fine of not exceeding two thousand dollars ($2,000), and shall not be released on probation, parole, or any other basis until he or she has served at least 10 days.
(3) If the defendant has been previously convicted two or more times of a violation of this section, by imprisonment in a county jail for a period of not less than 90 days or more than six months, or by both imprisonment and a fine of not exceeding two thousand dollars ($2,000), and shall not be released on probation, parole, or any other basis until he or she has served at least 90 days.
(e) Nothing in this section shall preclude or prohibit prosecution under any other provision of law.
(Added by Stats. 2006, Ch. 337, Sec. 28. Effective September 20, 2006.)
653d.
Every person who sells machinery used or to be used for mining purposes who fails to give to the buyer, at the time of sale, a bill of sale for the machinery, or who fails to keep a written record of the sale, giving the date thereof, describing the machinery, and showing the name and address of the buyer, and every buyer of such machinery, if in this State, who fails to keep a record of his purchase of such machinery, giving the name and address of the seller, describing the machinery, and showing the date of the purchase, is guilty of a misdemeanor.
(Added by Stats. 1959, Ch. 222.)
653f.
(a) Every person who, with the intent that the crime be committed, solicits another to offer, accept, or join in the offer or acceptance of a bribe, or to commit or join in the commission of carjacking, robbery, burglary, grand theft, receiving stolen property, extortion, perjury, subornation of perjury, forgery, kidnapping, arson or assault with a deadly weapon or instrument or by means of force likely to produce great bodily injury, or, by the use of force or a threat of force, to prevent or dissuade any person who is or may become a witness from attending upon, or testifying at, any trial, proceeding, or inquiry authorized by law, shall be punished by imprisonment in a county jail for not more than one year or pursuant to subdivision (h) of Section 1170, or by a fine of not more than ten thousand dollars ($10,000), or the amount which could have been assessed for commission of the offense itself, whichever is greater, or by both the fine and imprisonment.
(b) Every person who, with the intent that the crime be committed, solicits another to commit or join in the commission of murder shall be punished by imprisonment in the state prison for three, six, or nine years.
(c) Every person who, with the intent that the crime be committed, solicits another to commit rape by force or violence, sodomy by force or violence, oral copulation by force or violence, or any violation of Section 264.1, 288, or 289, shall be punished by imprisonment in the state prison for two, three, or four years.
(d) (1) Every person who, with the intent that the crime be committed, solicits another to commit an offense specified in Section 11352, 11379, 11379.5, 11379.6, or 11391 of the Health and Safety Code shall be punished by imprisonment in a county jail not exceeding six months. Every person who, having been convicted of soliciting another to commit an offense specified in this subdivision, is subsequently convicted of the proscribed solicitation, shall be punished by imprisonment in a county jail not exceeding one year, or pursuant to subdivision (h) of Section 1170.
(2) This subdivision does not apply where the term of imprisonment imposed under other provisions of law would result in a longer term of imprisonment.
(e) Every person who, with the intent that the crime be committed, solicits another to commit an offense specified in Section 14014 of the Welfare and Institutions Code shall be punished by imprisonment in a county jail for not exceeding six months. Every person who, having been convicted of soliciting another to commit an offense specified in this subdivision, is subsequently convicted of the proscribed solicitation, shall be punished by imprisonment in a county jail not exceeding one year, or pursuant to subdivision (h) of Section 1170.
(f) (1) Every person who, with the intent that the crime be committed, solicits another to commit an offense set forth in Section 502 shall be punished as set forth in paragraph (3).
(2) Every person who, with the intent that the crime be committed, offers to solicit assistance for another to conduct activities in violation of Section 502 shall be punished as set forth in paragraph (3). This includes persons operating Internet Web sites that offer to assist others in locating hacking services. For the purposes of this section "hacking services" means assistance in the unauthorized access to computers, computer systems, or data in violation of Section 502.
(3) Every person who violates this subdivision shall be punished by imprisonment in a county jail for a period not to exceed six months. Every subsequent violation of this subdivision by that same person shall be punished by imprisonment in a county jail not exceeding one year.
(g) An offense charged in violation of subdivision (a), (b), or (c) shall be proven by the testimony of two witnesses, or of one witness and corroborating circumstances. An offense charged in violation of subdivision (d), (e), or (f) shall be proven by the testimony of one witness and corroborating circumstances.
(h) Nothing in this section precludes prosecution under any other law that provides for a greater punishment.
(Amended by Stats. 2015, Ch. 552, Sec. 1. (AB 195) Effective January 1, 2016.)
653h.
(a) Every person is guilty of a public offense punishable as provided in subdivisions (b) and (c), who:
(1) Knowingly and willfully transfers or causes to be transferred any sounds that have been recorded on a phonograph record, disc, wire, tape, film or other article on which sounds are recorded, with intent to sell or cause to be sold, or to use or cause to be used for commercial advantage or private financial gain through public performance, the article on which the sounds are so transferred, without the consent of the owner.
(2) Transports for monetary or like consideration within this state or causes to be transported within this state any such article with the knowledge that the sounds thereon have been so transferred without the consent of the owner.
(b) Any person who has been convicted of a violation of subdivision (a), shall be punished by imprisonment in the county jail not to exceed one year, by imprisonment pursuant to subdivision (h) of Section 1170 for two, three, or five years, or by a fine not to exceed five hundred thousand dollars ($500,000), or by both that fine and imprisonment, if the offense involves the transfer or transportation, or conduct causing that transfer or transportation, of not less than 1,000 of the articles described in subdivision (a).
(c) Any person who has been convicted of any other violation of subdivision (a) not described in subdivision (b), shall be punished by imprisonment in the county jail not to

exceed one year, or by a fine of not more than fifty thousand dollars ($50,000), or by both that fine and imprisonment. A second or subsequent conviction under subdivision (a) not described in subdivision (b) shall be punished by imprisonment pursuant to subdivision (h) of Section 1170 or by a fine not to exceed two hundred thousand dollars ($200,000), or by both that fine and imprisonment.

(d) Every person who offers for sale or resale, or sells or resells, or causes the sale or resale, or rents, or possesses for these purposes, any article described in subdivision (a) with knowledge that the sounds thereon have been so transferred without the consent of the owner is guilty of a public offense.

(1) A violation of subdivision (d) involving not less than 100 of those articles shall be punishable by imprisonment in a county jail not to exceed one year or by a fine not to exceed twenty thousand dollars ($20,000), or by both that fine and imprisonment. A second or subsequent conviction for the conduct described in this paragraph shall be punishable by imprisonment in the county jail not to exceed one year or pursuant to subdivision (h) of Section 1170 or by a fine not to exceed fifty thousand dollars ($50,000), or by both that fine and imprisonment.

(2) A person who has been convicted of any violation of this subdivision not described in paragraph (1) shall be punished by imprisonment in the county jail not to exceed six months or by a fine not to exceed ten thousand dollars ($10,000), or by both that fine and imprisonment. A second conviction for the conduct described in this paragraph shall be punishable by imprisonment in the county jail not to exceed one year or by a fine not to exceed twenty thousand dollars ($20,000), or by both that fine and imprisonment. A third or subsequent conviction for the conduct described in this paragraph shall be punishable by imprisonment in the county jail not to exceed one year or pursuant to subdivision (h) of Section 1170, or by a fine not to exceed fifty thousand dollars ($50,000), or by both that fine and imprisonment.

(e) As used in this section, "person" means any individual, partnership, partnership's member or employee, corporation, limited liability company, association or corporation or association employee, officer or director; "owner" means the person who owns the original master recording embodied in the master phonograph record, master disc, master tape, master film or other article used for reproducing recorded sounds on phonograph records, discs, tapes, films or other articles on which sound is or can be recorded, and from which the transferred recorded sounds are directly or indirectly derived; and "master recording" means the original fixation of sounds upon a recording from which copies can be made.

(f) This section shall neither enlarge nor diminish the right of parties in private litigation.

(g) This section does not apply to any person engaged in radio or television broadcasting who transfers, or causes to be transferred, any such sounds (other than from the sound track of a motion picture) intended for, or in connection with, broadcast transmission or related uses, or for archival purposes.

(h) This section does not apply to any not-for-profit educational institution or any federal or state governmental entity, if the institution or entity has as a primary purpose the advancement of the public's knowledge and the dissemination of information regarding America's musical cultural heritage, provided that this purpose is clearly set forth in the institution's or entity's charter, bylaws, certificate of incorporation, or similar document, and the institution or entity has, prior to the transfer, made a good faith effort to identify and locate the owner or owners of the sound recordings to be transferred and, provided that the owner or owners could not be and have not been located. Nothing in this section shall be construed to relieve an institution or entity of its contractual or other obligation to compensate the owners of sound recordings to be transferred. In order to continue the exemption permitted by this subdivision, the institution or entity shall make continuing efforts to locate such owners and shall make an annual public notice of the fact of the transfers in newspapers of general circulation serving the jurisdictions where the owners were incorporated or doing business at the time of initial affixations. The institution or entity shall keep on file a record of the efforts made to locate such owners for inspection by appropriate governmental agencies.

(i) This section applies only to those articles that were initially mastered prior to February 15, 1972.

(Amended by Stats. 2011, Ch. 15, Sec. 433. (AB 109) Effective April 4, 2011. Operative October 1, 2011, by Sec. 636 of Ch. 15, as amended by Stats. 2011, Ch. 39, Sec. 68.)

653i.

Any person who is involved in a skiing accident and who leaves the scene of the accident knowing or having reason to believe that any other person involved in the accident is in need of medical and other assistance, except to notify the proper authorities or to obtain assistance, shall be guilty of an infraction punishable by fine not exceeding one thousand dollars ($1,000).

(Added by Stats. 1977, Ch. 870.)

653j.

(a) Every person 18 years of age or older who, in any voluntary manner, solicits, induces, encourages, or intimidates any minor with the intent that the minor shall commit a felony in violation of paragraph (1) of subdivision (c) of Section 136.1 or Section 187, 211, 215, 245, 246, 451, 459, or 520 of the Penal Code, or Section 10851 of the Vehicle Code, shall be punished by imprisonment pursuant to subdivision (h) of Section 1170 for a period of three, five, or seven years. If the minor is 16 years of age or older at the time of the offense, this section shall only apply when the adult is at least five years older than the minor at the time the offense is committed.

(b) In no case shall the court impose a sentence pursuant to subdivision (a) which exceeds the maximum penalty prescribed for the felony offense for which the minor was solicited, induced, encouraged, or intimidated to commit.

(c) Whenever a sentence is imposed under subdivision (a), the court shall consider the severity of the underlying crime as one of the circumstances in aggravation.

(Amended by Stats. 2011, Ch. 15, Sec. 434. (AB 109) Effective April 4, 2011. Operative October 1, 2011, by Sec. 636 of Ch. 15, as amended by Stats. 2011, Ch. 39, Sec. 68.)

653m.

(a) Every person who, with intent to annoy, telephones or makes contact by means of an electronic communication device with another and addresses to or about the other person any obscene language or addresses to the other person any threat to inflict injury to the person or property of the person addressed or any member of his or her family, is guilty of a misdemeanor. Nothing in this subdivision shall apply to telephone calls or electronic contacts made in good faith.

(b) Every person who, with intent to annoy or harass, makes repeated telephone calls or makes repeated contact by means of an electronic communication device, or makes any combination of calls or contact, to another person is, whether or not conversation ensues from making the telephone call or contact by means of an electronic communication device, guilty of a misdemeanor. Nothing in this subdivision shall apply to telephone calls or electronic contacts made in good faith or during the ordinary course and scope of business.

(c) Any offense committed by use of a telephone may be deemed to have been committed when and where the telephone call or calls were made or received. Any offense committed by use of an electronic communication device or medium, including the Internet, may be deemed to have been committed when and where the electronic communication or communications were originally sent or first viewed by the recipient.

(d) Subdivision (a) or (b) is violated when the person acting with intent to annoy makes a telephone call or contact by means of an electronic communication device requesting a return call and performs the acts prohibited under subdivision (a) or (b) upon receiving the return call.

(e) Subdivision (a) or (b) is violated when a person knowingly permits any telephone or electronic communication under the person's control to be used for the purposes prohibited by those subdivisions.

(f) If probation is granted, or the execution or imposition of sentence is suspended, for any person convicted under this section, the court may order as a condition of probation that the person participate in counseling.

(g) For purposes of this section, the term "electronic communication device" includes, but is not limited to, telephones, cellular phones, computers, video recorders, facsimile machines, pagers, personal digital assistants, smartphones, and any other device that transfers signs, signals, writing, images, sounds, or data. "Electronic communication device" also includes, but is not limited to, videophones, TTY/TDD devices, and all other devices used to aid or assist communication to or from deaf or disabled persons. "Electronic communication" has the same meaning as the term defined in Subsection 12 of Section 2510 of Title 18 of the United States Code.

(Amended by Stats. 2008, Ch. 109, Sec. 1. Effective January 1, 2009.)

653n.

Any person who installs or who maintains after April 1, 1970, any two-way mirror permitting observation of any restroom, toilet, bathroom, washroom, shower, locker room, fitting room, motel room, or hotel room, is guilty of a misdemeanor.

This section does not apply to such areas (a) in state or local public penal, correctional, custodial, or medical institutions which are used by, or for the treatment of, persons who are committed or voluntarily confined to such institutions or voluntarily receive treatment therein; (b) in private custodial or medical institutions, which are used by, or for the treatment of, persons who are committed or voluntarily confined to such institutions or voluntarily receive treatment therein; (c) in public or private treatment facilities which are used by, or for the treatment of, persons who are committed or voluntarily confined to such facilities or voluntarily receive treatment therein; (d) in buildings operated by state or local law enforcement agencies; or (e) in public or private educational institutions. "Two-way mirror" as used in this section means a mirror or other surface which permits any person on one side thereof to see through it under certain conditions of lighting, while any person on the other side thereof or other surface at that time can see only the usual mirror or other surface reflection.

(Added by Stats. 1969, Ch. 428.)

653o.

(a) It is unlawful to import into this state for commercial purposes, to possess with intent to sell, or to sell within the state, the dead body, or any part or product thereof, of a polar bear, leopard, ocelot, tiger, cheetah, jaguar, sable antelope, wolf (Canis lupus), zebra, whale, cobra, python, sea turtle, colobus monkey, kangaroo, vicuna, sea otter, free-roaming feral horse, dolphin or porpoise (Delphinidae), Spanish lynx, or elephant.

(b) (1) Commencing January 1, 2020, it shall be unlawful to import into this state for commercial purposes, to possess with intent to sell, or to sell within the state, the dead body, or any part or product thereof, of a crocodile or alligator.

(2) This subdivision shall not be construed to authorize the importation or sale of any alligator or crocodilian species, or any products thereof, that are listed as endangered under the federal Endangered Species Act, or to allow the importation or sale of any alligator or crocodilian species, or any products thereof, in violation of any federal law or international treaty to which the United States is a party.

(c) A person who violates this section is guilty of a misdemeanor and shall be subject to a fine of not less than one thousand dollars ($1,000) and not to exceed five thousand dollars ($5,000) or imprisonment in the county jail not to exceed six months, or both that fine and imprisonment, for each violation.

(d) The prohibitions against importation for commercial purposes, possession with intent to sell, and sale of the species listed in this section are severable. A finding of the invalidity of any one or more prohibitions shall not affect the validity of any remaining prohibitions.

(e) This section shall become operative on January 1, 2016.

(Amended (as amended by Stats. 2010, Ch. 412, Sec. 2) by Stats. 2014, Ch. 464, Sec. 2. (AB 2075) Effective January 1, 2015. Section operative January 1, 2016, by its own provisions.)

653p.

It is unlawful to possess with the intent to sell, or to sell, within the state, the dead body, or any part or product thereof, of any species or subspecies of any fish, bird, mammal, amphibian, reptile, mollusk, invertebrate, or plant, the importation of which is illegal under the Federal Endangered Species Act of 1973 (Title 16, United States Code Sec. 1531 et seq.) and subsequent amendments, or under the Marine Mammal Protection Act of 1972 (Title 16, United States Code Sec. 1361 et seq.), or which is listed in the Federal Register by the Secretary of the Interior pursuant to the above acts. The violation of any federal regulations adopted pursuant to the above acts shall also be deemed a violation of this section and shall be prosecuted by the appropriate state or local officials.

(Amended by Stats. 1976, Ch. 692.)

653q.

It is unlawful to import into this state for commercial purposes, to possess with intent to sell, or to sell within the state, the dead body, or any part or product thereof, of any seal.

Any person who violates any provision of this section is guilty of a misdemeanor and shall be subject to a fine of not less than one thousand dollars ($1,000) and not to exceed five thousand dollars ($5,000) or imprisonment in the county jail for not to exceed six months, or both such fine and imprisonment, for each violation.

(Added by Stats. 1971, Ch. 1200.)

653r.

Notwithstanding the provisions of Section 3 of Chapter 1557 of the Statutes of 1970, it shall be unlawful to possess with intent to sell, or to sell, within this state, after June 1, 1972, the dead body, or any part or product thereof, of any fish, bird, amphibian, reptile, or mammal specified in Section 653o or 653p.

Violation of this section constitutes a misdemeanor.

(Added by Stats. 1971, Ch. 1283.)

653s.

(a) Any person who transports or causes to be transported for monetary or other consideration within this state, any article containing sounds of a live performance with the knowledge that the sounds thereon have been recorded or mastered without the consent of the owner of the sounds of the live performance is guilty of a public offense punishable as provided in subdivision (g) or (h).

(b) As used in this section and Section 653u:

(1) "Live performance" means the recitation, rendering, or playing of a series of musical, spoken, or other sounds in any audible sequence thereof.

(2) "Article" means the original disc, wire, tape, film, phonograph record, or other recording device used to record or master the sounds of the live performance and any copy or reproduction thereof which duplicates, in whole or in part, the original.

(3) "Person" means any individual, partnership, partnership member or employee, corporation, association, or corporation or association employee, officer, or director, limited liability company, or limited liability company manager or officer.

(c) In the absence of a written agreement or operation of law to the contrary, the performer or performers of the sounds of a live performance shall be presumed to own the right to record or master those sounds.

(d) For purposes of this section, a person who is authorized to maintain custody and control over business records reflecting the consent of the owner to the recordation or master recording of a live performance shall be a proper witness in any proceeding regarding the issue of consent.

Any witness called pursuant to this section shall be subject to all rules of evidence relating to the competency of a witness to testify and the relevance and admissibility of the testimony offered.

(e) This section shall neither enlarge nor diminish the rights and remedies of parties to a recording or master recording which they might otherwise possess by law.

(f) This section shall not apply to persons engaged in radio or television broadcasting or cablecasting who record or fix the sounds of a live performance for, or in connection with, broadcast or cable transmission and related uses in educational television or radio programs, for archival purposes, or for news programs or purposes if the recordation or master recording is not commercially distributed independent of the broadcast or cablecast by or through the broadcasting or cablecasting entity to subscribers or the general public.

(g) Any person who has been convicted of a violation of subdivision (a), shall be punished by imprisonment in the county jail not to exceed one year, or by imprisonment pursuant to subdivision (h) of Section 1170 for two, three, or five years, or by a fine not to exceed five hundred thousand dollars ($500,000), or by both, if the offense involves the transportation or causing to be transported of not less than 1,000 articles described in subdivision (a).

(h) Any person who has been convicted of any other violation of subdivision (a) not described in subdivision (g) shall be punished by imprisonment in the county jail not to exceed one year, or by a fine not to exceed fifty thousand dollars ($50,000), or by both that fine and imprisonment. A second or subsequent conviction under subdivision (a) not described in subdivision (g) shall be punished by imprisonment in the county jail not to exceed one year or pursuant to subdivision (h) of Section 1170, or by a fine not to exceed two hundred thousand dollars ($200,000), or by both that fine and imprisonment.

(i) Every person who offers for sale or resale, or sells or resells, or causes the sale or resale, or rents, or possesses for these purposes, any article described in subdivision (a) with knowledge that the sounds thereon have been so recorded or mastered without the consent of the owner of the sounds of a live performance is guilty of a public offense.

(1) A violation of subdivision (i) involving not less than 100 of those articles shall be punishable by imprisonment in a county jail not to exceed one year or by a fine not to exceed twenty thousand dollars ($20,000), or by both that fine and imprisonment. A second or subsequent conviction for the conduct described in this paragraph shall be punishable by imprisonment in the county jail not to exceed one year or pursuant to subdivision (h) of Section 1170, or by a fine not to exceed fifty thousand dollars ($50,000), or by both.

(2) A person who has been convicted of any violation of this subdivision not described in paragraph (1) shall be punished by imprisonment in the county jail not to exceed six months or by a fine not to exceed ten thousand dollars ($10,000), or by both that fine and imprisonment. A second conviction for the conduct described in this paragraph shall be punishable by imprisonment in the county jail not to exceed one year or by a fine not to exceed twenty thousand dollars ($20,000), or by both that fine and imprisonment. A third or subsequent conviction for the conduct described in this paragraph shall be punishable by imprisonment in the county jail not to exceed one year or pursuant to subdivision (h) of Section 1170, or by a fine not to exceed fifty thousand dollars ($50,000), or by both that fine and imprisonment.

(Amended by Stats. 2011, Ch. 15, Sec. 435. (AB 109) Effective April 4, 2011. Operative October 1, 2011, by Sec. 636 of Ch. 15, as amended by Stats. 2011, Ch. 39, Sec. 68.)

653t.

(a) A person commits a public offense if the person knowingly and maliciously interrupts, disrupts, impedes, or otherwise interferes with the transmission of a communication over an amateur or a citizen's band radio frequency, the purpose of which communication is to inform or inquire about an emergency.

(b) For purposes of this section, "emergency" means a condition or circumstance in which an individual is or is reasonably believed by the person transmitting the communication to be in imminent danger of serious bodily injury, in which property is or is reasonably believed by the person transmitting the communication to be in imminent danger of extensive damage or destruction, or in which that injury or destruction has occurred and the person transmitting is attempting to summon assistance.

(c) A violation of subdivision (a) is a misdemeanor punishable by a fine not to exceed one thousand dollars ($1,000), by imprisonment in a county jail not to exceed six months, or by both, unless, as a result of the commission of the offense, serious bodily injury or property loss in excess of ten thousand dollars ($10,000) occurs, in which event the offense is a felony punishable by imprisonment pursuant to subdivision (h) of Section 1170.

(d) Any person who knowingly and maliciously interrupts, disrupts, impedes, or otherwise interferes with the transmission of an emergency communication over a public safety radio frequency, when the offense results in serious bodily injury or property loss in excess of ten thousand dollars ($10,000), is guilty of a felony punishable by imprisonment pursuant to subdivision (h) of Section 1170.

(Amended by Stats. 2011, Ch. 15, Sec. 436. (AB 109) Effective April 4, 2011. Operative October 1, 2011, by Sec. 636 of Ch. 15, as amended by Stats. 2011, Ch. 39, Sec. 68.)

653u.

(a) Any person who records or masters or causes to be recorded or mastered on any article with the intent to sell for commercial advantage or private financial gain, the sounds of a live performance with the knowledge that the sounds thereon have been recorded or mastered without the consent of the owner of the sounds of the live performance is guilty of a public offense punishable as provided in subdivisions (d) and (e).

(b) In the absence of a written agreement or operation of law to the contrary, the performer or performers of the sounds of a live performance shall be presumed to own the right to record or master those sounds.

(c) (1) For purposes of this section, a person who is authorized to maintain custody and control over business records reflecting the consent of the owner to the recordation or master recording of a live performance shall be a proper witness in any proceeding regarding the issue of consent.

(2) Any witness called pursuant to this section shall be subject to all rules of evidence relating to the competency of a witness to testify and the relevance and admissibility of the testimony offered.

(d) Any person who has been convicted of a violation of subdivision (a) shall be punished by imprisonment in the county jail not to exceed one year, or by imprisonment pursuant to subdivision (h) of Section 1170 for two, three, or five years, or by a fine not to exceed five hundred thousand dollars ($500,000), or by both that fine and imprisonment, if the offense involves the recording, mastering, or causing to be recorded or mastered at least 1,000 articles described in subdivision (a).

(e) Any person who has been convicted of any other violation of subdivision (a) not described in subdivision (d), shall be punished by imprisonment in the county jail not to exceed one year, or by a fine not to exceed fifty thousand dollars ($50,000), or by both that fine and imprisonment. A second or subsequent conviction under subdivision (a) not described in subdivision (d) shall be punished by imprisonment in the county jail not to exceed one year or pursuant to subdivision (h) of Section 1170 or by a fine not to exceed two hundred thousand dollars ($200,000), or by both that fine and imprisonment.

(Amended by Stats. 2011, Ch. 15, Sec. 437. (AB 109) Effective April 4, 2011. Operative October 1, 2011, by Sec. 636 of Ch. 15, as amended by Stats. 2011, Ch. 39, Sec. 68.)

653v.

Whenever any person is convicted of any violation of Section 653h, 653s, 653u, or 653w the court, in its judgment of conviction, shall, in addition to the penalty therein prescribed, order the forfeiture and destruction or other disposition of all articles, including, but not limited to, phonograph records, discs, wires, tapes, films, or any other article upon which sounds or images can be recorded or stored, and any and all electronic, mechanical, or other devices for manufacturing, reproducing or assembling these articles, which were used in connection with, or which were part of, any violation of Section 653h, 653s, 653u, or 653w.

(Amended by Stats. 1985, Ch. 364, Sec. 2.)

653w.

(a) (1) A person is guilty of failure to disclose the origin of a recording or audiovisual work if, for commercial advantage or private financial gain, he or she knowingly advertises or offers for sale or resale, or sells or resells, or causes the rental, sale, or resale of, or rents, or manufactures, or possesses for these purposes, any recording or audiovisual work, the outside cover, box, jacket, or label of which does not clearly and conspicuously disclose the actual true name and address of the manufacturer thereof and the name of the actual author, artist, performer, producer, programmer, or group thereon. This section does not require the original manufacturer or authorized licensees of software producers to disclose the contributing authors or programmers.

(2) As used in this section, "recording" means any tangible medium upon which information or sounds are recorded or otherwise stored, including, but not limited to, any phonograph record, disc, tape, audio cassette, wire, film, memory card, flash drive, hard drive, data storage device, or other medium on which information or sounds are recorded or otherwise stored, but does not include sounds accompanying a motion picture or other audiovisual work.

(3) As used in this section, "audiovisual works" are the physical embodiment of works that consist of related images that are intrinsically intended to be shown using machines or devices, such as projectors, viewers, or electronic equipment, together with accompanying sounds, if any, regardless of the nature of the material objects, such as films, tapes, discs, memory cards, flash drives, hard drives, data storage devices, or other devices, on which the works are embodied.

(b) A person who has been convicted of a violation of subdivision (a) shall be punished as follows:

(1) If the offense involves the advertisement, offer for sale or resale, sale, rental, manufacture, or possession for these purposes, of at least 100 articles of audio recordings or 100 articles of audiovisual works described in subdivision (a), or the commercial equivalent thereof, the person shall be punished by imprisonment in a county jail not to exceed one year, or by imprisonment pursuant to subdivision (h) of Section 1170 for two, three, or five years, or by a fine not to exceed five hundred thousand dollars ($500,000), or by both that fine and imprisonment.

(2) Any other violation of subdivision (a) not described in paragraph (1) shall, upon a first offense, be punished by imprisonment in a county jail not to exceed one year, or by a fine not to exceed fifty thousand dollars ($50,000), or by both that fine and imprisonment.

(3) A second or subsequent conviction under subdivision (a) not described in paragraph (1) shall be punished by imprisonment in a county jail not to exceed one year or pursuant to subdivision (h) of Section 1170, or by a fine of not less than one thousand dollars ($1,000), but not to exceed two hundred thousand dollars ($200,000), or by both that fine and imprisonment.

(Amended by Stats. 2017, Ch. 561, Sec. 181. (AB 1516) Effective January 1, 2018.)

653x.

(a) A person who telephones or uses an electronic communication device to initiate communication with the 911 emergency system with the intent to annoy or harass another person is guilty of a misdemeanor punishable by a fine of not more than one thousand dollars ($1,000), by imprisonment in a county jail for not more than six months, or by both the fine and imprisonment. Nothing in this section shall apply to telephone calls or communications using electronic devices made in good faith.

(b) An intent to annoy or harass is established by proof of repeated calls or communications over a period of time, however short, that are unreasonable under the circumstances.

(c) Upon conviction of a violation of this section, a person also shall be liable for all reasonable costs incurred by any unnecessary emergency response.

(Amended by Stats. 2016, Ch. 96, Sec. 1. (AB 1769) Effective January 1, 2017.)

653y.

(a) A person who knowingly allows the use or who uses the 911 emergency system for any reason other than because of an emergency is guilty of an infraction, punishable as follows:

(1) For a first violation, a written warning shall be issued to the violator by the public safety entity originally receiving the telephone call or the communication from an electronic device describing the punishment for subsequent violations. The written warning shall inform the recipient to notify the issuing agency that the warning was issued inappropriately if the recipient did not make, or knowingly allow the use of, the 911 emergency system for, the nonemergency 911 telephone call or the communication from an electronic device. The law enforcement agency may provide educational materials regarding the appropriate use of the 911 emergency system.

(2) For a second or subsequent violation, a citation may be issued by the public safety entity originally receiving the telephone call or the communication from an electronic device pursuant to which the violator shall be subject to the following penalties that may be reduced by a court upon consideration of the violator's ability to pay:

(A) For a second violation, a fine of fifty dollars ($50).

(B) For a third violation, a fine of one hundred dollars ($100).

(C) For a fourth or subsequent violation, a fine of two hundred and fifty dollars ($250).

(b) The parent or legal guardian having custody and control of an unemancipated minor who violates this section shall be jointly and severally liable with the minor for the fine imposed pursuant to this section.

(c) For purposes of this section, "emergency" means any condition in which emergency services will result in the saving of a life, a reduction in the destruction of property, quicker apprehension of criminals, or assistance with potentially life-threatening medical problems, a fire, a need for rescue, an imminent potential crime, or a similar situation in which immediate assistance is required.

(d) Notwithstanding subdivision (a), this section shall not apply to a telephone corporation or any other entity for acts or omissions relating to the routine maintenance, repair, or operation of the 911 emergency system or the 311 telephone system.

(Amended by Stats. 2016, Ch. 96, Sec. 2. (AB 1769) Effective January 1, 2017.)

653z.

(a) Every person who operates a recording device in a motion picture theater while a motion picture is being exhibited, for the purpose of recording a theatrical motion picture and without the express written authority of the owner of the motion picture theater, is guilty of a public offense and shall be punished by imprisonment in a county jail not exceeding one year, by a fine not exceeding five thousand dollars ($5,000), or by both that fine and imprisonment.

(b) For the purposes of this section, the following terms have the following meanings:

(1) "Recording device" means a photographic, digital or video camera, or other audio or video recording device capable of recording the sounds and images of a motion picture or any portion of a motion picture.

(2) "Motion picture theater" means a theater or other premises in which a motion picture is exhibited.

(c) Nothing in this section shall preclude prosecution under any other provision of law.

(Amended by Stats. 2010, Ch. 351, Sec. 7. (AB 819) Effective September 27, 2010.)

653aa.

(a) Any person, except a minor, who is located in California, who, knowing that a particular recording or audiovisual work is commercial, knowingly electronically disseminates all or substantially all of that commercial recording or audiovisual work to more than 10 other people without disclosing his or her e-mail address, and the title of the recording or audiovisual work is punishable by a fine not exceeding five thousand dollars ($5,000), imprisonment in a county jail for a period not exceeding one year, or by both that fine and imprisonment.

(b) Any minor who violates subdivision (a) is punishable by a fine not exceeding five hundred dollars ($500). Any minor who commits a third or subsequent violation of subdivision (a) is punishable by a fine not exceeding two thousand dollars ($2,000), imprisonment in a county jail for a period not to exceed one year, or by both that imprisonment and fine.

(c) Subdivisions (a) and (b) do not apply:

(1) To a person who electronically disseminates a commercial recording or audiovisual work to his or her immediate family, or within his or her personal network, defined as a restricted access network controlled by and accessible to only that person or people in his or her immediate household.

(2) If the copyright owner, or a person acting under the authority of the copyright owner, of a commercial recording or audiovisual work has explicitly given permission for all or substantially all of that recording or audiovisual work to be freely disseminated electronically by or to anyone without limitation.

(3) To a person who has been licensed either by the copyright owner or a person acting under the authority of the copyright owner to disseminate electronically all or substantially all of a commercial audiovisual work or recording.

(4) To the licensed electronic dissemination of a commercial audiovisual work or recording by means of a cable television service offered over a cable system or direct to home satellite service as defined in Title 47 of the United States Code.

(d) Nothing in this section shall restrict the copyright owner from disseminating his or her own copyrighted material.

(e) Upon conviction for a violation of this section, in addition to the penalty prescribed, the court shall order the permanent deletion or destruction of any electronic file containing a commercial recording or audiovisual work, the dissemination of which was the basis of the violation. This subdivision shall not apply to the copyright owner or to a person acting under the authority of the copyright owner.

(f) An Internet service provider does not violate, and does not aid and abet a violation of subdivision (a), and subdivision (a) shall not be enforced against an Internet service provider, to the extent that the Internet service provider enables a user of its service to electronically disseminate an audiovisual work or sound recording, if the Internet service provider maintains its valid e-mail address or other means of electronic notification on its Internet Web site in a location that is accessible to the public.

For the purposes of this section, "Internet service provider" means an entity, to the extent that the entity is transmitting, routing, or providing connections for Internet communications initiated by or at the direction of another person, between or among points specified by a user, of material placed online by a user, storing or hosting that material at the direction of a user, or referring or linking users to that material.

(g) For purposes of this section:

(1) "Recording" means the electronic or physical embodiment of any recorded images, sounds, or images and sounds, but does not include audiovisual works or sounds accompanying audiovisual works.

(2) "Audiovisual work" means the electronic or physical embodiment of motion pictures, television programs, video or computer games, or other audiovisual presentations that consist of related images that are intrinsically intended to be shown by the use of machines or devices such as projectors, viewers, or electronic equipment, or a computer program, software, or system, as defined in Section 502, together with accompanying sounds, if any.

(3) "Commercial recording or audiovisual work" means a recording or audiovisual work whose copyright owner, or assignee, authorized agent, or licensee, has made or intends to make available for sale, rental, or for performance or exhibition to the public under license, but does not include an excerpt consisting of less than substantially all of a recording or audiovisual work. A recording or audiovisual work may be commercial regardless of whether the person who electronically disseminates it seeks commercial advantage or private financial gain from that dissemination.

(4) "Electronic dissemination" means initiating a transmission of, making available, or otherwise offering, a commercial recording or audiovisual work for distribution on the Internet or other digital network, regardless of whether someone else had previously electronically disseminated the same commercial recording or audiovisual work.

(5) "E-mail address" means a valid e-mail address, or the valid e-mail address of the holder of the account from which the dissemination took place.

(6) "Disclosing" means providing information in, attached to, or discernable or available in or through the process of disseminating or obtaining a commercial recording or audiovisual work in a manner that is accessible by any person engaged in disseminating or receiving the commercial recording or audiovisual work.

(h) Nothing in this section shall preclude prosecution under any other provision of law.
(Amended by Stats. 2010, Ch. 351, Sec. 8. (AB 819) Effective September 27, 2010. Note: This amendment deleted the provision, in former subd. (i), that made this section inoperative on Jan. 1, 2010.)
653.1.

(a) No person or group shall release, outdoors, balloons made of electrically conductive material and filled with a gas lighter than air, as part of a public or civic event, promotional activity, or product advertisement.

(b) Any person who violates this section shall be guilty of an infraction punishable by a fine not exceeding one hundred dollars ($100). Any person who violates this section who has been previously convicted twice of violating this section shall be guilty of a misdemeanor.

(c) This section shall not apply to manned hot air balloons, or to balloons used in governmental or scientific research projects.
(Amended by Stats. 2018, Ch. 262, Sec. 2. (AB 2450) Effective January 1, 2019.)
653.2.

(a) Every person who, with intent to place another person in reasonable fear for his or her safety, or the safety of the other person's immediate family, by means of an electronic communication device, and without consent of the other person, and for the purpose of imminently causing that other person unwanted physical contact, injury, or harassment, by a third party, electronically distributes, publishes, e-mails, hyperlinks, or makes available for downloading, personal identifying information, including, but not limited to, a digital image of another person, or an electronic message of a harassing nature about another person, which would be likely to incite or produce that unlawful action, is guilty of a misdemeanor punishable by up to one year in a county jail, by a fine of not more than one thousand dollars ($1,000), or by both that fine and imprisonment.

(b) For purposes of this section, "electronic communication device" includes, but is not limited to, telephones, cell phones, computers, Internet Web pages or sites, Internet phones, hybrid cellular/Internet/wireless devices, personal digital assistants (PDAs), video recorders, fax machines, or pagers. "Electronic communication" has the same meaning as the term is defined in Section 2510(12) of Title 18 of the United States Code.

(c) For purposes of this section, the following terms apply:

(1) "Harassment" means a knowing and willful course of conduct directed at a specific person that a reasonable person would consider as seriously alarming, seriously annoying, seriously tormenting, or seriously terrorizing the person and that serves no legitimate purpose.

(2) "Of a harassing nature" means of a nature that a reasonable person would consider as seriously alarming, seriously annoying, seriously tormenting, or seriously terrorizing of the person and that serves no legitimate purpose.
(Amended by Stats. 2009, Ch. 140, Sec. 144. (AB 1164) Effective January 1, 2010.)

CHAPTER 2.5.
Loitering for the Purpose of Engaging in a Prostitution Offense [653.20 - 653.28]

(Chapter 2.5 added by Stats. 1995, Ch. 981, Sec. 4.)
653.20.
For purposes of this chapter, the following definitions apply:

(a) "Commit prostitution" means to engage in sexual conduct for money or other consideration, but does not include sexual conduct engaged in as a part of any stage performance, play, or other entertainment open to the public.

(b) "Public place" means an area open to the public, or an alley, plaza, park, driveway, or parking lot, or an automobile, whether moving or not, or a building open to the general public, including one which serves food or drink, or provides entertainment, or the doorways and entrances to a building or dwelling, or the grounds enclosing a building or dwelling.

(c) "Loiter" means to delay or linger without a lawful purpose for being on the property and for the purpose of committing a crime as opportunity may be discovered.
(Added by Stats. 1995, Ch. 981, Sec. 4. Effective January 1, 1996.)
653.22.

(a) (1) Except as specified in paragraph (2), it is unlawful for any person to loiter in any public place with the intent to commit prostitution. This intent is evidenced by acting in a manner and under circumstances that openly demonstrate the purpose of inducing, enticing, or soliciting prostitution, or procuring another to commit prostitution.

(2) Notwithstanding paragraph (1), this subdivision does not apply to a child under 18 years of age who is alleged to have engaged in conduct that would, if committed by an adult, violate this subdivision. A commercially exploited child under this paragraph may be adjudged a dependent child of the court pursuant to paragraph (2) of subdivision (b) of Section 300 of the Welfare and Institutions Code and may be taken into temporary custody pursuant to subdivision (a) of Section 305 of the Welfare and Institutions Code, if the conditions allowing temporary custody without warrant are met.

(b) Among the circumstances that may be considered in determining whether a person loiters with the intent to commit prostitution are that the person:

(1) Repeatedly beckons to, stops, engages in conversations with, or attempts to stop or engage in conversations with passersby, indicative of soliciting for prostitution.

(2) Repeatedly stops or attempts to stop motor vehicles by hailing the drivers, waving arms, or making any other bodily gestures, or engages or attempts to engage the drivers or passengers of the motor vehicles in conversation, indicative of soliciting for prostitution.

(3) Has been convicted of violating this section, subdivision (a) or (b) of Section 647, or any other offense relating to or involving prostitution, within five years of the arrest under this section.

(4) Circles an area in a motor vehicle and repeatedly beckons to, contacts, or attempts to contact or stop pedestrians or other motorists, indicative of soliciting for prostitution.

(5) Has engaged, within six months prior to the arrest under this section, in any behavior described in this subdivision, with the exception of paragraph (3), or in any other behavior indicative of prostitution activity.

(c) The list of circumstances set forth in subdivision (b) is not exclusive. The circumstances set forth in subdivision (b) should be considered particularly salient if they occur in an area that is known for prostitution activity. Any other relevant circumstances may be considered in determining whether a person has the requisite intent. Moreover, no one circumstance or combination of circumstances is in itself determinative of intent. Intent must be determined based on an evaluation of the particular circumstances of each case.
(Amended by Stats. 2016, Ch. 654, Sec. 2. (SB 1322) Effective January 1, 2017.)
653.23.

(a) It is unlawful for any person to do either of the following:

(1) Direct, supervise, recruit, or otherwise aid another person in the commission of a violation of subdivision (b) of Section 647 or subdivision (a) of Section 653.22.

(2) Collect or receive all or part of the proceeds earned from an act or acts of prostitution committed by another person in violation of subdivision (b) of Section 647.

(b) Among the circumstances that may be considered in determining whether a person is in violation of subdivision (a) are that the person does the following:

(1) Repeatedly speaks or communicates with another person who is acting in violation of subdivision (a) of Section 653.22.

(2) Repeatedly or continuously monitors or watches another person who is acting in violation of subdivision (a) of Section 653.22.

(3) Repeatedly engages or attempts to engage in conversation with pedestrians or motorists to solicit, arrange, or facilitate an act of prostitution between the pedestrians or motorists and another person who is acting in violation of subdivision (a) of Section 653.22.

(4) Repeatedly stops or attempts to stop pedestrians or motorists to solicit, arrange, or facilitate an act of prostitution between pedestrians or motorists and another person who is acting in violation of subdivision (a) of Section 653.22.

(5) Circles an area in a motor vehicle and repeatedly beckons to, contacts, or attempts to contact or stop pedestrians or other motorists to solicit, arrange, or facilitate an act of prostitution between the pedestrians or motorists and another person who is acting in violation of subdivision (a) of Section 653.22.

(6) Receives or appears to receive money from another person who is acting in violation of subdivision (a) of Section 653.22.

(7) Engages in any of the behavior described in paragraphs (1) to (6), inclusive, in regard to or on behalf of two or more persons who are in violation of subdivision (a) of Section 653.22.

(8) Has been convicted of violating this section, subdivision (a) or (b) of Section 647, subdivision (a) of Section 653.22, Section 266h, or 266i, or any other offense relating to or involving prostitution within five years of the arrest under this section.

(9) Has engaged, within six months prior to the arrest under subdivision (a), in any behavior described in this subdivision, with the exception of paragraph (8), or in any other behavior indicative of prostitution activity.

(c) The list of circumstances set forth in subdivision (b) is not exclusive. The circumstances set forth in subdivision (b) should be considered particularly salient if they occur in an area that is known for prostitution activity. Any other relevant circumstances may be considered. Moreover, no one circumstance or combination of circumstances is in itself determinative. A violation of subdivision (a) shall be determined based on an evaluation of the particular circumstances of each case.

(d) Nothing in this section shall preclude the prosecution of a suspect for a violation of Section 266h or 266i or for any other offense, or for a violation of this section in conjunction with a violation of Section 266h or 266i or any other offense.
(Added by Stats. 1998, Ch. 460, Sec. 1. Effective January 1, 1999.)
653.24.

If any section, subdivision, sentence, clause, phrase, or portion of this chapter is for any reason held invalid or unconstitutional by any court of competent jurisdiction, that portion shall be deemed a separate, distinct, and independent provision, and that holding shall not affect the validity of the remaining portion of the chapter.
(Added by Stats. 1995, Ch. 981, Sec. 4. Effective January 1, 1996.)
653.26.
A violation of any provision of this chapter is a misdemeanor.
(Added by Stats. 1995, Ch. 981, Sec. 4. Effective January 1, 1996.)
653.28.
Nothing in this chapter or Chapter 2 (commencing with Section 639) shall prevent a local governing body from adopting and enforcing laws consistent with these chapters relating to prostitution or prostitution-related activity. Where local laws duplicate or supplement this chapter or Chapter 2 (commencing with Section 639), these chapters shall be construed as providing alternative remedies and not to preempt the field.
(Added by Stats. 1995, Ch. 981, Sec. 4. Effective January 1, 1996.)

CHAPTER 3. Immigration Matters [653.55 - 653.61]

(Chapter 3 added by Stats. 1974, Ch. 999.)
653.55.
It is a misdemeanor for any person for compensation to knowingly make a false or misleading material statement or assertion of fact in the preparation of an immigration matter which statement or assertion is detrimentally relied upon by another. Such a misdemeanor is punishable by imprisonment in the county jail not exceeding six months, or by a fine not exceeding two thousand five hundred dollars ($2,500), or by both.
(Amended by Stats. 1976, Ch. 1125.)
653.56.
For purposes of this chapter:
(a) "Compensation" means money, property, or anything else of value.
(b) "Immigration matter" means any proceeding, filing, or action affecting the immigration or citizenship status of any person which arises under immigration and naturalization law, executive order or presidential proclamation, or action of the United States Immigration and Customs Enforcement, the United States Department of State, or the United States Department of Labor.
(c) "Person" means any individual, firm, partnership, corporation, limited liability company, association, other organization, or any employee or agent thereof.
(d) "Preparation" means giving advice on an immigration matter and includes drafting an application, brief, document, petition, or other paper, or completing a form provided by a federal or state agency in an immigration matter.
(Amended by Stats. 2011, Ch. 296, Sec. 210. (AB 1023) Effective January 1, 2012.)
653.57.
Any person violating the provisions of this chapter may be enjoined by any superior court of competent jurisdiction upon an action for injunction, brought by the Attorney General, or any district attorney, county counsel, city attorney, or city prosecutor in this state, and the superior court shall, after proof of violation, issue an injunction or other appropriate order restraining such conduct.
(Added by Stats. 1974, Ch. 999.)
653.58.
Any person who intentionally violates any injunction issued pursuant to Section 653.57 shall be liable for a civil penalty not to exceed two thousand five hundred dollars ($2,500) for each violation. Where the conduct constituting a violation is of a continuing nature, each day of such conduct is a separate and distinct violation.
(Amended by Stats. 1976, Ch. 1125.)
653.59.
Any person who violates any provision of this chapter shall be liable for a civil penalty not to exceed two thousand five hundred dollars ($2,500) for each violation, which shall be assessed and recovered in a civil action brought in the name of the people of the State of California by the Attorney General, or any district attorney, county counsel, city attorney, or city prosecutor in this state in any court of competent jurisdiction. If the civil action was brought by the Attorney General, one-half of the penalty collected shall be paid to the treasurer of the county in which the judgment was entered, and one-half to the State General Fund. If the civil action was brought by a district attorney or county counsel, the entire amount of the penalty collected shall be paid to the treasurer of the county in which the judgment was entered. If the civil action was brought by a city attorney or city prosecutor, one-half of the penalty shall be paid to the treasurer of the county in which the judgment was entered and one-half to the city.
The action may be brought upon the complaint of any person acting for the interests of itself, or members, or the general public.
(Added by Stats. 1974, Ch. 999.)
653.60.
Any person injured by violation of this chapter may recover: (a) his actual damages or five hundred dollars ($500), whichever is greater; and (b) the costs of the suit, including reasonable attorney's fees.
(Added by Stats. 1974, Ch. 999.)
653.61.
The remedies or penalties provided by this chapter are cumulative to each other and to the remedies or penalties available under all other laws of this state.
(Added by Stats. 1974, Ch. 999.)

CHAPTER 4. Crimes Committed while in Custody in Correctional Facilities [653.75- 653.75.]

(Chapter 4 added by Stats. 1987, Ch. 1005, Sec. 1.)
653.75.
Any person who commits any public offense while in custody in any local detention facility, as defined in Section 6031.4, or any state prison, as defined in Section 4504, is guilty of a crime. That crime shall be punished as provided in the section prescribing the punishment for that public offense.
(Added by Stats. 1987, Ch. 1005, Sec. 1.)

TITLE 16. GENERAL PROVISIONS [654 - 678]

(Title 16 enacted 1872.)
654.
(a) An act or omission that is punishable in different ways by different provisions of law shall be punished under the provision that provides for the longest potential term of imprisonment, but in no case shall the act or omission be punished under more than one provision. An acquittal or conviction and sentence under any one bars a prosecution for the same act or omission under any other.

(b) Notwithstanding subdivision (a), a defendant sentenced pursuant to subdivision (a) shall not be granted probation if any of the provisions that would otherwise apply to the defendant prohibits the granting of probation.
(Amended by Stats. 1997, Ch. 410, Sec. 1. Effective January 1, 1998.)
654.1.
It shall be unlawful for any person, acting individually or as an officer or employee of a corporation, or as a member of a copartnership or as a commission agent or employee of another person, firm or corporation, to sell or offer for sale or, to negotiate, provide or arrange for, or to advertise or hold himself out as one who sells or offers for sale or negotiates, provides or arranges for transportation of a person or persons on an individual fare basis over the public highways of the State of California unless such transportation is to be furnished or provided solely by, and such sale is authorized by, a carrier having a valid and existing certificate of convenience and necessity, or other valid and existing permit from the Public Utilities Commission of the State of California, or from the Interstate Commerce Commission of the United States, authorizing the holder of such certificate or permit to provide such transportation.
(Added by Stats. 1947, Ch. 1215.)
654.2.
The provisions of Section 654.1 of the Penal Code shall not apply to the selling, furnishing, or providing of transportation of any person or persons in any of the following circumstances:
(a) When no compensation is paid or to be paid, either directly or indirectly, for the transportation.
(b) For the furnishing or providing of transportation to or from work of employees engaged in farmwork on any farm of the State of California.
(c) For the furnishing or providing of transportation to and from work of employees of any nonprofit cooperative association, organized pursuant to any law of the State of California.
(d) For the transportation of persons wholly or substantially within the limits of a single municipality or of contiguous municipalities.
(e) For transportation of persons over a route wholly or partly within a national park or state park where the transportation is sold in conjunction with, or as part of, a rail trip or trip over a regularly operated motorbus transportation system or line.
(f) For the transportation of persons between home and work locations or of persons having a common work-related trip purpose in a vehicle having a seating capacity of 15 passengers or less, including the driver, which is used for the purpose of ridesharing, as defined in Section 522 of the Vehicle Code, when the ridesharing is incidental to another purpose of the driver. This exemption does not apply if the primary purpose for the transportation of those persons is to make a profit. "Profit," as used in this subdivision, does not include the recovery of the actual costs incurred in owning and operating a vanpool vehicle, as defined in Section 668 of the Vehicle Code.
(Amended by Stats. 1982, Ch. 185, Sec. 2.)
654.3.
Violation of Section 654.1 shall be a misdemeanor, and upon first conviction the punishment shall be a fine of not over five hundred dollars ($500), or imprisonment in jail for not over 90 days, or both such fine and imprisonment. Upon second conviction the punishment shall be imprisonment in jail for not less than 30 days and not more than 180 days. Upon a third or subsequent conviction the punishment shall be confinement in jail for not less than 90 days and not more than one year, and a person suffering three or more convictions shall not be eligible to probation, the provisions of any law to the contrary notwithstanding.
(Amended by Stats. 1983, Ch. 1092, Sec. 319. Effective September 27, 1983. Operative January 1, 1984, by Sec. 427 of Ch. 1092.)
655.
An act or omission declared punishable by this Code is not less so because it is also punishable under the laws of another State, Government, or country, unless the contrary is expressly declared.
(Enacted 1872.)
656.
Whenever on the trial of an accused person it appears that upon a criminal prosecution under the laws of the United States, or of another state or territory of the United States based upon the act or omission in respect to which he or she is on trial, he or she has been acquitted or convicted, it is a sufficient defense.
(Amended by Stats. 2004, Ch. 511, Sec. 1. Effective January 1, 2005.)
656.5.
Any person convicted of a crime based upon an act or omission for which he or she has been acquitted or convicted in another country shall be entitled to credit for any actual time served in custody in a penal institution in that country for the crime, and for any additional time credits that would have actually been awarded had the person been incarcerated in California.
(Added by Stats. 2004, Ch. 511, Sec. 2. Effective January 1, 2005.)
656.6.
No international treaties or laws shall be violated to secure the return of a person who has been convicted in another country of a crime committed in California in order to prosecute the person in California.
(Added by Stats. 2004, Ch. 511, Sec. 3. Effective January 1, 2005.)
657.
A criminal act is not the less punishable as a crime because it is also declared to be punishable as a contempt.
(Enacted 1872.)
658.
When it appears, at the time of passing sentence upon a person convicted upon indictment, that such person has already paid a fine or suffered an imprisonment for the act of which he stands convicted, under an order adjudging it a contempt, the Court authorized to pass sentence may mitigate the punishment to be imposed, in its discretion.
(Enacted 1872.)
659.
Whenever an act is declared a misdemeanor, and no punishment for counseling or aiding in the commission of such act is expressly prescribed by law, every person who counsels or aids another in the commission of such act is guilty of a misdemeanor.
(Enacted 1872.)
660.
In the various cases in which the sending of a letter is made criminal by this Code, the offense is deemed complete from the time when such letter is deposited in any Post Office or any other place, or delivered to any person, with intent that it shall be forwarded.
(Enacted 1872.)
661.
In addition to the penalty affixed by express terms, to every neglect or violation of official duty on the part of public officers, State, county, city, or township, where it is not so expressly provided, they may, in the discretion of the Court, be removed from office.
(Enacted 1872.)
662.
No person is punishable for an omission to perform an act, where such act has been performed by another person acting in his behalf and competent by law to perform it.
(Enacted 1872.)
663.

Any person may be convicted of an attempt to commit a crime, although it appears on the trial that the crime intended or attempted was perpetrated by such person in pursuance of such attempt, unless the Court, in its discretion, discharges the jury and directs such person to be tried for such crime.

(Enacted 1872.)

664.

Every person who attempts to commit any crime, but fails, or is prevented or intercepted in its perpetration, shall be punished where no provision is made by law for the punishment of those attempts, as follows:

(a) If the crime attempted is punishable by imprisonment in the state prison, or by imprisonment pursuant to subdivision (h) of Section 1170, the person guilty of the attempt shall be punished by imprisonment in the state prison or in a county jail, respectively, for one-half the term of imprisonment prescribed upon a conviction of the offense attempted. However, if the crime attempted is willful, deliberate, and premeditated murder, as defined in Section 189, the person guilty of that attempt shall be punished by imprisonment in the state prison for life with the possibility of parole. If the crime attempted is any other one in which the maximum sentence is life imprisonment or death, the person guilty of the attempt shall be punished by imprisonment in the state prison for five, seven, or nine years. The additional term provided in this section for attempted willful, deliberate, and premeditated murder shall not be imposed unless the fact that the attempted murder was willful, deliberate, and premeditated is charged in the accusatory pleading and admitted or found to be true by the trier of fact.

(b) If the crime attempted is punishable by imprisonment in a county jail, the person guilty of the attempt shall be punished by imprisonment in a county jail for a term not exceeding one-half the term of imprisonment prescribed upon a conviction of the offense attempted.

(c) If the offense so attempted is punishable by a fine, the offender convicted of that attempt shall be punished by a fine not exceeding one-half the largest fine which may be imposed upon a conviction of the offense attempted.

(d) If a crime is divided into degrees, an attempt to commit the crime may be of any of those degrees, and the punishment for the attempt shall be determined as provided by this section.

(e) Notwithstanding subdivision (a), if attempted murder is committed upon a peace officer or firefighter, as those terms are defined in paragraphs (7) and (9) of subdivision (a) of Section 190.2, a custodial officer, as that term is defined in subdivision (a) of Section 831 or subdivision (a) of Section 831.5, a custody assistant, as that term is defined in subdivision (a) of Section 831.7, or a nonsworn uniformed employee of a sheriff's department whose job entails the care or control of inmates in a detention facility, as defined in subdivision (c) of Section 289.6, and the person who commits the offense knows or reasonably should know that the victim is a peace officer, firefighter, custodial officer, custody assistant, or nonsworn uniformed employee of a sheriff's department engaged in the performance of his or her duties, the person guilty of the attempt shall be punished by imprisonment in the state prison for life with the possibility of parole.

This subdivision shall apply if it is proven that a direct but ineffectual act was committed by one person toward killing another human being and the person committing the act harbored express malice aforethought, namely, a specific intent to unlawfully kill another human being. The Legislature finds and declares that this paragraph is declaratory of existing law.

(f) Notwithstanding subdivision (a), if the elements of subdivision (e) are proven in an attempted murder and it is also charged and admitted or found to be true by the trier of fact that the attempted murder was willful, deliberate, and premeditated, the person guilty of the attempt shall be punished by imprisonment in the state prison for 15 years to life. Article 2.5 (commencing with Section 2930) of Chapter 7 of Title 1 of Part 3 shall not apply to reduce this minimum term of 15 years in state prison, and the person shall not be released prior to serving 15 years' confinement.

(Amended by Stats. 2011, Ch. 15, Sec. 439. (AB 109) Effective April 4, 2011. Operative October 1, 2011, by Sec. 636 of Ch. 15, as amended by Stats. 2011, Ch. 39, Sec. 68.)

665.

Sections 663 and 664 do not protect a person who, in attempting unsuccessfully to commit a crime, accomplishes the commission of another and different crime, whether greater or less in guilt, from suffering the punishment prescribed by law for the crime committed.

(Amended by Stats. 1987, Ch. 828, Sec. 45.)

666.

(a) Notwithstanding Section 490, any person described in subdivision (b) who, having been convicted of petty theft, grand theft, a conviction pursuant to subdivision (d) or (e) of Section 368, auto theft under Section 10851 of the Vehicle Code, burglary, carjacking, robbery, or a felony violation of Section 496, and having served a term of imprisonment therefor in any penal institution or having been imprisoned therein as a condition of probation for that offense, and who is subsequently convicted of petty theft, is punishable by imprisonment in the county jail not exceeding one year, or in the state prison.

(b) Subdivision (a) shall apply to any person who is required to register pursuant to the Sex Offender Registration Act, or who has a prior violent or serious felony conviction, as specified in clause (iv) of subparagraph (C) of paragraph (2) of subdivision (e) of Section 667, or has a conviction pursuant to subdivision (d) or (e) of Section 368.

(c) This section shall not be construed to preclude prosecution or punishment pursuant to subdivisions (b) to (i), inclusive, of Section 667, or Section 1170.12.

(Amended November 4, 2014, by initiative Proposition 47, Sec. 10.)

666.5.

(a) Every person who, having been previously convicted of a felony violation of Section 10851 of the Vehicle Code, or felony grand theft involving an automobile in violation of subdivision (d) of Section 487 or former subdivision (3) of Section 487, as that section read prior to being amended by Section 4 of Chapter 1125 of the Statutes of 1993, or felony grand theft involving a motor vehicle, as defined in Section 415 of the Vehicle Code, any trailer, as defined in Section 630 of the Vehicle Code, any special construction equipment, as defined in Section 565 of the Vehicle Code, or any vessel, as defined in Section 21 of the Harbors and Navigation Code in violation of former Section 487h, or a felony violation of Section 496d regardless of whether or not the person actually served a prior prison term for those offenses, is subsequently convicted of any of these offenses shall be punished by imprisonment pursuant to subdivision (h) of Section 1170 for two, three, or four years, or a fine of ten thousand dollars ($10,000), or both the fine and the imprisonment.

(b) For the purposes of this section, the terms "special construction equipment" and "vessel" are limited to motorized vehicles and vessels.

(c) The existence of any fact which would bring a person under subdivision (a) shall be alleged in the information or indictment and either admitted by the defendant in open court, or found to be true by the jury trying the issue of guilt or by the court where guilt is established by plea of guilty or nolo contendere or by trial by the court sitting without a jury.

(Amended by Stats. 2011, Ch. 15, Sec. 441. (AB 109) Effective April 4, 2011. Operative October 1, 2011, by Sec. 636 of Ch. 15, as amended by Stats. 2011, Ch. 39, Sec. 68.)

667.

(a) (1) Any person convicted of a serious felony who previously has been convicted of a serious felony in this state or of any offense committed in another jurisdiction which includes all of the elements of any serious felony, shall receive, in addition to the sentence imposed by the court for the present offense, a five-year enhancement for each such prior conviction on charges brought and tried separately. The terms of the present offense and each enhancement shall run consecutively.

(2) This subdivision shall not be applied when the punishment imposed under other provisions of law would result in a longer term of imprisonment. There is no requirement of prior incarceration or commitment for this subdivision to apply.

(3) The Legislature may increase the length of the enhancement of sentence provided in this subdivision by a statute passed by majority vote of each house thereof.

(4) As used in this subdivision, "serious felony" means a serious felony listed in subdivision (c) of Section 1192.7.

(5) This subdivision shall not apply to a person convicted of selling, furnishing, administering, or giving, or offering to sell, furnish, administer, or give to a minor any methamphetamine-related drug or any precursors of methamphetamine unless the prior conviction was for a serious felony described in subparagraph (24) of subdivision (c) of Section 1192.7.

(b) It is the intent of the Legislature in enacting subdivisions (b) to (i), inclusive, to ensure longer prison sentences and greater punishment for those who commit a felony and have been previously convicted of one or more serious or violent felony offenses.

(c) Notwithstanding any other law, if a defendant has been convicted of a felony and it has been pled and proved that the defendant has one or more prior serious or violent felony convictions as defined in subdivision (d), the court shall adhere to each of the following:

(1) There shall not be an aggregate term limitation for purposes of consecutive sentencing for any subsequent felony conviction.

(2) Probation for the current offense shall not be granted, nor shall execution or imposition of the sentence be suspended for any prior offense.

(3) The length of time between the prior serious or violent felony conviction and the current felony conviction shall not affect the imposition of sentence.

(4) There shall not be a commitment to any other facility other than the state prison. Diversion shall not be granted nor shall the defendant be eligible for commitment to the California Rehabilitation Center as provided in Article 2 (commencing with Section 3050) of Chapter 1 of Division 3 of the Welfare and Institutions Code.

(5) The total amount of credits awarded pursuant to Article 2.5 (commencing with Section 2930) of Chapter 7 of Title 1 of Part 3 shall not exceed one-fifth of the total term of imprisonment imposed and shall not accrue until the defendant is physically placed in the state prison.

(6) If there is a current conviction for more than one felony count not committed on the same occasion, and not arising from the same set of operative facts, the court shall sentence the defendant consecutively on each count pursuant to subdivision (e).

(7) If there is a current conviction for more than one serious or violent felony as described in paragraph (6), the court shall impose the sentence for each conviction consecutive to the sentence for any other conviction for which the defendant may be consecutively sentenced in the manner prescribed by law.

(8) Any sentence imposed pursuant to subdivision (e) will be imposed consecutive to any other sentence which the defendant is already serving, unless otherwise provided by law.

(d) Notwithstanding any other law and for the purposes of subdivisions (b) to (i), inclusive, a prior conviction of a serious and/or violent felony shall be defined as:

(1) Any offense defined in subdivision (c) of Section 667.5 as a violent felony or any offense defined in subdivision (c) of Section 1192.7 as a serious felony in this state. The determination of whether a prior conviction is a prior felony conviction for purposes of subdivisions (b) to (i), inclusive, shall be made upon the date of that prior conviction and is not affected by the sentence imposed unless the sentence automatically, upon the initial sentencing, converts the felony to a misdemeanor. None of the following dispositions shall affect the determination that a prior conviction is a prior felony for purposes of subdivisions (b) to (i), inclusive:

(A) The suspension of imposition of judgment or sentence.

(B) The stay of execution of sentence.

(C) The commitment to the State Department of Health Services as a mentally disordered sex offender following a conviction of a felony.

(D) The commitment to the California Rehabilitation Center or any other facility whose function is rehabilitative diversion from the state prison.

(2) A prior conviction in another jurisdiction for an offense that, if committed in California, is punishable by imprisonment in the state prison shall constitute a prior conviction of a particular serious and/or violent felony if the prior conviction in the other jurisdiction is for an offense that includes all of the elements of a particular violent felony as defined in subdivision (c) of Section 667.5 or serious felony as defined in subdivision (c) of Section 1192.7.

(3) A prior juvenile adjudication shall constitute a prior serious and/or violent felony conviction for purposes of sentence enhancement if:

(A) The juvenile was 16 years of age or older at the time he or she committed the prior offense.

(B) The prior offense is listed in subdivision (b) of Section 707 of the Welfare and Institutions Code or described in paragraph (1) or (2) as a serious or violent felony.

(C) The juvenile was found to be a fit and proper subject to be dealt with under the juvenile court law.

(D) The juvenile was adjudged a ward of the juvenile court within the meaning of Section 602 of the Welfare and Institutions Code because the person committed an offense listed in subdivision (b) of Section 707 of the Welfare and Institutions Code.

(e) For purposes of subdivisions (b) to (i), inclusive, and in addition to any other enhancement or punishment provisions which may apply, the following shall apply where a defendant has one or more prior serious or violent felony convictions:

(1) If a defendant has one prior serious or violent felony conviction as defined in subdivision (d) that has been pled and proved, the determinate term or minimum term for an indeterminate term shall be twice the term otherwise provided as punishment for the current felony conviction.

(2) (A) Except as provided in subparagraph (C), if a defendant has two or more prior serious or violent felony convictions as defined in subdivision (d) that have been pled and proved, the term for the current felony conviction shall be an indeterminate term of life imprisonment with a minimum term of the indeterminate sentence calculated as the greatest of:

(i) Three times the term otherwise provided as punishment for each current felony conviction subsequent to the two or more prior serious or violent felony convictions.

(ii) Imprisonment in the state prison for 25 years.

(iii) The term determined by the court pursuant to Section 1170 for the underlying conviction, including any enhancement applicable under Chapter 4.5 (commencing with Section 1170) of Title 7 of Part 2, or any period prescribed by Section 190 or 3046.

(B) The indeterminate term described in subparagraph (A) shall be served consecutive to any other term of imprisonment for which a consecutive term may be imposed by law. Any other term imposed subsequent to any indeterminate term described in subparagraph (A) shall not be merged therein but shall commence at the time the person would otherwise have been released from prison.

(C) If a defendant has two or more prior serious or violent felony convictions as defined in subdivision (c) of Section 667.5 or subdivision (c) of Section 1192.7 that have been pled and proved, and the current offense is not a serious or violent felony as defined in subdivision (d), the defendant shall be sentenced pursuant to paragraph (1) of subdivision (e) unless the prosecution pleads and proves any of the following:

(i) The current offense is a controlled substance charge, in which an allegation under Section 11370.4 or 11379.8 of the Health and Safety Code was admitted or found true.

(ii) The current offense is a felony sex offense, defined in subdivision (d) of Section 261.5 or Section 262, or any felony offense that results in mandatory registration as a sex offender pursuant to subdivision (c) of Section 290 except for violations of Sections 266 and 285, paragraph (1) of subdivision (b) and subdivision (e) of Section 286, paragraph (1) of subdivision (b) and subdivision (e) of Section 288a, Section 311.11, and Section 314.

(iii) During the commission of the current offense, the defendant used a firearm, was armed with a firearm or deadly weapon, or intended to cause great bodily injury to another person.

(iv) The defendant suffered a prior serious or violent felony conviction, as defined in subdivision (d) of this section, for any of the following felonies:

(I) A "sexually violent offense" as defined in subdivision (b) of Section 6600 of the Welfare and Institutions Code.

(II) Oral copulation with a child who is under 14 years of age, and who is more than 10 years younger than he or she as defined by Section 288a, sodomy with another person who is under 14 years of age and more than 10 years younger than he or she as defined by Section 286, or sexual penetration with another person who is under 14 years of age, and who is more than 10 years younger than he or she, as defined by Section 289.

(III) A lewd or lascivious act involving a child under 14 years of age, in violation of Section 288.

(IV) Any homicide offense, including any attempted homicide offense, defined in Sections 187 to 191.5, inclusive.

(V) Solicitation to commit murder as defined in Section 653f.

(VI) Assault with a machine gun on a peace officer or firefighter, as defined in paragraph (3) of subdivision (d) of Section 245.

(VII) Possession of a weapon of mass destruction, as defined in paragraph (1) of subdivision (a) of Section 11418.

(VIII) Any serious or violent felony offense punishable in California by life imprisonment or death.

(f) (1) Notwithstanding any other law, subdivisions (b) to (i), inclusive, shall be applied in every case in which a defendant has one or more prior serious or violent felony convictions as defined in subdivision (d). The prosecuting attorney shall plead and prove each prior serious or violent felony conviction except as provided in paragraph (2).

(2) The prosecuting attorney may move to dismiss or strike a prior serious or violent felony conviction allegation in the furtherance of justice pursuant to Section 1385, or if there is insufficient evidence to prove the prior serious or violent felony conviction. If upon the satisfaction of the court that there is insufficient evidence to prove the prior serious or violent felony conviction, the court may dismiss or strike the allegation. Nothing in this section shall be read to alter a court's authority under Section 1385.

(g) Prior serious or violent felony convictions shall not be used in plea bargaining as defined in subdivision (b) of Section 1192.7. The prosecution shall plead and prove all known prior felony serious or violent convictions and shall not enter into any agreement to strike or seek the dismissal of any prior serious and/or violent felony conviction allegation except as provided in paragraph (2) of subdivision (f).

(h) All references to existing statutes in subdivisions (c) to (g), inclusive, are to statutes as they existed on November 7, 2012.

(i) If any provision of subdivisions (b) to (h), inclusive, or the application thereof to any person or circumstance is held invalid, that invalidity shall not affect other provisions or applications of those subdivisions which can be given effect without the invalid provision or application, and to this end the provisions of those subdivisions are severable.

(j) The provisions of this section shall not be amended by the Legislature except by statute passed in each house by rollcall vote entered in the journal, two-thirds of the membership concurring, or by a statute that becomes effective only when approved by the electors.

(Amended by Stats. 2018, Ch. 1013, Sec. 1. (SB 1393) Effective January 1, 2019. Note: This section was added on June 8, 1982, by initiative Prop. 8.)

667.1.
Notwithstanding subdivision (h) of Section 667, for all offenses committed on or after November 7, 2012, all references to existing statutes in subdivisions (c) to (g), inclusive, of Section 667, are to those statutes as they existed on November 7, 2012.
(Amended November 6, 2012, by initiative Proposition 36, Sec. 3. Note: This section was added on March 7, 2000, by initiative Prop. 21.)

667.2.
(a) The Legislature finds and declares that assisting offenders released pursuant to Proposition 36, adopted at the November 6, 2012, statewide general election, with their transition back into communities will increase the offenders' likelihood of successful reintegration.

(b) Subject to the availability of funding for and space in the programs and services, the Department of Corrections and Rehabilitation may provide programs and services, including, but not limited to, transitional housing, mental health, and substance abuse treatment to an offender who is released from the department's custody and satisfies both of the following conditions:

(1) The offender is released pursuant to any of the following provisions, as they were amended or added by Sections 2 to 6, inclusive, of Proposition 36, as adopted at the November 6, 2012, statewide general election:

(A) Section 667.
(B) Section 667.1.
(C) Section 1170.12.
(D) Section 1170.125.
(E) Section 1170.126.

(2) The offender is not subject to either of the following:

(A) Parole pursuant to Article 3 (commencing with Section 3040) of Chapter 8 of Title 1 of Part 3.

(B) Postrelease community supervision pursuant to Title 2.05 (commencing with Section 3450) of Part 3.

(c) (1) The Department of Corrections and Rehabilitation, in consultation with the Administrative Office of the Courts, shall establish a referral process for offenders described in subdivision (b) to participate in programs and receive services that the department has existing contracts to provide.

(2) The Administrative Office of the Courts shall inform courts of the availability of the programs and services described in this section.
(Added by Stats. 2014, Ch. 26, Sec. 12. (AB 1468) Effective June 20, 2014.)

667.5.
Enhancement of prison terms for new offenses because of prior prison terms shall be imposed as follows:

(a) Where one of the new offenses is one of the violent felonies specified in subdivision (c), in addition to and consecutive to any other prison terms therefor, the court shall impose a three-year term for each prior separate prison term served by the defendant where the prior offense was one of the violent felonies specified in subdivision (c). However, no additional term shall be imposed under this subdivision for any prison term served prior to a period of 10 years in which the defendant remained free of both prison custody and the commission of an offense which results in a felony conviction.

(b) Except where subdivision (a) applies, where the new offense is any felony for which a prison sentence or a sentence of imprisonment in a county jail under subdivision (h) of Section 1170 is imposed or is not suspended, in addition and consecutive to any other sentence therefor, the court shall impose a one-year term for each prior separate prison term or county jail term imposed under subdivision (h) of Section 1170 or when sentence is not suspended for any felony; provided that no additional term shall be

imposed under this subdivision for any prison term or county jail term imposed under subdivision (h) of Section 1170 or when sentence is not suspended prior to a period of five years in which the defendant remained free of both the commission of an offense which results in a felony conviction, and prison custody or the imposition of a term of jail custody imposed under subdivision (h) of Section 1170 or any felony sentence that is not suspended. A term imposed under the provisions of paragraph (5) of subdivision (h) of Section 1170, wherein a portion of the term is suspended by the court to allow mandatory supervision, shall qualify as a prior county jail term for the purposes of the one-year enhancement.

(c) For the purpose of this section, "violent felony" shall mean any of the following:
(1) Murder or voluntary manslaughter.
(2) Mayhem.
(3) Rape as defined in paragraph (2) or (6) of subdivision (a) of Section 261 or paragraph (1) or (4) of subdivision (a) of Section 262.
(4) Sodomy as defined in subdivision (c) or (d) of Section 286.
(5) Oral copulation as defined in subdivision (c) or (d) of Section 287 or of former Section 288a.
(6) Lewd or lascivious act as defined in subdivision (a) or (b) of Section 288.
(7) Any felony punishable by death or imprisonment in the state prison for life.
(8) Any felony in which the defendant inflicts great bodily injury on any person other than an accomplice which has been charged and proved as provided for in Section 12022.7, 12022.8, or 12022.9 on or after July 1, 1977, or as specified prior to July 1, 1977, in Sections 213, 264, and 461, or any felony in which the defendant uses a firearm which use has been charged and proved as provided in subdivision (a) of Section 12022.3, or Section 12022.5 or 12022.55.
(9) Any robbery.
(10) Arson, in violation of subdivision (a) or (b) of Section 451.
(11) Sexual penetration as defined in subdivision (a) or (j) of Section 289.
(12) Attempted murder.
(13) A violation of Section 18745, 18750, or 18755.
(14) Kidnapping.
(15) Assault with the intent to commit a specified felony, in violation of Section 220.
(16) Continuous sexual abuse of a child, in violation of Section 288.5.
(17) Carjacking, as defined in subdivision (a) of Section 215.
(18) Rape, spousal rape, or sexual penetration, in concert, in violation of Section 264.1.
(19) Extortion, as defined in Section 518, which would constitute a felony violation of Section 186.22.
(20) Threats to victims or witnesses, as defined in Section 136.1, which would constitute a felony violation of Section 186.22.
(21) Any burglary of the first degree, as defined in subdivision (a) of Section 460, wherein it is charged and proved that another person, other than an accomplice, was present in the residence during the commission of the burglary.
(22) Any violation of Section 12022.53.
(23) A violation of subdivision (b) or (c) of Section 11418. The Legislature finds and declares that these specified crimes merit special consideration when imposing a sentence to display society's condemnation for these extraordinary crimes of violence against the person.

(d) For the purposes of this section, the defendant shall be deemed to remain in prison custody for an offense until the official discharge from custody, including any period of mandatory supervision, or until release on parole or postrelease community supervision, whichever first occurs, including any time during which the defendant remains subject to reimprisonment or custody in county jail for escape from custody or is reimprisoned on revocation of parole or postrelease community supervision. The additional penalties provided for prior prison terms shall not be imposed unless they are charged and admitted or found true in the action for the new offense.

(e) The additional penalties provided for prior prison terms shall not be imposed for any felony for which the defendant did not serve a prior separate term in state prison or in county jail under subdivision (h) of Section 1170.

(f) A prior conviction of a felony shall include a conviction in another jurisdiction for an offense which, if committed in California, is punishable by imprisonment in the state prison or in county jail under subdivision (h) of Section 1170 if the defendant served one year or more in prison for the offense in the other jurisdiction. A prior conviction of a particular felony shall include a conviction in another jurisdiction for an offense which includes all of the elements of the particular felony as defined under California law if the defendant served one year or more in prison for the offense in the other jurisdiction.

(g) A prior separate prison term for the purposes of this section shall mean a continuous completed period of prison incarceration imposed for the particular offense alone or in combination with concurrent or consecutive sentences for other crimes, including any reimprisonment on revocation of parole which is not accompanied by a new commitment to prison, and including any reimprisonment after an escape from incarceration.

(h) Serving a prison term includes any confinement time in any state prison or federal penal institution as punishment for commission of an offense, including confinement in a hospital or other institution or facility credited as service of prison time in the jurisdiction of the confinement.

(i) For the purposes of this section, a commitment to the State Department of Mental Health, or its successor the State Department of State Hospitals, as a mentally disordered sex offender following a conviction of a felony, which commitment exceeds one year in duration, shall be deemed a prior prison term.

(j) For the purposes of this section, when a person subject to the custody, control, and discipline of the Secretary of the Department of Corrections and Rehabilitation is incarcerated at a facility operated by the Division of Juvenile Justice, that incarceration shall be deemed to be a term served in state prison.

(k) (1) Notwithstanding subdivisions (d) and (g) or any other provision of law, where one of the new offenses is committed while the defendant is temporarily removed from prison pursuant to Section 2690 or while the defendant is transferred to a community facility pursuant to Section 3416, 6253, or 6263, or while the defendant is on furlough pursuant to Section 6254, the defendant shall be subject to the full enhancements provided for in this section.

(2) This subdivision shall not apply when a full, separate, and consecutive term is imposed pursuant to any other provision of law.
(Amended by Stats. 2018, Ch. 423, Sec. 65. (SB 1494) Effective January 1, 2019. Note: This section was amended on March 7, 2000, by initiative Prop. 21, and on Nov. 7, 2006, by initiative Prop. 83.)

667.51.
(a) Any person who is convicted of violating Section 288 or 288.5 shall receive a five-year enhancement for a prior conviction of an offense specified in subdivision (b).
(b) Section 261, 262, 264.1, 269, 285, 286, 287, 288, 288.5, or 289, former Section 288a, or any offense committed in another jurisdiction that includes all of the elements of any of the offenses specified in this subdivision.
(c) A violation of Section 288 or 288.5 by a person who has been previously convicted two or more times of an offense specified in subdivision (b) shall be punished by imprisonment in the state prison for 15 years to life.
(Amended by Stats. 2018, Ch. 423, Sec. 66. (SB 1494) Effective January 1, 2019. Note: This section was amended November 7, 2006, by initiative Proposition 83.)

667.6.
(a) Any person who is convicted of an offense specified in subdivision (e) and who has been convicted previously of any of those offenses shall receive a five-year enhancement for each of those prior convictions.

(b) Any person who is convicted of an offense specified in subdivision (e) and who has served two or more prior prison terms as defined in Section 667.5 for any of those offenses shall receive a 10-year enhancement for each of those prior terms.
(c) In lieu of the term provided in Section 1170.1, a full, separate, and consecutive term may be imposed for each violation of an offense specified in subdivision (e) if the crimes involve the same victim on the same occasion. A term may be imposed consecutively pursuant to this subdivision if a person is convicted of at least one offense specified in subdivision (e). If the term is imposed consecutively pursuant to this subdivision, it shall be served consecutively to any other term of imprisonment, and shall commence from the time the person otherwise would have been released from imprisonment. The term shall not be included in any determination pursuant to Section 1170.1. Any other term imposed subsequent to that term shall not be merged therein but shall commence at the time the person otherwise would have been released from prison.
(d) A full, separate, and consecutive term shall be imposed for each violation of an offense specified in subdivision (e) if the crimes involve separate victims or involve the same victim on separate occasions.
In determining whether crimes against a single victim were committed on separate occasions under this subdivision, the court shall consider whether, between the commission of one sex crime and another, the defendant had a reasonable opportunity to reflect upon his or her actions and nevertheless resumed sexually assaultive behavior. Neither the duration of time between crimes, nor whether or not the defendant lost or abandoned his or her opportunity to attack, shall be, in and of itself, determinative on the issue of whether the crimes in question occurred on separate occasions.
The term shall be served consecutively to any other term of imprisonment and shall commence from the time the person otherwise would have been released from imprisonment. The term shall not be included in any determination pursuant to Section 1170.1. Any other term imposed subsequent to that term shall not be merged therein but shall commence at the time the person otherwise would have been released from prison.
(e) This section shall apply to the following offenses:
(1) Rape, in violation of paragraph (2), (3), (6), or (7) of subdivision (a) of Section 261.
(2) Spousal rape, in violation of paragraph (1), (4), or (5) of subdivision (a) of Section 262.
(3) Rape, spousal rape, or sexual penetration, in concert, in violation of Section 264.1.
(4) Sodomy, in violation of paragraph (2) or (3) of subdivision (c), or subdivision (d) or (k), of Section 286.
(5) Lewd or lascivious act, in violation of subdivision (b) of Section 288.
(6) Continuous sexual abuse of a child, in violation of Section 288.5.
(7) Oral copulation, in violation of paragraph (2) or (3) of subdivision (c), or subdivision (d) or (k), of Section 287 or of former Section 288a.
(8) Sexual penetration, in violation of subdivision (a) or (g) of Section 289.
(9) As a present offense under subdivision (c) or (d), assault with intent to commit a specified sexual offense, in violation of Section 220.
(10) As a prior conviction under subdivision (a) or (b), an offense committed in another jurisdiction that includes all of the elements of an offense specified in this subdivision.
(f) In addition to any enhancement imposed pursuant to subdivision (a) or (b), the court may also impose a fine not to exceed twenty thousand dollars ($20,000) for anyone sentenced under those provisions. The fine imposed and collected pursuant to this subdivision shall be deposited in the Victim-Witness Assistance Fund to be available for appropriation to fund child sexual exploitation and child sexual abuse victim counseling centers and prevention programs established pursuant to Section 13837. If the court orders a fine to be imposed pursuant to this subdivision, the actual administrative cost of collecting that fine, not to exceed 2 percent of the total amount paid, may be paid into the general fund of the county treasury for the use and benefit of the county.
(Amended by Stats. 2018, Ch. 423, Sec. 67. (SB 1494) Effective January 1, 2019. Note: This section was amended November 7, 2006, by initiative Proposition 83.)

667.61.

(a) Except as provided in subdivision (j), (l), or (m), any person who is convicted of an offense specified in subdivision (c) under one or more of the circumstances specified in subdivision (d) or under two or more of the circumstances specified in subdivision (e) shall be punished by imprisonment in the state prison for 25 years to life.
(b) Except as provided in subdivision (a), (j), (l), or (m), any person who is convicted of an offense specified in subdivision (c) under one of the circumstances specified in subdivision (e) shall be punished by imprisonment in the state prison for 15 years to life.
(c) This section shall apply to any of the following offenses:
(1) Rape, in violation of paragraph (2) or (6) of subdivision (a) of Section 261.
(2) Spousal rape, in violation of paragraph (1) or (4) of subdivision (a) of Section 262.
(3) Rape, spousal rape, or sexual penetration, in concert, in violation of Section 264.1.
(4) Lewd or lascivious act, in violation of subdivision (b) of Section 288.
(5) Sexual penetration, in violation of subdivision (a) of Section 289.
(6) Sodomy, in violation of paragraph (2) or (3) of subdivision (c), or subdivision (d), of Section 286.
(7) Oral copulation, in violation of paragraph (2) or (3) of subdivision (c), or subdivision (d), of Section 287 or former Section 288a.
(8) Lewd or lascivious act, in violation of subdivision (a) of Section 288.
(9) Continuous sexual abuse of a child, in violation of Section 288.5.
(d) The following circumstances shall apply to the offenses specified in subdivision (c):
(1) The defendant has been previously convicted of an offense specified in subdivision (c), including an offense committed in another jurisdiction that includes all of the elements of an offense specified in subdivision (c).
(2) The defendant kidnapped the victim of the present offense and the movement of the victim substantially increased the risk of harm to the victim over and above that level of risk necessarily inherent in the underlying offense in subdivision (c).
(3) The defendant inflicted aggravated mayhem or torture on the victim or another person in the commission of the present offense in violation of Section 205 or 206.
(4) The defendant committed the present offense during the commission of a burglary of the first degree, as defined in subdivision (a) of Section 460, with intent to commit an offense specified in subdivision (c).
(5) The defendant committed the present offense in violation of Section 264.1, subdivision (d) of Section 286, or subdivision (d) of Section 287 or former Section 288a, and, in the commission of that offense, any person committed any act described in paragraph (2), (3), or (4) of this subdivision.
(6) The defendant personally inflicted great bodily injury on the victim or another person in the commission of the present offense in violation of Section 12022.53, 12022.7, or 12022.8.
(7) The defendant personally inflicted bodily harm on the victim who was under 14 years of age.
(e) The following circumstances shall apply to the offenses specified in subdivision (c):
(1) Except as provided in paragraph (2) of subdivision (d), the defendant kidnapped the victim of the present offense in violation of Section 207, 209, or 209.5.
(2) Except as provided in paragraph (4) of subdivision (d), the defendant committed the present offense during the commission of a burglary in violation of Section 459.
(3) The defendant personally used a dangerous or deadly weapon or a firearm in the commission of the present offense in violation of Section 12022, 12022.3, 12022.5, or 12022.53.
(4) The defendant has been convicted in the present case or cases of committing an offense specified in subdivision (c) against more than one victim.
(5) The defendant engaged in the tying or binding of the victim or another person in the commission of the present offense.
(6) The defendant administered a controlled substance to the victim in the commission of the present offense in violation of Section 12022.75.
(7) The defendant committed the present offense in violation of Section 264.1, subdivision (d) of Section 286, or subdivision (d) of Section 287 or former Section 288a, and, in the commission of that offense, any person committed any act described in paragraph (1), (2), (3), (5), or (6) of this subdivision or paragraph (6) of subdivision (d).
(f) If only the minimum number of circumstances specified in subdivision (d) or (e) that are required for the punishment provided in subdivision (a), (b), (j), (l), or (m) to apply have been pled and proved, that circumstance or those circumstances shall be used as the basis for imposing the term provided in subdivision (a), (b), (j), (l), or (m) whichever is greater, rather than being used to impose the punishment authorized under any other provision of law, unless another provision of law provides for a greater penalty or the punishment under another provision of law can be imposed in addition to the punishment provided by this section. However, if any additional circumstance or circumstances specified in subdivision (d) or (e) have been pled and proved, the minimum number of circumstances shall be used as the basis for imposing the term provided in subdivision (a), (j), or (l) and any other additional circumstance or circumstances shall be used to impose any punishment or enhancement authorized under any other provision of law.
(g) Notwithstanding Section 1385 or any other provision of law, the court shall not strike any allegation, admission, or finding of any of the circumstances specified in subdivision (d) or (e) for any person who is subject to punishment under this section.
(h) Notwithstanding any other provision of law, probation shall not be granted to, nor shall the execution or imposition of sentence be suspended for, any person who is subject to punishment under this section.
(i) For any offense specified in paragraphs (1) to (7), inclusive, of subdivision (c), or in paragraphs (1) to (6), inclusive, of subdivision (n), the court shall impose a consecutive sentence for each offense that results in a conviction under this section if the crimes involve separate victims or involve the same victim on separate occasions as defined in subdivision (d) of Section 667.6.
(j) (1) Any person who is convicted of an offense specified in subdivision (c), with the exception of a violation of subdivision (a) of Section 288, upon a victim who is a child under 14 years of age under one or more of the circumstances specified in subdivision (d) or under two or more of the circumstances specified in subdivision (e), shall be punished by imprisonment in the state prison for life without the possibility of parole. Where the person was under 18 years of age at the time of the offense, the person shall be punished by imprisonment in the state prison for 25 years to life.
(2) Any person who is convicted of an offense specified in subdivision (c) under one of the circumstances specified in subdivision (e), upon a victim who is a child under 14 years of age, shall be punished by imprisonment in the state prison for 25 years to life.
(k) As used in this section, "bodily harm" means any substantial physical injury resulting from the use of force that is more than the force necessary to commit an offense specified in subdivision (c).
(l) Any person who is convicted of an offense specified in subdivision (n) under one or more of the circumstances specified in subdivision (d) or under two or more of the circumstances specified in subdivision (e), upon a victim who is a minor 14 years of age or older shall be punished by imprisonment in the state prison for life without the possibility of parole. If the person who was convicted was under 18 years of age at the time of the offense, he or she shall be punished by imprisonment in the state prison for 25 years to life.
(m) Any person who is convicted of an offense specified in subdivision (n) under one of the circumstances specified in subdivision (e) against a minor 14 years of age or older shall be punished by imprisonment in the state prison for 25 years to life.
(n) Subdivisions (l) and (m) shall apply to any of the following offenses:
(1) Rape, in violation of paragraph (2) of subdivision (a) of Section 261.
(2) Spousal rape, in violation of paragraph (1) of subdivision (a) of Section 262.
(3) Rape, spousal rape, or sexual penetration, in concert, in violation of Section 264.1.
(4) Sexual penetration, in violation of paragraph (1) of subdivision (a) of Section 289.
(5) Sodomy, in violation of paragraph (2) of subdivision (c) of Section 286, or in violation of subdivision (d) of Section 286.
(6) Oral copulation, in violation of paragraph (2) of subdivision (c) of Section 287 or former Section 288a, or in violation of subdivision (d) of Section 287 or former Section 288a.
(o) The penalties provided in this section shall apply only if the existence of any circumstance specified in subdivision (d) or (e) is alleged in the accusatory pleading pursuant to this section, and is either admitted by the defendant in open court or found to be true by the trier of fact.
(Amended by Stats. 2018, Ch. 423, Sec. 68. (SB 1494) Effective January 1, 2019. Note: This section was amended on Nov. 7, 2006, by initiative Prop. 83.)

667.7.

(a) Any person convicted of a felony in which the person inflicted great bodily injury as provided in Section 12022.53 or 12022.7, or personally used force which was likely to produce great bodily injury, who has served two or more prior separate prison terms as defined in Section 667.5 for the crime of murder; attempted murder; voluntary manslaughter; mayhem; rape by force, violence, or fear of immediate and unlawful bodily injury on the victim or another person; oral copulation by force, violence, duress, menace, or fear of immediate and unlawful bodily injury on the victim or another person; sodomy by force, violence, duress, menace, or fear of immediate and unlawful bodily injury on the victim or another person; lewd acts on a child under the age of 14 years by use of force, violence, duress, menace, or fear of immediate and unlawful bodily injury on the victim or another person; a violation of subdivision (a) of Section 289 where the act is accomplished against the victim's will by means of force, violence, duress, menace, or fear of immediate and unlawful bodily injury on the victim or another person; kidnapping as punished in former subdivision (d) of Section 208, or for ransom, extortion, or robbery; robbery involving the use of force or a deadly weapon; carjacking involving the use of a deadly weapon; assault with intent to commit murder; assault with a deadly weapon; assault with a force likely to produce great bodily injury; assault with intent to commit rape, sodomy, oral copulation, sexual penetration in violation of Section 289, or lewd and lascivious acts on a child; arson of a structure; escape or attempted escape by an inmate with force or violence in violation of subdivision (a) of Section 4530, or of Section 4532; exploding a destructive device with intent to murder in violation of Section 18745; exploding a destructive device which causes bodily injury in violation of Section 18750, or mayhem or great bodily injury in violation of Section 18755; exploding a destructive device with intent to injure, intimidate, or terrify, in violation of Section 18740; any felony in which the person inflicted great bodily injury as provided in Section 12022.53 or 12022.7; or any felony punishable by death or life imprisonment with or without the possibility of parole is a habitual offender and shall be punished as follows:
(1) A person who served two prior separate prison terms shall be punished by imprisonment in the state prison for life and shall not be eligible for release on parole for 20 years, or the term determined by the court pursuant to Section 1170 for the underlying conviction, including any enhancement applicable under Chapter 4.5 (commencing with Section 1170) of Title 7 of Part 2, or any period prescribed by Section 190 or 3046, whichever is greatest. Article 2.5 (commencing with Section

2930) of Chapter 7 of Title 1 of Part 3 shall apply to reduce any minimum term in a state prison imposed pursuant to this section, but the person shall not otherwise be released on parole prior to that time.

(2) Any person convicted of a felony specified in this subdivision who has served three or more prior separate prison terms, as defined in Section 667.5, for the crimes specified in subdivision (a) of this section shall be punished by imprisonment in the state prison for life without the possibility of parole.

(b) This section shall not prevent the imposition of the punishment of death or imprisonment for life without the possibility of parole. No prior prison term shall be used for this determination which was served prior to a period of 10 years in which the person remained free of both prison custody and the commission of an offense which results in a felony conviction. As used in this section, a commitment to the Department of the Youth Authority after conviction for a felony shall constitute a prior prison term. The term imposed under this section shall be imposed only if the prior prison terms are alleged under this section in the accusatory pleading, and either admitted by the defendant in open court, or found to be true by the jury trying the issue of guilt or by the court where guilt is established by a plea of guilty or nolo contendere or by a trial by the court sitting without a jury.

(Amended by Stats. 2010, Ch. 178, Sec. 64. (SB 1115) Effective January 1, 2011. Operative January 1, 2012, by Sec. 107 of Ch. 178.)

667.70.

Any person who is convicted of murder, which was committed prior to June 3, 1998, and sentenced pursuant to paragraph (1) of subdivision (a) of Section 667.7, shall be eligible only for credit pursuant to subdivisions (a), (b), and (c) of Section 2931.

(Amended by Stats. 1999, Ch. 706, Sec. 8. Effective October 10, 1999.)

667.71.

(a) For the purpose of this section, a habitual sexual offender is a person who has been previously convicted of one or more of the offenses specified in subdivision (c) and who is convicted in the present proceeding of one of those offenses.

(b) A habitual sexual offender shall be punished by imprisonment in the state prison for 25 years to life.

(c) This section shall apply to any of the following offenses:

(1) Rape, in violation of paragraph (2) or (6) of subdivision (a) of Section 261.

(2) Spousal rape, in violation of paragraph (1) or (4) of subdivision (a) of Section 262.

(3) Rape, spousal rape, or sexual penetration, in concert, in violation of Section 264.1.

(4) Lewd or lascivious act, in violation of subdivision (a) or (b) of Section 288.

(5) Sexual penetration, in violation of subdivision (a) or (j) of Section 289.

(6) Continuous sexual abuse of a child, in violation of Section 288.5.

(7) Sodomy, in violation of subdivision (c) or (d) of Section 286.

(8) Oral copulation, in violation of subdivision (c) or (d) of Section 287 or of former Section 288a.

(9) Kidnapping, in violation of subdivision (b) of Section 207.

(10) Kidnapping, in violation of former subdivision (d) of Section 208 (kidnapping to commit specified sex offenses).

(11) Kidnapping, in violation of subdivision (b) of Section 209 with the intent to commit a specified sexual offense.

(12) Aggravated sexual assault of a child, in violation of Section 269.

(13) An offense committed in another jurisdiction that includes all of the elements of an offense specified in this subdivision.

(d) Notwithstanding Section 1385 or any other provision of law, the court shall not strike any allegation, admission, or finding of any prior conviction specified in subdivision (c) for any person who is subject to punishment under this section.

(e) Notwithstanding any other provision of law, probation shall not be granted to, nor shall the execution or imposition of sentence be suspended for, any person who is subject to punishment under this section.

(f) This section shall apply only if the defendant's status as a habitual sexual offender is alleged in the accusatory pleading, and either admitted by the defendant in open court, or found to be true by the trier of fact.

(Amended by Stats. 2018, Ch. 423, Sec. 69. (SB 1494) Effective January 1, 2019. Note: This section was amended November 7, 2006, by initiative Proposition 83.)

667.75.

Any person convicted of a violation of Section 11353, 11353.5, 11361, 11380, or 11380.5 of the Health and Safety Code who has previously served two or more prior separate prison terms, as defined in Section 667.5, for a violation of Section 11353, 11353.5, 11361, 11380, or 11380.5 of the Health and Safety Code, may be punished by imprisonment in the state prison for life and shall not be eligible for release on parole for 17 years, or the term determined by the court pursuant to Section 1170 for the underlying conviction, including any enhancement applicable under Chapter 4.5 (commencing with Section 1170) of Title 7 of Part 2, whichever is greatest. The provisions of Article 2.5 (commencing with Section 2930) of Chapter 7 of Title 1 of Part 3 shall apply to reduce any minimum term in a state prison imposed pursuant to this section, but the person shall not otherwise be released on parole prior to that time. No prior prison term shall be used for this determination which was served prior to a period of 10 years in which the person remained free of both prison custody and the commission of an offense which results in a felony conviction. As used in this section, a commitment to the Department of the Youth Authority after conviction for a felony shall constitute a prior prison term. The term imposed under this section shall be imposed only if the prior prison terms are alleged under this section in the accusatory pleading, and either admitted by the defendant in open court, or found to be true by the jury trying the issue of guilt or by the court where guilt is established by a plea of guilty or nolo contendere or by a trial by the court sitting without a jury.

(Added by Stats. 1987, Ch. 729, Sec. 1.)

667.8.

(a) Except as provided in subdivision (b), any person convicted of a felony violation of Section 261, 262, 264.1, 286, 287, or 289 or former Section 288a who, for the purpose of committing that sexual offense, kidnapped the victim in violation of Section 207 or 209, shall be punished by an additional term of nine years.

(b) Any person convicted of a felony violation of subdivision (c) of Section 286, subdivision (c) of Section 287 or former Section 288a, or Section 288 who, for the purpose of committing that sexual offense, kidnapped the victim, who was under the age of 14 years at the time of the offense, in violation of Section 207 or 209, shall be punished by an additional term of 15 years. This subdivision is not applicable to conduct proscribed by Section 277, 278, or 278.5.

(c) The following shall govern the imposition of an enhancement pursuant to this section:

(1) Only one enhancement shall be imposed for a victim per incident.

(2) If there are two or more victims, one enhancement can be imposed for each victim per incident.

(3) The enhancement may be in addition to the punishment for either, but not both, of the following:

(A) A violation of Section 207 or 209.

(B) A violation of the sexual offenses enumerated in this section.

(Amended by Stats. 2018, Ch. 423, Sec. 70. (SB 1494) Effective January 1, 2019.)

667.85.

Any person convicted of a violation of Section 207 or 209, who kidnapped or carried away any child under the age of 14 years with the intent to permanently deprive the parent or legal guardian custody of that child, shall be punished by imprisonment in the state prison for an additional five years.

(Amended by Stats. 1997, Ch. 817, Sec. 11. Effective January 1, 1998.)

667.9.

(a) Any person who commits one or more of the crimes specified in subdivision (c) against a person who is 65 years of age or older, or against a person who is blind, deaf, developmentally disabled, a paraplegic, or a quadriplegic, or against a person who is under the age of 14 years, and that disability or condition is known or reasonably should be known to the person committing the crime, shall receive a one-year enhancement for each violation.

(b) Any person who commits a violation of subdivision (a) and who has a prior conviction for any of the offenses specified in subdivision (c), shall receive a two-year enhancement for each violation in addition to the sentence provided under Section 667.

(c) Subdivisions (a) and (b) apply to the following crimes:

(1) Mayhem, in violation of Section 203 or 205.

(2) Kidnapping, in violation of Section 207, 209, or 209.5.

(3) Robbery, in violation of Section 211.

(4) Carjacking, in violation of Section 215.

(5) Rape, in violation of paragraph (2) or (6) of subdivision (a) of Section 261.

(6) Spousal rape, in violation of paragraph (1) or (4) of subdivision (a) of Section 262.

(7) Rape, spousal rape, or sexual penetration in concert, in violation of Section 264.1.

(8) Sodomy, in violation of paragraph (2) or (3) of subdivision (c), or subdivision (d), of Section 286.

(9) Oral copulation, in violation of paragraph (2) or (3) of subdivision (c), or subdivision (d), of Section 287 or of former Section 288a.

(10) Sexual penetration, in violation of subdivision (a) of Section 289.

(11) Burglary of the first degree, as defined in Section 460, in violation of Section 459.

(d) As used in this section, "developmentally disabled" means a severe, chronic disability of a person, which is all of the following:

(1) Attributable to a mental or physical impairment or a combination of mental and physical impairments.

(2) Likely to continue indefinitely.

(3) Results in substantial functional limitation in three or more of the following areas of life activity:

(A) Self-care.

(B) Receptive and expressive language.

(C) Learning.

(D) Mobility.

(E) Self-direction.

(F) Capacity for independent living.

(G) Economic self-sufficiency.

(Amended by Stats. 2018, Ch. 423, Sec. 71. (SB 1494) Effective January 1, 2019.)

667.95.

In sentencing a person convicted of a violent felony listed in subdivision (c) of Section 667.5, the court may consider, as a factor in aggravation, that the defendant willfully recorded a video of the commission of the violent felony with the intent to encourage or facilitate the offense.

(Added by Stats. 2017, Ch. 668, Sec. 1. (AB 1542) Effective January 1, 2018.)

667.10.

(a) Any person who has a prior conviction of the offense set forth in Section 289 and who commits that crime against a person who is 65 years of age or older, or against a person who is blind, deaf, developmentally disabled, as defined in subdivision (d) of Section 667.9, a paraplegic, or a quadriplegic, or against a person who is under the age of 14 years, and that disability or condition is known or reasonably should be known to the person committing the crime, shall receive a two-year enhancement for each violation in addition to the sentence provided under Section 289.

(b) The existence of any fact which would bring a person under subdivision (a) shall be alleged in the information or indictment and either admitted by the defendant in open court, or found to be true by the jury trying the issue of guilt or by the court where guilt is established by plea of guilty or nolo contendere or by trial by the court sitting without a jury.

(Amended by Stats. 1992, Ch. 265, Sec. 3. Effective January 1, 1993.)

667.15.

Any adult who, prior to or during the commission or attempted commission of a violation of Section 288 or 288.5, exhibits to the minor any matter, as defined in subdivision (d) of Section 311.11, the production of which involves the use of a person under the age of 14 years, knowing that the matter depicts a person under the age of 14 years personally engaging in or simulating sexual conduct, as defined in subdivision (d) of Section 311.4, with the intent of arousing, appealing to, or gratifying the lust, passions, or sexual desires of that person or of the minor, or with the intent, or for the purpose, of seducing the minor, shall be punished for a violation of this section as follows:

(a) If convicted of the commission or attempted commission of a violation of Section 288, the adult shall receive an additional term of one year, which punishment shall be imposed in addition and consecutive to the punishment imposed for the commission or attempted commission of a violation of Section 288.

(b) If convicted of the commission or attempted commission of a violation of Section 288.5, the adult shall receive an additional term of two years, which punishment shall be imposed in addition and consecutive to the punishment imposed for the commission or attempted commission of a violation of Section 288.5.

(Added by Stats. 1993, Ch. 591, Sec. 1. Effective January 1, 1994.)

667.16.

(a) Any person convicted of a felony violation of Section 470, 487, or 532 as part of a plan or scheme to defraud an owner of a residential or nonresidential structure, including a mobilehome or manufactured home, in connection with the offer or performance of repairs to the structure for damage caused by a natural disaster, shall receive a one-year enhancement in addition and consecutive to the penalty prescribed. The additional term shall not be imposed unless the allegation is charged in the accusatory pleading and admitted by the defendant or found to be true by the trier of fact.

(b) This enhancement applies to natural disasters for which a state of emergency is proclaimed by the Governor pursuant to Section 8625 of the Government Code or for which an emergency or major disaster is declared by the President of the United States.

(c) Notwithstanding any other law, the court may strike the additional term provided in subdivision (a) if the court determines that there are mitigating circumstances and states on the record the reasons for striking the additional punishment.

(Added by Stats. 1994, Ch. 175, Sec. 5. Effective July 11, 1994.)

667.17.

Any person who violates the provisions of Section 538d during the commission of a felony shall receive an additional one-year term of imprisonment to be imposed consecutive to the term imposed for the felony, in lieu of the penalty that would have been imposed under Section 538d.

(Added by Stats. 1998, Ch. 279, Sec. 2. Effective January 1, 1999.)

668.

Every person who has been convicted in any other state, government, country, or jurisdiction of an offense for which, if committed within this state, that person could have been punished under the laws of this state by imprisonment in the state prison, is punishable for any subsequent crime committed within this state in the manner prescribed by law and to the same extent as if that prior conviction had taken place in a court of this state. The application of this section includes, but is not limited to, all statutes that provide for an enhancement or a term of imprisonment based on a prior conviction or a prior prison term or a term pursuant to subdivision (h) of Section 1170.

(Amended by Stats. 2011, Ch. 15, Sec. 444. (AB 109) Effective April 4, 2011. Operative October 1, 2011, by Sec. 636 of Ch. 15, as amended by Stats. 2011, Ch. 39, Sec. 68.)
668.5.
An offense specified as a prior felony conviction by reference to a specific code section shall include any prior felony conviction under any predecessor statute of that specified offense that includes all of the elements of that specified offense. The application of this section includes, but is not limited to, all statutes that provide for an enhancement or a term of imprisonment based on a prior conviction or a prior prison term.
(Added by Stats. 1999, Ch. 350, Sec. 2. Effective September 7, 1999.)
669.
(a) When a person is convicted of two or more crimes, whether in the same proceeding or court or in different proceedings or courts, and whether by judgment rendered by the same judge or by different judges, the second or other subsequent judgment upon which sentence is ordered to be executed shall direct whether the terms of imprisonment or any of them to which he or she is sentenced shall run concurrently or consecutively. Life sentences, whether with or without the possibility of parole, may be imposed to run consecutively with one another, with any term imposed for applicable enhancements, or with any other term of imprisonment for a felony conviction. Whenever a person is committed to prison on a life sentence which is ordered to run consecutive to any determinate term of imprisonment, the determinate term of imprisonment shall be served first and no part thereof shall be credited toward the person's eligibility for parole as calculated pursuant to Section 3046 or pursuant to any other section of law that establishes a minimum period of confinement under the life sentence before eligibility for parole.
(b) In the event that the court at the time of pronouncing the second or other judgment upon that person had no knowledge of a prior existing judgment or judgments, or having knowledge, fails to determine how the terms of imprisonment shall run in relation to each other, then, upon that failure to determine, or upon that prior judgment or judgments being brought to the attention of the court at any time prior to the expiration of 60 days from and after the actual commencement of imprisonment upon the second or other subsequent judgments, the court shall, in the absence of the defendant and within 60 days of the notice, determine how the term of imprisonment upon the second or other subsequent judgment shall run with reference to the prior incompleted term or terms of imprisonment. Upon the failure of the court to determine how the terms of imprisonment on the second or subsequent judgment shall run, the term of imprisonment on the second or subsequent judgment shall run concurrently.
(c) The Department of Corrections and Rehabilitation shall advise the court pronouncing the second or other subsequent judgment of the existence of all prior judgments against the defendant, the terms of imprisonment of which have not been completely served.
(d) When a court imposes a concurrent term of imprisonment and imprisonment for one of the crimes is required to be served in the state prison, the term for all crimes shall be served in the state prison, even if the term for any other offense specifies imprisonment in a county jail pursuant to subdivision (h) of Section 1170.
(Amended by Stats. 2012, Ch. 43, Sec. 23. (SB 1023) Effective June 27, 2012.)
670.
(a) Any person who violates Section 7158 or 7159 of, or subdivision (b), (c), (d), or (e) of Section 7161 of, the Business and Professions Code or Section 470, 484, 487, or 532 of this code as part of a plan or scheme to defraud an owner or lessee of a residential or nonresidential structure in connection with the offer or performance of repairs to the structure for damage caused by a natural disaster specified in subdivision (b), shall be subject to the penalties and enhancements specified in subdivisions (c) and (d). The existence of any fact which would bring a person under this section shall be alleged in the information or indictment and either admitted by the defendant in open court, or found to be true by the jury trying the issue of guilt or by the court where guilt is established by a plea of guilty or nolo contendere or by trial by the court sitting without a jury.
(b) This section applies to natural disasters for which a state of emergency is proclaimed by the Governor pursuant to Section 8625 of the Government Code or for which an emergency or major disaster is declared by the President of the United States.
(c) The maximum or prescribed amounts of fines for offenses subject to this section shall be doubled. If the person has been previously convicted of a felony offense specified in subdivision (a), the person shall receive a one-year enhancement in addition to, and to run consecutively to, the term of imprisonment for any felony otherwise prescribed by this subdivision.
(d) Additionally, the court shall order any person sentenced pursuant to this section to make full restitution to the victim or to make restitution to the victim based on the person's ability to pay, as defined in subdivision (e) of Section 1203.1b. The payment of the restitution ordered by the court pursuant to this subdivision shall be made a condition of any probation granted by the court for an offense punishable under this section. Notwithstanding any other provision of law, the period of probation shall be at least five years or until full restitution is made to the victim, whichever first occurs.
(e) Notwithstanding any other provision of law, the prosecuting agency shall be entitled to recover its costs of investigation and prosecution from any fines imposed for a conviction under this section.
(Amended by Stats. 2016, Ch. 86, Sec. 226. (SB 1171) Effective January 1, 2017.)
672.
Upon a conviction for any crime punishable by imprisonment in any jail or prison, in relation to which no fine is herein prescribed, the court may impose a fine on the offender not exceeding one thousand dollars ($1,000) in cases of misdemeanors or ten thousand dollars ($10,000) in cases of felonies, in addition to the imprisonment prescribed.
(Amended by Stats. 1983, Ch. 1092, Sec. 320. Effective September 27, 1983. Operative January 1, 1984, by Sec. 427 of Ch. 1092.)
673.
It shall be unlawful to use in the reformatories, institutions, jails, state hospitals or any other state, county, or city institution any cruel, corporal or unusual punishment or to inflict any treatment or allow any lack of care whatever which would injure or impair the health of the prisoner, inmate, or person confined; and punishment by the use of the strait jacket, gag, thumbscrew, shower bath or the tricing up of a prisoner, inmate or person confined is hereby prohibited. Any person who violates the provisions of this section or who aids, abets, or attempts in any way to contribute to the violation of this section shall be guilty of a misdemeanor.
(Added by renumbering Section 681 (as added by Stats. 1913, Ch. 583) by Stats. 1953, Ch. 615.)
674.
(a) Any person who is a primary care provider in a day care facility and who is convicted of a felony violation of Section 261, 285, 286, 287, 288, or 289 or former Section 288a, where the victim of the crime was a minor entrusted to his or her care by the minor's parent or guardian, a court, any public agency charged with the provision of social services, or a probation department, may be punished by an additional term of two years.
(b) If the crime described in subdivision (a) was committed while voluntarily acting in concert with another, the person so convicted may be punished by an additional term of three years.
(c) The enhancements authorized by this section may be imposed in addition to any other required or authorized enhancement.
(Amended by Stats. 2018, Ch. 423, Sec. 72. (SB 1494) Effective January 1, 2019.)
675.

(a) Any person suffering a felony conviction for a violation of subdivision (c) or (d) of Section 261.5, paragraph (1) or (2) of subdivision (b) or paragraph (1) of subdivision (c) of Section 286, paragraph (1) or (2) of subdivision (b) or paragraph (1) of subdivision (c) of Section 287 or former Section 288a, or subdivision (a) or paragraph (1) of subdivision (c) of Section 288, where the offense was committed with a minor for money or other consideration, is punishable by an additional term of imprisonment in the state prison of one year.
(b) The enhancements authorized by this section may be imposed in addition to any other required or authorized enhancement.
(Amended by Stats. 2018, Ch. 423, Sec. 73. (SB 1494) Effective January 1, 2019.)
678.
Whenever in this code the character or grade of an offense, or its punishment, is made to depend upon the value of property, such value shall be estimated exclusively in lawful money of the United States.
(Amended by Stats. 1953, Ch. 616.)

TITLE 17. RIGHTS OF VICTIMS AND WITNESSES OF CRIME [679 - 680.4]

(Title 17 added by Stats. 1986, Ch. 1427, Sec. 1.)
679.
In recognition of the civil and moral duty of victims and witnesses of crime to fully and voluntarily cooperate with law enforcement and prosecutorial agencies, and in further recognition of the continuing importance of this citizen cooperation to state and local law enforcement efforts and the general effectiveness and well-being of the criminal justice system of this state, the Legislature declares its intent, in the enactment of this title, to ensure that all victims and witnesses of crime are treated with dignity, respect, courtesy, and sensitivity. It is the further intent that the rights enumerated in Section 679.02 relating to victims and witnesses of crime are honored and protected by law enforcement agencies, prosecutors, and judges in a manner no less vigorous than the protections afforded criminal defendants. It is the intent of the Legislature to add to Section 679.02 references to new rights as or as soon after they are created. The failure to enumerate in that section a right which is enumerated elsewhere in the law shall not be deemed to diminish the importance or enforceability of that right.
(Added by Stats. 1986, Ch. 1427, Sec. 1.)
679.01.
As used in this title, the following definitions shall control:
(a) "Crime" means an act committed in this state which, if committed by a competent adult, would constitute a misdemeanor or felony.
(b) "Victim" means a person against whom a crime has been committed.
(c) "Witness" means any person who has been or is expected to testify for the prosecution, or who, by reason of having relevant information, is subject to call or likely to be called as a witness for the prosecution, whether or not any action or proceeding has yet been commenced.
(Added by Stats. 1986, Ch. 1427, Sec. 1.)
679.015.
(a) It is the public policy of this state to protect the public from crime and violence by encouraging all persons who are victims of or witnesses to crimes, or who otherwise can give evidence in a criminal investigation, to cooperate with the criminal justice system and not to penalize these persons for being victims or for cooperating with the criminal justice system.
(b) Whenever an individual who is a victim of or witness to a crime, or who otherwise can give evidence in a criminal investigation, is not charged with or convicted of committing any crime under state law, a peace officer may not detain the individual exclusively for any actual or suspected immigration violation or turn the individual over to federal immigration authorities absent a judicial warrant.
(Added by Stats. 2017, Ch. 194, Sec. 1. (AB 493) Effective January 1, 2018.)
679.02.
(a) The following are hereby established as the statutory rights of victims and witnesses of crimes:
(1) To be notified as soon as feasible that a court proceeding to which he or she has been subpoenaed as a witness will not proceed as scheduled, provided the prosecuting attorney determines that the witness' attendance is not required.
(2) Upon request of the victim or a witness, to be informed by the prosecuting attorney of the final disposition of the case, as provided by Section 11116.10.
(3) For the victim, the victim's parents or guardian if the victim is a minor, or the next of kin of the victim if the victim has died, to be notified of all sentencing proceedings, and of the right to appear, to reasonably express his or her views, have those views preserved by audio or video means as provided in Section 1191.16, and to have the court consider his or her statements, as provided by Sections 1191.1 and 1191.15.
(4) For the victim, the victim's parents or guardian if the victim is a minor, or the next of kin of the victim if the victim has died, to be notified of all juvenile disposition hearings in which the alleged act would have been a felony if committed by an adult, and of the right to attend and to express his or her views, as provided by Section 656.2 of the Welfare and Institutions Code.
(5) Upon request by the victim or the next of kin of the victim if the victim has died, to be notified of any parole eligibility hearing and of the right to appear, either personally as provided by Section 3043 of this code, or by other means as provided by Sections 3043.2 and 3043.25 of this code, to reasonably express his or her views, and to have his or her statements considered, as provided by Section 3043 of this code and by Section 1767 of the Welfare and Institutions Code.
(6) Upon request by the victim or the next of kin of the victim if the crime was a homicide, to be notified of an inmate's placement in a reentry or work furlough program, or notified of the inmate's escape as provided by Section 11155.
(7) To be notified that he or she may be entitled to witness fees and mileage, as provided by Section 1329.1.
(8) For the victim, to be provided with information concerning the victim's right to civil recovery and the opportunity to be compensated from the Restitution Fund pursuant to Chapter 5 (commencing with Section 13959) of Part 4 of Division 3 of Title 2 of the Government Code and Section 1191.2 of this code.
(9) To the expeditious return of his or her property which has allegedly been stolen or embezzled, when it is no longer needed as evidence, as provided by Chapter 12 (commencing with Section 1407) and Chapter 13 (commencing with Section 1417) of Title 10 of Part 2.
(10) To an expeditious disposition of the criminal action.
(11) To be notified, if applicable, in accordance with Sections 679.03 and 3058.8 if the defendant is to be placed on parole.
(12) For the victim, upon request, to be notified of any pretrial disposition of the case, to the extent required by Section 28 of Article I of the California Constitution.
(A) A victim may request to be notified of a pretrial disposition.
(B) The victim may be notified by any reasonable means available.
Nothing in this paragraph is intended to affect the right of the people and the defendant to an expeditious disposition as provided in Section 1050.
(13) For the victim, to be notified by the district attorney's office of the right to request, upon a form provided by the district attorney's office, and receive a notice pursuant to paragraph (14), if the defendant is convicted of any of the following offenses:

(A) Assault with intent to commit rape, sodomy, oral copulation, or any violation of Section 264.1, 288, or 289, in violation of Section 220.

(B) A violation of Section 207 or 209 committed with the intent to commit a violation of Section 261, 262, 286, 287, 288, or 289, or former Section 288a.

(C) Rape, in violation of Section 261.

(D) Oral copulation, in violation of Section 287 or former Section 288a.

(E) Sodomy, in violation of Section 286.

(F) A violation of Section 288.

(G) A violation of Section 289.

(14) When a victim has requested notification pursuant to paragraph (13), the sheriff shall inform the victim that the person who was convicted of the offense has been ordered to be placed on probation, and give the victim notice of the proposed date upon which the person will be released from the custody of the sheriff.

(b) The rights set forth in subdivision (a) shall be set forth in the information and educational materials prepared pursuant to Section 13897.1. The information and educational materials shall be distributed to local law enforcement agencies and local victims' programs by the Victims' Legal Resource Center established pursuant to Chapter 11 (commencing with Section 13897) of Title 6 of Part 4.

(c) Local law enforcement agencies shall make available copies of the materials described in subdivision (b) to victims and witnesses.

(d) Nothing in this section is intended to affect the rights and services provided to victims and witnesses by the local assistance centers for victims and witnesses.

(e) The court shall not release statements, made pursuant to paragraph (3) or (4) of subdivision (a), to the public prior to the statement being heard in court.

(Amended by Stats. 2018, Ch. 423, Sec. 74. (SB 1494) Effective January 1, 2019.)

679.026.

(a) It is the intent of the people of the State of California in enacting this section to implement the rights of victims of crime established in Section 28 of Article I of the California Constitution to be informed of the rights of crime victims enumerated in the Constitution and in the statutes of this state.

(b) Every victim of crime has the right to receive without cost or charge a list of the rights of victims of crime recognized in Section 28 of Article I of the California Constitution. These rights shall be known as "Marsy Rights."

(c) (1) Every law enforcement agency investigating a criminal act and every agency prosecuting a criminal act shall, as provided herein, at the time of initial contact with a crime victim, during follow-up investigation, or as soon thereafter as deemed appropriate by investigating officers or prosecuting attorneys, provide or make available to each victim of the criminal act without charge or cost a "Marsy Rights" card described in paragraphs (3) and (4).

(2) The victim disclosures required under this section shall be available to the public at a state funded and maintained Web site authorized pursuant to Section 14260 of the Penal Code to be known as "Marsy's Page."

(3) The Attorney General shall design and make available in ".pdf" or other imaging format to every agency listed in paragraph (1) a "Marsy Rights" card, which shall contain the rights of crime victims described in subdivision (b) of Section 28 of Article I of the California Constitution, information on the means by which a crime victim can access the web page described in paragraph (2), and a toll-free telephone number to enable a crime victim to contact a local victim's assistance office.

(4) Every law enforcement agency which investigates criminal activity shall, if provided without cost to the agency by any organization classified as a nonprofit organization under paragraph (3) of subdivision (c) of Section 501 of the Internal Revenue Code, make available and provide to every crime victim a "Victims' Survival and Resource Guide" pamphlet and/or video that has been approved by the Attorney General. The "Victims' Survival and Resource Guide" and video shall include an approved "Marsy Rights" card, a list of government agencies, nonprofit victims' rights groups, support groups, and local resources that assist crime victims, and any other information which the Attorney General determines might be helpful to victims of crime.

(5) Any agency described in paragraph (1) may in its discretion design and distribute to each victim of a criminal act its own Victims' Survival and Resource Guide and video, the contents of which have been approved by the Attorney General, in addition to or in lieu of the materials described in paragraph (4).

(Added November 4, 2008, by initiative Proposition 9, Sec. 6.1. Note: Prop. 9 is titled the Victims' Bill of Rights Act of 2008: Marsy's Law.)

679.03.

(a) With respect to the conviction of a defendant involving a violent offense, as defined in Section 29905, the county district attorney, probation department, and victim-witness coordinator shall confer and establish an annual policy within existing resources to decide which one of their agencies shall inform each witness involved in the conviction who was threatened by the defendant following the defendant's arrest and each victim or next of kin of the victim of that offense of the right to request and receive a notice pursuant to Section 3058.8 or 3605. If no agreement is reached, the presiding judge shall designate the appropriate county agency or department to provide this notification.

(b) The Department of Corrections and Rehabilitation shall supply a form to the agency designated pursuant to subdivision (a) in order to enable persons specified in subdivision (a) to request and receive notification from the department of the release, escape, scheduled execution, or death of the violent offender. That agency shall give the form to the victim, witness, or next of kin of the victim for completion, explain to that person or persons the right to be so notified, and forward the completed form to the department. The department or the Board of Parole Hearings is responsible for notifying all victims, witnesses, or next of kin of victims who request to be notified of a violent offender's release or scheduled execution, as provided by Sections 3058.8 and 3605.

(c) All information relating to any person receiving notice pursuant to subdivision (b) shall remain confidential and is not subject to disclosure pursuant to the California Public Records Act (Chapter 3.5 (commencing with Section 6250) of Division 7 of Title 1 of the Government Code).

(d) Nothing in this section precludes a victim, witness, or next of kin of the victim from requesting notification using an automated electronic notification process, if available.

(Amended (as amended by Stats. 2010, Ch. 178) by Stats. 2011, Ch. 364, Sec. 2. (SB 852) Effective September 29, 2011. Amended version operative January 1, 2012, pursuant to Stats. 2010, Ch. 178, Sec. 107.)

679.04.

(a) A victim of sexual assault as the result of any offense specified in paragraph (1) of subdivision (b) of Section 264.2 has the right to have victim advocates and a support person of the victim's choosing present at any interview by law enforcement authorities, district attorneys, or defense attorneys. A victim retains this right regardless of whether he or she has waived the right in a previous medical evidentiary or physical examination or in a previous interview by law enforcement authorities, district attorneys, or defense attorneys. However, the support person may be excluded from an interview by law enforcement or the district attorney if the law enforcement authority or the district attorney determines that the presence of that individual would be detrimental to the purpose of the interview. As used in this section, "victim advocate" means a sexual assault counselor, as defined in Section 1035.2 of the Evidence Code, or a victim advocate working in a center established under Article 2 (commencing with Section 13835) of Chapter 4 of Title 6 of Part 4.

(b) (1) Prior to the commencement of the initial interview by law enforcement authorities or the district attorney pertaining to any criminal action arising out of a sexual assault, a victim of sexual assault as the result of any offense specified in Section 264.2 shall be notified in writing by the attending law enforcement authority or district attorney that he or she has the right to have victim advocates and a support person of the victim's

choosing present at the interview or contact, about any other rights of the victim pursuant to law in the card described in subdivision (a) of Section 680.2, and that the victim has the right to request to have a person of the same gender or opposite gender as the victim present in the room during any interview with a law enforcement official or district attorney, unless no such person is reasonably available. This subdivision applies to investigators and agents employed or retained by law enforcement or the district attorney.

(2) At the time the victim is advised of his or her rights pursuant to paragraph (1), the attending law enforcement authority or district attorney shall also advise the victim of the right to have victim advocates and a support person present at any interview by the defense attorney or investigators or agents employed by the defense attorney.

(3) The presence of a victim advocate shall not defeat any existing right otherwise guaranteed by law. A victim's waiver of the right to a victim advocate is inadmissible in court, unless a court determines the waiver is at issue in the pending litigation.

(4) The victim has the right to request to have a person of the same gender or opposite gender as the victim present in the room during any interview with a law enforcement official or district attorney, unless no such person is reasonably available. It is the intent of the Legislature to encourage every interviewer in this context to have trauma-based training.

(c) An initial investigation by law enforcement to determine whether a crime has been committed and the identity of the suspects shall not constitute a law enforcement interview for purposes of this section.

(d) A law enforcement official shall not, for any reason, discourage a victim of an alleged sexual assault from receiving a medical evidentiary or physical examination.

(Amended by Stats. 2017, Ch. 692, Sec. 2. (AB 1312) Effective January 1, 2018.)

679.05.

(a) A victim of domestic violence or abuse, as defined in Sections 6203 or 6211 of the Family Code, or Section 13700 of the Penal Code, has the right to have a domestic violence advocate and a support person of the victim's choosing present at any interview by law enforcement authorities, prosecutors, or defense attorneys. However, the support person may be excluded from an interview by law enforcement or the prosecutor if the law enforcement authority or the prosecutor determines that the presence of that individual would be detrimental to the purpose of the interview. As used in this section, "domestic violence advocate" means either a person employed by a program specified in Section 13835.2 for the purpose of rendering advice or assistance to victims of domestic violence, or a domestic violence counselor, as defined in Section 1037.1 of the Evidence Code. Prior to being present at any interview conducted by law enforcement authorities, prosecutors, or defense attorneys, a domestic violence advocate shall advise the victim of any applicable limitations on the confidentiality of communications between the victim and the domestic violence advocate.

(b) (1) Prior to the commencement of the initial interview by law enforcement authorities or the prosecutor pertaining to any criminal action arising out of a domestic violence incident, a victim of domestic violence or abuse, as defined in Section 6203 or 6211 of the Family Code, or Section 13700 of this code, shall be notified orally or in writing by the attending law enforcement authority or prosecutor that the victim has the right to have a domestic violence advocate and a support person of the victim's choosing present at the interview or contact. This subdivision applies to investigators and agents employed or retained by law enforcement or the prosecutor.

(2) At the time the victim is advised of his or her rights pursuant to paragraph (1), the attending law enforcement authority or prosecutor shall also advise the victim of the right to have a domestic violence advocate and a support person present at any interview by the defense attorney or investigators or agents employed by the defense attorney.

(c) An initial investigation by law enforcement to determine whether a crime has been committed and the identity of the suspects shall not constitute a law enforcement interview for purposes of this section.

(Amended by Stats. 2007, Ch. 206, Sec. 6. Effective January 1, 2008.)

679.08.

(a) (1) Whenever there has been a crime committed against a victim, the law enforcement officer assigned to the case may provide the victim of the crime with a "Victim's Rights Card," as specified in subdivision (b).

(2) This section shall be operative in a city or county only upon the adoption of a resolution by the city council or board of supervisors to that effect.

(3) This section shall not be interpreted as replacing or prohibiting any services currently offered to victims of crime by any agency or person affected by this section.

(b) A "Victim's Rights Card" means a card or paper that provides a printed notice with a disclaimer, in at least 10-point type, to a victim of a crime regarding potential services that may be available under existing state law to assist the victim. The printed notice shall include the following language or language substantially similar to the following: "California law provides crime victims with important rights. If you are a victim of crime, you may be entitled to the assistance of a victim advocate who can answer many of the questions you might have about the criminal justice system."

"Victim advocates can assist you with the following:

(1) Explaining what information you are entitled to receive while criminal proceedings are pending.

(2) Assisting you in applying for restitution to compensate you for crime-related losses.

(3) Communicating with the prosecution.

(4) Assisting you in receiving victim support services.

(5) Helping you prepare a victim impact statement before an offender is sentenced."

"To speak with a victim advocate, please call any of the following numbers:"

[Set forth the name and phone number, including area code, of all victim advocate agencies in the local jurisdiction]

"PLEASE NOTE THAT THIS INFORMATION IS PROVIDED IN AN ATTEMPT TO ASSIST THE VICTIM, BY NOTIFYING THE VICTIM ABOUT SOME, BUT NOT NECESSARILY ALL, SERVICES AVAILABLE TO THE VICTIM; THE PROVISION OF THIS INFORMATION AND THE INFORMATION CONTAINED THEREIN IS NOT LEGAL ADVICE AND IS NOT INTENDED TO CONSTITUTE A GUARANTEE OF ANY VICTIM'S RIGHTS OR OF A VICTIM'S ELIGIBILITY OR ENTITLEMENT TO ANY SPECIFIC BENEFITS OR SERVICES."

(c) Any act or omission covered by this section is a discretionary act pursuant to Section 820.2 of the Government Code.

(Added by Stats. 2006, Ch. 94, Sec. 1. Effective January 1, 2007.)

679.10.

(a) For purposes of this section, a "certifying entity" is any of the following:

(1) A state or local law enforcement agency.

(2) A prosecutor.

(3) A judge.

(4) Any other authority that has responsibility for the detection or investigation or prosecution of a qualifying crime or criminal activity.

(5) Agencies that have criminal detection or investigative jurisdiction in their respective areas of expertise, including, but not limited to, child protective services, the Department of Fair Employment and Housing, and the Department of Industrial Relations.

(b) For purposes of this section, a "certifying official" is any of the following:

(1) The head of the certifying entity.

(2) A person in a supervisory role who has been specifically designated by the head of the certifying entity to issue Form I-918 Supplement B certifications on behalf of that agency.

(3) A judge.

(4) Any other certifying official defined under Section 214.14 (a)(2) of Title 8 of the Code of Federal Regulations.

(c) "Qualifying criminal activity" means qualifying criminal activity pursuant to Section 101(a)(15)(U)(iii) of the federal Immigration and Nationality Act which includes, but is not limited to, the following crimes:
(1) Rape.
(2) Torture.
(3) Human trafficking.
(4) Incest.
(5) Domestic violence.
(6) Sexual assault.
(7) Abusive sexual conduct.
(8) Prostitution.
(9) Sexual exploitation.
(10) Female genital mutilation.
(11) Being held hostage.
(12) Peonage.
(13) Perjury.
(14) Involuntary servitude.
(15) Slavery.
(16) Kidnaping.
(17) Abduction.
(18) Unlawful criminal restraint.
(19) False imprisonment.
(20) Blackmail.
(21) Extortion.
(22) Manslaughter.
(23) Murder.
(24) Felonious assault.
(25) Witness tampering.
(26) Obstruction of justice.
(27) Fraud in foreign labor contracting.
(28) Stalking.
(d) A "qualifying crime" includes criminal offenses for which the nature and elements of the offenses are substantially similar to the criminal activity described in subdivision (c), and the attempt, conspiracy, or solicitation to commit any of those offenses.
(e) Upon the request of the victim or victim's family member, a certifying official from a certifying entity shall certify victim helpfulness on the Form I-918 Supplement B certification, when the victim was a victim of a qualifying criminal activity and has been helpful, is being helpful, or is likely to be helpful to the detection or investigation or prosecution of that qualifying criminal activity.
(f) For purposes of determining helpfulness pursuant to subdivision (e), there is a rebuttable presumption that a victim is helpful, has been helpful, or is likely to be helpful to the detection or investigation or prosecution of that qualifying criminal activity, if the victim has not refused or failed to provide information and assistance reasonably requested by law enforcement.
(g) The certifying official shall fully complete and sign the Form I-918 Supplement B certification and, regarding victim helpfulness, include specific details about the nature of the crime investigated or prosecuted and a detailed description of the victim's helpfulness or likely helpfulness to the detection or investigation or prosecution of the criminal activity.
(h) A certifying entity shall process a Form I-918 Supplement B certification within 90 days of request, unless the noncitizen is in removal proceedings, in which case the certification shall be processed within 14 days of request.
(i) A current investigation, the filing of charges, and a prosecution or conviction are not required for the victim to request and obtain the Form I-918 Supplement B certification from a certifying official.
(j) A certifying official may only withdraw the certification if the victim refuses to provide information and assistance when reasonably requested.
(k) A certifying entity is prohibited from disclosing the immigration status of a victim or person requesting the Form I-918 Supplement B certification, except to comply with federal law or legal process, or if authorized by the victim or person requesting the Form I-918 Supplement B certification.
(l) A certifying entity that receives a request for a Form I-918 Supplement B certification shall report to the Legislature, on or before January 1, 2017, and annually thereafter, the number of victims that requested Form I-918 Supplement B certifications from the entity, the number of those certification forms that were signed, and the number that were denied. A report pursuant to this subdivision shall comply with Section 9795 of the Government Code.
(Amended by Stats. 2016, Ch. 86, Sec. 227. (SB 1171) Effective January 1, 2017.)
679.11.
(a) For purposes of this section, a "certifying entity" is any of the following:
(1) A state or local law enforcement agency.
(2) A prosecutor.
(3) A judge.
(4) The Department of Industrial Relations.
(5) Any other state or local government agencies that have criminal, civil, or administrative investigative or prosecutorial authority relating to human trafficking.
(b) For purposes of this section, a "certifying official" is any of the following:
(1) The head of the certifying entity.
(2) A person in a supervisory role who has been specifically designated by the head of the certifying entity to issue Form I-914 Supplement B declarations on behalf of that agency.
(3) A judge.
(4) Any other certifying official defined under Section 214.14(a)(2) of Title 8 of the Code of Federal Regulations.
(c) "Human trafficking" means "severe forms of trafficking in persons" pursuant to Section 7102 of Title 22 of the United States Code and includes either of the following:
(1) Sex trafficking in which a commercial sex act is induced by force, fraud, or coercion, or in which the person induced to perform such act has not attained 18 years of age.
(2) The recruitment, harboring, transportation, provision, or obtaining of a person for labor or services, through the use of force, fraud, or coercion for the purpose of subjection to involuntary servitude, peonage, debt bondage, or slavery.
(d) "Human trafficking" also includes criminal offenses for which the nature and elements of the offenses are substantially similar to the criminal activity described in subdivision (c), and the attempt, conspiracy, or solicitation to commit any of those offenses.
(e) Upon the request of the victim or victim's family member, a certifying official from a certifying entity shall certify victim cooperation on the Form I-914 Supplement B declaration, when the victim was a victim of human trafficking and has been cooperative, is being cooperative, or is likely to be cooperative to the investigation or prosecution of human trafficking.
(f) For purposes of determining cooperation pursuant to subdivision (e), there is a rebuttable presumption that a victim is cooperative, has been cooperative, or is likely to be cooperative to the investigation or prosecution of human trafficking, if the victim has not refused or failed to provide information and assistance reasonably requested by law enforcement.
(g) The certifying official shall fully complete and sign the Form I-914 Supplement B declaration and, regarding victim cooperation, include specific details about the nature of the crime investigated or prosecuted and a detailed description of the victim's cooperation or likely cooperation to the detection, investigation, or prosecution of the criminal activity.
(h) A certifying entity shall process a Form I-914 Supplement B declaration within 90 days of request, unless the noncitizen is in removal proceedings, in which case the declaration shall be processed within 14 days of request.
(i) A current investigation, the filing of charges, or a prosecution or conviction is not required for the victim to request and obtain the Form I-914 Supplement B declaration from a certifying official.
(j) A certifying official may only withdraw the certification if the victim refuses to provide information and assistance when reasonably requested.
(k) A certifying entity is prohibited from disclosing the immigration status of a victim or person requesting the Form I-914 Supplement B declaration, except to comply with federal law or legal process, or if authorized by the victim or person requesting the Form I-914 Supplement B declaration.
(l) A certifying entity that receives a request for a Form I-914 Supplement B declaration shall report to the Legislature, on or before January 1, 2018, and annually thereafter, the number of victims who requested Form I-914 Supplement B declarations from the entity, the number of those declaration forms that were signed, and the number that were denied. A report pursuant to this subdivision shall comply with Section 9795 of the Government Code.
(Added by Stats. 2016, Ch. 749, Sec. 1. (AB 2027) Effective January 1, 2017.)
680.
(a) This section shall be known as and may be cited as the "Sexual Assault Victims' DNA Bill of Rights."
(b) The Legislature finds and declares all of the following:
(1) Deoxyribonucleic acid (DNA) and forensic identification analysis is a powerful law enforcement tool for identifying and prosecuting sexual assault offenders.
(2) Existing law requires an adult arrested for or charged with a felony and a juvenile adjudicated for a felony to submit DNA samples as a result of that arrest, charge, or adjudication.
(3) Victims of sexual assaults have a strong interest in the investigation and prosecution of their cases.
(4) Law enforcement agencies have an obligation to victims of sexual assaults in the proper handling, retention, and timely DNA testing of rape kit evidence or other crime scene evidence and to be responsive to victims concerning the developments of forensic testing and the investigation of their cases.
(5) The growth of the Department of Justice's Cal-DNA databank and the national databank through the Combined DNA Index System (CODIS) makes it possible for many sexual assault perpetrators to be identified after their first offense, provided that rape kit evidence is analyzed in a timely manner.
(6) Timely DNA analysis of rape kit evidence is a core public safety issue affecting men, women, and children in the State of California. It is the intent of the Legislature, in order to further public safety, to encourage DNA analysis of rape kit evidence within the time limits imposed by subparagraphs (A) and (B) of paragraph (1) of subdivision (g) of Section 803.
(7) In order to ensure that sexual assault forensic evidence is analyzed within the two-year timeframe required by subparagraphs (A) and (B) of paragraph (1) of subdivision (g) of Section 803 and to ensure the longest possible statute of limitations for sex offenses, including sex offenses designated pursuant to those subparagraphs, the following should occur:
(A) A law enforcement agency in whose jurisdiction a sex offense specified in Section 261, 261.5, 262, 286, 287, or 289 or former Section 288a occurred should do one of the following for any sexual assault forensic evidence received by the law enforcement agency on or after January 1, 2016:
(i) Submit sexual assault forensic evidence to the crime lab within 20 days after it is booked into evidence.
(ii) Ensure that a rapid turnaround DNA program is in place to submit forensic evidence collected from the victim of a sexual assault directly from the medical facility where the victim is examined to the crime lab within five days after the evidence is obtained from the victim.
(B) The crime lab should do one of the following for any sexual assault forensic evidence received by the crime lab on or after January 1, 2016.
(i) Process sexual assault forensic evidence, create DNA profiles when able, and upload qualifying DNA profiles into CODIS as soon as practically possible, but no later than 120 days after initially receiving the evidence.
(ii) Transmit the sexual assault forensic evidence to another crime lab as soon as practically possible, but no later than 30 days after initially receiving the evidence, for processing of the evidence for the presence of DNA. If a DNA profile is created, the transmitting crime lab should upload the profile into CODIS as soon as practically possible, but no longer than 30 days after being notified about the presence of DNA.
(C) This subdivision does not require a lab to test all items of forensic evidence obtained in a sexual assault forensic evidence examination. A lab is considered to be in compliance with the guidelines of this section when representative samples of the evidence are processed by the lab in an effort to detect the foreign DNA of the perpetrator.
(D) This section does not require a DNA profile to be uploaded into CODIS if the DNA profile does not meet federal guidelines regarding the uploading of DNA profiles into CODIS.
(E) For purposes of this section, a "rapid turnaround DNA program" is a program for the training of sexual assault team personnel in the selection of representative samples of forensic evidence from the victim to be the best evidence, based on the medical evaluation and patient history, the collection and preservation of that evidence, and the transfer of the evidence directly from the medical facility to the crime lab, which is adopted pursuant to a written agreement between the law enforcement agency, the crime lab, and the medical facility where the sexual assault team is based.
(8) For the purpose of this section, "law enforcement" means the law enforcement agency with the primary responsibility for investigating an alleged sexual assault.
(c) (1) Upon the request of a sexual assault victim, the law enforcement agency investigating a violation of Section 261, 261.5, 262, 286, 287, or 289 or of former Section 288a shall inform the victim of the status of the DNA testing of the rape kit evidence or other crime scene evidence from the victim's case. The law enforcement agency may, at its discretion, require that the victim's request be in writing. The law enforcement agency shall respond to the victim's request with either an oral or written communication, or by email, if an email address is available. Nothing in this subdivision requires that the law enforcement agency communicate with the victim or the victim's designee regarding the status of DNA testing absent a specific request from the victim or the victim's designee.
(2) Subject to the commitment of sufficient resources to respond to requests for information, sexual assault victims have the following rights:
(A) The right to be informed whether or not a DNA profile of the assailant was obtained from the testing of the rape kit evidence or other crime scene evidence from their case.
(B) The right to be informed whether or not the DNA profile of the assailant developed from the rape kit evidence or other crime scene evidence has been entered into the Department of Justice Data Bank of case evidence.
(C) The right to be informed whether or not there is a match between the DNA profile of the assailant developed from the rape kit evidence or other crime scene evidence and a DNA profile contained in the Department of Justice Convicted Offender DNA Data Base, provided that disclosure would not impede or compromise an ongoing investigation.

(3) This subdivision is intended to encourage law enforcement agencies to notify victims of information which is in their possession. It is not intended to affect the manner of or frequency with which the Department of Justice provides this information to law enforcement agencies.

(d) If the law enforcement agency does not analyze DNA evidence within six months prior to the time limits established by subparagraphs (A) and (B) of paragraph (1) of subdivision (g) of Section 803, a victim of a sexual assault offense specified in Section 261, 261.5, 262, 286, 287, or 289 or former Section 288a shall be informed, either orally or in writing, of that fact by the law enforcement agency.

(e) (1) If the law enforcement agency intends to destroy or dispose of rape kit evidence or other crime scene evidence from an unsolved sexual assault case, a victim of a violation of Section 261, 261.5, 262, 286, 287, or 289 or former Section 288a shall be given written notification by the law enforcement agency of that intention.

(2) A law enforcement agency shall not destroy or dispose of rape kit evidence or other crime scene evidence from an unsolved sexual assault case before at least 20 years, or if the victim was under 18 years of age at the time of the alleged offense, before the victim's 40th birthday.

(f) Written notification under subdivision (d) or (e) shall be made at least 60 days prior to the destruction or disposal of the rape kit evidence or other crime scene evidence from an unsolved sexual assault case.

(g) A sexual assault victim may designate a sexual assault victim advocate, or other support person of the victim's choosing, to act as a recipient of the above information required to be provided by this section.

(h) It is the intent of the Legislature that a law enforcement agency responsible for providing information under subdivision (c) do so in a timely manner and, upon request of the victim or the victim's designee, advise the victim or the victim's designee of any significant changes in the information of which the law enforcement agency is aware. In order to be entitled to receive notice under this section, the victim or the victim's designee shall keep appropriate authorities informed of the name, address, telephone number, and email address of the person to whom the information should be provided, and any changes of the name, address, telephone number, and email address, if an email address is available.

(i) A defendant or person accused or convicted of a crime against the victim shall have no standing to object to any failure to comply with this section. The failure to provide a right or notice to a sexual assault victim under this section may not be used by a defendant to seek to have the conviction or sentence set aside.

(j) The sole civil or criminal remedy available to a sexual assault victim for a law enforcement agency's failure to fulfill its responsibilities under this section is standing to file a writ of mandamus to require compliance with subdivision (d) or (e).
(Amended by Stats. 2018, Ch. 423, Sec. 75. (SB 1494) Effective January 1, 2019.)
680.1.
The Department of Justice, on or before July 1, 2018, and in consultation with law enforcement agencies and crime victims groups, shall establish a process by which victims of sexual assault may inquire regarding the location and information regarding their sexual assault evidence kits.
(Added by Stats. 2016, Ch. 884, Sec. 2. (AB 2499) Effective January 1, 2017.)
680.2.
(a) Upon the initial interaction with a sexual assault victim, a law enforcement officer or medical provider shall provide the victim with a card to be developed by every local law enforcement agency, in consultation with sexual assault experts, that explains all of the rights of sexual assault victims in clear language that is comprehensible to a person proficient in English at the fifth grade level, in at least 12-point font, and available in all major languages of the state. This card shall include, but is not limited to, all of the following:
(1) A clear statement that a sexual assault victim is not required to participate in the criminal justice system or to receive a medical evidentiary or physical examination in order to retain his or her rights under law.
(2) Telephone or Internet Web site contact information for a nearby rape crisis center and sexual assault counselor.
(3) Information about the types of law enforcement protection available to the sexual assault victim, including a temporary protection order, and the process to obtain that protection.
(4) Instructions for requesting the results of the analysis of the victim's sexual assault forensic evidence.
(5) Information about state and federal compensation funds for medical and other costs associated with the sexual assault and information on any municipal, state, or federal right to restitution for sexual assault victims if a criminal trial occurs.
(6) A clear statement that the victim has the right to have a sexual assault counselor and at least one other support person of the victim's choosing present at any initial medical evidentiary examination, physical examination, or investigative interview arising out of a sexual assault, and that a sexual assault counselor can be contacted 24 hours a day.
(7) Information about the rate of potential evidence degradation.
(8) A clear statement that if sexual assault forensic evidence will be tested, it should be transported to the crime laboratory and analyzed within the time limits imposed by subparagraphs (A) and (B) of paragraph (1) of subdivision (g) of Section 803.
(9) A clear statement that the law enforcement agency or crime laboratory will retain the sexual assault forensic evidence for at least 20 years, or if the victim was under 18 years of age at the time of the alleged offense, at least until the victim's 40th birthday.
(b) A law enforcement official shall, upon written request by a sexual assault victim, furnish a free copy of the initial crime report related to the sexual assault, regardless of whether the report has been closed by the law enforcement agency, to the victim. A law enforcement agency may redact personal, identifying information in the copy furnished to the victim.
(c) A prosecutor shall, pursuant to Section 290.46, upon written request by a sexual assault victim, provide the convicted defendant's information on a sex offender registry to the victim, if the defendant is required to register as a sex offender.
(d) The law enforcement agency shall provide sufficient copies of the card described in subdivision (a) to each provider in its jurisdiction of medical evidentiary examinations or physical examinations arising out of sexual assault.
(Added by Stats. 2017, Ch. 692, Sec. 4. (AB 1312) Effective January 1, 2018.)
680.3.
(a) Each law enforcement agency that has investigated a case involving the collection of sexual assault kit evidence shall, within 120 days of collection, create an information profile for the kit on the Department of Justice's SAFE-T database and report the following:
(1) If biological evidence samples from the kit were submitted to a DNA laboratory for analysis.
(2) If the kit generated a probative DNA profile.
(3) If evidence was not submitted to a DNA laboratory for processing, the reason or reasons for not submitting evidence from the kit to a DNA laboratory for processing.
(b) After 120 days following submission of rape kit biological evidence for processing, if a public DNA laboratory has not conducted DNA testing, that laboratory shall provide the reasons for the status in the appropriate SAFE-T data field. If the investigating law enforcement agency has contracted with a private laboratory to conduct DNA testing on rape kit evidence, the submitting law enforcement agency shall provide the 120-day update in SAFE-T. The process described in this subdivision shall take place every 120 days until DNA testing occurs, except as provided in subdivision (c).

(c) Upon expiration of a sexual assault case's statute of limitations, or if a law enforcement agency elects not to analyze the DNA or intends to destroy or dispose of the crime scene evidence pursuant to subdivision (f) of Section 680, the investigating law enforcement agency shall state in writing the reason the kit collected as part of that case's investigation was not analyzed. This written statement relieves the investigating law enforcement agency or public laboratory of any further duty to report information related to that kit pursuant to this section.

(d) The SAFE-T database shall not contain any identifying information about a victim or a suspect, shall not contain any DNA profiles, and shall not contain any information that would impair a pending criminal investigation.

(e) On an annual basis, the Department of Justice shall file a report to the Legislature in compliance with Section 9795 of the Government Code summarizing data entered into the SAFE-T database during that year. The report shall not reference individual victims, suspects, investigations, or prosecutions. The report shall be made public by the department.

(f) Except as provided in subdivision (e), in order to protect the confidentiality of the SAFE-T database information, SAFE-T database contents shall be confidential, and a participating law enforcement agency or laboratory shall not be compelled in a criminal or civil proceeding, except as required by Brady v. Maryland (1963) 373 U.S. 83, to provide any SAFE-T database contents to a person or party seeking those records or information.

(g) The requirements of this section shall only apply to sexual assault evidence kit evidence collected on or after January 1, 2018.
(Amended by Stats. 2018, Ch. 36, Sec. 15. (AB 1812) Effective June 27, 2018.)
680.4.
(a) Each law enforcement agency, medical facility, crime laboratory, and any other facility that receives, maintains, stores, or preserves sexual assault evidence kits shall conduct an audit of all untested sexual assault kits in their possession and shall, no later than July 1, 2019, submit a report to the Department of Justice containing the following information:
(1) The total number of untested sexual assault kits in their possession.
(2) For each kit, the following information:
(A) Whether or not the assault was reported to a law enforcement agency.
(B) For kits other than those described in subparagraph (C), the following data, as applicable:
(i) The date the kit was collected.
(ii) The date the kit was picked up by a law enforcement agency, for each law enforcement agency that has taken custody of the kit.
(iii) The date the kit was delivered to a crime laboratory.
(iv) The reason the kit has not been tested, if applicable.
(C) For kits where the victim has chosen not to pursue prosecution at the time of the audit, only the number of kits.
(b) The Department of Justice shall, by no later than July 1, 2020, prepare and submit a report to the Legislature summarizing the information received pursuant to subdivision (a).
(c) The report required by subdivision (b) shall be submitted in compliance with Section 9795 of the Government Code.
(d) Pursuant to Section 10231.5 of the Government Code, this section is repealed on July 1, 2024.
(Added by Stats. 2018, Ch. 950, Sec. 1. (AB 3118) Effective January 1, 2019. Repealed as of July 1, 2024, by its own provisions.)

PART 2. OF CRIMINAL PROCEDURE [681 - 1620]
(Part 2 enacted 1872.)

TITLE 1. OF THE PREVENTION OF PUBLIC OFFENSES [692 - 727]
(Title 1 enacted 1872.)

CHAPTER 1. Of Lawful Resistance [692 - 694]

(Chapter 1 enacted 1872.)
692.
Lawful resistance to the commission of a public offense may be made:
1. By the party about to be injured;
2. By other parties.
(Enacted 1872.)
693.
Resistance sufficient to prevent the offense may be made by the party about to be injured:
1. To prevent an offense against his person, or his family, or some member thereof.
2. To prevent an illegal attempt by force to take or injure property in his lawful possession.
(Enacted 1872.)
694.
Any other person, in aid or defense of the person about to be injured, may make resistance sufficient to prevent the offense.
(Enacted 1872.)

CHAPTER 2. Of the Intervention of the Officers of Justice [697 - 698]

(Chapter 2 enacted 1872.)
697.
Public offenses may be prevented by the intervention of the officers of justice:
1. By requiring security to keep the peace;
2. By forming a police in cities and towns, and by requiring their attendance in exposed places;
3. By suppressing riots.
(Enacted 1872.)
698.
When the officers of justice are authorized to act in the prevention of public offenses, other persons, who, by their command, act in their aid, are justified in so doing.
(Enacted 1872.)

CHAPTER 3. Security to Keep the Peace [701 - 714]

(Chapter 3 enacted 1872.)
701.
An information may be laid before any of the magistrates mentioned in Section 808, that a person has threatened to commit an offense against the person or property of another.
(Enacted 1872.)
701.5.
(a) Notwithstanding subdivision (b), no peace officer or agent of a peace officer shall use a person who is 12 years of age or younger as a minor informant.
(b) No peace officer or agent of a peace officer shall use a person under the age of 18 years as a minor informant, except as authorized pursuant to the Stop Tobacco Access to Kids Enforcement Act (Division 8.5 (commencing with Section 22950) of the Business and Professions Code) for the purposes of that act, unless the peace officer or agent of a peace officer has obtained an order from the court authorizing the minor's cooperation.
(c) Prior to issuing any order pursuant to subdivision (b), the court shall find, after consideration of (1) the age and maturity of the minor, (2) the gravity of the minor's alleged offense, (3) the safety of the public, and (4) the interests of justice, that the agreement to act as a minor informant is voluntary and is being entered into knowingly and intelligently.
(d) Prior to the court making the finding required in subdivision (c), all of the following conditions shall be satisfied:
(1) The court has found probable cause that the minor committed the alleged offense. The finding of probable cause shall only be for the purpose of issuing the order pursuant to subdivision (b), and shall not prejudice the minor in any future proceedings.
(2) The court has advised the minor of the mandatory minimum and maximum sentence for the alleged offense.
(3) The court has disclosed the benefit the minor may obtain by cooperating with the peace officer or agent of a peace officer.
(4) The minor's parent or guardian has consented to the agreement by the minor unless the parent or guardian is a suspect in the criminal investigation.
(e) For purposes of this section, "minor informant" means a minor who participates, on behalf of a law enforcement agency, in a prearranged transaction or series of prearranged transactions with direct face-to-face contact with any party, when the minor's participation in the transaction is for the purpose of obtaining or attempting to obtain evidence of illegal activity by a third party and where the minor is participating in the transaction for the purpose of reducing or dismissing a pending juvenile petition against the minor.
(Added by Stats. 1998, Ch. 833, Sec. 1. Effective September 25, 1998.)
702.
When the information is laid before such magistrate he must examine on oath the informer, and any witness he may produce, and must take their depositions in writing, and cause them to be subscribed by the parties making them.
(Enacted 1872.)
703.
If it appears from the depositions that there is just reason to fear the commission of the offense threatened, by the person so informed against, the magistrate must issue a warrant, directed generally to the sheriff of the county, or any marshal, or policeman in the state, reciting the substance of the information, and commanding the officer forthwith to arrest the person informed of and bring him or her before the magistrate.
(Amended by Stats. 1996, Ch. 872, Sec. 113. Effective January 1, 1997.)
704.
When the person informed against is brought before the magistrate, if the charge be controverted, the magistrate shall take testimony in relation thereto. The evidence shall be reduced to writing and subscribed by the witnesses. The magistrate may, in his or her discretion, order the testimony and proceedings to be taken down in shorthand, and for that purpose he or she may appoint a shorthand reporter. The deposition or testimony of the witnesses shall be authenticated in the form prescribed in Section 869.
(Amended by Stats. 1987, Ch. 828, Sec. 48.)
705.
If it appears that there is no just reason to fear the commission of the offense alleged to have been threatened, the person complained of must be discharged.
(Enacted 1872.)
706.
If, however, there is just reason to fear the commission of the offense, the person complained of may be required to enter into an undertaking in such sum, not exceeding five thousand dollars, as the magistrate may direct, to keep the peace towards the people of this state, and particularly towards the informer. The undertaking is valid and binding for six months, and may, upon the renewal of the information, be extended for a longer period, or a new undertaking may be required.
(Amended by Stats. 1982, Ch. 517, Sec. 315.)
707.
If the undertaking required by the last section is given, the party informed of must be discharged. If he does not give it, the magistrate must commit him to prison, specifying in the warrant the requirement to give security, the amount thereof, and the omission to give the same.
(Enacted 1872.)
708.
If the person complained of is committed for not giving the undertaking required, he may be discharged by any magistrate, upon giving the same.
(Enacted 1872.)
709.
The undertaking must be filed by the magistrate in the office of the Clerk of the county.
(Enacted 1872.)
710.
A person who, in the presence of a Court or magistrate, assaults or threatens to assault another, or to commit an offense against his person or property, or who contends with another with angry words, may be ordered by the Court or magistrate to give security, as in this Chapter provided, and if he refuse to do so, may be committed as provided in Section 707.
(Enacted 1872.)
711.
Upon the conviction of the person informed against of a breach of the peace, the undertaking is broken.
(Enacted 1872.)
712.
Upon the District Attorney's producing evidence of such conviction to the Superior Court of the county, the Court must order the undertaking to be prosecuted, and the District Attorney must thereupon commence an action upon it in the name of the people of this State.
(Amended by Code Amendments 1880, Ch. 56.)
713.
In the action the offense stated in the record of conviction must be alleged as a breach of the undertaking, and such record is conclusive evidence of the breach.

(Enacted 1872.)
714.
Security to keep the peace, or be of good behavior, cannot be required except as prescribed in this Chapter.
(Enacted 1872.)

CHAPTER 5. Suppression of Riots [723 - 727]

(Chapter 5 enacted 1872.)
723.
When a sheriff or other public officer authorized to execute process finds, or has reason to apprehend, that resistance will be made to the execution of the process, the officer may command as many able-bodied inhabitants of the officer's county as he or she may think proper to assist in overcoming the resistance and, if necessary, in seizing, arresting, and confining the persons resisting, and their aiders and abettors.
(Amended by Stats. 1988, Ch. 160, Sec. 128.)
724.
The officer must certify to the Court from which the process issued the names of the persons resisting, and their aiders and abettors, to the end that they may be proceeded against for their contempt of Court.
(Enacted 1872.)
726.
Where any number of persons, whether armed or not, are unlawfully or riotously assembled, the sheriff of the county and his or her deputies, the officials governing the town or city, or any of them, must go among the persons assembled, or as near to them as possible, and command them, in the name of the people of the state, immediately to disperse.
(Amended by Stats. 1998, Ch. 931, Sec. 355. Effective September 28, 1998.)
727.
If the persons assembled do not immediately disperse, such magistrates and officers must arrest them, and to that end may command the aid of all persons present or within the county.
(Enacted 1872.)

TITLE 2. MODE OF PROSECUTION [737 - 740]

(Title 2 added by Stats. 1951, Ch. 1674.)
737.
All felonies shall be prosecuted by indictment or information, except as provided in Section 859a. A proceeding pursuant to Section 3060 of the Government Code shall be prosecuted by accusation.
(Amended by Stats. 1998, Ch. 931, Sec. 356. Effective September 28, 1998.)
738.
Before an information is filed there must be a preliminary examination of the case against the defendant and an order holding him to answer made under Section 872. The proceeding for a preliminary examination must be commenced by written complaint, as provided elsewhere in this code.
(Added by Stats. 1951, Ch. 1674.)
739.
When a defendant has been examined and committed, as provided in Section 872, it shall be the duty of the district attorney of the county in which the offense is triable to file in the superior court of that county within 15 days after the commitment, an information against the defendant which may charge the defendant with either the offense or offenses named in the order of commitment or any offense or offenses shown by the evidence taken before the magistrate to have been committed. The information shall be in the name of the people of the State of California and subscribed by the district attorney.
(Added by Stats. 1951, Ch. 1674.)
740.
Except as otherwise provided by law, all misdemeanors and infractions must be prosecuted by written complaint under oath subscribed by the complainant. Such complaint may be verified on information and belief.
(Amended by Stats. 1998, Ch. 931, Sec. 357. Effective September 28, 1998.)

TITLE 2.5. NIGHTCOURT [750- 750.]

(Title 2.5 added by Stats. 1992, Ch. 284, Sec. 1.)
750.
Notwithstanding any other provision of law, in the event that the superior court of a county having a population in excess of six million has discontinued, on or after December 1, 1991, a nightcourt policy or program with respect to criminal cases, the policy or program shall, upon approval of the board of supervisors, be substantially reinstated, with at least the average level of staffing and session scheduling which occurred during the period of six months immediately prior to December 1, 1991.
(Added by Stats. 1992, Ch. 284, Sec. 1. Effective July 21, 1992.)

TITLE 3. ADDITIONAL PROVISIONS REGARDING CRIMINAL PROCEDURE [777 - 883]

(Heading of Title 3 amended by Stats. 1951, Ch. 1674.)

CHAPTER 1. Of the Local Jurisdiction of Public Offenses [777 - 795]

(Chapter 1 enacted 1872.)
777.
Every person is liable to punishment by the laws of this State, for a public offense committed by him therein, except where it is by law cognizable exclusively in the courts of the United States; and except as otherwise provided by law the jurisdiction of every public offense is in any competent court within the jurisdictional territory of which it is committed.
(Amended by Stats. 1951, Ch. 1674.)
777a.

If a parent violates the provisions of Section 270 of this code, the jurisdiction of such offense is in any competent court of either the jurisdictional territory in which the minor child is cared for or in which such parent is apprehended.
(Added by Stats. 1951, Ch. 1674.)
777b.
Perjury, in violation of Section 118, committed outside of the State of California is punishable in a competent court in the jurisdictional territory in this state in which occurs the act, transaction, matter, action, or proceeding, in relation to which the testimony, declaration, deposition, or certification was given or made.
(Added by Stats. 1980, Ch. 889, Sec. 4.)
778.
When the commission of a public offense, commenced without the State, is consummated within its boundaries by a defendant, himself outside the State, through the intervention of an innocent or guilty agent or any other means proceeding directly from said defendant, he is liable to punishment therefor in this State in any competent court within the jurisdictional territory of which the offense is consummated.
(Amended by Stats. 1951, Ch. 1674.)
778a.
(a) Whenever a person, with intent to commit a crime, does any act within this state in execution or part execution of that intent, which culminates in the commission of a crime, either within or without this state, the person is punishable for that crime in this state in the same manner as if the crime had been committed entirely within this state.
(b) Whenever a person who, within this state, kidnaps another person within the meaning of Sections 207 and 209, and thereafter carries the person into another state or country and commits any crime of violence or theft against that person in the other state or country, the person is punishable for that crime of violence or theft in this state in the same manner as if the crime had been committed within this state.
(Amended by Stats. 2001, Ch. 854, Sec. 39. Effective January 1, 2002.)
778b.
Every person who, being out of this state, causes, aids, advises, or encourages any person to commit a crime within this state, and is afterwards found within this state, is punishable in the same manner as if he had been within this state when he caused, aided, advised, or encouraged the commission of such crime.
(Added by Stats. 1905, Ch. 529.)
781.
Except as provided in Section 923, when a public offense is committed in part in one jurisdictional territory and in part in another jurisdictional territory, or the acts or effects thereof constituting or requisite to the consummation of the offense occur in two or more jurisdictional territories, the jurisdiction for the offense is in any competent court within either jurisdictional territory.
(Amended by Stats. 2013, Ch. 59, Sec. 2. (SB 514) Effective January 1, 2014.)
782.
When a public offense is committed on the boundary of two or more jurisdictional territories, or within 500 yards thereof, the jurisdiction of such offense is in any competent court within either jurisdictional territory.
(Amended by Stats. 1951, Ch. 1674.)
783.
When a public offense is committed in this State, on board a vessel navigating a river, bay, slough, lake, or canal, or lying therein, in the prosecution of its voyage, or on a railroad train or car, motor vehicle, common carrier transporting passengers or on an aircraft prosecuting its trip, the jurisdiction is in any competent court, through, on, or over the jurisdictional territory of which the vessel, train, car, motor vehicle, common carrier or aircraft passes in the course of its voyage or trip, or in the jurisdictional territory of which the voyage or trip terminates.
(Amended by Stats. 1951, Ch. 1674.)
783.5.
When a public offense is committed in a park situated in more than one county, the jurisdiction over such an offense is in any competent court in any county in which any part of the park is situated. "Park," as used in this section means any area of land, or water, or both, which has been designated as a park or recreation area by any public agency or political subdivision of this state.
(Added by Stats. 1965, Ch. 582.)
784.
The jurisdiction of a criminal action:
(a) For forcibly and without lawful authority seizing and confining another, or inveigling or kidnapping another, with intent, against his or her will, to cause him or her to be secretly confined or imprisoned in this state, or to be sent out of the state, or from one county to another, or to be sold as a slave, or in any way held to service;
(b) For inveigling, enticing, or taking away any person for the purpose of concubinage or prostitution, as defined in subdivision (b) of Section 647;
Is in any competent court within the jurisdictional territory in which the offense was committed, or in the jurisdictional territory out of which the person upon whom the offense was committed was taken or within the jurisdictional territory in which an act was done by the defendant in instigating, procuring, promoting, or aiding in the commission of the offense, or in abetting the parties concerned therein.
(Amended by Stats. 1983, Ch. 990, Sec. 6.)
784.5.
The jurisdiction of a criminal action for a violation of Section 277, 278, or 278.5 shall be in any one of the following jurisdictional territories:
(a) Any jurisdictional territory in which the victimized person resides, or where the agency deprived of custody is located, at the time of the taking or deprivation.
(b) The jurisdictional territory in which the minor child was taken, detained, or concealed.
(c) The jurisdictional territory in which the minor child is found.
When the jurisdiction lies in more than one jurisdictional territory, the district attorneys concerned may agree which of them will prosecute the case.
(Amended by Stats. 1984, Ch. 1207, Sec. 5.)
784.7.
(a) If more than one violation of Section 220, except assault with intent to commit mayhem, 261, 262, 264.1, 269, 286, 287, 288, 288.5, 288.7, or 289 or former Section 288a occurs in more than one jurisdictional territory, the jurisdiction of any of those offenses, and for any offenses properly joinable with that offense, is in any jurisdiction where at least one of the offenses occurred, subject to a hearing, pursuant to Section 954, within the jurisdiction of the proposed trial. At the Section 954 hearing, the prosecution shall present written evidence that all district attorneys in counties with jurisdiction of the offenses agree to the venue. Charged offenses from jurisdictions where there is not a written agreement from the district attorney shall be returned to that jurisdiction.
(b) If more than one violation of Section 243.4, 261.5, 273a, 273.5, or 646.9 occurs in more than one jurisdictional territory, and the defendant and the victim are the same for all of the offenses, the jurisdiction of any of those offenses and for any offenses properly joinable with that offense, is in any jurisdiction where at least one of the offenses occurred.
(c) If more than one violation of Section 236.1, 266h, or 266i occurs in more than one jurisdictional territory, the jurisdiction of any of those offenses, and for any offenses properly joinable with that offense, is in any jurisdiction where at least one of the offenses occurred, subject to a hearing pursuant to Section 954, within the jurisdiction of the proposed trial. At the Section 954 hearing, the prosecution shall present written evidence that all district attorneys in counties with jurisdiction of the offenses agree to

the venue. Charged offenses from jurisdictions where there is not a written agreement from the district attorney shall be returned to that jurisdiction. In determining whether all counts in the complaint should be joined in one county for prosecution, the court shall consider the location and complexity of the likely evidence, where the majority of the offenses occurred, the rights of the defendant and the people, and the convenience of, or hardship to, the victim or victims and witnesses.
(Amended by Stats. 2018, Ch. 962, Sec. 1.5. (AB 1746) Effective January 1, 2019.)
785.
When the offense of incest is committed in the jurisdictional territory of one competent court and the defendant is apprehended in the jurisdictional territory of another competent court the jurisdiction is in either court.
When the offense of bigamy is committed, the jurisdiction is in any competent court within the jurisdictional territory of which the marriage took place, or cohabitation occurred or the defendant was apprehended.
(Amended by Stats. 1951, Ch. 1674.)
786.
(a) If property taken in one jurisdictional territory by burglary, carjacking, robbery, theft, or embezzlement has been brought into another, or when property is received in one jurisdictional territory with the knowledge that it has been stolen or embezzled and the property was stolen or embezzled in another jurisdictional territory, the jurisdiction of the offense is in any competent court within either jurisdictional territory, or any contiguous jurisdictional territory if the arrest is made within the contiguous territory, the prosecution secures on the record the defendant's knowing, voluntary, and intelligent waiver of the right of vicinage, and the defendant is charged with one or more property crimes in the arresting territory.
(b) (1) The jurisdiction of a criminal action for unauthorized use, retention, or transfer of personal identifying information, as defined in subdivision (b) of Section 530.55, shall also include the county where the theft of the personal identifying information occurred, the county in which the victim resided at the time the offense was committed, or the county where the information was used for an illegal purpose. If multiple offenses of unauthorized use of personal identifying information, either all involving the same defendant or defendants and the same personal identifying information belonging to the one person, or all involving the same defendant or defendants and the same scheme or substantially similar activity, occur in multiple jurisdictions, then any of those jurisdictions is a proper jurisdiction for all of the offenses. Jurisdiction also extends to all associated offenses connected together in their commission to the underlying identity theft offense or identity theft offenses.
(2) When charges alleging multiple offenses of unauthorized use of personal identifying information occurring in multiple territorial jurisdictions are filed in one county pursuant to this section, the court shall hold a hearing to consider whether the matter should proceed in the county of filing, or whether one or more counts should be severed. The district attorney filing the complaint shall present evidence to the court that the district attorney in each county where any of the charges could have been filed has agreed that the matter should proceed in the county of filing. In determining whether all counts in the complaint should be joined in one county for prosecution, the court shall consider the location and complexity of the likely evidence, where the majority of the offenses occurred, whether or not the offenses involved substantially similar activity or the same scheme, the rights of the defendant and the people, and the convenience of, or hardship to, the victim and witnesses.
(3) When an action for unauthorized use, retention, or transfer of personal identifying information is filed in the county in which the victim resided at the time the offense was committed, and no other basis for the jurisdiction applies, the court, upon its own motion or the motion of the defendant, shall hold a hearing to determine whether the county of the victim's residence is the proper venue for trial of the case. In ruling on the matter, the court shall consider the rights of the parties, the access of the parties to evidence, the convenience to witnesses, and the interests of justice.
(c) (1) The jurisdiction of a criminal action for conduct specified in paragraph (4) of subdivision (j) of Section 647 shall also include the county in which the offense occurred, the county in which the victim resided at the time the offense was committed, or the county in which the intimate image was used for an illegal purpose. If multiple offenses of unauthorized distribution of an intimate image, either all involving the same defendant or defendants and the same intimate image belonging to the one person, or all involving the same defendant or defendants and the same scheme or substantially similar activity, occur in multiple jurisdictions, then any of those jurisdictions is a proper jurisdiction for all of the offenses. Jurisdiction also extends to all associated offenses connected together in their commission to the underlying unauthorized distribution of an intimate image.
(2) When charges alleging multiple offenses of unauthorized distribution of an intimate image occurring in multiple territorial jurisdictions are filed in one county pursuant to this section, the court shall hold a hearing to consider whether the matter should proceed in the county of filing, or whether one or more counts should be severed. The district attorney filing the complaint shall present evidence to the court that the district attorney in each county where any of the charges could have been filed has agreed that the matter should proceed in the county of filing. In determining whether all counts in the complaint should be joined in one county for prosecution, the court shall consider the location and complexity of the likely evidence, where the majority of the offenses occurred, whether the offenses involved substantially similar activity or the same scheme, the rights of the defendant and the people, and the convenience of, or hardship to, the victim and witnesses.
(3) When an action for unauthorized distribution of an intimate image is filed in the county in which the victim resided at the time the offense was committed, and no other basis for the jurisdiction applies, the court, upon its own motion or the motion of the defendant, shall hold a hearing to determine whether the county of the victim's residence is the proper venue for trial of the case. In ruling on the matter, the court shall consider the rights of the parties, the access of the parties to evidence, the convenience to witnesses, and the interests of justice.
(d) This section does not alter victims' rights under Section 530.6.
(Amended by Stats. 2015, Ch. 643, Sec. 1. (AB 1310) Effective January 1, 2016.)
786.5.
(a) The jurisdiction of a criminal action for theft, as defined in subdivision (a) of Section 484, or a violation of Section 490.4 or Section 496, shall also include the county where an offense involving the theft or receipt of the stolen merchandise occurred, the county in which the merchandise was recovered, or the county where any act was done by the defendant in instigating, procuring, promoting, or aiding in the commission of a theft offense or a violation of Section 490.4 or Section 496 or in abetting the parties concerned therein. If multiple offenses of theft or violations of Section 490.4 or Section 496, either all involving the same defendant or defendants and the same merchandise, or all involving the same defendant or defendants and the same scheme or substantially similar activity, occur in multiple jurisdictions, then any of those jurisdictions are a proper jurisdiction for all of the offenses. Jurisdiction also extends to all associated offenses connected together in their commission to the underlying theft offenses or violations of Section 490.4 or Section 496.
(b) This section shall remain in effect only until July 1, 2021, and as of that date is repealed.
(Amended by Stats. 2019, Ch. 25, Sec. 29. (SB 94) Effective June 27, 2019. Repealed as of July 1, 2021, by its own provisions.)
787.
When multiple offenses punishable under one or more of Sections 11418, 11418.5, and 11419 occur in more than one jurisdictional territory, and the offenses are part of a

single scheme or terrorist attack, the jurisdiction of any of those offenses is in any jurisdiction where at least one of those offenses occurred.
(Added by Stats. 2002, Ch. 64, Sec. 1. Effective June 21, 2002.)

788.

The jurisdiction of a criminal action for treason, when the overt act is committed out of the State, is in any county of the State.
(Amended by Code Amendments 1880, Ch. 47.)

789.

The jurisdiction of a criminal action for stealing or embezzling, in any other state, the property of another, or receiving it knowing it to have been stolen or embezzled, and bringing the same into this State, is in any competent court into or through the jurisdictional territory of which such stolen or embezzled property has been brought.
(Amended by Stats. 1951, Ch. 1674.)

790.

(a) The jurisdiction of a criminal action for murder or manslaughter is in the county where the fatal injury was inflicted or in the county in which the injured party died or in the county in which his or her body was found. However, if the defendant is indicted in the county in which the fatal injury was inflicted, at any time before his or her trial in another county, the sheriff of the other county shall, if the defendant is in custody, deliver the defendant upon demand to the sheriff of the county in which the fatal injury was inflicted. When the fatal injury was inflicted and the injured person died or his or her body was found within five hundred yards of the boundary of two or more counties, jurisdiction is in either county.
(b) If a defendant is charged with a special circumstance pursuant to paragraph (3) of subdivision (a) of Section 190.2, the jurisdiction for any charged murder, and for any crimes properly joinable with that murder, shall be in any county that has jurisdiction pursuant to subdivision (a) for one or more of the murders charged in a single complaint or indictment as long as the charged murders are "connected together in their commission," as that phrase is used in Section 954, and subject to a hearing in the jurisdiction where the prosecution is attempting to consolidate the charged murders. If the charged murders are not joined or consolidated, the murder that was charged outside of the county that has jurisdiction pursuant to subdivision (a) shall be returned to that county.
(Amended by Stats. 1999, Ch. 83, Sec. 148. Effective January 1, 2000.)

791.

In the case of an accessory, as defined in Section 32, in the commission of a public offense, the jurisdiction is in any competent court within the jurisdictional territory of which the offense of the accessory was committed, notwithstanding the principal offense was committed in another jurisdictional territory.
(Amended by Stats. 1951, Ch. 1674.)

792.

The jurisdiction of a criminal action against a principal in the commission of a public offense, when such principal is not present at the commission of the offense is in the same court it would be under this code if he were so present and aiding and abetting therein.
(Amended by Stats. 1951, Ch. 1674.)

793.

When an act charged as a public offense is within the jurisdiction of the United States, or of another state or territory of the United States, as well as of this state, a conviction or acquittal thereof in that other jurisdiction is a bar to the prosecution or indictment in this state.
(Amended by Stats. 2004, Ch. 511, Sec. 4. Effective January 1, 2005.)

793.5.

Any person convicted of a crime based upon an act or omission for which he or she has been acquitted or convicted in another country shall be entitled to credit for any actual time served in custody in a penal institution in that country for the crime.
(Added by Stats. 2004, Ch. 511, Sec. 5. Effective January 1, 2005.)

794.

Where an offense is within the jurisdiction of two or more courts, a conviction or acquittal thereof in one court is a bar to a prosecution therefor in another.
(Amended by Stats. 1951, Ch. 1674.)

795.

The jurisdiction of a violation of Sections 412, 413, or 414, or a conspiracy to violate any of said sections, is in any competent court within the jurisdictional territory of which:
First. Any act is done towards the commission of the offense; or,
Second. The offender passed, whether into, out of, or through it, to commit the offense; or,
Third. The offender is arrested.
(Amended by Stats. 1951, Ch. 1674.)

CHAPTER 2. Time of Commencing Criminal Actions [799 - 805]

(Chapter 2 repealed and added by Stats. 1984, Ch. 1270, Sec. 2.)

799.

(a) Prosecution for an offense punishable by death or by imprisonment in the state prison for life or for life without the possibility of parole, or for the embezzlement of public money, may be commenced at any time.
(b) (1) Prosecution for a felony offense described in paragraph (1), (2), (3), (4), (6) or (7) of subdivision (a) of Section 261, paragraph (1), (2), (3), (4), or (5) of subdivision (a) of Section 262, Section 264.1, paragraph (2) or (3) of subdivision (c) of, or subdivision (d), (f), (g), (i), or (k) of, Section 286, paragraph (2) or (3) of subdivision (c) of, or subdivision (d), (f), (g), (i), or (k) of, Section 287 or former Section 288a, subdivision (a) of Section 288 involving substantial sexual conduct as defined by in subdivision (b) of Section 1203.066, subdivision (b) of Section 288, Section 288.5, or subdivision (a), (b), (d), (e), or (g) of Section 289 may be commenced at any time.
(2) This subdivision applies to crimes that were committed on or after January 1, 2017, and to crimes for which the statute of limitations that was in effect prior to January 1, 2017, has not run as of January 1, 2017.
(c) This section shall apply in any case in which the defendant was a minor at the time of the commission of the offense and the prosecuting attorney could have petitioned the court for a fitness hearing pursuant to Section 707 of the Welfare and Institutions Code.
(Amended by Stats. 2018, Ch. 423, Sec. 77. (SB 1494) Effective January 1, 2019.)

800.

Except as provided in Section 799, prosecution for an offense punishable by imprisonment in the state prison for eight years or more or by imprisonment pursuant to subdivision (h) of Section 1170 for eight years or more shall be commenced within six years after commission of the offense.
(Amended (as amended by Stats. 2011, Ch. 39, Sec. 24) by Stats. 2011, 1st Ex. Sess., Ch. 12, Sec. 11. (AB 17 1x) Effective September 21, 2011. Operative October 1, 2011, by Sec. 46 of Ch. 12.)

801.

Except as provided in Sections 799 and 800, prosecution for an offense punishable by imprisonment in the state prison or pursuant to subdivision (h) of Section 1170 shall be commenced within three years after commission of the offense.
(Amended by Stats. 2011, Ch. 15, Sec. 446. (AB 109) Effective April 4, 2011. Operative October 1, 2011, by Sec. 636 of Ch. 15, as amended by Stats. 2011, Ch. 39, Sec. 68.)

801.1.

(a) (1) Notwithstanding any other limitation of time described in this chapter, prosecution for a felony offense described in Section 261, 286, 287, 288, 288.5, or 289, or former Section 288a, or Section 289.5, as enacted by Chapter 293 of the Statutes of 1991 relating to penetration by an unknown object, that is alleged to have been committed when the victim was under 18 years of age, may be commenced any time prior to the victim's 40th birthday.
(2) Paragraph (1) shall only apply to crimes that were committed on or after January 1, 2015, or for which the statute of limitations that was in effect prior to January 1, 2015, has not run as of January 1, 2015.
(b) Notwithstanding any other limitation of time described in this chapter, if either subdivision (a) of this section or subdivision (b) of Section 799 does not apply, prosecution for a felony offense described in subdivision (c) of Section 290 shall be commenced within 10 years after commission of the offense.
(Amended by Stats. 2018, Ch. 423, Sec. 78. (SB 1494) Effective January 1, 2019.)

801.2.

Notwithstanding any other limitation of time prescribed in this chapter, prosecution for a violation of subdivision (b) of Section 311.4 shall commence within 10 years of the date of production of the pornographic material.
(Added by Stats. 2006, Ch. 337, Sec. 35. Effective September 20, 2006.)

801.5.

Notwithstanding Section 801 or any other provision of law, prosecution for any offense described in subdivision (c) of Section 803 shall be commenced within four years after discovery of the commission of the offense, or within four years after the completion of the offense, whichever is later.
(Amended by Stats. 1995, Ch. 704, Sec. 1. Effective January 1, 1996.)

801.6.

Notwithstanding any other limitation of time described in this chapter, prosecution for any offense proscribed by Section 368, except for a violation of any provision of law proscribing theft or embezzlement, or for the failure of a mandated reporter to report an incident under Section 11166 known or reasonably suspected by the mandated reporter to be sexual assault as defined in Section 11165.1, may be filed at any time within five years from the date of occurrence of such offense.
(Amended by Stats. 2018, Ch. 943, Sec. 1. (AB 2302) Effective January 1, 2019.)

802.

(a) Except as provided in subdivision (b), (c), (d), or (e), prosecution for an offense not punishable by death or imprisonment in the state prison or pursuant to subdivision (h) of Section 1170 shall be commenced within one year after commission of the offense.
(b) Prosecution for a misdemeanor violation of Section 647.6 or former Section 647a committed with or upon a minor under the age of 14 years shall be commenced within three years after commission of the offense.
(c) Prosecution of a misdemeanor violation of Section 729 of the Business and Professions Code shall be commenced within two years after commission of the offense.
(d) Prosecution of a misdemeanor violation of Chapter 9 (commencing with Section 7000) of Division 3 of the Business and Professions Code shall be commenced as follows:
(1) With respect to Sections 7028.17, 7068.5, and 7068.7 of the Business and Professions Code, within one year of the commission of the offense.
(2) With respect to Sections 7027.1, 7028.1, 7028.15, 7118.4, 7118.5, 7118.6, 7126, 7153, 7156, 7157, 7158, 7159.5 (licensee only), 7159.14 (licensee only), 7161, and 7189 of the Business and Professions Code, within two years of the commission of the offense.
(3) With respect to Sections 7027.3 and 7028.16 of the Business and Professions Code, within three years of the commission of the offense.
(4) With respect to Sections 7028, 7159.5 (nonlicensee only), and 7159.14 (nonlicensee only) of the Business and Professions Code, within four years of the commission of the offense.
(e) Prosecution for a misdemeanor violation of Section 6126, 10085.6, 10139, or 10147.6 of the Business and Professions Code or Section 2944.6 or 2944.7 of the Civil Code shall be commenced within three years after discovery of the commission of the offense, or within three years after completion of the offense, whichever is later.
(Amended (as amended by Stats. 2012, Ch. 43) by Stats. 2012, Ch. 569, Sec. 4. (AB 1950) Effective January 1, 2013.)

802.5.

Notwithstanding Section 802 or any other provision of law, prosecution for the offense described in Section 18897.93 of the Business and Professions Code shall be commenced within three years after discovery of the commission of the offense.
(Added by Stats. 2011, Ch. 146, Sec. 2. (SB 238) Effective January 1, 2012.)

803.

(a) Except as provided in this section, a limitation of time prescribed in this chapter is not tolled or extended for any reason.
(b) No time during which prosecution of the same person for the same conduct is pending in a court of this state is a part of a limitation of time prescribed in this chapter.
(c) A limitation of time prescribed in this chapter does not commence to run until the discovery of an offense described in this subdivision. This subdivision applies to an offense punishable by imprisonment in the state prison or imprisonment pursuant to subdivision (h) of Section 1170, a material element of which is fraud or breach of a fiduciary obligation, the commission of the crimes of theft or embezzlement upon an elder or dependent adult, or the basis of which is misconduct in office by a public officer, employee, or appointee, including, but not limited to, the following offenses:
(1) Grand theft of any type, forgery, falsification of public records, or acceptance of, or asking, receiving, or agreeing to receive, a bribe, by a public official or a public employee, including, but not limited to, a violation of Section 68, 86, or 93.
(2) A violation of Section 72, 118, 118a, 132, 134, or 186.10.
(3) A violation of Section 25540, of any type, or Section 25541 of the Corporations Code.
(4) A violation of Section 1090 or 27443 of the Government Code.
(5) Felony welfare fraud or Medi-Cal fraud in violation of Section 11483 or 14107 of the Welfare and Institutions Code.
(6) Felony insurance fraud in violation of Section 548 or 550 of this code or former Section 1871.1, or Section 1871.4, of the Insurance Code.
(7) A violation of Section 580, 581, 582, 583, or 584 of the Business and Professions Code.
(8) A violation of Section 22430 of the Business and Professions Code.
(9) A violation of Section 103800 of the Health and Safety Code.
(10) A violation of Section 529a.
(11) A violation of subdivision (d) or (e) of Section 368.
(d) If the defendant is out of the state when or after the offense is committed, the prosecution may be commenced as provided in Section 804 within the limitations of time prescribed by this chapter, and no time up to a maximum of three years during which the defendant is not within the state shall be a part of those limitations.
(e) A limitation of time prescribed in this chapter does not commence to run until the offense has been discovered, or could have reasonably been discovered, with regard to offenses under Division 7 (commencing with Section 13000) of the Water Code, under Chapter 6.5 (commencing with Section 25100) of, Chapter 6.7 (commencing with Section 25280) of, or Chapter 6.8 (commencing with Section 25300) of, Division 20 of, or Part 4 (commencing with Section 41500) of Division 26 of, the Health and Safety

Code, or under Section 386, or offenses under Chapter 5 (commencing with Section 2000) of Division 2 of, Chapter 9 (commencing with Section 4000) of Division 2 of, Section 6126 of, Chapter 10 (commencing with Section 7301) of Division 3 of, or Chapter 19.5 (commencing with Section 22440) of Division 8 of, the Business and Professions Code.

(f) (1) Notwithstanding any other limitation of time described in this chapter, if subdivision (b) of Section 799 does not apply, a criminal complaint may be filed within one year of the date of a report to a California law enforcement agency by a person of any age alleging that he or she, while under 18 years of age, was the victim of a crime described in Section 261, 286, 287, 288, 288.5, or 289, former Section 288a, or Section 289.5, as enacted by Chapter 293 of the Statutes of 1991 relating to penetration by an unknown object.

(2) This subdivision applies only if all of the following occur:

(A) The limitation period specified in Section 800, 801, or 801.1, whichever is later, has expired.

(B) The crime involved substantial sexual conduct, as described in subdivision (b) of Section 1203.066, excluding masturbation that is not mutual.

(C) There is independent evidence that corroborates the victim's allegation. If the victim was 21 years of age or older at the time of the report, the independent evidence shall clearly and convincingly corroborate the victim's allegation.

(3) No evidence may be used to corroborate the victim's allegation that otherwise would be inadmissible during trial. Independent evidence does not include the opinions of mental health professionals.

(4) (A) In a criminal investigation involving any of the crimes listed in paragraph (1) committed against a child, when the applicable limitations period has not expired, that period shall be tolled from the time a party initiates litigation challenging a grand jury subpoena until the end of the litigation, including any associated writ or appellate proceeding, or until the final disclosure of evidence to the investigating or prosecuting agency, if that disclosure is ordered pursuant to the subpoena after the litigation.

(B) Nothing in this subdivision affects the definition or applicability of any evidentiary privilege.

(C) This subdivision shall not apply if a court finds that the grand jury subpoena was issued or caused to be issued in bad faith.

(g) (1) Notwithstanding any other limitation of time described in this chapter, a criminal complaint may be filed within one year of the date on which the identity of the suspect is conclusively established by DNA testing, if both of the following conditions are met:

(A) The crime is one that is described in subdivision (c) of Section 290.

(B) The offense was committed prior to January 1, 2001, and biological evidence collected in connection with the offense is analyzed for DNA type no later than January 1, 2004, or the offense was committed on or after January 1, 2001, and biological evidence collected in connection with the offense is analyzed for DNA type no later than two years from the date of the offense.

(2) For purposes of this section, "DNA" means deoxyribonucleic acid.

(h) For any crime, the proof of which depends substantially upon evidence that was seized under a warrant, but which is unavailable to the prosecuting authority under the procedures described in People v. Superior Court (Laff) (2001) 25 Cal.4th 703, People v. Superior Court (Bauman & Rose) (1995) 37 Cal.App.4th 1757, or subdivision (c) of Section 1524, relating to claims of evidentiary privilege or attorney work product, the limitation of time prescribed in this chapter shall be tolled from the time of the seizure until final disclosure of the evidence to the prosecuting authority. Nothing in this section otherwise affects the definition or applicability of any evidentiary privilege or attorney work product.

(i) Notwithstanding any other limitation of time described in this chapter, a criminal complaint may be filed within one year of the date on which a hidden recording is discovered related to a violation of paragraph (2) or (3) of subdivision (j) of Section 647.

(j) Notwithstanding any other limitation of time described in this chapter, if a person flees the scene of an accident that caused death or permanent, serious injury, as defined in subdivision (d) of Section 20001 of the Vehicle Code, a criminal complaint brought pursuant to paragraph (2) of subdivision (b) of Section 20001 of the Vehicle Code may be filed within the applicable time period described in Section 801 or 802 or one year after the person is initially identified by law enforcement as a suspect in the commission of the offense, whichever is later, but in no case later than six years after the commission of the offense.

(k) Notwithstanding any other limitation of time described in this chapter, if a person flees the scene of an accident, a criminal complaint brought pursuant to paragraph (1) or (2) of subdivision (c) of Section 192 may be filed within the applicable time period described in Section 801 or 802, or one year after the person is initially identified by law enforcement as a suspect in the commission of that offense, whichever is later, but in no case later than six years after the commission of the offense.

(l) A limitation of time prescribed in this chapter does not commence to run until the discovery of an offense involving the offering or giving of a bribe to a public official or public employee, including, but not limited to, a violation of Section 67, 67.5, 85, 92, or 165, or Section 35230 or 72530 of the Education Code.

(m) Notwithstanding any other limitation of time prescribed in this chapter, if a person actively conceals or attempts to conceal an accidental death in violation of Section 152, a criminal complaint may be filed within one year after the person is initially identified by law enforcement as a suspect in the commission of that offense, provided, however, that in any case a complaint may not be filed more than four years after the commission of the offense.

(Amended by Stats. 2018, Ch. 423, Sec. 79. (SB 1494) Effective January 1, 2019.)

803.5.
With respect to a violation of Section 115 or 530.5, a limitation of time prescribed in this chapter does not commence to run until the discovery of the offense.
(Added by Stats. 2003, Ch. 468, Sec. 10.5. Effective January 1, 2004.)

803.6.
(a) If more than one time period described in this chapter applies, the time for commencing an action shall be governed by that period that expires the latest in time.

(b) Any change in the time period for the commencement of prosecution described in this chapter applies to any crime if prosecution for the crime was not barred on the effective date of the change by the statute of limitations in effect immediately prior to the effective date of the change.

(c) This section is declaratory of existing law.
(Added by Stats. 2004, Ch. 368, Sec. 3. Effective January 1, 2005.)

804.
Except as otherwise provided in this chapter, for the purpose of this chapter, prosecution for an offense is commenced when any of the following occurs:

(a) An indictment or information is filed.

(b) A complaint is filed charging a misdemeanor or infraction.

(c) The defendant is arraigned on a complaint that charges the defendant with a felony.

(d) An arrest warrant or bench warrant is issued, provided the warrant names or describes the defendant with the same degree of particularity required for an indictment, information, or complaint.
(Amended by Stats. 2008, Ch. 110, Sec. 1. Effective January 1, 2009.)

805.
For the purpose of determining the applicable limitation of time pursuant to this chapter:

(a) An offense is deemed punishable by the maximum punishment prescribed by statute for the offense, regardless of the punishment actually sought or imposed. Any

enhancement of punishment prescribed by statute shall be disregarded in determining the maximum punishment prescribed by statute for an offense.

(b) The limitation of time applicable to an offense that is necessarily included within a greater offense is the limitation of time applicable to the lesser included offense, regardless of the limitation of time applicable to the greater offense.
(Added by Stats. 1984, Ch. 1270, Sec. 2.)

CHAPTER 3. Complaints Before Magistrates [806 - 810]

(Heading of Chapter 3 amended by Stats. 1951, Ch. 1674.)

806.
A proceeding for the examination before a magistrate of a person on a charge of a felony must be commenced by written complaint under oath subscribed by the complainant and filed with the magistrate. Such complaint may be verified on information and belief. When the complaint is used as a pleading to which the defendant pleads guilty under Section 859a of this code, the complaint shall contain the same allegations, including the charge of prior conviction or convictions of crime, as are required for indictments and informations and, wherever applicable, shall be construed and shall have substantially the same effect as provided in this code for indictments and informations.
(Amended by Stats. 1998, Ch. 931, Sec. 359. Effective September 28, 1998.)

807.
A magistrate is an officer having power to issue a warrant for the arrest of a person charged with a public offense.
(Enacted 1872.)

808.
The following persons are magistrates:

(a) The judges of the Supreme Court.

(b) The judges of the courts of appeal.

(c) The judges of the superior courts.
(Amended by Stats. 2003, Ch. 62, Sec. 229. Effective January 1, 2004.)

809.
The night-time commissioner of the Santa Clara County Superior Court shall be considered a magistrate for the purpose of conducting prompt probable cause hearings for persons arrested without an arrest warrant as mandated by law.
(Added by Stats. 1993, Ch. 909, Sec. 14. Effective January 1, 1994.)

810.
(a) The presiding judge of the superior court in a county shall, as often as is necessary, designate on a schedule not less than one judge of the court to be reasonably available on call as a magistrate for the setting of orders for discharge from actual custody upon bail, the issuance of search warrants, and for such other matters as may by the magistrate be deemed appropriate, at all times when a court is not in session in the county.

(b) The officer in charge of a jail, or a person the officer designates, in which an arrested person is held in custody shall assist the arrested person or the arrested person's attorney in contacting the magistrate on call as soon as possible for the purpose of obtaining release on bail.

(c) Any telephone call made pursuant to this section by an arrested person while in custody or by such person's attorney shall not count or be considered as a telephone call for purposes of Section 851.5 of the Penal Code.
(Amended by Stats. 2002, Ch. 784, Sec. 530. Effective January 1, 2003.)

CHAPTER 4. The Warrant of Arrest [813 - 829]

(Chapter 4 enacted 1872.)

813.
(a) When a complaint is filed with a magistrate charging a felony originally triable in the superior court of the county in which he or she sits, if, and only if, the magistrate is satisfied from the complaint that the offense complained of has been committed and that there is reasonable ground to believe that the defendant has committed it, the magistrate shall issue a warrant for the arrest of the defendant, except that, upon the request of the prosecutor, a summons instead of an arrest warrant shall be issued.

(b) A summons issued pursuant to this section shall be in substantially the same form as an arrest warrant and shall contain all of the following:

(1) The name of the defendant.

(2) The date and time the summons was issued.

(3) The city or county where the summons was issued.

(4) The signature of the magistrate, judge, justice, or other issuing authority who is issuing the summons with the title of his or her office and the name of the court or other issuing agency.

(5) The offense or offenses with which the defendant is charged.

(6) The time and place at which the defendant is to appear.

(7) Notification that the defendant is to complete the booking process on or before his or her first court appearance, as well as instructions for the defendant on completing the booking process.

(8) A provision for certification by the booking agency that the defendant has completed the booking process which shall be presented to the court by the defendant as proof of booking.

(c) If a defendant has been properly served with a summons and thereafter fails to appear at the designated time and place, a bench warrant for arrest shall issue. In the absence of proof of actual receipt of the summons by the defendant, a failure to appear shall not be used in any future proceeding.

(d) A defendant who responds to a summons issued pursuant to this section and who has not been booked as provided in subdivision (b) shall be ordered by the court to complete the booking process.

(e) The prosecutor shall not request the issuance of a summons in lieu of an arrest warrant as provided in this section under any of the following circumstances:

(1) The offense charged involves violence.

(2) The offense charged involves a firearm.

(3) The offense charged involves resisting arrest.

(4) There are one or more outstanding arrest warrants for the person.

(5) The prosecution of the offense or offenses with which the person is charged, or the prosecution of any other offense or offenses would be jeopardized.

(6) There is a reasonable likelihood that the offense or offenses would continue or resume, or that the safety of persons or property would be imminently endangered.

(7) There is reason to believe that the person would not appear at the time and place specified in the summons.
(Amended by Stats. 1998, Ch. 931, Sec. 362. Effective September 28, 1998.)

814.
A warrant of arrest issued under Section 813 may be in substantially the following form:
County of _____
The people of the State of California to any peace officer of said State:

Complaint on oath having this day been laid before me that the crime of _____ (designating it generally) has been committed and accusing _____ (naming defendant) thereof, you are therefore commanded forthwith to arrest the above named defendant and bring him or her before me at _____ (naming the place), or in case of my absence or inability to act, before the nearest or most accessible magistrate in this county.

Dated at (place) this day of , 20__.
(Signature and full official title of magistrate.)

(Amended by Stats. 2015, Ch. 303, Sec. 391. (AB 731) Effective January 1, 2016.)

815.

A warrant of arrest shall specify the name of the defendant or, if it is unknown to the magistrate, judge, justice, or other issuing authority, the defendant may be designated therein by any name. It shall also state the time of issuing it, and the city or county where it is issued, and shall be signed by the magistrate, judge, justice, or other issuing authority issuing it with the title of his office and the name of the court or other issuing agency.

(Amended by Stats. 1970, Ch. 1490.)

815a.

At the time of issuing a warrant of arrest, the magistrate shall fix the amount of bail which in his judgment in accordance with the provisions of section 1275 will be reasonable and sufficient for the appearance of the defendant following his arrest, if the offense is bailable, and said magistrate shall endorse upon said warrant a statement signed by him, with the name of his office, dated at the county, city or town where it is made to the following effect "The defendant is to be admitted to bail in the sum of _____ dollars" (stating the amount).

(Added by Stats. 1933, Ch. 242.)

816.

A warrant of arrest shall be directed generally to any peace officer, or to any public officer or employee authorized to serve process where the warrant is for a violation of a statute or ordinance which such person has the duty to enforce, in the state, and may be executed by any of those officers to whom it may be delivered.

When a warrant of arrest has been delivered to a peace officer and the person named in the warrant is otherwise lawfully in the custody of the peace officer, the warrant may be executed by the peace officer or by any clerk of a city or county jail authorized to act and acting under the peace officer's direction.

(Amended by Stats. 1969, Ch. 1205, Sec. 2.)

816a.

A summons issued pursuant to Section 813 shall be served by any peace officer, or any public officer or employee authorized to serve process when the summons is for a violation of a statute or ordinance which that person has the duty to enforce, within the state. Upon service of the summons, the officer or employee shall deliver one copy of the summons to the defendant and shall file a duplicate copy with the magistrate before whom the defendant is to appear.

(Added by Stats. 1988, Ch. 664, Sec. 2.)

817.

(a) (1) If a declaration of probable cause is made by a peace officer of this state, in accordance with subdivisions (b), (c), and (d), as applicable, the magistrate shall issue a warrant of probable cause for the arrest of the defendant only if he or she is satisfied after reviewing the declaration that there exists probable cause that the offense described in the declaration has been committed and that the defendant described therein has committed the offense.

(2) The warrant of probable cause for arrest shall not begin a complaint process pursuant to Section 740 or 813. The warrant of probable cause for arrest shall have the same authority for service as set forth in Section 840 and the same time limitations as that of an arrest warrant issued pursuant to Section 813.

(b) The declaration in support of the warrant of probable cause for arrest shall be a sworn statement made in writing. If the declarant transmits the proposed warrant and all affidavits and supporting documents to the magistrate using facsimile transmission equipment, email, or computer server, the conditions in subdivision (d) shall apply.

(c) In lieu of the written declaration required in subdivision (b), the magistrate may accept an oral statement made under penalty of perjury and recorded and transcribed. The transcribed statement shall be deemed to be the declaration for the purposes of this section. The recording of the sworn oral statement and the transcribed statement shall be certified by the magistrate receiving it and shall be filed with the clerk of the court. In the alternative, the sworn oral statement may be recorded by a certified court reporter who shall certify the transcript of the statement, after which the magistrate receiving it shall certify the transcript, which shall be filed with the clerk of the court.

(d) (1) The declarant shall sign under penalty of perjury his or her declaration in support of the warrant of probable cause for arrest. The declarant's signature shall be in the form of a digital signature or electronic signature if email or computer server is used for transmission to the magistrate. The proposed warrant and all supporting declarations and attachments shall be transmitted to the magistrate utilizing facsimile transmission equipment, email, or computer server.

(2) The magistrate shall verify that all the pages sent have been received, that all the pages are legible, and that the declarant's signature, digital signature, or electronic signature is genuine.

(e) A warrant of probable cause for arrest shall contain the information required pursuant to Sections 815 and 815a.

(f) A warrant of probable cause for arrest may be in substantially the following form:

County of _______, State of California.	
The people of the State of California to any peace officer of the STATE:	
Proof by declaration under penalty of perjury having been made this day to me by ______ (name of declarant) ______ ,	
I find that there is probable cause to believe that the crime(s) of ______ (designate the crime/s) ______ has (have) been committed by the defendant named and described below.	
Therefore, you are commanded to arrest ______ (name of defendant) ______ and to bring the defendant before any magistrate in ________ County pursuant to Sections 821, 825, 826, and 848 of the Penal Code.	
Defendant is admitted to bail in the amount of _______ dollars ($_______).	
Time Issued:	______ (Signature of the Judge) ______
Dated: Judge of the Court	

(g) Before issuing a warrant, the magistrate may examine under oath the person seeking the warrant and any witness the person may produce, take the written declaration of the person or witness, and cause the person or witness to subscribe the declaration. If the magistrate decides to issue the warrant, he or she shall do all of the following:

(1) Sign the warrant. The magistrate's signature may be in the form of a digital signature or electronic signature if email or computer server was used for transmission to the magistrate.

(2) Note on the warrant the date and time of the issuance of the warrant.

(3) Transmit via facsimile transmission equipment, email, or computer server the signed warrant to the declarant. The warrant, signed by the magistrate and received by the declarant, shall be deemed to be the original warrant.

(h) An original warrant of probable cause for arrest or the duplicate original warrant of probable cause for arrest is sufficient for booking a defendant into custody.

(i) After the defendant named in the warrant of probable cause for arrest has been taken into custody, the agency that obtained the warrant shall file a "certificate of service" with the clerk of the issuing court. The certificate of service shall contain all of the following:

(1) The date and time of service.

(2) The name of the defendant arrested.

(3) The location of the arrest.

(4) The location where the defendant was incarcerated.

(Amended by Stats. 2018, Ch. 176, Sec. 1. (AB 2710) Effective January 1, 2019.)

817.5.

(a) On or after June 30, 2001, upon the issuance of any arrest warrant, the issuing law enforcement agency may enter the warrant information into the Department of Justice's Wanted Persons System.

(b) Notwithstanding any other provision of law, any state or local governmental agency shall, upon request, provide to the Department of Justice, a court, or any California law enforcement agency, the address of any person represented by the department, the court, or the law enforcement agency to be a person for whom there is an outstanding arrest warrant.

(Added by Stats. 2000, Ch. 940, Sec. 2. Effective January 1, 2001.)

818.

In any case in which a peace officer serves upon a person a warrant of arrest for a misdemeanor offense under the Vehicle Code or under any local ordinance relating to stopping, standing, parking, or operation of a motor vehicle and where no written promise to appear has been filed and the warrant states on its face that a citation may be used in lieu of physical arrest, the peace officer may, instead of taking the person before a magistrate, prepare a notice to appear and release the person on his promise to appear, as prescribed by Sections 853. 6 through 853.8 of the Penal Code. Issuance of a notice to appear and securing of a promise to appear shall be deemed a compliance with the directions of the warrant, and the peace officer issuing such notice to appear and obtaining such promise to appear shall endorse on the warrant "Section 818, Penal Code, complied with" and return the warrant to the magistrate who issued it.

(Amended by Stats. 1980, Ch. 336, Sec. 1.)

821.

If the offense charged is a felony, and the arrest occurs in the county in which the warrant was issued, the officer making the arrest must take the defendant before the magistrate who issued the warrant or some other magistrate of the same county.

If the defendant is arrested in another county, the officer must, without unnecessary delay, inform the defendant in writing of his right to be taken before a magistrate in that county, note on the warrant that he has so informed defendant, and, upon being required by defendant, take him before a magistrate in that county, who must admit him to bail in the amount specified in the endorsement referred to in Section 815a, and direct the defendant to appear before the court or magistrate by whom the warrant was issued on or before a day certain which shall in no case be more than 25 days after such admittance to bail. If bail be forthwith given, the magistrate shall take the same and endorse thereon a memorandum of the aforesaid order for the appearance of the defendant, or, if the defendant so requires, he may be released on bail set on the warrant by the issuing court, as provided in Section 1269b of this code, without an appearance before a magistrate.

If the warrant on which the defendant is arrested in another county does not have bail set thereon, or if the defendant arrested in another county does not require the arresting officer to take him before a magistrate in that county for the purpose of being admitted to bail, or if such defendant, after being admitted to bail, does not forthwith give bail, the arresting officer shall immediately notify the law enforcement agency requesting the arrest in the county in which the warrant was issued that such defendant is in custody, and thereafter such law enforcement agency shall take custody of the defendant within five days, or five court days if the law enforcement agency requesting the arrest is more than 400 miles from the county in which the defendant is held in custody, in the county in which he was arrested and shall take such defendant before the magistrate who issued the warrant, or before some other magistrate of the same county.

(Amended by Stats. 1983, Ch. 1083, Sec. 1.)

822.

If the offense charged is a misdemeanor, and the defendant is arrested in another county, the officer must, without unnecessary delay, inform the defendant in writing of his right to be taken before a magistrate in that county, note on the warrant that he has so informed defendant, and, upon being required by defendant, take him before a magistrate in that county, who must admit him to bail in the amount specified in the indorsement referred to in Section 815a, or if no bail is specified, the magistrate may set bail; if the defendant is admitted to bail the magistrate shall direct the defendant to appear before the court or magistrate by whom the warrant was issued on or before a day certain which shall in no case be more than 25 days after such admittance to bail. If bail be forthwith given, the magistrate shall take the same and indorse thereon a memorandum of the aforesaid order for the appearance of the defendant.

If the defendant arrested in another county on a misdemeanor charge does not require the arresting officer to take him before a magistrate in that county for the purpose of being admitted to bail, or if such defendant, after being admitted to bail, does not forthwith give bail, the arresting officer shall immediately notify the law enforcement agency requesting the arrest in the county in which the warrant was issued that such defendant is in custody, and thereafter such law enforcement agency shall take custody of such defendant within five days in the county in which he was arrested and shall take such defendant before the magistrate who issued the warrant, or before some other magistrate of the same county.

If a defendant is arrested in another county on a warrant charging the commission of a misdemeanor, upon which warrant the amount of bail is indorsed as provided in Section 815a, and defendant is held in jail in the county of arrest pending appearance before a magistrate, the officer in charge of the jail shall, to the same extent as provided by Section 1269b, have authority to approve and accept bail from defendant in the amount indorsed on the warrant, to issue and sign an order for the release of the defendant, and, on posting of such bail, shall discharge defendant from custody.

(Amended by Stats. 1983, Ch. 236, Sec. 2.)

823.

On taking the bail, the magistrate must certify that fact on the warrant, and deliver the warrant to the officer having charge of the defendant. The magistrate shall issue to defendant a receipt for the undertaking of bail. The officer must then discharge the defendant from arrest, and must, without delay, deliver the warrant to the clerk of the court at which the defendant is required to appear. If the undertaking of bail is in the form of a bond, the magistrate shall forward the bond to the court at which defendant is required to appear. If the undertaking is in the form of cash, the magistrate shall deposit the cash in the county treasury, notifying the county auditor thereof, and the county auditor shall, by warrant, transmit the amount of the undertaking to the court at which the defendant is required to appear. If authorized by the county auditor, the magistrate may deposit the money in a bank account pursuant to Section 68084 of the Government Code, and by check drawn on such bank account transmit the amount of the undertaking to the court at which the defendant is required to appear.

(Amended by Stats. 1959, Ch. 133.)

824.

When an adult willfully misrepresents himself or herself to be a minor under 18 years of age when taken into custody and this misrepresentation effects a material delay in investigation which prevents the filing of a criminal complaint against him or her in a court of competent jurisdiction within 48 hours, the complaint shall be filed within 48 hours from the time the true age is determined, excluding nonjudicial days.

(Added by Stats. 1981, Ch. 205, Sec. 1.)

825.

(a) (1) Except as provided in paragraph (2), the defendant shall in all cases be taken before the magistrate without unnecessary delay, and, in any event, within 48 hours after his or her arrest, excluding Sundays and holidays.

(2) When the 48 hours prescribed by paragraph (1) expire at a time when the court in which the magistrate is sitting is not in session, that time shall be extended to include the duration of the next court session on the judicial day immediately following. If the 48-hour period expires at a time when the court in which the magistrate is sitting is in session, the arraignment may take place at any time during that session. However, when the defendant's arrest occurs on a Wednesday after the conclusion of the day's court session, and if the Wednesday is not a court holiday, the defendant shall be taken before the magistrate not later than the following Friday, if the Friday is not a court holiday.

(b) After the arrest, any attorney at law entitled to practice in the courts of record of California, may, at the request of the prisoner or any relative of the prisoner, visit the prisoner. Any officer having charge of the prisoner who willfully refuses or neglects to allow that attorney to visit a prisoner is guilty of a misdemeanor. Any officer having a prisoner in charge, who refuses to allow the attorney to visit the prisoner when proper application is made, shall forfeit and pay to the party aggrieved the sum of five hundred dollars ($500), to be recovered by action in any court of competent jurisdiction.

(Amended by Stats. 2003, Ch. 149, Sec. 66. Effective January 1, 2004.)

825.5.

Any physician and surgeon, including a psychiatrist, licensed to practice in this state, or any psychologist licensed to practice in this state who holds a doctoral degree and has at least two years of experience in the diagnosis and treatment of emotional and mental disorders, who is employed by the prisoner or his or her attorney to assist in the preparation of the defense, shall be permitted to visit the prisoner while he or she is in custody.

(Amended by Stats. 1984, Ch. 1123, Sec. 1.)

826.

If on a warrant issued under Section 813 or 817 the defendant is brought before a magistrate other than the one who issued the warrant, the complaint on which the warrant was issued must be sent to that magistrate, or if it cannot be procured, a new complaint may be filed before that magistrate.

(Amended by Stats. 1995, Ch. 563, Sec. 3. Effective January 1, 1996.)

827.

When a complaint is filed with a magistrate of the commission of a felony originally triable in the superior court of another county of the state than that in which the magistrate sits, but showing that the defendant is in the county where the complaint is filed, the same proceedings must be had as prescribed in this chapter, except that the warrant must require the defendant to be taken before the nearest or most accessible magistrate of the county in which the offense is triable, and the complaint must be delivered by the magistrate to the officer to whom the warrant is delivered.

(Amended by Stats. 1998, Ch. 931, Sec. 363. Effective September 28, 1998.)

827.1.

A person who is specified or designated in a warrant of arrest for a misdemeanor offense may be released upon the issuance of a citation, in lieu of physical arrest, unless one of the following conditions exists:

(a) The misdemeanor cited in the warrant involves violence.

(b) The misdemeanor cited in the warrant involves a firearm.

(c) The misdemeanor cited in the warrant involves resisting arrest.

(d) The misdemeanor cited in the warrant involves giving false information to a peace officer.

(e) The person arrested is a danger to himself or herself or others due to intoxication or being under the influence of drugs or narcotics.

(f) The person requires medical examination or medical care or was otherwise unable to care for his or her own safety.

(g) The person has other ineligible charges pending against him or her.

(h) There is reasonable likelihood that the offense or offenses would continue or resume, or that the safety of persons or property would be immediately endangered by the release of the person.

(i) The person refuses to sign the notice to appear.

(j) The person cannot provide satisfactory evidence of personal identification.

(k) The warrant of arrest indicates that the person is not eligible to be released on a citation.

The issuance of a citation under this section shall be undertaken in the manner set forth in Sections 853.6 to 853.8, inclusive.

(Amended by Stats. 1988, Ch. 403, Sec. 1.)

828.

The officer who executes the warrant must take the defendant before the nearest or most accessible magistrate of the county in which the offense is triable, and must deliver to him the complaint and the warrant, with his return endorsed thereon, and the magistrate must then proceed in the same manner as upon a warrant issued by himself.

(Amended by Stats. 1951, Ch. 1674.)

829.

When a complaint is filed with a magistrate of the commission of a misdemeanor or infraction triable in another county of the state than that in which the magistrate sits, but showing that the defendant is in the county where the complaint is filed, the officer must, upon being required by the defendant, take the defendant before a magistrate of the county in which the warrant was issued, who must admit the defendant to bail in the amount specified in the endorsement referred to in Section 815a, and immediately transmit the warrant, complaint, and undertaking to the clerk of the court in which the defendant is required to appear.

(Amended by Stats. 1998, Ch. 931, Sec. 364. Effective September 28, 1998.)

CHAPTER 4.2. Code Enforcement Officers [829.5- 829.5.]

(Chapter 4.2 added by Stats. 2010, Ch. 117, Sec. 1.)

829.5.

(a) "Code enforcement officer" means any person who is not described in Chapter 4.5 (commencing with Section 830) and who is employed by any governmental subdivision, public or quasi-public corporation, public agency, public service corporation, any town, city, county, or municipal corporation, whether incorporated or chartered, who has enforcement authority for health, safety, and welfare requirements, whose duties include enforcement of any statute, rule, regulation, or standard, and who is authorized to issue citations, or file formal complaints.

(b) "Code enforcement officer" also includes any person who is employed by the Department of Housing and Community Development who has enforcement authority for health, safety, and welfare requirements pursuant to the Employee Housing Act (Part 1 (commencing with Section 17000) of Division 13 of the Health and Safety Code); the State Housing Law (Part 1.5 (commencing with Section 17910) of Division 13 of the Health and Safety Code); the Manufactured Housing Act of 1980 (Part 2 (commencing with Section 18000) of Division 13 of the Health and Safety Code); the Mobilehome Parks Act (Part 2.1 (commencing with Section 18200) of Division 13 of the Health and Safety Code); and the Special Occupancy Parks Act (Part 2.3 (commencing with Section 18860) of Division 13 of the Health and Safety Code).

(Amended by Stats. 2011, Ch. 296, Sec. 211. (AB 1023) Effective January 1, 2012.)

CHAPTER 4.5. Peace Officers [830 - 832.18]

(Chapter 4.5 added by Stats. 1968, Ch. 1222.)

830.

Any person who comes within the provisions of this chapter and who otherwise meets all standards imposed by law on a peace officer is a peace officer, and notwithstanding any other provision of law, no person other than those designated in this chapter is a peace officer. The restriction of peace officer functions of any public officer or employee shall not affect his or her status for purposes of retirement.

(Amended by Stats. 1989, Ch. 1165, Sec. 19.)

830.1.

(a) Any sheriff, undersheriff, or deputy sheriff, employed in that capacity, of a county, any chief of police of a city or chief, director, or chief executive officer of a consolidated municipal public safety agency that performs police functions, any police officer, employed in that capacity and appointed by the chief of police or chief, director, or chief executive of a public safety agency, of a city, any chief of police, or police officer of a district, including police officers of the San Diego Unified Port District Harbor Police, authorized by statute to maintain a police department, any marshal or deputy marshal of a superior court or county, any port warden or port police officer of the Harbor Department of the City of Los Angeles, or any inspector or investigator employed in that capacity in the office of a district attorney, is a peace officer. The authority of these peace officers extends to any place in the state, as follows:

(1) As to any public offense committed or which there is probable cause to believe has been committed within the political subdivision that employs the peace officer or in which the peace officer serves.

(2) Where the peace officer has the prior consent of the chief of police or chief, director, or chief executive officer of a consolidated municipal public safety agency, or person authorized by him or her to give consent, if the place is within a city, or of the sheriff, or person authorized by him or her to give consent, if the place is within a county.

(3) As to any public offense committed or which there is probable cause to believe has been committed in the peace officer's presence, and with respect to which there is immediate danger to person or property, or of the escape of the perpetrator of the offense.

(b) The Attorney General and special agents and investigators of the Department of Justice are peace officers, and those assistant chiefs, deputy chiefs, chiefs, deputy directors, and division directors designated as peace officers by the Attorney General are peace officers. The authority of these peace officers extends to any place in the state where a public offense has been committed or where there is probable cause to believe one has been committed.

(c) Any deputy sheriff of the County of Los Angeles, and any deputy sheriff of the Counties of Butte, Calaveras, Colusa, Glenn, Humboldt, Imperial, Inyo, Kern, Kings, Lake, Lassen, Mariposa, Mendocino, Plumas, Riverside, San Benito, San Diego, San Luis Obispo, Santa Barbara, Santa Clara, Shasta, Siskiyou, Solano, Sonoma, Stanislaus, Sutter, Tehama, Trinity, Tulare, Tuolumne, and Yuba who is employed to perform duties exclusively or initially relating to custodial assignments with responsibilities for maintaining the operations of county custodial facilities, including the custody, care, supervision, security, movement, and transportation of inmates, is a peace officer whose authority extends to any place in the state only while engaged in the performance of the duties of his or her respective employment and for the purpose of carrying out the primary function of employment relating to his or her custodial assignments, or when performing other law enforcement duties directed by his or her employing agency during a local state of emergency.

(Amended by Stats. 2012, Ch. 66, Sec. 1. (SB 1254) Effective January 1, 2013.)

830.2.

The following persons are peace officers whose authority extends to any place in the state:

(a) Any member of the Department of the California Highway Patrol including those members designated under subdivision (a) of Section 2250.1 of the Vehicle Code, provided that the primary duty of the peace officer is the enforcement of any law relating to the use or operation of vehicles upon the highways, or laws pertaining to the provision of police services for the protection of state officers, state properties, and the occupants of state properties, or both, as set forth in the Vehicle Code and Government Code.

(b) A member of the University of California Police Department appointed pursuant to Section 92600 of the Education Code, provided that the primary duty of the peace officer shall be the enforcement of the law within the area specified in Section 92600 of the Education Code.

(c) A member of the California State University Police Departments appointed pursuant to Section 89560 of the Education Code, provided that the primary duty of the peace officer shall be the enforcement of the law within the area specified in Section 89560 of the Education Code.

(d) (1) Any member of the Office of Correctional Safety of the Department of Corrections and Rehabilitation, provided that the primary duties of the peace officer shall be the investigation or apprehension of inmates, wards, parolees, parole violators, or escapees from state institutions, the transportation of those persons, the investigation of any violation of criminal law discovered while performing the usual and authorized duties of employment, and the coordination of those activities with other criminal justice agencies.

(2) Any member of the Office of Internal Affairs of the Department of Corrections and Rehabilitation, provided that the primary duties shall be criminal investigations of Department of Corrections and Rehabilitation personnel and the coordination of those activities with other criminal justice agencies. For purposes of this subdivision, the member of the Office of Internal Affairs shall possess certification from the Commission on Peace Officer Standards and Training for investigators, or have completed training pursuant to Section 6126.1 of the Penal Code.

(e) Employees of the Department of Fish and Game designated by the director, provided that the primary duty of those peace officers shall be the enforcement of the law as set forth in Section 856 of the Fish and Game Code.

(f) Employees of the Department of Parks and Recreation designated by the director pursuant to Section 5008 of the Public Resources Code, provided that the primary duty of the peace officer shall be the enforcement of the law as set forth in Section 5008 of the Public Resources Code.

(g) The Director of Forestry and Fire Protection and employees or classes of employees of the Department of Forestry and Fire Protection designated by the director pursuant to Section 4156 of the Public Resources Code, provided that the primary duty of the peace officer shall be the enforcement of the law as that duty is set forth in Section 4156 of the Public Resources Code.

(h) Persons employed by the Department of Alcoholic Beverage Control for the enforcement of Division 9 (commencing with Section 23000) of the Business and Professions Code and designated by the Director of Alcoholic Beverage Control, provided that the primary duty of any of these peace officers shall be the enforcement of the laws relating to alcoholic beverages, as that duty is set forth in Section 25755 of the Business and Professions Code.

(i) Marshals and police appointed by the Board of Directors of the California Exposition and State Fair pursuant to Section 3332 of the Food and Agricultural Code, provided that the primary duty of the peace officers shall be the enforcement of the law as prescribed in that section.

(Amended by Stats. 2011, Ch. 36, Sec. 19. (SB 92) Effective June 30, 2011.)
830.3.
The following persons are peace officers whose authority extends to any place in the state for the purpose of performing their primary duty or when making an arrest pursuant to Section 836 as to any public offense with respect to which there is immediate danger to person or property, or of the escape of the perpetrator of that offense, or pursuant to Section 8597 or 8598 of the Government Code. These peace officers may carry firearms only if authorized and under those terms and conditions as specified by their employing agencies:

(a) Persons employed by the Division of Investigation of the Department of Consumer Affairs and investigators of the Dental Board of California, who are designated by the Director of Consumer Affairs, provided that the primary duty of these peace officers shall be the enforcement of the law as that duty is set forth in Section 160 of the Business and Professions Code.

(b) Voluntary fire wardens designated by the Director of Forestry and Fire Protection pursuant to Section 4156 of the Public Resources Code, provided that the primary duty of these peace officers shall be the enforcement of the law as that duty is set forth in Section 4156 of that code.

(c) Employees of the Department of Motor Vehicles designated in Section 1655 of the Vehicle Code, provided that the primary duty of these peace officers shall be the enforcement of the law as that duty is set forth in Section 1655 of that code.

(d) Investigators of the California Horse Racing Board designated by the board, provided that the primary duty of these peace officers shall be the enforcement of Chapter 4 (commencing with Section 19400) of Division 8 of the Business and Professions Code and Chapter 10 (commencing with Section 330) of Title 9 of Part 1.

(e) The State Fire Marshal and assistant or deputy state fire marshals appointed pursuant to Section 13103 of the Health and Safety Code, provided that the primary duty of these peace officers shall be the enforcement of the law as that duty is set forth in Section 13104 of that code.

(f) Inspectors of the food and drug section designated by the chief pursuant to subdivision (a) of Section 106500 of the Health and Safety Code, provided that the primary duty of these peace officers shall be the enforcement of the law as that duty is set forth in Section 106500 of that code.

(g) All investigators of the Division of Labor Standards Enforcement designated by the Labor Commissioner, provided that the primary duty of these peace officers shall be the enforcement of the law as prescribed in Section 95 of the Labor Code.

(h) All investigators of the State Departments of Health Care Services, Public Health, and Social Services, the Department of Toxic Substances Control, the Office of Statewide Health Planning and Development, and the Public Employees' Retirement System, provided that the primary duty of these peace officers shall be the enforcement of the law relating to the duties of his or her department or office. Notwithstanding any other law, investigators of the Public Employees' Retirement System shall not carry firearms.

(i) Either the Deputy Commissioner, Enforcement Branch of, or the Fraud Division Chief of, the Department of Insurance and those investigators designated by the deputy or the chief, provided that the primary duty of those investigators shall be the enforcement of Section 550.

(j) Employees of the Department of Housing and Community Development designated under Section 18023 of the Health and Safety Code, provided that the primary duty of these peace officers shall be the enforcement of the law as that duty is set forth in Section 18023 of that code.

(k) Investigators of the office of the Controller, provided that the primary duty of these investigators shall be the enforcement of the law relating to the duties of that office. Notwithstanding any other law, except as authorized by the Controller, the peace officers designated pursuant to this subdivision shall not carry firearms.

(l) Investigators of the Department of Business Oversight designated by the Commissioner of Business Oversight, provided that the primary duty of these investigators shall be the enforcement of the provisions of law administered by the Department of Business Oversight. Notwithstanding any other law, the peace officers designated pursuant to this subdivision shall not carry firearms.

(m) Persons employed by the Contractors' State License Board designated by the Director of Consumer Affairs pursuant to Section 7011.5 of the Business and Professions Code, provided that the primary duty of these persons shall be the enforcement of the law as that duty is set forth in Section 7011.5, and in Chapter 9 (commencing with Section 7000) of Division 3, of that code. The Director of Consumer Affairs may designate as peace officers not more than 12 persons who shall at the time of their designation be assigned to the special investigations unit of the board. Notwithstanding any other law, the persons designated pursuant to this subdivision shall not carry firearms.

(n) The Chief and coordinators of the Law Enforcement Branch of the Office of Emergency Services.

(o) Investigators of the office of the Secretary of State designated by the Secretary of State, provided that the primary duty of these peace officers shall be the enforcement of

the law as prescribed in Chapter 3 (commencing with Section 8200) of Division 1 of Title 2 of, and Section 12172.5 of, the Government Code. Notwithstanding any other law, the peace officers designated pursuant to this subdivision shall not carry firearms.

(p) The Deputy Director for Security designated by Section 8880.38 of the Government Code, and all lottery security personnel assigned to the California State Lottery and designated by the director, provided that the primary duty of any of those peace officers shall be the enforcement of the laws related to ensuring the integrity, honesty, and fairness of the operation and administration of the California State Lottery.

(q) Investigators employed by the Investigation Division of the Employment Development Department designated by the director of the department, provided that the primary duty of those peace officers shall be the enforcement of the law as that duty is set forth in Section 317 of the Unemployment Insurance Code. Notwithstanding any other law, the peace officers designated pursuant to this subdivision shall not carry firearms.

(r) The chief and assistant chief of museum security and safety of the California Science Center, as designated by the executive director pursuant to Section 4108 of the Food and Agricultural Code, provided that the primary duty of those peace officers shall be the enforcement of the law as that duty is set forth in Section 4108 of the Food and Agricultural Code.

(s) Employees of the Franchise Tax Board designated by the board, provided that the primary duty of these peace officers shall be the enforcement of the law as set forth in Chapter 9 (commencing with Section 19701) of Part 10.2 of Division 2 of the Revenue and Taxation Code.

(t) (1) Notwithstanding any other provision of this section, a peace officer authorized by this section shall not be authorized to carry firearms by his or her employing agency until that agency has adopted a policy on the use of deadly force by those peace officers, and until those peace officers have been instructed in the employing agency's policy on the use of deadly force.

(2) Every peace officer authorized pursuant to this section to carry firearms by his or her employing agency shall qualify in the use of the firearms at least every six months.

(u) Investigators of the Department of Managed Health Care designated by the Director of the Department of Managed Health Care, provided that the primary duty of these investigators shall be the enforcement of the provisions of laws administered by the Director of the Department of Managed Health Care. Notwithstanding any other law, the peace officers designated pursuant to this subdivision shall not carry firearms.

(v) The Chief, Deputy Chief, supervising investigators, and investigators of the Office of Protective Services of the State Department of Developmental Services, the Office of Protective Services of the State Department of State Hospitals, and the Office of Law Enforcement Support of the California Health and Human Services Agency, provided that the primary duty of each of those persons shall be the enforcement of the law relating to the duties of his or her department or office.

(Amended by Stats. 2017, Ch. 561, Sec. 182. (AB 1516) Effective January 1, 2018.)
830.31.
The following persons are peace officers whose authority extends to any place in the state for the purpose of performing their primary duty or when making an arrest pursuant to Section 836 as to any public offense with respect to which there is immediate danger to person or property, or of the escape of the perpetrator of that offense, or pursuant to Section 8597 or 8598 of the Government Code. These peace officers may carry firearms only if authorized, and under the terms and conditions specified, by their employing agency.

(a) A police officer of the County of Los Angeles, if the primary duty of the officer is the enforcement of the law in or about properties owned, operated, or administered by his or her employing agency or when performing necessary duties with respect to patrons, employees, and properties of his or her employing agency.

(b) A person designated by a local agency as a park ranger and regularly employed and paid in that capacity, if the primary duty of the officer is the protection of park and other property of the agency and the preservation of the peace therein.

(c) (1) A peace officer of the Department of General Services of the City of Los Angeles who was transferred to the Los Angeles Police Department and designated by the Chief of Police of the Los Angeles Police Department, or his or her designee, if the primary duty of the officer is the enforcement of the law in or about properties owned, operated, or administered by the City of Los Angeles or when performing necessary duties with respect to patrons, employees, and properties of the City of Los Angeles. For purposes of this section, "properties" means city offices, city buildings, facilities, parks, yards, and warehouses.

(2) A peace officer designated pursuant to this subdivision, and authorized to carry firearms by the Los Angeles Police Department, shall satisfactorily complete the introductory course of firearm training required by Section 832 and shall requalify in the use of firearms every six months.

(3) Notwithstanding any other provision of law, a peace officer designated pursuant to this subdivision who is authorized to carry a firearm by his or her employing agency while on duty shall not be authorized to carry a firearm when he or she is not on duty.

(d) A housing authority patrol officer employed by the housing authority of a city, district, county, or city and county or employed by the police department of a city and county, if the primary duty of the officer is the enforcement of the law in or about properties owned, operated, or administered by his or her employing agency or when performing necessary duties with respect to patrons, employees, and properties of his or her employing agency.

(Amended by Stats. 2012, Ch. 795, Sec. 1. (SB 1466) Effective January 1, 2013.)
830.32.
The following persons are peace officers whose authority extends to any place in the state for the purpose of performing their primary duty or when making an arrest pursuant to Section 836 as to any public offense with respect to which there is immediate danger to person or property, or of the escape of the perpetrator of that offense, or pursuant to Section 8597 or 8598 of the Government Code. Those peace officers may carry firearms only if authorized and under terms and conditions specified by their employing agency.

(a) Members of a California Community College police department appointed pursuant to Section 72330 of the Education Code, if the primary duty of the police officer is the enforcement of the law as prescribed in Section 72330 of the Education Code.

(b) Persons employed as members of a police department of a school district pursuant to Section 38000 of the Education Code, if the primary duty of the police officer is the enforcement of the law as prescribed in Section 38000 of the Education Code.

(c) Any peace officer employed by a K-12 public school district or California Community College district who has completed training as prescribed by subdivision (f) of Section 832.3 shall be designated a school police officer.

(Amended by Stats. 2000, Ch. 135, Sec. 135. Effective January 1, 2001.)
830.33.
The following persons are peace officers whose authority extends to any place in the state for the purpose of performing their primary duty or when making an arrest pursuant to Section 836 as to any public offense with respect to which there is immediate danger to person or property, or of the escape of the perpetrator of that offense, or pursuant to Section 8597 or 8598 of the Government Code. Those peace officers may carry firearms only if authorized and under terms and conditions specified by their employing agency.

(a) A member of the San Francisco Bay Area Rapid Transit District Police Department appointed pursuant to Section 28767.5 of the Public Utilities Code, if the primary duty of the peace officer is the enforcement of the law in or about properties owned, operated, or administered by the district or when performing necessary duties with respect to patrons, employees, and properties of the district.

(b) Harbor or port police regularly employed and paid in that capacity by a county, city, or district other than peace officers authorized under Section 830.1, if the primary duty of the peace officer is the enforcement of the law in or about the properties owned, operated, or administered by the harbor or port or when performing necessary duties with respect to patrons, employees, and properties of the harbor or port.
(c) Transit police officers or peace officers of a county, city, transit development board, or district, if the primary duty of the peace officer is the enforcement of the law in or about properties owned, operated, or administered by the employing agency or when performing necessary duties with respect to patrons, employees, and properties of the employing agency.
(d) Any person regularly employed as an airport law enforcement officer by a city, county, or district operating the airport or by a joint powers agency, created pursuant to Article 1 (commencing with Section 6500) of Chapter 5 of Division 7 of Title 1 of the Government Code, operating the airport, if the primary duty of the peace officer is the enforcement of the law in or about properties owned, operated, and administered by the employing agency or when performing necessary duties with respect to patrons, employees, and properties of the employing agency.
(e) (1) Any railroad police officer commissioned by the Governor pursuant to Section 8226 of the Public Utilities Code, if the primary duty of the peace officer is the enforcement of the law in or about properties owned, operated, or administered by the employing agency or when performing necessary duties with respect to patrons, employees, and properties of the employing agency.
(2) Notwithstanding any other provision of law, a railroad police officer who has met the current requirements of the Commission on Peace Officer Standards and Training necessary for exercising the powers of a peace officer, and who has been commissioned by the Governor as described herein, and the officer's employing agency, may apply for access to information from the California Law Enforcement Telecommunications System (CLETS) through a local law enforcement agency that has been granted direct access to CLETS, provided that, in addition to other review standards and conditions of eligibility applied by the Department of Justice, the CLETS Advisory Committee and the Attorney General, before access is granted the following are satisfied:
(A) The employing agency shall enter into a Release of CLETS Information agreement as provided for in the CLETS policies, practices, and procedures, and the required background check on the peace officer and other pertinent personnel has been completed, together with all required training.
(B) The Release of CLETS Information agreement shall be in substantially the same form as prescribed by the CLETS policies, practices, and procedures for public agencies of law enforcement who subscribe to CLETS services, and shall be subject to the provisions of Chapter 2.5 (commencing with Section 15150) of Title 2 of Division 3 of the Government Code and the CLETS policies, practices, and procedures.
(C) (i) The employing agency shall expressly waive any objections to jurisdiction in the courts of the State of California for any liability arising from use, abuse, or misuse of CLETS access or services or the information derived therefrom, or with respect to any legal actions to enforce provisions of California law relating to CLETS access, services, or information under this subdivision, and provided that this liability shall be in addition to that imposed by Public Utilities Code Section 8226.
(ii) The employing agency shall further agree to utilize CLETS access, services, or information only for law enforcement activities by peace officers who have met the current requirements of the Commission on Peace Officer Standards and Training necessary for exercising the powers of a peace officer, and who have been commissioned as described herein who are operating within the State of California, where the activities are directly related to investigations or arrests arising from conduct occurring within the State of California.
(iii) The employing agency shall further agree to pay to the Department of Justice and the providing local law enforcement agency all costs related to the provision of access or services, including, but not limited to, any and all hardware, interface modules, and costs for telephonic communications, as well as administrative costs.
(Amended by Stats. 2004, Ch. 510, Sec. 1. Effective January 1, 2005.)

830.34.

The following persons are peace officers whose authority extends to any place in the state for the purpose of performing their primary duty or when making an arrest pursuant to Section 836 as to any public offense with respect to which there is immediate danger to person or property, or of the escape of the perpetrator of that offense, or pursuant to Section 8597 or 8598 of the Government Code. Those peace officers may carry firearms only if authorized and under terms and conditions specified by their employing agency.
(a) Persons designated as a security officer by a municipal utility district pursuant to Section 12820 of the Public Utilities Code, if the primary duty of the officer is the protection of the properties of the utility district and the protection of the persons thereon.
(b) Persons designated as a security officer by a county water district pursuant to Section 30547 of the Water Code, if the primary duty of the officer is the protection of the properties of the county water district and the protection of the persons thereon.
(c) The security director of the public utilities commission of a city and county, if the primary duty of the security director is the protection of the properties of the commission and the protection of the persons thereon.
(d) Persons employed as a park ranger by a municipal water district pursuant to Section 71341.5 of the Water Code, if the primary duty of the park ranger is the protection of the properties of the municipal water district and the protection of the persons thereon.
(Amended by Stats. 2004, Ch. 799, Sec. 1. Effective September 27, 2004.)

830.35.

The following persons are peace officers whose authority extends to any place in the state for the purpose of performing their primary duty or when making an arrest pursuant to Section 836 as to any public offense with respect to which there is immediate danger to person or property, or of the escape of the perpetrator of that offense, or pursuant to Section 8597 or 8598 of the Government Code. Those peace officers may carry firearms only if authorized and under terms and conditions specified by their employing agency.
(a) A welfare fraud investigator or inspector, regularly employed and paid in that capacity by a county, if the primary duty of the peace officer is the enforcement of the provisions of the Welfare and Institutions Code.
(b) A child support investigator or inspector, regularly employed and paid in that capacity by a district attorney's office, if the primary duty of the peace officer is the enforcement of the provisions of the Family Code and Section 270.
(c) The coroner and deputy coroners, regularly employed and paid in that capacity, of a county, if the primary duty of the peace officer are those duties set forth in Sections 27469 and 27491 to 27491.4, inclusive, of the Government Code.
(Amended by Stats. 2000, Ch. 808, Sec. 110.3. Effective September 28, 2000.)

830.36.

The following persons are peace officers whose authority extends to any place in the state for the purpose of performing their primary duty or when making an arrest pursuant to Section 836 as to any public offense with respect to which there is immediate danger to person or property, or of the escape of the perpetrator of that offense, or pursuant to Section 8597 or 8598 of the Government Code. Those peace officers may carry firearms only if authorized and under terms and conditions specified by their employing agency.
(a) The Sergeant-at-Arms of each house of the Legislature, if the primary duty of the peace officer is the enforcement of the law in or about properties owned, operated, or administered by the employing agency or when performing necessary duties with respect to patrons, employees, and properties of the employing agency.
(b) Marshals of the Supreme Court and bailiffs of the courts of appeal, and coordinators of security for the judicial branch, if the primary duty of the peace officer is the enforcement of the law in or about properties owned, operated, or administered by the employing agency or when performing necessary duties with respect to patrons, employees, and properties of the employing agency.
(c) Court service officer in a county of the second class and third class, if the primary duty of the peace officer is the enforcement of the law in or about properties owned, operated, or administered by the employing agency or when performing necessary duties with respect to patrons, employees, and properties of the employing agency.
(Amended by Stats. 1999, Ch. 891, Sec. 30. Effective January 1, 2000.)

830.37.

The following persons are peace officers whose authority extends to any place in the state for the purpose of performing their primary duty or when making an arrest pursuant to Section 836 as to any public offense with respect to which there is immediate danger to person or property, or of the escape of the perpetrator of that offense, or pursuant to Section 8597 or 8598 of the Government Code. These peace officers may carry firearms only if authorized and under terms and conditions specified by their employing agency:
(a) Members of an arson-investigating unit, regularly paid and employed in that capacity, of a fire department or fire protection agency of a county, city, city and county, district, or the state, if the primary duty of these peace officers is the detection and apprehension of persons who have violated any fire law or committed insurance fraud.
(b) Members other than members of an arson-investigating unit, regularly paid and employed in that capacity, of a fire department or fire protection agency of a county, city, city and county, district, or the state, if the primary duty of these peace officers, when acting in that capacity, is the enforcement of laws relating to fire prevention or fire suppression.
(c) Voluntary fire wardens as are designated by the Director of Forestry and Fire Protection pursuant to Section 4156 of the Public Resources Code, provided that the primary duty of these peace officers shall be the enforcement of the law as that duty is set forth in Section 4156 of the Public Resources Code.
(d) Firefighter/security guards by the Military Department, if the primary duty of the peace officer is the enforcement of the law in or about properties owned, operated, or administered by the employing agency or when performing necessary duties with respect to patrons, employees, and properties of the employing agency.
(Amended by Stats. 1992, Ch. 427, Sec. 129. Effective January 1, 1993.)

830.38.

(a) The officers of a state hospital under the jurisdiction of the State Department of State Hospitals or the State Department of Developmental Services appointed pursuant to Section 4313 or 4493 of the Welfare and Institutions Code, are peace officers whose authority extends to any place in the state for the purpose of performing their primary duty or when making an arrest pursuant to Section 836 as to any public offense with respect to which there is immediate danger to person or property, or of the escape of the perpetrator of that offense, or pursuant to Section 8597 or 8598 of the Government Code provided that the primary duty of the peace officers shall be the enforcement of the law as set forth in Sections 4311, 4313, 4491, and 4493 of the Welfare and Institutions Code. Those peace officers may carry firearms only if authorized and under terms and conditions specified by their employing agency.
(b) By July 1, 2015, the California Health and Human Services Agency shall develop training protocols and policies and procedures for peace officers specified in subdivision (a). When appropriate, training protocols and policies and procedures shall be uniformly implemented in both state hospitals and developmental centers. Additional training protocols and policies and procedures shall be developed to address the unique characteristics of the residents in each type of facility.
(c) In consultation with system stakeholders, the agency shall develop recommendations to further improve the quality and stability of law enforcement and investigative functions at both developmental centers and state hospitals in a meaningful and sustainable manner. These recommendations shall be submitted to the budget committees and relevant policy committees of both houses of the Legislature no later than January 10, 2015.
(Amended by Stats. 2014, Ch. 26, Sec. 14. (AB 1468) Effective June 20, 2014.)

830.39.

(a) Any regularly employed law enforcement officer of the Oregon State Police, the Nevada Department of Motor Vehicles and Public Safety, or the Arizona Department of Public Safety is a peace officer in this state if all of the following conditions are met:
(1) The officer is providing, or attempting to provide, law enforcement services within this state on the state or county highways and areas immediately adjacent thereto, within a distance of up to 50 statute miles of the contiguous border of this state and the state employing the officer.
(2) The officer is providing, or attempting to provide, law enforcement services pursuant to either of the following:
(A) In response to a request for services initiated by a member of the California Highway Patrol.
(B) In response to a reasonable belief that emergency law enforcement services are necessary for the preservation of life, and a request for services by a member of the Department of the California Highway Patrol is impractical to obtain under the circumstances. In those situations, the officer shall obtain authorization as soon as practical.
(3) The officer is providing, or attempting to provide, law enforcement services for the purpose of assisting a member of the California Highway Patrol to provide emergency service in response to misdemeanor or felony criminal activity, pursuant to the authority of a peace officer as provided in subdivision (a) of Section 830.2, or, in the event of highway-related traffic accidents, emergency incidents or other similar public safety problems, whether or not a member of the California Highway Patrol is present at the scene of the event. Nothing in this section shall be construed to confer upon the officer the authority to enforce traffic or motor vehicle infractions.
(4) An agreement pursuant to Section 2403.5 of the Vehicle Code is in effect between the Department of the California Highway Patrol and the agency of the adjoining state employing the officer, the officer acts in accordance with that agreement, and the agreement specifies that the officer and employing agency of the adjoining state shall be subject to the same civil immunities and liabilities as a peace officer and his or her employing agency in this state.
(5) The officer receives no separate compensation from this state for providing law enforcement services within this state.
(6) The adjoining state employing the officer confers similar rights and authority upon a member of the California Highway Patrol who renders assistance within that state.
(b) Whenever, pursuant to Nevada law, a Nevada correctional officer is working or supervising Nevada inmates who are performing conservation-related projects or fire suppression duties within California, the correctional officer may maintain custody of the inmates in California, and retake any inmate who should escape in California, to the same extent as if the correctional officer were a peace officer in this state and the inmate had been committed to his or her custody in proceedings under California law.
(c) Notwithstanding any other provision of law, any person who is acting as a peace officer in this state in the manner described in this section shall be deemed to have met the requirements of Section 1031 of the Government Code and the selection and training standards of the Commission on Peace Officer Standards and Training if the officer has completed the basic training required for peace officers in his or her state.

(d) In no case shall a peace officer of an adjoining state be authorized to provide services within a California jurisdiction during any period in which the regular law enforcement agency of the jurisdiction is involved in a labor dispute.
(Amended by Stats. 1992, Ch. 131, Sec. 1. Effective January 1, 1993.)
830.4.
The following persons are peace officers whose authority extends to any place in the state for the purpose of performing their duties under the conditions as specified by statute. Those peace officers may carry firearms only if authorized and under terms and conditions specified by their employing agency.
(a) Members of the California National Guard have the powers of peace officers when they are involved in any or all of the following:
(1) Called or ordered into active state service by the Governor pursuant to the provisions of Section 143 or 146 of the Military and Veterans Code.
(2) Serving within the area wherein military assistance is required.
(3) Directly assisting civil authorities in any of the situations specified in Section 143 or 146.
The authority of the peace officer under this subdivision extends to the area wherein military assistance is required as to a public offense committed or which there is reasonable cause to believe has been committed within that area. The requirements of Section 1031 of the Government Code are not applicable under those circumstances.
(b) Security officers of the Department of Justice when performing assigned duties as security officers.
(c) Security officers of Hastings College of the Law. These officers shall have authority of peace officers only within the City and County of San Francisco. Notwithstanding any other law, the peace officers designated by this subdivision shall not be authorized by this subdivision to carry firearms either on or off duty. Notwithstanding any other law, the act which designated the persons described in this subdivision as peace officers shall serve only to define those persons as peace officers, the extent of their jurisdiction, and the nature and scope of their authority, powers, and duties, and their status shall not change for purposes of retirement, workers' compensation or similar injury or death benefits, or other employee benefits.
(Amended by Stats. 2012, Ch. 227, Sec. 4. (SB 1578) Effective January 1, 2013.)
830.41.
Notwithstanding any other provision of law, the City of Tulelake, California, is authorized to enter into a mutual aid agreement with the City of Malin, Oregon, for the purpose of permitting their police departments to provide mutual aid to each other when necessary. Before the effective date of the agreement, the agreement shall be reviewed and approved by the Commissioner of the California Highway Patrol.
(Amended by Stats. 2013, Ch. 76, Sec. 149. (AB 383) Effective January 1, 2014.)
830.5.
The following persons are peace officers whose authority extends to any place in the state while engaged in the performance of the duties of their respective employment and for the purpose of carrying out the primary function of their employment or as required under Sections 8597, 8598, and 8617 of the Government Code. Except as specified in this section, these peace officers may carry firearms only if authorized and under those terms and conditions specified by their employing agency:
(a) A parole officer of the Department of Corrections and Rehabilitation, or the Department of Corrections and Rehabilitation, Division of Juvenile Parole Operations, probation officer, deputy probation officer, or a board coordinating parole agent employed by the Juvenile Parole Board. Except as otherwise provided in this subdivision, the authority of these parole or probation officers shall extend only as follows:
(1) To conditions of parole, probation, mandatory supervision, or postrelease community supervision by any person in this state on parole, probation, mandatory supervision, or postrelease community supervision.
(2) To the escape of any inmate or ward from a state or local institution.
(3) To the transportation of persons on parole, probation, mandatory supervision, or postrelease community supervision.
(4) To violations of any penal provisions of law which are discovered while performing the usual or authorized duties of the officer's employment.
(5) (A) To the rendering of mutual aid to any other law enforcement agency.
(B) For the purposes of this subdivision, "parole agent" shall have the same meaning as parole officer of the Department of Corrections and Rehabilitation or of the Department of Corrections and Rehabilitation, Division of Juvenile Justice.
(C) Any parole officer of the Department of Corrections and Rehabilitation, or the Department of Corrections and Rehabilitation, Division of Juvenile Parole Operations, is authorized to carry firearms, but only as determined by the director on a case-by-case or unit-by-unit basis and only under those terms and conditions specified by the director or chairperson. The Department of Corrections and Rehabilitation, Division of Juvenile Justice, shall develop a policy for arming peace officers of the Department of Corrections and Rehabilitation, Division of Juvenile Justice, who comprise "high-risk transportation details" or "high-risk escape details" no later than June 30, 1995. This policy shall be implemented no later than December 31, 1995.
(D) The Department of Corrections and Rehabilitation, Division of Juvenile Justice, shall train and arm those peace officers who comprise tactical teams at each facility for use during "high-risk escape details."
(b) A correctional officer employed by the Department of Corrections and Rehabilitation, or of the Department of Corrections and Rehabilitation, Division of Juvenile Justice, having custody of wards or any employee of the Department of Corrections and Rehabilitation designated by the secretary or any correctional counselor series employee of the Department of Corrections and Rehabilitation or any medical technical assistant series employee designated by the secretary or designated by the secretary and employed by the State Department of State Hospitals or any employee of the Board of Parole Hearings designated by the secretary or employee of the Department of Corrections and Rehabilitation, Division of Juvenile Justice, designated by the secretary or any superintendent, supervisor, or employee having custodial responsibilities in an institution operated by a probation department, or any transportation officer of a probation department.
(c) The following persons may carry a firearm while not on duty: a parole officer of the Department of Corrections and Rehabilitation, or the Department of Corrections and Rehabilitation, Division of Juvenile Justice, a correctional officer or correctional counselor employed by the Department of Corrections and Rehabilitation, or an employee of the Department of Corrections and Rehabilitation, Division of Juvenile Justice, having custody of wards or any employee of the Department of Corrections and Rehabilitation designated by the secretary or any medical technical assistant series employee designated by the secretary or designated by the secretary and employed by the State Department of State Hospitals. A parole officer of the Juvenile Parole Board may carry a firearm while not on duty only when so authorized by the chairperson of the board and only under the terms and conditions specified by the chairperson. Nothing in this section shall be interpreted to require licensure pursuant to Section 25400. The director or chairperson may deny, suspend, or revoke for good cause a person's right to carry a firearm under this subdivision. That person shall, upon request, receive a hearing, as provided for in the negotiated grievance procedure between the exclusive employee representative and the Department of Corrections and Rehabilitation, Division of Juvenile Justice, or the Juvenile Parole Board, to review the director's or the chairperson's decision.
(d) Persons permitted to carry firearms pursuant to this section, either on or off duty, shall meet the training requirements of Section 832 and shall qualify with the firearm at least quarterly. It is the responsibility of the individual officer or designee to maintain their eligibility to carry concealable firearms off duty. Failure to maintain quarterly

qualifications by an officer or designee with any concealable firearms carried off duty shall constitute good cause to suspend or revoke that person's right to carry firearms off duty.
(e) The Department of Corrections and Rehabilitation shall allow reasonable access to its ranges for officers and designees of either department to qualify to carry concealable firearms off duty. The time spent on the range for purposes of meeting the qualification requirements shall be the person's own time during the person's off-duty hours.
(f) The secretary shall promulgate regulations consistent with this section.
(g) "High-risk transportation details" and "high-risk escape details" as used in this section shall be determined by the secretary, or the secretary's designee. The secretary, or the secretary's designee, shall consider at least the following in determining "high-risk transportation details" and "high-risk escape details": protection of the public, protection of officers, flight risk, and violence potential of the wards.
(h) "Transportation detail" as used in this section shall include transportation of wards outside the facility, including, but not limited to, court appearances, medical trips, and interfacility transfers.
(i) This section shall remain in effect only until July 1, 2020, and as of that date is repealed.
(Amended by Stats. 2019, Ch. 25, Sec. 30. (SB 94) Effective June 27, 2019. Repealed as of July 1, 2020, by its own provisions. See later operative version added by Sec. 31 of Stats. 2019, Ch. 25.)
830.5.
The following persons are peace officers whose authority extends to any place in the state while engaged in the performance of the duties of their respective employment and for the purpose of carrying out the primary function of their employment or as required under Sections 8597, 8598, and 8617 of the Government Code. Except as specified in this section, these peace officers may carry firearms only if authorized and under those terms and conditions specified by their employing agency:
(a) A parole officer of the Department of Corrections and Rehabilitation, probation officer, or deputy probation officer. Except as otherwise provided in this subdivision, the authority of these parole or probation officers shall extend only as follows:
(1) To conditions of parole, probation, mandatory supervision, or postrelease community supervision by any person in this state on parole, probation, mandatory supervision, or postrelease community supervision.
(2) To the escape of any inmate or ward from a state or local institution.
(3) To the transportation of persons on parole, probation, mandatory supervision, or postrelease community supervision.
(4) To violations of any penal provisions of law which are discovered while performing the usual or authorized duties of the officer's employment.
(5) (A) To the rendering of mutual aid to any other law enforcement agency.
(B) For the purposes of this subdivision, "parole agent" shall have the same meaning as parole officer of the Department of Corrections and Rehabilitation.
(C) Any parole officer of the Department of Corrections and Rehabilitation is authorized to carry firearms, but only as determined by the director on a case-by-case or unit-by-unit basis and only under those terms and conditions specified by the director or chairperson.
(b) A correctional officer employed by the Department of Corrections and Rehabilitation or any employee of the Department of Corrections and Rehabilitation designated by the secretary or any correctional counselor series employee of the Department of Corrections and Rehabilitation or any medical technical assistant series employee designated by the secretary or designated by the secretary and employed by the State Department of State Hospitals or any employee of the Board of Parole Hearings designated by the secretary or any superintendent, supervisor, or employee having custodial responsibilities in an institution operated by a probation department, or any transportation officer of a probation department.
(c) The following persons may carry a firearm while not on duty: a parole officer of the Department of Corrections and Rehabilitation, a correctional officer or correctional counselor employed by the Department of Corrections and Rehabilitation, any employee of the Department of Corrections and Rehabilitation designated by the secretary or any medical technical assistant series employee designated by the secretary or designated by the secretary and employed by the State Department of State Hospitals. This section does not require licensure pursuant to Section 25400. The secretary or chairperson may deny, suspend, or revoke for good cause a person's right to carry a firearm under this subdivision. That person shall, upon request, receive a hearing, as provided for in the negotiated grievance procedure between the exclusive employee representative and the Department of Corrections and Rehabilitation, to review the secretary's or the chairperson's decision.
(d) Persons permitted to carry firearms pursuant to this section, either on or off duty, shall meet the training requirements of Section 832 and shall qualify with the firearm at least quarterly. It is the responsibility of the individual officer or designee to maintain their eligibility to carry concealable firearms off duty. Failure to maintain quarterly qualifications by an officer or designee with any concealable firearms carried off duty shall constitute good cause to suspend or revoke that person's right to carry firearms off duty.
(e) The Department of Corrections and Rehabilitation shall allow reasonable access to its ranges for officers and designees of either department to qualify to carry concealable firearms off duty. The time spent on the range for purposes of meeting the qualification requirements shall be the person's own time during the person's off-duty hours.
(f) The secretary shall promulgate regulations consistent with this section.
(g) This section shall become operative July 1, 2020.
(Repealed (in Sec. 30) and added by Stats. 2019, Ch. 25, Sec. 31. (SB 94) Effective June 27, 2019. Section operative July 1, 2020, by its own provisions.)
830.53.
(a) A youth correctional officer employed by the Department of Youth and Community Restoration, having custody of individuals subject to its jurisdiction, a youth correctional counselor series employee of the Department of Youth and Community Restoration, an employee of the Department of Youth and Community Restoration designated by the director, an employee of the Board of Juvenile Hearings designated by the director, and any superintendent, supervisor, or employee having custodial responsibilities in an institution or camp operated by the Department of Youth and Community Restoration is a peace officer whose authority extends to any place in the state while engaged in the performance of the duties of their respective employment and for the purpose of carrying out the primary function of their employment or as required under Sections 8597, 8598, and 8617 of the Government Code.
(b) A correctional officer or correctional counselor employed by the Department of Youth and Community Restoration or an employee of the department having custody of wards may carry a firearm while not on duty. This section does not require licensure pursuant to Section 25400. The director may deny, suspend, or revoke for good cause a person's right to carry a firearm under this subdivision. That person shall, upon request, receive a hearing, as provided for in the negotiated grievance procedure between the exclusive employee representative and the Department of Youth and Community Restoration or the Board of Juvenile Hearings, to review the director's or chairperson's decision.
(c) The Department of Youth and Community Restoration shall develop and implement a policy for arming peace officers of the department who comprise "high-risk transportation details" or "high-risk escape details" no later than December 31, 2020.
(d) The Department of Youth and Community Restoration shall train and arm those peace officers who comprise tactical teams at each facility for use during "high-risk escape details."

(e) Persons permitted to carry firearms pursuant to this section, either on or off duty, shall meet the training requirements of Section 832 and shall qualify with the firearm at least quarterly. It is the responsibility of the individual officer or designee to maintain their eligibility to carry concealable firearms off duty. Failure to maintain quarterly qualifications by an officer or designee with any concealable firearms carried off duty shall constitute good cause to suspend or revoke that person's right to carry firearms off duty.

(f) The director shall promulgate regulations consistent with this section.

(g) "High-risk transportation details" and "high-risk escape details" as used in this section shall be determined by the Director of the Department of Youth and Community Restoration, or the director's designee. The director, or the director's designee, shall consider at least the protection of the public, protection of officers, flight risk, and violence potential of wards in determining "high-risk transportation details" and "high-risk escape details."

(h) "Transportation detail" as used in this section includes transportation of wards outside of the facility, including, but not limited to, court appearances, medical trips, and interfacility transfers.

(i) This section shall become operative July 1, 2020.

(Added by Stats. 2019, Ch. 25, Sec. 32. (SB 94) Effective June 27, 2019.)

830.55.

(a) (1) As used in this section, a correctional officer is a peace officer, employed by a city, county, or city and county that operates a facility described in Section 2910.5 of this code or Section 1753.3 of the Welfare and Institutions Code or facilities operated by counties pursuant to Section 6241 or 6242 of this code under contract with the Department of Corrections and Rehabilitation or the Division of Juvenile Justice within the department, who has the authority and responsibility for maintaining custody of specified state prison inmates or wards, and who performs tasks related to the operation of a detention facility used for the detention of persons who have violated parole or are awaiting parole back into the community or, upon court order, either for their own safekeeping or for the specific purpose of serving a sentence therein.

(2) As used in this section, a correctional officer is also a peace officer, employed by a city, county, or city and county that operates a facility described in Section 4115.55, who has the authority and responsibility for maintaining custody of inmates sentenced to or housed in that facility, and who performs tasks related to the operation of that facility.

(b) A correctional officer shall have no right to carry or possess firearms in the performance of his or her prescribed duties, except, under the direction of the superintendent of the facility, while engaged in transporting prisoners, guarding hospitalized prisoners, or suppressing riots, lynchings, escapes, or rescues in or about a detention facility established pursuant to Section 2910.5 or 4115.55 of this code or Section 1753.3 of the Welfare and Institutions Code.

(c) Each person described in this section as a correctional officer, within 90 days following the date of the initial assignment to that position, shall satisfactorily complete the training course specified in Section 832. In addition, each person designated as a correctional officer, within one year following the date of the initial assignment as an officer, shall have satisfactorily met the minimum selection and training standards prescribed by the Board of State and Community Corrections pursuant to Section 6035. Persons designated as correctional officers, before the expiration of the 90-day and one-year periods described in this subdivision, who have not yet completed the required training, may perform the duties of a correctional officer only while under the direct supervision of a correctional officer who has completed the training required in this section, and shall not carry or possess firearms in the performance of their prescribed duties.

(d) This section shall not be construed to confer any authority upon a correctional officer except while on duty.

(e) A correctional officer may use reasonable force in establishing and maintaining custody of persons delivered to him or her by a law enforcement officer, may make arrests for misdemeanors and felonies within the local detention facility pursuant to a duly issued warrant, and may make warrantless arrests pursuant to Section 836.5 only during the duration of his or her job.

(Amended by Stats. 2013, Ch. 76, Sec. 150. (AB 383) Effective January 1, 2014.)

830.6.

(a) (1) Whenever any qualified person is deputized or appointed by the proper authority as a reserve or auxiliary sheriff or city police officer, a reserve deputy sheriff, a reserve deputy marshal, a reserve police officer of a regional park district or of a transit district, a reserve park ranger, a reserve harbor or port police officer of a county, city, or district as specified in Section 663.5 of the Harbors and Navigation Code, a reserve deputy of the Department of Fish and Game, a reserve special agent of the Department of Justice, a reserve officer of a community service district which is authorized under subdivision (h) of Section 61600 of the Government Code to maintain a police department or other police protection, a reserve officer of a school district police department under Section 35021.5 of the Education Code, a reserve officer of a community college police department under Section 72330, a reserve officer of a police protection district formed under Part 1 (commencing with Section 20000) of Division 14 of the Health and Safety Code, or a reserve housing authority patrol officer employed by a housing authority defined in subdivision (d) of Section 830.31, and is assigned specific police functions by that authority, the person is a peace officer, if the person qualifies as set forth in Section 832.6. The authority of a person designated as a peace officer pursuant to this paragraph extends only for the duration of the person's specific assignment. A reserve park ranger or a transit, harbor, or port district reserve officer may carry firearms only if authorized by, and under those terms and conditions as are specified by, his or her employing agency.

(2) Whenever any qualified person is deputized or appointed by the proper authority as a reserve or auxiliary sheriff or city police officer, a reserve deputy sheriff, a reserve deputy marshal, a reserve park ranger, a reserve police officer of a regional park district, transit district, community college district, or school district, a reserve harbor or port police officer of a county, city, or district as specified in Section 663.5 of the Harbors and Navigation Code, a reserve officer of a community service district that is authorized under subdivision (h) of Section 61600 of the Government Code to maintain a police department or other police protection, or a reserve officer of a police protection district formed under Part 1 (commencing with Section 20000) of Division 14 of the Health and Safety Code, and is so designated by local ordinance or, if the local agency is not authorized to act by ordinance, by resolution, either individually or by class, and is assigned to the prevention and detection of crime and the general enforcement of the laws of this state by that authority, the person is a peace officer, if the person qualifies as set forth in paragraph (1) of subdivision (a) of Section 832.6. The authority of a person designated as a peace officer pursuant to this paragraph includes the full powers and duties of a peace officer as provided by Section 830.1. A transit, harbor, or port district reserve police officer, or a city or county reserve peace officer who is not provided with the powers and duties authorized by Section 830.1, has the powers and duties authorized in Section 830.33, or in the case of a reserve park ranger, the powers and duties that are authorized in Section 830.31, or in the case of a reserve housing authority patrol officer, the powers and duties that are authorized in subdivision (d) of Section 830.31, and a school district reserve police officer or a community college district reserve police officer has the powers and duties authorized in Section 830.32.

(b) Whenever any person designated by a Native American tribe recognized by the United States Secretary of the Interior is deputized or appointed by the county sheriff as a reserve or auxiliary sheriff or a reserve deputy sheriff, and is assigned to the prevention and detection of crime and the general enforcement of the laws of this state by the county sheriff, the person is a peace officer, if the person qualifies as set forth in

paragraph (1) of subdivision (a) of Section 832.6. The authority of a peace officer pursuant to this subdivision includes the full powers and duties of a peace officer as provided by Section 830.1.

(c) Whenever any person is summoned to the aid of any uniformed peace officer, the summoned person is vested with the powers of a peace officer that are expressly delegated to him or her by the summoning officer or that are otherwise reasonably necessary to properly assist the officer.

(Amended by Stats. 2007, Ch. 118, Sec. 1. Effective January 1, 2008.)

830.65.

(a) Any person who is a regularly employed police officer of a city or a regularly employed deputy sheriff of a county, or a reserve peace officer of a city or county and is appointed in the manner described in paragraph (1) or (2) of subdivision (a) of Section 832.6, may be appointed as a Campaign Against Marijuana Planting emergency appointee by the Attorney General pursuant to Section 5 of Chapter 1563 of the Statutes of 1985 to assist with a specific investigation, tactical operation, or search and rescue operation. When so appointed, the person shall be a peace officer of the Department of Justice, provided that the person's authority shall extend only for the duration of the specific assignment.

(b) Notwithstanding any other provision of law, any person who is appointed as a peace officer in the manner described in this section shall be deemed to have met the requirements of Section 1031 of the Government Code and the selection and training standards of the Commission on Peace Officer Standards and Training.

(Added by Stats. 1988, Ch. 1482, Sec. 4.)

830.7.

The following persons are not peace officers but may exercise the powers of arrest of a peace officer as specified in Section 836 during the course and within the scope of their employment, if they successfully complete a course in the exercise of those powers pursuant to Section 832:

(a) Persons designated by a cemetery authority pursuant to Section 8325 of the Health and Safety Code.

(b) Persons regularly employed as security officers for independent institutions of higher education, recognized under subdivision (b) of Section 66010 of the Education Code, if the institution has concluded a memorandum of understanding, permitting the exercise of that authority, with the sheriff or the chief of police within whose jurisdiction the institution lies.

(c) Persons regularly employed as security officers for health facilities, as defined in Section 1250 of the Health and Safety Code, that are owned and operated by cities, counties, and cities and counties, if the facility has concluded a memorandum of understanding, permitting the exercise of that authority, with the sheriff or the chief of police within whose jurisdiction the facility lies.

(d) Employees or classes of employees of the California Department of Forestry and Fire Protection designated by the Director of Forestry and Fire Protection, provided that the primary duty of the employee shall be the enforcement of the law as that duty is set forth in Section 4156 of the Public Resources Code.

(e) Persons regularly employed as inspectors, supervisors, or security officers for transit districts, as defined in Section 99213 of the Public Utilities Code, if the district has concluded a memorandum of understanding permitting the exercise of that authority, with, as applicable, the sheriff, the chief of police, or the Department of the California Highway Patrol within whose jurisdiction the district lies. For the purposes of this subdivision, the exercise of peace officer authority may include the authority to remove a vehicle from a railroad right-of-way as set forth in Section 22656 of the Vehicle Code.

(f) Nonpeace officers regularly employed as county parole officers pursuant to Section 3089.

(g) Persons appointed by the Executive Director of the California Science Center pursuant to Section 4108 of the Food and Agricultural Code.

(h) Persons regularly employed as investigators by the Department of Transportation for the City of Los Angeles and designated by local ordinance as public officers, to the extent necessary to enforce laws related to public transportation, and authorized by a memorandum of understanding with the chief of police, permitting the exercise of that authority. For the purposes of this subdivision, "investigator" means an employee defined in Section 53075.61 of the Government Code authorized by local ordinance to enforce laws related to public transportation. Transportation investigators authorized by this section shall not be deemed "peace officers" for purposes of Sections 241 and 243.

(i) Persons regularly employed by any department of the City of Los Angeles who are designated as security officers and authorized by local ordinance to enforce laws related to the preservation of peace in or about the properties owned, controlled, operated, or administered by any department of the City of Los Angeles and authorized by a memorandum of understanding with the Chief of Police of the City of Los Angeles permitting the exercise of that authority. Security officers authorized pursuant to this subdivision shall not be deemed peace officers for purposes of Sections 241 and 243.

(j) Illegal dumping enforcement officers or code enforcement officers, to the extent necessary to enforce laws related to illegal waste dumping or littering, and authorized by a memorandum of understanding with, as applicable, the sheriff or chief of police within whose jurisdiction the person is employed, permitting the exercise of that authority. An "illegal dumping enforcement officer or code enforcement officer" is defined, for purposes of this section, as a person employed full time, part time, or as a volunteer after completing training prescribed by law, by a city, county, or city and county, whose duties include illegal dumping enforcement and who is designated by local ordinance as a public officer. An illegal dumping enforcement officer or code enforcement officer may also be a person who is not regularly employed by a city, county, or city and county, but who has met all training requirements and is directly supervised by a regularly employed illegal dumping enforcement officer or code enforcement officer conducting illegal dumping enforcement. This person shall not have the power of arrest or access to summary criminal history information pursuant to this section. No person may be appointed as an illegal dumping enforcement officer or code enforcement officer if that person is disqualified pursuant to the criteria set forth in Section 1029 of the Government Code. Persons regularly employed by a city, county, or city and county designated pursuant to this subdivision may be furnished state summary criminal history information upon a showing of compelling need pursuant to subdivision (c) of Section 11105.

(Amended by Stats. 2012, Ch. 298, Sec. 1. (AB 801) Effective January 1, 2013.)

830.75.

(a) Notwithstanding subdivision (b) of Section 830.7, a person regularly employed as a security officer for an independent institution of higher education recognized under subdivision (b) of Section 66010 of the Education Code may be deputized or appointed by the sheriff or the chief of police of the jurisdiction in which the institution is located as a reserve deputy or officer pursuant to Section 830.6, notwithstanding that he or she is compensated by the institution of higher education or that the assigned specific law enforcement functions and duties may be of a recurring or continuous nature, if both of the following requirements are met:

(1) The person meets the requirements specified in paragraph (1) of subdivision (a) of Section 832.6.

(2) The institution of higher education and the appropriate local law enforcement agency have entered into a memorandum of understanding.

(b) The authority of a person designated as a peace officer pursuant to this section extends to any place in the state and applies only while he or she is engaged in the performance of his or her assigned duties for his or her institution of higher education pursuant to the memorandum entered into pursuant to paragraph (2) of subdivision (a). The primary duty of a person designated as a peace officer pursuant to this section shall be the enforcement of the law upon the campuses of his or her institution of higher education and within one mile of the exterior of those campuses, and in or about other grounds and properties owned, operated, controlled, or administered by that institution of higher education.

(c) Vehicles owned by an independent institution of higher education that are specifically designated for use by persons designated as peace officers pursuant to this section shall be deemed authorized emergency vehicles for all purposes of the law within the institution's jurisdiction.

(Added by Stats. 2016, Ch. 356, Sec. 1. (AB 2361) Effective January 1, 2017.)

830.8.

(a) Federal criminal investigators and law enforcement officers are not California peace officers, but may exercise the powers of arrest of a peace officer in any of the following circumstances:

(1) Any circumstances specified in Section 836 of this code or Section 5150 of the Welfare and Institutions Code for violations of state or local laws.

(2) When these investigators and law enforcement officers are engaged in the enforcement of federal criminal laws and exercise the arrest powers only incidental to the performance of these duties.

(3) When requested by a California law enforcement agency to be involved in a joint task force or criminal investigation.

(4) When probable cause exists to believe that a public offense that involves immediate danger to persons or property has just occurred or is being committed.

In all of these instances, the provisions of Section 847 shall apply. These investigators and law enforcement officers, prior to the exercise of these arrest powers, shall have been certified by their agency heads as having satisfied the training requirements of Section 832, or the equivalent thereof.

This subdivision does not apply to federal officers of the Bureau of Land Management or the United States Forest Service. These officers have no authority to enforce California statutes without the written consent of the sheriff or the chief of police in whose jurisdiction they are assigned.

(b) Duly authorized federal employees who comply with the training requirements set forth in Section 832 are peace officers when they are engaged in enforcing applicable state or local laws on property owned or possessed by the United States government, or on any street, sidewalk, or property adjacent thereto, and with the written consent of the sheriff or the chief of police, respectively, in whose jurisdiction the property is situated.

(c) National park rangers are not California peace officers but may exercise the powers of arrest of a peace officer as specified in Section 836 and the powers of a peace officer specified in Section 5150 of the Welfare and Institutions Code for violations of state or local laws provided these rangers are exercising the arrest powers incidental to the performance of their federal duties or providing or attempting to provide law enforcement services in response to a request initiated by California state park rangers to assist in preserving the peace and protecting state parks and other property for which California state park rangers are responsible. National park rangers, prior to the exercise of these arrest powers, shall have been certified by their agency heads as having satisfactorily completed the training requirements of Section 832.3, or the equivalent thereof.

(d) Notwithstanding any other provision of law, during a state of war emergency or a state of emergency, as defined in Section 8558 of the Government Code, federal criminal investigators and law enforcement officers who are assisting California law enforcement officers in carrying out emergency operations are not deemed California peace officers, but may exercise the powers of arrest of a peace officer as specified in Section 836 and the powers of a peace officer specified in Section 5150 of the Welfare and Institutions Code for violations of state or local laws. In these instances, the provisions of Section 847 of this code and of Section 8655 of the Government Code shall apply.

(e) (1) Any qualified person who is appointed as a Washoe tribal law enforcement officer is not a California peace officer, but may exercise the powers of a Washoe tribal peace officer when engaged in the enforcement of Washoe tribal criminal laws against any person who is an Indian, as defined in subsection (d) of Section 450b of Title 25 of the United States Code, on Washoe tribal land. The respective prosecuting authorities, in consultation with law enforcement agencies, may agree on who shall have initial responsibility for prosecution of specified infractions. This subdivision is not meant to confer cross-deputized status as California peace officers, nor to confer California peace officer status upon Washoe tribal law enforcement officers when enforcing state or local laws in the State of California. Nothing in this section shall be construed to impose liability upon or to require indemnification by the County of Alpine or the State of California for any act performed by an officer of the Washoe Tribe. Washoe tribal law enforcement officers shall have the right to travel to and from Washoe tribal lands within California in order to carry out tribal duties.

(2) Washoe tribal law enforcement officers are exempted from the provisions of subdivision (a) of Section 25400 and subdivision (a) and subdivisions (c) to (h), inclusive, of Section 25850 while performing their official duties on their tribal lands or while proceeding by a direct route to or from the tribal lands. Tribal law enforcement vehicles are deemed to be emergency vehicles within the meaning of Section 30 of the Vehicle Code while performing official police services.

(3) As used in this subdivision, the term "Washoe tribal lands" includes the following:

(A) All lands located in the County of Alpine within the limits of the reservation created for the Washoe Tribe of Nevada and California, notwithstanding the issuance of any patent and including rights-of-way running through the reservation and all tribal trust lands.

(B) All Indian allotments, the Indian titles to which have not been extinguished, including rights-of-way running through the same.

(4) As used in this subdivision, the term "Washoe tribal law" refers to the laws codified in the Law and Order Code of the Washoe Tribe of Nevada and California, as adopted by the Tribal Council of the Washoe Tribe of Nevada and California.

(Amended (as amended by Stats. 2010, Ch. 178, Sec. 67) by Stats. 2011, Ch. 296, Sec. 212. (AB 1023) Effective January 1, 2012.)

830.85.

Notwithstanding any other law, United States Immigration and Customs Enforcement officers and United States Customs and Border Protection officers are not California peace officers.

(Added by Stats. 2017, Ch. 116, Sec. 2. (AB 1440) Effective January 1, 2018.)

830.9.

Animal control officers are not peace officers but may exercise the powers of arrest of a peace officer as specified in Section 836 and the power to serve warrants as specified in Sections 1523 and 1530 during the course and within the scope of their employment, if those officers successfully complete a course in the exercise of those powers pursuant to Section 832. That part of the training course specified in Section 832 pertaining to the carrying and use of firearms shall not be required for any animal control officer whose employing agency prohibits the use of firearms.

For the purposes of this section, "firearms" includes capture guns, blowguns, carbon dioxide operated rifles and pistols, air guns, handguns, rifles, and shotguns.

(Amended by Stats. 1990, Ch. 82, Sec. 13. Effective May 3, 1990.)

830.95.

(a) Any person who wears the uniform of a peace officer while engaged in picketing, or other informational activities in a public place relating to a concerted refusal to work, is guilty of a misdemeanor, whether or not the person is a peace officer.

(b) This section shall not be construed to authorize or ratify any picketing or other informational activities not otherwise authorized by law.

(Added by Stats. 2010, Ch. 711, Sec. 3. (SB 1080) Effective January 1, 2011. Operative January 1, 2012, by Sec. 10 of Ch. 711.)

830.10.

Any uniformed peace officer shall wear a badge, nameplate, or other device which bears clearly on its face the identification number or name of the officer.

(Amended by Stats. 1989, Ch. 1165, Sec. 38.)

830.11.

(a) The following persons are not peace officers but may exercise the powers of arrest of a peace officer as specified in Section 836 and the power to serve warrants as specified in Sections 1523 and 1530 during the course and within the scope of their employment, if they receive a course in the exercise of those powers pursuant to Section 832. The authority and powers of the persons designated under this section extend to any place in the state:

(1) A person employed by the Department of Business Oversight designated by the Commissioner of Business Oversight, provided that the person's primary duty is the enforcement of, and investigations relating to, the provisions of law administered by the Commissioner of Business Oversight.

(2) A person employed by the Bureau of Real Estate designated by the Real Estate Commissioner, provided that the person's primary duty is the enforcement of the laws set forth in Part 1 (commencing with Section 10000) and Part 2 (commencing with Section 11000) of Division 4 of the Business and Professions Code. The Real Estate Commissioner may designate a person under this section who, at the time of his or her designation, is assigned to the Special Investigations Unit, internally known as the Crisis Response Team.

(3) A person employed by the State Lands Commission designated by the executive officer, provided that the person's primary duty is the enforcement of the law relating to the duties of the State Lands Commission.

(4) A person employed as an investigator of the Investigations Bureau of the Department of Insurance, who is designated by the Chief of the Investigations Bureau, provided that the person's primary duty is the enforcement of the Insurance Code and other laws relating to persons and businesses, licensed and unlicensed by the Department of Insurance, who are engaged in the business of insurance.

(5) A person employed as an investigator or investigator supervisor by the Public Utilities Commission, who is designated by the commission's executive director and approved by the commission, provided that the person's primary duty is the enforcement of the law as that duty is set forth in Section 308.5 of the Public Utilities Code.

(6) (A) A person employed by the State Board of Equalization, Investigations Division, who is designated by the board's executive director, provided that the person's primary duty is the enforcement of laws administered by the State Board of Equalization.

(B) A person designated pursuant to this paragraph is not entitled to peace officer retirement benefits.

(7) A person employed by the Department of Food and Agriculture and designated by the Secretary of Food and Agriculture as an investigator, investigator supervisor, or investigator manager, provided that the person's primary duty is enforcement of, and investigations relating to, the Food and Agricultural Code or Division 5 (commencing with Section 12001) or Division 10 (commencing with Section 26000) of the Business and Professions Code.

(8) The Inspector General and those employees of the Office of the Inspector General designated by the Inspector General, provided that the person's primary duty is the enforcement of the law relating to the duties of the Office of the Inspector General.

(b) Notwithstanding any other law, a person designated pursuant to this section may not carry a firearm.

(c) A person designated pursuant to this section shall be included as a "peace officer of the state" under paragraph (2) of subdivision (c) of Section 11105 for the purpose of receiving state summary criminal history information and shall be furnished that information on the same basis as other peace officers designated in paragraph (2) of subdivision (c) of Section 11105.

(Amended by Stats. 2018, Ch. 138, Sec. 1. (AB 873) Effective January 1, 2019.)

830.12.

Notwithstanding any other provision of law, persons designated by a local agency as litter control officers, vehicle abatement officers, registered sanitarians, and solid waste specialists, are not peace officers, may not exercise the powers of arrest of a peace officer, as specified in Section 836, and shall not be authorized to carry or use firearms within the scope and course of their employment. These persons may, however, be authorized by the governing board of the particular local agency to issue citations involving violations of laws relating to abandoned vehicles and littering.

(Added by Stats. 1988, Ch. 726, Sec. 1.)

830.13.

(a) The following persons are not peace officers but may exercise the power to serve warrants as specified in Sections 1523 and 1530 during the course and within the scope of their employment, if they receive a course in the exercise of that power pursuant to Section 832. The authority and power of the persons designated under this section shall extend to any place in the state:

(1) Persons employed as investigators of an auditor-controller or director of finance of any county or persons employed by a city and county who conduct investigations under the supervision of the controller of the city and county, who are regularly employed and paid in that capacity, provided that the primary duty of these persons shall be to engage in investigations related to the theft of funds or the misappropriation of funds or resources, or investigations related to the duties of the auditor-controller or finance director as set forth in Chapter 3.5 (commencing with Section 26880), Chapter 4 (commencing with Section 26900), Chapter 4.5 (commencing with Section 26970), and Chapter 4.6 (commencing with Section 26980) of Part 3 of Division 2 of Title 3 of the Government Code.

(2) Persons employed by the Department of Justice as investigative auditors, provided that the primary duty of these persons shall be to investigate financial crimes. Investigative auditors shall only serve warrants for the production of documentary evidence held by financial institutions, Internet service providers, telecommunications companies, and third parties who are not reasonably suspected of engaging or having engaged in criminal activity related to the documentary evidence for which the warrant is requested.

(b) Notwithstanding any other provision of law, persons designated pursuant to this section shall not carry firearms.

(c) Persons designated pursuant to this section shall be included as "peace officers of the state" under paragraph (2) of subdivision (c) of Section 11105 for the purpose of receiving state summary criminal history information and shall be furnished that information on the same basis as peace officers of the state designated in paragraph (2) of subdivision (c) of Section 11105.

(d) Unless otherwise specifically provided, this section confers to persons designated in this section the same authority and power to serve warrants as conferred by Section 830.11.

(Amended by Stats. 2008, Ch. 81, Sec. 1. Effective January 1, 2009.)

830.14.

(a) A local or regional transit agency or a joint powers agency operating rail service identified in an implementation program adopted pursuant to Article 10 (commencing with Section 130450) of Chapter 4 of Division 12 of the Public Utilities Code may authorize by contract designated persons as conductors performing fare inspection

duties who are employed by a railroad corporation that operates public rail commuter transit services for that agency to act as its agent in the enforcement of subdivisions (a) to (d), inclusive, of Section 640 relating to the operation of the rail service if they complete the training requirement specified in this section.
(b) The governing board of the Altamont Commuter Express Authority, a joint powers agency duly formed pursuant to Article 1 (commencing with Section 6500) of Chapter 5 of Division 7 of Title 1 of the Government Code, by and between the Alameda County Congestion Management Agency, the Santa Clara Valley Transportation Authority, and the San Joaquin Regional Rail Commission, may contract with designated persons to act as its agents in the enforcement of subdivisions (a) to (d), inclusive, of Section 640 relating to the operation of a public transportation system if these persons complete the training requirement specified in this section.
(c) The governing board of the Peninsula Corridor Joint Powers Board, a joint powers agency duly formed pursuant to Article 1 (commencing with Section 6500) of Chapter 5 of Division 7 of Title 1 of the Government Code, by and between the San Mateo County Transit District, the Santa Clara Valley Transportation Authority, and the City and County of San Francisco, may appoint designated persons to act as its agents in the enforcement of subdivisions (a) to (d), inclusive, of Section 640 relating to the operation of a public transportation system if these persons complete the training requirement specified in this section.
(d) The governing board of Foothill Transit, a joint powers agency duly formed pursuant to Article 1 (commencing with Section 6500) of Chapter 5 of Division 7 of Title 1 of the Government Code, by and between the Cities of Arcadia, Azusa, Baldwin Park, Bradbury, Claremont, Covina, Diamond Bar, Duarte, El Monte, Glendora, Industry, Irwindale, La Habra Heights, La Puente, La Verne, Monrovia, Pomona, San Dimas, South El Monte, Temple City, Walnut, West Covina, and the County of Los Angeles, may resolve to contract with designated persons to act as its agents in the enforcement of subdivisions (a) to (d), inclusive, of Section 640 relating to the operation of a public transportation system if these persons complete the training requirement specified in this section.
(e) The governing board of the Sacramento Regional Transit District, a transit district duly formed pursuant to Part 14 (commencing with Section 102000) of Division 10 of the Public Utilities Code, may designate persons regularly employed by the district as inspectors or supervisors to enforce subdivisions (a) to (d), inclusive, of Section 640, relating to the operation of a public transportation system, and any ordinance adopted by the district pursuant to subdivision (a) of Section 102122 of the Public Utilities Code, if these persons complete the training requirement specified in this section.
(f) The governing board of a transit district, as defined in subdivision (b) of Section 99170 of the Public Utilities Code, may designate employees, except for union-represented employees employed to drive revenue-generating transit vehicles, or security officers contracted by the transit district, to enforce subdivisions (a) to (d), inclusive, of Section 640, and Section 640.5, and violations of Section 99170 of the Public Utilities Code.
(g) Persons authorized pursuant to this section to enforce subdivisions (a) to (d), inclusive, of Section 640, or Section 640.5, or Section 99170 of the Public Utilities Code, shall complete a specialized fare compliance course that shall be provided by the authorizing agency. This training course shall include, but not be limited to, the following topics:
(1) An overview of barrier-free fare inspection concepts.
(2) The scope and limitations of inspector authority.
(3) Familiarization with the elements of the infractions enumerated in subdivisions (a) to (d), inclusive, of Section 640, and, as applicable, the crimes enumerated in Section 640.5, and Section 99170 of the Public Utilities Code.
(4) Techniques for conducting fare checks, including inspection procedures, demeanor, and contacting violators.
(5) Citation issuance and court appearances.
(6) Fare media recognition.
(7) Handling argumentative violators and diffusing conflict.
(8) The mechanics of law enforcement support and interacting with law enforcement for effective incident resolution.
(h) Persons described in this section are public officers, not peace officers, have no authority to carry firearms or any other weapon while performing the duties authorized in this section, and may not exercise the powers of arrest of a peace officer while performing the duties authorized in this section. These persons may be authorized by the agencies specified in this section to issue citations involving infractions relating to the operation of the rail service specified in this section.
(i) This section does not affect the retirement or disability benefits provided to employees described in this section or be in violation of any collective bargaining agreement between a labor organization and a railroad corporation.
(j) Notwithstanding any other provision of this section, the primary responsibility of a conductor of a commuter passenger train shall be functions related to safe train operation.
(Amended by Stats. 2015, Ch. 303, Sec. 392. (AB 731) Effective January 1, 2016.)

830.15.

(a) Notwithstanding subdivision (d) of Section 830.33, a person regularly employed as an airport law enforcement officer by Los Angeles World Airports is a peace officer for purposes of Section 830.1 if and when the Los Angeles Police Commission and the Los Angeles Board of Airport Commissioners enter into an agreement to enable the Inspector General of the Los Angeles Police Commission to conduct audits and investigations of the Los Angeles Airport Police Division.
(b) For purposes of this section, "Los Angeles World Airports" means the department of the City of Los Angeles that owns and operates the Los Angeles International Airport, the Ontario International Airport, the Palmdale Regional Airport, and the Van Nuys Airport.
(c) If the Los Angeles Police Commission and the Los Angeles Board of Airport Commissioners do not take the necessary actions provided in subdivision (a) and do not make a record of that action publicly available on or before April 1, 2014, this section shall become inoperative on that date and, as of January 1, 2015, is repealed, unless a later enacted statute that is enacted before January 1, 2015, deletes or extends the dates on which this section becomes inoperative and is repealed.
(Added by Stats. 2013, Ch. 783, Sec. 1. (AB 128) Effective January 1, 2014. Conditionally inoperative on April 1, 2014. Repealed conditionally on January 1, 2015, by its own provisions.)

831.

(a) A custodial officer is a public officer, not a peace officer, employed by a law enforcement agency of a city or county who has the authority and responsibility for maintaining custody of prisoners and performs tasks related to the operation of a local detention facility used for the detention of persons usually pending arraignment or upon court order either for their own safekeeping or for the specific purpose of serving a sentence in that facility.
(b) A custodial officer shall not carry or possess firearms in the performance of his or her official duties. A custodial officer may use a firearm that is a less lethal weapon, as defined in Section 16780, in the performance of his or her official duties, at the discretion of the employing sheriff or chief of police, as applicable, or his or her designee. A custodial officer who uses a less lethal weapon shall be trained in its use and shall comply with the policy on the use of less lethal weapons as set forth by the sheriff or chief of police.
(c) Each person described in this section as a custodial officer shall, within 90 days following the date of the initial assignment to the position, satisfactorily complete the training course specified in Section 832. In addition, each person designated as a custodial officer shall, within one year following the date of the initial assignment as a custodial officer, have satisfactorily met the minimum selection and training standards prescribed by the Board of State and Community Corrections pursuant to Section 6035. Persons designated as custodial officers, before the expiration of the 90-day and one-year periods described in this subdivision, who have not yet completed the required training, may perform the duties of a custodial officer only while under the direct supervision of a peace officer as described in Section 830.1, who has completed the training prescribed by the Commission on Peace Officer Standards and Training, or a custodial officer who has completed the training required by this section.
(d) At any time 20 or more custodial officers are on duty, there shall be at least one peace officer, as described in Section 830.1, on duty at the same time to supervise the performance of the custodial officers.
(e) This section does not confer any authority upon any custodial officer, except while he or she is on duty.
(f) A custodial officer may do all of the following:
(1) Use reasonable force in establishing and maintaining custody of persons delivered to him or her by a law enforcement officer.
(2) Make arrests for misdemeanors and felonies within the local detention facility pursuant to a duly issued warrant.
(3) Release without further criminal process persons arrested for intoxication.
(4) Release misdemeanants on citation to appear in lieu of or after booking.
(Amended by Stats. 2017, Ch. 73, Sec. 1. (SB 324) Effective January 1, 2018.)

831.4.

(a) (1) A sheriff's or police security officer is a public officer, employed by the sheriff of a county, a police chief of a city police department, or a police chief of a police division that is within a city department and that operates independently of the city police department commanded by the police chief of a city, whose primary duty is the security of locations or facilities as directed by the sheriff or police chief. The duties of a sheriff's or police security officer shall be limited to the physical security and protection of properties owned, operated, controlled, or administered by the county or city, or any municipality or special district contracting for police services from the county or city pursuant to Section 54981 of the Government Code, or necessary duties with respect to the patrons, employees, and properties of the employing county, city, or contracting entities.
(2) In addition to the duties in paragraph (1), the duties of a security officer employed by the Chief of Police of the City of Sacramento or the Sheriff of the County of Sacramento may also include the physical security and protection of any properties owned, operated, or administered by a public agency, privately owned company, or nonprofit entity contracting for security services from the City or County of Sacramento, whose primary business supports national defense, or whose facility is qualified as a national critical infrastructure under federal law or by a federal agency, or that stores or manufactures material that, if stolen, vandalized, or otherwise compromised, may compromise national security or pose a danger to residents within the County of Sacramento. A contract entered into pursuant to this paragraph shall provide for full reimbursement to the City or County of Sacramento of the actual costs of providing those services, as determined by the county auditor or auditor-controller, or by the city. Before contracting for services pursuant to this paragraph, the Sacramento County Board of Supervisors or the governing board of the City of Sacramento shall discuss the contract and the requirements of this paragraph at a duly noticed public hearing.
(b) A sheriff's or police security officer is neither a peace officer nor a public safety officer as defined in Section 3301 of the Government Code. A sheriff's or police security officer may carry or possess a firearm, baton, and other safety equipment and weapons authorized by the sheriff or police chief while performing the duties authorized in this section, and under the terms and conditions specified by the sheriff or police chief. These persons may not exercise the powers of arrest of a peace officer, but may issue citations for infractions if authorized by the sheriff or police chief.
(c) Each sheriff's or police security officer shall satisfactorily complete a course of training as specified in Section 832 before being assigned to perform his or her duties. This section does not preclude the sheriff or police chief from requiring additional training requirements.
(d) Notwithstanding any other law, this section does not confer any authority upon a sheriff's or police security officer except while on duty, or confer any additional retirement benefits to persons employed within this classification.
(Amended by Stats. 2018, Ch. 92, Sec. 164. (SB 1289) Effective January 1, 2019.)

831.5.

(a) As used in this section, a custodial officer is a public officer, not a peace officer, who is employed by a law enforcement agency of San Diego County, Fresno County, Kern County, Stanislaus County, Riverside County, Santa Clara County, Napa County, or a county having a population of 425,000 or less who has the authority and responsibility for maintaining custody of prisoners and performs tasks related to the operation of a local detention facility used for the detention of persons usually pending arraignment or upon court order either for their own safekeeping or for the specific purpose of serving a sentence in the local detention facility. Custodial officers of a county shall be employees of, and under the authority of, the sheriff, except in counties in which the sheriff, as of July 1, 1993, is not in charge of and the sole and exclusive authority to keep the county jail and the prisoners in it. A custodial officer includes a person designated as a correctional officer, jailer, or other similar title. The duties of a custodial officer may include the serving of warrants, court orders, writs, and subpoenas in the detention facility or under circumstances arising directly out of maintaining custody of prisoners and related tasks.
(b) A custodial officer has no right to carry or possess firearms in the performance of his or her prescribed duties, except, under the direction of the sheriff or chief of police, while engaged in transporting prisoners; guarding hospitalized prisoners; or suppressing jail riots, lynchings, escapes, or rescues in or about a detention facility falling under the care and custody of the sheriff or chief of police.
(c) A person described in this section as a custodial officer shall, within 90 days following the date of the initial assignment to that position, satisfactorily complete the training course specified in Section 832. In addition, a person designated as a custodial officer shall, within one year following the date of the initial assignment as a custodial officer, have satisfactorily met the minimum selection and training standards prescribed by the Board of State and Community Corrections pursuant to Section 6035. Persons designated as custodial officers, before the expiration of the 90-day and one-year periods described in this subdivision, who have not yet completed the required training, shall not carry or possess firearms in the performance of their prescribed duties, but may perform the duties of a custodial officer only while under the direct supervision of a peace officer, as described in Section 830.1, who has completed the training prescribed by the Commission on Peace Officer Standards and Training, or a custodial officer who has completed the training required in this section.
(d) At any time 20 or more custodial officers are on duty, there shall be at least one peace officer, as described in Section 830.1, on duty at the same time to supervise the performance of the custodial officers.
(e) This section does not confer any authority upon any custodial officer except while on duty.
(f) A custodial officer may use reasonable force in establishing and maintaining custody of persons delivered to him or her by a law enforcement officer; may make arrests for misdemeanors and felonies within the local detention facility pursuant to a duly issued warrant; may make warrantless arrests pursuant to Section 836.5 only during the duration of his or her job; may release without further criminal process persons arrested

for intoxication; and may release misdemeanants on citation to appear in lieu of or after booking.

(g) Custodial officers employed by the Santa Clara County Department of Correction are authorized to perform the following additional duties in the facility:

(1) Arrest a person without a warrant whenever the custodial officer has reasonable cause to believe that the person to be arrested has committed a misdemeanor or felony in the presence of the officer that is a violation of a statute or ordinance that the officer has the duty to enforce.

(2) Search property, cells, prisoners or visitors.

(3) Conduct strip or body cavity searches of prisoners pursuant to Section 4030.

(4) Conduct searches and seizures pursuant to a duly issued warrant.

(5) Segregate prisoners.

(6) Classify prisoners for the purpose of housing or participation in supervised activities. These duties may be performed at the Santa Clara Valley Medical Center, or at other health care facilities in the County of Santa Clara, as needed and only as they directly relate to guarding in-custody inmates. This subdivision does not authorize the performance of any law enforcement activity involving any person other than the inmate or his or her visitors.

(h) (1) Upon resolution by the Napa County Board of Supervisors, custodial officers employed by the Napa County Department of Corrections are authorized to perform all of the following duties in a facility located in that county:

(A) Arrest a person without a warrant whenever the custodial officer has reasonable cause to believe that the person to be arrested has committed a misdemeanor or felony in the presence of the officer that is a violation of a statute or ordinance that the officer has the duty to enforce.

(B) Search property, cells, prisoners, or visitors.

(C) Conduct strip or body cavity searches of prisoners pursuant to Section 4030.

(D) Conduct searches and seizures pursuant to a duly issued warrant.

(E) Segregate prisoners.

(F) Classify prisoners for the purpose of housing or participation in supervised activities.

(2) This subdivision does not authorize the performance of any law enforcement activity involving any person other than an inmate or his or her visitors.

(i) (1) Upon resolution by the County of Madera Board of Supervisors, custodial officers employed by the Madera County Department of Corrections are authorized to perform all of the following duties in a facility located in that county:

(A) Arrest a person without a warrant whenever the custodial officer has reasonable cause to believe that the person to be arrested has committed a misdemeanor or felony in the presence of the officer that is a violation of a statute or ordinance that the officer has the duty to enforce.

(B) Search property, cells, prisoners, or visitors.

(C) Conduct strip or body cavity searches of prisoners pursuant to Section 4030.

(D) Conduct searches and seizures pursuant to a duly issued warrant.

(E) Segregate prisoners.

(F) Classify prisoners for the purpose of housing or participation in supervised activities.

(2) This subdivision does not authorize the performance of any law enforcement activity involving any person other than an inmate or his or her visitors.

(j) This section does not authorize a custodial officer to carry or possess a firearm when the officer is not on duty.

(k) It is the intent of the Legislature that this section, as it relates to Santa Clara, Madera, and Napa Counties, enumerate specific duties of custodial officers known as "correctional officers" in Santa Clara, Madera, and Napa Counties and to clarify the relationships of the correctional officers and deputy sheriffs in those counties. These duties are the same duties of the custodial officers prior to the date of enactment of Chapter 635 of the Statutes of 1999 pursuant to local rules and judicial decisions. It is further the intent of the Legislature that all issues regarding compensation for custodial officers remain subject to the collective bargaining process between the counties and the authorized bargaining representative for the custodial officers. However, this section does not assert that the duties of custodial officers are equivalent to the duties of deputy sheriffs and does not affect the ability of the county to negotiate pay that reflects the different duties of custodial officers and deputy sheriffs.

(Amended by Stats. 2018, Ch. 19, Sec. 1. (AB 2197) Effective January 1, 2019.)

831.6.

(a) A transportation officer is a public officer, not a peace officer, appointed on a contract basis by a peace officer to transport a prisoner or prisoners.

(b) A transportation officer shall have the authority of a public officer, and shall have the right to carry or possess firearms, only while engaged in the transportation of a prisoner or prisoners for the duration of the contract.

(c) Each person described in this section as a transportation officer shall, prior to the transportation of any prisoner, have satisfactorily completed the training course specified in Section 832.

(d) A transportation officer may use reasonable force in establishing and maintaining custody of persons delivered to him or her by a peace officer.

(Added by Stats. 1982, Ch. 416, Sec. 1. Effective July 8, 1982.)

831.7.

(a) As used in this section, a custody assistant is a person who is a full-time employee, not a peace officer, employed by the county sheriff's department who assists peace officer personnel in maintaining order and security in a custody detention, court detention, or station jail facility of the sheriff's department. A custody assistant is responsible for maintaining custody of prisoners and performs tasks related to the operation of a local detention facility used for the detention of persons usually pending arraignment or upon court order either for their own safekeeping or for the specific purpose of serving a sentence therein. Custody assistants of the sheriff's department shall be employees of, and under the authority of, the sheriff.

(b) A custody assistant has no right to carry or possess firearms in the performance of his or her prescribed duties.

(c) Each person described in this section as a custody assistant shall satisfactorily complete a training course specified by the sheriff's department. In addition, each person designated as a custody assistant shall satisfactorily meet the minimum selection and training standards prescribed by the Department of Corrections and Rehabilitation pursuant to Section 6035.

(d) A custody assistant may use reasonable force in establishing and maintaining custody of persons housed at a local detention facility, court detention facility, or station jail facility.

(e) Custody assistants employed by the county sheriff's department are authorized to perform the following additional duties in a custody facility, court detention facility, or station jail facility:

(1) Assist in supervising the conduct of inmates in sleeping quarters, during meals and bathing, at recreation, and on work assignments.

(2) Assist in overseeing the work of, and instructing, a group of inmates assigned to various operational, maintenance, or other rehabilitative activities.

(3) Assist in the operation of main or dormitory control booths.

(4) Assist in processing inmates for court appearances.

(5) Control, or assist in the monitoring and control of, access to attorney rooms and visiting areas.

(6) Fingerprint, photograph, or operate livescan machines with respect to inmates, or assist in the fingerprinting or photographing of inmates.

(7) Obtain criminal history information relating to an inmate including any warrant or other hold, and update classification or housing information relating to an inmate, as necessary.

(8) Interview inmates and review records related to the classification process to determine the appropriate security level for an inmate or the eligibility of an inmate for transfer to another facility.

(9) Ensure compliance of a custody facility, court detention facility, or station jail facility with the provisions of Title 15 of the California Code of Regulations, or with any other applicable legislative or judicial mandate.

(10) Assist in receiving and processing inmates in a sheriff's station, court detention area, or type I jail facility.

(11) Secure inmates and their personal property and moneys as necessary in compliance with the rules and regulations of the sheriff's department.

(12) Order, inspect, or serve meals to inmates.

(13) Maintain sanitary conditions within a custody facility, court detention facility, or station jail facility.

(14) Respond to public inquiries regarding any inmate.

(f) Notwithstanding any other law, nothing in this section shall be construed to confer any authority upon a custody assistant except while on duty, or to grant any additional retirement benefits to persons employed within this classification.

(g) This section shall apply only in a county of the first class, as established by Sections 28020 and 28022 of the Government Code, but shall not be operative in a county until adopted by resolution of the board of supervisors.

(Added by Stats. 2006, Ch. 468, Sec. 2. Effective January 1, 2007. Applicable as provided in subd. (g).)

832.

(a) Every person described in this chapter as a peace officer shall satisfactorily complete an introductory training course prescribed by the Commission on Peace Officer Standards and Training. On or after July 1, 1989, satisfactory completion of the course shall be demonstrated by passage of an appropriate examination developed or approved by the commission. Training in the carrying and use of firearms shall not be required of a peace officer whose employing agency prohibits the use of firearms.

(b) (1) Every peace officer described in this chapter, prior to the exercise of the powers of a peace officer, shall have satisfactorily completed the training course described in subdivision (a).

(2) Every peace officer described in Section 13510 or in subdivision (a) of Section 830.2 may satisfactorily complete the training required by this section as part of the training prescribed pursuant to Section 13510.

(c) Persons described in this chapter as peace officers who have not satisfactorily completed the course described in subdivision (a), as specified in subdivision (b), shall not have the powers of a peace officer until they satisfactorily complete the course.

(d) A peace officer who, on March 4, 1972, possesses or is qualified to possess the basic certificate as awarded by the Commission on Peace Officer Standards and Training is exempted from this section.

(e) (1) A person completing the training described in subdivision (a) who does not become employed as a peace officer within three years from the date of passing the examination described in subdivision (a), or who has a three-year or longer break in service as a peace officer, shall pass the examination described in subdivision (a) prior to the exercise of the powers of a peace officer, except for a person described in paragraph (2).

(2) The requirement in paragraph (1) does not apply to a person who meets any of the following requirements:

(A) Is returning to a management position that is at the second level of supervision or higher.

(B) Has successfully requalified for a basic course through the Commission on Peace Officer Standards and Training.

(C) Has maintained proficiency through teaching the course described in subdivision (a).

(D) During the break in California service, was continuously employed as a peace officer in another state or at the federal level.

(E) Has previously met the requirements of subdivision (a), has been appointed as a peace officer under subdivision (c) of Section 830.1, and has been continuously employed as a custodial officer as defined in Section 831 or 831.5 by the agency making the peace officer appointment since completing the training prescribed in subdivision (a).

(f) The commission may charge appropriate fees for the examination required by subdivision (e), not to exceed actual costs.

(g) Notwithstanding any other law, the commission may charge appropriate fees for the examination required by subdivision (a) to each applicant who is not sponsored by a local or other law enforcement agency, or is not a peace officer employed by, or under consideration for employment by, a state or local agency, department, or district, or is not a custodial officer as defined in Sections 831 and 831.5. The fees shall not exceed actual costs.

(h) (1) When evaluating a certification request from a probation department for a training course described in this section, the commission shall deem there to be an identifiable and unmet need for the training course.

(2) A probation department that is a certified provider of the training course described in this section shall not be required to offer the course to the general public.

(Amended by Stats. 2015, Ch. 200, Sec. 1. (AB 546) Effective January 1, 2016.)

832.05.

(a) Each state or local department or agency that employs peace officers shall utilize a person meeting the requirements set forth in subdivision (f) of Section 1031 of the Government Code, applicable to emotional and mental examinations, for any emotional and mental evaluation done in the course of the department or agency's screening of peace officer recruits or the evaluation of peace officers to determine their fitness for duty.

(b) This section shall become operative on January 1, 2005.

(Added by Stats. 2003, Ch. 777, Sec. 5. Effective January 1, 2004. Section operative January 1, 2005, by its own provisions.)

832.1.

Any airport security officer, airport policeman, or airport special officer, regularly employed and paid by a city, county, city and county, or district who is a peace officer shall have completed a course of training relative to airport security approved by the Commission on Peace Officers Standards and Training. Any such airport officer so employed on the effective date of this section shall have completed the course of instruction required by this section by September 1, 1973. Any airport officer so employed after such effective date shall have completed the course of instruction within 90 days after such employment.

Any officer who has not satisfactorily completed such course within such prescribed time shall not continue to have the powers of a peace officer until they have satisfactorily completed such course.

(Amended by Stats. 1975, Ch. 168.)

832.2.

Every school police reserve officer, as described in Section 38000 of the Education Code, shall complete a course of training approved by the Commission on Peace Officer Standards and Training relating directly to the role of school police reserve officers. The school police reserve officer training course shall address guidelines and procedures for reporting offenses to other law enforcement agencies that deal with violence on campus and other school related matters, as determined by the Commission on Peace Officer Standards and Training.

(Amended by Stats. 1998, Ch. 745, Sec. 5. Effective January 1, 1999.)

832.25.

(a) Notwithstanding any other provision of law, all welfare fraud investigators or inspectors who are appointed as peace officers pursuant to subdivision (a) of Section 830.35 on or after January 1, 2001, shall attend and complete a specialized investigators basic course approved by the Commission on Peace Officer Standards and Training within one year of being hired as a welfare investigator or inspector. Any welfare fraud investigator or inspector appointed prior to January 1, 2001, shall not be required to attend and complete the training required by this section, provided that he or she has been continuously employed in that capacity prior to January 1, 2001, by the county that made the appointment.
(b) Any investigator or inspector who possesses a valid basic peace officer certificate as awarded by the Commission on Peace Officer Standards and Training or who has successfully completed the regular basic course certified by the Commission on Peace Officer Standards and Training basic course within three years prior to appointment shall be exempt from the training requirements of subdivision (a).
(Added by Stats. 2000, Ch. 633, Sec. 1. Effective January 1, 2001.)
832.3.
(a) Except as provided in subdivision (e), any sheriff, undersheriff, or deputy sheriff of a county, any police officer of a city, and any police officer of a district authorized by statute to maintain a police department, who is first employed after January 1, 1975, shall successfully complete a course of training prescribed by the Commission on Peace Officer Standards and Training before exercising the powers of a peace officer, except while participating as a trainee in a supervised field training program approved by the Commission on Peace Officer Standards and Training. Each police chief, or any other person in charge of a local law enforcement agency, appointed on or after January 1, 1999, as a condition of continued employment, shall complete the course of training pursuant to this subdivision within two years of appointment. The training course for a sheriff, an undersheriff, and a deputy sheriff of a county, and a police chief and a police officer of a city or any other local law enforcement agency, shall be the same.
(b) For the purpose of ensuring competent peace officers and standardizing the training required in subdivision (a), the commission shall develop a testing program, including standardized tests that enable (1) comparisons between presenters of the training and (2) assessments of trainee achievement. The trainees' test scores shall be used only for the purposes enumerated in this subdivision and those research purposes as shall be approved in advance by the commission. The commission shall take all steps necessary to maintain the confidentiality of the test scores, test items, scoring keys, and other examination data used in the testing program required by this subdivision. The commission shall determine the minimum passing score for each test and the conditions for retesting students who fail. Passing these tests shall be required for successful completion of the training required in subdivision (a). Presenters approved by the commission to provide the training required in subdivision (a) shall administer the standardized tests or, at the commission's option, shall facilitate the commission's administration of the standardized tests to all trainees.
(c) Community colleges may give preference in enrollment to employed law enforcement trainees who shall complete training as prescribed by this section. At least 15 percent of each presentation shall consist of non-law-enforcement trainees if they are available. Preference should only be given when the trainee could not complete the course within the time required by statute, and only when no other training program is reasonably available. Average daily attendance for these courses shall be reported for state aid.
(d) Prior to July 1, 1987, the commission shall make a report to the Legislature on academy proficiency testing scores. This report shall include an evaluation of the correlation between academy proficiency test scores and performance as a peace officer.
(e) (1) Any deputy sheriff described in subdivision (c) of Section 830.1 shall be exempt from the training requirements specified in subdivisions (a) and (b) as long as his or her assignments remain custodial related.
(2) Deputy sheriffs described in subdivision (c) of Section 830.1 shall complete the training for peace officers pursuant to subdivision (a) of Section 832, and within 120 days after the date of employment, shall complete the training required by the Board of State and Community Corrections for custodial personnel pursuant to Section 6035, and the training required for custodial personnel of local detention facilities pursuant to Subchapter 1 (commencing with Section 100) of Chapter 1 of Division 1 of Title 15 of the California Code of Regulations.
(3) Deputy sheriffs described in subdivision (c) of Section 830.1 shall complete the course of training pursuant to subdivision (a) prior to being reassigned from custodial assignments to duties with responsibility for the prevention and detection of crime and the general enforcement of the criminal laws of this state. A deputy sheriff who has completed the course of training pursuant to subdivision (a) and has been hired as a deputy sheriff described in subdivision (c) of Section 830.1 shall be eligible to be reassigned from custodial assignments to duties with the responsibility for the prevention and detection of crime and the general enforcement of the criminal laws of this state within three years of completing the training pursuant to subdivision (a). A deputy sheriff shall be eligible for reassignment within five years of having completed the training pursuant to subdivision (a) without having to complete a requalification for the regular basic course provided that all of the following are satisfied:
(A) The deputy sheriff remains continuously employed by the same department in which the deputy sheriff is being reassigned from custodial assignments to duties with the responsibility for the prevention and detection of crime and the general enforcement of the criminal laws of this state.
(B) The deputy sheriff maintains the perishable skills training required by the commission for peace officers assigned to duties with the responsibility for the prevention and detection of crime and the general enforcement of the criminal laws of this state.
(f) Any school police officer first employed by a K–12 public school district or California Community College district after July 1, 1999, shall successfully complete a basic course of training as prescribed by subdivision (a) before exercising the powers of a peace officer. A school police officer shall not be subject to this subdivision while participating as a trainee in a supervised field training program approved by the Commission on Peace Officer Standards and Training.
(g) The commission shall prepare a specialized course of instruction for the training of school peace officers, as defined in Section 830.32, to meet the unique safety needs of a school environment. This course is intended to supplement any other training requirements.
(h) Any school peace officer first employed by a K–12 public school district or California Community College district before July 1, 1999, shall successfully complete the specialized course of training prescribed in subdivision (g) no later than July 1, 2002. Any school police officer first employed by a K–12 public school district or California Community College district after July 1, 1999, shall successfully complete the specialized course of training prescribed in subdivision (g) within two years of the date of first employment.
(Amended (as amended by Stats. 2016, Ch. 86, Sec. 228) by Stats. 2018, Ch. 17, Sec. 1. (AB 1888) Effective January 1, 2019.)
832.4.
(a) Any undersheriff or deputy sheriff of a county, any police officer of a city, and any police officer of a district authorized by statute to maintain a police department, who is first employed after January 1, 1974, and is responsible for the prevention and detection of crime and the general enforcement of the criminal laws of this state, shall obtain the basic certificate issued by the Commission on Peace Officer Standards and Training within 18 months of his or her employment in order to continue to exercise the powers of a peace officer after the expiration of the 18-month period.
(b) Every peace officer listed in subdivision (a) of Section 830.1, except a sheriff, or elected marshal, or a deputy sheriff described in subdivision (c) of Section 830.1, who is employed after January 1, 1988, shall obtain the basic certificate issued by the Commission on Peace Officer Standards and Training upon completion of probation, but in no case later than 24 months after his or her employment, in order to continue to exercise the powers of a peace officer after the expiration of the 24-month period. Deputy sheriffs described in subdivision (c) of Section 830.1 shall obtain the basic certificate issued by the Commission on Peace Officer Standards and Training within 24 months after being reassigned from custodial duties to general law enforcement duties. In those cases where the probationary period established by the employing agency is 24 months, the peace officers described in this subdivision may continue to exercise the powers of a peace officer for an additional three-month period to allow for the processing of the certification application.
(c) Each police chief, or any other person in charge of a local law enforcement agency, appointed on or after January 1, 1999, as a condition of continued employment, shall obtain the basic certificate issued by the Commission on Peace Officer Standards and Training within two years of appointment.
(Amended by Stats. 1998, Ch. 931, Sec. 366.5. Effective September 28, 1998. Operative January 1, 1999, by Sec. 496 of Ch. 931.)
832.5.
(a) (1) Each department or agency in this state that employs peace officers shall establish a procedure to investigate complaints by members of the public against the personnel of these departments or agencies, and shall make a written description of the procedure available to the public.
(2) Each department or agency that employs custodial officers, as defined in Section 831.5, may establish a procedure to investigate complaints by members of the public against those custodial officers employed by these departments or agencies, provided however, that any procedure so established shall comply with the provisions of this section and with the provisions of Section 832.7.
(b) Complaints and any reports or findings relating to these complaints shall be retained for a period of at least five years. All complaints retained pursuant to this subdivision may be maintained either in the peace or custodial officer's general personnel file or in a separate file designated by the department or agency as provided by department or agency policy, in accordance with all applicable requirements of law. However, prior to any official determination regarding promotion, transfer, or disciplinary action by an officer's employing department or agency, the complaints described by subdivision (c) shall be removed from the officer's general personnel file and placed in separate file designated by the department or agency, in accordance with all applicable requirements of law.
(c) Complaints by members of the public that are determined by the peace or custodial officer's employing agency to be frivolous, as defined in Section 128.5 of the Code of Civil Procedure, or unfounded or exonerated, or any portion of a complaint that is determined to be frivolous, unfounded, or exonerated, shall not be maintained in that officer's general personnel file. However, these complaints shall be retained in other, separate files that shall be deemed personnel records for purposes of the California Public Records Act (Chapter 3.5 (commencing with Section 6250) of Division 7 of Title 1 of the Government Code) and Section 1043 of the Evidence Code.
(1) Management of the peace or custodial officer's employing agency shall have access to the files described in this subdivision.
(2) Management of the peace or custodial officer's employing agency shall not use the complaints contained in these separate files for punitive or promotional purposes except as permitted by subdivision (f) of Section 3304 of the Government Code.
(3) Management of the peace or custodial officer's employing agency may identify any officer who is subject to the complaints maintained in these files which require counseling or additional training. However, if a complaint is removed from the officer's personnel file, any reference in the personnel file to the complaint or to a separate file shall be deleted.
(d) As used in this section, the following definitions apply:
(1) "General personnel file" means the file maintained by the agency containing the primary records specific to each peace or custodial officer's employment, including evaluations, assignments, status changes, and imposed discipline.
(2) "Unfounded" means that the investigation clearly established that the allegation is not true.
(3) "Exonerated" means that the investigation clearly established that the actions of the peace or custodial officer that formed the basis for the complaint are not violations of law or department policy.
(Amended by Stats. 2002, Ch. 391, Sec. 5. Effective January 1, 2003.)
832.6.
(a) Every person deputized or appointed, as described in subdivision (a) of Section 830.6, shall have the powers of a peace officer only when the person is any of the following:
(1) A level I reserve officer deputized or appointed pursuant to paragraph (1) or (2) of subdivision (a) or subdivision (b) of Section 830.6 and assigned to the prevention and detection of crime and the general enforcement of the laws of this state, whether or not working alone, and the person has completed the basic training course for deputy sheriffs and police officers prescribed by the Commission on Peace Officer Standards and Training. For level I reserve officers appointed prior to January 1, 1997, the basic training requirement shall be the course that was prescribed at the time of their appointment. Reserve officers appointed pursuant to this paragraph shall satisfy the continuing professional training requirement prescribed by the commission.
(2) (A) A level II reserve officer assigned to the prevention and detection of crime and the general enforcement of the laws of this state while under the immediate supervision of a peace officer who has completed the basic training course for deputy sheriffs and police officers prescribed by the Commission on Peace Officer Standards and Training, and the level II reserve officer has completed the course required by Section 832 and any other training prescribed by the commission.
(B) Level II reserve officers appointed pursuant to this paragraph may be assigned, without immediate supervision, to those limited duties that are authorized for level III reserve officers pursuant to paragraph (3). Reserve officers appointed pursuant to this paragraph shall satisfy the continuing professional training requirement prescribed by the commission.
(3) Level III reserve officers may be deployed and are authorized only to carry out limited support duties not requiring general law enforcement powers in their routine performance. Those limited duties shall include traffic control, security at parades and sporting events, report taking, evidence transportation, parking enforcement, and other duties that are not likely to result in physical arrests. Level III reserve officers, while assigned these duties, shall be supervised in the accessible vicinity by a level I reserve officer or a full-time, regular peace officer employed by a law enforcement agency authorized to have reserve officers. Level III reserve officers may transport prisoners without immediate supervision. Those persons shall have completed the training required under Section 832 and any other training prescribed by the commission for those persons.
(4) A person assigned to the prevention and detection of a particular crime or crimes or to the detection or apprehension of a particular individual or individuals while working under the supervision of a California peace officer in a county adjacent to the state border who possesses a basic certificate issued by the Commission on Peace Officer Standards and Training, and the person is a law enforcement officer who is regularly employed by a local or state law enforcement agency in an adjoining state and has completed the basic training required for peace officers in his or her state.

(5) (A) For purposes of this section, a reserve officer who has previously satisfied the training requirements pursuant to this section and has served as a level I or II reserve officer within the three-year period prior to the date of a new appointment shall be deemed to remain qualified as to the Commission on Peace Officer Standards and Training requirements if that reserve officer accepts a new appointment at the same or lower level with another law enforcement agency. If the reserve officer has more than a three-year break in service, he or she shall satisfy current training requirements.
(B) This training shall fully satisfy any other training requirements required by law, including those specified in Section 832.
(C) In no case shall a peace officer of an adjoining state provide services within a California jurisdiction during any period in which the regular law enforcement agency of the jurisdiction is involved in a labor dispute.
(b) Notwithstanding subdivision (a), a person who is issued a level I reserve officer certificate before January 1, 1981, shall have the full powers and duties of a peace officer, as provided by Section 830.1, if so designated by local ordinance or, if the local agency is not authorized to act by ordinance, by resolution, either individually or by class, if the appointing authority determines the person is qualified to perform general law enforcement duties by reason of the person's training and experience. Persons who were qualified to be issued the level I reserve officer certificate before January 1, 1981, and who state in writing under penalty of perjury that they applied for, but were not issued, the certificate before January 1, 1981, may be issued the certificate before July 1, 1984. For purposes of this section, certificates that are issued shall be deemed to have the full force and effect of any level I reserve officer certificate issued prior to January 1, 1981.
(c) In carrying out this section, the commission:
(1) May use proficiency testing to satisfy reserve training standards.
(2) Shall provide for convenient training to remote areas in the state.
(3) Shall establish a professional certificate for reserve officers, as defined in paragraph (1) of subdivision (a), and may establish a professional certificate for reserve officers, as defined in paragraphs (2) and (3) of subdivision (a).
(4) Shall facilitate the voluntary transition of reserve officers to regular officers with no unnecessary redundancy between the training required for level I and level II reserve officers.
(d) In carrying out paragraphs (1) and (3) of subdivision (c), the commission may establish and levy appropriate fees, provided the fees do not exceed the cost for administering the respective services. These fees shall be deposited in the State Penalty Fund established by Section 1464.
(e) The commission shall include an amount in its annual budget request to carry out this section.
(Amended by Stats. 2018, Ch. 36, Sec. 16. (AB 1812) Effective June 27, 2018.)
832.7.
(a) Except as provided in subdivision (b), the personnel records of peace officers and custodial officers and records maintained by any state or local agency pursuant to Section 832.5, or information obtained from these records, are confidential and shall not be disclosed in any criminal or civil proceeding except by discovery pursuant to Sections 1043 and 1046 of the Evidence Code. This section shall not apply to investigations or proceedings concerning the conduct of peace officers or custodial officers, or an agency or department that employs those officers, conducted by a grand jury, a district attorney's office, or the Attorney General's office.
(b) (1) Notwithstanding subdivision (a), subdivision (f) of Section 6254 of the Government Code, or any other law, the following peace officer or custodial officer personnel records and records maintained by any state or local agency shall not be confidential and shall be made available for public inspection pursuant to the California Public Records Act (Chapter 3.5 (commencing with Section 6250) of Division 7 of Title 1 of the Government Code):
(A) A record relating to the report, investigation, or findings of any of the following:
(i) An incident involving the discharge of a firearm at a person by a peace officer or custodial officer.
(ii) An incident in which the use of force by a peace officer or custodial officer against a person resulted in death, or in great bodily injury.
(B) (i) Any record relating to an incident in which a sustained finding was made by any law enforcement agency or oversight agency that a peace officer or custodial officer engaged in sexual assault involving a member of the public.
(ii) As used in this subparagraph, "sexual assault" means the commission or attempted initiation of a sexual act with a member of the public by means of force, threat, coercion, extortion, offer of leniency or other official favor, or under the color of authority. For purposes of this definition, the propositioning for or commission of any sexual act while on duty is considered a sexual assault.
(iii) As used in this subparagraph, "member of the public" means any person not employed by the officer's employing agency and includes any participant in a cadet, explorer, or other youth program affiliated with the agency.
(C) Any record relating to an incident in which a sustained finding was made by any law enforcement agency or oversight agency of dishonesty by a peace officer or custodial officer directly relating to the reporting, investigation, or prosecution of a crime, or directly relating to the reporting of, or investigation of misconduct by, another peace officer or custodial officer, including, but not limited to, any sustained finding of perjury, false statements, filing false reports, destruction, falsifying, or concealing of evidence.
(2) Records that shall be released pursuant to this subdivision include all investigative reports; photographic, audio, and video evidence; transcripts or recordings of interviews; autopsy reports; all materials compiled and presented for review to the district attorney or to any person or body charged with determining whether to file criminal charges against an officer in connection with an incident, or whether the officer's action was consistent with law and agency policy for purposes of discipline or administrative action, or what discipline to impose or corrective action to take; documents setting forth findings or recommended findings; and copies of disciplinary records relating to the incident, including any letters of intent to impose discipline, any documents reflecting modifications of discipline due to the Skelly or grievance process, and letters indicating final imposition of discipline or other documentation reflecting implementation of corrective action.
(3) A record from a separate and prior investigation or assessment of a separate incident shall not be released unless it is independently subject to disclosure pursuant to this subdivision.
(4) If an investigation or incident involves multiple officers, information about allegations of misconduct by, or the analysis or disposition of an investigation of, an officer shall not be released pursuant to subparagraph (B) or (C) of paragraph (1), unless it relates to a sustained finding against that officer. However, factual information about that action of an officer during an incident, or the statements of an officer about an incident, shall be released if they are relevant to a sustained finding against another officer that is subject to release pursuant to subparagraph (B) or (C) of paragraph (1).
(5) An agency shall redact a record disclosed pursuant to this section only for any of the following purposes:
(A) To remove personal data or information, such as a home address, telephone number, or identities of family members, other than the names and work-related information of peace and custodial officers.
(B) To preserve the anonymity of complainants and witnesses.
(C) To protect confidential medical, financial, or other information of which disclosure is specifically prohibited by federal law or would cause an unwarranted invasion of personal privacy that clearly outweighs the strong public interest in records about misconduct and serious use of force by peace officers and custodial officers.

(D) Where there is a specific, articulable, and particularized reason to believe that disclosure of the record would pose a significant danger to the physical safety of the peace officer, custodial officer, or another person.
(6) Notwithstanding paragraph (5), an agency may redact a record disclosed pursuant to this section, including personal identifying information, where, on the facts of the particular case, the public interest served by not disclosing the information clearly outweighs the public interest served by disclosure of the information.
(7) An agency may withhold a record of an incident described in subparagraph (A) of paragraph (1) that is the subject of an active criminal or administrative investigation, in accordance with any of the following:
(A) (i) During an active criminal investigation, disclosure may be delayed for up to 60 days from the date the use of force occurred or until the district attorney determines whether to file criminal charges related to the use of force, whichever occurs sooner. If an agency delays disclosure pursuant to this clause, the agency shall provide, in writing, the specific basis for the agency's determination that the interest in delaying disclosure clearly outweighs the public interest in disclosure. This writing shall include the estimated date for disclosure of the withheld information.
(ii) After 60 days from the use of force, the agency may continue to delay the disclosure of records or information if the disclosure could reasonably be expected to interfere with a criminal enforcement proceeding against an officer who used the force. If an agency delays disclosure pursuant to this clause, the agency shall, at 180-day intervals as necessary, provide, in writing, the specific basis for the agency's determination that disclosure could reasonably be expected to interfere with a criminal enforcement proceeding. The writing shall include the estimated date for the disclosure of the withheld information. Information withheld by the agency shall be disclosed when the specific basis for withholding is resolved, when the investigation or proceeding is no longer active, or by no later than 18 months after the date of the incident, whichever occurs sooner.
(iii) After 60 days from the use of force, the agency may continue to delay the disclosure of records or information if the disclosure could reasonably be expected to interfere with a criminal enforcement proceeding against someone other than the officer who used the force. If an agency delays disclosure under this clause, the agency shall, at 180-day intervals, provide, in writing, the specific basis why disclosure could reasonably be expected to interfere with a criminal enforcement proceeding, and shall provide an estimated date for the disclosure of the withheld information. Information withheld by the agency shall be disclosed when the specific basis for withholding is resolved, when the investigation or proceeding is no longer active, or by no later than 18 months after the date of the incident, whichever occurs sooner, unless extraordinary circumstances warrant continued delay due to the ongoing criminal investigation or proceeding. In that case, the agency must show by clear and convincing evidence that the interest in preventing prejudice to the active and ongoing criminal investigation or proceeding outweighs the public interest in prompt disclosure of records about use of serious force by peace officers and custodial officers. The agency shall release all information subject to disclosure that does not cause substantial prejudice, including any documents that have otherwise become available.
(iv) In an action to compel disclosure brought pursuant to Section 6258 of the Government Code, an agency may justify delay by filing an application to seal the basis for withholding, in accordance with Rule 2.550 of the California Rules of Court, or any successor rule thereto, if disclosure of the written basis itself would impact a privilege or compromise a pending investigation.
(B) If criminal charges are filed related to the incident in which force was used, the agency may delay the disclosure of records or information until a verdict on those charges is returned at trial or, if a plea of guilty or no contest is entered, the time to withdraw the plea pursuant to Section 1018.
(C) During an administrative investigation into an incident described in subparagraph (A) of paragraph (1), the agency may delay the disclosure of records or information until the investigating agency determines whether the use of force violated a law or agency policy, but no longer than 180 days after the date of the employing agency's discovery of the use of force, or allegation of use of force, by a person authorized to initiate an investigation, or 30 days after the close of any criminal investigation related to the peace officer or custodial officer's use of force, whichever is later.
(8) A record of a civilian complaint, or the investigations, findings, or dispositions of that complaint, shall not be released pursuant to this section if the complaint is frivolous, as defined in Section 128.5 of the Code of Civil Procedure, or if the complaint is unfounded.
(c) Notwithstanding subdivisions (a) and (b), a department or agency shall release to the complaining party a copy of his or her own statements at the time the complaint is filed.
(d) Notwithstanding subdivisions (a) and (b), a department or agency that employs peace or custodial officers may disseminate data regarding the number, type, or disposition of complaints (sustained, not sustained, exonerated, or unfounded) made against its officers if that information is in a form which does not identify the individuals involved.
(e) Notwithstanding subdivisions (a) and (b), a department or agency that employs peace or custodial officers may release factual information concerning a disciplinary investigation if the officer who is the subject of the disciplinary investigation, or the officer's agent or representative, publicly makes a statement he or she knows to be false concerning the investigation or the imposition of disciplinary action. Information may not be disclosed by the peace or custodial officer's employer unless the false statement was published by an established medium of communication, such as television, radio, or a newspaper. Disclosure of factual information by the employing agency pursuant to this subdivision is limited to facts contained in the officer's personnel file concerning the disciplinary investigation or imposition of disciplinary action that specifically refute the false statements made public by the peace or custodial officer or his or her agent or representative.
(f) (1) The department or agency shall provide written notification to the complaining party of the disposition of the complaint within 30 days of the disposition.
(2) The notification described in this subdivision shall not be conclusive or binding or admissible as evidence in any separate or subsequent action or proceeding brought before an arbitrator, court, or judge of this state or the United States.
(g) This section does not affect the discovery or disclosure of information contained in a peace or custodial officer's personnel file pursuant to Section 1043 of the Evidence Code.
(h) This section does not supersede or affect the criminal discovery process outlined in Chapter 10 (commencing with Section 1054) of Title 6 of Part 2, or the admissibility of personnel records pursuant to subdivision (a), which codifies the court decision in Pitchess v. Superior Court (1974) 11 Cal.3d 531.
(i) Nothing in this chapter is intended to limit the public's right of access as provided for in Long Beach Police Officers Association v. City of Long Beach (2014) 59 Cal.4th 59.
(Amended by Stats. 2018, Ch. 988, Sec. 2. (SB 1421) Effective January 1, 2019.)
832.8.
As used in Section 832.7, the following words or phrases have the following meanings:
(a) "Personnel records" means any file maintained under that individual's name by his or her employing agency and containing records relating to any of the following:
(1) Personal data, including marital status, family members, educational and employment history, home addresses, or similar information.
(2) Medical history.
(3) Election of employee benefits.
(4) Employee advancement, appraisal, or discipline.

(5) Complaints, or investigations of complaints, concerning an event or transaction in which he or she participated, or which he or she perceived, and pertaining to the manner in which he or she performed his or her duties.

(6) Any other information the disclosure of which would constitute an unwarranted invasion of personal privacy.

(b) "Sustained" means a final determination by an investigating agency, commission, board, hearing officer, or arbitrator, as applicable, following an investigation and opportunity for an administrative appeal pursuant to Sections 3304 and 3304.5 of the Government Code, that the actions of the peace officer or custodial officer were found to violate law or department policy.

(c) "Unfounded" means that an investigation clearly establishes that the allegation is not true.

(Amended by Stats. 2018, Ch. 988, Sec. 3. (SB 1421) Effective January 1, 2019.)

832.9.

(a) A governmental entity employing a peace officer, as defined in Section 830, judge, court commissioner, or an attorney employed by the Department of Justice, the State Public Defender, or a county office of a district attorney or public defender shall reimburse the moving and relocation expenses of those employees, or any member of his or her immediate family residing with the officer in the same household or on the same property when it is necessary to move because the officer has received a credible threat that a life threatening action may be taken against the officer, judge, court commissioner, or an attorney employed by the Department of Justice, the State Public Defender, or a county office of the district attorney or public defender or his or her immediate family as a result of his or her employment.

(b) The person relocated shall receive actual and necessary moving and relocation expenses incurred both before and after the change of residence, including reimbursement for the costs of moving household effects either by a commercial household goods carrier or by the employee.

(1) Actual and necessary moving costs shall be those costs that are set forth in the Department of Human Resources rules governing promotional relocations while in the state service. The department shall not be required to administer this section.

(2) The public entity shall not be liable for any loss in value to a residence or for the decrease in value due to a forced sale.

(3) Except as provided in subdivision (c), peace officers, judges, court commissioners, and attorneys employed by the Department of Justice, the State Public Defender, or a county office of a district attorney or public defender shall receive approval of the appointing authority prior to incurring any cost covered by this section.

(4) Peace officers, judges, court commissioners, and attorneys employed by the Department of Justice, the State Public Defender, or a county office of a district attorney or public defender shall not be considered to be on duty while moving unless approved by the appointing authority.

(5) For a relocation to be covered by this section, the appointing authority shall be notified as soon as a credible threat has been received.

(6) Temporary relocation housing shall not exceed 60 days.

(7) The public entity ceases to be liable for relocation costs after 120 days of the original notification of a viable threat if the peace officer, judge, court commissioner, or attorney employed by the Department of Justice, the State Public Defender, or a county office of a district attorney or public defender has failed to relocate.

(c) (1) For purposes of the right to reimbursement of moving and relocation expenses pursuant to this section, judges shall be deemed to be employees of the State of California and a court commissioner is an employee of the court by which he or she is employed.

(2) For purposes of paragraph (3) of subdivision (b), a court commissioner shall receive approval by the presiding judge of the superior court in the county in which he or she is located.

(3) For purposes of paragraph (3) of subdivision (b), judges, including justices of the Supreme Court and the Courts of Appeal, shall receive approval from the Chief Justice, or his or her designee.

(d) As used in this section, "credible threat" means a verbal or written statement or a threat implied by a pattern of conduct or a combination of verbal or written statements and conduct made with the intent and the apparent ability to carry out the threat so as to cause the person who is the target of the threat to reasonably fear for his or her safety or the safety of his or her immediate family.

(e) As used in this section, "immediate family" means the spouse, parents, siblings, and children residing with the peace officer, judge, court commissioner, or attorney employed by the Department of Justice, the State Public Defender, or a county office of a district attorney or public defender.

(Amended by Stats. 2012, Ch. 665, Sec. 182. (SB 1308) Effective January 1, 2013.)

832.12.

(a) Each department or agency in this state that employs peace officers shall make a record of any investigations of misconduct involving a peace officer in his or her general personnel file or a separate file designated by the department or agency. A peace officer seeking employment with a department or agency in this state that employs peace officers shall give written permission for the hiring department or agency to view his or her general personnel file and any separate file designated by a department or agency.

(Added by Stats. 2018, Ch. 966, Sec. 1. (AB 2327) Effective January 1, 2019.)

832.15.

(a) On and after October 1, 1993, the Department of Justice shall notify a state or local agency as to whether an individual applying for a position as a peace officer, as defined by this chapter, a custodial officer authorized by the employing agency to carry a firearm pursuant to Section 831.5, or a transportation officer pursuant to Section 831.6 authorized by the employing agency to carry a firearm, is prohibited from possessing, receiving, owning, or purchasing a firearm pursuant to state or federal law. If the prohibition is temporary, the notice shall indicate the date that the prohibition expires. However, the notice shall not provide any other information with respect to the basis for the prohibition.

(b) Before providing the information specified in subdivision (a), the applicant shall provide the Department of Justice with fingerprints and other identifying information deemed necessary by the department.

(c) The Department of Justice may charge the applicant a fee sufficient to reimburse its costs for furnishing the information specified in subdivision (a).

(d) The notice required by this section shall not apply to persons receiving treatment under subdivision (a) of Section 8100 of the Welfare and Institutions Code.

(Amended by Stats. 2008, Ch. 698, Sec. 9. Effective January 1, 2009.)

832.16.

(a) On and after October 1, 1993, the Department of Justice shall notify a state or local agency employing a peace officer, as defined by this chapter, who is authorized by the employing agency to carry a firearm, as to whether a peace officer is prohibited from possessing, receiving, owning, or purchasing a firearm pursuant to state or federal law. If the prohibition is temporary, the notice shall indicate the date that the prohibition expires. However, the notice shall not provide any other information with respect to the basis for the prohibition.

(b) Before providing the information specified in subdivision (a), the agency employing the peace officer shall provide the Department of Justice with the officer's fingerprints and other identifying information deemed necessary by the department.

(c) The information specified in this section shall only be provided by the Department of Justice subject to the availability of funding.

(d) The notice required by this section shall not apply to persons receiving treatment under subdivision (a) of Section 8100 of the Welfare and Institutions Code.

(Amended by Stats. 2008, Ch. 698, Sec. 10. Effective January 1, 2009.)

832.17.

(a) Upon request by a state or local agency, the Department of Justice shall notify the state or local agency as to whether an individual employed as a custodial or transportation officer and authorized by the employing agency to carry a firearm, is prohibited or subsequently becomes prohibited from possessing, receiving, owning, or purchasing a firearm pursuant to state or federal law. If the prohibition is temporary, the notice shall indicate the date on which the prohibition expires. However, the notice shall not provide any other information with respect to the basis for the prohibition.

(b) Before the department provides the information specified in subdivision (a), the officer shall provide the department with his or her fingerprints and other identifying information deemed necessary by the department.

(c) The department may charge the officer a fee sufficient to reimburse its costs for furnishing the information specified in subdivision (a). A local law enforcement agency may pay this fee for the officer.

(d) The notice required by this section shall not apply to persons receiving treatment under subdivision (a) of Section 8100 of the Welfare and Institutions Code.

(Amended by Stats. 2008, Ch. 698, Sec. 11. Effective January 1, 2009.)

832.18.

(a) It is the intent of the Legislature to establish policies and procedures to address issues related to the downloading and storage data recorded by a body-worn camera worn by a peace officer. These policies and procedures shall be based on best practices.

(b) When establishing policies and procedures for the implementation and operation of a body-worn camera system, law enforcement agencies, departments, or entities shall consider the following best practices regarding the downloading and storage of body-worn camera data:

(1) Designate the person responsible for downloading the recorded data from the body-worn camera. If the storage system does not have automatic downloading capability, the officer's supervisor should take immediate physical custody of the camera and should be responsible for downloading the data in the case of an incident involving the use of force by an officer, an officer-involved shooting, or other serious incident.

(2) Establish when data should be downloaded to ensure the data is entered into the system in a timely manner, the cameras are properly maintained and ready for the next use, and for purposes of tagging and categorizing the data.

(3) Establish specific measures to prevent data tampering, deleting, and copying, including prohibiting the unauthorized use, duplication, or distribution of body-worn camera data.

(4) Categorize and tag body-worn camera video at the time the data is downloaded and classified according to the type of event or incident captured in the data.

(5) Specifically state the length of time that recorded data is to be stored.

(A) Unless subparagraph (B) or (C) applies, nonevidentiary data including video and audio recorded by a body-worn camera should be retained for a minimum of 60 days, after which it may be erased, destroyed, or recycled. An agency may keep data for more than 60 days to have it available in case of a civilian complaint and to preserve transparency.

(B) Evidentiary data including video and audio recorded by a body-worn camera under this section should be retained for a minimum of two years under any of the following circumstances:

(i) The recording is of an incident involving the use of force by a peace officer or an officer-involved shooting.

(ii) The recording is of an incident that leads to the detention or arrest of an individual.

(iii) The recording is relevant to a formal or informal complaint against a law enforcement officer or a law enforcement agency.

(C) If evidence that may be relevant to a criminal prosecution is obtained from a recording made by a body-worn camera under this section, the law enforcement agency should retain the recording for any time in addition to that specified in subparagraphs (A) and (B), and in the same manner as is required by law for other evidence that may be relevant to a criminal prosecution.

(D) In determining a retention schedule, the agency should work with its legal counsel to determine a retention schedule to ensure that storage policies and practices are in compliance with all relevant laws and adequately preserve evidentiary chains of custody.

(E) Records or logs of access and deletion of data from body-worn cameras should be retained permanently.

(6) State where the body-worn camera data will be stored, including, for example, an in-house server which is managed internally, or an online cloud database which is managed by a third-party vendor.

(7) If using a third-party vendor to manage the data storage system, the following factors should be considered to protect the security and integrity of the data:

(A) Using an experienced and reputable third-party vendor.

(B) Entering into contracts that govern the vendor relationship and protect the agency's data.

(C) Using a system that has a built-in audit trail to prevent data tampering and unauthorized access.

(D) Using a system that has a reliable method for automatically backing up data for storage.

(E) Consulting with internal legal counsel to ensure the method of data storage meets legal requirements for chain-of-custody concerns.

(F) Using a system that includes technical assistance capabilities.

(8) Require that all recorded data from body-worn cameras are property of their respective law enforcement agency and shall not be accessed or released for any unauthorized purpose, explicitly prohibit agency personnel from accessing recorded data for personal use and from uploading recorded data onto public and social media Internet Web sites, and include sanctions for violations of this prohibition.

(c) (1) For purposes of this section, "evidentiary data" refers to data of an incident or encounter that could prove useful for investigative purposes, including, but not limited to, a crime, an arrest or citation, a search, a use of force incident, or a confrontational encounter with a member of the public. The retention period for evidentiary data are subject to state evidentiary laws.

(2) For purposes of this section, "nonevidentiary data" refers to data that does not necessarily have value to aid in an investigation or prosecution, such as data of an incident or encounter that does not lead to an arrest or citation, or data of general activities the officer might perform while on duty.

(d) This section shall not be interpreted to limit the public's right to access recorded data under the California Public Records Act (Chapter 3.5 (commencing with Section 6250) of Division 7 of Title 1 of the Government Code).

(Amended by Stats. 2017, Ch. 561, Sec. 183. (AB 1516) Effective January 1, 2018.)

CHAPTER 5. Arrest, by Whom and How Made [833 - 851.92]

(Chapter 5 enacted 1872.)

833.

A peace officer may search for dangerous weapons any person whom he has legal cause to arrest, whenever he has reasonable cause to believe that the person possesses a dangerous weapon. If the officer finds a dangerous weapon, he may take

and keep it until the completion of the questioning, when he shall either return it or arrest the person. The arrest may be for the illegal possession of the weapon.
(Added by Stats. 1957, Ch. 2147.)

833.2.
(a) It is the intent of the Legislature to encourage law enforcement and county child welfare agencies to develop protocols in collaboration with other local entities, which may include local educational, judicial, correctional, and community-based organizations, when appropriate, regarding how to best cooperate in their response to the arrest of a caretaker parent or guardian of a minor child, to ensure the child's safety and well-being.
(b) The Legislature encourages the Department of Justice to apply to the federal government for a statewide training grant on behalf of California law enforcement agencies, with the purpose of enabling local jurisdictions to provide training for their law enforcement officers to assist them in developing protocols and adequately addressing issues related to child safety when a caretaker parent or guardian is arrested.
(Added by Stats. 2006, Ch. 729, Sec. 1. Effective January 1, 2007.)

833.5.
(a) In addition to any other detention permitted by law, if a peace officer has reasonable cause to believe that a person has a firearm or other deadly weapon with him or her in violation of any provision of law relating to firearms or deadly weapons the peace officer may detain that person to determine whether a crime relating to firearms or deadly weapons has been committed.
For purposes of this section, "reasonable cause to detain" requires that the circumstances known or apparent to the officer must include specific and articulable facts causing him or her to suspect that some offense relating to firearms or deadly weapons has taken place or is occurring or is about to occur and that the person he or she intends to detain is involved in that offense. The circumstances must be such as would cause any reasonable peace officer in like position, drawing when appropriate on his or her training and experience, to suspect the same offense and the same involvement by the person in question.
(b) Incident to any detention permitted pursuant to subdivision (a), a peace officer may conduct a limited search of the person for firearms or weapons if the peace officer reasonably concludes that the person detained may be armed and presently dangerous to the peace officer or others. Any firearm or weapon seized pursuant to a valid detention or search pursuant to this section shall be admissible in evidence in any proceeding for any purpose permitted by law.
(c) This section shall not be construed to otherwise limit the authority of a peace officer to detain any person or to make an arrest based on reasonable cause.
(d) This section shall not be construed to permit a peace officer to conduct a detention or search of any person at the person's residence or place of business absent a search warrant or other reasonable cause to detain or search.
(e) If a firearm or weapon is seized pursuant to this section and the person from whom it was seized owned the firearm or weapon and is convicted of a violation of any offense relating to the possession of such firearm or weapon, the court shall order the firearm or weapon to be deemed a nuisance and disposed of in the manner provided by Sections 18000 and 18005.
(Amended (as amended by Stats. 2010, Ch. 178, Sec. 68) by Stats. 2011, Ch. 296, Sec. 213. (AB 1023) Effective January 1, 2012.)

834.
An arrest is taking a person into custody, in a case and in the manner authorized by law. An arrest may be made by a peace officer or by a private person.
(Enacted 1872.)

834a.
If a person has knowledge, or by the exercise of reasonable care, should have knowledge, that he is being arrested by a peace officer, it is the duty of such person to refrain from using force or any weapon to resist such arrest.
(Added by Stats. 1957, Ch. 2147.)

834c.
(a) (1) In accordance with federal law and the provisions of this section, every peace officer, upon arrest and booking or detention for more than two hours of a known or suspected foreign national, shall advise the foreign national that he or she has a right to communicate with an official from the consulate of his or her country, except as provided in subdivision (d). If the foreign national chooses to exercise that right, the peace officer shall notify the pertinent official in his or her agency or department of the arrest or detention and that the foreign national wants his or her consulate notified.
(2) The law enforcement official who receives the notification request pursuant to paragraph (1) shall be guided by his or her agency's procedures in conjunction with the Department of State Guidelines Regarding Foreign Nationals Arrested or Detained in the United States, and make the appropriate notifications to the consular officers at the consulate of the arrestee.
(3) The law enforcement official in charge of the custodial facility where an arrestee subject to this subdivision is located shall ensure that the arrestee is allowed to communicate with, correspond with, and be visited by, a consular officer of his or her country.
(b) The 1963 Vienna Convention on Consular Relations Treaty was signed by 140 nations, including the United States, which ratified the agreement in 1969. This treaty guarantees that individuals arrested or detained in a foreign country must be told by police "without delay" that they have a right to speak to an official from their country's consulate and if an individual chooses to exercise that right a law enforcement official is required to notify the consulate.
(c) California law enforcement agencies shall ensure that policy or procedure and training manuals incorporate language based upon provisions of the treaty that set forth requirements for handling the arrest and booking or detention for more than two hours of a foreign national pursuant to this section prior to December 31, 2000.
(d) Countries requiring mandatory notification under Article 36 of the Vienna Convention shall be notified as set forth in this section without regard to an arrested or detained foreign national's request to the contrary. Those countries, as identified by the United States Department of State on July 1, 1999, are as follows:
(1) Antigua and Barbuda.
(2) Armenia.
(3) Azerbaijan.
(4) The Bahamas.
(5) Barbados.
(6) Belarus.
(7) Belize.
(8) Brunei.
(9) Bulgaria.
(10) China.
(11) Costa Rica.
(12) Cyprus.
(13) Czech Republic.
(14) Dominica.
(15) Fiji.
(16) The Gambia.
(17) Georgia.
(18) Ghana.
(19) Grenada.
(20) Guyana.
(21) Hong Kong.

(22) Hungary.
(23) Jamaica.
(24) Kazakhstan.
(25) Kiribati.
(26) Kuwait.
(27) Kyrgyzstan.
(28) Malaysia.
(29) Malta.
(30) Mauritius.
(31) Moldova.
(32) Mongolia.
(33) Nigeria.
(34) Philippines.
(35) Poland (nonpermanent residents only).
(36) Romania.
(37) Russia.
(38) Saint Kitts and Nevis.
(39) Saint Lucia.
(40) Saint Vincent and the Grenadines.
(41) Seychelles.
(42) Sierra Leone.
(43) Singapore.
(44) Slovakia.
(45) Tajikistan.
(46) Tanzania.
(47) Tonga.
(48) Trinidad and Tobago.
(49) Turkmenistan.
(50) Tuvalu.
(51) Ukraine.
(52) United Kingdom.
(53) U.S.S.R.
(54) Uzbekistan.
(55) Zambia.
(56) Zimbabwe.
However, any countries requiring notification that the above list does not identify because the notification requirement became effective after July 1, 1999, shall also be required to be notified.
(Added by Stats. 1999, Ch. 268, Sec. 1. Effective January 1, 2000.)

835.
An arrest is made by an actual restraint of the person, or by submission to the custody of an officer. The person arrested may be subjected to such restraint as is reasonable for his arrest and detention.
(Amended by Stats. 1957, Ch. 2147.)

835a.
Any peace officer who has reasonable cause to believe that the person to be arrested has committed a public offense may use reasonable force to effect the arrest, to prevent escape or to overcome resistance.
A peace officer who makes or attempts to make an arrest need not retreat or desist from his efforts by reason of the resistance or threatened resistance of the person being arrested; nor shall such officer be deemed an aggressor or lose his right to self-defense by the use of reasonable force to effect the arrest or to prevent escape or to overcome resistance.
(Added by Stats. 1957, Ch. 2147.)

836.
(a) A peace officer may arrest a person in obedience to a warrant, or, pursuant to the authority granted to him or her by Chapter 4.5 (commencing with Section 830) of Title 3 of Part 2, without a warrant, may arrest a person whenever any of the following circumstances occur:
(1) The officer has probable cause to believe that the person to be arrested has committed a public offense in the officer's presence.
(2) The person arrested has committed a felony, although not in the officer's presence.
(3) The officer has probable cause to believe that the person to be arrested has committed a felony, whether or not a felony, in fact, has been committed.
(b) Any time a peace officer is called out on a domestic violence call, it shall be mandatory that the officer make a good faith effort to inform the victim of his or her right to make a citizen's arrest, unless the peace officer makes an arrest for a violation of paragraph (1) of subdivision (e) of Section 243 or 273.5. This information shall include advising the victim how to safely execute the arrest.
(c) (1) When a peace officer is responding to a call alleging a violation of a domestic violence protective or restraining order issued under Section 527.6 of the Code of Civil Procedure, the Family Code, Section 136.2, 646.91, or paragraph (2) of subdivision (a) of Section 1203.097 of this code, Section 213.5 or 15657.03 of the Welfare and Institutions Code, or of a domestic violence protective or restraining order issued by the court of another state, tribe, or territory and the peace officer has probable cause to believe that the person against whom the order is issued has notice of the order and has committed an act in violation of the order, the officer shall, consistent with subdivision (b) of Section 13701, make a lawful arrest of the person without a warrant and take that person into custody whether or not the violation occurred in the presence of the arresting officer. The officer shall, as soon as possible after the arrest, confirm with the appropriate authorities or the Domestic Violence Protection Order Registry maintained pursuant to Section 6380 of the Family Code that a true copy of the protective order has been registered, unless the victim provides the officer with a copy of the protective order.
(2) The person against whom a protective order has been issued shall be deemed to have notice of the order if the victim presents to the officer proof of service of the order, the officer confirms with the appropriate authorities that a true copy of the proof of service is on file, or the person against whom the protective order was issued was present at the protective order hearing or was informed by a peace officer of the contents of the protective order.
(3) In situations where mutual protective orders have been issued under Division 10 (commencing with Section 6200) of the Family Code, liability for arrest under this subdivision applies only to those persons who are reasonably believed to have been the dominant aggressor. In those situations, prior to making an arrest under this subdivision, the peace officer shall make reasonable efforts to identify, and may arrest, the dominant aggressor involved in the incident. The dominant aggressor is the person determined to be the most significant, rather than the first, aggressor. In identifying the dominant aggressor, an officer shall consider (A) the intent of the law to protect victims of domestic violence from continuing abuse, (B) the threats creating fear of physical injury, (C) the history of domestic violence between the persons involved, and (D) whether either person involved acted in self-defense.
(d) Notwithstanding paragraph (1) of subdivision (a), if a suspect commits an assault or battery upon a current or former spouse, fiancé, fiancée, a current or former cohabitant as defined in Section 6209 of the Family Code, a person with whom the suspect currently is having or has previously had an engagement or dating relationship, as defined in paragraph (10) of subdivision (f) of Section 243, a person with whom the suspect has parented a child, or is presumed to have parented a child pursuant to the Uniform Parentage Act (Part 3 (commencing with Section 7600) of Division 12 of the Family Code), a child of the suspect, a child whose parentage by the suspect is the

subject of an action under the Uniform Parentage Act, a child of a person in one of the above categories, any other person related to the suspect by consanguinity or affinity within the second degree, or any person who is 65 years of age or older and who is related to the suspect by blood or legal guardianship, a peace officer may arrest the suspect without a warrant where both of the following circumstances apply:

(1) The peace officer has probable cause to believe that the person to be arrested has committed the assault or battery, whether or not it has in fact been committed.

(2) The peace officer makes the arrest as soon as probable cause arises to believe that the person to be arrested has committed the assault or battery, whether or not it has in fact been committed.

(e) In addition to the authority to make an arrest without a warrant pursuant to paragraphs (1) and (3) of subdivision (a), a peace officer may, without a warrant, arrest a person for a violation of Section 25400 when all of the following apply:

(1) The officer has reasonable cause to believe that the person to be arrested has committed the violation of Section 25400.

(2) The violation of Section 25400 occurred within an airport, as defined in Section 21013 of the Public Utilities Code, in an area to which access is controlled by the inspection of persons and property.

(3) The peace officer makes the arrest as soon as reasonable cause arises to believe that the person to be arrested has committed the violation of Section 25400.

(Amended by Stats. 2012, Ch. 867, Sec. 20. (SB 1144) Effective January 1, 2013.)

836.1.

When a person commits an assault or battery against the person of a firefighter, emergency medical technician, or mobile intensive care paramedic while that person is on duty engaged in the performance of his or her duties in violation of subdivision (b) of Section 241 or subdivision (b) of Section 243, a peace officer may, without a warrant, arrest the person who commits the assault or battery:

(a) Whenever the peace officer has reasonable cause to believe that the person to be arrested has committed the assault or battery, although the assault or battery was not committed in the peace officer's presence.

(b) Whenever the peace officer has reasonable cause to believe that the person to be arrested has committed the assault or battery, whether or not the assault or battery has in fact been committed.

(Added by Stats. 1995, Ch. 52, Sec. 1. Effective January 1, 1996.)

836.3.

A peace officer may make an arrest in obedience to a warrant delivered to him, or may, without a warrant, arrest a person who, while charged with or convicted of a misdemeanor, has escaped from any county or city jail, prison, industrial farm or industrial road camp or from the custody of the officer or person in charge of him while engaged on any county road or other county work or going to or returning from such county road or other county work or from the custody of any officer or person in whose lawful custody he is when such escape is not by force or violence.

(Added by Stats. 1955, Ch. 609.)

836.5.

(a) A public officer or employee, when authorized by ordinance, may arrest a person without a warrant whenever the officer or employee has reasonable cause to believe that the person to be arrested has committed a misdemeanor in the presence of the officer or employee that is a violation of a statute or ordinance that the officer or employee has the duty to enforce.

(b) There shall be no civil liability on the part of, and no cause of action shall arise against, any public officer or employee acting pursuant to subdivision (a) and within the scope of his or her authority for false arrest or false imprisonment arising out of any arrest that is lawful or that the public officer or employee, at the time of the arrest, had reasonable cause to believe was lawful. No officer or employee shall be deemed an aggressor or lose his or her right to self-defense by the use of reasonable force to effect the arrest, prevent escape, or overcome resistance.

(c) In any case in which a person is arrested pursuant to subdivision (a) and the person arrested does not demand to be taken before a magistrate, the public officer or employee making the arrest shall prepare a written notice to appear and release the person on his or her promise to appear, as prescribed by Chapter 5C (commencing with Section 853.5). The provisions of that chapter shall thereafter apply with reference to any proceeding based upon the issuance of a written notice to appear pursuant to this authority.

(d) The governing body of a local agency, by ordinance, may authorize its officers and employees who have the duty to enforce a statute or ordinance to arrest persons for violations of the statute or ordinance as provided in subdivision (a).

(e) For purposes of this section, "ordinance" includes an order, rule, or regulation of any air pollution control district.

(f) For purposes of this section, a "public officer or employee" includes an officer or employee of a nonprofit transit corporation wholly owned by a local agency and formed to carry out the purposes of the local agency.

(Amended by Stats. 1997, Ch. 324, Sec. 3. Effective January 1, 1998.)

836.6.

(a) It is unlawful for any person who is remanded by a magistrate or judge of any court in this state to the custody of a sheriff, marshal, or other police agency, to thereafter escape or attempt to escape from that custody.

(b) It is unlawful for any person who has been lawfully arrested by any peace officer and who knows, or by the exercise of reasonable care should have known, that he or she has been so arrested, to thereafter escape or attempt to escape from that peace officer.

(c) Any person who violates subdivision (a) or (b) is guilty of a misdemeanor, punishable by imprisonment in a county jail not to exceed one year. However, if the escape or attempted escape is by force or violence, and the person proximately causes a peace officer serious bodily injury, the person shall be punished by imprisonment in the state prison for two, three, or four years, or by imprisonment in a county jail not to exceed one year.

(Amended by Stats. 2012, Ch. 43, Sec. 26. (SB 1023) Effective June 27, 2012.)

837.

A private person may arrest another:

1. For a public offense committed or attempted in his presence.

2. When the person arrested has committed a felony, although not in his presence.

3. When a felony has been in fact committed, and he has reasonable cause for believing the person arrested to have committed it.

(Enacted 1872.)

838.

A magistrate may orally order a peace officer or private person to arrest any one committing or attempting to commit a public offense in the presence of such magistrate.

(Enacted 1872.)

839.

Any person making an arrest may orally summon as many persons as he deems necessary to aid him therein.

(Enacted 1872.)

840.

An arrest for the commission of a felony may be made on any day and at any time of the day or night. An arrest for the commission of a misdemeanor or an infraction cannot be made between the hours of 10 o'clock p.m. of any day and 6 o'clock a.m. of the succeeding day, unless:

(1) The arrest is made without a warrant pursuant to Section 836 or 837.

(2) The arrest is made in a public place.

(3) The arrest is made when the person is in custody pursuant to another lawful arrest.

(4) The arrest is made pursuant to a warrant which, for good cause shown, directs that it may be served at any time of the day or night.

(Amended by Stats. 1976, Ch. 436.)

841.

The person making the arrest must inform the person to be arrested of the intention to arrest him, of the cause of the arrest, and the authority to make it, except when the person making the arrest has reasonable cause to believe that the person to be arrested is actually engaged in the commission of or an attempt to commit an offense, or the person to be arrested is pursued immediately after its commission, or after an escape.

The person making the arrest must, on request of the person he is arresting, inform the latter of the offense for which he is being arrested.

(Amended by Stats. 1961, Ch. 1863.)

841.5.

(a) Except as otherwise required by Chapter 10 (commencing with Section 1054) of Title 7, or by the United States Constitution or the California Constitution, no law enforcement officer or employee of a law enforcement agency shall disclose to any arrested person, or to any person who may be a defendant in a criminal action, the address or telephone number of any person who is a victim or witness in the alleged offense.

(b) Nothing in this section shall impair or interfere with the right of a defendant to obtain information necessary for the preparation of his or her defense through the discovery process.

(c) Nothing in this section shall impair or interfere with the right of an attorney to obtain the address or telephone number of any person who is a victim of, or a witness to, an alleged offense where a client of that attorney has been arrested for, or may be a defendant in, a criminal action related to the alleged offense.

(d) Nothing in this section shall preclude a law enforcement agency from releasing the entire contents of an accident report as required by Section 20012 of the Vehicle Code.

(Added by Stats. 1992, Ch. 3, Sec. 2. Effective February 10, 1992.)

842.

An arrest by a peace officer acting under a warrant is lawful even though the officer does not have the warrant in his possession at the time of the arrest, but if the person arrested so requests it, the warrant shall be shown to him as soon as practicable.

(Amended by Stats. 1957, Ch. 2147.)

843.

When the arrest is being made by an officer under the authority of a warrant, after information of the intention to make the arrest, if the person to be arrested either flees or forcibly resists, the officer may use all necessary means to effect the arrest.

(Enacted 1872.)

844.

To make an arrest, a private person, if the offense is a felony, and in all cases a peace officer, may break open the door or window of the house in which the person to be arrested is, or in which they have reasonable grounds for believing the person to be, after having demanded admittance and explained the purpose for which admittance is desired.

(Amended by Stats. 1989, Ch. 1360, Sec. 112.)

845.

Any person who has lawfully entered a house for the purpose of making an arrest, may break open the door or window thereof if detained therein, when necessary for the purpose of liberating himself, and an officer may do the same, when necessary for the purpose of liberating a person who, acting in his aid, lawfully entered for the purpose of making an arrest, and is detained therein.

(Enacted 1872.)

846.

Any person making an arrest may take from the person arrested all offensive weapons which he may have about his person, and must deliver them to the magistrate before whom he is taken.

(Enacted 1872.)

847.

(a) A private person who has arrested another for the commission of a public offense must, without unnecessary delay, take the person arrested before a magistrate, or deliver him or her to a peace officer.

(b) There shall be no civil liability on the part of, and no cause of action shall arise against, any peace officer or federal criminal investigator or law enforcement officer described in subdivision (a) or (d) of Section 830.8, acting within the scope of his or her authority, for false arrest or false imprisonment arising out of any arrest under any of the following circumstances:

(1) The arrest was lawful, or the peace officer, at the time of the arrest, had reasonable cause to believe the arrest was lawful.

(2) The arrest was made pursuant to a charge made, upon reasonable cause, of the commission of a felony by the person to be arrested.

(3) The arrest was made pursuant to the requirements of Section 142, 837, 838, or 839.

(Amended by Stats. 2003, Ch. 468, Sec. 13. Effective January 1, 2004.)

847.5.

If a person has been admitted to bail in another state, escapes bail, and is present in this State, the bail bondsman or other person who is bail for such fugitive, may file with a magistrate in the county where the fugitive is present an affidavit stating the name and whereabouts of the fugitive, the offense with which the alleged fugitive was charged or of which he was convicted, the time and place of same, and the particulars in which the fugitive has violated the terms of his bail, and may request the issuance of a warrant for arrest of the fugitive, and the issuance, after hearing, of an order authorizing the affiant to return the fugitive to the jurisdiction from which he escaped bail. The magistrate may require such additional evidence under oath as he deems necessary to decide the issue. If he concludes that there is probable cause for believing that the person alleged to be a fugitive is such, he may issue a warrant for his arrest. The magistrate shall notify the district attorney of such action and shall direct him to investigate the case and determine the facts of the matter. When the fugitive is brought before him pursuant to the warrant, the magistrate shall set a time and place for hearing, and shall advise the fugitive of his right to counsel and to produce evidence at the hearing. He may admit the fugitive to bail pending the hearing. The district attorney shall appear at the hearing. If, after hearing, the magistrate is satisfied from the evidence that the person is a fugitive he may issue an order authorizing affiant to return the fugitive to the jurisdiction from which he escaped bail.

A bondsman or other person who is bail for a fugitive admitted to bail in another state who takes the fugitive into custody, except pursuant to an order issued under this section, is guilty of a misdemeanor.

(Added by Stats. 1961, Ch. 2185.)

848.

An officer making an arrest, in obedience to a warrant, must proceed with the person arrested as commanded by the warrant, or as provided by law.

(Enacted 1872.)

849.

(a) When an arrest is made without a warrant by a peace officer or private person, the person arrested, if not otherwise released, shall, without unnecessary delay, be taken before the nearest or most accessible magistrate in the county in which the offense is triable, and a complaint stating the charge against the arrested person shall be laid before the magistrate.

(b) A peace officer may release from custody, instead of taking the person before a magistrate, a person arrested without a warrant in the following circumstances:
(1) The officer is satisfied that there are insufficient grounds for making a criminal complaint against the person arrested.
(2) The person arrested was arrested for intoxication only, and no further proceedings are desirable.
(3) The person was arrested only for being under the influence of a controlled substance or drug and the person is delivered to a facility or hospital for treatment and no further proceedings are desirable.
(4) The person was arrested for driving under the influence of alcohol or drugs and the person is delivered to a hospital for medical treatment that prohibits immediate delivery before a magistrate.
(5) The person was arrested and subsequently delivered to a hospital or other urgent care facility, including, but not limited to, a facility for the treatment of co-occurring substance use disorders, for mental health evaluation and treatment, and no further proceedings are desirable.
(c) The record of arrest of a person released pursuant to paragraph (1), (3), or (5) of subdivision (b) shall include a record of release. Thereafter, the arrest shall not be deemed an arrest, but a detention only.
(Amended by Stats. 2017, Ch. 566, Sec. 1. (SB 238) Effective October 7, 2017.)
849.5.
In any case in which a person is arrested and released and no accusatory pleading is filed charging him with an offense, any record of arrest of the person shall include a record of release. Thereafter, the arrest shall not be deemed an arrest, but a detention only.
(Added by Stats. 1975, Ch. 1117.)
850.
(a) A telegraphic copy of a warrant or an abstract of a warrant may be sent by telegraph, teletype, or any other electronic devices, to one or more peace officers, and such copy or abstract is as effectual in the hands of any officer, and he shall proceed in the same manner under it, as though he held the original warrant issued by a magistrate or the issuing authority or agency.
(b) Except as otherwise provided in Section 1549.2 relating to Governor's warrants of extradition, an abstract of the warrant as herein referred to shall contain the following information: the warrant number, the charge, the court or agency of issuance, the subject's name, address and description, the bail, the name of the issuing magistrate or authority, and if the offense charged is a misdemeanor, whether the warrant has been certified for night service.
(c) When the subject of a written or telegraphic warrant or abstract of warrant is in custody on another charge, the custodial officer shall, immediately upon receipt of information as to the existence of any such warrant or abstract, obtain and deliver a written copy of the warrant or abstract to the subject and shall inform him of his rights under Section 1381, where applicable, to request a speedy trial and under Section 858.7 relating to Vehicle Code violations.
(Amended by Stats. 1983, Ch. 793, Sec. 1.)
851.
Every officer causing telegraphic copies or abstracts of warrants to be sent, must certify as correct, and file in the telegraphic office from which such copies are sent, a copy of the warrant, and must return the original with a statement of his action thereunder.
(Amended by Stats. 1965, Ch. 1990.)
851.5.
(a) (1) Immediately upon being booked and, except where physically impossible, no later than three hours after arrest, an arrested person has the right to make at least three completed telephone calls, as described in subdivision (b).
(2) The arrested person shall be entitled to make at least three calls at no expense if the calls are completed to telephone numbers within the local calling area or at his or her own expense if outside the local calling area.
(b) At any police facility or place where an arrestee is detained, a sign containing the following information in bold block type shall be posted in a conspicuous place:
The arrestee has the right to free telephone calls within the local calling area, or at his or her own expense if outside the local calling area, to three of the following:
(1) An attorney of his or her choice or, if he or she has no funds, the public defender or other attorney assigned by the court to assist indigents, whose telephone number shall be posted. This telephone call shall not be monitored, eavesdropped upon, or recorded.
(2) A bail bondsman.
(3) A relative or other person.
(c) As soon as practicable upon being arrested but, except where physically impossible, no later than three hours after arrest, the arresting or booking officer shall inquire as to whether the arrested person is a custodial parent with responsibility for a minor child. The arresting or booking officer shall notify the arrested person who is a custodial parent with responsibility for a minor child that he or she is entitled to, and may request to, make two additional telephone calls at no expense if the telephone calls are completed to telephone numbers within the local calling area, or at his or her own expense if outside the local calling area, to a relative or other person for the purpose of arranging for the care of the minor child or children in the parent's absence.
(d) At any police facility or place where an arrestee is detained, a sign containing the following information in bold block type shall be posted in a conspicuous place:
The arrestee, if he or she is a custodial parent with responsibility for a minor child, has the right to two additional telephone calls within the local dialing area, or at his or her own expense if outside the local area, for the purpose of arranging for the care of the minor child or children in the parent's absence.
(e) These telephone calls shall be given immediately upon request, or as soon as practicable.
(f) The signs posted pursuant to subdivisions (b) and (d) shall make the specified notifications in English and any non-English language spoken by a substantial number of the public, as specified in Section 7296.2 of the Government Code, who are served by the police facility or place of detainment.
(g) The rights and duties set forth in this section shall be enforced regardless of the arrestee's immigration status.
(h) This provision shall not abrogate a law enforcement officer's duty to advise a suspect of his or her right to counsel or of any other right.
(i) Any public officer or employee who willfully deprives an arrested person of any right granted by this section is guilty of a misdemeanor.
(Amended by Stats. 2012, Ch. 816, Sec. 1. (AB 2015) Effective January 1, 2013.)
851.6.
(a) In any case in which a person is arrested and released pursuant to paragraph (1), (3), or (5) of subdivision (b) of Section 849, the person shall be issued a certificate, signed by the releasing officer or his superior officer, describing the action as a detention.
(b) In any case in which a person is arrested and released and an accusatory pleading is not filed charging him or her with an offense, the person shall be issued a certificate by the law enforcement agency which arrested him or her describing the action as a detention.
(c) The Attorney General shall prescribe the form and content of the certificate.
(d) Any reference to the action as an arrest shall be deleted from the arrest records of the arresting agency and of the Department of Justice. Thereafter, any record of the action shall refer to it as a detention.
(Amended by Stats. 2017, Ch. 566, Sec. 2. (SB 238) Effective October 7, 2017.)
851.7.
(a) Any person who has been arrested for a misdemeanor, with or without a warrant, while a minor, may, during or after minority, petition the court in which the proceedings occurred or, if there were no court proceedings, the court in whose jurisdiction the arrest occurred, for an order sealing the records in the case, including any records of arrest and detention, if any of the following occurred:
(1) He was released pursuant to paragraph (1) of subdivision (b) of Section 849.
(2) Proceedings against him were dismissed, or he was discharged, without a conviction.
(3) He was acquitted.
(b) If the court finds that the petitioner is eligible for relief under subdivision (a), it shall issue its order granting the relief prayed for. Thereafter, the arrest, detention, and any further proceedings in the case shall be deemed not to have occurred, and the petitioner may answer accordingly any question relating to their occurrence.
(c) This section applies to arrests and any further proceedings that occurred before, as well as those that occur after, the effective date of this section.
(d) This section does not apply to any person taken into custody pursuant to Section 625 of the Welfare and Institutions Code, or to any case within the scope of Section 781 of the Welfare and Institutions Code, unless, after a finding of unfitness for the juvenile court or otherwise, there were criminal proceedings in the case, not culminating in conviction. If there were criminal proceedings not culminating in conviction, this section shall be applicable to such criminal proceedings if such proceedings are otherwise within the scope of this section.
(e) This section does not apply to arrests for, and any further proceedings relating to, any of the following:
(1) Offenses for which registration is required under Section 290.
(2) Offenses under Division 10 (commencing with Section 11000) of the Health and Safety Code.
(3) Offenses under the Vehicle Code or any local ordinance relating to the operation, stopping, standing, or parking of a vehicle.
(f) In any action or proceeding based upon defamation, a court, upon a showing of good cause, may order any records sealed under this section to be opened and admitted in evidence. The records shall be confidential and shall be available for inspection only by the court, jury, parties, counsel for the parties, and any other person who is authorized by the court to inspect them. Upon the judgment in the action or proceeding becoming final, the court shall order the records sealed.
(g) This section shall apply in any case in which a person was under the age of 21 at the time of the commission of an offense as to which this section is made applicable if such offense was committed prior to March 7, 1973.
(Amended by Stats. 1974, Ch. 401.)
851.8.
(a) In any case where a person has been arrested and no accusatory pleading has been filed, the person arrested may petition the law enforcement agency having jurisdiction over the offense to destroy its records of the arrest. A copy of the petition shall be served upon the prosecuting attorney of the county or city having jurisdiction over the offense. The law enforcement agency having jurisdiction over the offense, upon a determination that the person arrested is factually innocent, shall, with the concurrence of the prosecuting attorney, seal its arrest records, and the petition for relief under this section for three years from the date of the arrest and thereafter destroy its arrest records and the petition. The law enforcement agency having jurisdiction over the offense shall notify the Department of Justice, and any law enforcement agency that arrested the petitioner or participated in the arrest of the petitioner for an offense for which the petitioner has been found factually innocent under this subdivision, of the sealing of the arrest records and the reason therefor. The Department of Justice and any law enforcement agency so notified shall forthwith seal their records of the arrest and the notice of sealing for three years from the date of the arrest, and thereafter destroy their records of the arrest and the notice of sealing. The law enforcement agency having jurisdiction over the offense and the Department of Justice shall request the destruction of any records of the arrest which they have given to any local, state, or federal agency or to any other person or entity. Each agency, person, or entity within the State of California receiving the request shall destroy its records of the arrest and the request, unless otherwise provided in this section.
(b) If, after receipt by both the law enforcement agency and the prosecuting attorney of a petition for relief under subdivision (a), the law enforcement agency and prosecuting attorney do not respond to the petition by accepting or denying the petition within 60 days after the running of the relevant statute of limitations or within 60 days after receipt of the petition in cases where the statute of limitations has previously lapsed, then the petition shall be deemed to be denied. In any case where the petition of an arrestee to the law enforcement agency to have an arrest record destroyed is denied, petition may be made to the superior court that would have had territorial jurisdiction over the matter. A copy of the petition shall be served on the law enforcement agency and the prosecuting attorney of the county or city having jurisdiction over the offense at least 10 days prior to the hearing thereon. The prosecuting attorney and the law enforcement agency through the district attorney may present evidence to the court at the hearing. Notwithstanding Section 1538.5 or 1539, any judicial determination of factual innocence made pursuant to this section may be heard and determined upon declarations, affidavits, police reports, or any other evidence submitted by the parties which is material, relevant, and reliable. A finding of factual innocence and an order for the sealing and destruction of records pursuant to this section shall not be made unless the court finds that no reasonable cause exists to believe that the arrestee committed the offense for which the arrest was made. In any court hearing to determine the factual innocence of a party, the initial burden of proof shall rest with the petitioner to show that no reasonable cause exists to believe that the arrestee committed the offense for which the arrest was made. If the court finds that this showing of no reasonable cause has been made by the petitioner, then the burden of proof shall shift to the respondent to show that a reasonable cause exists to believe that the petitioner committed the offense for which the arrest was made. If the court finds the arrestee to be factually innocent of the charges for which the arrest was made, then the court shall order the law enforcement agency having jurisdiction over the offense, the Department of Justice, and any law enforcement agency which arrested the petitioner or participated in the arrest of the petitioner for an offense for which the petitioner has been found factually innocent under this section to seal their records of the arrest and the court order to seal and destroy the records, for three years from the date of the arrest and thereafter to destroy their records of the arrest and the court order to seal and destroy those records. The court shall also order the law enforcement agency having jurisdiction over the offense and the Department of Justice to request the destruction of any records of the arrest which they have given to any local, state, or federal agency, person or entity. Each state or local agency, person or entity within the State of California receiving such a request shall destroy its records of the arrest and the request to destroy the records, unless otherwise provided in this section. The court shall give to the petitioner a copy of any court order concerning the destruction of the arrest records.
(c) In any case where a person has been arrested, and an accusatory pleading has been filed, but where no conviction has occurred, the defendant may, at any time after dismissal of the action, petition the court that dismissed the action for a finding that the defendant is factually innocent of the charges for which the arrest was made. A copy of the petition shall be served on the prosecuting attorney of the county or city in which the accusatory pleading was filed at least 10 days prior to the hearing on the petitioner's factual innocence. The prosecuting attorney may present evidence to the court at the hearing. The hearing shall be conducted as provided in subdivision (b). If the court finds

the petitioner to be factually innocent of the charges for which the arrest was made, then the court shall grant the relief as provided in subdivision (b).

(d) In any case where a person has been arrested and an accusatory pleading has been filed, but where no conviction has occurred, the court may, with the concurrence of the prosecuting attorney, grant the relief provided in subdivision (b) at the time of the dismissal of the accusatory pleading.

(e) Whenever any person is acquitted of a charge and it appears to the judge presiding at the trial at which the acquittal occurred that the defendant was factually innocent of the charge, the judge may grant the relief provided in subdivision (b).

(f) In any case where a person who has been arrested is granted relief pursuant to subdivision (a) or (b), the law enforcement agency having jurisdiction over the offense or court shall issue a written declaration to the arrestee stating that it is the determination of the law enforcement agency having jurisdiction over the offense or court that the arrestee is factually innocent of the charges for which the person was arrested and that the arrestee is thereby exonerated. Thereafter, the arrest shall be deemed not to have occurred and the person may answer accordingly any question relating to its occurrence.

(g) The Department of Justice shall furnish forms to be utilized by persons applying for the destruction of their arrest records and for the written declaration that one person was found factually innocent under subdivisions (a) and (b).

(h) Documentation of arrest records destroyed pursuant to subdivision (a), (b), (c), (d), or (e) that are contained in investigative police reports shall bear the notation "Exonerated" whenever reference is made to the arrestee. The arrestee shall be notified in writing by the law enforcement agency having jurisdiction over the offense of the sealing and destruction of the arrest records pursuant to this section.

(i) (1) Any finding that an arrestee is factually innocent pursuant to subdivision (a), (b), (c), (d), or (e) shall not be admissible as evidence in any action.

(2) Notwithstanding paragraph (1), a finding that an arrestee is factually innocent pursuant to subdivisions (a) to (e), inclusive, shall be admissible as evidence at a hearing before the California Victim Compensation Board.

(j) Destruction of records of arrest pursuant to subdivision (a), (b), (c), (d), or (e) shall be accomplished by permanent obliteration of all entries or notations upon the records pertaining to the arrest, and the record shall be prepared again so that it appears that the arrest never occurred. However, where (1) the only entries on the record pertain to the arrest and (2) the record can be destroyed without necessarily affecting the destruction of other records, then the document constituting the record shall be physically destroyed.

(k) No records shall be destroyed pursuant to subdivision (a), (b), (c), (d), or (e) if the arrestee or a codefendant has filed a civil action against the peace officers or law enforcement jurisdiction which made the arrest or instituted the prosecution and if the agency which is the custodian of the records has received a certified copy of the complaint in the civil action, until the civil action has been resolved. Any records sealed pursuant to this section by the court in the civil actions, upon a showing of good cause, may be opened and submitted into evidence. The records shall be confidential and shall be available for inspection only by the court, jury, parties, counsel for the parties, and any other person authorized by the court. Immediately following the final resolution of the civil action, records subject to subdivision (a), (b), (c), (d), or (e) shall be sealed and destroyed pursuant to subdivision (a), (b), (c), (d), or (e).

(l) For arrests occurring on or after January 1, 1981, and for accusatory pleadings filed on or after January 1, 1981, petitions for relief under this section may be filed up to two years from the date of the arrest or filing of the accusatory pleading, whichever is later. Until January 1, 1983, petitioners can file for relief under this section for arrests which occurred or accusatory pleadings which were filed up to five years prior to the effective date of the statute. Any time restrictions on filing for relief under this section may be waived upon a showing of good cause by the petitioner and in the absence of prejudice.

(m) Any relief which is available to a petitioner under this section for an arrest shall also be available for an arrest which has been deemed to be or described as a detention under Section 849.5 or 851.6.

(n) This section shall not apply to any offense which is classified as an infraction.

(o) (1) This section shall be repealed on the effective date of a final judgment based on a claim under the California or United States Constitution holding that evidence that is relevant, reliable, and material may not be considered for purposes of a judicial determination of factual innocence under this section. For purposes of this subdivision, a judgment by the appellate division of a superior court is a final judgment if it is published and if it is not reviewed on appeal by a court of appeal. A judgment of a court of appeal is a final judgment if it is published and if it is not reviewed by the California Supreme Court.

(2) Any decision referred to in this subdivision shall be stayed pending appeal.

(3) If not otherwise appealed by a party to the action, any decision referred to in this subdivision which is a judgment by the appellate division of the superior court shall be appealed by the Attorney General.

(p) A judgment of the court under subdivision (b), (c), (d), or (e) is subject to the following appeal path:

(1) In a felony case, appeal is to the court of appeal.

(2) In a misdemeanor case, or in a case in which no accusatory pleading was filed, appeal is to the appellate division of the superior court.

(Amended by Stats. 2016, Ch. 31, Sec. 235. (SB 836) Effective June 27, 2016. Repealed conditionally as provided in subd. (o).)
851.85.
Whenever a person is acquitted of a charge and it appears to the judge presiding at the trial wherein such acquittal occurred that the defendant was factually innocent of the charge, the judge may order that the records in the case be sealed, including any record of arrest or detention, upon the written or oral motion of any party in the case or the court, and with notice to all parties to the case. If such an order is made, the court shall give to the defendant a copy of such order and inform the defendant that he may thereafter state that he was not arrested for such charge and that he was found innocent of such charge by the court.

(Added by Stats. 1980, Ch. 1172, Sec. 3. Effective September 29, 1980. Conditionally operative, upon repeal of Section 851.8, by Sec. 4 of Ch. 1172.)
851.86.
Whenever a person is convicted of a charge, and the conviction is set aside based upon a determination that the person was factually innocent of the charge, the judge shall order that the records in the case be sealed, including any record of arrest or detention, upon written or oral motion of any party in the case or the court, and with notice to all parties to the case. If such an order is made, the court shall give the defendant a copy of that order and inform the defendant that he or she may thereafter state he or she was not arrested for that charge and that he or she was not convicted of that charge, and that he or she was found innocent of that charge by the court. The court shall also inform the defendant of the availability of indemnity for persons erroneously convicted pursuant to Chapter 5 (commencing with Section 4900) of Title 6 of Part 3, and the time limitations for presenting those claims.

(Added by Stats. 2009, Ch. 432, Sec. 4. (AB 316) Effective January 1, 2010.)
851.865.
(a) If a person has secured a declaration of factual innocence from the court pursuant to Section 851.8 or 851.86, the finding shall be sufficient grounds for payment of compensation for a claim made pursuant to Section 4900. Upon application by the person, the California Victim Compensation Board shall, without a hearing, recommend to the Legislature that an appropriation be made and the claim paid pursuant to Section 4904.

(b) If the declaration of factual innocence is granted pursuant to a stipulation of the prosecutor, the duty of the board to, without a hearing, recommend to the Legislature payment of the claim, shall apply.

(Amended by Stats. 2016, Ch. 31, Sec. 236. (SB 836) Effective June 27, 2016.)
851.87.
(a) (1) In any case where a person is arrested and successfully completes a prefiling diversion program administered by a prosecuting attorney in lieu of filing an accusatory pleading, the person may petition the superior court that would have had jurisdiction over the matter to issue an order to seal the records pertaining to an arrest and the court may order those records sealed as described in Section 851.92. A copy of the petition shall be served on the law enforcement agency and the prosecuting attorney of the county or city having jurisdiction over the offense, who may request a hearing within 60 days of receipt of the petition. The court may hear the matter no less than 60 days from the date the law enforcement agency and the prosecuting attorney receive a copy of the petition. The prosecuting attorney and the law enforcement agency, through the prosecuting attorney, may present evidence to the court at the hearing.

(2) If the order is made, the court shall give a copy of the order to the person and inform the person that he or she may thereafter state that he or she was not arrested for the charge.

(3) The person may, except as specified in subdivisions (b) and (c), indicate in response to any question concerning the person's prior criminal record that the person was not arrested.

(4) Subject to subdivisions (b) and (c), a record pertaining to the arrest shall not, without the person's permission, be used in any way that could result in the denial of any employment, benefit, or certificate.

(b) The person shall be advised that, regardless of the person's successful completion of the program, the arrest shall be disclosed by the Department of Justice in response to any peace officer application request, and that, notwithstanding subdivision (a), this section does not relieve the person of the obligation to disclose the arrest in response to any direct question contained in any questionnaire or application for a position as a peace officer, as defined in Section 830.

(c) The person shall be advised that an order to seal records pertaining to an arrest made pursuant to this section has no effect on a criminal justice agency's ability to access and use those sealed records and information regarding sealed arrests, as described in Section 851.92.

(d) As used in this section, "prefiling diversion" is a diversion from prosecution that is offered to a person by the prosecuting attorney in lieu of, or prior to, the filing of an accusatory pleading in court as set forth in Section 950.

(Amended by Stats. 2017, Ch. 680, Sec. 1. (SB 393) Effective January 1, 2018.)
851.90.
(a) (1) Whenever a person is diverted pursuant to a drug diversion program administered by a superior court pursuant to Section 1000.5 or is admitted to a deferred entry of judgment program pursuant to Section 1000 or 1000.8, and the person successfully completes the program, the judge may order those records pertaining to the arrest to be sealed as described in Section 851.92, upon the written or oral motion of any party in the case, or upon the court's own motion, and with notice to all parties in the case.

(2) If the order is made, the court shall give a copy of the order to the defendant and inform the defendant that he or she may thereafter state that he or she was not arrested for the charge.

(3) The defendant may, except as specified in subdivisions (b) and (c), indicate in response to any question concerning the defendant's prior criminal record that the defendant was not arrested or granted statutorily authorized drug diversion or deferred entry of judgment for the offense.

(4) Subject to subdivisions (b) and (c), a record pertaining to an arrest resulting in the successful completion of a statutorily authorized drug diversion or deferred entry of judgment program shall not, without the defendant's permission, be used in any way that could result in the denial of any employment, benefit, or certificate.

(b) The defendant shall be advised that, regardless of the defendant's successful completion of a statutorily authorized drug diversion or deferred entry of judgment program, the arrest upon which the case was based shall be disclosed by the Department of Justice in response to any peace officer application request, and that, notwithstanding subdivision (a), this section does not relieve the defendant of the obligation to disclose the arrest in response to any direct question contained in any questionnaire or application for a position as a peace officer, as defined in Section 830.

(c) The defendant shall be advised that, regardless of the defendant's successful completion of a statutorily authorized drug diversion or deferred entry of judgment program, an order to seal records pertaining to an arrest made pursuant to this section has no effect on a criminal justice agency's ability to access and use those sealed records and information regarding sealed arrests, as described in Section 851.92.

(Amended by Stats. 2017, Ch. 680, Sec. 2. (SB 393) Effective January 1, 2018.)
851.91.
(a) A person who has suffered an arrest that did not result in a conviction may petition the court to have his or her arrest and related records sealed, as described in Section 851.92.

(1) For purposes of this section, an arrest did not result in a conviction if any of the following are true:

(A) The statute of limitations has run on every offense upon which the arrest was based and the prosecuting attorney of the city or county that would have had jurisdiction over the offense or offenses upon which the arrest was based has not filed an accusatory pleading based on the arrest.

(B) The prosecuting attorney filed an accusatory pleading based on the arrest, but, with respect to all charges, one or more of the following has occurred:

(i) No conviction occurred, the charge has been dismissed, and the charge may not be refiled.

(ii) No conviction occurred and the arrestee has been acquitted of the charges.

(iii) A conviction occurred, but has been vacated or reversed on appeal, all appellate remedies have been exhausted, and the charge may not be refiled.

(2) A person is not eligible for relief under this section in any of the following circumstances:

(A) He or she may still be charged with any of the offenses upon which the arrest was based.

(B) Any of the arrest charges, as specified by the law enforcement agency that conducted the arrest, or any of the charges in the accusatory pleading based on the arrest, if filed, is a charge of murder or any other offense for which there is no statute of limitations, except when the person has been acquitted or found factually innocent of the charge.

(C) The petitioner intentionally evaded law enforcement efforts to prosecute the arrest, including by absconding from the jurisdiction in which the arrest occurred. The existence of bench warrants or failures to appear that were adjudicated before the case closed with no conviction does not establish intentional evasion.

(D) The petitioner intentionally evaded law enforcement efforts to prosecute the arrest by engaging in identity fraud and was subsequently charged with a crime for that act of identity fraud.

(b) (1) A petition to seal an arrest shall:

(A) Be verified.

(B) Be filed in the court in which the accusatory pleading based on the arrest was filed or, if no accusatory pleading was filed, in a court with criminal jurisdiction in the city or county in which the arrest occurred.

(C) Be filed at least 15 days prior to the hearing on the petition.
(D) Be served, by copy, upon the prosecuting attorney of the city or county in which the arrest occurred and upon the law enforcement agency that made the arrest at least 15 days prior to the hearing on the petition.
(E) Include all of the following information:
(i) The petitioner's name and date of birth.
(ii) The date of the arrest for which sealing is sought.
(iii) The city and county where the arrest took place.
(iv) The law enforcement agency that made the arrest.
(v) Any other information identifying the arrest that is available from the law enforcement agency that conducted the arrest or from the court in which the accusatory pleading, if any, based on the arrest was filed, including, but not limited to, the case number for the police investigative report documenting the arrest, and the court number under which the arrest was reviewed by the prosecuting attorney or under which the prosecuting attorney filed an accusatory pleading.
(vi) The offenses upon which the arrest was based or, if an accusatory pleading was filed based on the arrest, the charges in the accusatory pleading.
(vii) A statement that the petitioner is entitled to have his or her arrest sealed as a matter of right or, if the petitioner is requesting to have his or her arrest sealed in the interests of justice, how the interests of justice would be served by granting the petition, accompanied by declarations made directly and verified by the petitioner, his or her supporting declarants, or both.
(2) The court may deny a petition for failing to meet any of the requirements described in paragraph (1).
(3) (A) The Judicial Council shall furnish forms to be utilized by a person applying to have his or her arrest sealed pursuant to this section. The petition form shall include all of the information required to be included in the petition by paragraph (1) of subdivision (b), shall be available in English, Spanish, Chinese, Vietnamese, and Korean, and shall include a statement that the petition form is available in additional languages and the Internet Web site where the form is available in alternative languages. The forms shall include notice of other means to address arrest records, including a determination of factual innocence under Section 851.8 and deeming an arrest a detention under Section 849.5.
(B) (i) A facility at which an arrestee is detained shall, at the request of an arrestee upon release, provide the forms furnished by Judicial Council pursuant to subparagraph (A) to the arrestee.
(ii) A facility at which an arrestee is detained shall post a sign containing the following information: "A person who has been arrested but not convicted may petition the court to have his or her arrest and related records sealed. The petition form is available on the Internet or upon request in this facility."
(c) A petition to seal an arrest record pursuant to this section may be granted as a matter of right or in the interests of justice.
(1) A petitioner who is eligible for relief under subdivision (a) is entitled to have his or her arrest sealed as a matter of right unless he or she is subject to paragraph (2).
(2) (A) (i) A petitioner may have his or her arrest sealed only upon a showing that the sealing would serve the interests of justice if any of the offenses upon which the arrest was based, as specified by the law enforcement agency that made the arrest, or, if an accusatory pleading was filed, any of the charges in the accusatory pleading, was one of the following:
(I) Domestic violence, if the petitioner's record demonstrates a pattern of domestic violence arrests, convictions, or both.
(II) Child abuse, if the petitioner's record demonstrates a pattern of child abuse arrests, convictions, or both.
(III) Elder abuse, if the petitioner's record demonstrates a pattern of elder abuse arrests, convictions, or both.
(ii) For purposes of this subparagraph, "pattern" means two or more convictions, or five or more arrests, for separate offenses occurring on separate occasions within three years from at least one of the other convictions or arrests.
(B) In determining whether the interests of justice would be served by sealing an arrest record pursuant to this section, the court may consider any relevant factors, including, but not limited to, any of the following:
(i) Hardship to the petitioner caused by the arrest that is the subject of the petition.
(ii) Declarations or evidence regarding the petitioner's good character.
(iii) Declarations or evidence regarding the arrest.
(iv) The petitioner's record of convictions.
(d) (1) At a hearing on a petition under this section, the petitioner, the prosecuting attorney, and, through the prosecuting attorney, the arresting agency may present evidence to the court. Notwithstanding Section 1538.5 or 1539, the hearing may be heard and determined upon declarations, affidavits, police investigative reports, copies of state summary criminal history information and local summary criminal history information, or any other evidence submitted by the parties that is material, relevant, and reliable.
(2) The petitioner has the initial burden of proof to show that he or she is entitled to have his or her arrest sealed as a matter of right or that sealing would serve the interests of justice. If the court finds that petitioner has satisfied his or her burden of proof, then the burden of proof shall shift to the respondent prosecuting attorney.
(e) If the court grants a petition pursuant to this section, the court shall do all of the following:
(1) Furnish a disposition report to the Department of Justice, pursuant to Section 13151, stating that relief was granted under this section.
(2) (A) Issue a written ruling and order to the petitioner, the prosecuting attorney, and to the law enforcement agency that made the arrest that states all of the following:
(B) The record of arrest has been sealed as to petitioner, the arrest is deemed not to have occurred, the petitioner may answer any question relating to the sealed arrest accordingly, and the petitioner is released from all penalties and disabilities resulting from the arrest, except as provided in Section 851.92 and as follows:
(i) The sealed arrest may be pleaded and proved in any subsequent prosecution of the petitioner for any other offense, and shall have the same effect as if it had not been sealed.
(ii) The sealing of an arrest pursuant to this section does not relieve the petitioner of the obligation to disclose the arrest, if otherwise required by law, in response to any direct question contained in a questionnaire or application for public office, for employment as a peace officer, for licensure by any state or local agency, or for contracting with the California State Lottery Commission.
(iii) The sealing of an arrest pursuant to this section does not affect petitioner's authorization to own, possess, or have in his or her custody or control any firearm, or his or her susceptibility to conviction under Chapter 2 (commencing with Section 29800) of Division 9 of Title 4 of Part 6, if the arrest would otherwise affect this authorization or susceptibility.
(iv) The sealing of an arrest pursuant to this section does not affect any prohibition from holding public office that would otherwise apply under law as a result of the arrest.
(Amended by Stats. 2018, Ch. 653, Sec. 1. (AB 2599) Effective January 1, 2019.)
851.92.
(a) This section applies when an arrest record is sealed pursuant to Sections 851.87, 851.90, 851.91, 1000.4, and 1001.9.
(b) When the court issues an order to seal an arrest, the sealing shall be accomplished as follows:
(1) The court shall provide copies of the order and a report on the disposition of the arrest, as follows:

(A) Upon issuing the order, the court shall provide a copy to the person whose arrest was sealed and to the prosecuting attorney.
(B) Within 30 days of issuing the order, the court shall forward a copy of the order to the law enforcement agency that made the arrest, to any other law enforcement agency that participated in the arrest, and to the law enforcement agency that administers the master local summary criminal history information that contains the arrest record for the sealed arrest.
(C) Within 30 days of issuing the order, the court shall furnish a disposition report to the Department of Justice indicating that relief has been ordered and providing the section of the Penal Code under which that relief was granted and the date that relief was granted.
(D) A sealing order made pursuant to this subdivision shall not be forwarded to the Department of Justice to be included or notated in the department's manual or electronic fingerprint image or criminal history record systems. Any sealing order made pursuant to this subdivision and received by the Department of Justice shall not be processed by the department.
(2) The arrest record shall be updated, as follows:
(A) The local summary criminal history information shall include, directly next to or below the entry or entries regarding the sealed arrest, a note stating "arrest sealed" and providing the date that the court issued the order, and the section pursuant to which the arrest was sealed. This note shall be included in all master copies of the arrest record, digital or otherwise.
(B) The state summary criminal history information shall include, directly next to or below the entry or entries regarding the sealed arrest, a note stating "arrest relief granted," providing the date that the court issued the order and the section of the Penal Code pursuant to which the relief was granted. This note shall be included in all master copies of the arrest record, digital or otherwise.
(3) A police investigative report related to the sealed arrest shall, only as to the person whose arrest was sealed, be stamped "ARREST SEALED: DO NOT RELEASE OUTSIDE THE CRIMINAL JUSTICE SECTOR," and shall note next to the stamp the date the arrest was sealed and the section pursuant to which the arrest was sealed. The responsible local law enforcement agency shall ensure that this note is included in all master copies, digital or otherwise, of the police investigative report related to the arrest that was sealed.
(4) Court records related to the sealed arrest shall, only as to the person whose arrest was sealed, be stamped "ARREST SEALED: DO NOT RELEASE OUTSIDE OF THE CRIMINAL JUSTICE SECTOR," and shall note next to the stamp the date of the sealing and the section pursuant to which the arrest was sealed. This stamp and note shall be included on all master court dockets, digital or otherwise, relating to the arrest.
(5) Arrest records, police investigative reports, and court records that are sealed under this section shall not be disclosed to any person or entity except the person whose arrest was sealed or a criminal justice agency. Nothing shall prohibit disclosure of information between criminal history providers.
(6) Notwithstanding the sealing of an arrest, a criminal justice agency may continue, in the regular course of its duties, to access, furnish to other criminal justice agencies, and use, including, but not limited to, by discussing in open court and in unsealed court filings, sealed arrests, sealed arrest records, sealed police investigative reports, sealed court records, and information relating to sealed arrests, to the same extent that would have been permitted for a criminal justice agency if the arrest had not been sealed.
(c) Unless specifically authorized by this section, a person or entity, other than a criminal justice agency or the person whose arrest was sealed, who disseminates information relating to a sealed arrest is subject to a civil penalty of not less than five hundred dollars ($500) and not more than two thousand five hundred dollars ($2,500) per violation. The civil penalty may be enforced by a city attorney, district attorney, or the Attorney General. This subdivision does not limit any existing private right of action. A civil penalty imposed under this section shall be cumulative to civil remedies or penalties imposed under any other law.
(d) As used in this section and Sections 851.87, 851.90, 851.91, 1000.4, and 1001.9, all of the following terms have the following meanings:
(1) "Arrest record" and "record pertaining to an arrest" mean information about the arrest or detention that is contained in either of the following:
(A) The master, or a copy of the master, local summary criminal history information, as defined in subdivision (a) of Section 13300.
(B) The master, or a copy of the master, state summary criminal history information as defined in subparagraph (A) of paragraph (2) of subdivision (a) of Section 11105.
(2) "Court records" means records, files, and materials created, compiled, or maintained by or for the court in relation to court proceedings, and includes, but is not limited to, indexes, registers of actions, court minutes, court orders, court filings, court exhibits, court progress and status reports, court history summaries, copies of state summary criminal history information and local summary criminal history information, and any other criminal history information contained in any of those materials.
(3) "Criminal history provider" means a person or entity that is not a criminal justice agency and that provides background screening services or criminal history information on identified individuals to the public or to those outside the criminal justice sector upon request, charge, or pursuant to a contractual agreement or that aggregates into databases that are open to the public or to those outside the criminal justice sector upon request or charge, or pursuant to a contractual agreement, that are not created or maintained by a criminal justice agency, criminal history information on identified individuals. For the purposes of this paragraph, a criminal history provider includes an investigative consumer reporting agency, as defined in Section 1786.2 of the Civil Code, a consumer credit reporting agency, as defined in Section 1785.3 of the Civil Code, and a consumer reporting agency, as defined in Section 603(f) of the Fair Credit Reporting Act (15 U.S.C. 1681a(f)).
(4) "Criminal justice agency" means an agency at any level of government that performs, as its principal function, activities relating to the apprehension, prosecution, defense, adjudication, incarceration, or correction of criminal suspects and criminal offenders. A criminal justice agency includes, but is not limited to, any of the following:
(A) A court of this state.
(B) A peace officer, as defined in Section 830.1, subdivisions (a) and (e) of Section 830.2, subdivision (a) of Section 830.3, subdivision (a) of Section 830.31, and subdivisions (a) and (b) of Section 830.5.
(C) A district attorney.
(D) A prosecuting city attorney.
(E) A city attorney pursuing civil gang injunctions pursuant to Section 186.22a or drug abatement actions pursuant to Section 3479 or 3480 of the Civil Code or Section 11571 of the Health and Safety Code.
(F) A probation officer.
(G) A parole officer.
(H) A public defender or an attorney representing a person, or a person representing himself or herself, in a criminal proceeding, a proceeding to revoke parole, mandatory supervision, or postrelease community supervision, or in proceeding described in Chapter 3.5 (commencing with Section 4852.01) of Title 6 of Part 3.
(I) An expert, investigator, or other specialist contracted by a prosecuting attorney or defense attorney to accomplish the purpose of the prosecution, defense, or representation in the criminal proceeding.
(J) A correctional officer.
(5) "Police investigative report" means intelligence, analytical, and investigative reports and files created, compiled, and maintained by a law enforcement criminal justice agency

and relating to a potential crime, violation of the law, arrest, detention, prosecution, or law enforcement investigation.
(Added by Stats. 2017, Ch. 680, Sec. 4. (SB 393) Effective January 1, 2018.)

CHAPTER 5A. Uniform Act on Fresh Pursuit [852 - 852.4]

{ Heading of Chapter 5A renumbered from Chapter 5a by Stats. 2015, Ch. 303, Sec. 393. }

852.
This chapter may be cited as the Uniform Act on Fresh Pursuit.
(Added by Stats. 1937, Ch. 301.)

852.1.
As used in this chapter:
(a) "State" means any State of the United States and the District of Columbia.
(b) "Peace officer" means any peace officer or member of any duly organized State, county, or municipal peace unit or police force of another State.
(c) "Fresh Pursuit" includes close pursuit and hot pursuit.
(Added by Stats. 1937, Ch. 301.)

852.2.
Any peace officer of another State, who enters this State in fresh pursuit, and continues within this State in fresh pursuit, of a person in order to arrest him on the ground that he has committed a felony in the other State, has the same authority to arrest and hold the person in custody, as peace officers of this State have to arrest and hold a person in custody on the ground that he has committed a felony in this State.
(Added by Stats. 1937, Ch. 301.)

852.3.
If an arrest is made in this State by a peace officer of another State in accordance with the provisions of section 852.2 of this code, he shall without unnecessary delay take the person arrested before a magistrate of the county in which the arrest was made, who shall conduct a hearing for the purpose of determining the lawfulness of the arrest. If the magistrate determines that the arrest was lawful, he shall commit the person arrested to await a reasonable time for the issuance of an extradition warrant by the Governor of this State or admit him to bail for such purpose. If the magistrate determines that the arrest was unlawful he shall discharge the person arrested.
(Added by Stats. 1937, Ch. 301.)

852.4.
Section 852.2 of this code shall not be construed so as to make unlawful any arrest in this State which would otherwise be lawful.
(Added by Stats. 1937, Ch. 301.)

CHAPTER 5B. Interstate Jurisdiction [853.1 - 853.4]

{ Heading of Chapter 5B amended by Stats. 1995, Ch. 526, Sec. 3. }

ARTICLE 1. Colorado River Crime Enforcement Compact [853.1 - 853.2]
{ Article 1 heading added by Stats. 1995, Ch. 526, Sec. 4. }

853.1.
(a) Pursuant to the authority vested in this state by Section 112 of Title 4 of the United States Code, the Legislature of the State of California hereby ratifies the Colorado River Crime Enforcement Compact as set forth in Section 853.2.
(b) The purpose of this compact is to promote the interests of justice with regard to crimes committed on the Colorado River by avoiding jurisdictional issues as to whether a criminal act sought to be prosecuted was committed on one side or the other of the exact boundary of the channel, and thus avoiding the risk that an offender may go free on technical grounds because neither state is able to establish that the offense was committed within its boundaries.
(c) This compact shall become operative when ratified by law in the State of Arizona; and shall remain in full force and effect so long as the provisions of this compact, as ratified by the State of Arizona, remain substantively the same as the provisions of this compact, as ratified by this section. This compact may be amended in the same manner as is required for it to be ratified to become operative.
(Added by Stats. 1985, Ch. 754, Sec. 1.)

853.2.
(a) All courts and officers now or hereafter having and exercising jurisdiction in any county which is now or may hereafter be formed in any part of this state bordering upon the Colorado River, or any lake formed by, or which is a part of, the Colorado River, shall have and exercise jurisdiction in all criminal cases upon those waters concurrently with the courts of and officers of the State of Arizona, so far and to the extent that any of these bodies of water form a common boundary between this state and the State of Arizona. In addition, the officers shall have concurrent jurisdiction with the officers of the State of Arizona on any land mass within 25 air miles of the Colorado River, or within 25 air miles of any lake formed by, or that is a part of, the Colorado River.
(b) This section applies only to those crimes which are established in common between the States of Arizona and California; and an acquittal or conviction and sentence by one state shall bar a prosecution for the same act or omission by the other.
(c) This compact shall not be construed to bar the enforcement of the penal laws of either state not established in common with the other, provided that the act or omission proscribed occurs on that state's side of the river channel boundary.
(d) This compact does not apply to Division 3.5 (commencing with Section 9840) of the Vehicle Code, relating to registration of vessels, or to Section 658.7 of the Harbors and Navigation Code, relating to the display of a ski flag.
(Amended by Stats. 1994, Ch. 348, Sec. 1. Effective January 1, 1995. Note: This section constitutes the primary text of the Colorado River Crime Enforcement Compact. Section 853.1 provides for ratification, operation, and amendment of the compact.)

ARTICLE 2. California-Nevada Compact for Jurisdiction on Interstate Waters [853.3 - 853.4]
{ Article 2 added by Stats. 1995, Ch. 526, Sec. 5. }

853.3.
(a) Pursuant to the authority vested in this state by Section 112 of Title 4 of the United States Code, the Legislature of the State of California hereby ratifies the California-Nevada Compact for Jurisdiction on Interstate Waters as set forth in Section 853.4.
(b) The Legislature finds that law enforcement has been impaired in sections of Lake Tahoe and Topaz Lake forming an interstate boundary between California and Nevada because of difficulty in determining precisely where a criminal act was committed.

(c) The Legislature intends that a person arrested for an act that is illegal in both states should not be freed merely because neither state could establish that a crime was committed within its boundaries.
(d) The California-Nevada Compact for Jurisdiction on Interstate Waters is enacted to provide for the enforcement of the laws of this state with regard to certain acts committed on Lake Tahoe or Topaz Lake, on either side of the boundary line between California and Nevada.
(Added by Stats. 1995, Ch. 526, Sec. 5. Effective January 1, 1996.)

853.4.
(a) As used in this compact, unless the context otherwise requires, "party state" means a state that has enacted this compact.
(b) If conduct is prohibited by the party states, courts and law enforcement officers in either state who have jurisdiction over criminal offenses committed in a county where Lake Tahoe or Topaz Lake forms a common interstate boundary have concurrent jurisdiction to arrest, prosecute, and try offenders for the prohibited conduct committed anywhere on the body of water forming a boundary between the two states.
(c) This section applies only to those crimes that are established in common between the States of Nevada and California, and an acquittal or conviction and sentence by one state shall bar a prosecution for the same act or omission by the other.
(d) This compact does not authorize any conduct prohibited by a party state.
(e) This compact shall become operative when ratified by law by the party states and shall remain in full force and effect so long as the provisions of this compact, as ratified by the State of Nevada, remain substantively the same as the provisions of this compact, as ratified by this section. This compact may be amended in the same manner as is required for it to become operative.
(Added by Stats. 1995, Ch. 526, Sec. 5. Effective January 1, 1996. [Note: This section constitutes the primary text of the California-Nevada Compact for Jurisdiction on Interstate Waters, with subd. (e) providing for its operation and amendment. Section 853.3 provides for ratification of the compact.])

CHAPTER 5C. Citations for Misdemeanors [853.5 - 853.85]

{ Heading of Chapter 5C amended by Stats. 1967, Ch. 816. }

853.5.
(a) Except as otherwise provided by law, in any case in which a person is arrested for an offense declared to be an infraction, the person may be released according to the procedures set forth by this chapter for the release of persons arrested for an offense declared to be a misdemeanor. In all cases, except as specified in Sections 40302, 40303, 40305, and 40305.5 of the Vehicle Code, in which a person is arrested for an infraction, a peace officer shall only require the arrestee to present his or her driver's license or other satisfactory evidence of his or her identity for examination and to sign a written promise to appear contained in a notice to appear. If the arrestee does not have a driver's license or other satisfactory evidence of identity in his or her possession, the officer may require the arrestee to place a right thumbprint, or a left thumbprint or fingerprint if the person has a missing or disfigured right thumb, on the notice to appear. Except for law enforcement purposes relating to the identity of the arrestee, no person or entity may sell, give away, allow the distribution of, include in a database, or create a database with, this print. Only if the arrestee refuses to sign a written promise, has no satisfactory identification, or refuses to provide a thumbprint or fingerprint may the arrestee be taken into custody.
(b) A person contesting a charge by claiming under penalty of perjury not to be the person issued the notice to appear may choose to submit a right thumbprint, or a left thumbprint if the person has a missing or disfigured right thumb, to the issuing court through his or her local law enforcement agency for comparison with the one placed on the notice to appear. A local law enforcement agency providing this service may charge the requester no more than the actual costs. The issuing court may refer the thumbprint submitted and the notice to appear to the prosecuting attorney for comparison of the thumbprints. When there is no thumbprint or fingerprint on the notice to appear, or when the comparison of thumbprints is inconclusive, the court shall refer the notice to appear or copy thereof back to the issuing agency for further investigation, unless the court finds that referral is not in the interest of justice.
(c) Upon initiation of the investigation or comparison process by referral of the court, the court shall continue the case and the speedy trial period shall be tolled for 45 days.
(d) Upon receipt of the issuing agency's or prosecuting attorney's response, the court may make a finding of factual innocence pursuant to Section 530.6 if the court determines that there is insufficient evidence that the person cited is the person charged and shall immediately notify the Department of Motor Vehicles of its determination. If the Department of Motor Vehicles determines the citation or citations in question formed the basis of a suspension or revocation of the person's driving privilege, the department shall immediately set aside the action.
(e) If the prosecuting attorney or issuing agency fails to respond to a court referral within 45 days, the court shall make a finding of factual innocence pursuant to Section 530.6, unless the court finds that a finding of factual innocence is not in the interest of justice.
(Amended by Stats. 2003, Ch. 467, Sec. 2. Effective January 1, 2004.)

853.6.
(a) (1) In any case in which a person is arrested for an offense declared to be a misdemeanor, including a violation of any city or county ordinance, and does not demand to be taken before a magistrate, that person shall, instead of being taken before a magistrate, be released according to the procedures set forth by this chapter, although nothing prevents an officer from first booking an arrestee pursuant to subdivision (g). If the person is released, the officer or the officer's superior shall prepare in duplicate a written notice to appear in court, containing the name and address of the person, the offense charged, and the time when, and place where, the person shall appear in court. If, pursuant to subdivision (i), the person is not released prior to being booked and the officer in charge of the booking or the officer's superior determines that the person should be released, the officer or the officer's superior shall prepare a written notice to appear in a court.
(2) In any case in which a person is arrested for a misdemeanor violation of a protective court order involving domestic violence, as defined in subdivision (b) of Section 13700, or arrested pursuant to a policy, as described in Section 13701, the person shall be taken before a magistrate instead of being released according to the procedures set forth in this chapter, unless the arresting officer determines that there is not a reasonable likelihood that the offense will continue or resume or that the safety of persons or property would be imminently endangered by release of the person arrested. Prior to adopting these provisions, each city, county, or city and county shall develop a protocol to assist officers to determine when arrest and release is appropriate, rather than taking the arrested person before a magistrate. The county shall establish a committee to develop the protocol, consisting of, at a minimum, the police chief or county sheriff within the jurisdiction, the district attorney, county counsel, city attorney, representatives from domestic violence shelters, domestic violence councils, and other relevant community agencies.
(3) This subdivision shall not apply to the crimes specified in Section 1270.1, including crimes defined in each of the following:
(A) Paragraph (1) of subdivision (e) of Section 243.

(B) Section 273.5.
(C) Section 273.6, if the detained person made threats to kill or harm, has engaged in violence against, or has gone to the residence or workplace of, the protected party.
(D) Section 646.9.
(4) Nothing in this subdivision shall be construed to affect a defendant's ability to be released on bail or on their own recognizance, except as specified in Section 1270.1.
(b) Unless waived by the person, the time specified in the notice to appear shall be at least 10 days after arrest if the duplicate notice is to be filed by the officer with the magistrate.
(c) The place specified in the notice shall be the court of the magistrate before whom the person would be taken if the requirement of taking an arrested person before a magistrate were complied with, or shall be an officer authorized by that court to receive a deposit of bail.
(d) The officer shall deliver one copy of the notice to appear to the arrested person, and the arrested person, in order to secure release, shall give their written promise to appear in court as specified in the notice by signing the duplicate notice which shall be retained by the officer, and the officer may require the arrested person, if the arrested person has no satisfactory identification, to place a right thumbprint, or a left thumbprint or fingerprint if the person has a missing or disfigured right thumb, on the notice to appear. Except for law enforcement purposes relating to the identity of the arrestee, no person or entity may sell, give away, allow the distribution of, include in a database, or create a database with, this print. Upon the signing of the duplicate notice, the arresting officer shall immediately release the person arrested from custody.
(e) The officer shall, as soon as practicable, file the duplicate notice, as follows:
(1) It shall be filed with the magistrate if the offense charged is an infraction.
(2) It shall be filed with the magistrate if the prosecuting attorney has previously directed the officer to do so.
(3) (A) The duplicate notice and underlying police reports in support of the charge or charges shall be filed with the prosecuting attorney in cases other than those specified in paragraphs (1) and (2).
(B) If the duplicate notice is filed with the prosecuting attorney, the prosecuting attorney, within their discretion, may initiate prosecution by filing the notice or a formal complaint with the magistrate specified in the duplicate notice within 25 days from the time of arrest. If the prosecution is not to be initiated, the prosecutor shall send notice to the person arrested at the address on the notice to appear. The failure by the prosecutor to file the notice or formal complaint within 25 days of the time of the arrest shall not bar further prosecution of the misdemeanor charged in the notice to appear. However, any further prosecution shall be preceded by a new and separate citation or an arrest warrant.
(C) Upon the filing of the notice with the magistrate by the officer, or the filing of the notice or formal complaint by the prosecutor, the magistrate may fix the amount of bail that in the magistrate's judgment, in accordance with Section 1275, is reasonable and sufficient for the appearance of the defendant and shall endorse upon the notice a statement signed by the magistrate in the form set forth in Section 815a. The defendant may, prior to the date upon which the defendant promised to appear in court, deposit with the magistrate the amount of bail set by the magistrate. At the time the case is called for arraignment before the magistrate, if the defendant does not appear, either in person or by counsel, the magistrate may declare the bail forfeited and may, in the magistrate's discretion, order that no further proceedings shall be had in the case, unless the defendant has been charged with a violation of Section 374.3 or 374.7 of this code or of Section 11357, 11360, or 13002 of the Health and Safety Code, or a violation punishable under Section 5008.7 of the Public Resources Code, and the defendant has previously been convicted of a violation of that section or a violation that is punishable under that section, except in cases where the magistrate finds that undue hardship will be imposed upon the defendant by requiring the defendant to appear, the magistrate may declare the bail forfeited and order that no further proceedings be had in the case.
(D) Upon the making of the order that no further proceedings be had, all sums deposited as bail shall immediately be paid into the county treasury for distribution pursuant to Section 1463.
(f) No warrant shall be issued for the arrest of a person who has given a written promise to appear in court, unless and until that person has violated that promise or has failed to deposit bail, to appear for arraignment, trial, or judgment or to comply with the terms and provisions of the judgment, as required by law.
(g) The officer may book the arrested person at the scene or at the arresting agency prior to release or indicate on the citation that the arrested person shall appear at the arresting agency to be booked or indicate on the citation that the arrested person shall appear at the arresting agency to be fingerprinted prior to the date the arrested person appears in court. If it is indicated on the citation that the arrested person shall be booked or fingerprinted prior to the date of the person's court appearance, the arresting agency at the time of booking or fingerprinting shall provide the arrested person with verification of the booking or fingerprinting by making an entry on the citation. If it is indicated on the citation that the arrested person is to be booked or fingerprinted, the magistrate, judge, or court shall, before the proceedings begin, order the defendant to provide verification that the defendant was booked or fingerprinted by the arresting agency. If the defendant cannot produce the verification, the magistrate, judge, or court shall require that the defendant be booked or fingerprinted by the arresting agency before the next court appearance, and that the defendant provide the verification at the next court appearance unless both parties stipulate that booking or fingerprinting is not necessary.
(h) A peace officer shall use the written notice to appear procedure set forth in this section for any misdemeanor offense in which the officer has arrested a person without a warrant pursuant to Section 836 or in which the officer has taken custody of a person pursuant to Section 847.
(i) Whenever any person is arrested by a peace officer for a misdemeanor, that person shall be released according to the procedures set forth by this chapter unless one or more of the following is a reason for nonrelease, in which case the arresting officer may release the person, except as provided in subdivision (a), or the arresting officer shall indicate, on a form to be established by the officer's employing law enforcement agency, which of the following was a reason for the nonrelease:
(1) The person arrested was so intoxicated that they could have been a danger to themselves or to others.
(2) The person arrested required medical examination or medical care or was otherwise unable to care for their own safety.
(3) The person was arrested under one or more of the circumstances listed in Sections 40302 and 40303 of the Vehicle Code.
(4) There were one or more outstanding arrest warrants or failures to appear in court on previous misdemeanor citations that have not been resolved for the person.
(5) The person could not provide satisfactory evidence of personal identification.
(6) The prosecution of the offense or offenses for which the person was arrested, or the prosecution of any other offense or offenses, would be jeopardized by immediate release of the person arrested.
(7) There was a reasonable likelihood that the offense or offenses would continue or resume, or that the safety of persons or property would be imminently endangered by release of the person arrested.
(8) The person arrested demanded to be taken before a magistrate or refused to sign the notice to appear.
(9) There is reason to believe that the person would not appear at the time and place specified in the notice. The basis for this determination shall be specifically stated. An arrest warrant or failure to appear that is pending at the time of the current offense shall constitute reason to believe that the person would not appear as specified in the notice.
(10) The person was subject to Section 1270.1.
(11) The person has been cited, arrested, or convicted for misdemeanor or felony theft from a store or from a vehicle in the previous six months.
(12) (A) There is probable cause to believe that the person arrested is guilty of committing organized retail theft, as defined in subdivision (a) of Section 490.4.
(B) The form shall be filed with the arresting agency as soon as practicable and shall be made available to any party having custody of the arrested person, subsequent to the arresting officer, and to any person authorized by law to release the arrested person from custody before trial.
(j) (1) Once the arresting officer has prepared the written notice to appear and has delivered a copy to the person arrested, the officer shall deliver the remaining original and all copies as provided by subdivision (e).
(2) Any person, including the arresting officer and any member of the officer's department or agency, or any peace officer, who alters, conceals, modifies, nullifies, or destroys, or causes to be altered, concealed, modified, nullified, or destroyed, the face side of the remaining original or any copy of a citation that was retained by the officer, for any reason, before it is filed with the magistrate or with a person authorized by the magistrate to receive deposit of bail, is guilty of a misdemeanor.
(3) If, after an arrested person has signed and received a copy of a notice to appear, the arresting officer determines that, in the interest of justice, the citation or notice should be dismissed, the arresting agency may recommend, in writing, to the magistrate that the charges be dismissed. The recommendation shall cite the reasons for the recommendation and shall be filed with the court.
(4) If the magistrate makes a finding that there are grounds for dismissal, the finding shall be entered in the record and the charges dismissed.
(5) Under no circumstances shall a personal relationship with any officer, public official, or law enforcement agency be grounds for dismissal.
(k) (1) A person contesting a charge by claiming under penalty of perjury not to be the person issued the notice to appear may choose to submit a right thumbprint, or a left thumbprint if the person has a missing or disfigured right thumb, to the issuing court through the person's local law enforcement agency for comparison with the one placed on the notice to appear. A local law enforcement agency providing this service may charge the requester no more than the actual costs. The issuing court may refer the thumbprint submitted and the notice to appear to the prosecuting attorney for comparison of the thumbprints. When there is no thumbprint or fingerprint on the notice to appear, or when the comparison of thumbprints is inconclusive, the court shall refer the notice to appear or copy thereof back to the issuing agency for further investigation, unless the court finds that referral is not in the interest of justice.
(2) Upon initiation of the investigation or comparison process by referral of the court, the court shall continue the case and the speedy trial period shall be tolled for 45 days.
(3) Upon receipt of the issuing agency's or prosecuting attorney's response, the court may make a finding of factual innocence pursuant to Section 530.6 if the court determines that there is insufficient evidence that the person cited is the person charged and shall immediately notify the Department of Motor Vehicles of its determination. If the Department of Motor Vehicles determines the citation or citations in question formed the basis of a suspension or revocation of the person's driving privilege, the department shall immediately set aside the action.
(4) If the prosecuting attorney or issuing agency fails to respond to a court referral within 45 days, the court shall make a finding of factual innocence pursuant to Section 530.6, unless the court finds that a finding of factual innocence is not in the interest of justice.
(5) The citation or notice to appear may be held by the prosecuting attorney or issuing agency for future adjudication should the arrestee who received the citation or notice to appear be found.
(l) For purposes of this section, the term "arresting agency" includes any other agency designated by the arresting agency to provide booking or fingerprinting services.
(m) This section shall remain in effect only until July 1, 2021, and as of that date is repealed.
(Amended (as amended by Stats. 2018, Ch. 803, Sec. 3) by Stats. 2019, Ch. 25, Sec. 33. (SB 94) Effective June 27, 2019. Repealed as of July 1 2021, by its own provisions. See later operative version amended by Stats. 2019, Ch. 25.)
853.6.
(a) (1) In any case in which a person is arrested for an offense declared to be a misdemeanor, including a violation of any city or county ordinance, and does not demand to be taken before a magistrate, that person shall, instead of being taken before a magistrate, be released according to the procedures set forth by this chapter, although nothing prevents an officer from first booking an arrestee pursuant to subdivision (g). If the person is released, the officer or the officer's superior shall prepare in duplicate a written notice to appear in court, containing the name and address of the person, the offense charged, and the time when, and place where, the person shall appear in court. If, pursuant to subdivision (i), the person is not released prior to being booked and the officer in charge of the booking or the officer's superior determines that the person should be released, the officer or the officer's superior shall prepare a written notice to appear in a court.
(2) In any case in which a person is arrested for a misdemeanor violation of a protective court order involving domestic violence, as defined in subdivision (b) of Section 13700, or arrested pursuant to a policy, as described in Section 13701, the person shall be taken before a magistrate instead of being released according to the procedures set forth in this chapter, unless the arresting officer determines that there is not a reasonable likelihood that the offense will continue or resume or that the safety of persons or property would be imminently endangered by release of the person arrested. Prior to adopting these provisions, each city, county, or city and county shall develop a protocol to assist officers to determine when arrest and release is appropriate, rather than taking the arrested person before a magistrate. The county shall establish a committee to develop the protocol, consisting of, at a minimum, the police chief or county sheriff within the jurisdiction, the district attorney, county counsel, city attorney, representatives from domestic violence shelters, domestic violence councils, and other relevant community agencies.
(3) This subdivision shall not apply to the crimes specified in Section 1270.1, including crimes defined in each of the following:
(A) Paragraph (1) of subdivision (e) of Section 243.
(B) Section 273.5.
(C) Section 273.6, if the detained person made threats to kill or harm, has engaged in violence against, or has gone to the residence or workplace of, the protected party.
(D) Section 646.9.
(4) Nothing in this subdivision shall be construed to affect a defendant's ability to be released on bail or on their own recognizance, except as specified in Section 1270.1.
(b) Unless waived by the person, the time specified in the notice to appear shall be at least 10 days after arrest if the duplicate notice is to be filed by the officer with the magistrate.
(c) The place specified in the notice shall be the court of the magistrate before whom the person would be taken if the requirement of taking an arrested person before a magistrate were complied with, or shall be an officer authorized by that court to receive a deposit of bail.
(d) The officer shall deliver one copy of the notice to appear to the arrested person, and the arrested person, in order to secure release, shall give their written promise to

appear in court as specified in the notice by signing the duplicate notice which shall be retained by the officer, and the officer may require the arrested person, if the arrested person has no satisfactory identification, to place a right thumbprint, or a left thumbprint or fingerprint if the person has a missing or disfigured right thumb, on the notice to appear. Except for law enforcement purposes relating to the identity of the arrestee, no person or entity may sell, give away, allow the distribution of, include in a database, or create a database with, this print. Upon the signing of the duplicate notice, the arresting officer shall immediately release the person arrested from custody.
(e) The officer shall, as soon as practicable, file the duplicate notice, as follows:
(1) It shall be filed with the magistrate if the offense charged is an infraction.
(2) It shall be filed with the magistrate if the prosecuting attorney has previously directed the officer to do so.
(3) (A) The duplicate notice and underlying police reports in support of the charge or charges shall be filed with the prosecuting attorney in cases other than those specified in paragraphs (1) and (2).
(B) If the duplicate notice is filed with the prosecuting attorney, the prosecuting attorney, within their discretion, may initiate prosecution by filing the notice or a formal complaint with the magistrate specified in the duplicate notice within 25 days from the time of arrest. If the prosecution is not to be initiated, the prosecutor shall send notice to the person arrested at the address on the notice to appear. The failure by the prosecutor to file the notice or formal complaint within 25 days of the time of the arrest shall not bar further prosecution of the misdemeanor charged in the notice to appear. However, any further prosecution shall be preceded by a new and separate citation or an arrest warrant.
(C) Upon the filing of the notice with the magistrate by the officer, or the filing of the notice or formal complaint by the prosecutor, the magistrate may fix the amount of bail that in the magistrate's judgment, in accordance with Section 1275, is reasonable and sufficient for the appearance of the defendant and shall endorse upon the notice a statement signed by the magistrate in the form set forth in Section 815a. The defendant may, prior to the date upon which the defendant promised to appear in court, deposit with the magistrate the amount of bail set by the magistrate. At the time the case is called for arraignment before the magistrate, if the defendant does not appear, either in person or by counsel, the magistrate may declare the bail forfeited, and may, in the magistrate's discretion, order that no further proceedings shall be had in the case, unless the defendant has been charged with a violation of Section 374.3 or 374.7 of this code or of Section 11357, 11360, or 13002 of the Health and Safety Code, or a violation punishable under Section 5008.7 of the Public Resources Code, and the defendant has previously been convicted of a violation of that section or a violation that is punishable under that section, except in cases where the magistrate finds that undue hardship will be imposed upon the defendant by requiring the defendant to appear, the magistrate may declare the bail forfeited and order that no further proceedings be had in the case.
(D) Upon the making of the order that no further proceedings be had, all sums deposited as bail shall immediately be paid into the county treasury for distribution pursuant to Section 1463.
(f) No warrant shall be issued for the arrest of a person who has given a written promise to appear in court, unless and until the person has violated that promise or has failed to deposit bail, to appear for arraignment, trial, or judgment or to comply with the terms and provisions of the judgment, as required by law.
(g) The officer may book the arrested person at the scene or at the arresting agency prior to release or indicate on the citation that the arrested person shall appear at the arresting agency to be booked or indicate on the citation that the arrested person shall appear at the arresting agency to be fingerprinted prior to the date the arrested person appears in court. If it is indicated on the citation that the arrested person shall be booked or fingerprinted prior to the date of the person's court appearance, the arresting agency at the time of booking or fingerprinting shall provide the arrested person with verification of the booking or fingerprinting by making an entry on the citation. If it is indicated on the citation that the arrested person is to be booked or fingerprinted, the magistrate, judge, or court shall, before the proceedings begin, order the defendant to provide verification that the defendant was booked or fingerprinted by the arresting agency. If the defendant cannot produce the verification, the magistrate, judge, or court shall require that the defendant be booked or fingerprinted by the arresting agency before the next court appearance, and that the defendant provide the verification at the next court appearance unless both parties stipulate that booking or fingerprinting is not necessary.
(h) A peace officer shall use the written notice to appear procedure set forth in this section for any misdemeanor offense in which the officer has arrested a person without a warrant pursuant to Section 836 or in which the officer has taken custody of a person pursuant to Section 847.
(i) Whenever any person is arrested by a peace officer for a misdemeanor, that person shall be released according to the procedures set forth by this chapter unless one of the following is a reason for nonrelease, in which case the arresting officer may release the person, except as provided in subdivision (a), or the arresting officer shall indicate, on a form to be established by the officer's employing law enforcement agency, which of the following was a reason for the nonrelease:
(1) The person arrested was so intoxicated that they could have been a danger to themselves or to others.
(2) The person arrested required medical examination or medical care or was otherwise unable to care for their own safety.
(3) The person was arrested under one or more of the circumstances listed in Sections 40302 and 40303 of the Vehicle Code.
(4) There were one or more outstanding arrest warrants for the person.
(5) The person could not provide satisfactory evidence of personal identification.
(6) The prosecution of the offense or offenses for which the person was arrested, or the prosecution of any other offense or offenses, would be jeopardized by immediate release of the person arrested.
(7) There was a reasonable likelihood that the offense or offenses would continue or resume, or that the safety of persons or property would be imminently endangered by release of the person arrested.
(8) The person arrested demanded to be taken before a magistrate or refused to sign the notice to appear.
(9) There is reason to believe that the person would not appear at the time and place specified in the notice. The basis for this determination shall be specifically stated.
(10) (A) The person was subject to Section 1270.1.
(B) The form shall be filed with the arresting agency as soon as practicable and shall be made available to any party having custody of the arrested person, subsequent to the arresting officer, and to any person authorized by law to release the arrested person from custody before trial.
(j) (1) Once the arresting officer has prepared the written notice to appear and has delivered a copy to the person arrested, the officer shall deliver the remaining original and all copies as provided by subdivision (e).
(2) Any person, including the arresting officer and any member of the officer's department or agency, or any peace officer, who alters, conceals, modifies, nullifies, or destroys, or causes to be altered, concealed, modified, nullified, or destroyed, the face side of the remaining original or any copy of a citation that was retained by the officer, for any reason, before it is filed with the magistrate or with a person authorized by the magistrate to receive deposit of bail, is guilty of a misdemeanor.
(3) If, after an arrested person has signed and received a copy of a notice to appear, the arresting officer determines that, in the interest of justice, the citation or notice should be dismissed, the arresting agency may recommend, in writing, to the magistrate that the charges be dismissed. The recommendation shall cite the reasons for the recommendation and shall be filed with the court.
(4) If the magistrate makes a finding that there are grounds for dismissal, the finding shall be entered in the record and the charges dismissed.
(5) Under no circumstances shall a personal relationship with any officer, public official, or law enforcement agency be grounds for dismissal.
(k) (1) A person contesting a charge by claiming under penalty of perjury not to be the person issued the notice to appear may choose to submit a right thumbprint, or a left thumbprint if the person has a missing or disfigured right thumb, to the issuing court through the person's local law enforcement agency for comparison with the one placed on the notice to appear. A local law enforcement agency providing this service may charge the requester no more than the actual costs. The issuing court may refer the thumbprint submitted and the notice to appear to the prosecuting attorney for comparison of the thumbprints. When there is no thumbprint or fingerprint on the notice to appear, or when the comparison of thumbprints is inconclusive, the court shall refer the notice to appear or copy thereof back to the issuing agency for further investigation, unless the court finds that referral is not in the interest of justice.
(2) Upon initiation of the investigation or comparison process by referral of the court, the court shall continue the case and the speedy trial period shall be tolled for 45 days.
(3) Upon receipt of the issuing agency's or prosecuting attorney's response, the court may make a finding of factual innocence pursuant to Section 530.6 if the court determines that there is insufficient evidence that the person cited is the person charged and shall immediately notify the Department of Motor Vehicles of its determination. If the Department of Motor Vehicles determines the citation or citations in question formed the basis of a suspension or revocation of the person's driving privilege, the department shall immediately set aside the action.
(4) If the prosecuting attorney or issuing agency fails to respond to a court referral within 45 days, the court shall make a finding of factual innocence pursuant to Section 530.6, unless the court finds that a finding of factual innocence is not in the interest of justice.
(5) The citation or notice to appear may be held by the prosecuting attorney or issuing agency for future adjudication should the arrestee who received the citation or notice to appear be found.
(l) For purposes of this section, the term "arresting agency" includes any other agency designated by the arresting agency to provide booking or fingerprinting services.
(m) This section shall become operative July 1, 2021.
(Amended (as added by Stats. 2018, Ch. 803, Sec. 4) by Stats. 2019, Ch. 25, Sec. 34. (SB 94) Effective June 27, 2019. Section operative July 1, 2021, by its own provisions.)

853.6a.

(a) Except as provided in subdivision (b), if the person arrested appears to be under the age of 18 years, and the arrest is for a violation listed in Section 256 of the Welfare and Institutions Code, other than an offense involving a firearm, the notice under Section 853.6 shall instead provide that the person shall appear before the juvenile court, a juvenile court referee, or a juvenile hearing officer within the county in which the offense charged is alleged to have been committed, and the officer shall instead, as soon as practicable, file the duplicate notice with the prosecuting attorney unless the prosecuting attorney directs the officer to file the duplicate notice with the clerk of the juvenile court, the juvenile court referee, or the juvenile hearing officer. If the notice is filed with the prosecuting attorney, within 48 hours before the date specified on the notice to appear, the prosecutor, within his or her discretion, may initiate proceedings by filing the notice or a formal petition with the clerk of the juvenile court, or the juvenile court referee or juvenile hearing officer, before whom the person is required to appear by the notice.
(b) A juvenile court may exercise the option of not requiring a mandatory appearance of the juvenile before the court for infractions contained in the Vehicle Code, except those related to drivers' licenses as specified in Division 6 (commencing with Section 12500), those related to financial responsibility as specified in Division 7 (commencing with Section 16000), those related to speeding violations as specified in Division 11 (commencing with Section 21000) in which the speed limit was violated by 15 or more miles per hour, and those involving the use or possession of alcoholic beverages as specified in Division 11.5 (commencing with Section 23500).
(c) In counties where an Expedited Youth Accountability Program is operative, as established under Section 660.5 of the Welfare and Institutions Code, a peace officer may issue a citation and written promise to appear in juvenile court or record the minor's refusal to sign the promise to appear and serve notice to appear in juvenile court, according to the requirements and procedures provided in that section.
(d) This section may not be construed to limit the discretion of a peace officer or other person with the authority to enforce laws pertaining to juveniles to take the minor into custody pursuant to Article 15 (commencing with Section 625) of the Welfare and Institutions Code.
(Amended by Stats. 2003, Ch. 149, Sec. 68. Effective January 1, 2004.)

853.7.

Any person who willfully violates his or her written promise to appear or a lawfully granted continuance of his or her promise to appear in court is guilty of a misdemeanor, regardless of the disposition of the charge upon which he or she was originally arrested.
(Amended by Stats. 1988, Ch. 403, Sec. 2.)

853.7a.

(a) In addition to the fees authorized or required by any other provision of law, a county may, by resolution of the board of supervisors, require the courts of that county to impose an assessment of fifteen dollars ($15) upon every person who violates his or her written promise to appear or a lawfully granted continuance of his or her promise to appear in court or before a person authorized to receive a deposit of bail, or who otherwise fails to comply with any valid court order for a violation of any provision of this code or local ordinance adopted pursuant to this code. This assessment shall apply whether or not a violation of Section 853.7 is concurrently charged or a warrant of arrest is issued pursuant to Section 853.8.
(b) The clerk of the court shall deposit the amounts collected under this section in the county treasury. All money so deposited shall be used first for the development and operation of an automated county warrant system. If sufficient funds are available after appropriate expenditures to develop, modernize, and maintain the automated warrant system, a county may use the balance to fund a warrant service task force for the purpose of serving all bench warrants within the county.
(Amended by Stats. 2002, Ch. 148, Sec. 1. Effective January 1, 2003.)

853.8.

When a person signs a written promise to appear at the time and place specified in the written promise to appear and has not posted bail as provided in Section 853.6, the magistrate shall issue and have delivered for execution a warrant for his or her arrest within 20 days after his or her failure to appear as promised or within 20 days after his or her failure to appear after a lawfully granted continuance of his or her promise to appear.
(Amended by Stats. 1988, Ch. 403, Sec. 3.)

853.85.

This chapter shall not apply in any case where a person is arrested for an offense declared to be a felony.
(Added by Stats. 1992, Ch. 1009, Sec. 1. Effective January 1, 1993.)

CHAPTER 5D. Filing Complaint After Citation [853.9- 853.9.]

(Chapter 5D added by Stats. 1963, Ch. 1569.)

853.9.

(a) (1) If written notice to appear has been prepared, delivered, and filed by an officer or the prosecuting attorney with the court pursuant to Section 853.6, an exact and legible duplicate copy of the notice when filed with the magistrate, in lieu of a verified complaint, shall constitute a complaint to which the defendant may plead "guilty" or "nolo contendere."

(2) If the defendant violates his or her promise to appear in court, or does not deposit lawful bail, or pleads other than "guilty" or "nolo contendere" to the offense charged, a complaint shall be filed which shall conform to the provisions of this code and which shall be deemed to be an original complaint; and thereafter proceedings shall be had as provided by law, except that a defendant may, by an agreement in writing, subscribed by him or her and filed with the court, waive the filing of a verified complaint and elect that the prosecution may proceed upon a written notice to appear.

(b) Notwithstanding subdivision (a), if the written notice to appear has been prepared on a form approved by the Judicial Council, an exact and legible duplicate copy of the notice when filed with the magistrate shall constitute a complaint to which the defendant may enter a plea and, if the notice to appear is verified, upon which a warrant may be issued. If the notice to appear is not verified, the defendant may, at the time of arraignment, request that a verified complaint be filed.

(c) If the notice to appear issued to and signed by the arrested person is being transmitted in electronic form, the copy of the notice to appear issued to the arrested person need not include the signature of the arrested person, unless specifically requested by the arrested person.

(Amended by Stats. 2016, Ch. 19, Sec. 1. (AB 1927) Effective January 1, 2017.)

CHAPTER 6. Retaking After an Escape or Rescue [854 - 855]

(Chapter 6 enacted 1872.)

854.

If a person arrested escape or is rescued, the person from whose custody he escaped or was rescued, may immediately pursue and retake him at any time and in any place within the State.

(Enacted 1872.)

855.

To retake the person escaping or rescued, the person pursuing may break open an outer or inner door or window of a dwelling house, if, after notice of his intention, he is refused admittance.

(Enacted 1872.)

CHAPTER 6. Retaking After an Escape or Rescue [854 - 855]

(Chapter 6 enacted 1872.)

854.

If a person arrested escape or is rescued, the person from whose custody he escaped or was rescued, may immediately pursue and retake him at any time and in any place within the State.

(Enacted 1872.)

855.

To retake the person escaping or rescued, the person pursuing may break open an outer or inner door or window of a dwelling house, if, after notice of his intention, he is refused admittance.

(Enacted 1872.)

CHAPTER 7. Examination of the Case, and Discharge of the Defendant, or Holding Him to Answer [858 - 883]

(Chapter 7 enacted 1872.)

858.

(a) When the defendant first appears for arraignment on a charge of having committed a public offense, the magistrate shall immediately inform the defendant of the charge against him or her, and of his or her right to the aid of counsel in every stage of the proceedings.

(b) If it appears that the defendant may be a minor, the magistrate shall ascertain whether that is the case, and if the magistrate concludes that it is probable that the defendant is a minor, and unless the defendant is a member of the Armed Forces of the United States and the offense charged is a misdemeanor, he or she shall immediately either notify the parent or guardian of the minor of the arrest or appoint counsel to represent the minor.

(c) For the purposes of this section, the Judicial Council shall revise its military service form to include information explaining the rights under Section 1170.9 and related statutes of individuals who have active duty or veteran status and shall include a space for the local court to provide the contact information for the county veterans service office. For purposes of this section, "active duty or veteran status" includes active military duty service, reserve duty status, national guard service, and veteran status.

(d) The court shall inform the defendant that there are certain provisions of law specifically designed for individuals who have active duty or veteran status and who have been charged with a crime. The court shall inform the defendant that if the defendant is on active duty in the United States military, or is a veteran of the United States military, the defendant may request a copy of the Judicial Council military form that explains those rights and may file that form with the court so that the defendant's active duty or veteran status is on file with the court. The court shall advise the defendant that the defendant should consult with counsel prior to submitting the form and that the defendant may, without penalty, decline to provide this information to the court.

(e) If the defendant acknowledges active duty or veteran status and submits the Judicial Council military service form to the court, the defendant shall file the form with the court and serve the form on the prosecuting attorney and defense counsel. The form may be used to assist in determining eligibility for services pursuant to Section 1170.9. The court shall transmit a copy of the form to the county veterans service officer for confirmation of the defendant's military service. The court shall also transmit a copy of the form to the Department of Veterans Affairs.

(Amended by Stats. 2014, Ch. 655, Sec. 1. (SB 1110) Effective January 1, 2015.)

858.5.

(a) In any case in which a defendant is, on his demand, brought before a magistrate pursuant to Section 822 after arrest for a misdemeanor Vehicle Code violation, the magistrate shall give such instructions to the defendant as required by law and inform the defendant of his rights under this section, and, if the defendant desires to plead guilty or nolo contendere to the charge in the complaint, he may so advise the magistrate. If the magistrate determines that such plea would be in the interest of justice, he shall direct the defendant to appear before a specified appropriate court in the county in which defendant has been arrested at a designated certain time, which in no case shall be more than 10 calendar days from the date of arrest, for plea and sentencing. The magistrate shall request the court in which the complaint has been filed to transmit a certified copy of the complaint and any citation and any factual report which may have been prepared by the law enforcement agency that investigated the case to the court in which defendant is to appear for plea and sentencing. If the court of which the request is made deems such action to be in the interest of justice, and the district attorney of the county in which that court sits, after notice from the court of the request it has received, does not object to such action, the court shall immediately transmit a certified copy of the complaint and the report of the law enforcement agency that investigated the case, and, if not, shall advise the requesting magistrate of its decision not to take such action.

When defendant appears for plea and sentencing, and if a copy of the complaint has been transmitted, the court shall read the copy of the complaint to him, and the defendant may plead guilty or nolo contendere. Such court shall have jurisdiction to accept the plea and impose a sentence. Such court shall notify the court in which the complaint was originally filed of the disposition of the case. If defendant does not plead guilty or nolo contendere, or if transmittal of a copy of the complaint has been refused or if a copy of the complaint has not been received, the court shall terminate the proceedings under this section and shall direct the defendant to appear before the court or magistrate by whom the warrant was issued on or before a certain day which in no case shall be more than five days after the date such direction is made.

(b) Any fines imposed by a court which is given authority to sentence pursuant to this section shall be remitted to the court in which the complaint was originally filed for disposition as required by law. The county of the sentencing court shall bear all costs incurred incident to acceptance of the plea and sentencing, and no part of such costs shall be deducted from the fine remitted to the court in which the complaint was filed.

(Added by Stats. 1965, Ch. 947.)

858.7.

(a) In any case in which the defendant has been convicted of a misdemeanor and is serving a sentence as a result of such conviction and there has been filed and is pending in another county a complaint charging him with a misdemeanor Vehicle Code violation, the defendant may appear before the court that sentenced him, and a magistrate of that court shall give such instructions to the defendant as required by law and inform the defendant of his rights under this section, and, if the defendant desires to plead guilty or nolo contendere to the charge in the complaint, he may so advise the magistrate. If the magistrate determines that such plea would be in the interest of justice, he shall direct the defendant to appear before a specified appropriate court in the county in which defendant is serving his sentence at a designated certain time for plea and sentencing. The magistrate shall request the court in which the complaint has been filed to transmit a certified copy of the complaint and any citation and any factual report which may have been prepared by the law enforcement agency that investigated the case to the court in which defendant is to appear for plea and sentencing. If the court of which the request is made deems such action to be in the interest of justice, and the district attorney of the county in which that court sits, after notice from the court of the request it has received, does not object to such action, the court shall immediately transmit a certified copy of the complaint and any report of the law enforcement agency that investigated the case, and, if not, shall advise the requesting magistrate of its decision not to take such action.

When defendant appears for plea and sentencing, and if a copy of the complaint has been transmitted, the court shall read the copy of the complaint to him, and the defendant may plead guilty or nolo contendere. Such court shall have jurisdiction to accept the plea and impose a sentence. Such court shall notify the court in which the complaint was originally filed of the disposition of the case. If defendant does not plead guilty or nolo contendere, or if transmittal of a copy of the complaint has been refused or if a copy of the complaint has not been received, the court shall terminate the proceedings under this section and shall direct the defendant to appear before the court in which the complaint was filed and is pending on or before a certain day.

(b) (1) Any fines imposed by a court which is given authority to sentence pursuant to this section shall be remitted to the court in which the complaint was originally filed for disposition as required by law. Except as otherwise provided in paragraph (2) of this subdivision, the county of the sentencing court shall bear all costs incurred incident to acceptance of the plea and sentencing, and no part of such costs shall be deducted from the fine remitted to the court in which the complaint was filed.

(2) In any case in which a defendant is sentenced to imprisonment pursuant to this section, and as a result of such sentence he is required to be imprisoned for a time in addition to, and not concurrent with, the time he is imprisoned as a result of the sentence he is otherwise serving, the county in which the complaint was originally filed shall bear the cost of such additional time of imprisonment that the defendant is required to serve. Such cost may be deducted from any fine required to be remitted pursuant to paragraph (1) of this subdivision to the court in which the complaint was originally filed.

(c) As used in this section, "complaint" includes, but is not limited to, a notice to appear which is within the provisions of Section 40513 of the Vehicle Code.

(Added by Stats. 1968, Ch. 973.)

859.

When the defendant is charged with the commission of a felony by a written complaint subscribed under oath and on file in a court within the county in which the felony is triable, he or she shall, without unnecessary delay, be taken before a magistrate of the court in which the complaint is on file. The magistrate shall immediately deliver to the defendant a copy of the complaint, inform the defendant that he or she has the right to have the assistance of counsel, ask the defendant if he or she desires the assistance of counsel, and allow the defendant reasonable time to send for counsel. However, in a capital case, the court shall inform the defendant that the defendant must be represented in court by counsel at all stages of the preliminary and trial proceedings and that the representation will be at the defendant's expense if the defendant is able to employ counsel or at public expense if he or she is unable to employ counsel, inquire of him or her whether he or she is able to employ counsel and, if so, whether the defendant desires to employ counsel of the defendant's choice or to have counsel assigned for him or her, and allow the defendant a reasonable time to send for his or her chosen or assigned counsel. If the defendant desires and is unable to employ counsel, the court shall assign counsel to defend him or her; in a capital case, if the defendant is able to employ counsel and either refuses to employ counsel or appears without counsel after having had a reasonable time to employ counsel, the court shall assign counsel to defend him or her. If it appears that the defendant may be a minor, the magistrate shall ascertain whether that is the case, and if the magistrate concludes that it is probable that the defendant is a minor, he or she shall immediately either notify

the parent or guardian of the minor, by telephone or messenger, of the arrest, or appoint counsel to represent the minor.
(Amended by Stats. 1998, Ch. 931, Sec. 368. Effective September 28, 1998. Note: This section was added on June 5, 1990, by initiative Prop. 115.)

859.1.

(a) In any criminal proceeding in which the defendant is charged with any offense specified in Section 868.8 on a minor under the age of 16 years, or a dependent person with a substantial cognitive impairment, as defined in paragraph (3) of subdivision (f) of Section 288, the court shall, upon motion of the prosecuting attorney, conduct a hearing to determine whether the testimony of, and testimony relating to, a minor or dependent person shall be closed to the public in order to protect the minor's or the dependent person's reputation.
(b) In making this determination, the court shall consider all of the following:
(1) The nature and seriousness of the offense.
(2) The age of the minor, or the level of cognitive development of the dependent person.
(3) The extent to which the size of the community would preclude the anonymity of the victim.
(4) The likelihood of public opprobrium due to the status of the victim.
(5) Whether there is an overriding public interest in having an open hearing.
(6) Whether the prosecution has demonstrated a substantial probability that the identity of the witness would otherwise be disclosed to the public during that proceeding, and demonstrated a substantial probability that the disclosure of his or her identity would cause serious harm to the witness.
(7) Whether the witness has disclosed information concerning the case to the public through press conferences, public meetings, or other means.
(8) Other factors the court may deem necessary to protect the interests of justice.
(Amended by Stats. 2004, Ch. 823, Sec. 11. Effective January 1, 2005.)

859.5.

(a) Except as otherwise provided in this section, a custodial interrogation of any person, including an adult or a minor, who is in a fixed place of detention, and suspected of committing murder, as listed in Section 187 or 189 of this code, or paragraph (1) of subdivision (b) of Section 707 of the Welfare and Institutions Code, shall be electronically recorded in its entirety. A statement that is electronically recorded as required pursuant to this section creates a rebuttable presumption that the electronically recorded statement was, in fact, given and was accurately recorded by the prosecution's witnesses, provided that the electronic recording was made of the custodial interrogation in its entirety and the statement is otherwise admissible.
(b) The requirement for the electronic recordation of a custodial interrogation pursuant to this section shall not apply under any of the following circumstances:
(1) Electronic recording is not feasible because of exigent circumstances. An explanation of the exigent circumstances shall be documented in the police report.
(2) The person to be interrogated states that he or she will speak to a law enforcement officer only if the interrogation is not electronically recorded. If feasible, that statement shall be electronically recorded. The requirement also does not apply if the person being interrogated indicates during interrogation that he or she will not participate in further interrogation unless electronic recording ceases. If the person being interrogated refuses to record any statement, the officer shall document that refusal in writing.
(3) The custodial interrogation occurred in another jurisdiction and was conducted by law enforcement officers of that jurisdiction in compliance with the law of that jurisdiction, unless the interrogation was conducted with intent to avoid the requirements of this section.
(4) The interrogation occurs when no law enforcement officer conducting the interrogation has knowledge of facts and circumstances that would lead an officer to reasonably believe that the individual being interrogated may have committed murder for which this section requires that a custodial interrogation be recorded. If during a custodial interrogation, the individual reveals facts and circumstances giving a law enforcement officer conducting the interrogation reason to believe that murder has been committed, continued custodial interrogation concerning that offense shall be electronically recorded pursuant to this section.
(5) A law enforcement officer conducting the interrogation or the officer's superior reasonably believes that electronic recording would disclose the identity of a confidential informant or jeopardize the safety of an officer, the individual being interrogated, or another individual. An explanation of the circumstances shall be documented in the police report.
(6) The failure to create an electronic recording of the entire custodial interrogation was the result of a malfunction of the recording device, despite reasonable maintenance of the equipment, and timely repair or replacement was not feasible.
(7) The questions presented to a person by law enforcement personnel and the person's responsive statements were part of a routine processing or booking of that person. Electronic recording is not required for spontaneous statements made in response to questions asked during the routine processing of the arrest of the person.
(8) The interrogation of a person who is in custody on a charge of a violation of Section 187 or 189 of this code or paragraph (1) of subdivision (b) of Section 707 of the Welfare and Institutions Code if the interrogation is not related to any of these offenses. If, during the interrogation, any information concerning one of these offenses is raised or mentioned, continued custodial interrogation concerning that offense shall be electronically recorded pursuant to this section.
(c) If the prosecution relies on an exception in subdivision (b) to justify a failure to make an electronic recording of a custodial interrogation, the prosecution shall show by clear and convincing evidence that the exception applies.
(d) A person's statements that were not electronically recorded pursuant to this section may be admitted into evidence in a criminal proceeding or in a juvenile court proceeding, as applicable, if the court finds that all of the following apply:
(1) The statements are admissible under applicable rules of evidence.
(2) The prosecution has proven by clear and convincing evidence that the statements were made voluntarily.
(3) Law enforcement personnel made a contemporaneous audio or audio and visual recording of the reason for not making an electronic recording of the statements. This provision does not apply if it was not feasible for law enforcement personnel to make that recording.
(4) The prosecution has proven by clear and convincing evidence that one or more of the circumstances described in subdivision (b) existed at the time of the custodial interrogation.
(e) Unless the court finds that an exception in subdivision (b) applies, all of the following remedies shall be granted as relief for noncompliance:
(1) Failure to comply with any of the requirements of this section shall be considered by the court in adjudicating motions to suppress a statement of a defendant made during or after a custodial interrogation.
(2) Failure to comply with any of the requirements of this section shall be admissible in support of claims that a defendant's statement was involuntary or is unreliable, provided the evidence is otherwise admissible.
(3) If the court finds that a defendant was subject to a custodial interrogation in violation of subdivision (a), the court shall provide the jury with an instruction, to be developed by the Judicial Council, that advises the jury to view with caution the statements made in that custodial interrogation.
(f) The interrogating entity shall maintain the original or an exact copy of an electronic recording made of a custodial interrogation until a conviction for any offense relating to the interrogation is final and all direct and habeas corpus appeals are exhausted or the prosecution for that offense is barred by law or, in a juvenile court proceeding, as otherwise provided in subdivision (b) of Section 626.8 of the Welfare and Institutions Code. The interrogating entity may make one or more true, accurate, and complete copies of the electronic recording in a different format.
(g) For the purposes of this section, the following terms have the following meanings:
(1) "Custodial interrogation" means any interrogation in a fixed place of detention involving a law enforcement officer's questioning that is reasonably likely to elicit incriminating responses, and in which a reasonable person in the subject's position would consider himself or herself to be in custody, beginning when a person should have been advised of his or her constitutional rights, including the right to remain silent, the right to have counsel present during any interrogation, and the right to have counsel appointed if the person is unable to afford counsel, and ending when the questioning has completely finished.
(2) (A) For the purposes of the custodial interrogation of a minor, pursuant to subdivision (a) or (b), "electronically recorded," "electronic recordation," and "electronic recording" refer to a video recording that accurately records a custodial interrogation.
(B) For the purposes of the custodial interrogation of an adult, pursuant to subdivision (a) or (b), "electronically recorded," "electronic recordation," and "electronic recording" refer to a video or audio recording that accurately records a custodial interrogation. The Legislature encourages law enforcement agencies to use video recording when available.
(3) "Fixed place of detention" means a fixed location under the control of a law enforcement agency where an individual is held in detention in connection with a criminal offense that has been, or may be, filed against that person, including a jail, police or sheriff's station, holding cell, correctional or detention facility, juvenile hall, or a facility of the Division of Juvenile Facilities.
(4) "Law enforcement officer" means a person employed by a law enforcement agency whose duties include enforcing criminal laws or investigating criminal activity, or any other person who is acting at the request or direction of that person.
(Amended by Stats. 2016, Ch. 791, Sec. 2. (SB 1389) Effective January 1, 2017.)

859.7.

(a) All law enforcement agencies and prosecutorial entities shall adopt regulations for conducting photo lineups and live lineups with eyewitnesses. The regulations shall be developed to ensure reliable and accurate suspect identifications. In order to ensure reliability and accuracy, the regulations shall comply with, at a minimum, the following requirements:
(1) Prior to conducting the identification procedure, and as close in time to the incident as possible, the eyewitness shall provide the description of the perpetrator of the offense.
(2) The investigator conducting the identification procedure shall use blind administration or blinded administration during the identification procedure.
(3) The investigator shall state in writing the reason that the presentation of the lineup was not conducted using blind administration, if applicable.
(4) An eyewitness shall be instructed of the following, prior to any identification procedure:
(A) The perpetrator may or may not be among the persons in the identification procedure.
(B) The eyewitness should not feel compelled to make an identification.
(C) An identification or failure to make an identification will not end the investigation.
(5) An identification procedure shall be composed so that the fillers generally fit the eyewitness' description of the perpetrator. In the case of a photo lineup, the photograph of the person suspected as the perpetrator should, if practicable, resemble his or her appearance at the time of the offense and not unduly stand out.
(6) In a photo lineup, writings or information concerning any previous arrest of the person suspected as the perpetrator shall not be visible to the eyewitness.
(7) Only one suspected perpetrator shall be included in any identification procedure.
(8) All eyewitnesses shall be separated when viewing an identification procedure.
(9) Nothing shall be said to the eyewitness that might influence the eyewitness' identification of the person suspected as the perpetrator.
(10) If the eyewitness identifies a person he or she believes to be the perpetrator, all of the following shall apply:
(A) The investigator shall immediately inquire as to the eyewitness' confidence level in the accuracy of the identification and record in writing, verbatim, what the eyewitness says.
(B) Information concerning the identified person shall not be given to the eyewitness prior to obtaining the eyewitness' statement of confidence level and documenting the exact words of the eyewitness.
(C) The officer shall not validate or invalidate the eyewitness' identification.
(11) An electronic recording shall be made that includes both audio and visual representations of the identification procedures. Whether it is feasible to make a recording with both audio and visual representations shall be determined on a case-by-case basis. When it is not feasible to make a recording with both audio and visual representations, audio recording may be used. When audio recording without video recording is used, the investigator shall state in writing the reason that video recording was not feasible.
(b) Nothing in this section is intended to affect policies for field show up procedures.
(c) For purposes of this section, the following terms have the following meanings:
(1) "Blind administration" means the administrator of an eyewitness identification procedure does not know the identity of the suspect.
(2) "Blinded administration" means the administrator of an eyewitness identification procedure may know who the suspect is, but does not know where the suspect, or his or her photo, as applicable, has been placed or positioned in the identification procedure through the use of any of the following:
(A) An automated computer program that prevents the administrator from seeing which photos the eyewitness is viewing until after the identification procedure is completed.
(B) The folder shuffle method, which refers to a system for conducting a photo lineup by placing photographs in folders, randomly numbering the folders, shuffling the folders, and then presenting the folders sequentially so that the administrator cannot see or track which photograph is being presented to the eyewitness until after the procedure is completed.
(C) Any other procedure that achieves neutral administration and prevents the lineup administrator from knowing where the suspect or his or her photo, as applicable, has been placed or positioned in the identification procedure.
(3) "Eyewitness" means a person whose identification of another person may be relevant in a criminal investigation.
(4) "Field show up" means a procedure in which a suspect is detained shortly after the commission of a crime and who, based on his or her appearance, his or her distance from the crime scene, or other circumstantial evidence, is suspected of having just committed a crime. In these situations, the victim or an eyewitness is brought to the scene of the detention and is asked if the detainee was the perpetrator.
(5) "Filler" means either a person or a photograph of a person who is not suspected of an offense and is included in an identification procedure.
(6) "Identification procedure" means either a photo lineup or a live lineup.
(7) "Investigator" means the person conducting the identification procedure.
(8) "Live lineup" means a procedure in which a group of persons, including the person suspected as the perpetrator of an offense and other persons not suspected of the offense, are displayed to an eyewitness for the purpose of determining whether the eyewitness is able to identify the suspect as the perpetrator.

(9) "Photo lineup" means a procedure in which an array of photographs, including a photograph of the person suspected as the perpetrator of an offense and additional photographs of other persons not suspected of the offense, are displayed to an eyewitness for the purpose of determining whether the eyewitness is able to identify the suspect as the perpetrator.

(d) Nothing in this section is intended to preclude the admissibility of any relevant evidence or to affect the standards governing the admissibility of evidence under the United States Constitution.

(e) This section shall become operative on January 1, 2020.

(Added by Stats. 2018, Ch. 977, Sec. 2. (SB 923) Effective January 1, 2019. Section operative January 1, 2020, by its own provisions.)

859a.

(a) If the public offense charged is a felony not punishable with death, the magistrate shall immediately upon the appearance of counsel for the defendant read the complaint to the defendant and ask him or her whether he or she pleads guilty or not guilty to the offense charged therein and to a previous conviction or convictions of crime if charged. While the charge remains pending before the magistrate and when the defendant's counsel is present, the defendant may plead guilty to the offense charged, or, with the consent of the magistrate and the district attorney or other counsel for the people, plead nolo contendere to the offense charged or plead guilty or nolo contendere to any other offense the commission of which is necessarily included in that with which he or she is charged, or to an attempt to commit the offense charged and to the previous conviction or convictions of crime if charged upon a plea of guilty or nolo contendere. The magistrate may then fix a reasonable bail as provided by this code, and upon failure to deposit the bail or surety, shall immediately commit the defendant to the sheriff. Upon accepting the plea of guilty or nolo contendere the magistrate shall certify the case, including a copy of all proceedings therein and any testimony that in his or her discretion he or she may require to be taken, to the court in which judgment is to be pronounced at the time specified under subdivision (b), and thereupon the proceedings shall be had as if the defendant had pleaded guilty in that court. This subdivision shall not be construed to authorize the receiving of a plea of guilty or nolo contendere from any defendant not represented by counsel. If the defendant subsequently files a written motion to withdraw the plea under Section 1018, the motion shall be heard and determined by the court before which the plea was entered.

(b) Notwithstanding Section 1191 or 1203, the magistrate shall, upon the receipt of a plea of guilty or nolo contendere and upon the performance of the other duties of the magistrate under this section, immediately appoint a time for pronouncing judgment in the superior court and refer the case to the probation officer if eligible for probation, as prescribed in Section 1191.

(Amended by Stats. 2002, Ch. 784, Sec. 533. Effective January 1, 2003.)

859b.

At the time the defendant appears before the magistrate for arraignment, if the public offense is a felony to which the defendant has not pleaded guilty in accordance with Section 859a, the magistrate, immediately upon the appearance of counsel, or if none appears, after waiting a reasonable time therefor as provided in Section 859, shall set a time for the examination of the case and shall allow not less than two days, excluding Sundays and holidays, for the district attorney and the defendant to prepare for the examination. The magistrate shall also issue subpoenas, duly subscribed, for witnesses within the state, required either by the prosecution or the defense.

Both the defendant and the people have the right to a preliminary examination at the earliest possible time, and unless both waive that right or good cause for a continuance is found as provided for in Section 1050, the preliminary examination shall be held within 10 court days of the date the defendant is arraigned or pleads, whichever occurs later, or within 10 court days of the date criminal proceedings are reinstated pursuant to Chapter 6 (commencing with Section 1367) of Title 10 of Part 2.

Whenever the defendant is in custody, the magistrate shall dismiss the complaint if the preliminary examination is set or continued beyond 10 court days from the time of the arraignment, plea, or reinstatement of criminal proceedings pursuant to Chapter 6 (commencing with Section 1367) of Title 10 of Part 2, and the defendant has remained in custody for 10 or more court days solely on that complaint, unless either of the following occur:

(a) The defendant personally waives his or her right to preliminary examination within the 10 court days.

(b) The prosecution establishes good cause for a continuance beyond the 10-court-day period.

For purposes of this subdivision, "good cause" includes, but is not limited to, those cases involving allegations that a violation of one or more of the sections specified in subdivision (a) of Section 11165.1 or in Section 11165.6 has occurred and the prosecuting attorney assigned to the case has another trial, preliminary hearing, or motion to suppress in progress in that court or another court. Any continuance under this paragraph shall be limited to a maximum of three additional court days.

If the preliminary examination is set or continued beyond the 10-court-day period, the defendant shall be released pursuant to Section 1318 unless:

(1) The defendant requests the setting of continuance of the preliminary examination beyond the 10-court-day period.

(2) The defendant is charged with a capital offense in a cause where the proof is evident and the presumption great.

(3) A witness necessary for the preliminary examination is unavailable due to the actions of the defendant.

(4) The illness of counsel.

(5) The unexpected engagement of counsel in a jury trial.

(6) Unforeseen conflicts of interest which require appointment of new counsel.

The magistrate shall dismiss the complaint if the preliminary examination is set or continued more than 60 days from the date of the arraignment, plea, or reinstatement of criminal proceedings pursuant to Chapter 6 (commencing with Section 1367) of Title 10 of Part 2, unless the defendant personally waives his or her right to a preliminary examination within the 60 days.

(Amended by Stats. 1996, Ch. 122, Sec. 1. Effective January 1, 1997.)

859c.

Procedures under this code that provide for superior court review of a challenged ruling or order made by a superior court judge or a magistrate shall be performed by a superior court judge other than the judge or magistrate who originally made the ruling or order, unless agreed to by the parties.

(Added by Stats. 1998, Ch. 931, Sec. 370. Effective September 28, 1998.)

860.

At the time set for the examination of the case, if the public offense is a felony punishable with death, or is a felony to which the defendant has not pleaded guilty in accordance with Section 859a of this code, then, if the defendant requires the aid of counsel, the magistrate must allow the defendant a reasonable time to send for counsel, and may postpone the examination for not less than two nor more than five days for that purpose. The magistrate must, immediately after the appearance of counsel, or if, after waiting a reasonable time therefor, none appears, proceed to examine the case; provided, however, that a defendant represented by counsel may when brought before the magistrate as provided in Section 858 or at any time subsequent thereto, waive the right to an examination before such magistrate, and thereupon it shall be the duty of the magistrate to make an order holding the defendant to answer, and it shall be the duty of the district attorney within 15 days thereafter, to file in the superior court of the county in which the offense is triable the information; provided, further, however, that nothing

contained herein shall prevent the district attorney nor the magistrate from requiring that an examination be held as provided in this chapter.

(Amended by Stats. 1998, Ch. 931, Sec. 371. Effective September 28, 1998.)

861.

(a) The preliminary examination shall be completed at one session or the complaint shall be dismissed, unless the magistrate, for good cause shown by affidavit, postpones it. The postponement shall not be for more than 10 court days, unless either of the following occur:

(1) The defendant personally waives his or her right to a continuous preliminary examination.

(2) The prosecution establishes good cause for a postponement beyond the 10-court-day period. If the magistrate postpones the preliminary examination beyond the 10-court-day period, and the defendant is in custody, the defendant shall be released pursuant to subdivision (b) of Section 859b.

(b) The preliminary examination shall not be postponed beyond 60 days from the date the motion to postpone the examination is granted, unless by consent or on motion of the defendant.

(c) Nothing in this section shall preclude the magistrate from interrupting the preliminary examination to conduct brief court matters so long as a substantial majority of the court's time is devoted to the preliminary examination.

(d) A request for a continuance of the preliminary examination that is made by the defendant or his or her attorney of record for the purpose of filing a motion pursuant to paragraph (2) of subdivision (f) of Section 1538.5 shall be deemed a personal waiver of the defendant's right to a continuous preliminary examination.

(Amended by Stats. 1997, Ch. 279, Sec. 2. Effective January 1, 1998.)

861.5.

Notwithstanding subdivision (a) of Section 861, the magistrate may postpone the preliminary examination for one court day in order to accommodate the special physical, mental, or emotional needs of a child witness who is 10 years of age or younger or a dependent person, as defined in paragraph (3) of subdivision (f) of Section 288. The magistrate shall admonish both the prosecution and defense against coaching the witness prior to the witness' next appearance in the preliminary examination.

(Amended by Stats. 2005, Ch. 279, Sec. 7. Effective January 1, 2006.)

862.

If a postponement is had, the magistrate must commit the defendant for examination, admit him to bail or discharge him from custody upon the deposit of money as provided in this Code, as security for his appearance at the time to which the examination is postponed.

(Enacted 1872.)

863.

The commitment for examination is made by an indorsement, signed by the magistrate on the warrant of arrest, to the following effect: "The within named A. B. having been brought before me under this warrant, is committed for examination to the Sheriff of _____." If the Sheriff is not present, the defendant may be committed to the custody of a peace officer.

(Enacted 1872.)

864.

At the examination, the magistrate must first read to the defendant the depositions of the witnesses examined on taking the information.

(Amended by Stats. 1963, Ch. 1174.)

865.

The witnesses must be examined in the presence of the defendant, and may be cross-examined in his behalf.

(Enacted 1872.)

866.

(a) When the examination of witnesses on the part of the people is closed, any witness the defendant may produce shall be sworn and examined.

Upon the request of the prosecuting attorney, the magistrate shall require an offer of proof from the defense as to the testimony expected from the witness. The magistrate shall not permit the testimony of any defense witness unless the offer of proof discloses to the satisfaction of the magistrate, in his or her sound discretion, that the testimony of that witness, if believed, would be reasonably likely to establish an affirmative defense, negate an element of a crime charged, or impeach the testimony of a prosecution witness or the statement of a declarant testified to by a prosecution witness.

(b) It is the purpose of a preliminary examination to establish whether there exists probable cause to believe that the defendant has committed a felony. The examination shall not be used for purposes of discovery.

(c) This section shall not be construed to compel or authorize the taking of depositions of witnesses.

(Amended June 5, 1990, by initiative Proposition 115, Sec. 16.)

866.5.

The defendant may not be examined at the examination, unless he is represented by counsel, or unless he waives his right to counsel after being advised at such examination of his right to aid of counsel.

(Added by Stats. 1953, Ch. 1482.)

867.

While a witness is under examination, the magistrate shall, upon motion of either party, exclude all potential and actual witness who have not been examined.

The magistrate shall also order the witnesses not to converse with each other until they are all examined. The magistrate may also order, where feasible, that the witnesses be kept separated from each other until they are all examined.

This section does not apply to the investigating officer or the investigator for the defendant, nor does it apply to officers having custody of persons brought before the magistrate.

Either party may challenge the exclusion of any person under this section. Upon motion of either party, the magistrate shall hold a hearing, on the record, to determine if the person sought to be excluded is, in fact, a person excludable under this section.

(Amended by Stats. 1986, Ch. 868, Sec. 1.)

868.

The examination shall be open and public. However, upon the request of the defendant and a finding by the magistrate that exclusion of the public is necessary in order to protect the defendant's right to a fair and impartial trial, the magistrate shall exclude from the examination every person except the clerk, court reporter and bailiff, the prosecutor and his or her counsel, the Attorney General, the district attorney of the county, the investigating officer, the officer having custody of a prisoner witness while the prisoner is testifying, the defendant and his or her counsel, the officer having the defendant in custody, and a person chosen by the prosecuting witness who is not himself or herself a witness but who is present to provide the prosecuting witness moral support, provided that the person so chosen shall not discuss prior to or during the preliminary examination the testimony of the prosecuting witness with any person, other than the prosecuting witness, who is a witness in the examination. Upon motion of the prosecution, members of the alleged victim's family shall be entitled to be present and seated during the examination. The court shall grant the motion unless the magistrate finds that the exclusion is necessary to protect the defendant's right to a fair and impartial trial, or unless information provided by the defendant or noticed by the court establishes that there is a reasonable likelihood that the attendance of members of the alleged victim's family poses a risk of affecting the content of the testimony of the victim or any other witness. The court shall admonish members of the alleged victim's family who are present and seated during the examination not to discuss any testimony with family members, witnesses, or the public. Nothing in this section shall affect the exclusion of witnesses as provided in Section 867 of the Penal Code.

For purposes of this section, members of the alleged victim's family shall include the alleged victim's spouse, parents, legal guardian, children, or siblings.

(Amended by Stats. 1988, Ch. 277, Sec. 2.)

868.4.

(a) If requested by either party in a criminal or juvenile hearing, and if a therapy or facility dog is available to the party within the jurisdiction of the judicial district in which the case is being adjudicated, the following individuals shall be afforded the opportunity to have a therapy or facility dog accompany him or her while testifying in court, subject to the approval of the court:

(1) A child witness in a court proceeding involving any serious felony, as defined in subdivision (c) of Section 1192.7, or any violent felony, as defined in subdivision (c) of Section 667.5.

(2) A victim who is entitled to support persons pursuant to Section 868.5, in addition to any support persons selected pursuant to that section.

(b) Before a therapy or facility dog may be used pursuant to subdivision (a), the party seeking to utilize the therapy or facility dog shall file a motion with the court, which shall include the following:

(1) The training or credentials of the therapy or facility dog.

(2) The training of the therapy or facility dog handler.

(3) Facts justifying that the presence of the therapy or facility dog may reduce anxiety or otherwise be helpful to the witness while testifying.

(c) If a party, pursuant to subdivision (b), makes a showing that the therapy or facility dog and handler are suitably qualified and will reasonably assist the testifying witness, the court may grant the motion, unless the court finds the use of a therapy or facility dog would cause undue prejudice to the defendant or would be unduly disruptive to the court proceeding.

(d) The court shall take appropriate measures to make the presence of the therapy or facility dog as unobtrusive and nondisruptive as possible, including requiring the dog to be accompanied by a handler in the courtroom at all times.

(e) If a therapy or facility dog is used during a criminal jury trial, the court shall, upon request, issue an appropriate jury instruction designed to prevent prejudice for or against any party.

(f) This section does not prevent the court from removing or excluding a therapy or facility dog from the courtroom to maintain order or to ensure the fair presentation of evidence, as stated on the record.

(g) (1) It is the intent of the Legislature in adding this section to codify the holding in People v. Chenault (2014) 227 Cal.App.4th 1503 with respect to allowing an individual witness to have a support dog accompany him or her when testifying in proceedings as provided in subdivision (a).

(2) Nothing in this section abrogates the holding in People v. Chenault regarding the need to present appropriate jury instructions.

(3) Nothing in this section limits the use of a service dog, as defined in Section 54.1 of the Civil Code, by a person with a disability.

(h) As used in this section, the following definitions shall apply:

(1) "Child witness" means any witness who is under the age of 18 at the time he or she testifies.

(2) "Facility dog" means a dog that has successfully completed a training program in providing emotional comfort in a high-stress environment for the purpose of enhancing the ability of a witness to speak in a judicial proceeding and reducing his or her stress level, provided by an assistance dog organization accredited by Assistance Dogs International or a similar nonprofit organization that sets standards of training for dogs, and that has passed a public access test for service animals.

(3) "Handler" means a person who has successfully completed training on offering an animal for assistance purposes from an organization accredited by Assistance Dogs International, Therapy Dogs Incorporated, or a similar nonprofit organization, and has received additional training on policies and protocols of the court and the responsibilities of a courtroom dog handler.

(4) "Therapy dog" means a dog that has successfully completed training, certification, or evaluation in providing emotional support therapy in settings including, but not limited to, hospitals, nursing homes, and schools, provided by the American Kennel Club, Therapy Dogs Incorporated, or a similar nonprofit organization, and has been performing the duties of a therapy dog for not less than one year.

(Added by Stats. 2017, Ch. 290, Sec. 1. (AB 411) Effective January 1, 2018.)

868.5.

(a) Notwithstanding any other law, a prosecuting witness in a case involving a violation or attempted violation of Section 187, 203, 205, or 207, subdivision (b) of Section 209, Section 211, 215, 220, 236.1, 240, 242, 243.4, 245, 261, 262, 266, 266a, 266b, 266c, 266d, 266e, 266f, 266g, 266h, 266i, 266j, 266k, 267, 269, 273a, 273d, 273.5, 273.6, 278, 278.5, 285, 286, 287, 288, 288.5, 288.7, 289, 311.1, 311.2, 311.3, 311.4, 311.5, 311.6, 311.10, 311.11, 422, 646.9, or 647.6, former Section 277, 288a, or 647a, subdivision (1) of Section 314, or subdivision (b), (d), or (e) of Section 368 when the prosecuting witness is the elder or dependent adult, shall be entitled, for support, to the attendance of up to two persons of his or her own choosing, one of whom may be a witness, at the preliminary hearing and at the trial, or at a juvenile court proceeding, during the testimony of the prosecuting witness. Only one of those support persons may accompany the witness to the witness stand, although the other may remain in the courtroom during the witness' testimony. The person or persons so chosen shall not be a person described in Section 1070 of the Evidence Code unless the person or persons are related to the prosecuting witness as a parent, guardian, or sibling and do not make notes during the hearing or proceeding.

(b) If the person or persons so chosen are also witnesses, the prosecution shall present evidence that the person's attendance is both desired by the prosecuting witness for support and will be helpful to the prosecuting witness. Upon that showing, the court shall grant the request unless information presented by the defendant or noticed by the court establishes that the support person's attendance during the testimony of the prosecuting witness would pose a substantial risk of influencing or affecting the content of that testimony. In the case of a juvenile court proceeding, the judge shall inform the support person or persons that juvenile court proceedings are confidential and may not be discussed with anyone not in attendance at the proceedings. In all cases, the judge shall admonish the support person or persons to not prompt, sway, or influence the witness in any way. Nothing in this section shall preclude a court from exercising its discretion to remove a person from the courtroom whom it believes is prompting, swaying, or influencing the witness.

(c) The testimony of the person or persons so chosen who are also witnesses shall be presented before the testimony of the prosecuting witness. The prosecuting witness shall be excluded from the courtroom during that testimony. Whenever the evidence given by that person or those persons would be subject to exclusion because it has been given before the corpus delicti has been established, the evidence shall be admitted subject to the court's or the defendant's motion to strike that evidence from the record if the corpus delicti is not later established by the testimony of the prosecuting witness.

(Amended by Stats. 2018, Ch. 423, Sec. 80. (SB 1494) Effective January 1, 2019.)

868.6.

(a) It is the purpose of this section to provide a nonthreatening environment for minors involved in the judicial system in order to better enable them to speak freely and accurately of the experiences that are the subject of judicial inquiry.

(b) Each county is encouraged to provide a room, located within, or within a reasonable distance from, the courthouse, for the use of minors under the age of 16. Should any such room reach full occupancy, preference shall be given to minors under the age of 16 whose appearance has been subpoenaed by the court. The room may be multipurpose in character. The county may seek the assistance of civic groups in the furnishing of the room and the provision of volunteers to aid in its operation and maintenance. If a county newly constructs, substantially remodels or refurbishes any courthouse or facility used as a courthouse on or after January 1, 1988, that courthouse or facility shall contain the room described in this subdivision.

(Added by Stats. 1986, Ch. 976, Sec. 1.)

868.7.

(a) Notwithstanding any other provision of law, the magistrate may, upon motion of the prosecutor, close the examination in the manner described in Section 868 during the testimony of a witness:

(1) Who is a minor or a dependent person, as defined in paragraph (3) of subdivision (f) of Section 288, with a substantial cognitive impairment and is the complaining victim of a sex offense, where testimony before the general public would be likely to cause serious psychological harm to the witness and where no alternative procedures, including, but not limited to, video recorded deposition or contemporaneous examination in another place communicated to the courtroom by means of closed-circuit television, are available to avoid the perceived harm.

(2) Whose life would be subject to a substantial risk in appearing before the general public, and where no alternative security measures, including, but not limited to, efforts to conceal his or her features or physical description, searches of members of the public attending the examination, or the temporary exclusion of other actual or potential witnesses, would be adequate to minimize the perceived threat.

(b) In any case where public access to the courtroom is restricted during the examination of a witness pursuant to this section, a transcript of the testimony of the witness shall be made available to the public as soon as is practicable.

(Amended by Stats. 2009, Ch. 88, Sec. 73. (AB 176) Effective January 1, 2010.)

868.8.

Notwithstanding any other provision of law, in any criminal proceeding in which the defendant is charged with a violation or attempted violation of subdivision (b) of Section 209, Section 220, 236.1, 243.4, 261, 269, 273a, 273d, 285, 286, 287, 288, 288.5, 288.7, or 289, subdivision (1) of Section 314, Section 422, 646.9, 647.6, or former Section 288a or 647a, or any crime that constitutes domestic violence defined in Section 13700, committed with or upon a person with a disability or a minor under 11 years of age, the court shall take special precautions to provide for the comfort and support of the person with a disability or minor and to protect him or her from coercion, intimidation, or undue influence as a witness, including, but not limited to, any of the following:

(a) In the court's discretion, the witness may be allowed reasonable periods of relief from examination and cross-examination during which he or she may retire from the courtroom. The judge may also allow other witnesses in the proceeding to be examined when the person with a disability or child witness retires from the courtroom.

(b) Notwithstanding Section 68110 of the Government Code, in his or her discretion, the judge may remove his or her robe if the judge believes that this formal attire intimidates the person with a disability or the minor.

(c) In the court's discretion the judge, parties, witnesses, support persons, and court personnel may be relocated within the courtroom to facilitate a more comfortable and personal environment for the person with a disability or the child witness.

(d) In the court's discretion, the taking of the testimony of the person with a disability or the minor may be limited to normal school hours if there is no good cause to take the testimony of the person with a disability or the minor during other hours.

(e) For the purposes of this section, the term "disability" is defined in subdivision (j) of Section 12926 of the Government Code.

(Amended by Stats. 2018, Ch. 423, Sec. 81. (SB 1494) Effective January 1, 2019.)

869.

The testimony of each witness in cases of homicide shall be reduced to writing, as a deposition, by the magistrate, or under his or her direction, and in other cases upon the demand of the prosecuting attorney, or the defendant, or his or her counsel. The magistrate before whom the examination is had may, in his or her discretion, order the testimony and proceedings to be taken down in shorthand in all examinations herein mentioned, and for that purpose he or she may appoint a shorthand reporter. The deposition or testimony of the witness shall be authenticated in the following form:

(a) It shall state the name of the witness, his or her place of residence, and his or her business or profession; except that if the witness is a peace officer, it shall state his or her name, and the address given in his or her testimony at the hearing.

(b) It shall contain the questions put to the witness and his or her answers thereto, each answer being distinctly read to him or her as it is taken down, and being corrected or added to until it conforms to what he or she declares is the truth, except in cases where the testimony is taken down in shorthand, the answer or answers of the witness need not be read to him or her.

(c) If a question put be objected to on either side and overruled, or the witness declines answering it, that fact, with the ground on which the question was overruled or the answer declined, shall be stated.

(d) The deposition shall be signed by the witness, or if he or she refuses to sign it, his or her reason for refusing shall be stated in writing, as he or she gives it, except in cases where the deposition is taken down in shorthand, it need not be signed by the witness.

(e) The reporter shall, within 10 days after the close of the examination, if the defendant be held to answer the charge of a felony, or in any other case if either the defendant or the prosecution orders the transcript, transcribe his or her shorthand notes, making an original and one copy and as many additional copies thereof as there are defendants (other than fictitious defendants), regardless of the number of charges or fictitious defendants included in the same examination, and certify and deliver the original and all copies to the clerk of the superior court in the county in which the defendant was examined. The reporter shall, before receiving any compensation as a reporter, file his or her affidavit setting forth that the transcript has been delivered within the time herein provided for. The compensation of the reporter for any services rendered by him or her as the reporter in any court of this state shall be reduced one-half if the provisions of this section as to the time of filing said transcript have not been complied with by him or her.

(f) In every case in which a transcript is delivered as provided in this section, the clerk of the court shall file the original of the transcript with the papers in the case, and shall deliver a copy of the transcript to the district attorney immediately upon his or her receipt thereof and shall deliver a copy of said transcript to each defendant (other than a fictitious defendant) at least five days before trial or upon earlier demand by him or her without cost to him or her; provided, that if any defendant be held to answer to two or more charges upon the same examination and thereafter the district attorney shall file separate informations upon said several charges, the delivery to each such defendant of one copy of the transcript of the examination shall be a compliance with this section as to all of those informations.

(g) If the transcript is delivered by the reporter within the time hereinbefore provided for, the reporter shall be entitled to receive the compensation fixed and allowed by law to reporters in the superior courts of this state.

(Amended by Stats. 2002, Ch. 784, Sec. 534. Effective January 1, 2003.)

870.

The magistrate or his or her clerk shall keep the depositions taken on the information or the examination, until they are returned to the proper court; and shall not permit them to be examined or copied by any person except a judge of a court having jurisdiction of the offense, or authorized to issue writs of habeas corpus, the Attorney General, district attorney, or other prosecuting attorney, and the defendant and his or her counsel; provided however, upon demand by the defendant or his or her attorney the magistrate shall order a transcript of the depositions taken on the information, or on the examination, to be immediately furnished the defendant or his or her attorney, after the commitment of the defendant as provided by Sections 876 and 877, and the reporter furnishing the depositions, shall receive compensation in accordance with Section 869.
(Amended by Stats. 2002, Ch. 784, Sec. 535. Effective January 1, 2003.)
871.
If, after hearing the proofs, it appears either that no public offense has been committed or that there is not sufficient cause to believe the defendant guilty of a public offense, the magistrate shall order the complaint dismissed and the defendant to be discharged, by an indorsement on the depositions and statement, signed by the magistrate, to the following effect: "There being no sufficient cause to believe the within named A. B. guilty of the offense within mentioned, I order that the complaint be dismissed and that he or she shall be discharged."
(Amended by Stats. 1980, Ch. 938, Sec. 3.)
871.5.
(a) When an action is dismissed by a magistrate pursuant to Section 859b, 861, 871, 1008, 1381, 1381.5, 1385, 1387, or 1389 of this code or Section 41403 of the Vehicle Code, or a portion thereof is dismissed pursuant to those same sections which may not be charged by information under Section 739, the prosecutor may make a motion in the superior court within 15 days to compel the magistrate to reinstate the complaint or a portion thereof and to reinstate the custodial status of the defendant under the same terms and conditions as when the defendant last appeared before the magistrate.
(b) Notice of the motion shall be made to the defendant and the magistrate. The only ground for the motion shall be that, as a matter of law, the magistrate erroneously dismissed the action or a portion thereof.
(c) The superior court shall hear and determine the motion on the basis of the record of the proceedings before the magistrate. If the motion is litigated to decision by the prosecutor, the prosecution is prohibited from refiling the dismissed action, or portion thereof.
(d) Within 10 days after the magistrate has dismissed the action or a portion thereof, the prosecuting attorney may file a written request for a transcript of the proceedings with the clerk of the magistrate. The reporter shall immediately transcribe his or her shorthand notes pursuant to Section 869 and file with the clerk of the superior court an original plus one copy, and as many copies as there are defendants (other than a fictitious defendant). The reporter shall be entitled to compensation in accordance with Section 869. The clerk of the superior court shall deliver a copy of the transcript to the prosecuting attorney immediately upon its receipt and shall deliver a copy of the transcript to each defendant (other than a fictitious defendant) upon his or her demand without cost.
(e) When a court has ordered the resumption of proceedings before the magistrate, the magistrate shall resume the proceedings and when so ordered, issue an order of commitment for the reinstated offense or offenses within 10 days after the superior court has entered an order to that effect or within 10 days after the remittitur is filed in the superior court. Upon receipt of the remittitur, the superior court shall forward a copy to the magistrate.
(f) Pursuant to paragraph (9) of subdivision (a) of Section 1238 the people may take an appeal from the denial of the motion by the superior court to reinstate the complaint or a portion thereof. If the motion to reinstate the complaint is granted, the defendant may seek review thereof only pursuant to Sections 995 and 999a. That review may only be sought in the event the defendant is held to answer pursuant to Section 872.
(g) Nothing contained herein shall preclude a magistrate, upon the resumption of proceedings, from considering a motion made pursuant to Section 1318.
If the superior court grants the motion for reinstatement and orders the magistrate to issue an order of commitment, the defendant, in lieu of resumed proceedings before the magistrate, may elect to waive his or her right to be committed by a magistrate, and consent to the filing of an amended or initial information containing the reinstated charge or charges. After arraignment thereon, he or she may adopt as a motion pursuant to Section 995, the record and proceedings of the motion taken pursuant to this section and the order issued pursuant thereto, and may seek review of the order in the manner prescribed in Section 999a.
(Amended by Stats. 1993, Ch. 542, Sec. 1. Effective January 1, 1994.)
871.6.
If in a felony case the magistrate sets the preliminary examination beyond the time specified in Section 859b, in violation of Section 859b, or continues the preliminary hearing without good cause and good cause is required by law for such a continuance, the people or the defendant may file a petition for writ of mandate or prohibition in the superior court seeking immediate appellate review of the ruling setting the hearing or granting the continuance. Such a petition shall have precedence over all other cases in the court to which the petition is assigned. If the superior court grants a peremptory writ, it shall issue the writ and a remittitur three court days after its decision becomes final as to the court if this action is necessary to prevent mootness or to prevent frustration of the relief granted, notwithstanding the rights of the parties to seek review in a court of appeal. When the superior court issues the writ and remittitur as provided in this section, the writ shall command the magistrate to proceed with the preliminary hearing without further delay, other than that reasonably necessary for the parties to obtain the attendance of their witnesses.
The court of appeal may stay or recall the issuance of the writ and remittitur. The failure of the court of appeal to stay or recall the issuance of the writ and remittitur shall not deprive the parties of any right they would otherwise have to appellate review or extraordinary relief.
(Added June 5, 1990, by initiative Proposition 115, Sec. 17.)
872.
(a) If, however, it appears from the examination that a public offense has been committed, and there is sufficient cause to believe that the defendant is guilty, the magistrate shall make or indorse on the complaint an order, signed by him or her, to the following effect: "It appearing to me that the offense in the within complaint mentioned (or any offense, according to the fact, stating generally the nature thereof), has been committed, and that there is sufficient cause to believe that the within named A. B. is guilty, I order that he or she be held to answer to the same."
(b) Notwithstanding Section 1200 of the Evidence Code, the finding of probable cause may be based in whole or in part upon the sworn testimony of a law enforcement officer or honorably retired law enforcement officer relating the statements of declarants made out of court offered for the truth of the matter asserted. An honorably retired law enforcement officer may only relate statements of declarants made out of court and offered for the truth of the matter asserted that were made when the honorably retired officer was an active law enforcement officer. Any law enforcement officer or honorably retired law enforcement officer testifying as to hearsay statements shall either have five years of law enforcement experience or have completed a training course certified by the Commission on Peace Officer Standards and Training that includes training in the investigation and reporting of cases and testifying at preliminary hearings.

(c) For purposes of subdivision (b), a law enforcement officer is any officer or agent employed by a federal, state, or local government agency to whom all of the following apply:
(1) Has either five years of law enforcement experience or who has completed a training course certified by the Commission on Peace Officer Standards and Training that includes training in the investigation and reporting of cases and testifying at preliminary hearings.
(2) Whose primary responsibility is the enforcement of any law, the detection and apprehension of persons who have violated any law, or the investigation and preparation for prosecution of cases involving violation of laws.
(Amended by Stats. 2013, Ch. 125, Sec. 1. (AB 568) Effective January 1, 2014. Note: This section was amended on June 5, 1990, by initiative Prop. 115.)
872.5.
Notwithstanding Article 1 (commencing with Section 1520) of Chapter 2 of Division 11 of the Evidence Code, in a preliminary examination the content of a writing may be proved by an otherwise admissible original or otherwise admissible secondary evidence.
(Repealed and added by Stats. 1998, Ch. 100, Sec. 7. Effective January 1, 1999.)
873.
If the offense is not bailable, the following words must be added to the indorsement: "And he is hereby committed to the Sheriff of the County of _____."
(Enacted 1872.)
875.
If the offense is bailable, and the defendant is admitted to bail, the following words must be added to the order, "and that he be admitted to bail in the sum of _____ dollars, and is committed to the Sheriff of the County of _____ until he gives such bail."
(Amended by Code Amendments 1880, Ch. 60.)
876.
If the magistrate order the defendant to be committed, he must make out a commitment, signed by him, with his name of office, and deliver it, with the defendant, to the officer to whom he is committed, or, if that officer is not present, to a peace officer, who must deliver the defendant into the proper custody, together with the commitment.
(Enacted 1872.)
877.
The commitment must be to the following effect except when it is made under the provisions of section 859a of this code.
County of _____ (as the case may be).
The people of the State of California to the sheriff of the county of _____:
An order having been this day made by me, that A. B. be held to answer upon a charge of (stating briefly the nature of the offense, and giving as near as may be the time when and the place where the same was committed), you are commanded to receive him into your custody and detain him until he is legally discharged.
Dated this _____ day of _____ nineteen _____.
(Amended by Stats. 1935, Ch. 217.)
877a.
When the commitment is made under the provisions of section 859a of this code, it must be made to the following effect:
County of _____ (as the case may be).
The people of the State of California to the sheriff of the county of _____.
A. B. having pleaded guilty to the offense of (stating briefly the nature of the offense, and giving as near as may be the time when and the place where the same was committed), you are commanded to receive him into your custody and detain him until he is legally discharged.
Dated this _____ day of _____ nineteen _____.
(Added by Stats. 1935, Ch. 217.)
878.
On holding the defendant to answer or on a plea of guilty where permitted by law, the magistrate may take from each of the material witnesses examined before him on the part of the people a written undertaking, to the effect that he will appear and testify at the court to which the depositions and statements or case are to be sent, or that he will forfeit the sum of five hundred dollars.
(Amended by Stats. 1935, Ch. 217.)
879.
When the magistrate or a Judge of the Court in which the action is pending is satisfied, by proof on oath, that there is reason to believe that any such witness will not appear and testify unless security is required, he may order the witness to enter into a written undertaking, with sureties, in such sum as he may deem proper, for his appearance as specified in the preceding section.
(Enacted 1872.)
880.
Infants who are material witnesses against the defendant may be required to procure sureties for their appearance, as provided in the last section.
(Amended by Stats. 1977, Ch. 579.)
881.
(a) If a witness, required to enter into an undertaking to appear and testify, either with or without sureties, refuses compliance with the order for that purpose, the magistrate shall commit him or her to prison until he or she complies or is legally discharged.
(b) If a witness fails to appear at the preliminary hearing in response to a subpoena, the court may hear evidence, including testimony or an affidavit from the arresting or interviewing officer, and if the court determines on the basis of the evidence that the witness is a material witness, the court shall issue a bench warrant for the arrest of the witness, and upon the appearance of the witness, may commit him or her into custody until the conclusion of the preliminary hearing, or until the defendant enters a plea of nolo contendere, or the witness is otherwise legally discharged.
The court may order the witness to enter into a written undertaking to the effect that he or she will appear and testify at the time and place ordered by the court or that he or she will forfeit an amount that the court deems proper.
(c) Once the material witness has been taken into custody on the bench warrant he or she shall be brought before the magistrate issuing the warrant, if available, within two court days for a hearing to determine if the witness should be released on security of appearance or maintained in custody.
(d) A material witness shall remain in custody under this section for no longer than 10 days.
(e) If a material witness is being held in custody under this section the prosecution is entitled to have the preliminary hearing proceed, as to this witness only, within 10 days of the arraignment of the defendant. Once this material witness has completed his or her testimony the defendant shall be entitled to a reasonable continuance.
(Amended by Stats. 1987, Ch. 828, Sec. 53.)
882.
When, however, it satisfactorily appears by examination, on oath of the witness, or any other person, that the witness is unable to procure sureties, he or she may be forthwith conditionally examined on behalf of the people. The examination shall be by question and answer, in the presence of the defendant, or after notice to him or her, if on bail, and conducted in the same manner as the examination before a committing magistrate is required by this code to be conducted, and the witness thereupon discharged; and the deposition may be used upon the trial of the defendant, except in cases of homicide, under the same conditions as mentioned in Section 1345; but this section does not apply to an accomplice in the commission of the offense charged.
(Amended by Stats. 1987, Ch. 828, Sec. 54.)
883.

When a magistrate has discharged a defendant, or has held him to answer, he must return, without delay, to the Clerk of the Court at which the defendant is required to appear, the warrant, if any, the depositions, and all undertakings of bail, or for the appearance of witnesses taken by him.
(Enacted 1872.)

TITLE 4. GRAND JURY PROCEEDINGS [888 - 939.91]

(Title 4 repealed and added by Stats. 1959, Ch. 501.)

CHAPTER 1. General Provisions [888 - 892]

(Chapter 1 added by Stats. 1959, Ch. 501.)
888.
A grand jury is a body of the required number of persons returned from the citizens of the county before a court of competent jurisdiction, and sworn to inquire of public offenses committed or triable within the county.
Each grand jury or, if more than one has been duly impaneled pursuant to Sections 904.5 to 904.9, inclusive, one grand jury in each county, shall be charged and sworn to investigate or inquire into county matters of civil concern, such as the needs of county officers, including the abolition or creation of offices for, the purchase, lease, or sale of equipment for, or changes in the method or system of, performing the duties of the agencies subject to investigation pursuant to Section 914.1.
(Amended by Stats. 1988, Ch. 1297, Sec. 1.)
888.2.
As used in this title as applied to a grand jury, "required number" means:
(a) Twenty-three in a county having a population exceeding 4,000,000.
(b) Eleven in a county having a population of 20,000 or less, upon the approval of the board of supervisors.
(c) Nineteen in all other counties.
(Amended by Stats. 1994, Ch. 295, Sec. 1. Effective January 1, 1995.)
889.
An indictment is an accusation in writing, presented by the grand jury to a competent court, charging a person with a public offense.
(Added by Stats. 1959, Ch. 501.)
890.
Unless a higher fee or rate of mileage is otherwise provided by statute or county or city and county ordinance, the fees for grand jurors are fifteen dollars ($15) a day for each day's attendance as a grand juror, and the mileage reimbursement applicable to county employees for each mile actually traveled in attending court as a grand juror.
(Amended by Stats. 2001, Ch. 218, Sec. 1. Effective January 1, 2002. Operative July 1, 2002, by Sec. 2 of Ch. 218.)
890.1.
The per diem and mileage of grand jurors where allowed by law shall be paid by the treasurer of the county out of the general fund of the county upon warrants drawn by the county auditor upon the written order of the judge of the superior court of the county.
(Added by Stats. 1959, Ch. 501.)
891.
Every person who, by any means whatsoever, willfully and knowingly, and without knowledge and consent of the grand jury, records, or attempts to record, all or part of the proceedings of any grand jury while it is deliberating or voting, or listens to or observes, or attempts to listen to or observe, the proceedings of any grand jury of which he is not a member while such jury is deliberating or voting is guilty of a misdemeanor. This section is not intended to prohibit the taking of notes by a grand juror in connection with and solely for the purpose of assisting him in the performance of his duties as such juror.
(Added by Stats. 1959, Ch. 501.)
892.
The grand jury may proceed against a corporation.
(Amended by Stats. 1973, Ch. 249.)

CHAPTER 2. Formation of Grand Jury [893 - 913]

(Chapter 2 added by Stats. 1959, Ch. 501.)
ARTICLE 1. Qualifications of Grand Jurors [893 - 894]
(Article 1 added by Stats. 1959, Ch. 501.)
893.
(a) A person is competent to act as a grand juror only if he possesses each of the following qualifications:
(1) He is a citizen of the United States of the age of 18 years or older who shall have been a resident of the state and of the county or city and county for one year immediately before being selected and returned.
(2) He is in possession of his natural faculties, of ordinary intelligence, of sound judgment, and of fair character.
(3) He is possessed of sufficient knowledge of the English language.
(b) A person is not competent to act as a grand juror if any of the following apply:
(1) The person is serving as a trial juror in any court of this state.
(2) The person has been discharged as a grand juror in any court of this state within one year.
(3) The person has been convicted of malfeasance in office or any felony or other high crime.
(4) The person is serving as an elected public officer.
(Amended by Stats. 1973, Ch. 416.)
894.
Sections 204, 218, and 219 of the Code of Civil Procedure specify the exemptions and the excuses which relieve a person from liability to serve as a grand juror.
(Amended by Stats. 1989, Ch. 1416, Sec. 37.)
ARTICLE 2. Listing and Selection of Grand Jurors [895 - 902]
(Article 2 added by Stats. 1959, Ch. 501.)
895.
During the month preceding the beginning of the fiscal year of the county, the superior court of each county shall make an order designating the estimated number of grand jurors that will, in the opinion of the court, be required for the transaction of the business of the court during the ensuing fiscal year as provided in Section 905.5.
(Amended by Stats. 1974, Ch. 393.)
896.
(a) Immediately after an order is made pursuant to Section 895, the court shall select the grand jurors required by personal interview for the purpose of ascertaining whether they possess the qualifications prescribed by subdivision (a) of Section 893. If a person

so interviewed, in the opinion of the court, possesses the necessary qualifications, in order to be listed the person shall sign a statement declaring that the person will be available for jury service for the number of hours usually required of a member of the grand jury in that county.
(b) The selections shall be made of men and women who are not exempt from serving and who are suitable and competent to serve as grand jurors pursuant to Sections 893, 898, and 899. The court shall list the persons so selected and required by the order to serve as grand jurors during the ensuing fiscal year of the county, or until a new list of grand jurors is provided, and shall at once place this list in the possession of the jury commissioner.
(Amended by Stats. 2003, Ch. 149, Sec. 69. Effective January 1, 2004.)
898.
The list of grand jurors made in a county having a population in excess of four million shall contain the number of persons which has been designated by the court in its order.
(Amended by Stats. 1963, Ch. 259.)
899.
The names for the grand jury list shall be selected from the different wards, judicial districts, or supervisorial districts of the respective counties in proportion to the number of inhabitants therein, as nearly as the same can be estimated by the persons making the lists. The grand jury list shall be kept separate and distinct from the trial jury list. In a county of the first class, the names for such list may be selected from the county at large.
(Amended by Stats. 1969, Ch. 64.)
900.
On receiving the list of persons selected by the court, the jury commissioner shall file it in the jury commissioner's office and have the list, which shall include the name of the judge who selected each person on the list, published one time in a newspaper of general circulation, as defined in Section 6000 of the Government Code, in the county. The jury commissioner shall then do either of the following:
(a) Write down the names on the list onto separate pieces of paper of the same size and appearance, fold each piece so as to conceal the name, and deposit the pieces in a box to be called the "grand jury box."
(b) Assign a number to each name on the list and place, in a box to be called the "grand jury box," markers of the same size, shape, and color, each containing a number which corresponds with a number on the list.
(Amended by Stats. 2003, Ch. 149, Sec. 70. Effective January 1, 2004.)
901.
(a) The persons whose names are so returned shall be known as regular jurors, and shall serve for one year and until other persons are selected and returned.
(b) If the superior court so decides, the presiding judge may name up to 10 regular jurors not previously so named, who served on the previous grand jury and who so consent, to serve for a second year.
(c) The court may also decide to select grand jurors pursuant to Section 908.2.
(Amended by Stats. 1988, Ch. 886, Sec. 1.)
902.
The names of persons drawn for grand jurors shall be drawn from the grand jury box by withdrawing either the pieces of paper placed therein pursuant to subdivision (a) of Section 900 or the markers placed therein pursuant to subdivision (b) of Section 900. If, at the end of the fiscal year of the county, there are the names of persons in the grand jury box who have not been drawn during the fiscal year to serve and have not served as grand jurors, the names of such persons may be placed on the list of grand jurors drawn for the succeeding fiscal year.
(Amended by Stats. 1974, Ch. 393.)
ARTICLE 3. Jury Commissioners [903.1 - 903.4]
(Article 3 added by Stats. 1959, Ch. 501.)
903.1.
Pursuant to written rules or instructions adopted by a majority of the judges of the superior court of the county, the jury commissioner shall furnish the judges of the court annually a list of persons qualified to serve as grand jurors during the ensuing fiscal year of the county, or until a new list of jurors is required. From time to time, a majority of the judges of the superior court may adopt such rules or instructions as may be necessary for the guidance of the jury commissioner, who shall at all times be under the supervision and control of the judges of the court. Any list of jurors prepared pursuant to this article must, however, meet the requirements of Section 899.
(Amended by Stats. 1974, Ch. 393.)
903.2.
The jury commissioner shall diligently inquire and inform himself or herself in respect to the qualifications of persons resident in his or her county who may be liable to be summoned for grand jury duty. He or she may require a person to answer, under oath to be administered by him or her, all questions as he or she may address to that person, touching his or her name, age, residence, occupation, and qualifications as a grand juror, and also all questions as to similar matters concerning other persons of whose qualifications for grand jury duty he or she has knowledge.
The commissioner and his or her assistants, referred to in Sections 69895 and 69896 of the Government Code, shall have the power to administer oaths and shall be allowed actual traveling expenses incurred in the performance of their duties. Those traveling expenses shall be audited, allowed, and paid out of the general fund of the county.
(Amended by Stats. 2008, Ch. 179, Sec. 179. Effective January 1, 2009.)
903.3.
Pursuant to the rules or instructions adopted by a majority of the judges of the superior court, the jury commissioner shall return to the judges the list of persons recommended by him for grand jury duty. The judges of the superior court shall examine the jury list so returned and from such list a majority of the judges may select, to serve as grand jurors in the superior court of the county during the ensuing year or until a new list of jurors is required, such persons as, in their opinion, should be selected for grand jury duty. The persons so selected shall, in the opinion of the judges selecting them, be persons suitable and competent to serve as jurors, as required by law.
(Added by Stats. 1959, Ch. 501.)
903.4.
The judges are not required to select any name from the list returned by the jury commissioner, but may, if in their judgment the due administration of justice requires, make every or any selection from among the body of persons in the county suitable and competent to serve as grand jurors regardless of the list returned by the jury commissioner.
(Amended by Stats. 2011, Ch. 296, Sec. 214. (AB 1023) Effective January 1, 2012.)
ARTICLE 4. Impaneling of Grand Jury [904 - 913]
(Article 4 added by Stats. 1959, Ch. 501.)
904.
Every superior court, whenever in its opinion the public interest so requires, shall make and file with the jury commissioner an order directing a grand jury to be drawn. The order shall designate the number of grand jurors to be drawn, which may not be less than 29 nor more than 40 in counties having a population exceeding four million and not less than 25 nor more than 30 in other counties.
(Amended by Stats. 2003, Ch. 149, Sec. 72. Effective January 1, 2004.)
904.4.
(a) In any county having a population of more than 370,000 but less than 400,000 as established by Section 28020 of the Government Code, the presiding judge of the

superior court, upon application by the district attorney, may order and direct the drawing and impanelment at any time of one additional grand jury.
(b) The presiding judge may select persons, at random, from the list of trial jurors in civil and criminal cases and shall examine them to determine if they are competent to serve as grand jurors. When a sufficient number of competent persons have been selected, they shall constitute the additional grand jury.
(c) Any additional grand jury which is impaneled pursuant to this section may serve for a period of one year from the date of impanelment, but may be discharged at any time within the one-year period by order of the presiding judge. In no event shall more than one additional grand jury be impaneled pursuant to this section at the same time.
(d) Whenever an additional grand jury is impaneled pursuant to this section, it may inquire into any matters that are subject to grand jury inquiry and shall have the sole and exclusive jurisdiction to return indictments, except for any matters that the regular grand jury is inquiring into at the time of its impanelment.
(e) If an additional grand jury is also authorized by another section, the county may impanel the additional grand jury authorized by this section, or by the other section, but not both.
(Added by Stats. 1991, Ch. 1109, Sec. 1.)
904.6.
(a) In any county or city and county, the presiding judge of the superior court, or the judge appointed by the presiding judge to supervise the grand jury, may, upon the request of the Attorney General or the district attorney or upon his or her own motion, order and direct the impanelment, of one additional grand jury pursuant to this section.
(b) The presiding judge or the judge appointed by the presiding judge to supervise the grand jury shall select persons, at random, from the list of trial jurors in civil and criminal cases and shall examine them to determine if they are competent to serve as grand jurors. When a sufficient number of competent persons have been selected, they shall constitute the additional grand jury.
(c) Any additional grand jury which is impaneled pursuant to this section may serve for a period of one year from the date of impanelment, but may be discharged at any time within the one-year period by order of the presiding judge or the judge appointed by the presiding judge to supervise the grand jury. In no event shall more than one additional grand jury be impaneled pursuant to this section at the same time.
(d) Whenever an additional grand jury is impaneled pursuant to this section, it may inquire into any matters which are subject to grand jury inquiry and shall have the sole and exclusive jurisdiction to return indictments, except for any matters which the regular grand jury is inquiring into at the time of its impanelment.
(e) It is the intent of the Legislature that all persons qualified for jury service shall have an equal opportunity to be considered for service as criminal grand jurors in the county in which they reside, and that they have an obligation to serve, when summoned for that purpose. All persons selected for the additional criminal grand jury shall be selected at random from a source or sources reasonably representative of a cross section of the population which is eligible for jury service in the county.
(Amended by Stats. 2005, Ch. 25, Sec. 1. Effective January 1, 2006.)
904.7.
(a) Notwithstanding subdivision (a) of Section 904.6 or any other provision, in the County of San Bernardino, the presiding judge of the superior court, or the judge appointed by the presiding judge to supervise the grand jury, may, upon the request of the Attorney General or the district attorney or upon his or her own motion, order and direct the impanelment of an additional civil grand jury pursuant to this section.
(b) The presiding judge or the judge appointed by the presiding judge to supervise the grand jury shall select persons, at random, from the list of trial jurors in civil and criminal cases and shall examine them to determine if they are competent to serve as grand jurors. When a sufficient number of competent persons have been selected, they shall constitute an additional grand jury.
(c) Any additional civil grand jury that is impaneled pursuant to this section may serve for a term as determined by the presiding judge or the judge appointed by the presiding judge to supervise the civil grand jury, but may be discharged at any time within the set term by order of the presiding judge or the judge appointed by the presiding judge to supervise the civil grand jury. In no event shall more than one additional civil grand jury be impaneled pursuant to this section at the same time.
(d) Whenever an additional civil grand jury is impaneled pursuant to this section, it may inquire into matters of oversight, conduct investigations, issue reports, and make recommendations, except for any matters that the regular grand jury is inquiring into at the time of its impanelment. Any additional civil grand jury impaneled pursuant to this section shall not have jurisdiction to issue indictments.
(e) It is the intent of the Legislature that, in the County of San Bernardino, all persons qualified for jury service shall have an equal opportunity to be considered for service as grand jurors within the county, and that they have an obligation to serve, when summoned for that purpose. All persons selected for an additional grand jury shall be selected at random from a source or sources reasonably representative of a cross section of the population that is eligible for jury service in the county.
(Amended by Stats. 2011, Ch. 304, Sec. 7. (SB 428) Effective January 1, 2012.)
904.8.
(a) Notwithstanding subdivision (a) of Section 904.6 or any other provision, in the County of Los Angeles, the presiding judge of the superior court, or the judge appointed by the presiding judge to supervise the grand jury, may, upon the request of the Attorney General or the district attorney or upon his or her own motion, order and direct the impanelment of up to two additional grand juries pursuant to this section.
(b) The presiding judge or the judge appointed by the presiding judge to supervise the grand jury shall select persons, at random, from the list of trial jurors in civil and criminal cases and shall examine them to determine if they are competent to serve as grand jurors. When a sufficient number of competent persons have been selected, they shall constitute an additional grand jury.
(c) Any additional grand juries that are impaneled pursuant to this section may serve for a period of one year from the date of impanelment, but may be discharged at any time within the one-year period by order of the presiding judge or the judge appointed by the presiding judge to supervise the grand jury. In no event shall more than two additional grand juries be impaneled pursuant to this section at the same time.
(d) Whenever additional grand juries are impaneled pursuant to this section, they may inquire into any matters that are subject to grand jury inquiry and shall have the sole and exclusive jurisdiction to return indictments, except for any matters that the regular grand jury is inquiring into at the time of its impanelment.
(e) It is the intent of the Legislature that, in the County of Los Angeles, all persons qualified for jury service shall have an equal opportunity to be considered for service as criminal grand jurors within the county, and that they have an obligation to serve, when summoned for that purpose. All persons selected for an additional criminal grand jury shall be selected at random from a source or sources reasonably representative of a cross section of the population that is eligible for jury service in the county.
(Added by Stats. 2007, Ch. 82, Sec. 1. Effective January 1, 2008.)
905.
In all counties there shall be at least one grand jury drawn and impaneled in each year.
(Amended by Stats. 1982, Ch. 1408, Sec. 3.)
905.5.
(a) Except as otherwise provided in subdivision (b), the grand jury shall be impaneled and serve during the fiscal year of the county in the manner provided in this chapter.
(b) The board of supervisors of a county may provide that the grand jury shall be impaneled and serve during the calendar year. The board of supervisors shall provide for an appropriate transition from fiscal year term to calendar year term or from calendar year term to fiscal year term for the grand jury. The provisions of subdivisions (a) and (b) of Section 901 shall not be deemed a limitation on any appropriate transition provisions as determined by resolution or ordinance; and, except as otherwise provided in this chapter, no transition grand jury shall serve more than 18 months.
(Amended by Stats. 1984, Ch. 344, Sec. 1. Effective July 10, 1984.)
906.
The order shall designate the time at which the drawing will take place. The names of the grand jurors shall be drawn, and the list of names certified and summoned, as is provided for drawing and summoning trial jurors. The names of any persons drawn, who are not impaneled upon the grand jury, may be again placed in the grand jury box.
(Added by Stats. 1959, Ch. 501.)
907.
Any grand juror summoned, who willfully and without reasonable excuse fails to attend, may be attached and compelled to attend and the court may also impose a fine not exceeding fifty dollars ($50), upon which execution may issue. If the grand juror was not personally served, the fine shall not be imposed until upon an order to show cause an opportunity has been offered the grand juror to be heard.
(Repealed and added by Stats. 1959, Ch. 501.)
908.
If the required number of the persons summoned as grand jurors are present and not excused, the required number shall constitute the grand jury. If more than the required number of persons are present, the jury commissioner shall write their names on separate ballots, which the jury commissioner shall fold so that the names cannot be seen, place them in a box, and draw out the required number of them. The persons whose names are on the ballots so drawn shall constitute the grand jury. If less than the required number of persons are present, the panel may be filled as provided in Section 211 of the Code of Civil Procedure. If more of the persons summoned to complete a grand jury attend than are required, the requisite number shall be obtained by writing the names of those summoned and not excused on ballots, depositing them in a box, and drawing as provided above.
(Amended by Stats. 2003, Ch. 149, Sec. 73. Effective January 1, 2004.)
908.1.
When, after the grand jury consisting of the required number of persons has been impaneled pursuant to law, the membership is reduced for any reason, vacancies within an existing grand jury may be filled, so as to maintain the full membership at the required number of persons, by the jury commissioner, in the presence of the court, drawing out sufficient names to fill the vacancies from the grand jury box, pursuant to law, or from a special venire as provided in Section 211 of the Code of Civil Procedure. A person selected as a grand juror to fill a vacancy pursuant to this section may not vote as a grand juror on any matter upon which evidence has been taken by the grand jury prior to the time of the person's selection.
(Amended by Stats. 2003, Ch. 149, Sec. 74. Effective January 1, 2004.)
908.2.
(a) Upon the decision of the superior court pursuant to Section 901 to adopt this method of selecting grand jurors, when the required number of persons have been impaneled as the grand jury pursuant to law, the jury commissioner shall write the names of each person on separate ballots. The jury commissioner shall fold the ballots so that the names cannot be seen, place them in a box, and draw out half of the ballots, or in a county where the number of grand jurors is uneven, one more than half. The persons whose names are on the ballots so drawn shall serve for 12 months until July 1 of the following year. The persons whose names are not on the ballots so drawn shall serve for six months until January 1 of the following year.
(b) Each subsequent year, on January 2 and July 2, a sufficient number of grand jurors shall be impaneled to replace those whose service concluded the previous day. Those persons impaneled on January 2 shall serve until January 1 of the following year. Those persons impaneled on July 2 shall serve until July 1 of the following year. A person may not serve on the grand jury for more than one year.
(c) The provisions of subdivisions (a) and (b) do not apply to the selection of grand jurors for an additional grand jury authorized pursuant to Section 904.6.
(Amended by Stats. 2003, Ch. 149, Sec. 75. Effective January 1, 2004.)
909.
Before accepting a person drawn as a grand juror, the court shall be satisfied that such person is duly qualified to act as such juror. When a person is drawn and found qualified he shall be accepted unless the court, on the application of the juror and before he is sworn, excuses him from such service for any of the reasons prescribed in this title or in Chapter 1 (commencing with Section 190), Title 3, Part 1 of the Code of Civil Procedure.
(Added by Stats. 1959, Ch. 501.)
910.
No challenge shall be made or allowed to the panel from which the grand jury is drawn, nor to an individual grand juror, except when made by the court for want of qualification, as prescribed in Section 909.
(Added by Stats. 1959, Ch. 501.)
911.
The following oath shall be taken by each member of the grand jury: "I do solemnly swear (affirm) that I will support the Constitution of the United States and of the State of California, and all laws made pursuant to and in conformity therewith, will diligently inquire into, and true presentment make, of all public offenses against the people of this state, committed or triable within this county, of which the grand jury shall have or can obtain legal evidence. Further, I will not disclose any evidence brought before the grand jury, nor anything which I or any other grand juror may say, nor the manner in which I or any other grand juror may have voted on any matter before the grand jury. I will keep the charge that will be given to me by the court."
(Amended by Stats. 1983, Ch. 111, Sec. 4.)
912.
From the persons summoned to serve as grand jurors and appearing, the court shall appoint a foreman. The court shall also appoint a foreman when the person already appointed is excused or discharged before the grand jury is dismissed.
(Added by Stats. 1959, Ch. 501.)
913.
If a grand jury is not in existence, the Attorney General may demand the impaneling of a grand jury by those charged with the duty to do so, and upon such demand by him, it shall be their duty to do so.
(Added by Stats. 1959, Ch. 501.)

CHAPTER 3. Powers and Duties of Grand Jury [914 - 939.91]

(Chapter 3 added by Stats. 1959, Ch. 501.)

ARTICLE 1. General Provisions [914 - 924.6]
(Article 1 added by Stats. 1959, Ch. 501.)

914.
(a) When the grand jury is impaneled and sworn, it shall be charged by the court. In doing so, the court shall give the grand jurors such information as it deems proper, or as is required by law, as to their duties, and as to any charges for public offenses returned to the court or likely to come before the grand jury.

(b) To assist a grand jury in the performance of its statutory duties regarding civil matters, the court, in consultation with the district attorney, the county counsel, and at least one former grand juror, shall ensure that a grand jury that considers or takes action on civil matters receives training that addresses, at a minimum, report writing, interviews, and the scope of the grand jury's responsibility and statutory authority.
(c) Any costs incurred by the court as a result of this section shall be absorbed by the court or the county from existing resources.
(Amended by Stats. 1997, Ch. 443, Sec. 3. Effective January 1, 1998.)

914.1.
When a grand jury is impaneled, for purposes which include the investigation of, or inquiry into, county matters of civil concern, the judge of the superior court of the county, in addition to other matters requiring action, shall call its attention to the provisions of Chapter 1 (commencing with Section 23000) of Division 1 of Title 3, and Sections 24054 and 26525 of the Government Code, and instruct it to ascertain by a careful and diligent investigation whether such provisions have been complied with, and to note the result of such investigation in its report. At such time the judge shall also inform and charge the grand jury especially as to its powers, duties, and responsibilities under Article 1 (commencing with Section 888) of Chapter 2, and Article 2 (commencing with Section 925), Article 3 (commencing with Section 934) of this chapter, Article 3 (commencing with Section 3060) of Chapter 7 of Division 4 of Title 1 of the Government Code, and Section 17006 of the Welfare and Institutions Code.
(Amended by Stats. 1988, Ch. 1297, Sec. 2.)

914.5.
The grand jury shall not spend money or incur obligations in excess of the amount budgeted for its investigative activities pursuant to this chapter by the county board of supervisors unless the proposed expenditure is approved in advance by the presiding judge of the superior court after the board of supervisors has been advised of the request.
(Added by Stats. 1970, Ch. 740.)

915.
When the grand jury has been impaneled, sworn, and charged, it shall retire to a private room, except when operating under a finding pursuant to Section 939.1, and inquire into the offenses and matters of civil concern cognizable by it. On the completion of the business before the grand jury or expiration of the term of prescribed service of one or more grand jurors, the court shall discharge it or the affected individual jurors.
(Amended by Stats. 1988, Ch. 1297, Sec. 3.)

916.
Each grand jury shall choose its officers, except the foreman, and shall determine its rules of proceeding. Adoption of its rules of procedure and all public actions of the grand jury, whether concerning criminal or civil matters unless otherwise prescribed in law, including adoption of final reports, shall be only with the concurrence of that number of grand jurors necessary to find an indictment pursuant to Section 940. Rules of procedure shall include guidelines for that grand jury to ensure that all findings included in its final reports are supported by documented evidence, including reports of contract auditors or consultants, official records, or interviews attended by no fewer than two grand jurors and that all problems identified in a final report are accompanied by suggested means for their resolution, including financial, when applicable.
(Amended by Stats. 1988, Ch. 1297, Sec. 4.)

916.1.
If the foreman of a grand jury is absent from any meeting or if he is disqualified to act, the grand jury may select a member of that body to act as foreman pro tempore, who shall perform the duties, and have all the powers, of the regularly appointed foreman in his absence or disqualification.
(Added by Stats. 1959, Ch. 501.)

916.2.
(a) Notwithstanding any other provision of law, a grand juror who is a current employee of, or a former or retired employee last employed within the prior three years by, an agency within the investigative jurisdiction of the civil grand jury shall inform the foreperson and court of that fact and shall recuse himself or herself from participating in any grand jury civil investigation of that agency, including any discussion or vote concerning a civil investigation of that agency.
(b) This section shall be in addition to any local policies or rules regarding conflict of interest for grand jurors.
(c) For purposes of this section, "agency" means a department or operational part of a government entity, such as a city, county, city and county, school district, or other local government body.
(Amended by Stats. 2012, Ch. 867, Sec. 21. (SB 1144) Effective January 1, 2013.)

917.
(a) The grand jury may inquire into all public offenses committed or triable within the county and present them to the court by indictment.
(b) Except as provided in Section 918, the grand jury shall not inquire into an offense that involves a shooting or use of excessive force by a peace officer described in Section 830.1, subdivision (a) of Section 830.2, or Section 830.39, that led to the death of a person being detained or arrested by the peace officer pursuant to Section 836.
(Amended by Stats. 2015, Ch. 175, Sec. 1. (SB 227) Effective January 1, 2016.)

918.
If a member of a grand jury knows, or has reason to believe, that a public offense, triable within the county, has been committed, he may declare it to his fellow jurors, who may thereupon investigate it.
(Amended by Stats. 1976, Ch. 895.)

919.
(a) The grand jury may inquire into the case of every person imprisoned in the jail of the county on a criminal charge and not indicted.
(b) The grand jury shall inquire into the condition and management of the public prisons within the county.
(c) The grand jury shall inquire into the willful or corrupt misconduct in office of public officers of every description within the county. Except as provided in Section 918, this subdivision does not apply to misconduct that involves a shooting or use of excessive force by a peace officer described in Section 830.1, subdivision (a) of Section 830.2, or Section 830.39, that led to the death of a person being detained or arrested by the peace officer pursuant to Section 836.
(Amended by Stats. 2015, Ch. 175, Sec. 2. (SB 227) Effective January 1, 2016.)

920.
The grand jury may investigate and inquire into all sales and transfers of land, and into the ownership of land, which, under the state laws, might or should escheat to the State of California. For this purpose, the grand jury may summon witnesses before it and examine them and the records. The grand jury shall direct that proper escheat proceedings be commenced when, in the opinion of the grand jury, the evidence justifies such proceedings.
(Amended by Stats. 1976, Ch. 895.)

921.
The grand jury is entitled to free access, at all reasonable times, to the public prisons, and to the examination, without charge, of all public records within the county.
(Added by Stats. 1959, Ch. 501.)

922.
The powers and duties of the grand jury in connection with proceedings for the removal of district, county, or city officers are prescribed in Article 3 (commencing with Section 3060), Chapter 7, Division 4, Title 1, of the Government Code.
(Added by Stats. 1959, Ch. 501.)

923.
(a) Whenever the Attorney General considers that the public interest requires, he or she may, with or without the concurrence of the district attorney, direct the grand jury to convene for the investigation and consideration of those matters of a criminal nature that he or she desires to submit to it. He or she may take full charge of the presentation of the matters to the grand jury, issue subpoenas, prepare indictments, and do all other things incident thereto to the same extent as the district attorney may do.
(b) Whenever the Attorney General considers that the public interest requires, he or she may, with or without the concurrence of the district attorney, petition the court to impanel a special grand jury to investigate, consider, or issue indictments for any of the activities subject to fine, imprisonment, or asset forfeiture under Section 14107 of the Welfare and Institutions Code. He or she may take full charge of the presentation of the matters to the grand jury, issue subpoenas, prepare indictments, and do all other things incident thereto to the same extent as the district attorney may do. If the evidence presented to the grand jury shows the commission of an offense or offenses for which venue would be in a county other than the county where the grand jury is impaneled, the Attorney General, with or without the concurrence of the district attorney in the county with jurisdiction over the offense or offenses, may petition the court to impanel a special grand jury in that county. Notwithstanding any other law, upon request of the Attorney General, a grand jury convened by the Attorney General pursuant to this subdivision may submit confidential information obtained by that grand jury, including, but not limited to, documents and testimony, to a second grand jury that has been impaneled at the request of the Attorney General pursuant to this subdivision in any other county where venue for an offense or offenses shown by evidence presented to the first grand jury is proper. All confidentiality provisions governing information, testimony, and evidence presented to a grand jury shall be applicable, except as expressly permitted by this subdivision. The Attorney General shall inform the grand jury that transmits confidential information and the grand jury that receives confidential information of any exculpatory evidence, as required by Section 939.71. The grand jury that transmits information to another grand jury shall include the exculpatory evidence disclosed by the Attorney General in the transmission of the confidential information. The Attorney General shall inform both the grand jury transmitting the confidential information and the grand jury receiving that information of their duties under Section 939.7. A special grand jury convened pursuant to this subdivision shall be in addition to the other grand juries authorized by this section, this chapter, or Chapter 2 (commencing with Section 893).
(c) Whenever the Attorney General considers that the public interest requires, he or she may, with or without the concurrence of the district attorney, impanel a special statewide grand jury to investigate, consider, or issue indictments in any matters in which there are two or more activities, in which fraud or theft is a material element, that have occurred in more than one county and were conducted either by a single defendant or multiple defendants acting in concert.
(1) This special statewide grand jury may be impaneled in the Counties of Fresno, Los Angeles, Sacramento, San Diego, or San Francisco, at the Attorney General's discretion. When impaneling a special statewide grand jury pursuant to this subdivision, the Attorney General shall use an existing regularly impaneled criminal grand jury within the period of its regular impanelment to serve as the special statewide grand jury and make arrangements with the grand jury coordinator in the applicable county, or with the presiding judge or whoever is charged with scheduling the grand jury hearings, in order to ensure orderly coordination and use of the grand jurors' time for both regular grand jury duties and special statewide grand jury duties. Whenever the Attorney General impanels a special statewide grand jury, the prosecuting attorney representing the Attorney General shall inform the special statewide grand jury at the outset of the case that the special statewide grand jury is acting as a special statewide grand jury with statewide jurisdiction.
(2) For special statewide grand juries impaneled pursuant to this subdivision, the Attorney General may issue subpoenas for documents and witnesses located anywhere in the state in order to obtain evidence to present to the special statewide grand jury. The special statewide grand jury may hear all evidence in the form of testimony or physical evidence presented to the special statewide grand jury, irrespective of the location of the witness or physical evidence prior to subpoena. The special statewide grand jury impaneled pursuant to this subdivision may indict a person or persons with charges for crimes that occurred in counties other than where the special statewide grand jury is impaneled. The indictment shall then be submitted to the court in any county in which any of the charges could otherwise have been properly brought. The court where the indictment is filed under this subdivision shall have proper jurisdiction over all counts in the indictment.
(3) Notwithstanding Section 944, an indictment found by a special statewide grand jury convened pursuant to this subdivision and endorsed as a true bill by the special statewide grand jury foreperson, may be presented to the court, as set forth in paragraph (2), solely by the Attorney General and within five court days of the endorsement of the indictment. For indictments presented to the court in this manner, the Attorney General shall also file with the court or court clerk, at the time of presenting the indictment, an affidavit signed by the special statewide grand jury foreperson attesting that all the jurors who voted on the indictment heard all of the evidence presented by the Attorney General, and that a proper number of jurors voted for the indictment pursuant to Section 940. The Attorney General's office shall be responsible for prosecuting an indictment produced by the special statewide grand jury.
(4) If a defendant makes a timely and successful challenge to the Attorney General's right to convene a special statewide grand jury by clearly demonstrating that the charges brought are not encompassed by this subdivision, the court shall dismiss the indictment without prejudice to the Attorney General, who may bring the same or other charges against the defendant at a later date by way of another special statewide grand jury, properly convened, or a regular grand jury, or by any other procedure available.
(5) The provisions of Section 939.71 shall apply to the special statewide grand jury.
(6) Unless otherwise set forth in this section, a law applying to a regular grand jury impaneled pursuant to Section 23 of Article I of the California Constitution shall apply to a special statewide grand jury unless the application of the law to a special statewide grand jury would substantially interfere with the execution of one or more of the provisions of this section. If there is substantial interference, the provision governing the special statewide grand jury will govern.
(d) Upon certification by the Attorney General, a statement of the costs directly related to the impanelment and activities of the grand jury pursuant to subdivisions (b) and (c) from the presiding judge of the superior court where the grand jury was impaneled shall be submitted for state reimbursement of the costs to the county or courts.
(Amended by Stats. 2012, Ch. 568, Sec. 2. (SB 1474) Effective January 1, 2013.)

924.
Every grand juror who willfully discloses the fact of an information or indictment having been made for a felony, until the defendant has been arrested, is guilty of a misdemeanor.
(Added by Stats. 1959, Ch. 501.)

924.1.
(a) Every grand juror who, except when required by a court, willfully discloses any evidence adduced before the grand jury, or anything which he himself or any other member of the grand jury has said, or in what manner he or she or any other grand juror has voted on a matter before them, is guilty of a misdemeanor.
(b) Every interpreter for the disabled appointed to assist a member of the grand jury pursuant to Section 939.11 who, except when required by a court, willfully discloses any evidence adduced before the grand jury, or anything which he or she or any member of

the grand jury has said, or in what manner any grand juror has voted on a matter before them, is guilty of a misdemeanor.
(Amended by Stats. 1986, Ch. 357, Sec. 1.)
924.2.
Each grand juror shall keep secret whatever he himself or any other grand juror has said, or in what manner he or any other grand juror has voted on a matter before them. Any court may require a grand juror to disclose the testimony of a witness examined before the grand jury, for the purpose of ascertaining whether it is consistent with that given by the witness before the court, or to disclose the testimony given before the grand jury by any person, upon a charge against such person for perjury in giving his testimony or upon trial therefor.
(Added by Stats. 1959, Ch. 501.)
924.3.
A grand juror cannot be questioned for anything he may say or any vote he may give in the grand jury relative to a matter legally pending before the jury, except for a perjury of which he may have been guilty in making an accusation or giving testimony to his fellow jurors.
(Added by Stats. 1959, Ch. 501.)
924.4.
Notwithstanding the provisions of Sections 924.1 and 924.2, any grand jury or, if the grand jury is no longer impaneled, the presiding judge of the superior court, may pass on and provide the succeeding grand jury with any records, information, or evidence acquired by the grand jury during the course of any investigation conducted by it during its term of service, except any information or evidence that relates to a criminal investigation or that could form part or all of the basis for issuance of an indictment. Transcripts of testimony reported during any session of the grand jury shall be made available to the succeeding grand jury upon its request.
(Amended by Stats. 2002, Ch. 784, Sec. 536. Effective January 1, 2003.)
924.6.
(a) If no indictment is returned, the court that impaneled the grand jury shall, upon application of either party, order disclosure of all or part of the testimony of a witness before the grand jury to a defendant and the prosecutor in connection with any pending or subsequent criminal proceeding before any court if the court finds following an in camera hearing, which shall include the court's review of the grand jury's testimony, that the testimony is relevant, and appears to be admissible.
(b) If a grand jury decides not to return an indictment in a grand jury inquiry into an offense that involves a shooting or use of excessive force by a peace officer described in Section 830.1, subdivision (a) of Section 830.2, or Section 830.39, that led to the death of a person being detained or arrested by the peace officer pursuant to Section 836, the court that impaneled the grand jury shall, upon application of the district attorney, a legal representative of the decedent, or a legal representative of the news media or public, and with notice to the district attorney and the affected witness involved, and an opportunity to be heard, order disclosure of all or part of the indictment proceeding transcript, excluding the grand jury's private deliberations and voting, to the movant, unless the court expressly finds, following an in camera hearing, that there exists an overriding interest that outweighs the right of public access to the record, the overriding interest supports sealing the record, a substantial probability exists that the overriding interest will be prejudiced if the record is not sealed, the proposed sealing is narrowly tailored, and no less restrictive means exist to achieve the overriding interest.
(Amended by Stats. 2017, Ch. 204, Sec. 1. (AB 1024) Effective January 1, 2018.)

ARTICLE 2. Investigation of County, City, and District Affairs [925 - 933.6]
(Heading of Article 2 amended by Stats. 1973, Ch. 1036.)
925.
The grand jury shall investigate and report on the operations, accounts, and records of the officers, departments, or functions of the county including those operations, accounts, and records of any special legislative district or other district in the county created pursuant to state law for which the officers of the county are serving in their ex officio capacity as officers of the districts. The investigations may be conducted on some selective basis each year, but the grand jury shall not duplicate any examination of financial statements which has been performed by or for the board of supervisors pursuant to Section 25250 of the Government Code; this provision shall not be construed to limit the power of the grand jury to investigate and report on the operations, accounts, and records of the officers, departments, or functions of the county. The grand jury may enter into a joint contract with the board of supervisors to employ the services of an expert as provided for in Section 926.
(Repealed and added by Stats. 1977, Ch. 107.)
925a.
The grand jury may at any time examine the books and records of any incorporated city or joint powers agency located in the county. In addition to any other investigatory powers granted by this chapter, the grand jury may investigate and report upon the operations, accounts, and records of the officers, departments, functions, and the method or system of performing the duties of any such city or joint powers agency and make such recommendations as it may deem proper and fit.
The grand jury may investigate and report upon the needs of all joint powers agencies in the county, including the abolition or creation of agencies and the equipment for, or the method or system of performing the duties of, the several agencies. It shall cause a copy of any such report to be transmitted to the governing body of any affected agency. As used in this section, "joint powers agency" means an agency described in Section 6506 of the Government Code whose jurisdiction encompasses all or part of a county.
(Amended by Stats. 1983, Ch. 590, Sec. 1.)
926.
(a) If, in the judgment of the grand jury, the services of one or more experts are necessary for the purposes of Sections 925, 925a, 928, 933.1, and 933.5 or any of them, the grand jury may employ one or more experts, at an agreed compensation, to be first approved by the court. If, in the judgment of the grand jury, the services of assistants to such experts are required, the grand jury may employ such assistants, at a compensation to be agreed upon and approved by the court. Expenditures for the services of experts and assistants for the purposes of Section 933.5 shall not exceed the sum of thirty thousand dollars ($30,000) annually, unless such expenditures shall also be approved by the board of supervisors.
(b) When making an examination of the books, records, accounts, and documents maintained and processed by the county assessor, the grand jury, with the consent of the board of supervisors, may employ expert auditors or appraisers to assist in the examination. Auditors and appraisers, while performing pursuant to the directive of the grand jury, shall have access to all records and documents that may be inspected by the grand jury subject to the same limitations on public disclosure as apply to the grand jury.
(c) Any contract entered into by a grand jury pursuant to this section may include services to be performed after the discharge of the jury, but in no event may a jury contract for services to be performed later than six months after the end of the fiscal year during which the jury was impaneled.
(d) Any contract entered into by a grand jury pursuant to this section shall stipulate that the product of that contract shall be delivered on or before a time certain to the then-current grand jury of that county for such use as that jury finds appropriate to its adopted objectives.
(Amended by Stats. 1988, Ch. 1297, Sec. 4.5.)
927.

A grand jury may, and when requested by the board of supervisors shall, investigate and report upon the needs for increase or decrease in salaries of the county-elected officials. A copy of such report shall be transmitted to the board of supervisors.
(Amended by Stats. 1976, Ch. 481.)
928.
Every grand jury may investigate and report upon the needs of all county officers in the county, including the abolition or creation of offices and the equipment for, or the method or system of performing the duties of, the several offices. Such investigation and report shall be conducted selectively each year. The grand jury shall cause a copy of such report to be transmitted to each member of the board of supervisors of the county.
(Amended by Stats. 1981, Ch. 800, Sec. 5.)
929.
As to any matter not subject to privilege, with the approval of the presiding judge of the superior court or the judge appointed by the presiding judge to supervise the grand jury, a grand jury may make available to the public part or all of the evidentiary material, findings, and other information relied upon by, or presented to, a grand jury for its final report in any civil grand jury investigation provided that the name of any person, or facts that lead to the identity of any person who provided information to the grand jury, shall not be released. Prior to granting approval pursuant to this section, a judge may require the redaction or masking of any part of the evidentiary material, findings, or other information to be released to the public including, but not limited to, the identity of witnesses and any testimony or materials of a defamatory or libelous nature.
(Added by Stats. 1998, Ch. 79, Sec. 1. Effective January 1, 1999.)
930.
If any grand jury shall, in the report above mentioned, comment upon any person or official who has not been indicted by such grand jury such comments shall not be deemed to be privileged.
(Added by Stats. 1959, Ch. 501.)
931.
All expenses of the grand jurors incurred under this article shall be paid by the treasurer of the county out of the general fund of the county upon warrants drawn by the county auditor upon the written order of the judge of the superior court of the county.
(Added by Stats. 1959, Ch. 501.)
932.
After investigating the books and accounts of the various officials of the county, as provided in the foregoing sections of this article, the grand jury may order the district attorney of the county to institute suit to recover any money that, in the judgment of the grand jury, may from any cause be due the county. The order of the grand jury, certified by the foreman of the grand jury and filed with the clerk of the superior court of the county, shall be full authority for the district attorney to institute and maintain any such suit.
(Amended by Stats. 2002, Ch. 784, Sec. 537. Effective January 1, 2003.)
933.
(a) Each grand jury shall submit to the presiding judge of the superior court a final report of its findings and recommendations that pertain to county government matters during the fiscal or calendar year. Final reports on any appropriate subject may be submitted to the presiding judge of the superior court at any time during the term of service of a grand jury. A final report may be submitted for comment to responsible officers, agencies, or departments, including the county board of supervisors, when applicable, upon finding of the presiding judge that the report is in compliance with this title. For 45 days after the end of the term, the foreperson and his or her designees shall, upon reasonable notice, be available to clarify the recommendations of the report.
(b) One copy of each final report, together with the responses thereto, found to be in compliance with this title shall be placed on file with the clerk of the court and remain on file in the office of the clerk. The clerk shall immediately forward a true copy of the report and the responses to the State Archivist who shall retain that report and all responses in perpetuity.
(c) No later than 90 days after the grand jury submits a final report on the operations of any public agency subject to its reviewing authority, the governing body of the public agency shall comment to the presiding judge of the superior court on the findings and recommendations pertaining to matters under the control of the governing body, and every elected county officer or agency head for which the grand jury has responsibility pursuant to Section 914.1 shall comment within 60 days to the presiding judge of the superior court, with an information copy sent to the board of supervisors, on the findings and recommendations pertaining to matters under the control of that county officer or agency head and any agency or agencies which that officer or agency head supervises or controls. In any city and county, the mayor shall also comment on the findings and recommendations. All of these comments and reports shall forthwith be submitted to the presiding judge of the superior court who impaneled the grand jury. A copy of all responses to grand jury reports shall be placed on file with the clerk of the public agency and the office of the county clerk, or the mayor when applicable, and shall remain on file in those offices. One copy shall be placed on file with the applicable grand jury final report by, and in the control of the currently impaneled grand jury, where it shall be maintained for a minimum of five years.
(d) As used in this section "agency" includes a department.
(Amended by Stats. 2002, Ch. 784, Sec. 538. Effective January 1, 2003.)
933.05.
(a) For purposes of subdivision (b) of Section 933, as to each grand jury finding, the responding person or entity shall indicate one of the following:
(1) The respondent agrees with the finding.
(2) The respondent disagrees wholly or partially with the finding, in which case the response shall specify the portion of the finding that is disputed and shall include an explanation of the reasons therefor.
(b) For purposes of subdivision (b) of Section 933, as to each grand jury recommendation, the responding person or entity shall report one of the following actions:
(1) The recommendation has been implemented, with a summary regarding the implemented action.
(2) The recommendation has not yet been implemented, but will be implemented in the future, with a timeframe for implementation.
(3) The recommendation requires further analysis, with an explanation and the scope and parameters of an analysis or study, and a timeframe for the matter to be prepared for discussion by the officer or head of the agency or department being investigated or reviewed, including the governing body of the public agency when applicable. This timeframe shall not exceed six months from the date of publication of the grand jury report.
(4) The recommendation will not be implemented because it is not warranted or is not reasonable, with an explanation therefor.
(c) However, if a finding or recommendation of the grand jury addresses budgetary or personnel matters of a county agency or department headed by an elected officer, both the agency or department head and the board of supervisors shall respond if requested by the grand jury, but the response of the board of supervisors shall address only those budgetary or personnel matters over which it has some decisionmaking authority. The response of the elected agency or department head shall address all aspects of the findings or recommendations affecting his or her agency or department.
(d) A grand jury may request a subject person or entity to come before the grand jury for the purpose of reading and discussing the findings of the grand jury report that relates to that person or entity in order to verify the accuracy of the findings prior to their release.

(e) During an investigation, the grand jury shall meet with the subject of that investigation regarding the investigation, unless the court, either on its own determination or upon request of the foreperson of the grand jury, determines that such a meeting would be detrimental.

(f) A grand jury shall provide to the affected agency a copy of the portion of the grand jury report relating to that person or entity two working days prior to its public release and after the approval of the presiding judge. No officer, agency, department, or governing body of a public agency shall disclose any contents of the report prior to the public release of the final report.

(Amended by Stats. 1997, Ch. 443, Sec. 5. Effective January 1, 1998.)

933.06.

(a) Notwithstanding Sections 916 and 940, in a county having a population of 20,000 or less, a final report may be adopted and submitted pursuant to Section 933 with the concurrence of at least 10 grand jurors if all of the following conditions are met:

(1) The grand jury consisting of 19 persons has been impaneled pursuant to law, and the membership is reduced from 19 to fewer than 12.

(2) The vacancies have not been filled pursuant to Section 908.1 within 30 days from the time that the clerk of the superior court is given written notice that the vacancy has occurred.

(3) A final report has not been submitted by the grand jury pursuant to Section 933.

(b) Notwithstanding Section 933, no responsible officers, agencies, or departments shall be required to comment on a final report submitted pursuant to this section.

(Amended by Stats. 2001, Ch. 854, Sec. 40. Effective January 1, 2002.)

933.1.

A grand jury may at any time examine the books and records of a redevelopment agency, a housing authority, created pursuant to Division 24 (commencing with Section 33000) of the Health and Safety Code, or a joint powers agency created pursuant to Chapter 5 (commencing with Section 6500) of Division 7 of Title 1 of the Government Code, and, in addition to any other investigatory powers granted by this chapter, may investigate and report upon the method or system of performing the duties of such agency or authority.

(Amended by Stats. 1986, Ch. 279, Sec. 1.)

933.5.

A grand jury may at any time examine the books and records of any special-purpose assessing or taxing district located wholly or partly in the county or the local agency formation commission in the county, and, in addition to any other investigatory powers granted by this chapter, may investigate and report upon the method or system of performing the duties of such district or commission.

(Amended by Stats. 1979, Ch. 306.)

933.6.

A grand jury may at any time examine the books and records of any nonprofit corporation established by or operated on behalf of a public entity the books and records of which it is authorized by law to examine, and, in addition to any other investigatory powers granted by this chapter, may investigate and report upon the method or system of performing the duties of such nonprofit corporation.

(Added by Stats. 1986, Ch. 279, Sec. 2.)

ARTICLE 3. Legal and Other Assistants for Grand Juries [934 - 938.4]
(Article 3 added by Stats. 1959, Ch. 501.)

934.

(a) The grand jury may, at all times, request the advice of the court, or the judge thereof, the district attorney, the county counsel, or the Attorney General. Unless advice is requested, the judge of the court, or county counsel as to civil matters, shall not be present during the sessions of the grand jury.

(b) The Attorney General may grant or deny a request for advice from the grand jury. If the Attorney General grants a request for advice from the grand jury, the Attorney General shall fulfill that request within existing financial and staffing resources.

(Amended by Stats. 1998, Ch. 230, Sec. 3. Effective January 1, 1999.)

935.

The district attorney of the county may at all times appear before the grand jury for the purpose of giving information or advice relative to any matter cognizable by the grand jury, and may interrogate witnesses before the grand jury whenever he thinks it necessary. When a charge against or involving the district attorney, or assistant district attorney, or deputy district attorney, or anyone employed by or connected with the office of the district attorney, is being investigated by the grand jury, such district attorney, or assistant district attorney, or deputy district attorney, or all or anyone or more of them, shall not be allowed to be present before such grand jury when such charge is being investigated, in an official capacity but only as a witness, and he shall only be present while a witness and after his appearance as such witness shall leave the place where the grand jury is holding its session.

(Added by Stats. 1959, Ch. 501.)

936.

When requested so to do by the grand jury of any county, the Attorney General may employ special counsel and special investigators, whose duty it shall be to investigate and present the evidence in such investigation to such grand jury.

The services of such special counsel and special investigators shall be a county charge of such county.

(Added by Stats. 1959, Ch. 501.)

936.5.

(a) When requested to do so by the grand jury of any county, the presiding judge of the superior court may employ special counsel and special investigators, whose duty it shall be to investigate and present the evidence of the investigation to the grand jury.

(b) Prior to the appointment, the presiding judge shall conduct an evidentiary hearing and find that a conflict exists that would prevent the local district attorney, the county counsel, and the Attorney General from performing such investigation. Notice of the hearing shall be given to each of them unless he or she is a subject of the investigation. The finding of the presiding judge may be appealed by the district attorney, the county counsel, or the Attorney General. The order shall be stayed pending the appeal made under this section.

(c) The authority to appoint is contingent upon the certification by the auditor-comptroller of the county, that the grand jury has funds appropriated to it sufficient to compensate the special counsel and investigator for services rendered pursuant to the court order. In the absence of a certification the court has no authority to appoint. In the event the county board of supervisors or a member thereof is under investigation, the county has an obligation to appropriate the necessary funds.

(Added by Stats. 1980, Ch. 290, Sec. 2.)

936.7.

(a) In a county of the eighth class, as defined by Sections 28020 and 28029 of the Government Code, upon a request by the grand jury, the presiding judge of the superior court may retain, in the name of the county, a special counsel to the grand jury. The request shall be presented to the presiding judge in camera, by an affidavit, executed by the foreperson of the grand jury, which specifies the reason for the request and the nature of the services sought, and which certifies that the appointment of the special counsel is reasonably necessary to aid the work of the grand jury. The affidavit shall be confidential and its contents may not be made public except by order of the presiding judge upon a showing of good cause. The special counsel shall be selected by the presiding judge following submission of the name of the nominee to the board of supervisors for comment.

The special counsel shall be retained under a contract executed by the presiding judge in the name of the county. The contract shall contain the following terms:

(1) The types of legal services to be rendered to the grand jury; provided, (i) that the special counsel's duties shall not include any legal advisory, investigative, or prosecutorial service which by statute is vested within the powers of the district attorney, and (ii) that the special counsel may not perform any investigative or prosecutorial service whatsoever except upon advance written approval by the presiding judge which specifies the number of hours of these services, the hourly rate therefor, and the subject matter of the inquiry.

(2) The hourly rate of compensation of the special counsel for legal advisory services delivered, together with a maximum contract amount payable for all services rendered under the contract during the term thereof, and all service authorizations issued pursuant thereto.

(3) That the contract may be canceled in advance of the expiration of its term by the presiding judge pursuant to service upon the special counsel of 10 days' advance written notice.

(b) The maximum contract amount shall be determined by the board of supervisors and included in the grand jury's annual operational budget. The maximum amount shall be subject to increase by the presiding judge through contract amendment during the term thereof, subject to and in compliance with the procedure prescribed by Section 914.5.

(c) The contract shall constitute a public record and shall be subject to public inspection and copying pursuant to the provisions of the California Public Records Act (Chapter 3.5 (commencing with Section 6250) of Division 7 of Title 1 of the Government Code). However, at the sole discretion of the board of supervisors, any or all of the following steps may be taken:

(1) The nomination by the presiding judge, and any or all actions by the board of supervisors in commenting upon the nominee and the comments, may be made confidential.

(2) The deliberations and actions may be undertaken in meetings from which the public is excluded, and the communication containing comments may constitute a confidential record which is not subject to public inspection or copying except at the sole discretion of the board of supervisors. Moreover, any written authorization by the presiding judge pursuant to paragraph (1) of subdivision (a) shall constitute a confidential record which is not subject to public inspection or copying except in connection with a dispute concerning compensation for services rendered.

(Added by Stats. 1988, Ch. 886, Sec. 2.)

937.

The grand jury or district attorney may require by subpoena the attendance of any person before the grand jury as interpreter. While his services are necessary, such interpreter may be present at the examination of witnesses before the grand jury. The compensation for services of such interpreter constitutes a charge against the county, and shall be fixed by the grand jury.

(Amended by Stats. 1976, Ch. 1264.)

938.

(a) Whenever criminal causes are being investigated before the grand jury, it shall appoint a competent stenographic reporter. He shall be sworn and shall report in shorthand the testimony given in such causes and shall transcribe the shorthand in all cases where an indictment is returned or accusation presented.

(b) At the request of the grand jury, the reporter shall also prepare transcripts of any testimony reported during any session of the immediately preceding grand jury.

(Amended by Stats. 1975, Ch. 298.)

938.1.

(a) If an indictment has been found or accusation presented against a defendant, such stenographic reporter shall certify and deliver to the clerk of the superior court in the county an original transcription of the reporter's shorthand notes and a copy thereof and as many additional copies as there are defendants, other than fictitious defendants, regardless of the number of charges or fictitious defendants included in the same investigation. The reporter shall complete the certification and delivery within 10 days after the indictment has been found or the accusation presented unless the court for good cause makes an order extending the time. The time shall not be extended more than 20 days. The clerk shall file the original of the transcript, deliver a copy of the transcript to the district attorney immediately upon receipt thereof and deliver a copy of such transcript to each such defendant or the defendant's attorney. If the copy of the testimony is not served as provided in this section, the court shall on motion of the defendant continue the trial to such time as may be necessary to secure to the defendant receipt of a copy of such testimony 10 days before such trial. If several criminal charges are investigated against a defendant on one investigation and thereafter separate indictments are returned or accusations presented upon said several charges, the delivery to such defendant or the defendant's attorney of one copy of the transcript of such investigation shall be a compliance with this section as to all of such indictments or accusations.

(b) The transcript shall not be open to the public until 10 days after its delivery to the defendant or the defendant's attorney. Thereafter the transcript shall be open to the public unless the court orders otherwise on its own motion or on motion of a party pending a determination as to whether all or part of the transcript should be sealed. If the court determines that there is a reasonable likelihood that making all or any part of the transcript public may prejudice a defendant's right to a fair and impartial trial, that part of the transcript shall be sealed until the defendant's trial has been completed.

(Amended by Stats. 2002, Ch. 784, Sec. 539. Effective January 1, 2003.)

938.2.

(a) For preparing any transcript in any case pursuant to subdivision (a) of Section 938.1, the stenographic reporter shall draw no salary or fees from the county for preparing such transcript in any case until all such transcripts of testimony in such case so taken by him are written up and delivered. Before making the order for payment to the reporter, the judge of the superior court shall require the reporter to show by affidavit or otherwise that he has written up and delivered all testimony taken by him, in accordance with subdivision (a) of Section 938 and Section 938.1.

(b) Before making the order for payment to a reporter who has prepared transcripts pursuant to subdivision (b) of Section 938, the judge of the superior court shall require the reporter to show by affidavit or otherwise that he has written up and delivered all testimony requested of him in accordance with that sudivision.

(Amended by Stats. 1975, Ch. 298.)

938.3.

The services of the stenographic reporter shall constitute a charge against the county, and the stenographic reporter shall be compensated for reporting and transcribing at the same rates as prescribed in Sections 69947 to 69954, inclusive, of the Government Code, to be paid out of the county treasury on a warrant of the county auditor when ordered by the judge of the superior court.

(Amended by Stats. 1987, Ch. 828, Sec. 56.)

938.4.

The superior court shall arrange for a suitable meeting room and other support as the court determines is necessary for the grand jury. Any costs incurred by the court as a result of this section shall be absorbed by the court or the county from existing resources.

(Added by Stats. 1997, Ch. 443, Sec. 6. Effective January 1, 1998.)

ARTICLE 4. Conduct of Investigations [939 - 939.91]
(Article 4 added by Stats. 1959, Ch. 501.)

939.

No person other than those specified in Article 3 (commencing with Section 934), and in Sections 939.1, 939.11, and 939.21, and the officer having custody of a prisoner witness while the prisoner is testifying, is permitted to be present during the criminal

sessions of the grand jury except the members and witnesses actually under examination. Members of the grand jury who have been excused pursuant to Section 939.5 shall not be present during any part of these proceedings. No persons other than grand jurors shall be permitted to be present during the expression of the opinions of the grand jurors, or the giving of their votes, on any criminal or civil matter before them.
(Amended by Stats. 1998, Ch. 755, Sec. 1. Effective January 1, 1999.)
939.1.
The grand jury acting through its foreman and the attorney general or the district attorney may make a joint written request for public sessions of the grand jury. The request shall be filed with the superior court. If the court, or the judge thereof, finds that the subject matter of the investigation affects the general public welfare, involving the alleged corruption, misfeasance, or malfeasance in office or dereliction of duty of public officials or employees or of any person allegedly acting in conjunction or conspiracy with such officials or employees in such alleged acts, the court or judge may make an order directing the grand jury to conduct its investigation in a session or sessions open to the public. The order shall state the finding of the court. The grand jury shall comply with the order.
The conduct of such investigation and the examination of witnesses shall be by the members of the grand jury and the district attorney.
The deliberation of the grand jury and its voting upon such investigation shall be in private session. The grand jury may find indictments based wholly or partially upon the evidence introduced at such public session.
(Added by Stats. 1959, Ch. 501.)
939.11.
Any member of the grand jury who has a hearing, sight, or speech disability may request an interpreter when his or her services are necessary to assist the juror to carry out his or her duties. The request shall be filed with the superior court. If the court, or the judge thereof, finds that an interpreter is necessary, the court shall make an order to that effect and may require by subpoena the attendance of any person before the grand jury as interpreter. If the services of an interpreter are necessary, the court shall instruct the grand jury and the interpreter that the interpreter is not to participate in the jury's deliberations in any manner except to facilitate communication between the disabled juror and the other jurors. The court shall place the interpreter under oath not to disclose any grand jury matters, including the testimony of any witness, statements of any grand juror, or the vote of any grand juror, except in the due course of judicial proceedings.
(Added by Stats. 1986, Ch. 357, Sec. 3.)
939.2.
A subpoena requiring the attendance of a witness before the grand jury may be signed and issued by the district attorney, his investigator or, upon request of the grand jury, by any judge of the superior court, for witnesses in the state, in support of the prosecution, for those witnesses whose testimony, in his opinion is material in an investigation before the grand jury, and for such other witnesses as the grand jury, upon an investigation pending before them, may direct.
(Amended by Stats. 1971, Ch. 1196.)
939.21.
(a) Any prosecution witness before the grand jury in a proceeding involving a violation of Section 243.4, 261, 273a, 273d, 285, 286, 287, 288, 288.5, or 289, subdivision (1) of Section 314, Section 368, 647.6, or former Section 288a or 647a, who is a minor or a dependent person, may, at the discretion of the prosecution, select a person of his or her own choice to attend the testimony of the prosecution witness for the purpose of providing support. The person chosen shall not be a witness in the same proceeding, or a person described in Section 1070 of the Evidence Code.
(b) The grand jury foreperson shall inform any person permitted to attend the grand jury proceedings pursuant to this section that grand jury proceedings are confidential and may not be discussed with anyone not in attendance at the proceedings. The foreperson also shall admonish that person not to prompt, sway, or influence the witness in any way. Nothing in this section shall preclude the presiding judge from exercising his or her discretion to remove a person from the grand jury proceeding whom the judge believes is prompting, swaying, or influencing the witness.
(Amended by Stats. 2018, Ch. 423, Sec. 82. (SB 1494) Effective January 1, 2019.)
939.3.
In any investigation or proceeding before a grand jury for any felony offense when a person refuses to answer a question or produce evidence of any other kind on the ground that he may be incriminated thereby, proceedings may be had under Section 1324.
(Added by Stats. 1959, Ch. 501.)
939.4.
The foreman may administer an oath to any witness appearing before the grand jury.
(Added by Stats. 1959, Ch. 501.)
939.5.
Before considering a charge against any person, the foreman of the grand jury shall state to those present the matter to be considered and the person to be charged with an offense in connection therewith. He shall direct any member of the grand jury who has a state of mind in reference to the case or to either party which will prevent him from acting impartially and without prejudice to the substantial rights of the party to retire. Any violation of this section by the foreman or any member of the grand jury is punishable by the court as a contempt.
(Added by Stats. 1959, Ch. 501.)
939.6.
(a) Subject to subdivision (b), in the investigation of a charge, the grand jury shall receive no other evidence than what is:
(1) Given by witnesses produced and sworn before the grand jury;
(2) Furnished by writings, material objects, or other things presented to the senses; or
(3) Contained in a deposition that is admissible under subdivision 3 of Section 686.
(b) Except as provided in subdivision (c), the grand jury shall not receive any evidence except that which would be admissible over objection at the trial of a criminal action, but the fact that evidence that would have been excluded at trial was received by the grand jury does not render the indictment void where sufficient competent evidence to support the indictment was received by the grand jury.
(c) Notwithstanding Section 1200 of the Evidence Code, as to the evidence relating to the foundation for admissibility into evidence of documents, exhibits, records, and other items of physical evidence, the evidence to support the indictment may be based in whole or in part upon the sworn testimony of a law enforcement officer relating the statement of a declarant made out of court and offered for the truth of the matter asserted. Any law enforcement officer testifying as to a hearsay statement pursuant to this subdivision shall have either five years of law enforcement experience or have completed a training course certified by the Commission on Peace Officer Standards and Training that includes training in the investigation and reporting of cases and testifying at preliminary hearings.
(Amended by Stats. 1998, Ch. 757, Sec. 4. Effective January 1, 1999.)
939.7.
The grand jury is not required to hear evidence for the defendant, but it shall weigh all the evidence submitted to it, and when it has reason to believe that other evidence within its reach will explain away the charge, it shall order the evidence to be produced, and for that purpose may require the district attorney to issue process for the witnesses.
(Added by Stats. 1959, Ch. 501.)
939.71.
(a) If the prosecutor is aware of exculpatory evidence, the prosecutor shall inform the grand jury of its nature and existence. Once the prosecutor has informed the grand jury of exculpatory evidence pursuant to this section, the prosecutor shall inform the grand jury of its duties under Section 939.7. If a failure to comply with the provisions of this section results in substantial prejudice, it shall be grounds for dismissal of the portion of the indictment related to that evidence.
(b) It is the intent of the Legislature by enacting this section to codify the holding in Johnson v. Superior Court, 15 Cal. 3d 248, and to affirm the duties of the grand jury pursuant to Section 939.7.
(Added by Stats. 1997, Ch. 22, Sec. 1. Effective January 1, 1998.)
939.8.
The grand jury shall find an indictment when all the evidence before it, taken together, if unexplained or uncontradicted, would, in its judgment, warrant a conviction by a trial jury.
(Added by Stats. 1959, Ch. 501.)
939.9.
A grand jury shall make no report, declaration, or recommendation on any matter except on the basis of its own investigation of the matter made by such grand jury. A grand jury shall not adopt as its own the recommendation of another grand jury unless the grand jury adopting such recommendation does so after its own investigation of the matter as to which the recommendation is made, as required by this section.
(Added by Stats. 1959, Ch. 501.)
939.91.
(a) A grand jury which investigates a charge against a person, and as a result thereof cannot find an indictment against such person, shall, at the request of such person and upon the approval of the court which impaneled the grand jury, report or declare that a charge against such person was investigated and that the grand jury could not as a result of the evidence presented find an indictment. The report or declaration shall be issued upon completion of the investigation of the suspected criminal conduct, or series of related suspected criminal conduct, and in no event beyond the end of the grand jury's term.
(b) A grand jury shall, at the request of the person called and upon the approval of the court which impaneled the grand jury, report or declare that any person called before the grand jury for a purpose, other than to investigate a charge against such person, was called only as a witness to an investigation which did not involve a charge against such person. The report or declaration shall be issued upon completion of the investigation of the suspected criminal conduct, or series of related suspected criminal conduct, and in no event beyond the end of the grand jury's term.
(Added by Stats. 1975, Ch. 467.)

TITLE 5. THE PLEADINGS [940 - 973]

(Heading of Title 5 amended by Stats. 1951, Ch. 1674.)

CHAPTER 1. Finding and Presentment of the Indictment [940 - 945]

(Chapter 1 enacted 1872.)
940.
An indictment cannot be found without concurrence of at least 14 grand jurors in a county in which the required number of members of the grand jury prescribed by Section 888.2 is 23, at least eight grand jurors in a county in which the required number of members is 11, and at least 12 grand jurors in all other counties. When so found it shall be endorsed, "A true bill," and the endorsement shall be signed by the foreman of the grand jury.
(Amended by Stats. 1994, Ch. 295, Sec. 2. Effective January 1, 1995.)
943.
When an indictment is found, the names of the witnesses examined before the Grand Jury, or whose depositions may have been read before them, must be inserted at the foot of the indictment, or indorsed thereon, before it is presented to the Court.
(Enacted 1872.)
944.
An indictment, when found by the grand jury, must be presented by their foreman, in their presence, to the court, and must be filed with the clerk. No recommendation as to the dollar amount of bail to be fixed shall be made to any court by any grand jury.
(Amended by Stats. 1974, Ch. 695.)
945.
When an indictment is found against a defendant not in custody, the same proceedings must be had as are prescribed in Sections 979 to 984, inclusive, against a defendant who fails to appear for arraignment.
(Enacted 1872.)

CHAPTER 2. Rules of Pleading [948 - 973]

(Heading of Chapter 2 amended by Stats. 1951, Ch. 1674.)
948.
All the forms of pleading in criminal actions, and the rules by which the sufficiency of pleadings is to be determined, are those prescribed by this Code.
(Enacted 1872.)
949.
The first pleading on the part of the people in the superior court in a felony case is the indictment, information, or the complaint in any case certified to the superior court under Section 859a. The first pleading on the part of the people in a misdemeanor or infraction case is the complaint except as otherwise provided by law. The first pleading on the part of the people in a proceeding pursuant to Section 3060 of the Government Code is an accusation.
(Amended by Stats. 1998, Ch. 931, Sec. 373. Effective September 28, 1998.)
950.
The accusatory pleading must contain:
1. The title of the action, specifying the name of the court to which the same is presented, and the names of the parties;
2. A statement of the public offense or offenses charged therein.
(Amended by Stats. 1951, Ch. 1674.)
951.
An indictment or information may be in substantially the following form: The people of the State of California against A. B. In the superior court of the State of California, in and for the county of ______. The grand jury (or the district attorney) of the county of ______ hereby accuses A. B. of a felony (or misdemeanor), to wit: (giving the name of the crime, as murder, burglary, etc.), in that on or about the _____ day of _____, 19__, in the county of ______, State of California, he (here insert statement of act or omission, as for example, "murdered C. D.").
(Amended by Stats. 1927, Ch. 613.)

952.
In charging an offense, each count shall contain, and shall be sufficient if it contains in substance, a statement that the accused has committed some public offense therein specified. Such statement may be made in ordinary and concise language without any technical averments or any allegations of matter not essential to be proved. It may be in the words of the enactment describing the offense or declaring the matter to be a public offense, or in any words sufficient to give the accused notice of the offense of which he is accused. In charging theft it shall be sufficient to allege that the defendant unlawfully took the labor or property of another.
(Amended by Stats. 1929, Ch. 159.)

953.
When a defendant is charged by a fictitious or erroneous name, and in any stage of the proceedings his true name is discovered, it must be inserted in the subsequent proceedings, referring to the fact of his being charged by the name mentioned in the accusatory pleading.
(Amended by Stats. 1951, Ch. 1674.)

954.
An accusatory pleading may charge two or more different offenses connected together in their commission, or different statements of the same offense or two or more different offenses of the same class of crimes or offenses, under separate counts, and if two or more accusatory pleadings are filed in such cases in the same court, the court may order them to be consolidated. The prosecution is not required to elect between the different offenses or counts set forth in the accusatory pleading, but the defendant may be convicted of any number of the offenses charged, and each offense of which the defendant is convicted must be stated in the verdict or the finding of the court; provided, that the court in which a case is triable, in the interests of justice and for good cause shown, may in its discretion order that the different offenses or counts set forth in the accusatory pleading be tried separately or divided into two or more groups and each of said groups tried separately. An acquittal of one or more counts shall not be deemed an acquittal of any other count.
(Amended by Stats. 1951, Ch. 1674.)

954.1.
In cases in which two or more different offenses of the same class of crimes or offenses have been charged together in the same accusatory pleading, or where two or more accusatory pleadings charging offenses of the same class of crimes or offenses have been consolidated, evidence concerning one offense or offenses need not be admissible as to the other offense or offenses before the jointly charged offenses may be tried together before the same trier of fact.
(Added June 5, 1990, by initiative Proposition 115, Sec. 19.)

955.
The precise time at which the offense was committed need not be stated in the accusatory pleading, but it may be alleged to have been committed at any time before the finding or filing thereof, except where the time is a material ingredient in the offense.
(Amended by Stats. 1951, Ch. 1674.)

956.
When an offense involves the commission of, or an attempt to commit a private injury, and is described with sufficient certainty in other respects to identify the act, an erroneous allegation as to the person injured, or intended to be injured, or of the place where the offense was committed, or of the property involved in its commission, is not material.
(Amended by Stats. 1927, Ch. 611.)

957.
The words used in an accusatory pleading are construed in their usual acceptance in common language, except such words and phrases as are defined by law, which are construed according to their legal meaning.
(Amended by Stats. 1951, Ch. 1674.)

958.
Words used in a statute to define a public offense need not be strictly pursued in the accusatory pleading, but other words conveying the same meaning may be used.
(Amended by Stats. 1951, Ch. 1674.)

959.
The accusatory pleading is sufficient if it can be understood therefrom:
1. That it is filed in a court having authority to receive it, though the name of the court be not stated.
2. If an indictment, that it was found by a grand jury of the county in which the court was held, or if an information, that it was subscribed and presented to the court by the district attorney of the county in which the court was held.
3. If a complaint, that it is made and subscribed by some natural person and sworn to before some officer entitled to administer oaths.
4. That the defendant is named, or if his name is unknown, that he is described by a fictitious name, with a statement that his true name is to the grand jury, district attorney, or complainant, as the case may be, unknown.
5. That the offense charged therein is triable in the court in which it is filed, except in case of a complaint filed with a magistrate for the purposes of a preliminary examination.
6. That the offense was committed at some time prior to the filing of the accusatory pleading.
(Amended by Stats. 1951, Ch. 1674.)

959.1.
(a) Notwithstanding Sections 740, 806, 949, and 959 or any other law to the contrary, a criminal prosecution may be commenced by filing an accusatory pleading in electronic form with the magistrate or in a court having authority to receive it.
(b) As used in this section, accusatory pleadings include, but are not limited to, the complaint, the information, and the indictment.
(c) A magistrate or court is authorized to receive and file an accusatory pleading in electronic form if all of the following conditions are met:
(1) The accusatory pleading is issued in the name of, and transmitted by, a public prosecutor or law enforcement agency filing pursuant to Chapter 5c (commencing with Section 853.5) or Chapter 5d (commencing with Section 853.9), or by a clerk of the court with respect to complaints issued for the offenses of failure to appear, pay a fine, or comply with an order of the court.
(2) The magistrate or court has the facility to electronically store the accusatory pleading for the statutory period of record retention.
(3) The magistrate or court has the ability to reproduce the accusatory pleading in physical form upon demand and payment of any costs involved.
An accusatory pleading shall be deemed to have been filed when it has been received by the magistrate or court.
When transmitted in electronic form, the accusatory pleading shall be exempt from any requirement that it be subscribed by a natural person. It is sufficient to satisfy any requirement that an accusatory pleading, or any part of it, be sworn to before an officer entitled to administer oaths, if the pleading, or any part of it, was in fact sworn to and the electronic form indicates which parts of the pleading were sworn to and the name of the officer who administered the oath.
(d) Notwithstanding any other law, a notice to appear issued on a form approved by the Judicial Council may be received and filed by a court in electronic form, if the following conditions are met:
(1) The notice to appear is issued and transmitted by a law enforcement agency prosecuting pursuant to Chapter 5c (commencing with Section 853.5) or Chapter 5d

(commencing with Section 853.9) of Title 3 of Part 2 of this code, or Chapter 2 (commencing with Section 40300) of Division 17 of the Vehicle Code.
(2) The court has all of the following:
(A) The ability to receive the notice to appear in electronic format.
(B) The facility to electronically store an electronic copy and the data elements of the notice to appear for the statutory period of record retention.
(C) The ability to reproduce the electronic copy of the notice to appear and those data elements in printed form upon demand and payment of any costs involved.
(3) The issuing agency has the ability to reproduce the notice to appear in physical form upon demand and payment of any costs involved.
(e) A notice to appear that is received under subdivision (d) is deemed to have been filed when it has been accepted by the court and is in the form approved by the Judicial Council.
(f) If transmitted in electronic form, the notice to appear is deemed to have been signed by the defendant if it includes a digitized facsimile of the defendant's signature on the notice to appear. A notice to appear filed electronically under subdivision (d) need not be subscribed by the citing officer. An electronically submitted notice to appear need not be verified by the citing officer with a declaration under penalty of perjury if the electronic form indicates which parts of the notice are verified by that declaration and the name of the officer making the declaration.
(Amended by Stats. 2006, Ch. 567, Sec. 23. Effective January 1, 2007.)

960.
No accusatory pleading is insufficient, nor can the trial, judgment, or other proceeding thereon be affected by reason of any defect or imperfection in matter of form which does not prejudice a substantial right of the defendant upon the merits.
(Amended by Stats. 1951, Ch. 1674.)

961.
Neither presumptions of law, nor matters of which judicial notice is authorized or required to be taken, need be stated in an accusatory pleading.
(Amended by Stats. 1965, Ch. 299.)

962.
In pleading a judgment or other determination of, or proceeding before, a Court or officer of special jurisdiction, it is not necessary to state the facts constituting jurisdiction; but the judgment or determination may be stated as given or made, or the proceedings had. The facts constituting jurisdiction, however, must be established on the trial.
(Enacted 1872.)

963.
In pleading a private statute, or an ordinance of a county or a municipal corporation, or a right derived therefrom, it is sufficient to refer to the statute or ordinance by its title and the day of its passage, and the court must thereupon take judicial notice thereof in the same manner that it takes judicial notice of matters listed in Section 452 of the Evidence Code.
(Amended by Stats. 1965, Ch. 299.)

964.
(a) In each county, the district attorney and the courts, in consultation with any local law enforcement agencies that may desire to provide information or other assistance, shall establish a mutually agreeable procedure to protect confidential personal information regarding any witness or victim contained in a police report, arrest report, or investigative report if one of these reports is submitted to a court by a prosecutor in support of a criminal complaint, indictment, or information, or by a prosecutor or law enforcement officer in support of a search warrant or an arrest warrant.
(b) For purposes of this section, "confidential personal information" includes, but is not limited to, an address, telephone number, driver's license or California Identification Card number, social security number, date of birth, place of employment, employee identification number, mother's maiden name, demand deposit account number, savings or checking account number, or credit card number.
(c) (1) This section may not be construed to impair or affect the provisions of Chapter 10 (commencing with Section 1054) of Title 6 of Part 2.
(2) This section may not be construed to impair or affect procedures regarding informant disclosure provided by Sections 1040 to 1042, inclusive, of the Evidence Code, or as altering procedures regarding sealed search warrant affidavits as provided by People v. Hobbs (1994) 7 Cal.4th 948.
(3) This section shall not be construed to impair or affect a criminal defense counsel's access to unredacted reports otherwise authorized by law, or the submission of documents in support of a civil complaint.
(4) This section applies as an exception to California Rule of Court 2.550, as provided by paragraph (2) of subdivision (a) of that rule.
(Amended by Stats. 2012, Ch. 867, Sec. 22. (SB 1144) Effective January 1, 2013.)

965.
When an instrument which is the subject of an indictment or information for forgery has been destroyed or withheld by the act or the procurement of the defendant, and the fact of such destruction or withholding is alleged in the indictment, or information, and established on the trial, the misdescription of the instrument is immaterial.
(Amended by Code Amendments 1880, Ch. 47.)

966.
In an accusatory pleading for perjury, or subornation of perjury, it is sufficient to set forth the substance of the controversy or matter in respect to which the offense was committed, and in what court and before whom the oath alleged to be false was taken, and that the court, or the person before whom it was taken, had authority to administer it, with proper allegations of the falsity of the matter on which the perjury is assigned; but the accusatory pleading need not set forth the pleadings, records, or proceedings with which the oath is connected, nor the commission or authority of the court or person before whom the perjury was committed.
(Amended by Stats. 1951, Ch. 1674.)

967.
In an accusatory pleading charging the theft of money, bank notes, certificates of stock or valuable securities, or a conspiracy to cheat or defraud a person of any such property, it is sufficient to allege the theft, or the conspiracy to cheat or defraud, to be of money, bank notes, certificates of stock or valuable securities without specifying the coin, number, denomination, or kind thereof.
(Amended by Stats. 1951, Ch. 1674.)

968.
An accusatory pleading charging exhibiting, publishing, passing, selling, or offering to sell, or having in possession, with such intent, any lewd or obscene book, pamphlet, picture, print, card, paper, or writing, need not set forth any portion of the language used or figures shown upon such book, pamphlet, picture, print, card, paper, or writing; but it is sufficient to state generally the fact of the lewdness or obscenity thereof.
(Amended by Stats. 1951, Ch. 1674.)

969.
In charging the fact of a previous conviction of felony, or of an attempt to commit an offense which, if perpetrated, would have been a felony, or of theft, it is sufficient to state, "That the defendant, before the commission of the offense charged herein, was in (giving the title of the court in which the conviction was had) convicted of a felony (or attempt, etc., or of theft)." If more than one previous conviction is charged, the date of the judgment upon each conviction may be stated, and all known previous convictions, whether in this State or elsewhere, must be charged.
(Amended by Stats. 1951, Ch. 1674.)

969a.

Whenever it shall be discovered that a pending indictment or information does not charge all prior felonies of which the defendant has been convicted either in this State or elsewhere, said indictment or information may be forthwith amended to charge such prior conviction or convictions, and if such amendment is made it shall be made upon order of the court, and no action of the grand jury (in the case of an indictment) shall be necessary. Defendant shall promptly be rearraigned on such information or indictment as amended and be required to plead thereto.
(Amended by Stats. 1957, Ch. 1617.)
969b.
For the purpose of establishing prima facie evidence of the fact that a person being tried for a crime or public offense under the laws of this State has been convicted of an act punishable by imprisonment in a state prison, county jail or city jail of this State, and has served a term therefor in any penal institution, or has been convicted of an act in any other state, which would be punishable as a crime in this State, and has served a term therefor in any state penitentiary, reformatory, county jail or city jail, or has been convicted of an act declared to be a crime by any act or law of the United States, and has served a term therefor in any penal institution, the records or copies of records of any state penitentiary, reformatory, county jail, city jail, or federal penitentiary in which such person has been imprisoned, when such records or copies thereof have been certified by the official custodian of such records, may be introduced as such evidence.
(Amended by Stats. 1949, Ch. 701.)
969e.
In charging the fact of a previous conviction for a violation of Section 5652 of the Fish and Game Code, or of Section 13001 or 13002 of the Health and Safety Code or of Section 374b or 374d of the Penal Code or of Section 23111, 23112, or 23113 of the Vehicle Code, it is sufficient to state, "That the defendant, before the commission of the offense charged herein, was in (giving the title of the court in which the conviction was had) convicted of a violation of (specifying the section violated)."
(Added by Stats. 1977, Ch. 1161. Note: Former termination clause was deleted by Stats. 1980, Ch. 364, Sec. 34.)
969f.
(a) Whenever a defendant has committed a serious felony as defined in subdivision (c) of Section 1192.7, the facts that make the crime constitute a serious felony may be charged in the accusatory pleading. However, the crime shall not be referred to as a serious felony nor shall the jury be informed that the crime is defined as a serious felony. This charge, if made, shall be added to and be a part of the count or each of the counts of the accusatory pleading which charged the offense. If the defendant pleads not guilty to the offense charged in any count which alleges that the defendant committed a serious felony, the question whether or not the defendant committed a serious felony as alleged shall be tried by the court or jury which tries the issue upon the plea of not guilty. If the defendant pleads guilty of the offense charged, the question whether or not the defendant committed a serious felony as alleged shall be separately admitted or denied by the defendant.
(b) In charging an act or acts that bring the defendant within the operation of paragraph (8) or (23) of subdivision (c) of Section 1192.7, it is sufficient for purposes of subdivision (a) if the pleading states the following:
"It is further alleged that in the commission and attempted commission of the foregoing offense, the defendant _____, personally [inflicted great bodily injury on another person, other than an accomplice] [used a firearm, to wit: _____,] [used a dangerous and deadly weapon, to wit: _____,] within the meaning of Sections 667 and 1192.7 of the Penal Code."
(Added by Stats. 1991, Ch. 249, Sec. 1.)
969.5.
(a) Whenever it shall be discovered that a pending complaint to which a plea of guilty has been made under Section 859a does not charge all prior felonies of which the defendant has been convicted either in this state or elsewhere, the complaint may be forthwith amended to charge the prior conviction or convictions and the amendments may and shall be made upon order of the court. The defendant shall thereupon be arraigned before the court to which the complaint has been certified and shall be asked whether he or she has suffered the prior conviction. If the defendant enters a denial, his or her answer shall be entered in the minutes of the court. The refusal of the defendant to answer is equivalent to a denial that he or she has suffered the prior conviction.
(b) Except as provided in subdivision (c), the question of whether or not the defendant has suffered the prior conviction shall be tried by a jury impaneled for that purpose unless a jury is waived, in which case it may be tried by the court.
(c) Notwithstanding the provisions of subdivision (b), the question of whether the defendant is the person who has suffered the prior conviction shall be tried by the court without a jury.
(Added by renumbering Section 969½ by Stats. 1998, Ch. 235, Sec. 1. Effective January 1, 1999.)
970.
When several defendants are named in one accusatory pleading, any one or more may be convicted or acquitted.
(Amended by Stats. 1951, Ch. 1674.)
971.
The distinction between an accessory before the fact and a principal, and between principals in the first and second degree is abrogated; and all persons concerned in the commission of a crime, who by the operation of other provisions of this code are principals therein, shall hereafter be prosecuted, tried and punished as principals and no other facts need be alleged in any accusatory pleading against any such person than are required in an accusatory pleading against a principal.
(Amended by Stats. 1951, Ch. 1674.)
972.
An accessory to the commission of a felony may be prosecuted, tried, and punished, though the principal may be neither prosecuted nor tried, and though the principal may have been acquitted.
(Amended by Code Amendments 1880, Ch. 47.)
973.
If the accusatory pleading in any criminal action has heretofore been lost or destroyed or shall hereafter be lost or destroyed, the court must, upon the application of the prosecuting attorney or of the defendant, order a copy of such pleading to be filed and substituted for the original, and when filed and substituted, as provided in this section, the copy shall have the same force and effect as if it were the original pleading.
(Added by Stats. 1951, Ch. 1674.)

TITLE 6. PLEADINGS AND PROCEEDINGS BEFORE TRIAL [976 - 1054.10]

(Heading of Title 6 amended by Stats. 1951, Ch. 1674.)

CHAPTER 1. Of the Arraignment of the Defendant [976 - 993]

(Chapter 1 enacted by Stats. 1872.)

976.
(a) When the accusatory pleading is filed, the defendant shall be arraigned thereon before the court in which it is filed, unless the action is transferred to some other court for trial. However, within any county, if the defendant is in custody, upon the approval of both the presiding judge of the court in which the accusatory pleading is filed and the presiding judge of the court nearest to the place in which he or she is held in custody the arraignment may be before the court nearest to that place of custody.
(b) A defendant arrested in another county shall have the right to be taken before a magistrate in the arresting county for the purpose of being admitted to bail, as provided in Section 821 or 822. The defendant shall be informed of this right.
(c) Prior to being taken from the place where he or she is in custody to the place where he or she is to be arraigned, the defendent shall be allowed to make three completed telephone calls, at no expense to the defendant, in addition to any other telephone calls which the defendant is entitled to make pursuant to law.
(Amended by Stats. 1982, Ch. 395, Sec. 1.)
977.
(a) (1) In all cases in which the accused is charged with a misdemeanor only, he or she may appear by counsel only, except as provided in paragraphs (2) and (3). If the accused agrees, the initial court appearance, arraignment, and plea may be by video, as provided by subdivision (c).
(2) If the accused is charged with a misdemeanor offense involving domestic violence, as defined in Section 6211 of the Family Code, or a misdemeanor violation of Section 273.6, the accused shall be present for arraignment and sentencing, and at any time during the proceedings when ordered by the court for the purpose of being informed of the conditions of a protective order issued pursuant to Section 136.2.
(3) If the accused is charged with a misdemeanor offense involving driving under the influence, in an appropriate case, the court may order a defendant to be present for arraignment, at the time of plea, or at sentencing. For purposes of this paragraph, a misdemeanor offense involving driving under the influence shall include a misdemeanor violation of any of the following:
(A) Subdivision (b) of Section 191.5.
(B) Section 23103 as specified in Section 23103.5 of the Vehicle Code.
(C) Section 23152 of the Vehicle Code.
(D) Section 23153 of the Vehicle Code.
(b) (1) Except as provided in subdivision (c), in all cases in which a felony is charged, the accused shall be personally present at the arraignment, at the time of plea, during the preliminary hearing, during those portions of the trial when evidence is taken before the trier of fact, and at the time of the imposition of sentence. The accused shall be personally present at all other proceedings unless he or she shall, with leave of court, execute in open court, a written waiver of his or her right to be personally present, as provided by paragraph (2). If the accused agrees, the initial court appearance, arraignment, and plea may be by video, as provided by subdivision (c).
(2) The accused may execute a written waiver of his or her right to be personally present, approved by his or her counsel, and the waiver shall be filed with the court. However, the court may specifically direct the defendant to be personally present at any particular proceeding or portion thereof. The waiver shall be substantially in the following form:
"Waiver of Defendant's Personal Presence"
"The undersigned defendant, having been advised of his or her right to be present at all stages of the proceedings, including, but not limited to, presentation of and arguments on questions of fact and law, and to be confronted by and cross-examine all witnesses, hereby waives the right to be present at the hearing of any motion or other proceeding in this cause. The undersigned defendant hereby requests the court to proceed during every absence of the defendant that the court may permit pursuant to this waiver, and hereby agrees that his or her interest is represented at all times by the presence of his or her attorney the same as if the defendant were personally present in court, and further agrees that notice to his or her attorney that his or her presence in court on a particular day at a particular time is required is notice to the defendant of the requirement of his or her appearance at that time and place."
(c) (1) The court may permit the initial court appearance and arraignment of defendants held in any state, county, or local facility within the county on felony or misdemeanor charges, except for those defendants who were indicted by a grand jury, to be conducted by two-way electronic audiovideo communication between the defendant and the courtroom in lieu of the physical presence of the defendant in the courtroom. If the defendant is represented by counsel, the attorney shall be present with the defendant at the initial court appearance and arraignment, and may enter a plea during the arraignment. However, if the defendant is represented by counsel at an arraignment on an information in a felony case, and if the defendant does not plead guilty or nolo contendere to any charge, the attorney shall be present with the defendant or if the attorney is not present with the defendant, the attorney shall be present in court during the hearing. The defendant shall have the right to make his or her plea while physically present in the courtroom if he or she so requests. If the defendant decides not to exercise the right to be physically present in the courtroom, he or she shall execute a written waiver of that right. A judge may order a defendant's personal appearance in court for the initial court appearance and arraignment. In a misdemeanor case, a judge may, pursuant to this subdivision, accept a plea of guilty or no contest from a defendant who is not physically in the courtroom. In a felony case, a judge may, pursuant to this subdivision, accept a plea of guilty or no contest from a defendant who is not physically in the courtroom if the parties stipulate thereto.
(2) (A) A defendant who does not wish to be personally present for noncritical portions of the trial when no testimonial evidence is taken may make an oral waiver in open court prior to the proceeding or may submit a written request to the court, which the court may grant in its discretion. The court may, when a defendant has waived the right to be personally present, require a defendant held in any state, county, or local facility within the county on felony or misdemeanor charges to be present for noncritical portions of the trial when no testimonial evidence is taken, including, but not limited to, confirmation of the preliminary hearing, status conferences, trial readiness conferences, discovery motions, receipt of records, the setting of the trial date, a motion to vacate the trial date, and motions in limine, by two-way electronic audiovideo communication between the defendant and the courtroom in lieu of the physical presence of the defendant in the courtroom. If the defendant is represented by counsel, the attorney shall not be required to be personally present with the defendant for noncritical portions of the trial, if the audiovideo conferencing system or other technology allows for private communication between the defendant and the attorney prior to and during the noncritical portion of trial. Any private communication shall be confidential and privileged pursuant to Section 952 of the Evidence Code.
(B) This paragraph does not expand or limit the right of a defendant to be personally present with his or her counsel at a particular proceeding as required by Section 15 of Article 1 of the California Constitution.
(Amended by Stats. 2014, Ch. 167, Sec. 1. (AB 2397) Effective January 1, 2015.)
977.1.
The resolution of questions of fact or issues of law by trial or hearing which can be made without the assistance or participation of the defendant is not prohibited by the existence of any pending proceeding to determine whether the defendant is or remains mentally incompetent or gravely disabled pursuant to the provisions of either this code or the Welfare and Institutions Code.
(Added by Stats. 1974, Ch. 1511.)
977.2.

(a) Notwithstanding Section 977 or any other law, in any case in which the defendant is charged with a misdemeanor or a felony and is currently incarcerated in the state prison, the Department of Corrections may arrange for all court appearances in superior court, except for the preliminary hearing, trial, judgment and sentencing, and motions to suppress, to be conducted by two-way electronic audiovideo communication between the defendant and the courtroom in lieu of the physical presence of the defendant in the courtroom. Nothing in this section shall be interpreted to eliminate the authority of the court to issue an order requiring the defendant to be physically present in the courtroom in those cases where the court finds circumstances that require the physical presence of the defendant in the courtroom. For those court appearances that the department determines to conduct by two-way electronic audiovideo communication, the department shall arrange for two-way electronic audiovideo communication between the superior court and any state prison facility located in the county. The department shall provide properly maintained equipment and adequately trained staff at the prison as well as appropriate training for court staff to ensure that consistently effective two-way communication is provided between the prison facility and the courtroom for all appearances that the department determines to conduct by two-way electronic audiovideo communication.
(b) If the defendant is represented by counsel, the attorney shall be present with the defendant at the initial court appearance and arraignment, and may enter a plea during the arraignment. However, if the defendant is represented by counsel at an arraignment on an information or indictment in a felony case, and if the defendant does not plead guilty or nolo contendere to any charge, the attorney shall be present with the defendant or if the attorney is not present with the defendant, the attorney shall be present in court during the hearing.
(c) In lieu of the physical presence of the defendant's counsel at the institution with the defendant, the court and the department shall establish a confidential telephone and facsimile transmission line between the court and the institution for communication between the defendant's counsel in court and the defendant at the institution. In this case, counsel for the defendant shall not be required to be physically present at the institution during any court appearance that is conducted via electronic audiovideo communication. Nothing in this section shall be construed to prohibit the physical presence of the defense counsel with the defendant at the state prison.
(Amended by Stats. 2007, Ch. 43, Sec. 19. Effective January 1, 2008.)
978.
When his personal appearance is necessary, if he is in custody, the Court may direct and the officer in whose custody he is must bring him before it to be arraigned.
(Enacted 1872.)
978.5.
(a) A bench warrant of arrest may be issued whenever a defendant fails to appear in court as required by law including, but not limited to, the following situations:
(1) If the defendant is ordered by a judge or magistrate to personally appear in court at a specific time and place.
(2) If the defendant is released from custody on bail and is ordered by a judge or magistrate, or other person authorized to accept bail, to personally appear in court at a specific time and place.
(3) If the defendant is released from custody on their own recognizance and promises to personally appear in court at a specific time and place.
(4) If the defendant is released from custody or arrest upon citation by a peace officer or other person authorized to issue citations and the defendant has signed a promise to personally appear in court at a specific time and place.
(5) If a defendant is authorized to appear by counsel and the court or magistrate orders that the defendant personally appear in court at a specific time and place.
(6) If an information or indictment has been filed in the superior court and the court has fixed the date and place for the defendant personally to appear for arraignment.
(7) If a defendant has been cited or arrested for misdemeanor or felony theft from a store or vehicle and has failed to appear in court in connection with that charge or those charges in the previous six months.
(b) The bench warrant may be served in any county in the same manner as a warrant of arrest.
(c) This section shall remain in effect only until July 1, 2021, and as of that date is repealed.
(Amended (as amended by Stats. 2018, Ch. 803, Sec. 5) by Stats. 2019, Ch. 25, Sec. 35. (SB 94) Effective June 27, 2019. Repealed as of July 1, 2021, by its own provisions. See later operative version amended by Stats. 2019, Ch. 25.)
978.5.
(a) A bench warrant of arrest may be issued whenever a defendant fails to appear in court as required by law including, but not limited to, the following situations:
(1) If the defendant is ordered by a judge or magistrate to personally appear in court at a specific time and place.
(2) If the defendant is released from custody on bail and is ordered by a judge or magistrate, or other person authorized to accept bail, to personally appear in court at a specific time and place.
(3) If the defendant is released from custody on their own recognizance and promises to personally appear in court at a specific time and place.
(4) If the defendant is released from custody or arrest upon citation by a peace officer or other person authorized to issue citations and the defendant has signed a promise to personally appear in court at a specific time and place.
(5) If a defendant is authorized to appear by counsel and the court or magistrate orders that the defendant personally appear in court at a specific time and place.
(6) If an information or indictment has been filed in the superior court and the court has fixed the date and place for the defendant personally to appear for arraignment.
(b) The bench warrant may be served in any county in the same manner as a warrant of arrest.
(c) This section shall become operative on July 1, 2021.
(Amended (as added by Stats. 2018, Ch. 803, Sec. 6) by Stats. 2019, Ch. 25, Sec. 36. (SB 94) Effective June 27, 2019. Section operative July 1, 2021, by its own provisions.)
979.
If the defendant has been discharged on bail or has deposited money or other property instead thereof, and does not appear to be arraigned when his personal presence is necessary, the court, in addition to the forfeiture of the undertaking of bail or of the money or other property deposited, may order the issuance of a bench warrant for his arrest.
(Amended by Stats. 1951, Ch. 1674.)
980.
(a) At any time after the order for a bench warrant is made, whether the court is sitting or not, the clerk may issue a bench warrant to one or more counties.
(b) The clerk shall require the appropriate agency to enter each bench warrant issued on a private surety-bonded felony case into the national warrant system (National Crime Information Center (NCIC)). If the appropriate agency fails to enter the bench warrant into the national warrant system (NCIC), and the court finds that this failure prevented the surety or bond agent from surrendering the fugitive into custody, prevented the fugitive from being arrested or taken into custody, or resulted in the fugitive's subsequent release from custody, the court having jurisdiction over the bail shall, upon petition, set aside the forfeiture of the bond and declare all liability on the bail bond to be exonerated.
(Amended by Stats. 1998, Ch. 520, Sec. 2. Effective January 1, 1999.)
981.
The bench warrant must be substantially in the following form:

County of _____. The People of the State of California to any Sheriff, Marshal, or Policeman in this State: An accusatory pleading having been filed on the _____ day of _____, A.D. _____, in the Superior Court of the County of _____, charging C. D. with the crime of _____ (designating it generally); you are, therefore, commanded forthwith to arrest the above named C. D., and bring him or her before that Court (or if the accusatory pleading has been sent to another Court, then before that Court, naming it), to answer said accusatory pleading, or if the Court is not in session, that you deliver him or her into the custody of the Sheriff of the County of _____.
Given under my hand, with the seal of said Court affixed, this _____ day of _____, A.D. _____.
By order of said Court.

[seal.]	E. F., Clerk.

(Amended by Stats. 2003, Ch. 468, Sec. 14. Effective January 1, 2004.)
982.
The defendant, when arrested under a warrant for an offense not bailable, must be held in custody by the Sheriff of the county in which the indictment is found or information filed, unless admitted to bail after an examination upon a writ of habeas corpus; but if the offense is bailable, there must be added to the body of the bench warrant a direction to the following effect: "Or, if he requires it, that you take him before any magistrate in that county, or in the county in which you arrest him, that he may give bail to answer to the indictment (or information);" and the Court, upon directing it to issue, must fix the amount of bail, and an indorsement must be made thereon and signed by the Clerk, to the following effect: "The defendant is to be admitted to bail in the sum of _____ dollars."
(Amended by Code Amendments 1880, Ch. 47.)
983.
The bench warrant may be served in any county in the same manner as a warrant of arrest.
(Amended by Stats. 1951, Ch. 1674.)
984.
If the defendant is brought before a magistrate of another county for the purpose of giving bail, the magistrate must proceed in respect thereto in the same manner as if the defendant had been brought before him upon a warrant of arrest, and the same proceedings must be had thereon.
(Enacted 1872.)
985.
When the information or indictment is for a felony, and the defendant, before the filing thereof, has given bail for his appearance to answer the charge, the Court to which the indictment or information is presented, or in which it is pending, may order the defendant to be committed to actual custody, unless he gives bail in an increased amount, to be specified in the order.
(Amended by Code Amendments 1880, Ch. 47.)
986.
If the defendant is present when the order is made, he must be forthwith committed. If he is not present, a bench warrant must be issued and proceeded upon in the manner provided in this chapter.
(Enacted 1872.)
987.
(a) In a noncapital case, if the defendant appears for arraignment without counsel, he or she shall be informed by the court that it is his or her right to have counsel before being arraigned, and shall be asked if he or she desires the assistance of counsel. If he or she desires and is unable to employ counsel the court shall assign counsel to defend him or her.
(b) In a capital case, if the defendant appears for arraignment without counsel, the court shall inform him or her that he or she shall be represented by counsel at all stages of the preliminary and trial proceedings and that the representation is at his or her expense if he or she is able to employ counsel or at public expense if he or she is unable to employ counsel, inquire of him or her whether he or she is able to employ counsel and, if so, whether he or she desires to employ counsel of his or her choice or to have counsel assigned, and allow him or her a reasonable time to send for his or her chosen or assigned counsel. If the defendant is unable to employ counsel, the court shall assign counsel to defend him or her. If the defendant is able to employ counsel and either refuses to employ counsel or appears without counsel after having had a reasonable time to employ counsel, the court shall assign counsel.
The court shall at the first opportunity inform the defendant's trial counsel, whether retained by the defendant or court-appointed, of the additional duties imposed upon trial counsel in any capital case as set forth in paragraph (1) of subdivision (b) of Section 1240.1.
(c) In order to assist the court in determining whether a defendant is able to employ counsel in any case, the court may require a defendant to file a financial statement or other financial information under penalty of perjury with the court or, in its discretion, order a defendant to appear before a county officer designated by the court to make an inquiry into the ability of the defendant to employ his or her own counsel. If a county officer is designated, the county officer shall provide to the court a written recommendation and the reason or reasons in support of the recommendation. The determination by the court shall be made on the record. Except as provided in Section 1214, the financial statement or other financial information obtained from the defendant shall be confidential and privileged and shall not be admissible in evidence in any criminal proceeding except the prosecution of an alleged offense of perjury based upon false material contained in the financial statement. The financial statement shall be made available to the prosecution only for purposes of investigation of an alleged offense of perjury based upon false material contained in the financial statement at the conclusion of the proceedings for which the financial statement was required to be submitted. The financial statement and other financial information obtained from the defendant shall not be confidential and privileged in a proceeding under Section 987.8.
(d) In a capital case, the court may appoint an additional attorney as a cocounsel upon a written request of the first attorney appointed. The request shall be supported by an affidavit of the first attorney setting forth in detail the reasons why a second attorney should be appointed. Any affidavit filed with the court shall be confidential and privileged. The court shall appoint a second attorney when it is convinced by the reasons stated in the affidavit that the appointment is necessary to provide the defendant with effective representation. If the request is denied, the court shall state on the record its reasons for denial of the request.
(e) This section shall become operative on January 1, 2000.
(Repealed (in Sec. 3) and added by Stats. 1998, Ch. 587, Sec. 4. Effective January 1, 1999. Section operative January 1, 2000, by its own provisions.)
987.05.
In assigning defense counsel in felony cases, whether it is the public defender or private counsel, the court shall only assign counsel who represents, on the record, that he or she will be ready to proceed with the preliminary hearing or trial, as the case may be, within the time provisions prescribed in this code for preliminary hearings and trials, except in those unusual cases where the court finds that, due to the nature of the case, counsel cannot reasonably be expected to be ready within the presecribed period if he or she were to begin preparing the case forthwith and continue to make diligent and constant efforts to be ready. In the case where the time of preparation for preliminary hearing or trial is deemed greater than the statutory time, the court shall set a reasonable time period for preparation. In making this determination, the court shall not

consider counsel's convenience, counsel's calendar conflicts, or counsel's other business. The court may allow counsel a reasonable time to become familiar with the case in order to determine whether he or she can be ready. In cases where counsel, after making representations that he or she will be ready for preliminary examination or trial, and without good cause is not ready on the date set, the court may relieve counsel from the case and may impose sanctions upon counsel, including, but not limited to, finding the assigned counsel in contempt of court, imposing a fine, or denying any public funds as compensation for counsel's services. Both the prosecuting attorney and defense counsel shall have a right to present evidence and argument as to a reasonable length of time for preparation and on any reasons why counsel could not be prepared in the set time.
(Added June 5, 1990, by initiative Proposition 115, Sec. 20.)

987.1.
Counsel at the preliminary examination shall continue to represent a defendant who has been ordered to stand trial for a felony until the date set for arraignment on the information unless relieved by the court upon the substitution of other counsel or for cause.
(Amended by Stats. 1998, Ch. 931, Sec. 377. Effective September 28, 1998.)

987.2.
(a) In any case in which a person, including a person who is a minor, desires but is unable to employ counsel, and in which counsel is assigned in the superior court to represent the person in a criminal trial, proceeding, or appeal, the following assigned counsel shall receive a reasonable sum for compensation and for necessary expenses, the amount of which shall be determined by the court, to be paid out of the general fund of the county:
(1) In a county or city and county in which there is no public defender.
(2) In a county of the first, second, or third class where there is no contract for criminal defense services between the county and one or more responsible attorneys.
(3) In a case in which the court finds that, because of a conflict of interest or other reasons, the public defender has properly refused.
(4) In a county of the first, second, or third class where attorneys contracted by the county are unable to represent the person accused.
(b) The sum provided for in subdivision (a) may be determined by contract between the court and one or more responsible attorneys after consultation with the board of supervisors as to the total amount of compensation and expenses to be paid, which shall be within the amount of funds allocated by the board of supervisors for the cost of assigned counsel in those cases.
(c) In counties that utilize an assigned private counsel system as either the primary method of public defense or as the method of appointing counsel in cases where the public defender is unavailable, the county, the courts, or the local county bar association working with the courts are encouraged to do all of the following:
(1) Establish panels that shall be open to members of the State Bar of California.
(2) Categorize attorneys for panel placement on the basis of experience.
(3) Refer cases to panel members on a rotational basis within the level of experience of each panel, except that a judge may exclude an individual attorney from appointment to an individual case for good cause.
(4) Seek to educate those panel members through an approved training program.
(5) Establish a cost-efficient plan to ensure maximum recovery of costs pursuant to Section 987.8.
(d) In a county of the first, second, or third class, the court shall first utilize the services of the public defender to provide criminal defense services for indigent defendants. In the event that the public defender is unavailable and the county and the courts have contracted with one or more responsible attorneys or with a panel of attorneys to provide criminal defense services for indigent defendants, the court shall utilize the services of the county-contracted attorneys prior to assigning any other private counsel. Nothing in this subdivision shall be construed to require the appointment of counsel in any case in which the counsel has a conflict of interest. In the interest of justice, a court may depart from that portion of the procedure requiring appointment of a county-contracted attorney after making a finding of good cause and stating the reasons therefor on the record.
(e) In a county of the first, second, or third class, the court shall first utilize the services of the public defender to provide criminal defense services for indigent defendants. In the event that the public defender is unavailable and the county has created a second public defender and contracted with one or more responsible attorneys or with a panel of attorneys to provide criminal defense services for indigent defendants, and if the quality of representation provided by the second public defender is comparable to the quality of representation provided by the public defender, the court shall next utilize the services of the second public defender and then the services of the county-contracted attorneys prior to assigning any other private counsel. Nothing in this subdivision shall be construed to require the appointment of counsel in any case in which the counsel has a conflict of interest. In the interest of justice, a court may depart from that portion of the procedure requiring appointment of the second public defender or a county-contracted attorney after making a finding of good cause and stating the reasons therefor on the record.
(f) In any case in which counsel is assigned as provided in subdivision (a), that counsel appointed by the court and any court-appointed licensed private investigator shall have the same rights and privileges to information as the public defender and the public defender investigator. It is the intent of the Legislature in enacting this subdivision to equalize any disparity that exists between the ability of private, court-appointed counsel and investigators, and public defenders and public defender investigators, to represent their clients. This subdivision is not intended to grant to private investigators access to any confidential Department of Motor Vehicles' information not otherwise available to them. This subdivision is not intended to extend to private investigators the right to issue subpoenas.
(g) Notwithstanding any other provision of this section, where an indigent defendant is first charged in one county and establishes an attorney-client relationship with the public defender, defense services contract attorney, or private attorney, and where the defendant is then charged with an offense in a second or subsequent county, the court in the second or subsequent county may appoint the same counsel as was appointed in the first county to represent the defendant when all of the following conditions are met:
(1) The offense charged in the second or subsequent county would be joinable for trial with the offense charged in the first if it took place in the same county, or involves evidence which would be cross-admissible.
(2) The court finds that the interests of justice and economy will be best served by unitary representation.
(3) Counsel appointed in the first county consents to the appointment.
(h) The county may recover costs of public defender services under Chapter 6 (commencing with Section 4750) of Title 5 of Part 3 for any case subject to Section 4750.
(i) Counsel shall be appointed to represent, in a misdemeanor case, a person who desires but is unable to employ counsel, when it appears that the appointment is necessary to provide an adequate and effective defense for the defendant. Appointment of counsel in an infraction case is governed by Section 19.6.
(j) As used in this section, "county of the first, second, or third class" means the county of the first class, county of the second class, and county of the third class as provided by Sections 28020, 28022, 28023, and 28024 of the Government Code.
(Amended by Stats. 2002, Ch. 784, Sec. 540. Effective January 1, 2003.)

987.3.

Whenever in this code a court-appointed attorney is entitled to reasonable compensation and necessary expenses, the judge of the court shall consider the following factors, no one of which alone shall be controlling:
(a) Customary fee in the community for similar services rendered by privately retained counsel to a nonindigent client.
(b) The time and labor required to be spent by the attorney.
(c) The difficulty of the defense.
(d) The novelty or uncertainty of the law upon which the decision depended.
(e) The degree of professional ability, skill, and experience called for and exercised in the performance of the services.
(f) The professional character, qualification, and standing of the attorney.
(Added by Stats. 1973, Ch. 101.)

987.4.
When the public defender or an assigned counsel represents a person who is a minor in a criminal proceeding, at the expense of a county, the court may order the parent or guardian of such minor to reimburse the county for all or any part of such expense, if it determines that the parent or guardian has the ability to pay such expense.
(Added by Stats. 1970, Ch. 723.)

987.5.
(a) Every defendant shall be assessed a registration fee not to exceed fifty dollars ($50) when represented by appointed counsel. Notwithstanding this subdivision, no fee shall be required of any defendant that is financially unable to pay the fee.
(b) At the time of appointment of counsel by the court, or upon commencement of representation by the public defender, if prior to court appointment, the defendant shall be asked if he or she is financially able to pay the registration fee or any portion thereof. If the defendant indicates that he or she is able to pay the fee or a portion thereof, the court or public defender shall make an assessment in accordance with ability to pay. No fee shall be assessed against any defendant who asserts that he or she is unable to pay the fee or any portion thereof. No other inquiry concerning the defendant's ability to pay shall be made until proceedings are held pursuant to Section 987.8.
(c) No defendant shall be denied the assistance of appointed counsel due solely to a failure to pay the registration fee. An order to pay the registration fee may be enforced in the manner provided for enforcement of civil judgments generally, but may not be enforced by contempt.
(d) The fact that a defendant has or has not been assessed a fee pursuant to this section shall have no effect in any later proceedings held pursuant to Section 987.8, except that the defendant shall be given credit for any amounts paid as a registration fee toward any lien or assessment imposed pursuant to Section 987.8.
(e) This section shall be operative in a county only upon the adoption of a resolution or ordinance by the board of supervisors electing to establish the registration fee and setting forth the manner in which the funds shall be collected and distributed. Collection procedures, accounting measures, and the distribution of the funds received pursuant to this section shall be within the discretion of the board of supervisors.
(Amended by Stats. 2009, Ch. 606, Sec. 4. (SB 676) Effective January 1, 2010.)

987.6.
(a) From any state moneys made available to it for such purpose, the Department of Finance shall, pursuant to this section, pay to the counties an amount not to exceed 10 percent of the amounts actually expended by the counties in providing counsel in accordance with the law whether by public defender, assigned counsel, or both, for persons charged with violations of state criminal law or involuntarily detained under the Lanterman-Petris-Short Act, Division 5 (commencing with Section 5000) of the Welfare and Institutions Code, who desire, but are unable to afford, counsel.
(b) Application for payment shall be made in such manner and at such times as prescribed by the Department of Finance and the department may adopt rules necessary or appropriate to carry out the purposes of this section.
(Added by renumbering Section 987b by Stats. 1970, Ch. 723.)

987.8.
(a) If the court finds that a defendant is entitled to counsel but is unable to employ counsel, the court may hold a hearing or, in its discretion, order the defendant to appear before a county officer designated by the court, to determine whether the defendant owns or has an interest in real property or other assets subject to attachment and not otherwise exempt by law. The court may impose a lien on any real property owned by the defendant, or in which the defendant has an interest to the extent permitted by law. The lien shall contain a legal description of the property, shall be recorded with the county recorder in the county or counties in which the property is located, and shall have priority over subsequently recorded liens or encumbrances. The county shall have the right to enforce its lien for the payment of providing legal assistance to an indigent defendant in the same manner as other lienholders by way of attachment, except that a county shall not enforce its lien on a defendant's principal place of residence pursuant to a writ of execution. No lien shall be effective as against a bona fide purchaser without notice of the lien.
(b) If a defendant is provided legal assistance, either through the public defender or private counsel appointed by the court, upon conclusion of the criminal proceedings in the trial court or upon the withdrawal of the public defender or appointed private counsel, the court may, after notice and a hearing, make a determination of the present ability of the defendant to pay all or a portion of the cost thereof. The court may, in its discretion, hold one such additional hearing within six months of the conclusion of the criminal proceedings. The court may, in its discretion, order the defendant to appear before a county officer designated by the court to make an inquiry into the ability of the defendant to pay all or a portion of the legal assistance provided.
(c) (1) If the defendant hires counsel replacing a publicly provided attorney; in which the public defender or appointed counsel was required by the court to proceed with the case after a determination by the public defender that the defendant is not indigent; or, in which the defendant, at the conclusion of the case, appears to have sufficient assets to repay, without undue hardship, all or a portion of the cost of the legal assistance provided to him or her, by monthly installments or otherwise; the court shall make a determination of the defendant's ability to pay as provided in subdivision (b), and may, in its discretion, make other orders as provided in that subdivision.
(2) This subdivision applies to a county only upon the adoption of a resolution by the board of supervisors to that effect.
(d) If the defendant, after having been ordered to appear before a county officer, has been given proper notice and fails to appear before a county officer within 20 working days, the county officer shall recommend to the court that the full cost of the legal assistance be ordered to be paid by the defendant. The notice to the defendant shall contain all of the following:
(1) A statement of the cost of the legal assistance provided to the defendant as determined by the court.
(2) The defendant's procedural rights under this section.
(3) The time limit within which the defendant's response is required.
(4) A warning that if the defendant fails to appear before the designated officer, the officer will recommend that the court order the defendant to pay the full cost of the legal assistance provided to him or her.
(e) (1) At a hearing, the defendant shall be entitled to, but shall not be limited to, all of the following rights:
(A) The right to be heard in person.
(B) The right to present witnesses and other documentary evidence.
(C) The right to confront and cross-examine adverse witnesses.
(D) The right to have the evidence against him or her disclosed to him or her.
(E) The right to a written statement of the findings of the court.

(2) If the court determines that the defendant has the present ability to pay all or a part of the cost, the court shall set the amount to be reimbursed and order the defendant to pay the sum to the county in the manner in which the court believes reasonable and compatible with the defendant's financial ability. Failure of a defendant who is not in custody to appear after due notice is a sufficient basis for an order directing the defendant to pay the full cost of the legal assistance determined by the court. The order to pay all or a part of the costs may be enforced in the manner provided for enforcement of money judgments generally but may not be enforced by contempt.

(3) An order entered under this subdivision is subject to relief under Section 473 of the Code of Civil Procedure.

(f) Prior to the furnishing of counsel or legal assistance by the court, the court shall give notice to the defendant that the court may, after a hearing, make a determination of the present ability of the defendant to pay all or a portion of the cost of counsel. The court shall also give notice that, if the court determines that the defendant has the present ability, the court shall order him or her to pay all or a part of the cost. The notice shall inform the defendant that the order shall have the same force and effect as a judgment in a civil action and shall be subject to enforcement against the property of the defendant in the same manner as any other money judgment.

(g) As used in this section:

(1) "Legal assistance" means legal counsel and supportive services including, but not limited to, medical and psychiatric examinations, investigative services, expert testimony, or any other form of services provided to assist the defendant in the preparation and presentation of his or her case.

(2) "Ability to pay" means the overall capability of the defendant to reimburse the costs, or a portion of the costs, of the legal assistance provided to him or her, and shall include, but not be limited to, all of the following:

(A) The defendant's present financial position.

(B) The defendant's reasonably discernible future financial position. In no event shall the court consider a period of more than six months from the date of the hearing for purposes of determining the defendant's reasonably discernible future financial position. Unless the court finds unusual circumstances, a defendant sentenced to state prison, or to county jail for a period longer than 364 days, including, but not limited to, a sentence imposed pursuant to subdivision (h) of Section 1170, shall be determined not to have a reasonably discernible future financial ability to reimburse the costs of his or her defense.

(C) The likelihood that the defendant shall be able to obtain employment within a six-month period from the date of the hearing.

(D) Any other factor or factors that may bear upon the defendant's financial capability to reimburse the county for the costs of the legal assistance provided to the defendant.

(h) At any time during the pendency of the judgment rendered according to the terms of this section, a defendant against whom a judgment has been rendered may petition the rendering court to modify or vacate its previous judgment on the grounds of a change in circumstances with regard to the defendant's ability to pay the judgment. The court shall advise the defendant of this right at the time it renders the judgment.

(i) This section shall apply to all proceedings, including contempt proceedings, in which the party is represented by a public defender or appointed counsel and is convicted of a felony or a misdemeanor.

(Amended by Stats. 2017, Ch. 62, Sec. 1. (SB 355) Effective January 1, 2018.)

987.81.

(a) If a defendant is provided legal assistance, either through the public defender or private counsel appointed by the court, upon conclusion of the criminal proceedings in the trial court, or upon the withdrawal of the public defender or appointed private counsel, the court shall consider the available information concerning the defendant's ability to pay the costs of legal assistance and may, after notice, as provided in subdivision (b), hold a hearing to make a determination of the present ability of the defendant to pay all or a portion of the cost thereof. Notwithstanding the above, if the court has ordered the probation officer to investigate and report to the court pursuant to subdivision (b) of Section 1203, the court may hold such a hearing. The court may, in its discretion, hold one such additional hearing within six months of the conclusion of the criminal proceedings.

(b) Concurrent with counsel or legal assistance being furnished by the court, the court may order the defendant to appear before a county officer designated by the court to make an inquiry into the ability of the defendant to pay all or a portion of the legal assistance provided. Prior to the furnishing of counsel or legal assistance by the court, the court shall give notice to the defendant that the court may, after a hearing, make a determination of the present ability of the defendant to pay all or a portion of the cost of counsel. The court shall also give notice that, if the court determines that the defendant has the present ability, the court shall order him or her to pay all or a part of the cost. The notice shall inform the defendant that the order shall have the same force and effect as a judgment in a civil action and shall be subject to enforcement against the property of the defendant in the same manner as any other money judgment.

(c) The provisions of this section shall apply only in a county in which the board of supervisors adopts a resolution which elects to proceed under this section.

(d) This section shall apply only when the defendant is convicted of a felony or a misdemeanor.

(Amended by Stats. 2017, Ch. 62, Sec. 2. (SB 355) Effective January 1, 2018.)

987.9.

(a) In the trial of a capital case or a case under subdivision (a) of Section 190.05, the indigent defendant, through the defendant's counsel, may request the court for funds for the specific payment of investigators, experts, and others for the preparation or presentation of the defense. The application for funds shall be by affidavit and shall specify that the funds are reasonably necessary for the preparation or presentation of the defense. The fact that an application has been made shall be confidential and the contents of the application shall be confidential. Upon receipt of an application, a judge of the court, other than the trial judge presiding over the case in question, shall rule on the reasonableness of the request and shall disburse an appropriate amount of money to the defendant's attorney. The ruling on the reasonableness of the request shall be made at an in camera hearing. In making the ruling, the court shall be guided by the need to provide a complete and full defense for the defendant.

(b) (1) The Controller shall not reimburse any county for costs that exceed Department of General Services' standards for travel and per diem expenses. The Controller may reimburse extraordinary costs in unusual cases if the county provides sufficient documentation of the need for those expenditures.

(2) At the termination of the proceedings, the attorney shall furnish to the court a complete accounting of all moneys received and disbursed pursuant to this section.

(c) The Controller shall adopt regulations pursuant to Chapter 3.5 (commencing with Section 11340) of Part 1 of Division 3 of Title 2 of the Government Code, controlling reimbursements under this section. The regulations shall consider compensation for investigators, expert witnesses, and other expenses that may or may not be reimbursable pursuant to this section. Notwithstanding the provisions of Chapter 3.5 (commencing with Section 11340) of Part 1 of Division 3 of Title 2 of the Government Code, the Controller shall follow any regulations adopted until final approval by the Office of Administrative Law.

(d) The confidentiality provided in this section shall not preclude any court from providing the Attorney General with access to documents protected by this section when the defendant raises an issue on appeal or collateral review where the recorded portion of the record, created pursuant to this section, relates to the issue raised. When the defendant raises that issue, the funding records, or relevant portions thereof, shall be provided to the Attorney General at the Attorney General's request. In this case, the

documents shall remain under seal and their use shall be limited solely to the pending proceeding.

(Amended by Stats. 2016, Ch. 31, Sec. 237. (SB 836) Effective June 27, 2016.)

988.

The arraignment must be made by the court, or by the clerk or prosecuting attorney under its direction, and consists in reading the accusatory pleading to the defendant and delivering to the defendant a true copy thereof, and of the endorsements thereon, if any, including the list of witnesses, and asking the defendant whether the defendant pleads guilty or not guilty to the accusatory pleading; provided, that where the accusatory pleading is a complaint charging a misdemeanor, a copy of the same need not be delivered to any defendant unless requested by the defendant.

(Amended by Stats. 1998, Ch. 931, Sec. 379. Effective September 28, 1998.)

989.

When the defendant is arraigned, he must be informed that if the name by which he is prosecuted is not his true name, he must then declare his true name, or be proceeded against by the name in the accusatory pleading. If he gives no other name, the court may proceed accordingly; but if he alleges that another name is his true name, the court must direct an entry thereof in the minutes of the arraignment, and the subsequent proceedings on the accusatory pleading may be had against him by that name, referring also to the name by which he was first charged therein.

(Amended by Stats. 1951, Ch. 1674.)

990.

If on the arraignment, the defendant requires it, the defendant must be allowed a reasonable time to answer, which shall be not less than one day in a felony case and not more than seven days in a misdemeanor or infraction case.

(Amended by Stats. 1998, Ch. 931, Sec. 380. Effective September 28, 1998.)

991.

(a) If the defendant is in custody at the time he appears before the magistrate for arraignment and, if the public offense is a misdemeanor to which the defendant has pleaded not guilty, the magistrate, on motion of counsel for the defendant or the defendant, shall determine whether there is probable cause to believe that a public offense has been committed and that the defendant is guilty thereof.

(b) The determination of probable cause shall be made immediately unless the court grants a continuance for good cause not to exceed three court days.

(c) In determining the existence of probable cause, the magistrate shall consider any warrant of arrest with supporting affidavits, and the sworn complaint together with any documents or reports incorporated by reference thereto, which, if based on information and belief, state the basis for such information, or any other documents of similar reliability.

(d) If, after examining these documents, the court determines that there exists probable cause to believe that the defendant has committed the offense charged in the complaint, it shall set the matter for trial.

If the court determines that no such probable cause exists, it shall dismiss the complaint and discharge the defendant.

(e) Within 15 days of the dismissal of a complaint pursuant to this section the prosecution may refile the complaint.

A second dismissal pursuant to this section is a bar to any other prosecution for the same offense.

(Added by Stats. 1980, Ch. 1379, Sec. 1.)

991.5.

(a) On or before July 1, 2017, three counties shall be selected to participate in a three-year pilot project that would require a court, upon request by the defendant in the case of a defendant charged with a misdemeanor who is not in custody, to make a finding at the arraignment as to whether probable cause exists to believe that a public offense has been committed and that the defendant is guilty thereof.

(b) The pilot counties shall be selected by a three-member committee. One member of the committee shall be selected by the California Public Defenders Association, one member of the committee shall be selected by the California District Attorneys Association, and one member of the committee shall be selected by the Judicial Council. The committee shall be convened by the California Public Defenders Association and the California District Attorneys Association. The committee shall select one small county, one medium county, and one large county to participate in the pilot project. The committee shall consult with the relevant local officials in the eligible counties in making its selections. A county selected for the pilot project shall have a county public defender's office. For purposes of this section, the following terms have the following meanings:

(1) A "small county" means a county with a population of not less than 250,000 residents and not more than 750,000 residents.

(2) A "medium county" means a county with a population of not less than 750,001 residents and not more than 2,600,000 residents.

(3) A "large county" means a county with a population of not less than 2,600,001 residents.

(c) The following arraignment procedure applies in the pilot project counties:

(1) When the defendant is out of custody at the time he or she appears before the magistrate for arraignment and the public offense is a misdemeanor to which the defendant has pleaded not guilty, the magistrate, on motion of counsel for the defendant or the defendant, shall determine whether there is probable cause to believe that a public offense has been committed and that the defendant is guilty thereof.

(2) The determination of probable cause shall be made immediately, unless the court grants a continuance for good cause not to exceed 15 court days.

(3) In determining the existence of probable cause, the magistrate shall consider any warrant of arrest with supporting affidavits, and the sworn complaint together with any documents or reports incorporated by reference thereto, which, if based on information and belief, state the basis for that information, or any other documents of similar reliability.

(4) If, after examining these documents, the court determines that there exists probable cause to believe that the defendant has committed the offense charged in the complaint, it shall maintain the trial date already calendared for the defendant.

(5) If the court determines that no probable cause exists, it shall dismiss the complaint and discharge the defendant.

(6) The prosecution may refile the complaint within 15 days of the dismissal of a complaint pursuant to this section.

(7) A second dismissal pursuant to this section is a bar to any other prosecution for the same offense.

(d) (1) No later than July 1, 2020, the Department of Justice shall provide information to the Assembly Committee on Budget, the Senate Committee on Budget and Fiscal Review, and the appropriate policy committees of the Legislature regarding the implementation of this section, including, but not limited to, the number of instances that a prompt probable cause determination made to an Out of Custody defendant facing a misdemeanor charge resulted in the defendant's early dismissal.

(2) A report submitted pursuant to paragraph (1) shall be submitted in compliance with Section 9795 of the Government Code.

(e) This section shall become inoperative on July 1, 2020, and, as of January 1, 2021, is repealed, unless a later enacted statute, that becomes operative on or before January 1, 2021, deletes or extends the dates on which it becomes inoperative and is repealed.

(Amended by Stats. 2017, Ch. 561, Sec. 185. (AB 1516) Effective January 1, 2018. Inoperative July 1, 2020. Repealed as of January 1, 2021, by its own provisions.)

992.

(a) (1) In any case in which the defendant is charged with a felony, the court shall require the defendant to provide a right thumbprint on a form developed for this purpose. Unless the court has obtained the thumbprint at an earlier proceeding, it shall do so at the arraignment on the information or indictment, or upon entry of a guilty or no contest plea under Section 859a. The fingerprint form shall include the name and superior court case number of the defendant, the date, and the printed name, position, and badge or serial number of the court bailiff who imprints the defendant's thumbprint. In the event the defendant is physically unable to provide a right thumbprint, the defendant shall provide a left thumbprint. In the event the defendant is physically unable to provide a left thumbprint, the court shall make a determination as to how the defendant might otherwise provide a suitable identifying characteristic to be imprinted on the judgment of conviction. The clerk shall note on the fingerprint form which digit, if any, of the defendant's was imprinted thereon. In the event that the defendant is convicted, this fingerprint form shall be attached to the minute order reflecting the defendant's sentence. The fingerprint form shall be permanently maintained in the superior court file.
(2) This thumbprint or fingerprint shall not be used to create a database. The Judicial Council shall develop a form to implement this section.
(b) In the event that a county implements a countywide policy in which every felony defendant's photograph and fingerprints are permanently maintained in the superior court file, the presiding judge of that county may elect, after consultation with the district attorney, to continue compliance with this section.
(Amended by Stats. 2011, Ch. 304, Sec. 8. (SB 428) Effective January 1, 2012.)
993.
(a) At the arraignment of a defendant who is charged with a felony and who is, or whom the court reasonably deems to be, the sole custodial parent of one or more minor children, the court shall provide the following to the defendant:
(1) Judicial Council Form GC-250, the "Guardianship Pamphlet."
(2) Information regarding a power of attorney for a minor child.
(3) Information regarding trustline background examinations pertaining to child care providers as provided in Chapter 3.35 (commencing with Section 1596.60) of Division 2 of the Health and Safety Code.
(b) If the defendant states, orally or in writing, at the arraignment that he or she is a sole custodial parent of one or more minor children, the court may reasonably deem the defendant to be a sole custodial parent of one or more minor children without further investigation. The court may, but is not required to, make that determination on the basis of information other than the defendant's statement.
(Added by Stats. 2016, Ch. 882, Sec. 1. (AB 2380) Effective January 1, 2017.)

CHAPTER 2. Setting Aside the Indictment or Information [995 - 999a]

(Heading of Chapter 2 amended by Stats. 1951, Ch. 1674.)
995.
(a) Subject to subdivision (b) of Section 995a, the indictment or information shall be set aside by the court in which the defendant is arraigned, upon his or her motion, in either of the following cases:
(1) If it is an indictment:
(A) Where it is not found, endorsed, and presented as prescribed in this code.
(B) That the defendant has been indicted without reasonable or probable cause.
(2) If it is an information:
(A) That before the filing thereof the defendant had not been legally committed by a magistrate.
(B) That the defendant had been committed without reasonable or probable cause.
(b) In cases in which the procedure set out in subdivision (b) of Section 995a is utilized, the court shall reserve a final ruling on the motion until those procedures have been completed.
(Amended by Stats. 1982, Ch. 1505, Sec. 3.)
995a.
(a) If the names of the witnesses examined before the grand jury are not inserted at the foot of the indictment or indorsed thereon, the court shall order them to be so inserted or indorsed; and if the information be not subscribed by the district attorney, the court may order it to be so subscribed.
(b) (1) Without setting aside the information, the court may, upon motion of the prosecuting attorney, order further proceedings to correct errors alleged by the defendant if the court finds that such errors are minor errors of omission, ambiguity, or technical defect which can be expeditiously cured or corrected without a rehearing of a substantial portion of the evidence. The court may remand the cause to the committing magistrate for further proceedings, or if the parties and the court agree, the court may itself sit as a magistrate and conduct further proceedings. When remanding the cause to the committing magistrate, the court shall state in its remand order which minor errors it finds could be expeditiously cured or corrected.
(2) Any further proceedings conducted pursuant to this subdivision may include the taking of testimony and shall be deemed to be a part of the preliminary examination.
(3) The procedure specified in this subdivision may be utilized only once for each information filed. Any further proceedings conducted pursuant to this subdivision shall not be deemed to extend the time within which a defendant must be brought to trial under Section 1382.
(Amended by Stats. 1982, Ch. 1505, Sec. 4.)
996.
If the motion to set aside the indictment or information is not made, the defendant is precluded from afterwards taking the objections mentioned in Section 995.
(Amended by Stats. 1967, Ch. 138.)
997.
The motion must be heard at the time it is made, unless for cause the court postpones the hearing to another time. The court may entertain such motion prior to trial whether or not a plea has been entered and such plea need not be set aside in order to consider the motion. If the motion is denied, and the accused has not previously answered the indictment or information, either by demurring or pleading thereto, he shall immediately do so. If the motion is granted, the court must order that the defendant, if in custody, be discharged therefrom; or, if admitted to bail, that his bail be exonerated; or, if he has deposited money, or if money has been deposited by another or others instead of bail for his appearance, that the same be refunded to him or to the person or persons found by the court to have deposited said money on behalf of said defendant, unless it directs that the case be resubmitted to the same or another grand jury, or that an information be filed by the district attorney; provided, that after such order of resubmission the defendant may be examined before a magistrate, and discharged or committed by him, as in other cases, if before indictment or information filed he has not been examined and committed by a magistrate.
(Amended by Stats. 1968, Ch. 1064.)
998.
If the court directs the case to be resubmitted, or an information to be filed, the defendant, if already in custody, shall remain, unless he or she is admitted to bail; or, if already admitted to bail, or money has been deposited instead thereof, the bail or money is answerable for the appearance of the defendant to answer a new indictment or information; and, unless a new indictment is found or information filed before the next

grand jury of the county is discharged, the court shall, on the discharge of such grand jury, make the order prescribed by Section 997.
(Amended by Stats. 1987, Ch. 828, Sec. 58.)
999.
An order to set aside an indictment or information, as provided in this chapter, is no bar to a future prosecution for the same offense.
(Amended by Code Amendments 1880, Ch. 47.)
999a.
A petition for a writ of prohibition, predicated upon the ground that the indictment was found without reasonable or probable cause or that the defendant had been committed on an information without reasonable or probable cause, or that the court abused its discretion in utilizing the procedure set out in subdivision (b) of Section 995a, must be filed in the appellate court within 15 days after a motion made under Section 995 to set aside the indictment on the ground that the defendant has been indicted without reasonable or probable cause or that the defendant had been committed on an information without reasonable or probable cause, has been denied by the trial court. A copy of such petition shall be served upon the district attorney of the county in which the indictment is returned or the information is filed. The alternative writ shall not issue until five days after the service of notice upon the district attorney and until he has had an opportunity to appear before the appellate court and to indicate to the court the particulars in which the evidence is sufficient to sustain the indictment or commitment.
(Amended by Stats. 1982, Ch. 1505, Sec. 5.)

CHAPTER 2. Setting Aside the Indictment or Information [995 - 999a]

(Heading of Chapter 2 amended by Stats. 1951, Ch. 1674.)
995.
(a) Subject to subdivision (b) of Section 995a, the indictment or information shall be set aside by the court in which the defendant is arraigned, upon his or her motion, in either of the following cases:
(1) If it is an indictment:
(A) Where it is not found, endorsed, and presented as prescribed in this code.
(B) That the defendant has been indicted without reasonable or probable cause.
(2) If it is an information:
(A) That before the filing thereof the defendant had not been legally committed by a magistrate.
(B) That the defendant had been committed without reasonable or probable cause.
(b) In cases in which the procedure set out in subdivision (b) of Section 995a is utilized, the court shall reserve a final ruling on the motion until those procedures have been completed.
(Amended by Stats. 1982, Ch. 1505, Sec. 3.)
995a.
(a) If the names of the witnesses examined before the grand jury are not inserted at the foot of the indictment or indorsed thereon, the court shall order them to be so inserted or indorsed; and if the information be not subscribed by the district attorney, the court may order it to be so subscribed.
(b) (1) Without setting aside the information, the court may, upon motion of the prosecuting attorney, order further proceedings to correct errors alleged by the defendant if the court finds that such errors are minor errors of omission, ambiguity, or technical defect which can be expeditiously cured or corrected without a rehearing of a substantial portion of the evidence. The court may remand the cause to the committing magistrate for further proceedings, or if the parties and the court agree, the court may itself sit as a magistrate and conduct further proceedings. When remanding the cause to the committing magistrate, the court shall state in its remand order which minor errors it finds could be expeditiously cured or corrected.
(2) Any further proceedings conducted pursuant to this subdivision may include the taking of testimony and shall be deemed to be a part of the preliminary examination.
(3) The procedure specified in this subdivision may be utilized only once for each information filed. Any further proceedings conducted pursuant to this subdivision shall not be deemed to extend the time within which a defendant must be brought to trial under Section 1382.
(Amended by Stats. 1982, Ch. 1505, Sec. 4.)
996.
If the motion to set aside the indictment or information is not made, the defendant is precluded from afterwards taking the objections mentioned in Section 995.
(Amended by Stats. 1967, Ch. 138.)
997.
The motion must be heard at the time it is made, unless for cause the court postpones the hearing to another time. The court may entertain such motion prior to trial whether or not a plea has been entered and such plea need not be set aside in order to consider the motion. If the motion is denied, and the accused has not previously answered the indictment or information, either by demurring or pleading thereto, he shall immediately do so. If the motion is granted, the court must order that the defendant, if in custody, be discharged therefrom; or, if admitted to bail, that his bail be exonerated; or, if he has deposited money, or if money has been deposited by another or others instead of bail for his appearance, that the same be refunded to him or to the person or persons found by the court to have deposited said money on behalf of said defendant, unless it directs that the case be resubmitted to the same or another grand jury, or that an information be filed by the district attorney; provided, that after such order of resubmission the defendant may be examined before a magistrate, and discharged or committed by him, as in other cases, if before indictment or information filed he has not been examined and committed by a magistrate.
(Amended by Stats. 1968, Ch. 1064.)
998.
If the court directs the case to be resubmitted, or an information to be filed, the defendant, if already in custody, shall remain, unless he or she is admitted to bail; or, if already admitted to bail, or money has been deposited instead thereof, the bail or money is answerable for the appearance of the defendant to answer a new indictment or information; and, unless a new indictment is found or information filed before the next grand jury of the county is discharged, the court shall, on the discharge of such grand jury, make the order prescribed by Section 997.
(Amended by Stats. 1987, Ch. 828, Sec. 58.)
999.
An order to set aside an indictment or information, as provided in this chapter, is no bar to a future prosecution for the same offense.
(Amended by Code Amendments 1880, Ch. 47.)
999a.
A petition for a writ of prohibition, predicated upon the ground that the indictment was found without reasonable or probable cause or that the defendant had been committed on an information without reasonable or probable cause, or that the court abused its discretion in utilizing the procedure set out in subdivision (b) of Section 995a, must be filed in the appellate court within 15 days after a motion made under Section 995 to set aside the indictment on the ground that the defendant has been indicted without reasonable or probable cause or that the defendant had been committed on an information without reasonable or probable cause, has been denied by the trial court. A

copy of such petition shall be served upon the district attorney of the county in which the indictment is returned or the information is filed. The alternative writ shall not issue until five days after the service of notice upon the district attorney and until he has had an opportunity to appear before the appellate court and to indicate to the court the particulars in which the evidence is sufficient to sustain the indictment or commitment.
(Amended by Stats. 1982, Ch. 1505, Sec. 5.)

CHAPTER 2.2. Career Criminals [999b - 999h]

(Heading of Chapter 2.2 renumbered from Chapter 2.3 by Stats. 1987, Ch. 56, Sec. 125.)
999b.
The Legislature hereby finds a substantial and disproportionate amount of serious crime is committed against the people of California by a relatively small number of multiple and repeat felony offenders, commonly known as career criminals. In enacting this chapter, the Legislature intends to support increased efforts by district attorneys' offices to prosecute career criminals through organizational and operational techniques that have been proven effective in selected counties in this and other states.
(Added by Stats. 1982, Ch. 42, Sec. 1. Effective February 17, 1982.)
999c.
(a) There is hereby established in the Office of Emergency Services a program of financial and technical assistance for district attorneys' offices, designated the California Career Criminal Prosecution Program. All funds appropriated to the office for the purposes of this chapter shall be administered and disbursed by the Director of Emergency Services, and shall to the greatest extent feasible be coordinated or consolidated with federal funds that may be made available for these purposes.
(b) The Director of Emergency Services is authorized to allocate and award funds to counties in which career criminal prosecution units are established in substantial compliance with the policies and criteria set forth below in Sections 999d, 999e, 999f, and 999g.
(c) The allocation and award of funds shall be made upon application executed by the county's district attorney and approved by its board of supervisors. Funds disbursed under this chapter shall not supplant local funds that would, in the absence of the California Career Criminal Prosecution Program, be made available to support the prosecution of felony cases. Funds available under this program shall not be subject to review as specified in Section 14780 of the Government Code.
(Amended by Stats. 2013, Ch. 352, Sec. 406. (AB 1317) Effective September 26, 2013. Operative July 1, 2013, by Sec. 543 of Ch. 352.)
999d.
Career criminal prosecution units receiving funds under this chapter shall concentrate enhanced prosecution efforts and resources upon individuals identified under selection criteria set forth in Section 999e. Enhanced prosecution efforts and resources shall include, but not be limited to:
(a) "Vertical" prosecutorial representation, whereby the prosecutor who makes the initial filing or appearance in a career criminal case will perform all subsequent court appearances on that particular case through its conclusion, including the sentencing phase;
(b) Assignment of highly qualified investigators and prosecutors to career criminal cases; and
(c) Significant reduction of caseloads for investigators and prosecutors assigned to career criminal cases.
(Added by Stats. 1982, Ch. 42, Sec. 1. Effective February 17, 1982.)
999e.
(a) An individual who is under arrest for the commission or attempted commission of one or more of the felonies listed in paragraph (1) and who is either being prosecuted for three or more separate offenses not arising out of the same transaction involving one or more of those felonies, or has been convicted during the preceding 10 years for any felony listed in paragraph (2) of this subdivision, or at least two convictions during the preceding 10 years for any felony listed in paragraph (3) of this subdivision shall be the subject of career criminal prosecution efforts.
(1) Murder, manslaughter, rape, sexual assault, child molestation, robbery, carjacking, burglary, arson, receiving stolen property, grand theft, grand theft auto, lewd and lascivious conduct upon a child, assault with a firearm, discharging a firearm into an inhabited structure or vehicle, owning, possessing, or having custody or control of a firearm, as specified in subdivision (a) or (b) of Section 29800, or any unlawful act relating to controlled substances in violation of Section 11351, 11351.5, 11352, or 11378 of the Health and Safety Code.
(2) Robbery of the first degree, carjacking, burglary of the first degree, arson as defined in Section 451, unlawfully causing a fire as defined in Section 452, forcible rape, sodomy or oral copulation committed with force, lewd or lascivious conduct committed upon a child, kidnapping as defined in Section 209 or 209.5, murder, or manslaughter.
(3) Grand theft, grand theft auto, receiving stolen property, robbery of the second degree, burglary of the second degree, kidnapping as defined in Section 207, assault with a deadly weapon or instrument, or any unlawful act relating to controlled substances in violation of Section 11351 or 11352 of the Health and Safety Code.
For purposes of this chapter, the 10-year periods specified in this section shall be exclusive of any time which the arrested person has served in state prison.
(b) In applying the career criminal selection criteria set forth above, a district attorney may elect to limit career criminal prosecution efforts to persons arrested for any one or more of the felonies listed in subdivision (a) of this section if crime statistics demonstrate that the incidence of one or more of these felonies presents a particularly serious problem in the county.
(c) In exercising the prosecutorial discretion granted by Section 999g, the district attorney shall consider the character, background, and prior criminal background of the defendant, and the number and the seriousness of the offenses currently charged against the defendant.
(Amended by Stats. 2010, Ch. 178, Sec. 70. (SB 1115) Effective January 1, 2011. Operative January 1, 2012, by Sec. 107 of Ch. 178.)
999f.
(a) Each district attorney's office establishing a career criminal prosecution unit and receiving state support under this chapter shall adopt and pursue the following policies for career criminal cases:
(1) A plea of guilty or a trial conviction will be sought on all the offenses charged in the accusatory pleading against an individual meeting career criminal selection criteria.
(2) All reasonable prosecutorial efforts will be made to resist the pretrial release of a charged defendant meeting career criminal selection criteria.
(3) All reasonable prosecutorial efforts will be made to persuade the court to impose the most severe authorized sentence upon a person convicted after prosecution as a career criminal.
(4) All reasonable prosecutorial efforts will be made to reduce the time between arrest and disposition of charge against an individual meeting career criminal selection criteria.
(b) The prosecution shall not negotiate a plea agreement with a defendant in a career criminal prosecution; and Sections 1192.1 to 1192.5, inclusive, shall not apply, nor shall any plea of guilty or nolo contendere authorized by any such section, or any plea of guilty or nolo contendere as a result of any plea agreement be approved by the court in a career criminal prosecution.

(c) For purposes of this section a "plea agreement" means an agreement by the defendant to plead guilty or nolo contendere in exchange for any or all of the following: a dismissal of charges, a reduction in the degree of a charge, a change of a charge to a lesser or different crime, a specific manner or extent of punishment.
(d) This section does not prohibit the reduction of the offense charged or dismissal of counts in the interest of justice when a written declaration by the prosecuting attorney stating the specific factual and legal basis for such reduction or dismissal is presented to the court and the court, in writing, acknowledges acceptance of such declaration. A copy of such declaration and acceptance shall be retained in the case file. The only basis upon which charges may be reduced or counts dismissed by the court shall be in cases where the prosecuting attorney decides that there is insufficient evidence to prove the people's case, the testimony of a material witness cannot be obtained, or a reduction or dismissal would not result in a substantial change in sentence.
In any case in which the court or magistrate grants the prosecuting attorney's motion for a reduction of charges or dismissal of counts because there would be no substantial change in sentence, the court or magistrate shall require the prosecuting attorney to put on the record in open court the following:
(1) The charges filed in the complaint or information and the maximum statutory penalty that could be given if the defendant were convicted of all such charges.
(2) The charges which would be filed against the defendant if the court or magistrate grants the prosecuting attorney's motion and the maximum statutory penalty which can be given for these charges.
(e) This section does not prohibit a plea agreement when there are codefendants, and the prosecuting attorney determines that the information or testimony of the defendant making the agreement is necessary for the conviction of one or more of the other codefendants. The court shall condition its acceptance of the plea agreement on the defendant giving the information or testimony.
Before the court can accept the plea agreement, the prosecuting attorney shall present a written declaration to the court, specifying the legal and factual reasons for the agreement, and the court shall acknowledge in writing its acceptance of that declaration. A copy of the declaration and acceptance shall be retained in the case file.
(Added by Stats. 1982, Ch. 42, Sec. 1. Effective February 17, 1982.)
999g.
The selection criteria set forth in Section 999e shall be adhered to for each career criminal case unless, in the reasonable exercise of prosecutor's discretion, extraordinary circumstances require the departure from such policies in order to promote the general purposes and intent of this chapter.
(Added by Stats. 1982, Ch. 42, Sec. 1. Effective February 17, 1982.)
999h.
The characterization of a defendant as a "career criminal" as defined by this chapter may not be communicated to the trier of fact.
(Added by Stats. 1982, Ch. 42, Sec. 1. Effective February 17, 1982.)

CHAPTER 2.3. Repeat Sexual Offenders [999i - 999p]

(Heading of Chapter 2.3 renumbered from Chapter 2.4 (as added by Stats. 1983, Ch. 1078) by Stats. 1987, Ch. 56, Sec. 126.)
999i.
The Legislature hereby finds that repeat sexual offenders present a clear and present danger to the mental and physical well-being of the citizens of the State of California, especially of its children. The Legislature further finds that the concept of vertical prosecution, in which one deputy district attorney is assigned to a case from its filing to its completion, is a proven way of demonstrably increasing the likelihood of convicting repeat sex offenders and ensuring appropriate sentences for such offenders. In enacting this chapter, the Legislature intends to support increased efforts by district attorneys' offices to prosecute repeat sexual offenders through organizational and operational techniques that have already proven their effectiveness in selected counties in this and other states, as demonstrated by the California Career Criminal Prosecution Program and the California Gang Violence Suppression Program, as well as sexual assault prosecution units in several counties.
(Added by Stats. 1983, Ch. 1078, Sec. 1.)
999j.
(a) There is hereby established in the Office of Emergency Services a program of financial and technical assistance for district attorneys' offices, designated the Repeat Sexual Offender Prosecution Program. All funds appropriated to the office for the purposes of this chapter shall be administered and disbursed by the Director of Emergency Services, and shall to the greatest extent feasible, be coordinated or consolidated with any federal or local funds that may be made available for these purposes.
The Office of Emergency Services shall establish guidelines for the provision of grant awards to proposed and existing programs prior to the allocation of funds under this chapter. These guidelines shall contain the criteria for the selection of agencies to receive funding, as developed in consultation with an advisory group to be known as the Repeat Sexual Offender Prosecution Program Steering Committee. The membership of the steering committee shall be designated by the secretary of the office.
A draft of the guidelines shall be developed and submitted to the Chairpersons of the Assembly Criminal Law and Public Safety Committee and the Senate Judiciary Committee within 60 days of the effective date of this chapter and issued within 90 days of the same effective date. These guidelines shall set forth the terms and conditions upon which the Office of Emergency Services is prepared to offer grants pursuant to statutory authority. The guidelines shall not constitute rules, regulations, orders, or standards of general application.
(b) The Director of Emergency Services is authorized to allocate and award funds to counties in which repeat sexual offender prosecution units are established or are proposed to be established in substantial compliance with the policies and criteria set forth below in Sections 999k, 999l, and 999m.
(c) The allocation and award of funds shall be made upon application executed by the county's district attorney and approved by its board of supervisors. Funds disbursed under this chapter shall not supplant local funds that would, in the absence of the California Repeat Sexual Offender Prosecution Program, be made available to support the prosecution of repeat sexual offender felony cases. Local grant awards made under this program shall not be subject to review as specified in Section 14780 of the Government Code.
(Amended by Stats. 2013, Ch. 352, Sec. 407. (AB 1317) Effective September 26, 2013. Operative July 1, 2013, by Sec. 543 of Ch. 352.)
999k.
Repeat sexual offender prosecution units receiving funds under this chapter shall concentrate enhanced prosecution efforts and resources upon individuals identified under selection criteria set forth in Section 999l. Enhanced prosecution efforts and resources shall include, but not be limited to:
(a) Vertical prosecutorial representation, whereby the prosecutor who makes the initial filing or appearance in a repeat sexual offender case will perform all subsequent court appearances on that particular case through its conclusion, including the sentencing phase.

(b) The assignment of highly qualified investigators and prosecutors to repeat sexual offender cases. "Highly qualified" for the purposes of this chapter shall be defined as: (1) individuals with one year of experience in the investigation and prosecution of felonies or specifically the felonies listed in subdivision (a) of Section 999l; or (2) individuals whom the district attorney has selected to receive training as set forth in Section 13836; or (3) individuals who have attended a program providing equivalent training as approved by the Office of Emergency Services.
(c) A significant reduction of caseloads for investigators and prosecutors assigned to repeat sexual offender cases.
(d) Coordination with local rape victim counseling centers, child abuse services programs, and victim witness assistance programs. Coordination shall include, but not be limited to: referrals of individuals to receive client services; participation in local training programs; membership and participation in local task forces established to improve communication between criminal justice system agencies and community service agencies; and cooperating with individuals serving as liaison representatives of local rape victim counseling centers and victim witness assistance programs.
(Amended by Stats. 2013, Ch. 352, Sec. 408. (AB 1317) Effective September 26, 2013. Operative July 1, 2013, by Sec. 543 of Ch. 352.)
999l.
(a) An individual shall be the subject of a repeat sexual offender prosecution effort who is under arrest for the commission or attempted commission of one or more of the following offenses: assault with intent to commit rape, sodomy, oral copulation or any violation of Section 264.1, Section 288, or Section 289; rape, in violation of Section 261; sexual battery, in violation of Section 243.4; sodomy, in violation of Section 286; lewd acts on a child under 14, in violation of Section 288; oral copulation, in violation of Section 287 or former Section 288a; sexual penetration, in violation of Section 289; and (1) who is being prosecuted for offenses involving two or more separate victims, or (2) who is being prosecuted for the commission or attempted commission of three or more separate offenses not arising out of the same transaction involving one or more of the above-listed offenses, or (3) who has suffered at least one conviction during the preceding 10 years for any of the above-listed offenses. For purposes of this chapter, the 10-year periods specified in this section shall be exclusive of any time which the arrested person has served in state prison or in a state hospital pursuant to a commitment as a mentally disordered sex offender.
(b) In applying the repeat sexual offender selection criteria set forth above: (1) a district attorney may elect to limit repeat sexual offender prosecution efforts to persons arrested for any one or more of the offenses listed in subdivision (a) if crime statistics demonstrate that the incidence of such one or more offenses presents a particularly serious problem in the county; (2) a district attorney shall not reject cases for filing exclusively on the basis that there is a family or personal relationship between the victim and the alleged offender.
(c) In exercising the prosecutorial discretion granted by Section 999n, the district attorney shall consider the following: (1) the character, the background, and prior criminal background of the defendant, and (2) the number and seriousness of the offenses currently charged against the defendant.
(Amended by Stats. 2018, Ch. 423, Sec. 83. (SB 1494) Effective January 1, 2019.)
999m.
Each district attorney's office establishing a repeat sexual offender prosecution unit and receiving state support under this chapter shall adopt and pursue the following policies for repeat sexual offender cases:
(a) All reasonable prosecutorial efforts will be made to resist the pretrial release of a charged defendant meeting repeat sexual offender selection criteria.
(b) All reasonable prosecutorial efforts will be made to persuade the court to impose the most severe authorized sentence upon a person convicted after prosecution as a repeat sexual offender. In the prosecution of an intrafamily sexual abuse case, discretion may be exercised as to the type and nature of sentence recommended to the court.
(c) All reasonable prosecutorial efforts will be made to reduce the time between arrest and disposition of charge against an individual meeting repeat sexual offender criteria.
(Added by Stats. 1983, Ch. 1078, Sec. 1.)
999n.
(a) The selection criteria set forth in Section 999l shall be adhered to for each repeat sexual offender case unless, in the reasonable exercise of prosecutor's discretion, extraordinary circumstances require departure from those policies in order to promote the general purposes and intent of this chapter.
(b) Each district attorney's office establishing a repeat sexual offender prosecution unit and receiving state support under this chapter shall submit the following information, on a quarterly basis, to the Office of Emergency Services:
(1) The number of sexual assault cases referred to the district attorney's office for possible filing.
(2) The number of sexual assault cases filed for felony prosecution.
(3) The number of sexual assault cases taken to trial.
(4) The percentage of sexual assault cases tried which resulted in conviction.
(Amended by Stats. 2013, Ch. 352, Sec. 409. (AB 1317) Effective September 26, 2013. Operative July 1, 2013, by Sec. 543 of Ch. 352.)
999o.
The characterization of a defendant as a "repeat sexual offender" as defined by this chapter shall not be communicated to the trier of fact.
(Added by Stats. 1983, Ch. 1078, Sec. 1.)
999p.
The Office of Emergency Services is encouraged to utilize any federal funds which may become available in order to implement the provisions of this chapter.
(Amended by Stats. 2013, Ch. 352, Sec. 410. (AB 1317) Effective September 26, 2013. Operative July 1, 2013, by Sec. 543 of Ch. 352.)

CHAPTER 2.4. Child Abusers [999q - 999y]

(Chapter 2.4 added by Stats. 1985, Ch. 1097, Sec. 1.)
999q.
The Legislature hereby finds that child abusers present a clear and present danger to the mental health and physical well-being of the citizens of the State of California, especially of its children. The Legislature further finds that the concept of vertical prosecution, in which a specially trained deputy district attorney or prosecution unit is assigned to a case from its filing to its completion, is a proven way of demonstrably increasing the likelihood of convicting child abusers and ensuring appropriate sentences for such offenders. In enacting this chapter, the Legislature intends to support increased efforts by district attorneys' offices to prosecute child abusers through organizational and operational techniques that have already proven their effectiveness in selected counties in this and other states, as demonstrated by the California Career Criminal Prosecution Program, the California Gang Violence Suppression Program, and the Repeat Sexual Offender Prosecution Program.
(Added by Stats. 1985, Ch. 1097, Sec. 1.)
999r.
(a) There is hereby established in the Office of Emergency Services a program of financial and technical assistance for district attorneys' offices, designated the Child Abuser Prosecution Program. All funds appropriated to the agency for the purposes of this chapter shall be administered and disbursed by the executive director of that

agency or agencies, and shall to the greatest extent feasible, be coordinated or consolidated with any federal or local funds that may be made available for these purposes.
The Office of Emergency Services shall establish guidelines for the provision of grant awards to proposed and existing programs prior to the allocation of funds under this chapter. These guidelines shall contain the criteria for the selection of agencies to receive funding and the terms and conditions upon which the agency is prepared to offer grants pursuant to statutory authority. The guidelines shall not constitute rules, regulations, orders, or standards of general application. The guidelines shall be submitted to the appropriate policy committees of the Legislature prior to their adoption.
(b) The Director of Emergency Services is authorized to allocate and award funds to counties in which child abuser offender prosecution units are established or are proposed to be established in substantial compliance with the policies and criteria set forth below in Sections 999s, 999t, and 999u.
(c) The allocation and award of funds shall be made upon application executed by the county's district attorney and approved by its board of supervisors. Funds disbursed under this chapter shall not supplant local funds that would, in the absence of the California Child Abuser Prosecution Program, be made available to support the prosecution of child abuser felony cases. Local grant awards made under this program shall not be subject to review as specified in Section 14780 of the Government Code.
(Amended by Stats. 2013, Ch. 352, Sec. 411. (AB 1317) Effective September 26, 2013. Operative July 1, 2013, by Sec. 543 of Ch. 352.)
999s.
Child abuser prosecution units receiving funds under this chapter shall concentrate enhanced prosecution efforts and resources upon individuals identified under selection criteria set forth in Section 999t. Enhanced prosecution efforts and resources shall include, but not be limited to:
(a) Vertical prosecutorial representation, whereby the prosecutor who, or prosecution unit which, makes the initial filing or appearance in a case performs all subsequent court appearances on that particular case through its conclusion, including the sentencing phase.
(b) The assignment of highly qualified investigators and prosecutors to child abuser cases. "Highly qualified" for the purposes of this chapter means: (1) individuals with one year of experience in the investigation and prosecution of felonies or specifically the felonies listed in subdivision (a) of Section 999l or 999t; or (2) individuals whom the district attorney has selected to receive training as set forth in Section 13836; or (3) individuals who have attended a program providing equivalent training as approved by the Office of Emergency Services.
(c) A significant reduction of caseloads for investigators and prosecutors assigned to child abuser cases.
(d) Coordination with local rape victim counseling centers, child abuse services programs, and victim witness assistance programs. That coordination shall include, but not be limited to: referrals of individuals to receive client services; participation in local training programs; membership and participation in local task forces established to improve communication between criminal justice system agencies and community service agencies; and cooperating with individuals serving as liaison representatives of child abuse and child sexual abuse programs, local rape victim counseling centers and victim witness assistance programs.
(Amended by Stats. 2013, Ch. 352, Sec. 412. (AB 1317) Effective September 26, 2013. Operative July 1, 2013, by Sec. 543 of Ch. 352.)
999t.
(a) An individual may be the subject of a child abuser prosecution effort who is under arrest for the sexual assault of a child, as defined in Section 11165, or a violation of subdivision (a) or (b) of Section 273a, or a violation of Section 273ab, or 273d, or a violation of Section 288.2 when committed in conjunction with any other violation listed in this subdivision.
(b) In applying the child abuser selection criteria set forth above: (1) a district attorney may elect to limit child abuser prosecution efforts to persons arrested for any one or more of the offenses described in subdivision (a) if crime statistics demonstrate that the incidence of such one or more offenses presents a particularly serious problem in the county; (2) a district attorney shall not reject cases for filing exclusively on the basis that there is a family or personal relationship between the victim and the alleged offender.
(c) In exercising the prosecutorial discretion granted by Section 999v, the district attorney shall consider the character, the background, and the prior criminal background of the defendant.
(Amended by Stats. 2001, Ch. 210, Sec. 1. Effective January 1, 2002.)
999u.
Each district attorney's office establishing a child abuser prosecution unit and receiving state support under this chapter shall adopt and pursue the following policies for child abuser cases:
(a) Except as provided in subdivision (b), all reasonable prosecutorial efforts will be made to resist the pretrial release of a charged defendant meeting child abuser selection criteria.
(b) Nothing in this chapter shall be construed to limit the application of diversion programs authorized by law. All reasonable efforts shall be made to utilize diversion alternatives in appropriate cases.
(c) All reasonable prosecutorial efforts will be made to reduce the time between arrest and disposition of charge against an individual meeting child abuser criteria.
(Added by Stats. 1985, Ch. 1097, Sec. 1.)
999v.
(a) The selection criteria set forth in Section 999t shall be adhered to for each child abuser case unless, in the reasonable exercise of prosecutor's discretion, extraordinary circumstances require departure from those policies in order to promote the general purposes and intent of this chapter.
(b) Each district attorney's office establishing a child abuser prosecution unit and receiving state support under this chapter shall submit the following information, on a quarterly basis, to the Office of Emergency Services:
(1) The number of child abuser cases referred to the district attorney's office for possible filing.
(2) The number of child abuser cases filed for felony prosecution.
(3) The number of sexual assault cases taken to trial.
(4) The number of child abuser cases tried which resulted in conviction.
(Amended by Stats. 2013, Ch. 352, Sec. 413. (AB 1317) Effective September 26, 2013. Operative July 1, 2013, by Sec. 543 of Ch. 352.)
999w.
The characterization of a defendant as a "child abuser" as defined by this chapter shall not be communicated to the trier of fact.
(Added by Stats. 1985, Ch. 1097, Sec. 1.)
999x.
The Office of Emergency Services is encouraged to utilize any federal funds which may become available in order to implement the provisions of this chapter.
(Amended by Stats. 2013, Ch. 352, Sec. 414. (AB 1317) Effective September 26, 2013. Operative July 1, 2013, by Sec. 543 of Ch. 352.)
999y.
The Office of Emergency Services shall report annually to the Legislature concerning the program established by this chapter. The office shall prepare and submit to the Legislature on or before December 15, 2002, and within six months of the completion of subsequent funding cycles for this program, an evaluation of the Child Abuser

Prosecution Program. This evaluation shall identify outcome measures to determine the effectiveness of the programs established under this chapter, which shall include, but not be limited to, both of the following, to the extent that data is available:

(a) Child abuse conviction rates of Child Abuser Prosecution Program units compared to those of nonfunded counties.

(b) Quantification of the annual per capita costs of the Child Abuser Prosecution Program compared to the costs of prosecuting child abuse crimes in nonfunded counties.

(Amended by Stats. 2013, Ch. 352, Sec. 415. (AB 1317) Effective September 26, 2013. Operative July 1, 2013, by Sec. 543 of Ch. 352.)

CHAPTER 2.5. Special Proceedings in Narcotics and Drug Abuse Cases [1000 - 1000.65]

(Chapter 2.5 added by Stats. 1972, Ch. 1255.)

1000.

(a) This chapter shall apply whenever a case is before any court upon an accusatory pleading for a violation of Section 11350, 11357, 11364, or 11365, paragraph (2) of subdivision (b) of Section 11375, Section 11377, or Section 11550 of the Health and Safety Code, or subdivision (b) of Section 23222 of the Vehicle Code, or Section 11358 of the Health and Safety Code if the marijuana planted, cultivated, harvested, dried, or processed is for personal use, or Section 11368 of the Health and Safety Code if the narcotic drug was secured by a fictitious prescription and is for the personal use of the defendant and was not sold or furnished to another, or subdivision (d) of Section 653f if the solicitation was for acts directed to personal use only, or Section 381 or subdivision (f) of Section 647 of the Penal Code, if for being under the influence of a controlled substance, or Section 4060 of the Business and Professions Code, and it appears to the prosecuting attorney that, except as provided in subdivision (b) of Section 11357 of the Health and Safety Code, all of the following apply to the defendant:

(1) Within five years prior to the alleged commission of the charged offense, the defendant has not suffered a conviction for any offense involving controlled substances other than the offenses listed in this subdivision.

(2) The offense charged did not involve a crime of violence or threatened violence.

(3) There is no evidence of a contemporaneous violation relating to narcotics or restricted dangerous drugs other than a violation of the offenses listed in this subdivision.

(4) The defendant has no prior felony conviction within five years prior to the alleged commission of the charged offense.

(b) The prosecuting attorney shall review his or her file to determine whether or not paragraphs (1) to (4), inclusive, of subdivision (a) apply to the defendant. If the defendant is found eligible, the prosecuting attorney shall file with the court a declaration in writing or state for the record the grounds upon which the determination is based, and shall make this information available to the defendant and his or her attorney. This procedure is intended to allow the court to set the hearing for pretrial diversion at the arraignment. If the defendant is found ineligible for pretrial diversion, the prosecuting attorney shall file with the court a declaration in writing or state for the record the grounds upon which the determination is based, and shall make this information available to the defendant and his or her attorney. The sole remedy of a defendant who is found ineligible for pretrial diversion is a postconviction appeal.

(c) All referrals for pretrial diversion granted by the court pursuant to this chapter shall be made only to programs that have been certified by the county drug program administrator pursuant to Chapter 1.5 (commencing with Section 1211) of Title 8, or to programs that provide services at no cost to the participant and have been deemed by the court and the county drug program administrator to be credible and effective. The defendant may request to be referred to a program in any county, as long as that program meets the criteria set forth in this subdivision.

(d) Pretrial diversion for an alleged violation of Section 11368 of the Health and Safety Code shall not prohibit any administrative agency from taking disciplinary action against a licensee or from denying a license. This subdivision does not expand or restrict the provisions of Section 1000.4.

(e) Any defendant who is participating in a program authorized in this section may be required to undergo analysis of his or her urine for the purpose of testing for the presence of any drug as part of the program. However, urinalysis results shall not be admissible as a basis for any new criminal prosecution or proceeding.

(Amended by Stats. 2017, Ch. 778, Sec. 1. (AB 208) Effective January 1, 2018.)

1000.1.

(a) If the prosecuting attorney determines that this chapter may be applicable to the defendant, he or she shall advise the defendant and his or her attorney in writing of that determination. This notification shall include all of the following:

(1) A full description of the procedures for pretrial diversion.

(2) A general explanation of the roles and authorities of the probation department, the prosecuting attorney, the program, and the court in the process.

(3) A clear statement that the court may grant pretrial diversion with respect to any offense specified in subdivision (a) of Section 1000 that is charged, provided that the defendant pleads not guilty to the charge or charges, waives the right to a speedy trial, to a speedy preliminary hearing, and to a trial by jury, if applicable, and that upon the defendant's successful completion of a program, as specified in subdivision (c) of Section 1000, the positive recommendation of the program authority and the motion of the defendant, prosecuting attorney, the court, or the probation department, but no sooner than 12 months and no later than 18 months from the date of the defendant's referral to the program, the court shall dismiss the charge or charges against the defendant.

(4) A clear statement that upon any failure of treatment or condition under the program, or any circumstance specified in Section 1000.3, the prosecuting attorney or the probation department or the court on its own may make a motion to the court to terminate pretrial diversion and schedule further proceedings as otherwise provided in this code.

(5) An explanation of criminal record retention and disposition resulting from participation in the pretrial diversion program and the defendant's rights relative to answering questions about his or her arrest and pretrial diversion following successful completion of the program.

(b) If the defendant consents and waives his or her right to a speedy trial, a speedy preliminary hearing, and to a trial by jury, if applicable, the court may refer the case to the probation department or the court may summarily grant pretrial diversion. When directed by the court, the probation department shall make an investigation and take into consideration the defendant's age, employment and service records, educational background, community and family ties, prior controlled substance use, treatment history, if any, demonstrable motivation, and other mitigating factors in determining whether the defendant is a person who would be benefited by education, treatment, or rehabilitation. The probation department shall also determine which programs the defendant would benefit from and which programs would accept the defendant. The probation department shall report its findings and recommendations to the court. The court shall make the final determination regarding education, treatment, or rehabilitation for the defendant. If the court determines that it is appropriate, the court shall grant pretrial diversion if the defendant pleads not guilty to the charge or charges and waives

the right to a speedy trial, to a speedy preliminary hearing, and to a trial by jury, if applicable.

(c) (1) No statement, or any information procured therefrom, made by the defendant to any probation officer or drug treatment worker, that is made during the course of any investigation conducted by the probation department or treatment program pursuant to subdivision (b), and prior to the reporting of the probation department's findings and recommendations to the court, shall be admissible in any action or proceeding brought subsequent to the investigation.

(2) No statement, or any information procured therefrom, with respect to the specific offense with which the defendant is charged, that is made to any probation officer or drug program worker subsequent to the granting of pretrial diversion shall be admissible in any action or proceeding.

(d) A defendant's participation in pretrial diversion pursuant to this chapter shall not constitute a conviction or an admission of guilt for any purpose.

(Amended by Stats. 2017, Ch. 778, Sec. 2. (AB 208) Effective January 1, 2018.)

1000.2.

(a) The court shall hold a hearing and, after consideration of any information relevant to its decision, shall determine if the defendant consents to further proceedings under this chapter and if the defendant should be granted pretrial diversion. If the defendant does not consent to participate in pretrial diversion, the proceedings shall continue as in any other case.

(b) At the time that pretrial diversion is granted, any bail bond or undertaking, or deposit in lieu thereof, on file by or on behalf of the defendant shall be exonerated, and the court shall enter an order so directing.

(c) The period during which pretrial diversion is granted shall be for no less than 12 months nor longer than 18 months. However, the defendant may request, and the court shall grant, for good cause shown, an extension of time to complete a program specified in subdivision (c) of Section 1000. Progress reports shall be filed by the probation department with the court as directed by the court.

(Amended by Stats. 2017, Ch. 778, Sec. 3. (AB 208) Effective January 1, 2018.)

1000.3.

(a) If it appears to the prosecuting attorney, the court, or the probation department that the defendant is performing unsatisfactorily in the assigned program, that the defendant is convicted of an offense that reflects the defendant's propensity for violence, or that the defendant is convicted of a felony, the prosecuting attorney, the court on its own, or the probation department may make a motion for termination from pretrial diversion.

(b) After notice to the defendant, the court shall hold a hearing to determine whether pretrial diversion shall be terminated.

(c) If the court finds that the defendant is not performing satisfactorily in the assigned program, or the court finds that the defendant has been convicted of a crime as indicated in subdivision (a), the court shall schedule the matter for further proceedings as otherwise provided in this code.

(d) If the defendant has completed pretrial diversion, at the end of that period, the criminal charge or charges shall be dismissed.

(e) Prior to dismissing the charge or charges or terminating pretrial diversion, the court shall consider the defendant's ability to pay and whether the defendant has paid a diversion restitution fee pursuant to Section 1001.90, if ordered, and has met his or her financial obligation to the program, if any. As provided in Section 1203.1b, the defendant shall reimburse the probation department for the reasonable cost of any program investigation or progress report filed with the court as directed pursuant to Sections 1000.1 and 1000.2.

(Amended by Stats. 2017, Ch. 778, Sec. 4. (AB 208) Effective January 1, 2018.)

1000.4.

(a) Any record filed with the Department of Justice shall indicate the disposition in those cases referred to pretrial diversion pursuant to this chapter. Upon successful completion of a pretrial diversion program, the arrest upon which the defendant was diverted shall be deemed to have never occurred and the court may issue an order to seal the records pertaining to the arrest as described in Section 851.92. The defendant may indicate in response to any question concerning his or her prior criminal record that he or she was not arrested or granted pretrial diversion for the offense, except as specified in subdivision (c). A record pertaining to an arrest resulting in successful completion of a pretrial diversion program shall not, without the defendant's consent, be used in any way that could result in the denial of any employment, benefit, license, or certificate, except that, as specified in Section 492 of the Business and Professions Code, successful completion of a pretrial diversion program shall not prohibit any agency established under Division 2 (commencing with Section 500) of the Business and Professions Code, or under any initiative act referred to in that division, from taking disciplinary action against a licensee or from denying a license for professional misconduct, notwithstanding that evidence of that misconduct may be recorded in a record pertaining to an arrest leading to successful completion of a pretrial diversion program.

(b) Notwithstanding any other law, any licensing agency listed in Section 144 of the Business and Professions Code may request, and is authorized to receive, from a local or state agency certified records regarding referral to, participation in, successful completion of, and termination from, diversion programs described in this section.

(c) The defendant shall be advised that, regardless of his or her successful completion of the pretrial diversion program, the arrest upon which the pretrial diversion was based may be disclosed by the Department of Justice in response to any peace officer application request and that, notwithstanding subdivision (a), this section does not relieve him or her of the obligation to disclose the arrest in response to any direct question contained in any questionnaire or application for a position as a peace officer, as defined in Section 830.

(d) The defendant shall be advised that, regardless of the defendant's successful completion of a pretrial diversion program, an order to seal records pertaining to an arrest made pursuant to this section has no effect on a criminal justice agency's ability to access and use those sealed records and information regarding sealed arrests, as described in Section 851.92.

(Amended by Stats. 2017, Ch. 778, Sec. 5.5. (AB 208) Effective January 1, 2018.)

1000.5.

(a) (1) The presiding judge of the superior court, or a judge designated by the presiding judge, together with the district attorney and the public defender, may agree in writing to establish and conduct a preguilty plea drug court program pursuant to the provisions of this chapter, wherein criminal proceedings are suspended without a plea of guilty for designated defendants. The drug court program shall include a regimen of graduated sanctions and rewards, individual and group therapy, urinalysis testing commensurate with treatment needs, close court monitoring and supervision of progress, educational or vocational counseling as appropriate, and other requirements as agreed to by the presiding judge or his or her designee, the district attorney, and the public defender. If there is no agreement in writing for a preguilty plea program by the presiding judge or his or her designee, the district attorney, and the public defender, the program shall be operated as a pretrial diversion program as provided in this chapter.

(2) A person charged with a misdemeanor under paragraph (3) of subdivision (b) of Section 11357.5 or paragraph (3) of subdivision (b) of Section 11375.5 of the Health and Safety Code shall be eligible to participate in a preguilty plea drug court program established pursuant to this chapter, as set forth in Section 11375.7 of the Health and Safety Code.

(b) The provisions of Section 1000.3 and Section 1000.4 regarding satisfactory and unsatisfactory performance in a program shall apply to preguilty plea programs, except as provided in Section 11375.7 of the Health and Safety Code. If the court finds that (1)

the defendant is not performing satisfactorily in the assigned program, (2) the defendant is not benefiting from education, treatment, or rehabilitation, (3) the defendant has been convicted of a crime specified in Section 1000.3, or (4) the defendant has engaged in criminal conduct rendering him or her unsuitable for the preguilty plea program, the court shall reinstate the criminal charge or charges. If the defendant has performed satisfactorily during the period of the preguilty plea program, at the end of that period, the criminal charge or charges shall be dismissed and the provisions of Section 1000.4 shall apply.
(Amended by Stats. 2017, Ch. 778, Sec. 6. (AB 208) Effective January 1, 2018.)
1000.6.
(a) A person who is participating in a pretrial diversion program or a preguilty plea program pursuant to this chapter is authorized under the direction of a licensed health care practitioner, to use medications including, but not limited to, methadone, buprenorphine, or levoalphacetylmethadol (LAAM) to treat substance use disorders if the participant allows release of his or her medical records to the court presiding over the participant's preguilty plea or pretrial diversion program for the limited purpose of determining whether or not the participant is using such medications under the direction of a licensed health care practitioner and is in compliance with the pretrial diversion or preguilty plea program rules.
(b) If the conditions specified in subdivision (a) are met, the use by a participant of medications to treat substance use disorders shall not be the sole reason for exclusion from a pretrial diversion or preguilty plea program. A patient who uses medications to treat substance use disorders and participates in a preguilty plea or pretrial diversion program shall comply with all court program rules.
(c) A person who is participating in a pretrial diversion program or preguilty plea program pursuant to this chapter who uses medications to treat substance use disorders shall present to the court a declaration from his or her health care practitioner, or his or her health care practitioner's authorized representative, that the person is currently under their care.
(d) Urinalysis results that only establish that a person described in this section has ingested medication duly prescribed to that person by his or her physician or psychiatrist, or medications used to treat substance use disorders, shall not be considered a violation of the terms of the pretrial diversion or preguilty plea program under this chapter.
(e) Except as provided in subdivisions (a) to (d), inclusive, this section does not affect any other law governing diversion programs.
(Amended by Stats. 2017, Ch. 778, Sec. 7. (AB 208) Effective January 1, 2018.)
1000.65.
This chapter does not affect a pretrial diversion program provided pursuant to Chapter 2.7 (commencing with Section 1001).
(Added by Stats. 2017, Ch. 778, Sec. 8. (AB 208) Effective January 1, 2018.)

CHAPTER 2.55. Deferred Entry of Judgment Pilot Program [1000.7- 1000.7.]

(Chapter 2.55 added by Stats. 2016, Ch. 865, Sec. 1.)
1000.7.
(a) The following counties may establish a pilot program pursuant to this section to operate a deferred entry of judgment pilot program for eligible defendants described in subdivision (b):
(1) County of Alameda.
(2) County of Butte.
(3) County of Napa.
(4) County of Nevada.
(5) County of Santa Clara.
(6) County of Ventura.
(b) A defendant may participate in a deferred entry of judgment pilot program within the county's juvenile hall if that person is charged with committing a felony offense, other than the offenses listed under subdivision (d), he or she pleads guilty to the charge or charges, and the probation department determines that the person meets all of the following requirements:
(1) Is 18 years of age or older, but under 21 years of age on the date the offense was committed.
(2) Is suitable for the program after evaluation using a risk assessment tool, as described in subdivision (c).
(3) Shows the ability to benefit from services generally reserved for delinquents, including, but not limited to, cognitive behavioral therapy, other mental health services, and age-appropriate educational, vocational, and supervision services, that are currently deployed under the jurisdiction of the juvenile court.
(4) Meets the rules of the juvenile hall developed in accordance with the applicable regulations set forth in Title 15 of the California Code of Regulations.
(5) Does not have a prior or current conviction for committing an offense listed under subdivision (c) of Section 1192.7 or subdivision (c) of Section 667.5, or subdivision (b) of Section 707 of the Welfare and Institutions Code.
(6) Is not required to register as a sex offender pursuant to Chapter 5.5 (commencing with Section 290) of Title 9 of Part 1.
(c) The probation department, in consultation with the superior court, district attorney, and sheriff of the county or the governmental body charged with operating the county jail, shall develop an evaluation process using a risk assessment tool to determine eligibility for the program.
(d) If the defendant is required to register as a sex offender pursuant to Chapter 5.5 (commencing with Section 290) of Title 9 of Part 1, or if he or she has been convicted of one or more of the following offenses, he or she is not eligible for the program:
(1) An offense listed under subdivision (c) of Section 1192.7.
(2) An offense listed under subdivision (c) of Section 667.5.
(3) An offense listed under subdivision (b) of Section 707 of the Welfare and Institutions Code.
(e) The court shall grant deferred entry of judgment if an eligible defendant consents to participate in the program, waives his or her right to a speedy trial or a speedy preliminary hearing, pleads guilty to the charge or charges, and waives time for the pronouncement of judgment.
(f) (1) If the probation department determines that the defendant is not eligible for the deferred entry of judgment pilot program or the defendant does not consent to participate in the program, the proceedings shall continue as in any other case.
(2) If it appears to the probation department that the defendant is performing unsatisfactorily in the program as a result of the commission of a new crime or the violation of any of the rules of the juvenile hall or that the defendant is not benefiting from the services in the program, the probation department may make a motion for entry of judgment. After notice to the defendant, the court shall hold a hearing to determine whether judgment should be entered. If the court finds that the defendant is performing unsatisfactorily in the program or that the defendant is not benefiting from the services in the program, the court shall render a finding of guilt to the charge or charges pleaded, enter judgment, and schedule a sentencing hearing as otherwise provided in this code, and the probation department, in consultation with the county sheriff, shall remove the defendant from the program and return him or her to custody in county jail. The mechanism of when and how the defendant is moved from custody in juvenile hall to custody in a county jail shall be determined by the local multidisciplinary team specified in paragraph (2) of subdivision (m).
(3) If the defendant has performed satisfactorily during the period in which deferred entry of judgment was granted, at the end of that period, the court shall dismiss the criminal charge or charges.
(g) A defendant shall serve no longer than one year in custody within a county's juvenile hall pursuant to the program.
(h) The probation department shall develop a plan for reentry services, including, but not limited to, housing, employment, and education services, as a component of the program.
(i) The probation department shall submit data relating to the effectiveness of the program to the Division of Recidivism Reduction and Re-Entry, within the Department of Justice, including recidivism rates for program participants as compared to recidivism rates for similar populations in the adult system within the county.
(j) A defendant participating in the program pursuant to this section shall not come into contact with minors within the juvenile hall for any purpose, including, but not limited to, housing, recreation, or education.
(k) Prior to establishing a pilot program pursuant to this section, the county shall apply to the Board of State and Community Corrections for approval of a county institution as a suitable place for confinement for the purpose of the pilot program. The board shall review and approve or deny the application of the county within 30 days of receiving notice of this proposed use. In its review, the board shall take into account the available programming, capacity, and safety of the institution as a place for the confinement and rehabilitation of individuals within the jurisdiction of the criminal court, and those within the jurisdiction of the juvenile court.
(l) The Board of State and Community Corrections shall review a county's pilot program to ensure compliance with requirements of the federal Juvenile Justice and Delinquency Prevention Act of 1974 (34 U.S.C. Sec. 11101 et seq.), as amended, relating to "sight and sound" separation between juveniles and adult inmates.
(m) (1) This section applies to a defendant who would otherwise serve time in custody in a county jail. Participation in a program pursuant to this section shall not be authorized as an alternative to a sentence involving community supervision.
(2) Each county shall establish a multidisciplinary team that shall meet periodically to review and discuss the implementation, practices, and impact of the program. The team shall include representatives from the following:
(A) Probation department.
(B) The district attorney's office.
(C) The public defender's office.
(D) The sheriff's department.
(E) Courts located in the county.
(F) The county board of supervisors.
(G) The county health and human services department.
(H) A youth advocacy group.
(n) (1) A county that establishes a pilot program pursuant to this section shall submit data regarding the pilot program to the Board of State and Community Corrections. The data submitted shall be used for the purposes of paragraph (2).
(2) The board shall conduct an evaluation of the pilot program's impact and effectiveness. The evaluation shall include, but not be limited to, evaluating each pilot program's impact on sentencing and impact on opportunities for community supervision, monitoring the program's effect on minors in the juvenile facility, if any, and its effectiveness with respect to program participants, including outcome-related data for program participants compared to young adult offenders sentenced for comparable crimes.
(3) Each evaluation shall be combined into a comprehensive report and submitted to the Assembly and Senate Committees on Public Safety, no later than December 31, 2020.
(4) The board may contract with an independent entity, including, but not limited to, the Regents of the University of California, for the purposes of carrying out the duties of the board pursuant to this subdivision.
(o) This chapter shall remain in effect only until January 1, 2022, and as of that date is repealed, unless a later enacted statute, that is enacted before January 1, 2022, deletes or extends that date.
(Amended by Stats. 2018, Ch. 1007, Sec. 1. (SB 1106) Effective January 1, 2019. Repealed as of January 1, 2022, by its own provisions. Note: Repeal affects Chapter 2.55, consisting of this section.)

CHAPTER 2.6. Deferred Entry of Judgment Reentry Program [1000.8 - 1000.10]

(Chapter 2.6 added by Stats. 2009, Ch. 372, Sec. 4.)
1000.8.
A superior court, with the concurrence of the prosecuting attorney of the county, may create a "Back on Track" deferred entry of judgment reentry program aimed at preventing recidivism among first-time nonviolent felony drug offenders. No defendant who has been convicted of a violation of an offense enumerated in subdivision (c) of Section 290 or in Section 1192.7 shall be eligible for the program established in this chapter. When creating this program, the prosecuting attorney, together with the presiding judge and a representative of the criminal defense bar selected by the presiding judge of the superior court may agree to establish a "Back on Track" deferred entry of judgment program pursuant to the provisions of this chapter. The agreement shall specify which low-level nonviolent felony drug offenses under the Health and Safety Code will be eligible for the program and a process for selecting participants. The program shall have the following characteristics:
(a) A dedicated calendar.
(b) Leadership by a superior court judicial officer who is assigned by the presiding judge.
(c) Clearly defined eligibility criteria to enter the program and clearly defined criteria for completion of the program.
(d) Legal incentives for defendants to successfully complete the program, including dismissal or reduction of criminal charges upon successful completion of the program.
(e) Close supervision to hold participants accountable to program compliance, including the use of graduated sanctions and frequent, ongoing appearances before the court regarding participants' program progress and compliance with all program terms and conditions. The court may use available legal mechanisms, including return to custody if necessary, for failure to comply with the supervised plan.
(f) Appropriate transitional programming for participants, based on available resources from county and community service providers and other agencies. The transitional programming may include, but is not limited to, any of the following:
(1) Vocational training, readiness, and placement.
(2) Educational training, including assistance with acquiring a G.E.D. or high school diploma and assistance with admission to college.
(3) Substance abuse treatment.
(4) Assistance with obtaining identification cards and driver's licenses.
(5) Parenting skills training and assistance in becoming compliant with child support obligations.

(g) The program may develop a local, public-private partnership between law enforcement, government agencies, private employers, and community-based organizations for the purpose of creating meaningful employment opportunities for participants and to take advantage of incentives for hiring program participants.
(Added by Stats. 2009, Ch. 372, Sec. 4. (AB 750) Effective January 1, 2010.)
1000.9.
The prosecuting attorney shall determine whether a defendant is eligible for participation in the deferred entry of judgment reentry program.
(a) If the prosecuting attorney determines that this section may be applicable to the defendant, he or she shall advise the defendant and his or her attorney in writing of that determination. This notification shall include the following:
(1) A full description of the procedures for deferred entry of judgment.
(2) A general explanation of the role and authority of the prosecuting attorney, the program, and the court in the process.
(3) A clear statement that in lieu of trial, the court may grant deferred entry of judgment with respect to the current crime or crimes charged if the defendant pleads guilty to each charge and waives time for the pronouncement of judgment, and that, upon the defendant's successful completion of the program and the motion of the prosecuting attorney, the court will dismiss the charge or charges against the defendant and the provisions of Sections 851.90 and 1203.4 will apply.
(4) A clear statement that failure to comply with any condition under the program may result in the prosecuting attorney or the court making a motion for entry of judgment, whereupon the court will render a finding of guilty to the charge or charges pled, enter judgment, and schedule a sentencing hearing as otherwise provided in this code.
(5) An explanation of criminal record retention and disposition resulting from participation in the deferred entry of judgment program and the defendant's rights relative to answering questions about his or her arrest and deferred entry of judgment following successful completion of the program.
(b) If the prosecuting attorney determines that the defendant is eligible for the program, the prosecuting attorney shall state for the record the grounds upon which the determination is based and shall make this information available to the defendant and his or her attorney. This procedure is intended to allow the court to set the hearing for deferred entry of judgment at the arraignment.
(c) If the prosecuting attorney determines that the defendant is ineligible for the program, the prosecuting attorney shall state for the record the grounds upon which the determination is based and shall make this information available to the defendant and his or her attorney. The sole remedy of a defendant who is found ineligible for deferred entry of judgment is a postconviction appeal. If the prosecuting attorney does not deem the defendant eligible, or the defendant does not consent to participate, the proceedings shall continue as in any other case.
(d) Upon a motion by the prosecuting attorney for an entry of judgment, before entering a judgment of guilty, the court may hold a hearing to determine whether the defendant has failed to comply with the program and should be terminated from the program.
(Added by Stats. 2009, Ch. 372, Sec. 4. (AB 750) Effective January 1, 2010.)
1000.10.
The following provisions apply to this chapter:
(a) A defendant's plea of guilty shall not constitute a conviction for any purpose unless a judgment of guilty is entered pursuant to Section 1000.3.
(b) Counties that opt to create a deferred entry of judgment reentry program pursuant to Section 1000.8 of the Penal Code shall not seek state reimbursement for costs associated with the implementation, development, or operation of that program.
(c) To the extent county resources beyond those of the superior court and the district attorney are needed to implement the program, those agencies shall consult with the county board of supervisors and other impacted county agencies to assess resources before program implementation.
(d) Local law enforcement agencies and counties administering the programs may seek federal or private funding for the purpose of implementing the provisions of this chapter.
(Added by Stats. 2009, Ch. 372, Sec. 4. (AB 750) Effective January 1, 2010.)

CHAPTER 2.65. Child Abuse and Neglect Counseling [1000.12 - 1000.17]

(Chapter 2.65 added by Stats. 1983, Ch. 804, Sec. 2.)
1000.12.
(a) It is the intent of the Legislature that nothing in this chapter deprive a prosecuting attorney of the ability to prosecute any person who is suspected of committing any crime in which a minor is a victim of an act of physical abuse or neglect to the fullest extent of the law, if the prosecuting attorney so chooses.
(b) In lieu of prosecuting a person suspected of committing any crime, involving a minor victim, of an act of physical abuse or neglect, the prosecuting attorney may refer that person to the county department in charge of public social services or the probation department for counseling or psychological treatment and such other services as the department deems necessary. The prosecuting attorney shall seek the advice of the county department in charge of public social services or the probation department in determining whether or not to make the referral.
(c) This section shall not apply to any person who is charged with sexual abuse or molestation of a minor victim, or any sexual offense involving force, violence, duress, menace, or fear of immediate and unlawful bodily injury on the minor victim or another person.
(Amended by Stats. 2005, Ch. 477, Sec. 3. Effective January 1, 2006.)
1000.17.
If the person is referred pursuant to this chapter he or she shall be responsible for paying the administrative cost of the referral and the expense of such counseling as determined by the county department responsible for public social services or the probation department. The administrative cost of the referral shall not exceed one hundred dollars ($100) for any person referred pursuant to this chapter for an offense punishable as a felony and shall not exceed fifty dollars ($50) for any person referred pursuant to the chapter for an offense punishable as a misdemeanor. The department shall take into consideration the ability of the referred party to pay and no such person shall be denied counseling services because of his or her inability to pay.
(Added by Stats. 1983, Ch. 804, Sec. 2.)

CHAPTER 2.7. Misdemeanor Diversion [1001 - 1001.9]

(Chapter 2.7 added by Stats. 1982, Ch. 42, Sec. 2.)
1001.
It is the intent of the Legislature that this chapter, Chapter 2.5 (commencing with Section 1000) of this title, or any other provision of law not be construed to preempt other current or future pretrial or precomplaint diversion programs. It is also the intent of the Legislature that current or future posttrial diversion programs not be preempted, except as provided in Section 13201 or 13352.5 of the Vehicle Code. Sections 1001.2

to 1001.9, inclusive, of this chapter apply only to pretrial diversion programs as defined in Section 1001.1.
(Amended by Stats. 2017, Ch. 537, Sec. 9. (SB 239) Effective January 1, 2018.)
1001.1.
As used in Sections 1001.2 to 1001.9, inclusive, of this chapter, pretrial diversion refers to the procedure of postponing prosecution of an offense filed as a misdemeanor either temporarily or permanently at any point in the judicial process from the point at which the accused is charged until adjudication.
(Amended by Stats. 2017, Ch. 537, Sec. 10. (SB 239) Effective January 1, 2018.)
1001.2.
(a) This chapter shall not apply to any pretrial diversion or posttrial programs for the treatment of problem drinking or alcoholism utilized for persons convicted of one or more offenses under Section 23152 or 23153 or former Section 23102 of the Vehicle Code or to pretrial diversion programs established pursuant to Chapter 2.5 (commencing with Section 1000) of this title nor shall this chapter be deemed to authorize any pretrial diversion or posttrial programs for persons alleged to have committed violation of Section 23152 or 23153 of the Vehicle Code.
(b) The district attorney of each county shall review annually any diversion program established pursuant to this chapter, and no program shall continue without the approval of the district attorney. No person shall be diverted under a program unless it has been approved by the district attorney. Nothing in this subdivision shall authorize the prosecutor to determine whether a particular defendant shall be diverted.
(Added by Stats. 1982, Ch. 42, Sec. 2. Effective February 17, 1982.)
1001.3.
At no time shall a defendant be required to make an admission of guilt as a prerequisite for placement in a pretrial diversion program.
(Added by Stats. 1982, Ch. 42, Sec. 2. Effective February 17, 1982.)
1001.4.
A divertee is entitled to a hearing, as set forth by law, before his or her pretrial diversion can be terminated for cause.
(Added by Stats. 1982, Ch. 42, Sec. 2. Effective February 17, 1982.)
1001.5.
No statement, or information procured therefrom, made by the defendant in connection with the determination of his or her eligibility for diversion, and no statement, or information procured therefrom, made by the defendant, subsequent to the granting of diversion or while participating in such program, and no information contained in any report made with respect thereto, and no statement or other information concerning the defendant's participation in such program shall be admissible in any action or proceeding. However, if a divertee is recommended for termination for cause, information regarding his or her participation in such program may be used for purposes of the termination proceedings.
(Added by Stats. 1982, Ch. 42, Sec. 2. Effective February 17, 1982.)
1001.6.
At such time that a defendant's case is diverted, any bail bond or undertaking, or deposit in lieu thereof, on file by or on behalf of the defendant shall be exonerated, and the court shall enter an order so directing.
(Added by Stats. 1982, Ch. 42, Sec. 2. Effective February 17, 1982.)
1001.7.
If the divertee has performed satisfactorily during the period of diversion, the criminal charges shall be dismissed at the end of the period of diversion.
(Added by Stats. 1982, Ch. 42, Sec. 2. Effective February 17, 1982.)
1001.8.
Any record filed with the Department of Justice shall indicate the disposition of those cases diverted pursuant to this chapter.
(Added by Stats. 1982, Ch. 42, Sec. 2. Effective February 17, 1982.)
1001.9.
(a) Any record filed with the Department of Justice shall indicate the disposition in those cases diverted pursuant to this chapter. Upon successful completion of a diversion program, the arrest upon which the diversion was based shall be deemed to have never occurred and the court may issue an order to seal the records pertaining to the arrest as described in Section 851.92. The divertee may indicate in response to any question concerning his or her prior criminal record that he or she was not arrested or diverted for the offense, except as specified in subdivision (b). A record pertaining to an arrest resulting in successful completion of a diversion program shall not, without the divertee's consent, be used in any way that could result in the denial of any employment, benefit, license, or certificate.
(b) The divertee shall be advised that, regardless of his or her successful completion of diversion, the arrest upon which the diversion was based may be disclosed by the Department of Justice in response to any peace officer application request and that, notwithstanding subdivision (a), this section does not relieve him or her of the obligation to disclose the arrest in response to any direct question contained in any questionnaire or application for a position as a peace officer, as defined in Section 830.
(c) The divertee shall be advised that, regardless of the defendant's successful completion of a deferred entry of judgment program, an order to seal records pertaining to an arrest made pursuant to this section has no effect on a criminal justice agency's ability to access and use those sealed records and information regarding sealed arrests, as described in Section 851.92.
(Amended by Stats. 2017, Ch. 680, Sec. 6. (SB 393) Effective January 1, 2018.)

CHAPTER 2.71. AIDS Prevention Program in Drug Abuse and Prostitution Cases

CHAPTER 2.75. Diversion Fees [1001.15 - 1001.16]

(Chapter 2.75 added by Stats. 1982, Ch. 1226, Sec. 1.)
1001.15.
(a) In addition to the fees authorized or required by other provisions of law, a judge may require the payment of an administrative fee, as part of an enrollment fee in a diversion program, by a defendant accused of a felony to cover the actual cost of any criminalistics laboratory analysis, the actual cost of processing a request or application for diversion, and the actual cost of supervising the divertee pursuant to Chapter 2.5 (commencing with Section 1000), not to exceed five hundred dollars ($500). The fee shall be payable at the time of enrollment in the diversion program. The court shall take into consideration the defendant's ability to pay, and no defendant shall be denied diversion because of his or her inability to pay.
(b) As used in this section, "criminalistics laboratory" means a laboratory operated by, or under contract with a city, county, or other public agency, including a criminalistics laboratory of the Department of Justice, which has not less than one regularly employed forensic scientist engaged in the analysis of solid dose material and body fluids for controlled substances, and which is registered as an analytical laboratory with the Drug Enforcement Administration of the United States Department of Justice for the processing of all scheduled controlled substances.

(c) In addition to the fees authorized or required by other provisions of law, a judge may require the payment of an administrative fee, as part of an enrollment fee in a diversion program, by a defendant accused of an act charged as, or reduced to, a misdemeanor to cover the actual cost of processing a request or application for diversion pursuant to Chapter 2.6 (commencing with Section 1000.6), the actual costs of reporting to the court on a defendant's eligibility and suitability for diversion, the actual cost of supervising the divertee, and for the actual costs of performing any duties required pursuant to Section 1000.9, not to exceed three hundred dollars ($300). The fee shall be payable at the time of enrollment in the diversion program. The fee shall be determined on a sliding scale according to the defendant's ability to pay, and no defendant shall be denied diversion because of his or her inability to pay.

(d) The fee established pursuant to this section may not exceed the actual costs required for the programs authorized to be reimbursed by this fee. All proceeds from the fee established pursuant to this section shall be allocated only for the programs authorized to be reimbursed by this fee.

(e) As used in this section, "diversion" also means deferred entry of judgment pursuant to Chapter 2.5 (commencing with Section 1000).

(Amended by Stats. 1997, Ch. 324, Sec. 4. Effective January 1, 1998.)

1001.16.

(a) In addition to the fees authorized or required by other provisions of law, a judge may require the payment of an administrative fee, as part of an enrollment fee in a diversion program, by a defendant accused of a misdemeanor to cover the actual cost of any criminalistics laboratory analysis in a case involving a violation of the California Uniform Controlled Substances Act under Division 10 (commencing with Section 11000) of the Health and Safety Code, the actual cost of processing a request or application for diversion, and the actual cost of supervising the divertee, not to exceed three hundred dollars ($300). The fee shall be payable at the time of enrollment in the diversion program. The court shall take into consideration the defendant's ability to pay, and no defendant shall be denied diversion because of his or her inability to pay.

(b) As used in this section, "criminalistics laboratory" means a laboratory operated by, or under contract with, a city, county, or other public agency, including a criminalistics laboratory of the Department of Justice, which has not less than one regularly employed forensic scientist engaged in the analysis of solid dose material and body fluids for controlled substances and which is registered as an analytical laboratory with the Drug Enforcement Administration of the United States Department of Justice for the processing of all scheduled controlled substances.

(c) This section shall apply to all deferred entry of judgment and misdemeanor pretrial diversion programs established pursuant to this title.

(d) The fee established pursuant to this section may not exceed the actual costs required for the programs authorized to be reimbursed by this fee. All proceeds from the fee established pursuant to this section shall be allocated only for the programs authorized to be reimbursed by this fee.

(e) As used in this section, "diversion" also means deferred entry of judgment pursuant to Chapter 2.5 (commencing with Section 1000).

(Amended by Stats. 1997, Ch. 324, Sec. 5. Effective January 1, 1998.)

CHAPTER 2.8.
Diversion of Defendants With Cognitive Developmental Disabilities [1001.20 - 1001.34]

(Heading of Chapter 2.8 amended by Stats. 2004, Ch. 290, Sec. 1.)

1001.20.

As used in this chapter:

(a) "Cognitive Developmental Disability" means any of the following:

(1) "Intellectual disability" means a condition of significantly subaverage general intellectual functioning existing concurrently with deficits in adaptive behavior and manifested during the developmental period.

(2) "Autism" means a diagnosed condition of markedly abnormal or impaired development in social interaction, in communication, or in both, with a markedly restricted repertoire of activity and interests.

(3) Disabling conditions found to be closely related to intellectual disability or autism, or that require treatment similar to that required for individuals with intellectual disability or autism, and that would qualify an individual for services provided under the Lanterman Developmental Disabilities Services Act.

(b) "Diversion-related treatment and habilitation" means, but is not limited to, specialized services or special adaptations of generic services, directed toward the alleviation of cognitive developmental disability or toward social, personal, physical, or economic habilitation or rehabilitation of an individual with a cognitive developmental disability, and includes, but is not limited to, diagnosis, evaluation, treatment, personal care, day care, domiciliary care, special living arrangements, physical, occupational, and speech therapy, training, education, sheltered employment, mental health services, recreation, counseling of the individual with this disability and of his or her family, protective and other social and sociolegal services, information and referral services, follow-along services, and transportation services necessary to ensure delivery of services to persons with cognitive developmental disabilities.

(c) "Regional center" means a regional center for the developmentally disabled established under the Lanterman Developmental Disabilities Services Act that is organized as a private nonprofit community agency to plan, purchase, and coordinate the delivery of services that cannot be provided by state agencies to developmentally disabled persons residing in a particular geographic catchment area, and that is licensed and funded by the State Department of Developmental Services.

(d) "Director of a regional center" means the executive director of a regional center for the developmentally disabled or his or her designee.

(e) "Agency" means the prosecutor, the probation department, and the regional center involved in a particular defendant's case.

(f) "Dual agency diversion" means a treatment and habilitation program developed with court approval by the regional center, administered jointly by the regional center and by the probation department, that is individually tailored to the needs of the defendant as derived from the defendant's individual program plan pursuant to Section 4646 of the Welfare and Institutions Code, and that includes, but is not limited to, treatment specifically addressed to the criminal offense charged, for a specified period of time as prescribed in Section 1001.28.

(g) "Single agency diversion" means a treatment and habilitation program developed with court approval by the regional center, administered solely by the regional center without involvement by the probation department, that is individually tailored to the needs of the defendant as derived from the defendant's individual program plan pursuant to Section 4646 of the Welfare and Institutions Code, and that includes, but is not limited to, treatment specifically addressed to the criminal offense charged, for a specified period of time as prescribed in Section 1001.28.

(Amended by Stats. 2013, Ch. 76, Sec. 151. (AB 383) Effective January 1, 2014.)

1001.21.

(a) This chapter shall apply whenever a case is before any court upon an accusatory pleading at any stage of the criminal proceedings, for any person who has been evaluated by a regional center for the developmentally disabled and who is determined to be a person with a cognitive developmental disability by the regional center, and who therefore is eligible for its services.

(b) This chapter applies to any offense which is charged as or reduced to a misdemeanor, except that diversion shall not be ordered when the defendant previously has been diverted under this chapter within two years prior to the present criminal proceedings.

(c) This chapter shall apply to persons who have a condition described in paragraph (2) or (3) of subdivision (a) of Section 1001.20 only if that person was a client of a regional center at the time of the offense for which he or she is charged.

(Amended by Stats. 2004, Ch. 290, Sec. 3. Effective January 1, 2005.)

1001.22.

The court shall consult with the prosecutor, the defense counsel, the probation department, and the appropriate regional center in order to determine whether a defendant may be diverted pursuant to this chapter. If the defendant is not represented by counsel, the court shall appoint counsel to represent the defendant. When the court suspects that a defendant may have a cognitive developmental disability, as defined in subdivision (a) of Section 1001.20, and the defendant consents to the diversion process and to his or her case being evaluated for eligibility for regional center services, and waives his or her right to a speedy trial, the court shall order the prosecutor, the probation department, and the regional center to prepare reports on specified aspects of the defendant's case. Each report shall be prepared concurrently.

(a) The regional center shall submit a report to the probation department within 25 judicial days of the court's order. The regional center's report shall include a determination as to whether the defendant has a cognitive developmental disability and is eligible for regional center diversion-related treatment and habilitation services, and the regional center shall also submit to the court a proposed diversion program, individually tailored to the needs of the defendant as derived from the defendant's individual program plan pursuant to Section 4646 of the Welfare and Institutions Code, which shall include, but not be limited to, treatment addressed to the criminal offense charged for a period of time as prescribed in Section 1001.28. The regional center's report shall also contain a statement whether such a proposed program is available for the defendant through the treatment and habilitation services of the regional centers pursuant to Section 4648 of the Welfare and Institutions Code.

(b) The prosecutor shall submit a report on specified aspects of the defendant's case, within 30 judicial days of the court's order, to the court, to each of the other agencies involved in the case, and to the defendant. The prosecutor's report shall include all of the following:

(1) A statement of whether the defendant's record indicates the defendant's diversion pursuant to this chapter within two years prior to the alleged commission of the charged divertible offense.

(2) If the prosecutor recommends that this chapter may be applicable to the defendant, he or she shall recommend either a dual or single agency diversion program and shall advise the court, the probation department, the regional center, and the defendant, in writing, of that determination within 20 judicial days of the court's order to prepare the report.

(3) If the prosecutor recommends against diversion, the prosecutor's report shall include a declaration in writing to state for the record the grounds upon which the recommendation was made, and the court shall determine, pursuant to Section 1001.23, whether the defendant shall be diverted.

(4) If dual agency diversion is recommended by the prosecutor, a copy of the prosecutor's report shall also be provided by the prosecutor to the probation department, the regional center, and the defendant within the above prescribed time period. This notification shall include all of the following:

(A) A full description of the proceedings for diversion and the prosecutor's investigation procedures.

(B) A general explanation of the role and authority of the probation department, the prosecutor, the regional center, and the court in the diversion program process.

(C) A clear statement that the court may decide in a hearing not to divert the defendant and that he or she may have to stand trial for the alleged offense.

(D) A clear statement that should the defendant fail in meeting the terms of his or her diversion, or if, during the period of diversion the defendant is subsequently charged with a felony, the defendant may be required, after a hearing, to stand trial for the original diverted offense.

(c) The probation department shall submit a report on specified aspects of the defendant's case within 30 judicial days of the court's order, to the court, to each of the other agencies involved in the case, and to the defendant. The probation department's report to the court shall be based upon an investigation by the probation department and consideration of the defendant's age, cognitive developmental disability, employment record, educational background, ties to community agencies and family, treatment history, criminal record if any, and demonstrable motivation and other mitigating factors in determining whether the defendant is a person who would benefit from a diversion-related treatment and habilitation program. The regional center's report in full shall be appended to the probation department's report to the court.

(Amended by Stats. 2004, Ch. 290, Sec. 4. Effective January 1, 2005.)

1001.23.

(a) Upon the court's receipt of the reports from the prosecutor, the probation department, and the regional center, and a determination by the regional center that the defendant does not have a cognitive developmental disability, the criminal proceedings for the offense charged shall proceed. If the defendant is found to have a cognitive developmental disability and to be eligible for regional center services, and the court determines from the various reports submitted to it that the proposed diversion program is acceptable to the court, the prosecutor, the probation department, and the regional center, and if the defendant consents to diversion and waives his or her right to a speedy trial, the court may order, without a hearing, that the diversion program be implemented for a period of time as prescribed in Section 1001.28.

(b) After consideration of the probation department's report, the report of the regional center, and the report of the prosecutor relating to his or her recommendation for or against diversion, and any other relevant information, the court shall determine if the defendant shall be diverted under either dual or single agency supervision, and referred for habilitation or rehabilitation diversion pursuant to this chapter. If the court does not deem the defendant a person who would benefit by diversion at the time of the hearing, the suspended criminal proceedings may be reinstituted, or any other disposition as authorized by law may be made, and diversion may be ordered at a later date.

(c) Where a dual agency diversion program is ordered by the court, the regional center shall submit a report to the probation department on the defendant's progress in the diversion program not less than every six months. Within five judicial days after receiving the regional center's report, the probation department shall submit its report on the defendant's progress in the diversion program, with the full report of the regional center appended, to the court and to the prosecutor. Where single agency diversion is ordered by the court, the regional center alone shall report the defendant's progress to the court and to the prosecutor not less than every six months.

(Amended by Stats. 2004, Ch. 290, Sec. 5. Effective January 1, 2005.)

1001.24.

No statement, or information procured therefrom, made by the defendant to any probation officer, the prosecutor, or any regional center designee during the course of the investigation conducted by either the regional center or the probation department pursuant to this chapter, and prior to the reporting to the probation department of the regional center's findings of eligibility and recommendations to the court, shall be admissible in any action or proceeding brought subsequent to this investigation.

(Added by Stats. 1980, Ch. 1253, Sec. 1.)
1001.25.
No statement, or information procured therefrom, with respect to the specific offense with which the defendant is charged, which is made to a probation officer, a prosecutor, or a regional center designee subsequent to the granting of diversion shall be admissible in any action or proceeding brought subsequent to the investigation.
(Added by Stats. 1980, Ch. 1253, Sec. 1.)
1001.26.
In the event that diversion is either denied or is subsequently revoked once it has been granted, neither the probation investigation nor the statements or other information divulged by the defendant during the investigation by the probation department or the regional center shall be used in any sentencing procedures.
(Added by Stats. 1980, Ch. 1253, Sec. 1.)
1001.27.
At such time as the defendant's case is diverted, any bail, bond, or undertaking, or deposit in lieu thereof, on file or on behalf of the defendant shall be exonerated, and the court shall enter an order so directing.
(Added by Stats. 1980, Ch. 1253, Sec. 1.)
1001.28.
The period during which criminal proceedings against the defendant may be diverted shall be no longer than two years. The responsible agency or agencies shall file reports on the defendant's progress in the diversion program with the court and with the prosecutor not less than every six months.
(a) Where dual agency diversion has been ordered, the probation department shall be responsible for the progress reports. The probation department shall append to its own report a copy of the regional center's assessment of the defendant's progress.
(b) Where single agency diversion has been ordered, the regional center alone shall be responsible for the progress reports.
(Added by Stats. 1980, Ch. 1253, Sec. 1.)
1001.29.
If it appears that the divertee is not meeting the terms and conditions of his or her diversion program, the court may hold a hearing and amend such program to provide for greater supervision by the responsible regional center alone, by the probation department alone, or by both the regional center and the probation department. However, notwithstanding any such modification of a diversion order, the court may hold a hearing to determine whether the diverted criminal proceedings should be reinstituted if it appears that the divertee's performance in the diversion program is unsatisfactory, or if the divertee is subsequently charged with a felony during the period of diversion.
(a) In cases of dual agency diversion, a hearing to reinstitute the diverted criminal proceedings may be initiated by either the court, the prosecutor, the regional center, or the probation department.
(b) In cases of single agency diversion, a hearing to reinstitute the diverted criminal proceedings may be initiated only by the court, the prosecutor, or the regional center.
(c) No hearing for either of these purposes shall be held unless the moving agency or the court has given the divertee prior notice of the hearing.
(d) Where the cause of the hearing is a subsequent charge of a felony against the divertee subsequent to the diversion order, any hearing to reinstitute the diverted criminal proceedings shall be delayed until such time as probable cause has been established in court to bind the defendant over for trial on the subsequently charged felony.
(Added by Stats. 1980, Ch. 1253, Sec. 1.)
1001.30.
At any time during which the defendant is participating in a diversion program, he or she may withdraw consent to further participate in the diversion program, and at such time as such consent is withdrawn, the suspended criminal proceedings may resume or such other disposition may be made as is authorized by law.
(Added by Stats. 1980, Ch. 1253, Sec. 1.)
1001.31.
If the divertee has performed satisfactorily during the period of diversion, the criminal charges shall be dismissed at the end of the diversion period.
(Added by Stats. 1980, Ch. 1253, Sec. 1.)
1001.32.
Any record filed with the State Department of Justice shall indicate the disposition of those cases diverted pursuant to this chapter.
(Added by Stats. 1980, Ch. 1253, Sec. 1.)
1001.33.
(a) Any record filed with the Department of Justice shall indicate the disposition in those cases diverted pursuant to this chapter. Upon successful completion of a diversion program, the arrest upon which the diversion was based shall be deemed to have never occurred. The divertee may indicate in response to any question concerning his or her prior criminal record that he or she was not arrested or diverted for the offense, except as specified in subdivision (b). A record pertaining to an arrest resulting in successful completion of a diversion program shall not, without the divertee's consent, be used in any way that could result in the denial of any employment, benefit, license, or certificate.
(b) The divertee shall be advised that, regardless of his or her successful completion of diversion, the arrest upon which the diversion was based may be disclosed by the Department of Justice in response to any peace officer application request and that, notwithstanding subdivision (a), this section does not relieve him or her of the obligation to disclose the arrest in response to any direct question contained in any questionnaire or application for a position as a peace officer, as defined in Section 830.
(Amended by Stats. 1996, Ch. 743, Sec. 3. Effective January 1, 1997.)
1001.34.
Notwithstanding any other provision of law, the diversion-related individual program plan shall be fully implemented by the regional centers upon court order and approval of the diversion-related treatment and habilitation plan.
(Added by Stats. 1980, Ch. 1253, Sec. 1.)

CHAPTER 2.8A. Diversion of Individuals with Mental Disorders [1001.35 - 1001.36]

(Chapter 2.8A added by Stats. 2018, Ch. 34, Sec. 24.)
1001.35.
The purpose of this chapter is to promote all of the following:
(a) Increased diversion of individuals with mental disorders to mitigate the individuals' entry and reentry into the criminal justice system while protecting public safety.
(b) Allowing local discretion and flexibility for counties in the development and implementation of diversion for individuals with mental disorders across a continuum of care settings.
(c) Providing diversion that meets the unique mental health treatment and support needs of individuals with mental disorders.
(Added by Stats. 2018, Ch. 34, Sec. 24. (AB 1810) Effective June 27, 2018.)
1001.36.
(a) On an accusatory pleading alleging the commission of a misdemeanor or felony offense, the court may, after considering the positions of the defense and prosecution, grant pretrial diversion to a defendant pursuant to this section if the defendant meets all of the requirements specified in paragraph (1) of subdivision (b).

(b) (1) Pretrial diversion may be granted pursuant to this section if all of the following criteria are met:
(A) The court is satisfied that the defendant suffers from a mental disorder as identified in the most recent edition of the Diagnostic and Statistical Manual of Mental Disorders, including, but not limited to, bipolar disorder, schizophrenia, schizoaffective disorder, or post-traumatic stress disorder, but excluding antisocial personality disorder, borderline personality disorder, and pedophilia. Evidence of the defendant's mental disorder shall be provided by the defense and shall include a recent diagnosis by a qualified mental health expert. In opining that a defendant suffers from a qualifying disorder, the qualified mental health expert may rely on an examination of the defendant, the defendant's medical records, arrest reports, or any other relevant evidence.
(B) The court is satisfied that the defendant's mental disorder was a significant factor in the commission of the charged offense. A court may conclude that a defendant's mental disorder was a significant factor in the commission of the charged offense if, after reviewing any relevant and credible evidence, including, but not limited to, police reports, preliminary hearing transcripts, witness statements, statements by the defendant's mental health treatment provider, medical records, records or reports by qualified medical experts, or evidence that the defendant displayed symptoms consistent with the relevant mental disorder at or near the time of the offense, the court concludes that the defendant's mental disorder substantially contributed to the defendant's involvement in the commission of the offense.
(C) In the opinion of a qualified mental health expert, the defendant's symptoms of the mental disorder motivating the criminal behavior would respond to mental health treatment.
(D) The defendant consents to diversion and waives his or her right to a speedy trial, unless a defendant has been found to be an appropriate candidate for diversion in lieu of commitment pursuant to clause (iv) of subparagraph (B) paragraph (1) of subdivision (a) of Section 1370 and, as a result of his or her mental incompetence, cannot consent to diversion or give a knowing and intelligent waiver of his or her right to a speedy trial.
(E) The defendant agrees to comply with treatment as a condition of diversion.
(F) The court is satisfied that the defendant will not pose an unreasonable risk of danger to public safety, as defined in Section 1170.18, if treated in the community. The court may consider the opinions of the district attorney, the defense, or a qualified mental health expert, and may consider the defendant's violence and criminal history, the current charged offense, and any other factors that the court deems appropriate.
(2) A defendant may not be placed into a diversion program, pursuant to this section, for the following current charged offenses:
(A) Murder or voluntary manslaughter.
(B) An offense for which a person, if convicted, would be required to register pursuant to Section 290, except for a violation of Section 314.
(C) Rape.
(D) Lewd or lascivious act on a child under 14 years of age.
(E) Assault with intent to commit rape, sodomy, or oral copulation, in violation of Section 220.
(F) Commission of rape or sexual penetration in concert with another person, in violation of Section 264.1.
(G) Continuous sexual abuse of a child, in violation of Section 288.5.
(H) A violation of subdivision (b) or (c) of Section 11418.
(3) At any stage of the proceedings, the court may require the defendant to make a prima facie showing that the defendant will meet the minimum requirements of eligibility for diversion and that the defendant and the offense are suitable for diversion. The hearing on the prima facie showing shall be informal and may proceed on offers of proof, reliable hearsay, and argument of counsel. If a prima facie showing is not made, the court may summarily deny the request for diversion or grant any other relief as may be deemed appropriate.
(c) As used in this chapter, "pretrial diversion" means the postponement of prosecution, either temporarily or permanently, at any point in the judicial process from the point at which the accused is charged until adjudication, to allow the defendant to undergo mental health treatment, subject to all of the following:
(1) (A) The court is satisfied that the recommended inpatient or outpatient program of mental health treatment will meet the specialized mental health treatment needs of the defendant.
(B) The defendant may be referred to a program of mental health treatment utilizing existing inpatient or outpatient mental health resources. Before approving a proposed treatment program, the court shall consider the request of the defense, the request of the prosecution, the needs of the defendant, and the interests of the community. The treatment may be procured using private or public funds, and a referral may be made to a county mental health agency, existing collaborative courts, or assisted outpatient treatment only if that entity has agreed to accept responsibility for the treatment of the defendant, and mental health services are provided only to the extent that resources are available and the defendant is eligible for those services.
(2) The provider of the mental health treatment program in which the defendant has been placed shall provide regular reports to the court, the defense, and the prosecutor on the defendant's progress in treatment.
(3) The period during which criminal proceedings against the defendant may be diverted shall be no longer than two years.
(4) Upon request, the court shall conduct a hearing to determine whether restitution, as defined in subdivision (f) of Section 1202.4, is owed to any victim as a result of the diverted offense and, if owed, order its payment during the period of diversion. However, a defendant's inability to pay restitution due to indigence or mental disorder shall not be grounds for denial of diversion or a finding that the defendant has failed to comply with the terms of diversion.
(d) If any of the following circumstances exists, the court shall, after notice to the defendant, defense counsel, and the prosecution, hold a hearing to determine whether the criminal proceedings should be reinstated, whether the treatment should be modified, or whether the defendant should be conserved and referred to the conservatorship investigator of the county of commitment to initiate conservatorship proceedings for the defendant pursuant to Chapter 3 (commencing with Section 5350) of Part 1 of Division 5 of the Welfare and Institutions Code:
(1) The defendant is charged with an additional misdemeanor allegedly committed during the pretrial diversion and that reflects the defendant's propensity for violence.
(2) The defendant is charged with an additional felony allegedly committed during the pretrial diversion.
(3) The defendant is engaged in criminal conduct rendering him or her unsuitable for diversion.
(4) Based on the opinion of a qualified mental health expert whom the court may deem appropriate, either of the following circumstances exists:
(A) The defendant is performing unsatisfactorily in the assigned program.
(B) The defendant is gravely disabled, as defined in subparagraph (B) of paragraph (1) of subdivision (h) of Section 5008 of the Welfare and Institutions Code. A defendant shall only be conserved and referred to the conservatorship investigator pursuant to this finding.
(e) If the defendant has performed satisfactorily in diversion, at the end of the period of diversion, the court shall dismiss the defendant's criminal charges that were the subject of the criminal proceedings at the time of the initial diversion. A court may conclude that the defendant has performed satisfactorily if the defendant has substantially complied with the requirements of diversion, has avoided significant new violations of law unrelated to the defendant's mental health condition, and has a plan in place for long-

term mental health care. If the court dismisses the charges, the clerk of the court shall file a record with the Department of Justice indicating the disposition of the case diverted pursuant to this section. Upon successful completion of diversion, if the court dismisses the charges, the arrest upon which the diversion was based shall be deemed never to have occurred, and the court shall order access to the record of the arrest restricted in accordance with Section 1001.9, except as specified in subdivisions (g) and (h). The defendant who successfully completes diversion may indicate in response to any question concerning his or her prior criminal record that he or she was not arrested or diverted for the offense, except as specified in subdivision (g).

(f) A record pertaining to an arrest resulting in successful completion of diversion, or any record generated as a result of the defendant's application for or participation in diversion, shall not, without the defendant's consent, be used in any way that could result in the denial of any employment, benefit, license, or certificate.

(g) The defendant shall be advised that, regardless of his or her completion of diversion, both of the following apply:

(1) The arrest upon which the diversion was based may be disclosed by the Department of Justice to any peace officer application request and that, notwithstanding subdivision (f), this section does not relieve the defendant of the obligation to disclose the arrest in response to any direct question contained in any questionnaire or application for a position as a peace officer, as defined in Section 830.

(2) An order to seal records pertaining to an arrest made pursuant to this section has no effect on a criminal justice agency's ability to access and use those sealed records and information regarding sealed arrests, as described in Section 851.92.

(h) A finding that the defendant suffers from a mental disorder, any progress reports concerning the defendant's treatment, or any other records related to a mental disorder that were created as a result of participation in, or completion of, diversion pursuant to this section or for use at a hearing on the defendant's eligibility for diversion under this section may not be used in any other proceeding without the defendant's consent, unless that information is relevant evidence that is admissible under the standards described in paragraph (2) of subdivision (f) of Section 28 of Article I of the California Constitution. However, when determining whether to exercise its discretion to grant diversion under this section, a court may consider previous records of participation in diversion under this section.

(i) The county agency administering the diversion, the defendant's mental health treatment providers, the public guardian or conservator, and the court shall, to the extent not prohibited by federal law, have access to the defendant's medical and psychological records, including progress reports, during the defendant's time in diversion, as needed, for the purpose of providing care and treatment and monitoring treatment for diversion or conservatorship.

(Amended by Stats. 2018, Ch. 1005, Sec. 1. (SB 215) Effective January 1, 2019.)

CHAPTER 2.81. Pretrial Diversion of Traffic Violators [1001.40- 1001.40.]

(Chapter 2.81 added by Stats. 1990, Ch. 1303, Sec. 1.)
1001.40.
Notwithstanding any other provision of law, a county acting on behalf of one or more individual courts may by ordinance establish a program that provides for pretrial diversion by the court of any person issued a notice to appear for a traffic violation to attend any traffic violator school licensed pursuant to Chapter 1.5 (commencing with Section 11200) of Division 5 of the Vehicle Code.
(Added by Stats. 1990, Ch. 1303, Sec. 1.)

CHAPTER 2.9. Diversion of Misdemeanor Offenders [1001.50 - 1001.55]

(Chapter 2.9 added by Stats. 1982, Ch. 1251, Sec. 2.)
1001.50.
(a) Notwithstanding any other provision of law, this chapter shall become operative in a county only if the board of supervisors adopts the provisions of this chapter by ordinance.

(b) The district attorney of each county shall review annually any diversion program established pursuant to this chapter, and no program shall continue without the approval of the district attorney. No person shall be diverted under a program unless it has been approved by the district attorney. Nothing in this subdivision shall authorize the prosecutor to determine whether a particular defendant shall be diverted.

(c) As used in this chapter, "pretrial diversion" means the procedure of postponing prosecution either temporarily or permanently at any point in the judicial process from the point at which the accused is charged until adjudication.
(Added by Stats. 1982, Ch. 1251, Sec. 2.)
1001.51.
(a) This chapter shall apply whenever a case is before any court upon an accusatory pleading concerning the commission of a misdemeanor, except a misdemeanor specified in subdivision (b), and it appears to the court that all of the following apply to the defendant:

(1) The defendant's record does not indicate that probation or parole has ever been revoked without thereafter being completed.

(2) The defendant's record does not indicate that he has been diverted pursuant to this chapter within five years prior to the filing of the accusatory pleading which charges the divertible offense.

(3) The defendant has never been convicted of a felony, and has not been convicted of a misdemeanor within five years prior to the filing of the accusatory pleading which charges the divertible offense.

(b) This chapter shall not apply to any pretrial diversion or posttrial program otherwise established by this code, nor shall this chapter be deemed to authorize any pretrial diversion or posttrial program for any person alleged to have committed a violation of Section 23152 or 23153 of the Vehicle Code.

(c) This chapter shall not apply whenever the accusatory pleading charges the commission of a misdemeanor:

(1) For which incarceration would be mandatory upon conviction of the defendant.

(2) For which registration would be required pursuant to Section 290 upon conviction of the defendant.

(3) Which the magistrate determines shall be prosecuted as a misdemeanor pursuant to paragraph (5) of subdivision (b) of Section 17.

(4) Which involves the use of force or violence against a person, unless the charge is of a violation of Section 241 or 243.

(5) For which the granting of probation is prohibited.

(6) Which is a driving offense punishable as a misdemeanor pursuant to the Vehicle Code.
(Added by Stats. 1982, Ch. 1251, Sec. 2.)
1001.52.

(a) If the defendant consents and waives his right to a speedy trial, the case shall be referred to the probation department. The probation department shall conduct such investigation as is necessary to determine whether the defendant qualifies for diversion under subdivision (a) of Section 1001.51, and whether he or she is a person who would be benefited by education, treatment or rehabilitation. The probation department shall also determine which educational, treatment or rehabilitative plan would benefit the defendant. The probation department shall report its findings and recommendation to the court. If the recommendation includes referral to a community program, the report shall contain a statement regarding the program's willingness to accept the defendant and the manner in which the services they offer can assist the defendant in completing the diversion program successfully.

(b) No statement, or any information procured therefrom, made by the defendant to any probation officer, which is made during the course of any investigation conducted by the probation department pursuant to subdivision (b), and prior to the reporting of the probation department's findings and recommendations to the court, shall be admissible in any action or proceeding brought subsequent to the investigation.

No statement, or any information procured therefrom, with respect to the specific offense with which the defendant is charged, which is made to any probation officer subsequent to the granting of diversion, shall be admissible in any action or proceeding. In the event that diversion is either denied, or is subsequently revoked once it has been granted, neither the probation investigation nor statements or information divulged during that investigation shall be used in any pretrial sentencing procedures.
(Added by Stats. 1982, Ch. 1251, Sec. 2.)
1001.53.
The court shall hold a hearing and, after consideration of the probation department's report, and any other relevant information, shall determine if the defendant consents to further proceedings under this chapter and waives his or her right to a speedy trial. If the court orders a defendant to be diverted, the court may make inquiry into the financial condition of the defendant, and upon a finding that the defendant is able in whole or in part, to pay the reasonable cost of diversion, the court may order him or her to pay all or part of such expense. The reasonable cost of diversion shall not exceed the amount determined to be the actual average cost of diversion services.

If the court does not deem the defendant to be a person who would be benefited by diversion, or if the defendant does not consent to participate, the proceedings shall continue as in any other case.

At such time that a defendant's case is diverted, any bail bond or undertaking, or deposit in lieu thereof, on file by or on behalf of the defendant shall be exonerated, and the court shall enter an order so directing.

The period during which the further criminal proceedings against the defendant may be diverted shall be for the length of time required to complete and verify the diversion program but in no case shall it exceed two years.
(Added by Stats. 1982, Ch. 1251, Sec. 2.)
1001.54.
If it appears to the probation department that the divertee is performing unsatisfactorily in the assigned program, or that the divertee is not benefiting from education, treatment or rehabilitation, or that the divertee is convicted of a misdemeanor in which force or violence is used, or if the divertee is convicted of a felony, after notice to the divertee, the court shall hold a hearing to determine whether the criminal proceedings should be reinstituted. If the court finds that the divertee is not performing satisfactorily in the assigned program, or that the divertee is not benefiting from diversion, or the court finds that the divertee has been convicted of a crime as indicated above, the criminal case shall be referred back to the court for resumption of the criminal proceedings. If the divertee has performed satisfactorily during the period of diversion, at the end of the period of diversion, the criminal charges shall be dismissed.
(Added by Stats. 1982, Ch. 1251, Sec. 2.)
1001.55.
(a) Any record filed with the Department of Justice shall indicate the disposition in those cases diverted pursuant to this chapter. Upon successful completion of a diversion program, the arrest upon which the diversion was based shall be deemed to have never occurred. The divertee may indicate in response to any question concerning his or her prior criminal record that he or she was not arrested or diverted for the offense, except as specified in subdivision (b). A record pertaining to an arrest resulting in successful completion of a diversion program shall not, without the divertee's consent, be used in any way that could result in the denial of any employment, benefit, license, or certificate.

(b) The divertee shall be advised that, regardless of his or her successful completion of diversion, the arrest upon which the diversion was based may be disclosed by the Department of Justice in response to any peace officer application request and that, notwithstanding subdivision (a), this section does not relieve him or her of the obligation to disclose the arrest in response to any direct question contained in any questionnaire or application for a position as a peace officer, as defined in Section 830.
(Amended by Stats. 1996, Ch. 743, Sec. 4. Effective January 1, 1997.)

CHAPTER 2.9A. Bad Check Diversion [1001.60 - 1001.67]

(Chapter 2.9A added by Stats. 1985, Ch. 1059, Sec. 1.)
1001.60.
Upon the adoption of a resolution by the board of supervisors declaring that there are sufficient funds available to fund the program, the district attorney may create within his or her office a diversion program pursuant to this chapter for persons who write bad checks. For purposes of this chapter, "writing a bad check" means making, drawing, uttering, or delivering any check or draft upon any bank or depository for the payment of money where there is probable cause to believe there has been a violation of Section 476a. The program may be conducted by the district attorney or by a private entity under contract with the district attorney.
(Amended by Stats. 2008, Ch. 264, Sec. 1. Effective January 1, 2009.)
1001.61.
The district attorney may refer a bad check case to the diversion program. Except as provided in Section 1001.64, this chapter does not limit the power of the district attorney to prosecute bad check complaints.
(Added by Stats. 1985, Ch. 1059, Sec. 1.)
1001.62.
On receipt of a bad check case, the district attorney shall determine if the case is one which is appropriate to be referred to the bad check diversion program. In determining whether to refer a case to the bad check diversion program, the district attorney shall consider, but is not limited to, all of the following:

(a) The amount of the bad check.

(b) If the person has a prior criminal record or has previously been diverted.

(c) The number of bad check grievances against the person previously received by the district attorney.

(d) Whether there are other bad check grievances currently pending against the person.

(e) The strength of the evidence, if any, of intent to defraud the victim.
(Added by Stats. 1985, Ch. 1059, Sec. 1.)
1001.63.

On referral of a bad check case to the diversion program, a notice shall be forwarded by mail to the person alleged to have written the bad check which contains all of the following:
(a) The date and amount of the bad check.
(b) The name of the payee.
(c) The date before which the person must contact the person designated by the district attorney concerning the bad check.
(d) A statement of the penalty for issuance of a bad check.
(Added by Stats. 1985, Ch. 1059, Sec. 1.)
1001.64.
The district attorney may enter into a written agreement with the person to forego prosecution on the bad check for a period to be determined by the district attorney, not to exceed six months, pending all of the following:
(a) Completion of a class or classes conducted by the district attorney or private entity under contract with the district attorney.
(b) Full restitution being made to the victim of the bad check to hold offenders accountable for victims' losses as a result of criminal conduct. For the purpose of this subdivision, "restitution" means the face value of the bad check or bad checks and any bank charges, as described in Section 1001.65.
(c) Full payment of the diversion fees, if any, specified in Section 1001.65.
(Amended by Stats. 2008, Ch. 264, Sec. 2. Effective January 1, 2009.)
1001.65.
(a) A district attorney may collect a processing fee if his or her office collects and processes a bad check. The amount of the fee shall not exceed fifty dollars ($50) for each bad check in addition to the actual amount of any bank charges, including the returned check fee, if any, incurred by the victim as a result of the offense.
(b) Notwithstanding subdivision (a), when a criminal complaint is filed in a bad check case after the maker of the check fails to comply with the terms of the bad check diversion program, the court, after conviction, may impose a bad check processing fee for the recovery and processing efforts by the district attorney of not more than fifty dollars ($50) for each bad check in addition to the actual amount of any bank charges incurred by the victim as a result of the offense, including the returned check fee, if any, not to exceed one thousand two hundred dollars ($1,200) in the aggregate. The court also may, as a condition of probation, require a defendant to participate in and successfully complete a check writing education class. If so required, the court shall make inquiry into the financial condition of the defendant and, upon a finding that the defendant is able in whole or part to pay the expense of the education class, the court may order him or her to pay for all or part of that expense.
(c) If the district attorney elects to collect any fee for bank charges incurred by the victim pursuant to this section, including any fee charged for a returned check, that fee shall be paid to the victim for any bank fees that the victim may have been assessed. In no event shall reimbursement of a bank charge to the victim pursuant to subdivision (a) or (b) exceed fifteen dollars ($15) per check.
(Amended by Stats. 2008, Ch. 264, Sec. 3. Effective January 1, 2009.)
1001.66.
At no time shall a defendant be required to make an admission of guilt as a prerequisite for placement in a precomplaint diversion program.
(Added by Stats. 1985, Ch. 1059, Sec. 1.)
1001.67.
No statement, or information procured therefrom, made by the defendant in connection with the determination of his or her eligibility for diversion, and no statement, or information procured therefrom, made by the defendant, subsequent to the granting of diversion or while participating in the program, and no information contained in any report made with respect thereto, and no statement or other information concerning the defendant's participation in the program shall be admissible in any action or proceeding.
(Added by Stats. 1985, Ch. 1059, Sec. 1.)

CHAPTER 2.9B. Parental Diversion [1001.70 - 1001.75]

(Chapter 2.9B added by Stats. 1988, Ch. 1256, Sec. 3.)
1001.70.
(a) Every local prosecutor with jurisdiction to prosecute violations of Section 272 shall review annually any diversion program established pursuant to this chapter, and no program shall commence or continue without the approval of the local prosecutor. No person shall be diverted under a program unless it has been approved by the local prosecutor. Nothing in this subdivision shall authorize the prosecutor to determine whether a particular defendant shall be diverted.
(b) As used in this chapter, "pretrial diversion" means the procedure of postponing prosecution either temporarily or permanently at any point in the judicial process from the point at which the accused is charged until adjudication.
(Added by Stats. 1988, Ch. 1256, Sec. 3. Effective September 26, 1988.)
1001.71.
This chapter shall apply whenever a case is before any court upon an accusatory pleading alleging a parent or legal guardian to have violated Section 272 with respect to his or her minor child, and all of the following apply to the defendant:
(a) The defendant's record does not indicate that probation or parole has ever been revoked without thereafter being completed.
(b) The defendant's record does not indicate that he or she has previously been diverted pursuant to this chapter.
(Amended by Stats. 1989, Ch. 144, Sec. 2.)
1001.72.
(a) If the defendant consents and waives his or her right to a speedy trial, the case shall be referred to the probation department. The probation department shall conduct an investigation as is necessary to determine whether the defendant qualifies for diversion under this chapter, and whether he or she is a person who would be benefited by education, treatment, or rehabilitation. The probation department shall also determine which education, treatment, or rehabilitative plan would benefit the defendant. The probation department shall report its findings and recommendations to the court. If the recommendation includes referral to a community program, the report shall contain a statement regarding the program's willingness to accept the defendant and the manner in which the services they offer can assist the defendant in completing the diversion program successfully.
(b) No statement, or any information procured therefrom, made by the defendant to any probation officer, which is made during the course of any investigation conducted by the probation department pursuant to subdivision (a), and prior to the reporting of the probation department's findings and recommendations to the court, shall be admissible in any action or proceeding brought subsequent to the investigation.
No statement, or any information procured therefrom, with respect to the specific offense with which the defendant is charged which is made to any probation officer subsequent to the granting of diversion, shall be admissible in any action or proceeding. In the event that diversion is either denied or is subsequently revoked once it has been granted, neither the probation investigation nor statements or information divulged during that investigation shall be used in any pretrial sentencing procedures.
(Added by Stats. 1988, Ch. 1256, Sec. 3. Effective September 26, 1988.)
1001.73.
The court shall hold a hearing and, after consideration of the probation department's report, and any other relevant information, shall determine if the defendant consents to further proceedings under this chapter and waives his or her right to a speedy trial. If the court orders a defendant to be diverted, the court may make inquiry into the financial condition of the defendant, and upon a finding that the defendant is able, in whole or in part, to pay the reasonable cost of diversion, the court may order him or her to pay all or part of the expense. The reasonable cost of diversion shall not exceed the amount determined to be the actual average cost of diversion services.
If the court does not deem the defendant to be a person who would be benefited by diversion or if the defendant does not consent to participate, the proceedings shall continue as in any other case.
At the time that a defendant's case is diverted, any bail bond or undertaking, or deposit in lieu thereof, on file by or on behalf of the defendant shall be exonerated, and the court shall enter an order so directing.
The period during which the further criminal proceedings against the defendant may be diverted shall be for the length of time required to complete and verify the diversion program but in no case shall it exceed two years.
(Added by Stats. 1988, Ch. 1256, Sec. 3. Effective September 26, 1988.)
1001.74.
If it appears to the probation department that the divertee is performing unsatisfactorily in the assigned program, or that the divertee is not benefiting from education, treatment, or rehabilitation, or that the divertee is convicted of a misdemeanor in which force or violence was used, or if the divertee is convicted of a felony, after notice to the divertee, the court shall hold a hearing to determine whether the criminal proceedings should be reinstituted. If the court finds that the divertee is not performing satisfactorily in the assigned program, or that the divertee has been convicted of a crime as indicated above, the criminal case shall be referred back to the court for resumption of the criminal proceedings. If the divertee has performed satisfactorily during the period of diversion, the criminal charges shall be dismissed.
(Added by Stats. 1988, Ch. 1256, Sec. 3. Effective September 26, 1988.)
1001.75.
(a) Any record filed with the Department of Justice shall indicate the disposition in those cases diverted pursuant to this chapter. Upon successful completion of a diversion program, the arrest upon which the diversion was based shall be deemed to have never occurred. The divertee may indicate in response to any question concerning his or her prior criminal record that he or she was not arrested or diverted for that offense, except as specified in subdivision (b). A record pertaining to an arrest resulting in successful completion of a diversion program shall not, without the divertee's consent, be used in any way that would result in the denial of any employment, benefit, license, or certificate.
(b) The divertee shall be advised that, regardless of his or her successful completion of diversion, the arrest upon which the diversion was based may be disclosed by the Department of Justice in response to any peace officer application request and that, notwithstanding subdivision (a), this section does not relieve him or her of the obligation to disclose the arrest in response to any direct question contained in any questionnaire or application for a position as a peace officer, as defined in Section 830.
(Amended by Stats. 1996, Ch. 743, Sec. 5. Effective January 1, 1997.)

CHAPTER 2.9C. Military Diversion Program [1001.80- 1001.80.]

(Chapter 2.9C added by Stats. 2014, Ch. 658, Sec. 1.)
1001.80.
(a) This chapter shall apply to a case before a court on an accusatory pleading alleging the commission of a misdemeanor offense if both of the following apply to the defendant:
(1) The defendant was, or currently is, a member of the United States military.
(2) The defendant may be suffering from sexual trauma, traumatic brain injury, post-traumatic stress disorder, substance abuse, or mental health problems as a result of his or her military service. The court may request, using existing resources, an assessment to aid in the determination that this paragraph applies to a defendant.
(b) If the court determines that a defendant charged with an applicable offense under this chapter is a person described in subdivision (a), the court, with the consent of the defendant and a waiver of the defendant's speedy trial right, may place the defendant in a pretrial diversion program, as defined in subdivision (k).
(c) If it appears to the court that the defendant is performing unsatisfactorily in the assigned program, or that the defendant is not benefiting from the treatment and services provided under the diversion program, after notice to the defendant, the court shall hold a hearing to determine whether the criminal proceedings should be reinstituted. If the court finds that the defendant is not performing satisfactorily in the assigned program, or that the defendant is not benefiting from diversion, the court may end the diversion and order resumption of the criminal proceedings. If the defendant has performed satisfactorily during the period of diversion, at the end of the period of diversion, the criminal charges shall be dismissed.
(d) If a referral is made to the county mental health authority as part of the pretrial diversion program, the county shall provide mental health treatment services only to the extent that resources are available for that purpose, as described in paragraph (5) of subdivision (b) of Section 5600.3 of the Welfare and Institutions Code. If mental health treatment services are ordered by the court, the county mental health agency shall coordinate appropriate referral of the defendant to the county veterans service officer, as described in paragraph (5) of subdivision (b) of Section 5600.3 of the Welfare and Institutions Code. The county mental health agency is not responsible for providing services outside its traditional scope of services. An order shall be made referring a defendant to a county mental health agency only if that agency has agreed to accept responsibility for all of the following:
(1) The treatment of the defendant.
(2) The coordination of appropriate referral to a county veterans service officer.
(3) The filing of reports pursuant to subdivision (h).
(e) When determining the requirements of a pretrial diversion program pursuant to this chapter, the court shall assess whether the defendant should be ordered to participate in a federal or community-based treatment service program with a demonstrated history of specializing in the treatment of mental health problems, including substance abuse, post-traumatic stress disorder, traumatic brain injury, military sexual trauma, and other related mental health problems.
(f) The court, in making an order pursuant to this section to commit a defendant to an established treatment program, shall give preference to a treatment program that has a history of successfully treating veterans who suffer from sexual trauma, traumatic brain injury, post-traumatic stress disorder, substance abuse, or mental health problems as a result of military service, including, but not limited to, programs operated by the United States Department of Defense or the United States Department of Veterans Affairs.
(g) The court and the assigned treatment program may collaborate with the Department of Veterans Affairs and the United States Department of Veterans Affairs to maximize benefits and services provided to a veteran.
(h) The period during which criminal proceedings against the defendant may be diverted shall be no longer than two years. The responsible agency or agencies shall file reports on the defendant's progress in the diversion program with the court and with the prosecutor not less than every six months.

(i) A record filed with the Department of Justice shall indicate the disposition of those cases diverted pursuant to this chapter. Upon successful completion of a diversion program, the arrest upon which the diversion was based shall be deemed to have never occurred. The defendant may indicate in response to a question concerning his or her prior criminal record that he or she was not arrested or diverted for the offense, except as specified in subdivision (j). A record pertaining to an arrest resulting in successful completion of a diversion program shall not, without the defendant's consent, be used in any way that could result in the denial of any employment, benefit, license, or certificate.

(j) The defendant shall be advised that, regardless of his or her successful completion of diversion, the arrest upon which the diversion was based may be disclosed by the Department of Justice in response to a peace officer application request and that, notwithstanding subdivision (i), this section does not relieve him or her of the obligation to disclose the arrest in response to a direct question contained in a questionnaire or application for a position as a peace officer, as defined in Section 830.

(k) (1) As used in this chapter, "pretrial diversion" means the procedure of postponing prosecution, either temporarily or permanently, at any point in the judicial process from the point at which the accused is charged until adjudication.

(2) A pretrial diversion program shall utilize existing resources available to current or former members of the United States military to address and treat those suffering from sexual trauma, traumatic brain injury, post-traumatic stress disorder, substance abuse, or mental health problems as a result of military service.

(l) Notwithstanding any other law, including Section 23640 of the Vehicle Code, a misdemeanor offense for which a defendant may be placed in a pretrial diversion program in accordance with this section includes a misdemeanor violation of Section 23152 or 23153 of the Vehicle Code. However, this section does not limit the authority of the Department of Motor Vehicles to take administrative action concerning the driving privileges of a person arrested for a violation of Section 23152 or 23153 of the Vehicle Code.

(Amended by Stats. 2017, Ch. 179, Sec. 1. (SB 725) Effective August 7, 2017.)

CHAPTER 2.9D. Repeat Theft Crimes Diversion or Deferred Entry of Judgment Program [1001.81 - 1001.82]

(Chapter 2.9D added by Stats. 2018, Ch. 803, Sec. 7.)
1001.81.
(a) The city or county prosecuting attorney or county probation department may create a diversion or deferred entry of judgment program pursuant to this section for persons who commit repeat theft offenses. The program may be conducted by the prosecuting attorney's office or the county probation department.

(b) Except as provided in subdivision (e), this chapter does not limit the power of the prosecuting attorney to prosecute repeat theft.

(c) If a county creates a diversion or deferred entry of judgment program for individuals committing repeat theft offenses, on receipt of a case or at arraignment, the prosecuting attorney shall either refer the case to the county probation department to conduct a prefiling investigation report to assess the appropriateness of program placement or, if the prosecuting attorney's office operates the program, determine if the case is one that is appropriate to be referred to the program. In determining whether to refer a case to the program, the probation department or prosecuting attorney shall consider, but is not limited to, all of the following factors:

(1) Any prefiling investigation report conducted by the county probation department or nonprofit contract agency operating the program that evaluates the individual's risk and needs and the appropriateness of program placement.

(2) If the person demonstrates a willingness to engage in community service, restitution, or other mechanisms to repair the harm caused by the criminal activity and address the underlying drivers of the criminal activity.

(3) If a risk and needs assessment identifies underlying substance abuse or mental health needs or other drivers of criminal activity that can be addressed through the diversion or deferred entry of judgment program.

(4) If the person has a violent or serious prior criminal record or has previously been referred to a diversion program and failed that program.

(5) Any relevant information concerning the efficacy of the program in reducing the likelihood of participants committing future offenses.

(d) On referral of a case to the program, a notice shall be provided to or forwarded by mail to the person alleged to have committed the offense with all of the following information:

(1) The date by which the person must contact the diversion program or deferred entry of judgment program in the manner designated by the supervising agency.

(2) A statement of the penalty for the offense or offenses with which that person has been charged.

(e) The prosecuting attorney may enter into a written agreement with the person to refrain from, or defer, prosecution on the offense or offenses on the following conditions:

(1) Completion of the program requirements such as community service or courses reasonably required by the prosecuting attorney.

(2) Making adequate restitution or an appropriate substitute for restitution to the establishment or person from which property was stolen at the face value of the stolen property, if required by the program.

(f) For the purposes of this section, "repeat theft offenses" means being cited or convicted for misdemeanor or felony theft from a store or from a vehicle two or more times in the previous 12 months and failing to appear in court when cited for these crimes or continuing to engage in these crimes after release or after conviction.

(Added by Stats. 2018, Ch. 803, Sec. 7. (AB 1065) Effective January 1, 2019. Repealed as of July 1, 2021, pursuant to Section 1001.82.)
1001.82.
This chapter shall remain in effect only until July 1, 2021, and as of that date is repealed.

(Amended by Stats. 2019, Ch. 25, Sec. 37. (SB 94) Effective June 27, 2019. Repealed as of July 1, 2021, by its own provisions. Note: Repeal affects Chapter 2.9D, commencing with Section 1001.81.)

CHAPTER 2.92. Law Enforcement Assisted Diversion (LEAD) Pilot Program [1001.85 - 1001.88]

(Chapter 2.92 added by Stats. 2016, Ch. 33, Sec. 17.)
1001.85.
(a) The Law Enforcement Assisted Diversion (LEAD) pilot program is hereby established. The purpose of the LEAD program is to improve public safety and reduce recidivism by increasing the availability and use of social service resources while reducing costs to law enforcement agencies and courts stemming from repeated incarceration.

(b) LEAD pilot programs shall be consistent with the following principles, implemented to address and reflect the priorities of the community in which the program exists:

(1) Providing intensive case management services and an individually tailored intervention plan that acts as a blueprint for assisting LEAD participants.

(2) Prioritizing temporary and permanent housing that includes individualized supportive services, without preconditions of drug or alcohol treatment or abstinence from drugs or alcohol.

(3) Employing human and social service resources in coordination with law enforcement in a manner that improves individual outcomes and community safety, and promotes community wellness.

(4) Participation in LEAD services shall be voluntary throughout the duration of the program and shall not require abstinence from drug or alcohol use as a condition of continued participation.

(Added by Stats. 2016, Ch. 33, Sec. 17. (SB 843) Effective June 27, 2016.)
1001.86.
(a) The LEAD program shall be administered by the Board of State and Community Corrections.

(b) The board shall award grants, on a competitive basis, to up to three jurisdictions as authorized by this chapter. The board shall establish minimum standards, funding schedules, and procedures for awarding grants, which shall take into consideration, but not be limited to, all of the following:

(1) Information from the applicant demonstrating a clear understanding of the program's purpose and the applicant's willingness and ability to implement the LEAD program as described in this chapter.

(2) Key local partners who would be committed to, and involved in, the development and successful implementation of a LEAD program, including, but not limited to, balanced representation from law enforcement agencies, prosecutorial agencies, public defenders and defense counsel, public health and social services agencies, case management service providers, and any other entities identified by the applicant as integral to the successful implementation of a LEAD program in the jurisdiction.

(3) The jurisdiction's capacity and commitment to coordinate social services, law enforcement efforts, and justice system decisionmaking processes, and to work to ensure that the discretionary decisions made by each participant in the administration of the program operates in a manner consistent with the purposes of this chapter.

(c) Successful grant applicants shall collect and maintain data pertaining to the effectiveness of the program as indicated by the board in the request for proposals.

(Added by Stats. 2016, Ch. 33, Sec. 17. (SB 843) Effective June 27, 2016.)
1001.87.
(a) LEAD programs funded pursuant to this chapter shall consist of a strategy of effective intervention for eligible participants consistent with the following gateways to services:

(1) Prebooking referral. As an alternative to arrest, a law enforcement officer may take or refer a person for whom the officer has probable cause for arrest for any of the offenses in subdivision (b) to a case manager to be screened for immediate crisis services and to schedule a complete assessment intake interview. Participation in LEAD shall be voluntary, and the person may decline to participate in the program at any time. Criminal charges based on the conduct for which a person is diverted to LEAD shall not be filed, provided that the person finishes the complete assessment intake interview within a period set by the local jurisdictional partners, but not to exceed 30 days after the referral.

(2) Social contact referral. A law enforcement officer may refer an individual to LEAD whom he or she believes is at high risk of arrest in the future for any of the crimes specified in subdivision (b), provided that the individual meets the criteria specified in this paragraph and expresses interest in voluntarily participating in the program. LEAD may accept these referrals if the program has capacity after responding to prebooking diversion referrals described in paragraph (1). All social contact referrals to LEAD shall meet the following criteria:

(A) Verification by law enforcement that the individual has had prior involvement with low-level drug activity or prostitution. Verification shall consist of any of the following:

(i) Criminal history records, including, but not limited to, prior police reports, arrests, jail bookings, criminal charges, or convictions indicating that he or she was engaged in low-level drug or prostitution activity.

(ii) Law enforcement has directly observed the individual's low-level drug or prostitution activity on prior occasions.

(iii) Law enforcement has a reliable basis of information to believe that the individual is engaged in low-level drug or prostitution activity, including, but not limited to, information provided by another first responder, a professional, or a credible community member.

(B) The individual's prior involvement with low-level drug or prostitution activity occurred within the LEAD pilot program area.

(C) The individual's prior involvement with low-level drug or prostitution activity occurred within 24 months of the date of referral.

(D) The individual does not have a pending case in drug court or mental health court.

(E) The individual is not prohibited, by means of an existing no-contact order, temporary restraining order, or antiharassment order, from making contact with a current LEAD participant.

(b) The following offenses are eligible for either prebooking diversion, social contact referral, or both:

(1) Possession for sale or transfer of a controlled substance or other prohibited substance where the circumstances indicate that the sale or transfer is intended to provide a subsistence living or to allow the person to obtain or afford drugs for his or her own consumption.

(2) Sale or transfer of a controlled substance or other prohibited substance where the circumstances indicate that the sale or transfer is intended to provide a subsistence living or to allow the person to obtain or afford drugs for his or her own consumption.

(3) Possession of a controlled substance or other prohibited substance.

(4) Being under the influence of a controlled substance or other prohibited substance.

(5) Being under the influence of alcohol and a controlled substance or other prohibited substance.

(6) Prostitution pursuant to subdivision (b) of Section 647.

(Amended by Stats. 2017, Ch. 561, Sec. 186. (AB 1516) Effective January 1, 2018.)
1001.88.
(a) Services provided pursuant to this chapter may include, but are not limited to, case management, housing, medical care, mental health care, treatment for alcohol or substance use disorders, nutritional counseling and treatment, psychological counseling, employment, employment training and education, civil legal services, and system navigation. Grant funding may be used to support any of the following:

(1) Project management and community engagement.

(2) Temporary services and treatment necessary to stabilize a participant's condition, including necessary housing.

(3) Outreach and direct service costs for services described in this section.

(4) Civil legal services for LEAD participants.

(5) Dedicated prosecutorial resources, including for coordinating any nondiverted criminal cases of LEAD participants.

(6) Dedicated law enforcement resources, including for overtime required for participation in operational meetings and training.

(7) Training and technical assistance from experts in the implementation of LEAD in other jurisdictions.

(8) Collecting and maintaining the data necessary for program evaluation.

(b) (1) The board shall contract with a nonprofit research entity, university, or college to evaluate the effectiveness of the LEAD program. The evaluation design shall include measures to assess the cost-benefit outcomes of LEAD programs compared to booking and prosecution, and may include evaluation elements such as comparing outcomes for LEAD participants to similarly situated offenders who are arrested and booked, the number of jail bookings, total number of jail days, the prison incarceration rate, subsequent felony and misdemeanor arrests or convictions, and costs to the criminal justice and court systems. Savings will be compared to costs of LEAD participation. By January 1, 2020, a report of the findings shall be submitted to the Governor and the Legislature pursuant to Section 9795 of the Government Code.
(2) The requirement for submitting a report pursuant to this subdivision is inoperative on January 1, 2024, pursuant to Section 10231.5 of the Government Code.
(c) The board may contract with experts in the implementation of LEAD in other jurisdictions for the purpose of providing technical assistance to participating jurisdictions.
(d) The sum of fifteen million dollars ($15,000,000) is hereby appropriated from the General Fund for the LEAD pilot program authorized in this chapter. The board may spend up to five hundred fifty thousand dollars ($550,000) of the amount appropriated in this subdivision for the contracts authorized in subdivisions (b) and (c).
(Added by Stats. 2016, Ch. 33, Sec. 17. (SB 843) Effective June 27, 2016.)

CHAPTER 2.95. Diversion Restitution Fee [1001.90- 1001.90.]

(Chapter 2.95 added by Stats. 1995, Ch. 313, Sec. 4.)
1001.90.
(a) For all persons charged with a felony or misdemeanor whose case is diverted by the court pursuant to this title, the court shall impose on the defendant a diversion restitution fee in addition to any other administrative fee provided or imposed under the law. This fee shall not be imposed upon persons whose case is diverted by the court pursuant to Chapter 2.8 (commencing with Section 1001.20).
(b) The diversion restitution fee imposed pursuant to this section shall be set at the discretion of the court and shall be commensurate with the seriousness of the offense, but shall not be less than one hundred dollars ($100), and not more than one thousand dollars ($1,000).
(c) The diversion restitution fee shall be ordered regardless of the defendant's present ability to pay. However, if the court finds that there are compelling and extraordinary reasons, the court may waive imposition of the fee. When the waiver is granted, the court shall state on the record all reasons supporting the waiver. Except as provided in this subdivision, the court shall impose the separate and additional diversion restitution fee required by this section.
(d) In setting the amount of the diversion restitution fee in excess of the one hundred dollar ($100) minimum, the court shall consider any relevant factors, including, but not limited to, the defendant's ability to pay, the seriousness and gravity of the offense and the circumstances of its commission, any economic gain derived by the defendant as a result of the crime, and the extent to which any other person suffered any losses as a result of the crime. Those losses may include pecuniary losses to the victim or his or her dependents as well as intangible losses, such as psychological harm caused by the crime. Consideration of a defendant's ability to pay may include his or her future earning capacity. A defendant shall bear the burden of demonstrating the lack of his or her ability to pay. Express findings by the court as to the factors bearing on the amount of the fee shall not be required. A separate hearing for the diversion restitution fee shall not be required.
(e) The court shall not limit the ability of the state to enforce the fee imposed by this section in the manner of a judgment in a civil action. The court shall not modify the amount of this fee except to correct an error in the setting of the amount of the fee imposed.
(f) The fee imposed pursuant to this section shall be immediately deposited in the Restitution Fund for use pursuant to Section 13967 of the Government Code.
(g) The board of supervisors of any county may impose a fee at its discretion to cover the actual administrative costs of collection of the restitution fee, not to exceed 10 percent of the amount ordered to be paid. Any fee imposed pursuant to this subdivision shall be deposited in the general fund of the county.
(h) The state shall pay the county agency responsible for collecting the diversion restitution fee owed to the Restitution Fund under this section, 10 percent of the funds so owed and collected by the county agency and deposited in the Restitution Fund. This payment shall be made only when the funds are deposited in the Restitution Fund within 45 days of the end of the month in which the funds are collected. Receiving 10 percent of the moneys collected as being owed to the Restitution Fund shall be considered an incentive for collection efforts and shall be used for furthering these collection efforts. The 10 percent rebates shall be used to augment the budgets for the county agencies responsible for collection of funds owed to the Restitution Fund as provided in this section. The 10 percent rebates shall not be used to supplant county funding.
(i) As used in this section, "diversion" also means deferred entry of judgment pursuant to Chapter 2.5 (commencing with Section 1000).
(Amended by Stats. 1997, Ch. 324, Sec. 6. Effective January 1, 1998.)

CHAPTER 3. Demurrer and Amendment [1002 - 1012]

(Heading of Chapter 3 amended by Stats. 1951, Ch. 1674.)
1002.
The only pleading on the part of the defendant is either a demurrer or a plea.
(Enacted 1872.)
1003.
Both the demurrer and plea must be put in, in open Court, either at the time of the arraignment or at such other time as may be allowed to the defendant for that purpose.
(Enacted 1872.)
1004.
The defendant may demur to the accusatory pleading at any time prior to the entry of a plea, when it appears upon the face thereof either:
1. If an indictment, that the grand jury by which it was found had no legal authority to inquire into the offense charged, or, if any information or complaint that the court has no jurisdiction of the offense charged therein;
2. That it does not substantially conform to the provisions of Sections 950 and 952, and also Section 951 in case of an indictment or information;
3. That more than one offense is charged, except as provided in Section 954;
4. That the facts stated do not constitute a public offense;
5. That it contains matter which, if true, would constitute a legal justification or excuse of the offense charged, or other legal bar to the prosecution.
(Amended by Stats. 1951, Ch. 1674.)
1005.

The demurrer must be in writing, signed either by the defendant or his counsel, and filed. It must distinctly specify the grounds of objection to the accusatory pleading or it must be disregarded.
(Amended by Stats. 1951, Ch. 1674.)
1006.
Upon the demurrer being filed, the argument upon the objections presented thereby must be heard immediately, unless for exceptional cause shown, the court shall grant a continuance. Such continuance shall be for no longer time than the ends of justice require, and the court shall enter in its minutes the facts requiring it.
(Amended by Stats. 1927, Ch. 609.)
1007.
Upon considering the demurrer, the court must make an order either overruling or sustaining it. If the demurrer to an indictment or information is overruled, the court must permit the defendant, at the defendant's election, to plead, which the defendant must do forthwith, unless the court extends the time. If the demurrer is sustained, the court must, if the defect can be remedied by amendment, permit the indictment or information to be amended, either forthwith or within such time, not exceeding 10 days, as it may fix, or, if the defect or insufficiency therein cannot be remedied by amendment, the court may direct the filing of a new information or the submission of the case to the same or another grand jury. If the demurrer to a complaint is sustained, the court must, if the defect can be remedied, permit the filing of an amended complaint within such time not exceeding 10 days as it may fix. The orders made under this section shall be entered in the docket or minutes of the court.
(Amended by Stats. 1998, Ch. 931, Sec. 382. Effective September 28, 1998.)
1008.
If the demurrer is sustained, and no amendment of the accusatory pleading is permitted, or, in case an amendment is permitted, no amendment is made or amended pleading is filed within the time fixed therefor, the action shall be dismissed, and, except as provided in Section 1010, the court must order, if the defendant is in custody, that he be discharged or if he has been admitted to bail, that his bail be exonerated, or, if money or other property has been deposited instead of bail for his appearance, that such money or other property be refunded to him or to the person or persons found by the court to have deposited such money or other property on his behalf.
(Amended by Stats. 1951, Ch. 1674.)
1009.
An indictment, accusation or information may be amended by the district attorney, and an amended complaint may be filed by the prosecuting attorney, without leave of court at any time before the defendant pleads or a demurrer to the original pleading is sustained. The court in which an action is pending may order or permit an amendment of an indictment, accusation or information, or the filing of an amended complaint, for any defect or insufficiency, at any stage of the proceedings, or if the defect in an indictment or information be one that cannot be remedied by amendment, may order the case submitted to the same or another grand jury, or a new information to be filed. The defendant shall be required to plead to such amendment or amended pleading forthwith, or, at the time fixed for pleading, if the defendant has not yet pleaded and the trial or other proceeding shall continue as if the pleading had been originally filed as amended, unless the substantial rights of the defendant would be prejudiced thereby, in which event a reasonable postponement, not longer than the ends of justice require, may be granted. An indictment or accusation cannot be amended so as to change the offense charged, nor an information so as to charge an offense not shown by the evidence taken at the preliminary examination. A complaint cannot be amended to charge an offense not attempted to be charged by the original complaint, except that separate counts may be added which might properly have been joined in the original complaint. The amended complaint must be verified but may be verified by some person other than the one who made oath to the original complaint.
(Amended by Stats. 1998, Ch. 931, Sec. 383. Effective September 28, 1998.)
1010.
When an indictment or information is dismissed after the sustaining of a demurrer, or at any other stage of the proceedings because of any defect or insufficiency of the indictment or information, if the court directs that the case be resubmitted to the same or another grand jury or that a new information be filed, the defendant shall not be discharged from custody, nor the defendant's bail exonerated nor money or other property deposited instead of bail on the defendant's behalf refunded, but the same proceedings must be had on such direction as are prescribed in Sections 997 and 998.
(Amended by Stats. 1998, Ch. 931, Sec. 384. Effective September 28, 1998.)
1012.
When any of the objections mentioned in Section 1004 appears on the face of the accusatory pleading, it can be taken only by demurrer, and failure so to take it shall be deemed a waiver thereof, except that the objection to the jurisdiction of the court and the objection that the facts stated do not constitute a public offense may be taken by motion in arrest of judgment.
(Amended by Stats. 1951, Ch. 1674.)

CHAPTER 4. Plea [1016 - 1027]

(Chapter 4 enacted 1872.)
1016.
There are six kinds of pleas to an indictment or an information, or to a complaint charging a misdemeanor or infraction:
1. Guilty.
2. Not guilty.
3. Nolo contendere, subject to the approval of the court. The court shall ascertain whether the defendant completely understands that a plea of nolo contendere shall be considered the same as a plea of guilty and that, upon a plea of nolo contendere, the court shall find the defendant guilty. The legal effect of such a plea, to a crime punishable as a felony, shall be the same as that of a plea of guilty for all purposes. In cases other than those punishable as felonies, the plea and any admissions required by the court during any inquiry it makes as to the voluntariness of, and factual basis for, the plea may not be used against the defendant as an admission in any civil suit based upon or growing out of the act upon which the criminal prosecution is based.
4. A former judgment of conviction or acquittal of the offense charged.
5. Once in jeopardy.
6. Not guilty by reason of insanity.
A defendant who does not plead guilty may enter one or more of the other pleas. A defendant who does not plead not guilty by reason of insanity shall be conclusively presumed to have been sane at the time of the commission of the offense charged; provided, that the court may for good cause shown allow a change of plea at any time before the commencement of the trial. A defendant who pleads not guilty by reason of insanity, without also pleading not guilty, thereby admits the commission of the offense charged.
(Amended by Stats. 1998, Ch. 931, Sec. 385. Effective September 28, 1998.)
1016.2.
The Legislature finds and declares all of the following:
(a) In Padilla v. Kentucky, 559 U.S. 356 (2010), the United States Supreme Court held that the Sixth Amendment requires defense counsel to provide affirmative and competent advice to noncitizen defendants regarding the potential immigration

consequences of their criminal cases. California courts also have held that defense counsel must investigate and advise regarding the immigration consequences of the available dispositions, and should, when consistent with the goals of and informed consent of the defendant, and as consistent with professional standards, defend against adverse immigration consequences (People v. Soriano, 194 Cal.App.3d 1470 (1987), People v. Barocio, 216 Cal.App.3d 99 (1989), People v. Bautista, 115 Cal.App.4th 229 (2004)).

(b) In Padilla v. Kentucky, the United States Supreme Court sanctioned the consideration of immigration consequences by both parties in the plea negotiating process. The court stated that "informed consideration of possible deportation can only benefit both the State and noncitizen defendants during the plea-bargaining process. By bringing deportation consequences into this process, the defense and prosecution may well be able to reach agreements that better satisfy the interests of both parties."

(c) In Padilla v. Kentucky, the United States Supreme Court found that for noncitizens, deportation is an integral part of the penalty imposed for criminal convictions. Deportation may result from serious offenses or a single minor offense. It may be by far the most serious penalty flowing from the conviction.

(d) With an accurate understanding of immigration consequences, many noncitizen defendants are able to plead to a conviction and sentence that satisfy the prosecution and court, but that have no, or fewer, adverse immigration consequences than the original charge.

(e) Defendants who are misadvised or not advised at all of the immigration consequences of criminal charges often suffer irreparable damage to their current or potential lawful immigration status, resulting in penalties such as mandatory detention, deportation, and permanent separation from close family. In some cases, these consequences could have been avoided had counsel provided informed advice and attempted to defend against such consequences.

(f) Once in removal proceedings, a noncitizen may be transferred to any of over 200 immigration detention facilities across the country. Many criminal offenses trigger mandatory detention, so that the person may not request bond. In immigration proceedings, there is no court-appointed right to counsel and as a result, the majority of detained immigrants go unrepresented. Immigration judges often lack the power to consider whether the person should remain in the United States in light of equitable factors such as serious hardship to United States citizen family members, length of time living in the United States, or rehabilitation.

(g) The immigration consequences of criminal convictions have a particularly strong impact in California. One out of every four persons living in the state is foreign-born. One out of every two children lives in a household headed by at least one foreign-born person. The majority of these children are United States citizens. It is estimated that 50,000 parents of California United States citizen children were deported in a little over two years. Once a person is deported, especially after a criminal conviction, it is extremely unlikely that he or she ever is permitted to return.

(h) It is the intent of the Legislature to codify Padilla v. Kentucky and related California case law and to encourage the growth of such case law in furtherance of justice and the findings and declarations of this section.
(Added by Stats. 2015, Ch. 705, Sec. 1. (AB 1343) Effective January 1, 2016.)

1016.3.
(a) Defense counsel shall provide accurate and affirmative advice about the immigration consequences of a proposed disposition, and when consistent with the goals of and with the informed consent of the defendant, and consistent with professional standards, defend against those consequences.

(b) The prosecution, in the interests of justice, and in furtherance of the findings and declarations of Section 1016.2, shall consider the avoidance of adverse immigration consequences in the plea negotiation process as one factor in an effort to reach a just resolution.

(c) This code section shall not be interpreted to change the requirements of Section 1016.5, including the requirement that no defendant shall be required to disclose his or her immigration status to the court.
(Added by Stats. 2015, Ch. 705, Sec. 2. (AB 1343) Effective January 1, 2016.)

1016.5.
(a) Prior to acceptance of a plea of guilty or nolo contendere to any offense punishable as a crime under state law, except offenses designated as infractions under state law, the court shall administer the following advisement on the record to the defendant:
If you are not a citizen, you are hereby advised that conviction of the offense for which you have been charged may have the consequences of deportation, exclusion from admission to the United States, or denial of naturalization pursuant to the laws of the United States.

(b) Upon request, the court shall allow the defendant additional time to consider the appropriateness of the plea in light of the advisement as described in this section. If, after January 1, 1978, the court fails to advise the defendant as required by this section and the defendant shows that conviction of the offense to which defendant pleaded guilty or nolo contendere may have the consequences for the defendant of deportation, exclusion from admission to the United States, or denial of naturalization pursuant to the laws of the United States, the court, on defendant's motion, shall vacate the judgment and permit the defendant to withdraw the plea of guilty or nolo contendere, and enter a plea of not guilty. Absent a record that the court provided the advisement required by this section, the defendant shall be presumed not to have received the required advisement.

(c) With respect to pleas accepted prior to January 1, 1978, it is not the intent of the Legislature that a court's failure to provide the advisement required by subdivision (a) of Section 1016.5 should require the vacation of judgment and withdrawal of the plea or constitute grounds for finding a prior conviction invalid. Nothing in this section, however, shall be deemed to inhibit a court, in the sound exercise of its discretion, from vacating a judgment and permitting a defendant to withdraw a plea.

(d) The Legislature finds and declares that in many instances involving an individual who is not a citizen of the United States charged with an offense punishable as a crime under state law, a plea of guilty or nolo contendere is entered without the defendant knowing that a conviction of such offense is grounds for deportation, exclusion from admission to the United States, or denial of naturalization pursuant to the laws of the United States. Therefore, it is the intent of the Legislature in enacting this section to promote fairness to such accused individuals by requiring in such cases that acceptance of a guilty plea or plea of nolo contendere be preceded by an appropriate warning of the special consequences for such a defendant which may result from the plea. It is also the intent of the Legislature that the court in such cases shall grant the defendant a reasonable amount of time to negotiate with the prosecuting agency in the event the defendant or the defendant's counsel was unaware of the possibility of deportation, exclusion from admission to the United States, or denial of naturalization as a result of conviction. It is further the intent of the Legislature that at the time of the plea no defendant shall be required to disclose his or her legal status to the court.
(Added by Stats. 1977, Ch. 1088.)

1017.
Every plea must be made in open court and, may be oral or in writing, shall be entered upon the minutes of the court, and shall be taken down in shorthand by the official reporter if one is present. All pleas of guilty or nolo contendere to misdemeanors or felonies shall be oral or in writing. The plea, whether oral or in writing, shall be in substantially the following form:
1. If the defendant plead guilty: "The defendant pleads that he or she is guilty of the offense charged."

2. If he or she plead not guilty: "The defendant pleads that he or she is not guilty of the offense charged."
3. If he or she plead a former conviction or acquittal: "The defendant pleads that he or she has already been convicted (or acquitted) of the offense charged, by the judgment of the court of _____ (naming it), rendered at _____ (naming the place), on the _____ day of _____."
4. If he or she plead once in jeopardy: "The defendant pleads that he or she has been once in jeopardy for the offense charged (specifying the time, place, and court)."
5. If he or she plead not guilty by reason of insanity: "The defendant pleads that he or she is not guilty of the offense charged because he or she was insane at the time that he or she is alleged to have committed the unlawful act."
(Amended by Stats. 1990, Ch. 632, Sec. 2.)

1018.
Unless otherwise provided by law, every plea shall be entered or withdrawn by the defendant himself or herself in open court. No plea of guilty of a felony for which the maximum punishment is death, or life imprisonment without the possibility of parole, shall be received from a defendant who does not appear with counsel, nor shall that plea be received without the consent of the defendant's counsel. No plea of guilty of a felony for which the maximum punishment is not death or life imprisonment without the possibility of parole shall be accepted from any defendant who does not appear with counsel unless the court shall first fully inform him or her of the right to counsel and unless the court shall find that the defendant understands the right to counsel and freely waives it, and then only if the defendant has expressly stated in open court, to the court, that he or she does not wish to be represented by counsel. On application of the defendant at any time before judgment or within six months after an order granting probation is made if entry of judgment is suspended, the court may, and in case of a defendant who appeared without counsel at the time of the plea the court shall, for a good cause shown, permit the plea of guilty to be withdrawn and a plea of not guilty substituted. Upon indictment or information against a corporation a plea of guilty may be put in by counsel. This section shall be liberally construed to effect these objects and to promote justice.
(Amended by Stats. 1991, Ch. 421, Sec. 1.)

1019.
The plea of not guilty puts in issue every material allegation of the accusatory pleading, except those allegations regarding previous convictions of the defendant to which an answer is required by Section 1025.
(Amended by Stats. 1951, Ch. 1674.)

1020.
All matters of fact tending to establish a defense other than one specified in the fourth, fifth, and sixth subdivisions of Section 1016, may be given in evidence under the plea of not guilty.
(Amended by Stats. 1968, Ch. 122.)

1021.
If the defendant was formerly acquitted on the ground of variance between the accusatory pleading and the proof or the accusatory pleading was dismissed upon an objection to its form or substance, or in order to hold the defendant for a higher offense, without a judgment of acquittal, it is not an acquittal of the same offense.
(Amended by Stats. 1951, Ch. 1674.)

1022.
Whenever the defendant is acquitted on the merits, he is acquitted of the same offense, notwithstanding any defect in form or substance in the accusatory pleading on which the trial was had.
(Amended by Stats. 1951, Ch. 1674.)

1023.
When the defendant is convicted or acquitted or has been once placed in jeopardy upon an accusatory pleading, the conviction, acquittal, or jeopardy is a bar to another prosecution for the offense charged in such accusatory pleading, or for an attempt to commit the same, or for an offense necessarily included therein, of which he might have been convicted under that accusatory pleading.
(Amended by Stats. 1951, Ch. 1674.)

1024.
If the defendant refuses to answer the accusatory pleading, by demurrer or plea, a plea of not guilty must be entered.
(Amended by Stats. 1951, Ch. 1674.)

1025.
(a) When a defendant who is charged in the accusatory pleading with having suffered a prior conviction pleads either guilty or not guilty of the offense charged against him or her, he or she shall be asked whether he or she has suffered the prior conviction. If the defendant enters an admission, his or her answer shall be entered in the minutes of the court, and shall, unless withdrawn by consent of the court, be conclusive of the fact of his or her having suffered the prior conviction in all subsequent proceedings. If the defendant enters a denial, his or her answer shall be entered in the minutes of the court. The refusal of the defendant to answer is equivalent to a denial that he or she has suffered the prior conviction.

(b) Except as provided in subdivision (c), the question of whether or not the defendant has suffered the prior conviction shall be tried by the jury that tries the issue upon the plea of not guilty, or in the case of a plea of guilty or nolo contendere, by a jury impaneled for that purpose, or by the court if a jury is waived.

(c) Notwithstanding the provisions of subdivision (b), the question of whether the defendant is the person who has suffered the prior conviction shall be tried by the court without a jury.

(d) Subdivision (c) shall not apply to prior convictions alleged pursuant to Section 190.2 or to prior convictions alleged as an element of a charged offense.

(e) If the defendant pleads not guilty, and answers that he or she has suffered the prior conviction, the charge of the prior conviction shall neither be read to the jury nor alluded to during trial, except as otherwise provided by law.

(f) Nothing in this section alters existing law regarding the use of prior convictions at trial.
(Amended by Stats. 1997, Ch. 95, Sec. 1. Effective January 1, 1998.)

1026.
(a) If a defendant pleads not guilty by reason of insanity, and also joins with it another plea or pleas, the defendant shall first be tried as if only the other plea or pleas had been entered, and in that trial the defendant shall be conclusively presumed to have been sane at the time the offense is alleged to have been committed. If the jury finds the defendant guilty, or if the defendant pleads only not guilty by reason of insanity, the question whether the defendant was sane or insane at the time the offense was committed shall be promptly tried, either before the same jury or before a new jury in the discretion of the court. In that trial, the jury shall return a verdict either that the defendant was sane at the time the offense was committed or was insane at the time the offense was committed. If the verdict or finding is that the defendant was sane at the time the offense was committed, the court shall sentence the defendant as provided by law. If the verdict or finding is that the defendant was insane at the time the offense was committed, the court, unless it appears to the court that the sanity of the defendant has been recovered fully, shall direct that the defendant be committed to the State Department of State Hospitals for the care and treatment of the mentally disordered or any other appropriate public or private treatment facility approved by the community program director, or the court may order the defendant placed on outpatient status pursuant to Title 15 (commencing with Section 1600) of Part 2.

(b) Prior to making the order directing that the defendant be committed to the State Department of State Hospitals or other treatment facility or placed on outpatient status, the court shall order the community program director or a designee to evaluate the defendant and to submit to the court within 15 judicial days of the order a written recommendation as to whether the defendant should be placed on outpatient status or committed to the State Department of State Hospitals or other treatment facility. A person shall not be admitted to a state hospital or other treatment facility or placed on outpatient status under this section without having been evaluated by the community program director or a designee. If, however, it appears to the court that the sanity of the defendant has been recovered fully, the defendant shall be remanded to the custody of the sheriff until the issue of sanity has been finally determined in the manner prescribed by law. A defendant committed to a state hospital or other treatment facility or placed on outpatient status pursuant to Title 15 (commencing with Section 1600) of Part 2 shall not be released from confinement, parole, or outpatient status unless and until the court that committed the person, after notice and hearing, finds and determines that the person's sanity has been restored, or meets the criteria for release pursuant to Section 4146 of the Welfare and Institutions Code. This section does not prohibit the transfer of the patient from one state hospital to any other state hospital by proper authority. This section does not prohibit the transfer of the patient to a hospital in another state in the manner provided in Section 4119 of the Welfare and Institutions Code.
(c) If the defendant is committed or transferred to the State Department of State Hospitals pursuant to this section, the court may, upon receiving the written recommendation of the medical director of the state hospital and the community program director that the defendant be transferred to a public or private treatment facility approved by the community program director, order the defendant transferred to that facility. If the defendant is committed or transferred to a public or private treatment facility approved by the community program director, the court may, upon receiving the written recommendation of the community program director, order the defendant transferred to the State Department of State Hospitals or to another public or private treatment facility approved by the community program director. If either the defendant or the prosecuting attorney chooses to contest either kind of order of transfer, a petition may be filed in the court requesting a hearing, which shall be held if the court determines that sufficient grounds exist. At that hearing, the prosecuting attorney or the defendant may present evidence bearing on the order of transfer. The court shall use the same procedures and standards of proof as used in conducting probation revocation hearings pursuant to Section 1203.2.
(d) Prior to making an order for transfer under this section, the court shall notify the defendant, the attorney of record for the defendant, the prosecuting attorney, and the community program director or a designee.
(e) When the court, after considering the placement recommendation of the community program director required in subdivision (b), orders that the defendant be committed to the State Department of State Hospitals or other public or private treatment facility, the court shall provide copies of the following documents prior to the admission of the defendant to the State Department of State Hospitals or other treatment facility where the defendant is to be committed:
(1) The commitment order, including a specification of the charges.
(2) A computation or statement setting forth the maximum term of commitment in accordance with Section 1026.5.
(3) A computation or statement setting forth the amount of credit for time served, if any, to be deducted from the maximum term of commitment.
(4) State summary criminal history information.
(5) Any arrest reports prepared by the police department or other law enforcement agency.
(6) Any court-ordered psychiatric examination or evaluation reports.
(7) The community program director's placement recommendation report.
(8) Any medical records.
(f) If the defendant is confined in a state hospital or other treatment facility as an inpatient, the medical director of the facility shall, at six-month intervals, submit a report in writing to the court and the community program director of the county of commitment, or a designee, setting forth the status and progress of the defendant. The court shall transmit copies of these reports to the prosecutor and defense counsel.
(g) For purposes of this section and Sections 1026.1 to 1026.6, inclusive, "community program director" means the person, agency, or entity designated by the State Department of State Hospitals pursuant to Section 1605 of this code and Section 4360 of the Welfare and Institutions Code.
(Amended by Stats. 2016, Ch. 715, Sec. 1. (SB 955) Effective January 1, 2017.)

1026.1.

A person committed to a state hospital or other treatment facility under the provisions of Section 1026 shall be released from the state hospital or other treatment facility only under one or more of the following circumstances:
(a) Pursuant to the provisions of Section 1026.2.
(b) Upon expiration of the maximum term of commitment as provided in subdivision (a) of Section 1026.5, except as such term may be extended under the provisions of subdivision (b) of Section 1026.5.
(c) As otherwise expressly provided in Title 15 (commencing with Section 1600) of Part 2.
(Amended by Stats. 1984, Ch. 1488, Sec. 2.)

1026.2.

(a) An application for the release of a person who has been committed to a state hospital or other treatment facility, as provided in Section 1026, upon the ground that sanity has been restored, may be made to the superior court of the county from which the commitment was made, either by the person, or by the medical director of the state hospital or other treatment facility to which the person is committed or by the community program director where the person is on outpatient status under Title 15 (commencing with Section 1600). The court shall give notice of the hearing date to the prosecuting attorney, the community program director or a designee, and the medical director or person in charge of the facility providing treatment to the committed person at least 15 judicial days in advance of the hearing date.
(b) Pending the hearing, the medical director or person in charge of the facility in which the person is confined shall prepare a summary of the person's programs of treatment and shall forward the summary to the community program director or a designee and to the court. The community program director or a designee shall review the summary and shall designate a facility within a reasonable distance from the court in which the person may be detained pending the hearing on the application for release. The facility so designated shall continue the program of treatment, shall provide adequate security, and shall, to the greatest extent possible, minimize interference with the person's program of treatment.
(c) A designated facility need not be approved for 72-hour treatment and evaluation pursuant to the Lanterman-Petris-Short Act (Part 1 (commencing with Section 5000) of Division 5 of the Welfare and Institutions Code). However, a county jail may not be designated unless the services specified in subdivision (b) are provided and accommodations are provided which ensure both the safety of the person and the safety of the general population of the jail. If there is evidence that the treatment program is not being complied with or accommodations have not been provided which ensure both the safety of the committed person and the safety of the general population of the jail, the court shall order the person transferred to an appropriate facility or make any other appropriate order, including continuance of the proceedings.
(d) No hearing upon the application shall be allowed until the person committed has been confined or placed on outpatient status for a period of not less than 180 days from the date of the order of commitment.
(e) The court shall hold a hearing to determine whether the person applying for restoration of sanity would be a danger to the health and safety of others, due to mental defect, disease, or disorder, if under supervision and treatment in the community. If the court at the hearing determines the applicant will not be a danger to the health and safety of others, due to mental defect, disease, or disorder, while under supervision and treatment in the community, the court shall order the applicant placed with an appropriate forensic conditional release program for one year. All or a substantial portion of the program shall include outpatient supervision and treatment. The court shall retain jurisdiction. The court at the end of the one year, shall have a trial to determine if sanity has been restored, which means the applicant is no longer a danger to the health and safety of others, due to mental defect, disease, or disorder. The court shall not determine whether the applicant has been restored to sanity until the applicant has completed the one year in the appropriate forensic conditional release program, unless the community program director sooner makes a recommendation for restoration of sanity and unconditional release as described in subdivision (h). The court shall notify the persons required to be notified in subdivision (a) of the hearing date.
(f) If the applicant is on parole or outpatient status and has been on it for one year or longer, then it is deemed that the applicant has completed the required one year in an appropriate forensic conditional release program and the court shall, if all other applicable provisions of law have been met, hold the trial on restoration of sanity as provided for in this section.
(g) Before placing an applicant in an appropriate forensic conditional release program, the community program director shall submit to the court a written recommendation as to what forensic conditional release program is the most appropriate for supervising and treating the applicant. If the court does not accept the community program director's recommendation, the court shall specify the reason or reasons for its order on the court record. Sections 1605 to 1610, inclusive, shall be applicable to the person placed in the forensic conditional release program unless otherwise ordered by the court.
(h) If the court determines that the person should be transferred to an appropriate forensic conditional release program, the community program director or a designee shall make the necessary placement arrangements, and, within 21 days after receiving notice of the court finding, the person shall be placed in the community in accordance with the treatment and supervision plan, unless good cause for not doing so is made known to the court.
During the one year of supervision and treatment, if the community program director is of the opinion that the person is no longer a danger to the health and safety of others due to a mental defect, disease, or disorder, the community program director shall submit a report of his or her opinion and recommendations to the committing court, the prosecuting attorney, and the attorney for the person. The court shall then set and hold a trial to determine whether restoration of sanity and unconditional release should be granted. The trial shall be conducted in the same manner as is required at the end of one full year of supervision and treatment.
(i) If at the trial for restoration of sanity the court rules adversely to the applicant, the court may place the applicant on outpatient status, pursuant to Title 15 (commencing with Section 1600) of Part 2, unless the applicant does not meet all of the requirements of Section 1603.
(j) If the court denies the application to place the person in an appropriate forensic conditional release program or if restoration of sanity is denied, no new application may be filed by the person until one year has elapsed from the date of the denial.
(k) In any hearing authorized by this section, the applicant shall have the burden of proof by a preponderance of the evidence.
(l) If the application for the release is not made by the medical director of the state hospital or other treatment facility to which the person is committed or by the community program director where the person is on outpatient status under Title 15 (commencing with Section 1600), no action on the application shall be taken by the court without first obtaining the written recommendation of the medical director of the state hospital or other treatment facility or of the community program director where the person is on outpatient status under Title 15 (commencing with Section 1600).
(m) This subdivision shall apply only to persons who, at the time of the petition or recommendation for restoration of sanity, are subject to a term of imprisonment with prison time remaining to serve or are subject to the imposition of a previously stayed sentence to a term of imprisonment. Any person to whom this subdivision applies who petitions or is recommended for restoration of sanity may not be placed in a forensic conditional release program for one year, and a finding of restoration of sanity may be made without the person being in a forensic conditional release program for one year. If a finding of restoration of sanity is made, the person shall be transferred to the custody of the California Department of Corrections to serve the term of imprisonment remaining or shall be transferred to the appropriate court for imposition of the sentence that is pending, whichever is applicable.
(Amended by Stats. 2003, Ch. 230, Sec. 43. Effective August 11, 2003.)

1026.3.

A person committed to a state hospital or other treatment facility under Section 1026, and a person placed pursuant to subdivision (e) of Section 1026.2 as amended by Section 3.5 of Chapter 1488 of the Statutes of 1984, may be placed on outpatient status from the commitment as provided in Title 15 (commencing with Section 1600) of Part 2.
(Amended by Stats. 1985, Ch. 260, Sec. 2.)

1026.4.

(a) Every person committed to a state hospital or other public or private mental health facility pursuant to the provisions of Section 1026, who escapes from or who escapes while being conveyed to or from the state hospital or facility, is punishable by imprisonment in the county jail not to exceed one year or in a state prison for a determinate term of one year and one day. The term of imprisonment imposed pursuant to this section shall be served consecutively to any other sentence or commitment.
(b) The medical director or person in charge of a state hospital or other public or private mental health facility to which a person has been committed pursuant to the provisions of Section 1026 shall promptly notify the chief of police of the city in which the hospital or facility is located, or the sheriff of the county if the hospital or facility is located in an unincorporated area, of the escape of the person, and shall request the assistance of the chief of police or sheriff in apprehending the person, and shall within 48 hours of the escape of the person orally notify the court that made the commitment, the prosecutor in the case, and the Department of Justice of the escape.
(Amended by Stats. 1989, Ch. 568, Sec. 1.)

1026.5.

(a) (1) In the case of any person committed to a state hospital or other treatment facility pursuant to Section 1026 or placed on outpatient status pursuant to Section 1604, who committed a felony on or after July 1, 1977, the court shall state in the commitment order the maximum term of commitment, and the person may not be kept in actual custody longer than the maximum term of commitment, except as provided in this section. For the purposes of this section, "maximum term of commitment" shall mean the longest term of imprisonment which could have been imposed for the offense or offenses of which the person was convicted, including the upper term of the base offense and any additional terms for enhancements and consecutive sentences which could have been imposed less any applicable credits as defined by Section 2900.5, and disregarding any credits which could have been earned pursuant to Article 2.5 (commencing with Section 2930) of Chapter 7 of Title 1 of Part 3.

(2) In the case of a person confined in a state hospital or other treatment facility pursuant to Section 1026 or placed on outpatient status pursuant to Section 1604, who committed a felony prior to July 1, 1977, and who could have been sentenced under Section 1168 or 1170 if the offense was committed after July 1, 1977, the Board of Prison Terms shall determine the maximum term of commitment which could have been imposed under paragraph (1), and the person may not be kept in actual custody longer than the maximum term of commitment, except as provided in subdivision (b). The time limits of this section are not jurisdictional.

In fixing a term under this section, the board shall utilize the upper term of imprisonment which could have been imposed for the offense or offenses of which the person was convicted, increased by any additional terms which could have been imposed based on matters which were found to be true in the committing court. However, if at least two of the members of the board after reviewing the person's file determine that a longer term should be imposed for the reasons specified in Section 1170.2, a longer term may be imposed following the procedures and guidelines set forth in Section 1170.2, except that any hearings deemed necessary by the board shall be held within 90 days of September 28, 1979. Within 90 days of the date the person is received by the state hospital or other treatment facility, or of September 28, 1979, whichever is later, the Board of Prison Terms shall provide each person with the determination of the person's maximum term of commitment or shall notify the person that a hearing will be scheduled to determine the term.

Within 20 days following the determination of the maximum term of commitment the board shall provide the person, the prosecuting attorney, the committing court, and the state hospital or other treatment facility with a written statement setting forth the maximum term of commitment, the calculations, and any materials considered in determining the maximum term.

(3) In the case of a person committed to a state hospital or other treatment facility pursuant to Section 1026 or placed on outpatient status pursuant to Section 1604 who committed a misdemeanor, the maximum term of commitment shall be the longest term of county jail confinement which could have been imposed for the offense or offenses which the person was found to have committed, and the person may not be kept in actual custody longer than this maximum term.

(4) Nothing in this subdivision limits the power of any state hospital or other treatment facility or of the committing court to release the person, conditionally or otherwise, for any period of time allowed by any other provision of law.

(b) (1) A person may be committed beyond the term prescribed by subdivision (a) only under the procedure set forth in this subdivision and only if the person has been committed under Section 1026 for a felony and by reason of a mental disease, defect, or disorder represents a substantial danger of physical harm to others.

(2) Not later than 180 days prior to the termination of the maximum term of commitment prescribed in subdivision (a), the medical director of a state hospital in which the person is being treated, or the medical director of the person's treatment facility or the local program director, if the person is being treated outside a state hospital setting, shall submit to the prosecuting attorney his or her opinion as to whether or not the patient is a person described in paragraph (1). If requested by the prosecuting attorney, the opinion shall be accompanied by supporting evaluations and relevant hospital records. The prosecuting attorney may then file a petition for extended commitment in the superior court which issued the original commitment. The petition shall be filed no later than 90 days before the expiration of the original commitment unless good cause is shown. The petition shall state the reasons for the extended commitment, with accompanying affidavits specifying the factual basis for believing that the person meets each of the requirements set forth in paragraph (1).

(3) When the petition is filed, the court shall advise the person named in the petition of the right to be represented by an attorney and of the right to a jury trial. The rules of discovery in criminal cases shall apply. If the person is being treated in a state hospital when the petition is filed, the court shall notify the community program director of the petition and the hearing date.

(4) The court shall conduct a hearing on the petition for extended commitment. The trial shall be by jury unless waived by both the person and the prosecuting attorney. The trial shall commence no later than 30 calendar days prior to the time the person would otherwise have been released, unless that time is waived by the person or unless good cause is shown.

(5) Pending the hearing, the medical director or person in charge of the facility in which the person is confined shall prepare a summary of the person's programs of treatment and shall forward the summary to the community program director or a designee, and to the court. The community program director or a designee shall review the summary and shall designate a facility within a reasonable distance from the court in which the person may be detained pending the hearing on the petition for extended commitment. The facility so designated shall continue the program of treatment, shall provide adequate security, and shall, to the greatest extent possible, minimize interference with the person's program of treatment.

(6) A designated facility need not be approved for 72-hour treatment and evaluation pursuant to the provisions of the Lanterman-Petris-Short Act (Part 1 (commencing with Section 5000) of Division 5 of the Welfare and Institutions Code). However, a county jail may not be designated unless the services specified in paragraph (5) are provided and accommodations are provided which ensure both the safety of the person and the safety of the general population of the jail. If there is evidence that the treatment program is not being complied with or accommodations have not been provided which ensure both the safety of the committed person and the safety of the general population of the jail, the court shall order the person transferred to an appropriate facility or make any other appropriate order, including continuance of the proceedings.

(7) The person shall be entitled to the rights guaranteed under the federal and State Constitutions for criminal proceedings. All proceedings shall be in accordance with applicable constitutional guarantees. The state shall be represented by the district attorney who shall notify the Attorney General in writing that a case has been referred under this section. If the person is indigent, the county public defender or State Public Defender shall be appointed. The State Public Defender may provide for representation of the person in any manner authorized by Section 15402 of the Government Code. Appointment of necessary psychologists or psychiatrists shall be made in accordance with this article and Penal Code and Evidence Code provisions applicable to criminal defendants who have entered pleas of not guilty by reason of insanity.

(8) If the court or jury finds that the patient is a person described in paragraph (1), the court shall order the patient recommitted to the facility in which the patient was confined at the time the petition was filed. This commitment shall be for an additional period of two years from the date of termination of the previous commitment, and the person may not be kept in actual custody longer than two years unless another extension of commitment is obtained in accordance with the provisions of this subdivision. Time spent on outpatient status, except when placed in a locked facility at the direction of the outpatient supervisor, shall not count as actual custody and shall not be credited toward the person's maximum term of commitment or toward the person's term of extended commitment.

(9) A person committed under this subdivision shall be eligible for release to outpatient status pursuant to the provisions of Title 15 (commencing with Section 1600) of Part 2.

(10) Prior to termination of a commitment under this subdivision, a petition for recommitment may be filed to determine whether the patient remains a person described in paragraph (1). The recommitment proceeding shall be conducted in accordance with the provisions of this subdivision.

(11) Any commitment under this subdivision places an affirmative obligation on the treatment facility to provide treatment for the underlying causes of the person's mental disorder.
(Amended by Stats. 1994, 1st Ex. Sess., Ch. 9, Sec. 1. Effective November 30, 1994.)
1026.6.
Whenever any person who has been committed to a state hospital pursuant to Section 1026 is released for any reason, including placement on outpatient status, the director of the hospital shall notify the community program director of the county, and the chief law enforcement officer of the jurisdiction, in which the person will reside upon release, if that information is available.
(Amended by Stats. 1985, Ch. 1232, Sec. 4. Effective September 30, 1985. Note: This text was suspended from Jan. 1, 1987, until Jan. 1, 1989, during operation of the temporary amendment by Stats. 1986, Ch. 64.)
1027.
(a) When a defendant pleads not guilty by reason of insanity the court shall select and appoint two, and may select and appoint three, psychiatrists, or licensed psychologists who have a doctoral degree in psychology and at least five years of postgraduate experience in the diagnosis and treatment of emotional and mental disorders, to examine the defendant and investigate his or her mental status. It is the duty of the psychiatrists or psychologists selected and appointed to make the examination and investigation, and to testify, whenever summoned, in any proceeding in which the sanity of the defendant is in question. The psychiatrists or psychologists appointed by the court shall be allowed, in addition to their actual traveling expenses, those fees that in the discretion of the court seem just and reasonable, having regard to the services rendered by the witnesses. The fees allowed shall be paid by the county where the indictment was found or in which the defendant was held for trial.
(b) Any report on the examination and investigation made pursuant to subdivision (a) shall include, but not be limited to, the psychological history of the defendant, the facts surrounding the commission of the acts forming the basis for the present charge used by the psychiatrist or psychologist in making his or her examination of the defendant, the present psychological or psychiatric symptoms of the defendant, if any, the substance abuse history of the defendant, the substance use history of the defendant on the day of the offense, a review of the police report for the offense, and any other credible and relevant material reasonably necessary to describe the facts of the offense.
(c) This section does not presume that a psychiatrist or psychologist can determine whether a defendant was sane or insane at the time of the alleged offense. This section does not limit a court's discretion to admit or exclude, pursuant to the Evidence Code, psychiatric or psychological evidence about the defendant's state of mind or mental or emotional condition at the time of the alleged offense.
(d) Nothing contained in this section shall be deemed or construed to prevent any party to any criminal action from producing any other expert evidence with respect to the mental status of the defendant. If expert witnesses are called by the district attorney in the action, they shall only be entitled to those witness fees as may be allowed by the court.
(e) Any psychiatrist or psychologist appointed by the court may be called by either party to the action or by the court, and shall be subject to all legal objections as to competency and bias and as to qualifications as an expert. When called by the court or by either party to the action, the court may examine the psychiatrist or psychologist, as deemed necessary, but either party shall have the same right to object to the questions asked by the court and the evidence adduced as though the psychiatrist or psychologist were a witness for the adverse party. When the psychiatrist or psychologist is called and examined by the court, the parties may cross-examine him or her in the order directed by the court. When called by either party to the action, the adverse party may examine him or her the same as in the case of any other witness called by the party.
(Amended by Stats. 2012, Ch. 150, Sec. 1. (SB 1281) Effective January 1, 2013.)

CHAPTER 5. Transmission of Certain Indictments and Information [1029- 1029.]

(Heading of Chapter 5 amended by Stats. 1979, Ch. 373.)
1029.
When an indictment is found or an information filed in the superior court against a judge thereof, a certificate of that fact must be transmitted by the clerk to the chairman of the Judicial Council, who shall thereupon designate and assign a judge of the superior court of another county to preside at the trial of such indictment or information, and hear and determine all pleas and motions affecting the defendant thereunder before and after judgment.
(Amended by Stats. 1935, Ch. 573.)

CHAPTER 6. Change of Venue [1033 - 1038]

(Chapter 6 repealed and added by Stats. 1971, Ch. 1476.)
1033.
In a criminal action pending in the superior court, the court shall order a change of venue:
(a) On motion of the defendant, to another county when it appears that there is a reasonable likelihood that a fair and impartial trial cannot be had in the county. When a change of venue is ordered by the superior court, it shall be for the trial itself. All proceedings before trial shall occur in the county of original venue, except when it is evident that a particular proceeding must be heard by the judge who is to preside over the trial.
(b) On its own motion or on motion of any party, to an adjoining county when it appears as a result of the exhaustion of all of the jury panels called that it will be impossible to secure a jury to try the cause in the county.
(Amended by Stats. 1983, Ch. 562, Sec. 1.)
1033.1.
In any criminal action or proceeding in which the place of trial has been changed for any of the reasons set forth in Section 1033, the court, upon its own motion or upon the motion of any party, may return the action or proceeding to the original place of trial if both of the following conditions apply:
(a) The action or proceeding is pending before the court after reversal of the original judgment by the appellate court.
(b) The court finds that the conditions which originally required the order to change venue, as set forth in Section 1033, no longer apply. Prior to making such a finding, the court shall conduct a hearing, upon notice to all parties. At the hearing, the burden shall be on the prosecution to establish that the conditions which originally required the order to change venue no longer apply, unless the defendant and his or her attorney consent to the return of the action or proceeding to the original place of trial.
(Added by Stats. 1993, Ch. 837, Sec. 1. Effective October 6, 1993.)
1035.
A defendant arrested, held, or present in a county other than that in which an indictment, information, felony complaint, or felony probation violation is pending against the defendant, may state in writing his or her agreement to plead guilty or nolo

contendere to some or all of the pending charges, to waive trial or hearing in the county in which the pleading is pending, and to consent to disposition of the case in the county in which that defendant was arrested, held, or present, subject to the approval of the district attorney for each county. Upon receipt of the defendant's statement and of the written approval of the district attorneys, the clerk of the court in which the pleading is pending shall transmit the papers in the proceeding or certified copies thereof to the clerk of the court for the county in which the defendant is arrested, held, or present, and the prosecution shall continue in that county. However, the proceedings shall be limited solely to the purposes of plea and sentencing and not for trial. If, after the proceeding has been transferred pursuant to this section, the defendant pleads not guilty, the clerk shall return the papers to the court in which the prosecution was commenced and the proceeding shall be restored to the docket of that court. The defendant's statement that the defendant wishes to plead guilty or nolo contendere may not be used against the defendant.
(Amended by Stats. 2003, Ch. 449, Sec. 32. Effective January 1, 2004.)

1036.
(a) Unless the court reserves jurisdiction to hear other pretrial motions, if a defendant is incarcerated and the court orders a change of venue to another county, the court shall direct the sheriff to deliver the defendant to the custody of the sheriff of the other county for the purpose of trial.
(b) If the defendant is incarcerated and the court orders that the jury be selected from the county to which the venue would otherwise have been transferred pursuant to Section 1036.7, the court shall direct the sheriff to deliver the defendant to the custody of the sheriff of that county for the purpose of jury selection.
(Amended by Stats. 1987, Ch. 780, Sec. 1.)

1036.5.
Following the resolution of pre-trial motions, and prior to the issuance of an order under Section 1036 or the transmittal of the case file for the purpose of trial to the court to which venue has been ordered transferred, the court may, upon its own motion or the motion of any party and on appropriate notice to the court to which venue has been transferred, set aside its order to change venue on the ground that the conditions which originally required the order to change venue, as set forth in Section 1033 or 1034, no longer apply.
(Added by Stats. 1983, Ch. 947, Sec. 7.)

1036.7.
When a change of venue is ordered and the court, upon motion to transfer a jury or on its own motion and upon unanimous consent of all defendants, determines that it would be in the interests of the administration of justice to move the jury rather than to move the pending action, a change of venue may be accomplished by the selection of a jury in the county or judicial district to which the venue would otherwise have been transferred, and the selected jury shall be moved to the court in which the criminal action is pending.
(Added by Stats. 1987, Ch. 780, Sec. 2.)

1037.
(a) When a court orders a change of venue to a court in another county, all costs incurred by the receiving court or county, that are not payable pursuant to Section 4750, shall be paid by the transferring court or county as provided in Sections 1037.1 and 1037.2. Those costs may include, but are not limited to, the expenses for the following:
(1) The transfer, preparation, and trial of the action.
(2) The guarding, keeping, and transportation of the prisoner.
(3) Any appeal or other proceeding relating to the action.
(4) Execution of the sentence.
(b) The term "all costs" means all reasonable and necessary costs incurred by the receiving court or county as a result of the change of venue that would not have been incurred but for the change of venue. "All costs" does not include normal salaries, overhead, and other expenses that would have been incurred by the receiving court or county if it did not receive the trial.
(Amended by Stats. 2005, Ch. 282, Sec. 1. Effective January 1, 2006.)

1037.1.
(a) Change of venue costs, as defined in Section 1037, that are court operations, as defined in Section 77003 of the Government Code and Rule 10.810 of the California Rules of Court, shall be considered court costs to be charged against and paid by the transferring court to the receiving court.
(b) The Judicial Council shall adopt financial policies and procedures to ensure the timely payment of court costs pursuant to this section. The policies and procedures shall include, but are not limited to, both of the following:
(1) The requirement that courts approve a budget and a timeline for reimbursement before the beginning of the trial.
(2) A process for the Administrative Office of the Courts to mediate any disputes regarding costs between transferring and receiving courts.
(c) (1) The presiding judge of the transferring court, or his or her designee, shall authorize the payment for the reimbursement of court costs out of the court operations fund of the transferring court.
(2) Payments for the reimbursement of court costs shall be deposited into the court operations fund of the receiving court.
(Amended by Stats. 2007, Ch. 130, Sec. 192. Effective January 1, 2008.)

1037.2.
(a) Change of venue costs, as defined in Section 1037, that are incurred by the receiving county and not defined as court operations under Section 77003 of the Government Code or Rule 10.810 of the California Rules of Court shall be considered to be county costs to be paid by the transferring county to the receiving county. County costs include, but are not limited to, alterations, including all construction-related costs, to a courthouse made that only resulted from the transfer of the trial, rental of furniture or equipment that only resulted from the transfer of the trial, inmate transportation provided by the county sheriff from the jail to the courthouse, security of the inmate or other participants in the trial, unique or extraordinary costs for the extended storage and safekeeping of evidence related to the trial, rental of jury parking lot, jury parking lot security and related costs, security expenses incurred by the county sheriff or a contracted agency that resulted only from the transfer of the trial, and information services for the court, jury, public, or media.
(b) Transferring counties shall approve a budget and a timeline for the payment of county costs before the beginning of trial.
(c) Claims for the costs described in subdivision (a) shall be forwarded to the treasurer and auditor of the transferring county on a monthly basis. The treasurer shall pay the amount of county costs out of the general funds of the transferring county within 30 days of receiving the claim for costs from the receiving county.
(d) (1) The transferring court may, in its sound discretion, determine the reasonable and necessary costs under this section.
(2) The transferring court's approval of costs shall become effective 10 days after the court has given written notice of the costs to the auditor of the transferring county.
(3) During the 10-day period specified in paragraph (2), the auditor of the transferring county may contest the costs approved by the transferring court.
(4) If the auditor of the transferring county fails to contest the costs within the 10-day period specified in paragraph (2), the transferring county shall be deemed to have waived the right to contest the imposition of these costs.
(Amended by Stats. 2007, Ch. 130, Sec. 193. Effective January 1, 2008.)

1038.
The Judicial Council shall adopt rules of practice and procedure for the change of venue in criminal actions.
(Amended by Stats. 2003, Ch. 449, Sec. 33. Effective January 1, 2004.)

CHAPTER 7. The Mode of Trial [1041 - 1045]

(Chapter 7 enacted 1872.)

1041.
An issue of fact arises:
1. Upon a plea of not guilty.
2. Upon a plea of a former conviction or acquittal of the same offense.
3. Upon a plea of once in jeopardy.
4. Upon a plea of not guilty by reason of insanity.
(Amended by Stats. 1949, Ch. 1314.)

1042.
Issues of fact shall be tried in the manner provided in Article I, Section 16 of the Constitution of this state.
(Amended by Stats. 2002, Ch. 787, Sec. 20. Effective January 1, 2003.)

1042.5.
Trial of an infraction shall be by the court, but when a defendant has been charged with an infraction and with a public offense for which there is a right to jury trial and a jury trial is not waived, the court may order that the offenses be tried together by jury or that they be tried separately with the infraction being tried by the court either in the same proceeding or a separate proceeding as may be appropriate.
(Added by Stats. 1968, Ch. 1192.)

1043.
(a) Except as otherwise provided in this section, the defendant in a felony case shall be personally present at the trial.
(b) The absence of the defendent in a felony case after the trial has commenced in his presence shall not prevent continuing the trial to, and including, the return of the verdict in any of the following cases:
(1) Any case in which the defendant, after he has been warned by the judge that he will be removed if he continues his disruptive behavior, nevertheless insists on conducting himself in a manner so disorderly, disruptive, and disrespectful of the court that the trial cannot be carried on with him in the courtroom.
(2) Any prosecution for an offense which is not punishable by death in which the defendant is voluntarily absent.
(c) Any defendant who is absent from a trial pursuant to paragraph (1) of subdivision (b) may reclaim his right to be present at the trial as soon as he is willing to conduct himself consistently with the decorum and respect inherent in the concept of courts and judicial proceedings.
(d) Subdivisions (a) and (b) shall not limit the right of a defendant to waive his right to be present in accordance with Section 977.
(e) If the defendant in a misdemeanor case fails to appear in person at the time set for trial or during the course of trial, the court shall proceed with the trial, unless good cause for a continuance exists, if the defendant has authorized his counsel to proceed in his absence pursuant to subdivision (a) of Section 977.
If there is no authorization pursuant to subdivision (a) of Section 977 and if the defendant fails to appear in person at the time set for trial or during the course of trial, the court, in its discretion, may do one or more of the following, as it deems appropriate:
(1) Continue the matter.
(2) Order bail forfeited or revoke release on the defendant's own recognizance.
(3) Issue a bench warrant.
(4) Proceed with the trial if the court finds the defendant has absented himself voluntarily with full knowledge that the trial is to be held or is being held.
Nothing herein shall limit the right of the court to order the defendant to be personally present at the trial for purposes of identification unless counsel stipulate to the issue of identity.
(Amended by Stats. 1977, Ch. 1152.)

1043.5.
(a) Except as otherwise provided in this section, the defendant in a preliminary hearing shall be personally present.
(b) The absence of the defendant in a preliminary hearing after the hearing has commenced in his presence shall not prevent continuing the hearing to, and including, holding to answer, filing an information, or discharging the defendant in any of the following cases:
(1) Any case in which the defendant, after he has been warned by the judge that he will be removed if he continued his disruptive behavior, nevertheless insists on conducting himself in a manner so disorderly, disruptive, and disrespectful of the court that the hearing cannot be carried on with him in the courtroom.
(2) Any prosecution for an offense which is not punishable by death in which the defendant is voluntarily absent.
(c) Any defendant who is absent from a preliminary hearing pursuant to paragraph (1) of subdivision (b) may reclaim his right to be present at the hearing as soon as he is willing to conduct himself consistently with the decorum and respect inherent in the concept of courts and judicial proceedings.
(d) Subdivisions (a) and (b) shall not limit the right of a defendant to waive his right to be present in accordance with Section 977.
(Added by Stats. 1980, Ch. 1379, Sec. 2.)

1044.
It shall be the duty of the judge to control all proceedings during the trial, and to limit the introduction of evidence and the argument of counsel to relevant and material matters, with a view to the expeditious and effective ascertainment of the truth regarding the matters involved.
(Added by Stats. 1927, Ch. 607.)

1045.
In any misdemeanor or infraction matter, where a verbatim record of the proceedings is not required to be made and where the right of a party to request a verbatim record is not provided for pursuant to any other provision of law or rule of court, if any party makes a request at least five days in advance and deposits the required fees, the court shall order that a verbatim record be made of all proceedings. Except as otherwise provided by law or rule the party requesting any reporting, recording, or transcript pursuant to this section shall pay the cost of such reporting, recording, or transcript. This section shall cease to be operative upon a final decision of an appellate court holding that there is a constitutional right or other requirement that a verbatim record or transcript be provided at public expense for indigent or any other defendants in cases subject to the provisions of this section.
(Added by Stats. 1980, Ch. 1200, Sec. 1.)

CHAPTER 8. Formation of the Trial Jury and theCalendar of Issues for Trial [1046 - 1051]

(Chapter 8 enacted 1872.)

1046.

Trial juries for criminal actions are formed in the same manner as trial juries in civil actions.
(Enacted 1872.)
1048.
(a) The issues on the calendar shall be disposed of in the following order, unless for good cause the court directs an action to be tried out of its order:
(1) Prosecutions for felony, when the defendant is in custody.
(2) Prosecutions for misdemeanor, when the defendant is in custody.
(3) Prosecutions for felony, when the defendant is on bail.
(4) Prosecutions for misdemeanor, when the defendant is on bail.
(b) Notwithstanding subdivision (a), all criminal actions in which (1) a minor is detained as a material witness or is the victim of the alleged offense, (2) a person who was 70 years of age or older at the time of the alleged offense or is a dependent adult, as defined in subdivision (h) of Section 368, was a witness to, or is the victim of, the alleged offense or (3) any person is a victim of an alleged violation of Section 261, 262, 264.1, 273a, 273d, 285, 286, 287, 288, or 289 or former Section 288a, committed by the use of force, violence, or the threat thereof, shall be given precedence over all other criminal actions in the order of trial. In those actions, continuations shall be granted by the court only after a hearing and determination of the necessity thereof, and in any event, the trial shall be commenced within 30 days after arraignment, unless for good cause the court shall direct the action to be continued, after a hearing and determination of the necessity of the continuance, and states the findings for a determination of good cause on the record.
(c) Nothing in this section shall be deemed to provide a statutory right to a trial within 30 days.
(Amended by Stats. 2018, Ch. 423, Sec. 84. (SB 1494) Effective January 1, 2019.)
1048.1.
(a) In scheduling a trial date at an arraignment in superior court involving any of the following offenses, reasonable efforts shall be made to avoid setting that trial, when that case is assigned to a particular prosecuting attorney, on the same day that another case is set for trial involving the same prosecuting attorney:
(1) Murder, as defined in subdivision (a) of Section 187.
(2) An alleged sexual assault offense, as described in subdivisions (a) and (b) of Section 11165.1.
(3) An alleged child abuse offense, as described in Section 11165.6.
(4) A case being handled in the Career Criminal Prosecution Program pursuant to Chapter 2.2 (commencing with Section 999b).
(5) An alleged offense against a person with a developmental disability.
(b) For purposes of this section, "developmental disability" has the same meaning as found in Section 4512 of the Welfare and Institutions Code.
(Amended by Stats. 2016, Ch. 91, Sec. 1. (AB 1272) Effective January 1, 2017.)
1048.2.
Notwithstanding subdivision (b) of Section 1048, for good cause shown, the court may grant priority to an action for an alleged violation of Section 236.1 as the court, in its discretion, may determine to be appropriate.
(Added by Stats. 2016, Ch. 644, Sec. 4. (AB 2498) Effective January 1, 2017.)
1049.
After his plea, the defendant is entitled to at least five days to prepare for trial.
(Amended by Stats. 1927, Ch. 606.)
1049.5.
In felony cases, the court shall set a date for trial which is within 60 days of the defendant's arraignment in the superior court unless, upon a showing of good cause as prescribed in Section 1050, the court lengthens the time. If the court, after a hearing as presecribed in Section 1050, finds that there is good cause to set the date for trial beyond the 60 days, it shall state on the record the facts proved that justify its finding. A statement of facts proved shall be entered in the minutes.
(Added June 5, 1990, by initiative Proposition 115, Sec. 21.)
1050.
(a) The welfare of the people of the State of California requires that all proceedings in criminal cases shall be set for trial and heard and determined at the earliest possible time. To this end, the Legislature finds that the criminal courts are becoming increasingly congested with resulting adverse consequences to the welfare of the people and the defendant. Excessive continuances contribute substantially to this congestion and cause substantial hardship to victims and other witnesses. Continuances also lead to longer periods of presentence confinement for those defendants in custody and the concomitant overcrowding and increased expenses of local jails. It is therefore recognized that the people, the defendant, and the victims and other witnesses have the right to an expeditious disposition, and to that end it shall be the duty of all courts and judicial officers and of all counsel, both for the prosecution and the defense, to expedite these proceedings to the greatest degree that is consistent with the ends of justice. In accordance with this policy, criminal cases shall be given precedence over, and set for trial and heard without regard to the pendency of, any civil matters or proceedings. In further accordance with this policy, death penalty cases in which both the prosecution and the defense have informed the court that they are prepared to proceed to trial shall be given precedence over, and set for trial and heard without regard to the pendency of, other criminal cases and any civil matters or proceedings, unless the court finds in the interest of justice that it is not appropriate.
(b) To continue any hearing in a criminal proceeding, including the trial, (1) a written notice shall be filed and served on all parties to the proceeding at least two court days before the hearing sought to be continued, together with affidavits or declarations detailing specific facts showing that a continuance is necessary and (2) within two court days of learning that he or she has a conflict in the scheduling of any court hearing, including a trial, an attorney shall notify the calendar clerk of each court involved, in writing, indicating which hearing was set first. A party shall not be deemed to have been served within the meaning of this section until that party actually has received a copy of the documents to be served, unless the party, after receiving actual notice of the request for continuance, waives the right to have the documents served in a timely manner. Regardless of the proponent of the motion, the prosecuting attorney shall notify the people's witnesses and the defense attorney shall notify the defense's witnesses of the notice of motion, the date of the hearing, and the witnesses' right to be heard by the court.
(c) Notwithstanding subdivision (b), a party may make a motion for a continuance without complying with the requirements of that subdivision. However, unless the moving party shows good cause for the failure to comply with those requirements, the court may impose sanctions as provided in Section 1050.5.
(d) When a party makes a motion for a continuance without complying with the requirements of subdivision (b), the court shall hold a hearing on whether there is good cause for the failure to comply with those requirements. At the conclusion of the hearing, the court shall make a finding whether good cause has been shown and, if it finds that there is good cause, shall state on the record the facts proved that justify its finding. A statement of the finding and a statement of facts proved shall be entered in the minutes. If the moving party is unable to show good cause for the failure to give notice, the motion for continuance shall not be granted.
(e) Continuances shall be granted only upon a showing of good cause. Neither the convenience of the parties nor a stipulation of the parties is in and of itself good cause.
(f) At the conclusion of the motion for continuance, the court shall make a finding whether good cause has been shown and, if it finds that there is good cause, shall state on the record the facts proved that justify its finding. A statement of facts proved shall be entered in the minutes.
(g) (1) When deciding whether or not good cause for a continuance has been shown, the court shall consider the general convenience and prior commitments of all witnesses, including peace officers. Both the general convenience and prior commitments of each witness also shall be considered in selecting a continuance date if the motion is granted. The facts as to inconvenience or prior commitments may be offered by the witness or by a party to the case.
(2) For purposes of this section, "good cause" includes, but is not limited to, those cases involving murder, as defined in subdivision (a) of Section 187, allegations that stalking, as defined in Section 646.9, a violation of one or more of the sections specified in subdivision (a) of Section 11165.1 or Section 11165.6, or domestic violence as defined in Section 13700, or a case being handled in the Career Criminal Prosecution Program pursuant to Sections 999b through 999h, or a hate crime, as defined in Title 11.6 (commencing with Section 422.6) of Part 1, has occurred and the prosecuting attorney assigned to the case has another trial, preliminary hearing, or motion to suppress in progress in that court or another court. A continuance under this paragraph shall be limited to a maximum of 10 additional court days.
(3) Only one continuance per case may be granted to the people under this subdivision for cases involving stalking, hate crimes, or cases handled under the Career Criminal Prosecution Program. Any continuance granted to the people in a case involving stalking or handled under the Career Criminal Prosecution Program shall be for the shortest time possible, not to exceed 10 court days.
(h) Upon a showing that the attorney of record at the time of the defendant's first appearance in the superior court on an indictment or information is a Member of the Legislature of this state and that the Legislature is in session or that a legislative interim committee of which the attorney is a duly appointed member is meeting or is to meet within the next seven days, the defendant shall be entitled to a reasonable continuance not to exceed 30 days.
(i) A continuance shall be granted only for that period of time shown to be necessary by the evidence considered at the hearing on the motion. Whenever any continuance is granted, the court shall state on the record the facts proved that justify the length of the continuance, and those facts shall be entered in the minutes.
(j) Whenever it shall appear that any court may be required, because of the condition of its calendar, to dismiss an action pursuant to Section 1382, the court must immediately notify the Chair of the Judicial Council.
(k) This section shall not apply when the preliminary examination is set on a date less than 10 court days from the date of the defendant's arraignment on the complaint, and the prosecution or the defendant moves to continue the preliminary examination to a date not more than 10 court days from the date of the defendant's arraignment on the complaint.
(l) This section is directory only and does not mandate dismissal of an action by its terms.
(Amended by Stats. 2003, Ch. 133, Sec. 1. Effective January 1, 2004.)
1050.1.
In any case in which two or more defendants are jointly charged in the same complaint, indictment, or information, and the court or magistrate, for good cause shown, continues the arraignment, preliminary hearing, or trial of one or more defendants, the continuance shall, upon motion of the prosecuting attorney, constitute good cause to continue the remaining defendants' cases so as to maintain joinder. The court or magistrate shall not cause jointly charged cases to be severed due to the unavailability or unpreparedness of one or more defendants unless it appears to the court or magistrate that it will be impossible for all defendants to be available and prepared within a reasonable period of time.
(Added June 5, 1990, by initiative Proposition 115, Sec. 22.)
1050.5.
(a) When, pursuant to subdivision (c) of Section 1050, the court imposes sanctions for failure to comply with the provisions of subdivision (b) of Section 1050, the court may impose one or both of the following sanctions when the moving party is the prosecuting or defense attorney:
(1) A fine not exceeding one thousand dollars ($1,000) upon counsel for the moving party.
(2) The filing of a report with an appropriate disciplinary committee.
(b) The authority to impose sanctions provided for by this section shall be in addition to any other authority or power available to the court, except that the court or magistrate shall not dismiss the case.
(Amended by Stats. 2003, Ch. 133, Sec. 2. Effective January 1, 2004.)
1051.
Upon a trial for any offense, if a defense witness testifies, there shall be good cause for a reasonable continuance unless the court finds that the prosecutor was or should, with due diligence, have been aware of such evidence. If the continuance is granted because of the defendant's testimony, it shall not exceed one day.
(Amended by Stats. 1983, Ch. 782, Sec. 1.)

CHAPTER 9. Postponement of the Trial [1053-1053.]

(Chapter 9 enacted 1872.)
1053.
If after the commencement of the trial of a criminal action or proceeding in any court the judge or justice presiding at the trial shall die, become ill, or for any other reason be unable to proceed with the trial, any other judge or justice of the court in which the trial is proceeding may proceed with and finish the trial; or if there be no other judge or justice of that court available, then the clerk, sheriff, or marshal shall adjourn the court and notify the Chairman of the Judicial Council of the facts, and shall continue the case from day to day until the time that the chairman shall designate and assign a judge or justice of some other court, and the judge or justice shall arrive, to proceed with and complete the trial, or until such time as by stipulation in writing between the prosecuting attorney and the attorney for the defendant, filed with the court, a judge or justice shall be agreed upon by them, and the judge or justice shall arrive to complete the trial. The judge or justice authorized by this section to proceed with and complete the trial shall have the same power, authority, and jurisdiction as if the trial had been commenced before that judge or justice.
(Amended by Stats. 1996, Ch. 872, Sec. 118. Effective January 1, 1997.)

CHAPTER 10. Discovery [1054 - 1054.10]

(Chapter 10 added June 5, 1990, by initiative Proposition 115, Sec. 23.)
1054.
This chapter shall be interpreted to give effect to all of the following purposes:
(a) To promote the ascertainment of truth in trials by requiring timely pretrial discovery.
(b) To save court time by requiring that discovery be conducted informally between and among the parties before judicial enforcement is requested.
(c) To save court time in trial and avoid the necessity for frequent interruptions and postponements.

(d) To protect victims and witnesses from danger, harassment, and undue delay of the proceedings.
(e) To provide that no discovery shall occur in criminal cases except as provided by this chapter, other express statutory provisions, or as mandated by the Constitution of the United States.
(Added June 5, 1990, by initiative Proposition 115.)
1054.1.
The prosecuting attorney shall disclose to the defendant or his or her attorney all of the following materials and information, if it is in the possession of the prosecuting attorney or if the prosecuting attorney knows it to be in the possession of the investigating agencies:
(a) The names and addresses of persons the prosecutor intends to call as witnesses at trial.
(b) Statements of all defendants.
(c) All relevant real evidence seized or obtained as a part of the investigation of the offenses charged.
(d) The existence of a felony conviction of any material witness whose credibility is likely to be critical to the outcome of the trial.
(e) Any exculpatory evidence.
(f) Relevant written or recorded statements of witnesses or reports of the statements of witnesses whom the prosecutor intends to call at the trial, including any reports or statements of experts made in conjunction with the case, including the results of physical or mental examinations, scientific tests, experiments, or comparisons which the prosecutor intends to offer in evidence at the trial.
(Added June 5, 1990, by initiative Proposition 115.)
1054.2.
(a) (1) Except as provided in paragraph (2), no attorney may disclose or permit to be disclosed to a defendant, members of the defendant's family, or anyone else, the address or telephone number of a victim or witness whose name is disclosed to the attorney pursuant to subdivision (a) of Section 1054.1, unless specifically permitted to do so by the court after a hearing and a showing of good cause.
(2) Notwithstanding paragraph (1), an attorney may disclose or permit to be disclosed the address or telephone number of a victim or witness to persons employed by the attorney or to persons appointed by the court to assist in the preparation of a defendant's case if that disclosure is required for that preparation. Persons provided this information by an attorney shall be informed by the attorney that further dissemination of the information, except as provided by this section, is prohibited.
(3) Willful violation of this subdivision by an attorney, persons employed by the attorney, or persons appointed by the court is a misdemeanor.
(b) If the defendant is acting as his or her own attorney, the court shall endeavor to protect the address and telephone number of a victim or witness by providing for contact only through a private investigator licensed by the Department of Consumer Affairs and appointed by the court or by imposing other reasonable restrictions, absent a showing of good cause as determined by the court.
(Amended by Stats. 1998, Ch. 485, Sec. 133. Effective January 1, 1999. Note: This section was added June 5, 1990, by initiative Prop. 115. Prop. 115 allows the Legislature to directly amend its provisions by 2/3 vote.)
1054.3.
(a) The defendant and his or her attorney shall disclose to the prosecuting attorney:
(1) The names and addresses of persons, other than the defendant, he or she intends to call as witnesses at trial, together with any relevant written or recorded statements of those persons, or reports of the statements of those persons, including any reports or statements of experts made in connection with the case, and including the results of physical or mental examinations, scientific tests, experiments, or comparisons which the defendant intends to offer in evidence at the trial.
(2) Any real evidence which the defendant intends to offer in evidence at the trial.
(b) (1) Unless otherwise specifically addressed by an existing provision of law, whenever a defendant in a criminal action or a minor in a juvenile proceeding brought pursuant to a petition alleging the juvenile to be within Section 602 of the Welfare and Institutions Code places in issue his or her mental state at any phase of the criminal action or juvenile proceeding through the proposed testimony of any mental health expert, upon timely request by the prosecution, the court may order that the defendant or juvenile submit to examination by a prosecution-retained mental health expert.
(A) The prosecution shall bear the cost of any such mental health expert's fees for examination and testimony at a criminal trial or juvenile court proceeding.
(B) The prosecuting attorney shall submit a list of tests proposed to be administered by the prosecution expert to the defendant in a criminal action or a minor in a juvenile proceeding. At the request of the defendant in a criminal action or a minor in a juvenile proceeding, a hearing shall be held to consider any objections raised to the proposed tests before any test is administered. Before ordering that the defendant submit to the examination, the trial court must make a threshold determination that the proposed tests bear some reasonable relation to the mental state placed in issue by the defendant in a criminal action or a minor in a juvenile proceeding. For the purposes of this subdivision, the term "tests" shall include any and all assessment techniques such as a clinical interview or a mental status examination.
(2) The purpose of this subdivision is to respond to Verdin v. Superior Court 43 Cal.4th 1096, which held that only the Legislature may authorize a court to order the appointment of a prosecution mental health expert when a defendant has placed his or her mental state at issue in a criminal case or juvenile proceeding pursuant to Section 602 of the Welfare and Institutions Code. Other than authorizing the court to order testing by prosecution-retained mental health experts in response to Verdin v. Superior Court, supra, it is not the intent of the Legislature to disturb, in any way, the remaining body of case law governing the procedural or substantive law that controls the administration of these tests or the admission of the results of these tests into evidence.
(Amended by Stats. 2009, Ch. 297, Sec. 1. (AB 1516) Effective January 1, 2010. Note: This section was added on June 5, 1990, by initiative Prop. 115.)
1054.4.
Nothing in this chapter shall be construed as limiting any law enforcement or prosecuting agency from obtaining nontestimonial evidence to the extent permitted by law on the effective date of this section.
(Added June 5, 1990, by initiative Proposition 115.)
1054.5.
(a) No order requiring discovery shall be made in criminal cases except as provided in this chapter. This chapter shall be the only means by which the defendant may compel the disclosure or production of information from prosecuting attorneys, law enforcement agencies which investigated or prepared the case against the defendant, or any other persons or agencies which the prosecuting attorney or investigating agency may have employed to assist them in performing their duties.
(b) Before a party may seek court enforcement of any of the disclosures required by this chapter, the party shall make an informal request of opposing counsel for the desired materials and information. If within 15 days the opposing counsel fails to provide the materials and information requested, the party may seek a court order. Upon a showing that a party has not complied with Section 1054.1 or 1054.3 and upon a showing that the moving party complied with the informal discovery procedure provided in this subdivision, a court may make any order necessary to enforce the provisions of this chapter, including, but not limited to, immediate disclosure, contempt proceedings, delaying or prohibiting the testimony of a witness or the presentation of real evidence, continuance of the matter, or any other lawful order. Further, the court may advise the jury of any failure or refusal to disclose and of any untimely disclosure.
(c) The court may prohibit the testimony of a witness pursuant to subdivision (b) only if all other sanctions have been exhausted. The court shall not dismiss a charge pursuant to subdivision (b) unless required to do so by the Constitution of the United States.
(Added June 5, 1990, by initiative Proposition 115.)
1054.6.
Neither the defendant nor the prosecuting attorney is required to disclose any materials or information which are work product as defined in subdivision (a) of Section 2018.030 of the Code of Civil Procedure, or which are privileged pursuant to an express statutory provision, or are privileged as provided by the Constitution of the United States.
(Amended by Stats. 2004, Ch. 182, Sec. 50. Effective January 1, 2005. Operative July 1, 2005, by Sec. 64 of Ch. 182. Note: This section was added on June 5, 1990, by initiative Prop. 115.)
1054.7.
The disclosures required under this chapter shall be made at least 30 days prior to the trial, unless good cause is shown why a disclosure should be denied, restricted, or deferred. If the material and information becomes known to, or comes into the possession of, a party within 30 days of trial, disclosure shall be made immediately, unless good cause is shown why a disclosure should be denied, restricted, or deferred. "Good cause" is limited to threats or possible danger to the safety of a victim or witness, possible loss or destruction of evidence, or possible compromise of other investigations by law enforcement.
Upon the request of any party, the court may permit a showing of good cause for the denial or regulation of disclosures, or any portion of that showing, to be made in camera. A verbatim record shall be made of any such proceeding. If the court enters an order granting relief following a showing in camera, the entire record of the showing shall be sealed and preserved in the records of the court, and shall be made available to an appellate court in the event of an appeal or writ. In its discretion, the trial court may after trial and conviction, unseal any previously sealed matter.
(Added June 5, 1990, by initiative Proposition 115.)
1054.8.
(a) No prosecuting attorney, attorney for the defendant, or investigator for either the prosecution or the defendant shall interview, question, or speak to a victim or witness whose name has been disclosed by the opposing party pursuant to Section 1054.1 or 1054.3 without first clearly identifying himself or herself, identifying the full name of the agency by whom he or she is employed, and identifying whether he or she represents, or has been retained by, the prosecution or the defendant. If the interview takes place in person, the party shall also show the victim or witness a business card, official badge, or other form of official identification before commencing the interview or questioning.
(b) Upon a showing that a person has failed to comply with this section, a court may issue any order authorized by Section 1054.5.
(Added by Stats. 1998, Ch. 630, Sec. 1. Effective January 1, 1999.)
1054.9.
(a) In a case involving a conviction of a serious felony or a violent felony resulting in a sentence of 15 years or more, upon the prosecution of a postconviction writ of habeas corpus or a motion to vacate a judgment, or in preparation to file that writ or motion, and on a showing that good faith efforts to obtain discovery materials from trial counsel were made and were unsuccessful, the court shall, except as provided in subdivision (b) or (d), order that the defendant be provided reasonable access to any of the materials described in subdivision (c).
(b) Notwithstanding subdivision (a), in a case in which a sentence other than death or life in prison without the possibility of parole has been imposed, if a court has entered a previous order granting discovery pursuant to this section, a subsequent order granting discovery pursuant to subdivision (a) may be made in the court's discretion. A request for discovery subject to this subdivision shall include a statement by the person requesting discovery as to whether he or she has previously been granted an order for discovery pursuant to this section.
(c) For purposes of this section, "discovery materials" means materials in the possession of the prosecution and law enforcement authorities to which the same defendant would have been entitled at time of trial.
(d) In response to a writ or motion satisfying the conditions in subdivision (a), the court may order that the defendant be provided access to physical evidence for the purpose of examination, including, but not limited to, any physical evidence relating to the investigation, arrest, and prosecution of the defendant only upon a showing that there is good cause to believe that access to physical evidence is reasonably necessary to the defendant's effort to obtain relief. The procedures for obtaining access to physical evidence for purposes of postconviction DNA testing are provided in Section 1405, and this section does not provide an alternative means of access to physical evidence for those purposes.
(e) The actual costs of examination or copying pursuant to this section shall be borne or reimbursed by the defendant.
(f) This section does not require the retention of any discovery materials not otherwise required by law or court order.
(g) In criminal matters involving a conviction for a serious or a violent felony resulting in a sentence of 15 years or more, trial counsel shall retain a copy of a former client's files for the term of his or her imprisonment. An electronic copy is sufficient only if every item in the file is digitally copied and preserved.
(h) As used in this section, a "serious felony" is a conviction of a felony enumerated in subdivision (c) of Section 1192.7.
(i) As used in this section, a "violent felony" is a conviction of a felony enumerated in subdivision (c) of Section 667.5.
(j) The changes made to this section by the act that added this subdivision are intended to only apply prospectively.
(Amended by Stats. 2018, Ch. 482, Sec. 2. (AB 1987) Effective January 1, 2019.)
1054.10.
(a) Except as provided in subdivision (b), no attorney may disclose or permit to be disclosed to a defendant, members of the defendant's family, or anyone else copies of child pornography evidence, unless specifically permitted to do so by the court after a hearing and a showing of good cause.
(b) Notwithstanding subdivision (a), an attorney may disclose or permit to be disclosed copies of child pornography evidence to persons employed by the attorney or to persons appointed by the court to assist in the preparation of a defendant's case if that disclosure is required for that preparation. Persons provided this material by an attorney shall be informed by the attorney that further dissemination of the material, except as provided by this section, is prohibited.
(Added by Stats. 2003, Ch. 238, Sec. 1. Effective August 11, 2003.)

CHAPTER 1. Challenging the Jury [1065 - 1089]

(Chapter 1 enacted 1872.)
1065.
If, either upon an exception to the challenge or a denial of the facts, the challenge is allowed, the Court must discharge the jury so far as the trial in question is concerned. If it is disallowed, the Court must direct the jury to be impaneled.
(Amended by Code Amendments 1880, Ch. 47.)
[1083.]

Section Ten Hundred and Eighty-three. The Court must allow or disallow the challenge, and its decision must be entered in the minutes of the Court.
(Amended by Code Amendments 1873-74, Ch. 614.)

1089.
Whenever, in the opinion of a judge of a superior court about to try a defendant against whom has been filed any indictment or information or complaint, the trial is likely to be a protracted one, the court may cause an entry to that effect to be made in the minutes of the court, and thereupon, immediately after the jury is impaneled and sworn, the court may direct the calling of one or more additional jurors, in its discretion, to be known as "alternate jurors."

The alternate jurors must be drawn from the same source, and in the same manner, and have the same qualifications as the jurors already sworn, and be subject to the same examination and challenges, provided that the prosecution and the defendant shall each be entitled to as many peremptory challenges to the alternate jurors as there are alternate jurors called. When two or more defendants are tried jointly each defendant shall be entitled to as many peremptory challenges to the alternate jurors as there are alternate jurors called. The prosecution shall be entitled to additional peremptory challenges equal to the number of all the additional separate challenges allowed the defendant or defendants to the alternate jurors.

The alternate jurors shall be seated so as to have equal power and facilities for seeing and hearing the proceedings in the case, and shall take the same oath as the jurors already selected, and must attend at all times upon the trial of the cause in company with the other jurors, and for a failure so to do are liable to be punished for contempt. They shall obey the orders of and be bound by the admonition of the court, upon each adjournment of the court; but if the regular jurors are ordered to be kept in the custody of the sheriff or marshal during the trial of the cause, the alternate jurors shall also be kept in confinement with the other jurors; and upon final submission of the case to the jury the alternate jurors shall be kept in the custody of the sheriff or marshal and shall not be discharged until the original jurors are discharged, except as hereinafter provided.

If at any time, whether before or after the final submission of the case to the jury, a juror dies or becomes ill, or upon other good cause shown to the court is found to be unable to perform his or her duty, or if a juror requests a discharge and good cause appears therefor, the court may order the juror to be discharged and draw the name of an alternate, who shall then take a place in the jury box, and be subject to the same rules and regulations as though the alternate juror had been selected as one of the original jurors.
(Amended by Stats. 2003, Ch. 62, Sec. 230. Effective January 1, 2004.)

CHAPTER 2. The Trial [1093 - 1130]

(Chapter 2 enacted 1872.)
1093.
The jury having been impaneled and sworn, unless waived, the trial shall proceed in the following order, unless otherwise directed by the court:
(a) If the accusatory pleading be for a felony, the clerk shall read it, and state the plea of the defendant to the jury, and in cases where it charges a previous conviction, and the defendant has confessed the same, the clerk in reading it shall omit therefrom all that relates to such previous conviction. In all other cases this formality may be dispensed with.
(b) The district attorney, or other counsel for the people, may make an opening statement in support of the charge. Whether or not the district attorney, or other counsel for the people, makes an opening statement, the defendant or his or her counsel may then make an opening statement, or may reserve the making of an opening statement until after introduction of the evidence in support of the charge.
(c) The district attorney, or other counsel for the people shall then offer the evidence in support of the charge. The defendant or his or her counsel may then offer his or her evidence in support of the defense.
(d) The parties may then respectively offer rebutting testimony only, unless the court, for good reason, in furtherance of justice, permit them to offer evidence upon their original case.
(e) When the evidence is concluded, unless the case is submitted on either side, or on both sides, without argument, the district attorney, or other counsel for the people, and counsel for the defendant, may argue the case to the court and jury; the district attorney, or other counsel for the people, opening the argument and having the right to close.
(f) The judge may then charge the jury, and shall do so on any points of law pertinent to the issue, if requested by either party; and the judge may state the testimony, and he or she may make such comment on the evidence and the testimony and credibility of any witness as in his or her opinion is necessary for the proper determination of the case and he or she may declare the law. At the beginning of the trial or from time to time during the trial, and without any request from either party, the trial judge may give the jury such instructions on the law applicable to the case as the judge may deem necessary for their guidance on hearing the case. Upon the jury retiring for deliberation, the court shall advise the jury of the availability of a written copy of the jury instructions. The court may, at its discretion, provide the jury with a copy of the written instructions given. However, if the jury requests the court to supply a copy of the written instructions, the court shall supply the jury with a copy.
(Amended by Stats. 1986, Ch. 1045, Sec. 2.)

1093.5.
In any criminal case which is being tried before the court with a jury, all requests for instructions on points of law must be made to the court and all proposed instructions must be delivered to the court before commencement of argument. Before the commencement of the argument, the court, on request of counsel, must: (1) decide whether to give, refuse, or modify the proposed instructions; (2) decide which instructions shall be given in addition to those proposed, if any; and (3) advise counsel of all instructions to be given. However, if, during the argument, issues are raised which have not been covered by instructions given or refused, the court may, on request of counsel, give additional instructions on the subject matter thereof.
(Added by Stats. 1957, Ch. 1698.)

1094.
When the state of the pleadings requires it, or in any other case, for good reasons, and in the sound discretion of the court, the order prescribed in Section 1093 may be departed from.
(Amended by Stats. 2009, Ch. 35, Sec. 11. (SB 174) Effective January 1, 2010.)

1095.
If the offense charged is punishable with death, two counsel on each side may argue the cause. In any other case the court may, in its discretion, restrict the argument to one counsel on each side.
(Amended by Stats. 1951, Ch. 1674.)

1096.
A defendant in a criminal action is presumed to be innocent until the contrary is proved, and in case of a reasonable doubt whether his or her guilt is satisfactorily shown, he or she is entitled to an acquittal, but the effect of this presumption is only to place upon the state the burden of proving him or her guilty beyond a reasonable doubt. Reasonable doubt is defined as follows: "It is not a mere possible doubt; because

everything relating to human affairs is open to some possible or imaginary doubt. It is that state of the case, which, after the entire comparison and consideration of all the evidence, leaves the minds of jurors in that condition that they cannot say they feel an abiding conviction of the truth of the charge."
(Amended by Stats. 1995, Ch. 46, Sec. 1. Effective July 3, 1995.)

1096a.
In charging a jury, the court may read to the jury Section 1096, and no further instruction on the subject of the presumption of innocence or defining reasonable doubt need be given.
(Amended by Stats. 1995, Ch. 46, Sec. 2. Effective July 3, 1995.)

1097.
When it appears that the defendant has committed a public offense, or attempted to commit a public offense, and there is reasonable ground of doubt in which of two or more degrees of the crime or attempted crime he is guilty, he can be convicted of the lowest of such degrees only.
(Amended by Stats. 1978, Ch. 1166.)

1098.
When two or more defendants are jointly charged with any public offense, whether felony or misdemeanor, they must be tried jointly, unless the court order separate trials. In ordering separate trials, the court in its discretion may order a separate trial as to one or more defendants, and a joint trial as to the others, or may order any number of the defendants to be tried at one trial, and any number of the others at different trials, or may order a separate trial for each defendant; provided, that where two or more persons can be jointly tried, the fact that separate accusatory pleadings were filed shall not prevent their joint trial.
(Amended by Stats. 1955, Ch. 103.)

1099.
When two or more defendants are included in the same accusatory pleading, the court may, at any time before the defendants have gone into their defense, on the application of the prosecuting attorney, direct any defendant to be discharged, that he may be a witness for the people.
(Amended by Stats. 1951, Ch. 1674.)

1100.
When two or more defendants are included in the same accusatory pleading, and the court is of opinion that in regard to a particular defendant there is not sufficient evidence to put him on his defense, it must order him to be discharged before the evidence is closed, that he may be a witness for his codefendant.
(Amended by Stats. 1951, Ch. 1674.)

1101.
The order mentioned in Sections 1099 and 1100 is an acquittal of the defendant discharged, and is a bar to another prosecution for the same offense.
(Amended by Stats. 1987, Ch. 828, Sec. 64.)

1102.
The rules of evidence in civil actions are applicable also to criminal actions, except as otherwise provided in this Code.
(Enacted 1872.)

1102.6.
The right of a victim of crime to be present during any criminal proceeding shall be secured as follows:
(a) Notwithstanding any other law, and except as specified in subdivision (d), a victim shall be entitled to be present and seated at all criminal proceedings where the defendant, the prosecuting attorney, and the general public are entitled to be present.
(b) A victim may be excluded from a criminal proceeding only if each of the following criteria are met:
(1) Any movant, including the defendant, who seeks to exclude the victim from any criminal proceeding demonstrates that there is a substantial probability that overriding interests will be prejudiced by the presence of the victim. "Overriding interests" may include, but are not limited to, the following:
(A) The defendant's right to a fair trial.
(B) The government's interest in inhibiting the disclosure of sensitive information.
(C) The protection of witnesses from harassment and physical harm.
(D) The court's interest in maintaining order.
(E) The protection of sexual offense victims from the trauma and embarrassment of testifying.
(F) Safeguarding the physical and psychological well-being of a minor.
(G) The preservation of trade secrets.
(2) The court considers reasonable alternatives to exclusion of the victim from the criminal proceeding.
(3) The exclusion of the victim from any criminal proceeding, or any limitation on his or her presence at any criminal proceeding, is narrowly tailored to serve the overriding interests identified by the movant.
(4) Following a hearing at which any victim who is to be excluded from a criminal proceeding is afforded an opportunity to be heard, the court makes specific factual findings that support the exclusion of the victim from, or any limitation on his or her presence at, the criminal proceeding.
(c) As used in this section, "victim" means (1) the alleged victim of the offense and one person of his or her choosing or however many more the court may allow under the particular circumstances surrounding the proceeding, (2) in the event that the victim is unable to attend the proceeding, two persons designated by the victim or however many more the court may allow under the particular circumstances surrounding the proceeding, or (3) if the victim is no longer living, two members of the victim's immediate family or however many more the court may allow under the particular circumstances surrounding the proceeding.
(d) Nothing in this section shall prevent a court from excluding a victim from a criminal proceeding, pursuant to Section 777 of the Evidence Code, when the victim is subpoenaed as a witness. An order of exclusion shall be consistent with the objectives of paragraphs (1) to (4), inclusive, of subdivision (b) to allow the victim to be present, whenever possible, at all proceedings.
(Repealed and added by Stats. 1995, Ch. 332, Sec. 3. Effective January 1, 1996.)

1108.
Upon a trial for procuring or attempting to procure an abortion, or aiding or assisting therein, or for inveigling, enticing, or taking away an unmarried female of previous chaste character, under the age of eighteen years, for the purpose of prostitution, or aiding or assisting therein, the defendant cannot be convicted upon the testimony of the woman upon or with whom the offense was committed, unless she is corroborated by other evidence.
(Amended by Stats. 1905, Ch. 533.)

1111.
A conviction can not be had upon the testimony of an accomplice unless it be corroborated by such other evidence as shall tend to connect the defendant with the commission of the offense; and the corroboration is not sufficient if it merely shows the commission of the offense or the circumstances thereof.
An accomplice is hereby defined as one who is liable to prosecution for the identical offense charged against the defendant on trial in the cause in which the testimony of the accomplice is given.
(Amended by Stats. 1915, Ch. 457.)

1111.5.
(a) A jury or judge may not convict a defendant, find a special circumstance true, or use a fact in aggravation based on the uncorroborated testimony of an in-custody informant.

The testimony of an in-custody informant shall be corroborated by other evidence that connects the defendant with the commission of the offense, the special circumstance, or the evidence offered in aggravation to which the in-custody informant testifies. Corroboration is not sufficient if it merely shows the commission of the offense or the special circumstance or the circumstance in aggravation. Corroboration of an in-custody informant shall not be provided by the testimony of another in-custody informant unless the party calling the in-custody informant as a witness establishes by a preponderance of the evidence that the in-custody informant has not communicated with another in-custody informant on the subject of the testimony.

(b) As used in this section, "in-custody informant" means a person, other than a codefendant, percipient witness, accomplice, or coconspirator, whose testimony is based on statements allegedly made by the defendant while both the defendant and the informant were held within a city or county jail, state penal institution, or correctional institution. Nothing in this section limits or changes the requirements for corroboration of accomplice testimony pursuant to Section 1111.

(Added by Stats. 2011, Ch. 153, Sec. 1. (SB 687) Effective January 1, 2012.)

1112.
Notwithstanding the provisions of subdivision (d) of Section 28 of Article I of the California Constitution, the trial court shall not order any prosecuting witness, complaining witness, or any other witness, or victim in any sexual assault prosecution to submit to a psychiatric or psychological examination for the purpose of assessing his or her credibility.

(Amended by Stats. 1984, Ch. 1101, Sec. 1. Effective September 13, 1984.)

1113.
The Court may direct the jury to be discharged where it appears that it has not jurisdiction of the offense, or that the facts charged do not constitute an offense punishable by law.

(Amended by Code Amendments 1880, Ch. 47.)

1114.
If the jury be discharged because the Court has not jurisdiction of the offense charged, and it appear that it was committed out of the jurisdiction of this State, the defendant must be discharged.

(Amended by Code Amendments 1880, Ch. 47.)

1115.
If the offense was committed within the exclusive jurisdiction of another county of this State, the Court must direct the defendant to be committed for such time as it deems reasonable, to await a warrant from the proper county for his arrest; or if the offense is a misdemeanor only, it may admit him to bail in an undertaking, with sufficient sureties, that he will, within such time as the Court may appoint, render himself amenable to a warrant for his arrest from the proper county; and, if not sooner arrested thereon, will attend at the office of the Sheriff of the county where the trial was had, at a certain time particularly specified in the undertaking, to surrender himself upon the warrant, if issued, or that his bail will forfeit such sum as the Court may fix, to be mentioned in the undertaking; and the Clerk must forthwith transmit a certified copy of the indictment or information, and of all the papers filed in the action, to the District Attorney of the proper county, the expense of which transmission is chargeable to that county.

(Amended by Code Amendments 1880, Ch. 47.)

1116.
If the defendant is not arrested on a warrant from the proper county, as provided in section 1115, he must be discharged from custody, or his bail in the action is exonerated, or money deposited instead of bail must be refunded to him or to the person or persons found by the court to have deposited said money on behalf of said defendant, as the case may be, and the sureties in the undertaking, as mentioned in that section, must be discharged. If he is arrested, the same proceedings must be had thereon as upon the arrest of a defendant in another county on a warrant of arrest issued by a magistrate.

(Amended by Stats. 1935, Ch. 657.)

1117.
If the jury is discharged because the facts as charged do not constitute an offense punishable by law, the court must order that the defendant, if in custody, be discharged; or if admitted to bail, that his bail be exonerated; or, if he has deposited money or if money has been deposited by another or others instead of bail for his appearance, that the money be refunded to him or to the person or persons found by the court to have deposited said money on behalf of said defendant, unless in its opinion a new indictment or information can be framed upon which the defendant can be legally convicted, in which case it may direct the district attorney to file a new information, or (if the defendant has not been committed by a magistrate) direct that the case be submitted to the same or another grand jury; and the same proceedings must be had thereon as are prescribed in section 998; provided, that after such order or submission the defendant may be examined before a magistrate, and discharged or committed by him as in other cases.

(Amended by Stats. 1935, Ch. 657.)

1118.
In a case tried by the court without a jury, a jury having been waived, the court on motion of the defendant or on its own motion shall order the entry of a judgment of acquittal of one or more of the offenses charged in the accusatory pleading after the evidence of the prosecution has been closed if the court, upon weighing the evidence then before it, finds the defendant not guilty of such offense or offenses. If such a motion for judgment of acquittal at the close of the evidence offered by the prosecution is not granted, the defendant may offer evidence without first having reserved that right.

(Repealed and added by Stats. 1967, Ch. 256.)

1118.1.
In a case tried before a jury, the court on motion of the defendant or on its own motion, at the close of the evidence on either side and before the case is submitted to the jury for decision, shall order the entry of a judgment of acquittal of one or more of the offenses charged in the accusatory pleading if the evidence then before the court is insufficient to sustain a conviction of such offense or offenses on appeal. If such a motion for judgment of acquittal at the close of the evidence offered by the prosecution is not granted, the defendant may offer evidence without first having reserved that right.

(Added by Stats. 1967, Ch. 256.)

1118.2.
A judgment of acquittal entered pursuant to the provisions of Section 1118 or 1118.1 shall not be appealable and is a bar to any other prosecution for the same offense.

(Added by Stats. 1967, Ch. 256.)

1119.
When, in the opinion of the court, it is proper that the jury should view the place in which the offense is charged to have been committed, or in which any other material fact occurred, or any personal property which has been referred to in the evidence and cannot conveniently be brought into the courtroom, it may order the jury to be conducted in a body, in the custody of the sheriff or marshal, as the case may be, to the place, or to the property, which must be shown to them by a person appointed by the court for that purpose; and the officer must be sworn to suffer no person to speak or communicate with the jury, nor to do so himself or herself, on any subject connected with the trial, and to return them into court without unnecessary delay, or at a specified time.

(Amended by Stats. 1996, Ch. 872, Sec. 119. Effective January 1, 1997.)

1120.
If a juror has any personal knowledge respecting a fact in controversy in a cause, he or she must declare the same in open court during the trial. If, during the retirement of the jury, a juror declares a fact that could be evidence in the cause, as of his or her own knowledge, the jury must return into court. In either of these cases, the juror making the statement must be sworn as a witness and examined in the presence of the parties in order that the court may determine whether good cause exists for his or her discharge as a juror.

(Amended by Stats. 2010, Ch. 328, Sec. 161. (SB 1330) Effective January 1, 2011.)

1121.
The jurors sworn to try an action may, in the discretion of the court, be permitted to separate or be kept in charge of a proper officer. Where the jurors are permitted to separate, the court shall properly admonish them. Where the jurors are kept in charge of a proper officer, the officer must be sworn to keep the jurors together until the next meeting of the court, to suffer no person to speak to them or communicate with them, nor to do so himself, on any subject connected with the trial, and to return them into court at the next meeting thereof.

(Amended by Stats. 1969, Ch. 520.)

1122.
(a) After the jury has been sworn and before the people's opening address, the court shall instruct the jury generally concerning its basic functions, duties, and conduct. The instructions shall include, among other matters, all of the following admonitions:
(1) That the jurors shall not converse among themselves, or with anyone else, conduct research, or disseminate information on any subject connected with the trial. The court shall clearly explain, as part of the admonishment, that the prohibition on conversation, research, and dissemination of information applies to all forms of electronic and wireless communication.
(2) That they shall not read or listen to any accounts or discussions of the case reported by newspapers or other news media.
(3) That they shall not visit or view the premises or place where the offense or offenses charged were allegedly committed or any other premises or place involved in the case.
(4) That prior to, and within 90 days of, discharge, they shall not request, accept, agree to accept, or discuss with any person receiving or accepting, any payment or benefit in consideration for supplying any information concerning the trial.
(5) That they shall promptly report to the court any incident within their knowledge involving an attempt by any person to improperly influence any member of the jury.
(b) The jury shall also, at each adjournment of the court before the submission of the cause to the jury, whether permitted to separate or kept in charge of officers, be admonished by the court that it is their duty not to conduct research, disseminate information, or converse among themselves, or with anyone else, on any subject connected with the trial, or to form or express any opinion about the case until the cause is finally submitted to them. The court shall clearly explain, as part of the admonishment, that the prohibition on research, dissemination of information, and conversation applies to all forms of electronic and wireless communication.

(Amended by Stats. 2011, Ch. 181, Sec. 5. (AB 141) Effective January 1, 2012.)

1122.5.
(a) The court, in its discretion, may, at each adjournment of the court before the submission of the cause to the jury, admonish the jury, whether permitted to be separate or kept in charge of officers, that, on pain of contempt of court, no juror shall, prior to discharge, accept, agree to accept, or benefit, directly or indirectly, from any payment or other consideration for supplying any information concerning the trial.
(b) In enacting this section, the Legislature recognizes that the appearance of justice, and justice itself, may be undermined by any juror who, prior to discharge, accepts, agrees to accept, or benefits from valuable consideration for providing information concerning a criminal trial.

(Amended by Stats. 1995, Ch. 91, Sec. 128. Effective January 1, 1996.)

1124.
The Court must decide all questions of law which arise in the course of a trial.

(Enacted 1872.)

1126.
In a trial for any offense, questions of law are to be decided by the court, and questions of fact by the jury. Although the jury has the power to find a general verdict, which includes questions of law as well as of fact, they are bound, nevertheless, to receive as law what is laid down as such by the court.

(Amended by Stats. 2008, Ch. 699, Sec. 12. Effective January 1, 2009.)

1127.
All instructions given shall be in writing, unless there is a phonographic reporter present and he takes them down, in which case they may be given orally; provided however, that in all misdemeanor cases oral instructions may be given pursuant to stipulation of the prosecuting attorney and counsel for the defendant. In charging the jury the court may instruct the jury regarding the law applicable to the facts of the case, and may make such comment on the evidence and the testimony and credibility of any witness as in its opinion is necessary for the proper determination of the case and in any criminal case, whether the defendant testifies or not, his failure to explain or to deny by his testimony any evidence or facts in the case against him may be commented upon by the court. The court shall inform the jury in all cases that the jurors are the exclusive judges of all questions of fact submitted to them and of the credibility of the witnesses. Either party may present to the court any written charge on the law, but not with respect to matters of fact, and request that it be given. If the court thinks it correct and pertinent, it must be given; if not, it must be refused. Upon each charge presented and given or refused, the court must endorse and sign its decision and a statement showing which party requested it. If part be given and part refused, the court must distinguish, showing by the endorsement what part of the charge was given and what part refused.

(Amended by Stats. 1951, Ch. 1674.)

1127a.
(a) As used in this section, an "in-custody informant" means a person, other than a codefendant, percipient witness, accomplice, or coconspirator whose testimony is based upon statements made by the defendant while both the defendant and the informant are held within a correctional institution.
(b) In any criminal trial or proceeding in which an in-custody informant testifies as a witness, upon the request of a party, the court shall instruct the jury as follows:
"The testimony of an in-custody informant should be viewed with caution and close scrutiny. In evaluating such testimony, you should consider the extent to which it may have been influenced by the receipt of, or expectation of, any benefits from the party calling that witness. This does not mean that you may arbitrarily disregard such testimony, but you should give it the weight to which you find it to be entitled in the light of all the evidence in the case."
(c) When the prosecution calls an in-custody informant as a witness in any criminal trial, contemporaneous with the calling of that witness, the prosecution shall file with the court a written statement setting out any and all consideration promised to, or received by, the in-custody informant.
The statement filed with the court shall not expand or limit the defendant's right to discover information that is otherwise provided by law. The statement shall be provided to the defendant or the defendant's attorney prior to trial and the information contained in the statement shall be subject to rules of evidence.
(d) For purposes of subdivision (c), "consideration" means any plea bargain, bail consideration, reduction or modification of sentence, or any other leniency, benefit, immunity, financial assistance, reward, or amelioration of current or future conditions of incarceration in return for, or in connection with, the informant's testimony in the criminal proceeding in which the prosecutor intends to call him or her as a witness.

(Added by Stats. 1989, Ch. 901, Sec. 1.)

1127b.

When, in any criminal trial or proceeding, the opinion of any expert witness is received in evidence, the court shall instruct the jury substantially as follows:

Duly qualified experts may give their opinions on questions in controversy at a trial. To assist the jury in deciding such questions, the jury may consider the opinion with the reasons stated therefor, if any, by the expert who gives the opinion. The jury is not bound to accept the opinion of any expert as conclusive, but should give to it the weight to which they shall find it to be entitled. The jury may, however, disregard any such opinion, if it shall be found by them to be unreasonable.

No further instruction on the subject of opinion evidence need be given.

(Added by Stats. 1929, Ch. 876.)

1127c.

In any criminal trial or proceeding where evidence of flight of a defendant is relied upon as tending to show guilt, the court shall instruct the jury substantially as follows:

The flight of a person immediately after the commission of a crime, or after he is accused of a crime that has been committed, is not sufficient in itself to establish his guilt, but is a fact which, if proved, the jury may consider in deciding his guilt or innocence. The weight to which such circumstance is entitled is a matter for the jury to determine.

No further instruction on the subject of flight need be given.

(Added by Stats. 1929, Ch. 875.)

1127d.

(a) In any criminal prosecution for the crime of rape, or for violation of Section 261.5, or for an attempt to commit, or assault with intent to commit, any such crime, the jury shall not be instructed that it may be inferred that a person who has previously consented to sexual intercourse with persons other than the defendant or with the defendant would be therefore more likely to consent to sexual intercourse again. However, if evidence was received that the victim consented to and did engage in sexual intercourse with the defendant on one or more occasions prior to that charged against the defendant in this case, the jury shall be instructed that this evidence may be considered only as it relates to the question of whether the victim consented to the act of intercourse charged against the defendant in the case, or whether the defendant had a good faith reasonable belief that the victim consented to the act of sexual intercourse. The jury shall be instructed that it shall not consider this evidence for any other purpose.

(b) A jury shall not be instructed that the prior sexual conduct in and of itself of the complaining witness may be considered in determining the credibility of the witness pursuant to Chapter 6 (commencing with Section 780) of Division 6 of the Evidence Code.

(Amended by Stats. 1990, Ch. 269, Sec. 1.)

1127e.

The term "unchaste character" shall not be used by any court in any criminal case in which the defendant is charged with a violation of Section 261, 261.5, or 262 of the Penal Code, or attempt to commit or assault with intent to commit any crime defined in any of these sections, in any instruction to the jury.

(Amended by Stats. 1994, Ch. 1188, Sec. 11. Effective January 1, 1995.)

1127f.

In any criminal trial or proceeding in which a child 10 years of age or younger testifies as a witness, upon the request of a party, the court shall instruct the jury, as follows:

In evaluating the testimony of a child you should consider all of the factors surrounding the child's testimony, including the age of the child and any evidence regarding the child's level of cognitive development. Although, because of age and level of cognitive development, a child may perform differently as a witness from an adult, that does not mean that a child is any more or less credible a witness than an adult. You should not discount or distrust the testimony of a child solely because he or she is a child.

(Added by Stats. 1986, Ch. 1051, Sec. 3.)

1127g.

In any criminal trial or proceeding in which a person with a developmental disability, or cognitive, mental, or communication impairment testifies as a witness, upon the request of a party, the court shall instruct the jury, as follows:

In evaluating the testimony of a person with a developmental disability, or cognitive, mental, or communication impairment, you should consider all of the factors surrounding the person's testimony, including their level of cognitive development. Although, because of his or her level of cognitive development, a person with a developmental disability, or cognitive, mental, or communication impairment may perform differently as a witness, that does not mean that a person with a developmental disability, or cognitive, mental, or communication impairment is any more or less credible a witness than another witness. You should not discount or distrust the testimony of a person with a developmental disability, or cognitive, mental, or communication impairment solely because he or she is a person with a developmental disability, or cognitive, mental, or communication impairment.

(Added by Stats. 2004, Ch. 823, Sec. 15. Effective January 1, 2005.)

1127h.

In any criminal trial or proceeding, upon the request of a party, the court shall instruct the jury substantially as follows:

"Do not let bias, sympathy, prejudice, or public opinion influence your decision. Bias includes bias against the victim or victims, witnesses, or defendant based upon his or her disability, gender, nationality, race or ethnicity, religion, gender identity, or sexual orientation."

(Added by Stats. 2006, Ch. 550, Sec. 3. Effective January 1, 2007.)

1128.

After hearing the charge, the jury may either decide in court or may retire for deliberation. If they do not agree without retiring for deliberation, an officer shall be sworn to keep them together for deliberation in some private and convenient place, and, during the deliberation, not to permit any person to speak to or communicate with them, including any form of electronic or wireless communication, nor to do so himself or herself, unless by order of the court, or to ask them whether they have agreed upon a verdict, and to return them into court when they have so agreed, or when ordered by the court. The court shall fix the time and place for deliberation. The jurors shall not deliberate on the case except under those circumstances. If the jurors are permitted by the court to separate, the court shall properly admonish them as provided in subdivision (b) of Section 1122. If the jury is composed of both men and women, and the jurors are not permitted by the court to separate, in the event that it becomes necessary to retire for the night, the women shall be kept in a room or rooms separate and apart from the men.

(Amended by Stats. 2011, Ch. 181, Sec. 6. (AB 141) Effective January 1, 2012.)

1129.

When a defendant who has given bail appears for trial, the Court may, in its discretion, at any time after his appearance for trial, order him to be committed to the custody of the proper officer of the county, to abide the judgment or further order of the court, and he must be committed and held in custody accordingly.

(Enacted 1872.)

1130.

If the prosecuting attorney fails to attend at the trial of a felony, the court must appoint an attorney at law to perform the duties of the prosecuting attorney on such trial.

(Amended by Stats. 1998, Ch. 931, Sec. 389. Effective September 28, 1998.)

CHAPTER 3. Conduct of the Jury After the Cause Is Submitted to Them [1137 - 1142]

(Chapter 3 enacted 1872.)

1137.

Upon retiring for deliberation, the jury may take with them all papers (except depositions) which have been received as evidence in the cause, or copies of such public records or private documents given in evidence as ought not, in the opinion of the court, to be taken from the person having them in possession. They may also take with them the written instructions given, and notes of the testimony or other proceedings on the trial, taken by themselves or any of them, but none taken by any other person. The court shall provide for the custody and safekeeping of such items.

(Amended by Stats. 1969, Ch. 520.)

1138.

After the jury have retired for deliberation, if there be any disagreement between them as to the testimony, or if they desire to be informed on any point of law arising in the case, they must require the officer to conduct them into court. Upon being brought into court, the information required must be given in the presence of, or after notice to, the prosecuting attorney, and the defendant or his counsel, or after they have been called.

(Amended by Stats. 1951, Ch. 1674.)

1138.5.

Except for good cause shown, the judge in his of her discretion need not be present in the court while testimony previously received in evidence is read to the jury.

(Added by Stats. 1987, Ch. 88, Sec. 2. Effective July 2, 1987.)

1140.

Except as provided by law, the jury cannot be discharged after the cause is submitted to them until they have agreed upon their verdict and rendered it in open court, unless by consent of both parties, entered upon the minutes, or unless, at the expiration of such time as the court may deem proper, it satisfactorily appears that there is no reasonable probability that the jury can agree.

(Amended by Stats. 1949, Ch. 1313.)

1141.

In all cases where a jury is discharged or prevented from giving a verdict by reason of an accident or other cause, except where the defendant is discharged during the progress of the trial, or after the cause is submitted to them, the cause may be again tried.

(Amended by Code Amendments 1880, Ch. 47.)

1142.

While the jury are absent the Court may adjourn from time to time, as to other business, but it must nevertheless be open for every purpose connected with the cause submitted to the jury until a verdict is rendered or the jury discharged.

(Enacted 1872.)

CHAPTER 4. The Verdict or Finding [1147 - 1168]

(Heading of Chapter 4 amended by Stats. 1951, Ch. 1674.)

1147.

When the jury have agreed upon their verdict, they must be conducted into court by the officer having them in charge. Their names must then be called, and if all do not appear, the rest must be discharged without giving a verdict. In that case the action may be again tried.

(Amended by Stats. 1905, Ch. 534.)

1148.

If charged with a felony the defendant must, before the verdict is received, appear in person, unless, after the exercise of reasonable diligence to procure the presence of the defendant, the court shall find that it will be in the interest of justice that the verdict be received in his absence. If for a misdemeanor, the verdict may be rendered in his absence.

(Amended by Stats. 1931, Ch. 124.)

1149.

When the jury appear they must be asked by the Court, or Clerk, whether they have agreed upon their verdict, and if the foreman answers in the affirmative, they must, on being required, declare the same.

(Enacted 1872.)

1150.

The jury must render a general verdict, except that in a felony case, when they are in doubt as to the legal effect of the facts proved, they may, except upon a trial for libel, find a special verdict.

(Amended by Stats. 1998, Ch. 931, Sec. 390. Effective September 28, 1998.)

1151.

A general verdict upon a plea of not guilty is either "guilty" or "not guilty," which imports a conviction or acquittal of the offense charged in the accusatory pleading. Upon a plea of a former conviction or acquittal of the offense charged, or upon a plea of once in jeopardy, the general verdict is either "for the people" or "for the defendant." When the defendant is acquitted on the ground of a variance between the accusatory pleading and the proof, the verdict is "not guilty by reason of variance between charge and proof."

(Amended by Stats. 1951, Ch. 1674.)

1152.

A special verdict is that by which the jury find the facts only, leaving the judgment to the Court. It must present the conclusions of fact as established by the evidence, and not the evidence to prove them, and these conclusions of fact must be so presented as that nothing remains to the Court but to draw conclusions of law upon them.

(Enacted 1872.)

1153.

The special verdict must be reduced to writing by the jury, or in their presence entered upon the minutes of the Court, read to the jury and agreed to by them, before they are discharged.

(Enacted 1872.)

1154.

The special verdict need not be in any particular form, but is sufficient if it presents intelligibly the facts found by the jury.

(Amended by Stats. 1987, Ch. 828, Sec. 65.)

1155.

The court must give judgment upon the special verdict as follows:

1. If the plea is not guilty, and the facts prove the defendant guilty of the offense charged in the indictment or information, or of any other offense of which he could be convicted under that indictment or information, judgment must be given accordingly. But if otherwise, judgment of acquittal must be given.

2. If the plea is a former conviction or acquittal or once in jeopardy of the same offense, the court must give judgment of acquittal or conviction, as the facts prove or fail to prove the former conviction or acquittal or jeopardy.

(Amended by Stats. 1951, Ch. 1674.)

1156.

If the jury do not, in a special verdict, pronounce affirmatively or negatively on the facts necessary to enable the court to give judgment, or if they find the evidence of facts merely, and not the conclusions of fact, from the evidence, as established to their satisfaction, the court shall direct the jury to retire and return another special verdict.

The court may explain to the jury the defect or insufficiency in the special verdict returned, and the form which the special verdict to be returned must take.
(Amended by Stats. 1927, Ch. 602.)

1157.

Whenever a defendant is convicted of a crime or attempt to commit a crime which is distinguished into degrees, the jury, or the court if a jury trial is waived, must find the degree of the crime or attempted crime of which he is guilty. Upon the failure of the jury or the court to so determine, the degree of the crime or attempted crime of which the defendant is guilty, shall be deemed to be of the lesser degree.
(Amended by Stats. 1978, Ch. 1166.)

1158.

Whenever the fact of a previous conviction of another offense is charged in an accusatory pleading, and the defendant is found guilty of the offense with which he is charged, the jury, or the judge if a jury trial is waived, must unless the answer of the defendant admits such previous conviction, find whether or not he has suffered such previous conviction. The verdict or finding upon the charge of previous conviction may be: "We (or I) find the charge of previous conviction true" or "We (or I) find the charge of previous conviction not true," according as the jury or the judge find that the defendant has or has not suffered such conviction. If more than one previous conviction is charged a separate finding must be made as to each.
(Amended by Stats. 1951, Ch. 1674.)

1158a.

(a) Whenever the fact that a defendant was armed with a weapon either at the time of his commission of the offense or at the time of his arrest, or both, is charged in accordance with section 969c of this code, in any count of the indictment or information to which the defendant has entered a plea of not guilty, the jury, if they find a verdict of guilty of the offense with which the defendant is charged, or of any offense included therein, must also find whether or not the defendant was armed as charged in the count to which the plea of not guilty was entered. The verdict of the jury upon a charge of being armed may be: "We find the charge of being armed contained in the _____ count true," or "We find the charge of being armed contained in the _____ count not true," as they find that the defendant was or was not armed as charged in any particular count of the indictment or information. A separate verdict upon the charge of being armed must be returned for each count which alleges that the defendant was armed.

(b) Whenever the fact that a defendant used a firearm is charged in accordance with Section 969d in any count of the indictment or information to which the defendant has entered a plea of not guilty, the jury if they find a verdict of guilty of the offense with which the defendant is charged must also find whether or not the defendant used a firearm as charged in the count to which the plea of not guilty was entered. A verdict of the jury upon a charge of using a firearm may be: "We find the charge of using a firearm contained in the _____ count true," or "We find the charge of using a firearm contained in the _____ count not true," as they find that the defendant used or did not use a firearm as charged in any particular count of the indictment or information. A separate verdict upon the charge of using a firearm shall be returned for each count which alleges that defendant used a firearm.
(Amended by Stats. 1972, Ch. 1131, Sec. 2.)

1159.

The jury, or the judge if a jury trial is waived, may find the defendant guilty of any offense, the commission of which is necessarily included in that with which he is charged, or of an attempt to commit the offense.
(Amended by Stats. 1951, Ch. 1674.)

1160.

On a charge against two or more defendants jointly, if the jury cannot agree upon a verdict as to all, they may render a verdict as to the defendant or defendants in regard to whom they do agree, on which a judgment must be entered accordingly, and the case as to the other may be tried again.

Where two or more offenses are charged in any accusatory pleading, if the jury cannot agree upon a verdict as to all of them, they may render a verdict as to the charge or charges upon which they do agree, and the charges on which they do not agree may be tried again.
(Amended by Stats. 1951, Ch. 1674.)

1161.

When there is a verdict of conviction, in which it appears to the Court that the jury have mistaken the law, the Court may explain the reason for that opinion and direct the jury to reconsider their verdict, and if, after the reconsideration, they return the same verdict, it must be entered; but when there is a verdict of acquittal, the Court cannot require the jury to reconsider it. If the jury render a verdict which is neither general nor special, the Court may direct them to reconsider it, and it cannot be recorded until it is rendered in some form from which it can be clearly understood that the intent of the jury is either to render a general verdict or to find the facts specially and to leave the judgment to the Court.
(Enacted 1872.)

1162.

If the jury persist in finding an informal verdict, from which, however, it can be clearly understood that their intention is to find in favor of the defendant upon the issue, it must be entered in the terms in which it is found, and the Court must give judgment of acquittal. But no judgment of conviction can be given unless the jury expressly find against the defendant upon the issue, or judgment is given against him on a special verdict.
(Enacted 1872.)

1163.

When a verdict is rendered, and before it is recorded, the jury may be polled, at the request of either party, in which case they must be severally asked whether it is their verdict, and if any one answer in the negative, the jury must be sent out for further deliberation.
(Enacted 1872.)

1164.

(a) When the verdict given is receivable by the court, the clerk shall record it in full upon the minutes, and if requested by any party shall read it to the jury, and inquire of them whether it is their verdict. If any juror disagrees, the fact shall be entered upon the minutes and the jury again sent out; but if no disagreement is expressed, the verdict is complete, and the jury shall, subject to subdivision (b), be discharged from the case.

(b) No jury shall be discharged until the court has verified on the record that the jury has either reached a verdict or has formally declared its inability to reach a verdict on all issues before it, including, but not limited to, the degree of the crime or crimes charged, and the truth of any alleged prior conviction whether in the same proceeding or in a bifurcated proceeding.
(Amended by Stats. 1990, Ch. 800, Sec. 1.)

1165.

Where a general verdict is rendered or a finding by the court is made in favor of the defendant, except on a plea of not guilty by reason of insanity, a judgment of acquittal must be forthwith given. If such judgment is given, or a judgment imposing a fine only, without imprisonment for nonpayment is given, and the defendant is not detained for any other legal cause, he must be discharged, if in custody, as soon as the judgment is given, except that where the acquittal is because of a variance between the pleading and the proof which may be obviated by a new accusatory pleading, the court may order his detention, to the end that a new accusatory pleading may be preferred, in the same manner and with like effect as provided in Section 1117.
(Amended by Stats. 1951, Ch. 1674.)

1166.

If a general verdict is rendered against the defendant, or a special verdict is given, he or she must be remanded, if in custody, or if on bail he or she shall be committed to the proper officer of the county to await the judgment of the court upon the verdict, unless, upon considering the protection of the public, the seriousness of the offense charged and proven, the previous criminal record of the defendant, the probability of the defendant failing to appear for the judgment of the court upon the verdict, and public safety, the court concludes the evidence supports its decision to allow the defendant to remain out on bail. When committed, his or her bail is exonerated, or if money is deposited instead of bail it must be refunded to the defendant or to the person or persons found by the court to have deposited said money on behalf of said defendant.
(Amended by Stats. 1999, Ch. 570, Sec. 1. Effective January 1, 2000.)

1167.

When a jury trial is waived, the judge or justice before whom the trial is had shall, at the conclusion thereof, announce his findings upon the issues of fact, which shall be in substantially the form prescribed for the general verdict of a jury and shall be entered upon the minutes.
(Added by Stats. 1951, Ch. 1674.)

1168.

(a) Every person who commits a public offense, for which any specification of three time periods of imprisonment in any state prison or imprisonment pursuant to subdivision (h) of Section 1170 is now prescribed by law or for which only a single term of imprisonment in state prison or imprisonment pursuant to subdivision (h) of Section 1170 is specified shall, unless such convicted person be placed on probation, a new trial granted, or the imposing of sentence suspended, be sentenced pursuant to Chapter 4.5 (commencing with Section 1170) of Title 7 of Part 2.

(b) For any person not sentenced under such provision, but who is sentenced to be imprisoned in the state prison or imprisonment pursuant to subdivision (h) of Section 1170, including imprisonment not exceeding one year and one day, the court imposing the sentence shall not fix the term or duration of the period of imprisonment.
(Amended by Stats. 2011, Ch. 15, Sec. 449. (AB 109) Effective April 4, 2011. Operative October 1, 2011, by Sec. 636 of Ch. 15, as amended by Stats. 2011, Ch. 39, Sec. 68.)

CHAPTER 4.5. Trial Court Sentencing [1170 - 1170.9]

(Chapter 4.5 added by Stats. 1976, Ch. 1139.)

ARTICLE 1. Initial Sentencing [1170 - 1170.95]

(Article 1 added by Stats. 1976, Ch. 1139.)

1170.

(a) (1) The Legislature finds and declares that the purpose of sentencing is public safety achieved through punishment, rehabilitation, and restorative justice. When a sentence includes incarceration, this purpose is best served by terms that are proportionate to the seriousness of the offense with provision for uniformity in the sentences of offenders committing the same offense under similar circumstances.

(2) The Legislature further finds and declares that programs should be available for inmates, including, but not limited to, educational, rehabilitative, and restorative justice programs that are designed to promote behavior change and to prepare all eligible offenders for successful reentry into the community. The Legislature encourages the development of policies and programs designed to educate and rehabilitate all eligible offenders. In implementing this section, the Department of Corrections and Rehabilitation is encouraged to allow all eligible inmates the opportunity to enroll in programs that promote successful return to the community. The Department of Corrections and Rehabilitation is directed to establish a mission statement consistent with these principles.

(3) In any case in which the sentence prescribed by statute for a person convicted of a public offense is a term of imprisonment in the state prison or a term pursuant to subdivision (h) of any specification of three time periods, the court shall sentence the defendant to one of the terms of imprisonment specified unless the convicted person is given any other disposition provided by law, including a fine, jail, probation, or the suspension of imposition or execution of sentence or is sentenced pursuant to subdivision (b) of Section 1168 because he or she had committed his or her crime prior to July 1, 1977. In sentencing the convicted person, the court shall apply the sentencing rules of the Judicial Council. The court, unless it determines that there are circumstances in mitigation of the sentence prescribed, shall also impose any other term that it is required by law to impose as an additional term. Nothing in this article shall affect any provision of law that imposes the death penalty, that authorizes or restricts the granting of probation or suspending the execution or imposition of sentence, or expressly provides for imprisonment in the state prison for life, except as provided in paragraph (2) of subdivision (d). In any case in which the amount of preimprisonment credit under Section 2900.5 or any other law is equal to or exceeds any sentence imposed pursuant to this chapter, except for the remaining portion of mandatory supervision pursuant to subparagraph (B) of paragraph (5) of subdivision (h), the entire sentence shall be deemed to have been served, except for the remaining period of mandatory supervision, and the defendant shall not be actually delivered to the custody of the secretary or to the custody of the county correctional administrator. The court shall advise the defendant that he or she shall serve an applicable period of parole, postrelease community supervision, or mandatory supervision, and order the defendant to report to the parole or probation office closest to the defendant's last legal residence, unless the in-custody credits equal the total sentence, including both confinement time and the period of parole, postrelease community supervision, or mandatory supervision. The sentence shall be deemed a separate prior prison term or a sentence of imprisonment in a county jail under subdivision (h) for purposes of Section 667.5, and a copy of the judgment and other necessary documentation shall be forwarded to the secretary.

(b) When a judgment of imprisonment is to be imposed and the statute specifies three possible terms, the choice of the appropriate term shall rest within the sound discretion of the court. At least four days prior to the time set for imposition of judgment, either party or the victim, or the family of the victim if the victim is deceased, may submit a statement in aggravation or mitigation. In determining the appropriate term, the court may consider the record in the case, the probation officer's report, other reports, including reports received pursuant to Section 1203.03, and statements in aggravation or mitigation submitted by the prosecution, the defendant, or the victim, or the family of the victim if the victim is deceased, and any further evidence introduced at the sentencing hearing. The court shall select the term which, in the court's discretion, best serves the interests of justice. The court shall set forth on the record the reasons for imposing the term selected and the court may not impose an upper term by using the fact of any enhancement upon which sentence is imposed under any provision of law. A term of imprisonment shall not be specified if imposition of sentence is suspended.

(c) The court shall state the reasons for its sentence choice on the record at the time of sentencing. The court shall also inform the defendant that as part of the sentence after expiration of the term he or she may be on parole for a period as provided in Section 3000 or 3000.08 or postrelease community supervision for a period as provided in Section 3451.

(d) (1) When a defendant subject to this section or subdivision (b) of Section 1168 has been sentenced to be imprisoned in the state prison or a county jail pursuant to

subdivision (h) and has been committed to the custody of the secretary or the county correctional administrator, the court may, within 120 days of the date of commitment on its own motion, or at any time upon the recommendation of the secretary or the Board of Parole Hearings in the case of state prison inmates, the county correctional administrator in the case of county jail inmates, or the district attorney of the county in which the defendant was sentenced, recall the sentence and commitment previously ordered and resentence the defendant in the same manner as if he or she had not previously been sentenced, provided the new sentence, if any, is no greater than the initial sentence. The court resentencing under this subdivision shall apply the sentencing rules of the Judicial Council so as to eliminate disparity of sentences and to promote uniformity of sentencing. The court resentencing under this paragraph may reduce a defendant's term of imprisonment and modify the judgment, including a judgment entered after a plea agreement, if it is in the interest of justice. The court may consider postconviction factors, including, but not limited to, the inmate's disciplinary record and record of rehabilitation while incarcerated, evidence that reflects whether age, time served, and diminished physical condition, if any, have reduced the inmate's risk for future violence, and evidence that reflects that circumstances have changed since the inmate's original sentencing so that the inmate's continued incarceration is no longer in the interest of justice. Credit shall be given for time served.
(2) (A) (i) When a defendant who was under 18 years of age at the time of the commission of the offense for which the defendant was sentenced to imprisonment for life without the possibility of parole has been incarcerated for at least 15 years, the defendant may submit to the sentencing court a petition for recall and resentencing.
(ii) Notwithstanding clause (i), this paragraph shall not apply to defendants sentenced to life without parole for an offense where it was pled and proved that the defendant tortured, as described in Section 206, his or her victim or the victim was a public safety official, including any law enforcement personnel mentioned in Chapter 4.5 (commencing with Section 830) of Title 3, or any firefighter as described in Section 245.1, as well as any other officer in any segment of law enforcement who is employed by the federal government, the state, or any of its political subdivisions.
(B) The defendant shall file the original petition with the sentencing court. A copy of the petition shall be served on the agency that prosecuted the case. The petition shall include the defendant's statement that he or she was under 18 years of age at the time of the crime and was sentenced to life in prison without the possibility of parole, the defendant's statement describing his or her remorse and work towards rehabilitation, and the defendant's statement that one of the following is true:
(i) The defendant was convicted pursuant to felony murder or aiding and abetting murder provisions of law.
(ii) The defendant does not have juvenile felony adjudications for assault or other felony crimes with a significant potential for personal harm to victims prior to the offense for which the sentence is being considered for recall.
(iii) The defendant committed the offense with at least one adult codefendant.
(iv) The defendant has performed acts that tend to indicate rehabilitation or the potential for rehabilitation, including, but not limited to, availing himself or herself of rehabilitative, educational, or vocational programs, if those programs have been available at his or her classification level and facility, using self-study for self-improvement, or showing evidence of remorse.
(C) If any of the information required in subparagraph (B) is missing from the petition, or if proof of service on the prosecuting agency is not provided, the court shall return the petition to the defendant and advise the defendant that the matter cannot be considered without the missing information.
(D) A reply to the petition, if any, shall be filed with the court within 60 days of the date on which the prosecuting agency was served with the petition, unless a continuance is granted for good cause.
(E) If the court finds by a preponderance of the evidence that one or more of the statements specified in clauses (i) to (iv), inclusive, of subparagraph (B) is true, the court shall recall the sentence and commitment previously ordered and hold a hearing to resentence the defendant in the same manner as if the defendant had not previously been sentenced, provided that the new sentence, if any, is not greater than the initial sentence. Victims, or victim family members if the victim is deceased, shall retain the rights to participate in the hearing.
(F) The factors that the court may consider when determining whether to resentence the defendant to a term of imprisonment with the possibility of parole include, but are not limited to, the following:
(i) The defendant was convicted pursuant to felony murder or aiding and abetting murder provisions of law.
(ii) The defendant does not have juvenile felony adjudications for assault or other felony crimes with a significant potential for personal harm to victims prior to the offense for which the defendant was sentenced to life without the possibility of parole.
(iii) The defendant committed the offense with at least one adult codefendant.
(iv) Prior to the offense for which the defendant was sentenced to life without the possibility of parole, the defendant had insufficient adult support or supervision and had suffered from psychological or physical trauma, or significant stress.
(v) The defendant suffers from cognitive limitations due to mental illness, developmental disabilities, or other factors that did not constitute a defense, but influenced the defendant's involvement in the offense.
(vi) The defendant has performed acts that tend to indicate rehabilitation or the potential for rehabilitation, including, but not limited to, availing himself or herself of rehabilitative, educational, or vocational programs, if those programs have been available at his or her classification level and facility, using self-study for self-improvement, or showing evidence of remorse.
(vii) The defendant has maintained family ties or connections with others through letter writing, calls, or visits, or has eliminated contact with individuals outside of prison who are currently involved with crime.
(viii) The defendant has had no disciplinary actions for violent activities in the last five years in which the defendant was determined to be the aggressor.
(G) The court shall have the discretion to resentence the defendant in the same manner as if the defendant had not previously been sentenced, provided that the new sentence, if any, is not greater than the initial sentence. The discretion of the court shall be exercised in consideration of the criteria in subparagraph (F). Victims, or victim family members if the victim is deceased, shall be notified of the resentencing hearing and shall retain their rights to participate in the hearing.
(H) If the sentence is not recalled or the defendant is resentenced to imprisonment for life without the possibility of parole, the defendant may submit another petition for recall and resentencing to the sentencing court when the defendant has been committed to the custody of the department for at least 20 years. If the sentence is not recalled or the defendant is resentenced to imprisonment for life without the possibility of parole under that petition, the defendant may file another petition after having served 24 years. The final petition may be submitted, and the response to that petition shall be determined, during the 25th year of the defendant's sentence.
(I) In addition to the criteria in subparagraph (F), the court may consider any other criteria that the court deems relevant to its decision, so long as the court identifies them on the record, provides a statement of reasons for adopting them, and states why the defendant does or does not satisfy the criteria.
(J) This subdivision shall have retroactive application.
(K) Nothing in this paragraph is intended to diminish or abrogate any rights or remedies otherwise available to the defendant.
(e) (1) Notwithstanding any other law and consistent with paragraph (1) of subdivision (a), if the secretary or the Board of Parole Hearings or both determine that a prisoner satisfies the criteria set forth in paragraph (2), the secretary or the board may recommend to the court that the prisoner's sentence be recalled.
(2) The court shall have the discretion to resentence or recall if the court finds that the facts described in subparagraphs (A) and (B) or subparagraphs (B) and (C) exist:
(A) The prisoner is terminally ill with an incurable condition caused by an illness or disease that would produce death within six months, as determined by a physician employed by the department.
(B) The conditions under which the prisoner would be released or receive treatment do not pose a threat to public safety.
(C) The prisoner is permanently medically incapacitated with a medical condition that renders him or her permanently unable to perform activities of basic daily living, and results in the prisoner requiring 24-hour total care, including, but not limited to, coma, persistent vegetative state, brain death, ventilator-dependency, loss of control of muscular or neurological function, and that incapacitation did not exist at the time of the original sentencing.
The Board of Parole Hearings shall make findings pursuant to this subdivision before making a recommendation for resentence or recall to the court. This subdivision does not apply to a prisoner sentenced to death or a term of life without the possibility of parole.
(3) Within 10 days of receipt of a positive recommendation by the secretary or the board, the court shall hold a hearing to consider whether the prisoner's sentence should be recalled.
(4) Any physician employed by the department who determines that a prisoner has six months or less to live shall notify the chief medical officer of the prognosis. If the chief medical officer concurs with the prognosis, he or she shall notify the warden. Within 48 hours of receiving notification, the warden or the warden's representative shall notify the prisoner of the recall and resentencing procedures, and shall arrange for the prisoner to designate a family member or other outside agent to be notified as to the prisoner's medical condition and prognosis, and as to the recall and resentencing procedures. If the inmate is deemed mentally unfit, the warden or the warden's representative shall contact the inmate's emergency contact and provide the information described in paragraph (2).
(5) The warden or the warden's representative shall provide the prisoner and his or her family member, agent, or emergency contact, as described in paragraph (4), updated information throughout the recall and resentencing process with regard to the prisoner's medical condition and the status of the prisoner's recall and resentencing proceedings.
(6) Notwithstanding any other provisions of this section, the prisoner or his or her family member or designee may independently request consideration for recall and resentencing by contacting the chief medical officer at the prison or the secretary. Upon receipt of the request, the chief medical officer and the warden or the warden's representative shall follow the procedures described in paragraph (4). If the secretary determines that the prisoner satisfies the criteria set forth in paragraph (2), the secretary or board may recommend to the court that the prisoner's sentence be recalled. The secretary shall submit a recommendation for release within 30 days in the case of inmates sentenced to determinate terms and, in the case of inmates sentenced to indeterminate terms, the secretary shall make a recommendation to the Board of Parole Hearings with respect to the inmates who have applied under this section. The board shall consider this information and make an independent judgment pursuant to paragraph (2) and make findings related thereto before rejecting the request or making a recommendation to the court. This action shall be taken at the next lawfully noticed board meeting.
(7) Any recommendation for recall submitted to the court by the secretary or the Board of Parole Hearings shall include one or more medical evaluations, a postrelease plan, and findings pursuant to paragraph (2).
(8) If possible, the matter shall be heard before the same judge of the court who sentenced the prisoner.
(9) If the court grants the recall and resentencing application, the prisoner shall be released by the department within 48 hours of receipt of the court's order, unless a longer time period is agreed to by the inmate. At the time of release, the warden or the warden's representative shall ensure that the prisoner has each of the following in his or her possession: a discharge medical summary, full medical records, state identification, parole or postrelease community supervision medications, and all property belonging to the prisoner. After discharge, any additional records shall be sent to the prisoner's forwarding address.
(10) The secretary shall issue a directive to medical and correctional staff employed by the department that details the guidelines and procedures for initiating a recall and resentencing procedure. The directive shall clearly state that any prisoner who is given a prognosis of six months or less to live is eligible for recall and resentencing consideration, and that recall and resentencing procedures shall be initiated upon that prognosis.
(11) The provisions of this subdivision shall be available to an inmate who is sentenced to a county jail pursuant to subdivision (h). For purposes of those inmates, "secretary" or "warden" shall mean the county correctional administrator and "chief medical officer" shall mean a physician designated by the county correctional administrator for this purpose.
(f) Notwithstanding any other provision of this section, for purposes of paragraph (3) of subdivision (h), any allegation that a defendant is eligible for state prison due to a prior or current conviction, sentence enhancement, or because he or she is required to register as a sex offender shall not be subject to dismissal pursuant to Section 1385.
(g) A sentence to the state prison for a determinate term for which only one term is specified, is a sentence to the state prison under this section.
(h) (1) Except as provided in paragraph (3), a felony punishable pursuant to this subdivision where the term is not specified in the underlying offense shall be punishable by a term of imprisonment in a county jail for 16 months, or two or three years.
(2) Except as provided in paragraph (3), a felony punishable pursuant to this subdivision shall be punishable by imprisonment in a county jail for the term described in the underlying offense.
(3) Notwithstanding paragraphs (1) and (2), where the defendant (A) has a prior or current felony conviction for a serious felony described in subdivision (c) of Section 1192.7 or a prior or current conviction for a violent felony described in subdivision (c) of Section 667.5, (B) has a prior felony conviction in another jurisdiction for an offense that has all the elements of a serious felony described in subdivision (c) of Section 1192.7 or a violent felony described in subdivision (c) of Section 667.5, (C) is required to register as a sex offender pursuant to Chapter 5.5 (commencing with Section 290) of Title 9 of Part 1, or (D) is convicted of a crime and as part of the sentence an enhancement pursuant to Section 186.11 is imposed, an executed sentence for a felony punishable pursuant to this subdivision shall be served in the state prison.
(4) Nothing in this subdivision shall be construed to prevent other dispositions authorized by law, including pretrial diversion, deferred entry of judgment, or an order granting probation pursuant to Section 1203.1.
(5) (A) Unless the court finds that, in the interests of justice, it is not appropriate in a particular case, the court, when imposing a sentence pursuant to paragraph (1) or (2), shall suspend execution of a concluding portion of the term for a period selected at the court's discretion.
(B) The portion of a defendant's sentenced term that is suspended pursuant to this paragraph shall be known as mandatory supervision, and, unless otherwise ordered by the court, shall commence upon release from physical custody or an alternative custody program, whichever is later. During the period of mandatory supervision, the defendant shall be supervised by the county probation officer in accordance with the terms,

conditions, and procedures generally applicable to persons placed on probation, for the remaining unserved portion of the sentence imposed by the court. The period of supervision shall be mandatory, and may not be earlier terminated except by court order. Any proceeding to revoke or modify mandatory supervision under this subparagraph shall be conducted pursuant to either subdivisions (a) and (b) of Section 1203.2 or Section 1203.3. During the period when the defendant is under that supervision, unless in actual custody related to the sentence imposed by the court, the defendant shall be entitled to only actual time credit against the term of imprisonment imposed by the court. Any time period which is suspended because a person has absconded shall not be credited toward the period of supervision.

(6) When the court is imposing a judgment pursuant to this subdivision concurrent or consecutive to a judgment or judgments previously imposed pursuant to this subdivision in another county or counties, the court rendering the second or other subsequent judgment shall determine the county or counties of incarceration and supervision of the defendant.

(7) The sentencing changes made by the act that added this subdivision shall be applied prospectively to any person sentenced on or after October 1, 2011.

(8) The sentencing changes made to paragraph (5) by the act that added this paragraph shall become effective and operative on January 1, 2015, and shall be applied prospectively to any person sentenced on or after January 1, 2015.

(i) This section shall remain in effect only until January 1, 2022, and as of that date is repealed, unless a later enacted statute, that is enacted before January 1, 2022, deletes or extends that date.

(Amended (as amended by Stats. 2018, Ch. 36, Sec. 17) by Stats. 2018, Ch. 1001, Sec. 1. (AB 2942) Effective January 1, 2019. Repealed as of January 1, 2022, by its own provisions. See later operative version, as amended by Sec. 2 of Stats. 2018, Ch. 1001.)

1170.

(a) (1) The Legislature finds and declares that the purpose of sentencing is public safety achieved through punishment, rehabilitation, and restorative justice. When a sentence includes incarceration, this purpose is best served by terms that are proportionate to the seriousness of the offense with provision for uniformity in the sentences of offenders committing the same offense under similar circumstances.

(2) The Legislature further finds and declares that programs should be available for inmates, including, but not limited to, educational, rehabilitative, and restorative justice programs that are designed to promote behavior change and to prepare all eligible offenders for successful reentry into the community. The Legislature encourages the development of policies and programs designed to educate and rehabilitate all eligible offenders. In implementing this section, the Department of Corrections and Rehabilitation is encouraged to allow all eligible inmates the opportunity to enroll in programs that promote successful return to the community. The Department of Corrections and Rehabilitation is directed to establish a mission statement consistent with these principles.

(3) In any case in which the sentence prescribed by statute for a person convicted of a public offense is a term of imprisonment in the state prison, or a term pursuant to subdivision (h), of any specification of three time periods, the court shall sentence the defendant to one of the terms of imprisonment specified unless the convicted person is given any other disposition provided by law, including a fine, jail, probation, or the suspension of imposition or execution of sentence or is sentenced pursuant to subdivision (b) of Section 1168 because he or she had committed his or her crime prior to July 1, 1977. In sentencing the convicted person, the court shall apply the sentencing rules of the Judicial Council. The court, unless it determines that there are circumstances in mitigation of the sentence prescribed, shall also impose any other term that it is required by law to impose as an additional term. Nothing in this article shall affect any provision of law that imposes the death penalty, that authorizes or restricts the granting of probation or suspending the execution or imposition of sentence, or expressly provides for imprisonment in the state prison for life, except as provided in paragraph (2) of subdivision (d). In any case in which the amount of preimprisonment credit under Section 2900.5 or any other provision of law is equal to or exceeds any sentence imposed pursuant to this chapter, except for a remaining portion of mandatory supervision imposed pursuant to subparagraph (B) of paragraph (5) of subdivision (h), the entire sentence shall be deemed to have been served, except for the remaining period of mandatory supervision, and the defendant shall not be actually delivered to the custody of the secretary or the county correctional administrator. The court shall advise the defendant that he or she shall serve an applicable period of parole, postrelease community supervision, or mandatory supervision and order the defendant to report to the parole or probation office closest to the defendant's last legal residence, unless the in-custody credits equal the total sentence, including both confinement time and the period of parole, postrelease community supervision, or mandatory supervision. The sentence shall be deemed a separate prior prison term or a sentence of imprisonment in a county jail under subdivision (h) for purposes of Section 667.5, and a copy of the judgment and other necessary documentation shall be forwarded to the secretary.

(b) When a judgment of imprisonment is to be imposed and the statute specifies three possible terms, the court shall order imposition of the middle term, unless there are circumstances in aggravation or mitigation of the crime. At least four days prior to the time set for imposition of judgment, either party or the victim, or the family of the victim if the victim is deceased, may submit a statement in aggravation or mitigation to dispute facts in the record or the probation officer's report, or to present additional facts. In determining whether there are circumstances that justify imposition of the upper or lower term, the court may consider the record in the case, the probation officer's report, other reports, including reports received pursuant to Section 1203.03, and statements in aggravation or mitigation submitted by the prosecution, the defendant, or the victim, or the family of the victim if the victim is deceased, and any further evidence introduced at the sentencing hearing. The court shall set forth on the record the facts and reasons for imposing the upper or lower term. The court may not impose an upper term by using the fact of any enhancement upon which sentence is imposed under any provision of law. A term of imprisonment shall not be specified if imposition of sentence is suspended.

(c) The court shall state the reasons for its sentence choice on the record at the time of sentencing. The court shall also inform the defendant that as part of the sentence after expiration of the term he or she may be on parole for a period as provided in Section 3000 or 3000.08 or postrelease community supervision for a period as provided in Section 3451.

(d) (1) When a defendant subject to this section or subdivision (b) of Section 1168 has been sentenced to be imprisoned in the state prison or a county jail pursuant to subdivision (h) and has been committed to the custody of the secretary or the county correctional administrator, the court may, within 120 days of the date of commitment on its own motion, or at any time upon the recommendation of the secretary or the Board of Parole Hearings in the case of state prison inmates, the county correctional administrator in the case of county jail inmates, or the district attorney of the county in which the defendant was sentenced, recall the sentence and commitment previously ordered and resentence the defendant in the same manner as if he or she had not previously been sentenced, provided the new sentence, if any, is no greater than the initial sentence. The court resentencing under this subdivision shall apply the sentencing rules of the Judicial Council so as to eliminate disparity of sentences and to promote uniformity of sentencing. The court resentencing under this paragraph may reduce a defendant's term of imprisonment and modify the judgment, including a judgment entered after a plea agreement, if it is in the interest of justice. The court may consider

postconviction factors, including, but not limited to, the inmate's disciplinary record and record of rehabilitation while incarcerated, evidence that reflects whether age, time served, and diminished physical condition, if any, have reduced the inmate's risk for future violence, and evidence that reflects that circumstances have changed since the inmate's original sentencing so that the inmate's continued incarceration is no longer in the interest of justice. Credit shall be given for time served.

(2) (A) (i) When a defendant who was under 18 years of age at the time of the commission of the offense for which the defendant was sentenced to imprisonment for life without the possibility of parole has been incarcerated for at least 15 years, the defendant may submit to the sentencing court a petition for recall and resentencing.

(ii) Notwithstanding clause (i), this paragraph shall not apply to defendants sentenced to life without parole for an offense where it was pled and proved that the defendant tortured, as described in Section 206, his or her victim or the victim was a public safety official, including any law enforcement personnel mentioned in Chapter 4.5 (commencing with Section 830) of Title 3, or any firefighter as described in Section 245.1, as well as any other officer in any segment of law enforcement who is employed by the federal government, the state, or any of its political subdivisions.

(B) The defendant shall file the original petition with the sentencing court. A copy of the petition shall be served on the agency that prosecuted the case. The petition shall include the defendant's statement that he or she was under 18 years of age at the time of the crime and was sentenced to life in prison without the possibility of parole, the defendant's statement describing his or her remorse and work towards rehabilitation, and the defendant's statement that one of the following is true:

(i) The defendant was convicted pursuant to felony murder or aiding and abetting murder provisions of law.

(ii) The defendant does not have juvenile felony adjudications for assault or other felony crimes with a significant potential for personal harm to victims prior to the offense for which the sentence is being considered for recall.

(iii) The defendant committed the offense with at least one adult codefendant.

(iv) The defendant has performed acts that tend to indicate rehabilitation or the potential for rehabilitation, including, but not limited to, availing himself or herself of rehabilitative, educational, or vocational programs, if those programs have been available at his or her classification level and facility, using self-study for self-improvement, or showing evidence of remorse.

(C) If any of the information required in subparagraph (B) is missing from the petition, or if proof of service on the prosecuting agency is not provided, the court shall return the petition to the defendant and advise the defendant that the matter cannot be considered without the missing information.

(D) A reply to the petition, if any, shall be filed with the court within 60 days of the date on which the prosecuting agency was served with the petition, unless a continuance is granted for good cause.

(E) If the court finds by a preponderance of the evidence that one or more of the statements specified in clauses (i) to (iv), inclusive, of subparagraph (B) is true, the court shall recall the sentence and commitment previously ordered and hold a hearing to resentence the defendant in the same manner as if the defendant had not previously been sentenced, provided that the new sentence, if any, is not greater than the initial sentence. Victims, or victim family members if the victim is deceased, shall retain the rights to participate in the hearing.

(F) The factors that the court may consider when determining whether to resentence the defendant to a term of imprisonment with the possibility of parole include, but are not limited to, the following:

(i) The defendant was convicted pursuant to felony murder or aiding and abetting murder provisions of law.

(ii) The defendant does not have juvenile felony adjudications for assault or other felony crimes with a significant potential for personal harm to victims prior to the offense for which the defendant was sentenced to life without the possibility of parole.

(iii) The defendant committed the offense with at least one adult codefendant.

(iv) Prior to the offense for which the defendant was sentenced to life without the possibility of parole, the defendant had insufficient adult support or supervision and had suffered from psychological or physical trauma, or significant stress.

(v) The defendant suffers from cognitive limitations due to mental illness, developmental disabilities, or other factors that did not constitute a defense, but influenced the defendant's involvement in the offense.

(vi) The defendant has performed acts that tend to indicate rehabilitation or the potential for rehabilitation, including, but not limited to, availing himself or herself of rehabilitative, educational, or vocational programs, if those programs have been available at his or her classification level and facility, using self-study for self-improvement, or showing evidence of remorse.

(vii) The defendant has maintained family ties or connections with others through letter writing, calls, or visits, or has eliminated contact with individuals outside of prison who are currently involved with crime.

(viii) The defendant has had no disciplinary actions for violent activities in the last five years in which the defendant was determined to be the aggressor.

(G) The court shall have the discretion to resentence the defendant in the same manner as if the defendant had not previously been sentenced, provided that the new sentence, if any, is not greater than the initial sentence. The discretion of the court shall be exercised in consideration of the criteria in subparagraph (F). Victims, or victim family members if the victim is deceased, shall be notified of the resentencing hearing and shall retain their rights to participate in the hearing.

(H) If the sentence is not recalled or the defendant is resentenced to imprisonment for life without the possibility of parole, the defendant may submit another petition for recall and resentencing to the sentencing court when the defendant has been committed to the custody of the department for at least 20 years. If the sentence is not recalled or the defendant is resentenced to imprisonment for life without the possibility of parole under that petition, the defendant may file another petition after having served 24 years. The final petition may be submitted, and the response to that petition shall be determined, during the 25th year of the defendant's sentence.

(I) In addition to the criteria in subparagraph (F), the court may consider any other criteria that the court deems relevant to its decision, so long as the court identifies them on the record, provides a statement of reasons for adopting them, and states why the defendant does or does not satisfy the criteria.

(J) This subdivision shall have retroactive application.

(K) Nothing in this paragraph is intended to diminish or abrogate any rights or remedies otherwise available to the defendant.

(e) (1) Notwithstanding any other law and consistent with paragraph (1) of subdivision (a), if the secretary or the Board of Parole Hearings or both determine that a prisoner satisfies the criteria set forth in paragraph (2), the secretary or the board may recommend to the court that the prisoner's sentence be recalled.

(2) The court shall have the discretion to resentence or recall if the court finds that the facts described in subparagraphs (A) and (B) or subparagraphs (B) and (C) exist:

(A) The prisoner is terminally ill with an incurable condition caused by an illness or disease that would produce death within six months, as determined by a physician employed by the department.

(B) The conditions under which the prisoner would be released or receive treatment do not pose a threat to public safety.

(C) The prisoner is permanently medically incapacitated with a medical condition that renders him or her permanently unable to perform activities of basic daily living, and results in the prisoner requiring 24-hour total care, including, but not limited to, coma, persistent vegetative state, brain death, ventilator-dependency, loss of control of muscular or neurological function, and that incapacitation did not exist at the time of the original sentencing.

The Board of Parole Hearings shall make findings pursuant to this subdivision before making a recommendation for resentence or recall to the court. This subdivision does not apply to a prisoner sentenced to death or a term of life without the possibility of parole.

(3) Within 10 days of receipt of a positive recommendation by the secretary or the board, the court shall hold a hearing to consider whether the prisoner's sentence should be recalled.

(4) Any physician employed by the department who determines that a prisoner has six months or less to live shall notify the chief medical officer of the prognosis. If the chief medical officer concurs with the prognosis, he or she shall notify the warden. Within 48 hours of receiving notification, the warden or the warden's representative shall notify the prisoner of the recall and resentencing procedures, and shall arrange for the prisoner to designate a family member or other outside agent to be notified as to the prisoner's medical condition and prognosis, and as to the recall and resentencing procedures. If the inmate is deemed mentally unfit, the warden or the warden's representative shall contact the inmate's emergency contact and provide the information described in paragraph (2).

(5) The warden or the warden's representative shall provide the prisoner and his or her family member, agent, or emergency contact, as described in paragraph (4), updated information throughout the recall and resentencing process with regard to the prisoner's medical condition and the status of the prisoner's recall and resentencing proceedings.

(6) Notwithstanding any other provisions of this section, the prisoner or his or her family member or designee may independently request consideration for recall and resentencing by contacting the chief medical officer at the prison or the secretary. Upon receipt of the request, the chief medical officer and the warden or the warden's representative shall follow the procedures described in paragraph (4). If the secretary determines that the prisoner satisfies the criteria set forth in paragraph (2), the secretary or board may recommend to the court that the prisoner's sentence be recalled. The secretary shall submit a recommendation for release within 30 days in the case of inmates sentenced to determinate terms and, in the case of inmates sentenced to indeterminate terms, the secretary shall make a recommendation to the Board of Parole Hearings with respect to the inmates who have applied under this section. The board shall consider this information and make an independent judgment pursuant to paragraph (2) and make findings related thereto before rejecting the request or making a recommendation to the court. This action shall be taken at the next lawfully noticed board meeting.

(7) Any recommendation for recall submitted to the court by the secretary or the Board of Parole Hearings shall include one or more medical evaluations, a postrelease plan, and findings pursuant to paragraph (2).

(8) If possible, the matter shall be heard before the same judge of the court who sentenced the prisoner.

(9) If the court grants the recall and resentencing application, the prisoner shall be released by the department within 48 hours of receipt of the court's order, unless a longer time period is agreed to by the inmate. At the time of release, the warden or the warden's representative shall ensure that the prisoner has each of the following in his or her possession: a discharge medical summary, full medical records, state identification, parole or postrelease community supervision medications, and all property belonging to the prisoner. After discharge, any additional records shall be sent to the prisoner's forwarding address.

(10) The secretary shall issue a directive to medical and correctional staff employed by the department that details the guidelines and procedures for initiating a recall and resentencing procedure. The directive shall clearly state that any prisoner who is given a prognosis of six months or less to live is eligible for recall and resentencing consideration, and that recall and resentencing procedures shall be initiated upon that prognosis.

(11) The provisions of this subdivision shall be available to an inmate who is sentenced to a county jail pursuant to subdivision (h). For purposes of those inmates, "secretary" or "warden" shall mean the county correctional administrator and "chief medical officer" shall mean a physician designated by the county correctional administrator for this purpose.

(f) Notwithstanding any other provision of this section, for purposes of paragraph (3) of subdivision (h), any allegation that a defendant is eligible for state prison due to a prior or current conviction, sentence enhancement, or because he or she is required to register as a sex offender shall not be subject to dismissal pursuant to Section 1385.

(g) A sentence to the state prison for a determinate term for which only one term is specified, is a sentence to state prison under this section.

(h) (1) Except as provided in paragraph (3), a felony punishable pursuant to this subdivision where the term is not specified in the underlying offense shall be punishable by a term of imprisonment in a county jail for 16 months, or two or three years.

(2) Except as provided in paragraph (3), a felony punishable pursuant to this subdivision shall be punishable by imprisonment in a county jail for the term described in the underlying offense.

(3) Notwithstanding paragraphs (1) and (2), where the defendant (A) has a prior or current felony conviction for a serious felony described in subdivision (c) of Section 1192.7 or a prior or current conviction for a violent felony described in subdivision (c) of Section 667.5, (B) has a prior felony conviction in another jurisdiction for an offense that has all the elements of a serious felony described in subdivision (c) of Section 1192.7 or a violent felony described in subdivision (c) of Section 667.5, (C) is required to register as a sex offender pursuant to Chapter 5.5 (commencing with Section 290) of Title 9 of Part 1, or (D) is convicted of a crime and as part of the sentence an enhancement pursuant to Section 186.11 is imposed, an executed sentence for a felony punishable pursuant to this subdivision shall be served in the state prison.

(4) Nothing in this subdivision shall be construed to prevent other dispositions authorized by law, including pretrial diversion, deferred entry of judgment, or an order granting probation pursuant to Section 1203.1.

(5) (A) Unless the court finds, in the interest of justice, that it is not appropriate in a particular case, the court, when imposing a sentence pursuant to paragraph (1) or (2), shall suspend execution of a concluding portion of the term for a period selected at the court's discretion.

(B) The portion of a defendant's sentenced term that is suspended pursuant to this paragraph shall be known as mandatory supervision, and, unless otherwise ordered by the court, shall commence upon release from physical custody or an alternative custody program, whichever is later. During the period of mandatory supervision, the defendant shall be supervised by the county probation officer in accordance with the terms, conditions, and procedures generally applicable to persons placed on probation, for the remaining unserved portion of the sentence imposed by the court. The period of supervision shall be mandatory, and may not be earlier terminated except by court order. Any proceeding to revoke or modify mandatory supervision under this subparagraph shall be conducted pursuant to either subdivisions (a) and (b) of Section 1203.2 or Section 1203.3. During the period when the defendant is under that supervision, unless in actual custody related to the sentence imposed by the court, the defendant shall be entitled to only actual time credit against the term of imprisonment imposed by the court. Any time period which is suspended because a person has absconded shall not be credited toward the period of supervision.

(6) When the court is imposing a judgment pursuant to this subdivision concurrent or consecutive to a judgment or judgments previously imposed pursuant to this subdivision in another county or counties, the court rendering the second or other subsequent

judgment shall determine the county or counties of incarceration and supervision of the defendant.

(7) The sentencing changes made by the act that added this subdivision shall be applied prospectively to any person sentenced on or after October 1, 2011.

(8) The sentencing changes made to paragraph (5) by the act that added this paragraph shall become effective and operative on January 1, 2015, and shall be applied prospectively to any person sentenced on or after January 1, 2015.

(i) This section shall become operative on January 1, 2022.

(Amended (as amended by Stats. 2018, Ch. 36, Sec. 18) by Stats. 2018, Ch. 1001, Sec. 2. (AB 2942) Effective January 1, 2019. Section operative January 1, 2022, by its own provisions.)

1170.02.

A prisoner is not eligible for resentence or recall pursuant to subdivision (e) of Section 1170 if he or she was convicted of first-degree murder if the victim was a peace officer, as defined in Section 830.1, 830.2, 830.3, 830.31, 830.32, 830.33, 830.34, 830.35, 830.36, 830.37, 830.4, 830.5, 830.6, 830.10, 830.11, or 830.12, who was killed while engaged in the performance of his or her duties, and the individual knew, or reasonably should have known, that the victim was a peace officer engaged in the performance of his or her duties, or the victim was a peace officer or a former peace officer under any of the above-enumerated sections, and was intentionally killed in retaliation for the performance of his or her official duties.

(Added by Stats. 2016, Ch. 886, Sec. 1. (SB 6) Effective January 1, 2017.)

1170.05.

(a) Notwithstanding any other law, the Secretary of the Department of Corrections and Rehabilitation is authorized to offer a program under which female inmates as specified in subdivision (c), who are not precluded by subdivision (d), and who have been committed to state prison may be allowed to participate in a voluntary alternative custody program as defined in subdivision (b) in lieu of their confinement in state prison. In order to qualify for the program an offender need not be confined in an institution under the jurisdiction of the Department of Corrections and Rehabilitation. Under this program, one day of participation in an alternative custody program shall be in lieu of one day of incarceration in the state prison. Participants in the program shall receive any sentence reduction credits that they would have received had they served their sentence in the state prison, and shall be subject to denial and loss of credit pursuant to subdivision (a) of Section 2932. The department may enter into contracts with county agencies, not-for-profit organizations, for-profit organizations, and others in order to promote alternative custody placements.

(b) As used in this section, an alternative custody program shall include, but not be limited to, the following:

(1) Confinement to a residential home during the hours designated by the department.

(2) Confinement to a residential drug or treatment program during the hours designated by the department.

(3) Confinement to a transitional care facility that offers appropriate services.

(c) Except as provided by subdivision (d), female inmates sentenced to state prison for a determinate term of imprisonment pursuant to Section 1170, and only those persons, are eligible to participate in the alternative custody program authorized by this section.

(d) An inmate committed to the state prison who meets any of the following criteria is not eligible to participate in the alternative custody program:

(1) The person has a current conviction for a violent felony as defined in Section 667.5.

(2) The person has a current conviction for a serious felony as defined in Sections 1192.7 and 1192.8.

(3) The person has a current or prior conviction for an offense that requires the person to register as a sex offender as provided in Chapter 5.5 (commencing with Section 290) of Title 9 of Part 1.

(4) The person was screened by the department using a validated risk assessment tool and determined to pose a high risk to commit a violent offense.

(5) The person has a history, within the last 10 years, of escape from a facility while under juvenile or adult custody, including, but not limited to, any detention facility, camp, jail, or state prison facility.

(e) An alternative custody program shall include the use of electronic monitoring, global positioning system devices, or other supervising devices for the purpose of helping to verify a participant's compliance with the rules and regulations of the program. The devices shall not be used to eavesdrop or record any conversation, except a conversation between the participant and the person supervising the participant, in which case the recording of such a conversation is to be used solely for the purposes of voice identification.

(f) (1) In order to implement alternative custody for the population specified in subdivision (c), the department shall create, and the participant shall agree to and fully participate in, an individualized treatment and rehabilitation plan. When available and appropriate for the individualized treatment and rehabilitation plan, the department shall prioritize the use of evidence-based programs and services that will aid in the successful reentry into society while she takes part in alternative custody. Case management services shall be provided to support rehabilitation and to track the progress and individualized treatment plan compliance of the inmate.

(2) For purposes of this section, "evidence-based practices" means supervision policies, procedures, programs, and practices demonstrated by scientific research to reduce recidivism among individuals under probation, parole, or postrelease community supervision.

(g) The secretary shall prescribe reasonable rules and regulations under which the alternative custody program shall operate. The department shall adopt regulations necessary to effectuate this section, including emergency regulations as provided under Section 5058.3 and adopted pursuant to the Administrative Procedure Act (Chapter 3.5 (commencing with Section 11340) of Part 1 of Division 3 of Title 2 of the Government Code). The participant shall be informed in writing that she shall comply with the rules and regulations of the program, including, but not limited to, the following rules:

(1) The participant shall remain within the interior premises of her residence during the hours designated by the secretary or his or her designee.

(2) The participant shall be subject to search and seizure by a peace officer at any time of the day or night, with or without cause. In addition, the participant shall admit any peace officer designated by the secretary or his or her designee into the participant's residence at any time for purposes of verifying the participant's compliance with the conditions of her detention. Prior to participation in the alternative custody program, all participants shall agree in writing to these terms and conditions.

(3) The secretary or his or her designee may immediately retake the participant into custody to serve the balance of her sentence if the electronic monitoring or supervising devices are unable for any reason to properly perform their function at the designated place of detention, if the participant fails to remain within the place of detention as stipulated in the agreement, or if the participant for any other reason no longer meets the established criteria under this section.

(h) Whenever a peace officer supervising a participant has reasonable suspicion to believe that the participant is not complying with the rules or conditions of the program, or that the electronic monitoring devices are unable to function properly in the designated place of confinement, the peace officer may, under general or specific authorization of the secretary or his or her designee, and without a warrant of arrest, retake the participant into custody to complete the remainder of the original sentence.

(i) This section does not require the secretary or his or her designee to allow an inmate to participate in this program if it appears from the record that the inmate has not satisfactorily complied with reasonable rules and regulations while in custody. An inmate is eligible for participation in an alternative custody program only if the secretary or his

or her designee concludes that the inmate meets the criteria for program participation established under this section and that the inmate's participation is consistent with any reasonable rules and regulations prescribed by the secretary.
(1) The rules and regulations and administrative policies of the program shall be written and shall be given or made available to the participant upon assignment to the alternative custody program.
(2) The secretary or his or her designee shall have the sole discretion concerning whether to permit program participation as an alternative to custody in state prison. A risk and needs assessment shall be completed on each inmate to assist in the determination of eligibility for participation and the type of alternative custody.
(3) An inmate's existing psychiatric or medical condition that requires ongoing care is not a basis for excluding the inmate from eligibility to participate in an alternative custody program authorized by this section.
(j) The secretary or his or her designee shall establish a timeline for the application process. The secretary or his or her designee shall respond to an applicant within two weeks of her application to inform the inmate that the application was received, and to notify the inmate of the eligibility criteria of the program. The secretary or his or her designee shall provide a written notice to the inmate of her acceptance or denial into the program. The individualized treatment and rehabilitation plan described in subdivision (f) shall be developed, in consultation with the inmate, after the applicant has been found potentially eligible for participation in the program and no later than 30 calendar days after the potential eligibility determination. Except as necessary to comply with any release notification requirements, the inmate shall be released to the program no later than seven business days following notice of acceptance into the program, or if this is not possible in the case of an inmate to be placed in a residential drug or treatment program or in a transitional care facility, the first day a contracted bed becomes available at the requested location. If the inmate is denied participation in the program, the notice of denial shall specify the reason the inmate was denied. The secretary or his or her designee shall maintain a record of the application and notice of denials for participation. The inmate may appeal the decision through normal grievance procedures or reapply for participation in the program 30 days after the notice of the denial.
(k) The secretary or his or her designee shall permit program participants to seek and retain employment in the community, attend psychological counseling sessions or educational or vocational training classes, participate in life skills or parenting training, utilize substance abuse treatment services, or seek medical and dental assistance based upon the participant's individualized treatment and release plan. Participation in other rehabilitative services and programs may be approved by the case manager if it is specified as a requirement of the inmate's individualized treatment and rehabilitative case plan. Willful failure of the program participant to return to the place of detention not later than the expiration of any period of time during which she is authorized to be away from the place of detention pursuant to this section, unauthorized departures from the place of detention, or tampering with or disabling, or attempting to tamper with or disable, an electronic monitoring device shall subject the participant to a return to custody pursuant to subdivisions (g) and (h). In addition, participants may be subject to forfeiture of credits pursuant to the provisions of Section 2932, or to discipline for violation of rules established by the secretary.
(l) (1) Notwithstanding any other law, the secretary or his or her designee shall provide the information specified in paragraph (2) regarding participants in an alternative custody program to the law enforcement agencies of the jurisdiction in which persons participating in an alternative custody program reside.
(2) The information required by paragraph (1) shall consist of the following:
(A) The participant's name, address, and date of birth.
(B) The offense committed by the participant.
(C) The period of time the participant will be subject to an alternative custody program.
(3) The information received by a law enforcement agency pursuant to this subdivision may be used for the purpose of monitoring the impact of an alternative custody program on the community.
(m) It is the intent of the Legislature that the alternative custody program established under this section maintain the highest public confidence, credibility, and public safety. In the furtherance of these standards, the secretary may administer an alternative custody program pursuant to written contracts with appropriate public agencies or entities to provide specified program services. No public agency or entity entering into a contract may itself employ any person who is in an alternative custody program. The department shall determine the recidivism rate of each participant in an alternative custody program.
(n) An inmate participating in this program shall voluntarily agree to all of the provisions of the program in writing, including that she may be returned to confinement at any time with or without cause, and shall not be charged fees or costs for the program.
(o) (1) The secretary or his or her designee shall assist an individual participating in the alternative custody program in obtaining health care coverage, including, but not limited to, assistance with having suspended Medi-Cal benefits reinstated, applying for Medi-Cal benefits, or obtaining health care coverage under a private health plan or policy.
(2) To the extent not covered by a participant's health care coverage, the state shall retain responsibility for the medical, dental, and mental health needs of individuals participating in the alternative custody program.
(p) The secretary shall adopt emergency regulations specifically governing participants in this program.
(q) If a phrase, clause, sentence, or provision of this section or application thereof to a person or circumstance is held invalid, that invalidity shall not affect any other phrase, clause, sentence, or provision or application of this section, which can be given effect without the invalid phrase, clause, sentence, or provision or application and to this end the provisions of this section are declared to be severable.
(Amended by Stats. 2015, Ch. 762, Sec. 1. (SB 219) Effective January 1, 2016.)
1170.06.
(a) Notwithstanding any other law, a sheriff or a county director of corrections is authorized to offer a program under which inmates as specified in subdivision (c), who are not precluded by subdivision (d), and who have been committed to a county jail may be allowed to participate in a voluntary alternative custody program as defined in subdivision (b) in lieu of their confinement in a county jail. Under this program, one day of participation is in lieu of one day of incarceration in a county jail. Participants in the program shall receive any sentence reduction credits that they would have received had they served their sentence in a county jail, and are subject to denial and loss of credit pursuant to subdivision (d) of Section 4019. The sheriff or the county director of corrections may enter into contracts with county agencies, not-for-profit organizations, for-profit organizations, and others in order to promote alternative custody placements.
(b) As used in this section, an alternative custody program shall include, but is not limited to, the following:
(1) Confinement to a residential home during the hours designated by the sheriff or the county director of corrections.
(2) Confinement to a residential drug or treatment program during the hours designated by the county sheriff or the county director of corrections.
(3) Confinement to a transitional care facility that offers appropriate services.
(4) Confinement to a mental health clinic or hospital that offers appropriate mental health services.
(c) Except as provided by subdivision (d), inmates sentenced to a county jail for a determinate term of imprisonment pursuant to a misdemeanor or a felony pursuant to subdivision (h) of Section 1170, and only those persons, are eligible to participate in the alternative custody program authorized by this section.
(d) An inmate committed to a county jail who meets any of the following criteria is not eligible to participate in the alternative custody program:
(1) The person was screened by the sheriff or the county director of corrections using a validated risk assessment tool and determined to pose a high risk to commit a violent offense.
(2) The person has a history, within the last 10 years, of escape from a facility while under juvenile or adult custody, including, but not limited to, any detention facility, camp, jail, or state prison facility.
(3) The person has a current or prior conviction for an offense that requires the person to register as a sex offender as provided in Chapter 5.5. (commencing with Section 290) of Title 9 of Part 1.
(e) An alternative custody program may include the use of electronic monitoring, global positioning system devices, or other supervising devices for the purpose of helping to verify a participant's compliance with the rules and regulations of the program. The devices shall not be used to eavesdrop or record any conversation, except a conversation between the participant and the person supervising the participant, in which case the recording of the conversation is to be used solely for the purposes of voice identification.
(f) (1) In order to implement alternative custody for the population specified in subdivision (c), the sheriff or the county director of corrections shall create, and the participant shall agree to and fully participate in, an individualized treatment and rehabilitation plan. When available and appropriate for the individualized treatment and rehabilitation plan, the sheriff or the county director of corrections shall prioritize the use of evidence-based programs and services that will aid in the participant's successful reentry into society while he or she takes part in alternative custody. Case management services shall be provided to support rehabilitation and to track the progress and individualized treatment plan compliance of the inmate.
(2) For purposes of this section, "evidence-based practices" means supervision policies, procedures, programs, and practices demonstrated by scientific research to reduce recidivism among individuals under probation, parole, or postrelease community supervision.
(g) The sheriff or the county director of corrections shall prescribe reasonable rules to govern the operation of the alternative custody program. Each participant shall be informed in writing that he or she is required to comply with the rules of the program, including, but not limited to, the following rules:
(1) The participant shall remain within the interior premises of his or her residence during the hours designated by the sheriff or his or her designee or the county director of corrections or his or her designee.
(2) The participant shall be subject to search and seizure by a peace officer at any time of the day or night, with or without cause. In addition, the participant shall admit any peace officer designated by the sheriff or his or her designee or the county director of corrections or his or her designee into the participant's residence at any time for purposes of verifying the participant's compliance with the conditions of his or her detention. Prior to participation in the alternative custody program, each participant shall agree in writing to these terms and conditions.
(3) The sheriff or his or her designee, or the county director of corrections or his or her designee, may immediately retake the participant into custody to serve the balance of his or her sentence if an electronic monitoring or supervising device is unable for any reason to properly perform its function at the designated place of detention, if the participant fails to remain within the place of detention as stipulated in the agreement, or if the participant for any other reason no longer meets the criteria under this section.
(h) Whenever a peace officer supervising a participant has reasonable suspicion to believe that the participant is not complying with the rules or conditions of the program, or that a required electronic monitoring device is unable to function properly in the designated place of confinement, the peace officer may, under general or specific authorization of the sheriff or his or her designee, or the county director of corrections or his or her designee, and without a warrant of arrest, retake the participant into custody to complete the remainder of the original sentence.
(i) This section shall not be construed to require a sheriff or his or her designee, or a county director of corrections or his or her designee, to allow an inmate to participate in this program if it appears from the record that the inmate has not satisfactorily complied with reasonable rules and regulations while in custody. An inmate shall be eligible for participation in an alternative custody program only if the sheriff or his or her designee or the county director of corrections or his or her designee concludes that the inmate meets the criteria for program participation established under this section and that the inmate's participation is consistent with any reasonable rules prescribed by the sheriff or the county director of corrections.
(1) The rules and administrative policies of the program shall be written and shall be given or made available to each participant upon assignment to the alternative custody program.
(2) The sheriff or his or her designee or the county director of corrections or his or her designee shall have the sole discretion concerning whether to permit program participation as an alternative to custody in a county jail. A risk and needs assessment shall be completed on each inmate to assist in the determination of eligibility for participation and the type of alternative custody.
(j) (1) The sheriff or his or her designee or the county director of corrections or his or her designee shall permit program participants to seek and retain employment in the community, attend psychological counseling sessions or educational or vocational training classes, participate in life skills or parenting training, utilize substance abuse treatment services, or seek medical, mental health, and dental assistance based upon the participant's individualized treatment and release plan. Participation in other rehabilitative services and programs may be approved by the case manager if it is specified as a requirement of the inmate's individualized treatment and rehabilitative case plan.
(2) Willful failure of the program participant to return to the place of detention prior to the expiration of any period of time during which he or she is authorized to be away from the place of detention, unauthorized departures from the place of detention, or tampering with or disabling, or attempting to tamper with or disable, an electronic monitoring device is punishable pursuant to Section 4532 and shall additionally subject the participant to a return to custody pursuant to subdivisions (g) and (h). In addition, participants may be subject to forfeiture of credits pursuant to the provisions of Section 4019, or to discipline for violation of rules established by the sheriff or the county director of corrections.
(k) (1) Notwithstanding any other law, the sheriff or his or her designee or the county director of corrections or his or her designee shall provide the information specified in paragraph (2) regarding participants in an alternative custody program to the law enforcement agencies of the jurisdiction in which persons participating in an alternative custody program reside.
(2) The information required by paragraph (1) shall consist of the following:
(A) The participant's name, address, and date of birth.
(B) The offense committed by the participant.
(C) The period of time the participant will be subject to an alternative custody program.
(3) The information received by a law enforcement agency pursuant to this subdivision may be used for the purpose of monitoring the impact of an alternative custody program on the community.
(l) It is the intent of the Legislature that the alternative custody programs established under this section maintain the highest public confidence, credibility, and public safety. In the furtherance of these standards, the sheriff or the county director of corrections may administer an alternative custody program pursuant to written contracts with

appropriate public agencies or entities to provide specified program services. No public agency or entity entering into a contract may itself employ any person who is in an alternative custody program. The sheriff or the county director of corrections shall determine the recidivism rate of each participant in an alternative custody program.

(m) An inmate participating in this program shall voluntarily agree to all of the provisions of the program in writing, including that he or she may be returned to confinement at any time with or without cause, and shall not be charged fees or costs for the program.

(n) If a phrase, clause, sentence, or provision of this section or application thereof to a person or circumstance is held invalid, that invalidity shall not affect any other phrase, clause, sentence, or provision or application of this section, which can be given effect without the invalid phrase, clause, sentence, or provision or application and to this end the provisions of this section are declared to be severable.

(Added by Stats. 2014, Ch. 26, Sec. 18. (AB 1468) Effective June 20, 2014.)

1170.1.

(a) Except as otherwise provided by law, and subject to Section 654, when any person is convicted of two or more felonies, whether in the same proceeding or court or in different proceedings or courts, and whether by judgment rendered by the same or by a different court, and a consecutive term of imprisonment is imposed under Sections 669 and 1170, the aggregate term of imprisonment for all these convictions shall be the sum of the principal term, the subordinate term, and any additional term imposed for applicable enhancements for prior convictions, prior prison terms, and Section 12022.1. The principal term shall consist of the greatest term of imprisonment imposed by the court for any of the crimes, including any term imposed for applicable specific enhancements. The subordinate term for each consecutive offense shall consist of one-third of the middle term of imprisonment prescribed for each other felony conviction for which a consecutive term of imprisonment is imposed, and shall include one-third of the term imposed for any specific enhancements applicable to those subordinate offenses. Whenever a court imposes a term of imprisonment in the state prison, whether the term is a principal or subordinate term, the aggregate term shall be served in the state prison, regardless as to whether or not one of the terms specifies imprisonment in a county jail pursuant to subdivision (h) of Section 1170.

(b) If a person is convicted of two or more violations of kidnapping, as defined in Section 207, involving separate victims, the subordinate term for each consecutive offense of kidnapping shall consist of the full middle term and shall include the full term imposed for specific enhancements applicable to those subordinate offenses.

(c) In the case of any person convicted of one or more felonies committed while the person is confined in the state prison or is subject to reimprisonment for escape from custody and the law either requires the terms to be served consecutively or the court imposes consecutive terms, the term of imprisonment for all the convictions that the person is required to serve consecutively shall commence from the time the person would otherwise have been released from prison. If the new offenses are consecutive with each other, the principal and subordinate terms shall be calculated as provided in subdivision (a). This subdivision shall be applicable in cases of convictions of more than one offense in the same or different proceedings.

(d) When the court imposes a sentence for a felony pursuant to Section 1170 or subdivision (b) of Section 1168, the court shall also impose, in addition and consecutive to the offense of which the person has been convicted, the additional terms provided for any applicable enhancements. If an enhancement is punishable by one of three terms, the court shall, in its discretion, impose the term that best serves the interest of justice, and state the reasons for its sentence choice on the record at the time of sentencing. The court shall also impose any other additional term that the court determines in its discretion or as required by law shall run consecutive to the term imposed under Section 1170 or subdivision (b) of Section 1168. In considering the imposition of the additional term, the court shall apply the sentencing rules of the Judicial Council.

(e) All enhancements shall be alleged in the accusatory pleading and either admitted by the defendant in open court or found to be true by the trier of fact.

(f) When two or more enhancements may be imposed for being armed with or using a dangerous or deadly weapon or a firearm in the commission of a single offense, only the greatest of those enhancements shall be imposed for that offense. This subdivision shall not limit the imposition of any other enhancements applicable to that offense, including an enhancement for the infliction of great bodily injury.

(g) When two or more enhancements may be imposed for the infliction of great bodily injury on the same victim in the commission of a single offense, only the greatest of those enhancements shall be imposed for that offense. This subdivision shall not limit the imposition of any other enhancements applicable to that offense, including an enhancement for being armed with or using a dangerous or deadly weapon or a firearm.

(h) For any violation of an offense specified in Section 667.6, the number of enhancements that may be imposed shall not be limited, regardless of whether the enhancements are pursuant to this section, Section 667.6, or some other provision of law. Each of the enhancements shall be a full and separately served term.

(i) This section shall remain in effect only until January 1, 2022, and as of that date is repealed, unless a later enacted statute, that is enacted before January 1, 2022, deletes or extends that date.

(Amended (as amended by Stats. 2013, Ch. 508, Sec. 7) by Stats. 2016, Ch. 887, Sec. 7. (SB 1016) Effective January 1, 2017. Repealed as of January 1, 2022, by its own provisions. See later operative version, as amended by Sec. 8 of Stats. 2016, Ch. 887.)

1170.1.

(a) Except as otherwise provided by law, and subject to Section 654, when any person is convicted of two or more felonies, whether in the same proceeding or court or in different proceedings or courts, and whether by judgment rendered by the same or by a different court, and a consecutive term of imprisonment is imposed under Sections 669 and 1170, the aggregate term of imprisonment for all these convictions shall be the sum of the principal term, the subordinate term, and any additional term imposed for applicable enhancements for prior convictions, prior prison terms, and Section 12022.1. The principal term shall consist of the greatest term of imprisonment imposed by the court for any of the crimes, including any term imposed for applicable specific enhancements. The subordinate term for each consecutive offense shall consist of one-third of the middle term of imprisonment prescribed for each other felony conviction for which a consecutive term of imprisonment is imposed, and shall include one-third of the term imposed for any specific enhancements applicable to those subordinate offenses. Whenever a court imposes a term of imprisonment in the state prison, whether the term is a principal or subordinate term, the aggregate term shall be served in the state prison, regardless as to whether or not one of the terms specifies imprisonment in a county jail pursuant to subdivision (h) of Section 1170.

(b) If a person is convicted of two or more violations of kidnapping, as defined in Section 207, involving separate victims, the subordinate term for each consecutive offense of kidnapping shall consist of the full middle term and shall include the full term imposed for specific enhancements applicable to those subordinate offenses.

(c) In the case of any person convicted of one or more felonies committed while the person is confined in the state prison or is subject to reimprisonment for escape from custody and the law either requires the terms to be served consecutively or the court imposes consecutive terms, the term of imprisonment for all the convictions that the person is required to serve consecutively shall commence from the time the person would otherwise have been released from prison. If the new offenses are consecutive with each other, the principal and subordinate terms shall be calculated as provided in subdivision (a). This subdivision shall be applicable in cases of convictions of more than one offense in the same or different proceedings.

(d) When the court imposes a sentence for a felony pursuant to Section 1170 or subdivision (b) of Section 1168, the court shall also impose, in addition and consecutive

to the offense of which the person has been convicted, the additional terms provided for any applicable enhancements. If an enhancement is punishable by one of three terms, the court shall impose the middle term unless there are circumstances in aggravation or mitigation, and state the reasons for its sentence choice, other than the middle term, on the record at the time of sentencing. The court shall also impose any other additional term that the court determines in its discretion or as required by law shall run consecutive to the term imposed under Section 1170 or subdivision (b) of Section 1168. In considering the imposition of the additional term, the court shall apply the sentencing rules of the Judicial Council.

(e) All enhancements shall be alleged in the accusatory pleading and either admitted by the defendant in open court or found to be true by the trier of fact.

(f) When two or more enhancements may be imposed for being armed with or using a dangerous or deadly weapon or a firearm in the commission of a single offense, only the greatest of those enhancements shall be imposed for that offense. This subdivision shall not limit the imposition of any other enhancements applicable to that offense, including an enhancement for the infliction of great bodily injury.

(g) When two or more enhancements may be imposed for the infliction of great bodily injury on the same victim in the commission of a single offense, only the greatest of those enhancements shall be imposed for that offense. This subdivision shall not limit the imposition of any other enhancements applicable to that offense, including an enhancement for being armed with or using a dangerous or deadly weapon or a firearm.

(h) For any violation of an offense specified in Section 667.6, the number of enhancements that may be imposed shall not be limited, regardless of whether the enhancements are pursuant to this section, Section 667.6, or some other provision of law. Each of the enhancements shall be a full and separately served term.

(i) This section shall become operative on January 1, 2022.

(Amended (as amended by Stats. 2013, Ch. 508, Sec. 8) by Stats. 2016, Ch. 887, Sec. 8. (SB 1016) Effective January 1, 2017. Section operative January 1, 2022, by its own provisions.)

1170.11.

As used in Section 1170.1, the term "specific enhancement" means an enhancement that relates to the circumstances of the crime. It includes, but is not limited to, the enhancements provided in Sections 186.10, 186.11, 186.22, 186.26, 186.33, 192.5, 273.4, 289.5, 290.4, 290.45, 290.46, 347, and 368, subdivisions (a) and (b) of Section 422.75, paragraphs (2), (3), (4), and (5) of subdivision (a) of Section 451.1, paragraphs (2), (3), and (4) of subdivision (a) of Section 452.1, subdivision (g) of Section 550, Sections 593a, 600, 667.8, 667.85, 667.9, 667.10, 667.15, 667.16, 667.17, 674, 675, 12021.5, 12022, 12022.2, 12022.3, 12022.4, 12022.5, 12022.53, 12022.55, 12022.6, 12022.7, 12022.75, 12022.8, 12022.85, 12022.9, 12022.95, 27590, 30600, and 30615 of this code, and in Sections 1522.01 and 11353.1, subdivision (b) of Section 11353.4, Sections 11353.6, 11356.5, 11370.4, 11379.7, 11379.8, 11379.9, 11380.1, 11380.7, 25189.5, and 25189.7 of the Health and Safety Code, and in Sections 20001 and 23558 of the Vehicle Code, and in Sections 10980 and 14107 of the Welfare and Institutions Code.

(Amended by Stats. 2010, Ch. 178, Sec. 71. (SB 1115) Effective January 1, 2011. Operative January 1, 2012, by Sec. 107 of Ch. 178.)

1170.12.

Aggregate and consecutive terms for multiple convictions; Prior conviction as prior felony; Commitment and other enhancements or punishment.

(a) Notwithstanding any other provision of law, if a defendant has been convicted of a felony and it has been pled and proved that the defendant has one or more prior serious and/or violent felony convictions, as defined in subdivision (b), the court shall adhere to each of the following:

(1) There shall not be an aggregate term limitation for purposes of consecutive sentencing for any subsequent felony conviction.

(2) Probation for the current offense shall not be granted, nor shall execution or imposition of the sentence be suspended for any prior offense.

(3) The length of time between the prior serious and/or violent felony conviction and the current felony conviction shall not affect the imposition of sentence.

(4) There shall not be a commitment to any other facility other than the state prison. Diversion shall not be granted nor shall the defendant be eligible for commitment to the California Rehabilitation Center as provided in Article 2 (commencing with Section 3050) of Chapter 1 of Division 3 of the Welfare and Institutions Code.

(5) The total amount of credits awarded pursuant to Article 2.5 (commencing with Section 2930) of Chapter 7 of Title 1 of Part 3 shall not exceed one-fifth of the total term of imprisonment imposed and shall not accrue until the defendant is physically placed in the state prison.

(6) If there is a current conviction for more than one felony count not committed on the same occasion, and not arising from the same set of operative facts, the court shall sentence the defendant consecutively on each count pursuant to this section.

(7) If there is a current conviction for more than one serious or violent felony as described in subdivision (b), the court shall impose the sentence for each conviction consecutive to the sentence for any other conviction for which the defendant may be consecutively sentenced in the manner prescribed by law.

(b) Notwithstanding any other provision of law and for the purposes of this section, a prior serious and/or violent conviction of a felony shall be defined as:

(1) Any offense defined in subdivision (c) of Section 667.5 as a violent felony or any offense defined in subdivision (c) of Section 1192.7 as a serious felony in this state. The determination of whether a prior conviction is a prior serious and/or violent felony conviction for purposes of this section shall be made upon the date of that prior conviction and is not affected by the sentence imposed unless the sentence automatically, upon the initial sentencing, converts the felony to a misdemeanor. None of the following dispositions shall affect the determination that a prior serious and/or violent conviction is a serious and/or violent felony for purposes of this section:

(A) The suspension of imposition of judgment or sentence.

(B) The stay of execution of sentence.

(C) The commitment to the State Department of Health Services as a mentally disordered sex offender following a conviction of a felony.

(D) The commitment to the California Rehabilitation Center or any other facility whose function is rehabilitative diversion from the state prison.

(2) A prior conviction in another jurisdiction for an offense that, if committed in California, is punishable by imprisonment in the state prison shall constitute a prior conviction of a particular serious and/or violent felony if the prior conviction in the other jurisdiction is for an offense that includes all of the elements of the particular violent felony as defined in subdivision (c) of Section 667.5 or serious felony as defined in subdivision (c) of Section 1192.7.

(3) A prior juvenile adjudication shall constitute a prior serious and/or violent felony conviction for the purposes of sentence enhancement if:

(A) The juvenile was sixteen years of age or older at the time he or she committed the prior offense, and

(B) The prior offense is

(i) listed in subdivision (b) of Section 707 of the Welfare and Institutions Code, or

(ii) listed in this subdivision as a serious and/or violent felony, and

(C) The juvenile was found to be a fit and proper subject to be dealt with under the juvenile court law, and

(D) The juvenile was adjudged a ward of the juvenile court within the meaning of Section 602 of the Welfare and Institutions Code because the person committed an offense listed in subdivision (b) of Section 707 of the Welfare and Institutions Code.

(c) For purposes of this section, and in addition to any other enhancements or punishment provisions which may apply, the following shall apply where a defendant has one or more prior serious and/or violent felony convictions:

(1) If a defendant has one prior serious and/or violent felony conviction as defined in subdivision (b) that has been pled and proved, the determinate term or minimum term for an indeterminate term shall be twice the term otherwise provided as punishment for the current felony conviction.

(2) (A) Except as provided in subparagraph (C), if a defendant has two or more prior serious and/or violent felony convictions, as defined in subdivision (b), that have been pled and proved, the term for the current felony conviction shall be an indeterminate term of life imprisonment with a minimum term of the indeterminate sentence calculated as the greatest of:

(i) three times the term otherwise provided as punishment for each current felony conviction subsequent to the two or more prior serious and/or violent felony convictions, or

(ii) twenty-five years or

(iii) the term determined by the court pursuant to Section 1170 for the underlying conviction, including any enhancement applicable under Chapter 4.5 (commencing with Section 1170) of Title 7 of Part 2, or any period prescribed by Section 190 or 3046.

(B) The indeterminate term described in subparagraph (A) of paragraph (2) of this subdivision shall be served consecutive to any other term of imprisonment for which a consecutive term may be imposed by law. Any other term imposed subsequent to any indeterminate term described in subparagraph (A) of paragraph (2) of this subdivision shall not be merged therein but shall commence at the time the person would otherwise have been released from prison.

(C) If a defendant has two or more prior serious and/or violent felony convictions as defined in subdivision (c) of Section 667.5 or subdivision (c) of Section 1192.7 that have been pled and proved, and the current offense is not a felony described in paragraph (1) of subdivision (b) of this section, the defendant shall be sentenced pursuant to paragraph (1) of subdivision (c) of this section, unless the prosecution pleads and proves any of the following:

(i) The current offense is a controlled substance charge, in which an allegation under Section 11370.4 or 11379.8 of the Health and Safety Code was admitted or found true.

(ii) The current offense is a felony sex offense, defined in subdivision (d) of Section 261.5 or Section 262, or any felony offense that results in mandatory registration as a sex offender pursuant to subdivision (c) of Section 290 except for violations of Sections 266 and 285, paragraph (1) of subdivision (b) and subdivision (e) of Section 286, paragraph (1) of subdivision (b) and subdivision (e) of Section 287, Section 314, and Section 311.11.

(iii) During the commission of the current offense, the defendant used a firearm, was armed with a firearm or deadly weapon, or intended to cause great bodily injury to another person.

(iv) The defendant suffered a prior conviction, as defined in subdivision (b) of this section, for any of the following serious and/or violent felonies:

(I) A "sexually violent offense" as defined by subdivision (b) of Section 6600 of the Welfare and Institutions Code.

(II) Oral copulation with a child who is under 14 years of age, and who is more than 10 years younger than he or she as defined by Section 287 or former Section 288a, sodomy with another person who is under 14 years of age and more than 10 years younger than he or she as defined by Section 286 or sexual penetration with another person who is under 14 years of age, and who is more than 10 years younger than he or she, as defined by Section 289.

(III) A lewd or lascivious act involving a child under 14 years of age, in violation of Section 288.

(IV) Any homicide offense, including any attempted homicide offense, defined in Sections 187 to 191.5, inclusive.

(V) Solicitation to commit murder as defined in Section 653f.

(VI) Assault with a machine gun on a peace officer or firefighter, as defined in paragraph (3) of subdivision (d) of Section 245.

(VII) Possession of a weapon of mass destruction, as defined in paragraph (1) of subdivision (a) of Section 11418.

(VIII) Any serious and/or violent felony offense punishable in California by life imprisonment or death.

(d) (1) Notwithstanding any other provision of law, this section shall be applied in every case in which a defendant has one or more prior serious and/or violent felony convictions as defined in this section. The prosecuting attorney shall plead and prove each prior serious and/or violent felony conviction except as provided in paragraph (2).

(2) The prosecuting attorney may move to dismiss or strike a prior serious and/or violent felony conviction allegation in the furtherance of justice pursuant to Section 1385, or if there is insufficient evidence to prove the prior serious and/or violent conviction. If upon the satisfaction of the court that there is insufficient evidence to prove the prior serious and/or violent felony conviction, the court may dismiss or strike the allegation. Nothing in this section shall be read to alter a court's authority under Section 1385.

(e) Prior serious and/or violent felony convictions shall not be used in plea bargaining, as defined in subdivision (b) of Section 1192.7. The prosecution shall plead and prove all known prior serious and/or violent felony convictions and shall not enter into any agreement to strike or seek the dismissal of any prior serious and/or violent felony conviction allegation except as provided in paragraph (2) of subdivision (d).

(f) If any provision of subdivisions (a) to (e), inclusive, or of Section 1170.126, or the application thereof to any person or circumstance is held invalid, that invalidity shall not affect other provisions or applications of those subdivisions which can be given effect without the invalid provision or application, and to this end the provisions of those subdivisions are severable.

(g) The provisions of this section shall not be amended by the Legislature except by statute passed in each house by rollcall vote entered in the journal, two-thirds of the membership concurring, or by a statute that becomes effective only when approved by the electors.

(Amended by Stats. 2018, Ch. 423, Sec. 85. (SB 1494) Effective January 1, 2019. Note: This section was added on Nov. 8, 1994, by initiative Prop. 184.)

1170.125.

Notwithstanding Section 2 of Proposition 184, as adopted at the November 8, 1994, General Election, for all offenses committed on or after November 7, 2012, all references to existing statutes in Sections 1170.12 and 1170.126 are to those sections as they existed on November 7, 2012.

(Amended November 6, 2012, by initiative Proposition 36, Sec. 5. Note: This section was added on March 7, 2000, by initiative Prop. 21.)

1170.126.

(a) The resentencing provisions under this section and related statutes are intended to apply exclusively to persons presently serving an indeterminate term of imprisonment pursuant to paragraph (2) of subdivision (e) of Section 667 or paragraph (2) of subdivision (c) of Section 1170.12, whose sentence under this act would not have been an indeterminate life sentence.

(b) Any person serving an indeterminate term of life imprisonment imposed pursuant to paragraph (2) of subdivision (e) of Section 667 or paragraph (2) of subdivision (c) of Section 1170.12 upon conviction, whether by trial or plea, of a felony or felonies that are not defined as serious and/or violent felonies by subdivision (c) of Section 667.5 or subdivision (c) of Section 1192.7, may file a petition for a recall of sentence, within two years after the effective date of the act that added this section or at a later date upon a

showing of good cause, before the trial court that entered the judgment of conviction in his or her case, to request resentencing in accordance with the provisions of subdivision (e) of Section 667, and subdivision (c) of Section 1170.12, as those statutes have been amended by the act that added this section.

(c) No person who is presently serving a term of imprisonment for a "second strike" conviction imposed pursuant to paragraph (1) of subdivision (e) of Section 667 or paragraph (1) of subdivision (c) of Section 1170.12, shall be eligible for resentencing under the provisions of this section.

(d) The petition for a recall of sentence described in subdivision (b) shall specify all of the currently charged felonies, which resulted in the sentence under paragraph (2) of subdivision (e) of Section 667 or paragraph (2) of subdivision (c) of Section 1170.12, or both, and shall also specify all of the prior convictions alleged and proved under subdivision (d) of Section 667 and subdivision (b) of Section 1170.12.

(e) An inmate is eligible for resentencing if:

(1) The inmate is serving an indeterminate term of life imprisonment imposed pursuant to paragraph (2) of subdivision (e) of Section 667 or subdivision (c) of Section 1170.12 for a conviction of a felony or felonies that are not defined as serious and/or violent felonies by subdivision (c) of Section 667.5 or subdivision (c) of Section 1192.7.

(2) The inmate's current sentence was not imposed for any of the offenses appearing in clauses (i) to (iii), inclusive, of subparagraph (C) of paragraph (2) of subdivision (e) of Section 667 or clauses (i) to (iii), inclusive, of subparagraph (C) of paragraph (2) of subdivision (c) of Section 1170.12.

(3) The inmate has no prior convictions for any of the offenses appearing in clause (iv) of subparagraph (C) of paragraph (2) of subdivision (e) of Section 667 or clause (iv) of subparagraph (C) of paragraph (2) of subdivision (c) of Section 1170.12.

(f) Upon receiving a petition for recall of sentence under this section, the court shall determine whether the petitioner satisfies the criteria in subdivision (e). If the petitioner satisfies the criteria in subdivision (e), the petitioner shall be resentenced pursuant to paragraph (1) of subdivision (e) of Section 667 and paragraph (1) of subdivision (c) of Section 1170.12 unless the court, in its discretion, determines that resentencing the petitioner would pose an unreasonable risk of danger to public safety.

(g) In exercising its discretion in subdivision (f), the court may consider:

(1) The petitioner's criminal conviction history, including the type of crimes committed, the extent of injury to victims, the length of prior prison commitments, and the remoteness of the crimes;

(2) The petitioner's disciplinary record and record of rehabilitation while incarcerated; and

(3) Any other evidence the court, within its discretion, determines to be relevant in deciding whether a new sentence would result in an unreasonable risk of danger to public safety.

(h) Under no circumstances may resentencing under this act result in the imposition of a term longer than the original sentence.

(i) Notwithstanding subdivision (b) of Section 977, a defendant petitioning for resentencing may waive his or her appearance in court for the resentencing, provided that the accusatory pleading is not amended at the resentencing, and that no new trial or retrial of the individual will occur. The waiver shall be in writing and signed by the defendant.

(j) If the court that originally sentenced the defendant is not available to resentence the defendant, the presiding judge shall designate another judge to rule on the defendant's petition.

(k) Nothing in this section is intended to diminish or abrogate any rights or remedies otherwise available to the defendant.

(l) Nothing in this and related sections is intended to diminish or abrogate the finality of judgments in any case not falling within the purview of this act.

(m) A resentencing hearing ordered under this act shall constitute a "post-conviction release proceeding" under paragraph (7) of subdivision (b) of Section 28 of Article I of the California Constitution (Marsy's Law).

(Added November 6, 2012, by initiative Proposition 36, Sec. 6. Note: Prop. 36 is titled the Three Strikes Reform Act of 2012.)

1170.127.

(a) A person who is committed to a state hospital after being found not guilty by reason of insanity pursuant to Section 1026 may petition the court to have his or her maximum term of commitment, as established by Section 1026.5, reduced to the length it would have been had Section 1170.126 been in effect at the time of the original determination. Both of the following conditions are required for the maximum term of commitment to be reduced:

(1) The person would have met all of the criteria for a reduction in sentence pursuant to Section 1170.126 had he or she been found guilty.

(2) The person files the petition for a reduction of the maximum term of commitment before January 1, 2021, or on a later date upon a showing of good cause.

(b) If a petitioner's maximum term of confinement is ordered reduced under this section, the new term of confinement must provide opportunity to meet requirements provided in subdivision (b) of Section 1026.5. If a petitioner's new maximum term of confinement ordered under this section does not provide sufficient time to meet requirements provided in subdivision (b) of Section 1026.5, the new maximum term of confinement may be extended, not more than 240 days from the date the petition is granted, in order to meet requirements provided in subdivision (b) of Section 1026.5.

(Added by Stats. 2017, Ch. 17, Sec. 25. (AB 103) Effective June 27, 2017.)

1170.13.

Notwithstanding subdivision (a) of Section 1170.1 which provides for the imposition of a subordinate term for a consecutive offense of one-third of the middle term of imprisonment, if a person is convicted pursuant to subdivision (b) of Section 139, the subordinate term for each consecutive offense shall consist of the full middle term.

(Amended by Stats. 1998, Ch. 926, Sec. 3. Effective January 1, 1999.)

1170.15.

Notwithstanding subdivision (a) of Section 1170.1 which provides for the imposition of a subordinate term for a consecutive offense of one-third of the middle term of imprisonment, if a person is convicted of a felony, and of an additional felony that is a violation of Section 136.1 or 137 and that was committed against the victim of, or a witness or potential witness with respect to, or a person who was about to give material information pertaining to, the first felony, or of a felony violation of Section 653f that was committed to dissuade a witness or potential witness to the first felony, the subordinate term for each consecutive offense that is a felony described in this section shall consist of the full middle term of imprisonment for the felony for which a consecutive term of imprisonment is imposed, and shall include the full term prescribed for any enhancements imposed for being armed with or using a dangerous or deadly weapon or a firearm, or for inflicting great bodily injury.

(Amended by Stats. 1998, Ch. 926, Sec. 4. Effective January 1, 1999.)

1170.16.

In lieu of the term provided in Section 1170.1, a full, separate, and consecutive term may be imposed for each violation of subdivision (a) of Section 192, whether or not the offenses were committed during a single transaction.

(Added by Stats. 1996, Ch. 421, Sec. 1. Effective January 1, 1997.)

1170.17.

(a) When a person is prosecuted for a criminal offense committed while he or she was under 18 years of age and the prosecution was lawfully initiated in a court of criminal jurisdiction without a prior finding that the person is not a fit and proper subject to be dealt with under the juvenile court law, upon subsequent conviction for any criminal offense, the person shall be subject to the same sentence as an adult convicted of the

identical offense, in accordance with subdivision (a) of Section 1170.19, except under the circumstances described in subdivision (b), (c), or (d).
(b) Where the conviction is for the type of offense which, in combination with the person's age at the time the offense was committed, makes the person eligible for transfer to a court of criminal jurisdiction, pursuant to a rebuttable presumption that the person is not a fit and proper subject to be dealt with under the juvenile court law, and the prosecution for the offense could not lawfully be initiated in a court of criminal jurisdiction, then either of the following shall apply:
(1) The person shall be subject to the same sentence as an adult convicted of the identical offense in accordance with the provisions set forth in subdivision (a) of Section 1170.19, unless the person prevails upon a motion brought pursuant to paragraph (2).
(2) Upon a motion brought by the person, the court shall order the probation department to prepare a written social study and recommendation concerning the person's fitness to be dealt with under the juvenile court law and the court shall either conduct a fitness hearing or suspend proceedings and remand the matter to the juvenile court to prepare a social study and make a determination of fitness. The person shall receive a disposition under the juvenile court law only if the person demonstrates, by a preponderance of the evidence, that he or she is a fit and proper subject to be dealt with under the juvenile court law, based upon each of the following five criteria:
(A) The degree of criminal sophistication exhibited by the person. This may include, but is not limited to, giving weight to the person's age, maturity, intellectual capacity, and physical, mental, and emotional health at the time of the offense, the person's impetuosity or failure to appreciate risks and consequences of criminal behavior, the effect of familial, adult, or peer pressure on the person's actions, and the effect of the person's family and community environment and childhood trauma on the person's criminal sophistication.
(B) Whether the person can be rehabilitated prior to the expiration of the juvenile court's jurisdiction. This may include, but is not limited to, giving weight to the minor's potential to grow and mature.
(C) The person's previous delinquent history. This may include, but is not limited to, giving weight to the seriousness of the person's previous delinquent history and the effect of the person's family and community environment and childhood trauma on the person's previous delinquent behavior.
(D) Success of previous attempts by the juvenile court to rehabilitate the person. This may include, but is not limited to, giving weight to an analysis of the adequacy of the services previously provided to address the person's needs.
(E) The circumstances and gravity of the offense for which the person has been convicted. This may include, but is not limited to, giving weight to the actual behavior of the person, the mental state of the person, the person's degree of involvement in the crime, the level of harm actually caused by the person, and the person's mental and emotional development.
If the court conducting the fitness hearing finds that the person is not a fit and proper subject for juvenile court jurisdiction, then the person shall be sentenced by the court where he or she was convicted, in accordance with paragraph (1). If the court conducting the hearing on fitness finds that the person is a fit and proper subject for juvenile court jurisdiction, then the person shall be subject to a disposition in accordance with subdivision (b) of Section 1170.19.
(c) Where the conviction is for the type of offense which, in combination with the person's age at the time the offense was committed, makes the person eligible for transfer to a court of criminal jurisdiction, pursuant to a rebuttable presumption that the person is a fit and proper subject to be dealt with under the juvenile court law, then the person shall be sentenced as follows:
(1) The person shall be subject to a disposition under the juvenile court law, in accordance with the provisions of subdivision (b) of Section 1170.19, unless the district attorney prevails upon a motion, as described in paragraph (2).
(2) Upon a motion brought by the district attorney, the court shall order the probation department to prepare a written social study and recommendation concerning whether the person is a fit and proper subject to be dealt with under the juvenile court law. The court shall either conduct a fitness hearing or suspend proceedings and remand the matter to the juvenile court for a determination of fitness. The person shall be subject to a juvenile disposition under the juvenile court law unless the district attorney demonstrates, by a preponderance of the evidence, that the person is not a fit and proper subject to be dealt with under the juvenile court law, based upon the five criteria set forth in paragraph (2) of subdivision (b). If the person is found to be not a fit and proper subject to be dealt with under the juvenile court law, then the person shall be sentenced in the court where he or she was convicted, in accordance with the provisions set forth in subdivision (a) of Section 1170.19. If the person is found to be a fit and proper subject to be dealt with under the juvenile court law, the person shall be subject to a disposition, in accordance with the provisions of subdivision (b) of Section 1170.19.
(d) Where the conviction is for the type of offense which, in combination with the person's age, does not make the person eligible for transfer to a court of criminal jurisdiction, the person shall be subject to a disposition in accordance with the provisions of subdivision (b) of Section 1170.19.
(Amended by Stats. 2015, Ch. 234, Sec. 1. (SB 382) Effective January 1, 2016.)
1170.18.
(a) A person who, on November 5, 2014, was serving a sentence for a conviction, whether by trial or plea, of a felony or felonies who would have been guilty of a misdemeanor under the act that added this section ("this act") had this act been in effect at the time of the offense may petition for a recall of sentence before the trial court that entered the judgment of conviction in his or her case to request resentencing in accordance with Sections 11350, 11357, or 11377 of the Health and Safety Code, or Section 459.5, 473, 476a, 490.2, 496, or 666 of the Penal Code, as those sections have been amended or added by this act.
(b) Upon receiving a petition under subdivision (a), the court shall determine whether the petitioner satisfies the criteria in subdivision (a). If the petitioner satisfies the criteria in subdivision (a), the petitioner's felony sentence shall be recalled and the petitioner resentenced to a misdemeanor pursuant to Sections 11350, 11357, or 11377 of the Health and Safety Code, or Section 459.5, 473, 476a, 490.2, 496, or 666 of the Penal Code, as those sections have been amended or added by this act, unless the court, in its discretion, determines that resentencing the petitioner would pose an unreasonable risk of danger to public safety. In exercising its discretion, the court may consider all of the following:
(1) The petitioner's criminal conviction history, including the type of crimes committed, the extent of injury to victims, the length of prior prison commitments, and the remoteness of the crimes.
(2) The petitioner's disciplinary record and record of rehabilitation while incarcerated.
(3) Any other evidence the court, within its discretion, determines to be relevant in deciding whether a new sentence would result in an unreasonable risk of danger to public safety.
(c) As used throughout this code, "unreasonable risk of danger to public safety" means an unreasonable risk that the petitioner will commit a new violent felony within the meaning of clause (iv) of subparagraph (C) of paragraph (2) of subdivision (e) of Section 667.
(d) A person who is resentenced pursuant to subdivision (b) shall be given credit for time served and shall be subject to parole for one year following completion of his or her sentence, unless the court, in its discretion, as part of its resentencing order, releases the person from parole. The person is subject to parole supervision by the Department of Corrections and Rehabilitation pursuant to Section 3000.08 and the jurisdiction of the court in the county in which the parolee is released or resides, or in which an alleged violation of supervision has occurred, for the purpose of hearing petitions to revoke parole and impose a term of custody.
(e) Resentencing pursuant to this section shall not result in the imposition of a term longer than the original sentence.
(f) A person who has completed his or her sentence for a conviction, whether by trial or plea, of a felony or felonies who would have been guilty of a misdemeanor under this act had this act been in effect at the time of the offense, may file an application before the trial court that entered the judgment of conviction in his or her case to have the felony conviction or convictions designated as misdemeanors.
(g) If the application satisfies the criteria in subdivision (f), the court shall designate the felony offense or offenses as a misdemeanor.
(h) Unless the applicant requests a hearing, a hearing is not necessary to grant or deny an application filed under subdivision (f).
(i) This section does not apply to a person who has one or more prior convictions for an offense specified in clause (iv) of subparagraph (C) of paragraph (2) of subdivision (e) of Section 667 or for an offense requiring registration pursuant to subdivision (c) of Section 290.
(j) Except as specified in subdivision (p), a petition or application under this section shall be filed on or before November 4, 2022, or at a later date upon showing of good cause.
(k) A felony conviction that is recalled and resentenced under subdivision (b) or designated as a misdemeanor under subdivision (g) shall be considered a misdemeanor for all purposes, except that resentencing shall not permit that person to own, possess, or have in his or her custody or control a firearm or prevent his or her conviction under Chapter 2 (commencing with Section 29800) of Division 9 of Title 4 of Part 6.
(l) If the court that originally sentenced the petitioner is not available, the presiding judge shall designate another judge to rule on the petition or application.
(m) This section does not diminish or abrogate any rights or remedies otherwise available to the petitioner or applicant.
(n) Resentencing pursuant to this section does not diminish or abrogate the finality of judgments in any case that does not come within the purview of this section.
(o) A resentencing hearing ordered under this section shall constitute a "post-conviction release proceeding" under paragraph (7) of subdivision (b) of Section 28 of Article I of the California Constitution (Marsy's Law).
(p) (1) A person who is committed to a state hospital after being found not guilty by reason of insanity pursuant to Section 1026 may petition the court to have his or her maximum term of commitment, as established by Section 1026.5, reduced to the length it would have been had the act that added this section been in effect at the time of the original determination. Both of the following conditions are required for the maximum term of commitment to be reduced.
(A) The person would have met all of the criteria for a reduction in sentence pursuant to this section had he or she been found guilty.
(B) The person files the petition for a reduction of the maximum term of commitment before January 1, 2021, or on a later date upon a showing of good cause.
(2) If a petitioner's maximum term of confinement is ordered reduced under this subdivision, the new term of confinement must provide opportunity to meet requirements provided in subdivision (b) of Section 1026.5. If a petitioner's new maximum term of confinement ordered under this section does not provide sufficient time to meet requirements provided in subdivision (b) of Section 1026.5, the new maximum term of confinement may be extended, not more than 240 days from the date the petition is granted, in order to meet requirements provided in subdivision (b) of Section 1026.5.
(Amended by Stats. 2017, Ch. 17, Sec. 26. (AB 103) Effective June 27, 2017. Note: This section was added on Nov. 4, 2014, by initiative Prop. 47.)
1170.19.
(a) Notwithstanding any other provision of law, the following shall apply to a person sentenced pursuant to Section 1170.17.
(1) The person may be committed to the Youth Authority only to the extent the person meets the eligibility criteria set forth in Section 1732.6 of the Welfare and Institutions Code.
(2) The person shall not be housed in any facility under the jurisdiction of the Department of Corrections, if the person is under the age of 16 years.
(3) The person shall have his or her criminal court records accorded the same degree of public access as the records pertaining to the conviction of an adult for the identical offense.
(4) Subject to the knowing and intelligent consent of both the prosecution and the person being sentenced pursuant to this section, the court may order a juvenile disposition under the juvenile court law, in lieu of a sentence under this code, upon a finding that such an order would serve the best interests of justice, protection of the community, and the person being sentenced. Prior to ordering a juvenile disposition, the court shall cause to be received into evidence a social study by the probation officer, prepared pursuant to Section 706 of the Welfare and Institutions Code, and shall state that the social study made by the probation officer has been read and considered by the court.
(b) Notwithstanding any other provision of law, the following shall apply to a person who is eligible to receive a juvenile disposition pursuant to Section 1170.17.
(1) The person shall be entitled a hearing on the proper disposition of the case, conducted in accordance with the provisions of Section 706 of the Welfare and Institutions Code. The court in which the conviction occurred shall order the probation department to prepare a written social study and recommendation concerning the proper disposition of the case, prior to conducting the hearing or remand the matter to the juvenile court for purposes of preparing the social study, conducting the disposition hearing pursuant to Section 706 of the Welfare and Institutions Code, and making a disposition order under the juvenile court law.
(2) The person shall have his or her conviction deemed to be a finding of delinquency wardship under Section 602 of the Welfare and Institutions Code.
(3) The person shall have his or her criminal court records accorded the same degree of confidentiality as if the matter had been initially prosecuted as a delinquency petition in the juvenile court.
(4) Subject to the knowing and intelligent consent of both the prosecution and the person being sentenced pursuant to this section, the court may impose an adult sentence under this code, in lieu of ordering a juvenile disposition under the juvenile court law, upon a finding that such an order would serve the best interests of justice, protection of the community, and the person being sentenced. Prior to ordering an adult sentence, the court shall cause to be received into evidence a social study by the probation officer, prepared pursuant to Section 706 of the Welfare and Institutions Code, and shall state that the social study prepared by the probation officer has been read and considered by the court.
(Added by Stats. 1999, Ch. 996, Sec. 12.1. Effective January 1, 2000.)
1170.2.
(a) In the case of any inmate who committed a felony prior to July 1, 1977, who would have been sentenced under Section 1170 if he or she had committed it after July 1, 1977, the Board of Prison Terms shall determine what the length of time of imprisonment would have been under Section 1170 without consideration of good-time credit and utilizing the middle term of the offense bearing the longest term of imprisonment of which the prisoner was convicted increased by any enhancements justified by matters found to be true and which were imposed by the court at the time of sentencing for such felony. These matters include: being armed with a deadly or

dangerous weapon as specified in Section 211a, 460, 3024, or 12022 prior to July 1, 1977, which may result in a one-year enhancement pursuant to the provisions of Section 12022; using a firearm as specified in Section 12022.5 prior to July 1, 1977, which may result in a two-year enhancement pursuant to the provisions of Section 12022.5; infliction of great bodily injury as specified in Section 213, 264, or 461 prior to July 1, 1977, which may result in a three-year enhancement pursuant to the provisions of Section 12022.7; any prior felony conviction as specified in any statute prior to July 1, 1977, which prior felony conviction is the equivalent of a prior prison term as defined in Section 667.5, which may result in the appropriate enhancement pursuant to the provisions of Section 667.5; and any consecutive sentence.

(b) If the calculation required under subdivision (a) is less than the time to be served prior to a release date set prior to July 1, 1977, or if a release date had not been set, the Board of Prison Terms shall establish the prisoner's parole date, subject to subdivision (d), on the date calculated under subdivision (a) unless at least two of the commissioners of the Board of Prison Terms after reviewing the prisoner's file, determine that due to the number of crimes of which the prisoner was convicted, or due to the number of prior convictions suffered by the prisoner, or due to the fact that the prisoner was armed with a deadly weapon when the crime was committed, or used a deadly weapon during the commission of the crime, or inflicted or attempted to inflict great bodily injury on the victim of the crime, the prisoner should serve a term longer than that calculated in subdivision (a), in which event the prisoner shall be entitled to a hearing before a panel consisting of at least two commissioners of the Board of Prison Terms as provided for in Section 3041.5. The Board of Prison Terms shall notify each prisoner who is scheduled for such a hearing within 90 days of July 1, 1977, or within 90 days of the date the prisoner is received by or returned to the custody of the Department of Corrections, whichever is later. The hearing shall be held before October 1, 1978, or within 120 days of receipt of the prisoner, whichever is later. It is the intent of the Legislature that the hearings provided for in this subdivision shall be accomplished in the most expeditious manner possible. At the hearing the prisoner shall be entitled to be represented by legal counsel, a release date shall be set, and the prisoner shall be informed in writing of the extraordinary factors specifically considered determinative and on what basis the release date has been calculated. In fixing a term under this section the board shall be guided by, but not limited to, the term which reasonably could be imposed on a person who committed a similar offense under similar circumstances on or after July 1, 1977, and further, the board shall be guided by the following finding and declaration hereby made by the Legislature: that the necessity to protect the public from repetition of extraordinary crimes of violence against the person is the paramount consideration.

(c) Nothing in this section shall be deemed to keep an inmate in the custody of the Department of Corrections for a period of time longer than he would have been kept in its custody under the provisions of law applicable to him prior to July 1, 1977. Nothing in this section shall be deemed to require the release of an inmate sentenced to consecutive sentences under the provisions of law applicable to him prior to July 1, 1977, earlier than if he had been sentenced to concurrent sentences.

(d) In the case of any prisoner who committed a felony prior to July 1, 1977, who would have been sentenced under Section 1170 if the felony was committed on or after July 1, 1977, the good behavior and participation provisions of Article 2.5 (commencing with Section 2930) of Chapter 7 of Title 1 of Part 3 shall apply from July 1, 1977, and thereafter.

(e) In the case of any inmate who committed a felony prior to July 1, 1977, who would have been sentenced under Section 1168 if the felony was committed on or after July 1, 1977, the Board of Prison Terms shall provide for release from prison as provided for by this code.

(f) In the case of any inmate who committed a felony prior to July 1, 1977, the length, conditions, revocation, and other incidents of parole shall be the same as if the prisoner had been sentenced for an offense committed on or after July 1, 1977.

(g) Nothing in this chapter shall affect the eligibility for parole under Article 3 (commencing with Section 3040) of Chapter 8 of Title 1 of Part 3 of an inmate sentenced pursuant to Section 1168 as operative prior to July 1, 1977, for a period of parole as specified in subdivision (b) of Section 3000.

(h) In fixing a term under this section, the Board of Prison Terms shall utilize the terms of imprisonment as provided in Chapter 1139 of the Statutes of 1976 and Chapter 165 of the Statutes of 1977.

(Amended by Stats. 1989, Ch. 568, Sec. 1.5.)

1170.21.
A conviction for a violation of Section 647f as it read on December 31, 2017, is invalid and vacated. All charges alleging violation of Section 647f are dismissed and all arrests for violation of Section 647f are deemed to have never occurred. An individual who was arrested, charged, or convicted for a violation of Section 647f may indicate in response to any question concerning his or her prior arrest, charge, or conviction under Section 647f that he or she was not arrested, charged, or convicted for a violation of Section 647f. Notwithstanding any other law, information pertaining to an individual's arrest, charge, or conviction for violation of Section 647f shall not, without the individual's consent, be used in any way adverse to his or her interests, including, but not limited to, denial of any employment, benefit, license, or certificate.

(Added by Stats. 2017, Ch. 537, Sec. 13. (SB 239) Effective January 1, 2018.)

1170.22.
(a) A person who is serving a sentence as a result of a violation of Section 647f as it read on December 31, 2017, whether by trial or by open or negotiated plea, may petition for a recall or dismissal of sentence before the trial court that entered the judgment of conviction in his or her case.

(b) If the court's records show that the petitioner was convicted for a violation of Section 647f as it read on December 31, 2017, the court shall vacate the conviction and resentence the person for any remaining counts.

(c) A person who is serving a sentence and resentenced pursuant to subdivision (b) shall be given credit for any time already served and shall be subject to whatever supervision time he or she would have otherwise been subject to after release, whichever is shorter, unless the court, in its discretion, as part of its resentencing order, releases the person from supervision.

(d) Under no circumstances may resentencing under this section result in the imposition of a term longer than the original sentence, or the reinstatement of charges dismissed pursuant to a negotiated plea agreement.

(e) Upon completion of sentence for a conviction under Section 647f as it read on December 31, 2017, the provisions of Section 1170.21 shall apply.

(f) Nothing in this and related sections is intended to diminish or abrogate the finality of judgments in any case not falling within the purview of this section.

(g) A resentencing hearing ordered under this section shall constitute a "post-conviction release proceeding" under paragraph (7) of subdivision (b) of Section 28 of Article I of the California Constitution.

(h) The provisions of this section apply to juvenile delinquency adjudications and dispositions under Section 602 of the Welfare and Institutions Code if the juvenile would not have been guilty of an offense or would not have been guilty of an offense governed by this section.

(i) The Judicial Council shall promulgate and make available all necessary forms to enable the filing of petitions and applications provided in this section.

(Added by Stats. 2017, Ch. 537, Sec. 14. (SB 239) Effective January 1, 2018.)

1170.3.
The Judicial Council shall seek to promote uniformity in sentencing under Section 1170 by:

(a) The adoption of rules providing criteria for the consideration of the trial judge at the time of sentencing regarding the court's decision to:

(1) Grant or deny probation.

(2) Impose the lower, middle, or upper prison term.

(3) Impose the lower, middle, or upper term pursuant to paragraph (1) or (2) of subdivision (h) of Section 1170.

(4) Impose concurrent or consecutive sentences.

(5) Determine whether or not to impose an enhancement where that determination is permitted by law.

(6) Deny a period of mandatory supervision in the interests of justice under paragraph (5) of subdivision (h) of Section 1170 or determine the appropriate period and conditions of mandatory supervision. The rules implementing this paragraph shall be adopted no later than January 1, 2015.

(7) Determine the county or counties of incarceration and supervision when the court is imposing a judgment pursuant to subdivision (h) of Section 1170 concurrent or consecutive to a judgment or judgments previously imposed pursuant to subdivision (h) of Section 1170 in a county or counties.

(b) The adoption of rules standardizing the minimum content and the sequential presentation of material in probation officer reports submitted to the court regarding probation and mandatory supervision under paragraph (5) of subdivision (h) of Section 1170.

(c) This section shall remain in effect only until January 1, 2022, and as of that date is repealed, unless a later enacted statute, that is enacted before January 1, 2022, deletes or extends that date.

(Amended (as amended by Stats. 2016, Ch. 887, Sec. 9) by Stats. 2017, Ch. 287, Sec. 3. (SB 670) Effective January 1, 2018. Repealed as of January 1, 2022, by its own provisions. See later operative version, as amended by Sec. 4 of Stats. 2017, Ch. 287.)

1170.3.
The Judicial Council shall seek to promote uniformity in sentencing under Section 1170 by:

(a) The adoption of rules providing criteria for the consideration of the trial judge at the time of sentencing regarding the court's decision to:

(1) Grant or deny probation.

(2) Impose the lower or upper prison term.

(3) Impose the lower or upper term pursuant to paragraph (1) or (2) of subdivision (h) of Section 1170.

(4) Impose concurrent or consecutive sentences.

(5) Determine whether or not to impose an enhancement where that determination is permitted by law.

(6) Deny a period of mandatory supervision in the interests of justice under paragraph (5) of subdivision (h) of Section 1170 or determine the appropriate period and conditions of mandatory supervision. The rules implementing this paragraph shall be adopted no later than January 1, 2015.

(7) Determine the county or counties of incarceration and supervision when the court is imposing a judgment pursuant to subdivision (h) of Section 1170 concurrent or consecutive to a judgment or judgments previously imposed pursuant to subdivision (h) of Section 1170 in a county or counties.

(b) The adoption of rules standardizing the minimum content and the sequential presentation of material in probation officer reports submitted to the court regarding probation and mandatory supervision under paragraph (5) of subdivision (h) of Section 1170.

(c) This section shall become operative on January 1, 2022.

(Amended (as amended by Stats. 2016, Ch. 887, Sec. 10) by Stats. 2017, Ch. 287, Sec. 4. (SB 670) Effective January 1, 2018. Section operative January 1, 2022, by its own provisions.)

1170.4.
The Judicial Council shall collect and analyze relevant information relating to sentencing practices in this state and other jurisdictions. Such information shall be taken into consideration by the Judicial Council in the adoption of rules pursuant to Section 1170.3.

(Amended by Stats. 1993, Ch. 909, Sec. 15. Effective January 1, 1994.)

1170.45.
The Judicial Council shall collect data on criminal cases statewide relating to the disposition of those cases according to the race and ethnicity of the defendant, and report annually thereon to the Legislature beginning no later than January 1, 1999. It is the intent of the Legislature to appropriate funds to the Judicial Council for this purpose.

(Added by Stats. 1997, Ch. 850, Sec. 48.5. Effective January 1, 1998.)

1170.5.
The Judicial Council shall conduct annual sentencing institutes for trial court judges pursuant to Section 68551 of the Government Code, toward the end of assisting the judge in the imposition of appropriate sentences.

(Added by Stats. 1976, Ch. 1139.)

1170.7.
Robbery or attempted robbery for the purpose of obtaining any controlled substance, as defined in Division 10 (commencing with Section 11000) of the Health and Safety Code, when committed against a pharmacist, pharmacy employee, or other person lawfully possessing controlled substances, shall be considered a circumstance in aggravation of the crime in imposing a term under subdivision (b) of Section 1170.

(Amended by Stats. 1987, Ch. 828, Sec. 67.)

1170.71.
The fact that a person who commits a violation of Section 288 has used obscene or harmful matter to induce, persuade, or encourage the minor to engage in a lewd or lascivious act shall be considered a circumstance in aggravation of the crime in imposing a term under subdivision (b) of Section 1170.

(Added by Stats. 1985, Ch. 165, Sec. 1.)

1170.72.
Upon conviction of a violation of Section 11353, 11353.5, 11353.7, 11354, 11361, or 11380 of the Health and Safety Code, or a finding of truth of an enhancing allegation pursuant to paragraph (3) of subdivision (a) of Section 11353.1, Section 11353.6, or paragraph (3) of subdivision (a) of Section 11380.1, the fact that the minor was 11 years of age or younger shall be considered a circumstance in aggravation when imposing a term under subdivision (b) of Section 1170.

(Added by Stats. 1993, Ch. 131, Sec. 1. Effective January 1, 1994.)

1170.73.
Upon conviction of a felony violation of Section 11377, 11378, or 11378.5 of the Health and Safety Code, the court shall consider the quantity of controlled substance involved in determining whether to impose an aggravated term under subdivision (b) of Section 1170.

(Added by Stats. 1990, Ch. 777, Sec. 1.)

1170.74.
Upon conviction of a felony violation of Section 11377, 11378, 11379, or 11379.6 of the Health and Safety Code, for an offense involving methamphetamine, the fact that the controlled substance is the crystalline form of methamphetamine shall be considered a circumstance in aggravation of the crime in imposing a term under subdivision (b) of Section 1170.

(Added by Stats. 1990, Ch. 952, Sec. 1.)

1170.76.
The fact that a defendant who commits or attempts to commit a violation of Section 243.4, 245, or 273.5 is or has been a member of the household of a minor or of the victim of the offense, or the defendant is a marital or blood relative of the minor or the

victim, or the defendant or the victim is the natural parent, adoptive parent, stepparent, or foster parent of the minor, and the offense contemporaneously occurred in the presence of, or was witnessed by, the minor shall be considered a circumstance in aggravation of the crime in imposing a term under subdivision (b) of Section 1170.
(Amended by Stats. 2005, Ch. 279, Sec. 9. Effective January 1, 2006.)

1170.78.
Upon a conviction of a violation of Section 451, the fact that the person committed the offense in retaliation against the owner or occupant of the property or structure burned, or against one believed by the person to be the owner or occupant of the property or structure burned, for any eviction or other legal action taken by the owner or occupant, or believed owner or occupant, shall be a circumstance in aggravation of the crime in imposing a term under subdivision (b) of Section 1170.
(Added by Stats. 1991, Ch. 602, Sec. 7.)

1170.8.
(a) The fact that a robbery or an assault with a deadly weapon or instrument or by means of any force likely to produce great bodily injury was committed against a person while that person was in a church, synagogue, or building owned and occupied by a religious educational institution, or any other place primarily used as a place of worship where religious services are regularly conducted, shall be considered a circumstance in aggravation of the crime in imposing a term under subdivision (b) of Section 1170.
(b) Upon conviction of any person for a violation of Section 451 or 453, the fact that the person intentionally burned, or intended to burn, a church, synagogue, or building owned and occupied by a religious educational institution, or any other place primarily used as a place of worship where religious services are regularly conducted, shall be considered a circumstance in aggravation of the crime in imposing a term under subdivision (b) of Section 1170.
(Added by Stats. 1982, Ch. 929, Sec. 1.)

1170.81.
The fact that the intended victim of an attempted life term crime was a peace officer, as described in subdivisions (a) and (b) of Section 830.1, or Section 830.2, 830.5 or 830.6, while the peace officer was engaged in the performance of his or her duties, and the defendant knew or reasonably should have known that the victim was a peace officer engaged in the performance of his or her duties, shall be considered a circumstance in aggravation of the crime in imposing a term under subdivision (b) of Section 1170.
(Added by Stats. 1990, Ch. 1031, Sec. 1.)

1170.82.
Upon a conviction of a violation of Section 11352, 11360, 11379, or 11379.5 of the Health and Safety Code, the fact that the person who committed the offense knew, or reasonably should have known, that any of the following circumstances existed with regard to the person to whom he or she unlawfully sold, furnished, administered, or gave away a controlled substance, shall be a circumstance in aggravation of the crime in imposing a term pursuant to subdivision (b) of Section 1170:
(a) The person was pregnant at the time of the selling, furnishing, administering, or giving away of the controlled substance.
(b) The person had been previously convicted of a violent felony, as defined in subdivision (c) of Section 667.5.
(c) The person was in psychological treatment for a mental disorder or for substance abuse at the time of the selling, furnishing, administering, or giving away of the controlled substance.
(Added by Stats. 1994, Ch. 352, Sec. 1. Effective January 1, 1995.)

1170.84.
Upon conviction of any serious felony, listed in subdivision (c) of Section 1192.7, it shall be considered a circumstance in aggravation of the crime in imposing a term under subdivision (b) of Section 1170 if, during the course of the serious felony, the person engaged in the tying, binding, or confining of any victim.
(Added by Stats. 1990, Ch. 1216, Sec. 1.)

1170.85.
(a) Upon conviction of any felony assault or battery offense, it shall be considered a circumstance in aggravation of the crime in imposing a term under subdivision (b) of Section 1170 if the offense was committed to prevent or dissuade a person who is or may become a witness from attending upon or testifying at any trial, proceeding, or inquiry authorized by law, or if the offense was committed because the person provided assistance or information to a law enforcement officer, or to a public prosecutor in a criminal or juvenile court proceeding.
(b) Upon conviction of any felony it shall be considered a circumstance in aggravation in imposing a term under subdivision (b) of Section 1170 if the victim of an offense is particularly vulnerable, or unable to defend himself or herself, due to age or significant disability.
(Amended by Stats. 1985, Ch. 1108, Sec. 3.)

1170.86.
Upon conviction of a felony violation of Section 220, 261, 261.5, 264.1, or 266j the fact that the felony was committed within a safe school zone, as defined in subdivision (c) of Section 626, against a victim who was a pupil currently attending school, shall be considered a circumstance in aggravation in imposing a term under subdivision (b) of Section 1170.
(Amended by Stats. 2005, Ch. 279, Sec. 10. Effective January 1, 2006.)

1170.89.
Where there is an applicable triad for an enhancement related to the possession of, being armed with, use of, or furnishing or supplying a firearm, set forth in Section 12021.5, 12022, 12022.2, 12022.3, 12022.4, 12022.5, or 12022.55 the fact that a person knew or had reason to believe that a firearm was stolen shall constitute a circumstance in aggravation of the enhancement justifying imposition of the upper term on that enhancement.
(Amended by Stats. 2005, Ch. 279, Sec. 11. Effective January 1, 2006.)

1170.9.
(a) In the case of any person convicted of a criminal offense who could otherwise be sentenced to county jail or state prison and who alleges that he or she committed the offense as a result of sexual trauma, traumatic brain injury, post-traumatic stress disorder, substance abuse, or mental health problems stemming from service in the United States military, the court shall, prior to sentencing, make a determination as to whether the defendant was, or currently is, a member of the United States military and whether the defendant may be suffering from sexual trauma, traumatic brain injury, post-traumatic stress disorder, substance abuse, or mental health problems as a result of his or her service. The court may request, through existing resources, an assessment to aid in that determination.
(b) (1) If the court concludes that a defendant convicted of a criminal offense is a person described in subdivision (a), and if the defendant is otherwise eligible for probation, the court shall consider the circumstances described in subdivision (a) as a factor in favor of granting probation.
(2) If the court places the defendant on probation, the court may order the defendant into a local, state, federal, or private nonprofit treatment program for a period not to exceed that period which the defendant would have served in state prison or county jail, provided the defendant agrees to participate in the program and the court determines that an appropriate treatment program exists.
(c) If a referral is made to the county mental health authority, the county shall be obligated to provide mental health treatment services only to the extent that resources are available for that purpose, as described in paragraph (5) of subdivision (b) of Section 5600.3 of the Welfare and Institutions Code. If mental health treatment services are ordered by the court, the county mental health agency shall coordinate appropriate

referral of the defendant to the county veterans service officer, as described in paragraph (5) of subdivision (b) of Section 5600.3 of the Welfare and Institutions Code. The county mental health agency shall not be responsible for providing services outside its traditional scope of services. An order shall be made referring a defendant to a county mental health agency only if that agency has agreed to accept responsibility for the treatment of the defendant.
(d) When determining the "needs of the defendant," for purposes of Section 1202.7, the court shall consider the fact that the defendant is a person described in subdivision (a) in assessing whether the defendant should be placed on probation and ordered into a federal or community-based treatment service program with a demonstrated history of specializing in the treatment of mental health problems, including substance abuse, post-traumatic stress disorder, traumatic brain injury, military sexual trauma, and other related mental health problems.
(e) A defendant granted probation under this section and committed to a residential treatment program shall earn sentence credits for the actual time the defendant serves in residential treatment.
(f) The court, in making an order under this section to commit a defendant to an established treatment program, shall give preference to a treatment program that has a history of successfully treating veterans who suffer from sexual trauma, traumatic brain injury, post-traumatic stress disorder, substance abuse, or mental health problems as a result of that service, including, but not limited to, programs operated by the United States Department of Defense or the United States Department of Veterans Affairs.
(g) The court and the assigned treatment program may collaborate with the Department of Veterans Affairs and the United States Department of Veterans Affairs to maximize benefits and services provided to the veteran.
(h) (1) It is in the interests of justice to restore a defendant who acquired a criminal record due to a mental health disorder stemming from service in the United States military to the community of law abiding citizens. The restorative provisions of this subdivision shall apply to cases in which a trial court or a court monitoring the defendant's performance of probation pursuant to this section finds at a public hearing, held after not less than 15 days' notice to the prosecution, the defense, and any victim of the offense, that all of the following describe the defendant:
(A) He or she was granted probation and was at the time that probation was granted a person described in subdivision (a).
(B) He or she is in substantial compliance with the conditions of that probation.
(C) He or she has successfully participated in court-ordered treatment and services to address the sexual trauma, traumatic brain injury, post-traumatic stress disorder, substance abuse, or mental health problems stemming from military service.
(D) He or she does not represent a danger to the health and safety of others.
(E) He or she has demonstrated significant benefit from court-ordered education, treatment, or rehabilitation to clearly show that granting restorative relief pursuant to this subdivision would be in the interests of justice.
(2) When determining whether granting restorative relief pursuant to this subdivision is in the interests of justice, the court may consider, among other factors, all of the following:
(A) The defendant's completion and degree of participation in education, treatment, and rehabilitation as ordered by the court.
(B) The defendant's progress in formal education.
(C) The defendant's development of career potential.
(D) The defendant's leadership and personal responsibility efforts.
(E) The defendant's contribution of service in support of the community.
(3) If the court finds that a case satisfies each of the requirements described in paragraph (1), then the court may take any of the following actions by a written order setting forth the reasons for so doing:
(A) Deem all conditions of probation to be satisfied, including fines, fees, assessment, and programs, and terminate probation prior to the expiration of the term of probation. This subparagraph does not apply to any court-ordered victim restitution.
(B) Reduce an eligible felony to a misdemeanor pursuant to subdivision (b) of Section 17.
(C) Grant relief in accordance with Section 1203.4.
(4) Notwithstanding anything to the contrary in Section 1203.4, a dismissal of the action pursuant to this subdivision has the following effect:
(A) Except as otherwise provided in this paragraph, a dismissal of the action pursuant to this subdivision releases the defendant from all penalties and disabilities resulting from the offense of which the defendant has been convicted in the dismissed action.
(B) A dismissal pursuant to this subdivision does not apply to any of the following:
(i) A conviction pursuant to subdivision (c) of Section 42002.1 of the Vehicle Code.
(ii) A felony conviction pursuant to subdivision (d) of Section 261.5.
(iii) A conviction pursuant to subdivision (c) of Section 286.
(iv) A conviction pursuant to Section 288.
(v) A conviction pursuant to subdivision (c) of Section 287 or former Section 288a.
(vi) A conviction pursuant to Section 288.5.
(vii) A conviction pursuant to subdivision (j) of Section 289.
(viii) The requirement to register pursuant to Section 290.
(C) The defendant is not obligated to disclose the arrest on the dismissed action, the dismissed action, or the conviction that was set aside when information concerning prior arrests or convictions is requested to be given under oath, affirmation, or otherwise. The defendant may indicate that he or she has not been arrested when his or her only arrest concerns the dismissed action, except when the defendant is required to disclose the arrest, the conviction that was set aside, and the dismissed action in response to any direct question contained in any questionnaire or application for any law enforcement position.
(D) A dismissal pursuant to this subdivision may, in the discretion of the court, order the sealing of police records of the arrest and court records of the dismissed action, thereafter viewable by the public only in accordance with a court order.
(E) The dismissal of the action pursuant to this subdivision shall be a bar to any future action based on the conduct charged in the dismissed action.
(F) In any subsequent prosecution for any other offense, a conviction that was set aside in the dismissed action may be pleaded and proved as a prior conviction and shall have the same effect as if the dismissal pursuant to this subdivision had not been granted.
(G) A conviction that was set aside in the dismissed action may be considered a conviction for the purpose of administratively revoking or suspending or otherwise limiting the defendant's driving privilege on the ground of two or more convictions.
(H) The defendant's DNA sample and profile in the DNA data bank shall not be removed by a dismissal pursuant to this subdivision.
(I) Dismissal of an accusation, information, or conviction pursuant to this section does not authorize a defendant to own, possess, or have in his or her custody or control any firearm or prevent his or her conviction pursuant to Chapter 2 (commencing with Section 29800) of Division 9 of Title 4 of Part 6.
(Amended by Stats. 2018, Ch. 423, Sec. 86. (SB 1494) Effective January 1, 2019.)

1170.91.
(a) If the court concludes that a defendant convicted of a felony offense is, or was, a member of the United States military who may be suffering from sexual trauma, traumatic brain injury, post-traumatic stress disorder, substance abuse, or mental health problems as a result of his or her military service, the court shall consider the circumstance as a factor in mitigation when imposing a term under subdivision (b) of Section 1170. This consideration does not preclude the court from considering similar trauma, injury, substance abuse, or mental health problems due to other causes, as evidence or factors in mitigation.

(b) (1) A person currently serving a sentence for a felony conviction, whether by trial or plea, who is, or was, a member of the United States military and who may be suffering from sexual trauma, traumatic brain injury, post-traumatic stress disorder, substance abuse, or mental health problems as a result of his or her military service may petition for a recall of sentence, before the trial court that entered the judgment of conviction in his or her case, to request resentencing pursuant to subdivision (a) if the person meets both of the following conditions:

(A) The circumstance of suffering from sexual trauma, traumatic brain injury, post-traumatic stress disorder, substance abuse, or mental health problems as a result of the person's military service was not considered as a factor in mitigation at the time of sentencing.

(B) The person was sentenced prior to January 1, 2015. This subdivision shall apply retroactively, whether or not the case was final as of January 1, 2015.

(2) If the court that originally sentenced the person is not available, the presiding judge shall designate another judge to rule on the petition.

(3) Upon receiving a petition under this subdivision, the court shall determine, at a public hearing held after not less than 15 days' notice to the prosecution, the defense, and any victim of the offense, whether the person satisfies the criteria in this subdivision. At that hearing, the prosecution shall have an opportunity to be heard on the petitioner's eligibility and suitability for resentencing. If the person satisfies the criteria, the court may, in its discretion, resentence the person following a resentencing hearing.

(4) A person who is resentenced pursuant to this subdivision shall be given credit for time served.

(5) Under no circumstances may resentencing under this subdivision result in the imposition of a term longer than the original sentence.

(6) This subdivision does not alter or diminish any rights conferred under Section 28 of Article I of the California Constitution (Marsy's Law).

(7) This subdivision does not diminish or abrogate any rights or remedies otherwise available to the person.

(8) This subdivision does not diminish or abrogate the finality of judgments in any case not falling within the purview of this subdivision.

(9) This subdivision does not impose an obligation on the Department of Corrections and Rehabilitation to provide medical or mental health assessments in order to identify potential service-related injuries.

(Amended by Stats. 2018, Ch. 523, Sec. 1. (AB 865) Effective January 1, 2019.)

1170.95.

(a) A person convicted of felony murder or murder under a natural and probable consequences theory may file a petition with the court that sentenced the petitioner to have the petitioner's murder conviction vacated and to be resentenced on any remaining counts when all of the following conditions apply:

(1) A complaint, information, or indictment was filed against the petitioner that allowed the prosecution to proceed under a theory of felony murder or murder under the natural and probable consequences doctrine.

(2) The petitioner was convicted of first degree or second degree murder following a trial or accepted a plea offer in lieu of a trial at which the petitioner could be convicted for first degree or second degree murder.

(3) The petitioner could not be convicted of first or second degree murder because of changes to Section 188 or 189 made effective January 1, 2019.

(b) (1) The petition shall be filed with the court that sentenced the petitioner and served by the petitioner on the district attorney, or on the agency that prosecuted the petitioner, and on the attorney who represented the petitioner in the trial court or on the public defender of the county where the petitioner was convicted. If the judge that originally sentenced the petitioner is not available to resentence the petitioner, the presiding judge shall designate another judge to rule on the petition. The petition shall include all of the following:

(A) A declaration by the petitioner that he or she is eligible for relief under this section, based on all the requirements of subdivision (a).

(B) The superior court case number and year of the petitioner's conviction.

(C) Whether the petitioner requests the appointment of counsel.

(2) If any of the information required by this subdivision is missing from the petition and cannot be readily ascertained by the court, the court may deny the petition without prejudice to the filing of another petition and advise the petitioner that the matter cannot be considered without the missing information.

(c) The court shall review the petition and determine if the petitioner has made a prima facie showing that the petitioner falls within the provisions of this section. If the petitioner has requested counsel, the court shall appoint counsel to represent the petitioner. The prosecutor shall file and serve a response within 60 days of service of the petition and the petitioner may file and serve a reply within 30 days after the prosecutor response is served. These deadlines shall be extended for good cause. If the petitioner makes a prima facie showing that he or she is entitled to relief, the court shall issue an order to show cause.

(d) (1) Within 60 days after the order to show cause has issued, the court shall hold a hearing to determine whether to vacate the murder conviction and to recall the sentence and resentence the petitioner on any remaining counts in the same manner as if the petitioner had not been previously been sentenced, provided that the new sentence, if any, is not greater than the initial sentence. This deadline may be extended for good cause.

(2) The parties may waive a resentencing hearing and stipulate that the petitioner is eligible to have his or her murder conviction vacated and for resentencing. If there was a prior finding by a court or jury that the petitioner did not act with reckless indifference to human life or was not a major participant in the felony, the court shall vacate the petitioner's conviction and resentence the petitioner.

(3) At the hearing to determine whether the petitioner is entitled to relief, the burden of proof shall be on the prosecution to prove, beyond a reasonable doubt, that the petitioner is ineligible for resentencing. If the prosecution fails to sustain its burden of proof, the prior conviction, and any allegations and enhancements attached to the conviction, shall be vacated and the petitioner shall be resentenced on the remaining charges. The prosecutor and the petitioner may rely on the record of conviction or offer new or additional evidence to meet their respective burdens.

(e) If petitioner is entitled to relief pursuant to this section, murder was charged generically, and the target offense was not charged, the petitioner's conviction shall be redesignated as the target offense or underlying felony for resentencing purposes. Any applicable statute of limitations shall not be a bar to the court's redesignation of the offense for this purpose.

(f) This section does not diminish or abrogate any rights or remedies otherwise available to the petitioner.

(g) A person who is resentenced pursuant to this section shall be given credit for time served. The judge may order the petitioner to be subject to parole supervision for up to three years following the completion of the sentence.

(Added by Stats. 2018, Ch. 1015, Sec. 4. (SB 1437) Effective January 1, 2019.)

CHAPTER 4.8. Pregnant and Parenting Women's Alternative Sentencing Program Act [1174 - 1174.9]

(Chapter 4.8 added by Stats. 1994, Ch. 63, Sec. 2.)

1174.

This chapter shall be known as the Pregnant and Parenting Women's Alternative Sentencing Program Act.

(Added by Stats. 1994, Ch. 63, Sec. 2. Effective May 9, 1994.)

1174.1.

For purposes of this chapter, the following definitions shall apply:

(a) "Agency" means the private agency selected by the department to operate this program.

(b) "Construction" means the purchase, new construction, reconstruction, remodeling, renovation, or replacement of facilities, or a combination thereof.

(c) "County" means each individual county as represented by the county board of supervisors.

(d) "Court" means the superior court sentencing the offender to the custody of the department.

(e) "Department" means the Department of Corrections.

(f) "Facility" means the nonsecure physical buildings, rooms, areas, and equipment.

(g) "Program" means an intensive substance abusing pregnant and parenting women's alternative sentencing program.

(Added by Stats. 1994, Ch. 63, Sec. 2. Effective May 9, 1994.)

1174.2.

(a) Notwithstanding any other law, the unencumbered balance of Item 5240-311-751 of Section 2 of the Budget Act of 1990 shall revert to the unappropriated surplus of the 1990 Prison Construction Fund. The sum of fifteen million dollars ($15,000,000) is hereby appropriated to the Department of Corrections from the 1990 Prison Construction Fund for site acquisition, site studies, environmental studies, master planning, architectural programming, schematics, preliminary plans, working drawings, construction, and long lead and equipment items for the purpose of constructing facilities for pregnant and parenting women's alternative sentencing programs. These funds shall not be expended for any operating costs, including those costs reimbursed by the department pursuant to subdivision (c) of Section 1174.3. Funds not expended pursuant to this chapter shall be used for planning, construction, renovation, or remodeling by, or under the supervision of, the Department of Corrections and Rehabilitation, of community-based facilities for programs designed to reduce drug use and recidivism, including, but not limited to, restitution centers, facilities for the incarceration and rehabilitation of drug offenders, multipurpose correctional centers, and centers for intensive programs for parolees. These funds shall not be expended until legislation authorizing the establishment of these programs is enacted. If the Legislature finds that the Department of Corrections and Rehabilitation has made a good faith effort to site community-based facilities, but funds designated for these community-based facilities are unexpended as of January 1, 1998, the Legislature may appropriate these funds for other Level I housing.

(b) The Department of Corrections and Rehabilitation shall purchase, design, construct, and renovate facilities in counties or multicounty areas with a population of more than 450,000 people pursuant to this chapter. The department shall target for selection, among other counties, Los Angeles County, San Diego County, and a bay area, central valley, and an inland empire county as determined by the Secretary of the Department of Corrections and Rehabilitation. The department, in consultation with the State Department of Health Care Services, shall design core alcohol and drug treatment programs, with specific requirements and standards. Residential facilities shall be licensed by the State Department of Health Care Services in accordance with provisions of the Health and Safety Code governing licensure of alcoholism or drug abuse recovery or treatment facilities. Residential and nonresidential programs shall be certified by the State Department of Health Care Services as meeting its standards for perinatal services. Funds shall be awarded to selected agency service providers based upon all of the following criteria and procedures:

(1) A demonstrated ability to provide comprehensive services to pregnant women or women with children who are substance abusers consistent with this chapter. Criteria shall include, but not be limited to, each of the following:

(A) The success records of the types of programs proposed based upon standards for successful programs.

(B) Expertise and actual experience of persons who will be in charge of the proposed program.

(C) Cost-effectiveness, including the costs per client served.

(D) A demonstrated ability to implement a program as expeditiously as possible.

(E) An ability to accept referrals and participate in a process with the probation department determining eligible candidates for the program.

(F) A demonstrated ability to seek and obtain supplemental funding as required in support of the overall administration of this facility from any county, state, or federal source that may serve to support this program, including the State Department of Health Care Services, the Office of Emergency Services, the State Department of Social Services, the State Department of State Hospitals, or any county public health department. In addition, the agency shall also attempt to secure other available funding from all county, state, or federal sources for program implementation.

(G) An ability to provide intensive supervision of the program participants to ensure complete daily programming.

(2) Staff from the department shall be available to selected agencies for consultation and technical services in preparation and implementation of the selected proposals.

(3) The department shall consult with existing program operators that are then currently delivering similar program services, the State Department of Health Care Services, and others it may identify in the development of the program.

(4) Funds shall be made available by the department to the agencies selected to administer the operation of this program.

(5) Agencies shall demonstrate an ability to provide offenders a continuing supportive network of outpatient drug treatment and other services upon the women's completion of the program and reintegration into the community.

(6) The department may propose any variation of types and sizes of facilities to carry out the purposes of this chapter.

(7) The department shall secure all other available funding for its eligible population from all county, state, or federal sources.

(8) Each program proposal shall include a plan for the required 12-month residential program, plus a 12-month outpatient transitional services program to be completed by participating women and children.

(Amended by Stats. 2013, Ch. 22, Sec. 77. (AB 75) Effective June 27, 2013. Operative July 1, 2013, by Sec. 110 of Ch. 22.)

1174.3.

(a) The department shall ensure that the facility designs provide adequate space to carry out this chapter, including the capability for nonsecure housing, programming, child care, food services, treatment services, educational or vocational services, intensive day treatment, and transitional living skills services.

(b) The agency selected to operate the program shall administer and operate the center and program consistent with the criteria set forth in this chapter and any criteria established by the department. These responsibilities shall include maintenance and compliance with all laws, regulations, and health standards. The department shall contract to reimburse the agency selected to operate this program for women who would otherwise be sentenced to state prison based upon actual costs not provided by other funding sources.

(c) Notwithstanding any other law, Division 13 (commencing with Section 21000) of the Public Resources Code shall not apply to any facility used for multiperson residential use

in the last five years, including, but not limited to, motels, hotels, long-term care facilities, apartment buildings, and rooming houses, or to any project for which facilities intended to house no more than 75 women and children are constructed or leased pursuant to this chapter.
(d) Proposals submitted pursuant to this chapter are exempt from approval and submittal of plans and specifications to the Joint Legislative Committee on Prison Construction Operations and other legislative fiscal committees.
(Added by Stats. 1994, Ch. 63, Sec. 2. Effective May 9, 1994.)
1174.4.
(a) Persons eligible for participation in this alternative sentencing program shall meet all of the following criteria:
(1) Pregnant women with an established history of substance abuse, or pregnant or parenting women with an established history of substance abuse who have one or more children under six years old at the time of entry into the program. For women with children, at least one eligible child shall reside with the mother in the facility.
(2) Never served a prior prison term for, nor been convicted in the present proceeding of, committing or attempting to commit, any of the following offenses:
(A) Murder or voluntary manslaughter.
(B) Mayhem.
(C) Rape.
(D) Kidnapping.
(E) Sodomy by force, violence, duress, menace, or fear of immediate and unlawful bodily injury on the victim or another person.
(F) Oral copulation by force, violence, duress, menace, or fear of immediate and unlawful bodily injury on the victim or another person.
(G) Lewd acts on a child under 14 years of age, as defined in Section 288.
(H) Any felony punishable by death or imprisonment in the state prison for life.
(I) Any felony in which the defendant inflicts great bodily injury on any person, other than an accomplice, that has been charged and proved as provided for in Section 12022.53, 12022.7, or 12022.9, or any felony in which the defendant uses a firearm, as provided in Section 12022.5, 12022.53, or 12022.55, in which the use has been charged and proved.
(J) Robbery.
(K) Any robbery perpetrated in an inhabited dwelling house or trailer coach as defined in the Vehicle Code, or in the inhabited portion of any other building, wherein it is charged and proved that the defendant personally used a deadly or dangerous weapon, as provided in subdivision (b) of Section 12022, in the commission of that robbery.
(L) Arson in violation of subdivision (a) of Section 451.
(M) Sexual penetration in violation of subdivision (a) of Section 289 if the act is accomplished against the victim's will by force, violence, duress, menace, or fear of immediate and unlawful bodily injury on the victim or another person.
(N) Rape or sexual penetration in concert, in violation of Section 264.1.
(O) Continual sexual abuse of a child in violation of Section 288.5.
(P) Assault with intent to commit mayhem, rape, sodomy, oral copulation, rape in concert with another, lascivious acts upon a child, or sexual penetration.
(Q) Assault with a deadly weapon or with force likely to produce great bodily injury in violation of subdivision (a) of Section 245.
(R) Any violent felony defined in Section 667.5.
(S) A violation of Section 12022.
(T) A violation of Section 18745.
(U) Burglary of the first degree.
(V) A violation of Section 11351, 11351.5, 11352, 11353, 11358, 11359, 11360, 11370.1, 11370.6, 11378, 11378.5, 11379, 11379.5, 11379.6, 11380, or 11383 of the Health and Safety Code.
(3) Has not been sentenced to state prison for a term exceeding 36 months.
(b) Prior to sentencing, if the court proposes to give consideration to a placement, the court shall consider a written evaluation by the probation department, which shall include the following:
(1) Whether the defendant is eligible for participation pursuant to this section.
(2) Whether participation by the defendant and her eligible children is deemed to be in the best interests of the children.
(3) Whether the defendant is amenable to treatment for substance abuse and would benefit from participation in the program.
(4) Whether the program is deemed to be in the best interests of an eligible child of the defendant, as determined by a representative of the appropriate child welfare services agency of the county if the child is a dependent child of the juvenile court pursuant to Section 300 of the Welfare and Institutions Code.
(c) The district attorney shall make a recommendation to the court as to whether or not the defendant would benefit from the program, which the court shall consider in making its decision. If the court's decision is without the concurrence of the district attorney, the court shall specify its reasons in writing and enter them into the record.
(d) If the court determines that the defendant may benefit from participation in this program, the court may impose a sentence of imprisonment pursuant to subdivision (h) of Section 1170 with the recommendation that the defendant participate in the program pursuant to this chapter. The court shall notify the department within 48 hours of imposition of this sentence.
(e) The Director of Corrections shall consider the court's recommendation in making a determination on the inmate's placement in the program.
(f) Women accepted for the program by the Director of Corrections shall be delivered by the county, pursuant to Section 1202a, to the facility selected by the department. Before the director accepts a woman for the program, the county shall provide to the director the necessary information to determine her eligibility and appropriate placement status. Priority for services and aftercare shall be given to inmates who are incarcerated in a county, or adjacent to a county, in which a program facility is located.
(g) Prior to being admitted to the program, each participant shall voluntarily sign an agreement specifying the terms and conditions of participation in the program.
(h) The department may refer inmates back to the sentencing court if the department determines that an eligible inmate has not been recommended for the program. The department shall refer the inmate to the court by an evaluative report so stating the department's assessment of eligibility, and requesting a recommendation by the court.
(i) Women who successfully complete the program, including the minimum of one year of transition services under intensive parole supervision, shall be discharged from parole. Women who do not successfully complete the program shall be returned to imprisonment pursuant to subdivision (h) of Section 1170 where they shall serve their original sentences. These persons shall receive full credit against their original sentences for the time served in the program, pursuant to Section 2933.
(Amended (as amended by Stats. 2010, Ch. 178) by Stats. 2011, Ch. 15, Sec. 453. (AB 109) Effective April 4, 2011. Amending action operative October 1, 2011, by Sec. 636 of Ch. 15, as amended by Stats. 2011, Ch. 39, Sec. 68. Amended version operative January 1, 2012, pursuant to Stats. 2010, Ch. 178, Sec. 107.)
1174.5.
The department shall be responsible for the funding and monitoring of the progress, activities, and performance of each program.
(Added by Stats. 1994, Ch. 63, Sec. 2. Effective May 9, 1994.)
1174.8.
(a) The department shall adopt regulations pursuant to the Administrative Procedure Act (Chapter 3.5 (commencing with Section 11340) of Part 1 of Division 3 of Title 2 of the Government Code) to implement this chapter.
(b) Notwithstanding subdivision (a) and any other law, and except as otherwise specifically provided in this chapter, until July 1, 1996, the Director of Corrections shall have the power to implement, interpret, and make specific the changes made in this chapter by issuing director's criteria. These criteria shall be exempt from the requirements of Articles 5 (commencing with Section 11346) and 6 (commencing with Section 11349) of the Administrative Procedure Act (Chapter 3.5 (commencing with Section 11340) of Part 1 of Division 3 of Title 2 of the Government Code) and shall remain in effect until July 1, 1996, unless terminated or replaced by, or readopted as, emergency regulations pursuant to subdivision (c).
(c) On or before July 1, 1995, the department shall file emergency regulations to implement this chapter with the Office of Administrative Law. These emergency regulations shall be considered by the office as necessary for the immediate preservation of the public peace, health and safety, or general welfare and shall remain in effect until July 1, 1996, unless terminated or replaced by, or readopted as, permanent regulations in compliance with Articles 5 (commencing with Section 11346) and 6 (commencing with Section 11349) of the Administrative Procedure Act (Chapter 3.5 (commencing with Section 11340) of Part 1 of Division 3 of Title 2 of the Government Code) pursuant to subdivision (d).
(d) The department shall file a certificate of compliance with the Office of Administrative Law to adopt permanent regulations on or before May 15, 1996.
(Added by Stats. 1994, Ch. 63, Sec. 2. Effective May 9, 1994.)
1174.9.
A program facility administered by the Department of Corrections pursuant to this chapter is exempt from the requirements and provisions of Chapter 3.4 (commencing with Section 1596.70), Chapter 3.5 (commencing with Section 1596.90), and Chapter 3.6 (commencing with Section 1597.30) of Division 2 of the Health and Safety Code.
(Added by Stats. 1995, Ch. 372, Sec. 4. Effective January 1, 1996.)

CHAPTER 5. Bills of Exception [1176- 1176.]

(Chapter 5 enacted 1872.)
1176.
When written instructions have been presented, and given, modified, or refused, or when the charge of the court has been taken down by the reporter, the questions presented in such instructions or charge need not be excepted to; but the judge must make and sign an indorsement upon such instructions, showing the action of the court thereon.
(Amended by Stats. 1945, Ch. 40.)

CHAPTER 6. New Trials [1179 - 1182]

(Chapter 6 enacted 1872.)
1179.
A new trial is a reëxamination of the issue in the same Court, before another jury, after a verdict has been given.
(Enacted 1872.)
1180.
The granting of a new trial places the parties in the same position as if no trial had been had. All the testimony must be produced anew, and the former verdict or finding cannot be used or referred to, either in evidence or in argument, or be pleaded in bar of any conviction which might have been had under the accusatory pleading.
(Amended by Stats. 1951, Ch. 1674.)
1181.
When a verdict has been rendered or a finding made against the defendant, the court may, upon his application, grant a new trial, in the following cases only:
1. When the trial has been had in his absence except in cases where the trial may lawfully proceed in his absence;
2. When the jury has received any evidence out of court, other than that resulting from a view of the premises, or of personal property;
3. When the jury has separated without leave of the court after retiring to deliberate upon their verdict, or been guilty of any misconduct by which a fair and due consideration of the case has been prevented;
4. When the verdict has been decided by lot, or by any means other than a fair expression of opinion on the part of all the jurors;
5. When the court has misdirected the jury in a matter of law, or has erred in the decision of any question of law arising during the course of the trial, and when the district attorney or other counsel prosecuting the case has been guilty of prejudicial misconduct during the trial thereof before a jury;
6. When the verdict or finding is contrary to law or evidence, but if the evidence shows the defendant to be not guilty of the degree of the crime of which he was convicted, but guilty of a lesser degree thereof, or of a lesser crime included therein, the court may modify the verdict, finding or judgment accordingly without granting or ordering a new trial, and this power shall extend to any court to which the cause may be appealed;
7. When the verdict or finding is contrary to law or evidence, but in any case wherein authority is vested by statute in the trial court or jury to recommend or determine as a part of its verdict or finding the punishment to be imposed, the court may modify such verdict or finding by imposing the lesser punishment without granting or ordering a new trial, and this power shall extend to any court to which the case may be appealed;
8. When new evidence is discovered material to the defendant, and which he could not, with reasonable diligence, have discovered and produced at the trial. When a motion for a new trial is made upon the ground of newly discovered evidence, the defendant must produce at the hearing, in support thereof, the affidavits of the witnesses by whom such evidence is expected to be given, and if time is required by the defendant to procure such affidavits, the court may postpone the hearing of the motion for such length of time as, under all circumstances of the case, may seem reasonable.
9. When the right to a phonographic report has not been waived, and when it is not possible to have a phonographic report of the trial transcribed by a stenographic reporter as provided by law or by rule because of the death or disability of a reporter who participated as a stenographic reporter at the trial or because of the loss or destruction, in whole or in substantial part, of the notes of such reporter, the trial court or a judge, thereof, or the reviewing court shall have power to set aside and vacate the judgment, order or decree from which an appeal has been taken or is to be taken and to order a new trial of the action or proceeding.
(Amended by Stats. 1973, Ch. 167.)
1182.
The application for a new trial must be made and determined before judgment, the making of an order granting probation, the commitment of a defendant for observation as a mentally disordered sex offender, or the commitment of a defendant for narcotics addiction or insanity, whichever first occurs, and the order granting or denying the application shall be immediately entered by the clerk in the minutes.
(Amended by Stats. 1980, Ch. 676, Sec. 252.)

CHAPTER 7. Arrest of Judgment [1185 - 1188]

(Chapter 7 enacted 1872.)

1185.
A motion in arrest of judgment is an application on the part of the defendant that no judgment be rendered on a plea, finding, or verdict of guilty, or on a finding or verdict against the defendant, on a plea of a former conviction, former acquittal or once in jeopardy. It may be founded on any of the defects in the accusatory pleading mentioned in Section 1004, unless the objection has been waived by a failure to demur, and must be made and determined before the judgment is pronounced. When determined, the order must be immediately entered in the minutes.
(Amended by Stats. 1951, Ch. 1674.)

1186.
The court may, on its own motion, at any time before judgment is pronounced, arrest the judgment for any of the defects in the accusatory pleading upon which a motion in arrest of judgment may be founded as provided in Section 1185, by order for that purpose entered upon its minutes.
(Amended by Stats. 1951, Ch. 1674.)

1187.
The effect of an order arresting judgment, in a felony case, is to place the defendant in the same situation in which the defendant was immediately before the indictment was found or information filed. In a misdemeanor or infraction case, the effect is to place the defendant in the situation in which the defendant was before the trial was had.
(Amended by Stats. 1998, Ch. 931, Sec. 391. Effective September 28, 1998.)

1188.
If, from the evidence on the trial, there is reason to believe the defendant guilty, and a new indictment or information can be framed upon which he may be convicted, the court may order him to be recommitted to the officer of the proper county, or admitted to bail anew, to answer the new indictment or information. If the evidence shows him guilty of another offense, he must be committed or held thereon, and in neither case shall the verdict be a bar to another prosecution. But if no evidence appears sufficient to charge him with any offense, he must, if in custody, be discharged; or if admitted to bail, his bail is exonerated; or if money has been deposited instead of bail, it must be refunded to the defendant or to the person or persons found by the court to have deposited said money on behalf of said defendant; and the arrest of judgment shall operate as an acquittal of the charge upon which the indictment or information was founded.
(Amended by Stats. 1935, Ch. 657.)

TITLE 8. OF JUDGMENT AND EXECUTION [1191 - 1234.5]

(Title 8 enacted 1872.)

CHAPTER 1. The Judgment [1191 - 1210.6]

(Chapter 1 enacted 1872.)

1191.
In a felony case, after a plea, finding, or verdict of guilty, or after a finding or verdict against the defendant on a plea of a former conviction or acquittal, or once in jeopardy, the court shall appoint a time for pronouncing judgment, which shall be within 20 judicial days after the verdict, finding, or plea of guilty, during which time the court shall refer the case to the probation officer for a report if eligible for probation and pursuant to Section 1203. However, the court may extend the time not more than 10 days for the purpose of hearing or determining any motion for a new trial, or in arrest of judgment, and may further extend the time until the probation officer's report is received and until any proceedings for granting or denying probation have been disposed of. If, in the opinion of the court, there is a reasonable ground for believing a defendant insane, the court may extend the time for pronouncing sentence until the question of insanity has been heard and determined, as provided in this code. If the court orders the defendant placed in a diagnostic facility pursuant to Section 1203.03, the time otherwise allowed by this section for pronouncing judgment is extended by a period equal to (1) the number of days which elapse between the date of the order and the date on which notice is received from the Director of Corrections advising whether or not the Department of Corrections will receive the defendant in the facility, and (2) if the director notifies the court that it will receive the defendant, the time which elapses until his or her return to the court from the facility.
(Amended by Stats. 1998, Ch. 931, Sec. 392. Effective September 28, 1998.)

1191.1.
The victim of any crime, or the parents or guardians of the victim if the victim is a minor, or the next of kin of the victim if the victim has died, have the right to attend all sentencing proceedings under this chapter and shall be given adequate notice by the probation officer of all sentencing proceedings concerning the person who committed the crime.
The victim, or up to two of the victim's parents or guardians if the victim is a minor, or the next of kin of the victim if the victim has died, have the right to appear, personally or by counsel, at the sentencing proceeding and to reasonably express his, her, or their views concerning the crime, the person responsible, and the need for restitution. The court in imposing sentence shall consider the statements of victims, parents or guardians, and next of kin made pursuant to this section and shall state on the record its conclusion concerning whether the person would pose a threat to public safety if granted probation.
The provisions of this section shall not be amended by the Legislature except by statute passed in each house by rollcall vote entered in the journal, two-thirds of the membership concurring, or by a statute that becomes effective only when approved by the electors.
(Amended by Stats. 1993, Ch. 338, Sec. 1. Effective January 1, 1994. Note: This section was added on June 8, 1982, by initiative Prop. 8.)

1191.10.
The definition of the term "victim" as used in Section 1191.1 includes any insurer or employer who was the victim of workers' compensation fraud for the crimes specified in Section 549 of this code, Sections 2314 and 6152 of the Business and Professions Code, Sections 1871.4, 11760, and 11880 of the Insurance Code, and Section 3215 of the Labor Code.
(Added by Stats. 1993, Ch. 120, Sec. 9. Effective July 16, 1993.)

1191.15.
(a) The court may permit the victim of any crime, his or her parent or guardian if the victim is a minor, or the next of kin of the victim if the victim has died, to file with the court a written, audiotaped, or videotaped statement, or statement stored on a CD-ROM, DVD, or any other recording medium acceptable to the court, expressing his or her views concerning the crime, the person responsible, and the need for restitution, in lieu of or in addition to the person personally appearing at the time of judgment and sentence. The court shall consider the statement filed with the court prior to imposing judgment and sentence.
Whenever an audio or video statement or statement stored on a CD-ROM, DVD, or other medium is filed with the court, a written transcript of the statement shall also be

provided by the person filing the statement, and shall be made available as a public record of the court after the judgment and sentence have been imposed.
(b) Whenever a written, audio, or video statement or statement stored on a CD-ROM, DVD, or other medium is filed with the court, it shall remain sealed until the time set for imposition of judgment and sentence except that the court, the probation officer, and counsel for the parties may view and listen to the statement not more than two court days prior to the date set for imposition of judgment and sentence.
(c) A person or a court shall not permit any person to duplicate, copy, or reproduce by audio or visual means a statement submitted to the court under the provisions of this section.
(d) Nothing in this section shall be construed to prohibit the prosecutor from representing to the court the views of the victim, his or her parent or guardian, the next of kin, or the California Victim Compensation Board.
(e) In the event the court permits an audio or video statement or statement stored on a CD-ROM, DVD, or other medium to be filed, the court shall not be responsible for providing any equipment or resources needed to assist the victim in preparing the statement.
(Amended by Stats. 2016, Ch. 31, Sec. 238. (SB 836) Effective June 27, 2016.)

1191.16.
The victim of any crime, or the parents or guardians of the victim if the victim is a minor, or the next of kin of the victim if the victim has died, who choose to exercise their rights with respect to sentencing proceedings as described in Section 1191.1 may, in any case where the defendant is subject to an indeterminate term of imprisonment, have their statements simultaneously recorded and preserved by means of videotape, videodisc, or any other means of preserving audio and video, if they notify the prosecutor in advance of the sentencing hearing and the prosecutor reasonably is able to provide the means to record and preserve the statement. If a video and audio record is developed, that record shall be maintained and preserved by the prosecution and used in accordance with the regulations of the Board of Prison Terms at any hearing to review parole suitability or the setting of a parole date.
(Added by Stats. 1997, Ch. 902, Sec. 2. Effective January 1, 1998.)

1191.2.
In providing notice to the victim pursuant to Section 1191.1, the probation officer shall also provide the victim with information concerning the victim's right to civil recovery against the defendant, the requirement that the court order restitution for the victim, the victim's right to receive a copy of the restitution order from the court and to enforce the restitution order as a civil judgment, the victim's responsibility to furnish the probation department, district attorney, and court with information relevant to his or her losses, and the victim's opportunity to be compensated from the Restitution Fund if eligible under Article 1 (commencing with Section 13959) of Chapter 5 of Part 4 of Division 3 of Title 2 of the Government Code. This information shall be in the form of written material prepared by the Judicial Council in consultation with the California Victim Compensation Board, shall include the relevant sections of the Penal Code, and shall be provided to each victim for whom the probation officer has a current mailing address.
(Amended by Stats. 2016, Ch. 31, Sec. 239. (SB 836) Effective June 27, 2016.)

1191.21.
(a) (1) The Office of Emergency Services shall develop and make available a "notification of eligibility" card for victims and derivative victims of crimes as defined in subdivision (c) of Section 13960 of the Government Code that includes, but is not limited to, the following information:
"If you have been the victim of a crime that meets the required definition, you or others may be eligible to receive payment from the California State Restitution Fund for losses directly resulting from the crime. To learn about eligibility and receive an application to receive payments, call the Victims of Crime Program at (800) 777-9229 or call your local county Victim Witness Assistance Center."
(2) At a minimum, the Office of Emergency Services shall develop a template available for downloading on its Internet Web site the information requested in subdivision (b).
(b) In a case involving a crime as defined in subdivision (c) of Section 13960 of the Government Code, the law enforcement officer with primary responsibility for investigating the crime committed against the victim and the district attorney may provide the "notification of eligibility" card to the victim and derivative victim of a crime.
(c) The terms "victim" and "derivative victim" shall be given the same meaning given those terms in Section 13960 of the Government Code.
(Amended by Stats. 2013, Ch. 352, Sec. 416. (AB 1317) Effective September 26, 2013. Operative July 1, 2013, by Sec. 543 of Ch. 352.)

1191.25.
The prosecution shall make a good faith attempt to notify any victim of a crime which was committed by, or is alleged to have been committed by, an in-custody informant, as defined in subdivision (a) of Section 1127a, within a reasonable time before the in-custody informant is called to testify. The notice shall include information concerning the prosecution's intention to offer the in-custody informant a modification or reduction in sentence or dismissal of the case or early parole in exchange for the in-custody informant's testimony in another case. The notification or attempt to notify the victim shall be made prior to the commencement of the trial in which the in-custody informant is to testify where the intention to call him or her is known at that time, but in no case shall the notice be made later than the time the in-custody informant is called to the stand.
Nothing contained in this section is intended to affect the right of the people and the defendant to an expeditious disposition of a criminal proceeding, as provided in Section 1050. The victim of any case alleged to have been committed by the in-custody informant may exercise his or her right to appear at the sentencing of the in-custody informant pursuant to Section 1191.1, but the victim shall not have a right to intervene in the trial in which the in-custody informant is called to testify.
(Added by Stats. 1989, Ch. 901, Sec. 2.)

1191.3.
(a) At the time of sentencing or pronouncement of judgment in which sentencing is imposed, the court shall make an oral statement that statutory law permits the award of conduct and worktime credits up to one-third or one-half of the sentence that is imposed by the court, that the award and calculation of credits is determined by the sheriff in cases involving imprisonment in county jails and by the Department of Corrections in cases involving imprisonment in the state prison, and that credit for presentence incarceration served by the defendant is calculated by the probation department under current state law.
As used in this section, "victim" means the victim of the offense, the victim's parent or guardian if the victim is a minor, or the victim's next of kin.
(b) The probation officer shall provide a general estimate of the credits to which the defendant may be entitled for previous time served, and conduct or worktime credits authorized under Sections 2931, 2933, or 4019, and shall inform the victim pursuant to Section 1191.1. The probation officer shall file this estimate with the court and it shall become a part of the court record.
(c) This section applies to all felony convictions.
(Added by Stats. 1987, Ch. 1247, Sec. 3.)

1192.
Upon a plea of guilty, or upon conviction by the court without a jury, of a crime or attempted crime distinguished or divided into degrees, the court must, before passing sentence, determine the degree. Upon the failure of the court to so determine, the degree of the crime or attempted crime of which the defendant is guilty, shall be deemed to be of the lesser degree.
(Amended by Stats. 1978, Ch. 1166.)

1192.1.
Upon a plea of guilty to an information or indictment accusing the defendant of a crime or attempted crime divided into degrees when consented to by the prosecuting attorney in open court and approved by the court, such plea may specify the degree thereof and in such event the defendant cannot be punished for a higher degree of the crime or attempted crime than the degree specified.
(Amended by Stats. 1978, Ch. 1166.)

1192.2.
Upon a plea of guilty before a committing magistrate as provided in Section 859a, to a crime or attempted crime divided into degrees, when consented to by the prosecuting attorney in open court and approved by such magistrate, such plea may specify the degree thereof and in such event, the defendant cannot be punished for a higher degree of the crime or attempted crime than the degree specified.
(Amended by Stats. 1978, Ch. 1166.)

1192.3.
(a) A plea of guilty or nolo contendere to an accusatory pleading charging a public offense, other than a felony specified in Section 1192.5 or 1192.7, which public offense did not result in damage for which restitution may be ordered, made on the condition that charges be dismissed for one or more public offenses arising from the same or related course of conduct by the defendant which did result in damage for which restitution may be ordered, may specify the payment of restitution by the defendant as a condition of the plea or any probation granted pursuant thereto, so long as the plea is freely and voluntarily made, there is factual basis for the plea, and the plea and all conditions are approved by the court.
(b) If restitution is imposed which is attributable to a count dismissed pursuant to a plea bargain, as described in this section, the court shall obtain a waiver pursuant to People v. Harvey (1979) 25 Cal. 3d 754 from the defendant as to the dismissed count.
(Added by Stats. 1988, Ch. 287, Sec. 1.)

1192.4.
If the defendant's plea of guilty pursuant to Section 1192.1 or 1192.2 is not accepted by the prosecuting attorney and approved by the court, the plea shall be deemed withdrawn and the defendant may then enter such plea or pleas as would otherwise have been available. The plea so withdrawn may not be received in evidence in any criminal, civil, or special action or proceeding of any nature, including proceedings before agencies, commissions, boards, and tribunals.
(Amended by Stats. 1970, Ch. 1123.)

1192.5.
Upon a plea of guilty or nolo contendere to an accusatory pleading charging a felony, other than a violation of paragraph (2), (3), or (6) of subdivision (a) of Section 261, paragraph (1) or (4) of subdivision (a) of Section 262, Section 264.1, Section 286 or 287 or former Section 288a by force, violence, duress, menace or threat of great bodily harm, subdivision (b) of Section 288, or subdivision (a) of Section 289, the plea may specify the punishment to the same extent as it may be specified by the jury on a plea of not guilty or fixed by the court on a plea of guilty, nolo contendere, or not guilty, and may specify the exercise by the court thereafter of other powers legally available to it. Where the plea is accepted by the prosecuting attorney in open court and is approved by the court, the defendant, except as otherwise provided in this section, cannot be sentenced on the plea to a punishment more severe than that specified in the plea and the court may not proceed as to the plea other than as specified in the plea.
If the court approves of the plea, it shall inform the defendant prior to the making of the plea that (1) its approval is not binding, (2) it may, at the time set for the hearing on the application for probation or pronouncement of judgment, withdraw its approval in the light of further consideration of the matter, and (3) in that case, the defendant shall be permitted to withdraw his or her plea if he or she desires to do so. The court shall also cause an inquiry to be made of the defendant to satisfy itself that the plea is freely and voluntarily made, and that there is a factual basis for the plea.
If the plea is not accepted by the prosecuting attorney and approved by the court, the plea shall be deemed withdrawn and the defendant may then enter the plea or pleas as would otherwise have been available.
If the plea is withdrawn or deemed withdrawn, it may not be received in evidence in any criminal, civil, or special action or proceeding of any nature, including proceedings before agencies, commissions, boards, and tribunals.
(Amended by Stats. 2018, Ch. 423, Sec. 87. (SB 1494) Effective January 1, 2019.)

1192.6.
(a) In each felony case in which the charges contained in the original accusatory pleading are amended or dismissed, the record shall contain a statement explaining the reason for the amendment or dismissal.
(b) In each felony case in which the prosecuting attorney seeks a dismissal of a charge in the complaint, indictment, or information, he or she shall state the specific reasons for the dismissal in open court, on the record.
(c) When, upon a plea of guilty or nolo contendere to an accusatory pleading charging a felony, whether or not that plea is entered pursuant to Section 1192.5, the prosecuting attorney recommends what punishment the court should impose or how it should exercise any of the powers legally available to it, the prosecuting attorney shall state the specific reasons for the recommendation in open court, on the record. The reasons for the recommendation shall be transcribed and made part of the court file.
(Added by Stats. 1981, Ch. 759, Sec. 1.)

1192.7.
(a) (1) It is the intent of the Legislature that district attorneys prosecute violent sex crimes under statutes that provide sentencing under a "one strike," "three strikes" or habitual sex offender statute instead of engaging in plea bargaining over those offenses.
(2) Plea bargaining in any case in which the indictment or information charges any serious felony, any felony in which it is alleged that a firearm was personally used by the defendant, or any offense of driving while under the influence of alcohol, drugs, narcotics, or any other intoxicating substance, or any combination thereof, is prohibited, unless there is insufficient evidence to prove the people's case, or testimony of a material witness cannot be obtained, or a reduction or dismissal would not result in a substantial change in sentence.
(3) If the indictment or information charges the defendant with a violent sex crime, as listed in subdivision (c) of Section 667.61, that could be prosecuted under Sections 269, 288.7, subdivisions (b) through (i) of Section 667, Section 667.61, or 667.71, plea bargaining is prohibited unless there is insufficient evidence to prove the people's case, or testimony of a material witness cannot be obtained, or a reduction or dismissal would not result in a substantial change in sentence. At the time of presenting the agreement to the court, the district attorney shall state on the record why a sentence under one of those sections was not sought.
(b) As used in this section "plea bargaining" means any bargaining, negotiation, or discussion between a criminal defendant, or his or her counsel, and a prosecuting attorney or judge, whereby the defendant agrees to plead guilty or nolo contendere, in exchange for any promises, commitments, concessions, assurances, or consideration by the prosecuting attorney or judge relating to any charge against the defendant or to the sentencing of the defendant.
(c) As used in this section, "serious felony" means any of the following:
(1) Murder or voluntary manslaughter; (2) mayhem; (3) rape; (4) sodomy by force, violence, duress, menace, threat of great bodily injury, or fear of immediate and unlawful bodily injury on the victim or another person; (5) oral copulation by force, violence, duress, menace, threat of great bodily injury, or fear of immediate and unlawful bodily injury on the victim or another person; (6) lewd or lascivious act on a child under 14 years of age; (7) any felony punishable by death or imprisonment in the state prison for

life; (8) any felony in which the defendant personally inflicts great bodily injury on any person, other than an accomplice, or any felony in which the defendant personally uses a firearm; (9) attempted murder; (10) assault with intent to commit rape or robbery; (11) assault with a deadly weapon or instrument on a peace officer; (12) assault by a life prisoner on a noninmate; (13) assault with a deadly weapon by an inmate; (14) arson; (15) exploding a destructive device or any explosive with intent to injure; (16) exploding a destructive device or any explosive causing bodily injury, great bodily injury, or mayhem; (17) exploding a destructive device or any explosive with intent to murder; (18) any burglary of the first degree; (19) robbery or bank robbery; (20) kidnapping; (21) holding of a hostage by a person confined in a state prison; (22) attempt to commit a felony punishable by death or imprisonment in the state prison for life; (23) any felony in which the defendant personally used a dangerous or deadly weapon; (24) selling, furnishing, administering, giving, or offering to sell, furnish, administer, or give to a minor any heroin, cocaine, phencyclidine (PCP), or any methamphetamine-related drug, as described in paragraph (2) of subdivision (d) of Section 11055 of the Health and Safety Code, or any of the precursors of methamphetamines, as described in subparagraph (A) of paragraph (1) of subdivision (f) of Section 11055 or subdivision (a) of Section 11100 of the Health and Safety Code; (25) any violation of subdivision (a) of Section 289 where the act is accomplished against the victim's will by force, violence, duress, menace, or fear of immediate and unlawful bodily injury on the victim or another person; (26) grand theft involving a firearm; (27) carjacking; (28) any felony offense, which would also constitute a felony violation of Section 186.22; (29) assault with the intent to commit mayhem, rape, sodomy, or oral copulation, in violation of Section 220; (30) throwing acid or flammable substances, in violation of Section 244; (31) assault with a deadly weapon, firearm, machinegun, assault weapon, or semiautomatic firearm or assault on a peace officer or firefighter, in violation of Section 245; (32) assault with a deadly weapon against a public transit employee, custodial officer, or school employee, in violation of Section 245.2, 245.3, or 245.5; (33) discharge of a firearm at an inhabited dwelling, vehicle, or aircraft, in violation of Section 246; (34) commission of rape or sexual penetration in concert with another person, in violation of Section 264.1; (35) continuous sexual abuse of a child, in violation of Section 288.5; (36) shooting from a vehicle, in violation of subdivision (c) or (d) of Section 26100; (37) intimidation of victims or witnesses, in violation of Section 136.1; (38) criminal threats, in violation of Section 422; (39) any attempt to commit a crime listed in this subdivision other than an assault; (40) any violation of Section 12022.53; (41) a violation of subdivision (b) or (c) of Section 11418; and (42) any conspiracy to commit an offense described in this subdivision.
(d) As used in this section, "bank robbery" means to take or attempt to take, by force or violence, or by intimidation from the person or presence of another any property or money or any other thing of value belonging to, or in the care, custody, control, management, or possession of, any bank, credit union, or any savings and loan association.
As used in this subdivision, the following terms have the following meanings:
(1) "Bank" means any member of the Federal Reserve System, and any bank, banking association, trust company, savings bank, or other banking institution organized or operating under the laws of the United States, and any bank the deposits of which are insured by the Federal Deposit Insurance Corporation.
(2) "Savings and loan association" means any federal savings and loan association and any "insured institution" as defined in Section 401 of the National Housing Act, as amended, and any federal credit union as defined in Section 2 of the Federal Credit Union Act.
(3) "Credit union" means any federal credit union and any state-chartered credit union the accounts of which are insured by the Administrator of the National Credit Union administration.
(e) The provisions of this section shall not be amended by the Legislature except by statute passed in each house by rollcall vote entered in the journal, two-thirds of the membership concurring, or by a statute that becomes effective only when approved by the electors.
(Amended by Stats. 2010, Ch. 178, Sec. 73. (SB 1115) Effective January 1, 2011. Operative January 1, 2012, by Sec. 107 of Ch. 178. Note: This section was added on June 8, 1982, by initiative Prop. 8, and amended on March 7, 2000, by initiative Prop. 21.)

1192.8.
(a) For purposes of subdivision (c) of Section 1192.7, "serious felony" also means any violation of Section 191.5, paragraph (1) of subdivision (c) of Section 192, subdivision (a), (b), or (c) of Section 192.5 of this code, or Section 2800.3, subdivision (b) of Section 23104, or Section 23153 of the Vehicle Code, when any of these offenses involve the personal infliction of great bodily injury on any person other than an accomplice, or the personal use of a dangerous or deadly weapon, within the meaning of paragraph (8) or (23) of subdivision (c) of Section 1192.7.
(b) It is the intent of the Legislature, in enacting subdivision (a), to codify the court decisions of People v. Gonzales, 29 Cal. App. 4th 1684, and People v. Bow, 13 Cal. App. 4th 1551, and to clarify that the crimes specified in subdivision (a) have always been, and continue to be, serious felonies within the meaning of subdivision (c) of Section 1192.7.
(Amended by Stats. 2007, Ch. 747, Sec. 9. Effective January 1, 2008.)

1193.
Judgment upon persons convicted of commission of crime shall be pronounced as follows:
(a) If the conviction is for a felony, the defendant shall be personally present when judgment is pronounced against him or her, unless the defendant, in open court and on the record, or in a notarized writing, requests that judgment be pronounced against him or her in his or her absence, and that he or she be represented by an attorney when judgment is pronounced, and the court approves his or her absence during the pronouncement of judgment, or unless, after the exercise of reasonable diligence to procure the presence of the defendant, the court shall find that it will be in the interest of justice that judgment be pronounced in his or her absence; provided, that when any judgment imposing the death penalty has been affirmed by the appellate court, sentence may be reimposed upon the defendant in his or her absence by the court from which the appeal was taken, and in the following manner: upon receipt by the superior court from which the appeal is taken of the certificate of the appellate court affirming the judgment, the judge of the superior court shall forthwith make and cause to be entered an order pronouncing sentence against the defendant, and a warrant signed by the judge, and attested by the clerk under the seal of the court, shall be drawn, and it shall state the conviction and judgment and appoint a day upon which the judgment shall be executed, which shall not be less than 60 days nor more than 90 days from the time of making the order; and that, within five days thereafter, a certified copy of the order, attested by the clerk under the seal of the court, and attached to the warrant, shall, for the purpose of execution, be transmitted by registered mail to the warden of the state prison having the custody of the defendant and certified copies thereof shall be transmitted by registered mail to the Governor; and provided further, that when any judgment imposing the death penalty has been affirmed and sentence has been reimposed as above provided there shall be no appeal from the order fixing the time for and directing the execution of the judgment as herein provided. If a pro se defendant requests that judgment in a noncapital case be pronounced against him or her in his or her absence, the court shall appoint an attorney to represent the defendant in the in absentia sentencing.
(b) If the conviction be of a misdemeanor, judgment may be pronounced against the defendant in his absence.
(Amended by Stats. 1986, Ch. 1222, Sec. 1.)

1194.
When the defendant is in custody, the Court may direct the officer in whose custody he is to bring him before it for judgment, and the officer must do so.
(Enacted 1872.)
1195.
If the defendant has been released on bail, or has deposited money or property instead thereof, and does not appear for judgment when his personal appearance is necessary, the court, in addition to the forfeiture of the undertaking of bail, or of the money or property deposited, must, on application of the prosecuting attorney, direct the issuance of a bench warrant for the arrest of the defendant.
If the defendant, who is on bail, does appear for judgment and judgment is pronounced upon him or probation is granted to him, then the bail shall be exonerated or, if money or property has been deposited instead of bail, it must be returned to the defendant or to the person or persons found by the court to have deposited said money or property on behalf of said defendant.
(Amended by Stats. 1959, Ch. 1187.)
1196.
(a) The clerk must, at any time after the order, issue a bench warrant into one or more counties.
(b) The clerk shall require the appropriate agency to enter each bench warrant issued on a private surety-bonded felony case into the national warrant system (National Crime Information Center (NCIC)). If the appropriate agency fails to enter the bench warrant into the national warrant system (NCIC), and the court finds that this failure prevented the surety or bond agent from surrendering the fugitive into custody, prevented the fugitive from being arrested or taken into custody, or resulted in the fugitive's subsequent release from custody, the court having jurisdiction over the bail shall, upon petition, set aside the forfeiture of the bond and declare all liability on the bail bond to be exonerated.
(Amended by Stats. 2007, Ch. 263, Sec. 27. Effective January 1, 2008.)
1197.
The bench warrant must be substantially in the following form:
County of ______
The people of the State of California to any peace officer in this State: _______ (name of defendant) having been on the _____ day of _____, 19_, duly convicted in the _____ court of _____ (naming the court) of the crime of _____ (designating it generally), you are therefore commanded forthwith to arrest the above named defendant and bring him before that court for judgment.
Given under my hand with the seal of said court affixed, this _____ day of _____, 19_.
By order of said court.

____
(seal)Clerk (or Judge, or Justice)
(Amended by Stats. 1951, Ch. 1674.)
1198.
The bench warrant may be served in any county in the same manner as a warrant of arrest.
(Amended by Stats. 1951, Ch. 1674.)
1199.
Whether the bench warrant is served in the county in which it was issued or in another county, the officer must arrest the defendant and bring him before the court, or deliver him to any peace officer of the county from which the warrant issued, who must bring him before said court according to the command thereof.
(Amended by Stats. 1951, Ch. 1674.)
1200.
When the defendant appears for judgment he must be informed by the Court, or by the Clerk, under its direction, of the nature of the charge against him and of his plea, and the verdict, if any thereon, and must be asked whether he has any legal cause to show why judgment should not be pronounced against him.
(Amended by Code Amendments 1880, Ch. 47.)
1201.
He or she may show, for cause against the judgment:
(a) That he or she is insane; and if, in the opinion of the court, there is reasonable ground for believing him or her insane, the question of insanity shall be tried as provided in Chapter 6 (commencing with Section 1367) of Title 10 of Part 2. If, upon the trial of that question, the jury finds that he or she is sane, judgment shall be pronounced, but if they find him or her insane, he or she shall be committed to the state hospital for the care and treatment of the insane, until he or she becomes sane; and when notice is given of that fact, as provided in Section 1372, he or she shall be brought before the court for judgment.
(b) That he or she has good cause to offer, either in arrest of judgment or for a new trial; in which case the court may, in its discretion, order the judgment to be deferred, and proceed to decide upon the motion in arrest of judgment or for a new trial.
(Amended by Stats. 1987, Ch. 828, Sec. 68.)
1201.3.
(a) Upon the conviction of a defendant for a sexual offense involving a minor victim or, in the case of a minor appearing in juvenile court, if a petition is admitted or sustained for a sexual offense involving a minor victim, the court is authorized to issue orders that would prohibit the defendant or juvenile, for a period up to 10 years, from harassing, intimidating, or threatening the victim or the victim's family members or spouse.
(b) No order issued pursuant to this section shall be interpreted to apply to counsel acting on behalf of the defendant or juvenile, or to investigators working on behalf of counsel, in an action relating to a conviction, petition in juvenile court, or any civil action arising therefrom, provided, however, that no counsel or investigator shall harass or threaten any person protected by an order issued pursuant to subdivision (a).
(c) Notice of the intent to request an order pursuant to this section shall be given to counsel for the defendant or juvenile by the prosecutor or the court at the time of conviction, or disposition of the petition in juvenile court, and counsel shall have adequate time in which to respond to the request before the order is made.
(d) A violation of an order issued pursuant to subdivision (a) is punishable as provided in Section 166.
(Amended by Stats. 2011, Ch. 296, Sec. 215. (AB 1023) Effective January 1, 2012.)
1201.5.
Any motions made subsequent to judgment must be made only upon written notice served upon the prosecution at least three days prior to the date of hearing thereon. No affidavit or other writing shall be presented or considered in support thereof unless a copy of the same has been duly served upon the prosecution at least three days prior to a hearing thereon. Any appeal from an order entered upon a motion made other than as herein provided, must be dismissed by the court.
(Added by Stats. 1937, Ch. 31.)
1202.
If no sufficient cause is alleged or appears to the court at the time fixed for pronouncing judgment, as provided in Section 1191, why judgment should not be pronounced, it shall thereupon be rendered; and if not rendered or pronounced within the time so fixed or to which it is continued under the provisions of Section 1191, then the defendant shall be entitled to a new trial. If the court shall refuse to hear a defendant's motion for a new trial or when made shall neglect to determine such motion before pronouncing judgment or the making of an order granting probation, then the defendant shall be entitled to a new trial.
(Amended by Stats. 1987, Ch. 828, Sec. 69.)
1202a.
If the judgment is for imprisonment in the state prison the judgment shall direct that the defendant be delivered into the custody of the Director of Corrections at the state prison or institution designated by the Director of Corrections as the place for the reception of persons convicted of felonies, except where the judgment is for death in which case the defendant shall be taken to the warden of the California State Prison at San Quentin. Unless a different place or places are so designated by the Director of Corrections, the judgment shall direct that the defendant be delivered into the custody of the Director of Corrections at the California State Prison at San Quentin. The Director of Corrections shall designate a place or places for the reception of persons convicted of felonies by order, which order or orders shall be served by registered mail, return receipt requested, upon each judge of each superior court in the state. The Director of Corrections may change the place or places of commitment by the issuance of a new order. Nothing contained in this section affects any provision of Section 3400.
(Amended by Stats. 1987, Ch. 828, Sec. 70.)
1202.05.
(a) Whenever a person is sentenced to the state prison on or after January 1, 1993, for violating Section 261, 264.1, 266c, 285, 286, 287, 288, 288.5, or 289, or former Section 288a, and the victim of one or more of those offenses is a child under the age of 18 years, the court shall prohibit all visitation between the defendant and the child victim. The court's order shall be transmitted to the Department of Corrections, to the parents, adoptive parents, or guardians, or a combination thereof, of the child victim, and to the child victim. If any parent, adoptive parent, or legal guardian of the child victim, or the child victim objects to the court's order, he or she may request a hearing on the matter. Any request for a hearing on the matter filed with the sentencing court shall be referred to the appropriate juvenile court pursuant to Section 362.6 of the Welfare and Institutions Code.
(b) The Department of Corrections is authorized to notify the sentencing court of persons who were sentenced to the state prison prior to January 1, 1993, for violating Section 261, 264.1, 266c, 285, 286, 288, 288.5, or 289, or former Section 288a, when the victim of one or more of those offenses was a child under the age of 18 years. Upon notification by the department pursuant to this subdivision, the sentencing court shall prohibit all visitation between the defendant and the child victim, according to the procedures specified in subdivision (a).
(Amended by Stats. 2018, Ch. 423, Sec. 88. (SB 1494) Effective January 1, 2019.)
1202.1.
(a) Notwithstanding Sections 120975 and 120990 of the Health and Safety Code, the court shall order every person who is convicted of, or adjudged by the court to be a person described by Section 601 or 602 of the Welfare and Institutions Code as provided in Section 725 of the Welfare and Institutions Code by reason of a violation of, a sexual offense listed in subdivision (e), whether or not a sentence or fine is imposed or probation is granted, to submit to a blood or oral mucosal transudate saliva test for evidence of antibodies to the probable causative agent of acquired immunodeficiency syndrome (AIDS) within 180 days of the date of conviction. Each person tested under this section shall be informed of the results of the blood or oral mucosal transudate saliva test.
(b) Notwithstanding Section 120980 of the Health and Safety Code, the results of the blood or oral mucosal transudate saliva test to detect antibodies to the probable causative agent of AIDS shall be transmitted by the clerk of the court to the Department of Justice and the local health officer.
(c) Notwithstanding Section 120980 of the Health and Safety Code, the Department of Justice shall provide the results of a test or tests as to persons under investigation or being prosecuted under Section 12022.85, if the results are on file with the department, to the defense attorney upon request and the results also shall be available to the prosecuting attorney upon request for the purpose of either preparing counts for a sentence enhancement under Section 12022.85 or complying with subdivision (d).
(d) (1) In every case in which a person is convicted of a sexual offense listed in subdivision (e) or adjudged by the court to be a person described by Section 601 or 602 of the Welfare and Institutions Code as provided in Section 725 of the Welfare and Institutions Code by reason of the commission of a sexual offense listed in subdivision (e), the prosecutor or the prosecutor's victim-witness assistance bureau shall advise the victim of his or her right to receive the results of the blood or oral mucosal transudate saliva test performed pursuant to subdivision (a). The prosecutor or the prosecutor's victim-witness assistance bureau shall refer the victim to the local health officer for counseling to assist him or her in understanding the extent to which the particular circumstances of the crime may or may not have placed the victim at risk of transmission of the human immunodeficiency virus (HIV) from the accused, to ensure that the victim understands the limitations and benefits of current tests for HIV, and to assist the victim in determining whether he or she should make the request.
(2) Notwithstanding any other law, upon the victim's request, the local health officer shall be responsible for disclosing test results to the victim who requested the test and the person who was tested. However, as specified in subdivision (g), positive test results shall not be disclosed to the victim or the person who was tested without offering or providing professional counseling appropriate to the circumstances as follows:
(A) To help the victim understand the extent to which the particular circumstances of the crime may or may not have put the victim at risk of transmission of HIV from the perpetrator.
(B) To ensure that the victim understands both the benefits and limitations of the current tests for HIV.
(C) To obtain referrals to appropriate health care and support services.
(e) For purposes of this section, "sexual offense" includes any of the following:
(1) Rape in violation of Section 261 or 264.1.
(2) Unlawful intercourse with a person under 18 years of age in violation of Section 261.5 or 266c.
(3) Rape of a spouse in violation of Section 262 or 264.1.
(4) Sodomy in violation of Section 266c or 286.
(5) Oral copulation in violation of Section 266c or 287, or former Section 288a.
(6) (A) Any of the following offenses if the court finds that there is probable cause to believe that blood, semen, or any other bodily fluid capable of transmitting HIV has been transferred from the defendant to the victim:
(i) Sexual penetration in violation of Section 264.1, 266c, or 289.
(ii) Aggravated sexual assault of a child in violation of Section 269.
(iii) Lewd or lascivious conduct with a child in violation of Section 288.
(iv) Continuous sexual abuse of a child in violation of Section 288.5.
(v) The attempt to commit any offense described in clauses (i) to (iv), inclusive.
(B) For purposes of this paragraph, the court shall note its finding on the court docket and minute order if one is prepared.
(f) Any blood or oral mucosal transudate saliva tested pursuant to subdivision (a) shall be subjected to appropriate confirmatory tests to ensure accuracy of the first test results, and under no circumstances shall test results be transmitted to the victim or the person who is tested unless any initially reactive test result has been confirmed by appropriate confirmatory tests for positive reactors.
(g) The local health officer shall be responsible for disclosing test results to the victim who requested the test and the person who was tested. However, positive test results shall not be disclosed to the victim or the person who was tested without offering or providing professional counseling appropriate to the circumstances.
(h) The local health officer and the victim shall comply with all laws and policies relating to medical confidentiality, subject to the disclosure authorized by subdivisions (g) and (i).

(i) Any victim who receives information from the local health officer pursuant to subdivision (g) may disclose the information as he or she deems necessary to protect his or her health and safety or the health and safety of his or her family or sexual partner.

(j) Any person who transmits test results or discloses information pursuant to this section shall be immune from civil liability for any action taken in compliance with this section.

(Amended by Stats. 2018, Ch. 423, Sec. 89. (SB 1494) Effective January 1, 2019.)

1202.4.

(a) (1) It is the intent of the Legislature that a victim of crime who incurs an economic loss as a result of the commission of a crime shall receive restitution directly from a defendant convicted of that crime.

(2) Upon a person being convicted of a crime in the State of California, the court shall order the defendant to pay a fine in the form of a penalty assessment in accordance with Section 1464.

(3) The court, in addition to any other penalty provided or imposed under the law, shall order the defendant to pay both of the following:

(A) A restitution fine in accordance with subdivision (b).

(B) Restitution to the victim or victims, if any, in accordance with subdivision (f), which shall be enforceable as if the order were a civil judgment.

(b) In every case where a person is convicted of a crime, the court shall impose a separate and additional restitution fine, unless it finds compelling and extraordinary reasons for not doing so and states those reasons on the record.

(1) The restitution fine shall be set at the discretion of the court and commensurate with the seriousness of the offense. If the person is convicted of a felony, the fine shall not be less than three hundred dollars ($300) and not more than ten thousand dollars ($10,000). If the person is convicted of a misdemeanor, the fine shall not be less than one hundred fifty dollars ($150) and not more than one thousand dollars ($1,000).

(2) In setting a felony restitution fine, the court may determine the amount of the fine as the product of the minimum fine pursuant to paragraph (1) multiplied by the number of years of imprisonment the defendant is ordered to serve, multiplied by the number of felony counts of which the defendant is convicted.

(c) The court shall impose the restitution fine unless it finds compelling and extraordinary reasons for not doing so and states those reasons on the record. A defendant's inability to pay shall not be considered a compelling and extraordinary reason not to impose a restitution fine. Inability to pay may be considered only in increasing the amount of the restitution fine in excess of the minimum fine pursuant to paragraph (1) of subdivision (b). The court may specify that funds confiscated at the time of the defendant's arrest, except for funds confiscated pursuant to Chapter 8 (commencing with Section 11469) of Division 10 of the Health and Safety Code, be applied to the restitution fine if the funds are not exempt for spousal or child support or subject to any other legal exemption.

(d) In setting the amount of the fine pursuant to subdivision (b) in excess of the minimum fine pursuant to paragraph (1) of subdivision (b), the court shall consider any relevant factors, including, but not limited to, the defendant's inability to pay, the seriousness and gravity of the offense and the circumstances of its commission, any economic gain derived by the defendant as a result of the crime, the extent to which any other person suffered losses as a result of the crime, and the number of victims involved in the crime. Those losses may include pecuniary losses to the victim or his or her dependents as well as intangible losses, such as psychological harm caused by the crime. Consideration of a defendant's inability to pay may include his or her future earning capacity. A defendant shall bear the burden of demonstrating his or her inability to pay. Express findings by the court as to the factors bearing on the amount of the fine shall not be required. A separate hearing for the fine shall not be required.

(e) The restitution fine shall not be subject to penalty assessments authorized in Section 1464 or Chapter 12 (commencing with Section 76000) of Title 8 of the Government Code, or the state surcharge authorized in Section 1465.7, and shall be deposited in the Restitution Fund in the State Treasury.

(f) Except as provided in subdivisions (q) and (r), in every case in which a victim has suffered economic loss as a result of the defendant's conduct, the court shall require that the defendant make restitution to the victim or victims in an amount established by court order, based on the amount of loss claimed by the victim or victims or any other showing to the court. If the amount of loss cannot be ascertained at the time of sentencing, the restitution order shall include a provision that the amount shall be determined at the direction of the court. The court shall order full restitution. The court may specify that funds confiscated at the time of the defendant's arrest, except for funds confiscated pursuant to Chapter 8 (commencing with Section 11469) of Division 10 of the Health and Safety Code, be applied to the restitution order if the funds are not exempt for spousal or child support or subject to any other legal exemption.

(1) The defendant has the right to a hearing before a judge to dispute the determination of the amount of restitution. The court may modify the amount, on its own motion or on the motion of the district attorney, the victim or victims, or the defendant. If a motion is made for modification of a restitution order, the victim shall be notified of that motion at least 10 days prior to the proceeding held to decide the motion. A victim at a restitution hearing or modification hearing described in this paragraph may testify by live, two-way audio and video transmission, if testimony by live, two-way audio and video transmission is available at the court.

(2) Determination of the amount of restitution ordered pursuant to this subdivision shall not be affected by the indemnification or subrogation rights of a third party. Restitution ordered pursuant to this subdivision shall be ordered to be deposited in the Restitution Fund to the extent that the victim, as defined in subdivision (k), has received assistance from the California Victim Compensation Board pursuant to Chapter 5 (commencing with Section 13950) of Part 4 of Division 3 of Title 2 of the Government Code.

(3) To the extent possible, the restitution order shall be prepared by the sentencing court, shall identify each victim and each loss to which it pertains, and shall be of a dollar amount that is sufficient to fully reimburse the victim or victims for every determined economic loss incurred as the result of the defendant's criminal conduct, including, but not limited to, all of the following:

(A) Full or partial payment for the value of stolen or damaged property. The value of stolen or damaged property shall be the replacement cost of like property, or the actual cost of repairing the property when repair is possible.

(B) Medical expenses.

(C) Mental health counseling expenses.

(D) Wages or profits lost due to injury incurred by the victim, and if the victim is a minor, wages or profits lost by the minor's parent, parents, guardian, or guardians, while caring for the injured minor. Lost wages shall include commission income as well as base wages. Commission income shall be established by evidence of commission income during the 12-month period prior to the date of the crime for which restitution is being ordered, unless good cause for a shorter time period is shown.

(E) Wages or profits lost by the victim, and if the victim is a minor, wages or profits lost by the minor's parent, parents, guardian, or guardians, due to time spent as a witness or in assisting the police or prosecution. Lost wages shall include commission income as well as base wages. Commission income shall be established by evidence of commission income during the 12-month period prior to the date of the crime for which restitution is being ordered, unless good cause for a shorter time period is shown.

(F) Noneconomic losses, including, but not limited to, psychological harm, for felony violations of Section 288, 288.5, or 288.7.

(G) Interest, at the rate of 10 percent per annum, that accrues as of the date of sentencing or loss, as determined by the court.

(H) Actual and reasonable attorney's fees and other costs of collection accrued by a private entity on behalf of the victim.

(I) Expenses incurred by an adult victim in relocating away from the defendant, including, but not limited to, deposits for utilities and telephone service, deposits for rental housing, temporary lodging and food expenses, clothing, and personal items. Expenses incurred pursuant to this section shall be verified by law enforcement to be necessary for the personal safety of the victim or by a mental health treatment provider to be necessary for the emotional well-being of the victim.

(J) Expenses to install or increase residential security incurred related to a violation of Section 273.5, or a violent felony as defined in subdivision (c) of Section 667.5, including, but not limited to, a home security device or system, or replacing or increasing the number of locks.

(K) Expenses to retrofit a residence or vehicle, or both, to make the residence accessible to or the vehicle operational by the victim, if the victim is permanently disabled, whether the disability is partial or total, as a direct result of the crime.

(L) Expenses for a period of time reasonably necessary to make the victim whole, for the costs to monitor the credit report of, and for the costs to repair the credit of, a victim of identity theft, as defined in Section 530.5.

(4) (A) If, as a result of the defendant's conduct, the Restitution Fund has provided assistance to or on behalf of a victim or derivative victim pursuant to Chapter 5 (commencing with Section 13950) of Part 4 of Division 3 of Title 2 of the Government Code, the amount of assistance provided shall be presumed to be a direct result of the defendant's criminal conduct and shall be included in the amount of the restitution ordered.

(B) The amount of assistance provided by the Restitution Fund shall be established by copies of bills submitted to the California Victim Compensation Board reflecting the amount paid by the board and whether the services for which payment was made were for medical or dental expenses, funeral or burial expenses, mental health counseling, wage or support losses, or rehabilitation. Certified copies of these bills provided by the board and redacted to protect the privacy and safety of the victim or any legal privilege, together with a statement made under penalty of perjury by the custodian of records that those bills were submitted to and were paid by the board, shall be sufficient to meet this requirement.

(C) If the defendant offers evidence to rebut the presumption established by this paragraph, the court may release additional information contained in the records of the board to the defendant only after reviewing that information in camera and finding that the information is necessary for the defendant to dispute the amount of the restitution order.

(5) Except as provided in paragraph (6), in any case in which an order may be entered pursuant to this subdivision, the defendant shall prepare and file a disclosure identifying all assets, income, and liabilities in which the defendant held or controlled a present or future interest as of the date of the defendant's arrest for the crime for which restitution may be ordered. The financial disclosure statements shall be made available to the victim and the board pursuant to Section 1214. The disclosure shall be signed by the defendant upon a form approved or adopted by the Judicial Council for the purpose of facilitating the disclosure. A defendant who willfully states as true a material matter that he or she knows to be false on the disclosure required by this subdivision is guilty of a misdemeanor, unless this conduct is punishable as perjury or another provision of law provides for a greater penalty.

(6) A defendant who fails to file the financial disclosure required in paragraph (5), but who has filed a financial affidavit or financial information pursuant to subdivision (c) of Section 987, shall be deemed to have waived the confidentiality of that affidavit or financial information as to a victim in whose favor the order of restitution is entered pursuant to subdivision (f). The affidavit or information shall serve in lieu of the financial disclosure required in paragraph (5), and paragraphs (7) to (10), inclusive, shall not apply.

(7) Except as provided in paragraph (6), the defendant shall file the disclosure with the clerk of the court no later than the date set for the defendant's sentencing, unless otherwise directed by the court. The disclosure may be inspected or copied as provided by subdivision (b), (c), or (d) of Section 1203.05.

(8) In its discretion, the court may relieve the defendant of the duty under paragraph (7) of filing with the clerk by requiring that the defendant's disclosure be submitted as an attachment to, and be available to, those authorized to receive the following:

(A) A report submitted pursuant to subparagraph (D) of paragraph (2) of subdivision (b) of Section 1203 or subdivision (g) of Section 1203.

(B) A stipulation submitted pursuant to paragraph (4) of subdivision (b) of Section 1203.

(C) A report by the probation officer, or information submitted by the defendant applying for a conditional sentence pursuant to subdivision (d) of Section 1203.

(9) The court may consider a defendant's unreasonable failure to make a complete disclosure pursuant to paragraph (5) as any of the following:

(A) A circumstance in aggravation of the crime in imposing a term under subdivision (b) of Section 1170.

(B) A factor indicating that the interests of justice would not be served by admitting the defendant to probation under Section 1203.

(C) A factor indicating that the interests of justice would not be served by conditionally sentencing the defendant under Section 1203.

(D) A factor indicating that the interests of justice would not be served by imposing less than the maximum fine and sentence fixed by law for the case.

(10) A defendant's failure or refusal to make the required disclosure pursuant to paragraph (5) shall not delay entry of an order of restitution or pronouncement of sentence. In appropriate cases, the court may do any of the following:

(A) Require the defendant to be examined by the district attorney pursuant to subdivision (h).

(B) If sentencing the defendant under Section 1170, provide that the victim shall receive a copy of the portion of the probation report filed pursuant to Section 1203.10 concerning the defendant's employment, occupation, finances, and liabilities.

(C) If sentencing the defendant under Section 1203, set a date and place for submission of the disclosure required by paragraph (5) as a condition of probation or suspended sentence.

(11) If a defendant has any remaining unpaid balance on a restitution order or fine 120 days prior to his or her scheduled release from probation or 120 days prior to his or her completion of a conditional sentence, the defendant shall prepare and file a new and updated financial disclosure identifying all assets, income, and liabilities in which the defendant holds or controls or has held or controlled a present or future interest during the defendant's period of probation or conditional sentence. The financial disclosure shall be made available to the victim and the board pursuant to Section 1214. The disclosure shall be signed and prepared by the defendant on the same form as described in paragraph (5). A defendant who willfully states as true a material matter that he or she knows to be false on the disclosure required by this subdivision is guilty of a misdemeanor, unless this conduct is punishable as perjury or another provision of law provides for a greater penalty. The financial disclosure required by this paragraph shall be filed with the clerk of the court no later than 90 days prior to the defendant's scheduled release from probation or completion of the defendant's conditional sentence.

(12) In cases where an employer is convicted of a crime against an employee, a payment to the employee or the employee's dependent that is made by the employer's workers' compensation insurance carrier shall not be used to offset the amount of the

restitution order unless the court finds that the defendant substantially met the obligation to pay premiums for that insurance coverage.

(g) A defendant's inability to pay shall not be a consideration in determining the amount of a restitution order.

(h) The district attorney may request an order of examination pursuant to the procedures specified in Article 2 (commencing with Section 708.110) of Chapter 6 of Division 2 of Title 9 of Part 2 of the Code of Civil Procedure, in order to determine the defendant's financial assets for purposes of collecting on the restitution order.

(i) A restitution order imposed pursuant to subdivision (f) shall be enforceable as if the order were a civil judgment.

(j) The making of a restitution order pursuant to subdivision (f) shall not affect the right of a victim to recovery from the Restitution Fund as otherwise provided by law, except to the extent that restitution is actually collected pursuant to the order. Restitution collected pursuant to this subdivision shall be credited to any other judgments for the same losses obtained against the defendant arising out of the crime for which the defendant was convicted.

(k) For purposes of this section, "victim" shall include all of the following:

(1) The immediate surviving family of the actual victim.

(2) A corporation, business trust, estate, trust, partnership, association, joint venture, government, governmental subdivision, agency, or instrumentality, or any other legal or commercial entity when that entity is a direct victim of a crime.

(3) A person who has sustained economic loss as the result of a crime and who satisfies any of the following conditions:

(A) At the time of the crime was the parent, grandparent, sibling, spouse, child, or grandchild of the victim.

(B) At the time of the crime was living in the household of the victim.

(C) At the time of the crime was a person who had previously lived in the household of the victim for a period of not less than two years in a relationship substantially similar to a relationship listed in subparagraph (A).

(D) Is another family member of the victim, including, but not limited to, the victim's fiancé or fiancée, and who witnessed the crime.

(E) Is the primary caretaker of a minor victim.

(4) A person who is eligible to receive assistance from the Restitution Fund pursuant to Chapter 5 (commencing with Section 13950) of Part 4 of Division 3 of Title 2 of the Government Code.

(5) A governmental entity that is responsible for repairing, replacing, or restoring public or privately owned property that has been defaced with graffiti or other inscribed material, as defined in subdivision (e) of Section 594, and that has sustained an economic loss as the result of a violation of Section 594, 594.3, 594.4, 640.5, 640.6, or 640.7.

(l) At its discretion, the board of supervisors of a county may impose a fee to cover the actual administrative cost of collecting the restitution fine, not to exceed 10 percent of the amount ordered to be paid, to be added to the restitution fine and included in the order of the court, the proceeds of which shall be deposited in the general fund of the county.

(m) In every case in which the defendant is granted probation, the court shall make the payment of restitution fines and orders imposed pursuant to this section a condition of probation. Any portion of a restitution order that remains unsatisfied after a defendant is no longer on probation shall continue to be enforceable by a victim pursuant to Section 1214 until the obligation is satisfied.

(n) If the court finds and states on the record compelling and extraordinary reasons why a restitution fine should not be required, the court shall order, as a condition of probation, that the defendant perform specified community service, unless it finds and states on the record compelling and extraordinary reasons not to require community service in addition to the finding that a restitution fine should not be required. Upon revocation of probation, the court shall impose the restitution fine pursuant to this section.

(o) The provisions of Section 13963 of the Government Code shall apply to restitution imposed pursuant to this section.

(p) The court clerk shall notify the California Victim Compensation and Government Claims Board within 90 days of an order of restitution being imposed if the defendant is ordered to pay restitution to the board due to the victim receiving compensation from the Restitution Fund. Notification shall be accomplished by mailing a copy of the court order to the board, which may be done periodically by bulk mail or email.

(q) Upon conviction for a violation of Section 236.1, the court shall, in addition to any other penalty or restitution, order the defendant to pay restitution to the victim in a case in which a victim has suffered economic loss as a result of the defendant's conduct. The court shall require that the defendant make restitution to the victim or victims in an amount established by court order, based on the amount of loss claimed by the victim or victims or another showing to the court. In determining restitution pursuant to this section, the court shall base its order upon the greater of the following: the gross value of the victim's labor or services based upon the comparable value of similar services in the labor market in which the offense occurred, or the value of the victim's labor as guaranteed under California law, or the actual income derived by the defendant from the victim's labor or services or any other appropriate means to provide reparations to the victim.

(r) (1) In addition to any other penalty or fine, the court shall order a person who has been convicted of a violation of Section 350, 653h, 653s, 653u, 653w, or 653aa that involves a recording or audiovisual work to make restitution to an owner or lawful producer, or trade association acting on behalf of the owner or lawful producer, of a phonograph record, disc, wire, tape, film, or other device or article from which sounds or visual images are derived that suffered economic loss resulting from the violation. The order of restitution shall be based on the aggregate wholesale value of lawfully manufactured and authorized devices or articles from which sounds or visual images are devised corresponding to the number of nonconforming devices or articles involved in the offense, unless a higher value can be proved in the case of (A) an unreleased audio work, or (B) an audiovisual work that, at the time of unauthorized distribution, has not been made available in copies for sale to the general public in the United States on a digital versatile disc. For purposes of this subdivision, possession of nonconforming devices or articles intended for sale constitutes actual economic loss to an owner or lawful producer in the form of displaced legitimate wholesale purchases. The order of restitution shall also include reasonable costs incurred as a result of an investigation of the violation undertaken by the owner, lawful producer, or trade association acting on behalf of the owner or lawful producer. "Aggregate wholesale value" means the average wholesale value of lawfully manufactured and authorized sound or audiovisual recordings. Proof of the specific wholesale value of each nonconforming device or article is not required.

(2) As used in this subdivision, "audiovisual work" and "recording" shall have the same meaning as in Section 653w.

(Amended by Stats. 2018, Ch. 142, Sec. 1. (AB 2226) Effective January 1, 2019.)
1202.41.

(a) (1) Notwithstanding Section 977 or any other law, if a defendant is currently incarcerated in a state prison with two-way audiovideo communication capability, the Department of Corrections, at the request of the California Victim Compensation Board, may collaborate with a court in any county to arrange for a hearing to impose or amend a restitution order, if the victim has received assistance pursuant to Article 5 (commencing with Section 13959) of Chapter 5 of Part 4 of Division 3 of Title 2 of the Government Code, to be conducted by two-way electronic audiovideo communication between the defendant and the courtroom in lieu of the defendant's physical presence in the courtroom, provided the county has agreed to make the necessary equipment available.

(2) Nothing in this subdivision shall be interpreted to eliminate the authority of the court to issue an order requiring the defendant to be physically present in the courtroom in those cases where the court finds circumstances that require the physical presence of the defendant in the courtroom.

(3) In lieu of the physical presence of the defendant's counsel at the institution with the defendant, the court and the Department of Corrections shall establish a confidential telephone and facsimile transmission line between the court and the institution for communication between the defendant's counsel in court and the defendant at the institution. In this case, counsel for the defendant shall not be required to be physically present at the institution during the hearing via electronic audiovideo communication. Nothing in this subdivision shall be construed to prohibit the physical presence of the defense counsel with the defendant at the state prison.

(b) If an inmate who is not incarcerated in a state prison with two-way audiovideo communication capability or ward does not waive his or her right to attend a restitution hearing for the amendment of a restitution order, the California Victim Compensation Board shall determine if the cost of holding the hearing is justified. If the board determines that the cost of holding the hearing is not justified, the amendment of the restitution order affecting that inmate or ward shall not be pursued at that time.

(c) Nothing in this section shall be construed to prohibit an individual or district attorney's office from independently pursuing the imposition or amendment of a restitution order that may result in a hearing, regardless of whether the victim has received assistance pursuant to Article 1 (commencing with Section 13959) of Chapter 5 of Part 4 of Division 3 of Title 2 of the Government Code.

(Amended by Stats. 2016, Ch. 31, Sec. 241. (SB 836) Effective June 27, 2016.)
1202.42.

Upon entry of a restitution order under subdivision (c) of Section 13967 of the Government Code, as operative on or before September 28, 1994, paragraph (3) of subdivision (a) of Section 1202.4 of this code, or Section 1203.04 as operative on or before August 2, 1995, the following shall apply:

(a) The court shall enter a separate order for income deduction upon determination of the defendant's ability to pay, regardless of the probation status, in accordance with Section 1203. Determination of a defendant's ability to pay may include his or her future earning capacity. A defendant shall bear the burden of demonstrating lack of his or her ability to pay. Express findings by the court as to the factors bearing on the amount of the fine shall not be required.

(b) (1) In any case in which the court enters a separate order for income deduction under this section, the order shall be stayed until the agency in the county responsible for collection of restitution determines that the defendant has failed to meet his or her obligation under the restitution order and the defendant has not provided the agency with good cause for the failure in accordance with paragraph (2).

(2) If the agency responsible for collection of restitution receives information that the defendant has failed to meet his or her obligation under the restitution order, the agency shall request the defendant to provide evidence indicating that timely payments have been made or provide information establishing good cause for the failure. If the defendant fails to either provide the agency with the evidence or fails to establish good cause within five days of the request, the agency shall immediately inform the defendant of that fact, and shall inform the clerk of the court in order that an income deduction order will be served pursuant to subdivision (f) following a 15-day appeal period. The defendant may apply for a hearing to contest the lifting of the stay pursuant to subdivision (f).

(c) The income deduction order shall direct a payer to deduct from all income due and payable to the defendant the amount required by the court to meet the defendant's obligation.

(d) The income deduction order shall be effective so long as the order for restitution upon which it is based is effective or until further order of the court.

(e) When the court orders the income deduction, the court shall furnish to the defendant a statement of his or her rights, remedies, and duties in regard to the income deduction order. The statement shall state all of the following:

(1) All fees or interest that will be imposed.

(2) The total amount of income to be deducted for each pay period.

(3) That the income deduction order applies to current and subsequent payers and periods of employment.

(4) That a copy of the income deduction order will be served on the defendant's payer or payers.

(5) That enforcement of the income deduction order may only be contested on the ground of mistake of fact regarding the amount of restitution owed.

(6) That the defendant is required to notify the clerk of the court within seven days after changes in the defendant's address, payers, and the addresses of his or her payers.

(7) That the court order will be stayed in accordance with subdivision (b) and that a hearing is available in accordance with subdivision (f).

(f) (1) Upon receiving the notice described in paragraph (2) of subdivision (b), the clerk of the court or officer of the agency responsible for collection of restitution shall serve an income deduction order and the notice to payer on the defendant's payer unless the defendant has applied for a hearing to contest the enforcement of the income deduction order.

(2) (A) Service by or upon any person who is a party to a proceeding under this section shall be made in the manner prescribed for service upon parties in a civil action.

(B) Service upon the defendant's payer or successor payer under this section shall be made by prepaid certified mail, return receipt requested.

(3) The defendant, within 15 days after being informed that the order staying the income deduction order will be lifted, may apply for a hearing to contest the enforcement of the income deduction order on the ground of mistake of fact regarding the amount of restitution owed or on the ground that the defendant has established good cause for the nonpayment. The timely request for a hearing shall stay the service of an income deduction order on all payers of the defendant until a hearing is held and a determination is made as to whether the enforcement of the income deduction order is proper.

(4) The notice to any payer required by this subdivision shall contain only information necessary for the payer to comply with the income deduction order. The notice shall do all of the following:

(A) Require the payer to deduct from the defendant's income the amount specified in the income deduction order, and to pay that amount to the clerk of the court.

(B) Instruct the payer to implement the income deduction order no later than the first payment date that occurs more than 14 days after the date the income deduction order was served on the payer.

(C) Instruct the payer to forward, within two days after each payment date, to the clerk of the court the amount deducted from the defendant's income and a statement as to whether the amount totally or partially satisfies the periodic amount specified in the income deduction order.

(D) Specify that if a payer fails to deduct the proper amount from the defendant's income, the payer is liable for the amount the payer should have deducted, plus costs, interest, and reasonable attorney's fees.

(E) Provide that the payer may collect up to five dollars ($5) against the defendant's income to reimburse the payer for administrative costs for the first income deduction and up to one dollar ($1) for each deduction thereafter.

(F) State that the income deduction order and the notice to payer are binding on the payer until further notice by the court or until the payer no longer provides income to the defendant.

(G) Instruct the payer that, when he or she no longer provides income to the defendant, he or she shall notify the clerk of the court and shall also provide the defendant's last known address and the name and address of the defendant's new payer, if known, and that, if the payer violates this provision, the payer is subject to a civil penalty not to exceed two hundred fifty dollars ($250) for the first violation or five hundred dollars ($500) for any subsequent violation.

(H) State that the payer shall not discharge, refuse to employ, or take disciplinary action against the defendant because of an income deduction order and shall state that a violation of this provision subjects the payer to a civil penalty not to exceed two hundred fifty dollars ($250) for the first violation or five hundred dollars ($500) for any subsequent violation.

(I) Inform the payer that when he or she receives income deduction orders requiring that the income of two or more defendants be deducted and sent to the same clerk of a court, he or she may combine the amounts that are to be paid to the depository in a single payment as long as he or she identifies that portion of the payment attributable to each defendant.

(J) Inform the payer that if the payer receives more than one income deduction order against the same defendant, he or she shall contact the court for further instructions.

(5) The clerk of the court shall enforce income deduction orders against the defendant's successor payer who is located in this state in the same manner prescribed in this subdivision for the enforcement of an income deduction order against a payer.

(6) A person may not discharge, refuse to employ, or take disciplinary action against an employee because of the enforcement of an income deduction order. An employer who violates this provision is subject to a civil penalty not to exceed two hundred fifty dollars ($250) for the first violation or five hundred dollars ($500) for any subsequent violation.

(7) When a payer no longer provides income to a defendant, he or she shall notify the clerk of the court and shall provide the defendant's last known address and the name and address of the defendant's new payer, if known. A payer who violates this provision is subject to a civil penalty not to exceed two hundred fifty dollars ($250) for the first violation or five hundred dollars ($500) for a subsequent violation.

(g) If the defendant has failed to meet his or her obligation under the restitution order and the defendant has not provided good cause for the failure in accordance with the process set forth in paragraph (2) of subdivision (b), the court may, upon the request of the prosecuting attorney, order that the prosecuting attorney be given authority to use lien procedures applicable to the defendant, including, but not limited to, a writ of attachment of property. This authority is in addition to any authority granted to the prosecuting attorney in subdivision (h).

(1) If the court authorizes a lien or other similar encumbrance on real property pursuant to this subdivision, the court shall, within 15 days, furnish to the defendant a statement of his or her rights, remedies, and duties in regard to the order. The statement shall state all of the following:

(A) That the lien is enforceable and collectible by execution issued by order of the court, except that a lien shall not be enforced by writ of execution on a defendant's principal place of residence.

(B) A legal description of the property to be encumbered.

(C) The total amount of restitution still owed by the defendant.

(D) That enforcement of the lien order may only be contested on the ground of mistake of fact regarding the amount of restitution owed or on the ground of mistake of fact regarding the defendant's ownership interest of the property to be encumbered.

(E) That a hearing is available in accordance with paragraph (2).

(F) That, upon paying the restitution order in full, the defendant may petition the court for a full release of any related encumbrance in accordance with paragraph (3).

(2) The defendant, within 15 days after being informed that a lien or other similar encumbrance on real property has been ordered, may apply for a hearing to contest the enforcement order on the ground of mistake of fact regarding the amount of restitution owed, on the ground of mistake of fact regarding the defendant's ownership interest of the property to be encumbered, or on the ground that the defendant has established good cause for the nonpayment. The timely request for a hearing shall stay any execution on the lien until a hearing is held and a determination is made as to whether the enforcement order is proper.

(3) Upon payment of the restitution order in full, the defendant may petition the court to issue an order directing the clerk of the court to execute a full reconveyance of title, a certificate of discharge, or a full release of any lien against real property created to secure performance of the restitution order.

(4) Neither a prosecutorial agency nor a prosecuting attorney shall be liable for an injury caused by an act or omission in exercising the authority granted by this subdivision.

(h) If there is no agency in the county responsible for the collection of restitution, the county probation office or the prosecuting attorney may carry out the functions and duties of such an agency as specified in subdivisions (b) and (f).

(i) A prosecuting attorney shall not make any collection against, or take any percentage of, the defendant's income or assets to reimburse the prosecuting attorney for administrative costs in carrying out any action authorized by this section.

(j) As used in this section, "good cause" for failure to meet an obligation or "good cause" for nonpayment means, but shall not be limited to, any of the following:

(1) That there has been a substantial change in the defendant's economic circumstances, such as involuntary unemployment, involuntary cost-of-living increases, or costs incurred as the result of medical circumstances or a natural disaster.

(2) That the defendant reasonably believes there has been an administrative error with regard to his or her obligation for payment.

(3) Any other similar and justifiable reasons.

(Amended by Stats. 2010, Ch. 582, Sec. 1. (AB 1847) Effective January 1, 2011.)
1202.43.

(a) The restitution fine imposed pursuant to subdivision (a) of Section 13967 of the Government Code, as operative on or before September 28, 1994, subparagraph (B) of paragraph (2) of subdivision (a) of Section 1203.04, as operative on or before August 2, 1995, or Section 1202.4 shall be payable to the clerk of the court, the probation officer, or any other person responsible for the collection of criminal fines. If the defendant is unable or otherwise fails to pay that fine in a felony case and there is an amount unpaid of one thousand dollars ($1,000) or more within 60 days after the imposition of sentence, or in a case in which probation is granted, within the period of probation, the clerk of the court, probation officer, or other person to whom the fine is to be paid shall forward to the Controller the abstract of judgment along with any information which may be relevant to the present and future location of the defendant and his or her assets, if any, and any verifiable amount which the defendant may have paid to the victim as a result of the crime.

(b) A restitution fine shall be deemed a debt of the defendant owing to the state for the purposes of Sections 12418 and 12419.5 of the Government Code, excepting any amounts the defendant has paid to the victim as a result of the crime. Upon request by the Controller, the district attorney of a county or the Attorney General may take any necessary action to recover amounts owing on a restitution fine. The amount of the recovery shall be increased by a sum sufficient to cover any costs incurred by any state or local agency in the administration of this section. The remedies provided by this subdivision are in addition to any other remedies provided by law for the enforcement of a judgment.

(Added by Stats. 2002, Ch. 1141, Sec. 15. Effective January 1, 2003.)
1202.44.

In every case in which a person is convicted of a crime and a conditional sentence or a sentence that includes a period of probation is imposed, the court shall, at the time of imposing the restitution fine pursuant to subdivision (b) of Section 1202.4, assess an additional probation revocation restitution fine in the same amount as that imposed pursuant to subdivision (b) of Section 1202.4. This additional probation revocation restitution fine shall become effective upon the revocation of probation or of a conditional sentence, and shall not be waived or reduced by the court, absent compelling and extraordinary reasons stated on record. Probation revocation restitution fines shall be deposited in the Restitution Fund in the State Treasury.

(Added by Stats. 2004, Ch. 223, Sec. 3. Effective August 16, 2004.)
1202.45.

(a) In every case where a person is convicted of a crime and his or her sentence includes a period of parole, the court shall, at the time of imposing the restitution fine pursuant to subdivision (b) of Section 1202.4, assess an additional parole revocation restitution fine in the same amount as that imposed pursuant to subdivision (b) of Section 1202.4.

(b) In every case where a person is convicted of a crime and is subject to either postrelease community supervision under Section 3451 or mandatory supervision under subparagraph (B) of paragraph (5) of subdivision (h) of Section 1170, the court shall, at the time of imposing the restitution fine pursuant to subdivision (b) of Section 1202.4, assess an additional postrelease community supervision revocation restitution fine or mandatory supervision revocation restitution fine in the same amount as that imposed pursuant to subdivision (b) of Section 1202.4, that may be collected by the agency designated pursuant to subdivision (b) of Section 2085.5 by the board of supervisors of the county in which the prisoner is incarcerated.

(c) The fines imposed pursuant to subdivisions (a) and (b) shall not be subject to penalty assessments authorized by Section 1464 or Chapter 12 (commencing with Section 76000) of Title 8 of the Government Code, or the state surcharge authorized by Section 1465.7, and shall be suspended unless the person's parole, postrelease community supervision, or mandatory supervision is revoked. Fine moneys shall be deposited in the Restitution Fund in the State Treasury.

(Amended by Stats. 2012, Ch. 762, Sec. 1. (SB 1210) Effective January 1, 2013.)
1202.46.

Notwithstanding Section 1170, when the economic losses of a victim cannot be ascertained at the time of sentencing pursuant to subdivision (f) of Section 1202.4, the court shall retain jurisdiction over a person subject to a restitution order for purposes of imposing or modifying restitution until such time as the losses may be determined. This section does not prohibit a victim, the district attorney, or a court on its own motion from requesting correction, at any time, of a sentence when the sentence is invalid due to the omission of a restitution order or fine pursuant to Section 1202.4.

(Amended by Stats. 2016, Ch. 37, Sec. 4. (AB 2295) Effective January 1, 2017.)
1202.5.

(a) In any case in which a defendant is convicted of any of the offenses enumerated in Section 211, 215, 459, 470, 484, 487, subdivision (a) of Section 487a, or Section 488, or 594, the court shall order the defendant to pay a fine of ten dollars ($10) in addition to any other penalty or fine imposed. If the court determines that the defendant has the ability to pay all or part of the fine, the court shall set the amount to be reimbursed and order the defendant to pay that sum to the county in the manner in which the court believes reasonable and compatible with the defendant's financial ability. In making a determination of whether a defendant has the ability to pay, the court shall take into account the amount of any other fine imposed upon the defendant and any amount the defendant has been ordered to pay in restitution.

(b) (1) All fines collected pursuant to this section shall be held in trust by the county collecting them, until transferred to the local law enforcement agency to be used exclusively for the jurisdiction where the offense took place. All moneys collected shall implement, support, and continue local crime prevention programs.

(2) All amounts collected pursuant to this section shall be in addition to, and shall not supplant funds received for crime prevention purposes from other sources.

(c) As used in this section, "law enforcement agency" includes, but is not limited to, police departments, sheriffs departments, and probation departments.

(Amended by Stats. 2013, Ch. 618, Sec. 10. (AB 924) Effective January 1, 2014.)
1202.51.

In any case in which a defendant is convicted of any of the offenses enumerated in Section 372, 373a, 374.3, 374.4, 374.7, or 374.8, the court shall order the defendant to pay a fine of one hundred dollars ($100) if the conviction is for an infraction or two hundred dollars ($200) if the conviction is for a misdemeanor, in addition to any other penalty or fine imposed. If the court determines that the defendant has the ability to pay all or part of the fine, the court shall set the amount to be paid and order the defendant to pay that sum to the city or, if not within a city, the county, where the violation occurred, to be used for the city's or county's illegal dumping enforcement program. Notwithstanding any other provision of law, no state or county penalty, assessment, fee, or surcharge shall be imposed on the fine ordered under this section.

(Added by Stats. 2007, Ch. 394, Sec. 1. Effective January 1, 2008.)
1202.6.

Notwithstanding Sections 120975, 120980, and 120990 of the Health and Safety Code, upon the first conviction of a person for a violation of subdivision (b) of Section 647, the court shall refer the defendant, where appropriate, to a program under Article 3.2 (commencing with Section 11320) of Chapter 2 of Part 3 of Division 9 of the Welfare and Institutions Code or to a drug diversion program, or to both.

(Repealed and added by Stats. 2017, Ch. 537, Sec. 17. (SB 239) Effective January 1, 2018.)
1202.7.

The Legislature finds and declares that the provision of probation services is an essential element in the administration of criminal justice. The safety of the public, which shall be a primary goal through the enforcement of court-ordered conditions of probation; the nature of the offense; the interests of justice, including punishment, reintegration of the offender into the community, and enforcement of conditions of probation; the loss to the victim; and the needs of the defendant shall be the primary considerations in the granting of probation. It is the intent of the Legislature that efforts be made with respect to persons who are subject to Section 290.011 who are on probation to engage them in treatment.

(Amended by Stats. 2007, Ch. 579, Sec. 42. Effective October 13, 2007.)
1202.8.

(a) Persons placed on probation by a court shall be under the supervision of the county probation officer who shall determine both the level and type of supervision consistent with the court-ordered conditions of probation.

(b) Commencing January 1, 2009, every person who has been assessed with the State Authorized Risk Assessment Tool for Sex Offenders (SARATSO) pursuant to Sections 290.04 to 290.06, inclusive, and who has a SARATSO risk level of high shall be continuously electronically monitored while on probation, unless the court determines that such monitoring is unnecessary for a particular person. The monitoring device used for these purposes shall be identified as one that employs the latest available proven effective monitoring technology. Nothing in this section prohibits probation authorities from using electronic monitoring technology pursuant to any other provision of law.

(c) Within 30 days of a court making an order to provide restitution to a victim or to the Restitution Fund, the probation officer shall establish an account into which any restitution payments that are not deposited into the Restitution Fund shall be deposited.

(d) Beginning January 1, 2009, and every two years thereafter, each probation department shall report to the Corrections Standards Authority all relevant statistics and relevant information regarding the effectiveness of continuous electronic monitoring of offenders pursuant to subdivision (b). The report shall include the costs of monitoring and the recidivism rates of those persons who have been monitored. The Corrections Standards Authority shall compile the reports and submit a single report to the Legislature and the Governor every two years through 2017.
(Amended by Stats. 2010, Ch. 328, Sec. 164. (SB 1330) Effective January 1, 2011.)
1203.
(a) As used in this code, "probation" means the suspension of the imposition or execution of a sentence and the order of conditional and revocable release in the community under the supervision of a probation officer. As used in this code, "conditional sentence" means the suspension of the imposition or execution of a sentence and the order of revocable release in the community subject to conditions established by the court without the supervision of a probation officer. It is the intent of the Legislature that both conditional sentence and probation are authorized whenever probation is authorized in any code as a sentencing option for infractions or misdemeanors.
(b) (1) Except as provided in subdivision (j), if a person is convicted of a felony and is eligible for probation, before judgment is pronounced, the court shall immediately refer the matter to a probation officer to investigate and report to the court, at a specified time, upon the circumstances surrounding the crime and the prior history and record of the person, which may be considered either in aggravation or mitigation of the punishment.
(2) (A) The probation officer shall immediately investigate and make a written report to the court of his or her findings and recommendations, including his or her recommendations as to the granting or denying of probation and the conditions of probation, if granted.
(B) Pursuant to Section 828 of the Welfare and Institutions Code, the probation officer shall include in his or her report any information gathered by a law enforcement agency relating to the taking of the defendant into custody as a minor, which shall be considered for purposes of determining whether adjudications of commissions of crimes as a juvenile warrant a finding that there are circumstances in aggravation pursuant to Section 1170 or to deny probation.
(C) If the person was convicted of an offense that requires him or her to register as a sex offender pursuant to Sections 290 to 290.023, inclusive, or if the probation report recommends that registration be ordered at sentencing pursuant to Section 290.006, the probation officer's report shall include the results of the State-Authorized Risk Assessment Tool for Sex Offenders (SARATSO) administered pursuant to Sections 290.04 to 290.06, inclusive, if applicable.
(D) The probation officer may also include in the report his or her recommendation of both of the following:
(i) The amount the defendant should be required to pay as a restitution fine pursuant to subdivision (b) of Section 1202.4.
(ii) Whether the court shall require, as a condition of probation, restitution to the victim or to the Restitution Fund and the amount thereof.
(E) The report shall be made available to the court and the prosecuting and defense attorneys at least five days, or upon request of the defendant or prosecuting attorney nine days, prior to the time fixed by the court for the hearing and determination of the report, and shall be filed with the clerk of the court as a record in the case at the time of the hearing. The time within which the report shall be made available and filed may be waived by written stipulation of the prosecuting and defense attorneys that is filed with the court or an oral stipulation in open court that is made and entered upon the minutes of the court.
(3) At a time fixed by the court, the court shall hear and determine the application, if one has been made, or, in any case, the suitability of probation in the particular case. At the hearing, the court shall consider any report of the probation officer, including the results of the SARATSO, if applicable, and shall make a statement that it has considered the report, which shall be filed with the clerk of the court as a record in the case. If the court determines that there are circumstances in mitigation of the punishment prescribed by law or that the ends of justice would be served by granting probation to the person, it may place the person on probation. If probation is denied, the clerk of the court shall immediately send a copy of the report to the Department of Corrections and Rehabilitation at the prison or other institution to which the person is delivered.
(4) The preparation of the report or the consideration of the report by the court may be waived only by a written stipulation of the prosecuting and defense attorneys that is filed with the court or an oral stipulation in open court that is made and entered upon the minutes of the court, except that a waiver shall not be allowed unless the court consents thereto. However, if the defendant is ultimately sentenced and committed to the state prison, a probation report shall be completed pursuant to Section 1203c.
(c) If a defendant is not represented by an attorney, the court shall order the probation officer who makes the probation report to discuss its contents with the defendant.
(d) If a person is convicted of a misdemeanor, the court may either refer the matter to the probation officer for an investigation and a report or summarily pronounce a conditional sentence. If the person was convicted of an offense that requires him or her to register as a sex offender pursuant to Sections 290 to 290.023, inclusive, or if the probation officer recommends that the court, at sentencing, order the offender to register as a sex offender pursuant to Section 290.006, the court shall refer the matter to the probation officer for the purpose of obtaining a report on the results of the State-Authorized Risk Assessment Tool for Sex Offenders administered pursuant to Sections 290.04 to 290.06, inclusive, if applicable, which the court shall consider. If the case is not referred to the probation officer, in sentencing the person, the court may consider any information concerning the person that could have been included in a probation report. The court shall inform the person of the information to be considered and permit him or her to answer or controvert the information. For this purpose, upon the request of the person, the court shall grant a continuance before the judgment is pronounced.
(e) Except in unusual cases where the interests of justice would best be served if the person is granted probation, probation shall not be granted to any of the following persons:
(1) Unless the person had a lawful right to carry a deadly weapon, other than a firearm, at the time of the perpetration of the crime or his or her arrest, any person who has been convicted of arson, robbery, carjacking, burglary, burglary with explosives, rape with force or violence, torture, aggravated mayhem, murder, attempt to commit murder, trainwrecking, kidnapping, escape from the state prison, or a conspiracy to commit one or more of those crimes and who was armed with the weapon at either of those times.
(2) Any person who used, or attempted to use, a deadly weapon upon a human being in connection with the perpetration of the crime of which he or she has been convicted.
(3) Any person who willfully inflicted great bodily injury or torture in the perpetration of the crime of which he or she has been convicted.
(4) Any person who has been previously convicted twice in this state of a felony or in any other place of a public offense which, if committed in this state, would have been punishable as a felony.
(5) Unless the person has never been previously convicted once in this state of a felony or in any other place of a public offense which, if committed in this state, would have been punishable as a felony, any person who has been convicted of burglary with explosives, rape with force or violence, torture, aggravated mayhem, murder, attempt to commit murder, trainwrecking, extortion, kidnapping, escape from the state prison, a violation of Section 286, 287, 288, or 288.5, or of former Section 288a, or a conspiracy to commit one or more of those crimes.

(6) Any person who has been previously convicted once in this state of a felony or in any other place of a public offense which, if committed in this state, would have been punishable as a felony, if he or she committed any of the following acts:
(A) Unless the person had a lawful right to carry a deadly weapon at the time of the perpetration of the previous crime or his or her arrest for the previous crime, he or she was armed with a weapon at either of those times.
(B) The person used, or attempted to use, a deadly weapon upon a human being in connection with the perpetration of the previous crime.
(C) The person willfully inflicted great bodily injury or torture in the perpetration of the previous crime.
(7) Any public official or peace officer of this state or any city, county, or other political subdivision who, in the discharge of the duties of his or her public office or employment, accepted or gave or offered to accept or give any bribe, embezzled public money, or was guilty of extortion.
(8) Any person who knowingly furnishes or gives away phencyclidine.
(9) Any person who intentionally inflicted great bodily injury in the commission of arson under subdivision (a) of Section 451 or who intentionally set fire to, burned, or caused the burning of, an inhabited structure or inhabited property in violation of subdivision (b) of Section 451.
(10) Any person who, in the commission of a felony, inflicts great bodily injury or causes the death of a human being by the discharge of a firearm from or at an occupied motor vehicle proceeding on a public street or highway.
(11) Any person who possesses a short-barreled rifle or a short-barreled shotgun under Section 33215, a machinegun under Section 32625, or a silencer under Section 33410.
(12) Any person who is convicted of violating Section 8101 of the Welfare and Institutions Code.
(13) Any person who is described in subdivision (b) or (c) of Section 27590.
(f) When probation is granted in a case which comes within subdivision (e), the court shall specify on the record and shall enter on the minutes the circumstances indicating that the interests of justice would best be served by that disposition.
(g) If a person is not eligible for probation, the judge shall refer the matter to the probation officer for an investigation of the facts relevant to determination of the amount of a restitution fine pursuant to subdivision (b) of Section 1202.4 in all cases where the determination is applicable. The judge, in his or her discretion, may direct the probation officer to investigate all facts relevant to the sentencing of the person. Upon that referral, the probation officer shall immediately investigate the circumstances surrounding the crime and the prior record and history of the person and make a written report to the court of his or her findings. The findings shall include a recommendation of the amount of the restitution fine as provided in subdivision (b) of Section 1202.4.
(h) If a defendant is convicted of a felony and a probation report is prepared pursuant to subdivision (b) or (g), the probation officer may obtain and include in the report a statement of the comments of the victim concerning the offense. The court may direct the probation officer not to obtain a statement if the victim has in fact testified at any of the court proceedings concerning the offense.
(i) A probationer shall not be released to enter another state unless his or her case has been referred to the Administrator of the Interstate Probation and Parole Compacts, pursuant to the Uniform Act for Out-of-State Probationer or Parolee Supervision (Article 3 (commencing with Section 11175) of Chapter 2 of Title 1 of Part 4) and the probationer has reimbursed the county that has jurisdiction over his or her probation case the reasonable costs of processing his or her request for interstate compact supervision. The amount and method of reimbursement shall be in accordance with Section 1203.1b.
(j) In any court where a county financial evaluation officer is available, in addition to referring the matter to the probation officer, the court may order the defendant to appear before the county financial evaluation officer for a financial evaluation of the defendant's ability to pay restitution, in which case the county financial evaluation officer shall report his or her findings regarding restitution and other court-related costs to the probation officer on the question of the defendant's ability to pay those costs.
Any order made pursuant to this subdivision may be enforced as a violation of the terms and conditions of probation upon willful failure to pay and at the discretion of the court, may be enforced in the same manner as a judgment in a civil action, if any balance remains unpaid at the end of the defendant's probationary period.
(k) Probation shall not be granted to, nor shall the execution of, or imposition of sentence be suspended for, any person who is convicted of a violent felony, as defined in subdivision (c) of Section 667.5, or a serious felony, as defined in subdivision (c) of Section 1192.7, and who was on probation for a felony offense at the time of the commission of the new felony offense.
(l) For any person granted probation prior to January 1, 2021, at the time the court imposes probation, the court may take a waiver from the defendant permitting flash incarceration by the probation officer, pursuant to Section 1203.35.
(Amended by Stats. 2018, Ch. 423, Sec. 90. (SB 1494) Effective January 1, 2019.)
1203.01.
(a) Immediately after judgment has been pronounced, the judge and the district attorney, respectively, may cause to be filed with the clerk of the court a brief statement of their views respecting the person convicted or sentenced and the crime committed, together with any reports the probation officer may have filed relative to the prisoner. The judge and district attorney shall cause those statements to be filed if no probation officer's report has been filed. The attorney for the defendant and the law enforcement agency that investigated the case may likewise file with the clerk of the court statements of their views respecting the defendant and the crime of which he or she was convicted. Immediately after the filing of those statements and reports, the clerk of the court shall mail a copy thereof, certified by that clerk, with postage prepaid, addressed to the Department of Corrections and Rehabilitation at the prison or other institution to which the person convicted is delivered. The clerk shall also mail a copy of any statement submitted by the court, district attorney, or law enforcement agency, pursuant to this section, with postage prepaid, addressed to the attorney for the defendant, if any, and to the defendant, in care of the Department of Corrections and Rehabilitation, and a copy of any statement submitted by the attorney for the defendant, with postage prepaid, shall be mailed to the district attorney.
(b) (1) In all cases in which the judgment imposed includes a sentence of death or an indeterminate term with or without the possibility of parole, the clerk shall, within 60 days after judgment has been pronounced, mail with postage prepaid, to the prison or other institution to which the person convicted is delivered, a copy of the charging documents, a copy of waiver and plea forms, if any, the transcript of the proceedings at the time of the defendant's guilty or nolo contendere plea, if the defendant pleaded guilty or nolo contendere, and the transcript of the proceedings at the time of sentencing.
(2) In all other cases not described in paragraph (1), the clerk shall mail with postage prepaid, to the prison or other institution to which the person convicted is delivered, a copy of the charging documents, a copy of the waiver and plea forms, if any, and upon written request by the Department of Corrections and Rehabilitation or by an inmate, or by his or her counsel, for, among other purposes on a particular case, appeals, review of custody credits and release dates, and restitution orders, the transcript of the proceedings at the time of the defendant's guilty or nolo contendere plea, if the defendant pleaded guilty or nolo contendere, and the transcript of the proceedings at the time of sentencing.
(Amended by Stats. 2011, Ch. 193, Sec. 7. (AB 110) Effective August 30, 2011.)
1203.016.

(a) Notwithstanding any other law, the board of supervisors of any county may authorize the correctional administrator, as defined in subdivision (h), to offer a program under which inmates committed to a county jail or other county correctional facility or granted probation, or inmates participating in a work furlough program, may voluntarily participate or involuntarily be placed in a home detention program during their sentence in lieu of confinement in a county jail or other county correctional facility or program under the auspices of the probation officer.

(b) The board of supervisors, in consultation with the correctional administrator, may prescribe reasonable rules and regulations under which a home detention program may operate. As a condition of participation in the home detention program, the inmate shall give his or her consent in writing to participate in the home detention program and shall in writing agree to comply or, for involuntary participation, the inmate shall be informed in writing that he or she shall comply, with the rules and regulations of the program, including, but not limited to, the following rules:

(1) The participant shall remain within the interior premises of his or her residence during the hours designated by the correctional administrator.

(2) The participant shall admit any person or agent designated by the correctional administrator into his or her residence at any time for purposes of verifying the participant's compliance with the conditions of his or her detention.

(3) The participant shall agree to the use of electronic monitoring, which may include Global Positioning System devices or other supervising devices for the purpose of helping to verify his or her compliance with the rules and regulations of the home detention program. The devices shall not be used to eavesdrop or record any conversation, except a conversation between the participant and the person supervising the participant which is to be used solely for the purposes of voice identification.

(4) The participant shall agree that the correctional administrator in charge of the county correctional facility from which the participant was released may, without further order of the court, immediately retake the person into custody to serve the balance of his or her sentence if the electronic monitoring or supervising devices are unable for any reason to properly perform their function at the designated place of home detention, if the person fails to remain within the place of home detention as stipulated in the agreement, if the person willfully fails to pay fees to the provider of electronic home detention services, as stipulated in the agreement, subsequent to the written notification of the participant that the payment has not been received and that return to custody may result, or if the person for any other reason no longer meets the established criteria under this section. A copy of the agreement shall be delivered to the participant and a copy retained by the correctional administrator.

(c) If the peace officer supervising a participant has reasonable cause to believe that the participant is not complying with the rules or conditions of the program, or that the electronic monitoring devices are unable to function properly in the designated place of confinement, the peace officer may, under general or specific authorization of the correctional administrator, and without a warrant of arrest, retake the person into custody to complete the remainder of the original sentence.

(d) Nothing in this section shall be construed to require the correctional administrator to allow a person to participate in this program if it appears from the record that the person has not satisfactorily complied with reasonable rules and regulations while in custody. A person shall be eligible for participation in a home detention program only if the correctional administrator concludes that the person meets the criteria for release established under this section and that the person's participation is consistent with any reasonable rules and regulations prescribed by the board of supervisors or the administrative policy of the correctional administrator.

(1) The rules and regulations and administrative policy of the program shall be written and reviewed on an annual basis by the county board of supervisors and the correctional administrator. The rules and regulations shall be given to or made available to any participant upon request.

(2) The correctional administrator, or his or her designee, shall have the sole discretionary authority to permit program participation as an alternative to physical custody. All persons referred or recommended by the court to participate in the home detention program pursuant to subdivision (e) who are denied participation or all persons removed from program participation shall be notified in writing of the specific reasons for the denial or removal. The notice of denial or removal shall include the participant's appeal rights, as established by program administrative policy.

(e) The court may recommend or refer a person to the correctional administrator for consideration for placement in the home detention program. The recommendation or referral of the court shall be given great weight in the determination of acceptance or denial. At the time of sentencing or at any time that the court deems it necessary, the court may restrict or deny the defendant's participation in a home detention program.

(f) The correctional administrator may permit home detention program participants to seek and retain employment in the community, attend psychological counseling sessions or educational or vocational training classes, or seek medical and dental assistance. Willful failure of the program participant to return to the place of home detention not later than the expiration of any period of time during which he or she is authorized to be away from the place of home detention pursuant to this section and unauthorized departures from the place of home detention are punishable as provided in Section 4532.

(g) The board of supervisors may prescribe a program administrative fee to be paid by each adult home detention participant who is over 21 years of age and under the jurisdiction of the criminal court that shall be determined according to his or her ability to pay. Inability to pay all or a portion of the program fees shall not preclude participation in the program, and eligibility shall not be enhanced by reason of ability to pay. All program administration and supervision fees shall be administered in compliance with Section 1208.2.

(h) As used in this section, "correctional administrator" means the sheriff, probation officer, or director of the county department of corrections.

(i) Notwithstanding any other law, the police department of a city where an office is located to which persons on an electronic monitoring program report may request the county correctional administrator to provide information concerning those persons. This information shall be limited to the name, address, date of birth, offense committed by the home detainee, and if available, at the discretion of the supervising agency and solely for investigatory purposes, current and historical GPS coordinates of the home detainee. A law enforcement department that does not have the primary responsibility to supervise participants in the electronic monitoring program that receives information pursuant to this subdivision shall not use the information to conduct enforcement actions based on administrative violations of the home detention program. A law enforcement department that has knowledge that the subject in a criminal investigation is a participant in an electronic monitoring program shall make reasonable efforts to notify the supervising agency prior to serving a warrant or taking any law enforcement action against a participant in an electronic monitoring program.

(j) It is the intent of the Legislature that home detention programs established under this section maintain the highest public confidence, credibility, and public safety. In the furtherance of these standards, the following shall apply:

(1) The correctional administrator, with the approval of the board of supervisors, may administer a home detention program pursuant to written contracts with appropriate public or private agencies or entities to provide specified program services. No public or private agency or entity may operate a home detention program in any county without a written contract with that county's correctional administrator. However, this does not apply to the use of electronic monitoring by the Department of Corrections and Rehabilitation. No public or private agency or entity entering into a contract may itself employ any person who is in the home detention program.

(2) Program acceptance shall not circumvent the normal booking process for sentenced offenders. All home detention program participants shall be supervised.

(3) (A) All privately operated home detention programs shall be under the jurisdiction of, and subject to the terms and conditions of the contract entered into with, the correctional administrator.

(B) Each contract shall include, but not be limited to, all of the following:

(i) A provision whereby the private agency or entity agrees to operate in compliance with any available standards promulgated by state correctional agencies and bodies, including the Corrections Standards Authority, and all statutory provisions and mandates, state and county, as appropriate and applicable to the operation of home detention programs and the supervision of sentenced offenders in a home detention program.

(ii) A provision that clearly defines areas of respective responsibility and liability of the county and the private agency or entity.

(iii) A provision that requires the private agency or entity to demonstrate evidence of financial responsibility, submitted and approved by the board of supervisors, in amounts and under conditions sufficient to fully indemnify the county for reasonably foreseeable public liability, including legal defense costs, that may arise from, or be proximately caused by, acts or omissions of the contractor. The contract shall provide for annual review by the correctional administrator to ensure compliance with requirements set by the board of supervisors and for adjustment of the financial responsibility requirements if warranted by caseload changes or other factors.

(iv) A provision that requires the private agency or entity to provide evidence of financial responsibility, such as certificates of insurance or copies of insurance policies, prior to commencing any operations pursuant to the contract or at any time requested by the board of supervisors or correctional administrator.

(v) A provision that permits the correctional administrator to immediately terminate the contract with a private agency or entity at any time that the contractor fails to demonstrate evidence of financial responsibility.

(C) All privately operated home detention programs shall comply with all appropriate, applicable ordinances and regulations specified in subdivision (a) of Section 1208.

(D) The board of supervisors, the correctional administrator, and the designee of the correctional administrator shall comply with Section 1090 of the Government Code in the consideration, making, and execution of contracts pursuant to this section.

(E) The failure of the private agency or entity to comply with statutory provisions and requirements or with the standards established by the contract and with the correctional administrator may be sufficient cause to terminate the contract.

(F) Upon the discovery that a private agency or entity with whom there is a contract is not in compliance pursuant to this paragraph, the correctional administrator shall give 60 days' notice to the director of the private agency or entity that the contract may be canceled if the specified deficiencies are not corrected.

(G) Shorter notice may be given or the contract may be canceled without notice whenever a serious threat to public safety is present because the private agency or entity has failed to comply with this section.

(k) For purposes of this section, "evidence of financial responsibility" may include, but is not limited to, certified copies of any of the following:

(1) A current liability insurance policy.

(2) A current errors and omissions insurance policy.

(3) A surety bond.

(Amended by Stats. 2017, Ch. 678, Sec. 2. (SB 190) Effective January 1, 2018.)

1203.017.

(a) Notwithstanding any other provision of law, upon determination by the correctional administrator that conditions in a jail facility warrant the necessity of releasing sentenced misdemeanor inmates prior to them serving the full amount of a given sentence due to lack of jail space, the board of supervisors of any county may authorize the correctional administrator to offer a program under which inmates committed to a county jail or other county correctional facility or granted probation, or inmates participating in a work furlough program, may be required to participate in an involuntary home detention program, which shall include electronic monitoring, during their sentence in lieu of confinement in the county jail or other county correctional facility or program under the auspices of the probation officer. Under this program, one day of participation shall be in lieu of one day of incarceration. Participants in the program shall receive any sentence reduction credits that they would have received had they served their sentences in a county correctional facility.

(b) The board of supervisors may prescribe reasonable rules and regulations under which an involuntary home detention program may operate. The inmate shall be informed in writing that he or she shall comply with the rules and regulations of the program, including, but not limited to, the following rules:

(1) The participant shall remain within the interior premises of his or her residence during the hours designated by the correctional administrator.

(2) The participant shall admit any peace officer designated by the correctional administrator into his or her residence at any time for purposes of verifying the participant's compliance with the conditions of his or her detention.

(3) The use of electronic monitoring may include global positioning system devices or other supervising devices for the purpose of helping to verify his or her compliance with the rules and regulations of the home detention program. The devices shall not be used to eavesdrop or record any conversation, except a conversation between the participant and the person supervising the participant which is to be used solely for the purposes of voice identification.

(4) The correctional administrator in charge of the county correctional facility from which the participant was released may, without further order of the court, immediately retake the person into custody to serve the balance of his or her sentence if the electronic monitoring or supervising devices are unable for any reason to properly perform their function at the designated place of home detention, if the person fails to remain within the place of home detention as stipulated in the agreement, or if the person for any other reason no longer meets the established criteria under this section.

(c) Whenever the peace officer supervising a participant has reasonable cause to believe that the participant is not complying with the rules or conditions of the program, or that the electronic monitoring devices are unable to function properly in the designated place of confinement, the peace officer may, under general or specific authorization of the correctional administrator, and without a warrant of arrest, retake the person into custody to complete the remainder of the original sentence.

(d) Nothing in this section shall be construed to require the correctional administrator to allow a person to participate in this program if it appears from the record that the person has not satisfactorily complied with reasonable rules and regulations while in custody. A person shall be eligible for participation in a home detention program only if the correctional administrator concludes that the person meets the criteria for release established under this section and that the person's participation is consistent with any reasonable rules and regulations prescribed by the board of supervisors or the administrative policy of the correctional administrator.

(1) The rules and regulations and administrative policy of the program shall be written and reviewed on an annual basis by the county board of supervisors and the correctional administrator. The rules and regulations shall be given to or made available to any participant upon request.

(2) The correctional administrator, or his or her designee, shall have the sole discretionary authority to permit program participation as an alternative to physical custody. All persons referred or recommended by the court to participate in the home detention program pursuant to subdivision (e) who are denied participation or all persons removed from program participation shall be notified in writing of the specific

reasons for the denial or removal. The notice of denial or removal shall include the participant's appeal rights, as established by program administrative policy.

(e) The court may recommend or refer a person to the correctional administrator for consideration for placement in the home detention program. The recommendation or referral of the court shall be given great weight in the determination of acceptance or denial. At the time of sentencing or at any time that the court deems it necessary, the court may restrict or deny the defendant's participation in a home detention program.

(f) The correctional administrator may permit home detention program participants to seek and retain employment in the community, attend psychological counseling sessions or educational or vocational training classes, or seek medical and dental assistance. Willful failure of the program participant to return to the place of home detention not later than the expiration of any period of time during which he or she is authorized to be away from the place of home detention pursuant to this section and unauthorized departures from the place of home detention are punishable as provided in Section 4532.

(g) As used in this section, "correctional administrator" means the sheriff, probation officer, or director of the county department of corrections.

(h) (1) Notwithstanding any other law, the correctional administrator shall provide the information specified in paragraph (2) regarding persons on involuntary home detention to the Corrections Standards Authority, and upon request, shall provide that information to the law enforcement agency of a city or unincorporated area where an office is located to which persons on involuntary home detention report.

(2) The information required by paragraph (1) shall consist of the following:

(A) The participant's name, address, and date of birth.

(B) The offense committed by the participant.

(C) The period of time the participant will be placed on home detention.

(D) Whether the participant successfully completed the prescribed period of home detention or was returned to a county correctional facility, and if the person was returned to a county correctional facility, the reason for that return.

(E) The gender and ethnicity of the participant.

(3) Any information received by a police department pursuant to this subdivision shall be used only for the purpose of monitoring the impact of home detention programs on the community.

(i) It is the intent of the Legislature that home detention programs established under this section maintain the highest public confidence, credibility, and public safety. In the furtherance of these standards, the following shall apply:

(1) The correctional administrator, with the approval of the board of supervisors, may administer a home detention program pursuant to written contracts with appropriate public or private agencies or entities to provide specified program services. No public or private agency or entity may operate a home detention program in any county without a written contract with that county's correctional administrator. However, this does not apply to the use of electronic monitoring by the Department of Corrections and Rehabilitation as established in Section 3004. No public or private agency or entity entering into a contract may itself employ any person who is in the home detention program.

(2) Program acceptance shall not circumvent the normal booking process for sentenced offenders. All home detention program participants shall be supervised.

(3) (A) All privately operated home detention programs shall be under the jurisdiction of, and subject to the terms and conditions of the contract entered into with, the correctional administrator.

(B) Each contract shall include, but not be limited to, all of the following:

(i) A provision whereby the private agency or entity agrees to operate in compliance with any available standards promulgated by state correctional agencies and bodies, including the Corrections Standards Authority, and all statutory provisions and mandates, state and county, as appropriate and applicable to the operation of home detention programs and the supervision of sentenced offenders in a home detention program.

(ii) A provision that clearly defines areas of respective responsibility and liability of the county and the private agency or entity.

(iii) A provision that requires the private agency or entity to demonstrate evidence of financial responsibility, submitted and approved by the board of supervisors, in amounts and under conditions sufficient to fully indemnify the county for reasonably foreseeable public liability, including legal defense costs, that may arise from, or be proximately caused by, acts or omissions of the contractor. The contract shall provide for annual review by the correctional administrator to ensure compliance with requirements set by the board of supervisors and for adjustment of the financial responsibility requirements if warranted by caseload changes or other factors.

(iv) A provision that requires the private agency or entity to provide evidence of financial responsibility, such as certificates of insurance or copies of insurance policies, prior to commencing any operations pursuant to the contract or at any time requested by the board of supervisors or correctional administrator.

(v) A provision that permits the correctional administrator to immediately terminate the contract with a private agency or entity at any time that the contractor fails to demonstrate evidence of financial responsibility.

(C) All privately operated home detention programs shall comply with all appropriate, applicable ordinances and regulations specified in subdivision (a) of Section 1208.

(D) The board of supervisors, the correctional administrator, and the designee of the correctional administrator shall comply with Section 1090 of the Government Code in the consideration, making, and execution of contracts pursuant to this section.

(E) The failure of the private agency or entity to comply with statutory provisions and requirements or with the standards established by the contract and with the correctional administrator may be sufficient cause to terminate the contract.

(F) Upon the discovery that a private agency or entity with whom there is a contract is not in compliance pursuant to this paragraph, the correctional administrator shall give 60 days' notice to the director of the private agency or entity that the contract may be canceled if the specified deficiencies are not corrected.

(G) Shorter notice may be given or the contract may be canceled without notice whenever a serious threat to public safety is present because the private agency or entity has failed to comply with this section.

(j) Inmates participating in this program shall not be charged fees or costs for the program.

(k) For purposes of this section, "evidence of financial responsibility" may include, but is not limited to, certified copies of any of the following:

(1) A current liability insurance policy.

(2) A current errors and omissions insurance policy.

(3) A surety bond.

(Added by Stats. 2007, Ch. 252, Sec. 1. Effective September 26, 2007.)

1203.018.

(a) Notwithstanding any other law, this section shall only apply to inmates being held in lieu of bail and on no other basis.

(b) Notwithstanding any other law, the board of supervisors of any county may authorize the correctional administrator, as defined in paragraph (1) of subdivision (k), to offer a program under which inmates being held in lieu of bail in a county jail or other county correctional facility may participate in an electronic monitoring program if the conditions specified in subdivision (c) are met.

(c) (1) In order to qualify for participation in an electronic monitoring program pursuant to this section, the inmate shall be an inmate with no holds or outstanding warrants to whom one of the following circumstances applies:

(A) The inmate has been held in custody for at least 30 calendar days from the date of arraignment pending disposition of only misdemeanor charges.

(B) The inmate has been held in custody pending disposition of charges for at least 60 calendar days from the date of arraignment.

(C) The inmate is appropriate for the program based on a determination by the correctional administrator that the inmate's participation would be consistent with the public safety interests of the community.

(2) All participants shall be subject to discretionary review for eligibility and compliance by the correctional administrator consistent with this section.

(d) The board of supervisors, after consulting with the sheriff and district attorney, may prescribe reasonable rules and regulations under which an electronic monitoring program pursuant to this section may operate. As a condition of participation in the electronic monitoring program, the participant shall give his or her consent in writing to participate and shall agree in writing to comply with the rules and regulations of the program, including, but not limited to, all of the following:

(1) The participant shall remain within the interior premises of his or her residence during the hours designated by the correctional administrator.

(2) The participant shall admit any person or agent designated by the correctional administrator into his or her residence at any time for purposes of verifying the participant's compliance with the conditions of his or her detention.

(3) The electronic monitoring may include global positioning system devices or other supervising devices for the purpose of helping to verify the participant's compliance with the rules and regulations of the electronic monitoring program. The electronic devices shall not be used to eavesdrop or record any conversation, except a conversation between the participant and the person supervising the participant to be used solely for the purposes of voice identification.

(4) The correctional administrator in charge of the county correctional facility from which the participant was released may, without further order of the court, immediately retake the person into custody if the electronic monitoring or supervising devices are unable for any reason to properly perform their function at the designated place of home detention, if the person fails to remain within the place of home detention as stipulated in the agreement, if the person willfully fails to pay fees to the provider of electronic home detention services, as stipulated in the agreement, subsequent to the written notification of the participant that the payment has not been received and that return to custody may result, or if the person for any other reason no longer meets the established criteria under this section.

(5) A copy of the signed consent to participate and a copy of the agreement to comply with the rules and regulations shall be provided to the participant and a copy shall be retained by the correctional administrator.

(e) The rules and regulations and administrative policy of the program shall be reviewed on an annual basis by the county board of supervisors and the correctional administrator. The rules and regulations shall be given to every participant.

(f) Whenever the peace officer supervising a participant has reasonable cause to believe that the participant is not complying with the rules or conditions of the program, or that the electronic monitoring devices are unable to function properly in the designated place of confinement, the peace officer may, under general or specific authorization of the correctional administrator, and without a warrant of arrest, retake the person into custody.

(g) (1) Nothing in this section shall be construed to require the correctional administrator to allow a person to participate in this program if it appears from the record that the person has not satisfactorily complied with reasonable rules and regulations while in custody. A person shall be eligible for participation in an electronic monitoring program only if the correctional administrator concludes that the person meets the criteria for release established under this section and that the person's participation is consistent with any reasonable rules and regulations prescribed by the board of supervisors or the administrative policy of the correctional administrator.

(2) The correctional administrator, or his or her designee, shall have discretionary authority consistent with this section to permit program participation as an alternative to physical custody. All persons approved by the correctional administrator to participate in the electronic monitoring program pursuant to subdivision (c) who are denied participation and all persons removed from program participation shall be notified in writing of the specific reasons for the denial or removal. The notice of denial or removal shall include the participant's appeal rights, as established by program administrative policy.

(h) The correctional administrator may permit electronic monitoring program participants to seek and retain employment in the community, attend psychological counseling sessions or educational or vocational training classes, or seek medical and dental assistance.

(i) Willful failure of the program participant to return to the place of home detention prior to the expiration of any period of time during which he or she is authorized to be away from the place of home detention pursuant to this section and unauthorized departures from the place of home detention is punishable pursuant to Section 4532.

(j) The board of supervisors may prescribe a program administrative fee to be paid by each electronic monitoring participant.

(k) For purposes of this section, the following terms have the following meanings:

(1) "Correctional administrator" means the sheriff, probation officer, or director of the county department of corrections.

(2) "Electronic monitoring program" includes, but is not limited to, home detention programs, work furlough programs, and work release programs.

(l) Notwithstanding any other law, upon request of a local law enforcement agency with jurisdiction over the location where a participant in an electronic monitoring program is placed, the correctional administrator shall provide the following information regarding participants in the electronic monitoring program:

(1) The participant's name, address, and date of birth.

(2) The offense or offenses alleged to have been committed by the participant.

(3) The period of time the participant will be placed on home detention.

(4) Whether the participant successfully completed the prescribed period of home detention or was returned to a county correctional facility, and if the person was returned to a county correctional facility, the reason for the return.

(5) The gender and ethnicity of the participant.

(m) Notwithstanding any other law, upon request of a local law enforcement agency with jurisdiction over the location where a participant in an electronic monitoring program is placed, the correctional administrator may, in his or her discretion and solely for investigatory purposes, provide current and historical GPS coordinates, if available.

(n) A law enforcement agency that does not have the primary responsibility to supervise participants in the electronic monitoring program that receives information pursuant to subdivision (l) shall not use the information to conduct enforcement actions based on administrative violations of the home detention program. An agency that has knowledge that the subject in a criminal investigation is a participant in an electronic monitoring program shall make reasonable efforts to notify the supervising agency prior to serving a warrant or taking any law enforcement action against a participant in an electronic monitoring program.

(o) It is the intent of the Legislature that electronic monitoring programs established under this section maintain the highest public confidence, credibility, and public safety. In the furtherance of these standards, the following shall apply:

(1) The correctional administrator, with the approval of the board of supervisors, may administer an electronic monitoring program as provided in this section pursuant to written contracts with appropriate public or private agencies or entities to provide specified program services. A public or private agency or entity shall not operate a home

detention program pursuant to this section in any county without a written contract with that county's correctional administrator. A public or private agency or entity entering into a contract pursuant to this subdivision shall not itself employ any person who is in the electronic monitoring program.
(2) Program participants shall undergo the normal booking process for arrestees entering the jail. All electronic monitoring program participants shall be supervised.
(3) (A) All privately operated electronic monitoring programs shall be under the jurisdiction of, and subject to the terms and conditions of the contract entered into with, the correctional administrator.
(B) Each contract specified in subparagraph (A) shall include, but not be limited to, all of the following:
(i) A provision whereby the private agency or entity agrees to operate in compliance with any available standards and all state and county laws applicable to the operation of electronic monitoring programs and the supervision of offenders in an electronic monitoring program.
(ii) A provision that clearly defines areas of respective responsibility and liability of the county and the private agency or entity.
(iii) A provision that requires the private agency or entity to demonstrate evidence of financial responsibility, submitted to and approved by the board of supervisors, in amounts and under conditions sufficient to fully indemnify the county for reasonably foreseeable public liability, including legal defense costs that may arise from, or be proximately caused by, acts or omissions of the contractor.
(iv) A provision that requires the private agency or entity to provide evidence of financial responsibility, such as certificates of insurance or copies of insurance policies, prior to commencing any operations pursuant to the contract or at any time requested by the board of supervisors or correctional administrator.
(v) A provision that requires an annual review by the correctional administrator to ensure compliance with requirements set by the board of supervisors and for adjustment of the financial responsibility requirements if warranted by caseload changes or other factors.
(vi) A provision that permits the correctional administrator to immediately terminate the contract with a private agency or entity at any time that the contractor fails to demonstrate evidence of financial responsibility.
(C) All privately operated electronic monitoring programs shall comply with all applicable ordinances and regulations specified in subdivision (a) of Section 1208.
(D) The board of supervisors, the correctional administrator, and the designee of the correctional administrator shall comply with Section 1090 of the Government Code in the consideration, making, and execution of contracts pursuant to this section.
(E) The failure of the private agency or entity to comply with state or county laws or with the standards established by the contract with the correctional administrator shall constitute cause to terminate the contract.
(F) Upon the discovery that a private agency or entity with which there is a contract is not in compliance with this paragraph, the correctional administrator shall give 60 days' notice to the director of the private agency or entity that the contract may be canceled if the specified deficiencies are not corrected.
(G) Shorter notice may be given or the contract may be canceled without notice whenever a serious threat to public safety is present because the private agency or entity has failed to comply with this section.
(H) For purposes of this section, "evidence of financial responsibility" may include, but is not limited to, certified copies of any of the following:
(i) A current liability insurance policy.
(ii) A current errors and omissions insurance policy.
(iii) A surety bond.
(Amended by Stats. 2014, Ch. 612, Sec. 4. (AB 2499) Effective January 1, 2015.)

1203.02.

The court, or judge thereof, in granting probation to a defendant convicted of any of the offenses enumerated in Section 290 of this code shall inquire into the question whether the defendant at the time the offense was committed was intoxicated or addicted to the excessive use of alcoholic liquor or beverages at that time or immediately prior thereto, and if the court, or judge thereof, believes that the defendant was so intoxicated, or so addicted, such court, or judge thereof, shall require as a condition of such probation that the defendant totally abstain from the use of alcoholic liquor or beverages.
(Amended by Stats. 1951, Ch. 1608.)

1203.03.

(a) In any case in which a defendant is convicted of an offense punishable by imprisonment in the state prison, the court, if it concludes that a just disposition of the case requires such diagnosis and treatment services as can be provided at a diagnostic facility of the Department of Corrections, may order that defendant be placed temporarily in such facility for a period not to exceed 90 days, with the further provision in such order that the Director of the Department of Corrections report to the court his diagnosis and recommendations concerning the defendant within the 90-day period.
(b) The Director of the Department of Corrections shall, within the 90 days, cause defendant to be observed and examined and shall forward to the court his diagnosis and recommendation concerning the disposition of defendant's case. Such diagnosis and recommendation shall be embodied in a written report and copies of the report shall be served only upon the defendant or his counsel, the probation officer, and the prosecuting attorney by the court receiving such report. After delivery of the copies of the report, the information contained therein shall not be disclosed to anyone else without the consent of the defendant. After disposition of the case, all copies of the report, except the one delivered to the defendant or his counsel, shall be filed in a sealed file and shall be available thereafter only to the defendant or his counsel, the prosecuting attorney, the court, the probation officer, or the Department of Corrections.
(c) Notwithstanding subdivision (b), the probation officer may retain a copy of the report for the purpose of supervision of the defendant if the defendant is placed on probation by the court. The report and information contained therein shall be confidential and shall not be disclosed to anyone else without the written consent of the defendant. Upon the completion or termination of probation, the copy of the report shall be returned by the probation officer to the sealed file prescribed in subdivision (b).
(d) The Department of Corrections shall designate the place to which a person referred to it under the provisions of this section shall be transported. After the receipt of any such person, the department may return the person to the referring court if the director of the department, in his discretion, determines that the staff and facilities of the department are inadequate to provide such services.
(e) The sheriff of the county in which an order is made placing a defendant in a diagnostic facility pursuant to this section, or any other peace officer designated by the court, shall execute the order placing such defendant in the center or returning him therefrom to the court. The expense of such sheriff or other peace officer incurred in executing such order is a charge upon the county in which the court is situated.
(f) It is the intention of the Legislature that the diagnostic facilities made available to the counties by this section shall only be used for the purposes designated and not in lieu of sentences to local facilities.
(g) Time spent by a defendant in confinement in a diagnostic facility of the Department of Corrections pursuant to this section or as an inpatient of the California Rehabilitation Center shall be credited on the term of imprisonment in state prison, if any, to which defendant is sentenced in the case.
(h) In any case in which a defendant has been placed in a diagnostic facility pursuant to this section and, in the course of his confinement, he is determined to be suffering from a remediable condition relevant to his criminal conduct, the department may, with the permission of defendant, administer treatment for such condition. If such treatment will require a longer period of confinement than the period for which defendant was placed in the diagnostic facility, the Director of Corrections may file with the court which placed defendant in the facility a petition for extension of the period of confinement, to which shall be attached a writing signed by defendant giving his consent to the extension. If the court finds the petition and consent in order, it may order the extension, and transmit a copy of the order to the Director of Corrections.
(Amended by Stats. 1977, Ch. 165.)

1203.045.

(a) Except in unusual cases where the interests of justice would best be served if the person is granted probation, probation shall not be granted to any person convicted of a crime of theft of an amount exceeding one hundred thousand dollars ($100,000).
(b) The fact that the theft was of an amount exceeding one hundred thousand dollars ($100,000) shall be alleged in the accusatory pleading, and either admitted by the defendant in open court, or found to be true by the jury trying the issue of guilt or by the court where guilt is established by plea of guilty or nolo contendere or by trial by the court sitting without a jury.
(c) When probation is granted, the court shall specify on the record and shall enter on the minutes the circumstances indicating that the interests of justice would best be served by such a disposition.
(Added by Stats. 1983, Ch. 327, Sec. 1.)

1203.046.

(a) Except in unusual cases where the interests of justice would best be served if the person is granted probation, probation shall not be granted to any person who is convicted of violating Section 653j by using, soliciting, inducing, encouraging, or intimidating a minor to commit a felony in violation of that section.
(b) When probation is granted pursuant to subdivision (a), the court shall specify on the record and shall enter into the minutes the circumstances indicating that the interests of justice would best be served by that disposition.
(Amended by Stats. 1989, Ch. 897, Sec. 37.5.)

1203.047.

A person convicted of a violation of paragraph (1), (2), (4), or (5) of subdivision (c) of Section 502, or of a felony violation of paragraph (3), (6), (7), or (8) of subdivision (c) of Section 502, or a violation of subdivision (b) of Section 502.7 may be granted probation, but, except in unusual cases where the ends of justice would be better served by a shorter period, the period of probation shall not be less than three years and the following terms shall be imposed. During the period of probation, that person shall not accept employment where that person would use a computer connected by any means to any other computer, except upon approval of the court and notice to and opportunity to be heard by the prosecuting attorney, probation department, prospective employer, and the convicted person. Court approval shall not be given unless the court finds that the proposed employment would not pose a risk to the public.
(Added by Stats. 1989, Ch. 1357, Sec. 3.)

1203.048.

(a) Except in unusual cases where the interests of justice would best be served if the person is granted probation, probation shall not be granted to any person convicted of a violation of Section 502 or subdivision (b) of Section 502.7 involving the taking of or damage to property with a value exceeding one hundred thousand dollars ($100,000).
(b) The fact that the value of the property taken or damaged was an amount exceeding one hundred thousand dollars ($100,000) shall be alleged in the accusatory pleading, and either admitted by the defendant in open court, or found to be true by the jury trying the issue of guilt or by the court where guilt is established by plea of guilt or nolo contendere or by trial by the court sitting without a jury.
(c) When probation is granted, the court shall specify on the record and shall enter on the minutes the circumstances indicating that the interests of justice would best be served by such a disposition.
(Added by Stats. 1989, Ch. 1357, Sec. 4.)

1203.049.

(a) Except in unusual cases where the interest of justice would best be served if the person is granted probation, probation shall not be granted to any person who violates subdivision (f) or (g) of Section 10980 of the Welfare and Institutions Code, when the violation has been committed by means of the electronic transfer of CalFresh benefits, and the amount of the electronically transferred CalFresh benefits exceeds one hundred thousand dollars ($100,000).
(b) The fact that the violation was committed by means of an electronic transfer of CalFresh benefits and the amount of the electronically transferred CalFresh benefits exceeds one hundred thousand dollars ($100,000) shall be alleged in the accusatory pleading, and either admitted by the defendant in open court, or found to be true by the jury trying the issue of guilt or by the court where guilt is established by a plea of guilty or nolo contendere or by trial by the court sitting without a jury.
(c) If probation is granted, the court shall specify on the record and shall enter on the minutes the circumstances indicating that the interests of justice would best be served by that disposition of the case.
(Amended by Stats. 2011, Ch. 227, Sec. 16. (AB 1400) Effective January 1, 2012.)

1203.05.

Any report of the probation officer filed with the court, including any report arising out of a previous arrest of the person who is the subject of the report, may be inspected or copied only as follows:
(a) By any person, from the date judgment is pronounced or probation granted or, in the case of a report arising out of a previous arrest, from the date the subsequent accusatory pleading is filed, to and including 60 days from the date judgment is pronounced or probation is granted, whichever is earlier.
(b) By any person, at any time, by order of the court, upon filing a petition therefor by the person.
(c) By the general public, if the court upon its own motion orders that a report or reports shall be open or that the contents of the report or reports shall be disclosed.
(d) By any person authorized or required by law to inspect or receive copies of the report.
(e) By the district attorney of the county at any time.
(f) By the subject of the report at any time.
(Amended by Stats. 1997, Ch. 128, Sec. 1. Effective January 1, 1998.)

1203.055.

(a) Notwithstanding any other law, in sentencing a person convicted of committing or of attempting to commit one or more of the offenses listed in subdivision (b) against a person who is a passenger, operator, driver, or other occupant of any public transit vehicle whether the offense or attempt is committed within the vehicle or directed at the vehicle, the court shall require that the person serve some period of confinement. If probation is granted, it shall be a condition of probation that the person shall be confined in the county jail for some period of time. If the time spent in jail prior to arraignment is less than 24 hours, it shall not be considered to satisfy the requirement that some period of confinement be imposed.
As used in this subdivision, "public transit vehicle" means any motor vehicle, streetcar, trackless trolley, bus, shuttle, light rail system, rapid transit system, subway, train, taxi cab, or jitney, which transports members of the public for hire.
(b) Subdivision (a) applies to the following crimes:
(1) Murder.
(2) A violation of Section 241, 241.3, 241.4, 244, 245, 245.2, or 246.
(3) Robbery, in violation of Section 211.
(4) Kidnapping, in violation of Section 207.
(5) Kidnapping, in violation of Section 209.

(6) Battery, in violation of Section 243, 243.1, or 243.3.

(7) Rape, in violation of Section 261, 262, 264, or 264.1.

(8) Assault with intent to commit rape or sodomy, in violation of Section 220.

(9) Any other offense in which the defendant inflicts great bodily injury on any person other than an accomplice. As used in this paragraph, "great bodily injury" means "great bodily injury" as defined in Section 12022.7.

(10) Grand theft, in violation of subdivision (1) of Section 487.

(11) Throwing of a hard substance or shooting a missile at a transit vehicle, in violation of Section 219.2.

(12) Unlawfully causing a fire, in violation of Section 452.

(13) Drawing, exhibiting, or using a firearm or deadly weapon, in violation of Section 417.

(14) A violation of Section 214.

(15) A violation of Section 215.

(16) Kidnapping, in violation of Section 209.5.

(c) Probation shall not be granted to, nor shall the execution or imposition of sentence be suspended for, any person convicted of a felony offense falling within this section if the person has been previously convicted and sentenced pursuant to this section.

(d) (1) The existence of any fact which would make a person ineligible for probation under subdivisions (a) and (c) shall be alleged in the accusatory pleading, and either admitted by the defendant in open court, or found to be true by the jury trying the issue of guilt or by the court where guilt is established by a plea of guilty or nolo contendere or by a trial by the court sitting without a jury.

A finding bringing the defendant within this section shall not be stricken pursuant to Section 1385 or any provision of law.

(2) This subdivision does not prohibit the adjournment of criminal proceedings pursuant to Division 3 (commencing with Section 3000) or Division 6 (commencing with Section 6000) of the Welfare and Institutions Code.

(e) The court shall require, as a condition of probation for any person convicted of committing a crime which took place on a public transit vehicle, except in any case in which the court makes a finding and states on the record clear and compelling reasons why the condition would be inappropriate, that the person make restitution to the victim. If restitution is found to be inappropriate, the court shall require as a condition of probation, except in any case in which the court makes a finding and states on the record its reasons that the condition would be inappropriate, that the defendant perform specified community service. Nothing in this subdivision shall be construed to limit the authority of a court to provide additional conditions of probation.

(f) In any case in which a person is convicted of committing a crime which took place on a public transit vehicle, the probation officer shall immediately investigate and report to the court at a specified time whether, as a result of the crime, property damage or loss or personal injury was caused by the defendant, the amount of the damage, loss, or injury, and the feasibility of requiring restitution to be made by the defendant. When a probation report is required pursuant to Section 1203 the information required by this subdivision shall be added to that probation report.

(Amended by Stats. 1994, Ch. 224, Sec. 3. Effective January 1, 1995.)

1203.06.

(a) Notwithstanding any other provision of law, probation shall not be granted to, nor shall the execution or imposition of sentence be suspended for, nor shall a finding bringing the defendant within this section be stricken pursuant to Section 1385 for, any of the following persons:

(1) Any person who personally used a firearm during the commission or attempted commission of any of the following crimes:

(A) Murder.

(B) Robbery, in violation of Section 211.

(C) Kidnapping, in violation of Section 207, 209, or 209.5.

(D) Lewd or lascivious act, in violation of Section 288.

(E) Burglary of the first degree, as defined in Section 460.

(F) Rape, in violation of Section 261, 262, or 264.1.

(G) Assault with intent to commit a specified sexual offense, in violation of Section 220.

(H) Escape, in violation of Section 4530 or 4532.

(I) Carjacking, in violation of Section 215.

(J) Aggravated mayhem, in violation of Section 205.

(K) Torture, in violation of Section 206.

(L) Continuous sexual abuse of a child, in violation of Section 288.5.

(M) A felony violation of Section 136.1 or 137.

(N) Sodomy, in violation of Section 286.

(O) Oral copulation, in violation of Section 287 or former Section 288a.

(P) Sexual penetration, in violation of Section 289 or 264.1.

(Q) Aggravated sexual assault of a child, in violation of Section 269.

(2) Any person previously convicted of a felony specified in paragraph (1), or assault with intent to commit murder under former Section 217, who is convicted of a subsequent felony and who was personally armed with a firearm at any time during its commission or attempted commission or was unlawfully armed with a firearm at the time of his or her arrest for the subsequent felony.

(3) Aggravated arson, in violation of Section 451.5.

(b) (1) The existence of any fact that would make a person ineligible for probation under subdivision (a) shall be alleged in the accusatory pleading, and either admitted by the defendant in open court, or found to be true by the trier of fact.

(2) As used in subdivision (a), "used a firearm" means to display a firearm in a menacing manner, to intentionally fire it, to intentionally strike or hit a human being with it, or to use it in any manner that qualifies under Section 12022.5.

(3) As used in subdivision (a), "armed with a firearm" means to knowingly carry or have available for use a firearm as a means of offense or defense.

(Amended by Stats. 2018, Ch. 423, Sec. 91. (SB 1494) Effective January 1, 2019. Note: This section was amended November 7, 2006, by initiative Proposition 83.)

1203.065.

(a) Notwithstanding any other law, probation shall not be granted to, nor shall the execution or imposition of sentence be suspended for, a person who is convicted of violating paragraph (2), (3), (4), or (6) of subdivision (a) of Section 261, Section 264.1, 266h, 266i, 266j, or 269, paragraph (2) or (3) of subdivision (c), or subdivision (d), (f), or (i) of Section 286, paragraph (2) or (3) of subdivision (c), or subdivision (d), (f), or (i) of Section 287 or former Section 288a, Section 288.7, subdivision (a), (d), or (e) of Section 289, or subdivision (b) of Section 311.4.

(b) (1) Except in unusual cases where the interests of justice would best be served if the person is granted probation, probation shall not be granted to a person who is convicted of violating paragraph (7) of subdivision (a) of Section 261, subdivision (k) of Section 286, subdivision (k) of Section 287 or former Section 288a, subdivision (g) of Section 289, or Section 220 for assault with intent to commit a specified sexual offense.

(2) If probation is granted, the court shall specify on the record and shall enter on the minutes the circumstances indicating that the interests of justice would best be served by the disposition.

(Amended by Stats. 2018, Ch. 423, Sec. 92. (SB 1494) Effective January 1, 2019. Note: This section was amended on Nov. 7, 2006, by initiative Prop. 83.)

1203.066.

(a) Notwithstanding Section 1203 or any other law, probation shall not be granted to, nor shall the execution or imposition of sentence be suspended for, nor shall a finding bringing the defendant within the provisions of this section be stricken pursuant to Section 1385 for, any of the following persons:

(1) A person who is convicted of violating Section 288 or 288.5 when the act is committed by the use of force, violence, duress, menace, or fear of immediate and unlawful bodily injury on the victim or another person.

(2) A person who caused bodily injury on the child victim in committing a violation of Section 288 or 288.5.

(3) A person who is convicted of a violation of Section 288 or 288.5 and who was a stranger to the child victim or befriended the child victim for the purpose of committing an act in violation of Section 288 or 288.5, unless the defendant honestly and reasonably believed the victim was 14 years of age or older.

(4) A person who used a weapon during the commission of a violation of Section 288 or 288.5.

(5) A person who is convicted of committing a violation of Section 288 or 288.5 and who has been previously convicted of a violation of Section 261, 262, 264.1, 266, 266c, 267, 285, 286, 287, 288, 288.5, or 289, or former Section 288a, or of assaulting another person with intent to commit a crime specified in this paragraph in violation of Section 220, or who has been previously convicted in another state of an offense which, if committed or attempted in this state, would constitute an offense enumerated in this paragraph.

(6) A person who violated Section 288 or 288.5 while kidnapping the child victim in violation of Section 207, 209, or 209.5.

(7) A person who is convicted of committing a violation of Section 288 or 288.5 against more than one victim.

(8) A person who, in violating Section 288 or 288.5, has substantial sexual conduct with a victim who is under 14 years of age.

(9) A person who, in violating Section 288 or 288.5, used obscene matter, as defined in Section 311, or matter, as defined in Section 311, depicting sexual conduct, as defined in Section 311.3.

(b) "Substantial sexual conduct" means penetration of the vagina or rectum of either the victim or the offender by the penis of the other or by any foreign object, oral copulation, or masturbation of either the victim or the offender.

(c) (1) Except for a violation of subdivision (b) of Section 288, this section shall only apply if the existence of any fact required in subdivision (a) is alleged in the accusatory pleading and is either admitted by the defendant in open court, or found to be true by the trier of fact.

(2) For the existence of any fact under paragraph (7) of subdivision (a), the allegation must be made pursuant to this section.

(d) (1) If a person is convicted of a violation of Section 288 or 288.5, and the factors listed in subdivision (a) are not pled or proven, probation may be granted only if the following terms and conditions are met:

(A) If the defendant is a member of the victim's household, the court finds that probation is in the best interest of the child victim.

(B) The court finds that rehabilitation of the defendant is feasible and that the defendant is amenable to undergoing treatment, and the defendant is placed in a recognized treatment program designed to deal with child molestation immediately after the grant of probation or the suspension of execution or imposition of sentence.

(C) If the defendant is a member of the victim's household, probation shall not be granted unless the defendant is removed from the household of the victim until the court determines that the best interests of the victim would be served by his or her return. While removed from the household, the court shall prohibit contact by the defendant with the victim, with the exception that the court may permit supervised contact, upon the request of the director of the court-ordered supervised treatment program, and with the agreement of the victim and the victim's parent or legal guardian, other than the defendant.

(D) If the defendant is not a member of the victim's household, the court shall prohibit the defendant from being placed or residing within one-half mile of the child victim's residence for the duration of the probation term unless the court, on the record, states its reasons for finding that this residency restriction would not serve the best interests of the victim.

(E) The court finds that there is no threat of physical harm to the victim if probation is granted.

(2) The court shall state its reasons on the record for whatever sentence it imposes on the defendant.

(3) The court shall order the psychiatrist or psychologist who is appointed pursuant to Section 288.1 to include a consideration of the factors specified in subparagraphs (A), (B), and (C) of paragraph (1) in making his or her report to the court.

(4) The court shall order the defendant to comply with all probation requirements, including the requirements to attend counseling, keep all program appointments, and pay program fees based upon ability to pay.

(5) No victim shall be compelled to participate in a program or counseling, and no program may condition a defendant's enrollment on participation by the victim.

(e) As used in subdivision (d), the following definitions apply:

(1) "Contact with the victim" includes all physical contact, being in the presence of the victim, communicating by any means, including by a third party acting on behalf of the defendant, or sending any gifts.

(2) "Recognized treatment program" means a program that consists of the following components:

(A) Substantial expertise in the treatment of child sexual abuse.

(B) A treatment regimen designed to specifically address the offense.

(C) The ability to serve indigent clients.

(D) Adequate reporting requirements to ensure that all persons who, after being ordered to attend and complete a program, may be identified for either failure to enroll in, or failure to successfully complete, the program, or for the successful completion of the program as ordered. The program shall notify the court and the probation department, in writing, within the period of time and in the manner specified by the court of any person who fails to complete the program. Notification shall be given if the program determines that the defendant is performing unsatisfactorily or if the defendant is not benefiting from the education, treatment, or counseling.

(Amended by Stats. 2018, Ch. 423, Sec. 93. (SB 1494) Effective January 1, 2019.)

1203.067.

(a) Notwithstanding any other law, before probation may be granted to any person convicted of a felony specified in Section 261, 262, 264.1, 286, 287, 288, 288.5, or 289, or former Section 288a, who is eligible for probation, the court shall do all of the following:

(1) Order the defendant evaluated pursuant to Section 1203.03, or similar evaluation by the county probation department.

(2) Conduct a hearing at the time of sentencing to determine if probation of the defendant would pose a threat to the victim. The victim shall be notified of the hearing by the prosecuting attorney and given an opportunity to address the court.

(3) Order any psychiatrist or psychologist appointed pursuant to Section 288.1 to include a consideration of the threat to the victim and the defendant's potential for positive response to treatment in making his or her report to the court. Nothing in this section shall be construed to require the court to order an examination of the victim.

(b) On or after July 1, 2012, the terms of probation for persons placed on formal probation for an offense that requires registration pursuant to Sections 290 to 290.023, inclusive, shall include all of the following:

(1) Persons placed on formal probation prior to July 1, 2012, shall participate in an approved sex offender management program, following the standards developed pursuant to Section 9003, for a period of not less than one year or the remaining term of probation if it is less than one year. The length of the period in the program is to be

determined by the certified sex offender management professional in consultation with the probation officer and as approved by the court. Participation in this program applies to every person described without regard to when his or her crime or crimes were committed.
(2) Persons placed on formal probation on or after July 1, 2012, shall successfully complete a sex offender management program, following the standards developed pursuant to Section 9003, as a condition of release from probation. The length of the period in the program shall be not less than one year, up to the entire period of probation, as determined by the certified sex offender management professional in consultation with the probation officer and as approved by the court. Participation in this program applies to each person without regard to when his or her crime or crimes were committed.
(3) Waiver of any privilege against self-incrimination and participation in polygraph examinations, which shall be part of the sex offender management program.
(4) Waiver of any psychotherapist-patient privilege to enable communication between the sex offender management professional and supervising probation officer, pursuant to Section 290.09.
(c) Any defendant ordered to be placed in an approved sex offender management program pursuant to subdivision (b) shall be responsible for paying the expense of his or her participation in the program as determined by the court. The court shall take into consideration the ability of the defendant to pay, and no defendant shall be denied probation because of his or her inability to pay.
(Amended by Stats. 2018, Ch. 423, Sec. 94. (SB 1494) Effective January 1, 2019.)
1203.07.
(a) Notwithstanding Section 1203, probation shall not be granted to, nor shall the execution or imposition of sentence be suspended for, any of the following persons:
(1) Any person who is convicted of violating Section 11351 of the Health and Safety Code by possessing for sale 14.25 grams or more of a substance containing heroin.
(2) Any person who is convicted of violating Section 11352 of the Health and Safety Code by selling or offering to sell 14.25 grams or more of a substance containing heroin.
(3) Any person convicted of violating Section 11351 of the Health and Safety Code by possessing heroin for sale or convicted of violating Section 11352 of the Health and Safety Code by selling or offering to sell heroin, and who has one or more prior convictions for violating Section 11351 or Section 11352 of the Health and Safety Code.
(4) Any person who is convicted of violating Section 11378.5 of the Health and Safety Code by possessing for sale 14.25 grams or more of any salt or solution of phencyclidine or any of its analogs as specified in paragraph (21), (22), or (23) of subdivision (d) of Section 11054 or in paragraph (3) of subdivision (e) of Section 11055 of the Health and Safety Code, or any of the precursors of phencyclidine as specified in paragraph (2) of subdivision (f) of Section 11055 of the Health and Safety Code.
(5) Any person who is convicted of violating Section 11379.5 of the Health and Safety Code by transporting for sale, importing for sale, or administering, or offering to transport for sale, import for sale, or administer, or by attempting to import for sale or transport for sale, phencyclidine or any of its analogs or precursors.
(6) Any person who is convicted of violating Section 11379.5 of the Health and Safety Code by selling or offering to sell phencyclidine or any of its analogs or precursors.
(7) Any person who is convicted of violating Section 11379.6 of the Health and Safety Code by manufacturing or offering to perform an act involving the manufacture of phencyclidine or any of its analogs or precursors.
As used in this section "manufacture" refers to the act of any person who manufactures, compounds, converts, produces, derives, processes, or prepares, either directly or indirectly by chemical extraction or independently by means of chemical synthesis.
(8) Any person who is convicted of violating Section 11380 of the Health and Safety Code by using, soliciting, inducing, encouraging, or intimidating a minor to act as an agent to manufacture, compound, or sell any controlled substance specified in subdivision (d) of Section 11054 of the Health and Safety Code, except paragraphs (13), (14), (15), (20), (21), (22), and (23) of subdivision (d), or specified in subdivision (d), (e), or (f) of Section 11055 of the Health and Safety Code, except paragraph (3) of subdivision (e) and subparagraphs (A) and (B) of paragraph (2) of subdivision (f).
(9) Any person who is convicted of violating Section 11380.5 of the Health and Safety Code by the use of a minor as an agent or who solicits, induces, encourages, or intimidates a minor with the intent that the minor shall violate the provisions of Section 11378.5, 11379.5, or 11379.6 of the Health and Safety Code insofar as the violation relates to phencyclidine or any of its analogs or precursors.
(10) Any person who is convicted of violating subdivision (b) of Section 11383 of the Health and Safety Code by possessing piperidine, pyrrolidine, or morpholine, and cyclohexanone, with intent to manufacture phencyclidine or any of its analogs.
(11) Any person convicted of violating Section 11351, 11351.5, or 11378 of the Health and Safety Code by possessing for sale cocaine base, cocaine, or methamphetamine, or convicted of violating Section 11352 or 11379 of the Health and Safety Code, by selling or offering to sell cocaine base, cocaine, or methamphetamine and who has one or more convictions for violating Section 11351, 11351.5, 11352, 11378, 11378.5, 11379, or 11379.5 of the Health and Safety Code. For purposes of prior convictions under Sections 11352, 11379, and 11379.5 of the Health and Safety Code, this subdivision shall not apply to the transportation, offering to transport, or attempting to transport a controlled substance.
(b) The existence of any fact which would make a person ineligible for probation under subdivision (a) shall be alleged in the information or indictment, and either admitted by the defendant in open court, or found to be true by the jury trying the issue of guilt or by the court where guilt is established by plea of guilty or nolo contendere or by trial by the court sitting without a jury.
(Amended by Stats. 1989, Ch. 1135, Sec. 2.)
1203.073.
(a) A person convicted of a felony specified in subdivision (b) may be granted probation only in an unusual case where the interests of justice would best be served. When probation is granted in such a case, the court shall specify on the record and shall enter in the minutes the circumstances indicating that the interests of justice would best be served by such a disposition.
(b) Except as provided in subdivision (a), probation shall not be granted to, nor shall the execution or imposition of sentence be suspended for, any of the following persons:
(1) Any person who is convicted of violating Section 11351 or 11351.5 of the Health and Safety Code by possessing for sale, or Section 11352 of the Health and Safety Code by selling, a substance containing 28.5 grams or more of cocaine as specified in paragraph (6) of subdivision (b) of Section 11055 of, or cocaine base as specified in paragraph (1) of subdivision (f) of Section 11054 of, the Health and Safety Code, or 57 grams or more of a substance containing at least five grams of cocaine as specified in paragraph (6) of subdivision (b) of Section 11055 of, or cocaine base as specified in paragraph (1) of subdivision (f) of Section 11054 of, the Health and Safety Code.
(2) Any person who is convicted of violating Section 11378 of the Health and Safety Code by possessing for sale, or Section 11379 of the Health and Safety Code by selling a substance containing 28.5 grams or more of methamphetamine or 57 grams or more of a substance containing methamphetamine.
(3) Any person who is convicted of violating subdivision (a) of Section 11379.6 of the Health and Safety Code, except those who manufacture phencyclidine, or who is convicted of an act which is punishable under subdivision (b) of Section 11379.6 of the Health and Safety Code, except those who offer to perform an act which aids in the manufacture of phencyclidine.
(4) Except as otherwise provided in Section 1203.07, any person who is convicted of violating Section 11353 or 11380 of the Health and Safety Code by using, soliciting, inducing, encouraging, or intimidating a minor to manufacture, compound, or sell heroin, cocaine base as specified in paragraph (1) of subdivision (f) of Section 11054 of the Health and Safety Code, cocaine as specified in paragraph (6) of subdivision (b) of Section 11055 of the Health and Safety Code, or methamphetamine.
(5) Any person convicted of violating Section 11379.6, 11382, or 11383 of the Health and Safety Code with respect to methamphetamine, if he or she has one or more prior convictions for a violation of Section 11378, 11379, 11379.6, 11380, 11382, or 11383 of the Health and Safety Code with respect to methamphetamine.
(c) As used in this section, the term "manufacture" refers to the act of any person who manufactures, compounds, converts, produces, derives, processes, or prepares, either directly or indirectly by chemical extraction or independently by means of chemical synthesis.
(d) The existence of any previous conviction or fact which would make a person ineligible for probation under this section shall be alleged in the information or indictment, and either admitted by the defendant in open court, or found to be true by the jury trying the issue of guilt or by the court where guilt is established by a plea of guilty or nolo contendere or by trial by the court sitting without a jury.
(Amended by Stats. 2014, Ch. 749, Sec. 5. (SB 1010) Effective January 1, 2015.)
1203.074.
(a) A person convicted of a felony specified in subdivision (b) may be granted probation only in an unusual case where the interests of justice would best be served; when probation is granted in such a case, the court shall specify on the record and shall enter in the minutes the circumstances indicating that the interests of justice would best be served by such a disposition.
(b) Except as provided in subdivision (a), probation shall not be granted to, nor shall the execution or imposition of sentence be suspended for, any person who is convicted of violating Section 11366.6 of the Health and Safety Code.
(Added by Stats. 1985, Ch. 1533, Sec. 3.)
1203.075.
(a) Notwithstanding any other provision of law, probation shall not be granted to, nor shall the execution or imposition of sentence be suspended for, nor shall a finding bringing the defendant within this section be stricken pursuant to Section 1385 for, any person who personally inflicts great bodily injury, as defined in Section 12022.7, on the person of another in the commission or attempted commission of any of the following crimes:
(1) Murder.
(2) Robbery, in violation of Section 211.
(3) Kidnapping, in violation of Section 207, 209, or 209.5.
(4) Lewd or lascivious act, in violation of Section 288.
(5) Burglary of the first degree, as defined in Section 460.
(6) Rape, in violation of Section 261, 262, or 264.1.
(7) Assault with intent to commit a specified sexual offense, in violation of Section 220.
(8) Escape, in violation of Section 4530 or 4532.
(9) Sexual penetration, in violation of Section 289 or 264.1.
(10) Sodomy, in violation of Section 286.
(11) Oral copulation, in violation of Section 287 or former Section 288a.
(12) Carjacking, in violation of Section 215.
(13) Continuous sexual abuse of a child, in violation of Section 288.5.
(14) Aggravated sexual assault of a child, in violation of Section 269.
(b) The existence of any fact that would make a person ineligible for probation under subdivision (a) shall be alleged in the accusatory pleading, and either admitted by the defendant in open court, or found to be true by the trier of fact.
(Amended by Stats. 2018, Ch. 423, Sec. 95. (SB 1494) Effective January 1, 2019. Note: This section was amended November 7, 2006, by initiative Proposition 83.)
1203.076.
Any person convicted of violating Section 11352 of the Health and Safety Code relating to the sale of cocaine, cocaine hydrochloride, or heroin, or Section 11379.5 of the Health and Safety Code, who is eligible for probation and who is granted probation shall, as a condition thereof, be confined in the county jail for at least 180 days. The imposition of the minimum 180-day sentence shall be imposed in every case where probation has been granted, except that the court may, in an unusual case where the interests of justice would best be served, absolve a person from spending the 180-day sentence in the county jail if the court specifies on the record and enters into the minutes, the circumstances indicating that the interests of justice would best be served by that disposition.
(Added by Stats. 1988, Ch. 1244, Sec. 1.)
1203.08.
(a) Notwithstanding any other law, probation shall not be granted to, nor shall the execution or imposition of sentence be suspended for, any adult person convicted of a designated felony who has been previously convicted as an adult under charges separately brought and tried two or more times of any designated felony or in any other place of a public offense which, if committed in this state, would have been punishable as a designated felony, if all the convictions occurred within a 10-year period. The 10-year period shall be calculated exclusive of any period of time during which the person has been confined in a state or federal prison.
(b) (1) The existence of any fact which would make a person ineligible for probation under subdivision (a) shall be alleged in the information or indictment, and either admitted by the defendant in open court, or found to be true by the jury trying the issue of guilt or by the court where guilt is established by plea of guilty or nolo contendere or by trial by the court sitting without a jury.
(2) Except where the existence of the fact was not admitted or found to be true pursuant to paragraph (1), or the court finds that a prior conviction was invalid, the court shall not strike or dismiss any prior convictions alleged in the information or indictment.
(3) This subdivision does not prohibit the adjournment of criminal proceedings pursuant to Division 3 (commencing with Section 3000) or Division 6 (commencing with Section 6000) of the Welfare and Institutions Code.
(c) As used in this section, "designated felony" means any felony specified in Section 187, 192, 207, 209, 209.5, 211, 215, 217, 245, 288, or paragraph (2), (6), or (7) of subdivision (a) of Section 261, paragraph (1), (4), or (5) of subdivision (a) of Section 262, subdivision (a) of Section 460, or when great bodily injury occurs in perpetration of an assault to commit robbery, mayhem, or rape, as defined in Section 220.
(Amended by Stats. 1994, Ch. 1188, Sec. 15. Effective January 1, 1995.)
1203.085.
(a) Any person convicted of an offense punishable by imprisonment in the state prison but without an alternate sentence to a county jail shall not be granted probation or have the execution or imposition of sentence suspended, if the offense was committed while the person was on parole from state prison pursuant to Section 3000, following a term of imprisonment imposed for a violent felony, as defined in subdivision (c) of Section 667.5, or a serious felony, as defined in subdivision (c) of Section 1192.7.
(b) Any person convicted of a violent felony, as defined in subdivision (c) of Section 667.5, or a serious felony, as defined in subdivision (c) of Section 1192.7, shall not be granted probation or have the execution or imposition of sentence suspended, if the offense was committed while the person was on parole from state prison pursuant to Section 3000.

(c) The existence of any fact that would make a person ineligible for probation under subdivision (a) or (b) shall be alleged in the information or indictment, and either admitted by the defendant in open court, or found to be true by the jury trying the issue of guilt or by the court where guilt is established by plea of guilty or nolo contendere or by trial by the court sitting without a jury.

(Amended by Stats. 1997, Ch. 160, Sec. 1. Effective January 1, 1998.)

1203.09.

(a) Notwithstanding any other law, probation shall not be granted to, nor shall the execution or imposition of sentence be suspended for, any person who commits or attempts to commit one or more of the crimes listed in subdivision (b) against a person who is 60 years of age or older; or against a person who is blind, a paraplegic, a quadriplegic, or a person confined to a wheelchair and that disability is known or reasonably should be known to the person committing the crime; and who during the course of the offense inflicts great bodily injury upon the person.

(b) Subdivision (a) applies to the following crimes:

(1) Murder.

(2) Robbery, in violation of Section 211.

(3) Kidnapping, in violation of Section 207.

(4) Kidnapping, in violation of Section 209.

(5) Burglary of the first degree, as defined in Section 460.

(6) Rape by force or violence, in violation of paragraph (2) or (6) of subdivision (a) of Section 261 or paragraph (1) or (4) of subdivision (a) of Section 262.

(7) Assault with intent to commit rape or sodomy, in violation of Section 220.

(8) Carjacking, in violation of Section 215.

(9) Kidnapping, in violation of Section 209.5.

(c) The existence of any fact which would make a person ineligible for probation under either subdivision (a) or (f) shall be alleged in the information or indictment, and either admitted by the defendant in open court, or found to be true by the jury trying the issue of guilt or by the court where guilt is established by plea of guilty or nolo contendere or by trial by the court sitting without a jury.

(d) As used in this section "great bodily injury" means "great bodily injury" as defined in Section 12022.7.

(e) This section shall apply in all cases, including those cases where the infliction of great bodily injury is an element of the offense.

(f) Except in unusual cases where the interests of justice would best be served if the person is granted probation, probation shall not be granted to, nor shall the execution or imposition of sentence be suspended for, any person convicted of having committed one or more of the following crimes against a person who is 60 years of age or older: assault with a deadly weapon or instrument, battery which results in physical injury which requires professional medical treatment, carjacking, robbery, or mayhem.

(Amended by Stats. 1994, Ch. 1188, Sec. 16. Effective January 1, 1995.)

1203.095.

(a) Except as provided in subdivision (b), but notwithstanding any other provision of law, if any person convicted of a violation of paragraph (2) of subdivision (a) of Section 245, of a violation of paragraph (1) of subdivision (d) of Section 245, of a violation of Section 246, or a violation of subdivision (c) of Section 417, is granted probation or the execution or imposition of sentence is suspended, it shall be a condition thereof that he or she be imprisoned for at least six months, and if any person convicted of a violation of paragraph (2) of subdivision (a) of Section 417 is granted probation or the execution or imposition of sentence is suspended, it shall be a condition thereof that he or she be imprisoned for at least three months.

(b) The provisions of subdivision (a) shall apply except in unusual cases where the interests of justice would best be served by granting probation or suspending the imposition or execution of sentence without the imprisonment required by subdivision (a), or by granting probation or suspending the imposition or execution of sentence with conditions other than those set forth in subdivision (a), in which case the court shall specify on the record and shall enter on the minutes the circumstances indicating that the interests of justice would best be served by such a disposition.

(c) This section does not prohibit the adjournment of criminal proceedings pursuant to Division 3 (commencing with Section 3000) or Division 6 (commencing with Section 6000) of the Welfare and Institutions Code.

(Amended by Stats. 1995, Ch. 377, Sec. 4. Effective January 1, 1996.)

1203.096.

(a) Upon conviction of any felony in which the defendant is sentenced to state prison and in which the court makes the findings set forth in subdivision (b), a court shall, in addition to any other terms of imprisonment, fine, and conditions, recommend in writing that the defendant participate in a counseling or education program having a substance abuse component while imprisoned.

(b) The court shall make the recommendation specified in subdivision (a) if it finds that any of the following are true:

(1) That the defendant at the time of the commission of the offense was under the influence of any alcoholic beverages.

(2) That the defendant at the time of the commission of the offense was under the influence of any controlled substance.

(3) That the defendant has a demonstrated history of substance abuse.

(4) That the offense or offenses for which the defendant was convicted are drug related.

(Added by Stats. 1991, Ch. 552, Sec. 1.)

1203.097.

(a) If a person is granted probation for a crime in which the victim is a person defined in Section 6211 of the Family Code, the terms of probation shall include all of the following:

(1) A minimum period of probation of 36 months, which may include a period of summary probation as appropriate.

(2) A criminal court protective order protecting the victim from further acts of violence, threats, stalking, sexual abuse, and harassment, and, if appropriate, containing residence exclusion or stay-away conditions.

(3) Notice to the victim of the disposition of the case.

(4) Booking the defendant within one week of sentencing if the defendant has not already been booked.

(5) (A) A minimum payment by the defendant of a fee of five hundred dollars ($500) to be disbursed as specified in this paragraph. If, after a hearing in open court, the court finds that the defendant does not have the ability to pay, the court may reduce or waive this fee. If the court exercises its discretion to reduce or waive the fee, it shall state the reason on the record.

(B) Two-thirds of the moneys deposited with the county treasurer pursuant to this section shall be retained by counties and deposited in the domestic violence programs special fund created pursuant to Section 18305 of the Welfare and Institutions Code, to be expended for the purposes of Chapter 5 (commencing with Section 18290) of Part 6 of Division 9 of the Welfare and Institutions Code. Of the moneys deposited in the domestic violence programs special fund, no more than 8 percent may be used for administrative costs, as specified in Section 18305 of the Welfare and Institutions Code.

(C) The remaining one-third of the moneys shall be transferred, once a month, to the Controller for deposit in equal amounts in the Domestic Violence Restraining Order Reimbursement Fund and in the Domestic Violence Training and Education Fund, which are hereby created, in an amount equal to one-third of funds collected during the preceding month. Moneys deposited into these funds pursuant to this section shall be available upon appropriation by the Legislature and shall be distributed each fiscal year as follows:

(i) Funds from the Domestic Violence Restraining Order Reimbursement Fund shall be distributed to local law enforcement or other criminal justice agencies for state-

mandated local costs resulting from the notification requirements set forth in subdivision (b) of Section 6380 of the Family Code, based on the annual notification from the Department of Justice of the number of restraining orders issued and registered in the state domestic violence restraining order registry maintained by the Department of Justice, for the development and maintenance of the domestic violence restraining order databank system.

(ii) Funds from the Domestic Violence Training and Education Fund shall support a statewide training and education program to increase public awareness of domestic violence and to improve the scope and quality of services provided to the victims of domestic violence. Grants to support this program shall be awarded on a competitive basis and be administered by the State Department of Public Health, in consultation with the statewide domestic violence coalition, which is eligible to receive funding under this section.

(D) The fee imposed by this paragraph shall be treated as a fee, not as a fine, and shall not be subject to reduction for time served as provided pursuant to Section 1205 or 2900.5.

(E) The fee imposed by this paragraph may be collected by the collecting agency, or the agency's designee, after the termination of the period of probation, whether probation is terminated by revocation or by completion of the term.

(6) Successful completion of a batterer's program, as defined in subdivision (c), or if none is available, another appropriate counseling program designated by the court, for a period not less than one year with periodic progress reports by the program to the court every three months or less and weekly sessions of a minimum of two hours class time duration. The defendant shall attend consecutive weekly sessions, unless granted an excused absence for good cause by the program for no more than three individual sessions during the entire program, and shall complete the program within 18 months, unless, after a hearing, the court finds good cause to modify the requirements of consecutive attendance or completion within 18 months.

(7) (A) (i) The court shall order the defendant to comply with all probation requirements, including the requirements to attend counseling, keep all program appointments, and pay program fees based upon the ability to pay.

(ii) The terms of probation for offenders shall not be lifted until all reasonable fees due to the counseling program have been paid in full, but in no case shall probation be extended beyond the term provided in subdivision (a) of Section 1203.1. If the court finds that the defendant does not have the ability to pay the fees based on the defendant's changed circumstances, the court may reduce or waive the fees.

(B) Upon request by the batterer's program, the court shall provide the defendant's arrest report, prior incidents of violence, and treatment history to the program.

(8) The court also shall order the defendant to perform a specified amount of appropriate community service, as designated by the court. The defendant shall present the court with proof of completion of community service and the court shall determine if the community service has been satisfactorily completed. If sufficient staff and resources are available, the community service shall be performed under the jurisdiction of the local agency overseeing a community service program.

(9) If the program finds that the defendant is unsuitable, the program shall immediately contact the probation department or the court. The probation department or court shall either recalendar the case for hearing or refer the defendant to an appropriate alternative batterer's program.

(10) (A) Upon recommendation of the program, a court shall require a defendant to participate in additional sessions throughout the probationary period, unless it finds that it is not in the interests of justice to do so, states its reasons on the record, and enters them into the minutes. In deciding whether the defendant would benefit from more sessions, the court shall consider whether any of the following conditions exists:

(i) The defendant has been violence free for a minimum of six months.

(ii) The defendant has cooperated and participated in the batterer's program.

(iii) The defendant demonstrates an understanding of and practices positive conflict resolution skills.

(iv) The defendant blames, degrades, or has committed acts that dehumanize the victim or puts at risk the victim's safety, including, but not limited to, molesting, stalking, striking, attacking, threatening, sexually assaulting, or battering the victim.

(v) The defendant demonstrates an understanding that the use of coercion or violent behavior to maintain dominance is unacceptable in an intimate relationship.

(vi) The defendant has made threats to harm anyone in any manner.

(vii) The defendant has complied with applicable requirements under paragraph (6) of subdivision (c) or subparagraph (C) to receive alcohol counseling, drug counseling, or both.

(viii) The defendant demonstrates acceptance of responsibility for the abusive behavior perpetrated against the victim.

(B) The program shall immediately report any violation of the terms of the protective order, including any new acts of violence or failure to comply with the program requirements, to the court, the prosecutor, and, if formal probation has been ordered, to the probation department. The probationer shall file proof of enrollment in a batterer's program with the court within 30 days of conviction.

(C) Concurrent with other requirements under this section, in addition to, and not in lieu of, the batterer's program, and unless prohibited by the referring court, the probation department or the court may make provisions for a defendant to use his or her resources to enroll in a chemical dependency program or to enter voluntarily a licensed chemical dependency recovery hospital or residential treatment program that has a valid license issued by the state to provide alcohol or drug services to receive program participation credit, as determined by the court. The probation department shall document evidence of this hospital or residential treatment participation in the defendant's program file.

(11) The conditions of probation may include, in lieu of a fine, but not in lieu of the fund payment required under paragraph (5), one or more of the following requirements:

(A) That the defendant make payments to a battered women's shelter, up to a maximum of five thousand dollars ($5,000).

(B) That the defendant reimburse the victim for reasonable expenses that the court finds are the direct result of the defendant's offense.

For any order to pay a fine, to make payments to a battered women's shelter, or to pay restitution as a condition of probation under this subdivision, the court shall make a determination of the defendant's ability to pay. Determination of a defendant's ability to pay may include his or her future earning capacity. A defendant shall bear the burden of demonstrating lack of his or her ability to pay. Express findings by the court as to the factors bearing on the amount of the fine shall not be required. In no event shall any order to make payments to a battered women's shelter be made if it would impair the ability of the defendant to pay direct restitution to the victim or court-ordered child support. When the injury to a married person is caused, in whole or in part, by the criminal acts of his or her spouse in violation of this section, the community property shall not be used to discharge the liability of the offending spouse for restitution to the injured spouse, as required by Section 1203.04, as operative on or before August 2, 1995, or Section 1202.4, or to a shelter for costs with regard to the injured spouse, until all separate property of the offending spouse is exhausted.

(12) If it appears to the prosecuting attorney, the court, or the probation department that the defendant is performing unsatisfactorily in the assigned program, is not benefiting from counseling, or has engaged in criminal conduct, upon request of the probation officer, the prosecuting attorney, or on its own motion, the court, as a priority calendar item, shall hold a hearing to determine whether further sentencing should proceed. The court may consider factors, including, but not limited to, any violence by the defendant against the former or a new victim while on probation and noncompliance

with any other specific condition of probation. If the court finds that the defendant is not performing satisfactorily in the assigned program, is not benefiting from the program, has not complied with a condition of probation, or has engaged in criminal conduct, the court shall terminate the defendant's participation in the program and shall proceed with further sentencing.

(b) If a person is granted formal probation for a crime in which the victim is a person defined in Section 6211 of the Family Code, in addition to the terms specified in subdivision (a), all of the following shall apply:

(1) The probation department shall make an investigation and take into consideration the defendant's age, medical history, employment and service records, educational background, community and family ties, prior incidents of violence, police report, treatment history, if any, demonstrable motivation, and other mitigating factors in determining which batterer's program would be appropriate for the defendant. This information shall be provided to the batterer's program if it is requested. The probation department shall also determine which community programs the defendant would benefit from and which of those programs would accept the defendant. The probation department shall report its findings and recommendations to the court.

(2) The court shall advise the defendant that the failure to report to the probation department for the initial investigation, as directed by the court, or the failure to enroll in a specified program, as directed by the court or the probation department, shall result in possible further incarceration. The court, in the interests of justice, may relieve the defendant from the prohibition set forth in this subdivision based upon the defendant's mistake or excusable neglect. Application for this relief shall be filed within 20 court days of the missed deadline. This time limitation may not be extended. A copy of any application for relief shall be served on the office of the prosecuting attorney.

(3) After the court orders the defendant to a batterer's program, the probation department shall conduct an initial assessment of the defendant, including, but not limited to, all of the following:

(A) Social, economic, and family background.

(B) Education.

(C) Vocational achievements.

(D) Criminal history.

(E) Medical history.

(F) Substance abuse history.

(G) Consultation with the probation officer.

(H) Verbal consultation with the victim, only if the victim desires to participate.

(I) Assessment of the future probability of the defendant committing murder.

(4) The probation department shall attempt to notify the victim regarding the requirements for the defendant's participation in the batterer's program, as well as regarding available victim resources. The victim also shall be informed that attendance in any program does not guarantee that an abuser will not be violent.

(c) The court or the probation department shall refer defendants only to batterer's programs that follow standards outlined in paragraph (1), which may include, but are not limited to, lectures, classes, group discussions, and counseling. The probation department shall design and implement an approval and renewal process for batterer's programs and shall solicit input from criminal justice agencies and domestic violence victim advocacy programs.

(1) The goal of a batterer's program under this section shall be to stop domestic violence. A batterer's program shall consist of the following components:

(A) Strategies to hold the defendant accountable for the violence in a relationship, including, but not limited to, providing the defendant with a written statement that the defendant shall be held accountable for acts or threats of domestic violence.

(B) A requirement that the defendant participate in ongoing same-gender group sessions.

(C) An initial intake that provides written definitions to the defendant of physical, emotional, sexual, economic, and verbal abuse, and the techniques for stopping these types of abuse.

(D) Procedures to inform the victim regarding the requirements for the defendant's participation in the intervention program as well as regarding available victim resources. The victim also shall be informed that attendance in any program does not guarantee that an abuser will not be violent.

(E) A requirement that the defendant attend group sessions free of chemical influence.

(F) Educational programming that examines, at a minimum, gender roles, socialization, the nature of violence, the dynamics of power and control, and the effects of abuse on children and others.

(G) A requirement that excludes any couple counseling or family counseling, or both.

(H) Procedures that give the program the right to assess whether or not the defendant would benefit from the program and to refuse to enroll the defendant if it is determined that the defendant would not benefit from the program, so long as the refusal is not because of the defendant's inability to pay. If possible, the program shall suggest an appropriate alternative program.

(I) Program staff who, to the extent possible, have specific knowledge regarding, but not limited to, spousal abuse, child abuse, sexual abuse, substance abuse, the dynamics of violence and abuse, the law, and procedures of the legal system.

(J) Program staff who are encouraged to utilize the expertise, training, and assistance of local domestic violence centers.

(K) A requirement that the defendant enter into a written agreement with the program, which shall include an outline of the contents of the program, the attendance requirements, the requirement to attend group sessions free of chemical influence, and a statement that the defendant may be removed from the program if it is determined that the defendant is not benefiting from the program or is disruptive to the program.

(L) A requirement that the defendant sign a confidentiality statement prohibiting disclosure of any information obtained through participating in the program or during group sessions regarding other participants in the program.

(M) Program content that provides cultural and ethnic sensitivity.

(N) A requirement of a written referral from the court or probation department prior to permitting the defendant to enroll in the program. The written referral shall state the number of minimum sessions required by the court.

(O) Procedures for submitting to the probation department all of the following uniform written responses:

(i) Proof of enrollment, to be submitted to the court and the probation department and to include the fee determined to be charged to the defendant, based upon the ability to pay, for each session.

(ii) Periodic progress reports that include attendance, fee payment history, and program compliance.

(iii) Final evaluation that includes the program's evaluation of the defendant's progress, using the criteria set forth in subparagraph (A) of paragraph (10) of subdivision (a), and recommendation for either successful or unsuccessful termination or continuation in the program.

(P) A sliding fee schedule based on the defendant's ability to pay. The batterer's program shall develop and utilize a sliding fee scale that recognizes both the defendant's ability to pay and the necessity of programs to meet overhead expenses. An indigent defendant may negotiate a deferred payment schedule, but shall pay a nominal fee, if the defendant has the ability to pay the nominal fee. Upon a hearing and a finding by the court that the defendant does not have the financial ability to pay the nominal fee, the court shall waive this fee. The payment of the fee shall be made a condition of probation if the court determines the defendant has the present ability to pay the fee. The fee shall be paid during the term of probation unless the program sets other conditions. The acceptance policies shall be in accordance with the scaled fee system.

(2) The court shall refer persons only to batterer's programs that have been approved by the probation department pursuant to paragraph (5). The probation department shall do both of the following:

(A) Provide for the issuance of a provisional approval, provided that the applicant is in substantial compliance with applicable laws and regulations and an urgent need for approval exists. A provisional approval shall be considered an authorization to provide services and shall not be considered a vested right.

(B) If the probation department determines that a program is not in compliance with standards set by the department, the department shall provide written notice of the noncompliant areas to the program. The program shall submit a written plan of corrections within 14 days from the date of the written notice on noncompliance. A plan of correction shall include, but not be limited to, a description of each corrective action and timeframe for implementation. The department shall review and approve all or any part of the plan of correction and notify the program of approval or disapproval in writing. If the program fails to submit a plan of correction or fails to implement the approved plan of correction, the department shall consider whether to revoke or suspend approval and, upon revoking or suspending approval, shall have the option to cease referrals of defendants under this section.

(3) No program, regardless of its source of funding, shall be approved unless it meets all of the following standards:

(A) The establishment of guidelines and criteria for education services, including standards of services that may include lectures, classes, and group discussions.

(B) Supervision of the defendant for the purpose of evaluating the person's progress in the program.

(C) Adequate reporting requirements to ensure that all persons who, after being ordered to attend and complete a program, may be identified for either failure to enroll in, or failure to successfully complete, the program or for the successful completion of the program as ordered. The program shall notify the court and the probation department, in writing, within the period of time and in the manner specified by the court of any person who fails to complete the program. Notification shall be given if the program determines that the defendant is performing unsatisfactorily or if the defendant is not benefiting from the education, treatment, or counseling.

(D) No victim shall be compelled to participate in a program or counseling, and no program may condition a defendant's enrollment on participation by the victim.

(4) In making referrals of indigent defendants to approved batterer's programs, the probation department shall apportion these referrals evenly among the approved programs.

(5) The probation department shall have the sole authority to approve a batterer's program for probation. The program shall be required to obtain only one approval but shall renew that approval annually.

(A) The procedure for the approval of a new or existing program shall include all of the following:

(i) The completion of a written application containing necessary and pertinent information describing the applicant program.

(ii) The demonstration by the program that it possesses adequate administrative and operational capability to operate a batterer's treatment program. The program shall provide documentation to prove that the program has conducted batterer's programs for at least one year prior to application. This requirement may be waived under subparagraph (A) of paragraph (2) if there is no existing batterer's program in the city, county, or city and county.

(iii) The onsite review of the program, including monitoring of a session to determine that the program adheres to applicable statutes and regulations.

(iv) The payment of the approval fee.

(B) The probation department shall fix a fee for approval not to exceed two hundred fifty dollars ($250) and for approval renewal not to exceed two hundred fifty dollars ($250) every year in an amount sufficient to cover its costs in administering the approval process under this section. No fee shall be charged for the approval of local governmental entities.

(C) The probation department has the sole authority to approve the issuance, denial, suspension, or revocation of approval and to cease new enrollments or referrals to a batterer's program under this section. The probation department shall review information relative to a program's performance or failure to adhere to standards, or both. The probation department may suspend or revoke an approval issued under this subdivision or deny an application to renew an approval or to modify the terms and conditions of approval, based on grounds established by probation, including, but not limited to, either of the following:

(i) Violation of this section by any person holding approval or by a program employee in a program under this section.

(ii) Misrepresentation of any material fact in obtaining the approval.

(6) For defendants who are chronic users or serious abusers of drugs or alcohol, standard components in the program shall include concurrent counseling for substance abuse and violent behavior, and in appropriate cases, detoxification and abstinence from the abused substance.

(7) The program shall conduct an exit conference that assesses the defendant's progress during his or her participation in the batterer's program.

(d) An act or omission relating to the approval of a batterer's treatment programs under paragraph (5) of subdivision (c) is a discretionary act pursuant to Section 820.2 of the Government Code.

(Amended (as amended by Stats. 2012, Ch. 628, Sec. 1.5) by Stats. 2013, Ch. 144, Sec. 2. (AB 139) Effective January 1, 2014.)

1203.098.

(a) Unless otherwise provided, a person who works as a facilitator in a batterers' intervention program that provides programs for batterers pursuant to subdivision (c) of Section 1203.097 shall complete the following requirements before being eligible to work as a facilitator in a batterers' intervention program:

(1) Forty hours of basic core training. A minimum of eight hours of this instruction shall be provided by a shelter-based or shelter-approved trainer. The core curriculum shall include the following components:

(A) A minimum of eight hours in basic domestic violence knowledge focusing on victim safety and the role of domestic violence shelters in a community-coordinated response.

(B) A minimum of eight hours in multicultural, cross-cultural, and multiethnic diversity and domestic violence.

(C) A minimum of four hours in substance abuse and domestic violence.

(D) A minimum of four hours in intake and assessment, including the history of violence and the nature of threats and substance abuse.

(E) A minimum of eight hours in group content areas focusing on gender roles and socialization, the nature of violence, the dynamics of power and control, and the effects of abuse on children and others as required by Section 1203.097.

(F) A minimum of four hours in group facilitation.

(G) A minimum of four hours in domestic violence and the law, ethics, all requirements specified by the probation department pursuant to Section 1203.097, and the role of batterers' intervention programs in a coordinated-community response.

(H) Any person that provides documentation of coursework, or equivalent training, that he or she has satisfactorily completed, shall be exempt from that part of the training that was covered by the satisfactorily completed coursework.

(I) The coursework that this person performs shall count toward the continuing education requirement.

(2) Fifty-two weeks or no less than 104 hours in six months, as a trainee in an approved batterers' intervention program with a minimum of a two-hour group each week. A training program shall include at least one of the following:

(A) Cofacilitation internship in which an experienced facilitator is present in the room during the group session.

(B) Observation by a trainer of the trainee conducting a group session via a one-way mirror.

(C) Observation by a trainer of the trainee conducting a group session via a video or audio recording.

(D) Consultation or supervision twice a week in a six-month program or once a week in a 52-week program.

(3) An experienced facilitator is one who has the following qualifications:

(A) Documentation on file, approved by the agency, evidencing that the experienced facilitator has the skills needed to provide quality supervision and training.

(B) Documented experience working with batterers for three years, and a minimum of two years working with batterers' groups.

(C) Documentation by January 1, 2003, of coursework or equivalent training that demonstrates satisfactory completion of the 40-hour basic core training.

(b) A facilitator of a batterers' intervention program shall complete, as a minimum continuing education requirement, 16 hours annually of continuing education in either domestic violence or a related field with a minimum of eight hours in domestic violence.

(c) A person or agency with a specific hardship may request the probation department, in writing, for an extension of time to complete the training or to complete alternative training options.

(d) (1) An experienced facilitator, as defined in paragraph (3) of subdivision (a), is not subject to the supervision requirements of this section, if he or she meets the requirements of subparagraph (C) of paragraph (3) of subdivision (a).

(2) This section does not apply to a person who provides batterers' treatment through a jail education program if the person in charge of that program determines that the person providing treatment has adequate education or training in domestic violence or a related field.

(e) A person who satisfactorily completes the training requirements of a county probation department whose training program is equivalent to or exceeds the training requirements of this act shall be exempt from the training requirements of this act.
(Amended by Stats. 2010, Ch. 328, Sec. 165. (SB 1330) Effective January 1, 2011.)

1203.099.
(a) The counties of Napa, San Luis Obispo, Santa Barbara, Santa Clara, Santa Cruz, and Yolo may offer a program for individuals convicted of domestic violence that does not comply with the requirement of the batterer's program in Sections 1203.097 and 1203.098 if the program meets all of the following conditions:

(1) The county develops the program in consultation with the domestic violence service providers and other relevant community partners.

(2) The county performs a risk and needs assessment utilizing an assessment demonstrated to be appropriate for domestic violence offenders for each offender entering the program.

(3) The offender's treatment within the program is based on the findings of the risk and needs assessment.

(4) The program includes components which are evidence-based or promising practices.

(5) The program has a comprehensive written curriculum that informs the operations of the program and outlines the treatment and intervention modalities.

(6) The offender's treatment within the program is for not less than one year in length, unless an alternative length is established by a validated risk and needs assessment completed by the probation department or an organization approved by the probation department.

(7) The county collects all of the following data for participants in the program:

(A) The offender's demographic information, including age, gender, race, ethnicity, marital status, familial status, and employment status.

(B) The offender's criminal history.

(C) The offender's risk level as determined by the risk and needs assessment.

(D) The treatment provided to the offender during the program and if the offender completed that treatment.

(E) The offender's outcome at the time of program completion, and six months after completion, including subsequent restraining order violations, arrests and convictions, and feedback provided by the victim if the victim desires to participate.

(8) The county reports all of the following information annually to the Legislature:

(A) The risk and needs assessment tool used for the program.

(B) The curriculum used by each program.

(C) The number of participants with a program length other than one year, and the alternative program lengths used.

(D) Individual data on the number of offenders participating in the program.

(E) Individual data for the items described in paragraph (7).

(b) Offenders who complete a program described in subdivision (a) shall be deemed to have met the batterer's program requirements set forth in Section 1203.097.

(c) As used in this section, the following definitions shall apply:

(1) "Evidence-based program or practice" means a program or practice that has a high level of research indicating its effectiveness, determined as a result of multiple rigorous evaluations including randomized controlled trials and evaluations that incorporate strong comparison group designs, or a single large multisite randomized study, and, typically, has specified procedures that allow for successful replication.

(2) "Promising program or practice" means a program or practice that has some research demonstrating its effectiveness but does not meet the full criteria for an evidence-based designation.

(d) A report to be submitted pursuant to paragraph (8) of subdivision (a) shall be submitted in compliance with Section 9795 of the Government Code.

(e) This section shall become operative on July 1, 2019.

(f) This section shall remain in effect only until July 1, 2022, and as of that date is repealed.
(Added by Stats. 2018, Ch. 290, Sec. 1. (AB 372) Effective January 1, 2019. Section operative July 1, 2019. Repealed as of July 1, 2022, by its own provisions.)

1203.1.
(a) The court, or judge thereof, in the order granting probation, may suspend the imposing or the execution of the sentence and may direct that the suspension may continue for a period of time not exceeding the maximum possible term of the sentence, except as hereinafter set forth, and upon those terms and conditions as it shall determine. The court, or judge thereof, in the order granting probation and as a condition thereof, may imprison the defendant in a county jail for a period not exceeding the maximum time fixed by law in the case.

However, where the maximum possible term of the sentence is five years or less, then the period of suspension of imposition or execution of sentence may, in the discretion of the court, continue for not over five years. The following shall apply to this subdivision:

(1) The court may fine the defendant in a sum not to exceed the maximum fine provided by law in the case.

(2) The court may, in connection with granting probation, impose either imprisonment in a county jail or a fine, both, or neither.

(3) The court shall provide for restitution in proper cases. The restitution order shall be fully enforceable as a civil judgment forthwith and in accordance with Section 1202.4 of the Penal Code.

(4) The court may require bonds for the faithful observance and performance of any or all of the conditions of probation.

(b) The court shall consider whether the defendant as a condition of probation shall make restitution to the victim or the Restitution Fund. Any restitution payment received by a court or probation department in the form of cash or money order shall be forwarded to the victim within 30 days from the date the payment is received by the department. Any restitution payment received by a court or probation department in the form of a check or draft shall be forwarded to the victim within 45 days from the date the payment is received, provided, that payment need not be forwarded to a victim until 180 days from the date the first payment is received, if the restitution payments for that victim received by the court or probation department total less than fifty dollars ($50). In cases where the court has ordered the defendant to pay restitution to multiple victims and where the administrative cost of disbursing restitution payments to multiple victims involves a significant cost, any restitution payment received by a probation department shall be forwarded to multiple victims when it is cost effective to do so, but in no event shall restitution disbursements be delayed beyond 180 days from the date the payment is received by the probation department.

(c) In counties or cities and counties where road camps, farms, or other public work is available the court may place the probationer in the road camp, farm, or other public work instead of in jail. In this case, Section 25359 of the Government Code shall apply to probation and the court shall have the same power to require adult probationers to work, as prisoners confined in the county jail are required to work, at public work. Each county board of supervisors may fix the scale of compensation of the adult probationers in that county.

(d) In all cases of probation the court may require as a condition of probation that the probationer go to work and earn money for the support of his or her dependents or to pay any fine imposed or reparation condition, to keep an account of his or her earnings, to report them to the probation officer and apply those earnings as directed by the court.

(e) The court shall also consider whether the defendant as a condition of probation shall make restitution to a public agency for the costs of an emergency response pursuant to Article 8 (commencing with Section 53150) of Chapter 1 of Part 1 of Division 2 of the Government Code.

(f) In all felony cases in which, as a condition of probation, a judge of the superior court sitting by authority of law elsewhere than at the county seat requires a convicted person to serve his or her sentence at intermittent periods the sentence may be served on the order of the judge at the city jail nearest to the place at which the court is sitting, and the cost of his or her maintenance shall be a county charge.

(g) (1) The court and prosecuting attorney shall consider whether any defendant who has been convicted of a nonviolent or nonserious offense and ordered to participate in community service as a condition of probation shall be required to engage in the removal of graffiti in the performance of the community service. For the purpose of this subdivision, a nonserious offense shall not include the following:

(A) Offenses in violation of the Dangerous Weapons Control Law, as defined in Section 23500.

(B) Offenses involving the use of a dangerous or deadly weapon, including all violations of Section 417.

(C) Offenses involving the use or attempted use of violence against the person of another or involving injury to a victim.

(D) Offenses involving annoying or molesting children.

(2) Notwithstanding subparagraph (A) of paragraph (1), any person who violates Chapter 1 (commencing with Section 29610) of Division 9 of Title 4 of Part 6 shall be ordered to perform not less than 100 hours and not more than 500 hours of community service as a condition of probation.

(3) The court and the prosecuting attorney need not consider a defendant pursuant to paragraph (1) if the following circumstances exist:

(A) The defendant was convicted of any offense set forth in subdivision (c) of Section 667.5 or subdivision (c) of Section 1192.7.

(B) The judge believes that the public safety may be endangered if the person is ordered to do community service or the judge believes that the facts or circumstances or facts and circumstances call for imposition of a more substantial penalty.

(h) The probation officer or his or her designated representative shall consider whether any defendant who has been convicted of a nonviolent and nonserious offense and ordered to participate in community service as a condition of probation shall be required to engage in the performance of house repairs or yard services for senior citizens and the performance of repairs to senior centers through contact with local senior service organizations in the performance of the community service.

(i) (1) Upon conviction of any offense involving child abuse or neglect, the court may require, in addition to any or all of the above-mentioned terms of imprisonment, fine, and other reasonable conditions, that the defendant shall participate in counseling or education programs, or both, including, but not limited to, parent education or parenting programs operated by community colleges, school districts, other public agencies, or private agencies.

(2) Upon conviction of any sex offense subjecting the defendant to the registration requirements of Section 290, the court may order as a condition of probation, at the request of the victim or in the court's discretion, that the defendant stay away from the victim and the victim's residence or place of employment, and that the defendant have no contact with the victim in person, by telephone or electronic means, or by mail.

(j) The court may impose and require any or all of the above-mentioned terms of imprisonment, fine, and conditions, and other reasonable conditions, as it may determine are fitting and proper to the end that justice may be done, that amends may be made to society for the breach of the law, for any injury done to any person resulting from that breach, and generally and specifically for the reformation and rehabilitation of the probationer, and that should the probationer violate any of the terms or conditions imposed by the court in the matter, it shall have authority to modify and change any and all the terms and conditions and to reimprison the probationer in the county jail within the limitations of the penalty of the public offense involved. Upon the defendant being released from the county jail under the terms of probation as originally granted or any modification subsequently made, and in all cases where confinement in a county jail has not been a condition of the grant of probation, the court shall place the defendant or probationer in and under the charge of the probation officer of the court, for the period or term fixed for probation. However, upon the payment of any fine imposed and the fulfillment of all conditions of probation, probation shall cease at the end of the term of probation, or sooner, in the event of modification. In counties and cities and counties in which there are facilities for taking fingerprints, those of each probationer shall be taken and a record of them kept and preserved.

(k) Notwithstanding any other provisions of law to the contrary, except as provided in Section 13967, as operative on or before September 28, 1994, of the Government Code and Section 13967.5 of the Government Code and Sections 1202.4, 1463.16, paragraph (1) of subdivision (a) of Section 1463.18, and Section 1464, and Section 1203.04, as operative on or before August 2, 1995, all fines collected by a county probation officer in any of the courts of this state, as a condition of the granting of probation or as a part of the terms of probation, shall be paid into the county treasury and placed in the general fund for the use and benefit of the county.

(l) If the court orders restitution to be made to the victim, the entity collecting the restitution may add a fee to cover the actual administrative cost of collection, but not to exceed 15 percent of the total amount ordered to be paid. The amount of the fee shall be set by the board of supervisors if it is collected by the county and the fee collected shall be paid into the general fund of the county treasury for the use and benefit of the county. The amount of the fee shall be set by the court if it is collected by the court and the fee collected shall be paid into the Trial Court Operations Fund or account established by Section 77009 of the Government Code for the use and benefit of the court.

(Amended by Stats. 2010, Ch. 178, Sec. 75. (SB 1115) Effective January 1, 2011. Operative January 1, 2012, by Sec. 107 of Ch. 178.)

1203.1a.
The probation officer of the county may authorize the temporary removal under custody or temporary release without custody of any inmate of the county jail, honor farm, or other detention facility, who is confined or committed as a condition of probation, after suspension of imposition of sentence or suspension of execution of sentence, for purposes preparatory to his return to the community, within 30 days prior to his release date, if he concludes that such an inmate is a fit subject therefor. Any such temporary removal shall not be for a period of more than three days. When an inmate is released for purposes preparatory to his return to the community, the probation officer may require the inmate to reimburse the county, in whole or in part, for expenses incurred by the county in connection therewith.

(Added by Stats. 1971, Ch. 1357.)

1203.1ab.
Upon conviction of any offense involving the unlawful possession, use, sale, or other furnishing of any controlled substance, as defined in Chapter 2 (commencing with Section 11053) of Division 10 of the Health and Safety Code, in addition to any or all of the terms of imprisonment, fine, and other reasonable conditions specified in or permitted by Section 1203.1, unless it makes a finding that this condition would not serve the interests of justice, the court, when recommended by the probation officer, shall require as a condition of probation that the defendant shall not use or be under the influence of any controlled substance and shall submit to drug and substance abuse testing as directed by the probation officer. If the defendant is an adult over 21 years of age and under the jurisdiction of the criminal court, is required to submit to testing, and has the financial ability to pay all or part of the costs associated with that testing, the court shall order the defendant to pay a reasonable fee, which shall not exceed the actual cost of the testing.

(Amended by Stats. 2017, Ch. 678, Sec. 3. (SB 190) Effective January 1, 2018.)

1203.1b.
(a) In any case in which a defendant is convicted of an offense and is the subject of any preplea or presentence investigation and report, whether or not probation supervision is ordered by the court, and in any case in which a defendant is granted probation, given a conditional sentence, or receives a term of mandatory supervision pursuant to subparagraph (B) of paragraph (5) of subdivision (h) of Section 1170, the probation officer, or his or her authorized representative, taking into account any amount that the defendant is ordered to pay in fines, assessments, and restitution, shall make a determination of the ability of the defendant to pay all or a portion of the reasonable cost of any probation supervision, conditional sentence, or term of mandatory supervision, of conducting any preplea investigation and preparing any preplea report pursuant to Section 1203.7, of conducting any presentence investigation and preparing any presentence report made pursuant to Section 1203, and of processing a jurisdictional transfer pursuant to Section 1203.9 or of processing a request for interstate compact supervision pursuant to Sections 11175 to 11179, inclusive, whichever applies. The reasonable cost of these services and of probation supervision, a conditional sentence, or mandatory supervision shall not exceed the amount determined to be the actual average cost thereof. A payment schedule for the reimbursement of the costs of preplea or presentence investigations based on income shall be developed by the probation department of each county and approved by the presiding judge of the superior court. The court shall order the defendant to appear before the probation officer, or his or her authorized representative, to make an inquiry into the ability of the defendant to pay all or a portion of these costs. The probation officer, or his or her authorized representative, shall determine the amount of payment and the manner in which the payments shall be made to the county, based upon the defendant's ability to pay. The probation officer shall inform the defendant that the defendant is entitled to a hearing, that includes the right to counsel, in which the court shall make a determination of the defendant's ability to pay and the payment amount. The defendant must waive the right to a determination by the court of his or her ability to pay and the payment amount by a knowing and intelligent waiver.

(b) When the defendant fails to waive the right provided in subdivision (a) to a determination by the court of his or her ability to pay and the payment amount, the probation officer shall refer the matter to the court for the scheduling of a hearing to determine the amount of payment and the manner in which the payments shall be made. The court shall order the defendant to pay the reasonable costs if it determines that the defendant has the ability to pay those costs based on the report of the probation officer, or his or her authorized representative. The following shall apply to a hearing conducted pursuant to this subdivision:

(1) At the hearing, the defendant shall be entitled to have, but shall not be limited to, the opportunity to be heard in person, to present witnesses and other documentary evidence, and to confront and cross-examine adverse witnesses, and to disclosure of the evidence against the defendant, and a written statement of the findings of the court or the probation officer, or his or her authorized representative.

(2) At the hearing, if the court determines that the defendant has the ability to pay all or part of the costs, the court shall set the amount to be reimbursed and order the defendant to pay that sum to the county in the manner in which the court believes reasonable and compatible with the defendant's financial ability.

(3) At the hearing, in making a determination of whether a defendant has the ability to pay, the court shall take into account the amount of any fine imposed upon the defendant and any amount the defendant has been ordered to pay in restitution.

(4) When the court determines that the defendant's ability to pay is different from the determination of the probation officer, the court shall state on the record the reason for its order.

(c) The court may hold additional hearings during the probationary, conditional sentence, or mandatory supervision period to review the defendant's financial ability to pay the amount, and in the manner, as set by the probation officer, or his or her authorized representative, or as set by the court pursuant to this section.

(d) If practicable, the court shall order or the probation officer shall set payments pursuant to subdivisions (a) and (b) to be made on a monthly basis. Execution may be issued on the order issued pursuant to this section in the same manner as a judgment in a civil action. The order to pay all or part of the costs shall not be enforced by contempt.

(e) The term "ability to pay" means the overall capability of the defendant to reimburse the costs, or a portion of the costs, of conducting the presentence investigation, preparing the preplea or presentence report, processing a jurisdictional transfer pursuant to Section 1203.9, processing requests for interstate compact supervision pursuant to Sections 11175 to 11179, inclusive, and probation supervision, conditional sentence, or mandatory supervision, and shall include, but shall not be limited to, the defendant's:

(1) Present financial position.

(2) Reasonably discernible future financial position. In no event shall the court consider a period of more than one year from the date of the hearing for purposes of determining reasonably discernible future financial position.

(3) Likelihood that the defendant shall be able to obtain employment within the one-year period from the date of the hearing.

(4) Any other factor or factors that may bear upon the defendant's financial capability to reimburse the county for the costs.

(f) At any time during the pendency of the judgment rendered according to the terms of this section, a defendant against whom a judgment has been rendered may petition the probation officer for a review of the defendant's financial ability to pay or the rendering court to modify or vacate its previous judgment on the grounds of a change of circumstances with regard to the defendant's ability to pay the judgment. The probation officer and the court shall advise the defendant of this right at the time of rendering of the terms of probation or the judgment.

(g) All sums paid by a defendant pursuant to this section shall be allocated for the operating expenses of the county probation department.

(h) The board of supervisors in any county, by resolution, may establish a fee for the processing of payments made in installments to the probation department pursuant to this section, not to exceed the administrative and clerical costs of the collection of those installment payments as determined by the board of supervisors, except that the fee shall not exceed seventy-five dollars ($75).

(i) This section shall be operative in a county upon the adoption of an ordinance to that effect by the board of supervisors.

(Amended by Stats. 2014, Ch. 468, Sec. 1. (AB 2199) Effective January 1, 2015.)

1203.1bb.
(a) The reasonable cost of probation determined under subdivision (a) of Section 1203.1b shall include the cost of purchasing and installing an ignition interlock device pursuant to Section 13386 of the Vehicle Code. Any defendant subject to this section shall pay the manufacturer of the ignition interlock device directly for the cost of its purchase and installation, in accordance with the payment schedule ordered by the court. If practicable, the court shall order payment to be made to the manufacturer of the ignition interlock device within a six-month period.

(b) This section does not require any county to pay the costs of purchasing and installing any ignition interlock devices ordered pursuant to Section 13386 of the Vehicle Code. The Office of Traffic Safety shall consult with the presiding judge or his or her designee in each county to determine an appropriate means, if any, to provide for installation of ignition interlock devices in cases in which the defendant has no ability to pay.

(Amended by Stats. 2002, Ch. 787, Sec. 21. Effective January 1, 2003.)

1203.1c.
(a) In any case in which a defendant is convicted of an offense and is ordered to serve a period of confinement in a county jail, city jail, or other local detention facility as a term of probation or a conditional sentence, the court may, after a hearing, make a determination of the ability of the defendant to pay all or a portion of the reasonable costs of such incarceration, including incarceration pending disposition of the case. The reasonable cost of such incarceration shall not exceed the amount determined by the board of supervisors, with respect to the county jail, and by the city council, with respect to the city jail, to be the actual average cost thereof on a per-day basis. The court may, in its discretion, hold additional hearings during the probationary period. The court may, in its discretion before such hearing, order the defendant to file a statement setting forth his or her assets, liability and income, under penalty of perjury, and may order the defendant to appear before a county officer designated by the board of supervisors to make an inquiry into the ability of the defendant to pay all or a portion of such costs. At the hearing, the defendant shall be entitled to have the opportunity to be heard in person or to be represented by counsel, to present witnesses and other evidence, and to confront and cross-examine adverse witnesses. A defendant represented by counsel appointed by the court in the criminal proceedings shall be entitled to such representation at any hearing held pursuant to this section. If the court determines that the defendant has the ability to pay all or a part of the costs, the court may set the amount to be reimbursed and order the defendant to pay that sum to the county, or to the city with respect to incarceration in the city jail, in the manner in which the court believes reasonable and compatible with the defendant's financial ability. Execution may be issued on the order in the same manner as on a judgment in a civil action. The order to pay all or part of the costs shall not be enforced by contempt.

If practicable, the court shall order payments to be made on a monthly basis and the payments shall be made payable to the county officer designated by the board of supervisors, or to a city officer designated by the city council with respect to incarceration in the city jail.

A payment schedule for reimbursement of the costs of incarceration pursuant to this section based upon income shall be developed by the county officer designated by the board of supervisors, or by the city council with respect to incarceration in the city jail, and approved by the presiding judge of the superior court in the county.

(b) "Ability to pay" means the overall capability of the defendant to reimburse the costs, or a portion of the costs, of incarceration and includes, but is not limited to, the defendant's:

(1) Present financial obligations, including family support obligations, and fines, penalties and other obligations to the court.

(2) Reasonably discernible future financial position. In no event shall the court consider a period of more than one year from the date of the hearing for purposes of determining reasonable discernible future position.

(3) Likelihood that the defendant shall be able to obtain employment within the one-year period from the date of the hearing.

(4) Any other factor or factors which may bear upon the defendant's financial ability to reimburse the county or city for the costs.

(c) All sums paid by a defendant pursuant to this section shall be deposited in the general fund of the county or city.

(d) This section shall be operative in a county upon the adoption of an ordinance to that effect by the board of supervisors, and shall be operative in a city upon the adoption of an ordinance to that effect by the city council. Such ordinance shall include a designation of the officer responsible for collection of moneys ordered pursuant to this section and shall include a determination, to be reviewed annually, of the average per-day costs of incarceration in the county jail, city jail, or other local detention facility.

(Amended by Stats. 2002, Ch. 784, Sec. 547. Effective January 1, 2003.)

1203.1d.
(a) In determining the amount and manner of disbursement under an order made pursuant to this code requiring a defendant to make reparation or restitution to a victim of a crime, to pay any money as reimbursement for legal assistance provided by the court, to pay any cost of probation or probation investigation, to pay any cost of jail or other confinement, or to pay any other reimbursable costs, the court, after determining the amount of any fine and penalty assessments, and a county financial evaluation officer when making a financial evaluation, shall first determine the amount of restitution to be ordered paid to any victim, and shall then determine the amount of the other reimbursable costs.

If payment is made in full, the payment shall be apportioned and disbursed in the amounts ordered by the court.

If reasonable and compatible with the defendant's financial ability, the court may order payments to be made in installments.

(b) With respect to installment payments and amounts collected by the Franchise Tax Board pursuant to Section 19280 of the Revenue and Taxation Code and subsequently transferred by the Controller pursuant to Section 19282 of the Revenue and Taxation Code, the board of supervisors shall provide that disbursements be made in the following order of priority:

(1) Restitution ordered to, or on behalf of, the victim pursuant to subdivision (f) of Section 1202.4.

(2) The state surcharge ordered pursuant to Section 1465.7.

(3) Any fines, penalty assessments, and restitution fines ordered pursuant to subdivision (b) of Section 1202.4. Payment of each of these items shall be made on a proportional basis to the total amount levied for all of these items.

(4) Any other reimbursable costs.

(c) The board of supervisors shall apply these priorities of disbursement to orders or parts of orders in cases where defendants have been ordered to pay more than one court order.

(d) Documentary evidence, such as bills, receipts, repair estimates, insurance payment statements, payroll stubs, business records, and similar documents relevant to the value of the stolen or damaged property, medical expenses, and wages and profits lost shall not be excluded as hearsay evidence.

(e) This section shall become operative on January 1, 2012.

(Repealed (in Sec. 27) and added by Stats. 2008, Ch. 311, Sec. 27.5. Effective January 1, 2009. Section operative January 1, 2012, by its own provisions.)

1203.1e.

(a) In any case in which a defendant is ordered to serve a period of confinement in a county jail or other local detention facility, and the defendant is eligible to be released on parole by the county board of parole commissioners, the court shall, after a hearing, make a determination of the ability of the person to pay all or a portion of the reasonable cost of providing parole supervision. The reasonable cost of those services shall not exceed the amount determined to be the actual average cost of providing parole supervision.

(b) If the court determines that the person has the ability to pay all or part of the costs, the court may set the amount to be reimbursed and order the person to pay that sum to the county in the manner in which the court believes reasonable and compatible with the person's financial ability. In making a determination of whether a person has the ability to pay, the court shall take into account the amount of any fine imposed upon the person and any amount the person has been ordered to pay in restitution.

If practicable, the court shall order payments to be made on a monthly basis as directed by the court. Execution may be issued on the order in the same manner as a judgment in a civil action. The order to pay all or part of the costs shall not be enforced by contempt.

(c) For the purposes of this section, "ability to pay" means the overall capability of the person to reimburse the costs, or a portion of the costs, of providing parole supervision and shall include, but shall not be limited to, consideration of all of the following factors:

(1) Present financial position.

(2) Reasonably discernible future financial position. In no event shall the board consider a period of more than six months from the date of the hearing for purposes of determining reasonably discernible future financial position.

(3) Likelihood that the person shall be able to obtain employment within the six-month period from the date of the hearing.

(4) Any other factor or factors which may bear upon the person's financial capability to reimburse the county for the costs.

(d) At any time during the pendency of the order made under this section, a person against whom an order has been made may petition the court to modify or vacate its previous order on the grounds of a change of circumstances with regard to the person's ability to pay. The court shall advise the person of this right at the time of making the order.

(e) All sums paid by any person pursuant to this section shall be deposited in the general fund of the county.

(f) The parole of any person shall not be denied or revoked in whole or in part based upon the inability or failure to pay under this section.

(g) The county board of parole commissioners shall not have access to offender financial data prior to the rendering of any parole decision.

(h) This section shall become operative on January 1, 1995.

(Repealed (Jan. 1, 1992) and added by Stats. 1991, Ch. 437, Sec. 2. Effective September 19, 1991. Section operative January 1, 1995, by its own provisions.)

1203.1f.

If practicable, the court shall consolidate the ability to pay determination hearings authorized by this code into one proceeding, and the determination of ability to pay made at the consolidated hearing may be used for all purposes.

(Amended by Stats. 2002, Ch. 198, Sec. 1. Effective January 1, 2003.)

1203.1g.

In any case in which a defendant is convicted of sexual assault on a minor, and the defendant is eligible for probation, the court, as a condition of probation, shall order him or her to make restitution for the costs of medical or psychological treatment incurred by the victim as a result of the assault and that he or she seek and maintain employment and apply that portion of his or her earnings specified by the court toward those costs.

As used in this section, "sexual assault" has the meaning specified in subdivisions (a) and (b) of Section 11165.1. The defendant is entitled to a hearing concerning any modification of the amount of restitution based on the costs of medical and psychological treatment incurred by the victim subsequent to the issuance of the order of probation.

(Amended by Stats. 1994, Ch. 146, Sec. 168. Effective January 1, 1995.)

1203.1h.

(a) In addition to any other costs which a court is authorized to require a defendant to pay, upon conviction of any offense involving child abuse or neglect, the court may require that the defendant pay to a law enforcement agency incurring the cost, the cost of any medical examinations conducted on the victim in order to determine the nature or extent of the abuse or neglect. If the court determines that the defendant has the ability to pay all or part of the medical examination costs, the court may set the amount to be reimbursed and order the defendant to pay that sum to the law enforcement agency in the manner in which the court believes reasonable and compatible with the defendant's financial ability. In making a determination of whether a defendant has the ability to pay, the court shall take into account the amount of any fine imposed upon the defendant and any amount the defendant has been ordered to pay in restitution.

(b) In addition to any other costs which a court is authorized to require a defendant to pay, upon conviction of any offense involving sexual assault or attempted sexual assault, including child molestation, the court may require that the defendant pay, to the law enforcement agency, county, or local governmental agency incurring the cost, the cost of any medical examinations conducted on the victim for the collection and preservation of evidence. If the court determines that the defendant has the ability to pay all or part of the cost of the medical examination, the court may set the amount to be reimbursed and order the defendant to pay that sum to the law enforcement agency, county, or local governmental agency, in the manner in which the court believes reasonable and compatible with the defendant's financial ability. In making the determination of whether a defendant has the ability to pay, the court shall take into account the amount of any fine imposed upon the defendant and any amount the defendant has been ordered to pay in restitution. In no event shall a court penalize an indigent defendant by imposing an additional period of imprisonment in lieu of payment.

(Amended by Stats. 1991, Ch. 377, Sec. 1.)

1203.1i.

(a) In any case in which a defendant is convicted of a violation of any building standards adopted by a local entity by ordinance or resolution, including, but not limited to, local health, fire, building, or safety ordinances or resolutions, or any other ordinance or resolution relating to the health and safety of occupants of buildings, by maintaining a substandard building, as specified in Section 17920.3 of the Health and Safety Code,

the court, or judge thereof, in making an order granting probation, in addition to any other orders, may order the defendant placed under house confinement, or may order the defendant to serve both a term of imprisonment in the county jail and to be placed under house confinement.

This section only applies to violations involving a dwelling unit occupied by persons specified in subdivision (a) of Section 1940 of the Civil Code who are not excluded by subdivision (b) of that section.

(b) If the court orders a defendant to serve all or part of his or her sentence under house confinement, pursuant to subdivision (a), he or she may also be ordered to pay the cost of having a police officer or guard stand guard outside the area in which the defendant has been confined under house confinement if it has been determined that the defendant is able to pay these costs.

(c) As used in this section, "house confinement" means confinement to a residence or location designated by the court and specified in the probation order.

(Added by Stats. 1987, Ch. 1063, Sec. 1.)

1203.1j.

In any case in which the defendant is convicted of assault, battery, or assault with a deadly weapon on a victim 65 years of age or older, and the defendant knew or reasonably should have known the elderly status of the victim, the court, as a condition of probation, shall order the defendant to make restitution for the costs of medical or psychological treatment incurred by the victim as a result of the crime, and that the defendant seek and maintain legitimate employment and apply that portion of his or her earnings specified by the court toward those costs.

The defendant shall be entitled to a hearing, concerning any modification of the amount of restitution, based on the costs of medical and psychological treatment incurred by the victim subsequent to the issuance of the order of probation.

(Amended by Stats. 1990, Ch. 45, Sec. 8.)

1203.1k.

For any order of restitution made under Section 1203.1, the court may order the specific amount of restitution and the manner in which restitution shall be made to a victim or the Restitution Fund, to the extent that the victim has received payment from the Victims of Crime Program, based on the probation officer's report or it may, with the consent of the defendant, order the probation officer to set the amount of restitution and the manner in which restitution shall be made to a victim or the Restitution Fund, to the extent that the victim has received payment from the Victims of Crime Program. The defendant shall have the right to a hearing before the judge to dispute the determinations made by the probation officer in regard to the amount or manner in which restitution is to be made to the victim or the Restitution Fund, to the extent that the victim has received payment from the Victims of Crime Program. If the court orders restitution to be made to the Restitution Fund, the court, and not the probation officer, shall determine the amount and the manner in which restitution is to be made to the Restitution Fund.

(Amended by Stats. 2000, Ch. 1016, Sec. 10. Effective January 1, 2001.)

1203.1l.

In any case in which, pursuant to Section 1203.1, the court orders the defendant, as a condition of probation, to make restitution to a public agency for the costs of an emergency response, all of the following shall apply:

(a) The probation department shall obtain the actual costs for an emergency response from a public agency, and shall include the public agency's documents supporting the actual costs for the emergency response in the probation department's sentencing report to the court.

(b) At the sentencing hearing, the defendant has the right to confront witnesses and present evidence in opposition to the amount claimed to be due to the public agency for its actual costs for the emergency response.

(c) The collection of the emergency response costs is the responsibility of the public agency seeking the reimbursement. If a defendant fails to make restitution payment when a payment is due, the public agency shall by verified declaration notify the probation department of the delinquency. The probation department shall make an investigation of the delinquency and shall make a report to the court of the delinquency. The report shall contain any recommendation that the probation officer finds to be relevant regarding the delinquency and future payments. The court, after a hearing on the delinquency, may make modifications to the existing order in the furtherance of justice.

(d) The defendant has the right to petition the court for a modification of the emergency response reimbursement order whenever he or she has sustained a substantial change in economic circumstances. The defendant has a right to a hearing on the proposed modification, and the court may make any modification to the existing order in the furtherance of justice.

(Added by renumbering Section 1203.1i (as added by Stats. 1987, Ch. 713) by Stats. 1989, Ch. 1360, Sec. 114.)

1203.1m.

(a) If a defendant is convicted of an offense and ordered to serve a period of imprisonment in the state prison, the court may, after a hearing, make a determination of the ability of the defendant to pay all or a portion of the reasonable costs of the imprisonment. The reasonable costs of imprisonment shall not exceed the amount determined by the Director of Corrections to be the actual average cost of imprisonment in the state prison on a per-day basis.

(b) The court may, in its discretion before any hearing, order the defendant to file a statement setting forth his or her assets, liability, and income, under penalty of perjury. At the hearing, the defendant shall have the opportunity to be heard in person or through counsel, to present witnesses and other evidence, and to confront and cross-examine adverse witnesses. A defendant who is represented by counsel appointed by the court in the criminal proceedings shall be entitled to representation at any hearing held pursuant to this section. If the court determines that the defendant has the ability to pay all or a part of the costs, the court shall set the amount to be reimbursed and order the defendant to pay that sum to the Department of Corrections for deposit in the General Fund in the manner in which the court believes reasonable and compatible with the defendant's financial ability. Execution may be issued on the order in the same manner as on a judgment in a civil action. The order to pay all or part of the costs shall not be enforced by contempt.

(c) At any time during the pendency of an order made under this section, a person against whom the order has been made may petition the court to modify or vacate its previous order on the grounds of a change of circumstances with regard to the person's ability to pay. The court shall advise the person of this right at the time of making the order.

(d) If the amount paid by the defendant for imprisonment exceeds the actual average cost of the term of imprisonment actually served by the defendant, the amount paid by the defendant in excess of the actual average cost shall be returned to the defendant within 60 days of his or her release from the state prison.

(e) For the purposes of this section, in determining a defendant's ability to pay, the court shall consider the overall ability of the defendant to reimburse all or a portion of the costs of imprisonment in light of the defendant's present and foreseeable financial obligations, including family support obligations, restitution to the victim, and fines, penalties, and other obligations to the court, all of which shall take precedence over a reimbursement order made pursuant to this section.

(f) For the purposes of this section, in determining a defendant's ability to pay, the court shall not consider the following:

(1) The personal residence of the defendant, if any, up to a maximum amount of the median home sales price in the county in which the residence is located.

(2) The personal motor vehicle of the defendant, if any, up to a maximum amount of ten thousand dollars ($10,000).

(3) Any other assets of the defendant up to a maximum amount of the median annual income in California.

(Added by Stats. 1994, Ch. 145, Sec. 3. Effective July 11, 1994.)
1203.2.

(a) At any time during the period of supervision of a person (1) released on probation under the care of a probation officer pursuant to this chapter, (2) released on conditional sentence or summary probation not under the care of a probation officer, (3) placed on mandatory supervision pursuant to subparagraph (B) of paragraph (5) of subdivision (h) of Section 1170, (4) subject to revocation of postrelease community supervision pursuant to Section 3455, or (5) subject to revocation of parole supervision pursuant to Section 3000.08, if any probation officer, parole officer, or peace officer has probable cause to believe that the supervised person is violating any term or condition of his or her supervision, the officer may, without warrant or other process and at any time until the final disposition of the case, rearrest the supervised person and bring him or her before the court or the court may, in its discretion, issue a warrant for his or her rearrest. Notwithstanding Section 3056, and unless the supervised person is otherwise serving a period of flash incarceration, whenever a supervised person who is subject to this section is arrested, with or without a warrant or the filing of a petition for revocation as described in subdivision (b), the court may order the release of a supervised person from custody under any terms and conditions the court deems appropriate. Upon rearrest, or upon the issuance of a warrant for rearrest. the court may revoke and terminate the supervision of the person if the interests of justice so require and the court, in its judgment, has reason to believe from the report of the probation or parole officer or otherwise that the person has violated any of the conditions of his or her supervision, has become abandoned to improper associates or a vicious life, or has subsequently committed other offenses, regardless of whether he or she has been prosecuted for those offenses. However, the court shall not terminate parole pursuant to this section. Supervision shall not be revoked for failure of a person to make restitution imposed as a condition of supervision unless the court determines that the defendant has willfully failed to pay and has the ability to pay. Restitution shall be consistent with a person's ability to pay. The revocation, summary or otherwise, shall serve to toll the running of the period of supervision.

(b) (1) Upon its own motion or upon the petition of the supervised person, the probation or parole officer, or the district attorney, the court may modify, revoke, or terminate supervision of the person pursuant to this subdivision, except that the court shall not terminate parole pursuant to this section. The court in the county in which the person is supervised has jurisdiction to hear the motion or petition, or for those on parole, either the court in the county of supervision or the court in the county in which the alleged violation of supervision occurred. A person supervised on parole or postrelease community supervision pursuant to Section 3455 may not petition the court pursuant to this section for early release from supervision, and a petition under this section shall not be filed solely for the purpose of modifying parole. This section does not prohibit the court in the county in which the person is supervised or in which the alleged violation of supervision occurred from modifying a person's parole when acting on the court's own motion or a petition to revoke parole. The court shall give notice of its motion, and the probation or parole officer or the district attorney shall give notice of his or her petition to the supervised person, his or her attorney of record, and the district attorney or the probation or parole officer, as the case may be. The supervised person shall give notice of his or her petition to the probation or parole officer and notice of any motion or petition shall be given to the district attorney in all cases. The court shall refer its motion or the petition to the probation or parole officer. After the receipt of a written report from the probation or parole officer, the court shall read and consider the report and either its motion or the petition and may modify, revoke, or terminate the supervision of the supervised person upon the grounds set forth in subdivision (a) if the interests of justice so require.

(2) The notice required by this subdivision may be given to the supervised person upon his or her first court appearance in the proceeding. Upon the agreement by the supervised person in writing to the specific terms of a modification or termination of a specific term of supervision, any requirement that the supervised person make a personal appearance in court for the purpose of a modification or termination shall be waived. Prior to the modification or termination and waiver of appearance, the supervised person shall be informed of his or her right to consult with counsel, and if indigent the right to secure court appointed counsel. If the supervised person waives his or her right to counsel a written waiver shall be required. If the supervised person consults with counsel and thereafter agrees to a modification, revocation, or termination of the term of supervision and waiver of personal appearance, the agreement shall be signed by counsel showing approval for the modification or termination and waiver.

(c) Upon any revocation and termination of probation the court may, if the sentence has been suspended, pronounce judgment for any time within the longest period for which the person might have been sentenced. However, if the judgment has been pronounced and the execution thereof has been suspended, the court may revoke the suspension and order that the judgment shall be in full force and effect. In either case, the person shall be delivered over to the proper officer to serve his or her sentence, less any credits herein provided for.

(d) In any case of revocation and termination of probation, including, but not limited to, cases in which the judgment has been pronounced and the execution thereof has been suspended, upon the revocation and termination, the court may, in lieu of any other sentence, commit the person to the Department of Corrections and Rehabilitation, Division of Juvenile Facilities if he or she is otherwise eligible for that commitment.

(e) If probation has been revoked before the judgment has been pronounced, the order revoking probation may be set aside for good cause upon motion made before pronouncement of judgment. If probation has been revoked after the judgment has been pronounced, the judgment and the order which revoked the probation may be set aside for good cause within 30 days after the court has notice that the execution of the sentence has commenced. If an order setting aside the judgment, the revocation of probation, or both is made after the expiration of the probationary period, the court may again place the person on probation for that period and with those terms and conditions as it could have done immediately following conviction.

(f) As used in this section, the following definitions shall apply:

(1) "Court" means a judge, magistrate, or revocation hearing officer described in Section 71622.5 of the Government Code.

(2) "Probation officer" means a probation officer as described in Section 1203 or an officer of the agency designated by the board of supervisors of a county to implement postrelease community supervision pursuant to Section 3451.

(3) "Supervised person" means a person who satisfies any of the following:

(A) He or she is released on probation subject to the supervision of a probation officer.

(B) He or she is released on conditional sentence or summary probation not under the care of a probation officer.

(C) He or she is subject to mandatory supervision pursuant to subparagraph (B) of paragraph (5) of subdivision (h) of Section 1170.

(D) He or she is subject to revocation of postrelease community supervision pursuant to Section 3455.

(E) He or she is subject to revocation of parole pursuant to Section 3000.08.

(g) This section does not affect the authority of the supervising agency to impose intermediate sanctions, including flash incarceration, to persons supervised on parole pursuant to Section 3000.8 or postrelease community supervision pursuant to Part 3 (commencing with Section 3450) of Title 2.05.

(Amended by Stats. 2015, Ch. 61, Sec. 1. (SB 517) Effective January 1, 2016.)
1203.2a.

If any defendant who has been released on probation is committed to a prison in this state or another state for another offense, the court which released him or her on probation shall have jurisdiction to impose sentence, if no sentence has previously been imposed for the offense for which he or she was granted probation, in the absence of the defendant, on the request of the defendant made through his or her counsel, or by himself or herself in writing, if such writing is signed in the presence of the warden of the prison in which he or she is confined or the duly authorized representative of the warden, and the warden or his or her representative attests both that the defendant has made and signed such request and that he or she states that he or she wishes the court to impose sentence in the case in which he or she was released on probation, in his or her absence and without him or her being represented by counsel.

The probation officer may, upon learning of the defendant's imprisonment, and must within 30 days after being notified in writing by the defendant or his or her counsel, or the warden or duly authorized representative of the prison in which the defendant is confined, report such commitment to the court which released him or her on probation. Upon being informed by the probation officer of the defendant's confinement, or upon receipt from the warden or duly authorized representative of any prison in this state or another state of a certificate showing that the defendant is confined in prison, the court shall issue its commitment if sentence has previously been imposed. If sentence has not been previously imposed and if the defendant has requested the court through counsel or in writing in the manner herein provided to impose sentence in the case in which he or she was released on probation in his or her absence and without the presence of counsel to represent him or her, the court shall impose sentence and issue its commitment, or shall make other final order terminating its jurisdiction over the defendant in the case in which the order of probation was made. If the case is one in which sentence has previously been imposed, the court shall be deprived of jurisdiction over defendant if it does not issue its commitment or make other final order terminating its jurisdiction over defendant in the case within 60 days after being notified of the confinement. If the case is one in which sentence has not previously been imposed, the court is deprived of jurisdiction over defendant if it does not impose sentence and issue its commitment or make other final order terminating its jurisdiction over defendant in the case within 30 days after defendant has, in the manner prescribed by this section, requested imposition of sentence.

Upon imposition of sentence hereunder the commitment shall be dated as of the date upon which probation was granted. If the defendant is then in a state prison for an offense committed subsequent to the one upon which he or she has been on probation, the term of imprisonment of such defendant under a commitment issued hereunder shall commence upon the date upon which defendant was delivered to prison under commitment for his or her subsequent offense. Any terms ordered to be served consecutively shall be served as otherwise provided by law.

In the event the probation officer fails to report such commitment to the court or the court fails to impose sentence as herein provided, the court shall be deprived thereafter of all jurisdiction it may have retained in the granting of probation in said case.

(Amended by Stats. 1989, Ch. 1420, Sec. 2.)
1203.3.

(a) The court shall have authority at any time during the term of probation to revoke, modify, or change its order of suspension of imposition or execution of sentence. The court may at any time when the ends of justice will be subserved thereby, and when the good conduct and reform of the person so held on probation shall warrant it, terminate the period of probation, and discharge the person so held. The court shall also have the authority at any time during the term of mandatory supervision pursuant to subparagraph (B) of paragraph (5) of subdivision (h) of Section 1170 to revoke, modify, or change the conditions of the court's order suspending the execution of the concluding portion of the supervised person's term.

(b) The exercise of the court's authority in subdivision (a) to revoke, modify, or change probation or mandatory supervision, or to terminate probation, is subject to the following:

(1) Before any sentence or term or condition of probation or condition of mandatory supervision is modified, a hearing shall be held in open court before the judge. The prosecuting attorney shall be given a two-day written notice and an opportunity to be heard on the matter, except that, as to modifying or terminating a protective order in a case involving domestic violence, as defined in Section 6211 of the Family Code, the prosecuting attorney shall be given a five-day written notice and an opportunity to be heard.

(A) If the sentence or term or condition of probation or the term or any condition of mandatory supervision is modified pursuant to this section, the judge shall state the reasons for that modification on the record.

(B) As used in this section, modification of sentence shall include reducing a felony to a misdemeanor.

(2) No order shall be made without written notice first given by the court or the clerk thereof to the proper probation officer of the intention to revoke, modify, or change its order.

(3) In all probation cases, if the court has not seen fit to revoke the order of probation and impose sentence or pronounce judgment, the defendant shall at the end of the term of probation or any extension thereof, be by the court discharged subject to the provisions of these sections.

(4) The court may modify the time and manner of the term of probation for purposes of measuring the timely payment of restitution obligations or the good conduct and reform of the defendant while on probation. The court shall not modify the dollar amount of the restitution obligations due to the good conduct and reform of the defendant, absent compelling and extraordinary reasons, nor shall the court limit the ability of payees to enforce the obligations in the manner of judgments in civil actions.

(5) Nothing in this section shall be construed to prohibit the court from modifying the dollar amount of a restitution order pursuant to subdivision (f) of Section 1202.4 at any time during the term of the probation.

(6) The court may limit or terminate a protective order that is a condition of probation or mandatory supervision in a case involving domestic violence, as defined in Section 6211 of the Family Code. In determining whether to limit or terminate the protective order, the court shall consider if there has been any material change in circumstances since the crime for which the order was issued, and any issue that relates to whether there exists good cause for the change, including, but not limited to, consideration of all of the following:

(A) Whether the probationer or supervised person has accepted responsibility for the abusive behavior perpetrated against the victim.

(B) Whether the probationer or supervised person is currently attending and actively participating in counseling sessions.

(C) Whether the probationer or supervised person has completed parenting counseling, or attended alcoholics or narcotics counseling.

(D) Whether the probationer or supervised person has moved from the state, or is incarcerated.

(E) Whether the probationer or supervised person is still cohabiting, or intends to cohabit, with any subject of the order.

(F) Whether the defendant has performed well on probation or mandatory supervision, including consideration of any progress reports.

(G) Whether the victim desires the change, and if so, the victim's reasons, whether the victim has consulted a victim advocate, and whether the victim has prepared a safety plan and has access to local resources.

(H) Whether the change will impact any children involved, including consideration of any child protective services information.
(I) Whether the ends of justice would be served by limiting or terminating the order.
(c) If a probationer is ordered to serve time in jail, and the probationer escapes while serving that time, the probation is revoked as a matter of law on the day of the escape.
(d) If probation is revoked pursuant to subdivision (c), upon taking the probationer into custody, the probationer shall be accorded a hearing or hearings consistent with the holding in the case of People v. Vickers (1972) 8 Cal.3d 451. The purpose of that hearing or hearings is not to revoke probation, as the revocation has occurred as a matter of law in accordance with subdivision (c), but rather to afford the defendant an opportunity to require the prosecution to establish that the alleged violation did in fact occur and to justify the revocation.
(e) This section does not apply to cases covered by Section 1203.2.
(Amended by Stats. 2012, Ch. 43, Sec. 31. (SB 1023) Effective June 27, 2012.)

1203.35.
(a) (1) In any case where the court grants probation or imposes a sentence that includes mandatory supervision, the county probation department is authorized to use flash incarceration for any violation of the conditions of probation or mandatory supervision if, at the time of granting probation or ordering mandatory supervision, the court obtains from the defendant a waiver to a court hearing prior to the imposition of a period of flash incarceration. Probation shall not be denied for refusal to sign the waiver.
(2) Each county probation department shall develop a response matrix that establishes protocols for the imposition of graduated sanctions for violations of the conditions of probation to determine appropriate interventions to include the use of flash incarceration.
(3) A supervisor shall approve the term of flash incarceration prior to the imposition of flash incarceration.
(4) Upon a decision to impose a period of flash incarceration, the probation department shall notify the court, public defender, district attorney, and sheriff of each imposition of flash incarceration.
(5) If the person on probation or mandatory supervision does not agree to accept a recommended period of flash incarceration, upon a determination that there has been a violation, the probation officer is authorized to address the alleged violation by filing a declaration or revocation request with the court.
(b) For purposes of this section, "flash incarceration" is a period of detention in a county jail due to a violation of an offender's conditions of probation or mandatory supervision. The length of the detention period may range between one and 10 consecutive days. Shorter, but if necessary more frequent, periods of detention for violations of an offender's conditions of probation or mandatory supervision shall appropriately punish an offender while preventing the disruption in a work or home establishment that typically arises from longer periods of detention. In cases where there are multiple violations in a single incident, only one flash incarceration booking is authorized and may range between one and 10 consecutive days.
(c) This section shall not apply to any defendant sentenced pursuant to Section 1210.1.
(d) This section shall remain in effect only until January 1, 2021, and as of that date is repealed, unless a later enacted statute, that is enacted before January 1, 2021, deletes or extends that date.
(Added by Stats. 2016, Ch. 706, Sec. 2. (SB 266) Effective January 1, 2017. Repealed as of January 1, 2021, by its own provisions.)

1203.4.
(a) (1) In any case in which a defendant has fulfilled the conditions of probation for the entire period of probation, or has been discharged prior to the termination of the period of probation, or in any other case in which a court, in its discretion and the interests of justice, determines that a defendant should be granted the relief available under this section, the defendant shall, at any time after the termination of the period of probation, if he or she is not then serving a sentence for any offense, on probation for any offense, or charged with the commission of any offense, be permitted by the court to withdraw his or her plea of guilty or plea of nolo contendere and enter a plea of not guilty; or, if he or she has been convicted after a plea of not guilty, the court shall set aside the verdict of guilty; and, in either case, the court shall thereupon dismiss the accusations or information against the defendant and except as noted below, he or she shall thereafter be released from all penalties and disabilities resulting from the offense of which he or she has been convicted, except as provided in Section 13555 of the Vehicle Code. The probationer shall be informed, in his or her probation papers, of this right and privilege and his or her right, if any, to petition for a certificate of rehabilitation and pardon. The probationer may make the application and change of plea in person or by attorney, or by the probation officer authorized in writing. However, in any subsequent prosecution of the defendant for any other offense, the prior conviction may be pleaded and proved and shall have the same effect as if probation had not been granted or the accusation or information dismissed. The order shall state, and the probationer shall be informed, that the order does not relieve him or her of the obligation to disclose the conviction in response to any direct question contained in any questionnaire or application for public office, for licensure by any state or local agency, or for contracting with the California State Lottery Commission.
(2) Dismissal of an accusation or information pursuant to this section does not permit a person to own, possess, or have in his or her custody or control any firearm or prevent his or her conviction under Chapter 2 (commencing with Section 29800) of Division 9 of Title 4 of Part 6.
(3) Dismissal of an accusation or information underlying a conviction pursuant to this section does not permit a person prohibited from holding public office as a result of that conviction to hold public office.
(4) This subdivision shall apply to all applications for relief under this section which are filed on or after November 23, 1970.
(b) Subdivision (a) of this section does not apply to any misdemeanor that is within the provisions of Section 42002.1 of the Vehicle Code, to any violation of subdivision (c) of Section 286, Section 288, subdivision (c) of Section 287 or of former Section 288a, Section 288.5, subdivision (j) of Section 289, Section 311.1, 311.2, 311.3, or 311.11, or any felony conviction pursuant to subdivision (d) of Section 261.5, or to any infraction.
(c) (1) Except as provided in paragraph (2), subdivision (a) does not apply to a person who receives a notice to appear or is otherwise charged with a violation of an offense described in subdivisions (a) to (e), inclusive, of Section 12810 of the Vehicle Code.
(2) If a defendant who was convicted of a violation listed in paragraph (1) petitions the court, the court in its discretion and in the interests of justice, may order the relief provided pursuant to subdivision (a) to that defendant.
(d) A person who petitions for a change of plea or setting aside of a verdict under this section may be required to reimburse the court for the actual costs of services rendered, whether or not the petition is granted and the records are sealed or expunged, at a rate to be determined by the court not to exceed one hundred fifty dollars ($150), and to reimburse the county for the actual costs of services rendered, whether or not the petition is granted and the records are sealed or expunged, at a rate to be determined by the county board of supervisors not to exceed one hundred fifty dollars ($150), and to reimburse any city for the actual costs of services rendered, whether or not the petition is granted and the records are sealed or expunged, at a rate to be determined by the city council not to exceed one hundred fifty dollars ($150). Ability to make this reimbursement shall be determined by the court using the standards set forth in paragraph (2) of subdivision (g) of Section 987.8 and shall not be a prerequisite to a person's eligibility under this section. The court may order reimbursement in any case in which the petitioner appears to have the ability to pay, without undue hardship, all or any portion of the costs for services established pursuant to this subdivision.
(e) (1) Relief shall not be granted under this section unless the prosecuting attorney has been given 15 days' notice of the petition for relief. The probation officer shall notify the prosecuting attorney when a petition is filed, pursuant to this section.
(2) It shall be presumed that the prosecuting attorney has received notice if proof of service is filed with the court.
(f) If, after receiving notice pursuant to subdivision (e), the prosecuting attorney fails to appear and object to a petition for dismissal, the prosecuting attorney may not move to set aside or otherwise appeal the grant of that petition.
(g) Notwithstanding the above provisions or any other provision of law, the Governor shall have the right to pardon a person convicted of a violation of subdivision (c) of Section 286, Section 288, subdivision (c) of Section 287 or of former Section 288a, Section 288.5, or subdivision (j) of Section 289, if there are extraordinary circumstances.
(Amended by Stats. 2018, Ch. 423, Sec. 96. (SB 1494) Effective January 1, 2019.)

1203.4a.
(a) Every defendant convicted of a misdemeanor and not granted probation, and every defendant convicted of an infraction shall, at any time after the lapse of one year from the date of pronouncement of judgment, if he or she has fully complied with and performed the sentence of the court, is not then serving a sentence for any offense and is not under charge of commission of any crime, and has, since the pronouncement of judgment, lived an honest and upright life and has conformed to and obeyed the laws of the land, be permitted by the court to withdraw his or her plea of guilty or nolo contendere and enter a plea of not guilty; or if he or she has been convicted after a plea of not guilty, the court shall set aside the verdict of guilty; and in either case the court shall thereupon dismiss the accusatory pleading against the defendant, who shall thereafter be released from all penalties and disabilities resulting from the offense of which he or she has been convicted, except as provided in Chapter 3 (commencing with Section 29900) of Division 9 of Title 4 of Part 6 of this code or Section 13555 of the Vehicle Code.
(b) If a defendant does not satisfy all the requirements of subdivision (a), after a lapse of one year from the date of pronouncement of judgment, a court, in its discretion and in the interests of justice, may grant the relief available pursuant to subdivision (a) to a defendant convicted of an infraction, or of a misdemeanor and not granted probation, or both, if he or she has fully complied with and performed the sentence of the court, is not then serving a sentence for any offense, and is not under charge of commission of any crime.
(c) (1) The defendant shall be informed of the provisions of this section, either orally or in writing, at the time he or she is sentenced. The defendant may make an application and change of plea in person or by attorney, or by the probation officer authorized in writing, provided that, in any subsequent prosecution of the defendant for any other offense, the prior conviction may be pleaded and proved and shall have the same effect as if relief had not been granted pursuant to this section.
(2) Dismissal of an accusatory pleading pursuant to this section does not permit a person to own, possess, or have in his or her custody or control any firearm or prevent his or her conviction under Chapter 2 (commencing with Section 29800) of Division 9 of Title 4 of Part 6.
(3) Dismissal of an accusatory pleading underlying a conviction pursuant to this section does not permit a person prohibited from holding public office as a result of that conviction to hold public office.
(d) This section applies to any conviction specified in subdivision (a) or (b) that occurred before, as well as those occurring after, the effective date of this section, except that this section does not apply to the following:
(1) A misdemeanor violation of subdivision (c) of Section 288.
(2) Any misdemeanor falling within the provisions of Section 42002.1 of the Vehicle Code.
(3) Any infraction falling within the provisions of Section 42001 of the Vehicle Code.
(e) A person who petitions for a dismissal of a charge under this section may be required to reimburse the county and the court for the cost of services rendered at a rate to be determined by the county board of supervisors for the county and by the court for the court, not to exceed sixty dollars ($60), and to reimburse any city for the cost of services rendered at a rate to be determined by the city council not to exceed sixty dollars ($60). Ability to make this reimbursement shall be determined by the court using the standards set forth in paragraph (2) of subdivision (g) of Section 987.8 and shall not be a prerequisite to a person's eligibility under this section. The court may order reimbursement in any case in which the petitioner appears to have the ability to pay, without undue hardship, all or any portion of the cost for services established pursuant to this subdivision.
(f) A petition for dismissal of an infraction pursuant to this section shall be by written declaration, except upon a showing of compelling need. Dismissal of an infraction shall not be granted under this section unless the prosecuting attorney has been given at least 15 days' notice of the petition for dismissal. It shall be presumed that the prosecuting attorney has received notice if proof of service is filed with the court.
(g) Any determination of amount made by a court under this section shall be valid only if either (1) made under procedures adopted by the Judicial Council or (2) approved by the Judicial Council.
(Amended by Stats. 2013, Ch. 76, Sec. 153.5. (AB 383) Effective January 1, 2014.)

1203.41.
(a) If a defendant is sentenced pursuant to paragraph (5) of subdivision (h) of Section 1170, the court, in its discretion and in the interests of justice, may order the following relief, subject to the conditions of subdivision (b):
(1) The court may permit the defendant to withdraw his or her plea of guilty or plea of nolo contendere and enter a plea of not guilty, or, if he or she has been convicted after a plea of not guilty, the court shall set aside the verdict of guilty, and, in either case, the court shall thereupon dismiss the accusations or information against the defendant and he or she shall thereafter be released from all penalties and disabilities resulting from the offense of which he or she has been convicted, except as provided in Section 13555 of the Vehicle Code.
(2) The relief available under this section may be granted only after the lapse of one year following the defendant's completion of the sentence, if the sentence was imposed pursuant to subparagraph (B) of paragraph (5) of subdivision (h) of Section 1170, or after the lapse of two years following the defendant's completion of the sentence, if the sentence was imposed pursuant to subparagraph (A) of paragraph (5) of subdivision (h) of Section 1170.
(3) The relief available under this section may be granted only if the defendant is not under supervision pursuant to subparagraph (B) of paragraph (5) of subdivision (h) of Section 1170, and is not serving a sentence for, on probation for, or charged with the commission of any offense.
(4) The defendant shall be informed, either orally or in writing, of the provisions of this section and of his or her right, if any, to petition for a certificate of rehabilitation and pardon at the time he or she is sentenced.
(5) The defendant may make the application and change of plea in person or by attorney, or by a probation officer authorized in writing.
(b) Relief granted pursuant to subdivision (a) is subject to the following conditions:
(1) In any subsequent prosecution of the defendant for any other offense, the prior conviction may be pleaded and proved and shall have the same effect as if the accusation or information had not been dismissed.

(2) The order shall state, and the defendant shall be informed, that the order does not relieve him or her of the obligation to disclose the conviction in response to any direct question contained in any questionnaire or application for public office, for licensure by any state or local agency, or for contracting with the California State Lottery Commission.

(3) Dismissal of an accusation or information pursuant to this section does not permit a person to own, possess, or have in his or her custody or control any firearm or prevent his or her conviction under Chapter 2 (commencing with Section 29800) of Division 9 of Title 4 of Part 6.

(4) Dismissal of an accusation or information underlying a conviction pursuant to this section does not permit a person prohibited from holding public office as a result of that conviction to hold public office.

(c) This section applies to any conviction specified in subdivision (a) that occurred before, on, or after January 1, 2014.

(d) A person who petitions for a change of plea or setting aside of a verdict under this section may be required to reimburse the court for the actual costs of services rendered, whether or not the petition is granted and the records are sealed or expunged, at a rate to be determined by the court not to exceed one hundred fifty dollars ($150), and to reimburse the county for the actual costs of services rendered, whether or not the petition is granted and the records are sealed or expunged, at a rate to be determined by the county board of supervisors not to exceed one hundred fifty dollars ($150), and to reimburse any city for the actual costs of services rendered, whether or not the petition is granted and the records are sealed or expunged, at a rate to be determined by the city council not to exceed one hundred fifty dollars ($150). Ability to make this reimbursement shall be determined by the court using the standards set forth in paragraph (2) of subdivision (g) of Section 987.8 and shall not be a prerequisite to a person's eligibility under this section. The court may order reimbursement in any case in which the petitioner appears to have the ability to pay, without undue hardship, all or any portion of the costs for services established pursuant to this subdivision.

(e) (1) Relief shall not be granted under this section unless the prosecuting attorney has been given 15 days' notice of the petition for relief. The probation officer shall notify the prosecuting attorney when a petition is filed, pursuant to this section.

(2) It shall be presumed that the prosecuting attorney has received notice if proof of service is filed with the court.

(f) If, after receiving notice pursuant to subdivision (e), the prosecuting attorney fails to appear and object to a petition for dismissal, the prosecuting attorney may not move to set aside or otherwise appeal the grant of that petition.

(Added by Stats. 2013, Ch. 787, Sec. 1. (AB 651) Effective January 1, 2014.)
1203.42.

(a) If a defendant was sentenced prior to the implementation of the 2011 Realignment Legislation for a crime for which he or she would otherwise have been eligible for sentencing pursuant to subdivision (h) of Section 1170, the court, in its discretion and in the interests of justice, may order the following relief, subject to the conditions of subdivision (b):

(1) The court may permit the defendant to withdraw his or her plea of guilty or plea of nolo contendere and enter a plea of not guilty, or, if he or she has been convicted after a plea of not guilty, the court shall set aside the verdict of guilty, and, in either case, the court shall thereupon dismiss the accusations or information against the defendant and he or she shall thereafter be released from all penalties and disabilities resulting from the offense of which he or she has been convicted, except as provided in Section 13555 of the Vehicle Code.

(2) The relief available under this section may be granted only after the lapse of two years following the defendant's completion of the sentence.

(3) The relief available under this section may be granted only if the defendant is not under supervised release, and is not serving a sentence for, on probation for, or charged with the commission of any offense.

(4) The defendant may make the application and change of plea in person or by attorney, or by a probation officer authorized in writing.

(b) Relief granted pursuant to subdivision (a) is subject to the following conditions:

(1) In any subsequent prosecution of the defendant for any other offense, the prior conviction may be pleaded and proved and shall have the same effect as if the accusation or information had not been dismissed.

(2) The order shall state, and the defendant shall be informed, that the order does not relieve him or her of the obligation to disclose the conviction in response to any direct question contained in any questionnaire or application for public office, for licensure by any state or local agency, or for contracting with the California State Lottery Commission.

(3) Dismissal of an accusation or information pursuant to this section does not permit a person to own, possess, or have in his or her custody or control any firearm or prevent his or her conviction under Chapter 2 (commencing with Section 29800) of Division 9 of Title 4 of Part 6.

(4) Dismissal of an accusation or information underlying a conviction pursuant to this section does not permit a person prohibited from holding public office as a result of that conviction to hold public office.

(c) A person who petitions for a change of plea or setting aside of a verdict under this section may be required to reimburse the court for the actual costs of services rendered, whether or not the petition is granted and the records are sealed or expunged, at a rate to be determined by the court not to exceed one hundred fifty dollars ($150), and to reimburse the county for the actual costs of services rendered, whether or not the petition is granted and the records are sealed or expunged, at a rate to be determined by the county board of supervisors not to exceed one hundred fifty dollars ($150), and to reimburse any city for the actual costs of services rendered, whether or not the petition is granted and the records are sealed or expunged, at a rate to be determined by the city council not to exceed one hundred fifty dollars ($150). Ability to make this reimbursement shall be determined by the court using the standards set forth in paragraph (2) of subdivision (g) of Section 987.8 and shall not be a prerequisite to a person's eligibility under this section. The court may order reimbursement in any case in which the petitioner appears to have the ability to pay, without undue hardship, all or any portion of the costs for services established pursuant to this subdivision.

(d) (1) Relief shall not be granted under this section unless the prosecuting attorney has been given 15 days' notice of the petition for relief. The probation officer shall notify the prosecuting attorney when a petition is filed, pursuant to this section.

(2) It shall be presumed that the prosecuting attorney has received notice if proof of service is filed with the court.

(e) If, after receiving notice pursuant to subdivision (d), the prosecuting attorney fails to appear and object to a petition for dismissal, the prosecuting attorney may not move to set aside or otherwise appeal the grant of that petition.

(Added by Stats. 2017, Ch. 207, Sec. 1. (AB 1115) Effective January 1, 2018.)
1203.43.

(a) (1) The Legislature finds and declares that the statement in Section 1000.4, that "successful completion of a deferred entry of judgment program shall not, without the defendant's consent, be used in any way that could result in the denial of any employment, benefit, license, or certificate" constitutes misinformation about the actual consequences of making a plea in the case of some defendants, including all noncitizen defendants, because the disposition of the case may cause adverse consequences, including adverse immigration consequences.

(2) Accordingly, the Legislature finds and declares that based on this misinformation and the potential harm, the defendant's prior plea is invalid.

(b) For the above-specified reason, in any case in which a defendant was granted deferred entry of judgment on or after January 1, 1997, has performed satisfactorily during the period in which deferred entry of judgment was granted, and for whom the criminal charge or charges were dismissed pursuant to Section 1000.3, the court shall, upon request of the defendant, permit the defendant to withdraw the plea of guilty or nolo contendere and enter a plea of not guilty, and the court shall dismiss the complaint or information against the defendant. If court records showing the case resolution are no longer available, the defendant's declaration, under penalty of perjury, that the charges were dismissed after he or she completed the requirements for deferred entry of judgment, shall be presumed to be true if the defendant has submitted a copy of his or her state summary criminal history information maintained by the Department of Justice that either shows that the defendant successfully completed the deferred entry of judgment program or that the record is incomplete in that it does not show a final disposition. For purposes of this section, a final disposition means that the state summary criminal history information shows either a dismissal after completion of the program or a sentence after termination of the program.

(Added by Stats. 2015, Ch. 646, Sec. 1. (AB 1352) Effective January 1, 2016.)
1203.45.

(a) In a case in which a person was under 18 years of age at the time of commission of a misdemeanor and is eligible for, or has previously received, the relief provided by Section 1203.4 or 1203.4a, that person, in a proceeding under Section 1203.4 or 1203.4a, or a separate proceeding, may petition the court for an order sealing the record of conviction and other official records in the case, including records of arrests resulting in the criminal proceeding and records relating to other offenses charged in the accusatory pleading, whether the defendant was acquitted or charges were dismissed. If the court finds that the person was under 18 years of age at the time of the commission of the misdemeanor, and is eligible for relief under Section 1203.4 or 1203.4a or has previously received that relief, it may issue its order granting the relief prayed for. Thereafter the conviction, arrest, or other proceeding shall be deemed not to have occurred, and the petitioner may answer accordingly any question relating to their occurrence.

(b) This section applies to convictions that occurred before, as well as those that occur after, the effective date of this section.

(c) This section shall not apply to offenses for which registration is required under Section 290, to violations of Division 10 (commencing with Section 11000) of the Health and Safety Code, or to misdemeanor violations of the Vehicle Code relating to operation of a vehicle or of a local ordinance relating to operation, standing, stopping, or parking of a motor vehicle.

(d) This section does not apply to a person convicted of more than one offense, whether the second or additional convictions occurred in the same action in which the conviction as to which relief is sought occurred or in another action, except in the following cases:

(1) One of the offenses includes the other or others.

(2) The other conviction or convictions were for the following:

(A) Misdemeanor violations of Chapters 1 (commencing with Section 21000) to 9 (commencing with Section 22500), inclusive, Chapter 12 (commencing with Section 23100), or Chapter 13 (commencing with Section 23250) of Division 11 of the Vehicle Code, other than Section 23103, 23104, 23105, 23152, 23153, or 23220.

(B) Violation of a local ordinance relating to the operation, stopping, standing, or parking of a motor vehicle.

(3) The other conviction or convictions consisted of any combination of paragraphs (1) and (2).

(e) This section shall apply in a case in which a person was under 21 years of age at the time of the commission of an offense as to which this section is made applicable if that offense was committed prior to March 7, 1973.

(f) In an action or proceeding based upon defamation, a court, upon a showing of good cause, may order the records sealed under this section to be opened and admitted into evidence. The records shall be confidential and shall be available for inspection only by the court, jury, parties, counsel for the parties, and any other person who is authorized by the court to inspect them. Upon the judgment in the action or proceeding becoming final, the court shall order the records sealed.

(g) A person who is 26 years of age or older and petitions for an order sealing a record under this section may be required to reimburse the court for the actual cost of services rendered, whether or not the petition is granted and the records are sealed or expunged, at a rate to be determined by the court, not to exceed one hundred fifty dollars ($150), and to reimburse the county for the actual cost of services rendered, whether or not the petition is granted and the records are sealed or expunged, at a rate to be determined by the county board of supervisors, not to exceed one hundred fifty dollars ($150), and to reimburse any city for the actual cost of services rendered, whether or not the petition is granted and the records are sealed or expunged, at a rate to be determined by the city council, not to exceed one hundred fifty dollars ($150). Ability to make this reimbursement shall be determined by the court using the standards set forth in paragraph (2) of subdivision (g) of Section 987.8 and shall not be a prerequisite to a person's eligibility under this section. The court may order reimbursement in a case in which the petitioner appears to have the ability to pay, without undue hardship, all or any portion of the cost for services established pursuant to this subdivision.

(Amended by Stats. 2015, Ch. 388, Sec. 1. (SB 504) Effective January 1, 2016.)
1203.47.

(a) A person who was found to be a person described in Section 602 of the Welfare and Institutions Code by reason of the commission of an offense described in subdivision (b) of Section 647 or in Section 653.22 may, upon reaching 18 years of age, petition the court to have his or her record sealed, as provided in Section 781 of the Welfare and Institutions Code, except that, as pertaining to any records regarding the commission of an offense described in subdivision (b) of Section 647 or in Section 653.22, it shall not be a requirement in granting the petition for the person to show that he or she has not been convicted of a felony or of any misdemeanor involving moral turpitude, or that rehabilitation has been attained to the satisfaction of the court. Upon granting the petition, all records relating to the violation or violations of subdivision (b) of Section 647 or of Section 653.22, or both, shall be sealed pursuant to Section 781 of the Welfare and Institutions Code.

(b) The relief provided by this section does not apply to a person adjudicated pursuant to subdivision (b) of Section 647 or of Section 653.22 who paid money or any other valuable thing, or attempted to pay money or any other valuable thing, to any person for the purpose of prostitution as defined in subdivision (b) of Section 647.

(c) This section applies to adjudications that occurred before, as well as those that occur after, the effective date of this section.

(d) A petition granted pursuant to this section does not authorize the sealing of any part of a person's record that is unrelated to a violation of subdivision (b) of Section 647, Section 653.22, or both.

(Amended by Stats. 2013, Ch. 59, Sec. 4. (SB 514) Effective January 1, 2014.)
1203.49.

If a defendant has been convicted of solicitation or prostitution, as described in subdivision (b) of Section 647, and if the defendant has completed any term of probation for that conviction, the defendant may petition the court for relief under this section. If the defendant can establish by clear and convincing evidence that the conviction was the result of his or her status as a victim of human trafficking, the court may issue an order that does all of the following:

(a) Sets forth a finding that the petitioner was a victim of human trafficking when he or she committed the crime.

(b) Orders any of the relief described in Section 1203.4.
(c) Notifies the Department of Justice that the petitioner was a victim of human trafficking when he or she committed the crime and the relief that has been ordered.
(Added by Stats. 2014, Ch. 708, Sec. 4. (AB 1585) Effective January 1, 2015.)
1203.5.
The chief probation officers, assistant probation officers, and deputy probation officers appointed in accordance with Chapter 16 (commencing with Section 27770) of Part 3 of Division 2 of Title 3 of the Government Code shall be ex officio adult chief probation officers, assistant adult probation officers, and deputy adult probation officers except in any county or city and county whose charter provides for the separate office of adult probation officer. When the separate office of adult probation officer has been established he or she shall perform all the duties of probation officers except for matters under the jurisdiction of the juvenile court.
(Repealed and added by Stats. 2017, Ch. 17, Sec. 28. (AB 103) Effective June 27, 2017.)
1203.7.
(a) Either at the time of the arrest for a crime of any person over 16 years of age, or at the time of the plea or verdict of guilty, the probation officer of the county of the jurisdiction of the crime shall, when so directed by the court, inquire into the antecedents, character, history, family environment and offense of that person. The probation officer shall report that information to the court and file a written report in the records of the court. The report shall contain his or her recommendation for or against the release of the person on probation.
(b) If that person is released on probation and committed to the care of the probation officer, the officer shall keep a complete and accurate record of the history of the case in court and of the name of the probation officer, and his or her acts in connection with the case. This information shall include the age, sex, nativity, residence, education, habits of temperance, marital status, and the conduct, employment, occupation, parents' occupation, and the condition of the person committed to his or her care during the term of probation, and the result of probation. This record shall constitute a part of the records of the court and shall at all times be open to the inspection of the court or any person appointed by the court for that purpose, as well as of all magistrates and the chief of police or other head of the police, unless otherwise ordered by the court.
(c) Five years after termination of probation in any case subject to this section, the probation officer may destroy any records and papers in his or her possession relating to the case.
(d) The probation officer shall furnish to each person released on probation and committed to his or her care, a written statement of the terms and conditions of probation, and shall report to the court or judge appointing him or her, any violation or breach of the terms and conditions imposed by the court on the person placed in his or her care.
(Amended by Stats. 2003, Ch. 296, Sec. 25.1. Effective January 1, 2004.)
1203.71.
Any of the duties of the probation officer may be performed by a deputy probation officer and shall be performed by him or her whenever detailed to perform those by the probation officer; and it shall be the duty of the probation officer to see that the deputy probation officer performs his or her duties.
The probation officer and each deputy probation officer shall have, as to the person so committed to the care of the probation officer or deputy probation officer, the powers of a peace officer.
The probation officers and deputy probation officers shall serve as such probation officers in all courts having original jurisdiction of criminal actions in this state.
(Added by Stats. 2001, Ch. 473, Sec. 10. Effective January 1, 2002.)
1203.72.
Except as provided in subparagraph (D) of paragraph (2) of subdivision (b) of Section 1203, no court shall pronounce judgment upon any defendant, as to whom the court has requested a probation report pursuant to Section 1203.7, unless a copy of the probation report has been made available to the court, the prosecuting attorney, and the defendant or his or her attorney, at least two days or, upon the request of the defendant, five days prior to the time fixed by the court for consideration of the report with respect to pronouncement of judgment. The report shall be filed with the clerk of the court as a record in the case at the time the court considers the report.
If the defendant is not represented by an attorney, the court, upon ordering the probation report, shall also order the probation officer who prepares the report to discuss its contents with the defendant.
(Amended by Stats. 2002, Ch. 787, Sec. 22. Effective January 1, 2003.)
1203.73.
The probation officers and deputy probation officers in all counties of the state shall be allowed those necessary incidental expenses incurred in the performance of their duties as required by any law of this state, as may be authorized by a judge of the superior court; and the same shall be a charge upon the county in which the court appointing them has jurisdiction and shall be paid out of the county treasury upon a warrant issued therefor by the county auditor upon the order of the court; provided, however, that in counties in which the probation officer is appointed by the board of supervisors, the expenses shall be authorized by the probation officer and claims therefor shall be audited, allowed and paid in the same manner as other county claims.
(Amended by Stats. 2002, Ch. 787, Sec. 23. Effective January 1, 2003.)
1203.74.
Upon a determination that, in his or her opinion, staff and financial resources available to him or her are insufficient to meet his or her statutory or court ordered responsibilities, the probation officer shall immediately notify the presiding judge of the superior court and the board of supervisors of the county, or city and county, in writing. The notification shall explain which responsibilities cannot be met and what resources are necessary in order that statutory or court ordered responsibilities can be properly discharged.
(Added by Stats. 2001, Ch. 473, Sec. 13. Effective January 1, 2002.)
1203.8.
(a) A county may develop a multiagency plan to prepare and enhance nonviolent felony offenders' successful reentry into the community. The plan shall be developed by, and have the concurrence of, the presiding judge, the chief probation officer, the district attorney, the local custodial agency, and the public defender, or their designees, and shall be submitted to the board of supervisors for its approval. The plan shall provide that when a report prepared pursuant to Section 1203.10 recommends a state prison commitment, the report shall also include, but not be limited to, the offender's treatment, literacy, and vocational needs. Any sentence imposed pursuant to this section shall include a recommendation for completion while in state prison, all relevant programs to address those needs identified in the assessment.
(b) The Department of Corrections and Rehabilitation is authorized to enter into an agreement with up to three counties to implement subdivision (a) and to provide funding for the purpose of the probation department carrying out the assessment. The Department of Corrections and Rehabilitation, to the extent feasible, shall provide to the offender all programs pursuant to the court's recommendation.
(Added by Stats. 2005, Ch. 603, Sec. 2. Effective January 1, 2006.)
1203.9.
(a) (1) Except as provided in paragraph (3), whenever a person is released on probation or mandatory supervision, the court, upon noticed motion, shall transfer the case to the superior court in any other county in which the person resides permanently, meaning with the stated intention to remain for the duration of probation or mandatory supervision, unless the transferring court determines that the transfer would be inappropriate and states its reasons on the record.
(2) Upon notice of the motion for transfer, the court of the proposed receiving county may provide comments for the record regarding the proposed transfer, following procedures set forth in rules of court developed by the Judicial Council for this purpose, pursuant to subdivision (f). The court and the probation department shall give the matter of investigating those transfers precedence over all actions or proceedings therein, except actions or proceedings to which special precedence is given by law, to the end that all those transfers shall be completed expeditiously.
(3) If victim restitution was ordered as a condition of probation or mandatory supervision, the transferring court shall determine the amount of restitution before the transfer unless the court finds that the determination cannot be made within a reasonable time from when the motion for transfer is made. If a case is transferred without a determination of the amount of restitution, the transferring court shall complete the determination as soon as practicable. In all other aspects, except as provided in subdivisions (d) and (e), the court of the receiving county shall have full jurisdiction over the matter upon transfer as provided in subdivision (b).
(b) The court of the receiving county shall accept the entire jurisdiction over the case effective the date that the transferring court orders the transfer.
(c) The order of transfer shall contain an order committing the probationer or supervised person to the care and custody of the probation officer of the receiving county and, if applicable, an order for reimbursement of reasonable costs for processing the transfer to be paid to the sending county in accordance with Section 1203.1b. A copy of the orders and any probation reports shall be transmitted to the court and probation officer of the receiving county within two weeks of the finding that the person does permanently reside in or has permanently moved to that county, and the receiving court shall have entire jurisdiction over the case, except as provided in subdivisions (d) and (e), with the like power to again request transfer of the case whenever it seems proper.
(d) (1) Notwithstanding subdivision (b) and except as provided in subdivision (e), if the transferring court has ordered the defendant to pay fines, fees, forfeitures, penalties, assessments, or restitution, the transfer order shall require that those and any other amounts ordered by the transferring court that are still unpaid at the time of transfer be paid by the defendant to the collection program for the transferring court for proper distribution and accounting once collected.
(2) The receiving court and receiving county probation department may impose additional local fees and costs as authorized, and shall notify the responsible collection program for the transferring court of those changes.
(3) Any local fees imposed pursuant to paragraph (2) shall be paid by the defendant to the collection program for the transferring court which shall remit the additional fees and costs to the receiving court for proper accounting and distribution.
(e) (1) Upon approval of a transferring court, a receiving court may elect to collect all of the court-ordered payments from a defendant attributable to the case under which the defendant is being supervised, provided, however, that the collection program for the receiving court transmits the revenue collected to the collection program for the transferring court for deposit, accounting, and distribution. A collection program for the receiving court shall not charge administrative fees for collections performed for the collection program for the transferring court without a written agreement with the other program.
(2) A collection program for a receiving court collecting funds for a collection program for a transferring court pursuant to paragraph (1) shall not report revenue owed or collected on behalf of the collection program for the transferring court as part of those collections required to be reported annually by the court to the Judicial Council.
(f) The Judicial Council shall promulgate rules of court for procedures by which the proposed receiving county shall receive notice of the motion for transfer and by which responsive comments may be transmitted to the court of the transferring county. The Judicial Council shall adopt rules providing factors for the court's consideration when determining the appropriateness of a transfer, including, but not limited to, the following:
(1) Permanency of residence of the offender.
(2) Local programs available for the offender.
(3) Restitution orders and victim issues.
(g) The Judicial Council shall consider adoption of rules of court as it deems appropriate to implement the collection, accounting, and disbursement requirements of subdivisions (d) and (e).
(Amended by Stats. 2015, Ch. 251, Sec. 1. (AB 673) Effective January 1, 2016.)
1203.10.
(a) At the time of the plea or verdict of guilty of any person over 18 years of age, a probation officer of the county of the jurisdiction of the criminal shall, when so directed by the court, inquire into the antecedents, character, history, family environment, and offense of such person, and must report the same to the court and file his or her report in writing in the records of such court. When directed, his or her report shall contain a recommendation for or against the release for the person on probation. If any such person shall be released on probation and committed to the supervision of a probation officer, such officer shall keep a complete and accurate record in suitable books of the history of the case and supervision, including the names of probation officers assigned to the case, and their actions in connection with the case; also the age, sex, nativity, residence, education, habit of temperance, whether married or single, and the conduct, employment and occupation, and parents' occupation, if relevant, and condition of such person during the term of the probation and the result of the probation. The record of the probation officer is a part of the records of the court, and shall at all times be open to the inspection of the court or of any person appointed by, or allowed access by order of, the court for that purpose, as well as of all magistrates, and the chief of police, or other heads of the police, and other probation agencies, unless otherwise ordered by the court.
(b) Five years after termination of probation in any case subject to this section, the probation officer may destroy any records and papers in his or her possession relating to such case.
(Amended by Stats. 2016, Ch. 59, Sec. 4. (SB 1474) Effective January 1, 2017.)
1203.11.
A probation or parole officer or parole agent of the Department of Corrections may serve any process regarding the issuance of a temporary restraining order or other protective order against a person committed to the care of the probation or parole officer or parole agent when the person appears for an appointment with the probation or parole officer or parole agent at their office.
(Added by Stats. 1991, Ch. 866, Sec. 5.)
1203.12.
The probation officer shall furnish to each person who has been released on probation, and committed to his care, a written statement of the terms and conditions of his probation unless such a statement has been furnished by the court, and shall report to the court, or judge, releasing such person on probation, any violation or breach of the terms and conditions imposed by such court on the person placed in his care.
(Amended by Stats. 1968, Ch. 1222.)
1203.13.
The probation officer of any county may establish, or assist in the establishment of, any public council or committee having as its object the prevention of crime, and may cooperate with or participate in the work of any such councils or committees for the purpose of preventing or decreasing crime, including the improving of recreational, health, and other conditions in the community.
(Added by Stats. 1947, Ch. 876.)

1203.14.

Notwithstanding any other provision of law, probation departments may engage in activities designed to prevent adult delinquency. These activities include rendering direct and indirect services to persons in the community. Probation departments shall not be limited to providing services only to those persons on probation being supervised under Section 1203.10, but may provide services to any adults in the community.

(Added by Stats. 1973, Ch. 512.)

1203a.

In all counties and cities and counties the courts therein, having jurisdiction to impose punishment in misdemeanor cases, shall have the power to refer cases, demand reports and to do and require all things necessary to carry out the purposes of Section 1203 of this code insofar as they are in their nature applicable to misdemeanors. Any such court shall have power to suspend the imposing or the execution of the sentence, and to make and enforce the terms of probation for a period not to exceed three years; provided, that when the maximum sentence provided by law exceeds three years imprisonment, the period during which sentence may be suspended and terms of probation enforced may be for a longer period than three years, but in such instance, not to exceed the maximum time for which sentence of imprisonment might be pronounced.

(Amended by Stats. 1949, Ch. 504.)

1203b.

All courts shall have power to suspend the imposition or execution of a sentence and grant a conditional sentence in misdemeanor and infraction cases without referring such cases to the probation officer. Unless otherwise ordered by the court, persons granted a conditional sentence in the community shall report only to the court and the probation officer shall not be responsible in any way for supervising or accounting for such persons.

(Amended by Stats. 1982, Ch. 247, Sec. 2. Effective June 9, 1982.)

1203c.

(a) (1) Notwithstanding any other law, whenever a person is committed to an institution under the jurisdiction of the Department of Corrections and Rehabilitation, whether probation has been applied for or not, or granted and revoked, it shall be the duty of the probation officer of the county from which the person is committed to send to the Department of Corrections and Rehabilitation a report of the circumstances surrounding the offense and the prior record and history of the defendant, as may be required by the Secretary of the Department of Corrections and Rehabilitation.

(2) If the person is being committed to the jurisdiction of the department for a conviction of an offense that requires him or her to register as a sex offender pursuant to Section 290, the probation officer shall include in the report the results of the State-Authorized Risk Assessment Tool for Sex Offenders (SARATSO) administered pursuant to Sections 290.04 to 290.06, inclusive, if applicable.

(b) These reports shall accompany the commitment papers. The reports shall be prepared in the form prescribed by the administrator following consultation with the Board of State and Community Corrections, except that if the defendant is ineligible for probation, a report of the circumstances surrounding the offense and the prior record and history of the defendant, prepared by the probation officer on request of the court and filed with the court before sentence, shall be deemed to meet the requirements of paragraph (1) of subdivision (a).

(c) In order to allow the probation officer an opportunity to interview, for the purpose of preparation of these reports, the defendant shall be held in the county jail for 48 hours, excluding Saturdays, Sundays, and holidays, subsequent to imposition of sentence and prior to delivery to the custody of the Secretary of the Department of Corrections and Rehabilitation, unless the probation officer has indicated the need for a different period of time.

(d) Whenever a person is committed to an institution under the jurisdiction of the Department of Corrections and Rehabilitation or a county jail pursuant to subdivision (h) of Section 1170, or is placed on postrelease community supervision or mandatory supervision, and the court has ordered the person to pay restitution to a victim, the following shall apply:

(1) If the victim consents, the probation officer of the county from which the person is committed may send the victim's contact information and a copy of the restitution order to the department or to the county agency designated by the board of supervisors to collect and distribute restitution for the sole purpose of distributing the restitution collected on behalf of the victim.

(2) Notwithstanding paragraph (1), the district attorney of the county from which the person is committed may send the victim's contact information and a copy of the restitution order to the department or to the county agency designated by the board of supervisors to collect and distribute restitution for the sole purpose of distributing the restitution collected on behalf of the victim if the district attorney finds it is in the best interest of the victim to send that information. If the victim affirmatively objects, the district attorney shall not send the victim's contact information. The district attorney shall not be required to inform the victim of the right to object.

(3) The victim's contact information shall remain confidential and shall not be made part of the court file or combined with any public document.

(Amended by Stats. 2014, Ch. 517, Sec. 1. (SB 1197) Effective January 1, 2015.)

1203d.

No court shall pronounce judgment upon any defendant, as to whom the court has requested a probation report pursuant to Section 1203.10, unless a copy of the probation report has been made available to the court, the prosecuting attorney, and the defendant or his or her attorney, at least two days or, upon the request of the defendant, five days prior to the time fixed by the court for consideration of the report with respect to pronouncement of judgment. The report shall be filed with the clerk of the court as a record in the case at the time the court considers the report.

If the defendant is not represented by an attorney, the court, upon ordering the probation report, shall also order the probation officer who prepares the report to discuss its contents with the defendant. Any waiver of the preparation of the report or the consideration of the report by the court shall be as provided in subdivision (b) of Section 1203, with respect to cases to which that subdivision applies.

The sentence recommendations of the report shall also be made available to the victim of the crime, or the victim's next of kin if the victim has died, through the district attorney's office. The victim or the victim's next of kin shall be informed of the availability of this information through the notice provided pursuant to Section 1191.1.

(Amended by Stats. 1996, Ch. 123, Sec. 2. Effective January 1, 1997.)

1203e.

(a) Commencing June 1, 2010, the probation department shall compile a Facts of Offense Sheet for every person convicted of an offense that requires him or her to register as a sex offender pursuant to Section 290 who is referred to the department pursuant to Section 1203. The Facts of Offense Sheet shall contain the following information concerning the offender: name; CII number; criminal history, including all arrests and convictions for any registerable sex offenses or any violent offense; circumstances of the offense for which registration is required, including, but not limited to, weapons used and victim pattern; and results of the State-Authorized Risk Assessment Tool for Sex Offenders (SARATSO), as set forth in Section 290.04, if required. The Facts of Offense Sheet shall be included in the probation officer's report.

(b) The defendant may move the court to correct the Facts of Offense Sheet. Any corrections to that sheet shall be made consistent with procedures set forth in Section 1204.

(c) The probation officer shall send a copy of the Facts of Offense Sheet to the Department of Justice within 30 days of the person's sex offense conviction, and it shall

be made part of the registered sex offender's file maintained by the Department of Justice. The Facts of Offense Sheet shall thereafter be made available to law enforcement by the Department of Justice, which shall post it with the offender's record on the Department of Justice Internet Web site maintained pursuant to Section 290.46, and shall be accessible only to law enforcement.

(d) If the registered sex offender is sentenced to a period of incarceration, at either the state prison or a county jail, the Facts of Offense Sheet shall be sent by the Department of Corrections and Rehabilitation or the county sheriff to the registering law enforcement agency in the jurisdiction where the registered sex offender will be paroled or will live on release, within three days of the person's release. If the registered sex offender is committed to the State Department of State Hospitals, the Facts of Offense Sheet shall be sent by the State Department of State Hospitals to the registering law enforcement agency in the jurisdiction where the person will live on release, within three days of release.

(Amended by Stats. 2016, Ch. 59, Sec. 5. (SB 1474) Effective January 1, 2017.)

1203f.

Every probation department shall ensure that all probationers under active supervision who are deemed to pose a high risk to the public of committing sex crimes, as determined by the State-Authorized Risk Assessment Tool for Sex Offenders, as set forth in Sections 290.04 to 290.06, inclusive, are placed on intensive and specialized probation supervision and are required to report frequently to designated probation officers. The probation department may place any other probationer convicted of an offense that requires him or her to register as a sex offender who is on active supervision to be placed on intensive and specialized supervision and require him or her to report frequently to designated probation officers.

(Added by Stats. 2006, Ch. 337, Sec. 41. Effective September 20, 2006.)

1203h.

If the court initiates an investigation pursuant to subdivision (a) or (d) of Section 1203 and the convicted person was convicted of violating any section of this code in which a minor is a victim of an act of abuse or neglect, then the investigation may include a psychological evaluation to determine the extent of counseling necessary for successful rehabilitation and which may be mandated by the court during the term of probation. Such evaluation may be performed by psychiatrists, psychologists, or licensed clinical social workers. The results of the examination shall be included in the probation officer's report to the court.

(Amended by Stats. 1982, Ch. 282, Sec. 1.)

1204.

The circumstances shall be presented by the testimony of witnesses examined in open court, except that when a witness is so sick or infirm as to be unable to attend, his deposition may be taken by a magistrate of the county, out of court, upon such notice to the adverse party as the court may direct. No affidavit or testimony, or representation of any kind, verbal or written, can be offered to or received by the court, or a judge thereof, in aggravation or mitigation of the punishment, except as provided in this and the preceding section. This section shall not be construed to prohibit the filing of a written report by a defendant or defendant's counsel on behalf of a defendant if such a report presents a study of his background and personality and suggests a rehabilitation program. If such a report is submitted, the prosecution or probation officer shall be permitted to reply to or to evaluate the program.

(Amended by Stats. 1971, Ch. 1080.)

1204.5.

(a) In any criminal action, after the filing of any complaint or other accusatory pleading and before a plea, finding, or verdict of guilty, no judge shall read or consider any written report of any law enforcement officer or witness to any offense, any information reflecting the arrest or conviction record of a defendant, or any affidavit or representation of any kind, verbal or written, without the defendant's consent given in open court, except as provided in the rules of evidence applicable at the trial, or as provided in affidavits in connection with the issuance of a warrant or the hearing of any law and motion matter, or in any application for an order fixing or changing bail, or a petition for a writ.

(b) This section does not preclude a judge, who is not the preliminary hearing or trial judge in the case, from considering any information about the defendant for the purpose of that judge adopting a pre-trial sentencing position or approving or disapproving a guilty plea entered pursuant to Section 1192.5, if all of the following occur:

(1) The defendant is represented by counsel, unless he or she expressly waives the right to counsel.

(2) Any information provided to the judge for either of those purposes is also provided to the district attorney and to the defense counsel at least five days prior to any hearing or conference held for the purpose of considering a proposed guilty plea or proposed sentence.

(3) At any hearing or conference held for either of those purposes, defense counsel or the district attorney is allowed to provide information, either on or off the record, to supplement or rebut the information provided pursuant to paragraph (2).

(Amended by Stats. 1995, Ch. 86, Sec. 1. Effective January 1, 1996.)

1205.

(a) A judgment that the defendant pay a fine, with or without other punishment, may also direct that he or she be imprisoned until the fine is satisfied and may further direct that the imprisonment begin at and continue after the expiration of any imprisonment imposed as a part of the punishment or of any other imprisonment to which the defendant may have been sentenced. The judgment shall specify the term of imprisonment for nonpayment of the fine, which shall not be more than one day for each one hundred twenty-five dollars ($125) of the base fine, nor exceed the term for which the defendant may be sentenced to imprisonment for the offense of which he or she has been convicted. A defendant held in custody for nonpayment of a fine shall be entitled to credit on the fine for each day he or she is held in custody, at the rate specified in the judgment. When the defendant has been convicted of a misdemeanor, a judgment that the defendant pay a fine may also direct that he or she pay the fine within a limited time or in installments on specified dates, and that in default of payment as stipulated he or she be imprisoned in the discretion of the court either until the defaulted installment is satisfied or until the fine is satisfied in full; but unless the direction is given in the judgment, the fine shall be payable. If an amount of the base fine is not satisfied by jail credits, or by community service, the penalties and assessments imposed on the base fine shall be reduced by the percentage of the base fine that was satisfied.

(b) Except as otherwise provided in case of fines imposed, as a condition of probation, the defendant shall pay the fine to the clerk of the court, or to the judge if there is no clerk, unless the defendant is taken into custody for nonpayment of the fine, in which event payments made while he or she is in custody shall be made to the officer who holds the defendant in custody, and all amounts paid shall be paid over by the officer to the court that rendered the judgment. The clerk shall report to the court every default in payment of a fine or any part of that fine, or if there is no clerk, the court shall take notice of the default. If time has been given for payment of a fine or it has been made payable in installments, the court shall, upon any default in payment, immediately order the arrest of the defendant and order him or her to show cause why he or she should not be imprisoned until the fine or installment is satisfied in full. If the fine or installment is payable forthwith and it is not paid, the court shall, without further proceedings, immediately commit the defendant to the custody of the proper officer to be held in custody until the fine or installment is satisfied in full.

(c) This section applies to any violation of any of the codes or statutes of this state punishable by a fine or by a fine and imprisonment.

(d) Nothing in this section shall be construed to prohibit the clerk of the court, or the judge if there is no clerk, from turning these accounts over to another county department or a collecting agency for processing and collection.

(e) The defendant shall pay to the clerk of the court or the collecting agency a fee for the processing of installment accounts. This fee shall equal the administrative and clerical costs, as determined by the board of supervisors, or by the court, depending on which entity administers the account. The defendant shall pay to the clerk of the court or the collecting agency the fee established for the processing of the accounts receivable that are not to be paid in installments. The fee shall equal the administrative and clerical costs, as determined by the board of supervisors, or by the court, depending on which entity administers the account, except that the fee shall not exceed thirty dollars ($30).

(f) This section shall not apply to restitution fines and restitution orders.

(Amended by Stats. 2016, Ch. 769, Sec. 1. (AB 2839) Effective January 1, 2017.)

1205.3.

In any case in which a defendant is convicted of an offense and granted probation, and the court orders the defendant either to pay a fine or to perform specified community service work as a condition of probation, the court shall specify that if community service work is performed, it shall be performed in place of the payment of all fines and restitution fines on a proportional basis, and the court shall specify in its order the amount of the fine and restitution fine and the number of hours of community service work that shall be performed as an alternative to payment of the fine.

(Amended by Stats. 1996, Ch. 1077, Sec. 23. Effective January 1, 1997.)

1207.

When judgment upon a conviction is rendered, the clerk must enter the judgment in the minutes, stating briefly the offense for which the conviction was had, and the fact of a prior conviction, if any. A copy of the judgment of conviction shall be filed with the papers in the case.

(Amended by Stats. 2007, Ch. 263, Sec. 28. Effective January 1, 2008.)

1208.

(a) (1) The provisions of this section, insofar as they relate to employment, shall be operative in any county in which the board of supervisors by ordinance finds, on the basis of employment conditions, the state of the county jail facilities, and other pertinent circumstances, that the operation of this section, insofar as it relates to employment, in that county is feasible. The provisions of this section, insofar as they relate to job training, shall be operative in any county in which the board of supervisors by ordinance finds, on the basis of job training conditions, the state of the county jail facilities, and other pertinent circumstances, that the operation of this section, insofar as it relates to job training, in that county is feasible. The provisions of this section, insofar as they relate to education, shall be operative in any county in which the board of supervisors by ordinance finds, on the basis of education conditions, the state of the county jail facilities, and other pertinent circumstances, that the operation of this section, insofar as it relates to education, in that county is feasible. In any ordinance the board shall prescribe whether the sheriff, the probation officer, the director of the county department of corrections, or the superintendent of a county industrial farm or industrial road camp in the county shall perform the functions of the work furlough administrator. The board may, in that ordinance, provide for the performance of any or all functions of the work furlough administrator by any one or more of those persons, acting separately or jointly as to any of the functions; and may, by a subsequent ordinance, revise the provisions within the authorization of this section. The board of supervisors may also terminate the operation of this section, either with respect to employment, job training, or education in the county, if the board finds by ordinance that because of changed circumstances, the operation of this section, either with respect to employment, job training, or education in that county, is no longer feasible.

(2) Notwithstanding any other law, the board of supervisors may by ordinance designate a facility for confinement of prisoners classified for the work furlough program and designate the work furlough administrator as the custodian of the facility. The work furlough administrator may operate the work furlough facility or, with the approval of the board of supervisors, administer the work furlough facility pursuant to written contracts with appropriate public or private agencies or private entities. No agency or private entity may operate a work furlough program or facility without a written contract with the work furlough administrator, and no agency or private entity entering into a written contract may itself employ any person who is in the work furlough program. The sheriff or director of the county department of corrections, as the case may be, is authorized to transfer custody of prisoners to the work furlough administrator to be confined in a facility for the period during which they are in the work furlough program.

(3) All privately operated local work furlough facilities and programs shall be under the jurisdiction of, and subject to the terms of a written contract entered into with, the work furlough administrator. Each contract shall include, but not be limited to, a provision whereby the private agency or entity agrees to operate in compliance with all appropriate state and local building, zoning, health, safety, and fire statutes, ordinances, and regulations and the minimum jail standards for Type IV facilities as established by regulations adopted by the Board of State and Community Corrections, and a provision whereby the private agency or entity agrees to operate in compliance with Section 1208.2, which provides that no eligible person shall be denied consideration for, or be removed from, participation in a work furlough program because of an inability to pay all or a portion of the program fees. The private agency or entity shall select and train its personnel in accordance with selection and training requirements adopted by the Board of State and Community Corrections as set forth in Subchapter 1 (commencing with Section 100) of Chapter 1 of Division 1 of Title 15 of the California Code of Regulations. Failure to comply with the appropriate health, safety, and fire laws or minimum jail standards adopted by the board may be cause for termination of the contract. Upon discovery of a failure to comply with these requirements, the work furlough administrator shall notify the privately operated program director that the contract may be canceled if the specified deficiencies are not corrected within 60 days.

(4) All private work furlough facilities and programs shall be inspected biennially by the Board of State and Community Corrections unless the work furlough administrator requests an earlier inspection pursuant to Section 6031.1. Each private agency or entity shall pay a fee to the Board of State and Community Corrections commensurate with the cost of those inspections and a fee commensurate with the cost of the initial review of the facility.

(b) When a person is convicted and sentenced to the county jail, or is imprisoned in the county jail for nonpayment of a fine, for contempt, or as a condition of probation for any criminal offense, the work furlough administrator may, if he or she concludes that the person is a fit subject to continue in his or her regular employment, direct that the person be permitted to continue in that employment, if that is compatible with the requirements of subdivision (c), or may authorize the person to secure employment for himself or herself, unless the court at the time of sentencing or committing has ordered that the person not be granted work furloughs. The work furlough administrator may, if he or she concludes that the person is a fit subject to continue in his or her job training program, direct that the person be permitted to continue in that job training program, if that is compatible with the requirements of subdivision (c), or may authorize the person to secure local job training for himself or herself, unless the court at the time of sentencing has ordered that person not be granted work furloughs. The work furlough administrator may, if he or she concludes that the person is a fit subject to continue in his or her regular educational program, direct that the person be permitted to continue in that educational program, if that is compatible with the requirements of subdivision (c), or may authorize the person to secure education for himself or herself, unless the court at the time of sentencing has ordered that person not be granted work furloughs.

(c) If the work furlough administrator so directs that the prisoner be permitted to continue in his or her regular employment, job training, or educational program, the administrator shall arrange for a continuation of that employment or for that job training or education, so far as possible without interruption. If the prisoner does not have regular employment or a regular job training or educational program, and the administrator has authorized the prisoner to secure employment, job training, or education for himself or herself, the prisoner may do so, and the administrator may assist the prisoner in doing so. Any employment, job training, or education so secured shall be suitable for the prisoner. The employment, and the job training or educational program if it includes earnings by the prisoner, shall be at a wage at least as high as the prevailing wage for similar work in the area where the work is performed and in accordance with the prevailing working conditions in that area. In no event may any employment, job training, or educational program involving earnings by the prisoner be permitted where there is a labor dispute in the establishment in which the prisoner is, or is to be, employed, trained, or educated.

(d) (1) Whenever the prisoner is not employed or being trained or educated and between the hours or periods of employment, training, or education, the prisoner shall be confined in the facility designated by the board of supervisors for work furlough confinement unless the work furlough administrator directs otherwise. If the prisoner is injured during a period of employment, job training, or education, the work furlough administrator shall have the authority to release him or her from the facility for continued medical treatment by private physicians or at medical facilities at the expense of the employer, workers' compensation insurer, or the prisoner. The release shall not be construed as assumption of liability by the county or work furlough administrator for medical treatment obtained.

(2) The work furlough administrator may release any prisoner classified for the work furlough program for a period not to exceed 72 hours for medical, dental, or psychiatric care, or for family emergencies or pressing business which would result in severe hardship if the release were not granted, or to attend those activities as the administrator deems may effectively promote the prisoner's successful return to the community, including, but not limited to, an attempt to secure housing, employment, entry into educational programs, or participation in community programs.

(e) The earnings of the prisoner may be collected by the work furlough administrator, and it shall be the duty of the prisoner's employer to transmit the wages to the administrator at the latter's request. Earnings levied upon pursuant to writ of execution or in other lawful manner shall not be transmitted to the administrator. If the administrator has requested transmittal of earnings prior to levy, that request shall have priority. In a case in which the functions of the administrator are performed by a sheriff, and the sheriff receives a writ of execution for the earnings of a prisoner subject to this section but has not yet requested transmittal of the prisoner's earnings pursuant to this section, the sheriff shall first levy on the earnings pursuant to the writ. When an employer or educator transmits earnings to the administrator pursuant to this subdivision, the sheriff shall have no liability to the prisoner for those earnings. From the earnings the administrator shall pay the prisoner's board and personal expenses, both inside and outside the jail, and shall deduct so much of the costs of administration of this section as is allocable to the prisoner or if the prisoner is unable to pay that sum, a lesser sum as is reasonable, and, in an amount determined by the administrator, shall pay the support of the prisoner's dependents, if any. If sufficient funds are available after making the foregoing payments, the administrator may, with the consent of the prisoner, pay, in whole or in part, the preexisting debts of the prisoner. Any balance shall be retained until the prisoner's discharge. Upon discharge the balance shall be paid to the prisoner.

(f) The prisoner shall be eligible for time credits pursuant to Sections 4018 and 4019.

(g) If the prisoner violates the conditions laid down for his or her conduct, custody, job training, education, or employment, the work furlough administrator may order the balance of the prisoner's sentence to be spent in actual confinement.

(h) Willful failure of the prisoner to return to the place of confinement not later than the expiration of any period during which he or she is authorized to be away from the place of confinement pursuant to this section is punishable as provided in Section 4532.

(i) The court may recommend or refer a person to the work furlough administrator for consideration for placement in the work furlough program or a particular work furlough facility. The recommendation or referral of the court shall be given great weight in the determination of acceptance or denial for placement in the work furlough program or a particular work furlough facility.

(j) As used in this section, the following definitions apply:

(1) "Education" includes vocational and educational training and counseling, and psychological, drug abuse, alcoholic, and other rehabilitative counseling.

(2) "Educator" includes a person or institution providing that training or counseling.

(3) "Employment" includes care of children, including the daytime care of children of the prisoner.

(4) "Job training" may include, but shall not be limited to, job training assistance.

(k) This section shall be known and may be cited as the "Cobey Work Furlough Law."

(Amended by Stats. 2014, Ch. 71, Sec. 127. (SB 1304) Effective January 1, 2015.)

1208.2.

(a) (1) This section shall apply to individuals authorized to participate in a work furlough program pursuant to Section 1208, or to individuals authorized to participate in an electronic home detention program pursuant to Section 1203.016 or 1203.018, or to individuals authorized to participate in a county parole program pursuant to Article 3.5 (commencing with Section 3074) of Chapter 8 of Title 1 of Part 3.

(2) As used in this section, as appropriate, "administrator" means the sheriff, probation officer, director of the county department of corrections, or county parole administrator.

(b) (1) A board of supervisors that implements programs identified in paragraph (1) of subdivision (a), may prescribe a program administrative fee and an application fee, that together shall not exceed the pro rata cost of the program to which the person is accepted, including equipment, supervision, and other operating costs, except as provided in paragraphs (2) and (3).

(2) With regard to a privately operated electronic home detention program pursuant to Section 1203.016 or 1203.018, the limitation, described in paragraph (1), in prescribing a program administrative fee and application fee shall not apply.

(3) With regard to an electronic home detention program operated pursuant to Section 1203.016, whether or not the program is privately operated, any administrative fee or application fee prescribed by a board of supervisors shall only apply to adults over 21 years of age and under the jurisdiction of the criminal court.

(c) The correctional administrator, or his or her designee, shall not have access to a person's financial data prior to granting or denying a person's participation in, or assigning a person to, any of the programs governed by this section.

(d) The correctional administrator, or his or her designee, shall not consider a person's ability or inability to pay all or a portion of the program fee for the purposes of granting or denying a person's participation in, or assigning a person to, any of the programs governed by this section.

(e) For purposes of this section, "ability to pay" means the overall capability of the person to reimburse the costs, or a portion of the costs, of providing supervision and shall include, but shall not be limited to, consideration of all of the following factors:

(1) Present financial position.

(2) Reasonably discernible future financial position. In no event shall the administrator, or his or her designee, consider a period of more than six months from the date of acceptance into the program for purposes of determining reasonably discernible future financial position.

(3) Likelihood that the person shall be able to obtain employment within the six-month period from the date of acceptance into the program.

(4) Any other factor that may bear upon the person's financial capability to reimburse the county for the fees fixed pursuant to subdivision (b).

(f) The administrator, or his or her designee, may charge a person the fee set by the board of supervisors or any portion of the fee and may determine the method and frequency of payment. Any fee the administrator, or his or her designee, charges pursuant to this section shall not in any case be in excess of the fee set by the board of supervisors and shall be based on the person's ability to pay. The administrator, or his or her designee, shall have the option to waive the fees for program supervision when deemed necessary, justified, or in the interests of justice. The fees charged for program supervision may be modified or waived at any time based on the changing financial position of the person. All fees paid by persons for program supervision shall be deposited into the general fund of the county.

(g) No person shall be denied consideration for, or be removed from, participation in any of the programs to which this section applies because of an inability to pay all or a portion of the program supervision fees. At any time during a person's sentence, the person may request that the administrator, or his or her designee, modify or suspend the payment of fees on the grounds of a change in circumstances with regard to the person's ability to pay.

(h) If the person and the administrator, or his or her designee, are unable to come to an agreement regarding the person's ability to pay, or the amount that is to be paid, or the method and frequency with which payment is to be made, the administrator, or his or her designee, shall advise the appropriate court of the fact that the person and administrator, or his or her designee, have not been able to reach agreement and the court shall then resolve the disagreement by determining the person's ability to pay, the amount that is to be paid, and the method and frequency with which payment is to be made.

(i) At the time a person is approved for any of the programs to which this section applies, the administrator, or his or her designee, shall furnish the person a written statement of the person's rights in regard to the program for which the person has been approved, including, but not limited to, both of the following:

(1) The fact that the person cannot be denied consideration for or removed from participation in the program because of an inability to pay.

(2) The fact that if the person is unable to reach agreement with the administrator, or his or her designee, regarding the person's ability to pay, the amount that is to be paid, or the manner and frequency with which payment is to be made, that the matter shall be referred to the court to resolve the differences.

(j) In all circumstances where a county board of supervisors has approved a program administrator, as described in Section 1203.016, 1203.018, or 1208, to enter into a contract with a private agency or entity to provide specified program services, the program administrator shall ensure that the provisions of this section are contained within any contractual agreement for this purpose. All privately operated home detention programs shall comply with all appropriate, applicable ordinances and regulations specified in subdivision (a) of Section 1208.

(Amended by Stats. 2017, Ch. 678, Sec. 4. (SB 190) Effective January 1, 2018.)
1208.3.
The administrator is not prohibited by subdivision (c) of Section 1208.2 from verifying any of the following:

(a) That the prisoner is receiving wages at a rate of pay not less than the prevailing minimum wage requirement as provided for in subdivision (c) of Section 1208.

(b) That the prisoner is working a specified minimum number of required hours.

(c) That the prisoner is covered under an appropriate or suitable workers' compensation insurance plan as may otherwise be required by law.

The purpose of the verification shall be solely to insure that the prisoner's employment rights are being protected, that the prisoner is not being taken advantage of, that the job is suitable for the prisoner, and that the prisoner is making every reasonable effort to make a productive contribution to the community.

(Added by Stats. 1999, Ch. 113, Sec. 2. Effective January 1, 2000.)
1208.5.
The boards of supervisors of two or more counties having work furlough programs may enter into agreements whereby a person sentenced to, or imprisoned in, the jail of one county, but regularly residing in another county or regularly employed in another county, may be transferred by the sheriff of the county in which he or she is confined to the jail of the county in which he or she resides or is employed, in order that he or she may be enabled to continue in his or her regular employment or education in the other county through the county's work furlough program. This agreement may make provision for the support of transferred persons by the county from which they are transferred. The board of supervisors of any county may, by ordinance, delegate the authority to enter into these agreements to the work furlough administrator.

This section shall become operative on January 1, 1999.

(Amended (as added by Stats. 1991, Ch. 437, Sec. 8) by Stats. 1994, Ch. 770, Sec. 5. Effective January 1, 1995. Section operative January 1, 1999, by its own provisions.)
1209.
Upon conviction of any criminal offense for which the court orders the confinement of a person in the county jail, or other suitable place of confinement, either as the final sentence or as a condition of any grant of probation, and allows the person so sentenced to continue in his or her regular employment by serving the sentence on weekends or similar periods during the week other than their regular workdays and by virtue of this schedule of serving the sentence the prisoner is ineligible for work furlough under Section 1208, the county may collect from the defendant according to the defendant's ability to pay so much of the costs of administration of this section as are allocable to such defendant. The amount of this fee shall not exceed the actual costs of such confinement and may be collected prior to completion of each weekly or monthly period of confinement until the entire sentence has been served, and the funds shall be deposited in the county treasury pursuant to county ordinance.

The court, upon allowing sentences to be served on weekends or other nonemployment days, shall conduct a hearing to determine if the defendant has the ability to pay all or a part of the costs of administration without resulting in unnecessary economic hardship to the defendant and his or her dependents. At the hearing, the defendant shall be entitled to have, but shall not be limited to, the opportunity to be heard in person, to present witnesses and other documentary evidence, and to confront and cross-examine adverse witnesses, and to disclosure of the evidence against the defendant, and a written statement of the findings of the court. If the court determines that the defendant has the ability to pay all or part of the costs of administration without resulting in unnecessary economic hardship to the defendant and his or her dependents, the court shall advise the defendant of the provisions of this section and order him or her to pay all or part of the fee as required by the sheriff, probation officer, or Director of the County Department of Corrections, whichever the case may be. In making a determination of whether a defendant has the ability to pay, the court shall take into account the amount of any fine imposed upon the defendant and any amount the defendant has been ordered to pay in restitution.

As used in this section, the term "ability to pay" means the overall capability of the defendant to reimburse the costs, or a portion of the costs, and shall include, but shall not be limited to, the following:

(a) The defendant's present financial position.

(b) The defendant's reasonably discernible future financial position. In no event shall the court consider a period of more than six months from the date of the hearing for purposes of determining reasonably discernible future financial position.

(c) Likelihood that the defendant shall be able to obtain employment within the six-month period from the date of the hearing.

(d) Any other factor or factors which may bear upon the defendant's financial capability to reimburse the county for the costs.

Execution may be issued on the order in the same manner as a judgment in a civil action.

The order to pay all or part shall not be enforced by contempt. At any time during the pendency of the judgment, a defendant against whom a judgment has been rendered may petition the rendering court to modify or vacate its previous judgment on the grounds of a change of circumstances with regard to the defendant's ability to pay the judgment. The court shall advise the defendant of this right at the time of making the judgment.

(Amended by Stats. 1983, Ch. 779, Sec. 1.)
1209.5.
(a) Notwithstanding any other law, the court shall permit a person convicted of an infraction, upon a showing that payment of the total fine would pose a hardship on the defendant or his or her family, to elect to perform community service in lieu of the total fine that would otherwise be imposed.

(b) For purposes of this section, the term "total fine" means the total bail, including the base fine and all assessments, penalties, and additional moneys to be paid by the defendant.

(c) (1) For purposes of this section, the hourly rate applicable to community service performed pursuant to this section shall be double the minimum wage set for the applicable calendar year, based on the schedule for an employer who employs 25 or fewer employees, as established in paragraph (2) of subdivision (b) of Section 1182.12 of the Labor Code.

(2) Notwithstanding paragraph (1), a court may by local rule increase the amount that is credited for each hour of community service performed pursuant to this section, to exceed the hourly rate described in paragraph (1).

(Amended by Stats. 2018, Ch. 280, Sec. 1. (AB 2532) Effective January 1, 2019.)
1210.
As used in Sections 1210.1 and 3063.1 of this code, and Division 10.8 (commencing with Section 11999.4) of the Health and Safety Code, the following definitions apply:

(a) The term "nonviolent drug possession offense" means the unlawful personal use, possession for personal use, or transportation for personal use of any controlled substance identified in Section 11054, 11055, 11056, 11057 or 11058 of the Health and Safety Code, or the offense of being under the influence of a controlled substance in violation of Section 11550 of the Health and Safety Code. The term "nonviolent drug possession offense" does not include the possession for sale, production, or manufacturing of any controlled substance and does not include violations of Section 4573.6 or 4573.8.

(b) The term "drug treatment program" or "drug treatment" means a state licensed or certified community drug treatment program, which may include one or more of the following: drug education, outpatient services, narcotic replacement therapy, residential treatment, detoxification services, and aftercare services. The term "drug treatment program" or "drug treatment" includes a drug treatment program operated under the direction of the Veterans Health Administration of the Department of Veterans Affairs or a program specified in Section 8001. That type of program shall be eligible to provide drug treatment services without regard to the licensing or certification provisions required by this subdivision. The term "drug treatment program" or "drug treatment" does not include drug treatment programs offered in a prison or jail facility.

(c) The term "successful completion of treatment" means that a defendant who has had drug treatment imposed as a condition of probation has completed the prescribed course of drug treatment as recommended by the treatment provider and ordered by the court and, as a result, there is reasonable cause to believe that the defendant will not abuse controlled substances in the future. Completion of treatment shall not require cessation of narcotic replacement therapy.

(d) The term "misdemeanor not related to the use of drugs" means a misdemeanor that does not involve (1) the simple possession or use of drugs or drug paraphernalia, being present where drugs are used, or failure to register as a drug offender, or (2) any activity similar to those listed in (1).

(Amended by Stats. 2006, Ch. 63, Sec. 6. Effective July 12, 2006. Note: This section was added on Nov. 7, 2000, by initiative Prop. 36.)
1210.1.
(a) Notwithstanding any other provision of law, and except as provided in subdivision (b), any person convicted of a nonviolent drug possession offense shall receive probation. As a condition of probation the court shall require participation in and completion of an appropriate drug treatment program. The court shall impose appropriate drug testing as a condition of probation. The court may also impose, as a condition of probation, participation in vocational training, family counseling, literacy training and/or community service. A court may not impose incarceration as an additional condition of probation. Aside from the limitations imposed in this subdivision, the trial court is not otherwise limited in the type of probation conditions it may impose. Probation shall be imposed by suspending the imposition of sentence. No person shall be denied the opportunity to benefit from the provisions of the Substance Abuse and Crime Prevention Act of 2000 based solely upon evidence of a co-occurring psychiatric or developmental disorder. To the greatest extent possible, any person who is convicted of, and placed on probation pursuant to this section for a nonviolent drug possession offense shall be monitored by the court through the use of a dedicated court calendar and the incorporation of a collaborative court model of oversight that includes close collaboration with treatment providers and probation, drug testing commensurate with treatment needs, and supervision of progress through review hearings.

In addition to any fine assessed under other provisions of law, the trial judge may require any person convicted of a nonviolent drug possession offense who is reasonably able to do so to contribute to the cost of his or her own placement in a drug treatment program.

(b) Subdivision (a) shall not apply to any of the following:

(1) Any defendant who previously has been convicted of one or more violent or serious felonies as defined in subdivision (c) of Section 667.5 or subdivision (c) of Section 1192.7, respectively, unless the nonviolent drug possession offense occurred after a period of five years in which the defendant remained free of both prison custody and the commission of an offense that results in a felony conviction other than a nonviolent drug possession offense, or a misdemeanor conviction involving physical injury or the threat of physical injury to another person.

(2) Any defendant who, in addition to one or more nonviolent drug possession offenses, has been convicted in the same proceeding of a misdemeanor not related to the use of drugs or any felony.

(3) Any defendant who, while armed with a deadly weapon, with the intent to use the same as a deadly weapon, unlawfully possesses or is under the influence of any controlled substance identified in Section 11054, 11055, 11056, 11057, or 11058 of the Health and Safety Code.

(4) Any defendant who refuses drug treatment as a condition of probation.

(5) Any defendant who has two separate convictions for nonviolent drug possession offenses, has participated in two separate courses of drug treatment pursuant to subdivision (a), and is found by the court, by clear and convincing evidence, to be unamenable to any and all forms of available drug treatment, as defined in subdivision (b) of Section 1210. Notwithstanding any other provision of law, the trial court shall sentence that defendant to 30 days in jail.

(c) (1) Any defendant who has previously been convicted of at least three non-drug-related felonies for which the defendant has served three separate prison terms within the meaning of subdivision (b) of Section 667.5 shall be presumed eligible for treatment under subdivision (a). The court may exclude the defendant from treatment under subdivision (a) where the court, pursuant to the motion of the prosecutor or its own motion, finds that the defendant poses a present danger to the safety of others and would not benefit from a drug treatment program. The court shall, on the record, state its findings, the reasons for those findings.
(2) Any defendant who has previously been convicted of a misdemeanor or felony at least five times within the prior 30 months shall be presumed to be eligible for treatment under subdivision (a). The court may exclude the defendant from treatment under subdivision (a) if the court, pursuant to the motion of the prosecutor, or on its own motion, finds that the defendant poses a present danger to the safety of others or would not benefit from a drug treatment program. The court shall, on the record, state its findings and the reasons for those findings.
(d) Within seven days of an order imposing probation under subdivision (a), the probation department shall notify the drug treatment provider designated to provide drug treatment under subdivision (a). Within 30 days of receiving that notice, the treatment provider shall prepare a treatment plan and forward it to the probation department for distribution to the court and counsel. The treatment provider shall provide to the probation department standardized treatment progress reports, with minimum data elements as determined by the department, including all drug testing results. At a minimum, the reports shall be provided to the court every 90 days, or more frequently, as the court directs.
(1) If at any point during the course of drug treatment the treatment provider notifies the probation department and the court that the defendant is unamenable to the drug treatment being provided, but may be amenable to other drug treatments or related programs, the probation department may move the court to modify the terms of probation, or on its own motion, the court may modify the terms of probation after a hearing to ensure that the defendant receives the alternative drug treatment or program.
(2) If at any point during the course of drug treatment the treatment provider notifies the probation department and the court that the defendant is unamenable to the drug treatment provided and all other forms of drug treatment programs pursuant to subdivision (b) of Section 1210, the probation department may move to revoke probation. At the revocation hearing, if it is proved that the defendant is unamenable to all drug treatment programs pursuant to subdivision (b) of Section 1210, the court may revoke probation.
(3) Drug treatment services provided by subdivision (a) as a required condition of probation may not exceed 12 months, unless the court makes a finding supported by the record, that the continuation of treatment services beyond 12 months is necessary for drug treatment to be successful. If that finding is made, the court may order up to two six-month extensions of treatment services. The provision of treatment services under the Substance Abuse and Crime Prevention Act of 2000 shall not exceed 24 months.
(e) (1) At any time after completion of drug treatment and the terms of probation, the court shall conduct a hearing, and if the court finds that the defendant successfully completed drug treatment, and substantially complied with the conditions of probation, including refraining from the use of drugs after the completion of treatment, the conviction on which the probation was based shall be set aside and the court shall dismiss the indictment, complaint, or information against the defendant. In addition, except as provided in paragraphs (2) and (3), both the arrest and the conviction shall be deemed never to have occurred. The defendant may additionally petition the court for a dismissal of charges at any time after completion of the prescribed course of drug treatment. Except as provided in paragraph (2) or (3), the defendant shall thereafter be released from all penalties and disabilities resulting from the offense of which he or she has been convicted.
(2) Dismissal of an indictment, complaint, or information pursuant to paragraph (1) does not permit a person to own, possess, or have in his or her custody or control any firearm capable of being concealed upon the person or prevent his or her conviction under Chapter 2 (commencing with Section 29800) of Division 9 of Title 4 of Part 6.
(3) Except as provided below, after an indictment, complaint, or information is dismissed pursuant to paragraph (1), the defendant may indicate in response to any question concerning his or her prior criminal record that he or she was not arrested or convicted for the offense. Except as provided below, a record pertaining to an arrest or conviction resulting in successful completion of a drug treatment program under this section may not, without the defendant's consent, be used in any way that could result in the denial of any employment, benefit, license, or certificate.
Regardless of his or her successful completion of drug treatment, the arrest and conviction on which the probation was based may be recorded by the Department of Justice and disclosed in response to any peace officer application request or any law enforcement inquiry. Dismissal of an information, complaint, or indictment under this section does not relieve a defendant of the obligation to disclose the arrest and conviction in response to any direct question contained in any questionnaire or application for public office, for a position as a peace officer as defined in Section 830, for licensure by any state or local agency, for contracting with the California State Lottery, or for purposes of serving on a jury.
(f) (1) If probation is revoked pursuant to the provisions of this subdivision, the defendant may be incarcerated pursuant to otherwise applicable law without regard to the provisions of this section. The court may modify or revoke probation if the alleged violation is proved.
(2) If a defendant receives probation under subdivision (a), and violates that probation either by committing an offense that is not a nonviolent drug possession offense, or by violating a non-drug-related condition of probation, and the state moves to revoke probation, the court may remand the defendant for a period not exceeding 30 days during which time the court may receive input from treatment, probation, the state, and the defendant, and the court may conduct further hearings as it deems appropriate to determine whether or not probation should be reinstated under this section. If the court reinstates the defendant on probation, the court may modify the treatment plan and any other terms of probation, and continue the defendant in a treatment program under the Substance Abuse and Crime Prevention Act of 2000. If the court reinstates the defendant on probation, the court may, after receiving input from the treatment provider and probation, if available, intensify or alter the treatment plan under subdivision (a), and impose sanctions, including jail sanctions not exceeding 30 days, a tool to enhance treatment compliance.
(3) (A) If a defendant receives probation under subdivision (a), and violates that probation either by committing a nonviolent drug possession offense, or a misdemeanor for simple possession or use of drugs or drug paraphernalia, being present where drugs are used, or failure to register as a drug offender, or any activity similar to those listed in subdivision (d) of Section 1210, or by violating a drug-related condition of probation, and the state moves to revoke probation, the court shall conduct a hearing to determine whether probation shall be revoked. The trial court shall revoke probation if the alleged probation violation is proved and the state proves by a preponderance of the evidence that the defendant poses a danger to the safety of others. If the court does not revoke probation, it may intensify or alter the drug treatment plan and in addition, if the violation does not involve the recent use of drugs as a circumstance of the violation, including, but not limited to, violations relating to failure to appear at treatment or court, noncompliance with treatment, and failure to report for drug testing, the court may impose sanctions including jail sanctions that may not exceed 48 hours of continuous custody as a tool to enhance treatment compliance and impose other changes in the terms and conditions of probation. The court shall consider, among other factors, the seriousness of the violation, previous treatment compliance, employment, education, vocational training, medical conditions, medical treatment, including narcotics replacement treatment, and including the opinion of the defendant's licensed and treating physician if immediately available and presented at the hearing, child support obligations, and family responsibilities. The court shall consider additional conditions of probation, which may include, but are not limited to, community service and supervised work programs. If one of the circumstances of the violation involves recent drug use, as well as other circumstances of violation, and the circumstance of recent drug use is demonstrated to the court by satisfactory evidence and a finding made on the record, the court may, after receiving input from treatment and probation, if available, direct the defendant to enter a licensed detoxification or residential treatment facility, and if there is no bed immediately available in that type of facility, the court may order that the defendant be confined in a county jail for detoxification purposes only, if the jail offers detoxification services, for a period not to exceed 10 days. The detoxification services must provide narcotic replacement therapy for those defendants presently actually receiving narcotic replacement therapy.
(B) If a defendant receives probation under subdivision (a), and for the second time violates that probation either by committing a nonviolent drug possession offense, or a misdemeanor for simple possession or use of drugs or drug paraphernalia, being present where drugs are used, or failure to register as a drug offender, or any activity similar to those listed in subdivision (d) of Section 1210, or by violating a drug-related condition of probation, and the state moves to revoke probation, the court shall conduct a hearing to determine whether probation shall be revoked. The trial court shall revoke probation if the alleged probation violation is proved and the state proves by a preponderance of the evidence either that the defendant poses a danger to the safety of others or is unamenable to drug treatment. In determining whether a defendant is unamenable to drug treatment, the court may consider, to the extent relevant, whether the defendant (i) has committed a serious violation of rules at the drug treatment program, (ii) has repeatedly committed violations of program rules that inhibit the defendant's ability to function in the program, or (iii) has continually refused to participate in the program or asked to be removed from the program. If the court does not revoke probation, it may intensify or alter the drug treatment plan, and may, in addition, if the violation does not involve the recent use of drugs as a circumstance of the violation, including, but not limited to, violations relating to failure to appear at treatment or court, noncompliance with treatment, and failure to report for drug testing, impose sanctions including jail sanctions that may not exceed 120 hours of continuous custody as a tool to enhance treatment compliance and impose other changes in the terms and conditions of probation. The court shall consider, among other factors, the seriousness of the violation, previous treatment compliance, employment, education, vocational training, medical conditions, medical treatment, including narcotics replacement treatment, and including the opinion of the defendant's licensed and treating physician if immediately available and presented at the hearing, child support obligations, and family responsibilities. The court shall consider additional conditions of probation, which may include, but are not limited to, community service and supervised work programs. If one of the circumstances of the violation involves recent drug use, as well as other circumstances of violation, and the circumstance of recent drug use is demonstrated to the court by satisfactory evidence and a finding made on the record, the court may, after receiving input from treatment and probation, if available, direct the defendant to enter a licensed detoxification or residential treatment facility, and if there is no bed immediately available in the facility, the court may order that the defendant be confined in a county jail for detoxification purposes only, if the jail offers detoxification services, for a period not to exceed 10 days. Detoxification services must provide narcotic replacement therapy for those defendants presently actually receiving narcotic replacement therapy.
(C) If a defendant receives probation under subdivision (a), and for the third or subsequent time violates that probation either by committing a nonviolent drug possession offense, or by violating a drug-related condition of probation, and the state moves for a third or subsequent time to revoke probation, the court shall conduct a hearing to determine whether probation shall be revoked. If the alleged probation violation is proved, the defendant is not eligible for continued probation under subdivision (a) unless the court determines that the defendant is not a danger to the community and would benefit from further treatment under subdivision (a). The court may then either intensify or alter the treatment plan under subdivision (a) or transfer the defendant to a highly structured drug court. If the court continues the defendant in treatment under subdivision (a), or drug court, the court may impose appropriate sanctions including jail sanctions as the court deems appropriate.
(D) If a defendant on probation at the effective date of this act for a nonviolent drug possession offense violates that probation either by committing a nonviolent drug possession offense, or a misdemeanor for simple possession or use of drugs or drug paraphernalia, being present where drugs are used, or failure to register as a drug offender, or any activity similar to those listed in subdivision (d) of Section 1210, or by violating a drug-related condition of probation, and the state moves to revoke probation, the court shall conduct a hearing to determine whether probation shall be revoked. The trial court shall revoke probation if the alleged probation violation is proved and the state proves by a preponderance of the evidence that the defendant poses a danger to the safety of others. If the court does not revoke probation, it may modify or alter the treatment plan, and in addition, if the violation does not involve the recent use of drugs as a circumstance of the violation, including, but not limited to, violations relating to failure to appear at treatment or court, noncompliance with treatment, and failure to report for drug testing, the court may impose sanctions including jail sanctions that may not exceed 48 hours of continuous custody as a tool to enhance treatment compliance and impose other changes in the terms and conditions of probation. The court shall consider, among other factors, the seriousness of the violation, previous treatment compliance, employment, education, vocational training, medical conditions, medical treatment, including narcotics replacement treatment, and including the opinion of the defendant's licensed and treating physician if immediately available and presented at the hearing, child support obligations, and family responsibilities. The court shall consider additional conditions of probation, which may include, but are not limited to, community service and supervised work programs. If one of the circumstances of the violation involves recent drug use, as well as other circumstances of violation, and the circumstance of recent drug use is demonstrated to the court by satisfactory evidence and a finding made on the record, the court may, after receiving input from treatment and probation, if available, direct the defendant to enter a licensed detoxification or residential treatment facility, and if there is no bed immediately available in that type of facility, the court may order that the defendant be confined in a county jail for detoxification purposes only, if the jail offers detoxification services, for a period not to exceed 10 days. The detoxification services must provide narcotic replacement therapy for those defendants presently actually receiving narcotic replacement therapy.
(E) If a defendant on probation at the effective date of this act for a nonviolent drug possession offense violates that probation a second time either by committing a nonviolent drug possession offense, or a misdemeanor for simple possession or use of drugs or drug paraphernalia, being present where drugs are used, or failure to register as a drug offender, or any activity similar to those listed in subdivision (d) of Section 1210, or by violating a drug-related condition of probation, and the state moves for a second time to revoke probation, the court shall conduct a hearing to determine whether probation shall be revoked. The trial court shall revoke probation if the alleged

probation violation is proved and the state proves by a preponderance of the evidence either that the defendant poses a danger to the safety of others or that the defendant is unamenable to drug treatment. If the court does not revoke probation, it may modify or alter the treatment plan, and in addition, if the violation does not involve the recent use of drugs as a circumstance of the violation, including, but not limited to, violations relating to failure to appear at treatment or court, noncompliance with treatment, and failure to report for drug testing, the court may impose sanctions including jail sanctions that may not exceed 120 hours of continuous custody as a tool to enhance treatment compliance and impose other changes in the terms and conditions of probation. The court shall consider, among other factors, the seriousness of the violation, previous treatment compliance, employment, education, vocational training, medical conditions, medical treatment including narcotics replacement treatment, and including the opinion of the defendant's licensed and treating physician if immediately available and presented at the hearing, child support obligations, and family responsibilities. The court shall consider additional conditions of probation, which may include, but are not limited to, community service and supervised work programs. If one of the circumstances of the violation involves recent drug use, as well as other circumstances of violation, and the circumstance of recent drug use is demonstrated to the court by satisfactory evidence and a finding made on the record, the court may, after receiving input from treatment and probation, if available, direct the defendant to enter a licensed detoxification or residential treatment facility, and if there is no bed immediately available in that type of facility, the court may order that the defendant be confined in a county jail for detoxification purposes only, if the jail offers detoxification services, for a period not to exceed 10 days. The detoxification services must provide narcotic replacement therapy for those defendants presently actually receiving narcotic replacement therapy.

(F) If a defendant on probation at the effective date of this act for a nonviolent drug offense violates that probation a third or subsequent time either by committing a nonviolent drug possession offense, or by violating a drug-related condition of probation, and the state moves for a third or subsequent time to revoke probation, the court shall conduct a hearing to determine whether probation shall be revoked. If the alleged probation violation is proved, the defendant is not eligible for continued probation under subdivision (a), unless the court determines that the defendant is not a danger to the community and would benefit from further treatment under subdivision (a). The court may then either intensify or alter the treatment plan under subdivision (a) or transfer the defendant to a highly structured drug court. If the court continues the defendant in treatment under subdivision (a), or drug court, the court may impose appropriate sanctions including jail sanctions.

(g) The term "drug-related condition of probation" shall include a probationer's specific drug treatment regimen, employment, vocational training, educational programs, psychological counseling, and family counseling.

(Amended by Stats. 2010, Ch. 178, Sec. 78. (SB 1115) Effective January 1, 2011. Operative January 1, 2012, by Sec. 107 of Ch. 178. Note: This section was added on Nov. 7, 2000, by initiative Prop. 36.)

1210.5.

In a case where a person has been ordered to undergo drug treatment as a condition of probation, any court ordered drug testing shall be used as a treatment tool. In evaluating a probationer's treatment program, results of any drug testing shall be given no greater weight than any other aspects of the probationer's individual treatment program.

(Added by Stats. 2001, Ch. 721, Sec. 4. Effective October 11, 2001.)

1210.6.

(a) (1) Upon appropriation by the Legislature, the Board of State and Community Corrections shall award funding for a grant program to four or more county superior courts or county probation departments to create demonstration projects to reduce the recidivism of high-risk misdemeanor probationers.

(2) The demonstration projects shall use risk assessments at sentencing when a misdemeanor conviction results in a term of probation to identify high-risk misdemeanants and to place these misdemeanants on formal probation that combines supervision with individually tailored programs, graduated sanctions, or incentives that address behavioral or treatment needs to achieve rehabilitation and successful completion of probation. The formal probation program may include incentives such as shortening probation terms as probationers complete the individually tailored program or probation requirements.

(3) The demonstration projects shall evaluate the probation completion and recidivism rates for project participants and may compare them to control groups to evaluate program efficacy. The Board of State and Community Corrections shall determine criteria for awarding the grants on a competitive basis that shall take into consideration the ability of a county to conduct a formal misdemeanor probation project for high-risk misdemeanor probationers, including components that align with evidence-based practices in reducing recidivism, including, but not limited to, risk and needs assessment, programming to help with drug or alcohol abuse, mental illness, or housing, and the support of the superior court if the application is from a county probation department.

(b) The Board of State and Community Corrections shall develop reporting requirements for each county receiving a grant to report to the board the results of the demonstration project. The reports may include, but are not limited to, the use of risk assessment, the formal probation program components, the number of individuals who were placed on formal probation, the number of individuals who were placed on informal probation, and the number of individuals in each group who were subsequently convicted of a new offense.

(c) (1) The Board of State and Community Corrections shall prepare a report that compiles the information it receives from each county receiving a grant, as described in subdivision (b). The report shall be completed and distributed to the Legislature and county criminal justice officials two years after an appropriation by the Legislature for this section.

(2) A report to be submitted pursuant to paragraph (1) shall be submitted in compliance with Section 9795 of the Government Code.

(d) This section shall remain in effect only until July 1, 2021, and as of that date is repealed.

(Amended by Stats. 2019, Ch. 25, Sec. 38. (SB 94) Effective June 27, 2019. Repealed as of July 1, 2021, by its own provisions.)

CHAPTER 1.4. Electronic Monitoring [1210.7 - 1210.16]

(Chapter 1.4 added by Stats. 2005, Ch. 484, Sec. 1.)

1210.7.

(a) Notwithstanding any other provisions of law, a county probation department may utilize continuous electronic monitoring to electronically monitor the whereabouts of persons on probation, as provided by this chapter.

(b) Any use of continuous electronic monitoring pursuant to this chapter shall have as its primary objective the enhancement of public safety through the reduction in the number of people being victimized by crimes committed by persons on probation.

(c) It is the intent of the Legislature in enacting this chapter to specifically encourage a county probation department acting pursuant to this chapter to utilize a system of continuous electronic monitoring that conforms with the requirements of this chapter.

(d) For purposes of this chapter, "continuous electronic monitoring" may include the use of worldwide radio navigation system technology, known as the Global Positioning System, or GPS. The Legislature finds that because of its capability for continuous surveillance, continuous electronic monitoring has been used in other parts of the country to monitor persons on formal probation who are identified as requiring a high level of supervision.

(e) The Legislature finds that continuous electronic monitoring has proven to be an effective risk management tool for supervising high-risk persons on probation who are likely to reoffend where prevention and knowledge of their whereabouts is a high priority for maintaining public safety.

(Added by Stats. 2005, Ch. 484, Sec. 1. Effective October 4, 2005.)

1210.8.

A county probation department may utilize a continuous electronic monitoring device pursuant to this section that has all of the following attributes:

(a) A device designed to be worn by a human being.

(b) A device that emits a signal as a person is moving or is stationary. The signal shall be capable of being received and tracked across large urban or rural areas, statewide, and being received from within structures, vehicles, and other objects to the degree technically feasible in light of the associated costs, design, and other considerations as are determined relevant by the county probation department.

(c) A device that functions 24 hours a day.

(d) A device that is resistant or impervious to unintentional or willful damage.

(Added by Stats. 2005, Ch. 484, Sec. 1. Effective October 4, 2005.)

1210.9.

(a) A continuous electronic monitoring system may have the capacity to immediately notify a county probation department of violations, actual or suspected, of the terms of probation that have been identified by the monitoring system if the requirement is deemed necessary by the county probation officer with respect to an individual person.

(b) The information described in subdivision (a), including geographic location and tampering, may be used as evidence to prove a violation of the terms of probation.

(Added by Stats. 2005, Ch. 484, Sec. 1. Effective October 4, 2005.)

1210.10.

A county probation department shall establish the following standards as are necessary to enhance public safety:

(a) Standards for the minimum time interval between transmissions of information about the location of the person under supervision. The standards shall be established after an evaluation of, at a minimum, all of the following:

(1) The resources of the county probation department.

(2) The criminal history of the person under supervision.

(3) The safety of the victim of the persons under supervision.

(b) Standards for the accuracy of the information identifying the location of the person under supervision. The standards shall be established after consideration of, at a minimum, all of the following:

(1) The need to identify the location of a person proximate to the location of a crime, including a violation of probation.

(2) Resources of the probation department.

(3) The need to avoid false indications of proximity to crimes.

(Added by Stats. 2005, Ch. 484, Sec. 1. Effective October 4, 2005.)

1210.11.

(a) A county probation department operating a system of continuous electronic monitoring pursuant to this section shall establish prohibitions against unauthorized access to, and use of, information by private or public entities as may be deemed appropriate. Unauthorized access to, and use of, electronic signals includes signals transmitted in any fashion by equipment utilized for continuous electronic monitoring.

(b) Devices used pursuant to this section shall not be used to eavesdrop or record any conversation, except a conversation between the participant and the person supervising the participant that is to be used solely for the purposes of voice identification.

(Added by Stats. 2005, Ch. 484, Sec. 1. Effective October 4, 2005.)

1210.12.

(a) A county chief probation officer shall have the sole discretion, consistent with the terms and conditions of probation, to decide which persons shall be supervised using continuous electronic monitoring administered by the county probation department. No individual shall be required to participate in continuous electronic monitoring authorized by this chapter for any period of time longer than the term of probation.

(b) The county chief probation officer shall establish written guidelines that identify those persons on probation subject to continuous electronic monitoring authorized by this chapter. These guidelines shall include the need for enhancing monitoring in comparison to other persons not subject to the enhanced monitoring and the public safety needs that will be served by the enhanced monitoring.

(Added by Stats. 2005, Ch. 484, Sec. 1. Effective October 4, 2005.)

1210.13.

A county chief probation officer may revoke, in his or her discretion, the continuous monitoring of any individual.

(Added by Stats. 2005, Ch. 484, Sec. 1. Effective October 4, 2005.)

1210.14.

Whenever a probation officer supervising an individual has reasonable cause to believe that the individual is not complying with the rules or conditions set forth for the use of continuous electronic monitoring as a supervision tool, the probation officer supervising the individual may, without a warrant of arrest, take the individual into custody for a violation of probation.

(Added by Stats. 2005, Ch. 484, Sec. 1. Effective October 4, 2005.)

1210.15.

(a) A chief probation officer may charge persons on probation for the costs of any form of supervision that utilizes continuous electronic monitoring devices that monitor the whereabouts of the person pursuant to this chapter, upon a finding of the ability to pay those costs. However, the department shall waive any or all of that payment upon a finding of an inability to pay. Inability to pay all or a portion of the costs of continuous electronic monitoring authorized by this chapter shall not preclude use of continuous electronic monitoring, and eligibility for probation shall not be enhanced by reason of ability to pay.

(b) A chief probation officer may charge a person on probation pursuant to subdivision (a) for the cost of continuous electronic monitoring in accordance with Section 1203.1b provided the person has first satisfied all other outstanding base fines, state and local penalties, restitution fines, and restitution orders imposed by a court.

(Added by Stats. 2005, Ch. 484, Sec. 1. Effective October 4, 2005.)

1210.16.

It is the intent of the Legislature that continuous electronic monitoring established pursuant to this chapter maintain the highest public confidence, credibility, and public safety. In the furtherance of these standards, the following shall apply:

(a) The chief probation officer may administer continuous electronic monitoring pursuant to written contracts and appropriate public or private agencies or entities to provide specified supervision services. No public or private agency or entity may operate a continuous electronic monitoring system as authorized by this section in any county without a written contract with the county's probation department. No public or private agency or entity entering into a contract may itself employ any person who is a participant in continuous electronic monitoring surveillance.

(b) The county board of supervisors, the chief probation officer, and designees of the chief probation officer shall comply with Section 1090 of the Government Code in the consideration, making, and execution of contracts pursuant to this section.

(Added by Stats. 2005, Ch. 484, Sec. 1. Effective October 4, 2005.)

CHAPTER 1.5. Certification of Drug Diversion Programs [1211- 1211.]

(Chapter 1.5 added by Stats. 1992, Ch. 1118, Sec. 4.)
1211.
(a) In order to ensure the quality of drug diversion programs provided pursuant to this chapter and Chapter 2.5 (commencing with Section 1000) of Title 6, and to expand the availability of these programs, the county drug program administrator in each county, in consultation with representatives of the court and the county probation department, shall establish minimum requirements, criteria, and fees for the successful completion of drug diversion programs which shall be approved by the county board of supervisors no later than January 1, 1995. These minimum requirements shall include, but not be limited to, all of the following:
(1) An initial assessment of each divertee, which may include all of the following:
(A) Social, economic, and family background.
(B) Education.
(C) Vocational achievements.
(D) Criminal history.
(E) Medical history.
(F) Drug history and previous treatment.
(2) A minimum of 20 hours of either effective education or counseling or any combination of both for each divertee.
(3) An exit conference which shall reflect the divertee's progress during his or her participation in the program.
(4) Fee exemptions for persons who cannot afford to pay.
(b) The county drug program administrator shall implement a certification procedure for drug diversion programs.
(c) The county drug program administrator shall recommend for approval by the county board of supervisors programs pursuant to this chapter. No program, regardless of how it is funded, may be approved unless it meets the standards established by the administrator, which shall include, but not be limited to, all of the following:
(1) Guidelines and criteria for education and treatment services, including standards of services which may include lectures, classes, group discussions, and individual counseling. However, any class or group discussion other than lectures, shall not exceed 15 persons at any one meeting.
(2) Established and approved supervision, either on a regular or irregular basis, of the person for the purpose of evaluating the person's progress.
(3) A schedule of fees to be charged for services rendered to each person under a county drug program plan in accordance with the following provisions:
(A) Fees shall be used only for the purposes set forth in this chapter.
(B) Fees for the treatment or rehabilitation of each participant receiving services under a certified drug diversion program shall not exceed the actual cost thereof, as determined by the county drug program administrator according to standard accounting practices.
(C) Actual costs shall include both of the following:
(i) All costs incurred by the providers of diversion programs.
(ii) All expenses incurred by the county for administration, certification, or management of the drug diversion program in compliance with this chapter.
(d) The county shall require, as a condition of certification, that the drug diversion program pay to the county drug program administrator all expenses incurred by the county for administration, certification, or management of the drug diversion program in compliance with this chapter. No fee shall be required by any county other than that county where the program is located.
(Amended by Stats. 1993, Ch. 850, Sec. 4. Effective January 1, 1994.)

CHAPTER 2. The Execution [1213 - 1227.5]

(Chapter 2 enacted 1872.)
1213.
(a) When a probationary order or a judgment, other than of death, has been pronounced, a copy of the entry of that portion of the probationary order ordering the defendant confined in a city or county jail as a condition of probation, or a copy of the entry of the judgment, or, if the judgment is for imprisonment in the state prison or imprisonment pursuant to subdivision (h) of Section 1170, either a copy of the minute order or an abstract of the judgment as provided in Section 1213.5, certified by the clerk of the court, and a Criminal Investigation and Identification (CII) number shall be forthwith furnished to the officer whose duty it is to execute the probationary order or judgment, and no other warrant or authority is necessary to justify or require its execution.
(b) If a copy of the minute order is used as the commitment document, the first page or pages shall be identical in form and content to that prescribed by the Judicial Council for an abstract of judgment, and other matters as appropriate may be added thereafter.
(Amended by Stats. 2011, Ch. 15, Sec. 457. (AB 109) Effective April 4, 2011. Operative October 1, 2011, by Sec. 636 of Ch. 15, as amended by Stats. 2011, Ch. 39, Sec. 68.)
1213.5.
The abstract of judgment provided for in Section 1213 shall be prescribed by the Judicial Council.
(Amended by Stats. 1986, Ch. 248, Sec. 164.)
1214.
(a) If the judgment is for a fine, including a restitution fine ordered pursuant to Section 1202.4, 1202.44, or 1202.45, or Section 1203.04 as operative on or before August 2, 1995, or Section 13967 of the Government Code, as operative on or before September 28, 1994, with or without imprisonment, or a diversion restitution fee ordered pursuant to Section 1001.90, the judgment may be enforced in the manner provided for the enforcement of money judgments generally. Any portion of a restitution fine or restitution fee that remains unsatisfied after a defendant is no longer on probation, parole, postrelease community supervision pursuant to Section 3451, or mandatory supervision pursuant to subparagraph (B) of paragraph (5) of subdivision (h) of Section 1170, after a term in custody pursuant to subparagraph (A) of paragraph (5) of subdivision (h) of Section 1170, or after completing diversion is enforceable by the California Victim Compensation Board pursuant to this section. Notwithstanding any other provision of law prohibiting disclosure, the state, as defined in Section 900.6 of the Government Code, a local public entity, as defined in Section 900.4 of the Government Code, or any other entity, may provide the California Victim Compensation Board any and all information to assist in the collection of unpaid portions of a restitution fine for terminated probation or parole cases, or of a restitution fee for completed diversion cases. For purposes of the preceding sentence, "state, as defined in Section 900.6 of the Government Code," and "any other entity" shall not include the Franchise Tax Board. A local collection program may continue to collect restitution fines and restitution orders once a defendant is no longer on probation, postrelease

community supervision, or mandatory supervision or after a term in custody pursuant to subparagraph (A) of paragraph (5) of subdivision (h) of Section 1170.
(b) In any case in which a defendant is ordered to pay restitution, the order to pay restitution (1) is deemed a money judgment if the defendant was informed of his or her right to have a judicial determination of the amount and was provided with a hearing, waived a hearing, or stipulated to the amount of the restitution ordered, and (2) shall be fully enforceable by a victim as if the restitution order were a civil judgment, and enforceable in the same manner as is provided for the enforcement of any other money judgment. Upon the victim's request, the court shall provide the victim in whose favor the order of restitution is entered with a certified copy of that order and a copy of the defendant's disclosure pursuant to paragraph (5) of subdivision (f) of Section 1202.4, affidavit or information pursuant to paragraph (6) of subdivision (f) of Section 1202.4, or report pursuant to paragraph (8) of subdivision (f) of Section 1202.4. The court also shall provide this information to the district attorney upon request in connection with an investigation or prosecution involving perjury or the veracity of the information contained within the defendant's financial disclosure. In addition, upon request, the court shall provide the California Victim Compensation Board with a certified copy of any order imposing a restitution fine or order and a copy of the defendant's disclosure pursuant to paragraph (5) of subdivision (f) of Section 1202.4, affidavit or information pursuant to paragraph (6) of subdivision (f) of Section 1202.4, or report pursuant to paragraph (8) of subdivision (f) of Section 1202.4. A victim shall have access to all resources available under the law to enforce the restitution order, including, but not limited to, access to the defendant's financial records, use of wage garnishment and lien procedures, information regarding the defendant's assets, and the ability to apply for restitution from any fund established for the purpose of compensating victims in civil cases. Any portion of a restitution order that remains unsatisfied after a defendant is no longer on probation, parole, postrelease community supervision under Section 3451, or mandatory supervision imposed pursuant to subparagraph (B) of paragraph (5) of subdivision (h) of Section 1170 or after a term in custody pursuant to subparagraph (A) of paragraph (5) of subdivision (h) of Section 1170 is enforceable by the victim pursuant to this section. Victims and the California Victim Compensation Board shall inform the court whenever an order to pay restitution is satisfied. A local collection program may continue to enforce victim restitution orders once a defendant is no longer on probation, postrelease community supervision, or mandatory supervision or after completion of a term in custody pursuant to subparagraph (A) of paragraph (5) of subdivision (h) of Section 1170.
(c) A defendant who owes a restitution fine, a restitution order, or any portion thereof, and who is released from the custody of a county jail facility after a term in custody pursuant to subparagraph (A) of paragraph (5) of subdivision (h) of Section 1170 shall have a continuing obligation to pay the restitution fine or restitution order in full.
(d) Except as provided in subdivision (d), and notwithstanding the amount in controversy limitation of Section 85 of the Code of Civil Procedure, a restitution order or restitution fine that was imposed pursuant to Section 1202.4 in any of the following cases may be enforced in the same manner as a money judgment in a limited civil case:
(1) In a misdemeanor case.
(2) In a case involving violation of a city or town ordinance.
(3) In a noncapital criminal case where the court has received a plea of guilty or nolo contendere.
(e) Chapter 3 (commencing with Section 683.010) of Division 1 of Title 9 of Part 2 of the Code of Civil Procedure shall not apply to any of the following:
(1) A judgment for court-ordered fines, forfeitures, penalties, fees, or assessments.
(2) A restitution fine or restitution order imposed pursuant to Section 1202.4, 1202.44, or 1202.45, or Section 1203.04, as operative on or before August 2, 1995, or Section 13967 of the Government Code, as operative on or before September 28, 1994.
(3) A diversion restitution fee ordered pursuant to Section 1001.90.
(Amended by Stats. 2016, Ch. 31, Sec. 242. (SB 836) Effective June 27, 2016.)
1214.1.
(a) In addition to any other penalty in infraction, misdemeanor, or felony cases, the court may impose a civil assessment of up to three hundred dollars ($300) against a defendant who fails, after notice and without good cause, to appear in court for a proceeding authorized by law or who fails to pay all or any portion of a fine ordered by the court or to pay an installment of bail as agreed to under Section 40510.5 of the Vehicle Code. This assessment shall be deposited in the Trial Court Trust Fund, as provided in Section 68085.1 of the Government Code.
(b) (1) The assessment imposed pursuant to subdivision (a) shall not become effective until at least 20 calendar days after the court mails a warning notice to the defendant by first-class mail to the address shown on the notice to appear or to the defendant's last known address. If the defendant appears within the time specified in the notice and shows good cause for the failure to appear or for the failure to pay a fine or installment of bail, the court shall vacate the assessment.
(2) Payment of bail, fines, penalties, fees, or a civil assessment shall not be required in order for the court to vacate the assessment at the time of appearance pursuant to paragraph (1). Payment of a civil assessment shall not be required to schedule a court hearing on a pending underlying charge.
(c) If a civil assessment is imposed pursuant to subdivision (a), no bench warrant or warrant of arrest shall be issued with respect to the failure to appear at the proceeding for which the assessment is imposed or the failure to pay the fine or installment of bail. An outstanding, unserved bench warrant or warrant of arrest for a failure to appear or for a failure to pay a fine or installment of bail shall be recalled prior to the subsequent imposition of a civil assessment.
(d) The assessment imposed pursuant to subdivision (a) shall be subject to the due process requirements governing defense and collection of civil money judgments generally.
(e) Each court and county shall maintain the collection program that was in effect on July 1, 2005, unless otherwise agreed to by the court and county. If a court and a county do not agree on a plan for the collection of civil assessments imposed pursuant to this section, or any other collections under Section 1463.010, after the implementation of Sections 68085.6 and 68085.7 of the Government Code, the court or the county may request arbitration by a third party mutually agreed upon by the Administrative Director of the Courts and the California State Association of Counties.
(Amended by Stats. 2015, Ch. 385, Sec. 1. (SB 405) Effective September 30, 2015.)
1214.2.
(a) Except as provided in subdivision (c), if a defendant is ordered to pay a fine as a condition of probation, the order to pay a fine may be enforced during the term of probation in the same manner as is provided for the enforcement of money judgments.
(b) Except as provided in subdivision (c), an order to pay a fine as a condition of probation may also be enforced as follows:
(1) With respect to a willful failure to pay during the term of probation, in the same manner as a violation of the terms and conditions of probation.
(2) If any balance remains unpaid at the end of the term of probation, in the same manner as a judgment in a civil action.
(c) If an order to pay a fine as a condition of probation is stayed, a writ of execution shall not issue until the stay is lifted.
(Added by Stats. 1987, Ch. 454, Sec. 1. Effective September 9, 1987.)
1214.5.
(a) In any case in which the defendant is ordered to pay more than fifty dollars ($50) in restitution as a condition of probation, the court may, as an additional condition of probation since the court determines that the defendant has the ability to pay, as

defined in subdivision (e) of Section 1203.1b, order the defendant to pay interest at the rate of 10 percent per annum on the principal amount remaining unsatisfied.

(b) (1) Except as provided in paragraph (2), interest commences to accrue on the date of entry of the judgment or order.

(2) Unless the judgment or order otherwise provides, if restitution is payable in installments, interest commences to accrue as to each installment on the date the installment becomes due.

(Amended by Stats. 2016, Ch. 86, Sec. 230. (SB 1171) Effective January 1, 2017.)

1215.

If the judgment is for imprisonment, or a fine and imprisonment until it be paid, the defendant must forthwith be committed to the custody of the proper officer and by him or her detained until the judgment is complied with. Where, however, the court has suspended sentence, or where, after imposing sentence, the court has suspended the execution thereof and placed the defendant on probation, as provided in Section 1203, the defendant, if over the age of 16 years, shall be placed under the care and supervision of the probation officer of the court committing him or her, until the expiration of the period of probation and the compliance with the terms and conditions of the sentence, or of the suspension thereof. Where, however, the probation has been terminated as provided in Section 1203, and the suspension of the sentence, or of the execution revoked, and the judgment pronounced, the defendant shall be committed to the custody of the proper officer and be detained until the judgment be complied with.

(Amended by Stats. 1987, Ch. 828, Sec. 80.)

1216.

If the judgment is for imprisonment in the state prison, the sheriff of the county shall, upon receipt of a certified abstract or minute order thereof, take and deliver the defendant to the warden of the state prison. The sheriff also shall deliver to the warden the certified abstract of the judgment or minute order, a Criminal Investigation and Identification (CII) number, a Confidential Medical/Mental Health Information Transfer Form indicating that the defendant is medically capable of being transported, and take from the warden a receipt for the defendant.

(Amended by Stats. 1998, Ch. 767, Sec. 1. Effective January 1, 1999.)

1217.

When judgment of death is rendered, a commitment signed by the judge, and attested by the clerk under the seal of the court must be drawn and delivered to the sheriff. It must state the conviction and judgment, and must direct the sheriff to deliver the defendant, within 10 days from the time of judgment, to the warden of the State prison of this State designated by the State Board of Prison Directors for the execution of the death penalty, to be held pending the decision upon his appeal.

(Amended by Stats. 1943, Ch. 107.)

1218.

The judge of the court at which a judgment of death is had, must, immediately after the judgment, transmit to the Governor, by mail or otherwise, a statement of the conviction and judgment, and a complete transcript of all the testimony given at the trial including any arguments made by respective counsel and a copy of the clerk's transcript.

(Amended by Stats. 1961, Ch. 1648.)

1219.

The Governor may thereupon require the opinion of the Justices of the Supreme Court and of the Attorney General, or any of them, upon the statement so furnished.

(Enacted 1872.)

1227.

(a) If for any reason other than the pendency of an appeal pursuant to subdivision (b) of Section 1239 of this code a judgment of death has not been executed, and it remains in force, the court in which the conviction was had shall, on application of the district attorney, or may upon its own motion, make and cause to be entered an order specifying a period of 10 days during which the judgment shall be executed. The 10-day period shall begin no less than 30 days after the order is entered and shall end no more than 60 days after the order is entered. Immediately after the order is entered, a certified copy of the order, attested by the clerk, under the seal of the court, shall, for the purpose of execution, be transmitted by registered mail to the warden of the state prison having the custody of the defendant; provided, that if the defendant be at large, a warrant for his apprehension may be issued, and upon being apprehended, he shall be brought before the court, whereupon the court shall make an order directing the warden of the state prison to whom the sheriff is instructed to deliver the defendant to execute the judgment within a period of 10 days, which shall not begin less than 30 days nor end more than 60 days from the time of making such order.

(b) From an order fixing the time for and directing the execution of such judgment as herein provided, there shall be no appeal.

(Amended November 8, 2016, by initiative Proposition 66, Sec. 4.)

1227.5.

Notwithstanding Section 1227, where a judgment of death has not been executed by reason of a stay or reprieve granted by the Governor, the execution shall be carried out on the day immediately after the period of the stay or reprieve without further judicial proceedings.

(Added by Stats. 1961, Ch. 1648.)

CHAPTER 3. California Community Corrections Performance Incentives [1228 - 1233.10]

(Chapter 3 added by Stats. 2009, Ch. 608, Sec. 2.)

1228.

The Legislature finds and declares all of the following:

(a) In 2007, nearly 270,000 felony offenders were subject to probation supervision in California's communities.

(b) In 2007, out of 46,987 new admissions to state prison, nearly 20,000 were felony offenders who were committed to state prison after failing probation supervision.

(c) Probation is a judicially imposed suspension of sentence that attempts to supervise, treat, and rehabilitate offenders while they remain in the community under the supervision of the probation department. Probation is a linchpin of the criminal justice system, closely aligned with the courts, and plays a central role in promoting public safety in California's communities.

(d) Providing sustainable funding for improved, evidence-based probation supervision practices and capacities will improve public safety outcomes among adult felons who are on probation. Improving felony probation performance, measured by a reduction in felony probationers who are sent to prison because they were revoked on probation or convicted of another crime while on probation, will reduce the number of new admissions to state prison, saving taxpayer dollars and allowing a portion of those state savings to be redirected to probation for investing in community corrections programs.

(Added by Stats. 2009, Ch. 608, Sec. 2. (SB 678) Effective January 1, 2010.)

1229.

As used in this chapter, the following definitions apply:

(a) "Community corrections" means the placement of persons convicted of a felony offense under probation supervision, mandatory supervision, or postrelease community supervision for a specified period.

(b) "Chief probation officer" or "CPO" means the chief probation officer for the county or city and county in which an adult offender is subject to probation for the conviction of a felony offense.

(c) "Community corrections program" means a program established pursuant to this act consisting of a system of services for felony offenders under local supervision dedicated to all of the following goals:

(1) Enhancing public safety through the management and reduction of offender risk while under local supervision and upon reentry from jail or prison into the community.

(2) Providing a range of supervision tools, sanctions, and services applied to felony offenders subject to local supervision based on a risk and needs assessment for the purpose of reducing criminal conduct and promoting behavioral change that results in reducing recidivism and promoting the successful reintegration of offenders into the community.

(3) Maximizing offender restitution, reconciliation, and restorative services to victims of crime.

(4) Holding offenders accountable for their criminal behaviors and for successful compliance with applicable court orders and conditions of supervision.

(5) Improving public safety outcomes for persons subject to local supervision for a felony offense, as measured by their successful completion of the period of local supervision and the commensurate reduction in the rate of offenders sent to prison as a result of a revocation of supervision or conviction of a new crime.

(d) "Evidence-based practices" refers to supervision policies, procedures, programs, and practices demonstrated by scientific research to reduce recidivism among individuals under local supervision.

(e) "Local supervision" means the supervision of an adult felony offender on probation, mandatory supervision, or postrelease community supervision.

(Amended by Stats. 2013, Ch. 31, Sec. 10. (SB 75) Effective June 27, 2013.)

1230.

(a) Each county is hereby authorized to establish in each county treasury a Community Corrections Performance Incentives Fund (CCPIF), to receive all amounts allocated to that county for purposes of implementing this chapter.

(b) Notwithstanding any other law, in any fiscal year for which a county receives moneys to be expended for the implementation of this chapter, the moneys, including any interest, shall be made available to the CPO of that county, within 30 days of the deposit of those moneys into the fund, for the implementation of the community corrections program authorized by this chapter.

(1) The community corrections program shall be developed and implemented by probation and advised by a local Community Corrections Partnership.

(2) The local Community Corrections Partnership shall be chaired by the CPO and comprised of the following membership:

(A) The presiding judge of the superior court, or his or her designee.

(B) A county supervisor or the chief administrative officer for the county or a designee of the board of supervisors.

(C) The district attorney.

(D) The public defender.

(E) The sheriff.

(F) A chief of police.

(G) The head of the county department of social services.

(H) The head of the county department of mental health.

(I) The head of the county department of employment.

(J) The head of the county alcohol and substance abuse programs.

(K) The head of the county office of education.

(L) A representative from a community-based organization with experience in successfully providing rehabilitative services to persons who have been convicted of a criminal offense.

(M) An individual who represents the interests of victims.

(3) Funds allocated to probation pursuant to this act shall be used to provide supervision and rehabilitative services for adult felony offenders subject to local supervision, and shall be spent on evidence-based community corrections practices and programs, as defined in subdivision (d) of Section 1229, which may include, but are not limited to, the following:

(A) Implementing and expanding evidence-based risk and needs assessments.

(B) Implementing and expanding intermediate sanctions that include, but are not limited to, electronic monitoring, mandatory community service, home detention, day reporting, restorative justice programs, work furlough programs, and incarceration in county jail for up to 90 days.

(C) Providing more intensive local supervision.

(D) Expanding the availability of evidence-based rehabilitation programs including, but not limited to, drug and alcohol treatment, mental health treatment, anger management, cognitive behavior programs, and job training and employment services.

(E) Evaluating the effectiveness of rehabilitation and supervision programs and ensuring program fidelity.

(4) Notwithstanding any other law, the CPO shall have discretion to spend funds on any of the above practices and programs consistent with this act but, at a minimum, shall devote at least 5 percent of all funding received to evaluate the effectiveness of those programs and practices implemented with the funds provided pursuant to this chapter. A CPO may petition the Judicial Council to have this restriction waived, and the Judicial Council shall have the authority to grant such a petition, if the CPO can demonstrate that the department is already devoting sufficient funds to the evaluation of these programs and practices.

(5) Each probation department receiving funds under this chapter shall maintain a complete and accurate accounting of all funds received pursuant to this chapter.

(Amended by Stats. 2015, Ch. 26, Sec. 14. (SB 85) Effective June 24, 2015.)

1230.1.

(a) Each county local Community Corrections Partnership established pursuant to subdivision (b) of Section 1230 shall recommend a local plan to the county board of supervisors for the implementation of the 2011 public safety realignment.

(b) The plan shall be voted on by an executive committee of each county's Community Corrections Partnership consisting of the chief probation officer of the county as chair, a chief of police, the sheriff, the District Attorney, the Public Defender, the presiding judge of the superior court, or his or her designee, and one department representative listed in either subparagraph (G), (H), or (J) of paragraph (2) of subdivision (b) of Section 1230, as designated by the county board of supervisors for purposes related to the development and presentation of the plan.

(c) The plan shall be deemed accepted by the county board of supervisors unless the board rejects the plan by a vote of four-fifths of the board, in which case the plan goes back to the Community Corrections Partnership for further consideration.

(d) Consistent with local needs and resources, the plan may include recommendations to maximize the effective investment of criminal justice resources in evidence-based correctional sanctions and programs, including, but not limited to, day reporting centers, drug courts, residential multiservice centers, mental health treatment programs, electronic and GPS monitoring programs, victim restitution programs, counseling programs, community service programs, educational programs, and work training programs.

(Amended (as added by Stats. 2011, Ch. 15) by Stats. 2011, Ch. 39, Sec. 33. (AB 117) Effective June 30, 2011. Addition and amendment operative October 1, 2011, pursuant to Secs. 68 and 69 of Ch. 39.)

1231.

(a) Community corrections programs funded pursuant to this chapter shall identify and track specific outcome-based measures consistent with the goals of this act.

(b) The Judicial Council, in consultation with the Chief Probation Officers of California, shall specify and define minimum required outcome-based measures, which shall include, but not be limited to, all of the following:
(1) The percentage of persons subject to local supervision who are being supervised in accordance with evidence-based practices.
(2) The percentage of state moneys expended for programs that are evidence based, and a descriptive list of all programs that are evidence based.
(3) Specification of supervision policies, procedures, programs, and practices that were eliminated.
(4) The percentage of persons subject to local supervision who successfully complete the period of supervision.
(c) Each CPO receiving funding pursuant to Sections 1233 to 1233.6, inclusive, shall provide an annual written report to the Judicial Council, evaluating the effectiveness of the community corrections program, including, but not limited to, the data described in subdivision (b).
(d) The Judicial Council, shall, in consultation with the CPO of each county and the Department of Corrections and Rehabilitation, provide a quarterly statistical report to the Department of Finance including, but not limited to, the following statistical information for each county:
(1) The number of felony filings.
(2) The number of felony convictions.
(3) The number of felony convictions in which the defendant was sentenced to the state prison.
(4) The number of felony convictions in which the defendant was granted probation.
(5) The adult felon probation population.
(6) The number of adult felony probationers who had their probation terminated and revoked and were sent to state prison for that revocation.
(7) The number of adult felony probationers sent to state prison for a conviction of a new felony offense, including when probation was revoked or terminated.
(8) The number of adult felony probationers who had their probation revoked and were sent to county jail for that revocation.
(9) The number of adult felony probationers sent to county jail for a conviction of a new felony offense, including when probation was revoked or terminated.
(10) The number of felons placed on postrelease community supervision, commencing January 1, 2012.
(11) The number of felons placed on mandatory supervision, commencing January 1, 2012.
(12) The mandatory supervision population, commencing January 1, 2012.
(13) The postrelease community supervision population, commencing January 1, 2012.
(14) The number of felons on postrelease community supervision sentenced to state prison for a conviction of a new felony offense, commencing January 1, 2012.
(15) The number of felons on mandatory supervision sentenced to state prison for a conviction of a new felony offense, commencing January 1, 2012.
(16) The number of felons who had their postrelease community supervision revoked and were sent to county jail for that revocation, commencing January 1, 2012. This number shall not include felons on postrelease community supervision who are subject to flash incarceration pursuant to Section 3453.
(17) The number of felons on postrelease community supervision sentenced to county jail for a conviction of a new felony offense, including when postrelease community supervision was revoked or terminated, commencing January 1, 2012.
(18) The number of felons who had their mandatory supervision revoked and were sentenced to county jail for that revocation, commencing January 1, 2012.
(19) The number of felons on mandatory supervision sentenced to county jail for a conviction of a new felony offense, including when mandatory supervision was revoked or terminated, commencing January 1, 2012.
(Amended by Stats. 2015, Ch. 26, Sec. 15. (SB 85) Effective June 24, 2015.)

1232.

Commencing no later than 18 months following the initial receipt of funding pursuant to this chapter and annually thereafter, the Judicial Council, in consultation with the Department of Corrections and Rehabilitation, the Department of Finance, and the Chief Probation Officers of California, shall submit to the Governor and the Legislature a comprehensive report on the implementation of this chapter. The report shall include, but not be limited to, all of the following information:
(a) The effectiveness of the community corrections program based on the reports of performance-based outcome measures required in Section 1231.
(b) The percentage of offenders subject to local supervision whose supervision was revoked and who were sent to prison for the year on which the report is being made.
(c) The percentage of offenders subject to local supervision who were convicted of crimes during their term of supervision for the year on which the report is being made.
(d) The impact of the moneys appropriated pursuant to this chapter to enhance public safety by reducing the percentage and number of offenders subject to local supervision whose supervision was revoked for the year being reported on for violations or new convictions, and to reduce the number of offenders subject to local supervision who are sentenced to prison for a new conviction for the year on which the report is being made.
(e) Any recommendations regarding resource allocations or additional collaboration with other state, regional, federal, or local entities for improvements to this chapter.
(Amended by Stats. 2015, Ch. 26, Sec. 16. (SB 85) Effective June 24, 2015.)

1233.1.

After the conclusion of each calendar year, the Director of Finance, in consultation with the Department of Corrections and Rehabilitation, the Joint Legislative Budget Committee, the Chief Probation Officers of California, and the Judicial Council, shall calculate the following for that calendar year:
(a) The cost to the state to incarcerate in a contract facility and supervise on parole an offender who fails local supervision and is sent to prison.
(b) The statewide probation failure rate shall be calculated as the total number of adult felony probationers statewide sent to state prison as a percentage of the average statewide adult felony probation population for that year.
(c) The probation failure rate for each county shall be calculated as the total number of adult felony probationers sent to state prison from that county, as a percentage of the county's average adult felony probation population for that year.
(d) An estimate of the number of adult felony probationers each county successfully prevented from being incarcerated in state prison. For each county, this estimate shall be calculated based on the reduction in the county's probation failure rate as calculated annually pursuant to subdivision (c) for that year and the county's probation failure rate from the previous year.
(e) In calculating probation failure to prison rates for the state and individual counties, the number of adult felony probationers sent to state prison shall include those adult felony probationers sent to state prison for a revocation of probation, as well as adult felony probationers sent to state prison for a conviction of a new felony offense. The calculation shall also include adult felony probationers who are sent to state prison for a conviction of a new crime and who simultaneously have their probation terms terminated.
(f) The statewide mandatory supervision failure to prison rate. The statewide mandatory supervision failure to prison rate shall be calculated as the total number of offenders supervised under mandatory supervision pursuant to subparagraph (B) of paragraph (5) of subdivision (h) of Section 1170, statewide, sent to prison in the previous calendar year as a percentage of the average statewide mandatory supervision population for that year.
(g) A mandatory supervision failure to prison rate for each county. Each county's mandatory supervision failure to prison rate shall be calculated as the number of offenders supervised under mandatory supervision pursuant to subparagraph (B) of paragraph (5) of subdivision (h) of Section 1170 sent to prison from that county in the previous calendar year as a percentage of the county's average mandatory supervision population for that year.
(h) An estimate of the number of felons on mandatory supervision each county successfully prevented from being incarcerated in state prison. For each county, this estimate shall be calculated based on the reduction in the county's mandatory supervision failure to prison rate as calculated annually pursuant to subdivision (g) for that year and the county's mandatory supervision failure to prison rate from the previous year.
(i) The statewide postrelease community supervision failure to prison rate. The statewide postrelease community supervision failure to prison rate shall be calculated as the total number of offenders supervised under postrelease community supervision pursuant to Title 2.05 (commencing with Section 3450) of Part 3, statewide, sent to prison in the previous calendar year as a percentage of the average statewide postrelease community supervision population for that year.
(j) A postrelease community supervision failure to prison rate for each county. Each county's postrelease community supervision failure to prison rate shall be calculated as the number of offenders supervised under postrelease community supervision pursuant to Title 2.05 (commencing with Section 3450) of Part 3 sent to prison from that county in the previous calendar year as a percentage of the county's average postrelease community supervision population for that year.
(k) An estimate of the number of felons on postrelease community supervision each county successfully prevented from being incarcerated in state prison. For each county, this estimate shall be calculated based on the reduction in the county's postrelease community supervision failure to prison rate as calculated annually pursuant to subdivision (i) for that year and the county's postrelease community supervision failure to prison rate from the previous year.
(l) The statewide return to prison rate. The statewide return to prison rate shall be calculated as the total number of offenders supervised by probation departments as felony probationers, or subject to mandatory supervision pursuant to subdivision (h) of Section 1170, or subject to postrelease community supervision, who were sent to prison, as a percentage of the average statewide adult felony probation, mandatory supervision, and postrelease community supervision population.
(m) The county return to prison rate. The combined individual county return to prison rate shall be calculated as the total number of offenders supervised by a county probation department as felony probationers, or subject to mandatory supervision pursuant to subdivision (h) of Section 1170, or subject to postrelease community supervision, who were sent to prison, as a percentage of the average adult felony probation, mandatory supervision, and postrelease community supervision population for that county.
(Amended by Stats. 2015, Ch. 26, Sec. 18. (SB 85) Effective June 24, 2015.)

1233.3.

Annually, the Director of Finance, in consultation with the Department of Corrections and Rehabilitation, the Joint Legislative Budget Committee, the Chief Probation Officers of California, and the Judicial Council, shall calculate a statewide performance incentive payment for each eligible county for the most recently completed calendar year, as follows:
(a) For a county identified as having a return to prison rate less than 1.5 percent, the incentive payment shall be equal to 100 percent of the highest year of funding that a county received for the California Community Incentive Grant Program from the 2011–12 fiscal year to the 2014–15 fiscal year, inclusive.
(b) For a county identified as having a return to prison rate of 1.5 percent or greater, but not exceeding 3.2 percent, the incentive payment shall be equal to 70 percent of the highest year of funding that a county received for the California Community Incentive Grant Program from the 2011–12 fiscal year to the 2014–15 fiscal year, inclusive.
(c) For a county identified as having a return to prison rate of more than 3.2 percent, not exceeding 5.5 percent, the incentive payment shall be equal to 60 percent of the highest year of funding that a county received for the California Community Incentive Grant Program from the 2011–12 fiscal year to the 2014–15 fiscal year, inclusive.
(d) For a county identified as having a return to prison rate of more than 5.5 percent, not exceeding 6.1 percent, the incentive payment shall be equal to 50 percent of the highest year of funding that a county received for the California Community Incentive Grant Program from the 2011–12 fiscal year to the 2014–15 fiscal year, inclusive.
(e) For a county identified as having a return to prison rate of more than 6.1 percent, not exceeding 7.9 percent, the incentive payment shall be equal to 40 percent of the highest year of funding that a county received for the California Community Incentive Grant Program from the 2011–12 fiscal year to the 2014–15 fiscal year, inclusive.
(f) A county that fails to provide information specified in Section 1231 to the Administrative Office of the Courts is not eligible for a statewide performance incentive payment.
(Amended by Stats. 2015, Ch. 26, Sec. 21. (SB 85) Effective June 24, 2015.)

1233.4.

The Director of Finance, in consultation with the Department of Corrections and Rehabilitation, the Joint Legislative Budget Committee, the Chief Probation Officers of California, and the Judicial Council, shall, for the most recently completed calendar year, annually calculate a county performance incentive payment for each eligible county. A county shall be eligible for compensation for each of the following:
(a) The estimated number of felons on probation that were successfully prevented from being incarcerated in the state prison as calculated in subdivision (d) of Section 1233.1, multiplied by 35 percent of the state's costs to incarcerate a prison felony offender in a contract facility, as defined in subdivision (a) of Section 1233.1.
(b) The estimated number of felons on mandatory supervision that were successfully prevented from being incarcerated in the state prison as calculated in subdivision (h) of Section 1233.1, multiplied by 35 percent of the state's costs to incarcerate a prison felony offender in a contract facility, as defined in subdivision (a) of Section 1233.1.
(c) The estimated number of felons on postrelease community supervision that were successfully prevented from being incarcerated in the state prison as calculated in subdivision (k) of Section 1233.1, multiplied by 35 percent of the state's costs to incarcerate a prison felony offender in a contract facility, as defined in subdivision (a) of Section 1233.1.
(Repealed and added by Stats. 2015, Ch. 26, Sec. 23. (SB 85) Effective June 24, 2015.)

1233.5.

If data of sufficient quality and of the types required for the implementation of this chapter are not available to the Director of Finance, the Director of Finance, in consultation with the Department of Corrections and Rehabilitation, the Joint Legislative Budget Committee, and Judicial Council, shall use the best available data to estimate the statewide performance incentive payments and county performance incentive payments utilizing a methodology that is as consistent with that described in this chapter as is reasonably possible.
(Amended by Stats. 2015, Ch. 26, Sec. 24. (SB 85) Effective June 24, 2015.)

1233.6.

(a) A statewide performance incentive payment calculated pursuant to Section 1233.3 and a county performance incentive payment calculated pursuant to Section 1233.4 for any calendar year shall be provided to a county in the following fiscal year. The total annual payment to a county shall be divided into four equal quarterly payments.

(b) The Department of Finance shall include an estimate of the total statewide performance incentive payments and county performance incentive payments to be provided to counties in the coming fiscal year as part of the Governor's proposed budget released no later than January 10 of each year. This estimate shall be adjusted by the Department of Finance, as necessary, to reflect the actual calculations of probation failure reduction incentive payments and high performance grants completed by the Director of Finance, in consultation with the Department of Corrections and Rehabilitation, the Joint Legislative Budget Committee, the Chief Probation Officers of California, and the Judicial Council. This adjustment shall occur as part of standard budget revision processes completed by the Department of Finance in April and May of each year.

(c) There is hereby established, in the State Treasury, the State Community Corrections Performance Incentives Fund, which is continuously appropriated. Moneys appropriated for purposes of statewide performance incentive payments and county performance incentive payments authorized in Sections 1230 to 1233.6, inclusive, shall be transferred into this fund from the General Fund. Any moneys transferred into this fund from the General Fund shall be administered by the Judicial Council and the share calculated for each county probation department shall be transferred to its Community Corrections Performance Incentives Fund authorized in Section 1230.

(d) For each fiscal year, the Director of Finance shall determine the total amount of the State Community Corrections Performance Incentives Fund and the amount to be allocated to each county, pursuant to this section and Sections 1230 to 1233.5, inclusive, and shall report those amounts to the Controller. The Controller shall make an allocation from the State Community Corrections Performance Incentives Fund authorized in subdivision (c) to each county in accordance with the amounts provided.

(e) Notwithstanding Section 13340 of the Government Code, commencing July 1, 2014, and each fiscal year thereafter, the amount of one million dollars ($1,000,000) is hereby continuously appropriated from the State Community Corrections Performance Incentives Fund to the Judicial Council for the costs of implementing and administering this program, pursuant to subdivision (c), and the 2011 realignment legislation addressing public safety.
(Amended by Stats. 2015, Ch. 26, Sec. 25. (SB 85) Effective June 24, 2015.)

1233.61.
(a) The Department of Finance shall increase to no more than two hundred thousand dollars ($200,000) the award amount for any county whose statewide performance incentive payment and county performance incentive payment, as calculated pursuant to Sections 1233.3 and 1233.4, totals less than two hundred thousand dollars ($200,000).

(b) The Department of Finance shall adjust the award amount up to two hundred thousand dollars ($200,000) per county, to those counties that did not receive a statewide performance incentive payment and county performance incentive payment, as calculated pursuant to Sections 1233.3 and 1233.4.

(c) Any county receiving funding through subdivision (b) shall submit a report to the Judicial Council and the Chief Probation Officers of California describing how it plans on using the funds to enhance its ability to be successful under this chapter. Commencing January 1, 2014, a county that fails to submit this report by March 1 annually shall not receive funding pursuant to subdivision (b) in the subsequent fiscal year.

(d) A county that fails to provide the information specified in Section 1231 to the Judicial Council shall not be eligible for payment pursuant to this section.
(Amended by Stats. 2015, Ch. 26, Sec. 26. (SB 85) Effective June 24, 2015.)

1233.7.
The moneys appropriated pursuant to this chapter shall be used to supplement, not supplant, any other state or county appropriation for a CPO or a probation department.
(Amended (as added by Stats. 2009, Ch. 608, Sec. 2) by Stats. 2010, Ch. 328, Sec. 172. (SB 1330) Effective January 1, 2011.)

1233.9.
(a) There is hereby created in the State Treasury the Recidivism Reduction Fund for moneys to be available upon appropriation by the Legislature, for activities designed to reduce the state's prison population, including, but not limited to, reducing recidivism. Funds available in the Recidivism Reduction Fund may be transferred to the State Community Corrections Performance Incentives Fund.

(b) Any funds in the Recidivism Reduction Fund not encumbered by June 30, 2016, shall revert to the General Fund upon order of the Department of Finance.

(c) The Recidivism Reduction Fund shall be abolished once all funds encumbered in the Recidivism Reduction Fund are liquidated.
(Amended by Stats. 2015, Ch. 26, Sec. 27. (SB 85) Effective June 24, 2015.)

1233.10.
(a) Upon agreement to accept funding from the Recidivism Reduction Fund, created in Section 1233.9, a county board of supervisors, in collaboration with the county's Community Corrections Partnership, shall develop, administer, and collect and submit data to the Board of State and Community Corrections regarding a competitive grant program intended to fund community recidivism and crime reduction services, including, but not limited to, delinquency prevention, homelessness prevention, and reentry services.

(1) Commencing with the 2014–15 fiscal year, the funding shall be allocated to counties by the State Controller's Office from Item 5227-101-3259 of Section 2.00 of the Budget Act of 2014 according to the following schedule:

Alameda	$ 250,000
Alpine	$ 10,000
Amador	$ 10,000
Butte	$ 50,000
Calaveras	$ 10,000
Colusa	$ 10,000
Contra Costa	$ 250,000
Del Norte	$ 10,000
El Dorado	$ 50,000
Fresno	$ 250,000
Glenn	$ 10,000

Humboldt	$ 50,000
Imperial	$ 50,000
Inyo	$ 10,000
Kern	$ 250,000
Kings	$ 50,000
Lake	$ 25,000
Lassen	$ 10,000
Los Angeles	$ 1,600,000
Madera	$ 50,000
Marin	$ 50,000
Mariposa	$ 10,000
Mendocino	$ 25,000
Merced	$ 50,000
Modoc	$ 10,000
Mono	$ 10,000
Monterey	$ 100,000
Napa	$ 50,000
Nevada	$ 25,000
Orange	$ 500,000
Placer	$ 50,000
Plumas	$ 10,000
Riverside	$ 500,000
Sacramento	$ 250,000
San Benito	$ 25,000
San Bernardino	$ 500,000
San Diego	$ 500,000
San Francisco	$ 250,000
San Joaquin	$ 250,000
San Luis Obispo	$ 50,000
San Mateo	$ 250,000
Santa Barbara	$ 100,000
Santa Clara	$ 500,000
Santa Cruz	$ 50,000
Shasta	$ 50,000
Sierra	$ 10,000
Siskiyou	$ 10,000
Solano	$ 100,000
Sonoma	$ 100,000
Stanislaus	$ 100,000

Sutter	$ 25,000
Tehama	$ 25,000
Trinity	$ 10,000
Tulare	$ 100,000
Tuolumne	$ 25,000
Ventura	$ 250,000
Yolo	$ 50,000
Yuba	$ 25,000

(2) Commencing with the 2015–16 fiscal year, the funding shall be allocated to counties by the State Controller's Office from Item 5227-101-3259 of Section 2.00 of the Budget Act of 2015 according to the following schedule:

Alameda	$ 125,000
Alpine	$ 5,000
Amador	$ 5,000
Butte	$ 25,000
Calaveras	$ 5,000
Colusa	$ 5,000
Contra Costa	$ 125,000
Del Norte	$ 5,000
El Dorado	$ 25,000
Fresno	$ 125,000
Glenn	$ 5,000
Humboldt	$ 25,000
Imperial	$ 25,000
Inyo	$ 5,000
Kern	$ 125,000
Kings	$ 25,000
Lake	$ 12,500
Lassen	$ 5,000
Los Angeles	$ 800,000
Madera	$ 25,000
Marin	$ 25,000
Mariposa	$ 5,000
Mendocino	$ 12,500
Merced	$ 25,000
Modoc	$ 5,000
Mono	$ 5,000
Monterey	$ 50,000
Napa	$ 25,000
Nevada	$ 12,500
Orange	$ 250,000
Placer	$ 25,000
Plumas	$ 5,000
Riverside	$ 250,000
Sacramento	$ 125,000
San Benito	$ 12,500
San Bernardino	$ 250,000
San Diego	$ 250,000
San Francisco	$ 125,000
San Joaquin	$ 125,000
San Luis Obispo	$ 25,000
San Mateo	$ 125,000
Santa Barbara	$ 50,000
Santa Clara	$ 250,000
Santa Cruz	$ 25,000
Shasta	$ 25,000
Sierra	$ 5,000
Siskiyou	$ 5,000
Solano	$ 50,000
Sonoma	$ 50,000
Stanislaus	$ 50,000
Sutter	$ 12,500
Tehama	$ 12,500
Trinity	$ 5,000
Tulare	$ 50,000
Tuolumne	$ 12,500
Ventura	$ 125,000
Yolo	$ 25,000
Yuba	$ 12,500

(b) For purposes of this section, "community recidivism and crime reduction service provider" means a nongovernmental entity or a consortium or coalition of nongovernmental entities, that provides community recidivism and crime reduction services, as described in paragraph (2) of subdivision (c), to persons who have been released from the state prison, a county jail, a juvenile detention facility, who are under the supervision of a parole or probation department, or any other person at risk of becoming involved in criminal activities.

(c) (1) A community recidivism and crime reduction service provider shall have a demonstrated history of providing services, as described in paragraph (2), to the target population during the five years immediately prior to the application for a grant awarded pursuant to this section.

(2) A community recidivism and crime reduction service provider shall provide services that are designed to enable persons to whom the services are provided to refrain from engaging in crime, reconnect with their family members, and contribute to their communities. Community recidivism and crime reduction services may include all of the following:

(A) Self-help groups.

(B) Individual or group assistance with basic life skills.

(C) Mentoring programs.

(D) Academic and educational services, including, but not limited to, services to enable the recipient to earn his or her high school diploma.

(E) Job training skills and employment.

(F) Truancy prevention programs.

(G) Literacy programs.

(H) Any other service that advances community recidivism and crime reduction efforts, as identified by the county board of supervisors and the Community Corrections Partnership.

(I) Individual or group assistance with referrals for any of the following:

(i) Mental and physical health assessments.

(ii) Counseling services.

(iii) Education and vocational programs.

(iv) Employment opportunities.
(v) Alcohol and drug treatment.
(vi) Health, wellness, fitness, and nutrition programs and services.
(vii) Personal finance and consumer skills programs and services.
(viii) Other personal growth and development programs to reduce recidivism.
(ix) Housing assistance.
(d) Pursuant to this section and upon agreement to accept funding from the Recidivism Reduction Fund, the board of supervisors, in collaboration with the county's Community Corrections Partnership, shall grant funds allocated to the county, as described in subdivision (a), to community recidivism and crime reduction service providers based on the needs of their community.
(e) (1) The amount awarded to each community recidivism and crime reduction service provider by a county shall be based on the population of the county, as projected by the Department of Finance, and shall not exceed the following for each Budget Act allocation:
(A) One hundred thousand dollars ($100,000) in a county with a population of over 4,000,000 people.
(B) Fifty thousand dollars ($50,000) in a county with a population of 700,000 or more people but less than 4,000,000 people.
(C) Twenty-five thousand dollars ($25,000) in a county with a population of 400,000 or more people but less than 700,000 people.
(D) Ten thousand dollars ($10,000) in a county with a population of less than 400,000 people.
(2) The total amount of grants awarded to a single community recidivism and crime reduction service provider by all counties pursuant to this section shall not exceed one hundred thousand dollars ($100,000) per Budget Act allocation.
(f) The board of supervisors, in collaboration with the county's Community Corrections Partnership, shall establish minimum requirements, funding criteria, and procedures for the counties to award grants consistent with the criteria established in this section.
(g) A community recidivism and crime reduction service provider that receives a grant under this section shall report to the county board of supervisors or the Community Corrections Partnership on the number of individuals served and the types of services provided, consistent with paragraph (2) of subdivision (c). The board of supervisors or the Community Corrections Partnership shall report to the Board of State and Community Corrections any information received under this subdivision from grant recipients.
(h) Of the total amount granted to a county, up to 5 percent may be withheld by the board of supervisors or the Community Corrections Partnership for the payment of administrative costs.
(i) Any funds allocated to a county under this section shall be available for expenditure for a period of four years and any unexpended funds shall revert to the state General Fund at the end of the four-year period.
(Amended by Stats. 2015, Ch. 323, Sec. 7. (SB 102) Effective September 22, 2015.)

CHAPTER 4. Supervised Population Workforce Training Grant Program [1234 - 1234.5]

(Chapter 4 added by Stats. 2014, Ch. 383, Sec. 2.)
1234.
For purposes of this chapter, the following terms have the following meanings:
(a) "California Workforce Development Board" means the California Workforce Development Board established pursuant to Article 1 (commencing with Section 14010) of Chapter 3 of Division 7 of the Unemployment Insurance Code.
(b) "Earn and learn" has the same meaning as in Section 14005 of the Unemployment Insurance Code.
(c) "Grant program" means the Supervised Population Workforce Training Grant Program.
(d) "Supervised population" means those persons who are on parole, probation, mandatory supervision, or postrelease community supervision and are supervised by, or are under the jurisdiction of, a county or the Department of Corrections and Rehabilitation.
(Amended by Stats. 2017, Ch. 96, Sec. 13. (SB 106) Effective July 21, 2017. Repealed as of January 1, 2021, pursuant to Section 1234.5.)
1234.1.
(a) This chapter establishes the Supervised Population Workforce Training Grant Program to be administered by the California Workforce Development Board.
(b) The grant program shall be developed and implemented in accordance with the criteria set forth in Section 1234.3. In developing the program, the California Workforce Development Board shall consult with public and private stakeholders, including local workforce development boards, local governments, and nonprofit community-based organizations that serve the supervised population.
(c) The grant program shall be funded, upon appropriation by the Legislature. Implementation of this program is contingent upon the director of the California Workforce Development Board notifying the Department of Finance that sufficient moneys have been appropriated for this specific grant program.
(d) The outcomes from the grant program shall be reported pursuant to Section 1234.4.
(Amended by Stats. 2016, Ch. 100, Sec. 3. (AB 2061) Effective January 1, 2017. Repealed as of January 1, 2021, pursuant to Section 1234.5.)
1234.2.
The California Workforce Development Board is responsible for setting the policy of the grant program and any funding for the program shall be appropriated directly to the board. The board shall administer the grant program as follows:
(a) Develop criteria for the selection of grant recipients through a public application process, including, but not limited to, the rating and ranking of applications that meet the threshold criteria set forth in this section.
(b) Design the grant program application process to ensure all of the following occurs:
(1) Outreach and technical assistance is made available to eligible applicants, especially to small population and rural counties.
(2) Grants are awarded on a competitive basis. Multiyear grants may be awarded.
(3) Small and rural counties are competitive in applying for funds.
(4) Applicants are encouraged to develop, pilot, or implement, or develop, pilot, and implement, evidence-based, best practices for serving the workforce development or training needs, or both development and training needs, of the supervised population.
(5) Nonprofit community-based organizations are competitive in applying for funds as the lead applicant or in partnership with other agencies and organizations.
(6) The workforce and training needs of one or both of the following are addressed:
(A) Individuals with some postsecondary education who can enter into programs and benefit from services that result in certifications, and placement on a middle skill career ladder.
(B) Individuals who require basic education, training, or earn and learn experience in order to obtain entry level jobs where there are opportunities for career advancement.
(7) Grants are allocated equitably among the grant partners based on services and activities provided in support of the success of participants.
(Amended by Stats. 2017, Ch. 96, Sec. 14. (SB 106) Effective July 21, 2017. Repealed as of January 1, 2021, pursuant to Section 1234.5.)

1234.3.
(a) Each application shall include a list of proposed partners and a partnership agreement outlining the actions each party agrees to undertake as part of the project proposed in the application. Partners may include a county or counties, one or more local workforce development boards, one or more community-based organizations that work directly with the supervised population, and any participating programs operated by the Department of Corrections and Rehabilitation. Partnerships shall be designated to effectively deliver the services specified in the grant so as to meet the needs of the supervised population.
(b) Each project proposed shall allocate grant funds that reflect the role each party plays in the proposed project.
(c) Eligible uses of grant funds include, but are not limited to, vocational training, stipends for trainees, and earn and learn opportunities for the supervised population. Supportive services and job readiness activities shall serve as bridge activities that lead to enrollment in employment or training programs, or both.
(d) Preference shall be awarded to applications for the following:
(1) An application that proposes matching funds, including, but not limited to, moneys committed by local workforce development boards, local governments, and private foundation funds for the express purpose of providing services to the supervised population.
(2) An application submitted by a partnership that currently administers or participates in a workforce training program for the supervised population.
(3) An application that proposes participation by one or more employers, including mission-driven social enterprises and nonprofit organizations with a track record of employing a workforce comprised of formerly incarcerated individuals, who have demonstrated interest in employing individuals in the supervised population, including, but not limited to, earn and learn opportunities and intent to hire individuals who have successfully completed the program.
(4) Applicants that use grant funds primarily to support the direct provision of workforce and training services to the supervised population.
(5) Applicants that propose projects that align with the California Workforce Development Board's strategic plan, regional workforce plans, or local workforce development board plans.
(e) An application shall meet the following requirements:
(1) Set a specific purpose for the use of the grant funds that aligns with the services to be provided and the role of each partner, as well as provide the baseline criteria and metrics by which the overall success of the grant project can be evaluated.
(2) Define the specific subset or subsets of the supervised population, among the eligible supervised population that the grant money will serve.
(3) Define the industry sector or sectors in which the targeted supervised population will be prepared, including the current and projected workforce within the region for those jobs, the range of wage rates, and the training, education, and experience requirements within those industry sectors.
(4) Define the general methodology and training or employment preparation methods proposed to be used and explain the manner in which the progress of the targeted supervised population will be monitored during the grant period.
(5) As appropriate, provide for a partnership with a lead community-based organization with a track record of success in effectively serving the supervised population.
(f) As a condition of receiving funds, a grant recipient shall agree to provide information to the California Workforce Development Board in sufficient detail to allow the California Workforce Development Board to meet the reporting requirements in Section 1234.4.
(Amended by Stats. 2017, Ch. 96, Sec. 15. (SB 106) Effective July 21, 2017. Repealed as of January 1, 2021, pursuant to Section 1234.5.)
1234.4.
(a) On at least an annual basis, and upon completion of the grant period, grant recipients shall report to the California Workforce Development Board regarding their use of the funds and workforce training program outcomes.
(b) By January 1, 2018, the California Workforce Development Board shall submit a report to the Legislature using the reports from the grant recipients. The report shall contain all the following information:
(1) The overall success of the grant program, based on the goals and metrics set in the awarded grants.
(2) An evaluation of the effectiveness of the grant program based on the goals and metrics set in the awarded grants.
(3) In considering the overall success and effectiveness of the grant program, the report shall include a discussion of all of the following:
(A) The education and workforce readiness of the supervised population at the time individual participants entered the program and how this impacted the types of services needed and offered.
(B) Whether the programs aligned with the workforce needs of high-demand sectors of the state and regional economies.
(C) Whether there was an active job market for the skills being developed where the member of the supervised population was likely to be released.
(D) Whether the program increased the number of members of the supervised population that obtained a marketable and industry or apprenticeship board-recognized certification, credential, or degree.
(E) Whether the program led to employment in occupations with a livable wage.
(F) Whether the metrics used to evaluate the individual grants were sufficiently aligned with the objectives of the program.
(c) (1) The requirement for submitting a report imposed under subdivision (b) is inoperative on January 1, 2021, pursuant to Section 10231.5 of the Government Code.
(2) A report to be submitted pursuant to subdivision (b) shall be submitted in compliance with Section 9795 of the Government Code.
(Amended by Stats. 2017, Ch. 96, Sec. 16. (SB 106) Effective July 21, 2017. Repealed as of January 1, 2021, pursuant to Section 1234.5.)
1234.5.
This chapter shall remain in effect only until January 1, 2021, and as of that date is repealed, unless a later enacted statute, that is enacted before January 1, 2021, deletes or extends that date.
(Added by Stats. 2014, Ch. 383, Sec. 2. (AB 2060) Effective January 1, 2015. Repealed as of January 1, 2021, by its own provisions. Note: Repeal affects Chapter 4, commencing with Section 1234.)

TITLE 9. APPEALS IN FELONY CASES [1235 - 1265]

(Heading of Title 9 amended by Stats. 1998, Ch. 931, Sec. 396.)

CHAPTER 1. Appeals, When Allowed and How Taken, and the Effect Thereof [1235 - 1246]

(Chapter 1 enacted 1872.)
1235.

(a) Either party to a felony case may appeal on questions of law alone, as prescribed in this title and in rules adopted by the Judicial Council. The provisions of this title apply only to such appeals.

(b) An appeal from the judgment or appealable order in a felony case is to the court of appeal for the district in which the court from which the appeal is taken is located.

(Amended by Stats. 1998, Ch. 931, Sec. 397. Effective September 28, 1998.)

1236.

The party appealing is known as the appellant, and the adverse party as the respondent, but the title of the action is not changed in consequence of the appeal.

(Enacted 1872.)

1237.

An appeal may be taken by the defendant from both of the following:

(a) Except as provided in Sections 1237.1, 1237.2, and 1237.5, from a final judgment of conviction. A sentence, an order granting probation, or the commitment of a defendant for insanity, the indeterminate commitment of a defendant as a mentally disordered sex offender, or the commitment of a defendant for controlled substance addiction shall be deemed to be a final judgment within the meaning of this section. Upon appeal from a final judgment the court may review any order denying a motion for a new trial.

(b) From any order made after judgment, affecting the substantial rights of the party.

(Amended by Stats. 2015, Ch. 194, Sec. 1. (AB 249) Effective January 1, 2016.)

1237.1.

No appeal shall be taken by the defendant from a judgment of conviction on the ground of an error in the calculation of presentence custody credits, unless the defendant first presents the claim in the trial court at the time of sentencing, or if the error is not discovered until after sentencing, the defendant first makes a motion for correction of the record in the trial court, which may be made informally in writing. The trial court retains jurisdiction after a notice of appeal has been filed to correct any error in the calculation of presentence custody credits upon the defendant's request for correction.

(Amended by Stats. 2015, Ch. 194, Sec. 2. (AB 249) Effective January 1, 2016.)

1237.2.

An appeal may not be taken by the defendant from a judgment of conviction on the ground of an error in the imposition or calculation of fines, penalty assessments, surcharges, fees, or costs unless the defendant first presents the claim in the trial court at the time of sentencing, or if the error is not discovered until after sentencing, the defendant first makes a motion for correction in the trial court, which may be made informally in writing. The trial court retains jurisdiction after a notice of appeal has been filed to correct any error in the imposition or calculation of fines, penalty assessments, surcharges, fees, or costs upon the defendant's request for correction. This section only applies in cases where the erroneous imposition or calculation of fines, penalty assessments, surcharges, fees, or costs are the sole issue on appeal.

(Added by Stats. 2015, Ch. 194, Sec. 3. (AB 249) Effective January 1, 2016.)

1237.5.

No appeal shall be taken by the defendant from a judgment of conviction upon a plea of guilty or nolo contendere, or a revocation of probation following an admission of violation, except where both of the following are met:

(a) The defendant has filed with the trial court a written statement, executed under oath or penalty of perjury showing reasonable constitutional, jurisdictional, or other grounds going to the legality of the proceedings.

(b) The trial court has executed and filed a certificate of probable cause for such appeal with the clerk of the court.

(Amended by Stats. 2002, Ch. 784, Sec. 550. Effective January 1, 2003.)

1238.

(a) An appeal may be taken by the people from any of the following:

(1) An order setting aside all or any portion of the indictment, information, or complaint.

(2) An order sustaining a demurrer to all or any portion of the indictment, accusation, or information.

(3) An order granting a new trial.

(4) An order arresting judgment.

(5) An order made after judgment, affecting the substantial rights of the people.

(6) An order modifying the verdict or finding by reducing the degree of the offense or the punishment imposed or modifying the offense to a lesser offense.

(7) An order dismissing a case prior to trial made upon motion of the court pursuant to Section 1385 whenever such order is based upon an order granting the defendant's motion to return or suppress property or evidence made at a special hearing as provided in this code.

(8) An order or judgment dismissing or otherwise terminating all or any portion of the action including such an order or judgment after a verdict or finding of guilty or an order or judgment entered before the defendant has been placed in jeopardy or where the defendant has waived jeopardy.

(9) An order denying the motion of the people to reinstate the complaint or a portion thereof pursuant to Section 871.5.

(10) The imposition of an unlawful sentence, whether or not the court suspends the execution of the sentence, except that portion of a sentence imposing a prison term which is based upon a court's choice that a term of imprisonment (A) be the upper, middle, or lower term, unless the term selected is not set forth in an applicable statute, or (B) be consecutive or concurrent to another term of imprisonment, unless an applicable statute requires that the term be consecutive. As used in this paragraph, "unlawful sentence" means the imposition of a sentence not authorized by law or the imposition of a sentence based upon an unlawful order of the court which strikes or otherwise modifies the effect of an enhancement or prior conviction.

(11) An order recusing the district attorney pursuant to Section 1424.

(b) If, pursuant to paragraph (8) of subdivision (a), the people prosecute an appeal to decision, or any review of such decision, it shall be binding upon them and they shall be prohibited from refiling the case which was appealed.

(c) When an appeal is taken pursuant to paragraph (7) of subdivision (a), the court may review the order granting the defendant's motion to return or suppress property or evidence made at a special hearing as provided in this code.

(d) Nothing contained in this section shall be construed to authorize an appeal from an order granting probation. Instead, the people may seek appellate review of any grant of probation, whether or not the court imposes sentence, by means of a petition for a writ of mandate or prohibition which is filed within 60 days after probation is granted. The review of any grant of probation shall include review of any order underlying the grant of probation.

(Amended by Stats. 1999, Ch. 344, Sec. 25. Effective September 7, 1999.)

1238.5.

Upon appeal by the prosecution pursuant to Section 1238, where the notice of appeal is filed after the expiration of the time available to defendant to seek review of an otherwise reviewable order or ruling and the appeal by the prosecution relates to a matter decided during the time available to the defendant to seek review of the otherwise reviewable order or ruling, the time for defendant to seek such review is reinstated to run from the date the notice of appeal was filed with proof of service upon defendant or his counsel.

The Judicial Council shall provide by rule for the consolidation of such petition for review with the prosecution appeal.

(Added by Stats. 1975, Ch. 1195.)

1239.

(a) Where an appeal lies on behalf of the defendant or the people, it may be taken by the defendant or his or her counsel, or by counsel for the people, in the manner provided in rules adopted by the Judicial Council.

(b) When upon any plea a judgment of death is rendered, an appeal is automatically taken by the defendant without any action by him or her or his or her counsel. The defendant's trial counsel, whether retained by the defendant or court appointed, shall continue to represent the defendant until completing the additional duties set forth in paragraph (1) of subdivision (e) of Section 1240.1.

(Amended (as added by Stats. 1982, Ch. 917, Sec. 4) by Stats. 1988, Ch. 551, Sec. 1.)

1239.1.

(a) It is the duty of the Supreme Court in a capital case to expedite the review of the case. The court shall appoint counsel for an indigent appellant as soon as possible. The court shall only grant extensions of time for briefing for compelling or extraordinary reasons.

(b) When necessary to remove a substantial backlog in appointment of counsel for capital cases, the Supreme Court shall require attorneys who are qualified for appointment to the most serious non-capital appeals and who meet the qualifications for capital appeals to accept appointment in capital cases as a condition for remaining on the court's appointment list. A "substantial backlog" exists for this purpose when the time from entry of judgment in the trial court to appointment of counsel for appeal exceeds 6 months over a period of 12 consecutive months.

(Added November 8, 2016, by initiative Proposition 66, Sec. 5.)

1240.

(a) When in a proceeding falling within the provisions of Section 15421 of the Government Code a person is not represented by a public defender acting pursuant to Section 27706 of the Government Code or other counsel and he is unable to afford the services of counsel, the court shall appoint the State Public Defender to represent the person except as follows:

(1) The court shall appoint counsel other than the State Public Defender when the State Public Defender has refused to represent the person because of conflict of interest or other reason.

(2) The court may, in its discretion, appoint either the State Public Defender or the attorney who represented the person at his trial when the person requests the latter to represent him on appeal and the attorney consents to the appointment. In unusual cases, where good cause exists, the court may appoint any other attorney.

(3) A court may appoint a county public defender, private attorney, or nonprofit corporation with which the State Public Defender has contracted to furnish defense services pursuant to Government Code Section 15402.

(4) When a judgment of death has been rendered the Supreme Court may, in its discretion, appoint counsel other than the State Public Defender or the attorney who represented the person at trial.

(b) If counsel other than the State Public Defender is appointed pursuant to this section, he may exercise the same authority as the State Public Defender pursuant to Chapter 2 (commencing with Section 15420) of Part 7 of Division 3 of Title 2 of the Government Code.

(Added by Stats. 1975, Ch. 1125.)

1240.1.

(a) In any noncapital criminal, juvenile court, or civil commitment case wherein the defendant would be entitled to the appointment of counsel on appeal if indigent, it shall be the duty of the attorney who represented the person at trial to provide counsel and advice as to whether arguably meritorious grounds exist for reversal or modification of the judgment on appeal. The attorney shall admonish the defendant that he or she is not able to provide advice concerning his or her own competency, and that the State Public Defender or other counsel should be consulted for advice as to whether an issue regarding the competency of counsel should be raised on appeal. The trial court may require trial counsel to certify that he or she has counseled the defendant as to whether arguably meritorious grounds for appeal exist at the time a notice of appeal is filed. Nothing in this section shall be construed to prevent any person having a right to appeal from doing so.

(b) It shall be the duty of every attorney representing an indigent defendant in any criminal, juvenile court, or civil commitment case to execute and file on his or her client's behalf a timely notice of appeal when the attorney is of the opinion that arguably meritorious grounds exist for a reversal or modification of the judgment or orders to be appealed from, and where, in the attorney's judgment, it is in the defendant's interest to pursue any relief that may be available to him or her on appeal; or when directed to do so by a defendant having a right to appeal.

With the notice of appeal the attorney shall file a brief statement of the points to be raised on appeal and a designation of any document, paper, pleading, or transcript of oral proceedings necessary to properly present those points on appeal when the document, paper, pleading, or transcript of oral proceedings would not be included in the normal record on appeal according to the applicable provisions of the California Rules of Court. The executing of the notice of appeal by the defendant's attorney shall not constitute an undertaking to represent the defendant on appeal unless the undertaking is expressly stated in the notice of appeal.

If the defendant was represented by appointed counsel on the trial level, or if it appears that the defendant will request the appointment of counsel on appeal by reason of indigency, the trial attorney shall also assist the defendant in preparing and submitting a motion for the appointment of counsel and any supporting declaration or affidavit as to the defendant's financial condition. These documents shall be filed with the trial court at the time of filing a notice of appeal, and shall be transmitted by the clerk of the trial court to the clerk of the appellate court within three judicial days of their receipt. The appellate court shall act upon that motion without unnecessary delay. An attorney's failure to file a motion for the appointment of counsel with the notice of appeal shall not foreclose the defendant from filing a motion at any time it becomes known to him or her that the attorney has failed to do so, or at any time he or she shall become indigent if he or she was not previously indigent.

(c) The State Public Defender shall, at the request of any attorney representing a prospective indigent appellant or at the request of the prospective indigent appellant himself or herself, provide counsel and advice to the prospective indigent appellant or attorney as to whether arguably meritorious grounds exist on which the judgment or order to be appealed from would be reversed or modified on appeal.

(d) The failure of a trial attorney to perform any duty prescribed in this section, assign any particular point or error in the notice of appeal, or designate any particular thing for inclusion in the record on appeal shall not foreclose any defendant from filing a notice of appeal on his or her own behalf or from raising any point or argument on appeal; nor shall it foreclose the defendant or his or her counsel on appeal from requesting the augmentation or correction of the record on appeal in the reviewing court.

(e) (1) In order to expedite certification of the entire record on appeal in all capital cases, the defendant's trial counsel, whether retained by the defendant or court-appointed, and the prosecutor shall continue to represent the respective parties. Each counsel's obligations extend to taking all steps necessary to facilitate the preparation and timely certification of the record of all trial court proceedings.

(2) The duties imposed on trial counsel in paragraph (1) shall not foreclose the defendant's appellate counsel from requesting additions or corrections to the record on appeal in either the trial court or the California Supreme Court in a manner provided by rules of court adopted by the Judicial Council.

(Amended by Stats. 2003, Ch. 62, Sec. 232. Effective January 1, 2004.)

1241.

In any case in which counsel other than a public defender has been appointed by the Supreme Court or by a court of appeal to represent a party to any appeal or proceeding, such counsel shall receive a reasonable sum for compensation and necessary expenses, the amount of which shall be determined by the court and paid from any funds appropriated to the Judicial Council for that purpose. Claim for the payment of such compensation and expenses shall be made on a form prescribed by the Judicial Council and presented by counsel to the clerk of the appointing court. After the court has made its order fixing the amount to be paid the clerk shall transmit a copy of the order to the State Controller who shall draw his warrant in payment thereof and transmit it to the payee.
(Amended by Stats. 1975, Ch. 1125.)
1242.
An appeal taken by the people in no case stays or affects the operation of a judgment in favor of the defendant, until judgment is reversed.
(Enacted 1872.)
1243.
An appeal to the Supreme Court or to a court of appeal from a judgment of conviction stays the execution of the judgment in all cases where a sentence of death has been imposed, but does not stay the execution of the judgment or order granting probation in any other case unless the trial or appellate court shall so order. The granting or refusal of such an order shall rest in the discretion of the court, except that a court shall not stay any duty to register as a sex offender pursuant to Section 290. If the order is made, the clerk of the court shall issue a certificate stating that the order has been made.
(Amended by Stats. 1998, Ch. 960, Sec. 3. Effective January 1, 1999.)
1244.
If the certificate provided for in the preceding section is filed, the Sheriff must, if the defendant be in his custody, upon being served with a copy thereof, keep the defendant in his custody without executing the judgment, and detain him to abide the judgment on appeal.
(Enacted 1872.)
1245.
If before the granting of the certificate, the execution of the judgment has commenced, the further execution thereof is suspended, and upon service of a copy of such certificate the defendant must be restored, by the officer in whose custody he is, to his original custody.
(Amended by Stats. 1905, Ch. 538.)
1246.
The record on appeal shall be made up and filed in such time and manner as shall be prescribed in rules adopted by the Judicial Council.
(Amended by Stats. 1945, Ch. 40.)

CHAPTER 1a. Judicial Council Rules [1247k-1247k.]

(Chapter 1a added by Stats. 1941, Ch. 562.)
1247k.
The Judicial Council shall have the power to prescribe by rules for the practice and procedure on appeal, and for the time and manner in which the records on such appeals shall be made up and filed, in all criminal cases in all courts of this state.
The rules shall take effect on July 1, 1943, and thereafter all laws in conflict therewith shall be of no further force or effect.
(Amended by Stats. 2004, Ch. 193, Sec. 143. Effective January 1, 2005.)

CHAPTER 2. Dismissing an Appeal for Irregularity [1248- 1248.]

(Chapter 2 enacted 1872.)
1248.
If the appeal is irregular in any substantial particular, but not otherwise, the appellate court may order it to be dismissed.
(Amended by Stats. 1945, Ch. 40.)

CHAPTER 3. Argument of the Appeal [1252 - 1256]

(Chapter 3 enacted 1872.)
1252.
On an appeal in a criminal case, no continuance shall be granted upon stipulation of counsel, and no continuance shall be granted for any longer period than the ends of justice shall require. On an appeal by a defendant, the appellate court shall, in addition to the issues raised by the defendant, consider and pass upon all rulings of the trial court adverse to the State which it may be requested to pass upon by the Attorney General.
(Amended by Stats. 1945, Ch. 40.)
1253.
The judgment may be affirmed if the appellant fail to appear, but can be reversed only after argument, though the respondent fail to appear.
(Enacted 1872.)
1254.
Upon the argument of the appeal, if the offense is punishable with death, two counsel must be heard on each side, if they require it. In any other case the Court may, in its discretion, restrict the argument to one counsel on each side.
(Enacted 1872.)
1255.
The defendant need not personally appear in the appellate Court.
(Enacted 1872.)
1256.
It shall be the duty of the district attorney to cooperate with and assist the attorney general in presenting all criminal matters on appeal.
(Added by Stats. 1927, Ch. 620.)

CHAPTER 4. Judgment Upon Appeal [1258 - 1265]

(Chapter 4 enacted 1872.)

1258.
After hearing the appeal, the Court must give judgment without regard to technical errors or defects, or to exceptions, which do not affect the substantial rights of the parties.
(Enacted 1872.)
1259.
Upon an appeal taken by the defendant, the appellate court may, without exception having been taken in the trial court, review any question of law involved in any ruling, order, instruction, or thing whatsoever said or done at the trial or prior to or after judgment, which thing was said or done after objection made in and considered by the lower court, and which affected the substantial rights of the defendant. The appellate court may also review any instruction given, refused or modified, even though no objection was made thereto in the lower court, if the substantial rights of the defendant were affected thereby.
(Amended by Stats. 1939, Ch. 1016.)
1260.
The court may reverse, affirm, or modify a judgment or order appealed from, or reduce the degree of the offense or attempted offense or the punishment imposed, and may set aside, affirm, or modify any or all of the proceedings subsequent to, or dependent upon, such judgment or order, and may, if proper, order a new trial and may, if proper, remand the cause to the trial court for such further proceedings as may be just under the circumstances.
(Amended by Stats. 1978, Ch. 1166.)
1261.
When a new trial is ordered it must be directed to be had in the Court of the county from which the appeal was taken.
(Enacted 1872.)
1262.
If a judgment against the defendant is reversed, such reversal shall be deemed an order for a new trial, unless the appellate court shall otherwise direct. If the appellate court directs a final disposition of the action in the defendant's favor, the court must, if he is in custody, direct him to be discharged therefrom; or if on bail that his bail may be exonerated; or if money or other property was deposited instead of bail, that it be refunded to the defendant or to the person or persons found by the court to have deposited said money or other property on behalf of said defendant. If a judgment against the defendant is reversed and the case is dismissed, or if the appellate court directs a final disposition of the action in defendant's favor, and defendant has theretofore paid a fine in the case, such act shall also be deemed an order of the court that the fine, including any penalty assessment thereon, be returned to defendant.
(Amended by Stats. 1963, Ch. 1609.)
1263.
If a judgment against the defendant is affirmed, the original judgment must be enforced.
(Enacted 1872.)
1265.
(a) After the certificate of the judgment has been remitted to the court below, the appellate court has no further jurisdiction of the appeal or of the proceedings thereon, and all orders necessary to carry the judgment into effect shall be made by the court to which the certificate is remitted. However, if a judgment has been affirmed on appeal no motion shall be made or proceeding in the nature of a petition for a writ of error coram nobis shall be brought to procure the vacation of that judgment, except in the court which affirmed the judgment on appeal. When a judgment is affirmed by a court of appeal and a hearing is not granted by the Supreme Court, the application for the writ shall be made to the court of appeal.
(b) Where it is necessary to obtain personal jurisdiction of the defendant in order to carry the judgment into effect, upon a satisfactory showing that other means such as contact by mail, phone, or notification by means of the defendant's counsel have failed to secure the defendant's appearance, the court to which the certificate has been remitted may issue a bench warrant.
(Amended by Stats. 1992, Ch. 128, Sec. 1. Effective July 7, 1992.)

TITLE 10. MISCELLANEOUS PROCEEDINGS [1268 - 1424.5]
(Title 10 enacted 1872.)

CHAPTER 1. Bail [1268 - 1320.6]

(Chapter 1 enacted 1872.)
ARTICLE 1. In What Cases the Defendant May Be Admitted to Bail [1268 - 1276.5]
(Article 1 enacted 1872.)
1268.
Admission to bail is the order of a competent Court or magistrate that the defendant be discharged from actual custody upon bail.
(Enacted 1872. Repealed pursuant to Section 1320.6 if and when that section takes effect.)
1269.
The taking of bail consists in the acceptance, by a competent court or magistrate, of the undertaking of sufficient bail for the appearance of the defendant, according to the terms of the undertaking, or that the bail will pay to the people of this state a specified sum. Upon filing, the clerk shall enter in the register of actions the date and amounts of such bond and the name or names of the surety or sureties thereon. In the event of the loss or destruction of such bond, such entries so made shall be prima facie evidence of the due execution of such bond as required by law.
Whenever any bail bond has been deposited in any criminal action or proceeding in a municipal or superior court or in any proceeding in habeas corpus in a superior court, and it is made to appear to the satisfaction of the court by affidavit or by testimony in open court that more than three years have elapsed since the exoneration or release of said bail, the court must direct that such bond be destroyed.
(Amended by Stats. 1998, Ch. 931, Sec. 398. Effective September 28, 1998. Repealed pursuant to Section 1320.6 if and when that section takes effect.)
1269a.
Except as otherwise provided by law, no defendant charged in a warrant of arrest with any public offense shall be discharged from custody upon bail except upon a written order of a competent court or magistrate admitting the defendant to bail in the amount specified in the indorsement referred to in Section 815a, and where an undertaking is furnished, upon a written order of such court or magistrate approving the undertaking. All such orders must be signed by such court or magistrate and delivered to the officer having custody of the defendant before the defendant is released. Any officer releasing any defendant upon bail otherwise than as herein provided shall be guilty of a misdemeanor.
(Amended by Stats. 1941, Ch. 366. Repealed pursuant to Section 1320.6 if and when that section takes effect.)
1269b.

(a) The officer in charge of a jail in which an arrested person is held in custody, an officer of a sheriff's department or police department of a city who is in charge of a jail or is employed at a fixed police or sheriff's facility and is acting under an agreement with the agency that keeps the jail in which an arrested person is held in custody, an employee of a sheriff's department or police department of a city who is assigned by the department to collect bail, the clerk of the superior court of the county in which the offense was alleged to have been committed, and the clerk of the superior court in which the case against the defendant is pending may approve and accept bail in the amount fixed by the warrant of arrest, schedule of bail, or order admitting to bail in cash or surety bond executed by a certified, admitted surety insurer as provided in the Insurance Code, to issue and sign an order for the release of the arrested person, and to set a time and place for the appearance of the arrested person before the appropriate court and give notice thereof.

(b) If a defendant has appeared before a judge of the court on the charge contained in the complaint, indictment, or information, the bail shall be in the amount fixed by the judge at the time of the appearance. If that appearance has not been made, the bail shall be in the amount fixed in the warrant of arrest or, if no warrant of arrest has been issued, the amount of bail shall be pursuant to the uniform countywide schedule of bail for the county in which the defendant is required to appear, previously fixed and approved as provided in subdivisions (c) and (d).

(c) It is the duty of the superior court judges in each county to prepare, adopt, and annually revise a uniform countywide schedule of bail for all bailable felony offenses and for all misdemeanor and infraction offenses except Vehicle Code infractions. The penalty schedule for infraction violations of the Vehicle Code shall be established by the Judicial Council in accordance with Section 40310 of the Vehicle Code.

(d) A court may, by local rule, prescribe the procedure by which the uniform countywide schedule of bail is prepared, adopted, and annually revised by the judges. If a court does not adopt a local rule, the uniform countywide schedule of bail shall be prepared, adopted, and annually revised by a majority of the judges.

(e) In adopting a uniform countywide schedule of bail for all bailable felony offenses the judges shall consider the seriousness of the offense charged. In considering the seriousness of the offense charged the judges shall assign an additional amount of required bail for each aggravating or enhancing factor chargeable in the complaint, including, but not limited to, additional bail for charges alleging facts that would bring a person within any of the following sections: Section 667.5, 667.51, 667.6, 667.8, 667.85, 667.9, 667.10, 12022, 12022.1, 12022.2, 12022.3, 12022.4, 12022.5, 12022.53, 12022.6, 12022.7, 12022.8, or 12022.9 of this code, or Section 11356.5, 11370.2, or 11370.4 of the Health and Safety Code.
In considering offenses in which a violation of Chapter 6 (commencing with Section 11350) of Division 10 of the Health and Safety Code is alleged, the judge shall assign an additional amount of required bail for offenses involving large quantities of controlled substances.

(f) The countywide bail schedule shall contain a list of the offenses and the amounts of bail applicable for each as the judges determine to be appropriate. If the schedule does not list all offenses specifically, it shall contain a general clause for designated amounts of bail as the judges of the county determine to be appropriate for all the offenses not specifically listed in the schedule. A copy of the countywide bail schedule shall be sent to the officer in charge of the county jail, to the officer in charge of each city jail within the county, to each superior court judge and commissioner in the county, and to the Judicial Council.

(g) Upon posting bail, the defendant or arrested person shall be discharged from custody as to the offense on which the bail is posted.
All money and surety bonds so deposited with an officer authorized to receive bail shall be transmitted immediately to the judge or clerk of the court by which the order was made or warrant issued or bail schedule fixed. If, in the case of felonies, an indictment is filed, the judge or clerk of the court shall transmit all of the money and surety bonds to the clerk of the court.

(h) If a defendant or arrested person so released fails to appear at the time and in the court so ordered upon his or her release from custody, Sections 1305 and 1306 apply.
(Amended by Stats. 2003, Ch. 149, Sec. 76. Effective January 1, 2004. Repealed pursuant to Section 1320.6 if and when that section takes effect.)
1269c.
If a defendant is arrested without a warrant for a bailable felony offense or for the misdemeanor offense of violating a domestic violence restraining order, and a peace officer has reasonable cause to believe that the amount of bail set forth in the schedule of bail for that offense is insufficient to ensure the defendant's appearance or to ensure the protection of a victim, or family member of a victim, of domestic violence, the peace officer shall prepare a declaration under penalty of perjury setting forth the facts and circumstances in support of his or her belief and file it with a magistrate, as defined in Section 808, or his or her commissioner, in the county in which the offense is alleged to have been committed or having personal jurisdiction over the defendant, requesting an order setting a higher bail. Except where the defendant is charged with an offense listed in subdivision (a) of Section 1270.1, the defendant, either personally or through his or her attorney, friend, or family member, also may make application to the magistrate for release on bail lower than that provided in the schedule of bail or on his or her own recognizance. The magistrate or commissioner to whom the application is made is authorized to set bail in an amount that he or she deems sufficient to ensure the defendant's appearance or to ensure the protection of a victim, or family member of a victim, of domestic violence, and to set bail on the terms and conditions that he or she, in his or her discretion, deems appropriate, or he or she may authorize the defendant's release on his or her own recognizance. If, after the application is made, no order changing the amount of bail is issued within eight hours after booking, the defendant shall be entitled to be released on posting the amount of bail set forth in the applicable bail schedule.
(Amended by Stats. 2010, Ch. 176, Sec. 1. (SB 1049) Effective January 1, 2011. Repealed pursuant to Section 1320.6 if and when that section takes effect.)
1270.
(a) Any person who has been arrested for, or charged with, an offense other than a capital offense may be released on his or her own recognizance by a court or magistrate who could release a defendant from custody upon the defendant giving bail, including a defendant arrested upon an out-of-county warrant. A defendant who is in custody and is arraigned on a complaint alleging an offense which is a misdemeanor, and a defendant who appears before a court or magistrate upon an out-of-county warrant arising out of a case involving only misdemeanors, shall be entitled to an own recognizance release unless the court makes a finding on the record, in accordance with Section 1275, that an own recognizance release will compromise public safety or will not reasonably assure the appearance of the defendant as required. Public safety shall be the primary consideration. If the court makes one of those findings, the court shall then set bail and specify the conditions, if any, whereunder the defendant shall be released.
(b) Article 9 (commencing with Section 1318) shall apply to any person who is released pursuant to this section.
(Amended by Stats. 1995, Ch. 51, Sec. 1. Effective January 1, 1996. Repealed pursuant to Section 1320.6 if and when that section takes effect.)
1270.1.
(a) Except as provided in subdivision (e), before any person who is arrested for any of the following crimes may be released on bail in an amount that is either more or less than the amount contained in the schedule of bail for the offense, or may be released on his or her own recognizance, a hearing shall be held in open court before the magistrate or judge:

(1) A serious felony, as defined in subdivision (c) of Section 1192.7, or a violent felony, as defined in subdivision (c) of Section 667.5, but not including a violation of subdivision (a) of Section 460 (residential burglary).
(2) A violation of Section 136.1 where punishment is imposed pursuant to subdivision (c) of Section 136.1, Section 262, 273.5, or 422 where the offense is punished as a felony, or Section 646.9.
(3) A violation of paragraph (1) of subdivision (e) of Section 243.
(4) A violation of Section 273.6 if the detained person made threats to kill or harm, has engaged in violence against, or has gone to the residence or workplace of, the protected party.
(b) The prosecuting attorney and defense attorney shall be given a two-court-day written notice and an opportunity to be heard on the matter. If the detained person does not have counsel, the court shall appoint counsel for purposes of this section only. The hearing required by this section shall be held within the time period prescribed in Section 825.
(c) At the hearing, the court shall consider evidence of past court appearances of the detained person, the maximum potential sentence that could be imposed, and the danger that may be posed to other persons if the detained person is released. In making the determination whether to release the detained person on his or her own recognizance, the court shall consider the potential danger to other persons, including threats that have been made by the detained person and any past acts of violence. The court shall also consider any evidence offered by the detained person regarding his or her ties to the community and his or her ability to post bond.
(d) If the judge or magistrate sets the bail in an amount that is either more or less than the amount contained in the schedule of bail for the offense, the judge or magistrate shall state the reasons for that decision and shall address the issue of threats made against the victim or witness, if they were made, in the record. This statement shall be included in the record.
(e) Notwithstanding subdivision (a), a judge or magistrate, pursuant to Section 1269c, may, with respect to a bailable felony offense or a misdemeanor offense of violating a domestic violence order, increase bail to an amount exceeding that set forth in the bail schedule without a hearing, provided an oral or written declaration of facts justifying the increase is presented under penalty of perjury by a sworn peace officer.
(Amended by Stats. 2010, Ch. 176, Sec. 2. (SB 1049) Effective January 1, 2011. Repealed pursuant to Section 1320.6 if and when that section takes effect.)
1270.2.
When a person is detained in custody on a criminal charge prior to conviction for want of bail, that person is entitled to an automatic review of the order fixing the amount of the bail by the judge or magistrate having jurisdiction of the offense. That review shall be held not later than five days from the time of the original order fixing the amount of bail on the original accusatory pleading. The defendant may waive this review.
(Added by Stats. 1986, Ch. 658, Sec. 1. Repealed pursuant to Section 1320.6 if and when that section takes effect.)
1270.5.
A defendant charged with an offense punishable with death cannot be admitted to bail, when the proof of his or her guilt is evident or the presumption thereof great. The finding of an indictment does not add to the strength of the proof or the presumptions to be drawn therefrom.
(Added by renumbering Section 1270 (as enacted in 1872) by Stats. 1986, Ch. 248, Sec. 165. Repealed pursuant to Section 1320.6 if and when that section takes effect.)
1271.
If the charge is for any other offense, he may be admitted to bail before conviction, as a matter of right.
(Enacted 1872. Repealed pursuant to Section 1320.6 if and when that section takes effect.)
1272.
After conviction of an offense not punishable with death, a defendant who has made application for probation or who has appealed may be admitted to bail:
1. As a matter of right, before judgment is pronounced pending application for probation in cases of misdemeanors, or when the appeal is from a judgment imposing a fine only.
2. As a matter of right, before judgment is pronounced pending application for probation in cases of misdemeanors, or when the appeal is from a judgment imposing imprisonment in cases of misdemeanors.
3. As a matter of discretion in all other cases, except that a person convicted of an offense subject to this subdivision, who makes a motion for release on bail subsequent to a sentencing hearing, shall provide notice of the hearing on the bail motion to the prosecuting attorney at least five court days prior to the hearing.
(Amended by Stats. 1984, Ch. 1202, Sec. 2. Effective September 17, 1984. Repealed pursuant to Section 1320.6 if and when that section takes effect.)
1272.1.
Release on bail pending appeal under subdivision (3) of Section 1272 shall be ordered by the court if the defendant demonstrates all the following:
(a) By clear and convincing evidence, the defendant is not likely to flee. Under this subdivision the court shall consider the following criteria:
(1) The ties of the defendant to the community, including his or her employment, the duration of his or her residence, the defendant's family attachments and his or her property holdings.
(2) The defendant's record of appearance at past court hearings or of flight to avoid prosecution.
(3) The severity of the sentence the defendant faces.
(b) By clear and convincing evidence, the defendant does not pose a danger to the safety of any other person or to the community.
Under this subdivision the court shall consider, among other factors, whether the crime for which the defendant was convicted is a violent felony, as defined in subdivision (c) of Section 667.5.
(c) The appeal is not for the purpose of delay and, based upon the record in the case, raises a substantial legal question which, if decided in favor of the defendant, is likely to result in reversal.
For purposes of this subdivision, a "substantial legal question" means a close question, one of more substance than would be necessary to a finding that it was not frivolous. In assessing whether a substantial legal question has been raised on appeal by the defendant, the court shall not be required to determine whether it committed error.
In making its decision on whether to grant defendants' motions for bail under subdivision (3) of Section 1272, the court shall include a brief statement of reasons in support of an order granting or denying a motion for bail on appeal. The statement need only include the basis for the order with sufficient specificity to permit meaningful review.
(Amended by Stats. 1989, Ch. 150, Sec. 1. Repealed pursuant to Section 1320.6 if and when that section takes effect.)
1273.
If the offense is bailable, the defendant may be admitted to bail before conviction:
First—For his appearance before the magistrate, on the examination of the charge, before being held to answer.
Second—To appear at the Court to which the magistrate is required to return the depositions and statement, upon the defendant being held to answer after examination.
Third—After indictment, either before the bench warrant is issued for his arrest, or upon any order of the Court committing him, or enlarging the amount of bail, or upon his being surrendered by his bail to answer the indictment in the Court in which it is found, or to which it may be transferred for trial.

And after conviction, and upon an appeal:

First—If the appeal is from a judgment imposing a fine only, on the undertaking of bail that he will pay the same, or such part of it as the appellate Court may direct, if the judgment is affirmed or modified, or the appeal is dismissed.

Second—If judgment of imprisonment has been given, that he will surrender himself in execution of the judgment, upon its being affirmed or modified, or upon the appeal being dismissed, or that in case the judgment be reversed, and that the cause be remanded for a new trial, that he will appear in the Court to which said cause may be remanded, and submit himself to the orders and process thereof.

(Amended by Code Amendments 1875-76, Ch. 80. Repealed pursuant to Section 1320.6 if and when that section takes effect.)

1274.

When the admission to bail is a matter of discretion, the Court or officer to whom the application is made must require reasonable notice thereof to be given to the District Attorney of the county.

(Enacted 1872. Repealed pursuant to Section 1320.6 if and when that section takes effect.)

1275.

(a) (1) In setting, reducing, or denying bail, a judge or magistrate shall take into consideration the protection of the public, the seriousness of the offense charged, the previous criminal record of the defendant, and the probability of his or her appearing at trial or at a hearing of the case. The public safety shall be the primary consideration. In setting bail, a judge or magistrate may consider factors such as the information included in a report prepared in accordance with Section 1318.1.

(2) In considering the seriousness of the offense charged, a judge or magistrate shall include consideration of the alleged injury to the victim, and alleged threats to the victim or a witness to the crime charged, the alleged use of a firearm or other deadly weapon in the commission of the crime charged, and the alleged use or possession of controlled substances by the defendant.

(b) In considering offenses wherein a violation of Chapter 6 (commencing with Section 11350) of Division 10 of the Health and Safety Code is alleged, a judge or magistrate shall consider the following: (1) the alleged amounts of controlled substances involved in the commission of the offense, and (2) whether the defendant is currently released on bail for an alleged violation of Chapter 6 (commencing with Section 11350) of Division 10 of the Health and Safety Code.

(c) Before a court reduces bail to below the amount established by the bail schedule approved for the county, in accordance with subdivisions (b) and (c) of Section 1269b, for a person charged with a serious felony, as defined in subdivision (c) of Section 1192.7, or a violent felony, as defined in subdivision (c) of Section 667.5, the court shall make a finding of unusual circumstances and shall set forth those facts on the record. For purposes of this subdivision, "unusual circumstances" does not include the fact that the defendant has made all prior court appearances or has not committed any new offenses.

(Amended by Stats. 2014, Ch. 71, Sec. 128. (SB 1304) Effective January 1, 2015. Repealed pursuant to Section 1320.6 if and when that section takes effect.)

1275.1.

(a) Bail, pursuant to this chapter, shall not be accepted unless a judge or magistrate finds that no portion of the consideration, pledge, security, deposit, or indemnification paid, given, made, or promised for its execution was feloniously obtained.

(b) A hold on the release of a defendant from custody shall only be ordered by a magistrate or judge if any of the following occurs:

(1) A peace officer, as defined in Section 830, files a declaration executed under penalty of perjury setting forth probable cause to believe that the source of any consideration, pledge, security, deposit, or indemnification paid, given, made, or promised for its execution was feloniously obtained.

(2) A prosecutor files a declaration executed under penalty of perjury setting forth probable cause to believe that the source of any consideration, pledge, security, deposit, or indemnification paid, given, made, or promised for its execution was feloniously obtained. A prosecutor shall have absolute civil immunity for executing a declaration pursuant to this paragraph.

(3) The magistrate or judge has probable cause to believe that the source of any consideration, pledge, security, deposit, or indemnification paid, given, made, or promised for its execution was feloniously obtained.

(c) Once a magistrate or judge has determined that probable cause exists, as provided in subdivision (b), a defendant bears the burden by a preponderance of the evidence to show that no part of any consideration, pledge, security, deposit, or indemnification paid, given, made, or promised for its execution was obtained by felonious means. Once a defendant has met such burden, the magistrate or judge shall release the hold previously ordered and the defendant shall be released under the authorized amount of bail.

(d) The defendant and his or her attorney shall be provided with a copy of the declaration of probable cause filed under subdivision (b) no later than the date set forth in Section 825.

(e) Nothing in this section shall prohibit a defendant from obtaining a loan of money so long as the loan will be funded and repaid with funds not feloniously obtained.

(f) At the request of any person providing any portion of the consideration, pledge, security, deposit, or indemnification paid, given, made, or promised for its execution, the magistrate or judge, at an evidentiary hearing to determine the source of the funds, may close it to the general public to protect the person's right to privacy in his or her financial affairs.

(g) If the declaration, having been filed with a magistrate or judge, is not acted on within 24 hours, the defendant shall be released from custody upon posting of the amount of bail set.

(h) Nothing in this code shall deny the right of the defendant, either personally or through his or her attorney, bail agent licensed by the Department of Insurance, admitted surety insurer licensed by the Department of Insurance, friend, or member of his or her family from making an application to the magistrate or judge for the release of the defendant on bail.

(i) The bail of any defendant found to have willfully misled the court regarding the source of bail may be increased as a result of the willful misrepresentation. The misrepresentation may be a factor considered in any subsequent bail hearing.

(j) If a defendant has met the burden under subdivision (c), and a defendant will be released from custody upon the issuance of a bail bond issued pursuant to authority of Section 1269 or 1269b by any admitted surety insurer or any bail agent, approved by the Insurance Commissioner, the magistrate or judge shall vacate the holding order imposed under subdivision (b) upon the condition that the consideration for the bail bond is approved by the court.

(k) As used in this section, "feloniously obtained" means any consideration, pledge, security, deposit, or indemnification paid, given, made, or promised for its execution which is possessed, received, or obtained through an unlawful act, transaction, or occurrence constituting a felony.

(Added by Stats. 1998, Ch. 726, Sec. 2. Effective January 1, 1999. Repealed pursuant to Section 1320.6 if and when that section takes effect.)

1276.

(a) A bail bond or undertaking of bail of an admitted surety insurer shall be accepted or approved by a court or magistrate without further acknowledgment if executed by a licensed bail agent of the insurer under penalty of perjury and issued in the name of the insurer by a person authorized to do so by an unrevoked power of attorney on file in the office of the clerk of the county in which the court or magistrate is located.

(b) One person may both execute and issue the bail bond or undertaking of bail if qualified as provided in this section.

(Added by Stats. 1982, Ch. 517, Sec. 316. Repealed pursuant to Section 1320.6 if and when that section takes effect.)

1276.5.

(a) At the time of an initial application to a bail bond licensee for a bail bond which is to be secured by a lien against real property, the bail bond licensee shall provide the property owner with a written disclosure statement in the following form:

"DISCLOSURE OF LIEN AGAINST REAL PROPERTY DO NOT SIGN THIS DOCUMENT UNTIL YOU READ AND UNDERSTAND IT!

THIS BAIL BOND WILL BE SECURED BY REAL PROPERTY YOU OWN OR IN WHICH YOU HAVE AN INTEREST. THE FAILURE TO PAY THE BAIL BOND PREMIUMS WHEN DUE OR THE FAILURE OF THE DEFENDANT TO COMPLY WITH THE CONDITIONS OF BAIL COULD RESULT IN THE LOSS OF YOUR PROPERTY!"

(b) The disclosure required in subdivision (a) shall be made in 14-point bold type by either of the following means:

(1) A separate and specific document attached to or accompanying the application.

(2) A clear and conspicuous statement on the face of the application.

(c) The property owner shall be given a completed copy of the disclosure statement and of the note and deed of trust or other instrument creating the lien against real property prior to the execution of any instrument creating a lien against real property. The failure to fully comply with subdivision (a) or (b), or this subdivision, shall render the deed of trust or other instrument creating the lien against real property voidable.

(d) Within 30 days after notice is given by any individual, agency, or entity to the surety or bail bond licensee of the expiration of the time for appeal of the order exonerating the bail bond, or within 30 days after the payment in full of all moneys owed on the bail bond obligation secured by any lien against real property, whichever is later in time, the bail bond licensee shall deliver to the property owner a fully executed and notarized reconveyance of title, a certificate of discharge, or a full release of any lien against real property to secure performance of the conditions of the bail bond. If a timely notice of appeal of the order exonerating the bail bond is filed with the court, that 30-day period shall begin on the date the determination of the appellate court affirming the order exonerating the bail bond becomes final. Upon the reconveyance, the licensee shall deliver to the property owner the original note and deed of trust, security agreement, or other instrument which secures the bail bond obligation. If the licensee fails to comply with this subdivision, the property owner may petition the superior court to issue an order directing the clerk of the superior court to execute a full reconveyance of title, a certificate of discharge, or a full release of any lien against real property created to secure performance of the conditions of the bail bond. The petition shall be verified and shall allege facts showing that the licensee has failed to comply with this subdivision.

(e) The violation of this section shall make the violator liable to the person affected by the violation for all damages which that person may sustain by reason of the violation plus statutory damages in the sum of three hundred dollars ($300). The property owner shall be entitled, if he or she prevails, to recover court costs and reasonable attorney's fees as determined by the court in any action brought to enforce this section.

(Added by Stats. 1991, Ch. 838, Sec. 1. Repealed pursuant to Section 1320.6 if and when that section takes effect.)

ARTICLE 2. Bail Upon Being Held to Answer Before Indictment [1277 - 1281a]

(Article 2 enacted 1872.)

1277.

When the defendant has been held to answer upon an examination for a public offense, the admission to bail may be by the magistrate by whom he is so held, or by any magistrate who has power to issue the writ of habeas corpus.

(Enacted 1872. Repealed pursuant to Section 1320.6 if and when that section takes effect.)

1278.

(a) Bail is put in by a written undertaking, executed by two sufficient sureties (with or without the defendant, in the discretion of the magistrate), and acknowledged before the court or magistrate, in substantially the following form:

An order having been made on the _____ day of _____, 20___, by _____, a judge of the _____ Court of _____ County, that _____ be held to answer upon a charge of (stating briefly the nature of the offense), upon which he or she has been admitted to bail in the sum of _____ dollars ($_____); we, _____ and _____, of _____ (stating their place of residence and occupation), hereby undertake that the above-named _____ will appear and answer any charge in any accusatory pleading based upon the acts supporting the charge above mentioned, in whatever court it may be prosecuted, and will at all times hold himself or herself amenable to the orders and process of the court, and if convicted, will appear for pronouncement of judgment or grant of probation, or if he or she fails to perform either of these conditions, that we will pay to the people of the State of California the sum of _____ dollars ($_____) (inserting the sum in which the defendant is admitted to bail). If the forfeiture of this bond be ordered by the court, judgment may be summarily made and entered forthwith against the said (naming the sureties), and the defendant if he or she be a party to the bond, for the amount of their respective undertakings herein, as provided by Sections 1305 and 1306.

(b) Every undertaking of bail shall contain the bail agent license number of the owner of the bail agency issuing the undertaking along with the name, address, and phone number of the agency, regardless of whether the owner is an individual, partnership, or corporation. The bail agency name on the undertaking shall be a business name approved by the Insurance Commissioner for use by the bail agency owner, and be so reflected in the public records of the commissioner. The license number of the bail agent appearing on the undertaking shall be in the same type size as the name, address, and phone number of the agency.

(Amended by Stats. 2004, Ch. 104, Sec. 1. Effective January 1, 2005. Repealed pursuant to Section 1320.6 if and when that section takes effect.)

1279.

The qualifications of bail are as follows:

1. Each of them must be a resident, householder, or freeholder within the state; but the court or magistrate may refuse to accept any person as bail who is not a resident of the county where bail is offered;

2. They must each be worth the amount specified in the undertaking, exclusive of property exempt from execution, except that if any of the sureties is not worth the amount specified in the undertaking, exclusive of property exempt from execution, but owns any equity in real property, a hearing must be held before the magistrate to determine the value of such equity. Witnesses may be called and examined at such hearing and if the magistrate is satisfied that the value of the equity is equal to twice the amount of the bond such surety is justified. In any case, the court or magistrate, on taking bail, may allow more than two sureties to justify severally in amounts less than that expressed in the undertaking, if the whole justification be equivalent to that of sufficient bail.

(Amended by Stats. 1931, Ch. 1172. Repealed pursuant to Section 1320.6 if and when that section takes effect.)

1280.

The bail must in all cases justify by affidavit taken before the magistrate, that they each possess the qualifications provided in the preceding section. The magistrate may further examine the bail upon oath concerning their sufficiency, in such manner as he may deem proper.

(Enacted 1872. Repealed pursuant to Section 1320.6 if and when that section takes effect.)

1280a.
All affidavits for the justification of bail shall set forth the amount of the bail undertaking, a notice that the affidavit shall constitute a lien upon the real property described in the affidavit immediately upon the recordation of the affidavit with the county recorder pursuant to Section 1280b, and the legal description and assessor's parcel numbers of the real estate owned by the bail, which is scheduled as showing that they each possess the qualifications provided in the preceding sections, the affidavit shall also show all encumbrances upon the real estate known to affiants and shall show the number of bonds, if any, on which each bail has qualified, within one year before the date of the affidavit, together with the amount of each such bond, the date on which, the county in which, and the name of the principal for whom each bond was executed.
The affidavit shall also state the amount of each bail's liability on bonds executed in previous years and not exonerated at the date of the execution of the affidavit and be signed and acknowledged by the owner of the real property.
(Amended by Stats. 1987, Ch. 828, Sec. 82. Repealed pursuant to Section 1320.6 if and when that section takes effect.)

1280b.
It shall be the duty of the judge or magistrate to file with the clerk of the court, within 24 hours after presentation to him or her, all affidavits for the justification of bail, by delivering or mailing them to the clerk of the court. Certified copies of the affidavits for justification of bail involving equity in real property may upon the written order of the judge or magistrate be recorded with the county recorder.
(Amended by Stats. 1988, Ch. 676, Sec. 1. Repealed pursuant to Section 1320.6 if and when that section takes effect.)

1280.1.
(a) From the time of recording an affidavit for the justification of bail, the affidavit shall constitute an attachment lien governed by Sections 488.500, 488.510 and 489.310 of the Code of Civil Procedure in the amount of the bail undertaking, until exonerated, released, or otherwise discharged. Any release of the undertaking shall be effected by an order of the court, filed with the clerk of the court, with a certified copy of the order recorded in the office of the county recorder.
(b) If the bail is forfeited and summary judgment is entered, pursuant to Sections 1305 and 1306, the lien shall have the force and effect of a judgment lien, by recordation of an abstract of judgment, which, may be enforced and satisfied pursuant to Section 1306 as well as through the applicable execution process set forth in Title 9 (commencing with Section 680.010) of Part 2 of the Code of Civil Procedure.
(Amended by Stats. 2001, Ch. 854, Sec. 45. Effective January 1, 2002. Repealed pursuant to Section 1320.6 if and when that section takes effect.)

1281.
Upon the allowance of bail and the execution and approval of the undertaking, the magistrate must, if the defendant is in custody, make and sign an order for his discharge, upon the delivery of which to the proper officer the defendant must be discharged.
(Amended by Stats. 1927, Ch. 733. Repealed pursuant to Section 1320.6 if and when that section takes effect.)

1281a.
A judge of the superior court within the county, wherein a cause is pending against any person charged with a felony, may justify and approve bail in the said cause, and may execute an order for the release of the defendant which shall authorize the discharge of the defendant by any officer having said defendant in custody.
(Amended by Stats. 2002, Ch. 784, Sec. 552. Effective January 1, 2003. Repealed pursuant to Section 1320.6 if and when that section takes effect.)

ARTICLE 3. Bail Upon an Indictment Before Conviction [1284 - 1289]

(Article 3 enacted 1872.)

1284.
When the offense charged is not punishable with death, the officer serving the bench warrant must, if required, take the defendant before a magistrate in the county in which it is issued, or in which he is arrested, for the purpose of giving bail. If the defendant appears before such magistrate without the bench warrant having been served upon him, the magistrate shall deliver him into the custody of the sheriff for the purpose of immediate booking and the recording of identification data, whereupon the sheriff shall deliver the defendant back before the magistrate for the purpose of giving bail.
(Amended by Stats. 1961, Ch. 2198. Repealed pursuant to Section 1320.6 if and when that section takes effect.)

1285.
If the offense charged is punishable with death, the officer arresting the defendant must deliver him into custody, according to the command of the bench warrant.
(Amended by Code Amendments 1880, Ch. 47. Repealed pursuant to Section 1320.6 if and when that section takes effect.)

1286.
When the defendant is so delivered into custody he must be held by the Sheriff, unless admitted to bail on examination upon a writ of habeas corpus.
(Enacted 1872. Repealed pursuant to Section 1320.6 if and when that section takes effect.)

1287.
(a) The bail shall be put in by a written undertaking, executed by two sufficient sureties (with or without the defendant, in the discretion of the court or magistrate), and acknowledged before the court or magistrate, in substantially the following form:
An indictment having been found on the _____ day of _____, 20___, in the Superior Court of the County of _____, charging _____ with the crime of _____ (designating it generally) and he or she having been admitted to bail in the sum of _____ dollars ($_____), we, _____ and _____, of _____ (stating their place of residence and occupation), hereby undertake that the above-named _____ will appear and answer any charge in any accusatory pleading based upon the acts supporting the indictment above mentioned, in whatever court it may be prosecuted, and will at all times render himself or herself amenable to the orders and process of the court, and, if convicted, will appear for pronouncement of judgment or grant of probation; or, if he or she fails to perform either of these conditions, that we will pay to the people of the State of California the sum of _____ dollars ($_____) (inserting the sum in which the defendant is admitted to bail). If the forfeiture of this bond be ordered by the court, judgment may be summarily made and entered forthwith against the said (naming the sureties, and the defendant if he or she be a party to the bond), for the amount of their respective undertakings herein, as provided by Sections 1305 and 1306.
(b) Every undertaking of bail shall contain the bail agent license number of the owner of the bail agency issuing the undertaking along with the name, address, and phone number of the agency, regardless of whether the owner is an individual, partnership, or corporation. The bail agency name on the undertaking shall be a business name approved by the Insurance Commissioner for use by the bail agency owner, and be so reflected in the public records of the commissioner. The license number of the bail agent appearing on the undertaking shall be in the same type size as the name, address, and phone number of the agency.
(Amended by Stats. 2004, Ch. 104, Sec. 2. Effective January 1, 2005. Repealed pursuant to Section 1320.6 if and when that section takes effect.)

1288.
The provisions contained in sections 1279, 1280, 1280a and 1281, in relation to bail before indictment, apply to bail after indictment.
(Amended by Stats. 1927, Ch. 736. Repealed pursuant to Section 1320.6 if and when that section takes effect.)

1289.
After a defendant has been admitted to bail upon an indictment or information, the Court in which the charge is pending may, upon good cause shown, either increase or reduce the amount of bail. If the amount be increased, the Court may order the defendant to be committed to actual custody, unless he give bail in such increased amount. If application be made by the defendant for a reduction of the amount, notice of the application must be served upon the District Attorney.
(Amended by Code Amendments 1880, Ch. 47. Repealed pursuant to Section 1320.6 if and when that section takes effect.)

ARTICLE 4. Bail on Appeal [1291 - 1292]

(Article 4 enacted 1872.)

1291.
In the cases in which defendant may be admitted to bail upon an appeal, the order admitting him to bail may be made by any Magistrate having the power to issue a writ of habeas corpus, or by the Magistrate before whom the trial was had.
(Amended by Code Amendments 1877-78, Ch. 89. Repealed pursuant to Section 1320.6 if and when that section takes effect.)

1292.
The bail must possess the qualifications, and must be put in, in all respects, as provided in Article II of this Chapter, except that the undertaking must be conditioned as prescribed in Section 1273, for undertakings of bail on appeal.
(Enacted 1872. Repealed pursuant to Section 1320.6 if and when that section takes effect.)

ARTICLE 5. Deposit Instead of Bail [1295 - 1298]

(Article 5 enacted 1872.)

1295.
(a) The defendant, or any other person, at any time after an order admitting defendant to bail or after the arrest and booking of a defendant for having committed a misdemeanor, instead of giving bail may deposit, with the clerk of the court in which the defendant is held to answer or notified to appear for arraignment, the sum mentioned in the order or, if no order, in the schedule of bail previously fixed by the judges of the court, and, upon delivering to the officer in whose custody defendant is a certificate of the deposit, the defendant must be discharged from custody.
(b) Where more than one deposit is made with respect to any charge in any accusatory pleading based upon the acts supporting the original charge as a result of which an earlier deposit was made, the defendant shall receive credit in the amount of any earlier deposit.
(c) The clerk of the court shall not accept a general assistance check for this deposit or any part thereof.
(Amended by Stats. 1997, Ch. 17, Sec. 104. Effective January 1, 1998. Repealed pursuant to Section 1320.6 if and when that section takes effect.)

1296.
If the defendant has given bail, he may, at any time before the forfeiture of the undertaking, in like manner deposit the sum mentioned in the recognizance, and upon the deposit being made the bail is exonerated.
(Enacted 1872. Repealed pursuant to Section 1320.6 if and when that section takes effect.)

1297.
When money has been deposited, a receipt shall be issued in the name of the depositor. If the money remains on deposit at the time of a judgment for the payment of a fine, the clerk shall, under the direction of the court, if the defendant be the depositor, apply the money in satisfaction thereof, and after satisfying restitution to the victim or the Restitution Fund, fines, and costs, shall refund the surplus, if any, to the defendant. If the person to whom the receipt for the deposit was issued was not the defendant, the deposit after judgment shall be returned to that person within 10 days after the person claims it by submitting the receipt, and, if a claim is not made within 10 days of the exoneration of bail, the clerk shall immediately notify the depositor of the exoneration of bail.
(Amended by Stats. 1995, Ch. 313, Sec. 11. Effective August 3, 1995. Repealed pursuant to Section 1320.6 if and when that section takes effect.)

1298.
In lieu of a deposit of money, the defendant or any other person may deposit bonds of the United States or of the State of California of the face value of the cash deposit required, and these bonds shall be treated in the same manner as a deposit of money or the defendant or any other person may give as security any equity in real property which he or she owns, provided that no charge is made to the defendant or any other person for the giving as security of any equity in real property. A hearing, at which witnesses may be called or examined, shall be held before the magistrate to determine the value of the equity and if the magistrate finds that the value of the equity is equal to twice the amount of the cash deposit required he or she shall allow the bail. The clerk shall, under order of the court, when occasion arises therefor, sell the bonds or the equity and apply the proceeds of the sale in the manner that a deposit of cash may be required to be applied.
(Amended by Stats. 2008, Ch. 699, Sec. 14. Effective January 1, 2009. Repealed pursuant to Section 1320.6 if and when that section takes effect.)

ARTICLE 5.5. Bail Fugitive Recovery Persons Act [1299 - 1299.12]

(Article 5.5 added by Stats. 2012, Ch. 747, Sec. 1.)

1299.
This article shall be known as the Bail Fugitive Recovery Persons Act.
(Added by Stats. 2012, Ch. 747, Sec. 1. (AB 2029) Effective January 1, 2013. Repealed pursuant to Section 1320.6 if and when that section takes effect.)

1299.01.
For purposes of this article, the following terms shall have the following meanings:
(a) "Bail fugitive" means a defendant in a pending criminal case who has been released from custody under a financially secured appearance, cash, or other bond and has had that bond declared forfeited, or a defendant in a pending criminal case who has violated a bond condition whereby apprehension and reincarceration are permitted.
(b) "Bail" means a person licensed by the Department of Insurance pursuant to Section 1800 of the Insurance Code.
(c) "Depositor of bail" means a person who or entity that has deposited money or bonds to secure the release of a person charged with a crime or offense.
(d) "Bail fugitive recovery person" means a person who is provided written authorization pursuant to Sections 1300 and 1301 by the bail or depositor of bail, and is contracted to investigate, surveil, locate, and arrest a bail fugitive for surrender to the appropriate court, jail, or police department, and any person who is employed to assist a bail or depositor of bail to investigate, surveil, locate, and arrest a bail fugitive for surrender to the appropriate court, jail, or police department.
(Added by Stats. 2012, Ch. 747, Sec. 1. (AB 2029) Effective January 1, 2013. Repealed pursuant to Section 1320.6 if and when that section takes effect.)

1299.02.
(a) No person, other than a certified law enforcement officer, shall be authorized to apprehend, detain, or arrest a bail fugitive unless that person meets one of the following conditions:
(1) Is a bail as defined in subdivision (b) of Section 1299.01 or a depositor of bail as defined in subdivision (c) of Section 1299.01.
(2) Is a bail fugitive recovery person as defined in subdivision (d) of Section 1299.01.
(3) Holds a bail license issued by a state other than California or is authorized by another state to transact and post bail and is in compliance with the provisions of Section 847.5 with respect to the arrest of a bail fugitive.

(4) Is licensed as a private investigator as provided in Chapter 11.3 (commencing with Section 7512) of Division 3 of the Business and Professions Code.
(5) Holds a private investigator license issued by another state, is authorized by the bail or depositor of bail to apprehend a bail fugitive, and is in compliance with the provisions of Section 847.5 with respect to the arrest of a bail fugitive.
(b) This article shall not prohibit an arrest pursuant to Sections 837, 838, and 839.
(Added by Stats. 2012, Ch. 747, Sec. 1. (AB 2029) Effective January 1, 2013. Repealed pursuant to Section 1320.6 if and when that section takes effect.)

1299.04.
(a) A bail fugitive recovery person, a bail agent, bail permittee, or bail solicitor who contracts his or her services to another bail agent or surety as a bail fugitive recovery person for the purposes specified in subdivision (d) of Section 1299.01, and any bail agent, bail permittee, or bail solicitor who obtains licensing after January 1, 2000, and who engages in the arrest of a defendant pursuant to Section 1301 shall comply with the following requirements:
(1) The person shall be at least 18 years of age.
(2) The person shall have completed a 40-hour power of arrest course certified by the Commission on Peace Officer Standards and Training pursuant to Section 832. Completion of the course shall be for educational purposes only and not intended to confer the power of arrest of a peace officer or public officer, or agent of any federal, state, or local government, unless the person is so employed by a governmental agency.
(3) The person shall have completed a minimum of 20 hours of classroom prelicensing education certified pursuant to Section 1810.7 of the Insurance Code. For those persons licensed by the department as a bail licensee prior to January 1, 1994, there is no prelicensing education requirement. For those persons licensed by the department as a bail licensee between January 1, 1994, and December 31, 2012, a minimum of 12 hours of classroom prelicensing education is required.
(4) The person shall not have been convicted of a felony, unless the person is licensed by the Department of Insurance pursuant to Section 1800 of the Insurance Code.
(b) Upon completion of any course or training program required by this section, an individual authorized by Section 1299.02 to apprehend a bail fugitive shall carry certificates of completion with him or her at all times in the course of performing his or her duties under this article.
(Amended by Stats. 2015, Ch. 348, Sec. 29. (AB 1515) Effective January 1, 2016. Repealed pursuant to Section 1320.6 if and when that section takes effect.)

1299.05.
In performing a bail fugitive apprehension, an individual authorized by Section 1299.02 to apprehend a bail fugitive shall comply with all laws applicable to that apprehension.
(Added by Stats. 2012, Ch. 747, Sec. 1. (AB 2029) Effective January 1, 2013. Repealed pursuant to Section 1320.6 if and when that section takes effect.)

1299.06.
Before apprehending a bail fugitive, an individual authorized by Section 1299.02 to apprehend a bail fugitive shall have in his or her possession proper documentation of authority to apprehend issued by the bail or depositor of bail as prescribed in Sections 1300 and 1301. The authority to apprehend document shall include all of the following information: the name of the individual authorized by Section 1299.02 to apprehend a bail fugitive and any fictitious name, if applicable; the address of the principal office of the individual authorized by Section 1299.02 to apprehend a bail fugitive; and the name and principal business address of the bail agency, surety company, or other party contracting with the individual authorized by Section 1299.02 to apprehend a bail fugitive.
(Added by Stats. 2012, Ch. 747, Sec. 1. (AB 2029) Effective January 1, 2013. Repealed pursuant to Section 1320.6 if and when that section takes effect.)

1299.07.
(a) An individual authorized by Section 1299.02 to apprehend a bail fugitive shall not represent himself or herself in any manner as being a sworn law enforcement officer.
(b) An individual authorized by Section 1299.02 to apprehend a bail fugitive shall not wear any uniform that represents himself or herself as belonging to any part or department of a federal, state, or local government. Any uniform shall not display the words United States, Bureau, Task Force, Federal, or other substantially similar words that a reasonable person may mistake for a government agency.
(c) An individual authorized by Section 1299.02 to apprehend a bail fugitive shall not wear or otherwise use a badge that represents himself or herself as belonging to any part or department of the federal, state, or local government.
(d) An individual authorized by Section 1299.02 to apprehend a bail fugitive shall not use a fictitious name that represents himself or herself as belonging to any federal, state, or local government.
(e) An individual authorized by Section 1299.02 to apprehend a bail fugitive may wear a jacket, shirt, or vest with the words "BAIL BOND RECOVERY AGENT," "BAIL ENFORCEMENT," or "BAIL ENFORCEMENT AGENT" displayed in letters at least two inches high across the front or back of the jacket, shirt, or vest and in a contrasting color to that of the jacket, shirt, or vest.
(Added by Stats. 2012, Ch. 747, Sec. 1. (AB 2029) Effective January 1, 2013. Repealed pursuant to Section 1320.6 if and when that section takes effect.)

1299.08.
(a) Except under exigent circumstances, an individual authorized by Section 1299.02 to apprehend a bail fugitive shall, prior to and no more than six hours before attempting to apprehend the bail fugitive, notify the local police department or sheriff's department of the intent to apprehend a bail fugitive in that jurisdiction by doing all of the following:
(1) Indicating the name of an individual authorized by Section 1299.02 to apprehend a bail fugitive entering the jurisdiction.
(2) Stating the approximate time an individual authorized by Section 1299.02 to apprehend a bail fugitive will be entering the jurisdiction and the approximate length of the stay.
(3) Stating the name and approximate location of the bail fugitive.
(b) If an exigent circumstance does arise and prior notification is not given as provided in subdivision (a), an individual authorized by Section 1299.02 to apprehend a bail fugitive shall notify the local police department or sheriff's department immediately after the apprehension, and upon request of the local jurisdiction, shall submit a detailed explanation of those exigent circumstances within three working days after the apprehension is made.
(c) This section shall not preclude an individual authorized by Section 1299.02 to apprehend a bail fugitive from making or attempting to make a lawful arrest of a bail fugitive on bond pursuant to Section 1300 or 1301. The fact that a bench warrant is not located or entered into a warrant depository or system shall not affect a lawful arrest of the bail fugitive.
(d) For the purposes of this section, notice may be provided to a local law enforcement agency by telephone prior to the arrest or, after the arrest has taken place, if exigent circumstances exist. In that case the name or operator number of the employee receiving the notice information shall be obtained and retained by the bail, depositor of bail, or bail fugitive recovery person.
(Added by Stats. 2012, Ch. 747, Sec. 1. (AB 2029) Effective January 1, 2013. Repealed pursuant to Section 1320.6 if and when that section takes effect.)

1299.09.
An individual, authorized by Section 1299.02 to apprehend a bail fugitive shall not forcibly enter a premises except as provided for in Section 844.
(Added by Stats. 2012, Ch. 747, Sec. 1. (AB 2029) Effective January 1, 2013. Repealed pursuant to Section 1320.6 if and when that section takes effect.)

1299.10.
An individual authorized by Section 1299.02 to apprehend a bail fugitive shall not carry a firearm or other weapon unless in compliance with the laws of the state.
(Added by Stats. 2012, Ch. 747, Sec. 1. (AB 2029) Effective January 1, 2013. Repealed pursuant to Section 1320.6 if and when that section takes effect.)

1299.11.
Any person who violates this act, or who conspires with another person to violate this act, or who hires an individual to apprehend a bail fugitive, knowing that the individual is not authorized by Section 1299.02 to apprehend a bail fugitive, is guilty of a misdemeanor punishable by a fine of five thousand dollars ($5,000) or by imprisonment in a county jail not to exceed one year, or by both that imprisonment and fine.
(Added by Stats. 2012, Ch. 747, Sec. 1. (AB 2029) Effective January 1, 2013. Repealed pursuant to Section 1320.6 if and when that section takes effect.)

1299.12.
Nothing in this article is intended to exempt from licensure persons otherwise required to be licensed as private investigators pursuant to Chapter 11.3 (commencing with Section 7512) of Division 3 of the Business and Professions Code.
(Added by Stats. 2012, Ch. 747, Sec. 1. (AB 2029) Effective January 1, 2013. Repealed pursuant to Section 1320.6 if and when that section takes effect.)

ARTICLE 6. Exoneration [1300 - 1304]
(Heading of Article 6 amended by Stats. 1971, Ch. 1790.)

1300.
(a) At any time before the forfeiture of their undertaking, or deposit by a third person, the bail or the depositor may surrender the defendant in their exoneration, or he may surrender himself, to the officer to whose custody he was committed at the time of giving bail, in the following manner:
(1) A certified copy of the undertaking of the bail, a certified copy of the certificate of deposit where a deposit is made, or an affidavit given by the bail licensee or surety company listing all that specific information that would be included on a certified copy of an undertaking of bail, must be delivered to the officer who must detain the defendant in his custody thereon as upon a commitment, and by a certificate in writing acknowledge the surrender.
(2) The bail or depositor, upon surrendering the defendant, shall make reasonable effort to give notice to the defendant's last attorney of record, if any, of such surrender.
(3) The officer to whom the defendant is surrendered shall, within 48 hours of the surrender, bring the defendant before the court in which the defendant is next to appear on the case for which he has been surrendered. The court shall advise the defendant of his right to move the court for an order permitting the withdrawal of any previous waiver of time and shall advise him of the authority of the court, as provided in subdivision (b), to order return of the premium paid by the defendant or other person, or any part of it.
(4) Upon the undertaking, or certificate of deposit, and the certificate of the officer, the court in which the action or appeal is pending may, upon notice of five days to the district attorney of the county, with a copy of the undertaking, or certificate of deposit, and the certificate of the officer, order that the bail or deposit be exonerated. However, if the defendant is released on his own recognizance or on another bond before the issuance of such an order, the court shall order that the bail or deposit be exonerated without prejudice to the court's authority under subdivision (b). On filing the order and papers used on the application, they are exonerated accordingly.
(b) Notwithstanding subdivision (a), if the court determines that good cause does not exist for the surrender of a defendant who has not failed to appear or has not violated any order of the court, it may, in its discretion, order the bail or the depositor to return to the defendant or other person who has paid the premium or any part of it, all of the money so paid or any part of it.
(Amended by Stats. 1998, Ch. 223, Sec. 1. Effective January 1, 1999. Repealed pursuant to Section 1320.6 if and when that section takes effect.)

1301.
For the purpose of surrendering the defendant, the bail or any person who has deposited money or bonds to secure the release of the defendant, at any time before such bail or other person is finally discharged, and at any place within the state, may himself arrest defendant, or by written authority indorsed on a certified copy of the undertaking or a certified copy of the certificate of deposit, may empower any person of suitable age to do so.
Any bail or other person who so arrests a defendant in this state shall, without unnecessary delay, and, in any event, within 48 hours of the arrest, deliver the defendant to the court or magistrate before whom the defendant is required to appear or to the custody of the sheriff or police for confinement in the appropriate jail in the county or city in which defendant is required to appear. Any bail or other person who arrests a defendant outside this state shall, without unnecessary delay after the time defendant is brought into this state, and, in any event, within 48 hours after defendant is brought into this state, deliver the defendant to the custody of the court or magistrate before whom the defendant is required to appear or to the custody of the sheriff or police for confinement in the appropriate jail in the county or city in which defendant is required to appear.
Any bail or other person who willfully fails to deliver a defendant to the court, magistrate, sheriff, or police as required by this section is guilty of a misdemeanor.
The provisions of this section relating to the time of delivery of a defendant are for his benefit and, with the consent of the bail, may be waived by him. To be valid, such waiver shall be in writing, signed by the defendant, and delivered to such bail or other person within 48 hours after the defendant's arrest or entry into this state, as the case may be. The defendant, at any time and in the same manner, may revoke said waiver. Whereupon, he shall be delivered as provided herein without unnecessary delay and, in any event within 48 hours from the time of such revocation.
If any 48-hour period specified in this section terminates on a Saturday, Sunday, or holiday, delivery of a defendant by a bail or other person to the court or magistrate or to the custody of the sheriff or police may, without violating this section, take place before noon on the next day following which is not a Saturday, Sunday, or holiday.
(Amended by Stats. 1965, Ch. 1859. Repealed pursuant to Section 1320.6 if and when that section takes effect.)

1302.
If money has been deposited instead of bail, and the defendant, at any time before the forfeiture thereof, surrenders himself or herself to the officer to whom the commitment was directed, in the manner provided in Sections 1300 and 1301, the court shall order a return of the deposit to the defendant or to the person or persons found by the court to have deposited said money on behalf of the defendant, upon the production of the certificate of the officer showing the surrender, and upon a notice of five days to the district attorney, with a copy of the certificate.
(Amended by Stats. 1987, Ch. 828, Sec. 84. Repealed pursuant to Section 1320.6 if and when that section takes effect.)

1303.
If an action or proceeding against a defendant who has been admitted to bail is dismissed, the bail shall not be exonerated until a period of 15 days has elapsed since the entry of the order of dismissal. If, within such period, the defendant is arrested and charged with a public offense arising out of the same act or omission upon which the action or proceeding was based, the bail shall be applied to the public offense. If an undertaking of bail is on file, the clerk of the court shall promptly mail notice to the surety on the bond and the bail agent who posted the bond whenever the bail is applied to a public offense pursuant to this section.
(Added by Stats. 1971, Ch. 1790. Repealed pursuant to Section 1320.6 if and when that section takes effect.)

1304.

Any bail, or moneys or bonds deposited in lieu of bail, or any equity in real property as security in lieu of bail, or any agreement whereby the defendant is released on his or her own recognizance shall be exonerated two years from the effective date of the initial bond, provided that the court is informed in writing at least 60 days prior to 2 years after the initial bond of the fact that the bond is to be exonerated, or unless the court determines otherwise and informs the party executing the bail of the reasons that the bail is not exonerated.

(Added by Stats. 1984, Ch. 284, Sec. 1. Repealed pursuant to Section 1320.6 if and when that section takes effect.)

ARTICLE 6. Exoneration [1300 - 1304]
(Heading of Article 6 amended by Stats. 1971, Ch. 1790.)

1300.

(a) At any time before the forfeiture of their undertaking, or deposit by a third person, the bail or the depositor may surrender the defendant in their exoneration, or he may surrender himself, to the officer to whose custody he was committed at the time of giving bail, in the following manner:

(1) A certified copy of the undertaking of the bail, a certified copy of the certificate of deposit where a deposit is made, or an affidavit given by the bail licensee or surety company listing all that specific information that would be included on a certified copy of an undertaking of bail, must be delivered to the officer who must detain the defendant in his custody thereon as upon a commitment, and by a certificate in writing acknowledge the surrender.

(2) The bail or depositor, upon surrendering the defendant, shall make reasonable effort to give notice to the defendant's last attorney of record, if any, of such surrender.

(3) The officer to whom the defendant is surrendered shall, within 48 hours of the surrender, bring the defendant before the court in which the defendant is next to appear on the case for which he has been surrendered. The court shall advise the defendant of his right to move the court for an order permitting the withdrawal of any previous waiver of time and shall advise him of the authority of the court, as provided in subdivision (b), to order return of the premium paid by the defendant or other person, or any part of it.

(4) Upon the undertaking, or certificate of deposit, and the certificate of the officer, the court in which the action or appeal is pending may, upon notice of five days to the district attorney of the county, with a copy of the undertaking, or certificate of deposit, and the certificate of the officer, order that the bail or deposit be exonerated. However, if the defendant is released on his own recognizance or on another bond before the issuance of such an order, the court shall order that the bail or deposit be exonerated without prejudice to the court's authority under subdivision (b). On filing the order and papers used on the application, they are exonerated accordingly.

(b) Notwithstanding subdivision (a), if the court determines that good cause does not exist for the surrender of a defendant who has not failed to appear or has not violated any order of the court, it may, in its discretion, order the bail or the depositor to return to the defendant or other person who has paid the premium or any part of it, all of the money so paid or any part of it.

(Amended by Stats. 1998, Ch. 223, Sec. 1. Effective January 1, 1999. Repealed pursuant to Section 1320.6 if and when that section takes effect.)

1301.

For the purpose of surrendering the defendant, the bail or any person who has deposited money or bonds to secure the release of the defendant, at any time before such bail or other person is finally discharged, and at any place within the state, may himself arrest defendant, or by written authority indorsed on a certified copy of the undertaking or a certified copy of the certificate of deposit, may empower any person of suitable age to do so.

Any bail or other person who so arrests a defendant in this state shall, without unnecessary delay, and, in any event, within 48 hours of the arrest, deliver the defendant to the court or magistrate before whom the defendant is required to appear or to the custody of the sheriff or police for confinement in the appropriate jail in the county or city in which defendant is required to appear. Any bail or other person who arrests a defendant outside this state shall, without unnecessary delay after the time defendant is brought into this state, and, in any event, within 48 hours after defendant is brought into this state, deliver the defendant to the custody of the court or magistrate before whom the defendant is required to appear or to the custody of the sheriff or police for confinement in the appropriate jail in the county or city in which defendant is required to appear.

Any bail or other person who willfully fails to deliver a defendant to the court, magistrate, sheriff, or police as required by this section is guilty of a misdemeanor.

The provisions of this section relating to the time of delivery of a defendant are for his benefit and, with the consent of the bail, may be waived by him. To be valid, such waiver shall be in writing, signed by the defendant, and delivered to such bail or other person within 48 hours after the defendant's arrest or entry into this state, as the case may be. The defendant, at any time and in the same manner, may revoke said waiver. Whereupon, he shall be delivered as provided herein without unnecessary delay and, in any event within 48 hours from the time of such revocation.

If any 48-hour period specified in this section terminates on a Saturday, Sunday, or holiday, delivery of a defendant by a bail or other person to the court or magistrate or to the custody of the sheriff or police may, without violating this section, take place before noon on the next day following which is not a Saturday, Sunday, or holiday.

(Amended by Stats. 1965, Ch. 1859. Repealed pursuant to Section 1320.6 if and when that section takes effect.)

1302.

If money has been deposited instead of bail, and the defendant, at any time before the forfeiture thereof, surrenders himself or herself to the officer to whom the commitment was directed, in the manner provided in Sections 1300 and 1301, the court shall order a return of the deposit to the defendant or to the person or persons found by the court to have deposited said money on behalf of the defendant, upon the production of the certificate of the officer showing the surrender, and upon a notice of five days to the district attorney, with a copy of the certificate.

(Amended by Stats. 1987, Ch. 828, Sec. 84. Repealed pursuant to Section 1320.6 if and when that section takes effect.)

1303.

If an action or proceeding against a defendant who has been admitted to bail is dismissed, the bail shall not be exonerated until a period of 15 days has elapsed since the entry of the order of dismissal. If, within such period, the defendant is arrested and charged with a public offense arising out of the same act or omission upon which the action or proceeding was based, the bail shall be applied to the public offense. If an undertaking of bail is on file, the clerk of the court shall promptly mail notice to the surety on the bond and the bail agent who posted the bond whenever the bail is applied to a public offense pursuant to this section.

(Added by Stats. 1971, Ch. 1790. Repealed pursuant to Section 1320.6 if and when that section takes effect.)

1304.

Any bail, or moneys or bonds deposited in lieu of bail, or any equity in real property as security in lieu of bail, or any agreement whereby the defendant is released on his or her own recognizance shall be exonerated two years from the effective date of the initial bond, provided that the court is informed in writing at least 60 days prior to 2 years after the initial bond of the fact that the bond is to be exonerated, or unless the court determines otherwise and informs the party executing the bail of the reasons that the bail is not exonerated.

(Added by Stats. 1984, Ch. 284, Sec. 1. Repealed pursuant to Section 1320.6 if and when that section takes effect.)

ARTICLE 7. Forfeiture of the Undertaking of Bail or of the Deposit of Money [1305 - 1308]
(Article 7 enacted 1872.)

1305.

(a) (1) A court shall in open court declare forfeited the undertaking of bail or the money or property deposited as bail if, without sufficient excuse, a defendant fails to appear for any of the following:

(A) Arraignment.

(B) Trial.

(C) Judgment.

(D) Any other occasion prior to the pronouncement of judgment if the defendant's presence in court is lawfully required.

(E) To surrender himself or herself in execution of the judgment after appeal.

(2) (A) Notwithstanding paragraph (1), except as provided in subparagraph (B), the court shall not have jurisdiction to declare a forfeiture and the bail shall be released of all obligations under the bond if the case is dismissed or if no complaint is filed within 15 days from the date of arraignment.

(B) The court's jurisdiction to declare a forfeiture and authority to release bail may be extended for not more than 90 days from the arraignment date originally set by the jailer pursuant to subdivision (a) of Section 1269b if either of the following occur:

(i) The prosecutor requests in writing or in open court that the arraignment be continued to allow the prosecutor time to file the complaint.

(ii) The defendant requests the extension in writing or in open court.

(b) (1) If the amount of the bond or money or property deposited exceeds four hundred dollars ($400), the clerk of the court shall, within 30 days of the forfeiture, mail notice of the forfeiture to the surety or the depositor of money posted instead of bail. At the same time, the court shall mail a copy of the forfeiture notice to the bail agent whose name appears on the bond. The clerk shall also execute a certificate of mailing of the forfeiture notice and shall place the certificate in the court's file. If the notice of forfeiture is required to be mailed pursuant to this section, the 180-day period provided for in this section shall be extended by a period of five days to allow for the mailing.

(2) If the surety is an authorized corporate surety, and if the bond plainly displays the mailing address of the corporate surety and the bail agent, then notice of the forfeiture shall be mailed to the surety at that address and to the bail agent, and mailing alone to the surety or the bail agent shall not constitute compliance with this section.

(3) The surety or depositor shall be released of all obligations under the bond if any of the following conditions apply:

(A) The clerk fails to mail the notice of forfeiture in accordance with this section within 30 days after the entry of the forfeiture.

(B) The clerk fails to mail the notice of forfeiture to the surety at the address printed on the bond.

(C) The clerk fails to mail a copy of the notice of forfeiture to the bail agent at the address shown on the bond.

(c) (1) If the defendant appears either voluntarily or in custody after surrender or arrest in court within 180 days of the date of forfeiture or within 180 days of the date of mailing of the notice if the notice is required under subdivision (b), the court shall, on its own motion at the time the defendant first appears in court on the case in which the forfeiture was entered, direct the order of forfeiture to be vacated and the bond exonerated. If the court fails to so act on its own motion, then the surety's or depositor's obligations under the bond shall be immediately vacated and the bond exonerated. An order vacating the forfeiture and exonerating the bond may be made on terms that are just and do not exceed the terms imposed in similar situations with respect to other forms of pretrial release.

(2) If, within the county where the case is located, the defendant is surrendered to custody by the bail or is arrested in the underlying case within the 180-day period, and is subsequently released from custody prior to an appearance in court, the court shall, on its own motion, direct the order of forfeiture to be vacated and the bond exonerated. If the court fails to so act on its own motion, then the surety's or depositor's obligations under the bond shall be immediately vacated and the bond exonerated. An order vacating the forfeiture and exonerating the bond may be made on terms that are just and do not exceed the terms imposed in similar situations with respect to other forms of pretrial release.

(3) If, outside the county where the case is located, the defendant is surrendered to custody by the bail or is arrested in the underlying case within the 180-day period, the court shall vacate the forfeiture and exonerate the bail.

(4) In lieu of exonerating the bond, the court may order the bail reinstated and the defendant released on the same bond if both of the following conditions are met:

(A) The bail is given prior notice of the reinstatement.

(B) The bail has not surrendered the defendant.

(d) In the case of a permanent disability, the court shall direct the order of forfeiture to be vacated and the bail or money or property deposited as bail exonerated if, within 180 days of the date of forfeiture or within 180 days of the date of mailing of the notice, if notice is required under subdivision (b), it is made apparent to the satisfaction of the court that both of the following conditions are met:

(1) The defendant is deceased or otherwise permanently unable to appear in the court due to illness, insanity, or detention by military or civil authorities.

(2) The absence of the defendant is without the connivance of the bail.

(e) (1) In the case of a temporary disability, the court shall order the tolling of the 180-day period provided in this section during the period of temporary disability, provided that it appears to the satisfaction of the court that the following conditions are met:

(A) The defendant is temporarily disabled by reason of illness, insanity, or detention by military or civil authorities.

(B) Based upon the temporary disability, the defendant is unable to appear in court during the remainder of the 180-day period.

(C) The absence of the defendant is without the connivance of the bail.

(2) The period of the tolling shall be extended for a reasonable period of time, at the discretion of the court, after the cessation of the disability to allow for the return of the defendant to the jurisdiction of the court.

(f) In all cases where a defendant is in custody beyond the jurisdiction of the court that ordered the bail forfeited, and the prosecuting agency elects not to seek extradition after being informed of the location of the defendant, the court shall vacate the forfeiture and exonerate the bond on terms that are just and do not exceed the terms imposed in similar situations with respect to other forms of pretrial release.

(g) In all cases of forfeiture where a defendant is not in custody and is beyond the jurisdiction of the state, is temporarily detained, by the bail agent, in the presence of a local law enforcement officer of the jurisdiction in which the defendant is located, and is positively identified by that law enforcement officer as the wanted defendant in an affidavit signed under penalty of perjury, and the prosecuting agency elects not to seek extradition after being informed of the location of the defendant, the court shall vacate the forfeiture and exonerate the bond on terms that are just and do not exceed the terms imposed in similar situations with respect to other forms of pretrial release.

(h) In cases arising under subdivision (g), if the bail agent and the prosecuting agency agree that additional time is needed to return the defendant to the jurisdiction of the court, and the prosecuting agency agrees to the tolling of the 180-day period, the court may, on the basis of the agreement, toll the 180-day period within which to vacate the forfeiture. The court may order tolling for up to the length of time agreed upon by the parties.

(i) As used in this section, "arrest" includes a hold placed on the defendant in the underlying case while he or she is in custody on other charges.

(j) A motion filed in a timely manner within the 180-day period may be heard within 30 days of the expiration of the 180-day period. The court may extend the 30-day period upon a showing of good cause. The motion may be made by the surety insurer, the bail agent, the surety, or the depositor of money or property, any of whom may appear in person or through an attorney.

(k) In addition to any other notice required by law, the moving party shall give the prosecuting agency a written notice at least 10 court days before a hearing held pursuant to subdivision (f), (g), or (j), as a condition precedent to granting the motion.
(Amended by Stats. 2016, Ch. 79, Sec. 1. (AB 2655) Effective January 1, 2017. Repealed pursuant to Section 1320.6 if and when that section takes effect.)

1305.1.
If the defendant fails to appear for arraignment, trial, judgment, or upon any other occasion when his or her appearance is lawfully required, but the court has reason to believe that sufficient excuse may exist for the failure to appear, the court may continue the case for a period it deems reasonable to enable the defendant to appear without ordering a forfeiture of bail or issuing a bench warrant.
If, after the court has made the order, the defendant, without sufficient excuse, fails to appear on or before the continuance date set by the court, the bail shall be forfeited and a warrant for the defendant's arrest may be ordered issued.
(Repealed and added by Stats. 1993, Ch. 524, Sec. 4. Effective January 1, 1994. Repealed pursuant to Section 1320.6 if and when that section takes effect.)

1305.2.
If an assessment is made a condition of the order to set aside the forfeiture of an undertaking, deposit, or bail under Section 1305, the clerk of the court shall within 30 days mail notice thereof to the surety or depositor at the address of its principal office, mail a copy to the bail agent whose name appears on the bond, and shall execute a certificate of mailing and place it in the court's file in the case. The time limit for payment shall in no event be less than 30 days after the date of mailing of the notice.
If the assessment has not been paid by the date specified, the court shall determine if a certificate of mailing has been executed, and if none has, the court shall cause a notice to be mailed to the surety, depositor, or bail agent whose name appears on the bond, and the surety, depositor, or bail agent whose name appears on the bond shall be allowed an additional 30 days to pay the assessment.
(Amended by Stats. 1995, Ch. 56, Sec. 2. Effective January 1, 1996. Repealed pursuant to Section 1320.6 if and when that section takes effect.)

1305.3.
The district attorney, county counsel, or applicable prosecuting agency, as the case may be, shall recover, out of the forfeited bail money, the costs and attorney's fees incurred in successfully opposing a motion to vacate the forfeiture and in collecting on the summary judgment prior to the division of the forfeited bail money between the cities and counties in accordance with Section 1463.001.
(Amended by Stats. 2016, Ch. 378, Sec. 1. (AB 1854) Effective January 1, 2017. Repealed pursuant to Section 1320.6 if and when that section takes effect.)

1305.4.
Notwithstanding Section 1305, the surety insurer, the bail agent, the surety, or the depositor may file a motion, based upon good cause, for an order extending the 180-day period provided in that section. The motion shall include a declaration or affidavit that states the reasons showing good cause to extend that period. The court, upon a hearing and a showing of good cause, may order the period extended to a time not exceeding 180 days from its order. A motion may be filed and calendared as provided in subdivision (j) of Section 1305. In addition to any other notice required by law, the moving party shall give the prosecuting agency a written notice at least 10 court days before a hearing held pursuant to this section as a condition precedent to granting the motion.
(Amended by Stats. 2013, Ch. 59, Sec. 6. (SB 514) Effective January 1, 2014. Repealed pursuant to Section 1320.6 if and when that section takes effect.)

1305.5.
Notwithstanding Sections 85, 580, 904.1, and 904.2 of the Code of Civil Procedure, the following rules apply to an appeal from an order of the superior court on a motion to vacate a bail forfeiture declared under Section 1305:
(a) If the amount in controversy exceeds twenty-five thousand dollars ($25,000), the appeal is to the court of appeal and shall be treated as an unlimited civil case.
(b) Except as provided in subdivision (c), if the amount in controversy does not exceed twenty-five thousand dollars ($25,000), the appeal is to the appellate division of the superior court and shall be treated as a limited civil case.
(c) If the bail forfeiture was in a felony case, or in a case in which both a felony and a misdemeanor were charged, and the forfeiture occurred at or after the sentencing hearing or after the indictment or the legal commitment by a magistrate, the appeal is to the court of appeal and shall be treated as an unlimited civil case.
(Added by Stats. 2012, Ch. 470, Sec. 49. (AB 1529) Effective January 1, 2013. Repealed pursuant to Section 1320.6 if and when that section takes effect.)

1305.6.
(a) If a person appears in court after the end of the 180-day period specified in Section 1305, the court may, in its discretion, vacate the forfeiture and exonerate the bond if both of the following conditions are met:
(1) The person was arrested on the same case within the county where the case is located, within the 180-day period.
(2) The person has been in continuous custody from the time of his or her arrest until the court appearance on that case.
(b) Upon a showing of good cause, a motion brought pursuant to paragraph (3) of subdivision (c) of Section 1305 may be filed within 20 days from the mailing of the notice of entry of judgment under Section 1306.
(c) In addition to any other notice required by law, the moving party shall give the applicable prosecuting agency written notice of the motion to vacate the forfeiture and exonerate the bond under this section at least 10 court days before the hearing.
(Added by Stats. 2012, Ch. 812, Sec. 1. (AB 1824) Effective January 1, 2013. Repealed pursuant to Section 1320.6 if and when that section takes effect.)

1306.
(a) When any bond is forfeited and the period of time specified in Section 1305 has elapsed without the forfeiture having been set aside, the court which has declared the forfeiture shall enter a summary judgment against each bondsman named in the bond in the amount for which the bondsman is bound. The judgment shall be the amount of the bond plus costs, and notwithstanding any other law, no penalty assessments shall be levied or added to the judgment.
(b) If a court grants relief from bail forfeiture, it shall impose a monetary payment as a condition of relief to compensate the people for the costs of returning a defendant to custody pursuant to Section 1305, except for cases where the court determines that in the best interest of justice no costs should be imposed. The amount imposed shall reflect the actual costs of returning the defendant to custody. Failure to act within the required time to make the payment imposed pursuant to this subdivision shall not be the basis for a summary judgment against any or all of the underlying amount of the bail. A summary judgment entered for failure to make the payment imposed under this subdivision is subject to the provisions of Section 1308, and shall apply only to the amount of the costs owing at the time the summary judgment is entered, plus administrative costs and interest.
(c) If, because of the failure of any court to promptly perform the duties enjoined upon it pursuant to this section, summary judgment is not entered within 90 days after the date upon which it may first be entered, the right to do so expires and the bail is exonerated.

(d) A dismissal of the complaint, indictment, or information after the default of the defendant shall not release or affect the obligation of the bail bond or undertaking.
(e) The district attorney or county counsel shall:
(1) Demand immediate payment of the judgment within 30 days after the summary judgment becomes final.
(2) If the judgment remains unpaid for a period of 20 days after demand has been made, shall forthwith enforce the judgment in the manner provided for enforcement of money judgments generally. If the judgment is appealed by the surety or bondsman, the undertaking required to be given in these cases shall be provided by a surety other than the one filing the appeal. The undertaking shall comply with the enforcement requirements of Section 917.1 of the Code of Civil Procedure. Notwithstanding Sections 85, 580, 904.1, and 904.2 of the Code of Civil Procedure, jurisdiction of the appeal, and treatment of the appeal as a limited civil case or an unlimited civil case, is governed by Section 1305.5.
(f) The right to enforce a summary judgment entered against a bondsman pursuant to this section shall expire two years after the entry of the judgment.
(Amended by Stats. 2012, Ch. 470, Sec. 50. (AB 1529) Effective January 1, 2013. Repealed pursuant to Section 1320.6 if and when that section takes effect.)

1306.1.
The provisions of Sections 1305 and 1306 shall not affect the payment of bail deposits into the city or county treasury, as the case may be, pursuant to Section 40512 of the Vehicle Code in those cases arising under Section 40500 of the Vehicle Code.
(Added by Stats. 1965, Ch. 1926. Repealed pursuant to Section 1320.6 if and when that section takes effect.)

1307.
If, by reason of the neglect of the defendant to appear, money deposited instead of bail is forfeited, and the forfeiture is not discharged or remitted, the clerk with whom it is deposited must, at the end of 180 days, unless the court has before that time discharged the forfeiture, pay over the money deposited to the county treasurer.
(Amended by Stats. 1965, Ch. 1926. Repealed pursuant to Section 1320.6 if and when that section takes effect.)

1308.
(a) No court or magistrate shall accept any person or corporation as surety on bail if any summary judgment against that person or corporation entered pursuant to Section 1306 remains unpaid after the expiration of 30 days after service of the notice of the entry of the summary judgment, provided that, if during the 30 days an action or proceeding available at law is initiated to determine the validity of the order of forfeiture or summary judgment rendered on it, this section shall be rendered inoperative until that action or proceeding has finally been determined, provided that, if an appeal is taken, an appeal bond is posted in compliance with Section 917.1 of the Code of Civil Procedure.
(b) The clerk of the court in which the judgment is rendered shall serve notice of the entry of judgment upon the judgment debtor within five days after the date of the entry of the summary judgment.
(Amended by Stats. 1999, Ch. 570, Sec. 4. Effective January 1, 2000. Inapplicable as prescribed in subd. (a). Repealed pursuant to Section 1320.6 if and when that section takes effect.)

ARTICLE 8. Recommitment of the Defendant, After Having Given Bail or Deposited Money Instead of Bail [1310 - 1317]
(Article 8 enacted 1872.)

1310.
The court to which the committing magistrate returns the depositions, or in which an indictment, information, or appeal is pending, or to which a judgment on appeal is remitted to be carried into effect, may, by an order entered upon its minutes, direct the arrest of the defendant and his or her commitment to the officer to whose custody he or she was committed at the time of giving bail, and his or her detention until legally discharged, in the following cases:
(a) When, by reason of his or her failure to appear, he or she has incurred a forfeiture of his or her bail, or of money deposited instead thereof.
(b) When it satisfactorily appears to the court that his or her bail, or either of them, are dead or insufficient, or have removed from the state.
(c) Upon an indictment being found or information filed in the cases provided in Section 985.
(Amended by Stats. 1987, Ch. 828, Sec. 85. Repealed pursuant to Section 1320.6 if and when that section takes effect.)

1311.
The order for the recommitment of the defendant must recite generally the facts upon which it is founded, and direct that the defendant be arrested by any sheriff, marshal, or policeman in this state, and committed to the officer in whose custody he or she was at the time he or she was admitted to bail, to be detained until legally discharged.
(Amended by Stats. 1996, Ch. 872, Sec. 120. Effective January 1, 1997. Repealed pursuant to Section 1320.6 if and when that section takes effect.)

1312.
The defendant may be arrested pursuant to the order, upon a certified copy thereof, in any county, in the same manner as upon a warrant of arrest, except that when arrested in another county the order need not be indorsed by a magistrate of that county.
(Enacted 1872. Repealed pursuant to Section 1320.6 if and when that section takes effect.)

1313.
If the order recites, as the ground upon which it is made, the failure of the defendant to appear for judgment upon conviction, the defendant must be committed according to the requirement of the order.
(Enacted 1872. Repealed pursuant to Section 1320.6 if and when that section takes effect.)

1314.
If the order be made for any other cause, and the offense is bailable, the Court may fix the amount of bail, and may cause a direction to be inserted in the order that the defendant be admitted to bail in the sum fixed, which must be specified in the order.
(Enacted 1872. Repealed pursuant to Section 1320.6 if and when that section takes effect.)

1315.
When the defendant is admitted to bail, the bail may be taken by any magistrate in the county, having authority in a similar case to admit to bail, upon the holding of the defendant to answer before an indictment, or by any other magistrate designated by the Court.
(Enacted 1872. Repealed pursuant to Section 1320.6 if and when that section takes effect.)

1316.
When bail is taken upon the recommitment of the defendant, the undertaking must be in substantially the following form:
An order having been made on the _____ day of _____, A.D. eighteen _____, by the Court (naming it), that A. B. be admitted to bail in the sum of _____ dollars, in an action pending in that Court against him in behalf of the people of the State of California, upon an (information, presentment, indictment, or appeal, as the case may be), we, C. D. and E. F., of (stating their places of residence and occupation), hereby undertake that the above named A. B. will appear in that or any other Court in which his appearance may be lawfully required upon that (information, presentment, indictment, or appeal, as the case may be), and will at all times render himself amenable to its orders and process, and appear for judgment and surrender himself in execution thereof; or if he fails to

perform either of these conditions, that we will pay to the people of the State of California the sum of _____ dollars (insert the sum in which the defendant is admitted to bail).
(Enacted 1872. Repealed pursuant to Section 1320.6 if and when that section takes effect.)

1317.
The bail must possess the qualifications, and must be put in, in all respects, in the manner prescribed in Article II of this Chapter.
(Enacted 1872. Repealed pursuant to Section 1320.6 if and when that section takes effect.)

ARTICLE 9. Procedure Relating to Release on Own Recognizance [1318 - 1319.5]
(Article 9 repealed (by Sec. 11) and added by Stats. 1979, Ch. 873, Sec. 12.)

1318.
(a) The defendant shall not be released from custody under an own recognizance until the defendant files with the clerk of the court or other person authorized to accept bail a signed release agreement which includes:
(1) The defendant's promise to appear at all times and places, as ordered by the court or magistrate and as ordered by any court in which, or any magistrate before whom the charge is subsequently pending.
(2) The defendant's promise to obey all reasonable conditions imposed by the court or magistrate.
(3) The defendant's promise not to depart this state without leave of the court.
(4) Agreement by the defendant to waive extradition if the defendant fails to appear as required and is apprehended outside of the State of California.
(5) The acknowledgment of the defendant that he or she has been informed of the consequences and penalties applicable to violation of the conditions of release.
(Amended (as amended by Stats. 1985, Ch. 1432) by Stats. 1988, Ch. 403, Sec. 4. Repealed pursuant to Section 1320.6 if and when that section takes effect.)

1318.1.
(a) A court, with the concurrence of the board of supervisors, may employ an investigative staff for the purpose of recommending whether a defendant should be released on his or her own recognizance.
(b) Whenever a court has employed an investigative staff pursuant to subdivision (a), an investigative report shall be prepared in all cases involving a violent felony, as described in subdivision (c) of Section 667.5, or a felony in violation of subdivision (a) of Section 23153 of the Vehicle Code, recommending whether the defendant should be released on his or her own recognizance. The report shall include all of the following:
(1) Written verification of any outstanding warrants against the defendant.
(2) Written verification of any prior incidents where the defendant has failed to make a court appearance.
(3) Written verification of the criminal record of the defendant.
(4) Written verification of the residence of the defendant during the past year.
After the report is certified pursuant to this subdivision, it shall be submitted to the court for review, prior to a hearing held pursuant to Section 1319.
(c) The salaries of the staff are a proper charge against the county.
(Amended by Stats. 1992, Ch. 1009, Sec. 2. Effective January 1, 1993. Repealed pursuant to Section 1320.6 if and when that section takes effect.)

1319.
(a) No person arrested for a violent felony, as described in subdivision (c) of Section 667.5, may be released on his or her own recognizance until a hearing is held in open court before the magistrate or judge, and until the prosecuting attorney is given notice and a reasonable opportunity to be heard on the matter. In all cases, these provisions shall be implemented in a manner consistent with the defendant's right to be taken before a magistrate or judge without unreasonable delay pursuant to Section 825.
(b) A defendant charged with a violent felony, as described in subdivision (c) of Section 667.5, shall not be released on his or her own recognizance where it appears, by clear and convincing evidence, that he or she previously has been charged with a felony offense and has willfully and without excuse from the court failed to appear in court as required while that charge was pending. In all other cases, in making the determination as to whether or not to grant release under this section, the court shall consider all of the following:
(1) The existence of any outstanding felony warrants on the defendant.
(2) Any other information presented in the report prepared pursuant to Section 1318.1. The fact that the court has not received the report required by Section 1318.1, at the time of the hearing to decide whether to release the defendant on his or her own recognizance, shall not preclude that release.
(3) Any other information presented by the prosecuting attorney.
(c) The judge or magistrate who, pursuant to this section, grants or denies release on a person's own recognizance, within the time period prescribed in Section 825, shall state the reasons for that decision in the record. This statement shall be included in the court's minutes. The report prepared by the investigative staff pursuant to subdivision (b) of Section 1318.1 shall be placed in the court file for that particular matter.
(Amended by Stats. 1992, Ch. 1009, Sec. 3. Effective January 1, 1993. Repealed pursuant to Section 1320.6 if and when that section takes effect.)

1319.5.
(a) A person described in subdivision (b) who is arrested for a new offense shall not be released on his or her own recognizance until a hearing is held in open court before the magistrate or judge.
(b) Subdivision (a) shall apply to the following:
(1) Any person who is currently on felony probation or felony parole.
(2) Any person who has failed to appear in court as ordered, resulting in a warrant being issued, three or more times over the three years preceding the current arrest, except for infractions arising from violations of the Vehicle Code, and who is arrested for any of the following offenses:
(A) Any violation of the California Street Terrorism Enforcement and Prevention Act (Chapter 11 (commencing with Section 186.20) of Title 7 of Part 1).
(B) Any violation of Chapter 9 (commencing with Section 240) of Title 8 of Part 1 (assault and battery).
(C) A violation of Section 459 (residential burglary).
(D) Any offense in which the defendant is alleged to have been armed with or to have personally used a firearm.
(E) Any offense involving domestic violence.
(F) Any offense in which the defendant is alleged to have caused great bodily injury to another person.
(G) Any other felony offense not described in subparagraphs (A) through (F), inclusive, unless the person is released pursuant to a court-operated pretrial release program or a pretrial release program with approval by the court, in which case subdivision (a) shall not apply.
(c) This section does not change the requirement under Section 1270.1 to hold a hearing in open court before the magistrate or judge in cases in which the person has been arrested for an offense specified in that section.
(d) This section does not alter or diminish the rights conferred under Section 28 of Article I of the California Constitution (Marsy's Law).
(Amended by Stats. 2017, Ch. 554, Sec. 1. (AB 789) Effective January 1, 2018. Repealed pursuant to Section 1320.6 if and when that section takes effect.)

ARTICLE 10. Violations [1320 - 1320.6]
(Article 10 added by Stats. 1979, Ch. 873, Sec. 13.)

1320.
(a) Every person who is charged with or convicted of the commission of a misdemeanor who is released from custody on his or her own recognizance and who in order to evade the process of the court willfully fails to appear as required, is guilty of a misdemeanor. It shall be presumed that a defendant who willfully fails to appear within 14 days of the date assigned for his or her appearance intended to evade the process of the court.
(b) Every person who is charged with or convicted of the commission of a felony who is released from custody on his or her own recognizance and who in order to evade the process of the court willfully fails to appear as required, is guilty of a felony, and upon conviction shall be punished by a fine not exceeding five thousand dollars ($5,000) or by imprisonment pursuant to subdivision (h) of Section 1170, or in the county jail for not more than one year, or by both that fine and imprisonment. It shall be presumed that a defendant who willfully fails to appear within 14 days of the date assigned for his or her appearance intended to evade the process of the court.
(Amended by Stats. 2011, Ch. 15, Sec. 459. (AB 109) Effective April 4, 2011. Operative October 1, 2011, by Sec. 636 of Ch. 15, as amended by Stats. 2011, Ch. 39, Sec. 68. Repealed pursuant to Section 1320.6 if and when that section takes effect.)

1320.5.
Every person who is charged with or convicted of the commission of a felony, who is released from custody on bail, and who in order to evade the process of the court willfully fails to appear as required, is guilty of a felony. Upon a conviction under this section, the person shall be punished by a fine not exceeding ten thousand dollars ($10,000) or by imprisonment pursuant to subdivision (h) of Section 1170, or in the county jail for not more than one year, or by both the fine and imprisonment. Willful failure to appear within 14 days of the date assigned for appearance may be found to have been for the purpose of evading the process of the court.
(Amended by Stats. 2011, Ch. 15, Sec. 460. (AB 109) Effective April 4, 2011. Operative October 1, 2011, by Sec. 636 of Ch. 15, as amended by Stats. 2011, Ch. 39, Sec. 68. Repealed pursuant to Section 1320.6 if and when that section takes effect.)

1320.6.
This chapter shall remain in effect only until October 1, 2019, and as of that date is repealed.
(Added by Stats. 2018, Ch. 244, Sec. 3. (SB 10) Effective date (January 1, 2019) suspended pursuant to referendum petition. Effective only if Ch. 244 is approved as a referendum measure at the November 3, 2020, election. Repealed by its own provisions on effective date of referendum measure, if approved. Note: Repeal affects Chapter 1, commencing with Section 1268.)

CHAPTER 1.5. Pretrial Custody Status [1320.7 - 1320.34]

(Chapter 1.5 added by Stats. 2018, Ch. 244, Sec. 4.)

ARTICLE 1. Definitions [1320.7- 1320.7.]
(Article 1 added by Stats. 2018, Ch. 244, Sec. 4.)

1320.7.
As used in this chapter, the following terms have the following meanings:
(a) "The court" as used in this chapter includes "subordinate judicial officers," if authorized by the particular superior court, as authorized in Section 22 of Article VI of the California Constitution and specified in Rule 10.703 of the California Rules of Court.
(b) "High risk" means that an arrested person, after determination of the person's risk following an investigation by Pretrial Assessment Services, including the use of a validated risk assessment tool, is categorized as having a significant level of risk of failure to appear in court as required or risk to public safety due to the commission of a new criminal offense while released on the current criminal offense.
(c) "Low risk" means that an arrested person, after determination of the person's risk following an investigation by Pretrial Assessment Services, including the use of a validated risk assessment tool, is categorized as having a minimal level of risk of failure to appear in court as required or risk to public safety due to the commission of a new criminal offense while released on the current criminal offense.
(d) "Medium risk" means that an arrested person, after determination of the person's risk following an investigation by Pretrial Assessment Services, including the use of a validated risk assessment tool, is categorized as having a moderate level of risk of failure to appear in court as required or risk to public safety due to the commission of a new criminal offense while released on the current criminal offense.
(e) "Own recognizance release" means the pretrial release of an arrested person who promises in writing to appear in court as required, and without supervision.
(f) "Pretrial risk assessment" means an assessment conducted by Pretrial Assessment Services with the use of a validated risk assessment tool, designed to provide information about the risk of a person's failure to appear in court as required or the risk to public safety due to the commission of a new criminal offense if the person is released before adjudication of his or her current criminal offense.
(g) "Pretrial Assessment Services" means an entity, division, or program that is assigned the responsibility, pursuant to Section 1320.26, to assess the risk level of persons charged with the commission of a crime, report the results of the risk determination to the court, and make recommendations for conditions of release of individuals pending adjudication of their criminal case, and as directed under statute or rule of court, implement risk-based determinations regarding release and detention. The entity, division, or program, at the option of the particular superior court, may be employees of the court, or employees of a public entity contracting with the court for those services as provided in Section 1320.26, and may include an entity, division, or program from an adjoining county or one that provides services as a member of a regional consortium. In all circumstances persons acting on behalf of the entity, division, or program shall be officers of the court. "Pretrial Assessment Services" does not include supervision of persons released under this chapter.
(h) "Risk" refers to the likelihood that a person will not appear in court as required or the likelihood that a person will commit a new crime if the person is released before adjudication of his or her current criminal offense.
(i) "Risk score" refers to a descriptive evaluation of a person's risk of failing to appear in court as required or the risk to public safety due to the commission of a new criminal offense if the person is released before adjudication of his or her current criminal offense, as a result of conducting an assessment with a validated risk assessment tool and may include a numerical value or terms such as "high," "medium," or "low" risk.
(j) "Supervised own recognizance release" means the pretrial release of an arrested person who promises in writing, but without posting money or a secured bond, to appear in court as required, and upon whom the court or Pretrial Assessment Services imposes specified conditions of release.
(k) "Validated risk assessment tool" means a risk assessment instrument, selected and approved by the court, in consultation with Pretrial Assessment Services or another entity providing pretrial risk assessments, from the list of approved pretrial risk assessment tools maintained by the Judicial Council. The assessment tools shall be demonstrated by scientific research to be accurate and reliable in assessing the risk of a person failing to appear in court as required or the risk to public safety due to the commission of a new criminal offense if the person is released before adjudication of his or her current criminal offense and minimize bias.

(l) "Witness" means any person who has testified or is expected to testify, or who, by reason of having relevant information, is subject to call or likely to be called as a witness in an action or proceeding for the current offense, whether or not any action or proceeding has yet been commenced, and whether or not the person is a witness for the defense or prosecution.

(Added by Stats. 2018, Ch. 244, Sec. 4. (SB 10) Effective date (January 1, 2019) suspended pursuant to referendum petition. Effective only if Ch. 244 is approved as a referendum measure at the November 3, 2020, election.)

ARTICLE 2. Book and Release [1320.8- 1320.8.]

(Article 2 added by Stats. 2018, Ch. 244, Sec. 4.)

1320.8.

A person arrested or detained for a misdemeanor, other than a misdemeanor listed in subdivision (e) of Section 1320.10, may be booked and released without being taken into custody or, if taken into custody, shall be released from custody without a risk assessment by Pretrial Assessment Services within 12 hours of booking. This section shall apply to any person who has been arrested for a misdemeanor other than those offenses or factors listed in subdivision (e) of Section 1320.10, whether arrested with or without a warrant.

(Added by Stats. 2018, Ch. 244, Sec. 4. (SB 10) Effective date (January 1, 2019) suspended pursuant to referendum petition. Effective only if Ch. 244 is approved as a referendum measure at the November 3, 2020, election.)

ARTICLE 3. Pretrial Assessment Services Investigation [1320.9- 1320.9.]

(Article 3 added by Stats. 2018, Ch. 244, Sec. 4.)

1320.9.

(a) Prior to arraignment, or prior to prearraignment review for those persons eligible for review, Pretrial Assessment Services shall obtain all of the following information regarding each detained person, other than those persons booked and released under Section 1320.8:

(1) The results of a risk assessment using a validated risk assessment instrument, including the risk score or risk level.

(2) The criminal charge for which the person was arrested and the criminal history of the person, including the person's history of failure to appear in court within the past three years.

(3) Any supplemental information reasonably available that directly addresses the arrested person's risk to public safety or risk of failure to appear in court as required.

(b) The district attorney shall make a reasonable effort to contact the victim for comment on the person's custody status.

(c) Prior to prearraignment review pursuant to subdivision (a) or (b) of Section 1320.10 or Section 1320.13, or prior to arraignment, Pretrial Assessment Services shall prepare a report containing information obtained in accordance with subdivisions (a) and (b), and any recommendations for conditions of the person's release. Options for conditions of release shall be established by the Judicial Council and set forth in the California Rules of Court. A copy of the report shall be served on the court and counsel.

(d) The report described in subdivision (c), including the results of a risk assessment using a validated risk assessment instrument, shall not be used for any purpose other than that provided for in this chapter.

(Added by Stats. 2018, Ch. 244, Sec. 4. (SB 10) Effective date (January 1, 2019) suspended pursuant to referendum petition. Effective only if Ch. 244 is approved as a referendum measure at the November 3, 2020, election.)

ARTICLE 4. Release by Pretrial Assessment Services [1320.10- 1320.10.]

(Article 4 added by Stats. 2018, Ch. 244, Sec. 4.)

1320.10.

(a) Pretrial Assessment Services shall conduct a prearraignment review of the facts and circumstances relevant to the arrested person's custody status, and shall consider any relevant and available information provided by law enforcement, the arrested person, any victim, and the prosecution or defense.

(b) Pretrial Assessment Services, using the information obtained pursuant to this section and Section 1320.9, and having assessed a person as having a low risk to public safety and low risk of failure to appear in court, shall release a low-risk person on his or her own recognizance, prior to arraignment, without review by the court, and with the least restrictive nonmonetary condition or combination of conditions that will reasonably assure public safety and the person's return to court. This subdivision does not apply to a person booked and released under Section 1320.8 or a person who is ineligible for consideration for release prior to arraignment as set forth in subdivision (e).

(c) Pretrial Assessment Services shall order the release or detention of medium-risk persons in accordance with the review and release standards set forth in the local rule of court authorized under Section 1320.11. A person released pursuant to the local rule of court shall be released on his or her own recognizance or on supervised own recognizance release, prior to arraignment, without review by the court, and with the least restrictive nonmonetary condition or combination of conditions that will reasonably assure public safety and the person's return to court. This subdivision shall not apply to a person booked and released under Section 1320.8 or a person ineligible for consideration prior to arraignment pursuant to subdivision (e) of this section. Pursuant to Section 1320.13, courts may conduct prearraignment reviews and make release decisions and may authorize subordinate judicial officers to conduct prearraignment reviews and make release decisions authorized by this chapter.

(d) A person shall not be required to pay for any nonmonetary condition or combination of conditions imposed pursuant to this section.

(e) Notwithstanding subdivisions (a) and (b), Pretrial Assessment Services shall not release:

(1) A person who has been assessed in the current case by Pretrial Assessment Services using a validated risk assessment tool pursuant to Section 1320.9 and is assessed as high risk.

(2) A person arrested for an offense listed in paragraph (2) or (3) of subdivision (d) of Section 290.

(3) A person arrested for any of the following misdemeanor offenses:

(A) A violation of Section 273.5.

(B) A violation of paragraph (1) of subdivision (e) of Section 243.

(C) A violation of Section 273.6 if the detained person is alleged to have made threats to kill or harm, engaged in violence against, or gone to the residence or the workplace of, the protected party.

(D) A violation of Section 646.9.

(4) A person arrested for a felony offense that includes, as an element of the crime for which the person was arrested, physical violence to another person, the threat of such violence, or the likelihood of great bodily injury, or a felony offense in which the person is alleged to have been personally armed with or personally used a deadly weapon or firearm in the commission of the crime, or alleged to have personally inflicted great bodily injury in the commission of the crime.

(5) A person arrested for a third offense within the past 10 years of driving under the influence of alcohol or drugs or any combination thereof, or for an offense of driving under the influence of alcohol or drugs with injury to another, or for an offense of driving with a blood alcohol level of .20 or above.

(6) A person arrested for a violation of any type of restraining order within the past five years.

(7) A person who has three or more prior warrants for failure to appear within the previous 12 months.

(8) A person who, at the time of arrest, was pending trial or pending sentencing for a misdemeanor or a felony.

(9) A person who, at the time of arrest, was on any form of postconviction supervision other than informal probation or court supervision.

(10) A person who has intimidated, dissuaded, or threatened retaliation against a witness or victim of the current crime.

(11) A person who has violated a condition of pretrial release within the past five years.

(12) A person who has been convicted of a serious felony, as defined in subdivision (c) of Section 1192.7, or a violent felony, as defined in subdivision (c) of Section 667.5, within the past five years.

(13) A person arrested with or without a warrant for a serious felony, as defined in subdivision (c) of Section 1192.7, or a "violent felony," as defined in subdivision (c) of Section 667.5.

(f) Review of the person's custody status and release pursuant to subdivision (b) or (c) shall occur without unnecessary delay, and no later than 24 hours of the person's booking. The 24-hour period may be extended for good cause, but shall not exceed an additional 12 hours.

(g) A person shall not be released on his or her own recognizance in accordance with subdivision (b) or (c) until the person signs a release agreement that includes, at a minimum, all of the following from the person:

(1) A promise to appear at all times and places, as ordered by the court.

(2) A promise not to depart this state without the permission of the court.

(3) Agreement to waive extradition if the person fails to appear as required and is apprehended outside of the State of California.

(4) Acknowledgment that he or she has been informed of the consequences and penalties applicable to violation of these conditions of release.

(5) Agreement to obey all laws and orders of the court.

(h) Persons not released pursuant to this section shall be detained until arraignment unless the court provides prearraignment review pursuant to Section 1320.13.

(Added by Stats. 2018, Ch. 244, Sec. 4. (SB 10) Effective date (January 1, 2019) suspended pursuant to referendum petition. Effective only if Ch. 244 is approved as a referendum measure at the November 3, 2020, election. Superseded on operative date of amendment by Stats. 2018, Ch. 980.)

1320.10.

(a) Pretrial Assessment Services shall conduct a prearraignment review of the facts and circumstances relevant to the arrested person's custody status, and shall consider any relevant and available information provided by law enforcement, the arrested person, any victim, and the prosecution or defense.

(b) Pretrial Assessment Services, using the information obtained pursuant to this section and Section 1320.9, and having assessed a person as having a low risk to public safety and low risk of failure to appear in court, shall release a low risk person on his or her own recognizance, prior to arraignment, without review by the court, and with the least restrictive nonmonetary condition or combination of conditions that will reasonably assure public safety and the person's return to court. This subdivision does not apply to a person booked and released under Section 1320.8 or a person who is ineligible for consideration for release prior to arraignment as set forth in subdivision (e).

(c) Pretrial Assessment Services shall order the release or detention of medium risk persons in accordance with the review and release standards set forth in the local rule of court authorized under Section 1320.11. A person released pursuant to the local rule of court shall be released on his or her own recognizance or on supervised own recognizance release, prior to arraignment, without review by the court, and with the least restrictive nonmonetary condition or combination of conditions that will reasonably assure public safety and the person's return to court. This subdivision shall not apply to a person booked and released under Section 1320.8 or a person ineligible for consideration prior to arraignment pursuant to subdivision (e) of this section. Pursuant to Section 1320.13, courts may conduct prearraignment reviews and make release decisions and may authorize subordinate judicial officers to conduct prearraignment reviews and make release decisions authorized by this chapter.

(d) A person shall not be required to pay for any nonmonetary condition or combination of conditions imposed pursuant to this section.

(e) Notwithstanding subdivisions (a) and (b), Pretrial Assessment Services shall not release:

(1) A person who has been assessed in the current case by Pretrial Assessment Services using a validated risk assessment tool pursuant to Section 1320.9 and is assessed as high risk.

(2) A person arrested for an offense listed in Section 290.

(3) A person arrested for any of the following misdemeanor offenses:

(A) A violation of Section 273.5.

(B) A violation of paragraph (1) of subdivision (e) of Section 243.

(C) A violation of Section 273.6 if the detained person is alleged to have made threats to kill or harm, engaged in violence against, or gone to the residence or the workplace of, the protected party.

(D) A violation of Section 646.9.

(4) A person arrested for a felony offense that includes, as an element of the crime for which the person was arrested, physical violence to another person, the threat of such violence, or the likelihood of great bodily injury, or a felony offense in which the person is alleged to have been personally armed with or personally used a deadly weapon or firearm in the commission of the crime, or alleged to have personally inflicted great bodily injury in the commission of the crime.

(5) A person arrested for a third offense within the past 10 years of driving under the influence of alcohol or drugs or any combination thereof, or for an offense of driving under the influence of alcohol or drugs with injury to another, or for an offense of driving with a blood alcohol level of .20 or above.

(6) A person arrested for a violation of any type of restraining order within the past five years.

(7) A person who has three or more prior warrants for failure to appear within the previous 12 months.

(8) A person who, at the time of arrest, was pending trial or pending sentencing for a misdemeanor or a felony.

(9) A person who, at the time of arrest, was on any form of postconviction supervision other than informal probation or court supervision.

(10) A person who has intimidated, dissuaded, or threatened retaliation against a witness or victim of the current crime.

(11) A person who has violated a condition of pretrial release within the past five years.

(12) A person who has been convicted of a serious felony, as defined in subdivision (c) of Section 1192.7, or a violent felony, as defined in subdivision (c) of Section 667.5, within the past five years.

(13) A person arrested with or without a warrant for a serious felony, as defined in subdivision (c) of Section 1192.7, or a "violent felony," as defined in subdivision (c) of Section 667.5.

(f) Review of the person's custody status and release pursuant to subdivision (b) or (c) shall occur without unnecessary delay, and no later than 24 hours of the person's booking. The 24-hour period may be extended for good cause, but shall not exceed an additional 12 hours.

(g) A person shall not be released on his or her own recognizance in accordance with subdivision (b) or (c) until the person signs a release agreement that includes, at a minimum, all of the following from the person:

(1) A promise to appear at all times and places, as ordered by the court.

(2) A promise not to depart this state without the permission of the court.

(3) Agreement to waive extradition if the person fails to appear as required and is apprehended outside of the State of California.

(4) Acknowledgment that he or she has been informed of the consequences and penalties applicable to violation of these conditions of release.

(5) Agreement to obey all laws and orders of the court.

(h) Persons not released pursuant to this section shall be detained until arraignment unless the court provides prearraignment review pursuant to Section 1320.13.

(Amended (as added by Stats. 2018, Ch. 244) by Stats. 2018, Ch. 980, Sec. 1. (SB 1054) Effective January 1, 2019. Pursuant to Sec. 3 of Stats. 2018, Ch. 980, this amendment is operative only if and when the addition of this section by Stats. 2018, Ch. 244, becomes effective.)

ARTICLE 5. Prearraignment Review by Pretrial Assessment Services or the Court [1320.11 - 1320.14]

(Article 5 added by Stats. 2018, Ch. 244, Sec. 4.)

1320.11.

(a) A superior court, in consultation with Pretrial Assessment Services and other stakeholders, shall adopt a local rule of court consistent with the California Rules of Court adopted by the Judicial Council, as described in subdivision (a) of Section 1320.25, that sets forth review and release standards for Pretrial Assessment Services for persons assessed as medium risk and eligible for prearraignment release on own recognizance or supervised own recognizance. The local rule of court shall provide for the release or detention of medium-risk defendants, support an effective and efficient pretrial release or detention system that protects public safety and respects the due process rights of defendants. The local rule shall provide Pretrial Assessment Services with authority to detain or release on own recognizance or supervised own recognizance defendants assessed as medium risk, consistent with the standards for release or detention set forth in the rule. The local rule may further expand the list of offenses and factors for which prearraignment release of persons assessed as medium risk is not permitted but shall not provide for the exclusion of release of all medium-risk defendants by Pretrial Assessment Services. The authority of the local rule of court shall be limited to determinations made pursuant to subdivision (c) of Section 1320.10. On an annual basis, superior courts shall consider the impact of the rule on public safety, the due process rights of defendants, and the preceding year's implementation of the rule.

(b) Pursuant to subdivision (d) of Rule 10.613 of the California Rules of Court, the court shall file with the Judicial Council an electronic copy of the rule and amendments to the rule adopted pursuant to this section in a format authorized by the Judicial Council.

(Added by Stats. 2018, Ch. 244, Sec. 4. (SB 10) Effective date (January 1, 2019) suspended pursuant to referendum petition. Effective only if Ch. 244 is approved as a referendum measure at the November 3, 2020, election.)

1320.13.

(a) The court may conduct prearraignment reviews, make release decisions, and may authorize subordinate judicial officers, as defined in Rule 10.703 of the California Rules of Court, to conduct prearraignment reviews and make release decisions authorized by this chapter.

(b) The authority for court prearraignment review and release granted by this section shall not apply to the following persons:

(1) Persons assessed as high risk.

(2) Persons charged with a serious felony, as defined in subdivision (c) of Section 1192.7, or a violent felony, as defined in subdivision (c) of Section 667.5.

(3) Persons who, at the time of arrest, were pending trial or sentencing in a felony matter.

(c) When making a prearraignment release or detention determination and ordering conditions of release, the information obtained under Section 1320.9 and any recommendations and options for conditions of release shall be considered, with significant weight given to the recommendations and assessment of Pretrial Assessment Services.

(d) The court shall consider any relevant and available information provided by law enforcement, the arrested person, any victim, and the prosecution or defense before making a pretrial release or detention determination.

(e) (1) If the court finds the person appropriate for prearraignment release, the arrested person shall be released on the person's own recognizance, or on supervised own recognizance, with the least restrictive nonmonetary condition or combination of conditions that will reasonably assure public safety and the arrested person's appearance in court as required.

(2) A person shall not be required to pay for any nonmonetary condition or combination of conditions imposed pursuant to this subdivision.

(f) A person released on his or her own recognizance shall sign a release agreement that includes, at a minimum, all of the following from the person:

(1) A promise to appear at all times and places, as ordered by the court.

(2) A promise not to depart this state without the permission of the court.

(3) Agreement to waive extradition if the person fails to appear as required and is apprehended outside of the State of California.

(4) Acknowledgment that he or she has been informed of the consequences and penalties applicable to violation of these conditions of release.

(5) Agreement to obey all laws and orders of the court.

(g) Options for conditions of release shall be established by the Judicial Council and set forth in the California Rules of Court.

(h) The court may decline to release a person pending arraignment if there is a substantial likelihood that no condition or combination of conditions of pretrial supervision will reasonably assure public safety or the appearance of the person as required.

(i) There shall be a presumption that no condition or combination of conditions of pretrial supervision will reasonably assure the safety of any other person and the community pending arraignment if it is shown that any of the following apply:

(1) The crime for which the person was arrested was committed with violence against a person, threatened violence or the likelihood of serious bodily injury, or one in which the person committing the offense was personally armed with or personally used a deadly weapon or firearm in the commission of the crime, or personally inflicted great bodily injury in the commission of the crime.

(2) At the time of arrest, the person was on any form of postconviction supervision, other than court supervision or informal probation.

(3) The arrested person intimidated, dissuaded, or threatened retaliation against a witness or victim of the current crime.

(4) The person is currently on pretrial release and has violated a condition of release.

(Added by Stats. 2018, Ch. 244, Sec. 4. (SB 10) Effective date (January 1, 2019) suspended pursuant to referendum petition. Effective only if Ch. 244 is approved as a referendum measure at the November 3, 2020, election.)

1320.14.

For good cause shown, the court may, at any time by its own motion, or upon ex parte application by the arrested person, the prosecution, or Pretrial Assessment Services, modify the conditions of release, with 24 hours' notice, unless time and circumstances do not permit notice within 24 hours.

(Added by Stats. 2018, Ch. 244, Sec. 4. (SB 10) Effective date (January 1, 2019) suspended pursuant to referendum petition. Effective only if Ch. 244 is approved as a referendum measure at the November 3, 2020, election.)

ARTICLE 6. Release or Detention Determination at Arraignment [1320.15 - 1320.18]

(Article 6 added by Stats. 2018, Ch. 244, Sec. 4.)

1320.15.

At or prior to the defendant's arraignment, Pretrial Assessment Services shall, if the defendant was not released pursuant to Section 1320.8, submit all of the following information for consideration by the court:

(a) The results of a risk assessment, including the risk score or risk level, or both, obtained using a validated risk assessment instrument.

(b) The criminal charge for which the person was arrested and the criminal history of the person, including the person's history of failure to appear in court within the past three years.

(c) Any supplemental information reasonably available that directly addresses the defendant's risk to public safety or risk of failure to appear in court as required.

(d) Recommendations to the court for conditions of release to impose upon a released defendant. Options for conditions of release shall be established by the Judicial Council and set forth in the California Rules of Court.

(Added by Stats. 2018, Ch. 244, Sec. 4. (SB 10) Effective date (January 1, 2019) suspended pursuant to referendum petition. Effective only if Ch. 244 is approved as a referendum measure at the November 3, 2020, election.)

1320.16.

(a) The victim of the crime for which the defendant was arrested shall be given notice of the arraignment by the prosecution and, if requested, any other hearing at which the custody status of the defendant will be determined. If requested by the victim, the victim shall be given a reasonable opportunity to be heard on the matter of the defendant's custody status.

(b) The prosecution shall make a reasonable effort to contact the victim for comment on the defendant's custody status.

(c) In instances where a victim cannot or does not wish to appear at the arraignment, the prosecution shall submit any of the victim's comments on the defendant's custody status in writing to the court.

(d) The appearance or nonappearance of the victim and any comments provided by the victim shall be included in the record.

(e) If requested by either party, the court may review and modify the conditions of the defendant's release at arraignment.

(Added by Stats. 2018, Ch. 244, Sec. 4. (SB 10) Effective date (January 1, 2019) suspended pursuant to referendum petition. Effective only if Ch. 244 is approved as a referendum measure at the November 3, 2020, election.)

1320.17.

At arraignment, the court shall order a defendant released on his or her own recognizance or supervised own recognizance with the least restrictive nonmonetary condition or combination of conditions that will reasonably assure public safety and the defendant's return to court unless the prosecution files a motion for preventive detention in accordance with Section 1320.18.

(Added by Stats. 2018, Ch. 244, Sec. 4. (SB 10) Effective date (January 1, 2019) suspended pursuant to referendum petition. Effective only if Ch. 244 is approved as a referendum measure at the November 3, 2020, election.)

1320.18.

(a) At the defendant's arraignment, or at any other time during the criminal proceedings, the prosecution may file a motion seeking detention of the defendant pending a trial, based on any of the following circumstances:

(1) The crime for which the person was arrested was committed with violence against a person, threatened violence, or the likelihood of serious bodily injury, or was one in which the person was personally armed with or personally used a deadly weapon or firearm in the commission of the crime, or was one in which he or she personally inflicted great bodily injury in the commission of the crime.

(2) At the time of arrest, the defendant was on any form of postconviction supervision other than informal probation or court supervision.

(3) At the time of arrest, the defendant was subject to a pending trial or sentencing on a felony matter.

(4) The defendant intimidated or threatened retaliation against a witness or victim of the current crime.

(5) There is substantial reason to believe that no nonmonetary condition or combination of conditions of pretrial supervision will reasonably assure protection of the public or a victim, or the appearance of the defendant in court as required.

(b) The court shall hold a preventive detention hearing as set forth in Section 1320.19.

(c) Upon the filing of a motion for preventive detention, the court shall make a determination regarding release or detention of the defendant pending the preventive detention hearing. When making the release or detention determination and ordering conditions of release pending the preventive detention hearing, the court shall consider the information provided by Pretrial Assessment Services, including recommendations on conditions of release and shall give significant weight to recommendations and assessment of Pretrial Assessment Services.

(d) If the court determines there is a substantial likelihood that no nonmonetary condition or combination of conditions of pretrial supervision will reasonably assure the appearance of the defendant at the preventive detention hearing or reasonably assure public safety prior to the preventive detention hearing, the court may detain the defendant pending a preventive detention hearing, and shall state the reasons for detention on the record.

(e) (1) If the court determines there is not a sufficient basis for detaining the defendant pending the preventive detention hearing, the court shall release the defendant on his or her own recognizance or on supervised own recognizance and impose the least restrictive nonmonetary condition or combination of conditions of pretrial release to reasonably assure public safety and the appearance of the defendant in court as required.

(2) A person shall not be required to pay for any nonmonetary condition or combination of conditions imposed pursuant to this subdivision.

(Added by Stats. 2018, Ch. 244, Sec. 4. (SB 10) Effective date (January 1, 2019) suspended pursuant to referendum petition. Effective only if Ch. 244 is approved as a referendum measure at the November 3, 2020, election.)

ARTICLE 7. Preventive Detention Hearing [1320.19 - 1320.23]

(Article 7 added by Stats. 2018, Ch. 244, Sec. 4.)

1320.19.

(a) If the defendant is detained in custody, the preventive detention hearing shall be held no later than three court days after the motion for preventive detention is filed. If the defendant is not detained in custody, the preventive detention hearing shall be held no later than three court days after the defendant is brought into custody as a result of a warrant issued in accordance with subdivision (c). If the defendant is not in custody at the time of the request for a preventive detention hearing and the court does not issue a warrant in connection with the request for a hearing, the preventive detention hearing shall be held within five court days of the request for the hearing. By stipulation of counsel and with agreement of the court, the preventive detention hearing may be held in conjunction with the arraignment, or within three days after arraignment.

(b) For good cause, the defense or the prosecution may seek a continuance of the preventive detention hearing. If a request for a continuance is granted, the continuance may not exceed three court days unless stipulated by the parties.

(c) The hearing shall be completed at one session, unless the defendant personally waives his or her right to a continuous preventive detention hearing. If the defendant is out of custody at the time the preventive detention hearing is requested, the court, upon the filing of an application for a warrant in conjunction with the motion for preventive detention, may issue a warrant requiring the defendant's placement in custody pending the completion of the preventive detention hearing.

(d) The defendant shall have the right to be represented by counsel at the hearing. If financially unable to obtain representation, the defendant has a right to have counsel appointed. The defendant has the right to be heard at the preventive detention hearing.

(e) Upon request of the victim of the crime, the victim shall be given notice by the prosecution of the preventive detention hearing. If requested, the victim shall be given a reasonable opportunity to be heard on the matter of the defendant's custody status.

(f) The prosecution shall make a reasonable effort to contact the victim for comment on the defendant's custody status. In instances where a victim cannot or does not wish to appear at the preventive detention hearing, the prosecution shall submit the victim's comments, if any, on the defendant's custody status in writing to the court and counsel.

(g) The appearance or nonappearance of a victim, and comments provided by a victim, shall be included in the record.

(Added by Stats. 2018, Ch. 244, Sec. 4. (SB 10) Effective date (January 1, 2019) suspended pursuant to referendum petition. Effective only if Ch. 244 is approved as a referendum measure at the November 3, 2020, election.)

1320.20.

(a) There shall be a rebuttable presumption that no condition or combination of conditions of pretrial supervision will reasonably assure public safety if the court finds probable cause to believe either of the following:

(1) The current crime is a violent felony as defined in subdivision (c) of Section 667.5, or was a felony offense committed with violence against a person, threatened violence, or with a likelihood of serious bodily injury, or one in which the defendant was personally armed with or personally used a deadly weapon or firearm in the commission of the crime, or was one in which he or she personally inflicted great bodily injury in the commission of the crime; or

(2) The defendant is assessed as "high risk" to the safety of the public or a victim and any of the following:

(A) The defendant was convicted of a serious felony as defined in subdivision (c) of Section 1192.7 or a violent felony as defined in subdivision (c) of Section 667.5, within the past 5 years.

(B) The defendant committed the current crime while pending sentencing for a crime described in paragraph (1) of subdivision (a).

(C) The defendant has intimidated, dissuaded, or threatened retaliation against a witness or victim of the current crime.

(D) At the time of arrest, the defendant was on any form of postconviction supervision other than informal probation or court supervision.

(b) The prosecution shall establish at the preventive detention hearing that there is probable cause to believe the defendant committed the charged crime or crimes in cases where there is no indictment, or if the defendant has not been held to answer following a preliminary hearing or waiver of a preliminary hearing, and the defendant challenges the sufficiency of the evidence showing that he or she committed the charged crime or crimes.

(c) The court shall make its decision regarding preventive detention, including the determination of probable cause to believe the defendant committed the charged crime or crimes, based on the statements, if any, of the defendant, offers of proof and argument of counsel, input from a victim, if any, and any evidence presented at the hearing. The court may consider reliable hearsay in making any decision under this section. The defendant shall have the right to testify at the hearing.

(d) (1) At the detention hearing, the court may order preventive detention of the defendant pending trial or other hearing only if the detention is permitted under the United States Constitution and under the California Constitution, and the court determines by clear and convincing evidence that no nonmonetary condition or combination of conditions of pretrial supervision will reasonably assure public safety or the appearance of the defendant in court as required. The court shall state the reasons for ordering preventive detention on the record.

(2) Upon the request of either party, a transcript of the hearing shall be provided within two court days after the request is made.

(3) If either party files a writ challenging the decision, the court of appeal shall expeditiously consider that writ.

(e) (1) If the court determines there is not a sufficient basis for detaining the defendant, the court shall release the defendant on his or her own recognizance or supervised own recognizance and impose the least restrictive nonmonetary condition or combination of conditions of pretrial release to reasonably assure public safety and the appearance of the defendant in court as required.

(2) A person shall not be required to pay for any nonmonetary condition or combination of conditions imposed pursuant to this subdivision.

(f) Solely for the purpose of determining whether the person should be detained or to establish the least restrictive nonmonetary conditions of pretrial release to impose, the court may take into consideration any relevant information, as set forth in a California Rule of Court, including, but not limited to, all of the following:

(1) The nature and circumstances of the crime charged.

(2) The weight of the evidence against the defendant, except that the court may consider the admissibility of any evidence sought to be excluded.

(3) The defendant's past conduct, family and community ties, criminal history, and record concerning appearance at court proceedings.

(4) Whether, at the time of the current crime or arrest, the defendant was on probation, parole, or on another form of supervised release pending trial, sentencing, appeal, or completion of sentence for an offense under federal law, or the law of this or any other state.

(5) The nature and seriousness of the risk to the safety of any other person or the community posed by the defendant's release, if applicable.

(6) The recommendation of Pretrial Assessment Services obtained using a validated risk assessment instrument.

(7) The impact of detention on the defendant's family responsibilities and community ties, employment, and participation in education.

(8) Any proposed plan of supervision.

(g) If a defendant is released from custody following a preventive detention hearing, the court, in the document authorizing the defendant's release, shall notify the defendant of both of the following:

(1) All the conditions, if any, to which the release is subject, in a manner sufficiently clear and specific to serve as a guide for the defendant's conduct.

(2) The penalties for and other consequences of violating a condition of release, which may include the immediate arrest or issuance of a warrant for the defendant's arrest.

(Added by Stats. 2018, Ch. 244, Sec. 4. (SB 10) Effective date (January 1, 2019) suspended pursuant to referendum petition. Effective only if Ch. 244 is approved as a referendum measure at the November 3, 2020, election.)

1320.21.

(a) Upon a showing of newly discovered evidence, facts, or material change in circumstances, the prosecution or defense may file a motion to reopen a preventive detention hearing or for a new hearing at any time before trial. The court, on its own motion, may reopen a preventive detention hearing based on newly discovered evidence, facts, or a material change in circumstances brought to the court's attention by Pretrial Assessment Services.

(b) Any motion for a hearing after the initial preventive detention hearing shall state the evidence or circumstances not known at the time of the preventive detention hearing or the material change in circumstances warranting a reopened or new preventive

detention hearing, including whether there are conditions of release that will reasonably assure public safety and the defendant's return to court as required.

(c) Upon request of the victim of the crime, the victim shall be given notice by the prosecution of the reopened preventive detention hearing. If requested, the victim shall be given a reasonable opportunity to be heard on the matter of the defendant's custody status.

(d) The court may grant the motion to reopen a preventive detention hearing or for a new hearing upon good cause shown.

(e) The court's determination regarding the custody status of the defendant shall be made in accordance with the provisions of this chapter.

(Added by Stats. 2018, Ch. 244, Sec. 4. (SB 10) Effective date (January 1, 2019) suspended pursuant to referendum petition. Effective only if Ch. 244 is approved as a referendum measure at the November 3, 2020, election.)

1320.22.

The court may issue a warrant for the defendant's arrest upon an ex parte application showing that the defendant has violated a condition of release imposed by the court. Upon the defendant's arrest, his or her custody status shall be reviewed in accordance with this chapter.

(Added by Stats. 2018, Ch. 244, Sec. 4. (SB 10) Effective date (January 1, 2019) suspended pursuant to referendum petition. Effective only if Ch. 244 is approved as a referendum measure at the November 3, 2020, election.)

1320.23.

(a) If the court issues an arrest warrant, or a bench warrant based upon a defendant's failure to appear in court as required, or upon allegations that the defendant has violated a condition of pretrial or postconviction supervision, the court may indicate on the face of the warrant whether, at the time the defendant is arrested on the warrant, the defendant should be booked and released, detained for an initial review, detained pending arraignment, or detained pending a hearing on the violation of supervision.

(b) If the prosecution, law enforcement, or supervising agency requests a warrant with a custody status for the defendant other than book and release, the agency shall provide the court with the factors justifying a higher level of supervision or detention.

(c) The court's release or detention indication on the warrant shall be binding on the arresting and booking agency and the custody facility, but is not binding on any subsequent decision by a court or Pretrial Assessment Services. The indication is, however, one factor that may be considered by Pretrial Assessment Services or the court when determining the person's custody status in subsequent proceedings.

(d) If the person is arrested on a misdemeanor warrant, the determination of the person's custody status shall start with the procedures set forth in Section 1320.8. If the person is arrested on a felony warrant, the determination of the person's custody status shall start with the procedures set forth in Section 1320.9.

(Added by Stats. 2018, Ch. 244, Sec. 4. (SB 10) Effective date (January 1, 2019) suspended pursuant to referendum petition. Effective only if Ch. 244 is approved as a referendum measure at the November 3, 2020, election.)

ARTICLE 8. Administrative Responsibilities of the Judicial Council [1320.24 - 1320.34]

(Article 8 added by Stats. 2018, Ch. 244, Sec. 4.)

1320.24.

(a) The Judicial Council shall adopt California Rules of Court and forms, as needed, to do all of the following:

(1) Prescribe the proper use of pretrial risk assessment information by the court when making pretrial release and detention decisions that take into consideration the safety of the public and victims, the due process rights of the defendant, specific characteristics or needs of the defendant, and availability of local resources to effectively supervise individuals while maximizing efficiency.

(2) Describe the elements of "validation," address the necessity and frequency of validation of risk assessment tools on local populations, and address the identification and mitigation of any implicit bias in assessment instruments.

(3) Prescribe standards for review, release, and detention by Pretrial Assessment Services and the court, that shall include a standard authorizing prearraignment detention if there is a substantial likelihood that no nonmonetary condition or combination of conditions of pretrial supervision will reasonably assure public safety or the appearance of the person as required.

(4) Prescribe the parameters of the local rule of court authorized in Section 1320.11, taking into consideration the safety of the public and the victims, the due process rights of the defendant, and availability of local resources to effectively supervise individuals while maximizing efficiency.

(5) Prescribe the imposition of pretrial release conditions, including the designation of risk levels or categories.

(b) The Judicial Council shall identify and define the minimum required data to be reported by each court. Courts shall submit data twice a year to the Judicial Council. Data will include, but not be limited to, the number of incidences in which individuals are:

(1) Assessed using a validated risk assessment tool, and the risk level of those individuals.

(2) Released on own recognizance or supervised own recognizance pursuant to:

(A) Subdivision (b) of Section 1320.10.

(B) Subdivision (c) of Section 1320.10.

(C) Section 1320.12, disaggregated by risk level.

(D) Section 1320.13, disaggregated by risk level.

(3) Detained at:

(A) Arraignment, disaggregated by risk level.

(B) A pretrial detention hearing, disaggregated by risk level.

(4) Released pretrial on own recognizance or on supervised own recognizance release who:

(A) Fail to appear at a required court appearance.

(B) Have charges filed for a new crime.

(5) Considered for release or detention at a preventive detention hearing.

(c) Pursuant to a contract under subdivision (a) of Section 1320.26, courts may require the entity providing pretrial assessment services to report the data in this section to the Judicial Council, where appropriate.

(d) On an annual basis, each court shall provide the following information to the Judicial Council:

(1) Whether the court conducts prearraignment reviews pursuant to Section 1320.13.

(2) The estimated amount of time required for making release and detention decisions at arraignment and preventive detention hearings.

(3) The validated risk assessment tool used by Pretrial Assessment Services.

(e) The Judicial Council shall do all of the following:

(1) Compile and maintain a list of validated pretrial risk assessment tools including those that are appropriate to assess for domestic violence, sex crimes, and other crimes of violence. The Judicial Council shall consult with Pretrial Assessment Services and other stakeholders in compiling the list of assessment tools.

(2) Collect data as prescribed in subdivision (b).

(3) Train judges on the use of pretrial risk assessment information when making pretrial release and detention decisions, and on the imposition of pretrial release conditions.

(4) In consultation with the Chief Probation Officers of California, assist courts in developing contracts with local public entities regarding the provision of pretrial assessment services.

(5) On or before January 1, 2021, and every other year thereafter, submit a report to the Governor and the Legislature documenting program implementation activities and providing data on program outputs and outcomes. The initial report shall focus on

program implementation, and subsequent reports shall contain the data described in subdivision (b). A report to be submitted pursuant to this paragraph shall be submitted in compliance with Section 9795 of the Government Code.

(6) Develop, in collaboration with the superior courts, an estimate of the amount of time taken at arraignment to make a release or detention determination when the determination is initially made at arraignment, and the estimated amount of time required for a preventive detention hearing.

(7) Convene a panel of subject matter experts and judicial officers to carry out the responsibilities described in subdivision (a) of Section 1320.25 and make the information available to courts.

(Added by Stats. 2018, Ch. 244, Sec. 4. (SB 10) Effective date (January 1, 2019) suspended pursuant to referendum petition. Effective only if Ch. 244 is approved as a referendum measure at the November 3, 2020, election.)

1320.25.
(a) The panel of experts and judicial officers as set forth in paragraph (7) of subdivision (e) of Section 1320.24 shall designate "low," " medium," and "high" risk levels based upon the scores or levels provided by the instrument for use by Pretrial Assessment Services in carrying out their responsibilities pursuant to Section 1320.9.

(b) The Chief Justice shall designate four individuals with specific subject matter expertise on scoring pretrial risk assessment instruments and three judicial officers with criminal law expertise, one of whom shall be the chair, to serve on this panel. At least one of the experts must have expertise in the potential impact of bias in risk assessment instruments in addition to scoring risk assessments.

(Added by Stats. 2018, Ch. 244, Sec. 4. (SB 10) Effective date (January 1, 2019) suspended pursuant to referendum petition. Effective only if Ch. 244 is approved as a referendum measure at the November 3, 2020, election.)

1320.26.
(a) The courts shall establish pretrial assessment services. The services may be performed by court employees or the court may contract for those services with a qualified local public agency with relevant experience.

(b) Before the court decides to not enter into a contract with a qualified local public agency, the court shall find that agency will not agree to perform this function with the resources available or does not have the capacity to perform the function.

(c) If no qualified local agency will agree to perform this pretrial assessment function for a superior court, and the court elects not to perform this function, the court may contract with a new local pretrial assessment services agency established to specifically perform this role.

(d) For the purpose of the provision of pretrial assessment services, the court may not contract with a qualified local public agency that has primary responsibility for making arrests and detentions within the jurisdiction.

(e) Pretrial assessment services shall be performed by public employees.

(f) Notwithstanding subdivision (h), the Superior Court of the County of Santa Clara may contract with the Office of Pretrial Services of the County of Santa Clara to provide pretrial assessment services within the County of Santa Clara and that office shall be eligible for funding allocations pursuant to subdivision (c) of Section 1320.27 and Section 1320.28.

(g) On or before February 1, 2019, the presiding judge of the superior court and the chief probation officer of each county, or the director of the County of Santa Clara's Office of Pretrial Services for that county, shall submit to the Judicial Council a letter confirming their intent to contract for pretrial assessment services pursuant to this section.

(h) For the purposes of this section:
(1) "Pretrial Assessment Services" does not include supervision of persons released under this chapter.
(2) A "qualified local public agency" is one with experience in all of the following:
(A) Relevant expertise in making risk-based determinations.
(B) Making recommendations to the courts pursuant to Section 1203.
(C) Supervising offenders in the community.
(D) Employing peace officers.

(Added by Stats. 2018, Ch. 244, Sec. 4. (SB 10) Effective date (January 1, 2019) suspended pursuant to referendum petition. Effective only if Ch. 244 is approved as a referendum measure at the November 3, 2020, election. Superseded on operative date of amendment by Stats. 2018, Ch. 980.)

1320.26.
(a) The courts shall establish pretrial assessment services. The services may be performed by court employees or the court may contract for those services with a qualified local public agency with relevant experience.

(b) Before the court decides to not enter into a contract with a qualified local public agency, the court shall find that agency will not agree to perform this function with the resources available or does not have the capacity to perform the function.

(c) If no qualified local agency will agree to perform this pretrial assessment function for a superior court, and the court elects not to perform this function, the court may contract with a new local pretrial assessment services agency established to specifically perform this role.

(d) For the purpose of the provision of pretrial assessment services, the court may not contract with a qualified local public agency that has primary responsibility for making arrests and detentions within the jurisdiction.

(e) Pretrial assessment services shall be performed by public employees.

(f) Notwithstanding subdivision (i), the Superior Court of the County of Santa Clara may contract with the Office of Pretrial Services of the County of Santa Clara to provide pretrial assessment services within the County of Santa Clara and that office shall be eligible for funding allocations pursuant to subdivision (c) of Section 1320.27 and Section 1320.28.

(g) Notwithstanding subdivision (e), until January 1, 2023, a qualified local public agency in the City and County of San Francisco may contract with the existing not-for-profit entity that is performing pretrial services in the city and county for pretrial assessment services to provide continuity and sufficient time to transition the entity's employees into public employment.

(h) On or before February 1, 2019, the presiding judge of the superior court and the chief probation officer of each county, or the director of the County of Santa Clara's Office of Pretrial Services for that county, shall submit to the Judicial Council a letter confirming their intent to contract for pretrial assessment services pursuant to this section.

(i) For the purposes of this section:
(1) "Pretrial Assessment Services" does not include supervision of persons released under this chapter.
(2) A "qualified local public agency" is one with experience in all of the following:
(A) Relevant expertise in making risk-based determinations.
(B) Making recommendations to the courts pursuant to Section 1203.
(C) Supervising offenders in the community.
(D) Employing peace officers.

(Amended (as added by Stats. 2018, Ch. 244) by Stats. 2018, Ch. 980, Sec. 2. (SB 1054) Effective January 1, 2019. Pursuant to Sec. 3 of Stats. 2018, Ch. 980, this amendment is operative only if and when the addition of this section by Stats. 2018, Ch. 244, becomes effective.)

1320.27.
(a) On or before January 10 of each year, the Department of Finance, in consultation with the Judicial Council and the Chief Probation Officers of California, shall estimate the level of funding needed to adequately support the pretrial assessment services provided

pursuant to this chapter. The estimate shall be based on a methodology developed by the Department of Finance, in consultation with the Judicial Council of California, that will incorporate the estimated number of defendants charged with a criminal offense who receive a risk assessment, direct and indirect costs associated with conducting risk assessments, and all costs associated with making release and detention decisions by the court and pretrial services. The estimate shall also reflect the direct and indirect cost of staff necessary to perform this function. The department shall publish its estimate and transmit it to the Legislature at the time of the submission of the Governor's Budget pursuant to Section 12 of Article IV of the California Constitution.

(b) Upon appropriation by the Legislature, the Judicial Council shall allocate funds to local courts for Pretrial Assessment Services. Funds shall be allocated after consultation with key stakeholders, including court executives, representatives of employees, and the Chief Probation Officers of California. As determined by the Judicial Council, the allocation shall include a base amount to support pretrial assessment services across the state and additional funding based on appropriate criteria. The Judicial Council shall consider regional variances in costs, pay scales, and other factors when making allocation determinations. The statewide allocation of the annual funding for pretrial services shall be adopted by the Judicial Council at a public meeting and shall be published publicly.

(c) All funds for pretrial assessment services shall be spent on direct and indirect costs exclusively related to the delivery of those services. Local courts contracting for pretrial assessment services entering into contracts pursuant to Section 1320.26 shall provide al funds received through this allocation directly to the contracting public entity.

(d) Local public entities receiving an allocation pursuant to this section shall separately account for these funds and annually certify that funds have been spent in accordance with relevant state law, including the requirements of this section.

(e) Funds allocated pursuant to this section shall supplement and not supplant current local funding to support pretrial assessment services.

(Added by Stats. 2018, Ch. 244, Sec. 4. (SB 10) Effective date (January 1, 2019) suspended pursuant to referendum petition. Effective only if Ch. 244 is approved as a referendum measure at the November 3, 2020, election.)

1320.28.
(a) By January 10 of each year, the Department of Finance, in consultation with the Judicial Council and the Chief Probation Officers of California, shall estimate the level of resources needed to adequately support the provision of pretrial supervision services provided pursuant to this chapter. The estimate shall reflect the number of individuals being supervised and the level of supervision required. The estimate shall also reflect the direct and indirect cost of personnel necessary to provide these services. The department shall publish its estimate and transmit it to the Legislature at the time of the submission of the Governor's Budget pursuant to Section 12 of Article IV of the California Constitution.

(b) Upon appropriation by the Legislature, the Department of Finance shall allocate funds to local probation departments for pretrial supervision services. For the purposes of this subdivision, the County of Santa Clara's Office of Pretrial Services shall be eligible for funding within that county. In allocating the funds, the department shall consider regional variances in costs, pay scales, and other factors when making allocation determinations. Allocations shall include a base portion to support pretrial supervision across the state, and an additional amount based at least in part on the county's population of adults between 18 and 50 years of age, and local arrest rates. The Department of Finance shall consult with the Judicial Council, the Chief Probation Officers of California, and key stakeholders, including representatives of employees, when adopting the annual allocation methodology.

(c) All funds for pretrial supervision shall be spent on direct and indirect costs exclusively related to the delivery of these services. All funds appropriated to support pretrial services shall be allocated to local entities to support pretrial supervision.

(d) Local public entities receiving an allocation pursuant to this section shall separately account for these funds and annually certify that funds have been spent in accordance with relevant state law, including the requirements of this section.

(e) Local public entities shall only be eligible for this funding when they contract with a court for the provision of pretrial assessment services.

(f) Funds allocated pursuant to this section shall supplement and not supplant current local funding to support pretrial assessment services.

(Added by Stats. 2018, Ch. 244, Sec. 4. (SB 10) Effective date (January 1, 2019) suspended pursuant to referendum petition. Effective only if Ch. 244 is approved as a referendum measure at the November 3, 2020, election.)

1320.29.
By January 10 of each year, the Department of Finance, in consultation with the Judicial Council, shall estimate the level of resources needed to adequately support the Judiciary's workload under this chapter. The estimate shall reflect the number of cases where the court is making detention determinations at arraignment, the volume of preventive detention hearings, the average amount of time required to make these determinations and to conduct the hearings, administrative costs associated with contracts for pretrial assessment services, and other factors relating to the Judiciary's workload pursuant to this act. The estimate shall also reflect average direct and indirect cost per minute of trial court proceedings. The department shall publish its estimate and transmit it to the Legislature at the time of the submission of the Governor's Budget pursuant to Section 12 of Article IV of the California Constitution.

(Added by Stats. 2018, Ch. 244, Sec. 4. (SB 10) Effective date (January 1, 2019) suspended pursuant to referendum petition. Effective only if Ch. 244 is approved as a referendum measure at the November 3, 2020, election.)

1320.30.
(a) Upon appropriation by the Legislature, the Board of State and Community Corrections shall contract with an academic institution, public policy center, or other research entity for an independent evaluation of the act that enacted this section, particularly of the impact of the act by race, ethnicity, gender, and income level. This evaluation shall be submitted to the Secretary of the State Senate and the Chief Clerk of the State Assembly by no later than January 1, 2024.

(b) Beginning in the 2019–20 fiscal year, state funds shall supplement, not supplant, local funds allocated to pretrial supervision, assessments, services or other purposes related to pretrial activities, excluding detention.

(Added by Stats. 2018, Ch. 244, Sec. 4. (SB 10) Effective date (January 1, 2019) suspended pursuant to referendum petition. Effective only if Ch. 244 is approved as a referendum measure at the November 3, 2020, election.)

1320.31.
(a) It is the intent of the Legislature that, to the extent practicable, priority for available jail capacity shall be for the postconviction population.

(b) The Legislature finds and declares that implementation of this chapter will require funds necessary to support pretrial risk assessment services, pretrial supervision, increased trial court workload, and necessary statewide activities to support effective implementation. These funds are reflected in the most recent longer term state spending plan and will be subject to appropriation in the annual Budget Act.

(Added by Stats. 2018, Ch. 244, Sec. 4. (SB 10) Effective date (January 1, 2019) suspended pursuant to referendum petition. Effective only if Ch. 244 is approved as a referendum measure at the November 3, 2020, election.)

1320.32.
Commencing October 1, 2019, all references in this code to "bail" shall refer to the procedures specified in this chapter.

(Added by Stats. 2018, Ch. 244, Sec. 4. (SB 10) Effective date (January 1, 2019) suspended pursuant to referendum petition. Effective only if Ch. 244 is approved as a referendum measure at the November 3, 2020, election.)

1320.33.
(a) Defendants released on bail before October 1, 2019, shall remain on bail pursuant to the terms of their release.
(b) Defendants in custody on October 1, 2019, shall be considered for release pursuant to Section 1320.8, and, if not released, shall receive a risk assessment and be considered for release or detention pursuant to this chapter.
(Added by Stats. 2018, Ch. 244, Sec. 4. (SB 10) Effective date (January 1, 2019) suspended pursuant to referendum petition. Effective only if Ch. 244 is approved as a referendum measure at the November 3, 2020, election.)
1320.34.
This chapter shall become operative on October 1, 2019.
(Added by Stats. 2018, Ch. 244, Sec. 4. (SB 10) Effective date (January 1, 2019) suspended pursuant to referendum petition. Effective only if Ch. 244 is approved as a referendum measure at the November 3, 2020, election.)

CHAPTER 2. Who May Be Witnesses in Criminal Actions [1321 - 1324.1]

(Chapter 2 enacted 1872.)
1321.
The rules for determining the competency of witnesses in civil actions are applicable also to criminal actions and proceedings, except as otherwise provided in this Code.
(Enacted 1872.)
1324.
In any felony proceeding or in any investigation or proceeding before a grand jury for any felony offense if a person refuses to answer a question or produce evidence of any other kind on the ground that he or she may be incriminated thereby, and if the district attorney of the county or any other prosecuting agency in writing requests the court, in and for that county, to order that person to answer the question or produce the evidence, a judge shall set a time for hearing and order the person to appear before the court and show cause, if any, why the question should not be answered or the evidence produced, and the court shall order the question answered or the evidence produced unless it finds that to do so would be clearly contrary to the public interest, or could subject the witness to a criminal prosecution in another jurisdiction, and that person shall comply with the order. After complying, and if, but for this section, he or she would have been privileged to withhold the answer given or the evidence produced by him or her, no testimony or other information compelled under the order or any information directly or indirectly derived from the testimony or other information may be used against the witness in any criminal case. But he or she may nevertheless be prosecuted or subjected to penalty or forfeiture for any perjury, false swearing or contempt committed in answering, or failing to answer, or in producing, or failing to produce, evidence in accordance with the order. Nothing in this section shall prohibit the district attorney or any other prosecuting agency from requesting an order granting use immunity or transactional immunity to a witness compelled to give testimony or produce evidence.
(Amended by Stats. 1996, Ch. 302, Sec. 1. Effective January 1, 1997.)
1324.1.
In any misdemeanor proceeding in any court, if a person refuses to answer a question or produce evidence of any other kind on the ground that he may be incriminated thereby, the person may agree in writing with the district attorney of the county, or the prosecuting attorney of a city, as the case may be, to testify voluntarily pursuant to this section. Upon written request of such district attorney, or prosecuting attorney, the court having jurisdiction of the proceeding shall approve such written agreement, unless the court finds that to do so would be clearly contrary to the public interest. If, after court approval of such agreement, and if, but for this section, the person would have been privileged to withhold the answer given or the evidence produced by him, that person shall not be prosecuted or subjected to penalty or forfeiture for or on account of any fact or act concerning which, in accordance with such agreement, he answered or produced evidence, but he may, nevertheless, be prosecuted or subjected to penalty or forfeiture for any perjury, false swearing or contempt committed in answering or in producing evidence in accordance with such agreement. If such person fails to give any answer or to produce any evidence in accordance with such agreement, that person shall be prosecuted or subjected to penalty or forfeiture in the same manner and to the same extent as he would be prosecuted or subjected to penalty or forfeiture but for this section.
(Added by Stats. 1968, Ch. 528.)

CHAPTER 3. Compelling the Attendance of Witnesses [1326 - 1332]

(Chapter 3 enacted 1872.)
1326.
(a) The process by which the attendance of a witness before a court or magistrate is required is a subpoena. It may be signed and issued by any of the following:
(1) A magistrate before whom a complaint is laid or his or her clerk, the district attorney or his or her investigator, or the public defender or his or her investigator, for witnesses in the state.
(2) The district attorney, his or her investigator, or, upon request of the grand jury, any judge of the superior court, for witnesses in the state, in support of an indictment or information, to appear before the court in which it is to be tried.
(3) The district attorney or his or her investigator, the public defender or his or her investigator, or the clerk of the court in which a criminal action is to be tried. The clerk shall, at any time, upon application of the defendant, and without charge, issue as many blank subpoenas, subscribed by him or her, for witnesses in the state, as the defendant may require.
(4) The attorney of record for the defendant.
(b) A subpoena issued in a criminal action that commands the custodian of records or other qualified witness of a business to produce books, papers, documents, or records shall direct that those items be delivered by the custodian or qualified witness in the manner specified in subdivision (b) of Section 1560 of the Evidence Code. Subdivision (e) of Section 1560 of the Evidence Code shall not apply to criminal cases.
(c) In a criminal action, no party, or attorney or representative of a party, may issue a subpoena commanding the custodian of records or other qualified witness of a business to provide books, papers, documents, or records, or copies thereof, relating to a person or entity other than the subpoenaed person or entity in any manner other than that specified in subdivision (b) of Section 1560 of the Evidence Code. When a defendant has issued a subpoena to a person or entity that is not a party for the production of books, papers, documents, or records, or copies thereof, the court may order an in camera hearing to determine whether or not the defense is entitled to receive the documents. The court may not order the documents disclosed to the prosecution except as required by Section 1054.3.

(d) This section shall not be construed to prohibit obtaining books, papers, documents, or records with the consent of the person to whom the books, papers, documents, or records relate.
(Amended by Stats. 2007, Ch. 263, Sec. 30. Effective January 1, 2008.)
1326.1.
(a) An order for the production of utility records in whatever form and however stored shall be issued by a judge only upon a written ex parte application by a peace officer showing specific and articulable facts that there are reasonable grounds to believe that the records or information sought are relevant and material to an ongoing investigation of a felony violation of Section 186.10 or of any felony subject to the enhancement set forth in Section 186.11. The ex parte application shall specify with particularity the records to be produced, which shall be only those of the individual or individuals who are the subject of the criminal investigation. The ex parte application and any subsequent judicial order shall be open to the public as a judicial record unless ordered sealed by the court, for a period of 60 days. The sealing of these records may be extended for 60-day periods upon a showing to the court that it is necessary for the continuance of the investigation. Sixty-day extensions may continue for up to one year or until termination of the investigation of the individual or individuals, whichever is sooner. The records ordered to be produced shall be returned to the peace officer applicant or his or her designee within a reasonable time period after service of the order upon the holder of the utility records.
(b) As used in subdivision (a), "utility records" include, but are not limited to, subscriber information, telephone or pager number information, toll call records, call detail records, automated message accounting records, billing statements, payment records, and applications for service in the custody of companies engaged in the business of providing telephone, pager, electric, gas, propane, water, or other like services. "Utility records" do not include the installation of, or the data collected from the installation of pen registers or trap-tracers, nor the contents of a wire or electronic communication.
(c) Nothing in this section shall preclude the holder of the utility records from notifying a customer of the receipt of the order for production of records unless a court orders the holder of the utility records to withhold notification to the customer upon a finding that this notice would impede the investigation. Where a court has made an order to withhold notification to the customer under this subdivision, the peace officer or law enforcement agency who obtained the utility records shall notify the customer by delivering a copy of the ex parte order to the customer within 10 days of the termination of the investigation.
(d) No holder of utility records, or any officer, employee, or agent thereof, shall be liable to any person for (A) disclosing information in response to an order pursuant to this section, or (B) complying with an order under this section not to disclose to the customer, the order or the dissemination of information pursuant to the order.
(e) Nothing in this section shall preclude the holder of the utility records from voluntarily disclosing information or providing records to law enforcement upon request.
(f) Utility records released pursuant to this section shall be used only for the purpose of criminal investigations and prosecutions.
(Added by Stats. 1998, Ch. 757, Sec. 5. Effective January 1, 1999.)
1326.2.
(a) An order for the production of escrow or title records in whatever form and however stored shall be issued by a judge only upon a written ex parte application by a peace officer showing specific and articulable facts that there are reasonable grounds to believe that the records or information sought are relevant and material to an ongoing investigation of a felony violation of Section 186.10 or of any felony subject to the enhancement set forth in Section 186.11. The ex parte application shall specify with particularity the records to be produced, which shall be only those of the individual or individuals who are the subject of the criminal investigation. The ex parte application and any subsequent judicial order shall be open to the public as a judicial record unless ordered sealed by the court, for a period of 60 days. The sealing of these records may be extended for 60-day periods upon a showing to the court that it is necessary for the continuance of the investigation. Sixty-day extensions may continue for up to one year or until termination of the investigation of the individual or individuals, whichever is sooner. The records ordered to be produced shall be returned to the peace officer applicant or his or her designee within a reasonable time period after service of the order upon the holder of the escrow or title records.
(b) As used in subdivision (a), "holder of escrow or title records" means a title insurer that engages in the "business of title insurance," as defined by Section 12340.3 of the Insurance Code, an underwritten title company, or an escrow company.
(c) Nothing in this section shall preclude the holder of the escrow or title records from notifying a customer of the receipt of the order for production of records unless a court orders the holder of the escrow or title records to withhold notification to the customer upon a finding that this notice would impede the investigation. Where a court has made an order to withhold notification to the customer under this subdivision, the peace officer or law enforcement agency who obtained the escrow or title records shall notify the customer by delivering a copy of the ex parte order to the customer within 10 days of the termination of the investigation.
(d) No holder of escrow or title records, or any officer, employee, or agent thereof, shall be liable to any person for (A) disclosing information in response to an order pursuant to this section, or (B) complying with an order under this section not to disclose to the customer, the order or the dissemination of information pursuant to the order.
(e) Nothing in this section shall preclude the holder of the escrow or title records from voluntarily disclosing information or providing records to law enforcement upon request.
(Added by Stats. 1998, Ch. 757, Sec. 6. Effective January 1, 1999.)
1327.
A subpoena authorized by Section 1326 shall be substantially in the following form:
The people of the State of California to A. B.:
You are commanded to appear before C. D., a judge of the _____ Court of _____ County, at (naming the place), on (stating the day and hour), as a witness in a criminal action prosecuted by the people of the State of California against E. F.
Given under my hand this _____ day of _____, A.D. 19_____. G. H., Judge of the _____ Court (or "J. K., District Attorney," or "J. K., District Attorney Investigator," or "D. E., Public Defender," or "D. E., Public Defender Investigator," or "F. G., Defense Counsel," or "By order of the court, L. M., Clerk," or as the case may be).

If books, papers, or documents are required, a direction to the following effect must be contained in the subpoena: "And you are required, also, to bring with you the following" (describing intelligibly the books, papers, or documents required).
(Amended by Stats. 1998, Ch. 931, Sec. 403. Effective September 28, 1998.)
1328.
(a) A subpoena may be served by any person, except that the defendant may not serve a subpoena in the criminal action to which he or she is a party, but a peace officer shall serve in his or her county any subpoena delivered to him or her for service, either on the part of the people or of the defendant, and shall, without delay, make a written return of the service, subscribed by him or her, stating the time and place of service. The service is made by delivering a copy of the subpoena to the witness personally.
(b) (1) If service is to be made on a minor, service shall be made on the minor's parent, guardian, conservator, or similar fiduciary, or if one of them cannot be located with reasonable diligence, then service shall be made on any person having the care or control of the minor or with whom the minor resides or by whom the minor is employed, unless the parent, guardian, conservator, or fiduciary or other specified person is the defendant, and on the minor if the minor is 12 years of age or older. The person served shall have the obligation of producing the minor at the time and place designated in the subpoena. A willful failure to produce the minor is punishable as a contempt pursuant to

Section 1218 of the Code of Civil Procedure. The person served shall be allowed the fees and expenses that are provided for subpoenaed witnesses.
(2) If the minor is alleged to come within the description of Section 300, 601, or 602 of the Welfare and Institutions Code, and the minor is not residing with a parent or guardian, regardless of the age of the minor, service shall also be made upon the designated agent for service of process at the county child welfare department or the probation department under whose jurisdiction the child has been placed.
(3) The court having jurisdiction of the case shall have the power to appoint a guardian ad litem to receive service of a subpoena of the child and shall have the power to produce the child ordered to court under this section.
(c) If any peace officer designated in Section 830 is required as a witness before any court or magistrate in any action or proceeding in connection with a matter regarding an event or transaction which he or she has perceived or investigated in the course of his or her duties, a criminal subpoena issued pursuant to this chapter requiring his or her attendance may be served either by delivering a copy to the peace officer personally or by delivering two copies to his or her immediate superior or agent designated by his or her immediate superior to receive the service or, in those counties where the local agencies have consented with the district attorney's office, marshal's office, or sheriff's office, where appropriate, to participate, by sending a copy by electronic means, including electronic mail, computer modem, facsimile, or other electronic means, to him or her personally, or to his or her immediate superior or agent designated by the immediate superior to receive the service. If the service is made by electronic means, the peace officer named in the subpoena, or his or her immediate superior or agency designated by his or her immediate superior shall acknowledge receipt of the subpoena by telephone or electronic means to the sender of origin. If service is made upon the immediate superior or agent designated by the immediate superior, the immediate superior or the agent shall deliver a copy of the subpoena to the peace officer as soon as possible and in no event later than a time which will enable the peace officer to comply with the subpoena.
(d) If the immediate superior or his or her designated agent upon whom service is attempted to be made knows he or she will be unable to deliver a copy of the subpoena to the peace officer within a time which will allow the peace officer to comply with the subpoena, the immediate superior or agent may refuse to accept service of process and is excused from any duty, liability, or penalty arising in connection with the service, upon notifying the server of that fact.
(e) If the immediate superior or his or her agent is tendered service of a subpoena less than five working days prior to the date of hearing, and he or she is not reasonably certain he or she can complete the service, he or she may refuse acceptance.
(f) If the immediate superior or agent upon whom service has been made, subsequently determines that he or she will be unable to deliver a copy of the subpoena to the peace officer within a time which will allow the peace officer to comply with the subpoena, the immediate superior or agent shall notify the server or his or her office or agent not less than 48 hours prior to the hearing date indicated on the subpoena, and is thereby excused from any duty, liability, or penalty arising because of his or her failure to deliver a copy of the subpoena to the peace officer. The server, so notified, is therewith responsible for preparing the written return of service and for notifying the originator of the subpoena if required.
(g) Notwithstanding subdivision (c), in the case of peace officers employed by the California Highway Patrol, if service is made upon the immediate superior or upon an agent designated by the immediate superior of the peace officer, the immediate superior or the agent shall deliver a copy of the subpoena to the peace officer on the officer's first workday following acceptance of service of process. In this case, failure of the immediate superior or the designated agent to deliver the subpoena shall not constitute a defect in service.
(Amended by Stats. 2016, Ch. 59, Sec. 6. (SB 1474) Effective January 1, 2017.)

1328.5.

Whenever any peace officer is a witness before any court or magistrate in any criminal action or proceeding in connection with a matter regarding an event or transaction which he has perceived or investigated in the course of his duties, where his testimony would become a matter of public record, and where he is required to state the place of his residence, he need not state the place of his residence, but in lieu thereof, he may state his business address.
(Added by Stats. 1971, Ch. 636.)

1328.6.

Whenever any criminalist, questioned document examiner, latent print analyst, polygraph examiner employed by the Department of Justice, a police department, a sheriff's office, or a district attorney's office, an intelligence specialist or other technical specialist employed by the Department of Justice, a custodial officer employed in a local detention facility, or an employee of the county welfare department or the department which administers the county public social services program, is a witness before any court or magistrate in any criminal action or proceeding in connection with a matter regarding an event or transaction which he or she has perceived or investigated in the course of his or her official duties, where his or her testimony would become a matter of public record, and where he or she is required to state the place of his or her residence, he or she need not state the place of his or her residence, but in lieu thereof, he or she may state his or her business address, unless the court finds, after an in camera hearing, that the probative value of the witness's residential address outweighs the creation of substantial danger to the witness.
Nothing in this section shall abridge or limit a defendant's right to discover or investigate this information. This section is not intended to apply to confidential informants.
(Amended by Stats. 1984, Ch. 535, Sec. 1.)

1328a.

A telegraphic copy of a subpoena for a witness in a criminal proceeding may be sent by telegraph or teletype to one or more peace officers, and such copy is as effectual in the hands of any officer, and he must proceed in the same manner under it, as though he held the original subpoena issued.
(Added by Stats. 1963, Ch. 803.)

1328b.

Every officer causing telegraphic copies of subpoenas to be sent, must certify as correct, and file in the telegraph office from which such copies are sent, a copy of the subpoena, and must return the original with a statement of his action thereunder.
(Added by Stats. 1963, Ch. 803.)

1328c.

A peace officer must serve in his county or city any subpoena delivered to him by telegraph or teletype for service and must without delay make a return of the service by telegraph or teletype. Any officer making a return of service of a subpoena by telegraph or teletype must certify as to his actions in making the service and file in the telegraph office from which the return is sent a written statement with his signature in the same form as the return on an original subpoena. The service of a teletype subpoena is made by showing the original teletype to the witness personally and informing him of its contents and delivering to him a copy of the teletype.
(Added by Stats. 1963, Ch. 803.)

1328d.

Notwithstanding Section 1328, a subpoena may be delivered by mail or messenger. Service shall be effected when the witness acknowledges receipt of the subpoena to the sender, by telephone, by mail, over the Internet by e-mail or by completion of the sender's online form, or in person, and identifies himself or herself by reference to his or her date of birth and his or her driver's license number or Department of Motor Vehicles identification card number. The sender shall make a written notation of the identifying information obtained during any acknowledgment by telephone or in person. The sender shall retain a copy of any acknowledgment received over the Internet until the court date for which the subpoena was issued or until any further date as specified by the court. A subpoena issued and acknowledged pursuant to this section shall have the same force and effect as a subpoena personally served. Failure to comply with a subpoena issued and acknowledged pursuant to this section may be punished as a contempt and the subpoena may so state; provided, that a warrant of arrest or a body attachment may not be issued based upon a failure to appear after being subpoenaed pursuant to this section.
A party requesting a continuance based upon the failure of a witness to appear in court at the time and place required for his or her appearance or testimony pursuant to a subpoena, shall prove to the court that the party has complied with the provisions of this section. Such a continuance shall only be granted for a period of time which would allow personal service of the subpoena and in no event longer than that allowed by law, including the requirements of Sections 861 and 1382.
(Amended by Stats. 2010, Ch. 709, Sec. 16. (SB 1062) Effective January 1, 2011.)

1329.

(a) When a person attends before a magistrate, grand jury, or court, as a witness in a criminal case, whether upon a subpoena or in pursuance of an undertaking, or voluntarily, the court, at its discretion, if the attendance of the witness be upon a trial may by an order upon its minutes, or in any criminal proceeding, by a written order, direct the county auditor to draw his warrant upon the county treasurer in favor of such witness for witness' fees at the rate of twelve dollars ($12) for each day's actual attendance and for a reasonable sum to be specified in the order for the necessary expenses of such witness. The court, in its discretion, may make an allowance under this section, or under any appropriate section in Chapter 1 (commencing with Section 68070), Title 8, of the Government Code, other than Section 68093. The allowances are county charges.
(b) The court, in its discretion, may authorize payment to such a witness, if he is employed and if his salary is not paid by his employer during the time he is absent from his employment because of being such a witness, of a sum equal to his gross salary for such time, but such sum shall not exceed eighteen dollars ($18) per day. The sum is a county charge.
A person compensated under the provisions of this subdivision may not receive the payment of witness' fees as provided for in subdivision (a).
(Amended by Stats. 1981, Ch. 184, Sec. 5.)

1329.1.

Any witness who is subpoenaed in any criminal action or proceeding shall be given written notice on the subpoena that the witness may be entitled to receive fees and mileage. Such notice shall indicate generally the manner in which a request or claim for fees and mileage should be made.
(Added by Stats. 1979, Ch. 67.)

1330.

No person is obliged to attend as a witness before a court or magistrate out of the county where the witness resides, or is served with the subpoena, unless the distance be less than 150 miles from his or her place of residence to the place of trial, or unless the judge of the court in which the offense is triable, or a justice of the Supreme Court, or a judge of a superior court, or, in the case of a minor concerning whom a petition has been filed pursuant to Article 16 (commencing with Section 650) of Chapter 2 of Part 1 of Division 2 of the Welfare and Institutions Code, by the judge of the juvenile court hearing the petition, upon an affidavit of the district attorney or prosecutor, or of the defendant, or his or her counsel, or in the case involving a minor in whose behalf a petition has been filed in the juvenile court, of the probation officer approving the filing of the petition or of any party to the action, or his or her counsel, stating that he or she believes the evidence of the witness is material, and his or her attendance at the examination, trial, or hearing is material and necessary, shall endorse on the subpoena an order for the attendance of the witness.
When a subpoena duces tecum is duly issued according to any other provision of law and is served upon a custodian of records or other qualified witness as provided in Article 4 (commencing with Section 1560) of Chapter 2 of Division 11 of the Evidence Code, and his or her personal attendance is not required by the terms of the subpoena, the limitations of this section shall not apply.
(Amended by Stats. 1987, Ch. 828, Sec. 86.)

1331.

Disobedience to a subpoena, or a refusal to be sworn or to testify as a witness, may be punished by the Court or magistrate as a contempt. A witness disobeying a subpoena issued on the part of the defendant, unless he show good cause for his nonattendance, is liable to the defendant in the sum of one hundred dollars, which may be recovered in a civil action.
(Enacted 1872.)

1331.5.

Any person who is subpoenaed to appear at a session of court, or at the trial of an issue therein, may, in lieu of appearance at the time specified in the subpoena, agree with the party at whose request the subpoena was issued, to appear at another time or upon such notice as may be agreed upon. Any failure to appear pursuant to such agreement may be punished as a contempt, and a subpoena shall so state. The facts establishing such agreement and the failure to appear may be shown by the affidavit of any person having personal knowledge of the facts and the court may grant such continuance as may be appropriate.
(Added by Stats. 1972, Ch. 393.)

1332.

(a) Notwithstanding the provisions of Sections 878 to 883, inclusive, when the court is satisfied, by proof on oath, that there is good cause to believe that any material witness for the prosecution or defense, whether the witness is an adult or a minor, will not appear and testify unless security is required, at any proceeding in connection with any criminal prosecution or in connection with a wardship petition pursuant to Section 602 of the Welfare and Institutions Code, the court may order the witness to enter into a written undertaking to the effect that he or she will appear and testify at the time and place ordered by the court or that he or she will forfeit an amount the court deems proper.
(b) If the witness required to enter into an undertaking to appear and testify, either with or without sureties, refuses compliance with the order for that purpose, the court may commit the witness, if an adult, to the custody of the sheriff, and if a minor, to the custody of the probation officer or other appropriate agency, until the witness complies or is legally discharged.
(c) When a person is committed pursuant to this section, he or she is entitled to an automatic review of the order requiring a written undertaking and the order committing the person, by a judge or magistrate having jurisdiction over the offense other than the one who issued the order. This review shall be held not later than two days from the time of the original order of commitment.
(d) If it is determined that the witness must remain in custody, the witness is entitled to a review of that order after 10 days.
(e) When a witness has entered into an undertaking to appear, upon his or her failure to do so the undertaking is forfeited in the same manner as undertakings of bail.
(Amended by Stats. 1987, Ch. 828, Sec. 87.)

CHAPTER 3. Compelling the Attendance of Witnesses [1326 - 1332]

(Chapter 3 enacted 1872.)

1326.

(a) The process by which the attendance of a witness before a court or magistrate is required is a subpoena. It may be signed and issued by any of the following:

(1) A magistrate before whom a complaint is laid or his or her clerk, the district attorney or his or her investigator, or the public defender or his or her investigator, for witnesses in the state.

(2) The district attorney, his or her investigator, or, upon request of the grand jury, any judge of the superior court, for witnesses in the state, in support of an indictment or information, to appear before the court in which it is to be tried.

(3) The district attorney or his or her investigator, the public defender or his or her investigator, or the clerk of the court in which a criminal action is to be tried. The clerk shall, at any time, upon application of the defendant, and without charge, issue as many blank subpoenas, subscribed by him or her, for witnesses in the state, as the defendant may require.

(4) The attorney of record for the defendant.

(b) A subpoena issued in a criminal action that commands the custodian of records or other qualified witness of a business to produce books, papers, documents, or records shall direct that those items be delivered by the custodian or qualified witness in the manner specified in subdivision (b) of Section 1560 of the Evidence Code. Subdivision (e) of Section 1560 of the Evidence Code shall not apply to criminal cases.

(c) In a criminal action, no party, or attorney or representative of a party, may issue a subpoena commanding the custodian of records or other qualified witness of a business to provide books, papers, documents, or records, or copies thereof, relating to a person or entity other than the subpoenaed person or entity in any manner other than that specified in subdivision (b) of Section 1560 of the Evidence Code. When a defendant has issued a subpoena to a person or entity that is not a party for the production of books, papers, documents, or records, or copies thereof, the court may order an in camera hearing to determine whether or not the defense is entitled to receive the documents. The court may not order the documents disclosed to the prosecution except as required by Section 1054.3.

(d) This section shall not be construed to prohibit obtaining books, papers, documents, or records with the consent of the person to whom the books, papers, documents, or records relate.

(Amended by Stats. 2007, Ch. 263, Sec. 30. Effective January 1, 2008.)

1326.1.

(a) An order for the production of utility records in whatever form and however stored shall be issued by a judge only upon a written ex parte application by a peace officer showing specific and articulable facts that there are reasonable grounds to believe that the records or information sought are relevant and material to an ongoing investigation of a felony violation of Section 186.10 or of any felony subject to the enhancement set forth in Section 186.11. The ex parte application shall specify with particularity the records to be produced, which shall be only those of the individual or individuals who are the subject of the criminal investigation. The ex parte application and any subsequent judicial order shall be open to the public as a judicial record unless ordered sealed by the court, for a period of 60 days. The sealing of these records may be extended for 60-day periods upon a showing to the court that it is necessary for the continuance of the investigation. Sixty-day extensions may continue for up to one year or until termination of the investigation of the individual or individuals, whichever is sooner. The records ordered to be produced shall be returned to the peace officer applicant or his or her designee within a reasonable time period after service of the order upon the holder of the utility records.

(b) As used in subdivision (a), "utility records" include, but are not limited to, subscriber information, telephone or pager number information, toll call records, call detail records, automated message accounting records, billing statements, payment records, and applications for service in the custody of companies engaged in the business of providing telephone, pager, electric, gas, propane, water, or other like services. "Utility records" do not include the installation of, or the data collected from the installation of pen registers or trap-tracers, nor the contents of a wire or electronic communication.

(c) Nothing in this section shall preclude the holder of the utility records from notifying a customer of the receipt of the order for production of records unless a court orders the holder of the utility records to withhold notification to the customer upon a finding that this notice would impede the investigation. Where a court has made an order to withhold notification to the customer under this subdivision, the peace officer or law enforcement agency who obtained the utility records shall notify the customer by delivering a copy of the ex parte order to the customer within 10 days of the termination of the investigation.

(d) No holder of utility records, or any officer, employee, or agent thereof, shall be liable to any person for (A) disclosing information in response to an order pursuant to this section, or (B) complying with an order under this section not to disclose to the customer, the order or the dissemination of information pursuant to the order.

(e) Nothing in this section shall preclude the holder of the utility records from voluntarily disclosing information or providing records to law enforcement upon request.

(f) Utility records released pursuant to this section shall be used only for the purpose of criminal investigations and prosecutions.

(Added by Stats. 1998, Ch. 757, Sec. 5. Effective January 1, 1999.)

1326.2.

(a) An order for the production of escrow or title records in whatever form and however stored shall be issued by a judge only upon a written ex parte application by a peace officer showing specific and articulable facts that there are reasonable grounds to believe that the records or information sought are relevant and material to an ongoing investigation of a felony violation of Section 186.10 or of any felony subject to the enhancement set forth in Section 186.11. The ex parte application shall specify with particularity the records to be produced, which shall be only those of the individual or individuals who are the subject of the criminal investigation. The ex parte application and any subsequent judicial order shall be open to the public as a judicial record unless ordered sealed by the court, for a period of 60 days. The sealing of these records may be extended for 60-day periods upon a showing to the court that it is necessary for the continuance of the investigation. Sixty-day extensions may continue for up to one year or until termination of the investigation of the individual or individuals, whichever is sooner. The records ordered to be produced shall be returned to the peace officer applicant or his or her designee within a reasonable time period after service of the order upon the holder of the escrow or title records.

(b) As used in subdivision (a), "holder of escrow or title records" means a title insurer that engages in the "business of title insurance," as defined by Section 12340.3 of the Insurance Code, an underwritten title company, or an escrow company.

(c) Nothing in this section shall preclude the holder of the escrow or title records from notifying a customer of the receipt of the order for production of records unless a court orders the holder of the escrow or title records to withhold notification to the customer upon a finding that this notice would impede the investigation. Where a court has made an order to withhold notification to the customer under this subdivision, the peace officer or law enforcement agency who obtained the escrow or title records shall notify the customer by delivering a copy of the ex parte order to the customer within 10 days of the termination of the investigation.

(d) No holder of escrow or title records, or any officer, employee, or agent thereof, shall be liable to any person for (A) disclosing information in response to an order pursuant to this section, or (B) complying with an order under this section not to disclose to the customer, the order or the dissemination of information pursuant to the order.

(e) Nothing in this section shall preclude the holder of the escrow or title records from voluntarily disclosing information or providing records to law enforcement upon request.

(Added by Stats. 1998, Ch. 757, Sec. 6. Effective January 1, 1999.)

1327.

A subpoena authorized by Section 1326 shall be substantially in the following form:

The people of the State of California to A. B.:

You are commanded to appear before C. D., a judge of the _____ Court of _____ County, at (naming the place), on (stating the day and hour), as a witness in a criminal action prosecuted by the people of the State of California against E. F.

Given under my hand this _____ day of _____, A.D. 19_____. G. H., Judge of the _____ Court (or "J. K., District Attorney," or "J. K., District Attorney Investigator," or "D. E., Public Defender," or "D. E., Public Defender Investigator," or "F. G., Defense Counsel," or "By order of the court, L. M., Clerk," or as the case may be).

If books, papers, or documents are required, a direction to the following effect must be contained in the subpoena: "And you are required, also, to bring with you the following" (describing intelligibly the books, papers, or documents required).

(Amended by Stats. 1998, Ch. 931, Sec. 403. Effective September 28, 1998.)

1328.

(a) A subpoena may be served by any person, except that the defendant may not serve a subpoena in the criminal action to which he or she is a party, but a peace officer shall serve in his or her county any subpoena delivered to him or her for service, either on the part of the people or of the defendant, and shall, without delay, make a written return of the service, subscribed by him or her, stating the time and place of service. The service is made by delivering a copy of the subpoena to the witness personally.

(b) (1) If service is to be made on a minor, service shall be made on the minor's parent, guardian, conservator, or similar fiduciary, or if one of them cannot be located with reasonable diligence, then service shall be made on any person having the care or control of the minor or with whom the minor resides or by whom the minor is employed, unless the parent, guardian, conservator, or fiduciary or other specified person is the defendant, and on the minor if the minor is 12 years of age or older. The person served shall have the obligation of producing the minor at the time and place designated in the subpoena. A willful failure to produce the minor is punishable as a contempt pursuant to Section 1218 of the Code of Civil Procedure. The person served shall be allowed the fees and expenses that are provided for subpoenaed witnesses.

(2) If the minor is alleged to come within the description of Section 300, 601, or 602 of the Welfare and Institutions Code, and the minor is not residing with a parent or guardian, regardless of the age of the minor, service shall also be made upon the designated agent for service of process at the county child welfare department or the probation department under whose jurisdiction the child has been placed.

(3) The court having jurisdiction of the case shall have the power to appoint a guardian ad litem to receive service of a subpoena of the child and shall have the power to produce the child ordered to court under this section.

(c) If any peace officer designated in Section 830 is required as a witness before any court or magistrate in any action or proceeding in connection with a matter regarding an event or transaction which he or she has perceived or investigated in the course of his or her duties, a criminal subpoena issued pursuant to this chapter requiring his or her attendance may be served either by delivering a copy to the peace officer personally or by delivering two copies to his or her immediate superior or agent designated by his or her immediate superior to receive the service or, in those counties where the local agencies have consented with the district attorney's office, marshal's office, or sheriff's office, where appropriate, to participate, by sending a copy by electronic means, including electronic mail, computer modem, facsimile, or other electronic means, to him or her personally, or to his or her immediate superior or agent designated by the immediate superior to receive the service. If the service is made by electronic means, the peace officer named in the subpoena, or his or her immediate superior or agency designated by his or her immediate superior shall acknowledge receipt of the subpoena by telephone or electronic means to the sender of origin. If service is made upon the immediate superior or agent designated by the immediate superior, the immediate superior or the agent shall deliver a copy of the subpoena to the peace officer as soon as possible and in no event later than a time which will enable the peace officer to comply with the subpoena.

(d) If the immediate superior or his or her designated agent upon whom service is attempted to be made knows he or she will be unable to deliver a copy of the subpoena to the peace officer within a time which will allow the peace officer to comply with the subpoena, the immediate superior or agent may refuse to accept service of process and is excused from any duty, liability, or penalty arising in connection with the service, upon notifying the server of that fact.

(e) If the immediate superior or his or her agent is tendered service of a subpoena less than five working days prior to the date of hearing, and he or she is not reasonably certain he or she can complete the service, he or she may refuse acceptance.

(f) If the immediate superior or agent upon whom service has been made, subsequently determines that he or she will be unable to deliver a copy of the subpoena to the peace officer within a time which will allow the peace officer to comply with the subpoena, the immediate superior or agent shall notify the server or his or her office or agent not less than 48 hours prior to the hearing date indicated on the subpoena, and is thereby excused from any duty, liability, or penalty arising because of his or her failure to deliver a copy of the subpoena to the peace officer. The server, so notified, is therewith responsible for preparing the written return of service and for notifying the originator of the subpoena if required.

(g) Notwithstanding subdivision (c), in the case of peace officers employed by the California Highway Patrol, if service is made upon the immediate superior or upon an agent designated by the immediate superior of the peace officer, the immediate superior or the agent shall deliver a copy of the subpoena to the peace officer on the officer's first workday following acceptance of service of process. In this case, failure of the immediate superior or the designated agent to deliver the subpoena shall not constitute a defect in service.

(Amended by Stats. 2016, Ch. 59, Sec. 6. (SB 1474) Effective January 1, 2017.)

1328.5.

Whenever any peace officer is a witness before any court or magistrate in any criminal action or proceeding in connection with a matter regarding an event or transaction which he has perceived or investigated in the course of his duties, where his testimony would become a matter of public record, and where he is required to state the place of his residence, he need not state the place of his residence, but in lieu thereof, he may state his business address.

(Added by Stats. 1971, Ch. 636.)

1328.6.

Whenever any criminalist, questioned document examiner, latent print analyst, polygraph examiner employed by the Department of Justice, a police department, a sheriff's office, or a district attorney's office, an intelligence specialist or other technical specialist employed by the Department of Justice, a custodial officer employed in a local detention facility, or an employee of the county welfare department or the department which administers the county public social services program, is a witness before any court or magistrate in any criminal action or proceeding in connection with a matter regarding an event or transaction which he or she has perceived or investigated in the course of his or her official duties, where his or her testimony would become a matter of public record, and where he or she is required to state the place of his or her residence, he or she need not state the place of his or her residence, but in lieu thereof, he or she may state his or her business address, unless the court finds, after an in camera hearing, that the probative value of the witness's residential address outweighs the creation of substantial danger to the witness.

Nothing in this section shall abridge or limit a defendant's right to discover or investigate this information. This section is not intended to apply to confidential informants.

(Amended by Stats. 1984, Ch. 535, Sec. 1.)

1328a.

A telegraphic copy of a subpoena for a witness in a criminal proceeding may be sent by telegraph or teletype to one or more peace officers, and such copy is as effectual in the hands of any officer, and he must proceed in the same manner under it, as though he held the original subpoena issued.

(Added by Stats. 1963, Ch. 803.)

1328b.

Every officer causing telegraphic copies of subpoenas to be sent, must certify as correct, and file in the telegraph office from which such copies are sent, a copy of the subpoena, and must return the original with a statement of his action thereunder.

(Added by Stats. 1963, Ch. 803.)

1328c.

A peace officer must serve in his county or city any subpoena delivered to him by telegraph or teletype for service and must without delay make a return of the service by telegraph or teletype. Any officer making a return of service of a subpoena by telegraph or teletype must certify as to his actions in making the service and file in the telegraph office from which the return is sent a written statement with his signature in the same form as the return on an original subpoena. The service of a teletype subpoena is made by showing the original teletype to the witness personally and informing him of its contents and delivering to him a copy of the teletype.

(Added by Stats. 1963, Ch. 803.)

1328d.

Notwithstanding Section 1328, a subpoena may be delivered by mail or messenger. Service shall be effected when the witness acknowledges receipt of the subpoena to the sender, by telephone, by mail, over the Internet by e-mail or by completion of the sender's online form, or in person, and identifies himself or herself by reference to his or her date of birth and his or her driver's license number or Department of Motor Vehicles identification card number. The sender shall make a written notation of the identifying information obtained during any acknowledgment by telephone or in person. The sender shall retain a copy of any acknowledgment received over the Internet until the court date for which the subpoena was issued or until any further date as specified by the court. A subpoena issued and acknowledged pursuant to this section shall have the same force and effect as a subpoena personally served. Failure to comply with a subpoena issued and acknowledged pursuant to this section may be punished as a contempt and the subpoena may so state; provided, that a warrant of arrest or a body attachment may not be issued based upon a failure to appear after being subpoenaed pursuant to this section.

A party requesting a continuance based upon the failure of a witness to appear in court at the time and place required for his or her appearance or testimony pursuant to a subpoena, shall prove to the court that the party has complied with the provisions of this section. Such a continuance shall only be granted for a period of time which would allow personal service of the subpoena and in no event longer than that allowed by law, including the requirements of Sections 861 and 1382.

(Amended by Stats. 2010, Ch. 709, Sec. 16. (SB 1062) Effective January 1, 2011.)

1329.

(a) When a person attends before a magistrate, grand jury, or court, as a witness in a criminal case, whether upon a subpoena or in pursuance of an undertaking, or voluntarily, the court, at its discretion, if the attendance of the witness be upon a trial may by an order upon its minutes, or in any criminal proceeding, by a written order, direct the county auditor to draw his warrant upon the county treasurer in favor of such witness for witness' fees at the rate of twelve dollars ($12) for each day's actual attendance and for a reasonable sum to be specified in the order for the necessary expenses of such witness. The court, in its discretion, may make an allowance under this section, or under any appropriate section in Chapter 1 (commencing with Section 68070), Title 8, of the Government Code, other than Section 68093. The allowances are county charges.

(b) The court, in its discretion, may authorize payment to such a witness, if he is employed and if his salary is not paid by his employer during the time he is absent from his employment because of being such a witness, of a sum equal to his gross salary for such time, but such sum shall not exceed eighteen dollars ($18) per day. The sum is a county charge.

A person compensated under the provisions of this subdivision may not receive the payment of witness' fees as provided for in subdivision (a).

(Amended by Stats. 1981, Ch. 184, Sec. 5.)

1329.1.

Any witness who is subpoenaed in any criminal action or proceeding shall be given written notice on the subpoena that the witness may be entitled to receive fees and mileage. Such notice shall indicate generally the manner in which a request or claim for fees and mileage should be made.

(Added by Stats. 1979, Ch. 67.)

1330.

No person is obliged to attend as a witness before a court or magistrate out of the county where the witness resides, or is served with the subpoena, unless the distance be less than 150 miles from his or her place of residence to the place of trial, or unless the judge of the court in which the offense is triable, or a justice of the Supreme Court, or a judge of a superior court, or, in the case of a minor concerning whom a petition has been filed pursuant to Article 16 (commencing with Section 650) of Chapter 2 of Part 1 of Division 2 of the Welfare and Institutions Code, by the judge of the juvenile court hearing the petition, upon an affidavit of the district attorney or prosecutor, or of the defendant, or his or her counsel, or in the case involving a minor in whose behalf a petition has been filed in the juvenile court, of the probation officer approving the filing of the petition or of any party to the action, or his or her counsel, stating that he or she believes the evidence of the witness is material, and his or her attendance at the examination, trial, or hearing is material and necessary, shall endorse on the subpoena an order for the attendance of the witness.

When a subpoena duces tecum is duly issued according to any other provision of law and is served upon a custodian of records or other qualified witness as provided in Article 4 (commencing with Section 1560) of Chapter 2 of Division 11 of the Evidence Code, and his or her personal attendance is not required by the terms of the subpoena, the limitations of this section shall not apply.

(Amended by Stats. 1987, Ch. 828, Sec. 86.)

1331.

Disobedience to a subpoena, or a refusal to be sworn or to testify as a witness, may be punished by the Court or magistrate as a contempt. A witness disobeying a subpoena issued on the part of the defendant, unless he show good cause for his nonattendance, is liable to the defendant in the sum of one hundred dollars, which may be recovered in a civil action.

(Enacted 1872.)

1331.5.

Any person who is subpoenaed to appear at a session of court, or at the trial of an issue therein, may, in lieu of appearance at the time specified in the subpoena, agree with the party at whose request the subpoena was issued, to appear at another time or upon such notice as may be agreed upon. Any failure to appear pursuant to such agreement may be punished as a contempt, and a subpoena shall so state. The facts establishing such agreement and the failure to appear may be shown by the affidavit of any person having personal knowledge of the facts and the court may grant such continuance as may be appropriate.

(Added by Stats. 1972, Ch. 393.)

1332.

(a) Notwithstanding the provisions of Sections 878 to 883, inclusive, when the court is satisfied, by proof on oath, that there is good cause to believe that any material witness for the prosecution or defense, whether the witness is an adult or a minor, will not appear and testify unless security is required, at any proceeding in connection with any criminal prosecution or in connection with a wardship petition pursuant to Section 602 of the Welfare and Institutions Code, the court may order the witness to enter into a written undertaking to the effect that he or she will appear and testify at the time and place ordered by the court or that he or she will forfeit an amount the court deems proper.

(b) If the witness required to enter into an undertaking to appear and testify, either with or without sureties, refuses compliance with the order for that purpose, the court may commit the witness, if an adult, to the custody of the sheriff, and if a minor, to the custody of the probation officer or other appropriate agency, until the witness complies or is legally discharged.

(c) When a person is committed pursuant to this section, he or she is entitled to an automatic review of the order requiring a written undertaking and the order committing the person, by a judge or magistrate having jurisdiction over the offense other than the one who issued the order. This review shall be held not later than two days from the time of the original order of commitment.

(d) If it is determined that the witness must remain in custody, the witness is entitled to a review of that order after 10 days.

(e) When a witness has entered into an undertaking to appear, upon his or her failure to do so the undertaking is forfeited in the same manner as undertakings of bail.

(Amended by Stats. 1987, Ch. 828, Sec. 87.)

CHAPTER 4. Examination of Witnesses Conditionally [1335 - 1345]

(Chapter 4 enacted 1872.)

1335.

(a) If a defendant has been charged with a public offense triable in a court, he or she in all cases, and the people in cases other than those for which the punishment may be death, may, if the defendant has been fully informed of his or her right to counsel as provided by law, have witnesses examined conditionally in his or her or their behalf, as prescribed in this chapter.

(b) If a defendant has been charged with a serious felony or in a case of domestic violence, the people or the defendant may, if the defendant has been fully informed of his or her right to counsel as provided by law, have a witness examined conditionally as prescribed in this chapter, if there is evidence that the life of the witness is in jeopardy.

(c) (1) If a defendant has been charged with human trafficking, pursuant to Section 236.1, and there is evidence that the victim or material witness has been or is being dissuaded by the defendant or a person acting on behalf of the defendant, by intimidation or physical threat, from cooperating with the prosecutor or testifying at trial, the people or the defendant may, if the defendant has been fully informed of his or her right to counsel as provided by law, have a witness examined conditionally as prescribed in this chapter.

(2) If a defendant has been charged with human trafficking, pursuant to Section 236.1, and the court finds that there is a reasonable basis to believe that the material witness will not attend the trial because he or she is under the direct control of the defendant or another person involved in human trafficking and, by virtue of this relationship, the defendant or other person seeks to prevent the witness or victim from testifying, and if the defendant has been fully informed of his or her right to counsel as provided by law, the court may have a witness examined conditionally as prescribed in this chapter.

(d) If a defendant has been charged with a case of domestic violence and there is evidence that a victim or material witness has been or is being dissuaded by the defendant or a person acting on behalf of the defendant, by intimidation or a physical threat, from cooperating with the prosecutor or testifying at trial, the people or the defendant may, if the defendant has been fully informed of his or her right to counsel as provided by law, have a witness examined conditionally as prescribed in this chapter.

(e) For the purposes of this section, the following definitions shall apply:

(1) "Domestic violence" means a public offense arising from acts of domestic violence as defined in Section 13700.

(2) "Serious felony" means a felony listed in subdivision (c) of Section 1192.7 or a violation of Section 11351, 11352, 11378, or 11379 of the Health and Safety Code.

(Amended by Stats. 2014, Ch. 709, Sec. 1. (AB 1610) Effective January 1, 2015.)

1336.

(a) When a material witness for the defendant, or for the people, is about to leave the state, or is so sick or infirm as to afford reasonable grounds for apprehension that he or she will be unable to attend the trial, or is a person 65 years of age or older, or a dependent adult, the defendant or the people may apply for an order that the witness be examined conditionally.

(b) When there is evidence that the life of a witness is in jeopardy, the defendant or the people may apply for an order that the witness be examined conditionally.

(c) As used in this section, "dependent adult" means a person, regardless of whether the person lives independently, who is between the ages of 18 and 65, who has physical or mental limitations which restrict his or her ability to carry out normal activities or to protect his or her rights, including, but not limited to, persons who have physical or developmental disabilities or whose physical or mental abilities have diminished because of age. "Dependent adult" includes any person between the ages of 18 and 65, who is admitted as an inpatient to a 24-hour facility, as defined in Sections 1250, 1250.2, and 1250.3 of the Health and Safety Code.

(Amended by Stats. 2018, Ch. 70, Sec. 4. (AB 1934) Effective January 1, 2019.)

1337.

The application shall be made upon affidavit stating all of the following:

(a) The nature of the offense charged.

(b) The state of the proceedings in the action.

(c) The name and residence of the witness, and that his or her testimony is material to the defense or the prosecution of the action.

(d) That any of the following are true:

(1) The witness is about to leave the state, or is so sick or infirm as to afford reasonable grounds for apprehending that he or she will not be able to attend the trial, or is a person 65 years of age or older, or a dependent adult, or that the life of the witness is in jeopardy.

(2) That the witness is a victim or a material witness in a human trafficking case who has been or is being intimidated or threatened, as described in paragraph (1) of subdivision (c) of Section 1335, from cooperating with the prosecutor or testifying at trial.

(3) That the witness is a victim or material witness in a domestic violence case who has been or is being intimidated or threatened, as described in subdivision (d) of Section 1335 from cooperating with the prosecutor or testifying at trial.
(Amended by Stats. 2014, Ch. 709, Sec. 2. (AB 1610) Effective January 1, 2015.)
1338.
The application may be made to the court or a judge thereof, and must be made upon three days' notice to the opposite party.
(Amended by Stats. 1905, Ch. 540.)
1339.
If the court or judge is satisfied that the examination of the witness is necessary, an order must be made that the witness be examined conditionally, at a specified time and place, and before a magistrate designated therein.
(Amended by Stats. 1905, Ch. 540.)
1340.
(a) The defendant has the right to be present in person and with counsel at the examination, and if the defendant is in custody, the officer in whose custody he or she is, must be informed of the time and place of the examination, and must take the defendant thereto, and keep him or her in the presence and hearing of the witness during the examination.
(b) If the court determines that the witness to be examined is so sick or infirm as to be unable to participate in the examination in person, the court may allow the examination to be conducted by a contemporaneous, two-way video conference system, in which the parties and the witness can see and hear each other via electronic communication.
(c) Nothing in this section is intended to require the court to acquire two-way video conference equipment for these purposes.
(Amended by Stats. 2008, Ch. 14, Sec. 1. Effective January 1, 2009.)
1341.
If, at the designated time and place, it is shown to the satisfaction of the magistrate that the stated ground for conditional examination is not true or that the application was made to avoid the examination of the witness at the trial, the examination cannot take place.
(Amended by Stats. 2009, Ch. 567, Sec. 3. (SB 197) Effective January 1, 2010.)
1342.
The attendance of the witness may be enforced by a subpoena, issued by the magistrate before whom the examination is to be taken.
(Enacted 1872.)
1343.
The testimony given by the witness shall be reduced to writing and authenticated in the same manner as the testimony of a witness taken in support of an information.
Additionally, the testimony may be video-recorded.
(Amended by Stats. 1997, Ch. 19, Sec. 1. Effective January 1, 1998.)
1344.
The deposition taken must, by the magistrate, be sealed up and transmitted to the Clerk of the Court in which the action is pending or may come for trial.
(Enacted 1872.)
1345.
The deposition, or a certified copy of it, may be read in evidence, or if the examination was video-recorded, that video-recording may be shown by either party at the trial if the court finds that the witness is unavailable as a witness within the meaning of Section 240 of the Evidence Code. The same objections may be taken to a question or answer contained in the deposition or video-recording as if the witness had been examined orally in court.
(Amended by Stats. 1997, Ch. 19, Sec. 2. Effective January 1, 1998.)

CHAPTER 4.5. Examination of Victims of Sexual Crimes [1346 - 1347.5]

(Chapter 4.5 added by Stats. 1982, Ch. 98, Sec. 1.)
1346.
(a) When a defendant has been charged with a violation of Section 220, 243.4, 261, 261.5, 264.1, 269, 273a, 273d, 285, 286, 287, 288, 288.5, 288.7, 289, or 647.6, or former Section 288a, and the victim either is a person 15 years of age or younger or is developmentally disabled as a result of an intellectual disability, as specified in subdivision (a) of Section 4512 of the Welfare and Institutions Code, the people may apply for an order that the victim's testimony at the preliminary hearing, in addition to being stenographically recorded, be video recorded and the video recording preserved.
(b) The application for the order shall be in writing and made three days prior to the preliminary hearing.
(c) Upon timely receipt of the application, the magistrate shall order that the testimony of the victim given at the preliminary hearing be taken and preserved as a video recording, in addition to being stenographically recorded. The video recording shall be transmitted to the clerk of the court in which the action is pending.
(d) If at the time of trial the court finds that further testimony would cause the victim emotional trauma so that the victim is medically unavailable or unavailable within the meaning of Section 240 of the Evidence Code, the court may admit the video recording of the victim's testimony at the preliminary hearing as former testimony under Section 1291 of the Evidence Code.
(e) A video recording that is taken pursuant to this section is subject to a protective order of the court for the purpose of protecting the privacy of the victim. This subdivision does not affect the provisions of subdivision (b) of Section 868.7.
(f) A video recording made pursuant to this section shall be made available to the prosecuting attorney, the defendant, and his or her attorney for viewing during ordinary business hours. A video recording that is made available pursuant to this section is subject to a protective order of the court for the purpose of protecting the privacy of the victim.
(g) The video recording shall be destroyed after five years have elapsed from the date of entry of judgment, except that if an appeal is filed, the video recording shall not be destroyed until a final judgment on appeal has been rendered.
(Amended by Stats. 2018, Ch. 423, Sec. 97. (SB 1494) Effective January 1, 2019.)
1346.1.
(a) When a defendant has been charged with a violation of Section 262 or subdivision (a) of Section 273.5, the people may apply for an order that the victim's testimony at the preliminary hearing, in addition to being stenographically recorded, be video recorded and the video recording preserved.
(b) The application for the order shall be in writing and made three days prior to the preliminary hearing.
(c) Upon timely receipt of the application, the magistrate shall order that the testimony of the victim given at the preliminary hearing be taken and preserved as a video recording, in addition to being stenographically recorded. The video recording shall be transmitted to the clerk of the court in which the action is pending.
(d) If the victim's prior testimony given at the preliminary hearing is admissible pursuant to the Evidence Code, then the video recording of that testimony may be introduced as evidence at trial.
(Amended by Stats. 2014, Ch. 160, Sec. 2. (AB 1900) Effective January 1, 2015.)
1347.

(a) It is the intent of the Legislature in enacting this section to provide the court with discretion to employ alternative court procedures to protect the rights of a child witness, the rights of the defendant, and the integrity of the judicial process. In exercising its discretion, the court necessarily will be required to balance the rights of the defendant or defendants against the need to protect a child witness and to preserve the integrity of the court's truthfinding function. This discretion is intended to be used selectively when the facts and circumstances in an individual case present compelling evidence of the need to use these alternative procedures.
(b) Notwithstanding any other law, the court in a criminal proceeding, upon written notice by the prosecutor made at least three days prior to the date of the preliminary hearing or trial date on which the testimony of the minor is scheduled, or during the course of the proceeding on the court's own motion, may order that the testimony of a minor 13 years of age or younger at the time of the motion be taken by contemporaneous examination and cross-examination in another place and out of the presence of the judge, jury, defendant or defendants, and attorneys, and communicated to the courtroom by means of closed-circuit television, if the court makes all of the following findings:
(1) The minor's testimony will involve a recitation of the facts of any of the following:
(A) An alleged sexual offense committed on or with the minor.
(B) An alleged violent felony, as defined in subdivision (c) of Section 667.5.
(C) An alleged felony offense specified in Section 273a or 273d of which the minor is a victim.
(2) The impact on the minor of one or more of the factors enumerated in subparagraphs (A) to (E), inclusive, is shown by clear and convincing evidence to be so substantial as to make the minor unavailable as a witness unless closed-circuit testimony is used.
(A) Testimony by the minor in the presence of the defendant would result in the child suffering serious emotional distress so that the child would be unavailable as a witness.
(B) The defendant used a deadly weapon in the commission of the offense.
(C) The defendant threatened serious bodily injury to the child or the child's family, threatened incarceration or deportation of the child or a member of the child's family, threatened removal of the child from the child's family, or threatened the dissolution of the child's family in order to prevent or dissuade the minor from attending or giving testimony at any trial or court proceeding, or to prevent the minor from reporting the alleged sexual offense, or from assisting in criminal prosecution.
(D) The defendant inflicted great bodily injury upon the child in the commission of the offense.
(E) The defendant or his or her counsel behaved during the hearing or trial in a way that caused the minor to be unable to continue his or her testimony.
In making the determination required by this section, the court shall consider the age of the minor, the relationship between the minor and the defendant or defendants, any handicap or disability of the minor, and the nature of the acts charged. The minor's refusal to testify shall not alone constitute sufficient evidence that the special procedure described in this section is necessary to obtain the minor's testimony.
(3) The equipment available for use of closed-circuit television would accurately communicate the image and demeanor of the minor to the judge, jury, defendant or defendants, and attorneys.
(c) If the court orders the use of closed-circuit television, two-way closed-circuit television shall be used, except that if the impact on the minor of one or more of the factors enumerated in subparagraphs (A) to (E), inclusive, of paragraph (2) of subdivision (b), is shown by clear and convincing evidence to be so substantial as to make the minor unavailable as a witness even if two-way closed-circuit television is used, one-way closed-circuit television may be used. The prosecution shall give the defendant or defendants at least 30 days' written notice of the prosecution's intent to seek the use of one-way closed-circuit television, unless the prosecution shows good cause to the court why this 30-day notice requirement should not apply.
(d) (1) The hearing on a motion brought pursuant to this section shall be conducted out of the presence of the jury.
(2) Notwithstanding Section 804 of the Evidence Code or any other law, the court, in determining the merits of the motion, shall not compel the minor to testify at the hearing, nor shall the court deny the motion on the ground that the minor has not testified.
(3) In determining whether the impact on an individual child of one or more of the five factors enumerated in paragraph (2) of subdivision (b) is so substantial that the minor is unavailable as a witness unless two-way or one-way closed-circuit television is used, the court may question the minor in chambers, or at some other comfortable place other than the courtroom, on the record for a reasonable period of time with the support person, the prosecutor, and defense counsel present. The defendant or defendants shall not be present. The court shall conduct the questioning of the minor and shall not permit the prosecutor or defense counsel to examine the minor. The prosecutor and defense counsel shall be permitted to submit proposed questions to the court prior to the session in chambers. Defense counsel shall be afforded a reasonable opportunity to consult with the defendant or defendants prior to the conclusion of the session in chambers.
(e) When the court orders the testimony of a minor to be taken in another place outside of the courtroom, the court shall do all of the following:
(1) Make a brief statement on the record, outside of the presence of the jury, of the reasons in support of its order. While the statement need not include traditional findings of fact, the reasons shall be set forth with sufficient specificity to permit meaningful review and to demonstrate that discretion was exercised in a careful, reasonable, and equitable manner.
(2) Instruct the members of the jury that they are to draw no inferences from the use of closed-circuit television as a means of facilitating the testimony of the minor.
(3) Instruct respective counsel, outside of the presence of the jury, that they are to make no comment during the course of the trial on the use of closed-circuit television procedures.
(4) Instruct the support witness, outside of the presence of the jury, that he or she is not to coach, cue, or in any way influence or attempt to influence the testimony of the minor.
(5) Order that a complete record of the examination of the minor, including the images and voices of all persons who in any way participate in the examination, be made and preserved as a video recording in addition to being stenographically recorded. The video recording shall be transmitted to the clerk of the court in which the action is pending and shall be made available for viewing to the prosecuting attorney, the defendant or defendants, and his or her attorney during ordinary business hours. The video recording shall be destroyed after five years have elapsed from the date of entry of judgment. If an appeal is filed, the video recording shall not be destroyed until a final judgment on appeal has been ordered. A video recording that is taken pursuant to this section is subject to a protective order of the court for the purpose of protecting the privacy of the witness. This subdivision does not affect the provisions of subdivision (b) of Section 868.7.
(f) When the court orders the testimony of a minor to be taken in another place outside the courtroom, only the minor, a support person designated pursuant to Section 868.5, a nonuniformed bailiff, any technicians necessary to operate the closed-circuit equipment, and, after consultation with the prosecution and the defense, a representative appointed by the court, shall be physically present for the testimony. A video recording device shall record the image of the minor and his or her testimony, and a separate video recording device shall record the image of the support person.

(g) When the court orders the testimony of a minor to be taken in another place outside the courtroom, the minor shall be brought into the judge's chambers prior to the taking of his or her testimony to meet for a reasonable period of time with the judge, the prosecutor, and defense counsel. A support person for the minor shall also be present. This meeting shall be for the purpose of explaining the court process to the child and to allow the attorneys an opportunity to establish rapport with the child to facilitate later questioning by closed-circuit television. No participant shall discuss the defendant or defendants or any of the facts of the case with the minor during this meeting.

(h) When the court orders the testimony of a minor to be taken in another place outside the courtroom, nothing in this section prohibits the court from ordering the minor to be brought into the courtroom for a limited purpose, including the identification of the defendant or defendants as the court deems necessary.

(i) The examination shall be under oath, and the defendant or defendants shall be able to see and hear the minor witness, and if two-way closed-circuit television is used, the defendant's image shall be transmitted live to the witness.

(j) Nothing in this section affects the disqualification of witnesses pursuant to Section 701 of the Evidence Code.

(k) The cost of examination by contemporaneous closed-circuit television ordered pursuant to this section shall be borne by the court out of its existing budget.

(l) Nothing in this section shall be construed to prohibit a defendant from being represented by counsel during any closed-circuit testimony.

(Amended by Stats. 2015, Ch. 155, Sec. 1. (SB 176) Effective January 1, 2016.)

1347.1.

(a) In any criminal proceeding in which a defendant is charged with a violation of Section 236.1, upon written notice by the prosecutor made at least three days prior to the date of the preliminary hearing or trial date on which the testimony of the minor is scheduled, or during the course of the proceeding on the court's own motion, may order that the testimony of a minor 15 years of age or younger at the time of the motion be taken by contemporaneous examination and cross-examination in another place and out of the presence of the judge, jury, defendant or defendants, and attorneys, and communicated to the courtroom by means of closed-circuit television, if the court makes all of the following findings:

(1) The minor's testimony will involve a recitation of the facts of an alleged offense of human trafficking, as defined in Section 236.1.

(2) (A) The impact on the minor of one or more of the factors enumerated in clauses (i) to (v), inclusive, is shown by clear and convincing evidence to be so substantial as to make the minor unavailable as a witness unless closed-circuit testimony is used.

(i) Testimony by the minor in the presence of the defendant would result in the minor suffering serious emotional distress so that the minor would be unavailable as a witness.

(ii) The defendant used a deadly weapon in the commission of the offense.

(iii) The defendant threatened serious bodily injury to the minor or the minor's family, threatened incarceration or deportation of the minor or a member of the minor's family, threatened removal of the minor from the minor's family, or threatened the dissolution of the minor's family in order to prevent or dissuade the minor from attending or giving testimony at any trial or court proceeding, or to prevent the minor from reporting the alleged offense, or from assisting in criminal prosecution.

(iv) The defendant inflicted great bodily injury upon the minor in the commission of the offense.

(v) The defendant or his or her counsel behaved during the hearing or trial in a way that caused the minor to be unable to continue his or her testimony.

(B) In making the determination required by this paragraph, the court shall consider the age of the minor, the relationship between the minor and the defendant or defendants, any handicap or disability of the minor, and the nature of the acts charged. The minor's refusal to testify shall not alone constitute sufficient evidence that the special procedure described in this section is necessary to obtain the minor's testimony.

(3) The equipment available for use of closed-circuit television would accurately communicate the image and demeanor of the minor to the judge, jury, defendant or defendants, and attorneys.

(b) If the court orders the use of closed-circuit television, two-way closed-circuit television shall be used, except that if the impact on the minor of one or more of the factors enumerated in clauses (i) to (v), inclusive, of subparagraph (A) of paragraph (2) of subdivision (a), is shown by clear and convincing evidence to be so substantial as to make the minor unavailable as a witness even if two-way closed-circuit television is used, one-way closed-circuit television may be used. The prosecution shall give the defendant or defendants at least 30 days' written notice of the prosecution's intent to seek the use of one-way closed-circuit television, unless the prosecution shows good cause to the court why this 30-day notice requirement should not apply.

(c) (1) The hearing on a motion brought pursuant to this section shall be conducted out of the presence of the jury.

(2) Notwithstanding Section 804 of the Evidence Code or any other law, the court, in determining the merits of the motion, shall not compel the minor to testify at the hearing, nor shall the court deny the motion on the ground that the minor has not testified.

(3) In determining whether the impact on an individual minor of one or more of the five factors enumerated in clauses (i) to (v), inclusive, of subparagraph (A) of paragraph (2) of subdivision (a) is so substantial that the minor is unavailable as a witness unless two-way or one-way closed-circuit television is used, the court may question the minor in chambers, or at some other comfortable place other than the courtroom, on the record for a reasonable period of time with the support person, the prosecutor, and defense counsel present. The defendant or defendants shall not be present. The court shall conduct the questioning of the minor and shall not permit the prosecutor or defense counsel to examine the minor. The prosecutor and defense counsel shall be permitted to submit proposed questions to the court prior to the session in chambers. Defense counsel shall be afforded a reasonable opportunity to consult with the defendant or defendants prior to the conclusion of the session in chambers.

(d) When the court orders the testimony of a minor to be taken in another place outside of the courtroom, the court shall do all of the following:

(1) Make a brief statement on the record, outside of the presence of the jury, of the reasons in support of its order. While the statement need not include traditional findings of fact, the reasons shall be set forth with sufficient specificity to permit meaningful review and to demonstrate that discretion was exercised in a careful, reasonable, and equitable manner.

(2) Instruct the members of the jury that they are to draw no inferences from the use of closed-circuit television as a means of facilitating the testimony of the minor.

(3) Instruct respective counsel, outside of the presence of the jury, that they are to make no comment during the course of the trial on the use of closed-circuit television procedures.

(4) Instruct the support witness, outside of the presence of the jury, that he or she is not to coach, cue, or in any way influence or attempt to influence the testimony of the minor.

(5) Order that a complete record of the examination of the minor, including the images and voices of all persons who in any way participate in the examination, be made and preserved as a video recording in addition to being stenographically recorded. The video recording shall be transmitted to the clerk of the court in which the action is pending and shall be made available for viewing to the prosecuting attorney, the defendant or defendants, and his or her attorney during ordinary business hours. The video recording shall be destroyed after five years have elapsed from the date of entry of judgment. If an appeal is filed, the video recording shall not be destroyed until a final judgment on appeal has been ordered. A video recording that is taken pursuant to this

section is subject to a protective order of the court for the purpose of protecting the privacy of the witness. This subdivision does not affect the provisions of subdivision (b) of Section 868.7.

(e) When the court orders the testimony of a minor to be taken in another place outside the courtroom, only the minor, a support person designated pursuant to Section 868.5, a nonuniformed bailiff, any technicians necessary to operate the closed-circuit equipment, and, after consultation with the prosecution and the defense, a representative appointed by the court, shall be physically present for the testimony. A video recording device shall record the image of the minor and his or her testimony, and a separate video recording device shall record the image of the support person.

(f) When the court orders the testimony of a minor to be taken in another place outside the courtroom, the minor shall be brought into the judge's chambers prior to the taking of his or her testimony to meet for a reasonable period of time with the judge, the prosecutor, and defense counsel. A support person for the minor shall also be present. This meeting shall be for the purpose of explaining the court process to the minor and to allow the attorneys an opportunity to establish rapport with the minor to facilitate later questioning by closed-circuit television. A participant shall not discuss the defendant or defendants or any of the facts of the case with the minor during this meeting.

(g) When the court orders the testimony of a minor to be taken in another place outside the courtroom, this section does not prohibit the court from ordering the minor to be brought into the courtroom for a limited purpose, including the identification of the defendant or defendants as the court deems necessary.

(h) The examination shall be under oath, and the defendant or defendants shall be able to see and hear the minor witness, and if two-way closed-circuit television is used, the defendant's image shall be transmitted live to the witness.

(i) This section does not affect the disqualification of witnesses pursuant to Section 701 of the Evidence Code.

(j) The cost of examination by contemporaneous closed-circuit television ordered pursuant to this section shall be borne by the court out of its existing budget.

(k) This section shall not be construed to prohibit a defendant from being represented by counsel during any closed-circuit testimony.

(Amended by Stats. 2017, Ch. 269, Sec. 9. (SB 811) Effective January 1, 2018.)

1347.5.

(a) It is the intent of the Legislature, in enacting this section, to provide the court with discretion to modify court procedures, as a reasonable accommodation, to ensure that adults and children with disabilities who have been victims of an alleged sexual or otherwise specified offense are able to participate effectively in criminal proceedings. In exercising its discretion, the court shall balance the rights of the defendant against the right of the victim who has a disability to full access and participation in the proceedings, while preserving the integrity of the court's truthfinding function.

(1) For purposes of this section, the term "disability" is defined in paragraphs (1) and (2) of subdivision (c) of Section 11135 of the Government Code.

(2) The right of the victim is not to confront the perpetrator, but derives under both Section 504 of the Rehabilitation Act of 1973 (29 U.S.C. Sec. 794) and the Americans with Disabilities Act of 1990 (42 U.S.C. Sec. 12101 et seq.) as a right to participate in or benefit from the same services or services that are equal or as effective as those enjoyed by persons without disabilities.

(b) Notwithstanding any other law, in any criminal proceeding in which the defendant is charged with a violation of Section 220, 243.4, 261, 261.5, 264.1, 273a, 273d, 285, 286, 287, 288, 288.5, or 289, or former Section 288a, subdivision (1) of Section 314, Section 368, 647.6, or with any attempt to commit a crime listed in this subdivision, committed with or upon a person with a disability, the court in its discretion may make accommodations to support the person with a disability, including, but not limited to, any of the following:

(1) Allow the person with a disability reasonable periods of relief from examination and cross-examination during which he or she may retire from the courtroom. The judge may also allow other witnesses in the proceeding to be examined when the person with a disability retires from the courtroom.

(2) Allow the person with a disability to utilize a support person pursuant to Section 868.5 or a regional center representative providing services to a developmentally disabled individual pursuant to Article 1 (commencing with Section 4620) or Article 2 (commencing with Section 4640) of Chapter 5 of Division 4.5 of the Welfare and Institutions Code. In addition to, or instead of, allowing the person with a disability to utilize a support person or regional center representative pursuant to this paragraph, the court may allow the person with a disability to utilize a person necessary to facilitate the communication or physical needs of the person with a disability.

(3) Notwithstanding Section 68110 of the Government Code, the judge may remove his or her robe if the judge believes that this formal attire prevents full participation of the person with a disability because it is intimidating to him or her.

(4) The judge, parties, witnesses, support persons, and court personnel may be relocated within the courtroom to facilitate a more comfortable and personal environment for the person with a disability as well as accommodating any specific requirements for communication by that person.

(c) The prosecutor may apply for an order that the testimony of the person with a disability at the preliminary hearing, in addition to being stenographically recorded, be video recorded and the video recording preserved.

(1) The application for the order shall be in writing and made three days prior to the preliminary hearing.

(2) Upon timely receipt of the application, the judge shall order that the testimony of the person with a disability given at the preliminary hearing be taken and preserved as a video recording, in addition to being stenographically recorded. The video recording shall be transmitted to the clerk of the court in which the action is pending.

(3) If at the time of trial the court finds that further testimony would cause the person with a disability emotional trauma so that he or she is medically unavailable or otherwise unavailable within the meaning of Section 240 of the Evidence Code, the court may admit the video recording of his or her testimony at the preliminary hearing as former testimony under Section 1291 of the Evidence Code.

(4) A video recording that is taken pursuant to this subdivision is subject to a protective order of the court for the purpose of protecting the privacy of the person with a disability. This subdivision does not affect the provisions of subdivision (b) of Section 868.7.

(d) Notwithstanding any other law, the court in any criminal proceeding, upon written notice of the prosecutor made at least three days prior to the date of the preliminary hearing or trial date on which the testimony of the person with a disability is scheduled, or during the course of the proceeding on the court's own motion, may order that the testimony of the person with a disability be taken by contemporaneous examination and cross-examination in another place and out of the presence of the judge, jury, and defendant, and communicated to the courtroom by means of two-way closed-circuit television, if the court makes all of the following findings:

(1) The person with a disability will be called on to testify concerning facts of an alleged sexual offense, or other crime as specified in subdivision (b), committed on or with that person.

(2) The impact on the person with a disability of one or more of the factors enumerated in subparagraphs (A) to (D), inclusive, is shown by clear and convincing evidence to be so substantial as to make the person with a disability unavailable as a witness unless closed-circuit television is used. The refusal of the person with a disability to testify shall not alone constitute sufficient evidence that the special procedure described in this subdivision is necessary in order to accommodate the disability. The court may take into

consideration the relationship between the person with a disability and the defendant or defendants.

(A) Threats of serious bodily injury to be inflicted on the person with a disability or a family member, of incarceration, institutionalization, or deportation of the person with a disability or a family member, or of removal of the person with a disability from his or her residence by withholding needed services when the threats come from a service provider, in order to prevent or dissuade the person with a disability from attending or giving testimony at any trial or court proceeding or to prevent that person from reporting the alleged offense or from assisting in criminal prosecution.

(B) Use of a firearm or any other deadly weapon during the commission of the crime.

(C) Infliction of great bodily injury upon the person with a disability during the commission of the crime.

(D) Conduct on the part of the defendant or defense counsel during the hearing or trial that causes the person with a disability to be unable to continue his or her testimony.

(e) (1) The hearing on the motion brought pursuant to this subdivision shall be conducted out of the presence of the jury.

(2) Notwithstanding Section 804 of the Evidence Code or any other law, the court, in determining the merits of the motion, shall not compel the person with a disability to testify at the hearing, nor shall the court deny the motion on the ground that the person with a disability has not testified.

(3) In determining whether the impact on an individual person with a disability of one or more of the factors enumerated under paragraph (2) of subdivision (d) is so substantial that the person is unavailable as a witness unless the closed-circuit television procedure is employed, the court may question the person with a disability in chambers, or at some other comfortable place other than the courtroom, on the record for a reasonable period of time with the support person described under paragraph (2) of subdivision (b), the prosecutor, and defense counsel present. At this time the court shall explain the process to the person with a disability. The defendant or defendants shall not be present; however, the defendant or defendants shall have the opportunity to contemporaneously observe the proceedings by closed-circuit television. Defense counsel shall be afforded a reasonable opportunity to consult with the defendant or defendants prior to the conclusion of the session in chambers.

(f) When the court orders the testimony of a victim who is a person with a disability to be taken in another place outside of the courtroom, the court shall do all of the following:

(1) Make a brief statement on the record, outside of the presence of the jury, of the reasons in support of its order. While the statement need not include traditional findings of fact, the reasons shall be set forth with sufficient specificity to permit meaningful review and to demonstrate that discretion was exercised in a careful, reasonable, and equitable manner.

(2) Instruct the members of the jury that they are to draw no inferences from the use of closed-circuit television as a means of ensuring the full participation of the victim who is a person with a disability by accommodating that individual's disability.

(3) Instruct respective counsel, outside of the presence of the jury, that they are to make no comment during the course of the trial on the use of closed-circuit television procedures.

(4) Instruct the support person, if the person is part of the court's accommodation of the disability, outside of the presence of the jury, that he or she is not to coach, cue, or in any way influence or attempt to influence the testimony of the person with a disability.

(5) Order that a complete record of the examination of the person with a disability, including the images and voices of all persons who in any way participate in the examination, be made and preserved as a video recording in addition to being stenographically recorded. The video recording shall be transmitted to the clerk of the court in which the action is pending and shall be made available for viewing to the prosecuting attorney, the defendant, and his or her attorney, during ordinary business hours. The video recording shall be destroyed after five years have elapsed from the date of entry of judgment. If an appeal is filed, the video recording shall not be destroyed until a final judgment on appeal has been ordered. A video recording that is taken pursuant to this section is subject to a protective order of the court for the purpose of protecting the privacy of the person with a disability. This subdivision does not affect the provisions of subdivision (b) of Section 868.7.

(g) When the court orders the testimony of a victim who is a person with a disability to be taken in another place outside the courtroom, nothing in this section shall prohibit the court from ordering the victim to appear in the courtroom for a limited purpose, including the identification of the defendant or defendants as the court deems necessary.

(h) The examination shall be under oath, and the defendant shall be able to see and hear the person with a disability. If two-way closed-circuit television is used, the defendant's image shall be transmitted live to the person with a disability.

(i) Nothing in this section shall affect the disqualification of witnesses pursuant to Section 701 of the Evidence Code.

(j) The cost of examination by contemporaneous closed-circuit television ordered pursuant to this section shall be borne by the court out of its existing budget.

(k) This section shall not be construed to obviate the need to provide other accommodations necessary to ensure accessibility of courtrooms to persons with disabilities nor prescribe a lesser standard of accessibility or usability for persons with disabilities than that provided by Title II of the Americans with Disabilities Act of 1990 (42 U.S.C. Sec. 12101 et seq.) and federal regulations adopted pursuant to that act.

(l) The Judicial Council shall report to the Legislature, no later than two years after the enactment of this subdivision, on the frequency of the use and effectiveness of admitting the videotape of testimony by means of closed-circuit television.

(Amended by Stats. 2018, Ch. 423, Sec. 98. (SB 1494) Effective January 1, 2019.)

CHAPTER 5. Examination of Witnesses on Commission [1349 - 1362]

(Chapter 5 enacted 1872.)

1349.
When an issue of fact is joined upon an indictment or information, the defendant may have any material witness, residing out of the state, examined in his behalf, as prescribed in this chapter, and not otherwise.
(Amended by Stats. 1980, Ch. 676, Sec. 253.)

1350.
When a material witness for the defendant resides out of the State, the defendant may apply for an order that the witness be examined on a commission.
(Enacted 1872.)

1351.
A commission is a process issued under the seal of the Court and the signature of the Clerk, directed to some person designated as Commissioner, authorizing him to examine the witness upon oath on interrogatories annexed thereto, to take and certify the deposition of the witness, and to return it according to the directions given with the commission.
(Enacted 1872.)

1352.
The application must be made upon affidavit, stating:
1. The nature of the offense charged;

2. The state of the proceedings in the action, and that an issue of fact has been joined therein;
3. The name of the witness, and that his testimony is material to the defense of the action;
4. That the witness resides out of the State.
(Enacted 1872.)

1353.
The application may be made to the Court, or a Judge thereof, and must be upon three days' notice to the District Attorney.
(Amended by Code Amendments 1880, Ch. 25.)

1354.
If the Court to whom the application is made is satisfied of the truth of the facts stated, and that the examination of the witness is necessary to the attainment of justice, an order must be made that a commission be issued to take his testimony; and the Court may insert in the order a direction that the trial be stayed for a specified time, reasonably sufficient for the execution and return of the commission.
(Amended by Code Amendments 1880, Ch. 47.)

1355.
When the commission is ordered, the defendant must serve upon the District Attorney, without delay, a copy of the interrogatories to be annexed thereto, with two days' notice of the time at which they will be presented to the Court or Judge. The District Attorney may in like manner serve upon the defendant or his counsel cross-interrogatories, to be annexed to the commission, with the like notice. In the interrogatories either party may insert any questions pertinent to the issue. When the interrogatories and cross-interrogatories are presented to the Court or Judge, according to the notice given, the Court or Judge must modify the questions so as to conform them to the rules of evidence, and must indorse upon them his allowance and annex them to the commission.
(Enacted 1872.)

1356.
Unless the parties otherwise consent, by an indorsement upon the commission, the Court or Judge must indorse thereon a direction as to the manner in which it must be returned, and may, in his discretion, direct that it be returned by mail or otherwise, addressed to the Clerk of the Court in which the action is pending, designating his name and the place where his office is kept.
(Enacted 1872.)

1357.
The commissioner, unless otherwise specially directed, may execute the commission in the following order:
(a) He or she shall publicly administer an oath to the witness that his or her answers given to the interrogatories shall be the truth, the whole truth, and nothing but the truth.
(b) He or she shall cause the examination of the witness to be reduced to writing and subscribed by the witness.
(c) He or she shall write the answers of the witness as near as possible in the language in which he or she gives them, and read to the witness each answer as it is taken down, and correct or add to it until it conforms to what he or she declares is the truth.
(d) If the witness declines to answer a question, that fact, with the reason assigned by him or her for declining, shall be stated.
(e) If any papers or documents are produced before him or her and proved by the witness, they, or copies of them, shall be annexed to the deposition subscribed by the witness and certified by the commissioner.
(f) The commissioner shall subscribe his or her name to each sheet of the deposition, and annex the deposition, with the papers and documents proved by the witness, or copies thereof, to the commission, and shall close it up under seal, and address it as directed by the indorsement thereon.
(g) If there is a direction on the commission to return it by mail, the commissioner shall immediately deposit it in the nearest post office. If any other direction is made by the written consent of the parties, or by the court or judge, on the commission, as to its return, the commissioner shall comply with the direction.
A copy of this section shall be annexed to the commission.
(Amended by Stats. 1989, Ch. 1360, Sec. 115.)

1358.
If the commission and return be delivered by the Commissioner to an agent, he must deliver the same to the Clerk to whom it is directed, or to the Judge of the Court in which the action is pending, by whom it may be received and opened, upon the agent making affidavit that he received it from the hands of the Commissioner, and that it has not been opened or altered since he received it.
(Amended by Code Amendments 1880, Ch. 47.)

1359.
If the agent is dead, or from sickness or other casualty unable personally to deliver the commission and return, as prescribed in the last section, it may be received by the Clerk or Judge from any other person, upon his making an affidavit that he received it from the agent; that the agent is dead, or from sickness or other casualty unable to deliver it; that it has not been opened or altered since the person making the affidavit received it; and that he believes it has not been opened or altered since it came from the hands of the Commissioner.
(Enacted 1872.)

1360.
The clerk or judge receiving and opening the commission and return shall immediately file it, with the affidavit mentioned in Sections 1358 and 1359, in the office of the clerk of the court in which the indictment is pending. If the commission and return is transmitted by mail, the clerk to whom it is addressed shall receive it from the post office, and open and file it in his or her office, where it must remain, unless otherwise directed by the court or judge.
(Amended by Stats. 1987, Ch. 828, Sec. 89.)

1361.
The commission and return must at all times be open to the inspection of the parties, who must be furnished by the Clerk with copies of the same or of any part thereof, on payment of his fees.
(Enacted 1872.)

1362.
The depositions taken under the commission may be read in evidence by either party on the trial if the court finds that the witness is unavailable as a witness within the meaning of Section 240 of the Evidence Code. The same objections may be taken to a question in the interrogatories or to an answer in the deposition as if the witness had been examined orally in court.
(Amended by Stats. 1965, Ch. 299.)

CHAPTER 6. Inquiry into the Competence of the Defendant Before Trial or After Conviction [1367 - 1376]

(Heading of Chapter 6 amended by Stats. 1980, Ch. 547, Sec. 6.5.)

1367.

(a) A person cannot be tried or adjudged to punishment or have his or her probation, mandatory supervision, postrelease community supervision, or parole revoked while that person is mentally incompetent. A defendant is mentally incompetent for purposes of this chapter if, as a result of mental disorder or developmental disability, the defendant is unable to understand the nature of the criminal proceedings or to assist counsel in the conduct of a defense in a rational manner.

(b) Section 1370 shall apply to a person who is charged with a felony or alleged to have violated the terms of probation for a felony or mandatory supervision and is incompetent as a result of a mental disorder. Section 1370.01 shall apply to a person who is charged with a misdemeanor or misdemeanors only, or a violation of formal or informal probation for a misdemeanor, and the judge finds reason to believe that the defendant is mentally disordered, and may, as a result of the mental disorder, be incompetent to stand trial. Section 1370.1 shall apply to a person who is incompetent as a result of a developmental disability and shall apply to a person who is incompetent as a result of a mental disorder, but is also developmentally disabled. Section 1370.02 shall apply to a person alleged to have violated the terms of his or her postrelease community supervision or parole.

(Amended by Stats. 2014, Ch. 759, Sec. 1. (SB 1412) Effective January 1, 2015.)
1368.

(a) If, during the pendency of an action and prior to judgment, or during revocation proceedings for a violation of probation, mandatory supervision, postrelease community supervision, or parole, a doubt arises in the mind of the judge as to the mental competence of the defendant, he or she shall state that doubt in the record and inquire of the attorney for the defendant whether, in the opinion of the attorney, the defendant is mentally competent. If the defendant is not represented by counsel, the court shall appoint counsel. At the request of the defendant or his or her counsel or upon its own motion, the court shall recess the proceedings for as long as may be reasonably necessary to permit counsel to confer with the defendant and to form an opinion as to the mental competence of the defendant at that point in time.

(b) If counsel informs the court that he or she believes the defendant is or may be mentally incompetent, the court shall order that the question of the defendant's mental competence is to be determined in a hearing which is held pursuant to Sections 1368.1 and 1369. If counsel informs the court that he or she believes the defendant is mentally competent, the court may nevertheless order a hearing. Any hearing shall be held in the superior court.

(c) Except as provided in Section 1368.1, when an order for a hearing into the present mental competence of the defendant has been issued, all proceedings in the criminal prosecution shall be suspended until the question of the present mental competence of the defendant has been determined.

If a jury has been impaneled and sworn to try the defendant, the jury shall be discharged only if it appears to the court that undue hardship to the jurors would result if the jury is retained on call.

If the defendant is declared mentally incompetent, the jury shall be discharged.

(Amended by Stats. 2014, Ch. 759, Sec. 3. (SB 1412) Effective January 1, 2015.)
1368.1.

(a) (1) If the action is on a complaint charging a felony, proceedings to determine mental competence shall be held prior to the filing of an information unless the counsel for the defendant requests a preliminary examination under Section 859b. At the preliminary examination, counsel for the defendant may either demur, move to dismiss the complaint on the ground that there is not reasonable cause to believe that a felony has been committed and that the defendant is guilty thereof, or make a motion under Section 1538.5. A proceeding to determine mental competence or a request for a preliminary examination pursuant to this paragraph does not preclude a request for a determination of probable cause pursuant to paragraph (2).

(2) If the action is on a complaint charging a felony involving death, great bodily harm, or a serious threat to the physical well-being of another person, the prosecuting attorney may, at any time before or after a defendant is determined incompetent to stand trial, request a determination of probable cause to believe the defendant committed the offense or offenses alleged in the complaint, solely for the purpose of establishing that the defendant is gravely disabled pursuant to subparagraph (B) of paragraph (1) of subdivision (h) of Section 5008 of the Welfare and Institutions Code, pursuant to procedures approved by the court. In making this determination, the court shall consider using procedures consistent with the manner in which a preliminary examination is conducted. A finding of probable cause shall only be made upon the presentation of evidence sufficient to satisfy the standard set forth in subdivision (a) of Section 872. The defendant shall be entitled to a preliminary hearing after the restoration of his or her competence. A request for a determination of probable cause pursuant to this paragraph does not preclude a proceeding to determine mental competence or a request for a preliminary examination pursuant to paragraph (1).

(b) If the action is on a complaint charging a misdemeanor, counsel for the defendant may either demur, move to dismiss the complaint on the ground that there is not reasonable cause to believe that a public offense has been committed and that the defendant is guilty thereof, or make a motion under Section 1538.5.

(c) If the proceeding involves an alleged violation of probation, mandatory supervision, postrelease community supervision, or parole, counsel for the defendant may move to reinstate supervision on the ground that there is not probable cause to believe that the defendant violated the terms of his or her supervision.

(d) In ruling upon any demurrer or motion described in subdivision (a), (b), or (c), the court may hear any matter which is capable of fair determination without the personal participation of the defendant.

(e) A demurrer or motion described in subdivision (a), (b), or (c) shall be made in the court having jurisdiction over the complaint. The defendant shall not be certified until the demurrer or motion has been decided.

(Amended by Stats. 2017, Ch. 246, Sec. 1. (SB 684) Effective January 1, 2018.)
1369.

Except as stated in subdivision (g), a trial by court or jury of the question of mental competence shall proceed in the following order:

(a) (1) The court shall appoint a psychiatrist or licensed psychologist, and any other expert the court may deem appropriate, to examine the defendant. If the defendant or the defendant's counsel informs the court that the defendant is not seeking a finding of mental incompetence, the court shall appoint two psychiatrists, licensed psychologists, or a combination thereof. One of the psychiatrists or licensed psychologists may be named by the defense and one may be named by the prosecution.

(2) The examining psychiatrists or licensed psychologists shall evaluate the nature of the defendant's mental disorder, if any, the defendant's ability or inability to understand the nature of the criminal proceedings or assist counsel in the conduct of a defense in a rational manner as a result of a mental disorder and, if within the scope of their licenses and appropriate to their opinions, whether or not treatment with antipsychotic medication is medically appropriate for the defendant and whether antipsychotic medication is likely to restore the defendant to mental competence. If an examining psychologist is of the opinion that antipsychotic medication may be medically appropriate for the defendant and that the defendant should be evaluated by a psychiatrist to determine if antipsychotic medication is medically appropriate, the psychologist shall inform the court of this opinion and his or her recommendation as to whether a psychiatrist should examine the defendant. The examining psychiatrists or licensed psychologists shall also address the issues of whether the defendant has capacity to make decisions regarding antipsychotic medication and whether the defendant is a danger to self or others. If the defendant is examined by a psychiatrist and the psychiatrist forms an opinion as to whether or not treatment with antipsychotic

medication is medically appropriate, the psychiatrist shall inform the court of his or her opinions as to the likely or potential side effects of the medication, the expected efficacy of the medication, possible alternative treatments, and whether it is medically appropriate to administer antipsychotic medication in the county jail.

(3) If it is suspected the defendant has a developmental disability, the court shall appoint the director of the regional center established under Division 4.5 (commencing with Section 4500) of the Welfare and Institutions Code, or the director's designee, to examine the defendant to determine whether he or she has a developmental disability. The regional center director or his or her designee shall determine whether the defendant has a developmental disability, as defined in Section 4512 of the Welfare and Institutions Code, and is therefore eligible for regional center services and supports. The regional center director or his or her designee shall provide the court with a written report informing the court of this determination.

(4) The regional center director shall recommend to the court a suitable residential facility or state hospital. Prior to issuing an order pursuant to this section, the court shall consider the recommendation of the regional center director. While the person is confined pursuant to order of the court under this section, he or she shall be provided with necessary care and treatment.

(b) (1) The counsel for the defendant shall offer evidence in support of the allegation of mental incompetence.

(2) If the defense declines to offer any evidence in support of the allegation of mental incompetence, the prosecution may do so.

(c) The prosecution shall present its case regarding the issue of the defendant's present mental competence.

(d) Each party may offer rebutting testimony, unless the court, for good reason in furtherance of justice, also permits other evidence in support of the original contention.

(e) When the evidence is concluded, unless the case is submitted without final argument, the prosecution shall make its final argument and the defense shall conclude with its final argument to the court or jury.

(f) In a jury trial, the court shall charge the jury, instructing them on all matters of law necessary for the rendering of a verdict. It shall be presumed that the defendant is mentally competent unless it is proved by a preponderance of the evidence that the defendant is mentally incompetent. The verdict of the jury shall be unanimous.

(g) Only a court trial is required to determine competency in a proceeding for a violation of probation, mandatory supervision, postrelease community supervision, or parole.

(h) (1) The State Department of State Hospitals, on or before July 1, 2017, shall adopt guidelines for education and training standards for a psychiatrist or licensed psychologist to be considered for appointment by the court pursuant to this section. To develop these guidelines, the State Department of State Hospitals shall convene a workgroup comprised of the Judicial Council and groups or individuals representing judges, defense counsel, district attorneys, counties, advocates for people with developmental and mental disabilities, state psychologists and psychiatrists, professional associations and accrediting bodies for psychologists and psychiatrists, and other interested stakeholders.

(2) When making an appointment pursuant to this section, the court shall appoint an expert who meets the guidelines established in accordance with this subdivision or an expert with equivalent experience and skills. If there is no reasonably available expert who meets the guidelines or who has equivalent experience and skills, the court may appoint an expert who does not meet the guidelines.

(Amended by Stats. 2018, Ch. 1008, Sec. 1. (SB 1187) Effective January 1, 2019.)
1369.1.

(a) As used in this chapter, "treatment facility" includes a county jail. Upon the concurrence of the county board of supervisors, the county mental health director, and the county sheriff, the jail may be designated to provide medically approved medication to defendants found to be mentally incompetent and unable to provide informed consent due to a mental disorder, pursuant to this chapter. In the case of Madera, Napa, and Santa Clara Counties, the concurrence shall be with the board of supervisors, the county mental health director, and the county sheriff or the chief of corrections. The provisions of Sections 1370, 1370.01, and 1370.02 shall apply to antipsychotic medications provided in a county jail, provided, however, that the maximum period of time a defendant may be treated in a treatment facility pursuant to this section shall not exceed six months.

(b) This section does not abrogate or limit any law enacted to ensure the due process rights set forth in Sell v. United States (2003) 539 U.S. 166.

(Amended by Stats. 2015, Ch. 26, Sec. 29. (SB 85) Effective June 24, 2015.)
1370.

(a) (1) (A) If the defendant is found mentally competent, the criminal process shall resume, the trial on the offense charged or hearing on the alleged violation shall proceed, and judgment may be pronounced.

(B) If the defendant is found mentally incompetent, the trial, the hearing on the alleged violation, or the judgment shall be suspended until the person becomes mentally competent.

(i) The court shall order that the mentally incompetent defendant be delivered by the sheriff to a State Department of State Hospitals facility, as defined in Section 4100 of the Welfare and Institutions Code, as directed by the State Department of State Hospitals, or to any other available public or private treatment facility, including a community-based residential treatment system established pursuant to Article 1 (commencing with Section 5670) of Chapter 2.5 of Part 2 of Division 5 of the Welfare and Institutions Code if the facility has a secured perimeter or a locked and controlled treatment facility, approved by the community program director that will promote the defendant's speedy restoration to mental competence, or placed on outpatient status as specified in Section 1600.

(ii) However, if the action against the defendant who has been found mentally incompetent is on a complaint charging a felony offense specified in Section 290, the prosecutor shall determine whether the defendant previously has been found mentally incompetent to stand trial pursuant to this chapter on a charge of a Section 290 offense, or whether the defendant is currently the subject of a pending Section 1368 proceeding arising out of a charge of a Section 290 offense. If either determination is made, the prosecutor shall notify the court and defendant in writing. After this notification, and opportunity for hearing, the court shall order that the defendant be delivered by the sheriff to a State Department of State Hospitals facility, as directed by the State Department of State Hospitals, or other secure treatment facility for the care and treatment of persons with a mental health disorder, unless the court makes specific findings on the record that an alternative placement would provide more appropriate treatment for the defendant and would not pose a danger to the health and safety of others.

(iii) If the action against the defendant who has been found mentally incompetent is on a complaint charging a felony offense specified in Section 290 and the defendant has been denied bail pursuant to subdivision (b) of Section 12 of Article I of the California Constitution because the court has found, based upon clear and convincing evidence, a substantial likelihood that the person's release would result in great bodily harm to others, the court shall order that the defendant be delivered by the sheriff to a State Department of State Hospitals facility, as directed by the State Department of State Hospitals, unless the court makes specific findings on the record that an alternative placement would provide more appropriate treatment for the defendant and would not pose a danger to the health and safety of others.

(iv) If, at any time after the court finds that the defendant is mentally incompetent and before the defendant is transported to a facility pursuant to this section, the court is provided with any information that the defendant may benefit from diversion pursuant to

Chapter 2.8A (commencing with Section 1001.35) of Title 6, the court may make a finding that the defendant is an appropriate candidate for diversion.

(v) If a defendant is found by the court to be an appropriate candidate for diversion pursuant to clause (iv), the defendant's eligibility shall be determined pursuant to Section 1001.36. A defendant granted diversion may participate for the lesser of the period specified in paragraph (1) of subdivision (c) or two years. If, during that period, the court determines that criminal proceedings should be reinstated pursuant to subdivision (d) of Section 1001.36, the court shall, pursuant to Section 1369, appoint a psychiatrist, licensed psychologist, or any other expert the court may deem appropriate, to determine the defendant's competence to stand trial.

(vi) Upon the dismissal of charges at the conclusion of the period of diversion, pursuant to subdivision (e) of Section 1001.36, a defendant shall no longer be deemed incompetent to stand trial pursuant to this section.

(vii) The clerk of the court shall notify the Department of Justice, in writing, of a finding of mental incompetence with respect to a defendant who is subject to clause (ii) or (iii) for inclusion in his or her state summary criminal history information.

(C) Upon the filing of a certificate of restoration to competence, the court shall order that the defendant be returned to court in accordance with Section 1372. The court shall transmit a copy of its order to the community program director or a designee.

(D) A defendant charged with a violent felony may not be delivered to a State Department of State Hospitals facility or treatment facility pursuant to this subdivision unless the State Department of State Hospitals facility or treatment facility has a secured perimeter or a locked and controlled treatment facility, and the judge determines that the public safety will be protected.

(E) For purposes of this paragraph, "violent felony" means an offense specified in subdivision (c) of Section 667.5.

(F) A defendant charged with a violent felony may be placed on outpatient status, as specified in Section 1600, only if the court finds that the placement will not pose a danger to the health or safety of others. If the court places a defendant charged with a violent felony on outpatient status, as specified in Section 1600, the court shall serve copies of the placement order on defense counsel, the sheriff in the county where the defendant will be placed, and the district attorney for the county in which the violent felony charges are pending against the defendant.

(G) If, at any time after the court has declared a defendant incompetent to stand trial pursuant to this section, counsel for the defendant or a jail medical or mental health staff provider provides the court with substantial evidence that the defendant's psychiatric symptoms have changed to such a degree as to create a doubt in the mind of the judge as to the defendant's current mental incompetence, the court may appoint a psychiatrist or a licensed psychologist to opine as to whether the defendant has regained competence. If, in the opinion of that expert, the defendant has regained competence, the court shall proceed as if a certificate of restoration of competence has been returned pursuant to paragraph (1) of subdivision (a) of Section 1372, except that a presumption of competency shall not apply and a hearing shall be held to determine whether competency has been restored.

(2) Prior to making the order directing that the defendant be committed to the State Department of State Hospitals or other treatment facility or placed on outpatient status, the court shall proceed as follows:

(A) The court shall order the community program director or a designee to evaluate the defendant and to submit to the court within 15 judicial days of the order a written recommendation as to whether the defendant should be required to undergo outpatient treatment, or be committed to the State Department of State Hospitals or to any other treatment facility. A person shall not be admitted to a State Department of State Hospitals facility or other treatment facility or placed on outpatient status under this section without having been evaluated by the community program director or a designee. The community program director or designee shall evaluate the appropriate placement for the defendant between a State Department of State Hospitals facility or the community-based residential treatment system based upon guidelines provided by the State Department of State Hospitals.

(B) The court shall hear and determine whether the defendant lacks capacity to make decisions regarding the administration of antipsychotic medication. The court shall consider opinions in the reports prepared pursuant to subdivision (a) of Section 1369, as applicable to the issue of whether the defendant lacks capacity to make decisions regarding the administration of antipsychotic medication, and shall proceed as follows:

(i) The court shall hear and determine whether any of the following is true:

(I) The defendant lacks capacity to make decisions regarding antipsychotic medication, the defendant's mental disorder requires medical treatment with antipsychotic medication, and, if the defendant's mental disorder is not treated with antipsychotic medication, it is probable that serious harm to the physical or mental health of the patient will result. Probability of serious harm to the physical or mental health of the defendant requires evidence that the defendant is presently suffering adverse effects to his or her physical or mental health, or the defendant has previously suffered these effects as a result of a mental disorder and his or her condition is substantially deteriorating. The fact that a defendant has a diagnosis of a mental disorder does not alone establish probability of serious harm to the physical or mental health of the defendant.

(II) The defendant is a danger to others, in that the defendant has inflicted, attempted to inflict, or made a serious threat of inflicting substantial physical harm on another while in custody, or the defendant had inflicted, attempted to inflict, or made a serious threat of inflicting substantial physical harm on another that resulted in his or her being taken into custody, and the defendant presents, as a result of mental disorder or mental defect, a demonstrated danger of inflicting substantial physical harm on others. Demonstrated danger may be based on an assessment of the defendant's present mental condition, including a consideration of past behavior of the defendant within six years prior to the time the defendant last attempted to inflict, inflicted, or threatened to inflict substantial physical harm on another, and other relevant evidence.

(III) The people have charged the defendant with a serious crime against the person or property, involuntary administration of antipsychotic medication is substantially likely to render the defendant competent to stand trial, the medication is unlikely to have side effects that interfere with the defendant's ability to understand the nature of the criminal proceedings or to assist counsel in the conduct of a defense in a reasonable manner, less intrusive treatments are unlikely to have substantially the same results, and antipsychotic medication is in the patient's best medical interest in light of his or her medical condition.

(ii) If the court finds any of the conditions described in clause (i) to be true, the court shall issue an order authorizing involuntary administration of antipsychotic medication to the defendant when and as prescribed by the defendant's treating psychiatrist at any facility housing the defendant for purposes of this chapter. The order shall be valid for no more than one year, pursuant to subparagraph (A) of paragraph (7). The court shall not order involuntary administration of psychotropic medication under subclause (III) of clause (i) unless the court has first found that the defendant does not meet the criteria for involuntary administration of psychotropic medication under subclause (I) of clause (i) and does not meet the criteria under subclause (II) of clause (i).

(iii) In all cases, the treating hospital, facility, or program may administer medically appropriate antipsychotic medication prescribed by a psychiatrist in an emergency as described in subdivision (m) of Section 5008 of the Welfare and Institutions Code.

(iv) If the court has determined that the defendant has the capacity to make decisions regarding antipsychotic medication, and if the defendant, with advice of his or her counsel, consents, the court order of commitment shall include confirmation that antipsychotic medication may be given to the defendant as prescribed by a treating psychiatrist pursuant to the defendant's consent. The commitment order shall also indicate that, if the defendant withdraws consent for antipsychotic medication, after the treating psychiatrist complies with the provisions of subparagraph (C), the defendant shall be returned to court for a hearing in accordance with subparagraphs (C) and (D) regarding whether antipsychotic medication shall be administered involuntarily.

(v) If the court has determined that the defendant has the capacity to make decisions regarding antipsychotic medication and if the defendant, with advice from his or her counsel, does not consent, the court order for commitment shall indicate that, after the treating psychiatrist complies with the provisions of subparagraph (C), the defendant shall be returned to court for a hearing in accordance with subparagraphs (C) and (D) regarding whether antipsychotic medication shall be administered involuntarily.

(vi) A report made pursuant to paragraph (1) of subdivision (b) shall include a description of antipsychotic medication administered to the defendant and its effects and side effects, including effects on the defendant's appearance or behavior that would affect the defendant's ability to understand the nature of the criminal proceedings or to assist counsel in the conduct of a defense in a reasonable manner. During the time the defendant is confined in a State Department of State Hospitals facility or other treatment facility or placed on outpatient status, either the defendant or the people may request that the court review any order made pursuant to this subdivision. The defendant, to the same extent enjoyed by other patients in the State Department of State Hospitals facility or other treatment facility, shall have the right to contact the patients' rights advocate regarding his or her rights under this section.

(C) If the defendant consented to antipsychotic medication as described in clause (iv) of subparagraph (B), but subsequently withdraws his or her consent, or, if involuntary antipsychotic medication was not ordered pursuant to clause (v) of subparagraph (B), and the treating psychiatrist determines that antipsychotic medication has become medically necessary and appropriate, the treating psychiatrist shall make efforts to obtain informed consent from the defendant for antipsychotic medication. If informed consent is not obtained from the defendant, and the treating psychiatrist is of the opinion that the defendant lacks capacity to make decisions regarding antipsychotic medication based on the conditions described in subclause (I) or (II) of clause (i) of subparagraph (B), the treating psychiatrist shall certify whether the lack of capacity and any applicable conditions described above exist. That certification shall contain an assessment of the current mental status of the defendant and the opinion of the treating psychiatrist that involuntary antipsychotic medication has become medically necessary and appropriate.

(D) (i) If the treating psychiatrist certifies that antipsychotic medication has become medically necessary and appropriate pursuant to subparagraph (C), antipsychotic medication may be administered to the defendant for not more than 21 days, provided, however, that, within 72 hours of the certification, the defendant is provided a medication review hearing before an administrative law judge to be conducted at the facility where the defendant is receiving treatment. The treating psychiatrist shall present the case for the certification for involuntary treatment and the defendant shall be represented by an attorney or a patients' rights advocate. The attorney or patients' rights advocate shall be appointed to meet with the defendant no later than one day prior to the medication review hearing to review the defendant's rights at the medication review hearing, discuss the process, answer questions or concerns regarding involuntary medication or the hearing, assist the defendant in preparing for the hearing and advocating for his or her interests at the hearing, review the panel's final determination following the hearing, advise the defendant of his or her right to judicial review of the panel's decision, and provide the defendant with referral information for legal advice on the subject. The defendant shall also have the following rights with respect to the medication review hearing:

(I) To be given timely access to the defendant's records.

(II) To be present at the hearing, unless the defendant waives that right.

(III) To present evidence at the hearing.

(IV) To question persons presenting evidence supporting involuntary medication.

(V) To make reasonable requests for attendance of witnesses on the defendant's behalf.

(VI) To a hearing conducted in an impartial and informal manner.

(ii) If the administrative law judge determines that the defendant either meets the criteria specified in subclause (I) of clause (i) of subparagraph (B), or meets the criteria specified in subclause (II) of clause (i) of subparagraph (B), antipsychotic medication may continue to be administered to the defendant for the 21-day certification period. Concurrently with the treating psychiatrist's certification, the treating psychiatrist shall file a copy of the certification and a petition with the court for issuance of an order to administer antipsychotic medication beyond the 21-day certification period. For purposes of this subparagraph, the treating psychiatrist shall not be required to pay or deposit any fee for the filing of the petition or other document or paper related to the petition.

(iii) If the administrative law judge disagrees with the certification, medication may not be administered involuntarily until the court determines that antipsychotic medication should be administered pursuant to this section.

(iv) The court shall provide notice to the prosecuting attorney and to the attorney representing the defendant, and shall hold a hearing, no later than 18 days from the date of the certification, to determine whether antipsychotic medication should be ordered beyond the certification period.

(v) If, as a result of the hearing, the court determines that antipsychotic medication should be administered beyond the certification period, the court shall issue an order authorizing the administration of that medication.

(vi) The court shall render its decision on the petition and issue its order no later than three calendar days after the hearing and, in any event, no later than the expiration of the 21-day certification period.

(vii) If the administrative law judge upholds the certification pursuant to clause (ii), the court may, for a period not to exceed 14 days, extend the certification and continue the hearing pursuant to stipulation between the parties or upon a finding of good cause. In determining good cause, the court may review the petition filed with the court, the administrative law judge's order, and any additional testimony needed by the court to determine if it is appropriate to continue medication beyond the 21-day certification and for a period of up to 14 days.

(viii) The district attorney, county counsel, or representative of a facility where a defendant found incompetent to stand trial is committed may petition the court for an order to administer involuntary medication pursuant to the criteria set forth in subclauses (II) and (III) of clause (i) of subparagraph (B). The order is reviewable as provided in paragraph (7).

(3) When the court orders that the defendant be committed to a State Department of State Hospitals facility or other public or private treatment facility, the court shall provide copies of the following documents prior to the admission of the defendant to the State Department of State Hospitals or other treatment facility where the defendant is to be committed:

(A) The commitment order, including a specification of the charges.

(B) A computation or statement setting forth the maximum term of commitment in accordance with subdivision (c).

(C) A computation or statement setting forth the amount of credit for time served, if any, to be deducted from the maximum term of commitment.

(D) State summary criminal history information.

(E) Arrest reports prepared by the police department or other law enforcement agency.

(F) Court-ordered psychiatric examination or evaluation reports.

(G) The community program director's placement recommendation report.

(H) Records of a finding of mental incompetence pursuant to this chapter arising out of a complaint charging a felony offense specified in Section 290 or a pending Section 1368 proceeding arising out of a charge of a Section 290 offense.

(I) Medical records.

(4) When the defendant is committed to a treatment facility pursuant to clause (i) of subparagraph (B) of paragraph (1) or the court makes the findings specified in clause (ii) or (iii) of subparagraph (B) of paragraph (1) to assign the defendant to a treatment facility other than a State Department of State Hospitals facility or other secure treatment facility, the court shall order that notice be given to the appropriate law enforcement agency or agencies having local jurisdiction at the placement facility of a finding of mental incompetence pursuant to this chapter arising out of a charge of a Section 290 offense.

(5) When directing that the defendant be confined in a State Department of State Hospitals facility pursuant to this subdivision, the court shall commit the patient to the State Department of State Hospitals.

(6) (A) If the defendant is committed or transferred to the State Department of State Hospitals pursuant to this section, the court may, upon receiving the written recommendation of the medical director of the State Department of State Hospitals facility and the community program director that the defendant be transferred to a public or private treatment facility approved by the community program director, order the defendant transferred to that facility. If the defendant is committed or transferred to a public or private treatment facility approved by the community program director, the court may, upon receiving the written recommendation of the community program director, transfer the defendant to the State Department of State Hospitals or to another public or private treatment facility approved by the community program director. In the event of dismissal of the criminal charges before the defendant recovers competence, the person shall be subject to the applicable provisions of the Lanterman-Petris-Short Act (Part 1 (commencing with Section 5000) of Division 5 of the Welfare and Institutions Code). If either the defendant or the prosecutor chooses to contest either kind of order of transfer, a petition may be filed in the court for a hearing, which shall be held if the court determines that sufficient grounds exist. At the hearing, the prosecuting attorney or the defendant may present evidence bearing on the order of transfer. The court shall use the same standards as are used in conducting probation revocation hearings pursuant to Section 1203.2.

Prior to making an order for transfer under this section, the court shall notify the defendant, the attorney of record for the defendant, the prosecuting attorney, and the community program director or a designee.

(B) If the defendant is initially committed to a State Department of State Hospitals facility or secure treatment facility pursuant to clause (ii) or (iii) of subparagraph (B) of paragraph (1) and is subsequently transferred to any other facility, copies of the documents specified in paragraph (3) shall be taken with the defendant to each subsequent facility to which the defendant is transferred. The transferring facility shall also notify the appropriate law enforcement agency or agencies having local jurisdiction at the site of the new facility that the defendant is a person subject to clause (ii) or (iii) of subparagraph (B) of paragraph (1).

(7) (A) An order by the court authorizing involuntary medication of the defendant shall be valid for no more than one year. The court shall review the order at the time of the review of the initial report and the six-month progress reports pursuant to paragraph (1) of subdivision (b) to determine if the grounds for the authorization remain. In the review, the court shall consider the reports of the treating psychiatrist or psychiatrists and the defendant's patients' rights advocate or attorney. The court may require testimony from the treating psychiatrist and the patients' rights advocate or attorney, if necessary. The court may continue the order authorizing involuntary medication for up to another six months, or vacate the order, or make any other appropriate order.

(B) Within 60 days before the expiration of the one-year involuntary medication order, the district attorney, county counsel, or representative of any facility where a defendant found incompetent to stand trial is committed may petition the committing court for a renewal, subject to the same conditions and requirements as in subparagraph (A). The petition shall include the basis for involuntary medication set forth in clause (i) of subparagraph (B) of paragraph (2). Notice of the petition shall be provided to the defendant, the defendant's attorney, and the district attorney. The court shall hear and determine whether the defendant continues to meet the criteria set forth in clause (i) of subparagraph (B) of paragraph (2). The hearing on a petition to renew an order for involuntary medication shall be conducted prior to the expiration of the current order.

(8) For purposes of subparagraph (D) of paragraph (2) and paragraph (7), if the treating psychiatrist determines that there is a need, based on preserving his or her rapport with the patient or preventing harm, the treating psychiatrist may request that the facility medical director designate another psychiatrist to act in the place of the treating psychiatrist. If the medical director of the facility designates another psychiatrist to act pursuant to this paragraph, the treating psychiatrist shall brief the acting psychiatrist of the relevant facts of the case and the acting psychiatrist shall examine the patient prior to the hearing.

(b) (1) Within 90 days of a commitment made pursuant to subdivision (a), the medical director of the State Department of State Hospitals facility or other treatment facility to which the defendant is confined shall make a written report to the court and the community program director for the county or region of commitment, or a designee, concerning the defendant's progress toward recovery of mental competence and whether the administration of antipsychotic medication remains necessary. If the defendant is on outpatient status, the outpatient treatment staff shall make a written report to the community program director concerning the defendant's progress toward recovery of mental competence. Within 90 days of placement on outpatient status, the community program director shall report to the court on this matter. If the defendant has not recovered mental competence, but the report discloses a substantial likelihood that the defendant will regain mental competence in the foreseeable future, the defendant shall remain in the State Department of State Hospitals facility or other treatment facility or on outpatient status. Thereafter, at six-month intervals or until the defendant becomes mentally competent, if the defendant is confined in a treatment facility, the medical director of the State Department of State Hospitals facility or person in charge of the facility shall report, in writing, to the court and the community program director or a designee regarding the defendant's progress toward recovery of mental competence and whether the administration of antipsychotic medication remains necessary. If the defendant is on outpatient status, after the initial 90-day report, the outpatient treatment staff shall report to the community program director on the defendant's progress toward recovery, and the community program director shall report to the court on this matter at six-month intervals. A copy of these reports shall be provided to the prosecutor and defense counsel by the court.

(A) If the report indicates that there is no substantial likelihood that the defendant will regain mental competence in the foreseeable future, the committing court shall order the defendant to be returned to the court for proceedings pursuant to paragraph (2) of subdivision (c) no later than 10 days following receipt of the report. The court shall transmit a copy of its order to the community program director or a designee.

(B) If the report indicates that there is no substantial likelihood that the defendant will regain mental competence in the foreseeable future, the medical director of the State Department of State Hospitals facility or other treatment facility to which the defendant is confined shall do both of the following:

(i) Promptly notify and provide a copy of the report to the defense counsel and the district attorney.

(ii) Provide a separate notification, in compliance with applicable privacy laws, to the committing county's sheriff that transportation will be needed for the patient.

(2) If the court has issued an order authorizing the treating facility to involuntarily administer antipsychotic medication to the defendant, the reports made pursuant to paragraph (1) concerning the defendant's progress toward regaining competency shall also consider the issue of involuntary medication. Each report shall include, but not be limited to, all of the following:

(A) Whether or not the defendant has the capacity to make decisions concerning antipsychotic medication.

(B) If the defendant lacks capacity to make decisions concerning antipsychotic medication, whether the defendant risks serious harm to his or her physical or mental health if not treated with antipsychotic medication.

(C) Whether or not the defendant presents a danger to others if he or she is not treated with antipsychotic medication.

(D) Whether the defendant has a mental disorder for which medications are the only effective treatment.

(E) Whether there are any side effects from the medication currently being experienced by the defendant that would interfere with the defendant's ability to collaborate with counsel.

(F) Whether there are any effective alternatives to medication.

(G) How quickly the medication is likely to bring the defendant to competency.

(H) Whether the treatment plan includes methods other than medication to restore the defendant to competency.

(I) A statement, if applicable, that no medication is likely to restore the defendant to competency.

(3) After reviewing the reports, the court shall determine whether or not grounds for the order authorizing involuntary administration of antipsychotic medication still exist and shall do one of the following:

(A) If the original grounds for involuntary medication still exist, the order authorizing the treating facility to involuntarily administer antipsychotic medication to the defendant shall remain in effect.

(B) If the original grounds for involuntary medication no longer exist, and there is no other basis for involuntary administration of antipsychotic medication, the order for the involuntary administration of antipsychotic medication shall be vacated.

(C) If the original grounds for involuntary medication no longer exist, and the report states that there is another basis for involuntary administration of antipsychotic medication, the court shall set a hearing within 21 days to determine whether the order for the involuntary administration of antipsychotic medication shall be vacated or whether a new order for the involuntary administration of antipsychotic medication shall be issued. The hearing shall proceed as set forth in subparagraph (B) of paragraph (2) of subdivision (a).

(4) If it is determined by the court that treatment for the defendant's mental impairment is not being conducted, the defendant shall be returned to the committing court. The court shall transmit a copy of its order to the community program director or a designee.

(5) At each review by the court specified in this subdivision, the court shall determine if the security level of housing and treatment is appropriate and may make an order in accordance with its determination. If the court determines that the defendant shall continue to be treated in the State Department of State Hospitals facility or on an outpatient basis, the court shall determine issues concerning administration of antipsychotic medication, as set forth in subparagraph (B) of paragraph (2) of subdivision (a).

(c) (1) At the end of two years from the date of commitment or a period of commitment equal to the maximum term of imprisonment provided by law for the most serious offense charged in the information, indictment, or misdemeanor complaint, or the maximum term of imprisonment provided by law for a violation of probation or mandatory supervision, whichever is shorter, but no later than 90 days prior to the expiration of the defendant's term of commitment, a defendant who has not recovered mental competence shall be returned to the committing court. The court shall notify the community program director or a designee of the return and of any resulting court orders.

(2) Whenever a defendant is returned to the court pursuant to paragraph (1) or (4) of subdivision (b) or paragraph (1) of this subdivision and it appears to the court that the defendant is gravely disabled, as defined in subparagraph (A) or (B) of paragraph (1) of subdivision (h) of Section 5008 of the Welfare and Institutions Code, the court shall order the conservatorship investigator of the county of commitment of the defendant to initiate conservatorship proceedings for the defendant pursuant to Chapter 3 (commencing with Section 5350) of Part 1 of Division 5 of the Welfare and Institutions Code. Hearings required in the conservatorship proceedings shall be held in the superior court in the county that ordered the commitment. The court shall transmit a copy of the order directing initiation of conservatorship proceedings to the community program director or a designee, the sheriff and the district attorney of the county in which criminal charges are pending, and the defendant's counsel of record. The court shall notify the community program director or a designee, the sheriff and district attorney of the county in which criminal charges are pending, and the defendant's counsel of record of the outcome of the conservatorship proceedings.

(3) If a change in placement is proposed for a defendant who is committed pursuant to subparagraph (A) or (B) of paragraph (1) of subdivision (h) of Section 5008 of the Welfare and Institutions Code, the court shall provide notice and an opportunity to be heard with respect to the proposed placement of the defendant to the sheriff and the district attorney of the county in which the criminal charges or revocation proceedings are pending.

(4) If the defendant is confined in a treatment facility, a copy of any report to the committing court regarding the defendant's progress toward recovery of mental competence shall be provided by the committing court to the prosecutor and to the defense counsel.

(d) With the exception of proceedings alleging a violation of mandatory supervision, the criminal action remains subject to dismissal pursuant to Section 1385. If the criminal action is dismissed, the court shall transmit a copy of the order of dismissal to the community program director or a designee. In a proceeding alleging a violation of mandatory supervision, if the person is not placed under a conservatorship as described in paragraph (2) of subdivision (c), or if a conservatorship is terminated, the court shall reinstate mandatory supervision and may modify the terms and conditions of supervision to include appropriate mental health treatment or refer the matter to a local mental health court, reentry court, or other collaborative justice court available for improving the mental health of the defendant.

(e) If the criminal action against the defendant is dismissed, the defendant shall be released from commitment ordered under this section, but without prejudice to the initiation of proceedings that may be appropriate under the Lanterman-Petris-Short Act (Part 1 (commencing with Section 5000) of Division 5 of the Welfare and Institutions Code).

(f) As used in this chapter, "community program director" means the person, agency, or entity designated by the State Department of State Hospitals pursuant to Section 1605 of this code and Section 4360 of the Welfare and Institutions Code.

(g) For the purpose of this section, "secure treatment facility" does not include, except for State Department of State Hospitals facilities, state developmental centers, and correctional treatment facilities, any facility licensed pursuant to Chapter 2 (commencing with Section 1250) of, Chapter 3 (commencing with Section 1500) of, or Chapter 3.2 (commencing with Section 1569) of, Division 2 of the Health and Safety Code, or any community board and care facility.

(h) This section does not preclude a defendant from filing a petition for habeas corpus to challenge the continuing validity of an order authorizing a treatment facility or outpatient program to involuntarily administer antipsychotic medication to a person being treated as incompetent to stand trial.
(Amended by Stats. 2018, Ch. 1008, Sec. 2. (SB 1187) Effective January 1, 2019.)
1370.01.
(a) (1) If the defendant is found mentally competent, the criminal process shall resume, the trial on the offense charged shall proceed, and judgment may be pronounced. If the defendant is found mentally incompetent, the trial, judgment, or hearing on the alleged violation shall be suspended until the person becomes mentally competent, and the court shall order that (A) in the meantime, the defendant be delivered by the sheriff to an available public or private treatment facility approved by the county mental health director that will promote the defendant's speedy restoration to mental competence, or placed on outpatient status as specified in this section, and (B) upon the filing of a certificate of restoration to competence, the defendant be returned to court in accordance with Section 1372. The court shall transmit a copy of its order to the county mental health director or his or her designee.
(2) If the defendant is found mentally incompetent, the court may make a finding that the defendant is an appropriate candidate for diversion pursuant to Chapter 2.8A (commencing with Section 1001.35) of Title 6, and may, if the defendant is eligible pursuant to Section 1001.36, grant diversion for a period not to exceed that set forth in paragraph (1) of subdivision (c). Upon the dismissal of charges at the conclusion of the period of diversion, pursuant to subdivision (e) of Section 1001.36, a defendant shall no longer be deemed incompetent to stand trial pursuant to this section.
(3) Prior to making the order directing that the defendant be confined in a treatment facility or placed on outpatient status, the court shall proceed as follows:
(A) The court shall order the county mental health director or his or her designee to evaluate the defendant and to submit to the court within 15 judicial days of the order a written recommendation as to whether the defendant should be required to undergo outpatient treatment, or committed to a treatment facility. No person shall be admitted to a treatment facility or placed on outpatient status under this section without having been evaluated by the county mental health director or his or her designee. No person shall be admitted to a state hospital under this section unless the county mental health director finds that there is no less restrictive appropriate placement available and the county mental health director has a contract with the State Department of State Hospitals for these placements.
(B) The court shall hear and determine whether the defendant, with advice of his or her counsel, consents to the administration of antipsychotic medication, and shall proceed as follows:
(i) If the defendant, with advice of his or her counsel, consents, the court order of commitment shall include confirmation that antipsychotic medication may be given to the defendant as prescribed by a treating psychiatrist pursuant to the defendant's consent. The commitment order shall also indicate that, if the defendant withdraws consent for antipsychotic medication, after the treating psychiatrist complies with the provisions of subparagraph (C), the defendant shall be returned to court for a hearing in accordance with this subdivision regarding whether antipsychotic medication shall be administered involuntarily.
(ii) If the defendant does not consent to the administration of medication, the court shall hear and determine whether any of the following is true:
(I) The defendant lacks capacity to make decisions regarding antipsychotic medication, the defendant's mental disorder requires medical treatment with antipsychotic medication, and, if the defendant's mental disorder is not treated with antipsychotic medication, it is probable that serious harm to the physical or mental health of the patient will result. Probability of serious harm to the physical or mental health of the defendant requires evidence that the defendant is presently suffering adverse effects to his or her physical or mental health, or the defendant has previously suffered these effects as a result of a mental disorder and his or her condition is substantially deteriorating. The fact that a defendant has a diagnosis of a mental disorder does not alone establish probability of serious harm to the physical or mental health of the defendant.
(II) The defendant is a danger to others, in that the defendant has inflicted, attempted to inflict, or made a serious threat of inflicting substantial physical harm on another while in custody, or the defendant had inflicted, attempted to inflict, or made a serious threat of inflicting substantial physical harm on another that resulted in his or her being taken into custody, and the defendant presents, as a result of mental disorder or mental defect, a demonstrated danger of inflicting substantial physical harm on others. Demonstrated danger may be based on an assessment of the defendant's present mental condition, including a consideration of past behavior of the defendant within six years prior to the time the defendant last attempted to inflict, inflicted, or threatened to inflict substantial physical harm on another, and other relevant evidence.
(III) The people have charged the defendant with a serious crime against the person or property; involuntary administration of antipsychotic medication is substantially likely to render the defendant competent to stand trial; the medication is unlikely to have side effects that interfere with the defendant's ability to understand the nature of the criminal proceedings or to assist counsel in the conduct of a defense in a reasonable manner; less intrusive treatments are unlikely to have substantially the same results; and antipsychotic medication is in the patient's best medical interest in light of his or her medical condition.
(iii) If the court finds any of the conditions described in clause (ii) to be true, the court shall issue an order authorizing the treatment facility to involuntarily administer antipsychotic medication to the defendant when and as prescribed by the defendant's treating psychiatrist. The court shall not order involuntary administration of psychotropic medication under subclause (III) of clause (ii) unless the court has first found that the defendant does not meet the criteria for involuntary administration of psychotropic medication under subclause (I) of clause (ii) and does not meet the criteria under subclause (II) of clause (ii).
(iv) In all cases, the treating hospital, facility, or program may administer medically appropriate antipsychotic medication prescribed by a psychiatrist in an emergency as described in subdivision (m) of Section 5008 of the Welfare and Institutions Code.
(v) Any report made pursuant to subdivision (b) shall include a description of any antipsychotic medication administered to the defendant and its effects and side effects, including effects on the defendant's appearance or behavior that would affect the defendant's ability to understand the nature of the criminal proceedings or to assist counsel in the conduct of a defense in a reasonable manner. During the time the defendant is confined in a state hospital or other treatment facility or placed on outpatient status, either the defendant or the people may request that the court review any order made pursuant to this subdivision. The defendant, to the same extent enjoyed by other patients in the state hospital or other treatment facility, shall have the right to contact the patients' rights advocate regarding his or her rights under this section.
(C) If the defendant consented to antipsychotic medication as described in clause (i) of subparagraph (B), but subsequently withdraws his or her consent, or, if involuntary antipsychotic medication was not ordered pursuant to clause (ii) of subparagraph (B), and the treating psychiatrist determines that antipsychotic medication has become medically necessary and appropriate, the treating psychiatrist shall make efforts to obtain informed consent from the defendant for antipsychotic medication. If informed consent is not obtained from the defendant, and the treating psychiatrist is of the opinion that the defendant lacks capacity to make decisions regarding antipsychotic medication as specified in subclause (I) of clause (ii) of subparagraph (B), or that the defendant is a danger to others as specified in subclause (II) of clause (ii) of

subparagraph (B), the committing court shall be notified of this, including an assessment of the current mental status of the defendant and the opinion of the treating psychiatrist that involuntary antipsychotic medication has become medically necessary and appropriate. The court shall provide copies of the report to the prosecuting attorney and to the attorney representing the defendant and shall set a hearing to determine whether involuntary antipsychotic medication should be ordered in the manner described in subparagraph (B).
(4) When the court, after considering the placement recommendation of the county mental health director required in paragraph (3), orders that the defendant be confined in a public or private treatment facility, the court shall provide copies of the following documents which shall be taken with the defendant to the treatment facility where the defendant is to be confined:
(A) The commitment order, including a specification of the charges.
(B) A computation or statement setting forth the maximum term of commitment in accordance with subdivision (c).
(C) A computation or statement setting forth the amount of credit for time served, if any, to be deducted from the maximum term of commitment.
(D) State summary criminal history information.
(E) Any arrest reports prepared by the police department or other law enforcement agency.
(F) Any court-ordered psychiatric examination or evaluation reports.
(G) The county mental health director's placement recommendation report.
(5) A person subject to commitment under this section may be placed on outpatient status under the supervision of the county mental health director or his or her designee by order of the court in accordance with the procedures contained in Title 15 (commencing with Section 1600) except that where the term "community program director" appears the term "county mental health director" shall be substituted.
(6) If the defendant is committed or transferred to a public or private treatment facility approved by the county mental health director, the court may, upon receiving the written recommendation of the county mental health director, transfer the defendant to another public or private treatment facility approved by the county mental health director. In the event of dismissal of the criminal charges before the defendant recovers competence, the person shall be subject to the applicable provisions of Part 1 (commencing with Section 5000) of Division 5 of the Welfare and Institutions Code. Where either the defendant or the prosecutor chooses to contest the order of transfer, a petition may be filed in the court for a hearing, which shall be held if the court determines that sufficient grounds exist. At the hearing, the prosecuting attorney or the defendant may present evidence bearing on the order of transfer. The court shall use the same standards as are used in conducting probation revocation hearings pursuant to Section 1203.2. Prior to making an order for transfer under this section, the court shall notify the defendant, the attorney of record for the defendant, the prosecuting attorney, and the county mental health director or his or her designee.
(b) Within 90 days of a commitment made pursuant to subdivision (a), the medical director of the treatment facility to which the defendant is confined shall make a written report to the court and the county mental health director or his or her designee, concerning the defendant's progress toward recovery of mental competence. Where the defendant is on outpatient status, the outpatient treatment staff shall make a written report to the county mental health director concerning the defendant's progress toward recovery of mental competence. Within 90 days of placement on outpatient status, the county mental health director shall report to the court on this matter. If the defendant has not recovered mental competence, but the report discloses a substantial likelihood that the defendant will regain mental competence in the foreseeable future, the defendant shall remain in the treatment facility or on outpatient status. Thereafter, at six-month intervals or until the defendant becomes mentally competent, where the defendant is confined in a treatment facility, the medical director of the hospital or person in charge of the facility shall report in writing to the court and the county mental health director or a designee regarding the defendant's progress toward recovery of mental competence. Where the defendant is on outpatient status, after the initial 90-day report, the outpatient treatment staff shall report to the county mental health director on the defendant's progress toward recovery, and the county mental health director shall report to the court on this matter at six-month intervals. A copy of these reports shall be provided to the prosecutor and defense counsel by the court. If the report indicates that there is no substantial likelihood that the defendant will regain mental competence in the foreseeable future, the committing court shall order the defendant to be returned to the court for proceedings pursuant to paragraph (2) of subdivision (c). The court shall transmit a copy of its order to the county mental health director or his or her designee.
(c) (1) If, at the end of one year from the date of commitment or a period of commitment equal to the maximum term of imprisonment provided by law for the most serious offense charged in the misdemeanor complaint, whichever is shorter, the defendant has not recovered mental competence, the defendant shall be returned to the committing court. The court shall notify the county mental health director or his or her designee of the return and of any resulting court orders.
(2) Whenever any defendant is returned to the court pursuant to subdivision (b) or paragraph (1) of this subdivision and it appears to the court that the defendant is gravely disabled, as defined in subparagraph (A) of paragraph (1) of subdivision (h) of Section 5008 of the Welfare and Institutions Code, the court shall order the conservatorship investigator of the county of commitment of the defendant to initiate conservatorship proceedings for the defendant pursuant to Chapter 3 (commencing with Section 5350) of Part 1 of Division 5 of the Welfare and Institutions Code. Any hearings required in the conservatorship proceedings shall be held in the superior court in the county that ordered the commitment. The court shall transmit a copy of the order directing initiation of conservatorship proceedings to the county mental health director or his or her designee and shall notify the county mental health director or his or her designee of the outcome of the proceedings.
(d) The criminal action remains subject to dismissal pursuant to Section 1385. If the criminal action is dismissed, the court shall transmit a copy of the order of dismissal to the county mental health director or his or her designee.
(e) If the criminal charge against the defendant is dismissed, the defendant shall be released from any commitment ordered under this section, but without prejudice to the initiation of any proceedings which may be appropriate under Part 1 (commencing with Section 5000) of Division 5 of the Welfare and Institutions Code.
(Amended by Stats. 2018, Ch. 34, Sec. 26. (AB 1810) Effective June 27, 2018.)
1370.015.
A person committed to the care of the State Department of State Hospitals because he or she is incompetent to stand trial or to be adjudged to punishment is eligible for compassionate release pursuant to Section 4146 of the Welfare and Institutions Code. In any case in which the criteria for compassionate release apply, the State Department of State Hospitals shall follow the procedures and standards in Section 4146 of the Welfare and Institutions Code to determine if the department should recommend to the court that the person's commitment for treatment and the underlying criminal charges be suspended for compassionate release.
(Added by Stats. 2016, Ch. 715, Sec. 2. (SB 955) Effective January 1, 2017.)
1370.02.
(a) If the defendant is found mentally competent during a postrelease community supervision or parole revocation hearing, the revocation proceedings shall resume. The formal hearing on the revocation shall occur within a reasonable time after resumption of the proceedings, but in no event may the defendant be detained in custody for over 180 days from the date of arrest.

(b) If the defendant is found mentally incompetent, the court shall dismiss the pending revocation matter and return the defendant to supervision. If the revocation matter is dismissed pursuant to this subdivision, the court may, using the least restrictive option to meet the mental health needs of the defendant, also do any of the following:
(1) Modify the terms and conditions of supervision to include appropriate mental health treatment.
(2) Refer the matter to any local mental health court, reentry court, or other collaborative justice court available for improving the mental health of the defendant.
(3) Refer the matter to the public guardian of the county of commitment to initiate conservatorship proceedings pursuant to Sections 5352 and 5352.5 of the Welfare and Institutions Code. The public guardian shall investigate all available alternatives to conservatorship pursuant to Section 5354 of the Welfare and Institutions Code. The court shall order the matter to the public guardian pursuant to this paragraph only if there are no other reasonable alternatives to the establishment of a conservatorship to meet the mental health needs of the defendant.
(c) (1) Notwithstanding any other law, if a person subject to parole pursuant to Section 3000.1 or paragraph (4) of subdivision (b) of Section 3000 is found mentally incompetent, the court shall order the parolee to undergo treatment pursuant to Section 1370 for restoring the person to competency, except that if the parolee is not restored to competency within the maximum period of confinement and the court dismisses the revocation, the court shall return the parolee to parole supervision.
(2) If the parolee is returned to parole supervision, the court may, using the least restrictive option to meet the mental health needs of the parolee, do any of the following:
(A) Modify the terms and conditions of parole to include appropriate mental health treatment.
(B) Refer the matter to any local mental health court, reentry court, or other collaborative justice court available for improving the mental health of the parolee.
(C) Refer the matter to the public guardian of the county of commitment to initiate conservatorship proceedings pursuant to Sections 5352 and 5352.5 of the Welfare and Institutions Code. The public guardian shall investigate all available alternatives to conservatorship pursuant to Section 5354 of the Welfare and Institutions Code. The court shall order the matter to the public guardian pursuant to this subparagraph only if there are no other reasonable alternatives to the establishment of a conservatorship to meet the mental health needs of the parolee.
(d) If a conservatorship is established for a defendant or parolee pursuant to subdivision (b) or (c), the county or the Department of Corrections and Rehabilitation shall not compassionately release the defendant or parolee or otherwise cause the termination of his or her supervision or parole based on the establishment of that conservatorship.
(Added by Stats. 2014, Ch. 759, Sec. 9. (SB 1412) Effective January 1, 2015.)
1370.1.
(a) (1) (A) If the defendant is found mentally competent, the criminal process shall resume, the trial on the offense charged or hearing on the alleged violation shall proceed, and judgment may be pronounced.
(B) If the defendant is found mentally incompetent and has been determined by a regional center to have a developmental disability, the trial or judgment shall be suspended until the defendant becomes mentally competent.
(i) Except as provided in clause (ii) or (iii), the court shall consider a recommendation for placement. The recommendation shall be made to the court by the director of a regional center or the director's designee. In the meantime, the court shall order that the mentally incompetent defendant be delivered by the sheriff or other person designated by the court to a state hospital, developmental center, or any other available residential facility approved by the director of a regional center established under Division 4.5 (commencing with Section 4500) of the Welfare and Institutions Code as will promote the defendant's speedy attainment of mental competence, or be placed on outpatient status pursuant to the provisions of Section 1370.4 and Title 15 (commencing with Section 1600).
(ii) When the action against a defendant who has been found mentally incompetent is on a complaint charging a felony offense specified in Section 290, the prosecutor shall determine whether the defendant previously has been found mentally incompetent to stand trial pursuant to this chapter on a charge of a Section 290 offense, or whether the defendant is currently the subject of a pending Section 1368 proceeding arising out of a charge of an offense specified in Section 290. If either determination is made, the prosecutor shall so notify the court and defendant in writing. After this notification, and opportunity for hearing, the court shall order that the defendant be delivered by the sheriff to a state hospital or other secure treatment facility for the care and treatment of persons with developmental disabilities unless the court makes specific findings on the record that an alternative placement would provide more appropriate treatment for the defendant and would not pose a danger to the health and safety of others.
(iii) If the action against the defendant who has been found mentally incompetent is on a complaint charging a felony offense specified in Section 290 and the defendant has been denied bail pursuant to subdivision (b) of Section 12 of Article I of the California Constitution because the court has found, based upon clear and convincing evidence, a substantial likelihood that the person's release would result in great bodily harm to others, the court shall order that the defendant be delivered by the sheriff to a state hospital for the care and treatment of persons with developmental disabilities unless the court makes specific findings on the record that an alternative placement would provide more appropriate treatment for the defendant and would not pose a danger to the health and safety of others.
(iv) The clerk of the court shall notify the Department of Justice, in writing, of a finding of mental incompetence with respect to a defendant who is subject to clause (ii) or (iii) for inclusion in his or her state summary criminal history information.
(C) Upon becoming competent, the court shall order that the defendant be returned to the committing court pursuant to the procedures set forth in paragraph (2) of subdivision (a) of Section 1372 or by another person designated by the court. The court shall further determine conditions under which the person may be absent from the placement for medical treatment, social visits, and other similar activities. Required levels of supervision and security for these activities shall be specified.
(D) The court shall transmit a copy of its order to the regional center director or the director's designee and to the Director of Developmental Services.
(E) A defendant charged with a violent felony may not be placed in a facility or delivered to a state hospital, developmental center, or residential facility pursuant to this subdivision unless the facility, state hospital, developmental center, or residential facility has a secured perimeter or a locked and controlled treatment facility, and the judge determines that the public safety will be protected.
(F) For purposes of this paragraph, "violent felony" means an offense specified in subdivision (c) of Section 667.5.
(G) A defendant charged with a violent felony may be placed on outpatient status, as specified in Section 1370.4 or 1600, only if the court finds that the placement will not pose a danger to the health or safety of others.
(H) As used in this section, "developmental disability" has the same meaning as in Section 4512 of the Welfare and Institutions Code.
(2) Prior to making the order directing that the defendant be confined in a state hospital, developmental center, or other residential facility, or be placed on outpatient status, the court shall order the regional center director or the director's designee to evaluate the defendant and to submit to the court, within 15 judicial days of the order, a written recommendation as to whether the defendant should be committed to a state hospital, a developmental center, or to any other available residential facility approved

by the regional center director. A person shall not be admitted to a state hospital, developmental center, or other residential facility or accepted for outpatient status under Section 1370.4 without having been evaluated by the regional center director or the director's designee.
(3) If the court orders that the defendant be confined in a state hospital or other secure treatment facility pursuant to clause (ii) or (iii) of subparagraph (B) of paragraph (1), the court shall provide copies of the following documents, which shall be taken with the defendant to the state hospital or other secure treatment facility where the defendant is to be confined:
(A) State summary criminal history information.
(B) Any arrest reports prepared by the police department or other law enforcement agency.
(C) Records of a finding of mental incompetence pursuant to this chapter arising out of a complaint charging a felony offense specified in Section 290 or a pending Section 1368 proceeding arising out of a charge of an offense specified in Section 290.
(4) When the defendant is committed to a residential facility pursuant to clause (i) of subparagraph (B) of paragraph (1) or the court makes the findings specified in clause (ii) or (iii) of subparagraph (B) of paragraph (1) to assign the defendant to a facility other than a state hospital or other secure treatment facility, the court shall order that notice be given to the appropriate law enforcement agency or agencies having local jurisdiction at the site of the placement facility of a finding of mental incompetence pursuant to this chapter arising out of a charge of an offense specified in Section 290.
(5) (A) If the defendant is committed or transferred to a state hospital or developmental center pursuant to this section, the court may, upon receiving the written recommendation of the executive director of the state hospital or developmental center and the regional center director that the defendant be transferred to a residential facility approved by the regional center director, order the defendant transferred to that facility. If the defendant is committed or transferred to a residential facility approved by the regional center director, the court may, upon receiving the written recommendation of the regional center director, transfer the defendant to a state hospital, a developmental center, or to another residential facility approved by the regional center director.
In the event of dismissal of the criminal action or revocation proceedings before the defendant recovers competence, the person shall be subject to the applicable provisions of the Lanterman-Petris-Short Act (Part 1 (commencing with Section 5000) of Division 5 of the Welfare and Institutions Code) or to commitment or detention pursuant to a petition filed pursuant to Section 6502 of the Welfare and Institutions Code.
The defendant or prosecuting attorney may contest either kind of order of transfer by filing a petition with the court for a hearing, which shall be held if the court determines that sufficient grounds exist. At the hearing, the prosecuting attorney or the defendant may present evidence bearing on the order of transfer. The court shall use the same standards as used in conducting probation revocation hearings pursuant to Section 1203.2.
Prior to making an order for transfer under this section, the court shall notify the defendant, the attorney of record for the defendant, the prosecuting attorney, and the regional center director or designee.
(B) If the defendant is committed to a state hospital or secure treatment facility pursuant to clause (ii) or (iii) of subparagraph (B) of paragraph (1) and is subsequently transferred to another facility, copies of the documents specified in paragraph (3) shall be taken with the defendant to the new facility. The transferring facility shall also notify the appropriate law enforcement agency or agencies having local jurisdiction at the site of the new facility that the defendant is a person subject to clause (ii) or (iii) of subparagraph (B) of paragraph (1).
(b) (1) Within 90 days of admission of a person committed pursuant to subdivision (a), the executive director or the director's designee of the state hospital, developmental center, or other facility to which the defendant is committed, shall make a written report to the committing court and the regional center director or a designee concerning the defendant's progress toward becoming mentally competent. If the defendant is placed on outpatient status, this report shall be made to the committing court by the regional center director or the director's designee. If the defendant has not become mentally competent, but the report discloses a substantial likelihood the defendant will become mentally competent within the next 90 days, the court may order that the defendant remain in the state hospital, developmental center, or other facility or on outpatient status for that period of time. Within 150 days of an admission made pursuant to subdivision (a), or if the defendant becomes mentally competent, the executive director or the director's designee of the state hospital, developmental center, or other facility to which the defendant is committed shall report to the court and the regional center director or the director's designee regarding the defendant's progress toward becoming mentally competent. If the defendant is placed on outpatient status, the regional center director or the director's designee shall make that report to the committing court. The court shall provide copies of all reports under this section to the prosecutor and defense counsel. If the report indicates that there is no substantial likelihood that the defendant has become mentally competent, the committing court shall order the defendant to be returned to the court for proceedings pursuant to paragraph (2) of subdivision (c). The court shall transmit a copy of its order to the regional center director or the director's designee and to the executive director of the developmental center.
(2) If it is determined by the court that treatment for the defendant's mental impairment is not being conducted, the defendant shall be returned to the committing court. A copy of this order shall be sent to the regional center director or the director's designee and to the executive director of the developmental center.
(3) At each review by the court specified in this subdivision, the court shall determine if the security level of housing and treatment is appropriate and may make an order in accordance with its determination.
(c) (1) (A) At the end of two years from the date of commitment or a period of commitment equal to the maximum term of imprisonment provided by law for the most serious offense charged in the information, indictment, or misdemeanor complaint, or the maximum term of imprisonment provided by law for a violation of probation or mandatory supervision, whichever is shorter, a defendant who has not become mentally competent shall be returned to the committing court.
(B) The court shall notify the regional center director or the director's designee and the executive director of the developmental center of that return and of any resulting court orders.
(2) (A) Except as provided in subparagraph (B), in the event of dismissal of the criminal charges before the defendant becomes mentally competent, the defendant shall be subject to the applicable provisions of the Lanterman-Petris-Short Act (Part 1 (commencing with Section 5000) of Division 5 of the Welfare and Institutions Code), or to commitment and detention pursuant to a petition filed pursuant to Section 6502 of the Welfare and Institutions Code. If it is found that the person is not subject to commitment or detention pursuant to the applicable provision of the Lanterman-Petris-Short Act (Part 1 (commencing with Section 5000) of Division 5 of the Welfare and Institutions Code) or to commitment or detention pursuant to a petition filed pursuant to Section 6502 of the Welfare and Institutions Code, the individual shall not be subject to further confinement pursuant to this article and the criminal action remains subject to dismissal pursuant to Section 1385. The court shall notify the regional center director and the executive director of the developmental center of any dismissal.
(B) In revocation proceedings alleging a violation of mandatory supervision in which the defendant remains incompetent upon return to court under subparagraph (A), the defendant shall be subject to the applicable provisions of the Lanterman-Petris-Short Act (Part 1 (commencing with Section 5000) of Division 5 of the Welfare and Institutions Code), or to commitment and detention pursuant to a petition filed pursuant to Section

6502 of the Welfare and Institutions Code. If it is found that the person is not subject to commitment or detention pursuant to the applicable provision of the Lanterman-Petris-Short Act (Part 1 (commencing with Section 5000) of Division 5 of the Welfare and Institutions Code) or to commitment or detention pursuant to a petition filed pursuant to Section 6502 of the Welfare and Institutions Code, the court shall reinstate mandatory supervision and modify the terms and conditions of supervision to include appropriate mental health treatment or refer the matter to a local mental health court, reentry court, or other collaborative justice court available for improving the mental health of the defendant. Actions alleging a violation of mandatory supervision are not subject to dismissal under Section 1385.

(d) Except as provided in subparagraph (B) of paragraph (2) of subdivision (c), the criminal action remains subject to dismissal pursuant to Section 1385. If at any time prior to the maximum period of time allowed for proceedings under this article, the regional center director concludes that the behavior of the defendant related to the defendant's criminal offense has been eliminated during time spent in court-ordered programs, the court may, upon recommendation of the regional center director, dismiss the criminal charges. The court shall transmit a copy of any order of dismissal to the regional center director and to the executive director of the developmental center.

(e) For the purpose of this section, "secure treatment facility" does not include, except for state mental hospitals, state developmental centers, and correctional treatment facilities, a facility licensed pursuant to Chapter 2 (commencing with Section 1250) of, Chapter 3 (commencing with Section 1500) of, or Chapter 3.2 (commencing with Section 1569) of, Division 2 of the Health and Safety Code, or a community board and care facility.

(Amended by Stats. 2018, Ch. 1008, Sec. 3. (SB 1187) Effective January 1, 2019.)
1370.2.

If a person is adjudged mentally incompetent pursuant to the provisions of this chapter, the superior court may dismiss any misdemeanor charge pending against the mentally incompetent person. Ten days notice shall be given to the district attorney of any motion to dismiss pursuant to this section. The court shall transmit a copy of any order dismissing a misdemeanor charge pursuant to this section to the community program director, the county mental health director, or the regional center director and the Director of Developmental Services, as appropriate.

(Amended by Stats. 1992, Ch. 722, Sec. 14. Effective September 15, 1992.)
1370.3.

A person committed to a state hospital or other treatment facility under the provisions of this chapter may be placed on outpatient status from such commitment as provided in Title 15 (commencing with Section 1600) of Part 2.

(Repealed and added by Stats. 1980, Ch. 547, Sec. 12.)
1370.4.

If, in the evaluation ordered by the court under Section 1370.1, the regional center director, or a designee, is of the opinion that the defendant is not a danger to the health and safety of others while on outpatient treatment and will benefit from such treatment, and has obtained the agreement of the person in charge of a residential facility and of the defendant that the defendant will receive and submit to outpatient treatment and that the person in charge of the facility will designate a person to be the outpatient supervisor of the defendant, the court may order the defendant to undergo outpatient treatment. All of the provisions of Title 15 (commencing with Section 1600) of Part 2 shall apply where a defendant is placed on outpatient status under this section, except that the regional center director shall be substituted for the community program director, the Director of Developmental Services for the Director of State Hospitals, and a residential facility for a treatment facility for the purposes of this section.

(Amended by Stats. 2012, Ch. 440, Sec. 36. (AB 1488) Effective September 22, 2012.)
1370.5.

(a) A person committed to a state hospital or other public or private mental health facility pursuant to the provisions of Section 1370, 1370.01, 1370.02, or 1370.1, who escapes from or who escapes while being conveyed to or from a state hospital or facility, is punishable by imprisonment in a county jail not to exceed one year or in the state prison for a determinate term of one year and one day. The term of imprisonment imposed pursuant to this section shall be served consecutively to any other sentence or commitment.

(b) The medical director or person in charge of a state hospital or other public or private mental health facility to which a person has been committed pursuant to the provisions of Section 1370, 1370.01, 1370.02, or 1370.1 shall promptly notify the chief of police of the city in which the hospital or facility is located, or the sheriff of the county if the hospital or facility is located in an unincorporated area, of the escape of the person, and shall request the assistance of the chief of police or sheriff in apprehending the person, and shall within 48 hours of the escape of the person orally notify the court that made the commitment, the prosecutor in the case, and the Department of Justice of the escape.

(Amended by Stats. 2014, Ch. 759, Sec. 11. (SB 1412) Effective January 1, 2015.)
1370.6.

(a) If a mentally incompetent defendant is admitted to a county jail treatment facility pursuant to Section 1370, the department shall provide restoration of competency treatment at the county jail treatment facility and shall provide payment to the county jail treatment facility for the reasonable costs of the bed during the restoration of competency treatment as well as for the reasonable costs of any necessary medical treatment not provided within the county jail treatment facility, unless otherwise agreed to by the department and the facility.

(1) If the county jail treatment facility is able to provide restoration of competency services, upon approval by the department and subject to funding appropriated in the annual Budget Act, the county jail treatment facility may provide those services and the State Department of State Hospitals may provide payment to the county jail treatment facility for the reasonable costs of the bed during the restoration of competency treatment as well as the reasonable costs of providing restoration of competency services and for any necessary medical treatment not provided within the county jail treatment facility, unless otherwise agreed to by the department and the facility.

(2) Transportation to a county jail treatment facility for admission and from the facility upon the filing of a certificate of restoration of competency, or for transfer of a person to another county jail treatment facility or to a state hospital, shall be provided by the committing county unless otherwise agreed to by the department and the facility.

(3) In the event the State Department of State Hospitals and a county jail treatment facility are determined to be comparatively at fault for any claim, action, loss, or damage which results from their respective obligations under such a contract, each shall indemnify the other to the extent of its comparative fault.

(4) The six-month limitation in Section 1369.1 shall not apply to individuals deemed incompetent to stand trial who are being treated to restore competency within a county jail treatment facility pursuant to this section.

(b) If the community-based residential system is selected by the court pursuant to Section 1370, the State Department of State Hospitals shall provide reimbursement to the community-based residential treatment system for the cost of restoration of competency treatment as negotiated with the State Department of State Hospitals.

(c) The State Department of State Hospitals may provide payment to either a county jail treatment facility or a community-based residential treatment system directly through invoice, or through a contract, at the discretion of the department in accordance with the terms and conditions of the contract or agreement.

(Amended by Stats. 2017, Ch. 17, Sec. 31. (AB 103) Effective June 27, 2017.)
1371.

The commitment of the defendant, as described in Section 1370, 1370.1, 1370.01, or 1370.02, exonerates his or her bail, or entitles a person, authorized to receive the property of the defendant, to a return of any money he or she may have deposited instead of bail, or gives, to the person or persons found by the court to have deposited any money instead of bail on behalf of the defendant, a right to the return of that money.

(Amended by Stats. 2014, Ch. 759, Sec. 12. (SB 1412) Effective January 1, 2015.)
1372.

(a) (1) If the medical director of a state hospital, a person designated by the State Department of State Hospitals at an entity contracted by the department to provide services to a defendant prior to placement in a treatment program or other facility to which the defendant is committed, or the community program director, county mental health director, or regional center director providing outpatient services, determines that the defendant has regained mental competence, the director or designee shall immediately certify that fact to the court by filing a certificate of restoration with the court by certified mail, return receipt requested, or by confidential electronic transmission. For purposes of this section, the date of filing shall be the date on the return receipt.

(2) The court's order committing an individual to a State Department of State Hospitals facility or other treatment facility pursuant to Section 1370 shall include direction that the sheriff shall redeliver the patient to the court without any further order from the court upon receiving from the state hospital or treatment facility a copy of the certificate of restoration.

(3) The defendant shall be returned to the committing court in the following manner:

(A) A patient who remains confined in a state hospital or other treatment facility shall be redelivered to the sheriff of the county from which the patient was committed. The sheriff shall immediately return the person from the state hospital or other treatment facility to the court for further proceedings.

(B) The patient who is on outpatient status shall be returned by the sheriff to court through arrangements made by the outpatient treatment supervisor.

(C) In all cases, the patient shall be returned to the committing court no later than 10 days following the filing of a certificate of restoration. The state shall only pay for 10 hospital days for patients following the filing of a certificate of restoration of competency. The State Department of State Hospitals shall report to the fiscal and appropriate policy committees of the Legislature on an annual basis in February, on the number of days that exceed the 10-day limit prescribed in this subparagraph. This report shall include, but not be limited to, a data sheet that itemizes by county the number of days that exceed this 10-day limit during the preceding year.

(b) If the defendant becomes mentally competent after a conservatorship has been established pursuant to the applicable provisions of the Lanterman-Petris-Short Act, Part 1 (commencing with Section 5000) of Division 5 of the Welfare and Institutions Code, and Section 1370, the conservator shall certify that fact to the sheriff and district attorney of the county in which the defendant's case is pending, defendant's attorney of record, and the committing court.

(c) When a defendant is returned to court with a certification that competence has been regained, the court shall notify either the community program director, the county mental health director, or the regional center director and the Director of Developmental Services, as appropriate, of the date of any hearing on the defendant's competence and whether or not the defendant was found by the court to have recovered competence.

(d) If the committing court approves the certificate of restoration to competence as to a person in custody, the court shall hold a hearing to determine whether the person is entitled to be admitted to bail or released on own recognizance status pending conclusion of the proceedings. If the superior court approves the certificate of restoration to competence regarding a person on outpatient status, unless it appears that the person has refused to come to court, that person shall remain released either on own recognizance status, or, in the case of a developmentally disabled person, either on the defendant's promise or on the promise of a responsible adult to secure the person's appearance in court for further proceedings. If the person has refused to come to court, the court shall set bail and may place the person in custody until bail is posted.

(e) A defendant subject to either subdivision (a) or (b) who is not admitted to bail or released under subdivision (d) may, at the discretion of the court, upon recommendation of the director of the facility where the defendant is receiving treatment, be returned to the hospital or facility of his or her original commitment or other appropriate secure facility approved by the community program director, the county mental health director, or the regional center director. The recommendation submitted to the court shall be based on the opinion that the person will need continued treatment in a hospital or treatment facility in order to maintain competence to stand trial or that placing the person in a jail environment would create a substantial risk that the person would again become incompetent to stand trial before criminal proceedings could be resumed.

(f) Notwithstanding subdivision (e), if a defendant is returned by the court to a hospital or other facility for the purpose of maintaining competency to stand trial and that defendant is already under civil commitment to that hospital or facility from another county pursuant to the Lanterman-Petris-Short Act (Part 1 (commencing with Section 5000) of Division 5 of the Welfare and Institutions Code) or as a developmentally disabled person committed pursuant to Article 2 (commencing with Section 6500) of Chapter 2 of Part 2 of Division 6 of the Welfare and Institutions Code, the costs of housing and treating the defendant in that facility following return pursuant to subdivision (e) shall be the responsibility of the original county of civil commitment.

(Amended by Stats. 2018, Ch. 34, Sec. 27. (AB 1810) Effective June 27, 2018.)
1373.

The expense of sending the defendant to the state hospital or other facility, and of bringing him or her back, are chargeable to the county in which the indictment was found, information was filed, or revocation proceeding was held; but the county may recover the expense from the estate of the defendant, if he or she has any, or from a relative, bound to provide for and maintain him or her.

(Amended by Stats. 2014, Ch. 759, Sec. 13. (SB 1412) Effective January 1, 2015.)
1373.5.

In every case where a claim is presented to the county for money due under the provisions of section 1373 of this code, interest shall be allowed from the date of rejection, if rejected and recovery is finally had thereon.

(Added by Stats. 1939, Ch. 441.)
1374.

When a defendant who has been found incompetent is on outpatient status under Title 15 (commencing with Section 1600) of Part 2 and the outpatient treatment staff is of the opinion that the defendant has recovered competence, the supervisor shall communicate such opinion to the community program director. If the community program director concurs, that opinion shall be certified by such director to the committing court. The court shall calendar the case for further proceeding pursuant to Section 1372.

(Amended by Stats. 1985, Ch. 1232, Sec. 9. Effective September 30, 1985.)
1375.

Claims by the state for all amounts due from any county by reason of the provisions of Section 1373 of this code shall be processed and paid by the county pursuant to the provisions of Chapter 4 (commencing with Section 29700) of Division 3 of Title 3 of the Government Code.

(Amended by Stats. 1965, Ch. 263.)
1375.5.

(a) Time spent by a person in a treatment facility or county jail as a result of proceedings under this chapter shall be credited against the sentence, if any, imposed in the underlying criminal case or revocation matter giving rise to the competency proceedings.

(b) As used in this section, "time spent in a treatment facility" includes days a person is treated as an outpatient pursuant to Title 15 (commencing with Section 1600) of Part 2.

(c) A person subject to this chapter shall receive credits pursuant to Section 4019 for all time during which he or she is confined in a county jail and for which he or she is otherwise eligible.

(Amended by Stats. 2018, Ch. 1008, Sec. 4. (SB 1187) Effective January 1, 2019.)

1376.

(a) As used in this section, "intellectual disability" means the condition of significantly subaverage general intellectual functioning existing concurrently with deficits in adaptive behavior and manifested before 18 years of age.

(b) (1) In any case in which the prosecution seeks the death penalty, the defendant may, at a reasonable time prior to the commencement of trial, apply for an order directing that a hearing to determine intellectual disability be conducted. Upon the submission of a declaration by a qualified expert stating his or her opinion that the defendant is a person with an intellectual disability, the court shall order a hearing to determine whether the defendant is a person with an intellectual disability. At the request of the defendant, the court shall conduct the hearing without a jury prior to the commencement of the trial. The defendant's request for a court hearing prior to trial shall constitute a waiver of a jury hearing on the issue of intellectual disability. If the defendant does not request a court hearing, the court shall order a jury hearing to determine if the defendant is a person with an intellectual disability. The jury hearing on intellectual disability shall occur at the conclusion of the phase of the trial in which the jury has found the defendant guilty with a finding that one or more of the special circumstances enumerated in Section 190.2 are true. Except as provided in paragraph (3), the same jury shall make a finding that the defendant is a person with an intellectual disability or that the defendant does not have an intellectual disability.

(2) For the purposes of the procedures set forth in this section, the court or jury shall decide only the question of the defendant's intellectual disability. The defendant shall present evidence in support of the claim that he or she is a person with an intellectual disability. The prosecution shall present its case regarding the issue of whether the defendant is a person with an intellectual disability. Each party may offer rebuttal evidence. The court, for good cause in furtherance of justice, may permit either party to reopen its case to present evidence in support of or opposition to the claim of intellectual disability. Nothing in this section shall prohibit the court from making orders reasonably necessary to ensure the production of evidence sufficient to determine whether or not the defendant is a person with an intellectual disability, including, but not limited to, the appointment of, and examination of the defendant by, qualified experts. A statement made by the defendant during an examination ordered by the court shall not be admissible in the trial on the defendant's guilt.

(3) At the close of evidence, the prosecution shall make its final argument, and the defendant shall conclude with his or her final argument. The burden of proof shall be on the defense to prove by a preponderance of the evidence that the defendant is a person with an intellectual disability. The jury shall return a verdict that either the defendant is a person with an intellectual disability or the defendant does not have an intellectual disability. The verdict of the jury shall be unanimous. In any case in which the jury has been unable to reach a unanimous verdict that the defendant is a person with an intellectual disability, and does not reach a unanimous verdict that the defendant does not have an intellectual disability, the court shall dismiss the jury and order a new jury impaneled to try the issue of intellectual disability. The issue of guilt shall not be tried by the new jury.

(c) In the event the hearing is conducted before the court prior to the commencement of the trial, the following shall apply:

(1) If the court finds that the defendant is a person with an intellectual disability, the court shall preclude the death penalty and the criminal trial thereafter shall proceed as in any other case in which a sentence of death is not sought by the prosecution. If the defendant is found guilty of murder in the first degree, with a finding that one or more of the special circumstances enumerated in Section 190.2 are true, the court shall sentence the defendant to confinement in the state prison for life without the possibility of parole. The jury shall not be informed of the prior proceedings or the findings concerning the defendant's claim of intellectual disability.

(2) If the court finds that the defendant does not have an intellectual disability, the trial court shall proceed as in any other case in which a sentence of death is sought by the prosecution. The jury shall not be informed of the prior proceedings or the findings concerning the defendant's claim of intellectual disability.

(d) In the event the hearing is conducted before the jury after the defendant is found guilty with a finding that one or more of the special circumstances enumerated in Section 190.2 are true, the following shall apply:

(1) If the jury finds that the defendant is a person with an intellectual disability, the court shall preclude the death penalty and shall sentence the defendant to confinement in the state prison for life without the possibility of parole.

(2) If the jury finds that the defendant does not have an intellectual disability, the trial shall proceed as in any other case in which a sentence of death is sought by the prosecution.

(e) In any case in which the defendant has not requested a court hearing as provided in subdivision (b), and has entered a plea of not guilty by reason of insanity under Sections 190.4 and 1026, the hearing on intellectual disability shall occur at the conclusion of the sanity trial if the defendant is found sane.

(Amended by Stats. 2012, Ch. 457, Sec. 42. (SB 1381) Effective January 1, 2013.)

CHAPTER 7. Compromising Certain Public Offenses by Leave of the Court [1377 - 1379]

(Chapter 7 enacted 1872.)

1377.

When the person injured by an act constituting a misdemeanor has a remedy by a civil action, the offense may be compromised, as provided in Section 1378, except when it is committed as follows:

(a) By or upon an officer of justice, while in the execution of the duties of his or her office.

(b) Riotously.

(c) With an intent to commit a felony.

(d) In violation of any court order as described in Section 273.6 or 273.65.

(e) By or upon any family or household member, or upon any person when the violation involves any person described in Section 6211 of the Family Code or subdivision (b) of Section 13700 of this code.

(f) Upon an elder, in violation of Section 368 of this code or Section 15656 of the Welfare and Institutions Code.

(g) Upon a child, as described in Section 647.6 or 11165.6.

(Amended by Stats. 1997, Ch. 243, Sec. 1. Effective January 1, 1998.)

1378.

If the person injured appears before the court in which the action is pending at any time before trial, and acknowledges that he has received satisfaction for the injury, the court

may, in its discretion, on payment of the costs incurred, order all proceedings to be stayed upon the prosecution, and the defendant to be discharged therefrom; but in such case the reasons for the order must be set forth therein, and entered on the minutes. The order is a bar to another prosecution for the same offense.

(Amended by Stats. 1957, Ch. 102.)

1379.

No public offense can be compromised, nor can any proceeding or prosecution for the punishment thereof upon a compromise be stayed, except as provided in this Chapter.

(Enacted 1872.)

CHAPTER 8. Dismissal of the Action for Want of Prosecution or Otherwise [1381 - 1388]

(Heading of Chapter 8 amended by Stats. 1951, Ch. 1674.)

1381.

Whenever a defendant has been convicted, in any court of this state, of the commission of a felony or misdemeanor and has been sentenced to and has entered upon a term of imprisonment in a state prison or has been sentenced to and has entered upon a term of imprisonment in a county jail for a period of more than 90 days or has been committed to and placed in a county jail for more than 90 days as a condition of probation or has been committed to and placed in an institution subject to the jurisdiction of the Department of the Youth Authority or whenever any person has been committed to the custody of the Director of Corrections pursuant to Chapter 1 (commencing with Section 3000) of Division 3 of the Welfare and Institutions Code and has entered upon his or her term of commitment, and at the time of the entry upon the term of imprisonment or commitment there is pending, in any court of this state, any other indictment, information, complaint, or any criminal proceeding wherein the defendant remains to be sentenced, the district attorney of the county in which the matters are pending shall bring the defendant to trial or for sentencing within 90 days after the person shall have delivered to said district attorney written notice of the place of his or her imprisonment or commitment and his or her desire to be brought to trial or for sentencing unless a continuance beyond the 90 days is requested or consented to by the person, in open court, and the request or consent entered upon the minutes of the court in which event the 90-day period shall commence to run anew from the date to which the consent or request continued the trial or sentencing. In the event that the defendant is not brought to trial or for sentencing within the 90 days the court in which the charge or sentencing is pending shall, on motion or suggestion of the district attorney, or of the defendant or person confined in the county jail or committed to the custody of the Director of Corrections or his or her counsel, or of the Department of Corrections, or of the Department of the Youth Authority, or on its own motion, dismiss the action. If a charge is filed against a person during the time the person is serving a sentence in any state prison or county jail of this state or while detained by the Director of Corrections pursuant to Chapter 1 (commencing with Section 3000) of Division 3 of the Welfare and Institutions Code or while detained in any institution subject to the jurisdiction of the Department of the Youth Authority it is hereby made mandatory upon the district attorney of the county in which the charge is filed to bring it to trial within 90 days after the person shall have delivered to said district attorney written notice of the place of his or her imprisonment or commitment and his or her desire to be brought to trial upon the charge, unless a continuance is requested or consented to by the person, in open court, and the request or consent entered upon the minutes of the court, in which event the 90-day period shall commence to run anew from the date to which the request or consent continued the trial. In the event the action is not brought to trial within the 90 days the court in which the action is pending shall, on motion or suggestion of the district attorney, or of the defendant or person committed to the custody of the Director of Corrections or to a county jail or his or her counsel, or of the Department of Corrections, or of the Department of the Youth Authority, or on its own motion, dismiss the charge. The sheriff, custodian, or jailer shall endorse upon the written notice of the defendant's desire to be brought to trial or for sentencing the cause of commitment, the date of commitment, and the date of release.

(Amended by Stats. 1987, Ch. 828, Sec. 91.)

1381.5.

Whenever a defendant has been convicted of a crime and has entered upon a term of imprisonment therefor in a federal correctional institution located in this state, and at the time of entry upon such term of imprisonment or at any time during such term of imprisonment there is pending in any court of this state any criminal indictment, information, complaint, or any criminal proceeding wherein the defendant remains to be sentenced the district attorney of the county in which such matters are pending, upon receiving from such defendant a request that he be brought to trial or for sentencing, shall promptly inquire of the warden or other head of the federal correctional institution in which such defendant is confined whether and when such defendant can be released for trial or for sentencing. If an assent from authorized federal authorities for release of the defendant for trial or sentencing is received by the district attorney he shall bring him to trial or sentencing within 90 days after receipt of such assent, unless the federal authorities specify a date of release after 90 days, in which event the district attorney shall bring the prisoner to trial or sentencing at such specified time, or unless the defendant requests, in open court, and receives, or, in open court, consents to, a continuance, in which event he may be brought to trial or sentencing within 90 days from such request or consent.

If a defendant is not brought to trial or for sentencing as provided by this section, the court in which the action is pending shall, on motion or suggestion of the district attorney, or representative of the United States, or the defendant or his counsel, dismiss the action.

(Amended by Stats. 1983, Ch. 793, Sec. 1.1.)

1382.

(a) The court, unless good cause to the contrary is shown, shall order the action to be dismissed in the following cases:

(1) When a person has been held to answer for a public offense and an information is not filed against that person within 15 days.

(2) In a felony case, when a defendant is not brought to trial within 60 days of the defendant's arraignment on an indictment or information, or reinstatement of criminal proceedings pursuant to Chapter 6 (commencing with Section 1367) of Title 10 of Part 2, or, in case the cause is to be tried again following a mistrial, an order granting a new trial from which an appeal is not taken, or an appeal from the superior court, within 60 days after the mistrial has been declared, after entry of the order granting the new trial, or after the filing of the remittitur in the trial court, or after the issuance of a writ or order which, in effect, grants a new trial, within 60 days after notice of the writ or order is filed in the trial court and served upon the prosecuting attorney, or within 90 days after notice of the writ or order is filed in the trial court and served upon the prosecuting attorney in any case where the district attorney chooses to resubmit the case for a preliminary examination after an appeal or the issuance of a writ reversing a judgment of conviction upon a plea of guilty prior to a preliminary hearing. However, an action shall not be dismissed under this paragraph if either of the following circumstances exists:

(A) The defendant enters a general waiver of the 60-day trial requirement. A general waiver of the 60-day trial requirement entitles the superior court to set or continue a trial date without the sanction of dismissal should the case fail to proceed on the date set for trial. If the defendant, after proper notice to all parties, later withdraws, in open

court, his or her waiver in the superior court, the defendant shall be brought to trial within 60 days of the date of that withdrawal. Upon the withdrawal of a general time waiver in open court, a trial date shall be set and all parties shall be properly notified of that date. If a general time waiver is not expressly entered, subparagraph (B) shall apply.
(B) The defendant requests or consents to the setting of a trial date beyond the 60-day period. In the absence of an express general time waiver from the defendant, or upon the withdrawal of a general time waiver, the court shall set a trial date. Whenever a case is set for trial beyond the 60-day period by request or consent, expressed or implied, of the defendant without a general waiver, the defendant shall be brought to trial on the date set for trial or within 10 days thereafter.
Whenever a case is set for trial after a defendant enters either a general waiver as to the 60-day trial requirement or requests or consents, expressed or implied, to the setting of a trial date beyond the 60-day period pursuant to this paragraph, the court may not grant a motion of the defendant to vacate the date set for trial and to set an earlier trial date unless all parties are properly noticed and the court finds good cause for granting that motion.
(3) Regardless of when the complaint is filed, when a defendant in a misdemeanor or infraction case is not brought to trial within 30 days after he or she is arraigned or enters his or her plea, whichever occurs later, if the defendant is in custody at the time of arraignment or plea, whichever occurs later, or in all other cases, within 45 days after the defendant's arraignment or entry of the plea, whichever occurs later, or in case the cause is to be tried again following a mistrial, an order granting a new trial from which no appeal is taken, or an appeal from a judgment in a misdemeanor or infraction case, within 30 days after the mistrial has been declared, after entry of the order granting the new trial, or after the remittitur is filed in the trial court, or within 30 days after the date of the reinstatement of criminal proceedings pursuant to Chapter 6 (commencing with Section 1367). However, an action shall not be dismissed under this subdivision if any of the following circumstances exists:
(A) The defendant enters a general waiver of the 30-day or 45-day trial requirement. A general waiver of the 30-day or 45-day trial requirement entitles the court to set or continue a trial date without the sanction of dismissal should the case fail to proceed on the date set for trial. If the defendant, after proper notice to all parties, later withdraws, in open court, his or her waiver in the superior court, the defendant shall be brought to trial within 30 days of the date of that withdrawal. Upon the withdrawal of a general time waiver in open court, a trial date shall be set and all parties shall be properly notified of that date. If a general time waiver is not expressly entered, subparagraph (B) shall apply.
(B) The defendant requests or consents to the setting of a trial date beyond the 30-day or 45-day period. In the absence of an express general time waiver from the defendant, or upon the withdrawal of a general time waiver the court shall set a trial date. Whenever a case is set for trial beyond the 30-day or 45-day period by request or consent, expressed or implied, of the defendant without a general waiver, the defendant shall be brought to trial on the date set for trial or within 10 days thereafter.
(C) The defendant in a misdemeanor case has been ordered to appear on a case set for hearing prior to trial, but the defendant fails to appear on that date and a bench warrant is issued, or the case is not tried on the date set for trial because of the defendant's neglect or failure to appear, in which case the defendant shall be deemed to have been arraigned within the meaning of this subdivision on the date of his or her subsequent arraignment on a bench warrant or his or her submission to the court.
(b) Whenever a defendant has been ordered to appear in superior court on a felony case set for trial or set for a hearing prior to trial after being held to answer, if the defendant fails to appear on that date and a bench warrant is issued, the defendant shall be brought to trial within 60 days after the defendant next appears in the superior court unless a trial date previously had been set which is beyond that 60-day period.
(c) If the defendant is not represented by counsel, the defendant shall not be deemed under this section to have consented to the date for the defendant's trial unless the court has explained to the defendant his or her rights under this section and the effect of his or her consent.
(Amended by Stats. 2009, Ch. 424, Sec. 1. (AB 250) Effective January 1, 2010.)
1383.
If the defendant is not charged or tried, as provided in Section 1382, and sufficient reason therefor is shown, the court may order the action to be continued from time to time, and in the meantime may discharge the defendant from custody on his or her own undertaking of bail for his or her appearance to answer the charge at the time to which the action is continued.
(Amended by Stats. 1987, Ch. 828, Sec. 92.)
1384.
If the judge or magistrate directs the action to be dismissed, the defendant must, if in custody, be discharged therefrom; or if admitted to bail, his bail is exonerated, or money deposited instead of bail must be refunded to him or to the person or persons found by the court to have deposited said money on behalf of said defendant.
(Amended by Stats. 1980, Ch. 938, Sec. 6.)
1385.
(a) The judge or magistrate may, either of his or her own motion or upon the application of the prosecuting attorney, and in furtherance of justice, order an action to be dismissed. The reasons for the dismissal shall be stated orally on the record. The court shall also set forth the reasons in an order entered upon the minutes if requested by either party or in any case in which the proceedings are not being recorded electronically or reported by a court reporter. A dismissal shall not be made for any cause that would be ground of demurrer to the accusatory pleading.
(b) (1) If the court has the authority pursuant to subdivision (a) to strike or dismiss an enhancement, the court may instead strike the additional punishment for that enhancement in the furtherance of justice in compliance with subdivision (a).
(2) This subdivision does not authorize the court to strike the additional punishment for any enhancement that cannot be stricken or dismissed pursuant to subdivision (a).
(Amended by Stats. 2018, Ch. 1013, Sec. 2. (SB 1393) Effective January 1, 2019.)
1385.1.
Notwithstanding Section 1385 or any other provision of law, a judge shall not strike or dismiss any special circumstance which is admitted by a plea of guilty or nolo contendere or is found by a jury or court as provided in Sections 190.1 to 190.5, inclusive.
(Added June 5, 1990, by initiative Proposition 115, Sec. 26.)
1386.
The entry of a nolle prosequi is abolished, and neither the Attorney General nor the district attorney can discontinue or abandon a prosecution for a public offense, except as provided in Section 1385.
(Amended by Stats. 1987, Ch. 828, Sec. 93.)
1387.
(a) An order terminating an action pursuant to this chapter, or Section 859b, 861, 871, or 995, is a bar to any other prosecution for the same offense if it is a felony or if it is a misdemeanor charged together with a felony and the action has been previously terminated pursuant to this chapter, or Section 859b, 861, 871, or 995, or if it is a misdemeanor not charged together with a felony, except in those felony cases, or those cases where a misdemeanor is charged with a felony, where subsequent to the dismissal of the felony or misdemeanor the judge or magistrate finds any of the following:
(1) That substantial new evidence has been discovered by the prosecution which would not have been known through the exercise of due diligence at, or prior to, the time of termination of the action.
(2) That the termination of the action was the result of the direct intimidation of a material witness, as shown by a preponderance of the evidence.
(3) That the termination of the action was the result of the failure to appear by the complaining witness, who had been personally subpoenaed in a prosecution arising under subdivision (e) of Section 243 or Section 262, 273.5, or 273.6. This paragraph shall apply only within six months of the original dismissal of the action, and may be invoked only once in each action. Nothing in this section shall preclude a defendant from being eligible for diversion.
(4) That the termination of the action was the result of the complaining witness being found in contempt of court as described in subdivision (b) of Section 1219 of the Code of Civil Procedure. This paragraph shall apply only within six months of the original dismissal of the action, and may be invoked only once in each action.
(b) Notwithstanding subdivision (a), an order terminating an action pursuant to this chapter is not a bar to another prosecution for the same offense if it is a misdemeanor charging an offense based on an act of domestic violence, as defined in subdivisions (a) and (b) of Section 13700, and the termination of the action was the result of the failure to appear by the complaining witness, who had been personally subpoenaed. This subdivision shall apply only within six months of the original dismissal of the action, and may be invoked only once in each action. Nothing in this subdivision shall preclude a defendant from being eligible for diversion.
(c) An order terminating an action is not a bar to prosecution if a complaint is dismissed before the commencement of a preliminary hearing in favor of an indictment filed pursuant to Section 944 and the indictment is based upon the same subject matter as charged in the dismissed complaint, information, or indictment.
However, if the previous termination was pursuant to Section 859b, 861, 871, or 995, the subsequent order terminating an action is not a bar to prosecution if:
(1) Good cause is shown why the preliminary examination was not held within 60 days from the date of arraignment or plea.
(2) The motion pursuant to Section 995 was granted because of any of the following reasons:
(A) Present insanity of the defendant.
(B) A lack of counsel after the defendant elected to represent himself or herself rather than being represented by appointed counsel.
(C) Ineffective assistance of counsel.
(D) Conflict of interest of defense counsel.
(E) Violation of time deadlines based upon unavailability of defense counsel.
(F) Defendant's motion to withdraw a waiver of the preliminary examination.
(3) The motion pursuant to Section 995 was granted after dismissal by the magistrate of the action pursuant to Section 871 and was recharged pursuant to Section 739.
(Amended by Stats. 2012, Ch. 510, Sec. 2. (AB 2051) Effective January 1, 2013.)
1387.1.
(a) Where an offense is a violent felony, as defined in Section 667.5 and the prosecution has had two prior dismissals, as defined in Section 1387, the people shall be permitted one additional opportunity to refile charges where either of the prior dismissals under Section 1387 were due solely to excusable neglect. In no case shall the additional refiling of charges provided under this section be permitted where the conduct of the prosecution amounted to bad faith.
(b) As used in this section, "excusable neglect" includes, but is not limited to, error on the part of the court, prosecution, law enforcement agency, or witnesses.
(Added by Stats. 1987, Ch. 1211, Sec. 47.5.)
1387.2.
Upon the express consent of both the people and the defendant, in lieu of issuing an order terminating an action the court may proceed on the existing accusatory pleading. For the purposes of Section 1387, the action shall be deemed as having been previously terminated. The defendant shall be rearraigned on the accusatory pleading and a new time period pursuant to Section 859b or 1382 shall commence.
(Added by Stats. 1992, Ch. 278, Sec. 2. Effective January 1, 1993.)
1388.
(a) In any case where an order for the dismissal of a felony action is made, as provided in this chapter, and where the defendant had been released on his own recognizance for that action, if the prosecutor files another accusatory pleading against the same defendant for the same offense, unless the defendant is present in court at the time of refiling, the district attorney shall send a letter to the defendant at his last known place of residence, and shall send a copy to the attorney of record, stating that the case has been refiled, and setting forth the date, time and place for rearraignment.
(b) If the defendant fails to appear for arraignment as stated, or at such time, date, and place as has been subsequently agreed to by defendant's counsel and the district attorney, then the court shall issue and have delivered for execution a warrant for his arrest within 20 days after his failure to appear.
(c) If the defendant was released on his own recognizance on the original charge, he shall, if he appears as provided in subdivisions (a) and (b), be released on his own recognizance on the refiled charge unless it is shown that changed conditions require a different disposition, in which case bail shall be set at the discretion of the judge.
(Added by Stats. 1976, Ch. 1024.)

CHAPTER 8.5. Agreement on Detainers [1389 - 1389.8]

(Chapter 8.5 added by Stats. 1963, Ch. 2115.)
1389.
The agreement on detainers is hereby enacted into law and entered into by this State with all other jurisdictions legally joining therein in the form substantially as follows:
The Agreement on Detainers
The contracting states solemnly agree that:
Article I
The party states find that charges outstanding against a prisoner, detainers based on untried indictments, informations or complaints, and difficulties in securing speedy trial of persons already incarcerated in other jurisdictions, produce uncertainties which obstruct programs of prisoner treatment and rehabilitation. Accordingly, it is the policy of the party states and the purpose of this agreement to encourage the expeditious and orderly disposition of such charges and determination of the proper status of any and all detainers based on untried indictments, informations or complaints. The party states also find that proceedings with reference to such charges and detainers, when emanating from another jurisdiction, cannot properly be had in the absence of cooperative procedures. It is the further purpose of this agreement to provide such cooperative procedures.
Article II
As used in this agreement:
(a) "State" shall mean a state of the United States; the United States of America; a territory or possession of the United States; the District of Columbia; the Commonwealth of Puerto Rico.
(b) "Sending state" shall mean a state in which a prisoner is incarcerated at the time that he initiates a request for final disposition pursuant to Article III hereof or at the time that a request for custody or availability is initiated pursuant to Article IV hereof.
(c) "Receiving state" shall mean the state in which trial is to be had on an indictment, information or complaint pursuant to Article III or Article IV hereof.

Article III

(a) Whenever a person has entered upon a term of imprisonment in a penal or correctional institution of a party state, and whenever during the continuance of the term of imprisonment there is pending in any other party state any untried indictment, information or complaint on the basis of which a detainer has been lodged against the prisoner, he shall be brought to trial within one hundred eighty days after he shall have caused to be delivered to the prosecuting officer and the appropriate court of the prosecuting officer's jurisdiction written notice of the place of his imprisonment and his request for a final disposition to be made of the indictment, information or complaint: provided that for good cause shown in open court, the prisoner or his counsel being present, the court having jurisdiction of the matter may grant any necessary or reasonable continuance. The request of the prisoner shall be accompanied by a certificate of the appropriate official having custody of the prisoner, stating the term of commitment under which the prisoner is being held, the time already served, the time remaining to be served on the sentence, the amount of good time earned, the time of parole eligibility of the prisoner, and any decisions of the state parole agency relating to the prisoner.

(b) The written notice and request for final disposition referred to in paragraph (a) hereof shall be given or sent by the prisoner to the warden, commissioner of corrections or other official having custody of him, who shall promptly forward it together with the certificate to the appropriate prosecuting official and court by registered or certified mail, return receipt requested.

(c) The warden, commissioner of corrections or other official having custody of the prisoner shall promptly inform him of the source and contents of any detainer lodged against him and shall also inform him of his right to make a request for final disposition of the indictment, information or complaint on which the detainer is based.

(d) Any request for final disposition made by a prisoner pursuant to paragraph (a) hereof shall operate as a request for final disposition of all untried indictments, informations or complaints on the basis of which detainers have been lodged against the prisoner from the state to whose prosecuting official the request for final disposition is specifically directed. The warden, commissioner of corrections or other official having custody of the prisoner shall forthwith notify all appropriate prosecuting officers and courts in the several jurisdictions within the state to which the prisoner's request for final disposition is being sent of the proceeding being initiated by the prisoner. Any notification sent pursuant to this paragraph shall be accompanied by copies of the prisoner's written notice, request, and the certificate. If trial is not had on any indictment, information or complaint contemplated hereby prior to the return of the prisoner to the original place of imprisonment, such indictment, information or complaint shall not be of any further force or effect, and the court shall enter an order dismissing the same with prejudice.

(e) Any request for final disposition made by a prisoner pursuant to paragraph (a) hereof shall also be deemed to be a waiver of extradition with respect to any charge or proceeding contemplated thereby or included therein by reason of paragraph (d) hereof, and a waiver of extradition to the receiving state to serve any sentence there imposed upon him, after completion of his term of imprisonment in the sending state. The request for final disposition shall also constitute a consent by the prisoner to the production of his body in any court where his presence may be required in order to effectuate the purposes of this agreement and a further consent voluntarily to be returned to the original place of imprisonment in accordance with the provisions of this agreement. Nothing in this paragraph shall prevent the imposition of a concurrent sentence if otherwise permitted by law.

(f) Escape from custody by the prisoner subsequent to his execution of the request for final disposition referred to in paragraph (a) hereof shall void the request.

Article IV

(a) The appropriate officer of the jurisdiction in which an untried indictment, information or complaint is pending shall be entitled to have a prisoner against whom he has lodged a detainer and who is serving a term of imprisonment in any party state made available in accordance with Article V (a) hereof upon presentation of a written request for temporary custody or availability to the appropriate authorities of the state in which the prisoner is incarcerated: provided that the court having jurisdiction of such indictment, information or complaint shall have duly approved, recorded and transmitted the request: and provided further that there shall be a period of thirty days after receipt by the appropriate authorities before the request be honored, within which period the governor of the sending state may disapprove the request for temporary custody or availability, either upon his own motion or upon motion of the prisoner.

(b) Upon receipt of the officer's written request as provided in paragraph (a) hereof, the appropriate authorities having the prisoner in custody shall furnish the officer with a certificate stating the term of commitment under which the prisoner is being held, the time already served, the time remaining to be served on the sentence, the amount of good time earned, the time of parole eligibility of the prisoner, and any decisions of the state parole agency relating to the prisoner. Said authorities simultaneously shall furnish all other officers and appropriate courts in the receiving state who have lodged detainers against the prisoner with similar certificates and with notices informing them of the request for custody or availability and of the reasons therefor.

(c) In respect of any proceeding made possible by this Article, trial shall be commenced within one hundred twenty days of the arrival of the prisoner in the receiving state, but for good cause shown in open court, the prisoner or his counsel being present, the court having jurisdiction of the matter may grant any necessary or reasonable continuance.

(d) Nothing contained in this Article shall be construed to deprive any prisoner of any right which he may have to contest the legality of his delivery as provided in paragraph (a) hereof, but such delivery may not be opposed or denied on the ground that the executive authority of the sending state has not affirmatively consented to or ordered such delivery.

(e) If trial is not had on any indictment, information or complaint contemplated hereby prior to the prisoner's being returned to the original place of imprisonment pursuant to Article V (e) hereof, such indictment, information or complaint shall not be of any further force or effect, and the court shall enter an order dismissing the same with prejudice.

Article V

(a) In response to a request made under Article III or Article IV hereof, the appropriate authority in a sending state shall offer to deliver temporary custody of such prisoner to the appropriate authority in the state where such indictment, information or complaint is pending against such person in order that speedy and efficient prosecution may be had. If the request for final disposition is made by the prisoner, the offer of temporary custody shall accompany the written notice provided for in Article III of this agreement. In the case of a federal prisoner, the appropriate authority in the receiving state shall be entitled to temporary custody as provided by this agreement or to the prisoner's presence in federal custody at the place for trial, whichever custodial arrangement may be approved by the custodian.

(b) The officer or other representative of a state accepting an offer of temporary custody shall present the following upon demand:

(1) Proper identification and evidence of his authority to act for the state into whose temporary custody the prisoner is to be given.

(2) A duly certified copy of the indictment, information or complaint on the basis of which the detainer has been lodged and on the basis of which the request for temporary custody of the prisoner has been made.

(c) If the appropriate authority shall refuse or fail to accept temporary custody of said person, or in the event that an action on the indictment, information or complaint on the basis of which the detainer has been lodged is not brought to trial within the period

provided in Article III or Article IV hereof, the appropriate court of the jurisdiction where the indictment, information or complaint has been pending shall enter an order dismissing the same with prejudice, and any detainer based thereon shall cease to be of any force or effect.

(d) The temporary custody referred to in this agreement shall be only for the purpose of permitting prosecution on the charge or charges contained in one or more untried indictments, informations or complaints which form the basis of the detainer or detainers or for prosecution on any other charge or charges arising out of the same transaction. Except for his attendance at court and while being transported to or from any place at which his presence may be required, the prisoner shall be held in a suitable jail or other facility regularly used for persons awaiting prosecution.

(e) At the earliest practicable time consonant with the purposes of this agreement, the prisoner shall be returned to the sending state.

(f) During the continuance of temporary custody or while the prisoner is otherwise being made available for trial as required by this agreement, time being served on the sentence shall continue to run but good time shall be earned by the prisoner only if, and to the extent that, the law and practice of the jurisdiction which imposed the sentence may allow.

(g) For all purposes other than that for which temporary custody as provided in this agreement is exercised, the prisoner shall be deemed to remain in the custody of and subject to the jurisdiction of the sending state and any escape from temporary custody may be dealt with in the same manner as an escape from the original place of imprisonment or in any other manner permitted by law.

(h) From the time that a party state receives custody of a prisoner pursuant to this agreement until such prisoner is returned to the territory and custody of the sending state, the state in which the one or more untried indictments, informations or complaints are pending or in which trial is being had shall be responsible for the prisoner and shall also pay all costs of transporting, caring for, keeping and returning the prisoner. The provisions of this paragraph shall govern unless the states concerned shall have entered into a supplementary agreement providing for a different allocation of costs and responsibilities as between or among themselves. Nothing herein contained shall be construed to alter or affect any internal relationship among the departments, agencies and officers of and in the government of a party state, or between a party state and its subdivisions, as to the payment of costs, or responsibilities therefor.

Article VI

(a) In determining the duration and expiration dates of the time periods provided in Articles III and IV of this agreement, the running of said time periods shall be tolled whenever and for as long as the prisoner is unable to stand trial, as determined by the court having jurisdiction of the matter.

(b) No provision of this agreement, and no remedy made available by this agreement, shall apply to any person who is adjudged to be mentally ill.

Article VII

Each state party to this agreement shall designate an officer who, acting jointly with like officers of other party states, shall promulgate rules and regulations to carry out more effectively the terms and provisions of this agreement, and who shall provide, within and without the state, information necessary to the effective operation of this agreement.

Article VIII

This agreement shall enter into full force and effect as to a party state when such state has enacted the same into law. A state party to this agreement may withdraw herefrom by enacting a statute repealing the same. However, the withdrawal of any state shall not affect the status of any proceedings already initiated by inmates or by state officers at the time such withdrawal takes effect, nor shall it affect their rights in respect thereof.

Article IX

This agreement shall be liberally construed so as to effectuate its purposes. The provisions of this agreement shall be severable and if any phrase, clause, sentence or provision of this agreement is declared to be contrary to the constitution of any party state or of the United States or the applicability thereof to any government, agency, person or circumstance is held invalid, the validity of the remainder of this agreement and the applicability thereof to any government, agency, person or circumstance shall not be affected thereby. If this agreement shall be held contrary to the constitution of any state party hereto, the agreement shall remain in full force and effect as to the remaining states and in full force and effect as to the state affected as to all severable matters.

(Added by Stats. 1963, Ch. 2115.)

1389.1.

The phrase "appropriate court" as used in the agreement on detainers shall, with reference to the courts of this State, means the court in which the indictment, information, or complaint is filed.

(Added by Stats. 1963, Ch. 2115.)

1389.2.

All courts, departments, agencies, officers, and employees of this State and its political subdivisions are hereby directed to enforce the agreement on detainer and to co-operate with one another and with other states in enforcing the agreement and effectuating its purpose.

(Added by Stats. 1963, Ch. 2115.)

1389.4.

Every person who has been imprisoned in a prison or institution in this State and who escapes while in the custody of an officer of this or another state in another state pursuant to the agreement on detainers is deemed to have violated Section 4530 and is punishable as provided therein.

(Added by Stats. 1963, Ch. 2115.)

1389.5.

It shall be lawful and mandatory upon the warden or other official in charge of a penal or correctional institution in this State to give over the person of any inmate thereof whenever so required by the operation of the agreement on detainer. Such official shall inform such inmate of his rights provided in paragraph (a) of Article IV of the Agreement on Detainers in Section 1389 of this code.

(Added by Stats. 1963, Ch. 2115.)

1389.6.

The Administrator, Interstate Probation and Parole Compacts, shall administer this agreement.

(Added by Stats. 1963, Ch. 2115.)

1389.7.

When, pursuant to the agreement on detainers or other provision of law, a person in actual confinement under sentence of another jurisdiction is brought before a California court and sentenced by the judge to serve a California sentence concurrently with the sentence of the other jurisdiction or has been transferred to another jurisdiction for concurrent service of previously imposed sentences, the Board of Prison Terms, and the panels and members thereof, may meet in such other jurisdiction, or enter into cooperative arrangements with corresponding agencies in the other jurisdiction, as necessary to carry out the term-fixing and parole functions.

(Amended by Stats. 1979, Ch. 255.)

1389.8.

It shall be the responsibility of the agent of the receiving state to return the prisoner to the sending state upon completion of the proceedings.

(Added by Stats. 1971, Ch. 1185.)

CHAPTER 9. Proceedings Against Corporations [1390 - 1397]

(Chapter 9 enacted 1872.)

1390.

Upon the filing of an accusatory pleading against a corporation, the court shall issue a summons, signed by the judge with his name of office, requiring the corporation to appear before him, at a specified time and place, to answer the charge, the time to be not less than 10 days after the issuing of the summons.

(Amended by Stats. 1971, Ch. 1591.)

1391.

The summons shall be substantially in the following form:

County of (as the case may be).

The people of the State of California to the (naming the corporation):

You are hereby summoned to appear before me at (naming the place), on (specifying the day and hour), to answer an accusatory pleading, for (designating the offense generally).

Dated this _____ day of _____, 19___.

G. H., Judge, (name of the court).

(Amended by Stats. 1971, Ch. 1591.)

1392.

The summons must be served at least five days before the day of appearance fixed therein, by delivering a copy thereof and showing the original to the president or other head of the corporation, or to the secretary, cashier, managing agent, or an agent of the corporation designated for service of civil process.

(Amended by Stats. 1973, Ch. 248.)

1393.

At the appointed time in the summons, the magistrate shall proceed with the charge in the same manner as in other cases.

(Amended by Stats. 1971, Ch. 1591.)

1396.

If an accusatory pleading is filed, the corporation may appear by counsel to answer the same, except that in the case of misdemeanors arising from operation of motor vehicles, or of infractions arising from operation of motor vehicles, a corporation may appear by its president, vice president, secretary or managing agent for the purpose of entering a plea of guilty. If it does not thus appear, a plea of not guilty shall be entered, and the same proceedings had thereon as in other cases.

(Amended by Stats. 1973, Ch. 718.)

1397.

When a fine is imposed upon a corporation on conviction, it may be collected by virtue of the order imposing it in the manner provided for enforcement of money judgments generally.

(Amended by Stats. 1982, Ch. 497, Sec. 140. Operative July 1, 1983, by Sec. 185 of Ch. 497.)

CHAPTER 10. Entitling Affidavits [1401- 1401.]

(Chapter 10 enacted 1872.)

1401.

It is not necessary to entitle an affidavit or deposition in the action, whether taken before or after indictment or information, or upon an appeal; but if made without a title, or with an erroneous title, it is as valid and effectual for every purpose as if it were duly entitled, if it intelligibly refer to the proceeding, indictment, information, or appeal in which it is made.

(Amended by Code Amendments 1880, Ch. 47.)

CHAPTER 11. Errors and Mistakes in Pleadings and Other Proceedings [1404 - 1405.1]

(Chapter 11 enacted 1872.)

1404.

Neither a departure from the form or mode prescribed by this Code in respect to any pleading or proceeding, nor an error or mistake therein, renders it invalid, unless it has actually prejudiced the defendant, or tended to his prejudice, in respect to a substantial right.

(Enacted 1872.)

1405.

(a) A person who was convicted of a felony and is currently serving a term of imprisonment may make a written motion, pursuant to subdivision (d), before the trial court that entered the judgment of conviction in his or her case, for performance of forensic deoxyribonucleic acid (DNA) testing.

(b) (1) An indigent convicted person may request appointment of counsel in order to prepare a motion pursuant to subdivision (d) by sending a written request to the court. The request shall include the person's statement that he or she was not the perpetrator of the crime and shall explain how the DNA testing is relevant to his or her assertion of innocence. The request also shall include the person's statement as to whether he or she previously has had counsel appointed under this section.

(2) If any of the information required in paragraph (1) is missing from the request, the court shall return the request to the convicted person and advise him or her that the matter cannot be considered without the missing information.

(3) (A) Upon a finding that the person is indigent, he or she has included the information required in paragraph (1), and counsel has not previously been appointed pursuant to this subdivision, the court shall appoint counsel to investigate and, if appropriate, to file a motion for DNA testing under this section and to represent the person solely for the purpose of obtaining DNA testing under this section.

(B) Upon a finding that the person is indigent, and counsel previously has been appointed pursuant to this subdivision, the court may, in its discretion, appoint counsel to investigate and, if appropriate, to file a motion for DNA testing under this section and to represent the person solely for the purpose of obtaining DNA testing under this section.

(4) This section does not provide for a right to the appointment of counsel in a postconviction collateral proceeding, or to set a precedent for any such right, in any context other than the representation being provided an indigent convicted person for the limited purpose of filing and litigating a motion for DNA testing pursuant to this section.

(c) Upon request of the convicted person or convicted person's counsel, the court may order the prosecutor to make all reasonable efforts to obtain, and police agencies and law enforcement laboratories to make all reasonable efforts to provide, the following documents that are in their possession or control, if the documents exist:

(1) Copies of DNA lab reports, with underlying notes, prepared in connection with the laboratory testing of biological evidence from the case, including presumptive tests for the presence of biological material, serological tests, and analyses of trace evidence.

(2) Copies of evidence logs, chain of custody logs and reports, including, but not limited to, documentation of current location of biological evidence, and evidence destruction logs and reports.

(3) If the evidence has been lost or destroyed, a custodian of record shall submit a report to the prosecutor and the convicted person or convicted person's counsel that sets forth the efforts that were made in an attempt to locate the evidence. If the last known or documented location of the evidence prior to its loss or destruction was in an area controlled by a law enforcement agency, the report shall include the results of a physical search of this area. If there is a record of confirmation of destruction of the evidence, the report shall include a copy of the record of confirmation of destruction in lieu of the results of a physical search of the area.

(d) (1) The motion for DNA testing shall be verified by the convicted person under penalty of perjury and shall include all of the following:

(A) A statement that he or she is innocent and not the perpetrator of the crime.

(B) Explain why the identity of the perpetrator was, or should have been, a significant issue in the case.

(C) Make every reasonable attempt to identify both the evidence that should be tested and the specific type of DNA testing sought.

(D) Explain, in light of all the evidence, how the requested DNA testing would raise a reasonable probability that the convicted person's verdict or sentence would be more favorable if the results of DNA testing had been available at the time of conviction.

(E) Reveal the results of any DNA or other biological testing that was conducted previously by either the prosecution or defense, if known.

(F) State whether any motion for testing under this section previously has been filed and the results of that motion, if known.

(2) Notice of the motion shall be served on the Attorney General, the district attorney in the county of conviction, and, if known, the governmental agency or laboratory holding the evidence sought to be tested. Responses, if any, shall be filed within 90 days of the date on which the Attorney General and the district attorney are served with the motion, unless a continuance is granted for good cause.

(e) If the court finds evidence was subjected to DNA or other forensic testing previously by either the prosecution or defense, it shall order the party at whose request the testing was conducted to provide all parties and the court with access to the laboratory reports, underlying data, and laboratory notes prepared in connection with the DNA or other biological evidence testing.

(f) If the court determines that the convicted person has met all of the requirements of subparagraphs (A) to (F), inclusive, of paragraph (1) of subdivision (d), the court may, as it deems necessary, order a hearing on the motion. The judge who conducted the trial, or accepted the convicted person's plea of guilty or nolo contendere, shall conduct the hearing unless the presiding judge determines that judge is unavailable. Upon request of either party, the court may order, in the interest of justice, that the convicted person be present at the hearing of the motion. Either party, upon request, may request an additional 60 days to brief issues raised in subdivision (g).

(g) The court shall grant the motion for DNA testing if it determines all of the following have been established:

(1) The evidence to be tested is available and in a condition that would permit the DNA testing requested in the motion.

(2) The evidence to be tested has been subject to a chain of custody sufficient to establish it has not been substituted, tampered with, replaced, or altered in any material aspect.

(3) The identity of the perpetrator of the crime was, or should have been, a significant issue in the case.

(4) The convicted person has made a prima facie showing that the evidence sought to be tested is material to the issue of the convicted person's identity as the perpetrator of, or accomplice to, the crime, special circumstance, or enhancement allegation that resulted in the conviction or sentence. The convicted person is only required to demonstrate that the DNA testing he or she seeks would be relevant to, rather than dispositive of, the issue of identity. The convicted person is not required to show a favorable result would conclusively establish his or her innocence.

(5) The requested DNA testing results would raise a reasonable probability that, in light of all the evidence, the convicted person's verdict or sentence would have been more favorable if the results of DNA testing had been available at the time of conviction. The court in its discretion may consider any evidence whether or not it was introduced at trial. In determining whether the convicted person is entitled to develop potentially exculpatory evidence, the court shall not decide whether, assuming a DNA test result favorable to the convicted person, he or she is entitled to some form of ultimate relief.

(6) The evidence sought to be tested meets either of the following conditions:

(A) The evidence was not tested previously.

(B) The evidence was tested previously, but the requested DNA test would provide results that are reasonably more discriminating and probative of the identity of the perpetrator or accomplice or have a reasonable probability of contradicting prior test results.

(7) The testing requested employs a method generally accepted within the relevant scientific community.

(8) The motion is not made solely for the purpose of delay.

(h) (1) If the court grants the motion for DNA testing, the court order shall identify the specific evidence to be tested and the DNA technology to be used.

(2) The testing shall be conducted by a laboratory that meets the FBI Director's Quality Assurance Standards and that is mutually agreed upon by the district attorney in a noncapital case, or the Attorney General in a capital case, and the person filing the motion. If the parties cannot agree, the court shall designate a laboratory that meets the FBI Director's Quality Assurance Standards. Laboratories accredited by the following entities have been determined to satisfy this requirement: the American Association for Laboratory Accreditation (A2LA), the American Society of Crime Laboratory Directors/Laboratory Accreditation Board (ASCLD/LAB), and Forensic Quality Services (ANSI-ASQ National Accreditation Board FQS).

(3) If the accredited laboratory selected by the parties or designated by the court to conduct DNA testing is not a National DNA Index System (NDIS) participating laboratory that takes or retains ownership of the DNA data for entry into the Combined DNA Index System (CODIS), the laboratory selected to perform DNA testing shall not initiate analysis for a specific case until documented approval has been obtained from an appropriate NDIS participating laboratory's technical leader of acceptance of ownership of the DNA data from the selected laboratory that may be entered into or searched in CODIS.

(i) In accordance with the court's order pursuant to subdivision (h), the laboratory may communicate with either party, upon request, during the testing process. The result of any testing ordered under this section shall be fully disclosed to the person filing the motion, the district attorney, and the Attorney General. If requested by any party, the court shall order production of the underlying laboratory data and notes.

(j) (1) The cost of DNA testing ordered under this section shall be borne by the state or the applicant, as the court may order in the interests of justice, if it is shown that the applicant is not indigent and possesses the ability to pay. However, the cost of any additional testing to be conducted by the district attorney or Attorney General shall not be borne by the convicted person.

(2) In order to pay the state's share of any testing costs, the laboratory designated in subdivision (h) shall present its bill for services to the superior court for approval and

payment. It is the intent of the Legislature to appropriate funds for this purpose in the 2000–01 Budget Act.
(k) An order granting or denying a motion for DNA testing under this section shall not be appealable, and shall be subject to review only through petition for writ of mandate or prohibition filed by the person seeking DNA testing, the district attorney, or the Attorney General. The petition shall be filed within 20 days after the court's order granting or denying the motion for DNA testing. In a noncapital case, the petition for writ of mandate or prohibition shall be filed in the court of appeal. In a capital case, the petition shall be filed in the California Supreme Court. The court of appeal or California Supreme Court shall expedite its review of a petition for writ of mandate or prohibition filed under this subdivision.
(l) DNA testing ordered by the court pursuant to this section shall be done as soon as practicable. However, if the court finds that a miscarriage of justice will otherwise occur and that it is necessary in the interests of justice to give priority to the DNA testing, a DNA laboratory shall be required to give priority to the DNA testing ordered pursuant to this section over the laboratory's other pending casework.
(m) DNA profile information from biological samples taken from a convicted person pursuant to a motion for postconviction DNA testing is exempt from any law requiring disclosure of information to the public.
(n) Notwithstanding any other provision of law, the right to file a motion for postconviction DNA testing provided by this section is absolute and shall not be waived. This prohibition applies to, but is not limited to, a waiver that is given as part of an agreement resulting in a plea of guilty or nolo contendere.
(o) The provisions of this section are severable. If any provision of this section or its application is held invalid, that invalidity shall not affect other provisions or applications that can be given effect without the invalid provision or application.
(Amended by Stats. 2014, Ch. 554, Sec. 1. (SB 980) Effective January 1, 2015.)
1405.1.
(a) When the court grants a motion for DNA testing pursuant to Section 1405 and a DNA profile of an unknown contributor is generated, the court may conduct a hearing to determine if the DNA profile should be uploaded into the State Index System, and if appropriate, the National DNA Index System. The court may issue an order directing the upload of the DNA profile into the State Index System, and if appropriate, the National DNA Index System, only if all of the following conditions are met:
(1) The source of the DNA profile is attributable to the putative perpetrator of the crime.
(2) The profile meets all requirements, whether technical or otherwise, for permanent inclusion into the State Index System, and if appropriate, the National DNA Index System, as determined by the Department of Justice, the Federal Bureau of Investigation, federal law, and California law.
(3) The convicted person or convicted person's counsel provides written notice to the California Combined DNA Index System (CODIS) State Administrator at the Department of Justice, the Attorney General, and the district attorney 30 court days prior to the hearing to determine if the DNA profile should be uploaded into the State Index System, and if appropriate, the National DNA Index System.
(b) A court shall not order an upload of a DNA profile into the State Index System or the National DNA Index System that violates any CODIS or state rule, policy, or regulation.
(Added by Stats. 2014, Ch. 554, Sec. 2. (SB 980) Effective January 1, 2015.)

CHAPTER 12. Disposal of Property Stolen or Embezzled [1407 - 1413]

(Chapter 12 enacted 1872.)
1407.
When property, alleged to have been stolen or embezzled, comes into the custody of a peace officer, he shall hold it subject to the provisions of this chapter relating to the disposal thereof.
(Amended by Stats. 1975, Ch. 774.)
1408.
On the application of the owner and on satisfactory proof of his ownership of the property, after reasonable notice and opportunity to be heard has been given to the person from whom custody of the property was taken and any other person as required by the magistrate, the magistrate before whom the complaint is laid, or who examines the charge against the person accused of stealing or embezzling it, shall order it to be delivered, without prejudice to the state, to the owner, on his paying the necessary expenses incurred in its preservation, to be certified by the magistrate. The order entitles the owner to demand and receive the property.
(Amended by Stats. 1971, Ch. 799.)
1409.
If property stolen or embezzled comes into the custody of the magistrate, it shall be delivered, without prejudice to the state, to the owner upon his application to the court and on satisfactory proof of his title, after reasonable notice and opportunity to be heard has been given to the person from whom custody of the property was taken and any other person as required by the magistrate, and on his paying the necessary expenses incurred in its preservation, to be certified by the magistrate.
(Amended by Stats. 1971, Ch. 799.)
1410.
If the property stolen or embezzled has not been delivered to the owner, the court before which a trial is had for stealing or embezzling it, upon the application of the owner to the court and on proof of his title, after reasonable notice and opportunity to be heard has been given to the person from whom custody of the property was taken and any other person as required by the court, may order it to be restored to the owner without prejudice to the state.
(Amended by Stats. 1971, Ch. 799.)
1411.
(a) If the ownership of the property stolen or embezzled and the address of the owner, and the address of the owner of a security interest therein, can be reasonably ascertained, the peace officer who took custody of the property shall notify the owner, and a person having a security interest therein, by letter of the location of the property and the method by which the owner may obtain it. This notice shall be given upon the conviction of a person for an offense involving the theft, embezzlement, or possession of the property, or if a conviction was not obtained, upon the making of a decision by the district attorney not to file the case or upon the termination of the proceedings in the case. Except as provided in Section 217 of the Welfare and Institutions Code, if the property stolen or embezzled is not claimed by the owner before the expiration of three months after the giving of this notice, or, in any case in which such a notice is not given, before the expiration of six months from the conviction of a person for an offense involving the theft, embezzlement, or possession of the property, or if a conviction was not obtained, then from the time the property came into the possession of the peace officer or the case involving the person from whom it was obtained is disposed of, whichever is later, the magistrate or other officer having it in custody may, on the payment of the necessary expenses incurred in its preservation, deliver it to the county treasurer or other proper county officer, by whom it shall be sold and the proceeds paid into the county treasury. However, notwithstanding any other law, if the person from whom custody of the property was taken is a secondhand dealer or licensed pawnbroker and reasonable but unsuccessful efforts have been made to notify the owner of the property and the property is no longer needed for the criminal proceeding, the property shall be returned to the secondhand dealer or pawnbroker who had custody of the property and be treated as regularly acquired property. If the property is transferred to the county purchasing agent it may be sold in the manner provided by Article 7 (commencing with Section 25500) of Chapter 5 of Part 2 of Division 2 of Title 3 of the Government Code for the sale of surplus personal property. If the county officer determines that any of the property transferred to him or her for sale is needed for a public use, the property may be retained by the county and need not be sold. The magistrate or other officer having the property in custody may, however, provide for the sale of the property in the manner provided for the sale of unclaimed property which has been held for at least three months pursuant to Section 2080.4 of the Civil Code.
(b) This section shall not govern the disposition of property placed on hold pursuant to Section 21647 of the Business and Professions Code, notwithstanding the current custodial status of the property, unless the licensed pawnbroker or secondhand dealer, after receipt of the written advisement required by subdivision (h) of Section 21647 of the Business and Professions Code, willfully refuses to consent to a statutory hold as provided by Section 21647 of the Business and Professions Code or a search warrant for the business of the licensed pawnbroker or secondhand dealer has resulted in the seizure of the property subject to this section.
(Amended by Stats. 2013, Ch. 318, Sec. 3. (SB 762) Effective January 1, 2014.)
1412.
When money or other property is taken from a defendant, arrested upon a charge of a public offense, the officer taking it must at the time give duplicate receipts therefor, specifying particularly the amount of money or the kind of property taken; one of which receipts he must deliver to the defendant and the other of which he must forthwith file with the Clerk of the Court to which the depositions and statement are to be sent. When such property is taken by a police officer of any incorporated city or town, he must deliver one of the receipts to the defendant, and one, with the property, at once to the Clerk or other person in charge of the police office in such city or town.
(Enacted 1872.)
1413.
(a) The clerk or person having charge of the property section for any police department in any incorporated city or town, or for any sheriff's department in any county, shall enter in a suitable book a description of every article of property alleged to be stolen or embezzled, and brought into the office or taken from the person of a prisoner, and shall attach a number to each article, and make a corresponding entry thereof. He may engrave or imbed an identification number in property described in Section 537e for the purposes thereof.
(b) The clerk or person in charge of the property section may, upon satisfactory proof of the ownership of property held pursuant to Section 1407, and upon presentation of proper personal identification, deliver it to the owner. Such delivery shall be without prejudice to the state or to the person from whom custody of the property was taken or to any other person who may have a claim against the property. Prior to such delivery such clerk or person in charge of the property section shall make and retain a complete photographic record of such property. The person to whom property is delivered shall sign, under penalty of perjury, a declaration of ownership, which shall be retained by the clerk or person in charge of the property section. This subdivision shall not apply to any property subject to forfeiture under any provision of law. This subdivision shall not apply unless the clerk or person in charge of the property section has served upon the person from whom custody of the property was taken a notice of a claim of ownership and a copy of the satisfactory proof of ownership tendered and has allowed such person reasonable opportunity to be heard as to why the property should not be delivered to the person claiming ownership.
If the person upon whom a notice of claim and proof of ownership has been served does not respond asserting a claim to the property within 15 days from the date of receipt of the service, the property may be disposed of in a manner not inconsistent with the provisions of this section.
(c) The magistrate before whom the complaint is laid, or who examines the charge against the person accused of stealing or embezzling the property, or the court before which a trial is had for stealing or embezzling it, shall upon application by the person from whom custody of the property was taken, review the determination of the clerk or person in charge of the property section, and may order the property taken into the custody of the court upon a finding that the person to whom the property was delivered is not entitled thereto. Such court shall make its determination in the same manner as a determination is made when the matter is before the court pursuant to Sections 1408 to 1410, inclusive.
(d) The clerk or person in charge of the property section is not liable in damages for any official action performed hereunder in good faith.
(Amended by Stats. 1981, Ch. 714, Sec. 332.)

CHAPTER 13. Disposition of Evidence in Criminal Cases [1417 - 1417.9]

(Chapter 13 repealed and added by Stats. 1985, Ch. 875, Sec. 3.)
1417.
All exhibits which have been introduced or filed in any criminal action or proceeding shall be retained by the clerk of the court who shall establish a procedure to account for the exhibits properly, subject to Sections 1417.2 and 1417.3 until final determination of the action or proceedings and the exhibits shall thereafter be distributed or disposed of as provided in this chapter.
(Amended by Stats. 1990, Ch. 382, Sec. 3.)
1417.1.
No order shall be made for the destruction of an exhibit prior to the final determination of the action or proceeding. For the purposes of this chapter, the date when a criminal action or proceeding becomes final is as follows:
(a) When no notice of appeal is filed, 30 days after the last day for filing that notice.
(b) When a notice of appeal is filed, 30 days after the date the clerk of the court receives the remittitur affirming the judgment.
(c) When an order for a rehearing, a new trial, or other proceeding is granted and the ordered proceedings have not been commenced within one year thereafter, one year after the date of that order.
(d) (1) In cases where the death penalty is imposed, 30 days after the date of execution of sentence.
(2) In cases where the death penalty is imposed and the defendant dies while awaiting execution, one year after the date of the defendant's death.
(Amended by Stats. 2012, Ch. 283, Sec. 2. (SB 1489) Effective January 1, 2013.)
1417.2.
Notwithstanding Section 1417.5, the court may, on application of the party entitled thereto or an agent designated in writing by the owner, order an exhibit delivered to that party at any time prior to the final determination of the action or proceeding, upon stipulation of the parties or upon notice and motion if both of the following requirements are met:
(a) No prejudice will be suffered by either party.
(b) A full and complete photographic record is made of the exhibits so released.
The party to whom the exhibit is being returned shall provide the photographic record.
This section shall not apply to any material, the release of which is prohibited by Section 1417.6.

(Added by Stats. 1985, Ch. 875, Sec. 3.)
1417.3.
(a) At any time prior to the final determination of the action or proceeding, exhibits offered by the state or defendant shall be returned to the party offering them by order of the court when an exhibit poses a security, storage, or safety problem, as recommended by the clerk of the court. If an exhibit by its nature is severable the court shall order the clerk to retain a portion of the exhibit not exceeding three pounds by weight or one cubic foot by volume and shall order the return of the balance of the exhibit to the district attorney. The clerk, upon court order, shall substitute a full and complete photographic record of any exhibit or part of any exhibit returned to the state under this section. The party to whom the exhibit is being returned shall provide the photographic record.
(b) Exhibits toxic by their nature that pose a health hazard to humans shall be introduced to the court in the form of a photographic record and a written chemical analysis certified by competent authority. Where the court finds that good cause exists to depart from this procedure, toxic exhibits may be brought into the courtroom and introduced. However, following introduction of the exhibit, the person or persons previously in possession of the exhibit shall take responsibility for it and the court shall not be required to store the exhibit.
(Amended by Stats. 1990, Ch. 382, Sec. 4.)
1417.5.
Except as provided in Section 1417.6, 60 days after the final determination of a criminal action or proceeding, the clerk of the court shall dispose of all exhibits introduced or filed in the case and remaining in the clerk's possession, as follows:
(a) If the name and address of the person from whom the exhibit was taken is contained in the court record, the clerk shall notify the person that he or she may make application to the court for release of the exhibits within 15 days of receipt of the notification.
(b) The court shall order the release of exhibits free of charge, without prejudice to the state, upon application, to the following:
(1) First, the person from whom the exhibits were taken into custody, provided that the person was in lawful possession of the exhibits.
(2) Second, a person establishing title to, or a right to possession of, the exhibits.
(c) If the party entitled to an exhibit fails to apply for the return of the exhibit prior to the date for disposition under this section, the following procedures shall apply:
(1) Exhibits of stolen or embezzled property other than money shall be disposed of pursuant to court order as provided in Section 1417.6.
(2) Exhibits of property other than property which is stolen or embezzled or property which consists of money or currency shall, except as otherwise provided in this paragraph and in paragraph (3), be transferred to the appropriate county agency for sale to the public in the same manner provided by Article 7 (commencing with Section 25500) of Chapter 5 of Part 2 of Division 2 of Title 3 of the Government Code for the sale of surplus personal property. If the county determines that any property is needed for a public use, the property may be retained by the county and need not be sold.
(3) Exhibits of property, other than money, currency, or stolen or embezzled property, that are determined by the court to have no value at public sale shall be destroyed or otherwise disposed of pursuant to court order.
(4) Exhibits of money or currency shall be disposed of pursuant to Section 1420.
(Amended by Stats. 1997, Ch. 133, Sec. 1. Effective January 1, 1998.)
1417.6.
(a) The provisions of Section 1417.5 shall not apply to any dangerous or deadly weapons, narcotic or poisonous drugs, explosives, or any property of any kind or character whatsoever the possession of which is prohibited by law and that was used by a defendant in the commission of the crime of which the defendant was convicted, or with which the defendant was armed or that the defendant had upon his or her person at the time of the defendant's arrest.
Any of this property introduced or filed as an exhibit shall be, by order of the trial court, destroyed or otherwise disposed of under the conditions provided in the order no sooner than 60 days following the final determination of the criminal action or proceeding.
(b) (1) Every person who knowingly has in his or her possession any tool or device that is seized and of a type used in the commission of a violation of Section 10801, 10802, or 10803 of the Vehicle Code, shall be subject to having the tool or device intended for the above purpose deemed a nuisance as provided in paragraph (2).
(2) An evidentiary hearing shall be held only upon conviction of the defendant for a violation of Section 10801, 10802, or 10803 of the Vehicle Code and after 15 days' notice is given to the defendant of the state's intent to declare as a nuisance any property that is described in paragraph (1). All relevant evidence shall be admissible at the hearing and the state shall prove by a preponderance of the evidence that the property seized is of a type used in facilitating the commission of the crime of which the defendant was convicted.
(3) If a person purports to be the lawful owner of any tool or device the state seeks to be declared a nuisance, the person shall show proof by a preponderance of the evidence at the hearing pursuant to paragraph (2), that he or she owns the tool or device, and the illegal use of the tool or device was without his or her knowledge or consent.
(4) Following a determination that the property shall be declared a nuisance, the property shall be disposed of as provided in paragraph (2) or (3) of subdivision (c) of Section 1417.5.
(Amended by Stats. 2010, Ch. 709, Sec. 17. (SB 1062) Effective January 1, 2011.)
1417.7.
Not less than 15 days before any proposed disposition of an exhibit pursuant to Section 1417.3, 1417.5, or 1417.6, the court shall notify the district attorney or other prosecuting attorney, the attorney of record for each party, and each party who is not represented by counsel of the proposed disposition. Before the disposition, any party, at his or her own expense, may cause to be prepared a photographic or digital record of all or part of the exhibit by a person who is not a party or attorney of a party. The clerk of the court shall observe the taking of the photographic or digital record and, upon receipt of a declaration of the person making the photographic or digital record that the duplicate delivered to the clerk is a true, unaltered, and unretouched duplicate of the photographic or digital record taken in the presence of the clerk, the clerk shall certify the photographic or digital record as such without charge and retain it unaltered for a period of 60 days following the final determination of the criminal action or proceeding. For purposes of this section, a "photographic record" of the exhibit means a photographic image of the exhibit or its equivalent stored in any form. For purposes of this section, a "duplicate" means a counterpart produced by a mechanical, photographic, chemical, electronic, or other equivalent process or technique that accurately reproduces the original. A certified photographic or digital record of exhibits shall not be deemed inadmissible pursuant to Section 1521 or 1522 of the Evidence Code.
(Amended by Stats. 2017, Ch. 566, Sec. 3. (SB 238) Effective October 7, 2017.)
1417.8.
(a) Notwithstanding any other provision of this chapter, the court shall direct that any photograph of any minor that has been found by the court to be harmful matter, as defined in Section 313, and introduced or filed as an exhibit in any criminal proceeding specified in subdivision (b) be handled as follows:
(1) Prior to the final determination of the action or proceeding, the photograph shall be available only to the parties or to a person named in a court order to receive the photograph.

(2) After the final determination of the action or proceeding, the photograph shall be preserved with the permanent record maintained by the clerk of the court. The photograph may be disposed of or destroyed after preservation through any appropriate photographic or electronic medium. If the photograph is disposed of, it shall be rendered unidentifiable before the disposal. No person shall have access to the photograph unless that person has been named in a court order to receive the photograph. Any copy, negative, reprint, or other duplication of the photograph in the possession of the state, a state agency, the defendant, or an agent of the defendant, shall be delivered to the clerk of the court for disposal whether or not the defendant was convicted of the offense.
(b) The procedure provided by subdivision (a) shall apply to actions listed under subdivision (c) of Section 290, and to acts under the following provisions:
(1) Section 261.5.
(2) Section 272.
(3) Chapter 7.5 (commencing with Section 311) of Title 9 of Part 1.
(4) Chapter 7.6 (commencing with Section 313) of Title 9 of Part 1.
(c) For the purposes of this section, "photograph" means any photographic image contained in a digital format or on any chemical, mechanical, magnetic, or electronic medium.
(Amended by Stats. 2007, Ch. 579, Sec. 43. Effective October 13, 2007.)
1417.9.
(a) Notwithstanding any other law and subject to subdivisions (b) and (c), the appropriate governmental entity shall retain any object or material that contains or includes biological material that is secured in connection with a criminal case for the period of time that any person remains incarcerated in connection with that case. The governmental entity shall have the discretion to determine how the evidence is retained pursuant to this section, provided that the evidence is retained in a condition suitable for deoxyribonucleic acid (DNA) testing.
(b) A governmental entity may dispose of any object or material that contains or includes biological material before the expiration of the period of time described in subdivision (a) if all of the conditions set forth below are met:
(1) The governmental entity notifies all of the following persons of the provisions of this section and of the intention of the governmental entity to dispose of the material:
(A) Any person, who as a result of a felony conviction in the case is currently serving a term of imprisonment and who remains incarcerated in connection with the case. This notification shall be sent to the current location where the person is incarcerated.
(B) Any counsel of record.
(C) The public defender in the county of conviction.
(D) The district attorney in the county of conviction.
(E) The Attorney General.
(2) The notifying entity does not receive, within 180 days of sending the notification, any of the following:
(A) A motion filed pursuant to Section 1405. However, upon filing of that motion, the governmental entity shall retain the material only until the time that the court's denial of the motion is final.
(B) A request under penalty of perjury that the material not be destroyed or disposed of because the declarant will file a motion for DNA testing pursuant to Section 1405 within one year, unless a request for an extension is requested by the convicted person and agreed to by the governmental entity in possession of the evidence.
(C) A declaration of innocence filed with the court under penalty of perjury. However, the court shall permit the destruction of the evidence upon a showing that the declaration is false or there is no issue of identity that would be affected by additional testing. The convicted person may be cross-examined on the declaration at any hearing conducted under this section or on an application by or on behalf of the convicted person filed pursuant to Section 1405.
(3) No other law requires that biological evidence be preserved or retained.
(c) Notwithstanding any other law, the right to receive notice pursuant to this section is absolute and shall not be waived. This prohibition applies to, but is not limited to, a waiver that is given as part of an agreement resulting in a plea of guilty or nolo contendere.
(Amended by Stats. 2018, Ch. 972, Sec. 1. (AB 2988) Effective January 1, 2019.)

CHAPTER 14. Disposition of Unclaimed Money Held by District Attorney or Court Clerk [1420 - 1422]

(Heading of Chapter 14 amended by Stats. 1985, Ch. 875, Sec. 4.)
1420.
All money received by a district attorney or clerk of the court in any criminal action or proceeding, the owner or owners of which are unknown, and which remains unclaimed in the possession of the district attorney or clerk of the court after final judgment in the criminal action or proceeding, shall be deposited with the county treasurer. Upon the expiration of two years after the deposit, the county treasurer shall cause a notice pursuant to Section 1421 to be published in the county once a week for two successive weeks in a newspaper of general circulation published in the county.
(Amended by Stats. 1985, Ch. 875, Sec. 5.)
1421.
The notice shall state the amount of money, the criminal action or proceeding in which the money was received by the district attorney or clerk of the court, the fund in which it is held and that it is proposed that the money will become the property of the county on a designated date not less than 45 days nor more than 60 days after the first publication of the notice.
(Amended by Stats. 1985, Ch. 875, Sec. 6.)
1422.
Unless some person files a verified complaint seeking to recover all, or a designated part, of the money in a court of competent jurisdiction within the county in which the notice is published, and serves a copy of the complaint and the summons issued thereon upon the county treasurer before the date designated in the notice, upon that date the money becomes the property of the county and shall be transferred by the treasurer to the general fund.
(Added by Stats. 1959. Ch. 2016.)

CHAPTER 15. Disqualification of Prosecuting Attorneys [1424 - 1424.5]

(Chapter 15 added by Stats. 1980, Ch. 780, Sec. 1.)
1424.
(a) (1) Notice of a motion to disqualify a district attorney from performing an authorized duty shall be served on the district attorney and the Attorney General at least 10 court days before the motion is heard. The notice of motion shall contain a statement of the facts setting forth the grounds for the claimed disqualification and the legal authorities relied upon by the moving party and shall be supported by affidavits of witnesses who

are competent to testify to the facts set forth in the affidavit. The district attorney or the Attorney General, or both, may file affidavits in opposition to the motion and may appear at the hearing on the motion and may file with the court hearing the motion a written opinion on the disqualification issue. The judge shall review the affidavits and determine whether or not an evidentiary hearing is necessary. The motion may not be granted unless the evidence shows that a conflict of interest exists that would render it unlikely that the defendant would receive a fair trial. An order recusing the district attorney from any proceeding may be reviewed by extraordinary writ or may be appealed by the district attorney or the Attorney General. The order recusing the district attorney shall be stayed pending any review authorized by this section. If the motion is brought at or before the preliminary hearing, it may not be renewed in the trial court on the basis of facts that were raised or could have been raised at the time of the original motion.
(2) An appeal from an order of recusal or from a case involving a charge punishable as a felony shall be made pursuant to Chapter 1 (commencing with Section 1235) of Title 9, regardless of the court in which the order is made. An appeal from an order of recusal in a misdemeanor case shall be made pursuant to Chapter 2 (commencing with Section 1466) of Title 11, regardless of the court in which the order is made.
(b) (1) Notice of a motion to disqualify a city attorney or city prosecutor from performing an authorized duty involving a criminal matter shall be served on the city attorney or city prosecutor and the district attorney at least 10 court days before the motion is heard. The notice of motion shall set forth a statement of the facts relevant to the claimed disqualification and the legal authorities relied on by the moving party. The district attorney may appear at the hearing on the motion and may file with the court hearing the motion a written opinion on the disqualification issue. The motion may not be granted unless the evidence shows that a conflict of interest exists that would render it unlikely that the defendant would receive a fair trial.
(2) An order recusing the city attorney or city prosecutor from a proceeding may be appealed by the city attorney or city prosecutor or the district attorney. The order recusing the city attorney or city prosecutor shall be stayed pending an appeal authorized by this section. An appeal from an order of disqualification in a misdemeanor case shall be made pursuant to Chapter 2 (commencing with Section 1466) of Title 11.
(c) Motions to disqualify the city attorney or city prosecutor and the district attorney shall be separately made.
(Amended by Stats. 2017, Ch. 299, Sec. 2. (AB 1418) Effective January 1, 2018.)

1424.5.
(a) (1) Upon receiving information that a prosecuting attorney may have deliberately and intentionally withheld relevant, material exculpatory evidence or information in violation of law, a court may make a finding, supported by clear and convincing evidence, that a violation occurred. If the court finds such a violation, the court shall inform the State Bar of California of that violation if the prosecuting attorney acted in bad faith and the impact of the withholding contributed to a guilty verdict, guilty or nolo contendere plea, or, if identified before conclusion of trial, seriously limited the ability of a defendant to present a defense.
(2) A court may hold a hearing to consider whether a violation occurred pursuant to paragraph (1).
(b) (1) If a court finds, pursuant to subdivision (a), that a violation occurred in bad faith, the court may disqualify an individual prosecuting attorney from a case.
(2) Upon a determination by a court to disqualify an individual prosecuting attorney pursuant to paragraph (1), the defendant or his or her counsel may file and serve a notice of a motion pursuant to Section 1424 to disqualify the prosecuting attorney's office if there is sufficient evidence that other employees of the prosecuting attorney's office knowingly and in bad faith participated in or sanctioned the intentional withholding of the relevant, material exculpatory evidence or information and that withholding is part of a pattern and practice of violations.
(c) This section does not limit the authority or discretion of, or any requirement placed upon, the court or other individuals to make reports to the State Bar of California regarding the same conduct, or otherwise limit other available legal authority, requirements, remedies, or actions.
(Amended by Stats. 2016, Ch. 59, Sec. 7. (SB 1474) Effective January 1, 2017.)

TITLE 11. PROCEEDINGS IN MISDEMEANOR AND INFRACTION CASES AND APPEALS FROM SUCH CASES [1427 - 1471]

(Heading of Title 11 amended by Stats. 1998, Ch. 931, Sec. 407.)

CHAPTER 1. Proceedings in Misdemeanor and Infraction Cases [1427 - 1465.8]

(Heading of Chapter 1 amended by Stats. 1998, Ch. 931, Sec. 408.)

1427.
(a) When a complaint is presented to a judge in a misdemeanor or infraction case appearing to be triable in the judge's court, the judge must, if satisfied therefrom that the offense complained of has been committed and that there is reasonable ground to believe that the defendant has committed it, issue a warrant, for the arrest of the defendant.
(b) Such warrant of arrest and proceedings upon it shall be in conformity to the provisions of this code regarding warrants of arrest, and it may be in the following form:
County of _____
The people of the State of California, to any peace officer in this state:
Complaint upon oath having been this day made before me that the offense of _____ (designating it generally) has been committed and accusing _____ (name of defendant) thereof you are therefore commanded forthwith to arrest the above-named defendant and bring the defendant forthwith before the _____ Court of _____ (stating full title of court) at _____ (naming place).
Witness my hand and the seal of said court this _____ day of _____, 19__.

_____ (Signed). _____ _____ Judge of said court _____

If it appears that the offense complained of has been committed by a corporation, no warrant of arrest shall issue, but the judge must issue a summons substantially in the form prescribed in Section 1391. Such summons must be served at the time and in the manner designated in Section 1392 except that if the offense complained of is a violation of the Vehicle Code or a local ordinance adopted pursuant to the Vehicle Code, such summons may be served by deposit by the clerk of the court in the United States mail of an envelope enclosing the summons, which envelope shall be addressed to a person authorized to accept service of legal process on behalf of the defendant, and which envelope shall be mailed by registered mail or certified mail with a return receipt requested. Promptly upon such mailing, the clerk of the court shall execute a certificate of such mailing and place it in the file of the court for that case. At the time stated in the summons the corporation may appear by counsel and answer the complaint, except that in the case of misdemeanors arising from operation of motor vehicles, or of infractions arising from operation of motor vehicles, a corporation may appear by its president, vice president, secretary or managing agent for the purpose of entering a plea of guilty. If it does not appear, a plea of not guilty shall be entered, and the same proceedings had therein as in other cases.
(Amended by Stats. 1998, Ch. 931, Sec. 409. Effective September 28, 1998.)

1428.
In misdemeanor and infraction cases, the clerk of the superior court may keep a docket, instead of minutes pursuant to Section 69844 of the Government Code and a register of actions pursuant to Section 69845 or 69845.5 of the Government Code. In the docket, the clerk shall enter the title of each criminal action or proceeding and under each title all the orders and proceedings in such action or proceeding. Wherever by any other section of this code made applicable to such court an entry of any judgment, order or other proceeding in the minutes or register of actions is required, an entry thereof in the docket shall be made and shall be deemed a sufficient entry in the minutes or register of actions for all purposes.
(Amended by Stats. 2002, Ch. 784, Sec. 553. Effective January 1, 2003.)

1429.
In a misdemeanor case the plea of the defendant may be made by the defendant or by the defendant's counsel. If such defendant pleads guilty, the court may, before entering such plea or pronouncing judgment, examine witnesses to ascertain the gravity of the offense committed; and if it appears to the court that a higher offense has been committed than the offense charged in the complaint, the court may order the defendant to be committed or admitted to bail, to answer any indictment which may be found against the defendant by the grand jury, or any complaint which may be filed charging the defendant with such higher offense.
(Amended by Stats. 1998, Ch. 931, Sec. 411. Effective September 28, 1998.)

1445.
When the defendant pleads guilty, or is convicted, either by the court, or by a jury, the court shall render judgment thereon of fine or imprisonment, or both, as the case may be.
(Amended by Stats. 1989, Ch. 1360, Sec. 117.)

1447.
When the defendant is acquitted in a misdemeanor or infraction case, if the court certifies in the minutes that the prosecution was malicious and without probable cause, the court may order the complainant to pay the costs of the action, or to give an undertaking to pay the costs within 30 days after the trial.
(Amended by Stats. 1998, Ch. 931, Sec. 413. Effective September 28, 1998.)

1448.
If the complainant does not pay the costs, or give an undertaking therefor, the court may enter judgment against the complainant for the amount of the costs, which may be enforced in the manner provided for enforcement of money judgments generally.
(Amended by Stats. 1983, Ch. 18, Sec. 25. Effective April 21, 1983.)

1449.
In a misdemeanor or infraction case, after a plea, finding, or verdict of guilty, or after a finding or verdict against the defendant on a plea of former conviction or acquittal, or once in jeopardy, the court shall appoint a time for pronouncing judgment which shall be not less than six hours, nor more than five days, after the verdict or plea of guilty, unless the defendant waives the postponement. The court may extend the time for not more than 10 days for the purpose of hearing or determining any motion for a new trial, or in arrest of judgment. The court also may extend the time for not more than 20 judicial days if probation is considered. Upon request of the defendant or the probation officer, that time may be further extended for not more than 90 additional days. In case of postponement, the court may hold the defendant to bail to appear for judgment. If, in the opinion of the court there is a reasonable ground for believing a defendant insane, the court may extend the time of pronouncing judgment and may commit the defendant to custody until the question of insanity has been heard and determined.
If the defendant is a veteran who was discharged from service for mental disability, upon his or her request, his or her case shall be referred to the probation officer, who shall secure a military medical history of the defendant and present it to the court together with a recommendation for or against probation.
(Amended by Stats. 1998, Ch. 931, Sec. 414. Effective September 28, 1998.)

1457.
Upon payment of the fine, the officer must discharge the defendant, if he is not detained for any other legal cause, and pay over the fine to the court which rendered the judgment.
(Amended by Stats. 1949, Ch. 1517. Note: The condition in Sec. 5 of Ch. 1517 was satisfied by adoption of Prop. 3 on Nov. 7, 1950.)

1458.
The provisions of this code relative to bail are applicable to bail in misdemeanor or infraction cases. The defendant, at any time after arrest and before conviction, may be admitted to bail. The undertaking of bail in such a case shall be in substantially the following form:
A complaint having been filed on the _____ day of _____, 19___, in the _____ Court of _____ County of _____ (stating title and location of court) charging _____ (naming defendant) as defendant with the crime of _____ (designating it generally) and the defendant having been admitted to bail in the sum of _____ dollars ($_____) (stating amount);
We, _____ and _____, of _____ (stating their places of residence and occupation), hereby undertake that the above-named defendant will appear and answer any charge in any accusatory pleading based upon the acts supporting the complaint above mentioned and all duly authorized amendments thereof, in whatever court it may be prosecuted, and will at all times hold himself or herself amenable to the orders and process of the court, and, if convicted, will appear for pronouncement of judgment or grant of probation or if the defendant fails to perform either of these conditions, that we will pay to the people of the State of California the sum of _____ dollars ($_____) (inserting the sum in which the defendant is admitted to bail). If the forfeiture of this bond is ordered by the court, judgment may be summarily made and entered forthwith against the said _____ (naming the sureties and the defendant if the defendant is a party to the bond) for the amount of their respective undertakings herein, as provided by Sections 1305 and 1306 of the California Penal Code.
(Amended by Stats. 1998, Ch. 931, Sec. 415. Effective September 28, 1998.)

1459.
Undertakings of bail filed by admitted surety insurers shall meet all other requirements of law and the obligation of the insurer shall be in the following form except to the extent a different form is otherwise provided by statute:
_____ (stating the title and the location of the court).
Defendant _____ (stating the name of the defendant) having been admitted to bail in the sum of _____ dollars ($_____) (stating the amount of bail fixed) and ordered to appear in the above-entitled court on _____, 19___ (stating the date for appearance in court), on _____ (stating only the word "misdemeanor" or the word "felony") charge/s;
Now, the _____ (stating the name of admitted surety insurer and state of incorporation) hereby undertakes that the above-named defendant will appear in the above-named court on the date above set forth to answer any charge in any accusatory pleading based upon the acts supporting the complaint filed against him/her and all duly authorized amendments thereof, in whatever court it may be prosecuted, and will at all times hold him/herself amenable to the orders and process of the court and, if

convicted, will appear for pronouncement of judgment or grant of probation or if he/she fails to perform either of these conditions, that the _____ (stating the name of admitted surety insurer and state of incorporation) will pay to the people of the State of California the sum of _____ dollars ($_____) (stating the amount of the undertaking of the admitted surety insurer.)

If the forfeiture of this bond be ordered by the court, judgment may be summarily made and entered forthwith against the said _____ (stating the name of admitted surety insurer and state of incorporation) for the amount of its undertaking herein, as provided by Sections 1305 and 1306 of the California Penal Code.

(Stating the name of admitted surety insurer and state of incorporation),
(Signature)
By Attorney-in-fact (Corporate seal)
(Jurat of notary public or other officer authorized to administer oaths.)

(Amended by Stats. 1998, Ch. 931, Sec. 416. Effective September 28, 1998.)
1462.2.
Except as otherwise provided in the Vehicle Code, the proper court for the trial of criminal cases amounting to misdemeanor shall be the superior court of the county within which the offense charged was committed.

If an action or proceeding is commenced in a court other than the court herein designated as the proper court for the trial, the action may, notwithstanding, be tried in the court where commenced, unless the defendant, at the time of pleading, requests an order transferring the action or proceeding to the proper court. If after that request it appears that the action or proceeding was not commenced in the proper court, the court shall order the action or proceeding transferred to the proper court. The judge shall, at the time of arraignment, inform the defendant of the right to be tried in the county where the offense was committed.

(Amended by Stats. 2003, Ch. 449, Sec. 35. Effective January 1, 2004.)
1462.25.
(a) A defendant formally charged with a violation of Vehicle Code Section 14601 in one court ("the first court"), against whom a formal charge of a violation of Vehicle Code Section 14601 is pending in one or more other courts, may state in writing his or her agreement to plead guilty or nolo contendere to some or all of the charges pending in the other courts, to waive trial or hearing in the other courts, and to consent to disposition of the case in the first court. The defendant's agreement is ineffective unless the district attorney for the other county approves in writing. Upon receipt of the defendant's agreement and the district attorney's approval, the clerk of court in the other court shall transfer the pending matter to the first court, and transmit the papers or certified copies. The prosecution of each transferred matter shall proceed in the first court as part of the case pending against the defendant there, but shall be limited to proceedings upon the defendant's plea of guilty or nolo contendere, and sentencing or probation. If the defendant pleads not guilty, the clerk shall retransfer the transferred case to the court of origin, and the prosecution shall be resumed in that court. The defendant's statement that the defendant agreed to plead guilty or nolo contendere shall not be used against the defendant.
(b) The procedure specified in subdivision (a) may be used only if the defendant is represented by counsel in the other courts, or the defendant has expressly waived his or her right to counsel in the other courts.
(c) A defendant may request appointment of counsel in the other courts by a written request. Upon receiving the defendant's written request, the other court shall appoint counsel to represent the defendant if he or she otherwise qualifies for appointed counsel.
(d) The appearance of the defendant in proceedings transferred pursuant to subdivision (a) shall not commence the running of time limits under Section 859b, 860, 861, or 1382.

(Added by Stats. 1994, Ch. 389, Sec. 20. Effective September 1, 1994.)
1462.5.
Each installment or partial payment of a fine, penalty, forfeiture, or fee shall be prorated among the state and local shares according to the trial court revenue distribution guidelines established by the Controller pursuant to Section 71380 of the Government Code. In cases subject to Section 1463.18 of the Penal Code, proration shall not occur until the minimum amounts have been transferred to the Restitution Fund as provided in that section.

(Amended by Stats. 2016, Ch. 703, Sec. 18. (AB 2881) Effective January 1, 2017.)
1463.
All fines and forfeitures imposed and collected for crimes shall be distributed in accordance with Section 1463.001.
The following definitions shall apply to terms used in this chapter:
(a) "Arrest" means any law enforcement action, including issuance of a notice to appear or notice of violation, which results in a criminal charge.
(b) "City" includes any city, city and county, district, including any enterprise special district, community service district, or community service area engaged in police protection activities as reported to the Controller for inclusion in the 1989–90 edition of the Financial Transactions Report Concerning Special Districts under the heading of Police Protection and Public Safety, authority, or other local agency (other than a county) which employs persons authorized to make arrests or to issue notices to appear or notices of violation which may be filed in court.
(c) "City arrest" means an arrest by an employee of a city, or by a California Highway Patrol officer within the limits of a city.
(d) "County" means the county in which the arrest took place.
(e) "County arrest" means an arrest by a California Highway Patrol officer outside the limits of a city, or any arrest by a county officer or by any other state officer.
(f) "Court" means the superior court or a juvenile forum established under Section 257 of the Welfare and Institutions Code, in which the case arising from the arrest is heard.
(g) "Division of moneys" means an allocation of base fine proceeds between agencies as required by statute, including, but not limited to, Sections 1463.003, 1463.9, 1463.23, and 1463.26 of this code, Sections 13001, 13002, and 13003 of the Fish and Game Code, and Section 11502 of the Health and Safety Code.
(h) "Offense" means any infraction, misdemeanor, or felony, and any act by a juvenile leading to an order to pay a financial sanction by reason of the act being defined as an infraction, misdemeanor, or felony, whether defined in this or any other code, except any parking offense as defined in subdivision (i).
(i) "Parking offense" means any offense charged pursuant to Article 3 (commencing with Section 40200) of Chapter 1 of Division 17 of the Vehicle Code, including registration and equipment offenses included on a notice of parking violation.

(j) "Penalty allocation" means the deposit of a specified part of moneys to offset designated processing costs, as provided by Section 1463.16 of this code and by Section 68090.8 of the Government Code.
(k) "Total parking penalty" means the total sum to be collected for a parking offense, whether as fine, forfeiture of bail, or payment of penalty to the Department of Motor Vehicles (DMV). It may include the following components:
(1) The base parking penalty as established pursuant to Section 40203.5 of the Vehicle Code.
(2) The DMV fees added upon the placement of a hold pursuant to Section 40220 of the Vehicle Code.
(3) The surcharges required by Section 76000 of the Government Code.
(4) The notice penalty added to the base parking penalty when a notice of delinquent parking violations is given.
(l) "Total fine or forfeiture" means the total sum to be collected upon a conviction, or the total amount of bail forfeited or deposited as cash bail subject to forfeiture. It may include, but is not limited to, the following components as specified for the particular offense:
(1) The "base fine" upon which the state penalty and additional county penalty is calculated.
(2) The "county penalty" required by Section 76000 of the Government Code.
(3) The "DNA penalty" required by Sections 76104.6 and 76104.7 of the Government Code.
(4) The "emergency medical services penalty" authorized by Section 76000.5 of the Government Code.
(5) The "service charge" permitted by Section 853.7 of the Penal Code and Section 40508.5 of the Vehicle Code.
(6) The "special penalty" dedicated for blood alcohol analysis, alcohol program services, traumatic brain injury research, and similar purposes.
(7) The "state penalty" required by Section 1464.

(Amended by Stats. 2007, Ch. 302, Sec. 16. Effective January 1, 2008.)
1463.001.
Except as otherwise provided in this section, all fines and forfeitures imposed and collected for crimes other than parking offenses resulting from a filing in a court shall as soon as practicable after receipt thereof, be deposited with the county treasurer, and each month the total fines and forfeitures which have accumulated within the past month shall be distributed, as follows:
(a) The state penalties, county penalties, special penalties, service charges, and penalty allocations shall be transferred to the proper funds as required by law.
(b) The base fines shall be distributed, as follows:
(1) Any base fines which are subject to specific distribution under any other section shall be distributed to the specified funds of the state or local agency.
(2) Base fines resulting from county arrest not included in paragraph (1), shall be transferred into the proper funds of the county.
(3) Base fines resulting from city arrests not included in paragraph (1), an amount equal to the applicable county percentages set forth in Section 1463.002, as modified by Section 1463.28, shall be transferred into the proper funds of the county. Until July 1, 1998, the remainder of base fines resulting from city arrests shall be divided between each city and county, with 50 percent deposited to the county's general fund, and 50 percent deposited to the treasury of the appropriate city, and thereafter the remainder of base fines resulting from city arrests shall be deposited to the treasury of the appropriate city.
(4) In a county that had an agreement as of March 22, 1977, that provides for city fines and forfeitures to accrue to the county in exchange for sales tax receipts, base fines resulting from city arrests not included in paragraph (1) shall be deposited into the proper funds of the county.
(c) Each county shall keep a record of its deposits to its treasury and its transmittal to each city treasury pursuant to this section.
(d) The distribution specified in subdivision (b) applies to all funds subject thereto distributed on or after July 1, 1992, regardless of whether the court has elected to allocate and distribute funds pursuant to Section 1464.8.
(e) Any amounts remitted to the county from amounts collected by the Franchise Tax Board upon referral by a county pursuant to Article 6 (commencing with Section 19280) of Chapter 5 of Part 10.2 of Division 2 of the Revenue and Taxation Code shall be allocated pursuant to this section.

(Amended by Stats. 1998, Ch. 146, Sec. 14.5. Effective July 13, 1998.)
1463.002.
The base fine amounts from city arrests shall be subject to distribution according to the following schedule:

County and city	Percentage
Alameda	
Alameda	18
Albany	29
Berkeley	19
Emeryville	13
Hayward	10
Livermore	7
Oakland	22
Piedmont	44
Pleasanton	17
San Leandro	9
County percentage	21
Amador	

County percentage	25
Kern	
Bakersfield	10
Delano	13
Maricopa	36
Shafter	15
Taft	19
Tehachapi	12
Wasco	28
County percentage	12
Kings	
Corcoran	31
Hanford	21
Lemoore	25
County percentage	25
Lake	
Lakeport	33
County percentage	33
Lassen	
Susanville	21
County percentage	21
Los Angeles	
Alhambra	13
Arcadia	11
Avalon	54
Azusa	11
Bell	11
Beverly Hills	14
Burbank	14
Claremont	5
Compton	16
Covina	11
Culver City	10
El Monte	11
El Segundo	11
Gardena	22
Glendale	16
Glendora	12
Hawthorne	7

Hermosa Beach	14
Huntington Park	12
Inglewood	16
La Verne	14
Long Beach	14
Los Angeles	8
Lynwood	9
Manhattan Beach	13
Maywood	15
Monrovia	11
Montebello	11
Monterey Park	11
Palos Verdes Estates	10
Pasadena	9
Pomona	12
Redondo Beach	15
San Fernando	17
San Gabriel	16
San Marino	5
Santa Monica	11
Sierra Madre	11
Signal Hill	24
South Gate	13
South Pasadena	9
Torrance	16
Vernon	25
West Covina	11
Whittier	11
County percentage	11
Madera	
Chowchilla	17
Madera	16
County percentage	17
Marin	
Belvedere	16
Corte Madera	12
Fairfax	30
Larkspur	30
Mill Valley	13

Ross	18
San Anselmo	11
San Rafael	13
Sausalito	21
County percentage	16
Mendocino	
Fort Bragg	19
Point Arena	40
Ukiah	10
Willits	24
County percentage	17
Merced	
Atwater	23
Dos Palos	21
Gustine	23
Livingston	14
Los Banos	13
Merced	18
County percentage	18
Modoc	
Alturas	42
County percentage	42
Monterey	
Carmel	17
Gonzales	10
Greenfield	13
King City	36
Monterey	13
Pacific Grove	22
Salinas	36
Soledad	16
County percentage	23
Napa	
Calistoga	37
Napa	11
St. Helena	12
County percentage	14
Nevada	
Grass Valley	7

Nevada City	17
County percentage	9
Orange	
County percentage	15
Placer	
Auburn	18
Colfax	8
Lincoln	26
Rocklin	16
Roseville	10
County percentage	14
Plumas	
Portola	19
County percentage	19
Riverside	
Banning	35
Beaumont	15
Blythe	9
Coachella	12
Corona	12
Elsinore	10
Hemet	35
Indio	16
Palm Springs	35
Perris	14
Riverside	16
San Jacinto	41
County percentage	35
Sacramento	
Folsom	31
Galt	25
Isleton	13
North Sacramento	10
Sacramento	21
County percentage	26
San Benito	
Hollister	9
San Juan Bautista	28
County percentage	11

San Bernardino	
Barstow	23
Chino	14
Colton	21
Fontana	15
Needles	33
Ontario	20
Redlands	28
Rialto	15
San Bernardino	20
Upland	14
County percentage	20
San Diego	
Carlsbad	8
Chula Vista	23
Coronado	25
Del Mar	8
El Cajon	17
Escondido	16
Imperial Beach	8
La Mesa	23
Lemon Grove	8
National City	14
Oceanside	15
San Marcos	8
Vista	8
San Diego	6
County percentage	25
San Joaquin	
Lodi	18
Manteca	8
Ripon	11
Stockton	14
Tracy	15
County percentage	14
San Luis Obispo	
Arroyo Grande	9
Paso Robles	26
Pismo Beach	8

San Luis Obispo	21
County percentage	16
San Mateo	
Atherton	27
Belmont	7
Burlingame	38
Colma	40
Daly City	24
Hillsborough	75
Menlo Park	12
Millbrae	16
Redwood City	27
San Bruno	13
San Carlos	8
San Mateo	42
South San Francisco	12
County percentage	21
Santa Barbara	
Guadalupe	28
Lompoc	16
Santa Barbara	11
Santa Maria	12
County percentage	13
Santa Clara	
Alviso	75
Campbell	16
Gilroy	28
Los Altos	16
Los Gatos	30
Morgan Hill	11
Mountain View	13
Palo Alto	21
San Jose	13
Santa Clara	16
Sunnyvale	26
County percentage	16
Santa Cruz	
Capitola	21
Santa Cruz	23

Watsonville	21
County percentage	22
Shasta	
Redding	22
County percentage	22
Sierra	
Loyalton	75
County percentage	75
Siskiyou	
Dorris	18
Dunsmuir	29
Etna	18
Fort Jones	46
Montague	75
Mount Shasta	37
Tulelake	33
Yreka	30
County percentage	29
Solano	
Benicia	17
Dixon	18
Fairfield	18
Rio Vista	19
Suisun	7
Vacaville	15
Vallejo	18
County percentage	19
Sonoma	
Cloverdale	40
Cotati	40
Healdsburg	40
Petaluma	24
Rohnert Park	40
Santa Rosa	40
Sebastopol	40
Sonoma	40
County percentage	40
Stanislaus	
Ceres	14

Modesto	15
Newman	10
Oakdale	15
Patterson	20
Riverbank	18
Turlock	19
County percentage	15
Sutter	
Live Oak	17
Yuba City	17
County percentage	17
Tehama	
Corning	26
Red Bluff	39
Tehama	10
County percentage	31
Tulare	
Dinuba	21
Exeter	23
Lindsay	24
Porterville	26
Tulare	20
Visalia	17
Woodlake	15
County percentage	21
Tuolumne	
Sonora	23
County percentage	23
Ventura	
Fillmore	16
Ojai	16
Oxnard	16
Port Hueneme	16
Santa Paula	16
Ventura	16
County percentage	16
Yolo	
Davis	22
Winters	19

Woodland	20
County percentage	20
Yuba	
Marysville	15
Wheatland	38
County percentage	15

With respect to any city arrest from a city which is not set forth in the above schedule, the county percentage shall apply. A county and city therein may, by mutual agreement, adjust these percentages. Where a county and a city have, prior to June 1, 1991, entered into an agreement to adjust the percentage specified in this section, or where a county and a city have entered into an agreement governing the distribution of revenue from parking penalties, those agreements shall remain in full force and effect until changed by mutual agreement.
(Added by Stats. 1991, Ch. 189, Sec. 20. Effective July 29, 1991.)
1463.004.
(a) If a sentencing judge specifies only the total fine or forfeiture, or if an automated case-processing system requires it, percentage calculations may be employed to establish the components of total fines or forfeitures, provided that the aggregate monthly distributions resulting from the calculations are the same as would be produced by strict observance of the statutory distributions.
(b) If a fund would receive less than one hundred dollars ($100) in monthly distributions of total fines and forfeitures by a particular court for at least 11 months of each year, the court may omit that fund from the system for calculating distributions, and shall instead apply the distribution provided for by Section 1463.001.
(Added by Stats. 1991, Ch. 189, Sec. 22. Effective July 29, 1991.)
1463.005.
Notwithstanding Section 1463.001, in a county subject to Section 77202.5 of the Government Code, of base fines resulting from arrests not subject to allocation under paragraph (1) of subdivision (b) of Section 1463.001, by a California Highway Patrol Officer on state highways constructed as freeways within the city whereon city police officers enforced the provisions of the Vehicle Code on April 1, 1965, 25 percent shall be deposited in the treasury of the appropriate city, 75 percent shall be deposited in the proper funds of the county.
(Amended by Stats. 1997, Ch. 850, Sec. 51. Effective January 1, 1998.)
1463.006.
Any money deposited with the court or with the clerk thereof which, by order of the court or for any other reason, should be returned, in whole or in part, to any person, or which is by law payable to the state or to any other public agency, shall be paid to that person or to the state or to the other public agency by warrant of the county auditor, which shall be drawn upon the requisition of the clerk of the court.
All money deposited as bail which has not been claimed within one year after the final disposition of the case in which the money was deposited, or within one year after an order made by the court for the return or delivery of the money to any person, shall be apportioned between the city and the county and paid or transferred in the manner provided by statute for the apportionment and payment of fines and forfeitures. This paragraph controls over any conflicting provisions of law.
(Added by Stats. 1991, Ch. 189, Sec. 23. Effective July 29, 1991.)
1463.007.
(a) Notwithstanding any other law, a county or court that operates a comprehensive collection program may deduct the costs of operating that program, excluding capital expenditures, from any revenues collected under that program. The costs shall be deducted before any distribution of revenues to other governmental entities required by any other law. A county or court operating a comprehensive collection program may establish a minimum base fee, fine, forfeiture, penalty, or assessment amount for inclusion in the program.
(b) Once debt becomes delinquent, it continues to be delinquent and may be subject to collection by a comprehensive collection program. Debt is delinquent and subject to collection by a comprehensive collection program if any of the following conditions is met:
(1) A defendant does not post bail or appear on or before the date on which he or she promised to appear, or any lawful continuance of that date, if that defendant was eligible to post and forfeit bail.
(2) A defendant does not pay the amount imposed by the court on or before the date ordered by the court, or any lawful continuance of that date.
(3) A defendant has failed to make an installment payment on the date specified by the court.
(c) For the purposes of this section, a "comprehensive collection program" is a separate and distinct revenue collection activity that meets each of the following criteria:
(1) The program identifies and collects amounts arising from delinquent court-ordered debt, whether or not a warrant has been issued against the alleged violator.
(2) The program complies with the requirements of subdivision (b) of Section 1463.010.
(3) The program engages in each of the following activities:
(A) Attempts telephone contact with delinquent debtors for whom the program has a telephone number to inform them of their delinquent status and payment options.
(B) Notifies delinquent debtors for whom the program has an address in writing of their outstanding obligation within 95 days of delinquency.
(C) Generates internal monthly reports to track collections data, such as age of debt and delinquent amounts outstanding.
(D) Uses Department of Motor Vehicles information to locate delinquent debtors.
(E) Accepts payment of delinquent debt by credit card.
(4) The program engages in at least five of the following activities:
(A) Sends delinquent debt to the Franchise Tax Board's Court-Ordered Debt Collections Program.
(B) Sends delinquent debt to the Franchise Tax Board's Interagency Intercept Collections Program.
(C) Initiates driver's license suspension or hold actions when appropriate for a failure to appear in court.
(D) Contracts with one or more private debt collectors to collect delinquent debt.
(E) Sends monthly bills or account statements to all delinquent debtors.
(F) Contracts with local, regional, state, or national skip tracing or locator resources or services to locate delinquent debtors.
(G) Coordinates with the probation department to locate debtors who may be on formal or informal probation.
(H) Uses Employment Development Department employment and wage information to collect delinquent debt.
(I) Establishes wage and bank account garnishments where appropriate.
(J) Places liens on real property owned by delinquent debtors when appropriate.

(K) Uses an automated dialer or automatic call distribution system to manage telephone calls.
(Amended by Stats. 2017, Ch. 17, Sec. 33. (AB 103) Effective June 27, 2017.)
1463.009.
Notwithstanding Section 1463, all bail forfeitures that are collected from any source in a case in which a defendant is charged and convicted of a violation of Section 261, 264.1, 286, 287, 288, 288.5, or 289, or former Section 288a, or of a violent felony as defined in subdivision (c) of Section 667.5 or a serious felony as defined in subdivision (c) of Section 1192.7, and that are required to be deposited with the county treasurer shall be allocated according to the following priority:
(a) The county shall be reimbursed for reasonable administrative costs for the collection of the forfeited property, the maintenance and preservation of the property, and the distribution of the property pursuant to this section.
(b) Out of the remainder of the forfeited bail money, a total of up to 50 percent shall be distributed in the amount necessary to satisfy any civil court judgment in favor of a victim as a result of the offense or a restitution order due to a criminal conviction to a victim who was under 18 years of age at the time of the commission of the offense if the defendant is convicted under Section 261, 264.1, 286, 287, 288, 288.5, or 289, or former Section 288a, and to a victim of any age if the defendant has been convicted of a violent felony as defined in subdivision (c) of Section 667.5 or a serious felony as defined in subdivision (c) of Section 1192.7.
(c) The balance of the amount collected shall be deposited pursuant to Section 1463.
(Amended by Stats. 2018, Ch. 423, Sec. 99. (SB 1494) Effective January 1, 2019.)
1463.010.
The uniform imposition and enforcement of court-ordered debts are recognized as an important element of California's judicial system. Prompt, efficient, and effective imposition and collection of court-ordered fees, fines, forfeitures, penalties, restitution, and assessments ensure the appropriate respect for court orders. The California State Association of Counties and the Administrative Office of the Courts are jointly committed to identifying, improving, and seeking to expand access to mechanisms and tools that will enhance efforts to collect court-ordered debt. To provide for this prompt, efficient, and effective collection:
(a) The Judicial Council shall adopt guidelines for a comprehensive program concerning the collection of moneys owed for fees, fines, forfeitures, penalties, and assessments imposed by court order. As part of its guidelines, the Judicial Council may establish standard agreements for entities to provide collection services. As part of its guidelines, the Judicial Council shall include provisions that promote competition by and between entities in providing collection services to courts and counties. The Judicial Council may delegate to the Administrative Director of the Courts the implementation of the aspects of this program to be carried out at the state level.
(b) The courts and counties shall maintain the collection program that was in place on January 1, 1996, unless otherwise agreed to in writing by the court and county. The program may wholly or partially be staffed and operated within the court itself, may be wholly or partially staffed and operated by the county, or may be wholly or partially contracted with a third party. In carrying out this collection program, each superior court and county shall develop a cooperative plan to implement the Judicial Council guidelines. In the event that a court and a county are unwilling or unable to enter into a cooperative plan pursuant to this section, prior to the arbitration procedures required by subdivision (e) of Section 1214.1, the court or the county may request the continuation of negotiations with mediation assistance as mutually agreed upon and provided by the Administrative Director of the Courts and the California State Association of Counties.
(c) The Judicial Council shall develop performance measures and benchmarks to review the effectiveness of the cooperative superior court and county collection programs operating pursuant to this section. Each superior court and county shall jointly report to the Judicial Council, as provided by the Judicial Council, information requested in a reporting template on or before September 1, 2009, and annually thereafter. The Judicial Council shall report to the Legislature on December 31, 2009, and annually thereafter, on all of the following:
(1) The extent to which each court or county is following best practices for its collection program.
(2) The performance of each collection program.
(3) Any changes necessary to improve performance of collection programs statewide.
(d) The Judicial Council may, when the efficiency and effectiveness of the collection process may be improved, facilitate a joint collection program between superior courts, between counties, or between superior courts and counties.
(e) The Judicial Council may establish, by court rule, a program providing for the suspension and nonrenewal of a business and professional license if the holder of the license has unpaid fees, fines, forfeitures, penalties, and assessments imposed upon them under a court order. The Judicial Council may provide that some or all of the superior courts or counties participate in the program. Any program established by the Judicial Council shall ensure that the licensee receives adequate and appropriate notice of the proposed suspension or nonrenewal of his or her license and has an opportunity to contest the suspension or nonrenewal. The opportunity to contest may not require a court hearing.
(f) Notwithstanding any other provision of law, the Judicial Council, after consultation with the Franchise Tax Board with respect to collections under Section 19280 of the Revenue and Taxation Code, may provide for an amnesty program involving the collection of outstanding fees, fines, forfeitures, penalties, and assessments, applicable either statewide or within one or more counties. The amnesty program shall provide that some or all of the interest or collections costs imposed on outstanding fees, fines, forfeitures, penalties, and assessments may be waived if the remaining amounts due are paid within the amnesty period.
(Amended by Stats. 2008, Ch. 311, Sec. 28. Effective January 1, 2009.)
1463.011.
(a) Notwithstanding any other provision of law, if a court, during the course of its routine process to collect fees, fines, forfeitures, or other penalties imposed by a court due to a citation issued for the violation of a state or local law, obtains information indicating that a person under 25 years of age, who has been issued a citation for truancy, loitering, curfew violations, or illegal lodging that is outstanding or unpaid, is homeless or has no permanent address, the court shall not garnish the wages or levy against bank accounts of that person until that person is 25 years of age or older, as that age is recorded by that person's credit report or other document already in the possession of, or previously provided to, the court.
(b) For purposes of this section a person is considered to be "homeless" or as having "no permanent address" if that person does not have a fixed, regular, adequate nighttime residence, or has a primary nighttime residence that is one of the following:
(1) A supervised publicly or privately operated shelter designed to provide temporary living accommodations, including, but not limited to, welfare hotels, congregate shelters, and transitional housing for the mentally ill.
(2) An institution that provides a temporary residence for individuals intended to be institutionalized.
(3) A public or private place not designed for, or ordinarily used as, a regular sleeping accommodation for human beings.
(c) Nothing in this section shall be construed to prevent a court from engaging in any other lawful debt collection activities.
(d) Nothing in this section shall be construed to require a court to perform any further investigation or financial screening into any matter beyond the scope of its regular duties.

(e) Nothing in this section shall be construed to prevent the Judicial Council from altering any best practices or recommendations for collection programs pursuant to Section 1463.010.

(f) Nothing in this section shall be construed to prevent a court from garnishing a person's wages or levying against a person's bank accounts if the court, subsequent to its initial determination that the person was a homeless youth exempt from wage garnishment or levy under this section, obtains evidence that the individual is no longer homeless.

(Added by Stats. 2011, Ch. 466, Sec. 2. (AB 1111) Effective January 1, 2012.)

1463.012.

(a) Notwithstanding any other law, if a court, during the course of its routine process to collect fees, fines, forfeitures, or other penalties imposed by a court due to a citation issued for the violation of a state or local law, obtains information indicating that a person who has been issued a citation for loitering, curfew violations, or illegal lodging that is outstanding or unpaid served in the military within the last eight years and is homeless or has no permanent address, the court shall not garnish the wages or levy against bank accounts of that person for five years from the date that the court obtained that information.

(b) For purposes of this section, a person is considered to be "homeless" or as having "no permanent address" if that person does not have a fixed, regular, adequate nighttime residence, or has a primary nighttime residence that is one of the following:

(1) A supervised publicly or privately operated shelter designed to provide temporary living accommodations, including, but not limited to, welfare hotels, congregate shelters, and transitional housing for the mentally ill.

(2) An institution that provides a temporary residence for individuals intended to be institutionalized.

(3) A public or private place not designed for, or ordinarily used as, a regular sleeping accommodation for human beings.

(c) Nothing in this section shall be construed to prevent a court from engaging in any other lawful debt collection activities.

(d) Nothing in this section shall be construed to require a court to perform any further investigation or financial screening into any matter beyond the scope of its regular duties.

(e) Nothing in this section shall be construed to prevent the Judicial Council from altering any best practices or recommendations for collection programs pursuant to Section 1463.010.

(f) Nothing in this section shall be construed to prevent a court from garnishing a person's wages or levying against a person's bank accounts if the court, subsequent to its initial determination that the person was a homeless veteran exempt from wage garnishment or levy under this section, obtains evidence that the individual is no longer homeless, or that the court had, on a previous occasion, suspended garnishment of that person's wages or levying against that person's bank accounts pursuant to subdivision (a).

(Added by Stats. 2013, Ch. 234, Sec. 2. (AB 508) Effective January 1, 2014.)

1463.02.

(a) On or before June 30, 2011, the Judicial Council shall establish a task force to evaluate criminal and traffic-related court-ordered debts imposed against adult and juvenile offenders. The task force shall be comprised of the following members:

(1) Two members appointed by the California State Association of Counties.

(2) Two members appointed by the League of California Cities.

(3) Two court executives, two judges, and two Administrative Office of the Courts employees appointed by the Judicial Council.

(4) One member appointed by the Controller.

(5) One member appointed by the Franchise Tax Board.

(6) One member appointed by the California Victim Compensation Board.

(7) One member appointed by the Department of Corrections and Rehabilitation.

(8) One member appointed by the Department of Finance.

(9) One member appointed by each house of the Legislature.

(10) A county public defender and a city attorney appointed by the Speaker of the Assembly.

(11) A defense attorney in private practice and a district attorney appointed by the Senate Committee on Rules.

(b) The Judicial Council shall designate a chairperson for the task force. The task force shall, among other duties, do all of the following:

(1) Identify all criminal and traffic-related court-ordered fees, fines, forfeitures, penalties, and assessments imposed under law.

(2) Identify the distribution of revenue derived from those debts and the expenditures made by those entities that benefit from the revenues.

(3) Consult with state and local entities that would be affected by a simplification and consolidation of criminal and traffic-related court-ordered debts.

(4) Evaluate and make recommendations to the Judicial Council and the Legislature for consolidating and simplifying the imposition of criminal and traffic-related court-ordered debts and the distribution of the revenue derived from those debts with the goal of improving the process for those entities that benefit from the revenues, and recommendations, if any, for adjustment to the court-ordered debts.

(c) The task force also shall document recent annual revenues from the various penalty assessments and surcharges and, to the extent feasible, evaluate the extent to which the amount of each penalty assessment and surcharge impacts total annual revenues, imposition of criminal sentences, and the actual amounts assessed.

(d) The task force also shall evaluate and make recommendations to the Judicial Council and the Legislature on or before June 30, 2011, regarding the priority in which court-ordered debts should be satisfied and the use of comprehensive collection programs authorized pursuant to Section 1463.007, including associated cost-recovery practices.

(Amended by Stats. 2016, Ch. 31, Sec. 243. (SB 836) Effective June 27, 2016.)

1463.04.

Notwithstanding Section 1463, out of the moneys deposited with the county treasurer pursuant to Section 1463, there shall be transferred once a month into the State Treasury to the credit of the Winter Recreation Fund an amount equal to 50 percent of all fines and forfeitures collected during the preceding month upon conviction or upon the forfeiture of bail from any person of any violation of Section 5091.15 of the Public Resources Code, and an amount equal to the remaining 50 percent shall be transferred to the county general fund and deposited in a special account which shall be used exclusively to pay for the cost of furthering the purposes of the California SNO-PARK Permit Program, including, but not limited to, the snow removal, maintenance, and development of designated parking areas.

(Added by Stats. 1991, Ch. 189, Sec. 25. Effective July 29, 1991.)

1463.07.

An administrative screening fee of twenty-five dollars ($25) shall be collected from each person arrested and released on his or her own recognizance upon conviction of any criminal offense related to the arrest other than an infraction. A citation processing fee in the amount of ten dollars ($10) shall be collected from each person cited and released by any peace officer in the field or at a jail facility upon conviction of any criminal offense, other than an infraction, related to the criminal offense cited in the notice to appear. However, the court may determine a lesser fee than otherwise provided in this subdivision upon a showing that the defendant is unable to pay the full amount. All fees collected pursuant to this subdivision shall be deposited by the county auditor in the general fund of the county. This subdivision applies only to convictions occurring on or after the effective date of the act adding this subdivision.

(Added by Stats. 1997, Ch. 850, Sec. 56. Effective January 1, 1998.)

1463.1.

Notwithstanding any other provisions of law except Section 77009 of the Government Code, any trial court may elect, with prior approval of the Administrative Director of the Courts, to deposit in a bank account pursuant to Section 53679 of the Government Code, all moneys deposited as bail with the court, or with the clerk thereof.

All moneys received and disbursed through the bank account shall be properly and uniformly accounted for under any procedures the Controller may deem necessary. The Judicial Council may regulate the bank accounts, provided that its regulations are not inconsistent with those of the Controller.

(Amended by Stats. 2001, Ch. 812, Sec. 25. Effective January 1, 2002.)

1463.5.

The distribution of funds required pursuant to Section 1463, and the distribution of assessments imposed and collected under Section 1464 and Section 42006 of the Vehicle Code, may be determined and made upon the basis of probability sampling. The sampling shall be procedural in nature and shall not substantively modify the distributions required pursuant to Sections 1463 and 1464 and Section 42006 of the Vehicle Code. The procedure for the sampling shall be prescribed by the county auditor and the procedure and its implementation shall be approved by the board of supervisors and a majority of the cities within a county. The reasonableness of the distribution shall be verified during the audit performed pursuant to Section 71383 of the Government Code.

(Amended by Stats. 1989, Ch. 897, Sec. 40.)

1463.7.

Funds transferred to the Regents of the University of California pursuant to Section 1462.3 may not be utilized to purchase land or to construct any parking facility. These funds shall be utilized for the development, enhancement, and operation of alternate methods of transportation of students and employees of the University of California and for the mitigation of the impact of off-campus student and employee parking in university communities.

(Added by Stats. 1991, Ch. 189, Sec. 26. Effective July 29, 1991.)

1463.9.

Notwithstanding the provisions of Section 1463, 50 percent of all fines and forfeitures collected upon conviction, or upon forfeiture of bail, for violations of Section 13002 of the Health and Safety Code, Sections 23111 and 23112, and subdivision (a) of Section 23113 of the Vehicle Code, and Section 374.3 of this code shall be kept separate and apart from any other fines and forfeitures. These fines and forfeitures shall, as soon as practicable after their receipt, be deposited with the county treasurer of the county in which the court is situated and shall be distributed as prescribed in Section 1463, except that the money distributed to any county or city shall be expended only for litter cleanup activities within that city or county.

(Added by Stats. 1991, Ch. 189, Sec. 27. Effective July 29, 1991.)

1463.10.

Notwithstanding Section 1463, fines and forfeitures which are collected for a conviction of a violation of Section 11366.7 of the Health and Safety Code and which are required to be deposited with the county treasurer pursuant to Section 1463 shall be allocated as follows:

(a) To reimburse any local agency for the reasonable costs of the removal and disposal, or storage, of any chemical or drug, or any laboratory apparatus or device, sold by a person convicted under Section 11366.7 of the Health and Safety Code.

(b) The balance of the amount collected, if any, shall be deposited by the county treasurer pursuant to Section 1463.

(Added by Stats. 1994, Ch. 979, Sec. 4. Effective January 1, 1995.)

1463.11.

Notwithstanding Sections 1463 and 1464 of this code and Section 76000 of the Government Code, moneys that are collected for a violation of subdivision (a) or (c) of Section 21453 of, subdivision (c) of Section 21454 of, or subdivision (a) of Section 21457 of, the Vehicle Code, and which are required to be deposited with the county treasurer pursuant to Section 1463 of this code shall be allocated as follows:

(a) The first 30 percent of the amount collected shall be allocated to the general fund of the city or county in which the offense occurred.

(b) The balance of the amount collected shall be deposited by the county treasurer under Sections 1463 and 1464.

(Added by Stats. 1997, Ch. 852, Sec. 2. Effective January 1, 1998.)

1463.12.

Notwithstanding Sections 1463 and 1464 of this code and Section 76000 of the Government Code, moneys that are collected for a violation of subdivision (c) of Section 21752 or Section 22450 of the Vehicle Code, involving railroad grade crossings, or Section 22451, 22452, or subdivision (c) of Section 22526 of the Vehicle Code, and that are required to be deposited with the county treasurer pursuant to Section 1463 of this code shall be allocated as follows:

(a) If the offense occurred in an area where a transit district or transportation commission or authority established under Division 12 (commencing with Section 130000) of the Public Utilities Code provides rail transportation, the first 30 percent of the amount collected shall be allocated to the general fund of that transit district or transportation commission or authority to be used only for public safety and public education purposes relating to railroad grade crossings.

(b) If there is no transit district or transportation commission or authority providing rail transportation in the area where the offense occurred, the first 30 percent of the amount collected shall be allocated to the general fund of the county in which the offense occurred, to be used only for public safety and public education purposes relating to railroad grade crossings.

(c) The balance of the amount collected shall be deposited by the county treasurer under Section 1463.

(d) A transit district, transportation commission or authority, or a county that is allocated funds pursuant to subdivision (a) or (b) shall provide public safety and public education relating to railroad grade crossings only to the extent that those purposes are funded by the allocations provided pursuant to subdivision (a) or (b).

(Amended by Stats. 2005, Ch. 716, Sec. 4. Effective January 1, 2006.)

1463.13.

(a) Each county may develop, implement, operate, and administer an alcohol and drug problem assessment program for persons convicted of a crime in which the court finds that alcohol or substance abuse was substantially involved in the commission of the crime. This program may be operated in coordination with the program developed under Article 6 (commencing with Section 23645) of Chapter 4 of Division 11.5 of the Vehicle Code.

(1) A portion of any program established pursuant to this section shall include a face-to-face interview with each program participant.

(2) No person convicted of driving under the influence of alcohol or a controlled substance or a related offense shall participate in any program established pursuant to this section.

(b) An alcohol and drug problem assessment report shall be made on each person who participates in the program. The report may be used to determine the appropriate sentence for the person. The report shall be submitted to the court within 14 days of the completion of the assessment.

(c) In any county in which the county operates an alcohol and drug problem assessment program under this section, a court may order any person convicted of a crime that involved the use of drugs or alcohol, including any person who is found to have been under the influence of drugs or alcohol during the commission of the crime, to participate in the assessment program.

(d) Notwithstanding any other provision of law, in addition to any other fine or penalty assessment, there shall be levied an assessment of not more than one hundred fifty dollars ($150) upon every fine, penalty, or forfeiture imposed and collected by the courts for a public offense wherein the court orders the offender to participate in a county alcohol and drug problem assessment program. The assessment shall only be levied in a county upon the adoption of a resolution by the board of supervisors of the county making that county subject to this section.

(e) The court shall determine if the defendant has the ability to pay the assessment. If the court determines that the defendant has the ability to pay the assessment then the court may set the amount to be reimbursed and order the defendant to pay that sum to the county in the manner which the court determines is reasonable and compatible with the defendant's financial ability. In making a determination of whether a defendant has the ability to pay, the court shall take into account the amount of any fine imposed upon the defendant and any amount the defendant has been ordered to pay in victim restitution.

(f) Notwithstanding Section 1463 or 1464 of the Penal Code or any other provision of law, all moneys collected pursuant to this section shall be deposited in a special account in the county treasury and shall be used exclusively to pay for the costs of developing, implementing, operating, maintaining, and evaluating alcohol and drug problem assessment and monitoring programs.

(g) On January 15 of each year, the treasurer of each county that administers an alcohol and drug problem assessment and monitoring program shall determine those moneys in the special account which were not expended during the preceding fiscal year, and shall transfer those moneys to the general fund of the county.
(Added by Stats. 2000, Ch. 165, Sec. 1. Effective January 1, 2001.)

1463.14.
(a) Notwithstanding the provisions of Section 1463, of the moneys deposited with the county treasurer pursuant to Section 1463, fifty dollars ($50) of each fine collected for each conviction of a violation of Section 23103, 23104, 23105, 23152, or 23153 of the Vehicle Code shall be deposited in a special account that shall be used exclusively to pay for the cost of performing for the county, or a city or special district within the county, analysis of blood, breath or urine for alcohol content or for the presence of drugs, or for services related to that testing. The sum shall not exceed the reasonable cost of providing the services for which the sum is intended.

On November 1 of each year, the treasurer of each county shall determine those moneys in the special account that were not expended during the preceding fiscal year, and shall transfer those moneys into the general fund of the county. The board of supervisors may, by resolution, assign the treasurer's duty to determine the amount of money that was not expended to the auditor or another county officer. The county may retain an amount of that money equal to its administrative cost incurred pursuant to this section, and shall distribute the remainder pursuant to Section 1463. If the account becomes exhausted, the public entity ordering a test performed pursuant to this subdivision shall bear the costs of the test.

(b) The board of supervisors of a county may, by resolution, authorize an additional penalty upon each defendant convicted of a violation of Section 23152 or 23153 of the Vehicle Code, of an amount equal to the cost of testing for alcohol content, less the fifty dollars ($50) deposited as provided in subdivision (a). The additional penalty authorized by this subdivision shall be imposed only in those instances where the defendant has the ability to pay, but in no case shall the defendant be ordered to pay a penalty in excess of fifty dollars ($50). The penalty authorized shall be deposited directly with the county, or city or special district within the county, that performed the test, in the special account described in subdivision (a), and shall not be the basis for an additional assessment pursuant to Section 1464, or Chapter 12 (commencing with Section 76010) of Title 8 of the Government Code.

For purposes of this subdivision, "ability to pay" means the overall capability of the defendant to pay the additional penalty authorized by this subdivision, taking into consideration all of the following:

(1) Present financial obligations, including family support obligations, and fines, penalties, and other obligations to the court.

(2) Reasonably discernible future financial position over the next 12 months.

(3) Any other factor or factors that may bear upon the defendant's financial ability to pay the additional penalty.

(c) The Department of Justice shall promulgate rules and regulations to implement the provisions of this section.
(Amended by Stats. 2007, Ch. 682, Sec. 5. Effective January 1, 2008.)

1463.15.
Notwithstanding Section 1463, if a county board of supervisors establishes a combined vehicle inspection and sobriety checkpoint program under Section 2814.1 of the Vehicle Code, thirty-five dollars ($35) of the money deposited with the county treasurer under Section 1463.001 and collected from each fine and forfeiture imposed under subdivision (b) of Section 42001.2 of the Vehicle Code shall be deposited in a special account to be used exclusively to pay the cost incurred by the county for establishing and conducting the combined vehicle inspection and sobriety checkpoint program. The money allocated to pay the cost incurred by the county for establishing and conducting the combined checkpoint program pursuant to this section may only be deposited in the special account after a fine imposed pursuant to subdivision (b) of Section 42001.2, and any penalty assessment thereon, has been collected.
(Added by Stats. 2003, Ch. 482, Sec. 2. Effective January 1, 2004.)

1463.16.
(a) Notwithstanding Section 1203.1 or 1463, fifty dollars ($50) of each fine collected for each conviction of a violation of Section 23103, 23104, 23105, 23152, or 23153 of the Vehicle Code shall be deposited with the county treasurer in a special account for exclusive allocation by the county for the county's alcoholism program, with approval of the board of supervisors, for alcohol programs and services for the general population. These funds shall be allocated through the local planning process and expenditures reported to the State Department of Health Care Services pursuant to subdivision (c) of Section 11798.2 and subdivision (a) of Section 11818.5 of the Health and Safety Code. Programs shall be certified by the State Department of Health Care Services or have made application for certification to be eligible for funding under this section. The county shall implement the intent and procedures of subdivision (b) of Section 11812 of the Health and Safety Code while distributing funds under this section.

(b) In a county of the 1st, 2nd, 3rd, 15th, 19th, 20th, or 24th class, notwithstanding Section 1463, of the moneys deposited with the county treasurer pursuant to Section 1463, fifty dollars ($50) for each conviction of a violation of Section 23103, 23104, 23105, 23152, or 23153 of the Vehicle Code shall be deposited in a special account for exclusive allocation by the administrator of the county's alcoholism program, with approval of the board of supervisors, for alcohol programs and services for the general population. These funds shall be allocated through the local planning process and expenditures reported to the State Department of Health Care Services pursuant to subdivision (c) of Section 11798.2 and subdivision (a) of Section 11818.5 of the Health and Safety Code. For those services for which standards have been developed and certification is available, programs shall be certified by the State Department of Health Care Services or shall apply for certification to be eligible for funding under this section. The county alcohol administrator shall implement the intent and procedures of subdivision (b) of Section 11812 of the Health and Safety Code while distributing funds under this section.

(c) The Board of Supervisors of Contra Costa County may, by resolution, authorize the imposition of a fifty dollar ($50) assessment by the court upon each defendant convicted of a violation of Section 23152 or 23153 of the Vehicle Code for deposit in

the account from which the fifty dollar ($50) distribution specified in subdivision (a) is deducted.

(d) It is the specific intent of the Legislature that funds expended under this part shall be used for ongoing alcoholism program services as well as for contracts with private nonprofit organizations to upgrade facilities to meet state certification and state licensing standards and federal nondiscrimination regulations relating to accessibility for handicapped persons.

(e) Counties may retain up to 5 percent of the funds collected to offset administrative costs of collection and disbursement.
(Amended by Stats. 2013, Ch. 22, Sec. 78. (AB 75) Effective June 27, 2013. Operative July 1, 2013, by Sec. 110 of Ch. 22.)

1463.17.
(a) In a county of the 19th class, notwithstanding any other provision of this chapter, of the moneys deposited with the county treasurer pursuant to Section 1463, fifty dollars ($50) for each conviction of a violation of Section 23103, 23104, 23105, 23152, or 23153 of the Vehicle Code shall be deposited in a special account to be used exclusively to pay the cost incurred by the county or a city or special district within the county, with approval of the board of supervisors, for performing analysis of blood, breath, or urine for alcohol content or for the presence of drugs, or for services related to the testing.

(b) The application of this section shall not reduce the county's remittance to the state specified in paragraph (2) of subdivision (b) of Section 77201, paragraph (2) of subdivision (b) of Section 77201.1, and paragraph (2) of subdivision (a) of Section 77201.3 of the Government Code.
(Amended by Stats. 2007, Ch. 682, Sec. 7.5. Effective January 1, 2008.)

1463.18.
(a) Notwithstanding the provisions of Section 1463, moneys which are collected for a conviction of a violation of Section 23152 or 23153 of the Vehicle Code and which are required to be deposited with the county treasurer pursuant to Section 1463 shall be allocated as follows:

(1) The first twenty dollars ($20) of any amount collected for a conviction shall be transferred to the Restitution Fund. This amount shall be aggregated by the county treasurer and transferred to the State Treasury once per month for deposit in the Restitution Fund.

(2) The balance of the amount collected, if any, shall be deposited by the county treasurer pursuant to Section 1463.

(b) The amount transferred to the Restitution Fund pursuant to this section shall be in addition to any amount of any additional fine or assessment imposed pursuant to Sections 1202.4 and 1203.04, as operative on or before August 3, 1995, or Section 13967, as operative on or before September 28, 1994, of the Government Code. The amount deposited to the Restitution Fund pursuant to this section shall be used for the purpose of indemnification of victims pursuant to Section 13965 of the Government Code, with priority given to victims of alcohol-related traffic offenses.
(Amended by Stats. 1996, Ch. 1077, Sec. 26. Effective January 1, 1997.)

1463.20.
Notwithstanding any other law, fifty dollars ($50) of every parking penalty received by a local entity pursuant to Section 42001.5 of the Vehicle Code may be deposited by the treasurer of the local entity in a special account to be used by the local entity for the sole purposes of altering existing public facilities to make them accessible to persons with disabilities in compliance with the Americans with Disabilities Act of 1990 (42 U.S.C. Sec. 12101, et seq.), and federal regulations adopted pursuant to that act, and covering the actual administrative cost of setting aside fifty dollars ($50) of every parking penalty received pursuant to Section 42001.5 of the Vehicle Code for that purpose.
(Added by Stats. 1993, Ch. 137, Sec. 1. Effective January 1, 1994.)

1463.22.
(a) Notwithstanding Section 1463, of the moneys deposited with the county treasurer pursuant to Section 1463, seventeen dollars and fifty cents ($17.50) for each conviction of a violation of Section 16028 of the Vehicle Code shall be deposited by the county treasurer in a special account and allocated to defray costs of municipal and superior courts incurred in administering Sections 16028, 16030, and 16031 of the Vehicle Code. Any moneys in the special account in excess of the amount required to defray those costs shall be redeposited and distributed by the county treasurer pursuant to Section 1463.

(b) Notwithstanding Section 1463, of the moneys deposited with the county treasurer pursuant to Section 1463, three dollars ($3) for each conviction for a violation of Section 16028 of the Vehicle Code shall be initially deposited by the county treasurer in a special account, and shall be transmitted once per month to the Controller for deposit in the Motor Vehicle Account in the State Transportation Fund. These moneys shall be available, when appropriated, to defray the administrative costs incurred by the Department of Motor Vehicles pursuant to Sections 16031, 16032, 16034, and 16035 of the Vehicle Code. It is the intent of this subdivision to provide sufficient revenues to pay for all of the department's costs in administering those sections of the Vehicle Code.

(c) Notwithstanding Section 1463, of the moneys deposited with the county treasurer pursuant to Section 1463, ten dollars ($10) upon the conviction of, or upon the forfeiture of bail from, any person arrested or notified for a violation of Section 16028 of the Vehicle Code shall be deposited by the county treasurer in a special account and shall be transmitted monthly to the Controller for deposit in the General Fund.
(Amended by Stats. 1998, Ch. 931, Sec. 422. Effective September 28, 1998.)

1463.25.
Notwithstanding Section 1203.1 or 1463, and in addition to any allocation under Section 1463.16, the moneys from alcohol abuse education and prevention penalty assessments collected pursuant to Section 23196 of the Vehicle Code shall be initially deposited by the county treasurer in a special county alcohol abuse and prevention fund for exclusive allocation by the county alcohol program administrator, subject to the approval of the board of supervisors, for the county's alcohol abuse education and prevention program pursuant to Section 11802 of the Health and Safety Code. A county shall not use more than 5 percent of the funds deposited in the special account for administrative costs.
(Added by Stats. 1991, Ch. 189, Sec. 33. Effective July 29, 1991.)

1463.26.
Notwithstanding Section 1463, out of moneys deposited with the county treasurer pursuant to Section 1463, there shall be transferred, once a month, to the traffic fund of the city, an amount equal to one-third of all fines and forfeitures collected during the preceding month upon the conviction of, or upon the forfeiture of bail by, any person charged with a violation of Section 21655.5 or 21655.8 of the Vehicle Code within that city, and an amount equal to one-third of those fines and forfeitures shall be transferred into the general fund of the county, and an amount equal to one-third of those fines and forfeitures shall be transferred to the agency whose approval is required for high-occupancy vehicle lanes on state highways pursuant to Section 21655.6 of the Vehicle Code. If the arrest for a violation of either Section 21655.5 or 21655.8 of the Vehicle Code was not within a city, then 50 percent of the fines and forfeitures shall be transferred to the general fund of the county and 50 percent shall be transferred to the agency having authority to approve high-occupancy vehicle lanes pursuant to Section 21655.6 of the Vehicle Code. Money received by the agency having the authority to approve high-occupancy vehicle lanes pursuant to Section 21655.6 of the Vehicle Code shall be used by that agency for the purposes of improving traffic flow and traffic operations upon the state highway system within the jurisdiction of that agency. In counties where there exists a county transportation commission created pursuant to

Division 12 (commencing with Section 130000) of the Public Utilities Code, that commission is the agency for purposes of this section.
(Added by Stats. 1991, Ch. 189, Sec. 34. Effective July 29, 1991.)
1463.27.
(a) Notwithstanding any other provision of law, in addition to any other fine or penalty assessment, the board of supervisors of a county may, by resolution, authorize a fee of not more than two hundred fifty dollars ($250) upon every fine, penalty, or forfeiture imposed and collected by the courts for a crime of domestic violence specified in paragraph (1) of subdivision (e) of Section 243 and in Section 273.5. Notwithstanding Section 1463 or 1464, money collected pursuant to this section shall be used to fund domestic violence prevention programs that focus on assisting immigrants, refugees, or persons who live in a rural community. Counties with existing domestic violence prevention programs that assist those persons may direct funds to those programs.
(b) The court shall determine if the defendant has the ability to pay the fee imposed under this section. In making that determination, the court shall take into account the total amount of fines and restitution that the defendant is subject to, and may waive payment of this additional fee.
(c) The court shall deposit the moneys collected pursuant to this section in a fund designated by the board of supervisors, to be used as specified in subdivision (a).
(Added by Stats. 2008, Ch. 241, Sec. 2. Effective January 1, 2009.)
1463.28.
(a) Notwithstanding any other provision of law, for each option county, as defined by Section 77004 of the Government Code, which has adopted the resolution specified in subdivision (b), that portion of fines and forfeitures, whether collected by the courts or by other processing agencies, which are attributable to an increase in the bail amounts adopted subsequent to the resolution pursuant to subdivision (c) of Section 1269b which would otherwise be divided between the county and cities within the county shall be deposited into the county general fund up to the annual limit listed in subdivision (b) for that county. Fine and forfeiture increments which exceed the specified annual limit shall be divided between the county and the cities within the county as otherwise provided by law. The scheduled bail amounts in such a county may exceed the bail amounts established by the Judicial Council pursuant to subdivision (c) of Section 1269b.
(b) The counties which may adopt a resolution directing that future increments in fines and forfeitures as specified in subdivision (a) be deposited in the county general fund and the annual limit applicable to those counties is as follows:

County	Annual Limit
Alpine	$ 300,000
Amador	200,000
Butte	900,000
Calaveras	300,000
Contra Costa	100,000
Del Norte	200,000
Fresno	700,000
Humboldt	200,000
Kings	300,000
Lake	400,000
Lassen	200,000
Los Angeles	15,000,000
Madera	600,000
Mariposa	200,000
Mendocino	600,000
Modoc	200,000
Mono	200,000
Plumas	200,000
San Benito	300,000
San Diego	5,200,000
San Joaquin	1,000,000
Santa Clara	3,200,000
Sierra	300,000
Stanislaus	1,900,000
Sutter	800,000

County	Annual Limit
Trinity	200,000
Tulare	2,000,000
Tuolumne	400,000
Yolo	700,000
Yuba	900,000

(c) Except as provided in Sections 40200.3 and 40200.4 of the Vehicle Code, this section does not apply to the collection of parking penalties.
(Amended by Stats. 2003, Ch. 149, Sec. 76.5. Effective January 1, 2004.)
1464.
(a) (1) Subject to Chapter 12 (commencing with Section 76000) of Title 8 of the Government Code, and except as otherwise provided in this section, there shall be levied a state penalty in the amount of ten dollars ($10) for every ten dollars ($10), or part of ten dollars ($10), upon every fine, penalty, or forfeiture imposed and collected by the courts for all criminal offenses, including all offenses, except parking offenses as defined in subdivision (i) of Section 1463, involving a violation of a section of the Vehicle Code or any local ordinance adopted pursuant to the Vehicle Code.
(2) Any bail schedule adopted pursuant to Section 1269b or bail schedule adopted by the Judicial Council pursuant to Section 40310 of the Vehicle Code may include the necessary amount to pay the penalties established by this section and Chapter 12 (commencing with Section 76000) of Title 8 of the Government Code, and the surcharge authorized by Section 1465.7, for all matters where a personal appearance is not mandatory and the bail is posted primarily to guarantee payment of the fine.
(3) The penalty imposed by this section does not apply to the following:
(A) Any restitution fine.
(B) Any penalty authorized by Chapter 12 (commencing with Section 76000) of Title 8 of the Government Code.
(C) Any parking offense subject to Article 3 (commencing with Section 40200) of Chapter 1 of Division 17 of the Vehicle Code.
(D) The state surcharge authorized by Section 1465.7.
(b) Where multiple offenses are involved, the state penalty shall be based upon the total fine or bail for each case. When a fine is suspended, in whole or in part, the state penalty shall be reduced in proportion to the suspension.
(c) When any deposited bail is made for an offense to which this section applies, and for which a court appearance is not mandatory, the person making the deposit shall also deposit a sufficient amount to include the state penalty prescribed by this section for forfeited bail. If bail is returned, the state penalty paid thereon pursuant to this section shall also be returned.
(d) In any case where a person convicted of any offense, to which this section applies, is in prison until the fine is satisfied, the judge may waive all or any part of the state penalty, the payment of which would work a hardship on the person convicted or his or her immediate family.
(e) After a determination by the court of the amount due, the clerk of the court shall collect the penalty and transmit it to the county treasury. The portion thereof attributable to Chapter 12 (commencing with Section 76000) of Title 8 of the Government Code shall be deposited in the appropriate county fund and 70 percent of the balance shall then be transmitted to the State Treasury, to be deposited in the State Penalty Fund, which is hereby created, and 30 percent to remain on deposit in the county general fund. The transmission to the State Treasury shall be carried out in the same manner as fines collected for the state by a county.
(f) Notwithstanding any other law, the Director of Finance shall provide a schedule to the Controller for all transfers of funds made available by the Budget Act from the State Penalty Fund in the current fiscal year.
(g) Upon the order of the Department of Finance, sufficient funds may be transferred by the Controller from the General Fund for cashflow needs of the State Penalty Fund. A cashflow loan made pursuant to this provision shall be short term and does not constitute a General Fund expenditure. A cashflow loan and the repayment of a cashflow loan does not affect the General Fund reserve.
(Amended by Stats. 2017, Ch. 17, Sec. 34. (AB 103) Effective June 27, 2017.)
1464.05.
Wherever the word "assessment" appears in any reference to Section 1464 in any law or regulation with regard to a fine, penalty, or bail forfeiture, it shall be deemed to refer to the penalty, state penalty, or additional penalty required by Section 1464.
(Added by Stats. 1990, Ch. 1293, Sec. 3.)
1464.8.
Notwithstanding any other provision of law, when an allocation and distribution of any fine, forfeiture, penalty, fee, or assessment collected in any criminal case is made, including, but not limited to, moneys collected pursuant to this chapter, Section 13003 of the Fish and Game Code, Chapter 12 (commencing with Section 76000) of Title 8 of the Government Code, and Sections 11372.5 and 11502 of the Health and Safety Code, the allocation and distribution of any payment may be based upon the law in effect during the accounting period when the payment is made.
(Amended by Stats. 1991, Ch. 189, Sec. 37. Effective July 29, 1991.)
1465.5.
An assessment of two dollars ($2) for every ten dollars ($10) or fraction thereof, for every fine, forfeiture, or parking penalty imposed and collected pursuant to Section 42001.13 of the Vehicle Code for violation of Section 22507.8 of the Vehicle Code, may be imposed by each county upon the adoption of a resolution by the board of supervisors. An assessment imposed by this section shall be collected and disbursed as provided in Section 9545 of the Welfare and Institutions Code.
(Amended by Stats. 2003, Ch. 555, Sec. 2. Effective January 1, 2004.)
1465.6.
(a) In addition to an assessment levied pursuant to Section 1465.5 of this code, or any other law, an additional assessment equal to 10 percent of the fine imposed under Section 42001.5, 42001.13, or 42002 of the Vehicle Code shall be imposed by each county for a criminal violation of the following:
(1) Subdivisions (b), (c), and (d) of Section 4461 of the Vehicle Code.
(2) Subdivision (c) of Section 4463 of the Vehicle Code.
(3) Section 22507.8 of the Vehicle Code.
(4) Section 22522 of the Vehicle Code.
(b) An assessment imposed pursuant to this section shall be deposited with the city or county where the violation occurred.
(Amended by Stats. 2009, Ch. 415, Sec. 1. (AB 144) Effective January 1, 2010.)
1465.7.
(a) A state surcharge of 20 percent shall be levied on the base fine used to calculate the state penalty assessment as specified in subdivision (a) of Section 1464.
(b) This surcharge shall be in addition to the state penalty assessed pursuant to Section 1464 of the Penal Code and may not be included in the base fine used to calculate the state penalty assessment as specified in subdivision (a) of Section 1464.

(c) After a determination by the court of the amount due, the clerk of the court shall cause the amount of the state surcharge collected to be transmitted to the General Fund.

(d) Notwithstanding Chapter 12 (commencing with Section 76000) of Title 8 of the Government Code and subdivision (b) of Section 68090.8 of the Government Code, the full amount of the surcharge shall be transmitted to the State Treasury to be deposited in the General Fund. Of the amount collected from the total amount of the fines, penalties, and surcharges imposed, the amount of the surcharge established by this section shall be transmitted to the State Treasury to be deposited in the General Fund.

(e) When any deposited bail is made for an offense to which this section applies, and for which a court appearance is not mandatory, the person making the deposit shall also deposit a sufficient amount to include the surcharge prescribed by this section.

(f) When amounts owed by an offender as a result of a conviction are paid in installment payments, payments shall be credited pursuant to Section 1203.1d. The amount of the surcharge established by this section shall be transmitted to the State Treasury prior to the county retaining or disbursing the remaining amount of the fines, penalties, and forfeitures imposed.

(g) Notwithstanding Sections 40512.6 and 42007 of the Vehicle Code, the term "total bail" as used in subdivision (a) of Section 42007 of the Vehicle Code does not include the surcharge set forth in this section. The surcharge set forth in this section shall be levied on what would have been the base fine had the provisions of Section 42007 not been invoked and the proceeds from the imposition of the surcharge shall be treated as otherwise set forth in this section.

(Amended by Stats. 2007, Ch. 176, Sec. 63. Effective August 24, 2007.)
1465.8.
(a) (1) To assist in funding court operations, an assessment of forty dollars ($40) shall be imposed on every conviction for a criminal offense, including a traffic offense, except parking offenses as defined in subdivision (i) of Section 1463, involving a violation of a section of the Vehicle Code or any local ordinance adopted pursuant to the Vehicle Code.

(2) For the purposes of this section, "conviction" includes the dismissal of a traffic violation on the condition that the defendant attend a court-ordered traffic violator school, as authorized by Sections 41501 and 42005 of the Vehicle Code. This court operations assessment shall be deposited in accordance with subdivision (d), and may not be included with the fee calculated and distributed pursuant to Section 42007 of the Vehicle Code.

(b) This assessment shall be in addition to the state penalty assessed pursuant to Section 1464 and may not be included in the base fine to calculate the state penalty assessment as specified in subdivision (a) of Section 1464. The penalties authorized by Chapter 12 (commencing with Section 76000) of Title 8 of the Government Code, and the state surcharge authorized by Section 1465.7, do not apply to this assessment.

(c) When bail is deposited for an offense to which this section applies, and for which a court appearance is not necessary, the person making the deposit shall also deposit a sufficient amount to include the assessment prescribed by this section.

(d) Notwithstanding any other law, the assessments collected pursuant to subdivision (a) shall all be deposited in a special account in the county treasury and transmitted therefrom monthly to the Controller for deposit in the Trial Court Trust Fund. The assessments collected pursuant to this section shall not be subject to subdivision (e) of Section 1203.1d, but shall be disbursed under subdivision (b) of Section 1203.1d.

(e) The Judicial Council shall provide for the administration of this section.

(Amended (as amended by Stats. 2011, Ch. 40, Sec. 6) by Stats. 2012, Ch. 41, Sec. 67. (SB 1021) Effective June 27, 2012.)

CHAPTER 2.
Appeals In Misdemeanor and Infraction Cases [1466 - 1469]

(Heading of Chapter 2 amended by Stats. 1998, Ch. 931, Sec. 423.)
1466.
An appeal may be taken from a judgment or order, in an infraction or misdemeanor case, to the appellate division of the superior court of the county in which the court from which the appeal is taken is located, in the following cases:

(a) By the people:

(1) From an order recusing the district attorney or city attorney pursuant to Section 1424.

(2) From an order or judgment dismissing or otherwise terminating all or any portion of the action, including such an order or judgment, entered after a verdict or finding of guilty or a verdict or judgment entered before the defendant has been placed in jeopardy or where the defendant has waived jeopardy.

(3) From sustaining a demurrer to any portion of the complaint or pleading.

(4) From an order granting a new trial.

(5) From an order arresting judgment.

(6) From any order made after judgment affecting the substantial rights of the people.

(7) From the imposition of an unlawful sentence, whether or not the court suspends the execution of sentence. As used in this paragraph, "unlawful sentence" means the imposition of a sentence not authorized by law or the imposition of a sentence based upon an unlawful order of the court that strikes or otherwise modifies the effect of an enhancement or prior conviction. A defendant shall have the right to counsel in the people's appeal of an unlawful sentence under the same circumstances that he or she would have a right to counsel under subdivision (a) of Section 1238.

(8) Nothing in this section shall be construed to authorize an appeal from an order granting probation. Instead, the people may seek appellate review of any grant of probation, whether or not the court imposes sentence, by means of a petition for a writ of mandate or prohibition that is filed within 60 days after probation is granted. The review of any grant of probation shall include review of any order underlying the grant of probation.

(b) By the defendant:

(1) From a final judgment of conviction. A sentence, an order granting probation, a conviction in a case in which before final judgment the defendant is committed for insanity or is given an indeterminate commitment as a mentally disordered sex offender, or the conviction of a defendant committed for controlled substance addiction shall be deemed to be a final judgment within the meaning of this section. Upon appeal from a final judgment or an order granting probation the court may review any order denying a motion for a new trial.

(2) From any order made after judgment affecting his or her substantial rights.

(Amended by Stats. 2011, Ch. 304, Sec. 11. (SB 428) Effective January 1, 2012.)
1467.
An appeal from a judgment of conviction does not stay the execution of the judgment in any case unless the trial or a reviewing court shall so order. The granting or refusal of such an order shall rest in the discretion of the court, except that a court shall not stay any duty to register as a sex offender pursuant to Section 290.

(Amended by Stats. 1998, Ch. 960, Sec. 6. Effective January 1, 1999.)
1468.
Appeals to the appellate divisions of superior courts shall be taken, heard and determined, the decisions thereon shall be remitted to the courts from which the

appeals are taken, and the records on such appeals shall be made up and filed in such time and manner as shall be prescribed in rules adopted by the Judicial Council.

(Amended by Stats. 1998, Ch. 931, Sec. 425. Effective September 28, 1998.)
1469.
Upon appeal by the people the reviewing court may review any question of law involved in any ruling affecting the judgment or order appealed from, without exception having been taken in the trial court. Upon an appeal by a defendant the court may, without exception having been taken in the trial court, review any question of law involved in any ruling, order, instruction, or thing whatsoever said or done at the trial or prior to or after judgment, which thing was said or done after objection made in and considered by the trial court and which affected the substantial rights of the defendant. The court may also review any instruction given, refused or modified, even though no objection was made thereto in the trial court if the substantial rights of the defendant were affected thereby. The reviewing court may reverse, affirm or modify the judgment or order appealed from, and may set aside, affirm or modify any or all of the proceedings subsequent to, or dependent upon, such judgment or order, and may, if proper, order a new trial. If a new trial is ordered upon appeal, it must be had in the court from which the appeal is taken.

(Amended by Stats. 1977, Ch. 1257.)

CHAPTER 3.
Transfer of Misdemeanor and Infraction Appeals [1471- 1471.]

(Heading of Chapter 3 amended by Stats. 1998, Ch. 931, Sec. 426.)
1471.
A court of appeal may order any case on appeal to a superior court in its district transferred to it for hearing and decision as provided by rules of the Judicial Council when the superior court certifies, or the court of appeal determines, that such transfer appears necessary to secure uniformity of decision or to settle important questions of law.

A court to which any such case is transferred shall have similar power to review any matter and make orders and judgments as the appellate division of the superior court by statute would have in such case, except as otherwise expressly provided.

(Amended by Stats. 1998, Ch. 931, Sec. 427. Effective September 28, 1998.)

TITLE 12. OF SPECIAL PROCEEDINGS OF A CRIMINAL NATURE [1473 - 1564]
(Title 12 enacted 1872.)

CHAPTER 1. Of the Writ of Habeas Corpus [1473 - 1509.1]

(Chapter 1 enacted 1872.)
1473.
(a) A person unlawfully imprisoned or restrained of his or her liberty, under any pretense, may prosecute a writ of habeas corpus to inquire into the cause of his or her imprisonment or restraint.

(b) A writ of habeas corpus may be prosecuted for, but not limited to, the following reasons:

(1) False evidence that is substantially material or probative on the issue of guilt or punishment was introduced against a person at a hearing or trial relating to his or her incarceration.

(2) False physical evidence, believed by a person to be factual, probative, or material on the issue of guilt, which was known by the person at the time of entering a plea of guilty, which was a material factor directly related to the plea of guilty by the person.

(3) (A) New evidence exists that is credible, material, presented without substantial delay, and of such decisive force and value that it would have more likely than not changed the outcome at trial.

(B) For purposes of this section, "new evidence" means evidence that has been discovered after trial, that could not have been discovered prior to trial by the exercise of due diligence, and is admissible and not merely cumulative, corroborative, collateral, or impeaching.

(c) Any allegation that the prosecution knew or should have known of the false nature of the evidence referred to in paragraphs (1) and (2) of subdivision (b) is immaterial to the prosecution of a writ of habeas corpus brought pursuant to paragraph (1) or (2) of subdivision (b).

(d) This section does not limit the grounds for which a writ of habeas corpus may be prosecuted or preclude the use of any other remedies.

(e) (1) For purposes of this section, "false evidence" includes opinions of experts that have either been repudiated by the expert who originally provided the opinion at a hearing or trial or that have been undermined by later scientific research or technological advances.

(2) This section does not create additional liabilities, beyond those already recognized, for an expert who repudiates his or her original opinion provided at a hearing or trial or whose opinion has been undermined by later scientific research or technological advancements.

(Amended by Stats. 2016, Ch. 785, Sec. 1. (SB 1134) Effective January 1, 2017.)
1473.5.
(a) A writ of habeas corpus also may be prosecuted on the basis that competent and substantial expert testimony relating to intimate partner battering and its effects, within the meaning of Section 1107 of the Evidence Code, was not presented to the trier of fact at the trial court proceedings and is of such substance that, had the competent and substantial expert testimony been presented, there is a reasonable probability, sufficient to undermine confidence in the judgment of conviction or sentence, that the result of the proceedings would have been different. Sections 1260 to 1262, inclusive, apply to the prosecution of a writ of habeas corpus pursuant to this section. As used in this section, "trial court proceedings" means those court proceedings that occur from the time the accusatory pleading is filed until and including judgment and sentence.

(b) This section is limited to violent felonies as specified in subdivision (c) of Section 667.5 that were committed before August 29, 1996, and that resulted in judgments of conviction or sentence after a plea or trial as to which expert testimony admissible pursuant to Section 1107 of the Evidence Code may be probative on the issue of culpability.

(c) A showing that expert testimony relating to intimate partner battering and its effects was presented to the trier of fact is not a bar to granting a petition under this section if that expert testimony was not competent or substantial. The burden of proof is on the petitioner to establish a sufficient showing that competent and substantial expert testimony, of a nature which would be competent using prevailing understanding of intimate partner battering and its effects, was not presented to the trier of fact, and had that evidence been presented, there is a reasonable probability that the result of the proceedings would have been different.

(d) If a petitioner for habeas corpus under this section has previously filed a petition for writ of habeas corpus, it is grounds for denial of the new petition if a court determined on the merits in the prior petition that the omission of expert testimony relating to battered women's syndrome or intimate partner battering and its effects at trial was not prejudicial and did not entitle the petitioner to the writ of habeas corpus.

(e) For purposes of this section, the changes that become effective on January 1, 2005, are not intended to expand the uses or applicability of expert testimony on battering and its effects that were in effect immediately prior to that date in criminal cases.
(Amended by Stats. 2012, Ch. 803, Sec. 1. (AB 593) Effective January 1, 2013.)

1473.6.

(a) Any person no longer unlawfully imprisoned or restrained may prosecute a motion to vacate a judgment for any of the following reasons:

(1) Newly discovered evidence of fraud by a government official that completely undermines the prosecution's case, is conclusive, and points unerringly to his or her innocence.

(2) Newly discovered evidence that a government official testified falsely at the trial that resulted in the conviction and that the testimony of the government official was substantially probative on the issue of guilt or punishment.

(3) Newly discovered evidence of misconduct by a government official committed in the underlying case that resulted in fabrication of evidence that was substantially material and probative on the issue of guilt or punishment. Evidence of misconduct in other cases is not sufficient to warrant relief under this paragraph.

(b) For purposes of this section, "newly discovered evidence" is evidence that could not have been discovered with reasonable diligence prior to judgment.

(c) The procedure for bringing and adjudicating a motion under this section, including the burden of producing evidence and the burden of proof, shall be the same as for prosecuting a writ of habeas corpus.

(d) A motion pursuant to this section must be filed within one year of the later of the following:

(1) The date the moving party discovered, or could have discovered with the exercise of due diligence, additional evidence of the misconduct or fraud by a government official beyond the moving party's personal knowledge.

(2) The effective date of this section.
(Added by Stats. 2002, Ch. 1105, Sec. 3. Effective January 1, 2003.)

1473.7.

(a) A person who is no longer in criminal custody may file a motion to vacate a conviction or sentence for either of the following reasons:

(1) The conviction or sentence is legally invalid due to prejudicial error damaging the moving party's ability to meaningfully understand, defend against, or knowingly accept the actual or potential adverse immigration consequences of a plea of guilty or nolo contendere. A finding of legal invalidity may, but need not, include a finding of ineffective assistance of counsel.

(2) Newly discovered evidence of actual innocence exists that requires vacation of the conviction or sentence as a matter of law or in the interests of justice.

(b) (1) Except as provided in paragraph (2), a motion pursuant to paragraph (1) of subdivision (a) shall be deemed timely filed at any time in which the individual filing the motion is no longer in criminal custody.

(2) A motion pursuant to paragraph (1) of subdivision (a) may be deemed untimely filed if it was not filed with reasonable diligence after the later of the following:

(A) The moving party receives a notice to appear in immigration court or other notice from immigration authorities that asserts the conviction or sentence as a basis for removal or the denial of an application for an immigration benefit, lawful status, or naturalization.

(B) Notice that a final removal order has been issued against the moving party, based on the existence of the conviction or sentence that the moving party seeks to vacate.

(c) A motion pursuant to paragraph (2) of subdivision (a) shall be filed without undue delay from the date the moving party discovered, or could have discovered with the exercise of due diligence, the evidence that provides a basis for relief under this section.

(d) All motions shall be entitled to a hearing. Upon the request of the moving party, the court may hold the hearing without the personal presence of the moving party provided that it finds good cause as to why the moving party cannot be present. If the prosecution has no objection to the motion, the court may grant the motion to vacate the conviction or sentence without a hearing.

(e) When ruling on the motion:

(1) The court shall grant the motion to vacate the conviction or sentence if the moving party establishes, by a preponderance of the evidence, the existence of any of the grounds for relief specified in subdivision (a). For a motion made pursuant to paragraph (1) of subdivision (a), the moving party shall also establish that the conviction or sentence being challenged is currently causing or has the potential to cause removal or the denial of an application for an immigration benefit, lawful status, or naturalization.

(2) There is a presumption of legal invalidity for the purposes of paragraph (1) of subdivision (a) if the moving party pleaded guilty or nolo contendere pursuant to a statute that provided that, upon completion of specific requirements, the arrest and conviction shall be deemed never to have occurred, where the moving party complied with these requirements, and where the disposition under the statute has been, or potentially could be, used as a basis for adverse immigration consequences.

(3) If the court grants the motion to vacate a conviction or sentence obtained through a plea of guilty or nolo contendere, the court shall allow the moving party to withdraw the plea.

(4) When ruling on a motion under paragraph (1) of subdivision (a), the only finding that the court is required to make is whether the conviction is legally invalid due to prejudicial error damaging the moving party's ability to meaningfully understand, defend against, or knowingly accept the actual or potential adverse immigration consequences of a plea of guilty or nolo contendere. When ruling on a motion under paragraph (2) of subdivision (a), the court shall specify the basis for its conclusion.

(f) An order granting or denying the motion is appealable under subdivision (b) of Section 1237 as an order after judgment affecting the substantial rights of a party.

(g) A court may only issue a specific finding of ineffective assistance of counsel as a result of a motion brought under paragraph (1) of subdivision (a) if the attorney found to be ineffective was given timely advance notice of the motion hearing by the moving party or the prosecutor, pursuant to Section 416.90 of the Code of Civil Procedure.
(Amended by Stats. 2018, Ch. 825, Sec. 2. (AB 2867) Effective January 1, 2019.)

1474.

Application for the writ is made by petition, signed either by the party for whose relief it is intended, or by some person in his behalf, and must specify:

1. That the person in whose behalf the writ is applied for is imprisoned or restrained of his liberty, the officer or person by whom he is so confined or restrained, and the place where, naming all the parties, if they are known, or describing them, if they are not known;

2. If the imprisonment is alleged to be illegal, the petition must also state in what the alleged illegality consists;

3. The petition must be verified by the oath or affirmation of the party making the application.
(Enacted 1872.)

1475.

The writ of habeas corpus may be granted in the manner provided by law. If the writ has been granted by any court or a judge thereof and after the hearing thereof the prisoner

---

has been remanded, he or she shall not be discharged from custody by the same or any other court of like general jurisdiction, or by a judge of the same or any other court of like general jurisdiction, unless upon some ground not existing in fact at the issuing of the prior writ. Should the prisoner desire to urge some point of law not raised in the petition for or at the hearing upon the return of the prior writ, then, in case the prior writ had been returned or returnable before a superior court or a judge thereof, no writ can be issued upon a second or other application except by the appropriate court of appeal or some judge thereof, or by the Supreme Court or some judge thereof, and in the event the writ must not be made returnable before any superior court or any judge thereof. In the event, however, that the prior writ was returned or made returnable before a court of appeal or any judge thereof, no writ can be issued upon a second or other application except by the Supreme Court or some judge thereof, and the writ must be made returnable before said Supreme Court or some judge thereof.

Every application for a writ of habeas corpus must be verified, and shall state whether any prior application or applications have been made for a writ in regard to the same detention or restraint complained of in the application, and if any prior application or applications have been made the later application must contain a brief statement of all proceedings had therein, or in any of them, to and including the final order or orders made therein, or in any of them, on appeal or otherwise.

Whenever the person applying for a writ of habeas corpus is held in custody or restraint by any officer of any court of this state or any political subdivision thereof, or by any peace officer of this state, or any political subdivision thereof, a copy of the application for the writ must in all cases be served upon the district attorney of the county wherein the person is held in custody or restraint at least 24 hours before the time at which said writ is made returnable and no application for the writ can be heard without proof of service in cases where the service is required.

If the person is in custody for violation of an ordinance of a city which has a city attorney, a copy of the application for the writ must also be served on the city attorney of the city whose ordinance is the basis for the charge at least 24 hours before the time at which the writ is made returnable, provided that failure to serve the city attorney shall not deprive the court of jurisdiction to hear the application. If a writ challenging a denial of parole or the applicant's suitability for parole is then made returnable, a copy of the application for the writ and the related order to show cause shall in all cases be served by the superior court upon the office of the Attorney General and the district attorney of the county in which the underlying judgment was rendered at least three business days before the time at which the writ is made returnable and no application for the writ can be heard without proof of such service.
(Amended by Stats. 2006, Ch. 274, Sec. 1. Effective January 1, 2007.)

1476.

Any court or judge authorized to grant the writ, to whom a petition therefor is presented, must endorse upon the petition the hour and date of its presentation and the hour and date of the granting or denial of the writ, and must, if it appear that the writ ought to issue, grant the same without delay; and if the person by or upon whose behalf the application for the writ is made be detained upon a criminal charge, may admit him to bail, if the offense is bailable, pending the determination of the proceeding.
(Amended by Stats. 1949, Ch. 1021.)

1477.

The writ must be directed to the person having custody of or restraining the person on whose behalf the application is made, and must command him to have the body of such person before the Court or Judge before whom the writ is returnable, at a time and place therein specified.
(Enacted 1872.)

1478.

If the writ is directed to the sheriff or other ministerial officer of the court out of which it issues, it must be delivered by the clerk to such officer without delay, as other writs are delivered for service. If it is directed to any other person, it must be delivered to the sheriff or a marshal, and be by him served upon such person by delivering the copy to him without delay, and make his return on the original to the court of issuance. If the person to whom the writ is directed cannot be found, or refuses admittance to the officer or person serving or delivering such writ, it may be served or delivered by leaving it at the residence of the person to whom it is directed, or by affixing it to some conspicuous place on the outside either of his dwelling house or of the place where the party is confined or under restraint.
(Amended by Stats. 1968, Ch. 479.)

1479.

If the person to whom the writ is directed refuses, after service, to obey the same, the Court or Judge, upon affidavit, must issue an attachment against such person, directed to the Sheriff or Coroner, commanding him forthwith to apprehend such person and bring him immediately before such Court or Judge; and upon being so brought, he must be committed to the jail of the county until he makes due return to such writ, or is otherwise legally discharged.
(Enacted 1872.)

1480.

The person upon whom the writ is served must state in his return, plainly and unequivocally:

1. Whether he has or has not the party in his custody, or under his power or restraint;

2. If he has the party in his custody or power, or under his restraint, he must state the authority and cause of such imprisonment or restraint;

3. If the party is detained by virtue of any writ, warrant, or other written authority, a copy thereof must be annexed to the return, and the original produced and exhibited to the Court or Judge on the hearing of such return;

4. If the person upon whom the writ is served had the party in his power or custody, or under his restraint, at any time prior or subsequent to the date of the writ of habeas corpus, but has transferred such custody or restraint to another, the return must state particularly to whom, at what time and place, for what cause, and by what authority such transfer took place;

5. The return must be signed by the person making the same, and, except when such person is a sworn public officer, and makes such return in his official capacity, it must be verified by his oath.
(Enacted 1872.)

1481.

The person to whom the writ is directed, if it is served, must bring the body of the party in his custody or under his restraint, according to the command of the writ, except in the cases specified in the next section.
(Enacted 1872.)

1482.

When, from sickness or infirmity of the person directed to be produced, he cannot, without danger, be brought before the Court or Judge, the person in whose custody or power he is may state that fact in his return to the writ, verifying the same by affidavit. If the Court or Judge is satisfied of the truth of such return, and the return to the writ is otherwise sufficient, the Court or Judge may proceed to decide on such return, and to dispose of the matter as if such party had been produced on the writ, or the hearing thereof may be adjourned until such party can be produced.
(Enacted 1872.)

1483.

The Court or Judge before whom the writ is returned must, immediately after the return, proceed to hear and examine the return, and such other matters as may be properly submitted to their hearing and consideration.
(Enacted 1872.)

1484.
The party brought before the Court or Judge, on the return of the writ, may deny or controvert any of the material facts or matters set forth in the return, or except to the sufficiency thereof, or allege any fact to show either that his imprisonment or detention is unlawful, or that he is entitled to his discharge. The Court or Judge must thereupon proceed in a summary way to hear such proof as may be produced against such imprisonment or detention, or in favor of the same, and to dispose of such party as the justice of the case may require, and have full power and authority to require and compel the attendance of witnesses, by process of subpoena and attachment, and to do and perform all other acts and things necessary to a full and fair hearing and determination of the case.
(Enacted 1872.)
1485.
If no legal cause is shown for such imprisonment or restraint, or for the continuation thereof, such Court or Judge must discharge such party from the custody or restraint under which he is held.
(Enacted 1872.)
1485.5.
(a) If the district attorney or Attorney General stipulates to or does not contest the factual allegations underlying one or more of the grounds for granting a writ of habeas corpus or a motion to vacate a judgment, the facts underlying the basis for the court's ruling or order shall be binding on the Attorney General, the factfinder, and the California Victim Compensation Board.
(b) The district attorney shall provide notice to the Attorney General prior to entering into a stipulation of facts that will be the basis for the granting of a writ of habeas corpus or a motion to vacate a judgment.
(c) In a contested or uncontested proceeding, the express factual findings made by the court, including credibility determinations, in considering a petition for habeas corpus, a motion to vacate judgment pursuant to Section 1473.6, or an application for a certificate of factual innocence, shall be binding on the Attorney General, the factfinder, and the California Victim Compensation Board.
(d) For the purposes of this section, "express factual findings" are findings established as the basis for the court's ruling or order.
(e) For purposes of this section, "court" is defined as a state or federal court.
(Amended by Stats. 2016, Ch. 785, Sec. 2. (SB 1134) Effective January 1, 2017.)
1485.55.
(a) In a contested proceeding, if the court has granted a writ of habeas corpus or when, pursuant to Section 1473.6, the court vacates a judgment, and if the court has found that the person is factually innocent, that finding shall be binding on the California Victim Compensation Board for a claim presented to the board, and upon application by the person, the board shall, without a hearing, recommend to the Legislature that an appropriation be made and the claim paid pursuant to Section 4904.
(b) In a contested or uncontested proceeding, if the court grants a writ of habeas corpus and did not find the person factually innocent in the habeas corpus proceedings, the petitioner may move for a finding of factual innocence by a preponderance of the evidence that the crime with which he or she was charged was either not committed at all or, if committed, was not committed by him or her.
(c) If the court vacates a judgment pursuant to Section 1473.6, on any ground, the petitioner may move for a finding of factual innocence by a preponderance of the evidence that the crime with which he or she was charged was either not committed at all or, if committed, was not committed by him or her.
(d) If the court makes a finding that the petitioner has proven his or her factual innocence by a preponderance of the evidence pursuant to subdivision (b) or (c), the board shall, without a hearing, recommend to the Legislature that an appropriation be made and any claim filed shall be paid pursuant to Section 4904.
(e) A presumption does not exist in any other proceeding for failure to make a motion or obtain a favorable ruling pursuant to subdivision (b) or (c).
(f) If a federal court, after granting a writ of habeas corpus, pursuant to a nonstatutory motion or request, finds a petitioner factually innocent by no less than a preponderance of the evidence that the crime with which he or she was charged was either not committed at all or, if committed, was not committed by him or her, the board shall, without a hearing, recommend to the Legislature that an appropriation be made and any claim filed shall be paid pursuant to Section 4904.
(Amended by Stats. 2016, Ch. 785, Sec. 3. (SB 1134) Effective January 1, 2017.)
1486.
The Court or Judge, if the time during which such party may be legally detained in custody has not expired, must remand such party, if it appears that he is detained in custody:
1. By virtue of process issued by any Court or Judge of the United States, in a case where such Court or Judge has exclusive jurisdiction; or,
2. By virtue of the final judgment or decree of any competent Court of criminal jurisdiction, or of any process issued upon such judgment or decree.
(Enacted 1872.)
1487.
If it appears on the return of the writ that the prisoner is in custody by virtue of process from any Court of this State, or Judge or officer thereof, such prisoner may be discharged in any of the following cases, subject to the restrictions of the last section:
1. When the jurisdiction of such Court or officer has been exceeded;
2. When the imprisonment was at first lawful, yet by some act, omission, or event which has taken place afterwards, the party has become entitled to a discharge;
3. When the process is defective in some matter of substance required by law, rendering such process void;
4. When the process, though proper in form, has been issued in a case not allowed by law;
5. When the person having the custody of the prisoner is not the person allowed by law to detain him;
6. Where the process is not authorized by any order, judgment, or decree of any Court, nor by any provision of law;
7. Where a party has been committed on a criminal charge without reasonable or probable cause.
(Enacted 1872.)
1488.
If any person is committed to prison, or is in custody of any officer on any criminal charge, by virtue of any warrant of commitment of a magistrate, such person must not be discharged on the ground of any mere defect of form in the warrant of commitment.
(Amended by Stats. 1951, Ch. 1608.)
1489.
If it appears to the Court or Judge, by affidavit or otherwise, or upon the inspection of the process or warrant of commitment, and such other papers in the proceedings as may be shown to the Court or Judge, that the party is guilty of a criminal offense, or ought not to be discharged, such Court or Judge, although the charge is defective or unsubstantially set forth in such process or warrant of commitment, must cause the complainant or other necessary witnesses to be subpoenaed to attend at such time as ordered, to testify before the Court or Judge; and upon the examination he may discharge such prisoner, let him to bail, if the offense be bailable, or recommit him to custody, as may be just and legal.
(Enacted 1872.)
1490.
When a person is imprisoned or detained in custody on any criminal charge, for want of bail, such person is entitled to a writ of habeas corpus for the purpose of giving bail, upon averring that fact in his petition, without alleging that he is illegally confined.
(Enacted 1872.)
1491.
Any judge before whom a person who has been committed upon a criminal charge may be brought on a writ of habeas corpus, if the same is bailable, may take an undertaking of bail from such person as in other cases, and file the same in the proper court.
Whenever a writ of habeas corpus is returned to a court for hearing and the petitioner is charged with an offense other than a crime of violence or committed with a deadly weapon or involving the forcible taking or destruction of the property of another, but the prisoner does not stand convicted of any offense, the amount of the bail must be set immediately if no bail has theretofore been fixed.
(Amended by Stats. 1933, Ch. 595.)
1492.
If a party brought before the Court or Judge on the return of the writ is not entitled to his discharge, and is not bailed, where such bail is allowable, the Court or Judge must remand him to custody or place him under the restraint from which he was taken, if the person under whose custody or restraint he was is legally entitled thereto.
(Enacted 1872.)
1493.
In cases where any party is held under illegal restraint or custody, or any other person is entitled to the restraint or custody of such party, the Judge or Court may order such party to be committed to the restraint or custody of such person as is by law entitled thereto.
(Enacted 1872.)
1494.
Until judgment is given on the return, the Court or Judge before whom any party may be brought on such writ may commit him to the custody of the Sheriff of the county, or place him in such care or under such custody as his age or circumstances may require.
(Enacted 1872.)
1495.
No writ of habeas corpus can be disobeyed for defect of form, if it sufficiently appear therefrom in whose custody or under whose restraint the party imprisoned or restrained is, the officer or person detaining him, and the Court or Judge before whom he is to be brought.
(Enacted 1872.)
1496.
No person who has been discharged by the order of the Court or Judge upon habeas corpus can be again imprisoned, restrained, or kept in custody for the same cause, except in the following cases:
1. If he has been discharged from custody on a criminal charge, and is afterwards committed for the same offense, by legal order or process;
2. If, after a discharge for defect of proof, or for any defect of the process, warrant, or commitment in a criminal case, the prisoner is again arrested on sufficient proof and committed by legal process for the same offense.
(Enacted 1872.)
1497.
When it appears to any court, or judge, authorized by law to issue the writ of habeas corpus, that any one is illegally held in custody, confinement, or restraint, and that there is reason to believe that the person will be carried out of the jurisdiction of the court or judge before whom the application is made, or will suffer some irreparable injury before compliance with the writ of habeas corpus can be enforced, the court or judge may cause a warrant to be issued, reciting the facts, and directed to any peace officer, commanding the peace officer to take the person held in custody, confinement, or restraint, and immediately bring him or her before the court or judge, to be dealt with according to law.
(Amended by Stats. 1983, Ch. 990, Sec. 8.)
1498.
The Court or Judge may also insert in such warrant a command for the apprehension of the person charged with such illegal detention and restraint.
(Enacted 1872.)
1499.
The officer to whom such warrant is delivered must execute it by bringing the person therein named before the Court or Judge who directed the issuing of such warrant.
(Enacted 1872.)
1500.
The person alleged to have such party under illegal confinement or restraint may make return to such warrant as in case of a writ of habeas corpus, and the same may be denied, and like allegations, proofs, and trial may thereupon be had as upon a return to a writ of habeas corpus.
(Enacted 1872.)
1501.
If such party is held under illegal restraint or custody, he must be discharged; and if not, he must be restored to the care or custody of the person entitled thereto.
(Enacted 1872.)
1502.
Any writ or process authorized by this Chapter may be issued and served on any day or at any time.
(Enacted 1872.)
1503.
All writs, warrants, process, and subpoenas authorized by the provisions of this Chapter must be issued by the Clerk of the Court, and, except subpoenas, must be sealed with the seal of such Court, and served and returned forthwith, unless the Court or Judge shall specify a particular time for any such return.
(Enacted 1872.)
1504.
All such writs and process, when made returnable before a Judge, must be returned before him at the county seat, and there heard and determined.
(Amended by Code Amendments 1880, Ch. 6.)
1505.
If the officer or person to whom a writ of habeas corpus is directed, refuses obedience to the command thereof, he shall forfeit and pay to the person aggrieved a sum not exceeding ten thousand dollars ($10,000), to be recovered by action in any court of competent jurisdiction.
(Amended by Stats. 1983, Ch. 1092, Sec. 322.5. Effective September 27, 1983. Operative January 1, 1984, by Sec. 427 of Ch. 1092.)
1506.
An appeal may be taken to the court of appeal by the people from a final order of a superior court made upon the return of a writ of habeas corpus discharging a defendant or otherwise granting all or any part of the relief sought, in all criminal cases, excepting criminal cases where judgment of death has been rendered, and in such cases to the Supreme Court; and in all criminal cases where an application for a writ of habeas corpus has been heard and determined in a court of appeal, either the defendant or the people may apply for a hearing in the Supreme Court. Such appeal shall be taken and such application for hearing in the Supreme Court shall be made in accordance with rules to be laid down by the Judicial Council. If the people appeal from an order granting the discharge or release of the defendant, or petition for hearing in either the court of appeal or the Supreme Court, the defendant shall be admitted to bail or released on his

own recognizance or any other conditions which the court deems just and reasonable, subject to the same limitations, terms, and conditions which are applicable to, or may be imposed upon, a defendant who is awaiting trial. If the order grants relief other than a discharge or release from custody, the trial court or the court in which the appeal or petition for hearing is pending may, upon application by the people, in its discretion, and upon such conditions as it deems just stay the execution of the order pending final determination of the matter.

(Amended by Stats. 1975, Ch. 1080.)

1507.

Where an application for a writ of habeas corpus has been made by or on behalf of any person other than a defendant in a criminal case, an appeal may be taken to the court of appeal from a final order of a superior court granting all or any part of the relief sought; and where such application has been heard and determined in a court of appeal, either on an application filed in that court or on appeal from a superior court, and all or any part of the relief sought has been granted, an application may be made for a hearing in the Supreme Court. Such appeal shall be taken and such application for hearing in the Supreme Court shall be made in accordance with rules to be laid down by the Judicial Council. The court which made the order granting relief or the court in which the appeal or petition for hearing is pending may, in its discretion, and upon such conditions as it deems just stay the execution of the order pending final determination of the matter.

(Amended by Stats. 1967, Ch. 17.)

1508.

(a) A writ of habeas corpus issued by the Supreme Court or a judge thereof may be made returnable before the issuing judge or his court, before any court of appeal or judge thereof, or before any superior court or judge thereof.

(b) A writ of habeas corpus issued by a court of appeal or a judge thereof may be made returnable before the issuing judge or his court or before any superior court or judge thereof located in that appellate district.

(c) A writ of habeas corpus issued by a superior court or a judge thereof may be made returnable before the issuing judge or his court.

(Added by Stats. 1969, Ch. 38.)

1509.

(a) This section applies to any petition for writ of habeas corpus filed by a person in custody pursuant to a judgment of death. A writ of habeas corpus pursuant to this section is the exclusive procedure for collateral attack on a judgment of death. A petition filed in any court other than the court which imposed the sentence should be promptly transferred to that court unless good cause is shown for the petition to be heard by another court. A petition filed in or transferred to the court which imposed the sentence shall be assigned to the original trial judge unless that judge is unavailable or there is other good cause to assign the case to a different judge.

(b) After the entry of a judgment of death in the trial court, that court shall offer counsel to the prisoner as provided in Section 68662 of the Government Code.

(c) Except as provided in subdivisions (d) and (g), the initial petition must be filed within one year of the order entered under Section 68662 of the Government Code.

(d) An initial petition which is untimely under subdivision (c) or a successive petition whenever filed shall be dismissed unless the court finds, by the preponderance of all available evidence, whether or not admissible at trial, that the defendant is actually innocent of the crime of which he or she was convicted or is ineligible for the sentence. A stay of execution shall not be granted for the purpose of considering a successive or untimely petition unless the court finds that the petitioner has a substantial claim of actual innocence or ineligibility. "Ineligible for the sentence of death" means that circumstances exist placing that sentence outside the range of the sentencer's discretion. Claims of ineligibility include a claim that none of the special circumstances in subdivision (a) of Section 190.2 is true, a claim that the defendant was under the age of 18 at the time of the crime, or a claim that the defendant has an intellectual disability, as defined in Section 1376. A claim relating to the sentencing decision under Section 190.3 is not a claim of actual innocence or ineligibility for the purpose of this section.

(e) A petitioner claiming innocence or ineligibility under subdivision (d) shall disclose all material information relating to guilt or eligibility in the possession of the petitioner or present or former counsel for petitioner. If the petitioner willfully fails to make the disclosure required by this subdivision and authorize disclosure by counsel, the petition may be dismissed.

(f) Proceedings under this section shall be conducted as expeditiously as possible, consistent with a fair adjudication. The superior court shall resolve the initial petition within one year of filing unless the court finds that a delay is necessary to resolve a substantial claim of actual innocence, but in no instance shall the court take longer than two years to resolve the petition. On decision of an initial petition, the court shall issue a statement of decision explaining the factual and legal basis for its decision.

(g) If a habeas corpus petition is pending on the effective date of this section, the court may transfer the petition to the court which imposed the sentence. In a case where a judgment of death was imposed prior to the effective date of this section, but no habeas corpus petition has been filed prior to the effective date of this section, a petition that would otherwise be barred by subdivision (c) may be filed within one year of the effective date of this section or within the time allowed under prior law, whichever is earlier.

(Added November 8, 2016, by initiative Proposition 66, Sec. 6.)

1509.1.

(a) Either party may appeal the decision of a superior court on an initial petition under Section 1509 to the court of appeal. An appeal shall be taken by filing a notice of appeal in the superior court within 30 days of the court's decision granting or denying the habeas petition. A successive petition shall not be used as a means of reviewing a denial of habeas relief.

(b) The issues considered on an appeal under subdivision (a) shall be limited to the claims raised in the superior court, except that the court of appeal may also consider a claim of ineffective assistance of trial counsel if the failure of habeas counsel to present that claim to the superior court constituted ineffective assistance. The court of appeal may, if additional findings of fact are required, make a limited remand to the superior court to consider the claim.

(c) The people may appeal the decision of the superior court granting relief on a successive petition. The petitioner may appeal the decision of the superior court denying relief on a successive petition only if the superior court or the court of appeal grants a certificate of appealability. A certificate of appealability may issue under this subdivision only if the petitioner has shown both a substantial claim for relief, which shall be indicated in the certificate, and a substantial claim that the requirements of subdivision (d) of Section 1509 have been met. An appeal under this subdivision shall be taken by filing a notice of appeal in the superior court within 30 days of the court's decision. The superior court shall grant or deny a certificate of appealability concurrently with a decision denying relief on the petition. The court of appeal shall grant or deny a request for a certificate of appealability within 10 days of an application for a certificate. The jurisdiction of the court of appeal is limited to the claims identified in the certificate and any additional claims added by the court of appeal within 60 days of the notice of appeal. An appeal under this subdivision shall have priority over all other matters and be decided as expeditiously as possible.

(Added November 8, 2016, by initiative Proposition 66, Sec. 7.)

CHAPTER 2. Pretrial Review [1510 - 1512]

(Chapter 2 added by Stats. 1971, Ch. 944.)

1510.

The denial of a motion made pursuant to Section 995 or 1538.5 may be reviewed prior to trial only if the motion was made by the defendant in the trial court not later than 45 days following defendant's arraignment on the complaint if a misdemeanor, or 60 days following defendant's arraignment on the information or indictment if a felony, unless within these time limits the defendant was unaware of the issue or had no opportunity to raise the issue.

(Added by Stats. 1971, Ch. 944.)

1511.

If in a felony case the superior court sets the trial beyond the period of time specified in Section 1049.5, in violation of Section 1049.5, or continues the hearing of any matter without good cause, and good cause is required by law for such a continuance, either party may file a petition for writ of mandate or prohibition in the court of appeal seeking immediate appellate review of the ruling setting the trial or granting the continuance. Such a petition shall have precedence over all other cases in the court to which the petition is assigned, including, but not limited to, cases that originated in the juvenile court. If the court of appeal grants a peremptory writ, it shall issue the writ and a remittitur three court days after its decision becomes final as to that court if such action is necessary to prevent mootness or to prevent frustration of the relief granted, notwithstanding the right of the parties to file a petition for review in the Supreme Court. When the court of appeal issues the writ and remittitur as provided herein, the writ shall command the superior court to proceed with the criminal case without further delay, other than that reasonbly necessary for the parties to obtain the attendance of their witnesses.

The Supreme Court may stay or recall the issuance of the writ and remittitur. The Supreme Court's failure to stay or recall the issuance of the writ and remittitur shall not deprive the respondent or the real party in interest of its right to file a petition for review in the Supreme Court.

(Added June 5, 1990, by initiative Proposition 115, Sec. 28.)

1512.

(a) In addition to petitions for a writ of mandate, prohibition, or review which the people are authorized to file pursuant to any other statute or pursuant to any court decision, the people may also seek review of an order granting a defendant's motion for severance or discovery by a petition for a writ of mandate or prohibition.

(b) In construing the legislative intent of subdivision (a), no inference shall be drawn from the amendment to Assembly Bill 1052 of the 1989–90 Regular Session of the Legislature which deleted reference to the case of People v. Superior Court, 69 Cal. 2d 491.

(Added by renumbering Section 1511 (as added by Stats. 1989, Ch. 560) by Stats. 2001, Ch. 854, Sec. 46. Effective January 1, 2002.)

CHAPTER 3. Of Search Warrants [1523 - 1542.5]

(Chapter 3 enacted 1872.)

1523.

A search warrant is an order in writing, in the name of the people, signed by a magistrate, directed to a peace officer, commanding him or her to search for a person or persons, a thing or things, or personal property, and, in the case of a thing or things or personal property, bring the same before the magistrate.

(Amended by Stats. 1996, Ch. 1078, Sec. 1.5. Effective January 1, 1997.)

1524.

(a) A search warrant may be issued upon any of the following grounds:

(1) When the property was stolen or embezzled.

(2) When the property or things were used as the means of committing a felony.

(3) When the property or things are in the possession of any person with the intent to use them as a means of committing a public offense, or in the possession of another to whom he or she may have delivered them for the purpose of concealing them or preventing them from being discovered.

(4) When the property or things to be seized consist of an item or constitute evidence that tends to show a felony has been committed, or tends to show that a particular person has committed a felony.

(5) When the property or things to be seized consist of evidence that tends to show that sexual exploitation of a child, in violation of Section 311.3, or possession of matter depicting sexual conduct of a person under 18 years of age, in violation of Section 311.11, has occurred or is occurring.

(6) When there is a warrant to arrest a person.

(7) When a provider of electronic communication service or remote computing service has records or evidence, as specified in Section 1524.3, showing that property was stolen or embezzled constituting a misdemeanor, or that property or things are in the possession of any person with the intent to use them as a means of committing a misdemeanor public offense, or in the possession of another to whom he or she may have delivered them for the purpose of concealing them or preventing their discovery.

(8) When the property or things to be seized include an item or evidence that tends to show a violation of Section 3700.5 of the Labor Code, or tends to show that a particular person has violated Section 3700.5 of the Labor Code.

(9) When the property or things to be seized include a firearm or other deadly weapon at the scene of, or at the premises occupied or under the control of the person arrested in connection with, a domestic violence incident involving a threat to human life or a physical assault as provided in Section 18250. This section does not affect warrantless seizures otherwise authorized by Section 18250.

(10) When the property or things to be seized include a firearm or other deadly weapon that is owned by, or in the possession of, or in the custody or control of, a person described in subdivision (a) of Section 8102 of the Welfare and Institutions Code.

(11) When the property or things to be seized include a firearm that is owned by, or in the possession of, or in the custody or control of, a person who is subject to the prohibitions regarding firearms pursuant to Section 6389 of the Family Code, if a prohibited firearm is possessed, owned, in the custody of, or controlled by a person against whom a protective order has been issued pursuant to Section 6218 of the Family Code, the person has been lawfully served with that order, and the person has failed to relinquish the firearm as required by law.

(12) When the information to be received from the use of a tracking device constitutes evidence that tends to show that either a felony, a misdemeanor violation of the Fish and Game Code, or a misdemeanor violation of the Public Resources Code has been committed or is being committed, tends to show that a particular person has committed a felony, a misdemeanor violation of the Fish and Game Code, or a misdemeanor violation of the Public Resources Code, or is committing a felony, a misdemeanor violation of the Fish and Game Code, or a misdemeanor violation of the Public Resources Code, or will assist in locating an individual who has committed or is committing a felony, a misdemeanor violation of the Fish and Game Code, or a misdemeanor violation of the Public Resources Code. A tracking device search warrant issued pursuant to this paragraph shall be executed in a manner meeting the requirements specified in subdivision (b) of Section 1534.

(13) When a sample of the blood of a person constitutes evidence that tends to show a violation of Section 23140, 23152, or 23153 of the Vehicle Code and the person from whom the sample is being sought has refused an officer's request to submit to, or has

failed to complete, a blood test as required by Section 23612 of the Vehicle Code, and the sample will be drawn from the person in a reasonable, medically approved manner. This paragraph is not intended to abrogate a court's mandate to determine the propriety of the issuance of a search warrant on a case-by-case basis.

(14) Beginning January 1, 2016, the property or things to be seized are firearms or ammunition or both that are owned by, in the possession of, or in the custody or control of a person who is the subject of a gun violence restraining order that has been issued pursuant to Division 3.2 (commencing with Section 18100) of Title 2 of Part 6, if a prohibited firearm or ammunition or both is possessed, owned, in the custody of, or controlled by a person against whom a gun violence restraining order has been issued, the person has been lawfully served with that order, and the person has failed to relinquish the firearm as required by law.

(15) Beginning January 1, 2018, the property or things to be seized include a firearm that is owned by, or in the possession of, or in the custody or control of, a person who is subject to the prohibitions regarding firearms pursuant to Section 29800 or 29805, and the court has made a finding pursuant to subdivision (c) of Section 29810 that the person has failed to relinquish the firearm as required by law.

(16) When the property or things to be seized are controlled substances or a device, contrivance, instrument, or paraphernalia used for unlawfully using or administering a controlled substance pursuant to the authority described in Section 11472 of the Health and Safety Code.

(17) (A) When all of the following apply:
(i) A sample of the blood of a person constitutes evidence that tends to show a violation of subdivision (b), (c), (d), (e), or (f) of Section 655 of the Harbors and Navigation Code.
(ii) The person from whom the sample is being sought has refused an officer's request to submit to, or has failed to complete, a blood test as required by Section 655.1 of the Harbors and Navigation Code.
(iii) The sample will be drawn from the person in a reasonable, medically approved manner.
(B) This paragraph is not intended to abrogate a court's mandate to determine the propriety of the issuance of a search warrant on a case-by-case basis.

(18) When the property or things to be seized consists of evidence that tends to show that a violation of paragraph (1), (2), or (3) of subdivision (j) of Section 647 has occurred or is occurring.

(b) The property, things, person, or persons described in subdivision (a) may be taken on the warrant from any place, or from any person in whose possession the property or things may be.

(c) Notwithstanding subdivision (a) or (b), a search warrant shall not be issued for any documentary evidence in the possession or under the control of any person who is a lawyer as defined in Section 950 of the Evidence Code, a physician as defined in Section 990 of the Evidence Code, a psychotherapist as defined in Section 1010 of the Evidence Code, or a member of the clergy as defined in Section 1030 of the Evidence Code, and who is not reasonably suspected of engaging or having engaged in criminal activity related to the documentary evidence for which a warrant is requested unless the following procedure has been complied with:
(1) At the time of the issuance of the warrant, the court shall appoint a special master in accordance with subdivision (d) to accompany the person who will serve the warrant. Upon service of the warrant, the special master shall inform the party served of the specific items being sought and that the party shall have the opportunity to provide the items requested. If the party, in the judgment of the special master, fails to provide the items requested, the special master shall conduct a search for the items in the areas indicated in the search warrant.
(2) (A) If the party who has been served states that an item or items should not be disclosed, they shall be sealed by the special master and taken to court for a hearing.
(B) At the hearing, the party searched shall be entitled to raise any issues that may be raised pursuant to Section 1538.5 as well as a claim that the item or items are privileged, as provided by law. The hearing shall be held in the superior court. The court shall provide sufficient time for the parties to obtain counsel and make motions or present evidence. The hearing shall be held within three days of the service of the warrant unless the court makes a finding that the expedited hearing is impracticable. In that case, the matter shall be heard at the earliest possible time.
(C) If an item or items are taken to court for a hearing, any limitations of time prescribed in Chapter 2 (commencing with Section 799) of Title 3 of Part 2 shall be tolled from the time of the seizure until the final conclusion of the hearing, including any associated writ or appellate proceedings.
(3) The warrant shall, whenever practicable, be served during normal business hours. In addition, the warrant shall be served upon a party who appears to have possession or control of the items sought. If, after reasonable efforts, the party serving the warrant is unable to locate the person, the special master shall seal and return to the court, for determination by the court, any item that appears to be privileged as provided by law.
(d) (1) As used in this section, a "special master" is an attorney who is a member in good standing of the California State Bar and who has been selected from a list of qualified attorneys that is maintained by the State Bar particularly for the purposes of conducting the searches described in this section. These attorneys shall serve without compensation. A special master shall be considered a public employee, and the governmental entity that caused the search warrant to be issued shall be considered the employer of the special master and the applicable public entity, for purposes of Division 3.6 (commencing with Section 810) of Title 1 of the Government Code, relating to claims and actions against public entities and public employees. In selecting the special master, the court shall make every reasonable effort to ensure that the person selected has no relationship with any of the parties involved in the pending matter. Information obtained by the special master shall be confidential and may not be divulged except in direct response to inquiry by the court.
(2) In any case in which the magistrate determines that, after reasonable efforts have been made to obtain a special master, a special master is not available and would not be available within a reasonable period of time, the magistrate may direct the party seeking the order to conduct the search in the manner described in this section in lieu of the special master.
(e) Any search conducted pursuant to this section by a special master may be conducted in a manner that permits the party serving the warrant or his or her designee to accompany the special master as he or she conducts his or her search. However, that party or his or her designee may not participate in the search nor shall he or she examine any of the items being searched by the special master except upon agreement of the party upon whom the warrant has been served.
(f) As used in this section, "documentary evidence" includes, but is not limited to, writings, documents, blueprints, drawings, photographs, computer printouts, microfilms, X-rays, files, diagrams, ledgers, books, tapes, audio and video recordings, films, and papers of any type or description.
(g) No warrant shall issue for any item or items described in Section 1070 of the Evidence Code.
(h) Notwithstanding any other law, no claim of attorney work product as described in Chapter 4 (commencing with Section 2018.010) of Title 4 of Part 4 of the Code of Civil Procedure shall be sustained where there is probable cause to believe that the lawyer is engaging or has engaged in criminal activity related to the documentary evidence for which a warrant is requested unless it is established at the hearing with respect to the documentary evidence seized under the warrant that the services of the lawyer were not sought or obtained to enable or aid anyone to commit or plan to commit a crime or a fraud.

(i) Nothing in this section is intended to limit an attorney's ability to request an in-camera hearing pursuant to the holding of the Supreme Court of California in People v. Superior Court (Laff) (2001) 25 Cal.4th 703.

(j) In addition to any other circumstance permitting a magistrate to issue a warrant for a person or property in another county, when the property or things to be seized consist of any item or constitute evidence that tends to show a violation of Section 530.5, the magistrate may issue a warrant to search a person or property located in another county if the person whose identifying information was taken or used resides in the same county as the issuing court.

(k) This section shall not be construed to create a cause of action against any foreign or California corporation, its officers, employees, agents, or other specified persons for providing location information.

(Amended by Stats. 2017, Ch. 342, Sec. 1. (AB 539) Effective January 1, 2018. Note: This section was amended on November 8, 2016, by initiative Prop. 63.)
1524.1.
(a) The primary purpose of the testing and disclosure provided in this section is to benefit the victim of a crime by informing the victim whether the defendant is infected with the HIV virus. It is also the intent of the Legislature in enacting this section to protect the health of both victims of crime and those accused of committing a crime. Nothing in this section shall be construed to authorize mandatory testing or disclosure of test results for the purpose of a charging decision by a prosecutor, nor, except as specified in subdivisions (g) and (i), shall this section be construed to authorize breach of the confidentiality provisions contained in Chapter 7 (commencing with Section 120975) of Part 4 of Division 105 of the Health and Safety Code.
(b) (1) Notwithstanding the provisions of Chapter 7 (commencing with Section 120975) of Part 4 of Division 105 of the Health and Safety Code, when a defendant has been charged by complaint, information, or indictment with a crime, or a minor is the subject of a petition filed in juvenile court alleging the commission of a crime, the court, at the request of the victim, may issue a search warrant for the purpose of testing the accused's blood or oral mucosal transudate saliva with any HIV test, as defined in Section 120775 of the Health and Safety Code only under the following circumstances: when the court finds, upon the conclusion of the hearing described in paragraph (3), or in those cases in which a preliminary hearing is not required to be held, that there is probable cause to believe that the accused committed the offense, and that there is probable cause to believe that blood, semen, or any other bodily fluid identified by the State Department of Health Services in appropriate regulations as capable of transmitting the human immunodeficiency virus has been transferred from the accused to the victim.
(2) Notwithstanding Chapter 7 (commencing with Section 120975) of Part 4 of Division 105 of the Health and Safety Code, when a defendant has been charged by complaint, information, or indictment with a crime under Section 220, 261, 261.5, 262, 264.1, 266c, 269, 286, 287, 288, 288.5, 289, or 289.5, or former Section 288a, or with an attempt to commit any of the offenses, and is the subject of a police report alleging the commission of a separate, uncharged offense that could be charged under Section 220, 261, 261.5, 262, 264.1, 266c, 269, 286, 287, 288, 288.5, 289, or 289.5, or former Section 288a, or of an attempt to commit any of the offenses, or a minor is the subject of a petition filed in juvenile court alleging the commission of a crime under Section 220, 261, 261.5, 262, 264.1, 266c, 269, 286, 287, 288, 288.5, 289, or 289.5, or former Section 288a, or of an attempt to commit any of the offenses, and is the subject of a police report alleging the commission of a separate, uncharged offense that could be charged under Section 220, 261, 261.5, 262, 264.1, 266c, 269, 286, 287, 288, 288.5, 289, or 289.5, or former Section 288a, or of an attempt to commit any of the offenses, the court, at the request of the victim of the uncharged offense, may issue a search warrant for the purpose of testing the accused's blood or oral mucosal transudate saliva with any HIV test, as defined in Section 120775 of the Health and Safety Code only under the following circumstances: when the court finds that there is probable cause to believe that the accused committed the uncharged offense, and that there is probable cause to believe that blood, semen, or any other bodily fluid identified by the State Department of Health Services in appropriate regulations as capable of transmitting the human immunodeficiency virus has been transferred from the accused to the victim. As used in this paragraph, "Section 289.5" refers to the statute enacted by Chapter 293 of the Statutes of 1991, penetration by an unknown object.
(3) (A) Prior to the issuance of a search warrant pursuant to paragraph (1), the court, where applicable and at the conclusion of the preliminary examination if the defendant is ordered to answer pursuant to Section 872, shall conduct a hearing at which both the victim and the defendant have the right to be present. During the hearing, only affidavits, counter affidavits, and medical reports regarding the facts that support or rebut the issuance of a search warrant under paragraph (1) shall be admissible.
(B) Prior to the issuance of a search warrant pursuant to paragraph (2), the court, where applicable, shall conduct a hearing at which both the victim and the defendant are present. During the hearing, only affidavits, counter affidavits, and medical reports regarding the facts that support or rebut the issuance of a search warrant under paragraph (2) shall be admissible.
(4) A request for a probable cause hearing made by a victim under paragraph (2) shall be made before sentencing in the superior court, or before disposition on a petition in a juvenile court, of the criminal charge or charges filed against the defendant.
(c) (1) In all cases in which the person has been charged by complaint, information, or indictment with a crime, or is the subject of a petition filed in a juvenile court alleging the commission of a crime, the prosecutor shall advise the victim of his or her right to make this request. To assist the victim of the crime to determine whether he or she should make this request, the prosecutor shall refer the victim to the local health officer for prerequest counseling to help that person understand the extent to which the particular circumstances of the crime may or may not have put the victim at risk of transmission of HIV from the accused, to ensure that the victim understands both the benefits and limitations of the current tests for HIV, to help the victim decide whether he or she wants to request that the accused be tested, and to help the victim decide whether he or she wants to be tested.
(2) The Department of Justice, in cooperation with the California District Attorneys Association, shall prepare a form to be used in providing victims with the notice required by paragraph (1).
(d) If the victim decides to request HIV testing of the accused, the victim shall request the issuance of a search warrant, as described in subdivision (b).
Neither the failure of a prosecutor to refer or advise the victim as provided in this subdivision, nor the failure or refusal by the victim to seek or obtain counseling, shall be considered by the court in ruling on the victim's request.
(e) The local health officer shall make provision for administering all HIV tests ordered pursuant to subdivision (b).
(f) Any blood or oral mucosal transudate saliva tested pursuant to subdivision (b) shall be subjected to appropriate confirmatory tests to ensure accuracy of the first test results, and under no circumstances shall test results be transmitted to the victim or the accused unless any initially reactive test result has been confirmed by appropriate confirmatory tests for positive reactors.
(g) The local health officer shall have the responsibility for disclosing test results to the victim who requested the test and to the accused who was tested. However, no positive test results shall be disclosed to the victim or to the accused without also providing or offering professional counseling appropriate to the circumstances.
(h) The local health officer and victim shall comply with all laws and policies relating to medical confidentiality subject to the disclosure authorized by subdivisions (g) and (i). Any individual who files a false report of sexual assault in order to obtain test result

information pursuant to this section shall, in addition to any other liability under law, be guilty of a misdemeanor punishable as provided in subdivision (c) of Section 120980 of the Health and Safety Code. Any individual as described in the preceding sentence who discloses test result information obtained pursuant to this section shall also be guilty of an additional misdemeanor punishable as provided for in subdivision (c) of Section 120980 of the Health and Safety Code for each separate disclosure of that information.
(i) Any victim who receives information from the health officer pursuant to subdivision (g) may disclose the test results as the victim deems necessary to protect his or her health and safety or the health and safety of his or her family or sexual partner.
(j) Any person transmitting test results or disclosing information pursuant to this section shall be immune from civil liability for any actions taken in compliance with this section.
(k) The results of any blood or oral mucosal transudate saliva tested pursuant to subdivision (b) shall not be used in any criminal proceeding as evidence of either guilt or innocence.
(Amended by Stats. 2018, Ch. 423, Sec. 100. (SB 1494) Effective January 1, 2019.)
1524.2.
(a) As used in this section, the following terms have the following meanings:
(1) The terms "electronic communication services" and "remote computing services" shall be construed in accordance with the Electronic Communications Privacy Act of 1986 in Chapter 121 (commencing with Section 2701) of Part I of Title 18 of the United States Code. This section does not apply to corporations that do not provide those services to the general public.
(2) An "adverse result" occurs when notification of the existence of a search warrant results in:
(A) Danger to the life or physical safety of an individual.
(B) A flight from prosecution.
(C) The destruction of or tampering with evidence.
(D) The intimidation of potential witnesses.
(E) Serious jeopardy to an investigation or undue delay of a trial.
(3) "Applicant" refers to the peace officer to whom a search warrant is issued pursuant to subdivision (a) of Section 1528.
(4) "California corporation" refers to any corporation or other entity that is subject to Section 102 of the Corporations Code, excluding foreign corporations.
(5) "Foreign corporation" refers to any corporation that is qualified to do business in this state pursuant to Section 2105 of the Corporations Code.
(6) "Properly served" means that a search warrant has been delivered by hand, or in a manner reasonably allowing for proof of delivery if delivered by United States mail, overnight delivery service, or facsimile to a person or entity listed in Section 2110 of the Corporations Code, or any other means specified by the recipient of the search warrant, including email or submission via an Internet Web portal that the recipient has designated for the purpose of service of process.
(b) The following provisions apply to any search warrant issued pursuant to this chapter allowing a search for records that are in the actual or constructive possession of a foreign corporation that provides electronic communication services or remote computing services to the general public, where those records would reveal the identity of the customers using those services, data stored by, or on behalf of, the customer, the customer's usage of those services, the recipient or destination of communications sent to or from those customers, or the content of those communications.
(1) When properly served with a search warrant issued by the California court, a foreign corporation subject to this section shall provide to the applicant, all records sought pursuant to that warrant within five business days of receipt, including those records maintained or located outside this state.
(2) If the applicant makes a showing and the magistrate finds that failure to produce records within less than five business days would cause an adverse result, the warrant may require production of records within less than five business days. A court may reasonably extend the time required for production of the records upon finding that the foreign corporation has shown good cause for that extension and that an extension of time would not cause an adverse result.
(3) A foreign corporation seeking to quash the warrant must seek relief from the court that issued the warrant within the time required for production of records pursuant to this section. The issuing court shall hear and decide that motion no later than five court days after the motion is filed.
(4) The foreign corporation shall verify the authenticity of records that it produces by providing an affidavit that complies with the requirements set forth in Section 1561 of the Evidence Code. Those records shall be admissible in evidence as set forth in Section 1562 of the Evidence Code.
(c) A California corporation that provides electronic communication services or remote computing services to the general public, when served with a warrant issued by another state to produce records that would reveal the identity of the customers using those services, data stored by, or on behalf of, the customer, the customer's usage of those services, the recipient or destination of communications sent to or from those customers, or the content of those communications, shall produce those records as if that warrant had been issued by a California court.
(d) A cause of action shall not lie against any foreign or California corporation subject to this section, its officers, employees, agents, or other specified persons for providing records, information, facilities, or assistance in accordance with the terms of a warrant issued pursuant to this chapter.
(Amended by Stats. 2016, Ch. 86, Sec. 231. (SB 1171) Effective January 1, 2017.)
1524.3.
(a) A provider of electronic communication service or remote computing service, as used in Chapter 121 (commencing with Section 2701) of Title 18 of the United States Code, shall disclose to a governmental prosecuting or investigating agency the name, address, local and long distance telephone toll billing records, telephone number or other subscriber number or identity, and length of service of a subscriber to or customer of that service, the types of services the subscriber or customer utilized, and the contents of communication originated by or addressed to the service provider when the governmental entity is granted a search warrant pursuant to paragraph (7) of subdivision (a) of Section 1524.
(b) The search warrant shall be limited to only that information necessary to achieve the objective of the warrant, including by specifying the target individuals or accounts, the applications or services, the types of information, and the time periods covered, as appropriate.
(c) Information obtained through the execution of a search warrant pursuant to this section that is unrelated to the objective of the warrant shall be sealed and not be subject to further review without an order from the court.
(d) (1) A governmental entity receiving subscriber records or information under this section shall provide notice to a subscriber or customer upon receipt of the requested records. The notification may be delayed by the court, in increments of 90 days, upon a showing that there is reason to believe that notification of the existence of the search warrant may have an adverse result.
(2) An "adverse result" for purposes of paragraph (1) means any of the following:
(A) Endangering the life or physical safety of an individual.
(B) Flight from prosecution.
(C) Tampering or destruction of evidence.
(D) Intimidation of a potential witness.
(E) Otherwise seriously jeopardizing an investigation or unduly delaying a trial.
(e) Upon the expiration of the period of delay for the notification, the governmental entity shall, by regular mail or email, provide a copy of the process or request and a notice, to the subscriber or customer. The notice shall accomplish all of the following:

(1) State the nature of the law enforcement inquiry with reasonable specificity.
(2) Inform the subscriber or customer that information maintained for the subscriber or customer by the service provider named in the process or request was supplied to or requested by the governmental entity, and the date upon which the information was supplied, and the request was made.
(3) Inform the subscriber or customer that notification to the subscriber or customer was delayed, and which court issued the order pursuant to which the notification was delayed.
(4) Provide a copy of the written inventory of the property that was taken that was provided to the court pursuant to Section 1537.
(f) A court issuing a search warrant pursuant to paragraph (7) of subdivision (a) of Section 1524, on a motion made promptly by the service provider, may quash or modify the warrant if the information or records requested are unusually voluminous in nature or compliance with the warrant otherwise would cause an undue burden on the provider.
(g) A provider of wire or electronic communication services or a remote computing service, upon the request of a peace officer, shall take all necessary steps to preserve records and other evidence in its possession pending the issuance of a search warrant or a request in writing and an affidavit declaring an intent to file a warrant to the provider. Records shall be retained for a period of 90 days, which shall be extended for an additional 90-day period upon a renewed request by the peace officer.
(h) No cause of action shall be brought against any provider, its officers, employees, or agents for providing information, facilities, or assistance in good faith compliance with a search warrant.
(Amended by Stats. 2015, Ch. 643, Sec. 2. (AB 1310) Effective January 1, 2016.)
1524.4.
(a) This section applies to a service provider that is subject to the Electronic Communications Privacy Act (Chapter 3.6 (commencing with Section 1546)) and that operates in California. This section does not apply to a service provider that does not offer services to the general public.
(b) (1) Every service provider described in subdivision (a) shall maintain a law enforcement contact process that meets the criteria set forth in paragraph (2).
(2) Every service provider described in subdivision (a) shall ensure, at a minimum, that its law enforcement contact process meets all of the following criteria:
(A) Provides a specific contact mechanism for law enforcement personnel.
(B) Provides continual availability of the law enforcement contact process.
(C) Provides a method to provide status updates to a requesting law enforcement agency on a request for assistance.
(3) Every service provider described in subdivision (a) shall, by July 1, 2017, file a statement with the Attorney General describing the law enforcement contact process maintained pursuant to paragraph (1). If a service provider makes a material change to its law enforcement contact process, the service provider shall, as soon as practicable, file a statement with the Attorney General describing its new law enforcement contact process.
(c) The Attorney General shall consolidate the statements received pursuant to this section into one discrete record and regularly make that record available to local law enforcement agencies.
(d) The exclusive remedy for a violation of this section shall be an action brought by the Attorney General for injunctive relief. Nothing in this section shall limit remedies available for a violation of any other state or federal law.
(e) A statement filed or distributed pursuant to this section is confidential and shall not be disclosed pursuant to any state law, including, but not limited to, the California Public Records Act (Chapter 3.5 (commencing with Section 6250) of Division 7 of Title 1 of the Government Code).
(Added by Stats. 2016, Ch. 514, Sec. 2. (AB 1993) Effective January 1, 2017.)
1525.
A search warrant cannot be issued but upon probable cause, supported by affidavit, naming or describing the person to be searched or searched for, and particularly describing the property, thing, or things and the place to be searched.
The application shall specify when applicable, that the place to be searched is in the possession or under the control of an attorney, physician, psychotherapist or clergyman.
(Amended by Stats. 1996, Ch. 1078, Sec. 3. Effective January 1, 1997.)
1526.
(a) Before issuing the search warrant, the magistrate may examine on oath the person seeking the warrant and any witnesses the person may produce, and shall take his or her affidavit or their affidavits in writing, and cause the affidavit or affidavits to be subscribed by the party or parties making them. If the affiant transmits the proposed search warrant and all affidavits and supporting documents to the magistrate using facsimile transmission equipment, email, or computer server, the conditions in subdivision (c) apply.
(b) In lieu of the written affidavit required in subdivision (a), the magistrate may take an oral statement under oath if the oath is made under penalty of perjury and recorded and transcribed. The transcribed statement shall be deemed to be an affidavit for the purposes of this chapter. The recording of the sworn oral statement and the transcribed statement shall be certified by the magistrate receiving it and shall be filed with the clerk of the court. In the alternative, the sworn oral statement shall be recorded by a certified court reporter and the transcript of the statement shall be certified by the reporter, after which the magistrate receiving it shall certify the transcript which shall be filed with the clerk of the court.
(c) (1) The affiant shall sign under penalty of perjury his or her affidavit in support of probable cause for issuance of a search warrant. The affiant's signature may be in the form of a digital signature or electronic signature if email or computer server is used for transmission to the magistrate.
(2) The magistrate shall verify that all the pages sent have been received, that all the pages are legible, and that the declarant's signature, digital signature, or electronic signature is genuine.
(3) If the magistrate decides to issue the search warrant, he or she shall do both of the following:
(A) Sign the warrant. The magistrate's signature may be in the form of a digital signature or electronic signature if email or computer server is used for transmission by the magistrate.
(B) Note on the warrant the date and time of the issuance of the warrant.
(4) The magistrate shall transmit via facsimile transmission equipment, email, or computer server the signed search warrant to the affiant. The search warrant signed by the magistrate and received by the affiant shall be deemed to be the original warrant. The original warrant and any affidavits or attachments in support thereof shall be returned as provided in Section 1534.
(Amended by Stats. 2018, Ch. 176, Sec. 2. (AB 2710) Effective January 1, 2019.)
1527.
The affidavit or affidavits must set forth the facts tending to establish the grounds of the application, or probable cause for believing that they exist.
(Amended by Stats. 1957, Ch. 1883.)
1528.
(a) If the magistrate is thereupon satisfied of the existence of the grounds of the application, or that there is probable cause to believe their existence, he or she must issue a search warrant, signed by him or her with his or her name of office, to a peace officer in his or her county, commanding him or her forthwith to search the person or place named for the property or things or person or persons specified, and to retain the property or things in his or her custody subject to order of the court as provided by Section 1536.

(b) The magistrate may orally authorize a peace officer to sign the magistrate's name on a duplicate original warrant. A duplicate original warrant shall be deemed to be a search warrant for the purposes of this chapter, and it shall be returned to the magistrate as provided for in Section 1537. The magistrate shall enter on the face of the original warrant the exact time of the issuance of the warrant and shall sign and file the original warrant and the duplicate original warrant with the clerk of the court as provided for in Section 1541.

(Amended by Stats. 1996, Ch. 1078, Sec. 4. Effective January 1, 1997.)

1529.

The warrant shall be in substantially the following form:

County of _____.

The people of the State of California to any peace officer in the County of _____: Proof, by affidavit, having been this day made before me by (naming every person whose affidavit has been taken), that (stating the grounds of the application, according to Section 1524, or, if the affidavit be not positive, that there is probable cause for believing that _____ stating the ground of the application in the same manner), you are therefore commanded, in the daytime (or at any time of the day or night, as the case may be, according to Section 1533), to make search on the person of C. D. (or in the house situated _____, describing it, or any other place to be searched, with reasonable particularity, as the case may be) for the following property, thing, things, or person: (describing the property, thing, things, or person with reasonable particularity); and, in the case of a thing or things or personal property, if you find the same or any part thereof, to bring the thing or things or personal property forthwith before me (or this court) at (stating the place).

Given under my hand, and dated this _____ day of _____, A.D. (year).

E. F., Judge of the (applicable) Court.

(Amended by Stats. 2005, Ch. 181, Sec. 1. Effective January 1, 2006.)

1530.

A search warrant may in all cases be served by any of the officers mentioned in its directions, but by no other person, except in aid of the officer on his requiring it, he being present and acting in its execution.

(Enacted 1872.)

1531.

The officer may break open any outer or inner door or window of a house, or any part of a house, or anything therein, to execute the warrant, if, after notice of his authority and purpose, he is refused admittance.

(Enacted 1872.)

1532.

He may break open any outer or inner door or window of a house, for the purpose of liberating a person who, having entered to aid him in the execution of the warrant, is detained therein, or when necessary for his own liberation.

(Enacted 1872.)

1533.

Upon a showing of good cause, the magistrate may, in his or her discretion, insert a direction in a search warrant that it may be served at any time of the day or night. In the absence of such a direction, the warrant shall be served only between the hours of 7 a.m. and 10 p.m.

When establishing "good cause" under this section, the magistrate shall consider the safety of the peace officers serving the warrant and the safety of the public as a valid basis for nighttime endorsements.

(Amended by Stats. 1986, Ch. 257, Sec. 1.)

1534.

(a) A search warrant shall be executed and returned within 10 days after date of issuance. A warrant executed within the 10-day period shall be deemed to have been timely executed and no further showing of timeliness need be made. After the expiration of 10 days, the warrant, unless executed, is void. The documents and records of the court relating to the warrant need not be open to the public until the execution and return of the warrant or the expiration of the 10-day period after issuance. Thereafter, if the warrant has been executed, the documents and records shall be open to the public as a judicial record.

(b) (1) A tracking device search warrant issued pursuant to paragraph (12) of subdivision (a) of Section 1524 shall identify the person or property to be tracked and shall specify a reasonable length of time, not to exceed 30 days from the date the warrant is issued, that the device may be used. The court may, for good cause, grant one or more extensions for the time that the device may be used, with each extension lasting for a reasonable length of time, not to exceed 30 days. The search warrant shall command the officer to execute the warrant by installing a tracking device or serving a warrant on a third-party possessor of the tracking data. The officer shall perform any installation authorized by the warrant during the daytime unless the magistrate, for good cause, expressly authorizes installation at another time. Execution of the warrant shall be completed no later than 10 days immediately after the date of issuance. A warrant executed within this 10-day period shall be deemed to have been timely executed and no further showing of timeliness need be made. After the expiration of 10 days, the warrant shall be void, unless it has been executed.

(2) An officer executing a tracking device search warrant shall not be required to knock and announce his or her presence before executing the warrant.

(3) No later than 10 calendar days after the use of the tracking device has ended, the officer executing the warrant shall file a return to the warrant.

(4) (A) No later than 10 calendar days after the use of the tracking device has ended, the officer who executed the tracking device warrant shall notify the person who was tracked or whose property was tracked pursuant to subdivision (a) of Section 1546.2.

(B) Notice under this paragraph may be delayed pursuant to subdivision (b) of Section 1546.2.

(5) An officer installing a device authorized by a tracking device search warrant may install and use the device only within California.

(6) As used in this section, "tracking device" means any electronic or mechanical device that permits the tracking of the movement of a person or object.

(7) As used in this section, "daytime" means the hours between 6 a.m. and 10 p.m. according to local time.

(c) If a duplicate original search warrant has been executed, the peace officer who executed the warrant shall enter the exact time of its execution on its face.

(d) A search warrant may be made returnable before the issuing magistrate or his or her court.

(Amended by Stats. 2016, Ch. 541, Sec. 1. (SB 1121) Effective January 1, 2017.)

1535.

When the officer takes property under the warrant, he must give a receipt for the property taken (specifying it in detail) to the person from whom it was taken by him, or in whose possession it was found; or, in the absence of any person, he must leave it in the place where he found the property.

(Enacted 1872.)

1536.

All property or things taken on a warrant must be retained by the officer in his custody, subject to the order of the court to which he is required to return the proceedings before him, or of any other court in which the offense in respect to which the property or things taken is triable.

(Amended by Stats. 1957, Ch. 1885.)

1536.5.

(a) If a government agency seizes business records from an entity pursuant to a search warrant, the entity from which the records were seized may file a demand on that government agency to produce copies of the business records that have been seized. The demand for production of copies of business records shall be supported by a declaration, made under penalty of perjury, that denial of access to the records in question will either unduly interfere with the entity's ability to conduct its regular course of business or obstruct the entity from fulfilling an affirmative obligation that it has under the law. Unless the government agency objects pursuant to subdivision (d), this declaration shall suffice if it makes a prima facie case that specific business activities or specific legal obligations faced by the entity would be impaired or impeded by the ongoing loss of records.

(b) (1) Except as provided in paragraph (2), when a government agency seizes business records from an entity and is subsequently served with a demand for copies of those business records pursuant to subdivision (a), the government agency in possession of those records shall make copies of those records available to the entity within 10 court days of the service of the demand to produce copies of the records.

(2) In the alternative, the agency in possession of the original records, may in its discretion, make the original records reasonably available to the entity within 10 court days following the service of the demand to produce records, and allow the entity reasonable time to copy the records.

(3) No agency shall be required to make records available at times other than normal business hours.

(4) If data is recorded in a tangible medium, copies of the data may be provided in that same medium, or any other medium of which the entity may make reasonable use. If the data is stored electronically, electromagnetically, or photo-optically, the entity may obtain either a copy made by the same process in which the data is stored, or in the alternative, by any other tangible medium through which the entity may make reasonable use of the data.

(5) A government agency granting the entity access to the original records for the purpose of making copies of the records, may take reasonable steps to ensure the integrity and chain of custody of the business records.

(6) If the seized records are too voluminous to be reviewed or be copied in the time period required by subdivision (a), the government agency that seized the records may file a written motion with the court for additional time to review the records or make the copies. This motion shall be made within 10 court days of the service of the demand for the records. An extension of time under this paragraph shall not be granted unless the agency establishes that reviewing or producing copies of the records within the 10 court day time period, would create a hardship on the agency. If the court grants the motion, it shall make an order designating a timeframe for the review and the duplication and return of the business records, deferring to the entity the priority of the records to be reviewed, duplicated, and returned first.

(c) If a court finds that a declaration made by an entity as provided in subdivision (a) is adequate to establish the specified prima facie case, a government agency may refuse to produce copies of the business records or to grant access to the original records only under one or both of the following circumstances:

(1) The court determines by the preponderance of the evidence standard that denial of access to the business records or copies of the business records will not unduly interfere with the entity's ability to conduct its regular course of business or obstruct the entity from fulfilling an affirmative obligation that it has under the law.

(2) The court determines by the preponderance of the evidence standard that possession of the business records by the entity will pose a significant risk of ongoing criminal activity, or that the business records are contraband, evidence of criminal conduct by the entity from which the records were seized, or depict a person under the age of 18 years personally engaging in or simulating sexual conduct, as defined in subdivision (d) of Section 311.4.

(d) A government agency that desires not to produce copies of, or grant access to, seized business records shall file a motion with the court requesting an order denying the entity copies of and access to the records. A motion under this paragraph shall be in writing, and filed and served upon the entity prior to the expiration of 10 court days following the service of the demand to produce records specified in subdivision (a), within any extension of that time period granted under paragraph (6) of subdivision (b), or as soon as reasonably possible after discovery of the risk of harm.

(e) A hearing on a motion under subdivision (d) shall be held within two court days of the filing of the motion, except upon agreement of the parties.

(f) (1) Upon filing a motion under subdivision (d) opposing a demand for copies of records, the government agency may file a request in writing, served upon the demanding entity, that any showings of why the material should not be copied and released occur in an ex parte, in camera hearing. If the government agency alleges in its request for an in camera hearing that the demanding entity is, or is likely to become, a target of the investigation resulting in the seizure of records, the court shall hold this hearing outside of the presence of the demanding entity, and any representatives or counsel of the demanding entity. If the government agency does not allege in its request for an in camera hearing that the demanding entity is, or is likely to become, a target of the investigation resulting in the seizure of records, the court shall hold the hearing in camera only upon a particular factual showing by the government agency in its pleadings that a hearing in open court would impede or interrupt an ongoing criminal investigation.

(2) At the in camera hearing, any evidence that the government agency may offer that the release of the material would pose a significant risk of ongoing criminal activity, impede or interrupt an ongoing criminal investigation, or both, shall be offered under oath. A reporter shall be present at the in camera hearing to transcribe the entirety of the proceedings.

(3) Any transcription of the proceedings at the in camera hearing, as well as any physical evidence presented at the hearing, shall be ordered sealed by the court, and only a court may have access to its contents, unless a court determines that the failure to disclose the contents of the hearing would deprive the defendant or the people of a fair trial.

(4) Following the conclusion of the in camera hearing, the court shall make its ruling in open court, after notice to the demanding entity.

(g) The reasonable and necessary costs of producing copies of business records under this section shall be borne by the entity requesting copies of the records. Either party may request the court to resolve any dispute regarding these costs.

(h) Any motion under this section shall be filed in the court that issued the search warrant.

(i) For purposes of this section, the following terms are defined as follows:

(1) "Seize" means obtaining actual possession of any property alleged by the entity to contain business records.

(2) "Business" means an entity, sole proprietorship, partnership, or corporation operating legally in the State of California, that sells, leases, distributes, creates, or otherwise offers products or services to customers.

(3) "Business records" means computer data, data compilations, accounts, books, reports, contracts, correspondence, inventories, lists, personnel files, payrolls, vendor and client lists, documents, or papers of the person or business normally used in the regular course of business, or any other material item of business recordkeeping that may become technologically feasible in the future.

(Added by Stats. 2004, Ch. 372, Sec. 1. Effective January 1, 2005.)

1537.

The officer must forthwith return the warrant to the magistrate, and deliver to him a written inventory of the property taken, made publicly or in the presence of the person from whose possession it was taken, and of the applicant for the warrant, if they are present, verified by the affidavit of the officer at the foot of the inventory, and taken before the magistrate at the time, to the following effect: "I, R. S., the officer by whom this warrant was executed, do swear that the above inventory contains a true and detailed account of all the property taken by me on the warrant."

(Enacted 1872.)

1538.

The magistrate must thereupon, if required, deliver a copy of the inventory to the person from whose possession the property was taken, and to the applicant for the warrant.

(Enacted 1872.)

1538.5.

(a) (1) A defendant may move for the return of property or to suppress as evidence any tangible or intangible thing obtained as a result of a search or seizure on either of the following grounds:

(A) The search or seizure without a warrant was unreasonable.

(B) The search or seizure with a warrant was unreasonable because any of the following apply:

(i) The warrant is insufficient on its face.

(ii) The property or evidence obtained is not that described in the warrant.

(iii) There was not probable cause for the issuance of the warrant.

(iv) The method of execution of the warrant violated federal or state constitutional standards.

(v) There was any other violation of federal or state constitutional standards.

(2) A motion pursuant to paragraph (1) shall be made in writing and accompanied by a memorandum of points and authorities and proof of service. The memorandum shall list the specific items of property or evidence sought to be returned or suppressed and shall set forth the factual basis and the legal authorities that demonstrate why the motion should be granted.

(b) When consistent with the procedures set forth in this section and subject to the provisions of Sections 170 to 170.6, inclusive, of the Code of Civil Procedure, the motion should first be heard by the magistrate who issued the search warrant if there is a warrant.

(c) (1) Whenever a search or seizure motion is made in the superior court as provided in this section, the judge or magistrate shall receive evidence on any issue of fact necessary to determine the motion.

(2) While a witness is under examination during a hearing pursuant to a search or seizure motion, the judge or magistrate shall, upon motion of either party, do any of the following:

(A) Exclude all potential and actual witnesses who have not been examined.

(B) Order the witnesses not to converse with each other until they are all examined.

(C) Order, where feasible, that the witnesses be kept separated from each other until they are all examined.

(D) Hold a hearing, on the record, to determine if the person sought to be excluded is, in fact, a person excludable under this section.

(3) Either party may challenge the exclusion of any person under paragraph (2).

(4) Paragraph (2) does not apply to the investigating officer or the investigator for the defendant, nor does it apply to officers having custody of persons brought before the court.

(d) If a search or seizure motion is granted pursuant to the proceedings authorized by this section, the property or evidence shall not be admissible against the movant at any trial or other hearing unless further proceedings authorized by this section, Section 871.5, 1238, or 1466 are utilized by the people.

(e) If a search or seizure motion is granted at a trial, the property shall be returned upon order of the court unless it is otherwise subject to lawful detention. If the motion is granted at a special hearing, the property shall be returned upon order of the court only if, after the conclusion of any further proceedings authorized by this section, Section 1238 or 1466, the property is not subject to lawful detention or if the time for initiating the proceedings has expired, whichever occurs last. If the motion is granted at a preliminary hearing, the property shall be returned upon order of the court after 10 days unless the property is otherwise subject to lawful detention or unless, within that time, further proceedings authorized by this section, Section 871.5 or 1238 are utilized; if they are utilized, the property shall be returned only if, after the conclusion of the proceedings, the property is no longer subject to lawful detention.

(f) (1) If the property or evidence relates to a felony offense initiated by a complaint, the motion shall be made only upon filing of an information, except that the defendant may make the motion at the preliminary hearing, but the motion shall be restricted to evidence sought to be introduced by the people at the preliminary hearing.

(2) The motion may be made at the preliminary examination only if, at least five court days before the date set for the preliminary examination, the defendant has filed and personally served on the people a written motion accompanied by a memorandum of points and authorities as required by paragraph (2) of subdivision (a). At the preliminary examination, the magistrate may grant the defendant a continuance for the purpose of filing the motion and serving the motion upon the people, at least five court days before resumption of the examination, upon a showing that the defendant or his or her attorney of record was not aware of the evidence or was not aware of the grounds for suppression before the preliminary examination.

(3) Any written response by the people to the motion described in paragraph (2) shall be filed with the court and personally served on the defendant or his or her attorney of record at least two court days prior to the hearing at which the motion is to be made.

(g) If the property or evidence relates to a misdemeanor complaint, the motion shall be made before trial and heard prior to trial at a special hearing relating to the validity of the search or seizure. If the property or evidence relates to a misdemeanor filed together with a felony, the procedure provided for a felony in this section and Sections 1238 and 1539 shall be applicable.

(h) If, prior to the trial of a felony or misdemeanor, opportunity for this motion did not exist or the defendant was not aware of the grounds for the motion, the defendant shall have the right to make this motion during the course of trial.

(i) If the property or evidence obtained relates to a felony offense initiated by complaint and the defendant was held to answer at the preliminary hearing, or if the property or evidence relates to a felony offense initiated by indictment, the defendant shall have the right to renew or make the motion at a special hearing relating to the validity of the search or seizure which shall be heard prior to trial and at least 10 court days after notice to the people, unless the people are willing to waive a portion of this time. Any written response by the people to the motion shall be filed with the court and personally served on the defendant or his or her attorney of record at least two court days prior to the hearing, unless the defendant is willing to waive a portion of this time. If the offense was initiated by indictment or if the offense was initiated by complaint and no motion was made at the preliminary hearing, the defendant shall have the right to fully litigate the validity of a search or seizure on the basis of the evidence presented at a special hearing. If the motion was made at the preliminary hearing, unless otherwise agreed to by all parties, evidence presented at the special hearing shall be limited to the transcript of the preliminary hearing and to evidence that could not reasonably have been presented at the preliminary hearing, except that the people may recall witnesses who testified at the preliminary hearing. If the people object to the presentation of evidence at the special hearing on the grounds that the evidence could reasonably have been presented at the preliminary hearing, the defendant shall be entitled to an in camera hearing to determine that issue. The court shall base its ruling on all evidence presented at the special hearing and on the transcript of the preliminary hearing, and the findings of the magistrate shall be binding on the court as to evidence or property not affected by evidence presented at the special hearing. After the special hearing is held, any review thereafter desired by the defendant prior to trial shall be by means of an

extraordinary writ of mandate or prohibition filed within 30 days after the denial of his or her motion at the special hearing.

(j) If the property or evidence relates to a felony offense initiated by complaint and the defendant's motion for the return of the property or suppression of the evidence at the preliminary hearing is granted, and if the defendant is not held to answer at the preliminary hearing, the people may file a new complaint or seek an indictment after the preliminary hearing, and the ruling at the prior hearing shall not be binding in any subsequent proceeding, except as limited by subdivision (p). In the alternative, the people may move to reinstate the complaint, or those parts of the complaint for which the defendant was not held to answer, pursuant to Section 871.5. If the property or evidence relates to a felony offense initiated by complaint and the defendant's motion for the return or suppression of the property or evidence at the preliminary hearing is granted, and if the defendant is held to answer at the preliminary hearing, the ruling at the preliminary hearing shall be binding upon the people unless, upon notice to the defendant and the court in which the preliminary hearing was held and upon the filing of an information, the people, within 15 days after the preliminary hearing, request a special hearing, in which case the validity of the search or seizure shall be relitigated de novo on the basis of the evidence presented at the special hearing, and the defendant shall be entitled, as a matter of right, to a continuance of the special hearing for a period of time up to 30 days. The people may not request relitigation of the motion at a special hearing if the defendant's motion has been granted twice. If the defendant's motion is granted at a special hearing, the people, if they have additional evidence relating to the motion and not presented at the special hearing, shall have the right to show good cause at the trial why the evidence was not presented at the special hearing and why the prior ruling at the special hearing should not be binding, or the people may seek appellate review as provided in subdivision (o), unless the court, prior to the time the review is sought, has dismissed the case pursuant to Section 1385. If the case has been dismissed pursuant to Section 1385, either on the court's own motion or the motion of the people after the special hearing, the people may file a new complaint or seek an indictment after the special hearing, and the ruling at the special hearing shall not be binding in any subsequent proceeding, except as limited by subdivision (p). If the property or evidence seized relates solely to a misdemeanor complaint, and the defendant made a motion for the return of property or the suppression of evidence in the superior court prior to trial, both the people and defendant shall have the right to appeal any decision of that court relating to that motion to the appellate division, in accordance with the California Rules of Court provisions governing appeals to the appellate division in criminal cases. If the people prosecute review by appeal or writ to decision, or any review thereof, in a felony or misdemeanor case, it shall be binding upon them.

(k) If the defendant's motion to return property or suppress evidence is granted and the case is dismissed pursuant to Section 1385, or the people appeal in a misdemeanor case pursuant to subdivision (j), the defendant shall be released pursuant to Section 1318 if he or she is in custody and not returned to custody unless the proceedings are resumed in the trial court and he or she is lawfully ordered by the court to be returned to custody.

If the defendant's motion to return property or suppress evidence is granted and the people file a petition for writ of mandate or prohibition pursuant to subdivision (o) or a notice of intention to file a petition, the defendant shall be released pursuant to Section 1318, unless (1) he or she is charged with a capital offense in a case where the proof is evident and the presumption great, or (2) he or she is charged with a noncapital offense defined in Chapter 1 (commencing with Section 187) of Title 8 of Part 1, and the court orders that the defendant be discharged from actual custody upon bail.

(l) If the defendant's motion to return property or suppress evidence is granted, the trial of a criminal case shall be stayed to a specified date pending the termination in the appellate courts of this state of the proceedings provided for in this section, Section 871.5, 1238, or 1466 and, except upon stipulation of the parties, pending the time for the initiation of these proceedings. Upon the termination of these proceedings, the defendant shall be brought to trial as provided by Section 1382, and, subject to the provisions of Section 1382, whenever the people have sought and been denied appellate review pursuant to subdivision (o), the defendant shall be entitled to have the action dismissed if he or she is not brought to trial within 30 days of the date of the order that is the last denial of the petition. Nothing contained in this subdivision shall prohibit a court, at the same time as it rules upon the search and seizure motion, from dismissing a case pursuant to Section 1385 when the dismissal is upon the court's own motion and is based upon an order at the special hearing granting the defendant's motion to return property or suppress evidence. In a misdemeanor case, the defendant shall be entitled to a continuance of up to 30 days if he or she intends to file a motion to return property or suppress evidence and needs this time to prepare for the special hearing on the motion. In case of an appeal by the defendant in a misdemeanor case from the denial of the motion, he or she shall be entitled to bail as a matter of right, and, in the discretion of the trial or appellate court, may be released on his or her own recognizance pursuant to Section 1318. In the case of an appeal by the defendant in a misdemeanor case from the denial of the motion, the trial court may, in its discretion, order or deny a stay of further proceedings pending disposition of the appeal.

(m) The proceedings provided for in this section, and Sections 871.5, 995, 1238, and 1466 shall constitute the sole and exclusive remedies prior to conviction to test the unreasonableness of a search or seizure where the person making the motion for the return of property or the suppression of evidence is a defendant in a criminal case and the property or thing has been offered or will be offered as evidence against him or her. A defendant may seek further review of the validity of a search or seizure on appeal from a conviction in a criminal case notwithstanding the fact that the judgment of conviction is predicated upon a plea of guilty. Review on appeal may be obtained by the defendant provided that at some stage of the proceedings prior to conviction he or she has moved for the return of property or the suppression of the evidence.

(n) This section establishes only the procedure for suppression of evidence and return of property, and does not establish or alter any substantive ground for suppression of evidence or return of property. Nothing contained in this section shall prohibit a person from making a motion, otherwise permitted by law, to return property, brought on the ground that the property obtained is protected by the free speech and press provisions of the United States and California Constitutions. Nothing in this section shall be construed as altering (1) the law of standing to raise the issue of an unreasonable search or seizure; (2) the law relating to the status of the person conducting the search or seizure; (3) the law relating to the burden of proof regarding the search or seizure; (4) the law relating to the reasonableness of a search or seizure regardless of any warrant that may have been utilized; or (5) the procedure and law relating to a motion made pursuant to Section 871.5 or 995, or the procedures that may be initiated after the granting or denial of a motion.

(o) Within 30 days after a defendant's motion is granted at a special hearing in a felony case, the people may file a petition for writ of mandate or prohibition in the court of appeal, seeking appellate review of the ruling regarding the search or seizure motion. If the trial of a criminal case is set for a date that is less than 30 days from the granting of a defendant's motion at a special hearing in a felony case, the people, if they have not filed a petition and wish to preserve their right to file a petition, shall file in the superior court on or before the trial date or within 10 days after the special hearing, whichever occurs last, a notice of intention to file a petition and shall serve a copy of the notice upon the defendant.

(p) If a defendant's motion to return property or suppress evidence in a felony matter has been granted twice, the people may not file a new complaint or seek an indictment in order to relitigate the motion or relitigate the matter de novo at a special hearing as otherwise provided by subdivision (j), unless the people discover additional evidence relating to the motion that was not reasonably discoverable at the time of the second suppression hearing. Relitigation of the motion shall be heard by the same judge who granted the motion at the first hearing if the judge is available.

(q) The amendments to this section enacted in the 1997 portion of the 1997–98 Regular Session of the Legislature shall apply to all criminal proceedings conducted on or after January 1, 1998.

(Amended by Stats. 2007, Ch. 302, Sec. 19. Effective January 1, 2008.)

1539.

(a) If a special hearing is held in a felony case pursuant to Section 1538.5, or if the grounds on which the warrant was issued are controverted and a motion to return property is made (i) by a defendant on grounds not covered by Section 1538.5, (ii) by a defendant whose property has not been offered or will not be offered as evidence against the defendant, or (iii) by a person who is not a defendant in a criminal action at the time the hearing is held, the judge or magistrate shall proceed to take testimony in relation thereto, and the testimony of each witness shall be reduced to writing and authenticated by a shorthand reporter in the manner prescribed in Section 869.

(b) The reporter shall forthwith transcribe the reporter's shorthand notes pursuant to this section if any party to a special hearing in a felony case files a written request for its preparation with the clerk of the court in which the hearing was held. The reporter shall forthwith file in the superior court an original and as many copies thereof as there are defendants (other than a fictitious defendant) or persons aggrieved. The reporter is entitled to compensation in accordance with the provisions of Section 869. In every case in which a transcript is filed as provided in this section, the clerk of the court shall deliver the original of the transcript so filed to the district attorney immediately upon receipt thereof and shall deliver a copy of the transcript to each defendant (other than a fictitious defendant) upon demand without cost to the defendant.

(c) Upon a motion by a defendant pursuant to this chapter, the defendant is entitled to discover any previous application for a search warrant in the case which was refused by a magistrate for lack of probable cause.

(Amended by Stats. 2002, Ch. 71, Sec. 7. Effective January 1, 2003.)

1540.

If it appears that the property taken is not the same as that described in the warrant, or that there is no probable cause for believing the existence of the grounds on which the warrant was issued, the magistrate must cause it to be restored to the person from whom it was taken.

(Enacted 1872.)

1541.

The magistrate must annex the affidavit, or affidavits, the search warrant and return, and the inventory, and if he has not power to inquire into the offense in respect to which the warrant was issued, he must at once file such warrant and return and such affidavit, or affidavits, and inventory with the clerk of the court having power to so inquire.

(Amended by Stats. 1957, Ch. 1881.)

1542.

When a person charged with a felony is supposed by the magistrate before whom he is brought to have on his person a dangerous weapon, or anything which may be used as evidence of the commission of the offense, the magistrate may direct him to be searched in his presence, and the weapon or other thing to be retained, subject to his order, or to the order of the Court in which the defendant may be tried.

(Enacted 1872.)

1542.5.

Notwithstanding any other law, with regards to a search warrant issued upon the grounds specified in paragraph (14) of subdivision (a) of Section 1524, the following shall apply:

(a) The law enforcement officer executing the warrant shall take custody of any firearm or ammunition that is in the restrained person's custody or control or possession or that is owned by the restrained person, which is discovered pursuant to a consensual or other lawful search.

(b) (1) If the location to be searched during the execution of the warrant is jointly occupied by the restrained person and one or more other persons and a law enforcement officer executing the warrant finds a firearm or ammunition in the restrained person's custody or control or possession, but that is owned by a person other than the restrained person, the firearm or ammunition shall not be seized if both of the following conditions are satisfied:

(A) The firearm or ammunition is removed from the restrained person's custody or control or possession and stored in a manner that the restrained person does not have access to or control of the firearm or ammunition.

(B) There is no evidence of unlawful possession of the firearm or ammunition by the owner of the firearm or ammunition.

(2) If the location to be searched during the execution of the warrant is jointly occupied by the restrained person and one or more other persons and a locked gun safe is located that is owned by a person other than the restrained person, the contents of the gun safe shall not be searched except in the owner's presence, and with his or her consent or with a valid search warrant for the gun safe.

(c) This section shall become operative on January 1, 2016.

(Added by Stats. 2014, Ch. 872, Sec. 2. (AB 1014) Effective January 1, 2015. Section operative January 1, 2016, by its own provisions.)

CHAPTER 3.5. Disclosure of Medical Records to Law Enforcement Agencies [1543 - 1545]

(Chapter 3.5 added by Stats. 1980, Ch. 1080, Sec. 1.)

1543.

(a) Records of the identity, diagnosis, prognosis, or treatment of any patient maintained by a health care facility which are not privileged records required to be secured by the special master procedure in Section 1524, or records required by law to be confidential, shall only be disclosed to law enforcement agencies pursuant to this section:

(1) In accordance with the prior written consent of the patient; or

(2) If authorized by an appropriate order of a court of competent jurisdiction in the county where the records are located, granted after application showing good cause therefor. In assessing good cause, the court:

(A) Shall weigh the public interest and the need for disclosure against the injury to the patient, to the physician-patient relationship, and to the treatment services;

(B) Shall determine that there is a reasonable likelihood that the records in question will disclose material information or evidence of substantial value in connection with the investigation or prosecution; or

(3) By a search warrant obtained pursuant to Section 1524.

(b) The prohibitions of this section continue to apply to records concerning any individual who has been a patient, irrespective of whether or when he or she ceases to be a patient.

(c) Except where an extraordinary order under Section 1544 is granted or a search warrant is obtained pursuant to Section 1524, any health care facility whose records are sought under this chapter shall be notified of the application and afforded an opportunity to appear and be heard thereon.

(d) Both disclosure and dissemination of any information from the records shall be limited under the terms of the order to assure that no information will be unnecessarily disclosed and that dissemination will be no wider than necessary.

This chapter shall not apply to investigations of fraud in the provision or receipt of Medi-Cal benefits, investigations of insurance fraud performed by the Department of Insurance or the California Highway Patrol, investigations of workers' compensation insurance fraud performed by the Department of Corrections and conducted by peace officers specified in paragraph (2) of subdivision (d) of Section 830.2, and investigations and research regarding occupational health and safety performed by or under agreement with the Department of Industrial Relations. Access to medical records in these investigations shall be governed by all laws in effect at the time access is sought.

(e) Nothing in this chapter shall prohibit disclosure by a medical facility or medical provider of information contained in medical records where disclosure to specific agencies is mandated by statutes or regulations.

(f) This chapter shall not be construed to authorize disclosure of privileged records to law enforcement agencies by the procedure set forth in this chapter, where the privileged records are required to be secured by the special master procedure set forth in subdivision (c) of Section 1524 or required by law to be confidential.

(Amended by Stats. 2004, Ch. 490, Sec. 2. Effective January 1, 2005.)

1544.

A law enforcement agency applying for disclosure of patient records under Section 1543 may petition the court for an extraordinary order delaying the notice of the application to the health care facility required by subdivision (f) of Section 1543 for a period of 30 days, upon a showing of good cause to believe that notice would seriously impede the investigation.

(Added by Stats. 1980, Ch. 1080, Sec. 1.)

1545.

For the purposes of this chapter:

(a) "Health care facility" means any clinic, health dispensary, or health facility, licensed pursuant to Division 2 (commencing with Section 1200) of the Health and Safety Code, or any mental hospital, drug abuse clinic, or detoxification center.

(b) "Law enforcement agency" means the Attorney General of the State of California, every district attorney, and every agency of the State of California expressly authorized by statute to investigate or prosecute law violators.

(Added by Stats. 1980, Ch. 1080, Sec. 1.)

CHAPTER 3.6. Electronic Communications Privacy Act [1546 - 1546.4]

(Chapter 3.6 added by Stats. 2015, Ch. 651, Sec. 1.)

1546.

For purposes of this chapter, the following definitions apply:

(a) An "adverse result" means any of the following:

(1) Danger to the life or physical safety of an individual.

(2) Flight from prosecution.

(3) Destruction of or tampering with evidence.

(4) Intimidation of potential witnesses.

(5) Serious jeopardy to an investigation or undue delay of a trial.

(b) "Authorized possessor" means the possessor of an electronic device when that person is the owner of the device or has been authorized to possess the device by the owner of the device.

(c) "Electronic communication" means the transfer of signs, signals, writings, images, sounds, data, or intelligence of any nature in whole or in part by a wire, radio, electromagnetic, photoelectric, or photo-optical system.

(d) "Electronic communication information" means any information about an electronic communication or the use of an electronic communication service, including, but not limited to, the contents, sender, recipients, format, or location of the sender or recipients at any point during the communication, the time or date the communication was created, sent, or received, or any information pertaining to any individual or device participating in the communication, including, but not limited to, an IP address. "Electronic communication information" does not include subscriber information as defined in this chapter.

(e) "Electronic communication service" means a service that provides to its subscribers or users the ability to send or receive electronic communications, including any service that acts as an intermediary in the transmission of electronic communications, or stores electronic communication information.

(f) "Electronic device" means a device that stores, generates, or transmits information in electronic form. An electronic device does not include the magnetic strip on a driver's license or an identification card issued by this state or a driver's license or equivalent identification card issued by another state.

(g) "Electronic device information" means any information stored on or generated through the operation of an electronic device, including the current and prior locations of the device.

(h) "Electronic information" means electronic communication information or electronic device information.

(i) "Government entity" means a department or agency of the state or a political subdivision thereof, or an individual acting for or on behalf of the state or a political subdivision thereof.

(j) "Service provider" means a person or entity offering an electronic communication service.

(k) "Specific consent" means consent provided directly to the government entity seeking information, including, but not limited to, when the government entity is the addressee or intended recipient or a member of the intended audience of an electronic communication. Specific consent does not require that the originator of the communication have actual knowledge that an addressee, intended recipient, or member of the specific audience is a government entity.

(l) "Subscriber information" means the name, street address, telephone number, email address, or similar contact information provided by the subscriber to the service provider to establish or maintain an account or communication channel, a subscriber or account number or identifier, the length of service, and the types of services used by a user of or subscriber to a service provider.

(Amended by Stats. 2016, Ch. 541, Sec. 2. (SB 1121) Effective January 1, 2017.)

1546.1.

(a) Except as provided in this section, a government entity shall not do any of the following:

(1) Compel the production of or access to electronic communication information from a service provider.

(2) Compel the production of or access to electronic device information from any person or entity other than the authorized possessor of the device.

(3) Access electronic device information by means of physical interaction or electronic communication with the electronic device. This section does not prohibit the intended recipient of an electronic communication from voluntarily disclosing electronic communication information concerning that communication to a government entity.

(b) A government entity may compel the production of or access to electronic communication information from a service provider, or compel the production of or access to electronic device information from any person or entity other than the authorized possessor of the device only under the following circumstances:

(1) Pursuant to a warrant issued pursuant to Chapter 3 (commencing with Section 1523) and subject to subdivision (d).

(2) Pursuant to a wiretap order issued pursuant to Chapter 1.4 (commencing with Section 629.50) of Title 15 of Part 1.

(3) Pursuant to an order for electronic reader records issued pursuant to Section 1798.90 of the Civil Code.

(4) Pursuant to a subpoena issued pursuant to existing state law, provided that the information is not sought for the purpose of investigating or prosecuting a criminal offense, and compelling the production of or access to the information via the subpoena is not otherwise prohibited by state or federal law. Nothing in this paragraph shall be construed to expand any authority under state law to compel the production of or access to electronic information.

(5) Pursuant to an order for a pen register or trap and trace device, or both, issued pursuant to Chapter 1.5 (commencing with Section 630) of Title 15 of Part 1.

(c) A government entity may access electronic device information by means of physical interaction or electronic communication with the device only as follows:

(1) Pursuant to a warrant issued pursuant to Chapter 3 (commencing with Section 1523) and subject to subdivision (d).

(2) Pursuant to a wiretap order issued pursuant to Chapter 1.4 (commencing with Section 629.50) of Title 15 of Part 1.

(3) Pursuant to a tracking device search warrant issued pursuant to paragraph (12) of subdivision (a) of Section 1524 and subdivision (b) of Section 1534.

(4) With the specific consent of the authorized possessor of the device.

(5) With the specific consent of the owner of the device, only when the device has been reported as lost or stolen.

(6) If the government entity, in good faith, believes that an emergency involving danger of death or serious physical injury to any person requires access to the electronic device information.

(7) If the government entity, in good faith, believes the device to be lost, stolen, or abandoned, provided that the government entity shall only access electronic device information in order to attempt to identify, verify, or contact the owner or authorized possessor of the device.

(8) Except where prohibited by state or federal law, if the device is seized from an inmate's possession or found in an area of a correctional facility or a secure area of a local detention facility where inmates have access, the device is not in the possession of an individual, and the device is not known or believed to be the possession of an authorized visitor. This paragraph shall not be construed to supersede or override Section 4576.

(9) Except where prohibited by state or federal law, if the device is seized from an authorized possessor of the device who is serving a term of parole under the supervision of the Department of Corrections and Rehabilitation or a term of postrelease community supervision under the supervision of county probation.

(10) Except where prohibited by state or federal law, if the device is seized from an authorized possessor of the device who is subject to an electronic device search as a clear and unambiguous condition of probation, mandatory supervision, or pretrial release.

(11) If the government entity accesses information concerning the location or the telephone number of the electronic device in order to respond to an emergency 911 call from that device.

(12) Pursuant to an order for a pen register or trap and trace device, or both, issued pursuant to Chapter 1.5 (commencing with Section 630) of Title 15 of Part 1.

(d) Any warrant for electronic information shall comply with the following:

(1) The warrant shall describe with particularity the information to be seized by specifying, as appropriate and reasonable, the time periods covered, the target individuals or accounts, the applications or services covered, and the types of information sought, provided, however, that in the case of a warrant described in paragraph (1) of subdivision (c), the court may determine that it is not appropriate to specify time periods because of the specific circumstances of the investigation, including, but not limited to, the nature of the device to be searched.

(2) The warrant shall require that any information obtained through the execution of the warrant that is unrelated to the objective of the warrant shall be sealed and shall not be subject to further review, use, or disclosure except pursuant to a court order or to comply with discovery as required by Sections 1054.1 and 1054.7. A court shall issue such an order upon a finding that there is probable cause to believe that the information is relevant to an active investigation, or review, use, or disclosure is required by state or federal law.

(3) The warrant shall comply with all other provisions of California and federal law, including any provisions prohibiting, limiting, or imposing additional requirements on the use of search warrants. If directed to a service provider, the warrant shall be accompanied by an order requiring the service provider to verify the authenticity of electronic information that it produces by providing an affidavit that complies with the requirements set forth in Section 1561 of the Evidence Code. Admission of that information into evidence shall be subject to Section 1562 of the Evidence Code.

(e) When issuing any warrant or order for electronic information, or upon the petition from the target or recipient of the warrant or order, a court may, at its discretion, do either or both of the following:

(1) Appoint a special master, as described in subdivision (d) of Section 1524, charged with ensuring that only information necessary to achieve the objective of the warrant or order is produced or accessed.

(2) Require that any information obtained through the execution of the warrant or order that is unrelated to the objective of the warrant be destroyed as soon as feasible after the termination of the current investigation and any related investigations or proceedings.

(f) A service provider may voluntarily disclose electronic communication information or subscriber information when that disclosure is not otherwise prohibited by state or federal law.

(g) If a government entity receives electronic communication information voluntarily provided pursuant to subdivision (f), it shall destroy that information within 90 days unless one or more of the following circumstances apply:

(1) The government entity has or obtains the specific consent of the sender or recipient of the electronic communications about which information was disclosed.

(2) The government entity obtains a court order authorizing the retention of the information. A court shall issue a retention order upon a finding that the conditions justifying the initial voluntary disclosure persist, in which case the court shall authorize the retention of the information only for so long as those conditions persist, or there is probable cause to believe that the information constitutes evidence that a crime has been committed.

(3) The government entity reasonably believes that the information relates to child pornography and the information is retained as part of a multiagency database used in the investigation of child pornography and related crimes.

(4) The service provider or subscriber is, or discloses the information to, a federal, state, or local prison, jail, or juvenile detention facility, and all participants to the electronic communication were informed, prior to the communication, that the service provider may disclose the information to the government entity.

(h) If a government entity obtains electronic information pursuant to an emergency involving danger of death or serious physical injury to a person, that requires access to the electronic information without delay, the government entity shall, within three court days after obtaining the electronic information, file with the appropriate court an application for a warrant or order authorizing obtaining the electronic information or a motion seeking approval of the emergency disclosures that shall set forth the facts giving rise to the emergency, and if applicable, a request supported by a sworn affidavit for an order delaying notification under paragraph (1) of subdivision (b) of Section 1546.2. The court shall promptly rule on the application or motion and shall order the immediate destruction of all information obtained, and immediate notification pursuant to subdivision (a) of Section 1546.2 if that notice has not already been given, upon a finding that the facts did not give rise to an emergency or upon rejecting the warrant or order application on any other ground. This subdivision does not apply if the government entity obtains information concerning the location or the telephone number of the electronic device in order to respond to an emergency 911 call from that device.

(i) This section does not limit the authority of a government entity to use an administrative, grand jury, trial, or civil discovery subpoena to do any of the following:

(1) Require an originator, addressee, or intended recipient of an electronic communication to disclose any electronic communication information associated with that communication.

(2) Require an entity that provides electronic communications services to its officers, directors, employees, or agents for the purpose of carrying out their duties, to disclose electronic communication information associated with an electronic communication to or from an officer, director, employee, or agent of the entity.

(3) Require a service provider to provide subscriber information.

(j) This section does not limit the authority of the Public Utilities Commission or the State Energy Resources Conservation and Development Commission to obtain energy or water supply and consumption information pursuant to the powers granted to them under the Public Utilities Code or the Public Resources Code and other applicable state laws.

(k) This chapter shall not be construed to alter the authority of a government entity that owns an electronic device to compel an employee who is authorized to possess the device to return the device to the government entity's possession.

(Amended by Stats. 2016, Ch. 541, Sec. 3.5. (SB 1121) Effective January 1, 2017.)

1546.2.

(a) (1) Except as otherwise provided in this section, any government entity that executes a warrant, or obtains electronic information in an emergency pursuant to Section 1546.1, shall serve upon, or deliver to by registered or first-class mail, electronic mail, or other means reasonably calculated to be effective, the identified targets of the warrant or emergency access, a notice that informs the recipient that information about the recipient has been compelled or obtained, and states with reasonable specificity the nature of the government investigation under which the information is sought. The notice shall include a copy of the warrant or a written statement setting forth facts giving rise to the emergency. The notice shall be provided contemporaneously with the execution of a warrant, or, in the case of an emergency, within three court days after obtaining the electronic information.

(2) Notwithstanding paragraph (1), notice is not required if the government entity accesses information concerning the location or the telephone number of an electronic device in order to respond to an emergency 911 call from that device.

(b) (1) When a warrant is sought or electronic information is obtained in an emergency under Section 1546.1, the government entity may submit a request supported by a sworn affidavit for an order delaying notification and prohibiting any party providing information from notifying any other party that information has been sought. The court shall issue the order if the court determines that there is reason to believe that notification may have an adverse result, but only for the period of time that the court finds there is reason to believe that the notification may have that adverse result, and not to exceed 90 days.

(2) The court may grant extensions of the delay of up to 90 days each on the same grounds as provided in paragraph (1).

(3) Upon expiration of the period of delay of the notification, the government entity shall serve upon, or deliver to by registered or first-class mail, electronic mail, or other means reasonably calculated to be effective as specified by the court issuing the order authorizing delayed notification, the identified targets of the warrant or emergency access, a document that includes the information described in subdivision (a), a copy of all electronic information obtained or a summary of that information, including, at a minimum, the number and types of records disclosed, the date and time when the earliest and latest records were created, and a statement of the grounds for the court's determination to grant a delay in notifying the individual.

(c) If there is no identified target of a warrant or emergency access at the time of its issuance, the government entity shall submit to the Department of Justice within three days of the execution of the warrant or issuance of the request all of the information required in subdivision (a). If an order delaying notice is obtained pursuant to subdivision (b), the government entity shall submit to the department upon the expiration of the period of delay of the notification all of the information required in paragraph (3) of subdivision (b). The department shall publish all those reports on its Internet Web site within 90 days of receipt. The department may redact names or other personal identifying information from the reports.

(d) Except as otherwise provided in this section, nothing in this chapter shall prohibit or limit a service provider or any other party from disclosing information about any request or demand for electronic information.

(Amended by Stats. 2017, Ch. 269, Sec. 10. (SB 811) Effective January 1, 2018.)

1546.4.

(a) Any person in a trial, hearing, or proceeding may move to suppress any electronic information obtained or retained in violation of the Fourth Amendment to the United States Constitution or of this chapter. The motion shall be made, determined, and be subject to review in accordance with the procedures set forth in subdivisions (b) to (q), inclusive, of Section 1538.5.

(b) The Attorney General may commence a civil action to compel any government entity to comply with the provisions of this chapter.

(c) An individual whose information is targeted by a warrant, order, or other legal process that is inconsistent with this chapter, or the California Constitution or the United States Constitution, or a service provider or any other recipient of the warrant, order, or other legal process may petition the issuing court to void or modify the warrant, order, or process, or to order the destruction of any information obtained in violation of this chapter, or the California Constitution, or the United States Constitution.

(d) A California or foreign corporation, and its officers, employees, and agents, are not subject to any cause of action for providing records, information, facilities, or assistance in accordance with the terms of a warrant, court order, statutory authorization, emergency certification, or wiretap order issued pursuant to this chapter.

(Added by Stats. 2015, Ch. 651, Sec. 1. (SB 178) Effective January 1, 2016.)

CHAPTER 3.6. Electronic Communications Privacy Act [1546 - 1546.4]

(Chapter 3.6 added by Stats. 2015, Ch. 651, Sec. 1.)

1546.

For purposes of this chapter, the following definitions apply:

(a) An "adverse result" means any of the following:

(1) Danger to the life or physical safety of an individual.

(2) Flight from prosecution.

(3) Destruction of or tampering with evidence.

(4) Intimidation of potential witnesses.

(5) Serious jeopardy to an investigation or undue delay of a trial.

(b) "Authorized possessor" means the possessor of an electronic device when that person is the owner of the device or has been authorized to possess the device by the owner of the device.

(c) "Electronic communication" means the transfer of signs, signals, writings, images, sounds, data, or intelligence of any nature in whole or in part by a wire, radio, electromagnetic, photoelectric, or photo-optical system.

(d) "Electronic communication information" means any information about an electronic communication or the use of an electronic communication service, including, but not limited to, the contents, sender, recipients, format, or location of the sender or recipients at any point during the communication, the time or date the communication was created, sent, or received, or any information pertaining to any individual or device participating in the communication, including, but not limited to, an IP address. "Electronic communication information" does not include subscriber information as defined in this chapter.

(e) "Electronic communication service" means a service that provides to its subscribers or users the ability to send or receive electronic communications, including any service that acts as an intermediary in the transmission of electronic communications, or stores electronic communication information.

(f) "Electronic device" means a device that stores, generates, or transmits information in electronic form. An electronic device does not include the magnetic strip on a driver's license or an identification card issued by this state or a driver's license or equivalent identification card issued by another state.

(g) "Electronic device information" means any information stored on or generated through the operation of an electronic device, including the current and prior locations of the device.

(h) "Electronic information" means electronic communication information or electronic device information.

(i) "Government entity" means a department or agency of the state or a political subdivision thereof, or an individual acting for or on behalf of the state or a political subdivision thereof.

(j) "Service provider" means a person or entity offering an electronic communication service.

(k) "Specific consent" means consent provided directly to the government entity seeking information, including, but not limited to, when the government entity is the addressee or intended recipient or a member of the intended audience of an electronic communication. Specific consent does not require that the originator of the communication have actual knowledge that an addressee, intended recipient, or member of the specific audience is a government entity.

(l) "Subscriber information" means the name, street address, telephone number, email address, or similar contact information provided by the subscriber to the service provider to establish or maintain an account or communication channel, a subscriber or account number or identifier, the length of service, and the types of services used by a user of or subscriber to a service provider.

(Amended by Stats. 2016, Ch. 541, Sec. 2. (SB 1121) Effective January 1, 2017.)

1546.1.

(a) Except as provided in this section, a government entity shall not do any of the following:

(1) Compel the production of or access to electronic communication information from a service provider.

(2) Compel the production of or access to electronic device information from any person or entity other than the authorized possessor of the device.

(3) Access electronic device information by means of physical interaction or electronic communication with the electronic device. This section does not prohibit the intended recipient of an electronic communication from voluntarily disclosing electronic communication information concerning that communication to a government entity.

(b) A government entity may compel the production of or access to electronic communication information from a service provider, or compel the production of or access to electronic device information from any person or entity other than the authorized possessor of the device only under the following circumstances:

(1) Pursuant to a warrant issued pursuant to Chapter 3 (commencing with Section 1523) and subject to subdivision (d).

(2) Pursuant to a wiretap order issued pursuant to Chapter 1.4 (commencing with Section 629.50) of Title 15 of Part 1.

(3) Pursuant to an order for electronic reader records issued pursuant to Section 1798.90 of the Civil Code.

(4) Pursuant to a subpoena issued pursuant to existing state law, provided that the information is not sought for the purpose of investigating or prosecuting a criminal offense, and compelling the production of or access to the information via the subpoena is not otherwise prohibited by state or federal law. Nothing in this paragraph shall be construed to expand any authority under state law to compel the production of or access to electronic information.

(5) Pursuant to an order for a pen register or trap and trace device, or both, issued pursuant to Chapter 1.5 (commencing with Section 630) of Title 15 of Part 1.

(c) A government entity may access electronic device information by means of physical interaction or electronic communication with the device only as follows:

(1) Pursuant to a warrant issued pursuant to Chapter 3 (commencing with Section 1523) and subject to subdivision (d).

(2) Pursuant to a wiretap order issued pursuant to Chapter 1.4 (commencing with Section 629.50) of Title 15 of Part 1.

(3) Pursuant to a tracking device search warrant issued pursuant to paragraph (12) of subdivision (a) of Section 1524 and subdivision (b) of Section 1534.

(4) With the specific consent of the authorized possessor of the device.

(5) With the specific consent of the owner of the device, only when the device has been reported as lost or stolen.

(6) If the government entity, in good faith, believes that an emergency involving danger of death or serious physical injury to any person requires access to the electronic device information.

(7) If the government entity, in good faith, believes the device to be lost, stolen, or abandoned, provided that the government entity shall only access electronic device information in order to attempt to identify, verify, or contact the owner or authorized possessor of the device.

(8) Except where prohibited by state or federal law, if the device is seized from an inmate's possession or found in an area of a correctional facility or a secure area of a local detention facility where inmates have access, the device is not in the possession of an individual, and the device is not known or believed to be the possession of an authorized visitor. This paragraph shall not be construed to supersede or override Section 4576.

(9) Except where prohibited by state or federal law, if the device is seized from an authorized possessor of the device who is serving a term of parole under the supervision of the Department of Corrections and Rehabilitation or a term of postrelease community supervision under the supervision of county probation.

(10) Except where prohibited by state or federal law, if the device is seized from an authorized possessor of the device who is subject to an electronic device search as a clear and unambiguous condition of probation, mandatory supervision, or pretrial release.

(11) If the government entity accesses information concerning the location or the telephone number of the electronic device in order to respond to an emergency 911 call from that device.

(12) Pursuant to an order for a pen register or trap and trace device, or both, issued pursuant to Chapter 1.5 (commencing with Section 630) of Title 15 of Part 1.

(d) Any warrant for electronic information shall comply with the following:

(1) The warrant shall describe with particularity the information to be seized by specifying, as appropriate and reasonable, the time periods covered, the target individuals or accounts, the applications or services covered, and the types of information sought, provided, however, that in the case of a warrant described in paragraph (1) of subdivision (c), the court may determine that it is not appropriate to specify time periods because of the specific circumstances of the investigation, including, but not limited to, the nature of the device to be searched.

(2) The warrant shall require that any information obtained through the execution of the warrant that is unrelated to the objective of the warrant shall be sealed and shall not be subject to further review, use, or disclosure except pursuant to a court order or to comply with discovery as required by Sections 1054.1 and 1054.7. A court shall issue such an order upon a finding that there is probable cause to believe that the information is relevant to an active investigation, or review, use, or disclosure is required by state or federal law.

(3) The warrant shall comply with all other provisions of California and federal law, including any provisions prohibiting, limiting, or imposing additional requirements on the use of search warrants. If directed to a service provider, the warrant shall be accompanied by an order requiring the service provider to verify the authenticity of electronic information that it produces by providing an affidavit that complies with the requirements set forth in Section 1561 of the Evidence Code. Admission of that information into evidence shall be subject to Section 1562 of the Evidence Code.

(e) When issuing any warrant or order for electronic information, or upon the petition from the target or recipient of the warrant or order, a court may, at its discretion, do either or both of the following:

(1) Appoint a special master, as described in subdivision (d) of Section 1524, charged with ensuring that only information necessary to achieve the objective of the warrant or order is produced or accessed.

(2) Require that any information obtained through the execution of the warrant or order that is unrelated to the objective of the warrant be destroyed as soon as feasible after the termination of the current investigation and any related investigations or proceedings.

(f) A service provider may voluntarily disclose electronic communication information or subscriber information when that disclosure is not otherwise prohibited by state or federal law.

(g) If a government entity receives electronic communication information voluntarily provided pursuant to subdivision (f), it shall destroy that information within 90 days unless one or more of the following circumstances apply:

(1) The government entity has or obtains the specific consent of the sender or recipient of the electronic communications about which information was disclosed.

(2) The government entity obtains a court order authorizing the retention of the information. A court shall issue a retention order upon a finding that the conditions justifying the initial voluntary disclosure persist, in which case the court shall authorize the retention of the information only for so long as those conditions persist, or there is probable cause to believe that the information constitutes evidence that a crime has been committed.

(3) The government entity reasonably believes that the information relates to child pornography and the information is retained as part of a multiagency database used in the investigation of child pornography and related crimes.

(4) The service provider or subscriber is, or discloses the information to, a federal, state, or local prison, jail, or juvenile detention facility, and all participants to the electronic communication were informed, prior to the communication, that the service provider may disclose the information to the government entity.

(h) If a government entity obtains electronic information pursuant to an emergency involving danger of death or serious physical injury to a person, that requires access to the electronic information without delay, the government entity shall, within three court days after obtaining the electronic information, file with the appropriate court an application for a warrant or order authorizing obtaining the electronic information or a motion seeking approval of the emergency disclosures that shall set forth the facts giving rise to the emergency, and if applicable, a request supported by a sworn affidavit for an order delaying notification under paragraph (1) of subdivision (b) of Section 1546.2. The court shall promptly rule on the application or motion and shall order the immediate destruction of all information obtained, and immediate notification pursuant to subdivision (a) of Section 1546.2 if that notice has not already been given, upon a finding that the facts did not give rise to an emergency or upon rejecting the warrant or order application on any other ground. This subdivision does not apply if the government entity obtains information concerning the location or the telephone number of the electronic device in order to respond to an emergency 911 call from that device.

(i) This section does not limit the authority of a government entity to use an administrative, grand jury, trial, or civil discovery subpoena to do any of the following:

(1) Require an originator, addressee, or intended recipient of an electronic communication to disclose any electronic communication information associated with that communication.

(2) Require an entity that provides electronic communications services to its officers, directors, employees, or agents for the purpose of carrying out their duties, to disclose electronic communication information associated with an electronic communication to or from an officer, director, employee, or agent of the entity.

(3) Require a service provider to provide subscriber information.

(j) This section does not limit the authority of the Public Utilities Commission or the State Energy Resources Conservation and Development Commission to obtain energy or water supply and consumption information pursuant to the powers granted to them under the Public Utilities Code or the Public Resources Code and other applicable state laws.

(k) This chapter shall not be construed to alter the authority of a government entity that owns an electronic device to compel an employee who is authorized to possess the device to return the device to the government entity's possession.

(Amended by Stats. 2016, Ch. 541, Sec. 3.5. (SB 1121) Effective January 1, 2017.)

1546.2.

(a) (1) Except as otherwise provided in this section, any government entity that executes a warrant, or obtains electronic information in an emergency pursuant to Section 1546.1, shall serve upon, or deliver to by registered or first-class mail, electronic mail, or other means reasonably calculated to be effective, the identified targets of the warrant or emergency access, a notice that informs the recipient that information about the recipient has been compelled or obtained, and states with reasonable specificity the nature of the government investigation under which the information is sought. The notice shall include a copy of the warrant or a written statement setting forth facts giving rise to the emergency. The notice shall be provided contemporaneously with the execution of a warrant, or, in the case of an emergency, within three court days after obtaining the electronic information.

(2) Notwithstanding paragraph (1), notice is not required if the government entity accesses information concerning the location or the telephone number of an electronic device in order to respond to an emergency 911 call from that device.

(b) (1) When a warrant is sought or electronic information is obtained in an emergency under Section 1546.1, the government entity may submit a request supported by a sworn affidavit for an order delaying notification and prohibiting any party providing information from notifying any other party that information has been sought. The court shall issue the order if the court determines that there is reason to believe that notification may have an adverse result, but only for the period of time that the court finds there is reason to believe that the notification may have that adverse result, and not to exceed 90 days.

(2) The court may grant extensions of the delay of up to 90 days each on the same grounds as provided in paragraph (1).

(3) Upon expiration of the period of delay of the notification, the government entity shall serve upon, or deliver to by registered or first-class mail, electronic mail, or other means reasonably calculated to be effective as specified by the court issuing the order authorizing delayed notification, the identified targets of the warrant or emergency access, a document that includes the information described in subdivision (a), a copy of all electronic information obtained or a summary of that information, including, at a minimum, the number and types of records disclosed, the date and time when the earliest and latest records were created, and a statement of the grounds for the court's determination to grant a delay in notifying the individual.

(c) If there is no identified target of a warrant or emergency access at the time of its issuance, the government entity shall submit to the Department of Justice within three days of the execution of the warrant or issuance of the request all of the information required in subdivision (a). If an order delaying notice is obtained pursuant to subdivision (b), the government entity shall submit to the department upon the expiration of the period of delay of the notification all of the information required in paragraph (3) of subdivision (b). The department shall publish all those reports on its Internet Web site within 90 days of receipt. The department may redact names or other personal identifying information from the reports.

(d) Except as otherwise provided in this section, nothing in this chapter shall prohibit or limit a service provider or any other party from disclosing information about any request or demand for electronic information.

(Amended by Stats. 2017, Ch. 269, Sec. 10. (SB 811) Effective January 1, 2018.)

1546.4.
(a) Any person in a trial, hearing, or proceeding may move to suppress any electronic information obtained or retained in violation of the Fourth Amendment to the United States Constitution or of this chapter. The motion shall be made, determined, and be subject to review in accordance with the procedures set forth in subdivisions (b) to (q), inclusive, of Section 1538.5.

(b) The Attorney General may commence a civil action to compel any government entity to comply with the provisions of this chapter.

(c) An individual whose information is targeted by a warrant, order, or other legal process that is inconsistent with this chapter, or the California Constitution or the United States Constitution, or a service provider or any other recipient of the warrant, order, or other legal process may petition the issuing court to void or modify the warrant, order, or process, or to order the destruction of any information obtained in violation of this chapter, or the California Constitution, or the United States Constitution.

(d) A California or foreign corporation, and its officers, employees, and agents, are not subject to any cause of action for providing records, information, facilities, or assistance in accordance with the terms of a warrant, court order, statutory authorization, emergency certification, or wiretap order issued pursuant to this chapter.

(Added by Stats. 2015, Ch. 651, Sec. 1. (SB 178) Effective January 1, 2016.)

CHAPTER 4. Proceedings Against Fugitives From Justice [1547 - 1558]

(Chapter 4 enacted 1872.)
1547.
(a) The Governor may offer a reward of not more than fifty thousand dollars ($50,000), payable out of the General Fund, for information leading to the arrest and conviction of any of the following:

(1) Any convict who has escaped from a state prison, prison camp, prison farm, or the custody of any prison officer or employee or as provided in Section 3059 or 4530.

(2) Any person who has committed, or is charged with the commission of, an offense punishable by death.

(3) (A) Any person engaged in the robbery or hijacking of, or any attempt to rob or hijack, any person upon or in charge of, in whole or in part, any public conveyance engaged at the time in carrying passengers within this state.

(B) As used in this paragraph, "hijacking" means an unauthorized person causing, or attempting to cause, by violence or threat of violence, a public conveyance to go to an unauthorized destination.

(4) Any person who attempts to murder either in the first or second degree, assaults with a deadly weapon, or inflicts serious bodily harm upon a peace officer or firefighter who is acting in the line of duty.

(5) Any person who has committed a crime involving the burning or bombing of public or private property, including any public hospital housed in a privately owned facility.

(6) Any person who has committed a crime involving the burning or bombing of any private hospital. A reward may be offered by the Governor in conjunction with that crime only if a reward in conjunction with the same crime is offered by the hospital, or any other public or private donor on its behalf. The amount of the reward offered by the Governor shall not exceed the aggregate amount offered privately, or fifty thousand dollars ($50,000), whichever is less. Nothing in this paragraph shall preclude a private hospital, or any public or private donor on its behalf, from offering a reward in an amount exceeding fifty thousand dollars ($50,000). If a person providing information for a reward under this paragraph so requests, his or her name and address shall remain confidential. This confidentiality, however, shall not preclude or obstruct the investigations of law enforcement authorities.

(7) Any person who commits a violation of Section 11413.

(8) Any person who commits a violation of Section 207.

(9) Any person who has committed a crime involving the burning or bombing of any bookstore or public or private library not subject to Section 11413. A reward may be offered by the Governor in conjunction with that crime only if a reward in conjunction with the same crime is offered by the bookstore or library, or any other public or private donor on its behalf. The amount of the reward offered by the Governor shall not exceed the aggregate amount offered privately, or fifty thousand dollars ($50,000), whichever is less. Nothing in this paragraph shall preclude a bookstore or public or private library, or any public or private donor on its behalf, from offering a reward in an amount exceeding fifty thousand dollars ($50,000). If a person providing information for a reward under this paragraph so requests, his or her name and address shall remain confidential. This confidentiality, however, shall not preclude or obstruct the investigations of law enforcement authorities.

(10) Any person who commits a violation of Section 454 or 463.

(11) Any person who willfully and maliciously sets fire to, or who attempts to willfully and maliciously set fire to, any property that is included within a hazardous fire area designated by the State Board of Forestry and Fire Protection pursuant to Section 4252 of the Public Resources Code or by the Director of Forestry and Fire Protection pursuant to Section 4253 of the Public Resources Code, if the fire, or attempt to set a fire, results in death or great bodily injury to anyone, including fire protection personnel, or if the fire causes substantial structural damage.

(12) Any person who has committed, or is charged with the commission of, a felony that is punishable under Section 422.75 and that resulted in serious bodily injury or in property damage of more than ten thousand dollars ($10,000).

(13) Any person who commits an act that violates Section 11411, if the Governor determines that the act is one in a series of similar or related acts committed in violation of that section by the same person or group.

(b) The Governor may offer a reward of not more than one hundred thousand dollars ($100,000) for information leading to the arrest and conviction of any person who kills a peace officer or firefighter who is acting in the line of duty.

(c) The Governor may offer a reward of not more than one hundred thousand dollars ($100,000), payable out of the General Fund, for information leading to the arrest and conviction of any person who commits arson upon a place of worship.

(d) The reward shall be paid to the person giving the information, promptly upon the conviction of the person so arrested, after a recommendation from the United States Attorney, or the California Attorney General, or the district attorney and the chief law enforcement officer, or his or her designate, in the jurisdiction where the crime occurred. Rewards shall only be paid to the person if the information is given voluntarily, at the person's own initiative. Rewards shall not be paid as part of any plea bargain.

(e) The reward may also be paid to the person giving the information if both of the following are met:

(1) The arrest or conviction of the person for an offense described in subdivision (a), (b), or (c) is rendered impossible by an intervening event, including, but not limited to, the death of the person during a pursuit by law enforcement, or while in custody.

(2) The appropriate law enforcement officials, after reviewing the evidence related to the crime or crimes, determine that the person is the individual responsible for the crime or crimes for which the reward was offered, and that the information would have reasonably led to the arrest and conviction of that person.

(f) If more than one claimant is eligible for any reward issued pursuant to this section, the Governor may apportion the reward money in a manner the Governor deems appropriate.

(Amended by Stats. 2002, Ch. 529, Sec. 1. Effective January 1, 2003.)

1548.
As used in this chapter:

(a) "Governor" means any person performing the functions of Governor by authority of the law of this State.

(b) "Executive authority" means the Governor or any person performing the functions of Governor in a State other than this State.

(c) "State," referring to a State other than the State of California, means any other State or Territory, organized or unorganized, of the United States of America.

(d) "Laws of the United States" means: (1) those laws of the United States passed by Congress pursuant to authority given to Congress by the Constitution of the United States where the laws of the United States are controlling, and (2) those laws of the United States not controlling the several States of the United States but which are not in conflict with the provisions of this chapter.

(Repealed and added by Stats. 1937, Ch. 554.)

1548.1.
Subject to the provisions of this chapter, the Constitution of the United States, and the laws of the United States, it is the duty of the Governor of this State to have arrested and delivered up to the executive authority of any other State any person charged in that State with treason, felony, or other crime, who has fled from justice and is found in this State.

(Added by Stats. 1937, Ch. 554.)

1548.2.
No demand for the extradition of a person charged with crime in another State shall be recognized by the Governor unless it is in writing alleging that the accused was present in the demanding State at the time of the commission of the alleged crime, and that thereafter he fled from that State. Such demand shall be accompanied by a copy of an indictment found or by information or by a copy of an affidavit made before a magistrate in the demanding State together with a copy of any warrant which was issued thereon; or such demand shall be accompanied by a copy of a judgment of conviction or of a sentence imposed in execution thereof, together with a statement by the executive authority of the demanding State that the person claimed has escaped from confinement or has violated the terms of his bail, probation or parole. The indictment, information, or affidavit made before the magistrate must substantially charge the person demanded with having committed a crime under the law of that State; and the copy of indictment, information, affidavit, judgment of conviction or sentence must be certified as authentic by the executive authority making the demand.

(Added by Stats. 1937, Ch. 554.)

1548.3.
When a demand is made upon the Governor of this State by the executive authority of another State for the surrender of a person so charged with crime, the Governor may call upon the Attorney General or any district attorney in this State to investigate or assist in investigating the demand, and to report to him the situation and circumstances of the person so demanded, and whether he ought to be surrendered according to the provision of this chapter.

(Added by Stats. 1937, Ch. 554.)

1549.
When it is desired to have returned to this state a person charged in this state with a crime, and the person is imprisoned or is held under criminal proceedings then pending against him or her in another state, the Governor of this state may agree with the executive authority of the other state for the extradition of the person before the conclusion of the proceedings or his or her term of sentence in the other state, upon the condition that the person be returned to the other state at the expense of this state as soon as the prosecution in this state is terminated.

The Governor of this state may also surrender on demand of the executive authority of any other state any person in this state who is charged in the manner provided in Section 1548.2 with having violated the laws of the demanding state even though such person left the demanding state involuntarily.

(Amended by Stats. 1987, Ch. 828, Sec. 101.)

1549.1.
The Governor of this state may also surrender, on demand of the executive authority of any other state, any person in this state charged in the other state in the manner provided in Section 1548.2 with committing an act in this state, or in a third state, intentionally resulting in a crime in the state whose executive authority is making the demand. The provisions of this chapter, not otherwise inconsistent, shall apply to those cases, even though the accused was not in the demanding state at the time of the commission of the crime, and has not fled therefrom. Neither the demand, the oath, nor any proceedings under this chapter pursuant to this section need state or show that the accused has fled from justice from, or at the time of the commission of the crime was in, the demanding or other state.

(Amended by Stats. 1987, Ch. 828, Sec. 102.)

1549.2.
If a demand conforms to the provisions of this chapter, the Governor or agent authorized in writing by the Governor whose authorization has been filed with the Secretary of State shall sign a warrant of arrest, which shall be sealed with the State Seal, and shall be directed to any peace officer or other person whom he may entrust with the execution thereof. The warrant must substantially recite the facts necessary to the validity of its issuance. The provisions of Section 850 shall be applicable to such warrant, except that it shall not be necessary to include a warrant number, address, or

description of the subject, provided that a complaint under Section 1551 is then pending against the subject.

(Amended by Stats. 1983, Ch. 793, Sec. 1.2.)

1549.3.

Such warrant shall authorize the peace officer or other person to whom it is directed:

(a) To arrest the accused at any time and any place where he may be found within the State;

(b) To command the aid of all peace officers or other persons in the execution of the warrant; and

(c) To deliver the accused, subject to the provisions of this chapter, to the duly authorized agent of the demanding State.

(Added by Stats. 1937, Ch. 554.)

1550.

Every peace officer or other person empowered to make the arrest hereunder shall have the same authority, in arresting the accused, to command assistance therefor as the persons designated in Section 150. Failure or refusal to render that assistance is a violation of Section 150.

(Amended by Stats. 1987, Ch. 828, Sec. 103.)

1550.1.

No person arrested upon such warrant shall be delivered over to the agent of the executive authority demanding him unless he is first taken forthwith before a magistrate, who shall inform him of the demand made for his surrender, and of the crime with which he is charged, and that he has the right to demand and procure counsel. If the accused or his counsel desires to test the legality of the arrest, the magistrate shall remand the accused to custody, and fix a reasonable time to be allowed him within which to apply for a writ of habeas corpus. If the writ is denied, and probable cause appears for an application for a writ of habeas corpus to another court, or justice or judge thereof, the order denying the writ shall remand the accused to custody, and fix a reasonable time within which the accused may again apply for a writ of habeas corpus. When an application is made for a writ of habeas corpus as contemplated by this section, a copy of the application shall be served as provided in Section 1475, upon the district attorney of the county in which the accused is in custody, and upon the agent of the demanding state. A warrant issued in accordance with the provisions of Section 1549.2 shall be presumed to be valid, and unless a court finds that the person in custody is not the same person named in the warrant, or that the person is not a fugitive from justice, or otherwise subject to extradition under Section 1549.1, or that there is no criminal charge or criminal proceeding pending against the person in the demanding state, or that the documents are not on their face in order, the person named in the warrant shall be held in custody at all times, and shall not be eligible for release on bail.

(Amended by Stats. 1983, Ch. 793, Sec. 2.)

1550.2.

Any officer or other person entrusted with a Governor's warrant who delivers to the agent of the demanding State a person in his custody under such Governor's warrant, in wilful disobedience to the preceding section, is guilty of a misdemeanor and, on conviction thereof, shall be fined not more than $1,000 or be imprisoned not more than six months, or both.

(Added by Stats. 1937, Ch. 554.)

1550.3.

The officer or persons executing the Governor's warrant of arrest, or the agent of the demanding State to whom the prisoner has been delivered may confine the prisoner in the jail of any county or city through which he may pass. The keeper of such jail must receive and safely keep the prisoner until the officer or person having charge of him is ready to proceed on his route. Such officer or person shall be charged with the expense of keeping the prisoner.

The officer or agent of a demanding State to whom a prisoner has been delivered following extradition proceedings in another State, or to whom a prisoner has been delivered after waiving extradition in such other State, and who is passing through this State with such a prisoner for the purpose of immediately returning such prisoner to the demanding State may confine the prisoner in the jail of any county or city through which he may pass. The keeper of such jail must receive and safely keep the prisoner until the officer or agent having charge of him is ready to proceed on his route. Such officer or agent shall be charged with the expense of keeping the prisoner. Such officer or agent shall produce and show to the keeper of such jail satisfactory written evidence of the fact that he is actually transporting such prisoner to the demanding State after a requisition by the executive authority thereof. Such prisoner shall not be entitled to demand a new requisition while in this State.

(Added by Stats. 1937, Ch. 554.)

1551.

(a) Whenever any person within this State is charged by a verified complaint before any magistrate of this State with the commission of any crime in any other State, or, with having been convicted of a crime in that State and having escaped from confinement, or having violated the terms of his bail, probation or parole; or (b) whenever complaint is made before any magistrate in this State setting forth on the affidavit of any credible person in another State that a crime has been committed in such other State and that the accused has been charged in such State with the commission of the crime, or that the accused has been convicted of a crime in that State and has escaped from bail, probation or parole and is believed to be in this State; then the magistrate shall issue a warrant directed to any peace officer commanding him to apprehend the person named therein, wherever he may be found in this State, and to bring him before the same or any other magistrate who is available in or convenient of access to the place where the arrest is made. A certified copy of the sworn charge or complaint and affidavit upon which the warrant is issued shall be attached to the warrant.

(Repealed and added by Stats. 1937, Ch. 554.)

1551.05.

(a) Any person on outpatient status pursuant to Title 15 (commencing with Section 1600) of Part 2 or pursuant to subdivision (d) of Section 2972 who leaves this state without complying with Section 1611, or who fails to return to this state on the date specified by the committing court, shall be subject to extradition in accordance with this section.

(b) If the return to this state is required by a person who is subject to extradition pursuant to subdivision (a), the Director of State Hospitals shall present to the Governor a written application for requisition for the return of that person. In the requisition application there shall be stated the name of the person, the type of judicial commitment the person is under, the nature of the underlying criminal act which was the basis for the judicial commitment, the circumstances of the noncompliance with Section 1611, and the state in which the person is believed to be, including the specific location of the person, if known.

(c) The application shall be verified, shall be executed in duplicate, and shall be accompanied by two certified copies of the court order of judicial commitment and of the court order authorizing outpatient status. The director may also attach any affidavits or other documents in duplicate as are deemed proper to be submitted with the application. One copy of the application, with the action of the Governor indicated by endorsement thereon, and one copy of the court orders shall be filed in the office of the Secretary of State. The other copies of all papers shall be forwarded with the Governor's requisition.

(d) Upon receipt of an application under this section, the Governor or agent authorized in writing by the Governor whose authorization has been filed with the Secretary of State, may sign a requisition for the return of the person.

(Amended by Stats. 2012, Ch. 440, Sec. 37. (AB 1488) Effective September 22, 2012.)

1551.1.

The arrest of a person may also be lawfully made by any peace officer, without a warrant, upon reasonable information that the accused stands charged in the courts of any other state with a crime punishable by death or imprisonment for a term exceeding one year, or that the person has been convicted of a crime punishable in the state of conviction by imprisonment for a term exceeding one year and thereafter escaped from confinement or violated the terms of his or her bail, probation or parole. When so arrested the accused shall be taken before a magistrate with all practicable speed and complaint shall be made against him or her under oath setting forth the ground for the arrest as in Section 1551.

(Amended by Stats. 1987, Ch. 828, Sec. 104.)

1551.2.

At the initial appearance of a person arrested under Section 1551 or 1551.1, he shall be informed of the reason for his arrest and of his right to demand and procure counsel. If the person denies that he is the same person charged with or convicted of a crime in the other state, a hearing shall be held within 10 days to determine whether there is probable cause to believe that he is the same person and whether he is charged with or convicted of a crime in the other state. At the hearing, the magistrate shall accept a certified copy of an indictment found, an information, a verified complaint, a judgment or sentence, or other judicial proceedings against that person in the state in which the crime is charged or the conviction occurred, and such copy shall constitute conclusive proof of its contents. Witnesses from the other state shall not be required to be present at the hearing.

(Amended by Stats. 1983, Ch. 793, Sec. 4.)

1551.3.

Immediately upon the arrest of the person charged, the magistrate must give notice thereof to the district attorney. The district attorney must immediately thereafter give notice to the executive authority of the State, or to the prosecuting attorney or presiding judge of the court of the city or county within the State having jurisdiction of the offense, to the end that a demand may be made for the arrest and surrender of the person charged.

(Added by Stats. 1937, Ch. 554.)

1552.

If at the hearing before the magistrate, it appears that the accused is the person charged with having committed the crime alleged, the magistrate must, by a warrant reciting the accusation, commit him to the county jail for such a time, not exceeding thirty days and specified in the warrant, as will enable the arrest of the accused to be made under a warrant of the Governor on a requisition of the executive authority of the State having jurisdiction of the offense, unless the accused give bail as provided in section 1552.1, or until he shall be legally discharged.

(Repealed and added by Stats. 1937, Ch. 554.)

1552.1.

Unless the offense with which the prisoner is charged, is shown to be an offense punishable by death or life imprisonment under the laws of the state in which it was committed, or it is shown that the prisoner is alleged to have escaped or violated the terms of his parole following conviction of a crime punishable in the state of conviction by imprisonment for a term exceeding one year, the magistrate may admit the person arrested to bail by bond or undertaking, with sufficient sureties, and in such sum as he deems proper, conditioned upon the appearance of such person before him at a time specified in such bond or undertaking, and for his surrender upon the warrant of the Governor of this state. Nothing in this section or in Section 1553 shall be deemed to prevent the immediate service of a Governor's warrant issued under Section 1549.2.

(Amended by Stats. 1983, Ch. 793, Sec. 5.)

1552.2.

If the accused is not arrested under warrant of the Governor by the expiration of the time specified in the warrant, bond, or undertaking, a magistrate may discharge him or may recommit him for a further period of 60 days. In the latter event a justice of the Supreme Court or court of appeal or a judge of the superior court may again take bail for his appearance and surrender, as provided in Section 1552.1 but within a period not to exceed 60 days after the date of such new bond or undertaking.

(Amended by Stats. 1967, Ch. 17.)

1553.

If the prisoner is admitted to bail, and fails to appear and surrender himself according to the conditions of his bond, the magistrate, by proper order, shall declare the bond forfeited and order his immediate arrest without warrant if he be within this State. Recovery may be had on such bond in the name of the people of the State as in the case of other bonds or undertakings given by a defendant in criminal proceedings.

(Repealed and added by Stats. 1937, Ch. 554.)

1553.1.

(a) If a criminal prosecution has been instituted against a person charged under Section 1551 under the laws of this state and is still pending, the Governor, with the consent of the Attorney General, may surrender the person on demand of the executive authority of another state or hold him or her until he or she has been tried and discharged or convicted and served his or her sentence in this state.

(b) If a criminal prosecution has been instituted under the laws of this state against a person charged under Section 1551, the restrictions on the length of commitment contained in Sections 1552 and 1552.2 shall not be applicable during the period that the criminal prosecution is pending in this state.

(Amended by Stats. 1983, Ch. 793, Sec. 6.)

1553.2.

The guilt or innocence of the accused as to the crime with which he is charged may not be inquired into by the Governor or in any proceeding after the demand for extradition accompanied by a charge of crime in legal form as above provided has been presented to the Governor, except as such inquiry may be involved in identifying the person held as the person charged with the crime.

(Added by Stats. 1937, Ch. 554.)

1554.

The Governor may recall his warrant of arrest or may issue another warrant whenever he deems it proper.

(Repealed and added by Stats. 1937, Ch. 554.)

1554.1.

Whenever the Governor of this State shall demand the return of a person charged with crime in this State or with escaping from confinement or violating the terms of his bail, probation or parole in this State, from the executive authority of any other State or of any foreign government or the chief justice or an associate justice of the Supreme Court of the District of Columbia authorized to receive such demand, he shall issue a warrant under the seal of this State to an agent, commanding him to receive the person so demanded and to convey him to the proper officer in the county in this State in which the offense was committed.

(Added by Stats. 1937, Ch. 554.)

1554.2.

(a) When the return to this state of a person charged with crime in this state is required, the district attorney shall present to the Governor his written application for a requisition for the return of the person charged. In such application there shall be stated the name of the person so charged, the crime charged against him, the approximate time, place and circumstances of its commission, and the state in which he is believed to be, including the location of the accused therein at the time the application is made. Such application shall certify that, in the opinion of the district attorney, the ends of justice require the arrest and return of the accused to this state for trial and that the proceeding is not instituted to enforce a private claim.

(b) When the return to this state is required of a person who has been convicted of a crime in this state and who has escaped from confinement or has violated the terms of his bail, probation or parole the district attorney of the county in which the offense was committed, the Board of Prison Terms, the Director of Corrections, the California Institution for Women, the Youth Authority, or the sheriff of the county from which escape from confinement was made, shall present to the Governor a written application for a requisition for the return of such person. In such application there shall be stated the name of the person, the crime of which he was convicted, the circumstances of his escape or of the violation of the terms of his bail, probation or parole, and the state in which he is believed to be, including the location of such person therein at the time application is made.

(c) The application shall be verified, shall be executed in duplicate, and shall be accompanied by two certified copies of the indictment, the information, or the verified complaint made to the magistrate stating the offense with which the accused is charged, or the judgment of conviction or the sentence. The officer or board requesting the requisition may also attach such affidavits and other documents in duplicate as are deemed proper to be submitted with such application. One copy of the application, with the action of the Governor indicated by endorsement thereon, and one of the certified copies of the indictment, verified complaint, information, or judgment of conviction or sentence shall be filed in the office of the Secretary of State. The other copies of all papers shall be forwarded with the Governor's requisition.

(d) Upon receipt of an application under this section, the Governor or agent authorized in writing by the Governor whose authorization has been filed with the Secretary of State, may sign a requisition for the return of the person charged and any other document incidental to that requisition or to the return of the person charged.
(Amended by Stats. 1983, Ch. 793, Sec. 7.)
1554.3.
After a person has been brought back to this state by extradition proceedings, the person shall be committed to a county jail with bail set in the amount of one hundred thousand dollars ($100,000) in addition to the amount of bail appearing on the warrant. A 48-hour noticed bail hearing, excluding weekends and holidays, is required to deviate from this prescribed bail amount. Nothing in this section is intended to preclude the application of subdivision (e) of Section 1270.1 to enhance the bail amount for the felony charge appearing on the warrant.
(Added by Stats. 2011, Ch. 67, Sec. 1. (SB 291) Effective January 1, 2012.)
1555.
A person brought into this State on, or after waiver of extradition based on a criminal charge shall not be subject to service of process in civil actions arising out of the same facts as the criminal proceedings for which he is returned, until he has been convicted in the criminal proceeding, or, if acquitted, until he has had reasonable opportunity to return to the State from which he was extradited.
(Repealed and added by Stats. 1937, Ch. 554.)
1555.1.
Any person arrested in this state charged with having committed any crime in another state or alleged to have escaped from confinement, or broken the terms of his or her bail, probation or parole may waive the issuance and service of the Governor's warrant provided for in this chapter and all other procedure incidental to extradition proceedings, by subscribing in the presence of a magistrate within this state a writing which states that he or she consents to return to the demanding state; provided, however, that before such waiver shall be subscribed by such person, the magistrate shall inform him or her of his or her rights to require the issuance and service of a warrant of extradition as provided in this chapter.
If such waiver is executed, it shall forthwith be forwarded to the office of the Governor of this state, and filed therein. The magistrate shall remand the person to custody without bail, unless otherwise stipulated by the district attorney with the concurrence of the other state, and shall direct the officer having such person in custody to deliver such person forthwith to the duly authorized agent of the demanding state, and shall deliver to such agent a copy of such waiver.
Nothing in this section shall be deemed to limit the rights of the accused person to return voluntarily and without formality to the demanding state, provided that state consents, nor shall this procedure of waiver be deemed to be an exclusive procedure or to limit the powers, rights or duties of the officers of the demanding state or of this state.
(Amended by Stats. 1983, Ch. 793, Sec. 8.)
1555.2.
(a) If the arrested person refuses to sign a waiver of extradition under Section 1555.1, a hearing shall be held, upon application of the district attorney, to determine whether the person is alleged to have violated the terms of his release within the past five years on bail or own recognizance while charged with a crime punishable in the charging state by imprisonment for a term exceeding one year, or on probation or parole following conviction of a crime punishable in the state of conviction by imprisonment for a term exceeding one year, and whether, as a condition of that release, the person was required to waive extradition.
(b) At the hearing, the district attorney shall present a certified copy of the order from the other state conditionally releasing the person, including the condition that he was required to waive extradition together with a certified copy of the order from the other state directing the return of the person for violating the terms of his conditional release. The magistrate shall accept these certified copies as conclusive proof of their contents and shall presume the validity of the extradition waiver condition.
(c) If the magistrate finds that there is probable cause to believe that the arrested person is the same person named in the conditional release order and the order commanding his return, the magistrate shall forthwith issue an order remanding the person to custody without bail and directing the delivery of the person to duly accredited agents of the other state.
(d) Notwithstanding the provisions of subdivision (c), the district attorney may stipulate, with the concurrence of the other state, that the arrested person may be released on bail or own recognizance pending the arrival of duly accredited agents from the other state.
(e) If the arrested person or his counsel desires to test the legality of the order issued under subdivision (c), the magistrate shall fix a reasonable time to be allowed him within which to apply for a writ of habeas corpus. If the writ is denied and probable cause appears for an application for a writ of habeas corpus to another court, or justice or judge thereof, the order denying the writ shall fix a reasonable time within which the accused may again apply for a writ of habeas corpus. Unless otherwise stipulated pursuant to subdivision (d), the arrested person shall remain in custody without bail.
(Added by Stats. 1983, Ch. 793, Sec. 10.)
1555.3.
Nothing in this chapter shall be deemed to constitute a waiver by this state of its right, power or privilege to try any demanded person for crime committed within this state, or of its right, power or privilege to regain custody of such person by extradition proceedings or otherwise for the purpose of trial, sentence or punishment for any crime committed within this state; nor shall any proceedings had under this chapter which result in, or fail to result in, extradition be deemed a waiver by this state of any of its rights, privileges or jurisdiction in any manner whatsoever.
(Added by renumbering Section 1555.2 by Stats. 1983, Ch. 793, Sec. 9.)
1556.

After a person has been brought back to this State by extradition proceedings, he may be tried in this State for other crimes which he may be charged with having committed in this State as well as for the crime or crimes specified in the requisition for his extradition.
(Repealed and added by Stats. 1937, Ch. 554.)
1556.1.
The provisions of this chapter shall be so interpreted and construed as to effectuate its general purposes to make uniform the law of those states which enact legislation based upon the Uniform Criminal Extradition Act.
(Added by Stats. 1937, Ch. 554.)
1556.2.
This chapter may be cited as the Uniform Criminal Extradition Act.
(Added by Stats. 1937, Ch. 554.)
1557.
(a) This section shall apply when this state or a city, county, or city and county employs a person to travel to a foreign jurisdiction outside this state for the express purpose of returning a fugitive from justice to this state when the Governor of this state, in the exercise of the authority conferred by Section 2 of Article IV of the United States Constitution, or by the laws of this state, has demanded the surrender of the fugitive from the executive authority of any state of the United States, or of any foreign government.
(b) Upon the approval of the Governor, the Controller shall audit and pay out of the State Treasury as provided in subdivision (c) or (d) the accounts of the person employed to bring back the fugitive, including any money paid by that person for all of the following:
(1) Money paid to the authorities of a sister state for statutory fees in connection with the detention and surrender of the fugitive.
(2) Money paid to the authorities of the sister state for the subsistence of the fugitive while detained by the sister state without payment of which the authorities of the sister state refuse to surrender the fugitive.
(3) Where it is necessary to present witnesses or evidence in the sister state, without which the sister state would not surrender the fugitive, the cost of producing the witnesses or evidence in the sister state.
(4) Where the appearance of witnesses has been authorized in advance by the Governor, who may authorize the appearance in unusual cases where the interests of justice would be served, the cost of producing witnesses to appear in the sister state on behalf of the fugitive in opposition to his or her extradition.
(c) No amount shall be paid out of the State Treasury to a city, county, or city and county except as follows:
(1) When a warrant has been issued by any magistrate after the filing of a complaint or the finding of an indictment and its presentation to the court and filing by the clerk, and the person named therein as defendant is a fugitive from justice who has been found and arrested in any state of the United States or in any foreign government, the county auditor shall draw his or her warrant and the county treasurer shall pay to the person designated to return the fugitive, the amount of expenses estimated by the district attorney to be incurred in the return of the fugitive.
(2) If the person designated to return the fugitive is a city officer, the city officer authorized to draw warrants on the city treasury shall draw his or her warrant and the city treasurer shall pay to that person the amount of expenses estimated by the district attorney to be incurred in the return of the fugitive.
(3) The person designated to return the fugitive shall make no disbursements from any funds advanced without a receipt being obtained therefor showing the amount, the purpose for which the sum is expended, the place, the date, and to whom paid.
(4) A receipt obtained pursuant to paragraph (3) shall be filed by the person designated to return the fugitive, with the county auditor or appropriate city officer or the Controller, as the case may be, together with an affidavit by the person that the expenditures represented by the receipts were necessarily made in the performance of duty, and when the advance has been made by the county or city treasurer to the person designated to return the fugitive, and has thereafter been audited by the Controller, the payment thereof shall be made by the State Treasurer to the county or city treasury that has advanced the funds.
(5) If the expenses of the person employed to bring back the fugitive are less than the amount advanced on the recommendation of the district attorney, the person employed to bring back the fugitive shall return to the county or city treasurer, as appropriate, the difference in amount between the aggregate amount of receipts so filed by him or her, and the amount advanced to the person upon the recommendation of the district attorney.
(6) When no advance has been made to the person designated to return the fugitive, the sums expended by him or her, when audited by the Controller, shall be paid by the State Treasurer to the person so designated.
(7) Any payments made out of the State Treasury pursuant to this section shall be made from appropriations for the fiscal year in which those payments are made.
(d) A city, county, or other jurisdiction shall not file, and the state shall not reimburse, a claim pursuant to this section that is presented to the Department of Corrections and Rehabilitation or to any other agency or department of the state more than six months after the close of the month in which the costs were incurred. Notwithstanding any other law, a person transporting a fugitive as authorized by the Governor pursuant to this section shall be reimbursed according to the rates in paragraphs (1) to (5), inclusive. Rates and rules for reimbursement of travel claims not specified in paragraphs (1) to (5), inclusive, shall be consistent with the rules of the Department of General Services.
(1) Reimbursement for breakfast is up to four dollars ($4).
(2) Reimbursement for lunch is up to seven dollars and twenty-five cents ($7.25).
(3) Reimbursement for dinner is up to twelve dollars ($12).
(4) Reimbursement for incidental expenses is up to three dollars and seventy-five cents ($3.75).
(5) Reimbursement for a meal for a prisoner, patient, ward, or fugitive is up to the amounts specified in paragraphs (1) to (3), inclusive.
(Amended by Stats. 2017, Ch. 17, Sec. 36. (AB 103) Effective June 27, 2017.)
1558.
No compensation, fee, profit, or reward of any kind can be paid to or received by a public officer of this state, a corporation or firm, or other person, for a service rendered in procuring from the Governor the demand mentioned in Section 1557, or the surrender of the fugitive, or for conveying him or her to this state, or detaining him or her therein, except as provided for in that section. Every person who violates any of the provisions of this section is guilty of a misdemeanor.
(Amended by Stats. 1990, Ch. 222, Sec. 1.)

CHAPTER 5. Miscellaneous Provisions Respecting Special Proceedings of a Criminal Nature [1562 - 1564]

(Chapter 5 enacted 1872.)
1562.
The party prosecuting a special proceeding of a criminal nature is designated in this Code as the complainant, and the adverse party as the defendant.

(Enacted 1872.)

1563.

The provisions of Section 1401, in respect to entitling affidavits, are applicable to such proceedings.

(Enacted 1872.)

1564.

The Courts and magistrates before whom such proceedings are prosecuted may issue subpoenas for witnesses, and punish their disobedience in the same manner as in a criminal action.

(Enacted 1872.)

TITLE 13. PROCEEDINGS FOR BRINGING PERSONS IMPRISONED IN THE STATE PRISON, OR THE JAIL OF ANOTHER COUNTY, BEFORE A COURT [1567- 1567.]

(Title 13 enacted 1872.)

1567.

When it is necessary to have a person imprisoned in the state prison brought before any court, or a person imprisoned in a county jail brought before a court sitting in another county, an order for that purpose may be made by the court and executed by the sheriff of the county where it is made. The order shall be signed by the judge or magistrate and sealed with the seal of the court, if any. The order shall be to the following effect:

County of _____ (as the case may be).

The people of the State of California to the warden of _____ (or sheriff of _____, as the case may be):

An order having been made this day by me, that A. B. be produced in this court as witness in the case of _____, you are commanded to deliver him or her into the custody of _____.

Dated this _____ day of _____, 19___.

(Amended by Stats. 1981, Ch. 714, Sec. 334.)

TITLE 15. OUTPATIENT STATUS FOR MENTALLY DISORDERED AND DEVELOPMENTALLY DISABLED OFFENDERS [1600 - 1620]

(Title 15 added by Stats. 1980, Ch. 547, Sec. 17.)

1600.

Any person committed to a state hospital or other treatment facility under the provisions of Section 1026, or Chapter 6 (commencing with Section 1367) of Title 10 of this code, or Section 6316 or 6321 of the Welfare and Institutions Code may be placed on outpatient status from that commitment subject to the procedures and provisions of this title, except that a developmentally disabled person may be placed on outpatient status from that commitment under the provisions of this title as modified by Section 1370.4. Any person committed as a sexually violent predator under the provisions of Article 4 (commencing with Section 6600) of Chapter 2 of Part 2 of Division 6 of the Welfare and Institutions Code may be placed on outpatient status from that commitment in accordance with the procedures described in Title 15 (commencing with Section 1600) of Part 2 of the Penal Code.

(Amended by Stats. 1996, Ch. 462, Sec. 1. Effective September 13, 1996.)

1600.5.

For a person committed as a mentally disordered sex offender under former Section 6316 or 6316.2 of the Welfare and Institutions Code, or committed pursuant to Section 1026 or 1026.5, or committed pursuant to Section 2972, who is placed on outpatient status under the provisions of this title, time spent on outpatient status, except when placed in a locked facility at the direction of the outpatient supervisor, shall not count as actual custody and shall not be credited toward the person's maximum term of commitment or toward the person's term of extended commitment. Nothing in this section shall be construed to extend the maximum period of parole of a mentally disordered offender.

(Amended by Stats. 2000, Ch. 324, Sec. 1. Effective January 1, 2001.)

1601.

(a) In the case of any person charged with and found incompetent on a charge of, convicted of, or found not guilty by reason of insanity of murder, mayhem, aggravated mayhem, a violation of Section 207, 209, or 209.5 in which the victim suffers intentionally inflicted great bodily injury, robbery or carjacking with a deadly or dangerous weapon or in which the victim suffers great bodily injury, a violation of subdivision (a) or (b) of Section 451, a violation of paragraph (2), (3), or (6) of subdivision (a) of Section 261, a violation of paragraph (1) or (4) of subdivision (a) of Section 262, a violation of Section 459 in the first degree, a violation of Section 220 in which the victim suffers great bodily injury, a violation of Section 288, a violation of Section 18715, 18725, 18740, 18745, 18750, or 18755, or any felony involving death, great bodily injury, or an act which poses a serious threat of bodily harm to another person, outpatient status under this title shall not be available until that person has actually been confined in a state hospital or other treatment facility for 180 days or more after having been committed under the provisions of law specified in Section 1600, unless the court finds a suitable placement, including, but not limited to, an outpatient placement program, that would provide the person with more appropriate mental health treatment and the court finds that the placement would not pose a danger to the health or safety of others, including, but not limited to, the safety of the victim and the victim's family.

(b) In the case of any person charged with, and found incompetent on a charge of, or convicted of, any misdemeanor or any felony other than those described in subdivision (a), or found not guilty of any misdemeanor by reason of insanity, outpatient status under this title may be granted by the court prior to actual confinement in a state hospital or other treatment facility under the provisions of law specified in Section 1600.

(Amended by Stats. 2014, Ch. 734, Sec. 1. (AB 2190) Effective January 1, 2015.)

1602.

(a) Before any person subject to the provisions of subdivision (b) of Section 1601 may be placed on outpatient status, the court shall consider all of the following criteria:

(1) In the case of a person who is an inpatient, whether the director of the state hospital or other treatment facility to which the person has been committed advises the court that the defendant will not be a danger to the health and safety of others while on outpatient status, and will benefit from such outpatient status.

(2) In all cases, whether the community program director or a designee advises the court that the defendant will not be a danger to the health and safety of others while on outpatient status, will benefit from such status, and identifies an appropriate program of supervision and treatment.

(b) Prior to determining whether to place the person on outpatient status, the court shall provide actual notice to the prosecutor and defense counsel, and to the victim, and shall hold a hearing at which the court may specifically order outpatient status for the person.

(c) The community program director or a designee shall prepare and submit the evaluation and the treatment plan specified in paragraph (2) of subdivision (a) to the court within 15 calendar days after notification by the court to do so, except that in the case of a person who is an inpatient, the evaluation and treatment plan shall be submitted within 30 calendar days after notification by the court to do so.

(d) Any evaluations and recommendations pursuant to paragraphs (1) and (2) of subdivision (a) shall include review and consideration of complete, available information regarding the circumstances of the criminal offense and the person's prior criminal history.

(Amended by Stats. 2014, Ch. 734, Sec. 2. (AB 2190) Effective January 1, 2015.)

1603.

(a) Before any person subject to subdivision (a) of Section 1601 may be placed on outpatient status the court shall consider all of the following criteria:

(1) Whether the director of the state hospital or other treatment facility to which the person has been committed advises the committing court and the prosecutor that the defendant would no longer be a danger to the health and safety of others, including himself or herself, while under supervision and treatment in the community, and will benefit from that status.

(2) Whether the community program director advises the court that the defendant will benefit from that status, and identifies an appropriate program of supervision and treatment.

(b) (1) Prior to release of a person under subdivision (a), the prosecutor shall provide notice of the hearing date and pending release to the victim or next of kin of the victim of the offense for which the person was committed where a request for the notice has been filed with the court, and after a hearing in court, the court shall specifically approve the recommendation and plan for outpatient status pursuant to Section 1604. The burden shall be on the victim or next of kin to the victim to keep the court apprised of the party's current mailing address.

(2) In any case in which the victim or next of kin to the victim has filed a request for notice with the director of the state hospital or other treatment facility, he or she shall be notified by the director at the inception of any program in which the committed person would be allowed any type of day release unattended by the staff of the facility.

(c) The community program director shall prepare and submit the evaluation and the treatment plan specified in paragraph (2) of subdivision (a) to the court within 30 calendar days after notification by the court to do so.

(d) Any evaluations and recommendations pursuant to paragraphs (1) and (2) of subdivision (a) shall include review and consideration of complete, available information regarding the circumstances of the criminal offense and the person's prior criminal history.

(Amended by Stats. 2014, Ch. 734, Sec. 3. (AB 2190) Effective January 1, 2015.)

1604.

(a) Upon receipt by the committing court of the recommendation of the director of the state hospital or other treatment facility to which the person has been committed that the person may be eligible for outpatient status as set forth in subdivision (a)(1) of Section 1602 or 1603, the court shall immediately forward such recommendation to the community program director, prosecutor, and defense counsel. The court shall provide copies of the arrest reports and the state summary criminal history information to the community program director.

(b) Within 30 calendar days the community program director or a designee shall submit to the court and, when appropriate, to the director of the state hospital or other treatment facility, a recommendation regarding the defendant's eligibility for outpatient status, as set forth in subdivision (a)(2) of Section 1602 or 1603 and the recommended plan for outpatient supervision and treatment. The plan shall set forth specific terms and conditions to be followed during outpatient status. The court shall provide copies of this report to the prosecutor and the defense counsel.

(c) The court shall calendar the matter for hearing within 15 judicial days of the receipt of the community program director's report and shall give notice of the hearing date to the prosecutor, defense counsel, the community program director, and, when appropriate, to the director of the state hospital or other facility. In any hearing conducted pursuant to this section, the court shall consider the circumstances and nature of the criminal offense leading to commitment and shall consider the person's prior criminal history.

(d) The court shall, after a hearing in court, either approve or disapprove the recommendation for outpatient status. If the approval of the court is given, the defendant shall be placed on outpatient status subject to the terms and conditions specified in the supervision and treatment plan. If the outpatient treatment occurs in a county other than the county of commitment, the court shall transmit a copy of the case record to the superior court in the county where outpatient treatment occurs, so that the record will be available if revocation proceedings are initiated pursuant to Section 1608 or 1609.

(Amended by Stats. 1985, Ch. 1232, Sec. 14. Effective September 30, 1985.)

1605.

(a) In accordance with Section 1615 of this code and Section 5709.8 of the Welfare and Institutions Code, the State Department of State Hospitals shall be responsible for the supervision of persons placed on outpatient status under this title. The State Department of State Hospitals shall designate, for each county or region comprised of two or more counties, a community program director who shall be responsible for administering the community treatment programs for persons committed from that county or region under the provisions specified in Section 1600.

(b) The State Department of State Hospitals shall notify in writing the superior court, the district attorney, the county public defender or public defense agency, and the county mental health director of each county as to the person designated to be the community program director for that county, and timely written notice shall be given whenever a new community program director is to be designated.

(c) The community program director shall be the outpatient treatment supervisor of persons placed on outpatient status under this title. The community program director may delegate the outpatient treatment supervision responsibility to a designee.

(d) The outpatient treatment supervisor shall, at 90-day intervals following the beginning of outpatient treatment, submit to the court, the prosecutor and defense counsel, and to the community program director, where appropriate, a report setting forth the status and progress of the defendant.

(Amended by Stats. 2012, Ch. 24, Sec. 30. (AB 1470) Effective June 27, 2012.)

1606.

Outpatient status shall be for a period not to exceed one year. At the end of the period of outpatient status approved by the court, the court shall, after actual notice to the prosecutor, the defense counsel, and the community program director, and after a hearing in court, either discharge the person from commitment under appropriate provisions of the law, order the person confined to a treatment facility, or renew its approval of outpatient status. Prior to such hearing, the community program director shall furnish a report and recommendation to the medical director of the state hospital, where appropriate, and to the court, which the court shall make available to the prosecutor and defense counsel. The person shall remain on outpatient status until the court renders its decision unless hospitalized under other provision of the law. The hearing pursuant to the provisions of this section shall be held no later than 30 days after the end of the one-year period of outpatient status unless good cause exists. The court shall transmit a copy of its order to the community program director or a designee.

(Amended by Stats. 1985, Ch. 1232, Sec. 16. Effective September 30, 1985.)

1607.

If the outpatient supervisor is of the opinion that the person has regained competence to stand trial, or is no longer insane, is no longer a mentally disordered offender, or is no longer a mentally disordered sex offender, the community program director shall submit his or her opinion to the medical director of the state hospital, where appropriate, and to the court which shall calendar the case for further proceedings under the provisions of Section 1372, 1026.2, or 2972 of this code or Section 6325 of the Welfare and Institutions Code.

(Amended by Stats. 2000, Ch. 324, Sec. 2. Effective January 1, 2001.)

1608.

If at any time during the outpatient period, the outpatient treatment supervisor is of the opinion that the person requires extended inpatient treatment or refuses to accept further outpatient treatment and supervision, the community program director shall notify the superior court in either the county which approved outpatient status or in the county where outpatient treatment is being provided of such opinion by means of a written request for revocation of outpatient status. The community program director shall furnish a copy of this request to the defense counsel and to the prosecutor in both counties if the request is made in the county of treatment rather than the county of commitment.

Within 15 judicial days, the court where the request was filed shall hold a hearing and shall either approve or disapprove the request for revocation of outpatient status. If the court approves the request for revocation, the court shall order that the person be confined in a state hospital or other treatment facility approved by the community program director. The court shall transmit a copy of its order to the community program director or a designee. Where the county of treatment and the county of commitment differ and revocation occurs in the county of treatment, the court shall enter the name of the committing county and its case number on the order of revocation and shall send a copy of the order to the committing court and the prosecutor and defense counsel in the county of commitment.

(Amended by Stats. 1985, Ch. 1232, Sec. 18. Effective September 30, 1985.)

1609.

If at any time during the outpatient period or placement with a local mental health program pursuant to subdivision (b) of Section 1026.2 the prosecutor is of the opinion that the person is a danger to the health and safety of others while on that status, the prosecutor may petition the court for a hearing to determine whether the person shall be continued on that status. Upon receipt of the petition, the court shall calendar the case for further proceedings within 15 judicial days and the clerk shall notify the person, the community program director, and the attorney of record for the person of the hearing date. Upon failure of the person to appear as noticed, if a proper affidavit of service and advisement has been filed with the court, the court may issue a body attachment for such person. If, after a hearing in court conducted using the same standards used in conducting probation revocation hearings pursuant to Section 1203.2, the judge determines that the person is a danger to the health and safety of others, the court shall order that the person be confined in a state hospital or other treatment facility which has been approved by the community program director.

(Amended by Stats. 1985, Ch. 1232, Sec. 19. Effective September 30, 1985.)

1610.

(a) Upon the filing of a request for revocation under Section 1608 or 1609 and pending the court's decision on revocation, the person subject to revocation may be confined in a facility designated by the community program director when it is the opinion of that director that the person will now be a danger to self or to another while on outpatient status and that to delay confinement until the revocation hearing would pose an imminent risk of harm to the person or to another. The facility so designated shall continue the patient's program of treatment, shall provide adequate security so as to ensure both the safety of the person and the safety of others in the facility, and shall, to the extent possible, minimize interference with the person's program of treatment. Upon the request of the community program director or a designee, a peace officer shall take, or cause to be taken, the person into custody and transport the person to a facility designated by the community program director for confinement under this section. Within one judicial day after the person is confined in a jail under this section, the community program director shall apply in writing to the court for authorization to confine the person pending the hearing under Section 1608 or Section 1609 or subdivision (c). The application shall be in the form of a declaration, and shall specify the behavior or other reason justifying the confinement of the person in a jail. Upon receipt of the application for confinement, the court shall consider and rule upon it, and if the court authorizes detention in a jail, the court shall actually serve copies of all orders and all documents filed by the community program director upon the prosecuting and defense counsel. The community program director shall notify the court in writing of the confinement of the person and of the factual basis for the opinion that the immediate confinement in a jail was necessary. The court shall supply a copy of these documents to the prosecutor and defense counsel.

(b) The facility designated by the community program director may be a state hospital, a local treatment facility, a county jail, or any other appropriate facility, so long as the facility can continue the person's program of treatment, provide adequate security, and minimize interference with the person's program of treatment. If the facility designated by the community program director is a county jail, the patient shall be separated from the general population of the jail. In the case of a sexually violent predator, as defined in Section 6600 of the Welfare and Institutions Code, who is held pending civil process under the sexually violent predator laws, the person may be housed as provided by Section 4002. The designated facility need not be approved for 72-hour treatment and evaluation pursuant to the provisions of the Lanterman-Petris-Short Act (Part 1 (commencing with Section 5000) of Division 5 of the Welfare and Institutions Code); however, a county jail may not be designated unless the services specified above are provided, and accommodations are provided which ensure both the safety of the person and the safety of the general population of the jail. Within three judicial days of the patient's confinement in a jail, the community program director shall report to the court regarding what type of treatment the patient is receiving in the facility. If there is evidence that the treatment program is not being complied with, or accommodations have not been provided which ensure both the safety of the committed person and the safety of the general population of the jail, the court shall order the person transferred to an appropriate facility, including an appropriate state hospital. Nothing in this subdivision shall be construed as authorizing jail facilities to operate as health facilities, as defined in Section 1250 of the Health and Safety Code, without complying with applicable requirements of law.

(c) A person confined under this section shall have the right to judicial review of his or her confinement in a jail under this section in a manner similar to that which is prescribed in Article 5 (commencing with Section 5275) of Chapter 2 of Part 1 of Division 5 of the Welfare and Institutions Code and to an explanation of rights in the manner prescribed in Section 5325 of the Welfare and Institutions Code. Nothing in this section shall prevent hospitalization pursuant to the provisions of Section 5150, 5250, 5350, or 5353 of the Welfare and Institutions Code.

(d) A person whose confinement in a treatment facility under Section 1608 or 1609 is approved by the court shall not be released again to outpatient status unless court approval is obtained under Section 1602 or 1603.

(Amended by Stats. 2001, Ch. 248, Sec. 1. Effective January 1, 2002.)

1611.

(a) No person who is on outpatient status pursuant to this title or Section 2972 shall leave this state without first obtaining prior written approval to do so from the committing court. The prior written approval of the court for the person to leave this state shall specify when the person may leave, when the person is required to return, and may specify other conditions or limitations at the discretion of the court. The written approval for the person to leave this state may be in a form and format chosen by the committing court.

In no event shall the court give written approval for the person to leave this state without providing notice to the prosecutor, the defense counsel, and the community program director. The court may conduct a hearing on the question of whether the person should be allowed to leave this state and what conditions or limitations, if any, should be imposed.

(b) Any person who violates subdivision (a) is guilty of a misdemeanor.

(Added by Stats. 1988, Ch. 74, Sec. 2.)

1612.

Any person committed to a state hospital or other treatment facility under the provisions of Section 1026, or Chapter 6 (commencing with Section 1367) of Title 10 of this code, or former Section 6316 or 6321 of the Welfare and Institutions Code shall not be released therefrom except as expressly provided in this title or Section 1026.2.

(Amended by Stats. 1984, Ch. 1488, Sec. 13.)

1614.

Persons ordered to undergo outpatient treatment under former Sections 1026.1 and 1374 of the Penal Code and subdivision (a) of Section 6325.1 of the Welfare and Institutions Code shall, on January 1, 1981, be considered as being on outpatient status under this title and this title shall apply to such persons.

(Added by Stats. 1980, Ch. 547, Sec. 17.)

1615.

Pursuant to Section 5709.8 of the Welfare and Institutions Code, the State Department of State Hospitals shall be responsible for the community treatment and supervision of judicially committed patients. These services shall be available on a county or regional basis. The department may provide these services directly or through contract with private providers or counties. The program or programs through which these services are provided shall be known as the Forensic Conditional Release Program.

The department shall contact all county mental health programs by January 1, 1986, to determine their interest in providing an appropriate level of supervision and treatment of judicially committed patients at reasonable cost. County mental health agencies may agree or refuse to operate such a program.

The State Department of State Hospitals shall ensure consistent data gathering and program standards for use statewide by the Forensic Conditional Release Program.

(Amended by Stats. 2012, Ch. 24, Sec. 31. (AB 1470) Effective June 27, 2012.)

1616.

The state shall contract with a research agency which shall determine the prevalence of severe mental disorder among the state prison inmates and parolees, including persons admitted to prison, the resident population, and those discharged to parole. An evaluation of the array of services shall be performed, including the correctional, state hospital, and local inpatient programs; residential-level care and partial day care within the institutions as well as in the community; and the individual and group treatment which may be provided within the correctional setting and in the community upon release. The review shall include the interrelationship between the security and clinical staff, as well as the architectural design which aids meeting the treatment needs of these mentally ill offenders while maintaining a secure setting. Administration of these programs within the institutions and in the community shall be reviewed by the contracting agency. The ability of treatment programs to prevent reoffenses by inmates with severe mental disorders shall also be addressed. The process for evaluating inmates and parolees to determine their need for treatment and the ability to differentiate those who will benefit from treatment and those who will not shall be reviewed.

The State Department of State Hospitals, the Department of Corrections and Rehabilitation, and the Department of Justice shall cooperate with the research agency conducting this study.

The research agency conducting this study shall consult with the State Department of State Hospitals, the Department of Corrections and Rehabilitation, the Department of Justice, and the Forensic Mental Health Association of California in the design of the study.

(Amended by Stats. 2012, Ch. 24, Sec. 32. (AB 1470) Effective June 27, 2012.)

1617.

The State Department of State Hospitals shall research the demographic profiles and other related information pertaining to persons receiving supervision and treatment in the Forensic Conditional Release Program. An evaluation of the program shall determine its effectiveness in successfully reintegrating these persons into society after release from state institutions. This evaluation of program effectiveness shall include, but not be limited to, a determination of the rates of reoffense while these persons are served by the program and after their discharge. This evaluation shall also address the effectiveness of the various treatment components of the program and their intensity. The State Department of State Hospitals may contract with an independent research agency to perform this research and evaluation project. Any independent research agency conducting this research shall consult with the Forensic Mental Health Association concerning the development of the research and evaluation design.

(Amended by Stats. 2012, Ch. 24, Sec. 33. (AB 1470) Effective June 27, 2012.)

1618.

The administrators and the supervision and treatment staff of the Forensic Conditional Release Program shall not be held criminally or civilly liable for any criminal acts committed by the persons on parole or judicial commitment status who receive supervision or treatment. This waiver of liability shall apply to employees of the State Department of State Hospitals, the Board of Parole Hearings, and the agencies or persons under contract to those agencies, who provide screening, clinical evaluation, supervision, or treatment to mentally ill parolees or persons under judicial commitment or considered for placement under a hold by the Board of Parole Hearings.

(Amended by Stats. 2012, Ch. 24, Sec. 34. (AB 1470) Effective June 27, 2012.)

1619.

The Department of Justice shall automate the criminal histories of all persons treated in the Forensic Conditional Release Program, as well as all persons committed as not guilty by reason of insanity pursuant to Section 1026, incompetent to stand trial pursuant to Section 1370 or 1370.2, any person currently under commitment as a mentally disordered sex offender, and persons treated pursuant to Section 1364 or 2684 or Article 4 (commencing with Section 2960) of Chapter 7 of Title 1 of Part 3.

(Amended by Stats. 1988, Ch. 37, Sec. 4.)

1620.

The Department of Justice shall provide mental health agencies providing treatment to patients pursuant to Sections 1600 to 1610, inclusive, or pursuant to Article 4 (commencing with Section 2960) of Chapter 7 of Title 1 of Part 3, with access to criminal histories of those mentally ill offenders who are receiving treatment and supervision. Treatment and supervision staff who have access to these criminal histories shall maintain the confidentiality of the information and shall sign a statement to be developed by the Department of Justice which informs them of this obligation.

(Amended by Stats. 1987, Ch. 687, Sec. 6.)

PART 3. OF IMPRISONMENT AND THE DEATH PENALTY [2000 - 10007]

(Part 3 repealed and added by Stats. 1941, Ch. 106.)

TITLE 1. IMPRISONMENT OF MALE PRISONERS IN STATE PRISONS [2000 - 3105]

(Title 1 repealed and added by Stats. 1941, Ch. 106.)

CHAPTER 1. Establishment of State Prisons [2000 - 2048.6]

(Chapter 1 added by Stats. 1941, Ch. 106.)

ARTICLE 1. California Institution for Men [2000 - 2002]
(Heading of Article 1 amended by Stats. 1941, Ch. 1192.)

2000.
There is and shall continue to be a State prison to be known as the California Institution for Men.
(Amended by Stats. 1941, Ch. 1192.)

2001.
The California Institution for Men shall be located at Chino, San Bernardino County, California.
(Amended by Stats. 1941, Ch. 1192.)

2002.
The primary purpose of the California Institution for Men shall be for the imprisonment of male offenders who, in the opinion of the department, seem capable of moral rehabilitation and restoration to good citizenship.
(Added by renumbering Section 2008 by Stats. 1957, Ch. 2256.)

ARTICLE 2. California State Prison at San Quentin [2020 - 2022]
(Article 2 added by Stats. 1941, Ch. 106.)

2020.
There is and shall continue to be a State prison to be known as the California State Prison at San Quentin.
(Added by Stats. 1941, Ch. 106.)

2021.
The California State Prison at San Quentin shall be located at San Quentin, in Marin County, California.
(Added by Stats. 1941, Ch. 106.)

2022.
The primary purpose of the California State Prison at San Quentin shall be to provide confinement, industrial and other training, treatment, and care to persons confined therein.
(Amended by Stats. 1965, Ch. 343.)

ARTICLE 3. California State Prison at Folsom [2030 - 2032]
(Article 3 added by Stats. 1941, Ch. 106.)

2030.
There is and shall continue to be a State prison to be known as the California State Prison at Folsom.
(Added by Stats. 1941, Ch. 106.)

2031.
The California State Prison at Folsom shall be located at Folsom, in Sacramento County, California.
(Added by Stats. 1941, Ch. 106.)

2032.
The primary purpose of the California State Prison at Folsom shall be to provide confinement, industrial and other training, treatment, and care to persons confined therein.
(Amended by Stats. 1965, Ch. 343.)

ARTICLE 4. The Deuel Vocational Institution [2035 - 2042]
(Heading of Article 4 amended by Stats. 1951, Ch. 1663.)

2035.
There is hereby established an institution for the confinement of males under the custody of the Director of Corrections and the Youth Authority to be known as the Deuel Vocational Institution.
(Amended by Stats. 1951, Ch. 1663.)

2037.
There may be transferred to and confined in the Deuel Vocational Institution any male, subject to the custody, control and discipline of the Director of Corrections, or any male, subject to the custody, control and discipline of the Youth Authority who has been committed to the Youth Authority under the provisions of Section 1731.5 of the Welfare and Institutions Code, who the Director of Corrections or Youth Authority, as the case may be, believes will be benefited by confinement in such an institution.
(Amended by Stats. 1987, Ch. 828, Sec. 107.)

2039.
The Governor, upon recommendation of the Director of Corrections, in accordance with Section 6050, shall appoint a warden for the Deuel Vocational Institution. The director shall appoint, subject to civil service, those other officers and employees as may be necessary.
The Director of Corrections may remove a warden at his or her own discretion at any time.
(Amended by Stats. 1992, Ch. 1279, Sec. 2. Effective January 1, 1993.)

2040.
The Director of Corrections shall construct and equip, in accordance with law, suitable buildings, structures, and facilities for the Deuel Vocational Institution.
(Amended by Stats. 1951, Ch. 1663.)

2041.
Part 3 (commencing with Section 2000) shall apply to the Deuel Vocational Institution and to the persons confined therein so far as those provisions may be applicable. Whenever the name California Vocational Institution appears in any statute, it shall be deemed for all purposes to refer to the Deuel Vocational Institution.
(Amended by Stats. 1987, Ch. 828, Sec. 108.)

2042.
Every minor person confined in the Deuel Vocational Institute who escapes or attempts to escape therefrom is guilty of a crime and shall be imprisoned in a state prison, or in the county jail for not exceeding one year.
(Amended by Stats. 1982, Ch. 1104, Sec. 1.)

ARTICLE 4.5. California Correctional Center [2043 - 2043.5]
(Article 4.5 added by Stats. 1977, Ch. 909.)

2043.
The Director of Corrections is authorized to establish a state prison for the confinement of males under the custody of the Director of Corrections to be known as the California Correctional Center at Susanville.
(Added by Stats. 1977, Ch. 909.)

2043.1.
The primary purpose of the state prison authorized to be established by Section 2043 shall be to provide custody and care, and industrial, vocational, and other training to persons confined therein.
(Added by Stats. 1977, Ch. 909.)

2043.2.
Any person under the custody of the Director of Corrections may be transferred to the California Correctional Center at Susanville in accordance with law.
(Added by Stats. 1977, Ch. 909.)

2043.4.
The warden of the California Correctional Center at Susanville shall be appointed pursuant to Section 6050 and the Director of Corrections shall appoint, subject to civil service, those other officials and employees as may be necessary.
(Amended by Stats. 1989, Ch. 1420, Sec. 4.)

2043.5.
Part 3 (commencing with Section 2000) shall apply to the California Correctional Center at Susanville and to the persons confined therein, insofar as those provisions may be applicable.
(Amended by Stats. 1987, Ch. 828, Sec. 109.)

ARTICLE 5. Correctional Training Facility [2045 - 2045.6]
(Heading of Article 5 amended by Stats. 1959, Ch. 936.)

2045.
The Director of Corrections with the approval of the Board of Corrections, is authorized to establish a State prison for the confinement of males under the custody of the Director of Corrections.
(Added by Stats. 1945, Ch. 75.)

2045.1.
The prison authorized to be established by Section 2045 shall be a medium security type institution. Its primary purpose shall be to provide custody, care, industrial, vocational, and other training to persons confined therein. However, the Director of Corrections may designate a portion or all of the prison to serve the same purposes and to have the same security standards as the institution provided for by Article 4 (commencing at Section 2035) of Chapter 1 of Title 1 of Part 3.
(Amended by Stats. 1987, Ch. 828, Sec. 110.)

2045.4.
The Governor, upon recommendation of the Director of Corrections, in accordance with Section 6050, shall appoint a warden for the California Training Facility. The director shall appoint, subject to civil service, those other officers and employees as may be necessary.
The Director of Corrections may remove a warden at his or her own discretion at any time.
(Amended by Stats. 1992, Ch. 1279, Sec. 3. Effective January 1, 1993.)

2045.5.
The Director of Corrections shall construct and equip in accordance with law, suitable buildings, structures and facilities for said institution.
(Added by Stats. 1945, Ch. 75.)

2045.6.
The provisions of Part 3 (commencing with Section 2000) apply to the institution and to the persons confined therein insofar as those provisions may be applicable.
(Amended by Stats. 1987, Ch. 828, Sec. 111.)

ARTICLE 5.5. California Correctional Institution in Monterey County [2045.10 - 2045.11]
(Article 5.5 added by Stats. 1992, Ch. 695, Sec. 11.)

2045.10.
The Director of Corrections is authorized to construct and establish a state prison for the confinement of males under the custody of the Director of Corrections.
(Added by Stats. 1992, Ch. 695, Sec. 11. Effective September 15, 1992.)

2045.11.
The facility authorized by Section 2045.10 shall be a combination 1,000-bed Level III and 1,000-bed Level IV prison together with a 200-bed Level I support services facility on the existing grounds of the Correctional Training Facility in Monterey County. The provisions of Division 13 (commencing with Section 21000) of the Public Resources Code that require consideration of alternatives for a proposed project shall not apply to the project authorized by Section 2045.10.
(Added by Stats. 1992, Ch. 695, Sec. 11. Effective September 15, 1992.)

ARTICLE 6. California Men's Colony [2046 - 2046.6]
(Heading of Article 6 amended by Stats. 1969, Ch. 421.)

2046.
The Director of Corrections is authorized to establish a state prison for the confinement of males under the custody of the Director of Corrections. It shall be a medium security institution and shall be known as the California Men's Colony.
(Amended by Stats. 1969, Ch. 421.)

2046.1.
The prison authorized to be established by Section 2046 shall be a medium security type institution. Its primary purpose shall be to provide custody, care, industrial, vocational, and other training to persons confined therein.
(Amended by Stats. 1987, Ch. 828, Sec. 112.)

2046.2.
Any person under the custody of the Director of Corrections may be transferred to the said prison in accordance with law.
(Added by Stats. 1949, Ch. 892.)

2046.4.
A warden for the said prison shall be appointed pursuant to Section 6050, and the Director of Corrections shall apoint, subject to civil service, such other officials and employees as may be necessary therefor, and shall fix their compensation.
(Added by Stats. 1949, Ch. 892.)

2046.5.
The Director of Corrections shall construct and equip in accordance with law, suitable buildings, structures, and facilities for the said prison.
(Added by Stats. 1949, Ch. 892.)

2046.6.
The provisions of this part shall apply to the prison and to the persons confined therein insofar as those provisions may be applicable.
(Amended by Stats. 1988, Ch. 160, Sec. 135.)

ARTICLE 7. California Correctional Institution at Tehachapi [2048 - 2048.6]
(Article 7 added by Stats. 1959, Ch. 1451.)

2048.
The Director of Corrections is authorized to establish a state prison for the confinement of males under the custody of the Director of Corrections, to be known as the California Correctional Institution at Tehachapi. The California Correctional Institution at Tehachapi shall be situated on such state land as is, as of the effective date of this article, the site of the Tehachapi Branch, California Institution for Men.
(Added by Stats. 1959, Ch. 1451.)

2048.1.
The primary purpose of the prison authorized to be established by Section 2048 shall be to provide custody and care, and industrial, vocational, and other training to persons confined therein.
(Added by Stats. 1959, Ch. 1451.)
2048.2.
Any person under the custody of the Director of Corrections may be transferred to the California Correctional Institution at Tehachapi in accordance with law.
(Added by Stats. 1959, Ch. 1451.)
2048.4.
The warden for the California Correctional Institution at Tehachapi shall be appointed pursuant to Section 6050, and the Director of Corrections shall appoint, subject to civil service, those other officers and employees as may be necessary.
The Director of Corrections may remove a warden at his or her own discretion at any time.
(Amended by Stats. 1992, Ch. 1279, Sec. 4. Effective January 1, 1993.)
2048.5.
The Director of Corrections shall construct and equip, in accordance with law, suitable buildings, structures, and facilities for the California Correctional Institution at Tehachapi.
(Added by Stats. 1959, Ch. 1451.)
2048.6.
The provisions of Part 3 (commencing with Section 2000) apply to the California Correctional Institution at Tehachapi and to the persons confined therein insofar as those provisions may be applicable.
(Amended by Stats. 1987, Ch. 828, Sec. 114.)

CHAPTER 2. Administration of State Prisons [2051 - 2541]

(Chapter 2 added by Stats. 1941, Ch. 106.)

ARTICLE 1. Miscellaneous Powers and Duties of Department and Director of Corrections [2051 - 2067]
(Heading of Article 1 amended by Stats. 1957, Ch. 2256.)
2051.
The department is hereby authorized to contract for provisions, clothing, medicines, forage, fuel, and all other staple supplies needed for the support of the prisons for any period of time, not exceeding one year, and such contracts shall be limited to bona fide dealers in the several classes of articles contracted for. Contracts for such articles as the department may desire to contract for, shall be given to the lowest bidder at a public letting thereof, if the price bid is a fair and reasonable one, and not greater than the usual value and prices.
Each bid shall be accompanied by such security as the department may require, conditional upon the bidder entering into a contract upon the terms of his bid, on notice of the acceptance thereof, and furnishing a penal bond with good and sufficient sureties in such sum as the department may require, and to its satisfaction that he will faithfully perform his contract.
If the proper officer of the prison reject any article, as not complying with the contract, or if a bidder fail to furnish the articles awarded to him when required, the proper officer of the prison may buy other articles of the kind rejected or called for, in the open market, and deduct the price thereof, over the contract price, from the amount due to the bidder, or charge the same up against him.
Notice of the time, place, and conditions of the letting of contracts shall be given for at least two consecutive weeks in two newspapers printed and published in the City and County of San Francisco, and in one newspaper printed and published in the County of Sacramento, and in the county where the prison to be supplied is situated.
If all the bids made at such letting are deemed unreasonably high, the department may, in its discretion, decline to contract and may again advertise for such time and in such papers as it sees proper for proposals, and may so continue to renew the advertisement until satisfactory contracts are made; and in the meantime the department may contract with anyone whose offer is regarded as just and equitable, or may purchase in the open market.
No bids shall be accepted, nor a contract entered into in pursuance thereof, when such bid is higher than any other bid at the same letting for the same class or schedule of articles, quality considered, and when a contract can be had at such lower bid.
When two or more bids for the same article or articles are equal in amount, the department may select the one which, all things considered, may by it be thought best for the interest of the State, or it may divide the contract between the bidders as in its judgment may seem proper and right.
The department shall have power to let a contract in the aggregate or they may segregate the items, and enter into a contract with the bidder or bidders who may bid lowest on the several articles.
The department shall have the power to reject the bid of any person who had a prior contract and who had not, in the opinion of the department, faithfully complied therewith.
(Amended by Stats. 1957, Ch. 2256.)
2052.
(a) The department shall have power to contract for the supply of electricity, gas and water for said prisons, upon such terms as the department shall deem to be for the best interests of the state, or to manufacture gas or electricity, or furnish water itself, at its option. It shall also have power to erect and construct or cause to be erected and constructed, electrical apparatus or other illuminating works in its discretion with or without contracting therefor, on such terms as it may deem just. The department shall have full power to erect any building or structure deemed necessary by it, or to alter or improve the same, and to pay for the same from the fund appropriated for the use or support of the prisons, or from the earnings thereof, without advertising or contracting therefor.
(b) With respect to any facility under the jurisdiction of the Prison Industry Authority, the Prison Industry Authority shall have the same powers which are vested in the department pursuant to subdivision (a).
(Amended by Stats. 1983, Ch. 669, Sec. 1.)
2053.
(a) The Legislature finds and declares that there is a correlation between prisoners who are functionally literate and those who successfully reintegrate into society upon release. It is therefore the intent of the Legislature, in enacting "The Prisoner Literacy Act," to raise the percentage of prisoners who are functionally literate, in order to provide for a corresponding reduction in the recidivism rate.
(b) The Department of Corrections shall determine the reading level of each prisoner upon commitment.
(Amended by Stats. 2004, Ch. 193, Sec. 144. Effective January 1, 2005.)
2053.1.
(a) The Secretary of the Department of Corrections and Rehabilitation shall implement in every state prison literacy programs that are designed to ensure that upon parole inmates are able to achieve the goals contained in this section. The department shall prepare an implementation plan for this program, and shall request the necessary funds to implement this program as follows:

(1) The department shall offer academic programming throughout an inmate's incarceration that shall focus on increasing the reading ability of an inmate to at least a 9th grade level.
(2) For an inmate reading at a 9th grade level or higher, the department shall focus on helping the inmate obtain a general education development certificate, or its equivalent, or a high school diploma.
(3) The department shall offer college programs through voluntary education programs or their equivalent.
(4) While the department shall offer education to target populations, priority shall be given to those with a criminogenic need for education, those who have a need based on their educational achievement level, or other factors as determined by the department.
(b) In complying with the requirements of this section, the department shall give strong consideration to the use of libraries and librarians, computer-assisted training, and other innovations that have proven to be effective in reducing illiteracy among disadvantaged adults.
(Amended by Stats. 2015, Ch. 798, Sec. 1. (SB 343) Effective January 1, 2016.)
2053.4.
The Secretary of the Department of Corrections and Rehabilitation shall appoint a Superintendent of Correctional Education, who shall oversee and administer all prison education programs. The Superintendent of Correctional Education shall set both short- and long-term goals for inmate literacy and testing and career technical education programs, and shall establish priorities for prison academic and career technical education programs.
(Amended by Stats. 2013, Ch. 789, Sec. 2. (AB 1019) Effective January 1, 2014.)
2053.5.
Consistent with the goals and priorities of the department, a career technical education program shall consider all of the following factors:
(a) Whether the program aligns with the workforce needs of high-demand sectors of the state and regional economies.
(b) Whether there is an active job market for the skills being developed where the inmate will likely be released.
(c) Whether the program increases the number of inmates who obtain a marketable and industry or apprenticeship board-recognized certification, credential, or degree.
(d) Whether there are formal or informal networks in the field that support finding employment upon release from prison.
(e) Whether the program will lead to employment in occupations with a livable wage.
(Added by Stats. 2013, Ch. 789, Sec. 3. (AB 1019) Effective January 1, 2014.)
2054.
(a) The Secretary of the Department of Corrections and Rehabilitation may establish and maintain classes for inmates by utilizing personnel of the Department of Corrections and Rehabilitation, or by entering into an agreement with the governing board of a school district or private school or the governing boards of school districts under which the district shall maintain classes for such inmates. The governing board of a school district or private school may enter into such an agreement regardless of whether the institution or facility at which the classes are to be established and maintained is within or without the boundaries of the school district.
(b) Any agreement entered into between the Secretary of the Department of Corrections and Rehabilitation and a school district or private school pursuant to this section may require the Department of Corrections and Rehabilitation to reimburse the school district or private school for the cost to the district or private school of maintaining such classes. "Cost" as used in this section includes contributions required of any school district to the State Teachers' Retirement System, but such cost shall not include an amount in excess of the amount expended by the district for salaries of the teachers for such classes, increased by one-fifth. Salaries of such teachers for the purposes of this section shall not exceed the salaries as set by the governing board for teachers in other classes for adults maintained by the district, or private schools.
(c) Attendance or average daily attendance in classes established pursuant to this section or in classes in trade and industrial education or vocational training for adult inmates of institutions or facilities under the jurisdiction of the Department of Corrections and Rehabilitation shall not be reported to the State Department of Education for apportionment and no apportionment from the State School Fund shall be made on account of average daily attendance in such classes.
(d) No school district or private school shall provide for the academic education of adult inmates of state institutions or facilities under the jurisdiction of the Department of Corrections and Rehabilitation except in accordance with this section.
(Amended by Stats. 2015, Ch. 798, Sec. 2. (SB 343) Effective January 1, 2016.)
2054.2.
The Department of Corrections and Rehabilitation shall determine and implement a system of incentives to increase inmate participation in, and completion of, academic and vocational education, consistent with the inmate's educational needs as identified in the assessment performed pursuant to Section 3020, including, but not limited to, a literacy level specified in Section 2053.1, a high school diploma or equivalent, completion of a community college or four-year academic degree, or a particular vocational job skill. These incentives may be consistent with other incentives provided to inmates who participate in work programs.
(Amended by Stats. 2015, Ch. 798, Sec. 4. (SB 343) Effective January 1, 2016.)
2055.
The Director of Corrections may, in his discretion, from time to time insure any or all products produced at any prison or institution under the jurisdiction of the Director of Corrections, whether the products are finished or unfinished, the materials from which such products are made or to be made, and the equipment necessary for the production thereof, against any or all risks of loss, wherever such products, materials, or equipment are located, while in the possession of the Department of Corrections and while in transit thereto or therefrom or in storage, in such amounts as the director deems proper. The cost of such insurance shall be paid from the Correctional Industries Revolving Fund.
(Amended by Stats. 1949, Ch. 887.)
2056.
If any of the shops or buildings in which convicts are employed require rebuilding or repair for any reason, they may be rebuilt or repaired immediately, under the direction of the Prison Industry Authority.
(Amended by Stats. 1983, Ch. 669, Sec. 2.)
2057.
Counties are authorized to contract with the Department of Corrections and Rehabilitation for the commitment to the department, of persons who have suffered a felony conviction. An offender sentenced to a county jail that serves his or her sentence in the state prison pursuant to this section shall be required to comply with the rules and regulations of the department consistent with Division 3 of Title 15 of the California Code of Regulations.
(Amended (as added by Stats. 2011, Ch. 15) by Stats. 2011, Ch. 39, Sec. 34. (AB 117) Effective June 30, 2011. Addition and amendment operative October 1, 2011, pursuant to Secs. 68 and 69 of Ch. 39.)
2059.
The department shall fix the compensation of its officers and employees, other than those of wardens and clerks, at a gross rate which shall include a cash allowance for board and lodging, but in no case shall the money compensation, exclusive of the cash allowance for board and lodging, be less than one hundred ten dollars ($110) per month. There shall be deducted from the gross salaries of the officers and employees of the prison the value of any board, lodging, services or supplies rendered or sold to each

such officer or employee. The deduction for board and lodging shall not exceed the cash allowance therefor.
(Amended by Stats. 1957, Ch. 2256.)

2060.
For the purposes of Sections 11009 and 11030 of the Government Code, the following constitute, among other proper purposes, state business for officers and employees of the department for which such officers and employees shall be allowed actual and necessary traveling expenses when the state travel and expense have been approved by the Governor and the Director of Finance as provided in that section.

Attending meetings of any national association or organization, having as its principal purpose the study of matters relating to penology, including prison management and paroles, or to a particular field thereof, conferring with officers or employees of the United States relative to problems relating to penology, including prison management and paroles, in California, conferring with officers or employees of other states engaged in the performance of similar duties, and obtaining information useful to the department in the conduct of its work.
(Amended by Stats. 1987, Ch. 828, Sec. 116.)

2061.
(a) The Department of Corrections and Rehabilitation shall develop and implement, by January 15, 2008, a plan to address management deficiencies within the department. The plan should, at a minimum, address all of the following:
(1) Filling vacancies in management positions within the department.
(2) Improving lines of accountability within the department.
(3) Standardizing processes to improve management.
(4) Improving communication within headquarters, between headquarters, institutions and parole offices, and between institutions and parole offices.
(5) Developing and implementing more comprehensive plans for management of the prison inmate and parole populations.
(b) The department may contract with an outside entity that has expertise in management of complex public and law enforcement organizations to assist in identifying and addressing deficiencies.
(Added by Stats. 2007, Ch. 7, Sec. 7. Effective May 3, 2007.)

2062.
(a) The Department of Corrections and Rehabilitation shall develop and implement a plan to obtain additional rehabilitation and treatment services for prison inmates and parolees. The plan shall include, but is not limited to, all of the following:
(1) Plans to fill vacant state staff positions that provide direct and indirect rehabilitation and treatment services to inmates and parolees.
(2) Plans to fill vacant staff positions that provide custody and supervision services for inmates and parolees.
(3) Plans to obtain from local governments and contractors services for parolees needing treatment while in the community and services that can be brought to inmates within prisons.
(4) Plans to enter into agreements with community colleges to accelerate training and education of rehabilitation and treatment personnel, and modifications to the licensing and certification requirements of state licensing agencies that can accelerate the availability and hiring of rehabilitation and treatment personnel.
(b) The department shall submit the plan and a schedule for implementation of its provisions to the Legislature by January 15, 2008.
(Added by Stats. 2007, Ch. 7, Sec. 8. Effective May 3, 2007.)

2063.
(a) It is the intent of the Legislature that the Department of Corrections and Rehabilitation shall regularly provide operational and fiscal information to the Legislature to allow it to better assess the performance of the department in critical areas of operations, including to both evaluate the effectiveness of department programs and activities, as well as assess how efficiently the department is using state resources.
(b) No later than January 10 of each year, the Department of Corrections and Rehabilitation shall provide to the Joint Legislative Budget Committee operational and fiscal information to be displayed in the Governor's proposed budget. This information shall include data for the three most recently ended fiscal years, and shall include, but is not limited to, the following:
(1) Per capita costs, average daily population, and offender to staff ratios for each of the following:
(A) Adult inmates housed in state prisons.
(B) Adult inmates housed in Community Correctional Facilities and out-of-state facilities.
(C) Adult parolees supervised in the community.
(D) Juvenile wards housed in state facilities.
(E) Juvenile parolees supervised in the community.
(2) Total expenditures and average daily population for each adult and juvenile institution.
(3) Number of established positions and percent of those positions vacant on June 30 for each of the following classifications within the department:
(A) Correctional officer.
(B) Correctional sergeant.
(C) Correctional lieutenant.
(D) Parole agent.
(E) Youth correctional counselor.
(F) Youth correctional officer.
(G) Physician.
(H) Registered nurse.
(I) Psychiatrist.
(J) Psychologist.
(K) Dentist.
(L) Teacher.
(M) Vocational instructor.
(N) Licensed vocational nurse.
(4) Average population of juvenile wards classified by board category.
(5) Average population of adult inmates classified by security level.
(6) Average population of adult parolees classified by supervision level.
(7) Number of new admissions from courts, parole violators with new terms, and parole violators returned to custody.
(8) Number of probable cause hearings, revocation hearings, and parole suitability hearings conducted.
(9) For both adult and juvenile facilities, the number of budgeted slots, actual enrollment, and average daily attendance for institutional academic and vocational education and substance abuse programs.
(10) Average population of mentally ill offenders classified by Correctional Clinical Case Management System or Enhanced Outpatient Program status, as well as information about mentally ill offenders in more acute levels of care.
(c) No later than January 10 of each year, the Department of Corrections and Rehabilitation shall provide to the Joint Legislative Budget Committee a supplemental report containing operational and fiscal information in addition to data provided in subdivision (b). To the extent possible and relevant, the department shall seek to keep the categories of information provided the same each year so as to provide consistency. This report shall contain information for the three most recently ended fiscal years, and shall include, but is not limited to, data on the operational level and outcomes associated with the following categories:
(1) Adult prison security operations, including use of disciplinary measures and special housing assignments such as placements in administrative segregation, Security

Housing Units, and sensitive needs yards, identifying these placements by offender categories such as security level and mental health classification.
(2) Adult prison education and treatment programs, including academic education, vocational training, prison industries, substance abuse treatment, and sex offender treatment.
(3) Adult prison health care operations, including medical, mental, and dental health.
(4) Adult parole operations, including number of discharges from parole supervision and provision of various treatment and sanction programs.
(5) Board of Parole Hearings, including the total number of parole suitability hearings scheduled for inmates serving life sentences each year, the number of parole suitability hearings postponed each year and the reasons for postponement, and the backlog of parole suitability hearings.
(5.1) Board of Parole Hearings, including the total number of adult parole revocation cases with probable cause hearings scheduled each year, the percent of parole revocation cases with probable cause hearings held within 10 business days, as well as the percent of adult parole revocation cases completed within 35 calendar days.
(6) Juvenile institution security operations, including use of disciplinary measures and special housing assignments such as special management programs, as well as the impact of time that adds or cuts the length of confinement.
(7) Juvenile institutional education and treatment programs, including academic education, vocational training, substance abuse treatment, and sex offender treatment.
(8) Juvenile institutional health care operations, including medical, mental, and dental health.
(9) Juvenile parole operations, including the number of juvenile parolees returned to state institutions and provision of various treatment and sanction programs.
(9.1) Juvenile Parole Board, including juvenile parole revocation hearings.
(d) To the extent any of the information in subdivision (b) or (c) falls under the purview of the federally appointed receiver over medical care services, the Department of Corrections and Rehabilitation shall, to the best of its ability, coordinate with the receiver in obtaining this information.
(Added by Stats. 2007, Ch. 175, Sec. 7. Effective August 24, 2007.)

2064.
(a) It is the intent of the Legislature that the Department of Corrections and Rehabilitation shall regularly provide to the Legislature information on the outcomes of department operations and activities to allow the Legislature to better assess the performance of the department, including both to evaluate the effectiveness of department programs and activities, as well as to assess how efficiently the department is using state resources.
(b) No later than January 10 each year, the Department of Corrections and Rehabilitation shall provide to the Joint Legislative Budget Committee an annual report on the outcomes of department operations and activities specified in the supplemental report of the annual Budget Act for the current fiscal year. At a minimum, for each performance measurement included in the supplemental report of the annual Budget Act for the current fiscal year, the department's report shall include data for the three most recently ended fiscal years, as well as establish target performance goals for each performance measurement for the current fiscal year identified in the supplemental report of the annual Budget Act and in the department's long-term strategic plan, if included in the strategic plan. If target performance goals stated in the prior department report have not been achieved, the annual department report for the current fiscal year shall include an explanation of why the target performance goals were not achieved. The supplemental report of the annual Budget Act may identify changes in the department's reporting requirements; however, if no changes are identified in the supplemental report of the annual Budget Act, the reporting requirements shall be the same as those for the prior fiscal year.
(c) The department shall also post the full annual report required by this section on its Internet Web site.
(Added by Stats. 2010, Ch. 729, Sec. 3. (AB 1628) Effective October 19, 2010.)

2064.1.
(a) On or before October 1 of each year, the Department of Corrections and Rehabilitation shall submit to the Legislature a report on the department's efforts to respond to and prevent suicides and attempted suicides among inmates. The information contained in the report shall include, but not be limited to, all of the following:
(1) A description of progress toward meeting the department's goals related to the completion of suicide risk evaluations in a sufficient manner.
(2) A description of progress toward meeting the department's goals related to the completion of 72 hour treatment plans in a sufficient manner.
(3) A description of the department's efforts to ensure that all required staff receive training related to suicide prevention and response.
(4) A description of the department's progress in implementing the recommendations made by the special master regarding inmate suicides and attempts, to include the results of any audits the department conducts, at the headquarters or regional level, as part of its planned audit process to measure the success of changes the department implements as a result of these recommendations.
(5) A description of the department's progress in identifying and implementing initiatives that are designed to reduce risk factors associated with suicide.
(6) A description of the department's efforts and progress to expand upon its process of notification pursuant to Section 5022, including expansion of those notifications in cases of suicide attempts when deemed appropriate by the department, and when inmates have consented to allow release of that information.
(b) The report shall be submitted to the Legislature pursuant to Section 9795 of the Government Code.
(c) The report shall also be posted on the department's Internet Web site in an easily accessible format.
(Added by Stats. 2018, Ch. 782, Sec. 1. (SB 960) Effective January 1, 2019.)

2065.
(a) The Department of Corrections and Rehabilitation shall complete all of the tasks associated with inmates granted medical parole pursuant to Section 3550 that are specified in this section. Subdivisions (c) and (d) shall apply only to the period of time that inmates are on medical parole.
(b) The department shall seek to enter into memoranda of understanding with federal, state, or county entities necessary to facilitate prerelease agreements to help inmates initiate benefits claims.
(c) This subdivision shall be implemented in a manner that is consistent with federal Medicaid law and regulations. The Director of Health Care Services shall seek any necessary federal approvals for the implementation of this subdivision. Claiming of federal Medicaid funds shall be implemented only to the extent that federal approval, if necessary, is obtained. If an inmate is granted medical parole and found to be eligible for Medi-Cal, all of the following shall apply:
(1) Hospitals, nursing facilities, and other providers providing services to medical parolees shall invoice the department in accordance with contracted rates of reimbursement or, if no contract is in place, pursuant to Section 5023.5.
(2) Upon receipt of an acceptable claim, the department shall reimburse hospitals, nursing facilities, and other providers for services provided to medical parolees in accordance with contracted rates of reimbursement or, if no contract is in place, pursuant to Section 5023.5.
(3) The department shall submit a quarterly invoice to the State Department of Health Care Services for medical parolees who are eligible for Medi-Cal for federal claiming and reimbursement of allowable federal Medicaid funds.

(4) The State Department of Health Care Services shall remit funds received for federal financial participation to the department.

(5) The department and the State Department of Health Care Services shall work together to do all of the following:

(A) Maximize federal financial participation for service costs, administrative costs, and targeted case management costs incurred pursuant to this section.

(B) Determine whether medical parolees shall be exempt from mandatory enrollment in managed health care, including county organized health plans, and determine the proper prior authorization process for individuals who have been granted medical parole.

(6) The department may submit retroactive Medi-Cal claims, in accordance with state and federal law and regulations to the State Department of Health Care Services for allowable certified public expenditures that have been reimbursed by the department. The department shall work with the Director of Health Care Services to ensure that any process established regarding the submission of retroactive claims shall be in compliance with state and federal law and regulations.

(d) If an inmate is granted medical parole and found to be ineligible for Medi-Cal, all of the following shall apply:

(1) The department shall consider the income and assets of a medical parolee to determine whether the individual has the ability to pay for the cost of his or her medical care.

(2) If the individual is unable to pay the cost of their medical care, the department shall establish contracts with appropriate medical providers and pay costs that are allowable pursuant to Section 5023.5.

(3) The department shall retain the responsibility to perform utilization review and cost management functions that it currently performs under existing contracts with health care facilities.

(4) The department shall directly provide, or provide reimbursement for, services associated with conservatorship or public guardianship.

(e) Notwithstanding the rulemaking provisions of Chapter 3.5 (commencing with Section 11340) of Part 1 of Division 2 of the Government Code, the department and the State Department of Health Care Services may implement this section by means of all-facility letters, all-county letters, or similar instructions, in addition to adopting regulations, as necessary.

(f) Notwithstanding any other state law, and only to the extent that federal law allows and federal financial participation is available, for the limited purpose of implementing this section, the department or its designees are authorized to act on behalf of an inmate for purposes of applying for redetermination of Medi-Cal eligibility and sharing and maintaining records with the State Department of Health Care Services.

(Amended by Stats. 2012, Ch. 41, Sec. 69. (SB 1021) Effective June 27, 2012.)

2066.

(a) Pursuant to Section 715 of the Military and Veterans Code, the Department of Veterans Affairs shall provide one employee, trained and accredited by the Department of Veterans Affairs, for every five state prisons to assist incarcerated veterans in applying for and receiving any federal or other veterans' benefits for which they or their families may be eligible.

(b) The department shall give a Department of Veterans Affairs' employee described in subdivision (a) access to the hardware, software, and those computer networks as are reasonably necessary to perform his or her duties while at the prison, while taking all necessary safety precautions.

(c) The department shall cooperate and collaborate with the Department of Veterans Affairs to ensure that a Department of Veterans Affairs' employee described in subdivision (a) has the greatest access and effectiveness practicable, while taking all necessary safety precautions, in order to assist veterans incarcerated within the state prisons.

(Added by Stats. 2017, Ch. 599, Sec. 2. (SB 776) Effective January 1, 2018.)

2067.

(a) As outlined in the Budget Act of 2018, it is anticipated that all California inmates will be returned from out-of-state contract correctional facilities by February 2019. To the extent that the adult offender population continues to decline, the Department of Corrections and Rehabilitation shall begin reducing private in-state male contract correctional facilities in a manner that maintains sufficient flexibility to comply with the federal court order to maintain the prison population at or below 137.5 percent of design capacity. The private in-state male contract correctional facilities that are primarily staffed by non-Department of Corrections and Rehabilitation personnel shall be prioritized for reduction over other in-state contract correctional facilities.

(b) As the population of offenders in private in-state male contract correctional facilities identified in subdivision (a) is reduced, and to the extent that the adult offender population continues to decline, the Department of Corrections and Rehabilitation shall accommodate the projected population decline by reducing the capacity of state-owned and operated prisons or in-state leased or contract correctional facilities, in a manner that maximizes long-term state facility savings, leverages long-term investments, and maintains sufficient flexibility to comply with the federal court order to maintain the prison population at or below 137.5 percent of design capacity. In reducing this additional capacity, the department shall take into consideration the following factors, including, but not limited to:

(1) The cost to operate at the capacity.

(2) Workforce impacts.

(3) Subpopulation and gender-specific housing needs.

(4) Long-term investment in state-owned and operated correctional facilities, including previous investments.

(5) Public safety and rehabilitation.

(6) The durability of the state's solution to prison overcrowding.

(Added by Stats. 2018, Ch. 36, Sec. 19. (AB 1812) Effective June 27, 2018.)

ARTICLE 2. Wardens [2078 - 2090]

(Article 2 added by Stats. 1941, Ch. 106.)

2078.

It shall be the duty of the department to prosecute all suits, at law or in equity, that may be necessary to protect the rights of the State in matters of property connected with the prisons and their management, such suits to be prosecuted in the name of the department.

(Amended by Stats. 1944, 3rd [1st] Ex. Sess., Ch. 2.)

2080.

A copy of the rules and regulations prescribing the duties and obligations of prisoners shall be furnished to each prisoner in a state prison or other facility under the jurisdiction of the Department of Corrections.

(Added by renumbering Section 2047 by Stats. 1959, Ch. 933.)

2081.

The director shall cause to be kept at each institution a register of institution violations and what kind of punishments, if any, are administered to prisoners or inmates; the offense committed; the rule or rules violated; the nature of punishment administered; the authority ordering such punishment; the duration of time during which the offender was subjected to punishment; and the condition of the prisoner's health.

(Amended by Stats. 1953, Ch. 1666.)

2081.5.

The Director of Corrections shall keep complete case records of all prisoners under custody of the department, which records shall be made available to the Board of Prison Terms at such times and in such form as the board may prescribe.

Case records shall include all information received by the Director of Corrections from the courts, probation officers, sheriffs, police departments, district attorneys, State Department of Justice, Federal Bureau of Investigation, and other interested agencies and persons. Case records shall also include a record of diagnostic findings, considerations, actions and dispositions with respect to classification, treatment, employment, training, and discipline as related to the institutional correctional program followed for each prisoner.

The director shall appoint, after consultation with the Board of Prison Terms, such employees of the various institutions under his control as may be necessary for the proper performance of the duties of the Board of Prison Terms, and when requested shall also have in attendance at hearings of the Board of Prison Terms, psychiatric or medical personnel. The director shall furnish, after consultation with the Board of Prison Terms and the Director of General Services, such hearing rooms and other physical facilities at such institutions as may be necessary for the proper performance of the duties of the Board of Prison Terms.

(Amended by Stats. 1979, Ch. 255.)

2082.

The Director of Corrections shall within 30 days after receiving persons convicted of crime and sentenced to serve terms in the respective prisons under the jurisdiction of the Director of Corrections, except those cases under juvenile court commitment, furnish to the Department of Justice two copies of a report containing the fingerprints and descriptions, including complete details of marks, scars, deformities, or other peculiarities, and a statement of the nature of the offense for which the person is committed. One copy shall be transmitted by the Department of Justice to the Federal Bureau of Investigation. The director shall notify the Department of Justice whenever any of the prisoners dies, escapes, is discharged, released on parole, transferred to or returned from a state hospital, taken out to court or returned therefrom, or whose custody is terminated in any other manner. The Director of Corrections may furnish to the Department of Justice such other fingerprints and information as may be useful for law enforcement purposes. Any expenditures incurred in carrying out the provisions of this section shall be paid for out of the appropriation made for the support of state's prisons or the Department of Corrections.

(Amended by Stats. 1983, Ch. 196, Sec. 1.)

2084.

(a) The department shall provide each prisoner with a bed, sufficient covering of blankets, and with garments of substantial material and of distinctive manufacture, and with sufficient plain and wholesome food of such variety as may be most conducive to good health and that shall include the availability of plant-based meals.

(b) The department shall develop a plan to make available the plant-based meals described in subdivision (a) on an overall cost-neutral basis.

(c) For the purposes of this section, "plant-based meals" shall mean entire meals that contain no animal products or byproducts, including meat, poultry, fish, dairy, or eggs.

(Amended by Stats. 2018, Ch. 512, Sec. 3. (SB 1138) Effective January 1, 2019.)

2085.

The department shall keep a correct account of all money and valuables upon the prisoner when delivered at the prison, and shall pay the amount, or the proceeds thereof, or return the same to the prisoner when discharged.

(Amended by Stats. 1949, Ch. 890.)

2085.5.

(a) If a prisoner owes a restitution fine imposed pursuant to subdivision (a) of Section 13967 of the Government Code, as operative prior to September 29, 1994, subdivision (b) of Section 730.6 of the Welfare and Institutions Code, or subdivision (b) of Section 1202.4 of this code, the secretary shall deduct a minimum of 20 percent or the balance owing on the fine amount, whichever is less, up to a maximum of 50 percent from the wages and trust account deposits of a prisoner, unless prohibited by federal law, and shall transfer that amount to the California Victim Compensation Board for deposit in the Restitution Fund. The amount deducted shall be credited against the amount owing on the fine. The sentencing court shall be provided a record of the payments.

(b) (1) If a prisoner is punished by imprisonment in a county jail pursuant to subdivision (h) of Section 1170 and owes a restitution fine imposed pursuant to subdivision (a) of Section 13967 of the Government Code, as operative prior to September 29, 1994, subdivision (b) of Section 730.6 of the Welfare and Institutions Code, or subdivision (b) of Section 1202.4 of this code, the agency designated by the board of supervisors in a county where the prisoner is incarcerated is authorized to deduct a minimum of 20 percent or the balance owing on the fine amount, whichever is less, up to a maximum of 50 percent from the county jail equivalent of wages and trust account deposits of a prisoner, unless prohibited by federal law, and shall transfer that amount to the California Victim Compensation Board for deposit in the Restitution Fund. The amount deducted shall be credited against the amount owing on the fine. The sentencing court shall be provided a record of the payments.

(2) If the board of supervisors designates the county sheriff as the collecting agency, the board of supervisors shall first obtain the concurrence of the county sheriff.

(c) If a prisoner owes a restitution order imposed pursuant to subdivision (c) of Section 13967 of the Government Code, as operative prior to September 29, 1994, subdivision (h) of Section 730.6 of the Welfare and Institutions Code, or subdivision (f) of Section 1202.4 of this code, the secretary shall deduct a minimum of 20 percent or the balance owing on the order amount, whichever is less, up to a maximum of 50 percent from the wages and trust account deposits of a prisoner, unless prohibited by federal law. The secretary shall transfer that amount to the California Victim Compensation Board for direct payment to the victim, or payment shall be made to the Restitution Fund to the extent that the victim has received assistance pursuant to that program. The sentencing court shall be provided a record of the payments made to victims and of the payments deposited to the Restitution Fund pursuant to this subdivision.

(d) If a prisoner is punished by imprisonment in a county jail pursuant to subdivision (h) of Section 1170 and owes a restitution order imposed pursuant to subdivision (c) of Section 13967 of the Government Code, as operative prior to September 29, 1994, subdivision (h) of Section 730.6 of the Welfare and Institutions Code, or subdivision (b) of Section 1202.4 of this code, the agency designated by the board of supervisors in the county where the prisoner is incarcerated is authorized to deduct a minimum of 20 percent or the balance owing on the order amount, whichever is less, up to a maximum of 50 percent from the county jail equivalent of wages and trust account deposits of a prisoner, unless prohibited by federal law. The agency shall transfer that amount to the California Victim Compensation Board for direct payment to the victim, or payment shall be made to the Restitution Fund to the extent that the victim has received assistance pursuant to that program, or may pay the victim directly. The sentencing court shall be provided a record of the payments made to the victims and of the payments deposited to the Restitution Fund pursuant to this subdivision.

(e) Except as provided in Section 2085.8, the secretary shall deduct and retain from the wages and trust account deposits of a prisoner, unless prohibited by federal law, an administrative fee to cover the actual administrative cost of collection, not to exceed 10 percent of the amount collected pursuant to subdivision (a) or (c). The secretary shall deposit the administrative fee moneys in a special deposit account for reimbursing administrative and support costs of the restitution program of the department. The secretary, at his or her discretion, may retain any excess funds in the special deposit account for future reimbursement of the department's administrative and support costs for the restitution program or may transfer all or part of the excess funds for deposit in the Restitution Fund.

(f) Except as provided in Section 2085.8, if a prisoner is punished by imprisonment in a county jail pursuant to subdivision (h) of Section 1170, the agency designated by the board of supervisors in a county where the prisoner is incarcerated may deduct and retain from the county jail equivalent of wages and trust account deposits of a prisoner, unless prohibited by federal law, an administrative fee to cover the actual administrative cost of collection, not to exceed 10 percent of the total amount collected, pursuant to subdivision (b) or (d). The agency shall deposit the administrative fee moneys in a special deposit account for reimbursing administrative and support costs of the restitution program of the agency. The agency may retain any excess funds in the special deposit account for future reimbursement of the agency's administrative and support costs for the restitution program or may transfer all or part of the excess funds for deposit in the Restitution Fund.

(g) In any case in which a parolee owes a restitution fine imposed pursuant to subdivision (a) of Section 13967 of the Government Code, as operative prior to September 29, 1994, subdivision (b) of Section 730.6 of the Welfare and Institutions Code, or subdivision (b) of Section 1202.4 of this code, either the secretary or, if a prisoner is punished by imprisonment in a county jail pursuant to subdivision (h) of Section 1170, the agency designated by the board of supervisors in the county where the prisoner is incarcerated may collect from the parolee any moneys owing on the restitution fine amount, unless prohibited by federal law. The secretary or the agency shall transfer that amount to the California Victim Compensation Board for deposit in the Restitution Fund. The amount deducted shall be credited against the amount owing on the fine. The sentencing court shall be provided a record of the payments.

(h) In any case in which a parolee owes a direct order of restitution, imposed pursuant to subdivision (c) of Section 13967 of the Government Code, as operative prior to September 29, 1994, subdivision (h) of Section 730.6 of the Welfare and Institutions Code, or paragraph (3) of subdivision (a) of Section 1202.4, either the secretary or, if a prisoner is punished by imprisonment in a county jail pursuant to subdivision (h) of Section 1170, the agency designated by the board of supervisors in the county where the prisoner is incarcerated or a local collection program may collect from the parolee any moneys owing, unless prohibited by federal law. The secretary or the agency shall transfer that amount to the California Victim Compensation Board for direct payment to the victim, or payment shall be made to the Restitution Fund to the extent that the victim has received assistance pursuant to that program, or the agency may pay the victim directly. The sentencing court shall be provided a record of the payments made by the offender pursuant to this subdivision.

(i) Except as provided in Section 2085.8, either the secretary or, if a prisoner is punished by imprisonment in a county jail pursuant to subdivision (h) of Section 1170, the agency designated by the board of supervisors in the county where the prisoner is incarcerated may deduct and retain from moneys collected from parolees an administrative fee to cover the actual administrative cost of collection, not to exceed 10 percent of the total amount collected pursuant to subdivision (g) or (h), unless prohibited by federal law. The secretary or the agency shall deposit the administrative fee moneys in a special deposit account for reimbursing administrative and support costs of the department or agency's restitution program, as applicable. The secretary, at his or her discretion, or the agency may retain any excess funds in the special deposit account for future reimbursement of the department's or agency's administrative and support costs for the restitution program or may transfer all or part of the excess funds for deposit in the Restitution Fund.

(j) If a prisoner has both a restitution fine and a restitution order from the sentencing court, the department shall collect the restitution order first pursuant to subdivision (c).

(k) If a prisoner is punished by imprisonment in a county jail pursuant to subdivision (h) of Section 1170 and that prisoner has both a restitution fine and a restitution order from the sentencing court, if the agency designated by the board of supervisors in the county where the prisoner is incarcerated collects the fine and order, the agency shall collect the restitution order first pursuant to subdivision (d).

(l) If a parolee has both a restitution fine and a restitution order from the sentencing court, either the department or, if the prisoner is punished by imprisonment in a county jail pursuant to subdivision (h) of Section 1170, the agency designated by the board of supervisors in the county where the prisoner is incarcerated may collect the restitution order first, pursuant to subdivision (h).

(m) If an inmate is housed at an institution that requires food to be purchased from the institution canteen for unsupervised overnight visits, and if the money for the purchase of this food is received from funds other than the inmate's wages, that money shall be exempt from restitution deductions. This exemption shall apply to the actual amount spent on food for the visit up to a maximum of fifty dollars ($50) for visits that include the inmate and one visitor, seventy dollars ($70) for visits that include the inmate and two or three visitors, and eighty dollars ($80) for visits that include the inmate and four or more visitors.

(n) (1) Amounts transferred to the California Victim Compensation Board for payment of direct orders of restitution shall be paid to the victim within 60 days from the date the restitution revenues are received by the California Victim Compensation Board. If the restitution payment to a victim is less than twenty-five dollars ($25), then payment need not be forwarded to that victim until the payment reaches twenty-five dollars ($25) or when the victim requests payment of the lesser amount.

(2) If a victim cannot be located, the restitution revenues received by the California Victim Compensation Board on behalf of the victim shall be held in trust in the Restitution Fund until the end of the state fiscal year subsequent to the state fiscal year in which the funds were deposited or until the time that the victim has provided current address information, whichever occurs sooner. Amounts remaining in trust at the end of the specified period of time shall revert to the Restitution Fund.

(3) (A) A victim failing to provide a current address within the period of time specified in paragraph (2) may provide documentation to the department, which shall verify that moneys were collected on behalf of the victim. Upon receipt of that verified information from the department, the California Victim Compensation Board shall transmit the restitution revenues to the victim in accordance with the provisions of subdivision (c) or (h).

(B) A victim failing to provide a current address within the period of time specified in paragraph (2) may provide documentation to the agency designated by the board of supervisors in the county where the prisoner punished by imprisonment in a county jail pursuant to subdivision (h) of Section 1170 is incarcerated, which may verify that moneys were collected on behalf of the victim. Upon receipt of that verified information from the agency, the California Victim Compensation Board shall transmit the restitution revenues to the victim in accordance with the provisions of subdivision (d) or (h).

(Amended by Stats. 2016, Ch. 718, Sec. 1. (SB 1054) Effective January 1, 2017.)
2085.6.
(a) When a prisoner who owes a restitution fine, or any portion thereof, is subsequently released from the custody of the Department of Corrections and Rehabilitation or a county jail facility, and is subject to postrelease community supervision under Section 3451 or mandatory supervision under subdivision (h) of Section 1170, he or she shall have a continuing obligation to pay the restitution fine in full. The restitution fine obligation and any portion left unsatisfied upon placement in postrelease community supervision or mandatory supervision is enforceable and may be collected, in a manner to be established by the county board of supervisors, by the department or county agency designated by the board of supervisors in the county where the prisoner is released. If a county elects to collect restitution fines, the department or county agency designated by the county board of supervisors shall transfer the amount collected to the California Victim Compensation Board for deposit in the Restitution Fund in the State Treasury.

(b) When a prisoner who owes payment for a restitution order, or any portion thereof, is released from the custody of the Department of Corrections and Rehabilitation or a county jail facility, and is subject to postrelease community supervision under Section 3451 or mandatory supervision under subdivision (h) of Section 1170, he or she shall have a continuing obligation to pay the restitution order in full. The restitution order obligation and any portion left unsatisfied upon placement in postrelease community supervision or mandatory supervision is enforceable and may be collected, in a manner to be established by the county board of supervisors, by the agency designated by the county board of supervisors in the county where the prisoner is released. If the county elects to collect the restitution order, the agency designated by the county board of supervisors for collection shall transfer the collected amount to the California Victim Compensation for deposit in the Restitution Fund in the State Treasury or may pay the victim directly. The sentencing court shall be provided a record of payments made to the victim and of the payments deposited into the Restitution Fund.

(c) Any portion of a restitution order or restitution fine that remains unsatisfied after an individual is released from postrelease community supervision or mandatory supervision shall continue to be enforceable by a victim pursuant to Section 1214 until the obligation is satisfied.

(d) At its discretion, a county board of supervisors may impose a fee upon the individual subject to postrelease community supervision or mandatory supervision to cover the actual administrative cost of collecting the restitution fine and the restitution order, not to exceed 10 percent of the amount collected, the proceeds of which shall be deposited into the general fund of the county.

(e) If a county elects to collect both a restitution fine and a restitution order, the amount owed on the restitution order shall be collected before the restitution fine.

(f) If a county elects to collect restitution fines and restitution orders pursuant to this section, the county shall coordinate efforts with the Franchise Tax Board pursuant to Section 19280 of the Revenue and Taxation Code.

(g) Pursuant to Section 1214, the county agency selected by a county board of supervisors to collect restitution fines and restitution orders may collect restitution fines and restitution orders after an individual is no longer on postrelease community supervision or mandatory supervision or after a term in custody pursuant to subparagraph (A) of paragraph (5) of subdivision (h) of Section 1170.

(h) For purposes of this section, the following definitions shall apply:

(1) "Restitution fine" means a fine imposed pursuant to subdivision (a) of Section 13967 of the Government Code, as operative prior to September 29, 1994, subdivision (b) of Section 730.6 of the Welfare and Institutions Code, or subdivision (b) of Section 1202.4.

(2) "Restitution order" means an order for restitution to the victim of a crime imposed pursuant to subdivision (c) of Section 13967 of the Government Code, as operative prior to September 29, 1994, subdivision (h) of Section 730.6 of the Welfare and Institutions Code, or subdivision (f) of Section 1202.4.

(Amended by Stats. 2016, Ch. 31, Sec. 248. (SB 836) Effective June 27, 2016.)
2085.7.
(a) When a prisoner who owes a restitution fine, or any portion thereof, is released from the custody of a county jail facility after completion of a term in custody pursuant to subparagraph (A) of paragraph (5) of subdivision (h) of Section 1170, he or she has a continuing obligation to pay the restitution fine in full. The balance of the restitution fine remaining unpaid after completion of a term in custody pursuant to subparagraph (A) of paragraph (5) of subdivision (h) of Section 1170 is enforceable and may be collected, in a manner to be established by the county board of supervisors, by the department or county agency designated by the board of supervisors in the county in which the prisoner is released. If a county elects to collect restitution fines, the department or county agency designated by the county board of supervisors shall transfer the amount collected to the California Victim Compensation Board for deposit in the Restitution Fund.

(b) When a prisoner who owes payment for a restitution order, or any portion thereof, is released from the custody of a county jail facility after completion of a term in custody pursuant to subparagraph (A) of paragraph (5) of subdivision (h) of Section 1170, he or she has a continuing obligation to pay the restitution order in full. The balance of the restitution order remaining unpaid after completion of a term in custody pursuant to subparagraph (A) of paragraph (5) of subdivision (h) of Section 1170 is enforceable and may be collected, in a manner to be established by the county board of supervisors, by the agency designated by the county board of supervisors in the county in which the prisoner is released. If the county elects to collect the restitution order, the agency designated by the county board of supervisors for collection shall transfer the collected amount to the California Victim Compensation Board for deposit in the Restitution Fund or may pay the victim directly. The sentencing court shall be provided a record of payments made to the victim and of the payments deposited into the Restitution Fund.

(c) The amount of a restitution order or restitution fine that remains unsatisfied after completion of a term in custody pursuant to subparagraph (A) of paragraph (5) of subdivision (h) of Section 1170 is to be enforceable by a victim pursuant to Section 1214 until the obligation is satisfied.

(d) Except as provided in Section 2085.8, at its discretion, a county board of supervisors may impose a fee upon the individual after completion of a term in custody pursuant to subparagraph (A) of paragraph (5) of subdivision (h) of Section 1170 to cover the actual administrative cost of collecting the restitution fine and the restitution order, in an amount not to exceed 10 percent of the amount collected, the proceeds of which shall be deposited into the general fund of the county.

(e) If a county elects to collect both a restitution fine and a restitution order, the amount owed on the restitution order shall be collected before the restitution fine.

(f) If a county elects to collect restitution fines and restitution orders pursuant to this section, the county shall coordinate efforts with the Franchise Tax Board pursuant to Section 19280 of the Revenue and Taxation Code.

(g) Pursuant to Section 1214, the county agency selected by a county board of supervisors to collect restitution fines and restitution orders may collect restitution fines and restitution orders after an individual has completed a term in custody pursuant to subparagraph (A) of paragraph (5) of subdivision (h) of Section 1170.

(h) For purposes of this section, the following definitions shall apply:

(1) "Restitution fine" means a fine imposed pursuant to subdivision (a) of Section 13967 of the Government Code, as operative prior to September 29, 1994, subdivision (b) of Section 730.6 of the Welfare and Institutions Code, or subdivision (b) of Section 1202.4.

(2) "Restitution order" means an order for restitution to the victim of a crime imposed pursuant to subdivision (c) of Section 13967 of the Government Code, as operative prior to September 29, 1994, subdivision (h) of Section 730.6 of the Welfare and Institutions Code, or subdivision (f) of Section 1202.4.

(Added by Stats. 2016, Ch. 718, Sec. 2. (SB 1054) Effective January 1, 2017.)
2085.8.
(a) Compensatory or punitive damages awarded by trial or settlement to any inmate, parolee, person placed on postrelease community supervision pursuant to Section 3451, or defendant on mandatory supervision imposed pursuant to subparagraph (B) of paragraph (5) of subdivision (h) of Section 1170 in connection with a civil action brought against a federal, state, or local jail, prison, or correctional facility, or any official or agent thereof, shall be paid directly, after payment of reasonable attorney's fees and litigation costs approved by the court, to satisfy any outstanding restitution orders or restitution fines against that person. The balance of the award shall be forwarded to the payee after full payment of all outstanding restitution orders and restitution fines, subject to subdivision (c).

(b) The department shall make all reasonable efforts to notify the victims of the crime for which that person was convicted concerning the pending payment of any compensatory or punitive damages. For any prisoner punished by imprisonment in a county jail pursuant to subdivision (h) of Section 1170, the agency may make all reasonable efforts to notify the victims of the crime for which that person was convicted concerning the pending payment of any compensatory or punitive damages.

(c) (1) The secretary shall deduct and retain from any prisoner or parolee settlement or trial award an administrative fee that totals 5 percent of any amount paid from the settlement or award to satisfy an outstanding restitution order or fine, unless prohibited by federal law.

(2) The agency may deduct and retain from any settlement or trial award of a person previously imprisoned in county jail an administrative fee that totals 5 percent of any amount paid from the settlement or award to satisfy an outstanding restitution order or fine, unless prohibited by federal law.

(3) The secretary or the agency shall deposit the administrative fee moneys in a special deposit account for reimbursing administrative and support costs of the department's or agency's restitution program, as applicable. The secretary, at his or her discretion, or the agency may either retain any excess funds in the special deposit account for future reimbursement of the department's or agency's administrative and support costs for the restitution program or may transfer all or part of the excess funds for deposit in the Restitution Fund.

(Added by Stats. 2016, Ch. 718, Sec. 3. (SB 1054) Effective January 1, 2017.)
2086.
The wardens may make temporary rules and regulations, in case of emergency, to remain in force until the department otherwise provides.
(Amended by Stats. 1944, 3rd Ex. Sess., Ch. 2.)
2087.
The wardens shall perform such other duties as may be prescribed by the department.
(Amended by Stats. 1957, Ch. 2256.)
2090.
The department is hereby authorized to receive from the Federal Government any federal prisoner and to charge and receive from the United States, for the use of the State, an amount sufficient for the support of each such federal prisoner, the cost of all clothing that may be furnished, and one dollar ($1) per month for the use of the prisoner. No other or further charges shall be made by any officer for or on account of such prisoners.
(Amended by Stats. 1957, Ch. 2256.)

ARTICLE 6. Prohibition Upon Wardens, Clerks, Officers and Employees [2540 - 2541]
(Article 6 added by Stats. 1941, Ch. 106.)
2540.
No officer or employee of the department shall receive directly, or indirectly, any compensation for his services other than that prescribed or authorized by law or the director; nor shall he receive any compensation whatever, directly or indirectly, for any act or service which he may do or perform for or on behalf of any contractor, or agent, or employee of a contractor. For any violation of the provisions of this section the officer or employee shall be discharged from his office or service; and every contractor, or employee, or agent of a contractor engaged therein, shall be expelled from the prison grounds, and not again permitted within the same as a contractor, agent, or employee.
(Amended by Stats. 1957, Ch. 2256.)
2541.
No officer or employee of the department, or contractor, or employee of a contractor, shall, without permission of the director, make any gift or present to a prisoner, or receive any from a prisoner, or have any barter or dealings with a prisoner. For every violation of the provisions of this section, the party engaged therein shall incur the same penalty as prescribed in the preceding section. No officer or employee of the prison shall be interested, directly or indirectly, in any contract or purchase made or authorized to be made by anyone for or on behalf of the prisons.
(Amended by Stats. 1957, Ch. 2256.)

CHAPTER 3. Civil Rights of Prisoners [2600 - 2643]

(Heading of Chapter 3 amended by Stats. 1975, Ch. 1175.)

ARTICLE 1. Civil Rights [2600 - 2604]
(Article 1 repealed and added by Stats. 1975, Ch. 1175.)
2600.
(a) A person sentenced to imprisonment in a state prison or to imprisonment pursuant to subdivision (h) of Section 1170 may during that period of confinement be deprived of such rights, and only such rights, as is reasonably related to legitimate penological interests.

(b) Nothing in this section shall be construed to overturn the decision in Thor v. Superior Court, 5 Cal. 4th 725.
(Amended (as amended by Stats. 2011, Ch. 15, Sec. 462) by Stats. 2011, Ch. 665, Sec. 1.5. (AB 1114) Effective January 1, 2012.)
2601.
Subject only to the provisions of that section, each person described in Section 2600 shall have the following civil rights:

(a) Except as provided in Section 2225 of the Civil Code, to inherit, own, sell, or convey real or personal property, including all written and artistic material produced or created by the person during the period of imprisonment. However, to the extent authorized in Section 2600, the Department of Corrections may restrict or prohibit sales or conveyances that are made for business purposes.

(b) To correspond, confidentially, with any member of the State Bar or holder of public office, provided that the prison authorities may open and inspect incoming mail to search for contraband.

(c) (1) To purchase, receive, and read any and all newspapers, periodicals, and books accepted for distribution by the United States Post Office. Pursuant to this section, prison authorities may exclude any of the following matter:

(A) Obscene publications or writings, and mail containing information concerning where, how, or from whom this matter may be obtained.

(B) Any matter of a character tending to incite murder, arson, riot, violent racism, or any other form of violence.

(C) Any matter concerning gambling or a lottery.

(2) Nothing in this section shall be construed as limiting the right of prison authorities to do the following:

(A) Open and inspect any and all packages received by an inmate.

(B) Establish reasonable restrictions as to the number of newspapers, magazines, and books that the inmate may have in his or her cell or elsewhere in the prison at one time.

(d) To initiate civil actions, subject to a three dollar ($3) filing fee to be collected by the Department of Corrections, in addition to any other filing fee authorized by law, and subject to Title 3a (commencing with Section 391) of the Code of Civil Procedure.

(e) To marry.

(f) To create a power of appointment.

(g) To make a will.

(h) To receive all benefits provided for in Sections 3370 and 3371 of the Labor Code and in Section 5069.
(Amended by Stats. 1996, Ch. 886, Sec. 3. Effective January 1, 1997.)

2602.
(a) Except as provided in subdivision (b), no person sentenced to imprisonment or housed in a state prison shall be administered any psychiatric medication without his or her prior informed consent.

(b) If a psychiatrist determines that an inmate should be treated with psychiatric medication, but the inmate does not consent, the inmate may be involuntarily treated with the medication. Treatment may be given on either a nonemergency basis as provided in subdivision (c), or on an emergency or interim basis as provided in subdivision (d).

(c) The Department of Corrections and Rehabilitation may seek to initiate involuntary medication on a nonemergency basis only if all of the following conditions have been met:

(1) A psychiatrist has determined that the inmate has a serious mental disorder.

(2) A psychiatrist has determined that, as a result of that mental disorder, the inmate is gravely disabled and does not have the capacity to refuse treatment with psychiatric medications or is a danger to self or others.

(3) A psychiatrist has prescribed one or more psychiatric medications for the treatment of the inmate's disorder, has considered the risks, benefits, and treatment alternatives to involuntary medication, and has determined that the treatment alternatives to involuntary medication are unlikely to meet the needs of the patient.

(4) The inmate has been advised of the risks and benefits of, and treatment alternatives to, the psychiatric medication and refuses or is unable to consent to the administration of the medication.

(5) The inmate is provided a hearing before an administrative law judge.

(6) The inmate is provided counsel at least 21 days prior to the hearing, unless emergency or interim medication is being administered pursuant to subdivision (d), in which case the inmate would receive expedited access to counsel. The hearing shall be held not more than 30 days after the filing of the notice with the Office of Administrative Hearings, unless counsel for the inmate agrees to extend the date of the hearing.

(7) The inmate and counsel are provided with written notice of the hearing at least 21 days prior to the hearing, unless emergency or interim medication is being administered pursuant to subdivision (d), in which case the inmate would receive an expedited hearing. The written notice shall do all of the following:

(A) Set forth the diagnosis, the factual basis for the diagnosis, the basis upon which psychiatric medication is recommended, the expected benefits of the medication, any potential side effects and risks to the inmate from the medication, and any alternatives to treatment with the medication.

(B) Advise the inmate of the right to be present at the hearing, the right to be represented by counsel at all stages of the proceedings, the right to present evidence, and the right to cross-examine witnesses. Counsel for the inmate shall have access to all medical records and files of the inmate, but shall not have access to the confidential section of the inmate's central file which contains materials unrelated to medical treatment.

(C) Inform the inmate of his or her right to contest the finding of an administrative law judge authorizing treatment with involuntary medication by filing a petition for writ of administrative mandamus pursuant to Section 1094.5 of the Code of Civil Procedure, and his or her right to file a petition for writ of habeas corpus with respect to any decision of the Department of Corrections and Rehabilitation to continue treatment with involuntary medication after the administrative law judge has authorized treatment with involuntary medication.

(8) An administrative law judge determines by clear and convincing evidence that the inmate has a mental illness or disorder, that as a result of that illness the inmate is gravely disabled and lacks the capacity to consent to or refuse treatment with psychiatric medications or is a danger to self or others if not medicated, that there is no less intrusive alternative to involuntary medication, and that the medication is in the inmate's best medical interest. Failure of the department to provide timely or adequate notice pursuant to this section shall be excused only upon a showing of good cause and the absence of prejudice to the inmate. In making this determination, the administrative law judge may consider factors, including, but not limited to, the ability of the inmate's counsel to adequately prepare the case and to confer with the inmate, the continuity of care, and, if applicable, the need for protection of the inmate or institutional staff that would be compromised by a procedural default.

(9) The historical course of the inmate's mental disorder, as determined by available relevant information about the course of the inmate's mental disorder, shall be considered when it has direct bearing on the determination of whether the inmate is a danger to self or others, or is gravely disabled and incompetent to refuse medication as the result of a mental disorder.

(10) An inmate is entitled to file one motion for reconsideration following a determination that he or she may receive involuntary medication, and may seek a hearing to present new evidence, upon good cause shown.

(d) This section does not prohibit a physician from taking appropriate action in an emergency. An emergency exists when there is a sudden and marked change in an inmate's mental condition so that action is immediately necessary for the preservation of life or the prevention of serious bodily harm to the inmate or others, and it is impractical, due to the seriousness of the emergency, to first obtain informed consent. If psychiatric medication is administered during an emergency, the medication shall only be that which is required to treat the emergency condition and shall be administered for only so long as the emergency continues to exist. If the Department of Corrections and Rehabilitation's clinicians identify a situation that jeopardizes the inmate's health or well-being as the result of a serious mental illness, and necessitates the continuation of medication beyond the initial 72 hours pending the full mental health hearing, the department shall give notice to the inmate and his or her counsel of the department's intention to seek an ex parte order to allow the continuance of medication pending the full hearing. The notice shall be served upon the inmate and counsel at the same time the inmate is given the written notice that the involuntary medication proceedings are being initiated and is appointed counsel as provided in subdivision (c). The order may be issued ex parte upon a showing that in the absence of the medication the emergency conditions are likely to recur. The request for an ex parte order shall be supported by an affidavit from the psychiatrist showing specific facts. The inmate and the inmate's appointed counsel shall have two business days to respond to the department's ex parte request to continue interim medication, and may present facts supported by an affidavit in opposition to the department's request. An administrative law judge shall review the ex parte request and shall have three business days to determine the merits of the department's request for an ex parte order. If an order is issued, the psychiatrist may continue the administration of the medication until the hearing described in paragraph (5) of subdivision (c) is held.

(1) The Department of Corrections and Rehabilitation shall file with the Office of Administrative Hearings, and serve on the inmate and his or her counsel, the written notice described in paragraph (7) of subdivision (c) within 72 hours of commencing medication pursuant to this subdivision, unless either of the following occurs:

(A) The inmate gives informed consent to continue the medication.

(B) A psychiatrist determines that the psychiatric medication is not necessary and administration of the medication is discontinued.

(2) If medication is being administered pursuant to this subdivision, the hearing described in paragraph (5) of subdivision (c) shall commence within 21 days of the filing and service of the notice, unless counsel for an inmate agrees to a different period of time.

(3) With the exception of the timeline provisions specified in paragraphs (1) and (2) for providing notice and commencement of the hearing pursuant to the conditions specified

in this subdivision, the inmate shall be entitled to and be given the same due process protections as specified in subdivision (c). The department shall prove the same elements supporting the involuntary administration of psychiatric medication and the administrative law judge shall be required to make the same findings described in subdivision (c).
(e) The determination that an inmate may receive involuntary medication shall be valid for one year from the date of the determination, regardless of whether the inmate subsequently gives his or her informed consent.
(f) If a determination has been made to involuntarily medicate an inmate pursuant to subdivision (c) or (d), the medication shall be discontinued one year after the date of that determination, unless the inmate gives his or her informed consent to the administration of the medication, or unless a new determination is made pursuant to the procedures set forth in subdivision (g).
(g) To renew an existing order allowing involuntary medication, the department shall file with the Office of Administrative Hearings, and shall serve on the inmate and his or her counsel, a written notice indicating the department's intent to renew the existing involuntary medication order.
(1) The request to renew the order shall be filed and served no later than 21 days prior to the expiration of the current order authorizing involuntary medication.
(2) The inmate shall be entitled to, and shall be given, the same due process protections as specified in subdivision (c).
(3) Renewal orders shall be valid for one year from the date of the hearing.
(4) An order renewing an existing order shall be granted based on clear and convincing evidence that the inmate has a serious mental disorder that requires treatment with psychiatric medication, and that, but for the medication, the inmate would revert to the behavior that was the basis for the prior order authorizing involuntary medication, coupled with evidence that the inmate lacks insight regarding his or her need for the medication, such that it is unlikely that the inmate would be able to manage his or her own medication and treatment regimen. No new acts need be alleged or proven.
(5) If the department wishes to add a basis to an existing order, the department shall give the inmate and the inmate's counsel notice in advance of the hearing via a renewal notice or supplemental petition. Within the renewal notice or supplemental petition, the department shall specify what additional basis is being alleged and what qualifying conduct within the past year supports that additional basis. The department shall prove the additional basis and conduct by clear and convincing evidence at a hearing as specified in subdivision (c).
(6) The hearing on any petition to renew an order for involuntary medication shall be conducted prior to the expiration of the current order.
(h) Pursuant to Section 5058, the Department of Corrections and Rehabilitation shall adopt regulations to fully implement this section.
(i) In the event of a conflict between the provisions of this section and the Administrative Procedure Act (Chapter 4.5 (commencing with Section 11400) of Part 1 of Division 3 of the Government Code), this section shall control.
(Amended by Stats. 2013, Ch. 76, Sec. 157. (AB 383) Effective January 1, 2014.)
2603.
(a) Except as provided in subdivision (b), an inmate confined in a county jail shall not be administered any psychiatric medication without his or her prior informed consent.
(b) If a psychiatrist determines that an inmate should be treated with psychiatric medication, but the inmate does not consent, the inmate may be involuntarily treated with the medication. Treatment may be given on either a nonemergency basis as provided in subdivision (c), or on an emergency or interim basis as provided in subdivision (d).
(c) A county department of mental health, or other designated county department, may administer involuntary medication on a nonemergency basis only if all of the following conditions have been met:
(1) A psychiatrist or psychologist has determined that the inmate has a serious mental disorder.
(2) A psychiatrist or psychologist has determined that, as a result of that mental disorder, the inmate is gravely disabled and does not have the capacity to refuse treatment with psychiatric medications, or is a danger to self or others.
(3) A psychiatrist has prescribed one or more psychiatric medications for the treatment of the inmate's disorder, has considered the risks, benefits, and treatment alternatives to involuntary medication, and has determined that the treatment alternatives to involuntary medication are unlikely to meet the needs of the patient.
(4) The inmate has been advised of the risks and benefits of, and treatment alternatives to, the psychiatric medication and refuses, or is unable to consent to, the administration of the medication.
(5) The jail has made a documented attempt to locate an available bed for the inmate in a community-based treatment facility in lieu of seeking to administer involuntary medication. The jail shall transfer that inmate to such a facility only if the facility can provide care for the mental health needs, and the physical health needs, if any, of the inmate and upon the agreement of the facility. In enacting the act that added this paragraph, it is the intent of the Legislature to recognize the lack of community-based beds and the inability of many facilities to accept transfers from correctional facilities.
(6) The inmate is provided a hearing before a superior court judge, a court-appointed commissioner or referee, or a court-appointed hearing officer, as specified in subdivision (c) of Section 5334 of the Welfare and Institutions Code.
(A) If the inmate is in custody awaiting trial, any hearing pursuant to this section shall be held before, and any requests for ex parte orders shall be submitted to, a judge in the superior court where the criminal case is pending.
(B) A superior court judge may consider whether involuntary medication would prejudice the inmate's defense.
(7) (A) The inmate is provided counsel at least 21 days prior to the hearing, unless emergency or interim medication is being administered pursuant to subdivision (d), in which case the inmate would receive expedited access to counsel.
(B) In the case of an inmate awaiting arraignment, the inmate is provided counsel within 48 hours of the filing of the notice of the hearing with the superior court, unless counsel has previously been appointed.
(C) The hearing shall be held not more than 30 days after the filing of the notice with the superior court, unless counsel for the inmate agrees to extend the date of the hearing.
(8) (A) The inmate and counsel are provided with written notice of the hearing at least 21 days prior to the hearing, unless emergency or interim medication is being administered pursuant to subdivision (d), in which case the inmate would receive an expedited hearing.
(B) The written notice shall do all of the following:
(i) Set forth the diagnosis, the factual basis for the diagnosis, the basis upon which psychiatric medication is recommended, the expected benefits of the medication, any potential side effects and risks to the inmate from the medication, and any alternatives to treatment with the medication.
(ii) Advise the inmate of the right to be present at the hearing, the right to be represented by counsel at all stages of the proceedings, the right to present evidence, and the right to cross-examine witnesses. Counsel for the inmate shall have access to all medical records and files of the inmate, but shall not have access to the confidential section of the inmate's central file which contains materials unrelated to medical treatment.
(iii) Inform the inmate of his or her right to appeal the determination to the superior court or the court of appeal as specified in subdivisions (e) and (f) of Section 5334 of the Welfare and Institutions Code, and his or her right to file a petition for writ of habeas corpus with respect to any decision of the county department of mental health, or other designated county department, to continue treatment with involuntary medication after the superior court judge, court-appointed commissioner or referee, or court-appointed hearing officer has authorized treatment with involuntary medication.
(9) (A) In the hearing described in paragraph (6), the superior court judge, a court-appointed commissioner or referee, or a court-appointed hearing officer determines by clear and convincing evidence that the inmate has a mental illness or disorder, that as a result of that illness the inmate is gravely disabled and lacks the capacity to consent to or refuse treatment with psychiatric medications or is a danger to self or others if not medicated, that there is no less intrusive alternative to involuntary medication, and that the medication is in the inmate's best medical interest.
(B) The superior court judge, court-appointed commissioner or referee, or a court-appointed hearing officer shall not make a finding pursuant to subparagraph (A) of this paragraph that there is no less intrusive alternative to involuntary medication and that the medication is in the inmate's best medical interest, without information from the jail to indicate that neither of the conditions specified in paragraph (5) is present.
(C) If the court makes the findings in subparagraph (A), that administration shall occur in consultation with a psychiatrist who is not involved in the treatment of the inmate at the jail, if available.
(D) In the event of any statutory notice issues with either initial or renewal filings by the county department of mental health, or other designated county department, the superior court judge, court-appointed commissioner or referee, or court-appointed hearing officer shall hear arguments as to why the case should be heard, and shall consider factors such as the ability of the inmate's counsel to adequately prepare the case and to confer with the inmate, the continuity of care, and, if applicable, the need for protection of the inmate or institutional staff that would be compromised by a procedural default.
(10) The historical course of the inmate's mental disorder, as determined by available relevant information about the course of the inmate's mental disorder, shall be considered when it has direct bearing on the determination of whether the inmate is a danger to self or others, or is gravely disabled and incompetent to refuse medication as the result of a mental disorder.
(11) An inmate is entitled to file one motion for reconsideration following a determination that he or she may receive involuntary medication, and may seek a hearing to present new evidence, upon good cause shown. This paragraph does not prevent a court from reviewing, modifying, or terminating an involuntary medication order for an inmate awaiting trial, if there is a showing that the involuntary medication is interfering with the inmate's due process rights in the criminal proceeding.
(d) (1) (A) This section does not prohibit a physician from taking appropriate action in an emergency. An emergency exists when both of the following criteria are met:
(i) There is a sudden and marked change in an inmate's mental condition so that action is immediately necessary for the preservation of life or the prevention of serious bodily harm to the inmate or others.
(ii) It is impractical, due to the seriousness of the emergency, to first obtain informed consent.
(B) If psychiatric medication is administered during an emergency, the medication shall only be that which is required to treat the emergency condition and shall be administered for only so long as the emergency continues to exist.
(2) (A) If the clinicians of the county department of mental health, or other designated county department, identify a situation that jeopardizes the inmate's health or well-being as the result of a serious mental illness, and necessitates the continuation of medication beyond the initial 72 hours pending the full mental health hearing, the county department may seek to continue the medication by giving notice to the inmate and his or her counsel of its intention to seek an ex parte order to allow the continuance of medication pending the full hearing, and filing an ex parte order within the initial 72-hour period. Treatment of the inmate in a facility pursuant to Section 4011.6 shall not be required in order to continue medication under this subdivision unless the treatment is otherwise medically necessary.
(B) The notice shall be served upon the inmate and counsel at the same time the inmate is given the written notice that the involuntary medication proceedings are being initiated and is appointed counsel as provided in subdivision (c).
(C) The order may be issued ex parte upon a showing that, in the absence of the medication, the emergency conditions are likely to recur. The request for an ex parte order shall be supported by an affidavit from the psychiatrist or psychologist showing specific facts.
(D) The inmate and the inmate's appointed counsel shall have two business days to respond to the county department's ex parte request to continue interim medication, and may present facts supported by an affidavit in opposition to the department's request. A superior court judge, a court-appointed commissioner or referee, or a court-appointed hearing officer shall review the ex parte request and shall have three business days to determine the merits of the department's request for an ex parte order.
(E) If an order is issued, the psychiatrist may continue the administration of the medication until the hearing described in paragraph (6) of subdivision (c) is held.
(3) If the county elects to seek an ex parte order pursuant to this subdivision, the county department of mental health, or other designated county department, shall file with the superior court, and serve on the inmate and his or her counsel, the written notice described in paragraph (8) of subdivision (c) within 72 hours of commencing medication pursuant to this subdivision, unless either of the following occurs:
(A) The inmate gives informed consent to continue the medication.
(B) A psychiatrist determines that the psychiatric medication is not necessary and administration of the medication is discontinued.
(4) If medication is being administered pursuant to this subdivision, the hearing described in paragraph (6) of subdivision (c) shall commence within 21 days of the filing and service of the notice, unless counsel for the inmate agrees to a different period of time.
(5) With the exception of the timeline provisions specified in paragraphs (3) and (4) for providing notice and commencement of the hearing in emergency or interim situations, the inmate shall be entitled to and be given the same due process protections as specified in subdivision (c). The county department of mental health, or other designated county department, shall prove the same elements supporting the involuntary administration of psychiatric medication and the superior court judge, court-appointed commissioner or referee, or court-appointed hearing officer shall be required to make the same findings described in subdivision (c).
(e) (1) (A) An order by the court authorizing involuntary medication of an inmate shall be valid for no more than one year after the date of determination.
(B) Notwithstanding subparagraph (A), in the case of an inmate who is awaiting arraignment, trial, or sentencing, the determination that an inmate may receive involuntary medication shall be valid for no more than 180 days. The court shall review the order at intervals of not more than 60 days to determine whether the grounds for the order remain. At each review, the psychiatrist shall file an affidavit with the court that ordered the involuntary medication affirming that the person who is the subject of the order continues to meet the criteria for involuntary medication. A copy of the affidavit shall be provided to the defendant and the defendant's attorney. In determining whether the criteria for involuntary medication still exist, the court shall consider the affidavit of the psychiatrist or psychiatrists and any supplemental information provided by the defendant's attorney. The court may also require the testimony from the psychiatrist, if necessary. The court, at each review, may continue the order authorizing involuntary medication, vacate the order, or make any other appropriate order.

(2) Notwithstanding subparagraph (A) of paragraph (1), any determination of an inmate's incapacity to refuse treatment with antipsychotic medication made pursuant to this section shall remain in effect only until one of the following occurs, whichever occurs first:

(A) The duration of the inmate's confinement ends.

(B) A court determines that the inmate no longer meets the criteria of subdivision (c) or (d), or by any other order of the court.

(3) An inmate's period of confinement may not be extended in order to provide treatment to the inmate with antipsychotic medication pursuant to this section.

(f) This section does not prohibit the court, upon making a determination that an inmate awaiting arraignment, preliminary hearing, trial, sentencing, or a postconviction proceeding to revoke or modify supervision may receive involuntary medication pursuant to subdivision (c) or (d), and, upon ex parte request of the defendant or counsel, from suspending all proceedings in the criminal prosecution, until the court determines that the defendant's medication will not interfere with his or her ability to meaningfully participate in the criminal proceedings.

(g) If a determination has been made to involuntarily medicate an inmate pursuant to subdivision (c) or (d), the medication shall be discontinued one year after the date of that determination, unless the inmate gives his or her informed consent to the administration of the medication, or unless a new determination is made pursuant to the procedures set forth in subdivision (h).

(h) To renew an existing order allowing involuntary medication, the county department of mental health, or other designated county department, shall file with the superior court, and shall serve on the inmate and his or her counsel, a written notice indicating the department's intent to renew the existing involuntary medication order.

(1) The request to renew the order shall be filed and served no later than 21 days prior to the expiration of the current order authorizing involuntary medication.

(2) The inmate shall be entitled to, and shall be given, the same due process protections as specified in subdivision (c).

(3) (A) Except as provided in subparagraph (B), renewal orders shall be valid for one year from the date of the hearing.

(B) In the case of an inmate awaiting arraignment, trial, or sentencing, the renewal order shall be valid for no more than 180 days. The court shall review the order at intervals of not more than 60 days to determine whether the grounds for the order remain. At each review, the psychiatrist shall file an affidavit with the court that ordered the involuntary medication affirming that the person who is the subject of the order continues to meet the criteria for involuntary medication. A copy of the affidavit shall be provided to the defendant and the defendant's attorney. In determining whether the criteria for involuntary medication still exist, the court shall consider the affidavit of the psychiatrist or psychiatrists and any supplemental information provided by the defendant's attorney. The court may also require the testimony from the psychiatrist, if necessary. The court, at each review, may continue the order authorizing involuntary medication, vacate the order, or make any other appropriate order.

(4) (A) An order renewing an existing order shall be granted based on clear and convincing evidence that the inmate has a serious mental disorder that requires treatment with psychiatric medication, and that, but for the medication, the inmate would revert to the behavior that was the basis for the prior order authorizing involuntary medication, coupled with evidence that the inmate lacks insight regarding his or her need for the medication, such that it is unlikely that the inmate would be able to manage his or her own medication and treatment regimen. No new acts need be alleged or proven.

(B) The superior court judge, court-appointed commissioner or referee, or a court-appointed hearing officer shall also make a finding that treatment of the inmate in a correctional setting continues to be necessary if neither of the criteria in paragraph (5) of subdivision (c) is present.

(5) If the county department of mental health, or other designated county department, wishes to add a basis to an existing order, it shall give the inmate and the inmate's counsel notice in advance of the hearing via a renewal notice or supplemental petition. Within the renewal notice or supplemental petition, as described in subdivision (h), the county department of mental health, or other designated county department, shall specify what additional basis is being alleged and what qualifying conduct within the past year supports that additional basis. The county department of mental health, or other designated county department, shall prove the additional basis and conduct by clear and convincing evidence at a hearing as specified in subdivision (c).

(6) The hearing on any petition to renew an order for involuntary medication shall be conducted prior to the expiration of the current order.

(i) In the event of a conflict between the provisions of this section and the Administrative Procedure Act (Chapter 4.5 (commencing with Section 11400) of Part 1 of Division 3 of the Government Code), this section shall control.

(j) As used in this section, "inmate" means a person confined in the county jail, including, but not limited to, a person sentenced to imprisonment in a county jail, a person housed in a county jail during or awaiting trial proceedings, and a person who has been booked into a county jail and is awaiting arraignment.

(k) This section does not apply to a person housed in a county jail solely on the basis of an immigration hold, except as it applies to medication provided on an emergency or interim basis as provided in subdivision (d).

(l) Each county that administers involuntary medication to an inmate awaiting arraignment, trial, or sentencing, shall file, by January 1, 2021, a written report with the Assembly Committees on Judiciary and Public Safety and the Senate Committee on Public Safety summarizing the following: the number of inmates who received involuntary medication while awaiting arraignment, trial, or sentencing between January 1, 2018, and July 1, 2020; the crime for which those inmates were arrested; the total time those inmates were detained while awaiting arraignment, trial, or sentencing; the duration of the administration of involuntary medication; the number of times, if any, that an existing order for the administration of involuntary medication was renewed; and the reason for termination of the administration of involuntary medication.

(m) This section shall remain in effect only until January 1, 2022, and as of that date is repealed, unless a later enacted statute, which is chaptered before that date, deletes or extends the date.

(Amended (as amended by Stats. 2017, Ch. 347, Sec. 2) by Stats. 2018, Ch. 423, Sec. 101. (SB 1494) Effective January 1, 2019. Repealed as of January 1, 2022, by its own provisions. See later operative version added by Sec. 3 of Stats. 2017, Ch. 347)

2603.

(a) Except as provided in subdivision (b), no person sentenced to imprisonment in a county jail shall be administered any psychiatric medication without his or her prior informed consent.

(b) If a psychiatrist determines that an inmate should be treated with psychiatric medication, but the inmate does not consent, the inmate may be involuntarily treated with the medication. Treatment may be given on either a nonemergency basis as provided in subdivision (c), or on an emergency or interim basis as provided in subdivision (d).

(c) A county department of mental health, or other designated county department, may seek to initiate involuntary medication on a nonemergency basis only if all of the following conditions have been met:

(1) A psychiatrist or psychologist has determined that the inmate has a serious mental disorder.

(2) A psychiatrist or psychologist has determined that, as a result of that mental disorder, the inmate is gravely disabled and does not have the capacity to refuse treatment with psychiatric medications, or is a danger to self or others.

(3) A psychiatrist has prescribed one or more psychiatric medications for the treatment of the inmate's disorder, has considered the risks, benefits, and treatment alternatives to involuntary medication, and has determined that the treatment alternatives to involuntary medication are unlikely to meet the needs of the patient.

(4) The inmate has been advised of the risks and benefits of, and treatment alternatives to, the psychiatric medication, and refuses, or is unable to consent to, the administration of the medication.

(5) The inmate is provided a hearing before a superior court judge, a court-appointed commissioner or referee, or a court-appointed hearing officer, as specified in subdivision (c) of Section 5334 of the Welfare and Institutions Code.

(6) The inmate is provided counsel at least 21 days prior to the hearing, unless emergency or interim medication is being administered pursuant to subdivision (d), in which case the inmate would receive expedited access to counsel. The hearing shall be held not more than 30 days after the filing of the notice with the superior court, unless counsel for the inmate agrees to extend the date of the hearing.

(7) The inmate and counsel are provided with written notice of the hearing at least 21 days prior to the hearing, unless emergency or interim medication is being administered pursuant to subdivision (d), in which case the inmate would receive an expedited hearing. The written notice shall do all of the following:

(A) Set forth the diagnosis, the factual basis for the diagnosis, the basis upon which psychiatric medication is recommended, the expected benefits of the medication, any potential side effects and risks to the inmate from the medication, and any alternatives to treatment with the medication.

(B) Advise the inmate of the right to be present at the hearing, the right to be represented by counsel at all stages of the proceedings, the right to present evidence, and the right to cross-examine witnesses. Counsel for the inmate shall have access to all medical records and files of the inmate, but shall not have access to the confidential section of the inmate's central file which contains materials unrelated to medical treatment.

(C) Inform the inmate of his or her right to appeal the determination to the superior court or the court of appeal as specified in subdivisions (e) and (f) of Section 5334 of the Welfare and Institutions Code, and of his or her right to file a petition for writ of habeas corpus with respect to any decision of the county department of mental health, or other designated county department, to continue treatment with involuntary medication after the superior court judge, court-appointed commissioner or referee, or court-appointed hearing officer has authorized treatment with involuntary medication.

(8) A superior court judge, a court-appointed commissioner or referee, or a court-appointed hearing officer determines by clear and convincing evidence that the inmate has a mental illness or disorder, that as a result of that illness the inmate is gravely disabled and lacks the capacity to consent to or refuse treatment with psychiatric medications or is a danger to self or others if not medicated, that there is no less intrusive alternative to involuntary medication, and that the medication is in the inmate's best medical interest. In the event of any statutory notice issues with either initial or renewal filings by the county department of mental health, or other designated county department, the superior court judge, court-appointed commissioner or referee, or court-appointed hearing officer shall hear arguments as to why the case should be heard, and shall consider factors such as the ability of the inmate's counsel to adequately prepare the case and to confer with the inmate, the continuity of care, and, if applicable, the need for protection of the inmate or institutional staff that would be compromised by a procedural default.

(9) The historical course of the inmate's mental disorder, as determined by available relevant information about the course of the inmate's mental disorder, shall be considered when it has direct bearing on the determination of whether the inmate is a danger to self or others, or is gravely disabled and incompetent to refuse medication as the result of a mental disorder.

(10) An inmate is entitled to file one motion for reconsideration following a determination that he or she may receive involuntary medication, and may seek a hearing to present new evidence, upon good cause shown.

(d) Nothing in this section is intended to prohibit a physician from taking appropriate action in an emergency. An emergency exists when there is a sudden and marked change in an inmate's mental condition so that action is immediately necessary for the preservation of life or the prevention of serious bodily harm to the inmate or others, and it is impractical, due to the seriousness of the emergency, to first obtain informed consent. If psychiatric medication is administered during an emergency, the medication shall only be that which is required to treat the emergency condition and shall be administered for only so long as the emergency continues to exist. If the clinicians of the county department of mental health, or other designated county department, identify a situation that jeopardizes the inmate's health or well-being as the result of a serious mental illness, and necessitates the continuation of medication beyond the initial 72 hours pending the full mental health hearing, the county department may seek to continue the medication by giving notice to the inmate and his or her counsel of its intention to seek an ex parte order to allow the continuance of medication pending the full hearing. Treatment of the inmate in a facility pursuant to Section 4011.6 shall not be required in order to continue medication under this subdivision unless the treatment is otherwise medically necessary. The notice shall be served upon the inmate and counsel at the same time the inmate is given the written notice that the involuntary medication proceedings are being initiated and is appointed counsel as provided in subdivision (c). The order may be issued ex parte upon a showing that, in the absence of the medication, the emergency conditions are likely to recur. The request for an ex parte order shall be supported by an affidavit from the psychiatrist or psychologist showing specific facts. The inmate and the inmate's appointed counsel shall have two business days to respond to the county department's ex parte request to continue interim medication, and may present facts supported by an affidavit in opposition to the department's request. A superior court judge, a court-appointed commissioner or referee, or a court-appointed hearing officer shall review the ex parte request and shall have three business days to determine the merits of the department's request for an ex parte order. If an order is issued, the psychiatrist may continue the administration of the medication until the hearing described in paragraph (5) of subdivision (c) is held.

(1) If the county elects to seek an ex parte order pursuant to this subdivision, the county department of mental health, or other designated county department, shall file with the superior court, and serve on the inmate and his or her counsel, the written notice described in paragraph (7) of subdivision (c) within 72 hours of commencing medication pursuant to this subdivision, unless either of the following occurs:

(A) The inmate gives informed consent to continue the medication.

(B) A psychiatrist determines that the psychiatric medication is not necessary and administration of the medication is discontinued.

(2) If medication is being administered pursuant to this subdivision, the hearing described in paragraph (5) of subdivision (c) shall commence within 21 days of the filing and service of the notice, unless counsel for the inmate agrees to a different period of time.

(3) With the exception of the timeline provisions specified in paragraphs (1) and (2) for providing notice and commencement of the hearing in emergency or interim situations, the inmate shall be entitled to and be given the same due process protections as specified in subdivision (c). The county department of mental health, or other designated county department, shall prove the same elements supporting the involuntary administration of psychiatric medication, and the superior court judge, court-appointed commissioner or referee, or court-appointed hearing officer shall be required to make the same findings described in subdivision (c).

(e) The determination that an inmate may receive involuntary medication shall be valid for one year from the date of the determination, regardless of whether the inmate subsequently gives his or her informed consent.
(f) If a determination has been made to involuntarily medicate an inmate pursuant to subdivision (c) or (d), the medication shall be discontinued one year after the date of that determination, unless the inmate gives his or her informed consent to the administration of the medication, or unless a new determination is made pursuant to the procedures set forth in subdivision (g).
(g) To renew an existing order allowing involuntary medication, the county department of mental health, or other designated county department, shall file with the superior court, and shall serve on the inmate and his or her counsel, a written notice indicating the department's intent to renew the existing involuntary medication order.
(1) The request to renew the order shall be filed and served no later than 21 days prior to the expiration of the current order authorizing involuntary medication.
(2) The inmate shall be entitled to, and shall be given, the same due process protections as specified in subdivision (c).
(3) Renewal orders shall be valid for one year from the date of the hearing.
(4) An order renewing an existing order shall be granted based on clear and convincing evidence that the inmate has a serious mental disorder that requires treatment with psychiatric medication, and that, but for the medication, the inmate would revert to the behavior that was the basis for the prior order authorizing involuntary medication, coupled with evidence that the inmate lacks insight regarding his or her need for the medication, such that it is unlikely that the inmate would be able to manage his or her own medication and treatment regimen. No new acts need be alleged or proven.
(5) If the county department of mental health, or other designated county department, wishes to add a basis to an existing order, it shall give the inmate and the inmate's counsel notice in advance of the hearing via a renewal notice or supplemental petition. Within the renewal notice or supplemental petition, as described in subdivision (g), the county department of mental health, or other designated county department, shall specify what additional basis is being alleged and what qualifying conduct within the past year supports that additional basis. The county department of mental health, or other designated county department, shall prove the additional basis and conduct by clear and convincing evidence at a hearing as specified in subdivision (c).
(6) The hearing on any petition to renew an order for involuntary medication shall be conducted prior to the expiration of the current order.
(h) In the event of a conflict between the provisions of this section and the Administrative Procedure Act (Chapter 4.5 (commencing with Section 11400) of Part 1 of Division 3 of Title 2 of the Government Code), this section shall control.
(i) This section shall become effective on January 1, 2022.
(Repealed (in Sec. 2) and added by Stats. 2017, Ch. 347, Sec. 3. (AB 720) Effective January 1, 2018. Section operative January 1, 2022, by its own provisions.)

<u>2604.</u>

(a) Except as provided in subdivision (b), an adult housed in state prison is presumed to have the capacity to give informed consent and make a health care decision, to give or revoke an advance health care directive, and to designate or disqualify a surrogate. This presumption is a presumption affecting the burden of proof.
(b) (1) Except as provided in Section 2602, a licensed physician or dentist may file a petition with the Office of Administrative Hearings to request that an administrative law judge make a determination as to a patient's capacity to give informed consent or make a health care decision, and request appointment of a surrogate decisionmaker, if all of the following conditions are satisfied:
(A) The licensed physician or dentist is treating a patient who is an adult housed in state prison.
(B) The licensed physician or dentist is unable to obtain informed consent from the inmate patient because the physician or dentist determines that the inmate patient appears to lack capacity to give informed consent or make a health care decision.
(C) There is no person with legal authority to provide informed consent for, or make decisions concerning the health care of, the inmate patient.
(2) Preference shall be given to the next of kin or a family member as a surrogate decisionmaker over other potential surrogate decisionmakers unless those individuals are unsuitable or unable to serve.
(c) The petition required by subdivision (b) shall allege all of the following:
(1) The inmate patient's current physical condition, describing the health care conditions currently afflicting the inmate patient.
(2) The inmate patient's current mental health condition resulting in the inmate patient's inability to understand the nature and consequences of his or her need for care such that there is a lack of capacity to give informed consent or make a health care decision.
(3) The deficit or deficits in the inmate patient's mental functions as listed in subdivision (a) of Section 811 of the Probate Code.
(4) An identification of a link, if any, between the deficits identified pursuant to paragraph (3) and an explanation of how the deficits identified pursuant to that paragraph result in the inmate patient's inability to participate in a decision about his or her health care either knowingly and intelligently or by means of a rational thought process.
(5) A discussion of whether the deficits identified pursuant to paragraph (3) are transient, fixed, or likely to change during the proposed year-long duration of the court order.
(6) The efforts made to obtain informed consent or refusal from the inmate patient and the results of those efforts.
(7) The efforts made to locate next of kin who could act as a surrogate decisionmaker for the inmate patient. If those individuals are located, all of the following shall also be included, so far as the information is known:
(A) The names and addresses of the individuals.
(B) Whether any information exists to suggest that any of those individuals would not act in the inmate patient's best interests.
(C) Whether any of those individuals are otherwise suitable to make health care decisions for the inmate patient.
(8) The probable impact on the inmate patient with, or without, the appointment of a surrogate decisionmaker.
(9) A discussion of the inmate patient's desires, if known, and whether there is an advance health care directive, Physicians Orders for Life Sustaining Treatment (POLST), or other documented indication of the inmate patient's directives or desires and how those indications might influence the decision to issue an order. Additionally, any known POLST or Advanced Health Care Directives executed while the inmate patient had capacity shall be disclosed.
(10) The petitioner's recommendation specifying a qualified and willing surrogate decisionmaker as described in subdivision (q), and the reasons for that recommendation.
(d) The petition shall be served on the inmate patient and his or her counsel, and filed with the Office of Administrative Hearings on the same day as it was served. The Office of Administrative Hearings shall issue a notice appointing counsel.
(e) (1) At the time the initial petition is filed, the inmate patient shall be provided with counsel and a written notice advising him or her of all of the following:
(A) His or her right to be present at the hearing.
(B) His or her right to be represented by counsel at all stages of the proceedings.
(C) His or her right to present evidence.
(D) His or her right to cross-examine witnesses.
(E) The right of either party to seek one reconsideration of the administrative law judge's decision per calendar year.
(F) His or her right to file a petition for writ of administrative mandamus in superior court pursuant to Section 1094.5 of the Code of Civil Procedure.
(G) His or her right to file a petition for writ of habeas corpus in superior court with respect to any decision.
(2) Counsel for the inmate patient shall have access to all relevant medical and central file records for the inmate patient, but shall not have access to materials unrelated to medical treatment located in the confidential section of the inmate patient's central file. Counsel shall also have access to all health care appeals filed by the inmate patient and responses to those appeals, and, to the extent available, any habeas corpus petitions or health care related litigation filed by, or on behalf of, the inmate patient.
(f) The inmate patient shall be provided with a hearing before an administrative law judge within 30 days of the date of filing the petition, unless counsel for the inmate patient agrees to extend the date of the hearing.
(g) The inmate patient, or his or her counsel, shall have 14 days from the date of filing of any petition to file a response to the petition, unless a shorter time for the hearing is sought by the licensed physician or dentist and ordered by the administrative law judge, in which case the judge shall set the time for filing a response. The response shall be served to all parties who were served with the initial petition and the attorney for the petitioner.
(h) In case of an emergency, as described in Section 3351 of Title 15 of the California Code of Regulations, the inmate patient's physician or dentist may administer a medical intervention that requires informed consent prior to the date of the administrative hearing. Counsel for the inmate patient shall be notified by the physician or dentist.
(i) In either an initial or renewal proceeding, the inmate patient has the right to contest the finding of an administrative law judge authorizing a surrogate decisionmaker by filing a petition for writ of administrative mandamus pursuant to Section 1094.5 of the Code of Civil Procedure.
(j) In either an initial or renewal proceeding, either party is entitled to file one motion for reconsideration per calendar year in front of the administrative law judge following a determination as to an inmate patient's capacity to give informed consent or make a health care decision. The motion may seek to review the decision for the necessity of a surrogate decisionmaker, the individual appointed under the order, or both. The motion for reconsideration shall not require a formal rehearing unless ordered by the administrative law judge following submission of the motion, or upon the granting of a request for formal rehearing by any party to the action based on a showing of good cause.
(k) (1) To renew an existing order appointing a surrogate decisionmaker, the current physician or dentist, or a previously appointed surrogate decisionmaker shall file a renewal petition. The renewal shall be for an additional year at a time. The renewal hearing on any order issued under this section shall be conducted prior to the expiration of the current order, but not sooner than 10 days after the petition is filed, at which time the inmate patient shall be brought before an administrative law judge for a review of his or her current medical and mental health condition.
(2) A renewal petition shall be served on the inmate patient and his or her counsel, and filed with the Office of Administrative Hearings on the same day as it was served. The Office of Administrative Hearings shall issue a written order appointing counsel.
(3) (A) The renewal hearing shall be held in accordance with subdivisions (d) to (g), inclusive.
(B) (i) At the time the renewal petition is filed, the inmate patient shall be provided with counsel and a written notice advising him or her of all of the following:
(I) His or her right to be present at the hearing.
(II) His or her right to be represented by counsel at all stages of the proceedings.
(III) His or her right to present evidence.
(IV) His or her right to cross-examine witnesses.
(V) The right of either party to seek one reconsideration of the administrative law judge's decision per calendar year.
(VI) His or her right to file a petition for writ of administrative mandamus in superior court pursuant to Section 1094.5 of the Code of Civil Procedure.
(VII) His or her right to file a petition for writ of habeas corpus in superior court with respect to any decision.
(ii) Counsel for the inmate patient shall have access to all relevant medical and central file records for the inmate patient, but shall not have access to materials unrelated to medical treatment located in the confidential section of the inmate patient's central file. Counsel shall also have access to all health care appeals filed by the inmate patient and responses to those appeals, and, to the extent available, any habeas corpus petitions or health care related litigation filed by, or on behalf of, the inmate patient.
(4) The renewal petition shall request the matter be reviewed by an administrative law judge, and allege all of the following:
(A) The current status of each of the elements set forth in paragraphs (1) to (8), inclusive, of subdivision (c).
(B) Whether the inmate patient still requires a surrogate decisionmaker.
(C) Whether the inmate patient continues to lack capacity to give informed consent or make a health care decision.
(l) A licensed physician or dentist who submits a petition pursuant to this section shall not be required to obtain a court order pursuant to Section 3201 of the Probate Code prior to administering care that requires informed consent.
(m) This section does not affect the right of an inmate patient who has been determined to lack capacity to give informed consent or make a health care decision and for whom a surrogate decisionmaker has been appointed to do either of the following:
(1) Seek appropriate judicial relief to review the determination or appointment by filing a petition for writ of administrative mandamus pursuant to Section 1094.5 of the Code of Civil Procedure.
(2) File a petition for writ of habeas corpus in superior court regarding the determination or appointment, or any treatment decision by the surrogate decisionmaker.
(n) A licensed physician or other health care provider whose actions under this section are in accordance with reasonable health care standards, a surrogate decisionmaker appointed pursuant to this section, and an administrative law judge shall not be liable for monetary damages or administrative sanctions for his or her decisions or actions consistent with this section and the known and documented desires of the inmate patient, or if unknown, the best interests of the inmate patient.
(o) The determinations required to be made pursuant to subdivisions (c) and (k), and the basis for those determinations, shall be documented in the inmate patient's medical record.
(p) (1) With regard to any petition filed pursuant to subdivision (c) or (k), the administrative law judge shall determine and provide a written order and findings setting forth whether there has been clear and convincing evidence that all of the following occurred:
(A) Adequate notice and an opportunity to be heard has been given to the inmate patient and his or her counsel.
(B) Reasonable efforts have been made to obtain informed consent from the inmate patient.
(C) As a result of one or more deficits in his or her mental functions, the inmate patient lacks capacity to give informed consent or make a health care decision and is unlikely to regain that capacity over the next year.
(D) Reasonable efforts have been made to identify family members or relatives who could serve as a surrogate decisionmaker for the inmate patient.
(2) The written decision shall also specify and describe any advance health care directives, POLST, or other documented indication of the inmate patient's directives or

desires regarding health care that were created and validly executed while the inmate patient had capacity.
(q) (1) If all findings required by subdivision (p) are made, the administrative law judge shall appoint a surrogate decisionmaker for health care for the inmate patient. In doing so, the administrative law judge shall consider all reasonable options presented, including those identified in the petition, and weigh how the proposed surrogate decisionmaker would represent the best interests of the inmate patient, the efficacy of achieving timely surrogate decisions, and the urgency of the situation. Family members or relatives of the inmate patient should be appointed when possible if such an individual is available and the administrative law judge determines the family member or relative will act in the inmate patient's best interests.
(2) An employee of the Department of Corrections and Rehabilitation, or other peace officer, shall not be appointed surrogate decisionmaker for health care for any inmate patient under this section, unless either of the following conditions apply:
(A) The individual is a family member or relative of the inmate patient and will, as determined by the administrative law judge, act in the inmate patient's best interests and consider the inmate patient's personal values and other wishes to the extent those values and wishes are known.
(B) The individual is a health care staff member in a managerial position and does not provide direct care to the inmate patient. A surrogate decisionmaker appointed under this subparagraph may be specified by his or her functional role at the institution, such as "Chief Physician and Surgeon" or "Chief Medical Executive" to provide clarity as to the active decisionmaker at the institution where the inmate patient is housed, and to anticipate potential personnel changes. When the surrogate decisionmaker is specified by position, rather than by name, the person occupying that specified role at the institution at which the inmate patient is currently housed shall be considered and act as the appointed surrogate decisionmaker.
(3) The order appointing the surrogate decisionmaker shall be written and state the basis for the decision by reference to the particular mandates of this subdivision. The order shall also state that the surrogate decisionmaker shall honor and follow any advance health care directive, POLST, or other documented indication of the inmate patient's directives or desires, and specify any such directive, order, or documented desire.
(4) The surrogate decisionmaker shall follow the inmate patient's personal values and other wishes to the extent those values and wishes are known.
(r) The administrative law judge's written decision and order appointing a surrogate decisionmaker shall be placed in the inmate patient's Department of Corrections and Rehabilitation health care record.
(s) An order entered under this section is valid for one year and the expiration date shall be written on the order. The order shall be valid at any state correctional facility within California. If the inmate patient is moved, the sending institution shall inform the receiving institution of the existence of an order entered under this section.
(t) (1) This section applies only to orders appointing a surrogate decisionmaker with authority to make a health care decision for an inmate patient who lacks capacity to give informed consent or make a health care decision.
(2) This section does not apply to existing law regarding health care to be provided in an emergency or existing law governing health care for unemancipated minors. This section shall not be used for the purposes of determining or directing an inmate patient's control over finances, marital status, or for convulsive treatment, as described in Section 5325 of the Welfare and Institutions Code, psychosurgery, as defined in Section 5325 of the Welfare and Institutions Code, sterilization, abortion, or involuntary administration of psychiatric medication, as described in Section 2602.
(u) The Secretary of the Department of Corrections and Rehabilitation may adopt regulations as necessary to carry out the purposes of this section.
(Added by Stats. 2015, Ch. 381, Sec. 2. (AB 1423) Effective January 1, 2016.)

ARTICLE 2. Prisoners as Witnesses [2620 - 2626]
(Article 2 added by Stats. 1941, Ch. 106.)

2620.
When it is necessary to have a person imprisoned in the state prison brought before any court to be tried for a felony, or for an examination before a grand jury or magistrate preliminary to such trial, or for the purpose of hearing a motion or other proceeding, to vacate a judgment, an order for the prisoner's temporary removal from said prison, and for the prisoner's production before such court, grand jury or magistrate, must be made by the superior court of the county in which said action, motion, or examination is pending or by a judge thereof; such order shall be made only upon the affidavit of the district attorney or defense attorney, stating the purpose for which said person is to be brought before the court, grand jury or magistrate or upon the court's own motion. The order shall be executed by the sheriff of the county in which it shall be made, whose duty it shall be to bring the prisoner before the proper court, grand jury or magistrate, to safely keep the prisoner, and when the prisoner's presence is no longer required to return the prisoner to the prison from whence the prisoner was taken; the expense of executing such order shall be a proper charge against, and shall be paid by, the county in which the order shall be made.
Such order shall recite the purposes for which said person is to be brought before the court, grand jury or magistrate, and shall be signed by the judge making the order and sealed with the seal of the court. The order must be to the following effect:
County of _____ (as the case may be).
The people of the State of California to the warden of _____:
An order having been made this day by me, that A.B. be produced in the _____ court (or before the grand jury, as the case may be) to be prosecuted or examined for the crime of _____, a felony (or to have said motion heard), you are commanded to deliver the prisoner into the custody of _____ for the purpose of (recite purposes).
Dated this _____ day of _____, 19___.
When a prisoner is removed from a state prison under this section the prisoner shall remain in the constructive custody of the warden thereof. During the prisoner's absence from the prison, the prisoner may be ordered to appear in other felony proceedings as a defendant or witness in the courts of the county from which the original order directing removal issued. A copy of the written order directing the prisoner to appear before any such court shall be forwarded by the district attorney to the warden of the prison having protective custody of the prisoner.
(Amended by Stats. 1998, Ch. 931, Sec. 429. Effective September 28, 1998.)

2621.
When the testimony of a material witness is required in a criminal action, before any court in this state, or in an examination before a grand jury or magistrate in a felony case and such witness is a prisoner in a state prison, an order for the prisoner's temporary removal from such prison, and for the prisoner's production before such court, grand jury or magistrate, may be made by the superior court of the county in which such action or examination is pending or by a judge thereof; but in case the prison is out of the county in which the application is made, such order shall be made only upon the affidavit of the district attorney or of the defendant or the defendant's counsel, showing that the testimony is material and necessary; and even then the granting of the order shall be in the discretion of said superior court or a judge thereof. The order shall be executed by the sheriff of the county in which it is made, whose duty it shall be to bring the prisoner before the proper court, grand jury or magistrate, to safely keep the prisoner, and when the prisoner is no longer required as a witness, to return the prisoner to the prison whence the prisoner was taken; the expense of executing such order shall be a proper charge against, and shall be paid by, the county in which the order shall be made. Such orders shall recite the purposes for which said person is to be brought before the court, grand jury or magistrate, and shall be signed by the magistrate or judge making the order, and sealed with the seal of the court, if any.
Such order must be to the following effect:
County of _____ (as the case may be).
The people of the State of California to the warden of _____:
An order having been made this day by me, that A. B. be produced in this court as witness in the case of _____, you are commanded to deliver the prisoner into the custody of _____ for the purpose of (recite purposes).
Dated this _____ day of _____, 19___.
When a prisoner is removed from a state prison under this section the prisoner shall remain in the constructive custody of the warden hereof. During the prisoner's absence from the prison, the prisoner may be ordered to appear in other felony proceedings as a defendant or witness in the courts of the county from which the original order directing removal issued. A copy of the written order directing the prisoner to appear before any such court shall be forwarded by the district attorney to the warden of the prison having protective custody of the prisoner.
(Amended by Stats. 1998, Ch. 931, Sec. 430. Effective September 28, 1998.)

2621.5.
The provisions of Sections 2620 and 2621 which impose a charge upon the counties shall not apply to cases coming within the provisions of Section 4750.
(Amended by Stats. 1986, Ch. 1310, Sec. 4.)

2622.
When the order for personal appearance is not made pursuant to Section 2620 or Section 2621 the deposition of the prisoner may be taken in the manner provided for in the case of a witness who is sick, and Chapter 4 (commencing with Section 1335) of Title 10 of Part 2 shall, so far as applicable, govern in the application for and in the taking and use of that deposition. The deposition may be taken before any magistrate or notary public of the county in which the prison is situated; or in case the defendant is unable to pay for taking the deposition, before an officer of the prison designated by the board, whose duty it shall be to act without compensation. Every officer before whom testimony shall be taken under this section, shall have authority to administer, and shall administer, an oath to the witness that his or her testimony shall be the truth, the whole truth, and nothing but the truth.
(Amended by Stats. 1987, Ch. 828, Sec. 119.)

2623.
If in a civil action or special proceeding a witness be a prisoner, confined in a state prison within this state, an order for the prisoner's examination in the prison by deposition may be made.
1. By the court itself in which the action or special proceeding is pending, unless it be a small claims court.
2. By a judge of the superior court of the county where the action or proceeding is pending, if pending before a small claims court or before a judge or other person out of court.
Such order can only be made on the motion of a party, upon affidavit showing the nature of the action or proceeding, the testimony expected from the witness, and its materiality. The deposition, when ordered, shall be taken in accordance with Section 2622.
(Amended by Stats. 1998, Ch. 931, Sec. 431. Effective September 28, 1998.)

2624.
(a) Notwithstanding any other provision of law, a court may, upon the submission of a written request by the party calling the witness, order an incarcerated witness to testify in legal proceedings via two-way electronic audiovisual communication.
(b) As used in this section, "legal proceedings" includes preliminary hearings, civil trials, and criminal trials.
(c) With reference to criminal trials only, the procedure described in this section shall only be used with the consent of both parties expressed in open court, and, in consultation with the defendant's counsel, upon a waiver by the defendant of his or her right to compel the physical presence of the witness, pursuant to the Sixth Amendment to the United States Constitution and Section 15 of Article I of the California Constitution. This waiver may be rescinded by the defendant upon a showing of good cause.
(d) No inducement shall be offered nor any penalty imposed in connection with a defendant's consent to allow a witness to testify via closed-circuit television.
(Added by Stats. 1998, Ch. 122, Sec. 1. Effective January 1, 1999.)

2625.
(a) For the purposes of this section only, the term "prisoner" includes any individual in custody in a state prison, the California Rehabilitation Center, or a county jail, or who is a ward of the Department of the Youth Authority or who, upon a verdict or finding that the individual was insane at the time of committing an offense, or mentally incompetent to be tried or adjudged to punishment, is confined in a state hospital for the care and treatment of the mentally disordered or in any other public or private treatment facility.
(b) In any proceeding brought under Part 4 (commencing with Section 7800) of Division 12 of the Family Code, and Section 366.26 of the Welfare and Institutions Code, where the proceeding seeks to terminate the parental rights of any prisoner, or any proceeding brought under Section 300 of the Welfare and Institutions Code, where the proceeding seeks to adjudicate the child of a prisoner a dependent child of the court, the superior court of the county in which the proceeding is pending, or a judge thereof, shall order notice of any court proceeding regarding the proceeding transmitted to the prisoner.
(c) Service of notice shall be made pursuant to Section 7881 or 7882 of the Family Code or Section 290.2, 291, or 294 of the Welfare and Institutions Code, as appropriate.
(d) Upon receipt by the court of a statement from the prisoner or his or her attorney indicating the prisoner's desire to be present during the court's proceedings, the court shall issue an order for the temporary removal of the prisoner from the institution, and for the prisoner's production before the court. No proceeding may be held under Part 4 (commencing with Section 7800) of Division 12 of the Family Code or Section 366.26 of the Welfare and Institutions Code and no petition to adjudge the child of a prisoner a dependent child of the court pursuant to subdivision (a), (b), (c), (d), (e), (f), (i), or (j) of Section 300 of the Welfare and Institutions Code may be adjudicated without the physical presence of the prisoner or the prisoner's attorney, unless the court has before it a knowing waiver of the right of physical presence signed by the prisoner or an affidavit signed by the warden, superintendent, or other person in charge of the institution, or his or her designated representative stating that the prisoner has, by express statement or action, indicated an intent not to appear at the proceeding.
(e) In any other action or proceeding in which a prisoner's parental or marital rights are subject to adjudication, an order for the prisoner's temporary removal from the institution and for the prisoner's production before the court may be made by the superior court of the county in which the action or proceeding is pending, or by a judge thereof. A copy of the order shall be transmitted to the warden, superintendent, or other person in charge of the institution not less than 15 days before the order is to be executed. The order shall be executed by the sheriff of the county in which it shall be made, whose duty it shall be to bring the prisoner before the proper court, to keep the prisoner safely, and when the prisoner's presence is no longer required, to return the prisoner to the institution from which he or she was taken. The expense of executing the order shall be a proper charge against, and shall be paid by, the county in which the order shall be made.
The order shall be to the following effect:
County of _____ (as the case may be).
The people of the State of California to the warden of _____:

An order having been made this day by me, that (name of prisoner) be produced in this court as a party in the case of _____, you are commanded to deliver (name of prisoner) into the custody of _____ for the purpose of (recite purposes).
Dated this _____ day of _____, 20___.

(f) When a prisoner is removed from the institution pursuant to this section, the prisoner shall remain in the constructive custody of the warden, superintendent, or other person in charge of the institution.

(g) A prisoner who is a parent of a child involved in a dependency hearing described in this section and who has either waived his or her right to physical presence at the hearing pursuant to subdivision (d) or who has not been ordered before the court may, at the court's discretion, in order to facilitate the parent's participation, be given the opportunity to participate in the hearing by videoconference, if that technology is available, and if that participation otherwise complies with the law. If videoconferencing technology is not available, teleconferencing may be utilized to facilitate parental participation. Because of the significance of dependency court hearings for parental rights and children's long-term care, physical attendance by the parent at the hearings is preferred to participation by videoconference or teleconference. This subdivision shall not be construed to limit a prisoner's right to physically attend a dependency hearing as provided in this section. This section does not authorize the use of videoconference or teleconference to replace in-person family visits with prisoners.

(h) It is the intent of the Legislature to maintain internal job placement opportunities and preserve earned privileges for prisoners, and prevent the removal of prisoners subject to this section from court-ordered courses as a result of their participation in the proceedings described in this section.

(i) Notwithstanding any other law, a court may not order the removal and production of a prisoner sentenced to death, whether or not that sentence is being appealed, in any action or proceeding in which the prisoner's parental rights are subject to adjudication.

(Amended by Stats. 2010, Ch. 482, Sec. 1. (SB 962) Effective January 1, 2011.)

2626.

(a) The Department of Corrections and Rehabilitation is authorized to accept donated materials and services related to videoconferencing and teleconferencing in order to implement a program, at a prison to be determined by the department, to facilitate the participation of incarcerated parents in dependency court hearings regarding their children.

(b) The implementation of this program is contingent upon the receipt of sufficient donations of materials and services by the department.

(Added by Stats. 2010, Ch. 482, Sec. 2. (SB 962) Effective January 1, 2011.)

ARTICLE 3. Sexual Abuse in Detention [2635 - 2644]

(Article 3 added by Stats. 2005, Ch. 303, Sec. 3.)

2635.

2635.The Department of Corrections and Rehabilitation shall review informational handbooks regarding sexual abuse in detention published by outside organizations. Upon approving the content thereof, handbooks provided by one or more outside organizations shall be made available to inmates and wards.

(Added by Stats. 2005, Ch. 303, Sec. 3. Effective January 1, 2006.)

2636.

For the purposes of this section, all references to classification of wards shall take effect upon the adoption of a classification system for wards developed by the Department of Corrections and Rehabilitation in compliance with Farrell v. Allen, Alameda County Superior Court Case No. RG 03079344.

The following practices shall be instituted to prevent sexual violence and promote inmate and ward safety in the Department of Corrections and Rehabilitation:

(a) The Department of Corrections and Rehabilitation inmate classification and housing assignment procedures shall take into account risk factors that can lead to inmates and wards becoming the target of sexual victimization or of being sexually aggressive toward others. Relevant considerations include:

(1) Age of the inmate or ward.

(2) Whether the offender is a violent or nonviolent offender.

(3) Whether the inmate or ward has served a prior term of commitment.

(4) Whether the inmate or ward has a history of mental illness.

(b) The Department of Corrections and Rehabilitation shall ensure that staff members intervene when an inmate or ward appears to be the target of sexual harassment or intimidation.

(Added by Stats. 2005, Ch. 303, Sec. 3. Effective January 1, 2006.)

2637.

The Department of Corrections and Rehabilitation shall ensure that its protocols for responding to sexual abuse include all of the following:

(a) The safety of an inmate or ward who alleges that he or she has been the victim of sexual abuse shall be immediately and discreetly ensured. Staff shall provide the safest possible housing options to inmates and wards who have experienced repeated abuse. Housing options may include discreet institution transfers.

(b) Inmates and wards who file complaints of sexual abuse shall not be punished, either directly or indirectly, for doing so. If a person is segregated for his or her own protection, segregation must be nondisciplinary.

(c) Any person who knowingly or willfully submits inaccurate or untruthful information in regards to sexual abuse is punishable pursuant to department regulations.

(d) Under no circumstances is it appropriate to suggest that an inmate should fight to avoid sexual violence or to suggest that the reported sexual abuse is not significant enough to be addressed by staff.

(e) Staff shall not discriminate in their response to inmates and wards who are gay, bisexual, or transgender who experience sexual aggression, or report that they have experienced sexual abuse.

(f) Retaliation against an inmate or ward for making an allegation of sexual abuse shall be strictly prohibited.

(Added by Stats. 2005, Ch. 303, Sec. 3. Effective January 1, 2006.)

2638.

Thoughtful, confidential standards of physical and mental health care shall be implemented to reduce the impact of sexual abuse on inmates and wards in the Department of Corrections and Rehabilitation that include all of the following:

(a) Victims shall receive appropriate acute-trauma care for rape victims, including, but not limited to, treatment of injuries, HIV/AIDS prophylactic measures, and, later, testing for sexually transmittable diseases.

(b) Health practitioners who conduct or encounter an inmate or ward suffering from problems that might indicate sexual abuse, such as trauma, sexually transmissible diseases, pregnancy, or chronic pain symptoms, shall ask whether the patient has experienced sexual abuse.

(c) Practitioners should strive to ask frank, straightforward questions about sexual incidents without shaming inmates or displaying embarrassment about the subject matter.

(d) Confidential mental health counseling intended to help the victim to cope with the aftermath of abuse shall be offered to those who report sexual abuse. Victims shall be monitored for suicidal impulses, posttraumatic stress disorder, depression, and other mental health consequences.

(e) Any adult inmate in mental health counseling for any reason shall be entitled to speak confidentially about sexual abuse.

(Added by Stats. 2005, Ch. 303, Sec. 3. Effective January 1, 2006.)

2639.

The Department of Corrections and Rehabilitation shall ensure that the following procedures are performed in the investigation and prosecution of sexual abuse incidents:

(a) The provision of safe housing options, medical care, and the like shall not be contingent upon the victim's willingness to press charges.

(b) Investigations into allegations of sexual abuse shall include, when deemed appropriate by the investigating agency, the use of forensic rape kits, questioning of suspects and witnesses, and gathering of other relevant evidence.

(c) Physical and testimonial evidence shall be carefully preserved for use in any future proceedings.

(d) Staff attitudes that inmates and wards cannot provide reliable information shall be discouraged.

(e) If an investigation confirms that any employee has sexually abused an inmate or ward, that employee shall be terminated. Administrators shall report criminal sexual abuse by staff to law enforcement authorities.

(f) Consensual sodomy and oral copulation among inmates is prohibited by subdivision (e) of Section 286 and subdivision (e) of Section 287 or former Section 288a, respectively. Without repealing those provisions, the increased scrutiny provided by this article shall apply only to nonconsensual sexual contact among inmates and custodial sexual misconduct.

(Amended by Stats. 2018, Ch. 423, Sec. 102. (SB 1494) Effective January 1, 2019.)

2640.

The Department of Corrections and Rehabilitation shall collect data as follows:

(a) The Department of Corrections and Rehabilitation shall keep statistics on the sexual abuse of inmates and wards. Sexual abuse incidents shall not be classified as "other" nor simply included in a broader category of general assaults.

(b) Statistics shall include whether the abuse was perpetrated by a staff member or other inmate, the results of the investigation and any resolution of the complaint by department officials and prosecution authorities.

The data shall be made available to the Office of the Sexual Abuse in Detention Elimination Ombudsperson.

(Added by Stats. 2005, Ch. 303, Sec. 3. Effective January 1, 2006.)

2641.

(a) The Office of the Sexual Abuse in Detention Elimination Ombudsperson is hereby created in state government to ensure the impartial resolution of inmate and ward sexual abuse complaints. The office shall be based within the Office of the Inspector General. The duties of this office may be contracted to outside nongovernmental experts.

(b) The ombudsperson shall have the authority to inspect all of the Department of Corrections and Rehabilitation institutions and to interview all inmates and wards.

(c) The Department of Corrections and Rehabilitation shall allow all inmates and wards to write confidential letters regarding sexual abuse to the ombudsperson.

(d) Information about how to confidentially contact the ombudsperson shall be clearly posted in all of the Department of Corrections and Rehabilitation institutions.

(e) The Office of the Inspector General shall investigate reports of the mishandling of incidents of sexual abuse, while maintaining the confidentiality of the victims of sexual abuse, if requested by the victim.

(Added by Stats. 2005, Ch. 303, Sec. 3. Effective January 1, 2006.)

2642.

The Department of Corrections and Rehabilitation shall:

Develop guidelines for allowing outside organizations and service agencies to offer resources to inmates and wards, including, but not limited to, the following:

(1) Rape crisis agencies.

(2) Hospitals.

(3) Gay rights organizations.

(4) HIV/AIDS service providers.

(5) Civil rights organizations.

(6) Human rights organizations.

(Added by Stats. 2005, Ch. 303, Sec. 3. Effective January 1, 2006.)

2643.

The provisions of this act are severable. If any provision of this act or its application is held invalid, that invalidity shall not affect other provisions or applications that can be given effect without the invalid provision or application.

(Added by Stats. 2005, Ch. 303, Sec. 3. Effective January 1, 2006.)

2644.

(a) A male correctional officer shall not conduct a pat down search of a female inmate unless the prisoner presents a risk of immediate harm to herself or others or risk of escape and there is not a female correctional officer available to conduct the search.

(b) A male correctional officer shall not enter into an area of the institution where female inmates may be in a state of undress, or be in an area where they can view female inmates in a state of undress, including, but not limited to, restrooms, shower areas, or medical treatment areas, unless an inmate in the area presents a risk of immediate harm to herself or others or if there is a medical emergency in the area. A male correctional officer shall not enter into an area prohibited under this subdivision if there is a female correctional officer who can resolve the situation in a safe and timely manner without his assistance. To prevent incidental viewing, staff of the opposite sex shall announce their presence when entering a housing unit.

(c) If a male correctional officer conducts a pat down search under an exception provided in subdivision (a) or enters a prohibited area under an exception provided in subdivision (b), the circumstances for and details of the exception shall be documented within three days of the incident. The documentation shall be reviewed by the warden and retained by the institution for reporting purposes.

(d) The department may promulgate regulations to implement this section.

(Added by Stats. 2018, Ch. 174, Sec. 1. (AB 2550) Effective January 1, 2019.)

CHAPTER 4. Treatment of Prisoners [2650 - 2695.5]

(Chapter 4 added by Stats. 1941, Ch. 106.)

ARTICLE 1. Mistreatment of Prisoners [2650 - 2657]

(Article 1 added by Stats. 1941, Ch. 106.)

2650.

The person of a prisoner sentenced to imprisonment in the state prison or to imprisonment pursuant to subdivision (h) of Section 1170 is under the protection of the law, and any injury to his person, not authorized by law, is punishable in the same manner as if he were not convicted or sentenced.

(Amended by Stats. 2011, Ch. 15, Sec. 463. (AB 109) Effective April 4, 2011. Operative October 1, 2011, by Sec. 636 of Ch. 15, as amended by Stats. 2011, Ch. 39, Sec. 68.)

2651.

No punishment, except as may be authorized by the Director of Corrections, shall be inflicted and then only by the order and under the direction of the wardens. Nothing in this section shall be construed as a limitation or impairment of the authority of the Board of Prison Terms in exercising its functions.

(Amended by Stats. 1979, Ch. 255.)

2652.

It shall be unlawful to use in the prisons, any cruel, corporal or unusual punishment or to inflict any treatment or allow any lack of care whatever which would injure or impair the health of the prisoner, inmate or person confined; and punishment by the use of the strait-jacket, gag, thumb-screw, shower-bath or the tricing up of prisoners, inmates or persons confined is hereby prohibited. Any person who violates the provisions of this section or who aids, abets, or attempts in any way to contribute to the violation of this section shall be guilty of a misdemeanor.

(Added by Stats. 1941, Ch. 106.)

2652.5.

No person employed by the Department of Corrections, the Department of the Youth Authority, or any city or county jail facility shall place any chain or other mechanical restraint around the neck of any prisoner for any purpose. Any violation of this section shall be a misdemeanor.

(Added by Stats. 1976, Ch. 1047.)

2653.

(a) If a physician employed by the Department of Corrections or the Department of the Youth Authority certifies in writing that a particular medical treatment is required to prevent a violation of Section 147, 673, 2650, or 2652, or is required to prevent serious and imminent harm to the health of a prisoner, the order for that particular medical treatment may not be modified or canceled by any employee of the department without the approval of the chief medical officer of the institution or the physician in attendance unless an inmate or ward has a known history of violent or otherwise disruptive behavior that requires additional measures to protect the safety and security of the institution specified in writing by the warden or superintendent, or unless immediate security needs require alternate or modified procedures. Following any necessary modified or alternate security procedures, treatment of the inmate or ward shall be effected as expeditiously as possible.

Nothing in this section shall be construed to prevent a registered nurse from questioning, or seeking clarification of, an order from a physician that in the professional judgment of that nurse endangers patient health or safety, or otherwise is contrary to the professional ethics of the registered nurse.

(b) Any person who violates this section shall be subject to appropriate disciplinary action by the department.

(Added by Stats. 1992, Ch. 602, Sec. 1. Effective January 1, 1993.)

2656.

(a) A person sentenced to incarceration or who is being held pursuant to a pending criminal matter in a county or city jail, or other county or city custodial correctional facility shall not be deprived of the possession or use of any orthopedic or prosthetic appliance, if such appliance has been prescribed or recommended and fitted by a physician.

(b) If, however, the person in charge of the county or city custodial or correctional facility has probable cause to believe possession of such orthopedic or prosthetic appliance constitutes an immediate risk of bodily harm to any person in the facility or threatens the security of the facility, such appliance may be removed.

If such appliance is removed, the prisoner shall be deprived of such appliance only during such time as the facts which constitute probable cause for its removal continue to exist; if such facts cease to exist, then the person in charge of the facility shall return such appliance to the prisoner.

When such appliance is removed, the prisoner shall be examined by a physician within 24 hours after such removal.

If the examining physician determines that removal is or will be injurious to the health or safety of the prisoner, he shall so inform the prisoner and the person in charge of the facility. Upon receipt of the physician's opinion, the person in charge of the facility shall either return the appliance to the prisoner or refuse to return such appliance to the prisoner, informing the physician and the prisoner of the reasons for such refusal and promptly providing the prisoner with a form, as specified in subdivision (c) of this section, by which the prisoner may petition the superior court of the county in which the facility is located for return of the appliance.

Upon petition by the prisoner, the court shall either order the appliance returned to the petitioner or within two judicial days after the petition is filed receive evidence relevant to the granting or denial of the petition. When evidence is received, the court shall consider the opinion of the physician who examined the prisoner and the opinion of the person in charge of the facility and all other evidence it deems relevant. A decision shall be promptly made and shall be based upon a weighing of the risk of immediate harm to persons within the facility and the threat to the security of the facility created by the appliance's presence in the facility as against the risk to the health and safety of the petitioner by its removal.

(c) The form for a request for return of an orthopedic or prosthetic appliance as required in subdivision (b) of this section shall be substantially as follows:

(Name of the facility) _____ day of _____ 19___

I, _____ (person in charge of the facility), have today received a request for the return of an orthopedic or prosthetic appliance, namely, _____ (description of appliance or device) from the undersigned prisoner.

_____	Signature or mark of prisoner making request for return of appliance or device

When the prisoner has signed or made his mark upon such form, the person in charge of the facility shall promptly file the completed form with the superior court.

(d) No person incarcerated in any facility of the Department of Corrections shall be deprived of the use or possession of any orthopedic or prosthetic appliance unless both the inmate's personal physician and a department physician concur in the professional opinion that such appliance is no longer needed.

(Added by Stats. 1974, Ch. 1352.)

2657.

(a) No person confined in a state prison, as defined in Section 4504, shall be subject to any institutional disciplinary action subsequent to an acquittal in a court of law upon criminal charges brought and tried for the act or omission which is the sole basis of the institutional disciplinary action.

(b) Where the act or omission resulting in acquittal is in any way referred to in any Department of Corrections file pertaining to the prisoner, the fact of acquittal by a court of law shall be clearly inscribed near each such reference.

(Added by Stats. 1975, Ch. 726.)

ARTICLE 2. Organic Therapy [2670 - 2680]
(Article 2 added by Stats. 1974, Ch. 1513.)

2670.

It is hereby recognized and declared that all persons, including all persons involuntarily confined, have a fundamental right against enforced interference with their thought processes, states of mind, and patterns of mentation through the use of organic therapies; that this fundamental right requires that no person with the capacity for

informed consent who refuses organic therapy shall be compelled to undergo such therapy; and that in order to justify the use of organic therapy upon a person who lacks the capacity for informed consent, other than psychosurgery as referred to in subdivision (c) of Section 2670.5 which is not to be administered to such persons, the state shall establish that the organic therapy would be beneficial to the person, that there is a compelling interest in administering such therapy, and that there are no less onerous alternatives to such therapy.

(Added by Stats. 1974, Ch. 1513.)

2670.5.

(a) No person confined or detained under Title 1 (commencing with Section 2000) and Title 2 (commencing with Section 3200) shall be administered or subjected to any organic therapy as defined in subdivision (c) without his or her informed consent, provided that:

(1) If the person gives his or her informed consent to organic therapy, it shall be administered only if there has been compliance with Sections 2675 to 2680, inclusive.

(2) If the person lacks the capacity for informed consent to organic therapy other than psychosurgery as referred to in subdivision (c), in order to proceed with the therapy, the warden shall secure an order from the superior court to authorize the administration of the therapy in accordance with Sections 2675 to 2680, inclusive.

(b) No person confined or detained under Title 1 (commencing with Section 2000) or Title 2 (commencing with Section 3200) who lacks the capacity for informed consent shall be administered or subjected to psychosurgery as referred to in subdivision (c).

(c) The term organic therapy refers to:

(1) Psychosurgery, including lobotomy, stereotactic surgery, electronic, chemical or other destruction of brain tissues, or implantation of electrodes into brain tissue.

(2) Shock therapy, including, but not limited to, any convulsive therapy and insulin shock treatments.

(3) The use of any drugs, electric shocks, electronic stimulation of the brain, or infliction of physical pain when used as an aversive or reinforcing stimulus in a program of aversive, classical, or operant conditioning.

(d) A person does not waive his or her right to refuse any organic therapy by having previously given his or her informed consent to the therapy, and the person may withdraw his or her consent at any time.

If required by sound medical-psychiatric practice, the attending physician shall, after the person withdraws his or her previously given informed consent, gradually phase the person out of the therapy if sudden cessation would create a serious risk of mental or physical harm to the person.

(e) Nothing in this article shall be construed to prevent the attending physician from administering nonorganic therapies such as psychotherapy, psychoanalysis, group therapy, milieu therapy, or other therapies or programs involving communication or interaction among physicians, patients, and others, with or without the use of drugs when used for purposes other than described in paragraph (3) of subdivision (c).

(f) Nothing in this article shall be construed to prevent the administration of drugs not connected with a program of conditioning and intended to cause negative physical reactions to ingestion of alcohol or drugs.

(Amended by Stats. 1989, Ch. 1420, Sec. 8.)

2671.

(a) Notwithstanding Section 2670.5, if a confined person has inflicted or attempted to inflict substantial physical harm upon the person of another or himself, or presents, as a result of mental disorder, an imminent threat of substantial harm to others or himself, the attending physician may in such emergency employ or authorize for no longer than seven days in any three-month period the immediate use of shock treatments in order to alleviate such danger.

(b) Notwithstanding Section 2670.5, if a confined person gives his informed consent to a program of shock therapy for a period not to exceed three months, the attending physician may administer such therapy for a period not to exceed three months in any one-year period without prior judicial authorization.

(Added by Stats. 1974, Ch. 1513.)

2672.

(a) For purposes of this article, "informed consent" means that a person must knowingly and intelligently, without duress or coercion, and clearly and explicitly manifest his consent to the proposed organic therapy to the attending physician.

(b) A person confined shall not be deemed incapable of informed consent solely by virtue of being diagnosed with a mental health disorder.

(c) A person confined shall be deemed incapable of informed consent if the person cannot understand, or knowingly and intelligently act upon, the information specified in Section 2673.

(d) A person confined shall be deemed incapable of informed consent if, for any reason, he or she cannot manifest his or her consent to the attending physician.

(Amended by Stats. 2014, Ch. 144, Sec. 47. (AB 1847) Effective January 1, 2015.)

2673.

(a) For purposes of this article, "informed consent" requires that the attending physician directly communicate with the person and clearly and explicitly provide all the following information prior to the person's decision:

(1) The nature and seriousness of the person's illness, disorder or defect.

(2) The nature of the proposed organic therapy and its intended duration.

(3) The likelihood of improvement or deterioration, temporary or permanent, without the administration of the proposed organic therapy.

(4) The likelihood and degree of improvement, remission, control, or cure resulting from the administration of such organic therapy, and the likelihood, nature, and extent of changes in and intrusions upon the person's personality and patterns of behavior and thought or mentation and the degree to which these changes may be irreversible. This information shall indicate the probable duration and intensity of such therapy and whether such therapy may have to be continued indefinitely for optimum therapeutic benefit.

(5) The likelihood, nature, extent, and duration of side effects of the proposed organic therapy, and how and to what extent they may be controlled, if at all.

(6) The uncertainty of the benefits and hazards of the proposed organic therapy because of the lack of sufficient data available to the medical profession, or any other reason for such uncertainty.

(7) The reasonable alternative organic therapy or psychotherapeutic modality of therapy, or nonorganic behavior modification programs, and why the organic therapy recommended is the therapy of choice. These alternatives shall be described and explained to the person in the manner specified in this section.

(8) Whether the proposed therapy is generally regarded as sound by the medical profession, or is considered experimental.

(Added by Stats. 1974, Ch. 1513.)

2674.

A written manifestation of informed consent shall be obtained in all cases by the attending physician and shall be preserved and available to the person, his attorney, his guardian, or his conservator.

(Added by Stats. 1974, Ch. 1513.)

2675.

(a) If the proposed organic therapy is not prohibited by subdivision (a) or (b) of Section 2670.5, then in order to administer the therapy the warden of the institution in which the person is confined shall petition the superior court of the county in which the person is confined for an order authorizing such organic therapy.

(b) The petition shall summarize the facts which the attending physician is required to communicate to the person pursuant to Section 2673, and shall state whether the person has the capacity for informed consent, and, if so, whether the person has given his or her informed consent to the proposed therapy. The petition shall clearly specify what organic therapy the institution proposes to administer to the person. The petition shall specify what mental illness, disorder, abnormality, or defect justifies the administration of such therapy. Copies of the petition shall be personally served upon the person and served upon his or her attorney, guardian or conservator on the same day as it is filed with the clerk of the superior court.

(c) The person confined, or his or her attorney, guardian, or conservator may file a response to the petition for organic therapy. The response shall be filed no later than 10 days after service of the petition unless the court grants a continuance not to exceed 10 additional days, and shall be served on the warden on the same day it is filed.

(Amended by Stats. 1989, Ch. 1420, Sec. 9.)

2676.

(a) Any person, or his or her attorney, guardian, or conservator may file a petition with the superior court of the county in which he or she is confined for an order to prohibit the administration upon him or her of an organic therapy. The filing of such a petition shall constitute a refusal of consent or withdrawal of any prior consent to an organic therapy. The clerk of the court shall serve a copy of the petition, on the same day it is filed, upon the warden.

(b) The warden shall file a response to the petition to prohibit the enforced administration of any organic therapy. The response shall be filed no later than 10 days after the filing of the petition, unless the court grants a continuance not to exceed 10 additional days, and shall be personally served upon the person and served upon his or her attorney, guardian, or conservator on the same day as it is filed with the clerk of the superior court. The response shall not constitute a petition for an order to proceed with any organic therapy pursuant to Section 2675, which shall be the exclusive procedure for authorization to administer any organic therapy.

(Amended by Stats. 1989, Ch. 1420, Sec. 10.)

2677.

At the time of filing of a petition pursuant to Section 2676 by the person, or pursuant to Section 2675 by the warden, the court shall appoint the public defender or other attorney to represent the person unless the person is financially able to provide his or her own attorney. The attorney shall advise the person of his or her rights in relation to the proceeding in question and shall represent him or her before the court.

The court shall also appoint an independent medical expert on the person's behalf to examine the person's medical, mental, or emotional condition and to testify thereon, unless the person is financially able to obtain the expert testimony. However, if the person has given his or her informed consent to the proposed organic therapy, other than psychosurgery as referred to in subdivision (c) of Section 2670.5, and his or her attorney concurs in the proposed administration of the organic therapy, the court may waive the requirement that an independent medical expert be appointed.

(Amended by Stats. 2001, Ch. 854, Sec. 47. Effective January 1, 2002.)

2678.

The court shall conduct the proceedings within 10 judicial days from the filing of the petition described in Section 2675 or 2676, whichever is filed earlier, unless the warden's attorney or the person's attorney requests a continuance, which may be for a maximum of 10 additional judicial days. The court shall conduct the proceedings in accordance with constitutional guarantees of due process of law and the procedures under Section 13 of Article I of the California Constitution.

(Amended by Stats. 1989, Ch. 1420, Sec. 12.)

2679.

(a) The court shall determine whether the state has proven, by clear and convincing evidence, that the confined person has the capacity for informed consent and has manifested his informed consent.

(b) If the court has determined that the person lacks the capacity for informed consent, the court shall determine by clear and convincing evidence that such therapy, other than psychosurgery as referred to in subdivision (c) of Section 2670.5, would be beneficial; that there is a compelling interest justifying the use of the organic therapy upon the person; that there are no less onerous alternatives to such organic therapy; and that such organic therapy is in accordance with sound medical-psychiatric practice. If the court so determines, then the court shall authorize the administration of the organic therapy for a period not to exceed six months.

(c) If the court has determined that the person has the capacity for informed consent and has manifested his informed consent to organic therapy, the court shall determine by clear and convincing evidence that such therapy would be beneficial; that there is a compelling interest justifying the use of the organic therapy upon the person; that there are no less onerous alternatives to such organic therapy; and that such organic therapy is in accordance with sound medical-psychiatric practice. If the court so determines then the court shall authorize the administration of the organic therapy for a period not to exceed six months.

(Added by Stats. 1974, Ch. 1513.)

2680.

(a) If it is determined by the attending physician that a confined person should be administered organic therapy, the person shall be advised and informed of his or her rights under this article, and he or she shall be provided a copy of this article.

(b) This article shall apply to prisoners confined under this part in public or private hospitals, sanitariums, and similar facilities, and to the personnel of the facilities.

(c) A person shall be entitled to communicate in writing and by visiting with his or her parents, guardian, or conservator regarding any proposed administration of any organic therapy. The communication shall not be censored. The person shall be entitled to communicate in writing with his or her attorney pursuant to Section 2600.

(d) This article shall not prohibit the attending physician from terminating organic therapy prior to the period authorized for that therapy by the court, pursuant to Section 2679.

(Amended by Stats. 1988, Ch. 160, Sec. 136.)

ARTICLE 3. Disposition of Insane Prisoners [2684 - 2685]
(Article 3 added by Stats. 1941, Ch. 106.)

2684.

(a) If, in the opinion of the Secretary of the Department of Corrections and Rehabilitation, the rehabilitation of any mentally ill, mentally deficient, or insane person confined in a state prison may be expedited by treatment at any one of the state hospitals under the jurisdiction of the State Department of State Hospitals or the State Department of Developmental Services, the Secretary of the Department of Corrections and Rehabilitation, with the approval of the Board of Parole Hearings for persons sentenced pursuant to subdivision (b) of Section 1168, shall certify that fact to the director of the appropriate department who shall evaluate the prisoner to determine if he or she would benefit from care and treatment in a state hospital. If the director of the appropriate department so determines, the superintendent of the hospital shall receive the prisoner and keep him or her until in the opinion of the superintendent the person has been treated to the extent that he or she will not benefit from further care and treatment in the state hospital.

(b) Whenever the Secretary of the Department of Corrections and Rehabilitation receives a recommendation from the court that a defendant convicted of a violation of Section 646.9 and sentenced to confinement in the state prison would benefit from treatment in a state hospital pursuant to subdivision (a), the secretary shall consider the recommendation. If appropriate, the secretary shall certify that the rehabilitation of the defendant may be expedited by treatment in a state hospital and subdivision (a) shall apply.

(Amended by Stats. 2012, Ch. 24, Sec. 35. (AB 1470) Effective June 27, 2012.)

2685.

Upon the receipt of a prisoner, as herein provided, the superintendent of the state hospital shall notify the Director of Corrections of that fact, giving his name, the date, the prison from which he was received, and from whose hands he was received. When in the opinion of the superintendent the mentally ill, mentally deficient or insane prisoner has been treated to such an extent that such person will not benefit by further care and treatment in the state hospital, the superintendent shall immediately notify the Director of Corrections of that fact. The Director of Corrections shall immediately send for, take and receive the prisoner back into prison. The time passed at the state hospital shall count as part of the prisoner's sentence.

(Amended by Stats. 1963, Ch. 372.)

ARTICLE 4. Temporary Removal of Prisoners [2690 - 2692]
(Article 4 added by Stats. 1941, Ch. 511.)

2690.

The Secretary of the Department of Corrections and Rehabilitation may authorize the temporary removal of an inmate from prison or any other institution for the detention of adults under the jurisdiction of the Department of Corrections and Rehabilitation, including removal for the purpose of attending college classes or permitting the inmate to participate in, or assist with, the gathering of evidence relating to crimes. The secretary may require that the temporary removal be under custody. Unless the inmate is removed for medical treatment, the removal shall not be for a period longer than three days. The secretary may require, except when the removal is for medical treatment or to assist with the gathering of evidence related to crimes, the inmate to reimburse the state, in whole or in part, for expenses incurred by the state in connection with the temporary removal.

(Amended (as amended by Stats. 2013, Ch. 181, Sec. 1) by Stats. 2014, Ch. 193, Sec. 1. (SB 1015) Effective August 15, 2014.)

2690.5.

(a) The superior court of the county in which a requesting district attorney or peace officer has jurisdiction may order the temporary removal of a prisoner from a state prison facility, and his or her transportation to a county or city jail, if a legitimate law enforcement purpose exists to move the prisoner. An order for the temporary removal of a prisoner may be issued, at the discretion of the court, upon a finding of good cause in an affidavit by the requesting district attorney or peace officer stating that the law enforcement purpose is legitimate and necessary. The order for the temporary removal of a prisoner to a county or city jail shall not exceed 30 days. Extensions of an order may be granted, but only upon application for an extension made in accordance with this section. The period of extension shall be no longer than the authorizing judge deems necessary to achieve the purposes for which it was granted, and shall not exceed an additional 30-day period beyond the initial period specified in the order for temporary removal.

(b) An order for the temporary removal of a prisoner shall include all of the following:
(1) A recitation of the purposes for which the prisoner is to be brought to the county or city jail.
(2) The affidavit of the requesting district attorney or peace officer stating that the law enforcement purpose is legitimate and necessary. The affidavit shall be supported by facts establishing good cause.
(3) The signature of the judge or magistrate making the order.
(4) The seal of the court, if any.

(c) Upon the request of a district attorney or peace officer for a court order for the temporary removal of a prisoner from a state prison facility pursuant to this section, the court may, for good cause, seal an order made pursuant to this section, unless a court determines that the failure to disclose the contents of the order would deny a fair trial to a charged defendant in a criminal proceeding.

(d) An order for the temporary removal of a prisoner shall be executed presumptively by the sheriff of the county in which the order is issued. It shall be the duty of the sheriff to bring the prisoner to the proper county or city jail, to safely retain the prisoner, and to return the prisoner to the state prison facility when he or she is no longer required for the stated law enforcement purpose. The prisoner shall be returned no later than 30 days after his or her removal from the state prison facility or no later than 30 days after the date of an order authorizing an extension pursuant to subdivision (a). The expense of executing the order shall be a proper charge against, and shall be paid by, the county in which the order is made. The presumption that the transfer will be effectuated by the sheriff of the county in which the transfer order is made may be overcome upon application of the investigating officer or prosecuting attorney stating the name of each peace officer who will conduct the transportation of the prisoner.

(e) If a prisoner is removed from a state prison facility pursuant to an order in accordance with this section, the prisoner shall remain at all times in the constructive custody of the warden of the state prison facility from which the prisoner was removed. During the temporary removal, the prisoner may be ordered to appear in other felony proceedings as a defendant or witness in the superior court of the county from which the original order for the temporary removal was issued. A copy of the written order directing the prisoner to appear before the superior court shall be forwarded by the district attorney to the warden of the prison having custody of the prisoner.

(f) The state is not liable for any claim of damage, or for the injury or death of any person, including a prisoner, that occurs during the period in which the prisoner is in the exclusive control of a local law enforcement agency pursuant to this section.

(Added by Stats. 2013, Ch. 56, Sec. 1. (SB 162) Effective January 1, 2014.)

2691.

No person imprisoned for a felony listed in Section 667.6 shall be removed or released under Section 2690 from the detention institution where he or she is confined for the purpose of attending college classes in any city or county nor shall that person be placed in a community correctional center pursuant to Chapter 9.5 (commencing with Section 6250) of Title 7 of Part 3. No person under the jurisdiction of the adult court and confined under the jurisdiction of the Department of the Youth Authority for conviction of a felony listed in Section 667.6 shall be removed or released from the place of confinement for attendance at any educational institution in any city or county.

(Amended by Stats. 1987, Ch. 828, Sec. 124.)

2692.

The Director of Corrections may enter into contracts with public or private agencies located either within or outside of the state for the housing, care, and treatment of inmates afflicted with acquired immune deficiency syndrome (AIDS) or AIDS-related complex (ARC).

(Added by Stats. 1986, Ch. 921, Sec. 1. Effective September 22, 1986.)

ARTICLE 5. Substance Abuse Treatment [2694 - 2694.5]
(Article 5 added by Stats. 2007, Ch. 7, Sec. 10.)

2694.

(a) The Department of Corrections and Rehabilitation shall expand substance abuse treatment services in prisons to accommodate at least 4,000 additional inmates who have histories of substance abuse. In determining the prisons in which these additional treatment services will be located, the department may consider efficiency and efficacy of treatment, availability of staff resources, availability of physical space, and availability of additional resources in surrounding communities to supplement the treatment. In addition, the department shall expand followup treatment services in the community in order to ensure that offenders who participate in substance abuse treatment while incarcerated in prison shall receive necessary followup treatment while on parole.

(b) (1) Notwithstanding any other law, unless there is a security or safety reason not to do so, a substance abuse treatment program funded by the Department of Corrections

and Rehabilitation and offered in a facility under the jurisdiction of the department pursuant to this section shall include a peer counseling component allowing prisoners to receive the necessary training within those facilities to become certified addiction counselors, including necessary course work and clinical hours.
(2) If the department determines that a peer counseling component shall not be included as part of a substance abuse treatment program offered in a facility under the department's jurisdiction, the department shall notify in writing on January 10, 2015, and January 10, 2016, the Assembly and Senate Committees on Budget and the relevant Assembly and Senate policy committees at the time the determination is made. The report shall include the reason for the determination and a description of the substance abuse treatment program being provided.
(3) For purposes of this section, "peer counseling" means counseling offered by a person sharing similar life experiences who provides advice and assistance to another individual with the intended outcome of overcoming addiction-related challenges.
(Amended by Stats. 2014, Ch. 26, Sec. 26. (AB 1468) Effective June 20, 2014.)
2694.5.
(a) The Department of Corrections and Rehabilitation, under the oversight of the Undersecretary of Health Care Services, shall establish a three-year pilot program at one or more institutions that will provide a medically assisted substance use disorder treatment model for treatment of inmates with a history of substance use problems. The program shall offer a continuum of evidenced-based care that is designed to meet the needs of the persons being served and that is appropriate for a correctional setting. In establishing the program, the department shall consider all of the following:
(1) Access to services during an inmate's enrollment in the pilot program.
(2) Access to subacute detoxification and medical detoxification, as necessary.
(3) Comprehensive pretreatment and posttreatment assessments.
(4) Ongoing evaluation of an inmate's program needs and progress at least every 90 days, and appropriate adjustment of treatment based on that evaluation.
(5) Services provided by professionals for whom substance use disorder treatment is within the scope of their practice.
(6) Referrals for medically assisted care and prescription of medication-assisted treatment.
(7) Provision of behavioral health services, including the capacity to treat cooccurring mental illness.
(8) Access to medication-assisted treatment throughout the period of incarceration up to and including immediately prior to release.
(9) Linkages to community-based treatment upon parole.
(b) (1) The department shall report to the fiscal and appropriate policy committees of the Legislature on March 1, 2017, and each March 1 thereafter during the tenure of the pilot project. The report shall include all of the following elements:
(A) The planned inmate capacity of the program.
(B) The number of persons enrolled in the program.
(C) The number of persons who leave the treatment program against medical advice and the number of persons who are discharged from the program prior to achieving their treatment goals.
(D) The percentage of participants with negative urine toxicology screens for illicit substances during treatment and posttreatment while incarcerated.
(E) The number of persons who are successfully linked to postrelease treatment.
(2) (A) The requirement for submitting a report imposed under this subdivision is inoperative on March 1, 2025, pursuant to Section 10231.5 of the Government Code.
(B) A report to be submitted pursuant to this subdivision shall be submitted in compliance with Section 9795 of the Government Code.
(Added by Stats. 2016, Ch. 33, Sec. 18. (SB 843) Effective June 27, 2016.)

ARTICLE 6. Veterans In State Prisons [2695 - 2695.5]

(Article 6 added by Stats. 2012, Ch. 407, Sec. 2.)
2695.
The Department of Corrections and Rehabilitation shall develop guidance policies relative to the release of veterans who are inmates. The policies shall be developed with the intent to assist veterans who are inmates in pursuing claims for federal veterans' benefits, or in establishing rights to any other privilege, preference, care, or compensation provided under federal or state law because of honorable service in the military. In developing the policies, the department may coordinate with the Department of Veterans Affairs and the county veterans service officer or veterans service organizations.
(Added by Stats. 2012, Ch. 407, Sec. 2. (AB 2490) Effective January 1, 2013.)
2695.1.
At each facility that is under the jurisdiction of the Department of Corrections and Rehabilitation, a veterans service organization may volunteer to serve as a veterans service advocate.
(Added by Stats. 2014, Ch. 652, Sec. 2. (AB 2263) Effective January 1, 2015.)
2695.2.
(a) The advocate shall be authorized to develop a veterans economic recidivism prevention plan for each inmate who is a veteran during the 180-day period preceding the inmate's release date.
(b) The veterans economic recidivism prevention plan for each inmate who is a veteran shall include, but not be limited to, the following:
(1) Facilitating access of the inmate to county veterans service officers, California Department of Veterans Affairs and United States Department of Veterans Affairs officers and personnel, so that the inmate may pursue claims for federal veterans' benefits or any other privilege, preference, care, or compensation provided under federal or state law because of the inmate's service in the military.
(2) Developing a plan for how the inmate will access earned veterans' benefits that he or she may be eligible for upon the inmate's release.
(c) In order to assist with the development and execution of the veterans economic recidivism prevention plan, the Department of Corrections and Rehabilitation shall do both of the following:
(1) (A) Facilitate access by the advocate to each inmate who is a veteran.
(B) Access by the advocate is subject to those department screening and clearance guidelines and training requirements that are imposed on other visitors and volunteers.
(C) Access by the advocate shall be allowed to the extent it does not pose a threat to the security or safety of the facility, or to inmates and staff.
(2) Provide the advocate with access to existing resources, including, but not limited to, computer and Internet access, that would assist the advocate in implementing the veterans economic recidivism prevention plan, to the extent it does not pose a threat to the security or safety of the facility, or to inmates and staff.
(d) A copy of the veterans economic recidivism prevention plan shall be provided to the inmate prior to the inmate's release.
(Added by Stats. 2014, Ch. 652, Sec. 3. (AB 2263) Effective January 1, 2015.)
2695.3.
The advocate shall coordinate with the United States Department of Veterans Affairs in order to provide each inmate who is a veteran with access to earned veterans' benefits.
(Added by Stats. 2014, Ch. 652, Sec. 4. (AB 2263) Effective January 1, 2015.)
2695.4.
The advocate shall coordinate with the California Department of Veterans Affairs and the county veterans service officer in the county in which the facility is located for advice, assistance, and training, and to evaluate the effectiveness of the veterans economic recidivism prevention plan.
(Added by Stats. 2014, Ch. 652, Sec. 5. (AB 2263) Effective January 1, 2015.)
2695.5.
For purposes of this article, the following definitions shall apply:
(a) "Advocate" means a veterans service organization that is federally certified and has volunteered to serve as a veterans service advocate pursuant to this article.
(b) "Veteran" means a person who has been discharged from the United States Army, United States Navy, United States Air Force, United States Marine Corps, United States Coast Guard, the National Guard of any state, or the Merchant Marine.
(Amended by Stats. 2016, Ch. 203, Sec. 1. (AB 2563) Effective January 1, 2017.)

CHAPTER 5. Employment of Prisoners [2700 - 2792]

(Heading of Chapter 5 amended by Stats. 1941, Ch. 893.)

ARTICLE 1. Employment of Prisoners Generally [2700 - 2717]

(Heading of Article 1 amended by Stats. 1941, Ch. 893.)
2700.
The Department of Corrections shall require of every able-bodied prisoner imprisoned in any state prison as many hours of faithful labor in each day and every day during his or her term of imprisonment as shall be prescribed by the rules and regulations of the Director of Corrections.
Whenever by any statute a price is required to be fixed for any services to be performed in connection with the work program of the Department of Corrections, the compensation paid to prisoners shall be included as an item of cost in fixing the final statutory price.
Prisoners not engaged on work programs under the jurisdiction of the Prison Industry Authority, but who are engaged in productive labor outside of such programs may be compensated in like manner. The compensation of such prisoners shall be paid either out of funds appropriated by the Legislature for that purpose or out of such other funds available to the Department of Corrections for expenditure, as the Director of Finance may direct.
When any prisoner escapes, the director shall determine what portion of his or her earnings shall be forfeited and such forfeiture shall be deposited in the State Treasury in a fund known as the Inmate Welfare Fund of the Department of Corrections.
(Amended by Stats. 1982, Ch. 1549, Sec. 6.)
2700.1.
Section 2700 applies to inmates sentenced to death, except as otherwise provided in this section.
Every person found guilty of murder, sentenced to death, and held by the Department of Corrections and Rehabilitation pursuant to Sections 3600 to 3602 shall be required to work as many hours of faithful labor each day he or she is so held as shall be prescribed the rules and regulations of the department.
Physical education and physical fitness programs shall not qualify as work for purposes of this section. The Department of Corrections and Rehabilitation may revoke the privileges of any condemned inmate who refuses to work as required by this section.
In any case where the condemned inmate owes a restitution fine or restitution order, the Secretary of the Department of Corrections and Rehabilitation shall deduct 70 percent or the balance owing, whichever is less, from the condemned inmate's wages and trust account deposits, regardless of the source of the income, and shall transfer those funds to the California Victim Compensation and Government Claims Board according to the rules and regulations of the Department of Corrections and Rehabilitation, pursuant to Sections 2085.5 and 2717.8.
(Added November 8, 2016, by initiative Proposition 66, Sec. 8.)
2701.
(a) The Department of Corrections is hereby authorized and empowered to cause the prisoners in the state prisons of this state to be employed in the rendering of services as are now, or may hereafter be, needed by the state, or any political subdivision thereof, or that may be needed for any state, county, district, municipal, school, or other public use, or that may be needed by any public institution of the state or of any political subdivision thereof, or that may be needed for use by the federal government, or any department, agency, or corporation thereof, or that may be needed for use by the government of any other state, or any department, agency, or corporation thereof, except for services provided by enterprises under the jurisdiction of the Prison Industry Authority. The Department of Corrections may enter into contracts for the purposes of this article.
(b) The Department of Corrections may cause prisoners in the prisons of this state to be employed in the rendering of emergency services for the preservation of life or property within the state, whether that property is owned by public entities or private citizens, when a county level state of emergency has been declared due to a natural disaster and the local governing board has requested the assistance of the Department of Corrections.
(Amended by Stats. 1994, Ch. 494, Sec. 1. Effective January 1, 1995.)
2702.
No person imprisoned after conviction of a violation of Section 502 or of subdivision (b) of Section 502.7 shall be permitted to work on or have access to any computer system of the department.
(Added by Stats. 1989, Ch. 1357, Sec. 5.)
2706.
All prisoners shall be employed under supervision of the wardens respectively, and such skilled foremen as they may deem necessary in the performance of work for the state.
(Amended by Stats. 1982, Ch. 1549, Sec. 10.)
2707.
The director is further authorized and empowered to purchase, install, and equip, such machinery, tools, supplies, materials, and equipment as may be necessary to carry out the provisions of this article.
(Amended by Stats. 1957, Ch. 2256.)
2708.
No inmate of any State prison shall be employed in the manufacture or production, of any article, intended for the private and personal use of any State officer, or officer, or employee, of any State institution; provided, that this act shall not prevent repairing of any kind nor the employment of such inmates in household or domestic work connected with such prison.
(Added by Stats. 1941, Ch. 106.)
2713.
Whenever an inmate is paid for his labor, performed under the supervision of the Department of Corrections or any other public agency, and is discharged, all sums due him shall be paid upon release. If an inmate is released on parole all sums due him shall be paid to the inmate as prescribed by the director.
(Added by Stats. 1963, Ch. 1200.)
2713.1.
In addition to any other payment to which he is entitled by law, each prisoner upon his release shall be paid the sum of two hundred dollars ($200), from such appropriations that may be made available for the purposes of this section.
The department may prescribe rules and regulations (a) to limit or eliminate any payments provided for in this section to prisoners who have not served for at least six consecutive months prior to their release in instances where the department determines that such a payment is not necessary for rehabilitation of the prisoner, (b) to establish

procedures for the payment of the sum of two hundred dollars ($200) within the first 60 days of a prisoner's release, and (c) to eliminate any payment provided for in this section to a parolee who upon release has not been paid the entire amount prescribed by this section and who willfully absconds after release on parole, but before any remaining balance of the two hundred dollar ($200) release funds has been paid. The provisions of this section shall not be applicable if a prisoner is released to the custody of another state or to the custody of the federal government.
(Amended by Stats. 1982, Ch. 1406, Sec. 1.)

2713.2.
The Department of Corrections and Rehabilitation shall examine and report to the Legislature on whether the provisions of existing law related to payments to inmates released from prison are hindering the success of parolees and resulting in their rapid return to prison for parole violations. The report shall specifically examine whether the costs of transportation of the inmate from prison to the parole location should be paid from the amounts specified in Section 2713.1 or whether it should be paid separately by the department. The department shall submit its findings and recommendations to the Legislature on or before January 15, 2008.
(Added by Stats. 2007, Ch. 7, Sec. 9. Effective May 3, 2007.)

2715.
Land belonging to the State of California may, with the approval of the Department of Finance, be transferred to the jurisdiction of the director for the purpose of establishing thereon a prison farm and prisoners in the state prisons may be transferred to such farm. Products from said farm shall first be used for supplying the state prisons, prison camps, or the prison farm and any surplus may be sold to any other state institution.
(Amended by Stats. 1957, Ch. 2256.)

2716.
(a) The Director of Corrections may enter into agreements with other state agencies for the use of inmates confined in the state prisons to perform work necessary and proper to be done by them in facilities of such state agencies for the purpose of vocational training and the improvement of job skills preparatory to release.
(b) The director shall determine which prisoners shall be eligible for such assignment and training.
(c) Suitable facilities for the housing, care, and feeding of the inmates may be provided by the agency for whom the work is performed at the location of such agency.
(d) The director shall have full jurisdiction over the discipline and control of the inmates assigned.
(e) The provisions of Title 5 (commencing with Section 4500) of Part 3 shall apply to all persons on such assignment.
(Amended by Stats. 1982, Ch. 1549, Sec. 16.)

2716.5.
(a) There is hereby established the Pre-Release Construction Trades Certificate Program, hereinafter referred to in this section as "the program," in the Department of Corrections and Rehabilitation, hereinafter referred to in this section as the "department," to increase employment opportunities in the construction trades for inmates upon release.
(b) The department shall establish a joint advisory committee for the purpose of implementation of the program. The committee shall be composed of representatives from building and construction trades employee organizations, the State Building and Construction Trades Council of California, joint apprenticeship training programs, the Prison Industry Authority, the Division of Apprenticeship Standards, the Labor and Workforce Development Agency, and any other representatives the department determines appropriate. The responsibilities of the committee shall include, but are not be limited to, the following:
(1) Develop guidelines for the participation of inmates in preapprenticeship training programs, as described in subdivision (e) of Section 14230 of the Unemployment Insurance Code. The guidelines shall provide for the integration, for all inmate preapprenticeship training programs in the building and construction trades, of the multicraft core curriculum implemented by the State Department of Education for its California Partnership Academies pilot project and by the California Workforce Development Board and local boards.
(2) Develop and implement a pre-release construction trades certification that validates that an inmate completed instruction, skills, and competencies required by and recognized by the participating building and construction trades.
(3) Ensure compliance with any applicable requirements and regulations of the Division of Apprenticeship Standards.
(4) Evaluate pre-release on-the-job training opportunities to compare and match competencies with those of registered apprentices in the building and construction trades.
(5) Explore the feasibility of the electronic tracking of each participating inmate's relevant activities to efficiently capture competencies related to the certification.
(6) Explore the pre-release awarding of formal credit for apprenticeship hours recognized by joint apprenticeship training programs and the Division of Apprenticeship Standards.
(7) Facilitate the admission of graduates of inmate preapprenticeship programs, after release, into state-approved apprenticeship programs and for apprenticeship programs to evaluate such individuals for admission with advanced standing based on prior coursework and work experience.
(Added by Stats. 2018, Ch. 53, Sec. 40. (SB 866) Effective June 27, 2018.)

2717.
The Department of Corrections shall require prisoners who are working outside the prison grounds in road cleanup crews pursuant to Article 4 (commencing with Section 2760) or fire crews pursuant to Article 5 (commencing with Section 2780) to wear distinctive clothing for identification purposes.
(Added by Stats. 2000, Ch. 525, Sec. 1. Effective January 1, 2001.)

ARTICLE 1.5. Joint Venture Program [2717.1 - 2717.9]
(Article 1.5 added November 6, 1990, by initiative Proposition 139, Sec. 5.)

2717.1.
Definitions.
(a) For the purposes of this section, joint venture program means a contract entered into between the Director of Corrections and any public entity, nonprofit or for profit entity, organization, or business for the purpose of employing inmate labor.
(b) Joint venture employer means any public entity, nonprofit or for profit entity, organization, or business which contracts with the Director of Corrections for the purpose of employing inmate labor.
(Added November 6, 1990, by initiative Proposition 139.)

2717.2.
The Director of Corrections shall establish joint venture programs within state prison facilities to allow joint venture employers to employ inmates confined in the state prison system for the purpose of producing goods or services. While recognizing the constraints of operating within the prison system, such programs will be patterned after operations outside of prison so as to provide inmates with the skills and work habits necessary to become productive members of society upon their release from state prison.
(Added November 6, 1990, by initiative Proposition 139.)

2717.3.
The Director of Corrections shall prescribe by rules and regulations provisions governing the operation and implementation of joint venture programs, which shall be in furtherance of the findings and declarations in the Prison Inmate Labor Initiative of 1990.

(Added November 6, 1990, by initiative Proposition 139.)

2717.4.
(a) There is hereby established within the Department of Corrections the Joint Venture Policy Advisory Board. The Joint Venture Policy Advisory Board shall consist of the Director of Corrections, who shall serve as chair, the Director of the Employment Development Department, and five members, to be appointed by the Governor, three of whom shall be public members, one of whom shall represent organized labor and one of whom shall represent industry. Five members shall constitute a quorum and a vote of the majority of the members in office shall be necessary for the transaction of the business of the board. Appointed members of the board shall be compensated at the rate of two hundred dollars ($200) for each day while on official business of the board and shall be reimbursed for necessary expenses. The initial terms of the members appointed by the Governor shall be for one year (one member), two years (two members), three years (one member), and four years (one member), as determined by the Governor. After the initial term, all members shall serve for four years.
(b) The board shall advise the Director of Corrections of policies that further the purposes of the Prison Inmate Labor Initiative of 1990 to be considered in the implementation of joint venture programs.
(Amended by Stats. 2001, Ch. 854, Sec. 48. Effective January 1, 2002. Note: This section was added on Nov. 6, 1990, by initiative Prop. 139.)

2717.5.
In establishing joint venture contracts the Director of Corrections shall consider the impact on the working people of California and give priority consideration to inmate employment which will retain or reclaim jobs in California, support emerging California industries, or create jobs for a deficient labor market.
(Added November 6, 1990, by initiative Proposition 139.)

2717.6.
(a) No contract shall be executed with a joint venture employer that will initiate employment by inmates in the same job classification as non-inmate employees of the same employer who are on strike, as defined in Section 1132.6 of the Labor Code, as it reads on January 1, 1990, or who are subject to lockout, as defined in Section 1132.8 of the Labor Code, as it reads on January 1, 1990.
(b) Total daily hours worked by inmates employed in the same job classification as non-inmate employees of the same joint venture employer who are on strike, as defined in Section 1132.6 of the Labor Code, as it reads on January 1, 1990, or who are subject to lockout, as defined in Section 1132.8 of the Labor Code, as it reads on January 1, 1990, shall not exceed, for the duration of the strike, the average daily hours worked for the preceding six months, or if the program has been in operation for less than six months, the average for the period of operation.
(c) The determination that a condition described in paragraph (b) above shall be made by the Director after notification by the union representing the workers on strike or subject to lockout. The limitation on work hours shall take effect 48 hours after receipt by the Director of written notice of the condition by the union.
(Added November 6, 1990, by initiative Proposition 139.)

2717.7.
Notwithstanding Section 2812 of the Penal Code or any other provision of law which restricts the sale of inmate-provided services or inmate-manufactured goods, services performed and articles manufactured by joint venture programs may be sold to the public.
(Added November 6, 1990, by initiative Proposition 139.)

2717.8.
The compensation of prisoners engaged in programs pursuant to contract between the Department of Corrections and joint venture employers for the purpose of conducting programs which use inmate labor shall be comparable to wages paid by the joint venture employer to non-inmate employees performing similar work for that employer. If the joint venture employer does not employ such non-inmate employees in similar work, compensation shall be comparable to wages paid for work of a similar nature in the locality in which the work is to be performed. Such wages shall be subject to deductions, as determined by the Director of Corrections, which shall not, in the aggregate, exceed 80 percent of gross wages and shall be limited to the following:
(1) Federal, state, and local taxes.
(2) Reasonable charges for room and board, which shall be remitted to the Director of Corrections.
(3) Any lawful restitution fine or contributions to any fund established by law to compensate the victims of crime of not more than 20 percent, but not less than 5 percent, of gross wages, which shall be remitted to the Director of Corrections for disbursement.
(4) Allocations for support of family pursuant to state statute, court order, or agreement by the prisoner.
(Added November 6, 1990, by initiative Proposition 139.)

2717.9.
Notwithstanding any other provision of law, a prisoner who participates in a joint venture program is ineligible for unemployment benefits upon his or her release from prison based upon participation in that program.
(Added by Stats. 1995, Ch. 440, Sec. 1. Approved in Proposition 194 at the March 26, 1996, election.)

ARTICLE 4. Employment at Road Camps [2760 - 2772]
(Article 4 added by Stats. 1941, Ch. 106.)

2760.
The Department of Transportation of the State of California may employ or cause to be employed, prisoners confined in the state prisons in the improvement and maintenance of any state highway.
(Amended by Stats. 1982, Ch. 1549, Sec. 19.)

2760.1.
"Department," as used in this article, means the Department of Transportation.
(Added by Stats. 1982, Ch. 681, Sec. 29.)

2761.
The Director of Corrections shall determine which prisoners shall be eligible for employment by the Department of Transportation in the improvement and maintenance of state highways, and shall establish lists of prisoners eligible for such employment. Upon the requisition of said department, the Director of Corrections shall send to the place and at the time designated the number of prisoners requisitioned or such number thereof as have been determined to be eligible for such employment and are available. The director may return to prison any prisoner transferred to camp pursuant to this section, when the need for such prisoner's labor has ceased or when the prisoner is guilty of any violation of the rules and regulations of the prison or camp.
(Amended by Stats. 1982, Ch. 1549, Sec. 20.)

2762.
The Director of Corrections shall fix a daily rate to be expended for convict labor, and when so fixed, the Department of Transportation shall monthly set aside funds to the director to pay for this labor from funds appropriated in the Budget Act for this purpose, and where no funds are available to the Department of Transportation the director may set aside the department's own funds to pay for this labor from funds appropriated in the Budget Act for this purpose. The Department of Corrections shall set up an account for each convict which shall be credited monthly with an amount computed by multiplying the daily rate by the number of days such convict actually performed labor during the month. Such account shall be debited monthly with the convict's proportionate share of expenses of camp maintenance, including the expenses for food, medicine, medical attendance, clerical and accounting personnel, and the expenses necessary to maintain

care and welfare facilities such as camp hospital for first aid, barbershop and cobbler shop, and the convict's personal expenses covering his drawings from the commissary for clothing, toilet articles, candy, and other personal items. The charge for camp maintenance may be made at a standard rate determined by the department maintaining the camps to be adequate to cover expenses and shall be adjusted periodically at the discretion of the department as needs of the camp require. No charge shall be made against such account for the costs of transporting prisoners to and from prison and camp or for the expense of guarding prisoners, which items shall be paid by the Department of Corrections from appropriations made for the support of the department. The director, by regulation, may fix the maximum amount, over and above all deductions, that a convict may receive. The Department of Corrections, in computing the debits to be made to the convict's accounts, may add not to exceed 10 percent on all items.
(Amended by Stats. 2004, Ch. 798, Sec. 3. Effective January 1, 2005. Operative July 1, 2005, by Sec. 9 of Ch. 798.)
2765.
When any prisoner shall wilfully violate the terms of his employment or the rules and regulations of the Department of Corrections, the Director of Corrections may in his discretion determine what portion of all moneys earned by the prisoner shall be forfeited by the said prisoner and such forfeiture shall be deposited in the State Treasury in a fund known as the Inmate Welfare Fund of the Department of Corrections.
(Amended by Stats. 1953, Ch. 1666.)
2766.
This article is not intended to restore, in whole or in part, the civil rights of any prisoner used hereunder, and such article shall not be so construed.
(Amended by Stats. 1976, Ch. 1347.)
2767.
No prisoner while engaged in such construction, maintenance and improvement of a state highway shall drive a motor truck or other vehicle or wagon outside of the limits established for the camp or construction work.
(Amended by Stats. 1947, Ch. 1380.)
2768.
Said prisoners when employed under the provisions of this article shall not be used for the purpose of building any bridge or structure of like character which requires the employment of skilled labor.
(Added by Stats. 1941, Ch. 106.)
2770.
The Department of Transportation shall designate and supervise all road work done under the provisions of this article. It shall provide, supervise and maintain necessary camps and commissariat, except that where no funds are available to the Department of Transportation, the director may provide, erect, and maintain the necessary camps.
(Amended by Stats. 1982, Ch. 1549, Sec. 24.)
2771.
The Director of Corrections shall have full jurisdiction at all times over the discipline and control of the prisoners employed on said roads.
(Amended by Stats. 1947, Ch. 1380.)
2772.
Any person who, without authority, interferes with or in any way interrupts the work of any prisoners employed pursuant to this article, and any person not authorized by law, who gives or attempts to give to any prisoner so employed any controlled substances or any intoxicating liquors of any kind whatever, or firearms, weapons or explosives of any kind, is guilty of a felony and upon conviction thereof shall be punished by imprisonment pursuant to subdivision (h) of Section 1170 and shall be disqualified from holding any state office or position in the employ of this state. Any person who interferes with the discipline or good conduct of any prisoner employed pursuant to this article, while that prisoner is in the confines or limits of the state prison road camp is guilty of a misdemeanor and upon conviction thereof shall be punished by imprisonment in the county jail for a term not more than six months, or by a fine of not more than two hundred dollars ($200), or by both that fine and imprisonment. Any peace officer or any officer or guard of any state prison or any superintendent of that road work, having in charge the prisoners employed upon such highways or state roads, may arrest without a warrant any person violating any provisions of this article.
(Amended by Stats. 2011, Ch. 15, Sec. 464. (AB 109) Effective April 4, 2011. Operative October 1, 2011, by Sec. 636 of Ch. 15, as amended by Stats. 2011, Ch. 39, Sec. 68.)

ARTICLE 5. Employment in Public Parks, Forests, etc. [2780 - 2792]
(Article 5 added by Stats. 1941, Ch. 363.)
2780.
Any department, division, bureau, commission or other agency of the State of California or the Federal Government may use or cause to be used convicts confined in the state prisons to perform work necessary and proper to be done by them at permanent, temporary, and mobile camps to be established under this article. The director may enter into contracts for the purposes of this article.
(Amended by Stats. 1959, Ch. 1583.)
2780.1.
Money received from the rendering of services under the prison camp work program shall be paid to the Treasurer monthly and shall be credited to the support appropriation of the prison rendering such services, in augmentation thereof. The appropriation to be credited shall be the appropriation current at the time of rendering the services. Nothing in this section shall apply to prison road camps established under Article 4 (commencing with Section 2760) of this chapter, except that, by mutual agreement between the Department of Transportation and the Department of Corrections, subject to the approval of the Department of Finance, such prison road camps may be administered, instead, under the provisions of this article.
(Amended by Stats. 1982, Ch. 1549, Sec. 27.)
2780.5.
The Director of Corrections may, during declared fire emergencies, allow the Director of the Department of Forestry and Fire Protection to use prisoners for fire suppression efforts outside of the boundaries of California, not to exceed a distance in excess of 25 miles from the California border, along the borders of Oregon, Nevada, or Arizona.
(Added by Stats. 1989, Ch. 419, Sec. 1.)
2781.
The Director of Corrections shall determine which prisoners shall be eligible for employment under Section 2780, and shall establish and modify lists of prisoners eligible for such employment. Upon the requisition of an agency mentioned in Section 2780, the Director of Corrections may send to the place and at the time designated the number of prisoners requisitioned or such number thereof as have been determined to be eligible for such employment and are available.
The director may return to prison any prisoner transferred to camp pursuant to this section, when the need for such prisoner's labor has ceased or when the prisoner is guilty of any violation of the rules and regulations of the prison or camp.
(Amended by Stats. 1953, Ch. 1666.)
2782.
The director may fix a daily rate to be expended for such convict labor, and when so fixed, the agency shall monthly set aside funds to the director to pay for such labor, and where no funds are available from the agency the director may set aside the department's own funds to pay for such labor. The director, by regulation, may authorize any or all deductions to be made from the pay due convicts as provided for convicts at road camps under Section 2762. The director, by regulation, may also fix the maximum amount, over and above all deductions, that a convict may receive.

(Amended by Stats. 1957, Ch. 2256.)
2785.
Whenever prisoners are paid for their labor under this article and a prisoner wilfully violates the terms of his employment or the rules of the camp or the Department of Corrections the Director of Corrections may in his discretion determine what portion of all moneys earned by the prisoner shall be forfeited by the prisoner and such forfeiture shall be deposited in the State Treasury in the fund known as the Inmate Welfare Fund of the Department of Corrections.
(Amended by Stats. 1953, Ch. 1666.)
2786.
All money received pursuant to this article in the Inmate Welfare Fund of the Department of Corrections and Rehabilitation is hereby appropriated for educational, recreational, and other purposes described in Section 5006 at the various prison camps established under this article and shall be expended by the secretary upon warrants drawn upon the State Treasury by the Controller after approval of the claims by the Department of General Services. It is the intent of the Legislature that moneys in this fund only be expended on services other than those that the department is required to provide to inmates.
(Amended by Stats. 2016, Ch. 31, Sec. 249. (SB 836) Effective June 27, 2016.)
2786.1.
The secretary shall make weight training equipment available to inmates assigned to fire suppression efforts pursuant to this article. The weight training equipment shall be used in accordance with the provisions of Section 5010.
(Added by Stats. 2007, Ch. 737, Sec. 1. Effective January 1, 2008.)
2787.
The agency providing work for convicts under this article shall designate and supervise all work done under the provisions of this article. The agency shall provide, erect and maintain the necessary camps, except that where no funds are available to the agency, the director may provide, erect and maintain the necessary camps. The director shall supervise and manage the necessary camps and commissariat.
(Amended by Stats. 1957, Ch. 2256.)
2788.
The director shall have full jurisdiction at all times over the discipline and control of the convicts performing work under this article.
(Amended by Stats. 1957, Ch. 2256.)
2790.
Any person, who, without authority, interferes with or in any way interrupts the work of any convict used pursuant to this article and any person not authorized by law, who gives or attempts to give to any state prison convict so employed any controlled substances, or any intoxicating liquors of any kind whatever, or firearms, weapons or explosives of any kind is guilty of a felony and upon conviction thereof shall be punished by imprisonment pursuant to subdivision (h) of Section 1170 and shall be disqualified from holding any state office or position in the employ of this state. Any person who interferes with the discipline or good conduct of any convict used pursuant to this article, while that convict is in such camps is guilty of a misdemeanor and upon conviction thereof shall be punished by imprisonment in the county jail for a term not more than six months, or by a fine of not more than four hundred dollars ($400), or by both that fine and imprisonment. Any peace officer or any officer or guard of any state prison or any superintendent of that work, having in charge the convicts used in those camps, may arrest without a warrant any person violating any provisions of this article.
(Amended by Stats. 2011, Ch. 15, Sec. 465. (AB 109) Effective April 4, 2011. Operative October 1, 2011, by Sec. 636 of Ch. 15, as amended by Stats. 2011, Ch. 39, Sec. 68.)
2791.
This article is not intended to restore, in whole or in part, the civil rights of any convict used hereunder, and such article shall not be so construed.
(Amended by Stats. 1976, Ch. 1347.)
2792.
Camps may be established under this article for the employment of paroled prisoners.
(Added by Stats. 1941, Ch. 363.)

CHAPTER 6. Sale of Prison-Made Goods [2800 - 2891]

(Heading of Chapter 6 renumbered from Chapter 7 by Stats. 1941, Ch. 893.)
ARTICLE 1. Prison Industry Authority [2800 - 2818]
(Article 1 added by Stats. 1982, Ch. 1549, Sec. 28.)
2800.
Commencing July 1, 2005, there is hereby continued in existence within the Department of Corrections and Rehabilitation the Prison Industry Authority. As used in this article, "authority" means the Prison Industry Authority. Commencing July 1, 2005, any reference to the Department of Corrections shall refer to the Department of Corrections and Rehabilitation.
(Amended by Stats. 2006, Ch. 538, Sec. 510. Effective January 1, 2007.)
2801.
The purposes of the authority are:
(a) To develop and operate industrial, agricultural, and service enterprises employing prisoners in institutions under the jurisdiction of the Department of Corrections, which enterprises may be located either within those institutions or elsewhere, all as may be determined by the authority.
(b) To create and maintain working conditions within the enterprises as much like those which prevail in private industry as possible, to assure prisoners employed therein the opportunity to work productively, to earn funds, and to acquire or improve effective work habits and occupational skills.
(c) To operate a work program for prisoners which will ultimately be self-supporting by generating sufficient funds from the sale of products and services to pay all the expenses of the program, and one which will provide goods and services which are or will be used by the Department of Corrections, thereby reducing the cost of its operation.
(1) This subdivision does not require immediate cash availability for funding retiree health care and pension liabilities above amounts established in the Budget Act, or as determined by the Board of Administration of the Public Employees' Retirement System, or the Director of Finance for the fiscal year.
(2) The Prison Industry Authority shall not establish cash reserves to support funding retiree health care and pension liabilities above the amounts specified in paragraph (1).
(Amended by Stats. 2017, Ch. 17, Sec. 37. (AB 103) Effective June 27, 2017.)
2802.
Commencing July 1, 2005, there is hereby continued in existence within the Department of Corrections and Rehabilitation a Prison Industry Board. The board shall consist of the following 11 members:
(a) The Secretary of the Department of Corrections and Rehabilitation, or his or her designee.
(b) The Director of the Department of General Services, or his or her designee.
(c) The Secretary of Transportation, or his or her designee.
(d) The Speaker of the Assembly shall appoint two members to represent the general public.

(e) The Senate Committee on Rules shall appoint two members to represent the general public.
(f) The Governor shall appoint four members. Of these, two shall be representatives of organized labor, and two shall be representatives of industry. The initial term of one of the members appointed by the Speaker of the Assembly shall be two years, and the initial term of the other shall be three years. The initial term of one of the members appointed by the Senate Committee on Rules shall be two years, and the initial term of the other shall be three years. The initial terms of the four members appointed by the Governor shall be four years. All subsequent terms of all members shall be for four years. Each member's term shall continue until the appointment and qualification of his or her successor.
(Amended by Stats. 2014, Ch. 401, Sec. 51. (AB 2763) Effective January 1, 2015.)

2803.

The Secretary of the Department Corrections and Rehabilitation shall be the chairperson of the board. The chairperson shall be the administrative head of the board and shall exercise all duties and functions necessary to insure that the responsibilities of the board are successfully discharged. The board shall hold meetings on the call of the chairperson or a majority of the board. Six members of the board, including the chairperson, shall constitute a quorum. The vote of a majority of the members serving on the board is necessary for the transaction of the business of the board.
(Amended by Stats. 2005, Ch. 10, Sec. 18. Effective May 10, 2005. Operative July 1, 2005, by Sec. 99 of Ch. 10.)

2804.

The appointed members of the board shall receive a per diem to be determined by the chairperson, but not less than the usual per diem rate allowed to the Department of Corrections and Rehabilitation employees during travel out of state. All members, including the chairperson, shall also receive their actual and necessary expenses of travel incurred in attending meetings of the commission and in making investigations, either as a board or individually as members of the board at the request of the chairperson. All the expenses shall be paid from the Prison Industries Revolving Fund.
(Amended by Stats. 2005, Ch. 10, Sec. 19. Effective May 10, 2005. Operative July 1, 2005, by Sec. 99 of Ch. 10.)

2805.

The authority shall assume jurisdiction over the operation of all industrial, agricultural, and service operations formerly under the jurisdiction of the Correctional Industries Commission. In addition, the authority shall have the power to establish new industrial, agricultural and service enterprises which it deems appropriate, to initiate and develop new vocational training programs, and to assume jurisdiction over existing vocational training programs. The authority shall have control over and the power to buy and sell all equipment, supplies and materials used in the operations over which it assumes control and jurisdiction.
(Added by Stats. 1982, Ch. 1549, Sec. 28.)

2806.

There is hereby constituted a permanent revolving fund in the sum of not less than seven hundred thirty thousand dollars ($730,000), to be known as the Prison Industries Revolving Fund, and to be used to meet the expenses necessary in the purchasing of materials and equipment, salaries, construction and cost of administration of the prison industries program. The fund may also be used to refund deposits either erroneously made or made in cases where delivery of products cannot be consummated. The fund shall at all times contain the amount of at least seven hundred thirty thousand dollars ($730,000), either in cash or in receivables, consisting of raw materials, finished or unfinished products, inventory at cost, equipment, or any combination of the above. Money received from the rendering of services or the sale of products in the prisons and institutions under the jurisdiction of the Department of Corrections and Rehabilitation pursuant to this article shall be paid to the State Treasurer monthly and shall be credited to the fund. At any time that the Secretary of the Department of Corrections and Rehabilitation and the Director of Finance jointly determine that the balance in that revolving fund is greater than is necessary to carry out the purposes of the authority, they shall so inform the Controller and request a transfer of the unneeded balance from the revolving fund to the General Fund of the State of California. The Controller is authorized to transfer balances upon request. Funds deposited in the revolving fund are not subject to annual appropriation by the Legislature and may be used without a time limit by the authority.
The Prison Industries Revolving Fund is not subject to the provisions of Articles 2 (commencing with Section 13320) and 3 (commencing with Section 13335) of Chapter 3 of Part 3 of Division 3 of Title 2 of the Government Code.
Any major capital outlay project undertaken by the authority pursuant to this article shall be subject to review by the Public Works Board pursuant to the provisions of Part 10.5 (commencing with Section 15752) of Division 3 of Title 2 of the Government Code.
(Amended by Stats. 2005, Ch. 10, Sec. 20. Effective May 10, 2005. Operative July 1, 2005, by Sec. 99 of Ch. 10.)

2807.

(a) The authority is hereby authorized and empowered to operate industrial, agricultural, and service enterprises which will provide products and services needed by the state, or any political subdivision thereof, or by the federal government, or any department, agency, or corporation thereof, or for any other public use. Products may be purchased by state agencies to be offered for sale to inmates of the department and to any other person under the care of the state who resides in state-operated institutional facilities. Fresh meat may be purchased by food service operations in state-owned facilities and sold for onsite consumption.
(b) All things authorized to be produced under subdivision (a) shall be purchased by the state, or any agency thereof, and may be purchased by any county, city, district, or political subdivision, or any agency thereof, or by any state agency to offer for sale to persons residing in state-operated institutions, at the prices fixed by the Prison Industry Authority. State agencies shall make maximum utilization of these products, and shall consult with the staff of the authority to develop new products and adapt existing products to meet their needs.
(c) All products and services provided by the authority may be offered for sale to a nonprofit organization, provided that all of the following conditions are met:
(1) The nonprofit organization is located in California and is exempt from taxation under Section 501(c)(3) of Title 26 of the United States Code.
(2) The nonprofit organization has entered into a memorandum of understanding with a local education agency. As used in this section, "local education agency" means a school district, county office of education, state special school, or charter school.
(3) The products and services are provided to public school students at no cost to the students or their families.
(Amended by Stats. 2011, Ch. 307, Sec. 1. (SB 608) Effective January 1, 2012.)

2808.

The board, in the exercise of its duties, shall have all of the powers and do all of the things that the board of directors of a private corporation would do, except as specifically limited in this article, including, but not limited to, all of the following:
(a) To enter into contracts and leases, execute leases, pledge the equipment, inventory, and supplies under the control of the authority and the anticipated future receipts of any enterprise under the jurisdiction of the authority as collateral for loans, and execute other necessary instruments and documents.
(b) To ensure that all funds received by the authority are kept in commercial accounts according to standard accounting practices.
(c) To arrange for an independent annual audit.
(d) To review and approve the annual budget for the authority, in order to ensure that the solvency of the Prison Industries Revolving Fund is maintained.
(1) This subdivision does not require immediate cash availability for funding retiree health care and pension liabilities above amounts established in the Budget Act, or as determined by the Board of Administration of the Public Employees' Retirement System, or the Director of Finance for the fiscal year.
(2) The Prison Industry Authority shall not establish cash reserves to support funding retiree health care and pension liabilities above the amounts specified in paragraph (1).
(e) To contract to employ a general manager to serve as the chief administrative officer of the authority. The general manager shall serve at the pleasure of the chairperson. The general manager shall have wide and successful experience with a productive enterprise, and have a demonstrated appreciation of the problems associated with prison management.
(f) To apply for and administer grants and contracts of all kinds.
(g) To establish, notwithstanding any other provision of law, procedures governing the purchase of raw materials, component parts, and any other goods and services which may be needed by the authority or in the operation of any enterprise under its jurisdiction. Those procedures shall contain provisions for appeal to the board from any action taken in connection with them.
(h) To establish, expand, diminish, or discontinue industrial, agricultural, and service enterprises under the authority's jurisdiction to enable it to operate as a self-supporting enterprise, to provide as much employment for inmates as is feasible, and to provide diversified work activities to minimize the impact on existing private industry in the state.
(i) To hold public hearings pursuant to subdivision (h) to provide an opportunity for persons or organizations who may be affected to appear and present testimony concerning the plans and activities of the authority. The authority shall ensure adequate public notice of those hearings. A new industrial, agricultural, or service enterprise that involves a gross annual production of more than fifty thousand dollars ($50,000) shall not be established unless and until a hearing concerning the enterprise has been held by a committee of persons designated by the board including at least two board members. The board shall take into consideration the effect of a proposed enterprise on California industry and shall not approve the establishment of the enterprise if the board determines it would have a comprehensive and substantial adverse impact on California industry that cannot be mitigated.
(j) To periodically determine the prices at which activities, supplies, and services shall be sold.
(k) To report to the Legislature in writing, on or before February 1 of each year, regarding:
(1) The financial activity and condition of each enterprise under its jurisdiction.
(2) The plans of the board regarding any significant changes in existing operations.
(3) The plans of the board regarding the development of new enterprises.
(4) A breakdown, by institution, of the number of prisoners at each institution, working in enterprises under the jurisdiction of the authority, said number to indicate the number of prisoners who are not working full time.
(Amended by Stats. 2018, Ch. 92, Sec. 166. (SB 1289) Effective January 1, 2019.)

2809.

Notwithstanding any other provision of law, commencing July 1, 2005, the authority may recruit and employ civilian staff that may be necessary to carry out the purposes of this article, and shall establish recruiting, testing, hiring, promotion, disciplinary, and dismissal procedures and practices which will meet the unique personnel needs of the authority. The practices may include incentives based on productivity, profit-sharing plans, or other criteria which will encourage civilian employee involvement in the productivity goals of the authority. The procedures and practices shall apply to all employees working in enterprises under the jurisdiction of the authority. The general manager shall be the appointing authority for all personnel of the authority other than the general manager.
(Amended by Stats. 2005, Ch. 10, Sec. 23. Effective May 10, 2005. Operative July 1, 2005, by Sec. 99 of Ch. 10.)

2810.

Commencing July 1, 2005, the general manager, with the approval of the Department of Finance, may authorize the borrowing of money by the authority for purposes of any of the following:
(a) Operating the business affairs of the authority.
(b) Purchasing new equipment, materials and supplies.
(c) Constructing new facilities, or repairing, remodeling, or demolishing old facilities.
Funds may be borrowed from private sources, upon those terms that the Department of Finance deems appropriate, including but not limited to, the use of equipment under the jurisdiction of the authority, and of the future income of an enterprise under the jurisdiction of the authority, as collateral to secure any loan.
(Amended by Stats. 2005, Ch. 10, Sec. 24. Effective May 10, 2005. Operative July 1, 2005, by Sec. 99 of Ch. 10.)

2810.5.

Notwithstanding any other provision of law, commencing July 1, 2005, the Pooled Money Investment Board, or its successor, may grant loans to the authority when money is appropriated for that purpose by the Legislature, upon application by the Secretary of the Department of Corrections and Rehabilitation, in order to finance the establishment of a new industrial, agricultural, or service enterprise. All loans shall bear the same interest rate as the pooled money market investment rate and shall have a maximum repayment period of 20 years from the date of approval of the loan.
Prior to making its decision to grant a loan, the Pooled Money Investment Board, or its successor, shall require the authority to demonstrate all of the following:
(a) The proposed industry project cannot be feasibly financed from private sources under Section 2810. The authority shall present proposed loan conditions from at least two private sources.
(b) The proposed industry project cannot feasibly be financed from proceeds from other Prison Industry Authority enterprises.
(c) The proceeds from the proposed project provide for a reasonable payback schedule to the General Fund.
(Amended by Stats. 2005, Ch. 10, Sec. 25. Effective May 10, 2005. Operative July 1, 2005, by Sec. 99 of Ch. 10.)

2811.

Commencing July 1, 2005, the general manager shall adopt and maintain a compensation schedule for inmate employees. That compensation schedule shall be based on quantity and quality of work performed and shall be required for its performance, but in no event shall that compensation exceed one-half the minimum wage provided in Section 1182 of the Labor Code, except as otherwise provided in this code. This compensation shall be credited to the account of the inmate.
Inmate compensation shall be paid from the Prison Industries Revolving Fund.
(Amended by Stats. 2005, Ch. 10, Sec. 26. Effective May 10, 2005. Operative July 1, 2005, by Sec. 99 of Ch. 10.)

2812.

It is unlawful for any person to sell, expose for sale, or offer for sale within this state, any article or articles manufactured wholly or in part by convict or other prison labor, except articles the sale of which is specifically sanctioned by law.
Every person selling, exposing for sale, or offering for sale any article manufactured in this state wholly or in part by convict or other prison labor, the sale of which is not specifically sanctioned by law, is guilty of a misdemeanor.
(Added by Stats. 1982, Ch. 1549, Sec. 28.)

2813.

The director may provide for the manufacture of small articles of handiwork by the prisoners out of raw materials purchased by the prisoners with their own funds or funds borrowed from the Inmates' Welfare Fund, or from raw materials furnished by the director without compensation therefor as provided in this section which articles may be sold to the public at the state prisons, in public buildings, at fairs, or on property operated by nonprofit associations. State-owned property shall not be given to prisoners for use under this section, unless all proceeds from the sale thereof shall be deposited in the Inmates' Welfare Fund. The director may provide that all or a part of the sale price of all other articles manufactured and sold under this section be deposited to the account of the prisoner manufacturing the article.
(Added by Stats. 1982, Ch. 1549, Sec. 28.)

2813.5.
Notwithstanding any other provision of this chapter except subdivision (i) of Section 2808, and notwithstanding subdivision (
l) of Section 22851.3 of the Vehicle Code, the Director of Corrections may provide for the inmates in trade and industrial education or vocational training classes established under Section 2054 to restore and rebuild donated salvageable and abandoned vehicles. If these vehicles comply with Section 24007.5 of the Vehicle Code, they may be sold at public auction to private persons. This activity shall be subject to the public hearing requirements of subdivision (i) of Section 2808 at any time that this activity involves a gross annual production of more than fifty thousand dollars ($50,000). The proceeds of the sale after deduction of the cost of materials shall be deposited in the Restitution Fund in the State Treasury and, upon appropriation by the Legislature, may be used for indemnification of victims of crimes.
(Amended by Stats. 1991, Ch. 1157, Sec. 1.)

2814.
Notwithstanding any provision of this chapter, products and byproducts of agricultural and animal husbandry enterprises, except nursery stock, may be sold to private persons, at public or private sale, under rules prescribed by the board.
(Added by Stats. 1983, Ch. 1150, Sec. 3.)

2815.
Commencing July 1, 2005, the authority may, under rules prescribed by the Secretary of the Department of Corrections and Rehabilitation, dispose of products developed from the operations of industrial enterprises in prisons and institutions under the jurisdiction of the authority by sale to foreign governments, corporations for distribution in foreign countries, and private persons or their agents in markets outside the United States and in countries which permit the importation of prison-made goods. All sales made pursuant to this section shall be reported to the Legislature in the general manager's annual report pursuant to Section 2808.
(Amended by Stats. 2005, Ch. 10, Sec. 27. Effective May 10, 2005. Operative July 1, 2005, by Sec. 99 of Ch. 10.)

2816.
(a) With the approval of the Department of Finance, there shall be transferred to, or deposited in, the Prison Industries Revolving Fund for purposes authorized by this section, money appropriated from any source including sources other than state appropriations.
(b) Notwithstanding subdivision (i) of Section 2808, the Secretary of the Department of Corrections and Rehabilitation may order any authorized public works project involving the construction, renovation, or repair of prison facilities to be performed by inmate labor or juvenile justice facilities to be performed by ward labor, when the total expenditure does not exceed the project limit established by the first paragraph of Section 10108 of the Public Contract Code. Projects entailing expenditure of greater than the project limit established by the first paragraph of Section 10108 of the Public Contract Code shall be reviewed and approved by the chairperson, in consultation with the board.
(c) Money so transferred or deposited shall be available for expenditure by the department for the purposes for which appropriated, contributed, or made available, without regard to fiscal years and irrespective of the provisions of Sections 13340 and 16304 of the Government Code. Money transferred or deposited pursuant to this section shall be used only for purposes authorized in this section.
(d) This section shall remain in effect only until July 1, 2020, and as of that date is repealed.
(Amended by Stats. 2019, Ch. 25, Sec. 39. (SB 94) Effective June 27, 2019. Repealed as of January 1, 2020, by its own provisions. See later operative version added by Sec. 40 of Stats. 2019, Ch. 25)

2816.
(a) With the approval of the Department of Finance, there shall be transferred to, or deposited in, the Prison Industries Revolving Fund for purposes authorized by this section, money appropriated from any source including sources other than state appropriations.
(b) Notwithstanding subdivision (i) of Section 2808, the Secretary of the Department of Corrections and Rehabilitation may order any authorized public works project involving the construction, renovation, or repair of prison facilities to be performed by inmate labor, and the Director of the Department of Youth and Community Restoration may request the Department of Corrections and Rehabilitation to order any authorized public work involving the construction, renovation, or repair of juvenile justice facilities to be performed by ward labor, when the total expenditure does not exceed the project limit established by the first paragraph of Section 10108 of the Public Contract Code. Projects entailing expenditure of greater than the project limit established by the first paragraph of Section 10108 of the Public Contract Code shall be reviewed and approved by the chairperson, in consultation with the board.
(c) Money so transferred or deposited shall be available for expenditure by the department for the purposes for which appropriated, contributed, or made available, without regard to fiscal years and irrespective of the provisions of Sections 13340 and 16304 of the Government Code. Money transferred or deposited pursuant to this section shall be used only for purposes authorized in this section.
(d) This section shall become operative July 1, 2020.
(Repealed (in Sec. 39) and added by Stats. 2019, Ch. 25, Sec. 40. (SB 94) Effective June 27, 2019. Section operative July 1, 2020, by its own provisions.)

2817.
The Inmate and Ward Construction Revolving Account is hereby created in the Prison Industries Revolving Fund, established in Section 2806, to receive funds transferred or deposited for the purposes described in Section 2816.
(Amended by Stats. 2008, Ch. 116, Sec. 2. Effective January 1, 2009.)

2818.
The New Industries Revolving Account is hereby created in the Prison Industries Revolving Fund to receive General Fund or other public money transferred or deposited for the purpose of financing new enterprises or the expansion of existing enterprises. Money in the fund may be disbursed by the board subject to the conditions prescribed in Section 2810.5.
(Added by Stats. 1985, Ch. 966, Sec. 3. Effective September 26, 1985. Operative October 1, 1985, by Sec. 4 of Ch. 966.)

ARTICLE 2. Sale of Prison Goods Made Outside California [2880 - 2891]
(Article 2 added by Stats. 1941, Ch. 106.)

2880.
To the extent and insofar as the same may be permitted under the provisions of the Constitution of the United States and the acts of Congress, all goods, wares, and merchandise manufactured, produced, or mined wholly or in part by prisoners (except prisoners on parole or probation) or manufactured, produced, or mined wholly or in part

in any state prison, transported into the State of California and remaining herein for use, consumption, sale, or storage, shall upon arrival and delivery in this state be subject to the operation and effect of the laws of this state to the same extent and in the same manner as though those commodities had been manufactured, produced, or mined in this state by prisoners or in any state prison, and shall not be exempt therefrom by reason of being introduced in the original package or otherwise.
(Amended by Stats. 1987, Ch. 828, Sec. 125.)

2881.
No person, firm, partnership, association or corporation within this State shall sell or offer, trade, consign, keep, expose or display for sale any goods, wares or merchandise manufactured, assembled, produced or mined in whole or in part by prisoners in any penitentiary, prison, reformatory or other establishment in which prison labor is employed, unless such prison-made goods, wares, or merchandise are plainly, legibly, conspicuously and indelibly branded, molded, embossed, stenciled or labeled with the words "Convict-made" in plain, bold letters followed by the name of such penitentiary, prison, reformatory or other establishment in which the goods, wares or merchandise were made.
(Added by Stats. 1941, Ch. 106.)

2882.
It is hereby specifically provided that any article of prison-made goods, wares or merchandise, as described in the preceding section, may be labeled by the attachment of a label not smaller than four inches long and two inches wide, upon which is printed the words "Convict-made" in plain, bold letters followed by the name of such penitentiary, prison, reformatory, or other establishment in which the goods, wares or merchandise were made; provided, that in the judgment of officials charged with the enforcement of this article such prison-made goods, wares or merchandise can not be legibly, conspicuously and indelibly branded, molded, embossed, stenciled or labeled as provided in said preceding section.
(Added by Stats. 1941, Ch. 106.)

2883.
The size and type of such stenciling or label must be consistent with the size and character of the merchandise to which such stenciling or label applies. The size, type and character of such stenciling or label will be subject to the approval of the officials of the State of California responsible for the enforcement of this article.
(Added by Stats. 1941, Ch. 106.)

2884.
No person, firm, partnership, association or corporation within this state shall sell or offer, trade, consign, keep, expose, or display for sale any goods, wares or merchandise manufactured, assembled, produced, or mined in whole or in part by prisoners in any penitentiary, prison, reformatory, or other establishment in which prison labor is employed, unless those prison-made goods, wares, or merchandise have first been disinfected or sterilized in a plant located in California and licensed by the State Department of Health Services in accordance with any regulations of the State Department of Health Services now in force or which later may be made effective. It is hereby further provided that certificate of that disinfection or sterilization must accompany, be stamped on or attached to those goods, wares, or merchandise in a manner or form prescribed by the officials of the State of California responsible for the enforcement of this article.
(Amended by Stats. 1987, Ch. 828, Sec. 126.)

2885.
No person, firm, partnership, association, or corporation within this State shall sell or offer, trade, consign, keep, expose or display for sale any goods, wares or merchandise manufactured, assembled, produced or mined in whole or in part by the prisoners in any penitentiary, prison, reformatory or other establishment in which prison labor is employed, unless such person, firm, partnership, association or corporation shall keep permanently and conspicuously displayed within the same inclosure and within 10 feet of the place where said prison-made goods, wares or merchandise are kept, exposed, displayed or offered for sale a suitable sign, at least 36 inches wide and 10 inches high, on which appear in legible letters not less than two inches high the following words: "Convict-made products on sale here."
(Added by Stats. 1941, Ch. 106.)

2886.
Any person, firm, partnership, association or corporation within this State, when advertising in any periodical or publication any goods, wares or merchandise made in whole or in part by prisoners in any penitentiary, prison, reformatory or other establishment in which prison labor is employed, must insert the words "Convict-made," in such advertisement in type or other letters conforming in size or shape to those used in the text of said periodical or publication.
(Added by Stats. 1941, Ch. 106.)

2887.
Any person, firm, partnership, association or corporation violating the provisions of this article shall be guilty of a misdemeanor and upon conviction thereof shall be punished by a fine of not less than fifty dollars ($50) or more than five hundred dollars ($500) for each offense, or by imprisonment in the county jail for not less than 30 days or more than six months or by both such fine and imprisonment.
(Added by Stats. 1941, Ch. 106.)

2888.
The State Superintendent of Weights and Measures or any deputy or inspector authorized by him, shall have access to any premises or any records held by any person, firm, partnership, association or corporation containing any information pertaining to the prison-made goods, wares or merchandise referred to herein.
(Added by Stats. 1941, Ch. 106.)

2889.
The enforcement of the provisions of this article shall be under the supervision of the State Superintendent of Weights and Measures.
(Added by Stats. 1941, Ch. 106.)

2890.
The provisions of this article shall not apply to any goods, wares or merchandise manufactured in any penitentiary or prison of this State.
(Added by Stats. 1941, Ch. 106.)

2891.
No person or corporation may sell, expose for sale or offer for sale any goods, wares or merchandise manufactured, produced or mined wholly or in part by prisoners (except prisoners on parole or probation) or manufactured, produced or mined wholly or in part in any State prison the sale of which is not specifically sanctioned by law; and any person or corporation violating any provision of this section is guilty of a misdemeanor.
(Added by Stats. 1941, Ch. 106.)

CHAPTER 7. Execution of Sentences of Imprisonment [2900 - 2985.5]

(Heading of Chapter 7 renumbered from Chapter 6 by Stats. 1941, Ch. 893.)

ARTICLE 1. Commencement of Term [2900 - 2905]
(Article 1 added by Stats. 1941, Ch. 106.)

2900.

(a) The term of imprisonment fixed by the judgment in a criminal action commences to run only upon the actual delivery of the defendant into the custody of the Director of Corrections at the place designated by the Director of Corrections as a place for the reception of persons convicted of felonies.

(b) Except as otherwise provided in this section, the place of reception shall be an institution under the jurisdiction of the Director of Corrections.

(1) As an emergency measure, the Director of Corrections may direct that persons convicted of felonies may be received and detained in jails or other facilities and that the judgment will commence to run upon the actual delivery of the defendant into such place and that any persons previously received and confined for conviction of a felony may be, as an emergency, temporarily housed at such place and the time during which such person is there shall be computed as a part of the term of judgment.

(2) In any case in which, pursuant to the agreement on detainers or other provision of law, a prisoner of another jurisdiction is, before completion of actual confinement in a penal or correctional institution of a jurisdiction other than the State of California, sentenced by a California court to a term of imprisonment for a violation of California law, and the judge of the California court orders that the California sentence shall run concurrently with the sentence which such person is already serving, the Director of Corrections shall designate the institution of the other jurisdiction as the place for reception of such person within the meaning of the preceding provisions of this section. He may also designate the place in California for reception of such person in the event that actual confinement under the prior sentence ends before the period of actual confinement required under the California sentence.

(3) In any case in which a person committed to the Director of Corrections is subsequently committed to a penal or correctional institution of another jurisdiction, the subsequent commitment is ordered to be served concurrently with the California commitment, the prisoner is placed in a penal or correctional institution of the other jurisdiction, and the prisoner is not received by the Director of Corrections pursuant to subdivision (a), the Director of Corrections shall designate the institution of the other jurisdiction as the place for reception and service of the California term.

(c) Except as provided in this section, all time served in an institution designated by the Director of Corrections shall be credited as service of the term of imprisonment.

(1) If a person is ordered released by a court from the custody and jurisdiction of the Director of Corrections pursuant to Section 1272 or 1506 or any other provision of law permitting the legal release of prisoners, time during which the person was released shall not be credited as service of the prison term.

(2) If a prisoner escapes from the custody and jurisdiction of the Director of Corrections, the prisoner shall be deemed an escapee and fugitive from justice, until the prisoner is available to return to the custody of the Director of Corrections or the State of California. Time during which the prisoner is an escapee shall not be credited as service of the prison term.

(d) The Department of Corrections may contract for the use of any facility of the state or political subdivision thereof to care for persons received in accordance with this section.
(Amended by Stats. 1987, Ch. 828, Sec. 127.)

2900.1.
Where a defendant has served any portion of his sentence under a commitment based upon a judgment which judgment is subsequently declared invalid or which is modified during the term of imprisonment, such time shall be credited upon any subsequent sentence he may receive upon a new commitment for the same criminal act or acts.
(Added by Stats. 1949, Ch. 519.)

2900.5.
(a) In all felony and misdemeanor convictions, either by plea or by verdict, when the defendant has been in custody, including, but not limited to, any time spent in a jail, camp, work furlough facility, halfway house, rehabilitation facility, hospital, prison, juvenile detention facility, or similar residential institution, all days of custody of the defendant, including days served as a condition of probation in compliance with a court order, credited to the period of confinement pursuant to Section 4019, and days served in home detention pursuant to Section 1203.016 or 1203.018, shall be credited upon his or her term of imprisonment, or credited to any base fine that may be imposed, at the rate of not less than one hundred twenty-five dollars ($125) per day, or more, in the discretion of the court imposing the sentence. If the total number of days in custody exceeds the number of days of the term of imprisonment to be imposed, the entire term of imprisonment shall be deemed to have been served. In any case where the court has imposed both a prison or jail term of imprisonment and a fine, any days to be credited to the defendant shall first be applied to the term of imprisonment imposed, and thereafter the remaining days, if any, shall be applied to the base fine. If an amount of the base fine is not satisfied by jail credits, or by community service, the penalties and assessments imposed on the base fine shall be reduced by the percentage of the base fine that was satisfied.

(b) For the purposes of this section, credit shall be given only where the custody to be credited is attributable to proceedings related to the same conduct for which the defendant has been convicted. Credit shall be given only once for a single period of custody attributable to multiple offenses for which a consecutive sentence is imposed.

(c) For the purposes of this section, "term of imprisonment" includes any period of imprisonment imposed as a condition of probation or otherwise ordered by a court in imposing or suspending the imposition of any sentence, and also includes any term of imprisonment, including any period of imprisonment prior to release on parole and any period of imprisonment and parole, prior to discharge, whether established or fixed by statute, by any court, or by any duly authorized administrative agency.

(d) It is the duty of the court imposing the sentence to determine the date or dates of any admission to, and release from, custody prior to sentencing and the total number of days to be credited pursuant to this section. The total number of days to be credited shall be contained in the abstract of judgment provided for in Section 1213.

(e) It is the duty of any agency to which a person is committed to apply the credit provided for in this section for the period between the date of sentencing and the date the person is delivered to the agency.

(f) If a defendant serves time in a camp, work furlough facility, halfway house, rehabilitation facility, hospital, juvenile detention facility, similar residential facility, or home detention program pursuant to Section 1203.016, 1203.017, or 1203.018, in lieu of imprisonment in a county jail, the time spent in these facilities or programs shall qualify as mandatory time in jail.

(g) Notwithstanding any other provision of this code as it pertains to the sentencing of convicted offenders, this section does not authorize the sentencing of convicted offenders to any of the facilities or programs mentioned herein.
(Amended by Stats. 2016, Ch. 769, Sec. 2. (AB 2839) Effective January 1, 2017.)

2901.
It is hereby made the duty of the wardens of the State prisons to receive persons sentenced to imprisonment in a State prison, and such persons shall be imprisoned until duly released according to law.
(Added by Stats. 1941, Ch. 106.)

2902.
All criminals sentenced to prison by the authority of the United States or of any state or territory of the United States, may be received by the Director of Corrections and imprisoned in California state prisons in accordance with the sentence of the court by which they were tried. The prisoners so confined shall be subject in all respects to discipline and treatment as though committed under the laws of this State and the Director of Corrections is authorized to enter into contracts with the proper agencies of the United States and of other states and territories of the United States with regard to

the per diem rate such agencies shall pay to the State of California for the keep of each prisoner.
(Amended by Stats. 1949, Ch. 1590.)

2903.
(a) In any case in which a woman offender can be sentenced to imprisonment in the county jail, or be required to serve a term of imprisonment therein as a condition of probation, or has already been so sentenced or imprisoned, the court which tried the offender may, with the consent of the offender and on application of the sheriff or on its own motion, with the consent of the offender, commit the offender to the sheriff with directions for placement in the California Institution for Women in lieu of placement in the county jail if the court finds that the local detention facilities are inadequate for the rehabilitation of the offenders and if the court concludes that the offender will benefit from that treatment and care as is available at that institution and the county has entered into a contract with the state under subdivision (b). The offenders may be received by the Director of Corrections and imprisoned in the California Institution for Women in accordance with the commitment of the court by which tried. The prisoners so confined shall be subject in all respects to discipline, diagnosis, and treatment as though committed under the laws of this state concerning felony prisoners.

(b) The Director of Corrections may enter into contracts, with the approval of the Director of General Services, with any county in this state, upon request of the board of supervisors thereof, wherein the Department of Corrections agrees to furnish diagnosis and treatment services and detention for selected women county prisoners. The county shall reimburse the state for the cost of the services, the cost to be determined by the Director of Finance. In any contract entered into pursuant to this subdivision, the county shall agree to pay that amount which is reasonably necessary for payment of an allowance to each released or paroled prisoner for transportation to the prisoner's county of residence or county where employment is available, and may agree to provide suitable clothing and a cash gratuity to the prisoners in the event that they are discharged from that institution because of parole or completion of the term for which they were sentenced. Each county auditor shall include in his state settlement report rendered to the Controller in the months of January and June the amounts due under any contract authorized by this section, and the county treasurer, at the time of settlement with the state in those months, shall pay to the State Treasurer upon order of the Controller, the amounts found to be due.

(c) The Department of Corrections shall accept the women county prisoners if it believes that they can be materially benefited by the confinement, care, treatment and employment and if adequate facilities to provide the care are available. None of those persons shall be transported to any facility under the jurisdiction of the Department of Corrections until the director has notified the referring court that the person may be transported to the California Institution for Women and the time at which she can be received.

(d) The sheriff of the county in which an order is made placing a woman county prisoner pursuant to this section, or any other peace officer designated by the court, shall execute the order placing the person in the institution or returning her therefrom to the court. The expenses of the peace officer incurred in executing the order is a charge upon the county in which the court is situated.

(e) The Director of Corrections may return to the committing authority any woman prisoner transferred pursuant to this section when that person is guilty of any violation of rules and regulations of the California Institution for Women or the Department of Corrections.

(f) No woman prisoner placed in the California Institution for Women pursuant to this section shall thereafter be deemed to have been guilty of a felony solely by virtue of such placement, and she shall have the same rights to parole and to time off for good behavior as she would have had if she had been confined in the county jail.
(Amended by Stats. 1981, Ch. 714, Sec. 335.)

2905.
(a) For purposes of this section, a "youth offender" is an individual committed to the Department of Corrections and Rehabilitation who is under 22 years of age.

(b) (1) The department shall conduct a youth offender Institutional Classification Committee review at reception to provide special classification consideration for every youth offender. The youth offender Institutional Classification Committee shall consist of the staff required by department regulations at any Institutional Classification Committee, however at least one member shall be a department staff member specially trained in conducting the reviews. Training shall include, but not be limited to, adolescent and young adult development and evidence-based interviewing processes employing positive and motivational techniques.

(2) The purpose of the youth offender Institutional Classification Committee review is to meet with the youth offender and assess the readiness of a youth offender for a lower security level or placement permitting increased access to programs and to encourage the youth offender to commit to positive change and self-improvement.

(c) A youth offender shall be considered for placement at a lower security level than corresponds with his or her classification score or placement in a facility that permits increased access to programs based on the Institutional Classification Committee review and factors including, but not limited to, the following:

(1) Recent in-custody behavior while housed in juvenile or adult facilities.

(2) Demonstrated efforts of progress toward self-improvement in juvenile or adult facilities.

(3) Family or community ties supportive of rehabilitation.

(4) Evidence of commitment to working toward self-improvement with a goal of being a law-abiding member of society upon release.

(d) If the department determines, based on the review described in subdivisions (b) and (c), that the youth offender may be appropriately placed at a lower security level, the department shall transfer the youth offender to a lower security level facility. If the youth offender is denied a lower security level, then he or she shall be considered for placement in a facility that permits increased access to programs. If the department determines a youth offender may appropriately be placed in a facility permitting increased access to programs, the youth offender shall be transferred to such a facility.

(e) If the youth offender demonstrates he or she is a safety risk to inmates, staff, or the public, and does not otherwise demonstrate a commitment to rehabilitation, the youth offender shall be reclassified and placed at a security level that is consistent with department regulations and procedures.

(f) A youth offender who at his or her initial youth offender Institutional Classification Committee review is denied a lower security level than corresponds with his or her placement score or did not qualify for a placement permitting increased access to programs due to previous incarceration history and was placed in the highest security level shall nevertheless be eligible to have his or her placement reconsidered pursuant to subdivisions (b) to (d), inclusive, at his or her annual review until reaching 25 years of age. If at an annual review it is determined that the youth offender has had no serious rule violations for one year, the department shall consider whether the youth would benefit from placement in a lower level facility or placement permitting increased access to programs.

(g) The department shall review and, as necessary, revise existing regulations and adopt new regulations regarding classification determinations made pursuant to this section, and provide for training for staff.

(h) This section shall become operative on July 1, 2015.
(Amended by Stats. 2015, Ch. 303, Sec. 395. (AB 731) Effective January 1, 2016.)

ARTICLE 1.5. Transfer of Prisoners [2910 - 2915]
(Heading of Article 1.5 amended by Stats. 1973, Ch. 187.)

2910.

(a) The Secretary of the Department of Corrections and Rehabilitation may enter into an agreement with a city, county, or city and county to permit transfer of prisoners in the custody of the secretary to a jail or other adult correctional facility of the city, county, or city and county, if the sheriff or corresponding official having jurisdiction over the facility has consented thereto. The agreement shall provide for contributions to the city, county, or city and county toward payment of costs incurred with reference to such transferred prisoners.

(b) For purposes of this section, a transfer of prisoners under subdivision (a) may include inmates who have been sentenced to the department but remain housed in a county jail. These prisoners shall be under the sole legal custody and jurisdiction of the sheriff or corresponding official having jurisdiction over the facility and shall not be under the legal custody or jurisdiction of the Department of Corrections and Rehabilitation.

(c) Notwithstanding any other law, for purposes of entering into agreements under subdivision (a), any process, regulation, requirement, including any state governmental reviews or approvals, or third-party approval that is required under, or implemented pursuant to, any statute that relates to entering into those agreements is hereby waived.

(d) When an agreement entered into pursuant to subdivision (a) or (c) is in effect with respect to a particular local facility, the secretary may transfer prisoners whose terms of imprisonment have been fixed and parole violators to the facility.

(e) Prisoners so transferred to a local facility may, with notice to the secretary, participate in programs of the facility, including, but not limited to, work furlough rehabilitation programs.

(f) The secretary, to the extent possible, shall select city, county, or city and county facilities in areas where medical, food, and other support services are available from nearby existing prison facilities.

(g) The secretary, with the approval of the Department of General Services, may enter into an agreement to lease state property for a period not in excess of 20 years to be used as the site for a facility operated by a city, county, or city and county authorized by this section.

(h) This section shall remain in effect only until January 1, 2020, and as of that date is repealed, unless a later enacted statute, that is enacted before January 1, 2020, deletes or extends that date.

(Amended (as amended by Stats. 2013, Ch. 310, Sec. 13) by Stats. 2016, Ch. 33, Sec. 19. (SB 843) Effective June 27, 2016. Repealed as of January 1, 2020, by its own provisions. See later operative version, as amended by Sec. 20 of Stats. 2016, Ch. 33.)
2910.

(a) The Secretary of the Department of Corrections and Rehabilitation may enter into an agreement with a city, county, or city and county to permit transfer of prisoners in the custody of the secretary to a jail or other adult correctional facility of the city, county, or city and county, if the sheriff or corresponding official having jurisdiction over the facility has consented thereto. The agreement shall provide for contributions to the city, county, or city and county toward payment of costs incurred with reference to such transferred prisoners.

(b) When an agreement entered into pursuant to subdivision (a) is in effect with respect to a particular local facility, the secretary may transfer prisoners whose terms of imprisonment have been fixed and parole violators to the facility.

(c) Prisoners so transferred to a local facility may, with approval of the secretary, participate in programs of the facility, including, but not limited to, work furlough rehabilitation programs.

(d) Prisoners transferred to such facilities are subject to the rules and regulations of the facility in which they are confined, but remain under the legal custody of the Department of Corrections and Rehabilitation and shall be subject at any time, pursuant to the rules and regulations of the secretary, to be detained in the county jail upon the exercise of a state parole or correctional officer's peace officer powers, as specified in Section 830.5, with the consent of the sheriff or corresponding official having jurisdiction over the facility.

(e) The secretary, to the extent possible, shall select city, county, or city and county facilities in areas where medical, food, and other support services are available from nearby existing prison facilities.

(f) The secretary, with the approval of the Department of General Services, may enter into an agreement to lease state property for a period not in excess of 20 years to be used as the site for a facility operated by a city, county, or city and county authorized by this section.

(g) An agreement shall not be entered into under this section unless the cost per inmate in the facility is no greater than the average costs of keeping an inmate in a comparable facility of the department, as determined by the secretary.

(h) This section shall become operative on January 1, 2020.

(Amended (as added by Stats. 2013, Ch. 310, Sec. 14) by Stats. 2016, Ch. 33, Sec. 20. (SB 843) Effective June 27, 2016. Section operative January 1, 2020, by its own provisions.)
2910.5.

(a) Pursuant to Section 2910, the Director of Corrections may enter into a long-term agreement not to exceed 20 years with a city, county, or city and county to place parole violators and other state inmates in a facility which is specially designed and built for the incarceration of parole violators and specified state prison inmates.

(b) The agreement shall provide that persons providing security at the facilities shall be peace officers as defined in Sections 830.1 and 830.55 who have satisfactorily met the minimum selection and training standards prescribed by the Board of Corrections for local correctional personnel established under Section 6035.

(c) A parole violator or other inmate may be confined in a facility established under this section.

(1) If convicted within the last 10 years of a violent felony, as defined in subdivision (c) of Section 667.5, or convicted of a crime, as defined in Sections 207, 210.5, 214, 217.1, or 220, or if that person has a history of escape or attempted escape, the Department of Corrections, prior to placing the parole violator or inmate in the facility, shall review each individual case to make certain that this placement is in keeping with the need to protect society.

(2) No inmate or parole violator who has received a sentence of life imprisonment within the past 20 years shall be eligible.

(3) The superintendent of the facility also shall review each individual case where the inmate or parolee has been convicted within the last 10 years of a crime specified in this subdivision and shall ascertain whether this is an appropriate placement. The superintendent shall reject those whom he or she determines are inappropriate due to their propensity for violence or escape and shall submit written findings for the rejection to the Department of Corrections.

(4) No parole violator who receives a revocation sentence greater than 12 months shall be confined in a facility established under this section.

(5) The Department of Corrections shall establish additional guidelines as to inmates eligible for the facilities.

(d) In determining the reimbursement rate pursuant to an agreement entered into pursuant to subdivision (a), the director shall take into consideration the costs incurred by the city, county, or city and county for services and facilities provided and any other factors that are necessary and appropriate to fix the obligations, responsibilities, and rights of the respective parties.

(e) Facilities operated by the county shall be under the supervision of the sheriff. Facilities operated by the city shall be under the supervision of a chief of police or a facility superintendent who shall have at least five years similar experience.

(f) Cities or counties contracting with the Department of Corrections for a facility pursuant to this section shall be responsible for managing and maintaining the security of the facility pursuant to the regulations and direction of the Director of Corrections. No city or county may contract with any private provider to manage, operate, or maintain the security of the facility.

(Amended by Stats. 1991, Ch. 1100, Sec. 4.)
2910.6.

The Director of Corrections may enter into an agreement consistent with applicable law for a city, county, or city and county to construct and operate community corrections programs, restitution centers, halfway houses, work furlough programs, or other correctional programs authorized by state law.

(Added by Stats. 1987, Ch. 1450, Sec. 2.5.)
2911.

(a) The Director of Corrections may enter into contracts, with the approval of the Director of General Services, with appropriate officials or agencies of the United States for the confinement, care, education, treatment, and employment of those persons convicted of criminal offenses in the courts of this state and committed to state prisons as the director believes can benefit by the confinement, care, education, treatment, and employment.

(b) Any contract entered into pursuant to subdivision (a) shall provide for (1) reimbursement to the United States government for the cost of those services, including any costs incurred by the government in transporting the prisoners, and (2) any other matters as may be necessary and appropriate to fix the obligations, responsibilities and rights of the respective parties to the contract.

(c) No inmate may be transferred from an institution within this state to a federal facility pursuant to a contract entered into pursuant to subdivision (a) unless he or she has executed, in the presence of the warden or other head of the institution in this state in which he or she is confined, a written consent to the transfer. The inmate shall have the right to a private consultation with an attorney of his or her choice, concerning his or her rights and obligations under this section, prior to his or her appearance before the warden or other head of the institution for the purpose of executing the written consent.

(d) Whenever a contract has been made pursuant to this section the director may direct the transfer of an inmate to the facility designated and shall thereafter deliver the inmate to the custody of the appropriate federal officials for transportation to that facility. An inmate so transferred shall at all times be subject to the jurisdiction of this state and may at any time be removed from the facility in which he or she is confined for return to this state, for transfer to another facility in which this state may have a contractual or other right to confine inmates, for release on probation or parole, for discharge, or for any other purpose permitted by the laws of this state; in all other respects, an inmate transferred to a federal facility shall be subject to all provisions of the law or regulations applicable to persons committed for violations of laws of the United States not inconsistent with the sentence imposed on the inmate.

(e) The Board of Prison Terms, and the panels and members thereof, may meet at the federal facility where an inmate is confined pursuant to this section or enter into cooperative arrangements with corresponding federal agencies or officials, as necessary to carry out the term-fixing and parole functions. Nothing in this subdivision shall be deemed to waive an inmate's right to personally appear before the Board of Prison Terms.

(f) Any inmate confined pursuant to a contract entered into pursuant to this section shall be released within the territory of this state unless the inmate, this state and the federal government shall agree upon release in some other place. This state shall bear the cost of return of the inmate to its territory.

(g) This section shall not apply to an inmate who is transferred by the Department of Corrections to the United States Immigration and Naturalization Service pursuant to Section 5025.

(Amended by Stats. 1994, Ch. 565, Sec. 3. Effective September 16, 1994. Superseded on operative date of amendment by Stats. 1994, Ch. 567.)
2911.

(a) The Director of Corrections may enter into contracts, with the approval of the Director of General Services, with appropriate officials or agencies of the United States for the confinement, care, education, treatment, and employment of persons convicted of criminal offenses in the courts of this state and committed to state prisons as the director believes can benefit by confinement, care, education, treatment, and employment.

(b) Any contract entered into pursuant to subdivision (a) shall provide for (1) reimbursement to the United States government for the cost of services, including any costs incurred by the federal government in transporting prisoners, and (2) other matters as may be necessary and appropriate to fix the obligations, responsibilities and rights of the respective parties to the contract.

(c) No inmate may be transferred from an institution within this state to a federal facility pursuant to a contract unless he or she has executed, in the presence of the warden or other head of the institution in this state in which he or she is confined, a written consent to the transfer. The inmate shall have the right to a private consultation with an attorney of his or her choice, concerning his or her rights and obligations under this section, prior to his or her appearance before the warden or other head of the institution for the purpose of executing the written consent.

(d) Whenever a contract has been made pursuant to this section the director may direct the transfer of an inmate to the facility designated and shall thereafter deliver the inmate to the custody of the appropriate federal officials for transportation to the facility. An inmate so transferred shall at all times be subject to the jurisdiction of this state and may at any time be removed from the facility in which he or she is confined for return to this state, for transfer to another facility in which this state may have a contractual or other right to confine inmates, for release on probation or parole, for discharge, or for any other purpose permitted by the laws of this state; in all other respects, an inmate transferred to a federal facility shall be subject to all provisions of the law or regulations applicable to persons committed for violations of laws of the United States not inconsistent with the sentence imposed on the inmate.

(e) The Board of Prison Terms, and the panels and members thereof, may meet at the federal facility where an inmate is confined pursuant to this section or enter into cooperative arrangements with corresponding federal agencies or officials, as necessary to carry out the term-fixing and parole functions. Nothing in this subdivision shall be deemed to waive an inmate's right to personally appear before the Board of Prison Terms.

(f) Any inmate confined pursuant to a contract entered into pursuant to this section shall be released within the territory of this state unless the inmate, this state and the federal government shall agree upon release in some other place. This state shall bear the cost of return of the inmate to his or her territory.

(g) This section shall not apply to any inmate or ward who is transferred by the Department of the Youth Authority or the Department of Corrections to the custody of the Attorney General of the United States pursuant to Section 5025.

(Amended by Stats. 1994, Ch. 567, Sec. 1. Effective January 1, 1995. Conditionally operative (upon enactment of federal legislation) as prescribed by Sec. 6 of Ch. 567.)
2912.

(a) Under its Foreign Prisoner Transfer Program, the Board of Prison Terms shall devise a method of notifying each foreign born inmate in a prison or reception center operated by the Department of Corrections that he or she may be eligible to serve his or her term of imprisonment in his or her nation of citizenship as provided in federal treaties.

(b) (1) The Board of Prison Terms shall actively encourage each eligible foreign born inmate to apply for return to his or her nation of citizenship as provided in federal

treaties and shall provide quarterly reports outlining its efforts under this section to the Chairperson of the Joint Legislative Budget Committee and the chairperson of each fiscal committee of the Legislature.
(2) The Board of Prison Terms shall adopt the model program developed by the State of Texas for encouraging participation in the federal repatriation program where appropriate.
(Amended by Stats. 2004, Ch. 924, Sec. 1. Effective January 1, 2005.)
2913.
A city shall give notice to, and consult with, the county prior to contracting with the state pursuant to Section 2910 of this code or Section 1753.3 of the Welfare and Institutions Code.
(Added by Stats. 1987, Ch. 1450, Sec. 2.6.)
2915.
(a) The Secretary of the Department of Corrections and Rehabilitation may enter into one or more agreements to obtain secure housing capacity within the state. These agreements may be entered into with private entities and may be in the form of a lease or an operating agreement. The secretary may procure and enter these agreements on terms and conditions he or she deems necessary and appropriate. Notwithstanding any other law, any process, regulation, requirement, including any state governmental reviews or approvals, or third-party approval that is required under statutes that relate to the procurement and implementation of those agreements is hereby waived, however, no agreement shall contain terms, either directly or indirectly, that involve the repayment of any debt issuance or other financing and, consistent with state law, shall provide that payment of that agreement is subject to appropriation.
(b) The Secretary of the Department of Corrections and Rehabilitation may enter into one or more agreements to obtain secure housing capacity in another state. These agreements may be entered into with private entities and may be in the form of an operating agreement or other contract. The secretary may procure and enter these agreements on terms and conditions he or she deems necessary and appropriate. Notwithstanding any other law, any process, regulation, requirement, including any state governmental reviews or approvals, or third-party approval that is required under statutes that relate to the procurement and implementation of those agreements is hereby waived, however, no agreement shall contain terms, either directly or indirectly, that involve the repayment of any debt issuance or other financing and, consistent with state law, shall provide that payment of that agreement is subject to appropriation. This subdivision does not authorize the department to operate a facility out of state.
(c) The provisions of Division 13 (commencing with Section 21000) of the Public Resources Code do not apply to this section.
(d) This section shall remain in effect only until January 1, 2020, and as of that date is repealed, unless a later enacted statute, that is enacted before January 1, 2020, deletes or extends that date.
(Amended by Stats. 2016, Ch. 33, Sec. 21. (SB 843) Effective June 27, 2016. Repealed as of January 1, 2020, by its own provisions.)
ARTICLE 2.5. Credit on Term of Imprisonment [2930 - 2936]
(Article 2.5 added by Stats. 1976, Ch. 1139.)
2930.
(a) The Department of Corrections shall inform every prisoner sentenced under Section 1170, for a crime committed prior to January 1, 1983, not later than 14 days after reception in prison, of all applicable prison rules and regulations including the possibility of receiving a one-third reduction of the sentence for good behavior and participation. Within 14 days of the prisoner's arrival at the institution to which the prisoner is ultimately assigned by the Department of Corrections, the prisoner shall be informed of the range of programs offered by that institution and their availability at that institution. The prisoner's central file shall reflect compliance with the provisions of this section not later than 90 days after reception in prison.
(b) The department shall, within 90 days after July 1, 1977, inform every prisoner who committed a felony before July 1, 1977, and who would have been sentenced under Section 1170 if the felony had been committed after July 1, 1977, of all applicable prison rules and regulations, which have not previously been provided, of the range of programs offered and their availability, and the possibility of receiving a reduction for good behavior and participation of one-third of the prisoner's remaining sentence after July 1, 1977. The prisoner's central file shall reflect compliance with the provisions of this section.
(Amended by Stats. 1982, Ch. 1234, Sec. 1.)
2931.
(a) In any case in which a prisoner was sentenced to the state prison pursuant to Section 1170, or if he committed a felony before July 1, 1977, and he would have been sentenced under Section 1170 if the felony had been committed after July 1, 1977, the Department of Corrections shall have the authority to reduce the term prescribed under such section by one-third for good behavior and participation consistent with subdivision (d) of Section 1170.2. A document shall be signed by a prison official and given to the prisoner, at the time of compliance with Section 2930, outlining the conditions which the prisoner shall meet to receive the credit. The conditions specified in such document may be modified upon any of the following:
(1) Mutual consent of the prisoner and the Department of Corrections.
(2) The transfer of the prisoner from one institution to another.
(3) The department's determination of the prisoner's lack of adaptability or success in a specific program or assignment. In such case the prisoner shall be entitled to a hearing regarding the department's decision.
(4) A change in custodial status.
(b) Total possible good behavior and participation credit shall result in a four-month reduction for each eight months served in prison or in a reduction based on this ratio for any lesser period of time. Three months of this four-month reduction, or a reduction based on this ratio for any lesser period, shall be based upon forbearance from any act for which the prisoner could be prosecuted in a court of law, either as a misdemeanor or a felony, or any act of misconduct described as a serious disciplinary infraction by the Department of Corrections.
(c) One month of this four-month reduction, or a reduction based on this ratio for a lesser period, shall be based solely upon participation in work, educational, vocational, therapeutic or other prison activities. Failure to succeed after demonstrating a reasonable effort in the specified activity shall not result in loss of participation credit. Failure to participate in the specified activities can result in a maximum loss of credit of 30 days for each failure to participate. However, those confined for other than behavior problems shall be given specified activities commensurate with the custodial status.
(d) This section shall not apply to any person whose crime was committed on or after January 1, 1983.
(Amended by Stats. 1982, Ch. 1234, Sec. 2.)
2932.
(a) (1) For any time credit accumulated pursuant to Section 2931 or 2933, not more than 360 days of credit may be denied or lost for a single act of murder, attempted murder, solicitation of murder, manslaughter, rape, sodomy, or oral copulation accomplished against the victim's will, attempted rape, attempted sodomy, or attempted oral copulation accomplished against the victim's will, assault or battery causing serious bodily injury, assault with a deadly weapon or caustic substance, taking of a hostage, escape with force or violence, or possession or manufacture of a deadly weapon or explosive device, whether or not prosecution is undertaken for purposes of this paragraph. Solicitation of murder shall be proved by the testimony of two witnesses, or of one witness and corroborating circumstances.
(2) Not more than 180 days of credit may be denied or lost for a single act of misconduct, except as specified in paragraph (1), which could be prosecuted as a felony whether or not prosecution is undertaken.
(3) Not more than 90 days of credit may be denied or lost for a single act of misconduct which could be prosecuted as a misdemeanor, whether or not prosecution is undertaken.
(4) Not more than 30 days of credit may be denied or lost for a single act of misconduct defined by regulation as a serious disciplinary offense by the Department of Corrections and Rehabilitation. Any person confined due to a change in custodial classification following the commission of any serious disciplinary infraction shall, in addition to any loss of time credits, be ineligible to receive participation or worktime credit for a period not to exceed the number of days of credit which have been lost for the act of misconduct or 180 days, whichever is less. Any person confined in a secure housing unit for having committed any misconduct specified in paragraph (1) in which great bodily injury is inflicted upon a nonprisoner shall, in addition to any loss of time credits, be ineligible to receive participation or worktime credit for a period not to exceed the number of days of credit which have been lost for that act of misconduct. In unusual cases, an inmate may be denied the opportunity to participate in a credit qualifying assignment for up to six months beyond the period specified in this subdivision if the Secretary of the Department of Corrections and Rehabilitation finds, after a hearing, that no credit qualifying program may be assigned to the inmate without creating a substantial risk of physical harm to staff or other inmates. At the end of the six-month period and of successive six-month periods, the denial of the opportunity to participate in a credit qualifying assignment may be renewed upon a hearing and finding by the director.
(5) The prisoner may appeal the decision through the department's review procedure, which shall include a review by an individual independent of the institution who has supervisorial authority over the institution.
(b) For any credit accumulated pursuant to Section 2931, not more than 30 days of participation credit may be denied or lost for a single failure or refusal to participate. Any act of misconduct described by the Department of Corrections and Rehabilitation as a serious disciplinary infraction if committed while participating in work, educational, vocational, therapeutic, or other prison activity shall be deemed a failure to participate.
(c) Any procedure not provided for by this section, but necessary to carry out the purposes of this section, shall be those procedures provided for by the Department of Corrections and Rehabilitation for serious disciplinary infractions if those procedures are not in conflict with this section.
(1) (A) The Department of Corrections and Rehabilitation shall, using reasonable diligence to investigate, provide written notice to the prisoner. The written notice shall be given within 15 days after the discovery of information leading to charges that may result in a possible denial of credit, except that if the prisoner has escaped, the notice shall be given within 15 days of the prisoner's return to the custody of the secretary. The written notice shall include the specific charge, the date, the time, the place that the alleged misbehavior took place, the evidence relied upon, a written explanation of the procedures that will be employed at the proceedings and the prisoner's rights at the hearing. The hearing shall be conducted by an individual who shall be independent of the case and shall take place within 30 days of the written notice.
(B) The Department of Corrections and Rehabilitation may delay written notice beyond 15 days when all of the following factors are true:
(i) An act of misconduct is involved which could be prosecuted as murder, attempted murder, or assault on a prison employee, whether or not prosecution is undertaken.
(ii) Further investigation is being undertaken for the purpose of identifying other prisoners involved in the misconduct.
(iii) Within 15 days after the discovery of information leading to charges that may result in a possible denial of credit, the investigating officer makes a written request to delay notifying that prisoner and states the reasons for the delay.
(iv) The warden of the institution approves of the delay in writing.
The period of delay under this paragraph shall not exceed 30 days. The prisoner's hearing shall take place within 30 days of the written notice.
(2) The prisoner may elect to be assigned an employee to assist in the investigation, preparation, or presentation of a defense at the disciplinary hearing if it is determined by the department that either of the following circumstances exist:
(A) The prisoner is illiterate.
(B) The complexity of the issues or the prisoner's confinement status makes it unlikely that the prisoner can collect and present the evidence necessary for an adequate comprehension of the case.
(3) The prisoner may request witnesses to attend the hearing and they shall be called unless the person conducting the hearing has specific reasons to deny this request. The specific reasons shall be set forth in writing and a copy of the document shall be presented to the prisoner.
(4) The prisoner has the right, under the direction of the person conducting the hearing, to question all witnesses.
(5) At the conclusion of the hearing the charge shall be dismissed if the facts do not support the charge, or the prisoner may be found guilty on the basis of a preponderance of the evidence.
(d) If found guilty the prisoner shall be advised in writing of the guilty finding and the specific evidence relied upon to reach this conclusion and the amount of time-credit loss. The prisoner may appeal the decision through the department's review procedure, and may, upon final notification of appeal denial, within 15 days of the notification demand review of the department's denial of credit to the Board of Parole Hearings, and the board may affirm, reverse, or modify the department's decision or grant a hearing before the board at which hearing the prisoner shall have the rights specified in Section 3041.5.
(e) Each prisoner subject to Section 2931 shall be notified of the total amount of good behavior and participation credit which may be credited pursuant to Section 2931, and his or her anticipated time-credit release date. The prisoner shall be notified of any change in the anticipated release date due to denial or loss of credits, award of worktime credit, under Section 2933, or the restoration of any credits previously forfeited.
(f) (1) If the conduct the prisoner is charged with also constitutes a crime, the department may refer the case to criminal authorities for possible prosecution. The department shall notify the prisoner, who may request postponement of the disciplinary proceedings pending the referral.
(2) The prisoner may revoke his or her request for postponement of the disciplinary proceedings up until the filing of the accusatory pleading. In the event of the revocation of the request for postponement of the proceeding, the department shall hold the hearing within 30 days of the revocation.
(3) Notwithstanding the notification requirements in this paragraph and subparagraphs (A) and (B) of paragraph (1) of subdivision (c), in the event the case is referred to criminal authorities for prosecution and the authority requests that the prisoner not be notified so as to protect the confidentiality of its investigation, no notice to the prisoner shall be required until an accusatory pleading is filed with the court, or the authority notifies the warden, in writing, that it will not prosecute or it authorizes the notification of the prisoner. The notice exceptions provided for in this paragraph shall only apply if the criminal authority requests of the warden, in writing, and within the 15 days provided in subparagraph (A) of paragraph (1) of subdivision (c), that the prisoner not be notified. Any period of delay of notice to the prisoner shall not exceed 30 days beyond the 15 days referred to in subdivision (c). In the event that no prosecution is undertaken, the procedures in subdivision (c) shall apply, and the time periods set forth in that

subdivision shall commence to run from the date the warden is notified in writing of the decision not to prosecute. In the event the authority either cancels its requests that the prisoner not be notified before it makes a decision on prosecution or files an accusatory pleading, the provisions of this paragraph shall apply as if no request had been received, beginning from the date of the cancellation or filing.

(4) In the case where the prisoner is prosecuted by the district attorney, the Department of Corrections and Rehabilitation shall not deny time credit where the prisoner is found not guilty and may deny credit if the prisoner is found guilty, in which case the procedures in subdivision (c) shall not apply.

(g) If time credit denial proceedings or criminal prosecution prohibit the release of a prisoner who would have otherwise been released, and the prisoner is found not guilty of the alleged misconduct, the amount of time spent incarcerated, in excess of what the period of incarceration would have been absent the alleged misbehavior, shall be deducted from the prisoner's parole period.

(h) Nothing in the amendments to this section made at the 1981–82 Regular Session of the Legislature shall affect the granting or revocation of credits attributable to that portion of the prisoner's sentence served prior to January 1, 1983.

(Amended by Stats. 2012, Ch. 162, Sec. 130. (SB 1171) Effective January 1, 2013.)

2932.5.

A prisoner who is found by a trial court to be a vexatious litigant as defined by Section 391 of the Code of Civil Procedure, shall be denied or lose 30 days of work time credit awarded under Section 2933.

(Added by Stats. 1996, Ch. 852, Sec. 1. Effective January 1, 1997.)

2933.

(a) It is the intent of the Legislature that persons convicted of a crime and sentenced to the state prison under Section 1170 serve the entire sentence imposed by the court, except for a reduction in the time served in the custody of the Secretary of the Department of Corrections and Rehabilitation pursuant to this section and Section 2933.05.

(b) For every six months of continuous incarceration, a prisoner shall be awarded credit reductions from his or her term of confinement of six months. A lesser amount of credit based on this ratio shall be awarded for any lesser period of continuous incarceration. Credit should be awarded pursuant to regulations adopted by the secretary. Prisoners who are denied the opportunity to earn credits pursuant to subdivision (a) of Section 2932 shall be awarded no credit reduction pursuant to this section. Under no circumstances shall any prisoner receive more than six months' credit reduction for any six-month period under this section.

(c) Credit is a privilege, not a right. Credit must be earned and may be forfeited pursuant to the provisions of Section 2932. Except as provided in subdivision (a) of Section 2932, every eligible prisoner shall have a reasonable opportunity to participate.

(d) Under regulations adopted by the Department of Corrections and Rehabilitation, which shall require a period of not more than one year free of disciplinary infractions, credit which has been previously forfeited may be restored by the secretary. The regulations shall provide for separate classifications of serious disciplinary infractions as they relate to restoration of credits, the time period required before forfeited credits or a portion thereof may be restored, and the percentage of forfeited credits that may be restored for these time periods. For credits forfeited as specified in paragraph (1) of subdivision (a) of Section 2932, the Department of Corrections and Rehabilitation may provide that up to 180 days of lost credit shall not be restored and up to 90 days of credit shall not be restored for a forfeiture resulting from conspiracy or attempts to commit one of those acts. No credits may be restored if they were forfeited for a serious disciplinary infraction in which the victim died or was permanently disabled. Upon application of the prisoner and following completion of the required time period free of disciplinary offenses, forfeited credits eligible for restoration under the regulations for disciplinary offenses other than serious disciplinary infractions punishable by a credit loss of more than 90 days shall be restored unless, at a hearing, it is found that the prisoner refused to accept or failed to perform in a credit qualifying assignment, or extraordinary circumstances are present that require that credits not be restored. "Extraordinary circumstances" shall be defined in the regulations adopted by the secretary. However, in any case in which credit was forfeited for a serious disciplinary infraction punishable by a credit loss of more than 90 days, restoration of credit shall be at the discretion of the secretary.

The prisoner may appeal the finding through the Department of Corrections and Rehabilitation's review procedure, which shall include a review by an individual independent of the institution who has supervisorial authority over the institution.

(e) The provisions of subdivision (d) shall also apply in cases of credit forfeited under Section 2931 for offenses and serious disciplinary infractions occurring on or after January 1, 1983.

(Amended by Stats. 2011, 1st Ex. Sess., Ch. 12, Sec. 16. (AB 17 1x) Effective September 21, 2011. Operative October 1, 2011, by Sec. 46 of Ch. 12.)

2933.05.

(a) In addition to any credit awarded pursuant to Section 2933, the department may also award a prisoner program credit reductions from his or her term of confinement as provided in this section. Within 90 days of the enactment of this section, the secretary shall promulgate regulations that provide for credit reductions for inmates who successfully complete specific program performance objectives for approved rehabilitative programming ranging from credit reduction of not less than one week to credit reduction of no more than six weeks for each performance milestone. Regulations promulgated pursuant to this subdivision shall specify the credit reductions applicable to distinct objectives in a schedule of graduated program performance objectives concluding with the successful completion of an in-prison rehabilitation program. Commencing upon the promulgation of those regulations, the department shall thereafter calculate and award credit reductions authorized by this section. However, a prisoner may not have his or her term of imprisonment reduced more than six weeks for credits awarded pursuant to this section during any 12-month period of continuous confinement.

(b) Program credit is a privilege, not a right. Prisoners shall have a reasonable opportunity to participate in program credit qualifying assignments in a manner consistent with institutional security and available resources. Assignments made to program credit qualifying programs shall be made in accordance with the prisoner's case plan, when available.

(c) As used in this section, "approved rehabilitation programming" shall include, but is not limited to, academic programs, vocational programs, vocational training, and core programs such as anger management and social life skills, and substance abuse programs.

(d) Credits awarded pursuant to this section may be forfeited pursuant to the provisions of Section 2932. Inmates shall not be eligible for program credits that result in an inmate overdue for release.

(e) The following prisoners shall not be eligible for program credits pursuant to this section:

(1) Any person serving a term of imprisonment for an offense specified in subdivision (c) of Section 667.5.

(2) Any person sentenced to state prison pursuant to Section 1170.12 or subdivisions (b) to (i), inclusive, of Section 667.

(3) Any person required to register as a sex offender pursuant to Chapter 5.5 (commencing with Section 290) of Title 9 of Part 1.

(4) Any person serving a term of imprisonment as a result of a violation of parole without a new term.

(Added by Stats. 2009, 3rd Ex. Sess., Ch. 28, Sec. 39. (SB 18 3x) Effective January 25, 2010.)

2933.1.

(a) Notwithstanding any other law, any person who is convicted of a felony offense listed in subdivision (c) of Section 667.5 shall accrue no more than 15 percent of worktime credit, as defined in Section 2933.

(b) The 15-percent limitation provided in subdivision (a) shall apply whether the defendant is sentenced under Chapter 4.5 (commencing with Section 1170) of Title 7 of Part 2 or sentenced under some other law. However, nothing in subdivision (a) shall affect the requirement of any statute that the defendant serve a specified period of time prior to minimum parole eligibility, nor shall any offender otherwise statutorily ineligible for credit be eligible for credit pursuant to this section.

(c) Notwithstanding Section 4019 or any other provision of law, the maximum credit that may be earned against a period of confinement in, or commitment to, a county jail, industrial farm, or road camp, or a city jail, industrial farm, or road camp, following arrest and prior to placement in the custody of the Director of Corrections, shall not exceed 15 percent of the actual period of confinement for any person specified in subdivision (a).

(d) This section shall only apply to offenses listed in subdivision (a) that are committed on or after the date on which this section becomes operative.

(Amended by Stats. 2002, Ch. 787, Sec. 25. Effective January 1, 2003.)

2933.2.

(a) Notwithstanding Section 2933.1 or any other law, any person who is convicted of murder, as defined in Section 187, shall not accrue any credit, as specified in Section 2933 or Section 2933.05.

(b) The limitation provided in subdivision (a) shall apply whether the defendant is sentenced under Chapter 4.5 (commencing with Section 1170) of Title 7 of Part 2 or sentenced under some other law.

(c) Notwithstanding Section 4019 or any other provision of law, no credit pursuant to Section 4019 may be earned against a period of confinement in, or commitment to, a county jail, industrial farm, or road camp, or a city jail, industrial farm, or road camp, following arrest for any person specified in subdivision (a).

(d) This section shall only apply to murder that is committed on or after the date on which this section becomes operative.

(Amended by Stats. 2009, 3rd Ex. Sess., Ch. 28, Sec. 40. (SB 18 3x) Effective January 25, 2010.)

2933.3.

(a) Notwithstanding any other law, any inmate assigned to a conservation camp by the Department of Corrections and Rehabilitation, who is eligible to earn one day of credit for every one day of incarceration pursuant to Section 2933 shall instead earn two days of credit for every one day of service. The enhanced credit authorized pursuant to this subdivision shall only apply to those prisoners eligible after January 1, 2003.

(b) Notwithstanding any other law, any inmate who has completed training for assignment to a conservation camp or to a correctional institution as an inmate firefighter or who is assigned to a correctional institution as an inmate firefighter and who is eligible to earn one day of credit for every one day of incarceration pursuant to Section 2933 shall instead earn two days of credit for every one day served in that assignment or after completing that training.

(c) In addition to credits granted pursuant to subdivision (a) or (b), inmates who have successfully completed training for firefighter assignments shall receive a credit reduction from his or her term of confinement pursuant to regulations adopted by the secretary.

(d) The credits authorized in subdivisions (b) and (c) shall only apply to inmates who are eligible after July 1, 2009.

(Amended by Stats. 2009, 3rd Ex. Sess., Ch. 28, Sec. 41. (SB 18 3x) Effective January 25, 2010.)

2933.5.

(a) (1) Notwithstanding any other law, every person who is convicted of any felony offense listed in paragraph (2), and who previously has been convicted two or more times, on charges separately brought and tried, and who previously has served two or more separate prior prison terms, as defined in subdivision (g) of Section 667.5, of any offense or offenses listed in paragraph (2), shall be ineligible to earn credit on his or her term of imprisonment pursuant to this article.

(2) As used in this subdivision, "felony offense" includes any of the following:

(A) Murder, as defined in Sections 187 and 189.

(B) Voluntary manslaughter, as defined in subdivision (a) of Section 192.

(C) Mayhem as defined in Section 203.

(D) Aggravated mayhem, as defined in Section 205.

(E) Kidnapping, as defined in Section 207, 209, or 209.5.

(F) Assault with vitriol, corrosive acid, or caustic chemical of any nature, as described in Section 244.

(G) Rape, as defined in paragraph (2) or (6) of subdivision (a) of Section 261 or paragraph (1) or (4) of subdivision (a) of Section 262.

(H) Sodomy by means of force, violence, duress, menace or fear of immediate and unlawful bodily injury on the victim or another person, as described in subdivision (c) of Section 286.

(I) Sodomy while voluntarily acting in concert, as described in subdivision (d) of Section 286.

(J) Lewd or lascivious acts on a child under the age of 14 years, as described in subdivision (b) of Section 288.

(K) Oral copulation by means of force, violence, duress, menace, or fear of immediate and unlawful bodily injury on the victim or another person, as described in subdivision (c) of Section 287 or of former Section 288a.

(L) Continuous sexual abuse of a child, as described in Section 288.5.

(M) Sexual penetration, as described in subdivision (a) of Section 289.

(N) Exploding a destructive device or explosive with intent to injure, as described in Section 18740, with intent to murder, as described in Section 18745, or resulting in great bodily injury or mayhem, as described in Section 18750.

(O) Any felony in which the defendant personally inflicted great bodily injury, as provided in Section 12022.53 or 12022.7.

(b) A prior conviction of an offense listed in subdivision (a) shall include a conviction in another jurisdiction for an offense which includes all of the elements of the particular felony as defined under California law.

(c) This section shall apply whenever the present felony is committed on or after the effective date of this section, regardless of the date of commission of the prior offense or offenses resulting in credit-earning ineligibility.

(d) This section shall be in addition to, and shall not preclude the imposition of, any applicable sentence enhancement terms, or probation ineligibility and habitual offender provisions authorized under any other section.

(Amended by Stats. 2018, Ch. 423, Sec. 103. (SB 1494) Effective January 1, 2019.)

2933.6.

The Department of Corrections and Rehabilitation shall, no later than July 1, 2017, establish regulations to allow specified inmates placed in segregation housing to earn credits pursuant to Section 2933 or 2933.05, or credits as otherwise specified in regulation, during the time he or she is in segregation housing. The regulations may establish separate classifications of serious disciplinary infractions to determine the rate of restoration of credits, the time period required before forfeited credits or a portion thereof may be restored, and the percentage of forfeited credits that may be restored for those time periods, not to exceed those percentages authorized for general

population inmates. The regulations shall provide for credit earning for inmates who successfully complete specific program performance objectives.
(Repealed and added by Stats. 2016, Ch. 191, Sec. 2. (SB 759) Effective January 1, 2017.)
2934.
Under rules prescribed by the Secretary of the Department of Corrections and Rehabilitation, a prisoner subject to the provisions of Section 2931 may waive the right to receive time credits as provided in Section 2931 and be subject to the provisions of Section 2933. In order to exercise a waiver under this section, a prisoner must apply in writing to the Department of Corrections. A prisoner exercising a waiver under this section shall retain only that portion of good behavior and participation credits, which have not been forfeited pursuant to Section 2932, attributable to the portion of the sentence served by the prisoner prior to the effective date of the waiver. A waiver under this section shall, if accepted by the department, become effective at a time to be determined by the Secretary of the Department of Corrections and Rehabilitation.
(Amended by Stats. 2009, 3rd Ex. Sess., Ch. 28, Sec. 45. (SB 18 3x) Effective January 25, 2010.)
2935.
Under the guidelines prescribed by the rules and regulations of the director, the Secretary of the Department of Corrections and Rehabilitation may grant up to 12 additional months of reduction of the sentence to a prisoner who has performed a heroic act in a life-threatening situation, or who has provided exceptional assistance in maintaining the safety and security of a prison.
(Amended by Stats. 2009, 3rd Ex. Sess., Ch. 28, Sec. 46. (SB 18 3x) Effective January 25, 2010.)
2936.
(a) The Department of Corrections and Rehabilitation shall submit a report to the relevant fiscal and policy committees of the Legislature and the Legislative Analyst's Office whenever the department proposes regulatory changes pursuant to Section 32 of Article I of the California Constitution that would affect inmate credit earning.
(b) A report required pursuant to subdivision (a) shall include both of the following:
(1) An explanation of the rationale for each of the proposed changes to credit earning.
(2) An estimate of the impact of the proposed changes to credit earning on the size of inmate and parolee populations.
(c) Reports required pursuant to subdivision (a) shall be submitted on or before the day that the regulatory changes are first submitted to the Office of Administrative Law.
(Added by Stats. 2019, Ch. 25, Sec. 41. (SB 94) Effective June 27, 2019.)

ARTICLE 3. Blacklist or Extortion of Discharged Prisoner [2947- 2947.]
(Article 3 repealed and added by Stats. 1977, Ch. 165.)
2947.
Any person who knowingly and willfully communicates to another, either orally or in writing, any statement concerning any person then or theretofore convicted of a felony, and then finally discharged, and which communication is made with the purpose and intent to deprive such person so convicted of employment, or to prevent him from procuring the same, or with the purpose and intent to extort from him any money or article of value; and any person who threatens to make any such communication with the purpose and intent to extort money or any article of value from such person so convicted of a felony is guilty of a misdemeanor.
(Repealed and added by Stats. 1977, Ch. 165.)

ARTICLE 4. Disposition of Mentally Disordered Prisoners Upon Discharge [2960 - 2981]
(Article 4 added by Stats. 1969, Ch. 872.)
2960.
The Legislature finds that there are prisoners who have a treatable, severe mental disorder that was one of the causes of, or was an aggravating factor in the commission of the crime for which they were incarcerated. Secondly, the Legislature finds that if the severe mental disorders of those prisoners are not in remission or cannot be kept in remission at the time of their parole or upon termination of parole, there is a danger to society, and the state has a compelling interest in protecting the public. Thirdly, the Legislature finds that in order to protect the public from those persons it is necessary to provide mental health treatment until the severe mental disorder which was one of the causes of or was an aggravating factor in the person's prior criminal behavior is in remission and can be kept in remission.
The Legislature further finds and declares the Department of Corrections should evaluate each prisoner for severe mental disorders during the first year of the prisoner's sentence, and that severely mentally disordered prisoners should be provided with an appropriate level of mental health treatment while in prison and when returned to the community.
(Amended by Stats. 1986, Ch. 858, Sec. 1.)
2962.
As a condition of parole, a prisoner who meets the following criteria shall be provided necessary treatment by the State Department of State Hospitals as follows:
(a) (1) The prisoner has a severe mental disorder that is not in remission or that cannot be kept in remission without treatment.
(2) The term "severe mental disorder" means an illness or disease or condition that substantially impairs the person's thought, perception of reality, emotional process, or judgment; or which grossly impairs behavior; or that demonstrates evidence of an acute brain syndrome for which prompt remission, in the absence of treatment, is unlikely. The term "severe mental disorder," as used in this section, does not include a personality or adjustment disorder, epilepsy, mental retardation or other developmental disabilities, or addiction to or abuse of intoxicating substances.
(3) The term "remission" means a finding that the overt signs and symptoms of the severe mental disorder are controlled either by psychotropic medication or psychosocial support. A person "cannot be kept in remission without treatment" if during the year prior to the question being before the Board of Parole Hearings or a trial court, he or she has been in remission and he or she has been physically violent, except in self-defense, or he or she has made a serious threat of substantial physical harm upon the person of another so as to cause the target of the threat to reasonably fear for his or her safety or the safety of his or her immediate family, or he or she has intentionally caused property damage, or he or she has not voluntarily followed the treatment plan. In determining if a person has voluntarily followed the treatment plan, the standard shall be whether the person has acted as a reasonable person would in following the treatment plan.
(b) The severe mental disorder was one of the causes of, or was an aggravating factor in, the commission of a crime for which the prisoner was sentenced to prison.
(c) The prisoner has been in treatment for the severe mental disorder for 90 days or more within the year prior to the prisoner's parole or release.
(d) (1) Prior to release on parole, the person in charge of treating the prisoner and a practicing psychiatrist or psychologist from the State Department of State Hospitals have evaluated the prisoner at a facility of the Department of Corrections and Rehabilitation, and a chief psychiatrist of the Department of Corrections and Rehabilitation has certified to the Board of Parole Hearings that the prisoner has a severe mental disorder, that the disorder is not in remission, or cannot be kept in remission without treatment, that the severe mental disorder was one of the causes or was an aggravating factor in the prisoner's criminal behavior, that the prisoner has been in treatment for the severe mental disorder for 90 days or more within the year prior to his or her parole release day, and that by reason of his or her severe mental disorder the prisoner represents a substantial danger of physical harm to others. For prisoners being treated by the State

Department of State Hospitals pursuant to Section 2684, the certification shall be by a chief psychiatrist of the Department of Corrections and Rehabilitation, and the evaluation shall be done at a state hospital by the person at the state hospital in charge of treating the prisoner and a practicing psychiatrist or psychologist from the Department of Corrections and Rehabilitation.
(2) If the professionals doing the evaluation pursuant to paragraph (1) do not concur that (A) the prisoner has a severe mental disorder, (B) that the disorder is not in remission or cannot be kept in remission without treatment, or (C) that the severe mental disorder was a cause of, or aggravated, the prisoner's criminal behavior, and a chief psychiatrist has certified the prisoner to the Board of Parole Hearings pursuant to this paragraph, then the Board of Parole Hearings shall order a further examination by two independent professionals, as provided for in Section 2978.
(3) If at least one of the independent professionals who evaluate the prisoner pursuant to paragraph (2) concurs with the chief psychiatrist's certification of the issues described in paragraph (2), this subdivision shall be applicable to the prisoner. The professionals appointed pursuant to Section 2978 shall inform the prisoner that the purpose of their examination is not treatment but to determine if the prisoner meets certain criteria to be involuntarily treated as a mentally disordered offender. It is not required that the prisoner appreciate or understand that information.
(e) The crime referred to in subdivision (b) meets both of the following criteria:
(1) The defendant received a determinate sentence pursuant to Section 1170 for the crime.
(2) The crime is one of the following:
(A) Voluntary manslaughter.
(B) Mayhem.
(C) Kidnapping in violation of Section 207.
(D) Any robbery wherein it was charged and proved that the defendant personally used a deadly or dangerous weapon, as provided in subdivision (b) of Section 12022, in the commission of that robbery.
(E) Carjacking, as defined in subdivision (a) of Section 215, if it is charged and proved that the defendant personally used a deadly or dangerous weapon, as provided in subdivision (b) of Section 12022, in the commission of the carjacking.
(F) Rape, as defined in paragraph (2) or (6) of subdivision (a) of Section 261 or paragraph (1) or (4) of subdivision (a) of Section 262.
(G) Sodomy by force, violence, duress, menace, or fear of immediate and unlawful bodily injury on the victim or another person.
(H) Oral copulation by force, violence, duress, menace, or fear of immediate and unlawful bodily injury on the victim or another person.
(I) Lewd acts on a child under 14 years of age in violation of Section 288.
(J) Continuous sexual abuse in violation of Section 288.5.
(K) The offense described in subdivision (a) of Section 289 where the act was accomplished against the victim's will by force, violence, duress, menace, or fear of immediate and unlawful bodily injury on the victim or another person.
(L) Arson in violation of subdivision (a) of Section 451, or arson in violation of any other provision of Section 451 or in violation of Section 455 where the act posed a substantial danger of physical harm to others.
(M) Any felony in which the defendant used a firearm which use was charged and proved as provided in Section 12022.5, 12022.53, or 12022.55.
(N) A violation of Section 18745.
(O) Attempted murder.
(P) A crime not enumerated in subparagraphs (A) to (O), inclusive, in which the prisoner used force or violence, or caused serious bodily injury as defined in paragraph (4) of subdivision (f) of Section 243.
(Q) A crime in which the perpetrator expressly or impliedly threatened another with the use of force or violence likely to produce substantial physical harm in such a manner that a reasonable person would believe and expect that the force or violence would be used. For purposes of this subparagraph, substantial physical harm shall not require proof that the threatened act was likely to cause great or serious bodily injury.
(f) For purposes of meeting the criteria set forth in this section, the existence or nature of the crime, as defined in paragraph (2) of subdivision (e), for which the prisoner has been convicted may be shown with documentary evidence. The details underlying the commission of the offense that led to the conviction, including the use of force or violence, causing serious bodily injury, or the threat to use force or violence likely to produce substantial physical harm, may be shown by documentary evidence, including, but not limited to, preliminary hearing transcripts, trial transcripts, probation and sentencing reports, and evaluations by the State Department of State Hospitals.
(g) As used in this chapter, "substantial danger of physical harm" does not require proof of a recent overt act.
(Amended by Stats. 2016, Ch. 430, Sec. 1. (SB 1295) Effective January 1, 2017.)
2963.
(a) Upon a showing of good cause, the Board of Parole Hearings may order that a person remain in custody for no more than 45 days beyond the person's scheduled release date for full evaluation pursuant to paragraph (1) of subdivision (d) of Section 2962 and any additional evaluations pursuant to paragraph (2) of subdivision (d) of Section 2962.
(b) For purposes of this section, good cause means circumstances where there is a recalculation of credits or a restoration of denied or lost credits, a resentencing by a court, the receipt of the prisoner into custody, or equivalent exigent circumstances which result in there being less than 45 days prior to the person's scheduled release date for the evaluations described in subdivision (d) of Section 2962.
(Added by Stats. 2010, Ch. 710, Sec. 2. (SB 1201) Effective January 1, 2011.)
2964.
(a) The treatment required by Section 2962 shall be inpatient unless the State Department of State Hospitals certifies to the Board of Parole Hearings that there is reasonable cause to believe the parolee can be safely and effectively treated on an outpatient basis, in which case the Board of Parole Hearings shall permit the State Department of State Hospitals to place the parolee in an outpatient treatment program specified by the State Department of State Hospitals. Any prisoner who is to be required to accept treatment pursuant to Section 2962 shall be informed in writing of his or her right to request a hearing pursuant to Section 2966. Prior to placing a parolee in a local outpatient program, the State Department of State Hospitals shall consult with the local outpatient program as to the appropriate treatment plan. Notwithstanding any other law, a parolee ordered to have outpatient treatment pursuant to this section may be placed in an outpatient treatment program used to provide outpatient treatment under Title 15 (commencing with Section 1600) of Part 2, but the procedural provisions of Title 15 shall not apply. The community program director or a designee of an outpatient program used to provide treatment under Title 15 in which a parolee is placed, may place the parolee, or cause the parolee to be placed, in a secure mental health facility if the parolee can no longer be safely or effectively treated in the outpatient program, and until the parolee can be safely and effectively treated in the program. Upon the request of the community program director or a designee, a peace officer shall take the parolee into custody and transport the parolee, or cause the parolee to be taken into custody and transported, to a facility designated by the community program director, or a designee, for confinement under this section. Within 15 days after placement in a secure facility the State Department of State Hospitals shall conduct a hearing on whether the parolee can be safely and effectively treated in the program unless the patient or the patient's attorney agrees to a continuance, or unless good cause exists that prevents the State Department of State Hospitals from conducting the hearing within that period of time. If good cause exists, the hearing shall be held within 21 days after placement in

a secure facility. For purposes of this section, "good cause" means the inability to secure counsel, an interpreter, or witnesses for the hearing within the 15-day time period. Before deciding to seek revocation of the parole of a parolee receiving mental health treatment pursuant to Section 2962, and return him or her to prison, the parole officer shall consult with the director of the parolee's outpatient program. Nothing in this section shall prevent hospitalization pursuant to Section 5150, 5250, or 5353 of the Welfare and Institutions Code.

(b) If the State Department of State Hospitals has not placed a parolee on outpatient treatment within 60 days after receiving custody of the parolee or after parole is continued pursuant to Section 3001, the parolee may request a hearing before the Board of Parole Hearings, and the board shall conduct a hearing to determine whether the prisoner shall be treated as an inpatient or an outpatient. At the hearing, the burden shall be on the State Department of State Hospitals to establish that the prisoner requires inpatient treatment as described in this subdivision. If the prisoner or any person appearing on his or her behalf at the hearing requests it, the board shall appoint two independent professionals as provided for in Section 2978.

(Amended by Stats. 2012, Ch. 24, Sec. 37. (AB 1470) Effective June 27, 2012.)

2966.

(a) A prisoner may request a hearing before the Board of Prison Terms, and the board shall conduct a hearing if so requested, for the purpose of proving that the prisoner meets the criteria in Section 2962. At the hearing, the burden of proof shall be on the person or agency who certified the prisoner under subdivision (d) of Section 2962. If the prisoner or any person appearing on his or her behalf at the hearing requests it, the board shall appoint two independent professionals as provided for in Section 2978. The prisoner shall be informed at the hearing of his or her right to request a trial pursuant to subdivision (b). The Board of Prison Terms shall provide a prisoner who requests a trial, a petition form and instructions for filing the petition.

(b) A prisoner who disagrees with the determination of the Board of Prison Terms that he or she meets the criteria of Section 2962, may file in the superior court of the county in which he or she is incarcerated or is being treated a petition for a hearing on whether he or she, as of the date of the Board of Prison Terms hearing, met the criteria of Section 2962. The court shall conduct a hearing on the petition within 60 calendar days after the petition is filed, unless either time is waived by the petitioner or his or her counsel, or good cause is shown. Evidence offered for the purpose of proving the prisoner's behavior or mental status subsequent to the Board of Prison Terms hearing shall not be considered. The order of the Board of Prison Terms shall be in effect until the completion of the court proceedings. The court shall advise the petitioner of his or her right to be represented by an attorney and of the right to a jury trial. The attorney for the petitioner shall be given a copy of the petition, and any supporting documents. The hearing shall be a civil hearing; however, in order to reduce costs, the rules of criminal discovery, as well as civil discovery, shall be applicable. The standard of proof shall be beyond a reasonable doubt, and if the trial is by jury, the jury shall be unanimous in its verdict. The trial shall be by jury unless waived by both the person and the district attorney. The court may, upon stipulation of both parties, receive in evidence the affidavit or declaration of any psychiatrist, psychologist, or other professional person who was involved in the certification and hearing process, or any professional person involved in the evaluation or treatment of the petitioner during the certification process. The court may allow the affidavit or declaration to be read and the contents thereof considered in the rendering of a decision or verdict in any proceeding held pursuant to subdivision (b) or (c), or subdivision (a) of Section 2972. If the court or jury reverses the determination of the Board of Prison Terms, the court shall stay the execution of the decision for five working days to allow for an orderly release of the prisoner.

(c) If the Board of Prison Terms continues a parolee's mental health treatment under Section 2962 when it continues the parolee's parole under Section 3001, the procedures of this section shall only be applicable for the purpose of determining if the parolee has a severe mental disorder, whether the parolee's severe mental disorder is not in remission or cannot be kept in remission without treatment, and whether by reason of his or her severe mental disorder, the parolee represents a substantial danger of physical harm to others.

(Amended by Stats. 1994, Ch. 706, Sec. 1. Effective January 1, 1995.)

2968.

If the prisoner's severe mental disorder is put into remission during the parole period, and can be kept in remission, the Director of State Hospitals shall notify the Board of Parole Hearings and the State Department of State Hospitals shall discontinue treating the parolee.

(Amended by Stats. 2012, Ch. 24, Sec. 38. (AB 1470) Effective June 27, 2012.)

2970.

(a) Not later than 180 days prior to the termination of parole, or release from prison if the prisoner refused to agree to treatment as a condition of parole as required by Section 2962, unless good cause is shown for the reduction of that 180-day period, if the parolee's or prisoner's severe mental disorder is not in remission or cannot be kept in remission without treatment, the medical director of the state hospital that is treating the parolee, or the community program director in charge of the parolee's outpatient program, or the Secretary of the Department of Corrections and Rehabilitation, shall submit to the district attorney of the county in which the parolee is receiving outpatient treatment, or for those in prison or in a state mental hospital, the district attorney of the county of commitment to prison, his or her written evaluation on remission. If requested by the district attorney, the written evaluation shall be accompanied by supporting affidavits.

(b) The district attorney may then file a petition with the superior court for continued involuntary treatment for one year. The petition shall be accompanied by affidavits specifying that treatment, while the prisoner was released from prison on parole, has been continuously provided by the State Department of State Hospitals either in a state hospital or in an outpatient program. The petition shall also specify that the prisoner has a severe mental disorder, that the severe mental disorder is not in remission or cannot be kept in remission if the person's treatment is not continued, and that, by reason of his or her severe mental disorder, the prisoner represents a substantial danger of physical harm to others.

(Amended by Stats. 2013, Ch. 705, Sec. 1. (AB 610) Effective January 1, 2014.)

2972.

(a) The court shall conduct a hearing on the petition under Section 2970 for continued treatment. The court shall advise the person of his or her right to be represented by an attorney and of the right to a jury trial. The attorney for the person shall be given a copy of the petition, and any supporting documents. The hearing shall be a civil hearing, however, in order to reduce costs the rules of criminal discovery, as well as civil discovery, shall be applicable.

The standard of proof under this section shall be proof beyond a reasonable doubt, and if the trial is by jury, the jury shall be unanimous in its verdict. The trial shall be by jury unless waived by both the person and the district attorney. The trial shall commence no later than 30 calendar days prior to the time the person would otherwise have been released, unless the time is waived by the person or unless good cause is shown.

(b) The people shall be represented by the district attorney. If the person is indigent, the county public defender shall be appointed.

(c) If the court or jury finds that the patient has a severe mental disorder, that the patient's severe mental disorder is not in remission or cannot be kept in remission without treatment, and that by reason of his or her severe mental disorder, the patient represents a substantial danger of physical harm to others, the court shall order the patient recommitted to the facility in which the patient was confined at the time the petition was filed, or recommitted to the outpatient program in which he or she was

being treated at the time the petition was filed, or committed to the State Department of State Hospitals if the person was in prison. The commitment shall be for a period of one year from the date of termination of parole or a previous commitment or the scheduled date of release from prison as specified in Section 2970. Time spent on outpatient status, except when placed in a locked facility at the direction of the outpatient supervisor, shall not count as actual custody and shall not be credited toward the person's maximum term of commitment or toward the person's term of extended commitment.

(d) A person shall be released on outpatient status if the committing court finds that there is reasonable cause to believe that the committed person can be safely and effectively treated on an outpatient basis. Except as provided in this subdivision, the provisions of Title 15 (commencing with Section 1600) of Part 2, shall apply to persons placed on outpatient status pursuant to this paragraph. The standard for revocation under Section 1609 shall be that the person cannot be safely and effectively treated on an outpatient basis.

(e) Prior to the termination of a commitment under this section, a petition for recommitment may be filed to determine whether the patient's severe mental disorder is not in remission or cannot be kept in remission without treatment, and whether by reason of his or her severe mental disorder, the patient represents a substantial danger of physical harm to others. The recommitment proceeding shall be conducted in accordance with the provisions of this section.

(f) Any commitment under this article places an affirmative obligation on the treatment facility to provide treatment for the underlying causes of the person's mental disorder.

(g) Except as provided in this subdivision, the person committed shall be considered to be an involuntary mental health patient and he or she shall be entitled to those rights set forth in Article 7 (commencing with Section 5325) of Chapter 2 of Part 1 of Division 5 of the Welfare and Institutions Code. Commencing January 1, 1986, the State Department of Mental Health, or its successor, the State Department of State Hospitals, may adopt regulations to modify those rights as is necessary in order to provide for the reasonable security of the inpatient facility in which the patient is being held. This subdivision and the regulations adopted pursuant thereto shall become operative on January 1, 1987, except that regulations may be adopted prior to that date.

(Amended by Stats. 2012, Ch. 24, Sec. 40. (AB 1470) Effective June 27, 2012.)

2972.1.

(a) Outpatient status for persons committed pursuant to Section 2972 shall be for a period not to exceed one year. Pursuant to Section 1606, at the end of a period of outpatient status approved by the court, the court shall, after actual notice to the prosecutor, the defense attorney, the community program director or a designee, the medical director of the facility that is treating the person, and the person on outpatient status, and after a hearing in court, either discharge the person from commitment under appropriate provisions of law, order the person confined to a treatment facility, or renew its approval of outpatient status.

(b) Prior to the hearing described in subdivision (a), the community program director or a designee shall furnish a report and recommendation to the court, the prosecution, the defense attorney, the medical director of the facility that is treating the person, and the person on outpatient status. If the recommendation is that the person continue on outpatient status or be confined to a treatment facility, the report shall also contain a statement that conforms with requirements of subdivision (c).

(c) (1) Upon receipt of a report prepared pursuant to Section 1606 that recommends confinement or continued outpatient treatment, the court shall direct prior defense counsel, or, if necessary, appoint new defense counsel, to meet and confer with the person who is on outpatient status and explain the recommendation contained therein. Following this meeting, both defense counsel and the person on outpatient status shall sign and return to the court a form which shall read as follows:

"Check One:

"_____ I do not believe that I need further treatment and I demand a jury trial to decide this question.

"_____ I accept the recommendation that I continue treatment."

(2) The signed form shall be returned to the court at least 10 days prior to the hearing described in subdivision (a). If the person on outpatient status refuses or is unable to sign the form, his or her counsel shall indicate, in writing, that the form and the report prepared pursuant to Section 1606 were explained to the person and the person refused or was unable to sign the form.

(d) If the person on outpatient status either requests a jury trial or fails to waive his or her right to a jury trial, a jury trial meeting all of the requirements of Section 2972 shall be set within 60 days of the initial hearing.

(e) The trier of fact, or the court if trial is waived, shall determine whether or not the requirements of subdivisions (c) and (d) of Section 2972 have been met. The court shall then make an appropriate disposition under subdivision (a) of this section.

(f) The court shall notify the community program director or a designee, the person on outpatient status, and the medical director or person in charge of the facility providing treatment of the person whether or not the person was found suitable for release.

(Added by Stats. 2000, Ch. 324, Sec. 4. Effective January 1, 2001.)

2974.

Before releasing any inmate or terminating supervision of any parolee who is a danger to self or others, or gravely disabled as a result of mental disorder, and who does not come within the provisions of Section 2962, the Director of Corrections may, upon probable cause, place, or cause to be placed, the person in a state hospital pursuant to the Lanterman-Petris-Short Act, Part 1 (commencing with Section 5000) of Division 5 of the Welfare and Institutions Code.

(Added by Stats. 1986, Ch. 858, Sec. 8.)

2976.

(a) The cost of inpatient or outpatient treatment under Section 2962 or 2972 shall be a state expense while the person is under the jurisdiction of the Department of Corrections and Rehabilitation or the State Department of State Hospitals.

(b) Any person placed outside of a facility of the Department of Corrections and Rehabilitation for the purposes of inpatient treatment under this article shall not be deemed to be released from imprisonment or from the custody of the Department of Corrections and Rehabilitation prior to the expiration of the maximum term of imprisonment of the person.

(Amended by Stats. 2012, Ch. 24, Sec. 41. (AB 1470) Effective June 27, 2012.)

2977.

A person committed to the care of the State Department of State Hospitals because he or she is a mentally disordered offender, including a person who is found not guilty by reason of insanity, is eligible for compassionate release pursuant to Section 4146 of the Welfare and Institutions Code. In any case in which the criteria for compassionate release apply, the State Department of State Hospitals shall follow the procedures and standards in Section 4146 of the Welfare and Institutions Code to determine if the department should recommend to the court that the person's commitment be suspended for compassionate release. This section applies to persons committed for treatment during parole and persons committed pursuant to Section 2970. If the person for whom compassionate release is recommended is on parole, notice shall be given to the Board of Parole Hearings.

(Added by Stats. 2016, Ch. 715, Sec. 3. (SB 955) Effective January 1, 2017.)

2978.

(a) Any independent professionals appointed by the Board of Parole Hearings for purposes of this article shall not be state government employees; shall have at least five years of experience in the diagnosis and treatment of mental disorders; and shall include psychiatrists, and licensed psychologists who have a doctoral degree in psychology.

(b) On July 1 of each year the Department of Corrections and Rehabilitation and the State Department of State Hospitals shall submit to the Board of Parole Hearings a list of 20 or more independent professionals on which both departments concur. The professionals shall not be state government employees and shall have at least five years of experience in the diagnosis and treatment of mental disorders and shall include psychiatrists and licensed psychologists who have a doctoral degree in psychology. For purposes of this article, when the Board of Parole Hearings receives the list, it shall only appoint independent professionals from the list. The list shall not be binding on the Board of Parole Hearings until it has received the list, and shall not be binding after June 30 following receipt of the list.

(Amended by Stats. 2012, Ch. 24, Sec. 42. (AB 1470) Effective June 27, 2012.)
2980.
This article applies to persons who committed their crimes on and after January 1, 1986.

(Amended by Stats. 1989, Ch. 228, Sec. 5. Effective July 27, 1989.)
2981.
For the purpose of proving the fact that a prisoner has received 90 days or more of treatment within the year prior to the prisoner's parole or release, the records or copies of records of any state penitentiary, county jail, federal penitentiary, or state hospital in which that person has been confined, when the records or copies thereof have been certified by the official custodian of those records, may be admitted as evidence.

(Added by Stats. 1987, Ch. 687, Sec. 11.)

ARTICLE 5. Supportive Housing Program for Mentally Ill Parolees [2985 - 2985.5]

(Article 5 added by Stats. 2012, Ch. 41, Sec. 70.)
2985.
It is the intent of the Legislature in enacting this article to provide evidence-based, comprehensive mental health and supportive services, including housing subsidies, to parolees who suffer from mental illness and are at risk of homelessness, in order to successfully reintegrate the parolees into the community, increase public safety, and reduce state costs of recidivism. It is further the intent of the Legislature to supplement existing parole outpatient clinic services by providing services to individuals who suffer from a severe mental illness, as defined in Section 5600.3 of the Welfare and Institutions Code, and who require services that cannot be provided by parole outpatient clinics, including services provided pursuant to Section 5806 of the Welfare and Institutions Code.

(Added by Stats. 2012, Ch. 41, Sec. 70. (SB 1021) Effective June 27, 2012.)
2985.1.
For purposes of this article, the following definitions shall apply:
(a) "Department" means the Department of Corrections and Rehabilitation.
(b) "Supportive housing" has the same meaning set forth in subdivision (b) of Section 50675.14 of the Health and Safety Code, and that, in addition, is decent, safe, and affordable.
(c) "Transitional housing" has the same meaning set forth in subdivision (h) of Section 50675.2 of the Health and Safety Code, and that, in addition, is decent, safe, and affordable.

(Added by Stats. 2012, Ch. 41, Sec. 70. (SB 1021) Effective June 27, 2012.)
2985.2.
(a) Pursuant to Section 3073, the Department of Corrections and Rehabilitation shall provide a supportive housing program that provides wraparound services to mentally ill parolees who are at risk of homelessness using funding appropriated by the Legislature for that purpose.
(b) Providers participating in this program shall comply with all of the following:
(1) Provide services and treatment based on best practices.
(2) Demonstrate that the program reduces recidivism and homelessness among program participants.
(3) Have prior experience working with county or regional mental health programs.
(c) (1) An inmate or parolee is eligible for participation in this program if all of the following are applicable:
(A) He or she has a serious mental disorder as defined in Section 5600.3 of the Welfare and Institutions Code and as identified by the department, and he or she has a history of mental health treatment in the prison's mental health services delivery system or in a parole outpatient clinic.
(B) The inmate or parolee voluntarily chooses to participate.
(C) Either of the following applies:
(i) He or she has been assigned a date of release within 60 to 180 days and is likely to become homeless upon release.
(ii) He or she is currently a homeless parolee.
(2) First priority for the program shall be given to the lowest functioning offenders in prison, as identified by the department, who are likely to become homeless upon release.
(3) For purposes of this subdivision, a person is "likely to become homeless upon release" if he or she has a history of "homelessness" as that term is used in Section 11302(a) of Title 42 of the United States Code and if he or she satisfies both of the following criteria:
(A) He or she has not identified a fixed, regular, and adequate nighttime residence for release.
(B) His or her only identified nighttime residence for release includes a supervised publicly or privately operated shelter designed to provide temporary living accommodations, or a public or private place not designed for, or is not ordinarily used as, a regular sleeping accommodation for human beings.

(Added by Stats. 2012, Ch. 41, Sec. 70. (SB 1021) Effective June 27, 2012.)
2985.3.
(a) Each provider shall offer services, in accordance with Section 5806 of the Welfare and Institutions Code, to obtain and maintain health and housing stability while participants are on parole, to enable the parolee to comply with the terms of parole, and to augment mental health treatment provided to other parolees. The services shall be offered to participants in their home, or be made as easily accessible to participants as possible and shall include, but are not limited to, all of the following:
(1) Case management services.
(2) Parole discharge planning.
(3) Housing location services, and, if needed, move-in cost assistance.
(4) Rental subsidies.
(5) Linkage to other services, such as vocational, educational, and employment services, as needed.
(6) Benefit entitlement application and appeal assistance.
(7) Transportation assistance to obtain services and health care needed.
(8) Assistance obtaining appropriate identification.
(b) For participants identified prior to release from state prison, upon the provider's receipt of referral and, in collaboration with the parole agent and, if appropriate, staff, the intake coordinator or case manager of the provider shall, when possible:
(1) Receive all prerelease assessments and discharge plans.
(2) Draft a plan for the participant's transition into housing that serves the participant's needs and is affordable, such as permanent supportive housing, or a transitional housing program that includes support services and demonstrates a clear transition pathway to permanent housing.
(3) Engage the participant to actively participate in services upon release.

(4) Assist in obtaining identification for the participant, if necessary.
(5) Assist in applying for any benefits for which the participant is eligible.
(c) (1) To facilitate the transition of participants identified prior to release into the community and participants identified during parole into supportive housing, each provider shall, on an ongoing basis, not less than quarterly, assess each participant's needs and include in each participant's assessment a plan to foster independence and a residence in permanent housing once parole is complete.
(2) Upon referral to the provider, the provider shall work to transition participants from the department's rental assistance to other mainstream rental assistance benefits if those benefits are necessary to enable the participant to remain in stable housing, and shall prioritize transitioning participants to these benefits in a manner that allows participants to remain housed, when possible, without moving. Mainstream rental assistance benefits may include, but are not limited to, federal Housing Choice Voucher assistance, Department of Housing and Urban Development-Veterans Affairs Supportive Housing vouchers, or other rental assistance programs.
(3) The participant's parole discharge plan and the assessments shall consider the need for and prioritize linkage to county mental health services and housing opportunities that are supported by the Mental Health Services Act, the Mental Health Services Act Housing Program, or other funding sources that finance permanent supportive housing for persons with mental illness, so that the participant may continue to achieve all recovery goals of the program and remain permanently housed once the term of parole ends.

(Added by Stats. 2012, Ch. 41, Sec. 70. (SB 1021) Effective June 27, 2012.)
2985.4.
(a) Providers shall identify and locate supportive housing and transitional housing opportunities for participants prior to release from state prison or as quickly upon release from state prison as possible, or as quickly as possible when participants are identified during parole.
(b) Housing identified pursuant to subdivision (a) shall satisfy both of the following:
(1) The housing is located in an apartment building, single-room occupancy buildings, townhouses, or single-family homes, including rent-subsidized apartments leased in the open market or set aside within privately owned buildings.
(2) The housing is not subject to community care licensing requirements or is exempt from licensing under Section 1504.5 of the Health and Safety Code.

(Added by Stats. 2012, Ch. 41, Sec. 70. (SB 1021) Effective June 27, 2012.)
2985.5.
(a) Each provider shall report to the department regarding the intended outcomes of the program, including all of the following:
(1) The number of participants served.
(2) The types of services that were provided to program participants.
(3) The outcomes for participants, including the number who graduated to independent living, the number who remain in or moved to permanent housing, the number who ceased to participate in the program, and the number who returned to state prison.
(4) The number of participants who successfully completed parole and transitioned to county mental health programs.
(b) The department shall prepare an analysis of the costs of the supportive housing program in comparison to the cost savings to the state as a result of reduced recidivism rates by participants using the information provided pursuant to subdivision (a). This analysis shall exclude from consideration any federal funds provided for services while the participant is on parole in order to ensure that the analysis accurately reflects only the costs to the state for the services provided to participants.
(c) The department shall annually submit, on or before February 1, the information collected pursuant to subdivision (a) and the analysis prepared pursuant to subdivision (b) to the chairs of the Joint Legislative Budget Committee, the Senate Committee on Budget and Fiscal Review, the Assembly Committee on Budget, the Senate and Assembly Committees on Public Safety, the Senate Committee on Transportation and Housing, and the Assembly Committee on Housing and Community Development.

(Added by Stats. 2012, Ch. 41, Sec. 70. (SB 1021) Effective June 27, 2012.)

CHAPTER 8. Length of Term of Imprisonment and Paroles [3000 - 3089]

(Heading of Chapter 8 renumbered from Chapter 7 by Stats. 1941, Ch. 893.)

ARTICLE 1. General Provisions [3000 - 3007.08]
(Article 1 repealed and added by Stats. 1976, Ch. 1139.)
3000.
(a) (1) The Legislature finds and declares that the period immediately following incarceration is critical to successful reintegration of the offender into society and to positive citizenship. It is in the interest of public safety for the state to provide for the effective supervision of and surveillance of parolees, including the judicious use of revocation actions, and to provide educational, vocational, family, and personal counseling necessary to assist parolees in the transition between imprisonment and discharge. A sentence resulting in imprisonment in the state prison pursuant to Section 1168 or 1170 shall include a period of parole supervision or postrelease community supervision, unless waived, or as otherwise provided in this article.
(2) The Legislature finds and declares that it is not the intent of this section to diminish resources allocated to the Department of Corrections and Rehabilitation for parole functions for which the department is responsible. It is also not the intent of this section to diminish the resources allocated to the Board of Parole Hearings to execute its duties with respect to parole functions for which the board is responsible.
(3) The Legislature finds and declares that diligent effort must be made to ensure that parolees are held accountable for their criminal behavior, including, but not limited to, the satisfaction of restitution fines and orders.
(4) For any person subject to a sexually violent predator proceeding pursuant to Article 4 (commencing with Section 6600) of Chapter 2 of Part 2 of Division 6 of the Welfare and Institutions Code, an order issued by a judge pursuant to Section 6601.5 of the Welfare and Institutions Code, finding that the petition, on its face, supports a finding of probable cause to believe that the individual named in the petition is likely to engage in sexually violent predatory criminal behavior upon his or her release, shall toll the period of parole of that person, from the date that person is released by the Department of Corrections and Rehabilitation as follows:
(A) If the person is committed to the State Department of State Hospitals as a sexually violent predator and subsequently a court orders that the person be unconditionally discharged, the parole period shall be tolled until the date the judge enters the order unconditionally discharging that person.
(B) If the person is not committed to the State Department of State Hospitals as a sexually violent predator, the tolling of the parole period shall be abrogated and the parole period shall be deemed to have commenced on the date of release from the Department of Corrections and Rehabilitation.
(5) Paragraph (4) applies to persons released by the Department of Corrections and Rehabilitation on or after January 1, 2012. Persons released by the Department of Corrections and Rehabilitation prior to January 1, 2012, shall continue to be subject to the law governing the tolling of parole in effect on December 31, 2011.

(b) Notwithstanding any provision to the contrary in Article 3 (commencing with Section 3040) of this chapter, the following shall apply to any inmate subject to Section 3000.08:

(1) In the case of any inmate sentenced under Section 1168 for a crime committed prior to July 1, 2013, the period of parole shall not exceed five years in the case of an inmate imprisoned for any offense other than first or second degree murder for which the inmate has received a life sentence, and shall not exceed three years in the case of any other inmate, unless in either case the Board of Parole Hearings for good cause waives parole and discharges the inmate from custody of the department. This subdivision shall also be applicable to inmates who committed crimes prior to July 1, 1977, to the extent specified in Section 1170.2. In the case of any inmate sentenced under Section 1168 for a crime committed on or after July 1, 2013, the period of parole shall not exceed five years in the case of an inmate imprisoned for any offense other than first or second degree murder for which the inmate has received a life sentence, and shall not exceed three years in the case of any other inmate, unless in either case the department for good cause waives parole and discharges the inmate from custody of the department.

(2) (A) For a crime committed prior to July 1, 2013, at the expiration of a term of imprisonment of one year and one day, or a term of imprisonment imposed pursuant to Section 1170 or at the expiration of a term reduced pursuant to Section 2931 or 2933, if applicable, the inmate shall be released on parole for a period not exceeding three years, except that any inmate sentenced for an offense specified in paragraph (3), (4), (5), (6), (11), or (18) of subdivision (c) of Section 667.5 shall be released on parole for a period not exceeding 10 years, unless a longer period of parole is specified in Section 3000.1.

(B) For a crime committed on or after July 1, 2013, at the expiration of a term of imprisonment of one year and one day, or a term of imprisonment imposed pursuant to Section 1170 or at the expiration of a term reduced pursuant to Section 2931 or 2933, if applicable, the inmate shall be released on parole for a period of three years, except that any inmate sentenced for an offense specified in paragraph (3), (4), (5), (6), (11), or (18) of subdivision (c) of Section 667.5 shall be released on parole for a period of 10 years, unless a longer period of parole is specified in Section 3000.1.

(3) Notwithstanding paragraphs (1) and (2), in the case of any offense for which the inmate has received a life sentence pursuant to subdivision (b) of Section 209, with the intent to commit a specified sex offense, or Section 667.51, 667.61, or 667.71, the period of parole shall be 10 years, unless a longer period of parole is specified in Section 3000.1.

(4) (A) Notwithstanding paragraphs (1) to (3), inclusive, in the case of a person convicted of and required to register as a sex offender for the commission of an offense specified in Section 261, 262, 264.1, 286, 287, paragraph (1) of subdivision (b) of Section 288, Section 288.5 or 289, or former Section 288a, in which one or more of the victims of the offense was a child under 14 years of age, the period of parole shall be 20 years and six months unless the board, for good cause, determines that the person will be retained on parole. The board shall make a written record of this determination and transmit a copy of it to the parolee.

(B) In the event of a retention on parole, the parolee shall be entitled to a review by the board each year thereafter.

(C) There shall be a board hearing consistent with the procedures set forth in Sections 3041.5 and 3041.7 within 12 months of the date of any revocation of parole to consider the release of the inmate on parole, and notwithstanding the provisions of paragraph (3) of subdivision (b) of Section 3041.5, there shall be annual parole consideration hearings thereafter, unless the person is released or otherwise ineligible for parole release. The panel or board shall release the person within one year of the date of the revocation unless it determines that the circumstances and gravity of the parole violation are such that consideration of the public safety requires a more lengthy period of incarceration or unless there is a new prison commitment following a conviction.

(D) The provisions of Section 3042 shall not apply to any hearing held pursuant to this subdivision.

(5) (A) The Board of Parole Hearings shall consider the request of any inmate whose commitment offense occurred prior to July 1, 2013, regarding the length of his or her parole and the conditions thereof.

(B) For an inmate whose commitment offense occurred on or after July 1, 2013, except for those inmates described in Section 3000.1, the department shall consider the request of the inmate regarding the length of his or her parole and the conditions thereof. For those inmates described in Section 3000.1, the Board of Parole Hearings shall consider the request of the inmate regarding the length of his or her parole and the conditions thereof.

(6) Upon successful completion of parole, or at the end of the maximum statutory period of parole specified for the inmate under paragraph (1), (2), (3), or (4), as the case may be, whichever is earlier, the inmate shall be discharged from custody. The date of the maximum statutory period of parole under this subdivision and paragraphs (1), (2), (3), and (4) shall be computed from the date of initial parole and shall be a period chronologically determined. Time during which parole is suspended because the prisoner has absconded or has been returned to custody as a parole violator shall not be credited toward any period of parole unless the prisoner is found not guilty of the parole violation. However, the period of parole is subject to the following:

(A) Except as provided in Section 3064, in no case may a prisoner subject to three years on parole be retained under parole supervision or in custody for a period longer than four years from the date of his or her initial parole.

(B) Except as provided in Section 3064, in no case may a prisoner subject to five years on parole be retained under parole supervision or in custody for a period longer than seven years from the date of his or her initial parole.

(C) Except as provided in Section 3064, in no case may a prisoner subject to 10 years on parole be retained under parole supervision or in custody for a period longer than 15 years from the date of his or her initial parole.

(7) The Department of Corrections and Rehabilitation shall meet with each inmate at least 30 days prior to his or her good time release date and shall provide, under guidelines specified by the parole authority or the department, whichever is applicable, the conditions of parole and the length of parole up to the maximum period of time provided by law. The inmate has the right to reconsideration of the length of parole and conditions thereof by the department or the parole authority, whichever is applicable. The Department of Corrections and Rehabilitation or the board may impose as a condition of parole that a prisoner make payments on the prisoner's outstanding restitution fines or orders imposed pursuant to subdivision (a) or (c) of Section 13967 of the Government Code, as operative prior to September 28, 1994, or subdivision (b) or (f) of Section 1202.4.

(8) For purposes of this chapter, and except as otherwise described in this section, the board shall be considered the parole authority.

(9) (A) On and after July 1, 2013, the sole authority to issue warrants for the return to actual custody of any state prisoner released on parole rests with the court pursuant to Section 1203.2, except for any escaped state prisoner or any state prisoner released prior to his or her scheduled release date who should be returned to custody, and Section 5054.1 shall apply.

(B) Notwithstanding subparagraph (A), any warrant issued by the Board of Parole Hearings prior to July 1, 2013, shall remain in full force and effect until the warrant is served or it is recalled by the board. All prisoners on parole arrested pursuant to a warrant issued by the board shall be subject to a review by the board prior to the department filing a petition with the court to revoke the parole of the petitioner.

(10) It is the intent of the Legislature that efforts be made with respect to persons who are subject to Section 290.011 who are on parole to engage them in treatment.
(Amended by Stats. 2018, Ch. 423, Sec. 104. (SB 1494) Effective January 1, 2019. Note: This section was amended on Nov. 7, 2006, by initiative Prop. 83.)

3000.03.
Notwithstanding any other provision of law, the Department of Corrections and Rehabilitation shall not return to prison, place a parole hold on pursuant to Section 3056, or report any parole violation to the Board of Parole Hearings or the court, as applicable, regarding any person to whom all of the following criteria apply:

(a) The person is not required to register as a sex offender pursuant to Chapter 5.5 (commencing with Section 290) of Title 9 of Part 1.

(b) The person was not committed to prison for a serious felony as defined in Sections 1192.7 and 1192.8, or a violent felony, as defined in Section 667.5, and does not have a prior conviction for a serious felony, as defined in Section 1192.7 and 1192.8, or a violent felony, as defined in Section 667.5.

(c) The person was not committed to prison for a sexually violent offense as defined in subdivision (b) of Section 6600 of the Welfare and Institutions Code and does not have a prior conviction for a sexually violent offense as defined in subdivision (b) of Section 6600 of the Welfare and Institutions Code.

(d) The person was not found guilty of a serious disciplinary offense, as defined in regulation by the department, during his or her current term of imprisonment.

(e) The person is not a validated prison gang member or associate, as defined in regulation by the department.

(f) The person did not refuse to sign any forms, or provide any samples, as required by Section 3060.5.

(g) The person was evaluated by the department using a validated risk assessment tool and was not determined to pose a high risk to reoffend.
(Amended by Stats. 2012, Ch. 43, Sec. 34. (SB 1023) Effective June 27, 2012.)

3000.05.
(a) The Department of Corrections and Rehabilitation may contract with a private debt collection agency or with the Franchise Tax Board, whichever is more cost-effective, to make collections, on behalf of a victim, from any person who is or has been under the jurisdiction of the department and who has failed to make restitution payments according to the terms and conditions specified by the department.

(b) If a debt is referred to a private debt collection agency or to the Franchise Tax Board pursuant to this section, the debtor shall be given notice of that fact, either by the department or the private debt collection agency in writing to his or her address of record, or by his or her parole officer.
(Amended by Stats. 2018, Ch. 423, Sec. 105. (SB 1494) Effective January 1, 2019.)

3000.07.
(a) Every inmate who has been convicted for any felony violation of a "registerable sex offense" described in subdivision (c) of Section 290 or any attempt to commit any of the above-mentioned offenses and who is committed to prison and released on parole pursuant to Section 3000 or 3000.1 shall be monitored by a global positioning system for the term of his or her parole, or for the duration or any remaining part thereof, whichever period of time is less.

(b) Any inmate released on parole pursuant to this section shall be required to pay for the costs associated with the monitoring by a global positioning system. However, the Department of Corrections and Rehabilitation shall waive any or all of that payment upon a finding of an inability to pay. The department shall consider any remaining amounts the inmate has been ordered to pay in fines, assessments and restitution fines, fees, and orders, and shall give priority to the payment of those items before requiring that the inmate pay for the global positioning monitoring. No inmate shall be denied parole on the basis of his or her inability to pay for those monitoring costs.
(Amended by Stats. 2007, Ch. 579, Sec. 45. Effective October 13, 2007. Note: This section was added on Nov. 7, 2006, by initiative Prop. 83.)

3000.08.
(a) A person released from state prison prior to or on or after July 1, 2013, after serving a prison term, or whose sentence has been deemed served pursuant to Section 2900.5, for any of the following crimes is subject to parole supervision by the Department of Corrections and Rehabilitation and the jurisdiction of the court in the county in which the parolee is released, resides, or in which an alleged violation of supervision has occurred, for the purpose of hearing petitions to revoke parole and impose a term of custody:

(1) A serious felony as described in subdivision (c) of Section 1192.7.

(2) A violent felony as described in subdivision (c) of Section 667.5.

(3) A crime for which the person was sentenced pursuant to paragraph (2) of subdivision (e) of Section 667 or paragraph (2) of subdivision (c) of Section 1170.12.

(4) Any crime for which the person is classified as a high-risk sex offender.

(5) Any crime for which the person is required, as a condition of parole, to undergo treatment by the State Department of State Hospitals pursuant to Section 2962.

(b) Notwithstanding any other law, all other offenders released from prison shall be placed on postrelease supervision pursuant to Title 2.05 (commencing with Section 3450).

(c) At any time during the period of parole of a person subject to this section, if any parole agent or peace officer has probable cause to believe that the parolee is violating any term or condition of his or her parole, the agent or officer may, without warrant or other process and at any time until the final disposition of the case, arrest the person and bring him or her before the court, or the court may, in its discretion, issue a warrant for that person's arrest pursuant to Section 1203.2. Notwithstanding Section 3056, and unless the parolee is otherwise serving a period of flash incarceration, whenever a supervised person who is subject to this section is arrested, with or without a warrant or the filing of a petition for revocation as described in subdivision (f), the court may order the release of the parolee from custody under any terms and conditions the court deems appropriate.

(d) Upon review of the alleged violation and a finding of good cause that the parolee has committed a violation of law or violated his or her conditions of parole, the supervising parole agency may impose additional and appropriate conditions of supervision, including rehabilitation and treatment services and appropriate incentives for compliance, and impose immediate, structured, and intermediate sanctions for parole violations, including flash incarceration in a city or a county jail. Periods of "flash incarceration," as defined in subdivision (e) are encouraged as one method of punishment for violations of a parolee's conditions of parole. This section does not preclude referrals to a reentry court pursuant to Section 3015.

(e) "Flash incarceration" is a period of detention in a city or a county jail due to a violation of a parolee's conditions of parole. The length of the detention period can range between one and 10 consecutive days. Shorter, but if necessary more frequent, periods of detention for violations of a parolee's conditions of parole shall appropriately punish a parolee while preventing the disruption in a work or home establishment that typically arises from longer periods of detention.

(f) If the supervising parole agency has determined, following application of its assessment processes, that intermediate sanctions up to and including flash incarceration are not appropriate, the supervising parole agency shall, pursuant to Section 1203.2, petition either the court in the county in which the parolee is being supervised or the court in the county in which the alleged violation of supervision occurred, to revoke parole. At any point during the process initiated pursuant to this section, a parolee may waive, in writing, his or her right to counsel, admit the parole violation, waive a court hearing, and accept the proposed parole modification or revocation. The petition shall include a written report that contains additional information

regarding the petition, including the relevant terms and conditions of parole, the circumstances of the alleged underlying violation, the history and background of the parolee, and any recommendations. The Judicial Council shall adopt forms and rules of court to establish uniform statewide procedures to implement this subdivision, including the minimum contents of supervision agency reports. Upon a finding that the person has violated the conditions of parole, the court shall have authority to do any of the following:
(1) Return the person to parole supervision with modifications of conditions, if appropriate, including a period of incarceration in a county jail.
(2) Revoke parole and order the person to confinement in a county jail.
(3) Refer the person to a reentry court pursuant to Section 3015 or other evidence-based program in the court's discretion.
(g) Confinement pursuant to paragraphs (1) and (2) of subdivision (f) shall not exceed a period of 180 days in a county jail.
(h) Notwithstanding any other law, if Section 3000.1 or paragraph (4) of subdivision (b) of Section 3000 applies to a person who is on parole and the court determines that the person has committed a violation of law or violated his or her conditions of parole, the person on parole shall be remanded to the custody of the Department of Corrections and Rehabilitation and the jurisdiction of the Board of Parole Hearings for the purpose of future parole consideration.
(i) Notwithstanding subdivision (a), any of the following persons released from state prison shall be subject to the jurisdiction of, and parole supervision by, the Department of Corrections and Rehabilitation for a period of parole up to three years or the parole term the person was subject to at the time of the commission of the offense, whichever is greater:
(1) The person is required to register as a sex offender pursuant to Chapter 5.5 (commencing with Section 290) of Title 9 of Part 1, and was subject to a period of parole exceeding three years at the time he or she committed a felony for which they were convicted and subsequently sentenced to state prison.
(2) The person was subject to parole for life pursuant to Section 3000.1 at the time of the commission of the offense that resulted in a conviction and state prison sentence.
(j) Parolees subject to this section who have a pending adjudication for a parole violation on July 1, 2013, are subject to the jurisdiction of the Board of Parole Hearings. Parole revocation proceedings conducted by the Board of Parole Hearings prior to July 1, 2013, if reopened on or after July 1, 2013, are subject to the jurisdiction of the Board of Parole Hearings.
(k) Except as described in subdivision (c), any person who is convicted of a felony that requires community supervision and who still has a period of state parole to serve shall discharge from state parole at the time of release to community supervision.
(l) Any person released to parole supervision pursuant to subdivision (a) shall, regardless of any subsequent determination that the person should have been released pursuant to subdivision (b), remain subject to subdivision (a) after having served 60 days under supervision pursuant to subdivision (a).
(Amended by Stats. 2016, Ch. 86, Sec. 236. (SB 1171) Effective January 1, 2017.)
3000.09.
(a) Notwithstanding any other law, any parolee who was paroled from state prison prior to October 1, 2011, shall be subject to this section.
(b) Parolees subject to this section shall remain under supervision by the Department of Corrections and Rehabilitation until one of the following occurs:
(1) Jurisdiction over the person is terminated by operation of law.
(2) The supervising agent recommends to the Board of Parole Hearings that the offender be discharged and the parole authority approves the discharge.
(3) The offender is subject to a period of parole of up to three years pursuant to paragraph (1) of subdivision (b) of Section 3000 and was not imprisoned for committing a violent felony, as defined in subdivision (c) of Section 667.5, a serious felony, as defined by subdivision (c) of Section 1192.7, or is required to register as a sex offender pursuant to Section 290, and completes six consecutive months of parole without violating their conditions, at which time the supervising agent shall review and make a recommendation on whether to discharge the offender to the Board of Parole Hearings and the Board of Parole Hearings approves the discharge.
(c) Parolees subject to this section who are being held for a parole violation in state prison on October 1, 2011, upon completion of a revocation term on or after November 1, 2011, shall either remain under parole supervision of the department pursuant to Section 3000.08 or shall be placed on postrelease community supervision pursuant to Title 2.05 (commencing with Section 3450). Any person placed on postrelease community supervision pursuant to Title 2.05 (commencing with Section 3450) after serving a term for a parole revocation pursuant to this subdivision shall serve a period of postrelease supervision that is no longer than the time period for which the person would have served if the person remained on parole. Notwithstanding Section 3000.08, any parolee who is in a county jail serving a term of parole revocation or being held pursuant to Section 3056 on October 1, 2011, and is released directly from county jail without returning to a state facility on or after October 1, 2011, shall remain under the parole supervision of the department. Any parolee that is pending final adjudication of a parole revocation charge prior to October 1, whether located in county jail or state prison, may be returned to state prison and shall be confined pursuant to subdivisions (a) to (d), inclusive, of Section 3057. Any subsequent parole revocations of a parolee on postrelease community supervision shall be served in county jail pursuant to Section 3056.
(d) Any parolee who was paroled prior to October 1, 2011, who commits a violation of parole shall, until July 1, 2013, be subject to parole revocation procedures in accordance with the rules and regulations of the department consistent with Division 2 of Title 15 of the California Code of Regulations. On and after July 1, 2013, any parolee who was paroled prior to October 1, 2011, shall be subject to the procedures established under Section 3000.08.
(Amended by Stats. 2012, Ch. 43, Sec. 36. (SB 1023) Effective June 27, 2012.)
3000.1.
(a) (1) In the case of any inmate sentenced under Section 1168 for any offense of first or second degree murder with a maximum term of life imprisonment, the period of parole, if parole is granted, shall be the remainder of the inmate's life.
(2) Notwithstanding any other law, in the case of any inmate sentenced to a life term under subdivision (b) of Section 209, if that offense was committed with the intent to commit a specified sexual offense, Section 269 or 288.7, subdivision (c) of Section 667.51, Section 667.71 in which one or more of the victims of the offense was a child under 14 years of age, or subdivision (j), (l), or (m) of Section 667.61, the period of parole, if parole is granted, shall be the remainder of the inmate's life.
(b) Notwithstanding any other law, when any person referred to in paragraph (1) of subdivision (a) has been released on parole from the state prison, and has been on parole continuously for seven years in the case of any person imprisoned for first degree murder, and five years in the case of any person imprisoned for second degree murder, since release from confinement, the board shall, within 30 days, discharge that person from parole, unless the board, for good cause, determines that the person will be retained on parole. The board shall make a written record of its determination and transmit a copy of it to the parolee.
(c) In the event of a retention on parole pursuant to subdivision (b), the parolee shall be entitled to a review by the board each year thereafter.
(d) There shall be a hearing as provided in Sections 3041.5 and 3041.7 within 12 months of the date of any revocation of parole of a person referred to in subdivision (a) to consider the release of the inmate on parole and, notwithstanding paragraph (3) of subdivision (b) of Section 3041.5, there shall be annual parole consideration hearings thereafter, unless the person is released or otherwise ineligible for parole release. The panel or board shall release the person within one year of the date of the revocation unless it determines that the circumstances and gravity of the parole violation are such that consideration of the public safety requires a more lengthy period of incarceration or unless there is a new prison commitment following a conviction.
(e) The provisions of Section 3042 shall not apply to any hearing held pursuant to this section.
(Amended by Stats. 2014, Ch. 280, Sec. 2. (AB 1438) Effective January 1, 2015.)
3001.
(a) (1) Notwithstanding any other provision of law, when any person referred to in paragraph (2) of subdivision (b) of Section 3000 who was not imprisoned for committing a violent felony, as defined in subdivision (c) of Section 667.5, not imprisoned for a serious felony, as defined by subdivision (c) of Section 1192.7, or is not required to register as a sex offender pursuant to Section 290, has been released on parole from the state prison, and has been on parole continuously for six months since release from confinement, within 30 days, that person shall be discharged from parole, unless the Department of Corrections and Rehabilitation recommends to the Board of Parole Hearings that the person be retained on parole and the board, for good cause, determines that the person will be retained.
(2) Notwithstanding any other provision of law, when any person referred to in paragraph (2) of subdivision (b) of Section 3000 who is required to register as a sex offender pursuant to the Sex Offender Registration Act or who was imprisoned for committing a serious felony described in either subdivision (c) of Section 1192.7 or subdivision (a) of Section 1192.8, has been released on parole from the state prison, and has been on parole continuously for one year since release from confinement, within 30 days, that person shall be discharged from parole, unless the Department of Corrections and Rehabilitation recommends to the Board of Parole Hearings that the person be retained on parole and the board, for good cause, determines that the person will be retained.
(3) Notwithstanding any other provision of law, when any person referred to in paragraph (2) of subdivision (b) of Section 3000 who was imprisoned for committing a violent felony, as defined in subdivision (c) of Section 667.5, has been released on parole from the state prison for a period not exceeding three years and has been on parole continuously for two years since release from confinement, or has been released on parole from the state prison for a period not exceeding five years and has been on parole continuously for three years since release from confinement, the department shall discharge, within 30 days, that person from parole, unless the department recommends to the board that the person be retained on parole and the board, for good cause, determines that the person will be retained. The board shall make a written record of its determination and the department shall transmit a copy thereof to the parolee.
(4) This subdivision shall apply only to those persons whose commitment offense occurred prior to the effective date of the act adding this paragraph.
(b) Notwithstanding any other provision of law, when any person referred to in paragraph (1) of subdivision (b) of Section 3000, with the exception of persons described in paragraph (2) of subdivision (a) of Section 3000.1, has been released on parole from the state prison, and has been on parole continuously for three years since release from confinement, the board shall discharge, within 30 days, the person from parole, unless the board, for good cause, determines that the person will be retained on parole. The board shall make a written record of its determination and the department shall transmit a copy of that determination to the parolee.
(c) Notwithstanding any other provision of law, when any person referred to in paragraph (3) of subdivision (b) of Section 3000 has been released on parole from the state prison, and has been on parole continuously for six years and six months since release from confinement, the board shall discharge, within 30 days, the person from parole, unless the board, for good cause, determines that the person will be retained on parole. The board shall make a written record of its determination and the department shall transmit a copy thereof to the parolee.
(d) In the event of a retention on parole, the parolee shall be entitled to a review by the Board of Parole Hearings each year thereafter until the maximum statutory period of parole has expired.
(e) The amendments to this section made during the 1987–88 Regular Session of the Legislature shall only be applied prospectively and shall not extend the parole period for any person whose eligibility for discharge from parole was fixed as of the effective date of those amendments.
(f) The Department of Corrections and Rehabilitation shall, within 60 days from the date that the act adding this subdivision is effective, submit to the Board of Parole Hearings recommendations pursuant to paragraph (2) of subdivision (a) for any person described in that paragraph who has been released from state prison from October 1, 2010, to the effective date of this subdivision, and who has been on parole continuously for one year since his or her release from confinement. A person who meets the criteria in this subdivision who are not retained on parole by the Board of Parole Hearings by the 91st day after the effective date of this subdivision shall be discharged from parole.
(g) The amendments made to subdivision (a) during the 2011–12 Regular Session and the First Extraordinary Session of the Legislature shall apply prospectively from October 1, 2011, and no person on parole prior to October 1, 2011, shall be discharged from parole pursuant to subdivision (a) unless one of the following circumstances exist:
(1) The person has been on parole continuously for six consecutive months after October 1, 2011, and the person is not retained by the Board of Parole Hearings for good cause.
(2) The person has, on or after October 1, 2011, been on parole for one year and the Board of Parole Hearings does not retain the person for good cause.
(Amended by Stats. 2012, Ch. 43, Sec. 38. (SB 1023) Effective June 27, 2012. Note: This section was amended on Nov. 7, 2006, by initiative Prop. 83.)
3002.
In considering the imposition of conditions of parole upon a prisoner convicted of violating any section of this code in which a minor is a victim of an act of abuse or neglect, the Department of Corrections shall provide for a psychological evaluation to be performed on the prisoner to determine the extent of counseling which may be mandated as a condition of parole. Such examination may be performed by psychiatrists, psychologists, or licensed clinical social workers.
(Added by renumbering Section 3001 by Stats. 1978, Ch. 582.)
3003.
(a) Except as otherwise provided in this section, an inmate who is released on parole or postrelease community supervision as provided by Title 2.05 (commencing with Section 3450) shall be returned to the county that was the last legal residence of the inmate prior to his or her incarceration. An inmate who is released on parole or postrelease community supervision as provided by Title 2.05 (commencing with Section 3450) and who was committed to prison for a sex offense for which registration is required pursuant to Section 290, shall, through all efforts reasonably possible, be returned to the city that was the last legal residence of the inmate prior to incarceration or a close geographic location in which he or she has family, social ties, or economic ties and access to reentry services, unless return to that location would violate any other law or pose a risk to his or her victim. For purposes of this subdivision, "last legal residence" shall not be construed to mean the county or city wherein the inmate committed an offense while confined in a state prison or local jail facility or while confined for treatment in a state hospital.
(b) Notwithstanding subdivision (a), an inmate may be returned to another county or city if that would be in the best interests of the public. If the Board of Parole Hearings

setting the conditions of parole for inmates sentenced pursuant to subdivision (b) of Section 1168, as determined by the parole consideration panel, or the Department of Corrections and Rehabilitation setting the conditions of parole for inmates sentenced pursuant to Section 1170, decides on a return to another county or city, it shall place its reasons in writing in the parolee's permanent record and include these reasons in the notice to the sheriff or chief of police pursuant to Section 3058.6. In making its decision, the paroling authority shall consider, among others, the following factors, giving the greatest weight to the protection of the victim and the safety of the community:

(1) The need to protect the life or safety of a victim, the parolee, a witness, or any other person.

(2) Public concern that would reduce the chance that the inmate's parole would be successfully completed.

(3) The verified existence of a work offer, or an educational or vocational training program.

(4) The existence of family in another county with whom the inmate has maintained strong ties and whose support would increase the chance that the inmate's parole would be successfully completed.

(5) The lack of necessary outpatient treatment programs for parolees receiving treatment pursuant to Section 2960.

(c) The Department of Corrections and Rehabilitation, in determining an out-of-county commitment, shall give priority to the safety of the community and any witnesses and victims.

(d) In making its decision about an inmate who participated in a joint venture program pursuant to Article 1.5 (commencing with Section 2717.1) of Chapter 5, the paroling authority shall give serious consideration to releasing him or her to the county where the joint venture program employer is located if that employer states to the paroling authority that he or she intends to employ the inmate upon release.

(e) (1) The following information, if available, shall be released by the Department of Corrections and Rehabilitation to local law enforcement agencies regarding a paroled inmate or inmate placed on postrelease community supervision pursuant to Title 2.05 (commencing with Section 3450) who is released in their jurisdictions:

(A) Last, first, and middle names.

(B) Birth date.

(C) Sex, race, height, weight, and hair and eye color.

(D) Date of parole or placement on postrelease community supervision and discharge.

(E) Registration status, if the inmate is required to register as a result of a controlled substance, sex, or arson offense.

(F) California Criminal Information Number, FBI number, social security number, and driver's license number.

(G) County of commitment.

(H) A description of scars, marks, and tattoos on the inmate.

(I) Offense or offenses for which the inmate was convicted that resulted in parole or postrelease community supervision in this instance.

(J) Address, including all of the following information:

(i) Street name and number. Post office box numbers are not acceptable for purposes of this subparagraph.

(ii) City and ZIP Code.

(iii) Date that the address provided pursuant to this subparagraph was proposed to be effective.

(K) Contact officer and unit, including all of the following information:

(i) Name and telephone number of each contact officer.

(ii) Contact unit type of each contact officer such as units responsible for parole, registration, or county probation.

(L) A digitized image of the photograph and at least a single digit fingerprint of the parolee.

(M) A geographic coordinate for the inmate's residence location for use with a Geographical Information System (GIS) or comparable computer program.

(2) Unless the information is unavailable, the Department of Corrections and Rehabilitation shall electronically transmit to the county agency identified in subdivision (a) of Section 3451 the inmate's tuberculosis status, specific medical, mental health, and outpatient clinic needs, and any medical concerns or disabilities for the county to consider as the offender transitions onto postrelease community supervision pursuant to Section 3450, for the purpose of identifying the medical and mental health needs of the individual. All transmissions to the county agency shall be in compliance with applicable provisions of the federal Health Insurance Portability and Accountability Act of 1996 (HIPAA) (Public Law 104-191), the federal Health Information Technology for Clinical Health Act (HITECH) (Public Law 111-005), and the implementing of privacy and security regulations in Parts 160 and 164 of Title 45 of the Code of Federal Regulations. This paragraph shall not take effect until the Secretary of the United States Department of Health and Human Services, or his or her designee, determines that this provision is not preempted by HIPAA.

(3) Except for the information required by paragraph (2), the information required by this subdivision shall come from the statewide parolee database. The information obtained from each source shall be based on the same timeframe.

(4) All of the information required by this subdivision shall be provided utilizing a computer-to-computer transfer in a format usable by a desktop computer system. The transfer of this information shall be continually available to local law enforcement agencies upon request.

(5) The unauthorized release or receipt of the information described in this subdivision is a violation of Section 11143.

(f) Notwithstanding any other law, if the victim or witness has requested additional distance in the placement of the inmate on parole, and if the Board of Parole Hearings or the Department of Corrections and Rehabilitation finds that there is a need to protect the life, safety, or well-being of the victim or witness, an inmate who is released on parole shall not be returned to a location within 35 miles of the actual residence of a victim of, or a witness to, any of the following crimes:

(1) A violent felony as defined in paragraphs (1) to (7), inclusive, and paragraphs (11) and (16) of subdivision (c) of Section 667.5.

(2) A felony in which the defendant inflicts great bodily injury on a person, other than an accomplice, that has been charged and proved as provided for in Section 12022.53, 12022.7, or 12022.9.

(3) A violation of paragraph (1), (3), or (4) of subdivision (a) of Section 261, subdivision (f), (g), or (i) of Section 286, subdivision (f), (g), or (i) of Section 288a, or subdivision (b), (d), or (e) of Section 289.

(g) Notwithstanding any other law, an inmate who is released on parole for a violation of Section 288 or 288.5 whom the Department of Corrections and Rehabilitation determines poses a high risk to the public shall not be placed or reside, for the duration of his or her parole, within one-half mile of a public or private school including any or all of kindergarten and grades 1 to 12, inclusive.

(h) Notwithstanding any other law, an inmate who is released on parole or postrelease community supervision for a stalking offense shall not be returned to a location within 35 miles of the victim's or witness' actual residence or place of employment if the victim or witness has requested additional distance in the placement of the inmate on parole or postrelease community supervision, and if the Board of Parole Hearings or the Department of Corrections and Rehabilitation, or the supervising county agency, as applicable, finds that there is a need to protect the life, safety, or well-being of the victim. If an inmate who is released on postrelease community supervision cannot be placed in his or her county of last legal residence in compliance with this subdivision, the

supervising county agency may transfer the inmate to another county upon approval of the receiving county.

(i) The authority shall give consideration to the equitable distribution of parolees and the proportion of out-of-county commitments from a county compared to the number of commitments from that county when making parole decisions.

(j) An inmate may be paroled to another state pursuant to any other law. The Department of Corrections and Rehabilitation shall coordinate with local entities regarding the placement of inmates placed out of state on postrelease community supervision pursuant to Title 2.05 (commencing with Section 3450).

(k) (1) Except as provided in paragraph (2), the Department of Corrections and Rehabilitation shall be the agency primarily responsible for, and shall have control over, the program, resources, and staff implementing the Law Enforcement Automated Data System (LEADS) in conformance with subdivision (e). County agencies supervising inmates released to postrelease community supervision pursuant to Title 2.05 (commencing with Section 3450) shall provide any information requested by the department to ensure the availability of accurate information regarding inmates released from state prison. This information may include the issuance of warrants, revocations, or the termination of postrelease community supervision. On or before August 1, 2011, county agencies designated to supervise inmates released to postrelease community supervision shall notify the department that the county agencies have been designated as the local entity responsible for providing that supervision.

(2) Notwithstanding paragraph (1), the Department of Justice shall be the agency primarily responsible for the proper release of information under LEADS that relates to fingerprint cards.

(l) In addition to the requirements under subdivision (k), the Department of Corrections and Rehabilitation shall submit to the Department of Justice data to be included in the supervised release file of the California Law Enforcement Telecommunications System (CLETS) so that law enforcement can be advised through CLETS of all persons on postrelease community supervision and the county agency designated to provide supervision. The data required by this subdivision shall be provided via electronic transfer.

(Amended by Stats. 2018, Ch. 226, Sec. 1. (SB 1199) Effective January 1, 2019. Note: This section was amended on Nov. 7, 2006, by initiative Prop. 83.)

3003.5.

(a) Notwithstanding any other provision of law, when a person is released on parole after having served a term of imprisonment in state prison for any offense for which registration is required pursuant to Section 290, that person may not, during the period of parole, reside in any single family dwelling with any other person also required to register pursuant to Section 290, unless those persons are legally related by blood, marriage, or adoption. For purposes of this section, "single family dwelling" shall not include a residential facility which serves six or fewer persons.

(b) Notwithstanding any other provision of law, it is unlawful for any person for whom registration is required pursuant to Section 290 to reside within 2000 feet of any public or private school, or park where children regularly gather.

(c) Nothing in this section shall prohibit municipal jurisdictions from enacting local ordinances that further restrict the residency of any person for whom registration is required pursuant to Section 290.

(Amended November 7, 2006, by initiative Proposition 83, Sec. 21.)

3003.6.

(a) Every person who is required to register pursuant to Section 290, based upon the commission of an offense against a minor, is prohibited from residing, except as a client, and from working or volunteering in any of the following:

(1) A child day care facility or children's residential facility that is licensed by the State Department of Social Services, a home certified by a foster family agency, or a home approved by a county child welfare services agency.

(2) A home or facility that receives a placement of a child who has been, or may be, declared a dependent child of the juvenile court pursuant to Section 300 of the Welfare and Institutions Code or who has been, or may be, declared a ward of the juvenile court pursuant to Section 601 or 602 of the Welfare and Institutions Code.

(b) Any person who violates this section is guilty of a misdemeanor.

(c) Nothing in this section shall limit the authority of the State Department of Social Services to deny a criminal record exemption request and to take an action to exclude an individual from residing, working, or volunteering in a licensed facility pursuant to Sections 1522, 1569.09, 1569.17, or 1596.871 of the Health and Safety Code.

(Added by Stats. 2013, Ch. 772, Sec. 1. (AB 1108) Effective January 1, 2014.)

3004.

(a) Notwithstanding any other law, the Board of Parole Hearings, the court, or the supervising parole authority may require, as a condition of release on parole or reinstatement on parole, or as an intermediate sanction in lieu of return to custody, that an inmate or parolee agree in writing to the use of electronic monitoring or supervising devices for the purpose of helping to verify his or her compliance with all other conditions of parole. The devices shall not be used to eavesdrop or record any conversation, except a conversation between the parolee and the agent supervising the parolee which is to be used solely for the purposes of voice identification.

(b) Every inmate who has been convicted for any felony violation of a "registerable sex offense" described in subdivision (c) of Section 290 or any attempt to commit any of the above-mentioned offenses and who is committed to prison and released on parole pursuant to Section 3000 or 3000.1 shall be monitored by a global positioning system for life.

(c) Any inmate released on parole pursuant to this section shall be required to pay for the costs associated with the monitoring by a global positioning system. However, the Department of Corrections and Rehabilitation shall waive any or all of that payment upon a finding of an inability to pay. The department shall consider any remaining amounts the inmate has been ordered to pay in fines, assessments and restitution fines, fees, and orders, and shall give priority to the payment of those items before requiring that the inmate pay for the global positioning monitoring.

(Amended by Stats. 2012, Ch. 43, Sec. 39. (SB 1023) Effective June 27, 2012. Note: This section was amended on Nov. 7, 2006, by initiative Prop. 83.)

3006.

(a) The Department of Corrections may require parolees participating in relapse prevention treatment programs or receiving medication treatments intended to prevent them from committing sex offenses to pay some or all of the costs associated with this treatment, subject to the person's ability to pay.

(b) For the purposes of this section, "ability to pay" means the overall capability of the person to reimburse the costs, or a portion of the costs, of providing sex offender treatment, and shall include, but shall not be limited to, consideration of all of the following factors:

(1) Present financial position.

(2) Reasonably discernible future financial position.

(3) Likelihood that the person shall be able to obtain employment after the date of parole.

(4) Any other factor or factors which may bear upon the person's financial capability to reimburse the department for the costs.

(Added by Stats. 2000, Ch. 127, Sec. 28. Effective July 10, 2000.)

3007.

The Department of Corrections and Rehabilitation shall require a research component for any sex offender treatment contract funded by the department. The research component shall enable the department's research unit or an independent contractor to evaluate the effectiveness of each contract on reducing the rate of recidivism of the

participants in the program funded by a contract. The research findings shall be compiled annually in a report due to the Legislature January 10 of each year.
(Added by Stats. 2007, Ch. 175, Sec. 8. Effective August 24, 2007.)
3007.05.
(a) The Department of Corrections and Rehabilitation and the Department of Motor Vehicles shall ensure that all eligible inmates released from state prisons have valid identification cards, issued pursuant to Article 5 (commencing with Section 13000) of Chapter 1 of Division 6 of the Vehicle Code.
(b) For purposes of this section, "eligible inmate" means an inmate who meets all of the following requirements:
(1) The inmate has previously held a California driver's license or identification card.
(2) The inmate has a usable photo on file with the Department of Motor Vehicles that is not more than 10 years old.
(3) The inmate has no outstanding fees due for a prior California identification card.
(4) The inmate has provided, and the Department of Motor Vehicles has verified, all of the following information:
(A) The inmate's true full name.
(B) The inmate's date of birth.
(C) The inmate's social security number.
(D) The inmate's legal presence in the United States.
(c) The Department of Corrections and Rehabilitation shall assist a person who is exonerated as to a conviction for which he or she is serving a state prison sentence at the time of exoneration with all of the following:
(1) Transitional services, including housing assistance, job training, and mental health services, as applicable. The services shall be offered within the first week of an individual's exoneration and again within the first 30 days of exoneration. Services shall be provided for a period of not less than six months and not more than one year from the date of release unless the exonerated person qualifies for services beyond one year under existing law.
(2) Enrollment in the Medi-Cal program established pursuant to Chapter 7 (commencing with Section 14000) of Part 3 of Division 9 of the Welfare and Institutions Code.
(3) (A) Enrollment in the CalFresh program established pursuant to Chapter 10 (commencing with Section 18900) of Part 6 of Division 9 of the Welfare and Institutions Code.
(B) Exonerated persons who are ineligible for CalFresh benefits pursuant to the federal Supplemental Nutrition Assistance Program limitation specified in subsection (o) of Section 2015 of Title 7 of the United States Code shall be given priority for receipt of the 15-percent exemption specified in paragraph (6) of subsection (o) of Section 2015 of Title 7 of the United States Code. The State Department of Social Services shall issue guidance to counties regarding that requirement.
(4) Referral to the Employment Development Department and applicable regional planning units for workforce services.
(5) Enrollment in the federal supplemental security income benefits program pursuant to Title XVI of the federal Social Security Act (42 U.S.C. Sec. 1381 et seq.) and state supplemental program pursuant to Title XVI of the federal Social Security Act and Chapter 3 (commencing with Section 12000) of Part 3 of Division 9 of the Welfare and Institutions Code.
(d) In addition to any other payment to which he or she is entitled to by law, each person who is exonerated shall be paid the sum of one thousand dollars ($1,000) upon his or her release, from funds to be made available upon appropriation by the Legislature for this purpose.
(e) For the purposes of this section, "exonerated" means the person has been convicted and subsequently one of the following occurred:
(1) A writ of habeas corpus concerning the person was granted on the basis that the evidence unerringly points to innocence, or the person's conviction was reversed on appeal on the basis of insufficient evidence.
(2) A writ of habeas corpus concerning the person was granted pursuant to Section 1473, either resulting in dismissal of the criminal charges for which he or she was incarcerated or following a determination that the person is entitled to release on his or her own recognizance, or to bail, pending retrial or pending appeal.
(3) The person was given an absolute pardon by the Governor on the basis that the person was innocent.
(Amended by Stats. 2018, Ch. 979, Sec. 2. (SB 1050) Effective January 1, 2019.)
3007.08.
(a) The Department of Corrections and Rehabilitation, Division of Juvenile Justice and the Department of Motor Vehicles shall ensure that an eligible juvenile offender released from a state juvenile facility has a valid identification card, issued pursuant to Article 3 (commencing with Section 12800) and Article 5 (commencing with Section 13000) of Chapter 1 of Division 6 of the Vehicle Code.
(b) The fee for an identification card issued pursuant to this section is eight dollars ($8). An eligible juvenile offender shall provide the Department of Motor Vehicles, upon application, with a verification of his or her eligibility that meets all of the following requirements:
(1) Is on state juvenile correctional facility letterhead.
(2) Is typed or computer generated.
(3) Contains the juvenile offender's name.
(4) Contains the juvenile offender's date of birth.
(5) Contains the original signature of an official from the state juvenile correctional facility.
(6) Is dated within 90 days of the application.
(c) The verification required by subdivision (b) may be used to attest to an applicant's residency in a facility operated by the department and shall be acceptable proof of California residency.
(d) (1) For purposes of this section, "eligible juvenile offender" means a juvenile offender who previously held a California driver's license or identification card, issued pursuant to Section 12801.5 of Article 3 (commencing with Section 12800) of Chapter 1 of Division 6 of the Vehicle Code, or a juvenile offender who provides acceptable proof of his or her:
(A) True full name.
(B) Date of birth.
(C) Social security number.
(D) Legal presence in the United States.
(E) California residency.
(2) A certified copy of a birth certificate issued by the Office of Vital Records of the State Department of Public Health is acceptable proof to satisfy the requirements of subparagraphs (A), (B), and (D) of paragraph (1).
(e) The Department of Corrections and Rehabilitation, Division of Juvenile Justice and the Department of Motor Vehicles shall enter into an interagency agreement to implement this section.
(Added by Stats. 2018, Ch. 36, Sec. 20. (AB 1812) Effective June 27, 2018.)

ARTICLE 1.5. Intensive Parole Supervision of Sex Offenders [3008- 3008.]
(Article 1.5 added by Stats. 2000, Ch. 142, Sec. 5.)
3008.
(a) The Department of Corrections and Rehabilitation shall ensure that all parolees under active supervision who are deemed to pose a high risk to the public of committing sex crimes, as determined by the State-Authorized Risk Assessment Tool for Sex Offenders (SARATSO), as set forth in Sections 290.04 to 290.06, inclusive, are placed on intensive and specialized parole supervision and are required to report frequently to designated parole officers. The department may place any other parolee convicted of an offense that requires him or her to register as a sex offender pursuant to Section 290 who is on active supervision on intensive and specialized supervision and require him or her to report frequently to designated parole officers.
(b) The department shall develop and, at the discretion of the secretary, and subject to an appropriation of the necessary funds, may implement a plan for the implementation of relapse prevention treatment programs, and the provision of other services deemed necessary by the department, in conjunction with intensive and specialized parole supervision, to reduce the recidivism of sex offenders.
(c) The department shall develop control and containment programming for sex offenders who have been deemed to pose a high risk to the public of committing a sex crime, as determined by the SARATSO, and shall require participation in appropriate programming as a condition of parole.
(d) On or after July 1, 2012, the parole conditions of a person released on parole for an offense that requires registration pursuant to Sections 290 to 290.023, inclusive, shall include all of the following:
(1) Persons placed on parole prior to July 1, 2012, shall participate in an approved sex offender management program, following the standards developed pursuant to Section 9003, for a period of not less than one year or the remaining term of parole if it is less than one year. The length of the period in the program is to be determined by the certified sex offender management professional in consultation with the parole officer and as approved by the court. Participation in this program applies to each person without regard to when his or her crime or crimes were committed.
(2) Persons placed on parole on or after July 1, 2012, shall successfully complete a sex offender management program, following the standards developed pursuant to Section 9003, as a condition of parole. The length of the period in the program shall be not less than one year, up to the entire period of parole, as determined by the certified sex offender management professional in consultation with the parole officer and as approved by the court. Participation in this program applies to every person described without regard to when his or her crime or crimes were committed.
(3) Waiver of any privilege against self-incrimination and participation in polygraph examinations, which shall be part of the sex offender management program.
(4) Waiver of any psychotherapist-patient privilege to enable communication between the sex offender management professional and supervising parole officer, pursuant to Section 290.09.
(e) Any defendant ordered to be placed in an approved sex offender management treatment program pursuant to subdivision (d) shall be responsible for paying the expense of his or her participation in the program. The department shall take into consideration the ability of the defendant to pay, and no defendant shall be denied discharge onto parole because of his or her inability to pay.
(Amended by Stats. 2014, Ch. 611, Sec. 2. (AB 2411) Effective September 26, 2014.)

ARTICLE 2. Electronic Monitoring [3010 - 3010.10]
(Article 2 added by Stats. 2005, Ch. 484, Sec. 2.)
3010.
(a) Notwithstanding any other provisions of law, the Department of Corrections and Rehabilitation may utilize continuous electronic monitoring to electronically monitor the whereabouts of persons on parole, as provided by this article.
(b) Any use of continuous electronic monitoring pursuant to this article shall have as its primary objective the enhancement of public safety through the reduction in the number of people being victimized by crimes committed by persons on parole.
(c) It is the intent of the Legislature in enacting this article to specifically expand the authority of the department acting pursuant to this article to utilize a system of continuous electronic monitoring that conforms with the requirements of this article.
(d) (1) For purposes of this article, "continuous electronic monitoring" may include the use of worldwide radio navigation system technology, known as the Global Positioning System, or GPS. The Legislature finds that because of its capability for continuous surveillance, continuous electronic monitoring has been used in other parts of the country to monitor persons on parole who are identified as requiring a high level of supervision.
(2) For purposes of this article, "department" means the Department of Corrections and Rehabilitation.
(e) The Legislature finds that continuous electronic monitoring has proven to be an effective risk management tool for supervising high-risk persons on parole who are likely to reoffend where prevention and knowledge of their whereabouts is a high priority for maintaining public safety.
(Added by Stats. 2005, Ch. 484, Sec. 2. Effective October 4, 2005.)
3010.1.
The department may utilize a continuous electronic monitoring device, as distinguished from an electronic monitoring device as described in Section 3004, pursuant to this section that has all of the following attributes:
(a) A device designed to be worn by a human being.
(b) A device that emits a signal as a person is moving or is stationary. The signal shall be capable of being received and tracked across large urban or rural areas, statewide, and being received from within structures, vehicles, and other objects to the degree technically feasible in light of the associated costs, design, and other considerations as are determined relevant by the department.
(c) A device that functions 24 hours a day.
(d) A device that is resistant or impervious to unintentional or willful damage.
(Added by Stats. 2005, Ch. 484, Sec. 2. Effective October 4, 2005.)
3010.2.
(a) A continuous electronic monitoring system may have the capacity to immediately notify the department of violations, actual or suspected, of the terms of parole that have been identified by the monitoring system if the requirement is deemed necessary by the parole officer with respect to an individual person.
(b) This information, including geographic location and tampering, may be used as evidence to prove a violation of the terms of parole.
(Added by Stats. 2005, Ch. 484, Sec. 2. Effective October 4, 2005.)
3010.3.
The department shall establish the following standards as are necessary to enhance public safety:
(a) Standards for the minimum time interval between transmissions of information about the location of the person under supervision. The standards shall be established after an evaluation of, at a minimum, all of the following:
(1) The resources of the department.
(2) The criminal history of the person under supervision.
(3) The safety of the victim of the persons under supervision.
(b) Standards for the accuracy of the information identifying the location of the person under supervision. The standards shall be established after consideration of, at a minimum, all of the following:
(1) The need to identify the location of a person proximate to the location of a crime, including a violation of parole.
(2) Resources of the department.
(3) The need to avoid false indications of proximity to crimes.
(Added by Stats. 2005, Ch. 484, Sec. 2. Effective October 4, 2005.)
3010.4.
(a) The department, operating a system of continuous electronic monitoring pursuant to this section, shall establish prohibitions against unauthorized access to, and use of, information by private or public entities as may be deemed appropriate. Unauthorized access to, and use of, electronic signals includes signals transmitted in any fashion by equipment utilized for continuous electronic monitoring.

(b) Devices used pursuant to this article shall not be used to eavesdrop or record any conversation, except a conversation between the participant and the person supervising the participant that is to be used solely for the purposes of voice identification.
(Added by Stats. 2005, Ch. 484, Sec. 2. Effective October 4, 2005.)
3010.5.
(a) The department shall have the sole discretion to decide which persons shall be supervised using continuous electronic monitoring administered by the department. No individual shall be required to participate in continuous electronic monitoring authorized by this article for any period of time longer than the term of parole.
(b) The department shall establish written guidelines that identify those persons on parole subject to continuous electronic monitoring authorized by this article. These guidelines shall include the need for enhancing monitoring in comparison to other persons not subject to the enhanced monitoring and the public safety needs that will be served by the enhanced monitoring.
(Added by Stats. 2005, Ch. 484, Sec. 2. Effective October 4, 2005.)
3010.6.
A parole officer may revoke, in his or her discretion, the continuous monitoring of any individual.
(Added by Stats. 2005, Ch. 484, Sec. 2. Effective October 4, 2005.)
3010.7.
Whenever a parole officer supervising an individual has reasonable cause to believe that the individual is not complying with the rules or conditions set forth for the use of continuous electronic monitoring as a supervision tool, the officer supervising the individual may, without a warrant of arrest, take the individual into custody for a violation of parole.
(Added by Stats. 2005, Ch. 484, Sec. 2. Effective October 4, 2005.)
3010.8.
(a) The department may charge persons on parole for the costs of any form of supervision that utilizes continuous electronic monitoring devices that monitor the whereabouts of the person pursuant to this article. Inability to pay all or a portion of the costs of continuous electronic monitoring authorized by this article shall not preclude use of continuous electronic monitoring and eligibility for parole shall not be enhanced by reason of ability to pay.
(b) Any person released on parole pursuant to subdivision (a) may be required to pay for that monitoring upon a finding of the ability to pay those costs. However, the department shall waive any or all of that payment upon a finding of an inability to pay. The department shall consider any remaining amounts the person has been ordered to pay in fines, assessments and restitution fines, fees, and orders, and shall give priority to the payment of those items before requiring that the person pay for the continuous electronic monitoring.
(Added by Stats. 2005, Ch. 484, Sec. 2. Effective October 4, 2005.)
3010.9.
It is the intent of the Legislature that continuous electronic monitoring established pursuant to this article maintain the highest public confidence, credibility, and public safety. In the furtherance of these standards, the following shall apply:
(a) The department may administer continuous electronic monitoring pursuant to written contracts and appropriate public or private agencies or entities to provide specified supervision services. No public or private agency or entity may operate a continuous electronic monitoring system as authorized by this section without a written contract with the department. No public or private agency or entity entering into a contract may itself employ any person who is a participant in continuous electronic monitoring surveillance.
(b) The department shall comply with Section 1090 of the Government Code in the consideration, making, and execution of contracts pursuant to this section.
(Added by Stats. 2005, Ch. 484, Sec. 2. Effective October 4, 2005.)
3010.10.
(a) A person who is required to register as a sex offender pursuant to Section 290 as a condition of parole shall report to his or her parole officer within one working day following release from custody, or as instructed by a parole officer to have an electronic, global positioning system (GPS), or other monitoring device affixed to his or her person.
(b) A person who is required to register as a sex offender pursuant to Section 290 shall not remove, disable, render inoperable, or knowingly circumvent the operation of, or permit another to remove, disable, render inoperable, or knowingly circumvent the operation of, an electronic, GPS, or other monitoring device affixed to his or her person as a condition of parole, when he or she knows that the device was affixed as a condition of parole.
(c) (1) This section does not apply if the removal, disabling, rendering inoperable, or circumvention of the electronic, GPS, or other monitoring device is performed by a physician, emergency medical services technician, or by any other emergency response or medical personnel when doing so is necessary during the course of medical treatment of the person subject to the electronic, GPS, or other monitoring device.
(2) This section does not apply if the removal, disabling, rendering inoperable, or knowingly circumventing the operation of the electronic, GPS, or other monitoring device is authorized or required by a court, or by the law enforcement, probation, parole authority, or other entity responsible for placing the electronic, GPS, or other monitoring device upon the person, or that has, at the time, the authority and responsibility to monitor the electronic, GPS, or other monitoring device.
(d) Unless the parole authority finds that in the interests of justice it is not appropriate in a particular case, upon a violation of subdivision (a), the parole authority shall revoke the person's parole and require that he or she be incarcerated in a county jail for 180 days.
(e) Upon a violation of subdivision (b), the parole authority shall revoke the person's parole and require that he or she be incarcerated in a county jail for 180 days.
(Amended by Stats. 2014, Ch. 603, Sec. 1. (AB 2121) Effective January 1, 2015.)

ARTICLE 2.3. Parole Reentry Accountability Program [3015- 3015.]
(Article 2.3 added by Stats. 2009, 3rd Ex. Sess., Ch. 28, Sec. 49.)
3015.
(a) The Secretary of the Department of Corrections and Rehabilitation shall establish a parole reentry accountability program for parolees who have been sentenced to a term of imprisonment under Section 1170. The purpose of the program is to promote public safety, hold parolees accountable, and reduce recidivism.
(b) The department shall employ a parole violation decisionmaking instrument to determine the most appropriate sanctions for these parolees who violate their conditions of parole.
(1) For purposes of this subdivision, a "parole violation decisionmaking instrument" means a standardized tool that provides ranges of appropriate sanctions for parole violators given relevant case factors, including, but not limited to, offense history, risk of reoffense based on a validated risk assessment tool, need for treatment services, the number and type of current and prior parole violations, and other relevant statutory requirements.
(2) The department shall adopt emergency regulations to implement this section initially, and shall subsequently adopt permanent regulations that make appropriate changes in policies and procedures to reflect the intent of this section.
(c) The secretary shall have the discretion to establish additional tools and standards to further the purposes of this section.
(d) Parolees who have been sentenced to a term of imprisonment under Section 1170 and offenders subject to postrelease supervision as established in the Postrelease Community Supervision Act of 2011 with a history of substance abuse or mental illness who violate their conditions of parole or postrelease supervision are eligible to participate in a reentry court program established pursuant to subdivision (e).

(1) A parolee or offender subject to postrelease supervision who is deemed eligible by the department or local supervising agency to participate in a reentry court program may be referred by his or her parole officer, local supervising agent, or a revocation hearing officer for participation in the program. The reentry court shall have the discretion to determine if the parolee or offender subject to postrelease supervision will be admitted into the program and, in making this determination, shall consider, among other factors, whether the offender will benefit from the program, the risk the offender poses to the community, and the history and nature of the committing offense.
(2) If the reentry court determines that the parolee or offender subject to postrelease supervision will be admitted into the program, the court, with the assistance of the participant's parole or local supervising agent, shall have exclusive authority to determine the appropriate conditions of parole or postrelease supervision, order rehabilitation and treatment services to be provided, determine appropriate incentives, order appropriate sanctions, lift parole holds, and hear and determine appropriate responses to alleged violations, unless and until the court terminates the participant's enrollment in the program authorized by subdivision (e).
(3) A reentry court program plan shall include, but not be limited to, all of the following:
(A) The anticipated number of parolees and offenders subject to postrelease supervision who will be served by the program.
(B) The method by which each parolee or offender subject to postrelease supervision who is eligible for the program shall be referred to the program.
(C) The method by which each parolee or offender subject to postrelease supervision is to be individually assessed as to his or her treatment and rehabilitative needs and the level of community and reentry court monitoring required by the program.
(D) The criteria for continued participation in, and successful completion of, the program, as well as the criteria for termination from the program and referral to the revocation process pursuant to Section 3000.08 for parolees and Section 3454 for offenders subject to postrelease supervision.
(E) A description of how the program shall be administered effectively.
(F) An established method by which to report outcome measures for program participants.
(G) The development of a program team, as well as a plan for ongoing training in utilizing the drug court and collaborative court nonadversarial model.
(e) (1) Subject to funding made available for this purpose, the secretary shall enter into a memorandum of understanding with the Administrative Office of the Courts for the purpose of the establishment and operation of reentry court programs. Only courts with existing drug and mental health courts or courts that otherwise demonstrate leadership and a commitment to conduct the reentry court authorized by this section may participate in this program. These reentry court programs shall, with the assistance of the participant's parole or postrelease supervision agent, direct the treatment and supervision of participants who would benefit from community drug treatment or mental health treatment. The purpose of reentry court programs created pursuant to this subdivision is to promote public safety, hold offenders accountable, and reduce recidivism. The program shall include key components of drug and collaborative courts using a highly structured model, including close supervision and monitoring, dedicated calendars, nonadversarial proceedings, frequent drug and alcohol testing, and close collaboration between the respective entities involved to improve the participant's likelihood of success on parole or postrelease supervision.
(2) The Judicial Council, in collaboration with the department, shall design and perform an evaluation of the program that will assess its effectiveness in reducing recidivism among parolees and offenders subject to postrelease supervision and reducing revocations.
(3) The Judicial Council, in collaboration with the department, shall submit a final report of the findings from its evaluation of the program to the Legislature and the Governor no later than 3 years after the establishment of a reentry court pursuant to this section.
(Amended by Stats. 2011, Ch. 39, Sec. 43. (AB 117) Effective June 30, 2011. Operative October 1, 2011, pursuant to Secs. 68 and 69 of Ch. 39.)

ARTICLE 2.4. Case Management Reentry Pilot Program [3016- 3016.]
(Article 2.4 added by Stats. 2014, Ch. 26, Sec. 27.)
3016.
(a) The Secretary of the Department of Corrections and Rehabilitation shall establish the Case Management Reentry Pilot Program for offenders under the jurisdiction of the department who have been sentenced to a term of imprisonment under Section 1170 and are likely to benefit from a case management reentry strategy designed to address homelessness, joblessness, mental disorders, and developmental disabilities among offenders transitioning from prison into the community. The purpose of the pilot program is to implement promising and evidence-based practices and strategies that promote improved public safety outcomes for offenders reentering society after serving a term in state prison and while released to parole.
(b) The program shall be initiated in at least three counties over three years, supported by department employees focusing primarily on case management services for eligible parolees selected for the pilot program. Department employees shall be experienced or trained to work as social workers with a parole population. Selection of a parolee for participation in the pilot program does not guarantee the availability of services.
(c) Case management social workers shall assist offenders on parole who are assigned to the program in managing basic needs, including housing, job training and placement, medical and mental health care, and any additional programming or responsibilities attendant to the terms of the offender's reentry requirements. Case management social workers also shall work closely with offenders to prepare, monitor, revise, and fulfill individualized offender reentry plans consistent with this section during the term of the program.
(d) Individualized offender reentry plans shall focus on connecting offenders to services for which the offender is eligible under existing federal, state, and local rules.
(e) Case management services shall be prioritized for offenders identified as potentially benefiting from assistance with the following:
(1) Food, including the immediate need and long-term planning for obtaining food.
(2) Clothing, including the immediate need to obtain appropriate clothing.
(3) Shelter, including obtaining housing consistent with the goals of the most independent, least restrictive and potentially durable housing in the local community and that are feasible for the circumstances of each reentering offender.
(4) Benefits, including, but not limited to, the California Work Opportunity and Responsibility to Kids program, general assistance, benefits administered by the federal Social Security Administration, Medi-Cal, and veterans benefits.
(5) Health services, including assisting parolee clients with accessing community mental health, medical, and dental treatment.
(6) Substance abuse services, including assisting parolee clients with obtaining community substance abuse treatment or related 12-step program information and locations.
(7) Income, including developing and implementing a feasible plan to obtain an income and employment reflecting the highest level of work appropriate for a reentering offender's abilities and experience.
(8) Identification cards, including assisting reentering offenders with obtaining state identification cards.
(9) Life skills, including assisting with the development of skills concerning money management, job interviewing, resume writing, and activities of daily living.
(10) Activities, including working with reentering offenders in choosing and engaging in suitable and productive activities.

(11) Support systems, including working with reentering offenders on developing a support system, which may consist of prosocial friends, family, and community groups and activities, such as religious activities, recovery groups, and other social events.
(12) Academic and vocational programs, including assisting reentering offenders in developing and implementing a realistic plan to achieve an academic education, or vocational training, or both.
(13) Discharge planning, including developing postparole plans to sustain parolees' achievements and goals to ensure long-term community success.
(f) The department shall contract for an evaluation of the pilot program that will assess its effectiveness in reducing recidivism among offenders transitioning from prison into the community.
(g) The department shall submit a final report of the findings from its evaluation of the pilot program to the Legislature and the Governor no later than July 31, 2017.
(h) Implementation of this article is contingent on the availability of funds and the pilot program may be limited in scope or duration based on the availability of funds.
(Amended by Stats. 2016, Ch. 86, Sec. 237. (SB 1171) Effective January 1, 2017.)

ARTICLE 2.5. Interdisciplinary Assessment of Inmates [3020 - 3021]

(Article 2.5 added by Stats. 2007, Ch. 7, Sec. 11.)

3020.
The Department of Corrections and Rehabilitation shall conduct assessments of all inmates that include, but are not limited to, data regarding the inmate's history of substance abuse, medical and mental health, education, family background, criminal activity, service in the United States military, and social functioning. The assessments shall be used to place the inmate in programs that will aid in his or her reentry to society and that will most likely reduce the inmate's chances of reoffending.
(Amended by Stats. 2014, Ch. 184, Sec. 1. (AB 2357) Effective January 1, 2015.)

3021.
A credentialed teacher, vice principal, or principal shall provide input relating to the academic or vocational education program placement of an inmate pursuant to Section 3375 of Title 15 of the California Code of Regulations, including, but not limited to, interviewing the inmate, verifying the inmate's education records and test scores, or being present at meetings relating to the academic or vocational education program placement.
(Added by Stats. 2012, Ch. 761, Sec. 1. (SB 1121) Effective January 1, 2013.)

ARTICLE 3. Paroles [3040 - 3073.1]

(Article 3 added by Stats. 1941, Ch. 106.)

3040.
The Board of Prison Terms shall have the power to allow prisoners imprisoned in the state prisons pursuant to subdivision (b) of Section 1168 to go upon parole outside the prison walls and enclosures. The board may parole prisoners in the state prisons to camps for paroled prisoners established under Section 2792.
(Amended by Stats. 1979, Ch. 255.)

3041.
(a) (1) In the case of any inmate sentenced pursuant to any law, other than Chapter 4.5 (commencing with Section 1170) of Title 7 of Part 2, the Board of Parole Hearings shall meet with each inmate during the sixth year before the inmate's minimum eligible parole date for the purposes of reviewing and documenting the inmate's activities and conduct pertinent to parole eligibility. During this consultation, the board shall provide the inmate information about the parole hearing process, legal factors relevant to his or her suitability or unsuitability for parole, and individualized recommendations for the inmate regarding his or her work assignments, rehabilitative programs, and institutional behavior. Within 30 days following the consultation, the board shall issue its positive and negative findings and recommendations to the inmate in writing.
(2) One year before the inmate's minimum eligible parole date a panel of two or more commissioners or deputy commissioners shall again meet with the inmate and shall normally grant parole as provided in Section 3041.5. No more than one member of the panel shall be a deputy commissioner.
(3) In the event of a tie vote, the matter shall be referred for an en banc review of the record that was before the panel that rendered the tie vote. Upon en banc review, the board shall vote to either grant or deny parole and render a statement of decision. The en banc review shall be conducted pursuant to subdivision (e).
(4) Upon a grant of parole, the inmate shall be released subject to all applicable review periods. However, an inmate shall not be released before reaching his or her minimum eligible parole date as set pursuant to Section 3046 unless the inmate is eligible for earlier release pursuant to his or her youth offender parole eligibility date or elderly parole eligible date.
(5) At least one commissioner of the panel shall have been present at the last preceding meeting, unless it is not feasible to do so or where the last preceding meeting was the initial meeting. Any person on the hearing panel may request review of any decision regarding parole for an en banc hearing by the board. In case of a review, a majority vote in favor of parole by the board members participating in an en banc review is required to grant parole to any inmate.
(b) (1) The panel or the board, sitting en banc, shall grant parole to an inmate unless it determines that the gravity of the current convicted offense or offenses, or the timing and gravity of current or past convicted offense or offenses, is such that consideration of the public safety requires a more lengthy period of incarceration for this individual.
(2) After July 30, 2001, any decision of the parole panel finding an inmate suitable for parole shall become final within 120 days of the date of the hearing. During that period, the board may review the panel's decision. The panel's decision shall become final pursuant to this subdivision unless the board finds that the panel made an error of law, or that the panel's decision was based on an error of fact, or that new information should be presented to the board, any of which when corrected or considered by the board has a substantial likelihood of resulting in a substantially different decision upon a rehearing. In making this determination, the board shall consult with the commissioners who conducted the parole consideration hearing.
(3) A decision of a panel shall not be disapproved and referred for rehearing except by a majority vote of the board, sitting en banc, following a public meeting.
(c) For the purpose of reviewing the suitability for parole of those inmates eligible for parole under prior law at a date earlier than that calculated under Section 1170.2, the board shall appoint panels of at least two persons to meet annually with each inmate until the time the person is released pursuant to proceedings or reaches the expiration of his or her term as calculated under Section 1170.2.
(d) It is the intent of the Legislature that, during times when there is no backlog of inmates awaiting parole hearings, life parole consideration hearings, or life rescission hearings, hearings will be conducted by a panel of three or more members, the majority of whom shall be commissioners. The board shall report monthly on the number of cases where an inmate has not received a completed initial or subsequent parole consideration hearing within 30 days of the hearing date required by subdivision (a) of Section 3041.5 or paragraph (2) of subdivision (b) of Section 3041.5, unless the inmate has waived the right to those timeframes. That report shall be considered the backlog of cases for purposes of this section, and shall include information on the progress toward eliminating the backlog, and on the number of inmates who have waived their right to the above timeframes. The report shall be made public at a regularly scheduled meeting of the board and a written report shall be made available to the public and transmitted to the Legislature quarterly.
(e) For purposes of this section, an en banc review by the board means a review conducted by a majority of commissioners holding office on the date the matter is heard by the board. An en banc review shall be conducted in compliance with the following:
(1) The commissioners conducting the review shall consider the entire record of the hearing that resulted in the tie vote.
(2) The review shall be limited to the record of the hearing. The record shall consist of the transcript or audiotape of the hearing, written or electronically recorded statements actually considered by the panel that produced the tie vote, and any other material actually considered by the panel. New evidence or comments shall not be considered in the en banc proceeding.
(3) The board shall separately state reasons for its decision to grant or deny parole.
(4) A commissioner who was involved in the tie vote shall be recused from consideration of the matter in the en banc review.
(Amended by Stats. 2017, Ch. 676, Sec. 1. (AB 1448) Effective January 1, 2018.)

3041.1.
(a) Any time before an inmate's release, the Governor may request review of a decision by a parole authority concerning the grant or denial of parole to any inmate in a state prison. The Governor shall state the reason or reasons for the request, and whether the request is based on a public safety concern, a concern that the gravity of current or past convicted offenses may have been given inadequate consideration, or on other factors.
(b) If a request has been made, the request shall be reviewed by a majority of commissioners specifically appointed to hear adult parole matters and who are holding office at the time. In case of a review, a vote in favor of parole by a majority of the commissioners reviewing the request shall be required to grant parole to any inmate. In carrying out any review, the board shall comply with this chapter.
(Amended by Stats. 2015, Ch. 470, Sec. 2. (SB 230) Effective January 1, 2016.)

3041.2.
(a) During the 30 days following the granting, denial, revocation, or suspension by the board of the parole of an inmate sentenced to an indeterminate prison term based upon a conviction of murder, the Governor, when reviewing the board's decision pursuant to subdivision (b) of Section 8 of Article V of the Constitution, shall review materials provided by the board.
(b) If the Governor decides to reverse or modify a parole decision of the board pursuant to subdivision (b) of Section 8 of Article V of the Constitution, he or she shall send a written statement to the inmate specifying the reasons for his or her decision.
(Amended by Stats. 2015, Ch. 470, Sec. 3. (SB 230) Effective January 1, 2016.)

3041.5.
(a) At all hearings for the purpose of reviewing an inmate's parole suitability, or the setting, postponing, or rescinding of parole, with the exception of en banc review of tie votes, the following shall apply:
(1) At least 10 days before any hearing by the Board of Parole Hearings, the inmate shall be permitted to review the file which will be examined by the board and shall have the opportunity to enter a written response to any material contained in the file.
(2) The inmate shall be permitted to be present, to ask and answer questions, and to speak on his or her own behalf. Neither the inmate nor the attorney for the inmate shall be entitled to ask questions of any person appearing at the hearing pursuant to subdivision (b) of Section 3043.
(3) Unless legal counsel is required by some other law, a person designated by the Department of Corrections and Rehabilitation shall be present to ensure that all facts relevant to the decision be presented, including, if necessary, contradictory assertions as to matters of fact that have not been resolved by departmental or other procedures.
(4) The inmate and any person described in subdivision (b) of Section 3043 shall be permitted to request and receive a stenographic record of all proceedings.
(5) If the hearing is for the purpose of postponing or rescinding parole, the inmate shall have the rights set forth in paragraphs (3) and (4) of subdivision (c) of Section 2932.
(6) The board shall set a date to reconsider whether an inmate should be released on parole that ensures a meaningful consideration of whether the inmate is suitable for release on parole.
(b) (1) Within 10 days following any decision granting parole, the board shall send the inmate a written statement setting forth the reason or reasons for granting parole, the conditions he or she must meet in order to be released, and the consequences of failure to meet those conditions.
(2) Within 20 days following any decision denying parole, the board shall send the inmate a written statement setting forth the reason or reasons for denying parole, and suggest activities in which he or she might participate that will benefit him or her while he or she is incarcerated.
(3) The board shall schedule the next hearing, after considering the views and interests of the victim, as follows:
(A) Fifteen years after any hearing at which parole is denied, unless the board finds by clear and convincing evidence that the criteria relevant to the decision denying parole are such that consideration of the public and victim's safety does not require a more lengthy period of incarceration for the inmate than 10 additional years.
(B) Ten years after any hearing at which parole is denied, unless the board finds by clear and convincing evidence that the criteria relevant to the decision denying parole are such that consideration of the public and victim's safety does not require a more lengthy period of incarceration for the inmate than seven additional years.
(C) Three years, five years, or seven years after any hearing at which parole is denied, because the criteria relevant to the decision denying parole are such that consideration of the public and victim's safety requires a more lengthy period of incarceration for the inmate, but does not require a more lengthy period of incarceration for the inmate than seven additional years.
(4) The board may in its discretion, after considering the views and interests of the victim, advance a hearing set pursuant to paragraph (3) to an earlier date, when a change in circumstances or new information establishes a reasonable likelihood that consideration of the public and victim's safety does not require the additional period of incarceration of the inmate provided in paragraph (3).
(5) Within 10 days of any board action resulting in the rescinding of parole, the board shall send the inmate a written statement setting forth the reason or reasons for that action, and shall schedule the inmate's next hearing in accordance with paragraph (3).
(c) The board shall conduct a parole hearing pursuant to this section as a de novo hearing. Findings made and conclusions reached in a prior parole hearing shall be considered in but shall not be deemed to be binding upon subsequent parole hearings for an inmate, but shall be subject to reconsideration based upon changed facts and circumstances. When conducting a hearing, the board shall admit the prior recorded or memorialized testimony or statement of a victim or witness, upon request of the victim or if the victim or witness has died or become unavailable. At each hearing the board shall determine the appropriate action to be taken based on the criteria set forth in paragraph (1) of subdivision (b) of Section 3041.
(d) (1) An inmate may request that the board exercise its discretion to advance a hearing set pursuant to paragraph (3) of subdivision (b) to an earlier date, by submitting a written request to the board, with notice, upon request, and a copy to the victim which shall set forth the change in circumstances or new information that establishes a reasonable likelihood that consideration of the public safety does not require the additional period of incarceration of the inmate.
(2) The board shall have sole jurisdiction, after considering the views and interests of the victim to determine whether to grant or deny a written request made pursuant to paragraph (1), and its decision shall be subject to review by a court or magistrate only for a manifest abuse of discretion by the board. The board shall have the power to summarily deny a request that does not comply with this subdivision or that does not set forth a change in circumstances or new information as required in paragraph (1) that in

the judgment of the board is sufficient to justify the action described in paragraph (4) of subdivision (b).

(3) An inmate may make only one written request as provided in paragraph (1) during each three-year period. Following either a summary denial of a request made pursuant to paragraph (1), or the decision of the board after a hearing described in subdivision (a) to deny parole, the inmate shall not be entitled to submit another request for a hearing pursuant to subdivision (a) until a three-year period of time has elapsed from the summary denial or decision of the board.

(Amended by Stats. 2015, Ch. 470, Sec. 4. (SB 230) Effective January 1, 2016. Note: This section was amended on Nov. 4, 2008, by initiative Prop. 9.)

3041.7.

At any hearing for the purpose of setting, postponing, or rescinding a parole release date of an inmate under a life sentence, the inmate shall be entitled to be represented by counsel and Section 3041.5 shall apply. The Board of Parole Hearings shall provide by rule for the invitation of the prosecutor of the county from which the inmate was committed, or his or her representative, to represent the interests of the people at the hearing. The Board of Parole Hearings shall notify the prosecutor and the Attorney General at least 30 days before the date of the hearing.

Notwithstanding Section 12550 of the Government Code, the prosecutor of the county from which the inmate was committed, or his or her representative, who shall not be the Attorney General, except in cases in which the Attorney General prosecuted the case at the trial level, shall be the sole representative of the interests of the people.

(Amended by Stats. 2015, Ch. 470, Sec. 5. (SB 230) Effective January 1, 2016.)

3042.

(a) (1) At least 30 days before the Board of Parole Hearings meets to review or consider the parole suitability of any inmate sentenced to a life sentence, the board shall send written notice thereof to each of the following persons: the judge of the superior court before whom the inmate was tried and convicted, the attorney who represented the defendant at trial, the district attorney of the county in which the offense was committed, the law enforcement agency that investigated the case, and if the inmate was convicted of the murder of a peace officer, the law enforcement agency that employed the peace officer at the time of the murder.

(2) If the inmate was convicted of the murder of a firefighter, the board or the Department of Corrections and Rehabilitation shall also send the written notice described in paragraph (1) to the fire department that employed the firefighter at the time of the murder, if that fire department registers with the board to receive that notification and provides the appropriate contact information.

(b) The Board of Parole Hearings shall record all of those hearings and transcribe recordings of those hearings within 30 days of any hearing. Those transcripts, including the transcripts of all prior hearings, shall be filed and maintained in the office of the Board of Parole Hearings and shall be made available to the public no later than 30 days from the date of the hearing. An inmate shall not be released on parole until 60 days from the date of the hearing have elapsed.

(c) At any hearing, the presiding hearing officer shall state his or her findings and supporting reasons on the record.

(d) Any statements, recommendations, or other materials considered shall be incorporated into the transcript of the hearing, unless the material is confidential in order to preserve institutional security and the security of others who might be endangered by disclosure.

(e) (1) The written notice to the judge of the superior court before whom the inmate was tried and convicted shall be sent by United States mail.

(2) The judge receiving this written notice may forward to the board any unprivileged information from the trial or sentencing proceeding regarding the inmate, witnesses, or victims, or other relevant persons, or any other information, that is pertinent to the question of whether the board should grant parole or under what conditions parole should be granted. The judge may also, in his or her discretion, include information given to him or her by victims, witnesses, or other persons that bear on the question of the inmate's suitability for parole.

(3) The board shall review and consider all information received from the judge or any other person and shall consider adjusting the conditions of parole to reflect the comments or concerns raised by this information, as appropriate.

(f) This section does not limit the type or content of information the judge or any other person may forward to the board for consideration under any other law.

(g) Any person who receives notice under subdivision (a) who is authorized to forward information for consideration in a parole suitability hearing for a person sentenced to a life sentence under this section, may forward that information either by facsimile or electronic mail. The Department of Corrections and Rehabilitation shall establish procedures for receiving the information by facsimile or electronic mail pursuant to this subdivision.

(Amended (as amended by Stats. 2015, Ch. 470, Sec. 6) by Stats. 2016, Ch. 161, Sec. 1. (AB 898) Effective January 1, 2017.)

3043.

(a) (1) Upon request to the Department of Corrections and Rehabilitation and verification of the identity of the requester, notice of any hearing to review or consider the parole suitability for any inmate in a state prison shall be given by telephone, certified mail, regular mail, or electronic mail, using the method of communication selected by the requesting party, if that method is available, by the Board of Parole Hearings at least 90 days before the hearing to any victim of any crime committed by the inmate, or to the next of kin of the victim if the victim has died, to include the commitment crimes, determinate term commitment crimes for which the inmate has been paroled, and any other felony crimes or crimes against the person for which the inmate has been convicted. The requesting party shall keep the board apprised of his or her current contact information in order to receive the notice.

(2) No later than 30 days before the date selected for the hearing, any person, other than the victim, entitled to attend the hearing shall inform the board of his or her intention to attend the hearing and the name and identifying information of any other person entitled to attend the hearing who will accompany him or her.

(3) No later than 14 days before the date selected for the hearing, the board shall notify every person entitled to attend the hearing confirming the date, time, and place of the hearing.

(b) (1) The victim, next of kin, members of the victim's family, and two representatives designated as provided in paragraph (2) of this subdivision have the right to appear, personally or by counsel, at the hearing and to adequately and reasonably express his, her, or their views concerning the inmate and the case, including, but not limited to the commitment crimes, determinate term commitment crimes for which the inmate has been paroled, any other felony crimes or crimes against the person for which the inmate has been convicted, the effect of the enumerated crimes on the victim and the family of the victim, the person responsible for these enumerated crimes, and the suitability of the inmate for parole.

(2) Any statement provided by a representative designated by the victim or next of kin may cover any subject about which the victim or next of kin has the right to be heard including any recommendation regarding the granting of parole. The representatives shall be designated by the victim or, in the event that the victim is deceased or incapacitated, by the next of kin. They shall be designated in writing for the particular hearing before the hearing.

(c) A representative designated by the victim or the victim's next of kin for purposes of this section may be any adult person selected by the victim or the family of the victim. The board shall permit a representative designated by the victim or the victim's next of kin to attend a particular hearing, to provide testimony at a hearing, and to submit a

statement to be included in the hearing as provided in Section 3043.2, even though the victim, next of kin, or a member of the victim's immediate family is present at the hearing, and even though the victim, next of kin, or a member of the victim's immediate family has submitted a statement as described in Section 3043.2.

(d) The board, in deciding whether to release the person on parole, shall consider the entire and uninterrupted statements of the victim or victims, next of kin, immediate family members of the victim, and the designated representatives of the victim or next of kin, if applicable, made pursuant to this section and shall include in its report a statement whether the person would pose a threat to public safety if released on parole.

(e) In those cases where there are more than two immediate family members of the victim who wish to attend any hearing covered in this section, the board shall allow attendance of additional immediate family members to include the following: spouse, children, parents, siblings, grandchildren, and grandparents.

(Amended by Stats. 2015, Ch. 470, Sec. 7. (SB 230) Effective January 1, 2016. Note: This section was added on June 8, 1982, by initiative Prop. 8, and amended on Nov. 4, 2008, by initiative Prop. 9.)

3043.1.

Notwithstanding any other law, a victim, his or her next of kin, or any immediate family member of the victim who appears at any hearing to review or consider the parole suitability of any inmate pursuant to Section 3043 shall be entitled to the attendance of one person of his or her own choosing at the hearing for support. The person so chosen shall not participate in the hearing nor make comments while in attendance.

(Amended by Stats. 2015, Ch. 470, Sec. 8. (SB 230) Effective January 1, 2016.)

3043.2.

(a) (1) In lieu of personal appearance at any hearing to review the parole suitability, the Board of Parole Hearings shall permit the victim, his or her next of kin, immediate family members, or two representatives designated for a particular hearing by the victim or next of kin in writing before the hearing to file with the board a written, audiotaped, or videotaped statement, or statement stored on a CD-ROM, DVD, or any other recording medium accepted by a court pursuant to Section 1191.15 or by the board, expressing his or her views concerning the crime and the person responsible. The statement may be personal messages from the person to the board made at any time or may be a statement made pursuant to Section 1191.16, or a combination of both, except that any statement provided by a representative designated by the victim or next of kin shall be limited to comments concerning the effect of the crime on the victim.

(2) A representative designated by the victim or the victim's next of kin for purposes of this section must be either a family or household member of the victim.

(3) The board shall consider any statement filed prior to reaching a decision, and shall include in its report a statement of whether the person would pose a threat to public safety if released on parole.

(b) Whenever an audio or video statement or a statement stored on a CD-ROM, DVD, or other medium is filed with the board, a written transcript of the statement shall also be provided by the person filing the statement.

(c) Nothing in this section shall be construed to prohibit the prosecutor from representing to the board the views of the victim, his or her immediate family members, or next of kin.

(d) In the event the board permits an audio or video statement or statement stored on a CD-ROM, DVD, or other medium to be filed, the board shall not be responsible for providing any equipment or resources needed to assist the victim in preparing the statement.

(Amended by Stats. 2015, Ch. 470, Sec. 9. (SB 230) Effective January 1, 2016.)

3043.25.

Any victim, next of kin, members of the victim's immediate family, or representatives designated for a particular hearing by the victim or next of kin in writing before the hearing who have the right to appear at a hearing to review parole suitability, either personally as provided in Section 3043, or by a written, audiotaped, or videotaped statement as provided in Section 3043.2, and any prosecutor who has the right to appear pursuant to Section 3041.7, shall also have the right to appear by means of videoconferencing, if videoconferencing is available at the hearing site. For the purposes of this section, "videoconferencing" means the live transmission of audio and video signals by any means from one physical location to another.

(Amended by Stats. 2015, Ch. 470, Sec. 10. (SB 230) Effective January 1, 2016.)

3043.3.

As used in Sections 3043, 3043.1, 3043.2, and 3043.25, the term "immediate family" shall include the victim's spouse, parent, grandparent, brother, sister, and children or grandchildren who are related by blood, marriage, or adoption. As used in Sections 3043 and 3043.2, the term "household member of the victim" means a person who lives, or was living at the time of the crime, in the victim's household, and who has, or for a deceased victim had at the time of the crime, an intimate or close relationship with the victim.

(Amended by Stats. 2004, Ch. 289, Sec. 4. Effective January 1, 2005.)

3043.5.

(a) This section shall be known as the "Condit-Nolan Public Participation in Parole Act of 1984."

(b) Any person interested in the grant or denial of parole to any prisoner in a state prison shall have the right to submit a statement of views in support of or in opposition to the granting of parole. The board, in deciding whether to release the person on parole, shall review all information received from the public to insure that the gravity and timing of all current or past convicted offenses have been given adequate consideration and to insure that the safety of the public has been adequately considered. Upon completion of its review, the board shall include in its report a statement that it has reviewed all information received from the public and its conclusion as to whether the person would pose a threat to the public safety if released on parole.

(Added by Stats. 1984, Ch. 805, Sec. 2.)

3043.6.

Any person authorized to appear at a parole hearing pursuant to Section 3043, or a prosecutor authorized to represent the views of the victim, his or her immediate family, or next of kin, pursuant to Section 3043.2, shall have the right to speak last before the board in regard to those persons appearing and speaking before the board at a parole hearing. Nothing in this section shall prohibit the person presiding at the hearing from taking any steps he or she deems appropriate to ensure that only accurate and relevant statements are considered in determining parole suitability as provided in law, including, but not limited to, the rebuttal of inaccurate statements made by any party.

(Added by Stats. 2004, Ch. 1, Sec. 4. Effective January 21, 2004.)

3044.

(a) Notwithstanding any other law, the Board of Parole Hearings or its successor in interest shall be the state's parole authority and shall be responsible for protecting victims' rights in the parole process. Accordingly, to protect a victim from harassment and abuse during the parole process, no person paroled from a California correctional facility following incarceration for an offense committed on or after the effective date of this act shall, in the event his or her parole is revoked, be entitled to procedural rights other than the following:

(1) A parolee shall be entitled to a probable cause hearing no later than 15 days following his or her arrest for violation of parole.

(2) A parolee shall be entitled to an evidentiary revocation hearing no later than 45 days following his or her arrest for violation of parole.

(3) A parolee shall, upon request, be entitled to counsel at state expense only if, considering the request on a case-by-case basis, the board or its hearing officers determine:

(A) The parolee is indigent; and

(B) Considering the complexity of the charges, the defense, or because the parolee's mental or educational capacity, he or she appears incapable of speaking effectively in his or her own defense.

(4) In the event the parolee's request for counsel, which shall be considered on a case-by-case basis, is denied, the grounds for denial shall be stated succinctly in the record.

(5) Parole revocation determinations shall be based upon a preponderance of evidence admitted at hearings including documentary evidence, direct testimony, or hearsay evidence offered by parole agents, peace officers, or a victim.

(6) Admission of the recorded or hearsay statement of a victim or percipient witness shall not be construed to create a right to confront the witness at the hearing.

(b) The board is entrusted with the safety of victims and the public and shall make its determination fairly, independently, and without bias and shall not be influenced by or weigh the state cost or burden associated with just decisions. The board must accordingly enjoy sufficient autonomy to conduct unbiased hearings, and maintain an independent legal and administrative staff. The board shall report to the Governor.

(Added November 4, 2008, by initiative Proposition 9, Sec. 5.3. Note: Prop. 9 is titled the Victims' Bill of Rights Act of 2008: Marsy's Law.)

3045.

Any sentence based on conviction of crime of which the person was previously pardoned on the express ground that he was not guilty shall not be counted as a previous conviction.

(Amended by Stats. 1951, Ch. 671.)

3046.

(a) An inmate imprisoned under a life sentence shall not be paroled until he or she has served the greater of the following:

(1) A term of at least seven calendar years.

(2) A term as established pursuant to any other law that establishes a minimum term or minimum period of confinement under a life sentence before eligibility for parole.

(b) If two or more life sentences are ordered to run consecutively to each other pursuant to Section 669, an inmate so imprisoned shall not be paroled until he or she has served the term specified in subdivision (a) on each of the life sentences that are ordered to run consecutively.

(c) Notwithstanding subdivisions (a) and (b), an inmate found suitable for parole pursuant to a youth offender parole hearing as described in Section 3051 or an elderly parole hearing as described in Section 3055 shall be paroled regardless of the manner in which the board set release dates pursuant to subdivision (a) of Section 3041, subject to subdivision (b) of Section 3041 and Sections 3041.1 and 3041.2, as applicable.

(d) The Board of Parole Hearings shall, in considering a parole for an inmate, consider all statements and recommendations which may have been submitted by the judge, district attorney, and sheriff, pursuant to Section 1203.01, or in response to notices given under Section 3042, and recommendations of other persons interested in the granting or denying of parole. The board shall enter on its order granting or denying parole to these inmates, the fact that the statements and recommendations have been considered by it.

(Amended by Stats. 2017, Ch. 676, Sec. 2. (AB 1448) Effective January 1, 2018.)

3049.

In all other cases not heretofore provided for, no prisoner sentenced prior to July 1, 1977 may be paroled until he has served the minimum term of imprisonment provided by law for the offense of which he was convicted, except that in cases where the prisoner was serving a sentence on December 31, 1947, and in which the minimum term of imprisonment is more than one year, he may be paroled at any time after the expiration of one-half of the minimum term, with benefit of credits, but in no case shall he be paroled until he has served one calendar year; provided, that any prisoner, received on or after January 1, 1948, at any state prison or institution under the jurisdiction of the Director of Corrections, whose minimum term of imprisonment is more than one year, may be paroled at any time after the expiration of one-third of the minimum term. In all other cases he may be paroled at any time after he has served the minimum term prescribed by law.

(Amended by Stats. 1976, Ch. 1139.)

3049.5.

Notwithstanding the provisions of Section 3049, any prisoner selected for inclusion in a specific research program approved by the Board of Corrections may be paroled upon completion of the diagnostic study provided for in Section 5079. The number of prisoners released in any year under this provision shall not exceed 5 percent of the total number of all prisoners released in the preceding year.

This section shall not apply to a prisoner who, while committing the offense for which he has been imprisoned, physically attacked any person by any means. A threat of attack is not a physical attack for the purposes of this section unless such threat was accompanied by an attempt to inflict physical harm upon some person.

(Amended by Stats. 2012, Ch. 728, Sec. 125. (SB 71) Effective January 1, 2013.)

3050.

(a) Notwithstanding any other provision of law, any inmate under the custody of the Department of Corrections and Rehabilitation who is not currently serving and has not served a prior indeterminate sentence or a sentence for a violent felony, a serious felony, or a crime that requires him or her to register as a sex offender pursuant to Section 290, who has successfully completed an in prison drug treatment program, upon release from state prison, shall, whenever possible, be entered into a 150-day residential aftercare drug treatment program sanctioned by the department.

(b) As a condition of parole, if the inmate successfully completes 150 days of residential aftercare treatment, as determined by the Department of Corrections and Rehabilitation and the aftercare provider, the parolee shall be discharged from parole supervision at that time.

(Amended by Stats. 2012, Ch. 728, Sec. 126. (SB 71) Effective January 1, 2013.)

3051.

(a) (1) A youth offender parole hearing is a hearing by the Board of Parole Hearings for the purpose of reviewing the parole suitability of any prisoner who was 25 years of age or younger, or was under 18 years of age as specified in paragraph (4) of subdivision (b), at the time of his or her controlling offense.

(2) For the purposes of this section, the following definitions shall apply:

(A) "Incarceration" means detention in a city or county jail, a local juvenile facility, a mental health facility, a Division of Juvenile Justice facility, or a Department of Corrections and Rehabilitation facility.

(B) "Controlling offense" means the offense or enhancement for which any sentencing court imposed the longest term of imprisonment.

(b) (1) A person who was convicted of a controlling offense that was committed when the person was 25 years of age or younger and for which the sentence is a determinate sentence shall be eligible for release on parole at a youth offender parole hearing by the board during his or her 15th year of incarceration, unless previously released pursuant to other statutory provisions.

(2) A person who was convicted of a controlling offense that was committed when the person was 25 years of age or younger and for which the sentence is a life term of less than 25 years to life shall be eligible for release on parole by the board during his or her 20th year of incarceration at a youth offender parole hearing, unless previously released or entitled to an earlier parole consideration hearing pursuant to other statutory provisions.

(3) A person who was convicted of a controlling offense that was committed when the person was 25 years of age or younger and for which the sentence is a life term of 25 years to life shall be eligible for release on parole by the board during his or her 25th year of incarceration at a youth offender parole hearing, unless previously released or entitled to an earlier parole consideration hearing pursuant to other statutory provisions.

(4) A person who was convicted of a controlling offense that was committed before the person had attained 18 years of age and for which the sentence is life without the possibility of parole shall be eligible for release on parole by the board during his or her 25th year of incarceration at a youth offender parole hearing, unless previously released or entitled to an earlier parole consideration hearing pursuant to other statutory provisions.

(c) An individual subject to this section shall meet with the board pursuant to subdivision (a) of Section 3041.

(d) The board shall conduct a youth offender parole hearing to consider release. At the youth offender parole hearing, the board shall release the individual on parole as provided in Section 3041, except that the board shall act in accordance with subdivision (c) of Section 4801.

(e) The youth offender parole hearing to consider release shall provide for a meaningful opportunity to obtain release. The board shall review and, as necessary, revise existing regulations and adopt new regulations regarding determinations of suitability made pursuant to this section, subdivision (c) of Section 4801, and other related topics, consistent with relevant case law, in order to provide that meaningful opportunity for release.

(f) (1) In assessing growth and maturity, psychological evaluations and risk assessment instruments, if used by the board, shall be administered by licensed psychologists employed by the board and shall take into consideration the diminished culpability of youth as compared to that of adults, the hallmark features of youth, and any subsequent growth and increased maturity of the individual.

(2) Family members, friends, school personnel, faith leaders, and representatives from community-based organizations with knowledge about the individual before the crime or his or her growth and maturity since the time of the crime may submit statements for review by the board.

(3) This section is not intended to alter the rights of victims at parole hearings.

(g) If parole is not granted, the board shall set the time for a subsequent youth offender parole hearing in accordance with paragraph (3) of subdivision (b) of Section 3041.5. In exercising its discretion pursuant to paragraph (4) of subdivision (b) and subdivision (d) of Section 3041.5, the board shall consider the factors in subdivision (c) of Section 4801. A subsequent youth offender parole hearing shall not be necessary if the offender is released pursuant to other statutory provisions prior to the date of the subsequent hearing.

(h) This section shall not apply to cases in which sentencing occurs pursuant to Section 1170.12, subdivisions (b) to (i), inclusive, of Section 667, or Section 667.61, or to cases in which an individual is sentenced to life in prison without the possibility of parole for a controlling offense that was committed after the person had attained 18 years of age. This section shall not apply to an individual to whom this section would otherwise apply, but who, subsequent to attaining 26 years of age, commits an additional crime for which malice aforethought is a necessary element of the crime or for which the individual is sentenced to life in prison.

(i) (1) The board shall complete all youth offender parole hearings for individuals who became entitled to have their parole suitability considered at a youth offender parole hearing prior to the effective date of the act that added paragraph (2) by July 1, 2015.

(2) (A) The board shall complete all youth offender parole hearings for individuals who were sentenced to indeterminate life terms and who become entitled to have their parole suitability considered at a youth offender parole hearing on the effective date of the act that added this paragraph by July 1, 2017.

(B) The board shall complete all youth offender parole hearings for individuals who were sentenced to determinate terms and who become entitled to have their parole suitability considered at a youth offender parole hearing on the effective date of the act that added this paragraph by July 1, 2021. The board shall, for all individuals described in this subparagraph, conduct the consultation described in subdivision (a) of Section 3041 before July 1, 2017.

(3) (A) The board shall complete all youth offender parole hearings for individuals who were sentenced to indeterminate life terms and who become entitled to have their parole suitability considered at a youth offender parole hearing on the effective date of the act that added this paragraph by January 1, 2020.

(B) The board shall complete all youth offender parole hearings for individuals who were sentenced to determinate terms and who become entitled to have their parole suitability considered at a youth offender parole hearing on the effective date of the act that added this paragraph by January 1, 2022. The board shall, for all individuals described in this subparagraph, conduct the consultation described in subdivision (a) of Section 3041 before January 1, 2019.

(4) The board shall complete, by July 1, 2020, all youth offender parole hearings for individuals who were sentenced to terms of life without the possibility of parole and who are or will be entitled to have their parole suitability considered at a youth offender parole hearing before July 1, 2020.

(Amended by Stats. 2017, Ch. 684, Sec. 1.5. (SB 394) Effective January 1, 2018.)

3051.1.

(a) Notwithstanding subdivision (i) of Section 3051, the board shall complete all youth offender parole hearings for individuals who were sentenced to indeterminate life terms and who become entitled to have their parole suitability considered at a youth offender parole hearing on the effective date of the act that added subparagraph (A) of paragraph (2) of subdivision (i) of Section 3051 by January 1, 2018.

(b) Notwithstanding subdivision (i) of Section 3051, the board shall complete all youth offender parole hearings for individuals who were sentenced to determinate terms and who become entitled to have their parole suitability considered at a youth offender parole hearing on the effective date of the act that added subparagraph (B) of paragraph (2) of subdivision (i) of Section 3051 by December 31, 2021. The board shall, for all individuals described in this subdivision, conduct the consultation described in subdivision (a) of Section 3041 before January 1, 2018.

(Added by Stats. 2015, Ch. 472, Sec. 1. (SB 519) Effective January 1, 2016.)

3052.

The Board of Parole Hearings shall have the power to establish and enforce rules and regulations under which inmates committed to state prisons may be allowed to go upon parole outside the prison buildings and enclosures when eligible for parole.

(Amended by Stats. 2015, Ch. 470, Sec. 12. (SB 230) Effective January 1, 2016.)

3053.

(a) The Board of Prison Terms upon granting any parole to any prisoner may also impose on the parole any conditions that it may deem proper.

(b) The Board of Prison Terms may impose as a condition of parole that any prisoner granted parole undergo an examination or test for tuberculosis when the board reasonably suspects that the parolee has, has had, or has been exposed to, tuberculosis in an infectious stage.

(c) For purposes of this section, an "examination or test for tuberculosis" means testing and followup examinations or treatment according to the Centers for Disease Control and American Thoracic Society recommendations in effect at the time of the initial examination.

(Amended by Stats. 1992, Ch. 1263, Sec. 1. Effective January 1, 1993.)

3053.2.

(a) Upon the request of the victim, or the victim's parent or legal guardian if the victim is a minor, the Board of Parole Hearings or the supervising parole agency shall impose the following condition on the parole of a person released from prison for an offense involving threatening, stalking, sexually abusing, harassing, or violent acts in which the victim is a person specified in Section 6211 of the Family Code:

Compliance with a protective order enjoining the parolee from threatening, stalking, sexually abusing, harassing, or taking further violent acts against the victim and, if appropriate, compliance with any or all of the following:

(1) An order prohibiting the parolee from having personal, telephonic, electronic, media, or written contact with the victim.

(2) An order prohibiting the parolee from coming within at least 100 yards of the victim or the victim's residence or workplace.

(3) An order excluding the parolee from the victim's residence.

(b) The Board of Parole Hearings or the supervising parole agency may impose the following condition on the parole of a person released from prison for an offense involving threatening, stalking, sexually abusing, harassing, or violent acts in which the victim is a person specified in Section 6211 of the Family Code:

For persons who committed the offense prior to January 1, 1997, participation in a batterer's program, as specified in this section, for the entire period of parole. For persons who committed the offense after January 1, 1997, successful completion of a batterer's program, which shall be a condition of release from parole. If no batterer's program is available, another appropriate counseling program designated by the parole agent or officer, for a period of not less than one year, with weekly sessions of a minimum of two hours of classroom time. The program director shall give periodic progress reports to the parole agent or officer at least every three months.

(c) The parole agent or officer shall refer the parolee only to a batterer's program that follows the standards outlined in Section 1203.097 and immediately following sections.

(d) The parolee shall file proof of enrollment in a batterer's program with the parole agent or officer within 30 days after the first meeting with his or her parole agent or officer, if he or she committed the offense after January 1, 1997, or within 30 days of receiving notice of this parole condition, if he or she committed the offense prior to January 1, 1997.

(e) The parole agent or officer shall conduct an initial assessment of the parolee, which information shall be provided to the batterer's program. The assessment shall include, but not be limited to, all of the following:

(1) Social, economic, and family background.

(2) Education.

(3) Vocational achievements.

(4) Criminal history, prior incidents of violence, and arrest reports.

(5) Medical history.

(6) Substance abuse history.

(7) Consultation with the probation officer.

(8) Verbal consultation with the victim, only if the victim desires to participate.

(f) Upon request of the victim, the victim shall be notified of the release of the parolee and the parolee's location and parole agent or officer. If the victim requests notification, he or she shall also be informed that attendance in any program does not guarantee that an abuser will not be violent.

(g) The parole agent or officer shall advise the parolee that the failure to enroll in a specified program, as directed, may be considered a parole violation that would result in possible further incarceration.

(h) The director of the batterer's program shall immediately report any violation of the terms of the protective order issued pursuant to paragraph (3) of subdivision (a), including any new acts of violence or failure to comply with the program requirements, to the parolee's parole agent or officer.

(i) Upon recommendation of the director of the batterer's program, a parole agent or officer may require a parolee to participate in additional sessions throughout the parole period, unless he or she finds that it is not in the interests of justice to do so. In deciding whether the parolee would benefit from more sessions, the parole agent or officer shall consider whether any of the following conditions exist:

(1) The parolee has been violence-free for a minimum of six months.

(2) The parolee has cooperated and participated in the batterer's program.

(3) The parolee demonstrates an understanding of, and practices, positive conflict resolution skills.

(4) The parolee blames, degrades, or has committed acts that dehumanize the victim or puts the victim's safety at risk, including, but not limited to, molesting, stalking, striking, attacking, threatening, sexually assaulting, or battering the victim.

(5) The parolee demonstrates an understanding that the use of coercion or violent behavior to maintain dominance is unacceptable in an intimate relationship.

(6) The parolee has made threats to harm another person in any manner.

(7) The parolee demonstrates acceptance of responsibility for the abusive behavior perpetrated against the victim.

(Amended by Stats. 2012, Ch. 43, Sec. 41. (SB 1023) Effective June 27, 2012.)

3053.4.

In the case of any person who is released from prison on parole or after serving a term of imprisonment for any felony offense committed against the person or property of another individual, private institution, or public agency because of the victim's actual or perceived race, color, ethnicity, religion, nationality, country of origin, ancestry, disability, gender, gender identity, gender expression, or sexual orientation, including, but not limited to, offenses defined in Section 422.6, 422.7, 422.75, 594.3, or 11411, the Board of Parole Hearings or the supervising parole agency, absent compelling circumstances, shall order the defendant as a condition of parole to refrain from further acts of violence, threats, stalking, or harassment of the victim, or known immediate family or domestic partner of the victim, including stay-away conditions when appropriate. In these cases, the parole authority may also order that the defendant be required as a condition of parole to complete a class or program on racial or ethnic sensitivity, or other similar training in the area of civil rights, or a one-year counseling program intended to reduce the tendency toward violent and antisocial behavior if that class, program, or training is available and was developed or authorized by the court or local agencies in cooperation with organizations serving the affected community.

(Amended by Stats. 2012, Ch. 43, Sec. 42. (SB 1023) Effective June 27, 2012.)

3053.5.

Upon granting parole to any prisoner convicted of any of the offenses enumerated in Section 290, the Board of Prison Terms shall inquire into the question whether the defendant at the time the offense was committed was intoxicated or addicted to the excessive use of alcoholic liquor or beverages at that time or immediately prior thereto, and if it is found that the person was so intoxicated or so addicted, it shall impose as a condition of parole that such prisoner shall totally abstain from the use of alcoholic liquor or beverages.

(Amended by Stats. 1979, Ch. 255.)

3053.6.

(a) Where a person committed to prison for a sex crime for which registration is required pursuant to Section 290 is to be released on parole, the department, in an appropriate case, shall make an order that the parolee not contact or communicate with the victim of the crime, or any of the victim's family members. In determining whether to make the order, the department shall consider the facts of the offense and the background of the parolee.

(b) Where a victim, or an immediate family member of a victim, requests that the parolee not contact him or her, the order shall be made. An immediate family member's request that the parolee not contact that person shall be granted even where the direct victim allows contact.

(c) Where the victim is a minor, the order that the parolee shall not contact or communicate with the victim shall be made where requested by the victim, or the parents or guardian of the victim. In the event of a dispute between the parents or guardians of a minor victim concerning whether a no-contact and no-communication order should be made, the board shall hold a hearing to resolve the dispute. The victim, or the parents or guardians, shall not be required to attend the hearing. The victim, or the parents of the victim, may submit a written statement to the board concerning the issue of whether a no-contact or no-communication order shall be made.

(d) The district attorney of the county that prosecuted the defendant for the sex crime for which the parolee was committed to prison may be available to facilitate and assist the victim, or victim's family member, in stating to the department whether or not the order that the parolee not contact or communicate with him or her shall be made.

(Added by Stats. 2006, Ch. 735, Sec. 1. Effective January 1, 2007.)

3053.8.

(a) Notwithstanding any other provision of law, when a person is released on parole after having served a term of imprisonment for any of the offenses specified in subdivision (b) in which one or more of the victims was under 14 years of age, and for which registration is required pursuant to the Sex Offender Registration Act, it shall be a condition of parole that the person may not, during his or her period of parole, enter any park where children regularly gather without the express permission of his or her parole agent.

(b) Subdivision (a) shall apply to persons released on parole after having served a term of imprisonment for an offense specified in Section 261, 262, 264.1, 269, 286, 287, 288.5, 288.7, or 289, paragraph (1) of subdivision (b) of Section 288, subdivision (c) of Section 667.51, subdivision (j), (k), or (l) of Section 667.61, Section 667.71, or former Section 288a.

(Amended by Stats. 2018, Ch. 423, Sec. 107. (SB 1494) Effective January 1, 2019.)

3054.

(a) (1) The Department of Corrections shall establish three pilot programs that provide intensive training and counseling programs for female parolees to assist in the successful reintegration of those parolees into the community upon release or discharge from prison and after completion of in-prison therapeutic community substance abuse treatment programs.

(2) The Director of Corrections shall determine the counties in which the pilot programs are established.

(b) (1) The services offered in the pilot programs may include, but shall not be limited to, drug and alcohol abuse treatment, cognitive skills development, education, life skills, job skills, victim impact awareness, anger management, family reunification, counseling, vocational training and support, residential care, and placement in affordable housing and employment opportunities.

(2) Ancillary services such as child care and reimbursement of transportation costs shall be provided to the extent necessary to permit full participation by female offenders in employment assistance, substance abuse treatment, and other program elements.

(3) The pilot programs shall include a case management component to assess the social services and other needs of participating in the social services, education, job training, and other programs most likely to result in their recovery and employment success.

(c) With respect to a female parolee who violates her parole, the Board of Prison Terms may order initial or continued participation in a program under this section, in lieu of revocation pursuant to Section 3060, provided the department approves the program participation, the parolee meets all eligibility criteria for the program, and the parole violation was nonviolent.

(d) (1) The Department of Corrections shall prepare an informational handout explaining the pilot programs created by this section.

(2) A copy of this informational handout shall be given to each female inmate eligible for any of the pilot programs and to each female parolee eligible for any of the pilot programs pursuant to subdivision (c).

(e) Subject to appropriation of funds, the department is authorized to enter into contracts, or amend existing contracts, for community residential treatment services for offenders and minor children in an offender's custody in order to carry out the goals stated in paragraph (1) of subdivision (a).

(f) (1) It is the intent of the Legislature that the programs demonstrate the cost-effectiveness of providing the enhanced services described in subdivision (b), based upon an annual evaluation of a representative sample of female parolees, in order to determine the impact of these services upon the criminal recidivism, employment, and welfare dependency of the offenders and their families.

(2) The department, with the assistance of an independent consultant with expertise in criminal justice programs, shall complete a report evaluating the cost-effectiveness of the pilot programs in regard to the effect of the programs (A) on the recidivism of participating female offenders compared with a comparable nonparticipating group of female offenders and (B) on the employment of female offenders and the welfare dependency of a female offender's family. The report shall be provided to the Governor and the Chairperson of the Joint Legislative Budget Committee and the chairpersons of the fiscal committees of both houses of the Legislature by January 1, 2002.

(Amended by Stats. 2002, Ch. 619, Sec. 1. Effective January 1, 2003.)

3055.

(a) The Elderly Parole Program is hereby established, to be administered by the Board of Parole Hearing, for purposes of reviewing the parole suitability of any inmate who is 60 years of age or older and has served a minimum of 25 years of continuous incarceration on his or her current sentence, serving either a determinate or indeterminate sentence.

(b) (1) For purposes of this code, the term "elderly parole eligible date" means the date on which an inmate who qualifies as an elderly offender is eligible for release from prison.

(2) For purposes of this section, "incarceration" means detention in a city or county jail, local juvenile facility, a mental health facility, a Division of Juvenile Justice facility, or a Department of Corrections and Rehabilitation facility.

(c) When considering the release of an inmate specified by subdivision (a) pursuant to Section 3041, the board shall give special consideration to whether age, time served, and diminished physical condition, if any, have reduced the elderly inmate's risk for future violence.

(d) When scheduling a parole suitability hearing date pursuant to subdivision (b) of Section 3041.5 or when considering a request for an advance hearing pursuant to subdivision (d) of Section 3041.5, the board shall consider whether the inmate meets or will meet the criteria specified in subdivision (a).

(e) An individual who is subject to this section shall meet with the board pursuant to subdivision (a) of Section 3041. If an inmate is found suitable for parole under the Elderly Parole Program, the board shall release the individual on parole as provided in Section 3041.

(f) If parole is not granted, the board shall set the time for a subsequent elderly parole hearing in accordance with paragraph (3) of subdivision (b) of Section 3041.5. No subsequent elderly parole hearing shall be necessary if the offender is released pursuant to other statutory provisions prior to the date of the subsequent hearing.

(g) This section shall not apply to cases in which sentencing occurs pursuant to Section 1170.12, subdivisions (b) to (i), inclusive, of Section 667, or in which an individual was sentenced to life in prison without the possibility of parole or death.

(h) This section does not apply if the person was convicted of first-degree murder if the victim was a peace officer, as defined in Section 830.1, 830.2, 830.3, 830.31, 830.32, 830.33, 830.34, 830.35, 830.36, 830.37, 830.4, 830.5, 830.6, 830.10, 830.11, or

830.12, who was killed while engaged in the performance of his or her duties, and the individual knew, or reasonably should have known, that the victim was a peace officer engaged in the performance of his or her duties, or the victim was a peace officer or a former peace officer under any of the above-enumerated sections, and was intentionally killed in retaliation for the performance of his or her official duties.
(i) This section does not alter the rights of victims at parole hearings.
(Added by Stats. 2017, Ch. 676, Sec. 3. (AB 1448) Effective January 1, 2018.)
3056.
(a) Prisoners on parole shall remain under the supervision of the department but shall not be returned to prison except as provided in subdivision (b) or as provided by subdivision (c) of Section 3000.09. A parolee awaiting a parole revocation hearing may be housed in a county jail while awaiting revocation proceedings. If a parolee is housed in a county jail, he or she shall be housed in the county in which he or she was arrested or the county in which a petition to revoke parole has been filed or, if there is no county jail in that county, in the housing facility with which that county has contracted to house jail inmates. Additionally, except as provided by subdivision (c) of Section 3000.09, upon revocation of parole, a parolee may be housed in a county jail for a maximum of 180 days per revocation. When housed in county facilities, parolees shall be under the sole legal custody and jurisdiction of local county facilities. A parolee shall remain under the sole legal custody and jurisdiction of the local county or local correctional administrator, even if placed in an alternative custody program in lieu of incarceration, including, but not limited to, work furlough and electronic home detention. When a parolee is under the legal custody and jurisdiction of a county facility awaiting parole revocation proceedings or upon revocation, he or she shall not be under the parole supervision or jurisdiction of the department. Unless otherwise serving a period of flash incarceration, whenever a parolee who is subject to this section has been arrested, with or without a warrant or the filing of a petition for revocation with the court, the court may order the release of the parolee from custody under any terms and conditions the court deems appropriate. When released from the county facility or county alternative custody program following a period of custody for revocation of parole or because no violation of parole is found, the parolee shall be returned to the parole supervision of the department for the duration of parole.
(b) Inmates paroled pursuant to Section 3000.1 may be returned to prison following the revocation of parole by the Board of Parole Hearings until July 1, 2013, and thereafter by a court pursuant to Section 3000.08.
(c) A parolee who is subject to subdivision (a), but who is under 18 years of age, may be housed in a facility of the Division of Juvenile Facilities, Department of Corrections and Rehabilitation.
(Amended by Stats. 2016, Ch. 86, Sec. 238. (SB 1171) Effective January 1, 2017.)
3057.
(a) Confinement pursuant to a revocation of parole in the absence of a new conviction and commitment to prison under other provisions of law, shall not exceed 12 months, except as provided in subdivision (c).
(b) Upon completion of confinement pursuant to parole revocation without a new commitment to prison, the inmate shall be released on parole for a period which shall not extend beyond that portion of the maximum statutory period of parole specified by Section 3000 which was unexpired at the time of each revocation.
(c) Notwithstanding the limitations in subdivision (a) and in Section 3060.5 upon confinement pursuant to a parole revocation, the parole authority may extend the confinement pursuant to parole revocation for a maximum of an additional 12 months for subsequent acts of misconduct committed by the parolee while confined pursuant to that parole revocation. Upon a finding of good cause to believe that a parolee has committed a subsequent act of misconduct and utilizing procedures governing parole revocation proceedings, the parole authority may extend the period of confinement pursuant to parole revocation as follows: (1) not more than 180 days for an act punishable as a felony, whether or not prosecution is undertaken, (2) not more than 90 days for an act punishable as a misdemeanor, whether or not prosecution is undertaken, and (3) not more than 30 days for an act defined as a serious disciplinary offense pursuant to subdivision (a) of Section 2932.
(d) (1) Except for parolees specified in paragraph (2), any revocation period imposed under subdivision (a) may be reduced in the same manner and to the same extent as a term of imprisonment may be reduced by worktime credits under Section 2933. Worktime credit must be earned and may be forfeited pursuant to the provisions of Section 2932.
Worktime credit forfeited shall not be restored.
(2) The following parolees shall not be eligible for credit under this subdivision:
(A) Parolees who are sentenced under Section 1168 with a maximum term of life imprisonment.
(B) Parolees who violated a condition of parole relating to association with specified persons, entering prohibited areas, attendance at parole outpatient clinics, or psychiatric attention.
(C) Parolees who were revoked for conduct described in, or that could be prosecuted under any of the following sections, whether or not prosecution is undertaken: Section 189, Section 191.5, subdivision (a) of Section 192, subdivision (a) of Section 192.5, Section 203, 207, 211, 215, 217.1, or 220, subdivision (b) of Section 241, Section 244, paragraph (1) or (2) of subdivision (a) of Section 245, paragraph (2) or (6) of subdivision (a) of Section 261, paragraph (1) or (4) of subdivision (a) of Section 262, Section 264.1, subdivision (c) or (d) of Section 286, subdivision (c) or (d) of Section 287 or of former Section 288a, Section 288, subdivision (a) of Section 289, 347, or 404, subdivision (a) of Section 451, Section 12022, 12022.5, 12022.53, 12022.7, 12022.8, or 25400, Chapter 2 (commencing with Section 29800) of Division 9 of Title 4 of Part 6, any provision listed in Section 16590, or Section 664 for any attempt to engage in conduct described in or that could be prosecuted under any of the above-mentioned sections.
(D) Parolees who were revoked for any reason if they had been granted parole after conviction of any of the offenses specified in subparagraph (C).
(E) Parolees who the parole authority finds at a revocation hearing to be unsuitable for reduction of the period of confinement because of the circumstances and gravity of the parole violation, or because of prior criminal history.
(e) Commencing October 1, 2011, this section shall only apply to inmates sentenced to a term of life imprisonment or parolees that on or before September 30, 2011, are pending a final adjudication of a parole revocation charge and subject to subdivision (c) of Section 3000.09.
(Amended by Stats. 2018, Ch. 423, Sec. 108. (SB 1494) Effective January 1, 2019.)
3058.
Any person who knowingly and wilfully communicates to another, either orally or in writing, any statement concerning any person then or theretofore convicted of a felony, and then on parole, and which communication is made with the purpose and intent to deprive said person so convicted of employment, or to prevent him from procuring the same, or with the purpose and intent to extort from him any money or article of value; and any person who threatens to make any said communication with the purpose and intent to extort money or any article of value from said person so convicted of a felony, is guilty of a misdemeanor.
(Added by Stats. 1941, Ch. 106.)
3058.4.
(a) All parole officers shall report to the appropriate child protective agency if a person paroled following a conviction of Section 273a, 273ab, or 273d, or any sex offense identified in statute as being perpetrated against a minor, has violated the terms or conditions of parole related specifically to restrictions on contact with the victim or the victim's family.
(b) The Department of Corrections shall annually provide to all parole officers a written summary describing the legal duties of parole officers to report information to local child protective agencies as required by Section 11166 and this section.
(Added by Stats. 1999, Ch. 957, Sec. 1. Effective January 1, 2000.)
3058.5.
The Department of Corrections shall provide within 10 days, upon request, to the chief of police of a city or the sheriff of a county, information available to the department, including actual, glossy photographs, no smaller than $3^1/_8$ x $3^1/_8$ inches in size, and, in conjunction with the Department of Justice, fingerprints, concerning persons then on parole who are or may be residing or temporarily domiciled in that city or county.
(Amended (as amended by Stats. 1983, Ch. 196, Sec. 2) by Stats. 1986, Ch. 600, Sec. 1.)
3058.6.
(a) Whenever any person confined to state prison is serving a term for the conviction of a violent felony listed in subdivision (c) of Section 667.5, the Board of Parole Hearings, with respect to inmates sentenced pursuant to subdivision (b) of Section 1168 or the Department of Corrections and Rehabilitation, with respect to inmates sentenced pursuant to Section 1170, shall notify the sheriff or chief of police, or both, and the district attorney, who has jurisdiction over the community in which the person was convicted and, in addition, the sheriff or chief of police, or both, and the district attorney, having jurisdiction over the community in which the person is scheduled to be released on parole or rereleased following a period of confinement pursuant to a parole revocation without a new commitment.
(b) (1) The notification shall be made by mail at least 60 days prior to the scheduled release date, except as provided in paragraph (3). In all cases, the notification shall include the name of the person who is scheduled to be released, whether or not the person is required to register with local law enforcement, and the community in which the person will reside. The notification shall specify the office within the Department of Corrections and Rehabilitation with the authority to make final determination and adjustments regarding parole location decisions.
(2) Notwithstanding any other provision of law, the Department of Corrections and Rehabilitation shall not restore credits nor take any administrative action resulting in an inmate being placed in a greater credit earning category that would result in notification being provided less than 60 days prior to an inmate's scheduled release date.
(3) When notification cannot be provided at least 60 days prior to release due to the unanticipated release date change of an inmate as a result of an order from the court, an action by the Board of Parole Hearings, the granting of an administrative appeal, or a finding of not guilty or dismissal of a disciplinary action, that affects the sentence of the inmate, or due to a modification of the department's decision regarding the community into which the person is scheduled to be released pursuant to paragraph (4), the department shall provide notification as soon as practicable, but in no case shall the department delay making the notification more than 24 hours from the time the final decision is made regarding where the parolee will be released.
(4) Those agencies receiving the notice referred to in this subdivision may provide written comment to the board or department regarding the impending release. Agencies that choose to provide written comments shall respond within 45 days prior to the inmate's scheduled release, unless an agency received less than 60 days' notice of the impending release, in which case the agency shall respond as soon as practicable prior to the scheduled release. Those comments shall be considered by the board or department which may, based on those comments, modify its decision regarding the community in which the person is scheduled to be released. The Department of Corrections and Rehabilitation shall respond in writing not less than 15 days prior to the scheduled release with a final determination as to whether to adjust the parole location and documenting the basis for its decision, unless the department received comments less than 45 days prior to the impending release, in which case the department shall respond as soon as practicable and prior to the scheduled release. The comments shall become a part of the inmate's file.
(c) If the court orders the immediate release of an inmate, the department shall notify the sheriff or chief of police, or both, and the district attorney, having jurisdiction over the community in which the person was convicted and, in addition, the sheriff or chief of police, or both, and the district attorney, having jurisdiction over the community in which the person is scheduled to be released on parole at the time of release.
(d) (1) The notification required by this section shall be made whether or not a request has been made under Section 3058.5.
(2) In no case shall notice required by this section to the appropriate agency be later than the day of release on parole. If, after the 60-day notice is given to law enforcement and to the district attorney relating to an out-of-county placement, there is a change of county placement, notice to the ultimate county of placement shall be made upon the determination of the county of placement.
(Amended by Stats. 2011, Ch. 355, Sec. 1. (AB 44) Effective January 1, 2012.)
3058.61.
Whenever any person confined to state prison is serving a term for a conviction of Section 646.9, the Department of Corrections shall notify by mail, at least 45 days prior to the person's scheduled release date, the sheriff or chief of police, or both, and the district attorney who has jurisdiction over the community in which the person was convicted, and the sheriff, chief of police, or both, and the district attorney having jurisdiction over the community in which the person is scheduled to be released on parole, or released following a period of confinement pursuant to a parole revocation without a new commitment. The notification shall indicate whether the victim has requested notification from the department pursuant to Section 646.92.
(Added by Stats. 2000, Ch. 561, Sec. 3. Effective January 1, 2001.)
3058.65.
(a) (1) Whenever any person confined in the state prison is serving a term for the conviction of child abuse, pursuant to Section 273a, 273ab, 273d, any sex offense specified as being perpetrated against a minor, or an act of domestic violence, or as ordered by a court, the Board of Prison Terms, with respect to inmates sentenced pursuant to subdivision (b) of Section 1168, or the Department of Corrections, with respect to inmates sentenced pursuant to Section 1170, shall notify the following parties that the person is scheduled to be released on parole, or rereleased following a period of confinement pursuant to a parole revocation without a new commitment, as specified in subdivision (b):
(A) The immediate family of the parolee who requests notification and provides the department with a current address.
(B) A county child welfare services agency that requests notification pursuant to Section 16507 of the Welfare and Institutions Code.
(2) For the purposes of this paragraph, "immediate family of the parolee" means the parents, siblings, and spouse of the parolee.
(b) (1) The notification shall be made by mail at least 60 days prior to the scheduled release date, except as provided in paragraph (2). In all cases, the notification shall include the name of the person who is scheduled to be released, the terms of that person's parole, whether or not that person is required to register with local law enforcement, and the community in which that person will reside. The notification shall specify the office within the Department of Corrections that has the authority to make the final determination and adjustments regarding parole location decisions.
(2) When notification cannot be provided within the 60 days due to the unanticipated release date change of an inmate as a result of an order from the court, an action by the Board of Prison Terms, the granting of an administrative appeal, or a finding of not

guilty or dismissal of a disciplinary action, that affects the sentence of the inmate, or due to a modification of the department's decision regarding the community into which the person is scheduled to be released pursuant to paragraph (3), the department shall provide notification to the parties and agencies specified in subdivision (a) as soon as practicable, but in no case less than 24 hours after the final decision is made regarding the location where the parolee will be released.

(3) Those agencies receiving the notice referred to in this subdivision may provide written comment to the board or department regarding the impending release. Agencies that choose to provide written comments shall respond within 30 days prior to the inmate's scheduled release, unless an agency received less than 60 days' notice of the impending release, in which case the agency shall respond as soon as practicable prior to the scheduled release. Those comments shall be considered by the board or department which may, based on those comments, modify its decision regarding the community in which the person is scheduled to be released. The board or department shall respond in writing not less than 15 days prior to the scheduled release with a final determination as to whether to adjust the parole location and documenting the basis for its decision, unless the department received comments less than 30 days prior to the impending release, in which case the department shall respond as soon as practicable prior to the scheduled release. The comments shall become a part of the inmate's file.

(c) In no case shall the notice required by this section be later than the day the person is released on parole.

(Amended by Stats. 2007, Ch. 571, Sec. 1. Effective January 1, 2008.)

3058.7.

(a) Whenever any sheriff or chief of police is notified of the pending release of a convicted violent felon pursuant to Section 3058.6, that sheriff or chief of police may notify any person designated by the sheriff or chief of police as an appropriate recipient of this notice.

(b) A law enforcement official authorized to provide notice pursuant to this section, and the public agency or entity employing the law enforcement official, shall not be liable for providing or failing to provide notice pursuant to this section.

(Added by Stats. 1995, Ch. 936, Sec. 1. Effective January 1, 1996.)

3058.8.

(a) At the time a notification is sent pursuant to subdivision (a) of Section 3058.6, the Board of Parole Hearings or the Department of Corrections and Rehabilitation, or the designated agency responsible for notification, as the case may be, shall also notify persons described in Section 679.03 who have requested a notice informing those persons of the fact that the person who committed the violent offense is scheduled to be released from the Department of Corrections and Rehabilitation or from the State Department of State Hospitals, including, but not limited to, conditional release, and specifying the proposed date of release. Notice of the community in which the person is scheduled to reside shall also be given if it is (1) in the county of residence of a witness, victim, or family member of a victim who has requested notification, or (2) within 100 miles of the actual residence of a witness, victim, or family member of a victim who has requested notification. If, after providing the witness, victim, or next of kin with the notice, there is any change in the release date or the community in which the person is to reside, the board or department shall provide the witness, victim, or next of kin with the revised information.

(b) In order to be entitled to receive the notice set forth in this section, the requesting party shall keep the department or board informed of his or her current contact information.

(c) The board or department, when sending out notices regarding an offender's release on parole, shall use the information provided by the requesting party pursuant to subdivision (b) of Section 679.03, unless that information is no longer current. If the information is no longer current, the department shall make a reasonable attempt to contact the person and to notify him or her of the impending release.

(Amended by Stats. 2012, Ch. 24, Sec. 46. (AB 1470) Effective June 27, 2012.)

3058.9.

(a) Whenever any person confined to state prison is serving a term for the conviction of child abuse pursuant to Section 273a, 273ab, 273d, or any sex offense identified in statute as being perpetrated against a minor victim, or as ordered by any court, the Board of Prison Terms, with respect to inmates sentenced pursuant to subdivision (b) of Section 1168 or the Department of Corrections, with respect to inmates sentenced pursuant to Section 1170, shall notify the sheriff or chief of police, or both, and the district attorney, having jurisdiction over the community in which the person was convicted and, in addition, the sheriff or chief of police, or both, and the district attorney having jurisdiction over the community in which the person is scheduled to be released on parole or rereleased following a period of confinement pursuant to a parole revocation without a new commitment.

(b) (1) The notification shall be made by mail at least 45 days prior to the scheduled release date, except as provided in paragraph (3). In all cases, the notification shall include the name of the person who is scheduled to be released, whether or not the person is required to register with local law enforcement, and the community in which the person will reside. The notification shall specify the office within the Department of Corrections with the authority to make final determination and adjustments regarding parole location decisions.

(2) Notwithstanding any other provision of law, the Department of Corrections shall not restore credits nor take any administrative action resulting in an inmate being placed in a greater credit earning category that would result in notification being provided less than 45 days prior to an inmate's scheduled release date.

(3) When notification cannot be provided within the 45 days due to the unanticipated release date change of an inmate as a result of an order from the court, an action by the Board of Prison Terms, the granting of an administrative appeal, or a finding of not guilty or dismissal of a disciplinary action, that affects the sentence of the inmate, or due to a modification of the department's decision regarding the community into which the person is scheduled to be released pursuant to paragraph (4), the department shall provide notification as soon as practicable, but in no case less than 24 hours after the final decision is made regarding where the parolee will be released.

(4) Those agencies receiving the notice referred to in this subdivision may provide written comment to the board or department regarding the impending release. Agencies that choose to provide written comments shall respond within 30 days prior to the inmate's scheduled release, unless an agency received less than 45 days' notice of the impending release, in which case the agency shall respond as soon as practicable prior to the scheduled release. Those comments shall be considered by the board or department, which may, based on those comments, modify its decision regarding the community in which the person is scheduled to be released. The Department of Corrections shall respond in writing not less than 15 days prior to the scheduled release with a final determination as to whether to adjust the parole location and documenting the basis for its decision, unless the department received comments less than 30 days prior to the impending release, in which case the department shall respond as soon as practicable prior to the scheduled release. The comments shall become a part of the inmate's file.

(c) If the court orders the immediate release of an inmate, the department shall notify the sheriff or chief of police, or both, and the district attorney, having jurisdiction over the community in which the person was convicted and, in addition, the sheriff or chief of police, or both, and the district attorney having jurisdiction over the community in which the person is scheduled to be released on parole or released following a period of confinement pursuant to a parole revocation without a new commitment.

(d) The notification required by this section shall be made whether or not a request has been made under Section 3058.5.

In no case shall notice required by this section to the appropriate agency be later than the day of release on parole. If, after the 45-day notice is given to law enforcement and to the district attorney relating to an out-of-county placement, there is change of county placement, notice to the ultimate county of placement shall be made upon the determination of the county of placement.

(e) The notice required by this section shall satisfy the notice required by Section 3058.6 for any person whose offense is identified in both sections.

(Amended by Stats. 2001, Ch. 854, Sec. 51. Effective January 1, 2002.)

3059.

If any paroled prisoner shall leave the state without permission of his or her supervising parole agency, he or she shall be held as an escaped prisoner and arrested as such.

(Amended by Stats. 2012, Ch. 43, Sec. 44. (SB 1023) Effective June 27, 2012.)

3060.1.

Upon the revocation of the parole of any prisoner who was ordered by the court to pay an additional restitution fine pursuant to Section 1202.45, but which was suspended by that section, the additional restitution fine shall be reinstated without the need for any further court proceeding.

(Added by Stats. 1995, Ch. 313, Sec. 14. Effective August 3, 1995.)

3060.5.

Notwithstanding any other provision of law, the parole authority shall revoke the parole of any prisoner who refuses to sign any form required by the Department of Justice stating that the duty of the prisoner to register under Section 290 has been explained to the prisoner, unless the duty to register has not been explained to the prisoner, or refuses to provide samples of blood or saliva as required by the DNA and Forensic Identification Data Base and Data Bank Act of 1998 (Chapter 6 (commencing with Section 295) of Title 9 of Part 1), and shall order the prisoner returned to prison. Confinement pursuant to any single revocation of parole under this section shall not, absent a new conviction and commitment to prison under other provisions of law, exceed six months, except as provided in subdivision (c) of Section 3057.

(Amended by Stats. 2012, Ch. 43, Sec. 45. (SB 1023) Effective June 27, 2012.)

3060.6.

Notwithstanding any other provision of law, on or after January 1, 2001, whenever any paroled person is returned to custody or has his or her parole revoked for conduct described in subdivision (c) of Section 290, the supervising parole agency shall report the circumstances that were the basis for the return to custody or revocation of parole to the law enforcement agency and the district attorney that has primary jurisdiction over the community in which the circumstances occurred and to the Department of Corrections and Rehabilitation. Upon the release of the paroled person, the Department of Corrections and Rehabilitation shall inform the law enforcement agency and the district attorney that has primary jurisdiction over the community in which the circumstances occurred and, if different, the county in which the person is paroled or discharged, of the circumstances that were the basis for the return to custody or revocation of parole.

(Amended by Stats. 2012, Ch. 43, Sec. 46. (SB 1023) Effective June 27, 2012.)

3060.7.

(a) (1) Notwithstanding any other law, the supervising parole agency shall notify any person released on parole or postrelease community supervision pursuant to Title 2.05 (commencing with Section 3450) of Part 3 who has been classified by the Department of Corrections and Rehabilitation as included within the highest control or risk classification that he or she shall be required to report to his or her assigned parole officer or designated local supervising agency within two days of release from the state prison.

(2) This section shall not prohibit the supervising parole agency or local supervising agency from requiring any person released on parole or postrelease community supervision to report to his or her assigned parole officer within a time period that is less than two days from the time of release.

(b) The supervising parole agency, within 24 hours of a parolee's failure to report as required by this section, shall issue a written order suspending the parole of that parolee, pending a hearing before the Board of Parole Hearings or the court, as applicable, and shall request that a warrant be issued for the parolee's arrest pursuant to subdivision (c) of Section 3000.08.

(c) Upon the issuance of an arrest warrant for a parolee who has been classified within the highest control or risk classification, the assigned parole officer shall continue to carry the parolee on his or her regular caseload and shall continue to search for the parolee's whereabouts.

(d) With regard to any inmate subject to this section, the Department of Corrections and Rehabilitation shall release an inmate sentenced prior to January 1, 1996, one or two days before his or her scheduled release date if the inmate's release date falls on the day before a holiday or weekend.

(e) With regard to any inmate subject to this section, the Department of Corrections and Rehabilitation shall release an inmate one or two days after his or her scheduled release date if the release date falls on the day before a holiday or weekend.

(Amended by Stats. 2014, Ch. 26, Sec. 28. (AB 1468) Effective June 20, 2014.)

3060.9.

(a) The Department of Corrections and Rehabilitation is hereby authorized to expand the use of parole programs or services to improve the rehabilitation of parolees, reduce recidivism, reduce prison overcrowding, and improve public safety through the following:

(1) The use of intermediate sanctions for offenders who commit a violation of parole.

(2) The use of parole programs or services, in addition to supervision, for any offender who is in need of services to reduce the parolee's likelihood to reoffend.

(b) For purposes of this section, the expansion of parole programs or services may include, but shall not be limited to, the following:

(1) Counseling.

(2) Electronic monitoring.

(3) Halfway house services.

(4) Home detention.

(5) Intensive supervision.

(6) Mandatory community service assignments.

(7) Increased drug testing.

(8) Participation in one or more components of the Preventing Parolee Crime Program pursuant to Section 3068.

(9) Rehabilitation programs, such as substance abuse treatment.

(10) Restitution.

(c) As used in this section:

(1) "Department" means the Department of Corrections and Rehabilitation.

(2) "Parole authority" means the Board of Parole Hearings.

(d) The department or the parole authority may assign the programs or services specified in subdivision (b) to offenders who meet the criteria of paragraph (1) or (2). This section shall not alter the existing discretion of the parole authority regarding the reporting by the department of parole violations or conditions of parole. In exercising its authority pursuant to paragraphs (2) and (3) of subdivision (e) and subdivision (f), the parole authority or the department in exercising its authority pursuant to paragraph (1) of subdivision (e) may determine an individual parolee's eligibility for parole programs or services by considering the totality of the circumstances including, but not limited to, the instant violation offense, the history of parole adjustment, current commitment offense, the risk needs assessment of the offender, and prior criminal history, with public safety and offender accountability as primary considerations.

(e) (1) Subject to the provisions of this section, the parole authority, in the absence of a new conviction and commitment of the parolee to the state prison under other provisions of law, may assign a parolee who violates a condition of his or her parole to parole programs or services in lieu of revocation of parole.

(2) In addition to the alternatives provided in this section, the parole authority may, as an alternative to ordering a revoked parolee returned to custody, suspend the period of revocation pending the parolee's successful completion of parole programs or services assigned by the parole authority.

(3) The department shall not establish a special condition of parole, assigning a parolee to parole programs or services in lieu of initiating revocation proceedings, if the department reasonably believes that the violation of the condition of parole involves commission of a serious felony, as defined in subdivision (c) of Section 1192.7, or a violent felony, as defined in subdivision (c) of Section 667.5, or involves the control or use of a firearm.

(f) A special condition of parole imposed pursuant to this section to participate in residential programs shall not be established without a hearing by the parole authority in accordance with Section 3068 and regulations of the parole authority. A special condition of parole providing an assignment to a parole program or service that does not consist of a residential component may be established without a hearing.

(g) Expansion of parole programs or services pursuant to this section by the department is subject to the appropriation of funding for this purpose as provided in the Budget Act of 2007, and subsequent budget acts.

(h) The department, in consultation with the Legislative Analyst's Office, shall, contingent upon funding, conduct an evaluation regarding the effect of parole programs or services on public safety, parolee recidivism, and prison and parole costs and report the results to the Legislature three years after funding is provided pursuant to subdivision (g). Until that date, the department shall report annually to the Legislature, beginning January 1, 2009, regarding the status of the expansion of parole programs or services and the number of offenders assigned and participating in parole programs or services in the preceding fiscal year.

(Added by Stats. 2007, Ch. 645, Sec. 1. Effective January 1, 2008.)

3062.
The Governor of the state shall have like power to revoke the parole of any prisoner. The written authority of the Governor shall likewise be sufficient to authorize any peace officer to retake and return any prisoner to the state prison. The Governor's written order revoking the parole shall have the same force and effect and be executed in like manner as the order of the parole authority.

(Amended by Stats. 1992, Ch. 695, Sec. 18. Effective September 15, 1992.)

3063.
No parole shall be suspended or revoked without cause, which cause must be stated in the order suspending or revoking the parole.

(Added by Stats. 1941, Ch. 106.)

3063.1.
(a) Notwithstanding any other provision of law, and except as provided in subdivision (d), parole shall not be suspended or revoked for commission of a nonviolent drug possession offense or for violating any drug-related condition of parole.

As an additional condition of parole for all such offenses or violations, the Parole Authority shall require participation in and completion of an appropriate drug treatment program. Vocational training, family counseling and literacy training may be imposed as additional parole conditions.

The Parole Authority may require any person on parole who commits a nonviolent drug possession offense or violates any drug-related condition of parole, and who is reasonably able to do so, to contribute to the cost of his or her own placement in a drug treatment program.

(b) Subdivision (a) does not apply to:

(1) Any parolee who has been convicted of one or more serious or violent felonies in violation of subdivision (c) of Section 667.5 or Section 1192.7.

(2) A parolee who, while on parole, commits one or more nonviolent drug possession offenses and is found to have concurrently committed a misdemeanor not related to the use of drugs or any felony.

(3) A parolee who refuses drug treatment as a condition of parole.

(c) Within seven days of a finding that the parolee has either committed a nonviolent drug possession offense or violated any drug-related condition of parole, the Department of Corrections and Rehabilitation, Division of Adult Parole Operations shall notify the treatment provider designated to provide drug treatment under subdivision (a). Within 30 days thereafter the treatment provider shall prepare an individualized drug treatment plan and forward it to the Parole Authority and to the California Department of Corrections and Rehabilitation, Division of Adult Parole Operations agent responsible for supervising the parolee. On a quarterly basis after the parolee begins drug treatment, the treatment provider shall prepare and forward a progress report on the individual parolee to these entities and individuals.

(1) If at any point during the course of drug treatment the treatment provider notifies the Department of Corrections and Rehabilitation, Division of Adult Parole Operations that the parolee is unamenable to the drug treatment provided, but amenable to other drug treatments or related programs, the Department of Corrections and Rehabilitation, Division of Adult Parole Operations may act to modify the terms of parole to ensure that the parolee receives the alternative drug treatment or program.

(2) If at any point during the course of drug treatment the treatment provider notifies the Department of Corrections and Rehabilitation, Division of Adult Parole Operations that the parolee is unamenable to the drug treatment provided and all other forms of drug treatment provided pursuant to subdivision (b) of Section 1210 and the amenability factors described in subparagraph (B) of paragraph (3) of subdivision (f) of Section 1210.1, the Department of Corrections and Rehabilitation, Division of Adult Parole Operations may act to revoke parole. At the revocation hearing, parole may be revoked if it is proved that the parolee is unamenable to all drug treatment.

(3) Drug treatment services provided by subdivision (a) as a required condition of parole may not exceed 12 months, unless the Department of Corrections and Rehabilitation, Division of Adult Parole Operations makes a finding supported by the record that the continuation of treatment services beyond 12 months is necessary for drug treatment to be successful. If that finding is made, the Department of Corrections and Rehabilitation, Division of Adult Parole Operations may order up to two six-month extensions of treatment services. The provision of treatment services under this act shall not exceed 24 months.

(d) (1) If parole is revoked pursuant to the provisions of this subdivision, the defendant may be incarcerated pursuant to otherwise applicable law without regard to the provisions of this section. Parole shall be revoked if the parole violation is proved and a preponderance of the evidence establishes that the parolee poses a danger to the safety of others.

(2) If a parolee receives drug treatment under subdivision (a), and during the course of drug treatment violates parole either by committing an offense other than a nonviolent drug possession offense, or by violating a non-drug-related condition of parole, and the Department of Corrections and Rehabilitation, Division of Adult Parole Operations acts to revoke parole, a hearing shall be conducted to determine whether parole shall be revoked.

Parole may be modified or revoked if the parole violation is proved.

(3) (A) If a parolee receives drug treatment under subdivision (a), and during the course of drug treatment violates parole either by committing a nonviolent drug possession offense, or a misdemeanor for simple possession or use of drugs or drug paraphernalia, being present where drugs are used, or failure to register as a drug offender, or any activity similar to those listed in subdivision (d) of Section 1210, or by violating a drug-related condition of parole, and the Department of Corrections and

Rehabilitation, Division of Adult Parole Operations acts to revoke parole, a hearing shall be conducted to determine whether parole shall be revoked. Parole shall be revoked if the parole violation is proved and a preponderance of the evidence establishes that the parolee poses a danger to the safety of others. If parole is not revoked, the conditions of parole may be intensified to achieve the goals of drug treatment.

(B) If a parolee receives drug treatment under subdivision (a), and during the course of drug treatment for the second time violates that parole either by committing a nonviolent drug possession offense, or by violating a drug-related condition of parole, and the Department of Corrections and Rehabilitation, Division of Adult Parole Operations acts for a second time to revoke parole, a hearing shall be conducted to determine whether parole shall be revoked. If the alleged parole violation is proved, the parolee is not eligible for continued parole under any provision of this section and may be reincarcerated.

(C) If a parolee already on parole at the effective date of this act violates that parole either by committing a nonviolent drug possession offense, or a misdemeanor for simple possession or use of drugs or drug paraphernalia, being present where drugs are used, or failure to register as a drug offender, or any activity similar to those listed in paragraph (1) of subdivision (d) of Section 1210, or by violating a drug-related condition of parole, and the Department of Corrections and Rehabilitation, Division of Adult Parole Operations acts to revoke parole, a hearing shall be conducted to determine whether parole shall be revoked. Parole shall be revoked if the parole violation is proved and a preponderance of the evidence establishes that the parolee poses a danger to the safety of others. If parole is not revoked, the conditions of parole may be modified to include participation in a drug treatment program as provided in subdivision (a). This paragraph does not apply to any parolee who at the effective date of this act has been convicted of one or more serious or violent felonies in violation of subdivision (c) of Section 667.5 or Section 1192.7.

(D) If a parolee already on parole at the effective date of this act violates that parole for the second time either by committing a nonviolent drug possession offense, or by violating a drug-related condition of parole, and the parole authority acts for a second time to revoke parole, a hearing shall be conducted to determine whether parole shall be revoked. If the alleged parole violation is proved, the parolee may be reincarcerated or the conditions of parole may be intensified to achieve the goals of drug treatment.

(e) The term "drug-related condition of parole" shall include a parolee's specific drug treatment regimen, and, if ordered by the Department of Corrections and Rehabilitation, Division of Adult Parole Operations pursuant to this section, employment, vocational training, educational programs, psychological counseling, and family counseling.

(Amended by Stats. 2015, Ch. 303, Sec. 398. (AB 731) Effective January 1, 2016. Note: This section was added on Nov. 7, 2000, by initiative Prop. 36.)

3063.2.
In a case where a parolee had been ordered to undergo drug treatment as a condition of parole pursuant to Section 3063.1, any drug testing of the parolee shall be used as a treatment tool. In evaluating a parolee's treatment program, results of any drug testing shall be given no greater weight than any other aspects of the parolee's individual treatment program.

(Added by Stats. 2001, Ch. 721, Sec. 6. Effective October 11, 2001.)

3063.5.
In parole revocation or revocation extension proceedings, a parolee or his or her attorney shall receive a copy of any police, arrest, and crime reports, criminal history information, and child abuse reports made pursuant to Sections 11166 and 11166.2 pertaining to those proceedings. Portions of those reports containing confidential information need not be disclosed if the parolee or his or her attorney has been notified that confidential information has not been disclosed. Portions of child abuse reports made pursuant to Sections 11166 and 11166.2 containing identifying information relating to the reporter shall not be disclosed. However, the parolee or his or her attorney shall be notified that information relating to the identity of the reporter has not been disclosed.

(Amended by Stats. 2005, Ch. 99, Sec. 1. Effective July 21, 2005.)

3063.6.
Parole revocation proceedings and parole revocation extension proceedings may be conducted by a panel of one person.

(Amended by Stats. 1992, Ch. 695, Sec. 19. Effective September 15, 1992.)

3064.
From and after the suspension or revocation of the parole of any prisoner and until his return to custody he is an escapee and fugitive from justice and no part of the time during which he is an escapee and fugitive from justice shall be part of his term.

(Amended by Stats. 1980, Ch. 676, Sec. 255.)

3065.
Except as otherwise provided in Section 1170.2 and Article 1 (commencing with Section 3000) of this chapter, the provisions of this article are to apply to all prisoners serving sentence in the state prisons on July 1, 1977, to the end that at all times the same provisions relating to sentence, imprisonments and paroles of prisoners shall apply to all the inmates thereof.

(Amended by Stats. 1977, Ch. 2.)

3066.
Notwithstanding Section 11425.10 of the Government Code, Chapter 4.5 (commencing with Section 11400) of Part 1 of Division 3 of Title 2 of the Government Code does not apply to a parole hearing or other adjudication concerning rights of an inmate or parolee conducted by the Department of Corrections or the Board of Prison Terms.

(Added by Stats. 1995, Ch. 938, Sec. 80. Effective January 1, 1996. Operative July 1, 1997, by Sec. 98 of Ch. 938.)

3067.
(a) Any inmate who is eligible for release on parole pursuant to this chapter or postrelease community supervision pursuant to Title 2.05 (commencing with Section 3450) of Part 3 shall be given notice that he or she is subject to terms and conditions of his or her release from prison.

(b) The notice shall include all of the following:

(1) The person's release date and the maximum period the person may be subject to supervision under this title.

(2) An advisement that if the person violates any law or violates any condition of his or her release that he or she may be incarcerated in a county jail or, if previously paroled pursuant to Section 3000.1 or paragraph (4) of subdivision (b) of Section 3000, returned to state prison, regardless of whether new charges are filed.

(3) An advisement that he or she is subject to search or seizure by a probation or parole officer or other peace officer at any time of the day or night, with or without a search warrant or with or without cause.

(c) This section shall only apply to an inmate who is eligible for release on parole for an offense committed on or after January 1, 1997.

(d) It is not the intent of the Legislature to authorize law enforcement officers to conduct searches for the sole purpose of harassment.

(e) This section does not affect the power of the Secretary of the Department of Corrections and Rehabilitation to prescribe and amend rules and regulations pursuant to Section 5058.

(Amended by Stats. 2012, Ch. 43, Sec. 49. (SB 1023) Effective June 27, 2012.)

3068.
(a) The Department of Corrections shall operate the Preventing Parolee Crime Program with various components, including, at a minimum, residential and nonresidential multiservice centers, literacy labs, drug treatment networks, and job placement assistance for parolees.

(b) The Department of Corrections shall, commencing in the 1998–99 fiscal year, initiate an expansion of the program to parole units now lacking some or all of the elements of the program, where doing so would be cost-effective, as determined by the Director of Corrections, to the extent that funding for the expansion becomes available.

(c) In addition to the assignment by the Department of Corrections of any other parolee to the Preventing Parolee Crime Program, the parole authority may assign a conditionally released or paroled prisoner to the Preventing Parolee Crime Program in lieu of the revocation of parole. The parole authority shall not assign a conditionally released or paroled prisoner to the Preventing Parolee Crime Program in lieu of the revocation of parole if the person has committed a parole violation involving a violent or serious felony. A special condition of parole that requires the parolee to participate in a live-in program shall not be imposed without a hearing by the Board of Prison Terms.

(d) (1) The Department of Corrections, in consultation with the Board of Prison Terms and the Legislative Analyst's office, shall, contingent upon funding, contract with an independent consultant to conduct an evaluation regarding the impact of an expansion of the Preventing Parolee Crime Program to additional parole units on public safety, parolee recidivism, and prison and parole costs, and report the results to the Legislature on or before January 1, 2004.

(2) The Department of Corrections shall sample several parole units in which the program has been added to examine the program's impact upon the supervision, control, and sanction of parolees under the jurisdiction of the sampled parole units. These results shall be compared with a control group of comparable parole populations that do not have Preventing Parolee Crime Program services.

(3) The report, whether in final or draft form, and all working papers and data, shall be available for immediate review upon request by the Legislative Analyst.

(4) The department in consultation with the Board of Prison Terms shall submit a multiyear evaluation plan for the program to the Legislature six months after an appropriation is made for the evaluation provided for in paragraph (1).

(Added by Stats. 1998, Ch. 526, Sec. 2. Effective September 16, 1998.)
3069.
(a) The Department of Corrections and Rehabilitation is hereby authorized to create the Parole Violation Intermediate Sanctions (PVIS) program. The purpose of the program shall be to improve the rehabilitation of parolees, reduce recidivism, reduce prison overcrowding, and improve public safety through the use of intermediate sanctions for offenders who violate parole. The PVIS program will allow the department to provide parole agents an early opportunity to intervene with parolees who are not in compliance with the conditions of parole and facing return to prison. The program will include key components used by drug and collaborative courts under a highly structured model, including close supervision and monitoring by a hearing officer, dedicated calendars, nonadversarial proceedings, frequent appearances before the hearing officer, utilization of incentives and sanctions, frequent drug and alcohol testing, immediate entry into treatment and rehabilitation programs, and close collaboration between the program, parole, and treatment to improve offender outcomes. The program shall be local and community based.

(b) As used in this section:

(1) "Department" means the Department of Corrections and Rehabilitation.

(2) "Parole authority" means the Board of Parole Hearings.

(3) "Program" means the Parole Violation Intermediate Sanctions program.

(c) (1) A parolee who is deemed eligible by the department to participate in this program, and who would otherwise be referred to the parole authority to have his or her parole revoked for a parole violation shall be referred by his or her parole officer for participation in the program in lieu of parole revocation.

(2) If the alleged violation of parole involves the commission of a serious felony, as defined in subdivision (c) of Section 1192.7, or a violent felony, as defined in subdivision (c) of Section 667.5, or involves the control or use of a firearm, the parolee shall not be eligible for referral to the program in lieu of revocation of parole.

(d) The department is authorized to establish local PVIS programs. Each local program may have, but shall not be limited to, the following characteristics:

(1) An assigned hearing officer who is a retired superior court judge or commissioner and who is experienced in using the drug court model and collaborative court model.

(2) The use of a dedicated calendar.

(3) Close coordination between the hearing officer, department, counsel, community treatment and rehabilitation programs participating in the program and adherence to a team approach in working with parolees.

(4) Enhanced accountability through the use of frequent program appearances by parolees in the program, at least one per month, with more frequent appearances in the time period immediately following the initial referral to the program and thereafter in the discretion of the hearing officer.

(5) Reviews of progress by the parolee as to his or her treatment and rehabilitation plan and abstinence from the use of drugs and alcohol through progress reports provided by the parole agent as well as all treatment and rehabilitation providers.

(6) Mandatory frequent drug and alcohol testing.

(7) Graduated in-custody sanctions may be imposed after a hearing in which it is found the parolee failed treatment and rehabilitation programs or continued in the use of drugs or alcohol while in the program.

(8) A problemsolving focus and team approach to decisionmaking.

(9) Direct interaction between the parolee and the hearing officer.

(10) Accessibility of the hearing officer to parole agents and parole employees as well as treatment and rehabilitation providers.

(e) Upon successful completion of the program, the parolee shall continue on parole, or be granted other relief as shall be determined in the sole discretion of the department or as authorized by law.

(f) The department is authorized to develop the programs. The parole authority is directed to convene in each county where the programs are selected to be established, all local stakeholders, including, but not limited to, a retired superior court judge or commissioner, designated by the Administrative Office of the Courts, who shall be compensated by the department at the present rate of pay for retired judges and commissioners, local parole agents and other parole employees, the district attorney, the public defender, an attorney actively representing parolees in the county and a private defense attorney designated by the public defenders association, the county director of alcohol and drug services, behavioral health, mental health, and any other local stakeholders deemed appropriate. Specifically, persons directly involved in the areas of substance abuse treatment, cognitive skills development, education, life skills, vocational training and support, victim impact awareness, anger management, family reunification, counseling, residential care, placement in affordable housing, employment development and placement are encouraged to be included in the meeting.

(g) The department, in consultation with local stakeholders, shall develop a plan that is consistent with this section. The plan shall address at a minimum the following components:

(1) The method by which each parolee eligible for the program shall be referred to the program.

(2) The method by which each parolee is to be individually assessed as to his or her treatment and rehabilitative needs and level of community and court monitoring required, participation of counsel, and the development of a treatment and rehabilitation plan for each parolee.

(3) The specific treatment and rehabilitation programs that will be made available to the parolees and the process to ensure that they receive the appropriate level of treatment and rehabilitative services.

(4) The criteria for continuing participation in, and successful completion of, the program, as well as the criteria for termination from the program and return to the parole revocation process.

(5) The development of a program team, as well as a plan for ongoing training in utilizing the drug court and collaborative court nonadversarial model.

(h) (1) If a parolee is referred to the program by his or her parole agent, as specified in this section, the hearing officer in charge of the local program to which the parolee is referred shall determine whether the parolee will be admitted to the program.

(2) A parolee may be excluded from admission to the program if the hearing officer determines that the parolee poses a risk to the community or would not benefit from the program. The hearing officer may consider the history of the offender, the nature of the committing offense, and the nature of the violation. The hearing officer shall state its findings, and the reasons for those findings, on the record.

(3) If the hearing officer agrees to admit the parolee into the program, any pending parole revocation proceedings shall be suspended contingent upon successful completion of the program as determined by the program hearing officer.

(i) A special condition of parole imposed as a condition of admission into the program consisting of a residential program shall not be established without a hearing in front of the hearing officer in accordance with Section 3068 and regulations of the parole authority. A special condition of parole providing an admission to the program that does not consist of a residential component may be established without a hearing.

(j) Implementation of this section by the department is subject to the appropriation of funding for this purpose as provided in the Budget Act of 2008, and subsequent budget acts.

(Added by Stats. 2007, Ch. 645, Sec. 2. Effective January 1, 2008.)
3069.5.
(a) The department, in consultation with the Legislative Analyst's Office, shall, contingent upon funding, conduct an evaluation of the PVIS program.

(b) A final report shall be due to the Legislature three years after funding is provided pursuant to subdivision (h) of Section 3069. Until that date, the department shall report annually to the Legislature, beginning January 1, 2009, regarding the status of implementation of the PVIS program and the number of offenders assigned and participating in the program in the preceding fiscal year.

(Added by Stats. 2007, Ch. 645, Sec. 3. Effective January 1, 2008.)
3070.
The Department of Corrections shall develop and report, utilizing existing resources, to the Legislature by December 31, 2000, a plan that would ensure by January 1, 2005, that all prisoners and parolees who are substance abusers receive appropriate treatment, including therapeutic community and academic programs. The plan shall include a range of options, estimated capital outlay and operating costs for the various options, and a recommended prioritization, including which persons shall receive priority for treatment, for phased implementation of the plan.

(Added by Stats. 1998, Ch. 526, Sec. 3. Effective September 16, 1998.)
3071.
The Department of Corrections shall implement, by January 1, 2002, a course of instruction for the training of parole officers in California in the management of parolees who were convicted of stalking pursuant to Section 646.9. The course shall include instruction in the appropriate protocol for notifying and interacting with stalking victims, especially in regard to a stalking offender's release from parole.

(Added by Stats. 2000, Ch. 564, Sec. 1. Effective January 1, 2001.)
3072.
(a) The Department of Corrections and Rehabilitation, subject to the legislative appropriation of the necessary funds, may establish and operate, after January 1, 2007, a specialized sex offender treatment pilot program for inmates whom the department determines pose a high risk to the public of committing violent sex crimes.

(b) (1) The program shall be based upon the relapse prevention model and shall include referral to specialized services, such as substance abuse treatment, for offenders needing those specialized services.

(2) Except as otherwise required under Section 645, the department may provide medication treatments for selected offenders, as determined by medical protocols, and only on a voluntary basis and with the offender's informed consent.

(c) (1) The program shall be targeted primarily at adult sex offenders who meet the following conditions:

(A) The offender is within five years of being released on parole. An inmate serving a life term may be excluded from treatment until he or she receives a parole date and is within five years of that parole date, unless the department determines that the treatment is necessary for the public safety.

(B) The offender has been clinically assessed.

(C) A review of the offender's criminal history indicates that the offender poses a high risk of committing new sex offenses upon his or her release on parole.

(D) Based upon the clinical assessment, the offender may be amenable to treatment.

(2) The department may include other appropriate offenders in the treatment program if doing so facilitates the effectiveness of the treatment program.

(3) Notwithstanding any other provision of law, inmates who are condemned to death or sentenced to life without the possibility of parole are ineligible to participate in treatment.

(d) The program under this section shall be established with the assistance and supervision of the staff of the department primarily by obtaining the services of specially trained sex offender treatment providers, as determined by the secretary of the department and the Director of State Hospitals.

(e) (1) The program under this section, upon full implementation, shall provide for the treatment of inmates who are deemed to pose a high risk to the public of committing sex crimes, as determined by the State-Authorized Risk Assessment Tool for Sex Offenders, pursuant to Sections 290.04 to 290.06, inclusive.

(2) To the maximum extent that is practical and feasible, offenders participating in the treatment program shall be held in a separate area of the prison facility, segregated from any non-sex offenders held at the same prison, and treatment in the pilot program shall be provided in program space segregated, to the maximum extent that is practical and feasible, from program space for any non-sex offenders held at the same prison.

(f) (1) The State Department of Mental Health, or its successor, the State Department of State Hospitals, by January 1, 2012, shall provide a report evaluating the program to the fiscal and public safety policy committees of both houses of the Legislature, and to the Joint Legislative Budget Committee.

(2) The report shall initially evaluate whether the program under this section is operating effectively, is having a positive clinical effect on participating sex offenders, and is cost effective for the state.

(3) In conducting its evaluation, the State Department of Mental Health, or its successor, the State Department of State Hospitals, shall consider the effects of treatment of offenders while in prison and while subsequently on parole.

(4) The State Department of Mental Health, or its successor, the State Department of State Hospitals, shall advise the Legislature as to whether the program should be continued past its expiration date, expanded, or concluded.

(Amended by Stats. 2012, Ch. 24, Sec. 47. (AB 1470) Effective June 27, 2012.)
3073.
The Department of Corrections and Rehabilitation is hereby authorized to obtain day treatment, and to contract for crisis care services, for parolees with mental health problems. Day treatment and crisis care services should be designed to reduce parolee recidivism and the chances that a parolee will return to prison. The department shall work with counties to obtain day treatment and crisis care services for parolees with the

goal of extending the services upon completion of the offender's period of parole, if needed.
(Added by Stats. 2007, Ch. 7, Sec. 12. Effective May 3, 2007.)
3073.1.
Counties are hereby authorized to contract with the Department of Corrections and Rehabilitation in order to obtain correctional clinical services for inmates with mental health problems who are released on postrelease community supervision with mental health problems.
(Amended by Stats. 2011, 1st Ex. Sess., Ch. 12, Sec. 26. (AB 17 1x) Effective September 21, 2011. Operative October 1, 2011, by Sec. 46 of Ch. 12.)

ARTICLE 3.5. County Boards of Parole Commissioners [3074 - 3089]
(Article 3.5 added by Stats. 1953, Ch. 1384.)
3074.
The Legislature finds and declares that the period immediately following incarceration is critical to successful reintegration of the offender into society and to positive citizenship. It is in the interest of public safety for a county to provide for the supervision of parolees, and to provide educational, vocational, family and personal counseling necessary to assist parolees in the transition between imprisonment and discharge.
(Added by Stats. 1978, Ch. 918.)
3075.
(a) There is in each county a board of parole commissioners, consisting of each of the following:
(1) The sheriff, or his or her designee, or, in a county with a department of corrections, the director of that department.
(2) The probation officer, or his or her designee.
(3) A member, not a public official, to be selected from the public by the presiding judge of the superior court.
(b) The public member of the county board of parole commissioners or his or her alternate shall be entitled to his or her actual traveling and other necessary expenses incurred in the discharge of his or her duties. In addition, the public member or his or her alternate shall be entitled to per diem at any rate that may be provided by the board of supervisors. The public member or his or her alternate shall hold office for a term of one year and in no event for a period exceeding three consecutive years. The term shall commence on the date of appointment.
(Amended by Stats. 2003, Ch. 149, Sec. 77. Effective January 1, 2004.)
3076.
(a) The board may make, establish and enforce rules and regulations adopted under this article.
(b) The board shall act at regularly called meetings at which two-thirds of the members are present, and shall make and establish rules and regulations in writing stating the reasons therefor under which any prisoner who is confined in or committed to any county jail, work furlough facility, industrial farm, or industrial road camp, or in any city jail, work furlough facility, industrial farm, or industrial road camp under a judgment of imprisonment or as a condition of probation for any criminal offense, unless the court at the time of committing has ordered that such prisoner confined as a condition of probation upon conviction of a felony not be granted parole, may be allowed to go upon parole outside of such jail, work furlough facility, industrial farm, or industrial road camp, but to remain, while on parole, in the legal custody and under the control of the board establishing the rules and regulations for the prisoner's parole, and subject at any time to be taken back within the enclosure of any such jail, work furlough facility, industrial farm, or industrial road camp.
(c) The board shall provide a complete copy of its written rules and regulations and reasons therefor and any amendments thereto to each of the judges of the superior court of the county.
The board shall provide to the persons in charge of the county's correctional facilities a copy of the sections of its written rules and regulations and any amendments thereto which govern eligibility for parole, and the name and telephone number of the person or agency to contact for additional information. Such rules and regulations governing eligibility either shall be conspicuously posted and maintained within each county correctional facility so that all prisoners have access to a copy, or shall be given to each prisoner.
(Amended by Stats. 2002, Ch. 784, Sec. 559. Effective January 1, 2003.)
3077.
Whenever a prisoner is sentenced in one county and incarcerated in another county, only the county in which he was sentenced shall have jurisdiction to grant parole.
(Added by Stats. 1978, Ch. 918.)
3078.
(a) The board shall notify the sentencing judge of an inmate's application for parole.
(b) The sentencing judge may make a recommendation regarding such application, and the board shall give careful consideration to such recommendation.
(Repealed and added by Stats. 1978, Ch. 918.)
3079.
(a) No application for parole shall be granted or denied except by a vote of the board at a meeting at which a quorum of its members are present. This paragraph shall not be applied to the denial of applicants who are ineligible by order of the superior court, or to the granting of parole in emergency situations.
(b) An applicant shall be permitted to appear and speak on his behalf at the meeting at which his application is considered by the board.
(Repealed and added by Stats. 1978, Ch. 918.)
3080.
If any paroled prisoner leaves the county in which he is imprisoned without permission from the board granting his parole, he shall be arrested as an escaped prisoner and held as such.
(Added by Stats. 1953, Ch. 1384.)
3081.
(a) Each county board may retake and imprison any prisoner upon parole granted under the provisions of this article.
(b) Each county board may release any prisoner on parole for a term not to exceed three years upon those conditions and under those rules and regulations as may seem fit and proper for his or her rehabilitation, and should the prisoner so paroled violate any of the conditions of his or her parole or any of the rules and regulations governing his or her parole, he or she shall, upon order of the parole commission, be returned to the jail from which he or she was paroled and be confined therein for the unserved portion of his or her sentence.
(c) The written order of each county board shall be a sufficient warrant for all officers named therein to authorize them, or any of them, to return to actual custody any conditionally released or paroled prisoner. All chiefs of police, marshals of cities, sheriffs, and all other police and peace officers of this state shall execute any such order in like manner as ordinary criminal process.
(d) In computing the unserved sentence of a person returned to jail because of the revocation of his or her parole no credit shall be granted for the time between his or her release from jail on parole and his or her return to jail because of the revocation of his or her parole.
(Amended by Stats. 2013, Ch. 456, Sec. 1. (AB 884) Effective January 1, 2014.)
3082.
Each county board may make and establish written rules and regulations for the unconditional release of and may unconditionally release any prisoner who is an alien and who voluntarily consents to return or to be returned to his native land and who actually returns or is returned thereto. The necessary expenses of the transportation of

such alien prisoner and officers or attendants in charge of such prisoner, may be paid by the county, upon order of the board of supervisors authorizing or ratifying the return of the prisoner at the expense of the county.
(Added by Stats. 1953, Ch. 1384.)
3083.
Whenever the board designates deputies to serve as temporary commissioners in considering applications for parole of prisoners, such temporary commissioners or deputies may also exercise all the powers granted by this article relative to the unconditional release of alien prisoners.
(Added by Stats. 1953, Ch. 1384.)
3084.
Each county board may release to the State Department of Corrections for return to a state prison or correctional institution any county or city jail inmate who is a state parole violator, when notified by the Board of Prison Terms.
(Amended by Stats. 1979, Ch. 255.)
3085.
The members of the board may for the purpose of considering applications for parole of prisoners from city or county jails, or industrial farms, or work furlough facilities, or industrial road camps, designate deputies of their respective offices to serve for them as temporary commissioners when they are unable to serve.
(Added by renumbering Section 3077 by Stats. 1978, Ch. 918.)
3086.
Each county board shall not require, when setting terms or discharge dates, an admission of guilt to any crime for which an inmate was committed.
(Added by Stats. 1976, Ch. 833.)
3087.
No prisoner shall be paroled without supervision.
(Added by Stats. 1979, Ch. 117.)
3088.
A prisoner who is released on parole pursuant to this article shall be supervised by a county parole officer of the county board of parole commissioners.
(Amended by Stats. 1991, Ch. 229, Sec. 2.)
3089.
(a) A county parole officer who is not a peace officer, as defined in Chapter 4.5 (commencing with Section 830) of Title 3 of Part 2, is a public officer who works at the direction of the County Board of Parole Commissioners, as provided for in Section 3075, and is responsible for supervising prisoners released on parole by the board.
(b) A county parole officer who is a public officer, as defined in subdivision (a), shall have no right to carry or possess firearms in the performance of his or her prescribed duties.
(c) A county parole officer, as defined in subdivision (a), shall comply with the standards for selection and training established by the Board of Corrections pursuant to Section 6035.
(Added by Stats. 1991, Ch. 229, Sec. 3.)

CHAPTER 9. Prison to Employment [3105- 3105.]

(Chapter 9 added by Stats. 2007, Ch. 7, Sec. 13.)
3105.
The Department of Corrections and Rehabilitation shall develop an Inmate Treatment and Prison-to-Employment Plan. The plan should evaluate and recommend changes to the Governor and the Legislature regarding current inmate education, treatment, and rehabilitation programs to determine whether the programs provide sufficient skills to inmates that will likely result in their successful employment in the community, and reduce their chances of returning to prison after release to parole. The department shall report the status of the development of the plan on or before October 1, 2007, again on or before January 15, 2008, and shall submit the final plan by April 1, 2008. The department may use resources of other state or local agencies, academic institutions, and other research organizations as necessary to develop the plan.
(Added by Stats. 2007, Ch. 7, Sec. 13. Effective May 3, 2007.)

TITLE 2. IMPRISONMENT OF FEMALE PRISONERS IN STATE INSTITUTIONS [3200 - 3440]
(Title 2 repealed and added by Stats. 1941, Ch. 106.)

CHAPTER 1. Establishment of Institution for Women [3200 - 3202]

(Heading of Chapter 1 amended by Stats. 1965, Ch. 238.)
3200.
There is and shall continue to be within the State an institution for the punishment, treatment, supervision, custody and care of females convicted of felonies to be known as "The California Institution for Women."
(Added by Stats. 1941, Ch. 106.)
3201.
The purpose of said institution shall be to provide custody, care, protection, industrial, vocational, and other training, and reformatory help, for women confined therein.
(Added by Stats. 1941, Ch. 106.)
3202.
As used in the sections of this Part 3 of the Penal Code providing for penal offenses and punishments therefor, the term "State prison" or "prison" shall refer to and include the California Institution for Women.
(Added by Stats. 1941, Ch. 106.)

CHAPTER 2. Administration of Institution [3325 - 3326]

(Chapter 2 added by Stats. 1941, Ch. 106.)

ARTICLE 1. Administration of Institution for Women [3325 - 3326]
(Heading of Article 1 renumbered from Article 2 by Stats. 1965, Ch. 238.)
3325.
The warden described in this chapter shall, subject to the control of the director, have those powers, perform those duties and exercise those functions, respecting females convicted of felonies, as the wardens now exercise over male prisoners.
(Amended by Stats. 1989, Ch. 1420, Sec. 15.)

3326.
The department is authorized to provide the necessary facilities, equipment, and personnel to operate a commissary at any institution under its jurisdiction for the sale of toilet articles, candy, gum, notions, and other sundries.
(Amended by Stats. 2004, Ch. 798, Sec. 4. Effective January 1, 2005. Operative July 1, 2005, by Sec. 9 of Ch. 798.)

CHAPTER 3. Prisoners [3400 - 3409]

(Chapter 3 added by Stats. 1941, Ch. 106.)
3400.
Upon the commitment or transfer of any woman to the institution it shall be the duty of the officer having custody of her or required to take custody of her, to deliver her to said institution, receiving therefor the fees payable for the transportation of prisoners to the state prisons. Such officer shall at the same time deliver to said institution a certified abstract of the judgment of conviction and of the order of commitment or order of transfer. Every woman so committed or transferred under this act shall be accompanied by a woman attendant from the place of commitment or transfer until delivered to said institution.
(Amended by Stats. 1951, Ch. 460.)
3402.
There shall be kept at said institution a record of the history and progress of every woman confined therein during the period of her confinement, and so far as practically possible, prior and subsequent thereto, and all judges, courts, officials and employees, district attorneys, sheriffs, chiefs of police and peace officers, shall furnish said institution with all data in their possession or knowledge relative to any inmate that said institution may request. If upon the arrest of any woman it be discovered that she was theretofore an inmate of said institution, the institution shall be promptly notified of her arrest.
(Added by Stats. 1941, Ch. 106.)
3403.
Every woman upon being committed to said institution shall be examined mentally and physically, and shall be given the care, treatment and training adapted to her particular condition. Such care, treatment and training shall be along the lines best suited to develop her mentality, character and industrial capacity; provided, however, no inmate shall be confined longer than the term of her commitment.
(Added by Stats. 1941, Ch. 106.)
3404.
When there is any reasonable grounds to believe that a prisoner may be forcibly removed from the California Institution for Women, the warden shall report the fact to the Governor, who may order the removal of the prisoner to any California State prison for safekeeping, and it is hereby made the duty of the warden of the prison to accept and detain the prisoner for the further execution of her sentence. The Governor may thereafter order the prisoner returned to the California Institution for Women for the further execution of her sentence according to law.
The necessary costs and expenses incurred in carrying out the provisions of this section shall be a proper charge against any fund hereafter appropriated as an emergency fund, or similar appropriation for contingencies, notwithstanding any limitations or restrictions that may be imposed upon the expenditure of any appropriation.
(Amended by Stats. 1989, Ch. 1420, Sec. 16.)
3405.
No condition or restriction upon the obtaining of an abortion by a prisoner, pursuant to the Therapeutic Abortion Act (Article 2 (commencing with Section 123400) of Chapter 2 of Part 2 of Division 106 of the Health and Safety Code), other than those contained in that act, shall be imposed. Prisoners found to be pregnant and desiring abortions, shall be permitted to determine their eligibility for an abortion pursuant to law, and if determined to be eligible, shall be permitted to obtain an abortion.
The rights provided for females by this section shall be posted in at least one conspicuous place to which all female prisoners have access.
(Amended by Stats. 1996, Ch. 1023, Sec. 394. Effective September 29, 1996.)
3406.
Any female prisoner shall have the right to summon and receive the services of any physician and surgeon of her choice in order to determine whether she is pregnant. The warden may adopt reasonable rules and regulations with regard to the conduct of examinations to effectuate this determination.
If the prisoner is found to be pregnant, she is entitled to a determination of the extent of the medical services needed by her and to the receipt of these services from the physician and surgeon of her choice. Any expenses occasioned by the services of a physician and surgeon whose services are not provided by the institution shall be borne by the prisoner.
Any physician providing services pursuant to this section shall possess a current, valid, and unrevoked certificate to engage in the practice of medicine issued pursuant to Chapter 5 (commencing with Section 2000) of Division 2 of the Business and Professions Code.
The rights provided for prisoners by this section shall be posted in at least one conspicuous place to which all female prisoners have access.
(Amended by Stats. 1989, Ch. 1420, Sec. 17.)
3407.
(a) An inmate known to be pregnant or in recovery after delivery shall not be restrained by the use of leg irons, waist chains, or handcuffs behind the body.
(b) A pregnant inmate in labor, during delivery, or in recovery after delivery, shall not be restrained by the wrists, ankles, or both, unless deemed necessary for the safety and security of the inmate, the staff, or the public.
(c) Restraints shall be removed when a professional who is currently responsible for the medical care of a pregnant inmate during a medical emergency, labor, delivery, or recovery after delivery determines that the removal of restraints is medically necessary.
(d) This section shall not be interpreted to require restraints in a case where restraints are not required pursuant to a statute, regulation, or correctional facility policy.
(e) Upon confirmation of an inmate's pregnancy, she shall be advised, orally or in writing, of the standards and policies governing pregnant inmates, including, but not limited to, the provisions of this chapter, the relevant regulations, and the correctional facility policies.
(f) For purposes of this section, "inmate" means an adult or juvenile who is incarcerated in a state or local correctional facility.
(Added by Stats. 2012, Ch. 726, Sec. 1. (AB 2530) Effective January 1, 2013.)
3409.
(a) Any incarcerated person in state prison who menstruates shall, upon request, have access to, and be allowed to use, materials necessary for personal hygiene with regard to their menstrual cycle and reproductive system. Any incarcerated person in state prison who is capable of becoming pregnant shall, upon request, have access to, and be allowed to obtain, contraceptive counseling and their choice of birth control methods, subject to the provisions of subdivision (b), unless medically contraindicated.
(b) (1) Except as provided in paragraph (2), all birth control methods and emergency contraception approved by the United States Food and Drug Administration (FDA) shall be made available to incarcerated persons who are capable of becoming pregnant, with the exception of sterilizing procedures prohibited by Section 3440.

(2) The California Correctional Health Care Services shall establish a formulary that consists of all FDA-approved birth control methods and that shall be available to persons specified in subdivision (a). If a birth control method has more than one FDA-approved therapeutic equivalent, only one version of that method shall be required to be made available, unless another version is specifically indicated by a prescribing provider and approved by the chief medical physician at the facility. Persons shall have access to nonprescription birth control methods without the requirement to see a licensed health care provider.
(c) (1) Any contraceptive service that requires a prescription, or any contraceptive counseling, provided to incarcerated persons who are capable of becoming pregnant, shall be furnished by a licensed health care provider who has been provided with training in reproductive health care and shall be nondirective, unbiased, and noncoercive. These services shall be furnished by the facility or by any other agency that contracts with the facility. Except as provided in paragraph (2), health care providers furnishing contraceptive services shall receive training in the following areas:
(A) The requirements of this section.
(B) Providing nondirective, unbiased, and noncoercive contraceptive counseling and services.
(2) Providers who attend an orientation program for the Family Planning, Access, Care, and Treatment Program shall be deemed to have met the training requirements described in paragraph (1).
(d) Any incarcerated person who is capable of becoming pregnant shall be furnished by the facility with information and education regarding the availability of family planning services and their right to receive nondirective, unbiased, and noncoercive contraceptive counseling and services. Each facility shall post this information in conspicuous places to which all incarcerated persons who are capable of becoming pregnant have access.
(e) Contraceptive counseling and family planning services shall be offered and made available to all incarcerated persons who are capable of becoming pregnant at least 60 days, but not longer than 180 days, prior to a scheduled release date.
(f) This section shall not be construed to limit an incarcerated person's access to any method of contraception that is prescribed or recommended for any medically indicated reason.
(Amended by Stats. 2017, Ch. 561, Sec. 191. (AB 1516) Effective January 1, 2018.)

CHAPTER 4. Community Treatment Programs [3410 - 3424]

(Chapter 4 added by Stats. 1978, Ch. 1054.)
3410.
The term "community" shall, for the purposes of this chapter, mean an environment away from the prison setting which is in an urban or suburban area.
(Added by Stats. 1978, Ch. 1054.)
3411.
The Department of Corrections shall on or before January 1, 1980, establish and implement a community treatment program under which women inmates sentenced to state prison pursuant to Section 1168 or 1170 who have one or more children under the age of six years, whether born prior to or after January 1, 1976, shall be eligible to participate within the provisions of this section. The community treatment program shall provide for the release of the mother and child or children to a public or private facility in the community suitable to the needs of the mother and child or children, and which will provide the best possible care for the mother and child. In establishing and operating such program, the department shall have as a prime concern the establishment of a safe and wholesome environment for the participating children.
(Amended by Stats. 1988, Ch. 1044, Sec. 1. Effective September 20, 1988.)
3412.
(a) The Department of Corrections shall provide pediatric care consistent with medical standards and, to the extent feasible, shall be guided by the need to provide the following:
(1) A stable, caregiving, stimulating environment for the children as developed and supervised by professional guidance in the area of child development.
(2) Programs geared to assure the stability of the parent-child relationship during and after participation in the program, to be developed and supervised by appropriate professional guidance. These programs shall, at a minimum, be geared to accomplish the following:
(A) The mother's mental stability.
(B) The mother's familiarity with good parenting and housekeeping skills.
(C) The mother's ability to function in the community, upon parole or release, as a viable member.
(D) The securing of adequate housing arrangements after participation in the program.
(E) The securing of adequate child care arrangements after participation in the program.
(3) Utilization of the least restrictive alternative to incarceration and restraint possible to achieve the objectives of correction and of this chapter consistent with public safety and justice.
(b) (1) The Department of Corrections shall ensure that the children and mothers residing in a community treatment program have access to, and are permitted by the community treatment program to participate in, available local Head Start, Healthy Start, and programs for early childhood development pursuant to the California Children and Families Program (Division 108 (commencing with Section 130100) of the Health and Safety Code).
(2) The community treatment program shall provide each mother with written information about the available local programs, including the telephone numbers for enrolling a child in a program.
(3) The community treatment program shall also provide transportation to program services and otherwise assist and facilitate enrollment and participation for eligible children.
(4) Nothing in this subdivision shall be construed as granting or requiring preferential access or enrollment for children of incarcerated mothers to any of the programs specified in this subdivision.
(Amended by Stats. 2004, Ch. 297, Sec. 1. Effective January 1, 2005.)
3413.
In determining how to implement this chapter, the Department of Corrections shall be guided by the need to utilize the most cost-efficient methods possible. Therefore, the Director of Corrections may enter into contracts, with the approval of the Director of General Services, with appropriate public or private agencies, to provide housing, sustenance, services as provided in subdivisions (a) and (b) of Section 3412, and supervision for such inmates as are eligible for placement in community treatment programs. Prisoners in the care of such agencies shall be subject to all provisions of law applicable to them.
(Amended by Stats. 1982, Ch. 42, Sec. 4. Effective February 17, 1982.)
3414.
The department shall establish reasonable rules and regulations concerning the operation of the program.
(Added by Stats. 1978, Ch. 1054.)
3415.

(a) The probation department shall, no later than the day that any woman is sentenced to the state prison, notify such woman of the provisions of this chapter, if the term of the state imprisonment does not exceed six years on the basis of either the probable release or parole date computed as if the maximum amount of good time credit would be granted. The probation department shall determine such term of state imprisonment at such time for the purposes of this section.

(b) The woman may, upon the receipt of such notice and upon sentencing to a term in state prison, give notice of her desire to be admitted to a program under this chapter. The probation department or the defendant shall transmit such notice to the Department of Corrections, and to the appropriate local social services agency that conducts investigations for child neglect and dependency hearings.

(Amended by Stats. 1982, Ch. 42, Sec. 5. Effective February 17, 1982.)

3416.

(a) If any woman received by or committed to the Department of Corrections has a child under six years of age, or gives birth to a child while an inmate under the jurisdiction of the Department of Corrections, the child and his or her mother shall, upon her request, be admitted to and retained in a community treatment program established by the Department of Corrections, subject to the provisions of this chapter.

(b) Women transferred to community treatment programs remain under the legal custody of the department and shall be subject at any time, pursuant to the rules and regulations of the Director of Corrections, to be detained in the county jail upon the exercise of a state parole or correctional officer's peace officer powers as specified in Section 830.5, with the consent of the sheriff or corresponding official having jurisdiction over the facility.

(Amended by Stats. 1984, Ch. 961, Sec. 2. Effective September 10, 1984.)

3417.

(a) Subject to reasonable rules and regulations adopted pursuant to Section 3414, the Department of Corrections and Rehabilitation shall admit to the program any applicant whose child was born prior to the receipt of the inmate by the department, whose child was born after the receipt of the inmate by the department, or who is pregnant, if all of the following requirements are met:

(1) The applicant has a probable release or parole date with a maximum time to be served of six years, calculated after deduction of any possible good time credit.

(2) The applicant was the primary caretaker of the infant prior to incarceration. "Primary caretaker" as used in this chapter means a parent who has consistently assumed responsibility for the housing, health, and safety of the child prior to incarceration. A parent who, in the best interests of the child, has arranged for temporary care for the child in the home of a relative or other responsible adult shall not for that reason be excluded from the category, "primary caretaker."

(3) The applicant had not been found to be an unfit parent in any court proceeding. An inmate applicant whose child has been declared a dependent of the juvenile court pursuant to Section 300 of the Welfare and Institutions Code shall be admitted to the program only after the court has found that participation in the program is in the child's best interest and that it meets the needs of the parent and child pursuant to paragraph (3) of subdivision (e) of Section 361.5 of the Welfare and Institutions Code. The fact that an inmate applicant's child has been found to come within Section 300 of the Welfare and Institutions Code shall not, in and of itself, be grounds for denying the applicant the opportunity to participate in the program.

(b) The Department of Corrections and Rehabilitation shall deny placement in the community treatment program if it determines that an inmate would pose an unreasonable risk to the public, or if any one of the following factors exist, except in unusual circumstances or if mitigating circumstances exist, including, but not limited to, the remoteness in time of the commission of the offense:

(1) The inmate has been convicted of any of the following:
(A) A sex offense listed in Section 667.6.
(B) A sex offense requiring registration pursuant to Section 290.
(C) A violent offense listed in subdivision (c) of Section 667.5, except that the Secretary of the Department of Corrections and Rehabilitation shall consider an inmate for placement in the community treatment program on a case-by-case basis if the violent offense listed in subdivision (c) of Section 667.5 was for robbery pursuant to paragraph (9) of subdivision (c) of Section 667.5 or burglary pursuant to paragraph (21) of subdivision (c) of Section 667.5.
(D) Arson as defined in Sections 450 to 455, inclusive.

(2) There is probability the inmate may abscond from the program as evidenced by any of the following:
(A) A conviction of escape, of aiding another person to escape, or of an attempt to escape from a jail or prison.
(B) The presence of an active detainer from a law enforcement agency, unless the detainer is based solely upon warrants issued for failure to appear on misdemeanor Vehicle Code violations.

(3) It is probable the inmate's conduct in a community facility will be adverse to herself or other participants in the program, as determined by the Secretary of the Department of Corrections and Rehabilitation or as evidenced by any of the following:
(A) The inmate's removal from a community program which resulted from violation of state laws, rules, or regulations governing Department of Corrections and Rehabilitation's inmates.
(B) A finding of the inmate's guilt of a serious rule violation, as defined by the Secretary of the Department of Corrections and Rehabilitation, which resulted in a credit loss on one occasion of 91 or more days or in a credit loss on more than one occasion of 31 days or more and the credit has not been restored.
(C) A current written opinion of a staff physician or psychiatrist that the inmate's medical or psychiatric condition is likely to cause an adverse effect upon the inmate or upon other persons if the inmate is placed in the program.

(c) The Secretary of the Department of Corrections and Rehabilitation shall consider the placement of the following inmates in the community treatment program on a case-by-case basis:
(1) An inmate convicted of the unlawful sale or possession for sale, manufacture, or transportation of controlled substances, as defined in Chapter 6 (commencing with Section 11350) of Division 10 of the Health and Safety Code, if large scale for profit as defined by the department, provided that an inmate convicted pursuant to Section 11358 or 11359 of the Health and Safety Code shall be admitted to the program pursuant to subdivision (a).
(2) An inmate with a United States Immigration and Customs Enforcement hold.

(d) A charged offense that did not result in a conviction shall not be used to exclude an applicant from the program.

(e) Nothing in this section shall be interpreted to limit the discretion of the Secretary of the Department of Corrections and Rehabilitation to deny or approve placement when subdivision (b) does not apply.

(f) The Department of Corrections and Rehabilitation shall determine if the applicant meets the requirements of this section within 30 days of the parent's application to the program. The department shall establish an appeal procedure for the applicant to appeal an adverse decision by the department.

(Amended by Stats. 2012, Ch. 41, Sec. 71. (SB 1021) Effective June 27, 2012.)

3418.

(a) In the case of any inmate who gave birth to a child after the date of sentencing, and in the case of any inmate who gave birth to a child prior to that date and meets the requirements of Section 3417 but has not yet made application for admission to a program, the department shall, at the earliest possible date, but in no case later than the birth of the child, or the receipt of the inmate to the custody of the Department of

Corrections, as the case may be, notify the inmate of the provisions of this chapter and provide her with a written application for the program described in this chapter.

(b) The notice provided by the department shall contain, but need not be limited to, guidelines for qualification for, and the timeframe for application to, the program and the process for appealing a denial of admittance.

(Amended by Stats. 2004, Ch. 297, Sec. 3. Effective January 1, 2005.)

3419.

(a) In the case of any inmate who gives birth after her receipt by the Department of Corrections and Rehabilitation, the department shall, subject to reasonable rules and regulations promulgated pursuant to Section 3414, provide notice of, and a written application for, the program described in this chapter, and upon her request, declare the inmate eligible to participate in a program pursuant to this chapter if all of the requirements of Section 3417 are met.

(b) The notice provided by the department shall contain, but need not be limited to, guidelines for qualification for, and the timeframe for application to, the program and the process for appealing a denial of admittance.

(c) Any community treatment program, in which an inmate who gives birth after her receipt by the Department of Corrections and Rehabilitation participates, shall include, but is not limited to, the following:
(1) Prenatal care.
(2) Access to prenatal vitamins.
(3) Childbirth education.
(4) Infant care.

(Amended by Stats. 2005, Ch. 608, Sec. 1. Effective January 1, 2006.)

3420.

(a) Within five days after the receipt of an inmate by the Department of Corrections who has already applied for admission to a program, or of her application for admission to a program, whichever is later, the department shall give notice of her application to the child's current caretaker or guardian, if any, and if it has not already been notified pursuant to Section 3415, the appropriate local social services agency that conducts investigations for child neglect and dependency hearings.

(b) The department and the individuals and agencies notified shall have five days from the date of notice to decide whether or not to challenge the appropriateness of the applicant's entry into the program. Lack of a petition filed by that time shall result in a presumption that the individuals and agencies notified do not challenge the appropriateness of the applicant's entry into the program.

(c) The local agency which has been notified pursuant to Section 3415 shall not initiate the process of considering whether or not to file until after the sentencing court has sentenced the applicant.

(d) The appropriate local agency that conducts investigations for child neglect and dependency hearings, the Department of Corrections, and the current guardian or caretaker of the child, shall have the authority to file for a fitness proceeding against the mother after the mother has applied in writing to participate in the program.

(e) The determination of whether or not to file shall be based in part on the likelihood of the mother being a fit parent for the child in question both during the program and afterwards. Program content shall be taken into account in this determination. There shall be a presumption affecting the burden of producing evidence in favor of filing for a fitness proceeding under the following circumstances:

(1) The applicant was convicted of one or more of the following violent felonies:
(A) Murder.
(B) Mayhem.
(C) Aggravated mayhem.
(D) Kidnapping as defined in Section 207 or 209.
(E) Lewd acts on a child under 14 as defined in Section 288.
(F) Any felony in which the defendant inflicts great bodily injury on a person other than accomplices which has been alleged and proven.
(G) Forcible rape in violation of subdivision (2), (3), or (4) of Section 261.
(H) Sodomy by force, violence, duress, menace, or threat of great bodily injury.
(I) Oral copulation by force, violence, duress, menace, or threat of great bodily injury.
(2) The applicant was convicted of child abuse in the current or any proceeding.

(f) Fitness petitions shall be resolved in the court of first instance as soon as possible for purposes of this section. Given the need to place the child as soon as possible, the first determination by the court as to the applicant's fitness as a mother shall determine her eligibility for the program for the current application. Outcomes of appeals shall not affect eligibility.

(Amended by Stats. 1994, Ch. 224, Sec. 8. Effective January 1, 1995.)

3421.

Children of women inmates may only participate in the program until they reach the age of six years, at which time the Board of Prison Terms may arrange for their care elsewhere under any procedure authorized by statute and transfer the mother to another placement under the jurisdiction of the Department of Corrections if necessary; and provided further, that at its discretion in exceptional cases, including, but not limited to cases where the mother's period of incarceration is extended, the board may retain such child and mother for a longer period of time.

(Amended by Stats. 1982, Ch. 42, Sec. 11. Effective February 17, 1982.)

3422.

The costs for care of any mother and child placed in a community treatment program pursuant to this section shall be paid for out of funds allocated to the department in the normal budgetary process. The department shall make diligent efforts to procure other funding sources for the program.

(Amended by Stats. 1982, Ch. 42, Sec. 12. Effective February 17, 1982.)

3423.

Any woman inmate who would give birth to a child during her term of imprisonment may be temporarily taken to a hospital outside the prison for the purposes of childbirth, and the charge for hospital and medical care shall be charged against the funds allocated to the institution. The inmate shall not be shackled by the wrists, ankles, or both during labor, including during transport to a hospital, during delivery, and while in recovery after giving birth, except as provided in Section 5007.7. The board shall provide for the care of any children so born and shall pay for their care until suitably placed, including, but not limited to, placement in a community treatment program.

(Amended by Stats. 2005, Ch. 608, Sec. 2. Effective January 1, 2006.)

3424.

A woman who is pregnant during her incarceration and who is not eligible for the program described in this chapter shall have access to complete prenatal health care. The department shall establish minimum standards for pregnant inmates in its custody who are not placed in a community treatment program including all of the following:
(a) A balanced, nutritious diet approved by a doctor.
(b) Prenatal and postpartum information and health care, including, but not limited to, access to necessary vitamins as recommended by a doctor.
(c) Information pertaining to childbirth education and infant care.
(d) A dental cleaning while in a state facility.

(Added by Stats. 2005, Ch. 608, Sec. 3. Effective January 1, 2006.)

CHAPTER 5. Gender Responsive Programs [3430-3430.]

(Chapter 5 added by Stats. 2007, Ch. 706, Sec. 1.)

3430.

The Department of Corrections and Rehabilitation shall do all of the following:

(a) Create a Female Offender Reform Master Plan, and shall present this plan to the Legislature by March 1, 2008.

(b) Create policies and operational practices that are designed to ensure a safe and productive institutional environment for female offenders.

(c) Contract with nationally recognized gender responsive experts in prison operational practices staffing, classification, substance abuse, trauma treatment services, mental health services, transitional services, and community corrections to do both of the following:

(1) Conduct a staffing analysis of all current job classifications assigned to each prison that houses only females. The department shall provide a plan to the Legislature by March 1, 2009, that incorporates those recommendations and details the changes that are needed to address any identified unmet needs of female inmates.

(2) Develop programs and training for department staff in correctional facilities.

(d) Create a gender responsive female classification system.

(e) Create a gender responsive staffing pattern for female institutions and community-based offender beds.

(f) Create a needs-based case and risk management tool designed specifically for female offenders. This tool shall include, but not be limited to, an assessment upon intake, and annually thereafter, that gauges an inmate's educational and vocational needs, including reading, writing, communication, and arithmetic skills, health care needs, mental health needs, substance abuse needs, and trauma-treatment needs. The initial assessment shall include projections for academic, vocational, health care, mental health, substance abuse, and trauma-treatment needs, and shall be used to determine appropriate programming and as a measure of progress in subsequent assessments of development.

(g) Design and implement evidence-based gender specific rehabilitative programs, including "wraparound" educational, health care, mental health, vocational, substance abuse and trauma treatment programs that are designed to reduce female offender recidivism. These programs shall include, but not be limited to, educational programs that include academic preparation in the areas of verbal communication skills, reading, writing, arithmetic, and the acquisition of high school diplomas and GEDs, and vocational preparation, including counseling and training in marketable skills, and job placement information.

(h) Build and strengthen systems of family support and family involvement during the period of the female's incarceration.

(i) Establish a family service coordinator at each prison that houses only females.

(Added by Stats. 2007, Ch. 706, Sec. 1. Effective January 1, 2008.)

CHAPTER 6. Sterilization of Inmates [3440-3440.]

(Chapter 6 added by Stats. 2014, Ch. 558, Sec. 2.)

3440.

(a) Sterilization for the purpose of birth control, including, but not limited to, during labor and delivery, of an individual under the control of the department or a county and imprisoned in the state prison or a reentry facility, community correctional facility, county jail, or any other institution in which an individual is involuntarily confined or detained under a civil or criminal statute, is prohibited.

(b) Sterilization of an individual under the control of the department or a county and imprisoned in the state prison or a reentry facility, community correctional facility, county jail, or any other institution in which an individual is involuntarily confined or detained under a civil or criminal statute, through tubal ligation, hysterectomy, oophorectomy, salpingectomy, or any other means rendering an individual permanently incapable of reproducing, is prohibited except in either of the following circumstances:

(1) The procedure is required for the immediate preservation of the individual's life in an emergency medical situation.

(2) The sterilizing procedure is medically necessary, as determined by contemporary standards of evidence-based medicine, to treat a diagnosed condition, and all of the following requirements are satisfied:

(A) Less invasive measures to address the medical need are nonexistent, are refused by the individual, or are first attempted and deemed unsuccessful by the individual, in consultation with his or her medical provider.

(B) A second physician, independent of, and not employed by, but authorized to provide services to individuals in the custody of, and to receive payment for those services from, the department or county department overseeing the confinement of the individual, conducts an in-person consultation with the individual and confirms the need for a medical intervention resulting in sterilization to address the medical need.

(C) Patient consent is obtained after the individual is made aware of the full and permanent impact the procedure will have on his or her reproductive capacity, that future medical treatment while under the control of the department or county will not be withheld should the individual refuse consent to the procedure, and the side effects of the procedure.

(c) If a sterilization procedure is performed pursuant to paragraph (1) or (2) of subdivision (b), presterilization and poststerilization psychological consultation and medical followup, including providing relevant hormone therapy to address surgical menopause, shall be made available to the individual sterilized while under the control of the department or the county.

(d) (1) The department shall, if a sterilization procedure is performed on one or more individuals under its control, annually publish on its Internet Web site data related to the number of sterilizations performed, disaggregated by race, age, medical justification, and method of sterilization.

(2) (A) Each county jail or other institution of confinement shall, if a sterilization procedure is performed on one or more individuals under its control, annually submit to the Board of State and Community Corrections data related to the number of sterilizations performed, disaggregated by race, age, medical justification, and method of sterilization.

(B) The Board of State and Community Corrections shall annually publish the data received pursuant to subparagraph (A) on its Internet Web site.

(e) The department and all county jails or other institutions of confinement shall provide notification to all individuals under their custody and to all employees who are involved in providing health care services of their rights and responsibilities under this section.

(f) An employee of the department or of a county jail or other institution of confinement who reports the sterilization of an individual performed in violation of this section is entitled to the protection available under subparagraphs (A) and (B) of paragraph (2) of subdivision (a) of Section 6129, or under the California Whistleblower Protection Act (Article 3 (commencing with Section 8547) of Chapter 6.5 of Division 1 of Title 2 of the Government Code) or the Whistleblower Protection Act (Article 10 (commencing with Section 9149.20) of Chapter 1.5 of Part 1 of Division 2 of Title 2 of the Government Code).

(Amended by Stats. 2015, Ch. 303, Sec. 399. (AB 731) Effective January 1, 2016.)

TITLE 2.05. Postrelease Community Supervision Act of 2011 [3450 - 3465]

(Title 2.05 added by Stats. 2011, Ch. 15, Sec. 479.)

3450.

(a) This act shall be known and may be cited as the Postrelease Community Supervision Act of 2011.

(b) The Legislature finds and declares all of the following:

(1) The Legislature reaffirms its commitment to reducing recidivism among criminal offenders.

(2) Despite the dramatic increase in corrections spending over the past two decades, national reincarceration rates for people released from prison remain unchanged or have worsened. National data show that about 40 percent of released individuals are reincarcerated within three years. In California, the recidivism rate for persons who have served time in prison is even greater than the national average.

(3) Criminal justice policies that rely on the reincarceration of parolees for technical violations do not result in improved public safety.

(4) California must reinvest its criminal justice resources to support community corrections programs and evidence-based practices that will achieve improved public safety returns on this state's substantial investment in its criminal justice system.

(5) Realigning the postrelease supervision of certain felons reentering the community after serving a prison term to local community corrections programs, which are strengthened through community-based punishment, evidence-based practices, and improved supervision strategies, will improve public safety outcomes among adult felon parolees and will facilitate their successful reintegration back into society.

(6) Community corrections programs require a partnership between local public safety entities and the county to provide and expand the use of community-based punishment for offenders paroled from state prison. Each county's local Community Corrections Partnership, as established in paragraph (2) of subdivision (b) of Section 1230, should play a critical role in developing programs and ensuring appropriate outcomes for persons subject to postrelease community supervision.

(7) Fiscal policy and correctional practices should align to promote a justice reinvestment strategy that fits each county. "Justice reinvestment" is a data-driven approach to reduce corrections and related criminal justice spending and reinvest savings in strategies designed to increase public safety. The purpose of justice reinvestment is to manage and allocate criminal justice populations more cost effectively, generating savings that can be reinvested in evidence-based strategies that increase public safety while holding offenders accountable.

(8) "Community-based punishment" means evidence-based correctional sanctions and programming encompassing a range of custodial and noncustodial responses to criminal or noncompliant offender activity. Intermediate sanctions may be provided by local public safety entities directly or through public or private correctional service providers and include, but are not limited to, the following:

(A) Short-term "flash" incarceration in jail for a period of not more than 10 days.

(B) Intensive community supervision.

(C) Home detention with electronic monitoring or GPS monitoring.

(D) Mandatory community service.

(E) Restorative justice programs, such as mandatory victim restitution and victim-offender reconciliation.

(F) Work, training, or education in a furlough program pursuant to Section 1208.

(G) Work, in lieu of confinement, in a work release program pursuant to Section 4024.2.

(H) Day reporting.

(I) Mandatory residential or nonresidential substance abuse treatment programs.

(J) Mandatory random drug testing.

(K) Mother-infant care programs.

(L) Community-based residential programs offering structure, supervision, drug treatment, alcohol treatment, literacy programming, employment counseling, psychological counseling, mental health treatment, or any combination of these and other interventions.

(9) "Evidence-based practices" refers to supervision policies, procedures, programs, and practices demonstrated by scientific research to reduce recidivism among individuals under probation, parole, or postrelease supervision.

(Amended by Stats. 2011, 1st Ex. Sess., Ch. 12, Sec. 27. (AB 17 1x) Effective September 21, 2011. Operative October 1, 2011, by Sec. 46 of Ch. 12.)

3451.

(a) Notwithstanding any other law and except for persons serving a prison term for any crime described in subdivision (b), all persons released from prison on and after October 1, 2011, or, whose sentence has been deemed served pursuant to Section 2900.5 after serving a prison term for a felony shall, upon release from prison and for a period not exceeding three years immediately following release, be subject to community supervision provided by the probation department of the county to which the person is being released, which is consistent with evidence-based practices, including, but not limited to, supervision policies, procedures, programs, and practices demonstrated by scientific research to reduce recidivism among individuals under postrelease supervision.

(b) This section shall not apply to any person released from prison after having served a prison term for any of the following:

(1) A serious felony described in subdivision (c) of Section 1192.7.

(2) A violent felony described in subdivision (c) of Section 667.5.

(3) A crime for which the person was sentenced pursuant to paragraph (2) of subdivision (e) of Section 667 or paragraph (2) of subdivision (c) of Section 1170.12.

(4) Any crime for which the person is classified as a high-risk sex offender.

(5) Any crime for which the person is required, as a condition of parole, to undergo treatment by the State Department of State Hospitals pursuant to Section 2962.

(c) (1) Postrelease supervision under this title shall be implemented by the county probation department according to a postrelease strategy designated by each county's board of supervisors.

(2) The Department of Corrections and Rehabilitation shall inform every prisoner subject to the provisions of this title, upon release from state prison, of the requirements of this title and of his or her responsibility to report to the county probation department. The department or probation department shall also inform persons serving a term of parole or postrelease community supervision for a felony offense who are subject to this section of the requirements of this title and of his or her responsibility to report to the county probation department. Thirty days prior to the release of any person subject to postrelease supervision by a county, the department shall notify the county of all information that would otherwise be required for parolees under subdivision (e) of Section 3003.

(d) A person released to postrelease community supervision pursuant to subdivision (a) shall, regardless of any subsequent determination that the person should have been released to parole pursuant to Section 3000.08, remain subject to subdivision (a) after having served 60 days under supervision pursuant to subdivision (a).

(Amended by Stats. 2015, Ch. 378, Sec. 5. (AB 1156) Effective January 1, 2016.)

3452.

(a) A person who is eligible for postrelease community supervision pursuant to this title shall be given notice that he or she is subject to postrelease community supervision prior to his or her release from prison. A person who is on parole and is then transferred to postrelease community supervision shall be given notice that he or she is subject to postrelease community supervision prior to his or her release from state prison.

(b) A postrelease community supervision notice shall specify the following:

(1) The person's release date and the maximum period the person may be subject to postrelease supervision under this title.

(2) The name, address, and telephone number of the county agency responsible for the person's postrelease supervision.

(3) An advisement that if a person breaks the law or violates the conditions of release, he or she can be incarcerated in a county jail regardless of whether or not new charges are filed.

(Amended by Stats. 2012, Ch. 43, Sec. 50. (SB 1023) Effective June 27, 2012.)

3453.

Postrelease community supervision shall include the following conditions:

(a) The person shall be informed of the conditions of release.

(b) The person shall obey all laws.

(c) The person shall report to the supervising county agency within two working days of release from custody.

(d) The person shall follow the directives and instructions of the supervising county agency.

(e) The person shall report to the supervising county agency as directed by that agency.

(f) The person, and his or her residence and possessions, shall be subject to search at any time of the day or night, with or without a warrant, by an agent of the supervising county agency or by a peace officer.

(g) The person shall waive extradition if found outside the state.

(h) (1) The person shall inform the supervising county agency of the person's place of residence and shall notify the supervising county agency of any change in residence, or the establishment of a new residence if the person was previously transient, within five working days of the change.

(2) For purposes of this section, "residence" means one or more locations at which a person regularly resides, regardless of the number of days or nights spent there, such as a shelter or structure that can be located by a street address, including, but not limited to, a house, apartment building, motel, hotel, homeless shelter, and recreational or other vehicle. If the person has no residence, he or she shall inform the supervising county agency that he or she is transient.

(i) (1) The person shall inform the supervising county agency of the person's place of employment, education, or training. The person shall inform the supervising agency of any pending or anticipated change in employment, education, or training.

(2) If the person enters into new employment, he or she shall inform the supervising county agency of the new employment within three business days of that entry.

(j) The person shall immediately inform the supervising county agency if he or she is arrested or receives a citation.

(k) The person shall obtain the permission of the supervising county agency to travel more than 50 miles from the person's place of residence.

(l) The person shall obtain a travel pass from the supervising county agency before he or she may leave the county or state for more than two days.

(m) The person shall not be in the presence of a firearm or ammunition, or any item that appears to be a firearm or ammunition.

(n) The person shall not possess, use, or have access to any weapon listed in Section 16140, subdivision (c) of Section 16170, Section 16220, 16260, 16320, 16330, or 16340, subdivision (b) of Section 16460, Section 16470, subdivision (f) of Section 16520, or Section 16570, 16740, 16760, 16830, 16920, 16930, 16940, 17090, 17125, 17160, 17170, 17180, 17190, 17200, 17270, 17280, 17330, 17350, 17360, 17700, 17705, 17710, 17715, 17720, 17725, 17730, 17735, 17740, 17745, 19100, 19200, 19205, 20200, 20310, 20410, 20510, 20610, 20611, 20710, 20910, 21110, 21310, 21810, 22010, 22015, 22210, 22215, 22410, 24310, 24410, 24510, 24610, 24680, 24710, 30210, 30215, 31500, 32310, 32400, 32405, 32410, 32415, 32420, 32425, 32430 32435, 32440, 32445, 32450, 32900, 33215, 33220, 33225, or 33600.

(o) (1) Except as provided in paragraph (2) and subdivision (p), the person shall not possess a knife with a blade longer than two inches.

(2) The person may possess a kitchen knife with a blade longer than two inches if the knife is used and kept only in the kitchen of the person's residence.

(p) The person may use a knife with a blade longer than two inches, if the use is required for that person's employment, the use has been approved in a document issued by the supervising county agency, and the person possesses the document of approval at all times and makes it available for inspection.

(q) The person shall waive any right to a court hearing prior to the imposition of a period of "flash incarceration" in a city or county jail of not more than 10 consecutive days for any violation of his or her postrelease supervision conditions.

(r) The person shall participate in rehabilitation programming as recommended by the supervising county agency.

(s) The person shall be subject to arrest with or without a warrant by a peace officer employed by the supervising county agency or, at the direction of the supervising county agency, by any peace officer when there is probable cause to believe the person has violated the terms and conditions of his or her release.

(t) The person shall pay court-ordered restitution and restitution fines in the same manner as a person placed on probation.

(Amended by Stats. 2017, Ch. 17, Sec. 39. (AB 103) Effective June 27, 2017.)

3454.

(a) Each supervising county agency, as established by the county board of supervisors pursuant to subdivision (a) of Section 3451, shall establish a review process for assessing and refining a person's program of postrelease supervision. Any additional postrelease supervision conditions shall be reasonably related to the underlying offense for which the offender spent time in prison, or to the offender's risk of recidivism, and the offender's criminal history, and be otherwise consistent with law.

(b) Each county agency responsible for postrelease supervision, as established by the county board of supervisors pursuant to subdivision (a) of Section 3451, may determine additional appropriate conditions of supervision listed in Section 3453 consistent with public safety, including the use of continuous electronic monitoring as defined in Section 1210.7, order the provision of appropriate rehabilitation and treatment services, determine appropriate incentives, and determine and order appropriate responses to alleged violations, which can include, but shall not be limited to, immediate, structured, and intermediate sanctions up to and including referral to a reentry court pursuant to Section 3015, or flash incarceration in a city or county jail. Periods of flash incarceration are encouraged as one method of punishment for violations of an offender's condition of postrelease supervision.

(c) As used in this title, "flash incarceration" is a period of detention in a city or county jail due to a violation of an offender's conditions of postrelease supervision. The length of the detention period can range between one and 10 consecutive days. Flash incarceration is a tool that may be used by each county agency responsible for postrelease supervision. Shorter, but if necessary more frequent, periods of detention for violations of an offender's postrelease supervision conditions shall appropriately punish an offender while preventing the disruption in a work or home establishment that typically arises from longer term revocations.

(Amended by Stats. 2013, Ch. 788, Sec. 3. (AB 986) Effective January 1, 2014.)

3455.

(a) If the supervising county agency has determined, following application of its assessment processes, that intermediate sanctions as authorized in subdivision (b) of Section 3454 are not appropriate, the supervising county agency shall petition the court

pursuant to Section 1203.2 to revoke, modify, or terminate postrelease community supervision. At any point during the process initiated pursuant to this section, a person may waive, in writing, his or her right to counsel, admit the violation of his or her postrelease community supervision, waive a court hearing, and accept the proposed modification of his or her postrelease community supervision. The petition shall include a written report that contains additional information regarding the petition, including the relevant terms and conditions of postrelease community supervision, the circumstances of the alleged underlying violation, the history and background of the violator, and any recommendations. The Judicial Council shall adopt forms and rules of court to establish uniform statewide procedures to implement this subdivision, including the minimum contents of supervision agency reports. Upon a finding that the person has violated the conditions of postrelease community supervision, the revocation hearing officer shall have authority to do all of the following:

(1) Return the person to postrelease community supervision with modifications of conditions, if appropriate, including a period of incarceration in a county jail.

(2) Revoke and terminate postrelease community supervision and order the person to confinement in a county jail.

(3) Refer the person to a reentry court pursuant to Section 3015 or other evidence-based program in the court's discretion.

(b) (1) At any time during the period of postrelease community supervision, if a peace officer has probable cause to believe a person subject to postrelease community supervision is violating any term or condition of his or her release, the officer may, without a warrant or other process, arrest the person and bring him or her before the supervising county agency established by the county board of supervisors pursuant to subdivision (a) of Section 3451. Additionally, an officer employed by the supervising county agency may seek a warrant and a court or its designated hearing officer appointed pursuant to Section 71622.5 of the Government Code shall have the authority to issue a warrant for that person's arrest.

(2) The court or its designated hearing officer shall have the authority to issue a warrant for a person who is the subject of a petition filed under this section who has failed to appear for a hearing on the petition or for any reason in the interests of justice, or to remand to custody a person who does appear at a hearing on the petition for any reason in the interests of justice.

(3) Unless a person subject to postrelease community supervision is otherwise serving a period of flash incarceration, whenever a person who is subject to this section is arrested, with or without a warrant or the filing of a petition for revocation, the court may order the release of the person under supervision from custody under any terms and conditions the court deems appropriate.

(c) The revocation hearing shall be held within a reasonable time after the filing of the revocation petition. Except as provided in paragraph (3) of subdivision (b), based upon a showing of a preponderance of the evidence that a person under supervision poses an unreasonable risk to public safety, or that the person may not appear if released from custody, or for any reason in the interests of justice, the supervising county agency shall have the authority to make a determination whether the person should remain in custody pending the first court appearance on a petition to revoke postrelease community supervision, and upon that determination, may order the person confined pending his or her first court appearance.

(d) Confinement pursuant to paragraphs (1) and (2) of subdivision (a) shall not exceed a period of 180 days in a county jail for each custodial sanction.

(e) A person shall not remain under supervision or in custody pursuant to this title on or after three years from the date of the person's initial entry onto postrelease community supervision, except when his or her supervision is tolled pursuant to Section 1203.2 or subdivision (b) of Section 3456.

(Amended by Stats. 2015, Ch. 61, Sec. 4. (SB 517) Effective January 1, 2016.)

3456.

(a) The county agency responsible for postrelease supervision, as established by the county board of supervisors pursuant to subdivision (a) of Section 3451, shall maintain postrelease supervision over a person under postrelease supervision pursuant to this title until one of the following events occurs:

(1) The person has been subject to postrelease supervision pursuant to this title for three years at which time the offender shall be immediately discharged from postrelease supervision.

(2) Any person on postrelease supervision for six consecutive months with no violations of his or her conditions of postrelease supervision that result in a custodial sanction may be considered for immediate discharge by the supervising county.

(3) The person who has been on postrelease supervision continuously for one year with no violations of his or her conditions of postrelease supervision that result in a custodial sanction shall be discharged from supervision within 30 days.

(4) Jurisdiction over the person has been terminated by operation of law.

(5) Jurisdiction is transferred to another supervising county agency.

(6) Jurisdiction is terminated by the revocation hearing officer upon a petition to revoke and terminate supervision by the supervising county agency.

(b) Time during which a person on postrelease supervision is suspended because the person has absconded shall not be credited toward any period of postrelease supervision.

(Amended by Stats. 2011, 1st Ex. Sess., Ch. 12, Sec. 31. (AB 17 1x) Effective September 21, 2011. Operative October 1, 2011, by Sec. 46 of Ch. 12.)

3456.5.

(a) (1) The local supervising agency, in coordination with the sheriff or local correctional administrator, may require any person that is to be released from county jail or a local correctional facility into postrelease community supervision to report to a supervising agent or designated local supervising agency within two days of release from the county jail or local correction facility.

(2) This section shall not prohibit the local supervising agency from requiring any person released on postrelease community supervision to report to his or her assigned supervising agent within a time period that is less than two days from the time of release.

(b) With regard to any inmate subject to this section, the sheriff or local correctional administrator may release an inmate sentenced prior to the effective date of the act adding this section one or two days before his or her scheduled release date if the inmate's release date falls on the day before a holiday or weekend.

(Added by Stats. 2012, Ch. 43, Sec. 53. (SB 1023) Effective June 27, 2012.)

3457.

The Department of Corrections and Rehabilitation shall have no jurisdiction over any person who is under postrelease community supervision pursuant to this title.

(Added by Stats. 2011, Ch. 15, Sec. 479. (AB 109) Effective April 4, 2011. Operative October 1, 2011, by Sec. 636 of Ch. 15, as amended by Stats. 2011, Ch. 39, Sec. 68.)

3458.

No person subject to this title shall be returned to prison for a violation of any condition of the person's postrelease supervision agreement.

(Added by Stats. 2011, Ch. 15, Sec. 479. (AB 109) Effective April 4, 2011. Operative October 1, 2011, by Sec. 636 of Ch. 15, as amended by Stats. 2011, Ch. 39, Sec. 68.)

3460.

(a) Whenever a supervising agency determines that a person subject to postrelease supervision pursuant to this chapter no longer permanently resides within its jurisdiction, and a change in residence was either approved by the supervising agency or did not violate the terms and conditions of postrelease supervision, the supervising agency shall transmit, within two weeks, any information the agency received from the Department of Corrections and Rehabilitation prior to the release of the person in that jurisdiction to the designated supervising agency in the county in which the person permanently resides.

(b) Upon verification of permanent residency, the receiving supervising agency shall accept jurisdiction and supervision of the person on postrelease supervision.

(c) For purposes of this section, residence means the place where the person customarily lives exclusive of employment, school, or other special or temporary purpose. A person may have only one residence.

(d) No supervising agency shall be required to transfer jurisdiction to another county unless the person demonstrates an ability to establish permanent residency within another county without violating the terms and conditions of postrelease supervision.

(Added by Stats. 2011, 1st Ex. Sess., Ch. 12, Sec. 32. (AB 17 1x) Effective September 21, 2011. Operative October 1, 2011, by Sec. 46 of Ch. 12.)

3465.

Every person placed on postrelease community supervision, and his or her residence and possessions, shall be subject to search or seizure at any time of the day or night, with or without a warrant, by an agent of the supervising county agency or by a peace officer.

(Added by Stats. 2011, 1st Ex. Sess., Ch. 12, Sec. 33. (AB 17 1x) Effective September 21, 2011. Operative October 1, 2011, by Sec. 46 of Ch. 12.)

TITLE 2.1. BIOMEDICAL AND BEHAVIORIAL RESEARCH [3500 - 3524]

(Title 2.1 added by Stats. 1977, Ch. 1250.)

CHAPTER 1. Definitions [3500- 3500.]

(Chapter 1 added by Stats. 1977, Ch. 1250.)

3500.

For purposes of this title:

(a) "Behavioral research" means studies involving, but not limited to, the investigation of human behavior, emotion, adaptation, conditioning, and response in a program designed to test certain hypotheses through the collection of objective data. Behavioral research does not include the accumulation of statistical data in the assessment of the effectiveness of programs to which inmates are routinely assigned, including, but not limited to, education, vocational training, productive work, counseling, recognized therapies, and programs that are not experimental in nature.

(b) "Biomedical research" means research relating to or involving biological, medical, or physical science. Biomedical research does not include the accumulation of statistical data in the assessment of the effectiveness of nonexperimental public health programs or treatment programs in which inmates routinely participate.

(c) "Psychotropic drug" means a drug that has the capability of changing or controlling mental functioning or behavior through direct pharmacological action. These drugs include, but are not limited to, antipsychotic, antianxiety, sedative, antidepressant, and stimulant drugs. Psychotropic drugs also include mind-altering and behavior-altering drugs that, in specified dosages, are used to alleviate certain physical disorders, and drugs that are ordinarily used to alleviate certain physical disorders but may, in specified dosages, have mind-altering or behavior-altering effects.

(d) "Research" means a class of activities designed to develop or contribute to generalizable knowledge, including theories, principles, or relationships, or the accumulation of data on which they may be based, that can be corroborated by accepted scientific observation and inferences.

(e) "Research protocol" means a formal document setting forth the explicit objectives of a research project and the procedures of investigation designed to reach those objectives.

(f) "Phase I drug" means a drug that is designated as a phase I drug for testing purposes under the federal Food and Drug Administration criteria in Part 312 of Subchapter D of Chapter I of Title 21 of the Code of Federal Regulations.

(Amended by Stats. 2016, Ch. 197, Sec. 1. (SB 1238) Effective January 1, 2017.)

CHAPTER 2. General Provisions and Prohibitions [3501 - 3509.5]

(Chapter 2 added by Stats. 1977, Ch. 1250.)

3501.

The Legislature affirms the fundamental right of competent adults to make decisions about their participation in behavioral research.

(Amended by Stats. 1985, Ch. 1553, Sec. 1.5.)

3502.

(a) Biomedical research shall not be conducted on any prisoner in this state.

(b) Notwithstanding subdivision (a), records-based biomedical research using existing information, without prospective interaction with human subjects, may be conducted consistent with this title. The use or disclosure of individually identifiable records pursuant to this subdivision shall only occur after both of the following requirements have been met:

(1) The research advisory committee established pursuant to Section 3369.5 of Title 15 of the California Code of Regulations approves of the use or disclosure.

(2) The prisoner provides written authorization for the use or disclosure, or the use or disclosure is permitted by Section 164.512 of Title 45 of the Code of Federal Regulations.

(Amended by Stats. 2016, Ch. 197, Sec. 2. (SB 1238) Effective January 1, 2017.)

3502.5.

(a) Notwithstanding Section 3502, any physician who provides medical care to prisoners may provide a patient who is a prisoner with a drug or treatment available only through a treatment protocol or treatment IND (investigational new drug), as defined in Section 312 of Title 21 of the Code of Federal Regulations, if the physician determines that access to that drug is in the best medical interest of the patient, and the patient has given informed consent under Section 3521.

(b) Notwithstanding any other provision of law, neither a public entity nor a public employee shall be liable for any injury caused by the administration of a drug pursuant to subdivision (a), where the administration is made in accordance with a treatment IND or a treatment protocol as defined in Section 312 of Title 21 of the Code of Federal Regulations.

(Amended by Stats. 1995, Ch. 70, Sec. 1. Effective January 1, 1996.)

3504.

Any physical or mental injury of a prisoner resulting from the participation in behavioral research, irrespective of causation of such injury, shall be treated promptly and on a continuing basis until the injury is cured.

(Amended by Stats. 1985, Ch. 1553, Sec. 5.)

3505.

Behavioral research shall be limited to studies of the possible causes, effects and processes of incarceration and studies of prisons as institutional structures or of prisoners as incarcerated persons which present minimal or no risk and no more than mere inconvenience to the subjects of the research. Informed consent shall not be required for participation in behavioral research when the department determines that it would be unnecessary or significantly inhibit the conduct of such research. In the absence of such determination, informed consent shall be required for participation in behavioral research.

(Amended by Stats. 1985, Ch. 1553, Sec. 6.)

3508.

Behavioral modification techniques shall be used only if such techniques are medically and socially acceptable means by which to modify behavior and if such techniques do not inflict permanent physical or psychological injury.

(Added by Stats. 1977, Ch. 1250.)

3509.5.

Nothing in this title is intended to diminish the authority of any official or agency to adopt and enforce rules pertaining to prisoners, so long as such rules are not inconsistent with this title.

(Added by Stats. 1977, Ch. 1250.)

CHAPTER 3. Administration [3515 - 3520]

(Chapter 3 added by Stats. 1977, Ch. 1250.)

3515.

The duties of the department are to determine:

(a) That the risks to the prisoners consenting to research are outweighed by the sum of benefits to the prisoners and the importance of the knowledge to be gained.

(b) That the rights and welfare of the prisoners are adequately protected, including the security of any confidential personal information.

(c) That the procedures for selection of prisoners are equitable and that subjects are not unjustly deprived of the opportunity to participate.

(d) That adequate provisions have been made for compensating research related injury.

(e) That the rate of remuneration is comparable to that received by nonprisoner volunteers in similar research.

(f) That the conduct of the activity will be reviewed at timely intervals.

(g) That legally effective informed consent will be obtained by adequate and appropriate methods.

(Amended by Stats. 1985, Ch. 1553, Sec. 15.)

3516.

No behavioral research shall be conducted on any prisoner in this state in the absence of a determination by the department consistent with this title.

(Amended by Stats. 1985, Ch. 1553, Sec. 16.)

3517.

The department shall promulgate rules and regulations reasonably necessary for the effective administration of the provisions of this title. Action on proposals submitted shall be taken within 60 days. The regulations shall be submitted to the Joint Legislative Prison Committee for review and shall not become operative until 60 days after submission.

(Amended by Stats. 1985, Ch. 1553, Sec. 17.)

3518.

The department shall promulgate rules and regulations prescribing procedures to be followed by any person who has a grievance concerning the operation of any particular research program conducted pursuant to this title.

(Amended by Stats. 1985, Ch. 1553, Sec. 18.)

3519.

The department shall evaluate the impact of research on human subjects approved and conducted pursuant to this title, including any adverse reactions.

(Amended by Stats. 1985, Ch. 1553, Sec. 19.)

3520.

The department shall make a report due on or before January 1 of each odd-numbered year containing a review of each research program which has been approved and conducted. The report shall be transmitted to the Legislature and shall be made available to the public.

(Amended by Stats. 2003, Ch. 468, Sec. 19. Effective January 1, 2004.)

CHAPTER 4. Prisoners' Rights as Research Subjects [3521 - 3523]

(Chapter 4 added by Stats. 1977, Ch. 1250.)

3521.

For the purposes of this title, a prisoner shall be deemed to have given his informed consent only if each of the following conditions are satisfied:

(a) Consent is given without duress, coercion, fraud, or undue influence.

(b) The prisoner is informed in writing of the potential risks or benefits, or both, of the proposed research.

(c) The prisoner is informed orally and in writing in the language in which the subject is fluent of each of the following:

(1) An explanation of the biomedical or behavioral research procedures to be followed and their purposes, including identification of any procedures which are experimental.

(2) A description of all known attendant discomfort and risks reasonably to be expected.

(3) A disclosure of any appropriate alternative biomedical or behavioral research procedures that might be advantageous for the subject.

(4) The nature of the information sought to be gained by the experiment.

(5) The expected recovery time of the subject after completion of the experiment.

(6) An offer to answer any inquiries concerning the applicable biomedical or behavioral research procedures.

(7) An instruction that the person is free to withdraw his consent and to discontinue participation in the research at any time without prejudice to the subject.

(Added by Stats. 1977, Ch. 1250.)

3522.

At the time of furnishing a prisoner the writing required by subdivision (b) of Section 3521, the prisoner shall also be given information as to (a) the amount of remuneration the prisoner will receive for the research and (b) the manner in which the prisoner may obtain prompt treatment for any research-related injuries. Such information shall be provided in writing on a form to be retained by the prisoner.

(Added by Stats. 1977, Ch. 1250.)

3523.

The amount of such remuneration shall be comparable to that which is paid to nonprisoner volunteers in similar research.

(Added by Stats. 1977, Ch. 1250.)

CHAPTER 5. Remedies [3524- 3524.]

(Chapter 5 added by Stats. 1977, Ch. 1250.)
3524.
(a) A prisoner may maintain an action for injury to such prisoner, including physical or mental injury, or both, caused by the wrongful or negligent act of a person during the course of the prisoner's participation in biomedical or behavioral research conducted pursuant to this title.
(b) In any action pursuant to this section, such damages may be awarded as under all of the circumstances of the case may be just.
(c) When the death of a prisoner is caused by the wrongful act or neglect of another, his or her heirs or personal representatives on their behalf may maintain an action for damages against the person causing the death, or if dead, such person's personal representatives.
(d) If an action arising out of the same wrongful act or neglect may be maintained pursuant to subdivision (c) for wrongful death to any such prisoner, the action authorized by subdivision (a) shall be consolidated therewith for trial on motion of any interested party.
(e) For the purposes of this section, "heirs" mean only the following:
(1) Those persons who would be entitled to succeed to the property of the decedent according to the provisions of Part 2 (commencing with Section 6400) of Division 6 of the Probate Code, and
(2) Whether or not qualified under paragraph (1), if they were dependent on the decedent, the putative spouse, children of the putative spouse, stepchildren, and parents. As used in this paragraph, "putative spouse" means the surviving spouse of a void or voidable marriage who is found by the court to have believed in good faith that the marriage to the decedent was valid.
(Amended by Stats. 1983, Ch. 842, Sec. 16. Operative January 1, 1985, by Sec. 58 of Ch. 842.)

TITLE 2.3. MEDICAL PAROLE [3550- 3550.]

(Title 2.3 added by Stats. 2010, Ch. 405, Sec. 2.)
3550.
(a) Notwithstanding any other law, except as provided in subdivision (b), if the head physician of an institution in which a prisoner is incarcerated determines, as provided in this section, that the prisoner is permanently medically incapacitated with a medical condition that renders him or her permanently unable to perform activities of basic daily living, and results in the prisoner requiring 24-hour care, and that incapacitation did not exist at the time of sentencing, the prisoner shall be granted medical parole if the Board of Parole Hearings determines that the conditions under which he or she would be released would not reasonably pose a threat to public safety.
(b) This section does not alter or diminish the rights conferred under the Victims' Bill of Rights Act of 2008 (Marsy's Law). Subdivision (a) does not apply to any of the following:
(1) A prisoner sentenced to death or life in prison without possibility of parole.
(2) A prisoner who is serving a sentence for which parole, pursuant to subdivision (a), is prohibited by any initiative statute.
(3) A prisoner who was convicted of first-degree murder if the victim was a peace officer, as defined in Section 830.1, 830.2, 830.3, 830.31, 830.32, 830.33, 830.34, 830.35, 830.36, 830.37, 830.4, 830.5, 830.6, 830.10, 830.11, or 830.12, who was killed while engaged in the performance of his or her duties, and the individual knew, or reasonably should have known, that the victim was a peace officer engaged in the performance of his or her duties, or the victim was a peace officer or a former peace officer under any of the above-enumerated sections, and was intentionally killed in retaliation for the performance of his or her official duties.
(c) When a physician employed by the Department of Corrections and Rehabilitation who is the primary care provider for a prisoner identifies a prisoner that he or she believes meets the medical criteria for medical parole specified in subdivision (a), the primary care physician shall recommend to the head physician of the institution where the prisoner is located that the prisoner be referred to the Board of Parole Hearings for consideration for medical parole. Within 30 days of receiving that recommendation, if the head physician of the institution concurs in the recommendation of the primary care physician, he or she shall refer the matter to the Board of Parole Hearings using a standardized form and format developed by the department, and if the head physician of the institution does not concur in the recommendation, he or she shall provide the primary care physician with a written explanation of the reasons for denying the referral.
(d) Notwithstanding any other provisions of this section, the prisoner or his or her family member or designee may independently request consideration for medical parole by contacting the head physician at the prison or the department. Within 30 days of receiving the request, the head physician of the institution shall, in consultation with the prisoner's primary care physician, make a determination regarding whether the prisoner meets the criteria for medical parole as specified in subdivision (a) and, if the head physician of the institution determines that the prisoner satisfies the criteria set forth in subdivision (a), he or she shall refer the matter to the Board of Parole Hearings using a standardized form and format developed by the department. If the head physician of the institution does not concur in the recommendation, he or she shall provide the prisoner or his or her family member or designee with a written explanation of the reasons for denying the application.
(e) The Department of Corrections and Rehabilitation shall complete parole plans for inmates referred to the Board of Parole Hearings for medical parole consideration. The parole plans shall include, but not be limited to, the inmate's plan for residency and medical care.
(f) Notwithstanding any other law, medical parole hearings shall be conducted by two-person panels consisting of at least one commissioner. In the event of a tie vote, the matter shall be referred to the full board for a decision. Medical parole hearings may be heard in absentia.
(g) Upon receiving a recommendation from the head physician of the institution where a prisoner is located for the prisoner to be granted medical parole pursuant to subdivision (c) or (d), the board, as specified in subdivision (f), shall make an independent judgment regarding whether the conditions under which the inmate would be released pose a reasonable threat to public safety, and make written findings related thereto.
(h) Notwithstanding any other law, the board or the Division of Adult Parole Operations shall have the authority to impose any reasonable conditions on prisoners subject to medical parole supervision pursuant to subdivision (a), including, but not limited to, the requirement that the parolee submit to electronic monitoring. As a further condition of medical parole, pursuant to subdivision (a), the parolee may be required to submit to an examination by a physician selected by the board for the purpose of diagnosing the parolee's current medical condition. In the event such an examination takes place, a report of the examination and diagnosis shall be submitted to the board by the examining physician. If the board determines, based on that medical examination, that the person's medical condition has improved to the extent that the person no longer qualifies for medical parole, the board shall return the person to the custody of the department.
(1) Notwithstanding any other law establishing maximum periods for parole, a prisoner sentenced to a determinate term who is placed on medical parole supervision prior to the earliest possible release date and who remains eligible for medical parole, shall remain on medical parole, pursuant to subdivision (a), until that earliest possible release

date, at which time the parolee shall commence serving that period of parole provided by, and under the provisions of, Chapter 8 (commencing with Section 3000) of Title 1.
(2) Notwithstanding any other law establishing maximum periods for parole, a prisoner sentenced to an indeterminate term who is placed on medical parole supervision prior to the prisoner's minimum eligible parole date, and who remains eligible for medical parole, shall remain on medical parole pursuant to subdivision (a) until that minimum eligible parole date, at which time the parolee shall be eligible for parole consideration under all other provisions of Chapter 8 (commencing with Section 3000) of Title 1.
(i) The Department of Corrections and Rehabilitation shall, at the time a prisoner is placed on medical parole supervision pursuant to subdivision (a), ensure that the prisoner has applied for any federal entitlement programs for which the prisoner is eligible, and has in his or her possession a discharge medical summary, full medical records, parole medications, and all property belonging to the prisoner that was under the control of the department. Any additional records shall be sent to the prisoner's forwarding address after release to health care-related parole supervision.
(j) The provisions for medical parole set forth in this title shall not affect an inmate's eligibility for any other form of parole or release provided by law.
(k) (1) Notwithstanding any other law, the Department of Corrections and Rehabilitation shall give notice to the county of commitment and the proposed county of release, if that county is different than the county of commitment, of any medical parole hearing as described in subdivision (f), and of any medical parole release as described in subdivision (g).
(2) Notice shall be made at least 30 days, or as soon as feasible, prior to the time any medical parole hearing or medical parole release is scheduled for an inmate receiving medical parole consideration, regardless of whether the inmate is sentenced either determinately or indeterminately.
(Amended by Stats. 2016, Ch. 886, Sec. 2. (SB 6) Effective January 1, 2017.)

TITLE 3. EXECUTION OF DEATH PENALTY [3600 - 3706]

(Title 3 added by Stats. 1941, Ch. 106.)

CHAPTER 1. Executing Death Penalty [3600 - 3607]

(Chapter 1 added by Stats. 1941, Ch. 106.)
3600.
Every male person, upon whom has been imposed the judgment of death, shall be delivered to the warden of the California state prison designated by the department for the execution of the death penalty. The inmate shall be kept in a California prison until execution of the judgment. The department may transfer the inmate to another prison which it determines to provide a level of security sufficient for that inmate. The inmate shall be returned to the prison designated for execution of the death penalty after an execution date has been set.
(Amended November 8, 2016, by initiative Proposition 66, Sec. 9.)
3601.
Every female person, upon whom has been imposed the judgment of death, shall be delivered to the warden of the Central California Women's Facility, there to be held pending decision upon appeal.
(Amended by Stats. 1991, Ch. 1016, Sec. 1.)
3602.
Upon the affirmance of her appeal, the female person sentenced to death shall thereafter be delivered to the warden of the California state prison designated by the department for the execution of the death penalty, not earlier than three days before the day upon which judgment is to be executed; provided, however, that in the event of a commutation of sentence said female prisoner shall be returned to the Central California Women's Facility, there to be confined pursuant to such commutation.
(Amended by Stats. 2005, Ch. 279, Sec. 14. Effective January 1, 2006.)
3603.
The judgment of death shall be executed within the walls of the California State Prison at San Quentin.
(Amended by Stats. 1992, Ch. 558, Sec. 1. Effective January 1, 1993.)
3604.
(a) The punishment of death shall be inflicted by the administration of a lethal gas or by an intravenous injection of a substance or substances in a lethal quantity sufficient to cause death, by standards established under the direction of the Department of Corrections and Rehabilitation.
(b) Persons sentenced to death prior to or after the operative date of this subdivision shall have the opportunity to elect to have the punishment imposed by lethal gas or lethal injection. This choice shall be made in writing and shall be submitted to the warden pursuant to regulations established by the Department of Corrections and Rehabilitation. If a person under sentence of death does not choose either lethal gas or lethal injection within 10 days after the warden's service upon the inmate of an execution warrant issued following the operative date of this subdivision, the penalty of death shall be imposed by lethal injection.
(c) Where the person sentenced to death is not executed on the date set for execution and a new execution date is subsequently set, the inmate again shall have the opportunity to elect to have punishment imposed by lethal gas or lethal injection, according to the procedures set forth in subdivision (b).
(d) Notwithstanding subdivision (b), if either manner of execution described in subdivision (a) is held invalid, the punishment of death shall be imposed by the alternative means specified in subdivision (a).
(e) The Department of Corrections and Rehabilitation, or any successor agency with the duty to execute judgments of death, shall maintain at all times the ability to execute such judgments.
(Amended November 8, 2016, by initiative Proposition 66, Sec. 10.)
3604.1.
(a) The Administrative Procedure Act shall not apply to standards, procedures, or regulations promulgated pursuant to Section 3604. The department shall make the standards adopted under subdivision (a) of that section available to the public and to inmates sentenced to death. The department shall promptly notify the Attorney General, the State Public Defender, and counsel for any inmate for whom an execution date has been set or for whom a motion to set an execution date is pending of any adoption or amendment of the standards. Noncompliance with this subdivision is not a ground for stay of an execution or an injunction against carrying out an execution unless the noncompliance has actually prejudiced the inmate's ability to challenge the standard, and in that event the stay shall be limited to a maximum of 10 days.
(b) Notwithstanding subdivision (a) of Section 3604, an execution by lethal injection may be carried out by means of an injection other than intravenous if the warden determines that the condition of the inmate makes intravenous injection impractical.
(c) The court which rendered the judgment of death has exclusive jurisdiction to hear any claim by the condemned inmate that the method of execution is unconstitutional or otherwise invalid. Such a claim shall be dismissed if the court finds its presentation was

delayed without good cause. If the method is found invalid, the court shall order the use of a valid method of execution. If the use of a method of execution is enjoined by a federal court, the Department of Corrections and Rehabilitation shall adopt, within 90 days, a method that conforms to federal requirements as found by that court. If the department fails to perform any duty needed to enable it to execute the judgment, the court which rendered the judgment of death shall order it to perform that duty on its own motion, on motion of the District Attorney or Attorney General, or on motion of any victim of the crime as defined in subdivision (e) of Section 28 of Article I of the California Constitution.
(Added November 8, 2016, by initiative Proposition 66, Sec. 11.)

3604.3.
(a) A physician may attend an execution for the purpose of pronouncing death and may provide advice to the department for the purpose of developing an execution protocol to minimize the risk of pain to the inmate.
(b) The purchase of drugs, medical supplies or medical equipment necessary to carry out an execution shall not be subject to the provisions of Chapter 9 (commencing with Section 4000) of Division 2 of the Business and Professions Code, and any pharmacist, or supplier, compounder, or manufacturer of pharmaceuticals is authorized to dispense drugs and supplies to the secretary or the secretary's designee, without prescription, for carrying out the provisions of this chapter.
(c) No licensing board, department, commission, or accreditation agency that oversees or regulates the practice of health care or certifies or licenses health care professionals may deny or revoke a license or certification, censure, reprimand, suspend, or take any other disciplinary action against any licensed health care professional for any action authorized by this section.
(Added November 8, 2016, by initiative Proposition 66, Sec. 12.)

3605.
(a) The warden of the state prison where the execution is to take place shall be present at the execution and shall, subject to any applicable requirement or definition set forth in subdivision (b), invite the presence of the Attorney General, the members of the immediate family of the victim or victims of the defendant, and at least 12 reputable citizens, to be selected by the warden. The warden shall, at the request of the defendant, permit those ministers of the Gospel, not exceeding two, as the defendant may name, and any persons, relatives or friends, not to exceed five, to be present at the execution, together with those peace officers or any other Department of Corrections employee as he or she may think expedient, to witness the execution. But no other persons than those specified in this section may be present at the execution, nor may any person under 18 years of age be allowed to witness the execution.
(b) (1) For purposes of an invitation required by subdivision (a) to members of the immediate family of the victim or victims of the defendant, the warden of the state prison where the execution is to take place shall make the invitation only if a member of the immediate family of the victim or victims of the defendant so requests in writing. In the event that a written request is made, the warden of the state prison where the execution is to take place shall automatically make the invitation 30 days prior to the date of an imminent execution or as close to this date as practicable.
(2) For purposes of this section, "immediate family" means those persons who are related by blood, adoption, or marriage, within the second degree of consanguinity or affinity.
(c) No physician or any other person invited pursuant to this section, whether or not employed by the Department of Corrections, shall be compelled to attend the execution, and any physician's attendance shall be voluntary. A physician's or any other person's refusal to attend the execution shall not be used in any disciplinary action or negative job performance citation.
(Amended by Stats. 2001, Ch. 71, Sec. 1. Effective January 1, 2002.)

3607.
After the execution, the warden must make a return upon the death warrant to the clerk of the court by which the judgment was rendered, showing the time, mode, and manner in which it was executed.
(Amended by Stats. 2002, Ch. 784, Sec. 561. Effective January 1, 2003.)

CHAPTER 2. Suspension of Execution of Death Penalty: Insanity: Pregnancy [3700 - 3706]

(Chapter 2 added by Stats. 1941, Ch. 106.)
3700.
No judge, court, or officer, other than the Governor, can suspend the execution of a judgment of death, except the warden of the State prison to whom he is delivered for execution, as provided in the six succeeding sections, unless an appeal is taken.
(Added by Stats. 1941, Ch. 106.)

3700.5.
Whenever a court makes and causes to be entered an order appointing a day upon which a judgment of death shall be executed upon a defendant, the warden of the state prison to whom such defendant has been delivered for execution or, if the defendant is a female, the warden of the Central California Women's Facility, shall notify the Director of Corrections who shall thereupon select and appoint three alienists, all of whom must be from the medical staffs of the Department of Corrections, to examine the defendant, under the judgment of death, and investigate his or her sanity. It is the duty of the alienists so selected and appointed to examine such defendant and investigate his or her sanity, and to report their opinions and conclusions thereon, in writing, to the Governor, to the warden of the prison at which the execution is to take place, or, if the defendant is female, the warden of the Central California Women's Facility, at least 20 days prior to the day appointed for the execution of the judgment of death upon the defendant. The warden shall furnish a copy of the report to counsel for the defendant upon his or her request.
(Amended by Stats. 2005, Ch. 279, Sec. 15. Effective January 1, 2006.)

3701.
If, after his delivery to the warden for execution, there is good reason to believe that a defendant, under judgment of death, has become insane, the warden must call such fact to the attention of the district attorney of the county in which the prison is situated, whose duty it is to immediately file in the superior court of such county a petition, stating the conviction and judgment, and the fact that the defendant is believed to be insane, and asking that the question of his sanity be inquired into. Thereupon the court must at once cause to be summoned and impaneled, from the regular jury list of the county, a jury of 12 persons to hear such inquiry.
(Added by Stats. 1941, Ch. 106.)

3702.
The district attorney must attend the hearing, and may produce witnesses before the jury, for which purpose he may issue process in the same manner as for witnesses to attend before the grand jury, and disobedience thereto may be punished in like manner as disobedience to process issued by the court.
(Added by Stats. 1941, Ch. 106.)

3703.
The verdict of the jury must be entered upon the minutes, and thereupon the court must make and cause to be entered an order reciting the fact of such inquiry and the result thereof, and when it is found that the defendant is insane, the order must direct that he

be taken to a medical facility of the Department of Corrections, and there kept in safe confinement until his reason is restored.
(Amended by Stats. 1971, Ch. 1136.)

3704.
If it is found that the defendant is sane, the warden must proceed to execute the judgment as specified in the warrant; if it is found that the defendant is insane, the warden must suspend the execution and transmit a certified copy of the order mentioned in the last section to the Governor, and deliver the defendant, together with a certified copy of such order, to the superintendent of the medical facility named in such order. When the defendant recovers his sanity, the superintendent of such medical facility must certify that fact to the judge of the superior court from which the defendant was committed as insane, who must thereupon fix a date upon which, after 10 days' written notice to the defendant and the district attorney of the county from which the defendant was originally sentenced and the district attorney of the county from which he was committed to the medical facility, a hearing shall be had before said judge sitting without a jury to determine whether or not the defendant has in fact recovered his sanity. If the defendant appears without counsel, the court shall appoint counsel to represent him at said hearing. If the judge should determine that the defendant has recovered his sanity he must certify that fact to the Governor, who must thereupon issue to the warden his warrant appointing a day for the execution of the judgment, and the warden shall thereupon return the defendant to the state prison pending the execution of the judgment. If, however, the judge should determine that the defendant has not recovered his sanity he shall direct the return of the defendant to a medical facility of the Department of Corrections, to be there kept in safe confinement until his sanity is restored.
(Amended by Stats. 1971, Ch. 1136.)

3704.5.
Any defendant who, on March 4, 1972, is in a state hospital under court order pursuant to Section 3703, as that section read on March 3, 1972, shall be transferred to a medical facility of the Department of Corrections, designated by the Director of Corrections, and there kept in safe confinement until his or her reason is restored. Section 3704 shall apply when the defendant recovers his or her sanity.
(Amended by Stats. 1988, Ch. 160, Sec. 137.)

3705.
If there is good reason to believe that a female against whom a judgment of death is rendered is pregnant, such proceedings must be had as are provided in Section 3701, except that instead of a jury, as therein provided, the court may summon three disinterested physicians, of good standing in their profession, to inquire into the supposed pregnancy, who shall, in the presence of the court, but with closed doors, if requested by the defendant, examine the defendant and hear any evidence that may be produced, and make a written finding and certificate of their conclusion, to be approved by the court and spread upon the minutes. The provisions of Section 3702 apply to the proceedings upon such inquiry.
(Amended by Stats. 1941, Ch. 1192.)

3706.
If it is found that the female is not pregnant, the warden must execute the judgment; if it is found that she is pregnant the warden must suspend the execution of the judgment, and transmit a certified copy of the finding and certificate to the Governor. When the Governor receives from the warden a certificate that the defendant is no longer pregnant, he must issue to the warden this warrant appointing a day for the execution of the judgment.
(Added by Stats. 1941, Ch. 106.)

TITLE 4. COUNTY JAILS, FARMS AND CAMPS [4000 - 4351]

(Heading of Title 4 amended by Stats. 1957, Ch. 50.)

CHAPTER 1. County Jails [4000 - 4032]

(Heading of Chapter 1 added by Stats. 1957, Ch. 50.)
4000.
The common jails in the several counties of this state are kept by the sheriffs of the counties in which they are respectively situated, and are used as follows:
1. For the detention of persons committed in order to secure their attendance as witnesses in criminal cases;
2. For the detention of persons charged with crime and committed for trial;
3. For the confinement of persons committed for contempt, or upon civil process, or by other authority of law;
4. For the confinement of persons sentenced to imprisonment therein upon a conviction for crime.
5. For the confinement of persons pursuant to subdivision (b) of Section 3454 for a violation of the terms and conditions of their postrelease community supervision.
(Amended by Stats. 2011, 1st Ex. Sess., Ch. 12, Sec. 34. (AB 17 1x) Effective September 21, 2011. Operative October 1, 2011, by Sec. 46 of Ch. 12.)

4000.5.
Notwithstanding any other provision of law, the sheriff of any county may transfer prisoners committed to any jail of the county to any industrial road camp maintained by the county.
(Added by Stats. 1989, Ch. 897, Sec. 44.)

4001.
Each county jail must contain a sufficient number of rooms to allow all persons belonging to either one of the following classes to be confined separately and distinctly from persons belonging to either of the other classes:
1. Persons committed on criminal process and detained for trial;
2. Persons already convicted of crime and held under sentence;
3. Persons detained as witnesses or held under civil process, or under an order imposing punishment for a contempt.
(Amended by Stats. 1975, Ch. 592.)

4001.1.
(a) No law enforcement or correctional official shall give, offer, or promise to give any monetary payment in excess of fifty dollars ($50) in return for an in-custody informant's testimony in any criminal proceeding. Nothing contained herein shall prohibit payments incidental to the informant's testimony such as expenses incurred for witness or immediate family relocation, lodging, housing, meals, phone calls, travel, or witness fees authorized by law, provided those payments are supported by appropriate documentation demonstrating that the money was used for the purposes for which it was given.
(b) No law enforcement agency and no in-custody informant acting as an agent for the agency, may take some action, beyond merely listening to statements of a defendant, that is deliberately designed to elicit incriminating remarks.
(c) As used in this section, an "in-custody informant" means a person described in subdivision (a) of Section 1127a.
(Added by Stats. 1989, Ch. 901, Sec. 3.)

4001.2.
(a) Each county jail shall, upon detention of a person, ask if the person has served in the United States military and document the person's response.
(b) The county jail shall make this information available to the person, his or her counsel, and the district attorney.
(c) This section shall become operative on January 1, 2020.
(Added by Stats. 2018, Ch. 281, Sec. 1. (AB 2568) Effective January 1, 2019. Section operative January 1, 2020, by its own provisions.)

4002.
(a) Persons committed on criminal process and detained for trial, persons convicted and under sentence, and persons committed upon civil process, shall not be kept or put in the same room, nor shall male and female prisoners, except spouses, sleep, dress or undress, bathe, or perform eliminatory functions in the same room. However, persons committed on criminal process and detained for trial may be kept or put in the same room with persons convicted and under sentence for the purpose of participating in supervised activities and for the purpose of housing, provided, that the housing occurs as a result of a classification procedure that is based upon objective criteria, including consideration of criminal sophistication, seriousness of crime charged, presence or absence of assaultive behavior, age, and other criteria that will provide for the safety of the prisoners and staff.
(b) Inmates who are held pending civil process under the sexually violent predator laws shall be held in administrative segregation. For purposes of this subdivision, administrative segregation means separate and secure housing that does not involve any deprivation of privileges other than what is necessary to protect the inmates and staff. Consistent with Section 1610, to the extent possible, the person shall continue in his or her course of treatment, if any. An alleged sexually violent predator held pending civil process may waive placement in secure housing by petitioning the court for a waiver. In order to grant the waiver, the court must find that the waiver is voluntary and intelligent, and that granting the waiver would not interfere with any treatment programming for the person requesting the waiver. A person granted a waiver shall be placed with inmates charged with similar offenses or with similar criminal histories, based on the objective criteria set forth in subdivision (a).
(c) Nothing in this section shall be construed to impose any requirement upon a county to confine male and female prisoners in the same or an adjoining facility or impose any duty upon a county to establish or maintain programs which involve the joint participation of male and female prisoners.
(Amended by Stats. 2016, Ch. 50, Sec. 74. (SB 1005) Effective January 1, 2017.)

4002.5.
(a) On or before January 1, 2020, the sheriff of each county or the administrator of each county jail shall develop and implement an infant and toddler breast milk feeding policy for lactating inmates detained in or sentenced to a county jail. The policy shall be based on currently accepted best practices. The policy shall include all of the following provisions:
(1) Procedures for providing medically appropriate support and care related to the cessation of lactation or weaning.
(2) Procedures providing for human milk expression, disposal, and same-day storage for later retrieval and delivery to an infant or toddler by an approved person, at the option of the lactating inmate and with the approval of the facility administrator.
(3) Procedures for conditioning an inmate's participation in the program upon the inmate undergoing drug screening.
(b) The infant and toddler breast milk feeding policy for lactating inmates shall be posted in all locations in the jail where medical care is provided and the provisions of the policy shall be communicated to all staff persons who interact with or oversee pregnant or lactating inmates.
(c) This section applies without regard to whether the jail is operated pursuant to a contract with a private contractor and without regard to whether the inmate has been charged with or convicted of a crime.
(Added by Stats. 2018, Ch. 944, Sec. 1. (AB 2507) Effective January 1, 2019.)

4003.
Whenever any weapon or other personal property is taken from an arrested person, it shall be the duty of the desk clerk or other proper officer of any city, county or city and county jail, to which such person is committed for detention, to give a receipt to such person without delay for the property taken.
(Added by Stats. 1941, Ch. 106.)

4004.
A prisoner committed to the county jail for examination, or upon conviction for a public offense, must be actually confined in the jail until legally discharged; and if the prisoner is permitted to go at large out of the jail, except by virtue of a legal order or process, it is an escape; provided, however, that during the pendency of a criminal proceeding, the court before which said proceeding is pending may make a legal order, good cause appearing therefor, for the removal of the prisoner from the county jail in custody of the sheriff. In courts where there is a marshal, the marshal shall maintain custody of such prisoner while the prisoner is in the court facility pursuant to such court order. The superior court of the county may make a legal order, good cause appearing therefor, for the removal of prisoners confined in the county jail, after conviction, in the custody of the sheriff.
If facilities are no longer available in the county jail due to crowded conditions, a sheriff may transfer a person committed to the county jail upon conviction for a public offense to facilities which are available in the city jail, as provided for in Section 4004.5.
(Amended by Stats. 1998, Ch. 931, Sec. 433. Effective September 28, 1998.)

4004.5.
(a) A city may furnish facilities to be used for holding prisoners held for examination or during trial without cost to the county or upon such terms as may be agreed upon by the governing body of the city and the board of supervisors, and the marshal may keep the prisoners in their custody in the city jail.
(b) A city may furnish facilities to be used for holding persons convicted of a public offense who have been transferred from the county jail by the sheriff due to crowded conditions upon those terms as may be agreed upon by the governing body of the city and the board of supervisors. The agreed terms may indicate that the facilities are to be provided free of charge to the county.
(Amended by Stats. 1996, Ch. 872, Sec. 123. Effective January 1, 1997.)

4005.
(a) Except as provided in subdivision (b), the sheriff shall receive, and keep in the county jail, any prisoner committed thereto by process or order issued under the authority of the United States, until he or she is discharged according to law, as if he or she had been committed under process issued under the authority of this state; provision being made by the United States for the support of the prisoner.
(b) The sheriff shall receive, and keep in the county jail, any prisoner committed thereto by process or order issued under the authority of the United States, until he or she is discharged according to law, as if he or she had been committed under process issued under the authority of this state, but only if the sheriff determines that adequate space in appropriate detention areas currently exists for this purpose. Provision shall be made by the United States for the support of the prisoner. This subdivision shall apply only in counties where a facility operated by the United States Bureau of Prisons exists within 200 miles of the county seat.
(Amended by Stats. 1986, Ch. 523, Sec. 1. Effective July 24, 1986.)

4006.

A sheriff, to whose custody a prisoner is committed as provided in the last section, is answerable for his safekeeping in the courts of the United States, according to the laws thereof.
(Added by Stats. 1941, Ch. 106.)

4006.5.
(a) Notwithstanding any other provision of law, a county board of supervisors or city council may enter into a contract with the federal government, or any department or agency thereof, to manage, control, and operate a federal prison located within the boundaries of that county or city.
(b) If a city or county enters into a contract pursuant to subdivision (a), the sheriff or chief of police, as appropriate, shall have sole and exclusive authority to keep the prison and the prisoners in it.
(c) If a city or county enters into a contract pursuant to subdivision (a), the employees working in the prison shall be employees of, and under the authority of, the sheriff or chief of police, as appropriate.
(Added by Stats. 1997, Ch. 468, Sec. 1. Effective January 1, 1998.)

4007.
When there is no jail in the county, or when the jail becomes unfit or unsafe for the confinement of prisoners, the judge of the superior court may, by a written order filed with the clerk of the court, designate the jail of a contiguous county for the confinement of any prisoner of his or her county, and may at any time modify or vacate the order. When there are reasonable grounds to believe that a prisoner may be forcibly removed from a county jail, the sheriff may remove the prisoner to any California state prison for safekeeping and it is the duty of the warden of the prison to accept and detain the prisoner in his or her custody until his or her removal is ordered by the superior court of the county from which he or she was delivered. Immediately upon receiving the prisoner the warden shall advise the Director of Corrections of that fact in writing.
When a county prisoner requires medical treatment necessitating hospitalization which cannot be provided at the county jail or county hospital because of lack of adequate detention facilities, and when the prisoner also presents a serious custodial problem because of his or her past or present behavior, the judge of the superior court may, on the request of the county sheriff and with the consent of the Director of Corrections, designate by written order the nearest state prison or correctional facility which would be able to provide the necessary medical treatment and secure confinement of the prisoner. The written order of the judge shall be filed with the clerk of the court. The court shall immediately calendar the matter for a hearing to determine whether the order shall continue or be rescinded. The hearing shall be held within 48 hours of the initial order or the next judicial day, whichever occurs later. The prisoner shall not be transferred to the state prison or correctional facility prior to the hearing, except upon a determination by the physician responsible for the prisoner's health care that a medical emergency exists which requires the transfer of the prisoner to the state prison or correctional facility prior to the hearing. The prisoner shall be entitled to be present at the hearing and to be represented by counsel. The prisoner may waive his or her right to this hearing in writing at any time. If the prisoner waives his or her right to the hearing, the county sheriff shall notify the prisoner's attorney of the transfer within 48 hours, or the next business day, whichever is later. The court may modify or vacate the order at any time.
The rate of compensation for the prisoner's medical treatment and confinement within a California state prison or correctional facility shall be established by the Department of Corrections, and shall be charged against the county making the request.
When there are reasonable grounds to believe that there is a prisoner in a county jail who is likely to be a threat to other persons in the facility or who is likely to cause substantial damage to the facility, the judge of the superior court may, on the request of the county sheriff and with the consent of the Director of Corrections, designate by written order the nearest state prison or correctional facility which would be able to secure confinement of the prisoner, subject to space available. The written order of the judge must be filed with the clerk of the court. The court shall immediately calendar the matter for a hearing to determine whether the order shall continue or be rescinded. The hearing shall be held within 48 hours of the initial order or the next judicial day, whichever occurs later. The prisoner shall be entitled to be present at the hearing and to be represented by counsel. The court may modify or vacate that order at any time. The rate of compensation for the prisoner's confinement within a California state prison or correctional facility shall be established by the Department of Corrections and shall be charged against the county making the request.
(Amended by Stats. 2002, Ch. 784, Sec. 562. Effective January 1, 2003.)

4008.
A copy of the appointment, certified by the clerk of the court, must be served on the sheriff or keeper of the jail designated, who must receive into the jail all prisoners authorized to be confined therein, pursuant to Section 4007, and who is responsible for the safekeeping of the persons so committed, in the same manner and to the same extent as if the sheriff or keeper of the jail were sheriff of the county for whose use the jail is designated, and with respect to the persons so committed the sheriff or keeper of the jail is deemed the sheriff of the county from which they were removed.
(Amended by Stats. 2002, Ch. 784, Sec. 563. Effective January 1, 2003.)

4009.
When a jail is erected in a county for the use of which the designation was made, or its jail is rendered fit and safe for the confinement of prisoners, the judge of the superior court of that county must, by a written revocation, filed with the clerk of the court, declare that the necessity for the designation has ceased, and that it is revoked.
(Amended by Stats. 2002, Ch. 784, Sec. 564. Effective January 1, 2003.)

4010.
The clerk of the court must immediately serve a copy of the revocation upon the sheriff of the county, who must thereupon remove the prisoners to the jail of the county from which the removal was had.
(Amended by Stats. 2002, Ch. 784, Sec. 565. Effective January 1, 2003.)

4011.
(a) When it is made to appear to any judge by affidavit of the sheriff or other official in charge of county correctional facilities or district attorney and oral testimony that a prisoner confined in any city or county jail within the jurisdiction of the court requires medical or surgical treatment necessitating hospitalization, which treatment cannot be furnished or supplied at such city or county jail, the court in its discretion may order the removal of such person or persons from such city or county jail to the county hospital in such county; provided, if there is no county hospital in such county, then to any hospital designated by such court; and it shall be the duty of the sheriff or other official in charge of county correctional facilities to maintain the necessary guards, who may be private security guards, for the safekeeping of such prisoner, the expense of which shall be a charge against the county.
(b) The cost of such medical services and such hospital care and treatment shall be charged against the county subject to subdivisions (c) and (d), in the case of a prisoner in or taken from the county jail, or against the city in the case of a prisoner in or taken from the city jail, and the city or county may recover the same by appropriate action from the person so served or cared for, or any person or agency responsible for his care and maintenance. If the prisoner is in the county jail under contract with a city or under some other arrangement with the city to keep the city prisoner in the county jail, then the city shall be charged, subject to subdivisions (c) and (d), for the prisoner's care and maintenance with the same right of recovery against any responsible person or any other agency.
(c) When such prisoner is poor and indigent the cost of such medical services and such hospital care and treatment shall, in the case of persons removed from the city jail be

paid out of the general fund of such city, and in the case of persons removed from the county jail to a hospital other than a county hospital, such cost shall be paid out of the general fund of such county or city and county. In the case of city jail prisoners removed to the county hospital, the cost of such hospital care and treatment to be paid by the city to the county, shall be the rate per day fixed by the board of supervisors of such county. Such board of supervisors may, but need not, fix different rates for different classes of patients, or for different wards, and any and all such rates may be changed by such board of supervisors at any time, but shall at all times approximate as nearly as may be, the average actual cost to the county of such hospital care and treatment either in such wards or for such classes of patients or otherwise.

(d) In the event such prisoner is financially able to pay for his care, support and maintenance, the medical superintendent of such hospital other than a county hospital may, with the approval of such judge, enter into a special agreement with such person, or with his relatives or friends, for his care, support, maintenance, and other hospital expenses.

Any prisoner may decline such care or treatment and provide other care and treatment for himself at his own expense.

(Amended by Stats. 1979, Ch. 124.)

4011.1.

(a) Notwithstanding Section 29602 of the Government Code and any other provisions of this chapter, a county, city or the Department of the Youth Authority is authorized to make claim for and recovery of the costs of necessary hospital, medical, surgical, dental, or optometric care rendered to any prisoner confined in a county or city jail or any juvenile confined in a detention facility, who would otherwise be entitled to that care under the Medi-Cal Act (Chapter 7 (commencing with Section 14000) Part 3, Division 9, of the Welfare and Institutions Code), and who is eligible for that care on the first day of confinement or detention, to the extent that federal financial participation is available, or under the provisions of any private program or policy for that care, and the county, city or the Department of the Youth Authority shall be liable only for the costs of that care as cannot be recovered pursuant to this section. No person who is eligible for Medi-Cal shall be eligible for benefits under the provisions of this section, and no county or city or the Department of the Youth Authority is authorized to make a claim for any recovery of costs for services for that person, unless federal financial participation is available for all or part of the costs of providing services to that person under the Medi-Cal Act. Notwithstanding any other provision of law, any county or city making a claim pursuant to this section and under the Medi-Cal Act shall reimburse the Health Care Deposit Fund for the state costs of paying those medical claims. Funds allocated to the county from the County Health Services Fund pursuant to Part 4.5 (commencing with Section 16700) of Division 9 of the Welfare and Institutions Code may be utilized by the county or city to make that reimbursement.

(b) Notwithstanding Section 29602 of the Government Code and any other provisions of this chapter, to the extent that recovery of costs of necessary hospital, medical, surgical, dental, or optometric care are not accomplished under subdivision (a), a county, city, or the Department of the Youth Authority is authorized to make claim for and recover from a prisoner or a person legally responsible for a prisoner's care and maintenance the costs of necessary hospital, medical, surgical, dental, or optometric care rendered to any prisoner confined in a county or city jail, or any juvenile confined in a detention facility, where the prisoner or the person legally responsible for the prisoner's care and maintenance is financially able to pay for the prisoner's care, support, and maintenance. Nothing in this subdivision shall be construed to authorize a city, a county, or the Department of the Youth Authority to make a claim against a spouse of a prisoner.

(c) Necessary hospital, medical, dental, or optometric care, as used in this section, does not include care rendered with respect to an injury occurring during confinement in a county or city jail or juvenile detention facility, nor does it include any care or testing mandated by law.

(d) Subdivisions (b) and (c) shall apply only where there has been a determination of the present ability of the prisoner or responsible third party to pay all or a portion of the cost of necessary hospital, medical, surgical, dental, or optometric care. The person legally responsible for the prisoner's care shall provide a financial disclosure statement, executed under penalty of perjury, based on his or her past year's income tax return, to the Department of the Youth Authority. The city, county, or Department of the Youth Authority may request that the prisoner appear before a designated hearing officer for an inquiry into the ability of the prisoner or responsible third party to pay all or part of the cost of the care provided.

(e) Notice of this request shall be provided to the prisoner or responsible third party, which shall contain the following:

(1) A statement of the cost of the care provided to the prisoner.

(2) The prisoner's or responsible third party's procedural rights under this section.

(3) The time limit within which the prisoner or responsible third party may respond.

(4) A warning that if the prisoner or responsible third party fails to appear before, or respond to, the designated officer, the officer may petition the court for an order requiring him or her to make payment of the full cost of the care provided to the prisoner.

(f) At the hearing, the prisoner or responsible third party shall be entitled to, but shall not be limited to, all of the following rights:

(1) The right to be heard in person.

(2) The right to present witnesses and documentary evidence.

(3) The right to confront and cross-examine adverse witnesses.

(4) The right to have adverse evidence disclosed to him or her.

(5) The right to a written statement of the findings of the designated hearing officer.

(g) If the hearing officer determines that the prisoner or responsible third party has the present ability to pay all or a part of the cost, the officer shall set the amount to be reimbursed, and shall petition the court to order the prisoner or responsible third party to pay the sum to the city, county, or state, in the manner in which it finds reasonable and compatible to the prisoner's or responsible third party's financial ability. The court's order shall be enforceable in the manner provided for money judgments in a civil action under the Code of Civil Procedure.

(h) At any time prior to satisfaction of the judgment rendered according to the terms of this section, a prisoner or responsible third party against whom a judgment has been rendered, may petition the rendering court for a modification of the previous judgment on the grounds of a change of circumstance with regard to his or her ability to pay the judgment. The prisoner or responsible third party shall be advised of this right at the time the original judgment is rendered.

(i) As used in this section, "ability to pay" means the overall capacity of the prisoner or responsible third party to reimburse the costs, or a portion of the costs, of the care provided to the prisoner, and shall include, but not be limited to, all of the following:

(1) The prisoner's or responsible third party's present financial position.

(2) The prisoner's or responsible third party's discernible future financial position.

(3) The likelihood that the prisoner or responsible third party will be able to obtain employment in the future.

(4) Any other factor or factors which may bear upon the prisoner's or responsible third party's financial position.

(Amended by Stats. 2001, Ch. 854, Sec. 52. Effective January 1, 2002.)

4011.2.

(a) Notwithstanding Section 4011.1, a sheriff, chief or director of corrections, or chief of police is authorized to charge a fee in the amount of three dollars ($3) for each inmate-initiated medical visit of an inmate confined in a county or city jail.

(b) The fee shall be charged to the inmate's personal account at the facility. If the inmate has no money in his or her personal account, there shall be no charge for the medical visit.

(c) An inmate shall not be denied medical care because of a lack of funds in his or her personal account at the facility.

(d) The medical provider may waive the fee for any inmate-initiated treatment and shall waive the fee in any life-threatening or emergency situation, defined as those health services required for alleviation of severe pain or for immediate diagnosis and treatment of unforeseen medical conditions that if not immediately diagnosed and treated could lead to disability or death.

(e) Followup medical visits at the direction of the medical staff shall not be charged to the inmate.

(f) All moneys received by a sheriff, chief or director of corrections, or chief of police pursuant to this section shall be transferred to the county or city general fund.

(Amended by Stats. 1995, Ch. 91, Sec. 132. Effective January 1, 1996.)

4011.5.

(a) If a sheriff or jailer determines that a prisoner in a county jail or a city jail under his or her charge is in need of immediate medical or hospital care, and that the health and welfare of the prisoner will be injuriously affected unless the prisoner is forthwith removed to a hospital, the sheriff or jailer may authorize the immediate removal of the prisoner under guard to a hospital, without first obtaining a court order as provided in Section 4011. If the condition of the prisoner prevents his or her return to the jail within 48 hours from the time of his or her removal, the sheriff or jailer shall apply to a judge of the superior court for an order authorizing the continued absence of the prisoner from the jail in the manner provided in Section 4011. The provisions of Section 4011 governing the cost of medical and hospital care of prisoners and the liability for those costs shall apply to the cost of, and the liability for, medical or hospital care of prisoners removed from jail pursuant to this section.

(b) For purposes of this section, "immediate medical or hospital care" includes, but is not limited to, critical specialty medical procedures or treatment, such as dialysis, which cannot be furnished, performed, or supplied at a county jail or city jail.

(Amended by Stats. 2016, Ch. 65, Sec. 1. (AB 1703) Effective January 1, 2017.)

4011.6.

In any case in which it appears to the person in charge of a county jail, city jail, or juvenile detention facility, or to any judge of a court in the county in which the jail or juvenile detention facility is located, that a person in custody in that jail or juvenile detention facility may be mentally disordered, he or she may cause the prisoner to be taken to a facility for 72-hour treatment and evaluation pursuant to Section 5150 of the Welfare and Institutions Code and he or she shall inform the facility in writing, which shall be confidential, of the reasons that the person is being taken to the facility. The local mental health director or his or her designee may examine the prisoner prior to transfer to a facility for treatment and evaluation. Upon transfer to a facility, Article 1 (commencing with Section 5150), Article 4 (commencing with Section 5250), Article 4.5 (commencing with Section 5260), Article 5 (commencing with Section 5275), Article 6 (commencing with Section 5300), and Article 7 (commencing with Section 5325) of Chapter 2 and Chapter 3 (commencing with Section 5350) of Part 1 of Division 5 of the Welfare and Institutions Code shall apply to the prisoner.

Where the court causes the prisoner to be transferred to a 72-hour facility, the court shall forthwith notify the local mental health director or his or her designee, the prosecuting attorney, and counsel for the prisoner in the criminal or juvenile proceedings about that transfer. Where the person in charge of the jail or juvenile detention facility causes the transfer of the prisoner to a 72-hour facility the person shall immediately notify the local mental health director or his or her designee and each court within the county where the prisoner has a pending proceeding about the transfer. Upon notification by the person in charge of the jail or juvenile detention facility the court shall forthwith notify counsel for the prisoner and the prosecuting attorney in the criminal or juvenile proceedings about that transfer.

If a prisoner is detained in, or remanded to, a facility pursuant to those articles of the Welfare and Institutions Code, the facility shall transmit a report, which shall be confidential, to the person in charge of the jail or juvenile detention facility or judge of the court who caused the prisoner to be taken to the facility and to the local mental health director or his or her designee, concerning the condition of the prisoner. A new report shall be transmitted at the end of each period of confinement provided for in those articles, upon conversion to voluntary status, and upon filing of temporary letters of conservatorship.

A prisoner who has been transferred to an inpatient facility pursuant to this section may convert to voluntary inpatient status without obtaining the consent of the court, the person in charge of the jail or juvenile detention facilty, or the local mental health director. At the beginning of that conversion to voluntary status, the person in charge of the facility shall transmit a report to the person in charge of the jail or juvenile detention facility or judge of the court who caused the prisoner to be taken to the facility, counsel for the prisoner, prosecuting attorney, and local mental health director or his or her designee.

If the prisoner is detained in, or remanded to, a facility pursuant to those articles of the Welfare and Institutions Code, the time passed in the facility shall count as part of the prisoner's sentence. When the prisoner is detained in, or remanded to, the facility, the person in charge of the jail or juvenile detention facility shall advise the professional person in charge of the facility of the expiration date of the prisoner's sentence. If the prisoner is to be released from the facility before the expiration date, the professional person in charge shall notify the local mental health director or his or her designee, counsel for the prisoner, the prosecuting attorney, and the person in charge of the jail or juvenile detention facility, who shall send for, take, and receive the prisoner back into the jail or juvenile detention facility.

A defendant, either charged with or convicted of a criminal offense, or a minor alleged to be within the jurisdiction of the juvenile court, may be concurrently subject to the Lanterman-Petris-Short Act (Part 1 (commencing with Section 5000) of Division 5 of the Welfare and Institutions Code).

If a prisoner is detained in a facility pursuant to those articles of the Welfare and Institutions Code and if the person in charge of the facility determines that arraignment or trial would be detrimental to the well-being of the prisoner, the time spent in the facility shall not be computed in any statutory time requirements for arraignment or trial in any pending criminal or juvenile proceedings. Otherwise, this section shall not affect any statutory time requirements for arraignment or trial in any pending criminal or juvenile proceedings.

For purposes of this section, the term "juvenile detention facility" includes any state, county, or private home or institution in which wards or dependent children of the juvenile court or persons awaiting a hearing before the juvenile court are detained.

(Amended by Stats. 1988, Ch. 160, Sec. 138.)

4011.7.

Notwithstanding the provisions of Sections 4011 and 4011.5, when it appears that the prisoner in need of medical or surgical treatment necessitating hospitalization or in need of medical or hospital care was arrested for, charged with, or convicted of an offense constituting a misdemeanor, the court in proceedings under Section 4011 or the sheriff or jailer in action taken under Section 4011.5 may direct that the guard be removed from the prisoner while he or she is in the hospital. If that direction is given, any prisoner who knowingly escapes or attempts to escape from that hospital shall upon conviction thereof be guilty of a misdemeanor and punishable by imprisonment for not to exceed one year in the county jail if the escape or attempt to escape was not by force or violence. However, if the escape is by force or violence the prisoner shall be guilty of

a felony and punishable by imprisonment pursuant to subdivision (h) of Section 1170, or in the county jail for not exceeding one year; provided, that when that second term of imprisonment is to be served in the county jail it shall commence from the time that prisoner would otherwise be discharged from that jail.
(Amended by Stats. 2011, Ch. 15, Sec. 480. (AB 109) Effective April 4, 2011. Operative October 1, 2011, by Sec. 636 of Ch. 15, as amended by Stats. 2011, Ch. 39, Sec. 68.)

4011.8.

A person in custody who has been charged with or convicted of a criminal offense may make voluntary application for inpatient or outpatient mental health services in accordance with Section 5003 of the Welfare and Institutions Code. If such services require absence from the jail premises, consent from the person in charge of the jail or from any judge of a court in the county in which the jail is located, and from the director of the county mental health program in which services are to be rendered, shall be obtained. The local mental health director or his designee may examine the prisoner prior to the transfer from the jail.
Where the court approves voluntary treatment for a jail inmate for whom criminal proceedings are pending, the court shall forthwith notify counsel for the prisoner and the prosecuting attorney about such approval. Where the person in charge of the jail approves voluntary treatment for a prisoner for whom criminal proceedings are pending, the person in charge of the jail shall immediately notify each court within the county where the prisoner has a pending proceeding about such approval; upon notification by the jailer the court shall forthwith notify the prosecuting attorney and counsel for the prisoner in the criminal proceedings about such transfer.
If the prisoner voluntarily obtains treatment in a facility or is placed on outpatient treatment pursuant to Section 5003 of the Welfare and Institutions Code, the time passed therein shall count as part of the prisoner's sentence. When the prisoner is permitted absence from the jail for voluntary treatment, the person in charge of the jail shall advise the professional person in charge of the facility of the expiration date of the prisoner's sentence. If the prisoner is to be released from the facility before such expiration date, the professional person in charge shall notify the local mental health director or his designee, counsel for the prisoner, the prosecuting attorney, and the person in charge of the jail, who shall send for, take, and receive the prisoner back into the jail.
A denial of an application for voluntary mental health services shall be reviewable only by mandamus.
(Added by Stats. 1975, Ch. 1258.)

4011.9.

Notwithstanding the provisions of Sections 4011 and 4011.5, when it appears that the prisoner in need of medical or surgical treatment necessitating hospitalization or in need of medical or hospital care was arrested for, charged with, or convicted of an offense constituting a felony, the court in proceedings under Section 4011 or the sheriff or jailer in action taken under Section 4011. 5 may direct that the guard be removed from the prisoner while he is in the hospital, if it reasonably appears that the prisoner is physically unable to effectuate an escape or the prisoner does not constitute a danger to life or property.
(Added by Stats. 1976, Ch. 80.)

4011.10.

(a) It is the intent of the Legislature in enacting this section to provide county sheriffs, chiefs of police, and directors or administrators of local detention facilities with an incentive to not engage in practices designed to avoid payment of legitimate health care costs for the treatment or examination of persons lawfully in their custody, and to promptly pay those costs as requested by the provider of services. Further, it is the intent of the Legislature to encourage county sheriffs, chiefs of police, and directors or administrators of local detention facilities to bargain in good faith when negotiating a service contract with hospitals providing health care services.
(b) Notwithstanding any other law, a county sheriff, police chief, or other public agency that contracts for health care services, may contract with providers of health care services for care to local law enforcement patients. Hospitals that do not contract for health care services with the county sheriff, police chief, or other public agency shall provide health care services to local law enforcement patients at a rate equal to 110 percent of the hospital's actual costs according to the most recent Hospital Annual Financial Data report issued by the Office of Statewide Health Planning and Development, as calculated using a cost-to-charge ratio, or, for claims that have not previously been paid or otherwise determined by local law enforcement, according to the most recently approved cost-to-charge ratio from the Medicare Program. The hospital, with the approval of the county sheriff, police chief, or other public agency responsible for providing health care services to local law enforcement patients, may choose the most appropriate cost-to-charge ratio and shall provide notice to the county sheriff, police chief, or other public agency, as applicable, of any change. If the hospital uses the cost-to-charge ratio from the Medicare Program, the hospital shall attach supporting Medicare documentation and an expected payment calculation to the claim. If a claim does not contain the supporting Medicare documentation and expected payment calculation, or if, within 60 days of the hospital's request for approval to use the cost-to-charge ratio from the Medicare Program, approval is not granted by the county sheriff, police chief, or other public agency responsible for providing health care services to local law enforcement patients, the Office of Statewide Health Planning and Development cost-to-charge ratio shall be used to calculate the payment.
(c) A county sheriff or police chief shall not request the release of an inmate from custody for the purpose of allowing the inmate to seek medical care at a hospital, and then immediately rearrest the same individual upon discharge from the hospital, unless the hospital determines this action would enable it to bill and collect from a third-party payment source.
(d) The California Hospital Association, the University of California, the California State Sheriffs' Association, and the California Police Chiefs Association shall, immediately upon enactment of this section, convene the Inmate Health Care and Medical Provider Fair Pricing Working Group. The working group shall consist of at least six members from the California Hospital Association and the University of California, and six members from the California State Sheriffs' Association and the California Police Chiefs Association. Each organization should give great weight and consideration to appointing members of the working group with diverse geographic and demographic interests. The working group shall meet as needed to identify and resolve industry issues that create fiscal barriers to timely and affordable inmate health care. In addition, the working group shall address issues, including, but not limited to, inmates being admitted for care and later rearrested and any other fiscal barriers to hospitals being able to enter into fair market contracts with public agencies. To the extent that the rate provisions of this statute result in a disproportionate share of local law enforcement patients being treated at any one hospital or system of hospitals, the working group shall address this issue. No reimbursement is required under this provision.
(e) This section does not require or encourage a hospital or public agency to replace any existing arrangements that any city police chief, county sheriff, or other public agency that contracts for health care services for local law enforcement patients has with health care providers.
(f) An entity that provides ambulance or any other emergency or nonemergency response service to a sheriff or police chief, and that does not contract with their departments for that service, shall be reimbursed for the service at the rate established by Medicare. Neither the sheriff nor the police chief shall reimburse a provider of any of these services that his or her department has not contracted with at a rate that exceeds the provider's reasonable and allowable costs, regardless of whether the provider is located within or outside of California.
(g) For the purposes of this section, "reasonable and allowable costs" shall be defined in accordance with Part 413 of Title 42 of the Code of Federal Regulations and federal Centers for Medicare and Medicaid Services Publication Numbers 15-1 and 15-2.
(h) For purposes of this section, in those counties in which the sheriff does not administer a jail facility, a director or administrator of a local department of corrections established pursuant to Section 23013 of the Government Code is the person who may contract for services provided to jail inmates in the facilities he or she administers in those counties.
(Amended by Stats. 2015, Ch. 119, Sec. 1. (AB 658) Effective January 1, 2016.)

4011.11.

(a) (1) The board of supervisors in each county, in consultation with the county sheriff, may designate an entity or entities to assist county jail inmates with submitting an application for a health insurance affordability program consistent with federal requirements.
(2) The board of supervisors shall not designate the county sheriff as an entity to assist with submitting an application for a health insurance affordability program for county jail inmates unless the county sheriff agrees to perform this function.
(3) If the board of supervisors designates a community-based organization as an entity to assist with submitting an application for a health insurance affordability program for county jail inmates, the designation shall be subject to approval by the jail administrator or his or her designee.
(b) The jail administrator, or his or her designee, may coordinate with an entity designated pursuant to subdivision (a).
(c) Consistent with federal law, a county jail inmate who is currently enrolled in the Medi-Cal program shall remain eligible for, and shall not be terminated from, the program due to his or her detention unless required by federal law, he or she becomes otherwise ineligible, or the inmate's suspension of benefits has ended pursuant to Section 14011.10 of the Welfare and Institutions Code.
(d) Notwithstanding any other state law, and only to the extent federal law allows and federal financial participation is available, an entity designated pursuant to subdivision (a) is authorized to act on behalf of a county jail inmate for the purpose of applying for, or determinations of, Medi-Cal eligibility for acute inpatient hospital services authorized by Section 14053.7 of the Welfare and Institutions Code. An entity designated pursuant to subdivision (a) shall not determine Medi-Cal eligibility or redetermine Medi-Cal eligibility, unless the entity is the county human services agency.
(e) The fact that an applicant is an inmate shall not, in and of itself, preclude a county human services agency from processing an application for the Medi-Cal program submitted to it by, or on behalf of, that inmate.
(f) For purposes of this section, "health insurance affordability program" means a program that is one of the following:
(1) The state's Medi-Cal program under Title XIX of the federal Social Security Act.
(2) The state's children's health insurance program (CHIP) under Title XXI of the federal Social Security Act.
(3) A program that makes coverage in a qualified health plan through the California Health Benefit Exchange established pursuant to Section 100500 of the Government Code with advance payment of the premium tax credit established under Section 36B of the Internal Revenue Code available to qualified individuals.
(4) A program that makes available coverage in a qualified health plan through the California Health Benefit Exchange established pursuant to Section 100500 of the Government Code with cost-sharing reductions established under Section 1402 of the federal Patient Protection and Affordable Care Act (Public Law 111-148) and any subsequent amendments to that act.
(g) Notwithstanding Chapter 3.5 (commencing with Section 11340) of Part 1 of Division 3 of Title 2 of the Government Code, the department may implement this section by means of all-county letters or similar instructions, without taking regulatory action.
(Added by Stats. 2013, Ch. 646, Sec. 2. (AB 720) Effective January 1, 2014.)

4012.

When a pestilence or contagious disease breaks out in or near a jail, and the physician thereof certifies that it is liable to endanger the health of the prisoners, the county judge may, by a written appointment, designate a safe and convenient place in the county, or the jail in a contiguous county, as the place of their confinement. The appointment must be filed in the office of the clerk of the court, and authorize the sheriff to remove the prisoners to the place or jail designated, and there confine them until they can be safely returned to the jail from which they were taken.
(Amended by Stats. 2002, Ch. 784, Sec. 566. Effective January 1, 2003.)

4013.

(a) A sheriff or jailer upon whom a paper in a judicial proceeding, directed to a prisoner in his or her custody, is served, shall forthwith deliver it to the prisoner, with a note thereon of the time of its service. For a neglect to do so, he or she is liable to the prisoner for all damages occasioned thereby.
(b) Service directed to a person who is incarcerated within any institution in this state may be served by any person who may lawfully serve process.
(Amended by Stats. 2005, Ch. 300, Sec. 8. Effective January 1, 2006.)

4014.

The sheriff, when necessary, may, with the assent in writing of the county judge, or in a city, of the mayor thereof, employ a temporary guard for the protection of the county jail, or for the safekeeping of prisoners, the expenses of which are a county charge.
(Added by Stats. 1941, Ch. 106.)

4015.

(a) The sheriff shall receive all persons committed to jail by competent authority. The board of supervisors shall provide the sheriff with necessary food, clothing, and bedding, for those prisoners, which shall be of a quality and quantity at least equal to the minimum standards and requirements prescribed by the Board of Corrections for the feeding, clothing, and care of prisoners in all county, city and other local jails and detention facilities. Except as provided in Section 4016, the expenses thereof shall be paid out of the county treasury.
(b) Nothing in this section shall be construed in a manner that would require the sheriff to receive a person who is in need of immediate medical care until the person has been transported to a hospital or medical facility so that his or her medical needs can be addressed prior to booking into county jail.
(c) Nothing in this section shall be construed or interpreted in a manner that would impose upon a city or its law enforcement agency any obligation to pay the cost of medical services rendered to any individual in need of immediate medical care who has been arrested by city law enforcement personnel and transported to a hospital or medical facility prior to being delivered to and received at the county jail or other detention facility for booking.
(d) It is the intent of the Legislature in enacting the act adding this subdivision to ensure that the costs associated with providing medical care to an arrested person are borne by the arrested person's private medical insurance or any other source of medical cost coverage for which the arrested person is eligible.
(Amended (as amended by Stats. 1992, Ch. 697) by Stats. 1992, Ch. 1369, Sec. 6. Effective October 27, 1992. Operative January 1, 1993, by Sec. 13 of Ch. 1369.)

4016.

Whenever a person is committed upon process in a civil action or proceeding, except when the people of this State are a party thereto, the sheriff is not bound to receive such person, unless security is given on the part of the party at whose instance the process is issued, by a deposit of money, to meet the expenses for him of necessary food, clothing, and bedding, or to detain such person any longer than these expenses

are provided for. This section does not apply to cases where a party is committed as a punishment for disobedience to the mandates, process, writs, or orders of court.
(Added by Stats. 1941, Ch. 106.)

4016.5.
A city or county shall be reimbursed by the Department of Corrections and Rehabilitation for costs incurred resulting from the detention of a state prisoner or a person sentenced or referred to the state prison when the detention meets any of the following conditions:
(a) (1) The detention results from a new commitment, or a referral pursuant to Section 1203.03, once the abstract of judgment has been completed, the department's intake control unit has been notified by the county that the prisoner is ready to be transported pursuant to Section 1216, and the department is unable to accept delivery of the prisoner. The reimbursement shall be provided for each day starting on the day following the fifth working day after the date of notification by the county, if the prisoner remains ready to be delivered and the department is unable to receive the prisoner. If a county delivers or attempts to deliver a person to the department without the prior notification required by this paragraph, the date of the delivery or attempted delivery shall be recognized as the notification date pursuant to this paragraph. The notification and verification required by the county for prisoners ready to be transported, and reimbursement provided to the county for prisoners that the department is unable to receive, shall be made pursuant to procedures established by the department.
(2) A city or county shall be reimbursed by the department from funds appropriated in Item 5240-001-0001 of the annual Budget Act for costs incurred pursuant to this subdivision.
(3) The reimbursement required by this section shall be expended for maintenance, upkeep, and improvement of jail conditions, facilities, and services. Before the county is reimbursed by the department, the total amount of all charges against that county authorized by law for services rendered by the department shall be first deducted from the gross amount of reimbursement authorized by this section. The net reimbursement shall be calculated and paid monthly by the department. The department shall withhold all or part of the net reimbursement to a county whose jail facility or facilities do not conform to minimum standards for local detention facilities as authorized by Section 6030 only if the county is failing to make reasonable efforts to correct differences, with consideration given to the resources available for those purposes.
(4) "Costs incurred resulting from the detention," as used in this section, shall include the same cost factors as are utilized by the Department of Corrections and Rehabilitation in determining the cost of prisoner care in state correctional facilities.
(b) No city, county, or other jurisdiction may file, and the state may not reimburse, a claim pursuant to this section that is presented to the Department of Corrections and Rehabilitation or to any other agency or department of the state more than six months after the close of the month in which the costs were incurred.
(c) The changes to this section made by the act that added this subdivision shall be effective on October 1, 2011.
(Amended as amended by Stats. 2011, Ch. 15) by Stats. 2011, Ch. 39, Sec. 52. (AB 117) Effective June 30, 2011. Operative October 1, 2011, pursuant to Secs. 68 and 69 of Ch. 39.)

4017.
All persons confined in the county jail, industrial farm, road camp, or city jail under a final judgment of imprisonment rendered in a criminal action or proceeding and all persons confined in the county jail, industrial farm, road camp, or city jail as a condition of probation after suspension of imposition of a sentence or suspension of execution of sentence may be required by an order of the board of supervisors or city council to perform labor on the public works or ways in the county or city, respectively, and to engage in the prevention and suppression of forest, brush and grass fires upon lands within the county or city, respectively, or upon lands in adjacent counties where the suppression of fires would afford fire protection to lands within the county.
Whenever any such person so in custody shall suffer injuries or death while working in the prevention or suppression of forest, brush or grass fires he shall be considered to be an employee of the county or city, respectively, for the purposes of compensation under the provisions of the Labor Code regarding workmen's compensation and such work shall be performed under the direct supervision of a local, state or federal employee whose duties include fire prevention and suppression work. A regularly employed member of an organized fire department shall not be required to directly supervise more than 20 such persons so in custody.
As used in this section, "labor on the public works" includes clerical and menial labor in the county jail, industrial farm, camps maintained for the labor of such persons upon the ways in the county, or city jail.
(Amended by Stats. 1971, Ch. 907.)

4017.1.
(a) (1) Except as provided in paragraph (2), any person confined in a county jail, industrial farm, road camp, or city jail who is required or permitted by an order of the board of supervisors or city council to perform work, and any person while performing community service in lieu of a fine or custody or who is assigned to work furlough, may not be employed to perform any function that provides access to personal information of private individuals, including, but not limited to, the following: addresses; telephone numbers; health insurance, taxpayer, school, or employee identification numbers; mothers' maiden names; demand deposit account, debit card, credit card, savings account, or checking account numbers, PINs, or passwords; social security numbers; places of employment; dates of birth; state- or government-issued driver's license or identification numbers; alien registration numbers; government passport numbers; unique biometric data, such as fingerprints, facial scan identifiers, voice prints, retina or iris images, or other similar identifiers; unique electronic identification numbers; address or routing codes; and telecommunication identifying information or access devices.
(2) Notwithstanding paragraph (1), persons assigned to work furlough programs may be permitted to work in situations that allow them to retain or look at a driver's license or credit card for no longer than the period of time needed to complete an immediate transaction. However, no person assigned to work furlough shall be placed in any position that may require the deposit of a credit card or driver's license as insurance or surety.
(b) Any person confined in a county jail, industrial farm, road camp, or city jail who has access to any personal information shall disclose that he or she is confined before taking any personal information from anyone.
(c) This section shall not apply to inmates in employment programs or public service facilities where incidental contact with personal information may occur.
(Amended by Stats. 2006, Ch. 538, Sec. 512. Effective January 1, 2007.)

4017.5.
In any case in which a person is confined to a city or county jail for a definite period of time for contempt pursuant to an action or proceeding other than a criminal action or proceeding, all of the provisions of law authorizing, requiring, or otherwise relating to, the performance of labor or work by persons sentenced to such facilities for like periods of time under a judgment of imprisonment, or a fine and imprisonment until the fine is paid or as a condition of probation after suspension of imposition of a sentence or suspension of execution of sentence, in a criminal action or proceeding, shall apply. Nothing in this section shall be construed to authorize the confinement of any prisoner contrary to the provisions of Section 4001.
(Added by Stats. 1976, Ch. 286.)

4018.
The board of supervisors making such order may prescribe and enforce the rules and regulations under which such labor is to be performed; and provide clothing of such a

distinctive character for said prisoners as such board, in its discretion, may deem proper.
(Amended by Stats. 1969, Ch. 380.)

4018.1.
Subject to the availability of adequate state funding for these purposes, the sheriff of each county shall provide inmates who have been sentenced for drug-related offenses with information about behavior that places a person at high risk for contracting the human immunodeficiency virus (HIV), and about the prevention of the transmission of acquired immune deficiency syndrome (AIDS). Each county sheriff or the chief county probation officer shall provide all inmates who have been sentenced for drug-related offenses, who are within one month of release, or who have been placed on probation, with information about behavior that places a person at high risk for contracting HIV, about the prevention of the transmission of AIDS, and about agencies and facilities that provide testing, counseling, medical, and support services for AIDS victims. Information about AIDS prevention shall be solicited by each county sheriff or chief county probation officer from the State Department of Health Services, the county health officer, or local agencies providing services to persons with AIDS. The Director of Health Services, or his or her designee, shall approve protocols pertaining to the information to be disseminated under this section.
(Added by Stats. 1988, Ch. 1301, Sec. 1.)

4018.5.
The sheriff or other official in charge of county correctional facilities may, subject to the approval of the board of supervisors, provide for the vocational training and rehabilitation of prisoners confined in the county jail, or any county industrial farm or county or joint county road camp. The sheriff or other official in charge of county correctional facilities may, subject to such approval, enter into an agreement with the governing board of any school district maintaining secondary schools, for the maintenance, by the district, for such prisoners, of adult education classes conducted pursuant to the Education Code.
(Amended by Stats. 1973, Ch. 167.)

4018.6.
The sheriff of the county may authorize the temporary removal under custody or temporary release without custody of any inmate of the county jail, honor farm, or other detention facility for family emergencies or for purposes preparatory to his return to the community, if the sheriff concludes that such inmate is a fit subject therefor. Any such temporary removal shall not be for a period of more than three days. When an inmate is released for purposes preparatory to his return to the community, the sheriff may require the inmate to reimburse the county, in whole or in part, for expenses incurred by the county in connection therewith.
(Added by Stats. 1975, Ch. 695.)

4019.
(a) The provisions of this section shall apply in all of the following cases:
(1) When a prisoner is confined in or committed to a county jail, industrial farm, or road camp or a city jail, industrial farm, or road camp, including all days of custody from the date of arrest to the date when the sentence commences, under a judgment of imprisonment or of a fine and imprisonment until the fine is paid in a criminal action or proceeding.
(2) When a prisoner is confined in or committed to a county jail, industrial farm, or road camp or a city jail, industrial farm, or road camp as a condition of probation after suspension of imposition of a sentence or suspension of execution of sentence in a criminal action or proceeding.
(3) When a prisoner is confined in or committed to a county jail, industrial farm, or road camp or a city jail, industrial farm, or road camp for a definite period of time for contempt pursuant to a proceeding other than a criminal action or proceeding.
(4) When a prisoner is confined in a county jail, industrial farm, or road camp or a city jail, industrial farm, or road camp following arrest and prior to the imposition of sentence for a felony conviction.
(5) When a prisoner is confined in a county jail, industrial farm, or road camp or a city jail, industrial farm, or road camp as part of custodial sanction imposed following a violation of postrelease community supervision or parole.
(6) When a prisoner is confined in a county jail, industrial farm, or road camp or a city jail, industrial farm, or road camp as a result of a sentence imposed pursuant to subdivision (h) of Section 1170.
(7) When a prisoner participates in a program pursuant to Section 1203.016 or Section 4024.2. Except for prisoners who have already been deemed eligible to receive credits for participation in a program pursuant to Section 1203.016 prior to January 1, 2015, this paragraph shall apply prospectively.
(8) When a prisoner is confined in or committed to a county jail treatment facility, as defined in Section 1369.1, in proceedings pursuant to Chapter 6 (commencing with Section 1367) of Title 10 of Part 2.
(b) Subject to the provisions of subdivision (d), for each four-day period in which a prisoner is confined in or committed to a facility as specified in this section, one day shall be deducted from his or her period of confinement unless it appears by the record that the prisoner has refused to satisfactorily perform labor as assigned by the sheriff, chief of police, or superintendent of an industrial farm or road camp.
(c) For each four-day period in which a prisoner is confined in or committed to a facility as specified in this section, one day shall be deducted from his or her period of confinement unless it appears by the record that the prisoner has not satisfactorily complied with the reasonable rules and regulations established by the sheriff, chief of police, or superintendent of an industrial farm or road camp.
(d) This section does not require the sheriff, chief of police, or superintendent of an industrial farm or road camp to assign labor to a prisoner if it appears from the record that the prisoner has refused to satisfactorily perform labor as assigned or that the prisoner has not satisfactorily complied with the reasonable rules and regulations of the sheriff, chief of police, or superintendent of an industrial farm or road camp.
(e) A deduction shall not be made under this section unless the person is committed for a period of four days or longer.
(f) It is the intent of the Legislature that if all days are earned under this section, a term of four days will be deemed to have been served for every two days spent in actual custody.
(g) The changes in this section as enacted by the act that added this subdivision shall apply to prisoners who are confined to a county jail, city jail, industrial farm, or road camp for a crime committed on or after the effective date of that act.
(h) The changes to this section enacted by the act that added this subdivision shall apply prospectively and shall apply to prisoners who are confined to a county jail, city jail, industrial farm, or road camp for a crime committed on or after October 1, 2011. Any days earned by a prisoner prior to October 1, 2011, shall be calculated at the rate required by the prior law.
(i) (1) This section shall not apply, and no credits may be earned, for periods of flash incarceration imposed pursuant to Section 3000.08 or 3454.
(2) Credits earned pursuant to this section for a period of flash incarceration pursuant to Section 1203.35 shall, if the person's probation or mandatory supervision is revoked, count towards the term to be served.
(j) This section shall remain in effect only until January 1, 2021, and as of that date is repealed, unless a later enacted statute, that is enacted before January 1, 2021, deletes or extends that date.
(Amended (as amended by Stats. 2016, Ch. 706, Sec. 3) by Stats. 2018, Ch. 1008, Sec. 5. (SB 1187) Effective January 1, 2019. Repealed as of January 1, 2021, by its

own provisions. See later operative version amended by Sec. 6 of Stats. 2018, Ch. 1008.)

4019.

(a) The provisions of this section shall apply in all of the following cases:

(1) When a prisoner is confined in or committed to a county jail, industrial farm, or road camp or a city jail, industrial farm, or road camp, including all days of custody from the date of arrest to the date when the sentence commences, under a judgment of imprisonment or of a fine and imprisonment until the fine is paid in a criminal action or proceeding.

(2) When a prisoner is confined in or committed to a county jail, industrial farm, or road camp or a city jail, industrial farm, or road camp as a condition of probation after suspension of imposition of a sentence or suspension of execution of sentence in a criminal action or proceeding.

(3) When a prisoner is confined in or committed to a county jail, industrial farm, or road camp or a city jail, industrial farm, or road camp for a definite period of time for contempt pursuant to a proceeding other than a criminal action or proceeding.

(4) When a prisoner is confined in a county jail, industrial farm, or road camp or a city jail, industrial farm, or road camp following arrest and prior to the imposition of sentence for a felony conviction.

(5) When a prisoner is confined in a county jail, industrial farm, or road camp or a city jail, industrial farm, or road camp as part of custodial sanction imposed following a violation of postrelease community supervision or parole.

(6) When a prisoner is confined in a county jail, industrial farm, or road camp or a city jail, industrial farm, or road camp as a result of a sentence imposed pursuant to subdivision (h) of Section 1170.

(7) When a prisoner participates in a program pursuant to Section 1203.016 or Section 4024.2. Except for prisoners who have already been deemed eligible to receive credits for participation in a program pursuant to Section 1203.016 prior to January 1, 2015, this paragraph shall apply prospectively.

(8) When a prisoner is confined in or committed to a county jail treatment facility, as defined in Section 1369.1, in proceedings pursuant to Chapter 6 (commencing with Section 1367) of Title 10 of Part 2.

(b) Subject to the provisions of subdivision (d), for each four-day period in which a prisoner is confined in or committed to a facility as specified in this section, one day shall be deducted from his or her period of confinement unless it appears by the record that the prisoner has refused to satisfactorily perform labor as assigned by the sheriff, chief of police, or superintendent of an industrial farm or road camp.

(c) For each four-day period in which a prisoner is confined in or committed to a facility as specified in this section, one day shall be deducted from his or her period of confinement unless it appears by the record that the prisoner has not satisfactorily complied with the reasonable rules and regulations established by the sheriff, chief of police, or superintendent of an industrial farm or road camp.

(d) This section does not require the sheriff, chief of police, or superintendent of an industrial farm or road camp to assign labor to a prisoner if it appears from the record that the prisoner has refused to satisfactorily perform labor as assigned or that the prisoner has not satisfactorily complied with the reasonable rules and regulations of the sheriff, chief of police, or superintendent of an industrial farm or road camp.

(e) A deduction shall not be made under this section unless the person is committed for a period of four days or longer.

(f) It is the intent of the Legislature that if all days are earned under this section, a term of four days will be deemed to have been served for every two days spent in actual custody.

(g) The changes in this section as enacted by the act that added this subdivision shall apply to prisoners who are confined to a county jail, city jail, industrial farm, or road camp for a crime committed on or after the effective date of that act.

(h) The changes to this section enacted by the act that added this subdivision shall apply prospectively and shall apply to prisoners who are confined to a county jail, city jail, industrial farm, or road camp for a crime committed on or after October 1, 2011. Any days earned by a prisoner prior to October 1, 2011, shall be calculated at the rate required by the prior law.

(i) This section shall not apply, and no credits may be earned, for periods of flash incarceration imposed pursuant to Section 3000.08 or 3454.

(j) This section shall become operative on January 1, 2021.

(Amended (as added by Stats. 2016, Ch. 706, Sec. 4) by Stats. 2018, Ch. 1008, Sec. 6. (SB 1187) Effective January 1, 2019. Section operative January 1, 2021, by its own provisions.)

4019.1.

(a) Notwithstanding any other law, the sheriff or county director of corrections may, at his or her discretion, award additional time credits to any inmate sentenced to the county jail who participates in an in-custody work or job training program other than those specified in Section 4019.2, and who is eligible to receive one day of credit for every one day of incarceration pursuant to Section 4019. The sheriff or county director of corrections may instead award one and one-half days of credit for every one day of incarceration while satisfactorily participating in work or job training subject to this section.

(b) As used in this section, a work or job training program includes, but is not limited to, any inmate working on an industrial farm or industrial road camp as authorized in Section 4101, an environmental improvement and preservation program, or projects such as forest and brush fire prevention, forest, brush, and watershed management, fish and game management, soil conservation, and forest and watershed revegetation.

(Added by Stats. 2013, Ch. 32, Sec. 12. (SB 76) Effective June 27, 2013.)

4019.2.

(a) Notwithstanding any other law, any inmate sentenced to county jail assigned to a conservation camp by a sheriff and who is eligible to earn one day of credit for every one day of incarceration pursuant to Section 4019 shall instead earn two days of credit for every one day of service.

(b) Notwithstanding any other law, any inmate who has completed training for assignment to a conservation camp or to a state or county facility as an inmate firefighter or who is assigned to a county or state correctional institution as an inmate firefighter and who is eligible to earn one day of credit for every one day of incarceration pursuant to Section 4019 shall instead earn two days of credit for every one day served in that assignment or after completing that training.

(c) In addition to credits granted pursuant to subdivision (a) or (b), inmates who have successfully completed training for firefighter assignments shall receive a credit reduction from his or her term of confinement.

(d) The credits authorized in subdivisions (b) and (c) shall only apply to inmates who are eligible after October 1, 2011.

(Added by Stats. 2011, 1st Ex. Sess., Ch. 12, Sec. 36. (AB 17 1x) Effective September 21, 2011. Operative October 1, 2011, by Sec. 46 of Ch. 12.)

4019.3.

The board of supervisors may provide that each prisoner confined in or committed to a county jail shall be credited with a sum not to exceed two dollars ($2) for each eight hours of work done by him in such county jail.

(Amended by Stats. 1975, Ch. 350.)

4019.4.

(a) (1) In addition to credit awarded pursuant to Section 4019, a sheriff or county director of corrections may also award an inmate program credit reductions from his or her term of confinement as provided in this section. A sheriff or county director of corrections who elects to participate in this credit reduction program shall create

guidelines that provide for credit reductions for inmates who successfully complete specific program performance objectives for approved rehabilitative programming, including, but not limited to, credit reduction of not less than one week to credit reduction of not more than six weeks for each performance milestone.

(2) Guidelines adopted by a sheriff or county director of corrections pursuant to this subdivision shall specify the credit reductions applicable to distinct objectives in a schedule of graduated program performance objectives concluding with the successful completion of an in-custody rehabilitation program. Upon adopting the guidelines, the sheriff or county director of corrections shall thereafter calculate and award credit reductions authorized by this section. An inmate may not have his or her term of imprisonment reduced by more than six weeks for credits awarded pursuant to this section during any 12-month period of continuous confinement.

(b) Program credit is a privilege, not a right. An inmate shall have a reasonable opportunity to participate in program credit qualifying assignments in a manner consistent with institutional security, available resources, and guidelines set forth by the sheriff or county director of corrections.

(c) As used in this section, "approved rehabilitation programming" includes, but is not limited to, academic programs, vocational programs, vocational training, substance abuse programs, and core programs such as anger management and social life skills.

(d) Credits awarded pursuant to this section may be forfeited pursuant to the provisions of Section 4019. An inmate shall not be eligible for program credits that result in him or her being overdue for release.

(e) This section applies to sentenced and unsentenced inmates confined in a county jail.

(f) (1) Nothing in this section shall prevent a person who has not been sentenced from participating in an approved rehabilitation program pursuant to this section.

(2) If a person is awarded credits prior to sentencing, the credits shall be applied to a sentence for the offense for which the person was awaiting sentence when the credits were awarded in the same manner as all other credits awarded.

(g) Evidence that an inmate has participated in, or attempted to participate in, an approved rehabilitation program eligible for credit pursuant to this section is not admissible in any proceeding as an admission of guilt.

(Amended by Stats. 2016, Ch. 36, Sec. 1. (AB 1597) Effective January 1, 2017.)

4019.5.

(a) "Kangaroo court" as used in this section means a mock court conducted by any prisoner or group of prisoners for the purpose of inflicting punishment upon any fellow prisoner in any prison, jail, jail camp, or other place of detention.

(b) "Sanitary committee" means a committee of prisoners formed ostensibly for the purpose of enforcing institutional sanitation but actually used for the purpose of inflicting punishment on any fellow prisoner, or group of prisoners in any prison, jail, jail camp, or other place of detention.

(c) It is unlawful for any sheriff, deputy sheriff, police officer, warden or keeper of a jail to delegate to any prisoner or group of prisoners, authority to exercise the right of punishment over any other prisoner or group of prisoners in any county or city prison, jail, jail camp, or other place of detention at which any person charged with or convicted of crime is detained.

(d) It is unlawful for any sheriff, deputy sheriff, police officer, warden or keeper of a jail to knowingly permit any prisoner or group of prisoners to assume authority over any other prisoner or group of prisoners by the operation of "kangaroo courts" or "sanitary committees."

(e) Every public official in charge of a prison, jail or other place of detention shall keep a record of all disciplinary infractions and punishment administered therefor.

(f) This section shall not prevent the use of skilled inmates, under adequate and proper supervision and guidance of jailers or other employed personnel, as instructors of other inmates in the performance of assigned work, if that relationship does not include the exercise of disciplinary authority.

(Amended by Stats. 1996, Ch. 872, Sec. 124. Effective January 1, 1997.)

4020.

Whenever the board of health of any city or county, or the board of supervisors of any county, or the county physician of any county of this State, presents, or causes to be presented to the sheriff, or other officer having charge of any county jail or prison in any county or city, in this State, a certificate, or order, in writing, to the effect that it is by them, or him, considered necessary for the purpose of protecting the public health, or to prevent the introduction or spreading of disease, or to protect or improve the health of criminals under sentence, that the hair of any criminal or criminals be cut, such sheriff, or other officer, must cut, or cause to be cut, the hair of any such person or persons in his charge convicted of a misdemeanor and sentenced to a longer term of imprisonment than 15 days, to a uniform length of one and one-half inches from the scalp of such person or persons so imprisoned.

(Added by Stats. 1941, Ch. 106.)

4020.4.

In every county having a population of more than 275,000, there shall be a female deputy sheriff in charge of female prisoners.

The sheriff of the county shall appoint the female deputy sheriff in charge of female prisoners.

(Amended by Stats. 1969, Ch. 643.)

4020.7.

The duties and powers of the female deputy sheriff or other suitable woman assigned to jail duty shall be as follows:

(a) She shall have free access at all reasonable times to the immediate presence of all female prisoners in the county jail to which she is assigned, including the right of personal visitation and conversation with them, and in all cases of searching the persons of female prisoners in such jail, the female deputy sheriff shall make such search;

(b) The female deputy sheriff or other suitable woman shall by example, advice, and admonition employ her best abilities to secure and promote the health, welfare, and reformation of all such prisoners.

(Amended by Stats. 1969, Ch. 643.)

4020.8.

No officer, deputy, jailer, keeper, guard, or person having charge or control of any such county jail shall refuse the duly appointed and qualified female deputy sheriff thereof, or other suitable woman having the care of female prisoners, free access at all reasonable times to the immediate presence of all female prisoners therein, including the right of visitation and conversation with them, or in such jail allow the searching of the person of a female prisoner to be made except by the female deputy sheriff of such jail or other suitable woman, or obstruct the performance by the female deputy sheriff, or other suitable woman, of her official duties.

(Amended by Stats. 1969, Ch. 643.)

4021.

(a) Whenever any female prisoner or prisoners are confined in any local detention facility in the state there shall be an appropriately trained female custodial person assigned, available, and accessible for the supervision of the female prisoners.

(b) It shall be unlawful for any officer, station officer, jailer, or custodial personnel to search the person of any prisoner of the opposite sex, or to enter into the room or cell occupied by any prisoner of the opposite sex, except in the company of an employee of the same sex as the prisoner. Except as provided herein, the provisions of this subdivision shall not be applied to discriminate against any employee by prohibiting appointment or work assignment on the basis of the sex of the employee.

As used in this subdivision "station officer" means an unarmed civilian employee who assists a peace officer in the processing of persons who have been arrested and who

performs duties including, but not limited to, booking and fingerprinting and maintaining custody and control of persons who have been arrested.
As used in this subdivision, "employee" means a deputy sheriff, correctional officer, custodial officer, medical staff person or designated civilian employee whose duties may include, but are not limited to, maintaining custody and control of persons who have been arrested or sentenced, or both.
(Amended by Stats. 1984, Ch. 986, Sec. 1.)
4022.
Whenever by the terms of this code, or of any other law of the state, it is provided that a prisoner shall be confined in any county jail, such provision shall be construed to authorize any prisoner convicted of a misdemeanor to be confined, with the consent of the city, in any city jail in the judicial district in which the offense was committed, and as to such prisoner so confined in such city jail, the designations, county jail and city jail shall be interchangeable, and in such case the obligations to which the county is liable in case of confinement in a county jail, shall become liabilities of the city where such prisoner is confined in a city jail.
(Amended by Stats. 1998, Ch. 931, Sec. 434. Effective September 28, 1998.)
4023.
Whenever the daily average of more than 100 persons are confined in any county or city jail there shall be available at all times a duly licensed and practicing physician for the care and treatment of all persons confined therein. Such daily average shall be determined by the number of persons confined in such jails during the last fiscal year. For county jails, such physician shall be designated by the sheriff. The salary of such physician shall be fixed by the supervisors of the county and shall be paid out of the same fund of the county as other claims against the county for salaries are paid. For city jails, such physician shall be designated and his salary fixed by the council of the city and shall be paid out of the general fund of such city. Any prisoner may decline such care or treatment and provide other care or treatment for himself at his own expense.
In the event a prisoner elects to decline treatment by the county or city jail physician and to provide medical treatment at his own expense, the sheriff or chief of police may have him removed from the county or city jail to a privately owned and operated medical facility or hospital located in the county approved by a judge of the superior court for such treatment. The prisoner shall be liable for the costs incurred by the county or city in providing the necessary custody and security of the prisoner only to the extent that such costs exceed the costs which would have been incurred by the county or city in providing such custody and security if it had provided treatment for him. The prisoner shall at all times remain in the location specified by the court and at no time be permitted to be housed or detained at any facility other than that designated.
(Amended by Stats. 1970, Ch. 683.)
4023.5.
(a) Any female confined in any local detention facility shall upon her request be allowed to continued to use materials necessary for (1) personal hygiene with regard to her menstrual cycle and reproductive system and (2) birth control measures as prescribed by her physician.
(b) Each and every female confined in any local detention facility shall be furnished by the county with information and education regarding the availability of family planning services.
(c) Family planning services shall be offered to each and every woman inmate at least 60 days prior to a scheduled release date. Upon request any woman inmate shall be furnished by the county with the services of a licensed physician or she shall be furnished by the county or by any other agency which contracts with the county with services necessary to meet her family planning needs at the time of her release.
(d) For the purposes of this section, "local detention facility" means any city, county, or regional facility used for the confinement of any female prisoner for more than 24 hours.
(Amended by Stats. 1975, Ch. 1146.)
4023.6.
Any female prisoner in any local detention facility shall have the right to summon and receive the services of any physician and surgeon of her choice in order to determine whether she is pregnant. The superintendent of such facility may adopt reasonable rules and regulations with regard to the conduct of examinations to effectuate such determination.
If the prisoner is found to be pregnant, she is entitled to a determination of the extent of the medical services needed by her and to the receipt of such services from the physician and surgeon of her choice. Any expenses occasioned by the services of a physician and surgeon whose services are not provided by the facility shall be borne by the prisoner.
For the purposes of this section, "local detention facility" means any city, county, or regional facility used for the confinement of any female prisoner for more than 24 hours.
Any physician providing services pursuant to this section shall possess a current, valid, and unrevoked certificate to engage in the practice of medicine issued pursuant to Chapter 5 (commencing with Section 2000) of Division 2 of the Business and Professions Code.
The rights provided for prisoners by this section shall be posted in at least one conspicuous place to which all female prisoners have access.
(Added by Stats. 1972, Ch. 1362.)
4024.
(a) The sheriff may discharge any prisoner from the county jail at such time on the last day such prisoner may be confined as the sheriff shall consider to be in the best interests of the prisoner.
(b) (1) Upon completion of a sentence served by a prisoner or the release of a prisoner ordered by the court to be effected the same day, including prisoners who are released on their own recognizance, have their charges dismissed by the court, are acquitted by a jury, are cited and released on a misdemeanor charge, have posted bail, or have the charges against them dropped by the prosecutor, the sheriff may offer a voluntary program to the prisoner that would allow that prisoner to stay in the custody facility for up to 16 additional hours or until normal business hours, whichever is shorter, in order to offer the prisoner the ability to be discharged to a treatment center or during daytime hours. The prisoner may revoke his or her consent and be discharged as soon as possible and practicable.
(2) This subdivision does not prevent the early release of prisoners as otherwise allowed by law or allow jails to retain prisoners any longer than otherwise required by law without the prisoner's express written consent.
(3) Offering this voluntary program is an act of discretion within the meaning of Section 820.2 of the Government Code.
(4) If a prisoner has posted bail and elects to participate in this program, he or she shall notify the bail agent as soon as possible and practicable of his or her decision to participate.
(5) A sheriff offering this program shall, whenever possible, allow the prisoner volunteering to participate in the program to make a telephone call to either arrange for transportation, or to notify the bail agent pursuant to paragraph (4), or both.
(Amended by Stats. 2014, Ch. 90, Sec. 2. (SB 833) Effective January 1, 2015.)
4024.1.
(a) The sheriff, chief of police, or any other person responsible for a county or city jail may apply to the presiding judge of the superior court to receive general authorization for a period of 30 days to release inmates pursuant to the provisions of this section.
(b) Whenever, after being authorized by a court pursuant to subdivision (a), the actual inmate count exceeds the actual bed capacity of a county or city jail, the sheriff, chief of police, or other person responsible for such county or city jail may accelerate the release, discharge, or expiration of sentence date of sentenced inmates up to a maximum of 30 days.
(c) The total number of inmates released pursuant to this section shall not exceed a number necessary to balance the inmate count and actual bed capacity.
(d) Inmates closest to their normal release, discharge, or expiration of sentence date shall be given accelerated release priority.
(e) The number of days that release, discharge, or expiration of sentence is accelerated shall in no case exceed 10 percent of the particular inmate's original sentence, prior to the application thereto of any other credits or benefits authorized by law.
(Amended by Stats. 2012, Ch. 43, Sec. 54. (SB 1023) Effective June 27, 2012.)
4024.2.
(a) Notwithstanding any other law, the board of supervisors of any county may authorize the sheriff or other official in charge of county correctional facilities to offer a voluntary program under which any person committed to the facility may participate in a work release program pursuant to criteria described in subdivision (b), in which one day of participation will be in lieu of one day of confinement.
(b) The criteria for a work release program are the following:
(1) The work release program shall consist of any of the following:
(A) Manual labor to improve or maintain levees or public facilities, including, but not limited to, streets, parks, and schools.
(B) Manual labor in support of nonprofit organizations, as approved by the sheriff or other official in charge of the correctional facilities. As a condition of assigning participants of a work release program to perform manual labor in support of nonprofit organizations pursuant to this section, the board of supervisors shall obtain workers' compensation insurance which shall be adequate to cover work-related injuries incurred by those participants, in accordance with Section 3363.5 of the Labor Code.
(C) Performance of graffiti cleanup for local governmental entities, including participation in a graffiti abatement program as defined in subdivision (f) of Section 594, as approved by the sheriff or other official in charge of the correctional facilities.
(D) Performance of weed and rubbish abatement on public and private property pursuant to Chapter 13 (commencing with Section 39501) of Part 2 of Division 3 of Title 4 of the Government Code, or Part 5 (commencing with Section 14875) or Part 6 (commencing with Section 14930) of Division 12 of the Health and Safety Code, as approved by the sheriff or other official in charge of the correctional facilities.
(E) Performance of house repairs or yard services for senior citizens and the performance of repairs to senior centers through contact with local senior service organizations, as approved by the sheriff or other official in charge of the correctional facilities. Where a work release participant has been assigned to this task, the sheriff or other official shall agree upon in advance with the senior service organization about the type of services to be rendered by the participant and the extent of contact permitted between the recipients of these services and the participant.
(F) Any person who is not able to perform manual labor as specified in this paragraph because of a medical condition, physical disability, or age, may participate in a work release program involving any other type of public sector work that is designated and approved by the sheriff or other official in charge of county correctional facilities.
(2) The sheriff or other official may permit a participant in a work release program to receive work release credit for documented participation in educational programs, vocational programs, substance abuse programs, life skills programs, or parenting programs. Participation in these programs shall be considered in lieu of performing labor in a work release program, with eight work-related hours to equal one day of custody credit.
(3) The work release program shall be under the direction of a responsible person appointed by the sheriff or other official in charge.
(4) The hours of labor to be performed pursuant to this section shall be uniform for all persons committed to a facility in a county and may be determined by the sheriff or other official in charge of county correctional facilities, and each day shall be a minimum of 8 and a maximum of 10 hours, in accordance with the normal working hours of county employees assigned to supervise the programs. However, reasonable accommodation may be made for participation in a program under paragraph (2).
As used in this section, "nonprofit organizations" means organizations established or operated for the benefit of the public or in support of a significant public interest, as set forth in Section 501(c)(3) of the Internal Revenue Code. Organizations established or operated for the primary purpose of benefiting their own memberships are excluded.
(c) The board of supervisors may prescribe reasonable rules and regulations under which a work release program is operated and may provide that participants wear clothing of a distinctive character while performing the work. As a condition of participating in a work release program, a person shall give his or her promise to appear for work or assigned activity by signing a notice to appear before the sheriff or at the education, vocational, or substance abuse program at a time and place specified in the notice and shall sign an agreement that the sheriff may immediately retake the person into custody to serve the balance of his or her sentence if the person fails to appear for the program at the time and place agreed to, does not perform the work or activity assigned, or for any other reason is no longer a fit subject for release under this section. A copy of the notice shall be delivered to the person and a copy shall be retained by the sheriff. Any person who willfully violates his or her written promise to appear at the time and place specified in the notice is guilty of a misdemeanor.
Whenever a peace officer has reasonable cause to believe the person has failed to appear at the time and place specified in the notice or fails to appear or work at the time and place agreed to or has failed to perform the work assigned, the peace officer may, without a warrant, retake the person into custody, or the court may issue an arrest warrant for the retaking of the person into custody, to complete the remainder of the original sentence. A peace officer may not retake a person into custody under this subdivision, without a warrant for arrest, unless the officer has a written order to do so, signed by the sheriff or other person in charge of the program, that describes with particularity the person to be retaken.
(d) This section does not require the sheriff or other official in charge to assign a person to a program pursuant to this section if it appears from the record that the person has refused to satisfactorily perform as assigned or has not satisfactorily complied with the reasonable rules and regulations governing the assignment or any other order of the court.
A person shall be eligible for work release under this section only if the sheriff or other official in charge concludes that the person is a fit subject therefor.
(e) The board of supervisors may prescribe a program administrative fee, not to exceed the pro rata cost of administration, to be paid by each person according to his or her ability to pay.
(Amended by Stats. 2013, Ch. 76, Sec. 160. (AB 383) Effective January 1, 2014.)
4024.3.
(a) Notwithstanding any other law, the board of supervisors of any county in which the average daily inmate population is 90 percent of the county's correctional system's mandated capacity may authorize the sheriff or other official in charge of county correctional facilities to operate a program under which any person committed to the facility is required to participate in a work release program pursuant to criteria described in subdivision (b) of Section 4024.2. Participants in this work release program shall receive any sentence reduction credits that they would have received had they served their sentences in a county correctional facility. Priority for participation in the work release program shall be given to inmates who volunteer to participate in the program.
(b) For purposes of this section, all of the following definitions apply:

(1) "County correctional system's mandated capacity" means the total capacity of all jails and other correctional facilities for the permanent housing of adult inmates within the county.
(2) "Mandated capacity" of any facility is the capacity for that facility as established by court order or the facility's rated capacity as established by the Board of Corrections, whichever is less.
(3) "Average daily jail population" is the average total number of inmates incarcerated within the county jail system computed on an annual basis.
(c) (1) The board of supervisors may prescribe reasonable rules and regulations under which a work release program authorized under this section is operated and may provide that participants wear clothing of a distinctive character while performing the work. A person shall be advised by written notice to appear before the sheriff or at the educational, vocational, or substance abuse program at a time and place specified in the notice and shall sign an acknowledgement that the sheriff may immediately retake the person into custody to serve the balance of his or her sentence if the person fails to appear for the program at the time and place designated in the notice, does not perform the work or activity assigned, or for any other reason is no longer a fit subject for release under this section. A copy of the notice and acknowledgement shall be delivered to the person and a copy shall be retained by the sheriff.
(2) Any person who willfully fails to appear at the time and place specified in the notice is guilty of a misdemeanor.
(3) Whenever a peace officer has reasonable cause to believe the person has failed to appear at the time and place specified in the notice or fails to appear or work at the time and place agreed to or has failed to perform the work assigned, the peace officer may, without a warrant, retake the person into custody, or the court may issue an arrest warrant for the retaking of the person into custody, to complete the remainder of the original sentence. A peace officer may not retake a person into custody under this subdivision, without a warrant for arrest, unless the officer has a written order to do so, signed by the sheriff or other person in charge of the work release program, that describes with particularity the person to be retaken.
(d) Nothing in this section shall be construed to require the sheriff or other official in charge to assign a person to a work release program pursuant to this section if it appears from the record that the person has refused to perform satisfactorily as assigned or has not satisfactorily complied with the reasonable rules and regulations governing the assignment or any other order of the court.
(e) A person shall be eligible for work release under this section only if the sheriff or other official in charge concludes that the person is a fit subject therefor.
(f) The board of supervisors may prescribe a program administrative fee, not to exceed the pro rata cost of administration, to be paid by each person according to his or her ability to pay.
(Added by Stats. 1995, Ch. 106, Sec. 2. Effective January 1, 1996.)

4024.4.

(a) The board of supervisors of each county, with the concurrence of the county sheriff before implementation, and the city council of each city, with the concurrence of the chief of police before implementation, may establish a notification procedure to provide notice of the release of any person incarcerated at, or arrested and released on bail from, a local detention facility under its jurisdiction to victims of crime who have requested to be so notified. A county or city and two or more counties or cities jointly may contract with a private entity to implement this procedure.
(b) Notwithstanding any other law, the sheriff, chief of police, or other official in charge of a local detention facility shall make available to any private entity under contract pursuant to subdivision (a) all information necessary to implement the notification procedure in a timely manner. The private entity under contract shall be responsible for retrieving the information and notifying the requester through computer or telephonic means and, if unable to notify the person requesting the information by these means, shall send written notification by mail.
(c) The sheriff, chief of police, or other official in charge of a local detention facility shall work cooperatively with law enforcement agencies within the county or city and local victim centers established under Section 13835 to implement the program.
(d) As used in this section, "local detention facility" means a facility specified in subdivision (a) or (b) of Section 6031.4.
(e) Notwithstanding any other provision of law, no public or private officer, employee, or entity may be held liable for any action or duty undertaken pursuant to this section.
(Added by Stats. 1996, Ch. 1060, Sec. 1. Effective January 1, 1997.)

4025.

(a) The sheriff of each county may establish, maintain and operate a store in connection with the county jail and for this purpose may purchase confectionery, tobacco and tobacco users' supplies, postage and writing materials, and toilet articles and supplies and sell these goods, articles, and supplies for cash to inmates in the jail.
(b) The sale prices of the articles offered for sale at the store shall be fixed by the sheriff. Any profit shall be deposited in an inmate welfare fund to be kept in the treasury of the county.
(c) There shall also be deposited in the inmate welfare fund 10 percent of all gross sales of inmate hobbycraft.
(d) There shall be deposited in the inmate welfare fund any money, refund, rebate, or commission received from a telephone company or pay telephone provider when the money, refund, rebate, or commission is attributable to the use of pay telephones which are primarily used by inmates while incarcerated.
(e) The money and property deposited in the inmate welfare fund shall be expended by the sheriff primarily for the benefit, education, and welfare of the inmates confined within the jail. Any funds that are not needed for the welfare of the inmates may be expended for the maintenance of county jail facilities. Maintenance of county jail facilities may include, but is not limited to, the salary and benefits of personnel used in the programs to benefit the inmates, including, but not limited to, education, drug and alcohol treatment, welfare, library, accounting, and other programs deemed appropriate by the sheriff. Inmate welfare funds shall not be used to pay required county expenses of confining inmates in a local detention system, such as meals, clothing, housing, or medical services or expenses, except that inmate welfare funds may be used to augment those required county expenses as determined by the sheriff to be in the best interests of inmates. An itemized report of these expenditures shall be submitted annually to the board of supervisors.
(f) The operation of a store within any other county adult detention facility which is not under the jurisdiction of the sheriff shall be governed by the provisions of this section, except that the board of supervisors shall designate the proper county official to exercise the duties otherwise allocated in this section to the sheriff.
(g) The operation of a store within any city adult detention facility shall be governed by the provisions of this section, except that city officials shall assume the respective duties otherwise outlined in this section for county officials.
(h) The treasurer may, pursuant to Article 1 (commencing with Section 53600), or Article 2 (commencing with Section 53630) of Chapter 4 of Part 1 of Division 2 of Title 5 of the Government Code, deposit, invest, or reinvest any part of the inmate welfare fund, in excess of that which the treasurer deems necessary for immediate use. The interest or increment accruing on these funds shall be deposited in the inmate welfare fund.
(i) The sheriff may expend money from the inmate welfare fund to provide indigent inmates, prior to release from the county jail or any other adult detention facility under the jurisdiction of the sheriff, with essential clothing and transportation expenses within the county or, at the discretion of the sheriff, transportation to the inmate's county of residence, if the county is within the state or within 500 miles from the county of incarceration. This subdivision does not authorize expenditure of money from the inmate welfare fund for the transfer of any inmate to the custody of any other law enforcement official or jurisdiction.
(Amended by Stats. 2007, Ch. 251, Sec. 1. Effective January 1, 2008.)

4025.5.

(a) There is hereby created a program in the Counties of Alameda, Kern, Los Angeles, Marin, Napa, Orange, Sacramento, San Bernardino, San Francisco, San Diego, San Luis Obispo, Santa Barbara, Santa Clara, Stanislaus, and Ventura. In each county, the sheriff or the county officer responsible for operating the jails may expend money from the inmate welfare fund to provide indigent inmates, after release from the county jail or any other adult detention facility under the jurisdiction of the sheriff or the county officer responsible for operating the jails, assistance with the reentry process within 30 days after the inmate's release. The assistance provided may include work placement, counseling, obtaining proper identification, education, and housing.
(b) This section does not authorize money from the inmate welfare fund to be used to provide any services that are required to be provided by the sheriff or the county. Money in the fund shall supplement existing services, and shall not be used to supplant any existing funding for services provided by the sheriff or the county.
(c) As part of the itemized report of expenditures required to be submitted to the board of supervisors pursuant to Section 4025, any sheriff or county officer responsible for operating a jail of a county that participates in the program shall include in the report all of the following:
(1) How much money was spent pursuant to this section.
(2) The number of inmates the program served.
(3) The types of assistance for which the funds were used.
(4) The average length of time an inmate used the program.
(Added by Stats. 2016, Ch. 178, Sec. 1. (AB 920) Effective August 25, 2016.)

4026.

The sheriff or other officer in charge of a county or city jail may provide for the manufacture of small articles of handiwork by prisoners out of raw materials purchased by the prisoners with their own funds or funds borrowed from the inmate welfare fund, which articles may be sold to the public at the county or city jails, in public buildings, at fairs, or on property operated by nonprofit associations. County- or city-owned property shall not be sold or given to prisoners for use under this section, except as expressly permitted by this section. The sheriff or other officer in charge shall comply with subdivision (c) of Section 4025 and provide that the balance of the sale price of the articles be deposited to the account of the prisoner manufacturing the article after repaying the inmate welfare fund any amount borrowed.
(Amended by Stats. 1970, Ch. 916.)

4027.

It is the intention of the Legislature that all prisoners confined in local detention facilities shall be afforded reasonable opportunities to exercise religious freedom.
As used in this section "local detention facility" means any city, county, or regional facility used for the confinement of prisoners for more than 24 hours.
(Added by Stats. 1972, Ch. 1349.)

4028.

No condition or restriction upon the obtaining of an abortion by a female detained in any local detention facility, pursuant to the Therapeutic Abortion Act (Article 2 (commencing with Section 123400) of Chapter 2 of Part 2 of Division 106 of the Health and Safety Code), other than those contained in that act, shall be imposed. Females found to be pregnant and desiring abortions shall be permitted to determine their eligibility for an abortion pursuant to law, and if determined to be eligible, shall be permitted to obtain an abortion.
For the purposes of this section, "local detention facility" means any city, county, or regional facility used for the confinement of any female person for more than 24 hours. The rights provided for females by this section shall be posted in at least one conspicuous place to which all female prisoners have access.
(Amended by Stats. 1996, Ch. 1023, Sec. 395. Effective September 29, 1996.)

4029.

(a) Whenever within any county adult detention facility or part of any county detention facility used for the confinement of adults, not including any city jail, any facility, including but not limited to any room or cell, vocational training facility, recreation area, rest area, dining room, store, or facility for the exercise of religious freedom, is provided for use by any prisoner for any purpose, a separate facility of equal quality, or separate use of the same facility, or joint use of the same facility where appropriate, shall be provided for prisoners of the opposite sex for such purpose.
(b) Whenever within any county adult detention facility or part of any county detention facility used for the confinement of adults, not including any city jail, any program, service or privilege, including but not limited to any general or vocational education, physical education or recreation, work furlough program, psychological counseling, work within the institution, visiting privileges, or medical treatment, is provided for any prisoner, such a program, service or privilege of equal quality shall be provided for prisoners of the opposite sex, except when the proportion of prisoners of one sex is so small that the cost of providing any program, service or privilege described in this subdivision, other than medical treatment or health maintenance, for such prisoners would not be justified in relation to the reduction in the level of any other program, service or privilege that would result from the diversion of funds for such purpose.
(c) Nothing in this section shall require the establishment of any facility for the use of, or the making available of any program, service or privilege to, any prisoner. Nothing in this section shall require any facility, program, service or privilege established or available prior or subsequent to January 1, 1975, to be made available to any particular male or female prisoner or number of such prisoners, except that any type of facility, program, service or privilege which is made accessible or available to all male or female prisoners in any class defined by subdivisions 1, 2, and 3 of Section 4001 shall be made accessible or available to all prisoners of the opposite sex in such class as provided in subdivisions (a) and (b), and any criterion other than the sex of the prisoner which is used for the selection of a particular prisoner or group of prisoners to have, or to have access to, any facility, program, service or privilege shall be equally applied to the selection of all prisoners, regardless of sex.
(d) Every county shall comply with subdivisions (a), (b), and (c) by January 1, 1979. Such compliance shall not be required unless the Legislature provides funds to assist in the accomplishment of such compliance. Every county shall report to the Legislature by January 1, 1976, as to whether such compliance can be accomplished, and stating the reasons why it cannot be accomplished if that be the case.
(e) Whenever within any county adult detention facility or part of any county detention facility used for the confinement of adults, not including any city jail, an inpatient psychiatric facility designated by the county mental health director to treat patients under Division 5 (commencing with Section 5000) and Division 6 (commencing with Section 6000) of the Welfare and Institutions Code, is provided for prisoners of one sex who may not depart from the detention facility for treatment elsewhere, and where the proportion of prisoners of the opposite sex requiring the same type of treatment is so small that the cost of providing a separate program of equal quality would not be justified in relation to the reduction in the level of another program, service, or privilege that would result from the diversion of funds for such purpose, the above designated mental health treatment program may treat prisoners of both sexes if each of the following conditions is met:
(1) The program is one that would be considered suitable for the treatment of patients of both sexes if it were located in a psychiatric treatment facility devoted to evaluation and treatment under Division 5 (commencing with Section 5000) and Division 6

(commencing with Section 6000) of the Welfare and Institutions Code for patients who are not prisoners.

(2) A female deputy sheriff or other suitable woman assigned to jail duty is assigned to the treatment program in accordance with Sections 4020.4, 4020.7, 4020.8, and 4021 of this code. Notwithstanding the provisions of Section 4020.4 of this code, in a county of any size, the sheriff may designate a female member of the mental health treatment staff for this assignment.

(Amended by Stats. 1980, Ch. 547, Sec. 17.5.)

4030.

(a) (1) The Legislature finds and declares that law enforcement policies and practices for conducting strip or body cavity searches of detained persons vary widely throughout California. Consequently, some people have been arbitrarily subjected to unnecessary strip and body cavity searches after arrests for minor misdemeanor and infraction offenses. Some present search practices violate state and federal constitutional rights to privacy and freedom from unreasonable searches and seizures.

(2) It is the intent of the Legislature in enacting this section to protect the state and federal constitutional rights of the people of California by establishing a statewide policy strictly limiting strip and body cavity searches.

(b) The provisions of this section shall apply only to prearraignment detainees arrested for infraction or misdemeanor offenses and to any minor detained prior to a detention hearing on the grounds that he or she is a person described in Section 300, 601, or 602 of the Welfare and Institutions Code alleged to have committed a misdemeanor or infraction offense. The provisions of this section shall not apply to a person in the custody of the Secretary of the Department of Corrections and Rehabilitation or the Director of the Division of Juvenile Justice in the Department of Corrections and Rehabilitation.

(c) As used in this section the following definitions shall apply:

(1) "Body cavity" only means the stomach or rectal cavity of a person, and vagina of a female person.

(2) "Physical body cavity search" means physical intrusion into a body cavity for the purpose of discovering any object concealed in the body cavity.

(3) "Strip search" means a search which requires a person to remove or arrange some or all of his or her clothing so as to permit a visual inspection of the underclothing, breasts, buttocks, or genitalia of such person.

(4) "Visual body cavity search" means visual inspection of a body cavity.

(d) (1) Notwithstanding any other law, including Section 40304.5 of the Vehicle Code, if a person is arrested and taken into custody, that person may be subjected to patdown searches, metal detector searches, body scanners, and thorough clothing searches in order to discover and retrieve concealed weapons and contraband substances prior to being placed in a booking cell.

(2) An agency that utilizes a body scanner pursuant to this subdivision shall endeavor to avoid knowingly using a body scanner to scan a woman who is pregnant.

(e) A person arrested and held in custody on a misdemeanor or infraction offense, except those involving weapons, controlled substances, or violence, or a minor detained prior to a detention hearing on the grounds that he or she is a person described in Section 300, 601, or 602 of the Welfare and Institutions Code, except for those minors alleged to have committed felonies or offenses involving weapons, controlled substances, or violence, shall not be subjected to a strip search or visual body cavity search prior to placement in the general jail population, unless a peace officer has determined there is reasonable suspicion, based on specific and articulable facts, to believe that person is concealing a weapon or contraband, and a strip search will result in the discovery of the weapon or contraband. A strip search or visual body cavity search, or both, shall not be conducted without the prior written authorization of the supervising officer on duty. The authorization shall include the specific and articulable facts and circumstances upon which the reasonable suspicion determination was made by the supervisor.

(f) (1) Except pursuant to the provisions of paragraph (2), a person arrested and held in custody on a misdemeanor or infraction offense not involving weapons, controlled substances, or violence, shall not be confined in the general jail population unless all of the following are true:

(A) The person is not cited and released.

(B) The person is not released on his or her own recognizance pursuant to Article 9 (commencing with Section 1318) of Chapter 1 of Title 10 of Part 2.

(C) The person is not able to post bail within a reasonable time, not less than three hours.

(2) A person shall not be housed in the general jail population prior to release pursuant to the provisions of paragraph (1) unless a documented emergency exists and there is no reasonable alternative to that placement. The person shall be placed in the general population only upon prior written authorization documenting the specific facts and circumstances of the emergency. The written authorization shall be signed by the uniformed supervisor of the facility or by a uniformed watch commander. A person confined in the general jail population pursuant to paragraph (1) shall retain all rights to release on citation, his or her own recognizance, or bail that were preempted as a consequence of the emergency.

(g) A person arrested on a misdemeanor or infraction offense, or a minor described in subdivision (b), shall not be subjected to a physical body cavity search except under the authority of a search warrant issued by a magistrate specifically authorizing the physical body cavity search.

(h) A copy of the prior written authorization required by subdivisions (e) and (f) and the search warrant required by subdivision (g) shall be placed in the agency's records and made available, on request, to the person searched or his or her authorized representative. With regard to a strip search or visual or physical body cavity search, the time, date, and place of the search, the name and sex of the person conducting the search, and a statement of the results of the search, including a list of items removed from the person searched, shall be recorded in the agency's records and made available, upon request, to the person searched or his or her authorized representative.

(i) Persons conducting a strip search or a visual body cavity search shall not touch the breasts, buttocks, or genitalia of the person being searched.

(j) A physical body cavity search shall be conducted under sanitary conditions, and only by a physician, nurse practitioner, registered nurse, licensed vocational nurse, or emergency medical technician Level II licensed to practice in this state. A physician engaged in providing health care to detainees and inmates of the facility may conduct physical body cavity searches.

(k) (1) A person conducting or otherwise present or within sight of the inmate during a strip search or visual or physical body cavity search shall be of the same sex as the person being searched, except for physicians or licensed medical personnel.

(2) A person within sight of the visual display of a body scanner depicting the body during a scan shall be of the same sex as the person being scanned, except for physicians or licensed medical personnel.

(l) All strip, visual, and physical body cavity searches shall be conducted in an area of privacy so that the search cannot be observed by persons not participating in the search. Persons are considered to be participating in the search if their official duties relative to search procedure require them to be present at the time the search is conducted.

(m) A person who knowingly and willfully authorizes or conducts a strip search or visual or physical body cavity search in violation of this section is guilty of a misdemeanor.

(n) This section does not limit the common law or statutory rights of a person regarding an action for damages or injunctive relief, or preclude the prosecution under another law of a peace officer or other person who has violated this section.

(o) Any person who suffers damage or harm as a result of a violation of this section may bring a civil action to recover actual damages, or one thousand dollars ($1,000), whichever is greater. In addition, the court may, in its discretion, award punitive damages, equitable relief as it deems necessary and proper, and costs, including reasonable attorney's fees.

(Amended by Stats. 2016, Ch. 162, Sec. 1. (AB 1705) Effective January 1, 2017.)

4031.

(a) This section applies to all minors detained in a juvenile detention center on the grounds that he or she is a person described in Section 300, 601, or 602 of the Welfare and Institutions Code, and all minors adjudged a ward of the court and held in a juvenile detention center on the grounds he or she is a person described in Section 300, 601, or 602 of the Welfare and Institutions Code.

(b) Persons conducting a strip search or a visual body cavity search shall not touch the breasts, buttocks, or genitalia of the person being searched.

(c) A physical body cavity search shall be conducted under sanitary conditions, and only by a physician, nurse practitioner, registered nurse, licensed vocational nurse, or emergency medical technician Level II licensed to practice in this state. A physician engaged in providing health care to detainees, wards, and inmates of the facility may conduct physical body cavity searches.

(d) A person conducting or otherwise present or within sight of the inmate during a strip search or visual or physical body cavity search shall be of the same sex as the person being searched, except for physicians or licensed medical personnel.

(e) All strip searches and visual and physical body cavity searches shall be conducted in an area of privacy so that the search cannot be observed by persons not participating in the search. Persons are considered to be participating in the search if their official duties relative to search procedure require them to be present at the time the search is conducted.

(f) A person who knowingly and willfully authorizes or conducts a strip search and visual or physical body cavity search in violation of this section is guilty of a misdemeanor.

(g) This section shall not be construed as limiting the common law or statutory rights of a person regarding an action for damages or injunctive relief, or as precluding the prosecution under another law of a peace officer or other person who has violated this section.

(h) Any person who suffers damage or harm as a result of a violation of this section may bring a civil action to recover actual damages, or one thousand dollars ($1,000), whichever is greater. In addition, the court may, in its discretion, award punitive damages, equitable relief as it deems necessary and proper, and costs, including reasonable attorney's fees.

(i) This section does not limit the protections granted by Section 4030 to individuals described in subdivision (b) of that section.

(Amended by Stats. 2016, Ch. 86, Sec. 240. (SB 1171) Effective January 1, 2017.)

4032.

(a) For purposes of this section, the following definitions shall apply:

(1) "In-person visit" means an on-site visit that may include barriers. In-person visits include interactions in which an inmate has physical contact with a visitor, the inmate is able to see a visitor through a barrier, or the inmate is otherwise in a room with a visitor without physical contact. "In-person visit" does not include an interaction between an inmate and a visitor through the use of an on-site, two-way, audio-video terminal.

(2) "Video visitation" means interaction between an inmate and a member of the public through the means of an audio-visual communication device when the member of the public is located at a local detention facility or at a remote location.

(3) "Local detention facility" has the same meaning as defined in Section 6031.4.

(b) A local detention facility that offered in-person visitation as of January 1, 2017, may not convert to video visitation only.

(c) A local detention facility shall not charge for visitation when visitors are onsite and participating in either in-person or video visitation. For purposes of this subdivision, "onsite" is defined as at the location where the inmate is housed.

(d) If a local detention facility offered video visitation only as of January 1, 2017, on-site video visitation shall be offered free of charge, and the first hour of remote video visitation per week shall be offered free of charge if the facility offers remote video visitation.

(Amended by Stats. 2017, Ch. 363, Sec. 8. (SB 112) Effective September 28, 2017.)

CHAPTER 1.5. Joint County Jails [4050 - 4067]

(Chapter 1.5 added by Stats. 1957, Ch. 1019.)

4050.

This chapter may be cited as the Joint County Jail Act.

(Added by Stats. 1957, Ch. 1019.)

4051.

Any two or more counties may form a district for the purpose of establishing and operating a joint county jail to serve such counties.

(Added by Stats. 1957, Ch. 1019.)

4052.

Any district organized under this chapter shall have and exercise the powers expressly granted in this chapter, together with such other powers as are reasonably implied therefrom and necessary and proper to carry out the objects and purposes of this chapter.

(Added by Stats. 1957, Ch. 1019.)

4053.

The board of supervisors of any county may initiate proceedings proposing the creation of a joint district for the purpose of maintaining a joint county jail under the provisions of this chapter to be composed of two or more counties by the adoption of a resolution reciting the following:

(1) That it will be beneficial to the public interest to create a joint district for the establishment or operation, or both, of a joint county jail to which persons from any of the counties proposed to be included in the proposed district may be committed.

(2) The names of the counties proposed to be included in the proposed district which will be benefited by the formation thereof.

(3) That it is proposed to create a joint district for the establishment or operation, or both, of a joint county jail under the provisions of this chapter for the counties so named.

(Added by Stats. 1957, Ch. 1019.)

4054.

When adopted, certified copies of the resolution provided for in Section 4053, shall be transmitted to the several clerks of the boards of supervisors in each of the counties named in the resolution other than that in which the proceedings are initiated.

Upon the adoption of the resolution provided for in Section 4053, the board of supervisors of the county adopting the same shall name and appoint two members of the board to represent the county upon the board of directors of the joint district proposed to be organized.

(Added by Stats. 1957, Ch. 1019.)

4055.

Upon receipt of the resolution adopted under Section 4053, the boards of supervisors of the counties affected and to whom the same may be directed shall consider the advisability of creating and organizing a joint district as proposed in said resolution and,

upon determining the facts involved therein, shall severally adopt resolutions either rejecting or approving the proposal to create such joint district. Each resolution of approval shall, in addition to the matters otherwise required therein, also name and appoint the members of the board of supervisors of the county adopting the resolution qualified to represent such county upon the board of directors of the proposed joint district. A certified copy of the resolution of approval shall be forthwith transmitted to the clerk of the board of supervisors initiating the proceedings.
(Added by Stats. 1957, Ch. 1019.)

4056.
The board of supervisors of any county initiating proceedings for the creation of a joint district under this chapter shall, after the receipt of a copy of the resolution approving the proposal to form such district as provided in Section 4055 from the board of supervisors of each county proposed to be included within any such joint district, adopt a resolution declaring the creation and organization of said joint district and setting forth the names of the counties composing said district. A certified copy of the resolution shall be transmitted to and filed with the Secretary of State, whereupon the joint district shall be deemed created and organized and shall exercise all the powers granted in this chapter and shall bear the name and designation of "Joint County Jail District No. _____ of the State of California."
(Added by Stats. 1957, Ch. 1019.)

4057.
All districts organized under this chapter shall be numbered in the order of their creation, the number to be assigned to said district forthwith upon the organization thereof by the Secretary of State, and the Secretary of State shall keep and maintain in his office a list and register showing the joint county jail districts organized under this chapter.
(Added by Stats. 1957, Ch. 1019.)

4058.
The Secretary of State shall furnish and transmit to the clerk of the board of supervisors of the county adopting the initial resolution for the organization of any district under this chapter a certificate of the organization of the same. Upon receipt of the certificate the clerk shall within 10 days send a certified copy of the certificate to each of the clerks of the several boards of supervisors of the counties constituting the district, and shall also within the time specified in this section notify each supervisor appointed as a member of the board of directors of the district of such fact and of the time and place of the first meeting of the board of directors of the district. The time and place of the meeting shall be fixed and determined by the clerk of the board adopting the initial resolution, but said time of meeting shall be within 30 days after the date of mailing notices thereof. The necessary expense incurred by supervisors in attending and in going to and coming from any meeting of the board of directors of the district shall constitute a county charge of their respective counties.
(Added by Stats. 1957, Ch. 1019.)

4059.
The body formed under Section 4058 shall be called the board of directors of such district.
(Added by Stats. 1957, Ch. 1019.)

4060.
The members of the board of directors may enter into an agreement for and on behalf of the counties appointing them binding said counties to the joint enterprise provided for in this chapter and apportioning the cost of establishing and maintaining a joint county jail.
(Added by Stats. 1957, Ch. 1019.)

4061.
All sums found due from any county according to the provisions of this chapter are a charge against said county, and may be collected in the manner provided by law by the board of directors of a district formed under this chapter, or, in its behalf by the board of supervisors of any county in the district by an action instituted and tried in any county in the district in which the same may be filed.
(Added by Stats. 1957, Ch. 1019.)

4062.
The board of directors may establish the joint county jail provided for in this chapter and shall provide for the feeding, care, and treatment of prisoners therein, and must conform to such standards for construction, feeding, clothing, bedding and programming as are imposed pursuant to law on county jails.
(Added by Stats. 1957, Ch. 1019.)

4063.
Each county in a district formed under this chapter shall pay from its general fund its proportionate share to the board of directors of such amount as the board may designate to constitute a cash revolving fund to carry on the work and expense of maintaining such joint county jail. Each month a statement of the expense of the joint county jail shall be sent to the board of supervisors of each county in the district, together with a claim for its proportionate share of expenses. Amounts when received shall be paid into the cash revolving fund.
(Added by Stats. 1957, Ch. 1019.)

4064.
Convicted persons may be committed to a joint county jail from a county comprising the district the same as if the commitment were to a jail maintained by that county alone.
(Added by Stats. 1957, Ch. 1019.)

4065.
The provisions of Chapter 1 (commencing at Section 4000) of this title shall, so far as appropriate, be applicable to a joint county jail established pursuant to this chapter, and the person appointed by the board of directors to superintend a joint county jail has such powers and duties as has a sheriff, with respect to county jails, under Chapter 1.
(Added by Stats. 1957, Ch. 1019.)

4066.
The board of directors may make rules and regulations for the government of a joint county jail not inconsistent with law.
(Added by Stats. 1957, Ch. 1019.)

4067.
A joint county jail district formed under this chapter may be dissolved in the following manner:
(a) The board or boards of supervisors of a county or counties containing more than fifty percent (50%) of the population of the entire district shall by a unanimous vote adopt a resolution stating that the existence of a joint county jail is no longer desirable for the public welfare and announcing the intention to withdraw therefrom and to dissolve said district.
(b) The resolution or resolutions so adopted shall be communicated to the clerks of the boards of supervisors of all the counties comprising the district and also to the Secretary of State.
(c) If it appears that the resolution was unanimously adopted by the board or boards of supervisors in the counties desiring to withdraw, and that such county or counties contain more than fifty percent (50%) of the entire population in the district, the Secretary of State shall thereupon certify to the clerks of the boards of supervisors of the counties composing the district that the district is dissolved.
(d) Thereupon the board of directors of the district shall within 90 days:
(1) Abolish the joint county jail;
(2) Return all prisoners therein to the custody of the sheriffs of their respective counties;
(3) Dispose of all equipment belonging to said joint county jail and the district;

(4) Render an accounting to the clerks of the boards of supervisors of the counties composing such district of all sums of money received and paid out since their last previous accounting, including the balance of revolving fund on hand at said last previous accounting;
(5) Apportion and repay to said counties all sums of money then remaining in their hands, and they shall thereupon be relieved of further responsibility in said matter.
(Added by Stats. 1957, Ch. 1019.)

CHAPTER 2. County Industrial Farms and Road Camps [4100 - 4305]

(Chapter 2 added by Stats. 1953, Ch. 69.)

ARTICLE 1. County Industrial Farms [4100 - 4137]
(Article 1 added by Stats. 1953, Ch. 69.)

4100.
It is the purpose of this article to make possible the substitution of constructive labor for profitless prison confinement in order that those who are charged with or convicted of public offenses and deprived of their liberty may become better citizens because of their disciplinary experience.
(Added by Stats. 1953, Ch. 69.)

4101.
In each county an industrial farm or industrial road camp may be established under the provisions of this article.
(Added by Stats. 1953, Ch. 69.)

4102.
Before establishing an industrial farm or industrial road camp in any county the board of supervisors thereof shall adopt a resolution of its intention so to do. The resolution shall state an amount per person per day for which persons from incorporated cities will be maintained on an industrial farm. Certified copies of the resolution shall be forwarded by the clerk of the board of supervisors to the clerks of all incorporated cities within the county.
(Amended by Stats. 1959, Ch. 1979.)

4103.
Upon receipt of the resolution as provided in Section 4102, the legislative body of any incorporated city wishing to avail itself of the use of a proposed industrial farm shall adopt a resolution setting forth the following matters:
1. The number of persons sentenced to imprisonment in the jail of such city during the fiscal year last preceding the adoption of the resolution of intention by the board of supervisors;
2. The total number of days for which all such persons were imprisoned in the jail of the city during such fiscal year;
3. A declaration of the desire of the city adopting the resolution to have the prisoners of the city cared for by the county on the industrial farm or industrial road camp and of the agreement of the city to pay the county quarterly for the care of the prisoners of the city at the rate set forth in the resolution of intention.
A certified copy of the resolution provided for in this section shall be forwarded to the clerk of the board of supervisors.
(Added by Stats. 1953, Ch. 69.)

4104.
Any board of supervisors having adopted a resolution of intention to establish an industrial farm or industrial road camp shall ascertain and enter in its minutes the following facts:
(a) The number of persons sentenced to imprisonment in the county jail during the fiscal year last preceding the adoption of the resolution of intention.
(b) The total number of days for which all persons were imprisoned in the county jail during that fiscal year.
(c) The number of persons sentenced from the superior court of the county to any state prison upon conviction of a violation of Section 270 or Section 270a during that fiscal year.
(d) The total number of days for which all persons so sentenced to state prisons were therein imprisoned during that fiscal year.
(Amended by Stats. 1987, Ch. 828, Sec. 135.)

4105.
Upon ascertaining the facts provided for in Sections 4102 to 4104, inclusive, the board of supervisors may proceed to establish an industrial farm or industrial road camp.
(Added by Stats. 1953, Ch. 69.)

4106.
For the purpose of establishing an industrial farm the board of supervisors may acquire by condemnation, purchase, lease or donation as many acres of land suitable for agriculture as may be necessary for the purposes of the farm. Such land may be situate within or without the county and may consist of separate parcels. If the land is without the county no industrial farm may be established thereon without the consent of the board of supervisors of the county in which the land is located. The board of supervisors shall erect on such land such buildings and structures and make such improvements and institute such industries as are necessary or convenient to carry out the purposes of this article.
(Added by Stats. 1953, Ch. 69.)

4107.
The board of supervisors shall secure by purchase or otherwise personal property convenient or necessary to carry out the purposes of this article. Stock, machinery, or any other property belonging to the county and in use on the county farm or elsewhere may be used on an industrial farm.
(Added by Stats. 1953, Ch. 69.)

4108.
The board of supervisors shall employ a superintendent of an industrial farm or camp and such other subordinate persons as may be necessary for the proper administration thereof and the keeping of the prisoners imprisoned thereon. As part of the compensation to be agreed upon for such superintendent and other persons board and lodging may be furnished.
(Added by Stats. 1953, Ch. 69.)

4109.
The board shall also adopt rules governing the administration of a farm or camp formed under the provisions of this article and discipline thereon in furtherance of the purposes of this article, which rules shall be enforced by the superintendent and those subordinate to him.
(Added by Stats. 1953, Ch. 69.)

4110.
If women are to be sentenced to an industrial farm, the board of supervisors establishing it shall provide thereon separate quarters for women prisoners, or may establish a separate industrial farm for women prisoners. Nothing in the section shall be construed to impose any requirement upon a county to confine male and female prisoners in the same or an adjoining facility or impose any duty upon a county to establish or maintain programs which involve the joint participation of male and female prisoners.
(Amended by Stats. 1975, Ch. 592.)

4111.
If a separate farm for women prisoners is established it shall be considered as a part of the industrial farm of the county within the meaning of all provisions of this article, except that none but women prisoners shall be admitted to it. A woman assistant to the superintendent of an industrial farm shall be in immediate charge of any farm established for women prisoners only.
(Added by Stats. 1953, Ch. 69.)

4112.
When land has been acquired and such buildings and structures erected and improvements made as may be immediately necessary for the carrying out of the purposes of this article or arrangements have been made for an industrial road camp or camps, the board of supervisors shall adopt a resolution proclaiming that an industrial farm or road camp has been established in the county and designating a day on and after which persons will be admitted to such farm or camp. Certified copies of the resolution shall be forwarded by the clerk of the board of supervisors to each superior court judge in the county.
(Amended by Stats. 2002, Ch. 784, Sec. 568. Effective January 1, 2003.)

4114.
Each county which establishes an industrial farm or camp shall provide a county classification committee, which shall function as follows:
(1) The sheriff shall appoint the members of this committee, which may include members of his staff and qualified citizens of the county. If there is a county jail physician, he shall be an ex officio member of this committee. All committee members shall serve without remuneration.
(2) The committee shall meet at least once weekly for the purpose of assigning each person who has been sentenced to the county jail to the proper degree of custody and treatment within one of the available adult detention facilities operated by the county. Any person assigned to medical treatment may decline such treatment and provide other care or treatment for himself at his own expense.
(3) Each county prisoner serving a jail sentence of over 30 days shall appear before the committee during the first third of his sentence.
(4) City prisoners who have been recommended to the committee by the chief of police may be transferred to the county industrial farm or camp at the option of the committee.
(Added by Stats. 1953, Ch. 69.)

4115.
The county jail shall serve as the initial place of detention for all adult persons committed to the custody of the sheriff, except city prisoners who are transferred to a farm or camp by the county classification committee.
(Added by Stats. 1953, Ch. 69.)

4115.5.
(a) The board of supervisors of a county where, in the opinion of the sheriff or the director of the county department of corrections, adequate facilities are not available for prisoners who would otherwise be confined in its county adult detention facilities, may enter into an agreement with the board or boards of supervisors of one or more counties whose county adult detention facilities are adequate for and accessible to the first county to permit commitment of sentenced misdemeanants, persons sentenced pursuant to subdivision (h) of Section 1170, and any persons required to serve a term of imprisonment in county adult detention facilities as a condition of probation, with the concurrence of that county's sheriff or director of its county department of corrections. When the agreement is in effect, commitments may be made by the court.
(b) A county entering into an agreement with another county pursuant to subdivision (a) shall report annually to the Board of State and Community Corrections on the number of offenders who otherwise would be under that county's jurisdiction but who are now being incarcerated in another county's facility pursuant to subdivision (a) and the reason for needing to incarcerate the offenders outside the county.
(c) This section shall become inoperative on July 1, 2021, and, as of January 1, 2022, is repealed, unless a later enacted statute, that becomes operative on or before January 1, 2022, deletes or extends the dates on which it becomes inoperative and is repealed.
(Amended (as amended by Stats. 2014, Ch. 44, Sec. 2) by Stats. 2018, Ch. 36, Sec. 21. (AB 1812) Effective June 27, 2018. Inoperative July 1, 2021. Repealed as of January 1, 2022, by its own provisions. See later operative version, as amended by Sec. 22 of Stats. 2018, Ch. 36.)

4115.5.
(a) The board of supervisors of a county where adequate facilities are not available for prisoners who would otherwise be confined in its county adult detention facilities may enter into an agreement with the board or boards of supervisors of one or more nearby counties whose county adult detention facilities are adequate and are readily accessible from the first county to permit commitment of misdemeanants, and any persons required to serve a term of imprisonment in county adult detention facilities as a condition of probation, to a jail in a county having adequate facilities that is a party to the agreement. That agreement shall make provision for the support of a person so committed or transferred by the county from which he or she is committed. When that agreement is in effect, commitments may be made by the court and support of a person so committed shall be a charge upon the county from which he or she is committed.
(b) This section shall become operative on July 1, 2021.
(Amended (as amended by Stats. 2014, Ch. 44, Sec. 3) by Stats. 2018, Ch. 36, Sec. 22. (AB 1812) Effective June 27, 2018. Section operative July 1, 2021, by its own provisions.)

4115.55.
(a) Upon agreement with the sheriff or director of the county department of corrections, a board of supervisors may enter into a contract with other public agencies to provide housing for inmates sentenced to a county jail in community correctional facilities created pursuant to Article 1.5 (commencing with Section 2910) of Chapter 7 of Title 1 or Chapter 9.5 (commencing with Section 6250) of Title 7.
(b) Facilities operated pursuant to agreements entered into under subdivision (a) shall comply with the minimum standards for local detention facilities as provided by Chapter 1 (commencing with Section 3000) of Division 3 of Title 15 of the California Code of Regulations.
(Amended by Stats. 2013, Ch. 76, Sec. 161. (AB 383) Effective January 1, 2014.)

4115.56.
(a) Upon agreement with the sheriff or director of the county department of corrections, a board of supervisors may enter into a contract with the Department of Corrections and Rehabilitation to house inmates who are within 60 days or less of release from the state prison to a county jail facility for the purpose of reentry and community transition purposes.
(b) When housed in county facilities, inmates shall be under the legal custody and jurisdiction of local county facilities and not under the jurisdiction of the Department of Corrections and Rehabilitation.
(Added by Stats. 2011, 1st Ex. Sess., Ch. 12, Sec. 37. (AB 17 1x) Effective September 21, 2011. Operative October 1, 2011, by Sec. 46 of Ch. 12.)

4116.
No person shall be committed directly by any court to a county industrial farm or camp except as provided in the Welfare and Institutions Code. All other commitments shall be made to the sheriff for placement in such county adult detention facility as the county classification committee may designate.
(Added by Stats. 1953, Ch. 69.)

4117.
No person shall be transferred to an industrial farm or camp unless he has appeared before the county classification committee and has been assigned to that facility.

(Added by Stats. 1953, Ch. 69.)

4118.
The legislative body of any incorporated city located in a county which has established an industrial farm or industrial road camp may adopt and forward to the board of supervisors a certified copy of a resolution stating that the city desires to have its prisoners cared for on the industrial farm or camp and agrees to pay therefor quarterly at a rate per prisoner per day, which rate shall be set forth in the resolution.
(Added by Stats. 1953, Ch. 69.)

4119.
At its option the board of supervisors may adopt a resolution stating that the county will care for the prisoners of the city on its industrial farm or camp at the rate set forth in the city's resolution specified in Section 4118. A certified copy of the resolution provided for in this section shall be forwarded to the clerk of the city named therein, who shall immediately notify the chief of police of the city.
Thereafter, the chief of police of the city, or his representative, shall meet regularly with the county classification committee for the purpose of determining the eligibility of certain city prisoners for transfer to a county industrial farm or camp. The committee shall consider for transfer only those city prisoners who have been selected and recommended for transfer by the chief of police. In each case, the committee may transfer or reject such prisoners as it sees fit.
(Added by Stats. 1953, Ch. 69.)

4120.
Upon the expiration of the sentence of any person imprisoned in any industrial farm or camp, he shall be discharged, and either furnished with transportation to the place where he was convicted or given a sum of money sufficient to pay his fare to such place.
(Added by Stats. 1953, Ch. 69.)

4121.
The cost of establishing and maintaining an industrial farm or industrial road camp formed under this article shall be paid out of the county general fund. Any revenue derived from such farm or camp, including that received from any city for the care of its prisoners on said farm, shall be paid into the county general fund.
(Added by Stats. 1953, Ch. 69.)

4122.
The cost of transporting city prisoners to an industrial farm or camp shall be borne by the city from whose courts they were committed. All other transportation charges shall be borne by the county and paid out of the general fund.
(Added by Stats. 1953, Ch. 69.)

4123.
Any person transferred from an industrial farm or camp to the county jail shall be maintained at the jail at the expense of the county as are other prisoners in such jail.
(Added by Stats. 1953, Ch. 69.)

4124.
Each county board of supervisors may specify a rate to be charged for the care of city prisoners, which rate shall not exceed the average cost to the county of caring for one prisoner per day. In calculating this average cost, the value of the farm products used in other county institutions and in supplying the needs of paupers, incompetents, poor and indigent persons and persons incapacitated by age, disease or accident shall be deducted from the cost of maintenance, and the cost of the original investment in establishing an industrial farm shall not be included. The reasonable value of services rendered by city prisoners to the extent that such services inure to the benefit of the county shall be deducted from the average cost of caring for city prisoners. Cities may, under terms and conditions suitable to the board of supervisors, be assigned prisoners for the purposes authorized by Section 36904 of the Government Code. By mutual agreement between cities and the county, the rate may be changed from time to time.
(Amended by Stats. 1959, Ch. 1979.)

4125.
Each person in custody on any industrial farm or industrial road camp who is found to have any person or persons dependent on him for support, as provided in Section 4127, shall be credited with a sum not to exceed two dollars ($2) for each day of eight hours work done by him on such farm or camp. Every other person in custody on an industrial farm or camp shall be credited with a sum not to exceed one dollar ($1) for each day of eight hours work done by him on such farm or camp.
(Amended by Stats. 1968, Ch. 495.)

4125.1.
The board of supervisors may contract with the United States or the State of California, or any department or agency thereof, for the performance of work and labor by any person in custody on any county industrial farm or industrial road camp or confined in the county jail or branch thereof under a final judgment of imprisonment rendered in a criminal action or proceeding or as a condition of probation in the suppression of fires within and upon the national forests, state parks, or other lands of the United States or the State of California, or within and upon such other lands, of whatever ownership, contiguous to, or adjacent to said state or federal lands, the suppression of fires upon which other lands affords fire protection to said state or federal lands. Such payments as may be so contracted for and to be paid by the United States or by the State of California for the work and labor so performed by any person so in custody may, by order of the board of supervisors, be credited in full or in part, and upon such terms and conditions as the board shall determine, to any such person so in custody and performing such work and labor, and all in addition to those credits hereinbefore provided in Section 4125 of this code.
Whenever any such person so in custody shall perform the services herein specified he shall be subject to workmen's compensation benefits to the same extent as a county employee, and the board of supervisors shall provide and cover any such person so in custody, while performing such services, with accident, death and compensation insurance as is otherwise regularly provided for employees of the county.
The term "suppression of fires" as herein used shall include the construction of firebreaks and other works of improvement for the prevention and suppression of fire whether or not constructed in the actual course of suppression of existing fires.
(Amended by Stats. 1959, Ch. 1660.)

4126.
The maximum amount per day to be credited to a person in custody on an industrial farm or camp shall be fixed from time to time by the board of supervisors and shall be as large as is justified by the production on the farm or camp but shall not exceed the sums mentioned in this article.
The superintendent of an industrial farm may by order cause an amount less than the maximum per day to be credited to any person because of lack of effort on the part of the person, the amount credited to be in proportion to the effort.
The sum to the credit of each person employed upon an industrial farm upon his discharge shall be paid him in addition to any transportation charge otherwise paid under this article. Any person may, by written order, direct the payment of any sums credited to him under this article to any person dependent upon him or to whom he is indebted.
(Added by Stats. 1953, Ch. 69.)

4127.
The court by whom any person was sentenced may at any time by written order direct payment of all or any part of the sums to be credited to any such person under this article to any person or persons dependent for support on the prisoner. At the time of sentencing the court shall by making inquiry or taking evidence find whether or not any person or persons are dependent upon the defendant for support. A copy of the finding of the court shall be transmitted to the county classification committee.

(Added by Stats. 1953, Ch. 69.)

4128.

Payments authorized under this article to be made to any person other than the prisoner may be made weekly on any day designated by the superintendent of the farm or camp.

(Added by Stats. 1953, Ch. 69.)

4129.

For the purpose of making the payments designated in this article the board of supervisors shall by order provide the superintendent with a revolving fund. Upon order of the board of supervisors the county auditor shall draw a warrant in favor of the superintendent of an industrial farm or camp and the county treasurer shall cash it. Thereafter the superintendent shall receive from the county general fund upon demands supported by receipts all sums paid out by him under the provisions of this section and shall return all sums so received to the revolving fund.

The provisions of Section 29323 of the Government Code are applicable to a revolving fund established pursuant to this section.

(Amended by Stats. 1965, Ch. 62.)

4130.

So far as practicable those in custody on an industrial farm shall be employed in productive labor. The products of an industrial farm shall be used: first, to maintain the prisoners and employees on such farm; second, to supply other county institutions having need of the same with the farm's products; third, to supply the needs of paupers, incompetents, poor and indigent persons and those incapacitated by age, disease or accident with whose relief and support the county is charged.

(Added by Stats. 1953, Ch. 69.)

4131.

Subject to regulations adopted by the board of supervisors the superintendent shall maintain discipline on an industrial farm. Whenever the superintendent reports to the county classification committee which assigned any prisoner to an industrial farm or camp that the prisoner refuses to abide by the rules of the farm or camp or refuses to work thereon, the committee may make an order transferring the prisoner to the county jail or city jail for the unexpired term of his sentence, and all sums credited to the prisoner shall be forfeited by him unless they have been ordered paid to some person dependent upon him. Thereafter the committee may reassign the person to the industrial farm or industrial road camp upon recommendation of the superintendent of the farm or camp.

(Added by Stats. 1953, Ch. 69.)

4133.

The boundary of every industrial farm established under the provisions of this article shall be marked by a fence, hedge or by some other visible line. Every person confined on any industrial farm who escapes therefrom or attempts to escape therefrom shall upon conviction thereof be imprisoned in a state prison, or in the county jail or industrial farm for not to exceed one year. Any such imprisonment shall begin at the expiration of the imprisonment in effect at the time of the escape.

(Amended by Stats. 1980, Ch. 1117, Sec. 18.)

4134.

Any board of supervisors which has established or desires to establish an industrial farm or industrial road camp may at any time appoint an advisory board to consist of not less than three nor more than five persons, one member of which shall be a penologist and one member a physician.

(Added by Stats. 1953, Ch. 69.)

4135.

The advisory board shall acquaint itself with the conduct of the jails in the county, keep itself informed about the administration of the industrial farm or industrial road camp, and report its recommendations and suggestions to the board of supervisors. It may visit any jail within the county, examine the records thereof, and ascertain whether or not there are any persons illegally committed to or detained at any jail.

The advisory board shall encourage recreational and educational activities on the industrial farm.

(Added by Stats. 1953, Ch. 69.)

4136.

Sections 4011, 4011.5, 4011.6 and 4011.7 are applicable to county industrial farms, county industrial road camps, and joint county road camps established pursuant to this chapter.

(Added by Stats. 1968, Ch. 517.)

4137.

The board of supervisors of any county in which a county industrial farm, industrial road camp, or honor camp has been established may, by ordinance, authorize the sheriff or any such person responsible to the board for the care, treatment, and custody of prisoners assigned to him as sentenced misdemeanants or felons, serving time as a condition of probation, to remove such prisoners from the facility to which they have been assigned under custody, without court order, for purposes such as: private medical, vision, or dental care, psychological care, vocational services, educational services, and funerals.

(Added by Stats. 1970, Ch. 133.)

ARTICLE 2. Joint County Road Camp Act [4200 - 4227]

(Article 2 added by Stats. 1953, Ch. 69.)

4200.

This article shall be known and may be cited as the Joint County Road Camp Act.

(Added by Stats. 1953, Ch. 69.)

4201.

Any two or more counties may form a district for the purpose of requiring all persons confined in the county jails of such counties, under a final judgment of imprisonment rendered in a criminal action or proceeding, to perform labor on the public works or public highways in all or any of such counties, and to maintain for that purpose one or more joint county road camps in which such jail prisoners of any or all of said counties may work together.

(Added by Stats. 1953, Ch. 69.)

4202.

Any district organized under this article shall have and exercise the powers expressly granted in this article, together with such other powers as are reasonably implied therefrom and necessary and proper to carry out the objects and purposes of this article.

(Added by Stats. 1953, Ch. 69.)

4203.

The board of supervisors of any county may initiate proceedings proposing the creation of a joint district for the purpose of maintaining a joint county road camp or camps under the provisions of this article to be composed of two or more counties having a combined population of not less than 50,000 persons, according to the official census next preceding the formation of such district, by the adoption of a resolution reciting the following:

(1) That it will be beneficial to the public interest to create a joint district wherein persons confined in any county jail within such district under a final judgment of imprisonment rendered in a criminal action or proceeding may be required to perform labor on the public works or ways within said district, and that a joint county road camp or camps be established and maintained for that purpose.

(2) The names of the counties proposed to be included in the proposed district which will be benefited by the formation thereof.

(3) That it is proposed to create a joint district for the establishment and maintenance of a joint county road camp under the provisions of this article composed of the counties so named.

(Added by Stats. 1953, Ch. 69.)

4204.

When adopted certified copies of the resolution provided for in Section 4203, shall be transmitted to the several clerks of the boards of supervisors in each of the counties named in the resolution other than that in which the proceedings are initiated.

Upon the adoption of the resolution provided for in Section 4203, the board of supervisors of the county adopting the same shall name and appoint a member of the board to represent the county upon the board of directors of the joint district proposed to be organized.

(Added by Stats. 1953, Ch. 69.)

4205.

Upon receipt of the resolution adopted under Section 4203, the boards of supervisors of the counties affected and to whom the same may be directed shall consider the advisability of creating and organizing a joint district as proposed in said resolution and, upon determining the facts involved therein, shall severally adopt resolutions either rejecting or approving the proposal to create such joint district. Each resolution of approval shall, in addition to the matter otherwise required therein, also name and appoint the member of the board of supervisors of the county adopting the resolution qualified to represent such county upon the board of directors of the proposed joint district. A certified copy of the resolution of approval shall be forthwith transmitted to the clerk of the board of supervisors initiating the proceedings.

(Added by Stats. 1953, Ch. 69.)

4206.

The board of supervisors of any county initiating proceedings for the creation of a joint district under this article shall, after the receipt of a copy of the resolution approving the proposal to form such district as provided in Section 4205 from the board of supervisors of each county proposed to be included within any such joint district, adopt a resolution declaring the creation and organization of said joint district and setting forth the names of the counties composing said district. A certified copy of the resolution shall be transmitted to and filed with the Secretary of State, whereupon the joint district shall be deemed created and organized and shall exercise all the powers granted in this article and shall bear the name and designation of "Joint County Road Camp District No. _____ of the State of California."

(Added by Stats. 1953, Ch. 69.)

4207.

All districts organized under this article shall be numbered in the order of their creation, the number to be assigned to said district forthwith upon the organization thereof by the Secretary of State, and the Secretary of State shall keep and maintain in his office a list and register showing the joint county road camp districts organized under this article.

(Added by Stats. 1953, Ch. 69.)

4208.

The Secretary of State shall furnish and transmit to the clerk of the board of supervisors of the county adopting the initial resolution for the organization of any district under this article a certificate of the organization of the same. Upon receipt of the certificate the clerk shall within 10 days send a certified copy of the certificate to each of the clerks of the several boards of supervisors of the counties constituting the district, and shall also within the time specified in this section notify each supervisor appointed as a member of the board of directors of the district of such fact and of the time and place of the first meeting of the board of directors of the district. The time and place of the meeting shall be fixed and determined by the clerk of the board adopting the initial resolution, but said time of meeting shall be within 30 days after the date of mailing notices thereof. The necessary expense incurred by supervisors in attending and in going to and coming from any meeting of the board of directors of the district shall constitute a county charge of their respective counties.

(Added by Stats. 1953, Ch. 69.)

4209.

The body formed under Section 4208 shall be called the board of directors of such district.

(Added by Stats. 1953, Ch. 69.)

4210.

The delegates from each county may enter into an agreement with the other counties for and on behalf of the county appointing them, binding said counties to the joint enterprise provided for in this article and apportioning the cost of establishing and maintaining a road camp or camps, such cost to be apportioned on the basis of the population of the respective counties as determined by the official declaration of the State Legislature determining the population of counties next preceding such apportionment.

(Added by Stats. 1953, Ch. 69.)

4211.

All sums found due from any county according to the provisions of this article are a debt against said county, and may be collected in the manner provided by law by the said board of directors of a district formed under this article, or, in its behalf, by the board of supervisors of any county in the district by an action instituted and tried in any county in the district in which the same may be first filed.

(Added by Stats. 1953, Ch. 69.)

4212.

The board of directors may establish the road camp or camps provided for in this article, and may furnish such camp or camps with the necessary personnel and equipment to transport, feed, clothe, shelter and lodge the prisoners who shall work therein and with the necessary hand tools and appliances for their work, and may employ one or more persons to supervise the camp and the work of the prisoners.

(Added by Stats. 1953, Ch. 69.)

4213.

Each county in a district formed under this article shall pay from its general fund its proportionate share to the board of directors of such amount as the board may designate to constitute a cash revolving fund to carry on the work and expense of maintaining such camp or camps. Each month a statement of the expense of the camp shall be sent to the board of supervisors of each county in the district, together with a claim for its proportionate share of expenses. Amounts when received shall be paid into the cash revolving fund.

(Added by Stats. 1953, Ch. 69.)

4214.

Within 15 days after any person is confined in the county jail of any county within a district under a final judgment of imprisonment rendered in a criminal action or proceeding, the county parole commissioners of such county shall meet and determine whether he should be paroled to work in the joint county road camps established under this article. If it appears to the commissioners that a prisoner is a fit subject for parole to a camp formed under this article, they shall forthwith parole him with the requirement that he perform labor in such joint county road camp wherever it may then be situated, or may thereafter be moved to during his term of imprisonment, and he shall forthwith be transferred by the sheriff of the county in which he is confined to said road camp at the expense of the county in which he was sentenced to imprisonment.

(Added by Stats. 1953, Ch. 69.)

4215.

The boards of directors of joint county road camp districts may contract with the State Department of Public Works for the employment of jail prisoners in the construction,

improvement, or maintenance of any portion of any state highway now existing, to be constructed, or under construction within said district and may also contract with any board of supervisors or with any supervisor of any road district, within said district, for the employment of jail prisoners on any county road or county public work within any county or road district lying within any district created under this article.
(Added by Stats. 1953, Ch. 69.)
4216.
When the prisoners of a road camp are engaged in the construction or maintenance of any portion of the state highway the expense of maintaining them together with the compensation of such prisoners fixed by the board of directors as provided in this article, and the expense of supervision and maintenance of the road camp and the prisoners thereof, shall be paid for by the district and the State Department of Public Works upon such terms and in such proportions as may be agreed upon by the Department of Public Works and the district.
(Added by Stats. 1953, Ch. 69.)
4217.
Any money expended by the Department of Public Works under the provisions of this article shall be taken from any funds available for the construction or maintenance of the highway upon which the prisoners of the district labor.
(Added by Stats. 1953, Ch. 69.)
4218.
The State Department of Public Works may contract with the boards of directors of the joint districts created under this article for all the purposes stated in this article.
(Added by Stats. 1953, Ch. 69.)
4219.
When a joint road camp, and the prisoners thereof, are employed in the construction or maintenance of any county way, road or public work, the total expense of maintenance, operation and supervision, of said camp, and the compensation of the prisoners thereof shall be paid for from any funds which may be available for the construction or maintenance of such road, highway or other public works on which said prisoners are employed, or from the county general fund upon a four-fifths vote of the board of supervisors of said county.
(Added by Stats. 1953, Ch. 69.)
4220.
All payments provided for in Section 4219 shall be made by warrants drawn on the proper fund in favor of "Joint County Road Camp District No. _____" (inserting the number assigned by the Secretary of State), and shall become a portion of the revolving fund provided for in this article.
(Added by Stats. 1953, Ch. 69.)
4221.
Whenever the revolving fund provided for in this article after payment of all bills due against a district exceeds twenty thousand dollars ($20,000) or exceeds such lesser sum as the board of directors shall determine to be a sufficient working fund for the purposes of this article, the board shall apportion such surplus to be repaid to the counties forming the district, in the same proportion in which they are required to contribute to the revolving fund in the first instance, the payments to go into the county general funds of such counties.
(Added by Stats. 1953, Ch. 69.)
4222.
The board of directors may make such rules as it deems proper for the government of camps and the conduct of prisoners therein and may fix a reasonable compensation, not to exceed seventy-five cents ($0.75) per day, for each prisoner performing labor in a camp.
(Added by Stats. 1953, Ch. 69.)
4223.
Each prisoner shall be charged with the cost of all tools and appliances for the performance of labor which are furnished to him, and upon his release or discharge from a camp, he shall deliver to the superintendent thereof all tools and appliances for which he is charged and shall thereupon be entitled to full credit for the cost of the tools and appliances so returned. The cost of any appliances and tools not returned as provided in this section shall be deducted from the compensation due the prisoner.
(Added by Stats. 1953, Ch. 69.)
4224.
All sums earned by any prisoner may be retained until he has completed his sentence, or until he is released or discharged, and shall thereupon be paid to him. If any prisoner has dependents, his compensation shall be paid to such dependents monthly as earned.
(Added by Stats. 1953, Ch. 69.)
4225.
The board of supervisors of any county not included within any joint county road camp district, and having a population of 150,000 or more persons, may establish and maintain a county road camp as provided in this article, and may provide a board of directors thereof, by passing the resolution and receiving the certificate of organization provided for in this article.
(Added by Stats. 1953, Ch. 69.)
4226.
The board of supervisors of any county covered by Section 4225 shall nominate three of its members to serve as directors of the district formed thereunder, and such directors shall have and exercise all the powers and perform all the duties granted to and imposed by this article upon boards of directors of joint county road camp districts, and such county shall constitute, and be recognized and dealt with in all respects as a joint county road camp district within the meaning of this article.
(Added by Stats. 1953, Ch. 69.)
4227.
A joint county road camp district formed under this article may be dissolved in the following manner:
1. The board or boards of supervisors of a county or counties containing more than fifty percent (50%) of the population of the entire district shall by a unanimous vote adopt a resolution stating that the existence of a county road camp is no longer desirable for the public welfare and announcing the intention to withdraw therefrom and to dissolve said district.
2. The resolution or resolutions so adopted shall be communicated to the clerks of the boards of supervisors of all the counties comprising the district and also to the Secretary of State.
3. If it appears that the resolution was unanimously adopted by the board or boards of supervisors in the counties desiring to withdraw, and that such county or counties contain more than fifty percent (50%) of the entire population in the district, the Secretary of State shall thereupon certify to the clerks of the boards of supervisors of the counties composing the district that the district is dissolved.
4. Thereupon the board of directors of the district shall within 90 days:
(a) Abolish the road camp or camps;
(b) Return all prisoners therein to their respective county jails;
(c) Dispose of all equipment belonging to said camp or camps and the district;
(d) Render an accounting to the clerks of the boards of supervisors of the counties composing such district of all sums of money received and paid out since their last previous accounting, including the balance of revolving fund on hand at said last previous accounting;
(e) Apportion and repay to said counties all sums of money then remaining in their hands, and they shall thereupon be relieved of further responsibility in said matter.
(Added by Stats. 1953, Ch. 69.)

ARTICLE 3. Advisory Committees for Adult Detention Facilities [4300 - 4305]

(Article 3 added by Stats. 1957, Ch. 349.)
4300.
The board of supervisors may establish in each county a county advisory committee on adult detention.
(Added by Stats. 1957, Ch. 349.)
4301.
There shall be 6, 9, or 12 members of the committee. One-third shall be appointed by the board of supervisors, one-third by the sheriff, and one-third by the presiding judge of the superior court. Of the members appointed by the presiding judge, one shall be a member of the State Bar.
(Amended by Stats. 2002, Ch. 784, Sec. 569. Effective January 1, 2003.)
4302.
The members of the committee shall hold office for four years, and until their successors are appointed and qualify. Of those first appointed by the sheriff, superior court judge, and the board of supervisors, one shall hold office for two years, and one for four years; and the respective terms of the members first appointed shall be determined by lot as soon as possible after their appointment. When a vacancy occurs in the committee by expiration of the term of office of any member thereof, his successor shall be appointed to hold office for a term of four years. When a vacancy occurs for any other reason, the appointee shall hold office for the unexpired term of his predecessor.
(Added by Stats. 1957, Ch. 349.)
4303.
Members of the committee shall serve without compensation, but shall be allowed their reasonable expenses as approved by the presiding judge of the superior court. The expenses shall be a charge upon the county in which the court has jurisdiction, and shall be paid out of the county treasury upon a written order of the presiding judge of the superior court directing the county auditor to draw a warrant upon the county treasurer for the specified amount of such expenses. All orders by the presiding judge upon the county treasurer shall be filed in duplicate with the county board of supervisors and sheriff.
(Amended by Stats. 2002, Ch. 784, Sec. 570. Effective January 1, 2003.)
4304.
The committee shall file a report within 90 days after the thirty-first day of December of the calendar year for which such report is made, copies of which shall be filed with the county board of supervisors, the presiding judge, the sheriff, the Board of Corrections, and the Attorney General.
(Amended by Stats. 2002, Ch. 784, Sec. 571. Effective January 1, 2003.)
4305.
The committee shall annually inspect the city and county adult detention facilities. Such inspection shall be concerned with the conditions of inmate employment, detention, care, custody, training, and treatment on the basis of, but not limited to, the minimum standards established by the Board of Corrections. A report of such visitations together with pertinent recommendations shall be annually filed in accordance with the provisions of Section 4304 of this code.
(Added by Stats. 1957, Ch. 349.)

CHAPTER 2.5. Jail Industry Authority [4325 - 4328]

(Heading of Chapter 2.5 amended by Stats. 2016, Ch. 452, Sec. 2.)
4325.
(a) The board of supervisors of the Counties of Lake, Los Angeles, Madera, Sacramento, San Diego, San Joaquin, San Luis Obispo, Sonoma, Stanislaus, Tulare, Tuolumne, and Ventura may authorize, by ordinance or resolution, the sheriff or county director of corrections to create a Jail Industry Authority within the county jail system.
(b) The purpose of the Jail Industry Authority includes all of the following:
(1) To develop and operate industrial, agricultural, or service enterprises or programs employing prisoners in county correctional facilities under the jurisdiction of the sheriff or county director of corrections.
(2) To create and maintain working conditions within the enterprises or programs as similar as possible to those that prevail in private industry.
(3) To ensure prisoners have the opportunity to work productively and earn funds, if approved by the board of supervisors pursuant to Section 4019.3, and to acquire or improve effective work habits and occupational skills.
(4) To allow inmates who participate in the enterprise or program the opportunity to earn additional time credits allowed under Section 4019.1 or 4019.4, if authorized by the sheriff or county director of corrections.
(5) To operate a work program for inmates in county correctional facilities that will ultimately be self-supporting by generating sufficient funds from the sale of products and services to pay all the expenses of the program and that will provide goods and services that are or will be used by the county correctional facilities, thereby reducing the cost of its operation.
(Repealed and added by Stats. 2016, Ch. 452, Sec. 4. (AB 2012) Effective January 1, 2017.)
4327.
Upon the establishment of the Jail Industry Program or Jail Industry Authority, the board of supervisors shall establish a Jail Industries Fund, which may be a revolving fund, for funding the operations of the program. All jail industry income shall be deposited in, and any prisoner compensation shall be paid to the account of the prisoner from, the Jail Industries Fund.
(Amended by Stats. 2016, Ch. 452, Sec. 6. (AB 2012) Effective January 1, 2017.)
4328.
Funds in a Jail Industries Fund may only be used for the operation or expansion of the jail industry program or to cover operating and construction costs of county detention facilities, and may not be transferred to the county general fund.
(Added by Stats. 1987, Ch. 1303, Sec. 3. Effective September 28, 1987.)

CHAPTER 3. Blood Donations [4350 - 4351]

(Chapter 3 added by Stats. 1957, Ch. 1428.)
4350.
This chapter applies to prisoners confined in city, county, or city and county jails, or industrial farms or road camps established pursuant to this title, who are under a sentence of 30 days or more.
(Added by renumbering Section 4250 by Stats. 1967, Ch. 138.)
4351.
Any prisoner, to whom this chapter applies, may voluntarily donate blood to a blood bank duly licensed by the State Department of Public Health. Prior to blood donation the prisoner shall be given an examination with all clothes removed by a physician and surgeon of the blood bank to whom blood is to be donated, and donations shall be

refused unless such physician shall find the prisoner to be a suitable person for blood donation. No more than one such donation shall be permitted during any 72-day period.
(Added by renumbering Section 4251 by Stats. 1967, Ch. 138.)

TITLE 4.7. COUNTY CORRECTIONAL FACILITY CAPITAL EXPENDITURE BOND ACT OF 1986 [4475 - 4495]

(Title 4.7 added by Stats. 1986, Ch. 12, Sec. 1.)

CHAPTER 1. Findings and Declarations [4475 - 4476]

(Chapter 1 added by Stats. 1986, Ch. 12, Sec. 1.)
4475.
This title shall be known and may be cited as the County Correctional Facility Capital Expenditure Bond Act of 1986.
(Added by Stats. 1986, Ch. 12, Sec. 1. Approved in Proposition 52 at the June 3, 1986, election.)
4476.
It is found and declared that:
(a) While the County Jail Capital Expenditure Bond Act of 1981 and the County Jail Capital Expenditure Bond Act of 1984 have helped eliminate many of the critically overcrowded conditions found in the 164 county jail facilities in the state, many problems remain.
(b) Numerous county jails and juvenile facilities throughout California are dilapidated and overcrowded.
(c) Capital improvements are necessary to protect life and safety of the persons confined or employed in jail facilities and to upgrade the health and sanitary conditions of those facilities.
(d) County jails are threatened with closure or the imposition of court supervision if health and safety deficiencies are not corrected immediately.
(e) Due to fiscal constraints associated with the loss of local property tax revenues, counties are unable to finance the construction of adequate jail and juvenile facilities.
(f) Local facilities for adults and juveniles are operating over capacity and the population of these facilities is still increasing. It is essential to the public safety that construction of new facilities proceed as expeditiously as possible to relieve overcrowding and to maintain public safety and security.
(Added by Stats. 1986, Ch. 12, Sec. 1. Approved in Proposition 52 at the June 3, 1986, election.)

CHAPTER 2. Fiscal Provisions [4480 - 4495]

(Chapter 2 added by Stats. 1986, Ch. 12, Sec. 1.)
4480.
The State General Obligation Bond Law is adopted for the purpose of the issuance, sale, and repayment of, and otherwise providing with respect to, the bonds authorized to be issued pursuant to this title, and the provisions of that law are included in this title as though set out in full in this chapter except that, notwithstanding anything in the State General Obligation Bond Law, the maximum maturity of the bonds shall not exceed 20 years from the date of each respective series. The maturity of each respective series shall be calculated from the date of these series.
(Added by Stats. 1986, Ch. 12, Sec. 1. Approved in Proposition 52 at the June 3, 1986, election.)
4481.
As used in this title, and for the purpose of this title, the following words shall have the following meanings:
(a) "Committee" means the 1986 County Correctional Facility Capital Expenditure Finance Committee created by Section 4483.
(b) "Fund" means the 1986 County Correctional Facility Expenditure Fund.
(c) "County juvenile facilities" means county juvenile halls, juvenile homes, ranches, or camps, and other juvenile detention facilities.
(Added by Stats. 1986, Ch. 12, Sec. 1. Approved in Proposition 52 at the June 3, 1986, election.)
4482.
There is in the State Treasury the 1986 County Correctional Facility Capital Expenditure Fund, which fund is hereby created.
(Added by Stats. 1986, Ch. 12, Sec. 1. Approved in Proposition 52 at the June 3, 1986, election.)
4483.
For the purpose of authorizing the issuance and sale, pursuant to the State General Obligation Bond Law, of the bonds authorized by this title, the 1986 County Correctional Facility Capital Expenditure Finance Committee is hereby created. The committee consists of the Governor or his or her designated representative, the Controller, the Treasurer, and the Director of Finance. The County Correctional Facility Capital Expenditure Committee shall be the "committee" as that term is used in the State General Obligation Bond Law, and the Treasurer shall serve as chairman of the Committee. The Board of Corrections is hereby designated as "the board" for purposes of this title and for the purposes of the State General Obligation Bond Law.
(Added by Stats. 1986, Ch. 12, Sec. 1. Approved in Proposition 52 at the June 3, 1986, election.)
4484.
The committee is hereby authorized and empowered to create a debt or debts, liability or liabilities, of the State of California, in the aggregate amount of four hundred ninety-five million dollars ($495,000,000), in the manner provided in this title. That debt or debts, liability or liabilities, shall be created for the purpose of providing the funds to be used for the object and work specified in Section 4485 and for administrative costs incurred in connection therewith.
(Added by Stats. 1986, Ch. 12, Sec. 1. Approved in Proposition 52 at the June 3, 1986, election.)
4485.
Moneys in the fund may be available for the construction, reconstruction, remodeling, and replacement of county jail facilities, including, but not limited to, separate facilities for care of mentally ill inmates and persons arrested because of intoxication, and the performance of deferred maintenance on county jail facilities except that up to twenty million dollars ($20,000,000) of the money in the fund shall be available for the construction, reconstruction, remodeling, and replacement of county juvenile facilities, and the performance of deferred maintenance on county juvenile facilities. However, deferred maintenance for jails and juvenile facilities shall only include items with a useful life of at least 10 years.

Expenditure shall be made only if county matching funds of 25 percent are provided as determined by the Legislature, except that this requirement may be modified or waived by the Legislature where it determines that it is necessary to facilitate the expeditious and equitable construction of state and local correctional facilities.
(Added by Stats. 1986, Ch. 12, Sec. 1. Approved in Proposition 52 at the June 3, 1986, election.)
4485.5.
During the design and planning stage for county jail facilities whose construction, reconstruction, or remodeling is financed by the fund, consideration shall be given to proper design to allow for areas where persons arrested for misdemeanors who are attempting to obtain release on bail can be safely accommodated without the necessity of unclothed body searches.
(Added by Stats. 1986, Ch. 12, Sec. 1. Approved in Proposition 52 at the June 3, 1986, election.)
4485.6.
In order to be eligible to receive funds derived from the issuance of General Obligation Bonds under this title, a county shall do all of the following:
(a) Adopt a plan to prohibit the detention of all juveniles in county jails unless otherwise authorized by law.
(b) Demonstrate that it has adequate facilities for mentally ill inmates or detainees and for those persons arrested because of inebriation, or demonstrate that it has a plan for the provision of services to these persons.
(c) Demonstrate that it has utilized, to the greatest practicable extent, alternatives to jail incarceration such as sheriff's work release under Section 4024. 2, own recognizance release, and weekend work programs.
(Added by Stats. 1986, Ch. 12, Sec. 1. Approved in Proposition 52 at the June 3, 1986, election.)
4485.7.
Moneys in the fund may be available for construction of joint-use correctional facilities housing county and state or federal prisoners or any combination thereof in proportion to the county's benefit.
(Added by Stats. 1986, Ch. 12, Sec. 1. Approved in Proposition 52 at the June 3, 1986, election.)
4486.
(a) When sold, the bonds authorized by this title shall constitute valid and legally binding general obligations of the State of California, and the full faith and credit of the State of California is hereby pledged for the punctual payment of both principal and interest thereon.
(b) There shall be collected annually in the same manner and at the same time as other state revenue is collected such a sum, in addition to the ordinary revenues of the state, as shall be required to pay the interest and principal on the bonds maturing each year, and it is hereby made the duty of all officers charged by law with any duty in regard to the collection of the revenue to do and perform each and every act which shall be necessary to collect that additional sum.
(c) All money deposited in the fund which has been derived from premium and accrued interest on bonds sold shall be available for transfer to the General Fund as a credit to expenditures for bond interest.
(Added by Stats. 1986, Ch. 12, Sec. 1. Approved in Proposition 52 at the June 3, 1986, election.)
4487.
All money deposited in the fund pursuant to any provision of law requiring repayments to the state for assistance financed by the proceeds of the bonds authorized by this title shall be available for transfer to the General Fund. When transferred to the General Fund, this money shall be applied as a reimbursement to the General Fund on account of principal and interest on the bonds which have been paid from the General Fund.
(Added by Stats. 1986, Ch. 12, Sec. 1. Approved in Proposition 52 at the June 3, 1986, election.)
4488.
There is hereby appropriated from the General Fund in the State Treasury for the purpose of this title such an amount as will equal the following:
(a) That sum annually as will be necessary to pay the principal of and the interest on the bonds issued and sold pursuant to the provisions of this title, as principal and interest become due and payable.
(b) That sum as is necessary to carry out the provisions of Section 4489, which sum is appropriated without regard to fiscal years.
(Added by Stats. 1986, Ch. 12, Sec. 1. Approved in Proposition 52 at the June 3, 1986, election.)
4489.
For the purpose of carrying out the provisions of this title, the Director of Finance may by executive order authorize the withdrawal from the General Fund of an amount or amounts not to exceed the amount of the unsold bonds which the committee has by resolution authorized to be sold for the purpose of carrying out this title. Any amounts withdrawn shall be deposited in the fund and shall be disbursed by the board in accordance with this title. Any money made available under this section to the board shall be returned by the board to the General Fund from moneys received from the sale of bonds sold for the purpose of carrying out this title. These withdrawals from the General Fund shall be returned to the General Fund with interest at the rate which would have otherwise been earned by these sums in the Pooled Money Investment Fund.
(Added by Stats. 1986, Ch. 12, Sec. 1. Approved in Proposition 52 at the June 3, 1986, election.)
4489.5.
Notwithstanding any other provision of this bond act, or of the State General Obligation Bond Law (Chapter 4 (commencing with Section 16720) of Part 3 of Division 4 of Title 2 of the Government Code), if the Treasurer sells bonds pursuant to this bond act that include a bond counsel opinion to the effect that the interest on the bonds is excluded from gross income for federal tax purposes under designated conditions, the Treasurer may maintain separate accounts for the bond proceeds invested and the investment earnings on those proceeds, and may use or direct the use of those proceeds or earnings to pay any rebate, penalty, or other payment required under federal law, or take any other action with respect to the investment and use of those bond proceeds, as may be required or desirable under federal law in order to maintain the tax-exempt status of those bonds and to obtain any other advantage under federal law on behalf of the funds of this state.
(Added by Stats. 1991, Ch. 652, Sec. 17.)
4490.
The committee may authorize the Treasurer to sell all or any part of the bonds herein authorized at such time or times as may be fixed by the Treasurer.
(Added by Stats. 1986, Ch. 12, Sec. 1. Approved in Proposition 52 at the June 3, 1986, election.)
4491.
All proceeds from the sale of bonds, except those derived from premiums and accrued interest, shall be available for the purpose provided in Section 4485 but shall not be available for transfer to the General Fund to pay principal and interest on bonds. The money in the fund may be expended only as herein provided.
(Added by Stats. 1986, Ch. 12, Sec. 1. Approved in Proposition 52 at the June 3, 1986, election.)
4492.

Notwithstanding Section 16305.7 of the Government Code, all interest or other increment resulting from the investment of moneys deposited in the fund shall be credited to the fund.
(Added by Stats. 1986, Ch. 12, Sec. 1. Approved in Proposition 52 at the June 3, 1986, election.)

4493.
Money in the fund may only be expended for projects specified in this title as allocated in appropriations made by the Legislature.
(Added by Stats. 1986, Ch. 12, Sec. 1. Approved in Proposition 52 at the June 3, 1986, election.)

4494.
(a) It is the intent of the people in enacting this bond act that jail authorization and construction proceed as quickly as possible. Due to the severe shortage of jail facilities and the need to begin construction of jail facilities as soon as possible, all decisions of the board regarding construction, reconstruction, remodeling, or replacement of jail facilities financed by this title shall be final.
(b) No court shall have jurisdiction over these decisions of the board absent a showing, beyond a reasonable doubt, of a gross abuse of discretion by the board.
(c) Should an action be commenced alleging gross abuse of discretion by the board, no court shall have jurisdiction to delay, prohibit, or interfere with the construction, reconstruction, remodeling, or replacement of the subject jail facilities. The sole remedy available to the court is a mandate that steps be taken to mitigate the abuse of discretion.
(d) Nothing in this title is intended in any way to delay, prohibit, or interfere with the construction of jail facilities.
(Added by Stats. 1986, Ch. 12, Sec. 1. Approved in Proposition 52 at the June 3, 1986, election.)

4495.
If any provision of this title, or the application thereof, is held to be invalid, that invalidity shall not affect the other provisions or applications of the title which can be given effect without the invalid provision or application, and to this end the provisions of this title are severable.
(Added by Stats. 1986, Ch. 12, Sec. 1. Approved in Proposition 52 at the June 3, 1986, election.)

TITLE 4.8. COUNTY CORRECTIONAL FACILITY CAPITAL EXPENDITURE AND YOUTH FACILITY BOND ACT OF 1988 [4496 - 4496.48]

(Title 4.8 added by Stats. 1988, Ch. 264, Sec. 1.)

CHAPTER 1. General Provisions [4496 - 4496.04]

(Chapter 1 added by Stats. 1988, Ch. 264, Sec. 1.)
4496.
This title shall be known and may be cited as the County Correctional Facility Capital Expenditure and Youth Facility Bond Act of 1988.
(Added by Stats. 1988, Ch. 264, Sec. 1. Approved in Proposition 86 at the November 8, 1988, election.)

4496.02.
The Legislature finds and declares all of the following:
(a) While the County Jail Capital Expenditure Bond Act of 1981, the County Jail Capital Expenditure Bond Act of 1984, and the County Correctional Facility Capital Expenditure Bond Act of 1986 have helped eliminate many of the critically overcrowded conditions found in county correctional facilities in the state, many problems remain.
(b) Numerous county jails and juvenile facilities throughout California are dilapidated and overcrowded.
(c) Capital improvements are necessary to protect life and safety of the persons confined or employed in jail facilities and to upgrade the health and sanitary conditions of those facilities.
(d) County jails are threatened with closure or the imposition of court supervision if health and safety deficiencies are not corrected immediately.
(e) Due to fiscal constraints associated with the loss of local property tax revenues, counties are unable to finance the construction of adequate jail and juvenile facilities.
(f) Local facilities for adults and juveniles are operating over capacity and the population of these facilities is still increasing. It is essential to the public safety that construction of new facilities proceed as expeditiously as possible to relieve overcrowding and to maintain public safety and security.
(Added by Stats. 1988, Ch. 264, Sec. 1. Approved in Proposition 86 at the November 8, 1988, election.)

4496.04.
As used in this title, the following terms have the following meanings:
(a) "Committee" means the 1988 County Correctional Facility Capital Expenditure and Youth Facility Finance Committee created pursuant to Section 4496.34.
(b) "Fund" means the 1988 County Correctional Facility Capital Expenditure and Youth Facility Bond Fund created pursuant to Section 4496.10.
(c) "County correctional facilities" means county jail facilities, including separate facilities for the care of mentally ill inmates and persons arrested because of intoxication, but does not include county juvenile facilities.
(d) "County juvenile facilities" means county juvenile halls, juvenile homes, ranches, or camps, and other juvenile detention facilities.
(e) "Youth center" means a facility where children, ages 6 to 17, inclusive, come together for programs and activities, including, but not limited to, recreation, health and fitness, delinquency prevention such as antigang programs and programs fostering resistance to peer group pressures, counseling for problems such as drug and alcohol abuse and suicide, citizenship and leadership development, and youth employment.
(f) "Youth shelter" means a facility that provides a variety of services to homeless minors living on the street or abused and neglected children to assist them with their immediate survival needs and to help reunite them with their parents or, as a last alternative, to find a suitable home.
(Added by Stats. 1988, Ch. 264, Sec. 1. Approved in Proposition 86 at the November 8, 1988, election.)

CHAPTER 2. Program [4496.10 - 4496.19]

(Chapter 2 added by Stats. 1988, Ch. 264, Sec. 1.)
4496.10.

The proceeds of bonds issued and sold pursuant to this chapter shall be deposited in the 1988 County Correctional Facility Capital Expenditure and Youth Facility Bond Fund, which is hereby created.
(Added by Stats. 1988, Ch. 264, Sec. 1. Approved in Proposition 86 at the November 8, 1988, election.)

4496.12.
(a) (1) Moneys in the fund, up to a limit of four hundred ten million dollars ($410,000,000), may be available for the construction, reconstruction, remodeling, and replacement of county correctional facilities, and the performance of deferred maintenance on county correctional facilities. However, deferred maintenance for facilities shall only include items with a useful life of at least 10 years.
(2) Moneys in the fund, up to a limit of sixty-five million dollars ($65,000,000), may be available for the construction, reconstruction, remodeling, and replacement of county juvenile facilities, and the performance of deferred maintenance on county juvenile facilities, but may only be used for the purpose of reducing overcrowding and eliminating health, fire, and life safety hazards.
(3) Expenditure shall be made only if county matching funds of 25 percent are provided as determined by the Legislature, except that this requirement may be modified or waived by the Legislature where it determines that it is necessary to facilitate the expeditious and equitable construction of state and local correctional facilities.
(b) Moneys in the fund, up to a limit of twenty-five million dollars ($25,000,000), may be available for the purpose of making awards to public or private nonprofit agencies or joint ventures, or a combination of those entities, for purpose of purchasing equipment and for acquiring, renovating, or constructing youth centers or youth shelters, as may be provided by statute. Fifteen million dollars ($15,000,000) shall be available for youth centers and ten million dollars ($10,000,000) shall be available for youth shelters and shall be distributed by the Department of the Youth Authority. However, any remaining money that has not been awarded under this subdivision within two years of the effective date of this title shall be available for both youth centers and youth shelters.
(Added by Stats. 1988, Ch. 264, Sec. 1. Approved in Proposition 86 at the November 8, 1988, election.)

4496.16.
In order to be eligible to receive funds for the purposes specified in subdivision (a) of Section 4496.12 derived from the issuance of bonds under this title, a county shall do all of the following:
(a) Adopt a plan to prohibit the detention of all juveniles in county jails unless otherwise authorized by law.
(b) Demonstrate that it has adequate facilities for mentally ill inmates or detainees and for those persons arrested because of inebriation, or demonstrate that it has a plan for the provision of services to these persons.
(c) Demonstrate that it has utilized, to the greatest practicable extent, alternatives to jail incarceration.
(Added by Stats. 1988, Ch. 264, Sec. 1. Approved in Proposition 86 at the November 8, 1988, election.)

4496.17.
The Department of the Youth Authority shall administer funds appropriated for juvenile facilities as specified in paragraph (2) of subdivision (a) of Section 4496.12.
(Added by Stats. 1989, Ch. 1130, Sec. 1. Effective September 30, 1989.)

4496.19.
Money in the fund may only be expended for projects specified in this chapter as allocated in appropriations made by the Legislature.
(Added by Stats. 1988, Ch. 264, Sec. 1. Approved in Proposition 86 at the November 8, 1988, election.)

CHAPTER 3. Fiscal Provisions [4496.30 - 4496.48]

(Chapter 3 added by Stats. 1988, Ch. 264, Sec. 1.)
4496.30.
Bonds in the total amount of five hundred million dollars ($500,000,000), exclusive of refunding bonds, or so much thereof as is necessary, may be issued and sold to provide a fund to be used for carrying out the purposes expressed in this title and to be used to reimburse the General Obligation Bond Expense Revolving Fund pursuant to Section 16724.5 of the Government Code. The bonds shall, when sold, be and constitute a valid and binding obligation of the State of California, and the full faith and credit of the State of California is hereby pledged for the punctual payment of both principal of, and interest on, the bonds as the principal and interest become due and payable.
(Added by Stats. 1988, Ch. 264, Sec. 1. Approved in Proposition 86 at the November 8, 1988, election.)

4496.32.
The bonds authorized by this title shall be prepared, executed, issued, sold, paid, and redeemed as provided in the State General Obligation Bond Law (Chapter 4 (commencing with Section 16720) of Part 3 of Division 4 of Title 2 of the Government Code), and all of the provisions of that law apply to the bonds and to this chapter and are hereby incorporated in this chapter as though set forth in full in this title.
(Added by Stats. 1988, Ch. 264, Sec. 1. Approved in Proposition 86 at the November 8, 1988, election.)

4496.34.
(a) Solely for the purpose of authorizing the issuance and sale, pursuant to the State General Obligation Bond Law, of the bonds authorized by this title, the 1988 County Correctional Facility Capital Expenditure and Youth Facility Finance Committee is hereby created. For purposes of this title, the finance committee is "the committee" as that term is used in the State General Obligation Bond Law. The committee consists of the Governor, the Controller, the Treasurer, the Director of Finance, or their designated representatives. A majority of the committee may act for the committee.
(b) For purposes of the State General Obligation Bond Law, the Board of Corrections is designated the "board."
(Added by Stats. 1988, Ch. 264, Sec. 1. Approved in Proposition 86 at the November 8, 1988, election.)

4496.36.
The committee shall determine whether or not it is necessary or desirable to issue bonds authorized pursuant to this chapter in order to carry out the actions specified in Section 4496.12 and, if so, the amount of bonds to be issued and sold. Successive issues of bonds may be authorized and sold to carry out those actions progressively, and it is not necessary that all of the bonds authorized to be issued be sold at any one time.
(Added by Stats. 1988, Ch. 264, Sec. 1. Approved in Proposition 86 at the November 8, 1988, election.)

4496.38.
There shall be collected each year and in the same manner and at the same time as other state revenue is collected, in addition to the ordinary revenues of the state, a sum in an amount required to pay the principal of, and interest on, the bonds each year, and it is the duty of all officers charged by law with any duty in regard to the collection of the revenue to do and perform each and every act which is necessary to collect that additional sum.

(Added by Stats. 1988, Ch. 264, Sec. 1. Approved in Proposition 86 at the November 8, 1988, election.)

4496.40.
Notwithstanding Section 13340 of the Government Code, there is hereby appropriated from the General Fund in the State Treasury, for the purposes of this chapter, an amount that will equal the total of the following:
(a) The sum annually necessary to pay the principal of, and interest on, bonds issued and sold pursuant to this chapter, as the principal and interest become due and payable.
(b) The sum which is necessary to carry out the provisions of Section 4496.42, appropriated without regard to fiscal years.
(Added by Stats. 1988, Ch. 264, Sec. 1. Approved in Proposition 86 at the November 8, 1988, election.)

4496.42.
For the purposes of carrying out this title, the Director of Finance may authorize the withdrawal from the General Fund of an amount or amounts not to exceed the amount of the unsold bonds which have been authorized by the committee to be sold for the purpose of carrying out this chapter. Any amounts withdrawn shall be deposited in the fund. Any money made available under this section, plus any interest that the amounts would have earned in the Pooled Money Investment Account, shall be returned to the General Fund from money received from the sale of bonds for the purpose of carrying out this title.
(Added by Stats. 1988, Ch. 264, Sec. 1. Approved in Proposition 86 at the November 8, 1988, election.)

4496.43.
Notwithstanding any other provision of this bond act, or of the State General Obligation Bond Law (Chapter 4 (commencing with Section 16720) of Part 3 of Division 4 of Title 2 of the Government Code), if the Treasurer sells bonds pursuant to this bond act that include a bond counsel opinion to the effect that the interest on the bonds is excluded from gross income for federal tax purposes under designated conditions, the Treasurer may maintain separate accounts for the bond proceeds invested and the investment earnings on those proceeds, and may use or direct the use of those proceeds or earnings to pay any rebate, penalty, or other payment required under federal law, or take any other action with respect to the investment and use of those bond proceeds, as may be required or desirable under federal law in order to maintain the tax-exempt status of those bonds and to obtain any other advantage under federal law on behalf of the funds of this state.
(Added by Stats. 1991, Ch. 652, Sec. 18.)

4496.44.
All money deposited in the fund which is derived from premium and accrued interest on bonds sold shall be reserved in the fund and shall be available for transfer to the General Fund as a credit to expenditures for bond interest.
(Added by Stats. 1988, Ch. 264, Sec. 1. Approved in Proposition 86 at the November 8, 1988, election.)

4496.46.
The bonds may be refunded in accordance with Article 6 (commencing with Section 16780) of Chapter 4 of Part 3 of Division 4 of Title 2 of the Government Code.
(Added by Stats. 1988, Ch. 264, Sec. 1. Approved in Proposition 86 at the November 8, 1988, election.)

4496.47.
The board may request the Pooled Money Investment Board to make a loan from the Pooled Money Investment Account, in accordance with Section 16312 of the Government Code, for the purposes of carrying out the provisions of this chapter. The amount of the request shall not exceed the amount of the unsold bonds which the committee has by resolution authorized to be sold for the purpose of carrying out this chapter. The board shall execute such documents as required by the Pooled Money Investment Board to obtain and repay the loan. Any amounts loaned shall be deposited in the fund to be allocated by the board in accordance with this chapter.
(Added by Stats. 1988, Ch. 264, Sec. 1. Approved in Proposition 86 at the November 8, 1988, election.)

4496.48.
The Legislature hereby finds and declares that, inasmuch as the proceeds from the sale of bonds authorized by this title are not "proceeds of taxes" as that term is used in Article XIII B of the California Constitution, the disbursement of these proceeds is not subject to the limitations imposed by that article.
(Added by Stats. 1988, Ch. 264, Sec. 1. Approved in Proposition 86 at the November 8, 1988, election.)

TITLE 4.85. COUNTY CORRECTIONAL FACILITIES CAPITAL EXPENDITURE AND YOUTH FACILITY BOND ACT OF 1988 ALLOCATIONS [4497 - 4497.56]

(Title 4.85 added by Stats. 1989, Ch. 1327, Sec. 5.)

CHAPTER 1. General [4497- 4497.]

(Chapter 1 added by Stats. 1989, Ch. 1327, Sec. 5.)
4497.
(a) The Legislature finds and declares that approval by the electors of the County Correctional Facilities Capital Expenditure and Youth Facility Bond Act of 1988 has made new funds available for the construction and renovation of county jails and county juvenile facilities. The Legislature hereby directs the Board of Corrections to allocate and administer the moneys intended in the County Correctional Facilities Capital Expenditure and Youth Facility Bond Act of 1988 for county jails, and the Department of the Youth Authority to allocate and administer the moneys intended in the County Correctional Facilities Capital Expenditure and Youth Facility Bond Act of 1988 for juvenile facilities, in accordance with the provisions of this title.
(b) Money appropriated for allocation under this title may be used for the renovation, replacement, reconstruction, or construction of county jail facilities, county medical facilities designated to house persons charged with or convicted of a crime and who are mentally ill, and county juvenile facilities. Money appropriated by this title may also be used for construction of separate local detention facility space for detoxification of persons arrested because of intoxication.
(c) It is the Legislature's intention to make the money appropriated for allocation under this title available to counties with established and documented needs for capital projects for jail and juvenile facilities. However, that money shall not be used to build facilities that the counties cannot afford to operate fully and safely.
(Added by Stats. 1989, Ch. 1327, Sec. 5. Effective October 2, 1989.)

CHAPTER 2. County Jails [4497.02 - 4497.16]

(Chapter 2 added by Stats. 1989, Ch. 1327, Sec. 5.)
4497.02.
(a) For the purpose of this chapter:
(1) "Board" means the Board of Corrections.
(2) "Fund" means the 1988 County Correctional Facilities Capital Expenditure and Youth Facility Fund.
(b) The Board of Corrections shall not itself be deemed a responsible agency, as defined by Section 21069 of the Public Resources Code, or otherwise be subject to the California Environmental Quality Act for any activities under this title, the County Jail Capital Expenditure Bond Acts of 1981 or 1984, or the County Facility Capital Expenditure Bond Act of 1986. This subdivision does not exempt any local agency from the requirements of the California Environmental Quality Act.
(Added by Stats. 1989, Ch. 1327, Sec. 5. Effective October 2, 1989.)

4497.04.
Money appropriated to the board for allocation pursuant to this chapter shall be allocated as follows:
(a) Funding shall be provided for those projects entitled to be funded under subdivision (c) of Section 3 of Chapter 444, Statutes of 1984, as amended, and Section 5 of Chapter 1519, Statutes of 1986, to the extent that those projects have not received full funding.
(b) The following additional amounts shall be allocated to the counties for the construction, reconstruction, replacement, or renovation of county jail facilities. These funds shall not be used to supplant local funds directed to previously approved state projects. Nor shall these funds be used to reimburse counties whose match on previously approved projects exceeded the required 25 percent. These funds may be used for allocations specified in subdivisions (c) and (d) of Chapter 444, Statutes of 1984, as amended, and Section 5, subdivision (b) of Chapter 1519, Statutes of 1986.

County	Allocation
Alameda	$ 6,441,198
Alpine	62,541
Amador	0
Butte	1,900,266
Calaveras	0
Colusa	0
Contra Costa	1,420,488
Del Norte	1,317,106
El Dorado	0
Fresno	4,326,606
Glenn	732,094
Humboldt	2,116,523
Imperial	0
Inyo	1,214,025
Kern	9,650,404
Kings	891,687
Lake	1,699,291
Lassen	727,717
Los Angeles	172,682,741
Madera	0
Marin	2,166,458
Mariposa	117,478
Mendocino	1,214,270
Merced	2,446,318
Modoc	181,761
Mono	120,421
Monterey	7,429,146
Napa	358,819

Nevada		1,179,930
Orange		21,723,387
Placer		2,022,123
Plumas		166,775
Riverside		10,476,076
Sacramento		6,299,898
San Benito		1,270,642
San Bernardino		10,874,718
San Diego		32,675,959
San Francisco		17,015,321
San Joaquin		12,377,292
San Luis Obispo		2,033,185
San Mateo		2,452,925
Santa Barbara		2,438,604
Santa Clara		11,780,710
Santa Cruz		2,889,829
Shasta		0
Sierra		119,234
Siskiyou		0
Solano		1,125,732
Sonoma		3,877,521
Stanislaus		3,649,178
Sutter		964,137
Tehama		532,947
Trinity		225,380
Tulare		2,513,889
Tuolumne		677,876
Ventura		14,733,637
Yolo		686,721
Yuba		1,844,691
TOTAL		$387,845,675

(c) If any county declares that it is unable to use the funds allocated to it under this section, or if any county is unable to satisfy the prerequisites for funding listed in Section 4494.10, the amount allocated to the county in this section shall revert to the state, to be reallocated by the board.

(d) If funds beyond those needed for the itemized amounts become available for reallocation, the board shall reallocate those funds under subdivision (e).

(e) Reverted funds under this chapter or subdivision (c) of Chapter 1519 of the Statutes of 1986 shall be reallocated to counties pursuant to the development and adoption of a new allocation plan as determined by an allocation advisory committee appointed by the board. The allocation advisory committee shall convene upon notification by the board that funds have been reverted. Reallocated funds shall be distributed three times. The first distribution shall occur on December 31, 1990; the second distribution shall occur on December 31, 1992, and the final distribution shall occur on December 31, 1993. If any county seeking funds has not completed architectural drawings at the time reallocation funds become available, the county shall be removed from reallocation consideration until it has completed architectural drawings.

(f) Any county that receives funds pursuant to this chapter or pursuant to Chapter 444 of the Statutes of 1984, as amended, or Chapter 1519 of the Statutes of 1986, that, in the aggregate, total ten million dollars ($10,000,000) or less may pool or combine those funds for the purpose of financing a jail construction project, subject to approval of the project pursuant to this chapter. However, under no circumstances shall the pooling of successive bond allocations relieve or exempt the county from its obligation to meet the 25 percent local match requirement.

This subdivision shall not be interpreted as an authorization to utilize allocated funds to reimburse counties whose match on previously approved and completed projects exceeded the required 25 percent.
(Added by Stats. 1989, Ch. 1327, Sec. 5. Effective October 2, 1989.)
4497.05.
Money in the 1986 County Correctional Facility Capital Expenditure Fund and money in the 1988 County Correctional Facility Capital Expenditure and Youth Facility Bond Fund may be used on the same project so long as the project is consistent with the purposes set forth in Sections 4485 and 4496.12 and is subject to the restrictions and requirements set forth in subdivision (f) of Section 4497.04. The deadlines applicable under this title shall be applicable to the joint use of funds under this section.
(Added by Stats. 1990, Ch. 619, Sec. 1.)
4497.06.
(a) The board shall administer the funds allocated in this chapter to adult jail facilities, according to existing County Correctional Facilities Capital Expenditure Fund regulations, except as those regulations may be amended to comply with the provisions of this chapter.
(b) The board shall apply its regulations in the approval or disapproval of county jail projects, except that the board may approve a project if the board finds, after conducting a public hearing, that although the county cannot possibly meet the regulations, the county will nonetheless comply with Section 4485.6.
(Added by Stats. 1989, Ch. 1327, Sec. 5. Effective October 2, 1989.)
4497.08.
No state moneys shall be encumbered in contracts with a county, nor released to a county, for construction or renovation of a local jail facility pursuant to this chapter until the conditions of this chapter have been fulfilled by the county.
(Added by Stats. 1989, Ch. 1327, Sec. 5. Effective October 2, 1989.)
4497.10.
To be eligible for funding consideration, a county shall, to the satisfaction of the board, do all of the following:
(a) Certify that juveniles are not housed in the county's adult detention facilities, except where authorized by law; and document the existence of, or plans for, separate housing for juveniles.
(b) Document the existence of, or plans for, separate housing for persons detained or arrested because of intoxication, which will prevent mixing of this category of prisoner with other prisoners. If the county has no existing provisions for detoxification housing, it shall make provisions for that housing as part of its proposed project.
(c) Document the existence of, or plans for, separate housing for mentally disordered defendants or convicted prisoners which will prevent mixing of this category of prisoner with other prisoners until the time that the responsible health authority or his or her designee clears specific prisoners for nonseparate housing, based on clinical judgment. If the county has no existing provisions for separate housing of mentally disordered prisoners, it shall make provisions for that housing as part of its proposed project.
(d) Submit a formal project proposal to the board on or before September 30, 1990. The project proposal shall describe the construction or renovation project to be undertaken and shall include an estimated budget for the project. The proposal shall also identify how county funding obligations, both for construction and operation of the facility, will be met. The project proposal shall be consistent with the needs and priorities identified in the needs assessment by the county.
Failure to submit a project proposal shall be deemed a declaration by the county that it does not intend to request its allocation under subdivisions (a) and (b) of Section 4497.04, and the amounts allocated in those subdivisions to the county shall be available for reallocation by the board. The board may waive this requirement for submission of a proposal within one year if it determines there are unavoidable delays in the county's preparation of a project proposal.
(e) Submit architectural drawings which shall be approved by the board for compliance with minimum jail standards and by the State Fire Marshal for compliance with fire safety requirements. If the board concludes that a county's proposed construction or renovation contains serious design deficiencies that, while they would not require a refusal to enter into the contract, would seriously impair the facility's functioning, it shall notify the sheriff and the board of supervisors of that county of the deficiencies and shall delay entering into a contract with the county for at least 30 days after mailing the letter. This letter shall be a public record.
(f) The county shall certify that it owns, or has long-term possession of, the construction site.
(g) The county shall have filed a final notice of determination on its environmental impact report with the board.
(h) The county has formally adopted a plan to finance the construction of the proposed facility.
(i) The county shall have submitted a preliminary staffing plan for the proposed facility, along with an analysis of other operating costs anticipated for the facility, to the board for review and comment. Prior to submission of the staffing plan and operating costs analysis of the board, the county board of supervisors shall have reviewed and approved the submittal in or following public hearings. The sheriff shall also have reviewed and commented on the preliminary staffing plan and the operating cost analysis. The board shall comment in writing to the sheriff and board of supervisors. This letter shall be a public record.
(j) The county shall submit either a major or minor needs assessment documenting the need for and purpose of the proposed project. The needs assessment shall meet all requirements listed in the applicable County Correctional Facility Capital Expenditure Fund regulations. The board may exempt a county from performing a new needs assessment if any of the following conditions exist:
(1) The board determines that a prior needs assessment is in substantial compliance and it justifies the project being funded in Section 4497.04.
(2) A county receives funds from this bond act in an amount of three hundred thousand dollars ($300,000) or less.
If exempted from performing a needs assessment, counties shall provide an analysis of specific jail deficiencies, including levels of security, program, including, but not limited to, medical and mental health care, housing, and administration. This analysis shall also include specific plans for correcting the deficiencies.
(k) Demonstrate to the board unless the county's sole project is a remodel of an existing adult detention facility which will not result in the addition of any beds, that it is using, to the greatest extent feasible, alternatives to incarceration based on the following measures: an incarceration rate of no more than one standard deviation above the mean for all counties and, either a pretrial misdemeanor incarceration rate of no more than one standard deviation above the mean for all counties or a sentenced prisoner alternatives percentage or 5 percent or more as related to total sentenced prisoner admissions.
(1) The data to be used in establishing the incarceration rate will be the 1989 calendar year average daily population as reported by each county to the board and the Department of Finance Report on Population by County.
(2) The pretrial misdemeanor incarceration rate will be based on an average of the daily pretrial misdemeanor jail population, developed from a four-day sample period in 1989 specified by the board.
(3) The sentenced prisoner alternatives percentage will be based on enrollment in three programs: Section 4024.2 of the Penal Code (work-in-lieu of jail), county parole, and home detention if the placement is made after some jail time is served.
(4) Counties failing to demonstrate adequate use of alternatives to incarcerations by the above measure by March 30, 1990, shall be reevaluated annually by the board. If any

county is unable to satisfy the requirements of this section by September 30, 1993, the amount allocated to the county shall revert to the state, to be reallocated by the board pursuant to subdivision (c) of Section 4497.04.

(l) Begin construction or renovation work within four years of the effective date of this title. If a county fails to meet this requirement, any allocations to the county under this chapter shall be deemed void and moneys allocated to the county shall revert to the board for reallocation. The board may waive this requirement if it determines that there are unavoidable delays in the initial construction activities.

(m) Counties shall provide for the construction of appropriate courtroom facilities and hearing room facilities within any jail construction plan submitted to the board. Those courtroom facilities and hearing room facilities shall be utilized for purposes of holding appropriate arraignments and bail hearings and for the conduct of parole revocation hearings. The board may waive this requirement where county specific circumstances dictate.

(Added by Stats. 1989, Ch. 1327, Sec. 5. Effective October 2, 1989.)
4497.12.
(a) County match on projects funded under this chapter shall be a minimum of 25 percent of the total project costs.

(b) The county match requirement imposed upon counties pursuant to the receipt of state moneys shall not be required to be made on a pro rata basis where the requirement would impede the expeditious and equitable construction of county correctional facilities. However, under no circumstances shall the county match for any county project be less than 25 percent.

(c) Costs eligible for state funding and as county match shall be those defined in applicable existing sections of the County Correctional Facilities Capital Expenditure Fund regulations, which regulations may be amended.

(Amended by Stats. 1990, Ch. 1057, Sec. 1.)
4497.14.
(a) The board shall not approve the expenditures of funds allocated under this act for the construction of county detention facilities until a master site plan for county detention facilities has been prepared and adopted by the board of supervisors of the county proposing to construct the facility. The board of supervisors shall determine the location of any detention facilities pursuant to a master plan, which determination shall not be subject to any initiative or ordinance adopted by initiative. In developing the plan, the board of supervisors shall consider alternatives to additional detention facilities and the specific concerns of incorporated cities and other community representatives, and shall give special consideration to existing federal, state, and local detention facilities in order to avoid over-concentration of inmates in one geographic area of the county. If the board of supervisors decides to locate new or expanded detention facilities near existing detention facilities, it shall publicly state its reasons for that decision.

The board shall only approve expenditure of funds allocated under this chapter for the construction of detention facilities in accordance with the plan adopted pursuant to this section. The board may exempt a county from this requirement if the master site plan remains unchanged from that approved under the provisions of the County Correctional Facilities Capital Expenditure Bond Act of 1986.

(b) The board shall establish construction costs controls and shall set forth in regulation procedures for setting maximum state funding levels for appropriate construction unit costs, including cost per cell for specified categories of facilities. These cost controls shall be based on average costs in recently constructed facilities in California that are comparable in size, use, location, and other relevant factors.

Allocations listed in Section 4497.04 notwithstanding, the state contribution shall be up to 75 percent of total project costs or up to 75 percent of the applicable construction cost norms, whichever is lower. Nothing in this section is intended, however, to prescribe maximum limits on county funding levels for the projects.

Prior to releasing any funds to a county, the board shall review construction cost levels in the funded projects for compliance with cost control regulations.

(c) Prior to entering into a contract with a county, the board shall review or approve or both review and approve the county submissions required by this chapter regarding the facility or facilities proposed for funding.

(d) The board shall collect annually from all counties information on county incarceration rates, average daily jail populations as a proportion of the total county population or total arrests or both; pretrial misdemeanant ratios, the percentage which unsentenced prisoners charged only with misdemeanors constitute the total average daily unsentenced jail population; and sentenced alternatives ratios, for example, average daily populations in work-in-lieu of jail programs and county parole as a percentage of the total average daily sentenced misdemeanant prisoner population. All counties that have received or will receive state funds for jail construction shall supply the board the information necessary to comply with this section.

(Added by Stats. 1989, Ch. 1327, Sec. 5. Effective October 2, 1989.)
4497.16.
If after a hearing, the board makes a finding that a county has failed to comply with a condition or plan approved by the board relating to the requirements of Section 4485.6, the board may require the county to pay an amount equal to the pro rata portion of the principal and interest, paid by the state on bonds the proceeds of which were allocated pursuant to this chapter to the county for the period of noncompliance. The repayment provisions shall not be applicable if the noncompliance with the condition or plan is the result of circumstances beyond the control of the county, or the board finds the county cannot reasonably comply under the circumstances.

(Added by Stats. 1989, Ch. 1327, Sec. 5. Effective October 2, 1989.)

CHAPTER 3. Juvenile Facilities [4497.20 - 4497.38]

(Chapter 3 added by Stats. 1989, Ch. 1327, Sec. 5.)
4497.20.
(a) The Department of the Youth Authority is hereby directed to administer the moneys intended for juvenile facilities in the County Correctional Facility Capital Expenditure and Youth Facility Bond Act of 1988, in accordance with the provisions of this chapter.

(b) It is the intention of the Legislature to make the money appropriated for allocation under this chapter available to counties with established and documented needs for capital projects for juvenile facilities.

(c) Counties that apply for funds to alleviate overcrowding shall submit a preliminary staffing plan for the proposed facility, along with an analysis of other operating costs anticipated for the facility, to the Department of the Youth Authority for review and comment. Prior to submission of the staffing plan and operating cost analysis to the department, the board of supervisors shall have reviewed and approved the submittal in or following public hearings. The chief probation officer shall also have reviewed and commented on the preliminary staffing plan and operating cost analysis. The department shall comment in writing to the chief probation officer and board of supervisors. This response shall be a public record.

(d) The Department of the Youth Authority shall conduct an assessment of the needs of counties for juvenile facilities in California which shall be submitted to the Legislature by June 30, 1990.

(Added by Stats. 1989, Ch. 1327, Sec. 5. Effective October 2, 1989.)
4497.22.

Funds appropriated to the Department of the Youth Authority for allocation under this chapter shall be allocated as provided by this chapter.

(Added by Stats. 1989, Ch. 1327, Sec. 5. Effective October 2, 1989.)
4497.24.
Two million three hundred fifty-seven thousand seven hundred seventy-eight dollars ($2,357,778) shall be set aside initially for the counties that did not have juvenile facilities on January 1, 1987. These funds shall be used to construct county juvenile facilities and are hereby allocated as follows:

Amador	$ 33,000
Calaveras	80,000
Colusa	218,928
Glenn	213,850
Inyo	846,000
Lassen	350,000
Mariposa	50,000
Modoc	126,000
Mono	18,000
Plumas	45,000
San Benito	243,000
Sierra	10,000
Trinity	30,000
Tuolumne	94,000

(Amended by Stats. 1992, Ch. 877, Sec. 1. Effective January 1, 1993.)
4497.26.
Ten million dollars ($10,000,000) shall be set aside initially for counties that do not have efficient and adequate facilities for youth with special problems. Two or more counties may apply jointly to construct those facilities regionally. No more than three million three hundred thousand dollars ($3,300,000) shall be awarded for the construction of each regional facility.

(Added by Stats. 1989, Ch. 1327, Sec. 5. Effective October 2, 1989.)
4497.28.
Forty-eight million nine hundred sixty-seven thousand two hundred twenty-two dollars ($48,967,222) shall be set aside initially for counties to alleviate overcrowding and eliminate health, fire, and life safety deficiencies in juvenile facilities or provide efficient and adequate facility for youth with special problems. These funds are hereby allocated to all counties except those listed in Section 4497.24, as follows:

Alameda	$ 2,378,878
Butte	303,787
Contra Costa	1,329,808
Del Norte	34,798
El Dorado	210,354
Fresno	1,064,299
Humboldt	201,133
Imperial	196,087
Kern	901,792
Kings	163,725
Lake	89,431
Los Angeles	14,970,647
Madera	143,542
Marin	400,004
Mendocino	132,407
Merced	297,871
Monterey	605,660

Napa	184,952
Nevada	134,321
Orange	3,934,095
Placer	272,121
Riverside	1,700,581
Sacramento	1,696,928
San Bernardino	2,235,602
San Diego	4,123,745
San Francisco	1,275,871
San Joaquin	794,440
San Luis Obispo	360,682
San Mateo	1,093,529
Santa Barbara	596,961
Santa Clara	2,488,758
Santa Cruz	393,914
Shasta	242,890
Siskiyou	75,338
Solano	544,764
Sonoma	636,457
Stanislaus	591,915
Sutter	107,352
Tehama	81,253
Tulare	517,621
Ventura	1,125,195
Yolo	234,887
Yuba	98,827

(Amended by Stats. 1992, Ch. 877, Sec. 2. Effective January 1, 1993.)
4497.30.
(a) Two million two hundred twenty-five thousand dollars ($2,225,000) shall be set aside initially for bond interest costs, and two hundred fifty thousand dollars ($250,000) shall be set aside to conduct a statewide assessment of the counties' needs for juvenile facilities.
(b) Notwithstanding Section 5.5 of Chapter 1130 of the Statutes of 1989, up to two hundred twenty-five thousand dollars ($225,000) shall be available for assistance to counties in planning and development of projects funded under Section 5 of Chapter 1327 of the Statutes of 1989 and in accordance with Section 4497.20.
(Amended by Stats. 1992, Ch. 877, Sec. 3. Effective January 1, 1993.)
4497.32.
(a) Funds which were set aside initially as provided by Sections 4497.24 to 4497.30, inclusive, that are not used and funds that were allocated under the provisions of the County Correctional Facility Capital Expenditure Bond Act of 1986 that are not used shall be allocated by the Department of the Youth Authority to those counties that received an allocation under Section 4497.28 which was not sufficient to fund the remaining portion of the total cost of the approved projects. The amount of each of those county's allocation shall be that county's per capita share of the total funds available for all counties with partially funded projects, or the amount needed to complete funding of that county's approved projects, whichever is less. At no time shall the allocation exceed 75 percent of the total eligible costs.
(b) The allocation procedure described in subdivision (a) shall be repeated until all of the available funds are awarded.
(c) Funds awarded by the Department of the Youth Authority under this section shall be used for the construction, reconstruction, remodeling, or replacement of county juvenile facilities, and for the performance of deferred maintenance on juvenile facilities, but may only be used for the purpose of reducing current overcrowding and eliminating health, fire, and life safety hazards.
(Added by Stats. 1989, Ch. 1327, Sec. 5. Effective October 2, 1989.)
4497.34.
(a) Counties with overcrowded juvenile facilities shall not be eligible to receive funds to construct, reconstruct, remodel, or replace juvenile facilities unless they have adopted a plan to correct overcrowded conditions within their facilities which includes the use of alternatives to detention. The corrective action plan shall provide for the use of five or

more methods or procedures to minimize the number of minors detained and shall be approved by the board of supervisors during or subsequent to a public hearing.
(b) To be eligible for funding under this chapter, the county shall enter into a contract with the Department of the Youth Authority and begin construction or renovation work within six years of the operative date of the regulations that implement this chapter. If a county fails to meet this requirement, any allocations or awards to that county under this chapter shall be deemed void and any moneys allocated or awarded to that county shall revert to the Department of the Youth Authority for reallocation to another county as provided by Section 4497.32. The department may waive this requirement if it determines that there are unavoidable delays in starting construction.
(c) To be eligible for funding for juvenile facilities under the County Correctional Facility Capital Expenditure Bond Act of 1986, the county shall enter into a contract with the Department of the Youth Authority and begin construction or renovation work by July 31, 1991. If a county fails to meet this requirement, all allocations or awards that have been made to that county under that act shall be deemed void and any moneys allocated or awarded to that county shall revert to the Department of the Youth Authority and are reappropriated for reallocation as provided by Section 4497.32. The department may waive this requirement if it determines that there are unavoidable delays in starting construction.
(d) Excluding moneys allocated for San Bernardino County, the Department of the Youth Authority shall immediately reallocate unused awards to eligible participating counties.
(Amended by Stats. 1995, Ch. 803, Sec. 1. Effective October 13, 1995.)
4497.36.
An application for funds shall be in the manner and form prescribed by the Department of the Youth Authority.
(Added by Stats. 1989, Ch. 1327, Sec. 5. Effective October 2, 1989.)
4497.38.
(a) Awards shall be made only if county matching funds of 25 percent are provided except as specified in subdivision (b).
(b) (1) A county or a consortium of counties may request the Director of the Department of the Youth Authority for a deferral of payment of the required matching funds for the construction of a juvenile detention facility. This request shall be approved if the county or consortium of counties meet all of the following criteria:
(A) The county or consortium of counties has plans for the construction of the facility approved by the Department of the Youth Authority.
(B) The facility to be built is located in Humboldt County.
(C) The county or consortium of counties submits to and receives approval by the Department of the Youth Authority, a plan and schedule for payment of the required match.
(2) Contribution of the county or consortium of counties matching requirement shall commence no later than three years from the date of occupation of any facility financed under this chapter.
(3) Under no circumstances shall the county match for any county juvenile project be less than 25 percent.
(Amended by Stats. 1996, Ch. 6, Sec. 1. Effective January 1, 1997.)

CHAPTER 4. Purchase of Correctional Industry Products For Correctional, Juvenile, and Youth Facilities [4497.50 - 4497.56]

(Chapter 4 added by Stats. 1989, Ch. 1327, Sec. 5.)
4497.50.
In order to be eligible to receive funds derived from the issuance of General Obligation Bonds under the County Correctional Facility Capital Expenditure and Youth Facility Bond Act of 1988, a county or city and county shall do all of the following:
(a) In the design and planning of facilities whose construction, reconstruction, or remodeling is financed under the County Correctional Facility Capital Expenditure and Youth Facility Bond Act of 1988, products for construction, renovation, equipment, and furnishings produced and sold by the Prison Industry Authority or local Jail Industry Authorities shall be utilized in the plans and specifications unless the county or city and county demonstrates either of the following to the satisfaction of the Board of State and Community Corrections or the Department of Corrections and Rehabilitation, Division of Juvenile Justice.
(1) The products cannot be produced and delivered without causing delay to the construction of the property.
(2) The products are not suitable for the facility or competitively priced and cannot otherwise be reasonably adapted.
(b) Counties and cities and counties shall consult with the staff of the Prison Industry Authority or local Jail Industry Authority to develop new products and adapt existing products to their needs.
(c) The Board of State and Community Corrections or the Department of Corrections and Rehabilitation, Division of Juvenile Justice, shall not enter into any contract with any county or city and county until that county's or city and county's plan for purchase from and consultation with the Prison Industry Authority or local jail industry program is reviewed and approved by the Board of State and Community Corrections or the Department of Corrections and Rehabilitation, Division of Juvenile Justice.
(Amended by Stats. 2016, Ch. 452, Sec. 8. (AB 2012) Effective January 1, 2017.)
4497.52.
Notwithstanding any other provision of law, a county or city and county may contract for the purchase of products as specified in Section 4497.50 with the Prison Industry Authority or local Jail Industry Authority without the formality of obtaining bids or otherwise complying with provisions of the Public Contract Code.
(Amended by Stats. 2016, Ch. 452, Sec. 9. (AB 2012) Effective January 1, 2017.)
4497.54.
The Prison Industry Authority shall designate an individual as County Jail and Juvenile Facility Liaison who shall work with counties to maximize the utilization of Prison Industry Authority products for construction, renovation, equipment, and furnishing, to ensure that manufactured products meet the contract specifications and delivery dates, and to assure consultation with counties for development of new products and adaption of existing products to meet their needs.
(Added by Stats. 1989, Ch. 1327, Sec. 5. Effective October 2, 1989.)
4497.56.
It is the intent of the Legislature to maximize the utilization of Prison Industry Authority products for jail construction, renovation, equipment, and furnishings to ensure that prisoners work productively and contribute to reducing the cost to the taxpayers of their incarceration.
(Added by Stats. 1989, Ch. 1327, Sec. 5. Effective October 2, 1989.)

TITLE 5. OFFENSES RELATING TO PRISONS AND PRISONERS [4500 - 4758]

(Title 5 added by Stats. 1941, Ch. 106.)

CHAPTER 1. Offenses by Prisoners [4500 - 4504]

(Heading of Chapter 1 amended by Stats. 1943, Ch. 173.)

4500.

Every person while undergoing a life sentence, who is sentenced to state prison within this state, and who, with malice aforethought, commits an assault upon the person of another with a deadly weapon or instrument, or by any means of force likely to produce great bodily injury is punishable with death or life imprisonment without possibility of parole. The penalty shall be determined pursuant to the provisions of Sections 190.3 and 190.4; however, in cases in which the person subjected to such assault does not die within a year and a day after such assault as a proximate result thereof, the punishment shall be imprisonment in the state prison for life without the possibility of parole for nine years.

For the purpose of computing the days elapsed between the commission of the assault and the death of the person assaulted, the whole of the day on which the assault was committed shall be counted as the first day.

Nothing in this section shall be construed to prohibit the application of this section when the assault was committed outside the walls of any prison if the person committing the assault was undergoing a life sentence and was serving a sentence to a state prison at the time of the commission of the assault and was not on parole, on probation, or released on bail pending an appeal.

(Amended by Stats. 1986, Ch. 1445, Sec. 1.)

4501.

(a) Except as provided in Section 4500, every person confined in the state prison of this state who commits an assault upon the person of another with a deadly weapon or instrument shall be guilty of a felony and shall be imprisoned in the state prison for two, four, or six years to be served consecutively.

(b) Except as provided in Section 4500, every person confined in the state prison of this state who commits an assault upon the person of another by any means of force likely to produce great bodily injury shall be guilty of a felony and shall be imprisoned in the state prison for two, four, or six years to be served consecutively.

(Amended by Stats. 2015, Ch. 303, Sec. 401. (AB 731) Effective January 1, 2016.)

4501.1.

(a) Every person confined in the state prison who commits a battery by gassing upon the person of any peace officer, as defined in Chapter 4.5 (commencing with Section 830) of Title 3 of Part 2, or employee of the state prison is guilty of aggravated battery and shall be punished by imprisonment in a county jail or by imprisonment in the state prison for two, three, or four years. Every state prison inmate convicted of a felony under this section shall serve his or her term of imprisonment as prescribed in Section 4501.5.

(b) For purposes of this section, "gassing" means intentionally placing or throwing, or causing to be placed or thrown, upon the person of another, any human excrement or other bodily fluids or bodily substances or any mixture containing human excrement or other bodily fluids or bodily substances that results in actual contact with the person's skin or membranes.

(c) The warden or other person in charge of the state prison shall use every available means to immediately investigate all reported or suspected violations of subdivision (a), including, but not limited to, the use of forensically acceptable means of preserving and testing the suspected gassing substance to confirm the presence of human excrement or other bodily fluids or bodily substances. If there is probable cause to believe that the inmate has violated subdivision (a), the chief medical officer of the state prison or his or her designee, may, when he or she deems it medically necessary to protect the health of an officer or employee who may have been subject to a violation of this section, order the inmate to receive an examination or test for hepatitis or tuberculosis or both hepatitis and tuberculosis on either a voluntary or involuntary basis immediately after the event, and periodically thereafter as determined to be necessary by the medical officer in order to ensure that further hepatitis or tuberculosis transmission does not occur. These decisions shall be consistent with an occupational exposure as defined by the Center for Disease Control and Prevention. The results of any examination or test shall be provided to the officer or employee who has been subject to a reported or suspected violation of this section. Nothing in this subdivision shall be construed to otherwise supersede the operation of Title 8 (commencing with Section 7500). Any person performing tests, transmitting test results, or disclosing information pursuant to this section shall be immune from civil liability for any action taken in accordance with this section.

(d) The warden or other person in charge of the state prison shall refer all reports for which there is probable cause to believe that the inmate has violated subdivision (a) to the local district attorney for prosecution.

(e) The Department of Corrections and Rehabilitation shall report to the Legislature, by January 1, 2000, its findings and recommendations on gassing incidents at the state prison and the medical testing authorized by this section. The report shall include, but not be limited to, all of the following:

(1) The total number of gassing incidents at each state prison facility up to the date of the report.

(2) The disposition of each gassing incident, including the administrative penalties imposed, the number of incidents that are prosecuted, and the results of those prosecutions, including any penalties imposed.

(3) A profile of the inmates who commit the aggravated batteries, including the number of inmates who have one or more prior serious or violent felony convictions.

(4) Efforts that the department has taken to limit these incidents, including staff training and the use of protective clothing and goggles.

(5) The results and costs of the medical testing authorized by this section.

(f) Nothing in this section shall preclude prosecution under both this section and any other provision of law.

(Amended (as amended by Stats. 2011, Ch. 15, Sec. 484) by Stats. 2011, 1st Ex. Sess., Ch. 12, Sec. 38. (AB 17 1x) Effective September 21, 2011. Operative October 1, 2011, by Sec. 46 of Ch. 12.)

4501.5.

Every person confined in a state prison of this state who commits a battery upon the person of any individual who is not himself a person confined therein shall be guilty of a felony and shall be imprisoned in the state prison for two, three, or four years, to be served consecutively.

(Amended by Stats. 1978, Ch. 579.)

4502.

(a) Every person who, while at or confined in any penal institution, while being conveyed to or from any penal institution, or while under the custody of officials, officers, or employees of any penal institution, possesses or carries upon his or her person or has under his or her custody or control any instrument or weapon of the kind commonly known as a blackjack, slungshot, billy, sandclub, sandbag, or metal knuckles, any explosive substance, or fixed ammunition, any dirk or dagger or sharp instrument, any pistol, revolver, or other firearm, or any tear gas or tear gas weapon, is guilty of a felony and shall be punished by imprisonment pursuant to subdivision (h) of Section 1170 for two, three, or four years, to be served consecutively.

(b) Every person who, while at or confined in any penal institution, while being conveyed to or from any penal institution, or while under the custody of officials, officers, or employees of any penal institution, manufactures or attempts to manufacture any instrument or weapon of the kind commonly known as a blackjack, slungshot, billy, sandclub, sandbag, or metal knuckles, any explosive substance, or fixed ammunition, any dirk or dagger or sharp instrument, any pistol, revolver, or other firearm, or any tear gas or tear gas weapon, is guilty of a felony and shall be punished by imprisonment pursuant to subdivision (h) of Section 1170 for 16 months, or two or three years, to be served consecutively.

(c) For purposes of this section, "penal institution" means the state prison, a prison road camp, prison forestry camp, or other prison camp or farm, or a county jail or county road camp.

(Amended by Stats. 2011, Ch. 15, Sec. 485. (AB 109) Effective April 4, 2011. Operative October 1, 2011, by Sec. 636 of Ch. 15, as amended by Stats. 2011, Ch. 39, Sec. 68.)

4503.

Any person confined therein who holds as hostage any person within any prison or facility under the jurisdiction of the Director of Corrections, or who by force or threat of force holds any person or persons against their will in defiance of official orders within any such prison or facility, shall be guilty of a felony and shall be imprisoned in the state prison for three, five, or seven years to be served consecutively.

(Amended by Stats. 1978, Ch. 579.)

4504.

For purposes of this chapter:

(a) A person is deemed confined in a "state prison" if he or she is confined in any of the prisons and institutions specified in Section 5003 by order made pursuant to law, including, but not limited to, commitments to the Department of Corrections and Rehabilitation or the Department of Corrections and Rehabilitation, Division of Juvenile Justice, regardless of the purpose of the confinement and regardless of the validity of the order directing the confinement, until a judgment of a competent court setting aside the order becomes final.

(b) A person is deemed "confined in" a prison although, at the time of the offense, he or she is temporarily outside its walls or bounds for the purpose of serving on a work detail, for the purpose of confinement in a local correctional institution pending trial, or for any other purpose for which a prisoner may be allowed temporarily outside the walls or bounds of the prison. A prisoner who has been released on parole is not deemed "confined in" a prison for purposes of this chapter.

(Amended by Stats. 2015, Ch. 499, Sec. 5. (SB 795) Effective January 1, 2016.)

CHAPTER 2. Escapes and Rescues [4530 - 4550]

(Chapter 2 added by Stats. 1941, Ch. 106.)

ARTICLE 1. Escapes [4530 - 4537]

(Article 1 added by Stats. 1941, Ch. 106.)

4530.

(a) Every prisoner confined in a state prison who, by force or violence, escapes or attempts to escape therefrom and every prisoner committed to a state prison who, by force or violence, escapes or attempts to escape while being conveyed to or from that prison or any other state prison, or any prison road camp, prison forestry camp, or other prison camp or prison farm or any other place while under the custody of prison officials, officers or employees; or who, by force or violence, escapes or attempts to escape from any prison road camp, prison forestry camp, or other prison camp or prison farm or other place while under the custody of prison officials, officers or employees; or who, by force or violence, escapes or attempts to escape while at work outside or away from prison under custody of prison officials, officers, or employees, is punishable by imprisonment in the state prison for a term of two, four, or six years. The second term of imprisonment of a person convicted under this subdivision shall commence from the time he or she would otherwise have been discharged from prison. No additional probation report shall be required with respect to that offense.

(b) Every prisoner who commits an escape or attempts an escape as described in subdivision (a), without force or violence, is punishable by imprisonment in the state prison for 16 months, or two or three years to be served consecutively. No additional probation report shall be required with respect to such offense.

(c) The willful failure of a prisoner who is employed or continuing his education, or who is authorized to secure employment or education, or who is temporarily released pursuant to Section 2690, 2910, or 6254, or Section 3306 of the Welfare and Institutions Code, to return to the place of confinement not later than the expiration of a period during which he or she is authorized to be away from the place of confinement, is an escape from the place of confinement punishable as provided in this section. A conviction of a violation of this subdivision, not involving force or violence, shall not be charged as a prior felony conviction in any subsequent prosecution for a public offense.

(Amended (as amended by Stats. 2011, Ch. 15, Sec. 486) by Stats. 2011, 1st Ex. Sess., Ch. 12, Sec. 39. (AB 17 1x) Effective September 21, 2011. Operative October 1, 2011, by Sec. 46 of Ch. 12.)

4530.5.

For the purposes of punishing escapes or attempts to escape under Section 4530, a person is deemed confined in a "state prison" if he is an adult prisoner confined in the Deuel Vocational Institution.

(Added by Stats. 1982, Ch. 1104, Sec. 2.)

4532.

(a) (1) Every prisoner arrested and booked for, charged with, or convicted of a misdemeanor, and every person committed under the terms of Section 5654, 5656, or 5677 of the Welfare and Institutions Code as an inebriate, who is confined in any county or city jail, prison, industrial farm, or industrial road camp, is engaged on any county road or other county work, is in the lawful custody of any officer or person, is employed or continuing in his or her regular educational program or authorized to secure employment or education away from the place of confinement, pursuant to the Cobey Work Furlough Law (Section 1208), is authorized for temporary release for family emergencies or for purposes preparatory to his or her return to the community pursuant to Section 4018.6, or is a participant in a home detention program pursuant to Section 1203.016, 1203.017, or 1203.018, and who thereafter escapes or attempts to escape from the county or city jail, prison, industrial farm, or industrial road camp or from the custody of the officer or person in charge of him or her while engaged in or going to or returning from the county work or from the custody of any officer or person in whose lawful custody he or she is, or from the place of confinement in a home detention program pursuant to Section 1203.016, 1203.017, or 1203.018 is guilty of a felony and, if the escape or attempt to escape was not by force or violence, is punishable by imprisonment in the state prison for a determinate term of one year and one day, or in a county jail not exceeding one year.

(2) If the escape or attempt to escape described in paragraph (1) is committed by force or violence, the person is guilty of a felony, punishable by imprisonment in the state prison for two, four, or six years to be served consecutively, or in a county jail not exceeding one year. When the second term of imprisonment is to be served in a county jail, it shall commence from the time the prisoner otherwise would have been discharged from jail.

(3) A conviction of a violation of this subdivision, or a violation of subdivision (b) involving a participant of a home detention program pursuant to Section 1203.016, 1203.017, or 1203.018 that is not committed by force or violence, shall not be charged as a prior felony conviction in any subsequent prosecution for a public offense.

(b) (1) Every prisoner arrested and booked for, charged with, or convicted of a felony, and every person committed by order of the juvenile court, who is confined in any county or city jail, prison, industrial farm, or industrial road camp, is engaged on any county road or other county work, is in the lawful custody of any officer or person, or is confined pursuant to Section 4011.9, is a participant in a home detention program pursuant to Section 1203.016, 1203.017, or 1203.018 who escapes or attempts to escape from a county or city jail, prison, industrial farm, or industrial road camp or from the custody of the officer or person in charge of him or her while engaged in or going to or returning from the county work or from the custody of any officer or person in whose lawful custody he or she is, or from confinement pursuant to Section 4011.9, or from the place of confinement in a home detention program pursuant to Section 1203.016, is guilty of a felony and, if the escape or attempt to escape was not by force or violence, is punishable by imprisonment in the state prison for 16 months, two years, or three years, to be served consecutively, or in a county jail not exceeding one year.

(2) If the escape or attempt to escape described in paragraph (1) is committed by force or violence, the person is guilty of a felony, punishable by imprisonment in the state prison for a full term of two, four, or six years to be served consecutively to any other term of imprisonment, commencing from the time the person otherwise would have been released from imprisonment and the term shall not be subject to reduction pursuant to subdivision (a) of Section 1170.1, or in a county jail for a consecutive term not to exceed one year, that term to commence from the time the prisoner otherwise would have been discharged from jail.

(c) Notwithstanding any other law, every inmate who is a participant in an alternative custody program pursuant to Section 1170.05 who escapes or attempts to escape from the program is guilty of a misdemeanor.

(d) (1) Except in unusual cases where the interests of justice would best be served if the person is granted probation, probation shall not be granted to any person who is convicted of a felony offense under this section in that he or she escaped or attempted to escape from a secure main jail facility, from a court building, or while being transported between the court building and the jail facility.

(2) In any case in which a person is convicted of a violation of this section designated as a misdemeanor, he or she shall be confined in a county jail for not less than 90 days nor more than one year except in unusual cases where the interests of justice would best be served by the granting of probation.

(3) For the purposes of this subdivision, "main jail facility" means the facility used for the detention of persons pending arraignment, after arraignment, during trial, and upon sentence or commitment. The facility shall not include an industrial farm, industrial road camp, work furlough facility, or any other nonsecure facility used primarily for sentenced prisoners. As used in this subdivision, "secure" means that the facility contains an outer perimeter characterized by the use of physically restricting construction, hardware, and procedures designed to eliminate ingress and egress from the facility except through a closely supervised gate or doorway.

(4) If the court grants probation under this subdivision, it shall specify the reason or reasons for that order on the court record.

(5) Any sentence imposed under this subdivision shall be served consecutive to any other sentence in effect or pending.

(e) The willful failure of a prisoner, whether convicted of a felony or a misdemeanor, to return to his or her place of confinement no later than the expiration of the period that he or she was authorized to be away from that place of confinement, is an escape from that place of confinement. This subdivision applies to a prisoner who is employed or continuing in his or her regular educational program, authorized to secure employment or education pursuant to the Cobey Work Furlough Law (Section 1208), authorized for temporary release for family emergencies or for purposes preparatory to his or her return to the community pursuant to Section 4018.6, or permitted to participate in a home detention program pursuant to Section 1203.016, 1203.017, or 1203.018. A prisoner convicted of a misdemeanor who willfully fails to return to his or her place of confinement under this subdivision shall be punished as provided in paragraph (1) of subdivision (a). A prisoner convicted of a felony who willfully fails to return to his or her place of confinement shall be punished as provided in paragraph (1) of subdivision (b). *(Amended by Stats. 2011, Ch. 15, Sec. 487. (AB 109) Effective April 4, 2011. Operative October 1, 2011, by Sec. 636 of Ch. 15, as amended by Stats. 2011, Ch. 39, Sec. 68.)*

4533.
Every keeper of a prison, sheriff, deputy sheriff, or jailer, or person employed as a guard, who fraudulently contrives, procures, aids, connives at, or voluntarily permits the escape of any prisoner in custody, is punishable by imprisonment pursuant to subdivision (h) of Section 1170, and fine not exceeding ten thousand dollars ($10,000). *(Amended by Stats. 2011, Ch. 15, Sec. 488. (AB 109) Effective April 4, 2011. Operative October 1, 2011, by Sec. 636 of Ch. 15, as amended by Stats. 2011, Ch. 39, Sec. 68.)*

4534.
Any person who willfully assists any paroled prisoner whose parole has been revoked, any escapee, any prisoner confined in any prison or jail, or any person in the lawful custody of any officer or person, to escape, or in an attempt to escape from such prison or jail, or custody, is punishable as provided in Section 4533. *(Amended by Stats. 1980, Ch. 676, Sec. 257.)*

4535.
Every person who carries or sends into a prison or jail anything useful to aid a prisoner or inmate in making his escape, with intent thereby to facilitate the escape of any prisoner or inmate confined therein, is guilty of a felony. *(Amended by Stats. 1976, Ch. 1139.)*

4536.
(a) Every person committed to a state hospital or other public or private mental health facility as a mentally disordered sex offender, who escapes from or who escapes while being conveyed to or from such state hospital or other public or private mental health facility, is punishable by imprisonment in the state prison or in the county jail not to exceed one year. The term imposed pursuant to this section shall be served consecutively to any other sentence or commitment.

(b) The medical director or person in charge of a state hospital or other public or private mental health facility to which a person has been committed as a mentally disordered sex offender shall promptly notify the chief of police of the city in which the hospital or facility is located, or the sheriff of the county if the hospital or facility is located in an unincorporated area, of the escape of the person, and shall request the assistance of the chief of police or sheriff in apprehending the person, and shall, within 48 hours of the escape of the person, orally notify the court that made the commitment, the prosecutor in the case, and the Department of Justice of the escape. *(Amended by Stats. 2012, Ch. 43, Sec. 56. (SB 1023) Effective June 27, 2012.)*

4536.5.
The medical director or person in charge of a state hospital or other public or private mental health facility to which a person has been committed under the provisions of Article 4 (commencing with Section 6600) of Chapter 2 of Part 2 of the Welfare and Institutions Code, shall promptly notify the Department of Corrections' Sexually Violent Predator Parole Coordinator, the chief of police of the city in which the hospital or facility is located, or the sheriff of the county if the hospital or facility is located in an unincorporated area, of the escape of the person, and shall request the assistance of the chief of police or sheriff in apprehending the person, and shall, within 48 hours of the escape of the person, orally notify the court that made the commitment, the prosecutor in the case, and the Department of Justice of the escape. *(Amended by Stats. 1999, Ch. 83, Sec. 156. Effective January 1, 2000.)*

4537.
(a) The person in charge of any secure detention facility, including, but not limited to, a prison, a juvenile hall, a county jail, or any institution under the jurisdiction of the

California Youth Authority, shall promptly notify the chief of police of the city in which the facility is located, or the sheriff of the county if the facility is located in an unincorporated area, of an escape by a person in its custody.

(b) The person in charge of any secure detention facility under the jurisdiction of the Department of Corrections or the Department of the Youth Authority shall release the name of, and any descriptive information about, any person who has escaped from custody to other law enforcement agencies, or to other persons if the release of the information would be necessary to assist in recapturing the person or to protect the public from substantial physical harm.

(c) In addition to the requirements of subdivisions (a) and (b), in cases of escape by persons in the custody of the Department of Corrections who have been convicted of a felony listed in subdivision (c) of Section 667.5 or who have effected the escape by force or violence as proscribed by subdivision (a) of Section 4530, prompt notification shall be given to the newspapers of general circulation within the county in which the escape occurred, and to television stations regularly broadcasting news into and within the county, accompanied by a photograph and description of the escapee. *(Amended by Stats. 1990, Ch. 819, Sec. 1.)*

ARTICLE 2. Rescues [4550- 4550.]

(Article 2 added by Stats. 1941, Ch. 106.)

4550.
Every person who rescues or attempts to rescue, or aids another person in rescuing or attempting to rescue any prisoner from any prison, or prison road camp or any jail or county road camp, or from any officer or person having him or her in lawful custody, is punishable as follows:

(a) If the prisoner was in custody upon a conviction of a felony punishable with death, by imprisonment pursuant to subdivision (h) of Section 1170 for two, three or four years.

(b) If the prisoner was in custody otherwise than as specified in subdivision (a), by imprisonment pursuant to subdivision (h) of Section 1170, or by imprisonment in the county jail not to exceed one year. *(Amended by Stats. 2011, Ch. 15, Sec. 490. (AB 109) Effective April 4, 2011. Operative October 1, 2011, by Sec. 636 of Ch. 15, as amended by Stats. 2011, Ch. 39, Sec. 68.)*

CHAPTER 3. Unauthorized Communications With Prisons and Prisoners [4570 - 4577]

(Chapter 3 added by Stats. 1941, Ch. 106.)

4570.
Every person who, without the permission of the warden or other officer in charge of any State prison, or prison road camp, or prison forestry camp, or other prison camp or prison farm or any other place where prisoners of the State prison are located under the custody of prison officials, officers or employees, or any jail, or any county road camp in this State, communicates with any prisoner or person detained therein, or brings therein or takes therefrom any letter, writing, literature, or reading matter to or from any prisoner or person confined therein, is guilty of a misdemeanor. *(Amended by Stats. 1943, Ch. 108.)*

4570.1.
Every person who, without permission of the peace officer or corrections officer in charge of any vehicle, bus, van or automobile used for the transportation of prisoners, delivers a written communication to any prisoner or person detained therein, or being escorted to or from that vehicle, or takes from or gives to the prisoner any item, is guilty of a misdemeanor. *(Added by Stats. 1982, Ch. 1134, Sec. 1.)*

4570.5.
Every person who falsely indentifies himself either verbally or by presenting any fraudulent written instrument to prison officials, officers, or employees of any state prison, prison road camp, or prison forestry camp, or other prison camp or prison farm, or any jail, or any county industrial farm, or any county road camp, for the purpose of securing admission to the premises or grounds of any such prison, camp, farm, or jail, and such person would not otherwise qualify for admission, is guilty of a misdemeanor. *(Added by Stats. 1969, Ch. 424.)*

4571.
Every person who, having been previously convicted of a felony and confined in any State prison in this State, without the consent of the warden or other officer in charge of any State prison or prison road camp, or prison forestry camp, or other prison camp or prison farm or any other place where prisoners of the State prison are located under the custody of prison officials, officers or employees, or any jail or any county road camp in this State, comes upon the grounds of any such institution, or lands belonging or adjacent thereto, is guilty of a felony. *(Amended by Stats. 1943, Ch. 108.)*

4573.
(a) Except when otherwise authorized by law, or when authorized by the person in charge of the prison or other institution referred to in this section or by an officer of the institution empowered by the person in charge of the institution to give the authorization, any person, who knowingly brings or sends into, or knowingly assists in bringing into, or sending into, any state prison, prison road camp, prison forestry camp, or other prison camp or prison farm or any other place where prisoners of the state are located under the custody of prison officials, officers or employees, or into any county, city and county, or city jail, road camp, farm or other place where prisoners or inmates are located under custody of any sheriff, chief of police, peace officer, probation officer or employees, or within the grounds belonging to the institution, any controlled substance, the possession of which is prohibited by Division 10 (commencing with Section 11000) of the Health and Safety Code, any device, contrivance, instrument, or paraphernalia intended to be used for unlawfully injecting or consuming a controlled substance, is guilty of a felony punishable by imprisonment pursuant to subdivision (h) of Section 1170 for two, three, or four years.

(b) The prohibitions and sanctions addressed in this section shall be clearly and prominently posted outside of, and at the entrance to, the grounds of all detention facilities under the jurisdiction of, or operated by, the state or any city, county, or city and county. *(Amended by Stats. 2011, Ch. 15, Sec. 491. (AB 109) Effective April 4, 2011. Operative October 1, 2011, by Sec. 636 of Ch. 15, as amended by Stats. 2011, Ch. 39, Sec. 68.)*

4573.5.
Any person who knowingly brings into any state prison or other institution under the jurisdiction of the Department of Corrections, or into any prison camp, prison farm, or any other place where prisoners or inmates of these institutions are located under the custody of prison or institution officials, officers, or employees, or into any county, city and county, or city jail, road camp, farm or any other institution or place where prisoners or inmates are being held under the custody of any sheriff, chief of police, peace officer, probation officer, or employees, or within the grounds belonging to any institution or place, any alcoholic beverage, any drugs, other than controlled substances, in any manner, shape, form, dispenser, or container, or any device, contrivance, instrument, or paraphernalia intended to be used for unlawfully injecting or consuming any drug other than controlled substances, without having authority so to do by the rules of the Department of Corrections, the rules of the prison, institution, camp, farm, place, or jail,

or by the specific authorization of the warden, superintendent, jailer, or other person in charge of the prison, jail, institution, camp, farm, or place, is guilty of a felony.
The prohibitions and sanctions addressed in this section shall be clearly and prominently posted outside of, and at the entrance to, the grounds of all detention facilities under the jurisdiction of, or operated by, the state or any city, county, or city and county.
(Amended by Stats. 1990, Ch. 1580, Sec. 3.)
4573.6.
(a) Any person who knowingly has in his or her possession in any state prison, prison road camp, prison forestry camp, or other prison camp or prison farm or any place where prisoners of the state are located under the custody of prison officials, officers, or employees, or in any county, city and county, or city jail, road camp, farm, or any place or institution, where prisoners or inmates are being held under the custody of any sheriff, chief of police, peace officer, probation officer, or employees, or within the grounds belonging to any jail, road camp, farm, place or institution, any controlled substances, the possession of which is prohibited by Division 10 (commencing with Section 11000) of the Health and Safety Code, any device, contrivance, instrument, or paraphernalia intended to be used for unlawfully injecting or consuming controlled substances, without being authorized to so possess the same by the rules of the Department of Corrections, rules of the prison or jail, institution, camp, farm or place, or by the specific authorization of the warden, superintendent, jailer, or other person in charge of the prison, jail, institution, camp, farm or place, is guilty of a felony punishable by imprisonment pursuant to subdivision (h) of Section 1170 for two, three, or four years.
(b) The prohibitions and sanctions addressed in this section shall be clearly and prominently posted outside of, and at the entrance to, the grounds of all detention facilities under the jurisdiction of, or operated by, the state or any city, county, or city and county.
(Amended by Stats. 2011, Ch. 15, Sec. 492. (AB 109) Effective April 4, 2011. Operative October 1, 2011, by Sec. 636 of Ch. 15, as amended by Stats. 2011, Ch. 39, Sec. 68.)
4573.8.
Any person who knowingly has in his or her possession in any state prison, prison road camp, prison forestry camp, or other prison camp or prison farm or any place where prisoners of the state are located under the custody of prison officials, officers, or employees, or in any county, city and county, or city jail, road camp, farm, or any place or institution, where prisoners or inmates are being held under the custody of any sheriff, chief of police, peace officer, probation officer, or employees, or within the grounds belonging to any jail, road camp, farm, place, or institution, drugs in any manner, shape, form, dispenser, or container, any device, contrivance, instrument, or paraphernalia intended to be used for unlawfully injecting or consuming drugs, or alcoholic beverages, without being authorized to possess the same by rules of the Department of Corrections, rules of the prison or jail, institution, camp, farm, or place, or by the specific authorization of the warden, superintendent, jailer, or other person in charge of the prison, jail, institution, camp, farm, or place, is guilty of a felony.
The prohibitions and sanctions addressed in this section shall be clearly and prominently posted outside of, and at the entrance to, the grounds of all detention facilities under the jurisdiction of, or operated by, the state or any city, county, or city and county.
(Added by Stats. 1990, Ch. 1580, Sec. 5.)
4573.9.
(a) Notwithstanding any other provision of law, any person, other than a person held in custody, who sells, furnishes, administers, or gives away, or offers to sell, furnish, administer, or give away to any person held in custody in any state prison or other institution under the jurisdiction of the Department of Corrections, or in any prison camp, prison farm, or any other place where prisoners or inmates of these institutions are located under the custody of prison institution officials, officers, or employees, or in any county, city and county, or city jail, road camp, farm, or any other institution or place where prisoners or inmates are being held under the custody of any sheriff, chief of police, peace officer, probation officer, or employees, or within the grounds belonging to any institution or place, any controlled substance, the possession of which is prohibited by Division 10 (commencing with Section 11000) of the Health and Safety Code, if the recipient is not authorized to possess the same by the rules of the Department of Corrections, rules of the prison or jail, institution, camp, farm, or place, or by the specific authorization of the warden, superintendent, jailer, or other person in charge of the prison, jail, institution, camp, farm, or place, is guilty of a felony punishable by imprisonment pursuant to subdivision (h) of Section 1170 for two, four, or six years.
(b) The prohibitions and sanctions addressed in this section shall be clearly and prominently posted outside of, and at the entrance to, the grounds of all detention facilities under the jurisdiction of, or operated by, the state or any city, county, or city and county.
(Amended by Stats. 2011, Ch. 15, Sec. 493. (AB 109) Effective April 4, 2011. Operative October 1, 2011, by Sec. 636 of Ch. 15, as amended by Stats. 2011, Ch. 39, Sec. 68.)
4574.
(a) Except when otherwise authorized by law, or when authorized by the person in charge of the prison or other institution referred to in this section or by an officer of the institution empowered by the person in charge of the institution to give such authorization, any person, who knowingly brings or sends into, or knowingly assists in bringing into, or sending into, any state prison or prison road camp or prison forestry camp, or other prison camp or prison farm or any other place where prisoners of the state prison are located under the custody of prison officials, officers or employees, or any jail or any county road camp in this state, or within the grounds belonging or adjacent to any such institution, any firearms, deadly weapons, or explosives, and any person who, while lawfully confined in a jail or county road camp possesses therein any firearm, deadly weapon, explosive, tear gas or tear gas weapon, is guilty of a felony and punishable by imprisonment pursuant to subdivision (h) of Section 1170 for two, three, or four years.
(b) Except as provided in subdivision (a), any person who knowingly brings or sends into those places any tear gas or tear gas weapons which results in the release of such tear gas or use of such weapon is guilty of a felony and punishable by imprisonment pursuant to subdivision (h) of Section 1170 for two, three, or four years.
(c) Except as provided in subdivision (a), any person who knowingly brings or sends into those places any tear gas or tear gas weapons is guilty of a misdemeanor and punishable by imprisonment in the county jail not exceeding six months, or by fine not exceeding one thousand dollars ($1,000), or by both such fine and imprisonment.
(Amended by Stats. 2011, Ch. 15, Sec. 494. (AB 109) Effective April 4, 2011. Operative October 1, 2011, by Sec. 636 of Ch. 15, as amended by Stats. 2011, Ch. 39, Sec. 68.)
4575.
(a) Any person in a local correctional facility who possesses a wireless communication device, including, but not limited to, a cellular telephone, pager, or wireless Internet device, who is not authorized to possess that item is guilty of a misdemeanor, punishable by a fine of not more than one thousand dollars ($1,000).
(b) Any person housed in a local correctional facility who possesses any tobacco products in any form, including snuff products, smoking paraphernalia, any device that is intended to be used for ingesting or consuming tobacco, or any container or dispenser used for any of those products, is guilty of an infraction, punishable by a fine not exceeding two hundred fifty dollars ($250).
(c) Money collected pursuant to this section shall be placed into the inmate welfare fund, as specified in Section 4025.
(d) Any person housed in a local correctional facility who possesses a handcuff key who is not authorized to possess that item is guilty of a misdemeanor, punishable by imprisonment in a county jail not exceeding six months, or by a fine of up to one

thousand dollars ($1,000), or by both that imprisonment and fine. As used in this subdivision, "handcuff key" means any device designed or intended to open or unlatch a handcuff.
(e) Subdivision (b) shall only apply to a person in a local correctional facility in a county in which the board of supervisors has adopted an ordinance or passed a resolution banning tobacco in its correctional facilities.
(Amended by Stats. 2008, Ch. 190, Sec. 1. Effective January 1, 2009.)
4576.
(a) Except as otherwise authorized by law, or when authorized by either the person in charge of the prison or other institution under the jurisdiction of the Department of Corrections and Rehabilitation or an officer of the institution empowered to give that authorization, a person who possesses with the intent to deliver, or delivers, to an inmate or ward in the custody of the department any cellular telephone or other wireless communication device or any component thereof, including, but not limited to, a subscriber identity module (SIM card) or memory storage device, is guilty of a misdemeanor, punishable by imprisonment in the county jail not exceeding six months, a fine not to exceed five thousand dollars ($5,000) for each device, or both that fine and imprisonment.
(b) (1) If a person visiting an inmate or ward in the custody of the department, upon being searched or subjected to a metal detector, is found to be in possession of a cellular telephone or other wireless communication device or any component thereof, including, but not limited to, a SIM card or memory storage device, that device or component shall be subject to confiscation but shall be returned on the same day the person visits the inmate or ward, unless the cellular telephone or other wireless communication device or any component thereof is held as evidence in a case where the person is cited for a violation of subdivision (a).
(2) If, upon investigation, it is determined that no prosecution will take place, the cellular telephone or other wireless communication device or any component thereof shall be returned to the owner at the owner's expense.
(3) Notice of this provision shall be posted in all areas where visitors are searched prior to visitation with an inmate or ward in the custody of the department.
(c) Any inmate who is found to be in possession of a wireless communication device shall be subject to time credit denial or loss of up to 90 days.
(d) A person who brings, without authorization, a wireless communication device within the secure perimeter of any prison or institution housing offenders under the jurisdiction of the department is deemed to have given his or her consent to the department using available technology to prevent that wireless device from sending or receiving telephone calls or other forms of electronic communication. Notice of this provision shall be posted at all public entry gates of the prison or institution.
(e) The department shall not access data or communications that have been captured using available technology from unauthorized use of a wireless communication device except after obtaining a valid search warrant.
(f) The department shall not capture data or communications from an authorized wireless communication device, except as already authorized under existing law.
(g) The department shall not access data or communications that have been captured using available technology from an authorized wireless communication device, except as already authorized under existing law.
(h) If the available technology to prevent wireless communications from sending and receiving telephone calls or other forms of electronic communication extends beyond the secure perimeter of the prison or institution, the department shall take all reasonable actions to correct the problem.
(i) Any contractor or employee of a contractor or the department who knowingly and willfully, without authorization, obtains, discloses, or uses confidential information in violation of subdivision (e), (f), or (g) shall be subject to an administrative fine or civil penalty not to exceed five thousand dollars ($5,000) for a first violation, or ten thousand dollars ($10,000) for a second violation, or twenty-five thousand dollars ($25,000) for a third or subsequent violation.
(j) Nothing in this section prohibits the department from obtaining electronic communications that the department could have lawfully obtained prior to the effective date of this section.
(Added by Stats. 2011, Ch. 500, Sec. 1. (SB 26) Effective October 6, 2011.)
4577.
(a) Except as provided in subdivisions (b), (c), and (d), a person who knowingly and intentionally operates an unmanned aircraft system on or above the grounds of a state prison, a jail, or a juvenile hall, camp, or ranch is guilty of an infraction, punishable by a fine of five hundred dollars ($500).
(b) This section does not apply to a person employed by the prison who operates the unmanned aircraft system within the scope of his or her employment, or a person who receives prior permission from the Department of Corrections and Rehabilitation to operate the unmanned aircraft system over the prison.
(c) This section does not apply to a person employed by the jail who operates the unmanned aircraft system within the scope of his or her employment, or a person who receives prior permission from the county sheriff to operate the unmanned aircraft system over the jail.
(d) This section does not apply to a person employed by the county department that operates the juvenile hall, camp, or ranch who operates the unmanned aircraft system within the scope of his or her employment, or a person who receives prior permission from the county department that operates the juvenile hall, camp, or ranch to operate the unmanned aircraft system over the juvenile hall, camp, or ranch.
(e) For purposes of this section, the following definitions apply:
(1) "Unmanned aircraft" means an aircraft that is operated without the possibility of direct human intervention from within or on the aircraft.
(2) "Unmanned aircraft system" means an unmanned aircraft and associated elements, including, but not limited to, communication links and the components that control the unmanned aircraft that are required for the pilot in command to operate safely and efficiently in the national airspace system.
(Added by Stats. 2018, Ch. 333, Sec. 1. (SB 1355) Effective January 1, 2019.)

CHAPTER 4. Demolishing Prisons and Jails [4600- 4600.]

(Chapter 4 added by Stats. 1941, Ch. 106.)
4600.
(a) Every person who willfully and intentionally breaks down, pulls down, or otherwise destroys or injures any jail, prison, or any public property in any jail or prison, is punishable by a fine not exceeding ten thousand dollars ($10,000), and by imprisonment pursuant to subdivision (h) of Section 1170, except that where the damage or injury to any city, city and county, or county jail property or prison property is determined to be nine hundred fifty dollars ($950) or less, that person is guilty of a misdemeanor.
(b) In any case in which a person is convicted of violating this section, the court may order the defendant to make restitution to the public entity that owns the property damaged by the defendant. The court shall specify in the order that the public entity that owns the property damaged by the defendant shall not enforce the order until the defendant satisfies all outstanding fines, penalties, assessments, restitution fines, and restitution orders.

(Amended by Stats. 2011, Ch. 15, Sec. 495. (AB 109) Effective April 4, 2011. Operative October 1, 2011, by Sec. 636 of Ch. 15, as amended by Stats. 2011, Ch. 39, Sec. 68.)

CHAPTER 5. Trials of Prisoners [4700.1 - 4703]

(Chapter 5 added by Stats. 1941, Ch. 106.)

4700.1.

For any trial or hearing referred to in Section 4750, the sheriff of the county where such trial or hearing is had and the person in charge of the prison may agree that the county shall transport prisoners in a state prison to and from such prison. Upon such agreement, the county, and not the Department of Corrections, shall perform the transportation referred to in this section.

(Amended by Stats. 1986, Ch. 1310, Sec. 6.)

4701.

The jurisdiction of a criminal action for escaping from any State prison is in any county of the State.

(Added by Stats. 1941, Ch. 106.)

4702.

Whenever any prisoner confined in a jail established and maintained by the sheriff in another county, is tried for any offense committed in such jail or for escaping or attempting to escape therefrom, the venue shall be in the county establishing and maintaining such jail and the costs shall be charged against that county.

(Added by Stats. 1941, Ch. 106.)

4703.

With the concurrence of the Attorney General, the district attorney may transfer the responsibility for the prosecution of any crime committed by prisoners in physical custody in the state prisons in the district attorney's county. As used in this section, crimes committed while in physical custody shall include escapes and attempted escapes but shall not include any crimes committed while a prisoner has been conditionally released from state prison on work furlough, parole, or upon any other conditional release where the inmate is in constructive but not actual physical custody.

(Amended by Stats. 1982, Ch. 147, Sec. 3. Effective April 5, 1982.)

CHAPTER 6. Local Expenses [4750 - 4758]

(Chapter 6 added by Stats. 1986, Ch. 1310, Sec. 8.)

4750.

A city, county, or superior court shall be entitled to reimbursement for reasonable and necessary costs connected with state prisons or prisoners in connection with any of the following:

(a) Any crime committed at a state prison, whether by a prisoner, employee, or other person.

With respect to a prisoner, "crime committed at a state prison" as used in this subdivision, includes, but is not limited to, crimes committed by the prisoner while detained in local facilities as a result of a transfer pursuant to Section 2910 or 6253, or in conjunction with any hearing, proceeding, or other activity for which reimbursement is otherwise provided by this section.

(b) Any crime committed by a prisoner in furtherance of an escape. Any crime committed by an escaped prisoner within 10 days after the escape and within 100 miles of the facility from which the escape occurred shall be presumed to have been a crime committed in furtherance of an escape.

(c) Any hearing on any return of a writ of habeas corpus prosecuted by or on behalf of a prisoner.

(d) Any trial or hearing on the question of the sanity of a prisoner.

(e) Any costs not otherwise reimbursable under Section 1557 or any other related provision in connection with any extradition proceeding for any prisoner released to hold.

(f) Any costs incurred by a coroner in connection with the death of a prisoner.

(g) Any costs incurred in transporting a prisoner within the host county or as requested by the prison facility or incurred for increased security while a prisoner is outside a state prison.

(h) Any crime committed by a state inmate at a state hospital for the care, treatment, and education of the mentally disordered, as specified in Section 7200 of the Welfare and Institutions Code.

(i) Commencing January 1, 2012, any nontreatment costs described in subdivision (b) of Section 4117 of the Welfare and Institutions Code.

(j) No city, county, or other jurisdiction may file, and the state may not reimburse, a claim pursuant to this section that is presented to the Department of Corrections and Rehabilitation or to any other agency or department of the state more than six months after the close of the month in which the costs were incurred.

(Amended by Stats. 2011, Ch. 660, Sec. 1. (AB 1016) Effective January 1, 2012.)

4751.

Costs incurred by a city or county include all of the following:

(a) Costs of law enforcement agencies in connection with any matter set forth in Section 4750, including the investigation or evaluation of any of those matters regardless of whether a crime has in fact occurred, a hearing held, or an offense prosecuted.

(b) Costs of participation in any trial or hearing of any matter set forth in Section 4750, including costs for the preparation for the trial, pretrial hearing, actual trial or hearing, expert witness fees, the costs of guarding or keeping the prisoner, the transportation of the prisoner, the costs of appeal, and the execution of the sentence. The cost of detention in a city or county correctional facility shall include the same cost factors as are utilized by the Department of Corrections in determining the cost of prisoner care in state correctional facilities.

(c) The costs of the prosecuting attorney in investigating, evaluating, or prosecuting cases related to any matter set forth in Section 4750, whether or not the prosecuting attorney decides to commence legal action.

(d) Costs incurred by the public defender or court-appointed attorney with respect to any matter set forth in Section 4750.

(e) Any costs incurred for providing training in the investigation or prosecution associated with any matter set forth in Section 4750.

(f) Any other costs reasonably incurred by a county in connection with any matter set forth in Section 4750.

(Amended by Stats. 2005, Ch. 54, Sec. 1. Effective January 1, 2006.)

4751.5.

Costs incurred by a superior court include all of the following:

(a) Costs of any trial or hearing of any matter set forth in Section 4750, including costs for the preparation of the trial, pretrial hearing, and the actual trial or hearing.

(b) Any other costs reasonably incurred by a superior court in connection with any matter set forth in Section 4750.

(Added by Stats. 2004, Ch. 227, Sec. 85. Effective August 16, 2004.)

4752.

As used in this chapter, reasonable and necessary costs shall be based upon all operating costs, including the cost of elected officials, except superior court judges, while serving in line functions and including all administrative costs associated with providing the necessary services and securing reimbursement therefor. Administrative costs include a proportional allowance for overhead determined in accordance with current accounting practices.

(Amended by Stats. 2004, Ch. 227, Sec. 86. Effective August 16, 2004.)

4753.

A city or county shall designate an officer or agency to prepare a statement of costs that shall be reimbursed under this chapter.

The statement shall be sent to the Controller for approval. The statement may not include any costs that are incurred by a superior court, as described in Section 4751.5.

The Controller shall reimburse the city or county within 60 days after receipt of the statement or provide a written statement as to the reason for not making reimbursement at that time. If sufficient funds are not available, the Controller shall request the Director of Finance to include any amounts necessary to satisfy the claims in a request for a deficiency appropriation.

(Amended by Stats. 2004, Ch. 227, Sec. 87. Effective August 16, 2004.)

4753.5.

A superior court shall prepare a statement of costs that shall be reimbursed under this chapter. The state may not include any costs that are incurred by a city or county, as described in Section 4751. The statement shall be sent to the Administrative Office of the Courts for approval and reimbursement.

(Added by Stats. 2004, Ch. 227, Sec. 88. Effective August 16, 2004.)

4754.

As used in this chapter, "prisoner" means any person committed to a state prison, including a person who has been transferred to any other facility, has escaped, or is otherwise absent, but does not include a person while on parole.

(Added by Stats. 1986, Ch. 1310, Sec. 8.)

4755.

Whenever a person has entered upon a term of imprisonment in a penal or correctional institution, and whenever during the continuance of the term of imprisonment there is a detainer lodged against the prisoner by a law enforcement or prosecutorial agency of the state or its subdivisions, the Department of Corrections may do either of the following:

(a) Release the inmate to the agency lodging the detainer, within five days, or five court days if the law enforcement agency lodging the detainer is more than 400 miles from the county in which the institution is located, prior to the scheduled release date provided the inmate is kept in custody until the scheduled release date.

(b) Retain the inmate in custody up to five days, or five court days if the law enforcement agency lodging the detainer is more than 400 miles from the county in which the institution is located, after the scheduled release date to facilitate pickup by the agency lodging the detainer.

If a person has been retained in custody under this subdivision in response to the issuance of a warrant of arrest charging a particular offense and the defendant is released from custody following the retention period without pickup by the agency lodging the detainer, a subsequent court order shall be issued before the arrest of that person for the same offense which was charged in the prior warrant.

As used in this section "detainer" means a warrant of arrest.

(Amended by Stats. 1987, Ch. 1303, Sec. 7. Effective September 28, 1987.)

4758.

(a) A county shall be entitled to reimbursement for reasonable and necessary costs incurred by the county with respect to an inmate housed and treated at a state hospital in that county pursuant to Section 2684, including, but not limited to, any trial costs related to a crime committed at the hospital by an inmate housed at the hospital.

(b) Where an inmate referred for treatment to a state hospital pursuant to Section 2684 commits a crime during transportation from prison to the hospital, or commits a crime during transportation from the hospital to the prison, a county that prosecutes the defendant shall be entitled to reimbursement for the costs of prosecution.

(c) No city, county, or other jurisdiction may file, and the state may not reimburse, a claim pursuant to this section that is presented to the Department of Corrections and Rehabilitation or to any other agency or department of the state more than six months after the close of the month in which the costs were incurred.

(Amended by Stats. 2007, Ch. 175, Sec. 11. Effective August 24, 2007.)

TITLE 6. REPRIEVES, PARDONS AND COMMUTATIONS [4800 - 4906]

(Title 6 added by Stats. 1941, Ch. 106.)

CHAPTER 1. Powers and Duties of Governor [4800 - 4813]

(Chapter 1 added by Stats. 1941, Ch. 106.)

4800.

The general authority to grant reprieves, pardons and commutations of sentence is conferred upon the Governor by Section 8 of Article V of the Constitution of the State of California.

(Amended by Stats. 1969, Ch. 43.)

4801.

(a) The Board of Parole Hearings may report to the Governor, from time to time, the names of any and all persons imprisoned in any state prison who, in its judgment, ought to have a commutation of sentence or be pardoned and set at liberty on account of good conduct, or unusual term of sentence, or any other cause, including evidence of intimate partner battering and its effects. For purposes of this section, "intimate partner battering and its effects" may include evidence of the nature and effects of physical, emotional, or mental abuse upon the beliefs, perceptions, or behavior of victims of domestic violence if it appears the criminal behavior was the result of that victimization.

(b) (1) The board, in reviewing a prisoner's suitability for parole pursuant to Section 3041.5, shall give great weight to any information or evidence that, at the time of the commission of the crime, the prisoner had experienced intimate partner battering, but was convicted of an offense that occurred prior to August 29, 1996. The board shall state on the record the information or evidence that it considered pursuant to this subdivision, and the reasons for the parole decision. The board shall annually report to the Legislature and the Governor on the cases the board considered pursuant to this subdivision during the previous year, including the board's decisions and the specific and detailed findings of its investigations of these cases.

(2) The report for the Legislature to be submitted pursuant to paragraph (1) shall be submitted pursuant to Section 9795 of the Government Code.

(3) The fact that a prisoner has presented evidence of intimate partner battering cannot be used to support a finding that the prisoner lacks insight into his or her crime and its causes.

(c) When a prisoner committed his or her controlling offense, as defined in subdivision (a) of Section 3051, when he or she was 25 years of age or younger, the board, in reviewing a prisoner's suitability for parole pursuant to Section 3041.5, shall give great weight to the diminished culpability of youth as compared to adults, the hallmark

features of youth, and any subsequent growth and increased maturity of the prisoner in accordance with relevant case law.
(Amended by Stats. 2017, Ch. 684, Sec. 2.5. (SB 394) Effective January 1, 2018.)
4802.
In the case of a person twice convicted of felony, the application for pardon or commutation of sentence shall be made directly to the Governor, who shall transmit all papers and documents relied upon in support of and in opposition to the application to the Board of Parole Hearings.
(Amended by Stats. 2011, Ch. 437, Sec. 2. (AB 648) Effective January 1, 2012.)
4802.5.
The Governor shall make the application for a pardon and the application for a commutation available on the Governor's Office Internet Web site and all applications for a direct pardon received by the Governor shall be promptly forwarded to the Board of Parole Hearings for an investigation and recommendation to the Governor. Applications supported by a certificate of rehabilitation may be granted by the Governor without investigation and recommendation by the Board of Parole Hearings in accordance with Section 4852.16.
(Added by Stats. 2018, Ch. 824, Sec. 3. (AB 2845) Effective January 1, 2019.)
4803.
When an application is made to the Governor for pardon or commutation of sentence, or when an application has been referred to the Board of Parole Hearings, the Governor or the board may require the judge of the court before which the conviction was had, or the district attorney by whom the action was prosecuted, to furnish the Governor or the board, without delay, with a summarized statement of the facts proved on the trial, and of any other facts having reference to the propriety of granting or refusing said application, together with his or her recommendation for or against the granting of the same and his or her reason for such recommendation.
(Amended by Stats. 2011, Ch. 437, Sec. 3. (AB 648) Effective January 1, 2012.)
4804.
At least 10 days before the Governor acts upon an application for a pardon, written notice of the intention to apply therefor, signed by the person applying, must be served upon the district attorney of the county where the conviction was had, and proof, by affidavit, of the service must be presented to the Governor.
(Added by Stats. 1941, Ch. 106.)
4805.
(a) At least 10 days before the Governor acts upon an application for a commutation of sentence, written notice of the intention to apply therefor, signed by the person applying, shall be served upon the district attorney of the county where the conviction was had, and proof, by affidavit, of the service shall be presented to the Governor.
(b) The district attorney may submit a written recommendation to the Governor for or against commutation of sentence.
(c) The district attorney shall make reasonable efforts to notify the victim or victims of the crime or crimes related to the application and the victims' families who may also submit a recommendation to the Governor for or against commutation of sentence.
(Added by Stats. 2011, Ch. 437, Sec. 4. (AB 648) Effective January 1, 2012.)
4806.
The provisions of Sections 4804 and 4805 are not applicable:
(a) When there is imminent danger of the death of the person convicted or imprisoned.
(b) When the term of imprisonment of the applicant is within 10 days of its expiration.
(Amended by Stats. 2011, Ch. 437, Sec. 5. (AB 648) Effective January 1, 2012.)
4807.
(a) At the beginning of every regular session of the Legislature, the Governor shall file a written report with the Legislature that shall include each application that was granted for each case of reprieve, pardon, or commutation by the Governor, or his or her predecessor in office, during the immediately preceding regular session of the Legislature, stating the name of the person convicted, the crime of which the person was convicted, the sentence and its date, the date of the reprieve, pardon, or commutation, and the reason for granting the same. The report shall be submitted in compliance with Section 9795 of the Government Code.
(b) Notwithstanding any other law, the written report filed with the Legislature pursuant to subdivision (a) shall be available to the public.
(Amended by Stats. 2012, Ch. 162, Sec. 133. (SB 1171) Effective January 1, 2013.)
4807.2.
Every application for pardon or commutation of sentence shall be accompanied by a full statement of any compensation being paid to any person for procuring or assisting in procuring the pardon or commutation or the pardon or commutation shall be denied.
(Added by Stats. 1943, Ch. 943.)
4807.3.
Every person who receives or agrees to receive any compensation or who receives any gift for procuring or assisting in procuring a pardon or commutation of sentence for any applicant must file with the Governor a full statement of the amount and character of such compensation or gift within 10 days of the receipt thereof. Any failure to file a full statement as required by this section is a misdemeanor.
(Added by Stats. 1943, Ch. 943.)
4810.
(a) The Board of Parole Hearings shall succeed to and shall exercise and perform all powers and duties granted to and imposed upon the Advisory Pardon Board by law.
(b) The Advisory Pardon Board is abolished.
(c) The report required of the Board of Parole Hearings by Section 4814 may be included in the report of the department.
(Amended by Stats. 2011, Ch. 437, Sec. 7. (AB 648) Effective January 1, 2012.)
4812.
(a) Upon request of the Governor, the Board of Parole Hearings shall investigate and report on all applications for reprieves, pardons, and commutations of sentence and shall make such recommendations to the Governor with reference thereto as it may seem advisable. To that end, the board shall examine and consider all applications so referred and all transcripts of judicial proceedings and all affidavits or other documents submitted in connection therewith, and shall have power to employ assistants and take testimony and to examine witnesses under oath and to do any and all things necessary to make a full and complete investigation of and concerning all applications referred to it. Members of the board and its administrative officer are, and each of them is, hereby authorized to administer oaths.
(b) The board may make recommendations to the Governor at any time regarding applications for pardon or commutation, and the Governor may request investigation into candidates for pardon or commutation at any time.
(c) If a petitioner indicates in the application an urgent need for the pardon or commutation, including, but not limited to, a pending deportation order or deportation proceeding, then the board shall consider expedited review of the application.
(d) The board shall provide electronic or written notification to an applicant after the board receives the application, and when the board has issued a recommendation on the application. Nothing in this section requires the board to notify the applicant as to the reasons for the board's recommendation, which shall remain confidential.
(e) An applicant is eligible for a pardon, commutation, or certificate of rehabilitation without regard to his or her immigration status.
(Amended by Stats. 2018, Ch. 824, Sec. 4. (AB 2845) Effective January 1, 2019.)
4813.
In the case of applications of persons twice convicted of a felony, the Board of Parole Hearings, after investigation, shall transmit its written recommendation upon such

application to the Governor, together with all papers filed in connection with the application.
(Amended by Stats. 2011, Ch. 437, Sec. 9. (AB 648) Effective January 1, 2012.)

CHAPTER 3. Duties of Supreme Court [4850 - 4852]

(Chapter 3 added by Stats. 1941, Ch. 106.)
4850.
An application that has not received a recommendation from the Board of Parole Hearings favorable to the applicant shall not be forwarded to the Clerk/Executive Officer of the Supreme Court, unless the Governor, notwithstanding the fact that the board has failed to make a recommendation favorable to the applicant, especially refers an application to the justices for their recommendation.
(Amended by Stats. 2017, Ch. 36, Sec. 18. (AB 452) Effective January 1, 2018.)
4851.
In all cases where the Board of Parole Hearings has made a recommendation favorable to the applicant and in those cases referred by the Governor, notwithstanding an adverse recommendation, the application, together with all papers and documents relied upon in support of and in opposition to the application, including prison records and recommendation of the Board of Prison Terms, shall be forwarded to the Clerk/Executive Officer of the Supreme Court for consideration of the justices.
(Amended by Stats. 2017, Ch. 36, Sec. 19. (AB 452) Effective January 1, 2018.)
4852.
If a majority of the justices recommend that clemency be granted, the Clerk/Executive Officer of the Supreme Court shall transmit the application, together with all papers and documents filed in the case, to the Governor; otherwise the documents shall remain in the files of the court.
(Amended by Stats. 2017, Ch. 36, Sec. 20. (AB 452) Effective January 1, 2018.)

CHAPTER 3.5. Procedure for Restoration of Rights and Application for Pardon [4852.01 - 4852.22]

(Chapter 3.5 added by Stats. 1943, Ch. 400.)
4852.01.
(a) A person convicted of a felony who is committed to a state prison or other institution or agency, including commitment to a county jail pursuant to subdivision (h) of Section 1170, may file a petition for a certificate of rehabilitation and pardon pursuant to the provisions of this chapter.
(b) A person convicted of a felony or a person who is convicted of a misdemeanor violation of any sex offense specified in Section 290, the accusatory pleading of which has been dismissed pursuant to Section 1203.4, may file a petition for certificate of rehabilitation and pardon pursuant to the provisions of this chapter if the petitioner has not been incarcerated in a prison, jail, detention facility, or other penal institution or agency since the dismissal of the accusatory pleading, is not on probation for the commission of any other felony, and the petitioner presents satisfactory evidence of five years' residence in this state prior to the filing of the petition.
(c) This chapter does not apply to persons serving a mandatory life parole, persons committed under death sentences, persons convicted of a violation of Section 269, subdivision (c) of Section 286, subdivision (c) of Section 287, Section 288, Section 288.5, Section 288.7, subdivision (j) of Section 289, or subdivision (c) of former Section 288a, or persons in military service.
(d) Notwithstanding any other law, the Governor has the right to pardon a person convicted of a violation of Section 269, subdivision (c) of Section 286, subdivision (c) of Section 287, Section 288, Section 288.5, Section 288.7, subdivision (j) of Section 289, or subdivision (c) of former Section 288a, if there are extraordinary circumstances.
(Amended by Stats. 2018, Ch. 423, Sec. 109. (SB 1494) Effective January 1, 2019.)
4852.03.
(a) The period of rehabilitation commences upon the discharge of the petitioner from custody due to his or her completion of the term to which he or she was sentenced or upon his or her release on parole, postrelease community supervision, mandatory supervision, or probation, whichever is sooner. For purposes of this chapter, the period of rehabilitation shall constitute five years' residence in this state, plus a period of time determined by the following rules:
(1) An additional four years in the case of a person convicted of violating Section 187, 209, 219, 4500, or 18755 of this code, or subdivision (a) of Section 1672 of the Military and Veterans Code, or of committing any other offense which carries a life sentence.
(2) An additional five years in the case of a person convicted of committing an offense or attempted offense for which sex offender registration is required pursuant to Section 290, except that in the case of a person convicted of a violation of subdivision (b), (c), or (d) of Section 311.2, or of Section 311.3, 311.10, or 314, an additional two years.
(3) An additional two years in the case of a person convicted of committing an offense that is not listed in paragraph (1) or paragraph (2) and that does not carry a life sentence.
(4) The trial court hearing the application for the certificate of rehabilitation may, if the defendant was ordered to serve consecutive sentences, order that the statutory period of rehabilitation be extended for an additional period of time which when combined with the time already served will not exceed the period prescribed by statute for the sum of the maximum penalties for all the crimes.
(b) Unless and until the period of rehabilitation required by subdivision (a) has passed, the petitioner shall be ineligible to file his or her petition for a certificate of rehabilitation with the court. A certificate of rehabilitation that is issued and under which the petitioner has not fulfilled the requirements of this chapter shall be void.
(c) A change of residence within this state does not interrupt the period of rehabilitation prescribed by this section.
(d) This section shall remain in effect only until July 1, 2021, and as of that date is repealed.
(Amended by Stats. 2017, Ch. 541, Sec. 13. (SB 384) Effective January 1, 2018. Repealed as of July 1, 2021, by its own provisions.)
4852.03.
(a) The period of rehabilitation commences upon the discharge of the petitioner from custody due to his or her completion of the term to which he or she was sentenced or upon his or her release on parole, postrelease community supervision, mandatory supervision, or probation, whichever is sooner. For purposes of this chapter, the period of rehabilitation shall constitute five years' residence in this state, plus a period of time determined by the following rules:
(1) An additional four years in the case of a person convicted of violating Section 187, 209, 219, 4500, or 18755 of this code, or subdivision (a) of Section 1672 of the Military and Veterans Code, or of committing any other offense which carries a life sentence.

(2) (A) An additional five years in the case of a person convicted of committing an offense or attempted offense for which sex offender registration is required pursuant to Sections 290 to 290.024, inclusive.

(B) A certificate of rehabilitation issued on or after July 1, 2021, does not relieve a person of the obligation to register as a sex offender unless the person obtains relief granted under Section 290.5.

(3) An additional two years in the case of a person convicted of committing an offense that is not listed in paragraph (1) or (2) and that does not carry a life sentence.

(4) The trial court hearing the application for the certificate of rehabilitation may, if the defendant was ordered to serve consecutive sentences, order that the statutory period of rehabilitation be extended for an additional period of time which when combined with the time already served will not exceed the period prescribed by statute for the sum of the maximum penalties for all the crimes.

(b) Unless and until the period of rehabilitation required by subdivision (a) has passed, the petitioner shall be ineligible to file his or her petition for a certificate of rehabilitation with the court. A certificate of rehabilitation that is issued and under which the petitioner has not fulfilled the requirements of this chapter shall be void.

(c) A change of residence within this state does not interrupt the period of rehabilitation prescribed by this section.

(d) This section shall become operative on July 1, 2021.

(Repealed (in Sec. 13) and added by Stats. 2017, Ch. 541, Sec. 14. (SB 384) Effective January 1, 2018. Section operative July 1, 2021, by its own provisions.)

4852.04.
Each person who may initiate the proceedings provided for in this chapter shall be entitled to receive counsel and assistance from all rehabilitative agencies, including the adult probation officer of the county and all state parole officers, and, in the case of persons under 30 years of age, from the Department of Corrections and Rehabilitation, Division of Juvenile Facilities.

(Amended by Stats. 2015, Ch. 378, Sec. 8. (AB 1156) Effective January 1, 2016.)

4852.05.
The person shall live an honest and upright life, shall conduct himself or herself with sobriety and industry, shall exhibit a good moral character, and shall conform to and obey the laws of the land.

(Amended by Stats. 1996, Ch. 981, Sec. 4. Effective January 1, 1997.)

4852.06.
After the expiration of the minimum period of rehabilitation a person who has complied with the requirements of Section 4852.05 may file in the superior court of the county in which he or she then resides or in which he or she was convicted of a felony or of a crime the accusatory pleading of which was dismissed pursuant to Section 1203.4, a petition for ascertainment and declaration of the fact of his or her rehabilitation and of matters incident thereto, and for a certificate of rehabilitation under this chapter. A petition shall not be filed until and unless the petitioner has continuously resided in this state, after leaving prison or jail, for a period of not less than five years immediately preceding the date of filing the petition.

(Amended by Stats. 2018, Ch. 824, Sec. 5. (AB 2845) Effective January 1, 2019.)

4852.07.
The petitioner shall give notice of the filing of the petition to the district attorney of the county in which the petition is filed, to the district attorney of each county in which the petitioner was convicted of a felony or of a crime the accusatory pleading of which was dismissed pursuant to Section 1203.4, and to the office of the Governor, together with notice of the time of the hearing of the petition, at least 30 days prior to the date set for such hearing.

(Amended by Stats. 1976, Ch. 434.)

4852.08.
During the proceedings upon the petition, the petitioner may be represented by counsel of his or her own selection. If the petitioner does not have counsel, he or she shall be represented by the public defender, if there is one in the county, and if there is none, by the adult probation officer of the county, or if in the opinion of the court the petitioner needs counsel, the court shall assign counsel to represent him or her.

(Amended by Stats. 2015, Ch. 303, Sec. 402. (AB 731) Effective January 1, 2016.)

4852.09.
No filing fee nor court fees of any kind shall be required of a petitioner in proceedings under this chapter.

(Added by Stats. 1943, Ch. 400.)

4852.1.
(a) The court in which the petition is filed may require testimony as it deems necessary, and the production, for the use of the court and without expense of any kind to the petitioner, of all records and reports relating to the petitioner and the crime of which he or she was convicted, including the following:

(1) The record of the trial.

(2) The report of the probation officer, if any.

(3) The records of the prison, jail, detention facility, or other penal institution from which the petitioner has been released showing his or her conduct during the time he or she was there, including the records of the penal institution, jail, or agency doctor and psychiatrist.

(4) The records of the parole officer concerning the petitioner if the petitioner was released on parole, records of the probation officer concerning the petitioner if the petitioner was released on postrelease community supervision or mandatory supervision, or the records of the Department of Corrections and Rehabilitation, Division of Juvenile Facilities concerning the petitioner if the petitioner had been committed to that authority.

(5) The written reports or records of any other law enforcement agency concerning the conduct of the petitioner since the petitioner's release on probation, parole, postrelease community supervision, or mandatory supervision, or discharge from custody.

(b) A person having custody of any of the records described in subdivision (a) shall make them available for the use of the court in the proceeding.

(Amended by Stats. 2015, Ch. 378, Sec. 10. (AB 1156) Effective January 1, 2016.)

4852.11.
A peace officer shall report to the court, upon receiving a request as provided in Section 4852.1, all known violations of law committed by the petitioner. Upon receiving satisfactory proof of a violation the court may deny the petition and determine a new period of rehabilitation not to exceed the original period of rehabilitation for the same crime. In that event, before granting the petition, the court may require the petitioner to fulfill all the requirements provided to be fulfilled before the granting of the certificate under the original petition.

(Amended by Stats. 2015, Ch. 303, Sec. 403. (AB 731) Effective January 1, 2016.)

4852.12.
(a) In a proceeding for the ascertainment and declaration of the fact of rehabilitation under this chapter, the court, upon the filing of the application for petition of rehabilitation, may request from the district attorney an investigation of the residence of the petitioner, the criminal record of the petitioner as shown by the records of the Department of Justice, any representation made to the court by the applicant, the conduct of the petitioner during the period of rehabilitation, including all matters mentioned in Section 4852.11, and any other information the court deems necessary in making its determination. The district attorney shall, upon request of the court, provide the court with a full and complete report of the investigations.

(b) In any proceeding for the ascertainment and declaration of the fact of rehabilitation under this chapter of a person convicted of a crime the accusatory pleading of which has been dismissed pursuant to Section 1203.4, the district attorney, upon request of

the court, shall deliver to the court the criminal record of petitioner as shown by the records of the Department of Justice. The district attorney may investigate any representation made to the court by petitioner and may file with the court a report of the investigation including all matters known to the district attorney relating to the conduct of the petitioner, the place and duration of residence of the petitioner during the period of rehabilitation, and all known violations of law committed by the petitioner.

(Amended by Stats. 2015, Ch. 303, Sec. 404. (AB 731) Effective January 1, 2016.)

4852.13.
(a) Except as otherwise provided in subdivision (b), if after hearing, the court finds that the petitioner has demonstrated by his or her course of conduct his or her rehabilitation and his or her fitness to exercise all of the civil and political rights of citizenship, the court may make an order declaring that the petitioner has been rehabilitated, and recommending that the Governor grant a full pardon to the petitioner. This order shall be filed with the clerk of the court, and shall be known as a certificate of rehabilitation.

(b) No certificate of rehabilitation shall be granted to a person convicted of any offense specified in Section 290 if the court determines that the petitioner presents a continuing threat to minors of committing any of the offenses specified in Section 290.

(c) A district attorney in either the county where the conviction was obtained or the county of residence of the recipient of the certificate of rehabilitation may petition the superior court to rescind a certificate if it was granted for any offense specified in Section 290. The petition shall be filed in either the county in which the person who has received the certificate of rehabilitation resides or the county in which the conviction was obtained. If the superior court finds that petitioner has demonstrated by a preponderance of the evidence that the person who has received the certificate presents a continuing threat to minors of committing any of the offenses specified in Section 290, the court shall rescind the certificate.

(Amended by Stats. 1996, Ch. 981, Sec. 6. Effective January 1, 1997.)

4852.14.
The clerk of the court shall immediately transmit certified copies of the certificate of rehabilitation to the Governor, to the Board of Parole Hearings and the Department of Justice, and, in the case of persons twice convicted of a felony, to the Supreme Court.

(Amended by Stats. 2015, Ch. 303, Sec. 405. (AB 731) Effective January 1, 2016.)

4852.15.
Nothing in this chapter shall be construed to abridge or impair the power or authority conferred by law on any officer, board, or tribunal to revoke or suspend any right, privilege, or franchise for any act or omission not involved in his or her conviction, or to require the reinstatement of the right or privilege to practice or carry on any profession or occupation the practice or conduct of which requires the possession or obtaining of a license, permit, or certificate. Nothing in this chapter shall affect any provision of Chapter 5 (commencing with Section 2000) of Division 2 of the Business and Professions Code or the power or authority conferred by law on the Board of Medical Examiners therein, or the power or authority conferred by law upon any board that issues a certificate permitting any person to practice or apply his or her art or profession on the person of another. Nothing in this chapter shall affect any provision of Chapter 4 (commencing with Section 6000) of Division 3 of the Business and Professions Code or the power or authority in relation to attorneys at law and the practice of the law in the State of California conferred by law upon or otherwise possessed by the courts, or the power or authority conferred by law upon the State Bar of California or any board or committee thereof.

(Amended by Stats. 1987, Ch. 828, Sec. 141.)

4852.16.
(a) The certified copy of a certificate of rehabilitation transmitted to the Governor shall constitute an application for a full pardon upon receipt of which the Governor may, without any further investigation, issue a pardon to the person named therein, except that, pursuant to Section 8 of Article V of the Constitution, the Governor shall not grant a pardon to any person twice convicted of felony, except upon the written recommendation of a majority of the judges of the Supreme Court.

(b) Subject to criteria established by the Governor, a certificate of rehabilitation issued by a court shall be reviewed by the Board of Parole Hearings within one year of receipt of the certificate, which shall issue a recommendation as to whether the Governor should pardon that individual. Any criteria established by the Governor shall be made publicly available, but shall be otherwise exempt from the requirements of Chapter 3.5 (commencing with Section 11340) of Part 1 of Division 3 of Title 2 of the Government Code.

(Amended by Stats. 2018, Ch. 824, Sec. 6. (AB 2845) Effective January 1, 2019.)

4852.17.
Whenever a person is issued a certificate of rehabilitation or granted a pardon from the Governor under this chapter, the fact shall be immediately reported to the Department of Justice by the court, Governor, officer, or governmental agency by whose official action the certificate is issued or the pardon granted. The Department of Justice shall immediately record the facts so reported on the former criminal record of the person, and transmit those facts to the Federal Bureau of Investigation at Washington, D.C. When the criminal record is thereafter reported by the department, it shall also report the fact that the person has received a certificate of rehabilitation, or pardon, or both. Whenever a person is granted a full and unconditional pardon by the Governor, based upon a certificate of rehabilitation, the pardon shall entitle the person to exercise thereafter all civil and political rights of citizenship, including, but not limited to: (1) the right to vote; (2) the right to own, possess, and keep any type of firearm that may lawfully be owned and possessed by other citizens; except that this right shall not be restored, and Sections 17800 and 23510 and Chapter 2 (commencing with Section 29800) of Division 9 of Title 4 of Part 6 shall apply, if the person was ever convicted of a felony involving the use of a dangerous weapon.

(Amended (as amended by Stats. 2010, Ch. 178, Sec. 85) by Stats. 2011, Ch. 296, Sec. 218. (AB 1023) Effective January 1, 2012.)

4852.18.
The Board of Parole Hearings shall furnish to the clerk of the superior court of each county a set of sample forms for a petition for certificate of rehabilitation and pardon, a notice of filing of petition for certificate of rehabilitation and pardon, and a certificate of rehabilitation. The clerk of the court shall have a sufficient number of these forms printed to meet the needs of the people of the county, shall post these forms on the court's Internet Web site, and shall make these forms available at no charge to persons requesting them.

(Amended by Stats. 2018, Ch. 824, Sec. 7. (AB 2845) Effective January 1, 2019.)

4852.19.
This chapter shall be construed as providing an additional, but not an exclusive, procedure for the restoration of rights and application for pardon. Nothing in this chapter shall be construed as repealing any other provision of law providing for restoration of rights or application for pardon.

(Added by Stats. 1943, Ch. 400.)

4852.2.
Every person, other than an individual who is licensed to practice law in the State of California, pursuant to Article 4 (commencing with Section 6060) of Chapter 4 of Division 3 of the Business and Professions Code and who is acting in that capacity, who solicits or accepts any fee, money, or anything of value for his or her services, or his or her purported services, in representing a petitioner in any proceeding under this chapter, or in any application to the Governor for a pardon under this chapter, is guilty of a misdemeanor.

(Amended by Stats. 1990, Ch. 632, Sec. 5.)

4852.21.

(a) A person to whom this chapter applies shall, prior to discharge or release on parole or postrelease community supervision from a state prison or other state penal institution or agency, or prior to discharge or release on mandatory supervision from a county jail, be informed in writing by the official in charge of the place of confinement of the person's right to petition for, and of the procedure for filing the petition for and obtaining, a certificate of rehabilitation and pardon pursuant to this chapter.

(b) Prior to dismissal of the accusatory pleading pursuant to Section 1203.4, the defendant shall be informed in writing by the clerk of the court dismissing the accusatory pleading of the defendant's right, if any, to petition for, and of the procedure for filing a petition for and obtaining, a certificate of rehabilitation and pardon pursuant to this chapter.

(Amended by Stats. 2015, Ch. 378, Sec. 11. (AB 1156) Effective January 1, 2016.)

4852.22.

Except in a case requiring registration pursuant to Section 290, a trial court hearing an application for a certificate of rehabilitation before the applicable period of rehabilitation has elapsed may grant the application if the court, in its discretion, believes relief serves the interests of justice.

(Added by Stats. 2013, Ch. 721, Sec. 2. (SB 530) Effective January 1, 2014.)

CHAPTER 4. Effect of Full Pardon [4853 - 4854]

(Chapter 4 added by Stats. 1941, Ch. 106.)

4853.

In all cases in which a full pardon has been granted by the Governor of this state or will hereafter be granted by the Governor to a person convicted of an offense to which the pardon applies, it shall operate to restore to the convicted person, all the rights, privileges, and franchises of which he or she has been deprived in consequence of that conviction or by reason of any matter involved therein; provided, that nothing herein contained shall abridge or impair the power or authority conferred by law on any board or tribunal to revoke or suspend any right, privilege or franchise for any act or omission not involved in the conviction; provided further, that nothing in this article shall affect any of the provisions of the Medical Practice Act (Chapter 5 (commencing with Section 2000) of Division 2 of the Business and Professions Code) or the power or authority conferred by law on the Board of Medical Examiners therein, or the power or authority conferred by law upon any board that issues a certificate which permits any person or persons to apply his or her or their art or profession on the person of another.

(Amended by Stats. 1987, Ch. 828, Sec. 143.)

4854.

In the granting of a pardon to a person, the Governor may provide that the person is entitled to exercise the right to own, possess, and keep any type of firearm that may lawfully be owned and possessed by other citizens; except that this right shall not be restored, and Sections 17800 and 23510 and Chapter 2 (commencing with Section 29800) of Division 9 of Title 4 of Part 6 shall apply, if the person was ever convicted of a felony involving the use of a dangerous weapon.

(Amended (as amended by Stats. 2010, Ch. 178, Sec. 86) by Stats. 2011, Ch. 296, Sec. 219. (AB 1023) Effective January 1, 2012.)

CHAPTER 5. Indemnity for Persons Erroneously Convicted and Pardoned [4900 - 4906]

(Chapter 5 added by Stats. 1941, Ch. 106.)

4900.

Any person who, having been convicted of any crime against the state amounting to a felony and imprisoned in the state prison or incarcerated in county jail pursuant to subdivision (h) of Section 1170 for that conviction, is granted a pardon by the Governor for the reason that the crime with which he or she was charged was either not committed at all or, if committed, was not committed by him or her, or who, being innocent of the crime with which he or she was charged for either of the foregoing reasons, shall have served the term or any part thereof for which he or she was imprisoned in state prison or incarcerated in county jail, may, under the conditions provided under this chapter, present a claim against the state to the California Victim Compensation Board for the pecuniary injury sustained by him or her through the erroneous conviction and imprisonment or incarceration.

(Amended by Stats. 2016, Ch. 31, Sec. 250. (SB 836) Effective June 27, 2016.)

4901.

(a) A claim under Section 4900, accompanied by a statement of the facts constituting the claim, verified in the manner provided for the verification of complaints in civil actions, is required to be presented by the claimant to the California Victim Compensation Board within a period of two years after judgment of acquittal or after pardon granted, or after release from custody, and no claim not so presented shall be considered by the California Victim Compensation Board.

(b) For purposes of subdivision (a), "release from custody" means release from imprisonment from state prison or from incarceration in county jail when there is no subsequent parole jurisdiction exercised by the Department of Correction and Rehabilitation or postrelease jurisdiction under a community corrections program, or when there is a parole period or postrelease period subject to jurisdiction of a community corrections program, when that period ends.

(c) A person may not file a claim under Section 4900 until 60 days have passed since the date of reversal of conviction or granting of the writ, or while the case is pending upon an initial refiling, or until a complaint or information has been dismissed a single time.

(Amended by Stats. 2016, Ch. 31, Sec. 251. (SB 836) Effective June 27, 2016.)

4902.

(a) If the provisions of Section 851.865 or 1485.55 apply in any claim, the California Victim Compensation Board shall, within 30 days of the presentation of the claim, calculate the compensation for the claimant pursuant to Section 4904 and recommend to the Legislature payment of that sum. As to any claim to which Section 851.865 or 1485.55 does not apply, the Attorney General shall respond to the claim within 60 days or request an extension of time, upon a showing of good cause.

(b) Upon receipt of a response from the Attorney General, the board shall fix a time and place for the hearing of the claim, and shall mail notice thereof to the claimant and to the Attorney General at least 15 days prior to the time fixed for the hearing. The board shall use reasonable diligence in setting the date for the hearing and shall attempt to set the date for the hearing at the earliest date convenient for the parties and the board.

(c) If the time period for response elapses without a request for extension or a response from the Attorney General pursuant to subdivision (a), the board shall fix a time and place for the hearing of the claim, mail notice thereof to the claimant at least 15 days prior to the time fixed for the hearing, and make a recommendation based on the claimant's verified claim and any evidence presented by him or her.

(Amended by Stats. 2016, Ch. 31, Sec. 252. (SB 836) Effective June 27, 2016.)

4903.

(a) At the hearing the claimant shall introduce evidence in support of the claim, and the Attorney General may introduce evidence in opposition thereto. The claimant shall prove the facts set forth in the statement constituting the claim, including the fact that the crime with which he or she was charged was either not committed at all, or, if committed, was not committed by him or her, and the pecuniary injury sustained by him or her through his or her erroneous conviction and imprisonment.

(b) In a hearing before the board, the factual findings and credibility determinations establishing the court's basis for granting a writ of habeas corpus, a motion for new trial pursuant to Section 1473.6, or an application for a certificate of factual innocence as described in Section 1485.5 shall be binding on the Attorney General, the factfinder, and the board.

(c) The board shall deny payment of any claim if the board finds by a preponderance of the evidence that a claimant pled guilty with the specific intent to protect another from prosecution for the underlying conviction for which the claimant is seeking compensation.

(Amended by Stats. 2013, Ch. 800, Sec. 7. (SB 618) Effective January 1, 2014.)

4904.

If the evidence shows that the crime with which the claimant was charged was either not committed at all, or, if committed, was not committed by the claimant, and that the claimant has sustained injury through his or her erroneous conviction and imprisonment, the California Victim Compensation Board shall report the facts of the case and its conclusions to the next Legislature, with a recommendation that the Legislature make an appropriation for the purpose of indemnifying the claimant for the injury. The amount of the appropriation recommended shall be a sum equivalent to one hundred forty dollars ($140) per day of incarceration served, and shall include any time spent in custody, including in a county jail, that is considered to be part of the term of incarceration. That appropriation shall not be treated as gross income to the recipient under the Revenue and Taxation Code.

(Amended by Stats. 2016, Ch. 31, Sec. 253. (SB 836) Effective June 27, 2016.)

4905.

The California Victim Compensation Board shall make up its report and recommendation and shall give to the Controller a statement showing its recommendations for appropriations under this chapter, as provided by law in cases of other claimants against the state for which no appropriations have been made.

(Amended by Stats. 2016, Ch. 31, Sec. 254. (SB 836) Effective June 27, 2016.)

4906.

The California Victim Compensation Board is hereby authorized to make all needful rules and regulations consistent with the law for the purpose of carrying into effect this chapter.

(Amended by Stats. 2016, Ch. 31, Sec. 255. (SB 836) Effective June 27, 2016.)

TITLE 7. ADMINISTRATION OF THE STATE CORRECTIONAL SYSTEM [5000 - 7445]

(Title 7 added by Stats. 1944, 3rd Ex. Sess., Ch. 2.)

CHAPTER 1. The Department of Corrections and Rehabilitation [5000 - 5031]

(Heading of Chapter 1 amended by Stats. 2005, Ch. 10, Sec. 31.)

5000.

Commencing July 1, 2005, any reference to the Department of Corrections in this or any other code refers to the Department of Corrections and Rehabilitation, Division of Adult Operations.

Nothing in the act enacted by Senate Bill 737 of the 2005-06 Regular Session shall be construed to alter the primary objective of adult incarceration under the reorganized Department of Corrections and Rehabilitation, which remains public safety as articulated in the legislative findings and declarations set forth in Section 1170.

(Amended by Stats. 2005, Ch. 10, Sec. 32. Effective May 10, 2005. Operative July 1, 2005, by Sec. 99 of Ch. 10.)

5001.

The Governor may request the State Personnel Board to use extensive recruitment and merit selection techniques and procedures to provide lists of persons qualified for appointment pursuant to Article 14 (commencing with Section 12838) of Chapter 1 of Part 2.5 of Division 3 of the Government Code. The Governor may appoint any person from the lists of qualified persons or may reject all names and appoint other persons who meet the requirements of the positions.

(Amended by Stats. 2006, Ch. 538, Sec. 519. Effective January 1, 2007.)

5002.

(a) The department shall succeed to and is hereby vested with all of the powers and duties exercised and performed by the following departments, boards, bureaus, commissions, and officers when such powers and duties are not otherwise vested by law:

(1) The Department of Penology.

(2) The State Board of Prison Directors.

(3) The Bureau of Paroles.

(4) The warden and the clerk of the California State Prison at San Quentin.

(5) The warden and the clerk of the California State Prison at Folsom.

(6) The warden of and the clerk of the California Institution for Men.

(7) The California Crime Commission.

(b) Whenever any designation of any of the departments, boards, bureaus, commissions, or officers mentioned in subdivision (a) is contained in any provision of law and this designation is expressly made to refer to the Department of Corrections, the Board of Corrections or the Board of Prison Terms, then the Department of Corrections, the Board of Corrections or the Board of Prison Terms, to whichever one the designation is made to refer, shall exercise the power or perform the duty heretofore exercised or performed by the particular departments, boards, bureaus, or officers mentioned in subdivision (a).

(c) The powers and duties of the State Board of Prison Directors and of the clerks of the state prisons and the California Institution for Men are transferred to and shall be exercised and performed by the Department of Corrections, except as may be otherwise expressly provided by law.

(d) The powers and duties of wardens of the state prisons and the California Institution for Men, presently or hereafter, expressly vested by law in them shall be exercised by them but such exercise shall be subject to the supervision and control of the Director of Corrections. All powers and duties not expressly vested in the wardens are transferred to and shall be exercised and performed by the Department of Corrections. When the designation of warden is expressly made to refer to the Department of Corrections, the department shall exercise the power and perform the duty heretofore exercised or performed by the warden.

(e) The Board of Prison Terms shall succeed to and is hereby vested with all of the powers and duties exercised and performed by the following boards when such powers and duties are not otherwise vested by law:

(1) The Board of Prison Terms and Paroles.

(2) The Advisory Pardon Board.
(3) The Adult Authority.
(4) The Women's Board of Terms and Paroles.
(5) The Community Release Board.
(Amended by Stats. 1989, Ch. 1420, Sec. 20.)
5003.
The department has jurisdiction over the following prisons and institutions:
(a) The California State Prison at San Quentin.
(b) The California State Prison at Folsom.
(c) The California Institution for Men.
(d) The California Institution for Women.
(e) The Deuel Vocational Institution.
(f) The California Medical Facility.
(g) The Correctional Training Facility.
(h) The California Men's Colony.
(i) The California Correctional Institution at Tehachapi.
(j) The California Rehabilitation Center.
(k) The California Correctional Center at Susanville.
(l) The Sierra Correctional Center.
(m) The Richard J. Donovan Correctional Facility at Rock Mountain.
(n) Mule Creek State Prison.
(o) Northern California Women's Facility.
(p) Pelican Bay State Prison.
(q) Avenal State Prison.
(r) California State Prison—King's County at Corcoran.
(s) Chuckawalla Valley State Prison.
(t) Those other institutions and prison facilities as the Department of Corrections or the Director of Corrections may be authorized by law to establish, including, but not limited to, prisons in Madera, Kern, Imperial, and Los Angeles Counties.
(Amended by Stats. 1990, Ch. 981, Sec. 11. Effective September 18, 1990.)
5003.2.
(a) The Secretary of the Department of Corrections and Rehabilitation, or his or her designee, shall provide written notification to any county impacted by the opening, closing, or changing of location of any reception center that accepts prisoners from county facilities, or by the opening, closing, or changing of the location of a parole office. Written notification of these changes shall also be provided to the California State Association of Counties, the California State Sheriffs' Association, and the Chief Probation Officers of California at least 90 days prior to the proposed change.
(b) The notification requirement in this section shall not apply to the opening, closing, or changing of location of a facility due to an emergency created by a riot, quarantine, or natural disaster.
(Added by Stats. 2013, Ch. 32, Sec. 13. (SB 76) Effective June 27, 2013.)
5003.5.
The Board of Parole Hearings is empowered to advise and recommend to the Secretary of the Department of Corrections and Rehabilitation on general and specific policies and procedures relating to the duties and functions of the secretary. The secretary is empowered to advise and recommend to the board on matters of general and specific policies and procedures, relating to the duties and functions of the board. The secretary and the board shall meet for purposes of exchange of information and advice.
(Amended by Stats. 2005, Ch. 10, Sec. 34. Effective May 10, 2005. Operative July 1, 2005, by Sec. 99 of Ch. 10.)
5004.
The Director of Corrections and the legislative body of any county or city may enter into agreements for mutual police aid. Pursuant to such agreements the director may authorize employees of state prisons and institutions to cooperate, anywhere within the State, with county and city peace officers in connection with any existing emergency. While so employed the employees shall have all the benefits of workmen's compensation laws, retirement laws, and all other similar laws and for such purposes shall be deemed to be performing services in the course of their regular official duties.
(Added by Stats. 1949, Ch. 870.)
5004.5.
The director shall require each state prison under the department's jurisdiction to develop a Mutual Aid Escape Pursuit Plan and Agreement with local law enforcement agencies. The plan, together with any supporting information, shall be submitted for annual review to the city council of the city containing or nearest to the institution and to the county board of supervisors of the county containing the prison.
Nothing in this section shall require the department to disclose any information which may threaten the security of an institution or the safety of the surrounding community.
(Added by Stats. 1984, Ch. 608, Sec. 1. Effective July 19, 1984.)
5004.7.
(a) The department shall establish a statewide policy on operational procedures for the handling of threats made by inmates or wards, and threats made by family members of inmates or wards, against department staff. The policy shall include methods to ensure that department staff members are advised of threats made against them by inmates, wards, or family members of inmates or wards, and shall require that all threats against department staff made by inmates, wards, or family members of inmates or wards are thoroughly investigated. A copy of the statewide policy shall be accessible to members of the public upon request.
(b) This section does not prohibit an individual institution within the department from developing a more detailed notification procedure for advising staff members of threats made against them. If an individual institution has a more detailed policy, the policy shall be accessible to every member of the staff of the institution.
(c) The department shall provide training on the policy developed pursuant to this section as part of its existing training programs.
(d) The policy developed pursuant to this section shall be fully implemented by July 1, 2016.
(Added by Stats. 2015, Ch. 195, Sec. 1. (AB 293) Effective August 13, 2015.)
5005.
The department may maintain a canteen at any prison or institution under its jurisdiction for the sale to persons confined therein of toilet articles, candy, notions, and other sundries, and may provide the necessary facilities, equipment, personnel, and merchandise for the canteen. The director shall specify what commodities shall be sold in the canteen. The sale prices of the articles offered for sale shall be fixed by the director at the amounts that will, as far as possible, render each canteen self-supporting. The department may undertake to insure against damage or loss of canteen and handicraft materials, supplies and equipment owned by the Inmate Welfare Fund of the Department of Corrections as provided in Section 5006.
The canteen operations at any prison or institution referred to in this section shall be audited biennially by the Department of Finance, and at the end of each intervening fiscal year, each prison or institution shall prepare a statement of operations. At least one copy of any audit report or statement of operations shall be posted at the canteen and at least one copy shall be available to inmates at the library of each prison or institution.
(Amended by Stats. 2004, Ch. 798, Sec. 5. Effective January 1, 2005. Operative July 1, 2005, by Sec. 9 of Ch. 798.)
5006.
(a) (1) All moneys now held for the benefit of inmates currently housed in Department of Corrections and Rehabilitation facilities including those known as the Inmate Canteen Fund of the California Institution for Men; the Inmate Welfare Fund of the California

Institution for Women; the Trust Contingent Fund of the California State Prison at Folsom; the S.P.L. Commissary, Canteen Account, Hobby Association, Camp Account, Library Fund, News Agency of the California State Prison at San Quentin, the Prisoners' Fund; and the Prisoners' Employment Fund, shall be deposited in the Inmate Welfare Fund of the Department of Corrections and Rehabilitation, in the State Treasury, which is hereby created. The money in the fund shall be used solely for the benefit and welfare of inmates of prisons and institutions under the jurisdiction of the Department of Corrections and Rehabilitation, including the following:
(A) The establishment, maintenance, employment of personnel for, and purchase of items for sale to inmates at canteens maintained at the state institutions.
(B) The establishment, maintenance, employment of personnel, and necessary expenses in connection with the operation of the hobby shops at institutions under the jurisdiction of the department.
(C) Educational programs, hobby and recreational programs, which may include physical education activities and hobby craft classes, inmate family visiting services, leisure-time activities, and assistance with obtaining photo identification from the Department of Motor Vehicles.
(D) Funding for innovative programming by not-for-profit organizations offering programs that have demonstrated success and focus on offender responsibility and restorative justice principles. All funding used for this purpose shall go directly to the not-for-profit organizations and shall not be used for department staff or administration of the programming.
(2) The warden of each institution, in collaboration with at least two representatives from local or state advocacy groups for inmates and two members of either the men's or women's advisory council or similar group within each institution, shall meet at least biannually to determine how the money in the fund shall be used to benefit the inmates of the respective institution. It is the intent of the Legislature that the funds only be expended on services other than those that the department is required to provide to inmates.
(b) There shall be deposited in the Inmate Welfare Fund all net proceeds from the operation of canteens and hobby shops and any moneys that may be assigned to the state prison by prisoners for deposit in the fund. The moneys in the fund shall constitute a trust held by the Secretary of the Department of Corrections and Rehabilitation for the benefit and welfare, as herein defined, of all of the inmates of institutions and prisons under the jurisdiction of the department.
(c) The Department of Finance shall conduct a biennial audit of the Inmate Welfare Fund to include an audit report which shall summarize expenditures from the fund by major categories. At the end of each intervening fiscal year, a statement of operations shall be prepared that shall contain the same information as would be provided in the biennial audit. At least one copy of any statement of operations or audit report shall be placed in each library maintained by the Department of Corrections and Rehabilitation and shall be available there to any inmate.
(Amended by Stats. 2014, Ch. 26, Sec. 29. (AB 1468) Effective June 20, 2014.)
5006.1.
(a) Notwithstanding any provision in Section 5006, money in the Inmate Welfare Fund shall not be expended to pay charges for any or all of the following purposes:
(1) Overtime for staff coverage of special events.
(2) Television repair.
(3) Original complement of television sets and replacement of television equipment.
(b) The department shall pay these charges out of any money appropriated for these purposes.
(Amended by Stats. 2012, Ch. 831, Sec. 3. (SB 542) Effective January 1, 2013.)
5007.
The Secretary of the Department of Corrections and Rehabilitation may invest money in the Inmate Welfare Fund that in his or her opinion is not necessary for immediate use, with the approval of the Department of Finance, and interest earned and other increment derived from investments made pursuant to this section shall be paid into the Inmate Welfare Fund of the Department of Corrections and Rehabilitation.
(Amended by Stats. 2012, Ch. 831, Sec. 4. (SB 542) Effective January 1, 2013.)
5007.3.
(a) (1) The department shall establish the California Reentry and Enrichment (CARE) Grant program to provide grants to community based organizations (CBOs) that provide rehabilitative services to incarcerated individuals.
(2) Grants shall be awarded by the steering committee established pursuant to subdivision (b) based on the following criteria:
(A) The steering committee shall prioritize the continuation, expansion, or replication of rehabilitative programs that have previously demonstrated success with incarcerated individuals within a correctional environment. This subparagraph does not disqualify a relatively new CBO that has programming that shows promise from applying for, or receiving, a grant.
(B) Grants shall be awarded to fund programs that provide insight-oriented restorative justice and offender accountability programs that can demonstrate that the approach has produced, or will produce, positive outcomes in department facilities, including, but not limited to:
(i) Increasing empathy and mindfulness.
(ii) Increasing resilience and reducing the impacts of stress and trauma.
(iii) Reducing violence in the form of physical aggression, verbal aggression, anger, and hostility.
(iv) Successfully addressing and treating the symptoms of post-traumatic stress disorder.
(v) Victim impacts and understanding.
(C) To the extent that the information is available, applicants shall provide evaluations and surveys, including qualitative and quantitative information, from current and former program participants and any program evaluation data conducted by an outside research organization.
(b) The department shall establish a CARE Grant program steering committee, which shall establish grant criteria, select grant recipients, and determine grant amounts and the number of grants. Members of the steering committee shall be chosen as a result of consultation with the Senate and Assembly, as follows:
(1) One member shall be an educator or trainer in the field of criminal justice, with specific knowledge and experience working with adult offenders.
(2) One member shall be a researcher with specific expertise evaluating the effectiveness of rehabilitative treatment for adult offenders.
(3) Two members shall be representatives for community based organizations with experience working with the department on CBO-led programs. The CBO representative is ineligible to apply for a grant and shall not receive any compensation from another nonprofit/CBO that receives a CARE grant.
(4) Two members shall have firsthand knowledge of rehabilitative CBO- or department-led programming through active participation and completion of courses within the preceding five years. These members are ineligible to apply for a grant and shall not receive any compensation from another nonprofit or CBO that receives a CARE grant.
(5) Two members shall be representatives of the Division of Rehabilitative Programs within the department who have had experience working directly with CBO programs.
(6) One member shall be a representative from the Division of Adult Institutions to provide insight and knowledge of the most effective CBO programs.
(7) One member shall be from the Office of the Inspector General who is familiar with the work and objectives of the California Rehabilitation Oversight Board.
(c) Members of the steering committee shall serve without compensation, but may be reimbursed for travel and other necessary expenses.

(Added by Stats. 2019, Ch. 25, Sec. 42. (SB 94) Effective June 27, 2019.)

5007.5.

(a) The Director of Corrections is authorized to charge a fee in the amount of five dollars ($5) for each inmate-initiated medical visit of an inmate confined in the state prison.
(b) The fee shall be charged to the prison account of the inmate. If the inmate has no money in his or her personal account, there shall be no charge for the medical visit.
(c) An inmate shall not be denied medical care because of a lack of funds in his or her prison account.
(d) The medical provider may waive the fee for any inmate-initiated treatment and shall waive the fee in any life-threatening or emergency situation, defined as those health services required for alleviation of severe pain or for immediate diagnosis and treatment of unforeseen medical conditions that if not immediately diagnosed and treated could lead to disability or death.
(e) Followup medical visits at the direction of the medical staff shall not be charged to the inmate.
(f) All moneys received by the Director of Corrections pursuant to this section shall, upon appropriation by the Legislature, be expended to reimburse the Department of Corrections for direct provision of inmate health care services.
(Amended by Stats. 1995, Ch. 749, Sec. 8. Effective October 10, 1995.)

5007.7.

An inmate who has maintained an inmate trust account with twenty-five dollars ($25) or less for 30 consecutive days shall be deemed indigent. An indigent inmate shall receive basic supplies necessary for maintaining personal hygiene. An indigent inmate shall be provided with sufficient resources to communicate with and access the courts, including, but not limited to, stamps, writing materials, envelopes, paper, and the services of a notary for the purpose of notarizing a signature on a document, as required.
(Added by Stats. 2018, Ch. 764, Sec. 1. (AB 2533) Effective January 1, 2019.)

5008.

The Secretary of the Department of Corrections and Rehabilitation shall deposit any funds of inmates in his or her possession in trust with the Treasurer pursuant to Section 16305.3 of the Government Code. However, the Secretary of the Department of Corrections and Rehabilitation, shall deposit those funds of inmates in interest-bearing bank accounts or invest or reinvest the funds in any of the securities that are described in Article 1 (commencing with Section 16430) of Chapter 3 of Part 2 of Division 4 of Title 2 of the Government Code and for the purposes of deposit or investment only may mingle the funds of any inmate with the funds of other inmates. Any interest or increment accruing on those funds, less expenses incurred in the investment, shall be deposited in individual inmate or parolee trust accounts on a proportional basis depending upon the amount of funds each individual inmate or parolee account has on deposit.
(Amended by Stats. 2008, Ch. 210, Sec. 1. Effective January 1, 2009.)

5008.1.

Subject to the availability of adequate state funding for these purposes, the Director of Corrections shall provide all inmates at each penal institution and prison facility under the jurisdiction of the department with information about behavior that places a person at high risk for contracting the human immunodeficiency virus (HIV), and about the prevention of transmission of acquired immune deficiency syndrome (AIDS). The director shall provide all inmates, who are within one month of release or being placed on parole, with information about agencies and facilities that provide testing, counseling, medical, and support services for AIDS victims. Information about AIDS prevention shall be solicited by the director from the State Department of Health Services, the county health officer, or local agencies providing services to persons with AIDS. The Director of Health Services, or his or her designee, shall approve protocols pertaining to the information to be disseminated under this section.
(Added by Stats. 1988, Ch. 1301, Sec. 2.)

5008.2.

(a) During the intake medical examination or intake health screening, or while providing general information during intake, the department shall provide all inmates with information on hepatitis C, including, but not limited to, methods of hepatitis C transmission and prevention, and information on opportunities for screening and treatment while incarcerated. This subdivision shall be implemented only to the extent that brochures, other printed information, or other media is provided at no charge to the department by public health agencies or any other organization promoting hepatitis C education.
(b) The department shall also provide hepatitis C screening to all inmates who request it, and offer it to inmates that have a history of intravenous drug use or other risk factors for hepatitis C. This testing shall be confidential. The medical copayment authorized in Section 5007.5 shall not be charged for hepatitis C testing, treatment, or any followup testing.
(Added by Stats. 2005, Ch. 524, Sec. 1. Effective January 1, 2006.)

5009.

(a) It is the intention of the Legislature that all prisoners shall be afforded reasonable opportunities to exercise religious freedom.
(b) (1) Except in extraordinary circumstances, upon the transfer of an inmate to another state prison institution, any member of the clergy or spiritual adviser who has been previously authorized by the Department of Corrections and Rehabilitation to visit that inmate shall be granted visitation privileges at the institution to which the inmate is transferred within 72 hours of the transfer.
(2) Visitations by members of the clergy or spiritual advisers shall be subject to the same rules, regulations, and policies relating to general visitations applicable at the institution to which the inmate is transferred.
(3) A departmental or volunteer chaplain who has ministered to or advised an inmate incarcerated in state prison may, voluntarily and without compensation, continue to minister to or advise the inmate while he or she is on parole, provided that the departmental or volunteer chaplain so notifies the warden and the parolee's parole agent in writing.
(c) Nothing in this section limits the department's ability to prohibit a departmental chaplain from ministering to a parolee, or to exclude a volunteer chaplain from department facilities, if either is found to be in violation of any law or regulation and that violation would ordinarily be grounds for adverse action or denial of access to a facility or person under the department's custody.
(Amended by Stats. 2006, Ch. 538, Sec. 520. Effective January 1, 2007.)

5010.

(a) The Legislature hereby finds and declares that the predominant purpose of exercise in correctional facilities should be for the maintenance of the general health and welfare of inmates and that exercise equipment and programs in correctional facilities should be consistent with this purpose.
The Legislature further finds and declares that in some cases it may be beneficial to provide access to weights for therapeutic or rehabilitative reasons under a doctor's order or for certain vocational activities such as firefighting.
(b) It is the intent of the Legislature that both the Department of Corrections and the Department of the Youth Authority eliminate or restrict access to weights and weight lifting equipment where it is determined that the particular type of equipment involved or the particular prison population or inmate involved poses a safety concern both in the correctional facility and to the public upon release. In those instances where inmates are allowed access to weights and weight lifting equipment, access shall be a privilege.
As a condition of inmate access to weights and weight lifting equipment, the departments may require inmates to participate in training in the proper use of weights and weight lifting equipment that emphasizes departmental rules and safety practices that must be observed when using weights and weight lifting equipment.
The directors of the departments, or their respective designees, may restrict individual or group access to weights and weight lifting equipment as deemed necessary for the orderly operation of the correctional facility.
(c) On or before July 1, 1995, both the Department of Corrections and the Department of the Youth Authority shall adopt regulations governing inmate access to weight lifting and weight training equipment in state prison and California Youth Authority facilities, respectively. In developing these regulations, the departments shall consider each of the following:
(1) Some prisoners may utilize weight equipment to develop strength and increase body mass and size rather than for the maintenance of general health. This use of weight equipment may create a risk of harm to other inmates, correctional officers, and staff and, upon release, to law enforcement officers and the general public.
(2) The improper use of weights and weight lifting equipment may result in injuries that require costly medical attention.
(3) Access to weights and weight lifting equipment by inmates may result in the use of the equipment by inmates to attack other inmates or correctional officers.
(Amended by Stats. 2004, Ch. 193, Sec. 148. Effective January 1, 2005.)

5011.

(a) The Department of Corrections shall not require, as a condition for any form of treatment or custody that the department offers, an admission of guilt to any crime for which an inmate was committed to the custody of the department.
(b) The Board of Prison Terms shall not require, when setting parole dates, an admission of guilt to any crime for which an inmate was committed.
(Amended by Stats. 1979, Ch. 255.)

5021.

(a) Any death that occurs in any facility operated by the Department of Corrections and Rehabilitation, the State Department of State Hospitals, a city, county, or city and county, including county juvenile facilities, or any facility which is under contract with any of these entities for the incarceration, rehabilitation, holding, or treatment of persons accused or convicted of crimes, shall be reported within a reasonable time, not to exceed two hours, of its discovery by authorities in the facility to the county sheriff, or his or her designated representative, and to the coroner's office, of the county in which the facility is located, as provided in Section 27491 of the Government Code. These deaths shall also be reported to the district attorney, or his or her designated representative, of the county in which the facility is located as soon as a representative of the district attorney's office is on duty. If the facility is located within the city limits of an incorporated city, the report shall also be made to the chief of police in that city, or to his or her designated representative, within a reasonable time, not to exceed two hours, of its discovery.
Any death of a person in a facility operated by the Department of Corrections and Rehabilitation shall also be reported to the Chief of Medical Services in the Central Office of the Department of Corrections and Rehabilitation, or his or her designated representative, as soon as a representative of that office is on duty.
(b) The initial report of the death of a person required in subdivision (a) may be transmitted by telephone, direct contact, or by written notification, and shall outline all pertinent facts known at the time the report is made and all persons to contact, in addition to any other information the reporting person or officer deems pertinent.
(c) The initial report of the death of a person as required in subdivision (a) shall be supplemented by a written report, which shall be submitted to the entities listed in subdivision (a) within eight hours of the discovery of the death. This written report shall include all circumstances and details of the death that were known at the time the report was prepared, and shall include the names of all persons involved in the death, and all persons with knowledge of the circumstances surrounding the death.
(Amended by Stats. 2012, Ch. 24, Sec. 49. (AB 1470) Effective June 27, 2012.)

5022.

(a) Upon the entry of a prisoner into a facility operated by the Department of Corrections, and at least every year thereafter, the Director of Corrections shall obtain from the prisoner the name and last known address and telephone number of any person or persons who shall be notified in the event of the prisoner's death or serious illness or serious injury, as determined by the physician in attendance, and who are authorized to receive his or her body. The persons shall be noted in the order of the prisoner's preference. The Director of Corrections shall provide the prisoner with the opportunity to modify or amend his or her notification list at any time.
(b) The Director of Corrections shall use all reasonable means to contact the person or persons set forth in the notification list upon the death or serious illness or serious injury, as determined by the physician in attendance, of the prisoner while confined in a facility operated by the Department of Corrections.
(Added by Stats. 1993, Ch. 211, Sec. 1. Effective July 26, 1993.)

5023.

(a) It is the intent of the Legislature that the Department of Corrections operate in the most cost-effective and efficient manner possible when purchasing health care services for inmates. To achieve this goal, it is desirable that the department have the benefit and experience of the California Medical Assistance Commission in planning and negotiating for the purchase of health care services.
(b) The Department of Corrections shall consult with the commission to assist the department in planning and negotiating contracts for the purchase of health care services. The commission shall advise the department, and may negotiate directly with providers on behalf of the department, as mutually agreed upon by the commission and the department.
(Amended by Stats. 1995, Ch. 749, Sec. 9. Effective October 10, 1995.)

5023.2.

(a) In order to promote the best possible patient outcomes, eliminate unnecessary medical and pharmacy costs, and ensure consistency in the delivery of health care services, the department shall maintain a statewide utilization management program that shall include, but not be limited to, all of the following:
(1) Objective, evidence-based medical necessity criteria and utilization guidelines.
(2) The review, approval, and oversight of referrals to specialty medical services.
(3) The management and oversight of community hospital bed usage and supervision of health care bed availability.
(4) Case management processes for high medical risk and high medical cost patients.
(5) A preferred provider organization (PPO) and related contract initiatives that improve the coverage, resource allocation, and quality of contract medical providers and facilities.
(b) The department shall develop and implement policies and procedures to ensure that all adult prisons employ the same statewide utilization management program established pursuant to subdivision (a) that supports the department's goals for cost-effective auditable patient outcomes, access to care, an effective and accessible specialty network, and prompt access to hospital and infirmary resources. The department shall provide a copy of these policies and procedures, by July 1, 2011, to the Joint Legislative Budget Committee, the Senate Committee on Appropriations, the Senate Committee on Budget and Fiscal Review, the Senate Committee on Health, the Senate Committee on Public Safety, the Assembly Committee on Appropriations, the Assembly Committee on Budget, the Assembly Committee on Health, and the Assembly Committee on Public Safety.
(c) (1) The department shall establish annual quantitative utilization management performance objectives to promote greater consistency in the delivery of contract health care services, enhance health care quality outcomes, and reduce unnecessary referrals

to contract medical services. On July 1, 2011, the department shall report the specific quantitative utilization management performance objectives it intends to accomplish statewide in each adult prison during the next 12 months to the Joint Legislative Budget Committee, the Senate Committee on Appropriations, the Senate Committee on Budget and Fiscal Review, the Senate Committee on Health, the Senate Committee on Public Safety, the Assembly Committee on Appropriations, the Assembly Committee on Budget, the Assembly Committee on Health, and the Assembly Committee on Public Safety.

(2) The requirement for submitting a report imposed under this subdivision is inoperative on January 1, 2015, pursuant to Section 10231.5 of the Government Code.

(d) On March 1, 2012, and each March 1 thereafter, the department shall report all of the following to the Joint Legislative Budget Committee, the Senate Committee on Appropriations, the Senate Committee on Budget and Fiscal Review, the Senate Committee on Health, the Senate Committee on Public Safety, the Assembly Committee on Appropriations, the Assembly Committee on Budget, the Assembly Committee on Health, and the Assembly Committee on Public Safety:

(1) The extent to which the department achieved the statewide quantitative utilization management performance objectives set forth in the report issued the previous March as well as the most significant reasons for achieving or not achieving those performance objectives.

(2) A list of adult prisons that achieved and a list of adult prisons that did not achieve their quantitative utilization management performance objectives and the significant reasons for the success or failure in achieving those performance objectives at each adult state prison.

(3) The specific quantitative utilization management performance objectives the department and each adult state prison intends to accomplish in the next 12 months.

(4) A description of planned and implemented initiatives necessary to accomplish the next 12 months' quantitative utilization management performance objectives statewide and for each adult state prison. The department shall describe initiatives that were considered and rejected and the reasons for their rejection.

(5) The costs for inmate health care for the previous fiscal year, both statewide and at each adult state prison, and a comparison of costs from the fiscal year prior to the fiscal year being reported both statewide and at each adult state prison.

(e) It is the intent of the Legislature that any activities the department undertakes to implement the provisions of this section shall result in no year-over-year net increase in state costs.

(f) The following definitions shall apply to this section:

(1) "Contract medical costs" mean costs associated with an approved contractual agreement for the purposes of providing direct and indirect specialty medical care services.

(2) "Specialty care" means medical services not delivered by primary care providers.

(3) "Utilization management program" means a strategy designed to ensure that health care expenditures are restricted to those that are needed and appropriate by reviewing patient-inmate medical records through the application of defined criteria or expert opinion, or both. Utilization management assesses the efficiency of the health care process and the appropriateness of decisionmaking in relation to the site of care, its frequency, and its duration through prospective, concurrent, and retrospective utilization reviews.

(4) "Community hospital" means an institution located within a city, county, or city and county which is licensed under all applicable state and local laws and regulations to provide diagnostic and therapeutic services for the medical diagnosis, treatment, and care of injured, disabled, or sick persons in need of acute inpatient medical, psychiatric, or psychological care.

(g) The requirement for submitting a report imposed under subdivision (d) is inoperative on March 1, 2016, pursuant to Section 10231.5 of the Government Code.

(Amended by Stats. 2011, Ch. 296, Sec. 220. (AB 1023) Effective January 1, 2012.)

5023.5.

(a) Notwithstanding any other law, the Department of Corrections and Rehabilitation may contract with providers of health care services and health care network providers, including, but not limited to, health plans, preferred provider organizations, and other health care network managers. Hospitals that do not contract with the department for emergency health care services shall provide these services to the department on the same basis as they are required to provide these services pursuant to Section 489.24 of Title 42 of the Code of Federal Regulations. The department may only reimburse a noncontract provider of hospital or physician services at a rate equal to or less than the amount payable under the Medicare Fee Schedule, regardless of whether the hospital is located within or outside of California.

(b) An entity that provides ambulance or any other emergency or nonemergency response service to the department, and that does not contract with the department for that service, shall be reimbursed for the service at the rate payable under the Medicare Fee Schedule, regardless of whether the provider is located within or outside of California.

(c) Until regulations or emergency regulations are adopted in accordance with subdivision (g), the department shall not reimburse a contract provider of hospital services at a rate that exceeds 130 percent of the amount payable under the Medicare Fee Schedule, a contract provider of physician services at a rate that exceeds 110 percent of the amount payable under the Medicare Fee Schedule, or a contract provider of ambulance services at a rate that exceeds 120 percent of the amount payable under the Medicare Fee Schedule. The maximum rates established by this subdivision shall not apply to reimbursement for administrative days, transplant services, services provided pursuant to competitively bid contracts, or services provided pursuant to a contract executed prior to September 1, 2009.

(d) The maximum rates set forth in this section shall not apply to contracts entered into through the department's designated health care network provider, if any. The rates for those contracts shall be negotiated at the lowest rate possible under the circumstances.

(e) The department and its designated health care network provider may enter into exclusive or nonexclusive contracts on a bid or negotiated basis for hospital, physician, and ambulance services contracts.

(f) The Secretary of the Department of Corrections and Rehabilitation may adopt regulations to implement this section. During the existence of the receivership established in United States District Court for the Northern District of California, Case No. C01-1351 TEH, Plata v. Schwarzenegger, the adoption, amendment, or repeal of a regulation authorized by this section is hereby exempted from the rulemaking provisions of the Administrative Procedure Act (Chapter 3.5 (commencing with Section 11340) of Part 1 of Division 3 of Title 2 of the Government Code).

(g) The secretary may change the maximum rates set forth in this section by regulation or emergency regulation, adopted in accordance with the Administrative Procedure Act, but no sooner than 30 days after notification to the Joint Legislative Budget Committee. Those changes may include, but are not limited to, increasing or decreasing rates, or adding location-based differentials such as those provided to small and rural hospitals as defined in Section 124840 of the Health and Safety Code. The adoption, amendment, repeal, or readoption of a regulation authorized by this section is deemed to address an emergency, for purposes of Sections 11346.1 and 11349.6 of the Government Code, and the secretary is hereby exempted for this purpose from the requirements of subdivision (b) of Section 11346.1 of the Government Code.

(h) During the existence of the receivership established in United States District Court for the Northern District of California, Case No. C01-1351 TEH, Plata v. Schwarzenegger, references in this section to the "secretary" shall mean the receiver appointed in that action.

(Amended by Stats. 2009, 4th Ex. Sess., Ch. 22, Sec. 31. Effective July 28, 2009.)

5023.6.

(a) The Department of Corrections and Rehabilitation shall, by January 1, 2011, do all of the following:

(1) Adopt industry standard claim forms for use by contract health care service providers.

(2) Be able to accept secure electronic submission of claims from contract health care service providers.

(3) Perform periodic audits of claims paid to contract health care providers.

(4) Provide secure, remote electronic access to claim status information to those contract health care service providers submitting claims electronically in the manner required by the department.

(b) The department may adopt policies and procedures for the purpose of enabling electronic health care claims management and processing. The adoption, amendment, or repeal of policies and procedures for this limited purpose are exempt from the rulemaking provisions of the Administrative Procedure Act (Chapter 3.5 (commencing with Section 11340) of Part 1 of Division 3 of Title 2 of the Government Code).

(Added by Stats. 2010, Ch. 669, Sec. 2. (AB 1985) Effective January 1, 2011.)

5023.7.

(a) Notwithstanding any other provision of law, money recovered prior to July 1, 2011, from an overpayment of a medical contract expenditure, under the authority of the federal health care receiver, shall be credited to the fiscal year in which the expenditure was drawn. An amount not to exceed the total amount of the funds recovered shall be augmented to the appropriation to the department for the 2010-11 fiscal year, upon approval of the Department of Finance.

(b) Money recovered on or after July 1, 2011, from an overpayment of a medical contract expenditure, under the authority of the federal health care receiver, shall be credited to the fiscal year in which the expenditure was drawn. An amount not to exceed the amount of the overpayment shall be augmented to the appropriation to the department for the fiscal year in which the recovered funds are received, upon approval of the Department of Finance.

(c) Any money recovered and any adjustments to appropriations made pursuant to subdivisions (a) and (b) shall be reported to the Joint Legislative Budget Committee within 30 days.

(d) The requirement for submitting a report imposed under subdivision (c) is inoperative on January 1, 2016, pursuant to Section 10231.5 of the Government Code.

(Added by Stats. 2011, Ch. 36, Sec. 28. (SB 92) Effective June 30, 2011.)

5024.

(a) The Legislature finds and declares that:

(1) State costs for purchasing drugs and medical supplies for the health care of offenders in state custody have grown rapidly in recent years and will amount to almost seventy-five million dollars ($75,000,000) annually in the 1999-2000 fiscal year.

(2) The California State Auditor's Office found in a January 2000 audit report that the state could save millions of dollars annually by improving its current processes for the procurement of drugs for inmate health care and by pursuing alternative procurement methods.

(3) It is the intent of the Legislature that the Department of Corrections and Rehabilitation, in cooperation with the Department of General Services and other appropriate state agencies, take prompt action to adopt cost-effective reforms in its drug and medical supply procurement processes by establishing a program to obtain rebates from drug manufacturers, implementing alternative contracting and procurement reforms, or by some combination of these steps.

(b) (1) The Secretary of the Department of Corrections and Rehabilitation, pursuant to the Administrative Procedure Act (Chapter 3.5 (commencing with Section 11340) of Part 1 of Division 3 of Title 2 of the Government Code) may adopt regulations requiring manufacturers of drugs to pay the department a rebate for the purchase of drugs for offenders in state custody that is at least equal to the rebate that would be applicable to the drug under Section 1927(c) of the federal Social Security Act (42 U.S.C. Sec. 1396r-8(c)). Any such regulation shall, at a minimum, specify the procedures for notifying drug manufacturers of the rebate requirements and for collecting rebate payments.

(2) If a rebate program is implemented, the secretary shall develop, maintain, and update as necessary a list of drugs to be provided under the rebate program, and establish a rate structure for reimbursement of each drug included in the rebate program. Rates shall not be less than the actual cost of the drug. However, the secretary may purchase a listed drug directly from the manufacturer and negotiate the most favorable bulk price for that drug. In order to minimize state administrative costs and maximize state benefits for the rebate program, the secretary may establish a program that focuses upon obtaining rebates for those drugs that it determines are purchased by the department in relatively large volumes.

(3) If a rebate program is implemented, the department shall submit an invoice, not less than two times per year, to each manufacturer for the amount of the rebate required by this subdivision. Drugs may be removed from the list for failure to pay the rebate required by this subdivision, unless the department determines that purchase of the drug is a medical necessity or that purchase of the drug is necessary to comply with a court order to ensure the appropriate provision of quality health care to offenders in state custody.

(4) In order to minimize state administrative costs and maximize state benefits for such a rebate program, if one is implemented, the Department of Corrections and Rehabilitation may enter into interagency agreements with the Department of General Services, the State Department of Health Care Services, the State Department of State Hospitals, or the State Department of Developmental Services, the University of California, another appropriate state department, or with more than one of those entities, for joint participation in a rebate program, collection and monitoring of necessary drug price and rebate data, the billing of manufacturers for rebates, the resolution of any disputes over rebates, and any other services necessary for the cost-effective operation of the rebate program.

(5) The Department of Corrections and Rehabilitation, separately or in cooperation with other state agencies, may contract for the services of a pharmaceutical benefits manager for any services necessary for the cost-effective operation of the rebate program, if one is implemented, or for other services to improve the contracting and procurement of drugs and medical supplies for inmate health care.

(c) Nothing in this section shall prohibit the department, as an alternative to or in addition to establishing a rebate program for drugs for inmate health care, from implementing, in cooperation with the Department of General Services and other appropriate state agencies, other cost-effective strategies for procurement of drugs and medical supplies for offenders in state custody, including, but not limited to:

(1) Improvements in the existing statewide master agreement procedures for purchasing contract and noncontract drugs at a discount from drug manufacturers.

(2) Participation by offenders in state custody infected with human immunodeficiency virus (HIV), the etiologic agent of acquired immune deficiency syndrome (AIDS), in the AIDS Drug Assistance Program.

(3) Membership in the Minnesota Multistate Contracting Alliance for Pharmacy (MMCAP) or other cooperative purchasing arrangements with other governmental entities.

(4) Greater centralization or standardization of procurement of drugs and medical supplies among individual prisons in the Department of Corrections and Rehabilitation prison system.

(d) The California State Auditor's Office shall report to the Legislature and the Governor by January 10, 2002, its findings in regard to:

(1) An evaluation of the trends in state costs for the procurement of drugs and medical supplies for offenders in state custody, and an assessment of the major factors affecting those trends.

(2) A summary of the steps taken by the Department of Corrections and Rehabilitation, the Department of General Services, and other appropriate state agencies to implement this section.

(3) An evaluation of the compliance by these state agencies with the findings and recommendations of the January 2000 California State Auditor's Office report for reform of procurement of drugs and medical supplies for offenders in state custody.

(4) Any further recommendations of the California State Auditor's Office for reform of state drug procurement practices, policies, or statutes.

(Amended by Stats. 2012, Ch. 281, Sec. 40. (SB 1395) Effective January 1, 2013.)

5024.2.

(a) The Department of Corrections and Rehabilitation is authorized to maintain and operate a comprehensive pharmacy services program for those facilities under the jurisdiction of the department that is both cost effective and efficient, and shall incorporate the following:

(1) A statewide pharmacy administration system with direct authority and responsibility for program administration and oversight.

(2) Medically necessary pharmacy services using professionally and legally qualified pharmacists, consistent with the size and the scope of medical services provided.

(3) Written procedures and operational practices pertaining to the delivery of pharmaceutical services.

(4) A multidisciplinary, statewide Pharmacy and Therapeutics Committee responsible for all of the following:

(A) Developing and managing a department formulary.

(B) Standardizing the strengths and dosage forms for medications used in department facilities.

(C) Maintaining and monitoring a system for the review and evaluation of corrective actions related to errors in prescribing, dispensing, and administering medications.

(D) Conducting regular therapeutic category reviews for medications listed in the department formulary.

(E) Evaluating medication therapies and providing input to the development of disease management guidelines used in the department.

(5) A requirement for the use of generic medications, when available, unless an exception is reviewed and approved in accordance with an established nonformulary approval process. The nonformulary approval process shall include a process whereby a prescriber may indicate on the face of the prescription "dispense as written" or other appropriate form for electronic prescriptions.

(6) Use of an enterprise-based pharmacy operating system that provides management with information on prescription workloads, medication utilization, prescribing data, and other key pharmacy information.

(b) The department is authorized to operate and maintain a centralized pharmacy distribution center to provide advantages of scale and efficiencies related to medication purchasing, inventory control, volume production, drug distribution, workforce utilization, and increased patient safety. It is the intent of the Legislature that the centralized pharmacy distribution center and institutional pharmacies be licensed as pharmacies by the California State Board of Pharmacy meeting all applicable regulations applying to a pharmacy.

(1) To the extent it is cost effective and efficient, the centralized pharmacy distribution center should include systems to do the following:

(A) Order and package bulk pharmaceuticals and prescription and stock orders for all department correctional facilities.

(B) Label medications as required to meet state and federal prescription requirements.

(C) Provide barcode validation matching the drug to the specific prescription or floor stock order.

(D) Sort completed orders for shipping and delivery to department facilities.

(2) Notwithstanding any other requirements, the department centralized pharmacy distribution center is authorized to do the following:

(A) Package bulk pharmaceuticals into both floor stock and patient-specific packs.

(B) Reclaim, for reissue, unused and unexpired medications.

(C) Distribute the packaged products to department facilities for use within the state corrections system.

(3) The centralized pharmacy distribution center should maintain a system of quality control checks on each process used to package, label, and distribute medications. The quality control system may include a regular process of random checks by a licensed pharmacist.

(c) The department may investigate and initiate potential systematic improvements in order to provide for the safe and efficient distribution and control of, and accountability for, drugs within the department's statewide pharmacy administration system, taking into account factors unique to the correctional environment.

(d) The department should ensure that there is a program providing for the regular inspection of all department pharmacies in the state to verify compliance with applicable law, rules, regulations, and other standards as may be appropriate to ensure the health, safety, and welfare of the department's inmate patients.

(e) On March 1, 2012, and each March 1 thereafter, the department shall report all of the following to the Joint Legislative Budget Committee, the Senate Committee on Appropriations, the Senate Committee on Budget and Fiscal Review, the Senate Committee on Health, the Senate Committee on Public Safety, the Assembly Committee on Appropriations, the Assembly Committee on Budget, the Assembly Committee on Health, and the Assembly Committee on Public Safety:

(1) The extent to which the Pharmacy and Therapeutics Committee has been established and achieved the objectives set forth in this section, as well as the most significant reasons for achieving or not achieving those objectives.

(2) The extent to which the department is achieving the objective of operating a fully functioning and centralized pharmacy distribution center, as set forth in this section, that distributes pharmaceuticals to every adult prison under the jurisdiction of the department, as well as the most significant reasons for achieving or not achieving that objective.

(3) The extent to which the centralized pharmacy distribution center is achieving cost savings through improved efficiency and distribution of unit dose medications.

(4) A description of planned or implemented initiatives to accomplish the next 12 months' objectives for achieving the goals set forth in this section, including a fully functioning and centralized pharmacy distribution center that distributes pharmaceuticals to every adult facility under the jurisdiction of the department.

(5) The costs for prescription pharmaceuticals for the previous fiscal year, both statewide and at each adult prison under the jurisdiction of the department, and a comparison of these costs with those of the prior fiscal year.

(f) The requirement for submitting a report imposed under subdivision (e) is inoperative on March 1, 2016, pursuant to Section 10231.5 of the Government Code.

(Amended by Stats. 2012, Ch. 41, Sec. 74. (SB 1021) Effective June 27, 2012.)

5024.5.

(a) The Department of Corrections shall adopt policies, procedures, and criteria to identify selected medication categories for the development of utilization protocols based on best practices, and the use of generic and therapeutic substitutes, as appropriate.

(b) The department shall develop utilization and treatment protocols for select medication categories based on defined priority criteria, including, but not limited to, the cost of the medications.

(c) On or before April 1, 2006, the department shall provide information, as part of the fiscal committee budget hearings for the 2006–07 budget year, on the impact of the adoption of these protocols.

(d) The department shall coordinate the implementation of this section with the Department of General Services' prescription drug bulk purchasing program pursuant to Chapter 12 (commencing with Section 14977) of Part 5.5 of Division 3 of Title 2 of the Government Code, in order to better achieve the goals and intent of that program.

(e) It is the intent of the Legislature that the department shall complete the implementation of this section utilizing the existing resources of the department.

(Added by Stats. 2004, Ch. 383, Sec. 1. Effective January 1, 2005.)

5025.

(a) On or before July 1, 1993, the Department of Corrections shall implement and maintain procedures to identify inmates serving terms in state prison who are undocumented aliens subject to deportation. This identification procedure shall be completed, as to each inmate, within 90 days of the Department of Corrections having taken custody of the inmate.

(b) The procedures implemented by the department, pursuant to subdivision (a), shall include, but not be limited to, the following criteria for determining the country of citizenship of any person serving a term in state prison:

(1) Country of citizenship.

(2) Place of birth.

(3) Inmate's statements.

(4) Prior parole records.

(5) Prior arrest records.

(6) Probation Officer's Report (POR).

(7) Information from the Department of Justice's Criminal Identification and Information Unit.

(8) Other legal documents.

(c) The Department of Corrections shall report annually to the Legislature the number of persons identified as undocumented aliens pursuant to subdivision (a). The reports shall contain the number of persons referred, the race, national origin, and national ancestry of persons referred, the offense or offenses for which the person was committed to state prison, and the disposition of the referral, if known.

(Amended by Stats. 1994, Ch. 565, Sec. 5. Effective September 16, 1994. Superseded on operative date of amendment by Stats. 1994, Ch. 567, as further amended by Stats. 1995, Ch. 91.)

5025.

(a) Immediately upon the effective date of the amendments to this section made at the 1993–94 First Extraordinary Session of the Legislature, the Department of Corrections and the Department of the Youth Authority shall implement and maintain procedures to identify, within 90 days of assuming custody, inmates serving terms in state prison or wards of the Department of the Youth Authority who are undocumented felons subject to deportation. The Department of Corrections and the Department of the Youth Authority shall refer to the United States Immigration and Naturalization Service the name and location of any inmate or ward who may be an undocumented alien and who may be subject to deportation for a determination of whether the inmate or ward is undocumented and subject to deportation. The Department of Corrections and the Department of the Youth Authority shall make case files available to the United States Immigration and Naturalization Service for purposes of investigation.

(b) The procedures implemented by the department pursuant to subdivision (a) shall include, but not be limited to, the following criteria for determining the country of citizenship of any person serving a term in the state prison:

(1) Country of citizenship.

(2) Place of birth.

(3) Inmate's statements.

(4) Prior parole records.

(5) Prior arrest records.

(6) Probation Officer's Report (POR).

(7) Information from the Department of Justice's Criminal Identification and Information Unit.

(8) Other legal documents.

(c) Within 48 hours of identifying an inmate or ward as an undocumented felon pursuant to subdivision (a), the Department of Corrections and the Department of the Youth Authority shall cause the inmate or ward to be transferred to the custody of the United States Attorney General for appropriate action. Once an inmate or ward has been identified as an undocumented felon by the United States Immigration and Naturalization Service, the inmate or ward shall not undergo any additional evaluation or classification procedures other than those required for the safety or security of the institution, the inmate or ward, or the public.

(d) The Department of Corrections shall report quarterly to the Legislature the number of persons referred to the United States Immigration and Naturalization Service pursuant to subdivision (a). The report shall contain the number of persons transported, the race, national origin, and national ancestry of persons transported, the offense or offenses for which the persons were committed to state prison, and the facilities to which the persons were transported.

(Amended (as amended by Stats. 1994, Ch. 567) by Stats. 1995, Ch. 91, Sec. 133. Effective January 1, 1996. Amendments not operative until enactment of federal legislation, as provided by Stats. 1994, Ch. 567, Sec. 6.)

5026.

The Department of Corrections shall cooperate with the United States Immigration and Naturalization Service by providing the use of prison facilities, transportation, and general support, as needed, for the purposes of conducting and expediting deportation hearings and subsequent placement of deportation holds on undocumented aliens who are incarcerated in state prison.

(Added by Stats. 1993, Ch. 124, Sec. 1. Effective January 1, 1994. Repealed conditionally by Stats. 1994, Ch. 567, Secs. 3 and 6, upon enactment of specified federal legislation.)

5027.

(a) Upon appropriation by the Legislature in the annual Budget Act, the Department of Corrections and Rehabilitation shall award funding for an innovative grant program to not-for-profit organizations to replicate their programs at institutions that the Director of the Division of Rehabilitative Programs has determined are underserved by volunteer and not-for-profit organizations. The director shall develop a formula for identifying target institutions based upon factors including, but not limited to, number of volunteers, number of inmates, number of volunteer-based programs, and the size of waiting lists for inmates wanting to participate in programs.

(b) Grant funding shall be provided to not-for-profit organizations wishing to expand programs that they are currently providing in other California state prisons that have demonstrated success and focus on offender responsibility and restorative justice principles. The grants shall be awarded for a three-year period and are designed to be one time in nature. The grants shall go to programs that demonstrate that they will become self-sufficient or will be funded in the long term by donations or another source of ongoing funding. All funding shall go directly to the not-for-profit organizations and shall not be used for custody staff or administration of the grant. Any unspent funds shall revert to the fund source authorized for this purpose at the end of three years.

(c) On or before January 1 of each year, the department shall report to the budget committees and public safety committees in both houses of the Legislature on the following information from the previous fiscal year's grants:

(1) The number of grants provided.

(2) The institutions receiving grants.

(3) A description of each program and level of funding provided, organized by institution.

(4) The start date of each program.

(5) Any feedback from inmates participating in the programs on the value of the programs.

(6) Any feedback from the program providers on their experience with each institution.

(7) The number of participants participating in each program.

(8) The number of participants completing each program.

(9) Waiting lists, if any, for each program.

(Added by Stats. 2016, Ch. 33, Sec. 22. (SB 843) Effective June 27, 2016.)

5028.

(a) Upon the entry of any person who is currently or was previously a foreign national into a facility operated by the Department of Corrections, the Director of Corrections shall inform the person that he or she may apply to be transferred to serve the remainder of his or her prison term in his or her current or former nation of citizenship. The director shall inform the person that he or she may contact his or her consulate and shall ensure that if notification is requested by the inmate, that the inmate's nearest consulate or embassy is notified without delay of his or her incarceration.

(b) Upon the request of a foreign consulate representing a nation that requires mandatory notification under Article 36 of the Vienna Convention on Consular Relations Treaty listed in subdivision (d) of Section 834c, the Department of Corrections shall provide the foreign consulate with a list of the names and locations of all inmates in its custody that have self-identified that nation as his or her place of birth.

(c) The Department of Corrections shall implement and maintain procedures to process applications for the transfer of prisoners to their current or former nations of citizenship under subdivision (a) and shall forward all applications to the Governor or his or her designee for appropriate action.

(Amended by Stats. 2004, Ch. 924, Sec. 2. Effective January 1, 2005.)

5029.

(a) The Director of Corrections shall ensure that documents, computers, or computer accessible media containing personal information relating to an employee of the Department of Corrections are not removed from the state prison without proper authorization from the warden or his or her designee.

(b) Any employee of the Department of Corrections who, without proper authorization, knowingly removes personal information relating to an employee of the Department of Corrections from the state prison in violation of subdivision (a), or who fails to provide the appropriate notice as required in subdivision (c), is subject to disciplinary action.

(c) (1) An employee who removes personal information shall, once the employee is aware that the information either is lost or stolen or cannot be accounted for, make a reasonable effort to immediately notify the warden, or his or her designee, of that fact.

(2) The warden, or his or her designee, shall attempt to notify the employee whose personal information either is lost or stolen or cannot be accounted for within 24 hours of receiving the notice under paragraph (1).

(d) For purposes of this section, "personal information" shall have the same meaning as set forth in Section 1798.3 of the Civil Code.

(e) It is not the intent of the Legislature, in enacting this section, to inhibit or prevent a person from making a disclosure of improper governmental activity that is protected by subparagraphs (A) and (B) of paragraph (2) of subdivision (a) of Section 6129, or by the California Whistleblower Protection Act, Article 3 (commencing with Section 8547) of Chapter 6.5 of Division 1 of Title 2 of the Government Code, or by the Whistleblower Protection Act, Article 10 (commencing with Section 9149.20) of Chapter 1.5 of Part 1 of Division 2 of Title 2 of the Government Code. Furthermore, nothing in this section shall be construed to interfere with the authority of the Office of the Inspector General pursuant to Section 6126.5 of this code, nor the authority of the State Auditor pursuant to Section 8545.2 of the Government Code.

(Added by Stats. 2002, Ch. 240, Sec. 1. Effective January 1, 2003.)

5030.1.

(a) The possession or use of tobacco products by inmates under the jurisdiction of the Department of Corrections is prohibited. The Director of Corrections shall adopt regulations to implement this prohibition, which shall include an exemption for departmentally approved religious ceremonies.

(b) The use of tobacco products by any person not included in subdivision (a) on the grounds of any institution or facility under the jurisdiction of the Department of Corrections is prohibited, with the exception of residential staff housing where inmates are not present.

(Added by Stats. 2004, Ch. 798, Sec. 6. Effective January 1, 2005. Operative July 1, 2005, by Sec. 9 of Ch. 798.)

5031.

(a) The department shall submit an estimate of expenditures for each state or contracted facility housing offenders and for the cost of supervising offenders on parole, by region, for inclusion in the annual Governor's Budget and the May Revision thereto. The department shall submit its preliminary estimates for the current and next fiscal years to the Department of Finance by October 1 of each year and revised estimates by April 1 of the following year. The Department of Finance shall approve, modify, or deny the assumptions underlying all estimates and the population estimates released for the annual Governor's Budget and the May Revision. The April 1 submission shall only be a revision of the October 1 estimates and may not include any new assumptions or estimates from those submitted in the October 1 estimate.

(b) The population estimate for each state or contracted adult or juvenile facility shall contain, at least, the following:

(1) The capacity, as measured by the number of beds, categorized by cells, dorms, and intended security level.

(2) The projected number of offenders, by security level.

(3) The actual number of offenders, by security level.

(4) The number of offenders in a security level that differ from the classification score.

(5) The number of offenders, by program, that could benefit from rehabilitative programming, as identified by an assessment of risk and criminogenic needs.

(6) The actual number of offenders, by program, that receive rehabilitative programming based on an assessment of risk and criminogenic needs.

(7) A comparison of the number of authorized positions, filled positions, and vacant positions, by classification.

(8) The budget authority, as displayed in the annual Budget Act by program, compared to fiscal year-to-date expenditures and projected expenditures for the fiscal year.

(c) The population estimate for the Division of Adult Parole Operations shall contain at least the following:

(1) The projected number of offenders in each subpopulation, by region, and the total number of offenders.

(2) The actual number of offenders in each subpopulation, by region, and the total number of offenders.

(3) The number of offenders, by region, that could benefit from rehabilitative programming, as identified by an assessment of risk and criminogenic needs.

(4) The actual number of offenders, by region, that receive rehabilitative programming based on an assessment of risk and criminogenic needs.

(5) The number of ratio-driven positions budgeted in each region.

(6) The number of nonratio positions budgeted in each region, by function.

(7) A comparison of the number of authorized positions, filled positions, and vacant positions, by region and function.

(8) The budget authority, as displayed in the annual Budget Act by program, compared to fiscal year-to-date expenditures and projected expenditures for the fiscal year.

(d) The estimates shall include fiscal charts that track appropriations from the Budget Act to the current Governor's Budget and the May Revision for all fund sources for the current year and budget year.

(e) In the event that the methodological steps employed to arrive at previous estimates differ from those proposed, the department shall submit a descriptive narrative of the revised methodology. This information shall be provided to the Department of Finance, the Joint Legislative Budget Committee, and the public safety policy committees and fiscal committees of the Legislature.

(f) On or after January 10, if the Department of Finance discovers a material error in the information provided pursuant to this section, the Department of Finance shall inform the consultants to the fiscal committees of the Legislature of the error in a timely manner.

(g) The departmental estimates, assumptions, and other supporting data prepared for purposes of this section shall be forwarded annually to the Joint Legislative Budget Committee and the public safety policy committees and fiscal committees of the Legislature.

(Added by Stats. 2012, Ch. 41, Sec. 75. (SB 1021) Effective June 27, 2012.)

CHAPTER 2. The Secretary of the Department of Corrections and Rehabilitation [5050 - 5072]

(Heading of Chapter 2 amended by Stats. 2005, Ch. 10, Sec. 35.)

5050.

Commencing July 1, 2005, any reference to the Director of Corrections in this or any other code refers to the Secretary of the Department of Corrections and Rehabilitation. As of that date, the office of the Director of Corrections is abolished.

(Amended by Stats. 2005, Ch. 10, Sec. 36. Effective May 10, 2005. Operative July 1, 2005, by Sec. 99 of Ch. 10.)

5051.2.

The Director of Corrections shall have wide and successful administrative experience in adult or youth correctional programs embodying rehabilitative concepts.

(Added by Stats. 1953, Ch. 1458.)

5052.

Any officer or employee of the Department of Corrections and Rehabilitation designated in writing by the secretary, shall have the power of a head of a department pursuant to Article 2 (commencing at Section 11180) of Chapter 2, Part 1, Division 3, Title 2, of the Government Code.

(Amended by Stats. 2005, Ch. 10, Sec. 39. Effective May 10, 2005. Operative July 1, 2005, by Sec. 99 of Ch. 10.)

5054.

Commencing July 1, 2005, the supervision, management and control of the state prisons, and the responsibility for the care, custody, treatment, training, discipline and employment of persons confined therein are vested in the Secretary of the Department of Corrections and Rehabilitation.

(Amended by Stats. 2005, Ch. 10, Sec. 41. Effective May 10, 2005. Operative July 1, 2005, by Sec. 99 of Ch. 10.)

5054.1.

The Secretary of the Department of Corrections and Rehabilitation has full power to order returned to custody any person under the secretary's jurisdiction. The written order of the secretary shall be sufficient warrant for any peace officer to return to actual custody any escaped state prisoner or any state prisoner released prior to his or her scheduled release date who should be returned to custody. All peace officers shall execute an order as otherwise provided by law.

(Amended by Stats. 2007, Ch. 579, Sec. 49. Effective October 13, 2007.)

5054.2.

Whenever a person is incarcerated in a state prison for violating Section 261, 264.1, 266c, 285, 286, 287, 288, 288.5, 289, or former Section 288a, and the victim of one or more of those offenses is a child under the age of 18 years, the Secretary of the Department of Corrections and Rehabilitation shall protect the interest of that child victim by prohibiting visitation between the incarcerated person and the child victim pursuant to Section 1202.05. The secretary shall allow visitation only when the juvenile court, pursuant to Section 362.6 of the Welfare and Institutions Code, finds that visitation between the incarcerated person and his or her child victim is in the best interests of the child victim.

(Amended by Stats. 2018, Ch. 423, Sec. 110. (SB 1494) Effective January 1, 2019.)

5055.

Commencing July 1, 2005, all powers and duties previously granted to and imposed upon the Department of Corrections shall be exercised by the Secretary of the Department of Corrections and Rehabilitation, except where those powers and duties are expressly vested by law in the Board of Parole Hearings.

Whenever a power is granted to the secretary or a duty is imposed upon the secretary, the power may be exercised or the duty performed by a subordinate officer to the secretary or by a person authorized pursuant to law by the secretary.

(Amended by Stats. 2005, Ch. 10, Sec. 42. Effective May 10, 2005. Operative July 1, 2005, by Sec. 99 of Ch. 10.)

5055.5.

(a) The Secretary of the Department of Corrections and Rehabilitation shall develop a Data Dashboard as described in subdivisions (b) and (c) for each institution on a quarterly basis and post those reports on the department's Internet Web site. The department shall post both current fiscal-year reports and reports for the immediately preceding three fiscal years for each institution. The department shall also post corrections made to inaccurate or incomplete data to current or previous reports.

(b) Each report shall include a brief biography of the warden, including whether he or she is an acting or permanent warden, and a brief description of the prison, including the total number and level of inmates.

(c) Each report shall be created using the following information already collected using the COMPSTAT (computer assisted statistics) reports for each prison and shall include, but not be limited to, all of the following indicators:

(1) Staff vacancies, overtime, sick leave, and number of authorized staff positions.

(2) Rehabilitation programs, including enrollment capacity, actual enrollment, and diploma and GED completion rate.

(3) Number of deaths, specifying homicides, suicides, unexpected deaths, and expected deaths.

(4) Number of use of force incidents.

(5) Number of inmate appeals, including the number being processed, overdue, dismissed, and upheld.

(6) Number of inmates in administrative segregation.

(7) Total contraband seized, specifying the number of cellular telephones and drugs.

(d) Each report shall also include the following information, which is not currently collected or displayed by COMPSTAT:

(1) Total budget, including actual expenditures.

(2) Number of days in lockdown.

(Added by Stats. 2015, Ch. 162, Sec. 2. (SB 601) Effective January 1, 2016.)

5056.

(a) Each state prison under the jurisdiction of the department shall have a citizens' advisory committee except that one committee may serve every prison located in the same city or community. Each committee shall consist of not more than 15 members appointed by the institution's warden, nine of whom shall be appointed from a list of nominations submitted to him or her as follows:

(1) Two persons from nominations submitted by the Assembly Member in whose district the prison is located.

(2) Two persons from nominations submitted by the Senator in whose district the prison is located.

(3) Two persons from nominations submitted by the city council of the city containing or nearest to the institution.

(4) Two persons from nominations submitted by the county board of supervisors of the county containing the institution.

(5) One person from nominations submitted by the chief of police of the city containing or nearest to the institution and the county sheriff of the county containing the institution.

(b) Where a citizens' advisory committee serves more than one prison, the warden of each prison served by this committee shall collaborate with every other warden of a prison served by the committee for the purpose of appointing committee members.

(c) Each committee shall select its own chairperson by a majority vote of its members. The term of office of all members shall be two years. In the event of a vacancy due to resignation, death, or absence from three consecutive meetings, the appointing power shall fill the vacancy following receipt of written notification that a vacancy has occurred.

(d) Each committee shall meet at least once every two months or as often, on the call of the chairperson, as necessary to carry out the purposes and duties of the committee. Meetings of the committee shall be open to the public. The warden of each institution shall meet with the committee at least four times each year.

The advisory committees of the several institutions shall have the power of visitation of prison facilities and personnel in furtherance of the goals of this section.

(e) Nothing in this section shall be construed to require the disclosure by the department of information which may threaten the security of an institution or the safety of the surrounding community, nor shall the power of visitation specified in subdivision (d) extend to situations where institutional security would be jeopardized.

(Amended by Stats. 1997, Ch. 942, Sec. 2. Effective October 12, 1997.)

5056.1.

(a) The Legislature finds and declares that due to the local conditions resulting in the Chino Valley Independent Fire District having within its area of service two state institutions under the jurisdiction of the Department of Corrections and Rehabilitation, the California Institution for Men and the California Institution for Women, special legislation is needed to address the need for the citizens' advisory committees responsible for those institutions to have an additional member representing the Chino Valley Independent Fire District.

(b) In addition to the members designated for the citizens' advisory committees that advise the California Institution for Men and the California Institution for Women pursuant to Section 5056, there shall be an additional member representing the Chino Valley Independent Fire District, nominated by the Chino Valley Independent Fire District, for selection by the warden, pursuant to Section 5056.

(Added by Stats. 2009, Ch. 108, Sec. 1. (AB 430) Effective January 1, 2010.)

5057.

(a) Subject to the powers of the Department of Finance under Section 13300 of the Government Code, the secretary shall establish an accounting and auditing system for all of the agencies and institutions including the prisons which comprise the department in whatever form that will best facilitate their operation, and may modify the system from time to time.

(b) The accounting and auditing system shall include those accounts and records that are necessary to properly account for all money and property of the inmates.

(c) Except where other disposition is provided by law, all money belonging to the state received by the department, shall be reported to the Controller and deposited in the State Treasury monthly.

(Amended by Stats. 2005, Ch. 10, Sec. 43. Effective May 10, 2005. Operative July 1, 2005, by Sec. 99 of Ch. 10.)

5057.5.

(a) Notwithstanding Section 11005 of the Government Code, the Director of Corrections may accept a gift or donation of goods or services to the state following a review and determination by the director that the gift or donation is not subject to illegal or discriminatory conditions, that it does not involve the expenditure of state funds, and that the acceptance of the gift is in the best interests of the state.

(b) Notwithstanding subdivision (a), the acceptance of a gift or donation that would involve any expenditure of state funds shall be subject to Section 11005 of the Government Code.

(c) It is the intent of the Legislature in enacting this section to recognize the significant contribution that private donors of goods and services can make in supporting the corrections system, and the development of effective vocational education and correctional industries in our prison system. With that objective in mind, the Director of Corrections is encouraged to further develop the current system of gifts and donations through the design of a prompt and efficient review procedure that will encourage donors and protect the interests of the state.

(Added by Stats. 1983, Ch. 574, Sec. 1.)

5058.

(a) The director may prescribe and amend rules and regulations for the administration of the prisons and for the administration of the parole of persons sentenced under Section 1170 except those persons who meet the criteria set forth in Section 2962. The rules and regulations shall be promulgated and filed pursuant to Chapter 3.5 (commencing with Section 11340) of Part 1 of Division 3 of Title 2 of the Government Code, except as otherwise provided in this section and Sections 5058.1 to 5058.3, inclusive. All rules and regulations shall, to the extent practical, be stated in language that is easily understood by the general public.

For any rule or regulation filed as regular rulemaking as defined in paragraph (5) of subdivision (a) of Section 1 of Title 1 of the California Code of Regulations, copies of the rule or regulation shall be posted in conspicuous places throughout each institution and shall be mailed to all persons or organizations who request them no less than 20 days prior to its effective date.

(b) The director shall maintain, publish and make available to the general public, a compendium of the rules and regulations promulgated by the director pursuant to this section and Sections 5058.1 to 5058.3, inclusive.

(c) The following are deemed not to be "regulations" as defined in Section 11342.600 of the Government Code:

(1) Rules issued by the director applying solely to a particular prison or other correctional facility, provided that the following conditions are met:

(A) All rules that apply to prisons or other correctional facilities throughout the state are adopted by the director pursuant to Chapter 3.5 (commencing with Section 11340) of Part 1 of Division 3 of Title 2 of the Government Code.

(B) All rules except those that are excluded from disclosure to the public pursuant to subdivision (f) of Section 6254 of the Government Code are made available to all inmates confined in the particular prison or other correctional facility to which the rules apply and to all members of the general public.

(2) Short-term criteria for the placement of inmates in a new prison or other correctional facility, or subunit thereof, during its first six months of operation, or in a prison or other correctional facility, or subunit thereof, planned for closing during its last six months of operation, provided that the criteria are made available to the public and that an estimate of fiscal impact is completed pursuant to Sections 6650 to 6670, inclusive, of the State Administrative Manual.

(3) Rules issued by the director that are excluded from disclosure to the public pursuant to subdivision (f) of Section 6254 of the Government Code.

(Amended by Stats. 2002, Ch. 787, Sec. 26. Effective January 1, 2003.)

5058.1.

(a) For the purposes of this section, "pilot program" means a program implemented on a temporary and limited basis in order to test and evaluate the effectiveness of the program, develop new techniques, or gather information.

(b) The adoption, amendment, or repeal of a regulation by the director to implement a legislatively mandated or authorized pilot program or a departmentally authorized pilot program, is exempt from Chapter 3.5 (commencing with Section 11340) of Part 1 of Division 3 of Title 2 of the Government Code, if the following conditions are met:

(1) A pilot program affecting male inmates affects no more than 10 percent of the total state male inmate population; a pilot program affecting female inmates affects no more than 10 percent of the total state female inmate population; and a pilot program affecting male and female inmates affects no more than 10 percent of the total state inmate population.

(2) The director certifies in writing that the regulations apply to a pilot program that qualifies for exemption under this section. The certification shall include a description of the pilot program and of the methods the department will use to evaluate the results of the pilot program.

(3) The certification and regulations are filed with the Office of Administrative Law and the regulations are made available to the public by publication pursuant to subparagraph (F) of paragraph (3) of subdivision (b) of Section 6 of Title 1 of the California Code of Regulations.

(4) An estimate of fiscal impact is completed pursuant to Sections 6650 to 6670, inclusive, of the State Administrative Manual.

(c) The adoption, amendment, or repeal of a regulation pursuant to this section becomes effective immediately upon filing with the Secretary of State.

(d) A regulation adopted pursuant to this section is repealed by operation of law, and the amendment or repeal of a regulation pursuant to this section is reversed by operation of law, two years after the commencement of the pilot program being implemented, unless the adoption, amendment, or repeal of the regulation is promulgated by the director pursuant to Chapter 3.5 (commencing with Section 11340) of Part 1 of Division 3 of Title 2 of the Government Code. For the purpose of this subdivision, a pilot program commences on the date the first regulatory change implementing the program is filed with the Secretary of State.

(Added by Stats. 2001, Ch. 141, Sec. 2. Effective January 1, 2002.)

5058.2.

(a) Chapter 3.5 (commencing with Section 11340) of Part 1 of Division 3 of Title 2 of the Government Code does not apply to a department action or policy implementing an action, that is based on a determination by the director that there is a compelling need for immediate action, and that unless the action is taken, serious injury, illness, or death is likely to result. The action, or the policy implementing the action, may be taken provided that the following conditions shall subsequently be met:

(1) A written determination of imminent danger shall be issued describing the compelling need and why the specific action or actions must be taken to address the compelling need.

(2) The written determination of imminent danger shall be mailed within 10 working days to every person who has filed a request for notice of regulatory actions with the department and to the Chief Clerk of the Assembly and the Secretary of the Senate for referral to the appropriate policy committees.

(b) Any policy in effect pursuant to a determination of imminent danger shall lapse by operation of law 15 calendar days after the date of the written determination of imminent danger unless an emergency regulation is filed with the Office of Administrative Law pursuant to Section 5058.3. This section shall in no way exempt the department from compliance with other provisions of law related to fiscal matters of the state.

(Added by Stats. 2001, Ch. 141, Sec. 3. Effective January 1, 2002.)

5058.3.

(a) Emergency adoption, amendment, or repeal of a regulation by the director shall be conducted pursuant to Chapter 3.5 (commencing with Section 11340) of Part 1 of Division 3 of Title 2 of the Government Code, except with respect to the following:

(1) Notwithstanding subdivision (e) of Section 11346.1 of the Government Code, the initial effective period for an emergency adoption, amendment, or repeal of a regulation shall be 160 days.

(2) Notwithstanding subdivision (b) of Section 11346.1 of the Government Code, no showing of emergency is necessary in order to adopt, amend, or repeal an emergency regulation if the director instead certifies, in a written statement filed with the Office of Administrative Law, that operational needs of the department require adoption, amendment, or repeal of the regulation on an emergency basis. The written statement shall include a description of the underlying facts and an explanation of the operational need to use the emergency rulemaking procedure. This paragraph provides an alternative to filing a statement of emergency pursuant to subdivision (b) of Section 11346.1 of the Government Code. It does not preclude filing a statement of emergency. This paragraph only applies to the initial adoption and one readoption of an emergency regulation.

(3) Notwithstanding subdivision (b) of Section 11349.6 of the Government Code, the adoption, amendment, or repeal of a regulation pursuant to paragraph (2) shall be reviewed by the Office of Administrative Law within 20 calendar days after its submission. In conducting its review, the Office of Administrative Law shall accept and consider public comments for the first 10 calendar days of the review period. Copies of any comments received by the Office of Administrative Law shall be provided to the department.

(4) Regulations adopted pursuant to paragraph (2) of subdivision (a) are not subject to the requirements of paragraph (2) of subdivision (a) of Section 11346.1 of the Government Code.

(b) It is the intent of the Legislature, in authorizing the deviations in this section from the requirements and procedures of Chapter 3.5 (commencing with Section 11340) of Part 1 of Division 3 of Title 2 of the Government Code, to authorize the department to expedite the exercise of its power to implement regulations as its unique operational circumstances require.

(Amended by Stats. 2006, Ch. 713, Sec. 7. Effective January 1, 2007.)

5058.4.

(a) The director shall provide for the development and implementation of a disciplinary matrix with offenses and associated punishments applicable to all department employees, in order to ensure notice and consistency statewide. The disciplinary matrix shall take into account aggravating and mitigating factors for establishing a just and proper penalty for the charged misconduct, as required by the California Supreme Court in Skelly v. State Personnel Board (1975) 15 Cal.3d 194. The presence of aggravating or mitigating factors may result in the imposition of a greater or a lesser penalty than might otherwise be mandated by the disciplinary matrix.

(b) The director shall adopt a code of conduct for all employees of the department.

(c) The director shall ensure that employees who have reported improper governmental activities and who request services from the department are informed of the services available to them.

(d) The department shall post the code of conduct in locations where employee notices are maintained. On July 1, 2005, and annually thereafter, the department shall send by

electronic mail to its employees who have authorized access to electronic mail, the following:
(1) Information regarding the code of conduct.
(2) The duty to report misconduct.
(3) How to report misconduct.
(4) The duty to fully cooperate during investigations.
(5) Assurances against retaliation.
(Added by Stats. 2004, Ch. 738, Sec. 2. Effective January 1, 2005.)
5058.5.
In addition to the services rendered by physicians and surgeons, including psychiatrists, or by psychologists, pursuant to Sections 5068 and 5079, physicians and surgeons, including psychiatrists and psychologists, employed by, or under contract to provide mental health services to, the Department of Corrections may also provide the following medically or psychologically necessary services: prescreening of mental disorders; determination of the mental competency of inmates to participate in classification hearings; evaluation of parolees during temporary detention; determining whether mental health treatment should be a condition of parole; and such other services as may be required which are consistent with their licensure.
(Added by Stats. 1984, Ch. 1123, Sec. 2.)
5058.6.
The Director of the Department of Corrections shall have the authority of a head of a department set forth in subdivision (e) of Section 11181 of the Government Code to issue subpoenas as provided in Article 2 (commencing with Section 11180) of Chapter 2 of Division 3 of Title 2 of the Government Code. The department shall adopt regulations on the policies and guidelines for the issuance of subpoenas.
(Added by renumbering Section 5058.5 (as added by Stats. 1992, Ch. 695) by Stats. 2001, Ch. 854, Sec. 53. Effective January 1, 2002.)
5059.
This title shall not affect the powers or jurisdiction of the Department of Transportation as to road camps pursuant to Article 4 (commencing with Section 2760) of Chapter 5 of Title 1 of Part 3.
(Amended by Stats. 1987, Ch. 828, Sec. 148.)
5060.
The Director of Corrections may assist persons discharged, paroled, or otherwise released from confinement in an institution of the department and may secure employment for them, and for such purposes he may employ necessary officers and employees, may purchase tools, and give any other assistance that, in his judgment, he deems proper for the purpose of carrying out the objects and spirit of this section. Repayment of cash assistance received under this section from the current, or any prior appropriation, shall be credited to the appropriation current at time of such repayment.
(Added by Stats. 1965, Ch. 1751.)
5061.
Whenever any person confined in any state institution subject to the jurisdiction of the Director of Corrections dies, and no demand or claim is made upon the director or his or her designee for the body of the deceased inmate by the inmate's next of kin or legally appointed representative, the director shall dispose of the body by cremation or burial no sooner than 10 calendar days after the inmate's death. The director or his or her designee may waive the 10-day waiting period for disposal of the deceased inmate's body if confirmation is received that the inmate's next of kin, or legally appointed representative, refuses to take possession of the body. If any personal funds or property of that person remains in the custody or possession of the Director of Corrections, the funds shall be applied to the payment of his or her cremation or burial expenses and related charges in an amount not exceeding those expenses and charges. If no demand or claim is made upon the director by the owner of the funds or property or his or her legally appointed representative, the director shall hold and dispose of those funds or property as follows:
(a) If the decedent leaves a will, the director shall, within 30 days after the date of death of the decedent, deliver the will to the clerk of the superior court having jurisdiction of the estate. If an executor is named in the will, the director shall furnish him or her written notice of the delivery of the will as provided in this section.
(b) All money or other personal property of the decedent remaining in the custody or possession of the director shall be held by him or her for a period of one year from the date of death of the decedent, for the benefit of the heirs, legatees or successors in interest of that decedent.
(c) Upon the expiration of the one-year period, any money remaining unclaimed in the custody or possession of the director shall be delivered by him or her to the Treasurer for deposit in the Unclaimed Property Fund under Article 1 (commencing with Section 1440) of Chapter 6 of Title 10 of Part 3 of the Code of Civil Procedure.
(d) Upon the expiration of the one-year period, all personal property and documents of the decedent, other than cash, remaining unclaimed in the custody or possession of the director, shall be disposed of as follows:
(1) All deeds, contracts, or assignments shall be filed by the director with the public administrator of the county of commitment of the decedent.
(2) All other personal property shall be sold by the director at public auction, or upon a sealed-bid basis, and the proceeds of the sale delivered by him or her to the Treasurer in the same manner as is provided in this section with respect to unclaimed money of the decedent. If he or she deems it expedient to do so, the director may accumulate the property of several decedents and sell the property in such lots as he or she may determine, provided that he or she makes a determination as to each decedent's share of the proceeds.
(3) If any personal property of the decedent is not salable at public auction, or upon a sealed-bid basis, or if it has no intrinsic value, or if its value is not sufficient to justify the deposit of the property in the State Treasury, the director may order it destroyed.
(4) All other unclaimed personal property of the decedent not disposed of as provided in paragraph (1), (2), or (3), shall be delivered by the director to the Controller for deposit in the State Treasury under Article 1 (commencing with Section 1440) of Chapter 6 of Title 10 of Part 3 of the Code of Civil Procedure.
(Amended by Stats. 1996, Ch. 805, Sec. 4. Effective January 1, 1997.)
5062.
Whenever any person confined in any state institution subject to the jurisdiction of the Director of Corrections escapes, or is discharged or paroled from that institution, and any personal funds or property of that person remains in the hands of the Director of Corrections, and no demand is made upon the director by the owner of the funds or property or his or her legally appointed representative, all money and other intangible personal property of the person, other than deeds, contracts, or assignments, remaining in the custody or possession of the director shall be held by him or her for a period of three years from the date of that escape, discharge, or parole, for the benefit of that person or his or her successors in interest.
Upon the expiration of the three-year period, any money and other intangible personal property, other than deeds, contracts, or assignments, remaining unclaimed in the custody or possession of the director shall be subject to Article 1 (commencing with Section 1500) of Chapter 7 of Title 10 of Part 3 of the Code of Civil Procedure.
Upon the expiration of one year from the date of that escape, discharge, or parole:
(a) All deeds, contracts, or assignments shall be filed by the director with the public administrator of the county of commitment of that person.
(b) All tangible personal property other than money, remaining unclaimed in his or her custody or possession, shall be sold by the director at public auction, or upon a sealed-bid basis, and the proceeds of the sale shall be held by him or her subject to Section 5008 and subject to Article 1 (commencing with Section 1500) of Chapter 7 of Title 10

of Part 3 of the Code of Civil Procedure. If he or she deems it expedient to do so, the director may accumulate the property of several inmates and may sell the property in lots as he or she may determine, provided that he or she makes a determination as to each inmate's share of the proceeds.
If any tangible personal property covered by this section is not salable at public auction or upon a sealed-bid basis, or if it has no intrinsic value, or if its value is not sufficient to justify its retention by the director to be offered for sale at public auction or upon a sealed-bid basis at a later date, the director may order it destroyed.
(Amended by Stats. 1992, Ch. 225, Sec. 1. Effective January 1, 1993.)
5063.
Before any money or other personal property or documents are delivered to the State Treasurer, State Controller, or public administrator, or sold at auction or upon a sealed-bid basis, or destroyed, under the provisions of Section 5061, and before any personal property or documents are delivered to the public administrator, or sold at auction or upon a sealed-bid basis, or destroyed, under the provisions of Section 5062, of this code, notice of said intended disposition shall be posted at least 30 days prior to the disposition, in a public place at the institution where the disposition is to be made, and a copy of such notice shall be mailed to the last known address of the owner or deceased owner, at least 30 days prior to such disposition. The notice prescribed by this section need not specifically describe each item of property to be disposed of.
(Amended by Stats. 1961, Ch. 1962.)
5064.
At the time of delivering any money or other personal property to the Treasurer or Controller under Section 5061 or of Article 1 (commencing with Section 1500) of Chapter 7 of Title 10 of Part 3 of the Code of Civil Procedure, the director shall deliver to the Controller a schedule setting forth a statement and description of all money and other personal property delivered, and the name and last known address of the owner or deceased owner.
(Amended by Stats. 1987, Ch. 828, Sec. 151.)
5065.
When any personal property has been destroyed as provided in Section 5061 or 5062, no suit shall thereafter be maintained by any person against the State or any officer thereof for or on account of such property.
(Added by Stats. 1951, Ch. 1708.)
5065.5.
(a) A person or entity that enters into a contract with a criminal offender for the sale of the story of a crime for which the offender was convicted shall notify the California Department of Corrections and Rehabilitation that the parties have entered into a contract for sale of the offender's story if both of the following conditions are met:
(1) The offender's conviction was for any offense specified in paragraph (1), except voluntary manslaughter, (2), (3), (4), (5), (6), (7), (9), (16), (17), (20), (22), (25), (34), or (35) of subdivision (c) of Section 1192.7.
(2) Subdivision (b) of Section 340.3 of the Code of Civil Procedure does not preclude commencement of a civil action against the criminal offender.
(b) Within 90 days of being notified, the California Department of Corrections and Rehabilitation shall notify the victim, or if the victim cannot be reasonably notified, a member of the victim's immediate family, who has requested notification of the existence of a contract described by this section.
(c) For purposes of this section, "member of the victim's immediate family" means a spouse, child, parent, sibling, grandchild, or grandparent.
(Amended by Stats. 2016, Ch. 86, Sec. 241. (SB 1171) Effective January 1, 2017.)
5066.
The Director of Corrections shall expand the existing prison ombudsman program to ensure the comprehensive deployment of ombudsmen throughout the state prison system with specific focus on the maximum security institutions.
(Amended by Stats. 2004, Ch. 193, Sec. 149. Effective January 1, 2005.)
5068.
The Director of Corrections shall cause each person who is newly committed to a state prison to be examined and studied. This includes the investigation of all pertinent circumstances of the person's life such as the existence of any strong community and family ties, the maintenance of which may aid in the person's rehabilitation, and the antecedents of the violation of law because of which he or she has been committed to prison. Any person may be reexamined to determine whether existing orders and dispositions should be modified or continued in force.
Upon the basis of the examination and study, the Director of Corrections shall classify prisoners; and when reasonable, the director shall assign a prisoner to the institution of the appropriate security level and gender population nearest the prisoner's home, unless other classification factors make such a placement unreasonable.
As used in this section, "reasonable" includes consideration of the safety of the prisoner and the institution, the length of term, and the availability of institutional programs and housing.
As used in this section, "prisoner's home" means a place where the prisoner's spouse, parents, or children reside at the time of commitment.
When the diagnostic study of any inmate committed under subdivision (b) of Section 1168 so indicates, the director shall cause a psychiatric or psychological report to be prepared for the Community Release Board prior to the release of the inmate. The report shall be prepared by a psychiatrist or psychologist licensed to practice in this state.
Before the release of any inmate committed under subdivision (b) of Section 1168, the director shall provide the Community Release Board with a written evaluation of the prisoner.
(Amended by Stats. 1989, Ch. 1061, Sec. 2.)
5068.5.
(a) Notwithstanding any other law, except as provided in subdivisions (b) and (c), any person employed or under contract to provide diagnostic, treatment, or other mental health services in the state or to supervise or provide consultation on these services in the state correctional system shall be a physician and surgeon, a psychologist, or other health professional, licensed to practice in this state.
(b) Notwithstanding Section 5068 or Section 704 of the Welfare and Institutions Code, the following persons are exempt from the requirements of subdivision (a), so long as they continue in employment in the same class and in the same department:
(1) Persons employed on January 1, 1985, as psychologists to provide diagnostic or treatment services, including those persons on authorized leave, but not including intermittent personnel.
(2) Persons employed on January 1, 1989, to supervise or provide consultation on the diagnostic or treatment services, including persons on authorized leave, but not including intermittent personnel.
(c) (1) The requirements of subdivision (a) may be waived by the secretary solely for persons in the professions of psychology or clinical social work who are gaining qualifying experience for licensure in those professions in this state. Providers working in a licensed health care facility operated by the department shall receive a waiver in accordance with Section 1277 of the Health and Safety Code.
(2) A waiver granted pursuant to this subdivision shall not exceed four years from commencement of the employment in this state, at which time licensure shall have been obtained or the employment shall be terminated, except that an extension of a waiver of licensure may be granted for one additional year, based on extenuating circumstances determined by the department pursuant to subdivision (d). For persons employed as psychologists or clinical social workers less than full time, an extension of a waiver of licensure may be granted for additional years proportional to the extent of part-time

employment, as long as the person is employed without interruption in service, but in no case shall the waiver of licensure exceed six years in the case of clinical social workers or five years in the case of psychologists. However, this durational limitation upon waivers shall not apply to active candidates for a doctoral degree in social work, social welfare, or social science who are enrolled at an accredited university, college, or professional school, but these limitations shall apply following completion of that training.

(3) A waiver pursuant to this subdivision shall be granted only to the extent necessary to qualify for licensure, except that personnel recruited for employment from outside this state and whose experience is sufficient to gain admission to a licensure examination shall nevertheless have one year from the date of their employment in California to become licensed, at which time licensure shall have been obtained or the employment shall be terminated, provided that the employee shall take the licensure examination at the earliest possible date after the date of his or her employment, and if the employee does not pass the examination at that time, he or she shall have a second opportunity to pass the next possible examination, subject to the one-year limit.

(d) The department shall grant a request for an extension of a waiver of licensure pursuant to subdivision (c) based on extenuating circumstances if any of the following circumstances exist:

(1) The person requesting the extension has experienced a recent catastrophic event that may impair the person's ability to qualify for and pass the licensure examination. Those events may include, but are not limited to, significant hardship caused by a natural disaster; serious and prolonged illness of the person; serious and prolonged illness or death of a child, spouse, or parent; or other stressful circumstances.

(2) The person requesting the extension has difficulty speaking or writing the English language, or other cultural and ethnic factors exist that substantially impair the person's ability to qualify for and pass the license examination.

(3) The person requesting the extension has experienced other personal hardship that the department, in its discretion, determines to warrant the extension.

(Amended by Stats. 2017, Ch. 151, Sec. 2. (AB 1456) Effective July 31, 2017.)

5069.

(a) The administrative director of the Division of Industrial Accidents shall formulate procedures for the selection and orderly referral of injured inmates of state penal or correctional institutions who may be benefited by rehabilitation services and retrained for other positions upon release from incarceration. The State Department of Rehabilitation shall cooperate in both designing and monitoring results of rehabilitation programs for the disabled inmates. The primary purpose of this section is to rehabilitate injured inmates in order that they might engage in suitable and gainful employment upon their release.

(b) The director shall notify the injured inmate of the availability of rehabilitation services in those cases where there is continuing disability of 28 days and beyond. A copy of such notification shall be forwarded to the State Department of Rehabilitation.

(c) The initiation of a rehabilitation plan shall be the responsibility of the director.

(d) Upon establishment of a rehabilitation plan, the injured inmate shall cooperate in carrying it out.

(e) The injured inmate shall receive such medical and vocational rehabilitative services as may be reasonably necessary to restore him to suitable employment.

(f) The injured inmate's rehabilitation benefit is an additional benefit and shall not be converted to or replace any workmen's compensation benefit available to him.

(Added by Stats. 1976, Ch. 1347.)

5070.

Notwithstanding any other provision of law, the sex of a prison inmate shall not prevent the Director of Corrections from assigning any prison inmate to academic or vocational training programs situated in correctional institutions established for the incarceration of offenders of the opposite sex.

(Added by Stats. 1978, Ch. 685.)

5071.

(a) The Secretary of the Department of Corrections and Rehabilitation shall not assign any prison inmate to employment that provides that inmate with access to personal information of private individuals, including, but not limited to, the following: addresses; telephone numbers; health insurance, taxpayer, school, or employee identification numbers; mothers' maiden names; demand deposit account, debit card, credit card, savings account, or checking account numbers, PINs, or passwords; social security numbers; places of employment; dates of birth; state- or government-issued driver's license or identification numbers; alien registration numbers; government passport numbers; unique biometric data, such as fingerprints, facial scan identifiers, voice prints, retina or iris images, or other similar identifiers; unique electronic identification numbers; address or routing codes; and telecommunication identifying information or access devices.

(b) Any person who is a prison inmate, and who has access to any personal information, shall disclose that he or she is a prison inmate before taking any personal information from anyone.

(c) This section shall not apply to inmates in employment programs or public service facilities where incidental contact with personal information may occur.

(Amended by Stats. 2006, Ch. 538, Sec. 521. Effective January 1, 2007.)

5072.

(a) Notwithstanding any other provision of law, the Department of Corrections and Rehabilitation and the State Department of Health Care Services may develop a process to maximize federal financial participation for the provision of acute inpatient hospital services rendered to individuals who, but for their institutional status as inmates, are otherwise eligible for Medi-Cal pursuant to Chapter 7 (commencing with Section 14000) of Part 3 of Division 9 of the Welfare and Institutions Code or a Low Income Health Program (LIHP) pursuant to Part 3.6 (commencing with Section 15909) of Division 9 of the Welfare and Institutions Code.

(b) Federal reimbursement for acute inpatient hospital services for inmates enrolled in Medi-Cal shall occur through the State Department of Health Care Services and federal reimbursement for acute inpatient hospital services for inmates not enrolled in Medi-Cal but who are eligible for a LIHP shall occur through a county LIHP.

(c) (1) The Secretary of the Department of Corrections and Rehabilitation, in conjunction with the State Department of Health Care Services, shall develop a process to claim federal financial participation and to reimburse the Department of Corrections and Rehabilitation for the federal share of the allowable Medicaid cost provision of acute inpatient hospital services rendered to inmates according to this section and for any administrative costs incurred in support of those services.

(2) Public or community hospitals shall invoice the Department of Corrections and Rehabilitation to obtain reimbursement for acute inpatient hospital services in accordance with contracted rates of reimbursement, or if no contract is in place, the rates pursuant to Section 5023.5. The Department of Corrections and Rehabilitation shall reimburse a public or community hospital for the delivery of acute inpatient hospital services rendered to an inmate pursuant to this section. For individuals eligible for Medi-Cal pursuant to this section, the Department of Corrections and Rehabilitation shall submit a quarterly invoice to the State Department of Health Care Services for claiming federal participation at the Medi-Cal rate for acute inpatient hospital services. For enrollees in the LIHP, the Department of Corrections and Rehabilitation shall submit a quarterly invoice to the county of last legal residence pursuant to Section 14053.7 of the Welfare and Institutions Code. The county shall submit the invoice to the State Department of Health Care Services for claiming federal financial participation for acute inpatient hospital services for individuals made eligible pursuant to this section, pursuant to Section 14053.7 of the Welfare and Institutions Code, and pursuant to the

process developed in subdivision (b). The State Department of Health Care Services shall claim federal participation for eligible services for LIHP enrolled inmates at the rate paid by the Department of Corrections and Rehabilitation. The State Department of Health Care Services and counties shall remit funds received for federal participation to the Department of Corrections and Rehabilitation for allowable costs incurred as a result of delivering acute inpatient hospital services allowable under this section.

(3) The county LIHPs shall not experience any additional net expenditures of county funds due to the provision of services under this section.

(4) The Department of Corrections and Rehabilitation shall reimburse the State Department of Health Care Services and counties for administrative costs that are not reimbursed by the federal government.

(5) The Department of Corrections and Rehabilitation shall reimburse the State Department of Health Care Services for any disallowance that is required to be returned to the Centers for Medicare and Medicaid Services for any litigation costs incurred due to the implementation of this section.

(d) (1) The state shall indemnify and hold harmless participating entities that operate a LIHP, including all counties, and all counties that operate in a consortium that participates as a LIHP, against any and all losses, including, but not limited to, claims, demands, liabilities, court costs, judgments, or obligations, due to the implementation of this section as directed by the secretary and the State Department of Health Care Services.

(2) The State Department of Health Care Services may at its discretion require a county, as a condition of participation as a LIHP, to enroll an eligible inmate into its LIHP if the county is the inmate's county of last legal residence.

(3) The county LIHPs shall be held harmless by the state for any disallowance or deferral if federal action is taken due to the implementation of this section in accord with the state's policies, directions, and requirements.

(e) (1) The Department of Corrections and Rehabilitation, in conjunction with the State Department of Health Care Services, shall develop a process to facilitate eligibility determinations for individuals who may be eligible for Medi-Cal or a LIHP pursuant to this section and Section 14053.7 of the Welfare and Institutions Code.

(2) The Department of Corrections and Rehabilitation shall assist inmates in completing either the Medi-Cal or LIHP application as appropriate and shall forward that application to the State Department of Health Care Services for processing.

(3) Notwithstanding any other state law, and only to the extent that federal law allows and federal financial participation is available, for the limited purpose of implementing this section, the department or its designee is authorized to act on behalf of an inmate for purposes of applying for or determinations of Medi-Cal or LIHP eligibility.

(f) (1) This section does not restrict or limit the eligibility or alter county responsibility for payment of any service delivered to a parolee who has been released from detention or incarceration and now resides in a county that participates in the LIHP. If otherwise eligible for the county's LIHP, the LIHP shall enroll the parolee.

(2) Notwithstanding paragraph (1), at the option of the state, for enrolled parolees who have been released from detention or incarceration and now reside in a county that participates in a LIHP, the LIHP shall reimburse providers for the delivery of services which are otherwise the responsibility of the state to provide. Payment for these medical services, including both the state and federal shares of reimbursement, shall be included as part of the reimbursement process described in paragraph (1) of subdivision (c).

(3) Enrollment of individuals in a LIHP under this subdivision shall be subject to any enrollment limitations described in subdivision (h) of Section 15910 of the Welfare and Institutions Code.

(g) The department shall be responsible to the LIHP for the nonfederal share of any reimbursement made for the provision of acute inpatient hospital services rendered to inmates pursuant to this section.

(h) Reimbursement pursuant to this section shall be limited to those acute inpatient hospital services for which federal financial participation pursuant to Title XIX of the federal Social Security Act is allowed.

(i) This section shall have no force or effect if there is a final judicial determination made by any state or federal court that is not appealed, or by a court of appellate jurisdiction that is not further appealed, in any action by any party, or a final determination by the administrator of the federal Centers for Medicare and Medicaid Services, that limits or affects the department's authority to select the hospitals used to provide inpatient hospital services to inmates.

(j) It is the intent of the Legislature that the implementation of this section will result in state General Fund savings for the funding of acute inpatient hospital services provided to inmates along with any related administrative costs.

(k) Any agreements entered into under this section for Medi-Cal or a LIHP to provide for reimbursement of acute inpatient hospital services and administrative expenditures as described in subdivision (c) shall not be subject to Part 2 (commencing with Section 10100) of Division 2 of the Public Contract Code.

(l) This section shall be implemented in a manner that is consistent with federal Medicaid law and regulations. The Director of the State Department of Health Care Services shall seek any federal approvals necessary for the implementation of this section. This section shall be implemented only when and to the extent that any necessary federal approval is obtained, and only to the extent that existing levels of federal financial participation are not otherwise jeopardized.

(m) To the extent that the Director of the State Department of Health Care Services determines that existing levels of federal financial participation are jeopardized, this section shall no longer be implemented.

(n) Notwithstanding Chapter 3.5 (commencing with Section 11340) of Part 1 of Division 3 of Title 2 of the Government Code, the State Department of Health Care Services may, without taking any further regulatory action, implement this section by means of all-county letters, provider bulletins, facility letters, or similar instructions.

(o) For purposes of this section, the following terms have the following meanings:

(1) The term "county of last legal residence" means the county in which the inmate resided at the time of arrest that resulted in conviction and incarceration in a state prison facility.

(2) The term "inmate" means an adult who is involuntarily residing in a state prison facility operated, administered, or regulated, directly or indirectly, by the department.

(3) During the existence of the receivership established in United States District Court for the Northern District of California, Case No. C01-1351 TEH, Plata v. Schwarzenegger, references in this section to the "secretary" shall mean the receiver appointed in that action, who shall implement portions of this section that would otherwise be within the secretary's responsibility.

(Amended by Stats. 2013, Ch. 76, Sec. 162. (AB 383) Effective January 1, 2014.)

CHAPTER 3. The Board of Parole Hearings [5075 - 5081]

(Heading of Chapter 3 amended by Stats. 2005, Ch. 10, Sec. 45.)

5075.

(a) There is hereby created the Board of Parole Hearings. Any reference to the Board of Prison Terms in this code or any other law refers to the Board of Parole Hearings. As of July 1, 2005, the Board of Prison Terms is abolished.

(b) (1) The Governor shall appoint 17 commissioners, subject to Senate confirmation, pursuant to this section. These commissioners shall be appointed and trained to hear only adult matters. Except as specified in paragraph (3), commissioners shall hold office for terms of three years, each term to commence on the expiration date of the predecessor. An appointment to a vacancy that occurs for any reason other than expiration of the term shall be for the remainder of the unexpired term. Commissioners are eligible for reappointment.

(2) The terms of the commissioners shall expire as follows:
(A) Five shall expire on July 1, 2020.
(B) Six shall expire on July 1, 2021.
(C) Six shall expire on July 1, 2022.
(3) The term for one of the commissioners whose position was created by the act that added this paragraph shall be for two years and shall begin on July 1, 2019. The term for the other commissioner whose position was created by the act that added this paragraph shall be for three years and shall begin on July 1, 2019.
(4) The selection of persons and their appointment by the Governor and confirmation by the Senate shall reflect as nearly as possible a cross section of the racial, sexual, economic, and geographic features of the population of the state.
(c) The chair of the board shall be designated by the Governor periodically. The Governor may appoint an executive officer of the board, subject to Senate confirmation, who shall hold office at the pleasure of the Governor. The executive officer shall be the administrative head of the board and shall exercise all duties and functions necessary to ensure that the responsibilities of the board are successfully discharged. The secretary shall be the appointing authority for all civil service positions of employment with the board.
(d) Each commissioner shall participate in hearings on each workday, except if it is necessary for a commissioner to attend training, en banc hearings or full board meetings, or other administrative business requiring the participation of the commissioner. For purposes of this subdivision, these hearings include parole consideration hearings and parole rescission hearings.
(Amended by Stats. 2019, Ch. 25, Sec. 43. (SB 94) Effective June 27, 2019.)
5075.1.
The Board of Parole Hearings shall do all of the following:
(a) Conduct parole consideration hearings, parole rescission hearings, and parole progress hearings for adults under the jurisdiction of the department.
(b) Conduct mentally disordered offender hearings.
(c) Conduct sexually violent predator hearings.
(d) Review inmates' requests for reconsideration of denial of good-time credit and setting of parole length or conditions, pursuant to Section 5077.
(e) Determine revocation of parole for adult offenders under the jurisdiction of the Division of Adult Parole Operations, pursuant to Section 5077.
(f) Conduct studies pursuant to Section 3150 of the Welfare and Institutions Code.
(g) Investigate and report on all applications for reprieves, pardons, and commutation of sentence, as provided in Title 6 (commencing with Section 4800) of Part 3.
(h) Exercise other powers and duties as prescribed by law.
(i) Effective January 1, 2007, all commissioners appointed and trained to hear juvenile parole matters, together with their duties prescribed by law as functions of the Board of Parole Hearings concerning wards under the jurisdiction of the Department of Corrections and Rehabilitation, are transferred to the Director of the Division of Juvenile Justice. All applicable regulations in effect at the time of transfer shall be deemed to apply to those commissioners until new regulations are adopted.
(Amended by Stats. 2016, Ch. 33, Sec. 25. (SB 843) Effective June 27, 2016.)
5075.5.
All commissioners and deputy commissioners who conduct hearings for the purpose of considering the parole suitability of prisoners or the setting of a parole release date for prisoners, shall receive initial training on domestic violence cases and intimate partner battering and its effects.
(Amended by Stats. 2005, Ch. 215, Sec. 4. Effective January 1, 2006.)
5075.6.
(a) Commissioners and deputy commissioners hearing matters concerning adults under the jurisdiction of the Department of Corrections and Rehabilitation shall have a broad background in criminal justice and an ability for appraisal of adult offenders, the crimes for which those persons are committed, and the evaluation of an individual's progress toward reformation. Insofar as practicable, commissioners and deputy commissioners shall have a varied interest in adult correction work, public safety, and shall have experience or education in the fields of corrections, sociology, law, law enforcement, medicine, mental health, or education.
(b) All commissioners and deputy commissioners who conduct hearings for the purpose of considering the parole suitability of inmates, the setting of a parole release date for inmates, or the revocation of parole for adult parolees, shall, within 60 days of appointment and annually thereafter undergo a minimum of 40 hours of training in the following areas:
(1) Treatment and training programs provided to inmates at Department of Corrections and Rehabilitation institutions, including, but not limited to, educational, vocational, mental health, medical, substance abuse, psychotherapeutic counseling, and sex offender treatment programs.
(2) Parole services.
(3) Commissioner duties and responsibilities.
(4) Knowledge of laws and regulations applicable to conducting parole hearings, including the rights of victims, witnesses, and inmates.
(Amended by Stats. 2016, Ch. 33, Sec. 26. (SB 843) Effective June 27, 2016.)
5076.
Each commissioner of the board shall devote his entire time to the duties of his office and shall receive an annual salary provided for by Chapter 6 (commencing with Section 11550) of Part 1 of Division 3 of Title 2 of the Government Code.
(Amended by Stats. 1986, Ch. 1446, Sec. 5.)
5076.1.
(a) The board shall meet at each of the state prisons and facilities under the jurisdiction of the Division of Adult Institutions. Meetings shall be held at whatever times may be necessary for a full and complete study of the cases of all inmates whose matters are considered. Other times and places of meeting may also be designated by the board. Each commissioner of the board shall receive his or her actual necessary traveling expenses incurred in the performance of his or her official duties. Where the board performs its functions by meeting en banc in either public or executive sessions to decide matters of general policy, at least seven members shall be present, and no action shall be valid unless it is concurred in by a majority vote of those present.
(b) The board may use deputy commissioners to whom it may assign appropriate duties, including hearing cases and making decisions. Those decisions shall be made in accordance with policies approved by a majority of the total membership of the board.
(c) The board may meet and transact business in panels. Each panel shall consist of two or more persons, subject to subdivision (d) of Section 3041. No action shall be valid unless concurred in by a majority vote of the persons present. In the event of a tie vote, the matter shall be referred to a randomly selected committee, comprised of a majority of the commissioners specifically appointed to hear adult parole matters and who are holding office at the time.
(d) Consideration of parole release for persons sentenced to life imprisonment pursuant to subdivision (b) of Section 1168 shall be heard by a panel of two or more commissioners or deputy commissioners, of which only one may be a deputy commissioner. A recommendation for recall of a sentence under subdivisions (d) and (e) of Section 1170 shall be made by a panel, a majority of whose commissioners are commissioners of the Board of Parole Hearings.

(Amended by Stats. 2016, Ch. 33, Sec. 27. (SB 843) Effective June 27, 2016.)
5076.2.
(a) Any rules and regulations, including any resolutions and policy statements, promulgated by the Board of Prison Terms, shall be promulgated and filed pursuant to Chapter 3.5 (commencing with Section 11340) of Part 1 of Division 3 of Title 2 of the Government Code, and shall, to the extent practical, be stated in language that is easily understood by the general public.
(b) The Board of Prison Terms shall maintain, publish and make available to the general public, a compendium of its rules and regulations, including any resolutions and policy statements, promulgated pursuant to this section.
(c) The exception specified in this subdivision to the procedures specified in this section shall apply to the Board of Prison Terms. The chairperson may specify an effective date that is any time more than 30 days after the rule or regulation is filed with the Secretary of State. However, no less than 20 days prior to that effective date, copies of the rule or regulation shall be posted in conspicuous places throughout each institution and shall be mailed to all persons or organizations who request them.
(Amended by Stats. 1988, Ch. 160, Sec. 142.)
5076.3.
The Chairman of the Board of Prison Terms shall have the authority of a head of a department set forth in subdivision (e) of Section 11181 of the Government Code to issue subpoenas as provided in Article 2 (commencing with Section 11180) of Chapter 2 of Division 3 of Title 2 of the Government Code. The board shall adopt regulations on the policies and guidelines for the issuance of subpoenas.
(Added by Stats. 1981, Ch. 792, Sec. 2.)
5077.
The Board of Prison Terms shall review the prisoners' requests for reconsideration of denial of good-time credit, and setting of parole length or conditions, and shall have the authority to modify the previously made decisions of the Department of Corrections as to these matters. The revocation of parole shall be determined by the Board of Prison Terms.
(Amended by Stats. 1996, Ch. 357, Sec. 2. Effective August 19, 1996.)
5078.
(a) The Board of Prison Terms shall succeed to and shall exercise and perform all powers and duties granted to, exercised by, and imposed upon the Adult Authority, the California Women's Board of Terms and Paroles, and the Community Release Board.
(b) The Adult Authority and California Women's Board of Terms and Paroles are abolished.
(Amended by Stats. 1979, Ch. 255.)
5079.
The Director of Corrections shall provide facilities and licensed professional personnel for a psychiatric and diagnostic clinic and such branches thereof as may be required at one or more of the state prisons or institutions under the jurisdiction of the Department of Corrections. The director shall have full administrative authority and responsibility for operation of the clinics. All required mental health treatment or diagnostic services shall be provided under the supervision of a psychiatrist licensed to practice in this state, or a psychologist licensed to practice in this state and who holds a doctoral degree and has at least two years of experience in the diagnosis and treatment of emotional and mental disorders. All such clinics shall be under the direction of such a psychiatrist or psychologist. A psychiatrist shall be available to assume responsibility for all acts of diagnosis or treatment which may only be performed by a licensed physician and surgeon.
The work of the clinic shall include a scientific study of each prisoner, his or her career and life history, the cause of his or her criminal acts and recommendations for his or her care, training, and employment with a view to his or her reformation and to the protection of society. The recommendation shall be submitted to the Director of Corrections and shall not be effective until approved by the director. The Director of Corrections may modify or reject the recommendations as he or she sees fit.
(Amended by Stats. 1984, Ch. 1123, Sec. 5.)
5080.
The Director of Corrections may transfer persons confined in one state prison institution or facility of the Department of Corrections to another. The Board of Prison Terms may request the Director of Corrections to transfer an inmate who is under its parole-granting jurisdiction if, after review of the case history in the course of routine procedures, such transfer is deemed advisable for the further diagnosis, and treatment of the inmate. The director shall as soon as practicable comply with such request, provided that, if facilities are not available he shall report that fact to the Board of Prison Terms and shall make the transfer as soon as facilities become available; provided further, that if in the opinion of the Director of Corrections such transfer would endanger security he may report that fact to the Board of Prison Terms and refuse to make such transfer.
When transferring an inmate from one state prison, institution, or facility of the Department of Corrections to another, the director may, as necessary or convenient, authorize transportation via a route that lies partly outside this state.
(Amended by Stats. 1979, Ch. 255.)
5081.
The Governor may remove any member of the Board of Prison Terms for misconduct, incompetency or neglect of duty after a full hearing by the Board of Corrections.
(Amended by Stats. 1979, Ch. 255.)

CHAPTER 3.5. The Robert Presley Center of Crime and Justice Studies [5085 - 5088]

(Chapter 3.5 repealed and added by Stats. 1993, Ch. 778, Sec. 2.)
5085.
The Robert Presley Institute of Corrections Research and Training, which provides and aggregates research on youth and adult corrections education and training, is hereby renamed the Robert Presley Center of Crime and Justice Studies and shall be transferred to the University of California. It is the intent of the Legislature that the center be maintained on the Riverside campus of the University of California.
(Repealed and added by Stats. 1993, Ch. 778, Sec. 2. Effective January 1, 1994.)
5086.
It is the intent of the Legislature that the university seek funding from federal, state, and private sources for research projects carried out by the center under the university's direction. The center shall have the following research goals:
(a) To better protect the public from crime by determining the causes of, and means of preventing, violence, crime, and criminal deviance.
(b) To identify the methods and practices necessary for the most beneficial operation of law enforcement and local and state youth and adult correctional institutions.
(c) To reduce violence and recidivism rates in prisons, jails, and youth facilities.
(Repealed and added by Stats. 1993, Ch. 778, Sec. 2. Effective January 1, 1994.)
5087.
The chancellor of the Riverside campus may appoint an advisory committee to assist in establishing research priorities. The university shall consult with the Department of Corrections, the Department of the Youth Authority, local law enforcement, probation, parole, and correctional agencies, and persons of experience or education in other higher education institutions in the field of corrections or related fields on the activities

of the center. These projects shall be related to the center's goals as specified in Section 5086 and may also include, but not be limited to, applied and theoretical research in the following areas:

(a) Methods of ensuring secure, cost-effective, safe, and gang-free incarceration in California's correctional institutions, including approaches to ameliorate overcrowding in those institutions.

(b) New approaches to reduce inmate and ward recidivism and consequent victimization of California citizens.

(c) Correctional facility management, planning, design, and construction.

(d) New approaches to rehabilitate inmates and wards during and after incarceration and to integrate offenders into society after incarceration.

(e) New approaches to inmate and ward diagnosis, classification, and treatment.

(f) At-risk youth and street gang activity.

(g) Law enforcement.

(Repealed and added by Stats. 1993, Ch. 778, Sec. 2. Effective January 1, 1994.)

5088.

The university shall negotiate and approve terms, services, and costs of contracts and research projects for purposes of this chapter.

(Repealed and added by Stats. 1993, Ch. 778, Sec. 2. Effective January 1, 1994.)

CHAPTER 4. Division of Juvenile Facilities [6001 - 6005]

(Heading of Chapter 4 amended by Stats. 2005, Ch. 10, Sec. 51.)

6001.

Commencing July 1, 2005, the establishment, organization, jurisdiction, powers, duties, responsibilities, and functions of the Youth Authority as provided in the Youth Authority Act (Chapter 1 (commencing with Section 1700) of Division 2.5 of the Welfare and Institutions Code), as it existed on June 30, 2005, are continued in the Department of Corrections and Rehabilitation, Division of Juvenile Facilities.

(Amended by Stats. 2005, Ch. 10, Sec. 52. Effective May 10, 2005. Operative July 1, 2005, by Sec. 99 of Ch. 10.)

6005.

(a) Whenever a person confined to a correctional institution under the supervision of the Department of Corrections and Rehabilitation is charged with a public offense committed within the confines of that institution and is tried for that public offense, a city, county, or superior court shall be entitled to reimbursement for reasonable and necessary costs connected with that matter.

(b) The appropriate financial officer or other designated official of a county or the city finance officer of a city incurring any costs in connection with that matter shall make out a statement of all the costs incurred by the county or city for the investigation, the preparation for the trial, participation in the actual trial of the case, all guarding and keeping of the person, and the execution of the sentence of the person, properly certified to by a judge of the superior court of the county. The statement may not include any costs that are incurred by the superior court pursuant to subdivision (c). The statement shall be sent to the department for its approval. After the approval the department must cause the amount of the costs to be paid out of the money appropriated for the support of the department to the county treasurer of the county or the city finance officer of the city incurring those costs.

(c) The superior court shall prepare a statement of all costs incurred by the court for the preparation of the trial and the actual trial of the case. The statement may not include any costs that are incurred by the city or county pursuant to subdivision (a). The statement shall be sent to the Administrative Office of the Courts for approval and reimbursement.

(d) No city, county, or other jurisdiction may file, and the state may not reimburse, a claim pursuant to this section that is presented to the Department of Corrections and Rehabilitation or to any other agency or department of the state more than six months after the close of the month in which the costs were incurred.

(Amended by Stats. 2007, Ch. 175, Sec. 12. Effective August 24, 2007.)

CHAPTER 4.5. Examination of Staff for Tuberculosis [6006 - 6009]

(Chapter 4.5 heading added by Stats. 1993, Ch. 932, Sec. 5.)

6006.

The Department of Corrections, Department of the Youth Authority, Board of Prison Terms, and Youthful Offender Parole Board, in conjunction with the State Department of Health Services, shall meet and confer with recognized employee organizations representing employees pursuant to the Ralph C. Dills Act, Chapter 10.3 (commencing with Section 3512) of Division 4 of Title 1 of the Government Code, to develop rules regarding the mandatory examination or testing for tuberculosis of the staff of the Department of Corrections, Department of the Youth Authority, Board of Prison Terms, and Youthful Offender Parole Board. These rules shall include mandated annual examination for tuberculosis of all employees with inmate contact and as a part of preemployment requirements. Except as provided in Section 6007, the confidentiality of the test results shall be maintained. However, statistical summaries which do not identify specific individuals may be prepared.

(Added by Stats. 1992, Ch. 1263, Sec. 2. Effective January 1, 1993.)

6006.5.

For purposes of this chapter, the following definitions shall apply:

(a) "Department" means the Department of Corrections, the Department of the Youth Authority, the Board of Prison Terms, or the Youthful Offender Parole Board.

(b) "Examination or test" means methods, processes, or other means, including a chest X-ray, conducted in accordance with the recommendations of the Centers for Disease Control and Prevention and as specified in the department's guidelines for tuberculosis control, to determine if a person has, has had, or has been exposed to tuberculosis.

(c) "Medical evaluation" means taking a history or gathering other information and may include, but is not limited to, listening to the chest or other examinations or tests, as specified in the department's guidelines for tuberculosis control, used to diagnose and assess the health conditions of the person.

(d) "Followup care" means the continued medical evaluations, monitoring, or care of a person after his or her initial visit, examination, or test, including, but not limited to, preventive therapy.

(e) "Certificate" means the official document developed and issued by the department that indicates the absence of tuberculosis in an infectious stage and that is signed by a physician and surgeon who is licensed by the Medical Board of California or the Osteopathic Medical Board of California under Division 2 (commencing with Section 500) of the Business and Professions Code or his or her designee. The certificate shall indicate that the examination, test, or evaluation was performed in accordance with the recommendations of the Centers for Disease Control and Prevention and as specified in the department's guidelines for tuberculosis control.

(f) "Negative skin test" shall have the same meaning as it is defined by the Centers for Disease Control and Prevention and the department's guidelines for tuberculosis control as the definition reads at the time of the examination.

(g) "Positive skin test" shall have the same meaning as it is defined by the Centers for Disease Control and Prevention and the department's guidelines for tuberculosis control as the definition reads at the time of the examination.

(h) "Institution" means any state prison, camp, center, office, or other facility under the jurisdiction of the Department of Corrections or the Department of the Youth Authority.

(i) "Infectious or contagious stage" means the period when a disease is capable of being transmitted from one person to another with or without contact.

(j) "Tuberculosis converter" shall have the same meaning as it is defined by the Centers for Disease Control and Prevention.

(Added by Stats. 1993, Ch. 932, Sec. 6. Effective October 8, 1993.)

6007.

(a) No person shall be employed initially by the department unless that person, after an offer of employment, completes an examination, a test, or a medical evaluation and is found to be free of tuberculosis in an infectious or contagious stage prior to assuming work duties.

(b) As a condition of continued employment with the department, those employees who are skin-test negative shall receive an examination or test at least once a year, or more often if directed by the department, for as long as the employee remains skin-test negative. If an employee has a documented positive skin test, the employee shall have a medical evaluation to determine the need for followup care. An employee with a positive skin test shall follow the department's guidelines for tuberculosis control.

(c) The department shall ensure that all examinations or tests and medical evaluations, as defined in subdivisions (b) and (c) of Section 6006.5, to diagnose and assess the health conditions of the person, meet the following conditions:

(1) Are made available to the employee promptly at a reasonable time and place.

(2) Are made available at no cost to the employee.

(3) Are performed by, or under the supervision of, a licensed health care professional.

(d) The examinations or tests or medical evaluations required pursuant to this chapter shall be offered by the department. The department may contract with a medical provider to administer the examinations or tests or medical evaluations. Employees who elect not to accept the department's offer shall obtain the examinations or tests or medical evaluations through their personal health care providers at no cost to the department.

The requirements of this section apply to the Department of Corrections and Rehabilitation and the Board of Parole Hearings. Notwithstanding any other provision of law, each department or board shall be responsible for the costs of the testing or evaluation required by this section for its own employees or potential employees.

(e) Followup care for tuberculosis infection or treatment for tuberculosis disease shall be pursued through the workers' compensation system as provided in Division 4 (commencing with Section 3200) and Division 5 (commencing with Section 6300) of the Labor Code for job-related incidents or through the employee's health insurance plan for non-job-related incidents. The department shall file a first report of injury for an employee whose examination or test for tuberculosis is positive. In addition, the department shall follow the guidelines, policies, and procedures of the workers' compensation early intervention program pursuant to Section 3214 of the Labor Code.

(f) Each employee, including employees who are employed initially, shall submit a signed certificate to the department annually that may be reviewed by the chief medical officer of the department.

(g) The department shall maintain a file containing an up-to-date certificate for each employee.

(h) Nothing in this section shall prevent the department from requiring and providing more extensive or more frequent examinations or tests.

(i) The department shall not discriminate against any employee because the employee tested positive for tuberculosis.

(j) All volunteers of the department shall be required to furnish the department with a certificate prior to assuming their volunteer duties and annually thereafter, showing that the volunteer has been examined and found to be free of tuberculosis in an infectious or contagious stage.

(k) The department shall maintain a file containing an up-to-date certificate for each volunteer.

(l) Employees from other state agencies, including, but not limited to, the State Department of State Hospitals and the Department of Forestry and Fire Protection, who are assigned to work in an institution, as defined in subdivision (h) of Section 6006.5, or who are assigned to work with inmates or wards on a regular basis, as defined in the department's guidelines, shall comply with the following requirements:

(1) Receive an examination or test prior to assuming their duties and at least once a year thereafter, or more often if directed by the department, for as long as the employee remains skin-test negative.

(2) Receive a medical evaluation to determine the need for followup care and follow the department's guidelines for tuberculosis control if an employee has a documented positive skin test.

(3) Submit a signed certificate to the department prior to assuming his or her duties and annually thereafter, showing that the employee has been found to be free of tuberculosis in an infectious or contagious state.

(4) Pursue followup care for tuberculosis infection or treatment for tuberculosis disease through the appropriate programs in their agency or department.

(m) The department shall offer the examinations, tests, or medical evaluations required pursuant to this chapter to employees of other state agencies or departments and may contract with a medical provider to administer the examinations, tests, or medical evaluations. Employees of other state agencies or departments who elect not to accept the department's offer shall obtain the examinations, tests, or medical evaluations from their personal health care provider at no cost to the department.

(n) The department shall maintain a file containing an up-to-date certificate for each employee from other state agencies who works in an institution.

(Amended by Stats. 2012, Ch. 24, Sec. 51. (AB 1470) Effective June 27, 2012.)

6008.

The Department of Corrections, the Department of the Youth Authority, the Board of Prison Terms, and the Youthful Offender Parole Board shall report to the State Department of Health Services the results of the tuberculosis examinations required by Section 6006.

(Amended by Stats. 2001, Ch. 854, Sec. 54. Effective January 1, 2002.)

6009.

In enacting this chapter, the Legislature hereby finds and declares that tuberculosis is a serious contagious disease. It is vital to the health and safety of inmates, employees, and the public at large, to conduct appropriate examinations and testing and to ensure that staff who test positive for tuberculosis obtain appropriate treatment in order to control the spread of tuberculosis in California's institutions.

(Added by Stats. 1993, Ch. 932, Sec. 8. Effective October 8, 1993.)

CHAPTER 5. The Corrections Standards Authority [6024 - 6046.3]

(Heading of Chapter 5 amended by Stats. 2005, Ch. 10, Sec. 55.)

ARTICLE 1. General Provisions [6024 - 6033]

(Heading of Article 1 added by Stats. 1979, Ch. 1148.)

6024.

(a) Commencing July 1, 2012, there is hereby established the Board of State and Community Corrections. The Board of State and Community Corrections shall be an entity independent of the Department of Corrections and Rehabilitation. The Governor may appoint an executive officer of the board, subject to Senate confirmation, who shall hold the office at the pleasure of the Governor. The executive officer shall be the administrative head of the board and shall exercise all duties and functions necessary to ensure that the responsibilities of the board are successfully discharged. As of July 1, 2012, any references to the Board of Corrections or the Corrections Standards Authority shall refer to the Board of State and Community Corrections. As of that date, the Corrections Standards Authority is abolished.

(b) The mission of the board shall include providing statewide leadership, coordination, and technical assistance to promote effective state and local efforts and partnerships in California's adult and juvenile criminal justice system, including addressing gang problems. This mission shall reflect the principle of aligning fiscal policy and correctional practices, including, but not limited to prevention, intervention, suppression, supervision, and incapacitation, to promote a justice investment strategy that fits each county and is consistent with the integrated statewide goal of improved public safety through cost-effective, promising, and evidence-based strategies for managing criminal justice populations.

(c) The board shall regularly seek advice from a balanced range of stakeholders and subject matter experts on issues pertaining to adult corrections, juvenile justice, and gang problems relevant to its mission. Toward this end, the board shall seek to ensure that its efforts (1) are systematically informed by experts and stakeholders with the most specific knowledge concerning the subject matter, (2) include the participation of those who must implement a board decision and are impacted by a board decision, and (3) promote collaboration and innovative problem solving consistent with the mission of the board. The board may create special committees, with the authority to establish working subgroups as necessary, in furtherance of this subdivision to carry out specified tasks and to submit its findings and recommendations from that effort to the board.

(d) The board shall act as the supervisory board of the state planning agency pursuant to federal acts. It shall annually review and approve, or review, revise, and approve, the comprehensive state plan for the improvement of criminal justice and delinquency and gang prevention activities throughout the state, shall establish priorities for the use of funds as are available pursuant to federal acts, and shall approve the expenditure of all funds pursuant to such plans or federal acts, provided that the approval of those expenditures may be granted to single projects or to groups of projects.

(e) It is the intent of the Legislature that any statutory authority conferred on the Corrections Standards Authority or the previously abolished Board of Corrections shall apply to the Board of State and Community Corrections on and after July 1, 2012, unless expressly repealed by the act which added this section. The Board of State and Community Corrections is the successor to the Corrections Standards Authority, and as of July 1, 2012, is vested with all of the authority's rights, powers, authority, and duties, unless specifically repealed by this act.

(f) For purposes of this chapter, "federal acts" means Subchapter V of Chapter 46 of the federal Omnibus Crime Control and Safe Streets Act of 1968 (Public Law 90-351, 82 Stat. 197; 42 U.S.C. Sec. 3750 et seq.), the federal Juvenile Justice and Delinquency Prevention Act of 1974 (42 U.S.C. Sec. 5601 et seq.), and any act or acts amendatory or supplemental thereto.

(Amended (as added by Stats. 2011, Ch. 36, Sec. 31) by Stats. 2012, Ch. 41, Sec. 79. (SB 1021) Effective June 27, 2012. Section operative July 1, 2012, pursuant to Stats. 2011, Ch. 36, Sec. 83 (which was amended by Stats. 2011, Ch. 136, with no impact on this section).)

6025.

(a) Commencing July 1, 2012, the Board of State and Community Corrections shall be composed of 12 members, as follows:

(1) The Chair of the Board of State and Community Corrections, who shall be the Secretary of the Department of Corrections and Rehabilitation.

(2) The Director of the Division of Adult Parole Operations for the Department of Corrections and Rehabilitation.

(3) A county sheriff in charge of a local detention facility which has a Corrections Standards Authority rated capacity of 200 or less inmates, appointed by the Governor, subject to Senate confirmation.

(4) A county sheriff in charge of a local detention facility which has a Corrections Standards Authority rated capacity of over 200 inmates, appointed by the Governor, subject to Senate confirmation.

(5) A county supervisor or county administrative officer. This member shall be appointed by the Governor, subject to Senate confirmation.

(6) A chief probation officer from a county with a population over 200,000, appointed by the Governor, subject to Senate confirmation.

(7) A chief probation officer from a county with a population under 200,000, appointed by the Governor, subject to Senate confirmation.

(8) A judge appointed by the Judicial Council of California.

(9) A chief of police, appointed by the Governor, subject to Senate confirmation.

(10) A community provider of rehabilitative treatment or services for adult offenders, appointed by the Speaker of the Assembly.

(11) A community provider or advocate with expertise in effective programs, policies, and treatment of at-risk youth and juvenile offenders, appointed by the Senate Committee on Rules.

(12) A public member, appointed by the Governor, subject to Senate confirmation.

(b) Commencing July 1, 2013, the Board of State and Community Corrections shall be composed of 13 members, as follows:

(1) The Chair of the Board of State and Community Corrections, who shall be appointed by the Governor, subject to Senate confirmation.

(2) The Secretary of the Department of Corrections and Rehabilitation.

(3) The Director of the Division of Adult Parole Operations for the Department of Corrections and Rehabilitation.

(4) The individuals listed in paragraphs (3) to (12), inclusive, of subdivision (a), who shall serve or continue to serve terms as provided in subdivision (d).

(c) The Chair of the Board of State and Community Corrections shall serve full time.

(d) The terms of the members appointed by the Governor shall expire as follows: three on July 1, 2014, and four on July 1, 2015, as specified by the Governor. The term of the member appointed by the Senate Committee on Rules shall expire on July 1, 2014. The term of the member appointed by the Speaker of the Assembly shall expire on July 1, 2015. The term of the member appointed by the Judicial Council shall expire on July 1, 2015. Successor members shall hold office for terms of three years, each term to commence on the expiration date of the predecessor. Any appointment to a vacancy that occurs for any reason other than expiration of the term shall be for the remainder of the unexpired term. Members are eligible for reappointment.

(e) The board shall select a vice chairperson from among its members, who shall be either a chief probation officer or a sheriff. Seven members of the board shall constitute a quorum.

(f) When the board is hearing charges against any member, the individual concerned shall not sit as a member of the board for the period of hearing of charges and the determination of recommendations to the Governor.

(g) If any appointed member is not in attendance for three meetings in any calendar year, the board shall inform the appointing authority, which may remove that member and make a new appointment, as provided in this section, for the remainder of the term.

(Amended by Stats. 2013, Ch. 30, Sec. 5. (SB 74) Effective June 27, 2013.)

6025.1.

(a) Members of the board, with the exception of the Chair of the Board of State and Community Corrections, shall receive no compensation, but shall be reimbursed for their actual and necessary travel expenses incurred in the performance of their duties. For purposes of compensation, attendance at meetings of the board shall be deemed performance by a member of the duties of his or her state or local governmental employment.

(b) For the purposes of Section 1090 of the Government Code, members of a committee created by the board pursuant to Section 6046.3 or a committee created with the primary purpose of administering grant funding from the Edward Byrne Memorial Justice Assistance Grant Program (42 U.S.C. Sec. 3751(a)), including a member of the board in his or her capacity as a member of a committee created by the board, have no financial interest in any contract made by the board, including a grant or bond financing transaction, based upon the receipt of compensation for holding public office or public employment.

(c) The Chair of the Board of State and Community Corrections shall serve full time. The Department of Human Resources shall fix the compensation of the Chair of the Board of State and Community Corrections.

(d) The amendments to this section by the act that added this subdivision are effective for grant awards made by the board on or after July 1, 2016.

(Amended by Stats. 2016, Ch. 33, Sec. 28. (SB 843) Effective June 27, 2016.)

6025.5.

The Director of Corrections, Board of Prison Terms, the Youthful Offender Parole Board, and the Director of the Youth Authority shall file with the Board of Corrections for information of the board or for review and advice to the respective agency as the board may determine, all rules, regulations and manuals relating to or in implementation of policies, procedures, or enabling laws.

(Amended by Stats. 1979, Ch. 860.)

6025.6.

The Board of Corrections may delegate any ministerial authority or duty conferred or imposed upon the board to a subordinate officer subject to those conditions as it may choose to impose.

(Added by Stats. 1991, Ch. 1017, Sec. 2.)

6026.

The Corrections Standards Authority shall be the means whereby the Department of Corrections and Rehabilitation may correlate its individual programs for adults and youths under its jurisdiction.

(Amended by Stats. 2005, Ch. 10, Sec. 58. Effective May 10, 2005. Operative July 1, 2005, by Sec. 99 of Ch. 10.)

6027.

(a) It shall be the duty of the Board of State and Community Corrections to collect and maintain available information and data about state and community correctional policies, practices, capacities, and needs, including, but not limited to, prevention, intervention, suppression, supervision, and incapacitation, as they relate to both adult corrections, juvenile justice, and gang problems. The board shall seek to collect and make publicly available up-to-date data and information reflecting the impact of state and community correctional, juvenile justice, and gang-related policies and practices enacted in the state, as well as information and data concerning promising and evidence-based practices from other jurisdictions.

(b) Consistent with subdivision (c) of Section 6024, the board shall also:

(1) Develop recommendations for the improvement of criminal justice and delinquency and gang prevention activity throughout the state.

(2) Identify, promote, and provide technical assistance relating to evidence-based programs, practices, and promising and innovative projects consistent with the mission of the board.

(3) Develop definitions of key terms, including, but not limited to, "recidivism," "average daily population," "treatment program completion rates," and any other terms deemed relevant in order to facilitate consistency in local data collection, evaluation, and implementation of evidence-based practices, promising evidence-based practices, and evidence-based programs. In developing these definitions, the board shall consult with the following stakeholders and experts:

(A) A county supervisor or county administrative officer, selected after conferring with the California State Association of Counties.

(B) A county sheriff, selected after conferring with the California State Sheriffs' Association.

(C) A chief probation officer, selected after conferring with the Chief Probation Officers of California.

(D) A district attorney, selected after conferring with the California District Attorneys Association.

(E) A public defender, selected after conferring with the California Public Defenders Association.

(F) The Secretary of the Department of Corrections and Rehabilitation.

(G) A representative from the Administrative Office of the Courts.

(H) A representative from a nonpartisan, nonprofit policy institute with experience and involvement in research and data relating to California's criminal justice system.

(I) A representative from a nonprofit agency providing comprehensive reentry services.

(4) Receive and disburse federal funds, and perform all necessary and appropriate services in the performance of its duties as established by federal acts.

(5) Develop comprehensive, unified, and orderly procedures to ensure that applications for grants are processed fairly, efficiently, and in a manner consistent with the mission of the board.

(6) Identify delinquency and gang intervention and prevention grants that have the same or similar program purpose, are allocated to the same entities, serve the same target populations, and have the same desired outcomes for the purpose of consolidating grant funds and programs and moving toward a unified single delinquency intervention and prevention grant application process in adherence with all applicable federal guidelines and mandates.

(7) Cooperate with and render technical assistance to the Legislature, state agencies, units of general local government, combinations of those units, or other public or private agencies, organizations, or institutions in matters relating to criminal justice and delinquency prevention.

(8) Develop incentives for units of local government to develop comprehensive regional partnerships whereby adjacent jurisdictions pool grant funds in order to deliver services, such as job training and employment opportunities, to a broader target population, including at-risk youth, and maximize the impact of state funds at the local level.

(9) Conduct evaluation studies of the programs and activities assisted by the federal acts.

(10) Identify and evaluate state, local, and federal gang and youth violence suppression, intervention, and prevention programs and strategies, along with funding for those efforts. The board shall assess and make recommendations for the coordination of the state's programs, strategies, and funding that address gang and youth violence in a manner that maximizes the effectiveness and coordination of those programs, strategies, and resources. By January 1, 2014, the board shall develop funding allocation policies to ensure that within three years no less than 70 percent of funding for gang and youth violence suppression, intervention, and prevention programs

and strategies is used in programs that utilize promising and proven evidence-based principles and practices. The board shall communicate with local agencies and programs in an effort to promote the best evidence-based principles and practices for addressing gang and youth violence through suppression, intervention, and prevention.

(11) The board shall collect from each county the plan submitted pursuant to Section 1230.1 within two months of adoption by the county boards of supervisors. Commencing January 1, 2013, and annually thereafter, the board shall collect and analyze available data regarding the implementation of the local plans and other outcome-based measures, as defined by the board in consultation with the Administrative Office of the Courts, the Chief Probation Officers of California, and the California State Sheriffs' Association. By July 1, 2013, and annually thereafter, the board shall provide to the Governor and the Legislature a report on the implementation of the plans described above.

(12) Commencing on and after July 1, 2012, the board, in consultation with the Administrative Office of the Courts, the California State Association of Counties, the California State Sheriffs' Association, and the Chief Probation Officers of California, shall support the development and implementation of first phase baseline and ongoing data collection instruments to reflect the local impact of Chapter 15 of the Statutes of 2011, specifically related to dispositions for felony offenders and postrelease community supervision. The board shall make any data collected pursuant to this paragraph available on the board's Internet Web site. It is the intent of the Legislature that the board promote collaboration and the reduction of duplication of data collection and reporting efforts where possible.

(c) The board may do either of the following:

(1) Collect, evaluate, publish, and disseminate statistics and other information on the condition and progress of criminal justice in the state.

(2) Perform other functions and duties as required by federal acts, rules, regulations, or guidelines in acting as the administrative office of the state planning agency for distribution of federal grants.

(d) Nothing in this chapter shall be construed to include, in the provisions set forth in this section, funds already designated to the Local Revenue Fund 2011 pursuant to Section 30025 of the Government Code.

(Amended by Stats. 2014, Ch. 601, Sec. 1. (AB 1920) Effective January 1, 2015.)

6028.

Upon request of the Board of Corrections or upon his own initiative, the Governor from time to time may create by executive order one or more special commissions to assist the Board of Corrections in the study of crime pursuant to Section 6027. Each such special commission shall consist of not less than three nor more than five members, who shall be appointed by the Governor. The members of any such special commission shall serve without compensation, except that they shall receive their actual and necessary expenses incurred in the discharge of their duties.

The executive order creating each special commission shall specify the subjects and scope of the study to be made by the commission, and shall fix a time within which the commission shall make its final report. Each commission shall cease to exist when it makes its final report.

(Repealed and added by Stats. 1947, Ch. 1181.)

6028.1.

Each such special commission may investigate any and all matters relating to the subjects specified in the order creating it. In the exercise of its powers the commission shall be subject to the following conditions and limitations:

(a) A witness at any hearing shall have the right to have present at such hearing counsel of his own choice, for the purpose of advising him concerning his constitutional rights.

(b) No hearing shall be televised or broadcast by radio, nor shall any mechanical, photographic or electronic record of the proceedings at any hearing be televised or broadcast by radio.

(Amended by Stats. 1951, Ch. 902.)

6028.2.

The Secretary of the Youth and Adult Correctional Agency may furnish for the use of any such commission such facilities, supplies, and personnel as may be available therefor.

(Amended by Stats. 1982, Ch. 1437, Sec. 5.)

6028.3.

All such special commissions shall make all their reports and recommendations to the Board of Corrections. The Board of Corrections shall consider such reports and recommendations, and shall transmit them to the Governor and the Legislature, together with its own comments and recommendations on the subject matter thereof, within the first 30 days of the next succeeding general or budget session of the Legislature. The Board of Corrections shall also file copies of such reports with the Attorney General, the State Library and such other state departments as may appear to have an official interest in the subject matter of the report or reports in question.

(Added by Stats. 1947, Ch. 1181.)

6028.4.

The Governor shall report to each regular session of the Legislature the names of any persons appointed under Section 6028 together with a statement of expenses incurred.

(Added by Stats. 1947, Ch. 1181.)

6029.

(a) The plans and specifications of every jail, prison, or other place of detention of persons charged with or convicted of crime or of persons detained pursuant to the Juvenile Court Law (Chapter 2 (commencing with Section 200) of Division 2 of the Welfare and Institutions Code) or the Youth Authority Act (Chapter 1 (commencing with Section 1700) of Division 2.5 of the Welfare and Institutions Code), if those plans and specifications involve construction, reconstruction, remodeling, or repairs of an aggregate cost in excess of fifteen thousand dollars ($15,000), shall be submitted to the board for its recommendations. Upon request of any city, city and county, or county, the board shall consider the entire program or group of detention facilities currently planned or under consideration by the city, city and county, or county, and make a study of the entire needs of the city, city and county, or county therefor, and make recommendations thereon. No state department or agency other than the board shall have authority to make recommendations in respect to plans and specifications for the construction of county jails or other county detention facilities or for alterations thereto, except such recommendations as the board may request from any such state department or agency.

(b) As used in this section, "place of detention" includes, but is not limited to, a correctional treatment center, as defined in subdivision (k) of Section 1250 of the Health and Safety Code, which is operated by a city, city and county, or county.

(Amended by Stats. 1989, Ch. 1327, Sec. 7. Effective October 2, 1989.)

6029.1.

(a) There is hereby created the County Jail Capital Expenditure Fund. Moneys in the County Jail Capital Expenditure Fund shall be expended by the Board of Corrections as specified in this section to assist counties to finance jail construction. Moneys in the County Jail Capital Expenditure Fund shall be available for encumbrance without regard to fiscal years, and notwithstanding any other provision of law, shall not revert to the General Fund or be transferred to any other fund or account in the State Treasury except for purposes of investment as provided in Article 4 (commencing with Section 16470) of Chapter 3 of Part 2 of Division 4 of Title 2 of the Government Code. All interest or other increment resulting from such investment shall be deposited in the County Jail Capital Expenditure Fund, notwithstanding Section 16305.7 of the Government Code.

(b) As used in this section, "construction" shall include, but not be limited to, reconstruction, remodeling, replacement of facilities, and the performance of deferred maintenance activities on facilities pursuant to rules and regulations regarding such activities as shall be adopted by the Board of Corrections.

(c) The Board of Corrections shall provide financial assistance to counties from the County Jail Capital Expenditure Fund according to policies, criteria, and procedures adopted by the board pursuant to recommendations made by the appropriate subcommittees of the Senate Committee on Criminal Procedure and the Assembly Committee on Public Safety and after consulting with a representative sample of county boards of supervisors and sheriffs.

(d) In performing the duties set forth in this section, the Board of Corrections and the policy committees of the Legislature shall consider the following:

(1) The extent to which the county requesting aid has exhausted all other available means of raising the requested funds for the capital improvements and the extent to which the funds from the County Jail Capital Expenditure Fund will be utilized to attract other sources of capital financing for county jail facilities;

(2) The extent to which a substantial county match shall be required and any circumstances under which the county match may be reduced or waived;

(3) The extent to which the county's match shall be based on the county's previous compliance with Board of Corrections standards;

(4) The extent to which the capital improvements are necessary to the life or safety of the persons confined or employed in the facility or the health and sanitary conditions of the facility;

(5) The extent to which the county has utilized reasonable alternatives to pre- and post-conviction incarceration, including, but not limited to, programs to facilitate release upon one's own recognizance where appropriate to individuals pending trial, sentencing alternatives to custody, and civil commitment or diversion programs consistent with public safety for those with drug- or alcohol-related problems or mental or developmental disabilities.

(Amended by Stats. 1996, Ch. 155, Sec. 4. Effective July 12, 1996.)

6029.5.

The Board of Corrections is authorized to expend money from the County Jail Capital Expenditure Fund, created pursuant to Sections 4412 and 6029.1, on joint use correctional facilities housing county and state or federal prisoners or any combination thereof in proportion to the county benefit.

(Added by Stats. 1983, Ch. 1101, Sec. 1.)

6030.

(a) The Board of State and Community Corrections shall establish minimum standards for local correctional facilities. The board shall review those standards biennially and make any appropriate revisions.

(b) The standards shall include, but not be limited to, the following areas: health and sanitary conditions, fire and life safety, security, rehabilitation programs, recreation, treatment of persons confined in local correctional facilities, and personnel training.

(c) The standards shall require that at least one person on duty at the facility is knowledgeable in the area of fire and life safety procedures.

(d) The standards shall also include requirements relating to the acquisition, storage, labeling, packaging, and dispensing of drugs.

(e) The standards shall require that inmates who are received by the facility while they are pregnant be notified, orally or in writing, of and provided all of the following:

(1) A balanced, nutritious diet approved by a doctor.

(2) Prenatal and post partum information and health care, including, but not limited to, access to necessary vitamins as recommended by a doctor.

(3) Information pertaining to childbirth education and infant care.

(4) A dental cleaning while in a state facility.

(f) The standards shall provide that a woman known to be pregnant or in recovery after delivery shall not be restrained, except as provided in Section 3407. The board shall develop standards regarding the restraint of pregnant women at the next biennial review of the standards after the enactment of the act amending this subdivision and shall review the individual facility's compliance with the standards.

(g) In establishing minimum standards, the board shall seek the advice of the following:

(1) For health and sanitary conditions:
The State Department of Public Health, physicians, psychiatrists, local public health officials, and other interested persons.

(2) For fire and life safety:
The State Fire Marshal, local fire officials, and other interested persons.

(3) For security, rehabilitation programs, recreation, and treatment of persons confined in correctional facilities:
The Department of Corrections and Rehabilitation, state and local juvenile justice commissions, state and local correctional officials, experts in criminology and penology, and other interested persons.

(4) For personnel training:
The Commission on Peace Officer Standards and Training, psychiatrists, experts in criminology and penology, the Department of Corrections and Rehabilitation, state and local correctional officials, and other interested persons.

(5) For female inmates and pregnant inmates in local adult and juvenile facilities:
The California State Sheriffs' Association and Chief Probation Officers' Association of California, and other interested persons.

(Amended by Stats. 2013, Ch. 76, Sec. 163. (AB 383) Effective January 1, 2014.)

6031.

The Board of State and Community Corrections shall, at a minimum, inspect each local detention facility in the state biennially.

(Amended by Stats. 2017, Ch. 17, Sec. 42. (AB 103) Effective June 27, 2017.)

6031.1.

(a) Inspections of local detention facilities shall, at a minimum, be made biennially. Inspections of privately operated work furlough facilities and programs shall be made biennially unless the work furlough administrator requests an earlier inspection. Inspections shall include, but not be limited to, the following:

(1) Health and safety inspections conducted pursuant to Section 101045 of the Health and Safety Code.

(2) Fire suppression preplanning inspections by the local fire department.

(3) Security, rehabilitation programs, recreation, treatment of persons confined in the facilities, and personnel training by the staff of the Board of State and Community Corrections.

(4) The types and availability of visitation, including, but not limited to, the mode of visitation, visitation hours, time inmates are allowed for visitation, and any restrictions on inmate visitation.

(5) Whether the county in which the facility is located received state funding for jail construction pursuant to Chapter 7 of the Statutes of 2007, Chapter 42 of the Statutes of 2012, Chapter 37 of the Statutes of 2014, or Chapter 34 of the Statutes of 2016. For counties that received funding, whether the county and facility are in compliance with the applicable requirements and restrictions of that funding.

(b) Reports of each facility's inspection shall be furnished to the official in charge of the local detention facility or, in the case of a privately operated facility, the work furlough administrator, the local governing body, the grand jury, and the presiding judge of the superior court in the county where the facility is located. These reports shall set forth the areas wherein the facility has complied and has failed to comply with the minimum standards established pursuant to Section 6030.

(c) All reports completed pursuant to this section shall be posted on the Board of State and Community Corrections' Internet Web site in a manner in which they are accessible to the public.

(Amended by Stats. 2017, Ch. 17, Sec. 43. (AB 103) Effective June 27, 2017.)
6031.2.
The Board of Corrections shall file with the Legislature on December 30, in each even-numbered year, reports to the Legislature which shall include information on all of the following:
(a) Inspection of those local detention facilities that have not complied with the minimum standards established pursuant to Section 6030. The reports shall specify those areas in which the facility has failed to comply and the estimated cost to the facility necessary to accomplish compliance with the minimum standards.
(b) Information regarding the progress and effectiveness of the standards and training program contained in Sections 6035 to 6037, inclusive.
(c) Status of funds expended, interest earned, actions implementing the prerequisites for funding, any reallocations of funds pursuant to Sections 4497.04 to 4497.16, inclusive, and a complete listing of funds allocated to each county.
(d) Inmate accounting system data to be maintained on an annual basis by the sheriff, chief of police, or other official in charge of operating the adult detention system in a county or city, including all of the following:
(1) Average daily population of sentenced and unsentenced prisoners classified according to gender and juvenile status.
(2) Jail admissions of sentenced and unsentenced prisoners, booking charge, date and time of booking, date and time of release, and operating expenses.
(3) Detention system capital and operating expenses.
(Amended by Stats. 1996, Ch. 805, Sec. 5. Effective January 1, 1997.)
6031.3.
The Board of Corrections is authorized to apply for any funds that may be available from the federal government to further the purposes of Sections 6030 to 6031.2, inclusive.
(Added by Stats. 1971, Ch. 1789.)
6031.4.
(a) For the purpose of this title, "local detention facility" means any city, county, city and county, or regional facility used for the confinement for more than 24 hours of adults, or of both adults and minors, but does not include that portion of a facility for the confinement of both adults and minors which is devoted only to the confinement of minors.
(b) In addition to those provided for in subdivision (a), for the purposes of this title, "local detention facility" also includes any city, county, city and county, or regional facility, constructed on or after January 1, 1978, used for the confinement, regardless of the length of confinement, of adults or of both adults and minors, but does not include that portion of a facility for the confinement of both adults and minors which is devoted only to the confinement of minors.
(c) "Local detention facility" also includes any adult detention facility, exclusive of any facility operated by the Department of Corrections and Rehabilitation or any facility holding inmates pursuant to Section 2910.5, Chapter 4 (commencing with Section 3410) of Title 2 of, Chapter 9.2 (commencing with Section 6220) of Title 7 of, Chapter 9.5 (commencing with Section 6250) of Title 7 of, or Chapter 9.6 (commencing with Section 6260) of Title 7 of, Part 3, that holds local prisoners under contract on behalf of a city, county, or city and county. Nothing in this subdivision shall be construed as affecting or authorizing the establishment of private detention facilities.
(d) "Local detention facility" also includes a court holding facility within a superior court that is operated by or supervised by personnel trained pursuant to Section 1024 of Title 15 of the California Code of Regulations. A court holding facility does not include an area within a courtroom or a public area in the courthouse.
(e) For purposes of this title, a local detention facility does not include those rooms that are used for holding persons for interviews, interrogations, or investigations, and are either separate from a jail or located in the administrative area of a law enforcement facility.
(Amended by Stats. 2018, Ch. 36, Sec. 23. (AB 1812) Effective June 27, 2018.)
6031.5.
For the purposes of this chapter, the term "correctional personnel" means either of the following:
(1) Any person described by subdivision (a) or (b) of Section 830.5, 830.55, 831, or 831.5.
(2) Any class of persons who perform supervision, custody, care, or treatment functions and are employed by the Department of Corrections, the Department of the Youth Authority, any correctional or detention facility, probation department, community-based correctional program, or other state or local public facility or program responsible for the custody, supervision, treatment, or rehabilitation of persons accused of, or adjudged responsible for, criminal or delinquent conduct.
(Amended by Stats. 1991, Ch. 1100, Sec. 5.)
6031.6.
(a) Any privately operated local detention facility responsible for the custody and control of any local prisoner shall, as required by subdivision (a) of Section 1208, operate pursuant to a contract with the city, county, or city and county, as appropriate.
(b) (1) Each contract shall include, but not be limited to, a provision whereby the private agency or entity agrees to operate in compliance with all appropriate state and local building, zoning, health, safety, and fire statutes, ordinances, and regulations, and with the minimum jail standards established by regulations adopted by the Board of Corrections, as set forth in Subchapter 4 (commencing with Section 1000) of Chapter 1 of Division 1 of Title 15 of the California Code of Regulations.
(2) The private agency or entity shall select and train its personnel in accordance with selection and training requirements adopted by the Board of Corrections as set forth in Subchapter 1 (commencing with Section 100) of Chapter 1 of Division 1 of Title 15 of the California Code of Regulations.
(3) The failure of a privately operated local detention facility to comply with the appropriate health, safety, and fire laws, or with the minimum jail standards adopted by the Board of Corrections, may constitute grounds for the termination of the contract.
(c) Upon the discovery of a failure of a privately operated local detention facility to comply with the requirements of subdivision (b), the local governmental entity shall notify the director of the facility that sanctions shall be applied or the contract shall be canceled if the specified deficiencies are not corrected within 60 days.
(Added by Stats. 1993, Ch. 787, Sec. 3. Effective January 1, 1994.)
6032.
(a) There is hereby established within the Board of State and Community Corrections the California Juvenile Justice Data Working Group. The purpose of the working group is to recommend options for coordinating and modernizing the juvenile justice data systems and reports that are developed and maintained by state and county agencies.
(b) (1) The working group shall include representatives from each of the following:
(A) The Department of Justice.
(B) The Board of State and Community Corrections.
(C) The Division of Juvenile Justice within the Department of Corrections and Rehabilitation.
(D) The Chief Probation Officers of California.
(E) The Judicial Council.
(F) The California State Association of Counties.
(G) Any other representatives that are deemed appropriate by the board.

(2) Members of the working group shall include persons that have experience or expertise related to the California juvenile justice system or the design and implementation of juvenile justice data systems, or both.
(c) (1) The working group shall analyze the capacities and limitations of the data systems and networks used to collect and report state and local juvenile caseload and outcome data. The analysis shall include all of the following:
(A) A review of the relevant data systems, studies, or models from California and other states having elements worthy of replication in California.
(B) Identify changes or upgrades to improve the capacity and utility of juvenile justice caseload and outcome data in California, including changes to support the gathering of juvenile justice outcome and recidivism information, and changes to improve performance outcome measurements for state-local juvenile justice grant programs.
(2) No later than January 1, 2016, the working group shall prepare and submit a report to the Legislature on the options for improving interagency coordination, modernization, and upgrading of state and local juvenile justice data and information systems. The report shall include, but not be limited to, all of the following:
(A) The additional collection and reporting responsibilities for agencies, departments, or providers that would be affected.
(B) Recommendations for the creation of a Web-based statewide clearinghouse or information center that would make relevant juvenile justice information on operations, caseloads, dispositions, and outcomes available in a user-friendly, query-based format for stakeholders and members of the public.
(C) An assessment of the feasibility of implementing the responsibilities identified in subparagraph (A) and the recommendations developed pursuant to subparagraph (B).
(3) The working group shall also recommend a plan for improving the current juvenile justice reporting requirements of Section 1961 of the Welfare and Institutions Code and Section 30061 of the Government Code, including streamlining and consolidating current requirements without sacrificing meaningful data collection. The working group shall submit its recommendations to the Board of State and Community Corrections no later than April 30, 2015.
(d) (1) The requirement for submitting a report imposed under subdivision (c) is inoperative on January 1, 2016, pursuant to Section 10231.5 of the Government Code.
(2) A report submitted to the Legislature pursuant to subdivision (c) shall be submitted in compliance with Section 9795 of the Government Code.
(Amended by Stats. 2014, Ch. 436, Sec. 1. (SB 1054) Effective January 1, 2015.)
6033.
The Board of State and Community Corrections shall, by January 1, 2018, develop recommendations for best practices and standardization for counties on how to disaggregate juvenile justice caseload and performance and outcome data by race and ethnicity.
(Added by Stats. 2016, Ch. 880, Sec. 3. (AB 1998) Effective January 1, 2017.)

ARTICLE 2. Standards and Training of Local Corrections and Probation Officers [6035 - 6036]
(Article 2 added by Stats. 1979, Ch. 1148.)
6035.
(a) For the purpose of raising the level of competence of local corrections and probation officers and other correctional personnel, the board shall adopt, and may from time to time amend, rules establishing minimum standards for the selection and training of these personnel employed by any city, county, or city and county who provide for the custody, supervision, treatment, or rehabilitation of persons accused of, or adjudged responsible for, criminal or delinquent conduct who are currently under local jurisdiction. All of these rules shall be adopted and amended pursuant to Chapter 3.5 (commencing with Section 11340) of Part 1 of Division 3 of Title 2 of the Government Code.
(b) Any city, county, or city and county may adhere to the standards for selection and training established by the board. The board may defer the promulgation of selection standards until necessary research for job relatedness is completed.
(c) Minimum training standards may include, but are not limited to, basic, entry, continuation, supervisory, management, and specialized assignments.
(Amended by Stats. 2003, Ch. 158, Sec. 3. Effective August 2, 2003.)
6036.
For purposes of implementing this article, the board shall have the following powers:
(a) Approve or certify, or both, training and education courses at institutions approved by the board.
(b) Develop and operate a professional certificate program which provides recognition of achievement for local corrections and probation officers whose agencies participate in the program.
(c) Adopt those regulations as are necessary to carry out the purposes of this chapter.
(d) Develop and present training courses for local corrections and probation officers.
(e) Perform those other activities and studies as would carry out the intent of this article.
(Amended by Stats. 2003, Ch. 158, Sec. 4. Effective August 2, 2003.)

ARTICLE 3. Corrections Training Fund [6040- 6040.]
(Article 3 added by Stats. 1979, Ch. 1148.)
6040.
There is hereby created in the State Treasury a Corrections Training Fund. Upon appropriation from the fund, moneys shall be used exclusively for the costs of administration, the development of appropriate standards, the development of training, and program evaluation, pursuant to this chapter. The fund is abolished on June 30, 2021, and any moneys remaining in the fund shall revert to the State Penalty Fund.
(Amended by Stats. 2018, Ch. 36, Sec. 24. (AB 1812) Effective June 27, 2018.)

ARTICLE 3.5. Council on Mentally Ill Offenders [6044- 6044.]
(Article 3.5 added by Stats. 2001, Ch. 860, Sec. 1.)
6044.
(a) The Council on Criminal Justice and Behavioral Health is hereby established within the Department of Corrections and Rehabilitation. The council shall be composed of 12 members, one of whom shall be the secretary of the department who shall be designated as the chairperson, one of whom shall be the Director of State Hospitals, one of whom shall be the Director of Health Care Services, and nine of whom shall be appointed. The Governor shall appoint three members, at least one of whom shall represent behavioral health. The Senate Committee on Rules shall appoint two members, one representing law enforcement and one representing behavioral health. The Speaker of the Assembly shall appoint two members, one representing law enforcement and one representing behavioral health. The Attorney General shall appoint one member. The Chief Justice of the California Supreme Court shall appoint one member who shall be a superior court judge. When selecting appointments, experience with the criminal justice or behavioral health systems, or both, either personally, as a family member, or as a caregiver, is encouraged.
(b) The council shall select a vice chairperson from among its members. Six members of the council shall constitute a quorum.
(c) The Director of State Hospitals and the Director of Health Care Services shall serve as the liaison to the California Health and Human Services Agency and any departments within that agency necessary to further the purposes of this article.
(d) Members of the council shall receive no compensation, but shall be reimbursed for actual and necessary travel expenses incurred in the performance of their duties. For purposes of compensation, attendance at meetings of the board shall be deemed performance by a member of the duties of his or her state or local government employment.

(e) The goal of the council shall be to investigate and promote cost-effective approaches to meeting the long-term needs of adults and juveniles with behavioral health disorders who are likely to become offenders or who have a history of offending. The council shall:

(1) Identify strategies for preventing adults and juveniles with behavioral health needs from becoming offenders.

(2) Identify strategies for improving the cost-effectiveness of services for adults and juveniles with behavioral health needs who have a history of offending.

(3) Identify incentives to encourage state and local criminal justice, juvenile justice, and behavioral health programs to adopt cost-effective approaches for serving adults and juveniles with behavioral health needs who are likely to offend or who have a history of offending.

(f) The council shall consider strategies that:

(1) Improve service coordination among state and local behavioral health, criminal justice, and juvenile justice programs.

(2) Improve the ability of adult and juvenile offenders with behavioral health needs to transition successfully between corrections-based, juvenile justice-based, and community-based treatment programs.

(g) The Secretary of the Department of Corrections and Rehabilitation, the Director of State Hospitals, and the Director of Health Care Services may furnish for the use of the council those facilities, supplies, and personnel as may be available therefor. The council may secure the assistance of any state agency, department, or instrumentality in the course of its work.

(h) (1) The Council on Criminal Justice and Behavioral Health shall file with the Legislature, not later than December 31 of each year, a report that shall provide details of the council's activities during the preceding year. The report shall include recommendations for improving the cost-effectiveness of behavioral health and criminal justice programs.

(2) After the first year of operation, the council may recommend to the Legislature and Governor modifications to its jurisdiction, composition, and membership that will further the purposes of this article.

(i) The Council on Criminal Justice and Behavioral Health is authorized to apply for any funds that may be available from the federal government or other sources to further the purposes of this article.

(j) (1) For purposes of this article, the council shall address the needs of adults and juveniles who meet the following criteria: persons who have been arrested, detained, incarcerated, or are at a significant risk of being arrested, detained, or incarcerated, and who have a mental disorder as defined in Section 1830.205 of Title 9 of the California Code of Regulations or who receive substance use disorder services as defined in Section 51341.1 of Title 22 of the California Code of Regulations that have been determined to be medically necessary pursuant to Section 51303 of Title 22 of the California Code of Regulations, or both.

(2) The council may expand its purview to allow it to identify strategies that are preventive in nature and could be directed to identifiable categories of adults and juveniles that fall outside of the above definitions.

(Amended by Stats. 2017, Ch. 269, Sec. 11. (SB 811) Effective January 1, 2018.)

ARTICLE 4. Mentally Ill Offender Crime Reduction Grants [6045 - 6045.9]
(Article 4 added by Stats. 2014, Ch. 26, Sec. 32.)

6045.

(a) The Board of State and Community Corrections shall administer mentally ill offender crime reduction grants on a competitive basis to counties that expand or establish a continuum of timely and effective responses to reduce crime and criminal justice costs related to mentally ill offenders. The grants administered under this article by the board shall be divided equally between adult and juvenile mentally ill offender crime reduction grants in accordance with the funds appropriated for each type of grant. The grants shall support prevention, intervention, supervision, and incarceration-based services and strategies to reduce recidivism and to improve outcomes for mentally ill juvenile and adult offenders.

(b) For purposes of this article, the following terms shall have the following meanings:

(1) "Board" means the Board of State and Community Corrections.

(2) "Mentally ill adult offenders" means persons described in subdivisions (b) and (c) of Section 5600.3 of the Welfare and Institutions Code.

(3) "Mentally ill juvenile offenders" means persons described in subdivision (a) of Section 5600.3 of the Welfare and Institutions Code.

(Amended by Stats. 2014, Ch. 436, Sec. 2. (SB 1054) Effective January 1, 2015.)

6045.2.

(a) A county shall be eligible to apply for either an adult mentally ill offender grant or a juvenile mentally ill offender grant or both in accordance with all other provisions of this article. The board shall provide a separate and competitive grant application and award process for each of the adult and juvenile mentally ill offender crime reduction grant categories. The board shall endeavor to assist counties that apply for grants in both categories in meeting any grant submission requirements that may overlap between the two categories of grants.

(b) (1) A county that applies for an adult mentally ill offender grant shall establish a strategy committee to design the grant application that includes, at a minimum, the sheriff or director of the county department of corrections in a county where the sheriff does not administer the county jail system, who shall chair the committee, and representatives from other local law enforcement agencies, the chief probation officer, the county mental health director, a superior court judge, a former offender who is or has been a client of a mental health treatment facility, and representatives from organizations that can provide or have provided treatment or stabilization services for mentally ill offenders, including treatment, housing, income or job support, and caretaking.

(2) A county that applies for a juvenile mentally ill offender grant shall establish a strategy committee that includes, at a minimum, the chief probation officer who shall chair the committee, representatives from local law enforcement agencies, the county mental health director, a superior court judge, a client or former offender who has received juvenile mental health services, and representatives from organizations that can provide or have provided treatment or support services for mentally ill juvenile offenders, including therapy, education, employment, housing, and caretaking services.

(3) A county that applies for both types of grants may convene a combined strategy committee that includes the sheriff or jail administrator and the chief probation officer as cochairs of the committee, as well as representation from the other agencies, departments, and disciplines designated in paragraphs (1) and (2) for both types of committees.

(c) The strategy committee shall develop and describe in its grant application a comprehensive county plan for providing a cost-effective continuum of responses and services for mentally ill adult offenders or mentally ill juvenile offenders, including prevention, intervention, and incarceration-based services, as appropriate. The plan shall describe how the responses and services included in the plan have been proven to be or are designed to be effective in addressing the mental health needs of the target offender population, while also reducing recidivism and custody levels for mentally ill offenders in adult or juvenile detention or correctional facilities. Strategies for prevention, intervention, and incarceration-based services in the plan shall include, but not be limited to, all of the following:

(1) Mental health and substance abuse treatment for mentally ill adult offenders or mentally ill juvenile offenders who are presently placed, incarcerated, or housed in a local adult or juvenile detention or correctional facility or who are under supervision by the probation department after having been released from a state or local adult or juvenile detention or correctional facility.

(2) Prerelease, reentry, continuing, and community-based services designed to provide long-term stability for juvenile or adult offenders outside of the facilities of the adult or juvenile justice systems, including services to support a stable source of income, a safe and decent residence, and a conservator or caretaker, as needed in appropriate cases.

(3) For mentally ill juvenile offender applications, one or more of the following strategies that has proven to be effective or has evidence-based support for effectiveness in the remediation of mental health disorders and the reduction of offending: short-term and family-based therapies, collaborative interagency service agreements, specialized court-based assessment and disposition tracks or programs, or other specialized mental health treatment and intervention models for juvenile offenders that are proven or promising from an evidence-based perspective.

(d) The plan as included in the grant application shall include the identification of specific outcome and performance measures and for annual reporting on grant performance and outcomes to the board that will allow the board to evaluate, at a minimum, the effectiveness of the strategies supported by the grant in reducing crime, incarceration, and criminal justice costs related to mentally ill offenders. The board shall, in the grant application process, provide guidance to counties on the performance measures and reporting criteria to be addressed in the application.

(Added by Stats. 2014, Ch. 26, Sec. 32. (AB 1468) Effective June 20, 2014.)

6045.4.

(a) The application submitted by a county shall describe a four-year plan for the programs, services, or strategies to be provided under the grant. The board shall award grants that provide funding for three years. Funding shall be used to supplement, rather than supplant, funding for existing programs. Funds may be used to fund specialized alternative custody and diversion programs that offer appropriate mental health treatment and services.

(b) A grant shall not be awarded unless the applicant makes available resources in accordance with the instructions of the board in an amount equal to at least 25 percent of the amount of the grant. Resources may include in-kind contributions from participating agencies.

(c) In awarding grants, priority or preference shall be given to those grant applications that include documented match funding that exceeds 25 percent of the total grant amount.

(Amended by Stats. 2015, Ch. 473, Sec. 1. (SB 621) Effective January 1, 2016.)

6045.6.

The board shall establish minimum requirements, funding criteria, and procedures for awarding grants, which shall take into consideration, but not be limited to, all of the following:

(a) The probable or potential impact of the grant on reducing the number or percent of mentally ill adult offenders or mentally ill juvenile offenders who are incarcerated or detained in local adult or juvenile correctional facilities and, as relevant for juvenile offenders, in probation out-of-home placements.

(b) Demonstrated ability to administer the program, including any past experience in the administration of a prior mentally ill offender crime reduction grant.

(c) Demonstrated ability to develop effective responses and to provide effective treatment and stability for mentally ill adult offenders or mentally ill juvenile offenders.

(d) Demonstrated ability to provide for interagency collaboration to ensure the effective coordination and delivery of the strategies, programs, or services described in the application.

(e) Likelihood that the program will continue to operate after state grant funding ends, including the applicant's demonstrated history of maximizing federal, state, local, and private funding sources to address the needs of the grant service population.

(Added by Stats. 2014, Ch. 26, Sec. 32. (AB 1468) Effective June 20, 2014.)

6045.8.

(a) The board shall create an evaluation design for adult and juvenile mentally ill offender crime reduction grants that assesses the effectiveness of the program in reducing crime, adult and juvenile offender incarceration and placement levels, early releases due to jail overcrowding, and local criminal and juvenile justice costs. The evaluation design may include outcome measures related to the service levels, treatment modes, and stability measures for juvenile and adult offenders participating in, or benefitting from, mentally ill offender crime reduction grant programs or services.

(b) Commencing on October 1, 2015, and annually thereafter, the board shall submit a report to the Legislature based on the evaluation design, with a final report due on December 31, 2018.

(c) The reports submitted pursuant to this section shall be submitted in compliance with Section 9795 of the Government Code.

(d) Pursuant to Section 10231.5 of the Government Code, this section shall be repealed as of January 1, 2024.

(Amended by Stats. 2014, Ch. 436, Sec. 4. (SB 1054) Effective January 1, 2015. Repealed as of January 1, 2024, by its own provisions.)

6045.9.

The board may use up to 5 percent of the funds appropriated for purposes of this article to administer this program, including technical assistance to counties and the development of the evaluation component.

(Added by Stats. 2014, Ch. 26, Sec. 32. (AB 1468) Effective June 20, 2014.)

ARTICLE 5. Second Chance Program [6046 - 6046.3]
(Article 5 added by Stats. 2015, Ch. 438, Sec. 4.)

6046.

(a) The purpose of this article is to build safer communities by investing in community-based programs, services, and initiatives for formerly incarcerated individuals in need of mental health and substance use treatment services.

(b) The program established pursuant to this article shall be restricted to supporting mental health treatment, substance use treatment, and diversion programs for persons in the criminal justice system, with an emphasis on programs that reduce recidivism of persons convicted of less serious crimes, such as those covered by the Safe Neighborhoods and Schools Act of 2014, and those who have substance use and mental health problems.

(c) The Board of State and Community Corrections shall administer a grant program established pursuant to this article.

(Added by Stats. 2015, Ch. 438, Sec. 4. (AB 1056) Effective January 1, 2016.)

6046.1.

For the purposes of this article, the following definitions shall apply:

(a) "Board" means the Board of State and Community Corrections.

(b) "Fund" means the Second Chance Fund established pursuant to Section 6046.2.

(c) "Public agency" means a county, city, whether a general law city or a chartered city, or city and county, the duly constituted governing body of an Indian reservation or rancheria, a school district, municipal corporation, district, political subdivision, or any board, commission, or agency thereof, entities that are legislative bodies of a local agency pursuant to subdivision (c) or (d) of Section 54952 of the Government Code, a housing authority organized pursuant to Part 2 (commencing with Section 34200) of Division 24 of the Health and Safety Code, a state agency, public district, or other political subdivision of the state, or any instrumentality thereof, which is authorized to engage in or assist in the development or operation of housing for persons and families of low or moderate income.

(d) "Recidivism" means a conviction of a new felony or misdemeanor committed within three years of release from custody or committed within three years of placement on supervision for a previous criminal conviction.

(Added by Stats. 2015, Ch. 438, Sec. 4. (AB 1056) Effective January 1, 2016.)
6046.2.

(a) The Second Chance Fund is hereby created in the State Treasury. The board shall be responsible for administering the fund. Moneys in the fund are hereby continuously appropriated without regard to fiscal year for the purposes of this article.

(b) (1) The Controller, upon order of the Director of Finance, shall transfer moneys available to the Board of State and Community Corrections pursuant to paragraph (3) of subdivision (a) of Section 7599.2 of the Government Code into the Second Chance Fund.

(2) The Second Chance Fund may receive moneys from any other federal, state, or local grant, or from any private donation or grant, for the purposes of this article.

(c) The board shall not spend more than 5 percent annually of the moneys in the fund for administrative costs.

(Added by Stats. 2015, Ch. 438, Sec. 4. (AB 1056) Effective January 1, 2016.)
6046.3.

(a) The board shall administer a competitive grant program to carry out the purposes of this article that focuses on community-based solutions for reducing recidivism. The grant program shall, at minimum, do all of the following:

(1) Restrict eligibility to proposals designed to serve people who have been arrested, charged with, or convicted of a criminal offense and have a history of mental health or substance use disorders.

(2) Restrict eligibility to proposals that offer mental health services, substance use disorder treatment services, misdemeanor diversion programs, or some combination thereof.

(3) Restrict eligibility to proposals that have a public agency as the lead applicant.

(b) The board shall form an executive steering committee that includes, but is not limited to, a balanced and diverse membership from relevant state and local government entities, community-based treatment and service providers, and the formerly incarcerated community. The committee shall have expertise in homelessness and housing, behavioral health and substance abuse treatment, and effective rehabilitative treatment for adults and juveniles. The committee shall make recommendations regarding the design, efficacy, and viability of proposals, and make recommendations on guidelines for the submission of proposals, including threshold or scoring criteria, or both, that do all of the following:

(1) Prioritize proposals that advance principles of restorative justice while demonstrating a capacity to reduce recidivism.

(2) Prioritize proposals that leverage other federal, state, and local funds or other social investments, such as the following sources of funding:

(A) The Drug Medi-Cal Treatment Program (22 Cal. Code Regs. 51341.1, 51490.1, and 51516.1).

(B) The Mental Health Services Act, enacted by Proposition 63 at the November 2, 2004, general election, as amended.

(C) Funds provided for in connection with the implementation of Chapter 15 of the Statutes of 2011.

(D) The Community Corrections Performance Incentives Act (Stats. 2009, Ch. 608; Chapter 3 (commencing with Section 1228) of Title 8 of Part 2).

(E) The tax credits established pursuant to Sections 12209, 17053.57, and 23657 of the Revenue and Taxation Code.

(F) The federal Department of Housing and Urban Development funds, such as the Emergency Solutions Grant program (42 U.S.C. Sec. 11371 et seq.).

(G) The federal Department of Veterans Affairs Supportive Services for Veteran Families program (38 U.S.C. Sec. 2044).

(H) Social Innovation Funds established by the Corporation for National and Community Service pursuant to Section 12653k of Title 42 of the United States Code.

(I) The Edward Byrne Memorial Justice Assistance Grant Program (42 U.S.C. Sec. 3750 et seq.).

(3) Prioritize proposals that provide for all of the following:

(A) Mental health services, substance use disorder treatment services, misdemeanor diversion programs, or some combination thereof.

(B) Housing-related assistance that utilizes evidence-based models, including, but not limited to, those recommended by the federal Department of Housing and Urban Development. Housing-related assistance may include, but is not limited to, the following:

(i) Financial assistance, including security deposits, utility payments, moving-cost assistance, and up to 24 months of rental assistance.

(ii) Housing stabilization assistance, including case management, relocation assistance, outreach and engagement, landlord recruitment, housing navigation and placement, and credit repair.

(C) Other community-based supportive services, such as job skills training, case management, and civil legal services.

(4) Prioritize proposals that leverage existing contracts, partnerships, memoranda of understanding, or other formal relationships to provide one or more of the services prioritized in paragraph (3).

(5) Prioritize proposals put forth by a public agency in partnership with a philanthropic or nonprofit organization.

(6) Prioritize proposals that promote interagency and regional collaborations.

(7) Consider ways to promote services for people with offenses identical or similar to those addressed by the Safe Neighborhoods and Schools Act of 2014, without precluding assistance to a person with other offenses in his or her criminal history.

(8) Consider geographic diversity.

(9) Consider appropriate limits for administrative costs and overhead.

(10) Consider proposals that provide services to juveniles.

(11) Permit proposals to expand the capacity of an existing program and prohibit proposals from using the fund to supplant funding for an existing program.

(Added by Stats. 2015, Ch. 438, Sec. 4. (AB 1056) Effective January 1, 2016.)

CHAPTER 6. Appointment of Personnel [6050 - 6055]

(Chapter 6 added by Stats. 1944, 3rd Ex. Sess., Ch. 2.)
6050.

(a) The Governor, upon recommendation of the secretary, shall appoint the wardens of the various state prisons. Each warden shall be subject to removal by the secretary. If the secretary removes him or her, the secretary's action shall be final. The wardens shall be exempt from civil service.

(b) The Department of Human Resources shall fix the compensation of the wardens of the state prisons.

(Amended by Stats. 2012, Ch. 665, Sec. 183. (SB 1308) Effective January 1, 2013.)
6053.

(a) All persons other than temporary appointees heretofore serving in the state civil service and engaged in the performance of a function transferred to the department or engaged in the administration of a law, the administration of which is transferred to the department, shall remain in the state civil service and are hereby transferred to the department on the effective date of this section, and their status, positions and rights shall not be affected by their transfer and shall continue to be retained by them pursuant to the State Civil Service Act. The director, pursuant to the State Civil Service

Act, shall be the appointing authority for the department for all civil service positions except those civil service positions in the Youth Authority. Positions not heretofore established, which are exclusively for the California Institution for Women or exclusively for the Youth Authority, shall be filled pursuant to the State Civil Service Act.

(b) Notwithstanding Section 18932 of the Government Code, the maximum age shall be 35 years for any open examination for the position of correctional officer, correctional program supervisor, and other custodial positions which normally afford entry into the Department of Corrections service, unless the applicant is already a "state safety" member for the purpose of retirement and disability benefits or was employed in a permanent, temporary, part-time, or intermittent capacity with the department after July 1, 1973, but before January 1, 1974.

(Amended by Stats. 1977, Ch. 165. Superseded on operative date of amendment by Stats. 1981, Ch. 453.)
6053.

(a) All persons other than temporary appointees heretofore serving in the state civil service and engaged in the performance of a function transferred to the department or engaged in the administration of a law the administration of which is transferred to the department shall remain in the state civil service and are hereby transferred to the department on the effective date of this section; and their status, positions and rights shall not be affected by their transfer and shall continue to be retained by them pursuant to the State Civil Service Act. The director, pursuant to the State Civil Service Act, shall be the appointing authority for the department for all civil service positions except those civil service positions in the Youth Authority. Positions not heretofore established which are exclusively for the California Institution for Women or exclusively for the Youth Authority shall be filled pursuant to the State Civil Service Act.

(b) Any open examination for the position of correctional officer, correctional program supervisor, and other custodial positions which normally afford entry into the Department of Corrections service shall require a demonstration of the physical ability to effectively carry out the duties and responsibilities of the position in a manner which would not inordinately endanger the health or safety of a custodial person or the health and safety of others.

(Amended by Stats. 1981, Ch. 453, Sec. 5. Conditionally operative as prescribed by Sec. 8 of Ch. 453.)
6055.

The Department of Corrections and the Department of the Youth Authority may provide time off with pay to security and treatment personnel who take courses approved by the departments on mental health treatment related to their jobs. The departments may also provide financial compensation to pay for the cost of such courses.

(Added by Stats. 1975, Ch. 1258.)

CHAPTER 6.5. Internal Investigations [6065-6065.]

(Chapter 6.5 added by Stats. 1998, Ch. 762, Sec. 2.)
6065.

(a) The Legislature finds and declares that investigations of the Department of Corrections and the Department of the Youth Authority that are conducted by their respective offices of internal affairs, or any successor to these offices, require appropriately trained personnel, who perform their duties with honesty, credibility, and without any conflicts of interest.

(b) To meet the objectives stated in subdivision (a), the following conditions shall be met:

(1) Prior to training any peace officer who is selected to conduct internal affairs investigations, the department shall conduct a complete and thorough background check. This background check shall be in addition to the original background screening that was conducted when the person was hired as a peace officer. Each person shall satisfactorily pass the second background check. Any person who has been the subject of a sustained, serious disciplinary action, including, but not limited to, termination, suspension, or demotion, shall not pass the background check.

(2) All internal affairs allegations or complaints, whether investigated or not, shall be logged and numbered sequentially on an annual basis. The log shall specify, but not be limited to, the following information: the sequential number of the allegation or complaint, the date of receipt of the allegation or complaint, the location or facility to which the allegation or complaint pertains, and the disposition of all actions taken, including any final action taken. The log shall be made available to the Inspector General.

(c) Consistent with the objectives expressed in subdivision (a), investigators shall conduct investigations and inquiries in a manner that provides a complete and thorough presentation of the facts regarding the allegation or complaint. All extenuating and mitigating facts shall be explored and reported. The role of the investigator is that of a factfinder. All reports prepared by an investigator shall provide the appointing authority with a complete recitation of the facts, and shall refrain from conjecture or opinion.

(1) Uncorroborated or anonymous allegations shall not constitute the sole basis for disciplinary action by the department, other than an investigation.

(2) All reports shall be submitted in a standard format, begin with a statement of the allegation or complaint, provide all relevant facts, and include the investigator's signature, certifying that the investigator has complied with the provisions of this section subject to compliance with Sections 118.1 and 148.6.

(Amended by Stats. 1999, Ch. 83, Sec. 159. Effective January 1, 2000.)

CHAPTER 7. Definitions [6080 - 6082]

(Chapter 7 added by Stats. 1944, 3rd [1st] Ex. Sess., Ch. 2.)
6080.

As used in his part, the following terms have the meanings described below:

(a) "Department" refers to the Department of Corrections.

(b) "Director" refers to the Director of Corrections.

(Added by Stats. 1944, 3rd [1st] Ex. Sess., Ch. 2.)
6081.

As used in this code, "prison" and "state prison" include the California Institution for Women.

(Amended by Stats. 1977, Ch. 165.)
6082.

References in this title and in Title 5 (commencing with Section 4500) to prisons refer to all facilities, camps, hospitals and institutions for the confinement, treatment, employment, training and discipline of persons in the legal custody of the Department of Corrections.

(Amended by Stats. 1987, Ch. 828, Sec. 163.)

CHAPTER 8. The Medical Facility [6100 - 6106]

(Chapter 8 added by Stats. 1945, Ch. 1491.)

6100.

There is hereby established an institution under the jurisdiction of the Department of Corrections to be known as the Medical Facility.

(Added by Stats. 1945, Ch. 1491.)

6101.

The Medical Facility shall be located in the northern part of the State.

(Amended by Stats. 1946, 1st Ex. Sess., Ch. 69.)

6102.

The primary purpose of the medical facility shall be the receiving, segregation, confinement, treatment and care of males under the custody of the Department of Corrections or any agency thereof who are any of the following:

(a) Mentally disordered.

(b) Developmentally disabled.

(c) Addicted to the use of controlled substances.

(d) Suffering from any other chronic disease or condition.

(Amended by Stats. 1986, Ch. 120, Sec. 1.)

6103.

The Director of Corrections shall construct and equip, in accordance with law, suitable buildings, structures, and facilities for the Medical Facility.

(Added by Stats. 1945, Ch. 1491.)

6104.

The Director of Corrections shall make rules and regulations for the government of the Medical Facility and the management of its affairs.

(Added by Stats. 1945, Ch. 1491.)

6105.

The Governor, upon the recommendation of the Director of Corrections, in accordance with Section 6050, shall appoint a warden for the medical facility. The director shall appoint, subject to civil service, those other officers and employees as may be necessary.

The Director of Corrections may remove a warden at his or her own discretion at any time.

(Amended by Stats. 1992, Ch. 1279, Sec. 6. Effective January 1, 1993.)

6106.

The supervision, management, and control of the Medical Facility and the responsibility for the care, custody, treatment, training, discipline and employment of persons confined therein are vested in the Director of Corrections. The provisions of Part 3 (commencing with Section 2000) apply to the institution as a prison under the jurisdiction of the Department of Corrections and to the persons confined therein insofar as those provisions may be applicable.

(Amended by Stats. 1987, Ch. 828, Sec. 164.)

CHAPTER 8.2. Office of the Inspector General [6125 - 6141]

(Chapter 8.2 added by Stats. 1994, Ch. 766, Sec. 1.)

6125.

There is hereby created the independent Office of the Inspector General which shall not be a subdivision of any other governmental entity. The Governor shall appoint, subject to confirmation by the Senate, the Inspector General to a six-year term. The Inspector General may not be removed from office during that term, except for good cause.

(Amended by Stats. 2009, Ch. 35, Sec. 13. (SB 174) Effective January 1, 2010.)

6126.

(a) The Inspector General shall be responsible for contemporaneous oversight of internal affairs investigations and the disciplinary process of the Department of Corrections and Rehabilitation, pursuant to Section 6133 under policies to be developed by the Inspector General.

(b) When requested by the Governor, the Senate Committee on Rules, or the Speaker of the Assembly, the Inspector General shall initiate an audit or review of policies, practices, and procedures of the department. The Inspector General may, under policies developed by the Inspector General, initiate an audit or review on the Inspector General's own accord. Following a completed audit or review, the Inspector General may perform a followup audit or review to determine what measures the department implemented to address the Inspector General's findings and to assess the effectiveness of those measures.

(c) (1) Upon completion of an audit or review pursuant to subdivision (b), the Inspector General shall prepare a complete written report, which may be held as confidential and disclosed in confidence, along with all underlying materials the Inspector General deems appropriate, to the Department of Corrections and Rehabilitation and to the requesting entity in subdivision (b), where applicable.

(2) The Inspector General shall also prepare a public report. When necessary, the public report shall differ from the complete written report in the respect that the Inspector General shall have the discretion to redact or otherwise protect the names of individuals, specific locations, or other facts that, if not redacted, might hinder prosecution related to the review, compromise the safety and security of staff, inmates, or members of the public, or where disclosure of the information is otherwise prohibited by law, and to decline to produce any of the underlying materials. Copies of public reports shall be posted on the Office of the Inspector General's internet website.

(d) The Inspector General shall, during the course of an audit or review, identify areas of full and partial compliance, or noncompliance, with departmental policies and procedures, specify deficiencies in the completion and documentation of processes, and recommend corrective actions, including, but not limited to, additional training, additional policies, or changes in policy, as well as any other findings or recommendations that the Inspector General deems appropriate.

(e) The Inspector General, pursuant to Section 6126.6, shall review the Governor's candidates for appointment to serve as warden for the state's adult correctional institutions and as superintendents for the state's juvenile facilities.

(f) The Inspector General shall conduct an objective, clinically appropriate, and metric-oriented medical inspection program to periodically review delivery of medical care at each state prison.

(g) The Inspector General shall conduct an objective, metric-oriented oversight and inspection program to periodically review delivery of the reforms identified in the document released by the Department of Corrections and Rehabilitation in April 2012, entitled The Future of California Corrections: A Blueprint to Save Billions of Dollars, End Federal Court Oversight, and Improve the Prison System (the blueprint), including, but not limited to, the following specific goals and reforms described by the blueprint:

(1) Whether the department has increased the percentage of inmates served in rehabilitative programs to 70 percent of the department's target population prior to their release.

(2) The establishment of an adherence to the standardized staffing model at each institution.

(3) The establishment of an adherence to the new inmate classification score system.

(4) The establishment of and adherence to the new prison gang management system, including changes to the department's current policies for identifying prison-based gang members and associates and the use and conditions associated with the department's security housing units.

(5) The implementation of and adherence to the Comprehensive Housing Plan described in the blueprint.

(h) The Inspector General shall, in consultation with the Department of Finance, develop a methodology for producing a workload budget to be used for annually adjusting the budget of the Office of the Inspector General, beginning with the budget for the 2005–06 fiscal year.

(i) The Inspector General shall provide contemporaneous oversight of grievances that fall within the department's process for reviewing and investigating inmate allegations of staff misconduct and other specialty grievances, examining compliance with regulations, department policy, and best practices. This contemporaneous oversight shall be completed within the Inspector General's budget excluding resources that, beginning in the Budget Act of 2019, were provided to restore the Inspector General's ability to initiate an audit or review pursuant to subdivision (a). The contemporaneous oversight shall be completed in a way that does not unnecessarily slow the department's review and investigation of inmate allegations of staff misconduct and other specialty grievances. The Inspector General shall issue reports annually, beginning in 2021.

(j) The Inspector General shall monitor the department's process for reviewing uses of force and shall issue reports annually.

(Amended by Stats. 2019, Ch. 364, Sec. 12. (SB 112) Effective September 27, 2019.)

6126.2.

The Inspector General shall not hire any person known to be considered a suspect or subject in an investigation being conducted by any federal, state, or local agency.

(Amended by Stats. 2019, Ch. 364, Sec. 13. (SB 112) Effective September 27, 2019.)

6126.3.

(a) The Inspector General shall not destroy any papers or memoranda used to support a completed review within three years after a report is released.

(b) Except as provided in subdivision (c), all books, papers, records, and correspondence of the office pertaining to its work are public records subject to Chapter 3.5 (commencing with Section 6250) of Division 7 of Title 1 of the Government Code and shall be filed at any of the regularly maintained offices of the Inspector General.

(c) The following books, papers, records, and correspondence of the Office of the Inspector General pertaining to its work are not public records subject to Chapter 3.5 (commencing with Section 6250) of Division 7 of Title 1 of the Government Code, nor shall they be subject to discovery pursuant to any provision of Title 3 (commencing with Section 1985) of Part 4 of the Code of Civil Procedure or Chapter 7 (commencing with Section 19570) of Part 2 of Division 5 of Title 2 of the Government Code in any manner:

(1) All reports, papers, correspondence, memoranda, electronic communications, or other documents that are otherwise exempt from disclosure pursuant to the provisions of subdivision (d) of Section 6126.5, Section 6126.6, subdivision (c) of Section 6128, subdivision (c) of Section 6126, or all other applicable laws regarding confidentiality, including, but not limited to, the California Public Records Act, the Public Safety Officers' Procedural Bill of Rights, the Information Practices Act of 1977, the Confidentiality of Medical Information Act of 1977, and the provisions of Section 832.7, relating to the disposition notification for complaints against peace officers.

(2) Any papers, correspondence, memoranda, electronic communications, or other documents pertaining to any audit or review that has not been completed.

(3) Any papers, correspondence, memoranda, electronic communications, or other documents pertaining to internal discussions between the Inspector General and the Inspector General's staff, or between staff members of the Inspector General, or any personal notes of the Inspector General or the Inspector General's staff.

(4) All identifying information, and any personal papers or correspondence from any person requesting assistance from the Inspector General, except in those cases where the Inspector General determines that disclosure of the information is necessary in the interests of justice.

(5) Any papers, correspondence, memoranda, electronic communications, or other documents pertaining to contemporaneous public oversight pursuant to Section 6133 or subdivision (i) or (j) of Section 6126.

(Amended by Stats. 2019, Ch. 364, Sec. 14. (SB 112) Effective September 27, 2019.)

6126.4.

It is a misdemeanor for the Inspector General or any employee or former employee of the Inspector General to divulge or make known in any manner not expressly permitted by law to any person not employed by the Inspector General any particulars of any record, document, or information the disclosure of which is restricted by law from release to the public. This prohibition is also applicable to any person who has been furnished a draft copy of any report for comment or review or any person or business entity that is contracting with or has contracted with the Inspector General and to the employees and former employees of that person or business entity or the employees of any state agency or public entity that has assisted the Inspector General in connection with duties authorized by this chapter.

(Amended by Stats. 2011, Ch. 36, Sec. 40. (SB 92) Effective June 30, 2011.)

6126.5.

(a) Notwithstanding any other law, the Inspector General during regular business hours or at any other time determined necessary by the Inspector General, shall have access to and authority to examine and reproduce any and all books, accounts, reports, vouchers, correspondence files, documents, and other records, and to examine the bank accounts, money, or other property of the Department of Corrections and Rehabilitation in connection with duties authorized by this chapter. Any officer or employee of any agency or entity having these records or property in their possession or under their control shall permit access to, and examination and reproduction thereof consistent with the provisions of this section, upon the request of the Inspector General or the Inspector General's authorized representative.

(b) In connection with duties authorized by this chapter, the Inspector General or the Inspector General's authorized representative shall have access to the records and property of any public or private entity or person subject to review or regulation by the public agency or public entity to the same extent that employees or officers of that agency or public entity have access. No provision of law, memorandum of understanding, or any other agreement entered into between the employing entity and the employee or the employee's representative providing for the confidentiality or privilege of any records or property shall prevent disclosure pursuant to subdivision (a). Access, examination, and reproduction consistent with the provisions of this section shall not result in the waiver of any confidentiality or privilege regarding any records or property.

(c) Any officer or person who fails or refuses to permit access, examination, or reproduction, as required by this section, is guilty of a misdemeanor.

(d) The Inspector General may require any employee of the Department of Corrections and Rehabilitation to be interviewed on a confidential basis. Any employee requested to be interviewed shall comply and shall have time afforded by the appointing authority for the purpose of an interview with the Inspector General or the Inspector General's designee. The Inspector General shall have the discretion to redact the name or other identifying information of any person interviewed from any public report issued by the Inspector General, where required by law or where the failure to redact the information may hinder prosecution or an action in a criminal, civil, or administrative proceeding, or where the Inspector General determines that disclosure of the information is not in the interests of justice. It is not the purpose of these communications to address disciplinary action or grievance procedures that may routinely occur. When conducting an investigation into allegations that an employee of the Department of Corrections and Rehabilitation engaged in misconduct, the Inspector General shall comply with Sections 3303, 3307, 3307.5, 3308, 3309, and subdivisions (a) to (d), inclusive, of Section 3309.5 of the Government Code, except that the Inspector General shall not be subject

to the provisions of any memorandum of understanding or other agreement entered into between the employing entity and the employee or the employee's representative that is in conflict with, or adds to the requirements of, Sections 3303, 3307, 3307.5, 3308, 3309, and subdivisions (a) to (d), inclusive, of Section 3309.5 of the Government Code.
(Amended by Stats. 2019, Ch. 364, Sec. 15. (SB 112) Effective September 27, 2019.)

6126.6.

(a) Prior to filling a vacancy for warden by appointment pursuant to Section 6050, or superintendent pursuant to Section 1049 of the Welfare and Institutions Code, the Governor shall first submit to the Inspector General the names of candidates for the position of warden or superintendent for review of their qualifications.
(b) (1) Upon receipt of the names of those candidates and their completed personal data questionnaires, the Inspector General shall employ appropriate confidential procedures to evaluate and determine the qualifications of each candidate with regard to his or her ability to discharge the duties of the office to which the appointment or nomination is made.
(2) Within 90 days of submission by the Governor of those names, the Inspector General shall advise in confidence to the Governor his or her recommendation whether the candidate is exceptionally well-qualified, well-qualified, qualified, or not qualified and the reasons therefore, and may report, in confidence, any other information that the Inspector General deems pertinent to the qualifications of the candidate.
(c) In reviewing the qualifications of a candidate for the position of warden or superintendent, the Inspector General shall consider, among other appropriate factors, his or her experience in effectively managing correctional facilities and inmate or ward populations; ability to deal effectively with employees, detained persons and other interested persons in addressing management, confinement, and safety issues in an effective, fair, and professional manner; and knowledge of correctional best practices.
(d) The Inspector General shall establish and adopt rules and procedures regarding the review of the qualifications of candidates for the position of warden or superintendent. Those rules and procedures shall establish appropriate, confidential methods for disclosing to the candidate the subject matter of substantial and credible adverse allegations received regarding the candidate's reputation and integrity which, unless rebutted, would be determinative of the candidate's unsuitability for appointment. A rule or procedure shall not be adopted that permits the disclosure to the candidate of information from which the candidate may infer the source, and information shall neither be disclosed to the candidate nor be obtainable by any process that would jeopardize the confidentiality of communications from persons whose opinion has been sought on the candidate's qualifications.
(e) All communications, written, verbal, or otherwise, of and to the Governor, the Governor's authorized agents or employees, including, but not limited to, the Governor's Legal Affairs Secretary and Appointments Secretary, or of and to the Inspector General in furtherance of the purposes of this section are absolutely privileged from disclosure and confidential, and any communication made in the discretion of the Governor or the Inspector General with a candidate or person providing information in furtherance of the purposes of this section shall not constitute a waiver of the privilege or a breach of confidentiality.
(f) When the Governor has appointed a person to the position of warden or superintendent who has been found not qualified by the Inspector General, the Inspector General shall make public that finding, after due notice to the appointee of his or her intention to do so. That notice and disclosure shall not constitute a waiver of privilege or breach of confidentiality with respect to communications of or to the Inspector General concerning the qualifications of the appointee.
(g) A person or entity shall not be liable for any injury caused by any act or failure to act, be it negligent, intentional, discretionary, or otherwise, in the furtherance of the purposes of this section, including, but not limited to, providing or receiving any information, making any recommendations, and giving any reasons therefore.
(h) As used in this section, the term "Inspector General" includes employees and agents of the Office of the Inspector General.
(i) At any time prior to the receipt of the review from the Inspector General specified in subdivision (b), the Governor may withdraw the name of any person submitted to the Inspector General for evaluation pursuant to this section.
(j) No candidate for the position of warden or superintendent may be appointed until the Inspector General has advised the Governor pursuant to this section, or until 90 days have elapsed after submission of the candidate's name to the Inspector General, whichever occurs earlier. The requirement of this subdivision shall not apply to any vacancy in the position of warden or superintendent occurring within the 90 days preceding the expiration of the Governor's term of office, provided, however, that with respect to those vacancies, the Governor shall be required to submit any candidate's name to the Inspector General in order to provide him or her an opportunity, if time permits, to review and make a report.
(k) This section shall not be construed as imposing an additional requirement for an appointment or nomination to the position of warden or superintendent, nor shall anything in this section be construed as adding any additional qualifications for the position of warden or superintendent.
(Amended by Stats. 2013, Ch. 30, Sec. 10. (SB 74) Effective June 27, 2013.)

6127.1.

The Inspector General shall be deemed to be a department head for the purpose of Section 11189 of the Government Code in connection with any duties authorized by this chapter. The Inspector General shall have authority to hire or retain counsel to provide confidential advice. If the Attorney General has a conflict of interest in representing the Inspector General in any litigation, the Inspector General shall have authority to hire or retain counsel to represent the Inspector General.
(Amended by Stats. 2011, Ch. 36, Sec. 42. (SB 92) Effective June 30, 2011.)

6127.3.

(a) In connection with duties authorized pursuant to this chapter, the Office of the Inspector General may do any of the following:
(1) Administer oaths.
(2) Certify to all official acts.
(3) Issue subpoenas for the attendance of witnesses and the production of papers, books, accounts, or documents in any medium, or for the making of oral or written sworn statements, in any interview conducted pursuant to duties authorized by this chapter.
(b) Any subpoena issued under this chapter extends as process to all parts of the state and may be served by any person authorized to serve process of courts of record or by any person designated for that purpose by the office. The person serving this process may receive compensation as is allowed by the office, not to exceed the fees prescribed by law for similar service.
(Amended by Stats. 2011, Ch. 36, Sec. 43. (SB 92) Effective June 30, 2011.)

6127.4.

(a) The superior court in the county in which any interview is held under the direction of the Inspector General, or his or her designee, pursuant to duties authorized by this chapter has jurisdiction to compel the attendance of witnesses, the making of oral or written sworn statements, and the production of papers, books, accounts, and documents, as required by any subpoena issued by the office.
(b) If any witness refuses to attend or testify or produce any papers required by the subpoena, the Inspector General, or his or her designee, may petition the superior court in the county in which the hearing is pending for an order compelling the person to attend and answer questions under penalty of perjury or produce the papers required by the subpoena before the person named in the subpoena. The petition shall set forth all of the following:
(1) That due notice of the time and place of attendance of the person or the production of the papers has been given.
(2) That the person has been subpoenaed in the manner prescribed in this chapter.
(3) That the person has failed and refused to attend or produce the papers required by subpoena before the office as named in the subpoena, or has refused to answer questions propounded to him or her in the course of the interview under penalty of perjury.
(c) Upon the filing of the petition, the court shall enter an order directing the person to appear before the court at a specified time and place and then and there show cause why he or she has not attended, answered questions under penalty of perjury, or produced the papers as required. A copy of the order shall be served upon him or her. If it appears to the court that the subpoena was regularly issued by the Inspector General, or his or her designee, the court shall enter an order that the person appear before the person named in the subpoena at the time and place fixed in the order and answer questions under penalty of perjury or produce the required papers. Upon failure to obey the order, the person shall be dealt with as for contempt of court.
(Amended by Stats. 2011, Ch. 36, Sec. 44. (SB 92) Effective June 30, 2011.)

6128.

(a) The Office of the Inspector General may receive communications from any individual, including those employed by any department, board, or authority who believes he or she may have information that may describe an improper governmental activity, as that term is defined in subdivision (c) of Section 8547.2 of the Government Code. It is not the purpose of these communications to redress any single disciplinary action or grievance that may routinely occur.
(b) In order to properly respond to any allegation of improper governmental activity, the Inspector General shall establish a toll-free public telephone number for the purpose of identifying any alleged wrongdoing by an employee of the Department of Corrections and Rehabilitation. This telephone number shall be posted by the department in clear view of all employees and the public. When requested pursuant to Section 6126, the Inspector General shall initiate a review of any alleged improper governmental activity.
(c) All identifying information, and any personal papers or correspondence from any person who initiated the review shall not be disclosed, except in those cases where the Inspector General determines that disclosure of the information is necessary in the interests of justice.
(Amended by Stats. 2011, Ch. 36, Sec. 45. (SB 92) Effective June 30, 2011.)

6129.

(a) (1) For purposes of this section, "employee" means any person employed by the Department of Corrections and Rehabilitation.
(2) For purposes of this section, "retaliation" means intentionally engaging in acts of reprisal, retaliation, threats, coercion, or similar acts against another employee who has done any of the following:
(A) Has disclosed or is disclosing to any employee at a supervisory or managerial level, what the employee, in good faith, believes to be improper governmental activities.
(B) Has cooperated or is cooperating with any investigation of improper governmental activities.
(C) Has refused to obey an illegal order or directive.
(b) (1) Upon receiving a complaint of retaliation from an employee against a member of management at the Department of Corrections and Rehabilitation, the Inspector General shall commence an inquiry into the complaint and conduct a formal investigation where a legally cognizable cause of action is presented. All investigations conducted pursuant to this section shall be performed in accordance with Sections 6126.5 and 6127.3. The Inspector General may refer all other matters for investigation by the appropriate employing entity, subject to oversight by the Inspector General. In a case in which the employing entity declines to investigate the complaint, it shall, within 30 days of receipt of the referral by the Inspector General, notify the Inspector General of its decision. The Inspector General shall thereafter, conduct his or her own inquiry into the complaint. If, after reviewing the complaint, the Inspector General determines that a legally cognizable cause of action has not been presented by the complaint, the Inspector General shall thereafter notify the complaining employee and the State Personnel Board that a formal investigation is not warranted.
(2) When investigating a complaint, in determining whether retaliation has occurred, the Inspector General or the employing entity shall consider, among other things, whether any of the following either actually occurred or were threatened:
(A) Unwarranted or unjustified staff changes.
(B) Unwarranted or unjustified letters of reprimand or other disciplinary actions, or unsatisfactory evaluations.
(C) Unwarranted or unjustified formal or informal investigations.
(D) Engaging in acts, or encouraging or permitting other employees to engage in acts, that are unprofessional, or foster a hostile work environment.
(E) Engaging in acts, or encouraging or permitting other employees to engage in acts, that are contrary to the rules, regulations, or policies of the workplace.
(3) In a case in which the complaining employee has also filed a retaliation complaint with the State Personnel Board pursuant to Sections 8547.8 and 19683 of the Government Code, the State Personnel Board shall have the discretion to toll any investigation, hearing, or other proceeding that would otherwise be conducted by the State Personnel Board in response to that complaint, pending either the completion of the Inspector General's or the employing entity's investigation, or until the complaint is rejected or otherwise dismissed by the Inspector General or the employing entity. An employee, however, may not be required to first file a retaliation complaint with the Inspector General prior to filing a complaint with the State Personnel Board.
(A) In a case in which the complaining employee has filed a retaliation complaint with the Inspector General but not with the State Personnel Board, the limitation period for filing a retaliation complaint with the State Personnel Board shall be tolled until the time the Inspector General or the employing entity either issues its report to the State Personnel Board, or until the complaint is rejected or otherwise dismissed by the Inspector General or the employing entity.
(B) In order to facilitate coordination of efforts between the Inspector General and the State Personnel Board, the Inspector General shall notify the State Personnel Board of the identity of any employee who has filed a retaliation complaint with the Inspector General, and the State Personnel Board shall notify the Inspector General of the identity of any employee who has filed a retaliation complaint with the State Personnel Board.
(c) (1) In a case in which the Inspector General determines, as a result of his or her own investigation, that an employee has been subjected to acts of reprisal, retaliation, threats, or similar acts in violation of this section, the Inspector General shall provide a copy of the report, together with all other underlying materials the Inspector General determines to be relevant, to the appropriate director or chair who shall take appropriate corrective action. In a case in which the Inspector General determines, based on an independent review of the investigation conducted by the employing entity, that an employee has been subjected to acts of reprisal, retaliation, threats, or similar acts in violation of this section, the Inspector General shall submit a written recommendation to the appropriate director or chair who shall take appropriate corrective action. If the hiring authority initiates disciplinary action as defined in Section 19570 of the Government Code, it shall provide the subject with all materials required by law.
(2) Any employee at any rank and file, supervisory, or managerial level, who intentionally engages in acts of reprisal, retaliation, threats, coercion, or similar acts against another employee, pursuant to paragraph (2) of subdivision (a), shall be disciplined by the employing entity by adverse action as provided in Section 19572 of the Government Code. The disciplinary action shall require, at a minimum, a suspension for not less than

30 days without pay, except in a case in which the employing entity determines that a lesser penalty is warranted. In that case, the employing entity shall, within 30 days of receipt of the report, provide written justification for that decision to the Inspector General. The employing entity shall also, within 30 days of receipt of the written report, notify the Inspector General in writing as to what steps, if any, it has taken to remedy the retaliatory conduct found to have been committed by any of its employees.

(d) (1) In an instance in which the appropriate director or chair declines to take adverse action against any employee found by the Inspector General to have engaged in acts of reprisal, retaliation, threats, or similar acts in violation of this section, the director or chair shall notify the Inspector General of that fact in writing within 30 days of receipt of the report from the Inspector General, and shall notify the Inspector General of the specific reasons why the director or chair declined to invoke adverse action proceedings against the employee.

(2) The Inspector General shall, thereafter, with the written consent of the complaining employee, forward an unredacted copy of the report, together with all other underlying materials the Inspector General deems to be relevant, to the State Personnel Board so that the complaining employee can request leave to file charges against the employee found to have engaged in acts of reprisal, retaliation, threats, or similar acts, in accordance with the provisions of Section 19583.5 of the Government Code. If the State Personnel Board accepts the complaint, the board shall provide the charged and complaining parties with a copy of all relevant materials.

(3) In addition to all other penalties provided by law, including Section 8547.8 of the Government Code or any other penalties that the sanctioning authority may determine to be appropriate, any state employee at any rank and file, supervisory, or managerial level found by the State Personnel Board to have intentionally engaged in acts of reprisal, retaliation, threats, or coercion shall be suspended for not less than 30 days without pay, and shall be liable in an action for damages brought against him or her by the injured party. If the State Personnel Board determines that a lesser period of suspension is warranted, the reasons for that determination must be justified in writing in the decision.

(e) Nothing in this section shall prohibit the employing entity from exercising its authority to terminate, suspend, or discipline an employee who engages in conduct prohibited by this section.

(Amended by Stats. 2013, Ch. 30, Sec. 11. (SB 74) Effective June 27, 2013.)
6132.
(a) Notwithstanding Section 10231.5 of the Government Code, the Inspector General shall report annually to the Governor and the Legislature a summary of its reports. The summary shall be posted on the office's Internet Web site and otherwise made available to the public upon its release to the Governor and the Legislature. The summary shall include, but not be limited to, significant problems discovered by the office, and whether recommendations the office has made have been implemented.

(b) A report pursuant to subdivision (a) shall be submitted in compliance with Section 9795 of the Government Code.

(Amended by Stats. 2011, Ch. 36, Sec. 48. (SB 92) Effective June 30, 2011.)
6133.
(a) The Office of the Inspector General shall be responsible for contemporaneous public oversight of the Department of Corrections and Rehabilitation investigations and staff grievance inquiries conducted by the Department of Corrections and Rehabilitation's Office of Internal Affairs. To facilitate oversight of the department's internal affairs investigations, the Office of the Inspector General shall have staff physically colocated with the Department of Corrections and Rehabilitation's Office of Internal Affairs, within a reasonable timeframe and without any undue delays. The Office of the Inspector General shall also be responsible for advising the public regarding the adequacy of each investigation, and whether discipline of the subject of the investigation is warranted. The Office of the Inspector General shall have discretion to provide public oversight of other Department of Corrections and Rehabilitation personnel investigations as needed.

(b) (1) The Office of the Inspector General shall issue regular reports, no less than annually, to the Governor and the Legislature summarizing its recommendations concerning its oversight of the Department of Corrections and Rehabilitation allegations of internal misconduct and use of force. The Office of the Inspector General shall also issue regular reports, no less than semiannually, summarizing its oversight of Office of Internal Affairs investigations pursuant to subdivision (a). The reports shall include, but not be limited to, all of the following:

(A) Data on the number, type, and disposition of complaints made against correctional officers and staff.

(B) A synopsis of each matter reviewed by the Office of the Inspector General.

(C) An assessment of the quality of the investigation, the appropriateness of any disciplinary charges, the Office of the Inspector General's recommendations regarding the disposition in the case and when founded, the level of discipline afforded, and the degree to which the agency's authorities agreed with the Office of the Inspector General recommendations regarding disposition and level of discipline.

(D) The report of any settlement and whether the Office of the Inspector General concurred with the settlement.

(E) The extent to which any discipline was modified after imposition.

(2) The reports shall be in a form that does not identify the agency employees involved in the alleged misconduct.

(3) The reports shall be posted on the Inspector General's internet website and otherwise made available to the public upon their release to the Governor and the Legislature.

(Amended by Stats. 2019, Ch. 364, Sec. 16. (SB 112) Effective September 27, 2019.)
6140.
There is in the Office of the Inspector General the California Rehabilitation Oversight Board (C-ROB). The board shall consist of the 11 members as follows:

(a) The Inspector General, who shall serve as chair.

(b) The Secretary of the Department of Corrections and Rehabilitation.

(c) The Superintendent of Public Instruction, or his or her designee.

(d) The Chancellor of the California Community Colleges, or his or her designee.

(e) The Director of Health Care Services, or his or her designee.

(f) The Director of State Hospitals, or his or her designee.

(g) A faculty member of the University of California who has expertise in rehabilitation of criminal offenders, appointed by the President of the University of California.

(h) A faculty member of the California State University, who has expertise in rehabilitation of criminal offenders, appointed by the Chancellor of the California State University.

(i) A county sheriff, appointed by the Governor.

(j) A county chief probation officer, appointed by the Senate Committee on Rules.

(k) A local government official who provides mental health, substance abuse, or educational services to criminal offenders, appointed by the Speaker of the Assembly.

(Amended by Stats. 2013, Ch. 22, Sec. 79. (AB 75) Effective June 27, 2013. Operative July 1, 2013, by Sec. 110 of Ch. 22.)
6141.
The California Rehabilitation Oversight Board shall meet at least twice annually, and shall regularly examine the various mental health, substance abuse, educational, and employment programs for inmates and parolees operated by the Department of Corrections and Rehabilitation. Beginning January 1, 2015, the board shall examine the department's effort to assist inmates and parolees to obtain postrelease health care coverage. The board shall report to the Governor and the Legislature annually, on September 15, and may submit other reports during the year if it finds they are necessary. The reports shall include, but are not limited to, findings on the effectiveness

of treatment efforts, rehabilitation needs of offenders, gaps in rehabilitation services in the department, and levels of offender participation and success in the programs. The board shall also make recommendations to the Governor and the Legislature with respect to modifications, additions, and eliminations of rehabilitation and treatment programs. In performing its duties, the board shall use the work products developed for the department as a result of the provisions of the 2006 Budget Act, including Provision 18 of Item 5225-001-0001.

(Amended by Stats. 2014, Ch. 822, Sec. 1. (AB 2570) Effective January 1, 2015.)

CHAPTER 9. Conservation Centers [6200 - 6208]

(Heading of Chapter 9 amended by Stats. 1963, Ch. 1431.)
6200.
There are hereby established, under the jurisdiction of the Director of Corrections, the Sierra Conservation Center, the North Coast Conservation Center and the Southern Conservation Center, hereafter referred to collectively as the "conservation centers."
(Amended by Stats. 1977, Ch. 909.)
6201.
The primary purpose of the conservation centers shall be the receiving, employment, care, custody and education of inmates in the custody of the Director of Corrections assigned thereto.
(Amended by Stats. 1963, Ch. 1431.)
6202.
Work of inmates assigned to the conservation centers may be performed at the conservation centers or branches thereof or in or from permanent, temporary, and mobile camps established pursuant to this chapter or pursuant to Article 5 (commencing with Section 2780) of Chapter 5 of Title 1 of Part 3. The provisions of Sections 2780.1 to 2786, inclusive, and Sections 2788 to 2791, inclusive, are applicable to camps established pursuant to this article as well as those established pursuant to that Article 5. The Director of Corrections may, at such times as the director deems proper and on such terms as the director deems wise, enter into contracts or cooperative agreements with any public agency, local, state, or federal, for the performance of other conservation projects which are appropriate for the public agencies under policies which shall be established by the Prison Industry Authority.

Inmates and wards may be assigned to perform public conservation projects, including, but not limited to, forest fire prevention and control, forest and watershed management, recreational area development, fish and game management, soil conservation, and forest watershed revegetation.

No productive industrial enterprise subject to the jurisdiction of the Prison Industry Authority shall be established at any center or branch thereof or camp established pursuant to this chapter except in compliance with Chapter 3.5 (commencing with Section 5085) of Title 7 of Part 3.

(Amended by Stats. 1983, Ch. 732, Sec. 1.)
6203.
The Director of Corrections shall, in accordance with law, construct and provide equipment for suitable buildings, structures, and facilities for the conservation centers, branches thereof, and permanent, temporary, and mobile camps operated therefrom. The director may, as necessary, lease equipment needed for the operation of mobile camps. The Sierra Conservation Center shall be located in the Tuolumne area of California. The North Coast Conservation Center shall be located in the North Coast area of California. The Southern Conservation Center shall be located on the grounds of the California Institution for Men at Chino. The director may establish such branches of the conservation centers as may be necessary.
(Amended by Stats. 1977, Ch. 909.)
6204.
The Director of Corrections shall make rules and regulations for the government of the conservation centers in the management of their affairs.
(Amended by Stats. 1963, Ch. 1431.)
6205.
Each conservation center shall be headed by a warden, appointed pursuant to Section 6050, and the Director of Corrections shall appoint, subject to civil service, other officers and employees as may be necessary.
(Amended by Stats. 1989, Ch. 1420, Sec. 24.)
6206.
The supervision, management, and control of the conservation centers and the responsibility for the care, custody, treatment, training, discipline, and employment of persons confined therein or in branches thereof or in permanent, temporary, and mobile camps operating therefrom are vested in the Director of Corrections.
(Amended by Stats. 1963, Ch. 1431.)
6207.
The provisions of Part 3 (commencing with Section 2000), insofar as applicable, apply to the conservation centers and branches thereof and any permanent, temporary, and mobile camps operating therefrom and to the persons confined therein.
(Amended by Stats. 1987, Ch. 828, Sec. 165.)
6208.
Any persons under the custody of the Director of Corrections may be transferred to the conservation centers in accordance with law.
(Amended by Stats. 1963, Ch. 1431.)

CHAPTER 9.2. Restitution Centers [6220 - 6236]

(Chapter 9.2 added by Stats. 1984, Ch. 1520, Sec. 1.)
6220.
The Director of Corrections may establish and operate facilities to be known as restitution centers.
(Added by Stats. 1984, Ch. 1520, Sec. 1.)
6221.
The purpose of restitution centers is to provide a means for those sentenced to prison to be able to pay their victims' financial restitution, which includes direct restitution to victims as well as other restitution fines and fees, as ordered by the sentencing court or as agreed upon by the defendant and his or her victims. Inmates who commit crimes involving a direct victim shall receive priority placement in restitution centers.
(Amended by Stats. 2010, Ch. 463, Sec. 2. (AB 2218) Effective January 1, 2011.)
6222.
The location for a restitution center or centers shall be determined by the Director of Corrections with approval from the county board of supervisors or city council in whose jurisdiction the center will be located.
(Added by Stats. 1984, Ch. 1520, Sec. 1.)
6223.
Restitution centers shall be located in areas which will maximize the employment opportunities of persons sentenced to the centers.
(Added by Stats. 1984, Ch. 1520, Sec. 1.)
6224.

The supervision, management, and control of the restitution centers and the responsibility for the care, custody, discipline, and employment of persons confined therein are vested in the Director of Corrections.
(Added by Stats. 1984, Ch. 1520, Sec. 1.)
6224.5.
The Director of Corrections may commingle inmates who have been assigned to a restitution center pursuant to Section 6227 with inmates who are in transit for community correctional reentry center placement.
(Added by Stats. 2000, Ch. 249, Sec. 1. Effective January 1, 2001.)
6225.
Supervision of inmates in the restitution centers may be by contract with private nonprofit or profit corporations, or by peace officer personnel of the Department of Corrections on a 24-hour basis. As a condition to any contract awarded by the state to a vendor for restitution center operations, a peace officer from the Department of Corrections shall be assigned to the site to provide daily oversight and guidance of custody and security activities. The peace officer also shall be the liaison between the vendor and the department. If the supervision is by a private entity, the per inmate cost of operating these facilities under contract shall be less than the per inmate cost of maintaining custody of inmates by the department.
(Amended by Stats. 1995, Ch. 372, Sec. 5. Effective January 1, 1996.)
6226.
The Director of Corrections in establishing a restitution center shall enter into an agreement with the county, city, or city and county in which the facility is located to reimburse the county, city, or city and county for any additional direct law enforcement costs that will occur as a result of the restitution center.
(Added by Stats. 1984, Ch. 1520, Sec. 1.)
6227.
The court may order the Department of Corrections to place an eligible defendant in a restitution center if the court makes a restitution order, or if a restitution agreement is entered into by the victims and the defendant. The Department of Corrections may send a defendant to a reception center for classification prior to placing the defendant in the restitution center.
(Added by Stats. 1984, Ch. 1520, Sec. 1.)
6227.5.
The Judicial Council shall provide information to sentencing courts to ensure that the judges responsible for sentencing are aware of the existence of the restitution center.
(Added by Stats. 2000, Ch. 249, Sec. 2. Effective January 1, 2001.)
6228.
A defendant is eligible for placement in a restitution center if the defendant does not have a criminal history of a conviction for the sale of drugs within the last five years, or for an offense requiring registration pursuant to Section 290, or a serious felony, as listed in Section 1192.7, or a violent felony, as listed in Section 667.5, the defendant did not receive a sentence of more than 60 months for the current offense or offenses, the defendant presents no unacceptable risk to the community, and the defendant is employable. The provisions of Article 2.5 (commencing with Section 2930) of Chapter 7 of Title 1 are applicable to prisoners in restitution centers.
(Amended by Stats. 2011, Ch. 296, Sec. 222. (AB 1023) Effective January 1, 2012.)
6229.
In each county, city, or city and county, in which a restitution center is established, there shall be a restitution center community advisory board to assist the Director of Corrections in establishing and promoting the restitution program of the center. The board shall include the sheriff or chief of police of the local jurisdiction, the district attorney, a superior court judge selected by the presiding superior court judge, the chief probation officer, a member of the city council or the board of supervisors of the local jurisdiction, selected by the council or board, and two public members chosen by the city council or board of supervisors. The public member shall serve for two years. All members shall receive only actual expenses approved by the Director of Corrections. The expenses shall be paid by the Department of Corrections.
(Added by Stats. 1984, Ch. 1520, Sec. 1.)
6230.
(a) Offenders shall perform all the labor necessary to maintain the restitution center and meet the offenders' needs unless the director finds that a particular task can be better performed by other persons.
(b) The director may employ and pay compensation to offenders to perform work at a center.
(Added by Stats. 1984, Ch. 1520, Sec. 1.)
6231.
(a) Wages earned by an offender, less any deductions for taxes, shall be paid directly to the Department of Corrections.
(b) Wage moneys received by the department shall be used to reimburse the offender for costs directly associated with continued employment, including transportation, special tools or clothing, meals away from the center, union dues, and other employee-mandated costs. The remaining wages shall be distributed as follows:
(1) One-third shall be transferred to the Department of Corrections to pay the costs of operating and maintaining the restitution center.
(2) One-third shall be used to pay restitution pursuant to the agreement or court order. After the restitution is paid these moneys shall be paid to the jurisdiction which prosecuted the offender to defray the court costs and attorney fees incurred in the offender's prosecution. If all restitution, court costs and attorney fees are paid, these moneys shall be paid to the local jurisdiction for crime prevention.
(3) One-third shall be placed in a savings account for the offender, to provide support for the offender's immediate family, to purchase items necessary for the offender's employment or to give to the offender to purchase personal accessories. Any moneys in the savings account or not expended pursuant to this paragraph at the time the offender is released from the restitution center shall be paid to the offender.
(Added by Stats. 1984, Ch. 1520, Sec. 1.)
6233.
(a) An offender shall not leave a restitution center except to go to work or when specifically authorized and shall return to the restitution center immediately after work or when required by the person in charge of the restitution center.
(b) An offender who violates this section is guilty of escape, and notwithstanding any other provision of law shall be punishable as provided in Section 4530.
(Added by Stats. 1984, Ch. 1520, Sec. 1.)
6234.
(a) The offender shall not be allowed to take employment if the rate of pay or other conditions of employment are less than those paid or provided for work of a similar nature in the locality in which the work is performed.
(b) To help in administering the restitution center programs, the director may use volunteer help.
(c) If an offender does not secure employment within three months after being sent to a restitution center, the director may, at any time thereafter, transfer the offender to another Department of Corrections facility if employment has not been obtained.
(d) If the offender violates any of the rules and regulations governing the restitution center, the director may transfer the offender to another Department of Corrections facility.
(Added by Stats. 1984, Ch. 1520, Sec. 1.)
6235.
The Department of Corrections shall, pursuant to Chapter 3.5 (commencing with Section 11340) of Part 1 of Division 3 of Title 2 of the Government Code, adopt regulations for administering restitution centers. To the extent practical, the rules and regulations shall be stated in language that is easily understood by the general public.
(Added by Stats. 1984, Ch. 1520, Sec. 1.)
6236.
This chapter shall be known as "Restitution Centers."
(Amended by Stats. 2001, Ch. 854, Sec. 56. Effective January 1, 2002.)

CHAPTER 9.2. Restitution Centers [6220 - 6236]

(Chapter 9.2 added by Stats. 1984, Ch. 1520, Sec. 1.)
6220.
The Director of Corrections may establish and operate facilities to be known as restitution centers.
(Added by Stats. 1984, Ch. 1520, Sec. 1.)
6221.
The purpose of restitution centers is to provide a means for those sentenced to prison to be able to pay their victims' financial restitution, which includes direct restitution to victims as well as other restitution fines and fees, as ordered by the sentencing court or as agreed upon by the defendant and his or her victims. Inmates who commit crimes involving a direct victim shall receive priority placement in restitution centers.
(Amended by Stats. 2010, Ch. 463, Sec. 2. (AB 2218) Effective January 1, 2011.)
6222.
The location for a restitution center or centers shall be determined by the Director of Corrections with approval from the county board of supervisors or city council in whose jurisdiction the center will be located.
(Added by Stats. 1984, Ch. 1520, Sec. 1.)
6223.
Restitution centers shall be located in areas which will maximize the employment opportunities of persons sentenced to the centers.
(Added by Stats. 1984, Ch. 1520, Sec. 1.)
6224.

The supervision, management, and control of the restitution centers and the responsibility for the care, custody, discipline, and employment of persons confined therein are vested in the Director of Corrections.
(Added by Stats. 1984, Ch. 1520, Sec. 1.)
6224.5.
The Director of Corrections may commingle inmates who have been assigned to a restitution center pursuant to Section 6227 with inmates who are in transit for community correctional reentry center placement.
(Added by Stats. 2000, Ch. 249, Sec. 1. Effective January 1, 2001.)
6225.
Supervision of inmates in the restitution centers may be by contract with private nonprofit or profit corporations, or by peace officer personnel of the Department of Corrections on a 24-hour basis. As a condition to any contract awarded by the state to a vendor for restitution center operations, a peace officer from the Department of Corrections shall be assigned to the site to provide daily oversight and guidance of custody and security activities. The peace officer also shall be the liaison between the vendor and the department. If the supervision is by a private entity, the per inmate cost of operating these facilities under contract shall be less than the per inmate cost of maintaining custody of inmates by the department.
(Amended by Stats. 1995, Ch. 372, Sec. 5. Effective January 1, 1996.)
6226.
The Director of Corrections in establishing a restitution center shall enter into an agreement with the county, city, or city and county in which the facility is located to reimburse the county, city, or city and county for any additional direct law enforcement costs that will occur as a result of the restitution center.
(Added by Stats. 1984, Ch. 1520, Sec. 1.)
6227.
The court may order the Department of Corrections to place an eligible defendant in a restitution center if the court makes a restitution order, or if a restitution agreement is entered into by the victims and the defendant. The Department of Corrections may send a defendant to a reception center for classification prior to placing the defendant in the restitution center.
(Added by Stats. 1984, Ch. 1520, Sec. 1.)
6227.5.
The Judicial Council shall provide information to sentencing courts to ensure that the judges responsible for sentencing are aware of the existence of the restitution center.
(Added by Stats. 2000, Ch. 249, Sec. 2. Effective January 1, 2001.)
6228.
A defendant is eligible for placement in a restitution center if the defendant does not have a criminal history of a conviction for the sale of drugs within the last five years, or for an offense requiring registration pursuant to Section 290, or a serious felony, as listed in Section 1192.7, or a violent felony, as listed in Section 667.5, the defendant did not receive a sentence of more than 60 months for the current offense or offenses, the defendant presents no unacceptable risk to the community, and the defendant is employable. The provisions of Article 2.5 (commencing with Section 2930) of Chapter 7 of Title 1 are applicable to prisoners in restitution centers.
(Amended by Stats. 2011, Ch. 296, Sec. 222. (AB 1023) Effective January 1, 2012.)
6229.
In each county, city, or city and county, in which a restitution center is established, there shall be a restitution center community advisory board to assist the Director of Corrections in establishing and promoting the restitution program of the center. The board shall include the sheriff or chief of police of the local jurisdiction, the district attorney, a superior court judge selected by the presiding superior court judge, the chief probation officer, a member of the city council or the board of supervisors of the local jurisdiction, selected by the council or board, and two public members chosen by the city council or board of supervisors. The public member shall serve for two years. All members shall receive only actual expenses approved by the Director of Corrections. The expenses shall be paid by the Department of Corrections.
(Added by Stats. 1984, Ch. 1520, Sec. 1.)
6230.
(a) Offenders shall perform all the labor necessary to maintain the restitution center and meet the offenders' needs unless the director finds that a particular task can be better performed by other persons.
(b) The director may employ and pay compensation to offenders to perform work at a center.
(Added by Stats. 1984, Ch. 1520, Sec. 1.)
6231.
(a) Wages earned by an offender, less any deductions for taxes, shall be paid directly to the Department of Corrections.
(b) Wage moneys received by the department shall be used to reimburse the offender for costs directly associated with continued employment, including transportation, special tools or clothing, meals away from the center, union dues, and other employee-mandated costs. The remaining wages shall be distributed as follows:
(1) One-third shall be transferred to the Department of Corrections to pay the costs of operating and maintaining the restitution center.

(2) One-third shall be used to pay restitution pursuant to the agreement or court order. After the restitution is paid these moneys shall be paid to the jurisdiction which prosecuted the offender to defray the court costs and attorney fees incurred in the offender's prosecution. If all restitution, court costs and attorney fees are paid, these moneys shall be paid to the local jurisdiction for crime prevention.

(3) One-third shall be placed in a savings account for the offender, to provide support for the offender's immediate family, to purchase items necessary for the offender's employment or to give to the offender to purchase personal accessories. Any moneys in the savings account or not expended pursuant to this paragraph at the time the offender is released from the restitution center shall be paid to the offender.

(Added by Stats. 1984, Ch. 1520, Sec. 1.)

6233.

(a) An offender shall not leave a restitution center except to go to work or when specifically authorized and shall return to the restitution center immediately after work or when required by the person in charge of the restitution center.

(b) An offender who violates this section is guilty of escape, and notwithstanding any other provision of law shall be punishable as provided in Section 4530.

(Added by Stats. 1984, Ch. 1520, Sec. 1.)

6234.

(a) The offender shall not be allowed to take employment if the rate of pay or other conditions of employment are less than those paid or provided for work of a similar nature in the locality in which the work is performed.

(b) To help in administering the restitution center programs, the director may use volunteer help.

(c) If an offender does not secure employment within three months after being sent to a restitution center, the director may, at any time thereafter, transfer the offender to another Department of Corrections facility if employment has not been obtained.

(d) If the offender violates any of the rules and regulations governing the restitution center, the director may transfer the offender to another Department of Corrections facility.

(Added by Stats. 1984, Ch. 1520, Sec. 1.)

6235.

The Department of Corrections shall, pursuant to Chapter 3.5 (commencing with Section 11340) of Part 1 of Division 3 of Title 2 of the Government Code, adopt regulations for administering restitution centers. To the extent practical, the rules and regulations shall be stated in language that is easily understood by the general public.

(Added by Stats. 1984, Ch. 1520, Sec. 1.)

6236.

This chapter shall be known as "Restitution Centers."

(Amended by Stats. 2001, Ch. 854, Sec. 56. Effective January 1, 2002.)

CHAPTER 9.4. Substance Abuse Community Correctional Detention Centers [6240 - 6246]

(Chapter 9.4 added by Stats. 1990, Ch. 1594, Sec. 1.)

6240.

The Legislature finds and declares the following:

(a) The number of people in state prisons whose primary commitment offense was for drug law violations represents approximately 24 percent of the inmate population. Based on a representative sample study of new felon admissions during 1988, it is estimated that approximately 76 percent of the new commitment admissions to prison have a known history of drug abuse.

The number of parole violators returned to prison for drug violations increased 2200 percent from 1980 to 1988. In fiscal year 1988–89, drug charges were a known contributing factor in over 64 percent of parolees returned to prison for parole violations.

(b) The relationship between public safety, recidivism, and substance abuse is undeniable and significant.

(c) As pointed out by the California Blue Ribbon Commission on Inmate Population Management in its January 1990 report, both state and local correction systems are presently lacking sufficient programs and strategies to intervene with substance abuse and other behaviors that contribute to criminality. Judges and parole authorities lack the options of community correctional facilities and programs with substance abuse intervention and treatment when managing parole violators, probationers, parolees, and nonviolent offenders with a history of substance abuse.

(d) There presently does not exist a model for a state and local center to house substance abusers, increase employability skills, provide counseling and support, and make treatment programs available to intervene and treat substance abuse, to reduce the crime problem and the social costs which these offenders bring upon society, themselves, and their families.

It is, therefore, the intent of the Legislature to provide for the establishment of substance abuse community correctional centers and programs to be operated locally in order to implement state-of-the-art rehabilitation programs commensurate with public safety considerations.

It is further the intent of the Legislature to focus these efforts in local communities in order to blend state and local efforts to achieve a higher success rate and lower recidivism, and to reduce the number of substance abusers and offenders who are currently being sent to state prison.

It is also the intent of the Legislature that these programs and housing facilities be built and operated in a manner providing maximum safety to the public commensurate with the purpose of the programming, and that the facilities be kept drug-free by whatever legal means are required.

The facilities and the programs shall be designed and operated in joint efforts by the state and counties, with primary funding from the state for construction of the facilities. It is the intent of the Legislature that funds disbursed pursuant to this chapter be used to construct the maximum possible number of community beds for this purpose commensurate with public safety requirements.

(Added by Stats. 1990, Ch. 1594, Sec. 1.)

6240.5.

This act shall be known, and may be cited, as the Substance Abuse Community Correctional Treatment Act.

(Added by Stats. 1990, Ch. 1594, Sec. 1.)

6240.6.

For purposes of this chapter, the following definitions shall apply:

(a) "Board" means the Board of Corrections.

(b) "Department" means the Department of Corrections.

(c) "Center" means a substance abuse community correctional detention center.

(d) "Construction" means new construction, reconstruction, remodeling, renovation, or replacement of facilities, or a combination thereof.

(e) "Facility" means the physical buildings, rooms, areas, and equipment used for the purpose of a substance abuse community correctional detention center.

(Added by Stats. 1990, Ch. 1594, Sec. 1.)

6241.

(a) The Substance Abuse Community Correctional Detention Centers Fund is hereby created within the State Treasury. The Board of Corrections is authorized to provide funds, as appropriated by the Legislature, for the purpose of establishing substance

abuse community correctional detention centers. These facilities shall be operated locally in order to manage parole violators, those select individuals sentenced to state prison for short periods of time, and other sentenced local offenders with a known history of substance abuse, and as further defined by this chapter.

(b) The facilities constructed with funds disbursed pursuant to this chapter in a county shall contain no less than 50 percent of total beds for use by the Department of Corrections and Rehabilitation.

(1) Upon agreement, the county and the department may negotiate any other mix of state and local bed space, providing the state's proportionate share shall not be less than 50 percent in the portion of the facilities financed through state funding.

(2) Nothing in this chapter shall prohibit the county from using county funds or nonrestricted jail bond funds to build and operate additional facilities in conjunction with the centers provided for in this chapter.

(c) Thirty million dollars ($30,000,000) in funds shall be provided from the 1990 Prison Construction Fund and the 1990–B Prison Construction Fund, with fifteen million dollars ($15,000,000) each from the June 1990 bond issue and the November 1990 bond issue, for construction purposes set forth in this chapter, provided that funding is appropriated in the state budget from the June and November 1990, prison bond issues for purposes of this chapter.

(d) Funds shall be awarded to counties based upon the following policies and criteria:

(1) Priority shall be given to urban counties with populations of 450,000 or more, as determined by Department of Finance figures. The board may allocate up to 10 percent of the funding to smaller counties or combinations of counties as pilot projects, if it concludes that proposals meet the requirements of this chapter, commensurate with the facilities and programming that a smaller county can provide.

(2) Upon application and submission of proposals by eligible counties, representatives of the board shall evaluate proposals and select recipients.

To help ensure that state-of-the-art drug rehabilitation and related programs are designed, implemented, and updated under this chapter, the board shall consult with not less than three authorities recognized nationwide with experience or expertise in the design or operation of successful programs in order to assist the board in all of the following:

(A) Drawing up criteria on which requests for proposals will be sought.

(B) Selecting proposals to be funded.

(C) Assisting the board in evaluation and operational problems of the programs, if those services are approved by the board.

Funding also shall be sought by the board from the federal government and private foundation sources in order to defray the costs of the board's responsibilities under this chapter.

(3) Preference shall be given to counties that can demonstrate a financial ability and commitment to operate the programs it is proposing for a period of at least three years and to make improvements as proposed by the department and the board.

(4) Applicants receiving awards under this chapter shall be selected from among those deemed appropriate for funding according to the criteria, policies, and procedures established by the board. Criteria shall include success records of the types of programs proposed based on nationwide standards for successful programs, if available, expertise and hands-on experience of persons who will be in charge of proposed programs, cost-effectiveness, including cost per bed, speed of construction, a demonstrated ability to construct the maximum number of beds which shall result in an overall net increase in the number of beds in the county for state and local offenders, comprehensiveness of services, location, participation by private or community-based organizations, and demonstrated ability to seek and obtain supplemental funding as required in support of the overall administration of this facility from sources such as the State Department of Health Care Services, the Office of Emergency Services, the National Institute of Corrections, the Department of Justice, and other state and federal sources.

(5) Funds disbursed under subdivision (c) shall be used for construction of substance abuse community correctional centers, with a level of security in each facility commensurate with public safety for the types of offenders being housed in or utilizing the facilities.

(6) Funds disbursed under this chapter shall not be used for the purchase of the site. Sites shall be provided by the county. However, a participating county may negotiate with the state for use of state land at nearby corrections facilities or other state facilities, provided that the locations fit in with the aims of the programs established by this chapter.

The county shall be responsible for ensuring the siting, acquisition, design, and construction of the center consistent with the California Environmental Quality Act pursuant to Division 13 (commencing with Section 21000) of the Public Resources Code.

(7) Staff of the department and the board, as well as persons selected by the board, shall be available to counties for consultation and technical services in preparation and implementation of proposals accepted by the board.

(8) The board also shall seek advice from the State Department of Health Care Services in exercising its responsibilities under this chapter.

(9) Funds shall be made available to the county and county agency which is selected to administer the program by the board of supervisors of that county.

(10) Area of greatest need can be a factor considered in awarding contracts to counties.

(11) Particular consideration shall be given to counties that can demonstrate an ability to provide continuing counseling and programming for offenders in programs established under this chapter, once the offenders have completed the programs and have returned to the community.

(12) A county may propose a variety of types and sizes of facilities to meet the needs of its plan and to provide the services for varying types of offenders to be served under this chapter. Funds granted to a county may be utilized for construction of more than one facility.

Any county wishing to use existing county-owned sites or facilities may negotiate those arrangements with the Department of Corrections and the Board of Corrections to meet the needs of its plan.

(Amended by Stats. 2013, Ch. 352, Sec. 417. (AB 1317) Effective September 26, 2013. Operative July 1, 2013, by Sec. 543 of Ch. 352.)

6241.5.

Because of the difficulties of finding locations for programs described in this chapter, the state shall assist in making state-owned lands available to counties for purposes of this chapter, so long as those efforts do not impede an agency's operations or planned expansions and are commensurate with public safety requirements.

(Added by Stats. 1990, Ch. 1594, Sec. 1.)

6242.

(a) The county shall assume full responsibility to administer and operate the center and program consistent with the criteria set forth in this chapter and those established by the board. This shall include maintenance and compliance with all codes, regulations, and health standards.

(b) The county shall select a local governmental department to operate the facility in accordance with the standards and oversight provided for in this chapter.

The facility shall be owned by the department for the duration of the payment of the bond used to finance construction of the facility. Upon completion of bond repayment, ownership of the facility shall be vested in the county. Ownership of a county facility renovated with funds awarded pursuant to this chapter shall be by the department for the period of bond repayment, after which ownership shall revert to the county. The department shall retain the option to lease from the county no less than 50 percent of inmate beds after completion of bond repayment.

If a county willfully terminates its participation in this act prior to completion of bond repayment or if its grant is terminated by the board for noncompliance with program regulations, ownership of the facility shall remain vested in the department. The department shall retain the option to lease as provided in this subdivision.

(c) Counties or the department shall operate all services and programs in secure facilities pursuant to this chapter with only county or state merit system employees, except that private nonprofit providers or individual professionals with demonstrated expertise and community experience also may be utilized to provide substance abuse treatment programs. Treatment programs outside secure facilities pursuant to this chapter may be provided only by county or state staff, by private nonprofit providers, or by individual professionals with demonstrated expertise and experience in providing services to this population of the community.

(d) Custody in secure facilities shall be provided by peace officers, as defined in Sections 830.1, 830.5, and 830.55, or custodial officers, as defined in Sections 831 and 831.5, who have satisfactorily met the minimum selection and training standards for corrections officers, as prescribed by the board under Section 6035.

(e) Parolees, parole violators, and state prisoners shall remain under overall supervision of state parole officers.

(f) The department shall contract to reimburse the county for allotted bed space and programming for state offenders based on actual cost plus a reasonable fee, but in no instance shall that amount exceed the average cost of housing an inmate in a state prison facility, as determined annually by the director.

(g) A county may bill the state for services provided to state parolees pursuant to this chapter on a pro rata basis of the cost of providing the programs and services, if requested by the department.

(h) The department and the board, as well as participating counties, shall seek funding from the federal government and from private foundation sources to help meet the costs of the programs outlined in this chapter.

(i) It shall be the responsibility of the board, the department, and the design and implementation panel to keep abreast of improvements in programs of the types established by this chapter, and to attempt to revise and update programs as state-of-the-art advances develop.

(j) Requests for proposals shall be ready for submission to eligible counties within nine months after the effective date of this chapter. Eligible counties shall submit proposals within six months after the request for proposals is submitted.

(k) An amount totaling no more than $1\frac{1}{2}$ percent of the total amount of funds to be disbursed under this chapter is hereby appropriated from the 1990 Prison Construction Fund and the 1990—B Prison Construction Fund to the board to be used for administrative costs.

(l) Following formal acceptance of proposals submitted by counties, the board shall have authority to modify, expand, or revise county programs, if requested by counties, or if the board concludes that changes should be made to improve, expand, or reduce the scope or approach of programs. This shall be done after formal notice to a county of proposed changes and opportunity for a county to submit evidence. The board also shall be able to recommend additional or reduced funding for a program, if funding becomes available upon appropriation by the Legislature.

(Amended by Stats. 1993, Ch. 589, Sec. 126. Effective January 1, 1994.)
6242.5.
(a) The board shall establish minimum standards, including security requirements, for the construction of facilities pursuant to this chapter.

(b) The board shall develop an architectural program describing the functions which the facility will be expected to serve, but which deemphasizes the correctional and detention nature of the exterior of the facilities in order to ease the difficulty in finding acceptable sites.

(c) Counties may substitute renovation of an existing structure for new construction, but renovation costs per bed shall not exceed the cost of new construction based on initial cost and useful life of the facility, and shall meet the program design standards established by the board. However, participation by a county or use of existing facilities for programs under this chapter shall not be utilized by a county to avoid meeting its needs for jail-bed construction and housing of jail inmates.

(d) Per-bed cost of secure facilities proposed by a county shall not exceed the cost of current similar construction by the department.

(e) The county shall lease the site on which the facility is located to the state for a term of not less than the period of bond repayment. The department shall pay to the county as lease the sum of one dollar ($1) per year beginning the first month after the first payment for the repayment of the bond to continue through the duration of the bond used to finance construction of the facility.

(Added by Stats. 1990, Ch. 1594, Sec. 1.)
6242.6.
(a) The board shall provide evaluation of the progress, activities, and performance of each center and participating county's progress established pursuant to this chapter and shall report the findings thereon to the Legislature two years after the operational onset of each facility.

(b) The board shall select an outside monitoring firm in cooperation with the Auditor General's office, to critique and evaluate the programs and their rates of success based on recidivism rates, drug use, and other factors it deems appropriate. Two years after the programs have begun operations, the report shall be provided to the Joint Legislative Prisons Committee, participating counties, the department, the State Department of Health Care Services, and other sources the board deems of value. Notwithstanding subdivision (k) of Section 6242, one hundred fifty thousand dollars ($150,000) is hereby appropriated from the funds disbursed under this chapter from the 1990 Prison Construction Fund to the Board of Corrections to be used for program evaluation under this subdivision.

(c) The department shall be responsible for the ongoing monitoring of contract compliance for state offenders placed in each center.

(Amended by Stats. 2013, Ch. 22, Sec. 81. (AB 75) Effective June 27, 2013. Operative July 1, 2013, by Sec. 110 of Ch. 22.)
6243.
Primary offender groups to be dealt with in the programs established by this chapter shall be probation or parole violators who would otherwise be returned to jail or prison. The following standards for selection shall apply:

(a) The Director of Corrections, or his or her designee, together with local parole officials, shall select offenders committed to state prison for placement in not less than 50 percent of the program beds established by this chapter. Eligible offenders shall be parole violators and felons committed to state prison who, after credit deduction for presentence incarceration and pursuant to Section 2933, would otherwise have served an actual term of six months or less in state prison. Offenders selected shall have a demonstrated history of alcohol or controlled substances abuse, or both, but shall not include any of the following:

(1) Offenders convicted at anytime of a violent felony, as defined in subdivision (c) of Section 667.5 whether in California or any other jurisdiction for an offense with the same elements.

(2) Offenders who have lost work credits while currently in prison for an offense listed in paragraph (1) of subdivision (a) of Section 2932, except for assault with a deadly weapon or a caustic substance.

(3) Offenders currently convicted of burglary of an inhabited dwelling.

(4) Offenders convicted on two or more separate occasions of violations of Section 11351, 11351.5, 11352, 11353, 11370.1, 11370.6, 11378.5, 11379, 11379.5, or 11379.6 of the Health and Safety Code for selling or transporting for sale, manufacturing for sale, processing for sale, importing for sale, or administering any controlled substance listed in these sections, or for attempting to commit any of these offenses for those purposes and who has served at least one term in prison for violating one of these sections.

(b) The maximum period of participation in a center program shall not exceed the maximum period for which the offender could have been incarcerated in county jail or state prison. Upon release from a center, a state offender shall be subject to the parole provisions of Section 3000. Local offenders shall be subject to all conditions of probation, if probation was imposed at the time of sentencing.

(c) The parole of an offender placed in a center following revocation of parole shall remain revoked during the period of participation in a center.

(d) Individuals eligible for this program who are deemed unfit for participation by either custodial or program staff at any time shall be transferred to a state prison or county facility to which they would otherwise have been committed and shall serve their remaining sentence minus the time served at the center.

(e) Except upon agreement between the county and the department, placement of state offenders in a center is limited to parolees on parole in that county and new commitments sentenced from that county.

(f) The county shall select local offenders for placement in up to 50 percent of the program beds established by this chapter. These offenders shall be persons convicted and sentenced to county jail, whether or not as a condition of probation, and who have a demonstrated history of abuse of alcohol or controlled substances, or both.

(g) State prisoners participating in these programs shall be eligible for work credit time reductions under provisions applicable to state prisoners committed to state prison.

(h) Primary emphasis in this program shall be toward parole violators and persons sentenced to prison or jail for short terms and for whom rehabilitation efforts should be provided.

(i) The department shall regularly notify the sheriff's department and the probation department of a participating county of offenders placed into the program or released from the program established by this chapter. The county shall likewise regularly notify local parole officials of persons placed into or released from its programs set up by this chapter.

The sheriff's department, probation and parole officials, and the Board of Prison Terms shall be permitted to recommend for or against placement of persons into these programs, as shall the judiciary of the county.

(j) Facilities may not serve as housing or parole or probation offices for offenders not a part of programs set up by this chapter.

(Added by Stats. 1990, Ch. 1594, Sec. 1.)
6245.
In submitting a proposal, a county's plan shall include at least all of the following elements that meet standards established by the board in its request for proposal, and demonstrate that its program will have strong links to the community organizations involved in providing those elements, and that those community organizations have helped in designing the proposal:

(a) A rigorous program of substance abuse testing.
(b) A drug-free environment.
(c) Substance abuse treatment.
(d) Employment services.
(e) Basic education services.
(f) Mental health services and family counseling.
(g) A strong linkage to probation and parole.
(Amended by Stats. 2004, Ch. 183, Sec. 273. Effective January 1, 2005.)
6246.
Each recipient county shall set up a program oversight committee, under rules and guidelines the Board of Corrections formulates, which shall include representatives from the following groups:

(a) Parole officials.
(b) Probation officials.
(c) Sheriff's department officials.
(d) County alcohol and drug abuse officials.
(e) Program contractors.
(f) Local judiciary personnel.
(g) Social welfare agency personnel.
(h) Local labor and employment representatives.
Responsibilities of the program oversight committee shall include, but not be limited to, regular reviews of program operations and criteria for offenders being placed into it, discussion and resolution of problems that may arise, costs, and other duties that may be assigned it by the Board of Corrections.
(Added by Stats. 1990, Ch. 1594, Sec. 1.)

CHAPTER 9.5. Community Correctional Centers [6250 - 6259]

(Chapter 9.5 added by Stats. 1965, Ch. 1931.)
6250.
(a) The Director of Corrections may establish and operate facilities to be known as community correctional centers. The director may enter into a long-term agreement, not to exceed 20 years, for transfer of prisoners to, or placement of prisoners in, community correctional centers.

(b) No later than 30 days after the department has designated a site as a potential site, the director shall notify the county board of supervisors or city council in whose jurisdiction the center may be located. The notification shall set forth the specifics of the site location, design, and operational characteristics for the facility. The department shall not contract for the facility until it has received and reviewed the comments of every local agency notified under this section or the expiration of 60 days after having given notice to the local agency, whichever occurs first.

Upon receipt of the notice, the city, county, or city and county may hold a public hearing concerning the impact of the facility on the community. At the conclusion of the public hearing, the city, county, or city and county may make a recommendation to the department as to the appropriateness of the proposed site, specific design and operational features to help make the facility more compatible with the community, and alternative locations, if appropriate.

Upon receipt of comments and recommendations, the department shall determine whether to proceed with the facility, to modify the proposal, or to select an alternative site. If the department selects a site recommended by the local agency after a hearing conducted pursuant to this section, no further review or hearings are required by this subdivision.

(c) The notice referred to in subdivision (b) may be delivered by hand or sent by any form of mail requiring a return receipt. Failure to provide the notice shall be grounds for extinguishing the contract upon motion of the board of supervisors or city council.

(d) The Director of Corrections shall not change the use of or significantly increase the capacity of a community correctional center established pursuant to subdivision (a) unless the director has first notified the county board of supervisors or city council in

whose jurisdiction the center is located at least 30 days prior to the change of use or capacity. Failure to provide the notice shall be grounds for enjoining the change in use or capacity.
(Amended by Stats. 1997, Ch. 643, Sec. 2. Effective January 1, 1998.)
6250.2.
(a) The Secretary of the Department of Corrections and Rehabilitation may enter into agreements for the transfer of prisoners to, or placement of prisoners in, community correctional centers. The secretary may enter into contracts to provide housing, sustenance, and supervision for inmates placed in community correctional centers.
(b) Notwithstanding any other law, for the purposes of entering into agreements under subdivision (a), any process, regulation, requirement, including any state government reviews or approvals, or third-party approval that is required under, or implemented pursuant to, any statute that relates to entering into those agreements is hereby waived.
(c) This section shall remain in effect only until January 1, 2020, and as of that date is repealed, unless a later enacted statute, that is enacted before January 1, 2020, deletes or extends that date.
(Amended by Stats. 2016, Ch. 33, Sec. 29. (SB 843) Effective June 27, 2016. Repealed as of January 1, 2020, by its own provisions.)
6250.5.
(a) The Director of Corrections may contract for the establishment and operation of community correctional facilities that offer programs for the treatment of addiction to alcohol or controlled substances based on the therapeutic community model, only if the cost per inmate of operating the facilities will be less than the cost per inmate of operating similar state facilities. The Legislature finds and declares that the purpose of a therapeutic community program, which emphasizes alcohol and controlled substance rehabilitation, is to substantially increase the likelihood of successful parole for those inmates.
(b) Each facility under contract pursuant to this section shall provide programs that prepare each inmate for successful reintegration into society. Those programs shall involve constant counseling in drug and alcohol abuse, employment skills, victim awareness, and family responsibility, and generally shall prepare each inmate for return to society. The programs also shall emphasize literacy training and use computer-supported training so that inmates may improve their reading and writing skills. The program shall include postincarceration counseling and care in order to ensure a greater opportunity for success.
(c) The department may enter into a long-term agreement, not to exceed 20 years, for transfer of prisoners to, or placement of prisoners in, facilities under contract pursuant to this section.
(d) The department shall provide for the review of any agreement entered into under this section to determine if the contractor is in compliance with the terms of this section. The review shall be conducted at least every five years. The department may revoke any agreement if the contractor is not in compliance with this section.
(e) Notwithstanding the Public Contract Code or Article 10 (commencing with Section 1200) of Title 15 of the California Code of Regulations, the Department of Corrections shall select an independent contractor to conduct an annual audit and cost comparison evaluation of any programs established under this section. Any contract for annual audits and evaluation shall provide that the annual report, whether in final or draft form, and all working papers and data, shall be available for immediate review upon request by the department.
(Added by Stats. 1997, Ch. 643, Sec. 3. Effective January 1, 1998.)
6251.
The primary purpose of such facilities is to provide housing, supervision, counseling, and other correctional programs for persons committed to the Department of Corrections.
(Added by Stats. 1965, Ch. 1931.)
6252.
The Director of Corrections shall make rules and regulations for the government of the community correctional centers in the management of their affairs.
(Added by Stats. 1965, Ch. 1931.)
6253.
(a) The Director of Corrections may transfer inmates whose terms of imprisonment have been fixed from the state prisons and facilities of the Department of Corrections to community correctional centers, and place parolees in the community correctional centers. The director may charge the resident reasonable fees, based on ability to pay, for room, board and so much of the costs of administration as are allocable to such resident. Fees may not exceed actual, demonstrable costs to the department. No fees shall be collected from an inmate or parolee after his or her residency in the center has terminated.
Notwithstanding any other provision of law, no inmate or parolee shall be denied placement in a community correctional center on the basis of inability to pay fees authorized by this section.
(b) Inmates transferred to community correctional centers remain under the legal custody of the department and shall be subject at any time, pursuant to the rules and regulations of the Director of Corrections, to be detained in the county jail upon the exercise of a state parole or correctional officer's peace officer powers as specified in Section 830.5, with the consent of the sheriff or corresponding official having jurisdiction over the facility.
(Amended by Stats. 1984, Ch. 961, Sec. 4. Effective September 10, 1984.)
6254.
The Director of Corrections may grant furloughs to residents of community correctional centers for the purpose of employment, education, including vocational training, or arranging a suitable employment and residence program.
(Amended by Stats. 1967, Ch. 772.)
6255.
The provisions of Title 5 (commencing with Section 4500) of Part 3 shall apply to all persons placed in a community correctional center by the Director of Corrections except that those persons who are on active parole shall be subject to the provisions of Article 3 (commencing with Section 3040) of Chapter 8, Title 1, Part 3.
(Added by Stats. 1965, Ch. 1931.)
6256.
The Director of Corrections may enter into contracts, with the approval of the Director of General Services, with appropriate public or private agencies, to provide housing, sustenance, and supervision for such inmates as are eligible for placement in community correctional centers. Prisoners in the care of such agencies shall be subject to all provisions of law applicable to them.
The Department of Corrections shall reimburse such agencies for their services from such funds as may be appropriated for the support of state prisoners.
(Added by Stats. 1972, Ch. 1168.)
6258.
(a) The Director of Corrections may contract for the establishment and operation of separate community correctional reentry centers for men and women, provided that the per-inmate cost for operating these facilities under contract will be less than the per-inmate cost of maintaining custody of the inmates by the department.
(b) The purpose of the community correctional reentry center is to provide an enhancement program to increase the likelihood of a successful parole. The objective of the program is to make the inmates aware of their responsibility to society, and to assist the inmates with educational and employment training to ensure employability once on parole.

(c) A community correctional reentry center shall prepare the inmate for reintegration into society. These centers shall provide counseling in the areas of drug and alcohol abuse, stress, employment skills, victim awareness, and shall, in general, prepare the inmate for return to society. The program shall also emphasize literacy training and utilize computer-supported training so that the inmate can read and write at least at a ninth grade level.
(d) In awarding contracts pursuant to this section, the director may entertain proposals for the establishment and operation of community correctional reentry centers from public and private entities and shall give preference to community correctional reentry centers located near large population centers.
(Added by Stats. 1989, Ch. 879, Sec. 1.)
6258.1.
An inmate shall not be transferred to a community correctional reentry facility unless all of the following conditions are met:
(a) The inmate applies for a transfer to a community correctional reentry facility.
(b) The inmate is not currently serving a sentence for conviction of any offense described in subdivision (c) of Section 667.5.
(c) The inmate has less than one year left to serve in a correctional facility.
(d) The inmate has not been convicted previously of an escape pursuant to Section 4532 of the Penal Code.
(e) The department determines that the inmate would benefit from the transfer.
(Amended by Stats. 2016, Ch. 33, Sec. 30. (SB 843) Effective June 27, 2016.)
6259.
(a) For the purposes of acquiring the 2,000 community correctional facility beds and notwithstanding any other provision of law, the procurement and performance of any contracts authorized pursuant to Chapter 9.5 (commencing with Section 6250) of Part 3 of Title 7 of the Penal Code shall be conducted under the provisions of Article 4 (commencing with Section 10335) of Part 2 of Division 2 of the Public Contract Code, as a contract for services.
(b) The procurement shall include requirements that the contractor provide to the state options to purchase all or a portion of the facilities and equipment used by the vendor in the performance of the contract and that the consideration of the proposals include the terms of these options. The contract shall provide specifications for the vendor's acquisition of sites, compliance with environmental requirements, preparation of plans and specifications for, and development and operation of, facilities, and such other matters as may be reasonably incidental to the development, operation, and potential future acquisition by the state pursuant to an option to purchase the facilities.
(c) The exercise of an option to purchase shall be subject to the jurisdiction of the State Public Works Board and the requirements of the master plan for prison construction, Chapter 11 (commencing with Section 7000) of Title 7 of Part 3 of the Penal Code, the State Contract Act, Chapter 1 (commencing with Section 10100) of Part 2 of Division 2 of the Public Contract Code, the State Building Construction Act of 1955, Part 10b (commencing with Section 15800) of Division 3 of the Government Code, and the Property Acquisition Law, and Part 11 (commencing with Section 15850) of Division 3 of the Government Code, but these provisions shall not apply to the procurement of the option to purchase or the procurement and performance of the contract.
(Added by Stats. 1998, Ch. 500, Sec. 3. Effective September 15, 1998.)

CHAPTER 9.6. Work Furlough Programs [6260 - 6266]

(Chapter 9.6 added by Stats. 1980, Ch. 596, Sec. 1.)
6260.
The Legislature finds and declares the following: that overcrowding in correctional institutions is not a desirable method of housing state inmates; that other methods of housing should be developed for appropriate state inmates, particularly if they can be less costly; that reentry programs for inmates who are nearing the completion of their term of incarceration provides a more normal environment and an opportunity to begin reintegrating into society; and that work furlough programs are appropriate only for specified types of inmates for a limited period of time prior to release back into society; and that existing law already recognizes the appropriateness of placing inmates in community facilities.
(Added by Stats. 1980, Ch. 596, Sec. 1.)
6261.
(a) To the extent that public and private nonprofit and profit corporations have available beds and satisfy the criteria specified in this chapter, the Department of Corrections shall contract with them to provide reentry work furlough programs for all inmates 120 days prior to scheduled release and who are not excluded under this chapter.
(b) The Department of Corrections shall contract with private nonprofit and profit corporations for at least $1/3$ of all reentry work furlough beds, unless the department determines these beds are not available or do not comply with this chapter. The department shall report annually in writing to the fiscal and appropriate policy committees of the Legislature of the actions performed to locate those beds or reasons for noncompliance. This provision shall not be interpreted to impair existing contracts.
(Amended by Stats. 1988, Ch. 1608, Sec. 5.)
6262.
The Department of Corrections may contract with a public or private nonprofit or profit corporation meeting all the following conditions:
(a) Availability of a work furlough facility in compliance with standards established by the Department of Corrections.
(b) Location of a facility in proximity to geographical areas providing employment opportunities and public transportation services.
(c) Cost proposals equal to or less than the per capita amount for housing in a correctional institution, including administrative costs.
(d) Criteria for placement that does not differ significantly from the policies of the Department of Corrections.
(e) Submission by the agency of operational guidelines that are approved by the Department of Corrections pursuant to its classification manual.
(f) Compliance with other requirements deemed appropriate by the Department of Corrections, including, but not limited to, visiting procedures, 24-hour security, and recreation.
(g) Efficient fiscal management and financially solvent.
(Added by Stats. 1980, Ch. 596, Sec. 1.)
6263.
(a) The Department of Corrections shall deny placement in a reentry work furlough program if it determines that an inmate would pose an unreasonable risk to the public, or if any one of the following factors exist, except in unusual circumstances, including, but not limited to, the remoteness in time of the commission of the offense:
(1) Conviction of a crime involving sex or arson.
(2) History of forced escape, or of drug use, sales, or addiction.
(3) Parole program or employment outside the area served by the facility.
(4) History of serious institutional misconduct.
(5) Prior placement in a protective housing unit within a correctional institution, except a person placed there while assisting a public entity in a civil or criminal matter.
(6) More than one conviction of a crime of violence.

(b) Nothing in this section shall be interpreted to limit the discretion of the Department of Corrections to deny placement when the provisions of subdivision (a) do not apply.
(c) Inmates transferred to reentry work furlough remain under the legal custody of the department and shall be subject at any time, pursuant to the rules and regulations of the Director of Corrections, to be detained in the county jail upon the exercise of a state parole or correctional officer's peace officer powers as specified in Section 830.5, with the consent of the sheriff or corresponding official having jurisdiction over the facility.
(Amended by Stats. 1984, Ch. 961, Sec. 5. Effective September 10, 1984.)

6264.
The Department of Corrections shall review each inmate for work furlough consideration at least 120 days prior to his or her scheduled parole date.
(Added by Stats. 1980, Ch. 596, Sec. 1.)

6265.
Any inmate violating the conditions of the work furlough prescribed by the Department of Corrections shall be subject to the disciplinary procedures identified in its classification manual.
(Added by Stats. 1980, Ch. 596, Sec. 1.)

6266.
The director may charge the inmate in a work furlough program reasonable fees, based on ability to pay for room, board, and so much of the costs of administration as are allocable to the inmate. Fees may not exceed the actual, demonstrable costs to the department. No fees shall be collected from an inmate after his or her tenure in a work furlough program is terminated.
Notwithstanding any other provision of law, no inmate shall be denied placement in a work furlough program on the basis of inability to pay fees authorized by this section.
(Added by Stats. 1983, Ch. 943, Sec. 2.)

CHAPTER 9.7. Special Facilities [6267- 6267.]

(Chapter 9.7 added by Stats. 2003, Ch. 708, Sec. 2.)

6267.
(a) (1) The Legislature finds and declares that the purpose of the program authorized under this section is to address the special needs of inmates with regard to the provision of long-term care in skilled nursing facilities.
(2) The department may contract with public or private entities for the establishment and operation of skilled nursing facilities for the incarceration and care of inmates who are limited in ability to perform activities of daily living and who are in need of skilled nursing services. The skilled nursing facility under contract pursuant to this section shall address the long-term care of inmates as needed. In addition, the facility shall be designed to maximize the personal security of inmates, to maximize the security of the facility, and to ensure the safety of the outside community at large.
(b) The department shall provide for the security of the facility in order to ensure the safety of the outside community at large.
(c) The department shall enter into an agreement for transfer of prisoners to, or placement of prisoners in, skilled nursing facilities pursuant to this section.
(d) The facility contractor shall ensure that the facility meets all licensing requirements by obtaining a license for the skilled nursing facility, as that term is defined in Section 1250 of the Health and Safety Code.
(e) The department shall provide for the review of any agreement entered into under this section to determine if the facility contractor is in compliance with the requirements of this section, and may revoke the agreement if the facility contractor is not in compliance.
(f) The Department of Corrections ombudsman program shall provide ombudsman services to prisoner residents of the department-contracted skilled nursing facilities.
(g) Notwithstanding the provisions of Chapter 11 (commencing with Section 9700) of Division 8.5 of the Welfare and Institutions Code, the Office of the State Long-Term Care Ombudsman shall be exempt from advocating on behalf of, or investigating complaints on behalf of residents of any skilled nursing facilities operated either directly or by contract by the Department of Corrections.
(h) As used in this section, "long-term care" means personal or supportive care services provided to people of all ages with physical or mental disabilities who need assistance with activities of daily living including bathing, eating, dressing, toileting, transferring, and ambulation.
(Added by Stats. 2003, Ch. 708, Sec. 2. Effective January 1, 2004.)

CHAPTER 10. Regional Jail Camps [6300 - 6304]

(Chapter 10 added by Stats. 1957, Ch. 1646.)

6300.
The Department of Corrections is authorized to establish and operate regional jail camps.
(Added by Stats. 1957, Ch. 1646.)

6301.
The primary purpose of the camps shall be the confinement, treatment, and care of persons sentenced to long jail terms, including persons so imprisoned as a condition of probation.
(Amended by Stats. 1987, Ch. 828, Sec. 166.)

6302.
The Director of Corrections shall make rules and regulations governing eligibility for commitment or transfer to such camps and rules and regulations for the government of such camps. Subject to the rules and regulations of the Director of Corrections, and if there is in effect for the county a contract entered into pursuant to Section 6303, a county prisoner may be committed to a regional jail camp in lieu of commitment to a county jail or other county detention facility.
(Added by Stats. 1957, Ch. 1646.)

6303.
(a) The director may enter into a contract, with the approval of the Director of General Services, with any county of the state, upon the request of the board of supervisors thereof, wherein the Director of Corrections agrees to furnish confinement, care, treatment, and employment of county prisoners. The county shall reimburse the state for the cost of such services, such cost to be determined by the Director of Finance. Each county auditor shall include in his state settlement report rendered to the Controller in the months of January and June the amounts due under any contract authorized by this section, and the county treasurer, at the time of settlement with the state in such months, shall pay to the State Treasurer upon order of the Controller, the amounts found to be due.
(b) The Department of Corrections shall accept such county prisoner if it believes that the prisoner can be materially benefited by such confinement, care, treatment, and employment, and if adequate facilities to provide such care are available. No such person shall be transported to any facility under the jurisdiction of the Department of Corrections until the director has notified the referring court of the place to which said person is to be transmitted and the time at which he can be received.
(c) The sheriff of the county in which such an order is made placing a misdemeanant in a jail camp pursuant to this chapter, or any other peace officer designated by the court, shall execute an order placing such county prisoner in the jail camp or returning him therefrom to the court. The expense of such sheriff or peace officer incurred in executing such order is a charge upon the county in which the court is situated.
(Amended by Stats. 1974, Ch. 1221.)

6304.
The Director of Corrections may return to the committing authority any person committed transferred to a regional jail camp pursuant to this chapter when there is no suitable employment or when such person is guilty of any violation of rules and regulations of the regional jail camp.
(Added by Stats. 1957, Ch. 1646.)

CHAPTER 10.5. Prison Visitor Services [6350 - 6356]

(Heading of Chapter 10.5 renumbered from Chapter 11 (as added by Stats. 1982, Ch. 17) by Stats. 1987, Ch. 56, Sec. 137.)

6350.
The Legislature finds and declares the following:
(a) Maintaining an inmate's family and community relationships is an effective correctional technique which reduces recidivism.
(b) Enhancing visitor services increases the frequency and quality of visits, thereby discouraging violent prisoner activity.
(c) The location of prisons and lack of services to assist visitors impedes visiting.
(Added by Stats. 1982, Ch. 17, Sec. 1.)

6351.
The Department of Corrections shall contract with a private nonprofit agency or agencies to establish and operate a visitor center outside each state adult prison in California which has a population of more than 300 inmates.
(Added by Stats. 1982, Ch. 17, Sec. 1.)

6352.
Each visitor center shall provide, at a minimum, each of the following services to prison visitors:
(a) Assistance to visitors with transportation between public transit terminals and prisons.
(b) Child care for visitors' children.
(c) Emergency clothing.
(d) Information on visiting regulations and processes.
(e) Referral to other agencies and services.
(f) A sheltered area, which is outside of the security perimeter, for visitors who are waiting before or after visits.
In addition, each center shall maintain working relations with the local community and institution.
(Amended by Stats. 1988, Ch. 160, Sec. 143.)

6353.
Each nonprofit agency which the department contracts with pursuant to Section 6351 shall submit to the department and to the Legislature an annual report which includes, but is not limited to, the following information:
(a) A description of the barriers to visiting.
(b) A quantitative and narrative description of the services which it rendered.
(c) A description of the impact of the centers which it provided on visiting.
(d) A description of areas for improvement of services or coordination with other public or private agencies.
(e) A description of the community resources which it utilized.
(Added by Stats. 1982, Ch. 17, Sec. 1.)

6354.
The Department of Corrections shall employ all the following criteria in selecting the agency or agencies with which it contracts pursuant to Section 6351:
(a) The number and quality of services proposed in comparison to direct program costs.
(b) Prior experience in establishing and operating prison visitor service centers in California.
(c) Prior experience in working cooperatively with the department, other correctional agencies, community programs, inmates, visitors, and the general public.
(d) The ability to use volunteers and other community resources to maximize the cost effectiveness of this program.
(e) The identified needs of visitors.
(Added by Stats. 1982, Ch. 17, Sec. 1.)

6355.
Nothing in this chapter is intended to limit the department in developing additional programs or making all reasonable efforts to promote visits to prisoners.
(Added by Stats. 1982, Ch. 17, Sec. 1.)

6356.
The department shall cooperate with the Department of Transportation in the development of public transportation services to prisons, pursuant to Section 14035.9 of the Government Code and Section 99317.9 of the Public Utilities Code.
(Added by Stats. 1987, Ch. 603, Sec. 2.)

CHAPTER 10.7. Prison Visitation [6400 - 6404]

(Chapter 10.7 added by Stats. 2002, Ch. 238, Sec. 1.)

6400.
Any amendments to existing regulations and any future regulations adopted by the Department of Corrections which may impact the visitation of inmates shall do all of the following:
(a) Recognize and consider the value of visiting as a means to improve the safety of prisons for both staff and inmates.
(b) Recognize and consider the important role of inmate visitation in establishing and maintaining a meaningful connection with family and community.
(c) Recognize and consider the important role of inmate visitation in preparing an inmate for successful release and rehabilitation.
(Added by Stats. 2002, Ch. 238, Sec. 1. Effective January 1, 2003.)

6402.
The Department of Corrections and Rehabilitation (CDCR) shall develop policies related to the department's contraband interdiction efforts for individuals entering CDCR detention facilities. When developed, these policies shall include, but not be limited to, the following specifications:
(a) Application to all individuals, including visitors, all department staff, including executive staff, volunteers, and contract employees.
(b) Use of methods to ensure that profiling is not practiced during random searches or searches of all individuals entering the prison at that time.
(c) Establishment of unpredictable, random search efforts and methods that ensures that no one, except department employees specifically designated to conduct the random search, shall have advance notice of when a random search is scheduled.

(d) All visitors attempting to enter a CDCR detention facility shall be informed that they may refuse to be searched by a passive alert dog.
(e) All visitors attempting to enter a CDCR detention facility who refuse to be searched by a passive alert dog shall be informed of options, including, but not limited to, the availability of a noncontact visit.
(f) All individuals attempting to enter a CDCR detention facility, who have a positive alert for contraband by an electronic drug detection device, a passive alert dog, or other technology, shall be informed of further potential search or visitation options.
(g) Establishment of a method by which an individual may demonstrate an authorized health-related use of a controlled substance when a positive alert is noted by an electronic drug detection device, a passive alert dog, or other technology.
(h) Establishment of specific requirements for additional search options when multiple positive alerts occur on an individual employee within a specified timeframe.
(i) In determining which additional search options to offer visitors and staff, CDCR shall consider the use of full-body scanners.
(j) CDCR shall conduct an evaluation of a policy described in this section and provide an interim report to the Legislature by June 30, 2016, and a final report to the Legislature on April 30, 2017. This evaluation shall include, but not be limited to, the impact of the policy on:
(1) The amount of contraband, including drugs and cellular phones, found in the prisons where the policy was implemented.
(2) The number of staff assaults that occurred in the prisons where the policy was implemented.
(3) The number of serious rules violation reports issued in prisons where the policy was implemented, including any reduction in offender violence.
(4) The rates of drug use by inmates in the prisons where the policy was implemented.
(k) (1) The requirement for submitting a report imposed under subdivision (j) is inoperative on June 30, 2020, pursuant to Section 10231.5 of the Government Code.
(2) The reports to be submitted pursuant to subdivision (j) shall be submitted in compliance with Section 9795 of the Government Code.
(Amended by Stats. 2016, Ch. 33, Sec. 31. (SB 843) Effective June 27, 2016.)
6402.5.
(a) It is the intent of the Legislature that the Contraband Interdiction Pilot Program at the California Substance Abuse Treatment Facility and State Prison, Corcoran authorized by the Budget Act of 2018 be designed in such a way as to provide the Legislature with reliable information about how contraband enters prisons and what strategies are most cost effective in reducing inmate drug use.
(b) The Department of Corrections and Rehabilitation shall design the pilot program and submit a report to the Legislature by February 1, 2021, that includes all of the following:
(1) An assessment of the relative cost-effectiveness in reducing inmate drug use of each contraband interdiction strategy used in the pilot program, including medication assisted treatment.
(2) Data on and analysis of instances of contraband entering the prison, including, but not limited to, the following:
(A) How the contraband was brought or attempted to be brought into the prison.
(B) When the violation occurred.
(C) Whether the person who is alleged to have committed the violation is an inmate, staff member, visitor, volunteer, contractor, or other.
(D) The type of contraband involved.
(E) How the violation was discovered.
(F) Data on and analysis of arrests resulting from the violation, including, but not limited to, the number and type of arrests.
(G) Data on and analysis of disciplinary actions taken against staff or inmates as a result of their participation in efforts to bring contraband into the prison.
(3) An assessment of whether the pilot program caused declines in or any other observable impact on visitation.
(4) An assessment of whether the pilot program caused changes in the prevalence of violence or lockdowns in the prison.
(5) Any other data the department determines has probative value as to the efficacy of the pilot program.
(c) The pilot program shall require that entrance screening be conducted on every individual and package entering the prison and take place 24 hours per day, seven days per week. The department shall track and report on the use of entrance screening technology and equipment throughout the pilot period. To the extent screening does not occur for any period of time on any given day, the department shall document the day of the week, date, and the length of time in which screening does not occur, including starting and ending times. The department shall also include the reason that screening was not conducted during that timeframe, including, but not limited to, technology failures and staffing issues.
(d) (1) A report to be submitted pursuant to subdivision (b) shall be submitted in compliance with Section 9795 of the Government Code.
(2) Pursuant to Section 10231.5 of the Government Code, this section is repealed on January 1, 2022.
(Added by Stats. 2018, Ch. 36, Sec. 25. (AB 1812) Effective June 27, 2018. Repealed as of January 1, 2022, by its own provisions.)
6404.
Inmates shall not be prohibited from family visits based solely on the fact that the inmate was sentenced to life without the possibility of parole or was sentenced to life and is without a parole date established by the Board of Parole Hearings.
(Added by Stats. 2016, Ch. 33, Sec. 32. (SB 843) Effective June 27, 2016.)

CHAPTER 10.9. Prisoner Protections for Family and Community Health Act [6500- 6500.]

(Chapter 10.9 added by Stats. 2014, Ch. 587, Sec. 2.)
6500.
Based on the recommendations contained in the "Evaluation of a Prisoner Condom Access Pilot Program Conducted in One California State Prison Facility" report, and in light of the successful pilot project conducted at California State Prison, Solano, the Department of Corrections and Rehabilitation shall develop a five-year plan to expand the availability of condoms in all California prisons.
(Added by Stats. 2014, Ch. 587, Sec. 2. (AB 966) Effective January 1, 2015.)

CHAPTER 11. Master Plan Construction [7000 - 7050]

(Chapter 11 added by Stats. 1981, Ch. 540, Sec. 6.)
7000.
(a) The Department of Corrections and Rehabilitation shall prepare plans for, and construct facilities and renovations included within, its master plan for which funds have been appropriated by the Legislature.
(b) "Master plan" means the department's "Facility Requirements Plan," dated April 7, 1980, and any subsequent revisions.
(Amended by Stats. 2007, Ch. 175, Sec. 15. Effective August 24, 2007.)
7001.
Any power, function, or jurisdiction for planning or construction of facilities or renovations pursuant to the master plan which is conferred by statute upon the Department of General Services shall be deemed to be conferred upon the department.
(Added by Stats. 1981, Ch. 540, Sec. 6. Effective September 17, 1981.)
7002.
The department may transfer the responsibility for undertaking any aspect of the master plan to the Department of General Services or the Office of the State Architect which, upon such transfer, shall perform those functions with all deliberate speed.
(Added by Stats. 1981, Ch. 540, Sec. 6. Effective September 17, 1981.)
7003.
For each facility or project included within its master plan, at least 30 days prior to submission of preliminary plans to the State Public Works Board, the department shall submit to the Joint Legislative Budget Committee all of the following:
(a) A preliminary plan submittal package, as defined by the State Administrative Manual.
(b) An estimate of the annual operating costs of the facility.
(c) A staffing plan for the operation of the facility.
(d) A plan for providing medical, mental health, and dental care to inmates.
(e) A plan for inmate programming at the facility, including education, work, and substance abuse programming.
If the committee fails to take any action with respect to the submitted plans within 45 days after submittal, this inaction shall be deemed to be approval for purposes of this section.
(Amended by Stats. 2007, Ch. 7, Sec. 18. Effective May 3, 2007.)
7003.5.
(a) The department shall provide the Joint Legislative Budget Committee with quarterly reports on the progress of funded projects consistent with the requirements outlined in the State Administrative Manual. This report shall include new prisons, projects to construct inmate housing and other buildings at, or within, existing prison facilities, prison medical, mental health, and dental facilities, reentry facilities, and infrastructure projects at existing prison facilities.
(b) On January 10 of each year, the department shall provide a report to the Joint Legislative Budget Committee that includes the status of each project that is part of the master plan, including projects planned, projects in preliminary planning, working, drawing and construction phases, and projects that have been completed. The report shall include new prisons; projects to construct inmate housing and other buildings at or within existing prison facilities; prison medical, mental health, and dental facilities; reentry facilities; and infrastructure projects at existing prison facilities.
(c) This section applies to regular prison facilities; projects to expand existing prison facilities; prison medical, mental health, and dental facilities; reentry facilities; and infrastructure projects at existing prison facilities, whether or not built or operated exclusively by the department.
(d) The report required in subdivision (b) shall include the following information for adult and juvenile facilities:
(1) The department's plans to remove temporary beds in dayrooms, gyms, and other areas, as well as plans to permanently close or change the mission of the facilities.
(2) The department's plans to construct new facilities, including reentry facilities.
(3) The department's plans to renovate existing facilities and renovate, improve, or expand infrastructure capacity at existing prison facilities.
(4) The scope of each project identified in the master plan.
(5) The budget for each project identified in the master plan.
(6) The schedule for each project identified in the master plan.
(7) A master schedule for the overall plan to deliver the department's capital outlay program including planned versus actual progress to date.
(8) Staffing plans for each project identified in the master plan, including program, custody, facilities management, administration, and health care.
(9) Total estimated cost of all projects in the master plan by funding source, including planned versus actual expenditures to date.
(10) Projected versus actual population plotted against projected versus actual housing capacity in aggregate and by security level.
(Amended by Stats. 2007, Ch. 175, Sec. 16. Effective August 24, 2007.)
7004.
The plans required pursuant to Section 7000 shall contain the department's plan for soliciting and receiving local public comment regarding the placement of a correctional facility in any particular community. The plan shall include provision for notice to a community, including the city, county, or city and county, under consideration for construction of a facility within 30 days after the department has identified a possible site for the proposed facility, public hearings on the proposed facility, and dissemination of the response of the department to comments of the community on the proposed facility.
The plan developed by the department concerning public comment on placement of correctional facilities shall be submitted to the Legislature and the Governor within 60 days of the effective date of this section. The plan shall be implemented as of the date of submission to the Governor and Legislature with respect to all prospective placements of correctional facilities. The Legislature and the Governor shall also be sent any subsequent changes or revisions of the plan by the department.
(Added by Stats. 1984, Ch. 365, Sec. 1. Effective July 10, 1984.)
7004.5.
The Department of Corrections and Rehabilitation shall meet with representatives of cities or, if the prison is located in an unincorporated location, counties, whenever the Legislature authorizes the planning, design, or construction of new permanent housing units. The meeting shall take place prior to the completion of the review required by Division 13 (commencing with Section 21000) of the Public Resources Code. The department shall describe the scope of the project and the project schedule, and shall consider comments from the city or county representatives regarding the project's impact.
(Added by Stats. 2007, Ch. 7, Sec. 20. Effective May 3, 2007.)
7005.
Notwithstanding any other provision of law, mitigation funding shall be distributed to any local education agency, or any city, county, or city and county as a result of the construction of new permanent prison housing facilities, the activation of temporary beds as part of the Emergency Bed Program authorized by the Budget Acts of 1995 and 1996, and any future emergency bed expansions by the Department of Corrections if funds for that purpose are appropriated to the department in the annual Budget Act or any other act approved by the Legislature.
(Amended by Stats. 1998, Ch. 593, Sec. 2. Effective January 1, 1999.)
7005.5.
(a) Any funds appropriated for mitigation costs pursuant to Section 7005 shall be divided as follows: one-half for allocation among any impacted local education agency, and one-half for allocation among any impacted city, county, or city and county.
(b) Any funds appropriated for mitigation of costs of a city, county, or city and county shall be divided among any city, county, or city and county impacted by the prison construction or expansion.
(c) Funds to be allocated among any impacted city, county, or city and county shall be paid directly to each impacted entity by the Department of Corrections upon receipt of resolutions adopted by the governing body of each impacted city, county, or city and

county indicating agreement by an entity regarding the specific allocations to that entity. Only a local impacted entity whose current approved sphere of influence includes the site of increased inmate housing capacity shall be deemed to be a jurisdiction eligible for mitigation pursuant to Section 7005.

(d) Funds to be allocated among any impacted local education agency shall be disbursed to the county superintendent of schools for allocation among any impacted local education agency.

(Amended by Stats. 1998, Ch. 593, Sec. 3. Effective January 1, 1999.)

7006.

(a) The Department of the Youth Authority is authorized to transfer to the Department of Corrections title to any property of the Preston School of Industry at Ione not currently being used by the Department of the Youth Authority.

(b) The Department of the Youth Authority is authorized to transfer to the Department of Corrections title to any property of the Northern California Youth Center near Stockton not currently being used by the Department of the Youth Authority.

(Amended by Stats. 1984, Ch. 1743, Sec. 3. Effective September 30, 1984.)

7008.

(a) Division 13 (commencing with Section 21000) of the Public Resources Code shall not apply to the addition of 150 Level I and Level II beds authorized by Section 5 of this act at San Gabriel Canyon, provided that the department has made the following finding with respect to that facility:

(1) The increase in bed capacity, if any, shall not exceed, 5 percent of the total capacity of the facility prior to the increase.

(2) Any modifications made to existing structures are internal only. No external additions to existing structures or construction of new structures shall be done. Modular structures used exclusively for prisoner program activity shall be exempt from this requirement.

(3) Any modifications to a facility shall not result in a significant depletion in water, sewage, or other environmental resources. The department shall present substantial evidence that this requirement has been met in the findings described in subdivision (b).

(b) The department shall make findings that the requirements of subdivision (a) have been met, and shall make the findings available to the public.

(Added by Stats. 1985, Ch. 933, Sec. 2. Effective September 25, 1985.)

7010.

(a) The Director of Corrections may solicit bids for any lease or lease-purchase for the establishment of a prison facility for a site in Los Angeles County.

(b) The director may not accept any lease or lease-purchase bid or execute any lease or lease-purchase agreement unless and until the bid or agreement is submitted for review and approval under the procedure described in Section 7003.

(c) Any lease or lease-purchase agreement executed pursuant to this section shall contain, as a condition of the agreement, stipulations requiring compliance with the provisions of Chapter 1 (commencing with Section 1720) of Part 7 of the Labor Code in the construction of any facility within the scope of the agreement.

(Added by Stats. 1984, Ch. 1742, Sec. 1.)

7011.

(a) The Department of Corrections shall submit to the Joint Legislative Prison Committee, the Kings County Board of Supervisors, the Corcoran City Council, and the State Public Works Board, at least 30 days prior to the acquisition of real property for a prison facility to be located in the vicinity of Corcoran in Kings County, an environmental assessment study, which shall include a discussion of impacts and mitigation measures, if necessary, for the following areas:

(1) Geology.

(2) Hydrology—groundwater.

(3) Water quality—surface waters.

(4) Plant and animal life—endangered and rare species.

(5) Air quality.

(6) Noise.

(7) Light and glare.

(8) Transportation and circulation.

(9) Utilities—gas, electricity, telephone, solid waste, sewage disposal, and drinking water.

(10) Archaeology.

(11) Energy.

(b) The factors set forth in subdivision (a) shall be assessed only as they relate to the direct impacts caused off the site as a result of the construction, operation, and maintenance of the prison facility upon completion and occupancy.

(c) Notwithstanding any other provisions of law, other than Section 7003 and those provisions of the Government Code that require the approval of the State Public Works Board, the Department of Finance, or the Director of Finance for capital outlay projects, the approval of the study by the State Public Works Board is the only approval required for the acquisition of real property, planning, design, and construction of the prison facility and the operation and maintenance of the facility. The State Public Works Board shall not act on the study until it receives a recommendation from the Joint Legislative Prison Committee. Approval of the study by the State Public Works Board shall be final and binding on all parties.

(d) If the committee does not, by a majority vote of the committee membership, take any action on the study within 30 days after submittal, that inaction shall be deemed to be a recommendation of concurrence for the purposes of this section.

(e) Prior to providing a recommendation to the State Public Works Board, but within the 30-day period specified in subdivision (d), the committee shall hold a public hearing in Corcoran. Notice of the hearing shall be published in a newspaper of general circulation in, or adjacent to, Corcoran. The notice shall be at least one-quarter page in size. The Corcoran City Council and the Kings County Board of Supervisors shall be invited to participate in the hearing.

(Added by Stats. 1985, Ch. 931, Sec. 2. Effective September 25, 1985.)

7012.

(a) The Department of Corrections shall submit to the Joint Legislative Prison Committee, the State Public Works Board, the appropriate county board of supervisors, and the local city council at least 30 days prior to the acquisition of real property for prison facilities to be located in Riverside and Del Norte Counties, an environmental assessment study, which shall include a discussion of impacts and mitigation measures, if necessary, for the following areas:

(1) Geology.

(2) Hydrology-groundwater.

(3) Water quality-surface waters.

(4) Plant and animal life-endangered and rare species.

(5) Air quality.

(6) Noise.

(7) Light and glare.

(8) Utilities-gas, electricity, telephone, solid waste, sewage disposal, and drinking water.

(9) Archaeology.

(10) Energy.

(b) The factors set forth in subdivision (a) shall be assessed only as they relate to the direct impacts caused off the site as a result of the construction, operation, and maintenance of the prison facility upon completion and occupancy.

(c) Notwithstanding any other provision of law, other than Section 7003, the approval of the study by the State Public Works Board is the only approval required for compliance with any applicable environmental requirements. The Public State Works Board shall not act on the study until it receives a recommendation from the Joint Legislative Prison

Committee. Approval of the study by the State Public Works Board shall be final and binding on all parties.

(d) If the committee does not, by a majority vote of the committee membership, take any action on the study within 30 days after submittal, that inaction shall be deemed to be a recommendation of concurrence for the purposes of this section.

(e) Prior to providing a recommendation to the State Public Works Board, but within the 30-day period specified in subdivision (d), the committee shall hold a public hearing in the community in the vicinity of the proposed site. Notice of the hearing shall be published in a newspaper of general circulation in, or adjacent to, that community. The notice shall be at least one-quarter page in size. The city council and the county board of supervisors shall be invited to participate in the hearing.

(Amended by Stats. 2001, Ch. 854, Sec. 57. Effective January 1, 2002.)

7013.

The Department of Corrections shall contract, or make a good-faith effort to contract, with the Department of Water Resources or the Bureau of Reclamation, or both, to secure a water supply for the prison at Avenal.

(Added by Stats. 1985, Ch. 931, Sec. 2.5. Effective September 25, 1985.)

7015.

(a) Except as provided in subdivision (b), the Department of Corrections may contract with the City of Folsom for the construction of a courthouse and related facilities, not to exceed one million nine hundred thousand dollars ($1,900,000) in costs. Under this contract, the Department of Corrections is authorized to make payments to the City of Folsom in consideration for the construction of the courthouse, provided that the sums paid to the city are realized from savings to the department by the location of the courthouse in the immediate proximity of Folsom Prison.

Under this contract, the Department of Corrections is authorized to make annual payments to the City of Folsom in an amount not to exceed the approximate savings realized in each fiscal year. These funds shall come from the operating budget of the department.

In negotiating this contract, the Department of Corrections shall note the extent to which the courthouse will serve the interests of the County of Sacramento independent of matters pertaining to individuals in state custody and shall seek appropriate participation in the funding of the courthouse from the county.

(b) The Department of Corrections may not contract with the City of Folsom for a court facility unless a majority of the members of the Sacramento County Board of Supervisors, the presiding judge of the Sacramento County Municipal Court, and the presiding judge of the Sacramento County Superior Court all agree, in writing, to operate a court facility in the City of Folsom as provided by subdivision (a).

(Added by Stats. 1988, Ch. 1393, Sec. 2.)

7016.

The Department of Corrections may contract with the County of Kern for the construction and financing of a courthouse and related facilities. Under this contract, the Department of Corrections is authorized to make payments to the County of Kern in consideration for the construction and financing of the courthouse and related facilities, provided that the sums paid to the county are realized from savings to the department by the location of the courthouse in the proximity of the California Correctional Facility in Tehachapi.

In accordance with the contract, the Department of Corrections is authorized to make annual payments to the County of Kern from the approximate savings realized in each fiscal year. These funds shall come from the operating budget of the department. In negotiating this contract, the Department of Corrections shall note the extent to which the courthouse will serve the interest of the County of Kern independent of matters pertaining to individuals in state custody, and seek appropriate county participation in funding.

(Added by Stats. 1988, Ch. 1400, Sec. 2.)

7050.

(a) (1) Section 28 of Chapter 7 of the Statutes of 2007 contains an appropriation of three hundred million dollars ($300,000,000) for capital outlay to be allocated to renovate, improve, or expand infrastructure capacity at existing prison facilities. The funds appropriated by that section may be used for land acquisition, environmental services, architectural programming, engineering assessments, schematic design, preliminary plans, working drawings, and construction.

(2) These funds may also be used to address deficiencies related to utility systems owned by local government entities and serving state prison facilities subject to the provisions of Section 54999 of the Government Code. The department shall report on any funds to be expended for this purpose to the Joint Legislative Budget Committee. If the committee fails to take any action with respect to each notification within 20 days after submittal, this inaction shall be deemed to be approval for purposes of this section.

(3) These funds may also be used for the design and construction of improvements to dental facilities at state prison facilities.

(4) These funds may also be used for the design and construction of improvements to medication distribution facilities at state prison facilities.

(5) These funds may also be used for the design and construction of projects in the Health Care Facility Improvement Program at state prison facilities.

(6) This subdivision authorizes the scope and cost of a single capital outlay project for purposes of calculating augmentations pursuant to Section 13332.11 or 13332.19.

(b) The scope and costs of the projects described in subdivision (a) of this section shall be subject to approval and administrative oversight by the State Public Works Board, including augmentations, pursuant to Section 13332.11 or 13332.19 of the Government Code. The availability of an augmentation for each individual project allocation shall be based on the total applicable capital outlay appropriation contained in Section 28 of Chapter 7 of the Statutes of 2007 and is not limited to 20 percent of the individual project allocation. These requirements shall be applied separately to each institution. All of the necessary infrastructure improvements at each institution may be treated as one project such that there would be one infrastructure improvement project at each institution. The scope and cost of each infrastructure improvement project shall be established by the board individually. The amount of the total appropriation in Section 28 of Chapter 7 of the Statutes of 2007 that is necessary for each infrastructure improvement project shall be allocated by institution. The appropriation may be allocated based on current estimates. These initial allocations may be adjusted commensurate to changes that occur during the progression of the projects. As allocations are made or adjusted, the anticipated deficit or savings shall be continuously tracked and reported. Once the total appropriation has been allocated, any augmentation necessary to fund an anticipated deficit shall be based on the total appropriation and allocated to each project as necessary. Concurrent with the request to the board to establish each project authorized pursuant to this section, the Department of Corrections and Rehabilitation shall report the associated scope, cost, and schedule information to the Joint Legislative Budget Committee.

(c) The projects authorized pursuant to this section shall be part of the Department of Corrections and Rehabilitation's master plan, as defined in Section 7000.

(d) The reporting requirements set forth in Sections 7000 to 7003.5, inclusive, shall apply separately to each project authorized pursuant to this section.

(Amended by Stats. 2014, Ch. 26, Sec. 35. (AB 1468) Effective June 20, 2014.)

CHAPTER 14. New Prison Construction Bond Act of 1986 [7300 - 7311]

(Chapter 14 added by Stats. 1986, Ch. 409, Sec. 1.)
7300.
This chapter shall be known and may be cited as the New Prison Construction Bond Act of 1986.
(Added by Stats. 1986, Ch. 409, Sec. 1. Approved in Proposition 54 at the November 4, 1986, election.)
7301.
The State General Obligation Bond Law is adopted for the purpose of the issuance, sale and repayment of, and otherwise providing with respect to, the bonds authorized to be issued by this chapter, and the provisions of that law are included in this chapter as though set out in full in this chapter except that, notwithstanding anything in the State General Obligation Bond Law, the maximum maturity of the bonds shall not exceed 20 years from the date of each respective series. The maturity of each respective series shall be calculated from the date of such series.
(Added by Stats. 1986, Ch. 409, Sec. 1. Approved in Proposition 54 at the November 4, 1986, election.)
7302.
There is in the State Treasury the 1986 Prison Construction Fund, which fund is hereby created. The proceeds of the sale of bonds authorized by this act shall be deposited in this fund and may be transferred upon request of the Department of Corrections and upon approval of the Director of Finance, to the 1984 Prison Construction Fund established by Section 7202. If the moneys are so transferred, "fund" means the 1984 Prison Construction Fund.
(Added by Stats. 1986, Ch. 409, Sec. 1. Approved in Proposition 54 at the November 4, 1986, election.)
7303.
The 1986 Prison Construction Committee is hereby created. The committee shall consist of the Controller, the State Treasurer, and the Director of Finance. That committee shall be the "committee," as that term is used in the State General Obligation Bond Law. The Department of Corrections is the "board" for the purpose of the State General Obligation Bond Law and this chapter.
(Added by Stats. 1986, Ch. 409, Sec. 1. Approved in Proposition 54 at the November 4, 1986, election.)
7304.
The committee is hereby authorized and empowered to create a debt or debts, liability or liabilities, of the State of California, in the aggregate of five hundred million dollars ($500,000,000), in the manner provided in this chapter. That debt or debts, liability or liabilities, shall be created for the purpose of providing the fund to be used for the object and work specified in Section 7306.
(Added by Stats. 1986, Ch. 409, Sec. 1. Approved in Proposition 54 at the November 4, 1986, election.)
7305.
The committee may determine whether or not it is necessary or desirable to issue any bonds authorized under this chapter, and if so, the amount of bonds then to be issued and sold. The committee may authorize the Treasurer to sell all or any part of the bonds herein authorized at such time or times as may be fixed by the Treasurer.
(Added by Stats. 1986, Ch. 409, Sec. 1. Approved in Proposition 54 at the November 4, 1986, election.)
7306.
The moneys in the fund shall be used for the acquisition, construction, renovation, remodeling, and deferred maintenance of state youth and adult corrections facilities.
(Added by Stats. 1986, Ch. 409, Sec. 1. Approved in Proposition 54 at the November 4, 1986, election.)
7307.
(a) All bonds herein authorized, which shall have been duly sold and delivered as herein provided, shall constitute valid and legally binding general obligations of the State of California, and the full faith and credit of the State of California is hereby pledged for the punctual payment of both principal and interest thereon.
(b) There shall be collected annually in the same manner and at the same time as other state revenue is collected such a sum, in addition to the ordinary revenues of the state, as shall be required to pay the principal and interest on those bonds, and it is hereby made the duty of all officers charged by law with any duty in regard to the collection of that revenue to do and perform each and every act which shall be necessary to collect that additional sum.
(c) All money deposited in the fund which has been derived from premium and accrued interest on bonds sold shall be available for transfer to the General Fund as a credit to expenditures for bond interest.
(d) All money deposited in the fund pursuant to any provision of law requiring repayments to the state which are financed by the proceeds of the bonds authorized by this chapter shall be available for transfer to the General Fund. When transferred to the General Fund that money shall be applied as a reimbursement to the General Fund on account of principal and interest on the bonds which has been paid from the General Fund.
(Added by Stats. 1986, Ch. 409, Sec. 1. Approved in Proposition 54 at the November 4, 1986, election.)
7308.
There is hereby appropriated from the General Fund in the State Treasury for the purpose of this chapter such an amount as will equal the following:
(a) That sum annually as will be necessary to pay the principal of and the interest on the bonds issued and sold pursuant to the provisions of this chapter.
(b) That sum as is necessary to carry out the provisions of Section 7309, which sum is appropriated without regard to fiscal years.
(Added by Stats. 1986, Ch. 409, Sec. 1. Approved in Proposition 54 at the November 4, 1986, election.)
7309.
For the purpose of carrying out the provisions of this chapter, the Director of Finance may by executive order authorize the withdrawal from the General Fund of an amount or amounts not to exceed the amount of the unsold bonds which the committee has by resolution authorized to be sold for the purpose of carrying out this chapter. Any amounts withdrawn shall be deposited in the fund and shall be disbursed by the committee in accordance with this chapter. Any money made available under this section to the board shall be returned by the board to the General Fund from moneys received from the sale of bonds sold for the purpose of carrying out this chapter. Those withdrawals from the General Fund shall be returned to the General Fund with interest at the rate which would otherwise have been earned by those sums in the Pooled Money Investment Fund.
(Added by Stats. 1986, Ch. 409, Sec. 1. Approved in Proposition 54 at the November 4, 1986, election.)
7309.5.
Notwithstanding any other provision of this bond act, or of the State General Obligation Bond Law (Chapter 4 (commencing with Section 16720) of Part 3 of Division 4 of Title 2 of the Government Code), if the Treasurer sells bonds pursuant to this bond act that include a bond counsel opinion to the effect that the interest on the bonds is excluded from gross income for federal tax purposes under designated conditions, the Treasurer may maintain separate accounts for the bond proceeds invested and the investment earnings on those proceeds, and may use or direct the use of those proceeds or earnings to pay any rebate, penalty, or other payment required under federal law, or take any other action with respect to the investment and use of those bond proceeds, as may be required or desirable under federal law in order to maintain the tax-exempt

status of those bonds and to obtain any other advantage under federal law on behalf of the funds of this state.
(Added by Stats. 1991, Ch. 652, Sec. 19.)
7310.
All proceeds from the sale of bonds, except those derived from premiums and accrued interest, shall be available for the purpose provided in Section 7306 but shall not be available for transfer to the General Fund to pay principal and interest on bonds. The money in the fund may be expended only as herein provided.
(Added by Stats. 1986, Ch. 409, Sec. 1. Approved in Proposition 54 at the November 4, 1986, election.)
7311.
Money in the fund may only be expended pursuant to appropriations by the Legislature.
(Added by Stats. 1986, Ch. 409, Sec. 1. Approved in Proposition 54 at the November 4, 1986, election.)

CHAPTER 15. New Prison Construction Bond Act of 1988 [7400 - 7414]

(Chapter 15 added by Stats. 1988, Ch. 43, Sec. 2.)
7400.
This chapter shall be known and may be cited as the New Prison Construction Bond Act of 1988.
(Added by Stats. 1988, Ch. 43, Sec. 2. Approved in Proposition 80 at the November 8, 1988, election.)
7401.
The State General Obligation Bond Law is adopted for the purpose of the issuance, sale and repayment of, and otherwise providing with respect to, the bonds authorized to be issued by this chapter, and the provisions of that law are included in this chapter as though set out in full in this chapter except that, notwithstanding anything in the State General Obligation Bond Law, the maximum maturity of the bonds shall not exceed 20 years from the date of each respective series. The maturity of each respective series shall be calculated from the date of that series.
(Added by Stats. 1988, Ch. 43, Sec. 2. Approved in Proposition 80 at the November 8, 1988, election.)
7402.
There is in the State Treasury the 1988 Prison Construction Fund, which fund is hereby created. The proceeds of the sale of bonds authorized by this act shall be deposited in the fund, and may be transferred upon request of the Department of Corrections and upon approval of the Director of Finance, to the New Prison Construction Fund established by Section 7102, the 1984 Prison Construction Fund established by Section 7202, or the 1986 Prison Construction Fund established by Section 7302, or any combination thereof. If the moneys are so transferred, "fund" means the New Prison Construction Fund, 1984 Prison Construction Fund, or 1986 Prison Construction Fund, or any combination thereof, as is appropriate. At least 30 days prior to requesting a transfer as authorized by this section, the Department of Corrections shall notify the chairpersons of the fiscal committees in each house of the Legislature, and the Chairperson and the Vice Chairperson of the Joint Legislative Budget Committee.
(Amended (as proposed to be added by Stats. 1988, Ch. 43) by Stats. 1988, Ch. 386, Sec. 3. Approved, in this amended form, in Proposition 80 at the November 8, 1988, election.)
7403.
The 1988 Prison Construction Committee is hereby created. The committee shall consist of the Controller, the Treasurer, and the Director of Finance. That committee shall be the "committee," as that term is used in the State General Obligation Bond Law. The Department of Corrections is the "board" for the purpose of the State General Obligation Bond Law and this chapter.
(Added by Stats. 1988, Ch. 43, Sec. 2. Approved in Proposition 80 at the November 8, 1988, election.)
7404.
The committee is hereby authorized and empowered to create a debt or debts, liability or liabilities, of the State of California, in the aggregate principal amount of eight hundred seventeen million dollars ($817,000,000), exclusive of refunding bonds, in the manner provided in this chapter. That debt or debts, liability or liabilities, shall be created for the purpose of providing the fund to be used for the object and work specified in Section 7406.
(Added by Stats. 1988, Ch. 43, Sec. 2. Approved in Proposition 80 at the November 8, 1988, election.)
7405.
The committee may determine whether or not it is necessary or desirable to issue any bonds authorized under this chapter, and if so, the amount of bonds then to be issued and sold. The committee may authorize the Treasurer to sell all or any part of the bonds herein authorized at such time or times as may be fixed by the Treasurer.
(Added by Stats. 1988, Ch. 43, Sec. 2. Approved in Proposition 80 at the November 8, 1988, election.)
7406.
(a) Except as provided in subdivision (b), the moneys in the fund shall be used for the acquisition, construction, renovation, remodeling, and deferred maintenance of state youth and adult correctional facilities.
(b) Of the moneys in the fund, forty million dollars ($40,000,000) is hereby appropriated to the Board of Corrections to fund those projects entitled to be funded under subdivision (c) of Section 3 of Chapter 444 of the Statutes of 1984, as amended, to the extent that those projects have not received full funding and for any costs associated with the sale of bonds and any administrative costs incurred by the Board of Corrections in the administration of the County Jail Capital Expenditure Bond Acts of 1981 and 1984 and the County Correctional Facility Capital Expenditure Bond Act of 1986.
(c) Notwithstanding subdivision (b) of Section 11 of Chapter 1519 of the Statutes of 1986 or any other provision of law to the contrary, and subject to the annual Budget Act appropriations by the Legislature, administrative costs shall not exceed 1 1/2 percent of the amount allocated for any costs incurred by the Board of Corrections in the administration of the County Jail Capital Expenditure Bond Acts of 1981 and 1984 and the County Correctional Facility Capital Expenditure Bond Act of 1986.
(Added by Stats. 1988, Ch. 43, Sec. 2. Approved in Proposition 80 at the November 8, 1988, election.)
7407.
(a) All bonds herein authorized, which shall have been duly sold and delivered as herein provided, shall constitute valid and legally binding general obligations of the State of California, and the full faith and credit of the State of California is hereby pledged for the punctual payment of both the principal thereof and interest thereon.
(b) There shall be collected annually in the same manner and at the same time as other state revenue is collected such a sum, in addition to the ordinary revenues of the state, as shall be required to pay the principal of and interest on those bonds, and it is hereby made the duty of all officers charged by law with any duty in regard to the collection of that revenue to do and perform each and every act which shall be necessary to collect that additional sum.

(c) All money deposited in the fund which has been derived from premiums or accrued interest on bonds sold shall be available for transfer to the General Fund as a credit to expenditures for bond interest.

(d) All money deposited in the fund pursuant to any provision of law requiring repayments to the state which are financed by the proceeds of the bonds authorized by this chapter shall be available for transfer to the General Fund. When transferred to the General Fund that money shall be applied as a reimbursement to the General Fund on account of the principal of and interest on the bonds which has been paid from the General Fund.

(Added by Stats. 1988, Ch. 43, Sec. 2. Approved in Proposition 80 at the November 8, 1988, election.)

7408.
Notwithstanding Section 13340 of the Government Code, there is hereby appropriated from the General Fund in the State Treasury for the purpose of this chapter such an amount as will equal the following:

(a) That sum annually as will be necessary to pay the principal of and the interest on the bonds issued and sold pursuant to this chapter.

(b) That sum as is necessary to carry out the provisions of Section 7409, which sum is appropriated without regard to fiscal years.

(Added by Stats. 1988, Ch. 43, Sec. 2. Approved in Proposition 80 at the November 8, 1988, election.)

7409.
For the purpose of carrying out this chapter, the Director of Finance may by executive order authorize the withdrawal from the General Fund of an amount or amounts not to exceed the amount of the unsold bonds which the committee has by resolution authorized to be sold for the purpose of carrying out this chapter. Any amounts withdrawn shall be deposited in the fund and shall be disbursed by the committee in accordance with this chapter. Any money made available under this section to the board shall be returned by the board to the General Fund from moneys received from the sale of bonds sold for the purpose of carrying out this chapter. Those withdrawals from the General Fund shall be returned to the General Fund with interest at the rate which would otherwise have been earned by those sums in the Pooled Money Investment Account.

(Added by Stats. 1988, Ch. 43, Sec. 2. Approved in Proposition 80 at the November 8, 1988, election.)

7409.5.
Notwithstanding any other provision of this bond act, or of the State General Obligation Bond Law (Chapter 4 (commencing with Section 16720) of Part 3 of Division 4 of Title 2 of the Government Code), if the Treasurer sells bonds pursuant to this bond act that include a bond counsel opinion to the effect that the interest on the bonds is excluded from gross income for federal tax purposes under designated conditions, the Treasurer may maintain separate accounts for the bond proceeds invested and the investment earnings on those proceeds, and may use or direct the use of those proceeds or earnings to pay any rebate, penalty, or other payment required under federal law, or take any other action with respect to the investment and use of those bond proceeds, as may be required or desirable under federal law in order to maintain the tax-exempt status of those bonds and to obtain any other advantage under federal law on behalf of the funds of this state.

(Added by Stats. 1991, Ch. 652, Sec. 20.)

7410.
The board may request the Pooled Money Investment Board to make a loan from the Pooled Money Investment Account, in accordance with Section 16312 of the Government Code, for the purposes of carrying out the provisions of this chapter. The amount of the request shall not exceed the amount of the unsold bonds which the committee has by resolution authorized to be sold for the purpose of carrying out this chapter. The board shall execute any documents required by the Pooled Money Investment Board to obtain and repay the loan. Any amounts loaned shall be deposited in the fund to be allocated by the board in accordance with this chapter.

(Added by Stats. 1988, Ch. 43, Sec. 2. Approved in Proposition 80 at the November 8, 1988, election.)

7411.
Any bonds issued and sold pursuant to this chapter may be refunded by the issuance of refunding bonds in accordance with Article 6 (commencing with Section 16780) of Chapter 4 of Part 3 of Division 2 of Title 2 of the Government Code. Approval by the electors of the state for the issuance of bonds shall include the approval of the issuance of any bonds issued to refund any bonds originally issued or any previously issued refunding bonds.

(Added by Stats. 1988, Ch. 43, Sec. 2. Approved in Proposition 80 at the November 8, 1988, election.)

7412.
All proceeds from the sale of bonds, except those derived from premiums and accrued interest, shall be available for the purpose provided in Section 7406 but shall not be available for transfer to the General Fund to pay the principal of and interest on bonds. The money in the fund may be expended only as herein provided.

(Added by Stats. 1988, Ch. 43, Sec. 2. Approved in Proposition 80 at the November 8, 1988, election.)

7413.
Money in the fund may only be expended pursuant to appropriations by the Legislature.

(Added by Stats. 1988, Ch. 43, Sec. 2. Approved in Proposition 80 at the November 8, 1988, election.)

7414.
The Legislature hereby finds and declares that, inasmuch as the proceeds from the sale of bonds authorized by this chapter are not "proceeds of taxes" as that term is used in Article XIII B of the California Constitution, the disbursement of these proceeds is not subject to the limitations imposed by that article.

(Added by Stats. 1988, Ch. 43, Sec. 2. Approved in Proposition 80 at the November 8, 1988, election.)

CHAPTER 16. New Prison Construction Bond Act of 1990 [7420 - 7434]

(Chapter 16 added by Stats. 1990, Ch. 5, Sec. 1.)

7420.
This chapter shall be known and may be cited as the New Prison Construction Bond Act of 1990.

(Added by Stats. 1990, Ch. 5, Sec. 1. Approved in Proposition 120 at the June 5, 1990, election.)

7421.
The State General Obligation Bond Law is adopted for the purpose of the issuance, sale and repayment of, and otherwise providing with respect to, the bonds authorized to be issued by this chapter, and the provisions of that law are included in this chapter as though set out in full in this chapter except that, notwithstanding anything in the State General Obligation Bond Law, the maximum maturity of the bonds shall not exceed 20 years from the date of each respective series. The maturity of each respective series shall be calculated from the date of that series.

(Added by Stats. 1990, Ch. 5, Sec. 1. Approved in Proposition 120 at the June 5, 1990, election.)

7422.
There is in the State Treasury the 1990 Prison Construction Fund, which fund is hereby created. The proceeds of the sale of bonds authorized by this chapter shall be deposited in the fund. Upon request of the Department of Corrections and upon approval of the Director of Finance, appropriations or augmentations to appropriations made from the 1984 Prison Construction Fund established by Section 7202, the 1986 Prison Construction Fund established by Section 7302, or the 1988 Prison Construction Fund established by Section 7402, or any combination thereof, may be funded from the 1990 Prison Construction Fund. If the moneys are so funded, "fund" means the 1984 Prison Construction Fund, the 1986 Prison Construction Fund, or the 1988 Prison Construction Fund, or any combination thereof, as is appropriate. At least 30 days prior to requesting funding for appropriations or augmentations to appropriations for other bond acts as authorized by this section, the Department of Corrections shall notify the chairpersons of the fiscal committees in each house of the Legislature, and the chairperson and the vice chairperson of the Joint Legislative Budget Committee.

(Added by Stats. 1990, Ch. 5, Sec. 1. Approved in Proposition 120 at the June 5, 1990, election.)

7423.
The 1990 Prison Construction Committee is hereby created. The committee shall consist of the Controller, the Treasurer, and the Director of Finance, or their designated representatives. A majority may act for the committee. The Treasurer shall chair the committee. That committee shall be the "committee," as that term is used in the State General Obligation Bond Law.

When funds are appropriated to the Department of Corrections, the Department of Corrections is the "board" for the purpose of the State General Obligation Bond Law and this chapter. When funds are appropriated to the Department of Youth Authority, the Department of Youth Authority is the "board" for the purpose of the State General Obligation Bond Law and this chapter.

(Added by Stats. 1990, Ch. 5, Sec. 1. Approved in Proposition 120 at the June 5, 1990, election.)

7424.
The committee is hereby authorized and empowered to create a debt or debts, liability or liabilities, of the State of California, in the aggregate principal amount of four hundred fifty million dollars ($450,000,000), exclusive of refunding bonds, in the manner provided in this chapter. That debt or debts, liability or liabilities, shall be created for the purpose of providing the fund to be used for the object and work specified in Section 7426.

(Added by Stats. 1990, Ch. 5, Sec. 1. Approved in Proposition 120 at the June 5, 1990, election.)

7425.
The committee may determine whether or not it is necessary or desirable to issue any bonds authorized under this chapter, and if so, the amount of bonds then to be issued and sold. The committee may authorize the Treasurer to sell all or any part of the bonds herein authorized at such time or times as may be fixed by the Treasurer.

(Added by Stats. 1990, Ch. 5, Sec. 1. Approved in Proposition 120 at the June 5, 1990, election.)

7426.
The moneys in the fund shall be used for the acquisition, construction, renovation, remodeling, and deferred maintenance of state youth and adult correctional facilities.

(Added by Stats. 1990, Ch. 5, Sec. 1. Approved in Proposition 120 at the June 5, 1990, election.)

7426.5.
Moneys deposited in the fund may also be used for the refinancing of interim debt incurred for any of the purposes specified in Section 7426.

(Added by Stats. 1990, Ch. 5, Sec. 1. Approved in Proposition 120 at the June 5, 1990, election.)

7427.
(a) All bonds herein authorized, which shall have been duly sold and delivered as herein provided, shall constitute valid and legally binding general obligations of the State of California, and the full faith and credit of the State of California is hereby pledged for the punctual payment of both the principal thereof and interest thereon.

(b) There shall be collected annually in the same manner and at the same time as other state revenue is collected that sum, in addition to the ordinary revenues of the state, that is required to pay the principal of and interest on those bonds, and it is hereby made the duty of all officers charged by law with any duty in regard to the collection of that revenue to do and perform each and every act which shall be necessary to collect that additional sum.

(c) All money deposited in the fund that has been derived from premiums or accrued interest on bonds sold shall be available for transfer to the General Fund as a credit to expenditures for bond interest.

(d) All money deposited in the fund pursuant to any provision of law requiring repayments to the state that is financed by the proceeds of the bonds authorized by this chapter shall be available for transfer to the General Fund. When transferred to the General Fund that money shall be applied as a reimbursement to the General Fund on account of the principal of and interest on the bonds which have been paid from the General Fund.

(Added by Stats. 1990, Ch. 5, Sec. 1. Approved in Proposition 120 at the June 5, 1990, election.)

7428.
Notwithstanding Section 13340 of the Government Code, there is hereby appropriated from the General Fund in the State Treasury for the purpose of this chapter such an amount as will equal the following:

(a) That sum annually as will be necessary to pay the principal of and the interest on the bonds issued and sold pursuant to this chapter.

(b) That sum as is necessary to carry out the provisions of Section 7429, which sum is appropriated without regard to fiscal years.

(Added by Stats. 1990, Ch. 5, Sec. 1. Approved in Proposition 120 at the June 5, 1990, election.)

7429.
For the purpose of carrying out this chapter, the Director of Finance may by executive order authorize the withdrawal from the General Fund of an amount or amounts not to exceed the amount of the unsold bonds which the committee has by resolution authorized to be sold for the purpose of carrying out this chapter. Any amounts withdrawn shall be deposited in the fund and shall be disbursed by the committee in accordance with this chapter. Any money made available under this section to the board shall be returned by the board to the General Fund from moneys received from the sale of bonds sold for the purpose of carrying out this chapter. Those withdrawals from the General Fund shall be returned to the General Fund with interest at the rate which would otherwise have been earned by those sums in the Pooled Money Investment Account.

(Added by Stats. 1990, Ch. 5, Sec. 1. Approved in Proposition 120 at the June 5, 1990, election.)

7430.
The board may request the Pooled Money Investment Board to make a loan from the Pooled Money Investment Account, in accordance with Section 16312 of the Government Code, for the purposes of carrying out the provisions of this chapter. The amount of the request shall not exceed the amount of the unsold bonds which the committee has by resolution authorized to be sold for the purpose of carrying out this chapter. The board shall execute any documents required by the Pooled Money

Investment Board to obtain and repay the loan. Any amounts loaned shall be deposited in the fund to be allocated by the board in accordance with this chapter.
(Added by Stats. 1990, Ch. 5, Sec. 1. Approved in Proposition 120 at the June 5, 1990, election.)
7431.
Any bonds issued and sold pursuant to this chapter may be refunded by the issuance of refunding bonds in accordance with Article 6 (commencing with Section 16780) of Chapter 4 of Part 3 of Division 2 of Title 2 of the Government Code. Approval by the electors of the state for the issuance of bonds shall include the approval of the issuance of any bonds issued to refund any bonds originally issued or any previously issued refunding bonds.
(Added by Stats. 1990, Ch. 5, Sec. 1. Approved in Proposition 120 at the June 5, 1990, election.)
7432.
All proceeds from the sale of bonds, except those derived from premiums and accrued interest, shall be available for the purpose provided in Section 7426 but shall not be available for transfer to the General Fund to pay the principal of and interest on bonds. The money in the fund may be expended only as herein provided.
Notwithstanding any provision of this chapter or the State General Obligation Bond Law set forth in Chapter 4 (commencing with Section 16720) of Part 3 of Division 4 of Title 2 of the Government Code, if the Treasurer sells bonds pursuant to this chapter the interest on which is intended to be excluded from gross income from federal tax purposes, the Treasurer is authorized to maintain separate accounts for the investment of bond proceeds and the investment earnings on the proceeds, and the Treasurer is authorized to use or direct the use of the proceeds or earnings to pay any rebate, penalty, or other payment required under federal law, or to take any other action with respect to the investment and use of bond proceeds required or desirable under federal law so as to maintain the tax-exempt status of those bonds and to obtain any other advantage under federal law on behalf of the funds of this state.
(Added by Stats. 1990, Ch. 5, Sec. 1. Approved in Proposition 120 at the June 5, 1990, election.)
7433.
Money in the fund may only be expended pursuant to appropriations by the Legislature.
(Amended by Stats. 2001, Ch. 745, Sec. 158.5. Effective October 12, 2001. Note: This section was added by Stats. 1990, Ch. 5, and approved in Prop. 120 on June 5, 1990.)
7434.
The Legislature hereby finds and declares that, inasmuch as the proceeds from the sale of bonds authorized by this chapter are not "proceeds of taxes" as that term is used in Article XIII B of the California Constitution, the disbursement of these proceeds is not subject to the limitations imposed by that article.
(Added by Stats. 1990, Ch. 5, Sec. 1. Approved in Proposition 120 at the June 5, 1990, election.)

CHAPTER 17. Children of Incarcerated Parents [7440 - 7445]

(Chapter 17 added by Stats. 2000, Ch. 965, Sec. 1.)
7440.
The California Research Bureau in the California State Library shall conduct a study of the children of women who are incarcerated in state prisons. The California Research Bureau shall design and complete the study, surveying selected state prisoners in cooperation with the Department of Corrections, and reviewing the records of local agencies to obtain outcome information about a sample of women prisoners' children.
(Added by Stats. 2000, Ch. 965, Sec. 1. Effective January 1, 2001.)
7441.
The purpose of the survey of state prisoners is to determine how many have children and to gather basic information about the children to include the following variables, among others:
(a) Number.
(b) Age.
(c) Siblings.
(d) Location.
(e) Caregiver.
(f) Grade and performance in school.
(g) Medical issues.
(h) Possible delinquency.
(i) Visitation.
(j) Possible involvement in the child welfare system.
(k) Other pertinent information.
(Added by Stats. 2000, Ch. 965, Sec. 1. Effective January 1, 2001.)
7442.
(a) The purpose of the review of local agency records, in a representative sample of California counties, is to obtain outcome information about the status of a sample of the children of incarcerated parents and their caregivers.
(b) Women prisoners who participate in the survey sample of state prisoners shall provide written permission allowing the California Research Bureau access to their children's records in regard to school performance, identity of the caretaker responsible for the child, child protective services records, public assistance records, juvenile justice records, and medical records including drug or alcohol use, and mental health. The California Research Bureau shall follow appropriate procedures to ensure confidentiality of the records and to protect the privacy of the survey participants and their children.
(c) County agencies, including members of multidisciplinary teams, and school districts shall permit the California Research Bureau to have reasonable access to records, pursuant to subdivision (b), to the extent permitted by federal law.
(d) Notwithstanding Section 10850 of the Welfare and Institutions Code, the survey required by this section is deemed to meet the research criteria identified in paragraph (3) of subdivision (c) of Section 11845.5 of the Health and Safety Code, and subdivision (e) of Section 5328 of the Welfare and Institutions Code. For purposes of this study, the research is deemed not to be harmful for the at-risk and vulnerable population of children of women prisoners.
(e) For purposes of the study only, the California Research Bureau is authorized to survey records, reports, and documents described in Section 827 and in paragraph (3) of subdivision (h) of Section 18986.4 of the Welfare and Institutions Code, and information relative to the incidence of child abuse, as provided by Section 11167, among children in the study sample.
(f) School districts shall permit reasonable access to directory information by the California Research Bureau for purposes of this study. The California Research Bureau is deemed an appropriate organization to conduct studies for legitimate educational interests, including improving instruction, for purposes of paragraph (4) of subdivision (b) of Section 4906 of the Education Code. School variables that the California Research Bureau shall survey shall include, but not be limited to, attendance patterns, truancy rates, achievement level, suspension and expulsion rates, and special education referrals.
(Amended by Stats. 2014, Ch. 71, Sec. 131. (SB 1304) Effective January 1, 2015.)
7443.

The California Research Bureau shall follow appropriate procedures to ensure confidentiality of the records and to protect the privacy of the survey participants and their children, and participating agencies. Data compiled from case files shall be coded under an assigned number and not identified by name. Survey questionnaires and coding forms shall be exempt from the public disclosure requirements prescribed by Chapter 3.4 (commencing with Section 6250) of Division 7 of Title 1 of the Government Code.
(Added by Stats. 2000, Ch. 965, Sec. 1. Effective January 1, 2001.)
7444.
The California Research Bureau shall convene an advisory group to assist in designing and administering the study.
(Added by Stats. 2000, Ch. 965, Sec. 1. Effective January 1, 2001.)
7445.
The California Research Bureau shall submit a report to the Legislature on or before January 1, 2003, analyzing the findings of its research, upon completion of the study.
(a) Of the funds identified in provision (2) of Item 6120-011-0001 of the 2000-01 State Budget, forty thousand dollars ($40,000) shall be made available, in consultation with the Assembly Rules Committee, to be used for the purposes of this act, including, but not limited to, contracts for outside researchers.
(b) Members of the advisory group convened pursuant to Section 7444 of the Penal Code, shall not receive compensation for their services but shall be reimbursed for travel and per diem expenses incurred while assisting in designing and administering the study required by this act. These expenses may be paid from the forty thousand dollars ($40,000) made available in subdivision (a).
(Added by Stats. 2000, Ch. 965, Sec. 1. Effective January 1, 2001.)

TITLE 8. MEDICAL TESTING OF PRISONERS [7500 - 7554]

(Title 8 added by Stats. 1988, Ch. 1579, Sec. 2.)

CHAPTER 1. General Provisions [7500 - 7505]

(Chapter 1 added by Stats. 1988, Ch. 1579, Sec. 2.)
7500.
The Legislature finds and declares all of the following:
(a) The public peace, health, and safety is endangered by the spread of the human immunodeficiency virus (HIV), acquired immunodeficiency syndrome (AIDS), and hepatitis B and C within state and local correctional institutions.
(b) The spread of AIDS and hepatitis B and C within prison and jail populations presents a grave danger to inmates within those populations, law enforcement personnel, and other persons in contact with a prisoner infected with the HIV virus as well as hepatitis B and C, both during and after the prisoner's confinement. Law enforcement personnel and prisoners are particularly vulnerable to this danger, due to the high number of assaults, violent acts, and transmissions of bodily fluids that occur within correctional institutions.
(c) HIV, as well as hepatitis B and C, have the potential of spreading more rapidly within the closed society of correctional institutions than outside these institutions. These major public health problems are compounded by the further potential of the rapid spread of communicable disease outside correctional institutions through contacts of an infected prisoner who is not treated and monitored upon his or her release, or by law enforcement employees who are unknowingly infected.
(d) New diseases of epidemic proportions such as AIDS may suddenly and tragically infect large numbers of people. This title primarily addresses a current problem of this nature, the spread of HIV, as well as hepatitis B and C, among those in correctional institutions and among the people of California.
(e) HIV, AIDS, and hepatitis B and C pose a major threat to the public health and safety of those governmental employees and others whose responsibilities bring them into direct contact with persons afflicted with those illnesses, and the protection of the health and safety of these personnel is of equal importance to the people of the State of California as the protection of the health of those afflicted with the diseases who are held in custodial situations.
(f) Testing described in this title of individuals housed within state and local correctional facilities for evidence of infection by HIV and hepatitis B and C would help to provide a level of information necessary for effective disease control within these institutions and would help to preserve the health of public employees, inmates, and persons in custody, as well as that of the public at large. This testing is not intended to be, and shall not be construed as, a prototypical method of disease control for the public at large.
(Amended by Stats. 2006, Ch. 800, Sec. 1. Effective January 1, 2007.)
7501.
In order to address the public health crisis described in Section 7500, it is the intent of the Legislature to do all of the following:
(a) Establish a procedure through which custodial and law enforcement personnel are required to report certain situations and may request and be granted a confidential test for HIV or for hepatitis B or C of an inmate convicted of a crime, or a person arrested or taken into custody, if the custodial or law enforcement officer has reason to believe that he or she has come into contact with the blood or semen of an inmate or in any other manner has come into contact with the inmate in a way that could result in HIV infection, or the transmission of hepatitis B or C, based on the latest determinations and conclusions by the federal Centers for Disease Control and Prevention and the State Department of Public Health on means for the transmission of AIDS or hepatitis B and C, and if appropriate medical authorities, as provided in this title, reasonably believe there is good medical reason for the test.
(b) Permit inmates to file similar requests stemming from contacts with other inmates.
(c) Require that probation and parole officers be notified when an inmate being released from incarceration is infected with AIDS or hepatitis B or C, and permit these officers to notify certain persons who will come into contact with the parolee or probationer, if authorized by law.
(d) Authorize prison medical staff authorities to require tests of a jail or prison inmate under certain circumstances, if they reasonably believe, based upon the existence of supporting evidence, that the inmate may be suffering from HIV infection or AIDS or hepatitis B or C and is a danger to other inmates or staff.
(e) Require supervisory and medical personnel of correctional institutions to which this title applies to notify staff if they are coming into close and direct contact with persons in custody who have tested positive or who have AIDS or hepatitis B or C, and provide appropriate counseling and safety equipment.
(Amended by Stats. 2007, Ch. 483, Sec. 44. Effective January 1, 2008.)
7502.
As used in this title, the following terms shall have the following meanings:
(a) "Correctional institution" means any state prison, county jail, city jail, Division of Juvenile Justice facility, county- or city-operated juvenile facility, including juvenile halls, camps, or schools, or any other state or local correctional institution, including a court facility.

(b) "Counseling" means counseling by a licensed physician and surgeon, registered nurse, or other health professional who meets guidelines which shall be established by the State Department of Public Health for purposes of providing counseling on AIDS and hepatitis B and C to inmates, persons in custody, and other persons pursuant to this title.

(c) "Law enforcement employee" means correctional officers, peace officers, and other staff of a correctional institution, California Highway Patrol officers, county sheriff's deputies, city police officers, parole officers, probation officers, and city, county, or state employees including but not limited to, judges, bailiffs, court personnel, prosecutors and staff, and public defenders and staff, who, as part of the judicial process involving an inmate of a correctional institution, or a person charged with a crime, including a minor charged with an offense for which he or she may be made a ward of the court under Section 602 of the Welfare and Institutions Code, are engaged in the custody, transportation, prosecution, representation, or care of these persons.

(d) "AIDS" means acquired immune deficiency syndrome.

(e) "Human immunodeficiency virus" or "HIV" means the etiologic virus of AIDS.

(f) "HIV test" or "HIV testing" means any clinical laboratory test approved by the federal Food and Drug Administration for HIV, component of HIV, or antibodies to HIV.

(g) "Inmate" means any of the following:

(1) A person in a state prison, or city and county jail, who has been either convicted of a crime or arrested or taken into custody, whether or not he or she has been charged with a crime.

(2) Any person in a Division of Juvenile Justice facility, or county- or city-operated juvenile facility, who has committed an act, or been charged with committing an act specified in Section 602 of the Welfare and Institutions Code.

(h) "Bodily fluids" means blood, semen, or any other bodily fluid identified by either the federal Centers for Disease Control and Prevention or State Department of Public Health in appropriate regulations as capable of transmitting HIV or hepatitis B or C.

(i) "Minor" means a person under 15 years of age.

(Amended by Stats. 2007, Ch. 483, Sec. 45. Effective January 1, 2008.)

7503.

The Department of Corrections, the Department of the Youth Authority, and county health officers shall adopt guidelines permitting a chief medical officer to delegate his or her medical responsibilities under this title to other qualified physicians and surgeons, and his or her nonmedical responsibilities to other qualified persons, as appropriate. The chief medical officer shall not, however, delegate the duty to determine whether mandatory testing is required as provided for in Chapter 2 (commencing with Section 7510) except to another qualified physician designated to act as chief medical officer in the chief medical officer's absence.

(Amended by Stats. 2004, Ch. 953, Sec. 2. Effective September 30, 2004.)

7504.

Actions taken pursuant to this title shall not be subject to subdivisions (a) to (c), inclusive, of Section 120980 of the Health and Safety Code. In addition, the requirements of subdivision (a) of Section 120990 of the Health and Safety Code, shall not apply to testing performed pursuant to this title.

(Amended by Stats. 1996, Ch. 1023, Sec. 397. Effective September 29, 1996.)

7505.

This title is intended to provide the authority for state and local correctional, custodial, and law enforcement agencies to perform medical testing of inmates and prisoners for the purposes specified herein. However, notwithstanding any other provision of this title, this title shall serve as authority for the HIV testing of prisoners in only those local facilities where the governing body has adopted a resolution affirming that it shall be operative in that city, county, or city and county. Testing within state correctional facilities under the jurisdiction of the Department of Corrections and state juvenile facilities under the jurisdiction of the Department of the Youth Authority shall not be affected by this requirement.

(Amended by Stats. 1996, Ch. 1107, Sec. 4. Effective January 1, 1997.)

CHAPTER 2. Procedures for Requiring HIV Testing [7510 - 7519]

(Chapter 2 added by Stats. 1988, Ch. 1579, Sec. 2.)

7510.

(a) A law enforcement employee who believes that he or she came into contact with bodily fluids of either an inmate of a correctional institution, a person not in a correctional institution who has been arrested or taken into custody whether or not the person has been charged with a crime, including a person detained for or charged with an offense for which he or she may be made a ward of the court under Section 602 of the Welfare and Institutions Code, a person charged with any crime, whether or not the person is in custody, on postrelease community supervision, mandatory supervision pursuant to paragraph (5) of subdivision (h) of Section 1170, or on probation or parole due to conviction of a crime, shall report the incident through the completion of a form provided by the State Department of Public Health. The form shall be directed to the chief medical officer, as defined in subdivision (c), who serves the applicable law enforcement employee. Utilizing this form the law enforcement employee may request a test for HIV or hepatitis B or C of the person who is the subject of the report. The forms may be combined with regular incident reports or other forms used by the correctional institution or law enforcement agency, however the processing of a form by the chief medical officer containing a request for HIV or hepatitis B or C testing of the subject person shall not be delayed by the processing of other reports or forms.

(b) The report required by subdivision (a) shall be submitted by the end of the law enforcement employee's shift during which the incident occurred, or if not practicable, as soon as possible, but no longer than two days after the incident, except that the chief medical officer may waive this filing period requirement if he or she finds that good cause exists. The report shall include names of witnesses to the incident, names of persons involved in the incident, and if feasible, any written statements from these parties. The law enforcement employee shall assist in the investigation of the incident, as requested by the chief medical officer.

(c) For purposes of this section, Section 7503, and Section 7511, "chief medical officer" means:

(1) In the case of a report filed by a staff member of a state prison, the chief medical officer of that facility.

(2) In the case of a parole officer filing a report, the chief medical officer of the nearest state prison.

(3) In the case of a report filed by an employee of the Division of Juvenile Justice, the chief medical officer of the facility.

(4) In the case of a report filed against a subject who is an inmate of a city or county jail or a county- or city-operated juvenile facility, or a court facility, or who has been arrested or taken into custody whether or not the person has been charged with a crime, but who is not in a correctional facility, including a person detained for, or charged with, an offense for which he or she may be made a ward of the court under Section 602 of the Welfare and Institutions Code, or a person charged with a crime, whether or not the person is in custody, the county health officer of the county in which the individual is jailed or charged with the crime.

(5) In the case of a report filed by a probation officer, a prosecutor or staff person, a public defender attorney or staff person, the county health officer of the county in which

the probation officer, prosecutor or staff person, a public defender attorney or staff person, is employed.

(6) In any instance where the chief medical officer, as determined pursuant to this subdivision, is not a physician and surgeon, the chief medical officer shall designate a physician and surgeon to perform his or her duties under this title.

(Amended by Stats. 2012, Ch. 43, Sec. 57. (SB 1023) Effective June 27, 2012.)

7511.

(a) The chief medical officer shall, regardless of whether a report filed pursuant to Section 7510 contains a request for HIV or hepatitis B or C testing, decide whether or not to require HIV or hepatitis B or C testing of the inmate or other person who is the subject of the report filed pursuant to Section 7510, within 24 hours of receipt of the report. If the chief medical officer decides to require HIV or hepatitis B or C testing, he or she shall specify in his or her decision the circumstances, if any, under which followup testing will also be required.

(b) The chief medical officer shall order an HIV or hepatitis B or C test only if he or she finds that, considering all of the facts and circumstances, there is a significant risk that HIV or hepatitis B or C was transmitted. In making this decision, the chief medical officer shall take the following factors into consideration:

(1) Whether an exchange of bodily fluids occurred which could have resulted in a significant risk of AIDS or hepatitis B or C infection, based on the latest written guidelines and standards established by the federal Centers for Disease Control and Prevention and the State Department of Health Services.

(2) Whether the person exhibits medical conditions or clinical findings consistent with HIV or hepatitis B or C infection.

(3) Whether the health of the institution staff or inmates may have been endangered as to HIV or hepatitis B or C infection resulting from the reported incident.

(c) Prior to reaching a decision, the chief medical officer may if needed receive written or oral testimony from the law enforcement employee filing the report, from the subject of the report, and from witnesses to the incident, as he or she deems necessary for a complete investigation. The decision shall be in writing and shall state the reasons for the decision. A copy shall be provided by the chief medical officer to the law enforcement employee who filed the report and to the subject of the report, and where the subject is a minor, to the parents or guardian of the minor, unless the parent or guardian of the minor cannot be located.

(Amended by Stats. 2006, Ch. 800, Sec. 5. Effective January 1, 2007.)

7512.

(a) An inmate of a correctional institution may request testing for HIV or hepatitis B or C of another inmate of that institution if he or she has reason to believe that he or she has come into contact with the bodily fluids of that inmate, in situations, which may include, but are not limited to, rape or sexual contact with a potentially infected inmate, tattoo- or drug-needle sharing, an incident involving injury in which bodily fluids are exchanged, or confinement with a cellmate under circumstances involving possible mingling of bodily fluids. A request may be filed under this section only within two calendar days of the date when the incident causing the request occurred, except that the chief medical officer may waive this filing period requirement when he or she finds that good cause exists.

(b) An inmate in a Division of Juvenile Justice facility or any county- or city-operated juvenile facility who is 15 years of age or older may file a request for a test of another inmate in that facility, in the same manner as an inmate in a state prison, and is subject to the same procedures and rights. An inmate in a Division of Juvenile Justice facility or a county- or city-operated juvenile facility who is a minor may file a request for testing through a staff member of the facility in which he or she is confined. A staff member may file this request on behalf of a minor on his or her own volition if he or she believes that a situation meeting the criteria specified in subdivision (a) has occurred warranting the request. The filing of a request by staff on behalf of an inmate of a Division of Juvenile Justice facility or a local juvenile facility shall be within two calendar days of its discovery by staff, except that the chief medical officer may waive this filing period requirement if he or she finds that good cause exists.

When a request is filed on behalf of a minor, the facility shall notify the parent or guardian of the minor of the request and seek permission from the parent or guardian for the test request to proceed. If the parent or guardian refuses to grant permission for the test, the Director of the Division of Juvenile Facilities may request the juvenile court in the county in which the facility is located, to rule on whether the test request procedure set forth in this title shall continue. The juvenile court shall make a ruling within five days of the case being brought before the court.

If the parent or guardian cannot be located, the superintendent of the facility shall approve or disapprove the request for a test.

(c) Upon receipt of a request for testing as provided in this section, a law enforcement employee shall submit the request to the chief medical officer, the identity of which shall be determined as if the request had been made by an employee of the facility. The chief medical officer shall follow the procedures set forth in Section 7511 with respect to investigating the request and reaching a decision as to mandatory testing of the inmate who is the subject of the request. The inmate submitting the request shall provide names or testimony of witnesses within the limits of his or her ability to do so. The chief medical officer shall make his or her decision based on the criteria set forth in Section 7511. A copy of the chief medical officer's decision shall be provided to the person submitting the request for HIV or hepatitis B or C testing, to the subject of the request, and to the superintendent of the correctional institution. In the case of a minor, a copy of the decision shall be provided to the parents or guardian of the minor, unless the parent or guardian of the minor cannot be located.

(Amended by Stats. 2006, Ch. 800, Sec. 6. Effective January 1, 2007.)

7512.5.

In the absence of the filing of a report pursuant to Section 7510 or a request pursuant to Section 7512, the chief medical officer may order a test of an inmate if he or she concludes there are clinical symptoms of HIV infection, AIDS, or hepatitis B or C, as recognized by the federal Centers for Disease Control and Prevention or the State Department of Health Services.

A copy of the decision shall be provided to the inmate, and where the inmate is a minor, to the parents or guardian of the minor, unless the parent or guardian of the minor cannot be located. Any decision made pursuant to this section shall not be appealable to a three-member panel provided for under Section 7515.

(Amended by Stats. 2006, Ch. 800, Sec. 7. Effective January 1, 2007.)

7513.

An inmate who is the subject of an HIV or hepatitis B or C test report filed pursuant to Section 7510 or an HIV or hepatitis B or C test report filed pursuant to Section 7512 shall receive, in conjunction with the decision of the chief medical officer to order a test, a copy of this title, a written description of the right to appeal the chief medical officer's decision which includes the applicable timelines, and notification of his or her right to receive pretest and posttest HIV counseling by staff that have been certified as HIV test counselors or to receive hepatitis B or C test results and counseling from a licensed medical professional.

(Amended by Stats. 2006, Ch. 800, Sec. 8. Effective January 1, 2007.)

7514.

(a) It shall be the chief medical officer's responsibility to see that personal counseling is provided to a law enforcement employee filing a report pursuant to Section 7510, an inmate filing a request pursuant to Section 7512, and any potential test subject, at the time the initial report or request for tests is made, at the time when tests are ordered, and at the time when test results are provided to the employee, inmate, or test subject.

(b) The chief medical officer may provide additional counseling to any of these individuals, upon his or her request, or whenever the chief medical officer deems advisable, and may arrange for the counseling to be provided in other jurisdictions. The chief medical officer shall encourage the subject of the report or request, the law enforcement employee who filed the report, the person who filed the request pursuant to Section 7512, or in the case of a minor, the minor on whose behalf the request was filed, to undergo voluntary HIV or hepatitis B or C testing if the chief medical officer deems it medically advisable. All testing required by this title or any voluntary testing resulting from the provisions of this title, shall be at the expense of the appropriate correctional institution.
(Amended by Stats. 2006, Ch. 800, Sec. 9. Effective January 1, 2007.)
7515.
(a) A decision of the chief medical officer made pursuant to Section 7511, 7512, or 7516 may be appealed, within three calendar days of receipt of the decision, to a three-person panel, either by the person required to be tested, his or her parent or guardian when the subject is a minor, the law enforcement employee filing a report pursuant to either Section 7510 or 7516, or the person requesting testing pursuant to Section 7512, whichever is applicable, or the chief medical officer, upon his or her own motion. If no request for appeal is filed under this subdivision, the chief medical officer's decision shall be final.
(b) Depending upon which entity has jurisdiction over the person requesting or appealing a test, the Department of Corrections and Rehabilitation, the Division of Juvenile Justice, the county, the city, or the county and city shall convene the appeal panel and shall ensure that the appeal is heard within seven calendar days.
(c) A panel required pursuant to subdivision (a) or (b) shall consist of three members, as follows:
(1) The chief medical officer making the original decision.
(2) A physician and surgeon who has knowledge in the diagnosis, treatment, and transmission of HIV or hepatitis B and C, selected by the Department of Corrections and Rehabilitation, the Division of Juvenile Justice, the county, the city, or the county and city. The physician and surgeon appointed pursuant to this paragraph shall preside at the hearing and serve as chairperson.
(3) A physician and surgeon not on the staff of, or under contract with, a state, county, city, or county and city correctional institution or with an employer of a law enforcement employee as defined in subdivision (b) of Section 7502, and who has knowledge of the diagnosis, treatment, and transmission of HIV or hepatitis B and C. The physician and surgeon appointed pursuant to this paragraph shall be selected by the State Department of Health Services from a list of persons to be compiled by that department. The State Department of Health Services shall adopt standards for selecting persons for the list required by this paragraph, as well as for their reimbursement, and shall, to the extent possible, utilize its normal process for selecting consultants in compiling this list. The Legislature finds and declares that the presence of a physician and surgeon on the panel who is selected by the State Department of Health Services enhances the objectivity of the panel, and it is the intent of the Legislature that the State Department of Health Services make every attempt to comply with this subdivision.
(d) The Department of Corrections and Rehabilitation, the county, the city, or the county and city shall notify the Office of AIDS in the State Department of Health Services when a panel must be convened under subdivision (a) wherein HIV testing has been requested or the State Department of Health Services when a test for hepatitis B or C has been requested. Within two calendar days of the notification, a physician and surgeon appointed under paragraph (3) of subdivision (c) shall reach agreement with the Department of Corrections, the county, the city, or the county and city on a date for the hearing that complies with subdivision (b).
(e) If the Office of AIDS in the State Department of Health Services or, in the case of a hepatitis B or C test, the State Department of Health Services, fails to comply with subdivision (d) or the physician and surgeon appointed under paragraph (3) of subdivision (c) fails to attend the scheduled hearing, the Department of Corrections and Rehabilitation, the county, the city, or the county and city shall appoint a physician and surgeon who has knowledge of the diagnosis, treatment, and transmission of HIV and hepatitis B and C to serve on the appeals panel to replace the physician and surgeon required under paragraph (3) of subdivision (c). The Department of Corrections and Rehabilitation, the county, the city, or the county and city shall have standards for selecting persons under this subdivision and for their reimbursement.
The Department of Corrections and Rehabilitation, the Division of Juvenile Justice, the county, the city, or the county and city shall, whenever feasible, create, and utilize ongoing panels to hear appeals under this section. The membership of the panel shall meet the requirements of paragraphs (1), (2), and (3) of subdivision (c).
No panel shall be created pursuant to this paragraph by a county, city, or county and city correctional institution except with the prior approval of the local health officer.
(f) A hearing conducted pursuant to this section shall be closed, except that each of the following persons shall have the right to attend the hearing, speak on the issues presented at the hearing, and call witnesses to testify at the hearing:
(1) The chief medical officer, who may also bring staff essential to the hearing, as well as the other two members of the panel.
(2) The subject of the chief medical officer's decision, except that a subject who is a minor may attend only with the consent of his or her parent or guardian and, if the subject is a minor, his or her parent or guardian.
(3) The law enforcement employee filing the report pursuant to Section 7510, or the person requesting HIV or hepatitis B or C testing pursuant to Section 7512, whichever is applicable and, if the person is a minor, his or her parent or guardian.
(g) The subject of the test, or the person requesting the test pursuant to Section 7512, or who filed the report pursuant to Section 7510, whichever is applicable, may appoint a representative to attend the hearing in order to assist him or her.
(h) When a hearing is sought pursuant to this section, or filed by a law enforcement employee pursuant to a request made under Section 7510, the decision shall be rendered within two days of the hearing. A unanimous vote of the panel shall be necessary in order to require that the subject of the hearing undergo HIV or hepatitis B or C testing.
The criteria specified in Section 7511 for use by the chief medical officer shall also be utilized by the panel in making its decision.
The decision shall be in writing, stating reasons for the decision, and shall be signed by the members. A copy shall be provided by the chief medical officer to the person requesting the test, or filing the report, whichever is applicable, to the subject of the test, and, when the subject is in a correctional institution, to the superintendent of the institution, except that, when the subject of the test or the person upon whose behalf the request for the test was made is a minor, copies shall also be provided to the parent or guardian of the minor, unless the parent or guardian cannot be located.
(Amended by Stats. 2006, Ch. 800, Sec. 10. Effective January 1, 2007.)
7516.
(a) When a custodial officer or staff person of a correctional institution, observes or is informed of activity in a correctional institution that is classified as causing, or known to cause, the transmission of the AIDS virus, as described in subdivision (b), he or she may file a written report with the facility's chief medical officer which, in the case of city or county jails, shall be the county health officer.
(b) Reportable activities within a correctional institution for which a report may be filed pursuant to subdivision (a) include, but are not limited to, all of the following activities, if they could result in the transmission of AIDS, according to the standards provided for in this chapter:
(1) Sexual activity resulting in exchange of bodily fluids.

(2) IV drug use.
(3) Incidents involving injury to inmates or staff in which bodily fluids are exchanged.
(4) Tampering with medical and food supplies or medical or food equipment.
(5) Tattooing among inmates.
(c) The medical officer may investigate the report, conduct interviews, and determine whether the situation reported caused the probable exchange of body fluids in a manner that could result in the transmission of HIV, utilizing the criteria set forth in Section 7511, and pose a danger to the health and safety of the institution's staff and inmate population.
If the chief medical officer concludes this may have occurred, he or she shall require HIV testing of any inmate which he or she deems necessary pursuant to the investigation. Whenever an inmate is required to undergo an HIV test pursuant to this subdivision, he or she may appeal that decision as provided for in Section 7515.
(d) Testing under this section may only be required by a unanimous vote of all three members of the panel. The rights guaranteed inmates under Section 7515 shall apply. When a hearing is convened pursuant to this section, the hearing shall be closed, except that both the person filing the original report and the chief medical officer as well as other panel members may also call witnesses to testify at the hearing.
When a hearing is sought pursuant to this section, the decision shall be rendered within 20 days of the date the hearing is sought by the medical officer.
(e) This section shall apply to situations involving individual inmates or group situations but shall not be utilized to require testing of all inmates in a correctional institution.
(f) The findings of the panel shall be set forth in writing, including reasons for the panel's decision, and shall be signed by the members of the panel. A copy of the decision shall be provided to the superintendent of the correctional institution, the subjects of the report and to any inmates or officers whom the panel concludes may have been exposed to HIV infection as established by provisions of this title.
(Added by Stats. 1988, Ch. 1579, Sec. 2. Effective September 30, 1988.)
7516.5.
Any decision by a panel pursuant to Section 7515 or 7516 may be appealed to the superior court, either by a law enforcement employee filing a report pursuant to Section 7510, a person requesting an HIV test pursuant to Section 7512, a medical officer convening a panel pursuant to Section 7516, or any person required to be tested pursuant to a panel's decision. A person required to be tested pursuant to Section 7512.5 may also appeal the decision to the superior court.
The court shall schedule a hearing as expeditiously as possible to review the decision of the panel or a decision made pursuant to Section 7512.5. The court shall uphold the decision being appealed if that decision is based upon substantial evidence.
(Added by Stats. 1988, Ch. 1579, Sec. 2. Effective September 30, 1988.)
7516.8.
It shall be the responsibility of the chief medical officer to see that copies of the hearing decision are distributed in accordance with requirements of this chapter.
(Added by Stats. 1988, Ch. 1579, Sec. 2. Effective September 30, 1988.)
7517.
Except as otherwise permitted by this title or any provision of law, any records, including decisions of a chief medical officer or an appeals panel, compiled pursuant to this chapter shall be confidential.
(Added by Stats. 1988, Ch. 1579, Sec. 2. Effective September 30, 1988.)
7518.
(a) The Department of Corrections and Rehabilitation and local health officers shall adopt guidelines for the making of decisions pursuant to this chapter in consultation with the Office of AIDS in the State Department of Health Services for HIV testing and with the State Department of Health Services for hepatitis B and C testing. The guidelines shall be based on the latest written guidelines of HIV or hepatitis B and C transmission and infection established by the federal Centers for Disease Control and Prevention and the State Department of Health Services.
(b) Oversight responsibility for implementation of the applicable provisions of this title, including the oversight of reports involving parole officers and the staff of state adult and youth correctional facilities shall be vested with the Chief of Medical Services in the Department of Corrections and Rehabilitation.
Oversight responsibility at the county, the city, or the county and city level shall rest with the local health officer.
(Amended by Stats. 2006, Ch. 800, Sec. 11. Effective January 1, 2007.)
7519.
(a) When an individual, including a minor charged with an offense for which he or she may be made a ward of the court under Section 602 of the Welfare and Institutions Code, has either been charged with a crime, but is not being held in a correctional institution due to his or her release, either through the granting of bail, a release on the individual's own recognizance, or for any other reason, or been convicted of a crime, but not held in a correctional institution due to the imposition of probation, a fine, or any other alternative sentence, and the individual is required to undergo initial or followup testing pursuant to this title, the failure of the individual to submit to the test may be grounds for revocation of the individual's release or probation or other sentence, whichever is applicable.
(b) Any refusal by a person on parole, probation, mandatory supervision pursuant to paragraph (5) of subdivision (h) of Section 1170, or postrelease community supervision to submit to testing required pursuant to this title may be ruled as a violation of the person's parole, probation, mandatory supervision, or postrelease community supervision.
(Amended by Stats. 2012, Ch. 43, Sec. 58. (SB 1023) Effective June 27, 2012.)

CHAPTER 3. Notification Requirement [7520 - 7523]

(Chapter 3 added by Stats. 1988, Ch. 1579, Sec. 2.)
7520.
(a) Upon the release of an inmate from a correctional institution, a medical representative of the institution shall notify the inmate's parole or probation officer, where it is the case, that the inmate has tested positive for infection with HIV, or has been diagnosed as having AIDS or hepatitis B and C. The representative of the correctional institution shall obtain the latest available medical information concerning any precautions which should be taken under the circumstances, and shall convey that information to the parole or probation officer.
(b) When a parole or probation officer learns from responsible medical authorities that a person on parole, probation, mandatory supervision pursuant to paragraph (5) of subdivision (h) of Section 1170, or postrelease community supervision under his or her jurisdiction has AIDS or has tested positive for HIV infection, or hepatitis B or C, the parole or probation officer shall be responsible for ensuring that the parolee or probationer contacts the county health department in order to be, or through his or her own physician and surgeon is, made aware of counseling and treatment for AIDS or hepatitis B or C, as appropriate commensurate with that available to the general population of that county.
(Amended by Stats. 2012, Ch. 43, Sec. 59. (SB 1023) Effective June 27, 2012.)
7521.
(a) When a parole or probation officer learns from responsible medical authorities that a supervised person in his or her custody has any of the conditions listed in Section 7520,

but that the supervised person has not properly informed his or her spouse, the officer may ensure that this information is relayed to the spouse only through either the chief medical officer of the institution from which the person was released or the physician and surgeon treating the spouse or the supervised person. The parole or probation officer shall seek to ensure that proper counseling accompanies release of this information to the spouse, through the person providing the information to the inmate's spouse.

(b) If a parole or probation officer has received information from appropriate medical authorities that one of his or her supervised persons is HIV infected or has AIDS or hepatitis B or C, and the supervised person has a record of assault on a peace officer, and the officer seeks the aid of local law enforcement officers to apprehend or take into custody the supervised person, he or she shall inform the officers assisting him or her in apprehending or taking into custody the supervised person, of the person's condition, to aid them in protecting themselves from contracting AIDS or hepatitis B or C.

(c) Local law enforcement officers receiving information pursuant to this subdivision shall maintain confidentiality of information received pursuant to subdivision (b). Willful use or disclosure of this information is a misdemeanor. Parole or probation officers who willfully or negligently disclose information about AIDS or hepatitis B or C infection, other than as prescribed under this title or any other provision of law, shall also be guilty of a misdemeanor.

(d) For purposes of this section, "supervised person" means a person on parole, probation, mandatory supervision pursuant to paragraph (5) of subdivision (h) of Section 1170, or postrelease community supervision.

(Amended by Stats. 2012, Ch. 43, Sec. 60. (SB 1023) Effective June 27, 2012.)
7522.
(a) Supervisory and medical personnel in correctional institutions shall notify all law enforcement employees when those employees have had direct contact with the bodily fluids of inmates or persons charged or in custody who either have tested positive for infection with HIV, or been diagnosed as having AIDS or hepatitis B or C.

(b) Supervisory and medical personnel at correctional institutions shall provide to employees covered by this section the latest medical information regarding precautions to be taken under the circumstances, and shall furnish proper protective clothing and other necessary protective devices or equipment, and instruct staff on the applicability of this title.

(c) The law enforcement employee who reported an incident pursuant to Section 7510 shall be notified of the results of any test administered to any person as a result of the reporting.

(Amended by Stats. 2006, Ch. 800, Sec. 14. Effective January 1, 2007.)
7523.
Information obtained by a law enforcement employee pursuant to this chapter shall be confidential, and shall not be disclosed except as specifically authorized by this chapter. Information obtained by a member of a panel pursuant to Section 7515 or 7516 shall not be disclosed except as authorized by this title.

(Added by Stats. 1988, Ch. 1579, Sec. 2. Effective September 30, 1988.)

CHAPTER 4. Testing Procedures [7530 - 7531]

(Chapter 4 added by Stats. 1988, Ch. 1579, Sec. 2.)
7530.
The following procedures shall apply to testing conducted under this title:
(a) The withdrawal of blood shall be performed in a medically approved manner. Only a physician, registered nurse, licensed vocational nurse, licensed medical technician, or licensed phlebotomist may withdraw blood specimens for the purposes of this title.

(b) The chief medical officer, as specified in Chapter 2 (commencing with Section 7510), shall order that the blood specimens be transmitted to a licensed medical laboratory which has been approved by the State Department of Health Services for the conducting of HIV testing, and that tests including all readily available confirmatory tests be conducted thereon for medically accepted indications of exposure to or infection with HIV. The State Department of Health Services shall adopt standards for the approval of medical laboratories for the conducting of HIV testing under this title. The State Department of Health Services shall adopt standards for the conducting of tests under Section 7530. Testing for hepatitis B or C may be conducted by any licensed medical laboratory approved by the chief medical officer.

(c) Copies of the test results shall be sent by the laboratory to the chief medical officer who made the decision under either Section 7511 or 7512 or who convened the panel under Section 7515 or 7516. The laboratory shall be responsible for protecting the confidentiality of these test results. Willful or negligent breach of this responsibility shall be grounds for a violation of the contract.

(d) The test results shall be sent by the chief medical officer to the designated recipients with the following disclaimer:
"The tests were conducted in a medically approved manner but tests cannot determine exposure to or infection by AIDS or other communicable diseases with absolute accuracy. Persons receiving this test result should continue to monitor their own health and should consult a physician as appropriate."

(e) If the person subject to the test is a minor, copies of the test result shall also be sent to the minor's parents or guardian.

(f) All persons, other than the test subject, who receive test results shall maintain the confidentiality of personal identifying data relating to the test results, except for disclosure which may be necessary to obtain medical or psychological care or advice, or to comply with this title.

(g) The specimens and the results of the tests shall not be admissible evidence in any criminal or disciplinary proceeding.

(h) Any person performing testing, transmitting test results, or disclosing information in accordance with this title shall be immune from civil liability for any action undertaken in accordance with this title.

(Amended by Stats. 2006, Ch. 800, Sec. 15. Effective January 1, 2007.)
7531.
Notwithstanding any other provision of law, no positive test results obtained pursuant to this title shall be disclosed to any person unless the initial positive test result has been confirmed by appropriate confirmatory tests for positive reactors.

(Added by Stats. 1988, Ch. 1579, Sec. 2. Effective September 30, 1988.)

CHAPTER 5. Penalties [7540- 7540.]

(Chapter 5 added by Stats. 1988, Ch. 1579, Sec. 2.)
7540.
A person committing any of the following acts shall be guilty of a misdemeanor:
(a) Willful false reporting in conjunction with a report or a request for testing under this title.

(b) Willful use or disclosure of test results or confidential information in violation of any of the provisions of this title.

(Added by Stats. 1988, Ch. 1579, Sec. 2. Effective September 30, 1988.)

CHAPTER 6. Miscellaneous Provisions [7550 - 7554]

(Chapter 6 added by Stats. 1988, Ch. 1579, Sec. 2.)
7550.
The State Department of Health Services shall prepare standardized forms for the reports, notices, and findings required by this title, and distribute these forms to the Department of Corrections, the Department of the Youth Authority, and to each county health officer within three months of the effective date of this title.
(Added by Stats. 1988, Ch. 1579, Sec. 2. Effective September 30, 1988.)
7551.
A correctional, custodial, or law enforcement agency to which this title applies shall be responsible for informing staff of the provisions of this title, and assisting in its implementation as it applies to the respective agency.
(Added by Stats. 1988, Ch. 1579, Sec. 2. Effective September 30, 1988.)
7552.
(a) It is recommended that every city or county correctional, custodial, and law enforcement agency to which this title applies have a comprehensive AIDS and HIV prevention and education program in operation by March 31, 1989. Recommended goals for the programs include all of the following:
(1) Education. Implementation of an educational plan which includes education and training for officers, support staff, and inmates on the prevention and transmission of HIV, with regular updates, at least every three months, with all persons held in custody for at least 12 hours in a correctional institution being provided at least with a pamphlet approved by the county health officer, and more detailed education for persons kept beyond three days.
(2) Body fluid precautions. Because all bodily fluids are considered as potentially infectious, supplying all employees of correctional institutions with the necessary equipment and supplies to follow accepted universal bodily fluids precautions, including gloves and devices to administer cardiopulmonary resuscitation, when dealing with infected persons or those in high-risk groups for HIV or hepatitis B or C.
(3) Separate housing for infected individuals. Making available adequate separate housing facilities for housing inmates who have tested positive for HIV infection and who continue to engage in activities which transmit HIV, with facilities comparable to those of other inmates with access to recreational and educational facilities, commensurate with the facilities available in the correctional institution.
(4) Adequate AIDS medical services. The provision of medical services appropriate for the diagnosis and treatment of HIV infection.
(5) These guidelines are advisory only and do not constitute a state mandate.
(b) The program shall require confidentiality of information in accordance with this title and other provisions of law.
(c) The Corrections Standards Authority and the State Department of Health Services shall assist in developing the programs.
(Amended by Stats. 2006, Ch. 800, Sec. 16. Effective January 1, 2007.)
7553.
With the approval of the county health officer, the State Department of Health Services, as it deems necessary for HIV detection and prevention, may conduct periodic anonymous unlinked serologic surveys of all or portions of the inmate population or persons under custody within a city or county.
(Added by Stats. 1988, Ch. 1579, Sec. 2. Effective September 30, 1988.)
7554.
(a) The purpose of this section is to establish the extent of peace officers' occupational exposure for HIV infection.
(b) The correctional, custodial, or law enforcement agency to which this title applies or the chief medical officer of a correctional, custodial, or law enforcement agency to which this title applies shall report each reportable incident involving a law enforcement employee under this title together with the disposition of each case to the State Department of Health Services.
The report shall include all of the following: the assignment of the law enforcement employee; the type of incident; the type of injury sustained; the treatment rendered to the injured employee; citations to criminal laws which were allegedly violated; and the identity of the employing agency. Under no circumstances shall the identity of the law enforcement employee or the source person be transmitted by the local law enforcement agency or the chief medical officer of the local agency to the State Department of Health Services.
(c) The State Department of Health Services shall release the data, upon written request, to any law enforcement agency or to any bona fide, nonprofit law enforcement research body primarily concerned with peace officer health issues, provided that the identity of any law enforcement employee, any person who is the subject of a report, or any tested person under this title shall remain anonymous. Any unauthorized release of information leading to the identity of a person whose identity is protected under this section shall constitute a misdemeanor.
(d) For purposes of this section, a "reportable incident" means an incident described in subdivision (a) of Section 7510. A "source person" means a person whose bodily fluids are believed to have contacted the bodily fluids of a law enforcement employee as described in subdivision (a) of Section 7510.
(Amended by Stats. 1992, Ch. 713, Sec. 26. Effective September 15, 1992.)

TITLE 8.7. EXAMINATION OF INMATES AND WARDS FOR TUBERCULOSIS [7570 - 7576]

(Title 8.7 repealed (comm. with Section 7580) and added by Stats. 1993, Ch. 932, Sec. 9.)
7570.
In enacting this chapter, the Legislature hereby finds and declares that tuberculosis is a serious contagious disease. It is vital to the health and safety of inmates, employees, and the public at large, to conduct appropriate examinations, testing, and treatment in order to control the spread of tuberculosis in California's institutions.
(Added by Stats. 1993, Ch. 932, Sec. 9. Effective October 8, 1993.)
7571.
For purposes of this title, the following definitions shall apply:
(a) "Chief medical officer" means the chief medical officer or acting chief medical officer of a state prison or any facility under the jurisdiction of the Department of Corrections or the Department of the Youth Authority.
(b) "Inmate or ward" means any person incarcerated within the jurisdiction of the Department of Corrections or the Department of the Youth Authority, with the exception of a person on parole.
(c) "Institution" means any state prison, camp, center, office, or other facility under the jurisdiction of the Department of Corrections or the Department of the Youth Authority.
(d) "Examination, test, or treatment" means methods, processes, or other means, including medical evaluations, testing, followup examinations, or treatment, in accordance with the recommendations of the Centers for Disease Control and Prevention and as specified in the guidelines for tuberculosis control of the Department of Corrections and the Department of the Youth Authority.

(e) "Medical evaluation" means taking a history or gathering other information and may include, but is not limited to, listening to the chest or other examinations or tests as specified in the guidelines for tuberculosis control of the Department of Corrections and the Department of the Youth Authority.

(f) "Department" means the Department of Corrections and the Department of the Youth Authority.

(g) "Chief of medical services" means the medical officer, acting medical officer, or designee responsible for all medical services of the Department of Corrections or the Department of the Youth authority.

(Added by Stats. 1993, Ch. 932, Sec. 9. Effective October 8, 1993.)

7572.

The chief of medical services, or his or her designee, shall use every available means to ascertain the existence of, and to immediately investigate all reported or suspected cases of, tuberculosis in the infectious stages and to ascertain the source or sources of the infections. In carrying out these investigations, the chief of medical services, or his or her designee, is hereby invested with full powers of inspection, examination, and quarantine or isolation of all inmates or wards known to be, or reasonably suspected to be, infected with tuberculosis in an infectious stage.

(Added by Stats. 1993, Ch. 932, Sec. 9. Effective October 8, 1993.)

7573.

(a) The chief medical officer shall order an inmate or ward to receive an examination or test, or may order an inmate or ward to receive treatment if the medical officer has a reasonable suspicion that the inmate or ward has, has had, or has been exposed to tuberculosis in an infectious stage and the chief medical officer has reasonable grounds to believe that it is necessary for the preservation and protection of staff and inmates or wards.

(b) The chief medical officer shall ensure that examinations or tests for tuberculosis on all inmates or wards are conducted upon incarceration and at least annually thereafter.

(Added by Stats. 1993, Ch. 932, Sec. 9. Effective October 8, 1993.)

7574.

Notwithstanding Section 2600 or 2601, or any other provision of law, any inmate or ward who refuses to submit to an examination, test, or treatment for tuberculosis as described in Section 7572 or 7573, or who refuses treatment for tuberculosis, or who, after notice, violates, or refuses or neglects to conform to, any rule, order, guideline, or regulation prescribed by the department with regard to tuberculosis control shall be tested involuntarily and may be treated involuntarily. This inmate or ward shall be subject to disciplinary action as described in Title 15 of the California Code of Regulations.

(Added by Stats. 1993, Ch. 932, Sec. 9. Effective October 8, 1993.)

7575.

To provide effective control of the spread of tuberculosis in institutions and to identify those among the inmate and ward populations with tuberculosis, the Department of Corrections shall operate pursuant to guidelines developed in consultation with the State Department of Health Services, which shall be adopted on or before July 1, 1994. The guidelines shall include, but not be limited to, establishing a reporting system which emphasizes standardized, uniform data collection, reporting, and assessment, as specified in Section 7576.

(Added by Stats. 1993, Ch. 932, Sec. 9. Effective October 8, 1993.)

7576.

(a) The Department of Corrections, the Department of the Youth Authority, the Board of Prison Terms, and the Youthful Offender Parole Board shall compile information through each department's respective reporting systems for individual institutions and each respective department as a whole and shall provide the results to the State Department of Health Services annually. The information reported shall consist of the following:

(1) Prevalence rates and conversion rates (tuberculin incidence) for tuberculosis infection for inmates or wards and staff in each institution.

(2) Case numbers and case rates for tuberculosis disease for inmates or wards in each institution.

(b) Subject to additional staffing resources provided through the state budget process, the departments described in subdivision (a) shall also compile the following information for individual institutions and each respective department as a whole and shall provide the results to the State Department of Health Services annually:

(1) Percentage of inmates and wards with tuberculosis disease who complete the prescribed course of directly observed curative therapy in accordance with the Centers for Disease Control and Prevention recommendations and as specified in the department's guidelines for tuberculosis control.

(2) Percentage of inmates and wards with culture positive sputum that convert to culture negative in accordance with the Centers for Disease Control and Prevention recommendations and as specified in the department's guidelines for tuberculosis control.

(3) Percentage of inmates and wards with tuberculosis who complete the prescribed INH (isoniazid) or other appropriate directly observed preventive therapy in accordance with the Centers for Disease Control and Prevention recommendations and as specified in the department's guidelines for tuberculosis control.

(Added by Stats. 1993, Ch. 932, Sec. 9. Effective October 8, 1993.)

TITLE 9. PUNISHMENT OPTIONS [8000 - 9003]

(Heading of Title 9 amended by Stats. 1994, 1st Ex. Sess., Ch. 41, Sec. 2.)

CHAPTER 1. Programs With Special Focus on Substance Abuse [8000 - 8002]

(Chapter 1 heading added by Stats. 1994, 1st Ex. Sess., Ch. 41, Sec. 3.)

8000.

The Legislature finds and declares that the existence of live-in alternative to incarceration rehabilitation programs with special focus on substance abusers provide a useful alternative to incarceration and promotes the resumption of useful lives by persons with impairments caused by drug or alcohol abuse, or persons with criminal records who, because of these impairments, cannot be absorbed into the competitive labor market, or who otherwise have little or no chance of rehabilitation.

(Added by Stats. 1990, Ch. 398, Sec. 1.)

8001.

For purposes of this title, a live-in alternative to incarceration rehabilitation program with special focus on substance abusers means any long-term (two-year minimum) private, nonprofit program that has operated and complied with the following conditions for at least five years prior to the effective date of this section:

(a) Participants live full time at the program site and receive room and board, and all necessary support at no cost to the participant.

(b) All necessary support shall include reasonable medical, dental, psychological, and legal services, counseling, entertainment, clothing, academic, life-skills, and interpersonal education, vocational training, rehabilitation, transportation, and recreation activities.

(c) Neither the directors nor the officers of the program shall be compensated in any manner other than the manner in which the participants of the program are compensated.

(d) The program shall not be operated with any public funds.

(Added by Stats. 1990, Ch. 398, Sec. 1.)

8002.

Notwithstanding any other provision of law, the participants, director, and staff of a live-in alternative to incarceration rehabilitation program with special focus on substance abusers, when participating in operations owned and operated by the program, are exempt from the wage and hour provisions and Section 1025 of the Labor Code, so long as all revenues generated by the operation are used for the support of the program. All providers who bid on public work shall include in their bid the prevailing wage rate as required by the request.

(Added by Stats. 1990, Ch. 398, Sec. 1.)

CHAPTER 2. Community-Based Punishment Act [8050 - 8093]

(Chapter 2 added by Stats. 1994, 1st Ex. Sess., Ch. 41, Sec. 4.)

ARTICLE 1. General Provisions [8050 - 8052]

(Article 1 added by Stats. 1994, 1st Ex. Sess., Ch. 41, Sec. 4.)

8050.

This chapter shall be known and may be cited as the Community-Based Punishment Act of 1994.

(Added by Stats. 1994, 1st Ex. Sess., Ch. 41, Sec. 4. Effective November 30, 1994.)

8051.

The Legislature hereby finds and declares as follows:

(a) Community-based punishment programs require a partnership between the state and local government to provide and expand the use of intermediate sanctions for specifically targeted offender populations.

(b) Community-based programs must operate to punish offenders while at the same time providing opportunities to change behavior.

(c) Community-based punishment programs provide appropriate means of managing select offenders but should not be viewed as the only solution to prison overcrowding.

(d) Community-based punishment programs target prison-bound and jail-bound nonviolent offenders because this group poses the least risk to the public and is the most amenable to the individualized programming and services offered by community-based programs.

(e) Community-based punishment programs emphasize reducing local jail populations, thereby making jail space available for new commitments, parole violators, and probation violators who are now being sent to jail and nonviolent felons who have already been sent to prison for short periods of time.

(f) Community-based punishment programs must be financed from a consistent, reliable, and separate funding source.

(g) Community-based punishment programs should be expanded incrementally with a variety of pilot approaches tested to determine their effectiveness prior to expansion.

(h) In order to effectively utilize available resources, to ensure appropriate management of the local offender population, each county utilizing community-based punishment programs must implement a locally coordinated planning process.

(i) Since successful community-based punishment programs are dependent on the coordinated efforts of, and successful working relationships between, state and local agencies, the Board of Corrections is the logical state agency to coordinate community punishment efforts because of its extensive experience with collaborative state and local programs.

(Added by Stats. 1994, 1st Ex. Sess., Ch. 41, Sec. 4. Effective November 30, 1994.)

8052.

As used in this chapter, the following definitions shall apply:

(a) "Board" means the Board of Corrections, unless otherwise indicated.

(b) "Chief correctional administrator" means the sheriff, chief probation officer, or director of the county department of corrections, who is designated by the board of supervisors to have administrative responsibility for county corrections operations and programs, including a community-based punishment program.

(c) "Community-based punishment" means a partnership between the state and a county or a collaboration of counties to manage and provide correctional services, especially those services considered to be intermediate sanctions at the local level of government for targeted, select offender populations pursuant to the community corrections plan of a county or a collaboration of counties.

(d) "Community-based punishment plan" means the proposal for a community-based punishment program promulgated by a county or a collaboration of counties that has been developed by the chief correctional administrator, in cooperation with the district attorney, public defender, and other concerned community representatives designated by the board of supervisors, to address correctional needs in that county or collaboration of counties.

(e) "Intermediate sanctions" means punishment options and sanctions other than simple incarceration in prison or jail or traditional routine probation supervision. Intermediate sanctions may be provided by correctional agencies directly or through community-based public or private correctional service providers, and include, but are not limited to, the following:

(1) Short-term "shock" incarceration in either jail or prison, for a period of not more than 60 days.

(2) Incarceration in a "boot camp" facility.

(3) Intensive supervision.

(4) Home detention with electronic monitoring.

(5) Mandatory community service.

(6) Restorative justice programs such as mandatory victim restitution and victim-offender reconciliation.

(7) Work, training, or education in a furlough program pursuant to Section 1208.

(8) Work, in lieu of confinement, in a work release program pursuant to Section 4024.2.

(9) Day reporting.

(10) Mandatory residential or nonresidential substance abuse treatment programs established pursuant to Chapter 9.4 (commencing with Section 6240) of Title 7.

(11) Mandatory random drug testing.

(12) Mother-infant care programs.

(13) Community-based residential programs offering structure, supervision, drug treatment, alcohol treatment, literacy programming, employment counseling, psychological counseling, or any combination of these and other interventions.

(f) "Nonviolent offender" means a person who is not currently charged with a violent crime, as defined in Section 667.5, does not have a criminal record that includes a violent crime, meets the National Institute of Corrections (NIC) Model Classification System guidelines for classification as a nonviolent offender, and does not pose a risk to the community, as determined by the correctional administrator.

(Added by Stats. 1994, 1st Ex. Sess., Ch. 41, Sec. 4. Effective November 30, 1994.)

ARTICLE 2. State Administration [8060 - 8061]

(Article 2 added by Stats. 1994, 1st Ex. Sess., Ch. 41, Sec. 4.)

8060.

This chapter shall be administered by the board. The board shall be responsible for ensuring that the policies and activities undertaken by state or local governmental units, or other organizations, in furtherance of the purposes of this chapter, are consistent with those purposes.
(Added by Stats. 1994, 1st Ex. Sess., Ch. 41, Sec. 4. Effective November 30, 1994.)
8061.
The board, in collaboration with state, local, and community-based departments, agencies, and organizations shall do the following:
(a) Describe the parameters of effective community-based punishment programs and the relationship between the state and local jurisdictions in meeting the purposes of this chapter.
(b) Develop and implement a process by which local jurisdictions are selected and can participate in pilot efforts initiated under this chapter.
(c) Develop and implement the process by which counties participating in accordance with this chapter annually submit their community-based punishment program proposals for approval, modification, or both.
(d) Design and implement a process for annually awarding funds to counties participating pursuant to this chapter to implement their community-based punishment program proposals, and administer and monitor the receipt, expenditure, and reporting of those funds by participating counties.
(e) Provide technical assistance and support to counties and community correctional administrators in determining whether to participate in community-based punishment programs, and in either developing or annually updating their punishment programs.
(f) Facilitate the sharing of information among counties and between county and state agencies relative to community-based punishment approaches and programs being initiated or already in existence, strengths and weaknesses of specific programs, specific offender groups appropriate for different programs, results of program evaluations and other data, and anecdotal material that may assist in addressing the purposes of this chapter.
(g) Adopt and periodically revise regulations necessary to implement this chapter.
(h) Design and provide for regular and rigorous evaluation of the community-based punishment programming undertaken pursuant to approved community-based punishment plans.
(i) Design and provide for analysis and evaluation of the pilot and any subsequent implementation of this chapter, with areas of analysis to include, at a minimum, the following:
(1) The relationship between the board and counties or collaborations of counties submitting county community-based punishment plans.
(2) The effectiveness of this chapter in encouraging the use of intermediate as well as traditional sanctions.
(3) The categories of offenders most suitable for specific intermediate sanctions, various aspects of community-based punishment programming, or both.
(4) The effectiveness of the programs implemented pursuant to this chapter in maintaining public safety.
(5) The cost-effectiveness of the programs implemented pursuant to this chapter.
(6) The effect of the programs implemented pursuant to this chapter on prison, jail, and Department of the Youth Authority populations.
(Amended by Stats. 2012, Ch. 728, Sec. 130. (SB 71) Effective January 1, 2013.)

ARTICLE 3. Community-Based Punishment Plan [8080- 8080.]
(Article 3 added by Stats. 1994, 1st Ex. Sess., Ch. 41, Sec. 4.)
8080.
Each county or collaboration of counties electing to operate a community-based punishment program under this chapter shall develop a community-based punishment plan describing the continuum of sanctions and services comprising its program. The plan shall be developed pursuant to guidelines established by the board and shall be updated annually or as determined by the board. The plan shall describe, at a minimum, the following:
(a) System design and administration, lines of authority, and responsible personnel, including, but not limited to, the chief correctional administrator and other relevant individuals.
(b) The extent and nature of citizen involvement in the development and promulgation of the community-based punishment plan, including, but not limited to, the following:
(1) Consultation with a citizens' advisory committee formed for the purpose of providing community input into the development and promulgation of a community-based punishment plan.
(2) Consultation with selected community leaders.
(3) Input derived from citizen testimony at public hearings or town hall meetings.
(c) The number and kind of offenders to participate in community-based punishment programs.
(d) Eligibility requirements.
(e) How offenders, including those coming from the courts and those who are probation and parole violators, are to be selected to participate.
(f) Community-based punishment program components, including, for example, which punishment options, intermediate sanctions, treatment options, or combinations are to be developed and used for which offenders.
(g) Responsibilities and relationships, including, but not limited to, the elements of community-based punishment programs that are administered by the sheriff's department, the probation department, or parole personnel, and when and how offenders are to be programmed.
(h) Criteria for transferring offenders from more restrictive to less restrictive sanctions.
(i) Criteria for disciplinary interventions, imposition of stricter sanctions, or return to prison or jail, when necessary.
(j) Anticipated costs and funding needs.
(Added by Stats. 1994, 1st Ex. Sess., Ch. 41, Sec. 4. Effective November 30, 1994.)

ARTICLE 4. Funding [8090 - 8093]
(Article 4 added by Stats. 1994, 1st Ex. Sess., Ch. 41, Sec. 4.)
8090.
Implementation of this chapter pursuant to Section 8060 is contingent upon the availability of funding. Funding for community-based punishment programs shall be administered by the board from funds appropriated by the Legislature. In addition to state funds appropriated in the annual Budget Act or other legislation, programs may be funded from a variety of sources, including, but not limited to, the following:
(a) Federal funds for community-based punishment programs.
(b) Private or corporate grants, or both.
(c) Service and administrative fees that may be charged to offenders who participate in community corrections programs, provided that no offender shall be denied entrance into a community-based punishment program solely for inability to pay fees.
(d) Income derived from community development corporations established as part of community-based punishment programs of a county or collaboration of counties, including, but not limited to, revenue generated by businesses owned and operated by community-based punishment programs, or by offender work programs, or by both, after the cost of operating and administering the business or work program has been paid.
(e) Other sources as may be identified as suitable for funding community corrections.
It is the intent of the Legislature that community corrections reduce the number of offenders who would be incarcerated in the state prison in the absence of a community-based punishment approach.
(Added by Stats. 1994, 1st Ex. Sess., Ch. 41, Sec. 4. Effective November 30, 1994.)

8091.
(a) From the amount of money appropriated for purposes of this chapter to the board, the board shall allocate block grants to counties or collaborations of counties that have passed a community corrections resolution, have applied for funding, and have complied with the administrative process as prescribed by the board.
(b) Each county or collaboration of counties shall maintain a complete and accurate accounting of all funds received pursuant to this section. These funds shall be used only for community-based punishment programs as authorized by this chapter and shall be used only as permitted by the regulations and guidelines established by the board.
(c) Unexpended funds provided to counties shall be returned to the board and may be reallocated by the board.
(Added by Stats. 1994, 1st Ex. Sess., Ch. 41, Sec. 4. Effective November 30, 1994.)
8092.
The board, in collaboration with its member and constituent agencies and departments, shall seek startup funding for community-based punishment planning and programming from public and private sources commencing as soon as practicable.
(Added by Stats. 1994, 1st Ex. Sess., Ch. 41, Sec. 4. Effective November 30, 1994.)
8093.
The board shall monitor the expenditures and funds of participating counties and collaborations of counties to determine whether the funds are being expended in accordance with all the requirements of this chapter. If the board finds that a participating county or collaboration of counties is not acting in accordance with all of the requirements of this chapter, it shall notify the county or collaboration of counties regarding the points of noncompliance, and the county or collaboration of counties shall have 60 days to explain or justify its actions in writing to the board. If the explanation is not satisfactory or if the point of noncompliance cannot be promptly cured in the opinion of the board, the board may issue a notice of noncompliance and may suspend payment of the funds to be allocated to the county or collaboration of counties under this chapter.
(Added by Stats. 1994, 1st Ex. Sess., Ch. 41, Sec. 4. Effective November 30, 1994.)

CHAPTER 3. Sex Offender Management Board [9000 - 9003]

(Chapter 3 added by Stats. 2006, Ch. 338, Sec. 1.)
9000.
As used in this chapter, the following definitions apply:
(a) "Board" means the Sex Offender Management Board created in this chapter.
(b) "Sex Offender" means any person who is required to register as a sex offender under Section 290 of the Penal Code.
(c) "Treatment" means a set of specialized interventions delivered by qualified mental health professionals and designed to address the multiple psychological and physiological factors found to be associated with sexual offending.
(d) "Management" means a comprehensive and collaborative team approach to regulating, controlling, monitoring, and otherwise influencing the current and, insofar as is possible, the future behavior of sex offenders who are living in the community and are directly under the authority of the criminal justice system or of another governmental agency performing similar functions. The overriding purpose of management of sex offenders is to enhance community safety by preventing future sexual victimization. Management includes supervision and specialized treatment as well as a variety of other interventions.
(e) "Supervision" means a specialized approach to the process of overseeing, insofar as authority to do so is granted to the supervising agency, all significant aspects of the lives of sex offenders who are being managed, as described in subdivision (d). This approach includes traditional methods as well as techniques and tools specifically designed to respond to the risks to community safety raised by sex offenders. Supervision is one component of management.
(Added by Stats. 2006, Ch. 338, Sec. 1. Effective September 20, 2006.)
9001.
(a) The Sex Offender Management Board which is hereby created under the jurisdiction of the Department of Corrections and Rehabilitation, shall consist of 17 members. The membership of the board shall reflect, to the extent possible, representation of northern, central, and southern California as well as both urban and rural areas. Each appointee to the board, regardless of the appointing authority, shall have the following characteristics:
(1) Substantial prior knowledge of issues related to sex offenders, at least insofar as related to his or her own agency's practices.
(2) Decisionmaking authority for, or direct access to those who have decisionmaking authority for, the agency or constituency he or she represents.
(3) A willingness to serve on the board and a commitment to contribute to the board's work.
(b) The membership of the board shall consist of the following persons:
(1) State government agencies:
(A) The Attorney General or his or her designee who shall be an authority in policy areas pertaining to sex offenders and shall have expertise in dealing with sex offender registration, notification, and enforcement.
(B) The Secretary of the Department of Corrections and Rehabilitation or his or her designee who has expertise in parole policies and practices.
(C) The Director of Adult Parole Services or his or her designee.
(D) One California state judge, appointed by the Judicial Council.
(E) The Director of State Hospitals or his or her designee who is a licensed mental health professional with recognized expertise in the treatment of sex offenders.
(2) Local government agencies:
(A) Three members who represent law enforcement, appointed by the Governor. One member shall possess investigative expertise and one member shall have law enforcement duties that include registration and notification responsibilities, and one shall be a chief probation officer.
(B) One member who represents prosecuting attorneys, appointed by the Senate Committee on Rules. He or she shall have expertise in dealing with adult sex offenders.
(C) One member who represents probation officers, appointed by the Speaker of the Assembly.
(D) One member who represents criminal defense attorneys, appointed by the Speaker of the Assembly.
(E) One member who is a county administrator, appointed by the Governor.
(F) One member who is a city manager or his or her designee, appointed by the Speaker of the Assembly.
(3) Nongovernmental agencies:
(A) Two members who are licensed mental health professionals with recognized experience in working with sex offenders and who can represent, through their established involvement in a formal statewide professional organization, those who provide evaluation and treatment for adult sex offenders, appointed by the Senate Committee on Rules.
(B) Two members who are recognized experts in the field of sexual assault and represent sexual assault victims, both adults and children, and rape crisis centers, appointed by the Governor.

(c) The board shall appoint a chair from among the members appointed pursuant to subdivision (b). The chair shall serve in that capacity at the pleasure of the board.
(d) Each member of the board who is appointed pursuant to this section shall serve without compensation.
(e) If a board member is unable to adequately perform his or her duties or is unable to attend more than three meetings in a single 12-month period, he or she is subject to removal from the board by a majority vote of the full board.
(f) Any vacancies on the board as a result of the removal of a member shall be filled by the appointing authority of the removed member within 30 days of the vacancy.
(g) The board may create, at its discretion, subcommittees or task forces to address specific issues. These may include board members as well as invited experts and other participants.
(h) The board shall hire a coordinator who has relevant experience in policy research. The board may hire other staff as funding permits.
(i) In the course of performing its duties, the board shall, when possible, make use of the available resources of research agencies such as the Legislative Analyst's Office, the California Research Bureau, the California State University system, including schools of public policy and criminology, and other similar sources of assistance.
(j) Staff support services for the board shall be provided by staff of the Department of Corrections and Rehabilitation as directed by the secretary.
(Amended by Stats. 2012, Ch. 440, Sec. 38. (AB 1488) Effective September 22, 2012.)
9002.
(a) The board shall address any issues, concerns, and problems related to the community management of sex offenders. The main objective of the board, which shall be used to guide the board in prioritizing resources and use of time, is to achieve safer communities by reducing victimization.
(b) The board shall conduct public hearings, as it deems necessary, to provide opportunities for gathering information and receiving input regarding the work of the board from concerned stakeholders and the public.
(c) The members of the board shall be immune from liability for good faith conduct under this chapter.
(Amended by Stats. 2017, Ch. 541, Sec. 15. (SB 384) Effective January 1, 2018.)
9003.
(a) On or before July 1, 2011, the board shall develop and update standards for certification of sex offender management professionals. All those professionals who provide sex offender management programs and risk assessments, pursuant to Section 290.09, shall be certified by the board according to these standards. The standards shall be published on the board's Internet Web site. Professionals may apply to the board for certification on or after August 1, 2011.
(1) (A) The board shall submit to the Department of Justice fingerprint images and related information required by the Department of Justice of all sex offender management applicants, as defined by subdivision (a), for the purposes of obtaining information as to the existence and content of a record of state or federal convictions and state or federal arrests and also information as to the existence and content of a record of state arrests or federal arrests for which the Department of Justice establishes that the person is free on bail or on his or her own recognizance pending trial or appeal.
(B) When received, the Department of Justice shall forward to the Federal Bureau of Investigation requests for federal summary criminal history information received pursuant to this section. The Department of Justice shall review the information returned from the Federal Bureau of Investigation and compile and disseminate a response to the board.
(C) The Department of Justice shall provide a state and federal response to the board pursuant to paragraph (1) of subdivision (l) of Section 11105.
(D) The board shall request from the Department of Justice subsequent arrest notification service, as provided pursuant to Section 11105.2, for persons described in subdivision (a).
(2) The board shall require any person who applies for certification under this section to submit information relevant to the applicant's fitness to provide sex offender management services. Any person who knowingly provides false information under this paragraph shall be subject to a civil penalty in an amount up to one thousand five hundred dollars ($1,500), in addition to any other remedies available to the board. An action for a civil penalty under this provision may be brought by any public prosecutor in the name of the people of the State of California.
(3) The board shall assess a fee to the applicant not to exceed one hundred eighty dollars ($180) per application. The board shall pay a fee to the Department of Justice sufficient to cover the cost of processing the criminal background request specified in this section.
(b) On or before July 1, 2011, the board shall develop and update standards for certification of sex offender management programs, which shall include treatment, as specified, and dynamic and future violence risk assessments pursuant to Section 290.09. The standards shall be published on the board's Internet Web site. All those programs shall include polygraph examinations by a certified polygraph examiner, which shall be conducted as needed during the period that the offender is in the sex offender management program. Only certified sex offender management professionals whose programs meet the standards set by the board are eligible to provide sex offender management programs pursuant to Section 290.09.
(c) Certified sex offender management professionals, who provide sex offender management programs and risk assessments pursuant to Section 290.09, shall not be held civilly liable for any criminal acts committed by the persons on parole, probation, or judicial commitment status who receive supervision or treatment. This waiver of liability shall apply to certified sex offender management professionals, administrators of the programs provided by those professionals, and to agencies or persons under contract to those professionals who provide screening, clinical evaluation, risk assessment, supervision, or treatment to sex offender parolees, probationers, or persons on conditional release pursuant to Article 4 (commencing with Section 6600) of Chapter 2 of Part 2 of Division 6 of the Welfare and Institutions Code.
(d) On or before July 1, 2011, the board shall develop and update standards for certification of polygraph examiners. The standards shall be published on the board's Internet Web site.
(Amended by Stats. 2011, Ch. 357, Sec. 7. (AB 813) Effective January 1, 2012.)

TITLE 10. GENERAL PROVISIONS [10000 – 10007]

(Title 10 added by Stats. 1941, Ch. 106.)
10000.
The provisions of Part 3 (commencing with Section 2000), insofar as they are substantially the same as existing provisions relating to the same subject matter, shall be construed as restatements and continuations thereof and not as new enactments.
(Amended by Stats. 1987, Ch. 828, Sec. 167.)
10001.
All persons who, at the time this act goes into effect, hold office under any of the acts repealed by this act, which offices are continued by this act, continue to hold the same according to the former tenure thereof.
(Added by Stats. 1941, Ch. 106.)
10002.

No action or proceeding commenced before this act takes effect, and no right accrued, is affected by the provisions of this act, but all procedure thereafter taken therein shall conform to the provisions of this act so far as possible.
(Added by Stats. 1941, Ch. 106.)
10003.
If any portion of Part 3 (commencing with Section 2000) is held unconstitutional, that decision shall not affect the validity of any other portion of Part 3 (commencing with Section 2000).
(Amended by Stats. 1987, Ch. 828, Sec. 168.)
10004.
Division, chapter, article, and section headings contained herein shall not be deemed to govern, limit, modify or in any manner affect the scope, meaning or intent of the provisions of any division, chapter, article or section hereof.
(Added by Stats. 1941, Ch. 106.)
10005.
Whenever, by the provisions of this act, a power is granted to a public officer or a duty imposed upon such an officer, the power may be exercised or the duty performed by a deputy of the officer or by a person authorized pursuant to law by the officer.
(Added by Stats. 1941, Ch. 106.)
10006.
(a) The Department of the Youth Authority and local juvenile halls and camps are prohibited from allowing a minor detained in any institution or facility under their respective jurisdiction to view a videotape or movie shown by the institution or facility that contains harmful matter, as specified in Chapter 7.6 (commencing with Section 313) of Title 9 of Part 1.
(b) The Department of Corrections, the Department of the Youth Authority, county juvenile halls and camps, and local adult detention facilities may promulgate regulations regarding the showing of videotapes and movies at any institution or facility under their respective jurisdiction in order to provide for the reasonable security of the institution or facility in which a minor or adult is confined and for the reasonable protection of the public consistent with Section 2600.
(Added by Stats. 1994, Ch. 323, Sec. 1. Effective January 1, 1995.)
10007.
The Department of Corrections and Rehabilitation may use portable or temporary buildings to provide rehabilitation, treatment, and educational services to inmates within its custody, or to house inmates, as long as that housing does not jeopardize inmate or staff safety.
(Added by Stats. 2007, Ch. 7, Sec. 23. Effective May 3, 2007.)

PART 4. PREVENTION OF CRIMES AND APPREHENSION OF CRIMINALS [11006 – 14315]

(Part 4 added by Stats. 1953, Ch. 1385.)

TITLE 1. INVESTIGATION AND CONTROL OF CRIMES AND CRIMINALS [11006 – 11482]

(Title 1 added by Stats. 1953, Ch. 1385.)

CHAPTER 1. Investigation, Identification, and Information Responsibilities of the Department of Justice [11006 – 11144]

(Heading of Chapter 1 amended by Stats. 1972, Ch. 1377.)
ARTICLE 1. Administration [11006 – 11010]
(Article 1 added by Stats. 1953, Ch. 1385.)
11006.
The Attorney General shall appoint such agents and other employees as he deems necessary to carry out the provisions of this chapter.
All persons employed after July 1, 1973, within the Department of Justice designated as peace officers and performing investigative duties shall be required by the department to obtain a certificate from the Commission on Peace Officer Standards and Training.
(Amended by Stats. 1973, Ch. 557.)
11008.
The Attorney General shall from time to time arrange for and organize schools at convenient centers in the State to train peace officers in their powers and duties and in the use of approved equipment and methods for detection, identification and apprehension of criminals.
(Added by Stats. 1953, Ch. 1385.)
11010.
(a) The Department of Justice shall adopt standards and guidelines regarding the handling of potential evidence arising out of the testing of substances that are suspected to be related to activities of terrorists, to be used by laboratories operated by or contracting with the Department of Justice, any state agency, or any local agency, and by any other laboratory in the state the department determines may test any material that may become evidence in a criminal prosecution for any crime committed in the commission of terrorist activities.
(b) The standards and guidelines adopted pursuant to this section shall include information on issues that may arise in the chain of custody and the employment of controls that are suitable for preserving evidence for use in the prosecution of a crime.
(c) In developing the standards for adoption pursuant to this section, the Department of Justice shall consult with appropriate laboratories of public agencies used by law enforcement agencies, law enforcement agencies, and the State Department of Health Services.
(d) The Department of Justice shall make the guidelines and standards adopted pursuant to this section available to the appropriate laboratories specified in subdivision (a).
(e) The provisions of this section shall be accomplished to the extent that funds are available.
(Added by Stats. 2002, Ch. 125, Sec. 1. Effective July 9, 2002.)
ARTICLE 2. Criminal Investigation [11050 – 11055]
(Article 2 added by Stats. 1953, Ch. 1385.)
11050.
In any crime of statewide importance, the Attorney General may, upon the request of any district attorney, sheriff or chief of police, assign to such officer so requesting, an investigator or investigators for the investigation or detection of crimes, and the apprehension or prosecution of criminals.
(Amended by Stats. 1972, Ch. 1377.)
11050.5.

(a) The Attorney General may, upon the request of any district attorney, sheriff, chief of police, or other local, state or federal law enforcement official, make available to such official so requesting, the department's laboratory facilities and personnel and the department's technical experts, including but not limited to such personnel as fingerprint examiners, criminalists, document examiners and intelligence specialists for the purpose of assisting in the investigation of criminal matters, the detection of crimes and the apprehension or prosecution of criminals.

(b) The Attorney General may, upon the request of any public defender or private defense counsel appointed by the court, make available to such public defender or such private appointed counsel, the department's laboratory facilities and personnel and the department's technical experts, including but not limited to such personnel as fingerprint examiners, criminalists, document examiners and intelligence specialists for the purpose of assisting in the representation by such public defender or private appointed counsel of persons in criminal proceedings. The Attorney General may contract with each county whose public defender or such private appointed counsel makes requests pursuant to this subdivision for the payment of the reasonable costs of time and material in making available information, services or facilities pursuant to this subdivision. No information, services or facilities shall be made available to such public defender or private appointed counsel unless the county so contracts with the Attorney General.

(c) A copy of any information, including the results of any analysis, furnished by the Attorney General to a public defender, or private defense counsel appointed by the court, pursuant to subdivision (b) shall be sent to the district attorney of the county in which the public defender is located. If this subdivision or its application to any person or circumstance is invalid, subdivision (b) shall not be operative.

(d) The Department of Justice may charge a fee for the laboratory services it performs.
(Amended by Stats. 1978, Ch. 1135.)

11051.
The Department of Justice shall perform duties in the investigation, detection, apprehension, prosecution or suppression of crimes as may be assigned by the Attorney General in the performance of his or her duties under Article V, Section 13 of the Constitution.
(Amended by Stats. 2002, Ch. 787, Sec. 27. Effective January 1, 2003.)

11052.
For the purpose of carrying out the provisions of this chapter, the investigators shall have all the powers conferred by law upon any peace officer of this State.
(Added by Stats. 1953, Ch. 1385.)

11053.
After the effective date of this chapter, and thereafter until the Governor finds and proclaims that an emergency no longer exists in preparing for the national defense, or whenever the United States is engaged in war, or whenever a war emergency has been declared to exist by the President of the United States, the Attorney General may appoint for the duration of the war or emergency, as the case may be, such additional special criminal investigators not to exceed nine in number as he deems necessary to carry out the provisions of this chapter. There shall not be more than 15 such investigators employed at any one time. The employment of such investigators shall terminate not later than 90 days after the conclusion of peace or the official termination of the emergency by the President or the Governor.
(Added by Stats. 1953, Ch. 1385.)

11054.
No investigation of the acts or conduct of any state agency or state official shall be initiated or made through or by the bureau or any employee thereof, without the authorization of the Attorney General particularly specifying the office, department or person to be investigated and the scope and purposes of the investigation.
(Added by Stats. 1953, Ch. 1385.)

11055.
(a) There is within the Department of Justice the Foreign Prosecution and Law Enforcement Unit designated with the responsibility for assisting local law enforcement agencies with foreign prosecutions, child abduction recoveries and returns under the Hague Convention on the Civil Aspects of International Child Abduction, and law enforcement investigative matters. The unit is also responsible for assisting local law enforcement in obtaining information from foreign officials on foreign prosecution matters.

(b) The Foreign Prosecution and Law Enforcement Unit shall do all of the following:
(1) For those countries having extraterritorial jurisdiction allowing for the prosecution of their citizens for crimes committed in California, the unit shall, upon request, provide informational assistance to local law enforcement on foreign prosecution protocols and provide technical assistance in preparing investigative materials for forwarding and filing in international jurisdictions. The unit shall provide information and assistance on the scope and uses of foreign prosecution to California prosecutors and law enforcement agencies. The unit shall be responsible for tracking foreign prosecution cases presented by California law enforcement agencies. The unit shall collect information on a statewide basis regarding foreign prosecution cases for the primary purpose of analyzing the information it collects and disseminating its conclusions to local law enforcement agencies. Local law enforcement agencies shall retain the authority to prepare and present foreign prosecution cases without the assistance of the unit.
(2) The unit shall assist district attorneys in recovering children from Mexico, and, where appropriate, other countries either in court-ordered returns pursuant to the Hague Convention or voluntary returns.
(3) The unit shall, upon request, assist local law enforcement agencies and foreign law enforcement in formal requests under the Mutual Legal Assistance Treaty. The unit shall, upon request, also assist California law enforcement agencies and foreign officials in informal requests for mutual legal assistance.
(4) The unit, under the direction of the Attorney General, shall provide information to local law enforcement on sensitive diplomatic issues.
(Amended by Stats. 2005, Ch. 22, Sec. 151. Effective January 1, 2006.)

ARTICLE 2.3. California Criminalistics Institute [11060 - 11062]
(Article 2.3 added by Stats. 1986, Ch. 1040, Sec. 1.)

11060.
There is hereby established in the Bureau of Forensic Services of the Department of Justice the California Criminalistics Institute.
The purposes of the institute shall include, but need not be limited to, the facilitation of a comprehensive and coordinated approach to meet the high technology forensic science needs of crime laboratories operated by the department and local law enforcement agencies, the provision of a statewide upgrading of advanced laboratory services incorporating new and developing technologies, the provision of training and methodology development for all law enforcement agencies, and the handling of advanced casework laboratory referral services.
The California Criminalistics Institute is intended for use by state and local forensic scientists and law enforcement personnel.
(Amended by Stats. 1993, Ch. 56, Sec. 28. Effective January 1, 1994.)

11061.
To meet the increasing statewide need for criminalists properly trained in DNA analysis, the Department of Justice, the California State University, and, upon agreement by the regents, the University of California, shall work together to enhance collaborative opportunities for DNA training of university students, graduates, and existing employees of crime laboratories.
(Added by Stats. 2001, Ch. 477, Sec. 2. Effective January 1, 2002.)

11061.5.

(a) The Department of Justice, through its California Criminalistics Institute, shall develop and coordinate an internship program in forensic DNA analysis for graduate-level students.
(1) Candidates for the program must possess at least a baccalaureate degree.
(2) The program shall be associated with graduate academic programs at accredited postsecondary institutions including the University of California and the California State University.
(3) The program shall include a one-year internship at a public forensic DNA laboratory for which the interns shall receive a stipend or fellowship funded by the Department of Justice.
(4) The program shall be designed to prepare students to meet national standards for DNA analysis, such as those established by the DNA Advisory Board (DAB) and the Scientific Working Group on DNA Analysis Methods (SWGDAM).
(5) In order to complete the program, interns shall be required to successfully complete a national certification examination like that administered in forensic molecular biology by the American Board of Criminalistics.
(b) Funding for the provisions of this measure shall be subject to both of the following conditions:
(1) The Department of Justice shall establish a working partnership and affiliation with accredited postsecondary institutions that can provide graduate-level academic programing.
(2) The Department of Justice shall submit a budgetary request for the internship program to the Director of the Department of Finance by May 15, 2002.
(c) The provisions of this act may only be implemented to the extent funds are appropriated for their purposes in the annual Budget Act.
(Added by Stats. 2001, Ch. 477, Sec. 3. Effective January 1, 2002.)

11062.
(a) The Department of Justice shall establish and chair a task force to conduct a review of California's crime laboratory system.
(b) The task force shall be known as the "Crime Laboratory Review Task Force." The composition of the task force shall, except as specified in paragraph (16), be comprised of one representative of each of the following entities:
(1) The Department of Justice.
(2) The California Association of Crime Laboratory Directors.
(3) The California Association of Criminalists.
(4) The International Association for Identification.
(5) The American Society of Crime Laboratory Directors.
(6) The Department of the California Highway Patrol.
(7) The California State Sheriffs' Association, from a department with a crime laboratory.
(8) The California District Attorneys Association, from an office with a crime laboratory.
(9) The California Police Chiefs Association, from a department with a crime laboratory.
(10) The California Peace Officers' Association.
(11) The California Public Defenders Association.
(12) A private criminal defense attorney organization.
(13) The Judicial Council, to be appointed by the Chief Justice.
(14) The Office of the Speaker of the Assembly.
(15) The Office of the President pro Tempore of the Senate.
(16) Two representatives to be appointed by the Governor.
(c) The task force shall review and make recommendations as to how best to configure, fund, and improve the delivery of state and local crime laboratory services in the future. To the extent feasible, the review and recommendations shall include, but are not limited to, addressing the following issues:
(1) With respect to organization and management of crime laboratory services, consideration of the following:
(A) If the existing mix of state and local crime laboratories is the most effective and efficient means to meet California's future needs.
(B) Whether laboratories should be further consolidated. If consolidation occurs, who should have oversight of crime laboratories.
(C) If management responsibilities for some laboratories should be transferred.
(D) Whether all laboratories should provide similar services.
(E) How other states have addressed similar issues.
(2) With respect to staff and training, consideration of the following:
(A) How to address recruiting and retention problems of laboratory staff.
(B) Whether educational and training opportunities are adequate to supply the needs of fully trained forensic criminalists in the future.
(C) Whether continuing education is available to ensure that forensic science personnel are up-to-date in their fields of expertise.
(D) If crime laboratory personnel should be certified, and, if so, the appropriate agency to assume this responsibility.
(E) The future educational role, if any, for the University of California or the California State University.
(3) With respect to funding, consideration of the following:
(A) Whether the current method of funding laboratories is predictable, stable, and adequate to meet future growth demands and to provide accurate and timely testing results.
(B) The adequacy of salary structures to attract and retain competent analysts and examiners.
(4) With respect to performance standards and equipment, consideration of the following:
(A) Whether workload demands are being prioritized properly and whether there are important workload issues not being addressed.
(B) If existing laboratories have the necessary capabilities, staffing, and equipment.
(C) If statewide standards should be developed for the accreditation of forensic laboratories, including minimum staffing levels, and if so, a determination regarding what entity should serve as the sanctioning body.
(d) The task force also shall seek input from specialized law enforcement disciplines, other state and local agencies, relevant advocacy groups, and the public. The final report also shall include a complete inventory of existing California crime laboratories. This inventory shall contain sufficient details on staffing, workload, budget, major instrumentation, and organizational placement within the controlling agency.
(e) The first meeting of the task force shall occur no later than December 9, 2007.
(f) On or before July 1, 2009, the task force shall submit a final report of its findings to the Department of Finance and to the budget and public safety committees of both houses of the Legislature.
(Amended by Stats. 2008, Ch. 179, Sec. 182. Effective January 1, 2009.)

ARTICLE 2.5. Criminal Record Dissemination [11075 - 11081]
(Article 2.5 added by Stats. 1972, Ch. 1437.)

11075.
(a) As used in this article, "criminal offender record information" means records and data compiled by criminal justice agencies for purposes of identifying criminal offenders and of maintaining as to each such offender a summary of arrests, pretrial proceedings, the nature and disposition of criminal charges, sentencing, incarceration, rehabilitation, and release.
(b) Such information shall be restricted to that which is recorded as the result of an arrest, detention, or other initiation of criminal proceedings or of any consequent proceedings related thereto.
(Added by Stats. 1972, Ch. 1437.)

11076.

Criminal offender record information shall be disseminated, whether directly or through any intermediary, only to such agencies as are, or may subsequently be, authorized access to such records by statute.
(Added by Stats. 1972, Ch. 1437.)
11077.
The Attorney General is responsible for the security of criminal offender record information. To this end, he or she shall:
(a) Establish regulations to assure the security of criminal offender record information from unauthorized access and disclosures by individuals and public and private agencies at all levels of operation in this state.
(b) Establish regulations to assure that this information is disseminated only in situations in which it is demonstrably required for the performance of an agency's or official's functions.
(c) Coordinate these activities with those of any interstate systems for the exchange of criminal offender record information.
(d) Cause to be initiated for employees of all agencies that maintain, receive, or are eligible to maintain or receive, criminal offender record information a continuing educational program in the proper use and control of criminal offender record information.
(e) Establish regulations as he or she finds appropriate to carry out his or her functions under this article.
(Amended by Stats. 2003, Ch. 470, Sec. 1. Effective January 1, 2004.)
11077.1.
(a) Commencing July 1, 2005, and except as provided by subdivision (b), the Department of Justice shall accept fingerprint images and related information to process criminal offender record information requests for employment, licensing, certification, custodial child placement, or adoption purposes, only if those images and related information are electronically transmitted. The department shall continually monitor the statewide availability of electronic transmission sights and work with public and private entities to ensure reasonable availability is maintained.
(b) The department shall, based on the regional unavailability of electronic transmission sites or when departmental processing procedures show a need, accept hard fingerprint cards in order to process criminal offender record information requests for employment, licensing, certification, custodial child placement, or adoption purposes.
(Added by Stats. 2003, Ch. 470, Sec. 2. Effective January 1, 2004.)
11077.2.
(a) The Attorney General shall establish a communication network that allows the transmission of requests from private service providers in California to the Department of Justice for criminal offender record information for purposes of employment, licensing, certification, custodial child placement or adoption. The communication network shall allow any entity that is approved by the department to connect directly to the department.
(b) Users of the communication network shall undergo initial and remedial training as determined by the department. Failure or refusal to comply with the training requirement shall terminate the connection to the communication network until the training is completed. The scope of the training and the entities' level of participation shall be determined by the department.
(c) Users of the communication network shall comply with any policy, practice, procedure, or requirement deemed necessary by the department to maintain network security and stability. Failure or refusal to comply shall terminate the connection to the communication network until the department determines that there is satisfactory compliance.
(d) Users of the communication network shall only use hardware and software in relation to or for connection to the communication network that is currently approved and certified by the department, the National Institute of Standards and Technology, and the Federal Bureau of Investigation.
(e) Users of the communication network shall be independently responsible for securing all hardware, software, and telecommunication service or linkage necessary to accomplish connection to the communication network, once they are authorized by the department.
(f) The communication network shall be implemented by July 1, 2004.
(g) Nothing in this section is intended to authorize any entity to access or receive criminal offender record information from the Department of Justice.
(Added by Stats. 2003, Ch. 470, Sec. 3. Effective January 1, 2004.)
11078.
Each agency holding or receiving criminal offender record information in a computerized system shall maintain, for such period as is found by the Attorney General to be appropriate, a listing of the agencies to which it has released or communicated such information.
(Added by Stats. 1972, Ch. 1437.)
11079.
(a) The Attorney General may conduct inquiries and investigations as he or she finds appropriate to carry out functions under this article. The Attorney General may for this purpose direct any agency, including a tribal court or tribal child welfare agency of a tribe or consortium of tribes that has entered into an agreement with the state pursuant to Section 10553.1 of the Welfare and Institutions Code, that maintains, or has received, or that is eligible to maintain or receive criminal offender records to produce for inspection statistical data, reports, and other information concerning the storage and dissemination of criminal offender record information. Each agency is authorized and directed to provide that data, reports, and other information.
(b) Notwithstanding any other law, any entity described in subdivision (a) that fails to comply with the requirements of this section shall lose access to criminal offender record information maintained by the Department of Justice until correction of the noncompliance is demonstrated.
(Amended by Stats. 2007, Ch. 583, Sec. 16. Effective January 1, 2008.)
11080.
Nothing in this article shall be construed to affect the right of access of any person or public agency to individual criminal offender record information that is authorized by any other provision of law.
(Added by Stats. 1972, Ch. 1437.)
11080.5.
A chief of police of a city or the sheriff of a county shall be authorized to request and receive relevant information concerning persons when on parole who are or may be residing or temporarily domiciled in that city or county and who have been convicted of a federal crime which could have been prosecuted as a felony under the penal provisions of this state.
(Added by Stats. 1982, Ch. 347, Sec. 1. Effective June 30, 1982.)
11081.
Nothing in this article shall be construed to authorize access of any person or public agency to individual criminal offender record information unless such access is otherwise authorized by law.
(Added by Stats. 1972, Ch. 1437.)

ARTICLE 3. Criminal Identification and Statistics [11100 - 11112]
(Article 3 added by Stats. 1953, Ch. 1385.)
11100.
The Attorney General shall provide for the installation of a proper system and file in the office of the bureau, cards containing an outline of the method of operation employed by criminals in the commission of crime.
(Added by Stats. 1953, Ch. 1385.)

11101.
The Attorney General shall procure from any available source, and file for record and report in the office of the bureau, all descriptions, information, photographs, and measurements of all persons convicted of a felony, or imprisoned for violating any of the military, naval, or criminal laws of the United States, and of all well-known and habitual criminals.
(Amended by Stats. 1993, Ch. 1270, Sec. 2. Effective January 1, 1994.)
11102.
The department may use the following systems of identification: the Bertillon, the fingerprint system, and any system of measurement that may be adopted by law in the various penal institutions of the state.
(Amended by Stats. 1972, Ch. 1377.)
11102.1.
(a) (1) Notwithstanding any other law, the Department of Justice shall establish, implement, and maintain a certification program to process fingerprint-based criminal background clearances on individuals who roll fingerprint impressions, manually or electronically, for non-law-enforcement purposes. Except as provided in paragraph (2), no person shall roll fingerprints for non-law-enforcement purposes unless certified.
(2) The following persons shall be exempt from this section if they have received training pertaining to applicant fingerprint rolling and have undergone a criminal offender record information background investigation:
(A) Law enforcement personnel and state employees.
(B) Employees of a tribal gaming agency or a tribal gaming operation, provided that the fingerprints are rolled and submitted to the Department of Justice for purposes of compliance with a tribal-state compact.
(3) The department shall not accept fingerprint impressions for non-law-enforcement purposes unless they were rolled by an individual certified or exempted pursuant to this section.
(b) Individuals who roll fingerprint impressions, either manually or electronically, for non-law-enforcement purposes, must submit to the Department of Justice fingerprint images and related information, along with the appropriate fees and documentation. The department shall retain one copy of the fingerprint impressions to process a state level criminal background clearance, and it shall submit one copy of the fingerprint impressions to the Federal Bureau of Investigation to process a federal level criminal background clearance.
(c) The department shall retain the fingerprint impressions for subsequent arrest notification pursuant to Section 11105.2.
(d) Every individual certified as a fingerprint roller shall meet the following criteria:
(1) Be a legal resident of this state at the time of certification.
(2) Be at least 18 years of age.
(3) Have satisfactorily completed a written application prescribed by the department to determine the fitness of the person to exercise the functions of a fingerprint roller.
(e) Prior to granting a certificate as a fingerprint roller, the department shall determine that the applicant possesses the required honesty, credibility, truthfulness, and integrity to fulfill the responsibilities of the position.
(f) (1) The department shall refuse to certify any individual as a fingerprint roller, and shall revoke the certification of any fingerprint roller, upon either of the following:
(A) Conviction of a felony offense.
(B) Conviction of any other offense that both involves moral turpitude, dishonesty, or fraud, and bears on the applicant's ability to perform the duties or responsibilities of a fingerprint roller.
(2) A conviction after a plea of nolo contendere is deemed to be a conviction for purposes of this subdivision.
(g) In addition to subdivision (f), the department may refuse to certify any individual as a fingerprint roller, and may revoke or suspend the certification of any fingerprint roller upon any of the following:
(1) Substantial and material misstatement or omission in the application submitted to the department.
(2) Arrest pending adjudication for a felony.
(3) Arrest pending adjudication for a lesser offense that both involves moral turpitude, dishonesty, or fraud, and bears on the applicant's ability to perform the duties or responsibilities of a fingerprint roller.
(4) Revocation, suspension, restriction, or denial of a professional license, if the revocation, suspension, restriction, or denial was for misconduct, dishonesty, or for any cause substantially related to the duties or responsibilities of a fingerprint roller.
(5) Failure to discharge fully and faithfully any of the duties or responsibilities required of a fingerprint roller.
(6) When adjudged liable for damages in any suit grounded in fraud, misrepresentation, or in violation of the state regulatory laws, or in any suit based upon a failure to discharge fully and faithfully the duties of a fingerprint roller.
(7) Use of false or misleading advertising in which the fingerprint roller has represented that he or she has duties, rights, or privileges that he or she does not possess by law.
(8) Commission of any act involving dishonesty, fraud, or deceit with the intent to substantially benefit the fingerprint roller or another, or to substantially injure another.
(9) Failure to submit any remittance payable upon demand by the department or failure to satisfy any court ordered money judgment, including restitution.
(h) The Department of Justice shall work with applicant regulatory entities to improve and make more efficient the criminal offender record information request process related to employment, licensing, and certification background investigations.
(i) The Department of Justice may adopt regulations as necessary to implement the provisions of this section.
(j) The department shall charge a fee sufficient to cover its costs under this section.
(Amended by Stats. 2009, Ch. 35, Sec. 25. (SB 174) Effective January 1, 2010.)
11102.2.
(a) (1) As used in this section, "custodian of records" means the individual designated by an agency as responsible for the security, storage, dissemination, and destruction of the criminal records furnished to the agency and who serves as the primary contact for the Department of Justice for any related issues.
(2) As used in this section, "agency" means any public or private entity that receives criminal history information from the Department of Justice.
(3) As used in this section, "department" means the Department of Justice.
(b) Commencing January 1, 2011, the department shall establish, implement, and maintain a confirmation program to process fingerprint-based criminal record background clearances on individuals designated by agencies as custodians of records. Commencing July 1, 2011, no person shall serve as an agency custodian of records unless confirmed by the department. Criminal justice agency personnel who have undergone a state and federal criminal record background check are exempt from the requirements of this section. The department shall charge a fee of thirty dollars ($30) to cover the costs of the confirmation program in addition to a fee sufficient to cover the cost of processing the appropriate state and federal level criminal record background check.
(c) Every agency must designate at least one custodian of records.
(1) The agency shall submit to the department the fingerprint images and related information of the individual or individuals designated by the agency to serve as the custodian or custodians of records, along with the appropriate fees and documentation. The department shall retain one copy of the fingerprint impressions to process a state level criminal record background check, and it shall submit one copy of the fingerprint impressions of each individual to the Federal Bureau of Investigation to process a federal level criminal record background check.

(2) The department shall retain the fingerprint impressions for subsequent arrest notification pursuant to Section 11105.2.

(d) Every individual confirmed as a custodian of records shall be at least 18 years of age and shall have completed and submitted a written application prescribed by the department.

(e) Prior to confirming an individual as a custodian of records, the department shall determine that the applicant possesses the required honesty, credibility, truthfulness, and integrity to fulfill the responsibilities of the position.

(f) The department shall not confirm any individual who has been convicted of a felony offense or any other offense that involves moral turpitude, dishonesty, or fraud, or that impacts the applicant's ability to perform the duties or responsibilities of a custodian of records. The confirmation shall be revoked if, at any time, the individual is convicted of either a felony offense, or any other offense that involves moral turpitude, dishonesty, or fraud, or that impacts the applicant's ability to perform the duties or responsibilities of a custodian of records.

(g) In addition to subdivision (f), the department may refuse to confirm any individual as a custodian of records or revoke or suspend the confirmation of any custodian of records if the individual has done any of the following:

(1) Made a substantial and material misstatement or omission in the application submitted to the department.

(2) Been convicted of an offense of a nature incompatible with the duties of a custodian of records. A conviction after a plea of nolo contendere is deemed to be a conviction within the meaning of this subdivision.

(3) Failed to discharge fully and faithfully any of the duties or responsibilities required of a custodian of records.

(4) Been adjudged liable for damages in any suit grounded in fraud, misrepresentation, or in violation of the state regulatory laws, or in any suit based upon a failure to discharge fully and faithfully the duties of a custodian of records.

(5) Committed any act involving dishonesty, fraud, or deceit.

(6) Failed to submit any remittance payable upon demand by the department under this section or failed to satisfy any court ordered money judgment, including restitution.

(h) The agency shall immediately notify the department when the designated custodian of records no longer serves in that capacity.

(Amended by Stats. 2014, Ch. 54, Sec. 15. (SB 1461) Effective January 1, 2015.)

11103.

The Attorney General shall keep on file in the office of the bureau a record consisting of duplicates of all measurements, processes, operations, signaletic cards, measurements, and descriptions of all persons confined in penal institutions of the state as far as possible, in accordance with whatever system or systems may be commonly used in the state.

(Amended by Stats. 1983, Ch. 196, Sec. 7.)

11104.

The Attorney General shall file all measurements, information and descriptions received and shall make a complete and systematic record and index, providing a method of convenience, consultation, and comparison.

(Amended by Stats. 1983, Ch. 196, Sec. 8.)

11105.

(a) (1) The Department of Justice shall maintain state summary criminal history information.

(2) As used in this section:

(A) "State summary criminal history information" means the master record of information compiled by the Attorney General pertaining to the identification and criminal history of a person, such as name, date of birth, physical description, fingerprints, photographs, dates of arrests, arresting agencies and booking numbers, charges, dispositions, sentencing information, and similar data about the person.

(B) "State summary criminal history information" does not refer to records and data compiled by criminal justice agencies other than the Attorney General, nor does it refer to records of complaints to or investigations conducted by, or records of intelligence information or security procedures of, the office of the Attorney General and the Department of Justice.

(b) The Attorney General shall furnish state summary criminal history information to the following, if needed in the course of their duties, provided that when information is furnished to assist an agency, officer, or official of state or local government, a public utility, or any other entity, in fulfilling employment, certification, or licensing duties, Chapter 1321 of the Statutes of 1974 and Section 432.7 of the Labor Code shall apply:

(1) The courts of the state.

(2) Peace officers of the state, as defined in Section 830.1, subdivisions (a) and (e) of Section 830.2, subdivision (a) of Section 830.3, subdivision (a) of Section 830.31, and subdivisions (a) and (b) of Section 830.5.

(3) District attorneys of the state.

(4) Prosecuting city attorneys or city prosecutors of a city within the state.

(5) City attorneys pursuing civil gang injunctions pursuant to Section 186.22a, or drug abatement actions pursuant to Section 3479 or 3480 of the Civil Code, or Section 11571 of the Health and Safety Code.

(6) Probation officers of the state.

(7) Parole officers of the state.

(8) A public defender or attorney of record when representing a person in proceedings upon a petition for a certificate of rehabilitation and pardon pursuant to Section 4852.08.

(9) A public defender or attorney of record when representing a person in a criminal case or a juvenile delinquency proceeding, including all appeals and postconviction motions, or a parole, mandatory supervision pursuant to paragraph (5) of subdivision (h) of Section 1170, or postrelease community supervision revocation or revocation extension proceeding, if the information is requested in the course of representation.

(10) An agency, officer, or official of the state if the state summary criminal history information is required to implement a statute or regulation that expressly refers to specific criminal conduct applicable to the subject person of the state summary criminal history information, and contains requirements or exclusions, or both, expressly based upon that specified criminal conduct. The agency, officer, or official of the state authorized by this paragraph to receive state summary criminal history information may also transmit fingerprint images and related information to the Department of Justice to be transmitted to the Federal Bureau of Investigation.

(11) A city or county, city and county, district, or an officer or official thereof if access is needed in order to assist that agency, officer, or official in fulfilling employment, certification, or licensing duties, and if the access is specifically authorized by the city council, board of supervisors, or governing board of the city, county, or district if the state summary criminal history information is required to implement a statute, ordinance, or regulation that expressly refers to specific criminal conduct applicable to the subject person of the state summary criminal history information, and contains requirements or exclusions, or both, expressly based upon that specified criminal conduct. The city or county, city and county, district, or the officer or official thereof authorized by this paragraph may also transmit fingerprint images and related information to the Department of Justice to be transmitted to the Federal Bureau of Investigation.

(12) The subject of the state summary criminal history information under procedures established under Article 5 (commencing with Section 11120).

(13) A person or entity when access is expressly authorized by statute if the criminal history information is required to implement a statute or regulation that expressly refers to specific criminal conduct applicable to the subject person of the state summary

criminal history information, and contains requirements or exclusions, or both, expressly based upon that specified criminal conduct.

(14) Health officers of a city, county, city and county, or district when in the performance of their official duties enforcing Section 120175 of the Health and Safety Code.

(15) A managing or supervising correctional officer of a county jail or other county correctional facility.

(16) A humane society, or society for the prevention of cruelty to animals, for the specific purpose of complying with Section 14502 of the Corporations Code for the appointment of humane officers.

(17) Local child support agencies established by Section 17304 of the Family Code. When a local child support agency closes a support enforcement case containing state summary criminal history information, the agency shall delete or purge from the file and destroy any documents or information concerning or arising from offenses for or of which the parent has been arrested, charged, or convicted, other than for offenses related to the parent's having failed to provide support for minor children, consistent with the requirements of Section 17531 of the Family Code.

(18) County child welfare agency personnel who have been delegated the authority of county probation officers to access state summary criminal history information pursuant to Section 272 of the Welfare and Institutions Code for the purposes specified in Section 16504.5 of the Welfare and Institutions Code. Information from criminal history records provided pursuant to this subdivision shall not be used for a purpose other than those specified in this section and Section 16504.5 of the Welfare and Institutions Code. When an agency obtains records both on the basis of name checks and fingerprint checks, final placement decisions shall be based only on the records obtained pursuant to the fingerprint check.

(19) The court of a tribe, or court of a consortium of tribes, that has entered into an agreement with the state pursuant to Section 10553.1 of the Welfare and Institutions Code. This information may be used only for the purposes specified in Section 16504.5 of the Welfare and Institutions Code and for tribal approval or tribal licensing of foster care or adoptive homes. Article 6 (commencing with Section 11140) shall apply to officers, members, and employees of a tribal court receiving state summary criminal history information pursuant to this section.

(20) Child welfare agency personnel of a tribe or consortium of tribes that has entered into an agreement with the state pursuant to Section 10553.1 of the Welfare and Institutions Code and to whom the state has delegated duties under paragraph (2) of subdivision (a) of Section 272 of the Welfare and Institutions Code. The purposes for use of the information shall be for the purposes specified in Section 16504.5 of the Welfare and Institutions Code and for tribal approval or tribal licensing of foster care or adoptive homes. When an agency obtains records on the basis of name checks and fingerprint checks, final placement decisions shall be based only on the records obtained pursuant to the fingerprint check. Article 6 (commencing with Section 11140) shall apply to child welfare agency personnel receiving criminal record offender information pursuant to this section.

(21) An officer providing conservatorship investigations pursuant to Sections 5351, 5354, and 5356 of the Welfare and Institutions Code.

(22) A court investigator providing investigations or reviews in conservatorships pursuant to Section 1826, 1850, 1851, or 2250.6 of the Probate Code.

(23) A person authorized to conduct a guardianship investigation pursuant to Section 1513 of the Probate Code.

(24) A humane officer pursuant to Section 14502 of the Corporations Code for the purposes of performing his or her duties.

(25) A public agency described in subdivision (b) of Section 15975 of the Government Code, for the purpose of oversight and enforcement policies with respect to its contracted providers.

(26) (A) A state entity, or its designee, that receives federal tax information. A state entity or its designee that is authorized by this paragraph to receive state summary criminal history information also may transmit fingerprint images and related information to the Department of Justice to be transmitted to the Federal Bureau of Investigation for the purpose of the state entity or its designee obtaining federal level criminal offender record information from the Department of Justice. This information shall be used only for the purposes set forth in Section 1044 of the Government Code.

(B) For purposes of this paragraph, "federal tax information," "state entity" and "designee" are as defined in paragraphs (1), (2), and (3), respectively, of subdivision (f) of Section 1044 of the Government Code.

(c) The Attorney General may furnish state summary criminal history information and, when specifically authorized by this subdivision, federal level criminal history information upon a showing of a compelling need to any of the following, provided that when information is furnished to assist an agency, officer, or official of state or local government, a public utility, or any other entity in fulfilling employment, certification, or licensing duties, Chapter 1321 of the Statutes of 1974 and Section 432.7 of the Labor Code shall apply:

(1) A public utility, as defined in Section 216 of the Public Utilities Code, that operates a nuclear energy facility when access is needed in order to assist in employing persons to work at the facility, provided that, if the Attorney General supplies the data, he or she shall furnish a copy of the data to the person to whom the data relates.

(2) To a peace officer of the state other than those included in subdivision (b).

(3) To an illegal dumping enforcement officer as defined in subdivision (j) of Section 830.7.

(4) To a peace officer of another country.

(5) To public officers, other than peace officers, of the United States, other states, or possessions or territories of the United States, provided that access to records similar to state summary criminal history information is expressly authorized by a statute of the United States, other states, or possessions or territories of the United States if the information is needed for the performance of their official duties.

(6) To a person when disclosure is requested by a probation, parole, or peace officer with the consent of the subject of the state summary criminal history information and for purposes of furthering the rehabilitation of the subject.

(7) The courts of the United States, other states, or territories or possessions of the United States.

(8) Peace officers of the United States, other states, or territories or possessions of the United States.

(9) To an individual who is the subject of the record requested if needed in conjunction with an application to enter the United States or a foreign nation.

(10) (A) (i) A public utility, as defined in Section 216 of the Public Utilities Code, or a cable corporation as defined in subparagraph (B), if receipt of criminal history information is needed in order to assist in employing current or prospective employees, contract employees, or subcontract employees who, in the course of their employment, may be seeking entrance to private residences or adjacent grounds. The information provided shall be limited to the record of convictions and arrests for which the person is released on bail or on his or her own recognizance pending trial.

(ii) If the Attorney General supplies the data pursuant to this paragraph, the Attorney General shall furnish a copy of the data to the current or prospective employee to whom the data relates.

(iii) State summary criminal history information is confidential and the receiving public utility or cable corporation shall not disclose its contents, other than for the purpose for which it was acquired. The state summary criminal history information in the possession of the public utility or cable corporation and all copies made from it shall be destroyed not more than 30 days after employment or promotion or transfer is denied or granted, except for those cases where a current or prospective employee is out on bail or on his or her own recognizance pending trial, in which case the state summary criminal history information and all copies shall be destroyed not more than 30 days after the case is resolved.

(iv) A violation of this paragraph is a misdemeanor, and shall give the current or prospective employee who is injured by the violation a cause of action against the public utility or cable corporation to recover damages proximately caused by the violations. A public utility's or cable corporation's request for state summary criminal history information for purposes of employing current or prospective employees who may be seeking entrance to private residences or adjacent grounds in the course of their employment shall be deemed a "compelling need" as required to be shown in this subdivision.

(v) This section shall not be construed as imposing a duty upon public utilities or cable corporations to request state summary criminal history information on current or prospective employees.

(B) For purposes of this paragraph, "cable corporation" means a corporation or firm that transmits or provides television, computer, or telephone services by cable, digital, fiber optic, satellite, or comparable technology to subscribers for a fee.

(C) Requests for federal level criminal history information received by the Department of Justice from entities authorized pursuant to subparagraph (A) shall be forwarded to the Federal Bureau of Investigation by the Department of Justice. Federal level criminal history information received or compiled by the Department of Justice may then be disseminated to the entities referenced in subparagraph (A), as authorized by law.

(11) To a campus of the California State University or the University of California, or a four-year college or university accredited by a regional accreditation organization approved by the United States Department of Education, if needed in conjunction with an application for admission by a convicted felon to a special education program for convicted felons, including, but not limited to, university alternatives and halfway houses. Only conviction information shall be furnished. The college or university may require the convicted felon to be fingerprinted, and any inquiry to the department under this section shall include the convicted felon's fingerprints and any other information specified by the department.

(12) To a foreign government, if requested by the individual who is the subject of the record requested, if needed in conjunction with the individual's application to adopt a minor child who is a citizen of that foreign nation. Requests for information pursuant to this paragraph shall be in accordance with the process described in Sections 11122 to 11124, inclusive. The response shall be provided to the foreign government or its designee and to the individual who requested the information.

(d) Whenever an authorized request for state summary criminal history information pertains to a person whose fingerprints are on file with the Department of Justice and the department has no criminal history of that person, and the information is to be used for employment, licensing, or certification purposes, the fingerprint card accompanying the request for information, if any, may be stamped "no criminal record" and returned to the person or entity making the request.

(e) Whenever state summary criminal history information is furnished as the result of an application and is to be used for employment, licensing, or certification purposes, the Department of Justice may charge the person or entity making the request a fee that it determines to be sufficient to reimburse the department for the cost of furnishing the information. In addition, the Department of Justice may add a surcharge to the fee to fund maintenance and improvements to the systems from which the information is obtained. Notwithstanding any other law, a person or entity required to pay a fee to the department for information received under this section may charge the applicant a fee sufficient to reimburse the person or entity for this expense. All moneys received by the department pursuant to this section, Sections 11105.3 and 26190, and former Section 13588 of the Education Code shall be deposited in a special account in the General Fund to be available for expenditure by the department to offset costs incurred pursuant to those sections and for maintenance and improvements to the systems from which the information is obtained upon appropriation by the Legislature.

(f) Whenever there is a conflict, the processing of criminal fingerprints and fingerprints of applicants for security guard or alarm agent registrations or firearms qualification permits submitted pursuant to Section 7583.9, 7583.23, 7596.3, or 7598.4 of the Business and Professions Code shall take priority over the processing of other applicant fingerprints.

(g) It is not a violation of this section to disseminate statistical or research information obtained from a record, provided that the identity of the subject of the record is not disclosed.

(h) It is not a violation of this section to include information obtained from a record in (1) a transcript or record of a judicial or administrative proceeding or (2) any other public record if the inclusion of the information in the public record is authorized by a court, statute, or decisional law.

(i) Notwithstanding any other law, the Department of Justice or a state or local law enforcement agency may require the submission of fingerprints for the purpose of conducting state summary criminal history information checks that are authorized by law.

(j) The state summary criminal history information shall include any finding of mental incompetence pursuant to Chapter 6 (commencing with Section 1367) of Title 10 of Part 2 arising out of a complaint charging a felony offense specified in Section 290.

(k) (1) This subdivision shall apply whenever state or federal summary criminal history information is furnished by the Department of Justice as the result of an application by an authorized agency or organization and the information is to be used for peace officer employment or certification purposes. As used in this subdivision, a peace officer is defined in Chapter 4.5 (commencing with Section 830) of Title 3 of Part 2.

(2) Notwithstanding any other law, whenever state summary criminal history information is initially furnished pursuant to paragraph (1), the Department of Justice shall disseminate the following information:

(A) Every conviction rendered against the applicant.

(B) Every arrest for an offense for which the applicant is presently awaiting trial, whether the applicant is incarcerated or has been released on bail or on his or her own recognizance pending trial.

(C) Every arrest or detention, except for an arrest or detention resulting in an exoneration, provided, however, that where the records of the Department of Justice do not contain a disposition for the arrest, the Department of Justice first makes a genuine effort to determine the disposition of the arrest.

(D) Every successful diversion.

(E) Every date and agency name associated with all retained peace officer or nonsworn law enforcement agency employee preemployment criminal offender record information search requests.

(F) Sex offender registration status of the applicant.

(G) Sentencing information, if present in the department's records at the time of the response.

(l) (1) This subdivision shall apply whenever state or federal summary criminal history information is furnished by the Department of Justice as the result of an application by a criminal justice agency or organization as defined in Section 13101, and the information is to be used for criminal justice employment, licensing, or certification purposes.

(2) Notwithstanding any other law, whenever state summary criminal history information is initially furnished pursuant to paragraph (1), the Department of Justice shall disseminate the following information:

(A) Every conviction rendered against the applicant.

(B) Every arrest for an offense for which the applicant is presently awaiting trial, whether the applicant is incarcerated or has been released on bail or on his or her own recognizance pending trial.

(C) Every arrest for an offense for which the records of the Department of Justice do not contain a disposition or which did not result in a conviction, provided that the Department of Justice first makes a genuine effort to determine the disposition of the arrest. However, information concerning an arrest shall not be disclosed if the records of the Department of Justice indicate or if the genuine effort reveals that the subject was exonerated, successfully completed a diversion or deferred entry of judgment program, or the arrest was deemed a detention, or the subject was granted relief pursuant to Section 851.91.

(D) Every date and agency name associated with all retained peace officer or nonsworn law enforcement agency employee preemployment criminal offender record information search requests.

(E) Sex offender registration status of the applicant.

(F) Sentencing information, if present in the department's records at the time of the response.

(m) (1) This subdivision shall apply whenever state or federal summary criminal history information is furnished by the Department of Justice as the result of an application by an authorized agency or organization pursuant to Section 1522, 1568.09, 1569.17, or 1596.871 of the Health and Safety Code, or a statute that incorporates the criteria of any of those sections or this subdivision by reference, and the information is to be used for employment, licensing, or certification purposes.

(2) Notwithstanding any other law, whenever state summary criminal history information is initially furnished pursuant to paragraph (1), the Department of Justice shall disseminate the following information:

(A) Every conviction of an offense rendered against the applicant, except a conviction for which relief has been granted pursuant to Section 1203.49.

(B) Every arrest for an offense for which the applicant is presently awaiting trial, whether the applicant is incarcerated or has been released on bail or on his or her own recognizance pending trial.

(C) Every arrest for an offense for which the Department of Social Services is required by paragraph (1) of subdivision (a) of Section 1522 of the Health and Safety Code to determine if an applicant has been arrested. However, if the records of the Department of Justice do not contain a disposition for an arrest, the Department of Justice shall first make a genuine effort to determine the disposition of the arrest.

(D) Sex offender registration status of the applicant.

(E) Sentencing information, if present in the department's records at the time of the response.

(3) Notwithstanding the requirements of the sections referenced in paragraph (1) of this subdivision, the Department of Justice shall not disseminate information about an arrest subsequently deemed a detention or an arrest that resulted in the successful completion of a diversion program, exoneration, or a grant of relief pursuant to Section 851.91.

(n) (1) This subdivision shall apply whenever state or federal summary criminal history information, to be used for employment, licensing, or certification purposes, is furnished by the Department of Justice as the result of an application by an authorized agency, organization, or individual pursuant to any of the following:

(A) Paragraph (10) of subdivision (c), when the information is to be used by a cable corporation.

(B) Section 11105.3 or 11105.4.

(C) Section 15660 of the Welfare and Institutions Code.

(D) A statute that incorporates the criteria of any of the statutory provisions listed in subparagraph (A), (B), or (C), or of this subdivision, by reference.

(2) With the exception of applications submitted by transportation companies authorized pursuant to Section 11105.3, and notwithstanding any other law, whenever state summary criminal history information is initially furnished pursuant to paragraph (1), the Department of Justice shall disseminate the following information:

(A) Every conviction, except a conviction for which relief has been granted pursuant to Section 1203.49, rendered against the applicant for a violation or attempted violation of an offense specified in subdivision (a) of Section 15660 of the Welfare and Institutions Code. However, with the exception of those offenses for which registration is required pursuant to Section 290, the Department of Justice shall not disseminate information pursuant to this subdivision unless the conviction occurred within 10 years of the date of the agency's request for information or the conviction is over 10 years old but the subject of the request was incarcerated within 10 years of the agency's request for information.

(B) Every arrest for a violation or attempted violation of an offense specified in subdivision (a) of Section 15660 of the Welfare and Institutions Code for which the applicant is presently awaiting trial, whether the applicant is incarcerated or has been released on bail or on his or her own recognizance pending trial.

(C) Sex offender registration status of the applicant.

(D) Sentencing information, if present in the department's records at the time of the response.

(o) (1) This subdivision shall apply whenever state or federal summary criminal history information is furnished by the Department of Justice as the result of an application by an authorized agency or organization pursuant to Section 379 or 550 of the Financial Code, or a statute that incorporates the criteria of either of those sections or this subdivision by reference, and the information is to be used for employment, licensing, or certification purposes.

(2) Notwithstanding any other law, whenever state summary criminal history information is initially furnished pursuant to paragraph (1), the Department of Justice shall disseminate the following information:

(A) Every conviction rendered against the applicant for a violation or attempted violation of an offense specified in Section 550 of the Financial Code, except a conviction for which relief has been granted pursuant to Section 1203.49.

(B) Every arrest for a violation or attempted violation of an offense specified in Section 550 of the Financial Code for which the applicant is presently awaiting trial, whether the applicant is incarcerated or has been released on bail or on his or her own recognizance pending trial.

(C) Sentencing information, if present in the department's records at the time of the response.

(p) (1) This subdivision shall apply whenever state or federal criminal history information is furnished by the Department of Justice as the result of an application by an agency, organization, or individual not defined in subdivision (k), (l), (m), (n), or (o), or by a transportation company authorized pursuant to Section 11105.3, or a statute that incorporates the criteria of that section or this subdivision by reference, and the information is to be used for employment, licensing, or certification purposes.

(2) Notwithstanding any other law, whenever state summary criminal history information is initially furnished pursuant to paragraph (1), the Department of Justice shall disseminate the following information:

(A) Every conviction rendered against the applicant, except a conviction for which relief has been granted pursuant to Section 1203.49.

(B) Every arrest for an offense for which the applicant is presently awaiting trial, whether the applicant is incarcerated or has been released on bail or on his or her own recognizance pending trial.

(C) Sex offender registration status of the applicant.

(D) Sentencing information, if present in the department's records at the time of the response.

(q) All agencies, organizations, or individuals defined in subdivisions (k), (l), (m), (n), (o), and (p) may contract with the Department of Justice for subsequent notification pursuant to Section 11105.2. This subdivision shall not supersede sections that mandate an agency, organization, or individual to contract with the Department of Justice for subsequent notification pursuant to Section 11105.2.

(r) This section does not require the Department of Justice to cease compliance with any other statutory notification requirements.

(s) The provisions of Section 50.12 of Title 28 of the Code of Federal Regulations are to be followed in processing federal criminal history information.

(t) Whenever state or federal summary criminal history information is furnished by the Department of Justice as the result of an application by an authorized agency, organization, or individual defined in subdivisions (k) to (p), inclusive, and the information is to be used for employment, licensing, or certification purposes, the authorized agency, organization, or individual shall expeditiously furnish a copy of the information to the person to whom the information relates if the information is a basis for an adverse employment, licensing, or certification decision. When furnished other than in person, the copy shall be delivered to the last contact information provided by the applicant.

(Amended by Stats. 2018, Ch. 965, Sec. 1. (AB 2133) Effective January 1, 2019.)
11105.01.
In addition to furnishing state summary criminal history information to the persons and entities set forth in Section 11105 and subject to the requirements and conditions set forth in that section, the Attorney General shall furnish state summary criminal history information to the Director, the Deputy Director for Security, and lottery security officers of the California State Lottery.

(Added by Stats. 1986, Ch. 55, Sec. 27. Effective April 16, 1986.)
11105.02.
In addition to furnishing state summary criminal history information to the persons and entities set forth in Section 11105 and subject to the requirements and conditions set forth in that section, the Attorney General shall furnish state summary criminal history information upon a showing of a compelling need to any city, county, city and county, or district, or any officer or official thereof, when needed to assist in the screening of a prospective concessionaire and their affiliates or associates, as these terms are defined in subdivision (k) of Section 432.7 of the Labor Code for purposes of consenting to, or approving of, the prospective concessionaire's application for, or acquisition of, any beneficial interest in a concession, lease, or other property interest.

Any local government's request for state summary criminal history information for purposes of screening a prospective concessionaire and their affiliates or associates before approving or denying an application for, or acquisition of, any beneficial interest in a concession, lease, or other property interest is deemed a "compelling need" as required by this section. However, only state summary criminal history information pertaining to criminal convictions, or to arrests for offenses for which the person being screened is incarcerated or has been released on bail or on his or her own recognizance pending trial, may be obtained pursuant to this section.

Any information obtained from the state summary criminal history information is confidential and the receiving local government shall not disclose its contents, other than for the purpose for which it was acquired. The state summary criminal history information in the possession of the local government and all copies made from it shall be destroyed not more than 30 days after the local government's final decision to grant or deny consent to, or approval of, the prospective concessionaire's application for, or acquisition of, a beneficial interest in a concession, lease, or other property interest. Nothing in this section shall be construed as imposing any duty upon a local government, or any officer or official thereof, to request state summary criminal history information on any current or prospective concessionaire or the affiliates or associates of that concessionaire.

(Amended by Stats. 2002, Ch. 627, Sec. 3. Effective January 1, 2003.)
11105.03.
(a) Subject to the requirements and conditions set forth in this section and Section 11105, local law enforcement agencies are hereby authorized to provide state criminal summary history information obtained through the California Law Enforcement Telecommunications System (CLETS) for the purpose of screening prospective participants and prospective and current staff of a regional, county, city, or other local public housing authority, at the request of the chief executive officer of the authority or his or her designee, upon a showing by that authority that the authority manages a Section 8 housing program pursuant to federal law (United States Housing Act of 1937), operates housing at which children under the age of 18 years reside, or operates housing for persons categorized as aged, blind, or disabled.

(b) The following requirements shall apply to information released by local law enforcement agencies pursuant to subdivision (a):

(1) Local law enforcement agencies shall not release any information unless it relates to a conviction for a serious felony, as defined in subdivision (c) of Section 1192.7, a conviction for any offense punishable under Section 273.5, 422.6, 422.7, 422.75, 422.9, or 422.76, or under Chapter 2 (commencing with Section 29800) or Chapter 3 (commencing with Section 29900) of Division 9 of Title 4 of Part 6, or under any provision listed in Section 16590, a conviction under Section 273.6 that involves a violation of a protective order, as defined in Section 6218 of the Family Code, or a conviction for any felony offense that involves controlled substances or alcoholic beverages, or any felony offense that involves any activity related to controlled substances or alcoholic beverages, or a conviction for any offense that involves domestic violence, as defined in Section 13700.

(2) Local law enforcement agencies shall not release information concerning an arrest for an offense that did not result in a conviction.

(3) Local law enforcement agencies shall not release information concerning an offense committed by a person who was under 18 years of age at the time he or she committed the offense.

(4) Local law enforcement agencies shall release any information concerning any conviction or release from custody that occurred within 10 years of the date on which the request for information is submitted to the Attorney General, unless the conviction was based upon a felony offense that involved controlled substances or alcoholic beverages or a felony offense that involved any activity related to controlled substances or alcoholic beverages. Where a conviction was based on any of these felony offenses, local law enforcement agencies shall release information concerning this conviction if the conviction occurred within five years of the date on which a request for the information was submitted.

(5) Notwithstanding paragraph (4), if information that meets the requirements of paragraphs (2) to (4), inclusive, is located and the information reveals a conviction of an offense specified in paragraph (1), local law enforcement agencies shall release all summary criminal history information concerning the person whether or not the information meets the requirements of paragraph (4), provided, however, that the information meets the requirements of paragraphs (1) to (3), inclusive.

(6) Information released to the local public housing authority pursuant to this section shall also be released to parole or probation officers at the same time.

(c) State summary criminal history information shall be used by the chief executive officer of the housing authority or a designee only for purposes of identifying prospective participants in subsidized programs and prospective and current staff who have access to residences, whose criminal history is likely to pose a risk to children under 18 years of age or persons categorized as aged, blind, or disabled living in the housing operated by the authority.

(d) If a housing authority obtains summary criminal history information for the purpose of screening a prospective participant pursuant to this section, it shall review and evaluate that information in the context of other available information and shall not evaluate the person's suitability as a prospective participant based solely on his or her past criminal history.

(e) If a housing authority determines that a prospective participant is not eligible as a resident, it shall promptly notify him or her of the basis for its determination and, upon request, shall provide him or her within a reasonable time after the determination is made with an opportunity for an informal hearing on the determination in accordance with Section 960.207 of Title 24 of the Code of Federal Regulations.

(f) Any information obtained from state summary criminal history information pursuant to this section is confidential and the recipient public housing authority shall not disclose or use the information for any purpose other than that authorized by this section. The state summary criminal history information in the possession of the authority and all copies made from it shall be destroyed not more than 30 days after the authority's final decision whether to act on the housing status of the individual to whom the information relates.

(g) The local public housing authority receiving state summary criminal history information pursuant to this section shall adopt regulations governing the receipt, maintenance, and use of the information. The regulations shall include provisions that require notice that the authority has access to criminal records of participants and employees who have access to programs.

(h) Use of this information is to be consistent with Title 24 of the Code of Federal Regulations and the current regulations adopted by the housing authority using the information.

(i) Nothing in this section shall be construed to require a housing authority to request and review an applicant's criminal history.

(j) The California Housing Authorities Association, after compiling data from all public housing authorities that receive summary criminal information pursuant to this chapter, shall report its findings based upon this data to the Legislature prior to January 1, 2000.

(Amended by Stats. 2012, Ch. 162, Sec. 135. (SB 1171) Effective January 1, 2013.)
11105.04.
(a) A designated Court Appointed Special Advocate (CASA) program may submit to the Department of Justice fingerprint images and related information of employment and volunteer candidates for the purpose of obtaining information as to the existence and nature of any record of child abuse investigations contained in the Child Abuse Central Index, state- or federal-level convictions, or state- or federal-level arrests for which the department establishes that the applicant was released on bail or on his or her own recognizance pending trial. Requests for federal-level criminal offender record information received by the department pursuant to this section shall be forwarded to the Federal Bureau of Investigation by the department.

(b) When requesting state-level criminal offender record information pursuant to this section, the designated CASA program shall request subsequent arrest notification, pursuant to Section 11105.2, for all employment and volunteer candidates.

(c) The department shall respond to the designated CASA program with information as delineated in subdivision (p) of Section 11105.

(d) (1) The department shall charge a fee sufficient to cover the cost of processing the requests for federal-level criminal offender record information.

(2) The department shall not charge a fee for state-level criminal offender record information.

(e) For purposes of this section, a designated CASA program is a local court-appointed special advocate program that has adopted and adheres to the guidelines established by the Judicial Council and which has been designated by the local presiding juvenile court judge to recruit, screen, select, train, supervise, and support lay volunteers to be appointed by the court to help define the best interests of children in juvenile court dependency and wardship proceedings. For purposes of this section, there shall be only one designated CASA program in each California county.

(Amended by Stats. 2017, Ch. 561, Sec. 192. (AB 1516) Effective January 1, 2018.)
11105.06.
The Department of Justice shall retain an individual's fingerprint images and related information submitted as part of a peace officer or nonsworn law enforcement agency employee preemployment criminal offender record information search request. When responding to preemployment criminal offender record information search requests pursuant to subdivision (k) or (l) of Section 11105, the department shall disseminate the request date and requesting agency name associated with all retained peace officer and nonsworn law enforcement agency employee information search requests.

(Added by Stats. 2009, Ch. 97, Sec. 2. (AB 297) Effective January 1, 2010.)
11105.07.
(a) An animal control officer, when necessary for performing his or her official duties, shall provide a compelling reason to an appropriate criminal justice agency to obtain state summary criminal history information.

(b) Upon a showing of compelling need, the criminal justice agency shall respond to the animal control officer with state summary criminal history information obtained through the California Law Enforcement Telecommunications Systems (CLETS). The criminal justice agency shall provide this information to the animal control officer in a timely manner. A criminal justice agency may charge a reasonable fee sufficient to cover the costs of providing information pursuant to this subdivision.

(c) An animal control officer who receives state summary criminal history information pursuant to this section shall not use that information for any purpose other than for the performance of his or her official duties.

(d) A law enforcement officer or other person authorized by law to provide or receive information obtained through CLETS pursuant to this section who knowingly furnishes the record or information to a person who is not authorized by law to receive that information is guilty of violating Section 11142.

(e) For the purposes of this section, an animal control officer is a person authorized to exercise the powers specified in Section 830.9.

(Added by Stats. 2014, Ch. 449, Sec. 1. (AB 1511) Effective January 1, 2015.)
11105.08.
(a) Notwithstanding any other law, a tribal agency may request from the Department of Justice state and federal level summary criminal history information for the purpose of approving a tribal home for the placement of an Indian child into foster or adoptive care.

(b) A tribal agency shall submit to the Department of Justice fingerprint images and related information required by the Department of Justice of an individual applying with the tribal agency as a prospective foster parent or adoptive parent, any adult who resides or is employed in the home of an applicant, any person who has a familial or intimate relationship with any person living in the home of an applicant, or employee of the child welfare agency who may have contact with a child, for the purposes of obtaining information as to the existence and content of a record of state or federal convictions and state or federal arrests and also information as to the existence and content of a record of state or federal arrests for which the Department of Justice establishes that the person is released on bail or on his or her own recognizance pending trial or appeal.

(c) Upon receipt of a request for federal summary criminal history information received pursuant to this section, the Department of Justice shall forward the request to the Federal Bureau of Investigation. The Department of Justice shall review the information returned from the Federal Bureau of Investigation and compile and disseminate a response to the requesting tribal child welfare agency.

(d) The Department of Justice shall provide a state and federal level response to a tribal child welfare agency pursuant to subdivision (m) of Section 11105 of the Penal Code.

(e) A tribal agency shall request from the Department of Justice subsequent notification service pursuant to Section 11105.2 for persons described in subdivision (b) of this section.

(f) The Department of Justice may charge a fee sufficient to cover the reasonable and appropriate costs of processing the request pursuant to this section.

(g) As used in this section a "tribal agency" means an entity designated by a federally recognized tribe as authorized to approve a home consistent with the federal Indian Child Welfare Act (25 U.S.C. Sec. 1901 et seq.), for the purpose of placement of an Indian child into foster or adoptive care, including the authority to conduct a criminal or child abuse background check of, and grant exemptions to, an individual who is a prospective foster or adoptive parent, an adult who resides or is employed in the home of an applicant for approval, any person who has a familial or intimate relationship with any person living in the home of an applicant, or an employee of a tribal child welfare agency who may have contact with a child.

(Amended by Stats. 2017, Ch. 561, Sec. 193. (AB 1516) Effective January 1, 2018.)

11105.1.

(a) The following persons shall be furnished with state summary criminal history information when needed in the course of their duties:

(1) The director of a state hospital or other treatment facility to which a person is committed for treatment under Sections 1026 and 1370 of the Penal Code, or Section 5250, if committed for being dangerous to others, or Section 5300, or former Section 6316 or 6321, of the Welfare and Institutions Code.

(2) The community program director or the director's designee under any of the following conditions:

(A) When ordered to evaluate a defendant for the court under paragraph (2) of subdivision (a) of Section 1370 and subdivision (b) of Section 1026 of the Penal Code, or paragraph (2) of subdivision (a) of former Section 6316 of the Welfare and Institutions Code.

(B) When ordered to provide outpatient treatment and supervision services under Title 15 (commencing with Section 1600) of Part 2 of the Penal Code.

(C) When a patient is committed for being dangerous to others under Section 5250 of the Welfare and Institutions Code.

(D) When the director or the director's designee provides evaluation, supervision, or treatment for a person under Section 2964 or 2972.

(3) The officer providing conservatorship investigation under Section 5354 of the Welfare and Institutions Code in cases where referral for conservatorship is made while the proposed conservatee is being treated under Section 1026 or 1370 of the Penal Code or Section 5250, if committed for being dangerous to others, or Section 5300, or former Section 6316 or 6321, of the Welfare and Institutions Code.

(b) In all instances pursuant to subdivision (a), the criminal history record shall be transmitted by the court with the request for evaluation or during the conservatorship investigation or with the order committing the person to a treatment facility or approving outpatient status, except that the director of a state hospital, the county mental health director, and the officer providing conservatorship investigation may receive the state summary criminal history information from the law enforcement agency that referred the person for evaluation and treatment under Section 5150 of the Welfare and Institutions Code if the person has been subsequently committed for being dangerous to others under Section 5250 of the Welfare and Institutions Code. Information obtained under this subdivision shall not be included in any document which will become part of a public record.

(Amended by Stats. 1988, Ch. 657, Sec. 3.)

11105.2.

(a) (1) The Department of Justice shall provide to the State Department of Social Services, the Medical Board of California, and the Osteopathic Medical Board of California, pursuant to state or federal law authorizing those departments to receive state or federal summary criminal history information, and may provide to any other entity authorized by state or federal law to receive state or federal summary criminal history information, subsequent state or federal arrest or disposition notification to assist in fulfilling employment, licensing, or certification duties, or the duties of approving relative caregivers, nonrelative extended family members, and resource families upon the arrest or disposition of any person whose fingerprints are maintained on file at the Department of Justice or the Federal Bureau of Investigation as the result of an application for licensing, employment, certification, or approval. This section does not authorize the notification of a subsequent disposition pertaining to a disposition that does not result in a conviction, unless the department has previously received notification of the arrest and has previously lawfully notified a receiving entity of the pending status of that arrest. If the department supplies subsequent arrest or disposition notification to a receiving entity, the entity shall, at the same time, expeditiously furnish a copy of the information to the person to whom it relates if the information is a basis for an adverse employment, licensing, or certification decision. If the copy is not furnished in person, the copy shall be delivered to the last contact information provided by the applicant.

(2) An entity that submits the fingerprints of applicants for licensing, employment, or certification, or approval to the Department of Justice for the purpose of establishing a record of the applicant to receive notification of subsequent state or federal arrests or dispositions pursuant to paragraph (1) shall comply with subdivision (d).

(b) For purposes of this section, "approval" means those duties described in subdivision (d) of Section 309 of the Welfare and Institutions Code for approving the home of a relative caregiver or of a nonrelative extended family member for placement of a child supervised by the juvenile court, and those duties in Section 16519.5 of the Welfare and Institutions Code for resource families.

(c) An entity, other than a law enforcement agency employing peace officers as defined in Section 830.1, subdivisions (a) and (e) of Section 830.2, subdivision (a) of Section 830.3, subdivisions (a) and (b) of Section 830.5, and subdivision (a) of Section 830.31, shall enter into a contract with the Department of Justice in order to receive notification of subsequent state or federal arrests or dispositions for licensing, employment, or certification purposes.

(d) An entity that submits the fingerprints of applicants for licensing, employment, certification, or approval to the Department of Justice for the purpose of establishing a record of the applicant to receive notification of subsequent state or federal arrests or dispositions shall immediately notify the department when the employment of the applicant is terminated, when the applicant's license or certificate is revoked, when the applicant may no longer renew or reinstate the license or certificate, or when a relative caregiver's or nonrelative extended family member's approval is terminated. The Department of Justice shall terminate state or federal subsequent notification on any applicant upon the request of the licensing, employment, certifying, or approving authority.

(e) An entity that receives a notification of a state or federal subsequent arrest or disposition for a person unknown to the entity, or for a person no longer employed by the entity, or no longer eligible to renew the certificate or license for which subsequent notification service was established shall immediately return the subsequent notification to the Department of Justice, informing the department that the entity is no longer interested in the applicant. The entity shall not record or otherwise retain any information received as a result of the subsequent notice.

(f) An entity that submits the fingerprints of an applicant for employment, licensing, certification, or approval to the Department of Justice for the purpose of establishing a record at the department or the Federal Bureau of Investigation to receive notification of

subsequent arrest or disposition shall immediately notify the department if the applicant is not subsequently employed, or if the applicant is denied licensing certification, or approval.

(g) An entity that fails to provide the Department of Justice with notification as set forth in subdivisions (c), (d), and (e) may be denied further subsequent notification service.

(h) Notwithstanding subdivisions (c), (d), and (f), subsequent notification by the Department of Justice and retention by the employing agency shall continue as to retired peace officers listed in subdivision (c) of Section 830.5.

(Amended by Stats. 2018, Ch. 300, Sec. 1. (AB 2461) Effective January 1, 2019.)

11105.3.

(a) Notwithstanding any other law, a human resource agency or an employer may request from the Department of Justice records of all convictions or any arrest pending adjudication involving the offenses specified in subdivision (a) of Section 15660 of the Welfare and Institutions Code of a person who applies for a license, employment, or volunteer position, in which he or she would have supervisory or disciplinary power over a minor or any person under his or her care. The department shall furnish the information to the requesting employer and shall also send a copy of the information to the applicant.

(b) Any request for records under subdivision (a) shall include the applicant's fingerprints, which may be taken by the requester, and any other data specified by the department. The request shall be on a form approved by the department, and the department may charge a fee to be paid by the employer, human resource agency, or applicant for the actual cost of processing the request. However, no fee shall be charged to a nonprofit organization. Requests received by the department for federal level criminal offender record information shall be forwarded to the Federal Bureau of Investigation by the department to be searched for any record of arrests or convictions.

(c) (1) When a request pursuant to this section reveals that a prospective employee or volunteer has been convicted of a violation or attempted violation of Section 220, 261.5, 262, 273a, 273d, or 273.5, or any sex offense listed in Section 290, except for the offense specified in subdivision (d) of Section 243.4, and where the agency or employer hires the prospective employee or volunteer, the agency or employer shall notify the parents or guardians of any minor who will be supervised or disciplined by the employee or volunteer. A conviction for a violation or attempted violation of an offense committed outside the State of California shall be included in this notice if the offense would have been a crime specified in this subdivision if committed in California. The notice shall be given to the parents or guardians with whom the child resides, and shall be given at least 10 days prior to the day that the employee or volunteer begins his or her duties or tasks. Notwithstanding any other law, any person who conveys or receives information in good faith and in conformity with this section is exempt from prosecution under Section 11142 or 11143 for that conveying or receiving of information. Notwithstanding subdivision (d), the notification requirements of this subdivision shall apply as an additional requirement of any other provision of law requiring criminal record access or dissemination of criminal history information.

(2) The notification requirement pursuant to paragraph (1) shall not apply to a misdemeanor conviction for violating Section 261.5 or to a conviction for violating Section 262 or 273.5. Nothing in this paragraph shall preclude an employer from requesting records of convictions for violating Section 261.5, 262, or 273.5 from the Department of Justice pursuant to this section.

(d) Nothing in this section supersedes any law requiring criminal record access or dissemination of criminal history information. In any conflict with another statute, dissemination of criminal history information shall be pursuant to the mandatory statute. This subdivision applies to, but is not limited to, requirements pursuant to Article 1 (commencing with Section 1500) of Chapter 3 of, and Chapter 3.2 (commencing with Section 1569) and Chapter 3.4 (commencing with Section 1596.70) of, Division 2 of, and Section 1522 of, the Health and Safety Code, and Sections 8712, 8811, and 8908 of the Family Code, and Section 16519.5 of the Welfare and Institutions Code.

(e) The department may adopt regulations to implement the provisions of this section as necessary.

(f) As used in this section, "employer" means any nonprofit corporation or other organization specified by the Attorney General that employs or uses the services of volunteers in positions in which the volunteer or employee has supervisory or disciplinary power over a child or children.

(g) As used in this section, "human resource agency" means a public or private entity, excluding any agency responsible for licensing of facilities pursuant to the California Community Care Facilities Act (Chapter 3 (commencing with Section 1500)), the California Residential Care Facilities for the Elderly Act (Chapter 3.2 (commencing with Section 1569)), Chapter 3.01 (commencing with Section 1568.01), and the California Child Day Care Facilities Act (Chapter 3.4 (commencing with Section 1596.70)) of Division 2 of the Health and Safety Code, responsible for determining the character and fitness of a person who is:

(1) Applying for a license, employment, or as a volunteer within the human services field that involves the care and security of children, the elderly, the handicapped, or the mentally impaired.

(2) Applying to be a volunteer who transports individuals impaired by drugs or alcohol.

(3) Applying to adopt a child or to be a foster parent.

(h) Except as provided in subdivision (c), any criminal history information obtained pursuant to this section is confidential and no recipient shall disclose its contents other than for the purpose for which it was acquired.

(i) As used in this subdivision, "community youth athletic program" means an employer having as its primary purpose the promotion or provision of athletic activities for youth under 18 years of age.

(j) A community youth athletic program, as defined in subdivision (i), may request state and federal level criminal history information pursuant to subdivision (a) for a volunteer coach or hired coach candidate. The director of the community youth athletic program shall be the custodian of records.

(k) The community youth athletic program may request from the Department of Justice subsequent arrest notification service, as provided in Section 11105.2, for a volunteer coach or a hired coach candidate.

(l) Compliance with this section does not remove or limit the liability of a mandated reporter pursuant to Section 11166.

(Amended by Stats. 2015, Ch. 773, Sec. 44. (AB 403) Effective January 1, 2016.)

11105.4.

(a) Notwithstanding any other provision of law, a contract or proprietary security organization may request any criminal history information concerning its prospective employees that may be furnished pursuant to subdivision (n) of Section 11105.

(b) The Department of Justice shall promulgate regulations to assure that criminal record information is not released to persons or entities not authorized to receive the information under this section.

(c) Any criminal history information obtained pursuant to this section shall be subject to the same requirements and conditions that the information is subject to when obtained by a human resource agency or a bank.

(d) The Legislature finds that contract security organizations and private security organizations often provide security service for financial institutions and human resource agencies, and, consequently, they have the same need for criminal history information as do those entities. Therefore, the Legislature intends to provide authority for contract security organizations and proprietary security organizations to obtain criminal history information to the extent that financial institutions and human resource agencies have that authority concerning their own employees.

(e) As used in this section, "contract security organization" means a person, business, or organization licensed to provide services as a private patrol operator, as defined in subdivision (a) of Section 7582.1 of the Business and Professions Code.

As used in this section, "proprietary security organization" means an organization within a business entity that has the primary responsibility of protecting the employees and property of its employer, and which allocates a substantial part of its annual budget to providing security and protective services for its employer, including providing qualifying and in-service training to members of the organization.

(f) Any criminal history information obtained pursuant to this section is confidential and no recipient shall disclose its contents other than for the purpose for which it was acquired.

(Amended by Stats. 2002, Ch. 627, Sec. 5. Effective January 1, 2003.)

11105.5.
When the Department of Justice receives a report that the record of a person has been sealed under Section 851.7, 851.8, or 1203.45, it shall send notice of that fact to all officers and agencies that it had previously notified of the arrest or other proceedings against the person.

(Amended by Stats. 1985, Ch. 106, Sec. 109.)

11105.6.
Upon the request of a licensed bail agent or bail bond licensee, as described in Sections 1276 and 1276.5, a local law enforcement agency may furnish an individual's known aliases and booking photograph, information identifying whether the individual has been convicted of any violent felony, as defined in subdivision (c) of Section 667.5, and an unaltered copy of the booking and property record, excluding any medical information, to the agent or licensee if all of the following circumstances exist:

(a) The information is from the record of a person for whom a bench warrant has been issued, or for whom a bail forfeiture has been ordered.

(b) The person described in subdivision (a) is a client of the agent or licensee.

(c) The agent or licensee pays to the law enforcement agency a fee equal to the cost of providing the information.

(d) Any information obtained pursuant to this section is confidential and the recipient bail agent or bail bond licensee shall not disclose its contents, other than for the purpose for which it was acquired. A violation of this subdivision is a misdemeanor.

(Amended by Stats. 1999, Ch. 33, Sec. 1. Effective January 1, 2000.)

11105.7.
(a) Notwithstanding any other provision of law, when a person is required to submit fingerprints or a fingerprint card to the Department of Justice for a criminal background investigation for purposes of employment, certification, or licensing, and the department determines either that it is impossible for the person to submit fingerprints or that the submitted fingerprints are not legible for identification purposes, the department, in its discretion, shall do either of the following:

(1) Make a determination that the person presently is unable to provide legible fingerprints, and therefore shall be deemed to have complied with the statutory requirement to submit fingerprints. The department, using available personal identifying data that the department deems appropriate, shall then conduct a search to determine if the person has a criminal history.

(2) Request that the person submit a second set of fingerprints or obtain verification from another law enforcement agency that he or she is unable to provide legible fingerprint impressions either manually or electronically. If the department requests law enforcement verification of the quality of fingerprints that the person is able to provide, it may designate the law enforcement agency that is to provide the verification and provide a form for the verification. If the second set of fingerprints is illegible or if the designated law enforcement agency verifies that the person is unable to submit legible fingerprints, the person shall be deemed to have complied with the statutory requirement to submit fingerprints, and the department, using available personal identifying data it deems appropriate, shall conduct a search to determine if the person has a criminal history.

(b) After a search of its data bases pursuant to subdivision (a), the department shall issue a certificate regarding the criminal history of the applicant to the employing, licensing, or certifying agency. This certificate shall indicate whether or not the applicant has any reportable criminal history for purposes of the employment, license, or certificate the applicant is seeking. The agency shall be entitled to receive information regarding any reportable offenses and may use this information to make a determination of eligibility.

(c) Whenever the department determines pursuant to this section that a person has a criminal record, the person shall be provided an opportunity to question the accuracy or completeness of any material matter contained in the record, under the procedures provided in Section 11126.

(d) It is the intent of the Legislature that this section shall only apply to those persons who are unable to supply legible fingerprints due to disability, illness, accident, or other circumstances beyond their control and does not apply to persons who are unable to provide fingerprints because of actions they have taken to avoid submitting their fingerprints.

(Added by Stats. 1998, Ch. 452, Sec. 1. Effective September 14, 1998.)

11105.75.
(a) (1) If, in the course of performing a criminal history background investigation for an agency or entity statutorily authorized to receive a criminal history, the Department of Justice determines that it appears that the applicant has criminal history record information that the requesting agency is statutorily authorized to receive, but the identity of the applicant cannot be verified with fingerprints, the department shall provide a copy of the criminal history record to the requesting agency or entity but shall note any entries as to which the identity of the subject has not been fingerprint verified.

(2) The department shall compare all available identifying characteristics of the applicant with those that appear in the criminal history information before responding to the requesting agency or entity with conviction disposition information that has not been fingerprint verified.

(b) If an agency or entity denies a license, certificate, or employment based upon information received from the department that is not fingerprint verified, the agency or entity shall notify the applicant of its decision and that he or she may challenge the identification. In that case, the applicant may appeal the decision of the agency or entity on the grounds that the applicant is not the person so identified.

(c) Neither the department nor any of its employees or any requesting agency or entity shall be liable to any applicant for misidentifications made pursuant to this section.

(Added by Stats. 2000, Ch. 623, Sec. 1. Effective January 1, 2001. Operative July 1, 2002, by Sec. 2 of Ch. 623.)

11105.8.
A nonprofit organization that is funded pursuant to subsection (a) of Section 3796h of Title 42 of the United States Code may be granted access to local, state, or federal criminal justice system information available to law enforcement agencies, including access to the California Law Enforcement Telecommunications System, provided that the nonprofit agency meets all other federal and state requirements for access to that information or system.

(Added by Stats. 2010, Ch. 719, Sec. 53. (SB 856) Effective October 19, 2010.)

11105.9.
(a) Notwithstanding subdivision (g) of Section 11105 and subdivision (a) of Section 13305, the Department of Corrections and Rehabilitation may provide the social security numbers of current or former inmates to the Employment Development Department, the California Workforce Development Board, or the California Workforce Development Board's designee for the purposes set forth in subdivision (i) of Section 14013 of the

Unemployment Insurance Code. The Employment Development Department, the California Workforce Development Board, and any board designee shall keep the social security numbers confidential and use them only to track the labor market and other employment outcomes of program participants, as described in subdivision (i) of Section 14013 of the Unemployment Insurance Code.

(b) The Employment Development Department, the California Workforce Development Board, and any board designee shall not disseminate social security numbers obtained pursuant to this section to an individual or public entity not identified in this section.

(Added by Stats. 2019, Ch. 25, Sec. 44. (SB 94) Effective June 27, 2019.)

11106.
(a) (1) In order to assist in the investigation of crime, the prosecution of civil actions by city attorneys pursuant to paragraph (3) of subdivision (b), the arrest and prosecution of criminals, and the recovery of lost, stolen, or found property, the Attorney General shall keep and properly file a complete record of all of the following:

(A) All copies of fingerprints.

(B) Copies of licenses to carry firearms issued pursuant to Section 26150, 26155, 26170, or 26215.

(C) Information reported to the Department of Justice pursuant to subdivision (e) of Section 18120, Section 26225, 27875, 27920, 29180, or 29830.

(D) Dealers' Records of Sales of firearms.

(E) Reports provided pursuant to Article 1 (commencing with Section 27500) of Chapter 4 of Division 6 of Title 4 of Part 6, or pursuant to any provision listed in subdivision (a) of Section 16585.

(F) Forms provided pursuant to Section 12084, as that section read prior to being repealed on January 1, 2006.

(G) Reports provided pursuant to Article 1 (commencing with Section 26700) and Article 2 (commencing with Section 26800) of Chapter 2 of Division 6 of Title 4 of Part 6, that are not dealers' records of sales of firearms.

(H) Information provided pursuant to Section 28255.

(I) Reports of stolen, lost, found, pledged, or pawned property in any city or county of this state.

(2) The Attorney General shall, upon proper application therefor, furnish the information to the officers referred to in Section 11105.

(b) (1) The Attorney General shall permanently keep and properly file and maintain all information reported to the Department of Justice pursuant to the following provisions as to firearms and maintain a registry thereof:

(A) Article 1 (commencing with Section 26700) and Article 2 (commencing with Section 26800) of Chapter 2 of Division 6 of Title 4 of Part 6.

(B) Article 1 (commencing with Section 27500) of Chapter 4 of Division 6 of Title 4 of Part 6.

(C) Chapter 5 (commencing with Section 28050) of Division 6 of Title 4 of Part 6.

(D) Any provision listed in subdivision (a) of Section 16585.

(E) Former Section 12084.

(F) Section 28255.

(G) Section 29180.

(H) Any other law.

(2) The registry shall consist of all of the following:

(A) The name, address, identification of, place of birth (state or country), complete telephone number, occupation, sex, description, and all legal names and aliases ever used by the owner or person being loaned the particular firearm as listed on the information provided to the department on the Dealers' Record of Sale, the Law Enforcement Firearms Transfer (LEFT), as defined in former Section 12084, or reports made to the department pursuant to any provision listed in subdivision (a) of Section 16585, Section 28255 or 29180, or any other law.

(B) The name and address of, and other information about, any person (whether a dealer or a private party) from whom the owner acquired or the person being loaned the particular firearm and when the firearm was acquired or loaned as listed on the information provided to the department on the Dealers' Record of Sale, the LEFT, or reports made to the department pursuant to any provision listed in subdivision (a) of Section 16585 or any other law.

(C) Any waiting period exemption applicable to the transaction which resulted in the owner of or the person being loaned the particular firearm acquiring or being loaned that firearm.

(D) The manufacturer's name if stamped on the firearm, model name or number if stamped on the firearm, and, if applicable, the serial number, other number (if more than one serial number is stamped on the firearm), caliber, type of firearm, if the firearm is new or used, barrel length, and color of the firearm, or, if the firearm is not a handgun and does not have a serial number or any identification number or mark assigned to it, that shall be noted.

(3) Information in the registry referred to in this subdivision shall, upon proper application therefor, be furnished to the officers referred to in Section 11105, to a city attorney prosecuting a civil action, solely for use in prosecuting that civil action and not for any other purpose, or to the person listed in the registry as the owner or person who is listed as being loaned the particular firearm.

(4) If any person is listed in the registry as the owner of a firearm through a Dealers' Record of Sale prior to 1979, and the person listed in the registry requests by letter that the Attorney General store and keep the record electronically, as well as in the record's existing photographic, photostatic, or nonerasable optically stored form, the Attorney General shall do so within three working days of receipt of the request. The Attorney General shall, in writing, and as soon as practicable, notify the person requesting electronic storage of the record that the request has been honored as required by this paragraph.

(c) (1) If the conditions specified in paragraph (2) are met, any officer referred to in paragraphs (1) to (6), inclusive, of subdivision (b) of Section 11105 may disseminate the name of the subject of the record, the number of the firearms listed in the record, and the description of any firearm, including the make, model, and caliber, from the record relating to any firearm's sale, transfer, registration, or license record, or any information reported to the Department of Justice pursuant to any of the following:

(A) Section 26225, 27875, or 27920.

(B) Article 1 (commencing with Section 26700) and Article 2 (commencing with Section 26800) of Chapter 2 of Division 6 of Title 4 of Part 6.

(C) Article 1 (commencing with Section 27500) of Chapter 4 of Division 6 of Title 4 of Part 6.

(D) Chapter 5 (commencing with Section 28050) of Division 6 of Title 4 of Part 6.

(E) Article 2 (commencing with Section 28150) of Chapter 6 of Division 6 of Title 4 of Part 6.

(F) Article 5 (commencing with Section 30900) of Chapter 2 of Division 10 of Title 4 of Part 6.

(G) Chapter 2 (commencing with Section 33850) of Division 11 of Title 4 of Part 6.

(H) Any provision listed in subdivision (a) of Section 16585.

(2) Information may be disseminated pursuant to paragraph (1) only if all of the following conditions are satisfied:

(A) The subject of the record has been arraigned for a crime in which the victim is a person described in subdivisions (a) to (f), inclusive, of Section 6211 of the Family Code and is being prosecuted or is serving a sentence for the crime, or the subject of the record is the subject of an emergency protective order, a temporary restraining order, or an order after hearing, which is in effect and has been issued by a family court under the Domestic Violence Prevention Act set forth in Division 10 (commencing with Section 6200) of the Family Code.

(B) The information is disseminated only to the victim of the crime or to the person who has obtained the emergency protective order, the temporary restraining order, or the order after hearing issued by the family court.

(C) Whenever a law enforcement officer disseminates the information authorized by this subdivision, that officer or another officer assigned to the case shall immediately provide the victim of the crime with a "Victims of Domestic Violence" card, as specified in subparagraph (H) of paragraph (9) of subdivision (c) of Section 13701.

(3) The victim or person to whom information is disseminated pursuant to this subdivision may disclose it as he or she deems necessary to protect himself or herself or another person from bodily harm by the person who is the subject of the record.

(Amended by Stats. 2018, Ch. 898, Sec. 2. (SB 1200) Effective January 1, 2019.)

11106.1.

Any system of microphotography, optical disk, or reproduction by other techniques that do not permit additions, deletions, or changes to the original document, may be used by the Department of Justice as a photographic reproduction process to record some or all instruments, papers, photographs, and notices that are required or permitted by law to be recorded or filed. All storage medium shall comply with minimum standards of quality approved by the National Institute of Standards and Technology.

(Amended by Stats. 1993, Ch. 1270, Sec. 4. Effective January 1, 1994.)

11106.2.

Any criminal justice agency may cause any or all files or records in its official custody to be microphotographed or otherwise reproduced pursuant to Section 11106.1, as in the case of original filings or recordings, or both. Every reproduction shall be deemed and considered an original, and as a transcript, exemplification or certified copy, as the case may be, of the original.

(Added by Stats. 1989, Ch. 257, Sec. 4.)

11106.3.

Fingerprints may be stored or created in an electronic format that does not permit additions, deletions or changes to the original fingerprints so long as the storage medium complies with the minimum standards of quality approved by the National Institute of Standards and Technology.

(Added by Stats. 2004, Ch. 65, Sec. 2. Effective January 1, 2005.)

11106.4.

(a) Every law enforcement agency shall develop, adopt, and implement written policies and standard protocols pertaining to the best manner to conduct a "welfare check," when the inquiry into the welfare or well-being of the person is motivated by a concern that the person may be a danger to himself or herself or to others. The policies shall encourage a peace officer, prior to conducting the welfare check and whenever possible and reasonable, to conduct a search of the Department of Justice Automated Firearms System via the California Law Enforcement Telecommunications System to determine whether the person is the registered owner of a firearm.

(b) For purposes of this section, "reasonable" as used in subdivision (a) means that the officer could conduct the firearm registry check without undue burden on the execution of the officer's other duties, that there are no exigent circumstances demanding immediate attention, and that the peace officer has access to, or can reasonably ascertain, relevant identifying information.

(Added by Stats. 2014, Ch. 918, Sec. 1. (SB 505) Effective January 1, 2015.)

11107.

Each sheriff or police chief executive shall furnish all of the following information to the Department of Justice on standard forms approved by the department:

Daily reports of those misdemeanors and felonies that are required to be reported by the Attorney General including, but not limited to, forgery, fraud-bunco, bombings, receiving or selling stolen property, safe and commercial burglary, grand theft, child abuse, homicide, threats, and offenses involving lost, stolen, found, pledged, or pawned property.

The reports required by this section shall describe the nature and character of each such crime and note all particular circumstances thereof and include all additional or supplemental data. The Attorney General may also require that the report shall indicate whether or not the submitting agency considers the information to be confidential because it was compiled for the purpose of a criminal investigation of suspected criminal activities. The term "criminal investigation" includes the gathering and maintenance of information pertaining to suspected criminal activity.

(Amended by Stats. 1984, Ch. 1613, Sec. 1. Effective September 30, 1984.)

11107.5.

The Attorney General shall report annually to the Legislature concerning the information pertaining to the sexual abuse of children reported to the Department of Justice pursuant to Sections 11107 and 11169. No confidential information shall be released in the reports submitted to the Legislature.

(Added by Stats. 1985, Ch. 592, Sec. 1.)

11108.

Each sheriff or police chief executive shall submit descriptions of serialized property, or nonserialized property that has been uniquely inscribed, which has been reported stolen, lost, found, recovered, held for safekeeping, or under observation, directly into the appropriate Department of Justice automated property system for stolen bicycles, stolen vehicles, or other property, as the case may be.

(Amended by Stats. 2018, Ch. 864, Sec. 1. (AB 2222) Effective January 1, 2019.)

11108.2.

(a) A law enforcement agency shall enter or cause to be entered into the Department of Justice Automated Firearms System each firearm that has been reported stolen, lost, found, recovered, held for safekeeping, or under observation, within seven calendar days after being notified of the precipitating event.

(b) Information about a firearm entered into the automated system for firearms shall remain in the system until the reported firearm has been found, recovered, is no longer under observation, or the record is determined to have been entered in error.

(c) Any costs incurred by the Department of Justice to implement subdivision (b) shall be reimbursed from funds other than fees charged and collected pursuant to Sections 28225 and 28230.

(d) As used in this section, "law enforcement agency" means a police or sheriff's department, or any department or agency of the state or any political subdivision thereof that employs any peace officer as defined in Section 830, including, but not limited to, the Department of the California Highway Patrol, the Department of Fish and Wildlife, the University of California or California State University Police Departments, and the police department of any school district, transit district, airport, and harbor, port, or housing authority.

(Added by Stats. 2018, Ch. 864, Sec. 2. (AB 2222) Effective January 1, 2019.)

11108.3.

(a) In addition to the requirements of Section 11108.2 that apply to a law enforcement agency's duty to report to the Department of Justice the recovery of a firearm, a law enforcement agency described in Section 11108.2 shall, and any other law enforcement agency or agent, including but not limited to a federal or tribal law enforcement agency or agent, may, report to the department in a manner determined by the Attorney General in consultation with the Bureau of Alcohol, Tobacco, Firearms and Explosives all available information necessary to identify and trace the history of all recovered firearms that are illegally possessed, have been used in a crime, or are suspected of having been used in a crime, within seven calendar days of obtaining the information.

(b) When the department receives information from a law enforcement agency pursuant to subdivision (a), it shall promptly forward this information to the National Tracing Center of the federal Bureau of Alcohol, Tobacco, Firearms and Explosives to the extent practicable.

(c) In implementing this section, the Attorney General shall ensure to the maximum extent practical that both of the following apply:

(1) The information he or she provides to the federal Bureau of Alcohol, Tobacco, Firearms and Explosives enables that agency to trace the ownership of the firearm described in subdivision (a).

(2) Law enforcement agencies can report all relevant information without being unduly burdened by this reporting function.

(d) Information collected pursuant to this section shall be maintained by the department for a period of not less than 10 years, and shall be available, under guidelines set forth by the Attorney General, for academic and policy research purposes.

(e) The Attorney General may issue regulations to further the purposes of this section.

(Amended by Stats. 2018, Ch. 864, Sec. 3. (AB 2222) Effective January 1, 2019.)

11108.5.

(a) If a law enforcement agency identifies serialized property or any property reported pursuant to Section 21628 of the Business and Professions Code that has been reported lost or stolen by the owner or a person entitled to possession of the property and the property has been entered into the appropriate Department of Justice automated property system pursuant to Section 11108 or 11108.2, the agency shall notify the owner or person claiming to be entitled to possession of the property of the location of the property within 15 days of making the identification. If the location of the property was reported by a licensed pawnbroker or secondhand dealer pursuant to Section 21630 of the Business and Professions Code, notwithstanding the method by which the property was identified, notice shall be given to the party who reported the property lost or stolen pursuant to Section 21647 of the Business and Professions Code.

(b) If the property is in the custody of the law enforcement agency and it is determined that the property is no longer required for use as evidence in a criminal case, the property shall be made available to the person entitled to possession pursuant to Section 1417.5 or if the property was found in the possession of a licensed pawnbroker or secondhand dealer, pursuant to Section 21647 of the Business and Professions Code.

(c) Subdivision (a) shall not apply to the return to an owner of a lost or stolen vehicle, as defined in Section 670 of the Vehicle Code if the report of theft or loss of the vehicle into the automated property system preceded the report of the acquisition of property as set forth in Section 21628 of the Business and Professions Code by a licensed pawnbroker.

(Amended by Stats. 2018, Ch. 864, Sec. 4. (AB 2222) Effective January 1, 2019.)

11108.9.

Each local law enforcement agency shall develop, in conjunction with and subject to the approval of the Department of Justice, a succinct Serial Number Restoration Plan setting forth the goals for reduction in the number of recovered firearms that cannot be traced due to obliterated serial numbers, and the methods that the local agency will follow in order to achieve these goals, including, but not limited to, establishing local programs for restoring serial numbers and accessing resources of the Department of Justice or the federal Bureau of Alcohol, Tobacco, Firearms and Explosives for restoring serial numbers. These plans shall be submitted to the Department of Justice by January 1, 2000.

(Amended by Stats. 2014, Ch. 103, Sec. 2. (AB 1798) Effective January 1, 2015.)

11108.10.

(a) In addition to the requirements of Sections 11108.2 and 11108.3, a local law enforcement agency may cause to be entered into the United States Department of Justice, National Integrated Ballistic Information Network (NIBIN) information to ensure that representative samples of fired bullets and cartridge cases collected at crime scenes, from test-fires of firearms recovered at crime scenes, and other firearm information needed to investigate crimes, are recorded into the NIBIN in accordance with the protocol set forth in subdivision (b).

(b) The Attorney General, in cooperation with those law enforcement agencies that choose to do so, shall develop a protocol for the implementation of this section.

(c) The Attorney General shall have the authority to issue guidelines to further the purposes of this section.

(Amended by Stats. 2018, Ch. 864, Sec. 5. (AB 2222) Effective January 1, 2019.)

11109.

Each coroner promptly shall furnish the Department of Justice with copies of fingerprints on standardized eight-inch by eight-inch cards, and descriptions and other identifying data, including date and place of death, of all deceased persons whose deaths are in classifications requiring inquiry by the coroner where the coroner is not satisfied with the decedent's identification. When it is not physically possible to furnish prints of the 10 fingers, prints or partial prints of any fingers, with other identifying data, shall be forwarded by the coroner to the department.

In all cases where there is a criminal record on file in the department for the decedent, the department shall notify the Federal Bureau of Investigation, and each California sheriff and chief of police in whose jurisdiction the decedent has been arrested, of the date and place of death of the decedent.

(Added by renumbering Section 11113 by Stats. 1996, Ch. 124, Sec. 86. Effective January 1, 1997.)

11111.

The Department of Justice shall maintain records relative to stolen and lost bicycles in the Criminal Justice Information System. Such records shall be accessible to authorized law enforcement agencies through the California Law Enforcement Telecommunications System.

(Amended by Stats. 1974, Ch. 971.)

11112.

The Department of Justice, in providing fingerprint clearances for employment purposes, shall facilitate the processing of fingerprint cards of employees of, and applicants for employment with, community care facilities, as defined in Section 1502 of the Health and Safety Code, which provide services to children, and child day care facilities, as defined in Section 1596.750 of the Health and Safety Code.

(Added by Stats. 1986, Ch. 927, Sec. 6. Effective September 22, 1986.)

ARTICLE 3.5. Fingerprints and Photographs [11112.1 - 11112.7]
(Heading of Article 3.5 amended by Stats. 1993, Ch. 1270, Sec. 5.)

11112.1.

As used in this article:

(a) "California Identification System" or "Cal-ID" means the automated system maintained by the Department of Justice for retaining fingerprint files and identifying latent fingerprints.

(b) "Remote Access Network" or "RAN" means a uniform statewide network of equipment and procedures allowing local law enforcement agencies direct access to the California Identification System.

(c) "Department" means the Department of Justice.

(d) "Cal-ID Telecommunications System" means a statewide telecommunications network dedicated to the transmission of fingerprint identification data in conjunction with Cal-ID for use by law enforcement agencies.

(Added by Stats. 1985, Ch. 1234, Sec. 3.)

11112.2.

The department shall develop a master plan recommending the type, number, and location of equipment necessary to implement RAN. The department shall also develop policy guidelines and administrative procedures to facilitate the implementation and use of RAN. The RAN master plan shall include reasonable interface specifications to access

Cal-ID and shall be provided to any supplier of automated fingerprint identification systems interested in bidding on RAN by May 15, 1986.

The master plan shall provide for the use of facsimile and direct image "live read" fingerprint equipment under RAN, including point-of-booking terminals.

The department shall amend the master plan to include additional processing, matching, and communications equipment at the Department of Justice, and to recommend the type, number, and location of equipment necessary to implement facsimile and direct image "live read" fingerprint equipment as part of RAN, including point-of-booking terminals. Funding shall be on a shared basis between the state and a region pursuant to Section 11112.5.

(Amended by Stats. 1988, Ch. 1263, Sec. 1.)

11112.3.

(a) The Attorney General shall appoint a RAN Advisory Committee to review the master plan, policy guidelines, and administrative procedures prepared by the department and advise the Attorney General of any modifications the committee deems necessary. Final approval and acceptance of the RAN Advisory Committee proposals shall be made by the Attorney General.

(b) The RAN Advisory Committee shall be composed of one representative from each of the following: The League of California Cities, California Peace Officers' Association, California District Attorneys' Association, California Police Chiefs' Association, California State Sheriffs' Association, County Supervisors' Association of California, Department of General Services, Office of Information Technology, and the Department of Justice. The members of the committee shall select a chairperson. The members shall serve without compensation, but reasonable and necessary travel and per diem expenses incurred by committee members shall be reimbursed by the department. The RAN Advisory Committee shall terminate January 1, 1989, unless extended by legislation enacted prior thereto.

(Added by Stats. 1985, Ch. 1234, Sec. 3.)

11112.4.

(a) Within each county or group of counties eligible to receive funding under the department's master plan for equipment, that elects to participate in the Remote Access Network, a local RAN board shall be established. Where a single county is eligible to receive funding, that county's RAN board shall be the local RAN board. Where a group of counties is eligible for funding, the local RAN board shall consist of a regional board. The RAN board shall determine the placement of RAN equipment within the county or counties, and coordinate acceptance, delivery, and installation of RAN equipment. The board shall also develop any procedures necessary to regulate the ongoing use and maintenance of that equipment, adhering to the policy guidelines and procedures adopted by the department. The local board shall consider placement of equipment on the basis of the following criteria:

(1) The crime rate of the jurisdiction or jurisdictions served by the agency.

(2) The number of criminal offenses reported by the agency or agencies to the department.

(3) The potential number of fingerprint cards and latent fingerprints processed.

(4) The number of sworn personnel of the agency or agencies.

(b) Except as provided in subdivision (c), each RAN board shall be composed of seven members, as follows: a member of the board of supervisors, the sheriff, the district attorney, the chief of police of the Cal-ID member department having the largest number of sworn personnel within the county, a second chief selected by all other police chiefs within the county, a mayor elected by the city selection committee established pursuant to Section 50270 of the Government Code, and a member-at-large chosen by the other members. In any county lacking two chiefs of police, a substitute member shall be selected by the other members on the board. Groups of counties forming a region shall establish a seven-member board with each county having equal representation on the board and at least one member-at-large. If the number of participating counties precludes equal representation on a seven-member board, the size of the board shall be expanded so that each county has at least two representatives and there is a single member-at-large.

(c) In any county with a population of 5,000,000 or more, each local board shall be composed of seven members, as follows: a member of the board of supervisors, the sheriff, the district attorney, the chief of police of the Cal-ID member department having the largest number of sworn personnel within the county, a second chief selected by all other police chiefs within the county, the mayor of the city with the greatest population within the county that has a Cal-ID member police department, and a member-at-large chosen by the other members. In any county lacking two chiefs of police, a substitute member shall be selected by the other members of the board.

(d) A county which is a part of a regional board may form a local RAN advisory board. The purpose of the local RAN advisory board shall be to provide advice and recommendations to the county's representatives on the regional RAN board. The local RAN advisory board may appoint alternate members to the regional RAN board from the local RAN advisory board to serve and work in the place of a regional RAN board member who is absent or who disqualifies himself or herself from participation in a meeting of the regional RAN board.

If a vacancy occurs in the office of a regional RAN board in a county which has established a local RAN advisory board, an alternate member selected by the local RAN advisory board may serve and vote in place of the former regional RAN board member until the appointment of a regional RAN board member is made to fill the vacancy.

(Amended by Stats. 2004, Ch. 73, Sec. 1. Effective January 1, 2005.)

11112.5.

(a) Costs for equipment purchases based upon the master plan approved by the Attorney General, including state sales tax, freight, insurance, and installation, shall be prorated between the state and local governmental entity. The state's share shall be 70 percent. The local government's share shall be 30 percent, paid in legal tender. Purchases may be made under the existing Cal-ID contract through the Department of General Services.

(b) Alternatively, at the discretion of the local board, an independent competitive procurement may be initiated under the following conditions:

(1) Prior to submitting a bid in an independent procurement, any prospective bidder must demonstrate the ability to meet or exceed performance levels established in the existing Cal-ID contract and demonstrate the ability to interface with Cal-ID and meet or exceed performance levels established in the existing Cal-ID contract without degrading the performance of the Cal-ID system.

(2) Both qualifying benchmarks will be at the prospective bidder's expense and will be conducted by the Department of Justice.

(3) In the event that no vendor other than the existing contract vendor qualifies to bid, purchases shall be made by the Department of General Services on behalf of local agencies pursuant to the existing Cal-ID contract.

(c) Competitive local procurements must adhere to the following guidelines:

(1) Administrative requirements contained within Section 5200 of the State Administrative Manual shall be met.

(2) Local procurements shall not increase the costs the state would otherwise be obligated to pay.

(3) Final bids submitted in an independent procurement shall contain a signed contract that represents an irrevocable offer that does not materially deviate from the terms and conditions of the existing Cal-ID contract.

(4) The selected vendor shall post a performance bond in an amount equal to 25 percent of the local equipment costs. The bond shall remain in effect until the local acceptance test has been successfully completed.

(5) Requests for tender, including contract language, shall be approved by the Department of General Services prior to release. The Department of General Services and the Department of Justice shall be represented on the evaluation and selection team.

(d) The local government agency shall be responsible for all costs related to conducting a local bid, site preparation, equipment maintenance, ongoing operational costs, file conversion over and above those records that are available on magnetic media from the Department of Justice, and equipment enhancements or systems design which exceed the basic design specifications of the Department of Justice. The state shall provide sufficient circuitry to each county, or group of counties to handle all fingerprint data traffic. The state shall provide for annual maintenance of that line.

(Amended by Stats. 2008, Ch. 699, Sec. 16. Effective January 1, 2009.)

11112.6.

(a) The Cal-ID Telecommunications System shall be under the direction of the Attorney General and shall be used exclusively for the official business of the state, and the official business of any city, county, city and county, or other public agency.

(b) The Cal-ID Telecommunications System shall provide telecommunication lines to one location in every participating county.

(c) The Cal-ID Telecommunications System shall be maintained at all times by the department with equipment and facilities adequate to meet the needs of law enforcement. The system shall be designed to accommodate present and future data transmission equipment.

(Added by Stats. 1985, Ch. 1234, Sec. 3.)

11112.7.

The Attorney General shall provide an annual status report to the Legislature beginning January 1, 1987, with the final report due January 1, 1990. The report shall include the status of the project to date, funds expended, and need, if any, for revision to the master plan.

(Amended by Stats. 1988, Ch. 1263, Sec. 3.)

ARTICLE 4. Criminal Records [11115 - 11117]
(Article 4 added by Stats. 1961, Ch. 1025.)

11115.

In any case in which a sheriff, police department or other law enforcement agency makes an arrest and transmits a report of the arrest to the Department of Justice or to the Federal Bureau of Investigation, it shall be the duty of such law enforcement agency to furnish a disposition report to such agencies whenever the arrested person is transferred to the custody of another agency or is released without having a complaint or accusation filed with a court. The disposition report in such cases shall be furnished to the appropriate agencies within 30 days of release or transfer to another agency. If either of the following dispositions is made, the disposition report shall so state:

(a) "Arrested for intoxication and released," when the arrested party is released pursuant to paragraph (2) of subdivision (b) of Section 849.

(b) "Detention only," when the detained party is released pursuant to paragraph (1) of subdivision (b) of Section 849 or issued a certificate pursuant to subdivision (b) of Section 851.6. In such cases the report shall state the specific reason for such release, indicating that there was no ground for making a criminal complaint because (1) further investigation exonerated the arrested party, (2) the complainant withdrew the complaint, (3) further investigation appeared necessary before prosecution could be initiated, (4) the ascertainable evidence was insufficient to proceed further, (5) the admissible or adducible evidence was insufficient to proceed further, or (6) other appropriate explanation for release.

(Amended by Stats. 1978, Ch. 152.)

11116.5.

Any dismissal and reason therefor provided by Section 11115 or 13151.1 may be used by the person subject to the disposition as an answer to any question regarding his arrest or detention history or any question regarding the outcome of a criminal proceeding against him.

(Amended by Stats. 1978, Ch. 152.)

11116.6.

The dispositions provided by Sections 11115 and 13151.1 must be entered on all appropriate records of the party arrested, detained, or against whom criminal proceedings are brought.

(Amended by Stats. 1978, Ch. 152.)

11116.7.

Whenever an accusatory pleading is filed in any court of this state alleging a public offense for which a defendant may be punished by incarceration, for a period in excess of 90 days, the court shall furnish upon request of the defendant named therein a certificate of disposition which describes the disposition of the accusatory pleading in that court when such disposition is one described in Section 13151.1. The certificate of disposition shall be signed by the judge, shall substantially conform with the requirements of Section 11116.8, and the seal of the court shall be affixed thereto. In the event that the initial disposition of the accusatory pleading is changed, a new disposition certificate showing the changed disposition shall be issued by the court changing the same upon request of the defendant or his counsel of record.

(Amended by Stats. 1978, Ch. 152.)

11116.8.

The certificate of disposition provided by Section 11116.7 shall describe the charge or charges set forth in the original and any amended accusatory pleading, together with the disposition of each charge in the original and any amended accusatory pleading.

(Amended by Stats. 1978, Ch. 152.)

11116.9.

The clerk of the court in which the disposition is made shall provide the defendant or his counsel of record with additional certified copies of the disposition certificate upon the payment of the fees provided by law for certified copies of court records.

(Added by Stats. 1972, Ch. 1279.)

11116.10.

(a) Upon the request of a victim or a witness of a crime, the prosecuting attorney shall, within 60 days of the final disposition of the case, inform the victim or witness by letter of such final disposition. Such notice shall state the information described in Section 13151.1.

(b) As used in this section, "victim" means any person alleged or found, upon the record, to have sustained physical or financial injury to person or property as a direct result of the crime charged.

(c) As used in this section, "witness" means any person who has been or is expected to testify for the prosecution, or who, by reason of having relevant information, is subject to call or likely to be called as a witness for the prosecution, whether or not any action or proceeding has yet been commenced.

(d) As used in this section, "final disposition," means an ultimate termination of the case at the trial level including, but not limited to, dismissal, acquittal, or imposition of sentence by the court, or a decision by the prosecuting attorney, for whatever reason, not to file the case.

(e) Subdivision (a) does not apply in any case where the offender or alleged offender is a minor unless the minor has been declared not a fit and proper subject to be dealt with under the juvenile court law.

(f) This section shall not apply to any case in which a disposition was made prior to the effective date of this section.

(Amended by Stats. 1986, Ch. 1427, Sec. 2.)

11117.

The Department of Justice shall prescribe and furnish the procedures and forms to be used for the disposition and other reports required in this article and in Sections 13151 and 13152. The department shall add the reports received to all appropriate criminal records.

Neither the reports required in this article nor those required in Sections 13151 and 13152 shall be admissible in evidence in any civil action.
(Amended by Stats. 1978, Ch. 152, Sec. 9.)

ARTICLE 5. Examination of Records [11120 - 11127]
(Article 5 added by Stats. 1971, Ch. 1439.)

11120.
As used in this article, "record" with respect to any person means the state summary criminal history information as defined in subdivision (a) of Section 11105, maintained under such person's name by the Department of Justice.
(Amended by Stats. 1975, Ch. 1222.)

11121.
It is the function and intent of this article to afford persons concerning whom a record is maintained in the files of the bureau an opportunity to obtain a copy of the record compiled from such files, and to refute any erroneous or inaccurate information contained therein.
(Amended by Stats. 1980, Ch. 939, Sec. 1.)

11122.
Any person desiring a copy of the record relating to himself shall obtain an application form furnished by the department which shall require his fingerprints in addition to such other information as the department shall specify. Applications may be obtained from police departments, sheriff departments, or the Department of Justice. The fingerprinting agency may fix a reasonable fee for affixing the applicant's fingerprints to the form, and shall retain such fee.
(Amended by Stats. 1980, Ch. 939, Sec. 2.)

11123.
The applicant shall submit the completed application directly to the department. The application shall be accompanied by a fee not to exceed twenty-five dollars ($25) that the department determines equals the costs of processing the application and providing a copy of the record to the applicant. All fees received by the department under this section are hereby appropriated without regard to fiscal years for the support of the Department of Justice in addition to such other funds as may be appropriated therefor by the Legislature. Any request for waiver of fee shall accompany the original request for the record and shall include a claim and proof of indigency.
(Amended by Stats. 1980, Ch. 939, Sec. 3.)

11124.
When an application is received by the department, the department shall determine whether a record pertaining to the applicant is maintained. If such record is maintained, the department shall furnish a copy of the record to the applicant or to an individual designated by the applicant. If no such record is maintained, the department shall so notify the applicant or an individual designated by the applicant. Delivery of the copy of the record, or notice of no record, may be by mail or other appropriate means agreed to by the applicant and the department.
(Amended by Stats. 1980, Ch. 939, Sec. 4.)

11125.
No person or agency shall require or request another person to furnish a copy of a record or notification that a record exists or does not exist, as provided in Section 11124. A violation of this section is a misdemeanor.
(Amended by Stats. 1992, Ch. 1227, Sec. 2. Effective January 1, 1993.)

11126.
(a) If the applicant desires to question the accuracy or completeness of any material matter contained in the record, he or she may submit a written request to the department in a form established by it. The request shall include a statement of the alleged inaccuracy or incompleteness in the record, and its materiality, and shall specify any proof or corroboration available. Upon receipt of the request, the department shall review the record to determine if the information correctly reflects the source document, and if it does not, the department shall make the necessary corrections and shall provide the applicant with a corrected copy of the record. If the accuracy of the source document is questioned, the department shall forward it to the person or agency which furnished the questioned information. This person or agency shall, within 30 days of receipt of the written request for clarification, review its information and forward to the department the results of the review.
(b) If the agency concurs in the allegations of inaccuracy or incompleteness in the record, and finds that the error is material, it shall correct its record and shall so inform the department, which shall correct the record accordingly. The department shall inform the applicant of its correction of the record under this subdivision within 30 days. The department and the agency shall notify all persons and agencies to which they have disseminated the incorrect record in the past 90 days of the correction of the record, and the applicant shall be informed that the notification has been given. The department and the agency shall also notify those persons or agencies to which the incorrect record has been disseminated which have been specifically requested by the applicant to receive notification of the correction of the record, and the applicant shall be informed that the notification has been given.
(c) If the department or the agency denies the allegations of inaccuracy or incompleteness in the record, the matter shall be referred for administrative adjudication in accordance with Chapter 5 (commencing with Section 11500) of Part 1, Division 3, Title 2 of the Government Code for a determination of whether material inaccuracy or incompleteness exists in the record. The department shall be the respondent in the hearing. If a material inaccuracy or incompleteness is found in any record, the department and the agency in charge of that record shall be directed to correct it accordingly. The department and the agency shall notify all persons and agencies to which they have disseminated the incorrect record in the past 90 days of the correction of the record, and the applicant shall be informed that the notification has been given. The department and the agency shall also notify those persons or agencies to which the incorrect record has been disseminated which have been specifically requested by the applicant to receive notification of the correction of the record, and the applicant shall be informed that the notification has been given. Judicial review of the decision shall be governed by Section 11523 of the Government Code. The applicant shall be informed of the decision within 30 days of its issuance in accordance with Section 11518 of the Government Code.
(Amended by Stats. 1992, Ch. 1227, Sec. 3. Effective January 1, 1993.)

11127.
The department shall adopt all regulations necessary to carry out the provisions of this article.
(Amended by Stats. 1972, Ch. 1377.)

ARTICLE 6. Unlawful Furnishing of State Summary Criminal History Information [11140 - 11144]
(Heading of Article 6 amended by Stats. 1975, Ch. 1222.)

11140.
As used in this article:
(a) "Record" means the state summary criminal history information as defined in subdivision (a) of Section 11105, or a copy thereof, maintained under a person's name by the Department of Justice.
(b) "A person authorized by law to receive a record" means any person or public agency authorized by a court, statute, or decisional law to receive a record.

(Amended by Stats. 1975, Ch. 1222.)

11141.
Any employee of the Department of Justice who knowingly furnishes a record or information obtained from a record to a person who is not authorized by law to receive the record or information is guilty of a misdemeanor.
(Added by Stats. 1974, Ch. 963.)

11142.
Any person authorized by law to receive a record or information obtained from a record who knowingly furnishes the record or information to a person who is not authorized by law to receive the record or information is guilty of a misdemeanor.
(Added by Stats. 1974, Ch. 963.)

11143.
Any person, except those specifically referred to in Section 1070 of the Evidence Code, who, knowing he is not authorized by law to receive a record or information obtained from a record, knowingly buys, receives, or possesses the record or information is guilty of a misdemeanor.
(Added by Stats. 1974, Ch. 963.)

11144.
(a) It is not a violation of this article to disseminate statistical or research information obtained from a record, provided that the identity of the subject of the record is not disclosed.
(b) It is not a violation of this article to disseminate information obtained from a record for the purpose of assisting in the apprehension of a person wanted in connection with the commission of a crime.
(c) It is not a violation of this article to include information obtained from a record in (1) a transcript or record of a judicial or administrative proceeding or (2) any other public record when the inclusion of the information in the public record is authorized by a court, statute, or decisional law.
(Added by Stats. 1974, Ch. 963.)

CHAPTER 1.5. National Search of Criminal Records [11145 - 11149.4]

(Chapter 1.5 added by Stats. 1982, Ch. 1222, Sec. 2.)

11145.
In lieu of a national check of fingerprint records conducted by the Federal Bureau of Investigation through the California Department of Justice, state agencies shall contract with an independent vendor to conduct a national search of the individuals' criminal records, as provided in this chapter.
(Added by Stats. 1982, Ch. 1222, Sec. 2. Effective September 22, 1982. Conditionally inoperative by Sec. 3 of Ch. 1222.)

11146.
This chapter applies to:
(a) The California Commission for Teacher Preparation and Licensing, in licensing of all teaching and services credential applicants, pursuant to Section 44341 of the Education Code.
(b) The State Department of Social Services in licensing those community care facility operators providing services to children as mandated in Section 1522 of the Health and Safety Code.
(c) The county welfare department in carrying out its approval authority for relative and nonrelative extended family member foster care placements pursuant to Section 309 of the Welfare and Institutions Code.
(Amended by Stats. 2002, Ch. 918, Sec. 2. Effective January 1, 2003. Conditionally inoperative by Sec. 3 of Ch. 1222.)

11147.
In order that a thorough search may be conducted, the agencies listed in Section 11146 shall require applicants, as a condition of employment or licensing, to provide (a) their social security and drivers' license numbers, (b) educational history, (c) three personal references, (d) a five-year employment and residence history, and, (e) if appropriate, any other names they may have been known under. This information shall be provided under penalty of perjury.
(Added by Stats. 1982, Ch. 1222, Sec. 2. Effective September 22, 1982. Conditionally inoperative by Sec. 3 of Ch. 1222.)

11148.
The agencies listed in Section 11146 may contract with any vendor demonstrating the capability to conduct such background searches in a timely manner and with the assurance of complete confidentiality. Any such vendor shall (a) be a licensed private investigator as defined in Section 7521 of the Business and Professions Code; (b) have been in business for at least five years; (c) be able to furnish bank references; (d) provide a minimum of one million dollars ($1,000,000) in liability insurance, with the contracting agency being named as an additional insured; and (e) be able to provide services, via subcontracts if necessary, in all areas of the state.
No contract shall be let unless it provides therein that the cost per applicant for a search, including administrative costs, shall not exceed forty dollars ($40). The state shall not be liable for any amount in excess of forty dollars ($40) per applicant.
(Added by Stats. 1982, Ch. 1222, Sec. 2. Effective September 22, 1982. Conditionally inoperative by Sec. 3 of Ch. 1222.)

11149.
In order to expedite the work of the vendor, all applications submitted to the vendor shall include the results of the fingerprint checks conducted by the California Department of Justice.
(Added by Stats. 1982, Ch. 1222, Sec. 2. Effective September 22, 1982. Conditionally inoperative by Sec. 3 of Ch. 1222.)

11149.1.
Vendors are exempted from any provisions of Chapter 1 (commencing with Section 1798) of Title 1.8 of Part 4 of Division 3 of the Civil Code which prevent the vendor from conducting the national search of individual criminal records required by this chapter.
(Added by Stats. 1982, Ch. 1222, Sec. 2. Effective September 22, 1982. Conditionally inoperative by Sec. 3 of Ch. 1222.)

11149.2.
Notwithstanding any other provision of law, applicants may be charged for the actual cost of the national search required by this statute, including administrative costs, not to exceed forty dollars ($40).
(Added by Stats. 1982, Ch. 1222, Sec. 2. Effective September 22, 1982. Conditionally inoperative by Sec. 3 of Ch. 1222.)

11149.3.
Any vendor or employee of a vendor who knowingly furnishes a record or information obtained from a record to a person who is not authorized by law to receive the record or information shall be guilty of a misdemeanor and fined not more than five thousand dollars ($5,000), or imprisoned in a county jail for not more than one year, or both.
(Added by Stats. 1982, Ch. 1222, Sec. 2. Effective September 22, 1982. Conditionally inoperative by Sec. 3 of Ch. 1222.)

11149.4.
Any vendor or employee of a vendor who intentionally discloses information, not otherwise public, which that person knows or should reasonably know was obtained from

confidential information, shall be subject to a civil action for invasion of privacy by the individual to whom the information pertains.

In any successful action brought under this section, the complainant, in addition to any special or general damages awarded, shall be awarded a minimum of two thousand five hundred dollars ($2,500) in exemplary damages as well as attorney's fees and other litigation costs reasonably incurred in the suit.

The right, remedy, and cause of action set forth in this section shall be nonexclusive and is in addition to all other rights, remedies, and causes of action for invasion of privacy, inherent in Section 1, Article I of the California Constitution.

(Added by Stats. 1982, Ch. 1222, Sec. 2. Effective September 22, 1982. Conditionally inoperative by Sec. 3 of Ch. 1222.)

CHAPTER 2. Control of Crimes and Criminals [11150 - 11199.5]

(Chapter 2 added by Stats. 1953, Ch. 70.)

ARTICLE 1. Release of Persons Convicted of Arson [11150 - 11152]
(Article 1 repealed and added by Stats. 1982, Ch. 919, Sec. 3.)

11150.

Prior to the release of a person convicted of arson from an institution under the jurisdiction of the Department of Corrections, the Director of Corrections shall notify in writing the State Fire Marshal and all police departments and the sheriff in the county in which the person was convicted and, if known, in the county in which he is to reside. The notice shall state the name of the person to be released, the county in which he was convicted and, if known, the county in which he will reside.

(Repealed and added by Stats. 1982, Ch. 919, Sec. 3.)

11151.

Within five days after release of a person convicted of arson from an institution under the jurisdiction of the State Department of State Hospitals, the Director of State Hospitals shall send the notice provided in Section 11150.

(Amended by Stats. 2014, Ch. 144, Sec. 48. (AB 1847) Effective January 1, 2015.)

11152.

Upon receipt of a notice as provided in Section 11150 or 11151, the State Fire Marshal shall notify all regularly organized fire departments in the county in which the person was convicted and, if known, in the county in which he is to reside.

(Repealed and added by Stats. 1982, Ch. 919, Sec. 3.)

ARTICLE 1.5. Reports of Disposition of Inmates [11155 - 11158]
(Article 1.5 added by Stats. 1982, Ch. 1048, Sec. 1.)

11155.

(a) As soon as placement of an inmate in any reentry or work furlough program is planned, but in no case less than 60 days prior to that placement, the Department of Corrections and Rehabilitation shall provide notice, if notice has been requested, to all of the following: (1) written notice to the chief of police of the city, if any, in which the inmate will reside, if known, or in which placement will be made, (2) written notice to the sheriff of the county in which the inmate will reside, if known, or in which placement will be made, and (3) notice, as provided in subdivision (d), to the victim, if any, of the crime for which the inmate was convicted or the next of kin of the victim if the crime was a homicide, if the victim or the next of kin has submitted a request for notice with the department. Information regarding victims or next of kin requesting the notice, and the notice, shall be confidential and not available to the inmate.

(b) In the event of an escape of an inmate from any facility under the jurisdiction of the department, the department shall immediately notify, by the most reasonable and expedient means available, the chief of police of the city, and the sheriff of the county, in which the inmate resided immediately prior to the inmate's arrest and conviction, and, if previously requested, to the victim, if any, of the crime for which the inmate was convicted, or to the next of kin of the victim if the crime was a homicide. If the inmate is recaptured, the department shall send written notice thereof to the chief of police and the sheriff, and notice to the victim, or next of kin of the victim, within 30 days after regaining custody of the inmate.

(c) Except as provided in subdivision (d), the department shall send the notices required by this section to the last address provided to the department by the requesting party. It is the responsibility of the requesting party to provide the department with a current address.

(d) Whenever the department provides the notice required by this section to a victim, or next of kin of the victim, it shall do so by telephone, certified mail, or electronic mail, using the method of communication selected by the victim or the next of kin of the victim, if that method is available. In the event the victim's or next of kin's contact information provided to the department is no longer current, the department shall make a diligent, good faith effort to learn the whereabouts of the victim in order to comply with these notification requirements.

(Amended by Stats. 2011, Ch. 364, Sec. 5. (SB 852) Effective September 29, 2011.)

11156.

The notice sent to the chief of police and county sheriff pursuant to Section 11155 shall include an actual glossy photograph no smaller than $3^1/_8$ x $3^1/_8$ inches in size, in conjunction with the Department of Justice, fingerprints of each inmate in the reentry or work furlough program.

(Amended by Stats. 1986, Ch. 600, Sec. 5.)

11157.

The victims may be notified of the opportunity to receive the notices provided by this article by means of adding a paragraph to the information contained on subpoena forms which are used in subpoenaing victims as material witnesses to any court proceedings resulting from the perpetration of the crime in which the victim was involved.

(Added by Stats. 1982, Ch. 1048, Sec. 1.)

11158.

As used in this article, "victim" means any person alleged or found, upon the record, to have sustained physical or financial injury to person or property as a direct result of the crime charged.

(Added by Stats. 1982, Ch. 1048, Sec. 1.)

ARTICLE 2. Reports of Injuries [11160 - 11163.6]
(Heading of Article 2 amended by Stats. 1993, Ch. 992, Sec. 1.)

11160.

(a) A health practitioner, as defined in subdivision (a) of Section 11162.5, employed by a health facility, clinic, physician's office, local or state public health department, local government agency, or a clinic or other type of facility operated by a local or state public health department who, in his or her professional capacity or within the scope of his or her employment, provides medical services for a physical condition to a patient whom he or she knows or reasonably suspects is a person described as follows, shall immediately make a report in accordance with subdivision (b):

(1) A person suffering from any wound or other physical injury inflicted by his or her own act or inflicted by another where the injury is by means of a firearm.

(2) A person suffering from any wound or other physical injury inflicted upon the person where the injury is the result of assaultive or abusive conduct.

(b) A health practitioner, as defined in subdivision (a) of Section 11162.5, employed by a health facility, clinic, physician's office, local or state public health department, local government agency, or a clinic or other type of facility operated by a local or state public

health department shall make a report regarding persons described in subdivision (a) to a local law enforcement agency as follows:

(1) A report by telephone shall be made immediately or as soon as practically possible.

(2) A written report shall be prepared on the standard form developed in compliance with paragraph (4) of this subdivision, and adopted by the Office of Emergency Services, or on a form developed and adopted by another state agency that otherwise fulfills the requirements of the standard form. The completed form shall be sent to a local law enforcement agency within two working days of receiving the information regarding the person.

(3) A local law enforcement agency shall be notified and a written report shall be prepared and sent pursuant to paragraphs (1) and (2) even if the person who suffered the wound, other injury, or assaultive or abusive conduct has expired, regardless of whether or not the wound, other injury, or assaultive or abusive conduct was a factor contributing to the death, and even if the evidence of the conduct of the perpetrator of the wound, other injury, or assaultive or abusive conduct was discovered during an autopsy.

(4) The report shall include, but shall not be limited to, the following:

(A) The name of the injured person, if known.

(B) The injured person's whereabouts.

(C) The character and extent of the person's injuries.

(D) The identity of any person the injured person alleges inflicted the wound, other injury, or assaultive or abusive conduct upon the injured person.

(c) For the purposes of this section, "injury" shall not include any psychological or physical condition brought about solely through the voluntary administration of a narcotic or restricted dangerous drug.

(d) For the purposes of this section, "assaultive or abusive conduct" shall include any of the following offenses:

(1) Murder, in violation of Section 187.

(2) Manslaughter, in violation of Section 192 or 192.5.

(3) Mayhem, in violation of Section 203.

(4) Aggravated mayhem, in violation of Section 205.

(5) Torture, in violation of Section 206.

(6) Assault with intent to commit mayhem, rape, sodomy, or oral copulation, in violation of Section 220.

(7) Administering controlled substances or anesthetic to aid in commission of a felony, in violation of Section 222.

(8) Battery, in violation of Section 242.

(9) Sexual battery, in violation of Section 243.4.

(10) Incest, in violation of Section 285.

(11) Throwing any vitriol, corrosive acid, or caustic chemical with intent to injure or disfigure, in violation of Section 244.

(12) Assault with a stun gun or taser, in violation of Section 244.5.

(13) Assault with a deadly weapon, firearm, assault weapon, or machinegun, or by means likely to produce great bodily injury, in violation of Section 245.

(14) Rape, in violation of Section 261.

(15) Spousal rape, in violation of Section 262.

(16) Procuring any female to have sex with another man, in violation of Section 266, 266a, 266b, or 266c.

(17) Child abuse or endangerment, in violation of Section 273a or 273d.

(18) Abuse of spouse or cohabitant, in violation of Section 273.5.

(19) Sodomy, in violation of Section 286.

(20) Lewd and lascivious acts with a child, in violation of Section 288.

(21) Oral copulation, in violation of Section 288a.

(22) Sexual penetration, in violation of Section 289.

(23) Elder abuse, in violation of Section 368.

(24) An attempt to commit any crime specified in paragraphs (1) to (23), inclusive.

(e) When two or more persons who are required to report are present and jointly have knowledge of a known or suspected instance of violence that is required to be reported pursuant to this section, and when there is an agreement among these persons to report as a team, the team may select by mutual agreement a member of the team to make a report by telephone and a single written report, as required by subdivision (b). The written report shall be signed by the selected member of the reporting team. Any member who has knowledge that the member designated to report has failed to do so shall thereafter make the report.

(f) The reporting duties under this section are individual, except as provided in subdivision (e).

(g) A supervisor or administrator shall not impede or inhibit the reporting duties required under this section and a person making a report pursuant to this section shall not be subject to any sanction for making the report. However, internal procedures to facilitate reporting and apprise supervisors and administrators of reports may be established, except that these procedures shall not be inconsistent with this article. The internal procedures shall not require any employee required to make a report under this article to disclose his or her identity to the employer.

(h) For the purposes of this section, it is the Legislature's intent to avoid duplication of information.

(i) For purposes of this section only, "employed by a local government agency" includes an employee of an entity under contract with a local government agency to provide medical services.

(Amended by Stats. 2018, Ch. 164, Sec. 1. (AB 1973) Effective January 1, 2019.)

11160.1.

(a) Any health practitioner employed in any health facility, clinic, physician's office, local or state public health department, or a clinic or other type of facility operated by a local or state public health department who, in his or her professional capacity or within the scope of his or her employment, performs a forensic medical examination on any person in the custody of law enforcement from whom evidence is sought in connection with the commission or investigation of a crime of sexual assault, as described in subdivision (d) of Section 11160, shall prepare a written report. The report shall be on a standard form developed by, or at the direction of, the Office of Emergency Services, and shall be immediately provided to the law enforcement agency who has custody of the individual examined.

(b) The examination and report is subject to the confidentiality requirements of the Confidentiality of Medical Information Act (Chapter 1 (commencing with Section 56) of Part 2.6 of Division 1 of the Civil Code), the physician-patient privilege pursuant to Article 6 (commencing with Section 990) of Chapter 4 of Division 8 of the Evidence Code, and the privilege of official information pursuant to Article 9 (commencing with Section 1040) of Chapter 4 of Division 8 of the Evidence Code.

(c) The report shall be released upon request, oral or written, to any person or agency involved in any related investigation or prosecution of a criminal case, including, but not limited to, a law enforcement officer, district attorney, city attorney, crime laboratory, county licensing agency, or coroner. The report may be released to defense counsel or another third party only through discovery of documents in the possession of a prosecuting agency or following the issuance of a lawful court order authorizing the release of the report.

(d) A health practitioner who makes a report in accordance with this section shall not incur civil or criminal liability. No person, agency, or their designee required or authorized to report pursuant to this section who takes photographs of a person suspected of being a person subject to a forensic medical examination as described in this section shall incur any civil or criminal liability for taking the photographs, causing the photographs to be taken, or disseminating the photographs to a law enforcement officer, district attorney, city attorney, crime laboratory, county licensing agency, or coroner with the reports required in accordance with this section. However, this subdivision shall not be deemed to grant immunity from civil or criminal liability with respect to any other use of the photographs.

(e) Section 11162 does not apply to this section.

(f) With the exception of any health practitioner who has entered into a contractual agreement to perform forensic medical examinations, no health practitioner shall be required to perform a forensic medical examination as part of his or her duties as a health practitioner.

(Amended by Stats. 2013, Ch. 352, Sec. 419. (AB 1317) Effective September 26, 2013. Operative July 1, 2013, by Sec. 543 of Ch. 352.)

11161.
Notwithstanding Section 11160, the following shall apply to every physician or surgeon who has under his or her charge or care any person described in subdivision (a) of Section 11160:

(a) The physician or surgeon shall make a report in accordance with subdivision (b) of Section 11160 to a local law enforcement agency.

(b) It is recommended that any medical records of a person about whom the physician or surgeon is required to report pursuant to subdivision (a) include the following:

(1) Any comments by the injured person regarding past domestic violence, as defined in Section 13700, or regarding the name of any person suspected of inflicting the wound, other physical injury, or assaultive or abusive conduct upon the person.

(2) A map of the injured person's body showing and identifying injuries and bruises at the time of the health care.

(3) A copy of the law enforcement reporting form.

(c) It is recommended that the physician or surgeon refer the person to local domestic violence services if the person is suffering or suspected of suffering from domestic violence, as defined in Section 13700.

(Repealed and added by Stats. 1993, Ch. 992, Sec. 5. Effective January 1, 1994.)

11161.2.
(a) The Legislature finds and declares that adequate protection of victims of domestic violence and elder and dependent adult abuse has been hampered by lack of consistent and comprehensive medical examinations. Enhancing examination procedures, documentation, and evidence collection will improve investigation and prosecution efforts.

(b) The Office of Emergency Services shall, in cooperation with the State Department of Public Health, the Department of Aging and the ombudsman program, the State Department of Social Services, law enforcement agencies, the Department of Justice, the California Association of Crime Lab Directors, the California District Attorneys Association, the California State Sheriffs' Association, the California Medical Association, the California Police Chiefs' Association, domestic violence advocates, the California Medical Training Center, adult protective services, and other appropriate experts:

(1) Establish medical forensic forms, instructions, and examination protocol for victims of domestic violence and elder and dependent adult abuse and neglect using as a model the form and guidelines developed pursuant to Section 13823.5. The form should include, but not be limited to, a place for a notation concerning each of the following:

(A) Notification of injuries and a report of suspected domestic violence or elder or dependent adult abuse and neglect to law enforcement authorities, Adult Protective Services, or the State Long-Term Care Ombudsmen, in accordance with existing reporting procedures.

(B) Obtaining consent for the examination, treatment of injuries, collection of evidence, and photographing of injuries. Consent to treatment shall be obtained in accordance with the usual hospital policy. A victim shall be informed that he or she may refuse to consent to an examination for evidence of domestic violence and elder and dependent adult abuse and neglect, including the collection of physical evidence, but that refusal is not a ground for denial of treatment of injuries and disease, if the person wishes to obtain treatment and consents thereto.

(C) Taking a patient history of domestic violence or elder or dependent adult abuse and neglect and other relevant medical history.

(D) Performance of the physical examination for evidence of domestic violence or elder or dependent adult abuse and neglect.

(E) Collection of physical evidence of domestic violence or elder or dependent adult abuse.

(F) Collection of other medical and forensic specimens, as indicated.

(G) Procedures for the preservation and disposition of evidence.

(H) Complete documentation of medical forensic exam findings.

(2) Determine whether it is appropriate and forensically sound to develop separate or joint forms for documentation of medical forensic findings for victims of domestic violence and elder and dependent adult abuse and neglect.

(3) The forms shall become part of the patient's medical record pursuant to guidelines established by the agency or agencies designated by the Office of Emergency Services advisory committee and subject to the confidentiality laws pertaining to release of medical forensic examination records.

(c) The forms shall be made accessible for use on the Internet.

(Amended by Stats. 2013, Ch. 352, Sec. 420. (AB 1317) Effective September 26, 2013. Operative July 1, 2013, by Sec. 543 of Ch. 352.)

11161.5.
(a) It is the intent of the Legislature that on or before January 1, 2006, the California District Attorneys Association, in conjunction with interested parties, including, but not limited to, the Department of Justice, the California Narcotic Officers' Association, the California Police Chiefs' Association, the California State Sheriffs' Association, the California Medical Association, the American Pain Society, the American Academy of Pain Medicine, the California Society of Anesthesiologists, the California Chapter of the American College of Emergency Physicians, the California Medical Board, the California Orthopedic Association, and other medical and patient advocacy entities specializing in pain control therapies, shall develop protocols for the development and implementation of interagency investigations in connection with a physician's prescription of medication to patients. The protocols are intended to assure the competent review of, and that relevant investigation procedures are followed for, the suspected undertreatment, undermedication, overtreatment, and overmedication of pain cases. Consideration shall be made for the special circumstances of urban and rural communities. The investigation protocol shall be designed to facilitate communication between the medical and law enforcement communities and the timely return of medical records pertaining to the identity, diagnosis, prognosis, or treatment of any patient that are seized by law enforcement from a physician who is suspected of engaging in or having engaged in criminal activity related to the documents.

(b) The costs incurred by the California District Attorneys Association in implementing this section shall be solicited and funded from nongovernmental entities.

(Added by Stats. 2004, Ch. 864, Sec. 2. Effective January 1, 2005.)

11161.8.
Every person, firm, or corporation conducting any hospital in the state, or the managing agent thereof, or the person managing or in charge of such hospital, or in charge of any ward or part of such hospital, who receives a patient transferred from a health facility, as defined in Section 1250 of the Health and Safety Code or from a community care facility, as defined in Section 1502 of the Health and Safety Code, who exhibits a physical injury or condition which, in the opinion of the admitting physician, reasonably appears to be the result of neglect or abuse, shall report such fact by telephone and in writing, within 36 hours, to both the local police authority having jurisdiction and the county health department.

Any registered nurse, licensed vocational nurse, or licensed clinical social worker employed at such hospital may also make a report under this section, if, in the opinion of such person, a patient exhibits a physical injury or condition which reasonably appears to be the result of neglect or abuse.

Every physician and surgeon who has under his charge or care any such patient who exhibits a physical injury or condition which reasonably appears to be the result of neglect or abuse shall make such report.

The report shall state the character and extent of the physical injury or condition.

No employee shall be discharged, suspended, disciplined, or harassed for making a report pursuant to this section.

No person shall incur any civil or criminal liability as a result of making any report authorized by this section.

(Amended by Stats. 1979, Ch. 1019.)

11161.9.
(a) A health practitioner who makes a report in accordance with this article shall not incur civil or criminal liability as a result of any report required or authorized by this article.

(b) (1) No person required or authorized to report pursuant to this article, or designated by a person required or authorized to report pursuant to this article, who takes photographs of a person suspected of being a person described in this article about whom a report is required or authorized shall incur any civil or criminal liability for taking the photographs, causing the photographs to be taken, or disseminating the photographs to local law enforcement with the reports required by this article in accordance with this article. However, this subdivision shall not be deemed to grant immunity from civil or criminal liability with respect to any other use of the photographs.

(2) A court may award attorney's fees to a commercial film and photographic print processor when a suit is brought against the processor because of a disclosure mandated by this article and the court finds that the suit is frivolous.

(c) A health practitioner who, pursuant to a request from an adult protective services agency or a local law enforcement agency, provides the requesting agency with access to the victim of a known or suspected instance of abuse shall not incur civil or criminal liability as a result of providing that access.

(d) No employee shall be discharged, suspended, disciplined, or harassed for making a report pursuant to this section.

(e) This section does not apply to mandated reporting of child abuse, as provided for in Article 2.5 (commencing with Section 11164).

(Added by Stats. 1993, Ch. 992, Sec. 6. Effective January 1, 1994.)

11162.
A violation of this article is a misdemeanor, punishable by imprisonment in a county jail not exceeding six months, or by a fine not exceeding one thousand dollars ($1,000), or by both that fine and imprisonment.

(Amended by Stats. 1993, Ch. 992, Sec. 7. Effective January 1, 1994.)

11162.5.
As used in this article, the following definitions shall apply:

(a) "Health practitioner" has the same meaning as provided in paragraphs (21) to (28), inclusive, of subdivision (a) of Section 11165.7.

(b) "Clinic" is limited to include any clinic specified in Sections 1204 and 1204.3 of the Health and Safety Code.

(c) "Health facility" has the same meaning as provided in Section 1250 of the Health and Safety Code.

(d) "Reasonably suspects" means that it is objectively reasonable for a person to entertain a suspicion, based upon facts that could cause a reasonable person in a like position, drawing, when appropriate, on his or her training and experience, to suspect.

(Amended by Stats. 2006, Ch. 701, Sec. 1. Effective January 1, 2007.)

11162.7.
This article shall not apply when a report is required to be made pursuant to the Child Abuse and Neglect Reporting Act (Article 2.5 (commencing with Section 11164)), and Chapter 11 (commencing with Section 15600) of Part 3 of Division 9 of the Welfare and Institutions Code.

(Added by Stats. 1993, Ch. 992, Sec. 9. Effective January 1, 1994.)

11163.
(a) The Legislature finds and declares that even though the Legislature has provided for immunity from liability, pursuant to Section 11161.9, for persons required or authorized to report pursuant to this article, that immunity does not eliminate the possibility that actions may be brought against those persons based upon required reports of abuse pursuant to other laws.

In order to further limit the financial hardship that those persons may incur as a result of fulfilling their legal responsibility, it is necessary that they not be unfairly burdened by legal fees incurred in defending those actions.

(b) (1) Therefore, a health practitioner may present a claim to the Department of General Services for reasonable attorney's fees incurred in any action against that person on the basis of that person reporting in accordance with this article if the court dismisses the action upon a demurrer or motion for summary judgment made by that person or if that person prevails in the action.

(2) The Department of General Services shall allow the claim pursuant to paragraph (1) if the requirements of paragraph (1) are met, and the claim shall be paid from an appropriation to be made for that purpose. Attorney's fees awarded pursuant to this section shall not exceed an hourly rate greater than the rate charged by the Attorney General at the time the award is made and shall not exceed an aggregate amount of fifty thousand dollars ($50,000).

(3) This subdivision shall not apply if a public entity has provided for the defense of the action pursuant to Section 995 of the Government Code.

(Amended by Stats. 2016, Ch. 31, Sec. 256. (SB 836) Effective June 27, 2016.)

11163.2.
(a) In any court proceeding or administrative hearing, neither the physician-patient privilege nor the psychotherapist privilege applies to the information required to be reported pursuant to this article.

(b) The reports required by this article shall be kept confidential by the health facility, clinic, or physician's office that submitted the report, and by local law enforcement agencies, and shall only be disclosed by local law enforcement agencies to those involved in the investigation of the report or the enforcement of a criminal law implicated by a report. In no case shall the person suspected or accused of inflicting the wound, other injury, or assaultive or abusive conduct upon the injured person or his or her attorney be allowed access to the injured person's whereabouts.

(c) For the purposes of this article, reports of suspected child abuse and information contained therein may be disclosed only to persons or agencies with whom investigations of child abuse are coordinated under the regulations promulgated under Section 11174.

(d) The Board of Prison Terms may subpoena reports that are not unfounded and reports that concern only the current incidents upon which parole revocation proceedings are pending against a parolee.

(Added by Stats. 1993, Ch. 992, Sec. 11. Effective January 1, 1994.)

11163.3.
(a) A county may establish an interagency domestic violence death review team to assist local agencies in identifying and reviewing domestic violence deaths, including homicides and suicides, and facilitating communication among the various agencies involved in domestic violence cases. Interagency domestic violence death review teams have been used successfully to ensure that incidents of domestic violence and abuse are recognized and that agency involvement is reviewed to develop recommendations for

policies and protocols for community prevention and intervention initiatives to reduce and eradicate the incidence of domestic violence.

(b) For purposes of this section, "abuse" has the meaning set forth in Section 6203 of the Family Code and "domestic violence" has the meaning set forth in Section 6211 of the Family Code.

(c) A county may develop a protocol that may be used as a guideline to assist coroners and other persons who perform autopsies on domestic violence victims in the identification of domestic violence, in the determination of whether domestic violence contributed to death or whether domestic violence had occurred prior to death, but was not the actual cause of death, and in the proper written reporting procedures for domestic violence, including the designation of the cause and mode of death.

(d) County domestic violence death review teams shall be comprised of, but not limited to, the following:

(1) Experts in the field of forensic pathology.

(2) Medical personnel with expertise in domestic violence abuse.

(3) Coroners and medical examiners.

(4) Criminologists.

(5) District attorneys and city attorneys.

(6) Domestic violence shelter service staff and battered women's advocates.

(7) Law enforcement personnel.

(8) Representatives of local agencies that are involved with domestic violence abuse reporting.

(9) County health department staff who deal with domestic violence victims' health issues.

(10) Representatives of local child abuse agencies.

(11) Local professional associations of persons described in paragraphs (1) to (10), inclusive.

(e) An oral or written communication or a document shared within or produced by a domestic violence death review team related to a domestic violence death review is confidential and not subject to disclosure or discoverable by a third party. An oral or written communication or a document provided by a third party to a domestic violence death review team, or between a third party and a domestic violence death review team, is confidential and not subject to disclosure or discoverable by a third party. Notwithstanding the foregoing, recommendations of a domestic violence death review team upon the completion of a review may be disclosed at the discretion of a majority of the members of the domestic violence death review team.

(f) Each organization represented on a domestic violence death review team may share with other members of the team information in its possession concerning the victim who is the subject of the review or any person who was in contact with the victim and any other information deemed by the organization to be pertinent to the review. Any information shared by an organization with other members of a team is confidential. This provision shall permit the disclosure to members of the team of any information deemed confidential, privileged, or prohibited from disclosure by any other statute.

(g) Written and oral information may be disclosed to a domestic violence death review team established pursuant to this section. The team may make a request in writing for the information sought and any person with information of the kind described in paragraph (2) may rely on the request in determining whether information may be disclosed to the team.

(1) An individual or agency that has information governed by this subdivision shall not be required to disclose information. The intent of this subdivision is to allow the voluntary disclosure of information by the individual or agency that has the information.

(2) The following information may be disclosed pursuant to this subdivision:

(A) Notwithstanding Section 56.10 of the Civil Code, medical information.

(B) Notwithstanding Section 5328 of the Welfare and Institutions Code, mental health information.

(C) Notwithstanding Section 15633.5 of the Welfare and Institutions Code, information from elder abuse reports and investigations, except the identity of persons who have made reports, which shall not be disclosed.

(D) Notwithstanding Section 11167.5 of the Penal Code, information from child abuse reports and investigations, except the identity of persons who have made reports, which shall not be disclosed.

(E) State summary criminal history information, criminal offender record information, and local summary criminal history information, as defined in Sections 11075, 11105, and 13300 of the Penal Code.

(F) Notwithstanding Section 11163.2 of the Penal Code, information pertaining to reports by health practitioners of persons suffering from physical injuries inflicted by means of a firearm or of persons suffering physical injury where the injury is a result of assaultive or abusive conduct, and information relating to whether a physician referred the person to local domestic violence services as recommended by Section 11161 of the Penal Code.

(G) Notwithstanding Section 827 of the Welfare and Institutions Code, information in any juvenile court proceeding.

(H) Information maintained by the Family Court, including information relating to the Family Conciliation Court Law pursuant to Section 1818 of the Family Code, and Mediation of Custody and Visitation Issues pursuant to Section 3177 of the Family Code.

(I) Information provided to probation officers in the course of the performance of their duties, including, but not limited to, the duty to prepare reports pursuant to Section 1203.10 of the Penal Code, as well as the information on which these reports are based.

(J) Notwithstanding Section 10850 of the Welfare and Institutions Code, records of in-home supportive services, unless disclosure is prohibited by federal law.

(3) The disclosure of written and oral information authorized under this subdivision shall apply notwithstanding Sections 2263, 2918, 4982, and 6068 of the Business and Professions Code, or the lawyer-client privilege protected by Article 3 (commencing with Section 950) of Chapter 4 of Division 8 of the Evidence Code, the physician-patient privilege protected by Article 6 (commencing with Section 990) of Chapter 4 of Division 8 of the Evidence Code, the psychotherapist-patient privilege protected by Article 7 (commencing with Section 1010) of Chapter 4 of Division 8 of the Evidence Code, the sexual assault counselor-victim privilege protected by Article 8.5 (commencing with Section 1035) of Chapter 4 of Division 8 of the Evidence Code, the domestic violence counselor-victim privilege protected by Article 8.7 (commencing with Section 1037) of Chapter 4 of Division 8 of the Evidence Code, and the human trafficking caseworker-victim privilege protected by Article 8.8 (commencing with Section 1038) of Chapter 4 of Division 8 of the Evidence Code.

(Amended by Stats. 2014, Ch. 913, Sec. 27. (AB 2747) Effective January 1, 2015.)
11163.4.

Subject to available funding, the Attorney General, working with the state domestic violence coalition, shall develop a protocol for the development and implementation of interagency domestic violence death review teams for use by counties, which shall include relevant procedures for both urban and rural counties. The protocol shall be designed to facilitate communication among persons who perform autopsies and the various persons and agencies involved in domestic violence cases so that incidents of domestic violence and deaths related to domestic violence are recognized and surviving nonoffending family and household members and domestic partners receive the appropriate services.

(Added by Stats. 1995, Ch. 710, Sec. 2. Effective January 1, 1996.)
11163.5.

(a) The purpose of this section is to coordinate and integrate state and local efforts to address fatal domestic violence, and to create a body of information to prevent domestic violence deaths.

(b) (1) The Department of Justice is hereby authorized to carry out the purpose of this section with the cooperation of the State Department of Social Services, the State Department of Health Services, the California State Coroner's Association, the County Welfare Directors Association, and the state domestic violence coalition.

(2) The Department of Justice, after consulting with the agencies and organizations specified in paragraph (1), may consult with other representatives of other agencies and private organizations to accomplish the purpose of this section.

(c) To accomplish the purpose of this section, the Department of Justice and agencies and organizations involved may engage in the following activities:

(1) Collect, analyze, and interpret state and local data on domestic violence death in an annual report to be available upon request. The report may contain, but need not be limited to, information provided by state agencies and the county domestic violence death review teams for the preceding year.

(2) Develop a state and local data base on domestic violence deaths.

(A) The state data may include the Department of Justice statistics, the State Department of Health Services Vital Statistics, and information obtained by other relevant state agencies.

(B) The Department of Justice, in consultation with the agencies and organizations specified in paragraph (1) of subdivision (b), may develop a model minimal local data set and request data from local teams for inclusion in the annual report.

(3) Distribute a copy of the report to public officials in the state who deal with domestic violence issues and to those agencies responsible for domestic violence death review investigation in each county.

(d) The Department of Justice may direct the creation of a statewide domestic violence death review team directory, which shall contain the names of the members of the agencies and private organizations participating under this section, the members of local domestic violence death review teams, and the local liaisons to those teams. The department may maintain and update the directory annually.

(e) The agencies or private organizations participating under this section shall participate without reimbursement from the state. Costs incurred by participants for travel or per diem shall be borne by the participant agency or organization. Any reports prepared by the Department of Justice pursuant to this section shall be in consultation with the state domestic violence coalition.

(Added by Stats. 1995, Ch. 710, Sec. 3. Effective January 1, 1996.)
11163.6.

In order to ensure consistent and uniform results, data may be collected and summarized by the domestic violence death review teams to show the statistical occurrence of domestic violence deaths in the team's county that occur under the following circumstances:

(a) The deceased was a victim of a homicide committed by a current or former spouse, fiancé, or dating partner.

(b) The deceased was the victim of a suicide, was the current or former spouse, fiancé, or dating partner of the perpetrator and was also the victim of previous acts of domestic violence.

(c) The deceased was the perpetrator of the homicide of a former or current spouse, fiancé, or dating partner and the perpetrator was also the victim of a suicide.

(d) The deceased was the perpetrator of the homicide of a former or current spouse, fiancé, or dating partner and the perpetrator was also the victim of a homicide related to the domestic homicide incident.

(e) The deceased was a child of either the homicide victim or the perpetrator, or both.

(f) The deceased was a current or former spouse, fiancé, or dating partner of the current or former spouse, fiancé, or dating partner of the perpetrator.

(g) The deceased was a law enforcement officer, emergency medical personnel, or other agency responding to a domestic violence incident.

(h) The deceased was a family member, other than identified above, of the perpetrator.

(i) The deceased was the perpetrator of the homicide of a family member, other than identified above.

(j) The deceased had a disability and the homicide was related to domestic violence.

(k) The deceased was a person not included in the above categories and the homicide was related to domestic violence.

(Amended by Stats. 2010, Ch. 617, Sec. 4. (SB 110) Effective January 1, 2011.)

ARTICLE 2.5. Child Abuse and Neglect Reporting Act [11164 - 11174.3]
(Heading of Article 2.5 amended by Stats. 1987, Ch. 1444, Sec. 1.)
11164.

(a) This article shall be known and may be cited as the Child Abuse and Neglect Reporting Act.

(b) The intent and purpose of this article is to protect children from abuse and neglect. In any investigation of suspected child abuse or neglect, all persons participating in the investigation of the case shall consider the needs of the child victim and shall do whatever is necessary to prevent psychological harm to the child victim.

(Amended by Stats. 2000, Ch. 916, Sec. 1. Effective January 1, 2001.)
11165.

As used in this article "child" means a person under the age of 18 years.

(Repealed and added by Stats. 1987, Ch. 1459, Sec. 2.)
11165.1.

As used in this article, "sexual abuse" means sexual assault or sexual exploitation as defined by the following:

(a) "Sexual assault" means conduct in violation of one or more of the following sections: Section 261 (rape), subdivision (d) of Section 261.5 (statutory rape), Section 264.1 (rape in concert), Section 285 (incest), Section 286 (sodomy), Section 287 or former Section 288a (oral copulation), subdivision (a) or (b), or paragraph (1) of subdivision (c) of Section 288 (lewd or lascivious acts upon a child), Section 289 (sexual penetration), or Section 647.6 (child molestation).

(b) Conduct described as "sexual assault" includes, but is not limited to, all of the following:

(1) Penetration, however slight, of the vagina or anal opening of one person by the penis of another person, whether or not there is the emission of semen.

(2) Sexual contact between the genitals or anal opening of one person and the mouth or tongue of another person.

(3) Intrusion by one person into the genitals or anal opening of another person, including the use of an object for this purpose, except that, it does not include acts performed for a valid medical purpose.

(4) The intentional touching of the genitals or intimate parts, including the breasts, genital area, groin, inner thighs, and buttocks, or the clothing covering them, of a child, or of the perpetrator by a child, for purposes of sexual arousal or gratification, except that it does not include acts which may reasonably be construed to be normal caretaker responsibilities; interactions with, or demonstrations of affection for, the child; or acts performed for a valid medical purpose.

(5) The intentional masturbation of the perpetrator's genitals in the presence of a child.

(c) "Sexual exploitation" refers to any of the following:

(1) Conduct involving matter depicting a minor engaged in obscene acts in violation of Section 311.2 (preparing, selling, or distributing obscene matter) or subdivision (a) of Section 311.4 (employment of minor to perform obscene acts).

(2) A person who knowingly promotes, aids, or assists, employs, uses, persuades, induces, or coerces a child, or a person responsible for a child's welfare, who knowingly permits or encourages a child to engage in, or assist others to engage in, prostitution

or a live performance involving obscene sexual conduct, or to either pose or model alone or with others for purposes of preparing a film, photograph, negative, slide, drawing, painting, or other pictorial depiction, involving obscene sexual conduct. For the purpose of this section, "person responsible for a child's welfare" means a parent, guardian, foster parent, or a licensed administrator or employee of a public or private residential home, residential school, or other residential institution.

(3) A person who depicts a child in, or who knowingly develops, duplicates, prints, downloads, streams, accesses through any electronic or digital media, or exchanges, a film, photograph, videotape, video recording, negative, or slide in which a child is engaged in an act of obscene sexual conduct, except for those activities by law enforcement and prosecution agencies and other persons described in subdivisions (c) and (e) of Section 311.3.

(d) "Commercial sexual exploitation" refers to either of the following:
(1) The sexual trafficking of a child, as described in subdivision (c) of Section 236.1.
(2) The provision of food, shelter, or payment to a child in exchange for the performance of any sexual act described in this section or subdivision (c) of Section 236.1.

(Amended by Stats. 2018, Ch. 423, Sec. 112. (SB 1494) Effective January 1, 2019.)

11165.2.
As used in this article, "neglect" means the negligent treatment or the maltreatment of a child by a person responsible for the child's welfare under circumstances indicating harm or threatened harm to the child's health or welfare. The term includes both acts and omissions on the part of the responsible person.
(a) "Severe neglect" means the negligent failure of a person having the care or custody of a child to protect the child from severe malnutrition or medically diagnosed nonorganic failure to thrive. "Severe neglect" also means those situations of neglect where any person having the care or custody of a child willfully causes or permits the person or health of the child to be placed in a situation such that his or her person or health is endangered, as proscribed by Section 11165.3, including the intentional failure to provide adequate food, clothing, shelter, or medical care.
(b) "General neglect" means the negligent failure of a person having the care or custody of a child to provide adequate food, clothing, shelter, medical care, or supervision where no physical injury to the child has occurred.
For the purposes of this chapter, a child receiving treatment by spiritual means as provided in Section 16509.1 of the Welfare and Institutions Code or not receiving specified medical treatment for religious reasons, shall not for that reason alone be considered a neglected child. An informed and appropriate medical decision made by parent or guardian after consultation with a physician or physicians who have examined the minor does not constitute neglect.

(Repealed and added by Stats. 1987, Ch. 1459, Sec. 7.)

11165.3.
As used in this article, "the willful harming or injuring of a child or the endangering of the person or health of a child," means a situation in which any person willfully causes or permits any child to suffer, or inflicts thereon, unjustifiable physical pain or mental suffering, or having the care or custody of any child, willfully causes or permits the person or health of the child to be placed in a situation in which his or her person or health is endangered.

(Amended by Stats. 2004, Ch. 842, Sec. 1. Effective January 1, 2005.)

11165.4.
As used in this article, "unlawful corporal punishment or injury" means a situation where any person willfully inflicts upon any child any cruel or inhuman corporal punishment or injury resulting in a traumatic condition. It does not include an amount of force that is reasonable and necessary for a person employed by or engaged in a public school to quell a disturbance threatening physical injury to person or damage to property, for purposes of self-defense, or to obtain possession of weapons or other dangerous objects within the control of the pupil, as authorized by Section 49001 of the Education Code. It also does not include the exercise of the degree of physical control authorized by Section 44807 of the Education Code. It also does not include an injury caused by reasonable and necessary force used by a peace officer acting within the course and scope of his or her employment as a peace officer.

(Amended by Stats. 1993, Ch. 346, Sec. 1. Effective January 1, 1994.)

11165.5.
As used in this article, the term "abuse or neglect in out-of-home care" includes physical injury or death inflicted upon a child by another person by other than accidental means, sexual abuse as defined in Section 11165.1, neglect as defined in Section 11165.2, unlawful corporal punishment or injury as defined in Section 11165.4, or the willful harming or injuring of a child or the endangering of the person or health of a child, as defined in Section 11165.3, where the person responsible for the child's welfare is a licensee, administrator, or employee of any facility licensed to care for children, or an administrator or employee of a public or private school or other institution or agency. "Abuse or neglect in out-of-home care" does not include an injury caused by reasonable and necessary force used by a peace officer acting within the course and scope of his or her employment as a peace officer.

(Amended by Stats. 2007, Ch. 393, Sec. 1. Effective January 1, 2008.)

11165.6.
As used in this article, the term "child abuse or neglect" includes physical injury or death inflicted by other than accidental means upon a child by another person, sexual abuse as defined in Section 11165.1, neglect as defined in Section 11165.2, the willful harming or injuring of a child or the endangering of the person or health of a child, as defined in Section 11165.3, and unlawful corporal punishment or injury as defined in Section 11165.4. "Child abuse or neglect" does not include a mutual affray between minors. "Child abuse or neglect" does not include an injury caused by reasonable and necessary force used by a peace officer acting within the course and scope of his or her employment as a peace officer.

(Amended by Stats. 2007, Ch. 393, Sec. 2. Effective January 1, 2008.)

11165.7.
(a) As used in this article, "mandated reporter" is defined as any of the following:
(1) A teacher.
(2) An instructional aide.
(3) A teacher's aide or teacher's assistant employed by a public or private school.
(4) A classified employee of a public school.
(5) An administrative officer or supervisor of child welfare and attendance, or a certificated pupil personnel employee of a public or private school.
(6) An administrator of a public or private day camp.
(7) An administrator or employee of a public or private youth center, youth recreation program, or youth organization.
(8) An administrator, board member, or employee of a public or private organization whose duties require direct contact and supervision of children, including a foster family agency.
(9) An employee of a county office of education or the State Department of Education whose duties bring the employee into contact with children on a regular basis.
(10) A licensee, an administrator, or an employee of a licensed community care or child day care facility.
(11) A Head Start program teacher.
(12) A licensing worker or licensing evaluator employed by a licensing agency, as defined in Section 11165.11.
(13) A public assistance worker.
(14) An employee of a child care institution, including, but not limited to, foster parents, group home personnel, and personnel of residential care facilities.

(15) A social worker, probation officer, or parole officer.
(16) An employee of a school district police or security department.
(17) A person who is an administrator or presenter of, or a counselor in, a child abuse prevention program in a public or private school.
(18) A district attorney investigator, inspector, or local child support agency caseworker, unless the investigator, inspector, or caseworker is working with an attorney appointed pursuant to Section 317 of the Welfare and Institutions Code to represent a minor.
(19) A peace officer, as defined in Chapter 4.5 (commencing with Section 830) of Title 3 of Part 2, who is not otherwise described in this section.
(20) A firefighter, except for volunteer firefighters.
(21) A physician and surgeon, psychiatrist, psychologist, dentist, resident, intern, podiatrist, chiropractor, licensed nurse, dental hygienist, optometrist, marriage and family therapist, clinical social worker, professional clinical counselor, or any other person who is currently licensed under Division 2 (commencing with Section 500) of the Business and Professions Code.
(22) An emergency medical technician I or II, paramedic, or other person certified pursuant to Division 2.5 (commencing with Section 1797) of the Health and Safety Code.
(23) A psychological assistant registered pursuant to Section 2913 of the Business and Professions Code.
(24) A marriage and family therapist trainee, as defined in subdivision (c) of Section 4980.03 of the Business and Professions Code.
(25) An unlicensed associate marriage and family therapist registered under Section 4980.44 of the Business and Professions Code.
(26) A state or county public health employee who treats a minor for venereal disease or any other condition.
(27) A coroner.
(28) A medical examiner or other person who performs autopsies.
(29) A commercial film and photographic print or image processor as specified in subdivision (e) of Section 11166. As used in this article, "commercial film and photographic print or image processor" means a person who develops exposed photographic film into negatives, slides, or prints, or who makes prints from negatives or slides, or who prepares, publishes, produces, develops, duplicates, or prints any representation of information, data, or an image, including, but not limited to, any film, filmstrip, photograph, negative, slide, photocopy, videotape, video laser disc, computer hardware, computer software, computer floppy disk, data storage medium, CD-ROM, computer-generated equipment, or computer-generated image, for compensation. The term includes any employee of that person; it does not include a person who develops film or makes prints or images for a public agency.
(30) A child visitation monitor. As used in this article, "child visitation monitor" means a person who, for financial compensation, acts as a monitor of a visit between a child and another person when the monitoring of that visit has been ordered by a court of law.
(31) An animal control officer or humane society officer. For the purposes of this article, the following terms have the following meanings:
(A) "Animal control officer" means a person employed by a city, county, or city and county for the purpose of enforcing animal control laws or regulations.
(B) "Humane society officer" means a person appointed or employed by a public or private entity as a humane officer who is qualified pursuant to Section 14502 or 14503 of the Corporations Code.
(32) A clergy member, as specified in subdivision (d) of Section 11166. As used in this article, "clergy member" means a priest, minister, rabbi, religious practitioner, or similar functionary of a church, temple, or recognized denomination or organization.
(33) Any custodian of records of a clergy member, as specified in this section and subdivision (d) of Section 11166.
(34) An employee of any police department, county sheriff's department, county probation department, or county welfare department.
(35) An employee or volunteer of a Court Appointed Special Advocate program, as defined in Rule 5.655 of the California Rules of Court.
(36) A custodial officer, as defined in Section 831.5.
(37) A person providing services to a minor child under Section 12300 or 12300.1 of the Welfare and Institutions Code.
(38) An alcohol and drug counselor. As used in this article, an "alcohol and drug counselor" is a person providing counseling, therapy, or other clinical services for a state licensed or certified drug, alcohol, or drug and alcohol treatment program. However, alcohol or drug abuse, or both alcohol and drug abuse, is not, in and of itself, a sufficient basis for reporting child abuse or neglect.
(39) A clinical counselor trainee, as defined in subdivision (g) of Section 4999.12 of the Business and Professions Code.
(40) An associate professional clinical counselor registered under Section 4999.42 of the Business and Professions Code.
(41) An employee or administrator of a public or private postsecondary educational institution, whose duties bring the administrator or employee into contact with children on a regular basis, or who supervises those whose duties bring the administrator or employee into contact with children on a regular basis, as to child abuse or neglect occurring on that institution's premises or at an official activity of, or program conducted by, the institution. Nothing in this paragraph shall be construed as altering the lawyer-client privilege as set forth in Article 3 (commencing with Section 950) of Chapter 4 of Division 8 of the Evidence Code.
(42) An athletic coach, athletic administrator, or athletic director employed by any public or private school that provides any combination of instruction for kindergarten, or grades 1 to 12, inclusive.
(43) (A) A commercial computer technician as specified in subdivision (e) of Section 11166. As used in this article, "commercial computer technician" means a person who works for a company that is in the business of repairing, installing, or otherwise servicing a computer or computer component, including, but not limited to, a computer part, device, memory storage or recording mechanism, auxiliary storage recording or memory capacity, or any other material relating to the operation and maintenance of a computer or computer network system, for a fee. An employer who provides an electronic communications service or a remote computing service to the public shall be deemed to comply with this article if that employer complies with Section 2258A of Title 18 of the United States Code.
(B) An employer of a commercial computer technician may implement internal procedures for facilitating reporting consistent with this article. These procedures may direct employees who are mandated reporters under this paragraph to report materials described in subdivision (e) of Section 11166 to an employee who is designated by the employer to receive the reports. An employee who is designated to receive reports under this subparagraph shall be a commercial computer technician for purposes of this article. A commercial computer technician who makes a report to the designated employee pursuant to this subparagraph shall be deemed to have complied with the requirements of this article and shall be subject to the protections afforded to mandated reporters, including, but not limited to, those protections afforded by Section 11172.
(44) Any athletic coach, including, but not limited to, an assistant coach or a graduate assistant involved in coaching, at public or private postsecondary educational institutions.
(45) An individual certified by a licensed foster family agency as a certified family home, as defined in Section 1506 of the Health and Safety Code.
(46) An individual approved as a resource family, as defined in Section 1517 of the Health and Safety Code and Section 16519.5 of the Welfare and Institutions Code.

(b) Except as provided in paragraph (35) of subdivision (a), volunteers of public or private organizations whose duties require direct contact with and supervision of children are not mandated reporters but are encouraged to obtain training in the identification and reporting of child abuse and neglect and are further encouraged to report known or suspected instances of child abuse or neglect to an agency specified in Section 11165.9.

(c) Except as provided in subdivision (d), employers are strongly encouraged to provide their employees who are mandated reporters with training in the duties imposed by this article. This training shall include training in child abuse and neglect identification and training in child abuse and neglect reporting. Whether or not employers provide their employees with training in child abuse and neglect identification and reporting, the employers shall provide their employees who are mandated reporters with the statement required pursuant to subdivision (a) of Section 11166.5.

(d) Pursuant to Section 44691 of the Education Code, school districts, county offices of education, state special schools and diagnostic centers operated by the State Department of Education, and charter schools shall annually train their employees and persons working on their behalf specified in subdivision (a) in the duties of mandated reporters under the child abuse reporting laws. The training shall include, but not necessarily be limited to, training in child abuse and neglect identification and child abuse and neglect reporting.

(e) (1) On and after January 1, 2018, pursuant to Section 1596.8662 of the Health and Safety Code, a child care licensee applicant shall take training in the duties of mandated reporters under the child abuse reporting laws as a condition of licensure, and a child care administrator or an employee of a licensed child day care facility shall take training in the duties of mandated reporters during the first 90 days when he or she is employed by the facility.

(2) A person specified in paragraph (1) who becomes a licensee, administrator, or employee of a licensed child day care facility shall take renewal mandated reporter training every two years following the date on which he or she completed the initial mandated reporter training. The training shall include, but not necessarily be limited to, training in child abuse and neglect identification and child abuse and neglect reporting.

(f) Unless otherwise specifically provided, the absence of training shall not excuse a mandated reporter from the duties imposed by this article.

(g) Public and private organizations are encouraged to provide their volunteers whose duties require direct contact with and supervision of children with training in the identification and reporting of child abuse and neglect.

(Amended by Stats. 2017, Ch. 573, Sec. 77. (SB 800) Effective January 1, 2018.)

11165.9.

Reports of suspected child abuse or neglect shall be made by mandated reporters, or in the case of reports pursuant to Section 11166.05, may be made, to any police department or sheriff's department, not including a school district police or security department, county probation department, if designated by the county to receive mandated reports, or the county welfare department. Any of those agencies shall accept a report of suspected child abuse or neglect whether offered by a mandated reporter or another person, or referred by another agency, even if the agency to whom the report is being made lacks subject matter or geographical jurisdiction to investigate the reported case, unless the agency can immediately electronically transfer the call to an agency with proper jurisdiction. When an agency takes a report about a case of suspected child abuse or neglect in which that agency lacks jurisdiction, the agency shall immediately refer the case by telephone, fax, or electronic transmission to an agency with proper jurisdiction. Agencies that are required to receive reports of suspected child abuse or neglect may not refuse to accept a report of suspected child abuse or neglect from a mandated reporter or another person unless otherwise authorized pursuant to this section, and shall maintain a record of all reports received.

(Amended by Stats. 2006, Ch. 701, Sec. 2. Effective January 1, 2007.)

11165.11.

As used in this article, "licensing agency" means the State Department of Social Services office responsible for the licensing and enforcement of the California Community Care Facilities Act (Chapter 3 (commencing with Section 1500) of Division 2 of the Health and Safety Code), the California Child Day Care Act (Chapter 3.4 (commencing with Section 1596.70) of Division 2 of the Health and Safety Code), and Chapter 3.5 (commencing with Section 1596.90) of Division 2 of the Health and Safety Code), or the county licensing agency which has contracted with the state for performance of those duties.

(Added by Stats. 1987, Ch. 1459, Sec. 18.)

11165.12.

As used in this article, the following definitions shall control:

(a) "Unfounded report" means a report that is determined by the investigator who conducted the investigation to be false, to be inherently improbable, to involve an accidental injury, or not to constitute child abuse or neglect, as defined in Section 11165.6.

(b) "Substantiated report" means a report that is determined by the investigator who conducted the investigation to constitute child abuse or neglect, as defined in Section 11165.6, based upon evidence that makes it more likely than not that child abuse or neglect, as defined, occurred. A substantiated report shall not include a report where the investigator who conducted the investigation found the report to be false, inherently improbable, to involve an accidental injury, or to not constitute child abuse or neglect as defined in Section 11165.6.

(c) "Inconclusive report" means a report that is determined by the investigator who conducted the investigation not to be unfounded, but the findings are inconclusive and there is insufficient evidence to determine whether child abuse or neglect, as defined in Section 11165.6, has occurred.

(Amended by Stats. 2011, Ch. 468, Sec. 1. (AB 717) Effective January 1, 2012.)

11165.13.

For purposes of this article, a positive toxicology screen at the time of the delivery of an infant is not in and of itself a sufficient basis for reporting child abuse or neglect. However, any indication of maternal substance abuse shall lead to an assessment of the needs of the mother and child pursuant to Section 123605 of the Health and Safety Code. If other factors are present that indicate risk to a child, then a report shall be made. However, a report based on risk to a child which relates solely to the inability of the parent to provide the child with regular care due to the parent's substance abuse shall be made only to a county welfare or probation department, and not to a law enforcement agency.

(Amended by Stats. 2000, Ch. 916, Sec. 11. Effective January 1, 2001.)

11165.14.

The appropriate local law enforcement agency shall investigate a child abuse complaint filed by a parent or guardian of a pupil with a school or an agency specified in Section 11165.9 against a school employee or other person that commits an act of child abuse, as defined in this article, against a pupil at a schoolsite and shall transmit a substantiated report, as defined in Section 11165.12, of that investigation to the governing board of the appropriate school district or county office of education. A substantiated report received by a governing board of a school district or county office of education shall be subject to the provisions of Section 44031 of the Education Code.

(Amended by Stats. 2000, Ch. 916, Sec. 12. Effective January 1, 2001.)

11165.15.

For the purposes of this article, the fact that a child is homeless or is classified as an unaccompanied youth, as defined in Section 11434a of the federal McKinney-Vento Homeless Assistance Act (42 U.S.C. Sec. 11301 et seq.), is not, in and of itself, a sufficient basis for reporting child abuse or neglect. This section shall not limit a mandated reporter, as defined in Section 11165.7, from making a report pursuant to

Section 11166 whenever the mandated reporter has knowledge of or observes an unaccompanied minor whom the mandated reporter knows or reasonably suspects to be the victim of abuse or neglect.

(Amended by Stats. 2014, Ch. 71, Sec. 132. (SB 1304) Effective January 1, 2015.)

11166.

(a) Except as provided in subdivision (d), and in Section 11166.05, a mandated reporter shall make a report to an agency specified in Section 11165.9 whenever the mandated reporter, in the mandated reporter's professional capacity or within the scope of the mandated reporter's employment, has knowledge of or observes a child whom the mandated reporter knows or reasonably suspects has been the victim of child abuse or neglect. The mandated reporter shall make an initial report by telephone to the agency immediately or as soon as is practicably possible, and shall prepare and send, fax, or electronically transmit a written followup report within 36 hours of receiving the information concerning the incident. The mandated reporter may include with the report any nonprivileged documentary evidence the mandated reporter possesses relating to the incident.

(1) For purposes of this article, "reasonable suspicion" means that it is objectively reasonable for a person to entertain a suspicion, based upon facts that could cause a reasonable person in a like position, drawing, when appropriate, on the person's training and experience, to suspect child abuse or neglect. "Reasonable suspicion" does not require certainty that child abuse or neglect has occurred nor does it require a specific medical indication of child abuse or neglect; any "reasonable suspicion" is sufficient. For purposes of this article, the pregnancy of a minor does not, in and of itself, constitute a basis for a reasonable suspicion of sexual abuse.

(2) The agency shall be notified and a report shall be prepared and sent, faxed, or electronically transmitted even if the child has expired, regardless of whether or not the possible abuse was a factor contributing to the death, and even if suspected child abuse was discovered during an autopsy.

(3) A report made by a mandated reporter pursuant to this section shall be known as a mandated report.

(b) If, after reasonable efforts, a mandated reporter is unable to submit an initial report by telephone, the mandated reporter shall immediately or as soon as is practicably possible, by fax or electronic transmission, make a one-time automated written report on the form prescribed by the Department of Justice, and shall also be available to respond to a telephone followup call by the agency with which the mandated reporter filed the report. A mandated reporter who files a one-time automated written report because the mandated reporter was unable to submit an initial report by telephone is not required to submit a written followup report.

(1) The one-time automated written report form prescribed by the Department of Justice shall be clearly identifiable so that it is not mistaken for a standard written followup report. In addition, the automated one-time report shall contain a section that allows the mandated reporter to state the reason the initial telephone call was not able to be completed. The reason for the submission of the one-time automated written report in lieu of the procedure prescribed in subdivision (a) shall be captured in the Child Welfare Services/Case Management System (CWS/CMS). The department shall work with stakeholders to modify reporting forms and the CWS/CMS as is necessary to accommodate the changes enacted by these provisions.

(2) This subdivision shall not become operative until the CWS/CMS is updated to capture the information prescribed in this subdivision.

(3) This subdivision shall become inoperative three years after this subdivision becomes operative or on January 1, 2009, whichever occurs first.

(4) This section does not supersede the requirement that a mandated reporter first attempt to make a report via telephone, or that agencies specified in Section 11165.9 accept reports from mandated reporters and other persons as required.

(c) A mandated reporter who fails to report an incident of known or reasonably suspected child abuse or neglect as required by this section is guilty of a misdemeanor punishable by up to six months confinement in a county jail or by a fine of one thousand dollars ($1,000) or by both that imprisonment and fine. If a mandated reporter intentionally conceals the mandated reporter's failure to report an incident known by the mandated reporter to be abuse or severe neglect under this section, the failure to report is a continuing offense until an agency specified in Section 11165.9 discovers the offense.

(d) (1) A clergy member who acquires knowledge or a reasonable suspicion of child abuse or neglect during a penitential communication is not subject to subdivision (a). For the purposes of this subdivision, "penitential communication" means a communication, intended to be in confidence, including, but not limited to, a sacramental confession, made to a clergy member who, in the course of the discipline or practice of the clergy member's church, denomination, or organization, is authorized or accustomed to hear those communications, and under the discipline, tenets, customs, or practices of the clergy member's church, denomination, or organization, has a duty to keep those communications secret.

(2) Nothing in this subdivision shall be construed to modify or limit a clergy member's duty to report known or suspected child abuse or neglect when the clergy member is acting in some other capacity that would otherwise make the clergy member a mandated reporter.

(3) (A) On or before January 1, 2004, a clergy member or any custodian of records for the clergy member may report to an agency specified in Section 11165.9 that the clergy member or any custodian of records for the clergy member, prior to January 1, 1997, in the clergy member's professional capacity or within the scope of the clergy member's employment, other than during a penitential communication, acquired knowledge or had a reasonable suspicion that a child had been the victim of sexual abuse and that the clergy member or any custodian of records for the clergy member did not previously report the abuse to an agency specified in Section 11165.9. The provisions of Section 11172 shall apply to all reports made pursuant to this paragraph.

(B) This paragraph shall apply even if the victim of the known or suspected abuse has reached the age of majority by the time the required report is made.

(C) The local law enforcement agency shall have jurisdiction to investigate any report of child abuse made pursuant to this paragraph even if the report is made after the victim has reached the age of majority.

(e) (1) A commercial film, photographic print, or image processor who has knowledge of or observes, within the scope of that person's professional capacity or employment, any film, photograph, videotape, negative, slide, or any representation of information, data, or an image, including, but not limited to, any film, filmstrip, photograph, negative, slide, photocopy, videotape, video laser disc, computer hardware, computer software, computer floppy disk, data storage medium, CD-ROM, computer-generated equipment, or computer-generated image depicting a child under 16 years of age engaged in an act of sexual conduct, shall, immediately or as soon as practicably possible, telephonically report the instance of suspected abuse to the law enforcement agency located in the county in which the images are seen. Within 36 hours of receiving the information concerning the incident, the reporter shall prepare and send, fax, or electronically transmit a written followup report of the incident with a copy of the image or material attached.

(2) A commercial computer technician who has knowledge of or observes, within the scope of the technician's professional capacity or employment, any representation of information, data, or an image, including, but not limited to, any computer hardware, computer software, computer file, computer floppy disk, data storage medium, CD-ROM, computer-generated equipment, or computer-generated image that is retrievable in perceivable form and that is intentionally saved, transmitted, or organized on an electronic medium, depicting a child under 16 years of age engaged in an act of sexual

conduct, shall immediately, or as soon as practicably possible, telephonically report the instance of suspected abuse to the law enforcement agency located in the county in which the images or materials are seen. As soon as practicably possible after receiving the information concerning the incident, the reporter shall prepare and send, fax, or electronically transmit a written followup report of the incident with a brief description of the images or materials.
(3) For purposes of this article, "commercial computer technician" includes an employee designated by an employer to receive reports pursuant to an established reporting process authorized by subparagraph (B) of paragraph (43) of subdivision (a) of Section 11165.7.
(4) As used in this subdivision, "electronic medium" includes, but is not limited to, a recording, CD-ROM, magnetic disk memory, magnetic tape memory, CD, DVD, thumbdrive, or any other computer hardware or media.
(5) As used in this subdivision, "sexual conduct" means any of the following:
(A) Sexual intercourse, including genital-genital, oral-genital, anal-genital, or oral-anal, whether between persons of the same or opposite sex or between humans and animals.
(B) Penetration of the vagina or rectum by any object.
(C) Masturbation for the purpose of sexual stimulation of the viewer.
(D) Sadomasochistic abuse for the purpose of sexual stimulation of the viewer.
(E) Exhibition of the genitals, pubic, or rectal areas of a person for the purpose of sexual stimulation of the viewer.
(f) Any mandated reporter who knows or reasonably suspects that the home or institution in which a child resides is unsuitable for the child because of abuse or neglect of the child shall bring the condition to the attention of the agency to which, and at the same time as, the mandated reporter makes a report of the abuse or neglect pursuant to subdivision (a).
(g) Any other person who has knowledge of or observes a child whom the person knows or reasonably suspects has been a victim of child abuse or neglect may report the known or suspected instance of child abuse or neglect to an agency specified in Section 11165.9. For purposes of this section, "any other person" includes a mandated reporter who acts in the person's private capacity and not in the person's professional capacity or within the scope of the person's employment.
(h) When two or more persons, who are required to report, jointly have knowledge of a known or suspected instance of child abuse or neglect, and when there is agreement among them, the telephone report may be made by a member of the team selected by mutual agreement and a single report may be made and signed by the selected member of the reporting team. Any member who has knowledge that the member designated to report has failed to do so shall thereafter make the report.
(i) (1) The reporting duties under this section are individual, and no supervisor or administrator may impede or inhibit the reporting duties, and no person making a report shall be subject to any sanction for making the report. However, internal procedures to facilitate reporting and apprise supervisors and administrators of reports may be established provided that they are not inconsistent with this article. An internal policy shall not direct an employee to allow the employee's supervisor to file or process a mandated report under any circumstances.
(2) The internal procedures shall not require any employee required to make reports pursuant to this article to disclose the employee's identity to the employer.
(3) Reporting the information regarding a case of possible child abuse or neglect to an employer, supervisor, school principal, school counselor, coworker, or other person shall not be a substitute for making a mandated report to an agency specified in Section 11165.9.
(j) (1) A county probation or welfare department shall immediately, or as soon as practicably possible, report by telephone, fax, or electronic transmission to the law enforcement agency having jurisdiction over the case, to the agency given the responsibility for investigation of cases under Section 300 of the Welfare and Institutions Code, and to the district attorney's office every known or suspected instance of child abuse or neglect, as defined in Section 11165.6, except acts or omissions coming within subdivision (b) of Section 11165.2, or reports made pursuant to Section 11165.13 based on risk to a child that relates solely to the inability of the parent to provide the child with regular care due to the parent's substance abuse, which shall be reported only to the county welfare or probation department. A county probation or welfare department also shall send, fax, or electronically transmit a written report thereof within 36 hours of receiving the information concerning the incident to any agency to which it makes a telephone report under this subdivision.
(2) A county probation or welfare department shall immediately, and in no case in more than 24 hours, report to the law enforcement agency having jurisdiction over the case after receiving information that a child or youth who is receiving child welfare services has been identified as the victim of commercial sexual exploitation, as defined in subdivision (d) of Section 11165.1.
(3) When a child or youth who is receiving child welfare services and who is reasonably believed to be the victim of, or is at risk of being the victim of, commercial sexual exploitation, as defined in Section 11165.1, is missing or has been abducted, the county probation or welfare department shall immediately, or in no case later than 24 hours from receipt of the information, report the incident to the appropriate law enforcement authority for entry into the National Crime Information Center database of the Federal Bureau of Investigation and to the National Center for Missing and Exploited Children.
(k) A law enforcement agency shall immediately, or as soon as practicably possible, report by telephone, fax, or electronic transmission to the agency given responsibility for investigation of cases under Section 300 of the Welfare and Institutions Code and to the district attorney's office every known or suspected instance of child abuse or neglect reported to it, except acts or omissions coming within subdivision (b) of Section 11165.2, which shall be reported only to the county welfare or probation department. A law enforcement agency shall report to the county welfare or probation department every known or suspected instance of child abuse or neglect reported to it which is alleged to have occurred as a result of the action of a person responsible for the child's welfare, or as the result of the failure of a person responsible for the child's welfare to adequately protect the minor from abuse when the person responsible for the child's welfare knew or reasonably should have known that the minor was in danger of abuse. A law enforcement agency also shall send, fax, or electronically transmit a written report thereof within 36 hours of receiving the information concerning the incident to any agency to which it makes a telephone report under this subdivision.
(Amended by Stats. 2019, Ch. 27, Sec. 16. (SB 80) Effective June 27, 2019.)

11166.01.

(a) Except as provided in subdivision (b), any supervisor or administrator who violates paragraph (1) of subdivision (i) of Section 11166 shall be punished by not more than six months in a county jail, by a fine of not more than one thousand dollars ($1,000), or by both that fine and imprisonment.
(b) Notwithstanding Section 11162 or subdivision (c) of Section 11166, any mandated reporter who willfully fails to report abuse or neglect, or any person who impedes or inhibits a report of abuse or neglect, in violation of this article, where that abuse or neglect results in death or great bodily injury, shall be punished by not more than one year in a county jail, by a fine of not more than five thousand dollars ($5,000), or by both that fine and imprisonment.
(Amended by Stats. 2006, Ch. 901, Sec. 10. Effective January 1, 2007.)

11166.02.

(a) A county welfare agency, as determined in Section 10612.5 of the Welfare and Institutions Code, may develop a pilot program for Internet-based reporting of child abuse and neglect. The pilot program may receive reports by mandated reporters, as specified in paragraph (5), of suspected child abuse or neglect and shall meet all of the following conditions:
(1) The suspected child abuse or neglect does not indicate that the child is subject to an immediate risk of abuse, neglect, or exploitation or that the child is in imminent danger of severe harm or death.
(2) The agency provides an Internet form that includes standardized safety assessment qualifying questions in order to obtain necessary information required to assess the need for child welfare services and a response. The State Department of Social Services shall provide guidance through written directives to counties participating in the pilot program to incorporate qualifying questions in the online report that would indicate the need to redirect the mandated reporter to perform a telephone report.
(3) The mandated reporter is required to complete all required fields, including identity and contact information of the mandated reporter, in order to submit the report.
(4) The agency provides an Internet-based reporting system that has appropriate security protocols to preserve the confidentiality of the reports and any documents or photographs submitted through the system.
(5) The system can only be used by mandated reporters who are any of the following:
(A) A peace officer, as defined in Chapter 4.5 (commencing with Section 830) of Title 3 of Part 2.
(B) A probation officer or social worker, as defined in Section 215 of the Welfare and Institutions Code.
(C) A school teacher, counselor, or administrator.
(D) A physician and surgeon, psychologist, licensed nurse, or clinical social worker licensed pursuant to Division 2 (commencing with Section 500) of the Business and Professions Code.
(E) A coroner.
(6) Nothing in this section shall be construed as changing current statutory or regulatory requirements regarding timely review, assessment, and response to reports of possible abuse or neglect.
(b) (1) In a county where the pilot program is active, a mandated reporter listed in paragraph (5) of subdivision (a) may use the Internet-based reporting tool in lieu of the required initial telephone report required by subdivision (a) of Section 11166. A mandated reporter listed in paragraph (5) of subdivision (a) submitting an Internet-based report in accordance with this subdivision shall, as soon as practically possible, cooperate with the agency on any requests for additional information if needed to investigate the report, subject to applicable confidentiality requirements.
(2) In a county where the pilot program is active, a mandated reporter who submits the initial report through the Internet-based reporting tool in lieu of the required initial telephone report is not required to submit the written followup report required pursuant to subdivision (a) of Section 11166.
(c) This section shall remain in effect only until January 1, 2021, and as of that date is repealed, unless a later enacted statute, that is enacted before January 1, 2021, deletes or extends that date.
(Added by Stats. 2015, Ch. 490, Sec. 1. (SB 478) Effective January 1, 2016. Repealed as of January 1, 2021, by its own provisions.)

11166.05.

Any mandated reporter who has knowledge of or who reasonably suspects that a child is suffering serious emotional damage or is at a substantial risk of suffering serious emotional damage, evidenced by states of being or behavior, including, but not limited to, severe anxiety, depression, withdrawal, or untoward aggressive behavior toward self or others, may make a report to an agency specified in Section 11165.9.
(Amended by Stats. 2004, Ch. 842, Sec. 9. Effective January 1, 2005.)

11166.1.

(a) When an agency receives a report pursuant to Section 11166 that contains either of the following, it shall, within 24 hours, notify the licensing office with jurisdiction over the facility:
(1) A report of abuse alleged to have occurred in facilities licensed to care for children by the State Department of Social Services.
(2) A report of the death of a child who was, at the time of death, living at, enrolled in, or regularly attending a facility licensed to care for children by the State Department of Social Services, unless the circumstances of the child's death are clearly unrelated to the child's care at the facility.
The agency shall send the licensing agency a copy of its investigation and any other pertinent materials.
(b) Any employee of an agency specified in Section 11165.9 who has knowledge of, or observes in his or her professional capacity or within the scope of his or her employment, a child in protective custody whom he or she knows or reasonably suspects has been the victim of child abuse or neglect shall, within 36 hours, send or have sent to the attorney who represents the child in dependency court, a copy of the report prepared in accordance with Section 11166. The agency shall maintain a copy of the written report. All information requested by the attorney for the child or the child's guardian ad litem shall be provided by the agency within 30 days of the request.
(Amended by Stats. 2000, Ch. 916, Sec. 17. Effective January 1, 2001.)

11166.2.

In addition to the reports required under Section 11166, any agency specified in Section 11165.9 shall immediately or as soon as practically possible report by telephone, fax, or electronic transmission to the appropriate licensing agency every known or suspected instance of child abuse or neglect when the instance of abuse or neglect occurs while the child is being cared for in a child day care facility, involves a child day care licensed staff person, or occurs while the child is under the supervision of a community care facility or involves a community care facility licensee or staff person. The agency shall also send, fax, or electronically transmit a written report thereof within 36 hours of receiving the information concerning the incident to any agency to which it makes a telephone report under this subdivision. The agency shall send the licensing agency a copy of its investigation report and any other pertinent materials.
(Amended by Stats. 2001, Ch. 133, Sec. 7. Effective July 31, 2001.)

11166.3.

(a) The Legislature intends that in each county the law enforcement agencies and the county welfare or probation department shall develop and implement cooperative arrangements in order to coordinate existing duties in connection with the investigation of suspected child abuse or neglect cases. The local law enforcement agency having jurisdiction over a case reported under Section 11166 shall report to the county welfare or probation department that it is investigating the case within 36 hours after starting its investigation. The county welfare department or probation department shall, in cases where a minor is a victim of actions specified in Section 288 of this code and a petition has been filed pursuant to Section 300 of the Welfare and Institutions Code with regard to the minor, evaluate what action or actions would be in the best interest of the child victim. Notwithstanding any other provision of law, the county welfare department or probation department shall submit in writing its findings and the reasons therefor to the district attorney on or before the completion of the investigation. The written findings and the reasons therefor shall be delivered or made accessible to the defendant or his or her counsel in the manner specified in Section 859.
(b) The local law enforcement agency having jurisdiction over a case reported under Section 11166 shall report to the district office of the State Department of Social Services any case reported under this section if the case involves a facility specified in paragraph (5) or (6) of subdivision (a) of Section 1502, Section 1596.750 or 1596.76 of the Health and Safety Code, and the licensing of the facility has not been delegated to a county agency. The law enforcement agency shall send a copy of its investigation

report and any other pertinent materials to the licensing agency upon the request of the licensing agency.

(Amended by Stats. 2001, Ch. 133, Sec. 8. Effective July 31, 2001.)

11166.5.

(a) (1) On and after January 1, 1985, any mandated reporter as specified in Section 11165.7, with the exception of child visitation monitors, prior to commencing his or her employment, and as a prerequisite to that employment, shall sign a statement on a form provided to him or her by his or her employer to the effect that he or she has knowledge of the provisions of Section 11166 and will comply with those provisions. The statement shall inform the employee that he or she is a mandated reporter and inform the employee of his or her reporting obligations under Section 11166 and of his or her confidentiality rights under subdivision (d) of Section 11167. The employer shall provide a copy of Sections 11165.7, 11166, and 11167 to the employee.

On and after January 1, 1993, any person who acts as a child visitation monitor, as defined in paragraph (31) of subdivision (a) of Section 11165.7, prior to engaging in monitoring the first visit in a case, shall sign a statement on a form provided to him or her by the court which ordered the presence of that third person during the visit, to the effect that he or she has knowledge of the provisions of Section 11166 and will comply with those provisions.

(2) The signed statements shall be retained by the employer or the court, as the case may be. The cost of printing, distribution, and filing of these statements shall be borne by the employer or the court.

(3) This subdivision is not applicable to persons employed by public or private youth centers, youth recreation programs, and youth organizations as members of the support staff or maintenance staff and who do not work with, observe, or have knowledge of children as part of their official duties.

(b) On and after January 1, 1986, when a person is issued a state license or certificate to engage in a profession or occupation, the members of which are required to make a report pursuant to Section 11166, the state agency issuing the license or certificate shall send a statement substantially similar to the one contained in subdivision (a) to the person at the same time as it transmits the document indicating licensure or certification to the person. In addition to the requirements contained in subdivision (a), the statement also shall indicate that failure to comply with the requirements of Section 11166 is a misdemeanor, punishable by up to six months in a county jail, by a fine of one thousand dollars ($1,000), or by both that imprisonment and fine.

(c) As an alternative to the procedure required by subdivision (b), a state agency may cause the required statement to be printed on all application forms for a license or certificate printed on or after January 1, 1986.

(d) On and after January 1, 1993, any child visitation monitor, as defined in paragraph (31) of subdivision (a) of Section 11165.7, who desires to act in that capacity shall have received training in the duties imposed by this article, including training in child abuse identification and child abuse reporting. The person, prior to engaging in monitoring the first visit in a case, shall sign a statement on a form provided to him or her by the court which ordered the presence of that third person during the visit, to the effect that he or she has received this training. This statement may be included in the statement required by subdivision (a) or it may be a separate statement. This statement shall be filed, along with the statement required by subdivision (a), in the court file of the case for which the visitation monitoring is being provided.

(e) Any person providing services to a minor child, as described in paragraph (38) of subdivision (a) of Section 11165.7, shall not be required to make a report pursuant to Section 11166 unless that person has received training, or instructional materials in the appropriate language, on the duties imposed by this article, including identifying and reporting child abuse and neglect.

(Amended by Stats. 2012, Ch. 518, Sec. 2. (SB 1264) Effective January 1, 2013.)

11167.

(a) Reports of suspected child abuse or neglect pursuant to Section 11166 or Section 11166.05 shall include the name, business address, and telephone number of the mandated reporter; the capacity that makes the person a mandated reporter; and the information that gave rise to the reasonable suspicion of child abuse or neglect and the source or sources of that information. If a report is made, the following information, if known, shall also be included in the report: the child's name, the child's address, present location, and, if applicable, school, grade, and class; the names, addresses, and telephone numbers of the child's parents or guardians; and the name, address, telephone number, and other relevant personal information about the person or persons who might have abused or neglected the child. The mandated reporter shall make a report even if some of this information is not known or is uncertain to him or her.

(b) Information relevant to the incident of child abuse or neglect and information relevant to a report made pursuant to Section 11166.05 may be given to an investigator from an agency that is investigating the known or suspected case of child abuse or neglect.

(c) Information relevant to the incident of child abuse or neglect, including the investigation report and other pertinent materials, and information relevant to a report made pursuant to Section 11166.05 may be given to the licensing agency when it is investigating a known or suspected case of child abuse or neglect.

(d) (1) The identity of all persons who report under this article shall be confidential and disclosed only among agencies receiving or investigating mandated reports, to the prosecutor in a criminal prosecution or in an action initiated under Section 602 of the Welfare and Institutions Code arising from alleged child abuse, or to counsel appointed pursuant to subdivision (c) of Section 317 of the Welfare and Institutions Code, or to the county counsel or prosecutor in a proceeding under Part 4 (commencing with Section 7800) of Division 12 of the Family Code or Section 300 of the Welfare and Institutions Code, or to a licensing agency when abuse or neglect in out-of-home care is reasonably suspected, or when those persons waive confidentiality, or by court order.

(2) No agency or person listed in this subdivision shall disclose the identity of any person who reports under this article to that person's employer, except with the employee's consent or by court order.

(e) Notwithstanding the confidentiality requirements of this section, a representative of a child protective services agency performing an investigation that results from a report of suspected child abuse or neglect made pursuant to Section 11166 or Section 11166.05, at the time of the initial contact with the individual who is subject to the investigation, shall advise the individual of the complaints or allegations against him or her, in a manner that is consistent with laws protecting the identity of the reporter under this article.

(f) Persons who may report pursuant to subdivision (g) of Section 11166 are not required to include their names.

(Amended by Stats. 2010, Ch. 95, Sec. 1. (AB 2339) Effective January 1, 2011.)

11167.5.

(a) The reports required by Sections 11166 and 11166.2, or authorized by Section 11166.05, and child abuse or neglect investigative reports that result in a summary report being filed with the Department of Justice pursuant to subdivision (a) of Section 11169 shall be confidential and may be disclosed only as provided in subdivision (b). Any violation of the confidentiality provided by this article is a misdemeanor punishable by imprisonment in a county jail not to exceed six months, by a fine of five hundred dollars ($500), or by both that imprisonment and fine.

(b) Reports of suspected child abuse or neglect and information contained therein may be disclosed only to the following:

(1) Persons or agencies to whom disclosure of the identity of the reporting party is permitted under Section 11167.

(2) Persons or agencies to whom disclosure of information is permitted under subdivision (b) of Section 11170 or subdivision (a) of Section 11170.5.

(3) Persons or agencies with whom investigations of child abuse or neglect are coordinated under the regulations promulgated under Section 11174.

(4) Multidisciplinary personnel teams as defined in subdivision (d) of Section 18951 of the Welfare and Institutions Code.

(5) Persons or agencies responsible for the licensing of facilities which care for children, as specified in Section 11165.7.

(6) The State Department of Social Services or any county, as specified in paragraph (4) of subdivision (b) of Section 11170, when an individual has applied for a license to operate a community care facility or child day care facility, or for a certificate of approval to operate a certified family home or resource family home, or for employment or presence in a licensed facility, certified family home, or resource family home, or when a complaint alleges child abuse or neglect by a licensee or employee of, or individual approved to be present in, a licensed facility, certified family home, or resource family home.

(7) Hospital scan teams. As used in this paragraph, "hospital scan team" means a team of three or more persons established by a hospital, or two or more hospitals in the same county, consisting of health care professionals and representatives of law enforcement and child protective services, the members of which are engaged in the identification of child abuse or neglect. The disclosure authorized by this section includes disclosure among all hospital scan teams.

(8) Coroners and medical examiners when conducting a post mortem examination of a child.

(9) The Board of Parole Hearings, which may subpoena an employee of a county welfare department who can provide relevant evidence and reports that both (A) are not unfounded, pursuant to Section 11165.12, and (B) concern only the current incidents upon which parole revocation proceedings are pending against a parolee charged with child abuse or neglect. The reports and information shall be confidential pursuant to subdivision (d) of Section 11167.

(10) Personnel from an agency responsible for making a placement of a child pursuant to Section 361.3 of, and Article 7 (commencing with Section 305) of Chapter 2 of Part 1 of Division 2 of, the Welfare and Institutions Code.

(11) Persons who have been identified by the Department of Justice as listed in the Child Abuse Central Index pursuant to paragraph (7) of subdivision (b) of Section 11170 or subdivision (c) of Section 11170, or persons who have verified with the Department of Justice that they are listed in the Child Abuse Central Index as provided in subdivision (f) of Section 11170. Disclosure under this paragraph is required notwithstanding the California Public Records Act, Chapter 3.5 (commencing with Section 6250) of Division 7 of Title 1 of the Government Code. Nothing in this paragraph shall preclude a submitting agency prior to disclosure from redacting any information necessary to maintain confidentiality as required by law.

(12) Out-of-state law enforcement agencies conducting an investigation of child abuse or neglect only when an agency makes the request for reports of suspected child abuse or neglect in writing and on official letterhead, or as designated by the Department of Justice, identifying the suspected abuser or victim by name and date of birth or approximate age. The request shall be signed by the department supervisor of the requesting law enforcement agency. The written request shall cite the out-of-state statute or interstate compact provision that requires that the information contained within these reports is to be disclosed only to law enforcement, prosecutorial entities, or multidisciplinary investigative teams, and shall cite the safeguards in place to prevent unlawful disclosure provided by the requesting state or the applicable interstate compact provision.

(13) Out-of-state agencies responsible for approving prospective foster or adoptive parents for placement of a child only when the agency makes the request in compliance with the Adam Walsh Child Protection and Safety Act of 2006 (Public Law 109-248). The request shall also cite the safeguards in place to prevent unlawful disclosure provided by the requesting state or the applicable interstate compact provision and indicate that the requesting state shall maintain continual compliance with the requirement in paragraph (20) of subdivision (a) of Section 671 of Title 42 of the United States Code that requires the state have in place safeguards to prevent the unauthorized disclosure of information in any child abuse and neglect registry maintained by the state and prevent the information from being used for a purpose other than the conducting of background checks in foster or adoptive placement cases.

(14) Each chairperson of a county child death review team, or his or her designee, to whom disclosure of information is permitted under this article, relating to the death of one or more children and any prior child abuse or neglect investigation reports maintained involving the same victim, siblings, or suspects. Local child death review teams may share any relevant information regarding case reviews involving child death with other child death review teams.

(c) Authorized persons within county health departments shall be permitted to receive copies of any reports made by health practitioners, as defined in paragraphs (21) to (28), inclusive, of subdivision (a) of Section 11165.7, and pursuant to Section 11165.13, and copies of assessments completed pursuant to Sections 123600 and 123605 of the Health and Safety Code, to the extent permitted by federal law. Any information received pursuant to this subdivision is protected by subdivision (e).

(d) Nothing in this section requires the Department of Justice to disclose information contained in records maintained under Section 11170 or under the regulations promulgated pursuant to Section 11174, except as otherwise provided in this article.

(e) This section shall not be interpreted to allow disclosure of any reports or records relevant to the reports of child abuse or neglect if the disclosure would be prohibited by any other provisions of state or federal law applicable to the reports or records relevant to the reports of child abuse or neglect.

(Amended by Stats. 2017, Ch. 732, Sec. 41. (AB 404) Effective January 1, 2018.)

11168.

The written reports required by Section 11166 shall be submitted on forms adopted by the Department of Justice after consultation with representatives of the various professional medical associations and hospital associations and county probation or welfare departments. Those forms shall be distributed by the agencies specified in Section 11165.9.

(Amended by Stats. 2000, Ch. 916, Sec. 26. Effective January 1, 2001.)

11169.

(a) An agency specified in Section 11165.9 shall forward to the Department of Justice a report in writing of every case it investigates of known or suspected child abuse or severe neglect that is determined to be substantiated, other than cases coming within subdivision (b) of Section 11165.2. An agency shall not forward a report to the Department of Justice unless it has conducted an active investigation and determined that the report is substantiated, as defined in Section 11165.12. If a report has previously been filed which subsequently proves to be not substantiated, the Department of Justice shall be notified in writing of that fact and shall not retain the report. The reports required by this section shall be in a form approved by the Department of Justice and may be sent by fax or electronic transmission. An agency specified in Section 11165.9 receiving a written report from another agency specified in Section 11165.9 shall not send that report to the Department of Justice.

(b) On and after January 1, 2012, a police department or sheriff's department specified in Section 11165.9 shall no longer forward to the Department of Justice a report in writing of any case it investigates of known or suspected child abuse or severe neglect.

(c) At the time an agency specified in Section 11165.9 forwards a report in writing to the Department of Justice pursuant to subdivision (a), the agency shall also notify in

writing the known or suspected child abuser that he or she has been reported to the Child Abuse Central Index (CACI).The notice required by this section shall be in a form approved by the Department of Justice. The requirements of this subdivision shall apply with respect to reports forwarded to the department on or after the date on which this subdivision becomes operative.
(d) Subject to subdivision (e), any person who is listed on the CACI has the right to a hearing before the agency that requested his or her inclusion in the CACI to challenge his or her listing on the CACI. The hearing shall satisfy due process requirements. It is the intent of the Legislature that the hearing provided for by this subdivision shall not be construed to be inconsistent with hearing proceedings available to persons who have been listed on the CACI prior to the enactment of the act that added this subdivision.
(e) A hearing requested pursuant to subdivision (d) shall be denied when a court of competent jurisdiction has determined that suspected child abuse or neglect has occurred, or when the allegation of child abuse or neglect resulting in the referral to the CACI is pending before the court. A person who is listed on the CACI and has been denied a hearing pursuant to this subdivision has a right to a hearing pursuant to subdivision (d) only if the court's jurisdiction has terminated, the court has not made a finding concerning whether the suspected child abuse or neglect was substantiated, and a hearing has not previously been provided to the listed person pursuant to subdivision (d).
(f) Any person listed in the CACI who has reached 100 years of age shall have his or her listing removed from the CACI.
(g) Any person listed in the CACI as of January 1, 2013, who was listed prior to reaching 18 years of age, and who is listed once in CACI with no subsequent listings, shall be removed from the CACI 10 years from the date of the incident resulting in the CACI listing.
(h) If, after a hearing pursuant to subdivision (d) or a court proceeding described in subdivision (e), it is determined the person's CACI listing was based on a report that was not substantiated, the agency shall notify the Department of Justice of that result and the department shall remove that person's name from the CACI.
(i) Agencies, including police departments and sheriff's departments, shall retain child abuse or neglect investigative reports that result or resulted in a report filed with the Department of Justice pursuant to subdivision (a) for the same period of time that the information is required to be maintained on the CACI pursuant to this section and subdivision (a) of Section 11170. Nothing in this section precludes an agency from retaining the reports for a longer period of time if required by law.
(j) The immunity provisions of Section 11172 shall not apply to the submission of a report by an agency pursuant to this section. However, nothing in this section shall be construed to alter or diminish any other immunity provisions of state or federal law.
(Amended by Stats. 2012, Ch. 848, Sec. 1. (AB 1707) Effective January 1, 2013.)
11170.
(a) (1) The Department of Justice shall maintain an index of all reports of child abuse and severe neglect submitted pursuant to Section 11169. The index shall be continually updated by the department and shall not contain any reports that are determined to be not substantiated. The department may adopt rules governing recordkeeping and reporting pursuant to this article.
(2) The department shall act only as a repository of reports of suspected child abuse and severe neglect to be maintained in the Child Abuse Central Index (CACI) pursuant to paragraph (1). The submitting agencies are responsible for the accuracy, completeness, and retention of the reports described in this section. The department shall be responsible for ensuring that the CACI accurately reflects the report it receives from the submitting agency.
(3) Only information from reports that are reported as substantiated shall be filed pursuant to paragraph (1), and all other determinations shall be removed from the central list. If a person listed in the CACI was under 18 years of age at the time of the report, the information shall be deleted from the CACI 10 years from the date of the incident resulting in the CACI listing, if no subsequent report concerning the same person is received during that time period.
(b) The provisions of subdivision (c) of Section 11169 apply to any information provided pursuant to this subdivision.
(1) The Department of Justice shall immediately notify an agency that submits a report pursuant to Section 11169, or a prosecutor who requests notification, of any information maintained pursuant to subdivision (a) that is relevant to the known or suspected instance of child abuse or severe neglect reported by the agency. The agency shall make that information available to the reporting health care practitioner who is treating a person reported as a possible victim of known or suspected child abuse. The agency shall make that information available to the reporting child custodian, Child Abuse Prevention and Treatment Act guardian ad litem appointed under Rule 5.662 of the California Rules of Court, or counsel appointed under Section 317 or 318 of the Welfare and Institutions Code, or the appropriate licensing agency, if he or she or the licensing agency is handling or investigating a case of known or suspected child abuse or severe neglect.
(2) When a report is made pursuant to subdivision (a) of Section 11166, or Section 11166.05, the investigating agency, upon completion of the investigation or after there has been a final disposition in the matter, shall inform the person required or authorized to report of the results of the investigation and of any action the agency is taking with regard to the child or family.
(3) The Department of Justice shall make relevant information from the CACI available to a law enforcement agency, county welfare department, tribal agency pursuant to Section 10553.12 of the Welfare and Institutions Code, or county probation department that is conducting a child abuse investigation.
(4) The department shall make available to the State Department of Social Services, to any county licensing agency that has contracted with the state for the performance of licensing duties, to a county approving resource families pursuant to Section 16519.5 of the Welfare and Institutions Code, or to a tribal court or tribal child welfare agency of a tribe, consortium of tribes, or tribal organization that has entered into an agreement with the state pursuant to Section 10553.1 of the Welfare and Institutions Code, information regarding a known or suspected child abuser maintained pursuant to this section and subdivision (a) of Section 11169 concerning any person who is an applicant for licensure or approval, or any adult who resides or is employed in the home of an applicant for licensure or approval, or who is an applicant for employment in a position having supervisorial or disciplinary power over a child or children, or who will provide 24-hour care for a child or children in a residential home or facility, pursuant to Section 1522.1 or 1596.877 of the Health and Safety Code, or Section 8714, 8802, 8912, or 9000 of the Family Code, or Section 11403.2 or 16519.5 of the Welfare and Institutions Code.
(5) The Department of Justice shall make available to a Court Appointed Special Advocate program that is conducting a background investigation of an applicant seeking employment with the program or a volunteer position as a Court Appointed Special Advocate, as defined in Section 101 of the Welfare and Institutions Code, information contained in the index regarding known or suspected child abuse by the applicant.
(6) For purposes of child death review, the Department of Justice shall make available to the chairperson, or the chairperson's designee, for each county child death review team, or the State Child Death Review Council, information for investigative purposes only that is maintained in the CACI pursuant to subdivision (a) relating to the death of one or more children and any prior child abuse or neglect investigation reports maintained involving the same victims, siblings, or suspects. Local child death review teams may share any relevant information regarding case reviews involving child death with other child death review teams.
(7) The department shall make available to investigative agencies or probation officers, or court investigators acting pursuant to Section 1513 of the Probate Code, responsible for placing children or assessing the possible placement of children pursuant to Article 6 (commencing with Section 300), Article 7 (commencing with Section 305), Article 10 (commencing with Section 360), or Article 14 (commencing with Section 601) of Chapter 2 of Part 1 of Division 2 of the Welfare and Institutions Code, or Article 2 (commencing with Section 1510) or Article 3 (commencing with Section 1540) of Chapter 1 of Part 2 of Division 4 of the Probate Code, information regarding a known or suspected child abuser contained in the index concerning any adult residing in the home where the child may be placed, when this information is requested for purposes of ensuring that the placement is in the best interest of the child. Upon receipt of relevant information concerning child abuse or neglect investigation reports contained in the CACI from the Department of Justice pursuant to this subdivision, the agency or court investigator shall notify, in writing, the person listed in the CACI that he or she is in the index. The notification shall include the name of the reporting agency and the date of the report.
(8) Pursuant to Section 10553.12 of the Welfare and Institutions Code, the department shall make available to a tribal agency information regarding a known or suspected child abuser maintained pursuant to this section or subdivision (a) of Section 11169 who is being considered as a prospective foster or adoptive parent, an adult who resides or is employed in the home of an applicant for approval, any person who has a familial or intimate relationship with any person living in the home of an applicant, or an employee of the tribal agency who may have contact with children.
(9) The Department of Justice shall make available to a government agency conducting a background investigation pursuant to Section 1031 of the Government Code of an applicant seeking employment as a peace officer, as defined in Section 830, information regarding a known or suspected child abuser maintained pursuant to this section concerning the applicant.
(10) The Department of Justice shall make available to a county child welfare agency or delegated county adoption agency, as defined in Section 8515 of the Family Code, conducting a background investigation, or a government agency conducting a background investigation on behalf of one of those agencies, information regarding a known or suspected child abuser maintained pursuant to this section and subdivision (a) of Section 11169 concerning any applicant seeking employment or volunteer status with the agency who, in the course of his or her employment or volunteer work, will have direct contact with children who are alleged to have been, are at risk of, or have suffered, abuse or neglect.
(11) (A) Persons or agencies, as specified in subdivision (b), if investigating a case of known or suspected child abuse or neglect, or the State Department of Social Services or any county licensing agency pursuant to paragraph (4), or a Court Appointed Special Advocate (CASA) program conducting a background investigation for employment or volunteer candidates pursuant to paragraph (5), or an investigative agency, probation officer, or court investigator responsible for placing children or assessing the possible placement of children pursuant to paragraph (7), or a government agency conducting a background investigation of an applicant seeking employment as a peace officer pursuant to paragraph (9), or a county child welfare agency or delegated county adoption agency conducting a background investigation of an applicant seeking employment or volunteer status who, in the course of his or her employment or volunteer work, will have direct contact with children who are alleged to have been, are at risk of, or have suffered, abuse or neglect, pursuant to paragraph (10), to whom disclosure of any information maintained pursuant to subdivision (a) is authorized, are responsible for obtaining the original investigative report from the reporting agency, and for drawing independent conclusions regarding the quality of the evidence disclosed, and its sufficiency for making decisions regarding investigation, prosecution, licensing, placement of a child, employment or volunteer positions with a CASA program, or employment as a peace officer.
(B) If CACI information is requested by an agency for the temporary placement of a child in an emergency situation pursuant to Article 7 (commencing with Section 305) of Chapter 2 of Part 1 of Division 2 of the Welfare and Institutions Code, the department is exempt from the requirements of Section 1798.18 of the Civil Code if compliance would cause a delay in providing an expedited response to the agency's inquiry and if further delay in placement may be detrimental to the child.
(12) (A) Whenever information contained in the Department of Justice files is furnished as the result of an application for employment or licensing or volunteer status pursuant to paragraph (4), (5), (8), (9), or (10), the Department of Justice may charge the person or entity making the request a fee. The fee shall not exceed the reasonable costs to the department of providing the information. The only increase shall be at a rate not to exceed the legislatively approved cost-of-living adjustment for the department. In no case shall the fee exceed fifteen dollars ($15).
(B) All moneys received by the department pursuant to this section to process trustline applications for purposes of Chapter 3.35 (commencing with Section 1596.60) of Division 2 of the Health and Safety Code shall be deposited in a special account in the General Fund that is hereby established and named the Department of Justice Child Abuse Fund. Moneys in the fund shall be available, upon appropriation by the Legislature, for expenditure by the department to offset the costs incurred to process trustline automated child abuse or neglect system checks pursuant to this section.
(C) All moneys, other than those described in subparagraph (B), received by the department pursuant to this paragraph shall be deposited in a special account in the General Fund which is hereby created and named the Department of Justice Sexual Habitual Offender Fund. The funds shall be available, upon appropriation by the Legislature, for expenditure by the department to offset the costs incurred pursuant to Chapter 9.5 (commencing with Section 13885) and Chapter 10 (commencing with Section 13890) of Title 6 of Part 4, and the DNA and Forensic Identification Data Base and Data Bank Act of 1998 (Chapter 6 (commencing with Section 295) of Title 9 of Part 1), and for maintenance and improvements to the statewide Sexual Habitual Offender Program and the California DNA offender identification file (CAL-DNA) authorized by Chapter 9.5 (commencing with Section 13885) of Title 6 of Part 4 and the DNA and Forensic Identification Data Base and Data Bank Act of 1998 (Chapter 6 (commencing with Section 295) of Title 9 of Part 1).
(c) (1) The Department of Justice shall make available to any agency responsible for placing children pursuant to Article 7 (commencing with Section 305) of Chapter 2 of Part 1 of Division 2 of the Welfare and Institutions Code, upon request, relevant information concerning child abuse or neglect reports contained in the index, when making a placement with a responsible relative pursuant to Sections 281.5, 305, and 361.3 of the Welfare and Institutions Code. Upon receipt of relevant information concerning child abuse or neglect reports contained in the index from the Department of Justice pursuant to this subdivision, the agency shall also notify in writing the person listed in the CACI that he or she is in the index. The notification shall include the location of the original investigative report and the submitting agency. The notification shall be submitted to the person listed at the same time that all other parties are notified of the information, and no later than the actual judicial proceeding that determines placement.
(2) If information is requested by an agency for the placement of a child with a responsible relative in an emergency situation pursuant to Article 7 (commencing with Section 305) of Chapter 2 of Part 1 of Division 2 of the Welfare and Institutions Code, the department is exempt from the requirements of Section 1798.18 of the Civil Code if compliance would cause a delay in providing an expedited response to the child protective agency's inquiry and if further delay in placement may be detrimental to the child.

(d) The department shall make available any information maintained pursuant to subdivision (a) to out-of-state law enforcement agencies conducting investigations of known or suspected child abuse or neglect only when an agency makes the request for information in writing and on official letterhead, or as designated by the department, identifying the suspected abuser or victim by name and date of birth or approximate age. The request shall be signed by the department supervisor of the requesting law enforcement agency. The written requests shall cite the out-of-state statute or interstate compact provision that requires that the information contained within these reports shall be disclosed only to law enforcement, prosecutorial entities, or multidisciplinary investigative teams, and shall cite the safeguards in place to prevent unlawful disclosure of any confidential information provided by the requesting state or the applicable interstate compact provision.

(e) (1) The department shall make available to an out-of-state agency, for purposes of approving a prospective foster or adoptive parent in compliance with the Adam Walsh Child Protection and Safety Act of 2006 (Public Law 109-248), information regarding a known or suspected child abuser maintained pursuant to subdivision (a) concerning the prospective foster or adoptive parent, and any other adult living in the home of the prospective foster or adoptive parent. The department shall make that information available only when the out-of-state agency makes the request indicating that continual compliance will be maintained with the requirement in paragraph (20) of subsection (a) of Section 671 of Title 42 of the United States Code that requires the state to have in place safeguards to prevent the unauthorized disclosure of information in any child abuse and neglect registry maintained by the state and prevent the information from being used for a purpose other than the conducting of background checks in foster or adoption placement cases.

(2) With respect to any information provided by the department in response to the out-of-state agency's request, the out-of-state agency is responsible for obtaining the original investigative report from the reporting agency, and for drawing independent conclusions regarding the quality of the evidence disclosed and its sufficiency for making decisions regarding the approval of prospective foster or adoptive parents.

(3) (A) Whenever information contained in the index is furnished pursuant to this subdivision, the department shall charge the out-of-state agency making the request a fee. The fee shall not exceed the reasonable costs to the department of providing the information. The only increase shall be at a rate not to exceed the legislatively approved cost-of-living adjustment for the department. In no case shall the fee exceed fifteen dollars ($15).

(B) All moneys received by the department pursuant to this subdivision shall be deposited in the Department of Justice Child Abuse Fund, established under subparagraph (B) of paragraph (12) of subdivision (b). Moneys in the fund shall be available, upon appropriation by the Legislature, for expenditure by the department to offset the costs incurred to process requests for information pursuant to this subdivision.

(f) (1) Any person may determine if he or she is listed in the CACI by making a request in writing to the Department of Justice. The request shall be notarized and include the person's name, address, date of birth, and either a social security number or a California identification number. Upon receipt of a notarized request, the Department of Justice shall make available to the requesting person information identifying the date of the report and the submitting agency. The requesting person is responsible for obtaining the investigative report from the submitting agency pursuant to paragraph (11) of subdivision (b) of Section 11167.5.

(2) No person or agency shall require or request another person to furnish a copy of a record concerning himself or herself, or notification that a record concerning himself or herself exists or does not exist, pursuant to paragraph (1).

(g) If a person is listed in the CACI only as a victim of child abuse or neglect, and that person is 18 years of age or older, that person may have his or her name removed from the index by making a written request to the Department of Justice. The request shall be notarized and include the person's name, address, social security number, and date of birth.

(Amended by Stats. 2017, Ch. 732, Sec. 42. (AB 404) Effective January 1, 2018.)

11170.5.

(a) Notwithstanding paragraph (4) of subdivision (b) of Section 11170, the Department of Justice shall make available to a licensed adoption agency, as defined in Section 8530 of the Family Code, information regarding a known or suspected child abuser maintained in the Child Abuse Central Index, pursuant to subdivision (a) of Section 11170, concerning any person who has submitted to the agency an application for adoption.

(b) A licensed adoption agency, to which disclosure of any information pursuant to subdivision (a) is authorized, is responsible for obtaining the original investigative report from the reporting agency, and for drawing independent conclusions regarding the quality of the evidence disclosed and the sufficiency of the evidence for making decisions when evaluating an application for adoption.

(c) Whenever information contained in the Department of Justice files is furnished as the result of an application for adoption pursuant to subdivision (a), the Department of Justice may charge the agency making the request a fee. The fee shall not exceed the reasonable costs to the department of providing the information. The only increase shall be at a rate not to exceed the legislatively approved cost-of-living adjustment for the department. In no case shall the fee exceed fifteen dollars ($15).

All moneys received by the department pursuant to this subdivision shall be deposited in the Department of Justice Sexual Habitual Offender Fund pursuant to subparagraph (C) of paragraph (9) of subdivision (b) of Section 11170.

(Amended by Stats. 2004, Ch. 842, Sec. 19. Effective January 1, 2005.)

11171.

(a) (1) The Legislature hereby finds and declares that adequate protection of victims of child physical abuse or neglect has been hampered by the lack of consistent and comprehensive medical examinations.

(2) Enhancing examination procedures, documentation, and evidence collection relating to child abuse or neglect will improve the investigation and prosecution of child abuse or neglect as well as other child protection efforts.

(b) The Office of Emergency Services shall, in cooperation with the State Department of Social Services, the Department of Justice, the California Association of Crime Lab Directors, the California District Attorneys Association, the California State Sheriffs' Association, the California Peace Officers Association, the California Medical Association, the California Police Chiefs' Association, child advocates, the California Medical Training Center, child protective services, and other appropriate experts, establish medical forensic forms, instructions, and examination protocols for victims of child physical abuse or neglect using as a model the form and guidelines developed pursuant to Section 13823.5.

(c) The forms shall include, but not be limited to, a place for notation concerning each of the following:

(1) Any notification of injuries or any report of suspected child physical abuse or neglect to law enforcement authorities or children's protective services, in accordance with existing reporting procedures.

(2) Addressing relevant consent issues, if indicated.

(3) The taking of a patient history of child physical abuse or neglect that includes other relevant medical history.

(4) The performance of a physical examination for evidence of child physical abuse or neglect.

(5) The collection or documentation of any physical evidence of child physical abuse or neglect, including any recommended photographic procedures.

(6) The collection of other medical or forensic specimens, including drug ingestion or toxication, as indicated.

(7) Procedures for the preservation and disposition of evidence.

(8) Complete documentation of medical forensic exam findings with recommendations for diagnostic studies, including blood tests and X-rays.

(9) An assessment as to whether there are findings that indicate physical abuse or neglect.

(d) The forms shall become part of the patient's medical record pursuant to guidelines established by the advisory committee of the Office of Emergency Services and subject to the confidentiality laws pertaining to the release of medical forensic examination records.

(e) The forms shall be made accessible for use on the Internet.

(Amended by Stats. 2013, Ch. 352, Sec. 421. (AB 1317) Effective September 26, 2013. Operative July 1, 2013, by Sec. 543 of Ch. 352.)

11171.2.

(a) A physician and surgeon or dentist or their agents and by their direction may take skeletal X-rays of the child without the consent of the child's parent or guardian, but only for purposes of diagnosing the case as one of possible child abuse or neglect and determining the extent of the child abuse or neglect.

(b) Neither the physician-patient privilege nor the psychotherapist-patient privilege applies to information reported pursuant to this article in any court proceeding or administrative hearing.

(Added by renumbering Section 11171 by Stats. 2002, Ch. 249, second Sec. 3. Effective January 1, 2003.)

11171.5.

(a) If a peace officer, in the course of an investigation of child abuse or neglect, has reasonable cause to believe that the child has been the victim of physical abuse, the officer may apply to a magistrate for an order directing that the victim be X-rayed without parental consent.

Any X-ray taken pursuant to this subdivision shall be administered by a physician and surgeon or dentist or their agents.

(b) With respect to the cost of an X-ray taken by the county coroner or at the request of the county coroner in suspected child abuse or neglect cases, the county may charge the parent or legal guardian of the child-victim the costs incurred by the county for the X-ray.

(c) No person who administers an X-ray pursuant to this section shall be entitled to reimbursement from the county for any administrative cost that exceeds 5 percent of the cost of the X-ray.

(Amended by Stats. 2000, Ch. 916, Sec. 30. Effective January 1, 2001.)

11172.

(a) No mandated reporter shall be civilly or criminally liable for any report required or authorized by this article, and this immunity shall apply even if the mandated reporter acquired the knowledge or reasonable suspicion of child abuse or neglect outside of his or her professional capacity or outside the scope of his or her employment. Any other person reporting a known or suspected instance of child abuse or neglect shall not incur civil or criminal liability as a result of any report authorized by this article unless it can be proven that a false report was made and the person knew that the report was false or was made with reckless disregard of the truth or falsity of the report, and any person who makes a report of child abuse or neglect known to be false or with reckless disregard of the truth or falsity of the report is liable for any damages caused. No person required to make a report pursuant to this article, nor any person taking photographs at his or her direction, shall incur any civil or criminal liability for taking photographs of a suspected victim of child abuse or neglect, or causing photographs to be taken of a suspected victim of child abuse or neglect, without parental consent, or for disseminating the photographs, images, or material with the reports required by this article. However, this section shall not be construed to grant immunity from this liability with respect to any other use of the photographs.

(b) Any person, who, pursuant to a request from a government agency investigating a report of suspected child abuse or neglect, provides the requesting agency with access to the victim of a known or suspected instance of child abuse or neglect shall not incur civil or criminal liability as a result of providing that access.

(c) Any commercial computer technician, and any employer of any commercial computer technician, who, pursuant to a warrant from a law enforcement agency investigating a report of suspected child abuse or neglect, provides the law enforcement agency with a computer or computer component which contains possible evidence of a known or suspected instance of child abuse or neglect, shall not incur civil or criminal liability as a result of providing that computer or computer component to the law enforcement agency.

(d) (1) The Legislature finds that even though it has provided immunity from liability to persons required or authorized to make reports pursuant to this article, that immunity does not eliminate the possibility that actions may be brought against those persons based upon required or authorized reports. In order to further limit the financial hardship that those persons may incur as a result of fulfilling their legal responsibilities, it is necessary that they not be unfairly burdened by legal fees incurred in defending those actions. Therefore, a mandated reporter may present a claim to the Department of General Services for reasonable attorney's fees and costs incurred in any action against that person on the basis of making a report required or authorized by this article if the court has dismissed the action upon a demurrer or motion for summary judgment made by that person, or if he or she prevails in the action. The Department of General Services shall allow that claim if the requirements of this subdivision are met, and the claim shall be paid from an appropriation to be made for that purpose.

Attorney's fees awarded pursuant to this section shall not exceed an hourly rate greater than the rate charged by the Attorney General of the State of California at the time the award is made and shall not exceed an aggregate amount of fifty thousand dollars ($50,000).

(2) This subdivision shall not apply if a public entity has provided for the defense of the action pursuant to Section 995 of the Government Code.

(e) A court may award attorney's fees and costs to a commercial film and photographic print processor when a suit is brought against the processor because of a disclosure mandated by this article and the court finds this suit to be frivolous.

(Amended by Stats. 2016, Ch. 31, Sec. 257. (SB 836) Effective June 27, 2016.)

11174.

The Department of Justice, in cooperation with the State Department of Social Services, shall prescribe by regulation guidelines for the investigation of abuse in out-of-home care, as defined in Section 11165.5, and shall ensure that the investigation is conducted in accordance with the regulations and guidelines.

(Amended by Stats. 1988, Ch. 269, Sec. 5.)

11174.1.

(a) The Department of Justice, in cooperation with the State Department of Social Services, shall prescribe by regulation guidelines for the investigation of child abuse or neglect, as defined in Section 11165.6, in facilities licensed to care for children, and shall ensure that the investigation is conducted in accordance with the regulations and guidelines.

(b) For community treatment facilities, day treatment facilities, group homes, and foster family agencies, the State Department of Social Services shall prescribe the following regulations:

(1) Regulations designed to assure that all licensees and employees of community treatment facilities, day treatment facilities, group homes, and foster family agencies licensed to care for children have had appropriate training, as determined by the State

Department of Social Services, in consultation with representatives of licensees, on the provisions of this article.
(2) Regulations designed to assure the community treatment facilities, day treatment facilities, group homes, and foster family agencies licensed to care for children maintain a written protocol for the investigation and reporting of child abuse or neglect, as defined in Section 11165.6, alleged to have occurred involving a child placed in the facility.
(c) The State Department of Social Services shall provide such orientation and training as it deems necessary to assure that its officers, employees, or agents who conduct inspections of facilities licensed to care for children are knowledgeable about the reporting requirements of this article and have adequate training to identify conditions leading to, and the signs of, child abuse or neglect, as defined in Section 11165.6.
(Amended by Stats. 2000, Ch. 916, Sec. 32. Effective January 1, 2001.)
11174.3.
(a) Whenever a representative of a government agency investigating suspected child abuse or neglect or the State Department of Social Services deems it necessary, a suspected victim of child abuse or neglect may be interviewed during school hours, on school premises, concerning a report of suspected child abuse or neglect that occurred within the child's home or out-of-home care facility. The child shall be afforded the option of being interviewed in private or selecting any adult who is a member of the staff of the school, including any certificated or classified employee or volunteer aide, to be present at the interview. A representative of the agency investigating suspected child abuse or neglect or the State Department of Social Services shall inform the child of that right prior to the interview.
The purpose of the staff person's presence at the interview is to lend support to the child and enable him or her to be as comfortable as possible. However, the member of the staff so elected shall not participate in the interview. The member of the staff so present shall not discuss the facts or circumstances of the case with the child. The member of the staff so present, including, but not limited to, a volunteer aide, is subject to the confidentiality requirements of this article, a violation of which is punishable as specified in Section 11167.5. A representative of the school shall inform a member of the staff so selected by a child of the requirements of this section prior to the interview. A staff member selected by a child may decline the request to be present at the interview. If the staff person selected agrees to be present, the interview shall be held at a time during school hours when it does not involve an expense to the school. Failure to comply with the requirements of this section does not affect the admissibility of evidence in a criminal or civil proceeding.
(b) The Superintendent of Public Instruction shall notify each school district and each agency specified in Section 11165.9 to receive mandated reports, and the State Department of Social Services shall notify each of its employees who participate in the investigation of reports of child abuse or neglect, of the requirements of this section.
(Amended by Stats. 2000, Ch. 916, Sec. 33. Effective January 1, 2001.)

ARTICLE 2.6. Child Death Review Teams [11174.32 - 11174.35]

(Article 2.6 heading added by Stats. 2004, Ch. 842, Sec. 22.)
11174.32.
(a) Each county may establish an interagency child death review team to assist local agencies in identifying and reviewing suspicious child deaths and facilitating communication among persons who perform autopsies and the various persons and agencies involved in child abuse or neglect cases. Interagency child death review teams have been used successfully to ensure that incidents of child abuse or neglect are recognized and other siblings and nonoffending family members receive the appropriate services in cases where a child has expired.
(b) Each county may develop a protocol that may be used as a guideline by persons performing autopsies on children to assist coroners and other persons who perform autopsies in the identification of child abuse or neglect, in the determination of whether child abuse or neglect contributed to death or whether child abuse or neglect had occurred prior to but was not the actual cause of death, and in the proper written reporting procedures for child abuse or neglect, including the designation of the cause and mode of death.
(c) In developing an interagency child death review team and an autopsy protocol, each county, working in consultation with local members of the California State Coroners Association and county child abuse prevention coordinating councils, may solicit suggestions and final comments from persons, including, but not limited to, the following:
(1) Experts in the field of forensic pathology.
(2) Pediatricians with expertise in child abuse.
(3) Coroners and medical examiners.
(4) Criminologists.
(5) District attorneys.
(6) Child protective services staff.
(7) Law enforcement personnel.
(8) Representatives of local agencies which are involved with child abuse or neglect reporting.
(9) County health department staff who deals with children's health issues.
(10) Local professional associations of persons described in paragraphs (1) to (9), inclusive.
(d) Records exempt from disclosure to third parties pursuant to state or federal law shall remain exempt from disclosure when they are in the possession of a child death review team.
(e) Written and oral information pertaining to the child's death as requested by a child death review team may be disclosed to a child death review team established pursuant to this section. The team may make a request, in writing, for the information sought and any person with information of the kind described in paragraph (2) may rely on the request in determining whether information may be disclosed to the team.
(1) An individual or agency that has information governed by this subdivision shall not be required to disclose information. The intent of this subdivision is to allow the voluntary disclosure of information by the individual or agency that has the information.
(2) The following information may be disclosed pursuant to this subdivision:
(A) Notwithstanding Section 56.10 of the Civil Code, medical information, unless disclosure is prohibited by federal law.
(B) Notwithstanding Section 5328 of the Welfare and Institutions Code, mental health information.
(C) Notwithstanding Section 11167.5, information from child abuse reports and investigations, except the identity of the person making the report, which shall not be disclosed.
(D) State summary criminal history information, criminal offender record information, and local summary criminal history information, as defined in Sections 11105, 11075, and 13300, respectively.
(E) Notwithstanding Section 11163.2, information pertaining to reports by health practitioners of persons suffering from physical injuries inflicted by means of a firearm or of persons suffering physical injury where the injury is a result of assaultive or abusive conduct.
(F) Notwithstanding Section 10850 of the Welfare and Institutions Code, records of in-home supportive services, unless disclosure is prohibited by federal law.
(3) Written or oral information disclosed to a child death review team pursuant to this subdivision shall remain confidential, and shall not be subject to disclosure or discovery by a third party unless otherwise required by law.
(f) (1) No less than once each year, each child death review team shall make available to the public findings, conclusions, and recommendations of the team, including aggregate statistical data on the incidences and causes of child deaths.
(2) In its report, the child death review team shall withhold the last name of the child that is subject to a review or the name of the deceased child's siblings unless the name has been publicly disclosed or is required to be disclosed by state law, federal law, or court order.
(Amended by Stats. 2017, Ch. 561, Sec. 195. (AB 1516) Effective January 1, 2018.)
11174.33.
Subject to available funding, the Attorney General, working with the California Consortium of Child Abuse Councils, shall develop a protocol for the development and implementation of interagency child death teams for use by counties, which shall include relevant procedures for both urban and rural counties. The protocol shall be designed to facilitate communication among persons who perform autopsies and the various persons and agencies involved in child abuse or neglect cases so that incidents of child abuse or neglect are recognized and other siblings and nonoffending family members receive the appropriate services in cases where a child has expired. The protocol shall be completed on or before January 1, 1991.
(Added by renumbering Section 11166.8 by Stats. 2004, Ch. 842, Sec. 12. Effective January 1, 2005.)
11174.34.
(a) (1) The purpose of this section shall be to coordinate and integrate state and local efforts to address fatal child abuse or neglect, and to create a body of information to prevent child deaths.
(2) It is the intent of the Legislature that the California State Child Death Review Council, the Department of Justice, the State Department of Social Services, the State Department of Health Services, and state and local child death review teams shall share data and other information necessary from the Department of Justice Child Abuse Central Index and Supplemental Homicide File, the State Department of Health Services Vital Statistics and the Department of Social Services Child Welfare Services/Case Management System files to establish accurate information on the nature and extent of child abuse- or neglect-related fatalities in California as those documents relate to child fatality cases. Further, it is the intent of the Legislature to ensure that records of child abuse- or neglect-related fatalities are entered into the State Department of Social Services, Child Welfare Services/Case Management System. It is also the intent that training and technical assistance be provided to child death review teams and professionals in the child protection system regarding multiagency case review.
(b) (1) It shall be the duty of the California State Child Death Review Council to oversee the statewide coordination and integration of state and local efforts to address fatal child abuse or neglect and to create a body of information to prevent child deaths. The Department of Justice, the State Department of Social Services, the State Department of Health Care Services, the California Coroner's Association, the County Welfare Directors Association, Prevent Child Abuse California, the California Homicide Investigators Association, the Office of Emergency Services, the Inter-Agency Council on Child Abuse and Neglect/National Center on Child Fatality Review, the California Conference of Local Health Officers, the California Conference of Local Directors of Maternal, Child, and Adolescent Health, the California Conference of Local Health Department Nursing Directors, the California District Attorneys Association, and at least three regional representatives, chosen by the other members of the council, working collaboratively for the purposes of this section, shall be known as the California State Child Death Review Council. The council shall select a chairperson or cochairpersons from the members.
(2) The Department of Justice is hereby authorized to carry out the purposes of this section by coordinating council activities and working collaboratively with the agencies and organizations in paragraph (1), and may consult with other representatives of other agencies and private organizations, to help accomplish the purpose of this section.
(c) Meetings of the agencies and organizations involved shall be convened by a representative of the Department of Justice. All meetings convened between the Department of Justice and any organizations required to carry out the purpose of this section shall take place in this state. There shall be a minimum of four meetings per calendar year.
(d) To accomplish the purpose of this section, the Department of Justice and agencies and organizations involved shall engage in the following activities:
(1) Analyze and interpret state and local data on child death in an annual report to be submitted to local child death review teams with copies to the Governor and the Legislature, no later than July 1 each year. Copies of the report shall also be distributed to public officials in the state who deal with child abuse issues and to those agencies responsible for child death investigation in each county. The report shall contain, but not be limited to, information provided by state agencies and the county child death review teams for the preceding year.
The state data shall include the Department of Justice Child Abuse Central Index and Supplemental Homicide File, the State Department of Health Services Vital Statistics, and the State Department of Social Services Child Welfare Services/Case Management System.
(2) In conjunction with the Office of Emergency Services, coordinate statewide and local training for county death review teams and the members of the teams, including, but not limited to, training in the application of the interagency child death investigation protocols and procedures established under Sections 11166.7 and 11166.8 to identify child deaths associated with abuse or neglect.
(e) The State Department of Public Health, in collaboration with the California State Child Death Review Council, shall design, test and implement a statewide child abuse or neglect fatality tracking system incorporating information collected by local child death review teams. The department shall:
(1) Establish a minimum case selection criteria and review protocols of local child death review teams.
(2) Develop a standard child death review form with a minimum core set of data elements to be used by local child death review teams, and collect and analyze that data.
(3) Establish procedural safeguards in order to maintain appropriate confidentiality and integrity of the data.
(4) Conduct annual reviews to reconcile data reported to the State Department of Health Services Vital Statistics, Department of Justice Homicide Files and Child Abuse Central Index, and the State Department of Social Services Child Welfare Services/Case Management System data systems, with data provided from local child death review teams.
(5) Provide technical assistance to local child death review teams in implementing and maintaining the tracking system.
(6) This subdivision shall become operative on July 1, 2000, and shall be implemented only to the extent that funds are appropriated for its purposes in the Budget Act.
(f) Local child death review teams shall participate in a statewide child abuse or neglect fatalities monitoring system by:
(1) Meeting the minimum standard protocols set forth by the State Department of Public Health in collaboration with the California State Child Death Review Council.
(2) Using the standard data form to submit information on child abuse or neglect fatalities in a timely manner established by the State Department of Public Health.
(g) The California State Child Death Review Council shall monitor the implementation of the monitoring system and incorporate the results and findings of the system and review into an annual report.
(h) The Department of Justice shall direct the creation, maintenance, updating, and distribution electronically and by paper, of a statewide child death review team directory,

which shall contain the names of the members of the agencies and private organizations participating under this section, and the members of local child death review teams and local liaisons to those teams. The department shall work in collaboration with members of the California State Child Death Review Council to develop a directory of professional experts, resources, and information from relevant agencies and organizations and local child death review teams, and to facilitate regional working relationships among teams. The Department of Justice shall maintain and update these directories annually.

(i) The agencies or private organizations participating under this section shall participate without reimbursement from the state. Costs incurred by participants for travel or per diem shall be borne by the participant agency or organization. The participants shall be responsible for collecting and compiling information to be included in the annual report. The Department of Justice shall be responsible for printing and distributing the annual report using available funds and existing resources.

(j) The Office of Emergency Services, in coordination with the State Department of Social Services, the Department of Justice, and the California State Child Death Review Council shall contract with state or nationally recognized organizations in the area of child death review to conduct statewide training and technical assistance for local child death review teams and relevant organizations, develop standardized definitions for fatal child abuse or neglect, develop protocols for the investigation of fatal child abuse or neglect, and address relevant issues such as grief and mourning, data collection, training for medical personnel in the identification of child abuse or neglect fatalities, domestic violence fatality review, and other related topics and programs. The provisions of this subdivision shall only be implemented to the extent that the agency can absorb the costs of implementation within its current funding, or to the extent that funds are appropriated for its purposes in the Budget Act.

(k) Law enforcement and child welfare agencies shall cross-report all cases of child death suspected to be related to child abuse or neglect whether or not the deceased child has any known surviving siblings.

(l) County child welfare agencies shall create a record in the Child Welfare Services/Case Management System (CWS/CMS) on all cases of child death suspected to be related to child abuse or neglect, whether or not the deceased child has any known surviving siblings. Upon notification that the death was determined not to be related to child abuse or neglect, the child welfare agency shall enter that information into the Child Welfare Services/Case Management System.

(Amended by Stats. 2013, Ch. 352, Sec. 422. (AB 1317) Effective September 26, 2013. Operative July 1, 2013, by Sec. 543 of Ch. 352.)
11174.35.
The State Department of Social Services shall work with state and local child death review teams and child protective services agencies in order to identify child death cases that were, or should have been, reported to or by county child protective services agencies. Findings made pursuant to this section shall be used to determine the extent of child abuse or neglect fatalities occurring in families known to child protective services agencies and to define child welfare training needs for reporting, cross-reporting, data integration, and involvement by child protective services agencies in multiagency review in child deaths. The State Department of Social Services, the State Department of Health Services, and the Department of Justice shall develop a plan to track and maintain data on child deaths from abuse or neglect, and submit this plan, not later than December 1, 1997, to the Senate Committee on Health and Human Services, the Assembly Committee on Human Services, and the chairs of the fiscal committees of the Legislature.
(Added by renumbering Section 11166.95 by Stats. 2004, Ch. 842, Sec. 14. Effective January 1, 2005.)

ARTICLE 2.7. Elder and Dependent Adult Death Review Teams [11174.4 - 11174.9]

(Heading of Article 2.7 amended by Stats. 2010, Ch. 617, Sec. 5.)
11174.4.
The following definitions shall govern the construction of this article, unless the context requires otherwise:
(a) "Elder" means any person who is 65 years of age or older.
(b) (1) "Abuse" means any of the conduct described in Article 2 (commencing with Section 15610) of Chapter 11 of Part 3 of Division 9 of the Welfare and Institutions Code.
(2) Abuse does not include the use of any reasonable and necessary force that may result in an injury used by a peace officer acting within the course of his or her employment as a peace officer.
(Amended (as added by Stats. 2001, Ch. 301) by Stats. 2002, Ch. 664, Sec. 174. Effective January 1, 2003.)
11174.5.
(a) Each county may establish an interagency elder and dependent adult death review team to assist local agencies in identifying and reviewing suspicious elder and dependent adult deaths and facilitating communication among persons who perform autopsies and the various persons and agencies involved in elder and dependent adult abuse or neglect cases.
(b) Each county may develop a protocol that may be used as a guideline by persons performing autopsies on elders and dependent adults to assist coroners and other persons who perform autopsies in the identification of elder and dependent adult abuse or neglect, in the determination of whether elder or dependent adult abuse or neglect contributed to death or whether elder or dependent adult abuse or neglect had occurred prior to, but was not the actual cause of, death, and in the proper written reporting procedures for elder and dependent adult abuse or neglect, including the designation of the cause and mode of death.
(c) As used in this section, the term "dependent adult" has the same meaning as in Section 368, and applies regardless of whether the person lived independently.
(Amended by Stats. 2010, Ch. 617, Sec. 6. (SB 110) Effective January 1, 2011.)
11174.6.
County elder death review teams may be comprised of, but not limited to, the following:
(a) Experts in the field of forensic pathology.
(b) Medical personnel with expertise in elder abuse and neglect.
(c) Coroners and medical examiners.
(d) District attorneys and city attorneys.
(e) County or local staff including, but not limited to:
(1) Adult protective services staff.
(2) Public administrator, guardian, and conservator staff.
(3) County health department staff who deal with elder health issues.
(4) County counsel.
(f) County and state law enforcement personnel.
(g) Local long-term care ombudsman.
(h) Community care licensing staff and investigators.
(i) Geriatric mental health experts.
(j) Criminologists.
(k) Representatives of local agencies that are involved with oversight of adult protective services and reporting elder abuse or neglect.
(l) Local professional associations of persons described in subdivisions (a) to (k), inclusive.
(Added by Stats. 2001, Ch. 301, Sec. 2. Effective January 1, 2002.)
11174.7.
(a) An oral or written communication or a document shared within or produced by an elder and dependent adult death review team related to an elder or dependent adult death review is confidential and not subject to disclosure or discoverable by another third party.

(b) An oral or written communication or a document provided by a third party to an elder and dependent adult death review team, or between a third party and an elder and dependent adult death review team, is confidential and not subject to disclosure or discoverable by a third party.
(c) Notwithstanding subdivisions (a) and (b), recommendations of an elder and dependent adult death review team upon the completion of a review may be disclosed at the discretion of a majority of the members of the elder and dependent adult death review team.
(Amended by Stats. 2010, Ch. 617, Sec. 7. (SB 110) Effective January 1, 2011.)
11174.8.
(a) Each organization represented on an elder death review team may share with other members of the team information in its possession concerning the decedent who is the subject of the review or any person who was in contact with the decedent and any other information deemed by the organization to be pertinent to the review. Any information shared by an organization with other members of a team is confidential. The intent of this subdivision is to permit the disclosure to members of the team of any information deemed confidential, privileged, or prohibited from disclosure by any other provision of law.
(b) (1) Written and oral information may be disclosed to an elder death review team established pursuant to this section. The team may make a request in writing for the information sought and any person with information of the kind described in paragraph (3) may rely on the request in determining whether information may be disclosed to the team.
(2) No individual or agency that has information governed by this subdivision shall be required to disclose information. The intent of this subdivision is to allow the voluntary disclosure of information by the individual or agency that has the information.
(3) The following information may be disclosed pursuant to this subdivision:
(A) Notwithstanding Section 56.10 of the Civil Code, medical information.
(B) Notwithstanding Section 5328 of the Welfare and Institutions Code, mental health information.
(C) Notwithstanding Section 15633.5 of the Welfare and Institutions Code, information from elder abuse reports and investigations, except the identity of persons who have made reports, which shall not be disclosed.
(D) State summary criminal history information, criminal offender record information, and local summary criminal history information, as defined in Sections 11075, 11105, and 13300.
(E) Notwithstanding Section 11163.2, information pertaining to reports by health practitioners of persons suffering from physical injuries inflicted by means of a firearm or of persons suffering physical injury where the injury is a result of assaultive or abusive conduct.
(F) Information provided to probation officers in the course of the performance of their duties, including, but not limited to, the duty to prepare reports pursuant to Section 1203.10, as well as the information on which these reports are based.
(G) Notwithstanding Section 10825 of the Welfare and Institutions Code, records relating to in-home supportive services, unless disclosure is prohibited by federal law.
(c) Written and oral information may be disclosed under this section notwithstanding Sections 2263, 2918, 4982, and 6068 of the Business and Professions Code, the lawyer-client privilege protected by Article 3 (commencing with Section 950) of Chapter 4 of Division 8 of the Evidence Code, the physician-patient privilege protected by Article 6 (commencing with Section 990) of Chapter 4 of Division 8 of the Evidence Code, and the psychotherapist-patient privilege protected by Article 7 (commencing with Section 1010) of Chapter 4 of Division 8 of the Evidence Code.
(Added by Stats. 2001, Ch. 301, Sec. 2. Effective January 1, 2002.)
11174.9.
Information gathered by the elder death review team and any recommendations made by the team shall be used by the county to develop education, prevention, and if necessary, prosecution strategies that will lead to improved coordination of services for families and the elder population.
(Added by Stats. 2001, Ch. 301, Sec. 2. Effective January 1, 2002.)

ARTICLE 3. Uniform Act for Out-of-State Parolee Supervision [11175 - 11179]

(Article 3 added by Stats. 1953, Ch. 1384.)
11175.
This article may be cited as the Uniform Act for Out-of-State Probationer or Parolee Supervision.
(Amended by Stats. 1955, Ch. 309.)
11176.
Pursuant to the authority vested in this State by that certain act of Congress, approved June 6, 1934, and entitled "An act granting the consent of Congress to any two or more states to enter into agreements or compacts for cooperative effort and mutual assistance in the prevention of crime, and for other purposes," the Governor is hereby authorized and directed to enter into a compact or compacts on behalf of this State with any of the United States legally joining therein.
(Added by Stats. 1953, Ch. 1384.)
11177.
The compact or compacts authorized by Section 11176 shall be in substantially the following form:
A compact entered into by and among the contracting states, signatories hereto, with the consent of the Congress of the United States of America, granted by an act entitled "An act granting the consent of Congress to any two or more states to enter into agreements or compacts for cooperative effort and mutual assistance in the prevention of crime and for other purposes."
The contracting states solemnly agree:
(1) That it shall be competent for the duly constituted judicial and administrative authorities of a state party to this compact (herein called "sending state"), to permit any person convicted of an offense within such state and placed on probation or released on parole to reside in any other state party to this compact (herein called "receiving state") while on probation or parole, if
(a) Such person is in fact a resident of or has his family residing within the receiving state and can obtain employment there;
(b) Though not a resident of the receiving state and not having his family residing there, the receiving state consents to such person being sent there.
Before granting such permission, opportunity shall be granted to the receiving state to investigate the home and prospective employment of such person.
A resident of the receiving state, within the meaning of this section, is one who has been an actual inhabitant of such state continuously for more than one year prior to his coming to the sending state and has not resided within the sending state more than six continuous months immediately preceding the commission of the offense for which he has been convicted.
(2) That each receiving state will assume the duties of visitation of and supervision over probationers or parolees of any sending state and in the exercise of those duties will be governed by the same standards that prevail for its own probationers and parolees.
(3) That duly accredited officers of a sending state may at all times enter a receiving state and there apprehend and retake any person on probation or parole. For that purpose no formalities will be required other than establishing the authority of the officer and the identity of the person to be retaken. All legal requirements to obtain extradition of fugitives from justice are hereby expressly waived on the part of states party hereto, as to such persons. The decision of the sending state to retake a person on probation or parole shall be conclusive upon and not reviewable within the receiving state. If at the

time when a state seeks to retake a probationer or parolee there should be pending against him within the receiving state any criminal charge, or he should be suspected of having committed within such state a criminal offense, he shall not be retaken without the consent of the receiving state until discharged from prosecution or from imprisonment for such offense.

(4) That the duly accredited officers of the sending state will be permitted to transport prisoners being retaken through any and all states parties to this compact, without interference.

(5) That the governor of each state may designate an officer who, acting jointly with like officers of other contracting states, if and when appointed, shall promulgate such rules and regulations as may be deemed necessary to more effectively carry out the terms of this compact.

(6) That this compact shall become operative immediately upon its ratification by any state as between it and any other state or states so ratifying. When ratified it shall have the full force and effect of law within such state, the form of ratification to be in accordance with the laws of the ratifying state.

(7) That this compact shall continue in force and remain binding upon each ratifying state until renounced by it. The duties and obligations hereunder of a renouncing state shall continue as to parolees or probationers residing therein at the time of withdrawal until retaken or finally discharged by the sending state. Renunciation of this compact shall be by the same authority which ratified it, by sending six months' notice in writing of its intention to withdraw from the compact to the other states party hereto.
(Added by Stats. 1953, Ch. 1384.)

11177.1.
(a) Before a probationer or parolee may be returned to the sending state under this compact, he shall have a right to counsel and to a hearing before a magistrate to determine whether he is in fact a probationer or parolee who was allowed to reside in this or any other state pursuant to this compact, whether his return to the sending state has been ordered, and whether there is probable cause to believe he is the same person whose return is sought. At the hearing, the magistrate shall accept certified copies of probation or parole documents showing that this compact has been invoked and that the probationer or parolee has been ordered returned to the sending state, and these documents shall constitute conclusive proof of their contents. If the magistrate concludes that the probationer or parolee is subject to the terms of this compact, an order shall be issued forthwith directing the delivery to the sending state of the probationer or parolee.

(b) If the probationer or parolee or his counsel desires to test the legality of the order issued under subdivision (a), the magistrate shall fix a reasonable time to be allowed him within which to apply for a writ of habeas corpus. If the writ is denied and probable cause appears for an application for a writ of habeas corpus to another court, or justice or judge thereof, the order denying the writ shall fix a reasonable time within which the accused may again apply for a writ of habeas corpus.
(Added by Stats. 1983, Ch. 793, Sec. 11.)

11177.2.
(a) No parolee or inmate may be released on parole to reside in any other receiving state if the parolee or inmate is subject to an unsatisfied order of restitution to a victim or a restitution fine within the sending state.

(b) A parolee or inmate may be granted an exception to the prohibition in subdivision (a) if the parolee or inmate posts a bond for the amount of the restitution order.

(c) A parolee or inmate may petition the court for a hearing to determine whether, in the interests of justice, the prohibition against leaving the state should be waived. This section shall not be construed to allow the reduction or waiver of a restitution order or fine.
(Amended by Stats. 1998, Ch. 587, Sec. 10. Effective January 1, 1999.)

11177.5.
The officer designated by the Governor pursuant to subdivision 5 of Section 11177 of this code may deputize any person regularly employed by another state to act as an officer and agent of this State in effecting the return of any person who has violated the terms and conditions of parole or probation as granted by this State. In any matter relating to the return of such a person, any agent so deputized shall have all the powers of a police officer of this State.
Any deputization pursuant to this section shall be in writing and any person authorized to act as an agent of this State pursuant hereto shall carry formal evidence of his deputization and shall produce the same upon demand.
(Added by Stats. 1955, Ch. 657.)

11177.6.
The officer designated by the Governor pursuant to subdivision 5 of Section 11177 of this code may, subject to the approval of the Department of General Services, enter into contracts with similar officials of any other state or states for the purpose of sharing an equitable portion of the cost of effecting the return of any person who has violated the terms and conditions of parole or probation as granted by this state.
(Amended by Stats. 1965, Ch. 371.)

11178.
If any portion of this article is held unconstitutional, such decision shall not affect the validity of any other portions of this act.
(Added by Stats. 1953, Ch. 1384.)

11179.
This article and compacts made pursuant thereto shall be construed as separate and distinct from any act or acts of this State relating to the extradition of fugitives from justice.
(Added by Stats. 1953, Ch. 1384.)

ARTICLE 3.5. Interstate Compact for Adult Offender Supervision [11180 - 11181]

(Article 3.5 added by Stats. 2000, Ch. 658, Sec. 1.)
11180.
The Interstate Compact for Adult Offender Supervision as contained herein is hereby enacted into law and entered into on behalf of the state with any and all other states legally joining therein in a form substantially as follows:
Preamble
Whereas:The interstate compact for the supervision of Parolees and Probationers was established in 1937. It is the earliest corrections "compact" established among the states and has not been amended since its adoption over 62 years ago.
Whereas:This compact is the only vehicle for the controlled movement of adult parolees and probationers across state lines and it currently has jurisdiction over more than a quarter of a million offenders.
Whereas:The complexities of the compact have become more difficult to administer, and many jurisdictions have expanded supervision expectations to include currently unregulated practices such as victim input, victim notification requirements, and sex offender registration.
Whereas:After hearings, national surveys, and a detailed study by a task force appointed by the National Institute of Corrections, the overwhelming recommendation has been to amend the document to bring about an effective management capacity that addresses public safety concerns and offender accountability.
Whereas:Upon the adoption of this Interstate Compact for Adult Offender Supervision, it is the intention of the Legislature to repeal the previous Interstate Compact for the Supervision of Parolees and Probationers as to those states that have ratified this compact.
Be it enacted by the General Assembly (Legislature) of the state of California.

Short title:This Act may be cited as The Interstate Compact for Adult Offender Supervision.
Article I.Purpose
The compacting states to this Interstate Compact recognize that each state is responsible for the supervision of adult offenders in the community who are authorized pursuant to the Bylaws and Rules of this compact to travel across state lines both to and from each compacting state in a manner so as to track the location of offenders, transfer supervision authority in an orderly and efficient manner, and when necessary return offenders to the originating jurisdictions. The compacting states also recognize that Congress, by enacting the Crime Control Act, 4 U.S.C. Section 112 (1965), has authorized and encouraged compacts for cooperative efforts and mutual assistance in the prevention of crime. It is the purpose of this compact and the Interstate Commission created hereunder, through means of joint and cooperative action among the compacting states: to provide the framework for the promotion of public safety and protect the rights of victims through the control and regulation of the interstate movement of offenders in the community; to provide for the effective tracking, supervision, and rehabilitation of these offenders by the sending and receiving states; and to equitably distribute the costs, benefits, and obligations of the compact among the compacting states. In addition, this compact will: create an Interstate Commission which will establish uniform procedures to manage the movement between states of adults placed under community supervision and released to the community under the jurisdiction of courts, paroling authorities, corrections or other criminal justice agencies which will promulgate rules to achieve the purpose of this compact; ensure an opportunity for input and timely notice to victims and to jurisdictions where defined offenders are authorized to travel or to relocate across state lines; establish a system of uniform data collection, access to information on active cases by authorized criminal justice officials, and regular reporting of Compact activities to heads of state councils, state executive, judicial, and legislative branches and criminal justice administrators; monitor compliance with rules governing interstate movement of offenders and initiate interventions to address and correct non-compliance; and coordinate training and education regarding regulations of interstate movement of offenders for officials involved in these types of activities. The compacting states recognize that there is no "right" of any offender to live in another state and that duly accredited officers of a sending state may at all times enter a receiving state and there apprehend and retake any offender under supervision subject to the provisions of this compact and Bylaws and Rules promulgated hereunder. It is the policy of the compacting states that the activities conducted by the Interstate Commission created herein are the formation of public policies and are therefore public business.
Article II.Definitions
As used in this compact, unless the context clearly requires a different construction:
"Adult" means both individuals legally classified as adults and juveniles treated as adults by court order, statute, or operation of law.
"By-laws" mean those by-laws established by the Interstate Commission for its governance, or for directing or controlling the Interstate Commission's actions or conduct.
"Compact Administrator" means the individual in each compacting state appointed pursuant to the terms of this compact responsible for the administration and management of the state's supervision and transfer of offenders subject to the terms of this compact, the rules adopted by the Interstate Commission and policies adopted by the State Council under this compact.
"Compacting state" means any state which has enacted the enabling legislation for this compact.
"Commissioner" means the voting representative of each compacting state appointed pursuant to Article III of this compact.
"Interstate Commission" means the Interstate Commission for Adult Offender Supervision established by this compact.
"Member" means the commissioner of a compacting state or designee, who shall be a person officially connected with the commissioner.
"Non Compacting state" means any state which has not enacted the enabling legislation for this compact.
"Offender" means an adult placed under, or subject to, supervision as the result of the commission of a criminal offense and released to the community under the jurisdiction of courts, paroling authorities, corrections, or other criminal justice agencies.
"Person" means any individual, corporation, business enterprise, or other legal entity, either public or private.
"Rules" means acts of the Interstate Commission, duly promulgated pursuant to Article VIII of this compact, substantially affecting interested parties in addition to the Interstate Commission, which shall have the force and effect of law in the compacting states.
"State" means a state of the United States, the District of Columbia, and any other territorial possessions of the United States.
"State Council" means the resident members of the State Council for Interstate Adult Offender Supervision created by each state under Article III of this compact.
Article III.The Compact Commission
The compacting states hereby create the "Interstate Commission for Adult Offender Supervision."
The Interstate Commission shall be a body corporate and joint agency of the compacting states.
The Interstate Commission shall have all the responsibilities, powers, and duties set forth herein, including the power to sue and be sued, and whatever additional powers as may be conferred upon it by subsequent action of the respective legislatures of the compacting states in accordance with the terms of this compact.
The Interstate Commission shall consist of Commissioners selected and appointed by resident members of the State Council for Interstate Adult Offender Supervision for each state. In addition to the Commissioners who are the voting representatives of each state, the Interstate Commission shall include individuals who are not commissioners but who are members of interested organizations; these noncommissioner members must include a member of the national organizations of governors, legislators, state chief justices, attorneys general and crime victims. All noncommissioner members of the Interstate Commission shall be ex-officio (nonvoting) members. The Interstate Commission may provide in its by-laws for these additional, ex-officio, nonvoting members as it deems necessary. Each compacting state represented at any meeting of the Interstate Commission is entitled to one vote. A majority of the compacting states shall constitute a quorum for the transaction of business, unless a larger quorum is required by the by-laws of the Interstate Commission. The Interstate Commission shall meet at least once each calendar year. The chairperson may call additional meetings and, upon the request of 27 or more compacting states, shall call additional meetings. Public notice shall be given of all meetings and meetings shall be open to the public. The Interstate Commission shall establish an Executive Committee which shall include commission officers, members and others as shall be determined by the By-laws. The Executive Committee shall have the power to act on behalf of the Interstate Commission during periods when the Interstate Commission is not in session, with the exception of rulemaking and/or amendment to the Compact. The Executive Committee oversees the day-to-day activities managed by the Executive Director and Interstate Commission staff; administers enforcement and compliance with the provisions of the compact, its by-laws and as directed by the Interstate Commission and performs other duties as directed by the Commission or set forth in the By-laws.
Article IV.The State Council
Each member state shall create a State Council for Interstate Adult Offender Supervision which shall be responsible for the appointment of the commissioner who shall serve on

the Interstate Commission from that state. Each state council shall appoint as its commissioner the Compact Administrator from that state to serve on the Interstate Commission in this capacity under or pursuant to applicable law of the member state. While each member state may determine the membership of its own state council, its membership must include at least one representative from the legislative, judicial, and executive branches of government, victims groups and compact administrators. Each compacting state retains the right to determine the qualifications of the Compact Administrator who shall be appointed by the state council or by the Governor in consultation with the Legislature and the Judiciary. In addition to appointment of its commissioner to the National Interstate Commission, each state council shall exercise oversight and advocacy concerning its participation in Interstate Commission activities and other duties as may be determined by each member state, including, but not limited to, development of policy concerning operations and procedures of the compact within that state.

Article V.Powers and Duties of the Interstate Commission
The Interstate Commission shall have the following powers:
To adopt a seal and suitable by-laws governing the management and operation of the Interstate Commission.
To promulgate rules which shall have the force and effect of statutory law and shall be binding in the compacting states to the extent and in the manner provided in this compact.
To oversee, supervise and coordinate the interstate movement of offenders subject to the terms of this compact and any by-laws adopted and rules promulgated by the compact commission.
To enforce compliance with compact provisions, Interstate Commission rules, and by-laws, using all necessary and proper means, including, but not limited to, the use of judicial process.
To establish and maintain offices.
To purchase and maintain insurance and bonds.
To borrow, accept, or contract for services of personnel, including, but not limited to, members and their staffs.
To establish and appoint committees and hire staff which it deems necessary for the carrying out of its functions including, but not limited to, an executive committee as required by Article III which shall have the power to act on behalf of the Interstate Commission in carrying out its powers and duties hereunder.
To elect or appoint officers, attorneys, employees, agents, or consultants, and to fix their compensation, define their duties and determine their qualifications; and to establish the Interstate Commission's personnel policies and programs relating to, among other things, conflicts of interest, rates of compensation, and qualifications of personnel.
To accept any and all donations and grants of money, equipment, supplies, materials, and services, and to receive, utilize, and dispose of same.
To lease, purchase, accept contributions or donations of, or otherwise to own, hold, improve or use any property, real, personal, or mixed.
To sell, convey, mortgage, pledge, lease, exchange, abandon, or otherwise dispose of any property, real, personal or mixed.
To establish a budget and make expenditures and levy dues as provided in Article X of this compact.
To sue and be sued.
To provide for dispute resolution among Compacting States.
To perform whatever functions as may be necessary or appropriate to achieve the purposes of this compact.
To report annually to the legislatures, governors, judiciary, and state councils of the compacting states concerning the activities of the Interstate Commission during the preceding year. These reports shall also include any recommendations that may have been adopted by the Interstate Commission.
To coordinate education, training and public awareness regarding the interstate movement of offenders for officials involved in these activities.
To establish uniform standards for the reporting, collecting, and exchanging of data.
Article VI.Organization and Operation of the Interstate Commission
Section A.By-laws
The Interstate Commission shall, by a majority of the Members, within twelve months of the first Interstate Commission meeting, adopt By-laws to govern its conduct as may be necessary or appropriate to carry out the purposes of the Compact, including, but not limited to:
Establishing the fiscal year of the Interstate Commission.
Establishing an executive committee and other committees as may be necessary.
Providing reasonable standards and procedures:
(i) For the establishment of committees.
(ii) Governing any general or specific delegation of any authority or function of the Interstate Commission; providing reasonable procedures for calling and conducting meetings of the Interstate Commission, and ensuring reasonable notice of each meeting; establishing the titles and responsibilities of the officers of the Interstate Commission; providing reasonable standards and procedures for the establishment of the personnel policies and programs of the Interstate Commission. Notwithstanding any civil service or other similar laws of any Compacting State, the By-laws shall exclusively govern the personnel policies and programs of the Interstate Commission; and providing a mechanism for winding up the operations of the Interstate Commission and the equitable return of any surplus funds that may exist upon the termination of the Compact after the payment and/or reserving of all of its debts and obligations; providing transition rules for "start up" administration of the compact; establishing standards and procedures for compliance and technical assistance in carrying out the compact.
Section B.Officers and Staff
The Interstate Commission shall, by a majority of the Members, elect from among its Members a chairperson and a vice chairperson, each of whom shall have authorities and duties as may be specified in the By-laws. The chairperson, or in his or her absence or disability, the vice chairperson, shall preside at all meetings of the Interstate Commission. The Officers so elected shall serve without compensation or remuneration from the Interstate Commission; provided that, subject to the availability of budgeted funds, the officers shall be reimbursed for any actual and necessary costs and expenses incurred by them in the performance of their duties and responsibilities as officers of the Interstate Commission.
The Interstate Commission shall, through its executive committee, appoint or retain an executive director for a period, upon terms and conditions and for compensation as the Interstate Commission may deem appropriate. The executive director shall serve as secretary to the Interstate Commission, and hire and supervise other staff as may be authorized by the Interstate Commission, but shall not be a member.
Section C.Corporate Records of the Interstate Commission
The Interstate Commission shall maintain its corporate books and records in accordance with the By-laws.
Section D.Qualified Immunity, Defense and Indemnification
The Members, officers, executive director and employees of the Interstate Commission shall be immune from suit and liability, either personally or in their official capacity, for any claim for damage to or loss of property or personal injury or other civil liability caused or arising out of any actual or alleged act, error or omission that occurred within the scope of Interstate Commission employment, duties or responsibilities; provided, that nothing in this paragraph shall be construed to protect anyone from suit and/or liability for any damage, loss, injury or liability caused by their intentional or willful and wanton misconduct. The Interstate Commission shall defend the Commissioner of a

Compacting State, or his or her representatives or employees, or the Interstate Commission's representatives or employees, in any civil action seeking to impose liability, arising out of any actual or alleged act, error or omission that occurred within the scope of Interstate Commission employment, duties or responsibilities, or that the defendant had a reasonable basis for believing occurred within the scope of Interstate Commission employment, duties or responsibilities; provided, that the actual or alleged act, error or omission did not result from intentional wrongdoing on the part of that person.
The Interstate Commission shall indemnify and hold the Commissioner of a Compacting State, the appointed designee or employees, or the Interstate Commission's representatives or employees, harmless in the amount of any settlement or judgment obtained against any person arising out of any actual or alleged act, error, or omission that occurred within the scope of Interstate Commission employment, duties, or responsibilities, or that the person had a reasonable basis for believing occurred within the scope of Interstate Commission employment, duties, or responsibilities, provided, that the actual or alleged act, error, or omission did not result from gross negligence or intentional wrongdoing on the part of the person.
Article VII.Activities of the Interstate Commission
The Interstate Commission shall meet and take whatever actions as are consistent with the provisions of this Compact.
Except as otherwise provided in this Compact and unless a greater percentage is required by the By-laws, in order to constitute an act of the Interstate Commission, the act shall have been taken at a meeting of the Interstate Commission and shall have received an affirmative vote of a majority of the members present.
Each Member of the Interstate Commission shall have the right and power to cast a vote to which that Compacting State is entitled and to participate in the business and affairs of the Interstate Commission. A Member shall vote in person on behalf of the state and shall not delegate a vote to another member state. However, a State Council shall appoint another authorized representative, in the absence of the commissioner from that state, to cast a vote on behalf of the member state at a specified meeting. The By-laws may provide for Members' participation in meetings by telephone or other means of telecommunication or electronic communication. Any voting conducted by telephone, or other means of telecommunication or electronic communication shall be subject to the same quorum requirements of meetings where members are present in person.
The Interstate Commission shall meet at least once during each calendar year. The chairperson of the Interstate Commission may call additional meetings at any time and, upon the request of a majority of the Members, shall call additional meetings.
The Interstate Commission's By-laws shall establish conditions and procedures under which the Interstate Commission shall make its information and official records available to the public for inspection or copying. The Interstate Commission may exempt from disclosure any information or official records to the extent they would adversely affect personal privacy rights or proprietary interests. In promulgating the Rules, the Interstate Commission may make available to law enforcement agencies records and information otherwise exempt from disclosure, and may enter into agreements with law enforcement agencies to receive or exchange information or records subject to nondisclosure and confidentiality provisions.
Public notice shall be given of all meetings and all meetings shall be open to the public, except as set forth in the Rules or as otherwise provided in the Compact. The Interstate Commission shall promulgate Rules consistent with the principles contained in the "Government in Sunshine Act," 5 U.S.C. Section 552(b), as may be amended. The Interstate Commission and any of its committees may close a meeting to the public where it determines by two-thirds vote that an open meeting would be likely to:
Relate solely to the Interstate Commission's internal personnel practices and procedures.
Disclose matters specifically exempted from disclosure by statute.
Disclose trade secrets or commercial or financial information which is privileged or confidential.
Involve accusing any person of a crime, or formally censuring any person.
Disclose information of a personal nature where disclosure would constitute a clearly unwarranted invasion of personal privacy.
Disclose investigatory records compiled for law enforcement purposes.
Disclose information contained in or related to examination, operating or condition reports prepared by, or on behalf of or for the use of, the Interstate Commission with respect to a regulated entity for the purpose of regulation or supervision of the entity.
Disclose information, the premature disclosure of which would significantly endanger the life of a person or the stability of a regulated entity.
Specifically relate to the Interstate Commission's issuance of a subpoena, or its participation in a civil action or proceeding.
For every meeting closed pursuant to this provision, the Interstate Commission's chief legal officer shall publicly certify that, in his or her opinion, the meeting may be closed to the public, and shall reference each relevant exemptive provision. The Interstate Commission shall keep minutes which shall fully and clearly describe all matters discussed in any meeting and shall provide a full and accurate summary of any actions taken, and the reasons therefor, including a description of each of the views expressed on any item and the record of any rollcall vote (reflected in the vote of each Member on the question). All documents considered in connection with any action shall be identified in the minutes. The Interstate Commission shall collect standardized data concerning the interstate movement of offenders as directed through its By-laws and Rules which shall specify the data to be collected, the means of collection and data exchange and reporting requirements.
Article VIII.Rulemaking Functions of the Interstate Commission
The Interstate Commission shall promulgate Rules in order to effectively and efficiently achieve the purposes of the Compact including transition rules governing administration of the compact during the period in which it is being considered and enacted by the states.
Rulemaking shall occur pursuant to the criteria set forth in this Article and the By-laws and Rules adopted pursuant thereto. Rulemaking shall substantially conform to the principles of the federal Administrative Procedure Act, 5 U.S.C.S. section 551 et seq., and the Federal Advisory Committee Act, 5 U.S.C.S. app. 2, section 1 et seq., as may be amended (hereinafter "APA"). All Rules and amendments shall become binding as of the date specified in each Rule or amendment.
If a majority of the legislatures of the Compacting States rejects a Rule, by enactment of a statute or resolution in the same manner used to adopt the compact, then the Rule shall have no further force and effect in any Compacting State.
When promulgating a Rule, the Interstate Commission shall:
Publish the proposed Rule stating with particularity the text of the Rule which is proposed and the reason for the proposed Rule.
Allow persons to submit written data, facts, opinions and arguments, which information shall be publicly available.
Provide an opportunity for an informal hearing.
Promulgate a final Rule and its effective date, if appropriate, based on the rulemaking record.
Not later than sixty days after a Rule is promulgated, any interested person may file a petition in the United States District Court for the District of Columbia or in the Federal District Court where the Interstate Commission's principal office is located for judicial review of the Rule. If the court finds that the Interstate Commission's action is not supported by substantial evidence, (as defined in the APA), in the rulemaking record, the court shall hold the Rule unlawful and set it aside. Subjects to be addressed within 12 months after the first meeting must at a minimum include:

Notice to victims and opportunity to be heard.
Offender registration and compliance.
Violations/returns.
Transfer procedures and forms.
Eligibility for transfer.
Collection of restitution and fees from offenders.
Data collection and reporting.
The level of supervision to be provided by the receiving state.
Transition rules governing the operation of the compact and the Interstate Commission during all or part of the period between the effective date of the compact and the date on which the last eligible state adopts the compact.
Mediation, arbitration and dispute resolution.
The existing rules governing the operation of the previous compact superseded by this Act shall be null and void twelve (12) months after the first meeting of the Interstate Commission created hereunder.
Upon determination by the Interstate Commission that an emergency exists, it may promulgate an emergency rule which shall become effective immediately upon adoption, provided that the usual rulemaking procedures provided hereunder shall be retroactively applied to said rule as soon as reasonably possible, in no event later than 90 days after the effective date of the rule.
Article IX.Oversight, Enforcement, and Dispute Resolution by the Interstate Commission
Section A.Oversight
The Interstate Commission shall oversee the interstate movement of adult offenders in the compacting states and shall monitor the activities being administered in Non-compacting States which may significantly affect Compacting States.
The courts and executive agencies in each Compacting State shall enforce this Compact and shall take all actions necessary and appropriate to effectuate the Compact's purposes and intent. In any judicial or administrative proceeding in a Compacting State pertaining to the subject matter of this Compact which may affect the powers, responsibilities or actions of the Interstate Commission, the Interstate Commission shall be entitled to receive all service of process in any proceeding, and shall have standing to intervene in the proceeding for all purposes.
Section B.Dispute Resolution
The Compacting States shall report to the Interstate Commission on issues or activities of concern to them, and cooperate with and support the Interstate Commission in the discharge of its duties and responsibilities.
The Interstate Commission shall attempt to resolve any disputes or other issues which are subject to the Compact and which may arise among Compacting States and Non-compacting States.
The Interstate Commission shall enact a By-law or promulgate a Rule providing for both mediation and binding dispute resolution for disputes among the Compacting States.
Section C.Enforcement
The Interstate Commission, in the reasonable exercise of its discretion, shall enforce the provisions of this compact using any or all means set forth in Article XII, Section B, of this compact.
Article X.Finance
The Interstate Commission shall pay or provide for the payment of the reasonable expenses of its establishment, organization and ongoing activities.
The Interstate Commission shall levy on and collect an annual assessment from each Compacting State to cover the cost of the internal operations and activities of the Interstate Commission and its staff which must be in a total amount sufficient to cover the Interstate Commission's annual budget as approved each year. The aggregate annual assessment amount shall be allocated based upon a formula to be determined by the Interstate Commission, taking into consideration the population of the state and the volume of interstate movement of offenders in each Compacting State and shall promulgate a Rule binding upon all Compacting States which governs said assessment. The Interstate Commission shall not incur any obligations of any kind prior to securing the funds adequate to meet the same; nor shall the Interstate Commission pledge the credit of any of the compacting states, except by and with the authority of the compacting state. The Interstate Commission shall keep accurate accounts of all receipts and disbursements. The receipts and disbursements of the Interstate Commission shall be subject to the audit and accounting procedures established under its By-laws. However, all receipts and disbursements of funds handled by the Interstate Commission shall be audited yearly by a certified or licensed public accountant and the report of the audit shall be included in and become part of the annual report of the Interstate Commission.
Article XI.Compacting States, Effective Date and Amendment
Any state, as defined in Article II of this compact, is eligible to become a Compacting State. The Compact shall become effective and binding upon legislative enactment of the Compact into law by no less than 35 of the States. The initial effective date shall be the later of July 1, 2001, or upon enactment into law by the 35th jurisdiction. Thereafter, it shall become effective and binding, as to any other Compacting State, upon enactment of the Compact into law by that State. The governors of Non-member states or their designees will be invited to participate in Interstate Commission activities on a non-voting basis prior to adoption of the compact by all states and territories of the United States.
Amendments to the Compact may be proposed by the Interstate Commission for enactment by the Compacting States. No amendment shall become effective and binding upon the Interstate Commission and the Compacting States unless and until it is enacted into law by unanimous consent of the Compacting States.
Article XII.Withdrawal, Default, Termination, and Judicial Enforcement
Section A.Withdrawal
Once effective, the Compact shall continue in force and remain binding upon each and every Compacting State; provided, that a Compacting State may withdraw from the Compact ("Withdrawing State") by enacting a statute specifically repealing the statute which enacted the Compact into law.
The effective date of withdrawal is the effective date of the repeal. The Withdrawing State shall immediately notify the Chairperson of the Interstate Commission in writing upon the introduction of legislation repealing this Compact in the Withdrawing State. The Interstate Commission shall notify the other Compacting States of the Withdrawing State's intent to withdraw within 60 days of its receipt thereof. The Withdrawing State is responsible for all assessments, obligations and liabilities incurred through the effective date of withdrawal, including any obligations, the performance of which extend beyond the effective date of withdrawal.
Reinstatement following withdrawal of any Compacting State shall occur upon the Withdrawing State reenacting the Compact or upon a later date as determined by the Interstate Commission.
Section B.Default
If the Interstate Commission determines that any Compacting State has at any time defaulted ("Defaulting State") in the performance of any of its obligations or responsibilities under this Compact, the By-laws or any duly promulgated Rules the Interstate Commission may impose any or all of the following penalties: Fines, fees and costs in amounts as are deemed to be reasonable as fixed by the Interstate Commission. Remedial training and technical assistance as directed by the Interstate Commission; suspension and termination of membership in the compact. Suspension shall be imposed only after all other reasonable means of securing compliance under the By-laws and Rules have been exhausted. Immediate notice of suspension shall be given by the Interstate Commission to the Governor, the Chief Justice or Chief Judicial

Officer of the state, the majority and minority leaders of the defaulting state's legislature, and the State Council.
The grounds for default include, but are not limited to, failure of a Compacting State to perform the obligations or responsibilities imposed upon it by this compact, Interstate Commission By-laws, or duly promulgated Rules. The Interstate Commission shall immediately notify the Defaulting State in writing of the penalty imposed by the Interstate Commission on the Defaulting State pending a cure of the default. The Interstate Commission shall stipulate the conditions and the time period within which the Defaulting State must cure its default. If the Defaulting State fails to cure the default within the time period specified by the Interstate Commission, in addition to any other penalties imposed herein, the Defaulting State may be terminated from the Compact upon an affirmative vote of a majority of the Compacting States and all rights, privileges and benefits conferred by this Compact shall be terminated from the effective date of suspension. Within 60 days of the effective date of termination of a Defaulting State, the Interstate Commission shall notify the Governor, the Chief Justice or Chief Judicial Officer and the Majority and Minority Leaders of the Defaulting State's legislature and the state council of the termination.
The Defaulting State is responsible for all assessments, obligations and liabilities incurred through the effective date of termination including any obligations, the performance of which extends beyond the effective date of termination.
The Interstate Commission shall not bear any costs relating to the Defaulting State unless otherwise mutually agreed upon between the Interstate Commission and the Defaulting State. Reinstatement following termination of any Compacting State requires both a reenactment of the Compact by the Defaulting State and the approval of the Interstate Commission pursuant to the Rules.
Section C.Judicial Enforcement
The Interstate Commission may, by majority vote of the Members, initiate legal action in the United States District Court for the District of Columbia or, at the discretion of the Interstate Commission, in the Federal District where the Interstate Commission has its offices to enforce compliance with the provisions of the Compact, its duly promulgated Rules and By-laws, against any Compacting State in default. In the event judicial enforcement is necessary the prevailing party shall be awarded all litigation costs including reasonable attorneys fees.
Section D.Dissolution of Compact
The Compact dissolves effective upon the date of the withdrawal or default of the Compacting State which reduces membership in the Compact to one Compacting State. Upon the dissolution of this Compact, the Compact becomes null and void and shall be of no further force or effect, and the business and affairs of the Interstate Commission shall be wound up and any surplus funds shall be distributed in accordance with the By-laws.
Article XIII.Severability and Construction
The provisions of this Compact shall be severable, and if any phrase, clause, sentence or provision is deemed unenforceable, the remaining provisions of the Compact shall be enforceable.
The provisions of this Compact shall be liberally constructed to effectuate its purposes.
Article XIV.Binding Effect of Compact and Other Laws
Section A.Other Laws
Nothing herein prevents the enforcement of any other law of a Compacting State that is not inconsistent with this Compact.
All Compacting States' laws conflicting with this Compact are superseded to the extent of the conflict.
Section B.Binding Effect of the Compact
All lawful actions of the Interstate Commission, including all Rules and By-laws promulgated by the Interstate Commission, are binding upon the Compacting States.
All agreements between the Interstate Commission and the Compacting States are binding in accordance with their terms.
Upon the request of a party to a conflict over meaning or interpretation of Interstate Commission actions, and upon a majority vote of the Compacting States, the Interstate Commission may issue advisory opinions regarding meaning or interpretation.
In the event any provision of this Compact exceeds the constitutional limits imposed on the legislature of any Compacting State, the obligations, duties, powers or jurisdiction sought to be conferred by the provision upon the Interstate Commission shall be ineffective and the obligations, duties, powers or jurisdiction shall remain in the Compacting State and shall be exercised by the agency thereof to which the obligations, duties, powers or jurisdiction are delegated by law in effect at the time this Compact becomes effective.
(Amended by Stats. 2011, Ch. 296, Sec. 223. (AB 1023) Effective January 1, 2012.)
__11181.__
(a) There is hereby established the California Council for Interstate Adult Offender Supervision.
(b) The council shall exercise oversight and advocacy concerning its participation in Interstate Commission activities, and other duties as may be determined by the Legislature or Governor, including but not limited to, development of policy concerning operations and procedures of the compact within the state.
(c) There shall be seven members of the council. The Director of Corrections, or his or her designee, shall be a member and serve as the commissioner, who shall represent California and serve on the Interstate Commission for Adult Offender Supervision. The commissioner shall also be the Compact Administrator for the State of California for purposes of the Interstate Compact for Adult Offender Supervision. The Governor shall appoint three members, one of whom shall represent victims rights groups, and one of whom shall represent chief probation officers. One member each shall be appointed by the Senate Committee on Rules and the Speaker of the Assembly. The Judicial Council shall appoint one superior court judge as a member.
(d) With the exception of the commissioner, each member of the council shall serve for a term of four years. Council members shall not be compensated, except for reasonable per diem expenses related to their work for council purposes.
(e) The council shall, not later than July 1, 2005, submit a report to the Legislature on the status of implementing the Interstate Compact for Adult Offender Supervision in California. The report shall clearly differentiate the role and responsibilities of the state Compact Administrator from local supervisory agencies and shall articulate the interdependence between the state Compact Administrator and other related entities, including, but not limited to, local supervisory agencies. Additionally, the report shall identify the process by which the State Council communicates with county probation offices and Superior courts to ensure the state's compliance with the Interstate Compact for Adult Offender Supervision.
(Amended by Stats. 2002, Ch. 1078, Sec. 2. Effective January 1, 2003.)

ARTICLE 4. Interstate Corrections Compacts [11189 - 11198]
(Heading of Article 4 amended by Stats. 1976, Ch. 667.)
__11189.__
The Interstate Corrections Compact as set forth in this section is hereby adopted and entered into with all other jurisdictions joining therein. The provisions of the interstate compact are as follows:
INTERSTATE CORRECTIONS COMPACT
This section may be cited as the Interstate Corrections Compact.
The Interstate Corrections Compact is hereby enacted into law and entered into by this state with any other states legally joining therein in the form substantially as follows:
Interstate Corrections Compact
Article I

Purpose and Policy

The party states, desiring by common action to fully utilize and improve their institutional facilities and provide adequate programs for the confinement, treatment and rehabilitation of various types of offenders, declare that it is the policy of each of the party states to provide such facilities and programs on a basis of cooperation with one another, thereby serving the best interests of such offenders and of society and effecting economies in capital expenditures and operational costs. The purpose of this compact is to provide for the mutual development and execution of such programs of cooperation for the confinement, treatment and rehabilitation of offenders with the most economical use of human and material resources.

Article II

Definitions

As used in this compact, unless the context clearly requires otherwise:

(a) "State" means a state of the United States; the United States of America; a territory or possession of the United States; the District of Columbia; the Commonwealth of Puerto Rico.

(b) "Sending state" means a state party to this compact in which conviction or court commitment was had.

(c) "Receiving state" means a state party to this compact to which an inmate is sent for confinement other than a state in which conviction or court commitment was had.

(d) "Inmate" means a male or female offender who is committed, under sentence to or confined in a penal or correctional institution.

(e) "Institution" means any penal or correctional facility, including but not limited to a facility for the mentally ill or mentally defective, in which inmates as defined in (d) above may lawfully be confined.

Article III

Contracts

(a) Each party state may make one or more contracts with any one or more of the other party states for the confinement of inmates on behalf of a sending state in institutions situated within receiving states. Any such contract shall provide for:

1. Its duration.

2. Payments to be made to the receiving state by the sending state for inmate maintenance, extraordinary medical and dental expenses, and any participation in or receipt by inmates of rehabilitative or correctional services, facilities, programs or treatment not reasonably included as part of normal maintenance.

3. Participation in programs of inmate employment, if any; the disposition or crediting of any payments received by inmates on account thereof; and the crediting of proceeds from or disposal of any products resulting therefrom.

4. Delivery and retaking of inmates.

5. Such other matters as may be necessary and appropriate to fix the obligations, responsibilities and rights of the sending and receiving states.

(b) The terms and provisions of this compact shall be a part of any contract entered into by the authority of or pursuant thereto, and nothing in any such contract shall be inconsistent therewith.

Article IV

Procedures and Rights

(a) Whenever the duly constituted authorities in a state party to this compact, and which has entered into a contract pursuant to Article III, shall decide that confinement in, or transfer of an inmate to, an institution within the territory of another party state is necessary or desirable in order to provide adequate quarters and care or an appropriate program of rehabilitation or treatment, said officials may direct that the confinement be within an institution within the territory of said other party state, the receiving state to act in that regard solely as agent for the sending state.

(b) The appropriate officials of any state party to this compact shall have access, at all reasonable times, to any institution in which it has a contractual right to confine inmates for the purpose of inspecting the facilities thereof and visiting such of its inmates as may be confined in the institution.

(c) Inmates confined in an institution pursuant to the terms of this compact shall at all times be subject to the jurisdiction of the sending state and may at any time be removed therefrom for transfer to a prison or other institution within the sending state, for transfer to another institution in which the sending state may have a contractual or other right to confine inmates, for release on probation or parole, for discharge, or for any other purpose permitted by the laws of the sending state; provided that the sending state shall continue to be obligated to such payments as may be required pursuant to the terms of any contract entered into under the terms of Article III.

(d) Each receiving state shall provide regular reports to each sending state on the inmates of that sending state in institutions pursuant to this compact including a conduct record of each inmate and certify said record to the official designated by the sending state, in order that each inmate may have official review of his or her record in determining and altering the disposition of said inmate in accordance with the law which may obtain in the sending state and in order that the same may be a source of information for the sending state.

(e) All inmates who may be confined in an institution pursuant to the provisions of this compact shall be treated in a reasonable and humane manner and shall be treated equally with such similar inmates of the receiving state as may be confined in the same institution. The fact of confinement in a receiving state shall not deprive any inmate so confined of any legal rights which said inmate would have had if confined in an appropriate institution of the sending state.

(f) Any hearing or hearings to which an inmate confined pursuant to this compact may be entitled by the laws of the sending state may be had before the appropriate authorities of the sending state, or of the receiving state if authorized by the sending state. The receiving state shall provide adequate facilities for such hearings as may be conducted by the appropriate officials of a sending state. In the event such hearing or hearings are had before officials of the receiving state, the governing law shall be that of the sending state and a record of the hearing or hearings as prescribed by the sending state shall be made. Said record together with any recommendations of the hearing officials shall be transmitted forthwith to the official or officials before whom the hearing would have been had if it had taken place in the sending state. In any and all proceedings had pursuant to the provisions of this subdivision, the officials of the receiving state shall act solely as agents of the sending state and no final determination shall be made in any matter except by the appropriate officials of the sending state.

(g) Any inmate confined pursuant to this compact shall be released within the territory of the sending state unless the inmate, and the sending and receiving states, shall agree upon release in some other place. The sending state shall bear the cost of such return to its territory.

(h) Any inmate confined pursuant to the terms of this compact shall have any and all rights to participate in and derive any benefits or incur or be relieved of any obligations or have such obligations modified or his status changed on account of any action or proceeding in which he could have participated if confined in any appropriate institution of the sending state located within such state.

(i) The parent, guardian, trustee, or other person or persons entitled under the laws of the sending state to act for, advise, or otherwise function with respect to any inmate shall not be deprived of or restricted in his exercise of any power in respect of any inmate confined pursuant to the terms of this compact.

Article V

Acts Not Reviewable in Receiving State: Extradition

(a) Any decision of the sending state in respect of any matter over which it retains jurisdiction pursuant to this compact shall be conclusive upon and not reviewable within the receiving state, but if at the time the sending state seeks to remove an inmate from an institution in the receiving state there is pending against the inmate within such state any criminal charge or if the inmate is formally accused of having committed within such state a criminal offense, the inmate shall not be returned without the consent of the receiving state until discharged from prosecution or other form of proceeding, imprisonment or detention for such offense. The duly accredited officers of the sending state shall be permitted to transport inmates pursuant to this compact through any and all states party to this compact without interference.

(b) An inmate who escapes from an institution in which he is confined pursuant to this compact shall be deemed a fugitive from the sending state and from the state in which the institution is situated. In the case of an escape to a jurisdiction other than the sending or receiving state, the responsibility for institution of extradition or rendition proceedings shall be that of the sending state, but nothing contained herein shall be construed to prevent or affect the activities of officers and agencies of any jurisdiction directed toward the apprehension and return of an escapee.

Article VI

Federal Aid

Any state party to this compact may accept federal aid for use in connection with any institution or program, the use of which is or may be affected by this compact or any contract pursuant hereto and any inmate in a receiving state pursuant to this compact may participate in any such federally aided program or activity for which the sending and receiving states have made contractual provision, provided that if such program or activity is not part of the customary correctional regimen, the express consent of the appropriate official of the sending state shall be required therefor.

Article VII

Entry Into Force

This compact shall enter into force and become effective and binding upon the states so acting when it has been enacted into law by any two states. Thereafter, this compact shall enter into force and become effective and binding as to any other of said states upon similar action by such state.

Article VIII

Withdrawal and Termination

This compact shall continue in force and remain binding upon a party state until it shall have enacted a statute repealing the same and providing for the sending of formal written notice of withdrawal from the compact to the appropriate officials of all other party states. An actual withdrawal shall not take effect until one year after the notices provided in said statute have been sent. Such withdrawal shall not relieve the withdrawing state from its obligations assumed hereunder prior to the effective date of withdrawal. Before the effective date of withdrawal, a withdrawing state shall remove to its territory, at its own expense, such inmates as it may have confined pursuant to the provisions of this compact.

Article IX

Other Arrangements Unaffected

Nothing contained in this compact shall be construed to abrogate or impair any agreement or other arrangement which a party state may have with a nonparty state for the confinement, rehabilitation or treatment of inmates nor to repeal any other laws of a party state authorizing the making of cooperative institutional arrangements.

Article X

Construction and Severability

The provisions of this compact shall be liberally construed and shall be severable. If any phrase, clause, sentence or provision of this compact is declared to be contrary to the constitution of any participating state or of the United States or the applicability thereof to any government, agency, person or circumstance is held invalid, the validity of the remainder of this compact and the applicability thereof to any government, agency, person or circumstance shall not be affected thereby. If this compact shall be held contrary to the constitution of any state participating therein, the compact shall remain in full force and effect as to the remaining states and in full force and effect as to the state affected as to all severable matters.

(Added by Stats. 1976, Ch. 667.)

11190.

The Western Interstate Corrections Compact as contained herein is hereby enacted into law and entered into on behalf of this State with any and all other states legally joining therein in a form substantially as follows:

Western Interstate Corrections Compact

Article I

Purpose and Policy

The party states, desiring by common action to improve their institutional facilities and provide programs of sufficiently high quality for the confinement, treatment and rehabilitation of various types of offenders, declare that it is the policy of each of the party states to provide such facilities and programs on a basis of co-operation with one another, thereby serving the best interests of such offenders and of society. The purpose of this compact is to provide for the development and execution of such programs of co-operation for the confinement, treatment and rehabilitation of offenders.

Article II

Definitions

As used in this compact, unless the context clearly requires otherwise:

(a) "State" means a state of the United States, or, subject to the limitation contained in Article VII, Guam.

(b) "Sending state" means a state party to this compact in which conviction was had.

(c) "Receiving state" means a state party to this compact to which an inmate is sent for confinement other than a state in which conviction was had.

(d) "Inmate" means a male or female offender who is under sentence to or confined in a prison or other correctional institution.

(e) "Institution" means any prison, reformatory or other correctional facility (including but not limited to a facility for the mentally ill or mentally defective) in which inmates may lawfully be confined.

Article III

Contracts

(a) Each party state may make one or more contracts with any one or more of the other party states for the confinement of inmates on behalf of a sending state in institutions situated within receiving states. Any such contract shall provide for:

1. Its duration.

2. Payments to be made to the receiving state by the sending state for inmate maintenance, extraordinary medical and dental expenses, and any participation in or receipt by inmates of rehabilitative or correctional services, facilities, programs or treatment not reasonably included as part of normal maintenance.

3. Participation in programs of inmate employment, if any; the disposition or crediting of any payments received by inmates on accounts thereof; and the crediting of proceeds from or disposal of any products resulting therefrom.

4. Delivery and retaking of inmates.

5. Such other matters as may be necessary and appropriate to fix the obligations, responsibilities and rights of the sending and receiving states.

(b) Prior to the construction or completion of construction of any institution or addition thereto by a party state, any other party state or states may contract therewith for the enlargement of the planned capacity of the institution or addition thereto, or for the inclusion therein of particular equipment or structures, and for the reservation of a specific per centum of the capacity of the institution to be kept available for use by inmates of the sending state or states so contracting. Any sending state so contracting may, to the extent that moneys are legally available therefor, pay to the receiving state, a reasonable sum as consideration for such enlargement of capacity, or provision of equipment or structures, and reservation of capacity. Such payment may be in a lump sum or in installments as provided in the contract.

(c) The terms and provisions of this compact shall be a part of any contract entered into by the authority of or pursuant thereto, and nothing in any such contract shall be inconsistent therewith.

Article IV

Procedures and Rights

(a) Whenever the duly constituted judicial or administrative authorities in a state party to this compact, and which has entered into a contract pursuant to Article III, shall decide that confinement in, or transfer of an inmate to, an institution within the territory of another party state is necessary in order to provide adequate quarters and care or desirable in order to provide an appropriate program of rehabilitation or treatment, said officials may direct that the confinement be within an institution within the territory of said other party state, the receiving state to act in that regard solely as agent for the sending state.

(b) The appropriate officials of any state party to this compact shall have access, at all reasonable times, to any institution in which it has a contractual right to confine inmates for the purpose of inspecting the facilities thereof and visiting such of its inmates as may be confined in the institution.

(c) Inmates confined in an institution pursuant to the terms of this compact shall at all times be subject to the jurisdiction of the sending state and may at any time be removed therefrom for transfer to a prison or other institution within the sending state, for transfer to another institution in which the sending state may have a contractual or other right to confine inmates, for release on probation or parole, for discharge, or for any other purpose permitted by the laws of the sending state; provided that the sending state shall continue to be obligated to such payments as may be required pursuant to the terms of any contract entered into under the terms of Article III.

(d) Each receiving state shall provide regular reports to each sending state on the inmates of that sending state in institutions pursuant to this compact including a conduct record of each inmate and certify said record to the official designated by the sending state, in order that each inmate may have the benefit of his or her record in determining and altering the disposition of said inmate in accordance with the law which may obtain in the sending state and in order that the same may be a source of information for the sending state.

(e) All inmates who may be confined in an institution pursuant to the provisions of this compact shall be treated in a reasonable and humane manner and shall be cared for and treated equally with such similar inmates of the receiving state as may be confined in the same institution. The fact of confinement in a receiving state shall not deprive any inmate so confined of any legal rights which said inmate would have had if confined in an appropriate institution of the sending state.

(f) Any hearing or hearings to which an inmate confined pursuant to this compact may be entitled by the laws of the sending state may be had before the appropriate authorities of the sending state, or of the receiving state if authorized by the sending state. The receiving state shall provide adequate facilities for such hearings as may be conducted by the appropriate officials of a sending state. In the event such hearing or hearings are had before officials of the receiving state, the governing law shall be that of the sending state and a record of the hearing or hearings as prescribed by the sending state shall be made. Said record together with any recommendations of the hearing officials shall be transmitted forthwith to the official or officials before whom the hearing would have been had if it had taken place in the sending state. In any and all proceedings had pursuant to the provisions of this subdivision, the officials of the receiving state shall act solely as agents of the sending state and no final determination shall be made in any matter except by the appropriate officials of the sending state. Costs of records made pursuant to this subdivision shall be borne by the sending state.

(g) Any inmate confined pursuant to this compact shall be released within the territory of the sending state unless the inmate, and the sending and receiving states, shall agree upon release in some other place. The sending state shall bear the cost of such return to its territory.

(h) Any inmate confined pursuant to the terms of this compact shall have any and all rights to participate in and derive any benefits or incur or be relieved of any obligations or have such obligations modified or his status changed on account of any action or proceeding in which he could have participated if confined in any appropriate institution of the sending state located within such state.

(i) The parent, guardian, trustee, or other person or persons entitled under the laws of the sending state to act for, advise, or otherwise function with respect to any inmate shall not be deprived of or restricted in his exercise of any power in respect of any inmate confined pursuant to the terms of this compact.

Article V

Acts Not Reviewable in Receiving State; Extradition

(a) Any decision of the sending state in respect of any matter over which it retains jurisdiction pursuant to this compact shall be conclusive upon and not reviewable within the receiving state, but if at the time the sending state seeks to remove an inmate from an institution in the receiving state there is pending against the inmate within such state any criminal charge or if the inmate is suspected of having committed within such state a criminal offense, the inmate shall not be returned without the consent of the receiving state until discharged from prosecution or other form of proceeding, imprisonment or detention for such offense. The duly accredited officers of the sending state shall be permitted to transport inmates pursuant to this compact through any and all states party to this compact without interference.

(b) An inmate who escapes from an institution in which he is confined pursuant to this compact shall be deemed a fugitive from the sending state and from the state in which the institution is situated. In the case of an escape to a jurisdiction other than the sending or receiving state, the responsibility for institution of extradition proceedings shall be that of the sending state, but nothing contained herein shall be construed to prevent or affect the activities of officers and agencies of any jurisdiction directed toward the apprehension and return of an escapee.

Article VI

Federal Aid

Any state party to this compact may accept federal aid for use in connection with any institution or program, the use of which is or may be affected by this compact or any contract pursuant hereto and any inmate in a receiving state pursuant to this compact may participate in any such federally aided program or activity for which the sending and

receiving states have made contractual provision provided that if such program or activity is not part of the customary correctional regimen the express consent of the appropriate official of the sending state shall be required therefor.

Article VII

Entry Into Force

This compact shall enter into force and become effective and binding upon the states so acting when it has been enacted into law by any two contiguous states from among the States of Alaska, Arizona, California, Colorado, Hawaii, Idaho, Montana, Nebraska, Nevada, New Mexico, Oregon, Utah, Washington and Wyoming. For the purpose of this article, Alaska and Hawaii shall be deemed contiguous to each other; to any and all of the States of California, Oregon and Washington; and to Guam. Thereafter, this compact shall enter into force and become effective and binding as to any other of said states, or any other state contiguous to at least one party state upon similar action by such state. Guam may become party to this compact by taking action similar to that provided for joinder by any other eligible party state and upon the consent of Congress to such joinder. For the purposes of this article, Guam shall be deemed contiguous to Alaska, Hawaii, California, Oregon and Washington.

Article VIII

Withdrawal and Termination

This compact shall continue in force and remain binding upon a party state until it shall have enacted a statute repealing the same and providing for the sending of formal written notice of withdrawal from the compact to the appropriate officials of all other party states. An actual withdrawal shall not take effect until two years after the notices provided in said statute have been sent. Such withdrawal shall not relieve the withdrawing state from its obligations assumed hereunder prior to the effective date of withdrawal. Before the effective date of withdrawal, a withdrawing state shall remove to its territory, at its own expense, such inmates as it may have confined pursuant to the provisions of this compact.

Article IX

Other Arrangements Unaffected

Nothing contained in this compact shall be construed to abrogate or impair any agreement or other arrangement which a party state may have with a nonparty state for the confinement, rehabilitation or treatment of inmates nor to repeal any other laws of a party state authorizing the making of co-operative institutional arrangements.

Article X

Construction and Severability

The provisions of this compact shall be liberally construed and shall be severable. If any phrase, clause, sentence or provision of this compact is declared to be contrary to the constitution of any participating state or of the United States or the applicability thereof to any government, agency, person or circumstance is held invalid, the validity of the remainder of this compact and the applicability thereof to any government, agency, person or circumstance shall not be affected thereby. If this compact shall be held contrary to the constitution of any state participating therein, the compact shall remain in full force and effect as to the remaining states and in full force and effect as to the state affected as to all severable matters.

(Added by Stats. 1961, Ch. 1397.)

11191.

(a) Any court or other agency or officer of this state having power to commit or transfer an inmate, as defined in Article II (d) of the Interstate Corrections Compact or of the Western Interstate Corrections Compact, to any institution for confinement may commit or transfer that inmate to any institution within or without this state if this state has entered into a contract or contracts for the confinement of inmates in that institution pursuant to Article III of the Interstate Corrections Compact or of the Western Interstate Corrections Compact.

(b) An inmate sentenced under California law shall not be committed or transferred to an institution outside of this state, unless he or she has executed a written consent to the transfer. The inmate shall have the right to a private consultation with an attorney of his choice, or with a public defender if the inmate cannot afford counsel, concerning his rights and obligations under this section, and shall be informed of those rights prior to executing the written consent. At any time more than five years after the transfer, the inmate shall be entitled to revoke his consent and to transfer to an institution in this state. In such cases, the transfer shall occur within the next 30 days.

(c) Notwithstanding the requirements in this section or Section 11194, the secretary may transfer an inmate to a facility in another state without the consent of the inmate.

(d) Inmates who volunteer by submitting a request to transfer and are otherwise eligible shall receive first priority under this section.

(e) This section shall remain in effect only until January 1, 2020, and as of that date is repealed, unless a later enacted statute, that is enacted before January 1, 2020, deletes or extends that date.

(Amended (as amended by Stats. 2013, Ch. 310, Sec. 17) by Stats. 2016, Ch. 33, Sec. 33. (SB 843) Effective June 27, 2016. Repealed as of January 1, 2020, by its own provisions. See later operative version, as amended by Sec. 34 of Stats. 2016, Ch. 33.)

11191.

(a) Any court or other agency or officer of this state having power to commit or transfer an inmate, as defined in Article II(d) of the Interstate Corrections Compact or of the Western Interstate Corrections Compact, to any institution for confinement may commit or transfer that inmate to any institution within or outside of this state if this state has entered into a contract or contracts for the confinement of inmates in that institution pursuant to Article III of the Interstate Corrections Compact or of the Western Interstate Corrections Compact.

(b) No inmate sentenced under California law may be committed or transferred to an institution outside of this state, unless he or she has executed a written consent to the transfer. The inmate shall have the right to a private consultation with an attorney of his choice, or with a public defender if the inmate cannot afford counsel, concerning his rights and obligations under this section, and shall be informed of those rights prior to executing the written consent. At any time more than five years after the transfer, the inmate shall be entitled to revoke his consent and to transfer to an institution in this state. In such cases, the transfer shall occur within the next 30 days.

(c) This section shall become operative on January 1, 2020.

(Amended (as added by Stats. 2013, Ch. 310, Sec. 18) by Stats. 2016, Ch. 33, Sec. 34. (SB 843) Effective June 27, 2016. Section operative January 1, 2020, by its own provisions.)

11192.

The courts, departments, agencies and officers of this State and its subdivisions shall enforce this compact and shall do all things appropriate to the effectuation of its purposes and intent which may be within their respective jurisdictions including but not limited to the making and submission of such reports as are required by the compact.

(Added by Stats. 1961, Ch. 1397.)

11193.

Any inmate sentenced under California law who is imprisoned in another state, pursuant to a compact, shall be entitled to all hearings, within 120 days of the time and under the same standards, which are normally accorded to persons similarly sentenced who are confined in institutions in this state. If the inmate consents in writing, such hearings may be conducted by the corresponding agencies or officials of such other jurisdiction. The Board of Prison Terms or its duly authorized representative is hereby authorized and

directed to hold such hearings as may be requested by such other jurisdiction or the inmate pursuant to this section or to Article IV (f) of the Interstate Corrections Compact or of the Western Interstate Corrections Compact.
(Amended by Stats. 1979, Ch. 255.)

11194.
The Director of Corrections is hereby empowered to enter into such contracts on behalf of this state as may be appropriate to implement the participation of this state in the Interstate Corrections Compact and the Western Interstate Corrections Compact pursuant to Article III thereof. No such contract shall be of any force or effect until approved by the Director of General Services. Such contracts may authorize confinement of inmates in, or transfer of inmates from, only such institutions in this state as are under the jurisdiction of the Department of Corrections, and no such contract may provide for transfer out of this state of any person committed to the custody of the Director of the Youth Authority. No such contract may authorize the confinement of an inmate, who is in the custody of the Director of Corrections, in an institution of a state other than a state that is a party to the Interstate Corrections Compact or to the Western Interstate Corrections Compact. The Director of Corrections, subject to the approval of the Board of Prison Terms, must first determine, on the basis of an inspection made by his direction, that such institution of another state is a suitable place for confinement of prisoners committed to his custody before entering into a contract permitting such confinement, and shall, at least annually, redetermine the suitability of such confinement. In determining the suitability of such institution of another state, the director shall assure himself that such institution maintains standards of care and discipline not incompatible with those of the State of California and that all inmates therein are treated equitably, regardless of race, religion, color, creed or national origin.
(Amended by Stats. 1979, Ch. 255.)

11194.5.
(a) At the request of the board of supervisors of any county that is adjacent to another state, the county sheriff shall negotiate with the appropriate officials of the adjacent state to contract pursuant to the authority of Article III of a compact executed under Section 11189 or 11190 for the confinement of county jail prisoners in corresponding facilities located in the adjacent state. The sheriff shall determine that the corresponding facilities are a suitable place of confinement of prisoners submitted to his or her custody and shall at least annually redetermine the suitability as a precondition to any contract under this section. In determining the suitability of the facilities of the other states, the sheriff shall assure himself or herself that it maintains standards of care and discipline not incompatible with those of this state and that all inmates therein are treated equally, regardless of race, religion, color, creed, or national origin.
(b) With the approval of the board of supervisors including agreement as to terms for payments to be made for prisoner maintenance and expenses, the county sheriff may enter into a contract negotiated under subdivision (a).
(c) No prisoner may be transferred to an institution outside of this state under this section unless he or she has executed a written consent to the transfer.
(d) Any person who was sent to another state from a county under the authority of this section shall be released within the territory of the county unless the person, the sheriff of the sending county, and the corresponding official or agency of the other state shall agree upon release in another place. The county shall bear the cost of transporting the person to the place of release.
(Added by Stats. 1986, Ch. 860, Sec. 1. Effective September 17, 1986.)

11195.
Every prisoner released from a prison without this state to which he has been committed or transferred from this state pursuant to this article shall be entitled to the same benefits, including, but not limited to money and tools, as are allowed to a prisoner released from a prison in this state. Any person who has been sent to another state for confinement pursuant to this article shall be released within the territory of this state unless the person, the Director of Corrections of California, and the corresponding agency or official of the other state shall agree upon release in some other place. This state shall bear the cost of transporting the person to the place of release.
(Amended by Stats. 1976, Ch. 667.)

11196.
The provisions of this article shall be severable and if any phrase, clause, sentence, or provision of this article is declared to be unconstitutional or the applicability thereof to any state, agency, person or circumstance is held invalid, the constitutionality of this article and the applicability thereof to any other state, agency, person or circumstance shall, with respect to all severable matters, not be affected thereby. It is the legislative intent that the provisions of this article be reasonably and liberally construed.
(Added by Stats. 1961, Ch. 1397.)

11197.
No person sentenced under California law who is committed or transferred to an institution outside of this state shall be competent to testify for the prosecution in any criminal proceeding in this state unless counsel for each defendant in such proceeding is notified that the prosecution may call the person as a witness and is given an opportunity to interview the person no less than 10 days before the commencement of the proceeding or, in the event the prosecution is not at that time considering the possibility of using such testimony, the notice and opportunity for interview shall be given at the earliest possible time. Nothing in this section shall be construed to compel the prisoner to submit to such an interview.
(Added by Stats. 1976, Ch. 667.)

11198.
(a) Except as authorized by California statute, no city, county, city and county, or private entity shall cause to be brought into, housed in, confined in, or detained in this state any person sentenced to serve a criminal commitment under the authority of any jurisdiction outside of California.
(b) It is the intent of the Legislature that this act shall neither prohibit nor authorize the confinement of federal prisoners in this state.
(Added by Stats. 1999, Ch. 707, Sec. 2. Effective January 1, 2000.)

ARTICLE 5. Reports of Animal Cruelty, Abuse, or Neglect [11199- 11199.]
(Article 5 added by Stats. 2002, Ch. 134, Sec. 1.)
11199.
(a) Any employee of a county child or adult protective services agency, while acting in his or her professional capacity or within the scope of his or her employment, who has knowledge of or observes an animal whom he or she knows or reasonably suspects has been the victim of cruelty, abuse, or neglect, may report the known or reasonably suspected animal cruelty, abuse, or neglect to the entity or entities that investigate reports of animal cruelty, abuse, and neglect in that county.
(b) The report may be made within two working days of receiving the information concerning the animal by facsimile transmission of a written report presented in the form described in subdivision (e) or by telephone if all of the information that is required to be provided pursuant to subdivision (e) is furnished. In cases where an immediate response may be necessary in order to protect the health and safety of the animal or others, the report may be made by telephone as soon as possible.
(c) Nothing in this section shall be construed to impose a duty to investigate known or reasonably suspected animal cruelty, abuse, or neglect.
(d) As used in this section, the terms "animal," "cruelty," "abuse," "neglect," "reasonable suspicion," and "owner" are defined as follows:
(1) "Animal" includes every dumb creature.
(2) "Cruelty," "abuse," and "neglect" include every act, omission, or neglect whereby unnecessary or unjustifiable physical pain or suffering is caused or permitted.

(3) "Reasonable suspicion" means that it is objectively reasonable for a person to entertain a suspicion, based upon facts that could cause a reasonable person in a like position, drawing, when appropriate, on his or her training and experience, to suspect animal cruelty, abuse, or neglect.
(4) "Owner" means any person who is the legal owner, keeper, harborer, possessor, or the actual custodian of an animal. "Owner" includes corporations as well as individuals.
(e) Reports made pursuant to this section may be made on a preprinted form prepared by the entity or entities that investigate reports of animal cruelty, abuse, and neglect in that county that includes the definitions contained in subdivision (d), and a space for the reporter to include each of the following:
(1) His or her name and title.
(2) His or her business address and telephone number.
(3) The name, if known, of the animal owner or custodian.
(4) The location of the animal and the premises on which the known or reasonably suspected animal cruelty, abuse, or neglect took place.
(5) A description of the location of the animal and the premises.
(6) Type and numbers of animals involved.
(7) A description of the animal and its condition.
(8) The date, time, and a description of the observation or incident which led the reporter to suspect animal cruelty, abuse, or neglect and any other information the reporter believes may be relevant.
(f) When two or more employees of a county child or adult protective services agency are present and jointly have knowledge of known or reasonably suspected animal cruelty, abuse, or neglect, and where there is agreement among them, a report may be made by one person by mutual agreement. Any reporter who has knowledge that the person designated to report has failed to do so may thereafter make the report.
(Amended by Stats. 2003, Ch. 62, Sec. 236. Effective January 1, 2004.)

ARTICLE 6. Reports of Metal Theft [11199.5- 11199.5.]
(Article 6 added by Stats. 2014, Ch. 608, Sec. 4.)
11199.5.
Local law enforcement agencies are encouraged to report thefts of commodity metals, including, but not limited to, ferrous metal, copper, brass, aluminum, nickel, stainless steel, and alloys, that have occurred within their jurisdiction to the theft alert system maintained by the Institute of Scrap Recycling Industries, Inc., or its successor, in order to ensure that persons using that system receive timely and thorough information regarding metal thefts. The institute or its successor shall not sell subscribers' information received pursuant to this section to third parties.
(Added by Stats. 2014, Ch. 608, Sec. 4. (AB 2312) Effective January 1, 2015.)

CHAPTER 3. Prevention and Abatement of Unlawful Activities [11200 - 11482]

(Chapter 3 added by Stats. 1953, Ch. 35.)
ARTICLE 1. Unlawful Liquor Sale Abatement Law [11200 - 11207]
(Article 1 added by Stats. 1953, Ch. 35.)
11200.
Every building or place used for the purpose of unlawfully selling, serving or giving away any spirituous, vinous, malt or other alcoholic liquor, and every building or place in or upon which such liquors are unlawfully sold, served or given away, is a nuisance which shall be enjoined, abated and prevented, whether it is a public or private nuisance.
(Added by Stats. 1953, Ch. 35.)

11201.
Whenever there is reason to believe that a nuisance as defined in this article is kept, maintained or exists in any county, the district attorney, in the name of the people of the State of California, shall, or the city attorney of an incorporated city, or any citizen of the state resident within the county, in his or her own name may, maintain an action in equity to abate and prevent the nuisance and to perpetually enjoin the person or persons conducting or maintaining it, and the owner, lessee or agent of the building, or place, in or upon which the nuisance exists, from directly or indirectly maintaining or permitting it.
The complaint in the action shall be verified unless filed by the district attorney.
(Amended by Stats. 1987, Ch. 1076, Sec. 5.)

11202.
Whenever the existence of a nuisance is shown in an action brought under this article to the satisfaction of the court or judge thereof, either by verified complaint or affidavit, and the court or judge is satisfied that the owner of the property has received written notice of the existence of the nuisance, signed by the complainant or the district attorney at least two weeks prior to the filing of the complaint, the court or judge shall allow a temporary writ of injunction to abate and prevent the continuance or recurrence of the nuisance. On granting such writ the court or judge shall require an undertaking on the part of the applicant to the effect that the applicant will pay to the party enjoined such damages, not exceeding an amount to be specified, as the opposing party may sustain by reason of the injunction, if the court finally decides that the applicant was not entitled to the injunction.
(Amended by Stats. 1982, Ch. 517, Sec. 319.)

11203.
Actions brought under this article shall have precedence over all other actions, excepting criminal proceedings, election contests and hearings on injunctions. If a complaint is filed under this article by a citizen, it shall not be dismissed by the plaintiff or for want of prosecution except upon a sworn statement made by the complainant and his attorney, setting forth the reasons why the action should be dismissed, and the dismissal ordered by the court. In case of failure to prosecute any such action with reasonable diligence, or at the request of the plaintiff, the court, in its discretion, may substitute any other citizen consenting thereto for the plaintiff. If the action is brought by a citizen and the court finds there was no reasonable ground or cause therefor, the costs shall be taxed against such citizen.
(Added by Stats. 1953, Ch. 35.)

11204.
If the existence of a nuisance is established in an action as provided in this article, an order of abatement shall be entered as part of the judgment in the case, and plaintiff's costs in such action are a lien upon the building and place, enforceable and collectible by execution issued by order of the court.
(Added by Stats. 1953, Ch. 35.)

11205.
Any violation or disobedience of an injunction or order expressly provided for in this article is punishable as a contempt of court by a fine of not less than two hundred dollars ($200) nor more than one thousand dollars ($1,000), or by imprisonment in the county jail for not less than one nor more than six months, or by both.
(Added by Stats. 1953, Ch. 35.)

11206.
Whenever the owner of a building or place upon which an act or acts constituting a contempt as defined in this article has been committed is guilty of a contempt of court, and is fined therefor in any proceedings under this article, the fine is a lien upon such building and place to the extent of the interest of such person therein, enforceable and collectible by execution issued by order of the court.

(Added by Stats. 1953, Ch. 35.)
11207.
"Person," as used in this article, means individuals, corporations, associations, partnerships, limited liability companies, trustees, lessees, agents and assignees.
(Amended by Stats. 1994, Ch. 1010, Sec. 199. Effective January 1, 1995.)

ARTICLE 2. Red Light Abatement Law [11225 - 11235]
(Article 2 added by Stats. 1953, Ch. 35.)

11225.
(a) (1) Every building or place used for the purpose of illegal gambling as defined by state law or local ordinance, lewdness, assignation, or prostitution, and every building or place in or upon which acts of illegal gambling as defined by state law or local ordinance, lewdness, assignation, or prostitution, are held or occur, is a nuisance which shall be enjoined, abated, and prevented, and for which damages may be recovered, whether it is a public or private nuisance.
(2) Nothing in this subdivision shall be construed to apply the definition of a nuisance to a private residence where illegal gambling is conducted on an intermittent basis and without the purpose of producing profit for the owner or occupier of the premises.
(b) (1) Notwithstanding any other law, every building or place used for the purpose of human trafficking, and every building or place in or upon which acts of human trafficking are held or occur, is a nuisance which shall be enjoined, abated, and prevented, and for which damages may be recovered, whether it is a public or private nuisance.
(2) For purposes of this subdivision, human trafficking is defined in Section 236.1.
(c) (1) Every building or place used as a bathhouse which as a primary activity encourages or permits conduct that according to the guidelines of the federal Centers for Disease Control and Prevention can transmit AIDS, including, but not limited to, anal intercourse, oral copulation, or vaginal intercourse, is a nuisance which shall be enjoined, abated, and prevented, and for which damages may be recovered, whether it is a public or private nuisance.
(2) For purposes of this subdivision, a "bathhouse" means a business which, as its primary purpose, provides facilities for a spa, whirlpool, communal bath, sauna, steam bath, mineral bath, mud bath, or facilities for swimming.
(Amended by Stats. 2012, Ch. 254, Sec. 2. (AB 2212) Effective January 1, 2013.)
11226.
If there is reason to believe that a nuisance, as defined in this article or as set forth in Section 17800 of the Business and Professions Code, is kept, maintained, or is in existence in any county, the district attorney or county counsel, in the name of the people of the State of California, or the city attorney of an incorporated city or any city and county may, or any citizen of the state resident within the county in his or her own name may, maintain an action in equity to abate and prevent the nuisance and to perpetually enjoin the person conducting or maintaining it, and the owner, lessee, or agent of the building or place, in or upon which the nuisance exists, from directly or indirectly maintaining or permitting it.
The complaint in the action shall be verified unless filed by the district attorney, county counsel, or the city attorney.
(Amended by Stats. 2010, Ch. 570, Sec. 4. (AB 1502) Effective January 1, 2011.)
11227.
(a) Whenever the existence of a nuisance is shown in an action brought under this article to the satisfaction of the court or judge thereof, either by verified complaint or affidavit, the court or judge shall allow a temporary restraining order or injunction to abate and prevent the continuance or recurrence of the nuisance.
(b) A temporary restraining order or injunction may enjoin subsequent owners, commercial lessees, or agents who acquire the building or place where the nuisance exists with notice of the order or injunction, specifying that the owner of the property subject to the temporary restraining order or injunction shall notify any prospective purchaser, commercial lessee, or other successor in interest of the existence of the order or injunction, and of its application to successors in interest, prior to entering into any agreement to sell or lease the property. The temporary restraining order or injunction shall not constitute a title defect, lien, or encumbrance on the real property.
(Amended by Stats. 2002, Ch. 1057, Sec. 6. Effective January 1, 2003.)
11228.
Actions brought under this article have precedence over all actions, excepting criminal proceedings, election contests and hearings on injunctions, and in such actions evidence of the general reputation of a place is admissible for the purpose of proving the existence of a nuisance. If the complaint is filed by a citizen, it shall not be dismissed by the plaintiff or for want of prosecution except upon a sworn statement made by the complainant and his attorney, setting forth the reasons why the action should be dismissed, and the dismissal ordered by the court. In case of failure to prosecute any such action with reasonable diligence, or at the request of the plaintiff, the court, in its discretion, may substitute any other citizen consenting thereto for the plaintiff. If the action is brought by a citizen and the court finds there was no reasonable ground or cause therefor, the costs shall be taxed against such citizen.
(Added by Stats. 1953, Ch. 35.)
11229.
Any violation or disobedience of an injunction or order expressly provided for by this article is punishable as a contempt of court by a fine of not less than two hundred dollars ($200) nor more than one thousand dollars ($1,000), by imprisonment in the county jail for not less than one nor more than six months, or by both.
(Added by Stats. 1953, Ch. 35.)
11230.
(a) (1) If the existence of a nuisance is established in an action as provided in this article, an order of abatement shall be entered as a part of the judgment in the case, directing the removal from the building or place of all fixtures, musical instruments and movable property used in conducting, maintaining, aiding, or abetting the nuisance, and directing the sale thereof in the manner provided for the sale of chattels under execution, and the effectual closing of the building or place against its use for any purpose, and that it be kept closed for a period of one year, unless sooner released. If the court finds that any vacancy resulting from closure of the building or place may create a nuisance or that closure is otherwise harmful to the community, in lieu of ordering the building or place closed, the court may order the person who is responsible for the existence of the nuisance to pay damages in an amount equal to the fair market rental value of the building or place for one year to the city or county in whose jurisdiction the nuisance is located. The actual amount of rent being received for the rental of the building or place, or the existence of any vacancy therein, may be considered, but shall not be the sole determinant of the fair market rental value. Expert testimony may be used to determine the fair market rental value.
(2) While the order remains in effect as to closing, the building or place is and shall remain in the custody of the court.
(3) For removing and selling the movable property, the officer is entitled to charge and receive the same fees as he or she would for levying upon and selling like property on execution.
(4) For closing the premises and keeping them closed, a reasonable sum shall be allowed by the court.
(b) The court may assess a civil penalty not to exceed twenty-five thousand dollars ($25,000) against any and all of the defendants, based upon the severity of the nuisance and its duration.
(c) Except as otherwise specified by subdivision (d), one-half of the civil penalties collected pursuant to this section shall be deposited in the Restitution Fund in the State Treasury, the proceeds of which shall be available for appropriation by the Legislature to indemnify persons filing claims pursuant to Article 1 (commencing with Section 13959)

of Chapter 5 of Part 4 of Division 3 of Title 2 of the Government Code, and one-half of the civil penalties collected shall be paid to the city in which the judgment was entered, if the action was brought by the city attorney or city prosecutor. If the action was brought by a district attorney, one-half of the civil penalties collected shall be paid to the treasurer of the county in which the judgment was entered.
(d) In cases involving human trafficking, one-half of the civil penalties collected pursuant to this section shall be deposited in the Victim-Witness Assistance Fund to be available for appropriation by the Legislature to the California Emergency Management Agency to fund grants for human trafficking victim services and prevention programs provided by community-based organizations. The community-based organizations shall have trained human trafficking caseworkers, as defined by Section 1038.2 of the Evidence Code. The other one-half of the civil penalties shall be paid to the city in which judgment was entered, if the action was brought by a city attorney or city prosecutor. If the action was brought by a district attorney, the one-half of the civil penalty shall, instead, be paid to the treasurer of the county in which judgment was entered.
(Amended by Stats. 2012, Ch. 254, Sec. 3. (AB 2212) Effective January 1, 2013.)
11231.
The proceeds of the sale of the property, as provided in Section 11230, shall be applied as follows:
1. To the fees and costs of removal and sale;
2. To the allowances and costs of closing and keeping closed the building or place;
3. To the payment of plaintiff's costs in the action;
4. The balance, if any, shall be paid to the owner of the property so sold.
If the proceeds of the sale do not fully discharge all such costs, fees and allowances, the building and place shall also be sold under execution issued upon the order of the court or judge and the proceeds of such sale applied in like manner.
(Added by Stats. 1953, Ch. 35.)
11232.
If the owner of the building or place is not guilty of any contempt of court in the proceedings, and appears and pays all costs, fees and allowances which are a lien on the building or place and files a bond in the full value of the property, to be ascertained by the court, conditioned that the owner will immediately abate any nuisance that may exist at the building or place and prevent the nuisance from being established or kept thereat within a period of one year thereafter, the court, or judge thereof, may, if satisfied of the owner's good faith, order the premises closed under the order of abatement, to be delivered to the owner, and the order of abatement canceled so far as the order relates to the property. The release of the property under the provisions of this section does not release it from any judgment, lien, penalty or liability to which it may be subject by law.
(Amended by Stats. 1982, Ch. 517, Sec. 320.)
11233.
Whenever the owner of a building or place upon which an act or acts constituting a contempt as defined in this article has been committed, is guilty of a contempt of court and fined therefor under this article, the fine shall be a lien upon the building and place to the extent of the interest of such person therein, enforceable and collectible by execution issued by the order of the court.
(Added by Stats. 1953, Ch. 35.)
11234.
"Person" as used in this article means individuals, corporations, associations, partnerships, limited liability companies, trustees, lessees, agents and assignees.
(Amended by Stats. 1994, Ch. 1010, Sec. 200. Effective January 1, 1995.)
11235.
"Building" as used in this article means so much of any building or structure of any kind as is or may be entered through the same outside entrance.
(Added by Stats. 1953, Ch. 35.)

ARTICLE 3. Control of Gambling Ships [11300 - 11319]
(Article 3 added by Stats. 1953, Ch. 35.)

11300.
It is unlawful for any person, within this State, to solicit, entice, induce, persuade or procure, or to aid in soliciting, enticing, inducing, persuading or procuring any person to visit any gambling ship, whether such gambling ship be within or without the jurisdiction of the State.
(Added by Stats. 1953, Ch. 35.)
11301.
As used in this article "craft" includes every boat, ship, vessel, craft, barge, hulk, float or other thing capable of floating.
(Added by Stats. 1953, Ch. 35.)
11302.
It is unlawful for any person, within this State, to solicit, entice, induce, persuade or procure, or to aid in soliciting, enticing, inducing, persuading or procuring any person to visit any craft, whether such craft is within or without the jurisdiction of the State, from which craft any person is transported, conveyed or carried to any gambling ship, whether such gambling ship is within or without the jurisdiction of the State.
(Added by Stats. 1953, Ch. 35.)
11303.
It is unlawful for any person, firm, association or corporation to transport, convey or carry, or to aid in transporting, conveying or carrying any person to any gambling ship, whether such gambling ship is within or without the jurisdiction of the State.
(Added by Stats. 1953, Ch. 35.)
11304.
It is unlawful for any person, firm, association or corporation to transport, convey or carry, or to aid in transporting, conveying or carrying any person to any craft, whether such craft is within or without the jurisdiction of the State, from which craft any person is transported, conveyed, or carried to any gambling ship, whether such gambling ship is within or without the jurisdiction of the State.
(Added by Stats. 1953, Ch. 35.)
11305.
Any boat, ship, vessel, watercraft, barge, airplane, seaplane or aircraft, hereinafter called "means of conveyance," used for the purpose of transporting, conveying or carrying persons in violation of this article is a public nuisance which shall be enjoined, abated and prevented.
(Added by Stats. 1953, Ch. 35.)
11306.
Whenever there is reason to believe that a nuisance as defined in this article is kept, maintained or exists in any county, the district attorney, in the name of the people, shall, or any citizen of the State resident in the county, in his own name, may, maintain an action to abate and prevent the nuisance and perpetually to enjoin the person or persons conducting or maintaining it, whether as principal, agent, servant, employee or otherwise, from directly or indirectly maintaining or permitting the nuisance.
Unless filed by the district attorney, the complaint in the action shall be verified.
In any such action the plaintiff, at the time of issuing the summons, or at any time afterward, may have the means of conveyance, with its tackle, apparel and furniture, seized and kept as security for the satisfaction of any judgment that may be entered in the action.
(Added by Stats. 1953, Ch. 35.)
11307.
When any means of conveyance is seized pursuant to Section 11306, the owner thereof or any other person otherwise entitled to possession thereof may apply to the court in which the action is pending for leave to file bond and regain possession of the means of

conveyance during the pendency of the proceedings. The bond shall be in an amount determined by the judge to be the actual value of the means of conveyance at the time of its release. Upon giving said bond conditioned upon compliance with the terms of any temporary writ of injunction entered in the action and upon the return of the means of conveyance to the custody of the court in the event the same is ordered forfeited, the person on whose behalf such bond is given shall be put in possession of said means of conveyance and may use it until it is finally ordered delivered up and forfeited, if such be the judgment of the court.
(Added by Stats. 1953, Ch. 35.)

11308.
If the existence of a nuisance as defined in this article is shown in any action brought under this article to the satisfaction of the court or judge, either by verified complaint or affidavit, the court or judge shall allow a temporary writ of injunction to abate and prevent the continuance or recurrence of the nuisance. On granting the temporary writ the court or judge shall require an undertaking on the part of the applicant to the effect that the applicant will pay to the defendant enjoined such damages, not exceeding an amount to be specified, as the defendant sustains by reason of the injunction if the court finally decides that the applicant was not entitled to it.
(Amended by Stats. 1982, Ch. 517, Sec. 321.)

11309.
Actions brought under this article shall have precedence over all other actions, except criminal proceedings, election contests and hearings on injunctions.
If the complaint is filed by a citizen it shall not be dismissed by him or for want of prosecution except upon a sworn statement made by him and his attorney, setting forth the reasons why the action should be dismissed, and by dismissal ordered by the court.
In case of failure to prosecute the action with reasonable diligence, or at the request of the plaintiff, the court, in its discretion, may substitute any other citizen consenting thereto for the plaintiff.
If the action is brought by a citizen and the court finds there was no reasonable ground or cause therefor, the costs shall be taxed against him.
(Added by Stats. 1953, Ch. 35.)

11310.
If the existence of a nuisance as defined in this article is established in an action brought thereunder, an order of abatement shall be entered as part of the judgment in the case, and plaintiff's costs in the action are a lien upon the means of conveyance, and upon its tackle, apparel and furniture. The lien is enforceable and collectible by execution issued by order of the court.
(Added by Stats. 1953, Ch. 35.)

11311.
A violation or disobedience of an injunction or order for abatement provided for in this article is punishable as a contempt of court by a fine of not less than two hundred dollars ($200) or more than one thousand dollars ($1,000), or by imprisonment in the county jail for not less than one nor more than six months, or by both.
(Added by Stats. 1953, Ch. 35.)

11312.
If the existence of a nuisance as defined in this article is established in an action brought thereunder, an order of abatement shall be entered as a part of the judgment, which order shall direct the seizure and forfeiture of the means of conveyance with its tackle, apparel and furniture, and the sale thereof in the manner provided for the sale of like chattels under execution.
While the order of abatement remains in effect, the means of conveyance is in the custody of the court.
For seizing and selling the means of conveyance, the officer is entitled to charge and receive the same fees as he would for levying upon and selling like property on execution.
(Added by Stats. 1953, Ch. 35.)

11313.
The proceeds of the sale of the means of conveyance shall be applied as follows:
First—To the fees and costs of the seizure and sale.
Second—To the payment of the plaintiff's costs in the action.
Third—The balance, if any, shall be paid into the State Treasury to the credit of the General Fund.
(Added by Stats. 1953, Ch. 35.)

11314.
If the owner of the means of conveyance has not been guilty of any contempt of court in a proceeding brought under this article, and appears and pays all costs, fees, and allowances that are a lien on the means of conveyance and files a bond in the full value of the means of conveyance, to be ascertained by the court, conditioned that the owner will immediately abate the nuisance and prevent it from being established or resumed within a period of one year thereafter, the court or judge may, if satisfied of the owner's good faith, order the means of conveyance to be delivered to the owner, and the order of abatement canceled so far as it may relate thereto. The release of such means of conveyance under the provisions of this section does not release it from any judgment, lien, penalty, or liability to which it may be subject.
(Amended by Stats. 1982, Ch. 517, Sec. 322.)

11315.
Whenever the owner of the means of conveyance, or the owner of any interest therein, has been guilty of a contempt of court, and fined in any proceeding under this article, the fine is a lien upon the property to the extent of his interest in it. The lien is enforceable and collectible by execution issued by order of the court.
(Added by Stats. 1953, Ch. 35.)

11316.
Any person, firm, association or corporation, either as principal, agent, servant, employee or otherwise, who violates any of the provisions of this article is guilty of a misdemeanor.
(Added by Stats. 1953, Ch. 35.)

11317.
The term "gambling ship" as used in this article means any boat, ship, vessel, watercraft or barge kept, operated or maintained for the purpose of gambling, whether within or without the jurisdiction of the State, and whether it is anchored, lying to, or navigating.
(Added by Stats. 1953, Ch. 35.)

11318.
If any section, subsection, paragraph, sentence or clause of this article is for any reason held to be invalid, the Legislature hereby declares that had it known of the invalidity of that portion at the time of this enactment, it would have passed the remainder of the article without the invalid portion and that it is the intention of the Legislature that the remainder of the article operate in the event of the invalidity of any portion thereof.
(Added by Stats. 1953, Ch. 35.)

11319.
It is unlawful for any person to do any of the following:
(a) Violate any provision of Chapter 9 (commencing with Section 319), Chapter 10 (commencing with Section 330), or Chapter 10.5 (commencing with Section 337.1) of Title 9 of Part 1 on a craft that embarks from any point within the state, and disembarks at the same or another point within the state, during which time the person intentionally causes or knowingly permits gambling activity to be conducted, whether within or without the waters of the state.
(b) Manage, supervise, control, operate, or own any craft that embarks from any point within the state, and disembarks at the same or another point within the state, during which time the person intentionally causes or knowingly permits gambling activity which

would violate any provision of Chapter 9 (commencing with Section 319), Chapter 10 (commencing with Section 330), or Chapter 10.5 (commencing with Section 337.1) of Title 9 of Part 1 to be conducted, whether within or without the waters of the state.
(c) This section shall not apply to gambling activity conducted on United States-flagged or foreign-flagged craft during travel from a foreign nation or another state or possession of the United States up to the point of first entry into California waters or during travel to a foreign nation or another state or possession of the United States from the point of departure from California waters, provided that nothing herein shall preclude prosecution for any other offense under this article.
(Added by Stats. 1992, Ch. 276, Sec. 2. Effective January 1, 1993.)

ARTICLE 4.5. Terrorizing [11410 - 11414]
(Article 4.5 added by Stats. 1982, Ch. 1624, Sec. 2.)

11410.
(a) The Legislature finds and declares that it is the right of every person regardless of actual or perceived disability, gender, gender identity, gender expression, nationality, race or ethnicity, religion, sexual orientation, or association with a person or group with these actual or perceived characteristics, to be secure and protected from fear, intimidation, and physical harm caused by the activities of violent groups and individuals. It is not the intent of this chapter to interfere with the exercise of rights protected by the Constitution of the United States. The Legislature recognizes the constitutional right of every citizen to harbor and express beliefs on any subject whatsoever and to associate with others who share similar beliefs. The Legislature further finds however, that the advocacy of unlawful violent acts by groups against other persons or groups under circumstances where death or great bodily injury is likely to result is not constitutionally protected, poses a threat to public order and safety, and should be subject to criminal and civil sanctions.
(b) For purposes of this section, the following definitions shall apply:
(1) "Association with a person or group with these actual or perceived characteristics" includes advocacy for, identification with, or being on the ground owned or rented by, or adjacent to, any of the following: a community center, educational facility, family, individual, office, meeting hall, place of worship, private institution, public agency, library, or other entity, group, or person that has, or is identified with people who have, one or more of those characteristics listed in the definition of "hate crime" under paragraphs (1) to (6), inclusive, of subdivision (a) of Section 422.55.
(2) "Disability" includes mental disability and physical disability as defined in Section 12926 of the Government Code.
(3) "Gender" means sex, and includes a person's gender identity and gender expression. "Gender expression" means a person's gender-related appearance and behavior whether or not stereotypically associated with the person's assigned sex at birth.
(4) "Nationality" includes citizenship, country of origin, and national origin.
(5) "Race or ethnicity" includes ancestry, color, and ethnic background.
(6) "Religion" includes all aspects of religious belief, observance, and practice and includes agnosticism and atheism.
(7) "Sexual orientation" means heterosexuality, homosexuality, or bisexuality.
(Amended by Stats. 2011, Ch. 719, Sec. 34. (AB 887) Effective January 1, 2012.)

11411.
(a) Any person who hangs a noose, knowing it to be a symbol representing a threat to life, on the private property of another, without authorization, for the purpose of terrorizing the owner or occupant of that private property or in reckless disregard of the risk of terrorizing the owner or occupant of that private property, or who hangs a noose, knowing it to be a symbol representing a threat to life, on the property of a primary school, junior high school, high school, college campus, public park, or place of employment, for the purpose of terrorizing any person who attends or works at the school, park, or place of employment, or who is otherwise associated with the school, park, or place of employment, shall be punished by imprisonment in a county jail not to exceed one year, or by a fine not to exceed five thousand dollars ($5,000), or by both the fine and imprisonment for the first conviction or by imprisonment in a county jail not to exceed one year, or by a fine not to exceed fifteen thousand dollars ($15,000), or by both the fine and imprisonment for any subsequent conviction.
(b) Any person who places or displays a sign, mark, symbol, emblem, or other physical impression, including, but not limited to, a Nazi swastika, on the private property of another, without authorization, for the purpose of terrorizing the owner or occupant of that private property or in reckless disregard of the risk of terrorizing the owner or occupant of that private property shall be punished by imprisonment in a county jail not to exceed one year, by a fine not to exceed five thousand dollars ($5,000), or by both the fine and imprisonment for the first conviction and by imprisonment in a county jail not to exceed one year, by a fine not to exceed fifteen thousand dollars ($15,000), or by both the fine and imprisonment for any subsequent conviction.
(c) Any person who engages in a pattern of conduct for the purpose of terrorizing the owner or occupant of private property or in reckless disregard of terrorizing the owner or occupant of that private property, by placing or displaying a sign, mark, symbol, emblem, or other physical impression, including, but not limited to, a Nazi swastika, on the private property of another on two or more occasions, shall be punished by imprisonment pursuant to subdivision (h) of Section 1170 for 16 months or two or three years, by a fine not to exceed ten thousand dollars ($10,000), or by both the fine and imprisonment, or by imprisonment in a county jail not to exceed one year, by a fine not to exceed five thousand dollars ($5,000), or by both the fine and imprisonment. A violation of this subdivision shall not constitute felonious conduct for purposes of Section 186.22.
(d) Any person who burns or desecrates a cross or other religious symbol, knowing it to be a religious symbol, on the private property of another without authorization for the purpose of terrorizing the owner or occupant of that private property or in reckless disregard of the risk of terrorizing the owner or occupant of that private property, or who burns, desecrates, or destroys a cross or other religious symbol, knowing it to be a religious symbol, on the property of a primary school, junior high school, or high school for the purpose of terrorizing any person who attends or works at the school or who is otherwise associated with the school, shall be punished by imprisonment pursuant to subdivision (h) of Section 1170 for 16 months or two or three years, by a fine of not more than ten thousand dollars ($10,000), or by both the fine and imprisonment, or by imprisonment in a county jail not to exceed one year, by a fine not to exceed five thousand dollars ($5,000), or by both the fine and imprisonment for the first conviction and by imprisonment pursuant to subdivision (h) of Section 1170 for 16 months or two or three years, by a fine of not more than ten thousand dollars ($10,000), or by both the fine and imprisonment, or by imprisonment in a county jail not to exceed one year, by a fine not to exceed fifteen thousand dollars ($15,000), or by both the fine and imprisonment for any subsequent conviction.
(e) As used in this section, "terrorize" means to cause a person of ordinary emotions and sensibilities to fear for personal safety.
(f) The provisions of this section are severable. If any provision of this section or its application is held invalid, that invalidity shall not affect other provisions or applications that can be given effect without the invalid provision or application.
(Amended by Stats. 2011, Ch. 15, Sec. 496. (AB 109) Effective April 4, 2011. Operative October 1, 2011, by Sec. 636 of Ch. 15, as amended by Stats. 2011, Ch. 39, Sec. 68.)

11412.
Any person who, with intent to cause, attempts to cause or causes another to refrain from exercising his or her religion or from engaging in a religious service by means of a threat, directly communicated to such person, to inflict an unlawful injury upon any

person or property, and it reasonably appears to the recipient of the threat that such threat could be carried out is guilty of a felony.
(Added by Stats. 1984, Ch. 1119, Sec. 1.)

11413.
(a) Any person who explodes, ignites, or attempts to explode or ignite any destructive device or any explosive, or who commits arson, in or about any of the places listed in subdivision (b), for the purpose of terrorizing another or in reckless disregard of terrorizing another is guilty of a felony, and shall be punished by imprisonment pursuant to subdivision (h) of Section 1170 for three, five, or seven years, and a fine not exceeding ten thousand dollars ($10,000).
(b) Subdivision (a) applies to the following places:
(1) Any health facility licensed under Chapter 2 (commencing with Section 1250) of Division 2 of the Health and Safety Code, or any place where medical care is provided by a licensed health care professional.
(2) Any church, temple, synagogue, mosque, or other place of worship.
(3) The buildings, offices, and meeting sites of organizations that counsel for or against abortion or among whose major activities are lobbying, publicizing, or organizing with respect to public or private issues relating to abortion.
(4) Any place at which a lecture, film-showing, or other private meeting or presentation that educates or propagates with respect to abortion practices or policies, whether on private property or at a meeting site authorized for specific use by a private group on public property, is taking place.
(5) Any bookstore or public or private library.
(6) Any building or facility designated as a courthouse.
(7) The home or office of a judicial officer.
(8) Any building or facility regularly occupied by county probation department personnel in which the employees perform official duties of the probation department.
(9) Any private property, if the property was targeted in whole or in part because of any of the actual or perceived characteristics of the owner or occupant of the property listed in subdivision (a) of Section 422.55.
(10) Any public or private school providing instruction in kindergarten or grades 1 to 12, inclusive.
(c) As used in this section, "judicial officer" means a magistrate, judge, justice, commissioner, referee, or any person appointed by a court to serve in one of these capacities, of any state or federal court located in this state.
(d) As used in this section, "terrorizing" means to cause a person of ordinary emotions and sensibilities to fear for personal safety.
(e) Nothing in this section shall be construed to prohibit the prosecution of any person pursuant to Section 18740 or any other provision of law in lieu of prosecution pursuant to this section.
(Amended (as amended by Stats. 2010, Ch. 178) by Stats. 2011, Ch. 15, Sec. 498. (AB 109) Effective April 4, 2011. Amending action operative October 1, 2011, by Sec. 636 of Ch. 15, as amended by Stats. 2011, Ch. 39, Sec. 68. Amended version operative January 1, 2012, pursuant to Stats. 2010, Ch. 178, Sec. 107.)

11414.
(a) Any person who intentionally harasses the child or ward of any other person because of that person's employment shall be punished by imprisonment in a county jail not exceeding one year, or by a fine not exceeding ten thousand dollars ($10,000), or by both that fine and imprisonment.
(b) For purposes of this section, the following definitions shall apply:
(1) "Child" and "ward" mean a person under 16 years of age.
(2) "Harasses" means knowing and willful conduct directed at a specific child or ward that seriously alarms, annoys, torments, or terrorizes the child or ward, and that serves no legitimate purpose, including, but not limited to, that conduct occurring during the course of any actual or attempted recording of the child's or ward's image or voice, or both, without the express consent of the parent or legal guardian of the child or ward, by following the child's or ward's activities or by lying in wait. The conduct must be such as would cause a reasonable child to suffer substantial emotional distress, and actually cause the victim to suffer substantial emotional distress.
(3) "Employment" means the job, vocation, occupation, or profession of the parent or legal guardian of the child or ward.
(c) A second conviction under this section shall be punished by a fine not exceeding twenty thousand dollars ($20,000) and by imprisonment in a county jail for not less than five days but not exceeding one year. A third or subsequent conviction under this section shall be punished by a fine not exceeding thirty thousand dollars ($30,000) and by imprisonment in a county jail for not less than 30 days but not exceeding one year.
(d) Upon a violation of this section, the parent or legal guardian of an aggrieved child or ward may bring a civil action against the violator on behalf of the child or ward. The remedies in that civil action shall be limited to one or more of the following: actual damages, punitive damages, reasonable attorney's fees, costs, disgorgement of any compensation from the sale; license, or dissemination of a child's image or voice received by the individual who, in violation of this section, recorded the child's image or voice, and injunctive relief against further violations of this section by the individual.
(e) The act of transmitting, publishing, or broadcasting a recording of the image or voice of a child does not constitute a violation of this section.
(f) This section does not preclude prosecution under any section of law that provides for greater punishment.
(Amended by Stats. 2013, Ch. 348, Sec. 1. (SB 606) Effective January 1, 2014.)

ARTICLE 4.6. The Hertzberg-Alarcon California Prevention of Terrorism Act [11415 - 11419]
(Article 4.6 added by Stats. 1999, Ch. 563, Sec. 1.)

11415.
This article shall be known and may be cited as the Hertzberg-Alarcon California Prevention of Terrorism Act.
(Added by Stats. 1999, Ch. 563, Sec. 1. Effective January 1, 2000.)

11416.
The Legislature hereby finds and declares that the threat of terrorism involving weapons of mass destruction, including, but not limited to, chemical, biological, nuclear, or radiological agents, is a significant public safety concern. The Legislature also recognizes that terrorism involving weapons of mass destruction could result in an intentional disaster placing residents of California in great peril. The Legislature also finds it necessary to sanction the possession, manufacture, use, or threatened use of chemical, biological, nuclear, or radiological weapons, as well as the intentional use or threatened use of industrial or commercial chemicals as weapons against persons or animals.
(Added by Stats. 1999, Ch. 563, Sec. 1. Effective January 1, 2000.)

11417.
(a) For the purposes of this article, the following terms have the following meanings:
(1) "Weapon of mass destruction" includes chemical warfare agents, weaponized biological or biologic warfare agents, restricted biological agents, nuclear agents, radiological agents, or the intentional release of industrial agents as a weapon, or an aircraft, vessel, or vehicle, as described in Section 34500 of the Vehicle Code, which is used as a destructive weapon.
(2) "Chemical Warfare Agents" includes, but is not limited to, the following weaponized agents, or any analog of these agents:
(A) Nerve agents, including Tabun (GA), Sarin (GB), Soman (GD), GF, and VX.
(B) Choking agents, including Phosgene (CG) and Diphosgene (DP).
(C) Blood agents, including Hydrogen Cyanide (AC), Cyanogen Chloride (CK), and Arsine (SA).

(D) Blister agents, including mustards (H, HD [sulfur mustard], HN-1, HN-2, HN-3 [nitrogen mustard]), arsenicals, such as Lewisite (L), urticants, such as CX; and incapacitating agents, such as BZ.
(3) "Weaponized biological or biologic warfare agents" include weaponized pathogens, such as bacteria, viruses, rickettsia, yeasts, fungi, or genetically engineered pathogens, toxins, vectors, and endogenous biological regulators (EBRs).
(4) "Nuclear or radiological agents" includes any improvised nuclear device (IND) which is any explosive device designed to cause a nuclear yield; any radiological dispersal device (RDD) which is any explosive device utilized to spread radioactive material; or a simple radiological dispersal device (SRDD) which is any act or container designed to release radiological material as a weapon without an explosion.
(5) "Vector" means a living organism or a molecule, including a recombinant molecule, or a biological product that may be engineered as a result of biotechnology, that is capable of carrying a biological agent or toxin to a host.
(6) "Weaponization" is the deliberate processing, preparation, packaging, or synthesis of any substance for use as a weapon or munition. "Weaponized agents" are those agents or substances prepared for dissemination through any explosive, thermal, pneumatic, or mechanical means.
(7) For purposes of this section, "used as a destructive weapon" means to use with the intent of causing widespread great bodily injury or death by causing a fire or explosion or the release of a chemical, biological, or radioactive agent.
(b) The intentional release of a dangerous chemical or hazardous material generally utilized in an industrial or commercial process shall be considered use of a weapon of mass destruction when a person knowingly utilizes those agents with the intent to cause harm and the use places persons or animals at risk of serious injury, illness, or death, or endangers the environment.
(c) The lawful use of chemicals for legitimate mineral extraction, industrial, agricultural, or commercial purposes is not proscribed by this article.
(d) No university, research institution, private company, individual, or hospital engaged in scientific or public health research and, as required, registered with the Centers for Disease Control and Prevention (CDC) pursuant to Part 113 (commencing with Section 113.1) of Subchapter E of Chapter 1 of Title 9 or pursuant to Part 72 (commencing with Section 72.1) of Subchapter E of Chapter 1 of Title 42 of the Code of Federal Regulations, or any successor provisions, shall be subject to this article.
(Amended by Stats. 2002, Ch. 611, Sec. 1. Effective September 17, 2002.)

11418.
(a) (1) Any person, without lawful authority, who possesses, develops, manufactures, produces, transfers, acquires, or retains any weapon of mass destruction, shall be punished by imprisonment pursuant to subdivision (h) of Section 1170 for 4, 8, or 12 years.
(2) Any person who commits a violation of paragraph (1) and who has been previously convicted of Section 11411, 11412, 11413, 11418, 11418.1, 11418.5, 11419, 11460, 18715, 18725, or 18740 shall be punished by imprisonment pursuant to subdivision (h) of Section 1170 for 5, 10, or 15 years.
(b) (1) Any person who uses or directly employs against another person a weapon of mass destruction in a form that may cause widespread, disabling illness or injury in human beings shall be punished by imprisonment in the state prison for life.
(2) Any person who uses or directly employs against another person a weapon of mass destruction in a form that may cause widespread great bodily injury or death and causes the death of any human being shall be punished by imprisonment in the state prison for life without the possibility of parole. Nothing in this paragraph shall prevent punishment instead under Section 190.2.
(3) Any person who uses a weapon of mass destruction in a form that may cause widespread damage to or disruption of the food supply or "source of drinking water" as defined in subdivision (d) of Section 25249.11 of the Health and Safety Code shall be punished by imprisonment in the state prison for 5, 8, or 12 years and by a fine of not more than one hundred thousand dollars ($100,000).
(4) Any person who maliciously uses against animals, crops, or seed and seed stock, a weapon of mass destruction in a form that may cause widespread damage to or substantial diminution in the value of stock animals or crops, including seeds used for crops or product of the crops, shall be punished by imprisonment in the state prison for 4, 8, or 12 years and by a fine of not more than one hundred thousand dollars ($100,000).
(c) Any person who uses a weapon of mass destruction in a form that may cause widespread and significant damage to public natural resources, including coastal waterways and beaches, public parkland, surface waters, ground water, and wildlife, shall be punished by imprisonment in the state prison for three, four, or six years.
(d) (1) Any person who uses recombinant technology or any other biological advance to create new pathogens or more virulent forms of existing pathogens for use in any crime described in subdivision (b) shall be punished by imprisonment in the state prison for 4, 8, or 12 years and by a fine of not more than two hundred fifty thousand dollars ($250,000).
(2) Any person who uses recombinant technology or any other biological advance to create new pathogens or more virulent forms of existing pathogens for use in any crime described in subdivision (c) shall be punished by imprisonment in the state prison for three, six, or nine years and by a fine of not more than two hundred fifty thousand dollars ($250,000).
(e) Nothing in this section shall be construed to prevent punishment instead pursuant to any other provision of law that imposes a greater or more severe punishment.
(Amended (as amended by Stats. 2011, Ch. 15, Sec. 500) by Stats. 2011, Ch. 39, Sec. 55. (AB 117) Effective June 30, 2011. Amending action (succeeding amendment by Stats. 2010, Ch. 178) operative October 1, 2011, pursuant to Secs. 68 and 69 of Ch. 39. Amended version operative January 1, 2012, pursuant to Stats. 2010, Ch. 178, Sec. 107.)

11418.1.
Any person who gives, mails, sends, or causes to be sent any false or facsimile of a weapon of mass destruction to another person, or places, causes to be placed, or possesses any false or facsimile of a weapon of mass destruction, with the intent to cause another person to fear for his or her own safety, or for the personal safety of others, is guilty of a misdemeanor. If the person's conduct causes another person to be placed in sustained fear, the person shall be punished by imprisonment in a county jail for not more than one year or in the state prison for 16 months, or two or three years and by a fine of not more than two hundred fifty thousand dollars ($250,000). For purposes of this section, "sustained fear" has the same meaning as in Section 11418.5.
(Added by Stats. 2002, Ch. 606, Sec. 6. Effective September 17, 2002.)

11418.5.
(a) Any person who knowingly threatens to use a weapon of mass destruction, with the specific intent that the statement as defined in Section 225 of the Evidence Code or a statement made by means of an electronic communication device, is to be taken as a threat, even if there is no intent of actually carrying it out, which, on its face and under the circumstances in which it is made, is so unequivocal, immediate, and specific as to convey to the person threatened, a gravity of purpose and an immediate prospect of execution of the threat, and thereby causes that person reasonably to be in sustained fear for his or her own safety, or for his or her immediate family's safety shall be punished by imprisonment in a county jail for up to one year or in the state prison for 3, 4, or 6 years, and by a fine of not more than two hundred fifty thousand dollars ($250,000).
(b) For the purposes of this section, "sustained fear" can be established by, but is not limited to, conduct such as evacuation of any building by any occupant, evacuation of

any school by any employee or student, evacuation of any home by any resident or occupant, any isolation, quarantine, or decontamination effort.

(c) The fact that the person who allegedly violated this section did not actually possess a biological agent, toxin, or chemical weapon does not constitute a defense to the crime specified in this section.

(d) Nothing in this section shall be construed to prevent punishment instead pursuant to any other provision of law that imposes a greater or more severe punishment.

(Amended by Stats. 2002, Ch. 611, Sec. 2. Effective September 17, 2002.)

11419.

(a) Any person or entity possessing any of the restricted biological agents enumerated in subdivision (b) shall be punished by imprisonment pursuant to subdivision (h) of Section 1170 for 4, 8, or 12 years, and by a fine of not more than two hundred fifty thousand dollars ($250,000).

(b) For the purposes of this section, "restricted biological agents" means the following:

(1) Viruses: Crimean-Congo hemorrhagic fever virus, eastern equine encephalitis virus, ebola viruses, equine morbilli virus, lassa fever virus, marburg virus, Rift Valley fever virus, South African hemorrhagic fever viruses (Junin, Machupo, Sabia, Flexal, Guanarito), tick-borne encephalitis complex viruses, variola major virus (smallpox virus), Venezuelan equine encephalitis virus, viruses causing hantavirus pulmonary syndrome, yellow fever virus.

(2) Bacteria: bacillus anthracis (commonly known as anthrax), brucella abortus, brucella melitensis, brucella suis, burkholderia (pseudomonas) mallei, burkholderia (pseudomonas) pseudomallei, clostridium botulinum, francisella tularensis, yersinia pestis (commonly known as plague).

(3) Rickettsiae: coxiella burnetii, rickettsia prowazekii, rickettsia rickettsii.

(4) Fungi: coccidioides immitis.

(5) Toxins: abrin, aflatoxins, botulinum toxins, clostridium perfringens epsilon toxin, conotoxins, diacetoxyscirpenol, ricin, saxitoxin, shigatoxin, staphylococcal enterotoxins, tabtoxin, tetrodotoxin, T-2 toxin.

(6) Any other microorganism, virus, infectious substance, or biological product that has the same characteristics as, or is substantially similar to, the substances prohibited in this section.

(c) (1) This section shall not apply to any physician, veterinarian, pharmacist, or licensed medical practitioner authorized to dispense a prescription under Section 11026 of the Health and Safety Code, or universities, research institutions, or pharmaceutical corporations, or any person possessing the agents pursuant to a lawful prescription issued by a person defined in Section 11026 of the Health and Safety Code, if the person possesses vaccine strains of the viral agents Junin virus strain #1, Rift Valley fever virus strain MP-12, Venezuelan equine encephalitis virus strain TC-83 and yellow fever virus strain 17-D; any vaccine strain described in Section 78.1 of Subpart A of Part 78 of Subchapter C of Chapter 1 of Title 9 of the Code of Federal Regulations, or any successor provisions, and any toxin for medical use, inactivated for use as vaccines, or toxin preparation for biomedical research use at a median lethal dose for vertebrates of more than 100 ng/kg, as well as any national standard toxin required for biologic potency testing as described in Part 113 (commencing with Section 113.1) of Subchapter E of Chapter 1 of Title 9 of the Code of Federal Regulations, or any successor provisions.

(2) For the purposes of this section, no person shall be deemed to be in possession of an agent if the person is naturally exposed to, or innocently infected or contaminated with, the agent.

(d) Any peace officer who encounters any of the restricted agents mentioned above shall immediately notify and consult with a local public health officer to ensure proper consideration of any public health risk.

(e) Nothing in this section shall be construed to prevent punishment instead pursuant to any other provision of law that imposes a greater or more severe punishment.

(Amended by Stats. 2011, Ch. 15, Sec. 501. (AB 109) Effective April 4, 2011. Operative October 1, 2011, by Sec. 636 of Ch. 15, as amended by Stats. 2011, Ch. 39, Sec. 68.)

ARTICLE 6. Paramilitary Organizations [11460- 11460.]

(Article 6 added by Stats. 1965, Ch. 1221.)

11460.

(a) Any two or more persons who assemble as a paramilitary organization for the purpose of practicing with weapons shall be punished by imprisonment in a county jail for not more than one year or by a fine of not more than one thousand dollars ($1,000), or by both that fine and imprisonment.

As used in this subdivision, "paramilitary organization" means an organization which is not an agency of the United States government or of the State of California, or which is not a private school meeting the requirements set forth in Section 48222 of the Education Code, but which engages in instruction or training in guerrilla warfare or sabotage, or which, as an organization, engages in rioting or the violent disruption of, or the violent interference with, school activities.

(b) (1) Any person who teaches or demonstrates to any other person the use, application, or making of any firearm, explosive, or destructive device, or technique capable of causing injury or death to persons, knowing or having reason to know or intending that these objects or techniques will be unlawfully employed for use in, or in the furtherance of a civil disorder; or any person who assembles with one or more other persons for the purpose of training with, practicing with, or being instructed in the use of any firearm, explosive, or destructive device, or technique capable of causing injury or death to persons, with the intent to cause or further a civil disorder, shall be punished by imprisonment in the county jail for not more than one year or by a fine of not more than one thousand dollars ($1,000), or by both that fine and imprisonment.

Nothing in this subdivision shall make unlawful any act of any peace officer or a member of the military forces of this state or of the United States, performed in the lawful course of his or her official duties.

(2) As used in this section:

(A) "Civil disorder" means any disturbance involving acts of violence which cause an immediate danger of or results in damage or injury to the property or person of any other individual.

(B) "Destructive device" has the same meaning as in Section 16460.

(C) "Explosive" has the same meaning as in Section 12000 of the Health and Safety Code.

(D) "Firearm" means any device designed to be used as a weapon, or which may readily be converted to a weapon, from which is expelled a projectile by the force of any explosion or other form of combustion, or the frame or receiver of this weapon.

(E) "Peace officer" means any peace officer or other officer having the powers of arrest of a peace officer, specified in Chapter 4.5 (commencing with Section 830) of Title 3 of Part 2.

(Amended by Stats. 2010, Ch. 178, Sec. 93. (SB 1115) Effective January 1, 2011. Operative January 1, 2012, by Sec. 107 of Ch. 178.)

ARTICLE 7. Interruption of Communication [11470 - 11482]

(Article 7 added by Stats. 2017, Ch. 322, Sec. 1.)

11470.

For the purposes of this article, the following terms have the following meanings:

(a) "Communication service" means any communication service that interconnects with the public switched telephone network and is required by the Federal Communications Commission to provide customers with 911 access to emergency services.

(b) "Government entity" means every local government, including a city, county, city and county, a transit, joint powers, special, or other district, the state, and every agency,

department, commission, board, bureau, or other political subdivision of the state, or any authorized agent thereof.

(c) "Interrupt communication service" means to knowingly or intentionally suspend, disconnect, interrupt, or disrupt a communication service to one or more particular customers or all customers in a geographical area.

(d) "Judicial officer" means a magistrate, judge, commissioner, referee, or any person appointed by a court to serve in one of these capacities, of a superior court.

(e) "Service provider" means a person or entity, including a government entity, that offers a communication service.

(Added by Stats. 2017, Ch. 322, Sec. 1. (AB 1034) Effective January 1, 2018.)

11471.

(a) Except as authorized by this article, no government entity, and no service provider acting at the request of a government entity, shall interrupt a communication service for either of the following purposes:

(1) To prevent the communication service from being used for an illegal purpose.

(2) To protect public health, safety, or welfare.

(b) A government entity may interrupt a communication service for a purpose stated in subdivision (a) in any of the following circumstances:

(1) The interruption is authorized by a court order pursuant to Section 11473.

(2) The government entity reasonably determines that (A) the interruption is required to address an extreme emergency situation that involves immediate danger of death or great bodily injury, (B) there is insufficient time, with due diligence, to first obtain a court order under Section 11473, and (C) the interruption meets the grounds for issuance of a court order under Section 11473. A government entity acting pursuant to this paragraph shall comply with Section 11475.

(3) Notwithstanding Section 591, 631, or 632, or Section 7906 of the Public Utilities Code, a supervising law enforcement official with jurisdiction may require that a service provider interrupt a communication service that is available to a person if (A) the law enforcement official has probable cause to believe that the person is holding hostages and is committing a crime, or is barricaded and is resisting apprehension through the use or threatened use of force, and (B) the purpose of the interruption is to prevent the person from communicating with anyone other than a peace officer or a person authorized by a peace officer. This paragraph does not authorize the interruption of communication service to a wireless device other than a wireless device used or available for use by the person or persons involved in a hostage or barricade situation.

(Added by Stats. 2017, Ch. 322, Sec. 1. (AB 1034) Effective January 1, 2018.)

11472.

(a) An application by a government entity for a court order authorizing the interruption of a communication service shall be made in writing upon the personal oath or affirmation of the chief executive of the government entity or his or her designee, to the presiding judge of the superior court or a judicial officer designated by the presiding judge for that purpose.

(b) Each application shall include all of the following information:

(1) The identity of the government entity making the application.

(2) A statement attesting to a review of the application and the circumstances in support of the application by the chief executive officer of the government entity making the application, or his or her designee. This statement shall state the name and office of the person who effected this review.

(3) A full and complete statement of the facts and circumstances relied on by the government entity to justify a reasonable belief that the order should be issued, including the facts and circumstances that support the statements made in paragraphs (4) to (7), inclusive.

(4) A statement that probable cause exists to believe that the communication service to be interrupted is being used or will be used for an unlawful purpose or to assist in a violation of the law. The statement shall expressly identify the unlawful purpose or violation of the law.

(5) A statement that immediate and summary action is needed to avoid serious, direct, and immediate danger to public health, safety, or welfare.

(6) A statement that the proposed interruption is narrowly tailored to the specific circumstances under which the order is made and would not interfere with more communication than is necessary to achieve the purposes of the order.

(7) A statement that the proposed interruption would leave open ample alternative means of communication.

(8) A statement that the government entity has considered the practical disadvantages of the proposed interruption, including any disruption of emergency communication service.

(9) A description of the scope and duration of the proposed interruption. The application shall clearly describe the specific communication service to be interrupted with sufficient detail as to customer, cell sector, central office, or geographical area affected.

(c) The judicial officer may require the applicant to furnish additional testimony or documentary evidence in support of an application for an order under this section.

(d) The judicial officer shall accept a facsimile copy of the signature of any person required to give a personal oath or affirmation pursuant to subdivision (a) as an original signature to the application.

(Added by Stats. 2017, Ch. 322, Sec. 1. (AB 1034) Effective January 1, 2018.)

11473.

Upon application made under Section 11472, the judicial officer may enter an ex parte order, as requested or modified, authorizing interruption of a communication service in the territorial jurisdiction in which the judicial officer is sitting, if the judicial officer determines, on the basis of the facts submitted by the applicant, that all of the following requirements are satisfied:

(a) There is probable cause that the communication service is being or will be used for an unlawful purpose or to assist in a violation of the law.

(b) Absent immediate and summary action to interrupt the communication service, serious, direct, and immediate danger to public health, safety, or welfare will result.

(c) The interruption of communication service is narrowly tailored to prevent unlawful infringement of speech that is protected by the First Amendment to the United States Constitution or Section 2 of Article I of the California Constitution, or a violation of any other rights under federal or state law.

(d) The interruption of a communication service would leave open ample alternative means of communication.

(Added by Stats. 2017, Ch. 322, Sec. 1. (AB 1034) Effective January 1, 2018.)

11474.

An order authorizing an interruption of a communication service shall include all of the following:

(a) A statement of the court's findings required by Section 11473.

(b) A clear description of the communication service to be interrupted, with specific detail as to the affected service, service provider, and customer or geographical area.

(c) A statement of the period of time during which the interruption is authorized. The order may provide for a fixed duration or require that the government end the interruption when it determines that the interruption is no longer reasonably necessary because the danger that justified the interruption has abated. If the judicial officer finds that probable cause exists that a particular communication service is being used or will be used as part of a continuing criminal enterprise, the court may order the permanent termination of that service and require that the terminated service not be referred to another communication service.

(d) A requirement that the government entity immediately serve notice on the service provider when the interruption is to cease.

(Added by Stats. 2017, Ch. 322, Sec. 1. (AB 1034) Effective January 1, 2018.)
11475.
A government entity that interrupts a communication service pursuant to paragraph (2) of subdivision (b) of Section 11471 shall take all of the following steps:
(a) Apply for a court order under Section 11472 without delay. If possible, the application shall be filed within six hours after commencement of the interruption. If that is not possible, the application shall be filed at the first reasonably available opportunity, but in no event later than 24 hours after commencement of an interruption of a communication service. If an application is filed more than six hours after commencement of an interruption of a communication service, the application shall include a declaration, made under penalty of perjury, stating the reason for the delay.
(b) Prepare a signed statement of intent to apply for a court order. The statement of intent shall clearly describe the extreme emergency situation and the specific communication service to be interrupted. If a government entity does not apply for a court order within six hours, the government entity shall submit a copy of the signed statement of intent to the court within six hours.
(c) Provide conspicuous notice of the application for a court order on the government entity's Internet Web site without delay, unless the circumstances that justify an interruption of a communication service without first obtaining a court order also justify not providing the notice.
(Added by Stats. 2017, Ch. 322, Sec. 1. (AB 1034) Effective January 1, 2018.)
11476.
(a) If an order issued pursuant to Section 11473 or a signed statement of intent prepared pursuant to Section 11475 would authorize the interruption of a communication service for all customers of the interrupted communication service within a geographical area, the government entity shall serve the order or statement on the Governor's Office of Emergency Services.
(b) The Governor's Office of Emergency Services shall have policy discretion on whether to request that the federal government authorize and effect the proposed interruption.
(Added by Stats. 2017, Ch. 322, Sec. 1. (AB 1034) Effective January 1, 2018.)
11477.
If an order issued pursuant to Section 11473 or a signed statement of intent prepared pursuant to Section 11475 is not governed by Section 11476, the government entity shall serve the order or statement on both of the following persons:
(a) The appropriate service provider's contact for receiving requests from law enforcement, including receipt of state or federal warrants, orders, or subpoenas.
(b) The affected customer, if the identity of the customer is known. When serving an affected customer, the government entity shall provide notice of the opportunity for judicial review under Section 11479.
(Added by Stats. 2017, Ch. 322, Sec. 1. (AB 1034) Effective January 1, 2018.)
11478.
(a) Good faith reliance by a service provider on a court order issued pursuant to Section 11473, a signed statement of intent prepared pursuant to Section 11475, or the instruction of a supervising law enforcement officer acting pursuant to paragraph (3) of subdivision (b) of Section 11471 shall constitute a complete defense for the service provider against any action brought as a result of the interruption of a communication service authorized by that court order, statement of intent, or instruction.
(b) A communications service provider shall designate a security employee and an alternate security employee, to provide all required assistance to law enforcement officials to carry out the purposes of this article.
(c) A service provider that intentionally interrupts communication service pursuant to this article shall comply with any rule or notification requirement of the Public Utilities Commission or Federal Communications Commission, or both, and any other applicable provision or requirement of state or federal law.
(Added by Stats. 2017, Ch. 322, Sec. 1. (AB 1034) Effective January 1, 2018.)
11479.
(a) A person whose communication service has been interrupted pursuant to this article may petition the superior court to contest the grounds for the interruption and restore the interrupted service.
(b) The remedy provided in this section is not exclusive. Other laws may provide a remedy for a person who is aggrieved by an interruption of a communication service authorized by this chapter.
(Added by Stats. 2017, Ch. 322, Sec. 1. (AB 1034) Effective January 1, 2018.)
11480.
The Legislature finds and declares that ensuring that California users of any communication service not have that service interrupted, and thereby be deprived of 911 access to emergency services or a means to engage in constitutionally protected expression, is a matter of statewide concern and not a municipal affair, as that term is used in Section 5 of Article XI of the California Constitution.
(Added by Stats. 2017, Ch. 322, Sec. 1. (AB 1034) Effective January 1, 2018.)
11481.
(a) This article does not apply to any of the following actions:
(1) The interruption of a communication service with the consent of the affected customer.
(2) The interruption of a communication service pursuant to a customer service agreement, contract, or tariff.
(3) The interruption of a communication service to protect the security of the communication network or other computing resources of a government entity or service provider.
(4) The interruption of a communication service to prevent unauthorized wireless communication by a prisoner in a state or local correctional facility, including a juvenile facility.
(5) The interruption of a communication service to transmit an emergency notice that includes, but is not limited to, an Amber Alert, a message transmitted through the federal Emergency Alert System, or a message transmitted through the federal Wireless Emergency Alert System.
(6) An interruption of a communication service pursuant to a statute that expressly authorizes an interruption of a communication service, including Sections 149 and 7099.10 of the Business and Professions Code and Sections 2876, 5322, and 5371.6 of the Public Utilities Code.
(7) An interruption of communication service that results from the execution of a search warrant.
(b) Nothing in this section provides authority for an action of a type listed in subdivision (a) or limits any remedy that may be available under law if an action of a type listed in subdivision (a) is taken unlawfully.
(Added by Stats. 2017, Ch. 322, Sec. 1. (AB 1034) Effective January 1, 2018.)
11482.
This article does not restrict, expand, or otherwise modify the authority of the Public Utilities Commission.
(Added by Stats. 2017, Ch. 322, Sec. 1. (AB 1034) Effective January 1, 2018.)

TITLE 1.5. STATEWIDE PROGRAMS OF EDUCATION, TRAINING, AND RESEARCH FOR LOCAL PUBLIC PROSECUTORS AND PUBLIC DEFENDERS [11500 - 11504]

(Title 1.5 added by Stats. 1982, Ch. 116, Sec. 1.)
11500.
The purpose of this title is to improve the administration of criminal justice by providing funding for statewide programs of education, training, and research for local public prosecutors and public defenders.
(Added by Stats. 1982, Ch. 116, Sec. 1. Effective March 16, 1982.)
11501.
(a) There is hereby established in the Office of Emergency Services, a program of financial assistance to provide for statewide programs of education, training, and research for local public prosecutors and public defenders. All funds made available to the office for the purposes of this chapter shall be administered and distributed by the Director of Emergency Services.
(b) The Director of Emergency Services is authorized to allocate and award funds to public agencies or private nonprofit organizations for purposes of establishing statewide programs of education, training, and research for public prosecutors and public defenders, which programs meet criteria established pursuant to Section 11502.
(Amended by Stats. 2013, Ch. 352, Sec. 423. (AB 1317) Effective September 26, 2013. Operative July 1, 2013, by Sec. 543 of Ch. 352.)
11502.
(a) Criteria for selection of education, training, and research programs for local public prosecutors and public defenders shall be developed by the Office of Emergency Services in consultation with an advisory group entitled the Prosecutors and Public Defenders Education and Training Advisory Committee.
(b) The Prosecutors and Public Defenders Education and Training Advisory Committee shall be composed of six local public prosecutors and six local public defender representatives, all of whom are appointed by the Director of Emergency Services, who shall provide staff services to the advisory committee. In appointing the members of the committee, the director shall invite the Attorney General, the State Public Defender, the Speaker of the Assembly, and the Senate President pro Tempore to participate as ex officio members of the committee.
(c) The Office of Emergency Services, in consultation with the advisory committee, shall develop specific guidelines including criteria for selection of organizations to provide education, training, and research services.
(d) In determining the equitable allocation of funds between prosecution and defense functions, the Office of Emergency Services and the advisory committee shall give consideration to the amount of local government expenditures on a statewide basis for the support of those functions.
(e) The administration of the overall program shall be performed by the Office of Emergency Services. The office may, out of any appropriation for this program, expend an amount not to exceed 7.5 percent for any fiscal year for those purposes.
(f) No funds appropriated pursuant to this title shall be used to support a legislative advocate.
(g) To the extent necessary to meet the requirements of the State Bar of California relating to certification of training for legal specialists, the executive director shall ensure that, where appropriate, all programs funded under this title are open to all members of the State Bar of California. The program guidelines established pursuant to subdivision (c) shall provide for the reimbursement of costs for all participants deemed eligible by the Office of Emergency Services, in conjunction with the Legal Training Advisory Committee, by means of course attendance.
(Amended by Stats. 2013, Ch. 352, Sec. 424. (AB 1317) Effective September 26, 2013. Operative July 1, 2013, by Sec. 543 of Ch. 352.)
11503.
There is hereby created in the State Treasury the Local Public Prosecutors and Public Defenders Training Fund for the support of the Prosecutors and Public Defenders Education and Training Program, established pursuant to this title.
(Added by Stats. 1986, Ch. 40, Sec. 1. Effective March 31, 1986.)
11504.
To the extent funds are appropriated from the Assessment Fund to the Local Public Prosecutors and Public Defenders Training Fund established pursuant to Section 11503, the Office of Emergency Services shall allocate financial resources for statewide programs of education, training, and research for local public prosecutors and public defenders.
(Amended by Stats. 2013, Ch. 352, Sec. 425. (AB 1317) Effective September 26, 2013. Operative July 1, 2013, by Sec. 543 of Ch. 352.)

TITLE 2. SENTENCE ENHANCEMENTS [12001 - 12022.95]

(Title 2 repealed and added by Stats. 2010, Ch. 711, Sec. 5.)
12001.
As used in this title, "firearm" has the meaning provided in subdivision (a) of Section 16520.
(Added by Stats. 2010, Ch. 711, Sec. 5. (SB 1080) Effective January 1, 2011. Operative January 1, 2012, by Sec. 10 of Ch. 711.)
12003.
If any section, subdivision, paragraph, subparagraph, sentence, clause, or phrase of this title or any other provision listed in Section 16580 is for any reason held to be unconstitutional, that decision shall not affect the validity of the remaining portions of this title or any other provision listed in Section 16580. The Legislature hereby declares that it would have passed this title and any other provision listed in Section 16580, and each section, subdivision, paragraph, subparagraph, sentence, clause, and phrase thereof, irrespective of the fact that any one or more other sections, subdivisions, paragraphs, subparagraphs, sentences, clauses, or phrases be declared unconstitutional.
(Amended (as added by Stats. 2010, Ch. 711) by Stats. 2011, Ch. 285, Sec. 24. (AB 1402) Effective January 1, 2012.)
12021.5.
(a) Every person who carries a loaded or unloaded firearm on his or her person, or in a vehicle, during the commission or attempted commission of any street gang crimes described in subdivision (a) or (b) of Section 186.22, shall, upon conviction of the felony or attempted felony, be punished by an additional term of imprisonment in the state prison for one, two, or three years. The court shall select the sentence enhancement that, in the court's discretion, best serves the interests of justice and shall state the reasons for its choice on the record at the time of sentence, in accordance with subdivision (d) of Section 1170.1.
(b) Every person who carries a loaded or unloaded firearm together with a detachable shotgun magazine, a detachable pistol magazine, a detachable magazine, or a belt-feeding device on his or her person, or in a vehicle, during the commission or attempted commission of any street gang crimes described in subdivision (a) or (b) of Section

186.22, shall, upon conviction of the felony or attempted felony, be punished by an additional term of imprisonment in the state prison for two, three, or four years. The court shall select the sentence enhancement that, in the court's discretion, best serves the interests of justice and shall state the reasons for its choice on the record at the time of sentence, in accordance with subdivision (d) of Section 1170.1.
(c) As used in this section, the following definitions shall apply:
(1) "Detachable magazine" means a device that is designed or redesigned to do all of the following:
(A) To be attached to a rifle that is designed or redesigned to fire ammunition.
(B) To be attached to, and detached from, a rifle that is designed or redesigned to fire ammunition.
(C) To feed ammunition continuously and directly into the loading mechanism of a rifle that is designed or redesigned to fire ammunition.
(2) "Detachable pistol magazine" means a device that is designed or redesigned to do all of the following:
(A) To be attached to a semiautomatic firearm that is not a rifle or shotgun that is designed or redesigned to fire ammunition.
(B) To be attached to, and detached from, a firearm that is not a rifle or shotgun that is designed or redesigned to fire ammunition.
(C) To feed ammunition continuously and directly into the loading mechanism of a firearm that is not a rifle or a shotgun that is designed or redesigned to fire ammunition.
(3) "Detachable shotgun magazine" means a device that is designed or redesigned to do all of the following:
(A) To be attached to a firearm that is designed or redesigned to fire a fixed shotgun shell through a smooth or rifled bore.
(B) To be attached to, and detached from, a firearm that is designed or redesigned to fire a fixed shotgun shell through a smooth bore.
(C) To feed fixed shotgun shells continuously and directly into the loading mechanism of a firearm that is designed or redesigned to fire a fixed shotgun shell.
(4) "Belt-feeding device" means a device that is designed or redesigned to continuously feed ammunition into the loading mechanism of a machinegun or a semiautomatic firearm.
(5) "Rifle" shall have the same meaning as specified in Section 17090.
(6) "Shotgun" shall have the same meaning as specified in Section 17190.
(d) This section shall remain in effect only until January 1, 2022, and as of that date is repealed, unless a later enacted statute, that is enacted before January 1, 2022, deletes or extends that date.
(Amended (as amended by Stats. 2016, Ch. 887, Sec. 11) by Stats. 2017, Ch. 561, Sec. 196. (AB 1516) Effective January 1, 2018. Repealed as of January 1, 2022, by its own provisions. See later operative version, as amended by Sec. 12 of Stats. 2016, Ch. 887.)

12021.5.

(a) Every person who carries a loaded or unloaded firearm on his or her person, or in a vehicle, during the commission or attempted commission of any street gang crimes described in subdivision (a) or (b) of Section 186.22, shall, upon conviction of the felony or attempted felony, be punished by an additional term of imprisonment pursuant to subdivision (h) of Section 1170 for one, two, or three years in the court's discretion. The court shall impose the middle term unless there are circumstances in aggravation or mitigation. The court shall state the reasons for its enhancement choice on the record at the time of sentence.
(b) Every person who carries a loaded or unloaded firearm together with a detachable shotgun magazine, a detachable pistol magazine, a detachable magazine, or a belt-feeding device on his or her person, or in a vehicle, during the commission or attempted commission of any street gang crimes described in subdivision (a) or (b) of Section 186.22, shall, upon conviction of the felony or attempted felony, be punished by an additional term of imprisonment in the state prison for two, three, or four years in the court's discretion. The court shall impose the middle term unless there are circumstances in aggravation or mitigation. The court shall state the reasons for its enhancement choice on the record at the time of sentence.
(c) As used in this section, the following definitions shall apply:
(1) "Detachable magazine" means a device that is designed or redesigned to do all of the following:
(A) To be attached to a rifle that is designed or redesigned to fire ammunition.
(B) To be attached to, and detached from, a rifle that is designed or redesigned to fire ammunition.
(C) To feed ammunition continuously and directly into the loading mechanism of a rifle that is designed or redesigned to fire ammunition.
(2) "Detachable pistol magazine" means a device that is designed or redesigned to do all of the following:
(A) To be attached to a semiautomatic firearm that is not a rifle or shotgun that is designed or redesigned to fire ammunition.
(B) To be attached to, and detached from, a firearm that is not a rifle or shotgun that is designed or redesigned to fire ammunition.
(C) To feed ammunition continuously and directly into the loading mechanism of a firearm that is not a rifle or a shotgun that is designed or redesigned to fire ammunition.
(3) "Detachable shotgun magazine" means a device that is designed or redesigned to do all of the following:
(A) To be attached to a firearm that is designed or redesigned to fire a fixed shotgun shell through a smooth or rifled bore.
(B) To be attached to, and detached from, a firearm that is designed or redesigned to fire a fixed shotgun shell through a smooth bore.
(C) To feed fixed shotgun shells continuously and directly into the loading mechanism of a firearm that is designed or redesigned to fire a fixed shotgun shell.
(4) "Belt-feeding device" means a device that is designed or redesigned to continuously feed ammunition into the loading mechanism of a machinegun or a semiautomatic firearm.
(5) "Rifle" shall have the same meaning as specified in Section 17090.
(6) "Shotgun" shall have the same meaning as specified in Section 17190.
(d) This section shall become operative on January 1, 2022.
(Amended (as amended by Stats. 2013, Ch. 508, Sec. 12) by Stats. 2016, Ch. 887, Sec. 12. (SB 1016) Effective January 1, 2017. Section operative January 1, 2022, by its own provisions.)

12022.

(a) (1) Except as provided in subdivisions (c) and (d), a person who is armed with a firearm in the commission of a felony or attempted felony shall be punished by an additional and consecutive term of imprisonment pursuant to subdivision (h) of Section 1170 for one year, unless the arming is an element of that offense. This additional term shall apply to a person who is a principal in the commission of a felony or attempted felony if one or more of the principals is armed with a firearm, whether or not the person is personally armed with a firearm.
(2) Except as provided in subdivision (c), and notwithstanding subdivision (d), if the firearm is an assault weapon, as defined in Section 30510 or 30515, or a machinegun, as defined in Section 16880, or a .50 BMG rifle, as defined in Section 30530, the additional and consecutive term described in this subdivision shall be three years imprisonment pursuant to subdivision (h) of Section 1170 whether or not the arming is an element of the offense of which the person was convicted. The additional term provided in this paragraph shall apply to any person who is a principal in the commission of a felony or attempted felony if one or more of the principals is armed with an assault weapon, machinegun, or a .50 BMG rifle, whether or not the person is personally armed with an assault weapon, machinegun, or a .50 BMG rifle.
(b) (1) A person who personally uses a deadly or dangerous weapon in the commission of a felony or attempted felony shall be punished by an additional and consecutive term of imprisonment in the state prison for one year, unless use of a deadly or dangerous weapon is an element of that offense.
(2) If the person described in paragraph (1) has been convicted of carjacking or attempted carjacking, the additional term shall be in the state prison for one, two, or three years.
(3) When a person is found to have personally used a deadly or dangerous weapon in the commission of a felony or attempted felony as provided in this subdivision and the weapon is owned by that person, the court shall order that the weapon be deemed a nuisance and disposed of in the manner provided in Sections 18000 and 18005.
(c) Notwithstanding the enhancement set forth in subdivision (a), a person who is personally armed with a firearm in the commission of a violation or attempted violation of Section 11351, 11351.5, 11352, 11366.5, 11366.6, 11378, 11378.5, 11379, 11379.5, or 11379.6 of the Health and Safety Code shall be punished by an additional and consecutive term of imprisonment pursuant to subdivision (h) of Section 1170 for three, four, or five years.
(d) Notwithstanding the enhancement set forth in subdivision (a), a person who is not personally armed with a firearm who, knowing that another principal is personally armed with a firearm, is a principal in the commission of an offense or attempted offense specified in subdivision (c), shall be punished by an additional and consecutive term of imprisonment pursuant to subdivision (h) of Section 1170 for one, two, or three years.
(e) For purposes of imposing an enhancement under Section 1170.1, the enhancements under this section shall count as a single enhancement.
(f) Notwithstanding any other provision of law, the court may strike the additional punishment for the enhancements provided in subdivision (c) or (d) in an unusual case where the interests of justice would best be served, if the court specifies on the record and enters into the minutes the circumstances indicating that the interests of justice would best be served by that disposition.
(Amended by Stats. 2013, Ch. 76, Sec. 166. (AB 383) Effective January 1, 2014.)

12022.1.

(a) For the purposes of this section only:
(1) "Primary offense" means a felony offense for which a person has been released from custody on bail or on his or her own recognizance prior to the judgment becoming final, including the disposition of any appeal, or for which release on bail or his or her own recognizance has been revoked. In cases where the court has granted a stay of execution of a county jail commitment or state prison commitment, "primary offense" also means a felony offense for which a person is out of custody during the period of time between the pronouncement of judgment and the time the person actually surrenders into custody or is otherwise returned to custody.
(2) "Secondary offense" means a felony offense alleged to have been committed while the person is released from custody for a primary offense.
(b) Any person arrested for a secondary offense that was alleged to have been committed while that person was released from custody on a primary offense shall be subject to a penalty enhancement of an additional two years, which shall be served consecutive to any other term imposed by the court.
(c) The enhancement allegation provided in subdivision (b) shall be pleaded in the information or indictment which alleges the secondary offense, or in the information or indictment of the primary offense if a conviction has already occurred in the secondary offense, and shall be proved as provided by law. The enhancement allegation may be pleaded in a complaint but need not be proved at the preliminary hearing or grand jury hearing.
(d) Whenever there is a conviction for the secondary offense and the enhancement is proved, and the person is sentenced on the secondary offense prior to the conviction of the primary offense, the imposition of the enhancement shall be stayed pending imposition of the sentence for the primary offense. The stay shall be lifted by the court hearing the primary offense at the time of sentencing for that offense and shall be recorded in the abstract of judgment. If the person is acquitted of the primary offense the stay shall be permanent.
(e) If the person is convicted of a felony for the primary offense, is sentenced to state prison for the primary offense, and is convicted of a felony for the secondary offense, any sentence for the secondary offense shall be consecutive to the primary sentence and the aggregate term shall be served in the state prison, even if the term for the secondary offense specifies imprisonment in county jail pursuant to subdivision (h) of Section 1170.
(f) If the person is convicted of a felony for the primary offense, is granted probation for the primary offense, and is convicted of a felony for the secondary offense, any sentence for the secondary offense shall be enhanced as provided in subdivision (b).
(g) If the primary offense conviction is reversed on appeal, the enhancement shall be suspended pending retrial of that felony. Upon retrial and reconviction, the enhancement shall be reimposed. If the person is no longer in custody for the secondary offense upon reconviction of the primary offense, the court may, at its discretion, reimpose the enhancement and order him or her recommitted to custody.
(Amended by Stats. 2013, Ch. 76, Sec. 167. (AB 383) Effective January 1, 2014.)

12022.2.

(a) A person who, while armed with a firearm in the commission or attempted commission of any felony, has in his or her immediate possession ammunition for the firearm designed primarily to penetrate metal or armor, shall, upon conviction of that felony or attempted felony, in addition and consecutive to the punishment prescribed for the felony or attempted felony, be punished by an additional term of 3, 4, or 10 years. The court shall select the sentence enhancement that, in the court's discretion, best serves the interests of justice and shall state the reasons for its choice on the record at the time of the sentence in accordance with subdivision (d) of Section 1170.1.
(b) A person who wears a body vest in the commission or attempted commission of a violent offense, as defined in Section 29905, shall, upon conviction of that felony or attempted felony, in addition and consecutive to the punishment prescribed for the felony or attempted felony of which he or she has been convicted, be punished by an additional term of one, two, or five years. The court shall select the sentence enhancement that, in the court's discretion, best serves the interests of justice and shall state the reasons for its choice on the record at the time of the sentence in accordance with subdivision (d) of Section 1170.1.
(c) As used in this section, "body vest" means any bullet-resistant material intended to provide ballistic and trauma protection for the wearer.
(d) This section shall remain in effect only until January 1, 2022, and as of that date is repealed, unless a later enacted statute, that is enacted before January 1, 2022, deletes or extends that date.
(Amended (as amended by Stats. 2016, Ch. 887, Sec. 13) by Stats. 2017, Ch. 561, Sec. 197. (AB 1516) Effective January 1, 2018. Repealed as of January 1, 2022, by its own provisions. See later operative version, as amended by Sec. 14 of Stats. 2016, Ch. 887.)

12022.2.

(a) Any person who, while armed with a firearm in the commission or attempted commission of any felony, has in his or her immediate possession ammunition for the firearm designed primarily to penetrate metal or armor, shall upon conviction of that felony or attempted felony, in addition and consecutive to the punishment prescribed for the felony or attempted felony, be punished by an additional term of 3, 4, or 10 years. The court shall order the middle term unless there are circumstances in aggravation or mitigation. The court shall state the reasons for its enhancement choice on the record at the time of the sentence.

(b) Any person who wears a body vest in the commission or attempted commission of a violent offense, as defined in Section 29905, shall, upon conviction of that felony or attempted felony, in addition and consecutive to the punishment prescribed for the felony or attempted felony of which he or she has been convicted, be punished by an additional term of one, two, or five years. The court shall order the middle term unless there are circumstances in aggravation or mitigation. The court shall state the reasons for its enhancement choice on the record at the time of the sentence.

(c) As used in this section, "body vest" means any bullet-resistant material intended to provide ballistic and trauma protection for the wearer.

(d) This section shall become operative on January 1, 2022.

(Amended (as amended by Stats. 2013, Ch. 508, Sec. 14) by Stats. 2016, Ch. 887, Sec. 14. (SB 1016) Effective January 1, 2017. Section operative January 1, 2022, by its own provisions.)

12022.3.

For each violation of Section 220 involving a specified sexual offense, or for each violation or attempted violation of Section 261, 262, 264.1, 286, 287, 288, or 289, or former Section 288a, and in addition to the sentence provided, any person shall receive the following:

(a) A 3-, 4-, or 10-year enhancement if the person uses a firearm or a deadly weapon in the commission of the violation.

(b) A one-, two-, or five-year enhancement if the person is armed with a firearm or a deadly weapon.

(Amended by Stats. 2018, Ch. 423, Sec. 113. (SB 1494) Effective January 1, 2019.)

12022.4.

(a) A person who, during the commission or attempted commission of a felony, furnishes or offers to furnish a firearm to another for the purpose of aiding, abetting, or enabling that person or any other person to commit a felony shall, in addition and consecutive to the punishment prescribed by the felony or attempted felony of which the person has been convicted, be punished by an additional term of one, two, or three years in the state prison. The court shall select the sentence enhancement that, in the court's discretion, best serves the interests of justice and shall state the reasons for its choice on the record at the time of the sentence, in accordance with subdivision (d) of Section 1170.1. The additional term provided in this section shall not be imposed unless the fact of the furnishing is charged in the accusatory pleading and admitted or found to be true by the trier of fact.

(b) This section shall remain in effect only until January 1, 2022, and as of that date is repealed, unless a later enacted statute, that is enacted before January 1, 2022, deletes or extends that date.

(Amended (as amended by Stats. 2016, Ch. 887, Sec. 15) by Stats. 2017, Ch. 561, Sec. 198. (AB 1516) Effective January 1, 2018. Repealed as of January 1, 2022, by its own provisions. See later operative version, as amended by Sec. 16 of Stats. 2016, Ch. 887.)

12022.4.

(a) Any person who, during the commission or attempted commission of a felony, furnishes or offers to furnish a firearm to another for the purpose of aiding, abetting, or enabling that person or any other person to commit a felony shall, in addition and consecutive to the punishment prescribed by the felony or attempted felony of which the person has been convicted, be punished by an additional term of one, two, or three years in the state prison. The court shall order the middle term unless there are circumstances in aggravation or mitigation. The court shall state the reasons for its enhancement choice on the record at the time of the sentence. The additional term provided in this section shall not be imposed unless the fact of the furnishing is charged in the accusatory pleading and admitted or found to be true by the trier of fact.

(b) This section shall become operative on January 1, 2022.

(Amended (as amended by Stats. 2013, Ch. 508, Sec. 16) by Stats. 2016, Ch. 887, Sec. 16. (SB 1016) Effective January 1, 2017. Section operative January 1, 2022, by its own provisions.)

12022.5.

(a) Except as provided in subdivision (b), any person who personally uses a firearm in the commission of a felony or attempted felony shall be punished by an additional and consecutive term of imprisonment in the state prison for 3, 4, or 10 years, unless use of a firearm is an element of that offense.

(b) Notwithstanding subdivision (a), any person who personally uses an assault weapon, as specified in Section 30510 or 30515, or a machinegun, as defined in Section 16880, in the commission of a felony or attempted felony, shall be punished by an additional and consecutive term of imprisonment in the state prison for 5, 6, or 10 years.

(c) The court may, in the interest of justice pursuant to Section 1385 and at the time of sentencing, strike or dismiss an enhancement otherwise required to be imposed by this section. The authority provided by this subdivision applies to any resentencing that may occur pursuant to any other law.

(d) Notwithstanding the limitation in subdivision (a) relating to being an element of the offense, the additional term provided by this section shall be imposed for any violation of Section 245 if a firearm is used, or for murder if the killing is perpetrated by means of shooting a firearm from a motor vehicle, intentionally at another person outside of the vehicle with the intent to inflict great bodily injury or death.

(e) When a person is found to have personally used a firearm, an assault weapon, a machinegun, or a .50 BMG rifle, in the commission of a felony or attempted felony as provided in this section and the firearm, assault weapon, machinegun, or a .50 BMG rifle, is owned by that person, the court shall order that the firearm be deemed a nuisance and disposed of in the manner provided in Sections 18000 and 18005.

(f) For purposes of imposing an enhancement under Section 1170.1, the enhancements under this section shall count as one single enhancement.

(Amended by Stats. 2017, Ch. 682, Sec. 1. (SB 620) Effective January 1, 2018.)

12022.53.

(a) This section applies to the following felonies:

(1) Section 187 (murder).

(2) Section 203 or 205 (mayhem).

(3) Section 207, 209, or 209.5 (kidnapping).

(4) Section 211 (robbery).

(5) Section 215 (carjacking).

(6) Section 220 (assault with intent to commit a specified felony).

(7) Subdivision (d) of Section 245 (assault with a firearm on a peace officer or firefighter).

(8) Section 261 or 262 (rape).

(9) Section 264.1 (rape or sexual penetration in concert).

(10) Section 286 (sodomy).

(11) Section 287 or former Section 288a (oral copulation).

(12) Section 288 or 288.5 (lewd act on a child).

(13) Section 289 (sexual penetration).

(14) Section 4500 (assault by a life prisoner).

(15) Section 4501 (assault by a prisoner).

(16) Section 4503 (holding a hostage by a prisoner).

(17) Any felony punishable by death or imprisonment in the state prison for life.

(18) Any attempt to commit a crime listed in this subdivision other than an assault.

(b) Notwithstanding any other provision of law, any person who, in the commission of a felony specified in subdivision (a), personally uses a firearm, shall be punished by an

additional and consecutive term of imprisonment in the state prison for 10 years. The firearm need not be operable or loaded for this enhancement to apply.

(c) Notwithstanding any other provision of law, any person who, in the commission of a felony specified in subdivision (a), personally and intentionally discharges a firearm, shall be punished by an additional and consecutive term of imprisonment in the state prison for 20 years.

(d) Notwithstanding any other provision of law, any person who, in the commission of a felony specified in subdivision (a), Section 246, or subdivision (c) or (d) of Section 26100, personally and intentionally discharges a firearm and proximately causes great bodily injury, as defined in Section 12022.7, or death, to any person other than an accomplice, shall be punished by an additional and consecutive term of imprisonment in the state prison for 25 years to life.

(e) (1) The enhancements provided in this section shall apply to any person who is a principal in the commission of an offense if both of the following are pled and proved:

(A) The person violated subdivision (b) of Section 186.22.

(B) Any principal in the offense committed any act specified in subdivision (b), (c), or (d).

(2) An enhancement for participation in a criminal street gang pursuant to Chapter 11 (commencing with Section 186.20) of Title 7 of Part 1 shall not be imposed on a person in addition to an enhancement imposed pursuant to this subdivision, unless the person personally used or personally discharged a firearm in the commission of the offense.

(f) Only one additional term of imprisonment under this section shall be imposed per person for each crime. If more than one enhancement per person is found true under this section, the court shall impose upon that person the enhancement that provides the longest term of imprisonment. An enhancement involving a firearm specified in Section 12021.5, 12022, 12022.3, 12022.4, 12022.5, or 12022.55 shall not be imposed on a person in addition to an enhancement imposed pursuant to this section. An enhancement for great bodily injury as defined in Section 12022.7, 12022.8, or 12022.9 shall not be imposed on a person in addition to an enhancement imposed pursuant to subdivision (d).

(g) Notwithstanding any other provision of law, probation shall not be granted to, nor shall the execution or imposition of sentence be suspended for, any person found to come within the provisions of this section.

(h) The court may, in the interest of justice pursuant to Section 1385 and at the time of sentencing, strike or dismiss an enhancement otherwise required to be imposed by this section. The authority provided by this subdivision applies to any resentencing that may occur pursuant to any other law.

(i) The total amount of credits awarded pursuant to Article 2.5 (commencing with Section 2930) of Chapter 7 of Title 1 of Part 3 or pursuant to Section 4019 or any other provision of law shall not exceed 15 percent of the total term of imprisonment imposed on a defendant upon whom a sentence is imposed pursuant to this section.

(j) For the penalties in this section to apply, the existence of any fact required under subdivision (b), (c), or (d) shall be alleged in the accusatory pleading and either admitted by the defendant in open court or found to be true by the trier of fact. When an enhancement specified in this section has been admitted or found to be true, the court shall impose punishment for that enhancement pursuant to this section rather than imposing punishment authorized under any other provision of law, unless another enhancement provides for a greater penalty or a longer term of imprisonment.

(k) When a person is found to have used or discharged a firearm in the commission of an offense that includes an allegation pursuant to this section and the firearm is owned by that person, a coparticipant, or a coconspirator, the court shall order that the firearm be deemed a nuisance and disposed of in the manner provided in Sections 18000 and 18005.

(l) The enhancements specified in this section shall not apply to the lawful use or discharge of a firearm by a public officer, as provided in Section 196, or by any person in lawful self-defense, lawful defense of another, or lawful defense of property, as provided in Sections 197, 198, and 198.5.

(Amended by Stats. 2018, Ch. 423, Sec. 114. (SB 1494) Effective January 1, 2019.)

12022.55.

Notwithstanding Section 12022.5, any person who, with the intent to inflict great bodily injury or death, inflicts great bodily injury, as defined in Section 12022.7, or causes the death of a person, other than an occupant of a motor vehicle, as a result of discharging a firearm from a motor vehicle in the commission of a felony or attempted felony, shall be punished by an additional and consecutive term of imprisonment in the state prison for 5, 6, or 10 years.

(Repealed and added by Stats. 2010, Ch. 711, Sec. 5. (SB 1080) Effective January 1, 2011. Operative January 1, 2012, by Sec. 10 of Ch. 711.)

12022.7.

(a) Any person who personally inflicts great bodily injury on any person other than an accomplice in the commission of a felony or attempted felony shall be punished by an additional and consecutive term of imprisonment in the state prison for three years.

(b) Any person who personally inflicts great bodily injury on any person other than an accomplice in the commission of a felony or attempted felony which causes the victim to become comatose due to brain injury or to suffer paralysis of a permanent nature shall be punished by an additional and consecutive term of imprisonment in the state prison for five years. As used in this subdivision, "paralysis" means a major or complete loss of motor function resulting from injury to the nervous system or to a muscular mechanism.

(c) Any person who personally inflicts great bodily injury on a person who is 70 years of age or older, other than an accomplice, in the commission of a felony or attempted felony shall be punished by an additional and consecutive term of imprisonment in the state prison for five years.

(d) Any person who personally inflicts great bodily injury on a child under the age of five years in the commission of a felony or attempted felony shall be punished by an additional and consecutive term of imprisonment in the state prison for four, five, or six years.

(e) Any person who personally inflicts great bodily injury under circumstances involving domestic violence in the commission of a felony or attempted felony shall be punished by an additional and consecutive term of imprisonment in the state prison for three, four, or five years. As used in this subdivision, "domestic violence" has the meaning provided in subdivision (b) of Section 13700.

(f) As used in this section, "great bodily injury" means a significant or substantial physical injury.

(g) This section shall not apply to murder or manslaughter or a violation of Section 451 or 452. Subdivisions (a), (b), (c), and (d) shall not apply if infliction of great bodily injury is an element of the offense.

(h) The court shall impose the additional terms of imprisonment under either subdivision (a), (b), (c), or (d), but may not impose more than one of those terms for the same offense.

(Amended (as added by Stats. 2010, Ch. 711, Sec. 5) by Stats. 2011, Ch. 296, Sec. 226. (AB 1023) Effective January 1, 2012.)

12022.75.

(a) Except as provided in subdivision (b), any person who, for the purpose of committing a felony, administers by injection, inhalation, ingestion, or any other means, any controlled substance listed in Section 11054, 11055, 11056, 11057, or 11058 of the Health and Safety Code, against the victim's will by means of force, violence, or fear of immediate and unlawful bodily injury to the victim or another person, shall, in addition and consecutive to the penalty provided for the felony or attempted felony of which he or she has been convicted, be punished by an additional term of three years.

(b) (1) Any person who, in the commission or attempted commission of any offense specified in paragraph (2), administers any controlled substance listed in Section 11054, 11055, 11056, 11057, or 11058 of the Health and Safety Code to the victim shall be punished by an additional and consecutive term of imprisonment in the state prison for five years.
(2) This subdivision shall apply to the following offenses:
(A) Rape, in violation of paragraph (3) or (4) of subdivision (a) of Section 261.
(B) Sodomy, in violation of subdivision (f) or (i) of Section 286.
(C) Oral copulation, in violation of subdivision (f) or (i) of Section 287 or of former Section 288a.
(D) Sexual penetration, in violation of subdivision (d) or (e) of Section 289.
(E) Any offense specified in subdivision (c) of Section 667.61.
(Amended by Stats. 2018, Ch. 423, Sec. 115. (SB 1494) Effective January 1, 2019. Note: Section 12022.75 was amended on Nov. 7, 2006, by initiative Prop. 83.)
12022.8.
Any person who inflicts great bodily injury, as defined in Section 12022.7, on any victim in a violation of Section 220 involving a specified sexual offense, or a violation or attempted violation of paragraph (2), (3), or (6) of subdivision (a) of Section 261, paragraph (1) or (4) of subdivision (a) of Section 262, Section 264.1, subdivision (b) of Section 288, subdivision (a) of Section 289, or sodomy or oral copulation by force, violence, duress, menace, or fear of immediate and unlawful bodily injury on the victim or another person as provided in Section 286 or 287, or former Section 288a, shall receive a five-year enhancement for each violation in addition to the sentence provided for the felony conviction.
(Amended by Stats. 2018, Ch. 423, Sec. 116. (SB 1494) Effective January 1, 2019.)
12022.85.
(a) Any person who violates one or more of the offenses listed in subdivision (b) with knowledge that he or she has acquired immune deficiency syndrome (AIDS) or with the knowledge that he or she carries antibodies of the human immunodeficiency virus at the time of the commission of those offenses shall receive a three-year enhancement for each violation in addition to the sentence provided under those sections.
(b) Subdivision (a) applies to the following crimes:
(1) Rape in violation of Section 261.
(2) Unlawful intercourse with a person under 18 years of age in violation of Section 261.5.
(3) Rape of a spouse in violation of Section 262.
(4) Sodomy in violation of Section 286.
(5) Oral copulation in violation of Section 287 or former Section 288a.
(c) For purposes of proving the knowledge requirement of this section, the prosecuting attorney may use test results received under subdivision (c) of Section 1202.1 or subdivision (g) of Section 1202.6.
(Amended by Stats. 2018, Ch. 423, Sec. 117. (SB 1494) Effective January 1, 2019.)
12022.9.
Any person who, during the commission of a felony or attempted felony, knows or reasonably should know that the victim is pregnant, and who, with intent to inflict injury, and without the consent of the woman, personally inflicts injury upon a pregnant woman that results in the termination of the pregnancy shall be punished by an additional and consecutive term of imprisonment in the state prison for five years. The additional term provided in this subdivision shall not be imposed unless the fact of that injury is charged in the accusatory pleading and admitted or found to be true by the trier of fact.
Nothing in this section shall be construed as affecting the applicability of subdivision (a) of Section 187.
(Amended (as amended by Stats. 2011, Ch. 15, Sec. 510) by Stats. 2011, Ch. 39, Sec. 62. (AB 117) Effective June 30, 2011. Amending action (succeeding the addition by Stats. 2010, Ch. 711) operative October 1, 2011, pursuant to Secs. 68 and 69 of Ch. 39. Section operative January 1, 2012, pursuant to Stats. 2010, Ch. 711, Sec. 10.)
12022.95.
Any person convicted of a violation of Section 273a, who under circumstances or conditions likely to produce great bodily harm or death, willfully causes or permits any child to suffer, or inflicts thereon unjustifiable physical pain or injury that results in death, or having the care or custody of any child, under circumstances likely to produce great bodily harm or death, willfully causes or permits that child to be injured or harmed, and that injury or harm results in death, shall receive a four-year enhancement for each violation, in addition to the sentence provided for that conviction. Nothing in this paragraph shall be construed as affecting the applicability of subdivision (a) of Section 187 or Section 192. This section shall not apply unless the allegation is included within an accusatory pleading and admitted by the defendant or found to be true by the trier of fact.
(Repealed and added by Stats. 2010, Ch. 711, Sec. 5. (SB 1080) Effective January 1, 2011. Operative January 1, 2012, by Sec. 10 of Ch. 711.)

TITLE 3. CRIMINAL STATISTICS [13000 - 13326]

(Title 3 added by Stats. 1955, Ch. 1128.)

CHAPTER 1. Department Of Justice [13000 - 13023]

(Heading of Chapter 1 amended by Stats. 1986, Ch. 248, Sec. 169.)

ARTICLE 1. Duties of the Department [13000 - 13014]
(Heading of Article 1 renumbered from Article 2 by Stats. 1986, Ch. 248, Sec. 170.)
13000.
(a) All statewide automated fingerprint identification systems shall be maintained by the Department of Justice. For purposes of this section, "automated fingerprint identification system" means electronic comparison of fingerprints to a data base of known persons.
(b) Any state agency is exempted from this section if the agency's director finds that the automated identification system needed to meet programmatic requirements is less costly than an identical system available through an interagency agreement with the Department of Justice, or is not provided by the Department of Justice.
(c) Information contained in these systems shall be released to state agencies only on a need-to-know basis pursuant to any of the following:
(1) Statutory authorization to the extent permitted by federal law.
(2) A court order or decision that requires release of the information.
(3) An interagency agreement with the Department of Justice to develop and operate a system.
(d) The department may charge a fee to be paid by the agency for the actual cost of supporting the service.
(Added by Stats. 1994, Ch. 875, Sec. 1. Effective January 1, 1995.)
13010.
It shall be the duty of the department:
(a) To collect data necessary for the work of the department from all persons and agencies mentioned in Section 13020 and from any other appropriate source.

(b) To prepare and distribute to all those persons and agencies cards, forms, or electronic means used in reporting data to the department. The cards, forms, or electronic means may, in addition to other items, include items of information needed by federal bureaus or departments engaged in the development of national and uniform criminal statistics.
(c) To recommend the form and content of records that must be kept by those persons and agencies in order to ensure the correct reporting of data to the department.
(d) To instruct those persons and agencies in the installation, maintenance, and use of those records and in the reporting of data therefrom to the department.
(e) To process, tabulate, analyze, and interpret the data collected from those persons and agencies.
(f) To supply, at their request, to federal bureaus or departments engaged in the collection of national criminal statistics data they need from this state.
(g) To make available to the public, through the department's OpenJustice Web portal, information relating to criminal statistics, to be updated at least once per year, and to present at other times as the Attorney General may approve reports on special aspects of criminal statistics. A sufficient number of copies of a downloadable summary of this information shall be annually prepared to enable the Attorney General to send a copy to the Governor and to all public officials in the state dealing with criminals and to distribute them generally in channels where they will add to the public enlightenment. This subdivision shall not be construed to require more frequent reporting by local agencies than what is required by any other law.
(h) To periodically review the requirements of units of government using criminal justice statistics, and to make recommendations for changes it deems necessary in the design of criminal justice statistics systems, including new techniques of collection and processing made possible by automation.
(i) To evaluate, on an annual basis, the progress of California's transition from summary crime reporting to incident-based crime reporting, in alignment with the federal National Incident-Based Reporting System, and report its findings to the Legislature annually through 2019, pursuant to Section 9795 of the Government Code.
(Amended by Stats. 2016, Ch. 418, Sec. 5. (AB 2524) Effective January 1, 2017.)
13010.5.
(a) The department shall collect data pertaining to the juvenile justice system for criminal history and statistical purposes. This information shall serve to assist the department, through its bureau whose mission is to protect the rights of children, in complying with the reporting requirement of paragraphs (3) and (4) of subdivision (a) of Section 13012, measuring the extent of juvenile delinquency, determining the need for, and effectiveness of, relevant legislation, and identifying long-term trends in juvenile delinquency. Any data collected pursuant to this section may include criminal history information that may be used by the department to comply with the requirements of Section 602.5 of the Welfare and Institutions Code.
(b) Statistical data collected pursuant to this section shall be made available to the public through the OpenJustice Web portal. The department may make available data collected pursuant to this section in the same manner as data collected pursuant to Section 13202.
(Amended by Stats. 2016, Ch. 418, Sec. 6. (AB 2524) Effective January 1, 2017.)
13011.
The department may serve as statistical and research agency to the Department of Corrections, the Board of Prison Terms, the Board of Corrections, the Department of the Youth Authority, and the Youthful Offender Parole Board.
(Amended by Stats. 1979, Ch. 860.)
13012.
(a) The information published on the OpenJustice Web portal pursuant to Section 13010 shall contain statistics showing all of the following:
(1) The amount and the types of offenses known to the public authorities.
(2) The personal and social characteristics of criminals and delinquents.
(3) The administrative actions taken by law enforcement, judicial, penal, and correctional agencies or institutions, including those in the juvenile justice system, in dealing with criminals or delinquents.
(4) The administrative actions taken by law enforcement, prosecutorial, judicial, penal, and correctional agencies or institutions, including those in the juvenile justice system, in dealing with minors who are the subject of a petition or hearing in the juvenile court to transfer their case to the jurisdiction of an adult criminal court or whose cases are directly filed or otherwise initiated in an adult criminal court.
(5) (A) The total number of each of the following:
(i) Civilian complaints received by law enforcement agencies under Section 832.5.
(ii) Civilian complaints alleging criminal conduct of either a felony or a misdemeanor.
(iii) Civilian complaints alleging racial or identity profiling, as defined in subdivision (e) of Section 13519.4. These statistics shall be disaggregated by the specific type of racial or identity profiling alleged, including, but not limited to, based on a consideration of race, color, ethnicity, national origin, religion, gender identity or expression, sexual orientation, or mental or physical disability.
(B) The statistics reported pursuant to this paragraph shall provide, for each category of complaint identified under subparagraph (A), the number of complaints within each of the following disposition categories:
(i) "Sustained," which means that the investigation disclosed sufficient evidence to prove the truth of allegation in the complaint by preponderance of the evidence.
(ii) "Exonerated," which means that the investigation clearly established that the actions of the personnel that formed the basis of the complaint are not a violation of law or agency policy.
(iii) "Not sustained," which means that the investigation failed to disclose sufficient evidence to clearly prove or disprove the allegation in the complaint.
(iv) "Unfounded," which means that the investigation clearly established that the allegation is not true.
(C) The reports under subparagraphs (A) and (B) shall be made available to the public and disaggregated for each individual law enforcement agency.
(b) The department shall give adequate interpretation of the statistics and present the information so that it may be of value in guiding the policies of the Legislature and of those in charge of the apprehension, prosecution, and treatment of criminals and delinquents, or those concerned with the prevention of crime and delinquency. This interpretation shall be presented in clear and informative formats on the OpenJustice Web portal. The Web portal shall also include statistics that are comparable with national uniform criminal statistics published by federal bureaus or departments.
(c) Each year, on an annual basis, the Racial and Identity Profiling Advisory Board (RIPA), established pursuant to paragraph (1) of subdivision (j) of Section 13519.4, shall analyze the statistics reported pursuant to subparagraphs (A) and (B) of paragraph (5) of subdivision (a) of this section. RIPA's analysis of the complaints shall be incorporated into its annual report as required by paragraph (3) of subdivision (j) of Section 13519.4 and shall be published on the OpenJustice Web portal. The reports shall not disclose the identity of peace officers.
(Amended by Stats. 2017, Ch. 328, Sec. 2. (AB 1518) Effective January 1, 2018.)
13012.5.
(a) The annual report published by the department under Section 13010 shall, in regard to the contents required by paragraph (4) of subdivision (a) of Section 13012, include the following statewide information:
(1) The annual number of fitness hearings held in the juvenile courts under Section 707 of the Welfare and Institutions Code, and the outcomes of those hearings including orders to remand to adult criminal court, cross-referenced with information about the

age, gender, ethnicity, and offense of the minors whose cases are the subject of those fitness hearings.
(2) The annual number of minors whose cases are filed directly in adult criminal court under Sections 602.5 and 707 of the Welfare and Institutions Code, cross-referenced with information about the age, gender, ethnicity, and offense of the minors whose cases are filed directly to the adult criminal court.
(3) The outcomes of cases involving minors who are prosecuted in adult criminal courts, regardless of how adult court jurisdiction was initiated, including whether the minor was acquitted or convicted, or whether the case was dismissed and returned to juvenile court, including sentencing outcomes, cross-referenced with the age, gender, ethnicity, and offense of the minors subject to these court actions.
(b) The department's annual report published under Section 13010 shall include the information described in paragraph (4) of subdivision (a) of Section 13012, as further delineated by this section, beginning with the report due on July 1, 2003, for the preceding calendar year.
(Amended by Stats. 2016, Ch. 99, Sec. 6. (AB 1953) Effective January 1, 2017.)
13012.6.
The data published by the department on the OpenJustice Web portal pursuant to Section 13010 shall include information concerning arrests for violations of Section 530.5.
(Amended by Stats. 2016, Ch. 418, Sec. 8. (AB 2524) Effective January 1, 2017.)
13012.8.
The annual report published by the department pursuant to Section 13010 shall include information concerning arrests for violations of Section 597.
(Added by Stats. 2016, Ch. 237, Sec. 1. (SB 1200) Effective January 1, 2017.)
13013.
The department shall maintain a data set, updated annually, that contains the number of crimes reported, number of clearances, and clearance rates in California as reported by individual law enforcement agencies. The data set shall be made available through the OpenJustice Web portal. This section shall not be construed to require reporting any crimes other than those required by Section 13012.
(Amended by Stats. 2016, Ch. 418, Sec. 9. (AB 2524) Effective January 1, 2017.)
13014.
(a) The Department of Justice shall perform the following duties concerning the investigation and prosecution of homicide cases:
(1) Collect information, as specified in subdivision (b), on all persons who are the victims of, and all persons who are charged with, homicide.
(2) Adopt and distribute, as a written form or by electronic means, to all state and governmental entities that are responsible for the investigation and prosecution of homicide cases, forms that will include information to be provided to the department pursuant to subdivision (b).
(3) Compile, collate, index, and maintain an electronic file of the information required by subdivision (b). The file shall be available to the general public during the normal business hours of the department, as well as on the OpenJustice Web portal, and the department shall at least annually update the information required by this section, which shall also be available to the general public.
The department shall perform the duties specified in this subdivision within its existing budget.
(b) Every state or local governmental entity responsible for the investigation and prosecution of a homicide case shall provide the department with demographic information about the victim and the person or persons charged with the crime, including age, gender, race, and ethnic background.
(Amended by Stats. 2016, Ch. 418, Sec. 10. (AB 2524) Effective January 1, 2017.)

ARTICLE 2. Duties of Public Agencies and Officers [13020 - 13023]

(Heading of Article 2 renumbered from Article 3 by Stats. 1986, Ch. 248, Sec. 171.)
13020.
It shall be the duty of every city marshal, chief of police, railroad and steamship police, sheriff, coroner, district attorney, city attorney and city prosecutor having criminal jurisdiction, probation officer, county board of parole commissioners, work furlough administrator, the Department of Justice, Health and Welfare Agency, Department of Corrections, Department of Youth Authority, Youthful Offender Parole Board, Board of Prison Terms, State Department of Health, Department of Benefit Payments, State Fire Marshal, Liquor Control Administrator, constituent agencies of the State Department of Investment, and every other person or agency dealing with crimes or criminals or with delinquency or delinquents, when requested by the Attorney General:
(a) To install and maintain records needed for the correct reporting of statistical data required by him or her.
(b) To report statistical data to the department at those times and in the manner that the Attorney General prescribes.
(c) To give to the Attorney General, or his or her accredited agent, access to statistical data for the purpose of carrying out this title.
(Amended by Stats. 1996, Ch. 872, Sec. 126. Effective January 1, 1997.)
13021.
Local law enforcement agencies shall report to the Department of Justice such information as the Attorney General may by regulation require relative to misdemeanor violations of Chapter 7.5 (commencing with Section 311) of Title 9 of Part 1 of this code.
(Amended by Stats. 1972, Ch. 1377.)
13022.
Each sheriff and chief of police shall annually furnish the Department of Justice, in the manner prescribed by the Attorney General, a report of all justifiable homicides committed in his or her jurisdiction. In cases where both a sheriff and chief of police would be required to report a justifiable homicide under this section, only the chief of police shall report the homicide.
(Amended by Stats. 2004, Ch. 405, Sec. 21. Effective January 1, 2005.)
13023.
(a) Subject to the availability of adequate funding, the Attorney General shall direct local law enforcement agencies to report to the Department of Justice, in a manner to be prescribed by the Attorney General, any information that may be required relative to hate crimes. This information may include any general orders or formal policies on hate crimes and the hate crime pamphlet required pursuant to Section 422.92.
(b) On or before July 1 of each year, the Department of Justice shall update the OpenJustice Web portal with the information obtained from local law enforcement agencies pursuant to this section. The department shall submit its analysis of this information to the Legislature in the manner described in subdivision (g) of Section 13010.
(c) For purposes of this section, "hate crime" has the same meaning as in Section 422.55.
(Amended by Stats. 2016, Ch. 418, Sec. 11. (AB 2524) Effective January 1, 2017.)

CHAPTER 1.5. Reports to the Bureau of Livestock Identification [13050 - 13051]

(Chapter 1.5 added by Stats. 1994, Ch. 431, Sec. 3.)
13050.
Each sheriff or other officer to whom a complaint that relates to the loss or theft of any equine animal is made shall, in a timely manner, transmit to the Bureau of Livestock Identification a report pursuant to Section 24104 of the Food and Agricultural Code.
(Added by Stats. 1994, Ch. 431, Sec. 3. Effective January 1, 1995.)
13051.
The Bureau of Livestock Identification shall compile a report on information received pursuant to Section 24104 of the Food and Agricultural Code. The bureau shall distribute the report to all county sheriffs' departments in a timely manner.
(Added by Stats. 1994, Ch. 431, Sec. 3. Effective January 1, 1995.)

CHAPTER 2. Criminal Offender Record Information [13100 - 13326]

(Chapter 2 added by Stats. 1973, Ch. 992.)

ARTICLE 1. Legislative Findings and Definitions [13100 - 13104]

(Article 1 added by Stats. 1973, Ch. 992.)
13100.
The Legislature finds and declares as follows:
(a) That the criminal justice agencies in this state require, for the performance of their official duties, accurate and reasonably complete criminal offender record information.
(b) That the Legislature and other governmental policymaking or policy-researching bodies, and criminal justice agency management units require greatly improved aggregate information for the performance of their duties.
(c) That policing agencies and courts require speedy access to information concerning all felony and selected misdemeanor arrests and final dispositions of such cases.
(d) That criminal justice agencies may require regular access to detailed criminal histories relating to any felony arrest that is followed by the filing of a complaint.
(e) That, in order to achieve the above improvements, the recording, reporting, storage, analysis, and dissemination of criminal offender record information in this state must be made more uniform and efficient, and better controlled and coordinated.
(Added by Stats. 1973, Ch. 992.)
13100.1.
(a) The Attorney General shall appoint an advisory committee to the California-Criminal Index and Identification (Cal-CII) system to assist in the ongoing management of the system with respect to operating policies, criminal records content, and records retention. The committee shall serve at the pleasure of the Attorney General, without compensation, except for reimbursement of necessary expenses.
(b) The committee shall consist of the following representatives:
(1) One representative from the California Police Chiefs' Association.
(2) One representative from the California Peace Officers' Association.
(3) Three representatives from the California State Sheriffs' Association.
(4) One trial judge appointed by the Judicial Council.
(5) One representative from the California District Attorneys Association.
(6) One representative from the California Court Clerks' Association.
(7) One representative from the Office of Emergency Services.
(8) One representative from the Chief Probation Officers' Association.
(9) One representative from the Department of Corrections and Rehabilitation.
(10) One representative from the Department of the California Highway Patrol.
(11) One member of the public, appointed by the Senate Committee on Rules, who is knowledgeable and experienced in the process of utilizing background clearances.
(12) One member of the public, appointed by the Speaker of the Assembly, who is knowledgeable and experienced in the process of utilizing background clearances.
(Amended by Stats. 2013, Ch. 352, Sec. 426. (AB 1317) Effective September 26, 2013. Operative July 1, 2013, by Sec. 543 of Ch. 352.)
13100.2.
(a) The designee of the Attorney General shall serve as chair of the committee.
(b) The Department of Justice shall provide staff and support for the committee.
(c) The committee shall meet at least twice annually. Subcommittees shall be formed and meet as necessary. All meetings shall be open to the public and reports shall be made available to the Legislature and other interested parties.
(Added by Stats. 1998, Ch. 841, Sec. 2. Effective January 1, 1999.)
13101.
As used in this chapter, "criminal justice agencies" are those agencies at all levels of government which perform as their principal functions, activities which either:
(a) Relate to the apprehension, prosecution, adjudication, incarceration, or correction of criminal offenders; or
(b) Relate to the collection, storage, dissemination or usage of criminal offender record information.
(Added by Stats. 1973, Ch. 992.)
13102.
As used in this chapter, "criminal offender record information" means records and data compiled by criminal justice agencies for purposes of identifying criminal offenders and of maintaining as to each such offender a summary of arrests, pretrial proceedings, the nature and disposition of criminal charges, sentencing, incarceration, rehabilitation, and release.
Such information shall be restricted to that which is recorded as the result of an arrest, detention, or other initiation of criminal proceedings or of any consequent proceedings related thereto. It shall be understood to include, where appropriate, such items for each person arrested as the following:
(a) Personal indentification.
(b) The fact, date, and arrest charge; whether the individual was subsequently released and, if so, by what authority and upon what terms.
(c) The fact, date, and results of any pretrial proceedings.
(d) The fact, date, and results of any trial or proceeding, including any sentence or penalty.
(e) The fact, date, and results of any direct or collateral review of that trial or proceeding; the period and place of any confinement, including admission, release; and, where appropriate, readmission and rerelease dates.
(f) The fact, date, and results of any release proceedings.
(g) The fact, date, and authority of any act of pardon or clemency.
(h) The fact and date of any formal termination to the criminal justice process as to that charge or conviction.
(i) The fact, date, and results of any proceeding revoking probation or parole.
It shall not include intelligence, analytical, and investigative reports and files, nor statistical records and reports in which individuals are not identified and from which their identities are not ascertainable.
(Added by Stats. 1973, Ch. 992.)
13103.
Notwithstanding any other provisions of law relating to retention of public records, any criminal justice agency may cause the original records filed pursuant to this chapter to be destroyed if all of the following requirements are met:
(a) The records have been reproduced onto microfilm or optical disk, or by any other techniques which do not permit additions, deletions, or changes to the original document.

(b) If the records have been reproduced onto optical disk, at least one year has elapsed since the date of registration of the records.

(c) The nonerasable storage medium used meets the minimum standards recommended by the National Institute of Standards and Technology for permanent record purposes.

(d) Adequate provisions are made to ensure that the nonerasable storage medium reflects additions or corrections to the records.

(e) A copy of the nonerasable storage medium is maintained in a manner which permits it to be used for all purposes served by the original record.

(f) A copy of the nonerasable storage medium has been stored at a separate physical location in a place and manner which will reasonably assure its preservation indefinitely against loss or destruction.

(Added by Stats. 1989, Ch. 257, Sec. 5.)

13104.

Any certified reproduction of any record stored on a nonerasable storage medium under the provisions of this chapter shall be deemed to be a certification of the original record.

(Added by Stats. 1989, Ch. 257, Sec. 6.)

ARTICLE 2. Recording Information [13125 - 13128]
(Article 2 added by Stats. 1973, Ch. 992.)

13125.

All basic information stored in state or local criminal offender record information systems shall be recorded, when applicable and available, in the form of the following standard data elements:

The following personal identification data:
Name—(full name)
Aliases
Monikers
Race
Sex
Date of birth
Place of birth (state or country)
Height
Weight
Hair color
Eye color
CII number
FBI number
Social security number
California operator's license number
Fingerprint classification number
Henry
NCIC
Address
The following arrest data:
Arresting agency
Booking number
Date of arrest
Offenses charged
Statute citations
Literal descriptions
Police disposition
Released
Cited and released
Turned over to

Complaint filed
The following misdemeanor or infraction data or preliminary hearing data:
County and court name
Date complaint filed
Original offenses charged in a complaint or citation
Held to answer
Certified plea
Disposition
Not convicted
Dismissed
Acquitted
Court trial
Jury trial
Convicted
Plea
Court trial
Jury trial
Date of disposition
Convicted offenses
Sentence
Sentence enhancement data elements
Proceedings suspended
Reason suspended
The following superior court data:
County
Date complaint filed
Type of proceeding
Indictment
Information
Certification
Original offenses charged in indictment or information
Disposition
Not convicted
Dismissed
Acquitted
Court trial
Jury trial
On transcript

Convicted—felony, misdemeanor

Plea

Court trial

Jury trial

On transcript

Date of disposition

Convicted offenses

Sentence

Sentence enhancement data elements

Proceedings suspended

Reason suspended

Source of reopened cases

The following corrections data:

Adult probation

County

Type of court

Court number

Offense

Date on probation

Date removed

Reason for removal

Jail (unsentenced prisoners only)

Offenses charged

Name of jail or institution

Date received

Date released

Reason for release

Bail on own recognizance

Bail

Other

Committing agency

County jail (sentenced prisoners only)

Name of jail, camp, or other

Convicted offense

Sentence

Sentence enhancement data elements

Date received

Date released

Reason for release

Committing agency

Division of Juvenile Justice

County

Type of court

Court number

Division of Juvenile Justice number

Date received

Convicted offense

Type of receipt

Original commitment

Parole violator

Date released

Type of release

Custody

Supervision

Date terminated

Department of Corrections and Rehabilitation

County

Type of court

Court number

Department of Corrections and Rehabilitation number

Date received

Convicted offense

Type of receipt

Original commitment

Parole violator

Date released

Type of release

Custody

Supervision

Date terminated

Mentally disordered sex offenders

County

Hospital number

Date received

Date discharged

Recommendation

(Amended by Stats. 2017, Ch. 541, Sec. 16. (SB 384) Effective January 1, 2018.)

13127.
Each recording agency shall insure that each portion of a criminal offender record that it originates shall include, for all felonies and reportable misdemeanors, the state or local unique and permanent fingerprint identification number, within 72 hours of origination of such records, excluding Saturday, Sunday, and holidays.

(Added by Stats. 1973, Ch. 992.)
13128.

For purposes of the maintenance of criminal records pursuant to Chapter 4 (commencing with Section 653.75) of Title 15, whenever a person is arrested for a public offense committed while in custody in any local detention facility, as defined in Section 6031.4, or any state prison, as defined in Section 4504, the state summary criminal history record shall include the section number of the public offense violated and information related to the "in custody" status of that person.
(Added by Stats. 1987, Ch. 1005, Sec. 2.)

ARTICLE 3. Reporting Information [13150 - 13155]
(Article 3 added by Stats. 1973, Ch. 992.)
13150.

For each arrest made, the reporting agency shall report to the Department of Justice, concerning each arrest, the applicable identification and arrest data described in Section 13125 and fingerprints, except as otherwise provided by law or as prescribed by the Department of Justice.
(Amended by Stats. 1978, Ch. 152.)
13151.

The superior court that disposes of a case for which an arrest was required to be reported to the Department of Justice pursuant to Section 13150 or for which fingerprints were taken and submitted to the Department of Justice by order of the court shall assure that a disposition report of such case containing the applicable data elements enumerated in Section 13125, or Section 13151.1 if such disposition is one of dismissal, is furnished to the Department of Justice within 30 days according to the procedures and on a format prescribed by the department. The court shall also furnish a copy of such disposition report to the law enforcement agency having primary jurisdiction to investigate the offense alleged in the complaint or accusation. Whenever a court shall order any action subsequent to the initial disposition of a case, the court shall similarly report such proceedings to the department.
(Amended by Stats. 2002, Ch. 784, Sec. 574. Effective January 1, 2003.)
13151.1.

When a disposition described in Section 13151 is one of dismissal of the charge, the disposition report shall state one of the following reasons, as appropriate:
(a) Dismissal in furtherance of justice, pursuant to Section 1385 of the Penal Code. In addition to this dismissal label, the court shall set forth the particular reasons for dismissal.
(b) Case compromised; defendant discharged because restitution or other satisfaction was made to the injured person, pursuant to Sections 1377 and 1378.
(c) Court found insufficient cause to believe defendant guilty of a public offense; defendant discharged without trial pursuant to Section 871.
(d) Dismissal due to delay; action against defendant dismissed because the information was not filed or the action was not brought to trial within the time allowed by Section 1381, 1381.5, or 1382.
(e) Accusation set aside pursuant to Section 995. In addition to this dismissal label, the court shall set forth the particular reasons for the dismissal.
(f) Defective accusation; defendant discharged pursuant to Section 1008, when the action is dismissed pursuant to that section after demurrer is sustained, because no amendment of the accusatory pleading is permitted or amendment is not made or filed within the time allowed.
(g) Defendant became a witness for the people and was discharged pursuant to Section 1099.
(h) Defendant discharged at trial because of insufficient evidence, in order to become a witness for his codefendant pursuant to Section 1100.
(i) Judgment arrested; defendant discharged, when the court finds defects in the accusatory pleading pursuant to Sections 1185 to 1187, inclusive, and defendant is released pursuant to Section 1188.
(j) Judgment arrested; defendant recommitted, when the court finds defects in the accusatory pleading pursuant to Sections 1185 to 1187, inclusive, and defendant is recommitted to answer a new indictment or information pursuant to Section 1188.
(k) Mistrial; defendant discharged. In addition to this dismissal label, the court shall set forth the particular reasons for its declaration of a mistrial.
(l) Mistrial; defendant recommitted. In addition to this dismissal label, the court shall set forth the particular reasons for its declaration of a mistrial.
(m) Any other dismissal by which the case was terminated. In addition to the dismissal label, the court shall set forth the particular reasons for the disposition.
(Added by Stats. 1978, Ch. 152.)
13152.

Both admission and release from detention facilities shall be reported by the detention agency to the Department of Justice within 30 days of that action.
(Amended by Stats. 2018, Ch. 814, Sec. 1. (AB 2080) Effective January 1, 2019.)
13153.

Criminal offender record information relating to arrests for being found in any public place under the influence of intoxicating liquor under subdivision (f) of Section 647 shall not be reported or maintained by the Department of Justice without special individual justification.
(Amended by Stats. 1974, Ch. 790.)
13154.

Each reporting agency shall report to the Department of Justice each arrest for the commission of a public offense while in custody in any local detention facility, or any state prison, as provided in Chapter 4 (commencing with Section 653.75) of Title 15, for inclusion in that person's state summary criminal history record. The report shall include the public offense committed and a reference indicating that the offense occurred while the person was in custody in a local detention facility or state prison.
(Added by Stats. 1987, Ch. 1005, Sec. 3.)
13155.

Commencing January 1, 2013, the Administrative Office of the Courts shall collect from trial courts information regarding the implementation of the 2011 Realignment Legislation. That information shall include statistics for each county regarding the dispositions of felonies at sentencing and petitions to revoke probation, postrelease community supervision, mandatory supervision, and, commencing July 1, 2013, parole. The data shall be provided not less frequently than twice a year by the trial courts to the Administrative Office of the Courts. Funds provided to the trial courts for the implementation of criminal justice realignment may be used for the purpose of collecting the information and providing it to the Administrative Office of the Courts. The Administrative Office of the Courts shall make this data available to the Department of Finance, the Board of State and Community Corrections, and the Joint Legislative Budget Committee on or before September 1, 2013, and annually thereafter. It is the intent of the Legislature that the Administrative Office of the Courts promote collaboration and the reduction of duplication of data collection and reporting efforts where possible.
(Added by Stats. 2012, Ch. 41, Sec. 83. (SB 1021) Effective June 27, 2012.)

ARTICLE 4. Information Service [13175 - 13177]
(Article 4 added by Stats. 1973, Ch. 992.)
13175.

When a criminal justice agency supplies fingerprints, or a fingerprint identification number, or such other personal identifiers as the Department of Justice deems appropriate, to the Department of Justice, such agency shall, upon request, be provided with identification, arrest, and, where applicable, final disposition data relating to such person within 72 hours of receipt by the Department of Justice.

(Added by Stats. 1973, Ch. 992.)
13176.

When a criminal justice agency entitled to such information supplies fingerprints, or a fingerprint identification number, or such other personal identifiers as the Department of Justice deems appropriate, to the Department of Justice, such agency shall, upon request, be provided with the criminal history of such person, or the needed portion thereof, within 72 hours of receipt by the Department of Justice.
(Added by Stats. 1973, Ch. 992.)
13177.

Nothing in this chapter shall be construed to prohibit the Department of Justice from requiring criminal justice agencies to report any information which is required by any other statute to be reported to the department.
(Amended by Stats. 1974, Ch. 790.)

ARTICLE 5. Access to Information [13200 - 13203]
(Article 5 added by Stats. 1973, Ch. 992.)
13200.

Nothing in this chapter shall be construed to affect the right of access of any person or public agency to individual criminal offender record information that is authorized by any other provision of law.
(Added by Stats. 1973, Ch. 992.)
13201.

Nothing in this chapter shall be construed to authorize access of any person or public agency to individual criminal offender record information unless such access is otherwise authorized by law.
(Added by Stats. 1973, Ch. 992.)
13202.

Notwithstanding subdivision (g) of Section 11105 and subdivision (a) of Section 13305, every public agency or bona fide research body immediately concerned with the prevention or control of crime, the quality of criminal justice, or the custody or correction of offenders may be provided with such criminal offender record information as is required for the performance of its duties, provided that any material identifying individuals is not transferred, revealed, or used for other than research or statistical activities and reports or publications derived therefrom do not identify specific individuals, and provided that such agency or body pays the cost of the processing of such data as determined by the Attorney General.
(Amended by Stats. 2009, Ch. 35, Sec. 29. (SB 174) Effective January 1, 2010.)
13203.

(a) Any criminal justice agency may release, within five years of the arrest, information concerning an arrest or detention of a peace officer or applicant for a position as a peace officer, as defined in Section 830, which did not result in conviction, and for which the person did not complete a postarrest diversion program, to a government agency employer of that peace officer or applicant.
(b) Any criminal justice agency may release information concerning an arrest of a peace officer or applicant for a position as a peace officer, as defined in Section 830, which did not result in conviction but for which the person completed a postarrest diversion program or a deferred entry of judgment program, or information concerning a referral to and participation in any postarrest diversion program or a deferred entry of judgment program to a government agency employer of that peace officer or applicant.
(c) Notwithstanding subdivision (a) or (b), a criminal justice agency shall not release information under the following circumstances:
(1) Information concerning an arrest for which diversion or deferred entry of judgment has been ordered without attempting to determine whether diversion or a deferred entry of judgment program has been successfully completed.
(2) Information concerning an arrest or detention followed by a dismissal or release without attempting to determine whether the individual was exonerated.
(3) Information concerning an arrest without a disposition without attempting to determine whether diversion or a deferred entry of judgment program has been successfully completed or the individual was exonerated.
(Amended by Stats. 1996, Ch. 743, Sec. 6. Effective January 1, 1997.)

ARTICLE 6. Local Summary Criminal History Information [13300 - 13305]
(Article 6 added by Stats. 1975, Ch. 1222.)
13300.

(a) As used in this section:
(1) "Local summary criminal history information" means the master record of information compiled by any local criminal justice agency pursuant to Chapter 2 (commencing with Section 13100) of Title 3 of Part 4 pertaining to the identification and criminal history of any person, such as name, date of birth, physical description, dates of arrests, arresting agencies and booking numbers, charges, dispositions, and similar data about the person.
(2) "Local summary criminal history information" does not refer to records and data compiled by criminal justice agencies other than that local agency, nor does it refer to records of complaints to or investigations conducted by, or records of intelligence information or security procedures of, the local agency.
(3) "Local agency" means a local criminal justice agency.
(b) A local agency shall furnish local summary criminal history information to any of the following, when needed in the course of their duties, provided that when information is furnished to assist an agency, officer, or official of state or local government, a public utility, or any entity, in fulfilling employment, certification, or licensing duties, Chapter 1321 of the Statutes of 1974 and Section 432.7 of the Labor Code shall apply:
(1) The courts of the state.
(2) Peace officers of the state, as defined in Section 830.1, subdivisions (a) and (d) of Section 830.2, subdivisions (a), (b), and (j) of Section 830.3, and subdivisions (a), (b), and (c) of Section 830.5.
(3) District attorneys of the state.
(4) Prosecuting city attorneys of any city within the state.
(5) City attorneys pursuing civil gang injunctions pursuant to Section 186.22a, or drug abatement actions pursuant to Section 3479 or 3480 of the Civil Code, or Section 11571 of the Health and Safety Code.
(6) Probation officers of the state.
(7) Parole officers of the state.
(8) A public defender or attorney of record when representing a person in proceedings upon a petition for a certificate of rehabilitation and pardon pursuant to Section 4852.08.
(9) A public defender or attorney of record when representing a person in a criminal case, or a parole, mandatory supervision, or postrelease community supervision revocation or revocation extension hearing, and when authorized access by statutory or decisional law.
(10) Any agency, officer, or official of the state when the local summary criminal history information is required to implement a statute, regulation, or ordinance that expressly refers to specific criminal conduct applicable to the subject person of the local summary criminal history information, and contains requirements or exclusions, or both, expressly based upon the specified criminal conduct.
(11) Any city, county, city and county, or district, or any officer or official thereof, when access is needed in order to assist the agency, officer, or official in fulfilling employment, certification, or licensing duties, and when the access is specifically authorized by the city council, board of supervisors, or governing board of the city, county, or district when the local summary criminal history information is required to implement a statute, regulation, or ordinance that expressly refers to specific criminal conduct applicable to

the subject person of the local summary criminal history information, and contains requirements or exclusions, or both, expressly based upon the specified criminal conduct.

(12) The subject of the local summary criminal history information.

(13) Any person or entity when access is expressly authorized by statute when the local summary criminal history information is required to implement a statute, regulation, or ordinance that expressly refers to specific criminal conduct applicable to the subject person of the local summary criminal history information, and contains requirements or exclusions, or both, expressly based upon the specified criminal conduct.

(14) Any managing or supervising correctional officer of a county jail or other county correctional facility.

(15) Local child support agencies established by Section 17304 of the Family Code. When a local child support agency closes a support enforcement case containing summary criminal history information, the agency shall delete or purge from the file and destroy any documents or information concerning or arising from offenses for or of which the parent has been arrested, charged, or convicted, other than for offenses related to the parents having failed to provide support for the minor children, consistent with Section 17531 of the Family Code.

(16) County child welfare agency personnel who have been delegated the authority of county probation officers to access state summary criminal information pursuant to Section 272 of the Welfare and Institutions Code for the purposes specified in Section 16504.5 of the Welfare and Institutions Code.

(17) A humane officer appointed pursuant to Section 14502 of the Corporations Code, for the purposes of performing his or her duties. A local agency may charge a reasonable fee sufficient to cover the costs of providing information pursuant to this paragraph.

(c) The local agency may furnish local summary criminal history information, upon a showing of a compelling need, to any of the following, provided that when information is furnished to assist an agency, officer, or official of state or local government, a public utility, or any entity, in fulfilling employment, certification, or licensing duties, Chapter 1321 of the Statutes of 1974 and Section 432.7 of the Labor Code shall apply:

(1) Any public utility, as defined in Section 216 of the Public Utilities Code, which operates a nuclear energy facility when access is needed to assist in employing persons to work at the facility, provided that, if the local agency supplies the information, it shall furnish a copy of this information to the person to whom the information relates.

(2) To a peace officer of the state other than those included in subdivision (b).

(3) An animal control officer, authorized to exercise powers specified in Section 830.9, for the purposes of performing his or her official duties. A local agency may charge a reasonable fee sufficient to cover the costs of providing information pursuant to this paragraph.

(4) To a peace officer of another country.

(5) To public officers, other than peace officers, of the United States, other states, or possessions or territories of the United States, provided that access to records similar to local summary criminal history information is expressly authorized by a statute of the United States, other states, or possessions or territories of the United States when this information is needed for the performance of their official duties.

(6) To any person when disclosure is requested by a probation, parole, or peace officer with the consent of the subject of the local summary criminal history information and for purposes of furthering the rehabilitation of the subject.

(7) The courts of the United States, other states, or territories or possessions of the United States.

(8) Peace officers of the United States, other states, or territories or possessions of the United States.

(9) To any individual who is the subject of the record requested when needed in conjunction with an application to enter the United States or any foreign nation.

(10) Any public utility, as defined in Section 216 of the Public Utilities Code, when access is needed to assist in employing persons who will be seeking entrance to private residences in the course of their employment. The information provided shall be limited to the record of convictions and any arrest for which the person is released on bail or on his or her own recognizance pending trial.

If the local agency supplies the information pursuant to this paragraph, it shall furnish a copy of the information to the person to whom the information relates.

Any information obtained from the local summary criminal history is confidential and the receiving public utility shall not disclose its contents, other than for the purpose for which it was acquired. The local summary criminal history information in the possession of the public utility and all copies made from it shall be destroyed 30 days after employment is denied or granted, including any appeal periods, except for those cases where an employee or applicant is out on bail or on his or her own recognizance pending trial, in which case the state summary criminal history information and all copies shall be destroyed 30 days after the case is resolved, including any appeal periods.

A violation of any of the provisions of this paragraph is a misdemeanor, and shall give the employee or applicant who is injured by the violation a cause of action against the public utility to recover damages proximately caused by the violation.

Nothing in this section shall be construed as imposing any duty upon public utilities to request local summary criminal history information on any current or prospective employee.

Seeking entrance to private residences in the course of employment shall be deemed a "compelling need" as required to be shown in this subdivision.

(11) Any city, county, city and county, or district, or any officer or official thereof, if a written request is made to a local law enforcement agency and the information is needed to assist in the screening of a prospective concessionaire, and any affiliate or associate thereof, as these terms are defined in subdivision (k) of Section 432.7 of the Labor Code, for the purposes of consenting to, or approving of, the prospective concessionaire's application for, or acquisition of, any beneficial interest in a concession, lease, or other property interest.

Any local government's request for local summary criminal history information for purposes of screening a prospective concessionaire and their affiliates or associates before approving or denying an application for, or acquisition of, any beneficial interest in a concession, lease, or other property interest is deemed a "compelling need" as required by this subdivision. However, only local summary criminal history information pertaining to criminal convictions may be obtained pursuant to this paragraph.

Any information obtained from the local summary criminal history is confidential and the receiving local government shall not disclose its contents, other than for the purpose for which it was acquired. The local summary criminal history information in the possession of the local government and all copies made from it shall be destroyed not more than 30 days after the local government's final decision to grant or deny consent to, or approval of, the prospective concessionaire's application for, or acquisition of, a beneficial interest in a concession, lease, or other property interest. Nothing in this section shall be construed as imposing any duty upon a local government, or any officer or official thereof, to request local summary criminal history information on any current or prospective concessionaire or their affiliates or associates.

(12) A public agency described in subdivision (b) of Section 15975 of the Government Code, for the purpose of oversight and enforcement policies with respect to its contracted providers.

(d) Whenever an authorized request for local summary criminal history information pertains to a person whose fingerprints are on file with the local agency and the local agency has no criminal history of that person, and the information is to be used for employment, licensing, or certification purposes, the fingerprint card accompanying the

request for information, if any, may be stamped "no criminal record" and returned to the person or entity making the request.

(e) A local agency taking fingerprints of a person who is an applicant for licensing, employment, or certification may charge a fee to cover the cost of taking the fingerprints and processing the required documents.

(f) Whenever local summary criminal history information furnished pursuant to this section is to be used for employment, licensing, or certification purposes, the local agency shall charge the person or entity making the request a fee which it determines to be sufficient to reimburse the local agency for the cost of furnishing the information, provided that no fee shall be charged to any public law enforcement agency for local summary criminal history information furnished to assist it in employing, licensing, or certifying a person who is applying for employment with the agency as a peace officer or criminal investigator. Any state agency required to pay a fee to the local agency for information received under this section may charge the applicant a fee sufficient to reimburse the agency for the expense.

(g) Whenever there is a conflict, the processing of criminal fingerprints shall take priority over the processing of applicant fingerprints.

(h) It is not a violation of this article to disseminate statistical or research information obtained from a record, provided that the identity of the subject of the record is not disclosed.

(i) It is not a violation of this article to include information obtained from a record in (1) a transcript or record of a judicial or administrative proceeding or (2) any other public record when the inclusion of the information in the public record is authorized by a court, statute, or decisional law.

(j) Notwithstanding any other law, a public prosecutor may, in response to a written request made pursuant to Section 6253 of the Government Code, provide information from a local summary criminal history, if release of the information would enhance public safety, the interest of justice, or the public's understanding of the justice system and the person making the request declares that the request is made for a scholarly or journalistic purpose. If a person in a declaration required by this subdivision willfully states as true any material fact that he or she knows to be false, he or she shall be subject to a civil penalty not exceeding ten thousand dollars ($10,000). The requestor shall be informed in writing of this penalty. An action to impose a civil penalty under this subdivision may be brought by any public prosecutor and shall be enforced as a civil judgment.

(k) Notwithstanding any other law, the Department of Justice or any state or local law enforcement agency may require the submission of fingerprints for the purpose of conducting summary criminal history information record checks which are authorized by law.

(l) Any local criminal justice agency may release, within five years of the arrest, information concerning an arrest or detention of a peace officer or applicant for a position as a peace officer, as defined in Section 830, which did not result in conviction, and for which the person did not complete a postarrest diversion program or a deferred entry of judgment program, to a government agency employer of that peace officer or applicant.

(m) Any local criminal justice agency may release information concerning an arrest of a peace officer or applicant for a position as a peace officer, as defined in Section 830, which did not result in conviction but for which the person completed a postarrest diversion program or a deferred entry of judgment program, or information concerning a referral to and participation in any postarrest diversion program or a deferred entry of judgment program to a government agency employer of that peace officer or applicant.

(n) Notwithstanding subdivision (l) or (m), a local criminal justice agency shall not release information under the following circumstances:

(1) Information concerning an arrest for which diversion or a deferred entry of judgment program has been ordered without attempting to determine whether diversion or a deferred entry of judgment program has been successfully completed.

(2) Information concerning an arrest or detention followed by a dismissal or release without attempting to determine whether the individual was exonerated.

(3) Information concerning an arrest without a disposition without attempting to determine whether diversion has been successfully completed or the individual was exonerated.

(Amended by Stats. 2014, Ch. 449, Sec. 2. (AB 1511) Effective January 1, 2015.)

13301.

As used in this article:

(a) "Record" means the master local summary criminal history information as defined in subdivision (a) of Section 13300, or a copy thereof.

(b) "A person authorized by law to receive a record" means any person or public agency authorized by a court, statute, or decisional law to receive a record.

(Amended by Stats. 1981, Ch. 714, Sec. 339.)

13302.

An employee of the local criminal justice agency who knowingly furnishes a record or information obtained from a record to a person who is not authorized by law to receive the record or information is guilty of a misdemeanor. Nothing in this section shall prohibit a public prosecutor from accessing and obtaining information from the public prosecutor's case management database to respond to a request for publicly disclosable information pursuant to the California Public Records Act (Chapter 3.5 (commencing with Section 6250) of Division 7 of Title 1 of the Government Code).

(Amended by Stats. 2012, Ch. 84, Sec. 1. (AB 2222) Effective January 1, 2013.)

13303.

Any person authorized by law to receive a record or information obtained from a record who knowingly furnishes the record or information to a person who is not authorized by law to receive the record or information is guilty of a misdemeanor.

(Added by Stats. 1975, Ch. 1222.)

13304.

Any person, except those specifically referred to in Section 1070 of the Evidence Code, who, knowing he is not authorized by law to receive a record or information obtained from a record, knowingly buys, receives, or possesses the record or information is guilty of a misdemeanor.

(Added by Stats. 1975, Ch. 1222.)

13305.

(a) It is not a violation of this article to disseminate statistical or research information obtained from a record, provided that the identity of the subject of the record is not disclosed.

(b) It is not a violation of this article to disseminate information obtained from a record for the purpose of assisting in the apprehension of a person wanted in connection with the commission of a crime.

(c) It is not a violation of this article to include information obtained from a record in (1) a transcript or record of a judicial or administrative proceeding or (2) any other public record when the inclusion of the information in the public record is authorized by a court, statute, or decisional law.

(Added by Stats. 1975, Ch. 1222.)

ARTICLE 7. Examinations of Local Records [13320 - 13326]
(Article 7 added by Stats. 1979, Ch. 849.)

13320.

(a) As used in this article, "record" with respect to any person means the local summary criminal history information as defined in subdivision (a) of Section 13300, maintained under such person's name by the local criminal justice agency.

(b) As used in this article, "agency" means any agency or consortium of agencies.

(c) It is the function and intent of this article to afford persons concerning whom a record is maintained in the files of the local criminal justice agency a reasonable opportunity to examine the record compiled from such files, and to refute any erroneous or inaccurate information contained therein.
(Added by Stats. 1979, Ch. 849.)
13321.
Any person desiring to examine a record relating to himself shall make application to the agency maintaining the record in the form prescribed by that agency which may require the submission of fingerprints.
(Added by Stats. 1979, Ch. 849.)
13322.
The agency may require the application be accompanied by a fee not to exceed twenty-five dollars ($25) that the agency determines is equal to the cost of processing the application and making a record available for examination.
(Added by Stats. 1979, Ch. 849.)
13323.
When an application is received by the agency, the agency shall upon verification of the applicant's identity determine whether a record pertaining to the applicant is maintained. If such record is maintained, the agency shall at its discretion either inform the applicant by mail of the existence of the record and specify a time when the record may be examined at a suitable facility of the agency or shall mail the subject a copy of the record.
(Added by Stats. 1979, Ch. 849.)
13324.
(a) If the applicant desires to question the accuracy or completeness of any material matter contained in the record, he may submit a written request to the agency in the form established by it. The request shall include a statement of the alleged inaccuracy or incompleteness in the record, its materiality, and shall specify any proof or corroboration available. Upon receipt of such request, the agency shall, within 60 days of receipt of such written request for clarification, review its information and forward to the applicant the results of such review.
(b) If the agency concurs in the allegations of inaccuracy or incompleteness in the record and finds that the error is material, it shall correct its record, and the agency shall inform the applicant of its correction of any material error in the record under this subdivision within 60 days. The agency shall notify all criminal justice agencies to which it has disseminated the incorrect record from an automated system in the past two years of the correction of the record.
The agency shall furnish the applicant with a list of all the noncriminal justice agencies to which the incorrect record has been disseminated from an automated system in the past two years unless it interferes with the conduct of an authorized investigation.
(c) If the agency denies the allegations of inaccuracy or incompleteness in the record, the matter shall at the option of the applicant be referred for administrative adjudication in accordance with the rules of the local governing body.
(Added by Stats. 1979, Ch. 849.)
13325.
The agency shall adopt all regulations necessary to carry out the provisions of this article.
(Added by Stats. 1979, Ch. 849.)
13326.
No person shall require an employee or prospective employee to obtain a copy of a record or notification that a record exists as provided in Section 13323. A violation of this section is a misdemeanor.
(Added by Stats. 1979, Ch. 849.)

TITLE 4. STANDARDS AND TRAINING OF LOCAL LAW ENFORCEMENT OFFICERS [13500 - 13553]

(Title 4 added by Stats. 1959, Ch. 1823.)

CHAPTER 1. Commission on Peace Officer Standards and Training [13500 - 13553]

(Chapter 1 added by Stats. 1959, Ch. 1823.)
ARTICLE 1. Administration [13500 - 13509]
(Article 1 added by Stats. 1959, Ch. 1823.)
13500.
(a) There is in the Department of Justice a Commission on Peace Officer Standards and Training, hereafter referred to in this chapter as the commission. The commission consists of 15 members appointed by the Governor, after consultation with, and with the advice of, the Attorney General and with the advice and consent of the Senate. Racial, gender, and ethnic diversity shall be considered for all appointments to the commission.
(b) The commission shall be composed of the following members:
(1) Two members shall be (i) sheriffs or chiefs of police or peace officers nominated by their respective sheriffs or chiefs of police, (ii) peace officers who are deputy sheriffs or city police officers, or (iii) any combination thereof.
(2) Three members shall be sheriffs or chiefs of police or peace officers nominated by their respective sheriffs or chiefs of police.
(3) Four members shall be peace officers of the rank of sergeant or below with a minimum of five years' experience as a deputy sheriff, city police officer, marshal, or state-employed peace officer for whom the commission sets standards. Each member shall have demonstrated leadership in the recognized employee organization having the right to represent the member, as set forth in the Meyers-Milias-Brown Act (Chapter 10 (commencing with Section 3500)) and the Ralph C. Dills Act (Chapter 10.5 (commencing with Section 3525)) of Division 4 of Title 1 of the Government Code.
(4) One member shall be an elected officer or chief administrative officer of a county in this state.
(5) One member shall be an elected officer or chief administrative officer of a city in this state.
(6) Two members shall be public members who shall not be peace officers.
(7) One member shall be an educator or trainer in the field of criminal justice.
(8) One member shall be a peace officer in California of the rank of sergeant or below with a minimum of five years experience as a deputy sheriff, city police officer, marshal, or state-employed peace officer for whom the commission sets standards. This member shall have demonstrated leadership in a California-based law enforcement association that is also a presenter of POST-certified law enforcement training that advances the professionalism of peace officers in California.
(c) The Attorney General shall be an ex officio member of the commission.
(d) Of the members first appointed by the Governor, three shall be appointed for a term of one year, three for a term of two years, and three for a term of three years. Their successors shall serve for a term of three years and until appointment and qualification

of their successors, each term to commence on the expiration date of the term of the predecessor.
(e) The additional member provided for by the Legislature in its 1973–74 Regular Session shall be appointed by the Governor on or before January 15, 1975, and shall serve for a term of three years.
(f) The additional member provided for by the Legislature in its 1977–78 Regular Session shall be appointed by the Governor on or after July 1, 1978, and shall serve for a term of three years.
(g) The additional members provided for by the Legislature in its 1999–2000 Regular Session shall be appointed by the Governor on or before July 1, 2000, and shall serve for a term of three years.
(h) The additional member provided for by the Legislature in its 2007–08 Regular Session shall be appointed by the Governor on or before January 31, 2008, and shall serve for a term of three years.
(Amended by Stats. 2007, Ch. 409, Sec. 1. Effective January 1, 2008.)
13501.
The Governor shall designate the chair of the commission from among the members of the commission. The person designated as the chair shall serve at the pleasure of the Governor. The commission shall annually select a vice chair from among its members. A majority of the members of the commission shall constitute a quorum.
(Amended by Stats. 2016, Ch. 33, Sec. 35. (SB 843) Effective June 27, 2016.)
13502.
Members of the commission shall receive no compensation, but shall be reimbursed for their actual and necessary travel expenses incurred in the performance of their duties. For purposes of compensation, attendance at meetings of the commission shall be deemed performance by a member of the duties of his local governmental employment.
(Added by Stats. 1959, Ch. 1823.)
13503.
In carrying out its duties and responsibilities, the commission shall have all of the following powers:
(a) To meet at those times and places as it may deem proper.
(b) To employ an executive secretary and, pursuant to civil service, those clerical and technical assistants as may be necessary.
(c) To contract with other agencies, public or private, or persons as it deems necessary, for the rendition and affording of those services, facilities, studies, and reports to the commission as will best assist it to carry out its duties and responsibilities.
(d) To cooperate with and to secure the cooperation of county, city, city and county, and other local law enforcement agencies in investigating any matter within the scope of its duties and responsibilities, and in performing its other functions.
(e) To develop and implement programs to increase the effectiveness of law enforcement and when those programs involve training and education courses to cooperate with and secure the cooperation of state-level officers, agencies, and bodies having jurisdiction over systems of public higher education in continuing the development of college-level training and education programs.
(f) To cooperate with and secure the cooperation of every department, agency, or instrumentality in the state government.
(g) To do any and all things necessary or convenient to enable it fully and adequately to perform its duties and to exercise the power granted to it.
(h) The commission shall not have the authority to adopt or carry out a regulation that authorizes the withdrawal or revocation of a certificate previously issued to a peace officer pursuant to this chapter.
(i) Except as specifically provided by law, the commission shall not have the authority to cancel a certificate previously issued to a peace officer pursuant to this chapter.
(Amended by Stats. 2003, Ch. 297, Sec. 2. Effective January 1, 2004.)
13503.5.
(a) Commencing February 1, 2020, and each year thereafter, the commission shall submit an annual report to the Legislature, in compliance with Section 9795 of the Government Code, on the overall effectiveness of any additional funding appropriated by the Legislature on or after July 1, 2019, in improving peace officer training. For the purpose of this section, "additional funding" does not include General Fund resources provided to backfill declines in non-General Fund revenue in the 2019 Budget Act.
(b) At minimum, the reporting described in subdivision (a) shall include both of the following:
(1) The number of peace officers trained by law enforcement agency, by course, and by how training was delivered.
(2) The training provided and the descriptions of the training, including the duration of the training and the skills addressed in the training.
(c) To the extent that information required in subdivision (b) is not yet available for a particular annual report, the commission shall report on how it plans to measure and report that information in the future. The commission also shall specify the date by which it anticipates that the information will be available for reporting.
(Added by Stats. 2019, Ch. 25, Sec. 45. (SB 94) Effective June 27, 2019.)
13504.
The Attorney General shall, so far as compatible with other demands upon the personnel in the Department of Justice, make available to the commission the services of such personnel to assist the commission in the execution of the duties imposed upon it by this chapter.
(Added by Stats. 1959, Ch. 1823.)
13505.
In exercising its functions, the commission shall endeavor to minimize costs of administration so that a maximum of funds will be expended for the purpose of providing training and other services to local law enforcement agencies. All expenses shall be a proper charge against the revenue accruing under Article 3 (commencing with Section 13520).
(Amended by Stats. 1985, Ch. 106, Sec. 112.)
13506.
The commission may adopt those regulations as are necessary to carry out the purposes of this chapter. The commission shall not have the authority to adopt or carry out a regulation that authorizes the withdrawal or revocation of a certificate previously issued to a peace officer pursuant to this chapter. Except as specifically provided by law, the commission shall not have the authority to adopt regulations providing for the cancellation of a certificate.
(Amended by Stats. 2003, Ch. 297, Sec. 3. Effective January 1, 2004.)
13507.
As used in this chapter, "district" means any of the following:
(a) A regional park district.
(b) A district authorized by statute to maintain a police department.
(c) The University of California.
(d) The California State University and Colleges.
(e) A community college district.
(f) A school district.
(g) A transit district.
(h) A harbor district.
(Amended by Stats. 1989, Ch. 950, Sec. 3.)
13507.1.
As used in this chapter, "joint powers agency" means any agency, entity, or authority formed pursuant to Article 1 (commencing with Section 6500) of Chapter 5 of Division 7 of Title 1 of the Government Code.
(Added by Stats. 2013, Ch. 59, Sec. 8. (SB 514) Effective January 1, 2014.)

13508.
(a) The commission shall do each of the following:
(1) Establish a learning technology laboratory that would conduct pilot projects with regard to needed facilities and otherwise implement modern instructional technology to improve the effectiveness of law enforcement training.
(2) Develop an implementation plan for the acquisition of law enforcement facilities and technology. In developing this plan, the commission shall consult with appropriate law enforcement and training organizations. The implementation plan shall include each of the following items:
(A) An evaluation of pilot and demonstration projects.
(B) Recommendations for the establishment of regional skills training centers, training conference centers, and the use of modern instructional technology.
(C) A recommended financing structure.
(b) The commission may enter into joint powers agreements with other governmental agencies for the purpose of developing and deploying needed technology and facilities.
(c) Any pilot project conducted pursuant to this section shall terminate on or before January 1, 1995, unless funding is provided for the project continuation.
(Amended by Stats. 2004, Ch. 193, Sec. 155. Effective January 1, 2005.)
13509.
(a) There is hereby established the Innovations Grant Program within the Commission on Peace Officer Standards and Training to, upon an appropriation of funds for the purposes described in this section, grant funds on a competitive basis to qualified public and private entities for the purpose of fostering innovations in training and procedures for law enforcement officers with the goal of reducing the number of officer-involved shootings statewide.
(b) The commission shall develop and implement the program described in this section, including, but not limited to, application procedures, selection criteria, and reporting requirements.
(c) In developing the program, the commission shall hold no less than two public hearings during which public and private stakeholders, community-based organizations that work on policing-related issues, and other interested parties can provide public comment or submit written public comment on the development and administration of the program.
(d) Grants issued pursuant to this section shall support one or more of the following purposes:
(1) Developing and providing training and workshops for law enforcement officers addressing issues of implicit bias.
(2) Developing and providing training and workshops for law enforcement officers on use of force and deescalation.
(3) Developing and providing training and workshops for law enforcement officers on cultural diversity and awareness.
(4) Developing and providing training and workshops for law enforcement officers on community policing.
(5) Developing and providing wellness programs for law enforcement officers.
(e) Grants issued pursuant to this section shall, at minimum, comply with the following guidelines:
(1) Priority shall be given to agencies that have the highest per-officer incidence rate of officer-involved shootings and to the organizations that serve those agencies or are located in the communities served by those agencies.
(2) Sixty-five percent of available funding shall be awarded to community-based nonprofit organizations with the remaining funds awarded to other categories of applicants, including, but not limited to, law enforcement agencies, educational or law enforcement training institutions, and private for-profit organizations.
(3) Grant recipients shall be awarded no more than two hundred thousand dollars ($200,000) and no less than twenty-five thousand dollars ($25,000).
(4) Grant recipients shall be required to report back to the commission on the use of grant funds, including, but not limited to, the number of officers that received training.
(f) Any costs incurred by the commission in connection with the development or administration of the program shall be deducted from the amount appropriated before awarding any grants, not to exceed 5 percent of the amount appropriated.
(g) (1) The commission shall, no later than January 31, 2023, prepare and submit a report to the Legislature summarizing the expenditure of Innovations Grant Program funds, including, but not limited to, recipients and award amounts, summaries of training programs that were developed, the number of officers who received training, and any measurable outcomes.
(2) The report required by paragraph (1) shall be submitted in compliance with Section 9795 of the Government Code.
(3) Pursuant to Section 10231.5 of the Government Code, this section is repealed on January 1, 2025.
(Added by Stats. 2018, Ch. 36, Sec. 26. (AB 1812) Effective June 27, 2018. Repealed as of January 1, 2025, by its own provisions.)

ARTICLE 2. Field Services and Standards for Recruitment and Training [13510 - 13519.15]

(Heading of Article 2 amended by Stats. 1967, Ch. 1640.)
13510.
(a) For the purpose of raising the level of competence of local law enforcement officers, the commission shall adopt, and may from time to time amend, rules establishing minimum standards relating to physical, mental, and moral fitness that shall govern the recruitment of any city police officers, peace officer members of a county sheriff's office, marshals or deputy marshals, peace officer members of a county coroner's office notwithstanding Section 13526, reserve officers, as defined in subdivision (a) of Section 830.6, police officers of a district authorized by statute to maintain a police department, peace officer members of a police department operated by a joint powers agency established by Article 1 (commencing with Section 6500) of Chapter 5 of Division 7 of Title 1 of the Government Code, regularly employed and paid inspectors and investigators of a district attorney's office, as defined in Section 830.1, who conduct criminal investigations, peace officer members of a district, safety police officers and park rangers of the County of Los Angeles, as defined in subdivisions (a) and (b) of Section 830.31, or housing authority police departments.
The commission also shall adopt, and may from time to time amend, rules establishing minimum standards for training of city police officers, peace officer members of county sheriff's offices, marshals or deputy marshals, peace officer members of a county coroner's office notwithstanding Section 13526, reserve officers, as defined in subdivision (a) of Section 830.6, police officers of a district authorized by statute to maintain a police department, peace officer members of a police department operated by a joint powers agency established by Article 1 (commencing with Section 6500) of Chapter 5 of Division 7 of Title 1 of the Government Code, regularly employed and paid inspectors and investigators of a district attorney's office, as defined in Section 830.1, who conduct criminal investigations, peace officer members of a district, safety police officers and park rangers of the County of Los Angeles, as defined in subdivisions (a) and (b) of Section 830.31, and housing authority police departments.
These rules shall apply to those cities, counties, cities and counties, and districts receiving state aid pursuant to this chapter and shall be adopted and amended pursuant to Chapter 3.5 (commencing with Section 11340) of Part 1 of Division 3 of Title 2 of the Government Code.
(b) The commission shall conduct research concerning job-related educational standards and job-related selection standards to include vision, hearing, physical ability, and emotional stability. Job-related standards that are supported by this research shall be adopted by the commission prior to January 1, 1985, and shall apply to those peace officer classes identified in subdivision (a). The commission shall consult with local entities during the conducting of related research into job-related selection standards.
(c) For the purpose of raising the level of competence of local public safety dispatchers, the commission shall adopt, and may from time to time amend, rules establishing minimum standards relating to the recruitment and training of local public safety dispatchers having a primary responsibility for providing dispatching services for local law enforcement agencies described in subdivision (a), which standards shall apply to those cities, counties, cities and counties, and districts receiving state aid pursuant to this chapter. These standards also shall apply to consolidated dispatch centers operated by an independent public joint powers agency established pursuant to Article 1 (commencing with Section 6500) of Chapter 5 of Division 7 of Title 1 of the Government Code when providing dispatch services to the law enforcement personnel listed in subdivision (a). Those rules shall be adopted and amended pursuant to Chapter 3.5 (commencing with Section 11340) of Part 1 of Division 3 of Title 2 of the Government Code. As used in this section, "primary responsibility" refers to the performance of law enforcement dispatching duties for a minimum of 50 percent of the time worked within a pay period.
(d) Nothing in this section shall prohibit a local agency from establishing selection and training standards that exceed the minimum standards established by the commission.
(Amended by Stats. 2010, Ch. 212, Sec. 12. (AB 2767) Effective January 1, 2011.)
13510.1.
(a) The commission shall establish a certification program for peace officers specified in Sections 13510 and 13522 and for the California Highway Patrol. Certificates of the commission established pursuant to this section shall be considered professional certificates.
(b) Basic, intermediate, advanced, supervisory, management, and executive certificates shall be established for the purpose of fostering professionalization, education, and experience necessary to adequately accomplish the general police service duties performed by peace officer members of city police departments, county sheriffs' departments, districts, university and state university and college departments, or by the California Highway Patrol.
(c) (1) Certificates shall be awarded on the basis of a combination of training, education, experience, and other prerequisites, as determined by the commission.
(2) In determining whether an applicant for certification has the requisite education, the commission shall recognize as acceptable college education only the following:
(A) Education provided by a community college, college, or university which has been accredited by the department of education of the state in which the community college, college, or university is located or by a recognized national or regional accrediting body.
(B) Until January 1, 1998, educational courses or degrees provided by a nonaccredited but state-approved college that offers programs exclusively in criminal justice.
(d) Persons who are determined by the commission to be eligible peace officers may make application for the certificates, provided they are employed by an agency which participates in the Peace Officer Standards and Training (POST) program.
(e) The commission shall have the authority to cancel any certificate that has been obtained through misrepresentation or fraud or that was issued as the result of an administrative error on the part of the commission or the employing agency.
(Amended by Stats. 2003, Ch. 297, Sec. 4. Effective January 1, 2004.)
13510.2.
Any person who knowingly commits any of the following acts is guilty of a misdemeanor, and for each offense is punishable by a fine of not more than one thousand dollars ($1,000) or imprisonment in the county jail not to exceed one year, or by both a fine and imprisonment:
(a) Presents or attempts to present as the person's own the certificate of another.
(b) Knowingly permits another to use his or her certificate.
(c) Knowingly gives false evidence of any material kind to the commission, or to any member thereof, including the staff, in obtaining a certificate.
(d) Uses, or attempts to use, a canceled certificate.
(Added by Stats. 1984, Ch. 43, Sec. 3.)
13510.3.
(a) The commission shall establish, by December 31, 1997, and in consultation with representatives of law enforcement organizations, a voluntary professional certification program for law enforcement records supervisors who have primary responsibility for providing records supervising services for local law enforcement agencies. The certificate or certificates shall be based upon standards related to the education, training, and experience of law enforcement records supervisors and shall serve to foster professionalism and recognition of achievement and competency.
(b) As used in this section, "primary responsibility" refers to the performance of law enforcement records supervising duties for a minimum of 50 percent of the time worked within a pay period.
(Added by Stats. 1996, Ch. 591, Sec. 1. Effective January 1, 1997.)
13510.4.
(a) A peace officer trainee who, based on the commission's investigative findings, knowingly cheats, assists in cheating, or aids, abets, or knowingly conceals efforts by others to cheat in any manner on a basic course examination mandated by the commission shall be liable for a civil fine of not more than one thousand dollars ($1,000) per occurrence.
(b) For purposes of this section, "cheating" means any attempt or act by a peace officer trainee to gain an unfair advantage or give an unfair advantage to another peace officer trainee or group of trainees taking a POST-mandated basic course examination.
(c) For purposes of this section, "peace officer trainee" means an applicant for a basic course examination who has not been hired by a department or agency and who has not been sworn as a peace officer.
(Added by Stats. 2012, Ch. 372, Sec. 1. (AB 2285) Effective January 1, 2013.)
13510.5.
For the purpose of maintaining the level of competence of state law enforcement officers, the commission shall adopt, and may, from time to time amend, rules establishing minimum standards for training of peace officers as defined in Chapter 4.5 (commencing with Section 830) of Title 3 of Part 2, who are employed by any railroad company, the University of California police department, a California State University police department, the Department of Alcoholic Beverage Control, the Division of Investigation of the Department of Consumer Affairs, the Wildlife Protection Branch of the Department of Fish and Wildlife, the Department of Forestry and Fire Protection, including the Office of the State Fire Marshal, the Department of Motor Vehicles, the California Horse Racing Board, the Food and Drug Section of the State Department of Public Health, the Division of Labor Standards Enforcement, the Director of Parks and Recreation, the State Department of Health Care Services, the Department of Toxic Substances Control, the State Department of Social Services, the State Department of State Hospitals, the State Department of Developmental Services, the Office of Statewide Health Planning and Development, and the Department of Justice. All rules shall be adopted and amended pursuant to Chapter 3.5 (commencing with Section 11340) of Part 1 of Division 3 of Title 2 of the Government Code.
(Amended by Stats. 2015, Ch. 303, Sec. 408. (AB 731) Effective January 1, 2016.)
13510.7.
(a) Whenever any person holding a certificate issued pursuant to Section 13510.1 is determined to be disqualified from holding office or being employed as a peace officer for the reasons set forth in subdivision (a) of Section 1029 of the Government Code, the commission shall cause the following to be entered in the commission's training record for that person: "THIS PERSON IS INELIGIBLE TO BE A PEACE OFFICER IN CALIFORNIA PURSUANT TO GOVERNMENT CODE SECTION 1029(a)."

(b) Whenever any person who is required to possess a basic certificate issued by the commission pursuant to Section 832.4 or who is subject to subdivision (a) of Section 13510.1 is determined to be disqualified from holding office or being employed as a peace officer for the reasons set forth in subdivision (a) of Section 1029 of the Government Code, the commission shall notify the law enforcement agency that employs the person that the person is ineligible to be a peace officer in California pursuant to subdivision (a) of Section 1029 of the Government Code.

(c) After the time for filing a notice of appeal has passed, or where the remittitur has been issued following the filing of a notice of appeal, in a criminal case establishing the ineligibility of a person to be a peace officer as specified in subdivision (c), or in the event a conviction of the offense requiring or accompanying ineligibility is subsequently overturned or reversed by the action of a court of competent jurisdiction, the person shall notify the commission in writing and provide documentation of the court's action.

(d) Upon written request of a person who is eligible for reinstatement pursuant to paragraph (2) of subdivision (b) of Section 1029 of the Government Code because of successful completion of probation pursuant to Section 1210.1 of the Penal Code, and who has provided court documentation that he or she has had eligibility restored, the commission shall remove the notation "THIS PERSON IS INELIGIBLE TO BE A PEACE OFFICER IN CALIFORNIA PURSUANT TO GOVERNMENT CODE SECTION 1029(a)" in the commission's training record for that person. The removal of this notation of ineligibility in the person's training record shall not create a mandate that the person be hired by any agency.

(Amended by Stats. 2018, Ch. 423, Sec. 118. (SB 1494) Effective January 1, 2019.)
13511.
(a) In establishing standards for training, the commission shall, so far as consistent with the purposes of this chapter, permit required training to be obtained at institutions approved by the commission.

(b) In those instances where individuals have acquired prior comparable peace officer training, the commission shall, adopt regulations providing for alternative means for satisfying the training required by Section 832.3. The commission shall charge a fee to cover administrative costs associated with the testing conducted under this subdivision.

(Amended by Stats. 2000, Ch. 354, Sec. 1. Effective January 1, 2001.)
13511.3.
The commission may evaluate and approve pertinent training previously completed by any jurisdiction's law enforcement officers as meeting current training requirements prescribed by the commission pursuant to this chapter. The evaluations performed by the commission shall conform to the standards established under this chapter.

(Added by Stats. 1994, Ch. 43, Sec. 2. Effective January 1, 1995.)
13511.5.
Each applicant for admission to a basic course of training certified by the Commission on Peace Officer Standards and Training that includes the carrying and use of firearms, as prescribed by subdivision (a) of Section 832 and subdivision (a) of Section 832.3, who is not sponsored by a local or other law enforcement agency, or is not a peace officer employed by a state or local agency, department, or district, shall be required to submit written certification from the Department of Justice pursuant to Sections 11122, 11123, and 11124 that the applicant has no criminal history background which would disqualify him or her, pursuant to state or federal law, from owning, possessing, or having under his or her control a firearm.

(Amended by Stats. 2008, Ch. 698, Sec. 27. Effective January 1, 2009.)
13512.
The commission shall make such inquiries as may be necessary to determine whether every city, county, city and county, and district receiving state aid pursuant to this chapter is adhering to the standards for recruitment and training established pursuant to this chapter.

(Amended by Stats. 1969, Ch. 1072.)
13513.
Upon the request of a local jurisdiction, the commission shall provide a counseling service to such local jurisdiction for the purpose of improving the administration, management or operations of a police agency and may aid such jurisdiction in implementing improved practices and techniques.

(Added by Stats. 1967, Ch. 1640.)
13514.
The commission shall prepare a course of instruction for the training of peace officers in the use of tear gas. Such course of instruction may be given, upon approval by the commission, by any agency or institution engaged in the training or instruction of peace officers.

(Added by Stats. 1969, Ch. 1231.)
13514.1.
(a) On or before July 1, 2005, the commission shall develop and disseminate guidelines and standardized training recommendations for all law enforcement officers, supervisors, and managers whose agency assigns them to perform, supervise, or manage Special Weapons and Tactics (SWAT) operations. The guidelines and standardized training recommendations shall be available for use by law enforcement agencies that conduct SWAT operations.

(b) The training and guidelines shall be developed in consultation with law enforcement officers, the Attorney General's office, supervisors, and managers, SWAT trainers, legal advisers, and others selected by the commission. Development of the training and guidelines shall include consideration of the recommendations contained in the Attorney General's Commission on Special Weapons and Tactics (S.W.A.T.) Final Report of 2002.

(c) The standardized training recommendations shall at a minimum include initial training requirements for SWAT operations, refresher or advanced training for experienced SWAT members, and supervision and management of SWAT operations.

(d) The guidelines shall at minimum address legal and practical issues of SWAT operations, personnel selection, fitness requirements, planning, hostage negotiation, tactical issues, safety, rescue methods, after-action evaluation of operations, logistical and resource needs, uniform and firearms requirements, risk assessment, policy considerations, and multijurisdictional SWAT operations. The guidelines may also address tactical casualty care.

(e) The guidelines shall provide procedures for approving the prior training of officers, supervisors, and managers that meet the standards and guidelines developed by the commission pursuant to this section, in order to avoid duplicative training.

(Amended by Stats. 2014, Ch. 668, Sec. 5. (AB 1598) Effective January 1, 2015.)
13514.5.
(a) The commission shall implement on or before July 1, 1999, a course or courses of instruction for the training of law enforcement officers in the handling of acts of civil disobedience and adopt guidelines that may be followed by police agencies in responding to acts of civil disobedience.

(b) The course of training for law enforcement officers shall include adequate consideration of all of the following subjects:
(1) Reasonable use of force.
(2) Dispute resolution.
(3) Nature and extent of civil disobedience, whether it be passive or active resistance.
(4) Media relations.
(5) Public and officer safety.
(6) Documentation, report writing, and evidence collection.
(7) Crowd control.

(c) (1) All law enforcement officers who have received their basic training before July 1, 1999, may participate in supplementary training on responding to acts of civil disobedience, as prescribed and certified by the commission.

(2) Law enforcement agencies are encouraged to include, as part of their advanced officer training program, periodic updates and training on responding to acts of civil disobedience. The commission shall assist these agencies where possible.

(d) (1) The course of instruction, the learning and performance objectives, the standards for the training and the guidelines shall be developed by the commission in consultation with appropriate groups and individuals having expertise in responding to acts of civil disobedience. The groups and individuals shall include, but not be limited to, law enforcement agencies, police academy instructors, subject matter experts, and members of the public. Different regional interests such as rural, suburban, and urban interests may be represented by the participating parties.

(2) The commission, in consultation with the groups and individuals described in paragraph (1), shall review existing training programs to determine in what ways civil disobedience training may be included as part of ongoing programs.

(e) As used in this section, "law enforcement officer" means any peace officer as defined in Chapter 4.5 (commencing with Section 830) of Title 3.

(f) It is the intent of the Legislature in enacting this section to provide law enforcement officers with additional training so as to control acts of civil disobedience with reasonable use of force and to ensure public and officer safety with minimum disruption to commerce and community affairs.

(g) It is also the intent of the Legislature in enacting this section that the guidelines to be developed by the commission should take into consideration the roles and responsibilities of all law enforcement officers responding to acts of civil disobedience.

(Added by Stats. 1998, Ch. 207, Sec. 1. Effective January 1, 1999.)
13515.
(a) Every city police officer or deputy sheriff at a supervisory level and below who is assigned field or investigative duties shall complete an elder and dependent adult abuse training course certified by the Commission on Peace Officer Standards and Training within 18 months of assignment to field duties. Completion of the course may be satisfied by telecourse, video training tape, or other instruction. The training shall, at a minimum, include all of the following subjects:
(1) Relevant laws.
(2) Recognition of elder and dependent adult abuse.
(3) Reporting requirements and procedures.
(4) Neglect of elders and dependent adults.
(5) Fraud of elders and dependent adults.
(6) Physical abuse of elders and dependent adults.
(7) Psychological abuse of elders and dependent adults.
(8) The role of the local adult protective services and public guardian offices.
(9) The legal rights of, and remedies available to, victims of elder or dependent adult abuse pursuant to Section 15657.03 of the Welfare and Institutions Code, including emergency protective orders and the option to request a simultaneous move-out order, and temporary restraining orders.

(b) When producing new or updated training materials pursuant to this section, the commission shall consult with the Bureau of Medi-Cal Fraud and Elder Abuse, local adult protective services offices, the Office of the State Long-Term Care Ombudsman, and other subject matter experts. Any new or updated training materials shall address all of the following:
(1) The jurisdiction and responsibility of law enforcement agencies pursuant to Section 368.5.
(2) The fact that the protected classes of "dependent person" as defined in Section 288 and "dependent adult" as defined in Section 368 include many persons with disabilities, regardless of the fact that most of those persons live independently.
(3) Other relevant information and laws.

(c) The commission also may inform the law enforcement agencies of other relevant training materials.

(Amended by Stats. 2014, Ch. 823, Sec. 1. (AB 2623) Effective January 1, 2015.)
13515.25.
(a) The Commission on Peace Officer Standards and Training shall establish and keep updated a continuing education classroom training course relating to law enforcement interaction with persons with mental disabilities. The training course shall be developed by the commission in consultation with appropriate community, local, and state organizations and agencies that have expertise in the area of mental illness and developmental disability, and with appropriate consumer and family advocate groups. In developing the course, the commission shall also examine existing courses certified by the commission that relate to persons with mental disabilities. The commission shall make the course available to law enforcement agencies in California.

(b) The course described in subdivision (a) shall consist of classroom instruction and shall utilize interactive training methods to ensure that the training is as realistic as possible. The course shall include, at a minimum, core instruction in all of the following:
(1) The cause and nature of mental illnesses and developmental disabilities.
(2) How to identify indicators of mental disability and how to respond appropriately in a variety of common situations.
(3) Conflict resolution and de-escalation techniques for potentially dangerous situations involving a person with a mental disability.
(4) Appropriate language usage when interacting with a person with a mental disability.
(5) Alternatives to lethal force when interacting with potentially dangerous persons with mental disabilities.
(6) Community and state resources available to serve persons with mental disabilities and how these resources can be best utilized by law enforcement to benefit the mentally disabled community.
(7) The fact that a crime committed in whole or in part because of an actual or perceived disability of the victim is a hate crime punishable under Title 11.6 (commencing with Section 422.55) of Part 1.

(c) The course described in subdivision (a) shall be shared with the State Fire Marshal, who may revise the course as appropriate to the firefighter training environment.

(d) The Legislature encourages law enforcement agencies to include the course created in this section, and any other course certified by the commission relating to persons with mental disabilities, as part of their advanced officer training program.

(e) It is the intent of the Legislature to reevaluate the extent to which law enforcement officers are receiving adequate training in how to interact with persons with mental disabilities.

(Amended by Stats. 2016, Ch. 367, Sec. 1. (SB 1221) Effective January 1, 2017.)
13515.26.
(a) The commission shall review the training module in the regular basic course relating to persons with a mental illness, intellectual disability, or substance use disorder, and analyze existing training curricula in order to identify areas where additional training is needed to better prepare law enforcement to effectively address incidents involving mentally disabled persons.

(b) Upon identifying what additional training is needed, the commission shall update the training in consultation with appropriate community, local, and state organizations and agencies that have expertise in the area of mental illness, intellectual disability, and substance use disorders, and with appropriate consumer and family advocate groups.

(c) The training shall address issues related to stigma, shall be culturally relevant and appropriate, and shall include all of the following topics:
(1) Recognizing indicators of mental illness, intellectual disability, and substance use disorders.
(2) Conflict resolution and deescalation techniques for potentially dangerous situations.
(3) Use of force options and alternatives.

(4) The perspective of individuals or families who have experiences with persons with mental illness, intellectual disability, and substance use disorders.
(5) Mental health resources available to the first responders to events that involve mentally disabled persons.
(d) The course of instruction shall be at least 15 hours, and shall include training scenarios and facilitated learning activities relating to law enforcement interaction with persons with mental illness, intellectual disability, and substance use disorders.
(e) The course shall be presented within the existing hours allotted for the regular basic course.
(f) The commission shall implement this section on or before August 1, 2016.
(Added by Stats. 2015, Ch. 468, Sec. 1. (SB 11) Effective January 1, 2016.)
13515.27.
(a) The commission shall establish and keep updated a classroom-based continuing training course that includes instructor-led active learning, such as scenario-based training, relating to behavioral health and law enforcement interaction with persons with mental illness, intellectual disability, and substance use disorders.
(b) This course shall be at least three consecutive hours, may include training scenarios and facilitated learning activities, shall address issues related to stigma, shall be culturally relevant and appropriate, and shall include all of the following topics:
(1) The cause and nature of mental illness, intellectual disability, and substance use disorders.
(2) Indicators of mental illness, intellectual disability, and substance use disorders.
(3) Appropriate responses to a variety of situations involving persons with mental illness, intellectual disability, and substance use disorders.
(4) Conflict resolution and deescalation techniques for potentially dangerous situations.
(5) Appropriate language usage when interacting with potentially emotionally distressed persons.
(6) Resources available to serve persons with mental illness or intellectual disability.
(7) The perspective of individuals or families who have experiences with persons with mental illness, intellectual disability, and substance use disorders.
(c) The course described in subdivisions (a) and (b) shall be made available by the commission to each law enforcement officer with a rank of supervisor or below and who is assigned to patrol duties or to supervise officers who are assigned to patrol duties.
(d) The commission shall implement this section on or before August 1, 2016.
(Added by Stats. 2015, Ch. 468, Sec. 2. (SB 11) Effective January 1, 2016.)
13515.28.
(a) (1) The commission shall require the field training officers who provide instruction in the field training program to have at least eight hours of crisis intervention behavioral health training to better train new peace officers on how to effectively interact with persons with mental illness or intellectual disability. This course shall include classroom instruction and instructor-led active learning, such as scenario-based training, and shall be taught in segments that are at least four hours long.
(2) If a field training officer has completed eight hours of crisis intervention behavioral health training within the past 24 months, or if a field training officer has completed 40 hours of crisis intervention behavioral health training, the requirement described in paragraph (1) shall not apply.
(b) The crisis intervention behavioral health training shall address issues relating to stigma, shall be culturally relevant and appropriate, and shall include all of the following topics:
(1) The cause and nature of mental illnesses and intellectual disabilities.
(2) (A) How to identify indicators of mental illness, intellectual disability, and substance use disorders.
(B) How to distinguish between mental illness, intellectual disability, and substance use disorders.
(C) How to respond appropriately in a variety of situations involving persons with mental illness, intellectual disability, and substance use disorders.
(3) Conflict resolution and deescalation techniques for potentially dangerous situations.
(4) Appropriate language usage when interacting with potentially emotionally distressed persons.
(5) Community and state resources available to serve persons with mental illness or intellectual disability, and how these resources can be best utilized by law enforcement.
(6) The perspective of individuals or families who have experiences with persons with mental illness, intellectual disability, and substance use disorders.
(c) Field training officers assigned or appointed before January 1, 2017, shall complete the crisis intervention behavioral health training by June 30, 2017. Field training officers assigned or appointed on or after January 1, 2017, shall complete the crisis intervention behavioral health training within 180 days of assignment or appointment.
(d) This section does not prevent an agency from requiring its field training officers to complete additional hours of crisis intervention behavioral health training or requiring its field training officers to complete that training earlier than as required by this section.
(Added by Stats. 2015, Ch. 469, Sec. 1. (SB 29) Effective January 1, 2016.)
13515.29.
(a) The commission shall establish and keep updated a field training officer course relating to competencies of the field training program and police training program that addresses how to interact with persons with mental illness or intellectual disability.
(b) This course shall consist of at least four hours of classroom instruction and instructor-led active learning, such as scenario-based training, shall address issues related to stigma, and shall be culturally relevant and appropriate.
(c) All prospective field training officers shall complete the course described in subdivisions (a) and (b) as part of the existing field training officer program.
(d) The commission shall implement the provisions of this section on or before August 1, 2016.
(Added by Stats. 2015, Ch. 469, Sec. 2. (SB 29) Effective January 1, 2016.)
13515.295.
(a) The commission shall, by May 1, 2016, conduct a review and evaluation of the required competencies of the field training program and police training program to identify areas where additional training is necessary to better prepare law enforcement officers to effectively address incidents involving persons with a mental illness or intellectual disability.
(b) Upon identifying what additional training is needed, the commission shall update the training in consultation with appropriate community, local, and state organizations, and agencies that have expertise in the area of mental illness, intellectual disabilities, and substance abuse disorders, and with appropriate consumer and family advocate groups.
(c) The training shall address issues related to stigma, shall be culturally relevant and appropriate, and shall include all of the following topics:
(1) How to identify indicators of mental illness, intellectual disability, substance use disorders, neurological disorders, traumatic brain injury, post-traumatic stress disorder, and dementia.
(2) Autism spectrum disorder.
(3) Genetic disorders, including, but not limited to, Down syndrome.
(4) Conflict resolution and deescalation techniques for potentially dangerous situations.
(5) Alternatives to the use of force when interacting with potentially dangerous persons with mental illness or intellectual disabilities.
(6) The perspective of individuals or families who have experiences with persons with mental illness, intellectual disability, and substance use disorders.
(7) Involuntary holds.
(8) Community and state resources available to serve persons with mental illness or intellectual disability, and how these resources can be best utilized by law enforcement.
(Added by Stats. 2015, Ch. 469, Sec. 3. (SB 29) Effective January 1, 2016.)

13515.30.
(a) By July 1, 2015, the Commission on Peace Officer Standards and Training shall establish and keep updated a continuing education training course relating to law enforcement interaction with mentally disabled and developmentally disabled persons living within a state mental hospital or state developmental center. The training course shall be developed by the commission in consultation with appropriate community, local, and state organizations and agencies that have expertise in the area of mental illness and developmental disability, and with appropriate consumer and family advocate groups. In developing the course, the commission shall also examine existing courses certified by the commission that relate to mentally disabled and developmentally disabled persons. The commission shall make the course available to all law enforcement agencies in California, and the course shall be required for law enforcement personnel serving in law enforcement agencies with jurisdiction over state mental hospitals and state developmental centers, as part of the agency's officer training program.
(b) The course described in subdivision (a) may consist of video-based or classroom instruction. The course shall include, at a minimum, core instruction in all of the following:
(1) The prevalence, cause, and nature of mental illnesses and developmental disabilities.
(2) The unique characteristics, barriers, and challenges of individuals who may be a victim of abuse or exploitation living within a state mental hospital or state developmental center.
(3) How to accommodate, interview, and converse with individuals who may require assistive devices in order to express themselves.
(4) Capacity and consent of individuals with cognitive and intellectual barriers.
(5) Conflict resolution and deescalation techniques for potentially dangerous situations involving mentally disabled or developmentally disabled persons.
(6) Appropriate language usage when interacting with mentally disabled or developmentally disabled persons.
(7) Community and state resources and advocacy support and services available to serve mentally disabled or developmentally disabled persons, and how these resources can be best utilized by law enforcement to benefit the mentally disabled or developmentally disabled community.
(8) The fact that a crime committed in whole or in part because of an actual or perceived disability of the victim is a hate crime punishable under Title 11.6 (commencing with Section 422.55) of Part 1.
(9) Information on the state mental hospital system and the state developmental center system.
(10) Techniques in conducting forensic investigations within institutional settings where jurisdiction may be shared.
(11) Examples of abuse and exploitation perpetrated by caregivers, staff, contractors, or administrators of state mental hospitals and state developmental centers, and how to conduct investigations in instances where a perpetrator may also be a caregiver or provider of therapeutic or other services.
(Added by Stats. 2013, Ch. 673, Sec. 1. (AB 602) Effective January 1, 2014.)
13515.35.
(a) The commission shall, upon the next regularly scheduled review of a training module relating to persons with disabilities, create and make available on DVD and may distribute electronically a course on how to recognize and interact with persons with autistic spectrum disorders. This course shall be designed for, and made available to, peace officers who are first responders to emergency situations.
(b) The training course shall be developed by the commission in consultation with the Department of Developmental Services and appropriate community, local, or other state organizations and agencies that have expertise in the area of autism spectrum disorders. The commission shall make the course available to law enforcement agencies in California.
(c) In addition to the duties contained in subdivisions (a) and (b), the commission shall distribute, as necessary, a training bulletin via the Internet to law enforcement agencies participating in the commission's program on the topic of autism spectrum disorders.
(Added by Stats. 2008, Ch. 621, Sec. 1. Effective January 1, 2009.)
13515.36.
(a) The commission shall meet with the Department of Veterans Affairs and community, local, or other state organizations and agencies that have expertise in the area of traumatic brain injury (TBI) and post-traumatic stress disorder (PTSD) in order to assess the training needed by peace officers, who are first responders in emergency situations, on the topic of returning veterans or other persons suffering from TBI or PTSD.
(b) Should the commission determine that there is an unfulfilled need for training on TBI and PTSD, the commission shall determine the training format that is both fiscally responsible and meets the training needs of the greatest number of officers.
(c) Should the commission determine that there is an unfulfilled need for training on TBI and PTSD, the commission shall, upon the next regularly scheduled review of a training module relating to persons with disabilities, create and make available on DVD and may distribute electronically, or provide by means of another form or method of training, a course on how to recognize and interact with returning veterans or other persons suffering from TBI or PTSD. This course shall be designed for, and made available to, peace officers who are first responders to emergency situations.
(d) The training course shall be developed by the commission in consultation with the Department of Veterans Affairs and appropriate community, local, or other state organizations and agencies that have expertise in the area of TBI and PTSD. The commission shall make the course available to law enforcement agencies in California.
(e) In addition to the duties contained in subdivisions (a), (b),(c), and (d), the commission shall distribute, as necessary, a training bulletin via the Internet to law enforcement agencies participating in the commission's program on the topic of TBI and PTSD.
(f) The commission shall report to the Legislature, no later than June 30, 2012, on the extent to which peace officers are receiving adequate training in how to interact with persons suffering from TBI or PTSD.
(g) (1) The requirement for submitting a report imposed under subdivision (f) is inoperative on June 30, 2016, pursuant to Section 10231.5 of the Government Code.
(2) A report to be submitted pursuant to subdivision (f) shall be submitted in compliance with Section 9795 of the Government Code.
(Added by Stats. 2010, Ch. 490, Sec. 1. (SB 1296) Effective January 1, 2011.)
13515.55.
Every city police officer or deputy sheriff at a supervisory level who is assigned field or investigative duties shall complete a high technology crimes and computer seizure training course certified by the Commission on Peace Officer Standards and Training by January 1, 2000, or within 18 months of assignment to supervisory duties. Completion of the course may be satisfied by telecourse, video training tape, or other instruction. This training shall be offered to all city police officers and deputy sheriffs as part of continuing professional training. The training shall, at a minimum, address relevant laws, recognition of high technology crimes, and computer evidence collection and preservation.
(Amended by Stats. 1999, Ch. 83, Sec. 165. Effective January 1, 2000.)
13516.
(a) The commission shall prepare guidelines establishing standard procedures which may be followed by police agencies in the investigation of sexual assault cases, and

cases involving the sexual exploitation or sexual abuse of children, including, police response to, and treatment of, victims of these crimes.
(b) The course of training leading to the basic certificate issued by the commission shall, on and after July 1, 1977, include adequate instruction in the procedures described in subdivision (a). No reimbursement shall be made to local agencies based on attendance on or after that date at any course which does not comply with the requirements of this subdivision.
(c) The commission shall prepare and implement a course for the training of specialists in the investigation of sexual assault cases, child sexual exploitation cases, and child sexual abuse cases. Officers assigned to investigation duties which include the handling of cases involving the sexual exploitation or sexual abuse of children, shall successfully complete that training within six months of the date the assignment was made.
(d) It is the intent of the Legislature in the enactment of this section to encourage the establishment of sex crime investigation units in police agencies throughout the state, which units shall include, but not be limited to, investigating crimes involving the sexual exploitation and sexual abuse of children.
(e) It is the further intent of the Legislature in the enactment of this section to encourage the establishment of investigation guidelines that take into consideration the sensitive nature of the sexual exploitation and sexual abuse of children with respect to both the accused and the alleged victim.
(Amended by Stats. 1986, Ch. 32, Sec. 3. Effective March 21, 1986.)
13516.5.
(a) The commission shall develop and implement a course or courses of instruction for the training of peace officers in California on commercial sexual exploitation of children (CSEC) and victims of human trafficking that shall include, but not be limited to, the following topics and activities:
(1) The dynamics of commercial sexual exploitation of children.
(2) The impact of trauma on child development and manifestations of trauma in victims of commercial sexual exploitation.
(3) Strategies to identify potential victims of commercial sexual exploitation, including indicators that a youth is being exploited.
(4) Mandatory reporting requirements related to commercial sexual exploitation.
(5) Appropriate interviewing, engagement, and intervention techniques that avoid retraumatizing the victim and promote collaboration with victim-serving agencies.
(6) Introduction to the purpose, scope, and use of specialized child victim interview resources.
(7) Local and state resources that are available to first responders.
(8) Perspectives of victims and their families.
(9) Issues of stigma.
(10) Any other critical topics identified by subject matter experts.
(b) The course of instruction shall be equivalent to a course that the commission produces for officers as part of continuing professional training and shall include facilitated discussions and learning activities, including scenario training exercises.
(c) The training described in subdivision (a) shall be developed with input from survivors of commercial sexual exploitation, the appropriate local and state agencies, and advocates that have expertise in CSEC and human trafficking. These shall include, but not be limited to, the California Child Welfare Council's CSEC Action Team, organizations that provide services specifically to sexually exploited children, and public agencies leading or participating in interagency responses to commercially sexually exploited children.
(Added by Stats. 2018, Ch. 973, Sec. 1. (AB 2992) Effective January 1, 2019.)
13517.
(a) The commission shall prepare guidelines establishing standard procedures which may be followed by police agencies in the detection, investigation, and response to cases in which a minor is a victim of an act of abuse or neglect prohibited by this code. The guidelines shall include procedures for determining whether or not a child should be taken into protective custody. The guidelines shall also include procedures for minimizing the number of times a child is interviewed by law enforcement personnel.
(b) The course of training leading to the basic certificate issued by the commission shall, not later than July 1, 1979, include adequate instruction in the procedures described in subdivision (a).
(c) The commission shall prepare and implement an optional course of training of specialists in the investigation of cases in which a minor is a victim of an act of abuse or neglect prohibited by this code.
(d) The commission shall consult with the State Office of Child Abuse Prevention in developing the guidelines and optional course of training.
(Amended by Stats. 1985, Ch. 672, Sec. 1.)
13517.5.
The commission shall prepare guidelines establishing standard procedures which may be followed by police agencies and prosecutors in interviewing minor witnesses.
(Added by Stats. 1987, Ch. 612, Sec. 1.)
13517.7.
(a) The commission shall develop guidelines and training for use by state and local law enforcement officers to address issues related to child safety when a caretaker parent or guardian is arrested.
(b) The guidelines and training shall, at a minimum, address the following subjects:
(1) Procedures to ensure that officers and custodial employees inquire whether an arrestee has minor dependent children without appropriate supervision.
(2) Authorizing additional telephone calls by arrestees so that they may arrange for the care of minor dependent children.
(3) Use of county child welfare services, as appropriate, and other similar service providers to assist in the placement of dependent children when the parent or guardian is unable or unwilling to arrange suitable care for the child or children.
(4) Identification of local government or nongovernmental agencies able to provide appropriate custodial services.
(5) Temporary supervision of minor children to ensure their safety and well-being.
(6) Sample procedures to assist state and local law enforcement agencies to develop ways to ensure the safety and well-being of children when the parent or guardian has been arrested.
(c) The commission shall use appropriate subject matter experts, including representatives of law enforcement and county child welfare agencies, in developing the guidelines and training required by this section.
(Added by Stats. 2006, Ch. 729, Sec. 2. Effective January 1, 2007.)
13518.
(a) Every city police officer, sheriff, deputy sheriff, marshal, deputy marshal, peace officer member of the Department of the California Highway Patrol, and police officer of a district authorized by statute to maintain a police department, except those whose duties are primarily clerical or administrative, shall meet the training standards prescribed by the Emergency Medical Services Authority for the administration of first aid and cardiopulmonary resuscitation. This training shall include instruction in the use of a portable manual mask and airway assembly designed to prevent the spread of communicable diseases. In addition, satisfactory completion of periodic refresher training or appropriate testing in cardiopulmonary resuscitation and other first aid as prescribed by the Emergency Medical Services Authority shall also be required.
(b) The course of training leading to the basic certificate issued by the commission shall include adequate instruction in the procedures described in subdivision (a). No reimbursement shall be made to local agencies based on attendance at any such course which does not comply with the requirements of this subdivision.
(c) As used in this section, "primarily clerical or administrative" means the performance of clerical or administrative duties for a minimum of 90 percent of the time worked within a pay period.
(Amended by Stats. 1996, Ch. 305, Sec. 57. Effective January 1, 1997.)
13518.1.
In order to prevent the spread of communicable disease, a law enforcement agency employing peace officers described in subdivision (a) of Section 13518 may provide to each of these peace officers an appropriate portable manual mask and airway assembly for use when applying cardiopulmonary resuscitation.
(Amended by Stats. 2013, Ch. 28, Sec. 46. (SB 71) Effective June 27, 2013.)
13518.5.
(a) Each peace officer in California who meets the criteria specified in subdivision (b) shall complete a course in basic maritime operations for law enforcement officers. The course of instruction shall include boat handling, chart reading, navigation rules, and comprehensive training regarding maritime boardings, arrest procedures, vessel identification, searches, and counterterrorism practices and procedures. The curriculum shall be consistent with applicable federal standards and tactical training.
(b) Subdivision (a) shall apply to a peace officer who meets all of the following criteria:
(1) Is employed by a city, county, city and county, or district that has adopted a resolution pursuant to paragraph (2) of subdivision (c).
(2) Is within a classification identified in the resolution adopted pursuant to paragraph (2) of subdivision (c).
(3) Is assigned in a jurisdiction that includes navigable waters.
(4) Serves as a crew member on a waterborne law enforcement vessel.
(c) This section shall become operative in a city, county, city and county, or district when both of the following apply:
(1) The federal Department of Homeland Security has provided funding to a law enforcement agency in a city, county, city and county, or district to implement this section.
(2) The governing body of the city, county, city and county, or district, such as the board of supervisors of a county or the city council, has adopted a resolution agreeing to implement this section and identifying the specific classifications of peace officers in the jurisdiction that will be subject to training pursuant to this section.
(Added by Stats. 2013, Ch. 619, Sec. 1. (AB 979) Effective January 1, 2014.)
13519.
(a) The commission shall implement by January 1, 1986, a course or courses of instruction for the training of law enforcement officers in California in the handling of domestic violence complaints and also shall develop guidelines for law enforcement response to domestic violence. The course or courses of instruction and the guidelines shall stress enforcement of criminal laws in domestic violence situations, availability of civil remedies and community resources, and protection of the victim. When appropriate, the training presenters shall include domestic violence experts with expertise in the delivery of direct services to victims of domestic violence, including utilizing the staff of shelters for battered women in the presentation of training.
(b) As used in this section, "law enforcement officer" means any officer or employee of a local police department or sheriff's office, any peace officer of the Department of Parks and Recreation, as defined in subdivision (f) of Section 830.2, any peace officer of the University of California Police Department, as defined in subdivision (b) of Section 830.2, any peace officer of the California State University Police Departments, as defined in subdivision (c) of Section 830.2, a peace officer, as defined in subdivision (d) of Section 830.31, or a peace officer as defined in subdivisions (a) and (b) of Section 830.32.
(c) The course of basic training for law enforcement officers shall include adequate instruction in the procedures and techniques described below:
(1) The provisions set forth in Title 5 (commencing with Section 13700) relating to response, enforcement of court orders, and data collection.
(2) The legal duties imposed on peace officers to make arrests and offer protection and assistance including guidelines for making felony and misdemeanor arrests.
(3) Techniques for handling incidents of domestic violence that minimize the likelihood of injury to the officer and that promote the safety of the victim.
(4) The nature and extent of domestic violence.
(5) The signs of domestic violence.
(6) The assessment of lethality or signs of lethal violence in domestic violence situations.
(7) The legal rights of, and remedies available to, victims of domestic violence.
(8) The use of an arrest by a private person in a domestic violence situation.
(9) Documentation, report writing, and evidence collection.
(10) Domestic violence diversion as provided in Chapter 2.6 (commencing with Section 1000.6) of Title 6 of Part 2.
(11) Tenancy issues and domestic violence.
(12) The impact on children of law enforcement intervention in domestic violence.
(13) The services and facilities available to victims and batterers.
(14) The use and applications of this code in domestic violence situations.
(15) Verification and enforcement of temporary restraining orders when (A) the suspect is present and (B) the suspect has fled.
(16) Verification and enforcement of stay-away orders.
(17) Cite and release policies.
(18) Emergency assistance to victims and how to assist victims in pursuing criminal justice options.
(d) The guidelines developed by the commission shall also incorporate the foregoing factors.
(e) (1) All law enforcement officers who have received their basic training before January 1, 1986, shall participate in supplementary training on domestic violence subjects, as prescribed and certified by the commission.
(2) Except as provided in paragraph (3), the training specified in paragraph (1) shall be completed no later than January 1, 1989.
(3) (A) The training for peace officers of the Department of Parks and Recreation, as defined in subdivision (g) of Section 830.2, shall be completed no later than January 1, 1992.
(B) The training for peace officers of the University of California Police Department and the California State University Police Departments, as defined in Section 830.2, shall be completed no later than January 1, 1993.
(C) The training for peace officers employed by a housing authority, as defined in subdivision (d) of Section 830.31, shall be completed no later than January 1, 1995.
(4) Local law enforcement agencies are encouraged to include, as a part of their advanced officer training program, periodic updates and training on domestic violence. The commission shall assist where possible.
(f) (1) The course of instruction, the learning and performance objectives, the standards for the training, and the guidelines shall be developed by the commission in consultation with appropriate groups and individuals having an interest and expertise in the field of domestic violence. The groups and individuals shall include, but shall not be limited to, the following: one representative each from the California Peace Officers' Association, the Peace Officers' Research Association of California, the State Bar of California, the California Women Lawyers' Association, and the State Commission on the Status of Women and Girls; two representatives from the commission; two representatives from the California Partnership to End Domestic Violence; two peace officers, recommended by the commission, who are experienced in the provision of domestic violence training; and two domestic violence experts, recommended by the California Partnership to End Domestic Violence, who are experienced in the provision of direct services to victims of

domestic violence and at least one representative of service providers serving the lesbian, gay, bisexual, and transgender community in connection with domestic violence. At least one of the persons selected shall be a former victim of domestic violence.

(2) The commission, in consultation with these groups and individuals, shall review existing training programs to determine in what ways domestic violence training might be included as a part of ongoing programs.

(g) Each law enforcement officer below the rank of supervisor who is assigned to patrol duties and would normally respond to domestic violence calls or incidents of domestic violence shall complete, every two years, an updated course of instruction on domestic violence that is developed according to the standards and guidelines developed pursuant to subdivision (d). The instruction required pursuant to this subdivision shall be funded from existing resources available for the training required pursuant to this section. It is the intent of the Legislature not to increase the annual training costs of local government entities.

(Amended by Stats. 2018, Ch. 137, Sec. 1. (SB 1331) Effective January 1, 2019.)

13519.05.

(a) The commission shall implement by January 1, 2002, a course or courses of instruction for the training of law enforcement officers in California in the handling of stalking complaints and also shall develop guidelines for law enforcement response to stalking. The course or courses of instruction and the guidelines shall stress enforcement of criminal laws in stalking situations, availability of civil remedies and community resources, and protection of the victim. Where appropriate, the training presenters shall include stalking experts with expertise in the delivery of direct services to victims of stalking. Completion of the course may be satisfied by telecommunication, video training tape, or other instruction.

(b) (1) As used in this section, "law enforcement officer" means any officer or employee of a local police department or sheriff's office, any peace officer of the Department of Parks and Recreation, as defined in subdivision (f) of Section 830.2, any peace officer of the University of California Police Department, as defined in subdivision (b) of Section 830.2, any peace officer of the California State University Police Departments, as defined in subdivision (c) of Section 830.2, a peace officer, as defined in subdivision (d) of Section 830.31, or a peace officer as defined in subdivisions (a) and (b) of Section 830.32.

(2) As used in this section, "stalking" means the offense defined in Section 646.9.

(c) (1) The course of instruction, the learning and performance objectives, the standards for the training, and the guidelines shall be developed by the commission in consultation with appropriate groups and individuals having an interest and expertise in the field of stalking.

(2) The commission, in consultation with these groups and individuals, shall review existing training programs to determine in what ways stalking training might be included as a part of ongoing programs.

(d) Participation in the course or courses specified in this section by peace officers or the agencies employing them, is voluntary.

(Added by Stats. 2000, Ch. 564, Sec. 2. Effective January 1, 2001.)

13519.07.

(a) The Department of Justice shall make accessible to law enforcement agencies, via a department bulletin and the California Law Enforcement Web, the commission's "Guidelines For Handling Missing Persons Investigations" or any subsequent similar guidelines created by the commission, relating to the investigation of missing persons.

(b) By January 1, 2012, law enforcement agencies shall adopt a checklist document directing peace officers on investigation guidelines and resources available to them in the early hours of a missing person investigation. The commission's "Guidelines For Handling Missing Persons Investigations" should be used as a model policy or example in developing the checklist document.

(c) By January 1, 2012, law enforcement agencies shall adopt a policy, regulations, or guidelines on missing persons investigations that are consistent with state and federal law. The commission's "Guidelines For Handling Missing Persons Investigations" should be used as a model policy or example in developing the policy, regulations, or guidelines.

(d) By January 1, 2012, law enforcement agencies shall utilize, at a minimum, the department's missing person reporting form for the initial contact with the parent or family member reporting a missing person.

(e) As necessary and appropriate, the commission shall modify its missing persons investigations guidelines and curriculum with contemporary information. Specifically, the commission should consider including and revising their guidelines to include both of the following:

(1) Steps for law enforcement agencies in the first few hours after the reporting of a missing person.

(2) Information on the availability of the department task forces, the SAFE Task Force Regional Teams, and other entities that can assist in the search for a missing person.

(Added by Stats. 2010, Ch. 224, Sec. 2. (AB 33) Effective January 1, 2011.)

13519.1.

(a) The commission shall implement by July 1, 1988, a course or courses of instruction for the training of law enforcement officers and law enforcement dispatchers in the handling of missing person and runaway cases and shall also develop guidelines for law enforcement response to missing person and runaway cases. The course or courses of instruction and the guidelines shall include, but not be limited to, timeliness and priority of response, assisting persons who make missing person reports to contact the appropriate law enforcement agency in the jurisdiction of the residence address of the missing person or runaway and the appropriate law enforcement agency in the jurisdiction where the missing person or runaway was last seen, and coordinating law enforcement agencies for the purpose of efficiently and effectively taking and investigating missing person reports.

As used in this section, "law enforcement" includes any officers or employees of a local police or sheriff's office or of the California Highway Patrol.

(b) The course of basic training for law enforcement officers and law enforcement dispatchers shall, not later than January 1, 1989, include adequate instruction in the handling of missing person and runaway cases developed pursuant to subdivision (a).

(c) All law enforcement officers and law enforcement dispatchers who have received their basic training before January 1, 1989, shall participate in supplementary training on missing person and runaway cases, as prescribed and certified by the commission. The training required by this subdivision shall be completed not later than January 1, 1991.

(Added by Stats. 1987, Ch. 705, Sec. 3.)

13519.2.

(a) The commission shall, on or before July 1, 1990, include in the basic training course for law enforcement officers, adequate instruction in the handling of persons with developmental disabilities or mental illness, or both. Officers who complete the basic training prior to July 1, 1990, shall participate in supplementary training on this topic. This supplementary training shall be completed on or before July 1, 1992. Further training courses to update this instruction shall be established, as deemed necessary by the commission.

(b) The course of instruction relating to the handling of developmentally disabled or mentally ill persons shall be developed by the commission in consultation with appropriate groups and individuals having an interest and expertise in this area. In addition to providing instruction on the handling of these persons, the course shall also include information on the cause and nature of developmental disabilities and mental illness, as well as the community resources available to serve these persons.

(Added by Stats. 1988, Ch. 593, Sec. 1.)

13519.3.

(a) Effective July 1, 1990, the commission shall establish, for those peace officers specified in subdivision (a) of Section 13510 who are assigned to patrol or investigations, a course on the nature of sudden infant death syndrome and the handling of cases involving the sudden deaths of infants. The course shall include information on the community resources available to assist families and child care providers who have lost a child to sudden infant death syndrome. Officers who are employed after January 1, 1990, shall complete a course in sudden infant death syndrome prior to the issuance of the Peace Officer Standards and Training basic certificate, and shall complete training on this topic on or before July 1, 1992.

(b) The commission, in consultation with experts in the field of sudden infant death syndrome, shall prepare guidelines establishing standard procedures which may be followed by law enforcement agencies in the investigation of cases involving sudden deaths of infants.

(c) The course relating to sudden infant death syndrome and the handling of cases of sudden infant deaths shall be developed by the commission in consultation with experts in the field of sudden infant death syndrome. The course shall include instruction in the standard procedures developed pursuant to subdivision (b). In addition, the course shall include information on the nature of sudden infant death syndrome which shall be taught by experts in the field of sudden infant death syndrome.

(d) The commission shall review and modify the basic course curriculum to include sudden infant death syndrome awareness as part of death investigation training.

(e) When the instruction and training are provided by a local agency, a fee shall be charged sufficient to defray the entire cost of instruction and training.

(Added by Stats. 1989, Ch. 1111, Sec. 7.)

13519.4.

(a) The commission shall develop and disseminate guidelines and training for all peace officers in California as described in subdivision (a) of Section 13510 and who adhere to the standards approved by the commission, on the racial and cultural differences among the residents of this state. The course or courses of instruction and the guidelines shall stress understanding and respect for racial, identity, and cultural differences, and development of effective, noncombative methods of carrying out law enforcement duties in a diverse racial, identity, and cultural environment.

(b) The course of basic training for peace officers shall include adequate instruction on racial, identity, and cultural diversity in order to foster mutual respect and cooperation between law enforcement and members of all racial, identity, and cultural groups. In developing the training, the commission shall consult with appropriate groups and individuals having an interest and expertise in the field of racial, identity, and cultural awareness and diversity.

(c) For the purposes of this section the following shall apply:

(1) "Disability," "gender," "nationality," "religion," and "sexual orientation" have the same meaning as in Section 422.55.

(2) "Culturally diverse" and "cultural diversity" include, but are not limited to, disability, gender, nationality, religion, and sexual orientation issues.

(3) "Racial" has the same meaning as "race or ethnicity" in Section 422.55.

(4) "Stop" has the same meaning as in paragraph (2) of subdivision (g) of Section 12525.5 of the Government Code.

(d) The Legislature finds and declares as follows:

(1) The working men and women in California law enforcement risk their lives every day. The people of California greatly appreciate the hard work and dedication of peace officers in protecting public safety. The good name of these officers should not be tarnished by the actions of those few who commit discriminatory practices.

(2) Racial or identity profiling is a practice that presents a great danger to the fundamental principles of our Constitution and a democratic society. It is abhorrent and cannot be tolerated.

(3) Racial or identity profiling alienates people from law enforcement, hinders community policing efforts, and causes law enforcement to lose credibility and trust among the people whom law enforcement is sworn to protect and serve.

(4) Pedestrians, users of public transportation, and vehicular occupants who have been stopped, searched, interrogated, and subjected to a property seizure by a peace officer for no reason other than the color of their skin, national origin, religion, gender identity or expression, housing status, sexual orientation, or mental or physical disability are the victims of discriminatory practices.

(5) It is the intent of the Legislature in enacting the changes to this section made by the act that added this paragraph that additional training is required to address the pernicious practice of racial or identity profiling and that enactment of this section is in no way dispositive of the issue of how the state should deal with racial or identity profiling.

(e) "Racial or identity profiling," for purposes of this section, is the consideration of, or reliance on, to any degree, actual or perceived race, color, ethnicity, national origin, age, religion, gender identity or expression, sexual orientation, or mental or physical disability in deciding which persons to subject to a stop or in deciding upon the scope or substance of law enforcement activities following a stop, except that an officer may consider or rely on characteristics listed in a specific suspect description. The activities include, but are not limited to, traffic or pedestrian stops, or actions during a stop, such as asking questions, frisks, consensual and nonconsensual searches of a person or any property, seizing any property, removing vehicle occupants during a traffic stop, issuing a citation, and making an arrest.

(f) A peace officer shall not engage in racial or identity profiling.

(g) Every peace officer in this state shall participate in expanded training as prescribed and certified by the Commission on Peace Officers Standards and Training.

(h) The curriculum shall be evidence-based and shall include and examine evidence-based patterns, practices, and protocols that make up racial or identity profiling, including implicit bias. This training shall prescribe evidence-based patterns, practices, and protocols that prevent racial or identity profiling. In developing the training, the commission shall consult with the Racial and Identity Profiling Advisory Board established pursuant to subdivision (j). The course of instruction shall include, but not be limited to, significant consideration of each of the following subjects:

(1) Identification of key indices and perspectives that make up racial, identity, and cultural differences among residents in a local community.

(2) Negative impact of intentional and implicit biases, prejudices, and stereotyping on effective law enforcement, including examination of how historical perceptions of discriminatory enforcement practices have harmed police-community relations and contributed to injury, death, disparities in arrest detention and incarceration rights, and wrongful convictions.

(3) The history and role of the civil and human rights movement and struggles and their impact on law enforcement.

(4) Specific obligations of peace officers in preventing, reporting, and responding to discriminatory or biased practices by fellow peace officers.

(5) Perspectives of diverse, local constituency groups and experts on particular racial, identity, and cultural and police-community relations issues in a local area.

(6) The prohibition against racial or identity profiling in subdivision (f).

(i) Once the initial basic training is completed, each peace officer in California as described in subdivision (a) of Section 13510 who adheres to the standards approved by the commission shall be required to complete a refresher course every five years thereafter, or on a more frequent basis if deemed necessary, in order to keep current with changing racial, identity, and cultural trends.

(j) (1) Beginning July 1, 2016, the Attorney General shall establish the Racial and Identity Profiling Advisory Board (RIPA) for the purpose of eliminating racial and identity profiling, and improving diversity and racial and identity sensitivity in law enforcement.

(2) RIPA shall include the following members:

(A) The Attorney General, or his or her designee.

(B) The President of the California Public Defenders Association, or his or her designee.

(C) The President of the California Police Chiefs Association, or his or her designee.

(D) The President of the California State Sheriffs' Association, or his or her designee.

(E) The President of the Peace Officers Research Association of California, or his or her designee.

(F) The Commissioner of the California Highway Patrol, or his or her designee.

(G) A university professor who specializes in policing, and racial and identity equity.

(H) Two representatives of human or civil rights tax-exempt organizations who specialize in civil or human rights.

(I) Two representatives of community organizations who specialize in civil or human rights and criminal justice, and work with victims of racial and identity profiling. At least one representative shall be between 16 and 24 years of age.

(J) Two religious clergy members who specialize in addressing and reducing racial and identity bias toward individuals and groups.

(K) Up to two other members that the Governor may prescribe.

(L) Up to two other members that the President pro Tempore of the Senate may prescribe.

(M) Up to two other members that the Speaker of the Assembly may prescribe.

(3) Each year, on an annual basis, RIPA shall do the following:

(A) Analyze the data reported pursuant to Section 12525.5 of the Government Code and Section 13012 of this code.

(B) Analyze law enforcement training under this section.

(C) Work in partnership with state and local law enforcement agencies to review and analyze racial and identity profiling policies and practices across geographic areas in California.

(D) Conduct, and consult available, evidence-based research on intentional and implicit biases, and law enforcement stop, search, and seizure tactics.

(E) Issue a report that provides RIPA's analysis under subparagraphs (A) to (D), inclusive, and detailed findings on the past and current status of racial and identity profiling, and makes policy recommendations for eliminating racial and identity profiling. RIPA shall post the report on its Internet Web site. Each report shall include disaggregated statistical data for each reporting law enforcement agency. The report shall include, at minimum, each reporting law enforcement agency's total results for each data collection criterion under subdivision (b) of Section 12525.5 of the Government Code for each calendar year. The reports shall be retained and made available to the public by posting those reports on the Department of Justice's OpenJustice Web portal. The first annual report shall be issued no later than January 1, 2018. The reports are public records within the meaning of subdivision (d) of Section 6252 of the Government Code and are open to public inspection pursuant to Sections 6253, 6256, 6257, and 6258 of the Government Code.

(F) Hold at least three public meetings annually to discuss racial and identity profiling, and potential reforms to prevent racial and identity profiling. Each year, one meeting shall be held in northern California, one in central California, and one in southern California. RIPA shall provide the public with notice of at least 60 days before each meeting.

(4) Pursuant to subdivision (e) of Section 12525.5 of the Government Code, RIPA shall advise the Attorney General in developing regulations for the collection and reporting of stop data, and ensuring uniform reporting practices across all reporting agencies.

(5) Members of RIPA shall not receive compensation, nor per diem expenses, for their services as members of RIPA.

(6) No action of RIPA shall be valid unless agreed to by a majority of its members.

(7) The initial terms of RIPA members shall be four years.

(8) Each year, RIPA shall elect two of its members as cochairpersons.

(Amended by Stats. 2016, Ch. 418, Sec. 12. (AB 2524) Effective January 1, 2017.)

13519.41.

(a) The commission shall develop and implement a course of training regarding sexual orientation and gender identity minority groups in this state. In developing the training, the commission shall consult with sexual orientation and gender identity minority members of law enforcement and the community who have expertise in the area of sexual orientation and gender identity, including at least one male, one female, and one transgender person.

(b) The course of training for officers and dispatchers described in subdivision (a) shall be incorporated into the course or courses of basic training for law enforcement officers and dispatchers and shall include, but not be limited to, the following:

(1) The difference between sexual orientation and gender identity and how these two aspects of identity relate to each other and to race, culture, and religion.

(2) The terminology used to identify and describe sexual orientation and gender identity.

(3) How to create an inclusive workplace within law enforcement for sexual orientation and gender identity minorities.

(4) Important moments in history related to sexual orientation and gender identity minorities and law enforcement.

(5) How law enforcement can respond effectively to domestic violence and hate crimes involving sexual orientation and gender identity minorities.

(c) Law enforcement officers, administrators, executives, and dispatchers may participate in supplementary training that includes all of the topics described in this section. The supplementary training shall fulfill the Commission on Peace Officer Standards and Training requirements for continuing professional training and shall include facilitated discussions and learning activities, including scenario training exercises. Additional training courses to update this instruction shall be established as deemed necessary by the commission.

(Added by Stats. 2018, Ch. 969, Sec. 1. (AB 2504) Effective January 1, 2019.)

13519.5.

The commission shall, on or before July 1, 1991, implement a course or courses of instruction to provide ongoing training to the appropriate peace officers on methods of gang and drug law enforcement.

(Added by Stats. 1990, Ch. 333, Sec. 2.)

13519.6.

(a) The commission shall develop guidelines and a course of instruction and training for law enforcement officers who are employed as peace officers, or who are not yet employed as a peace officer but are enrolled in a training academy for law enforcement officers, addressing hate crimes. "Hate crimes," for purposes of this section, has the same meaning as in Section 422.55.

(b) The course shall make maximum use of audio and video communication and other simulation methods and shall include instruction in each of the following:

(1) Indicators of hate crimes.

(2) The impact of these crimes on the victim, the victim's family, and the community, and the assistance and compensation available to victims.

(3) Knowledge of the laws dealing with hate crimes and the legal rights of, and the remedies available to, victims of hate crimes.

(4) Law enforcement procedures, reporting, and documentation of hate crimes.

(5) Techniques and methods to handle incidents of hate crimes in a noncombative manner.

(6) Multimission criminal extremism, which means the nexus of certain hate crimes, antigovernment extremist crimes, anti-reproductive-rights crimes, and crimes committed in whole or in part because of the victims' actual or perceived homelessness.

(7) The special problems inherent in some categories of hate crimes, including gender-bias crimes, disability-bias crimes, including those committed against homeless persons with disabilities, anti-immigrant crimes, and anti-Arab and anti-Islamic crimes, and techniques and methods to handle these special problems.

(8) Preparation for, and response to, possible future anti-Arab/Middle Eastern and anti-Islamic hate crimewaves, and any other future hate crime waves that the Attorney General determines are likely.

(c) The guidelines developed by the commission shall incorporate the procedures and techniques specified in subdivision (b), and shall include a framework and possible content of a general order or other formal policy on hate crimes that all state law enforcement agencies shall adopt and the commission shall encourage all local law enforcement agencies to adopt. The elements of the framework shall include, but not be limited to, the following:

(1) A message from the law enforcement agency's chief executive officer to the agency's officers and staff concerning the importance of hate crime laws and the agency's commitment to enforcement.

(2) The definition of "hate crime" in Section 422.55.

(3) References to hate crime statutes including Section 422.6.

(4) A title-by-title specific protocol that agency personnel are required to follow, including, but not limited to, the following:

(A) Preventing and preparing for likely hate crimes by, among other things, establishing contact with persons and communities who are likely targets, and forming and cooperating with community hate crime prevention and response networks.

(B) Responding to reports of hate crimes, including reports of hate crimes committed under the color of authority.

(C) Accessing assistance, by, among other things, activating the Department of Justice hate crime rapid response protocol when necessary.

(D) Providing victim assistance and followup, including community followup.

(E) Reporting.

(d) (1) The course of training leading to the basic certificate issued by the commission shall include the course of instruction described in subdivision (a).

(2) Every state law enforcement and correctional agency, and every local law enforcement and correctional agency to the extent that this requirement does not create a state-mandated local program cost, shall provide its peace officers with the basic course of instruction as revised pursuant to the act that amends this section in the 2003–04 session of the Legislature, beginning with officers who have not previously received the training. Correctional agencies shall adapt the course as necessary.

(e) As used in this section, "peace officer" means any person designated as a peace officer by Section 830.1 or 830.2.

(f) The additional training requirements imposed under this section by legislation adopted in 2004 shall be implemented by July 1, 2007.

(Amended by Stats. 2004, Ch. 700, Sec. 29. Effective January 1, 2005.)

13519.64.

(a) The Legislature finds and declares that research, including "Special Report to the Legislature on Senate Resolution 18: Crimes Committed Against Homeless Persons" by the Department of Justice and "Hate, Violence, and Death: A Report on Hate Crimes Against People Experiencing Homelessness from 1999–2002" by the National Coalition for the Homeless demonstrate that California has had serious and unaddressed problems of crime against homeless persons, including homeless persons with disabilities.

(b) (1) By July 1, 2005, the Commission on Peace Officer Standards and Training, using available funding, shall develop a two-hour telecourse to be made available to all law enforcement agencies in California on crimes against homeless persons and on how to deal effectively and humanely with homeless persons, including homeless persons with disabilities. The telecourse shall include information on multimission criminal extremism, as defined in Section 13519.6. In developing the telecourse, the commission shall consult subject-matter experts including, but not limited to, homeless and formerly homeless persons in California, service providers and advocates for homeless persons in California, experts on the disabilities that homeless persons commonly suffer, the California Council of Churches, the National Coalition for the Homeless, the Senate Office of Research, and the Criminal Justice Statistics Center of the Department of Justice.

(2) Every state law enforcement agency, and every local law enforcement agency, to the extent that this requirement does not create a state-mandated local program cost, shall provide the telecourse to its peace officers.

(Added by Stats. 2004, Ch. 700, Sec. 30. Effective January 1, 2005.)

13519.7.

(a) On or before August 1, 1994, the commission shall develop complaint guidelines to be followed by city police departments, county sheriffs' departments, districts, and state university departments, for peace officers who are victims of sexual harassment in the workplace. In developing the complaint guidelines, the commission shall consult with appropriate groups and individuals having an expertise in the area of sexual harassment.

(b) The course of basic training for law enforcement officers shall, no later than January 1, 1995, include instruction on sexual harassment in the workplace. The training shall include, but not be limited to, the following:

(1) The definition of sexual harassment.

(2) A description of sexual harassment, utilizing examples.

(3) The illegality of sexual harassment.

(4) The complaint process, legal remedies, and protection from retaliation available to victims of sexual harassment.

In developing this training, the commission shall consult with appropriate groups and individuals having an interest and expertise in the area of sexual harassment.

(c) All peace officers who have received their basic training before January 1, 1995, shall receive supplementary training on sexual harassment in the workplace by January 1, 1997.

(Added by Stats. 1993, Ch. 126, Sec. 1. Effective January 1, 1994.)

13519.8.

(a) (1) The commission shall implement a course or courses of instruction for the regular and periodic training of law enforcement officers in the handling of high-speed vehicle pursuits and shall also develop uniform, minimum guidelines for adoption and promulgation by California law enforcement agencies for response to high-speed vehicle pursuits. The guidelines and course of instruction shall stress the importance of vehicle safety and protecting the public at all times, include a regular assessment of law enforcement's vehicle pursuit policies, practices, and training, and recognize the need to balance the known offense and the need for immediate capture against the risks to officers and other citizens of a high-speed pursuit. These guidelines shall be a resource for each agency executive to use in the creation of a specific pursuit policy that the agency is encouraged to adopt and promulgate, and that reflects the needs of the agency, the jurisdiction it serves, and the law.

(2) As used in this section, "law enforcement officer" includes any peace officer of a local police or sheriff's department or the California Highway Patrol, or of any other law enforcement agency authorized by law to conduct vehicular pursuits.

(b) The course or courses of basic training for law enforcement officers and the guidelines shall include adequate consideration of each of the following subjects:

(1) When to initiate a pursuit.

(2) The number of involved law enforcement units permitted.

(3) Responsibilities of primary and secondary law enforcement units.
(4) Driving tactics.
(5) Helicopter assistance.
(6) Communications.
(7) Capture of suspects.
(8) Termination of a pursuit.
(9) Supervisory responsibilities.
(10) Blocking, ramming, boxing, and roadblock procedures.
(11) Speed limits.
(12) Interjurisdictional considerations.
(13) Conditions of the vehicle, driver, roadway, weather, and traffic.
(14) Hazards to uninvolved bystanders or motorists.
(15) Reporting and postpursuit analysis.
(c) (1) All law enforcement officers who have received their basic training before January 1, 1995, shall participate in supplementary training on high-speed vehicle pursuits, as prescribed and certified by the commission.
(2) Law enforcement agencies are encouraged to include, as part of their advanced officer training program, periodic updates and training on high-speed vehicle pursuit. The commission shall assist where possible.
(d) (1) The course or courses of instruction, the learning and performance objectives, the standards for the training, and the guidelines shall be developed by the commission in consultation with appropriate groups and individuals having an interest and expertise in the field of high-speed vehicle pursuits. The groups and individuals shall include, but not be limited to, law enforcement agencies, police academy instructors, subject matter experts, and members of the public.
(2) The commission, in consultation with these groups and individuals, shall review existing training programs to determine the ways in which high-speed pursuit training may be included as part of ongoing programs.
(e) It is the intent of the Legislature that each law enforcement agency adopt, promulgate, and require regular and periodic training consistent with an agency's specific pursuit policy that, at a minimum, complies with the guidelines developed under subdivisions (a) and (b).
(Amended by Stats. 2005, Ch. 485, Sec. 4. Effective January 1, 2006.)

13519.9.
(a) On or before January 1, 1995, the commission shall establish the Robert Presley Institute of Criminal Investigation which will make available to criminal investigators of California's law enforcement agencies an advanced training program to meet the needs of working investigators in specialty assignments, such as arson, auto theft, homicide, and narcotics.
(b) The institute shall provide an array of investigation training, including the following:
(1) Core instruction in matters common to all investigative activities.
(2) Advanced instruction through foundation specialty courses in the various investigative specialties.
(3) Completion of a variety of elective courses pertaining to investigation.
(c) (1) Instruction in core foundation and specialty courses shall be designed not only to impart new knowledge, but to evoke from students the benefit of their experience and ideas in a creative and productive instructional design environment.
(2) Instructors shall be skilled and knowledgeable both in subject matter and in the use of highly effective instructional strategies.
(d) (1) The commission shall design and operate the institute to constantly improve the effectiveness of instruction.
(2) The institute shall make use of the most modern instructional design and equipment, including computer-assisted instruction, scenarios, and case studies.
(3) The institute shall ensure that proper facilities, such as crime scene training areas, are available for use by students.
(Added by Stats. 1994, Ch. 43, Sec. 3. Effective January 1, 1995.)

13519.12.
(a) Pursuant to Section 13510, the Commission on Peace Officer Standards and Training shall establish training standards and develop a course of instruction that includes the criteria for the curriculum content recommended by the Curriculum Development Advisory Committee established pursuant to Section 8588.10 of the Government Code, involving the responsibilities of first responders to terrorism incidents. The course of instruction shall address the training needs of peace officers at a managerial or supervisory level and below who are assigned to field duties. The training shall be developed in consultation with the Department of Justice and other individuals knowledgeable about terrorism and address current theory, terminology, historical issues, and procedures necessary to appropriately respond to and effectively mitigate the effects of a terrorism incident. The training standards and course of instruction may, if appropriate, include coordination with emergency medical services providers that respond to an incident, tactical casualty care, and other standards of emergency care as established pursuant to Section 1799.50 of the Health and Safety Code by the Commission on Emergency Medical Services.
(b) The commission shall expedite the delivery of this training to law enforcement through maximum use of its local and regional delivery systems.
(c) To maximize the availability and delivery of training, the commission shall develop a course of instruction to train trainers and first responders dealing with terrorism incidents using a variety of formats.
(d) Every police chief and sheriff, the Commissioner of the Highway Patrol, and other general law enforcement agency executives may determine the members of their agency to receive the emergency response to terrorism incidents training developed by the commission under this section. The persons to be trained may include, but are not limited to, peace officers that perform general law enforcement duties at a managerial or supervisory level or below and are assigned to field duties.
(e) For purposes of this section, a "terrorism incident" includes, but is not limited to, an active shooter incident. An "active shooter incident" is an incident where an individual is actively engaged in killing or attempting to kill people.
(Amended by Stats. 2014, Ch. 668, Sec. 6. (AB 1598) Effective January 1, 2015.)

13519.14.
(a) The commission shall implement by January 1, 2007, a course or courses of instruction for the training of law enforcement officers in California in the handling of human trafficking complaints and also shall develop guidelines for law enforcement response to human trafficking. The course or courses of instruction and the guidelines shall stress the dynamics and manifestations of human trafficking, identifying and communicating with victims, providing documentation that satisfy the Law Enforcement Agency (LEA) endorsement required by federal law, collaboration with federal law enforcement officials, therapeutically appropriate investigative techniques, the availability of civil and immigration remedies and community resources, and protection of the victim. Where appropriate, the training presenters shall include human trafficking experts with experience in the delivery of direct services to victims of human trafficking. Completion of the course may be satisfied by telecommunication, video training tape, or other instruction.
(b) As used in this section, "law enforcement officer" means any officer or employee of a local police department or sheriff's office, and any peace officer of the Department of the California Highway Patrol, as defined by subdivision (a) of Section 830.2.
(c) The course of instruction, the learning and performance objectives, the standards for the training, and the guidelines shall be developed by the commission in consultation with appropriate groups and individuals having an interest and expertise in the field of human trafficking.
(d) The commission, in consultation with these groups and individuals, shall review existing training programs to determine in what ways human trafficking training may be included as a part of ongoing programs. .
(e) Every law enforcement officer who is assigned field or investigative duties shall complete a minimum of two hours of training in a course or courses of instruction pertaining to the handling of human trafficking complaints as described in subdivision (a) by July 1, 2014, or within six months of being assigned to that position, whichever is later.
(Amended November 6, 2012, by initiative Proposition 35, Sec. 14.)

13519.15.
The commission shall prepare guidelines establishing standard procedures which may be followed by law enforcement agencies in the investigation and reporting of cases involving anti-reproductive-rights crimes. In developing the guidelines, the commission shall consider recommendations 1 to 12, inclusive, 14, and 15 of the report prepared by the Department of Justice and submitted to the Legislature pursuant to the Reproductive Rights Law Enforcement Act (Title 5.7 (commencing with Section 13775)).
(Added by Stats. 2008, Ch. 206, Sec. 1. Effective January 1, 2009.)

ARTICLE 3. Peace Officers' Training Fund and Allocations Therefrom [13520 - 13526.3]

(Article 3 added by Stats. 1959, Ch. 1823.)

13520.
(a) There is hereby created in the State Treasury a Peace Officers' Training Fund, which is hereby appropriated, without regard to fiscal years, exclusively for costs of administration and for grants to local governments and districts pursuant to this chapter. The fund is abolished on January 1, 2020, and any moneys remaining in the fund shall revert to the State Penalty Fund.
(b) Notwithstanding any other law, the State Penalty Fund is the successor fund to the Peace Officers' Training Fund. All assets, liabilities, revenues, and expenditures of the Peace Officers' Training Fund shall be transferred to, and become a part of, the State Penalty Fund, as provided in Section 16346 of the Government Code. Any references in state law to the Peace Officers' Training Fund shall be construed to refer to the State Penalty Fund.
(Amended by Stats. 2019, Ch. 25, Sec. 46. (SB 94) Effective June 27, 2019.)

13522.
Any city, county, city and county, district, or joint powers agency, that desires to receive state aid pursuant to this chapter shall make application to the commission for the aid. The initial application shall be accompanied by a certified copy of an ordinance, or in the case of the University of California, the California State University, and agencies not authorized to act by ordinance, by a resolution, adopted by its governing body providing that while receiving any state aid pursuant to this chapter, the city, county, city and county, district, or joint powers agency will adhere to the standards for recruitment and training established by the commission. The application shall contain any information the commission may request.
(Amended by Stats. 2013, Ch. 59, Sec. 9. (SB 514) Effective January 1, 2014.)

13523.
(a) The commission shall annually allocate and the State Treasurer shall periodically pay from the Peace Officers' Training Fund, at intervals specified by the commission, to each city, county, district, or joint powers agency, that has applied and qualified for aid pursuant to this chapter an amount determined by the commission pursuant to standards set forth in its regulations. The commission shall grant aid only on a basis that is equally proportionate among cities, counties, districts, and joint powers agencies. State aid shall only be provided for training expenses of full-time regularly paid employees, as defined by the commission, of eligible agencies from cities, counties, districts, or joint powers agencies.
(b) In no event shall any allocation be made to any city, county, district, or joint power agency that is not adhering to the standards established by the commission as applicable to that city, county, district, or joint powers agency.
(c) This section shall become inoperative on July 1, 2019, and, as of January 1, 2020, is repealed.
(Amended by Stats. 2018, Ch. 36, Sec. 27. (AB 1812) Effective June 27, 2018. Inoperative July 1, 2019. Repealed as of January 1, 2020, by its own provisions. See later operative version as added by Sec. 28, Stats. 2018, Ch. 36.)

13523.
(a) The commission shall annually allocate and the State Treasurer shall periodically pay from the State Penalty Fund, at intervals specified by the commission, to each city, county, district, or joint powers agency that has applied and qualified for aid pursuant to this chapter an amount determined by the commission pursuant to standards set forth in its regulations. The commission shall grant aid only on a basis that is equally proportionate among cities, counties, districts, and joint powers agencies. State aid shall only be provided for training expenses of full-time regularly paid employees, as defined by the commission, of eligible agencies from cities, counties, districts, or joint powers agencies.
(b) An allocation shall not be made to any city, county, district, or joint power agency that is not adhering to the standards established by the commission as applicable to that city, county, district, or joint powers agency.
(c) This section shall become operative on July 1, 2019.
(Added by Stats. 2018, Ch. 36, Sec. 28. (AB 1812) Effective June 27, 2018. Section operative July 1, 2019, by its own provisions.)

13524.
Any county wishing to receive state aid pursuant to this chapter for the training of regularly employed and paid inspectors and investigators of a district attorney's office, as defined in Section 830.1 who conduct criminal investigations, shall include such request for aid in its application to the commission pursuant to Sections 13522 and 13523.
(Added by Stats. 1981, Ch. 710, Sec. 3.)

13525.
Any city, county, city and county, district, or joint powers agency which desires to receive state aid pursuant to this chapter for the training of regularly employed and paid local public safety dispatchers, as described in subdivision (c) of Section 13510, shall include that request for aid in its application to the commission pursuant to Sections 13522 and 13523.
(Amended by Stats. 1990, Ch. 333, Sec. 4.)

13526.
An allocation shall not be made from the State Penalty Fund, pursuant to this article, to a local government agency if the agency was not entitled to receive funding under any of the provisions of this article, as they read on December 31, 1989.
(Amended by Stats. 2019, Ch. 25, Sec. 47. (SB 94) Effective June 27, 2019.)

13526.1.
(a) It is the intent of the Legislature in adding this section that effect be given to amendments made by Chapter 950 of the Statutes of 1989. The Legislature recognizes those amendments were intended to make port wardens and special officers of the Harbor Department of the City of Los Angeles entitled to allocations from the State Penalty Fund for state aid pursuant to this chapter, notwithstanding the amendments made by Chapter 1165 of the Statutes of 1989, which added Section 13526 to this code.
(b) Notwithstanding Section 13526, for the purposes of this chapter, the port wardens and special officers of the Harbor Department of the City of Los Angeles shall be entitled to receive funding from the State Penalty Fund.
(Amended by Stats. 2019, Ch. 25, Sec. 48. (SB 94) Effective June 27, 2019.)

13526.2.
Notwithstanding Section 13526, for the purposes of this chapter, the housing authority police departments of the City of Los Angeles and the City of Oakland shall be entitled to receive funding from the State Penalty Fund, pursuant to this article.
(Amended by Stats. 2019, Ch. 25, Sec. 49. (SB 94) Effective June 27, 2019.)

13526.3.
Notwithstanding Section 13526, for the purposes of this chapter, joint powers agencies formed pursuant to Article 1 (commencing with Section 6500) of Chapter 5 of Division 7 of Title 1 of the Government Code shall be entitled to receive funding from the State Penalty Fund, pursuant to this article. This section is declaratory of existing law.
(Amended by Stats. 2019, Ch. 25, Sec. 50. (SB 94) Effective June 27, 2019.)

ARTICLE 4. Peace Officers [13540 - 13542]
(Article 4 added by Stats. 1989, Ch. 1165, Sec. 41.)

13540.
(a) Any person or persons desiring peace officer status under Chapter 4.5 (commencing with Section 830) of Title 3 of Part 2 who, on January 1, 1990, were not entitled to be designated as peace officers under that chapter shall request the Commission on Peace Officer Standards and Training to undertake a feasibility study regarding designating that person or persons as peace officers. The request and study shall be undertaken in accordance with regulations adopted by the commission. The commission may charge any person requesting a study, a fee, not to exceed the actual cost of undertaking the study. Nothing in this article shall apply to or otherwise affect the authority of the Director of Corrections, the Director of the Youth Authority, the Director of the Youthful Offender Parole Board, or the Secretary of the Youth and Adult Correctional Agency to designate peace officers as provided for in Section 830.5.
(b) Any person or persons who are designated as peace officers under Chapter 4.5, (commencing with Section 830) of Title 3 of Part 2, and who desire a change in peace officer designation or status, shall request the Commission on Peace Officer Standards and Training to undertake a study to assess the need for a change in designation or status. The request and study shall be undertaken in accordance with regulations adopted by the commission. The commission may charge any person, agency, or organization requesting a study, a fee, not to exceed the actual cost of undertaking the study.
(Amended by Stats. 2000, Ch. 96, Sec. 1. Effective July 7, 2000.)

13541.
(a) Any study undertaken under this article shall include, but shall not be limited to, the current and proposed duties and responsibilities of persons employed in the category seeking the designation change, their field law enforcement duties and responsibilities, their supervisory and management structure, and their proposed training methods and funding sources.
(b) A study undertaken pursuant to subdivision (b) of Section 13540 shall include, but shall not be limited to, the current and proposed duties and responsibilities of the persons employed in the category seeking the designation change and their field law enforcement duties and responsibilities, and the extent to which their current duties and responsibilities require additional peace officer powers and authority.
(Amended by Stats. 2000, Ch. 96, Sec. 2. Effective July 7, 2000.)

13542.
(a) In order for the commission to give a favorable recommendation as to a change in designation to peace officer status, the person or persons desiring the designation change shall be employed by an agency with a supervisory structure consisting of a chief law enforcement officer, the agency shall agree to comply with the training requirements set forth in Section 832, and shall be subject to the funding restriction set forth in Section 13526. The commission shall issue the study and its recommendations to the requesting person or agency within 18 months of the mutual acceptance of a contract between the requesting person or agency and the commission. A copy of that study and recommendations shall also be submitted to the Legislature.
(b) (1) In order for the commission to give a favorable recommendation as to a change in peace officer designation or status, the person or persons desiring the change in peace officer designation or status shall be employed by an agency that is currently participating in the Peace Officer Standard Training program.
(2) If the designation change is moving the person or persons into Section 830.1, the person or persons shall obtain the basic certificate issued by the Commission on Peace Officer Standards and Training, set forth in Section 832.4.
(3) The commission shall issue the study and its recommendations, as specified in subdivision (b) of Section 13540, to the requesting person or persons, within 12 months of the mutual acceptance of a contract between the requesting person or agency and the commission, or as soon as possible thereafter if the commission shows good cause as to the need for an extension of the 12-month time period.
(4) A copy of that study and recommendation shall also be submitted to the Legislature.
(Amended by Stats. 2000, Ch. 96, Sec. 3. Effective July 7, 2000.)

ARTICLE 5. Local Law Enforcement Accreditation [13550 - 13553]
(Article 5 added by Stats. 1992, Ch. 1249, Sec. 5.)

13550.
For the purposes of this article the following terms apply:
(a) "Local law enforcement" means city police and county sheriffs' departments.
(b) "Accreditation" means meeting and maintaining standards that render the agency eligible for certification by ascribing to publicly recognized principles for the professional operation of local law enforcement agencies.
(Added by Stats. 1992, Ch. 1249, Sec. 5. Effective January 1, 1993.)

13551.
(a) The Commission on Peace Officer Standards and Training shall develop regulations and professional standards for the law enforcement accreditation program when funding for this purpose from nongeneral funds is approved by the Legislature. The program shall provide standards for the operation of law enforcement agencies and shall be available as soon as practical after funding becomes available. The standards shall serve as a basis for the uniform operation of law enforcement agencies throughout the state to best serve the interests of the people of this state.
(b) The commission may, from time to time, amend the regulations and standards or adopt new standards relating to the accreditation program.
(Amended by Stats. 1996, Ch. 591, Sec. 2. Effective January 1, 1997.)

13552.
(a) Participation in this accreditation program is limited to police departments, sheriffs' departments, and the California Highway Patrol. Other law enforcement agencies shall be eligible for accreditation after January 1, 1998.
(b) Participation shall be voluntary and shall be initiated upon the application of the chief executive officer of each agency.
(Amended by Stats. 1994, Ch. 43, Sec. 5. Effective January 1, 1995.)

13553.
Nothing in this article shall prohibit a law enforcement agency from establishing standards that exceed the minimum accreditation standards set by the commission.
(Added by Stats. 1992, Ch. 1249, Sec. 5. Effective January 1, 1993.)

TITLE 4.5. COMMISSION ON CORRECTIONAL PEACE OFFICER STANDARDS AND TRAINING [13600 - 13603]
(Title 4.5 heading added by Stats. 2011, Ch. 136, Sec. 8.)

13600.
(a) (1) The Legislature finds and declares that peace officers of the state correctional system, including youth and adult correctional facilities, fulfill responsibilities that require creation and application of sound selection criteria for applicants and standards for their training prior to assuming their duties. For the purposes of this section, correctional peace officers are peace officers as defined in Section 830.5 and employed or designated by the Department of Corrections and Rehabilitation.
(2) The Legislature further finds that sound applicant selection and training are essential to public safety and in carrying out the missions of the Department of Corrections and Rehabilitation in the custody and care of the state's offender population. The greater degree of professionalism which will result from sound screening criteria and a significant training curriculum will greatly aid the department in maintaining smooth, efficient, and safe operations and effective programs.
(b) There is within the Department of Corrections and Rehabilitation a Commission on Correctional Peace Officer Standards and Training, hereafter referred to, for purposes of this title, as the CPOST.
(c) (1) The executive board of the CPOST shall be composed of six voting members.
(A) Three members from, appointed by, and representing the management of, the Department of Corrections and Rehabilitation, one of whom shall represent the Division of Juvenile Justice or the Division of Rehabilitative Programs.
(B) Three members from, and appointed by the Governor upon recommendation by, and representing the membership of, the California Correctional Peace Officers' Association. Two members shall be rank-and-file persons from State Bargaining Unit 6 and one member shall be supervisory.
(C) Appointments shall be for four years.
(D) Promotion of a member of the CPOST shall invalidate the appointment of that member and shall require the recommendation and appointment of a new member if the member was appointed from rank and file or from supervisory personnel and promoted out of his or her respective rank and file or supervisory position during his or her term on the CPOST.
(2) Each appointing authority shall appoint one alternate member for each regular member who it appoints pursuant to paragraph (1). Every alternate member shall possess the same qualifications as a regular member and shall substitute for, and vote in place of, a regular member who was appointed by the same appointing authority whenever a regular member is absent.
(d) The rules for voting on the executive board of the CPOST shall be as follows:
(1) Decisions shall be made by a majority vote.
(2) Proxy voting shall not be permitted.
(3) Tentative approval of a decision by the CPOST may be taken by a telephone vote. The CPOST members' decision shall be documented in writing and submitted to the CPOST for confirmation at the next scheduled CPOST meeting so as to become a part of the permanent record.
(e) The executive board of the CPOST shall adopt rules as it deems necessary for efficient operations, including, but not limited to, the appointment of advisory members for forming whatever committees it deems necessary to conduct its business. These rules shall conform to the State Personnel Board's rules and regulations, the Department of Human Resources' rules and regulations, and the provisions of the State Bargaining Unit 6 memorandum of understanding.
(f) The executive board shall seek advice from national experts, including university and college institutions and correctional associations, on issues pertaining to adult corrections, juvenile justice, and the training of the Department of Corrections and Rehabilitation staff that are relevant to its mission. To this end, the executive board shall seek information from experts with the most specific knowledge concerning the subject matter.
(g) This section shall be operative on July 1, 2015.
(Amended by Stats. 2018, Ch. 903, Sec. 21. (SB 1504) Effective January 1, 2019.)

13601.
(a) (1) The CPOST shall develop, approve, and monitor standards for the selection and training of state correctional peace officer apprentices.
(2) Any standard for selection established under this subdivision shall be subject to approval by the Department of Human Resources. Using the psychological and screening standards approved by the Department of Human Resources, the Department of Human Resources or the Department of Corrections and Rehabilitation shall ensure that, prior to training, each applicant who has otherwise qualified in all physical and other testing requirements to be a peace officer the Department of Corrections and Rehabilitation, is determined to be free from emotional or mental conditions that might adversely affect the exercise of his or her duties and powers as a peace officer pursuant to the standards developed by CPOST.
(3) When developing, approving, and monitoring the standards for training of state correctional peace officer apprentices, the CPOST shall consider including additional training in the areas of mental health and rehabilitation, as well as coursework on the theory and history of corrections.
(b) The CPOST may approve standards for a course in the carrying and use of firearms for correctional peace officers that is different from that prescribed pursuant to Section 832. The standards shall take into consideration the different circumstances presented within the institutional setting from that presented to other law enforcement agencies outside the correctional setting.
(c) Notwithstanding Section 3078 of the Labor Code, the length of the probationary period for correctional peace officer apprentices shall be determined by the CPOST subject to approval by the State Personnel Board, pursuant to Section 19170 of the Government Code.
(d) The CPOST shall develop, approve, and monitor standards for advanced rank-and-file and supervisory state correctional peace officer and training programs for the Department of Corrections and Rehabilitation. When a correctional peace officer is promoted within the department, he or she shall be provided with and be required to complete these secondary training experiences.
(e) The CPOST shall develop, approve, and monitor standards for the training of state correctional peace officers in the department in the handling of stress associated with their duties.
(f) Toward the accomplishment of the objectives of this section, the CPOST may confer with, and may avail itself of the assistance and recommendations of, other state and local agencies, boards, or commissions.
(g) Notwithstanding the authority of the CPOST, the department shall design and deliver training programs, shall conduct validation studies, and shall provide program support. The CPOST shall monitor program compliance by the department.
(h) The CPOST may disapprove any training courses created by the department pursuant to the standards developed by CPOST if it determines that the courses do not meet the prescribed standards. Training may continue with existing curriculum pending resolution.

(i) The CPOST shall annually submit an estimate of costs to conduct those inquiries and audits as may be necessary to determine whether the department and each of its institutions and parole regions are adhering to the standards developed by the CPOST, and shall conduct those inquiries and audits consistent with the annual Budget Act.
(j) The CPOST shall establish and implement procedures for reviewing and issuing decisions concerning complaints or recommendations from interested parties regarding the CPOST rules, regulations, standards, or decisions.
(Amended by Stats. 2016, Ch. 33, Sec. 36. (SB 843) Effective June 27, 2016.)
13602.
(a) The Department of Corrections and Rehabilitation may use the training academy at Galt or the training center in Stockton. The academy at Galt shall be known as the Richard A. McGee Academy. The training divisions, in using the funds, shall endeavor to minimize costs of administration so that a maximum amount of the funds will be used for providing training and support to correctional peace officers while being trained by the department.
(b) Notwithstanding subdivision (a), and pursuant to Section 13602.1, the Department of Corrections and Rehabilitation may use a training academy established for the California City Correctional Center. This academy, in using the funds, shall endeavor to minimize costs of administration so that a maximum amount of the funds will be used for providing training and support to correctional employees who are being trained by the department.
(c) Each new cadet who attends an academy shall complete the course of training, pursuant to standards approved by the CPOST before he or she may be assigned to a post or job as a peace officer. Every newly appointed first-line or second-line supervisor in the Department of Corrections and Rehabilitation shall complete the course of training, pursuant to standards approved by the CPOST for that position.
(d) The Department of Corrections and Rehabilitation shall make every effort to provide training prior to commencement of supervisorial duties. If this training is not completed within six months of appointment to that position, any first-line or second-line supervisor shall not perform supervisory duties until the training is completed.
(Amended (as amended by Stats. 2013, Ch. 310, Sec. 19) by Stats. 2015, Ch. 26, Sec. 37. (SB 85) Effective June 24, 2015.)
13602.1.
The Department of Corrections and Rehabilitation may establish a training academy for correctional peace officers in southern California.
(Amended by Stats. 2015, Ch. 26, Sec. 39. (SB 85) Effective June 24, 2015.)
13603.
(a) The Department of Corrections and Rehabilitation shall, until January 1, 2019, provide 480 hours of training to each correctional peace officer cadet. The department shall provide 520 hours of training to each correctional peace officer cadet who commences training on or after January 1, 2019. This training shall be completed by the cadet prior to his or her assignment to a post or position as a correctional peace officer.
(b) The CPOST shall determine the on-the-job training requirements for correctional peace officers.
(c) The department shall provide a minimum of two weeks of training to each newly appointed first-line supervisor.
(d) Training standards previously established pursuant to this section shall remain in effect until training requirements are established by the CPOST pursuant to Section 13602.
(Amended by Stats. 2018, Ch. 36, Sec. 29. (AB 1812) Effective June 27, 2018.)

TITLE 4.7. Law Enforcement Agency Regulations [13650- 13650.]

(Title 4.7 added by Stats. 2018, Ch. 978, Sec. 2.)
13650.
Commencing January 1, 2020, the Commission on Peace Officer Standards and Training and each local law enforcement agency shall conspicuously post on their Internet Web sites all current standards, policies, practices, operating procedures, and education and training materials that would otherwise be available to the public if a request was made pursuant to the California Public Records Act (Chapter 3.5 (commencing with Section 6250) of Division 7 of Title 1 of the Government Code).
(Added by Stats. 2018, Ch. 978, Sec. 2. (SB 978) Effective January 1, 2019.)

TITLE 5. LAW ENFORCEMENT RESPONSE TO DOMESTIC VIOLENCE [13700 - 13732]

(Title 5 added by Stats. 1984, Ch. 1609, Sec. 3.)

CHAPTER 1. General Provisions [13700 - 13702]

(Chapter 1 added by Stats. 1984, Ch. 1609, Sec. 3.)
13700.
As used in this title:
(a) "Abuse" means intentionally or recklessly causing or attempting to cause bodily injury, or placing another person in reasonable apprehension of imminent serious bodily injury to himself or herself, or another.
(b) "Domestic violence" means abuse committed against an adult or a minor who is a spouse, former spouse, cohabitant, former cohabitant, or person with whom the suspect has had a child or is having or has had a dating or engagement relationship. For purposes of this subdivision, "cohabitant" means two unrelated adult persons living together for a substantial period of time, resulting in some permanency of relationship. Factors that may determine whether persons are cohabiting include, but are not limited to, (1) sexual relations between the parties while sharing the same living quarters, (2) sharing of income or expenses, (3) joint use or ownership of property, (4) whether the parties hold themselves out as spouses, (5) the continuity of the relationship, and (6) the length of the relationship.
(c) "Officer" means any officer or employee of a local police department or sheriff's office, and any peace officer of the Department of the California Highway Patrol, the Department of Parks and Recreation, the University of California Police Department, or the California State University and College Police Departments, as defined in Section 830.2, a peace officer of the Department of General Services of the City of Los Angeles, as defined in subdivision (c) of Section 830.31, a housing authority patrol officer, as defined in subdivision (d) of Section 830.31, a peace officer as defined in subdivisions (a) and (b) of Section 830.32, or a peace officer as defined in subdivision (a) of Section 830.33.
(d) "Victim" means a person who is a victim of domestic violence.
(Amended by Stats. 2016, Ch. 50, Sec. 75. (SB 1005) Effective January 1, 2017.)
13701.
(a) Every law enforcement agency in this state shall develop, adopt, and implement written policies and standards for officers' responses to domestic violence calls by January 1, 1986. These policies shall reflect that domestic violence is alleged criminal conduct. Further, they shall reflect existing policy that a request for assistance in a

situation involving domestic violence is the same as any other request for assistance where violence has occurred.
(b) The written policies shall encourage the arrest of domestic violence offenders if there is probable cause that an offense has been committed. These policies also shall require the arrest of an offender, absent exigent circumstances, if there is probable cause that a protective order issued under Chapter 4 (commencing with Section 2040) of Part 1 of Division 6, Division 10 (commencing with Section 6200), or Chapter 6 (commencing with Section 7700) of Part 3 of Division 12, of the Family Code, or Section 136.2 of this code, or by a court of any other state, a commonwealth, territory, or insular possession subject to the jurisdiction of the United States, a military tribunal, or a tribe has been violated. These policies shall discourage, when appropriate, but not prohibit, dual arrests. Peace officers shall make reasonable efforts to identify the dominant aggressor in any incident. The dominant aggressor is the person determined to be the most significant, rather than the first, aggressor. In identifying the dominant aggressor, an officer shall consider the intent of the law to protect victims of domestic violence from continuing abuse, the threats creating fear of physical injury, the history of domestic violence between the persons involved, and whether either person acted in self-defense. These arrest policies shall be developed, adopted, and implemented by July 1, 1996. Notwithstanding subdivision (d), law enforcement agencies shall develop these policies with the input of local domestic violence agencies.
(c) These existing local policies and those developed shall be in writing and shall be available to the public upon request and shall include specific standards for the following:
(1) Felony arrests.
(2) Misdemeanor arrests.
(3) Use of citizen arrests.
(4) Verification and enforcement of temporary restraining orders when (A) the suspect is present and (B) the suspect has fled.
(5) Verification and enforcement of stay-away orders.
(6) Cite and release policies.
(7) Emergency assistance to victims, such as medical care, transportation to a shelter, or a hospital for treatment when necessary, and police standbys for removing personal property and assistance in safe passage out of the victim's residence.
(8) Assisting victims in pursuing criminal options, such as giving the victim the report number and directing the victim to the proper investigation unit.
(9) Furnishing written notice to victims at the scene, including, but not limited to, all of the following information:
(A) A statement informing the victim that despite official restraint of the person alleged to have committed domestic violence, the restrained person may be released at any time.
(B) A statement that, "For further information about a shelter you may contact ____."
(C) A statement that, "For information about other services in the community, where available, you may contact ____."
(D) A statement that, "For information about the California Victims' Compensation Program, you may contact 1-800-777-9229."
(E) A statement informing the victim of domestic violence that he or she may ask the district attorney to file a criminal complaint.
(F) A statement informing the victim of the right to go to the superior court and file a petition requesting any of the following orders for relief:
(i) An order restraining the attacker from abusing the victim and other family members.
(ii) An order directing the attacker to leave the household.
(iii) An order preventing the attacker from entering the residence, school, business, or place of employment of the victim.
(iv) An order awarding the victim or the other parent custody of or visitation with a minor child or children.
(v) An order restraining the attacker from molesting or interfering with minor children in the custody of the victim.
(vi) An order directing the party not granted custody to pay support of minor children, if that party has a legal obligation to do so.
(vii) An order directing the defendant to make specified debit payments coming due while the order is in effect.
(viii) An order directing that either or both parties participate in counseling.
(G) A statement informing the victim of the right to file a civil suit for losses suffered as a result of the abuse, including medical expenses, loss of earnings, and other expenses for injuries sustained and damage to property, and any other related expenses incurred by the victim or any agency that shelters the victim.
(H) In the case of an alleged violation of subdivision (e) of Section 243 or Section 261, 261.5, 262, 273.5, 286, 287, or 289, or former Section 288a, a "Victims of Domestic Violence" card which shall include, but is not limited to, the following information:
(i) The names and phone numbers of or local county hotlines for, or both the phone numbers of and local county hotlines for, local shelters for battered women and rape victim counseling centers within the county, including those centers specified in Section 13837, and their 24-hour counseling service telephone numbers.
(ii) A simple statement on the proper procedures for a victim to follow after a sexual assault.
(iii) A statement that sexual assault by a person who is known to the victim, including sexual assault by a person who is the spouse of the victim, is a crime.
(iv) A statement that domestic violence or assault by a person who is known to the victim, including domestic violence or assault by a person who is the spouse of the victim, is a crime.
(I) A statement informing the victim that strangulation may cause internal injuries and encouraging the victim to seek medical attention.
(10) Writing of reports.
(d) In the development of these policies and standards, each local department is encouraged to consult with domestic violence experts, such as the staff of the local shelter for battered women and their children. Departments may use the response guidelines developed by the commission in developing local policies.
(Amended by Stats. 2018, Ch. 423, Sec. 119. (SB 1494) Effective January 1, 2019.)
13702.
Every law enforcement agency in this state shall develop, adopt, and implement written policies and standards for dispatchers' response to domestic violence calls by July 1, 1991. These policies shall reflect that calls reporting threatened, imminent, or ongoing domestic violence, and the violation of any protection order, including orders issued pursuant to Section 136.2, and restraining orders, shall be ranked among the highest priority calls. Dispatchers are not required to verify the validity of the protective order before responding to the request for assistance.
(Added by Stats. 1990, Ch. 1692, Sec. 4.)

CHAPTER 2. Restraining Orders [13710 - 13711]

(Chapter 2 added by Stats. 1984, Ch. 1609, Sec. 3.)
13710.
(a) (1) Law enforcement agencies shall maintain a complete and systematic record of all protection orders with respect to domestic violence incidents, including orders which have not yet been served, issued pursuant to Section 136.2, restraining orders, and proofs of service in effect. This shall be used to inform law enforcement officers

responding to domestic violence calls of the existence, terms, and effective dates of protection orders in effect.
(2) The police department of a community college or school district described in subdivision (a) or (b) of Section 830.32 shall notify the sheriff or police chief of the city in whose jurisdiction the department is located of any protection order served by the department pursuant to this section.
(b) The terms and conditions of the protection order remain enforceable, notwithstanding the acts of the parties, and may be changed only by order of the court.
(c) Upon request, law enforcement agencies shall serve the party to be restrained at the scene of a domestic violence incident or at any time the party is in custody.
(Amended by Stats. 2013, Ch. 161, Sec. 2. (AB 81) Effective August 27, 2013.)
13711.
Whenever a protection order with respect to domestic violence incidents, including orders issued pursuant to Section 136.2 and restraining orders, is applied for or issued, it shall be the responsibility of the clerk of the superior court to distribute a pamphlet to the person who is to be protected by the order that includes the following:
(a) Information as specified in subdivision (i) of Section 13701.
(b) Notice that it is the responsibility of the victim to request notification of an inmate's release.
(c) Notice that the terms and conditions of the protection order remain enforceable, notwithstanding any acts of the parties, and may be changed only by order of the court.
(d) Notice that the protection order is enforceable in any state, in a commonwealth, territory, or insular possession subject to the jurisdiction of the United States, or on a reservation, and general information about agencies in other jurisdictions that may be contacted regarding enforcement of a protective order issued by a court of this state.
(Amended by Stats. 1999, Ch. 661, Sec. 12. Effective January 1, 2000.)

CHAPTER 4. Data Collection [13730 - 13732]

(Chapter 4 added by Stats. 1984, Ch. 1609, Sec. 3.)
13730.
(a) Each law enforcement agency shall develop a system, by January 1, 1986, for recording all domestic violence-related calls for assistance made to the department, including whether weapons are involved, or whether the incident involved strangulation or suffocation. All domestic violence-related calls for assistance shall be supported with a written incident report, as described in subdivision (c), identifying the domestic violence incident. Monthly, the total number of domestic violence calls received and the numbers of those cases involving weapons or strangulation or suffocation shall be compiled by each law enforcement agency and submitted to the Attorney General.
(b) The Attorney General shall report annually to the Governor, the Legislature, and the public the total number of domestic violence-related calls received by California law enforcement agencies, the number of cases involving weapons, the number of cases involving strangulation or suffocation, and a breakdown of calls received by agency, city, and county.
(c) Each law enforcement agency shall develop an incident report form that includes a domestic violence identification code by January 1, 1986. In all incidents of domestic violence, a report shall be written and shall be identified on the face of the report as a domestic violence incident. The report shall include at least all of the following:
(1) A notation of whether the officer or officers who responded to the domestic violence call observed any signs that the alleged abuser was under the influence of alcohol or a controlled substance.
(2) A notation of whether the officer or officers who responded to the domestic violence call determined if any law enforcement agency had previously responded to a domestic violence call at the same address involving the same alleged abuser or victim.
(3) A notation of whether the officer or officers who responded to the domestic violence call found it necessary, for the protection of the peace officer or other persons present, to inquire of the victim, the alleged abuser, or both, whether a firearm or other deadly weapon was present at the location, and, if there is an inquiry, whether that inquiry disclosed the presence of a firearm or other deadly weapon. Any firearm or other deadly weapon discovered by an officer at the scene of a domestic violence incident shall be subject to confiscation pursuant to Division 4 (commencing with Section 18250) of Title 2 of Part 6.
(4) A notation of whether there were indications that the incident involved strangulation or suffocation. This includes whether any witness or victim reported any incident of strangulation or suffocation, whether any victim reported symptoms of strangulation or suffocation, or whether the officer observed any signs of strangulation or suffocation.
(Amended by Stats. 2017, Ch. 331, Sec. 2. (SB 40) Effective January 1, 2018.)
13731.
(a) The San Diego Association of Governments may serve as the regional clearinghouse for criminal justice data involving domestic violence. The association may obtain monthly crime statistics from all law enforcement agencies in San Diego County. These law enforcement agencies may include their domestic violence supplements in the monthly crime reports that are supplied to the association. The association may obtain client-based data regarding clients or victims of domestic violence who seek protection in San Diego County shelters.
(b) Contingent upon the appropriation of funds therefor, the association shall do all of the following:
(1) Create a standardized, uniform intake form, to be referred to as a Compilation of Research and Evaluation Intake Instrument, also known as C.O.R.E., for use in San Diego County's domestic violence shelters. This form shall be completed and ready to use in the field for data collection purposes not later than March 31, 1997. The C.O.R.E. intake form shall be standardized to compile the same information from all clients for all shelters.
(2) Collect and analyze the standardized, uniform intake form in order to compile information including, but not limited to, victim sociodemographic characteristics, descriptions of domestic violence incidents pertaining to each victim and services needed by domestic violence shelter clients within San Diego County.
(3) Use the collected client-based data to describe the nature and scope of violence from the perspective of domestic violence shelter clients and to determine the service needs of clients and what gaps in service delivery exist, so that resources can be appropriately targeted and allocated. All data supplied to the association shall be stripped of any information regarding the personal identity of an individual to protect the privacy of domestic violence shelter clients.
(4) Establish an advisory committee in order to facilitate the research effort and to assess the value of the research project. The advisory committee shall consist of representation from the shelters, as well as members of the San Diego County Domestic Violence Council, local justice administrators, and the principal investigator. The advisory committee shall meet at least four times before April 30, 1999, to review the progress of the research, including research methodology, data collection instruments, preliminary analyses, and work product as they are drafted. Advisory committee members shall evaluate the final research product in terms of applicability and utility of findings and recommendations.
(Amended by Stats. 2001, Ch. 745, Sec. 163. Effective October 12, 2001.)
13732.
(a) The Legislature finds and declares that a substantial body of research demonstrates a strong connection between domestic violence and child abuse. However, despite this connection, child abuse and domestic violence services and agencies often fail to coordinate appropriately at the local level. It is the intent of the Legislature in enacting this section to improve preventative and supportive services to families experiencing violence in order to prevent further abuse of children and the victims of domestic violence. It is the further intent of this section that child protective services agencies develop a protocol which clearly sets forth the criteria for a child protective services response to a domestic violence related incident in a home in which a child resides.
(b) Commencing January 1, 2003, child protective services agencies, law enforcement, prosecution, child abuse and domestic violence experts, and community-based organizations serving abused children and victims of domestic violence shall develop, in collaboration with one another, protocols as to how law enforcement and child welfare agencies will cooperate in their response to incidents of domestic violence in homes in which a child resides. The requirements of this section shall not apply to counties where protocols consistent with this section already have been developed.
(Added by Stats. 2002, Ch. 187, Sec. 3. Effective January 1, 2003.)

TITLE 5.3. Family Justice Centers and Multidisciplinary Teams [13750 - 13753]

(Heading of Title 5.3 amended by Stats. 2018, Ch. 802, Sec. 1.)

CHAPTER 1. Family Justice Centers [13750 - 13753]

(Chapter 1 heading added by Stats. 2018, Ch. 802, Sec. 2.)
13750.
(a) A city, county, city and county, or community-based nonprofit organization may each establish a multiagency, multidisciplinary family justice center to assist victims of domestic violence, sexual assault, elder or dependent adult abuse, and human trafficking, to ensure that victims of abuse are able to access all needed services in one location in order to enhance victim safety, increase offender accountability, and improve access to services for victims of domestic violence, sexual assault, elder or dependent adult abuse, and human trafficking.
(b) For purposes of this title, the following terms have the following meanings:
(1) "Abuse" has the same meaning as set forth in Section 6203 of the Family Code.
(2) "Domestic violence" has the same meaning as set forth in Section 6211 of the Family Code.
(3) "Sexual assault" means an act or attempt made punishable by Section 220, 261, 261.5, 262, 264.1, 266c, 269, 285, 286, 287, 288, 288.5, 289, or 647.6, or former Section 288a.
(4) "Elder or dependent adult abuse" means an act made punishable by Section 368.
(5) "Human trafficking" has the same meaning as set forth in Section 236.1.
(c) For purposes of this title, family justice centers shall be defined as multiagency, multidisciplinary service centers where public and private agencies assign staff members on a full-time or part-time basis in order to provide services to victims of domestic violence, sexual assault, elder or dependent adult abuse, or human trafficking from one location in order to reduce the number of times victims must tell their story, reduce the number of places victims must go for help, and increase access to services and support for victims and their children. Staff members at a family justice center may be comprised of, but are not limited to, the following:
(1) Law enforcement personnel.
(2) Medical personnel.
(3) District attorneys and city attorneys.
(4) Victim-witness program personnel.
(5) Domestic violence shelter service staff.
(6) Community-based rape crisis, domestic violence, and human trafficking advocates.
(7) Social service agency staff members.
(8) Child welfare agency social workers.
(9) County health department staff.
(10) City or county welfare and public assistance workers.
(11) Nonprofit agency counseling professionals.
(12) Civil legal service providers.
(13) Supervised volunteers from partner agencies.
(14) Other professionals providing services.
(d) Nothing in this section is intended to abrogate existing laws regarding privacy or information sharing. Family justice center staff members shall comply with the laws governing their respective professions.
(e) Victims of crime shall not be denied services on the grounds of criminal history. No criminal history search shall be conducted of a victim at a family justice center without the victim's written consent unless the criminal history search is pursuant to a criminal investigation.
(f) Victims of crime shall not be required to participate in the criminal justice system or cooperate with law enforcement in order to receive counseling, medical care, or other services at a family justice center.
(g) (1) Each family justice center shall consult with community-based domestic violence, sexual assault, elder or dependent adult abuse, and human trafficking agencies in partnership with survivors of violence and abuse and their advocates in the operations process of the family justice center, and shall establish procedures for the ongoing input, feedback, and evaluation of the family justice center by survivors of violence and abuse and community-based crime victim service providers and advocates.
(2) Each family justice center shall develop policies and procedures, in collaboration with local community-based crime victim service providers and local survivors of violence and abuse, to ensure coordinated services are provided to victims and to enhance the safety of victims and professionals at the family justice center who participate in affiliated survivor-centered support or advocacy groups. Each family justice center shall maintain a formal client feedback, complaint, and input process to address client concerns about services provided or the conduct of any family justice center professionals, agency partners, or volunteers providing services in the family justice center.
(h) (1) Each family justice center shall maintain a client consent policy and shall be in compliance with all state and federal laws protecting the confidentiality of the types of information and documents that may be in a victim's file, including, but not limited to, medical, legal, and victim counselor records. Each family justice center shall have a designated privacy officer to develop and oversee privacy policies and procedures consistent with state and federal privacy laws and the Fair Information Practice Principles promulgated by the United States Department of Homeland Security. At no time shall a victim be required to sign a client consent form to share information in order to access services.
(2) Each family justice center is required to obtain informed, written, reasonably time limited, consent from the victim before sharing information obtained from the victim with any staff member or agency partner, except as provided in paragraphs (3) and (4).
(3) A family justice center is not required to obtain consent from the victim before sharing information obtained from the victim with any staff member or agency partner if the person is a mandated reporter, a peace officer, or a member of the prosecution team and is required to report or disclose specific information or incidents. These

persons shall inform the victim that they may share information obtained from the victim without the victim's consent.

(4) Each family justice center is required to inform the victim that information shared with staff members or partner agencies at a family justice center may be shared with law enforcement professionals without the victim's consent if there is a mandatory duty to report, or the client is a danger to himself or herself, or others. Each family justice center shall obtain written acknowledgment that the victim has been informed of this policy.

(5) Consent by a victim for sharing information within a family justice center pursuant to this section shall not be construed as a universal waiver of any existing evidentiary privilege that makes confidential any communications or documents between the victim and any service provider, including, but not limited to, any lawyer, advocate, sexual assault or domestic violence counselor as defined in Section 1035.2 or 1037.1 of the Evidence Code, human trafficking caseworker as defined in Section 1038.2 of the Evidence Code, therapist, doctor, or nurse. Any oral or written communication or any document authorized by the victim to be shared for the purposes of enhancing safety and providing more effective and efficient services to the victim of domestic violence, sexual assault, elder or dependent adult abuse, or human trafficking shall not be disclosed to any third party, unless that third-party disclosure is authorized by the victim, or required by other state or federal law or by court order.

(i) An individual staff member, volunteer, or agency that has victim information governed by this section shall not be required to disclose that information unless the victim has consented to the disclosure or it is otherwise required by other state or federal law or by court order.

(j) A disclosure of information consented to by the victim in a family justice center, made for the purposes of clinical assessment, risk assessment, safety planning, or service delivery, shall not be deemed a waiver of any privilege or confidentiality provision contained in Sections 2263, 2918, 4982, and 6068 of the Business and Professions Code, the lawyer-client privilege protected by Article 3 (commencing with Section 950) of Chapter 4 of Division 8 of the Evidence Code, the physician-patient privilege protected by Article 6 (commencing with Section 990) of Chapter 4 of Division 8 of the Evidence Code, the psychotherapist-patient privilege protected by Article 7 (commencing with Section 1010) of Chapter 4 of Division 8 of the Evidence Code, the sexual assault counselor-victim privilege protected by Article 8.5 (commencing with Section 1035) of Chapter 4 of Division 8 of the Evidence Code, or the domestic violence counselor-victim privilege protected by Article 8.7 (commencing with Section 1037) of Chapter 4 of Division 8 of the Evidence Code.

(Amended by Stats. 2018, Ch. 423, Sec. 120. (SB 1494) Effective January 1, 2019.)

13751.
Each family justice center established pursuant to subdivision (a) of Section 13750 shall maintain a formal training program with mandatory training for all staff members, volunteers, and agency professionals of not less than eight hours per year on subjects, including, but not limited to, privileges and confidentiality, information sharing, risk assessment, safety planning, victim advocacy, and high-risk case response.

(Added by Stats. 2014, Ch. 85, Sec. 1. (AB 1623) Effective January 1, 2015.)

CHAPTER 2. Multidisciplinary Teams [13752 - 13753]

(Chapter 2 added by Stats. 2018, Ch. 802, Sec. 3.)

13752.
(a) Notwithstanding any other law, a city, county, city and county, or community-based nonprofit organization may establish a domestic violence multidisciplinary personnel team consisting of two or more persons who are trained in the prevention, identification, management, or treatment of domestic violence cases and who are qualified to provide a broad range of services related to domestic violence.

(b) A domestic violence multidisciplinary team may include, but need not be limited to, any of the following:
(1) Law enforcement personnel.
(2) Medical personnel.
(3) Psychiatrists, psychologists, marriage and family therapists, or other trained counseling personnel.
(4) District attorneys and city attorneys.
(5) Victim-witness program personnel.
(6) Sexual assault counselors, as defined in Section 1035.2 of the Evidence Code.
(7) Domestic violence counselors, as defined in Section 1037.1 of the Evidence Code.
(8) Social service agency staff members.
(9) Child welfare agency social workers.
(10) County health department staff.
(11) City or county welfare and public assistance workers.
(12) Nonprofit agency counseling professionals.
(13) Civil legal service providers.
(14) Human trafficking caseworkers, as defined in Section 1038.2 of the Evidence Code.
(c) (1) Notwithstanding any other law, following a report of suspected domestic violence, members of a domestic violence multidisciplinary personnel team engaged in the prevention, identification, and treatment of domestic violence may disclose to and exchange with one another information and writings that relate to any incident of domestic violence that may also be designated as confidential under state law if the member of the team having that information or writing reasonably believes it is generally relevant to the prevention, identification, or treatment of domestic violence. Any discussion relative to the disclosure or exchange of the information or writings during a team meeting is confidential, and testimony concerning that discussion is not admissible in any criminal, civil, or juvenile court proceeding unless required by law.
(2) Disclosure and exchange of information pursuant to this section may occur telephonically or electronically if there is adequate verification of the identity of the domestic violence multidisciplinary personnel who are involved in that disclosure or exchange of information.
(3) Disclosure and exchange of information pursuant to this section shall not be made to anyone other than members of the domestic violence multidisciplinary personnel team and those qualified to receive information as set forth in subdivision (d).
(d) The domestic violence multidisciplinary personnel team may designate persons qualified pursuant to subdivision (b) to be a member of the team for a particular case. A person designated as a team member pursuant to this subdivision may receive and disclose relevant information and records, subject to the confidentiality provisions of subdivision (g).
(e) (1) The sharing of information permitted under subdivision (c) shall be governed by protocols developed in each county describing how and what information may be shared by the domestic violence multidisciplinary team to ensure that confidential information gathered by the team is not disclosed in violation of state or federal law. A copy of the protocols shall be distributed to each participating agency and to persons in those agencies who participate in the domestic violence multidisciplinary team.
(2) Members of the team that have confidential information obtained from an individual shall not disclose that information to and with one another unless the member has obtained that individual's informed, written, reasonably time-limited consent to the disclosure, in accordance with all applicable state and federal confidentiality laws, or it is otherwise required by other state or federal law or by court order. Before that consent

is obtained, a member of the team is required to inform the individual that the information may be shared with law enforcement professionals or other entities without that individual's consent if required by law.
(3) A disclosure of information consented to by an individual shall not be deemed a waiver of any privilege or confidentiality provision, including those contained in Sections 2263, 2918, 4982, and 6068 of the Business and Professions Code and in Chapter 4 of Division 8 of the Evidence Code.
(f) Every member of the domestic violence multidisciplinary personnel team who receives information or records regarding children or families in his or her capacity as a member of the team shall be under the same privacy and confidentiality obligations and subject to the same confidentiality penalties as the person disclosing or providing the information or records. The information or records obtained shall be maintained in a manner that ensures the maximum protection of privacy and confidentiality rights.
(g) This section shall not be construed to restrict guarantees of confidentiality provided under state or federal law.
(h) Information and records communicated or provided to the team members by providers and agencies, as well as information and records created in the course of a domestic violence investigation, shall be deemed private and confidential and shall be protected from discovery and disclosure by applicable statutory and common law protections, except where disclosure is required by law. Existing civil and criminal penalties shall apply to the inappropriate disclosure of information held by the team members.

(Added by Stats. 2018, Ch. 802, Sec. 3. (AB 998) Effective January 1, 2019.)

13753.
(a) Notwithstanding any other law, a city, county, city and county, or community-based nonprofit organization may establish a human trafficking multidisciplinary personnel team consisting of two or more persons who are trained in the prevention, identification, management, or treatment of human trafficking cases and who are qualified to provide a broad range of services related to human trafficking.

(b) A human trafficking multidisciplinary team may include, but need not be limited to, any of the following:
(1) Law enforcement personnel.
(2) Medical personnel.
(3) Psychiatrists, psychologists, marriage and family therapists, or other trained counseling personnel.
(4) District attorneys and city attorneys.
(5) Victim-witness program personnel.
(6) Sexual assault counselors, as defined in Section 1035.2 of the Evidence Code.
(7) Domestic violence counselors, as defined in Section 1037.1 of the Evidence Code.
(8) Social service agency staff members.
(9) Child welfare agency social workers.
(10) County health department staff.
(11) City or county welfare and public assistance workers.
(12) Nonprofit agency counseling professionals.
(13) Civil legal service providers.
(14) Human trafficking caseworkers, as defined in Section 1038.2 of the Evidence Code.
(c) (1) Notwithstanding any other law, following a report of suspected human trafficking, members of a human trafficking multidisciplinary personnel team engaged in the prevention, identification, and treatment of human trafficking may disclose to and exchange with one another information and writings that relate to any incident of human trafficking that may also be designated as confidential under state law if the member of the team having that information or writing reasonably believes it is generally relevant to the prevention, identification, or treatment of human trafficking. Any discussion relative to the disclosure or exchange of the information or writings during a team meeting is confidential, and testimony concerning that discussion is not admissible in any criminal, civil, or juvenile court proceeding unless required by law.
(2) Disclosure and exchange of information pursuant to this section may occur telephonically or electronically if there is adequate verification of the identity of the human trafficking multidisciplinary personnel who are involved in that disclosure or exchange of information.
(3) Disclosure and exchange of information pursuant to this section shall not be made to anyone other than members of the human trafficking multidisciplinary personnel team and those qualified to receive information as set forth in subdivision (d).
(d) The human trafficking multidisciplinary personnel team may designate persons qualified pursuant to subdivision (b) to be a member of the team for a particular case. A person designated as a team member pursuant to this subdivision may receive and disclose relevant information and records, subject to the confidentiality provisions of subdivision (g).
(e) (1) The sharing of information permitted under subdivision (c) shall be governed by protocols developed in each county describing how and what information may be shared by the human trafficking multidisciplinary team to ensure that confidential information gathered by the team is not disclosed in violation of state or federal law. A copy of the protocols shall be distributed to each participating agency and to persons in those agencies who participate in the human trafficking multidisciplinary team.
(2) Members of the team that have confidential information obtained from an individual shall not disclose that information to and with one another unless the member has obtained that individual's informed, written, reasonably time-limited consent to the disclosure, in accordance with all applicable state and federal confidentiality laws, or it is otherwise required by other state or federal law or by court order. Before such consent is obtained, a member of the team is required to inform the individual that the information may be shared with law enforcement professionals or other entities without that individual's consent if required by law.
(3) A disclosure of information consented to by an individual shall not be deemed a waiver of any privilege or confidentiality provision, including those contained in Sections 2263, 2918, 4982, and 6068 of the Business and Professions Code and in Chapter 4 of Division 8 of the Evidence Code.
(f) Every member of the human trafficking multidisciplinary personnel team who receives information or records regarding children or families in his or her capacity as a member of the team shall be under the same privacy and confidentiality obligations and subject to the same confidentiality penalties as the person disclosing or providing the information or records. The information or records obtained shall be maintained in a manner that ensures the maximum protection of privacy and confidentiality rights.
(g) This section shall not be construed to restrict guarantees of confidentiality provided under state or federal law.
(h) Information and records communicated or provided to the team members by providers and agencies, as well as information and records created in the course of a domestic violence investigation, shall be deemed private and confidential and shall be protected from discovery and disclosure by applicable statutory and common law protections, except where disclosure is required by law. Existing civil and criminal penalties shall apply to the inappropriate disclosure of information held by the team members.

(Added by Stats. 2018, Ch. 802, Sec. 3. (AB 998) Effective January 1, 2019.)

TITLE 5.7. REPRODUCTIVE RIGHTS LAW ENFORCEMENT ACT [13775 - 13778]
(Title 5.7 added by Stats. 2001, Ch. 899, Sec. 3.)

13775.
This title shall be known and may be cited as the Reproductive Rights Law Enforcement Act.
(Added by Stats. 2001, Ch. 899, Sec. 3. Effective January 1, 2002.)
13776.
The following definitions apply for the purposes of this title:
(a) "Anti-reproductive-rights crime" means a crime committed partly or wholly because the victim is a reproductive health services client, provider, or assistant, or a crime that is partly or wholly intended to intimidate the victim, any other person or entity, or any class of persons or entities from becoming or remaining a reproductive health services client, provider, or assistant. "Anti-reproductive-rights crime" includes, but is not limited to, a violation of subdivision (a) or (c) of Section 423.2.
(b) "Subject matter experts" includes, but is not limited to, the Commission on the Status of Women and Girls, law enforcement agencies experienced with anti-reproductive-rights crimes, including the Attorney General and the Department of Justice, and organizations such as the American Civil Liberties Union, the American College of Obstetricians and Gynecologists, the California Council of Churches, the California Medical Association, the Feminist Majority Foundation, NARAL Pro-Choice California, the National Abortion Federation, the California National Organization for Women, the Planned Parenthood Federation of America, Planned Parenthood Affiliates of California, and the Women's Health Specialists clinic that represent reproductive health services clients, providers, and assistants.
(c) "Crime of violence," "nonviolent," "reproductive health services;" "reproductive health services client, provider, or assistant;" and "reproductive health services facility" each has the same meaning as set forth in Section 423.1.
(Amended by Stats. 2012, Ch. 46, Sec. 117. (SB 1038) Effective June 27, 2012.)
13777.
(a) Except as provided in subdivision (d), the Attorney General shall do each of the following:
(1) Collect information relating to anti-reproductive-rights crimes, including, but not limited to, the threatened commission of these crimes and persons suspected of committing these crimes or making these threats.
(2) Direct local law enforcement agencies to provide to the Department of Justice, in a manner that the Attorney General prescribes, any information that may be required relative to anti-reproductive-rights crimes. The report of each crime that violates Section 423.2 shall note the subdivision that prohibits the crime. The report of each crime that violates any other law shall note the code, section, and subdivision that prohibits the crime. The report of any crime that violates both Section 423.2 and any other law shall note both the subdivision of Section 423.2 and the other code, section, and subdivision that prohibits the crime.
(3) Develop a plan to prevent, apprehend, prosecute, and report anti-reproductive-rights crimes, and to carry out the legislative intent expressed in subdivisions (c), (d), (e), and (f) of Section 1 of the act that enacts this title in the 2001–02 Regular Session of the Legislature.
(b) In carrying out his or her responsibilities under this section, the Attorney General shall consult the Governor, the Commission on Peace Officer Standards and Training, and other subject matter experts.
(c) The Attorney General shall implement this section to the extent the Legislature appropriates funds in the Budget Act or another statute for this purpose.
(Amended by Stats. 2012, Ch. 728, Sec. 133. (SB 71) Effective January 1, 2013.)
13777.2.
(a) The Commission on the Status of Women and Girls shall convene an advisory committee consisting of one person appointed by the Attorney General and one person appointed by each of the organizations named in subdivision (b) of Section 13776 that chooses to appoint a member, and any other subject matter experts the commission may appoint. The advisory committee shall elect its chair and any other officers of its choice.
(b) The advisory committee shall make two reports, the first by December 31, 2007, and the second by December 31, 2011, to the Committees on Health, Judiciary, and Public Safety of the Senate and Assembly, to the Attorney General, the Commission on Peace Officer Standards and Training, and the Commission on the Status of Women and Girls. The reports shall evaluate the implementation of Chapter 899 of the Statutes of 2001 and any subsequent amendments made to this title and the effectiveness of the plan developed by the Attorney General pursuant to paragraph (4) of subdivision (a) of Section 13777. The reports shall also include recommendations concerning whether the Legislature should extend or repeal the sunset dates in Section 13779, recommendations regarding any other legislation, and recommendations for any other actions by the Attorney General, Commission on Peace Officer Standards and Training, or the Commission on the Status of Women and Girls.
(c) The Commission on the Status of Women and Girls shall transmit the reports of the advisory committee to the appropriate committees of the Legislature, including, but not limited to, the Committees on Health, Judiciary, and Public Safety in the Senate and Assembly, and make the reports available to the public, including by posting them on the Commission on the Status of Women and Girls' Internet Web site. To avoid production and distribution costs, the Commission on the Status of Women and Girls may submit the reports electronically or as part of any other report that the Commission on the Status of Women and Girls submits to the Legislature.
(d) The Commission on Peace Officer Standards and Training shall make the telecourse that it produced in 2002 pursuant to subdivision (a) of Section 13778 available to the advisory committee. However, before providing the telecourse to the advisory committee or otherwise making it public, the commission shall remove the name and face of any person who appears in the telecourse as originally produced who informs the commission in writing that he or she has a reasonable apprehension that making the telecourse public without the removal will endanger his or her life or physical safety.
(e) Nothing in this section requires any state agency to pay for compensation, travel, or other expenses of any advisory committee member.
(Amended by Stats. 2012, Ch. 46, Sec. 118. (SB 1038) Effective June 27, 2012.)
13778.
(a) The Commission on Peace Officer Standards and Training, utilizing available resources, shall develop a two-hour telecourse on anti-reproductive-rights crimes and make the telecourse available to all California law enforcement agencies as soon as practicable after chaptering of the act that enacts this title in the 2001–2002 session of the Legislature.
(b) Persons and organizations, including, but not limited to, subject-matter experts, may make application to the commission, as outlined in Article 3 (commencing with Section 1051) of Division 2 of Title 11 of the California Code of Regulations, for certification of a course designed to train law enforcement officers to carry out the legislative intent expressed in paragraph (1) of subdivision (d) of Section 1 of the act that enacts this title in the 2001–02 Regular Session.
(c) In developing the telecourse required by subdivision (a), and in considering any applications pursuant to subdivision (b), the commission, utilizing available resources, shall consult the Attorney General and other subject matter experts, except where a subject matter expert has submitted, or has an interest in, an application pursuant to subdivision (b).
(d) In addition to producing and making available the telecourse described in subdivision (a), the commission shall distribute, as necessary, training bulletins, via the internet, to law enforcement agencies participating in training offered pursuant to this section.
(Amended by Stats. 2008, Ch. 206, Sec. 3. Effective January 1, 2009.)

TITLE 6. CALIFORNIA COUNCIL ON CRIMINAL JUSTICE [13800 - 13899.1]
(Title 6 repealed and added by Stats. 1973, Ch. 1047.)

CHAPTER 1. General Provisions and Definitions [13800 - 13801]

(Chapter 1 added by Stats. 1973, Ch. 1047.)
13800.
Unless otherwise required by context, as used in this title:
(a) "Agency" means the Office of Emergency Services.
(b) "Board" means the Board of State and Community Corrections.
(c) "Federal acts" means Subchapter V of Chapter 46 of the federal Omnibus Crime Control and Safe Streets Act of 1968 (42 U.S.C. Sec. 3750 et seq.), the federal Juvenile Justice and Delinquency Prevention Act of 1974 (42 U.S.C. Sec. 5601 et seq.), and any act or acts amendatory or supplemental thereto.
(d) "Local boards" means local criminal justice planning boards.
(e) "Executive director" means the Executive Director of the Board of State and Community Corrections.
(f) This section shall become operative on July 1, 2012.
(Amended by Stats. 2013, Ch. 352, Sec. 427. (AB 1317) Effective September 26, 2013. Operative July 1, 2013, by Sec. 543 of Ch. 352.)
13801.
Nothing in this title shall be construed as authorizing the board, or the local boards to undertake direct operational criminal justice responsibilities.
(Amended by Stats. 2011, Ch. 36, Sec. 55.5. (SB 92) Effective June 30, 2011.)

CHAPTER 2. California Council on Criminal Justice [13812- 13812.]

(Chapter 2 added by Stats. 1973, Ch. 1047.)
13812.
(a) The Advisory Committee on Juvenile Justice and Delinquency Prevention appointed by the Governor pursuant to federal law may be reimbursed by the agency or agencies designated by the Director of Finance pursuant to Section 13820 for expenses necessarily incurred by the members. Staff support for the committee will be provided by the agency or agencies designated by the Director of Finance pursuant to Section 13820.
(b) This section shall become operative January 1, 2012.
(Repealed (in Sec. 28) and added by Stats. 2011, Ch. 136, Sec. 29. (AB 116) Effective July 27, 2011. Section operative January 1, 2012, by its own provisions.)

CHAPTER 2. California Council on Criminal Justice [13812- 13812.]

(Chapter 2 added by Stats. 1973, Ch. 1047.)
13812.
(a) The Advisory Committee on Juvenile Justice and Delinquency Prevention appointed by the Governor pursuant to federal law may be reimbursed by the agency or agencies designated by the Director of Finance pursuant to Section 13820 for expenses necessarily incurred by the members. Staff support for the committee will be provided by the agency or agencies designated by the Director of Finance pursuant to Section 13820.
(b) This section shall become operative January 1, 2012.
(Repealed (in Sec. 28) and added by Stats. 2011, Ch. 136, Sec. 29. (AB 116) Effective July 27, 2011. Section operative January 1, 2012, by its own provisions.)

CHAPTER 2. California Council on Criminal Justice [13812- 13812.]

(Chapter 2 added by Stats. 1973, Ch. 1047.)
13812.
(a) The Advisory Committee on Juvenile Justice and Delinquency Prevention appointed by the Governor pursuant to federal law may be reimbursed by the agency or agencies designated by the Director of Finance pursuant to Section 13820 for expenses necessarily incurred by the members. Staff support for the committee will be provided by the agency or agencies designated by the Director of Finance pursuant to Section 13820.
(b) This section shall become operative January 1, 2012.
(Repealed (in Sec. 28) and added by Stats. 2011, Ch. 136, Sec. 29. (AB 116) Effective July 27, 2011. Section operative January 1, 2012, by its own provisions.)

CHAPTER 3. Criminal Justice Planning [13820 - 13825]

(Heading of Chapter 3 amended by Stats. 2010, Ch. 618, Sec. 216.)
13820.
(a) The Office of Criminal Justice Planning is hereby abolished. The duties and obligations of that office, and all powers and authority formerly exercised by that office, shall be transferred to and assumed by the Office of Emergency Services, with the exception of the duties described in Section 6024, which shall be assumed by the Board of State and Community Corrections.
(b) Except for this section, the phrase "Office of Criminal Justice Planning" or any reference to that phrase in this code shall be construed to mean or refer to the Office of Emergency Services. Any reference to the executive director of the Office of Criminal Justice Planning in this code shall be construed to mean the Director of Emergency Services.
(Amended by Stats. 2013, Ch. 352, Sec. 428. (AB 1317) Effective September 26, 2013. Operative July 1, 2013, by Sec. 543 of Ch. 352.)
13821.

(a) For the 2011–12 fiscal year, the Controller shall allocate 9 percent of the amount deposited in the Local Law Enforcement Services Account in the Local Revenue Fund 2011 to the Office of Emergency Services. The Controller shall allocate these funds on a quarterly basis beginning on October 1. These funds shall be allocated by the Controller pursuant to a schedule provided by the Office of Emergency Services which shall be developed according to the office's existing programmatic guidelines and the following percentages:

(1) The California Multi-Jurisdictional Methamphetamine Enforcement Teams shall receive 47.52 percent in the 2011–12 fiscal year.

(2) The Multi-Agency Gang Enforcement Consortium shall receive 0.2 percent in the 2011–12 fiscal year.

(3) The Sexual Assault Felony Enforcement Teams, authorized by Section 13887, shall receive 12.48 percent in the 2011–12 fiscal year.

(4) The High Technology Theft Apprehension and Prosecution Program, authorized by Section 13848.2, shall receive 26.83 percent in the 2011–12 fiscal year.

(5) The Gang Violence Suppression Program authorized by Section 13826.1, shall receive 3.91 percent in the 2011–12 fiscal year.

(6) The Central Valley and Central Coast Rural Crime Prevention Programs, authorized by Sections 14170 and 14180, shall receive 9.06 percent in the 2011–12 fiscal year.

(b) For the 2011–12 fiscal year, the Office of Emergency Services may be reimbursed up to five hundred eleven thousand dollars ($511,000) from the funds allocated in subdivision (a) for program administrative costs.

(c) Commencing with the 2012–13 fiscal year, subsequent to the allocation described in subdivision (c) of Section 29552 of the Government Code, and commencing with the 2013–14 fiscal year, subsequent to the allocation described in subdivision (d) of Section 29552 of the Government Code, the Controller shall allocate 8.99758189 percent of the remaining amount deposited in the Enhancing Law Enforcement Activities Subaccount in the Local Revenue Fund 2011 and shall distribute the moneys as follows:

(1) Commencing with the 2012–13 fiscal year, the California Multi-Jurisdictional Methamphetamine Enforcement Teams shall receive 47.52015636 percent and shall be allocated by the Controller according to the following schedule:

Alameda County	1.7109%
Alpine County	0.6327%
Amador County	0.6327%
Butte County	1.6666%
Calaveras County	0.8435%
Colusa County	0.1623%
Contra Costa County	1.3163%
Del Norte County	0.2167%
El Dorado County	1.3716%
Fresno County	5.3775%
Glenn County	0.2130%
Humboldt County	1.0198%
Imperial County	2.5510%
Inyo County	0.6327%
Kern County	5.6938%
Kings County	0.9701%
Lake County	0.6604%
Lassen County	0.2643%
Los Angeles County	5.3239%
Madera County	0.9701%
Marin County	0.6292%
Mariposa County	0.6327%
Mendocino County	0.6846%
Merced County	1.8136%
Modoc County	0.0734%
Mono County	0.6327%
Monterey County	0.9018%
Napa County	0.6803%

Nevada County	0.7482%
Orange County	1.5661%
Placer County	2.6395%
Plumas County	0.1516%
Riverside County	5.6395%
Sacramento County	10.0169%
San Benito County	0.8404%
San Bernardino County	8.9364%
San Diego County	2.5510%
San Francisco County	1.0034%
San Joaquin County	4.6394%
San Luis Obispo County	1.3483%
San Mateo County	1.1224%
Santa Barbara County	1.3483%
Santa Clara County	2.0612%
Santa Cruz County	0.8333%
Shasta County	1.3426%
Sierra County	0.0245%
Siskiyou County	0.3401%
Solano County	1.8979%
Sonoma County	1.1610%
Stanislaus County	3.6272%
Sutter County	0.7177%
Tehama County	0.4808%
Trinity County	0.1044%
Tulare County	2.5306%
Tuolumne County	0.6327%
Ventura County	1.3483%
Yolo County	1.5215%
Yuba County	0.5466%

(2) Commencing with the 2013–14 fiscal year, the California Multi-Jurisdictional Methamphetamine Enforcement Teams shall receive 47.52015636 percent and shall be allocated in monthly installments by the Controller according to the following schedule:

Alameda County	1.7109%
Alpine County	0.6327%
Amador County	0.6327%
Butte County	1.6666%
Calaveras County	0.8435%
Colusa County	0.1623%
Contra Costa County	1.3163%
Del Norte County	0.2167%

El Dorado County	1.3716%
Fresno County	5.3775%
Glenn County	0.2130%
Humboldt County	1.0198%
Imperial County	2.5510%
Inyo County	0.6327%
Kern County	5.6938%
Kings County	0.9701%
Lake County	0.6604%
Lassen County	0.2643%
Los Angeles County	5.3239%
Madera County	0.9701%
Marin County	0.6292%
Mariposa County	0.6327%
Mendocino County	0.6846%
Merced County	1.8136%
Modoc County	0.0734%
Mono County	0.6327%
Monterey County	0.9018%
Napa County	0.6803%
Nevada County	0.7482%
Orange County	1.5661%
Placer County	2.6395%
Plumas County	0.1516%
Riverside County	5.6395%
Sacramento County	10.0169%
San Benito County	0.8404%
San Bernardino County	8.9364%
San Diego County	2.5510%
San Francisco County	1.0034%
San Joaquin County	4.6394%
San Luis Obispo County	1.3483%
San Mateo County	1.1224%
Santa Barbara County	1.3483%
Santa Clara County	2.0612%
Santa Cruz County	0.8333%
Shasta County	1.3426%
Sierra County	0.0245%
Siskiyou County	0.3401%

Solano County	1.8979%
Sonoma County	1.1610%
Stanislaus County	3.6272%
Sutter County	0.7177%
Tehama County	0.4808%
Trinity County	0.1044%
Tulare County	2.5306%
Tuolumne County	0.6327%
Ventura County	1.3483%
Yolo County	1.5215%
Yuba County	0.5466%

(3) Commencing with the 2012–13 fiscal year, the Multi-Agency Gang Enforcement Consortium shall receive 0.19545566 percent and shall be allocated by the Controller to Fresno County.

(4) Commencing with the 2013–14 fiscal year, the Multi-Agency Gang Enforcement Consortium shall receive 0.19545566 percent and shall be allocated in monthly installments by the Controller to Fresno County.

(5) Commencing with the 2012–13 fiscal year, the Sexual Assault Felony Enforcement Teams, authorized by Section 13887, shall receive 12.48473003 percent and shall be allocated by the Controller according to the following schedule:

Los Angeles County	21.0294%
Riverside County	12.8778%
Sacramento County	14.0198%
San Luis Obispo County	12.0168%
Santa Clara County	17.0238%
Shasta County	12.0168%
Tulare County	11.0156%

(6) Commencing with the 2013–14 fiscal year, the Sexual Assault Felony Enforcement Teams, authorized by Section 13887, shall receive 12.48473003 percent and shall be allocated by the Controller in monthly installments according to the following schedule:

Los Angeles County	21.0294%
Riverside County	12.8778%
Sacramento County	14.0198%
San Luis Obispo County	12.0168%
Santa Clara County	17.0238%
Shasta County	12.0168%
Tulare County	11.0156%

(7) Commencing with the 2012–13 fiscal year, the High Technology Theft Apprehension and Prosecution Program, authorized by Section 13848.2, shall receive 26.82628878 percent and shall be allocated by the Controller according to the following schedule:

Los Angeles County	18.25%
Marin County	18.25%
Marin County, for use by the Department of Justice in implementing subdivision (b) of Section 13848.4	7.00%
Marin County, for use by the California District Attorneys Association in implementing subdivision (b) of Section 13848.4	1.75%
Sacramento County	18.25%
San Diego County	18.25%
Santa Clara County	18.25%

(8) Commencing with the 2013–14 fiscal year, the High Technology Theft Apprehension and Prosecution Program, authorized by Section 13848.2, shall receive 26.82628878 percent and shall be allocated by the Controller in monthly installments according to the following schedule:

Los Angeles County	18.25%
Marin County	18.25%
Marin County, for use by the Department of Justice in implementing subdivision (b) of Section 13848.4	7.00%
Marin County, for use by the California District Attorneys Association in implementing subdivision (b) of Section 13848.4	1.75%
Sacramento County	18.25%
San Diego County	18.25%
Santa Clara County	18.25%

(9) Commencing with the 2012–13 fiscal year, the Gang Violence Suppression Program, authorized by Section 13826.1, shall receive 3.90911312 percent and shall be allocated by the Controller according to the following schedule:

Alameda County	9.6775%
Los Angeles County	22.5808%
Monterey County	9.6775%
Napa County	17.7417%
City of Oxnard	17.7417%
City of Sacramento	22.5808%

(10) Commencing with the 2013–14 fiscal year, the Gang Violence Suppression Program, authorized by Section 13826.1, shall receive 3.90911312 percent and shall be allocated by the Controller in monthly installments according to the following schedule:

Alameda County	9.6775%
Los Angeles County	22.5808%
Monterey County	9.6775%
Napa County	17.7417%
City of Oxnard	17.7417%
City of Sacramento	22.5808%

(11) Commencing with the 2012–13 fiscal year, the Central Valley and Central Coast Rural Crime Prevention Programs, authorized by Sections 14170 and 14180, shall receive 9.06425605 percent and shall be allocated by the Controller according to the following schedule:

Fresno County	18.5588%
Kern County	13.7173%
Kings County	6.8587%
Madera County	4.4380%
Merced County	6.8587%
Monterey County	7.2411%
San Benito County	4.8273%
San Joaquin County	6.8587%
San Luis Obispo County	2.1723%
Santa Barbara County	3.6206%
Santa Cruz County	1.4482%
Stanislaus County	6.8587%
Tulare County	16.5415%

(12) Commencing with the 2013–14 fiscal year, the Central Valley and Central Coast Rural Crime Prevention Programs, authorized by Sections 14170 and 14180, shall receive 9.06425605 percent and shall be allocated by the Controller in monthly installments according to the following schedule:

Fresno County	18.5588%
Kern County	13.7173%
Kings County	6.8587%
Madera County	4.4380%
Merced County	6.8587%
Monterey County	7.2411%
San Benito County	4.8273%
San Joaquin County	6.8587%
San Luis Obispo County	2.1723%
Santa Barbara County	3.6206%
Santa Cruz County	1.4482%
Stanislaus County	6.8587%
Tulare County	16.5415%

(d) For any of the programs described in this section, funding will be distributed by local agencies as would otherwise have occurred pursuant to Section 1 of Chapter 13 of the Statutes of 2011, First Extraordinary Session.
(Amended by Stats. 2014, Ch. 26, Sec. 36. (AB 1468) Effective June 20, 2014.)
13823.2.
(a) The Legislature hereby finds and declares all of the following:
(1) That violent and serious crimes are being committed against the elderly on an alarmingly regular basis.
(2) That in 1985, the United States Department of Justice reported that approximately 1 in every 10 elderly households in the nation would be touched by crime.
(3) That the California Department of Justice, based upon limited data received from local law enforcement agencies, reported that approximately 10,000 violent crimes were committed against elderly victims in 1985.
(4) That while the elderly may not be the most frequent targets of crime, when they are victimized the impact of each vicious attack has long-lasting effects. Injuries involving, for example, a broken hip may never heal properly and often leave the victim physically impaired. The loss of money used for food and other daily living expenses for these costs may be life-threatening for the older citizen on a fixed income. In addition, stolen or damaged property often cannot be replaced.
(5) Although the State of California currently funds programs to provide assistance to victims of crime and to provide general crime prevention information, there are limited specialized efforts to respond directly to the needs of elderly victims or to provide prevention services tailored for the senior population.
(b) It is the intent of the Legislature that victim services, crime prevention, and criminal justice training programs funded by the Office of Emergency Services shall include, consistent with available resources, specialized components that respond to the diverse needs of elderly citizens residing in the state.
(Amended by Stats. 2013, Ch. 352, Sec. 430. (AB 1317) Effective September 26, 2013. Operative July 1, 2013, by Sec. 543 of Ch. 352.)
13823.3.
The Office of Emergency Services may expend funds for local domestic violence programs, subject to the availability of funds therefor.
(Amended by Stats. 2013, Ch. 352, Sec. 431. (AB 1317) Effective September 26, 2013. Operative July 1, 2013, by Sec. 543 of Ch. 352.)
13823.4.
(a) The Legislature finds the problem of family violence to be of serious and increasing magnitude. The Legislature also finds that acts of family violence often result in other crimes and social problems.
(b) There is in the Office of Emergency Services, a Family Violence Prevention Program. This program shall provide financial and technical assistance to local domestic and family violence centers in implementing family violence prevention programs.
The goals and functions of the program shall include all of the following:
(1) Promotion of community involvement through public education geared specifically toward reaching and educating the friends and neighbors of members of violent families.
(2) Development and dissemination of model protocols for the training of criminal justice system personnel in domestic violence intervention and prevention.
(3) Increasing citizen involvement in family violence prevention.
(4) Identification and testing of family violence prevention models.
(5) Replication of successful models, as appropriate, through the state.
(6) Identification and testing of domestic violence model protocols and intervention systems in major service delivery institutions.
(7) Development of informational materials and seminars to enable emulation or adaptation of the models by other communities.
(8) Provision of domestic violence prevention education and skills to students in schools.
(c) The Director of Emergency Services shall allocate funds to local centers meeting the criteria for funding that shall be established by the Office of Emergency Services in consultation with practitioners and experts in the field of family violence prevention. All centers receiving funds pursuant to this section shall have had an ongoing recognized program, supported by either public or private funds, dealing with an aspect of family violence, for at least two years prior to the date specified for submission of applications for funding pursuant to this section. All centers funded pursuant to this section shall utilize volunteers to the greatest extent possible.
The centers may seek, receive, and make use of any funds which may be available from all public and private sources to augment any state funds received pursuant to this section. Sixty percent of the state funds received pursuant to this section shall be used to develop and implement model program protocols and materials. Forty percent of the state funds received pursuant to this section shall be allocated to programs to

disseminate model program protocols and materials. Dissemination shall include training for domestic violence agencies in California. Each of the programs funded under this section shall focus on no more than two targeted areas. These targeted model areas shall be determined by the Office of Emergency Services in consultation with practitioners and experts in the field of domestic violence, using the domestic violence model priorities survey of the California Alliance Against Domestic Violence. Centers receiving funding shall provide matching funds of at least 10 percent of the funds received pursuant to this section.

(d) The Office of Emergency Services shall develop and disseminate throughout the state information and materials concerning family violence prevention, including, but not limited to, a procedures manual on prevention models. The Office of Emergency Services shall also establish a resource center for the collection, retention, and distribution of educational materials related to family violence and its prevention.

(Amended by Stats. 2013, Ch. 352, Sec. 432. (AB 1317) Effective September 26, 2013. Operative July 1, 2013, by Sec. 543 of Ch. 352.)

13823.5.

(a) The Office of Emergency Services, with the assistance of the advisory committee established pursuant to Section 13836, shall establish a protocol for the examination and treatment of victims of sexual assault and attempted sexual assault, including child molestation, and the collection and preservation of evidence therefrom. The protocol shall contain recommended methods for meeting the standards specified in Section 13823.11.

(b) In addition to the protocol, the Office of Emergency Services shall develop informational guidelines, containing general reference information on evidence collection and examination of victims of, and psychological and medical treatment for victims of, sexual assault and attempted sexual assault, including child molestation.

In developing the protocol and the informational guidelines, the Office of Emergency Services and the advisory committee shall seek the assistance and guidance of organizations assisting victims of sexual assault; qualified health care professionals, criminalists, and administrators who are familiar with emergency room procedures; victims of sexual assault; and law enforcement officials.

(c) The Office of Emergency Services, in cooperation with the State Department of Public Health and the Department of Justice, shall adopt a standard and a complete form or forms for the recording of medical and physical evidence data disclosed by a victim of sexual assault or attempted sexual assault, including child molestation.

Each qualified health care professional who conducts an examination for evidence of a sexual assault or an attempted sexual assault, including child molestation, shall use the standard form or forms adopted pursuant to this section, and shall make those observations and perform those tests as may be required for recording of the data required by the form. The forms shall be subject to the same principles of confidentiality applicable to other medical records.

The Office of Emergency Services shall make copies of the standard form or forms available to every public or private general acute care hospital, as requested.

The standard form shall be used to satisfy the reporting requirements specified in Sections 11160 and 11161 in cases of sexual assault, and may be used in lieu of the form specified in Section 11168 for reports of child abuse.

(d) The Office of Emergency Services shall distribute copies of the protocol and the informational guidelines to every general acute care hospital, law enforcement agency, and prosecutor's office in the state.

(e) As used in this chapter, "qualified health care professional" means a physician and surgeon currently licensed pursuant to Chapter 5 (commencing with Section 2000) of Division 2 of the Business and Professions Code, or a nurse currently licensed pursuant to Chapter 6 (commencing with Section 2700) of Division 2 of the Business and Professions Code and working in consultation with a physician and surgeon who conducts examinations or provides treatment as described in Section 13823.9 in a general acute care hospital or in a physician and surgeon's office.

(Amended by Stats. 2013, Ch. 352, Sec. 433. (AB 1317) Effective September 26, 2013. Operative July 1, 2013, by Sec. 543 of Ch. 352.)

13823.6.

The Office of Emergency Services may secure grants, donations, or other funding for the purpose of funding any statewide task force on sexual assault of children that may be established and administered by the Department of Justice.

(Amended by Stats. 2013, Ch. 352, Sec. 434. (AB 1317) Effective September 26, 2013. Operative July 1, 2013, by Sec. 543 of Ch. 352.)

13823.7.

The protocol adopted pursuant to Section 13823.5 for the medical treatment of victims of sexual assault, which includes the examination and treatment of victims of sexual assault or attempted sexual assault, including child molestation, and the collection and preservation of evidence therefrom shall include provisions for all of the following:

(a) Notification of injuries and a report of suspected child sexual abuse to law enforcement authorities.

(b) Obtaining consent for the examination, for the treatment of injuries, for the collection of evidence, and for the photographing of injuries.

(c) Taking a patient history of sexual assault and other relevant medical history.

(d) Performance of the physical examination for evidence of sexual assault.

(e) Collection of physical evidence of assault.

(f) Collection of other medical specimens.

(g) Procedures for the preservation and disposition of physical evidence.

(Amended by Stats. 2011, Ch. 360, Sec. 2. (SB 534) Effective January 1, 2012.)

13823.9.

(a) Every public or private general acute care hospital that examines a victim of sexual assault or attempted sexual assault, including child molestation, shall comply with the standards specified in Section 13823.11 and the protocol and guidelines adopted pursuant to Section 13823.5.

(b) Each county with a population of more than 100,000 shall arrange that professional personnel trained in the examination of victims of sexual assault, including child molestation, shall be present or on call either in the county hospital which provides emergency medical services or in any general acute care hospital which has contracted with the county to provide emergency medical services. In counties with a population of 1,000,000 or more, the presence of these professional personnel shall be arranged in at least one general acute care hospital for each 1,000,000 persons in the county.

(c) Each county shall designate at least one general acute care hospital to perform examinations on victims of sexual assault, including child molestation.

(d) (1) The protocol published by the Office of Emergency Services shall be used as a guide for the procedures to be used by every public or private general acute care hospital in the state for the examination and treatment of victims of sexual assault and attempted sexual assault, including child molestation, and the collection and preservation of evidence therefrom.

(2) The informational guide developed by the Office of Emergency Services shall be consulted where indicated in the protocol, as well as to gain knowledge about all aspects of examination and treatment of victims of sexual assault and child molestation.

(Amended by Stats. 2013, Ch. 352, Sec. 435. (AB 1317) Effective September 26, 2013. Operative July 1, 2013, by Sec. 543 of Ch. 352.)

13823.93.

(a) For purposes of this section, the following definitions apply:

(1) "Medical personnel" includes physicians, nurse practitioners, physician assistants, nurses, and other health care providers, as appropriate.

(2) To "perform a medical evidentiary examination" means to evaluate, collect, preserve, and document evidence, interpret findings, and document examination results.

(b) To ensure the delivery of standardized curriculum, essential for consistent examination procedures throughout the state, one hospital-based training center shall be established through a competitive bidding process, to train medical personnel on how to perform medical evidentiary examinations for victims of child abuse or neglect, sexual assault, domestic violence, elder abuse, and abuse or assault perpetrated against persons with disabilities. The center also shall provide training for investigative and court personnel involved in dependency and criminal proceedings, on how to interpret the findings of medical evidentiary examinations.

The training provided by the training center shall be made available to medical personnel, law enforcement, and the courts throughout the state.

(c) The training center shall meet all of the following criteria:

(1) Recognized expertise and experience in providing medical evidentiary examinations for victims of child abuse or neglect, sexual assault, domestic violence, elder abuse, and abuse or assault perpetrated against persons with disabilities.

(2) Recognized expertise and experience implementing the protocol established pursuant to Section 13823.5.

(3) History of providing training, including, but not limited to, the clinical supervision of trainees and the evaluation of clinical competency.

(4) Recognized expertise and experience in the use of advanced medical technology and training in the evaluation of victims of child abuse or neglect, sexual assault, domestic violence, elder abuse, and abuse or assault perpetrated against persons with disabilities.

(5) Significant history in working with professionals in the field of criminalistics.

(6) Established relationships with local crime laboratories, clinical laboratories, law enforcement agencies, district attorneys' offices, child protective services, victim advocacy programs, and federal investigative agencies.

(7) The capacity for developing a telecommunication network between primary, secondary, and tertiary medical providers.

(8) History of leadership in working collaboratively with medical forensic experts, criminal justice experts, investigative social worker experts, state criminal justice, social services, health and mental health agencies, and statewide professional associations representing the various disciplines, especially those specified in paragraph (6) of subdivision (d).

(9) History of leadership in working collaboratively with state and local victim advocacy organizations, especially those addressing sexual assault and domestic violence.

(10) History and experience in the development and delivery of standardized curriculum for forensic medical experts, criminal justice professionals, and investigative social workers.

(11) History of research, particularly involving databases, in the area of child physical and sexual abuse, sexual assault, elder abuse, or domestic violence.

(d) The training center shall do all of the following:

(1) Develop and implement a standardized training program for medical personnel that has been reviewed and approved by a multidisciplinary peer review committee.

(2) Develop a telecommunication system network between the training center and other areas of the state, including rural and midsized counties. This service shall provide case consultation to medical personnel, law enforcement, and the courts and provide continuing medical education.

(3) Provide ongoing basic, advanced, and specialized training programs.

(4) Develop guidelines for the reporting and management of child physical abuse and neglect, domestic violence, and elder abuse.

(5) Develop guidelines for evaluating the results of training for the medical personnel performing examinations.

(6) Provide standardized training for law enforcement officers, district attorneys, public defenders, investigative social workers, and judges on medical evidentiary examination procedures and the interpretation of findings. This training shall be developed and implemented in collaboration with the Peace Officer Standards and Training Program, the California District Attorneys Association, the California Peace Officers Association, the California Police Chiefs Association, the California State Sheriffs' Association, the California Association of Crime Laboratory Directors, the California Sexual Assault Investigators Association, the California Alliance Against Domestic Violence, the Statewide California Coalition for Battered Women, the Family Violence Prevention Fund, child victim advocacy organizations, the California Welfare Directors Association, the California Coalition Against Sexual Assault, the Department of Justice, the agency, the Child Welfare Training Program, and the University of California extension programs.

(7) Promote an interdisciplinary approach in the assessment and management of child abuse and neglect, sexual assault, elder abuse, domestic violence, and abuse or assault against persons with disabilities.

(8) Provide training in the dynamics of victimization, including, but not limited to, rape trauma syndrome, intimate partner battering and its effects, the effects of child abuse and neglect, and the various aspects of elder abuse. This training shall be provided by individuals who are recognized as experts within their respective disciplines.

(e) Nothing in this section shall be construed to change the scope of practice for any health care provider, as defined in other provisions of law.

(Amended by Stats. 2010, Ch. 618, Sec. 225. (AB 2791) Effective January 1, 2011.)

13823.95.

(a) No costs incurred by a qualified health care professional, hospital, or other emergency medical facility for the medical evidentiary examination portion of the examination of the victim of a sexual assault, as described in the protocol developed pursuant to Section 13823.5, when the examination is performed pursuant to Sections 13823.5 and 13823.7, shall be charged directly or indirectly to the victim of the assault.

(b) Any victim of a sexual assault who seeks a medical evidentiary examination, as that term is used in Section 13823.93, shall be provided with a medical evidentiary examination. A victim of a sexual assault shall not be required to participate or to agree to participate in the criminal justice system, either prior to the examination or at any other time.

(c) The cost of a medical evidentiary examination performed by a qualified health care professional, hospital, or other emergency medical facility for a victim of a sexual assault shall be treated as a local cost and charged to the local law enforcement agency in whose jurisdiction the alleged offense was committed; provided, however, that the local law enforcement agency may seek reimbursement, as provided in subdivision (d), for the cost of conducting the medical evidentiary examination portion of a medical examination of a sexual assault victim who does not participate in the criminal justice system.

(d) The amount that may be charged by a qualified health care professional, hospital, or other emergency medical facility to perform the medical evidentiary examination portion of a medical examination of a victim of a sexual assault shall not exceed three hundred dollars ($300). The Office of Emergency Services shall use the discretionary funds from federal grants awarded to the agency pursuant to the federal Violence Against Women and Department of Justice Reauthorization Act of 2005 and the federal Violence Against Women Reauthorization Act of 2013 through the federal Office of Violence Against Women, specifically, the STOP (Services, Training, Officers, and Prosecutors) Violence Against Women Formula Grant Program, to cover the cost of the medical evidentiary examination portion of a medical examination of a sexual assault victim.

(Amended by Stats. 2017, Ch. 692, Sec. 6. (AB 1312) Effective January 1, 2018.)

13823.11.

The minimum standards for the examination and treatment of victims of sexual assault or attempted sexual assault, including child molestation, and the collection and preservation of evidence therefrom include all of the following:

(a) Law enforcement authorities shall be notified.

(b) In conducting the physical examination, the outline indicated in the form adopted pursuant to subdivision (c) of Section 13823.5 shall be followed.
(c) Consent for a physical examination, treatment, and collection of evidence shall be obtained.
(1) Consent to an examination for evidence of sexual assault shall be obtained before the examination of a victim of sexual assault and shall include separate written documentation of consent to each of the following:
(A) Examination for the presence of injuries sustained as a result of the assault.
(B) Examination for evidence of sexual assault and collection of physical evidence.
(C) Photographs of injuries.
(2) Consent to treatment shall be obtained in accordance with usual hospital policy.
(3) A victim of sexual assault shall be informed that he or she may refuse to consent to an examination for evidence of sexual assault, including the collection of physical evidence, but that a refusal is not a ground for denial of treatment of injuries and for possible pregnancy and sexually transmitted diseases, if the person wishes to obtain treatment and consents thereto.
(4) Pursuant to Chapter 3 (commencing with Section 6920) of Part 4 of Division 11 of the Family Code, a minor may consent to hospital, medical, and surgical care related to a sexual assault without the consent of a parent or guardian.
(5) In cases of known or suspected child abuse, the consent of the parents or legal guardian is not required. In the case of suspected child abuse and nonconsenting parents, the consent of the local agency providing child protective services or the local law enforcement agency shall be obtained. Local procedures regarding obtaining consent for the examination and treatment of, and the collection of evidence from, children from child protective authorities shall be followed.
(d) A history of sexual assault shall be taken.
The history obtained in conjunction with the examination for evidence of sexual assault shall follow the outline of the form established pursuant to subdivision (c) of Section 13823.5 and shall include all of the following:
(1) A history of the circumstances of the assault.
(2) For a child, any previous history of child sexual abuse and an explanation of injuries, if different from that given by parent or person accompanying the child.
(3) Physical injuries reported.
(4) Sexual acts reported, whether or not ejaculation is suspected, and whether or not a condom or lubricant was used.
(5) Record of relevant medical history.
(e) (1) If indicated by the history of contact, a female victim of sexual assault shall be provided with the option of postcoital contraception by a physician or other health care provider.
(2) Postcoital contraception shall be dispensed by a physician or other health care provider upon the request of the victim at no cost to the victim.
(f) Each adult and minor victim of sexual assault who consents to a medical examination for collection of evidentiary material shall have a physical examination which includes, but is not limited to, all of the following:
(1) Inspection of the clothing, body, and external genitalia for injuries and foreign materials.
(2) Examination of the mouth, vagina, cervix, penis, anus, and rectum, as indicated.
(3) Documentation of injuries and evidence collected.
Prepubertal children shall not have internal vaginal or anal examinations unless absolutely necessary. This does not preclude careful collection of evidence using a swab.
(g) The collection of physical evidence shall conform to the following procedures:
(1) Each victim of sexual assault who consents to an examination for collection of evidence shall have the following items of evidence collected, except where he or she specifically objects:
(A) Clothing worn during the assault.
(B) Foreign materials revealed by an examination of the clothing, body, external genitalia, and pubic hair combings.
(C) Swabs and slides from the mouth, vagina, rectum, and penis, as indicated, to determine the presence or absence of semen.
(D) If indicated by the history of contact, the victim's urine and blood sample, for toxicology purposes, to determine if drugs or alcohol were used in connection with the assault. Toxicology results obtained pursuant to this paragraph shall not be admissible in any criminal or civil action or proceeding against any victim who consents to the collection of physical evidence pursuant to this paragraph. Except for purposes of prosecuting or defending the crime or crimes necessitating the examination specified by this section, any toxicology results obtained pursuant to this paragraph shall be kept confidential, may not be further disclosed, and shall not be required to be disclosed by the victim for any purpose not specified in this paragraph. The victim shall specifically be informed of the immunity and confidentiality safeguards provided herein.
(2) Each victim of sexual assault who consents to an examination for the collection of evidence shall have reference specimens taken, except when he or she specifically objects thereto. A reference specimen is a standard from which to obtain baseline information (for example: pubic and head hair, blood, and saliva for DNA comparison and analysis). Reference specimens may also be collected at a later time if they are needed. These specimens shall be taken in accordance with the standards of the local criminalistics laboratory.
(3) A baseline gonorrhea culture, and syphilis serology, shall be taken, if indicated by the history of contact. Specimens for a pregnancy test shall be taken, if indicated by the history of contact.
(4) (A) If indicated by the history of contact, a female victim of sexual assault shall be provided with the option of postcoital contraception by a physician or other health care provider.
(B) Postcoital contraception shall be dispensed by a physician or other health care provider upon the request of the victim at no cost to the victim.
(h) Preservation and disposition of physical evidence shall conform to the following procedures:
(1) All swabs and slides shall be air-dried before packaging.
(2) All items of evidence including laboratory specimens shall be clearly labeled as to the identity of the source and the identity of the person collecting them.
(3) The evidence shall have a form attached which documents its chain of custody and shall be properly sealed.
(4) The evidence shall be turned over to the proper law enforcement agency.
(Amended by Stats. 2017, Ch. 692, Sec. 5. (AB 1312) Effective January 1, 2018.)
13823.12.
Failure to comply fully with Section 13823.11 or with the protocol or guidelines, or to utilize the form established by the Office of Emergency Services or the standardized sexual assault forensic medical evidence kit described in Section 13823.14, shall not constitute grounds to exclude evidence, nor shall the court instruct or comment to the trier of fact in any case that less weight may be given to the evidence based on the failure to comply.
(Amended by Stats. 2016, Ch. 857, Sec. 1. (AB 1744) Effective January 1, 2017.)
13823.13.
(a) The Office of Emergency Services shall develop a course of training for qualified health care professionals relating to the examination and treatment of victims of sexual assault. In developing the curriculum for the course, the Office of Emergency Services shall consult with health care professionals and appropriate law enforcement agencies. The Office of Emergency Services shall also obtain recommendations from the same health care professionals and appropriate law enforcement agencies on the best means

to disseminate the course of training on a statewide basis. The Office of Emergency Services is encouraged to designate a course of training for qualified health care professionals, as described in this section, and shall partner with other allied professionals training courses, such as sexual assault investigator training administered by the Peace Officer Standards and Training (POST), sexual assault prosecutor training as administered by the California District Attorneys Association (CDAA), or sexual assault advocate training as administered by the California Coalition Against Sexual Assault (CalCASA).
(b) The training course developed pursuant to subdivision (a) shall be designed to train qualified health care professionals to do all of the following:
(1) Perform a health assessment of victims of sexual assault in accordance with any applicable minimum standards set forth in Section 13823.11.
(2) Collect and document physical and laboratory evidence in accordance with any applicable minimum standards set forth in Section 13823.11.
(3) Provide information and referrals to victims of sexual assault to enhance the continuity of care of victims.
(4) Present testimony in court.
(c) As used in this section, "qualified health care professional" means a physician and surgeon currently licensed pursuant to Chapter 5 (commencing with Section 2000) of Division 2 of the Business and Professions Code, or a nurse currently licensed pursuant to Chapter 6 (commencing with Section 2700) of Division 2 of the Business and Professions Code who works in consultation with a physician and surgeon or who conducts examinations described in Section 13823.9 in a general acute care hospital or in the office of a physician and surgeon, a nurse practitioner currently licensed pursuant to Chapter 6 (commencing with Section 2834) of Division 2 of the Business and Professions Code, or a physician assistant licensed pursuant to Chapter 7.7 (commencing with Section 3500) of Division 2 of the Business and Professions Code.
(d) As used in this section, "appropriate law enforcement agencies" may include, but shall not be limited to, the Attorney General of the State of California, any district attorney, and any agency of the State of California expressly authorized by statute to investigate or prosecute law violators.
(Amended by Stats. 2013, Ch. 352, Sec. 437. (AB 1317) Effective September 26, 2013. Operative July 1, 2013, by Sec. 543 of Ch. 352.)
13823.14.
(a) The Department of Justice's Bureau of Forensic Services, the California Association of Crime Laboratory Directors, and the California Association of Criminalists shall provide leadership and work collaboratively with public crime laboratories to develop a standardized sexual assault forensic medical evidence kit for use by all California jurisdictions. The packaging and appearance of the kit may vary, but the kit shall contain a minimum number of basic components and also clearly permit swabs or representative evidence samples to be earmarked for a rapid turnaround DNA program, as defined in subparagraph (E) of paragraph (7) of subdivision (b) of Section 680, when applicable.
(b) The collaboration to establish the basic components for a standardized sexual assault forensic medical evidence kit should be completed by January 30, 2018, and shall be conducted in conjunction with the California Clinical Forensic Medical Training Center, authorized by Section 13823.93, that is responsible for the development of sexual assault forensic medical examination procedures and sexual assault standardized forensic medical report forms and for providing training programs.
(c) On or before May 30, 2019, the California Clinical Forensic Medical Training Center, in coordination with the Department of Justice's Bureau of Forensic Services, the California Association of Crime Laboratory Directors, and the California Association of Criminalists, shall issue guidelines pertaining to the use of the standardized sexual assault kit components throughout the state.
(d) Every local and state agency shall remain responsible for its own costs in purchasing a standardized sexual assault forensic medical evidence kit.
(Added by Stats. 2016, Ch. 857, Sec. 2. (AB 1744) Effective January 1, 2017.)
13823.15.
(a) The Legislature finds the problem of domestic violence to be of serious and increasing magnitude. The Legislature also finds that existing domestic violence services are underfunded and that some areas of the state are unserved or underserved. Therefore, it is the intent of the Legislature that a goal or purpose of the Office of Emergency Services shall be to ensure that all victims of domestic violence served by the Office of Emergency Services Comprehensive Statewide Domestic Violence Program receive comprehensive, quality services.
(b) There is in the Office of Emergency Services a Comprehensive Statewide Domestic Violence Program. The goals of the program shall be to provide local assistance to existing service providers, to maintain and expand services based on a demonstrated need, and to establish a targeted or directed program for the development and establishment of domestic violence services in currently unserved and underserved areas. The Office of Emergency Services shall provide financial and technical assistance to local domestic violence centers in implementing all of the following services:
(1) Twenty-four-hour crisis hotlines.
(2) Counseling.
(3) Business centers.
(4) Emergency "safe" homes or shelters for victims and families.
(5) Emergency food and clothing.
(6) Emergency response to calls from law enforcement.
(7) Hospital emergency room protocol and assistance.
(8) Emergency transportation.
(9) Supportive peer counseling.
(10) Counseling for children.
(11) Court and social service advocacy.
(12) Legal assistance with temporary restraining orders, devices, and custody disputes.
(13) Community resource and referral.
(14) Household establishment assistance.
Priority for financial and technical assistance shall be given to emergency shelter programs and "safe" homes for victims of domestic violence and their children.
(c) Except as provided in subdivision (f), the Office of Emergency Services and the advisory committee established pursuant to Section 13823.16 shall collaboratively administer the Comprehensive Statewide Domestic Violence Program, and shall allocate funds to local centers meeting the criteria for funding. All organizations funded pursuant to this section shall utilize volunteers to the greatest extent possible.
The centers may seek, receive, and make use of any funds which may be available from all public and private sources to augment state funds received pursuant to this section. Centers receiving funding shall provide cash or an in-kind match of at least 10 percent of the funds received pursuant to this section.
(d) The Office of Emergency Services shall conduct statewide training workshops on domestic violence for local centers, law enforcement, and other service providers designed to enhance service programs. The workshops shall be planned in conjunction with practitioners and experts in the field of domestic violence prevention. The workshops shall include a curriculum component on lesbian, gay, bisexual, and transgender specific domestic abuse.
(e) The Office of Emergency Services shall develop and disseminate throughout the state information and materials concerning domestic violence. The Office of Emergency Services shall also establish a resource center for the collection, retention, and distribution of educational materials related to domestic violence. The Office of Emergency Services may utilize and contract with existing domestic violence technical assistance centers in this state in complying with the requirements of this subdivision.

(f) The funding process for distributing grant awards to domestic violence shelter service providers (DVSSPs) shall be administered by the Office of Emergency Services as follows:

(1) The Office of Emergency Services shall establish each of the following:

(A) The process and standards for determining whether to grant, renew, or deny funding to any DVSSP applying or reapplying for funding under the terms of the program.

(B) For DVSSPs applying for grants under the request for proposal process described in paragraph (2), a system for grading grant applications in relation to the standards established pursuant to subparagraph (A), and an appeal process for applications that are denied. A description of this grading system and appeal process shall be provided to all DVSSPs as part of the application required under the RFP process.

(C) For DVSSPs reapplying for funding under the request for application process described in paragraph (4), a system for grading the performance of DVSSPs in relation to the standards established pursuant to subparagraph (A), and an appeal process for decisions to deny or reduce funding. A description of this grading system and appeal process shall be provided to all DVSSPs receiving grants under this program.

(2) Grants for shelters that were not funded in the previous cycle shall be awarded as a result of a competitive request for proposal (RFP) process. The RFP process shall comply with all applicable state and federal statutes for domestic violence shelter funding and, to the extent possible, the response to the RFP shall not exceed 25 narrative pages, excluding attachments.

(3) Grants shall be awarded to DVSSPs that propose to maintain shelters or services previously granted funding pursuant to this section, to expand existing services or create new services, or to establish new domestic violence shelters in underserved or unserved areas. Each grant shall be awarded for a three-year term.

(4) DVSSPs reapplying for grants shall not be subject to a competitive grant process, but shall be subject to a request for application (RFA) process. The RFA process shall consist in part of an assessment of the past performance history of the DVSSP in relation to the standards established pursuant to paragraph (1). The RFA process shall comply with all applicable state and federal statutes for domestic violence center funding and, to the extent possible, the response to the RFA shall not exceed 10 narrative pages, excluding attachments.

(5) A DVSSP funded through this program in the previous grant cycle, including a DVSSP funded by Chapter 707 of the Statutes of 2001, shall be funded upon reapplication, unless, pursuant to the assessment required under the RFA process, its past performance history fails to meet the standards established by the Office of Emergency Services pursuant to paragraph (1).

(6) The Office of Emergency Services shall conduct a minimum of one site visit every three years for each DVSSP funded pursuant to this subdivision. The purpose of the site visit shall be to conduct a performance assessment of, and provide subsequent technical assistance for, each shelter visited. The performance assessment shall include, but need not be limited to, a review of all of the following:

(A) Progress in meeting program goals and objectives.

(B) Agency organization and facilities.

(C) Personnel policies, files, and training.

(D) Recordkeeping, budgeting, and expenditures.

(E) Documentation, data collection, and client confidentiality.

(7) After each site visit conducted pursuant to paragraph (6), the Office of Emergency Services shall provide a written report to the DVSSP summarizing the performance of the DVSSP, deficiencies noted, corrective action needed, and a deadline for corrective action to be completed. The Office of Emergency Services shall also develop a corrective action plan for verifying the completion of corrective action required. The Office of Emergency Services shall submit its written report to the DVSSP no more than 60 days after the site visit. No grant under the RFA process shall be denied if the DVSSP has not received a site visit during the previous three years, unless the Office of Emergency Services is aware of criminal violations relative to the administration of grant funding.

(8) If an agency receives funding from both the Comprehensive Statewide Domestic Violence Program in the Office of Emergency Services and the Maternal, Child, and Adolescent Health Division of the State Department of Public Health during any grant cycle, the Comprehensive Statewide Domestic Violence Program and the Maternal, Child, and Adolescent Health Division shall, to the extent feasible, coordinate agency site visits and share performance assessment data with the goal of improving efficiency, eliminating duplication, and reducing administrative costs.

(9) DVSSPs receiving written reports of deficiencies or orders for corrective action after a site visit shall be given no less than six months' time to take corrective action before the deficiencies or failure to correct may be considered in the next RFA process. However, the Office of Emergency Services shall have the discretion to reduce the time to take corrective action in cases where the deficiencies present a significant health or safety risk or when other severe circumstances are found to exist. If corrective action is deemed necessary, and a DVSSP fails to comply, or if other deficiencies exist that, in the judgment of the Office of Emergency Services, cannot be corrected, the Office of Emergency Services shall determine, using its grading system, whether continued funding for the DVSSP should be reduced or denied altogether. If a DVSSP has been determined to be deficient, the Office of Emergency Services may, at any point during the DVSSP's funding cycle following the expiration of the period for corrective action, deny or reduce further funding.

(10) If a DVSSP applies or reapplies for funding pursuant to this section and that funding is denied or reduced, the decision to deny or reduce funding shall be provided in writing to the DVSSP, along with a written explanation of the reasons for the reduction or denial made in accordance with the grading system for the RFP or RFA process. Except as otherwise provided, an appeal of the decision to deny or reduce funding shall be made in accordance with the appeal process established by the Office of Emergency Services. The appeal process shall allow a DVSSP a minimum of 30 days to appeal after a decision to deny or reduce funding. All pending appeals shall be resolved before final funding decisions are reached.

(11) It is the intent of the Legislature that priority for additional funds that become available shall be given to currently funded, new, or previously unfunded DVSSPs for expansion of services. However, the Office of Emergency Services may determine when expansion is needed to accommodate underserved or unserved areas. If supplemental funding is unavailable, the Office of Emergency Services shall have the authority to lower the base level of grants to all currently funded DVSSPs in order to provide funding for currently funded, new, or previously unfunded DVSSPs that will provide services in underserved or unserved areas. However, to the extent reasonable, funding reductions shall be reduced proportionately among all currently funded DVSSPs. After the amount of funding reductions has been determined, DVSSPs that are currently funded and those applying for funding shall be notified of changes in the available level of funding prior to the next application process. Funding reductions made under this paragraph shall not be subject to appeal.

(12) Notwithstanding any other provision of this section, Office of Emergency Services may reduce funding to a DVSSP funded pursuant to this section if federal funding support is reduced. Funding reductions as a result of a reduction in federal funding shall not be subject to appeal.

(13) Nothing in this section shall be construed to supersede any function or duty required by federal acts, rules, regulations, or guidelines for the distribution of federal grants.

(14) As a condition of receiving funding pursuant to this section, DVSSPs shall do all of the following:

(A) Provide matching funds or in-kind contributions equivalent to not less than 10 percent of the grant they would receive. The matching funds or in-kind contributions may come from other governmental or private sources.

(B) Ensure that appropriate staff and volunteers having client contact meet the definition of "domestic violence counselor" as specified in subdivision (a) of Section 1037.1 of the Evidence Code. The minimum training specified in paragraph (2) of subdivision (a) of Section 1037.1 of the Evidence Code shall be provided to those staff and volunteers who do not meet the requirements of paragraph (1) of subdivision (a) of Section 1037.1 of the Evidence Code.

(15) The following definitions shall apply for purposes of this subdivision:

(A) "Domestic violence" means the infliction or threat of physical harm against past or present adult or adolescent intimate partners, including physical, sexual, and psychological abuse against the partner, and is a part of a pattern of assaultive, coercive, and controlling behaviors directed at achieving compliance from or control over that person.

(B) "Domestic violence shelter service provider" or "DVSSP" means a victim services provider that operates an established system of services providing safe and confidential emergency housing on a 24-hour basis for victims of domestic violence and their children, including, but not limited to, hotel or motel arrangements, haven, and safe houses.

(C) "Emergency shelter" means a confidential or safe location that provides emergency housing on a 24-hour basis for victims of domestic violence and their children.

(g) The Office of Emergency Services may hire the support staff and utilize all resources necessary to carry out the purposes of this section. The Office of Emergency Services shall not utilize more than 10 percent of funds appropriated for the purpose of the program established by this section for the administration of that program.

(Amended by Stats. 2013, Ch. 352, Sec. 438. (AB 1317) Effective September 26, 2013. Operative July 1, 2013, by Sec. 543 of Ch. 352.)

13823.16.

(a) The Comprehensive Statewide Domestic Violence Program established pursuant to Section 13823.15 shall be collaboratively administered by the Office of Emergency Services and an advisory council. The membership of the Office of Emergency Services Domestic Violence Advisory Council shall consist of experts in the provision of either direct or intervention services to victims of domestic violence and their children, within the scope and intention of the Comprehensive Statewide Domestic Violence Assistance Program.

(b) The membership of the council shall consist of domestic violence victims' advocates, battered women service providers, at least one representative of service providers serving the lesbian, gay, bisexual, and transgender community in connection with domestic violence, and representatives of women's organizations, law enforcement, and other groups involved with domestic violence. At least one-half of the council membership shall consist of domestic violence victims' advocates or battered women service providers. It is the intent of the Legislature that the council membership reflect the ethnic, racial, cultural, and geographic diversity of the state, including people with disabilities. The council shall be composed of no more than 13 voting members and two nonvoting ex officio members who shall be appointed, as follows:

(1) Seven voting members shall be appointed by the Governor, including at least one person recommended by the federally recognized state domestic violence coalition.

(2) Three voting members shall be appointed by the Speaker of the Assembly.

(3) Three voting members shall be appointed by the Senate Committee on Rules.

(4) Two nonvoting ex officio members shall be Members of the Legislature, one appointed by the Speaker of the Assembly and one appointed by the Senate Committee on Rules. Any Member of the Legislature appointed to the council shall meet with the council and participate in its activities to the extent that participation is not incompatible with his or her position as a Member of the Legislature.

(c) The Office of Emergency Services shall collaborate closely with the council in developing funding priorities, framing the request for proposals, and soliciting proposals.

(Amended by Stats. 2014, Ch. 153, Sec. 1. (AB 1547) Effective January 1, 2015.)

13823.17.

(a) The Legislature finds the problem of domestic violence in the gay, lesbian, bisexual, and transgender community to be of serious and increasing magnitude. The Legislature also finds that existing domestic violence services for this population are underfunded and that members of this population are unserved or underserved in the state. Therefore, it is the intent of the Legislature that a goal of the Office of Emergency Services shall be to increase access to domestic violence education, prevention, and services specifically for the gay, lesbian, bisexual, and transgender community.

(b) The goal of this section is to establish a targeted or directed grant program for the development and support of domestic violence programs and services for the gay, lesbian, bisexual, and transgender community. The Office of Emergency Services shall use funds from the Equality in Prevention and Services for Domestic Abuse Fund to award grants annually to qualifying organizations, with at least one in southern California and one in northern California, to fund domestic violence programs and services that are specific to the lesbian, gay, bisexual, and transgender community, including, but not limited to, any of the following:

(1) Counseling.

(2) Legal assistance with temporary restraining orders, devices, and custody disputes.

(3) Court and social service advocacy.

(4) Batterers intervention.

(5) Educational workshops and publications.

(6) Community resource and referral.

(7) Emergency housing.

(8) Hotline or warmline.

(9) Household establishment assistance.

(c) Each grant shall be awarded for a three-year term, as funds are available, for the purposes of this section.

(d) In order to be eligible to receive funds under this section, qualified organizations shall provide matching funds of at least 10 percent of the funds to be received under the section unless this requirement is waived by the Director of Emergency Services, at his or her discretion.

(e) As a condition of receiving funding pursuant to this section, grant recipients shall ensure that appropriate staff and volunteers having client contact meet the definition of "domestic violence counselor," as specified in subdivision (a) of Section 1037.1 of the Evidence Code. The minimum training specified in paragraph (2) of subdivision (a) of Section 1037.1 of the Evidence Code shall be provided to those staff and volunteers who do not meet the requirements of paragraph (1) of subdivision (a) of Section 1037.1 of the Evidence Code.

(f) In order to qualify for a grant award under this section, the recipient shall be a California nonprofit organization with a demonstrated history of working in the area of domestic violence intervention, education, and prevention and serving the lesbian, gay, bisexual, and transgender community.

(g) The funding process for distributing grant awards to qualifying organizations shall be administered by the Office of Emergency Services as follows:

(1) Grant funds shall be awarded to qualifying organizations as a result of a competitive request for proposal (RFP) process. The RFP process shall comply with all applicable state and federal statutes and to the extent possible, the response to the RFP shall not exceed 15 narrative pages, excluding attachments.

(2) The following criteria shall be used to evaluate grant proposals:

(A) Whether the proposed program or services would further the purpose of promoting healthy, nonviolent relationships in the lesbian, gay, bisexual, and transgender community.
(B) Whether the proposed program or services would reach a significant number of people in, and have the support of, the lesbian, gay, bisexual, and transgender community.
(C) Whether the proposed program or services are grounded in a firm understanding of lesbian, gay, bisexual, and transgender domestic violence and represent an innovative approach to addressing the issue.
(D) Whether the proposed program or services would reach unique and underserved sectors of the lesbian, gay, bisexual, and transgender community, such as youth, people of color, immigrants, and transgender persons.
(3) Grant funds shall not be used to support any of the following:
(A) Scholarships.
(B) Awards to individuals.
(C) Out-of-state travel.
(D) Projects that are substantially completed before the anticipated date of the grant award.
(E) Fundraising activities.
(h) Grant recipients may seek, receive, and make use of any funds that may be available from all public and private sources to augment any funds received pursuant to this section.
(i) The Office of Emergency Services may adopt rules as necessary to implement the grant program created under this section.
(j) The Office of Emergency Services may hire the support staff and utilize all resources necessary to carry out the purposes of this section.
(k) The Office of Emergency Services shall consult with the State Department of Public Health to consider the consolidation of their respective domestic violence programs and report conclusions to the Legislature no later than June 30, 2011.
(l) For purposes of this section, "domestic violence" means the infliction or threat of physical harm against past or present adult or adolescent intimate partners, including physical, sexual, and psychological abuse against the person, and is a part of a pattern of assaultive, coercive, and controlling behavior directed at achieving compliance from or control over that person.
(Amended by Stats. 2013, Ch. 352, Sec. 440. (AB 1317) Effective September 26, 2013. Operative July 1, 2013, by Sec. 543 of Ch. 352.)
13824.
A brief description of all projects eligible for a commitment of council funds shall be made available to the public through a publication of the council having statewide circulation at least 30 days in advance of the meeting at which funds for such project can be committed by vote of the council.
(Added by Stats. 1973, Ch. 1047.)
13825.
The State Graffiti Clearinghouse is hereby created in the Office of Emergency Services. The State Graffiti Clearinghouse shall do all of the following, subject to federal funding:
(a) Assess and estimate the present costs to state and local agencies for graffiti abatement.
(b) Award grants to state and local agencies that have demonstrated implementation of effective graffiti reduction and abatement programs.
(c) Receive and disburse funds to effectuate the purposes of the clearinghouse.
(Amended by Stats. 2013, Ch. 352, Sec. 441. (AB 1317) Effective September 26, 2013. Operative July 1, 2013, by Sec. 543 of Ch. 352.)

CHAPTER 3.1. The California Gang, Crime, and Violence Prevention Partnership Program [13825.1 - 13825.6]

(Chapter 3.1 added by Stats. 1997, Ch. 885, Sec. 3.)
13825.1.
This chapter shall be known and may be cited as the California Gang, Crime, and Violence Prevention Partnership Program.
(Added by Stats. 1997, Ch. 885, Sec. 3. Effective January 1, 1998.)
13825.2.
(a) The California Gang, Crime, and Violence Prevention Partnership Program shall be administered by the Department of Justice for the purposes of reducing gang, criminal activity, and youth violence to the extent authorized pursuant to this chapter in communities with a high incidence of gang violence, including, but not limited to, the communities of Fresno, Glendale, Long Beach, Los Angeles, Oakland, Riverside, Santa Ana, Santa Cruz, San Bernardino, San Diego, San Jose, San Francisco, San Mateo, Santa Monica, and Venice. The department shall also consider communities that meet any one of the following criteria:
(1) An at-risk youth population, as defined in subdivision (c) of Section 13825.4, that is significantly disproportionate to the general youth population of that community.
(2) A juvenile arrest rate that is significantly disproportionate to the general youth population of that community.
(3) Significant juvenile gang problems or a high number of juvenile gang-affiliated acts of violence.
(b) All state and local juvenile detention facilities, including, but not limited to, facilities, juvenile halls, youth ranches, and youth camps of the Department of the Youth Authority, shall also be considered eligible to receive services through community-based organizations or nonprofit agencies that are operating programs funded under this chapter.
(Amended by Stats. 1998, Ch. 842, Sec. 1. Effective September 25, 1998.)
13825.3.
All funds made available to the Department of Justice for purposes of this chapter shall be disbursed in accordance with this chapter to community-based organizations and nonprofit agencies that comply with the program requirements of Section 13825.4 and the funding criteria of Section 13825.5 of this chapter.
(a) Funds disbursed under this chapter may enhance, but shall not supplant local, state, or federal funds that would, in the absence of the California Gang, Crime, and Violence Prevention Partnership Program, be made available for the prevention or intervention of youth involvement in gangs, crime, or violence.
(b) The applicant community-based organization or nonprofit agency may enter into interagency agreements between it and a fiscal agent that will allow the fiscal agent to manage the funds awarded to the community-based organization or nonprofit agency.
(c) Before April 15, 1998, the department shall prepare and file administrative guidelines and procedures for the California Gang, Crime, and Violence Prevention Partnership Program consistent with this chapter.
(d) Before July 1, 1998, the department shall issue a "request for funding proposal" that informs applicants of the purposes and availability of funds to be awarded under this chapter and solicits proposals from community-based organizations and nonprofit agencies to provide services consistent with this chapter.
(e) The department shall conduct an evaluation of the California Gang, Crime, and Violence Prevention Partnership Program after two years of program operation and each year thereafter, for purposes of identifying the effectiveness and results of the

program. The evaluation shall be conducted by staff or an independent body that has experience in evaluating programs operated by community-based organizations or nonprofit agencies.
(f) After two years of program operation, and each year thereafter, the department shall prepare and submit an annual report to the Legislature describing in detail the operation of the program and the results obtained from the California Gang, Crime, and Violence Prevention Partnership Program receiving funds under this chapter. The report shall also list the full costs applicable to the department for processing and reviewing applications, and for administering the California Gang, Crime, and Violence Prevention Partnership Program. The department shall be required to submit an annual report to the Legislature only in years in which the California Gang, Crime, and Violence Prevention Partnership Program receives funds under this chapter.
(Amended by Stats. 2008, Ch. 699, Sec. 22. Effective January 1, 2009.)
13825.4.
Community-based organizations and nonprofit agencies that receive funds under this chapter shall utilize the funds to provide services and activities designed to prevent or deter at-risk youth from participating in gangs, criminal activity, or violent behavior.
(a) These prevention and intervention efforts shall include, but not be limited to, any of the following:
(1) Services and activities designed to do any of the following:
(A) Teach alternative methods for resolving conflicts and responding to violence, drugs, and crime.
(B) Develop positive and life-affirming attitudes and behaviors.
(C) Build self-esteem.
(2) Recreational, educational or cultural activities.
(3) Counseling or mentoring services.
(4) Economic development activities.
(b) Funds allocated under this chapter may not be used for services or activities related to suppression, law enforcement, incarceration, or other purposes not related to the prevention and deterrence of gangs, crime, and violence.
Nothing in this paragraph shall prevent funds allocated under this chapter from being used for violence prevention and gang crime deterrence services provided by community-based organizations and nonprofit agencies to youths incarcerated in juvenile detention facilities.
(c) Services and activities provided with funds under this chapter shall be used for at-risk youth who are defined as persons from age 5 to 20 years of age and who fall into one or more of the following categories:
(1) Live in a high-crime or high-violence neighborhood as identified by local or federal law enforcement agencies.
(2) Live in a low-economic neighborhood as identified by the U.S. Census or come from an impoverished family.
(3) Are excessively absent from school or are doing poorly in school as identified by personnel from the youth's school.
(4) Come from a socially dysfunctional family as identified by local or state social service agencies.
(5) Have had one or more contacts with the police.
(6) Have entered the juvenile justice system.
(7) Are identified by the juvenile justice system as being at risk.
(8) Are current or former gang members.
(9) Have one or more family members living at home who are current or former members of a gang.
(10) Are identified as wards of the court, as defined in Section 601 of the Welfare and Institutions Code.
(d) Except as provided in subdivision (e), in carrying out a program of prevention and intervention services and activities with funds received under this chapter, community-based organizations and nonprofit agencies shall do all of the following:
(1) Collaborate with other local community-based organizations, nonprofit agencies or local agencies providing similar services, local schools, local law enforcement agencies, residents and families of the local community, private businesses in the local community, and charitable or religious organizations, for purposes of developing plans to provide a program of prevention and intervention services and activities with funds provided under this chapter.
(2) Identify other community-based organizations, nonprofit agencies, local agencies, and charitable or religious organizations in the local community that can serve as a resource in providing services and activities under this chapter.
(3) Follow the public health model approach in developing and carrying out a program to prevent, deter or reduce youth gangs, crime or violence by (A) identifying risk factors of the particular population to be targeted, (B) implementing protective factors to prevent or reduce gangs, crime or violence in the particular community to be serviced, and (C) designing community guidelines for prevention and intervention.
(4) Provide referral services to at-risk youth who are being served under this chapter to appropriate organizations and agencies where the community-based organization or nonprofit agency can readily identify a need for counseling, tutorial, family support, or other types of services.
(5) Provide the parents and family of the at-risk youth with support, information, and services to cope with the problems the at-risk youth, the parents, and the family are confronting.
(6) Involve members of the at-risk target population in the development, coordination, implementation, and evaluation of their program of services and activities.
(7) Objectively evaluate the effectiveness of their services and activities to determine changes in attitudes or behaviors of the at-risk youth being served under this chapter towards gangs, crime, and violence.
(e) Providers of programs that operate in juvenile detention facilities shall not be required to meet the criteria specified in paragraph (5) of subdivision (d) for those programs offered only in those facilities.
(Amended by Stats. 1998, Ch. 842, Sec. 2. Effective September 25, 1998.)
13825.5.
To be eligible for funding under this chapter, community-based organizations and nonprofit agencies shall submit a request for funding proposal in compliance with this chapter to conduct a program that meets the requirements of Section 13825.4. The Department of Justice shall establish the minimum standards, funding schedules, and procedures for awarding grants that shall take into consideration, but not be limited to, all of the following:
(a) A demonstrated showing of at least two years of experience in administering a program providing prevention or prevention and intervention services that have positively affected the attitudes or behaviors of at-risk youth, as defined in this chapter, toward gangs, crime, or violence.
(b) New programs, services, or staff that would augment the existing programs, services, and activities already being provided the community-based organization or nonprofit agency.
(c) The size of the eligible at-risk youth population that would be served by the community-based organization or nonprofit agency.
(d) The likelihood that the program will continue to operate after state grant funding ends.
(e) The ability of the community-based organization or nonprofit agency to objectively evaluate itself and a demonstrated showing of its plan to evaluate itself if funds are awarded. For purposes of this chapter, community-based organizations and nonprofit agencies do not include libraries, community service organizations, and city, county, and state-operated departments of parks and recreation.

(Added by Stats. 1997, Ch. 885, Sec. 3. Effective January 1, 1998.)
13825.6.
Funding for the California Gang, Crime, and Violence Prevention Partnership Program shall be subject to the following:
(a) 2 percent of the amounts appropriated in the Budget Act shall be transferred each year upon the approval of the Director of Finance, for expenditure as necessary for the Department of Justice to administer this program.
(b) 3 percent of the amounts appropriated in the Budget Act shall be transferred each year upon the approval of the Director of Finance, for expenditure as necessary for the department to provide technical assistance to community-based organizations and nonprofit agencies providing services under this chapter. Nothing in this chapter precludes the department from providing technical assistance services through an independent agency or organization.
(Amended by Stats. 1998, Ch. 842, Sec. 3. Effective September 25, 1998.)

CHAPTER 3.5. Gang Violence Suppression [13826 - 13826.7]

(Chapter 3.5 added by Stats. 1981, Ch. 1030, Sec. 1.)
13826.
The Legislature finds and declares all of the following:
(a) That violent activity by gangs is a serious and growing problem in the State of California.
(b) There is an increasing percentage of school age pupils involved in gang activity.
(c) There are many schools that serve a disproportionate number of youth involved in gang activity which are unable to effectively implement programs designed to prevent youth from becoming involved in gang activity. There is no statewide funded educational program developed for this purpose.
(d) There is evidence that gang involvement among youth begins at an early age.
(e) There is evidence that the parents of gang members lack appropriate parenting skills.
(f) There is evidence that drug activity is increasing among youth involved in gang activity.
(g) There is evidence that gang members have no contact with positive role models.
(h) There is evidence that most gang members lack basic educational skills.
In enacting this chapter, the Legislature intends to support increased efforts by district attorneys' offices to prosecute the perpetrators of gang violence, support increased efforts by local law enforcement agencies to identify, investigate, and apprehend perpetrators of gang violence, support increased efforts by county probation departments to intensively supervise gang members who are on court-ordered probation, support gang violence prevention and intervention efforts by school districts and county offices of education, and support gang violence suppression efforts by community-based organizations.
(Repealed and added by Stats. 1986, Ch. 929, Sec. 2.)
13826.1.
(a) There is hereby established in the Board of State and Community Corrections, the Gang Violence Suppression Program, a program of financial and technical assistance for district attorneys' offices, local law enforcement agencies, county probation departments, school districts, county offices of education, or any consortium thereof, and community-based organizations which are primarily engaged in the suppression of gang violence.
(b) Funds made available pursuant to this chapter are intended to ensure the highest quality provision of services and to reduce unnecessary duplication. Funds disbursed under this chapter shall not be used by local agencies to supplant other funding for Public Safety Services, as defined in Section 36 of Article XIII of the California Constitution. Funds awarded under this program as local assistance grants shall not be subject to review as specified in Section 10295 of the Public Contract Code.
(Amended by Stats. 2014, Ch. 26, Sec. 37. (AB 1468) Effective June 20, 2014.)
13826.11.
(a) The Legislature hereby finds and declares the following:
(1) There is a greater threat to public safety resulting from gang- and drug-related activity in and near California's inner cities.
(2) Young people, especially at-risk youth, are more vulnerable to gang- and drug-related activity during the potentially unsupervised hours between the end of school and the time their parents or guardians return home from work.
(3) Without local prevention and treatment efforts, hard drugs will continue to threaten and destroy families and communities in and near the inner cities. Drug-related violence may then escalate dramatically in every community, and thereby burden the criminal justice system to the point that it cannot function effectively.
(4) Los Angeles currently leads the nation in the number of gang members and gang sites, the consumption of drugs, the amount of drugs confiscated, drug-related violent crimes, and has the greatest number of young people between 6 and 18 years of age who are "at risk."
(5) It is the intent of the Legislature that a pilot program, the "After School Alternative Program" (ASAP), be established and implemented within a specified Los Angeles community. This community program would utilize the public schools, businesses, and community facilities to provide supportive programs and activities to young people during the time between the end of school and the return home of their parents or guardians (from approximately 3 p.m. to 7 p.m.).
(Added by Stats. 1990, Ch. 1625, Sec. 1.)
13826.15.
(a) The Legislature hereby finds and declares that the implementation of the Gang Violence Suppression Program, as provided in this chapter, has made a positive impact in the battle against crimes committed by gang members in California.
(b) The Legislature further finds and declares that the program, when it was originally created in 1981, provided financial and technical assistance only for district attorneys' offices. Since that time, however, the provisions of the program have been amended by the Legislature to enable additional public entities and community-based organizations to participate in the program.
(Amended (as amended by Stats. 2011, Ch. 36, Sec. 63) by Stats. 2012, Ch. 43, Sec. 68. (SB 1023) Effective June 27, 2012. Amended version operative July 1, 2012, pursuant to Stats. 2011, Ch. 136, Sec. 32.)
13826.2.
Gang violence prosecution units receiving funds under this chapter are encouraged to concentrate enhanced prosecution efforts and resources upon cases identified under the suggested criteria set forth in Section 13826.3. Enhanced prosecution efforts may include, but not be limited to:
(a) "Vertical" prosecutorial representation, whereby the prosecutor who makes the initial filing or appearance in a gang-related case will perform all subsequent court appearances on that particular case through its conclusion, including the sentencing phase.
(b) Assignment of highly qualified investigators and prosecutors to gang-related cases.
(c) Significant reduction of caseloads for investigators and prosecutors assigned to gang-related cases.

(d) Measures taken in coordination with law enforcement agencies to protect cooperating witnesses from intimidation or retribution at the hands of gang members or associates.
(Amended by Stats. 2012, Ch. 43, Sec. 69. (SB 1023) Effective June 27, 2012.)
13826.3.
(a) An individual is subject to gang violence prosecution efforts if he or she is under arrest for the commission or the attempted commission of any gang-related violent crime where the individual is (1) a known member of a gang, and (2) has exhibited a prior criminal background.
(b) For purposes of this chapter, "gang-related" means that the suspect or victim of the crime is a known member of a gang.
(c) For purposes of this chapter, gang violence prosecution includes both criminal prosecutions and proceedings in Juvenile Court in which a petition is filed pursuant to Section 602 of the Welfare and Institutions Code.
(Amended by Stats. 2012, Ch. 43, Sec. 70. (SB 1023) Effective June 27, 2012.)
13826.4.
Law enforcement agencies receiving funds under this chapter are encouraged to concentrate enhanced law enforcement efforts and resources upon cases identified under criteria set forth in Section 13826.3. Enhanced law enforcement criteria efforts may include, but not be limited to:
(a) The formation of a specialized gang violence unit whose staff shall be composed of the most highly qualified and trained personnel.
(b) The efforts of the gang violence unit may include, but not be limited to:
(1) Increased efforts to apprehend, prosecute, and convict violent "hard core" target gang members.
(2) Increasing the clearance rate of reported crimes which are targeted as gang related.
(3) Establishing more positive relations with, and encouraging the support of local citizens, community-based organizations, business representatives, and other criminal agencies.
(4) Aiding and assisting other criminal justice and governmental agencies in protecting cooperating witnesses from intimidation or retribution at the hands of gang members and their associates.
(c) Law enforcement agencies receiving funds under this program shall maintain a crime analysis capability which provides the following type of information:
(1) Identification of active gang members who have exhibited a prior criminal background.
(2) Identification of evolving or existing crime patterns that are gang related.
(3) Providing investigative leads.
(4) Maintaining statistical information pertaining to gang related criminal activity.
(Amended by Stats. 2012, Ch. 43, Sec. 71. (SB 1023) Effective June 27, 2012.)
13826.5.
County probation departments receiving funding under this chapter shall strictly enforce court-ordered conditions of probation for gang members.
(a) County probation departments supported under the Gang Violence Suppression Program may implement the following activities:
(1) A Gang Violence Intensive Supervision Unit dealing with gang members may be established.
(2) Criteria used to determine which probationer may be assigned to the Gang Violence Intensive Supervision Unit may be approved by the district attorney having a Gang Violence Prosecution Unit described in Section 13826.2.
(3) County probation departments are encouraged to inform probationers whose cases are assigned to the intensive supervision unit of what types of behavior are prescribed or forbidden. The counties are encouraged to provide notice in both oral and written form.
(4) County probation departments are encouraged to inform probationers whose cases are assigned to the intensive supervision unit, in writing, that all court-ordered conditions of probation will be strictly enforced.
(5) County probation departments are encouraged to ensure that deputy probation officers in the intensive supervision unit have reduced probationer caseloads and coordinate their supervision efforts with law enforcement and prosecution personnel. The coordination is encouraged to include informing law enforcement and prosecution personnel of the conditions set for probationers and of the strict enforcement procedures to be implemented.
(6) Deputy probation officers in the intensive supervision unit are encouraged to coordinate with the district attorney in ensuring that court-ordered conditions of probation are consistently enforced.
(7) Intensive supervision unit deputy probation officers are encouraged to coordinate, whenever feasible, with community-based organizations in seeking to ensure that probationers adhere to their court-ordered conditions.
(b) County probation departments may implement the California TEAM (Together Each Achieves More) Sports Camp Program, as described in Article 23.5 (commencing with Section 875) of Chapter 2 of Part 1 of Division 2 of the Welfare and Institutions Code.
(Amended by Stats. 2012, Ch. 43, Sec. 72. (SB 1023) Effective June 27, 2012.)
13826.6.
For purposes of this chapter, a "community-based" organization is defined as a nonprofit operation established to serve gang members, their families, schools, and the community with programs of community supervision and service that maintain community participation in the planning, operation, and evaluation of their programs. "Community-based" organization also includes public park and recreation agencies, public libraries, and public community services departments that provide gang suppression activities, either alone or in cooperation with other public agencies or other community-based organizations.
(a) Unless funded pursuant to subdivision (c), community-based organizations supported under the Gang Violence Suppression Program may implement the following activities:
(1) Providing information to law enforcement agencies concerning gang related activities in the community.
(2) Providing information to school administrators and staff concerning gang related activities in the community.
(3) Providing conflict resolution by means of intervention or mediation to prevent and limit gang crisis situations.
(4) Increasing witness cooperation through coordination with local law enforcement and prosecutors and by education of the community about the roles of these government agencies and the availability of witness protection services.
(b) Community-based organizations funded pursuant to subdivision (a) may also implement the following activities:
(1) Maintaining a 24-hour public telephone message center for the receipt of information and to assist individuals seeking services from the organization.
(2) Maintaining a "rumor control" public telephone service to provide accurate and reliable information to concerned citizens.
(3) Providing technical assistance and training concerning gang related activities to school staff members, law enforcement personnel, and community members, including parental groups. This training and assistance may include coverage of how to prevent and minimize intergang confrontations.
(4) Providing recreational activities for gang members or potential gang members.
(5) Providing job training and placement services for youth.
(6) Referring gang members, as needed, to appropriate agencies for the treatment of health, psychological, and drug-related problems.
(7) Administration of the Urban Corps Program pursuant to Section 13826.62.

(8) Mobilizing the community to share joint responsibility with local criminal justice personnel to prevent and suppress gang violence.

(c) Community-based organizations funded under the Gang Violence Suppression Program for specialized school prevention and intervention activities shall only be required to implement activities in the schools which are designed to discourage students from joining gangs and which offer or encourage students to participate in alternative programs.

(d) Community-based organizations funded pursuant to the Gang Violence Suppression Program as of January 1, 1997, shall receive preference over public agencies in any future funding awards.

(Amended by Stats. 2012, Ch. 43, Sec. 73. (SB 1023) Effective June 27, 2012.)

13826.62.

(a) There is hereby established in the Office of Emergency Services the Urban Corps Program. The Urban Corps Program is established as an optional activity under Section 13826.6. Community-based organizations receiving grants to participate in the Urban Corps Program may implement the following activities:

(1) Identification of publicly and privately administered programs in the county dealing with the suppression or prevention of criminal gang activities, or both.

(2) Maintenance of a listing of programs within the county identified as dealing with the suppression or prevention of criminal gang activities, or both.

(3) Surveying gang suppression and prevention organizations for the types of services and activities each is engaged in, and identifying needs among these organizations for resources to provide services and fulfill their activities.

(4) Recruitment of volunteers, identification of their skills, abilities, and interests, and matching volunteers with the resource needs of gang prevention and suppression organizations.

(5) Establishment of an urban respite program for the purpose of preventing self-destructive activities and diverting (A) identified youth gang members, and (B) youths who are at risk of becoming gang members, for the purposes of reducing or eliminating incentives for those youths to participate in gang-related crime activities.

(b) The Urban Corps Program shall operate within the Office of Emergency Services for two years following the establishment of a contract with a community-based organization to administer the program.

(c) This section shall be implemented to the extent that funds are available to the Office of Emergency Services for this purpose.

(Amended by Stats. 2013, Ch. 352, Sec. 442. (AB 1317) Effective September 26, 2013. Operative July 1, 2013, by Sec. 543 of Ch. 352.)

13826.65.

School districts, county offices of education, or any consortium thereof, receiving funding under this chapter shall develop or adopt and implement a gang violence prevention curriculum, provide gang violence prevention and intervention services for school-aged children, and shall be encouraged to do all of the following:

(a) Establish a local steering committee comprised of representatives of each local program funded under this chapter, corporations, small businesses, and other appropriate local, county, and community organization knowledgeable in the area of youth gang violence.

(b) Develop and distribute information concerning parent education and parenting classes, including methods whereby parents may recognize youth gang involvement.

(c) Identify and utilize the resources of appropriate community-based organizations involved in the coordination of after school activities for school-aged youth.

(d) Establish contact between positive role models and youth involved in gang activity through adopt-a-youth programs and similar programs.

(e) Incorporate into gang prevention activities references to the relationship between drug abuse and gang violence.

(f) Develop partnerships between schools and businesses for the purpose of enhancing pupil achievement through such methods as tutorial services, field trips, role modeling, and other supportive services.

(g) Develop methods of assuring followup services for children receiving the initial gang violence prevention and intervention services.

(Added by Stats. 1986, Ch. 929, Sec. 4.)

13826.7.

The Board of State and Community Corrections is encouraged to utilize any federal funds that may become available for purposes of this chapter. This chapter becomes operative only if federal funds are made available for its implementation.

(Amended by Stats. 2011, Ch. 36, Sec. 64. (SB 92) Effective June 30, 2011. Amendment operative July 1, 2012, by Sec. 83 of Ch. 36, as amended by Stats. 2011, Ch. 136, Sec. 32. Note: This section makes conditional the operation of Chapter 3.5, commencing with Section 13826.)

CHAPTER 3.6. Office of Gang and Youth Violence Policy [13827- 13827.]

(Chapter 3.6 added by Stats. 2007, Ch. 459, Sec. 2.)

13827.

(a) The Office of Gang and Youth Violence Policy is hereby abolished. The duties and obligations of that office, and all powers and authority formerly exercised by that office, shall be transferred to and assumed by the Board of State and Community Corrections.

(b) Except for this section, the phrase "Office of Gang and Youth Violence Policy" or any reference to that phrase in this code shall be construed to mean the board. Any reference to the executive director of the Office of Gang and Youth Violence Policy in this code shall be construed to mean the board.

(Added by Stats. 2012, Ch. 41, Sec. 85. (SB 1021) Effective June 27, 2012)

CHAPTER 3.7. Judicial Training Programs for Child Sexual Abuse Cases [13828 - 13828.1]

(Chapter 3.7 added by Stats. 1986, Ch. 792, Sec. 1.)

13828.

The Legislature hereby finds and declares that there is a need to develop and provide training programs regarding the handling of judicial proceedings involving the victims of child sexual abuse. It is the intent of the Legislature in enacting this chapter to provide training programs which will ensure that children who are the victims of sexual abuse shall be treated with special consideration during all proceedings related to allegations of child sexual abuse, including all trials and administrative hearings.

(Added by Stats. 1986, Ch. 792, Sec. 1.)

13828.1.

From funds appropriated for those purposes, the Judicial Council shall establish and maintain an ongoing program to provide training for the judicial branch of government relating to the handling of child sexual abuse cases.

(Added by Stats. 1986, Ch. 792, Sec. 1.)

CHAPTER 4. Criminal Justice Planning Committee for State Judicial System [13830 - 13838]

(Chapter 4 added by Stats. 1973, Ch. 1047.)

ARTICLE 1. General Provisions [13830 - 13833]
(Heading of Article 1 added by Stats. 1977, Ch. 1256.)

13830.

There is hereby created in state government a Judicial Criminal Justice Planning Committee of seven members. The Judicial Council shall appoint the members of the committee who shall hold office at its pleasure. In this respect the Legislature finds as follows:

(a) The California court system has a constitutionally established independence under the judicial and separation of power clauses of the State Constitution.

(b) The California court system has a statewide structure created under the Constitution, state statutes, and state court rules, and the Judicial Council of California is the constitutionally established state agency having responsibility for the operation of that structure.

(c) The California court system will be directly affected by the criminal justice planning that will be done under this title and by the federal grants that will be made to implement that planning.

(d) For effective planning and implementation of court projects it is essential that the Office of Emergency Services have the advice and assistance of a state judicial system planning committee.

(Amended by Stats. 2013, Ch. 352, Sec. 443. (AB 1317) Effective September 26, 2013. Operative July 1, 2013, by Sec. 543 of Ch. 352.)

13833.

The expenses necessarily incurred by the members of the Judicial Criminal Justice Planning Committee in the performance of their duties under this title shall be paid by the Judicial Council, but it shall be reimbursed by the Office of Emergency Services to the extent that federal funds can be made available for that purpose. Staff support for the committee's activities shall be provided by the Judicial Council, but the cost of that staff support shall be reimbursed by the Office of Emergency Services to the extent that federal funds can be made available for that purpose.

(Amended by Stats. 2013, Ch. 352, Sec. 444. (AB 1317) Effective September 26, 2013. Operative July 1, 2013, by Sec. 543 of Ch. 352.)

ARTICLE 2. Local Assistance Centers for Victims and Witnesses [13835 - 13835.10]
(Article 2 repealed and added by Stats. 1983, Ch. 1312, Sec. 2.)

13835.

The Legislature finds and declares as follows:

(a) That there is a need to develop methods to reduce the trauma and insensitive treatment that victims and witnesses may experience in the wake of a crime, since all too often citizens who become involved with the criminal justice system, either as victims or witnesses to crime, are further victimized by that system.

(b) That when a crime is committed, the chief concern of criminal justice agencies has been apprehending and dealing with the criminal, and that after police leave the scene of the crime, the victim is frequently forgotten.

(c) That victims often become isolated and receive little practical advice or necessary care.

(d) That witnesses must make arrangements to appear in court regardless of their own schedules, child care responsibilities, or transportation problems, and that they often find long waits, crowded courthouse hallways, confusing circumstances and, after testifying, receive no information as to the disposition of the case.

(e) That a large number of victims and witnesses are unaware of both their rights and obligations.

(f) That although the State of California has a fund for needy victims of violent crimes, and compensation is available for medical expenses, lost income or wages, and rehabilitation costs, the application process may be difficult, complex, and time-consuming, and victims may not be aware that the compensation provisions exist.

It is, therefore, the intent of the Legislature to provide services to meet the needs of both victims and witnesses of crime through the funding of local comprehensive centers for victim and witness assistance.

(Repealed and added by Stats. 1983, Ch. 1312, Sec. 2.)

13835.2.

(a) Funds appropriated from the Victim-Witness Assistance Fund shall be made available through the Office of Emergency Services to any public or private nonprofit agency for the assistance of victims and witnesses that meets all of the following requirements:

(1) It provides comprehensive services to victims and witnesses of all types of crime. It is the intent of the Legislature to make funds available only to programs that do not restrict services to victims and witnesses of a particular type of crime, and do not restrict services to victims of crime in which there is a suspect in the case.

(2) It is recognized by the board of supervisors as the major provider of comprehensive services to victims and witnesses in the county.

(3) It is selected by the board of supervisors as the agency to receive funds pursuant to this article.

(4) It assists victims of crime in the preparation, verification, and presentation of their claims to the California Victim Compensation Board for indemnification pursuant to Article 1 (commencing with Section 13959) of Part 4 of Division 3 of Title 2 of the Government Code.

(5) It cooperates with the California Victim Compensation Board in verifying the data required by Article 1 (commencing with Section 13959) of Part 4 of Division 3 of Title 2 of the Government Code.

(b) The Office of Emergency Services shall consider the following factors, together with any other circumstances it deems appropriate, in awarding funds to public or private nonprofit agencies designated as victim and witness assistance centers:

(1) The capability of the agency to provide comprehensive services as defined in this article.

(2) The stated goals and objectives of the center.

(3) The number of people to be served and the needs of the community.

(4) Evidence of community support.

(5) The organizational structure of the agency that will operate the center.

(6) The capability of the agency to provide confidentiality of records.

(Amended by Stats. 2016, Ch. 31, Sec. 258. (SB 836) Effective June 27, 2016.)

13835.4.

In order to ensure the effective delivery of comprehensive services to victims and witnesses, a center established by an agency receiving funds pursuant to this article shall carry out all of the following activities in connection with both primary and optional services:

(a) Translation services for non-English-speaking victims and witnesses or the deaf or hard of hearing.

(b) Follow-up contact to determine whether the client received the necessary assistance.

(c) Field visits to a client's home, place of business, or other location, whenever necessary to provide services.

(d) Service to victims and witnesses of all types of crime.

(e) Volunteer participation to encourage community involvement.

(f) Services for elderly victims of crime, appropriate to their special needs.

(Amended by Stats. 2017, Ch. 561, Sec. 199. (AB 1516) Effective January 1, 2018.)

13835.5.

(a) Comprehensive services shall include all of the following primary services:

(1) Crisis intervention, providing timely and comprehensive responses to the individual needs of victims.

(2) Emergency assistance, directly or indirectly providing food, housing, clothing, and, when necessary, cash.

(3) Resource and referral counseling to agencies within the community which are appropriate to meet the victim's needs.

(4) Direct counseling of the victim on problems resulting from the crime.

(5) Assistance in the processing, filing, and verifying of claims filed by victims of crime pursuant to Article 1 (commencing with Section 13959) of Part 4 of Division 3 of Title 2 of the Government Code.

(6) Assistance in obtaining the return of a victim's property held as evidence by law enforcement agencies, if requested.

(7) Orientation to the criminal justice system.

(8) Court escort.

(9) Presentations to and training of criminal justice system agencies.

(10) Public presentations and publicity.

(11) Monitoring appropriate court cases to keep victims and witnesses apprised of the progress and outcome of their case.

(12) Notification to friends, relatives, and employers of the occurrence of the crime and the victim's condition, upon request of the victim.

(13) Notification to the employer of the victim or witness, if requested by the victim or witness, informing the employer that the employee was a victim of or witness to a crime and asking the employer to minimize any loss of pay or other benefits which may result because of the crime or the employee's participation in the criminal justice system.

(14) Upon request of the victim, assisting in obtaining restitution for the victim, in ascertaining the victim's economic loss, and in providing the probation department, district attorney, and court with information relevant to his or her losses prior to the imposition of sentence.

(b) Comprehensive services may include the following optional services, if their provision does not preclude the efficient provision of primary services:

(1) Employer intervention.

(2) Creditor intervention.

(3) Child care.

(4) Notification to witnesses of any change in the court calendar.

(5) Funeral arrangements.

(6) Crime prevention information.

(7) Witness protection, including arranging for law enforcement protection or relocating witnesses in new residences.

(8) Assistance in obtaining temporary restraining orders.

(9) Transportation.

(10) Provision of a waiting area during court proceedings separate from defendants and families and friends of defendants.

(Amended by Stats. 1996, Ch. 629, Sec. 6. Effective January 1, 1997.)

13835.6.

(a) The Office of Emergency Services, in cooperation with representatives from local victim and witness assistance centers, shall develop standards defining the activities and services enumerated in this article.

(b) The Office of Emergency Services, in cooperation with representatives from local victim and witness assistance centers, shall develop a method of evaluating the activities and performance of centers established pursuant to this article.

(Amended by Stats. 2013, Ch. 352, Sec. 446. (AB 1317) Effective September 26, 2013. Operative July 1, 2013, by Sec. 543 of Ch. 352.)

13835.7.

There is in the State Treasury the Victim-Witness Assistance Fund. Funds appropriated thereto shall be dispensed to the Office of Emergency Services exclusively for the purposes specified in this article, for any other purpose that supports victims, and for the support of the centers specified in Section 13837.

(Amended by Stats. 2014, Ch. 28, Sec. 74. (SB 854) Effective June 20, 2014.)

13835.10.

(a) The Legislature finds and declares all of the following:

(1) That the provision of quality services for victims of crime is of high priority.

(2) That existing victim service programs do not have sufficient financial resources to consistently recruit and employ fully trained personnel.

(3) That there is no consistency in the training provided to the various agencies serving victims.

(4) That comprehensive training for victim service agencies is geographically limited or unavailable.

(5) That there is currently no statewide comprehensive training system in place for the state to ensure that all service providers receive adequate training to provide quality services to victims of crime.

(6) It is the intention of the Legislature to establish a statewide training program within the Office of Emergency Services to provide comprehensive standardized training to victim service providers.

(b) The Office of Emergency Services shall establish a statewide victim-assistance training program, the purpose of which is to develop minimum training and selection standards, certify training courses, and provide funding to enable local victim service providers to acquire the required training.

(c)(1) For the purpose of raising the level of competence of local victim service providers, the Office of Emergency Services shall adopt guidelines establishing minimum standards of training for employees of victim-witness and sexual assault programs funded by the office to provide services to victims of crime. The Office of Emergency Services shall establish an advisory committee composed of recognized statewide victim service organizations, representatives of local victim service programs, and others selected at the discretion of the executive director to consult on the research and development of the training, selection, and equivalency standards.

(2) Any local unit of government, community-based organization, or any other public or private nonprofit entity funded by the Office of Emergency Services as a victim-witness or sexual assault program to provide services to victims of crime shall adhere to the training and selection standards established by the Office of Emergency Services. The standards for sexual assault victim service programs developed by the advisory committee established pursuant to Section 13836 shall be the standards for purposes of this section. With the exception of the sexual assault standards, the Office of Emergency Services shall conduct or contract with an appropriate firm or entity for research on validated standards pursuant to this section in consultation with the advisory committee established pursuant to paragraph (1). The Office of Emergency Services may defer the adoption of the selection standards until the necessary research is completed. Until the standards are adopted, affected victim service programs may receive state funding from the Office of Emergency Services upon certification of their willingness to adhere to the training standards adopted by the Office of Emergency Services.

(3) Minimum training and selection standards may include, but shall not be limited to, basic entry, continuation, supervisory, management, specialized curricula, and confidentiality.

(4) Training and selection standards shall apply to all victim service and management personnel of the victim-witness and sexual assault agencies funded by the Office of Emergency Services to provide services to victims of crime. Exemptions from this requirement may be made by the Office of Emergency Services. A victim service agency which, despite good faith efforts, is unable to meet the standards established pursuant to this section, may apply to the Office of Emergency Services for an exemption. For the purpose of exemptions, the Office of Emergency Services may establish procedures that allow for partial adherence. The Office of Emergency Services may develop equivalency standards which recognize professional experience, education, training, or a combination of the above, for personnel hired before July 1, 1987.

(5) Nothing in this section shall prohibit a victim service agency, funded by the Office of Emergency Services to provide services to victims of crime, from establishing training and selection standards which exceed the minimum standards established by the Office of Emergency Services pursuant to this section.

(d) For purposes of implementing this section, the Office of Emergency Services has all of the following powers:

(1) To approve or certify, or both, training courses selected by the agency.

(2) To make those inquiries which may be necessary to determine whether every local unit of government, community-based organization, or any other public or private entity receiving state aid from the Office of Emergency Services as a victim-witness or sexual assault program for the provision of services to victims of crime, is adhering to the standards for training and selection established pursuant to this section.

(3) To adopt those guidelines which are necessary to carry out the purposes of this section.

(4) To develop or present, or both, training courses for victim service providers, or to contract with coalitions, councils, or other designated entities, to develop or present, or both, those training courses.

(5) To perform other activities and studies necessary to carry out the intent of this section.

(e) (1) The Office of Emergency Services may utilize any funds that may become available from the Victim-Witness Assistance Fund to fund the cost of training staff of victim service agencies which are funded by the Office of Emergency Services from the fund. The Office of Emergency Services may utilize federal or other state funds that may become available to fund the cost of training staff of victim service agencies which are not eligible for funding from the Victim-Witness Assistance Fund.

(2) Peace officer personnel whose jurisdictions are eligible for training subvention pursuant to Chapter 1 (commencing with Section 13500) of Title 4 of this part and correctional or probation personnel whose jurisdictions are eligible for state aid pursuant to Article 2 (commencing with Section 6035) of Chapter 5 of Title 7 of Part 3 are not eligible to receive training reimbursements under this section unless the person receiving the training is assigned to provide victim services in accordance with a grant award agreement with the Office of Emergency Services and is attending training to meet the established standards.

(Amended by Stats. 2013, Ch. 352, Sec. 448. (AB 1317) Effective September 26, 2013. Operative July 1, 2013, by Sec. 543 of Ch. 352.)

ARTICLE 3. Training of Sexual Assault Investigators [13836 - 13836.2]

(Article 3 added by Stats. 1980, Ch. 917, Sec. 5.)

13836.

The Office of Emergency Services shall establish an advisory committee which shall develop a course of training for district attorneys in the investigation and prosecution of sexual assault cases, child sexual exploitation cases, and child sexual abuse cases and shall approve grants awarded pursuant to Section 13837. The courses shall include training in the unique emotional trauma experienced by victims of these crimes.

It is the intent of the Legislature in the enactment of this chapter to encourage the establishment of sex crime prosecution units, which shall include, but not be limited to, child sexual exploitation and child sexual abuse cases, in district attorneys' offices throughout the state.

(Amended by Stats. 2013, Ch. 352, Sec. 449. (AB 1317) Effective September 26, 2013. Operative July 1, 2013, by Sec. 543 of Ch. 352.)

13836.1.

The committee shall consist of 11 members. Five shall be appointed by the Director of Emergency Services, and shall include three district attorneys or assistant or deputy district attorneys, one representative of a city police department or a sheriff or a representative of a sheriff's department, and one public defender or assistant or deputy public defender of a county. Six shall be public members appointed by the Commission on the Status of Women and Girls, and shall include one representative of a rape crisis center, and one medical professional experienced in dealing with sexual assault trauma victims. The committee members shall represent the points of view of diverse ethnic and language groups.

Members of the committee shall receive no compensation for their services but shall be reimbursed for their expenses actually and necessarily incurred by them in the performance of their duties. Staff support for the committee shall be provided by the Office of Emergency Services.

(Amended by Stats. 2013, Ch. 352, Sec. 450. (AB 1317) Effective September 26, 2013. Operative July 1, 2013, by Sec. 543 of Ch. 352.)

13836.2.

(a) The office shall reimburse each county for the costs of salaries and transportation to the extent necessary to permit up to 10 percent of the staff of the district attorney to complete the course of training established pursuant to this chapter. The office shall prescribe the manner in which the training shall be obtained. The training shall be offered at least twice each year in both northern and southern California.

(b) The office shall seek certification from the State Bar of the course as a course which may be taken to complete the Criminal Law Specialist Certificate.

(Amended by Stats. 1985, Ch. 1262, Sec. 6.)

ARTICLE 4. Rape Victim Counseling Centers [13837 - 13838]

(Article 4 added by Stats. 1980, Ch. 917, Sec. 6.)

13837.

(a) The California Emergency Management Agency (Cal EMA) shall provide grants to proposed and existing child sexual exploitation and child sexual abuse victim counseling centers and prevention programs, including programs for minor victims of human trafficking. Grant recipients shall provide appropriate in-person counseling and referral services during normal business hours, and maintain other standards or services which shall be determined to be appropriate by the advisory committee established pursuant to Section 13836 as grant conditions. The advisory committee shall identify the criteria to be utilized in awarding the grants provided by this chapter before any funds are allocated.

In order to be eligible for funding pursuant to this chapter, the centers shall demonstrate an ability to receive and make use of any funds available from governmental, voluntary, philanthropic, or other sources which may be used to augment any state funds appropriated for purposes of this chapter. Each center receiving funds pursuant to this chapter shall make every attempt to qualify for any available federal funding.

State funds provided to establish centers shall be utilized when possible, as determined by the advisory committee, to expand the program and shall not be expended to reduce fiscal support from other public or private sources. The centers shall maintain quarterly and final fiscal reports in a form to be prescribed by the administering agency. In granting funds, the advisory committee shall give priority to centers which are operated in close proximity to medical treatment facilities.

(b) (1) It is the intent of the Legislature that a goal or purpose of the Cal EMA shall be to ensure that all victims of sexual assault and rape receive comprehensive, quality services, and to decrease the incidence of sexual assault through school and community education and prevention programs.

(2) The Cal EMA and the advisory committee established pursuant to Section 13836 shall collaboratively administer sexual assault/rape crisis center victim services programs and provide grants to proposed and existing sexual assault services programs (SASPs) operating local rape victim centers and prevention programs. All SASPs shall provide the services in subparagraphs (A) to (G), inclusive, and to the extent federal funding is made available, shall also provide the service described in subparagraph (H). The Cal EMA shall provide financial and technical assistance to SASPs in implementing the following services:

(A) Crisis intervention, 24 hours per day, seven days per week.

(B) Followup counseling services.

(C) In-person counseling, including group counseling.

(D) Accompaniment services.

(E) Advocacy services.

(F) Information and referrals to victims and the general public.

(G) Community education presentations.

(H) Rape prevention presentations and self-defense programs.

(3) The funding process for distributing grant awards to SASPs shall be administered as follows:

(A) The Cal EMA and the advisory committee established pursuant to Section 13836 shall collaboratively adopt each of the following:

(i) The process and standards for determining whether to grant, renew, or deny funding to any SASP applying or reapplying for funding under the terms of the program.

(ii) For SASPs applying for grants under the RFP process described in subparagraph (B), a system for grading grant applications in relation to the standards established pursuant to clause (i), and an appeal process for applications that are denied. A description of this grading system and appeal process shall be provided to all SASPs as part of the application required under the RFP process.

(iii) For SASPs reapplying for funding under the RFA process described in subparagraph (D), a system for grading the performance of SASPs in relation to the standards established pursuant to clause (i), and an appeal process for decisions to deny or reduce funding. A description of this grading system and appeal process shall be provided to all SASPs receiving grants under this program.

(B) Grants for centers that have previously not been funded or were not funded in the previous cycle shall be awarded as a result of a competitive request for proposal (RFP) process. The RFP process shall comply with all applicable state and federal statutes for sexual assault/rape crisis center funding, and to the extent possible, the response to the RFP shall not exceed 25 narrative pages, excluding attachments.

(C) Grants shall be awarded to SASPs that propose to maintain services previously granted funding pursuant to this section, to expand existing services or create new services, or to establish new sexual assault/rape crisis centers in underserved or unserved areas. Each grant shall be awarded for a three-year term.

(D) SASPs reapplying for grants shall not be subject to a competitive bidding grant process, but shall be subject to a request for application (RFA) process. The RFA process for a SASP reapplying for grant funds shall consist in part of an assessment of the past performance history of the SASP in relation to the standards established pursuant to subparagraph (A). The RFA process shall comply with all applicable state and federal statutes for sexual assault/rape crisis center funding, and to the extent possible, the response to the RFA shall not exceed 10 narrative pages, excluding attachments.

(E) Any SASP funded through this program in the previous grant cycle shall be funded upon reapplication, unless its past performance history fails to meet the standards established pursuant to clause (i) of subparagraph (A).

(F) The Cal EMA shall conduct a minimum of one site visit every three years for each agency funded to provide sexual assault/rape crisis centers. The purpose of the site visit shall be to conduct a performance assessment of, and provide subsequent technical assistance for, each center visited. The performance assessment shall include, but need not be limited to, a review of all of the following:

(i) Progress in meeting program goals and objectives.

(ii) Agency organization and facilities.

(iii) Personnel policies, files, and training.

(iv) Recordkeeping, budgeting, and expenditures.

(v) Documentation, data collection, and client confidentiality.

(G) After each site visit conducted pursuant to subparagraph (F), the Cal EMA shall provide a written report to the SASP summarizing the performance of the SASP, any deficiencies noted, any corrective action needed, and a deadline for corrective action to be completed. The Cal EMA shall also develop a corrective action plan for verifying the completion of any corrective action required. The Cal EMA shall submit its written report to the SASP no more than 60 days after the site visit. No grant under the RFA process shall be denied if the SASP did not receive a site visit during the previous three years, unless the Cal EMA is aware of criminal violations relative to the administration of grant funding.

(H) SASPs receiving written reports of deficiencies or orders for corrective action after a site visit shall be given no less than six months' time to take corrective action before the deficiencies or failure to correct may be considered in the next RFA process. However, the Cal EMA shall have the discretion to reduce the time to take corrective action in cases where the deficiencies present a significant health or safety risk or when other severe circumstances are found to exist. If corrective action is deemed necessary, and a SASP fails to comply, or if other deficiencies exist that, in the judgment of the Cal EMA, cannot be corrected, the Cal EMA shall determine, using its grading system, whether continued funding for the SASP should be reduced or denied altogether. If a SASP has been determined to be deficient, the Cal EMA may, at any point during the SASP's funding cycle following the expiration of the period for corrective action, deny or reduce any further funding.

(I) If a SASP applies or reapplies for funding pursuant to this section and that funding is denied or reduced, the decision to deny or reduce funding shall be provided in writing to the SASP, along with a written explanation of the reasons for the reduction or denial made in accordance with the grading system for the RFP or RFA process. Except as otherwise provided, any appeal of the decision to deny or reduce funding shall be made in accordance with the appeal process established by the Cal EMA. The appeal process shall allow a SASP a minimum of 30 days to appeal after a decision to deny or reduce funding. All pending appeals shall be resolved before final funding decisions are reached.

(J) It is the intent of the Legislature that priority for additional funds that become available shall be given to currently funded, new, or previously unfunded SASPs for expansion of services. However, the Cal EMA may determine when expansion is needed to accommodate underserved or unserved areas. If supplemental funding is unavailable, the Cal EMA shall have the authority to lower the base level of grants to all currently funded SASPs in order to provide funding for currently funded, new, or previously unfunded SASPs that will provide services in underserved or unserved areas. However, to the extent reasonable, funding reductions shall be reduced proportionately among all currently funded SASPs. After the amount of funding reductions has been determined, SASPs that are currently funded and those applying for funding shall be notified of changes in the available level of funding prior to the next application process. Funding reductions made under this paragraph shall not be subject to appeal.

(K) Notwithstanding any other provision of this section, the Cal EMA may reduce funding to a SASP funded pursuant to this section if federal funding support is reduced. Funding reductions as a result of a reduction in federal funding shall not be subject to appeal.

(L) Nothing in this section shall be construed to supersede any function or duty required by federal acts, rules, regulations, or guidelines for the distribution of federal grants.

(M) As a condition of receiving funding pursuant to this section, a SASP shall do each of the following:

(i) Demonstrate an ability to receive and make use of any funds available from governmental, voluntary, philanthropic, or other sources that may be used to augment any state funds appropriated for purposes of this chapter.

(ii) Make every attempt to qualify for any available federal funding.

(N) For the purposes of this paragraph, "sexual assault" means an act or attempt made punishable by Section 220, 261, 261.5, 262, 264.1, 266c, 285, 286, 287, 288, or 647.6, or former Section 288a.

(O) For the purposes of this paragraph, "sexual assault services program" or "SASP" means an agency operating a sexual assault/rape crisis center.

(Amended by Stats. 2018, Ch. 423, Sec. 121. (SB 1494) Effective January 1, 2019.)

13838.

"Peer counselor" means a provider of mental health counseling services who has completed a specialized course in rape crisis counseling skills development, participates in continuing education in rape crisis counseling skills development, and provides rape crisis counseling in consultation with a mental health practitioner licensed within the State of California.

(Added by Stats. 1987, Ch. 1357, Sec. 4.)

CHAPTER 5. California Community Crime Resistance Program [13840 - 13846]

(Chapter 5 added by Stats. 1982, Ch. 1291, Sec. 1.)

13840.

The Legislature hereby finds the resistance to crime and juvenile delinquency requires the cooperation of both community and law enforcement officials; and that successful crime resistance programs involving the participation of citizen volunteers and community leaders shall be identified and given recognition. In enacting this chapter, the Legislature intends to recognize successful crime resistance and prevention programs, disseminate successful techniques and information and to encourage local agencies to involve citizen volunteers in efforts to combat crime and related problems.

(Added by Stats. 1982, Ch. 1291, Sec. 1.)

13841.

As used in this chapter:

(a) "Community" means city or county governments or portions or combinations thereof.

(b) "Elderly or senior citizen" means individuals 55 years of age or older.

(c) "Teenagers and young adults" means individuals between the ages of 15 and 24 years of age.

(d) "Community policing" means the coalescing of community organizations, residents, law enforcement, public social services, education, churches, and local governmental entities to unitedly combat illegal drug activity within a designated neighborhood, and create employment opportunity for neighborhood residents. In no case shall "community policing" include expenditures for the purchase of law enforcement equipment which would have been purchased from existing resources in the normal course of business.

(Amended by Stats. 1990, Ch. 1419, Sec. 1.)

13843.

(a) Allocation and award of funds made available under this chapter shall be made upon application to the Office of Emergency Services. All applications shall be reviewed and evaluated by the Office of Emergency Services.

(b) The Director of Emergency Services may allocate and award funds to communities developing and providing ongoing citizen involvement and crime resistance programs in compliance with the established policies and criteria of the agency. Applications receiving funding under this section shall be selected from among those deemed appropriate for funding according to the criteria, policy, and procedures established by the Office of Emergency Services.

(c) With the exception of funds awarded for programs authorized under paragraph (2) of subdivision (b) of Section 13844, no single award of funds under this chapter shall exceed a maximum of two hundred fifty thousand dollars ($250,000) for a 12-month grant period.

(d) Funds disbursed under this chapter shall not supplant local funds that would, in the absence of the California Community Crime Resistance Program, be made available to support crime resistance programs.

(e) Funds disbursed under this chapter shall be supplemented with local funds constituting, at a minimum, 10 percent of the total crime resistance program budget during the initial year and 20 percent in subsequent periods of funding.

(f) Annually, up to a maximum of 10 percent of the total funds appropriated to the Community Crime Resistance Program may be used by the Office of Emergency Services to support statewide technical assistance, training, and public awareness activities relating to crime prevention.

(g) Funds awarded under this program as local assistance grants shall not be subject to review as specified in Section 14780 of the Government Code.

(h) Guidelines shall set forth the terms and conditions upon which the Office of Emergency Services is prepared to offer grants of funds pursuant to statutory authority. The guidelines do not constitute rules, regulations, orders, or standards of general application.

(Amended by Stats. 2013, Ch. 352, Sec. 451. (AB 1317) Effective September 26, 2013. Operative July 1, 2013, by Sec. 543 of Ch. 352.)

13844.

(a) Use of funds granted under the California Community Crime Resistance Program are restricted to the following activities:

(1) Further the goal of a statewide crime prevention network by supporting the initiation or expansion of local crime prevention efforts.

(2) Provide information and encourage the use of new and innovative refinements to the traditional crime prevention model in localities that currently maintain a well-established crime prevention program.

(3) Support the development of a coordinated service network, including information exchange and case referral between such programs as local victim-witness assistance programs, sexual assault programs, gang violence reduction programs, drug suppression programs, elderly care custodians, state and local elderly service programs, or any other established and recognizable local programs devoted to the lessening of crime and the promotion of the community's well-being.

(b) With respect to the initiation or expansion of local crime prevention efforts, projects supported under the California Community Crime Resistance Program shall do either of the following:

(1) Carry out as many of the following activities as deemed, in the judgment of the Office of Emergency Services, to be consistent with available resources:

(A) Crime prevention programs using tailored outreach techniques in order to provide effective and consistent services for the elderly in the following areas:

(i) Crime prevention information to elderly citizens regarding personal safety, fraud, theft, grand theft, burglary, and elderly abuse.

(ii) Services designed to respond to the specific and diverse crime prevention needs of elderly residential communities.

(iii) Specific services coordinated to assist in the installation of security devices or provision of escort services and victim assistance.

(B) Programs to provide training, information, and prevention literature to peace officers, elderly care custodians, health practitioners, and social service providers regarding physical abuse and neglect within residential health care facilities for the elderly.

(C) Programs to promote neighborhood involvement such as, but not limited to, block clubs and other community or resident-sponsored anticrime programs.

(D) Personal safety programs.

(E) Domestic violence prevention programs.

(F) Crime prevention programs specifically geared to youth in schools and school district personnel.

(G) Programs which make available to residents and businesses information on locking devices, building security, and related crime resistance approaches.

(H) In cooperation with the Commission on Peace Officer Standards and Training, support for the training of peace officers in crime prevention and its effects on the relationship between citizens and law enforcement.

(I) Efforts to address the crime prevention needs of communities with high proportions of teenagers and young adults, low-income families, and non-English-speaking residents, including juvenile delinquency diversion, social service referrals, and making available crime resistance literature in appropriate languages other than English.

(2) Implement a community policing program in targeted neighborhoods that are drug infested. The goal of this program shall be to empower the people against illegal drug activity. A program funded pursuant to this chapter shall be able to target one or more neighborhoods within the grant period. In order to be eligible for funding, the program shall have the commitment of the community, local law enforcement, school districts, and community service groups; and shall be supported by either the city council or the board of supervisors, whichever is applicable.

(c) With respect to the support of new and innovative techniques, communities taking part in the California Crime Resistance Program shall carry out those activities, as determined by the Office of Emergency Services, that conform to local needs and are consistent with available expertise and resources. These techniques may include, but are not limited to, community policing programs or activities involving the following:

(1) Programs to reinforce the security of "latchkey" children, including neighborhood monitoring, special contact telephone numbers, emergency procedure training for the children, daily telephone checks for the children's well-being, and assistance in developing safe alternatives to unsupervised conditions for children.

(2) Programs dedicated to educating parents in procedures designed to do all of the following:

(A) Minimize or prevent the abduction of children.

(B) Assist children in understanding the risk of child abduction.

(C) Maximize the recovery of abducted children.

(3) Programs devoted to developing automated systems for monitoring and tracking crimes within organized neighborhoods.

(4) Programs devoted to developing timely "feedback mechanisms" whose goals would be to alert residents to new crime problems and to reinforce household participation in neighborhood security organizations.

(5) Programs devoted to creating and packaging special crime prevention approaches tailored to the special needs and characteristics of California's cultural and ethnic minorities.

(6) Research into the effectiveness of local crime prevention efforts including the relationships between crime prevention activities, participants' economic and demographic characteristics, project costs, local or regional crime rate, and law enforcement planning and staff deployment.

(7) Programs devoted to crime and delinquency prevention through the establishment of partnership initiatives utilizing elderly and juvenile volunteers.

(d) All approved programs shall utilize volunteers to assist in implementing and conducting community crime resistance programs. Programs providing elderly crime prevention programs shall recruit senior citizens to assist in providing services.

(e) Programs funded pursuant to this chapter shall demonstrate a commitment to support citizen involvement with local funds after the program has been developed and implemented with state moneys.

(Amended by Stats. 2013, Ch. 352, Sec. 452. (AB 1317) Effective September 26, 2013. Operative July 1, 2013, by Sec. 543 of Ch. 352.)

13845.

Selection of communities to receive funding shall include consideration of, but need not be limited to, the following:

(1) Compliance with subdivisions (a), (b), and (c) of Section 13844.

(2) The rate of reported crime, by type, including, but not limited to, the seven major offenses, in the community making the application.

(3) The number of elderly citizens residing in the community compared to the degree of service to be offered by the program for the elderly population.

(4) The number and ratio of elderly crime victims compared to the total senior citizen population in that community.

(5) The number of teenagers and young adults residing in the community.

(6) The number and ratio of crimes committed by teenagers and young adults.

(7) The proportion of families with an income below the federally established poverty level in the community.

(8) The proportion of non-English-speaking citizens in the community.

(9) The display of efforts of cooperation between the community and their local law enforcement agency in dealing with the crime problem.

(10) Demonstrated effort on the part of the applicant to show how funds that may be awarded under this program may be coordinated or consolidated with other local, state or federal funds available for the activities set forth in Section 13844.

(11) Applicant must be a city or county government, or portion or combinations thereof.

(Amended by Stats. 1987, Ch. 1462, Sec. 5.)

13845.5.

Notwithstanding Section 13845, the selection of communities to receive funding pursuant to paragraph (2) of subdivision (b) of Section 13844 shall include consideration of, but is not limited to, the following:

(a) The rate of reported drug crime within the community making the application.

(b) The degree to which the program proposes to empower the people within the targeted neighborhoods to combat drug crime.

(c) The display of efforts of cooperation between the community and its local law enforcement agency in dealing with the drug crime problem.

(d) The commitment of the targeted neighborhoods to fight the drug problem.

(e) The commitment of local governmental entities to join with law enforcement and the citizens to fight the drug problem. At a minimum, this commitment shall be demonstrated by the school districts, parks and recreation departments, public social services, and code enforcement agencies.

(f) The approval of the program by either the city council or the county board of supervisors.

(g) Demonstrated effort on the part of the applicant to show how funds that may be awarded under this program may be coordinated or consolidated with other local, state, or federal funds available for the activities set forth in Section 13844.

(h) Applicant shall be a city or county law enforcement agency, or portion, or combination thereof.

(Added by Stats. 1990, Ch. 1419, Sec. 4.)

13846.

(a) Evaluation and monitoring of all grants made under this section shall be the responsibility of the office. The office shall issue standard reporting forms for reporting the level of activities and number of crimes reported in participating communities.

(b) Information on successful programs shall be made available and relayed to other California communities through the technical assistance procedures of the office.

(Amended by Stats. 2013, Ch. 352, Sec. 453. (AB 1317) Effective September 26, 2013. Operative July 1, 2013, by Sec. 543 of Ch. 352.)

CHAPTER 5.5. Rural Indian Crime Prevention Program [13847 - 13847.2]

(Chapter 5.5 added by Stats. 1990, Ch. 132, Sec. 1.)

13847.

(a) There is hereby established in the Office of Emergency Services a program of financial and technical assistance for local law enforcement, called the Rural Indian Crime Prevention Program. The program shall target the relationship between law enforcement and Native American communities to encourage and to strengthen cooperative efforts and to implement crime suppression and prevention programs.

(b) The Director of Emergency Services may allocate and award funds to those local units of government, or combinations thereof, in which a special program is established in law enforcement agencies that meets the criteria set forth in Sections 13847.1 and 13847.2.

(c) The allocation and award of funds shall be made upon application executed by the chief law enforcement officer of the applicant unit of government and approved by the legislative body. Funds disbursed under this chapter shall not supplant local funds that would, in the absence of the Rural Indian Crime Prevention Program, be made available to support the suppression and prevention of crime on reservations and rancherias.

(d) The Director of Emergency Services shall prepare and issue administrative guidelines and procedures for the Rural Indian Crime Prevention Program consistent with this chapter.

(e) The guidelines shall set forth the terms and conditions upon which the Office of Emergency Services is prepared to offer grants of funds pursuant to statutory authority. The guidelines do not constitute rules, regulations, orders, or standards of general application.

(Amended by Stats. 2013, Ch. 352, Sec. 454. (AB 1317) Effective September 26, 2013. Operative July 1, 2013, by Sec. 543 of Ch. 352.)

13847.1.

Law enforcement agencies receiving funds under this chapter shall meet the following criteria:

(a) Training of law enforcement personnel to be culturally sensitive in the delivery of services to the Native American communities. This training shall include, but shall not be limited to, all of the following:

(1) The creation of an Indian community officer position.

(2) The recruiting and training of Native American volunteers to assist in implementing and conducting reservation or rancheria crime prevention programs.

(b) Increasing community crime awareness by establishing community involvement programs, such as community or neighborhood watch programs, tailored for reservations and rancherias.

(c) Establishing drug traffic intervention programs on reservations through the increased use of law enforcement and special assignment officers.

(d) Developing a delinquency prevention or diversion program for Indian teenagers and young adults.

(Added by Stats. 1990, Ch. 132, Sec. 1. Effective June 11, 1990.)

13847.2.

(a) The Rural Indian and Law Enforcement Local Advisory Committee shall be composed of a chief executive of a law enforcement agency, two tribal council members, two tribal elders, one Indian law enforcement officer, one Indian community officer, one representative of the Bureau of Indian Affairs, and any additional members that may prove to be crucial to the committee. All members of the advisory committee shall be designated by the Director of Emergency Services, who shall provide staff services to the advisory committee.

(b) The Director of Emergency Services, in consultation with the advisory committee, shall develop specific guidelines, and administrative procedures, for the selection of projects to be funded by the Rural Indian Crime Prevention Program which guidelines shall include the selection criteria described in this chapter.

(c) Administration of the overall program and the evaluation and monitoring of all grants made under this chapter shall be performed by the Office of Emergency Services, provided that funds expended for these functions shall not exceed 5 percent of the total annual amount made available for the purpose of this chapter.

(Amended by Stats. 2013, Ch. 352, Sec. 455. (AB 1317) Effective September 26, 2013. Operative July 1, 2013, by Sec. 543 of Ch. 352.)

CHAPTER 5.7.
High Technology Theft Apprehension and Prosecution Program [13848 - 13848.4]

(Chapter 5.7 added by Stats. 1997, Ch. 906, Sec. 2.)

13848.

(a) It is the intent of the Legislature in enacting this chapter to provide local law enforcement and district attorneys with the tools necessary to successfully interdict the promulgation of high technology crime. According to the federal Law Enforcement Training Center, it is expected that states will see a tremendous growth in high technology crimes over the next few years as computers become more available and computer users more skilled in utilizing technology to commit these faceless crimes. High technology crimes are those crimes in which technology is used as an instrument in committing, or assisting in the commission of, a crime, or which is the target of a criminal act.

(b) Funds provided under this program are intended to ensure that law enforcement is equipped with the necessary personnel and equipment to successfully combat high technology crime which includes, but is not limited to, the following offenses:

(1) White-collar crime, such as check, automated teller machine, and credit card fraud, committed by means of electronic or computer-related media.

(2) Unlawful access, destruction of or unauthorized entry into and use of private, corporate, or government computers and networks, including wireless and wireline communications networks and law enforcement dispatch systems, and the theft, interception, manipulation, destruction, or unauthorized disclosure of data stored within those computers and networks.

(3) Money laundering accomplished with the aid of computer networks or electronic banking transfers.
(4) Theft and resale of telephone calling codes, theft of telecommunications service, theft of wireless communication service, and theft of cable television services by manipulation of the equipment used to receive those services.
(5) Software piracy and other unlawful duplication of information.
(6) Theft and resale of computer components and other high technology products produced by the high technology industry.
(7) Remarking and counterfeiting of computer hardware and software.
(8) Theft of trade secrets.
(c) This program is also intended to provide support to law enforcement agencies by providing technical assistance to those agencies with respect to the seizure and analysis of computer systems used to commit high technology crimes or store evidence relating to those crimes.
(Amended by Stats. 1998, Ch. 555, Sec. 2. Effective September 18, 1998.)
13848.2.
There is hereby established a program of financial and technical assistance for law enforcement and district attorneys' offices, designated the High Technology Theft Apprehension and Prosecution Program.
(Amended by Stats. 2012, Ch. 43, Sec. 75. (SB 1023) Effective June 27, 2012.)
13848.4.
(a) Moneys allocated for the High Technology Theft Apprehension and Prosecution Program pursuant to Section 13821 shall be expended to fund programs to enhance the capacity of local law enforcement and prosecutors to deter, investigate, and prosecute high technology related crimes. Funds shall be expended to fund programs to enhance the capacity of local law enforcement, state police, and local prosecutors to deter, investigate, and prosecute high technology related crimes. Any funds distributed under this chapter shall be expended for the exclusive purpose of deterring, investigating, and prosecuting high technology related crimes.
(b) The funds allocated to the Department of Justice pursuant to paragraph (4) of subdivision (c) of Section 13821 shall be used for developing and maintaining a statewide database on high technology crime for use in developing and distributing intelligence information to participating law enforcement agencies. The funds allocated to the California District Attorneys Association pursuant to paragraph (4) of subdivision (c) of Section 13821, shall be used for the purposes of establishing statewide programs of education, training, and research for public prosecutors, investigators, and law enforcement officers relating to deterring, investigating, and prosecuting high technology related crimes.
(c) Any regional task force receiving funds under this section may elect to have the Department of Justice administer the regional task force program. The department may be reimbursed for any expenditures incurred for administering a regional task force from funds given to local law enforcement pursuant to subdivision (b).
(Amended by Stats. 2012, Ch. 43, Sec. 76. (SB 1023) Effective June 27, 2012.)

CHAPTER 5.7.
High Technology Theft Apprehension and Prosecution Program [13848 - 13848.4]

(Chapter 5.7 added by Stats. 1997, Ch. 906, Sec. 2.)
13848.
(a) It is the intent of the Legislature in enacting this chapter to provide local law enforcement and district attorneys with the tools necessary to successfully interdict the promulgation of high technology crime. According to the federal Law Enforcement Training Center, it is expected that states will see a tremendous growth in high technology crimes over the next few years as computers become more available and computer users more skilled in utilizing technology to commit these faceless crimes. High technology crimes are those crimes in which technology is used as an instrument in committing, or assisting in the commission of, a crime, or which is the target of a criminal act.
(b) Funds provided under this program are intended to ensure that law enforcement is equipped with the necessary personnel and equipment to successfully combat high technology crime which includes, but is not limited to, the following offenses:
(1) White-collar crime, such as check, automated teller machine, and credit card fraud, committed by means of electronic or computer-related media.
(2) Unlawful access, destruction of or unauthorized entry into and use of private, corporate, or government computers and networks, including wireless and wireline communications networks and law enforcement dispatch systems, and the theft, interception, manipulation, destruction, or unauthorized disclosure of data stored within those computers and networks.
(3) Money laundering accomplished with the aid of computer networks or electronic banking transfers.
(4) Theft and resale of telephone calling codes, theft of telecommunications service, theft of wireless communication service, and theft of cable television services by manipulation of the equipment used to receive those services.
(5) Software piracy and other unlawful duplication of information.
(6) Theft and resale of computer components and other high technology products produced by the high technology industry.
(7) Remarking and counterfeiting of computer hardware and software.
(8) Theft of trade secrets.
(c) This program is also intended to provide support to law enforcement agencies by providing technical assistance to those agencies with respect to the seizure and analysis of computer systems used to commit high technology crimes or store evidence relating to those crimes.
(Amended by Stats. 1998, Ch. 555, Sec. 2. Effective September 18, 1998.)
13848.2.
There is hereby established a program of financial and technical assistance for law enforcement and district attorneys' offices, designated the High Technology Theft Apprehension and Prosecution Program.
(Amended by Stats. 2012, Ch. 43, Sec. 75. (SB 1023) Effective June 27, 2012.)
13848.4.
(a) Moneys allocated for the High Technology Theft Apprehension and Prosecution Program pursuant to Section 13821 shall be expended to fund programs to enhance the capacity of local law enforcement and prosecutors to deter, investigate, and prosecute high technology related crimes. Funds shall be expended to fund programs to enhance the capacity of local law enforcement, state police, and local prosecutors to deter, investigate, and prosecute high technology related crimes. Any funds distributed under this chapter shall be expended for the exclusive purpose of deterring, investigating, and prosecuting high technology related crimes.
(b) The funds allocated to the Department of Justice pursuant to paragraph (4) of subdivision (c) of Section 13821 shall be used for developing and maintaining a statewide database on high technology crime for use in developing and distributing intelligence information to participating law enforcement agencies. The funds allocated to the California District Attorneys Association pursuant to paragraph (4) of subdivision (c) of Section 13821, shall be used for the purposes of establishing statewide programs of education, training, and research for public prosecutors, investigators, and law

enforcement officers relating to deterring, investigating, and prosecuting high technology related crimes.
(c) Any regional task force receiving funds under this section may elect to have the Department of Justice administer the regional task force program. The department may be reimbursed for any expenditures incurred for administering a regional task force from funds given to local law enforcement pursuant to subdivision (b).
(Amended by Stats. 2012, Ch. 43, Sec. 76. (SB 1023) Effective June 27, 2012.)

CHAPTER 7. Suppression of Drug Abuse in Schools [13860 - 13864]

(Chapter 7 added by Stats. 1983, Ch. 952, Sec. 1.)
13860.
The Legislature finds and declares that a substantial drug abuse and drug trafficking problem exists among school-age children on and around school campuses in the State of California. By enacting this chapter, it is the intention of the Legislature to support increased efforts by local law enforcement agencies, working in conjunction with school districts and county drug offices to suppress trafficking and prevent drug abuse among school age children on and around school campuses through the development of innovative and model programs by local law enforcement agencies and schools and drug abuse agencies. As used in this chapter, drugs are defined as marijuana, inhalants, narcotics, dangerous drugs, pharmaceuticals, glue and alcohol. It is the further intention of the Legislature to establish a program of financial and technical assistance for local law enforcement and school districts.
(Added by Stats. 1983, Ch. 952, Sec. 1. Effective September 20, 1983.)
13861.
There is hereby created in the Office of Emergency Services the Suppression of Drug Abuse in Schools Program. All funds made available to the Office of Emergency Services for the purposes of this chapter shall be administered and disbursed by the Director of Emergency Services in consultation with the State Suppression of Drug Abuse in Schools Advisory Committee established pursuant to Section 13863.
(a) The Director of Emergency Services, in consultation with the State Suppression of Drug Abuse in Schools Advisory Committee, is authorized to allocate and award funds to local law enforcement agencies and public schools jointly working to develop drug abuse prevention and drug trafficking suppression programs in substantial compliance with the policies and criteria set forth in Sections 13862 and 13863.
(b) The allocation and award of funds shall be made upon the joint application by the chief law enforcement officer of the coapplicant law enforcement agency and approved by the law enforcement agency's legislative body and the superintendent and board of the school district coapplicant. The joint application of the law enforcement agency and the school district shall be submitted for review to the Local Suppression of Drug Abuse in Schools Advisory Committee established pursuant to paragraph (4) of subdivision (a) of Section 13862. After review, the application shall be submitted to the Office of Emergency Services. Funds disbursed under this chapter may enhance but shall not supplant local funds that would, in the absence of the Suppression of Drug Abuse in Schools Program, be made available to suppress and prevent drug abuse among schoolage children and to curtail drug trafficking in and around school areas.
(c) The coapplicant local law enforcement agency and the coapplicant school district may enter into interagency agreements between themselves which will allow the management and fiscal tasks created pursuant to this chapter and assigned to both the law enforcement agency and the school district to be performed by only one of them.
(d) Within 90 days of the effective date of this chapter, the Director of Emergency Services, in consultation with the State Suppression of Drug Abuse in Schools Advisory Committee established pursuant to Section 13863, shall prepare and issue administrative guidelines and procedures for the Suppression of Drug Abuse in Schools Program consistent with this chapter. In addition to all other formal requirements that may apply to the enactment of these guidelines and procedures, a complete and final draft shall be submitted within 60 days of the effective date of this chapter to the Chairpersons of the Committee on Criminal Law and Public Safety of the Assembly and the Judiciary Committee of the Senate of the California Legislature.
(Amended by Stats. 2013, Ch. 352, Sec. 458. (AB 1317) Effective September 26, 2013. Operative July 1, 2013, by Sec. 543 of Ch. 352.)
13862.
Law enforcement agencies and school districts receiving funds under this chapter shall concentrate enhanced apprehension, prevention, and education efforts and resources on drug abuse and drug trafficking in and around school campuses.
(a) These enhanced apprehension, prevention, and education efforts shall include, but not be limited to:
(1) Drug traffic intervention programs.
(2) School and classroom-oriented programs, using tested drug abuse education curriculum that provides indepth and accurate information on drugs, which may include the participation of local law enforcement agencies and qualified drug abuse prevention specialists and which are designed to increase teachers' and students' awareness of drugs and their effects.
(3) Family oriented programs aimed at preventing drug abuse which may include the participation of community-based organizations experienced in the successful operation of such programs.
(4) The establishment of a Local Suppression of Drug Abuse in Schools Advisory Committee. The committee shall be established and appointed by the board of supervisors of each county and city and county. However, if the agency receiving funds under this chapter is a city agency and the program does not involve any county agency, or if a county agency is involved and the county board of supervisors consents, the committee shall be established and appointed by the city council. The committee may be a newly created committee or an existing local drug abuse committee as designated by the board or city council. The committee shall be composed of, at a minimum, the following:
(A) Local law enforcement executives.
(B) School district executives.
(C) Schoolsite staff, which includes administrators, teachers, or other credentialed personnel.
(D) Parents.
(E) Students.
(F) School peace officers.
(G) County drug program administrators designated pursuant to Section 11962 of the Health and Safety Code.
(H) Drug prevention program executives.
(5) Development and distribution of appropriate written and audio-visual aids for training of school and law enforcement staff for handling drug-related problems and offenses. Appropriate existing aids may be utilized in lieu of development of new materials.
(6) Development of prevention and intervention programs for elementary school teachers and students, including utilization of existing prevention and intervention programs.
(7) Development of a coordinated intervention system that identifies students with chronic drug abuse problems and facilitates their referral to a drug abuse treatment program.

(b) Enhanced apprehension, prevention, and education efforts commenced under this section shall be a joint effort between local law enforcement and local school districts in cooperation with county drug program offices. These efforts shall include, but not be limited to, the concentration of apprehension efforts in "problem" areas identified by local school authorities.

(c) Funds appropriated pursuant to this chapter may be used in part to support state-level development and statewide distribution of appropriate written and audio-visual aids for public awareness and training of school and law enforcement staff for handling drug-related problems and offenses. When existing aids can be identified, these aids may be utilized in lieu of the development of new aids.

(Amended by Stats. 1988, Ch. 935, Sec. 2.)

13864.

There is hereby created in the Office of Emergency Services the Comprehensive Alcohol and Drug Prevention Education component of the Suppression of Drug Abuse in Schools Program in public elementary schools in grades 4 to 6, inclusive. Notwithstanding Section 13861 or any other provision in this code. all Comprehensive Alcohol and Drug Prevention Education component funds made available to the Office of Emergency Services in accordance with the Classroom Instructional Improvement and Accountability Act shall be administered by and disbursed to county superintendents of schools in this state by the Director of Emergency Services. All applications for that funding shall be reviewed and evaluated by the Office of Emergency Services, in consultation with the State Department of Health Care Services and the State Department of Education.

(a) The Director of Emergency Services is authorized to allocate and award funds to county department superintendents of schools for allocation to individual school districts or to a consortium of two or more school districts. Applications funded under this section shall comply with the criteria, policies, and procedures established under subdivision (b) of this section.

(b) As a condition of eligibility for the funding described in this section, the school district or consortium of school districts shall have entered into an agreement with a local law enforcement agency to jointly implement a comprehensive alcohol and drug abuse prevention, intervention, and suppression program developed by the Office of Emergency Services, in consultation with the State Department of Health Care Services and the State Department of Education, containing all of the following components:

(1) A standardized age-appropriate curriculum designed for pupils in grades 4 to 6, inclusive, specifically tailored and sensitive to the socioeconomic and ethnic characteristics of the target pupil population. Although new curricula shall not be required to be developed, existing curricula may be modified and adapted to meet local needs. The elements of the standardized comprehensive alcohol and drug prevention education program curriculum shall be defined and approved by the Governor's Policy Council on Drug and Alcohol Abuse, as established by Executive Order No. D-70-80.

(2) A planning process that includes assessment of the school district's characteristics, resources, and the extent of problems related to juvenile drug abuse, and input from local law enforcement agencies.

(3) A school district governing board policy that provides for a coordinated intervention system that, at a minimum, includes procedures for identification, intervention, and referral of at-risk alcohol- and drug-involved youth, and identifies the roles and responsibilities of law enforcement, school personnel, parents, and pupils.

(4) Early intervention activities that include, but are not limited to, the identification of pupils who are high risk or have chronic drug abuse problems, assessment, and referral for appropriate services, including ongoing support services.

(5) Parent education programs to initiate and maintain parental involvement, with an emphasis for parents of at-risk pupils.

(6) Staff and in-service training programs, including both indepth training for the core team involved in providing program services and general awareness training for all school faculty and administrative, credentialed, and noncredentialed school personnel.

(7) In-service training programs for local law enforcement officers.

(8) School, law enforcement, and community involvement to ensure coordination of program services. Pursuant to that coordination, the school district or districts and other local agencies are encouraged to use a single community advisory committee or task force for drug, alcohol, and tobacco abuse prevention programs, as an alternative to the creation of a separate group for that purpose under each state or federally funded program.

(c) The application of the county superintendent of schools shall be submitted to the Office of Emergency Services. Funds made available to the Office of Emergency Services for allocation under this section are intended to enhance, but shall not supplant, local funds that would, in the absence of the Comprehensive Alcohol and Drug Prevention Education component, be made available to prevent, intervene in, or suppress drug abuse among schoolage children. For districts that are already implementing a comprehensive drug abuse prevention program for pupils in grades 4 to 6, inclusive, the county superintendent shall propose the use of the funds for drug prevention activities in school grades other than 4 to 6, inclusive, compatible with the program components of this section. The expenditure of funds for that alternative purpose shall be approved by the Director of Emergency Services.

(1) Unless otherwise authorized by the Office of Emergency Services, each county superintendent of schools shall be the fiscal agent for any Comprehensive Alcohol and Drug Prevention Education component award, and shall be responsible for ensuring that each school district within that county receives the allocation prescribed by the Office of Emergency Services. Each county superintendent shall develop a countywide plan that complies with program guidelines and procedures established by the Office of Emergency Services pursuant to subdivision (d). A maximum of 5 percent of the county's allocation may be used for administrative costs associated with the project.

(2) Each county superintendent of schools shall establish and chair a local coordinating committee to assist the superintendent in developing and implementing a countywide implementation plan. This committee shall include the county drug administrator, law enforcement executives, school district governing board members and administrators, school faculty, parents, and drug prevention and intervention program executives selected by the superintendent and approved by the county board of supervisors.

(d) The Director of Emergency Services, in consultation with the State Department of Health Care Services and the State Department of Education, shall prepare and issue guidelines and procedures for the Comprehensive Alcohol and Drug Prevention Education component consistent with this section.

(e) The Comprehensive Alcohol and Drug Prevention Education component guidelines shall set forth the terms and conditions upon which the Office of Emergency Services is prepared to award grants of funds pursuant to this section. The guidelines shall not constitute rules, regulations, orders, or standards of general application.

(f) Funds awarded under the Comprehensive Alcohol and Drug Prevention Education Program shall not be subject to Section 10318 of the Public Contract Code.

(g) Funds available pursuant to Item 8100-111-001 and Provision 1 of Item 8100-001-001 of the Budget Act of 1989, or the successor provision of the appropriate Budget Act, shall be allocated to implement this section.

(h) The Director of Emergency Services shall collaborate, to the extent possible, with other state agencies that administer drug, alcohol, and tobacco abuse prevention education programs to streamline and simplify the process whereby local educational agencies apply for drug, alcohol, and tobacco education funding under this section and under other state and federal programs. The Office of Emergency Services, the State Department of Health Care Services, the State Department of Education, and other state agencies, to the extent possible, shall develop joint policies and collaborate planning in the administration of drug, alcohol, and tobacco abuse prevention education programs.

(Amended by Stats. 2013, Ch. 352, Sec. 459. (AB 1317) Effective September 26, 2013. Operative July 1, 2013, by Sec. 543 of Ch. 352.)

CHAPTER 8. Information on Racial, Ethnic and Religious Crimes [13872- 13872.]

(Chapter 8 added by Stats. 1984, Ch. 1482, Sec. 1.)

13872.

The crimes that shall be the focus of this chapter shall include a wide variety of incidents, which reflect obvious racial, ethnic, or religious motivations, ranging from vandalizing a place of worship to assaults between members of gangs, including, but not limited to, incidents that occur on school grounds and between gang members and any other incidents that law enforcement officers on a case-by-case basis identify as having a racial, ethnic or religious motivation. They shall not include incidents of discrimination in employment.

(Added by Stats. 1984, Ch. 1482, Sec. 1.)

CHAPTER 8.6.
Law Enforcement Response to Drug Endangered C hildren [13879.80 - 13879.81]

(Chapter 8.6 added by Stats. 2003, Ch. 75, Sec. 1.)

13879.80.

(a) Every law enforcement and social services agency in this state is encouraged to develop, adopt, and implement written policies and standards for their response to narcotics crime scenes where a child is either immediately present or where there is evidence that a child lives, by January 1, 2005. These policies shall reflect the fact that exposing a child to the manufacturing, trafficking, and use of narcotics is criminal conduct and that a response coordinated by law enforcement and social services agencies is essential to the child's health and welfare.

(b) The needs of a drug endangered child are best served with written policies encouraging the arrest of an individual for child endangerment where there is probable cause that an offense has been committed coordinated with an appropriate investigation of the child's welfare by child protective agencies. Protocols that encourage a dependency investigation contemporaneous with a law enforcement investigation at a narcotics crime scene, when appropriate, are consistent with a child's best interest.

(Added by Stats. 2003, Ch. 75, Sec. 1. Effective January 1, 2004.)

13879.81.

Communities are encouraged to form multijurisdictional groups that include law enforcement officers, prosecutors, public health professionals, and social workers to address the welfare of children endangered by parental drug use. These coordinated groups should develop standards and protocols, evidenced by memorandums of understanding, that address the following:

(a) Felony and misdemeanor arrests.

(b) Immediate response of protective social workers to a narcotics crime scene involving a child.

(c) Outsourcing protective social workers to law enforcement.

(d) Dependency investigations.

(e) Forensic drug testing and interviewing.

(f) Decontamination of a child found in a lab setting.

(g) Medical examinations and developmental evaluations.

(h) Creation of two hours of P.O.S.T. drug endangered children awareness training.

(Amended by Stats. 2004, Ch. 405, Sec. 24. Effective January 1, 2005.)

CHAPTER 9. California Major Narcotic Vendors Prosecution Law [13880 - 13884]

(Chapter 9 added by Stats. 1984, Ch. 1424, Sec. 1.)

13880.

(a) The Legislature finds and declares that the production and sale of narcotics is an ever increasing problem because of the substantial illicit profits derived therefrom. The Legislature further finds and declares that a substantial and disproportionate amount of serious crime is associated with the cultivation, processing, manufacturing, and sale of narcotics.

(b) The Legislature finds and declares that the level of production, distribution, and sale of narcotics in small counties in this state threatens the well-being not only of citizens of those counties, but of the rest of the state as well. Since many of these counties have experienced less growth in their general purpose revenues than the rest of the state, and yet are required to bear the burden of funding disproportionate criminal justice costs associated with the production, distribution, and sale of narcotics, the Legislature recognizes the need to provide financial assistance for these counties.

(c) The Legislature intends to support intensified efforts by district attorneys' offices to prosecute drug producers and sellers through organizational and operational techniques that have been proven effective in selected jurisdictions in this and other states.

(Amended by Stats. 1987, Ch. 306, Sec. 1.)

13881.

(a) There is hereby established in the office a program of financial and technical assistance for district attorneys' offices, designated the California Major Narcotic Vendors Prosecution Law. All funds appropriated to the office for the purposes of this chapter shall be administered and disbursed by the director in consultation with the California Council on Criminal Justice, and shall to the greatest extent feasible be coordinated or consolidated with federal funds that may be made available for these purposes.

(b) The director is authorized to allocate and award funds to counties in which the California Major Narcotic Vendors Prosecution Law is implemented in substantial compliance with the policies and criteria set forth in this chapter.

(c) The allocation and award of funds shall be made upon application executed by the county's district attorney and approved by its board of supervisors. Funds disbursed under this chapter shall not supplant local funds that would, in the absence of the California Major Narcotic Vendors Prosecution Law, be made available to support the prosecution of felony drug cases. Funds available under this program shall not be subject to review, as specified in Section 14780 of the Government Code.

(d) The director shall prepare and issue written program and administrative guidelines and procedures for the California Major Narcotic Vendors Prosecution Program consistent with this chapter, which shall be submitted to the Chairpersons of the Assembly Committee on Public Safety and the Senate Committee on Criminal Procedure. These guidelines shall permit the selection of a county for the allocation and award of

funds only on a finding by the office that the county is experiencing a proportionately significant increase in major narcotic cases. Further, the guidelines shall provide for the allocation and award of funds to small county applicants, as designated by the director. The guidelines shall also provide that any funds received by a county under this chapter shall be used only for the prosecution of cases involving major narcotic dealers. For purposes of this subdivision, "small county" means a county having a population of 200,000 or less.
(Amended by Stats. 2013, Ch. 352, Sec. 460. (AB 1317) Effective September 26, 2013. Operative July 1, 2013, by Sec. 543 of Ch. 352.)
13882.
California major narcotic vendors prosecution units receiving funds under this chapter shall concentrate enhanced prosecution efforts and resources upon individuals identified under selection criteria set forth in Section 13883. Enhanced prosecution efforts and resources shall include, but not be limited to, all of the following:
(a) "Vertical" prosecutorial representation, whereby the prosecutor who makes the initial filing or appearance in a drug case will perform all subsequent court appearances on that particular case through its conclusion, including the sentencing phase.
(b) Assignment of highly qualified investigators and prosecutors to drug cases.
(c) Significant reduction of caseloads for investigators and prosecutors assigned to drug cases.
(Added by Stats. 1984, Ch. 1424, Sec. 1. Effective September 26, 1984.)
13883.
(a) An individual may be the subject of the California Major Narcotic Vendors Prosecution Law prosecution efforts who is under arrest for the commission or attempted commission of one or more felonies relating to controlled substances in violation of Section 11351, 11352, 11358, 11378, 11378.5, 11379, 11379.5, or 11383 of the Health and Safety Code.
(b) In applying the criteria set forth in subdivision (a), a district attorney may, consistent with the provisions of subdivision (d) of Section 13881, elect to limit drug prosecution efforts to persons arrested for any one or more of the felonies listed in subdivision (a) if crime statistics demonstrate that the incidence of that felony or felonies presents a particularly serious problem in the county.
(c) In exercising the prosecutorial discretion granted by this section, the district attorney shall consider (1) the character, background, and prior criminal background of the defendant, and (2) the number and the seriousness of the offenses currently charged against the defendant.
(Added by Stats. 1984, Ch. 1424, Sec. 1. Effective September 26, 1984.)
13884.
(a) Each district attorney's office establishing a California major narcotic vendors prosecution unit and receiving state support under this chapter shall adopt and pursue the following policies for the California Major Narcotic Vendors Prosecution Law cases:
(1) All reasonable prosecutorial efforts shall be made to resist the pretrial release of a charged defendant selected for prosecution under the California Major Narcotic Vendors Prosecution Law.
(2) All reasonable prosecutorial efforts shall be made to persuade the court to impose the most severe authorized sentence upon a person convicted after prosecution under the California Major Narcotic Vendors Prosecution Law.
(3) All reasonable prosecutorial efforts shall be made to reduce the time between arrest and disposition of charge against an individual selected for prosecution under the California Major Narcotic Vendors Prosecution Law.
(b) The selection criteria set forth in Section 13883 shall be adhered to for each California Major Narcotic Vendors Prosecution Law case unless, in the reasonable exercise of prosecutor's discretion, extraordinary circumstances require the departure from those policies in order to promote the general purposes and intent of this chapter.
(Added by Stats. 1984, Ch. 1424, Sec. 1. Effective September 26, 1984.)

CHAPTER 9.5.
Statewide Sexual Predator Apprehension Team [13885 - 13885.8]

(Heading of Chapter 9.5 amended by Stats. 2003, Ch. 27, Sec. 1.)
13885.
The Legislature hereby finds that a substantial and disproportionate amount of sexual offenses are committed against the people of California by a relatively small number of multiple and repeat sex offenders. In enacting this chapter, the Legislature intends to support efforts of the criminal justice community through a focused effort by law enforcement and prosecuting agencies to identify, locate, apprehend, and prosecute sex offenders.
(Amended by Stats. 2010, Ch. 709, Sec. 20. (SB 1062) Effective January 1, 2011.)
13885.1.
The Attorney General shall maintain, upon appropriation of funds by the Legislature, a statewide Sexual Predator Apprehension Team force. The Sexual Predator Apprehension Team force shall be comprised of special agent teams throughout California. The teams shall focus on repeat sex offenders, and perform the following activities:
(a) Coordinate state and local investigative resources to apprehend high risk sex offenders and persons required to register under Section 290 who violate the law or conditions of probation or parole.
(b) Target and monitor chronic repeat violent sex offenders before the commission of additional sexual offenses.
(c) Develop profiles in unsolved sexual assault cases.
(Amended by Stats. 2012, Ch. 867, Sec. 27. (SB 1144) Effective January 1, 2013.)
13885.15.
(a) The special agent teams established pursuant to Section 13885.1 shall also take a proactive role in the investigation and prosecution of preferential child molesters and sexual exploiters.
(b) For purposes of this section, "preferential child molester" means a person whose primary sex drive is directed toward children. A preferential child molester is distinguished from a situational child molester, who will use children sexually in times of stress because of a lack of impulse control or as a result of circumstances.
(Added by Stats. 1994, Ch. 876, Sec. 2. Effective January 1, 1995.)
13885.2.
The Attorney General, subject to the availability of funds, shall establish in the Department of Justice the High Risk Sex Offender Program, which is hereby created, which shall receive the Facts of Offense Sheets, pursuant to Section 1203e. The program shall use the scores of sex offenders reported on the Facts of Offense Sheets for the purpose of identifying, assessing, monitoring, and containing those sex offenders at a high risk of reoffending. This shall be a statewide program.
It is the intent of the Legislature that this statewide program shall not affect the operation of the Serious Habitual Offender Program authorized by Chapter 10 (commencing with Section 13890) involving the Counties of San Francisco, San Mateo, Santa Clara, Santa Cruz, Alameda, Contra Costa, Napa, Sonoma, Solano, and Marin which shall become inoperative on July 1, 1994.
(Amended by Stats. 2010, Ch. 709, Sec. 22. (SB 1062) Effective January 1, 2011.)
13885.4.

As used in this chapter, "high risk sex offenders" means those persons who are required to register as sex offenders pursuant to the Sex Offender Registration Act and who have been assessed with a score indicating a "high risk" on the SARATSO identified for that person's specific population as set forth in Section 290.04, or who are identified as being at a high risk of reoffending by the Department of Justice, based on the person's SARATSO score when considered in combination with other, empirically based risk factors.
(Amended by Stats. 2010, Ch. 709, Sec. 23. (SB 1062) Effective January 1, 2011.)
13885.6.
The Department of Justice shall establish and maintain a comprehensive file of existing information maintained by law enforcement agencies, probation departments, the Department of Corrections and Rehabilitation, the State Department of State Hospitals, the Department of Motor Vehicles, and the Department of Justice. The Department of Justice may request the Department of Corrections and Rehabilitation, the State Department of State Hospitals, the Department of Motor Vehicles, law enforcement agencies, and probation departments to provide existing information from their files regarding persons identified by the Department of Justice as high risk sex offenders pursuant to Section 13885.4. The Department of Corrections and Rehabilitation, the State Department of State Hospitals, the Department of Motor Vehicles, law enforcement agencies, and probation departments, when requested by the Department of Justice, shall provide copies of existing information maintained in their files regarding persons identified by the Department of Justice as high risk sex offenders and shall provide followup information to the Department of Justice as it becomes available, unless otherwise prohibited by federal law. This information shall include, but is not limited to, criminal histories, Facts of Offense Sheets, sex offender registration records, police reports, probation and presentencing reports, judicial records and case files, juvenile records, psychological evaluations and psychological hospital reports, and sexually violent predator treatment program reports. This information shall also include records that have been sealed. This information shall be provided to the Department of Justice in a manner and format jointly approved by the submitting department and the Department of Justice. This high risk sex offender file shall be maintained by the Department of Justice High Risk Sex Offender Program and shall contain a complete physical description and method of operation of the high risk sex offender, information describing his or her interaction with criminal justice agencies, and his or her prior criminal record. The Department of Justice also shall prepare a bulletin on each high risk sex offender for distribution to law enforcement agencies.
(Amended by Stats. 2012, Ch. 24, Sec. 54. (AB 1470) Effective June 27, 2012.)
13885.8.
The Department of Justice shall electronically provide a bulletin on each high risk sex offender to law enforcement agencies via the California Sex Offender Registry database and the California Law Enforcement Web (CLEW).
Upon request, the department shall provide the complete file of information on a high risk sex offender to law enforcement agencies, district attorneys, and the courts for the purpose of identifying, apprehending, prosecuting, and sentencing high risk sex offenders.
(Amended by Stats. 2010, Ch. 709, Sec. 25. (SB 1062) Effective January 1, 2011.)

CHAPTER 9.7.
County Sexual Assault Felony Enforcement (SAFE)Team Program [13887 - 13887.4]

(Chapter 9.7 added by Stats. 2002, Ch. 1090, Sec. 2.)
13887.
(a) Any county may establish and implement a sexual assault felony enforcement (SAFE) team program pursuant to the provisions of this chapter.
(b) The Legislature finds and declares that identifying and developing reliable and sustainable funding for SAFE teams established by this chapter, including those established in rural and regional areas, is critical for reducing sexual assaults in California.
(Amended by Stats. 2010, Ch. 219, Sec. 24. (AB 1844) Effective September 9, 2010.)
13887.1.
(a) The mission of this program shall be to reduce violent sexual assault offenses in the county through proactive surveillance and arrest of habitual sexual offenders, as defined in Section 667.71, and strict enforcement of registration requirements for sex offenders pursuant to Section 290.
(b) The proactive surveillance and arrest authorized by this chapter shall be conducted within the limits of existing statutory and constitutional law.
(c) The mission of this program shall also be to provide community education regarding the purposes of Chapter 5.5 (commencing with Section 290) of Title 9 of Part 2. The goal of community education is to do all of the following:
(1) Provide information to the public about ways to protect themselves and families from sexual assault.
(2) Emphasize the importance of using the knowledge of the presence of registered sex offenders in the community to enhance public safety.
(3) Explain that harassment or vigilantism against registrants may cause them to disappear and attempt to live without supervision, or to register as transients, which would defeat the purpose of sex offender registration.
(Amended by Stats. 2006, Ch. 337, Sec. 51. Effective September 20, 2006.)
13887.2.
The regional SAFE teams may consist of officers and agents from the following law enforcement agencies:
(a) Police departments.
(b) Sheriff's departments.
(c) The Bureau of Investigations of the Office of the District Attorney.
(d) County probation departments.
(e) To the extent that these agencies have available resources, the following law enforcement agencies:
(1) The Department of Justice.
(2) The Department of the California Highway Patrol.
(3) The Department of Corrections and Rehabilitation.
(4) The Federal Bureau of Investigation.
(Amended by Stats. 2012, Ch. 867, Sec. 28. (SB 1144) Effective January 1, 2013.)
13887.3.
The program established pursuant to this chapter shall have the following objectives:
(a) To identify, monitor, arrest, and assist in the prosecution of habitual sexual offenders who violate the terms and conditions of their probation or parole, who fail to comply with the registration requirements of Section 290, or who commit new sexual assault offenses.
(b) To collect data to determine if the proactive law enforcement procedures adopted by the program are effective in reducing violent sexual assault offenses.
(c) To develop procedures for operating a multijurisdictional regional task force.
(Added by Stats. 2002, Ch. 1090, Sec. 2. Effective January 1, 2003.)
13887.4.
Nothing in this chapter shall be construed to authorize the otherwise unlawful violation of any person's rights under the law.

(Added by Stats. 2002, Ch. 1090, Sec. 2. Effective January 1, 2003.)

CHAPTER 10.
California Forensic Science Laboratory Enhancement Program [13890 - 13891]

(Chapter 10 added by Stats. 1997, Ch. 931, Sec. 1.)
13890.
It is the intent of the Legislature to review the needs assessment report, as provided for in Section 13892, prior to providing additional funds for support of local forensic laboratory services or improvements.
(Added by Stats. 1997, Ch. 931, Sec. 1. Effective January 1, 1998.)
13891.
This chapter shall be known and may be cited as the California Forensic Science Laboratory Enhancement Act.
(Added by Stats. 1997, Ch. 931, Sec. 1. Effective January 1, 1998.)

CHAPTER 11. Victims' Legal Resource Center [13897 - 13897.3]

(Chapter 11 added by Stats. 1985, Ch. 1443, Sec. 1.)
13897.
The Legislature finds and declares each of the following:
(a) The citizens of California have expressed great concern for the plight of crime victims.
(b) It is in the best interest, not only of the victims and their families, but also of all the citizens of California to ensure that crime victims receive comprehensive assistance in overcoming the effects of victimization.
(c) While many options and rights exist for the crime victim, including providing financial assistance pursuant to Chapter 5 (commencing with Section 13959) of Part 4 of Division 3 of Title 2 of the Government Code, participation in sentencing and parole eligibility hearings of criminal perpetrators, civil litigation against the perpetrator and third parties, assistance from victim-witness programs, and private support and counseling services, research indicates that many crime victims suffer needlessly because they are not aware of these options and rights, or are apprehensive or uncertain about where to go for assistance or how to exercise their rights.
(d) It is thus necessary to provide a resource center, statewide in scope, where victims of crime, their families, and providers of services to victims of crime can receive referral information, assistance, and legal guidance in order to deal effectively with the needs of victims of crime and minimize the continuing victimization process, which often results from a complex justice system. This resource center shall be independent, offer victims assistance in understanding and effectively exercising their legal rights, provide information about their rights and the workings of the criminal justice system, and direct them to appropriate local resources and agencies which can offer further assistance. The resource center shall provide, on a statewide basis, information assistance for all crime victims without charge and shall complement the efforts of various local programs, including victim-witness programs, rape crisis units, domestic violence projects, and child abuse centers.
(Amended by Stats. 1988, Ch. 1640, Sec. 1.)
13897.1.
There shall be established a resource center which shall operate a statewide, toll-free information service, consisting of legal and other information, for crime victims and providers of services to crime victims. The center shall provide information and educational materials discussing victims' legal rights. The center shall distribute these materials to administrative agencies, law enforcement agencies, victim-service programs, local, regional, and statewide education systems, appropriate human service agencies, and political, social, civic, and religious leaders and organizations.
As used in this chapter, "provider of services to crime victims" means any hospital, doctor, attorney, local or statewide rape crisis center, domestic violence center, child abuse counseling center, or victims' witness center that seeks to assist crime victims in understanding and exercising their legal rights, including those under Chapter 5 (commencing with Section 13959) of Part 4 of Division 3 of Title 2 of the Government Code.
(Amended by Stats. 1988, Ch. 1640, Sec. 2.)
13897.2.
(a) The Office of Emergency Services shall grant an award to an appropriate private, nonprofit organization, to provide a statewide resource center, as described in Section 13897.1.
(b) The center shall:
(1) Provide callers with information about victims' legal rights to compensation pursuant to Chapter 5 (commencing with Section 13959) of Part 4 of Division 3 of Title 2 of the Government Code and, where appropriate, provide victims with guidance in exercising these rights.
(2) Provide callers who provide services to victims of crime with legal information regarding the legal rights of victims of crime.
(3) Advise callers about any potential civil causes of action and, where appropriate, provide callers with references to local legal aid and lawyer referral services.
(4) Advise and assist callers in understanding and implementing their rights to participate in sentencing and parole eligibility hearings as provided by statute.
(5) Advise callers about victims' rights in the criminal justice system, assist them in overcoming problems, including the return of property, and inform them of any procedures protecting witnesses.
(6) Refer callers, as appropriate, to local programs, which include victim-witness programs, rape crisis units, domestic violence projects, and child sexual abuse centers.
(7) Refer callers to local resources for information about appropriate public and private benefits and the means of obtaining aid.
(8) Publicize the existence of the toll-free service through the print and electronic media, including public service announcements, brochures, press announcements, various other educational materials, and agreements for the provision of publicity, by private entities.
(9) Compile comprehensive referral lists of local resources that include the following: victims' assistance resources, including legal and medical services, financial assistance, personal counseling and support services, and victims' support groups.
(10) Produce promotional materials for distribution to law enforcement agencies, state and local agencies, print, radio, and television media outlets, and the general public. These materials shall include placards, video and audio training materials, written handbooks, and brochures for public distribution. Distribution of these materials shall be coordinated with the local victims' service programs.
(11) Research, compile, and maintain a library of legal information concerning crime victims and their rights.

(12) Provide a 20-percent minimum cash match for all funds appropriated pursuant to this chapter which match may include federal and private funds in order to supplement any funds appropriated by the Legislature.
(c) The resource center shall be located so as to assure convenient and regular access between the center and those state agencies most concerned with crime victims. The entity receiving the grant shall be a private, nonprofit organization, independent of law enforcement agencies, and have qualified staff knowledgeable in the legal rights of crime victims and the programs and services available to victims throughout the state. The subgrantee shall have an existing statewide, toll-free information service and have demonstrated substantial capacity and experience serving crime victims in areas required by this act.
(d) The services of the resource center shall not duplicate the victim service activities of the Office of Emergency Services or those activities of local victim programs funded through the Office of Emergency Services.
(e) The subgrantee shall be compensated at its federally approved indirect cost rate, if any. For the purposes of this section, "federally approved indirect cost rate" means that rate established by the federal Department of Health and Human Services or other federal agency for the subgrantee. Nothing in this section shall be construed as requiring the Office of Emergency Services to permit the use of federally approved indirect cost rates for other subgrantees of other grants administered by the Office of Emergency Services.
(f) All information and records retained by the center in the course of providing services under this chapter shall be confidential and privileged pursuant to Article 3 (commencing with Section 950) of Chapter 4 of Division 8 of the Evidence Code and Article 4 (commencing with Section 6060) of Chapter 4 of Division 3 of the Business and Professions Code. Nothing in this subdivision shall prohibit compilation and distribution of statistical data by the center.
(Amended by Stats. 2013, Ch. 352, Sec. 461. (AB 1317) Effective September 26, 2013. Operative July 1, 2013, by Sec. 543 of Ch. 352.)
13897.3.
The Office of Emergency Services shall develop written guidelines for funding and performance standards for monitoring the effectiveness of the resource center program. The program shall be evaluated by a public or private nonprofit entity under a contract with the Office of Emergency Services.
(Amended by Stats. 2013, Ch. 352, Sec. 462. (AB 1317) Effective September 26, 2013. Operative July 1, 2013, by Sec. 543 of Ch. 352.)

CHAPTER 12. County Sexual Assault Response Team (SART) Program [13898 - 13898.2]

(Chapter 12 added by Stats. 2015, Ch. 210, Sec. 1.)
13898.
(a) Each county may establish and implement an interagency sexual assault response team (SART) program for the purpose of providing a forum for interagency cooperation and coordination, to assess and make recommendations for the improvement in the local sexual assault intervention system, and to facilitate improved communication and working relationships to effectively address the problem of sexual assault in California.
(b) Each SART program shall be established and implemented pursuant to the provisions of this chapter.
(Added by Stats. 2015, Ch. 210, Sec. 1. (AB 1475) Effective January 1, 2016.)
13898.1.
(a) Each SART may consist of representatives of the following public and private agencies or organizations:
(1) Law enforcement agencies.
(2) County district attorneys' offices.
(3) Rape crisis centers.
(4) Local sexual assault forensic examination teams.
(5) Crime laboratories.
(b) Dependent upon local needs and goals, each SART may include representatives of the following public and private agencies or organizations:
(1) Child protective services.
(2) Local victim and witness assistance centers.
(3) County public health departments.
(4) County mental health services departments.
(5) Forensic interview centers.
(6) University and college Title IX coordinators.
(7) University and college police departments.
(Added by Stats. 2015, Ch. 210, Sec. 1. (AB 1475) Effective January 1, 2016.)
13898.2.
The program established pursuant to this chapter shall have the following objectives:
(a) Review of local sexual assault intervention undertaken by all disciplines to promote effective intervention and best practices.
(b) Assessment of relevant trends, including drug-facilitated sexual assault, the incidence of predatory date rape, and human sex trafficking.
(c) Evaluation of the cost-effectiveness and feasibility of a per capita funding model for local sexual assault forensic examination teams to achieve stability for this component of the SART program.
(d) Evaluation of the effectiveness of individual agency and interagency protocols and systems by conducting case reviews of cases involving sexual assault.
(e) Plan and implement effective prevention strategies and collaborate with other agencies and educational institutions to address sexual assault perpetrated by strangers, sexual assault perpetrated by persons known to the victim, including, but not limited to, a friend, family member, or general acquaintance of the victim, predatory date rape, risks associated with binge alcohol drinking, and drug-facilitated sexual assault.
(Added by Stats. 2015, Ch. 210, Sec. 1. (AB 1475) Effective January 1, 2016.)

CHAPTER 13. Retail Theft Prevention Program [13899 - 13899.1]

(Chapter 13 added by Stats. 2018, Ch. 803, Sec. 9.)
13899.
The Department of the California Highway Patrol shall, in coordination with the Department of Justice, convene a regional property crimes task force to assist local law enforcement in counties identified by the Department of the California Highway Patrol as having elevated levels of property crime, including, but not limited to, organized retail theft and vehicle burglary. The task force shall provide local law enforcement in the identified region with logistical support and other law enforcement resources, including, but not limited to, personnel and equipment, as determined to be appropriate by the Commissioner of the California Highway Patrol in consultation with task force members.
(Added by Stats. 2018, Ch. 803, Sec. 9. (AB 1065) Effective January 1, 2019. Repealed as of July 1, 2021, pursuant to section 13889.1.)
13899.1.

This chapter shall remain in effect only until July 1, 2021, and as of that date is repealed.

(Amended by Stats. 2019, Ch. 25, Sec. 51. (SB 94) Effective June 27, 2019. Repealed as of July 1, 2021, by its own provisions. Note: Repeal affects Chapter 13, commencing with Section 13899.)

TITLE 6.5. LOCAL CRIMINAL JUSTICE PLANNING [13900 - 13908]

(Title 6.5 added by Stats. 1973, Ch. 1047.)

13900.
The Legislature finds and declares:
(a) That crime is a local problem that must be dealt with by state and local governments if it is to be controlled effectively.
(b) That criminal justice needs and problems vary greatly among the different local jurisdictions of this state.
(c) That effective planning and coordination can be accomplished only through the direct, immediate and continuing cooperation of local officials charged with general governmental and criminal justice agency responsibilities.
(d) That planning for the efficient use of criminal justice resources requires a permanent coordinating effort on the part of local governments and local criminal justice and delinquency prevention agencies.
(Amended by Stats. 1975, Ch. 1230.)

13901.
(a) For the purposes of coordinating local criminal justice activities and planning for the use of state and federal action funds made available through any grant programs, criminal justice and delinquency prevention planning districts shall be established.
(b) On January 1, 1976, all planning district boundaries shall remain as they were immediately prior to that date. Thereafter, the number and boundaries of those planning districts may be altered from time to time pursuant to this section; provided that no county shall be divided into two or more districts, nor shall two or more counties which do not comprise a contiguous area form a single district.
(c) Prior to taking any action to alter the boundaries of any planning district, the council shall adopt a resolution indicating its intention to take the action and, at least 90 days prior to the taking of the action, shall forward a copy of the resolution to all units of government directly affected by the proposed action.
(d) If any county or a majority of the cities directly affected by the proposed action objects thereto, and a copy of the resolution of each board of supervisors or city council stating its objection is delivered to the Director of Emergency Services within 30 days following the giving of the notice of the proposed action, the director shall conduct a public meeting within the boundaries of the district as they are proposed to be determined. Notice of the time and place of the meeting shall be given to the public and to all units of local government directly affected by the proposed action, and reasonable opportunity shall be given to members of the public and representatives of those units to present their views on the proposed action.
(Amended by Stats. 2013, Ch. 352, Sec. 463. (AB 1317) Effective September 26, 2013. Operative July 1, 2013, by Sec. 543 of Ch. 352.)

13902.
Each county placed within a single county planning district may constitute a planning district upon execution of a joint powers agreement or arrangement acceptable to the county and to at least that one-half of the cities in the district which contain at least one-half of the population of the district. Counties placed within a multicounty planning district may constitute a planning district upon execution of a joint powers agreement or other arrangement acceptable to the participating counties and to at least that one-half of the cities in such district which contain at least one-half of the population of such district. If no combination of one-half of the cities of a district contains at least one-half of the population of the district, then agreement of any half of the cities in such district is sufficient to enable execution of joint powers agreements or other acceptable arrangements for constituting planning districts.
(Repealed and added by Stats. 1975, Ch. 1230.)

13903.
Planning districts may be the recipients of criminal justice and delinquency prevention planning or coordinating funds made available to units of general local government or combinations of units of general local government by federal or state law. Such planning districts shall establish local criminal justice and delinquency prevention planning boards, but shall not be obligated to finance their activities in the event that federal or state support of such activities is lacking.
(Amended by Stats. 1975, Ch. 1230.)

13904.
(a) The membership of each local board shall be consistent with state and federal statutes and guidelines; shall be representative of a broad range of community interests and viewpoints; and shall be balanced in terms of racial, sexual, age, economic, and geographic factors. Each local board shall consist of not less than 21 and not more than 30 members, a majority of whom shall be locally elected officials.
(b) The California Council on Criminal Justice shall promulgate standards to ensure that the composition of each board complies with subdivision (a). The council shall annually review the composition of each board, and if it finds that the composition of a local board complies with the standards, it shall so certify. Certification shall be effective for one year; provided that if the membership of a board changes by more than 25 percent during a period of certification, the council may withdraw the certificate prior to its expiration.
(c) If the council determines that the composition of a local board does not comply with the standards, it shall direct the appropriate appointing authority to reappoint the local board and shall again review the composition pursuant to this section after such reappointments are made. The council may void decisions made by such board after such finding and due notice. The council may approve the allocation of planning or action funds only to those districts which have been certified pursuant to this section.
(Repealed and added by Stats. 1975, Ch. 1230.)

13905.
Except as otherwise provided in Section 13904, representatives of the public shall be appointed to local criminal justice and delinquency prevention planning boards, of a number not to exceed the number of representatives of government on that board. At least one-fifth of the membership of such boards shall be representatives of citizens, professional and community organizations, including organizations directly related to delinquency prevention.
(Amended by Stats. 1975, Ch. 1230.)

13906.
Planning boards may contract with other public or private entities for the performance of services, may appoint an executive officer and other employees, and may receive and expend funds in order to carry out planning and coordinating responsibility.
(Added by Stats. 1973, Ch. 1047.)

13908.
(a) The Office of Criminal Justice Planning shall undertake a study to determine whether it would be feasible to develop a state-operated center on computer forensics for the purpose of collecting, compiling, and analyzing information, including evidence seized in connection with criminal proceedings, in computer formats to provide assistance to state and local law enforcement agencies in the investigation and prosecution of crimes involving computer technology.
(b) The office shall involve state and local law enforcement agencies as well as representatives of the computer industry in the development of the feasibility study required by this section.
(c) The office shall report its findings and conclusions to the Legislature on or before June 30, 2000.
(Added by renumbering Section 13980 by Stats. 2015, Ch. 303, Sec. 409. (AB 731) Effective January 1, 2016.)

TITLE 7.5. THE HERTZBERG-LESLIE WITNESS PROTECTION ACT [14020 - 14033]

(Title 7.5 added by Stats. 1997, Ch. 507, Sec. 1.)

14020.
There is hereby established the Witness Relocation and Assistance Program.
(Amended by Stats. 2007, Ch. 455, Sec. 1. Effective January 1, 2008.)

14021.
As used in this title:
(a) "Witness" means any person who has been summoned, or is reasonably expected to be summoned, to testify in a criminal matter, including grand jury proceedings, for the people whether or not formal legal proceedings have been filed. Active or passive participation in the criminal matter does not disqualify an individual from being a witness. "Witness" may also apply to family, friends, or associates of the witness who are deemed by local or state prosecutors to be endangered.
(b) "Credible evidence" means evidence leading a reasonable person to believe that substantial reliability should be attached to the evidence.
(c) "Protection" means formal admission into a witness protection program established by this title memorialized by a written agreement between local or state prosecutors and the witness.
(Amended by Stats. 2002, Ch. 210, Sec. 3. Effective January 1, 2003.)

14022.
The program shall be administered by the Attorney General. In any criminal proceeding within this state, when the action is brought by local or state prosecutors, where credible evidence exists of a substantial danger that a witness may suffer intimidation or retaliatory violence, the Attorney General may reimburse state and local agencies for the costs of providing witness protection services.
(Amended by Stats. 2002, Ch. 210, Sec. 4. Effective January 1, 2003.)

14023.
The Attorney General shall give priority to matters involving organized crime, gang activities, drug trafficking, human trafficking, and cases involving a high degree of risk to the witness. Special regard shall also be given to the elderly, the young, battered, victims of domestic violence, the infirm, the handicapped, and victims of hate incidents.
(Amended by Stats. 2005, Ch. 240, Sec. 12. Effective January 1, 2006.)

14024.
The Attorney General shall coordinate the efforts of state and local agencies to secure witness protection, relocation, and assistance services and then reimburse those state and local agencies for the costs of the services that he or she determines to be necessary to protect a witness from bodily injury, assure the witness's safe transition into a new environment, and otherwise to assure the health, safety, and welfare of the witness. The Attorney General may reimburse the state or local agencies that provide witnesses with any of the following:
(a) Armed protection or escort by law enforcement officials or security personnel before, during, or subsequent to, legal proceedings.
(b) Physical relocation to an alternate residence.
(c) Housing expense.
(d) Appropriate documents to establish a new identity.
(e) Transportation or storage of personal possessions.
(f) Basic living expenses, including, but not limited to, food, transportation, utility costs, and health care.
(g) Support, advocacy, and other services to provide for witnesses' safe transition into a new environment.
(h) Other services as needed and approved by the Attorney General.
(Amended by Stats. 2007, Ch. 455, Sec. 2. Effective January 1, 2008.)

14025.
The witness protection agreement shall be in writing, and shall specify the responsibilities of the protected person that establish the conditions for local or state prosecutors providing protection. The protected person shall agree to all of the following:
(a) If a witness or potential witness, to testify in and provide information to all appropriate law enforcement officials concerning all appropriate proceedings.
(b) To refrain from committing any crime.
(c) To take all necessary steps to avoid detection by others of the facts concerning the protection provided to that person under this title.
(d) To comply with legal obligations and civil judgments against that person.
(e) To cooperate with all reasonable requests of officers and employees of this state who are providing protection under this title.
(f) To designate another person to act as agent for the service of process.
(g) To make a sworn statement of all outstanding legal obligations, including obligations concerning child custody and visitation.
(h) To disclose any probation or parole responsibilities, and if the person is on probation or parole.
(i) To regularly inform the appropriate program official of his or her activities and current address.
(Amended by Stats. 2002, Ch. 210, Sec. 5. Effective January 1, 2003.)

14025.5.
The State of California, the counties and cities within the state, and their respective officers and employees shall not be liable for any condition in the witness protection agreement that cannot reasonably be met due to a witness committing a crime during participation in the program.
(Amended by Stats. 2002, Ch. 210, Sec. 6. Effective January 1, 2003.)

14026.
Funds available to implement this title may be used for any of the following:
(a) To protect witnesses where credible evidence exists that they may be in substantial danger of intimidation or retaliatory violence because of their testimony.
(b) To provide temporary and permanent relocation of witnesses and provide for their transition and well-being into a safe and secure environment.
(c) To pay the costs of administering the program.
(Added by Stats. 1997, Ch. 507, Sec. 1. Effective January 1, 1998.)

14026.5.
For the purposes of this title, notwithstanding Article 1 (commencing with Section 13959) of Chapter 5 of Part 4 of Division 3 of Title 2 of the Government Code, a witness, as defined in subdivision (a) of Section 14021, selected by local or state prosecutors to receive services under the program established pursuant to this title

because he or she has been or may be victimized due to the testimony he or she will give, shall be deemed a victim.
(Amended by Stats. 2002, Ch. 210, Sec. 7. Effective January 1, 2003.)
14027.
The Attorney General shall issue appropriate guidelines and may adopt regulations to implement this title. These guidelines shall include:
(a) A process whereby state and local agencies shall apply for reimbursement of the costs of providing witness protection services.
(b) A 25-percent match that shall be required of local agencies. The Attorney General may also establish a process through which to waive the required local match when appropriate.
(Amended by Stats. 2007, Ch. 176, Sec. 65. Effective August 24, 2007.)
14028.
The State of California, the counties and cities within the state, and their respective officers and employees shall have immunity from civil liability for any decision declining or revoking protection to a witness under this title.
(Added by Stats. 1997, Ch. 507, Sec. 1. Effective January 1, 1998.)
14029.
All information relating to any witness participating in the program established pursuant to this title shall remain confidential and is not subject to disclosure pursuant to the California Public Records Act (Chapter 3.5 (commencing with Section 6250) of Division 7 of Title 1 of the Government Code) and, if a change of name has been approved by the program, the order to show cause is not subject to the publication requirement of Section 1277 of the Code of Civil Procedure.
(Amended by Stats. 2000, Ch. 688, Sec. 19. Effective January 1, 2001.)
14029.5.
(a) (1) No person or private entity shall post on the Internet the home address, the telephone number, or personal identifying information that discloses the location of any witness or witness' family member participating in the Witness Relocation and Assistance Program (WRAP) with the intent that another person imminently use that information to commit a crime involving violence or a threat of violence against that witness or witness' family member.
(2) A violation of this subdivision is a misdemeanor punishable by a fine of up to two thousand five hundred dollars ($2,500), or imprisonment of up to six months in a county jail, or by both that fine and imprisonment.
(3) A violation of this subdivision that leads to the bodily injury of the witness, or of any of the witness' family members who are participating in the program, is a misdemeanor punishable by a fine of up to five thousand dollars ($5,000), or imprisonment of up to one year in a county jail, or by both that fine and imprisonment.
(b) Upon admission to WRAP, local or state prosecutors shall give each participant a written opt-out form for submission to relevant Internet search engine companies or entities. This form shall notify entities of the protected person and prevent the inclusion of the participant's addresses and telephone numbers in public Internet search databases.
(c) A business, state or local agency, private entity, or person that receives the opt-out form of a WRAP participant pursuant to this section shall remove the participant's personal information from public display on the Internet within two business days of delivery of the opt-out form, and shall continue to ensure that this information is not reposted on the same Internet Web site, a subsidiary site, or any other Internet Web site maintained by the recipient of the opt-out form. No business, state or local agency, private entity, or person that has received an opt-out form from a WRAP participant shall solicit, sell, or trade on the Internet the home address or telephone number of that participant.
(d) A business, state or local agency, private entity, or person that violates subdivision (c) shall be subject to a civil penalty for each violation in the amount of five thousand dollars ($5,000). An action for a civil penalty under this subdivision may be brought by any public prosecutor in the name of the people of the State of California and the penalty imposed shall be enforceable as a civil judgment.
(e) A witness whose home address or telephone number is made public as a result of a violation of subdivision (c) may bring an action seeking injunctive or declaratory relief in any court of competent jurisdiction. If a jury or court finds that a violation has occurred, it may grant injunctive or declaratory relief and shall award the witness court costs and reasonable attorney's fees.
(f) Notwithstanding any other provision of law, a witness whose home address or telephone number is solicited, sold, or traded in violation of subdivision (c) may bring an action in any court of competent jurisdiction. If a jury or court finds that a violation has occurred, it shall award damages to that witness in an amount up to a maximum of three times the actual damages, but in no case less than four thousand dollars ($4,000).
(g) Nothing in this section shall preclude prosecution under any other provision of law.
(Amended by Stats. 2010, Ch. 328, Sec. 183. (SB 1330) Effective January 1, 2011.)
14030.
(a) The Attorney General shall establish a liaison with the United States Marshal's office in order to facilitate the legal processes over which the federal government has sole authority, including, but not limited to, those processes included in Section 14024. The liaison shall coordinate all requests for federal assistance relating to witness protection as established by this title.
(b) The Attorney General shall pursue all federal sources that may be available for implementing this program. For that purpose, the Attorney General shall establish a liaison with the United States Department of Justice.
(c) The Attorney General, with the California Victim Compensation Board, shall establish procedures to maximize federal funds for witness protection services.
(Amended by Stats. 2016, Ch. 31, Sec. 259. (SB 836) Effective June 27, 2016.)
14031.
Commencing one year after the effective date of this title, the Attorney General shall make an annual report to the Legislature no later than January 1 on the fiscal and operational status of the program. This report shall include the amount of funding sought by each county, the amount of funding provided to each county, and the amount of the county match.
(Amended by Stats. 2007, Ch. 176, Sec. 66. Effective August 24, 2007.)
14032.
The administrative costs of the Attorney General for the purposes of administering this title shall be limited to 5 percent of all costs incurred pursuant to this title.
(Added by Stats. 1997, Ch. 507, Sec. 1. Effective January 1, 1998.)
14033.
(a) The Governor's budget shall specify the estimated amount in the Restitution Fund that is in excess of the amount needed to pay claims pursuant to Sections 13960 to 13965, inclusive, of the Government Code, to pay administrative costs for increasing restitution funds, and to maintain a prudent reserve.
(b) It is the intent of the Legislature that, notwithstanding Government Code Section 13967, in the annual Budget Act, funds be appropriated to the Attorney General from those funds that are in excess of the amount specified pursuant to subdivision (a) for the purposes of this title.
(Added by Stats. 1997, Ch. 507, Sec. 1. Effective January 1, 1998.)

TITLE 8. BUILDING SECURITY [14051-14051.]

(Title 8 added by Stats. 1971, Ch. 1662.)
14051.
The chief law enforcement and fire officials of every city shall consult with the chief officer of their city who is charged with the enforcement of laws or ordinances regulating the erection, construction, or alteration of buildings within their jurisdiction for the purpose of developing local security standards and regulations supplemental to those adopted as part of Title 24 of the California Administrative Code, relating to building standards. The chief law enforcement and fire officials of every county shall consult with the chief officer of their county who is charged with the enforcement of laws or ordinances regulating the erection, construction, or alteration of buildings within their jurisdiction for the purpose of developing local security standards and regulations supplemental to those adopted as part of Title 24 of the California Administrative Code, relating to building standards. No provision of this or any other code shall prevent a city or county from enacting building security standards stricter than those enacted by the state.
(Added by Stats. 1971, Ch. 1662.)

TITLE 10. COMMUNITY VIOLENCE PREVENTION AND CONFLICT RESOLUTION [14110 - 14121]

(Title 10 added by Stats. 1984, Ch. 1709, Sec. 1.)
14110.
The Legislature finds the following:
(a) The incidence of violence in our state continues to present an increasing and dominating societal problem that must be addressed at its root causes in order to reduce significantly its effects upon our society.
(b) As an initial step toward that goal, the Legislature passed Assembly Bill No. 23 of the 1979–80 Regular Session which created the California Commission on Crime Control and Violence Prevention which was charged with compiling the latest research on root causes of violence, in order to lay the foundation for a credible, effective violence eradication program.
(c) The commission produced a final report in 1982 entitled "Ounces of Prevention," which established that long-term prevention is a valuable and viable public policy and demonstrated that there are reachable root causes of violence in our society.
(d) The report contains comprehensive findings and recommendations in 10 broad categorical areas for the removal of individual, familial, and societal causal factors of crime and violence in California.
(e) The recommendations in the report are feasible and credible, propose an effective means of resolving conflict and removing the root causes of violence in our society, and should be implemented, so that their value may be provided to our citizenry.
(Added by Stats. 1984, Ch. 1709, Sec. 1.)
14111.
The Legislature further finds that:
(a) It is in the public interest to translate the findings of the California Commission on Crime Control and Violence Prevention into community-empowering, community-activated violence prevention efforts that would educate, inspire, and inform the citizens of California about, coordinate existing programs relating to, and provide direct services addressing the root causes of, violence in California.
(b) The recommendations in the report of the commission can serve as both the foundation and guidelines for short-, intermediate-, and long-term programs to address and alleviate violence in California.
(c) It is in the public interest to facilitate the highest degree of coordination between, cooperation among, and utilization of public, nonprofit, and private sector resources, programs, agencies, organizations, and institutions toward maximally successful violence prevention and crime control efforts.
(d) Prevention is a sound fiscal, as well as social, policy objective. Crime and violence prevention programs can and should yield substantially beneficial results with regard to the exorbitant costs of both violence and crime to the public and private sectors.
(e) The Office of Emergency Services is the appropriate state agency to contract for programs addressing the root causes of violence.
(Amended by Stats. 2013, Ch. 352, Sec. 464. (AB 1317) Effective September 26, 2013. Operative July 1, 2013, by Sec. 543 of Ch. 352.)
14112.
The Legislature therefore intends:
(a) To develop community violence prevention and conflict resolution programs, in the state, based upon the recommendations of the California Commission on Crime Control and Violence Prevention, that would present a balanced, comprehensive educational, intellectual, and experiential approach toward eradicating violence in our society.
(b) That these programs shall be regulated, and funded pursuant to contracts with the Office of Emergency Services.
(Amended by Stats. 2013, Ch. 352, Sec. 465. (AB 1317) Effective September 26, 2013. Operative July 1, 2013, by Sec. 543 of Ch. 352.)
14113.
Unless otherwise required by context, as used in this title:
(a) "Agency" or "office" means the Office of Emergency Services.
(b) "Secretary" or "director" means the Director of Emergency Services.
(Amended by Stats. 2013, Ch. 352, Sec. 466. (AB 1317) Effective September 26, 2013. Operative July 1, 2013, by Sec. 543 of Ch. 352.)
14114.
(a) First priority shall be given to programs that provide community education, outreach, and coordination, and include creative and effective ways to translate the recommendations of the California Commission on Crime Control and Violence Prevention into practical use in one or more of the following subject areas:
(1) Parenting, birthing, early childhood development, self-esteem, and family violence, to include child, spousal, and elderly abuse.
(2) Economic factors and institutional racism.
(3) Schools and educational factors.
(4) Alcohol, diet, drugs, and other biochemical and biological factors.
(5) Conflict resolution.
(6) The media.
(b) At least three of the programs shall do all of the following:
(1) Use the recommendations of the California Commission on Crime Control and Violence Prevention and incorporate as many of those recommendations as possible into its program.
(2) Develop an intensive community-level educational program directed toward violence prevention. This educational component shall incorporate the commission's works "Ounces of Prevention" and "Taking Root," and shall be designed appropriately to reach the educational, ethnic, and socioeconomic individuals, groups, agencies, and institutions in the community.
(3) Include the imparting of conflict resolution skills.

(4) Coordinate with existing community-based, public and private, programs, agencies, organizations, and institutions, local, regional, and statewide public educational systems, criminal and juvenile justice systems, mental and public health agencies, appropriate human service agencies, and churches and religious organizations.
(5) Seek to provide specific resource and referral services to individuals, programs, agencies, organizations, and institutions confronting problems with violence and crime if the service is not otherwise available to the public.
(6) Reach all local ethnic, cultural, linguistic, and socioeconomic groups in the service area to the maximum extent feasible.
(Amended by Stats. 2001, Ch. 115, Sec. 33. Effective January 1, 2002.)
14114.5.
Other programs shall include subdivisions (a) and (f) of Section 14114 and may include public lectures or sponsoring of conferences, or both.
(Added by Stats. 1984, Ch. 1709, Sec. 1.)
14115.
(a) First priority programs may additionally provide specific direct services or contract for those services in one or more of the program areas as necessary to carry out the recommendations of the commission when those services are not otherwise available in the community and existing agencies do not furnish them. Direct services may include, but are not limited to, any of the following:
(1) Training seminars for law enforcement and human service agencies and operatives.
(2) Crisis intervention training and counseling.
(3) Casework and program consultation with local human service providers.
(4) Drug and alcohol counseling and treatment referral.
(5) Conflict resolution training and services, including the principles and practices of conflict mediation, arbitration, and "citizen tribunal" programs.
(b) All direct services are subject to Section 5328 of the Welfare and Institutions Code.
(Added by Stats. 1984, Ch. 1709, Sec. 1.)
14116.
Second priority shall be given to programs that conform to the requirements of Section 14114, except that the educational component of subdivision (f) of that section shall not be mandatory in each subject area, but shall be provided in at least three of those areas, and the programs shall provide specific direct services or contract for services in one or more program areas.
(Added by Stats. 1984, Ch. 1709, Sec. 1.)
14117.
(a) Each program shall have a governing board or an interagency coordinating team, or both, of at least nine members representing a cross section of existing and recipient, community-based, public and private persons, programs, agencies, organizations, and institutions. Each team shall do all of the following:
(1) As closely as possible represent the socioeconomic, ethnic, linguistic, and cultural makeup of the community and shall evidence an interest in and commitment to the categorical areas of violence prevention and conflict resolution.
(2) Be responsible for the implementation, evaluation, and operation of the program and all its constituent elements, including those specific direct services as may be provided pursuant to Section 14115.
(3) Be accountable for the distribution of all funds.
(4) Designate and appoint a responsible administrative authority acceptable to the Office of Emergency Services prior to the receipt of a grant.
(5) Submit an annual report to the Office of Emergency Services, which shall include information on all of the following:
(A) The number of learning events.
(B) The number of persons trained.
(C) An overview of the changing level of information regarding root causes of violence.
(D) An overview of the changing level of attitude regarding root causes of violence.
(E) The changing level of behavior regarding root causes of violence.
(F) The degree to which the program has been successful in satisfying the requirements set forth in subdivisions (e) and (f) of Section 14114.
(G) Other measures of program efficacy as specified by the Office of Emergency Services.
(b) Coordinating teams established under this section may adopt local policies, procedures, and bylaws consistent with this title.
(Amended by Stats. 2013, Ch. 352, Sec. 467. (AB 1317) Effective September 26, 2013. Operative July 1, 2013, by Sec. 543 of Ch. 352.)
14118.
(a) The Office of Emergency Services shall prepare and issue written program, fiscal, and administrative guidelines for the contracted programs that are consistent with this title, including guidelines for identifying recipient programs, agencies, organizations, and institutions, and organizing the coordinating teams. The Office of Emergency Services shall then issue a request for proposals. The responses to the request for proposals shall be rated according to the priorities set forth in subdivision (b) and additional criteria established by the guidelines. The highest rated responses shall be selected. The Office of Emergency Services shall do all of the following:
(1) Subject the proposed program and administrative guidelines to a 30-day period of broad public evaluation with public hearings commencing in May 1985, prior to adoption, including specific solicitation of input from culturally, geographically, socioeconomically, educationally, and ethnically diverse persons, programs, agencies, organizations, and institutions.
(2) Provide adequate public notice of the public evaluation around the state in major metropolitan and rural newspapers and related media outlets, and to local public, private, and nonprofit human service executives and advisory boards, and other appropriate persons and organizations.
(3) Establish a mechanism for obtaining, evaluating, and incorporating when appropriate and feasible, public input regarding the written program and administrative guidelines prior to adoption.
(b) Applicants for contracts under this title may be existing community-based public and nonprofit programs, agencies, organizations, and institutions, newly developed nonprofit corporations, or joint proposals from combinations of either or both of the above.
(Amended by Stats. 2013, Ch. 352, Sec. 468. (AB 1317) Effective September 26, 2013. Operative July 1, 2013, by Sec. 543 of Ch. 352.)
14119.
(a) The Office of Emergency Services shall promote, organize, and conduct a series of one-day crime and violence prevention training workshops around the state. The Office of Emergency Services shall seek participation in the workshops from ethnically, linguistically, culturally, educationally, and economically diverse persons, agencies, organizations, and institutions.
(b) The training workshops shall have all of the following goals:
(1) To identify phenomena which are thought to be root causes of crime and violence.
(2) To identify local manifestations of those root causes.
(3) To examine the findings and recommendations of the California Commission on Crime Control and Violence Prevention.
(4) To focus on team building and interagency cooperation and coordination toward addressing the local problems of crime and violence.
(5) To examine the merits and necessity of a local crime and violence prevention effort.
(c) There shall be at least three workshops.
(Amended by Stats. 2013, Ch. 352, Sec. 469. (AB 1317) Effective September 26, 2013. Operative July 1, 2013, by Sec. 543 of Ch. 352.)
14120.
(a) Programs shall be funded, depending upon the availability of funds, for a period of two years.
(b) The Office of Emergency Services shall provide 50 percent of the program costs, to a maximum amount of fifty thousand dollars ($50,000) per program per year. The recipient shall provide the remaining 50 percent with other resources which may include in-kind contributions and services. The administrative expenses for the pilot programs funded under Section 14120 shall not exceed 10 percent.
(c) Programs should be seeking private sector moneys and developing ways to become self-sufficient upon completion of pilot program funding.
(d) The recipient programs shall be responsible for a yearend independent audit.
(e) The Office of Emergency Services shall do an interim evaluation of the programs, commencing in July 1986, and shall report to the Legislature and the people with the results of the evaluation prior to October 31, 1986. The evaluation shall include, but not be limited to, an assessment and inventory of all of the following:
(1) The number of learning events.
(2) The number of persons trained.
(3) The changing level of information regarding root causes of violence.
(4) The changing level of attitude regarding root causes of violence.
(5) The changing level of behavior regarding root causes of violence.
(6) The reduced level of violence in our society.
(7) The degree to which the program has succeeded in reaching and impacting positively upon local ethnic, cultural, and socioeconomic groups in the service area.
A final evaluation shall be made with a report prior to October 31, 1987, which shall also include specific recommendations to the Legislature and the people of this state regarding methods and means by which these violence prevention and crime control programmatic efforts can be enhanced and improved.
(Amended by Stats. 2013, Ch. 352, Sec. 470. (AB 1317) Effective September 26, 2013. Operative July 1, 2013, by Sec. 543 of Ch. 352.)
14121.
The Office of Emergency Services may hire support staff and utilize resources necessary to carry out the purposes of this title.
(Amended by Stats. 2013, Ch. 352, Sec. 471. (AB 1317) Effective September 26, 2013. Operative July 1, 2013, by Sec. 543 of Ch. 352.)

TITLE 10.5. VIOLENT CRIMES AGAINST WOMEN [14140 - 14143]

(Title 10.5 added by Stats. 1992, Ch. 995, Sec. 1.)
14140.
(a) Each county is authorized and encouraged to create a county task force on violent crimes against women. The board of supervisors of a county which elects to create a task force under this section shall notify the Office of Emergency Services that the county is establishing, by appointment, a countywide task force. Each county task force shall develop a countywide policy on violent crimes against women.
(b) The Office of Emergency Services may provide technical assistance to, and collect and disseminate information on, the county task forces established under this section.
(Amended by Stats. 2013, Ch. 352, Sec. 472. (AB 1317) Effective September 26, 2013. Operative July 1, 2013, by Sec. 543 of Ch. 352.)
14141.
The purpose of each county task force may be as follows:
(a) To promote a countywide policy on violent crimes against women.
(b) To make recommendations on how to reduce violent crime.
(c) To prepare and place counties in a strong position to compete for federal and state funds that may become available for the purposes of this title.
(d) To facilitate coordination of services and responses between governmental agencies and between governmental agencies and nonprofit agencies serving women who are victims of violent crimes.
(e) To initiate local domestic violence prevention planning and priorities for the use of federal and state domestic violence prevention grants.
(Added by Stats. 1992, Ch. 995, Sec. 1. Effective January 1, 1993.)
14142.
Each county task force may evaluate and make recommendations regarding the following:
(a) The adequacy of current law enforcement efforts at the local level to reduce the rate of violent crimes against women.
(b) The responsiveness of local prosecutors and the courts to violent crimes against women.
(c) Local government efforts to reduce violent crimes against women.
(d) Public awareness and public dissemination of information essential to the prevention of violent crimes against women.
(e) The information collection and government statistics on the incidence and prevalence of violent crimes against women.
(f) The adequacy of federal, state, and local laws on sexual assault and domestic violence and the need for more uniform statutory responses to sex offenses and domestic violence.
(g) The need for services, including counseling, shelter, legal services, victim advocacy, and other supportive services, for women who are victims of violent crime.
(Added by Stats. 1992, Ch. 995, Sec. 1. Effective January 1, 1993.)
14143.
Every effort shall be made to ensure that the ethnic and racial composition of each task force is reflective of the ethnic and racial distribution of the persons and families in the community. Each county task force shall include, to the extent possible, but not be limited to, the following:
(a) A criminal court judge.
(b) A domestic relations or civil court judge.
(c) A prosecuting attorney.
(d) A city council person or other elected local governmental official.
(e) Representatives from the Council of Cities, the Police Chief Association, the County Office of Education, the Public Defender Program, the County Bar Association, the Domestic Violence Coalition, health services, social services, probation, a women's organization, each of the battered women's shelters serving the county, each of the rape crisis centers serving the county, a legal services program, a homeless program serving women, other nonprofit community-based organizations whose primary focus is to assist the women who are victims of violent crimes, the Native Tribal Councils, and the county Commission on the Status of Women.
(Added by Stats. 1992, Ch. 995, Sec. 1. Effective January 1, 1993.)

TITLE 10.6. COMMUNITY CONFLICT RESOLUTION PROGRAMS [14150 - 14156]

(Heading of Title 10.6 renumbered from Title 10.5 (as added by Stats. 1992, Ch. 696) by Stats. 2001, Ch. 854, Sec. 64.)
14150.
The Legislature hereby finds and declares:

(a) Over the last 10 years, criminal case filings, including misdemeanor filings, have been increasing faster than any other type of filing in California's courts. Between 1981 and 1991, nontraffic misdemeanor and infraction filings in municipal and justice courts increased by 35 percent.
(b) These misdemeanor cases add to the workload which is now straining the California court system. In addition, many of these cases are ill-suited to complete resolution through the criminal justice system because they involve underlying disputes which may result in continuing conflict and criminal conduct within the community.
(c) Many victims of misdemeanor criminal conduct feel excluded from the criminal justice process. Although they were the direct victims of the offenders' criminal conduct, the process does not currently provide them with a direct role in holding the offender accountable for this conduct.
(d) Community conflict resolution programs utilizing alternative dispute resolution (ADR) processes such as mediation and arbitration have been effectively used in California and elsewhere to resolve conflicts involving conduct that could be charged as a misdemeanor. These programs can assist in reducing the number of cases burdening the court system. By utilizing ADR processes, these programs also provide an opportunity for direct participation by the victims of the conduct, thereby increasing victims' satisfaction with the criminal justice process. In addition, by bringing the parties together, these programs may reduce conflict within the community by facilitating the settlement of disputes which are causing repeated misdemeanor criminal conduct and may increase compliance with restitution agreements by encouraging the offender to accept personal responsibility.
(e) As of the effective date of this section, the San Francisco and Contra Costa district attorney offices refer between 1,000 and 1,500 cases per year involving conduct which could be charged as a misdemeanor to California Community Dispute Services, which provides ADR services. Between 70 and 75 percent of these cases are successfully resolved through the ADR process, and the rate of compliance with the agreements reached is between 80 and 93 percent.
(f) The State of New York has developed a substantial statewide alternative dispute resolution program in which 65 percent of the cases using the services are of a criminal nature. These cases are referred to arbitration, conciliation, and mediation. Of the criminal misdemeanor cases that were mediated, 82 percent reached an agreement through the mediation process.
(g) It is in the public interest for community dispute resolution programs to be established to provide ADR services in cases involving conduct which could be charged as a misdemeanor and for district attorneys and courts to be authorized to refer cases to these programs.
(Added by Stats. 1992, Ch. 696, Sec. 91. Effective September 15, 1992.)
14151.
The district attorney may establish a community conflict resolution program pursuant to this title to provide alternative dispute resolution (ADR) services, such as mediation, arbitration, or a combination of both mediation and arbitration (med-arb) in cases, including those brought by a city prosecutor, involving conduct which could be charged as a misdemeanor. The district attorney may contract with a private entity to provide these services and may establish minimum training requirements for the neutral persons conducting the ADR processes.
(Added by Stats. 1992, Ch. 696, Sec. 91. Effective September 15, 1992.)
14152.
(a) The district attorney may refer cases involving conduct which could be charged as a misdemeanor to the community conflict resolution program. In determining whether to refer a case to the community conflict resolution program, the district attorney shall consider, but is not limited to considering, all of the following:
(1) The nature of the conduct in question.
(2) The nature of the relationship between the alleged victim and the person alleged to have committed the conduct.
(3) Whether referral to the community conflict resolution program is likely to help resolve underlying issues which are likely to result in additional conduct which could be the subject of criminal charges.
(b) No case where there has been a history of child abuse, sexual assault, or domestic violence, as that term is defined in Section 6211 of the Family Code, between the alleged victim and the person alleged to have committed the conduct, or where a protective order, as defined in Section 6218 of the Family Code, is in effect, shall be referred to the community conflict resolution program.
(Amended by Stats. 1993, Ch. 219, Sec. 222.7. Effective January 1, 1994.)
14153.
Both the alleged victim and the person alleged to have committed the conduct shall knowingly and voluntarily consent to participate in the ADR process conducted by the community conflict resolution program.
(Added by Stats. 1992, Ch. 696, Sec. 91. Effective September 15, 1992.)
14154.
In a county in which the district attorney has established a community conflict resolution program, the superior court may, with the consent of the district attorney and the defendant, refer misdemeanor cases, including those brought by a city prosecutor, to that program. In determining whether to refer a case to the community conflict resolution program, the court shall consider, but is not limited to considering, all of the following:
(a) The factors listed in Section 14152.
(b) Any other referral criteria established by the district attorney for the program.
The court shall not refer any case to the community conflict resolution program which was previously referred to that program by the district attorney.
(Amended by Stats. 2002, Ch. 784, Sec. 575. Effective January 1, 2003.)
14155.
(a) If the alleged victim or the person alleged to have committed the conduct does not agree to participate in the community conflict resolution program or the case is not resolved through the ADR process provided by that program, the community conflict resolution program shall promptly refer the case back to the district attorney or to the court that made the referral for appropriate action.
(b) If the community conflict resolution program determines that a case referred to it prior to the filing of a complaint has been resolved through that referral, the program shall recommend to the district attorney that the case not be prosecuted.
(c) If a case referred to the community conflict resolution program after the filing of a complaint but prior to adjudication is resolved through that referral, the court may dismiss the action pursuant to Section 1378 or 1385.
(Added by Stats. 1992, Ch. 696, Sec. 91. Effective September 15, 1992.)
14156.
It is the intent of the Legislature that neither this title nor any other provision of law be construed to preempt other precomplaint or pretrial diversion programs. It is also the intent of the Legislature that this title not preempt other posttrial diversion programs.
(Added by Stats. 1992, Ch. 696, Sec. 91. Effective September 15, 1992.)

TITLE 11. RECORDS AND REPORTS OF MONETARY INSTRUMENT TRANSACTIONS [14160 - 14167]

(Title 11 added by Stats. 1986, Ch. 1039, Sec. 3.)
14160.
(a) It is the purpose of this title to require certain reports or records of transactions involving monetary instruments as defined herein where those reports or records have a high degree of usefulness in criminal investigations or proceedings.
(b) The Attorney General shall adopt rules and regulations for the administration and enforcement of this title.
(c) It is the intent of the Legislature that the rules and regulations prescribed by the Attorney General for the administration and enforcement of this title shall be designed to minimize the cost and difficulty of compliance and shall, to the greatest extent possible, result in report and record-keeping forms consistent with those in use for compliance with Sections 5311 et seq. of Title 31 of the United States Code, Section 6050 I of Title 26 of the United States Code, and regulations adopted thereunder.
(d) Nothing in this title shall be construed to give rise to a private cause of action for relief or damages.
(Added by Stats. 1986, Ch. 1039, Sec. 3.)
14161.
As used in this title:
(a) "Financial institution" means, when located or doing business in this state, any national bank or banking association, state bank or banking association, commercial bank or trust company organized under the laws of the United States or any state, any private bank, industrial savings bank, savings bank or thrift institution, savings and loan association, or building and loan association organized under the laws of the United States or any state, any insured institution as defined in Section 401 of the National Housing Act, any credit union organized under the laws of the United States or any state, any national banking association or corporation acting under Chapter 6 (commencing with Section 601) of Title 12 of the United States Code, any foreign bank, any currency dealer or exchange, any person or business engaged primarily in the cashing of checks, any person or business who regularly engages in the issuing, selling, or redeeming of traveler's checks, money orders, or similar instruments, any broker or dealer in securities registered or required to be registered with the Securities and Exchange Commission under the Securities Exchange Act of 1934, any licensed sender of money, any investment banker or investment company, any insurance company, any dealer in coins, precious metals, stones, or jewelry, any pawnbroker, any telegraph company, any person or business engaged in controlled gambling within the meaning of subdivision (e) of Section 19805 of the Business and Professions Code, whether registered or licensed to do so or not, and any person or business defined as a "bank," "financial agency," or "financial institution" by Section 5312 of Title 31 of the United States Code or Section 103.11 of Title 31 of the Code of Federal Regulations and any successor provisions thereto.
(b) "Transaction" includes the deposit, withdrawal, transfer, bailment, loan, payment, or exchange of currency, or a monetary instrument, as defined by subdivision (c), by, through, or to, a financial institution, as defined by subdivision (a). "Transaction" does not include the purchase of gold, silver, or platinum bullion or coins, or diamonds, emeralds, rubies, or sapphires by a bona fide dealer therein, and does not include the sale of gold, silver, or platinum bullion or coins, or diamonds, emeralds, rubies, or sapphires by a bona fide dealer therein in exchange for other than a monetary instrument, and does not include the exchange of gold, silver, or platinum bullion or coins, or diamonds, emeralds, rubies, or sapphires by a bona fide dealer therein for gold, silver, or platinum bullion or coins, or diamonds, emeralds, rubies, or sapphires.
(c) "Monetary instrument" means United States currency and coin; the currency and coin of any foreign country; and any instrument defined as a "monetary instrument" by Section 5312 of Title 31 of the United States Code or Section 103.11 of Title 31 of the Code of Federal Regulations, or the successor of either. Notwithstanding any other provision of this subdivision, "monetary instrument" does not include bank checks, cashier's checks, traveler's checks, personal checks, or money orders made payable to the order of a named party that have not been endorsed or that bear restrictive endorsements.
(d) "Department" means the Department of Justice.
(e) "Criminal justice agency" means the Department of Justice and any district attorney's office, sheriff's department, police department, or city attorney's office of this state.
(f) "Currency" means United States currency or coin, the currency or coin of any foreign country, and any legal tender or coin defined as currency by Section 103.11 of Title 31 of the Code of Federal Regulations or any succeeding provision.
(Amended by Stats. 1997, Ch. 867, Sec. 60. Effective January 1, 1998.)
14162.
(a) A financial institution shall make and keep a record of each transaction by, through, or to, the financial institution that involves currency of more than ten thousand dollars ($10,000). A financial institution shall file a report of the transaction with the department in a form and at the time that the department, by regulation, shall require. The filing with the department within the time specified in its regulations of a duplicate copy of a report of the transaction required by Section 6050I of Title 26 of the United States Code, and any regulations adopted thereunder, shall satisfy the reporting requirements of this subdivision. This subdivision does not apply to a financial institution, as defined in Section 5312 of Title 31 of the United States Code and Section 103.11 of Title 31 of the Code of Federal Regulations and any successor provisions thereto.
(b) A financial institution, as defined in Section 5312 of Title 31 of the United States Code and Section 103.11 of Title 31 of the Code of Federal Regulations and any successor provisions, shall file with the department, at any time as the department by regulation shall require, a duplicate copy of each report required by Sections 5313 and 5314 of Title 31 of the United States Code and by Sections 103.22 and 103.23 of Title 31 of the Code of Federal Regulations, and any successor provisions thereto. The filing pursuant to this subdivision shall satisfy all reporting and recordkeeping requirements of this title.
(c) (1) A financial institution with actual knowledge of the requirements of this section that knowingly and willfully fails to comply with the requirements of this section shall be liable for a civil penalty.
(2) The court may impose a civil penalty for each violation. However, in the first civil proceeding against a financial institution, the civil penalties for all violations shall not exceed a total sum of ten thousand dollars ($10,000). If a civil penalty was imposed in a prior civil proceeding, the civil penalties for all violations shall not exceed a total sum of twenty-five thousand dollars ($25,000). If a civil penalty was imposed in two or more prior civil proceedings, the civil penalties for all violations shall not exceed a total sum of one hundred thousand dollars ($100,000).
(3) A proceeding for a civil penalty under this subdivision may be brought only by the Attorney General of California or the district attorney for the county in which the violation is alleged to have occurred. The proceeding shall be governed by the Code of Civil Procedure.
(4) This subdivision shall not apply to any case where the financial institution is criminally prosecuted in federal or state court for conduct related to a violation of this section.
(Amended by Stats. 1992, Ch. 672, Sec. 4. Effective January 1, 1993.)
14163.
Except as otherwise provided, a financial institution may exempt from the reporting requirements of Section 14162 monetary instrument transactions exempted from the reporting requirements of Section 5313 of Title 31 of the United States Code. However, the exemption shall be approved in writing and with the signature of two or more officers of the financial institution and subject to review and disapproval for reasonable cause by the department. An exemption disapproved by the department in writing shall be effective to require reporting pursuant to Section 14162 within five business days of the time the disapproval is communicated to the financial institution. The department may require, by regulation, the maintenance, and may provide for the inspection, of records of exemptions granted under this section.
(Added by Stats. 1986, Ch. 1039, Sec. 3.)
14164.

(a) A financial institution, or any officer, employee, or agent thereof, that keeps and files a record in reliance on Section 14162, shall not be liable to its customer, to a state or local agency, or to any person for any loss or damage caused in whole or in part by the making, filing, or governmental use of the report, or any information contained therein.
(b) This title does not preclude a financial institution, in its discretion, from instituting contact with, and thereafter communicating with and disclosing customer financial records to, appropriate federal, state, or local law enforcement agencies when the financial institution has reason to suspect that the records or information demonstrate that the customer has violated any provision of this title or Section 186.10.
(Added by Stats. 1986, Ch. 1039, Sec. 3.)
14165.
(a) The department shall analyze the reports required by Section 14162 and shall report any possible violations indicated by this analysis to the appropriate criminal justice agency.
(b) The department, in the discretion of the Attorney General, may make a report or information contained in a report filed under Section 14162 available to a district attorney or a deputy district attorney in this state, upon request made by the district attorney or his or her designee. The report or information shall be available only for a purpose consistent with this title and subject to regulations prescribed by the Attorney General, which shall require the district attorney or his or her designee seeking the report or information contained in the report to specify in writing the specific reasons for believing that a provision of this title or Section 186.10 has been violated.
(c) The department shall destroy a report filed with it under Section 14162 at the end of the fifth calendar year after receipt of the report, unless the report or information contained in the report is known by the department to be the subject of an existing criminal proceeding or investigation.
(Amended by Stats. 1997, Ch. 578, Sec. 3. Effective January 1, 1998.)
14166.
Any person (a) who willfully violates any provision of this title or any regulation adopted to implement Section 14162, (b) who, knowingly and with the intent either (1) to disguise the fact that a monetary instrument was derived from criminal activity or (2) to promote, manage, establish, carry on, or facilitate the promotion, management, establishment, or carrying on of any criminal activity, furnishes or provides to a financial institution or any officer, employee, or agent thereof or to the department, any false, inaccurate, or incomplete information or conceals a material fact in connection with a transaction for which a report is required to be filed pursuant to either Section 14162 of this code or Section 5313 of Title 31 of the United States Code, or in connection with an exemption prescribed in Section 14163, or (c) who, knowingly and with the intent either (1) to disguise the fact that a monetary instrument was derived from criminal activity or (2) to promote, manage, establish, carry on, or facilitate the promotion, management, establishment, or carrying on of any criminal activity, conducts a monetary instrument transaction or series of transactions by or through one or more financial institutions as part of a scheme and with the intent to avoid the making or filing of a report required under either Section 14162 of this code or Section 5313 of Title 31 of the United States Code, shall be punished by imprisonment in the county jail for not more than one year or in the state prison, by a fine of not more than the greater of two hundred fifty thousand dollars ($250,000) or twice the monetary value of the financial transaction or transactions, or by both that imprisonment and fine.
Notwithstanding any other provision of law, any violation of this section as to each monetary instrument transaction or exemption constitutes a separate, punishable offense.
(Amended by Stats. 1994, Ch. 1187, Sec. 5. Effective January 1, 1995.)
14167.
Any report, record, information, analysis, or request obtained by the department or any agency pursuant to this title is not a public record as defined in Section 6252 of the Government Code and is not subject to disclosure under Section 6253 of the Government Code.
(Amended by Stats. 1996, Ch. 809, Sec. 4. Effective January 1, 1997.)

TITLE 11.5. CENTRAL VALLEY RURAL CRIME PREVENTION PROGRAM [14170 - 14174]

(Heading of Title 11.5 amended by Stats. 2002, Ch. 719, Sec. 1.)
14170.
(a) It is the intent of the Legislature in enacting this measure to enhance crime prevention efforts by establishing a pilot program to strengthen the ability of law enforcement agencies in rural areas to detect and monitor agricultural- and rural-based crimes.
(b) The County of Tulare has developed the Rural Crime Demonstration Project administered by the Tulare County District Attorney's office under a joint powers agreement with the Tulare County Sheriff's office entered into pursuant to Chapter 5 (commencing with Section 6500) of Division 7 of Title 1 of the Government Code. The parties to that agreement formed a task force to include the office of the Tulare County Agricultural Commissioner. The task force is an interactive team working together to develop problem solving and crime control techniques, to encourage timely reporting of crimes, and to evaluate the results of these activities. The task force conducts joint operations in order to facilitate investigative coordination. The task force consults with experts from the United States military, the California Military Department, the Department of Justice, other law enforcement entities, and various other state and private organizations as deemed necessary to maximize the effectiveness of the task force. Media and community support have been solicited to promote the task force. The Rural Crime Demonstration Project has proven its cost effectiveness. It is appropriate that the project be expanded into a program that will allow the County of Tulare to continue to operate the task force formed under the above described joint powers agreement, and to permit the Counties of Fresno, Kern, Kings, Madera, Merced, San Joaquin, and Stanislaus to establish their own programs, pursuant to the provisions of this title, and to collectively establish a task force for the prevention of rural crime in those counties.
(c) The Legislature finds and declares that California has experienced an escalation in agricultural crimes in general, both property and personal, and that there has been no concentrated effort applied to the prevention of crimes against the agricultural industry. Currently, no national or state agency keeps track of statistics on agricultural and rural crime. According to media reports, this state lost millions of dollars worth of crops, livestock, and equipment in 1994 and 1995. A majority of these crimes occurred in agricultural-based counties. However, there has been no effort on the part of any state or local agency to accurately record these types of crimes.
The Legislature further finds and declares that there are no state or local law enforcement agencies in this state with programs that are specially designed to detect or monitor agricultural- and rural-based criminal activities. In addition, local law enforcement agencies do not possess the jurisdictional authority, investigative facilities, or data systems to coordinate a comprehensive approach to the state's agricultural and rural crime problem.
The Legislature additionally finds and declares that the proliferation of agricultural and rural crime in the various rural counties of this state is a threat to the vitality of our rich agrarian tradition. Agricultural and rural crime, if left unchecked, endangers an entire industry that is vital to America's continued economic role in the world, and therefore requires a proactive response from the Legislature. The intent of the Legislature in

authorizing the Central Valley Rural Crime Prevention Program pursuant to this act is to provide for the protection and safety of the state's agriculture industry by creating statewide standards and methods of detecting and tracking agrarian and rural crime.
(Amended by Stats. 2002, Ch. 719, Sec. 2. Effective September 20, 2002.)
14171.
(a) Each of the Counties of Fresno, Kern, Kings, Madera, Merced, San Joaquin, Stanislaus, and Tulare may develop within its respective jurisdiction a Central Valley Rural Crime Prevention Program, which shall be administered by the county district attorney's office or the county sheriff's department of each respective county under a joint powers agreement entered into pursuant to Chapter 5 (commencing with Section 6500) of Division 7 of Title 1 of the Government Code.
(b) The parties to each agreement shall form a regional task force that shall be known as the Central Valley Rural Crime Task Force, that may include the respective county office of the county agricultural commissioner, the county district attorney, the county sheriff, and interested property owner groups or associations. The task force shall be an interactive team working together to develop crime prevention, problem solving, and crime control techniques, to encourage timely reporting of crimes, and to evaluate the results of these activities. The task force may operate from a joint facility in order to facilitate investigative coordination. The task force may also consult with experts from the United States military, the California Military Department, the Department of Justice, other law enforcement entities, and various other state and private organizations as deemed necessary to maximize the effectiveness of this program. Media and community support may be solicited to promote this program. Each of the participating designated counties shall adopt rules and regulations for the implementation and administration of this program.
(1) In order to receive funds for this program, each designated county shall agree to participate in a regional task force, to be known as the Central Valley Rural Crime Task Force, and shall appoint a representative to that task force.
(2) The Central Valley Rural Crime Task Force may develop rural crime prevention programs containing a system for reporting rural crimes that enables the swift recovery of stolen goods and the apprehension of criminal suspects for prosecution. The task force may develop computer software and use communication technology to implement the reporting system, although the task force is not limited to the use of these means to achieve the stated goals.
(3) The Central Valley Rural Crime Task Force may develop a uniform procedure for all participating counties to collect, and each participating county may collect, data on agricultural crimes. The task force may also establish a central database for the collection and maintenance of data on agricultural crimes and designate one participating county to maintain the database. State funds the counties receive to operate their rural crime prevention programs may be used to implement the requirements of this paragraph. This paragraph does not prohibit counties from using their own funds to implement the paragraph's provisions, however, it is the Legislature's intent that this paragraph shall not be construed as creating a state-mandated local program.
(c) The staff for each program may consist of the personnel designated by the district attorney and sheriff for each county in accordance with the joint powers agreement.
(Amended by Stats. 2012, Ch. 43, Sec. 79. (SB 1023) Effective June 27, 2012.)
14173.
Funds appropriated to the Central Valley Rural Crime Prevention Program shall be allocated by the Controller and distributed according to the following schedule:

Fresno County	23%
Kern County	17%
Kings County	8.5%
Madera County	5.5%
Merced County	8.5%
San Joaquin County	8.5%
Stanislaus County	8.5%
Tulare County	20.5%

(Amended by Stats. 2012, Ch. 43, Sec. 80. (SB 1023) Effective June 27, 2012.)
14174.
Funds appropriated for the purposes of this title shall be allocated based on the counties' compliance with paragraph (3) of subdivision (b) of Section 14171.
(Added by renumbering Section 14174.3 by Stats. 2005, Ch. 497, Sec. 6. Effective October 4, 2005.)

TITLE 11.7. CENTRAL COAST RURAL CRIME PREVENTION PROGRAM [14180 - 14182]

(Title 11.7 added by Stats. 2003, Ch. 18, Sec. 1.)
14180.
The Legislature encourages the Counties of Monterey, San Benito, Santa Barbara, Santa Cruz, and San Luis Obispo to develop, adopt, and implement a Central Coast Rural Crime Prevention Program based upon the Central Valley Rural Crime Prevention Program established by Title 11.5 (commencing with Section 14170) of Part 4.
(Added by Stats. 2003, Ch. 18, Sec. 1. Effective January 1, 2004.)
14181.
(a) The Counties of Monterey, San Luis Obispo, Santa Barbara, Santa Cruz, and San Benito may each develop within its respective jurisdiction a Central Coast Rural Crime Prevention Program, which shall be administered in San Benito County, Santa Barbara County, Santa Cruz County, and San Luis Obispo County by the county district attorney's office or the county sheriff's office under a joint powers agreement entered into pursuant to Chapter 5 (commencing with Section 6500) of Division 7 of Title 1 of the Government Code.
(b) The parties to each agreement shall form a regional task force that shall be known as the Central Coast Rural Crime Task Force, that includes the respective county office of the county agricultural commissioner, the county district attorney, the county sheriff, and interested property owner groups or associations. The task force shall be an interactive team working together to develop crime prevention, problem solving, and crime control techniques, to encourage timely reporting of crimes, and to evaluate the results of these activities. The task force may operate from a joint facility in order to facilitate investigative coordination. The task force may also consult with experts from the United States military, other law enforcement entities, and various private organizations as

deemed necessary to maximize the effectiveness of this program. Media and community support may be solicited to promote this program. Each of the participating designated counties shall adopt rules and regulations for the implementation and administration of this program.
(1) The Central Coast Rural Crime Task Force may develop rural crime prevention programs containing a system for reporting rural crimes that enables the swift recovery of stolen goods and the apprehension of criminal suspects for prosecution. The task force may develop computer software and use communication technology to implement the reporting system, although the task force is not limited to the use of these means to achieve the stated goals.
(2) The Central Coast Rural Crime Task Force may develop a uniform procedure for all participating counties to collect, and each participating county may collect, data on agricultural crimes. The task force may also establish a central database for the collection and maintenance of data on agricultural crimes and designate one participating county to maintain the database.
(c) The staff for each program shall consist of the personnel designated by the district attorney and sheriff for each county in accordance with the joint powers agreement.
(Amended by Stats. 2012, Ch. 43, Sec. 82. (SB 1023) Effective June 27, 2012.)
14182.
Sources of funding for the program may include, but shall not be limited to, appropriations from local government and private contributions.
(Added by Stats. 2003, Ch. 18, Sec. 1. Effective January 1, 2004.)

TITLE 12. VIOLENT CRIME INFORMATION CENTER [14200 - 14216]

(Title 12 added by Stats. 1988, Ch. 1456, Sec. 5.)
14200.
(a) The Attorney General shall establish and maintain the Violent Crime Information Center to assist in the identification and the apprehension of persons responsible for specific violent crimes and for the disappearance and exploitation of persons, particularly children and at-risk adults.
(b) The center shall establish and maintain programs which include, but are not limited to, all of the following:
(1) Developing violent offender profiles.
(2) Assisting local law enforcement agencies and county district attorneys by providing investigative information on persons responsible for specific violent crimes and missing person cases.
(3) Providing physical description information and photographs, if available, of missing persons to county district attorneys, nonprofit missing persons organizations, and schools.
(4) Providing statistics on missing at-risk adults and on missing children, including, as may be applicable, family abductions, nonfamily abductions, voluntary missing, and lost children or lost at-risk adults.
(c) The Attorney General shall provide training on the services provided by the center to line personnel, supervisors, and investigators in the following fields: law enforcement, district attorneys' offices, the Department of Corrections and Rehabilitation, probation departments, court mediation services, and the judiciary.
(Amended by Stats. 2014, Ch. 437, Sec. 9. (SB 1066) Effective January 1, 2015.)
14201.
The Attorney General shall establish and maintain, upon appropriation of funds by the Legislature, the Violent Crime Information Network within the center to enable the Department of Justice crime analysts with expertise in child abuse, missing persons, child abductions, and sexual assaults to electronically share their data, analysis, and findings on violent crime cases with each other, and to electronically provide law enforcement agencies with information to assist in the identification, tracking, and apprehension of violent offenders. The Violent Crime Information Network shall integrate existing state, federal, and civilian databases into a single comprehensive network.
(Added by renumbering Section 14201.1 by Stats. 2014, Ch. 437, Sec. 11. (SB 1066) Effective January 1, 2015.)
14201.2.
Notwithstanding any other law, a law enforcement agency may request a copy of information or data maintained by the Department of Justice pursuant to this title, for the purpose of linking an unsolved missing or unidentified person case with another case that was previously unknown to be related to that case, or for the purpose of resolving an unsolved missing or unidentified person case. This section does not supersede subdivision (b) of Section 14204 or subdivision (f) of Section 14205.
(Added by Stats. 2014, Ch. 432, Sec. 2.5. (SB 846) Effective January 1, 2015.)
14202.
The Attorney General shall establish and maintain, upon appropriation of funds by the Legislature, within the center the Violent Crime Information System to track and monitor violent offenders and their activities. The Violent Crime Information System shall use computer technology to compare unsolved crime scenes and methods of operation information against the file of known violent sexual assault, kidnapping, and homicide offenders. The system shall provide local law enforcement agencies with investigative leads to assist in the resolution of violent crimes.
(Added by renumbering Section 14202.1 by Stats. 2014, Ch. 437, Sec. 17. (SB 1066) Effective January 1, 2015.)
14203.
(a) The Attorney General shall establish and maintain within the center an investigative support unit and an automated violent crime method of operation system to facilitate the identification and apprehension of persons responsible for murder, kidnap, including parental abduction, false imprisonment, or sexual assault. This unit shall be responsible for identifying perpetrators of violent felonies collected from the center and analyzing and comparing data on missing persons in order to determine possible leads which could assist local law enforcement agencies. This unit shall only release information about active investigations by police and sheriffs' departments to local law enforcement agencies.
(b) The Attorney General shall make available to the investigative support unit files organized by category of offender or victim and shall seek information from other files as needed by the unit. This set of files may include, among others, the following:
(1) Missing or unidentified, deceased persons' dental files filed pursuant to this title, Section 27521 of the Government Code, or Section 102870 of the Health and Safety Code.
(2) Child abuse reports filed pursuant to Section 11169.
(3) Sex offender registration files maintained pursuant to Section 290.
(4) State summary criminal history information maintained pursuant to Section 11105.
(5) Information obtained pursuant to the parent locator service maintained pursuant to Section 11478.1 of the Welfare and Institutions Code.
(6) Information furnished to the Department of Justice pursuant to Section 11107.
(7) Other Attorney General's office files as requested by the investigative support unit.
(c) The investigative support unit shall make available, within two hours of a reported stranger abduction of a child, a list of persons required to register as sex offenders based upon the modus operandi, if available, or the specified geographical location from which the child was abducted.
(Added by renumbering Section 14202 by Stats. 2014, Ch. 437, Sec. 16. (SB 1066) Effective January 1, 2015.)
14204.
(a) The Attorney General shall establish within the center and shall maintain an online, automated computer system designed to effect an immediate law enforcement response to reports of missing persons. The Attorney General shall design the computer system, using any existing system, including the California Law Enforcement Telecommunications System, to include an active file of information concerning persons reported to it as missing and who have not been reported as found. The computer system shall also include a confidential historic database. The Attorney General shall develop a system of cataloging missing person reports according to a variety of characteristics in order to facilitate locating particular categories of reports as needed.
(b) The Attorney General's active files described in subdivision (a) shall be made available to law enforcement agencies. The Attorney General shall provide to these agencies the name and personal description data of the missing person including, but not limited to, the person's date of birth, color of eyes and hair, sex, height, weight, and race, the time and date he or she was reported missing, the reporting agency, and any other data pertinent to the purpose of locating missing persons. However, the Attorney General shall not release the information if the reporting agency requests the Attorney General in writing not to release the information because it would impair a criminal investigation.
(c) The Attorney General shall distribute a missing children and at-risk adults bulletin on a quarterly basis to local law enforcement agencies, district attorneys, and public schools. The Attorney General shall also make this information accessible to other parties involved in efforts to locate missing children and at-risk adults and to those other persons as the Attorney General deems appropriate.
(Added by renumbering Section 14201 by Stats. 2014, Ch. 437, Sec. 10. (SB 1066) Effective January 1, 2015.)
14205.
(a) The online missing persons registry shall accept and generate complete information on a missing person.
(b) The information on a missing person shall be retrievable by any of the following:
(1) The person's name.
(2) The person's date of birth.
(3) The person's social security number.
(4) Whether a dental chart has been received, coded, and entered into the National Crime Information Center Missing Person System by the Attorney General.
(5) The person's physical description, including hair and eye color and body marks.
(6) The person's known associates.
(7) The person's last known location.
(8) The name or assumed name of the abductor, if applicable, other pertinent information relating to the abductor or the assumed abductor, or both.
(9) Any other information, as deemed appropriate by the Attorney General.
(c) The Attorney General, in consultation with local law enforcement agencies and other user groups, shall develop the form in which information shall be entered into the system.
(d) The Attorney General shall establish and maintain within the center a separate, confidential historic database relating to missing children and at-risk adults. The historic database may be used only by the center for statistical and research purposes. The historic database shall be set up to categorize cases relating to missing children and at-risk adults by type. These types shall include the following:
(1) Runaways.
(2) Voluntary missing.
(3) Lost.
(4) Abduction involving movement of the victim in the commission of the crime or sexual exploitation.
(5) Nonfamily abduction.
(6) Family abduction.
(7) Any other categories as determined by the Attorney General.
(e) In addition, the data shall include the number of missing children and missing at-risk adults in this state and the category of each case.
(f) The center may supply information about specific cases from the historic database to a local police department, sheriff's department, or district attorney, only in connection with an investigation by the police department, sheriff's department, or district attorney of a missing person case or a violation or attempted violation of Section 220, 261.5, 262, 273a, 273d, or 273.5, or any sex offense listed in Section 290, except for the offense specified in subdivision (d) of Section 243.4.
(Added by renumbering Section 14203 by Stats. 2014, Ch. 437, Sec. 19. (SB 1066) Effective January 1, 2015.)
14206.
(a) The Attorney General shall establish within the Department of Justice the Missing and Exploited Children's Recovery Network by July 31, 1995.
(b) This network shall consist of an automated computerized system that shall have the capability to electronically transmit to all state and local law enforcement agencies, and all cooperating news media services, either by facsimile or computer modem, a missing child poster that includes the name, personal description data, and picture of the missing child. The information contained in this poster shall include, but not be limited to, the child's date of birth, color of eyes and hair, sex, height, weight, race, the time and date he or she was reported missing, the reporting agency, including contact person at reporting agency if known, and any other data pertinent to the purpose of locating missing persons.
(c) The Department of Justice shall work in cooperation with the National Center for Missing and Exploited Children to develop and implement a network that can electronically interface with the National Missing and Exploited Children's Network.
(d) The Attorney General shall implement this network within existing Department of Justice resources.
(Added by renumbering Section 14201.5 by Stats. 2014, Ch. 437, Sec. 13. (SB 1066) Effective January 1, 2015.)
14207.
(a) The Department of Justice shall establish and maintain a publicly accessible computer Internet directory of information relating to the following:
(1) Persons for whom an arrest warrant has been issued pursuant to an alleged violation of any offense defined as a violent felony in subdivision (c) of Section 667.5.
(2) At-risk missing persons.
(3) Unsolved homicides and unidentified persons.
(b) The Attorney General may determine the extent of information and the priority of cases to be included in the directory.
(c) The department shall keep confidential, and not enter into the directory, either of the following:
(1) Information regarding any case for which the Attorney General has determined that disclosure pursuant to this section would endanger the safety of a person involved in an investigation or the successful completion of the investigation or a related investigation.
(2) Information regarding an arrest warrant for which the issuing magistrate has determined that disclosure pursuant to this section would endanger the safety of a person involved in an investigation or the successful completion of the investigation or a related investigation.
(Added by renumbering Section 14201.6 by Stats. 2014, Ch. 437, Sec. 14. (SB 1066) Effective January 1, 2015.)
14208.

(a) There shall be within the Department of Justice a director responsible for coordinating California's response to missing persons. This position is hereby established for all of the following purposes:
(1) To assist law enforcement agencies, at their request, with the timely search and recovery of missing children.
(2) To maintain up-to-date knowledge and expertise of those protocols, best practices, and technologies that are most effective for recovering missing children in a timely manner.
(3) To maintain relationships with federal, state, and local law enforcement agencies and other entities responsible for the investigation of missing persons in the state.
(4) To maintain records and make the Commission on Peace Officer Standards and Training Guidelines for Handling Missing Persons Investigations document available to law enforcement agencies upon request.
(b) The director shall utilize existing resources and expertise within the Attorney General's office to the maximum extent possible to accomplish the purposes specified in subdivision (a).
(Added by renumbering Section 14201.8 by Stats. 2014, Ch. 437, Sec. 15. (SB 1066) Effective January 1, 2015.)

14209.

The center shall make accessible to the National Missing and Unidentified Persons System specific information authorized for dissemination and as determined appropriate by the center that is contained in law enforcement reports regarding missing or unidentified persons. The information shall be accessible in a manner and format approved by the center and shall be used to assist in the search for the missing person or persons. The center shall not permit the transmission or sharing of information, or portions of information, to the National Missing and Unidentified Persons System unless the reporting agency, as specified in Section 14211, or the reporting party, with respect to the information submitted to the center, submits authorization to the center to transmit or share that information.
(Added by renumbering Section 14201.3 by Stats. 2014, Ch. 437, Sec. 12. (SB 1066) Effective January 1, 2015.)

14210.

(a) The Department of Justice shall operate a statewide, toll-free telephone hotline 24 hours per day, seven days per week to receive information regarding missing children and at-risk adults and relay this information to the appropriate law enforcement authorities.
(b) The Department of Justice shall select up to six persons per month from the missing persons publicly accessible computer Internet directory maintained pursuant to Section 14207 and shall produce posters with photographs and information regarding these persons, including the hotline telephone number and reward information. The department shall make these posters available to parties as prescribed and as the department deems appropriate.
(c) The Department of Justice shall provide appropriate local reporting agencies with a list of persons still listed as missing who are under 21 years of age, and with an appropriate waiver form in order to assist the reporting agency in obtaining a photograph of each of the missing children.
(d) Local reporting agencies shall attempt to obtain the most recent photograph available for persons still listed as missing and forward those photographs to the Department of Justice.
(e) The department shall include these photographs, as they become available, in the quarterly bulletins pursuant to subdivision (c) of Section 14204.
(f) State and local elected officials, agencies, departments, boards, and commissions may enclose in their mailings information regarding missing children or at-risk adults obtainable from the Department of Justice or any organization that is recognized as a nonprofit, tax-exempt organization under state or federal law and that has an ongoing missing children program. Elected officials, agency secretaries, and directors of departments, boards, and commissions are urged to develop policies to enclose missing children or at-risk adults information in mailings if it will not increase postage costs and is otherwise deemed appropriate.
(Added by renumbering Section 14208 by Stats. 2014, Ch. 437, Sec. 24. (SB 1066) Effective January 1, 2015.)

14211.

(a) All local police and sheriffs' departments shall accept any report, by any party, including any telephonic report, of a missing person, including runaways, without delay and shall give priority to the handling of these reports over the handling of reports relating to crimes involving property.
(b) In cases where the person making a report of a missing person or runaway, contacts, including by telephone, the Department of the California Highway Patrol, the Department of the California Highway Patrol may take the report, and shall immediately advise the person making the report of the name and telephone number of the police or sheriff's department having jurisdiction of the residence address of the missing person and of the name and telephone number of the police or sheriff's department having jurisdiction of the place where the person was last seen.
(c) In cases of reports involving missing persons, including, but not limited to, runaways, the local police or sheriff's department shall immediately take the report and make an assessment of reasonable steps to be taken to locate the person by using the report forms, checklists, and guidelines required under Section 13519.07.
(d) If the missing person is under 21 years of age, or there is evidence that the person is at risk, the police department or sheriff's department shall broadcast a "Be On the Lookout" bulletin, without delay, within its jurisdiction.
(e) If the person reported missing is under 21 years of age, or if there is evidence that the person is at risk, the law enforcement agency receiving the report shall, within two hours after the receipt of the report, electronically transmit the report to the Department of Justice via the California Law Enforcement Telecommunications System for inclusion in the Violent Crime Information Center and the National Crime Information Center databases.
(f) Information not immediately available for electronic transmission to the department shall be obtained by the investigating agency and provided as a supplement to the original entry as soon as possible, but in no event later than 60 days after the original electronic entry. Supplemental information may include, but is not limited to, the following:
(1) Dental records and treatment notes.
(2) Fingerprints.
(3) Photographs.
(4) Description of physical characteristics.
(5) Description of clothing the person was wearing when last seen.
(6) Vehicle information.
(7) Other information describing any person or vehicle believed to be involved in taking, abducting, or retaining the missing person.
(g) In cases where the report is taken by a department, other than that of the city or county of residence of the missing person or runaway, the department, or division of the Department of the California Highway Patrol taking the report shall, without delay, and, in the case of persons under 21 years of age or where there was evidence that the missing person was at risk, within no more than 24 hours, notify, and forward a copy of the report to the police or sheriff's department or departments having jurisdiction of the residence address of the missing person or runaway and of the place where the person was last seen. The report shall also be submitted by the department or division of the Department of the California Highway Patrol which took the report to the center. The initial California Law Enforcement Telecommunications System record may only be removed after the receiving agency has accepted the report.
(h) The requirements imposed by this section on local police and sheriffs' departments shall not be operative if the governing body of that local agency, by a majority vote of the members of that body, adopts a resolution expressly making those requirements inoperative.
(Added by renumbering Section 14205 by Stats. 2014, Ch. 437, Sec. 21. (SB 1066) Effective January 1, 2015.)

14212.

(a) When any person makes a report of a missing person to a police department, sheriff's department, district attorney's office, Department of the California Highway Patrol, or other law enforcement agency, the agency shall use the Attorney General's form as required under Section 13519.07. That form shall include a statement authorizing the release of the dental or skeletal X-rays, or both, and treatment notes, of the person reported missing and authorizing the release of a recent photograph of a person reported missing who is under 18 years of age.
(b) Included with the form shall be instructions which state that if the person reported missing is still missing 30 days after the report is made, the release form signed by a member of the family or next of kin of the missing person shall be taken by the family member or next of kin to the dentist, physician and surgeon, or medical facility in order to obtain the release of the dental or skeletal X-rays, or both, and treatment notes, of that person or may be taken by a peace officer, if others fail to take action, to secure those X-rays and treatment notes.
(c) Notwithstanding any other provision of law, dental or skeletal X-rays, or both, and treatment notes, shall be released by the dentist, physician and surgeon, or medical facility to the person presenting the request and shall be submitted within 10 days by that person to the police or sheriff's department or other law enforcement agency having jurisdiction over the investigation.
(d) When the person reported missing has been determined by the agency to be an at-risk person, and has not been found within 30 days, the law enforcement agency may execute a written declaration, stating that an active investigation seeking the location of the missing person is being conducted, and that the dental or skeletal X-rays, or both, and treatment notes, are necessary for the exclusive purpose of furthering the investigation.
(e) Notwithstanding any other provision of law, the written declaration, signed by a peace officer, is sufficient authority for the dentist, physician and surgeon, or medical facility to immediately release the missing person's dental or skeletal X-rays, or both, or treatment notes.
(f) The Attorney General's office shall code and enter the dental or skeletal X-rays, or both, into the center's database, which shall serve as the statewide database for those X-rays, and shall forward the information to the National Crime Information Center.
(g) When a person reported missing has not been found within 30 days, the sheriff, chief of police, or other law enforcement agency conducting the investigation for the missing person may confer with the coroner or medical examiner prior to the preparation of a missing person report. The coroner or medical examiner shall cooperate with the law enforcement agency. After conferring with the coroner or medical examiner, the sheriff, chief of police, or other law enforcement agency initiating and conducting the investigation for the missing person may submit a missing person report and the dental or skeletal X-rays, or both, and photograph received pursuant to subdivision (a) to the Attorney General's office in a format acceptable to the Attorney General.
(h) Nothing in this section prohibits a parent or guardian of a child, reported to a law enforcement agency as missing, from voluntarily submitting fingerprints, and other documents, to the law enforcement agency accepting the report for inclusion in the report which is submitted to the Attorney General.
(i) The requirements imposed by this section on local police and sheriff's departments shall not be operative if the governing body of that local agency, by a majority vote of the members of that body, adopts a resolution expressly making those requirements inoperative.
(Added by renumbering Section 14206 by Stats. 2014, Ch. 437, Sec. 22. (SB 1066) Effective January 1, 2015.)

14213.

(a) When a person reported missing has been found, the sheriff, chief of police, coroner or medical examiner, or the law enforcement agency locating the missing person shall immediately report that information to the Attorney General's office. The Attorney General's office shall then notify the National Crime Information Center that the missing person has been found.
(b) When a missing person is found, the report indicating that the person is found shall be made not later than 24 hours after the person is found to the law enforcement agency that made the initial missing person report.
(c) In the event that a missing person is found alive or dead in less than 24 hours and the local police or sheriff's department has reason to believe that the person had been abducted, the department shall submit a report to the center in a format established by the Attorney General. In the event that a missing person has been found before he or she has been reported missing to the center, the information related to the incident shall be submitted to the center.
(d) A law enforcement agency shall not establish or maintain any policy that requires the removal of a missing person entry from the center database or the National Crime Information Center database based solely on the age of the missing person.
(Added by renumbering Section 14207 by Stats. 2014, Ch. 437, Sec. 23. (SB 1066) Effective January 1, 2015.)

14214.

(a) The Legislature finds and declares that it is the duty of all law enforcement agencies to immediately assist any person who is attempting to make a report of a missing person or runaway.
(b) The Department of the California Highway Patrol shall continue to implement the written policy, required to be developed and adopted pursuant to former Section 11114.3, for the coordination of each of its divisions with the police and sheriffs' departments located within each division in taking, transmitting, and investigating reports of missing persons, including runaways.
(Added by renumbering Section 14210 by Stats. 2014, Ch. 437, Sec. 26. (SB 1066) Effective January 1, 2015.)

14215.

(a) As used in this title, "missing person" includes, but is not limited to, any of the following:
(1) An at-risk adult.
(2) A child who has been taken, detained, concealed, enticed away, or retained by a parent in violation of Chapter 4 (commencing with Section 277) of Title 9 of Part 1.
(3) A child who is missing voluntarily or involuntarily, or under circumstances not conforming to his or her ordinary habits or behavior and who may be in need of assistance.
(b) As used in this title, "at-risk" means there is evidence of, or there are indications of, any of the following:
(1) The person missing is the victim of a crime or foul play.
(2) The person missing is in need of medical attention.
(3) The person missing has no pattern of running away or disappearing.
(4) The person missing may be the victim of parental abduction.
(5) The person missing is mentally impaired, including cognitively impaired or developmentally disabled.

(c) As used in this title, "child" is any person under 18 years of age.
(d) As used in this title, "center" means the Violent Crime Information Center.
(e) As used in this title, "dental or medical records or X-rays" include all those records or X-rays which are in the possession of a dentist, physician and surgeon, or medical facility.
(f) As used in this title, "unidentified person" means a person, living or deceased, whose identity the local investigative agency is unable to determine.
(Amended by Stats. 2016, Ch. 544, Sec. 1. (SB 1330) Effective January 1, 2017.)
14216.
(a) The Department of Justice, in conjunction with the Department of Corrections and Rehabilitation, shall update any supervised release file that is available to law enforcement on the California Law Enforcement Telecommunications System every 10 days to reflect the most recent inmates paroled from facilities under the jurisdiction of the Department of Corrections and Rehabilitation.
(b) Commencing on July 1, 2001, the Department of Justice, in consultation with the State Department of Mental Health, or its successor, the State Department of State Hospitals, shall also update any supervised release file that is available to law enforcement on the California Law Enforcement Telecommunications System every 10 days to reflect patients undergoing community mental health treatment and supervision through the Forensic Conditional Release Program administered by the State Department of Mental Health, or its successor, the State Department of State Hospitals, other than individuals committed as incompetent to stand trial pursuant to Chapter 6 (commencing with Section 1367) of Title 10 of Part 2.
(Added by renumbering Section 14202.2 by Stats. 2014, Ch. 437, Sec. 18. (SB 1066) Effective January 1, 2015.)

TITLE 12.2. California Firearm Violence Research Act [14230 - 14232]

(Title 12.2 added by Stats. 2016, Ch. 24, Sec. 30.)
14230.
The Legislature finds and declares the following:
(a) Firearm violence is a significant public health and public safety problem in California and nationwide. Nationally, rates of fatal firearm violence have remained essentially unchanged for more than a decade, as declines in homicide have been offset by increases in suicide.
(b) California has been the site of some of the nation's most infamous mass shootings, such as those at a McDonald's in San Ysidro, at Cleveland Elementary School in Stockton, near the University of California, Santa Barbara in Isla Vista, and most recently at the Inland Regional Center in San Bernardino. Yet public mass shootings account for less than 1 percent of firearm violence. In 2014, there were 2,939 firearm-related deaths in California, including 1,582 suicides, 1,230 homicides, 89 deaths by legal intervention, and 38 unintentional or undetermined deaths. In communities where firearm violence is a frequent occurrence, the very structure of daily life is affected.
(c) Nationwide, the annual societal cost of firearm violence was estimated at $229,000,000,000 in 2012. A significant share of this burden falls on California. In 2013, the Office of Statewide Health Planning and Development noted that government-sponsored insurance programs covered nearly two-thirds of the costs of hospitalizations for firearm assaults in California, and about one-half of the costs of hospitalizations for unintentional injuries or those resulting from deliberate self-harm.
(d) California has been a leader in responding to this continuing crisis. However, although rates of fatal firearm violence in California are well below average for the 50 states, they are not low enough.
(e) Too little is known about firearm violence and its prevention. This is in substantial part because too little research has been done. The need for more research and more sophisticated research has repeatedly been emphasized. Because there has been so little support for research, only a small number of trained investigators are available.
(f) When confronted by other major health and social problems, California and the nation have mounted effective responses, coupling an expanded research effort with policy reform in the public's interest. Motor vehicle accidents, cancer, heart disease, and tobacco use are all examples of the benefits of this approach.
(g) Federal funding for firearm violence research through the federal Centers for Disease Control and Prevention has been virtually eliminated by Congress since 1996, leaving a major gap that must be filled by other sources.
(Added by Stats. 2016, Ch. 24, Sec. 30. (AB 1602) Effective June 27, 2016.)
14231.
(a) It is the intent of the Legislature to establish a center for research into firearm-related violence. It is the intent of the Legislature that the center be administered by the University of California pursuant to the following principles:
(1) Interdisciplinary work of the center shall address the following:
(A) The nature of firearm violence, including individual and societal determinants of risk for involvement in firearm violence, whether as a victim or a perpetrator.
(B) The individual, community, and societal consequences of firearm violence.
(C) Prevention and treatment of firearm violence at the individual, community, and societal levels.
(2) The center shall conduct basic, translational, and transformative research with a mission to provide the scientific evidence on which sound firearm violence prevention policies and programs can be based. Its research shall include, but not be limited to, the effectiveness of existing laws and policies intended to reduce firearm violence, including the criminal misuse of firearms, and efforts to promote the responsible ownership and use of firearms.
(3) The center shall work on a continuing basis with policymakers in the Legislature and state agencies to identify, implement, and evaluate innovative firearm violence prevention policies and programs.
(4) To help ensure a long-term and successful effort to understand and prevent firearm violence, the center shall recruit and provide specialized training opportunities for new researchers, including experienced investigators in related fields who are beginning work on firearm violence, young investigators who have completed their education, postdoctoral scholars, doctoral students, and undergraduates.
(5) As a supplement to its own research, the center may administer a small grant program for research on firearm violence. All research funds shall be awarded on the basis of scientific merit as determined by an open, competitive peer review process that assures objectivity, consistency, and high quality. All qualified investigators, regardless of institutional affiliation, shall have equal access and opportunity to compete for the funds.
(6) The peer review process for the selection of grants awarded under this program shall be modeled on the process used by the National Institutes of Health in its grantmaking process.
(b) It is further the intent of the Legislature that on or before December 31, 2017, and every five years thereafter, the University of California transmit programmatic, as well as financial, reports to the state, including a report on the grants made, pending grants, program accomplishments, and the future direction of the program. The report shall be submitted in compliance with Section 9795 of the Government Code.
(c) Subject to the conditions and requirements established elsewhere in statute, state agencies, including, but not limited to, the Department of Justice, the State Department of Public Health, the State Department of Health Care Services, the Office of Statewide Health Planning and Development, and the Department of Motor Vehicles, shall provide

to the center, upon proper request, the data necessary for the center to conduct its research.
(d) The center and all recipients of grants shall provide copies of their research publications to the Legislature and to agencies supplying data used in the conduct of that research as soon as is practicable following publication. These submissions shall be submitted in compliance with Section 9795 of the Government Code.
(e) Toward these ends, the Legislature requests that the Regents of the University of California establish a Firearm Violence Research Center and administer the center and grant program pursuant to, and consistent with, the principles and goals stated herein.
(Added by Stats. 2016, Ch. 24, Sec. 30. (AB 1602) Effective June 27, 2016.)
14231.5.
Notwithstanding any other law, the Department of Justice shall make information relating to gun violence restraining orders that is maintained in the California Restraining and Protective Order System, or any similar database maintained by the department, available to researchers affiliated with the University of California Firearm Violence Research Center, or, at the department's discretion, to any other nonprofit educational institution or public agency immediately concerned with the study and prevention of violence, for academic and policy research purposes, provided that any material identifying individuals is not transferred, revealed, or used for other than research or statistical activities and reports or publications derived therefrom shall not identify specific individuals.
(Added by Stats. 2017, Ch. 810, Sec. 1. (SB 536) Effective January 1, 2018.)
14232.
This article shall apply to the University of California only to the extent that the Regents of the University of California, by resolution, make any of these provisions applicable to the university.
(Added by Stats. 2016, Ch. 24, Sec. 30. (AB 1602) Effective June 27, 2016.)

TITLE 12.5. DNA [14250 - 14251]

(Title 12.5 added by Stats. 2000, Ch. 822, Sec. 2.)
14250.
(a) (1) The Department of Justice shall develop a DNA database for all cases involving the report of an unidentified deceased person or a high-risk missing person.
(2) The database required in paragraph (1) shall be comprised of DNA data from genetic markers that are appropriate for human identification, but have no capability to predict biological function other than gender. These markers shall be selected by the department and may change as the technology for DNA typing progresses. The results of DNA typing shall be compatible with and uploaded into the CODIS DNA database established by the Federal Bureau of Investigation. The sole purpose of this database shall be to identify missing persons and shall be kept separate from the database established under Chapter 6 (commencing with Section 295) of Title 9 of Part 1.
(3) The Department of Justice shall compare DNA samples taken from the remains of unidentified deceased persons with DNA samples taken from personal articles belonging to the missing person, or from the parents or appropriate relatives of high-risk missing persons.
(4) For the purpose of this database, "high-risk missing person" means a person missing as a result of a stranger abduction, a person missing under suspicious circumstances, a person missing under unknown circumstances, or where there is reason to assume that the person is in danger, or deceased, and that person has been missing more than 30 days, or less than 30 days in the discretion of the investigating agency.
(b) The department shall develop standards and guidelines for the preservation and storage of DNA samples. Any agency that is required to collect samples from unidentified remains for DNA testing shall follow these standards and guidelines. These guidelines shall address all scientific methods used for the identification of remains, including DNA, anthropology, odontology, and fingerprints.
(c) (1) A coroner shall collect samples for DNA testing from the remains of all unidentified persons and shall send those samples to the Department of Justice for DNA testing and inclusion in the DNA databank. After the department has taken a sample from the remains for DNA analysis and completed all DNA testing, the remaining evidence shall be returned to the appropriate local coroner.
(2) After a report has been made of a person missing under high-risk circumstances, the responsible investigating law enforcement agency shall inform the parents or other appropriate relatives that they may give a voluntary sample for DNA testing or may collect a DNA sample from a personal article belonging to the missing person if available. The samples shall be taken by the appropriate law enforcement agency in a manner prescribed by the Department of Justice. The responsible investigating law enforcement agency shall wait no longer than 30 days after a report has been made to inform the parents or other relatives of their right to give a sample.
(3) The Department of Justice shall develop a standard release form that authorizes a mother, father, or other relative to voluntarily provide the sample. The release shall explain that DNA is to be used only for the purpose of identifying the missing person and that the DNA sample and profile will be destroyed upon request. No incentive or coercion shall be used to compel a parent or relative to provide a sample.
(4) The Department of Justice shall develop a model kit that law enforcement shall use when taking samples from parents and relatives.
(5) Before submitting the sample to the department for analysis, law enforcement shall reverify the status of the missing person. After 30 days has elapsed from the date the report was filed, law enforcement shall send the sample to the department for DNA testing and inclusion in the DNA database, with a copy of the crime report, and any supplemental information.
(6) All retained samples and DNA extracted from a living person, and profiles developed therefrom, shall be used solely for the purpose of identification of the deceased's remains. All samples and DNA extracted from a living person, and profiles developed therefrom, shall be destroyed after a positive identification with the deceased's remains is made and a report is issued, unless any of the following has occurred:
(A) The coroner has made a report to a law enforcement agency pursuant to Section 27491.1 of the Government Code, that he or she has a reasonable ground to suspect that the identified person's death has been occasioned by another by criminal means.
(B) A law enforcement agency makes a determination that the identified person's death has been occasioned by another by criminal means.
(C) The evidence is needed in an active criminal investigation to determine whether the identified person's death has been occasioned by another by criminal means.
(D) A governmental entity is required to retain the material pursuant to Section 1417.9.
(7) Notwithstanding any other provisions of this section, upon the request of any living person who submits his or her DNA sample and profile pursuant to this section, including the parent or guardian of a child who submits a DNA sample of the child, the DNA sample shall be removed from the DNA database.
(d) All DNA samples and profiles developed therefrom shall be confidential and shall only be disclosed to personnel of the Department of Justice, law enforcement officers, coroners, medical examiners, district attorneys, and persons who need access to a DNA sample for purposes of the prosecution or defense of a criminal case, except that a law enforcement officer or agency may publicly disclose the fact of a DNA profile match after taking reasonable measures to first notify the family of an unidentified deceased person or the family of a high-risk missing person that there has been an identification.

(e) All DNA, forensic identification profiles, and other identification information retained by the Department of Justice pursuant to this section are exempt from any law requiring disclosure of information to the public.

(f) (1) Any person who knowingly discloses DNA or other forensic identification information developed pursuant to this section to an unauthorized individual or agency, or for any purpose other than for identification or for use in a criminal investigation, prosecution, or defense, is guilty of a misdemeanor.

(2) A person who collects, processes, or stores DNA or DNA samples from a living person that are used for DNA testing pursuant to this section who does either of the following is liable in civil damages to the donor of the DNA in the amount of five thousand dollars ($5,000) for each violation, plus attorney's fees and costs:

(A) Fails to destroy samples or DNA extracted from a living person pursuant to paragraph (6) of subdivision (c).

(B) Discloses DNA samples in violation of subdivision (d).

(g) (1) If a disclosure or failure to destroy samples described in paragraph (2) of subdivision (f) is made by an employee of the Department of Justice, the department shall be liable for those actions of its employee.

(2) Notwithstanding any other law, the remedy in this section shall be the sole and exclusive remedy against the department and its employees available to the donor of the DNA against the department and its employees.

(3) The department employee disclosing DNA or other forensic identification information or otherwise violating this section shall be absolutely immune from civil liability under this or any other law.

(h) It is not an unauthorized disclosure or violation of this section to release DNA and other forensic identification information as part of a judicial or administrative proceeding, to a jury or grand jury, or in a document filed with a court or administrative agency, or for this information to become part of the public transcript or record of proceedings.

(i) In order to maintain computer system security, the computer software and database structures used by the DNA laboratory of the Department of Justice to implement this chapter are confidential.

(Amended by Stats. 2009, Ch. 228, Sec. 1. (AB 275) Effective October 11, 2009.)

14251.

(a) The "Missing Persons DNA Database" shall be funded by a two dollar ($2) fee increase on death certificates issued by a local governmental agency or by the State of California. The issuing agencies may retain up to 5 percent of the funds from the fee increase for administrative costs.

(b) Funds shall be directed on a quarterly basis to the "Missing Persons DNA Data Base Fund," hereby established, to be administered by the department for establishing and maintaining laboratory infrastructure, DNA sample storage, DNA analysis, and labor costs for cases of missing persons and unidentified remains. Funds may also be distributed by the department to various counties for the purposes of pathology and exhumation consistent with this title. The department may also use those funds to publicize the database for the purpose of contacting parents and relatives so that they may provide a DNA sample for training law enforcement officials about the database and DNA sampling and for outreach.

(c) The identification of any backlog of human remain samples or samples donated by a family member or from a personal article belonging to the missing person may be outsourced to other laboratories at the department's discretion.

(d) (1) The Department of Justice shall retain the authority to prioritize case analysis, giving priority to those cases involving children and those involving homicide victims.

(2) If federal funding is made available, it shall be used to assist in the identification of the backlog of high-risk missing person cases and long-term unidentified remains.

(Amended by Stats. 2009, Ch. 228, Sec. 2. (AB 275) Effective October 11, 2009.)

TITLE 13. LOCAL ENVIRONMENTAL ENFORCEMENT AND TRAINING PROGRAMS [14300 - 14315]

(Heading of Title 13 amended by Stats. 2002, Ch. 1000, Sec. 2.)

CHAPTER 1. General Provisions [14300 - 14303]

(Chapter 1 added by Stats. 1992, Ch. 743, Sec. 3.)

14300.

(a) The Legislature finds and declares all of the following:

(1) The enforcement of California's environmental laws is essential to protect human health, the environment, and the state's economy.

(2) Fair and uniform enforcement of laws and regulations governing the environment benefits law abiding businesses, firms, and individuals.

(3) There is a need to better integrate enforcement of environmental laws into California's established criminal justice system.

(4) Local and state enforcement agencies can play an increasingly important role in protecting human health, the environment, and the state's economy through greater involvement in the enforcement of environmental laws.

(5) Prosecuting violators of environmental laws often requires special training to detect violations, understand complex laws, and prepare and present complicated enforcement cases.

(6) There is a need to support programs that assist local and state enforcement officials in prosecuting violations of environmental laws through the training of peace officers, investigators, firefighters, public prosecutors, and state and local environmental regulators.

(7) Fair and uniform enforcement of environmental laws is multidisciplinary and involves law enforcement, fire departments, state and local environmental regulators, and the offices of local and state public prosecutors.

(b) For purposes of this title, the following definitions shall apply:

(1) "Account" means the Environmental Enforcement and Training Account created pursuant to Section 14303.

(2) "Commission" means the Commission on Peace Officer Standards and Training.

(3) "Agency" means the California Environmental Protection Agency.

(4) "Secretary" means the Agency Secretary for the California Environmental Protection Agency or his or her designee.

(5) "Environmental laws" means state and federal environmental laws and regulations that impact public health and the environment, including, but not limited to, those that regulate toxic and carcinogenic materials, water quality, air quality, waste management, pesticides, and wildlife resources.

(6) "Public prosecutor" means district attorneys, city attorneys, city prosecutors, county counsels, and the Attorney General and his or her deputies.

(7) "Environmental regulator" means an employee of any state or local agency whose jurisdiction includes implementation, enforcement, or both implementation and enforcement of environmental laws.

(8) "Environmental enforcement" means the enforcement of environmental laws.

(c) This title shall be known and may be cited as the Environmental Enforcement and Training Act of 2002.

(d) It is the intent of the Legislature that the funds to implement this title, as specified in Section 14314, come from public and private contributions, and from the proceeds from any contributed state or federal court judgments, and that no funds be expended from the General Fund, other than from the Environmental Enforcement and Training Account, or other funds appropriated to, or authorized for expenditure by, the agency, to implement this title. It is the intent of the Legislature that the funds to implement this title shall be expended only from the account. It is the intent of the Legislature that funding provided from the account shall supplement, not supplant existing funding.

(Amended by Stats. 2002, Ch. 1000, Sec. 3. Effective January 1, 2003.)

14301.

(a) There is hereby established in the agency, a program of financial assistance to do all of the following:

(1) Provide for statewide education and training programs in the enforcement of environmental laws for peace officers, investigators, state and local environmental regulators, and public prosecutors.

(2) Establish enhanced local environmental enforcement efforts.

(3) All funds made available to the agency for the purposes of this title shall be administered and distributed by the secretary.

(b) Not later than 12 months after the date when this title may be implemented, as specified in Section 14314, the secretary shall prepare and issue regulations, which shall, at a minimum, describe how grants are to be allocated or awarded pursuant to this title, the procedures for applying for these grants, the criteria to be used in determining which applications will be funded, and the administrative and fiscal requirements governing the receipt and expenditure of these grants.

(c) The secretary shall allocate and award funds to public agencies or private nonprofit organizations for purposes of supporting statewide environmental enforcement education and training programs for peace officers, investigators, state and local environmental regulators, and public prosecutors pursuant to Chapter 2 (commencing with Section 14304) and Chapter 3 (commencing with Section 14306), which meet the criteria established pursuant to those chapters. To ensure that these programs are coordinated with existing peace officer training, the commission shall be consulted prior to the allocation of funds to peace officer education and training programs.

(d) The secretary shall allocate and award funds to support the Environmental Circuit Prosecutor Project pursuant to Chapter 4 (commencing with Section 14309) for the purpose of improving enforcement of environmental laws by enhancing the investigation and prosecution of violations of those laws.

(Amended by Stats. 2002, Ch. 1000, Sec. 4. Effective January 1, 2003.)

14303.

(a) There is hereby created, in the General Fund, the Environmental Enforcement and Training Account and up to two million dollars ($2,000,000) in the account may be expended annually by the agency, upon appropriation by the Legislature, for the purposes of this title.

(b) The agency may accept and receive any contribution of funds from a public or private organization or an individual, including the proceeds from a judgment in state or federal court, when the funds are contributed or the judgment specifies that the proceeds are to be used to carry out the purposes of this title. Private contributors shall not have the authority to further influence or direct the use of their contributions.

(c) The agency shall immediately deposit any funds contributed pursuant to subdivision (b) in the account.

(d) As of January 1, 2003, all unallocated funds in the Hazardous Materials Enforcement and Training Account created pursuant to Chapter 743 of the Statutes of 1992 that derive from court judgments specifying that the funds may be used only for purposes of this title shall be transferred to the Environmental Enforcement and Training Account.

(e) (1) Any funds that are appropriated by the Legislature pursuant to subdivision (a), allocated pursuant to Section 14314, and declined by the commission, shall be reallocated by the secretary as described in Section 14314.

(2) This subdivision applies to funds that are appropriated for the 2011–12 fiscal year and each fiscal year thereafter.

(Amended by Stats. 2011, Ch. 304, Sec. 12. (SB 428) Effective January 1, 2012.)

CHAPTER 2.
Peace Officer Environmental Enforcement Training [14304- 14304.]

(Heading of Chapter 2 amended by Stats. 2002, Ch. 1000, Sec. 6.)

14304.

(a) The commission shall develop or review and certify, not later than 12 months after the date when this title may be implemented, as specified in Section 14314, a course or courses of instruction for training local and state peace officers in the detection of violations, and in the apprehension of suspected violators, of state and local environmental laws.

(b) The course or courses of instruction shall, at a minimum, include training on all of the following:

(1) Understanding environmental laws.

(2) Detecting violations of environmental laws.

(3) Knowing steps to take when violations are discovered in order to protect public health and facilitate prosecution of violators.

(Amended by Stats. 2002, Ch. 1000, Sec. 7. Effective January 1, 2003.)

CHAPTER 3.
Environmental Training And Enforcement [14306 - 14308]

(Heading of Chapter 3 amended by Stats. 2002, Ch. 1000, Sec. 8.)

14306.

(a) The secretary shall provide funding to the California District Attorneys' Association to develop and implement, not later than 12 months after the receipt of funds, a course or courses of instruction for the training of public prosecutors in the enforcement of state and local environmental laws.

(b) The course or courses of instruction shall, at a minimum, do all of the following:

(1) Provide an understanding of the requirements of environmental laws.

(2) Teach prosecution techniques that will facilitate prosecution of environmental law violations.

(3) Provide environmental enforcement training materials.

(Amended by Stats. 2002, Ch. 1000, Sec. 9. Effective January 1, 2003.)

14307.

(a) The secretary shall provide funding to the California District Attorneys' Association to develop and implement, not later than 12 months after the receipt of funds, a course or courses of instruction for the training of investigators from the offices of public prosecutors, fire departments, and state and local environmental regulators.

(b) With the concurrence of the commission, peace officers may participate in the course or courses of training.
(c) The course or courses of instruction shall, at a minimum, do all of the following:
(1) Provide an understanding of the requirements of environmental laws.
(2) Teach enforcement investigative techniques that will facilitate the prosecution of environmental law violations.
(3) Provide environmental enforcement training materials.
(Amended by Stats. 2002, Ch. 1000, Sec. 10. Effective January 1, 2003.)
14308.
(a) The secretary may award grants to public and private entities for training public prosecutors, peace officers, firefighters, and state or local environmental regulators in the investigation and enforcement of environmental laws.
(b) The secretary may award local assistance grants to local environmental regulators for the enforcement of environmental laws.
(Added by Stats. 2002, Ch. 1000, Sec. 11. Effective January 1, 2003.)

CHAPTER 4. Environmental Circuit Prosecutor Project [14309- 14309.]

(Chapter 4 repealed and added by Stats. 2002, Ch. 1000, Sec. 13.)
14309.
(a) The Environmental Circuit Prosecutor Project, a cooperative project of the California Environmental Protection Agency and the California District Attorneys Association, is hereby established.
(b) The Environmental Circuit Prosecutor Project shall have the following purposes:
(1) Discourage the commission of violations of environmental laws by demonstrating the effective response of the criminal justice system to these violations, including, but not limited to, assisting district attorneys, particularly in rural counties, in the prosecution of criminal violations of environmental laws and regulations, where a district attorney has requested assistance.
(2) Establish model environmental crime prevention, enforcement, and prosecution techniques with statewide application for fair, uniform, and effective application.
(3) Increase the awareness and effectiveness of efforts to enforce environmental laws and to better integrate environmental prosecution into California's established criminal justice system by providing on the job education and training to local peace officers and prosecutors and to local and state environmental regulators.
(4) Promote, through uniform and effective prosecution and local assistance, the effective enforcement of environmental laws and regulations.
(c) (1) The secretary shall award project grants and administer funding from the account to the California District Attorneys Association for the purpose of providing for the day-to-day operations of the project.
(2) The award may only be used to fund the costs of prosecutors, investigators, and research attorney staff, including salary, benefits, and expenses.
(3) Circuit prosecutor project employees may be either employees of the California District Attorneys Association or employees on loan from local, state, or federal governmental agencies.
(d) (1) A district attorney may request the assistance of a circuit prosecutor from the Environmental Circuit Prosecutor Project for any of the following purposes:
(A) Assistance with the investigation and development of environmental cases.
(B)Consultation concerning whether an environmental case merits filing.
(C) Litigation support, including, but not limited to, the actual prosecution of the case. A district attorney shall, as appropriate, deputize a circuit prosecutor to prosecute cases within his or her jurisdiction.
(2) The authority of a deputized circuit prosecutor shall be consistent with and shall not exceed the authority of the elected district attorney or his or her deputies.
(3) Violations of city or county ordinances may be prosecuted by circuit prosecutors when there is an environmental nexus between the ordinance and a violation of state law, federal law, or both state and federal law.
(4) Participating district attorney offices shall provide matching funds or in-kind contributions equivalent to, but not less than, 20 percent of the expense of the deputized environmental circuit prosecutor.
(Amended by Stats. 2003, Ch. 468, Sec. 25. Effective January 1, 2004.)

CHAPTER 5. Implementation and Funding Priorities [14314 - 14315]

(Heading of Chapter 5 renumbered from Chapter 6 by Stats. 2002, Ch. 1000, Sec. 15.)
14314.
Notwithstanding any other provision of this title, the agency shall not implement this title until there is an amount of one hundred thousand dollars ($100,000) in the account. Funds in the account shall be divided as follows:
(a) Twenty-five percent or one hundred thousand dollars ($100,000) to the commission, whichever is less. The commission may decline all or part of the funds allocated to it pursuant to this subdivision. Any funds so declined shall be reallocated by the secretary to any of the entities listed in subdivisions (b), (c), and (d) for the training of peace officers consistent with this title.
(b) Twenty-five percent to the secretary for allocation to the Environmental Circuit Prosecutor Project pursuant to Chapter 4 (commencing with Section 14309).
(c) Twenty-five percent to the secretary for allocation to the California District Attorneys Association for training and assistance pursuant to Chapter 3 (commencing with Section 14306).
(d) (1) The balance to the secretary for grants awarded to programs pursuant to Chapter 3 (commencing with Section 14306) or Chapter 4 (commencing with Section 14309) based on need or in order to sustain the current level of presence and enforcement for those programs.
(2) Notwithstanding paragraph (1), the commission may also seek additional funding from the money allocated in this subdivision based on need if the environmental law enforcement training is mandated or if there are substantial changes in the law that require the commission to revise its environmental law courses.
(e) The secretary shall develop an application process for awarding funds to programs pursuant to subdivisions (b), (c), and (d).
(Amended by Stats. 2011, Ch. 304, Sec. 13. (SB 428) Effective January 1, 2012.)
14315.
Not later than 36 months after the date when this title may be implemented, as specified in Section 14314, the secretary shall post on the agency's Web site, updated no later than July 1, annually, a description of the operation and accomplishments of the training programs and the environmental enforcement and prosecution projects funded by this title. The commission shall prepare the section of the report pertaining to the course of instruction authorized in Section 14304 and submit it to the secretary for inclusion in the report.
(Amended by Stats. 2004, Ch. 644, Sec. 27. Effective January 1, 2005.)

PART 5. PEACE OFFICERS' MEMORIAL [15001 - 15003]

(Part 5 added by Stats. 1985, Ch. 1518, Sec. 1.)
15001.
(a) The construction of a memorial to California peace officers on the grounds of the State Capitol is hereby authorized. For purposes of this part, the grounds of the State Capitol are that property in the City of Sacramento bounded by Ninth, Fifteenth, "L," and "N" Streets. The actual site for the memorial shall be selected by the commission after consultation with the Department of General Services and the State Office of Historic Preservation.
(b) Funds for the construction of the memorial shall be provided through private contributions for this purpose.
(Added by Stats. 1985, Ch. 1518, Sec. 1.)
15003.
Peace officer memorial ceremonies, including the dedication of the memorial and any subsequent ceremonies, shall be conducted by the California Peace Officers' Memorial Foundation, Inc.
(Amended by Stats. 2016, Ch. 86, Sec. 242. (SB 1171) Effective January 1, 2017.)

PART 6. CONTROL OF DEADLY WEAPONS [16000 - 34370]

(Part 6 added by Stats. 2010, Ch. 711, Sec. 6.)

TITLE 1. PRELIMINARY PROVISIONS [16000 - 17360]

(Title 1 added by Stats. 2010, Ch. 711, Sec. 6.)

DIVISION 1. GENERAL PROVISIONS [16000 - 16025]

(Division 1 added by Stats. 2010, Ch. 711, Sec. 6.)
16000.
This act recodifies the provisions of former Title 2 (commencing with Section 12000) of Part 4, which was entitled "Control of Deadly Weapons." The act shall be known and may be cited as the "Deadly Weapons Recodification Act of 2010."
(Added by Stats. 2010, Ch. 711, Sec. 6. (SB 1080) Effective January 1, 2011. Operative January 1, 2012, by Sec. 10 of Ch. 711.)
16005.
Nothing in the Deadly Weapons Recodification Act of 2010 is intended to substantively change the law relating to deadly weapons. The act is intended to be entirely nonsubstantive in effect. Every provision of this part, of Title 2 (commencing with Section 12001) of Part 4, and every other provision of this act, including, without limitation, every cross-reference in every provision of the act, shall be interpreted consistent with the nonsubstantive intent of the act.
(Added by Stats. 2010, Ch. 711, Sec. 6. (SB 1080) Effective January 1, 2011. Operative January 1, 2012, by Sec. 10 of Ch. 711.)
16010.
(a) A provision of this part or of Title 2 (commencing with Section 12001) of Part 4, or any other provision of the Deadly Weapons Recodification Act of 2010, insofar as it is substantially the same as a previously existing provision relating to the same subject matter, shall be considered as a restatement and continuation thereof and not as a new enactment.
(b) A reference in a statute to a previously existing provision that is restated and continued in this part or in Title 2 (commencing with Section 12001) of Part 4, or in any other provision of the Deadly Weapons Recodification Act of 2010, shall, unless a contrary intent appears, be deemed a reference to the restatement and continuation.
(c) A reference in a statute to a provision of this part or of Title 2 (commencing with Section 12001) of Part 4, or any other provision of the Deadly Weapons Recodification Act of 2010, which is substantially the same as a previously existing provision, shall, unless a contrary intent appears, be deemed to include a reference to the previously existing provision.
(Added by Stats. 2010, Ch. 711, Sec. 6. (SB 1080) Effective January 1, 2011. Operative January 1, 2012, by Sec. 10 of Ch. 711.)
16015.
If a previously existing provision is restated and continued in this part, or in Title 2 (commencing with Section 12001) of Part 4, or in any other provision of the Deadly Weapons Recodification Act of 2010, a conviction under that previously existing provision shall, unless a contrary intent appears, be treated as a prior conviction under the restatement and continuation of that provision.
(Added by Stats. 2010, Ch. 711, Sec. 6. (SB 1080) Effective January 1, 2011. Operative January 1, 2012, by Sec. 10 of Ch. 711.)
16020.
(a) A judicial decision interpreting a previously existing provision is relevant in interpreting any provision of this part, of Title 2 (commencing with Section 12001) of Part 4, or any other provision of the Deadly Weapons Recodification Act of 2010, which restates and continues that previously existing provision.
(b) However, in enacting the Deadly Weapons Recodification Act of 2010, the Legislature has not evaluated the correctness of any judicial decision interpreting a provision affected by the act.
(c) The Deadly Weapons Recodification Act of 2010 is not intended to, and does not, reflect any assessment of any judicial decision interpreting any provision affected by the act.
(Added by Stats. 2010, Ch. 711, Sec. 6. (SB 1080) Effective January 1, 2011. Operative January 1, 2012, by Sec. 10 of Ch. 711.)
16025.
(a) A judicial decision determining the constitutionality of a previously existing provision is relevant in determining the constitutionality of any provision of this part, of Title 2 (commencing with Section 12001) of Part 4, or any other provision of the Deadly Weapons Recodification Act of 2010, which restates and continues that previously existing provision.
(b) However, in enacting the Deadly Weapons Recodification Act of 2010, the Legislature has not evaluated the constitutionality of any provision affected by the act, or the correctness of any judicial decision determining the constitutionality of any provision affected by the act.
(c) The Deadly Weapons Recodification Act of 2010 is not intended to, and does not, reflect any determination of the constitutionality of any provision affected by the act.
(Added by Stats. 2010, Ch. 711, Sec. 6. (SB 1080) Effective January 1, 2011. Operative January 1, 2012, by Sec. 10 of Ch. 711.)

DIVISION 2. DEFINITIONS [16100 - 17360]

(Division 2 added by Stats. 2010, Ch. 711, Sec. 6.)

16100.
Use of the term ".50 BMG cartridge" is governed by Section 30525.
(Added by Stats. 2010, Ch. 711, Sec. 6. (SB 1080) Effective January 1, 2011. Operative January 1, 2012, by Sec. 10 of Ch. 711.)

16110.
Use of the term ".50 BMG rifle" is governed by Section 30530.
(Added by Stats. 2010, Ch. 711, Sec. 6. (SB 1080) Effective January 1, 2011. Operative January 1, 2012, by Sec. 10 of Ch. 711.)

16120.
As used in this part, "abuse" means any of the following:
(a) Intentionally or recklessly to cause or attempt to cause bodily injury.
(b) Sexual assault.
(c) To place a person in reasonable apprehension of imminent serious bodily injury to that person or to another.
(d) To molest, attack, strike, stalk, destroy personal property, or violate the terms of a domestic violence protective order issued pursuant to Part 4 (commencing with Section 6300) of Division 10 of the Family Code.
(Added by Stats. 2010, Ch. 711, Sec. 6. (SB 1080) Effective January 1, 2011. Operative January 1, 2012, by Sec. 10 of Ch. 711.)

16130.
As used in Section 26915, "agent" means an employee of the licensee.
(Added by Stats. 2010, Ch. 711, Sec. 6. (SB 1080) Effective January 1, 2011. Operative January 1, 2012, by Sec. 10 of Ch. 711.)

16140.
As used in this part, "air gauge knife" means a device that appears to be an air gauge but has concealed within it a pointed, metallic shaft that is designed to be a stabbing instrument which is exposed by mechanical action or gravity which locks into place when extended.
(Added by Stats. 2010, Ch. 711, Sec. 6. (SB 1080) Effective January 1, 2011. Operative January 1, 2012, by Sec. 10 of Ch. 711.)

16150.
(a) As used in this part, except in subdivision (a) of Section 30305 and in Section 30306, "ammunition" means one or more loaded cartridges consisting of a primed case, propellant, and with one or more projectiles. "Ammunition" does not include blanks.
(b) As used in subdivision (a) of Section 30305 and in Section 30306, "ammunition" includes, but is not limited to, any bullet, cartridge, magazine, clip, speed loader, autoloader, or projectile capable of being fired from a firearm with a deadly consequence. "Ammunition" does not include blanks.
(c) This section shall remain in effect only until July 1, 2020, and as of that date is repealed.
(Amended by Stats. 2018, Ch. 780, Sec. 2. (SB 746) Effective January 1, 2019. Repealed as of July 1, 2020, by its own provisions. See later operative version added by Stats. 2018, Ch. 780. Note: This section was amended November 8, 2016, by initiative Proposition 63.)

16150.
(a) As used in this part, except in subdivision (a) of Section 30305 and in Section 30306, "ammunition" means one or more loaded cartridges consisting of a primed case, propellant, and with one or more projectiles. "Ammunition" does not include blanks.
(b) As used in subdivision (a) of Section 30305 and in Section 30306, "ammunition" includes, but is not limited to, any bullet, cartridge, magazine, clip, speed loader, autoloader, ammunition feeding device, or projectile capable of being fired from a firearm with a deadly consequence. "Ammunition" does not include blanks.
(c) This section shall become operative on July 1, 2020.
(Repealed and added by Stats. 2018, Ch. 780, Sec. 3. (SB 746) Effective January 1, 2019. Section operative July 1, 2020, by its own provisions.)

16151.
(a) As used in this part, commencing January 1, 2018, "ammunition vendor" means any person, firm, corporation, or other business enterprise that holds a current ammunition vendor license issued pursuant to Section 30385.
(b) Commencing January 1, 2018, a firearms dealer licensed pursuant to Sections 26700 to 26915, inclusive, shall automatically be deemed a licensed ammunition vendor, provided the dealer complies with the requirements of Articles 2 (commencing with Section 30300) and 3 (commencing with Section 30342) of Chapter 1 of Division 10 of Title 4.
(Added November 8, 2016, by initiative Proposition 63, Sec. 8.2.)

16160.
As used in this part, "antique cannon" means any cannon manufactured before January 1, 1899, which has been rendered incapable of firing or for which ammunition is no longer manufactured in the United States and is not readily available in the ordinary channels of commercial trade.
(Added by Stats. 2010, Ch. 711, Sec. 6. (SB 1080) Effective January 1, 2011. Operative January 1, 2012, by Sec. 10 of Ch. 711.)

16170.
(a) As used in Sections 30515 and 30530, "antique firearm" means any firearm manufactured before January 1, 1899.
(b) As used in Section 16520, Section 16650, subdivision (a) of Section 23630, paragraph (1) of subdivision (b) of Section 27505, and subdivision (a) of Section 31615, "antique firearm" has the same meaning as in Section 921(a)(16) of Title 18 of the United States Code.
(c) As used in Section 17700, "antique firearm" means either of the following:
(1) Any firearm not designed or redesigned for using rimfire or conventional center fire ignition with fixed ammunition and manufactured in or before 1898. This includes any matchlock, flintlock, percussion cap, or similar type of ignition system or replica thereof, whether actually manufactured before or after the year 1898.
(2) Any firearm using fixed ammunition manufactured in or before 1898, for which ammunition is no longer manufactured in the United States and is not readily available in the ordinary channels of commercial trade.
(Added by Stats. 2010, Ch. 711, Sec. 6. (SB 1080) Effective January 1, 2011. Operative January 1, 2012, by Sec. 10 of Ch. 711.)

16180.
As used in this part, "antique rifle" means a firearm conforming to the definition of an "antique firearm" in Section 479.11 of Title 27 of the Code of Federal Regulations.
(Added by Stats. 2010, Ch. 711, Sec. 6. (SB 1080) Effective January 1, 2011. Operative January 1, 2012, by Sec. 10 of Ch. 711.)

16190.
As used in this part, "application to purchase" means either of the following:
(a) The initial completion of the register by the purchaser, transferee, or person being loaned a firearm, as required by Section 28210.
(b) The initial completion and transmission to the Department of Justice of the record of electronic or telephonic transfer by the dealer on the purchaser, transferee, or person being loaned a firearm, as required by Section 28215.
(Amended by Stats. 2014, Ch. 103, Sec. 3. (AB 1798) Effective January 1, 2015.)

16200.
Use of the term "assault weapon" is governed by Sections 30510 and 30515.

(Added by Stats. 2010, Ch. 711, Sec. 6. (SB 1080) Effective January 1, 2011. Operative January 1, 2012, by Sec. 10 of Ch. 711.)

16220.
As used in this part, "ballistic knife" means a device that propels a knifelike blade as a projectile by means of a coil spring, elastic material, or compressed gas. Ballistic knife does not include any device that propels an arrow or a bolt by means of any common bow, compound bow, crossbow, or underwater speargun.
(Added by Stats. 2010, Ch. 711, Sec. 6. (SB 1080) Effective January 1, 2011. Operative January 1, 2012, by Sec. 10 of Ch. 711.)

16230.
As used in this part, "ballistics identification system" includes, but is not limited to, any automated image analysis system that is capable of storing firearm ballistic markings and tracing those markings to the firearm that produced them.
(Added by Stats. 2010, Ch. 711, Sec. 6. (SB 1080) Effective January 1, 2011. Operative January 1, 2012, by Sec. 10 of Ch. 711.)

16240.
As used in this part, "basic firearms safety certificate" means a certificate issued before January 1, 2003, by the Department of Justice pursuant to former Article 8 (commencing with Section 12800) of Chapter 6 of Title 2 of Part 4, as that article read at any time from when it became operative on January 1, 1992, to when it was repealed on January 1, 2003.
(Added by Stats. 2010, Ch. 711, Sec. 6. (SB 1080) Effective January 1, 2011. Operative January 1, 2012, by Sec. 10 of Ch. 711.)

16250.
(a) As used in this part, "BB device" means any instrument that expels a projectile, such as a BB or a pellet, through the force of air pressure, gas pressure, or spring action, or any spot marker gun.
(b) This section shall be operative on January 1, 2016.
(Repealed (in Sec. 1) and added by Stats. 2014, Ch. 915, Sec. 2. (SB 199) Effective January 1, 2015. Section operative January 1, 2016, by its own provisions.)

16260.
As used in this part, "belt buckle knife" is a knife that is made an integral part of a belt buckle and consists of a blade with a length of at least two and one-half inches.
(Added by Stats. 2010, Ch. 711, Sec. 6. (SB 1080) Effective January 1, 2011. Operative January 1, 2012, by Sec. 10 of Ch. 711.)

16270.
As used in this part, "blowgun" means a hollow tube designed and intended to be used as a tube through which a dart is propelled by the force of the breath of the user.
(Added by Stats. 2010, Ch. 711, Sec. 6. (SB 1080) Effective January 1, 2011. Operative January 1, 2012, by Sec. 10 of Ch. 711.)

16280.
As used in this part, "blowgun ammunition" means a dart designed and intended for use in a blowgun.
(Added by Stats. 2010, Ch. 711, Sec. 6. (SB 1080) Effective January 1, 2011. Operative January 1, 2012, by Sec. 10 of Ch. 711.)

16288.
As used in Section 31360, "body armor" means any bullet-resistant material intended to provide ballistic and trauma protection for the person wearing the body armor.
(Added by Stats. 2010, Ch. 711, Sec. 6. (SB 1080) Effective January 1, 2011. Operative January 1, 2012, by Sec. 10 of Ch. 711.)

16290.
As used in this part, "body vest" or "body shield" means any bullet-resistant material intended to provide ballistic and trauma protection for the wearer or holder.
(Added by Stats. 2010, Ch. 711, Sec. 6. (SB 1080) Effective January 1, 2011. Operative January 1, 2012, by Sec. 10 of Ch. 711.)

16300.
As used in this part, "bona fide evidence of identity" or "bona fide evidence of majority and identity" means a document issued by a federal, state, county, or municipal government, or subdivision or agency thereof, including, but not limited to, a motor vehicle operator's license, state identification card, identification card issued to a member of the armed forces, or other form of identification that bears the name, date of birth, description, and picture of the person.
(Added by Stats. 2010, Ch. 711, Sec. 6. (SB 1080) Effective January 1, 2011. Operative January 1, 2012, by Sec. 10 of Ch. 711.)

16310.
As used in this part, "boobytrap" means any concealed or camouflaged device designed to cause great bodily injury when triggered by an action of any unsuspecting person coming across the device. Boobytraps may include, but are not limited to, guns, ammunition, or explosive devices attached to trip wires or other triggering mechanisms, sharpened stakes, and lines or wire with hooks attached.
(Added by Stats. 2010, Ch. 711, Sec. 6. (SB 1080) Effective January 1, 2011. Operative January 1, 2012, by Sec. 10 of Ch. 711.)

16320.
(a) As used in this part, "camouflaging firearm container" means a container that meets all of the following criteria:
(1) It is designed and intended to enclose a firearm.
(2) It is designed and intended to allow the firing of the enclosed firearm by external controls while the firearm is in the container.
(3) It is not readily recognizable as containing a firearm.
(b) "Camouflaging firearm container" does not include any camouflaging covering used while engaged in lawful hunting or while going to or returning from a lawful hunting expedition.
(Added by Stats. 2010, Ch. 711, Sec. 6. (SB 1080) Effective January 1, 2011. Operative January 1, 2012, by Sec. 10 of Ch. 711.)

16330.
As used in this part, "cane gun" means any firearm mounted or enclosed in a stick, staff, rod, crutch, or similar device, designed to be, or capable of being used as, an aid in walking, if the firearm may be fired while mounted or enclosed therein.
(Added by Stats. 2010, Ch. 711, Sec. 6. (SB 1080) Effective January 1, 2011. Operative January 1, 2012, by Sec. 10 of Ch. 711.)

16340.
As used in this part, "cane sword" means a cane, swagger stick, stick, staff, rod, pole, umbrella, or similar device, having concealed within it a blade that may be used as a sword or stiletto.
(Added by Stats. 2010, Ch. 711, Sec. 6. (SB 1080) Effective January 1, 2011. Operative January 1, 2012, by Sec. 10 of Ch. 711.)

16350.
As used in Section 30515, "capacity to accept more than 10 rounds" means capable of accommodating more than 10 rounds. The term does not apply to a feeding device that has been permanently altered so that it cannot accommodate more than 10 rounds.
(Added by Stats. 2010, Ch. 711, Sec. 6. (SB 1080) Effective January 1, 2011. Operative January 1, 2012, by Sec. 10 of Ch. 711.)

16360.
As used in this part, "CCW" means "carry concealed weapons."
(Added by Stats. 2010, Ch. 711, Sec. 6. (SB 1080) Effective January 1, 2011. Operative January 1, 2012, by Sec. 10 of Ch. 711.)

16370.

As used in Sections 31610 to 31700, inclusive, "certified instructor" or "DOJ Certified Instructor" means a person designated as a handgun safety instructor by the Department of Justice pursuant to subdivision (a) of Section 31635.
(Added by Stats. 2010, Ch. 711, Sec. 6. (SB 1080) Effective January 1, 2011. Operative January 1, 2012, by Sec. 10 of Ch. 711.)
16380.
As used in this part, "chamber load indicator" means a device that plainly indicates that a cartridge is in the firing chamber. A device satisfies this definition if it is readily visible, has incorporated or adjacent explanatory text or graphics, or both, and is designed and intended to indicate to a reasonably foreseeable adult user of the pistol, without requiring the user to refer to a user's manual or any other resource other than the pistol itself, whether a cartridge is in the firing chamber.
(Added by Stats. 2010, Ch. 711, Sec. 6. (SB 1080) Effective January 1, 2011. Operative January 1, 2012, by Sec. 10 of Ch. 711.)
16400.
As used in this part, "clear evidence of the person's identity and age" means either of the following:
(a) A valid California driver's license.
(b) A valid California identification card issued by the Department of Motor Vehicles.
(Added by Stats. 2010, Ch. 711, Sec. 6. (SB 1080) Effective January 1, 2011. Operative January 1, 2012, by Sec. 10 of Ch. 711.)
16405.
As used in this part, "composite knuckles" means any device or instrument made wholly or partially of composite materials, other than a medically prescribed prosthetic, that is not metal knuckles, that is worn for purposes of offense or defense in or on the hand, and that either protects the wearer's hand while striking a blow or increases the force of impact from the blow or injury to the individual receiving the blow.
(Added by Stats. 2010, Ch. 711, Sec. 6. (SB 1080) Effective January 1, 2011. Operative January 1, 2012, by Sec. 10 of Ch. 711.)
16410.
As used in this part, "consultant-evaluator" means a consultant or evaluator who, in the course of that person's profession is loaned firearms from a person licensed pursuant to Chapter 44 (commencing with Section 921) of Title 18 of the United States Code and the regulations issued pursuant thereto, for research or evaluation, and has a current certificate of eligibility issued pursuant to Section 26710.
(Added by Stats. 2010, Ch. 711, Sec. 6. (SB 1080) Effective January 1, 2011. Operative January 1, 2012, by Sec. 10 of Ch. 711.)
16420.
Use of the term "dagger" is governed by Section 16470.
(Added by Stats. 2010, Ch. 711, Sec. 6. (SB 1080) Effective January 1, 2011. Operative January 1, 2012, by Sec. 10 of Ch. 711.)
16430.
As used in Division 4 (commencing with Section 18250) of Title 2, "deadly weapon" means any weapon, the possession or concealed carrying of which is prohibited by any provision listed in Section 16590.
(Added by Stats. 2010, Ch. 711, Sec. 6. (SB 1080) Effective January 1, 2011. Operative January 1, 2012, by Sec. 10 of Ch. 711.)
16440.
Use of the term "dealer" is governed by Section 26700.
(Added by Stats. 2010, Ch. 711, Sec. 6. (SB 1080) Effective January 1, 2011. Operative January 1, 2012, by Sec. 10 of Ch. 711.)
16450.
As used in Sections 31610 to 31700, inclusive, in Chapter 2 (commencing with Section 29030) of Division 7 of Title 4, and in Article 3 (commencing with Section 30345) of Chapter 1 of Division 10 of Title 4, "department" means the Department of Justice.
(Added by Stats. 2010, Ch. 711, Sec. 6. (SB 1080) Effective January 1, 2011. Operative January 1, 2012, by Sec. 10 of Ch. 711.)
16460.
(a) As used in Sections 16510, 16520, and 16780, and in Chapter 1 (commencing with Section 18710) of Division 5 of Title 2, "destructive device" includes any of the following weapons:
(1) Any projectile containing any explosive or incendiary material or any other chemical substance, including, but not limited to, that which is commonly known as tracer or incendiary ammunition, except tracer ammunition manufactured for use in shotguns.
(2) Any bomb, grenade, explosive missile, or similar device or any launching device therefor.
(3) Any weapon of a caliber greater than 0.60 caliber which fires fixed ammunition, or any ammunition therefor, other than a shotgun (smooth or rifled bore) conforming to the definition of a "destructive device" found in subsection (b) of Section 479.11 of Title 27 of the Code of Federal Regulations, shotgun ammunition (single projectile or shot), antique rifle, or an antique cannon.
(4) Any rocket, rocket-propelled projectile, or similar device of a diameter greater than 0.60 inch, or any launching device therefor, and any rocket, rocket-propelled projectile, or similar device containing any explosive or incendiary material or any other chemical substance, other than the propellant for that device, except those devices as are designed primarily for emergency or distress signaling purposes.
(5) Any breakable container that contains a flammable liquid with a flashpoint of 150 degrees Fahrenheit or less and has a wick or similar device capable of being ignited, other than a device which is commercially manufactured primarily for the purpose of illumination.
(6) Any sealed device containing dry ice (CO_2) or other chemically reactive substances assembled for the purpose of causing an explosion by a chemical reaction.
(b) A bullet containing or carrying an explosive agent is not a destructive device as that term is used in subdivision (a).
(Added by Stats. 2010, Ch. 711, Sec. 6. (SB 1080) Effective January 1, 2011. Operative January 1, 2012, by Sec. 10 of Ch. 711.)
16470.
As used in this part, "dirk" or "dagger" means a knife or other instrument with or without a handguard that is capable of ready use as a stabbing weapon that may inflict great bodily injury or death. A nonlocking folding knife, a folding knife that is not prohibited by Section 21510, or a pocketknife is capable of ready use as a stabbing weapon that may inflict great bodily injury or death only if the blade of the knife is exposed and locked into position.
(Added by Stats. 2010, Ch. 711, Sec. 6. (SB 1080) Effective January 1, 2011. Operative January 1, 2012, by Sec. 10 of Ch. 711.)
16480.
Use of the term "DOJ Certified Instructor" is governed by Section 16370.
(Added by Stats. 2010, Ch. 711, Sec. 6. (SB 1080) Effective January 1, 2011. Operative January 1, 2012, by Sec. 10 of Ch. 711.)
16490.
As used in this part, "domestic violence" means abuse perpetrated against any of the following persons:
(a) A spouse or former spouse.
(b) A cohabitant or former cohabitant, as defined in Section 6209 of the Family Code.
(c) A person with whom the respondent is having or has had a dating or engagement relationship.
(d) A person with whom the respondent has had a child, where the presumption applies that the male parent is the father of the child of the female parent under the Uniform

Parentage Act (Part 3 (commencing with Section 7600) of Division 12 of the Family Code).
(e) A child of a party or a child who is the subject of an action under the Uniform Parentage Act, where the presumption applies that the male parent is the father of the child to be protected.
(f) Any other person related by consanguinity or affinity within the second degree.
(Added by Stats. 2010, Ch. 711, Sec. 6. (SB 1080) Effective January 1, 2011. Operative January 1, 2012, by Sec. 10 of Ch. 711.)
16500.
Use of the phrase "drop safety requirement for handguns" is governed by Section 31900.
(Added by Stats. 2010, Ch. 711, Sec. 6. (SB 1080) Effective January 1, 2011. Operative January 1, 2012, by Sec. 10 of Ch. 711.)
16505.
For purposes of Chapter 7 (commencing with Section 26400) of Division 5 of Title 4, a firearm is "encased" when that firearm is enclosed in a case that is expressly made for the purpose of containing a firearm and that is completely zipped, snapped, buckled, tied, or otherwise fastened with no part of that firearm exposed.
(Added by Stats. 2012, Ch. 700, Sec. 4. (AB 1527) Effective January 1, 2013.)
16510.
As used in subdivision (a) of Section 16460 and Chapter 1 (commencing with Section 18710) of Division 5 of Title 2, "explosive" means any substance, or combination of substances, the primary or common purpose of which is detonation or rapid combustion, and which is capable of a relatively instantaneous or rapid release of gas and heat, or any substance, the primary purpose of which, when combined with others, is to form a substance capable of a relatively instantaneous or rapid release of gas and heat. "Explosive" includes, but is not limited to, any explosive as defined in Section 841 of Title 18 of the United States Code and published pursuant to Section 555.23 of Title 27 of the Code of Federal Regulations, and any of the following:
(a) Dynamite, nitroglycerine, picric acid, lead azide, fulminate of mercury, black powder, smokeless powder, propellant explosives, detonating primers, blasting caps, or commercial boosters.
(b) Substances determined to be division 1.1, 1.2, 1.3, or 1.6 explosives as classified by the United States Department of Transportation.
(c) Nitro carbo nitrate substances (blasting agent) classified as division 1.5 explosives by the United States Department of Transportation.
(d) Any material designated as an explosive by the State Fire Marshal. The designation shall be made pursuant to the classification standards established by the United States Department of Transportation. The State Fire Marshal shall adopt regulations in accordance with the Government Code to establish procedures for the classification and designation of explosive materials or explosive devices that are not under the jurisdiction of the United States Department of Transportation pursuant to provisions of Section 841 of Title 18 of the United States Code and published pursuant to Section 555.23 of Title 27 of the Code of Federal Regulations that define explosives.
(e) Certain division 1.4 explosives as designated by the United States Department of Transportation when listed in regulations adopted by the State Fire Marshal.
(f) As used in Section 16460 and Chapter 1 (commencing with Section 18710) of Division 5 of Title 2, "explosive" does not include any destructive device, nor does it include ammunition or small arms primers manufactured for use in shotguns, rifles, and pistols.
(Added by Stats. 2010, Ch. 711, Sec. 6. (SB 1080) Effective January 1, 2011. Operative January 1, 2012, by Sec. 10 of Ch. 711.)
16520.
(a) As used in this part, "firearm" means a device, designed to be used as a weapon, from which is expelled through a barrel, a projectile by the force of an explosion or other form of combustion.
(b) As used in the following provisions, "firearm" includes the frame or receiver of the weapon:
(1) Section 16550.
(2) Section 16730.
(3) Section 16960.
(4) Section 16990.
(5) Section 17070.
(6) Section 17310.
(7) Sections 26500 to 26588, inclusive.
(8) Sections 26600 to 27140, inclusive.
(9) Sections 27400 to 28000, inclusive.
(10) Section 28100.
(11) Sections 28400 to 28415, inclusive.
(12) Sections 29010 to 29150, inclusive.
(13) Section 29180.
(14) Sections 29610 to 29750, inclusive.
(15) Sections 29800 to 29905, inclusive.
(16) Sections 30150 to 30165, inclusive.
(17) Section 31615.
(18) Sections 31705 to 31830, inclusive.
(19) Sections 34355 to 34370, inclusive.
(20) Sections 8100, 8101, and 8103 of the Welfare and Institutions Code.
(c) As used in the following provisions, "firearm" also includes a rocket, rocket propelled projectile launcher, or similar device containing an explosive or incendiary material, whether or not the device is designed for emergency or distress signaling purposes:
(1) Section 16750.
(2) Subdivision (b) of Section 16840.
(3) Section 25400.
(4) Sections 25850 to 26025, inclusive.
(5) Subdivisions (a), (b), and (c) of Section 26030.
(6) Sections 26035 to 26055, inclusive.
(d) As used in the following provisions, "firearm" does not include an unloaded antique firearm:
(1) Subdivisions (a) and (c) of Section 16730.
(2) Section 16550.
(3) Section 16960.
(4) Section 17310.
(5) Chapter 6 (commencing with Section 26350) of Division 5 of Title 4.
(6) Chapter 7 (commencing with Section 26400) of Division 5 of Title 4.
(7) Sections 26500 to 26588, inclusive.
(8) Sections 26700 to 26915, inclusive.
(9) Section 27510.
(10) Section 27530.
(11) Section 27540.
(12) Section 27545.
(13) Sections 27555 to 27585, inclusive.
(14) Sections 29010 to 29150, inclusive.
(15) Section 25135.
(16) Section 29180.
(e) As used in Sections 34005 and 34010, "firearm" does not include a destructive device.
(f) As used in Sections 17280 and 24680, "firearm" has the same meaning as in Section 922 of Title 18 of the United States Code.

(g) As used in Sections 29010 to 29150, inclusive, "firearm" includes the unfinished frame or receiver of a weapon that can be readily converted to the functional condition of a finished frame or receiver.

(Amended by Stats. 2016, Ch. 60, Sec. 2. (AB 857) Effective January 1, 2017.)

16530.
(a) As used in this part, the terms "firearm capable of being concealed upon the person," "pistol," and "revolver" apply to and include any device designed to be used as a weapon, from which is expelled a projectile by the force of any explosion, or other form of combustion, and that has a barrel less than 16 inches in length. These terms also include any device that has a barrel 16 inches or more in length which is designed to be interchanged with a barrel less than 16 inches in length.
(b) Nothing shall prevent a device defined as a "firearm capable of being concealed upon the person," "pistol," or "revolver" from also being found to be a short-barreled rifle or a short-barreled shotgun.

(Added by Stats. 2010, Ch. 711, Sec. 6. (SB 1080) Effective January 1, 2011. Operative January 1, 2012, by Sec. 10 of Ch. 711.)

16535.
(a) As used in this part, "firearm safety certificate" means a certificate issued by the Department of Justice pursuant to Sections 31610 to 31700, inclusive, or pursuant to former Article 8 (commencing with Section 12800) of Chapter 6 of Title 2 of Part 4, as that article was operative at any time from January 1, 2003, until it was repealed by the Deadly Weapons Recodification Act of 2010.
(b) This section shall become operative on January 1, 2015.

(Added by Stats. 2013, Ch. 761, Sec. 1. (SB 683) Effective January 1, 2014. Section operative January 1, 2015, by its own provisions.)

16540.
As used in this part, "firearm safety device" means a device other than a gun safe that locks and is designed to prevent children and unauthorized users from firing a firearm. The device may be installed on a firearm, be incorporated into the design of the firearm, or prevent access to the firearm.

(Amended by Stats. 2014, Ch. 103, Sec. 4. (AB 1798) Effective January 1, 2015.)

16550.
As used in this part, "firearm transaction record" is a record containing the same information referred to in subdivision (a) of Section 478.124, Section 478.124a, and subdivision (e) of Section 478.125 of Title 27 of the Code of Federal Regulations.

(Added by Stats. 2010, Ch. 711, Sec. 6. (SB 1080) Effective January 1, 2011. Operative January 1, 2012, by Sec. 10 of Ch. 711.)

16560.
Use of the phrase "firing requirement for handguns" is governed by Section 31905.

(Added by Stats. 2010, Ch. 711, Sec. 6. (SB 1080) Effective January 1, 2011. Operative January 1, 2012, by Sec. 10 of Ch. 711.)

16570.
As used in this part, "flechette dart" means a dart, capable of being fired from a firearm, that measures approximately one inch in length, with tail fins that take up approximately five-sixteenths of an inch of the body.

(Added by Stats. 2010, Ch. 711, Sec. 6. (SB 1080) Effective January 1, 2011. Operative January 1, 2012, by Sec. 10 of Ch. 711.)

16575.
(a) Except as stated in subdivision (c), the following provisions are continuations of provisions that were included in former Article 4 (commencing with Section 12070) of Chapter 1 of Title 2 of Part 4, entitled "Licenses to Sell Firearms," when that article was repealed by the Deadly Weapons Recodification Act of 2010:
(1) Section 16130.
(2) Subdivision (b) of Section 16170, to the extent that it continues former Sections 12078 and 12085, as those sections read when they were repealed by the Deadly Weapons Recodification Act of 2010.
(3) Section 16230.
(4) Section 16400.
(5) Section 16450, to the extent that it continues subdivision (a) of former Section 12086, as that subdivision read when it was repealed by the Deadly Weapons Recodification Act of 2010.
(6) Subdivisions (b) and (d) of Section 16520, to the extent that they continue subdivision (e) of former Section 12085, as that subdivision read when it was repealed by the Deadly Weapons Recodification Act of 2010.
(7) Subdivision (g) of Section 16520.
(8) Section 16550.
(9) Section 16620.
(10) Section 16720.
(11) Section 16730.
(12) Section 16740, to the extent that it continues subdivision (b) of former Section 12079, as that subdivision read when it was repealed by the Deadly Weapons Recodification Act of 2010.
(13) Section 16800.
(14) Section 16810.
(15) Section 16960.
(16) Section 16990.
(17) Section 17110.
(18) Section 17310.
(19) Sections 26500 to 26588, inclusive.
(20) Sections 26600 to 29150, inclusive.
(21) Chapter 2 (commencing with Section 29500) of Division 8 of Title 4.
(22) Section 30105.
(23) Sections 30150 to 30165, inclusive.
(24) Sections 31705 to 31830, inclusive.
(25) Section 32315.
(26) Section 34205.
(27) Sections 34350 to 34370, inclusive.
(b) Except as stated in subdivision (c), the provisions listed in subdivision (a) may be referred to as "former Article 4 of Chapter 1 provisions."
(c) Subdivision (a) does not include any provision that was first codified in one of the specified numerical ranges after the effective date of the Deadly Weapons Recodification Act of 2010.

(Added by Stats. 2010, Ch. 711, Sec. 6. (SB 1080) Effective January 1, 2011. Operative January 1, 2012, by Sec. 10 of Ch. 711.)

16580.
(a) Except as stated in subdivision (c), the following provisions are continuations of provisions that were included in former Chapter 1 (commencing with Section 12000) of Title 2 of Part 4, entitled "Firearms," when that chapter was repealed by the Deadly Weapons Recodification Act of 2010:
(1) Sections 12001 to 12022.95, inclusive.
(2) Sections 16120 to 16140, inclusive.
(3) Subdivision (b) of Section 16170, to the extent it continues former Sections 12001, 12060, 12078, 12085, and 12088.8, as those sections read when they were repealed by the Deadly Weapons Recodification Act of 2010.
(4) Subdivision (c) of Section 16170.
(5) Section 16190.
(6) Sections 16220 to 16240, inclusive.
(7) Section 16250, to the extent it continues former Section 12001, as that section read when it was repealed by the Deadly Weapons Recodification Act of 2010.

(8) Section 16260.
(9) Sections 16320 to 16340, inclusive.
(10) Section 16360.
(11) Sections 16400 to 16410, inclusive.
(12) Section 16430.
(13) Section 16450, to the extent it continues former Sections 12060 and 12086, as those sections read when they were repealed by the Deadly Weapons Recodification Act of 2010.
(14) Subdivision (b) of Section 16460.
(15) Section 16470.
(16) Section 16490.
(17) Subdivision (a) of Section 16520, to the extent it continues former Section 12001, as that section read when it was repealed by the Deadly Weapons Recodification Act of 2010.
(18) Subdivisions (b) to (g), inclusive, of Section 16520.
(19) Sections 16530 to 16550, inclusive.
(20) Section 16570.
(21) Sections 16600 to 16640, inclusive.
(22) Section 16650, to the extent it continues former Section 12060, as that section read when it was repealed by the Deadly Weapons Recodification Act of 2010.
(23) Section 16662, to the extent it continues former Section 12060, as that section read when it was repealed by the Deadly Weapons Recodification Act of 2010.
(24) Sections 16670 to 16690, inclusive.
(25) Sections 16720 to 16760, inclusive.
(26) Sections 16800 and 16810.
(27) Sections 16830 to 16870, inclusive.
(28) Sections 16920 to 16960, inclusive.
(29) Sections 16990 and 17000.
(30) Sections 17020 to 17070, inclusive.
(31) Section 17090, to the extent it continues former Section 12020, as that section read when it was repealed by the Deadly Weapons Recodification Act of 2010.
(32) Section 17110.
(33) Section 17125.
(34) Section 17160.
(35) Sections 17170 to 17200, inclusive.
(36) Sections 17270 to 17290, inclusive.
(37) Sections 17310 and 17315.
(38) Sections 17330 to 17505, inclusive.
(39) Sections 17515 to 18500, inclusive.
(40) Sections 19100 to 19290, inclusive.
(41) Sections 20200 to 21390, inclusive.
(42) Sections 21790 to 22490, inclusive.
(43) Sections 23500 to 30290, inclusive.
(44) Sections 30345 to 30365, inclusive.
(45) Sections 31500 to 31590, inclusive.
(46) Sections 31705 to 31830, inclusive.
(47) Sections 32310 to 32450, inclusive.
(48) Sections 32900 to 33320, inclusive.
(49) Sections 33600 to 34370, inclusive.
(b) Except as stated in subdivision (c), the provisions listed in subdivision (a) may be referred to as "former Chapter 1 provisions."
(c) Subdivision (a) does not include any provision that was first codified in one of the specified numerical ranges after the effective date of the Deadly Weapons Recodification Act of 2010.

(Added by Stats. 2010, Ch. 711, Sec. 6. (SB 1080) Effective January 1, 2011. Operative January 1, 2012, by Sec. 10 of Ch. 711.)

16585.
(a) Except as stated in subdivision (d), the following provisions are continuations of provisions that were included in former Section 12078, as that section read when it was repealed by the Deadly Weapons Recodification Act of 2010:
(1) Subdivision (b) of Section 16170, as it pertains to former Section 12078, as that section read when it was repealed by the Deadly Weapons Recodification Act of 2010.
(2) Section 16720.
(3) Subdivision (a) of Section 16730, as it pertains to former Section 12078, as that section read when it was repealed by the Deadly Weapons Recodification Act of 2010.
(4) Subdivision (b) of Section 16730.
(5) Section 16990.
(6) Sections 26600 to 26615, inclusive.
(7) Sections 26950 to 27140, inclusive.
(8) Sections 27400 to 27415, inclusive.
(9) Subdivision (b) of Section 27505, as it pertains to former Section 12078, as that section read when it was repealed by the Deadly Weapons Recodification Act of 2010.
(10) Sections 27600 to 28000, inclusive.
(11) Sections 28400 to 28415, inclusive.
(12) Sections 30150 to 30165, inclusive.
(13) Sections 31705 to 31830, inclusive.
(14) Sections 34355 to 34370, inclusive.
(b) Except as stated in subdivision (d), the provisions listed in subdivision (a) may be referred to as "former Section 12078 provisions."
(c) Except as stated in subdivision (d), the following provisions are continuations of provisions that were included in subdivision (a) of former Section 12078, as that subdivision read when it was repealed by the Deadly Weapons Recodification Act of 2010:
(1) Sections 26600 to 26615, inclusive.
(2) Section 26950.
(3) Sections 27050 to 27065, inclusive.
(4) Sections 27400 to 27415, inclusive.
(5) Sections 27600 to 27615, inclusive.
(6) Section 27650.
(7) Sections 27850 to 27860, inclusive.
(8) Sections 28400 to 28415, inclusive.
(9) Sections 30150 to 30165, inclusive.
(10) Sections 31705 to 31735, inclusive.
(11) Sections 34355 to 34370, inclusive.
(d) Subdivisions (a) and (c) do not include any provision that was first codified in one of the specified numerical ranges after the effective date of the Deadly Weapons Recodification Act of 2010.

(Added by Stats. 2010, Ch. 711, Sec. 6. (SB 1080) Effective January 1, 2011. Operative January 1, 2012, by Sec. 10 of Ch. 711.)

16590.
As used in this part, "generally prohibited weapon" means any of the following:
(a) An air gauge knife, as prohibited by Section 20310.
(b) Ammunition that contains or consists of a flechette dart, as prohibited by Section 30210.
(c) A ballistic knife, as prohibited by Section 21110.
(d) A belt buckle knife, as prohibited by Section 20410.
(e) A bullet containing or carrying an explosive agent, as prohibited by Section 30210.
(f) A camouflaging firearm container, as prohibited by Section 24310.
(g) A cane gun, as prohibited by Section 24410.

(h) A cane sword, as prohibited by Section 20510.
(i) A concealed dirk or dagger, as prohibited by Section 21310.
(j) A concealed explosive substance, other than fixed ammunition, as prohibited by Section 19100.
(k) A firearm that is not immediately recognizable as a firearm, as prohibited by Section 24510.
(l) A large-capacity magazine, as prohibited by Section 32310.
(m) A leaded cane or an instrument or weapon of the kind commonly known as a billy, blackjack, sandbag, sandclub, sap, or slungshot, as prohibited by Section 22210.
(n) A lipstick case knife, as prohibited by Section 20610.
(o) Metal knuckles, as prohibited by Section 21810.
(p) A metal military practice handgrenade or a metal replica handgrenade, as prohibited by Section 19200.
(q) A multiburst trigger activator, as prohibited by Section 32900.
(r) A nunchaku, as prohibited by Section 22010.
(s) A shobi-zue, as prohibited by Section 20710.
(t) A short-barreled rifle or short-barreled shotgun, as prohibited by Section 33215.
(u) A shuriken, as prohibited by Section 22410.
(v) An unconventional pistol, as prohibited by Section 31500.
(w) An undetectable firearm, as prohibited by Section 24610.
(x) A wallet gun, as prohibited by Section 24710.
(y) A writing pen knife, as prohibited by Section 20910.
(z) A zip gun, as prohibited by Section 33600.
(Added by Stats. 2010, Ch. 711, Sec. 6. (SB 1080) Effective January 1, 2011. Operative January 1, 2012, by Sec. 10 of Ch. 711.)

16600.
As used in Chapter 2 (commencing with Section 25100) of Division 4 of Title 4, "great bodily injury" means a significant or substantial physical injury.
(Added by Stats. 2010, Ch. 711, Sec. 6. (SB 1080) Effective January 1, 2011. Operative January 1, 2012, by Sec. 10 of Ch. 711.)

16610.
As used in this part, "gun safe" means a locking container that fully contains and secures one or more firearms, and that meets the standards for gun safes adopted pursuant to Section 23650.
(Added by Stats. 2010, Ch. 711, Sec. 6. (SB 1080) Effective January 1, 2011. Operative January 1, 2012, by Sec. 10 of Ch. 711.)

16620.
As used in this part, "Gun Show Trader" means a person described in Section 26525.
(Added by Stats. 2010, Ch. 711, Sec. 6. (SB 1080) Effective January 1, 2011. Operative January 1, 2012, by Sec. 10 of Ch. 711.)

16630.
As used in this part, "gunsmith" means any person who is licensed as a dealer pursuant to Chapter 44 (commencing with Section 921) of Title 18 of the United States Code and the regulations issued pursuant thereto, who is engaged primarily in the business of repairing firearms, or making or fitting special barrels, stocks, or trigger mechanisms to firearms, or the agent or employee of that person.
(Added by Stats. 2010, Ch. 711, Sec. 6. (SB 1080) Effective January 1, 2011. Operative January 1, 2012, by Sec. 10 of Ch. 711.)

16640.
(a) As used in this part, "handgun" means any pistol, revolver, or firearm capable of being concealed upon the person.
(b) Nothing shall prevent a device defined as a "handgun" from also being found to be a short-barreled rifle or a short-barreled shotgun.
(Added by Stats. 2010, Ch. 711, Sec. 6. (SB 1080) Effective January 1, 2011. Operative January 1, 2012, by Sec. 10 of Ch. 711.)

16650.
(a) As used in this part, "handgun ammunition" means ammunition principally for use in pistols, revolvers, and other firearms capable of being concealed upon the person, notwithstanding that the ammunition may also be used in some rifles.
(b) As used in Section 30312 and in Article 3 (commencing with Section 30345) of Chapter 1 of Division 10 of Title 4, "handgun ammunition" does not include either of the following:
(1) Ammunition designed and intended to be used in an antique firearm.
(2) Blanks.
(Added by Stats. 2010, Ch. 711, Sec. 6. (SB 1080) Effective January 1, 2011. Operative January 1, 2012, by Sec. 10 of Ch. 711.)

16660.
As used in this part, "handgun ammunition designed primarily to penetrate metal or armor" means any ammunition, except a shotgun shell or ammunition primarily designed for use in a rifle, that is designed primarily to penetrate a body vest or body shield, and has either of the following characteristics:
(a) Has projectile or projectile core constructed entirely, excluding the presence of traces of other substances, from one or a combination of tungsten alloys, steel, iron, brass, beryllium copper, or depleted uranium, or any equivalent material of similar density or hardness.
(b) Is primarily manufactured or designed, by virtue of its shape, cross-sectional density, or any coating applied thereto, including, but not limited to, ammunition commonly known as "KTW ammunition," to breach or penetrate a body vest or body shield when fired from a pistol, revolver, or other firearm capable of being concealed upon the person.
(Added by Stats. 2010, Ch. 711, Sec. 6. (SB 1080) Effective January 1, 2011. Operative January 1, 2012, by Sec. 10 of Ch. 711.)

16670.
As used in this part, "handgun safety certificate" means a certificate issued by the Department of Justice pursuant to Sections 31610 to 31700, inclusive, or pursuant to former Article 8 (commencing with Section 12800) of Chapter 6 of Title 2 of Part 4, as that article was operative at any time from January 1, 2003, until it was repealed by the Deadly Weapons Recodification Act of 2010.
(Added by Stats. 2010, Ch. 711, Sec. 6. (SB 1080) Effective January 1, 2011. Operative January 1, 2012, by Sec. 10 of Ch. 711.)

16680.
As used in this part, "hard wooden knuckles" means any device or instrument made wholly or partially of wood or paper products that is not metal knuckles, that is worn for purposes of offense or defense in or on the hand, and that either protects the wearer's hand while striking a blow, or increases the force of impact from the blow or injury to the individual receiving the blow. The composite materials, wood, or paper products contained in the device may help support the hand or fist, provide a shield to protect it, or consist of projections or studs that would contact the individual receiving a blow.
(Added by Stats. 2010, Ch. 711, Sec. 6. (SB 1080) Effective January 1, 2011. Operative January 1, 2012, by Sec. 10 of Ch. 711.)

16690.
(a) As used in Sections 25650 and 26020, Article 2 (commencing with Section 25450) of Chapter 2 of Division 5 of Title 4, Article 3 (commencing with Section 25900) of Chapter 3 of Division 5 of Title 4, and Section 32406, as added by Chapter 58 of the Statutes of 2016 and as added by Proposition 63, "honorably retired" includes:
(1) A peace officer who has qualified for, and has accepted, a service or disability retirement.
(2) A retired level I reserve officer who meets the requirements specified in paragraph (2) of subdivision (c) of Section 26300.
(b) As used in this section, "honorably retired" does not include an officer who has agreed to a service retirement in lieu of termination.
(Amended by Stats. 2018, Ch. 63, Sec. 1. (AB 1192) Effective January 1, 2019.)

16700.
(a) (1) As used in this part, "imitation firearm" means any BB device, toy gun, replica of a firearm, or other device that is so substantially similar in coloration and overall appearance to an existing firearm as to lead a reasonable person to perceive that the device is a firearm.
(2) "Imitation firearm" also includes, but is not limited to, a protective case for a cellular telephone that is so substantially similar in coloration and overall appearance to an existing firearm as to lead a reasonable person to perceive that the case is a firearm.
(b) As used in Section 20165, "imitation firearm" does not include any of the following:
(1) A nonfiring collector's replica that is historically significant, and is offered for sale in conjunction with a wall plaque or presentation case.
(2) A spot marker gun which expels a projectile that is greater than 10mm caliber.
(3) A BB device that expels a projectile, such as a BB or pellet, that is other than 6mm or 8mm caliber.
(4) A BB device that is an airsoft gun that expels a projectile, such as a BB or pellet, that is 6mm or 8mm caliber which meets the following:
(A) If the airsoft gun is configured as a handgun, in addition to the blaze orange ring on the barrel required by federal law, the airsoft gun has a trigger guard that has fluorescent coloration over the entire guard, and there is a two centimeter wide adhesive band around the circumference of the protruding pistol grip that has fluorescent coloration.
(B) If the airsoft gun is configured as a rifle or long gun, in addition to the blaze orange ring on the barrel required by federal law, the airsoft gun has a trigger guard that has fluorescent coloration over the entire guard, and there is a two centimeter wide adhesive band with fluorescent coloring around the circumference of any two of the following:
(i) The protruding pistol grip.
(ii) The buttstock.
(iii) A protruding ammunition magazine or clip.
(5) A device where the entire exterior surface of the device is white, bright red, bright orange, bright yellow, bright green, bright blue, bright pink, or bright purple, either singly or as the predominant color in combination with other colors in any pattern, or where the entire device is constructed of transparent or translucent materials which permits unmistakable observation of the device's complete contents.
(c) The adhesive bands described in paragraph (4) of subdivision (b) shall be applied in a manner not intended for removal, and shall be in place on the airsoft gun prior to sale to a customer.
(Amended by Stats. 2016, Ch. 198, Sec. 1. (AB 1798) Effective January 1, 2017.)

16720.
As used in this part, "immediate family member" means either of the following relationships:
(a) Parent and child.
(b) Grandparent and grandchild.
(Added by Stats. 2010, Ch. 711, Sec. 6. (SB 1080) Effective January 1, 2011. Operative January 1, 2012, by Sec. 10 of Ch. 711.)

16730.
(a) As used in Section 31815 and in Division 6 (commencing with Section 26500) of Title 4, "infrequent" means:
(1) For handguns, less than six transactions per calendar year.
(2) For firearms other than handguns, occasional and without regularity.
(b) As used in Section 27900, the term "infrequent" shall not be construed to prohibit different local chapters of the same nonprofit corporation from conducting auctions or similar events, provided the individual local chapter conducts the auctions or similar events infrequently. It is the intent of the Legislature that different local chapters, representing different localities, be entitled to invoke the exemption created by Section 27900, notwithstanding the frequency with which other chapters of the same nonprofit corporation may conduct auctions or similar events.
(c) As used in this section, "transaction" means a single sale, lease, or transfer of any number of handguns.
(Added by Stats. 2010, Ch. 711, Sec. 6. (SB 1080) Effective January 1, 2011. Operative January 1, 2012, by Sec. 10 of Ch. 711.)

16740.
As used in this part, "large-capacity magazine" means any ammunition feeding device with the capacity to accept more than 10 rounds, but shall not be construed to include any of the following:
(a) A feeding device that has been permanently altered so that it cannot accommodate more than 10 rounds.
(b) A .22 caliber tube ammunition feeding device.
(c) A tubular magazine that is contained in a lever-action firearm.
(Added by Stats. 2010, Ch. 711, Sec. 6. (SB 1080) Effective January 1, 2011. Operative January 1, 2012, by Sec. 10 of Ch. 711.)

16750.
(a) As used in Section 25400, "lawful possession of the firearm" means that the person who has possession or custody of the firearm either lawfully owns the firearm or has the permission of the lawful owner or a person who otherwise has apparent authority to possess or have custody of the firearm. A person who takes a firearm without the permission of the lawful owner or without the permission of a person who has lawful custody of the firearm does not have lawful possession of the firearm.
(b) As used in Article 2 (commencing with Section 25850), Article 3 (commencing with Section 25900), and Article 4 (commencing with Section 26000) of Chapter 3 of Division 5 of Title 4, Chapter 6 (commencing with Section 26350) of Division 5 of Title 4, and Chapter 7 (commencing with Section 26400) of Division 5 of Title 4, "lawful possession of the firearm" means that the person who has possession or custody of the firearm either lawfully acquired and lawfully owns the firearm or has the permission of the lawful owner or person who otherwise has apparent authority to possess or have custody of the firearm. A person who takes a firearm without the permission of the lawful owner or without the permission of a person who has lawful custody of the firearm does not have lawful possession of the firearm.
(Amended by Stats. 2012, Ch. 700, Sec. 6. (AB 1527) Effective January 1, 2013.)

16760.
As used in this part, a "leaded cane" means a staff, crutch, stick, rod, pole, or similar device, unnaturally weighted with lead.
(Added by Stats. 2010, Ch. 711, Sec. 6. (SB 1080) Effective January 1, 2011. Operative January 1, 2012, by Sec. 10 of Ch. 711.)

16770.
As used in this part, "less lethal ammunition" means any ammunition that satisfies both of the following requirements:
(a) It is designed to be used in any less lethal weapon or any other kind of weapon (including, but not limited to, any firearm, pistol, revolver, shotgun, rifle, or spring, compressed air, or compressed gas weapon).
(b) When used in a less lethal weapon or other weapon, it is designed to immobilize, incapacitate, or stun a human being through the infliction of any less than lethal impairment of physical condition, function, or senses, including physical pain or discomfort.
(Added by Stats. 2010, Ch. 711, Sec. 6. (SB 1080) Effective January 1, 2011. Operative January 1, 2012, by Sec. 10 of Ch. 711.)

16780.

As used in this part:

(a) "Less lethal weapon" means any device that is designed to or that has been converted to expel or propel less lethal ammunition by any action, mechanism, or process for the purpose of incapacitating, immobilizing, or stunning a human being through the infliction of any less than lethal impairment of physical condition, function, or senses, including physical pain or discomfort. It is not necessary that a weapon leave any lasting or permanent incapacitation, discomfort, pain, or other injury or disability in order to qualify as a less lethal weapon.

(b) Less lethal weapon includes the frame or receiver of any weapon described in subdivision (a), but does not include any of the following unless the part or weapon has been converted as described in subdivision (a):

(1) Pistol, revolver, or firearm.

(2) Machinegun.

(3) Rifle or shotgun using fixed ammunition consisting of standard primer and powder and not capable of being concealed upon the person.

(4) A pistol, rifle, or shotgun that is a firearm having a barrel less than 0.18 inches in diameter and that is designed to expel a projectile by any mechanical means or by compressed air or gas.

(5) When used as designed or intended by the manufacturer, any weapon that is commonly regarded as a toy gun, and that as a toy gun is incapable of inflicting any impairment of physical condition, function, or senses.

(6) A destructive device.

(7) A tear gas weapon.

(8) A bow or crossbow designed to shoot arrows.

(9) A device commonly known as a slingshot.

(10) A device designed for the firing of stud cartridges, explosive rivets, or similar industrial ammunition.

(11) A device designed for signaling, illumination, or safety.

(12) An assault weapon.

(Added by Stats. 2010, Ch. 711, Sec. 6. (SB 1080) Effective January 1, 2011. Operative January 1, 2012, by Sec. 10 of Ch. 711.)

16790.

As used in Article 5 (commencing with Section 30900) and Article 7 (commencing with Section 31050) of Chapter 2 of Division 10 of Title 4, "licensed gun dealer" means a person who is licensed pursuant to Sections 26700 to 26915, inclusive, and who has a permit to sell assault weapons or .50 BMG rifles pursuant to Section 31005.

(Added by Stats. 2010, Ch. 711, Sec. 6. (SB 1080) Effective January 1, 2011. Operative January 1, 2012, by Sec. 10 of Ch. 711.)

16800.

As used in this part, "licensed gun show producer" means a person who has been issued a certificate of eligibility by the Department of Justice pursuant to Section 27200. No regulations shall be required to implement this section.

(Added by Stats. 2010, Ch. 711, Sec. 6. (SB 1080) Effective January 1, 2011. Operative January 1, 2012, by Sec. 10 of Ch. 711.)

16810.

As used in Article 1 (commencing with Section 26700) and Article 2 (commencing with Section 26800) of Chapter 2 of Division 6 of Title 4, "licensed premises," "licensee's business premises," or "licensee's place of business" means the building designated in the license.

(Added by Stats. 2010, Ch. 711, Sec. 6. (SB 1080) Effective January 1, 2011. Operative January 1, 2012, by Sec. 10 of Ch. 711.)

16820.

(a) For purposes of the provisions listed in Section 16580, use of the term "licensee" is governed by Section 26700.

(b) For purposes of Chapter 2 (commencing with Section 29030) of Division 7 of Title 4, use of the term "licensee" is governed by Section 29030.

(Added by Stats. 2010, Ch. 711, Sec. 6. (SB 1080) Effective January 1, 2011. Operative January 1, 2012, by Sec. 10 of Ch. 711.)

16822.

Use of the term "licensee's business premises" is governed by Section 16810.

(Added by Stats. 2010, Ch. 711, Sec. 6. (SB 1080) Effective January 1, 2011. Operative January 1, 2012, by Sec. 10 of Ch. 711.)

16824.

Use of the term "licensee's place of business" is governed by Section 16810.

(Added by Stats. 2010, Ch. 711, Sec. 6. (SB 1080) Effective January 1, 2011. Operative January 1, 2012, by Sec. 10 of Ch. 711.)

16830.

As used in this part, a "lipstick case knife" means a knife enclosed within and made an integral part of a lipstick case.

(Added by Stats. 2010, Ch. 711, Sec. 6. (SB 1080) Effective January 1, 2011. Operative January 1, 2012, by Sec. 10 of Ch. 711.)

16840.

(a) As used in Section 25800, a firearm shall be deemed to be "loaded" whenever both the firearm and the unexpended ammunition capable of being discharged from the firearm are in the immediate possession of the same person.

(b) As used in Chapter 2 (commencing with Section 25100) of Division 4 of Title 4, in subparagraph (A) of paragraph (6) of subdivision (c) of Section 25400, and in Sections 25850 to 26055, inclusive,

(1) A firearm shall be deemed to be "loaded" when there is an unexpended cartridge or shell, consisting of a case that holds a charge of powder and a bullet or shot, in, or attached in any manner to, the firearm, including, but not limited to, in the firing chamber, magazine, or clip thereof attached to the firearm.

(2) Notwithstanding paragraph (1), a muzzle-loader firearm shall be deemed to be loaded when it is capped or primed and has a powder charge and ball or shot in the barrel or cylinder.

(Added by Stats. 2010, Ch. 711, Sec. 6. (SB 1080) Effective January 1, 2011. Operative January 1, 2012, by Sec. 10 of Ch. 711.)

16850.

As used in this part, "locked container" means a secure container that is fully enclosed and locked by a padlock, keylock, combination lock, or similar locking device. The term "locked container" does not include the utility or glove compartment of a motor vehicle.

(Amended by Stats. 2014, Ch. 103, Sec. 5. (AB 1798) Effective January 1, 2015.)

16860.

As used in Sections 16850, 25105, and 25205, "locking device" means a device that is designed to prevent a firearm from functioning and, when applied to the firearm, renders the firearm inoperable.

(Added by Stats. 2010, Ch. 711, Sec. 6. (SB 1080) Effective January 1, 2011. Operative January 1, 2012, by Sec. 10 of Ch. 711.)

16865.

As used in Section 26860, "long gun" means any firearm that is not a handgun or a machinegun.

(Added by Stats. 2013, Ch. 761, Sec. 2. (SB 683) Effective January 1, 2014.)

16870.

As used in this part, "long-gun safe" means a locking container designed to fully contain and secure a rifle or shotgun, which has a locking system consisting of either a mechanical combination lock or an electronic combination lock that has at least 1,000 possible unique combinations consisting of a minimum of three numbers, letters, or

symbols per combination, and is not listed on the roster maintained pursuant to Section 23655.

(Added by Stats. 2010, Ch. 711, Sec. 6. (SB 1080) Effective January 1, 2011. Operative January 1, 2012, by Sec. 10 of Ch. 711.)

16880.

(a) As used in this part, "machinegun" means any weapon that shoots, is designed to shoot, or can readily be restored to shoot, automatically more than one shot, without manual reloading, by a single function of the trigger.

(b) The term "machinegun" also includes the frame or receiver of any weapon described in subdivision (a), any part designed and intended solely and exclusively, or combination of parts designed and intended, for use in converting a weapon into a machinegun, and any combination of parts from which a machinegun can be assembled if those parts are in the possession or under the control of a person.

(c) The term "machinegun" also includes any weapon deemed by the federal Bureau of Alcohol, Tobacco, Firearms and Explosives as readily convertible to a machinegun under Chapter 53 (commencing with Section 5801) of Title 26 of the United States Code.

(Amended by Stats. 2011, Ch. 296, Sec. 228. (AB 1023) Effective January 1, 2012.)

16890.

As used in Section 30515, "magazine" means any ammunition feeding device.

(Added by Stats. 2010, Ch. 711, Sec. 6. (SB 1080) Effective January 1, 2011. Operative January 1, 2012, by Sec. 10 of Ch. 711.)

16900.

As used in this part, "magazine disconnect mechanism" means a mechanism that prevents a semiautomatic pistol that has a detachable magazine from operating to strike the primer of ammunition in the firing chamber when a detachable magazine is not inserted in the semiautomatic pistol.

(Added by Stats. 2010, Ch. 711, Sec. 6. (SB 1080) Effective January 1, 2011. Operative January 1, 2012, by Sec. 10 of Ch. 711.)

16920.

As used in this part, "metal knuckles" means any device or instrument made wholly or partially of metal that is worn for purposes of offense or defense in or on the hand and that either protects the wearer's hand while striking a blow or increases the force of impact from the blow or injury to the individual receiving the blow. The metal contained in the device may help support the hand or fist, provide a shield to protect it, or consist of projections or studs which would contact the individual receiving a blow.

(Added by Stats. 2010, Ch. 711, Sec. 6. (SB 1080) Effective January 1, 2011. Operative January 1, 2012, by Sec. 10 of Ch. 711.)

16930.

(a) As used in this part, a "multiburst trigger activator" means either of the following:

(1) A device designed or redesigned to be attached to, built into, or used in conjunction with, a semiautomatic firearm, which allows the firearm to discharge two or more shots in a burst by activating the device.

(2) A manual or power-driven trigger activating device constructed and designed so that when attached to, built into, or used in conjunction with, a semiautomatic firearm it increases the rate of fire of that firearm.

(b) "Multiburst trigger activator" includes, but is not limited to, any of the following devices:

(1) A device that uses a spring, piston, or similar mechanism to push back against the recoil of a firearm, thereby moving the firearm in a back-and-forth motion and facilitating the rapid reset and activation of the trigger by a stationary finger. These devices are commonly known as bump stocks, bump fire stocks, or bump fire stock attachments.

(2) A device placed within the trigger guard of a firearm that uses a spring to push back against the recoil of the firearm causing the finger in the trigger guard to move back and forth and rapidly activate the trigger. These devices are commonly known as burst triggers.

(3) A mechanical device that activates the trigger of the firearm in rapid succession by turning a crank. These devices are commonly known as trigger cranks, gat cranks, gat triggers, or trigger actuators.

(4) Any aftermarket trigger or trigger system that, if installed, allows more than one round to be fired with a single depression of the trigger.

(Amended by Stats. 2018, Ch. 795, Sec. 1. (SB 1346) Effective January 1, 2019.)

16940.

As used in this part, "nunchaku" means an instrument consisting of two or more sticks, clubs, bars, or rods to be used as handles, connected by a rope, cord, wire, or chain, in the design of a weapon used in connection with the practice of a system of self-defense such as karate.

(Added by Stats. 2010, Ch. 711, Sec. 6. (SB 1080) Effective January 1, 2011. Operative January 1, 2012, by Sec. 10 of Ch. 711.)

16950.

As used in Chapter 6 (commencing with Section 26350) of Division 5 of Title 4, a handgun shall be deemed to be carried openly or exposed if the handgun is not carried concealed within the meaning of Section 25400.

(Added by Stats. 2011, Ch. 725, Sec. 7. (AB 144) Effective January 1, 2012.)

16960.

As used in Article 1 (commencing with Section 26500) of Chapter 1 of Division 6 of Title 4, "operation of law" includes, but is not limited to, any of the following:

(a) The executor or administrator of an estate, if the estate includes a firearm.

(b) A secured creditor or an agent or employee of a secured creditor when a firearm is possessed as collateral for, or as a result of, a default under a security agreement under the Commercial Code.

(c) A levying officer, as defined in Section 481.140, 511.060, or 680.260 of the Code of Civil Procedure.

(d) A receiver performing the functions of a receiver, if the receivership estate includes a firearm.

(e) A trustee in bankruptcy performing the duties of a trustee, if the bankruptcy estate includes a firearm.

(f) An assignee for the benefit of creditors performing the functions of an assignee, if the assignment includes a firearm.

(g) A transmutation of property between spouses pursuant to Section 850 of the Family Code.

(h) A firearm received by the family of a police officer or deputy sheriff from a local agency pursuant to Section 50081 of the Government Code.

(i) The transfer of a firearm by a law enforcement agency to the person who found the firearm where the delivery is to the person as the finder of the firearm pursuant to Article 1 (commencing with Section 2080) of Chapter 4 of Title 6 of Part 4 of Division 3 of the Civil Code.

(Added by Stats. 2010, Ch. 711, Sec. 6. (SB 1080) Effective January 1, 2011. Operative January 1, 2012, by Sec. 10 of Ch. 711.)

16965.

As used in this part, "passenger's or driver's area" means that part of a motor vehicle which is designed to carry the driver and passengers, including any interior compartment or space therein.

(Added by Stats. 2010, Ch. 711, Sec. 6. (SB 1080) Effective January 1, 2011. Operative January 1, 2012, by Sec. 10 of Ch. 711.)

16970.

(a) As used in Sections 16790, 17505, and 30600, "person" means an individual, partnership, corporation, limited liability company, association, or any other group or entity, regardless of how it was created.

(b) As used in Chapter 2 (commencing with Section 30500) of Division 10 of Title 4, except for Section 30600, "person" means an individual.
(Amended by Stats. 2014, Ch. 71, Sec. 134. (SB 1304) Effective January 1, 2015.)
16980.
Use of the term "person licensed pursuant to Sections 26700 to 26915, inclusive" is governed by Section 26700.
(Added by Stats. 2010, Ch. 711, Sec. 6. (SB 1080) Effective January 1, 2011. Operative January 1, 2012, by Sec. 10 of Ch. 711.)
16990.
As used in any provision listed in subdivision (a) of Section 16585, the phrase "a person taking title or possession of a firearm by operation of law" includes, but is not limited to, any of the following instances in which an individual receives title to, or possession of, a firearm:
(a) The executor or administrator of an estate, if the estate includes a firearm.
(b) A secured creditor or an agent or employee of a secured creditor when the firearm is possessed as collateral for, or as a result of, a default under a security agreement under the Commercial Code.
(c) A levying officer, as defined in Section 481.140, 511.060, or 680.260 of the Code of Civil Procedure.
(d) A receiver performing the functions of a receiver, if the receivership estate includes a firearm.
(e) A trustee in bankruptcy performing the duties of a trustee, if the bankruptcy estate includes a firearm.
(f) An assignee for the benefit of creditors performing the functions of an assignee, if the assignment includes a firearm.
(g) A transmutation of property consisting of a firearm pursuant to Section 850 of the Family Code.
(h) A firearm passing to a surviving spouse pursuant to Chapter 1 (commencing with Section 13500) of Part 2 of Division 8 of the Probate Code.
(i) A firearm received by the family of a police officer or deputy sheriff from a local agency pursuant to Section 50081 of the Government Code.
(j) The transfer of a firearm by a law enforcement agency to the person who found the firearm where the delivery is to the person as the finder of the firearm pursuant to Article 1 (commencing with Section 2080) of Chapter 4 of Division 3 of the Civil Code.
(Added by Stats. 2010, Ch. 711, Sec. 6. (SB 1080) Effective January 1, 2011. Operative January 1, 2012, by Sec. 10 of Ch. 711.)
17000.
(a) As used in this part, until January 1, 2014, any reference to the term "personal firearm importer" shall be deemed to mean "personal handgun importer" and, on and after January 1, 2014, any reference to the term "personal handgun importer" shall be deemed to mean "personal firearm importer." A "personal handgun importer," until January 1, 2014, and commencing January 1, 2014, a "personal firearm importer" means an individual who meets all of the following criteria:
(1) The individual is not a person licensed pursuant to Article 1 (commencing with Section 26700) and Article 2 (commencing with Section 26800) of Chapter 2 of Division 6 of Title 4.
(2) The individual is not a licensed manufacturer of firearms pursuant to Chapter 44 (commencing with Section 921) of Title 18 of the United States Code.
(3) The individual is not a licensed importer of firearms pursuant to Chapter 44 (commencing with Section 921) of Title 18 of the United States Code and the regulations issued pursuant thereto.
(4) The individual is the owner of a firearm.
(5) The individual acquired that firearm outside of California.
(6) The individual moved into this state on or after January 1, 1998, in the case of a handgun, or in the case of a firearm that is not a handgun, on or after January 1, 2014, as a resident of this state.
(7) The individual intends to possess that handgun within this state on or after January 1, 1998, or in the case of a firearm that is not a handgun, he or she intends to possess that firearm within this state on or after January 1, 2014.
(8) The firearm was not delivered to the individual by a person licensed pursuant to Article 1 (commencing with Section 26700) and Article 2 (commencing with Section 26800) of Chapter 2 of Division 6 of Title 4, who delivered that firearm following the procedures set forth in Section 27540 and Article 1 (commencing with Section 26700) and Article 2 (commencing with Section 26800) of Chapter 2 of Division 6 of Title 4.
(9) The individual, while a resident of this state, had not previously reported ownership of that firearm to the Department of Justice in a manner prescribed by the department that included information concerning the individual and a description of the firearm.
(10) The firearm is not a firearm that is prohibited by any provision listed in Section 16590.
(11) The firearm is not an assault weapon.
(12) The firearm is not a machinegun.
(13) The person is 18 years of age or older.
(14) The firearm is not a .50 BMG rifle.
(15) The firearm is not a destructive device.
(b) For purposes of paragraph (6) of subdivision (a):
(1) Except as provided in paragraph (2), residency shall be determined in the same manner as is the case for establishing residency pursuant to Section 12505 of the Vehicle Code.
(2) In the case of a member of the Armed Forces of the United States, residency shall be deemed to be established when the individual was discharged from active service in this state.
(Amended by Stats. 2011, Ch. 745, Sec. 3. (AB 809) Effective January 1, 2012.)
17010.
Use of the term "pistol" is governed by Section 16530.
(Added by Stats. 2010, Ch. 711, Sec. 6. (SB 1080) Effective January 1, 2011. Operative January 1, 2012, by Sec. 10 of Ch. 711.)
17020.
For purposes of this part, a city or county may be considered an applicant's "principal place of employment or business" only if the applicant is physically present in the jurisdiction during a substantial part of the applicant's working hours for purposes of that employment or business.
(Added by Stats. 2010, Ch. 711, Sec. 6. (SB 1080) Effective January 1, 2011. Operative January 1, 2012, by Sec. 10 of Ch. 711.)
17030.
As used in this part, "prohibited area" means any place where it is unlawful to discharge a weapon.
(Added by Stats. 2010, Ch. 711, Sec. 6. (SB 1080) Effective January 1, 2011. Operative January 1, 2012, by Sec. 10 of Ch. 711.)
17040.
As used in Chapter 6 (commencing with Section 26350) of Division 5 of Title 4, "public place" has the same meaning as in Section 25850.
(Added by Stats. 2011, Ch. 725, Sec. 8. (AB 144) Effective January 1, 2012.)
17060.
As used in Section 25135, "residence" means any structure intended or used for human habitation, including, but not limited to, houses, condominiums, rooms, motels, hotels, time-shares, and recreational or other vehicles where human habitation occurs.
(Added by Stats. 2013, Ch. 737, Sec. 5. (AB 500) Effective January 1, 2014.)
17070.

As used in this part, "responsible adult" means a person at least 21 years of age who is not prohibited by state or federal law from possessing, receiving, owning, or purchasing a firearm.
(Added by Stats. 2010, Ch. 711, Sec. 6. (SB 1080) Effective January 1, 2011. Operative January 1, 2012, by Sec. 10 of Ch. 711.)
17080.
Use of the term "revolver" is governed by Section 16530.
(Added by Stats. 2010, Ch. 711, Sec. 6. (SB 1080) Effective January 1, 2011. Operative January 1, 2012, by Sec. 10 of Ch. 711.)
17090.
As used in Sections 16530, 16640, 16650, 16660, 16870, and 17170, Sections 17720 to 17730, inclusive, Section 17740, subdivision (f) of Section 27555, Article 2 (commencing with Section 30300) of Chapter 1 of Division 10 of Title 4, and Article 1 (commencing with Section 33210) of Chapter 8 of Division 10 of Title 4, "rifle" means a weapon designed or redesigned, made or remade, and intended to be fired from the shoulder and designed or redesigned and made or remade to use the energy of the explosive in a fixed cartridge to fire only a single projectile through a rifled bore for each single pull of the trigger.
(Added by Stats. 2010, Ch. 711, Sec. 6. (SB 1080) Effective January 1, 2011. Operative January 1, 2012, by Sec. 10 of Ch. 711.)
17110.
As used in Section 26890, "secure facility" means a building that meets all of the following specifications:
(a) All perimeter doorways shall meet one of the following:
(1) A windowless steel security door equipped with both a dead bolt and a doorknob lock.
(2) A windowed metal door that is equipped with both a dead bolt and a doorknob lock. If the window has an opening of five inches or more measured in any direction, the window shall be covered with steel bars of at least one-half inch diameter or metal grating of at least nine gauge affixed to the exterior or interior of the door.
(3) A metal grate that is padlocked and affixed to the licensee's premises independent of the door and doorframe.
(b) All windows are covered with steel bars.
(c) Heating, ventilating, air-conditioning, and service openings are secured with steel bars, metal grating, or an alarm system.
(d) Any metal grates have spaces no larger than six inches wide measured in any direction.
(e) Any metal screens have spaces no larger than three inches wide measured in any direction.
(f) All steel bars shall be no further than six inches apart.
(Added by Stats. 2010, Ch. 711, Sec. 6. (SB 1080) Effective January 1, 2011. Operative January 1, 2012, by Sec. 10 of Ch. 711.)
17111.
For purposes of Chapter 2 (commencing with Section 29030) of Division 7 of Title 4, use of the term "secure facility" is governed by Sections 29141 and 29142.
(Added by Stats. 2010, Ch. 711, Sec. 6. (SB 1080) Effective January 1, 2011. Operative January 1, 2012, by Sec. 10 of Ch. 711.)
17125.
As used in this part, "Security Exemplar" has the same meaning as in Section 922 of Title 18 of the United States Code.
(Added by Stats. 2010, Ch. 711, Sec. 6. (SB 1080) Effective January 1, 2011. Operative January 1, 2012, by Sec. 10 of Ch. 711.)
17140.
As used in Sections 16900 and 31910, "semiautomatic pistol" means a pistol with an operating mode that uses the energy of the explosive in a fixed cartridge to extract a fired cartridge and chamber a fresh cartridge with each single pull of the trigger.
(Added by Stats. 2010, Ch. 711, Sec. 6. (SB 1080) Effective January 1, 2011. Operative January 1, 2012, by Sec. 10 of Ch. 711.)
17160.
As used in this part, a "shobi-zue" means a staff, crutch, stick, rod, or pole concealing a knife or blade within it, which may be exposed by a flip of the wrist or by a mechanical action.
(Added by Stats. 2010, Ch. 711, Sec. 6. (SB 1080) Effective January 1, 2011. Operative January 1, 2012, by Sec. 10 of Ch. 711.)
17170.
As used in this part, "short-barreled rifle" means any of the following:
(a) A rifle having a barrel or barrels of less than 16 inches in length.
(b) A rifle with an overall length of less than 26 inches.
(c) Any weapon made from a rifle (whether by alteration, modification, or otherwise) if that weapon, as modified, has an overall length of less than 26 inches or a barrel or barrels of less than 16 inches in length.
(d) Any device that may be readily restored to fire a fixed cartridge which, when so restored, is a device defined in subdivisions (a) to (c), inclusive.
(e) Any part, or combination of parts, designed and intended to convert a device into a device defined in subdivisions (a) to (c), inclusive, or any combination of parts from which a device defined in subdivisions (a) to (c), inclusive, may be readily assembled if those parts are in the possession or under the control of the same person.
(Amended by Stats. 2014, Ch. 103, Sec. 6. (AB 1798) Effective January 1, 2015.)
17180.
As used in this part, "short-barreled shotgun" means any of the following:
(a) A firearm that is designed or redesigned to fire a fixed shotgun shell and has a barrel or barrels of less than 18 inches in length.
(b) A firearm that has an overall length of less than 26 inches and that is designed or redesigned to fire a fixed shotgun shell.
(c) Any weapon made from a shotgun (whether by alteration, modification, or otherwise) if that weapon, as modified, has an overall length of less than 26 inches or a barrel or barrels of less than 18 inches in length.
(d) Any device that may be readily restored to fire a fixed shotgun shell which, when so restored, is a device defined in subdivisions (a) to (c), inclusive.
(e) Any part, or combination of parts, designed and intended to convert a device into a device defined in subdivisions (a) to (c), inclusive, or any combination of parts from which a device defined in subdivisions (a) to (c), inclusive, can be readily assembled if those parts are in the possession or under the control of the same person.
(Amended by Stats. 2014, Ch. 103, Sec. 7. (AB 1798) Effective January 1, 2015.)
17190.
As used in Sections 16530, 16640, 16870, and 17180, Sections 17720 to 17730, inclusive, Section 17740, Section 30215, and Article 1 (commencing with Section 33210) of Chapter 8 of Division 10 of Title 4, "shotgun" means a weapon designed or redesigned, made or remade, and intended to be fired from the shoulder and designed or redesigned and made or remade to use the energy of the explosive in a fixed shotgun shell to fire through a smooth bore either a number of projectiles (ball shot) or a single projectile for each pull of the trigger.
(Amended by Stats. 2014, Ch. 103, Sec. 8. (AB 1798) Effective January 1, 2015.)
17200.
As used in this part, a "shuriken" means any instrument, without handles, consisting of a metal plate having three or more radiating points with one or more sharp edges and designed in the shape of a polygon, trefoil, cross, star, diamond, or other geometric shape, for use as a weapon for throwing.

(Added by Stats. 2010, Ch. 711, Sec. 6. (SB 1080) Effective January 1, 2011. Operative January 1, 2012, by Sec. 10 of Ch. 711.)
17210.
As used in Chapter 9 (commencing with Section 33410) of Division 10 of Title 4, "silencer" means any device or attachment of any kind designed, used, or intended for use in silencing, diminishing, or muffling the report of a firearm. The term "silencer" also includes any combination of parts, designed or redesigned, and intended for use in assembling a silencer or fabricating a silencer and any part intended only for use in assembly or fabrication of a silencer.
(Added by Stats. 2010, Ch. 711, Sec. 6. (SB 1080) Effective January 1, 2011. Operative January 1, 2012, by Sec. 10 of Ch. 711.)
17220.
Use of the term "SKS rifle" is governed by Section 30710.
(Added by Stats. 2010, Ch. 711, Sec. 6. (SB 1080) Effective January 1, 2011. Operative January 1, 2012, by Sec. 10 of Ch. 711.)
17230.
As used in this part, "stun gun" means any item, except a less lethal weapon, used or intended to be used as either an offensive or defensive weapon that is capable of temporarily immobilizing a person by the infliction of an electrical charge.
(Added by Stats. 2010, Ch. 711, Sec. 6. (SB 1080) Effective January 1, 2011. Operative January 1, 2012, by Sec. 10 of Ch. 711.)
17235.
As used in this part, "switchblade knife" means a knife having the appearance of a pocketknife and includes a spring-blade knife, snap-blade knife, gravity knife, or any other similar type knife, the blade or blades of which are two or more inches in length and which can be released automatically by a flick of a button, pressure on the handle, flip of the wrist or other mechanical device, or is released by the weight of the blade or by any type of mechanism whatsoever. "Switchblade knife" does not include a knife that opens with one hand utilizing thumb pressure applied solely to the blade of the knife or a thumb stud attached to the blade, provided that the knife has a detent or other mechanism that provides resistance that must be overcome in opening the blade, or that biases the blade back toward its closed position.
(Added by Stats. 2010, Ch. 711, Sec. 6. (SB 1080) Effective January 1, 2011. Operative January 1, 2012, by Sec. 10 of Ch. 711.)
17240.
(a) As used in this part, "tear gas" applies to and includes any liquid, gaseous or solid substance intended to produce temporary physical discomfort or permanent injury through being vaporized or otherwise dispersed in the air.
(b) Notwithstanding subdivision (a), "tear gas" does not apply to, and does not include, any substance registered as an economic poison as provided in Chapter 2 (commencing with Section 12751) of Division 7 of the Food and Agricultural Code, provided that the substance is not intended to be used to produce discomfort or injury to human beings.
(Added by Stats. 2010, Ch. 711, Sec. 6. (SB 1080) Effective January 1, 2011. Operative January 1, 2012, by Sec. 10 of Ch. 711.)
17250.
As used in this part, "tear gas weapon" applies to and includes:
(a) Any shell, cartridge, or bomb capable of being discharged or exploded, when the discharge or explosion will cause or permit the release or emission of tear gas.
(b) Any revolver, pistol, fountain pen gun, billy, or other form of device, portable or fixed, intended for the projection or release of tear gas, except those regularly manufactured and sold for use with firearm ammunition.
(Added by Stats. 2010, Ch. 711, Sec. 6. (SB 1080) Effective January 1, 2011. Operative January 1, 2012, by Sec. 10 of Ch. 711.)
17270.
As used in this part, an "unconventional pistol" means a firearm with both of the following characteristics:
(a) It does not have a rifled bore.
(b) It has a barrel or barrels of less than 18 inches in length or has an overall length of less than 26 inches.
(Added by Stats. 2010, Ch. 711, Sec. 6. (SB 1080) Effective January 1, 2011. Operative January 1, 2012, by Sec. 10 of Ch. 711.)
17280.
As used in this part, "undetectable firearm" means any weapon that meets either of the following requirements:
(a) After removal of grips, stocks, and magazines, the weapon is not as detectable as the Security Exemplar, by a walk-through metal detector calibrated and operated to detect the Security Exemplar.
(b) Any major component of the weapon, as defined in Section 922 of Title 18 of the United States Code, when subjected to inspection by the types of X-ray machines commonly used at airports, does not generate an image that accurately depicts the shape of the component. Barium sulfate or other compounds may be used in the fabrication of the component.
(Added by Stats. 2010, Ch. 711, Sec. 6. (SB 1080) Effective January 1, 2011. Operative January 1, 2012, by Sec. 10 of Ch. 711.)
17290.
As used in this part, "undetectable knife" means any knife or other instrument, with or without a handguard, that satisfies all of the following requirements:
(a) It is capable of ready use as a stabbing weapon that may inflict great bodily injury or death.
(b) It is commercially manufactured to be used as a weapon.
(c) It is not detectable by a metal detector or magnetometer, either handheld or otherwise, which is set at standard calibration.
(Added by Stats. 2010, Ch. 711, Sec. 6. (SB 1080) Effective January 1, 2011. Operative January 1, 2012, by Sec. 10 of Ch. 711.)
17295.
(a) For purposes of Chapter 6 (commencing with Section 26350) of Division 5 of Title 4, a handgun shall be deemed "unloaded" if it is not "loaded" within the meaning of subdivision (b) of Section 16840.
(b) For purposes of Chapter 7 (commencing with Section 26400) of Division 5 of Title 4, a firearm that is not a handgun shall be deemed "unloaded" if it is not "loaded" within the meaning of subdivision (b) of Section 16840.
(Amended by Stats. 2012, Ch. 700, Sec. 8. (AB 1527) Effective January 1, 2013.)
17300.
Use of the phrase "unsafe handgun" is governed by Section 31910.
(Added by Stats. 2010, Ch. 711, Sec. 6. (SB 1080) Effective January 1, 2011. Operative January 1, 2012, by Sec. 10 of Ch. 711.)
17310.
As used in this part, "used firearm" means a firearm that has been sold previously at retail and is more than three years old.
(Added by Stats. 2010, Ch. 711, Sec. 6. (SB 1080) Effective January 1, 2011. Operative January 1, 2012, by Sec. 10 of Ch. 711.)
17315.
As used in Articles 2 through 5 of Chapter 1 of Division 10 of Title 4, "vendor" means an ammunition vendor.
(Amended November 8, 2016, by initiative Proposition 63, Sec. 8.4.)
17320.
For purposes of Section 31360 only, "violent felony" refers to the specific crimes listed in subdivision (c) of Section 667.5, and to crimes defined under the applicable laws of the United States or any other state, government, or country that are reasonably equivalent to the crimes listed in subdivision (c) of Section 667.5.
(Added by Stats. 2010, Ch. 711, Sec. 6. (SB 1080) Effective January 1, 2011. Operative January 1, 2012, by Sec. 10 of Ch. 711.)
17330.
As used in this part, "wallet gun" means any firearm mounted or enclosed in a case, resembling a wallet, designed to be or capable of being carried in a pocket or purse, if the firearm may be fired while mounted or enclosed in the case.
(Added by Stats. 2010, Ch. 711, Sec. 6. (SB 1080) Effective January 1, 2011. Operative January 1, 2012, by Sec. 10 of Ch. 711.)
17340.
(a) As used in this part, "wholesaler" means any person who is licensed as a dealer pursuant to Chapter 44 (commencing with Section 921) of Title 18 of the United States Code and the regulations issued pursuant thereto, who sells, transfers, or assigns firearms, or parts of firearms, to persons who are licensed as manufacturers, importers, or gunsmiths pursuant to Chapter 44 (commencing with Section 921) of Title 18 of the United States Code, or persons licensed pursuant to Sections 26700 to 26915, inclusive, and includes persons who receive finished parts of firearms and assemble them into completed or partially completed firearms in furtherance of that purpose.
(b) "Wholesaler" shall not include a manufacturer, importer, or gunsmith who is licensed to engage in those activities pursuant to Chapter 44 (commencing with Section 921) of Title 18 of the United States Code or a person licensed pursuant to Sections 26700 to 26915, inclusive, and the regulations issued pursuant thereto. A wholesaler also does not include a person dealing exclusively in grips, stocks, and other parts of firearms that are not frames or receivers thereof.
(Added by Stats. 2010, Ch. 711, Sec. 6. (SB 1080) Effective January 1, 2011. Operative January 1, 2012, by Sec. 10 of Ch. 711.)
17350.
As used in this part, "writing pen knife" means a device that appears to be a writing pen but has concealed within it a pointed, metallic shaft that is designed to be a stabbing instrument which is exposed by mechanical action or gravity which locks into place when extended or the pointed, metallic shaft is exposed by the removal of the cap or cover on the device.
(Added by Stats. 2010, Ch. 711, Sec. 6. (SB 1080) Effective January 1, 2011. Operative January 1, 2012, by Sec. 10 of Ch. 711.)
17360.
As used in this part, "zip gun" means any weapon or device that meets all of the following criteria:
(a) It was not imported as a firearm by an importer licensed pursuant to Chapter 44 (commencing with Section 921) of Title 18 of the United States Code and the regulations issued pursuant thereto.
(b) It was not originally designed to be a firearm by a manufacturer licensed pursuant to Chapter 44 (commencing with Section 921) of Title 18 of the United States Code and the regulations issued pursuant thereto.
(c) No tax was paid on the weapon or device nor was an exemption from paying tax on that weapon or device granted under Section 4181 and Subchapters F (commencing with Section 4216) and G (commencing with Section 4221) of Chapter 32 of Title 26 of the United States Code, as amended, and the regulations issued pursuant thereto.
(d) It is made or altered to expel a projectile by the force of an explosion or other form of combustion.
(Added by Stats. 2010, Ch. 711, Sec. 6. (SB 1080) Effective January 1, 2011. Operative January 1, 2012, by Sec. 10 of Ch. 711.)

TITLE 2. WEAPONS GENERALLY [17500 - 19405]

(Title 2 added by Stats. 2010, Ch. 711, Sec. 6.)

DIVISION 1. MISCELLANEOUS RULES RELATING TO WEAPONS GENERALLY [17500 - 17515]

(Division 1 added by Stats. 2010, Ch. 711, Sec. 6.)
17500.
Every person having upon the person any deadly weapon, with intent to assault another, is guilty of a misdemeanor.
(Added by Stats. 2010, Ch. 711, Sec. 6. (SB 1080) Effective January 1, 2011. Operative January 1, 2012, by Sec. 10 of Ch. 711.)
17505.
It shall be unlawful for any person, as defined in Section 16970, to advertise the sale of any weapon or device, the possession of which is prohibited by Section 18710, 20110, 30315, 30320, 32625, or 33410, by Article 2 (commencing with Section 30600) of Chapter 2 of Division 10 of Title 4, or by any provision listed in Section 16590, in any newspaper, magazine, circular, form letter, or open publication that is published, distributed, or circulated in this state, or on any billboard, card, label, or other advertising medium, or by means of any other advertising device.
(Added by Stats. 2010, Ch. 711, Sec. 6. (SB 1080) Effective January 1, 2011. Operative January 1, 2012, by Sec. 10 of Ch. 711.)
17510.
(a) Any person who does any of the following acts while engaged in picketing, or other informational activities in a public place relating to a concerted refusal to work, is guilty of a misdemeanor:
(1) Carries concealed upon the person, or within any vehicle which is under the person's control or direction, any pistol, revolver, or other firearm capable of being concealed upon the person.
(2) Carries a loaded firearm upon the person or within any vehicle that is under the person's control or direction.
(3) Carries a deadly weapon.
(b) This section shall not be construed to authorize or ratify any picketing or other informational activities not otherwise authorized by law.
(c) The following provisions shall not be construed to authorize any conduct described in paragraph (1) of subdivision (a):
(1) Article 2 (commencing with Section 25450) of Chapter 2 of Division 5 of Title 4.
(2) Sections 25615 to 25655, inclusive.
(d) Sections 25900 to 26020, inclusive, shall not be construed to authorize any conduct described in paragraph (2) of subdivision (a).
(Added by Stats. 2010, Ch. 711, Sec. 6. (SB 1080) Effective January 1, 2011. Operative January 1, 2012, by Sec. 10 of Ch. 711.)
17512.
It is a misdemeanor for a driver of any motor vehicle or the owner of any motor vehicle, whether or not the owner of the vehicle is occupying the vehicle, to knowingly permit any other person to carry into or bring into the vehicle a firearm in violation of Section 26350.
(Added by Stats. 2011, Ch. 725, Sec. 10. (AB 144) Effective January 1, 2012.)
17515.
Nothing in any provision listed in Section 16580 prohibits a police officer, special police officer, peace officer, or law enforcement officer from carrying any equipment authorized for the enforcement of law or ordinance in any city or county.

(Added by Stats. 2010, Ch. 711, Sec. 6. (SB 1080) Effective January 1, 2011. Operative January 1, 2012, by Sec. 10 of Ch. 711.)

CHAPTER 2. Miscellaneous Provisions [17800-17800.]

(Chapter 2 added by Stats. 2010, Ch. 711, Sec. 6.)
17800.
For purposes of the provisions listed in Section 16590, a violation as to each firearm, weapon, or device enumerated in any of those provisions shall constitute a distinct and separate offense.
(Added by Stats. 2010, Ch. 711, Sec. 6. (SB 1080) Effective January 1, 2011. Operative January 1, 2012, by Sec. 10 of Ch. 711.)

DIVISION 3. SURRENDER, DISPOSAL, AND ENJOINING OF WEAPONS CONSTITUTING A NUISANCE [18000 - 18010]

(Division 3 added by Stats. 2010, Ch. 711, Sec. 6.)
18000.
(a) Any weapon described in Section 19190, 21390, 21590, or 25700, or, upon conviction of the defendant or upon a juvenile court finding that an offense that would be a misdemeanor or felony if committed by an adult was committed or attempted by the juvenile with the use of a firearm, any weapon described in Section 29300, shall be surrendered to one of the following:
(1) The sheriff of a county.
(2) The chief of police or other head of a municipal police department of any city or city and county.
(3) The chief of police of any campus of the University of California or the California State University.
(4) The Commissioner of the California Highway Patrol.
(b) For purposes of this section, the Commissioner of the California Highway Patrol shall receive only weapons that were confiscated by a member of the California Highway Patrol.
(c) A finding that the defendant was guilty of the offense but was insane at the time the offense was committed is a conviction for the purposes of this section.
(Added by Stats. 2010, Ch. 711, Sec. 6. (SB 1080) Effective January 1, 2011. Operative January 1, 2012, by Sec. 10 of Ch. 711.)
18005.
(a) An officer to whom weapons are surrendered under Section 18000, except upon the certificate of a judge of a court of record, or of the district attorney of the county, that the retention thereof is necessary or proper to the ends of justice, may annually, between the 1st and 10th days of July, in each year, offer the weapons, which the officer in charge of them considers to have value with respect to sporting, recreational, or collection purposes, for sale at public auction to persons licensed pursuant to Sections 26700 to 26915, inclusive, to engage in businesses involving any weapon purchased.
(b) If any weapon has been stolen and is thereafter recovered from the thief or the thief's transferee, or is used in a manner as to constitute a nuisance under Section 19190, 21390, 21590, or 29300, or subdivision (a) of Section 25700 without the prior knowledge of its lawful owner that it would be so used, it shall not be offered for sale under subdivision (a) but shall be restored to the lawful owner, as soon as its use as evidence has been served, upon the lawful owner's identification of the weapon and proof of ownership, and after the law enforcement agency has complied with Chapter 2 (commencing with Section 33850) of Division 11 of Title 4.
(c) If, under this section, a weapon is not of the type that can be sold to the public, generally, or is not sold under subdivision (a), the weapon, in the month of July, next succeeding, or sooner, if necessary to conserve local resources, including space and utilization of personnel who maintain files and security of those weapons, shall be destroyed so that it can no longer be used as a weapon subject to surrender under Section 18000, except upon the certificate of a judge of a court of record, or of the district attorney of the county, that the retention of it is necessary or proper to the ends of justice.
(d) No stolen weapon shall be sold or destroyed pursuant to subdivision (a) or (c) unless reasonable notice is given to its lawful owner, if the lawful owner's identity and address can be reasonably ascertained.
(Added by Stats. 2010, Ch. 711, Sec. 6. (SB 1080) Effective January 1, 2011. Operative January 1, 2012, by Sec. 10 of Ch. 711.)
18010.
(a) The Attorney General, district attorney, or city attorney may bring an action to enjoin the manufacture of, importation of, keeping for sale of, offering or exposing for sale, giving, lending, or possession of, any item that constitutes a nuisance under any of the following provisions:
(1) Section 19290, relating to metal handgrenades.
(2) Section 20390, relating to an air gauge knife.
(3) Section 20490, relating to a belt buckle knife.
(4) Section 20590, relating to a cane sword.
(5) Section 20690, relating to a lipstick case knife.
(6) Section 20790, relating to a shobi-zue.
(7) Section 20990, relating to a writing pen knife.
(8) Section 21190, relating to a ballistic knife.
(9) Section 21890, relating to metal knuckles.
(10) Section 22090, relating to a nunchaku.
(11) Section 22290, relating to a leaded cane or an instrument or weapon of the kind commonly known as a billy, blackjack, sandbag, sandclub, sap, or slungshot.
(12) Section 22490, relating to a shuriken.
(13) Section 24390, relating to a camouflaging firearm container.
(14) Section 24490, relating to a cane gun.
(15) Section 24590, relating to a firearm not immediately recognizable as a firearm.
(16) Section 24690, relating to an undetectable firearm.
(17) Section 24790, relating to a wallet gun.
(18) Section 30290, relating to flechette dart ammunition and to a bullet with an explosive agent.
(19) Section 31590, relating to an unconventional pistol.
(20) Section 32390, relating to a large-capacity magazine.
(21) Section 32990, relating to a multiburst trigger activator.
(22) Section 33290, relating to a short-barreled rifle or a short-barreled shotgun.
(23) Section 33690, relating to a zip gun.
(b) These weapons shall be subject to confiscation and summary destruction whenever found within the state.
(c) These weapons shall be destroyed in the same manner described in Section 18005, except that upon the certification of a judge or of the district attorney that the ends of justice will be served thereby, the weapon shall be preserved until the necessity for its use ceases.
(Added by Stats. 2010, Ch. 711, Sec. 6. (SB 1080) Effective January 1, 2011. Operative January 1, 2012, by Sec. 10 of Ch. 711.)

DIVISION 3.2. Gun Violence Restraining Orders [18100 - 18205]

(Division 3.2 added by Stats. 2014, Ch. 872, Sec. 3.)

CHAPTER 1. General [18100 - 18122]

(Chapter 1 added by Stats. 2014, Ch. 872, Sec. 3.)
18100.
(a) A gun violence restraining order is an order, in writing, signed by the court, prohibiting and enjoining a named person from having in his or her custody or control, owning, purchasing, possessing, or receiving any firearms or ammunition. This division establishes a civil restraining order process to accomplish that purpose.
(b) For purposes of this chapter, the term "ammunition" includes a "magazine" as defined in Section 16890.
(Amended by Stats. 2018, Ch. 898, Sec. 3. (SB 1200) Effective January 1, 2019.)
18105.
The Judicial Council shall prescribe the form of the petitions and orders and any other documents, and shall promulgate any rules of court, necessary to implement this division. These forms, orders, and documents shall refer to any order issued pursuant to this chapter as a gun violence restraining order.
(Amended by Stats. 2018, Ch. 898, Sec. 4. (SB 1200) Effective January 1, 2019.)
18107.
A petition for a gun violence restraining order shall describe the number, types, and locations of any firearms and ammunition presently believed by the petitioner to be possessed or controlled by the subject of the petition.
(Added by Stats. 2014, Ch. 872, Sec. 3. (AB 1014) Effective January 1, 2015. Section operative January 1, 2016, pursuant to Section 18122.)
18109.
Nothing in this division shall be interpreted to require a law enforcement agency or a law enforcement officer to seek a gun violence restraining order in any case, including, but not limited to, in a case in which the agency or officer concludes, after investigation, that the criteria for issuance of a gun violence restraining order are not satisfied.
(Added by Stats. 2014, Ch. 872, Sec. 3. (AB 1014) Effective January 1, 2015. Section operative January 1, 2016, pursuant to Section 18122.)
18110.
Prior to a hearing on the issuance, renewal, or termination of an order under Chapter 3 (commencing with Section 18150) or Chapter 4 (commencing with Section 18170), the court shall ensure that a search as described in subdivision (a) of Section 6306 of the Family Code is conducted. After issuing its ruling, the court shall provide the advisement described in subdivision (c) of Section 6306 of the Family Code and shall keep information obtained from a search conducted pursuant to this section confidential in accordance with subdivision (d) of Section 6306 of the Family Code.
(Added by Stats. 2014, Ch. 872, Sec. 3. (AB 1014) Effective January 1, 2015. Section operative January 1, 2016, pursuant to Section 18122.)
18115.
(a) The court shall notify the Department of Justice when a gun violence restraining order has been issued or renewed under this division no later than one court day after issuing or renewing the order.
(b) The court shall notify the Department of Justice when a gun violence restraining order has been dissolved or terminated under this division no later than five court days after dissolving or terminating the order. Upon receipt of either a notice of dissolution or a notice of termination of a gun violence restraining order, the Department of Justice shall, within 15 days, document the updated status of any order issued under this division.
(c) The notices required to be submitted to the Department of Justice pursuant to this section shall be submitted in an electronic format, in a manner prescribed by the department.
(d) When notifying the Department of Justice pursuant to subdivision (a) or (b), the court shall indicate in the notice whether the person subject to the gun violence restraining order was present in court to be informed of the contents of the order or if the person failed to appear. The person's presence in court constitutes proof of service of notice of the terms of the order.
(e) (1) Within one business day of service, a law enforcement officer who served a gun violence restraining order shall submit the proof of service directly into the California Restraining and Protective Order System, including his or her name and law enforcement agency, and shall transmit the original proof of service form to the issuing court.
(2) Within one business day of receipt of proof of service by a person other than a law enforcement officer, the clerk of the court shall submit the proof of service of a gun violence restraining order directly into the California Restraining and Protective Order System, including the name of the person who served the order. If the court is unable to provide this notification to the Department of Justice by electronic transmission, the court shall, within one business day of receipt, transmit a copy of the proof of service to a local law enforcement agency. The local law enforcement agency shall submit the proof of service directly into the California Restraining and Protective Order System within one business day of receipt from the court.
(Amended by Stats. 2015, Ch. 303, Sec. 411. (AB 731) Effective January 1, 2016.)
18120.
(a) A person subject to a gun violence restraining order issued pursuant to this division shall not have in his or her custody or control, own, purchase, possess, or receive any firearms or ammunition while that order is in effect.
(b) (1) Upon issuance of a gun violence restraining order issued pursuant to this division, the court shall order the restrained person to surrender all firearms and ammunition in the restrained person's custody or control, or which the restrained person possesses or owns pursuant to paragraph (2).
(2) The surrender ordered pursuant to paragraph (1) shall occur by immediately surrendering all firearms and ammunition in a safe manner, upon request of any law enforcement officer, to the control of the officer, after being served with the restraining order. A law enforcement officer serving a gun violence restraining order that indicates that the restrained person possesses any firearms or ammunition shall request that all firearms and ammunition be immediately surrendered. Alternatively, if no request is made by a law enforcement officer, the surrender shall occur within 24 hours of being served with the order, by surrendering all firearms and ammunition in a safe manner to the control of the local law enforcement agency, selling all firearms and ammunition to a licensed firearms dealer, or transferring all firearms and ammunition to a licensed firearms dealer in accordance with Section 29830. The law enforcement officer or licensed firearms dealer taking possession of any firearms or ammunition pursuant to this subdivision shall issue a receipt to the person surrendering the firearm or firearms or ammunition or both at the time of surrender. A person ordered to surrender all firearms and ammunition pursuant to this subdivision shall, within 48 hours after being served with the order, do both of the following:
(A) File with the court that issued the gun violence restraining order the original receipt showing all firearms and ammunition have been surrendered to a local law enforcement agency or sold or transferred to a licensed firearms dealer. Failure to timely file a receipt shall constitute a violation of the restraining order.

(B) File a copy of the receipt described in subparagraph (A) with the law enforcement agency that served the gun violence restraining order. Failure to timely file a copy of the receipt shall constitute a violation of the restraining order.

(c) (1) Except as provided in paragraph (2), any firearms or ammunition surrendered to a law enforcement officer or law enforcement agency pursuant to this section shall be retained by the law enforcement agency until the expiration of any gun violence restraining order that has been issued against the restrained person. Upon expiration of any order, any firearms or ammunition shall be returned to the restrained person in accordance with the provisions of Chapter 2 (commencing with Section 33850) of Division 11 of Title 4. Firearms or ammunition that are not claimed are subject to the requirements of Section 34000.

(2) A restrained person who owns any firearms or ammunition that are in the custody of a law enforcement agency pursuant to this section is entitled to sell any firearms or ammunition to a licensed firearms dealer or transfer any firearms or ammunition to a licensed firearms dealer in accordance with Section 29830, provided that the firearm or firearms or ammunition are otherwise legal to own or possess and the restrained person otherwise has right to title of the firearm or firearms or ammunition.

(d) If a person other than the restrained person claims title to any firearms or ammunition surrendered pursuant to this section, and he or she is determined by the law enforcement agency to be the lawful owner of the firearm or firearms or ammunition, the firearm or firearms or ammunition shall be returned to him or her pursuant to Chapter 2 (commencing with Section 33850) of Division 11 of Title 4.

(e) Within one business day of receiving the receipt referred to in paragraph (2) of subdivision (b), the court that issued the order shall transmit a copy of the receipt to the Department of Justice in a manner and pursuant to a process prescribed by the department.
(Amended by Stats. 2018, Ch. 898, Sec. 5. (SB 1200) Effective January 1, 2019.)
18121.
There is no filing fee for an application, a responsive pleading, or an order to show cause that seeks to obtain, modify, or enforce a gun violence restraining order or other order authorized by this division if the request for the other order is necessary to obtain or give effect to a gun violence restraining order or other order authorized by this division. There is no fee for a subpoena filed in connection with that application, responsive pleading, or order to show cause.
(Added by Stats. 2018, Ch. 898, Sec. 6. (SB 1200) Effective January 1, 2019.)
18122.
This division shall become operative on January 1, 2016.
(Added by Stats. 2014, Ch. 872, Sec. 3. (AB 1014) Effective January 1, 2015. Note: This section prescribes a delayed operative date (Jan. 1, 2016) for Division 3.2, commencing with Section 18100.)

CHAPTER 2. Temporary Emergency Gun Violence Restraining Order [18125 - 18148]

(Chapter 2 added by Stats. 2014, Ch. 872, Sec. 3.)
18125.
(a) A temporary emergency gun violence restraining order may be issued on an ex parte basis only if a law enforcement officer asserts, and a judicial officer finds, that there is reasonable cause to believe both of the following:
(1) The subject of the petition poses an immediate and present danger of causing personal injury to himself, herself, or another by having in his or her custody or control, owning, purchasing, possessing, or receiving a firearm or ammunition.
(2) A temporary emergency gun violence restraining order is necessary to prevent personal injury to the subject of the petition or another because less restrictive alternatives either have been tried and found to be ineffective, or have been determined to be inadequate or inappropriate for the circumstances of the subject of the petition.
(b) A temporary emergency gun violence restraining order issued pursuant to this chapter shall prohibit the subject of the petition from having in his or her custody or control, owning, purchasing, possessing, or receiving, or attempting to purchase or receive, a firearm or ammunition, and shall expire 21 days from the date the order is issued.
(Amended by Stats. 2018, Ch. 898, Sec. 7. (SB 1200) Effective January 1, 2019.)
18130.
A temporary emergency gun violence restraining order is valid only if it is issued by a judicial officer after making the findings required by Section 18125 and pursuant to a specific request by a law enforcement officer.
(Added by Stats. 2014, Ch. 872, Sec. 3. (AB 1014) Effective January 1, 2015. Section operative January 1, 2016, pursuant to Section 18122.)
18135.
(a) A temporary emergency gun violence restraining order issued under this chapter shall include all of the following:
(1) A statement of the grounds supporting the issuance of the order.
(2) The date and time the order expires.
(3) The address of the superior court for the county in which the restrained party resides.
(4) The following statement:
"To the restrained person: This order will last until the date and time noted above. You are required to surrender all firearms, ammunition, and magazines that you own or possess in accordance with Section 18120 of the Penal Code and you may not have in your custody or control, own, purchase, possess, or receive, or attempt to purchase or receive any firearm, ammunition, or magazine while this order is in effect. However, a more permanent gun violence restraining order may be obtained from the court. You may seek the advice of an attorney as to any matter connected with the order. The attorney should be consulted promptly so that the attorney may assist you in any matter connected with the order."
(b) When serving a temporary emergency gun violence restraining order, a law enforcement officer shall verbally ask the restrained person if he or she has any firearm, ammunition, or magazine in his or her possession or under his or her custody or control.
(Amended by Stats. 2018, Ch. 898, Sec. 8. (SB 1200) Effective January 1, 2019.)
18140.
A law enforcement officer who requests a temporary emergency gun violence restraining order shall do all of the following:
(a) If the request is made orally, sign a declaration under penalty of perjury reciting the oral statements provided to the judicial officer and memorialize the order of the court on the form approved by the Judicial Council.
(b) Serve the order on the restrained person, if the restrained person can reasonably be located.
(c) File a copy of the order with the court as soon as practicable after issuance.
(d) Have the order entered into the computer database system for protective and restraining orders maintained by the Department of Justice.
(Amended by Stats. 2018, Ch. 873, Sec. 1. (AB 2526) Effective January 1, 2019.)
18145.
(a) (1) A judicial officer may issue a temporary emergency gun violence restraining order orally based on the statements of a law enforcement officer made in accordance with subdivision (a) of Section 18140.

(2) If time and circumstances permit, a temporary emergency gun violence restraining order may be obtained in writing and based on a declaration signed under penalty of perjury.
(b) The presiding judge of the superior court of each county shall designate at least one judge, commissioner, or referee who shall be reasonably available to issue temporary emergency gun violence restraining orders when the court is not in session.
(Amended by Stats. 2018, Ch. 873, Sec. 2. (AB 2526) Effective January 1, 2019.)
18148.
Within 21 days after the date on the order, the court that issued the order or another court in the same jurisdiction, shall hold a hearing pursuant to Section 18175 to determine if a gun violence restraining order should be issued pursuant to Chapter 4 (commencing with Section 18170) after notice and hearing.
(Added by Stats. 2018, Ch. 898, Sec. 9. (SB 1200) Effective January 1, 2019.)

CHAPTER 3. Ex Parte Gun Violence Restraining Order [18150 - 18165]

(Chapter 3 added by Stats. 2014, Ch. 872, Sec. 3.)
18150.
(a) (1) An immediate family member of a person or a law enforcement officer may file a petition requesting that the court issue an ex parte gun violence restraining order enjoining the subject of the petition from having in his or her custody or control, owning, purchasing, possessing, or receiving a firearm or ammunition.
(2) For purposes of this subdivision, "immediate family member" has the same meaning as in paragraph (3) of subdivision (b) of Section 422.4.
(b) A court may issue an ex parte gun violence restraining order if the petition, supported by an affidavit made in writing and signed by the petitioner under oath, or an oral statement taken pursuant to subdivision (a) of Section 18155, and any additional information provided to the court shows that there is a substantial likelihood that both of the following are true:
(1) The subject of the petition poses a significant danger, in the near future, of causing personal injury to himself, herself, or another by having in his or her custody or control, owning, purchasing, possessing, or receiving a firearm as determined by considering the factors listed in Section 18155.
(2) An ex parte gun violence restraining order is necessary to prevent personal injury to the subject of the petition or another because less restrictive alternatives either have been tried and found to be ineffective, or are inadequate or inappropriate for the circumstances of the subject of the petition.
(c) An affidavit supporting a petition for the issuance of an ex parte gun violence restraining order shall set forth the facts tending to establish the grounds of the petition, or the reason for believing that they exist.
(d) An ex parte order under this chapter shall be issued or denied on the same day that the petition is submitted to the court, unless the petition is filed too late in the day to permit effective review, in which case the order shall be issued or denied on the next day of judicial business in sufficient time for the order to be filed that day with the clerk of the court.
(Amended by Stats. 2015, Ch. 303, Sec. 412. (AB 731) Effective January 1, 2016.)
18155.
(a) (1) The court, before issuing an ex parte gun violence restraining order, shall examine on oath, the petitioner and any witness the petitioner may produce.
(2) In lieu of examining the petitioner and any witness the petitioner may produce, the court may require the petitioner and any witness to submit a written affidavit signed under oath.
(b) (1) In determining whether grounds for a gun violence restraining order exist, the court shall consider all evidence of the following:
(A) A recent threat of violence or act of violence by the subject of the petition directed toward another.
(B) A recent threat of violence or act of violence by the subject of the petition directed toward himself or herself.
(C) A violation of an emergency protective order issued pursuant to Section 646.91 or Part 3 (commencing with Section 6240) of Division 10 of the Family Code that is in effect at the time the court is considering the petition.
(D) A recent violation of an unexpired protective order issued pursuant to Part 4 (commencing with Section 6300) of Division 10 of the Family Code, Section 136.2, Section 527.6 of the Code of Civil Procedure, or Section 213.5 or 15657.03 of the Welfare and Institutions Code.
(E) A conviction for any offense listed in Section 29805.
(F) A pattern of violent acts or violent threats within the past 12 months, including, but not limited to, threats of violence or acts of violence by the subject of the petition directed toward himself, herself, or another.
(2) In determining whether grounds for a gun violence restraining order exist, the court may consider any other evidence of an increased risk for violence, including, but not limited to, evidence of any of the following:
(A) The unlawful and reckless use, display, or brandishing of a firearm by the subject of the petition.
(B) The history of use, attempted use, or threatened use of physical force by the subject of the petition against another person.
(C) A prior arrest of the subject of the petition for a felony offense.
(D) A history of a violation by the subject of the petition of an emergency protective order issued pursuant to Section 646.91 or Part 3 (commencing with Section 6240) of Division 10 of the Family Code.
(E) A history of a violation by the subject of the petition of a protective order issued pursuant to Part 4 (commencing with Section 6300) of Division 10 of the Family Code, Section 136.2, Section 527.6 of the Code of Civil Procedure, or Section 213.5 or 15657.03 of the Welfare and Institutions Code.
(F) Documentary evidence, including, but not limited to, police reports and records of convictions, of either recent criminal offenses by the subject of the petition that involve controlled substances or alcohol or ongoing abuse of controlled substances or alcohol by the subject of the petition.
(G) Evidence of recent acquisition of firearms, ammunition, or other deadly weapons.
(3) For the purposes of this subdivision, "recent" means within the six months prior to the date the petition was filed.
(c) If the court determines that the grounds to issue an ex parte gun violence restraining order exist, it shall issue an ex parte gun violence restraining order that prohibits the subject of the petition from having in his or her custody or control, owning, purchasing, possessing, or receiving, or attempting to purchase or receive, a firearm or ammunition, and expires no later than 21 days from the date of the order.
(Amended by Stats. 2015, Ch. 303, Sec. 413. (AB 731) Effective January 1, 2016.)
18160.
(a) An ex parte gun violence restraining order issued under this chapter shall include all of the following:
(1) A statement of the grounds supporting the issuance of the order.
(2) The date and time the order expires.
(3) The address of the superior court in which any responsive pleading should be filed.
(4) The date and time of the scheduled hearing.
(5) The following statement:

"To the restrained person: This order is valid until the expiration date and time noted above. You are required to surrender all firearms, ammunition, and magazines that you own or possess in accordance with Section 18120 of the Penal Code and you may not have in your custody or control, own, purchase, possess, or receive, or attempt to purchase or receive any firearm, ammunition, or magazine while this order is in effect. A hearing will be held on the date and at the time noted above to determine if a more permanent gun violence restraining order should be issued. Failure to appear at that hearing may result in a court making an order against you that is valid for a year. You may seek the advice of an attorney as to any matter connected with the order. The attorney should be consulted promptly so that the attorney may assist you in any matter connected with the order."

(b) (1) An ex parte gun violence restraining order shall be personally served on the restrained person by a law enforcement officer, or any person who is at least 18 years of age and not a party to the action, as provided in Section 414.10 of the Code of Civil Procedure, if the restrained person can reasonably be located.

(2) When serving a gun violence restraining order, a law enforcement officer shall inform the restrained person of the hearing scheduled pursuant to Section 18165.

(3) When serving a gun violence restraining order, a law enforcement officer shall verbally ask the restrained person if he or she has any firearm, ammunition, or magazine in his or her possession or under his or her custody or control.

(Amended by Stats. 2018, Ch. 898, Sec. 10. (SB 1200) Effective January 1, 2019.)

18165.

Within 21 days after the date on the order, before the court that issued the order or another court in the same jurisdiction, the court shall hold a hearing pursuant to Section 18175 to determine if a gun violence restraining order should be issued under Chapter 4 (commencing with Section 18170).

(Added by Stats. 2014, Ch. 872, Sec. 3. (AB 1014) Effective January 1, 2015. Section operative January 1, 2016, pursuant to Section 18122.)

CHAPTER 4. Gun Violence Restraining Order Issued After Notice and Hearing [18170 - 18197]

(Chapter 4 added by Stats. 2014, Ch. 872, Sec. 3.)

18170.

(a) An immediate family member of a person or a law enforcement officer may request that a court, after notice and a hearing, issue a gun violence restraining order enjoining the subject of the petition from having in his or her custody or control, owning, purchasing, possessing, or receiving a firearm or ammunition for a period of one year.

(b) For purposes of this subdivision, "immediate family member" has the same meaning as in paragraph (3) of subdivision (b) of Section 422.4.

(Added by Stats. 2014, Ch. 872, Sec. 3. (AB 1014) Effective January 1, 2015. Section operative January 1, 2016, pursuant to Section 18122.)

18175.

(a) In determining whether to issue a gun violence restraining order under this chapter, the court shall consider evidence of the facts identified in paragraph (1) of subdivision (b) of Section 18155 and may consider any other evidence of an increased risk for violence, including, but not limited to, evidence of the facts identified in paragraph (2) of subdivision (b) of Section 18155.

(b) At the hearing, the petitioner shall have the burden of proving, by clear and convincing evidence, that both of the following are true:

(1) The subject of the petition, or a person subject to an ex parte gun violence restraining order, as applicable, poses a significant danger of causing personal injury to himself, herself, or another by having in his or her custody or control, owning, purchasing, possessing, or receiving a firearm or ammunition.

(2) A gun violence restraining order is necessary to prevent personal injury to the subject of the petition, or the person subject to an ex parte gun violence restraining order, as applicable, or another because less restrictive alternatives either have been tried and found to be ineffective, or are inadequate or inappropriate for the circumstances of the subject of the petition, or the person subject to an ex parte gun violence restraining order, as applicable.

(c) (1) If the court finds that there is clear and convincing evidence to issue a gun violence restraining order, the court shall issue a gun violence restraining order that prohibits the subject of the petition from having in his or her custody or control, owning, purchasing, possessing, or receiving, or attempting to purchase or receive, a firearm or ammunition.

(2) If the court finds that there is not clear and convincing evidence to support the issuance of a gun violence restraining order, the court shall dissolve any temporary emergency or ex parte gun violence restraining order then in effect.

(d) A gun violence restraining order issued under this chapter has a duration of one year, subject to termination by further order of the court at a hearing held pursuant to Section 18185 and renewal by further order of the court pursuant to Section 18190.

(Amended by Stats. 2015, Ch. 303, Sec. 414. (AB 731) Effective January 1, 2016.)

18180.

(a) A gun violence restraining order issued pursuant to this chapter shall include all of the following:

(1) A statement of the grounds supporting the issuance of the order.

(2) The date and time the order expires.

(3) The address of the superior court for the county in which the restrained party resides.

(4) The following statement:

"To the restrained person: This order will last until the date and time noted above. If you have not done so already, you must surrender all firearms, ammunition, and magazines that you own or possess in accordance with Section 18120 of the Penal Code. You may not have in your custody or control, own, purchase, possess, or receive, or attempt to purchase or receive a firearm, ammunition, or magazine, while this order is in effect. Pursuant to Section 18185, you have the right to request one hearing to terminate this order at any time during its effective period. You may seek the advice of an attorney as to any matter connected with the order."

(b) When the court issues a gun violence restraining order under this chapter, the court shall inform the restrained person that he or she is entitled to one hearing to request a termination of the order, pursuant to Section 18185, and shall provide the restrained person with a form to request a hearing.

(Amended by Stats. 2018, Ch. 898, Sec. 11. (SB 1200) Effective January 1, 2019.)

18185.

(a) A person subject to a gun violence restraining order issued under this chapter may submit one written request at any time during the effective period of the order for a hearing to terminate the order.

(b) If the court finds after the hearing that there is no longer clear and convincing evidence to believe that paragraphs (1) and (2) of subdivision (b) of Section 18175 are true, the court shall terminate the order.

(Added by Stats. 2014, Ch. 872, Sec. 3. (AB 1014) Effective January 1, 2015. Section operative January 1, 2016, pursuant to Section 18122.)

18190.

(a) (1) An immediate family member of a restrained person or a law enforcement officer may request a renewal of a gun violence restraining order at any time within the three months before the expiration of a gun violence restraining order.

(2) For purposes of this subdivision, "immediate family member" has the same meaning as in paragraph (3) of subdivision (b) of Section 422.4.

(b) A court may, after notice and a hearing, renew a gun violence restraining order issued under this chapter if the petitioner proves, by clear and convincing evidence, that paragraphs (1) and (2) of subdivision (b) of Section 18175 continue to be true.

(c) In determining whether to renew a gun violence restraining order issued under this chapter, the court shall consider evidence of the facts identified in paragraph (1) of subdivision (b) of Section 18155 and any other evidence of an increased risk for violence, including, but not limited to, evidence of any of the facts identified in paragraph (2) of subdivision (b) of Section 18155.

(d) At the hearing, the petitioner shall have the burden of proving, by clear and convincing evidence, that paragraphs (1) and (2) of subdivision (b) of Section 18175 are true.

(e) If the renewal petition is supported by clear and convincing evidence, the court shall renew the gun violence restraining order issued under this chapter.

(f) The renewal of a gun violence restraining order issued pursuant to this section shall have a duration of one year, subject to termination by further order of the court at a hearing held pursuant to Section 18185 and further renewal by further order of the court pursuant to this section.

(g) A gun violence restraining order renewed pursuant to this section shall include the information identified in subdivision (a) of Section 18180.

(Added by Stats. 2014, Ch. 872, Sec. 3. (AB 1014) Effective January 1, 2015. Section operative January 1, 2016, pursuant to Section 18122.)

18195.

Any hearing held pursuant to this chapter may be continued upon a showing of good cause. Any existing order issued pursuant to this division shall remain in full force and effect during the period of continuance.

(Added by Stats. 2014, Ch. 872, Sec. 3. (AB 1014) Effective January 1, 2015. Section operative January 1, 2016, pursuant to Section 18122.)

18197.

If a person subject to a gun violence restraining order issued or renewed pursuant to this chapter was not present in court at the time the order was issued or renewed, the gun violence restraining order shall be personally served on the restrained person by a law enforcement officer or any person who is at least 18 years of age and not a party to the action, as provided in Section 414.10 of the Code of Civil Procedure, if the restrained person can reasonably be located.

(Added by Stats. 2014, Ch. 872, Sec. 3. (AB 1014) Effective January 1, 2015. Section operative January 1, 2016, pursuant to Section 18122.)

CHAPTER 5. Offenses [18200 - 18205]

(Chapter 5 added by Stats. 2014, Ch. 872, Sec. 3.)

18200.

Every person who files a petition for an ex parte gun violence restraining order pursuant to Chapter 3 (commencing with Section 18150) or a gun violence restraining order issued after notice and a hearing pursuant to Chapter 4 (commencing with Section 18170), knowing the information in the petition to be false or with the intent to harass, is guilty of a misdemeanor.

(Added by Stats. 2014, Ch. 872, Sec. 3. (AB 1014) Effective January 1, 2015. Section operative January 1, 2016, pursuant to Section 18122.)

18205.

Every person who owns or possesses a firearm or ammunition with knowledge that he or she is prohibited from doing so by a temporary emergency gun violence restraining order issued pursuant to Chapter 2 (commencing with Section 18125), an ex parte gun violence restraining order issued pursuant to Chapter 3 (commencing with Section 18150), or a gun violence restraining order issued after notice and a hearing issued pursuant to Chapter 4 (commencing with Section 18170), is guilty of a misdemeanor and shall be prohibited from having in his or her custody or control, owning, purchasing, possessing, or receiving, or attempting to purchase or receive, a firearm or ammunition for a five-year period, to commence upon the expiration of the existing gun violence restraining order.

(Added by Stats. 2014, Ch. 872, Sec. 3. (AB 1014) Effective January 1, 2015. Section operative January 1, 2016, pursuant to Section 18122.)

DIVISION 4. SEIZURE OF FIREARM OR OTHER DEADLY WEAPON AT SCENE OF DOMESTIC VIOLENCE [18250 - 18500]

(Division 4 added by Stats. 2010, Ch. 711, Sec. 6.)

CHAPTER 1. Seizure and Subsequent Procedures [18250 - 18275]

(Chapter 1 added by Stats. 2010, Ch. 711, Sec. 6.)

18250.

(a) If any of the following persons is at the scene of a domestic violence incident involving a threat to human life or a physical assault, is serving a protective order as defined in Section 6218 of the Family Code, or is serving a gun violence restraining order issued pursuant to Division 3.2 (commencing with Section 18100), that person shall take temporary custody of any firearm or other deadly weapon in plain sight or discovered pursuant to a consensual or other lawful search as necessary for the protection of the peace officer or other persons present:

(1) A sheriff, undersheriff, deputy sheriff, marshal, deputy marshal, or police officer of a city, as defined in subdivision (a) of Section 830.1.

(2) A peace officer of the Department of the California Highway Patrol, as defined in subdivision (a) of Section 830.2.

(3) A member of the University of California Police Department, as defined in subdivision (b) of Section 830.2.

(4) An officer listed in Section 830.6, while acting in the course and scope of the officer's employment as a peace officer.

(5) A member of a California State University Police Department, as defined in subdivision (c) of Section 830.2.

(6) A peace officer of the Department of Parks and Recreation, as defined in subdivision (f) of Section 830.2.

(7) A peace officer, as defined in subdivision (d) of Section 830.31.

(8) A peace officer, as defined in subdivisions (a) and (b) of Section 830.32.

(9) A peace officer, as defined in Section 830.5.

(10) A sworn member of the Department of Justice who is a peace officer, as defined in Section 830.1.

(11) A member of the San Francisco Bay Area Rapid Transit District Police Department, as defined in subdivision (a) of Section 830.33.

(b) This section shall become operative on January 1, 2016.

(Repealed (in Sec. 4.5) and added by Stats. 2014, Ch. 872, Sec. 5.5. (AB 1014) Effective January 1, 2015. Section operative January 1, 2016, by its own provisions.)
18255.
(a) Upon taking custody of a firearm or other deadly weapon pursuant to this division, the officer shall give the owner or person who possessed the firearm or other deadly weapon a receipt.

(b) The receipt shall describe the firearm or other deadly weapon and list any identification or serial number on the firearm.

(c) The receipt shall indicate where the firearm or other deadly weapon can be recovered, the time limit for recovery as required by this division, and the date after which the owner or possessor can recover the firearm or other deadly weapon.

(d) The receipt shall include the name and residential mailing address of the owner or person who possessed the firearm or other deadly weapon.

(Amended by Stats. 2018, Ch. 185, Sec. 1. (AB 2176) Effective January 1, 2019.)
18260.
Any peace officer, as defined in subdivisions (a) and (b) of Section 830.32, who takes custody of a firearm or other deadly weapon pursuant to this division, shall deliver the firearm or other deadly weapon within 24 hours to the city police department or county sheriff's office in the jurisdiction where the college or school is located.

(Amended by Stats. 2018, Ch. 185, Sec. 2. (AB 2176) Effective January 1, 2019.)
18265.
(a) No firearm or other deadly weapon taken into custody pursuant to this division shall be held less than 48 hours.

(b) Except as provided in Section 18400, if a firearm or other deadly weapon is not retained for use as evidence related to criminal charges brought as a result of the domestic violence incident or is not retained because it was illegally possessed, the firearm or other deadly weapon shall be made available to the owner or person who was in lawful possession 48 hours after the seizure, or as soon thereafter as possible, but no later than five business days after the owner or person who was in lawful possession demonstrates compliance with Chapter 2 (commencing with Section 33850) of Division 11 of Title 4.

(c) In any civil action or proceeding for the return of any firearm, ammunition, or other deadly weapon seized by any state or local law enforcement agency and not returned within five business days after the initial seizure, except as provided in Section 18270, the court shall allow reasonable attorney's fees to the prevailing party.

(Added by Stats. 2010, Ch. 711, Sec. 6. (SB 1080) Effective January 1, 2011. Operative January 1, 2012, by Sec. 10 of Ch. 711.)
18270.
If a firearm or other deadly weapon has been stolen and has been taken into custody pursuant to this division, it shall be restored to the lawful owner upon satisfaction of all of the following conditions:

(a) Its use for evidence has been served.

(b) The owner identifies the firearm or other deadly weapon and provides proof of ownership.

(c) The law enforcement agency has complied with Chapter 2 (commencing with Section 33850) of Division 11 of Title 4.

(Added by Stats. 2010, Ch. 711, Sec. 6. (SB 1080) Effective January 1, 2011. Operative January 1, 2012, by Sec. 10 of Ch. 711.)
18275.
(a) Any firearm or other deadly weapon that has been taken into custody and held by any of the following law enforcement authorities for longer than 12 months, and has not been recovered by the owner or person who had lawful possession at the time it was taken into custody, shall be considered a nuisance and sold or destroyed as provided in subdivisions (a) and (b) of Section 18000 and subdivisions (a) and (b) of Section 18005:

(1) A police, university police, or sheriff's department.

(2) A marshal's office.

(3) A peace officer of the Department of the California Highway Patrol, as defined in subdivision (a) of Section 830.2.

(4) A peace officer of the Department of Parks and Recreation, as defined in subdivision (f) of Section 830.2.

(5) A peace officer, as defined in subdivision (d) of Section 830.31.

(6) A peace officer, as defined in Section 830.5.

(b) If a firearm or other deadly weapon is not recovered within 12 months due to an extended hearing process as provided in Section 18420, it is not subject to destruction until the court issues a decision, and then only if the court does not order the return of the firearm or other deadly weapon to the owner.

(Added by Stats. 2010, Ch. 711, Sec. 6. (SB 1080) Effective January 1, 2011. Operative January 1, 2012, by Sec. 10 of Ch. 711.)

CHAPTER 2. Procedure Where Agency Believes Return of Weapon Would Create Danger [18400 - 18420]

(Chapter 2 added by Stats. 2010, Ch. 711, Sec. 6.)
18400.
(a) When a law enforcement agency has reasonable cause to believe that the return of a firearm or other deadly weapon seized under this division would be likely to result in endangering the victim or the person who reported the assault or threat, the agency shall so advise the owner of the firearm or other deadly weapon, and within 60 days of the date of seizure, initiate a petition in superior court to determine if the firearm or other deadly weapon should be returned.

(b) The law enforcement agency may make an ex parte application stating good cause for an order extending the time to file a petition.

(c) Including any extension of time granted in response to an ex parte request, a petition must be filed within 90 days of the date of seizure of the firearm or other deadly weapon.

(Added by Stats. 2010, Ch. 711, Sec. 6. (SB 1080) Effective January 1, 2011. Operative January 1, 2012, by Sec. 10 of Ch. 711.)
18405.
(a) If a petition is filed under Section 18400, the law enforcement agency shall inform the owner or person who had lawful possession of the firearm or other deadly weapon, at that person's last known address, by registered mail, return receipt requested, that the person has 30 days from the date of receipt of the notice to respond to the court clerk to confirm the person's desire for a hearing, and that the failure to respond shall result in a default order forfeiting the confiscated firearm or other deadly weapon.

(b) For purposes of this section, the person's last known address shall be presumed to be the address provided to the law enforcement officer by that person at the time of the domestic violence incident.

(c) In the event the person whose firearm or other deadly weapon was seized does not reside at the last address provided to the agency, the agency shall make a diligent, good faith effort to learn the whereabouts of the person and to comply with these notification requirements.

(Amended by Stats. 2018, Ch. 185, Sec. 3. (AB 2176) Effective January 1, 2019.)
18410.

(a) If the person who receives a petition under Section 18405 requests a hearing, the court clerk shall set a hearing no later than 30 days from receipt of that request.

(b) The court clerk shall notify the person, the law enforcement agency involved, and the district attorney of the date, time, and place of the hearing.

(c) Unless it is shown by a preponderance of the evidence that the return of the firearm or other deadly weapon would result in endangering the victim or the person reporting the assault or threat, the court shall order the return of the firearm or other deadly weapon and shall award reasonable attorney's fees to the prevailing party.

(Added by Stats. 2010, Ch. 711, Sec. 6. (SB 1080) Effective January 1, 2011. Operative January 1, 2012, by Sec. 10 of Ch. 711.)
18415.
If the person who receives a petition under Section 18405 does not request a hearing or does not otherwise respond within 30 days of the receipt of the notice, the law enforcement agency may file a petition for an order of default and may dispose of the firearm or other deadly weapon as provided in Sections 18000 and 18005.

(Added by Stats. 2010, Ch. 711, Sec. 6. (SB 1080) Effective January 1, 2011. Operative January 1, 2012, by Sec. 10 of Ch. 711.)
18420.
(a) If, at a hearing under Section 18410, the court does not order the return of the firearm or other deadly weapon to the owner or person who had lawful possession, that person may petition the court for a second hearing within 12 months from the date of the initial hearing.

(b) If there is a petition for a second hearing, unless it is shown by clear and convincing evidence that the return of the firearm or other deadly weapon would result in endangering the victim or the person reporting the assault or threat, the court shall order the return of the firearm or other deadly weapon and shall award reasonable attorney's fees to the prevailing party.

(c) If the owner or person who had lawful possession does not petition the court within this 12-month period for a second hearing or is unsuccessful at the second hearing in gaining return of the firearm or other deadly weapon, the firearm or other deadly weapon may be disposed of as provided in Sections 18000 and 18005.

(Added by Stats. 2010, Ch. 711, Sec. 6. (SB 1080) Effective January 1, 2011. Operative January 1, 2012, by Sec. 10 of Ch. 711.)

CHAPTER 3. Liability [18500- 18500.]

(Chapter 3 added by Stats. 2010, Ch. 711, Sec. 6.)
18500.
The law enforcement agency, or the individual law enforcement officer, shall not be liable for any act in the good faith exercise of this division.

(Added by Stats. 2010, Ch. 711, Sec. 6. (SB 1080) Effective January 1, 2011. Operative January 1, 2012, by Sec. 10 of Ch. 711.)

DIVISION 5. DESTRUCTIVE DEVICES, EXPLOSIVES, AND SIMILAR WEAPONS [18710 - 19290]

(Division 5 added by Stats. 2010, Ch. 711, Sec. 6.)

CHAPTER 1. Destructive Devices and Explosives Generally [18710 - 19000]

(Chapter 1 added by Stats. 2010, Ch. 711, Sec. 6.)
ARTICLE 1. Prohibited Acts [18710 - 18780]
(Article 1 added by Stats. 2010, Ch. 711, Sec. 6.)
18710.
(a) Except as provided by this chapter, any person, firm, or corporation who, within this state, possesses any destructive device, other than fixed ammunition of a caliber greater than .60 caliber, is guilty of a public offense.

(b) A person, firm, or corporation who is convicted of an offense under subdivision (a) shall be punished by imprisonment in the county jail for a term not to exceed one year, or in state prison, or by a fine not to exceed ten thousand dollars ($10,000), or by both this fine and imprisonment.

(Added by Stats. 2010, Ch. 711, Sec. 6. (SB 1080) Effective January 1, 2011. Operative January 1, 2012, by Sec. 10 of Ch. 711.)
18715.
(a) Every person who recklessly or maliciously has in possession any destructive device or any explosive in any of the following places is guilty of a felony:

(1) On a public street or highway.

(2) In or near any theater, hall, school, college, church, hotel, or other public building.

(3) In or near any private habitation.

(4) In, on, or near any aircraft, railway passenger train, car, cable road, cable car, or vessel engaged in carrying passengers for hire.

(5) In, on, or near any other public place ordinarily passed by human beings.

(b) An offense under subdivision (a) is punishable by imprisonment pursuant to subdivision (h) of Section 1170 for a period of two, four, or six years.

(Amended by Stats. 2011, Ch. 15, Sec. 531. (AB 109) Effective April 4, 2011. Amending action operative October 1, 2011, by Sec. 636 of Ch. 15, as amended by Stats. 2011, Ch. 39, Sec. 68. Section operative January 1, 2012, pursuant to Stats. 2010, Ch. 711, Sec. 10.)
18720.
Every person who possesses any substance, material, or any combination of substances or materials, with the intent to make any destructive device or any explosive without first obtaining a valid permit to make that destructive device or explosive, is guilty of a felony, and is punishable by imprisonment pursuant to subdivision (h) of Section 1170 for two, three, or four years.

(Amended by Stats. 2011, Ch. 15, Sec. 532. (AB 109) Effective April 4, 2011. Amending action operative October 1, 2011, by Sec. 636 of Ch. 15, as amended by Stats. 2011, Ch. 39, Sec. 68. Section operative January 1, 2012, pursuant to Stats. 2010, Ch. 711, Sec. 10.)
18725.
Every person who willfully does any of the following is guilty of a felony and is punishable by imprisonment pursuant to subdivision (h) of Section 1170 for two, four, or six years:

(a) Carries any destructive device or any explosive on any vessel, aircraft, car, or other vehicle that transports passengers for hire.

(b) While on board any vessel, aircraft, car, or other vehicle that transports passengers for hire, places or carries any destructive device or any explosive in any hand baggage, roll, or other container.

(c) Places any destructive device or any explosive in any baggage that is later checked with any common carrier.

(Amended by Stats. 2011, Ch. 15, Sec. 533. (AB 109) Effective April 4, 2011. Amending action operative October 1, 2011, by Sec. 636 of Ch. 15, as amended by

Stats. 2011, Ch. 39, Sec. 68. Section operative January 1, 2012, pursuant to Stats. 2010, Ch. 711, Sec. 10.)

18730.

Except as provided by this chapter, any person, firm, or corporation who, within this state, sells, offers for sale, or knowingly transports any destructive device, other than fixed ammunition of a caliber greater than .60 caliber, is guilty of a felony and is punishable by imprisonment pursuant to subdivision (h) of Section 1170 for two, three, or four years.

(Amended by Stats. 2011, Ch. 15, Sec. 534. (AB 109) Effective April 4, 2011. Amending action operative October 1, 2011, by Sec. 636 of Ch. 15, as amended by Stats. 2011, Ch. 39, Sec. 68. Section operative January 1, 2012, pursuant to Stats. 2010, Ch. 711, Sec. 10.)

18735.

(a) Except as provided by this chapter, any person, firm, or corporation who, within this state, sells, offers for sale, possesses or knowingly transports any fixed ammunition of a caliber greater than .60 caliber is guilty of a public offense.

(b) Upon conviction of an offense under subdivision (a), a person, firm, or corporation shall be punished by imprisonment in the county jail for a term not to exceed six months or by a fine not to exceed one thousand dollars ($1,000), or by both this fine and imprisonment.

(c) A second or subsequent conviction shall be punished by imprisonment in the county jail for a term not to exceed one year, or by imprisonment pursuant to subdivision (h) of Section 1170, or by a fine not to exceed three thousand dollars ($3,000), or by both this fine and imprisonment.

(Amended by Stats. 2011, Ch. 15, Sec. 535. (AB 109) Effective April 4, 2011. Amending action operative October 1, 2011, by Sec. 636 of Ch. 15, as amended by Stats. 2011, Ch. 39, Sec. 68. Section operative January 1, 2012, pursuant to Stats. 2010, Ch. 711, Sec. 10.)

18740.

Every person who possesses, explodes, ignites, or attempts to explode or ignite any destructive device or any explosive with intent to injure, intimidate, or terrify any person, or with intent to wrongfully injure or destroy any property, is guilty of a felony, and shall be punished by imprisonment pursuant to subdivision (h) of Section 1170 for a period of three, five, or seven years.

(Amended by Stats. 2011, Ch. 15, Sec. 536. (AB 109) Effective April 4, 2011. Amending action operative October 1, 2011, by Sec. 636 of Ch. 15, as amended by Stats. 2011, Ch. 39, Sec. 68. Section operative January 1, 2012, pursuant to Stats. 2010, Ch. 711, Sec. 10.)

18745.

Every person who explodes, ignites, or attempts to explode or ignite any destructive device or any explosive with intent to commit murder is guilty of a felony, and shall be punished by imprisonment in the state prison for life with the possibility of parole.

(Added by Stats. 2010, Ch. 711, Sec. 6. (SB 1080) Effective January 1, 2011. Operative January 1, 2012, by Sec. 10 of Ch. 711.)

18750.

Every person who willfully and maliciously explodes or ignites any destructive device or any explosive that causes bodily injury to any person is guilty of a felony, and shall be punished by imprisonment in the state prison for a period of five, seven, or nine years.

(Added by Stats. 2010, Ch. 711, Sec. 6. (SB 1080) Effective January 1, 2011. Operative January 1, 2012, by Sec. 10 of Ch. 711.)

18755.

(a) Every person who willfully and maliciously explodes or ignites any destructive device or any explosive that causes the death of any person is guilty of a felony, and shall be punished by imprisonment in the state prison for life without the possibility of parole.

(b) Every person who willfully and maliciously explodes or ignites any destructive device or any explosive that causes mayhem or great bodily injury to any person is guilty of a felony, and shall be punished by imprisonment in the state prison for life.

(Added by Stats. 2010, Ch. 711, Sec. 6. (SB 1080) Effective January 1, 2011. Operative January 1, 2012, by Sec. 10 of Ch. 711.)

18780.

A person convicted of a violation of this chapter shall not be granted probation, and the execution of the sentence imposed upon that person shall not be suspended by the court.

(Added by Stats. 2010, Ch. 711, Sec. 6. (SB 1080) Effective January 1, 2011. Operative January 1, 2012, by Sec. 10 of Ch. 711.)

ARTICLE 2. Exemptions [18800- 18800.]

(Article 2 added by Stats. 2010, Ch. 711, Sec. 6.)

18800.

(a) Nothing in this chapter prohibits the sale to, purchase by, or possession, transportation, storage, or use of, a destructive device or explosive by any of the following:

(1) Any peace officer listed in Section 830.1 or 830.2, or any peace officer in the Department of Justice authorized by the Attorney General, while on duty and acting within the scope and course of employment.

(2) Any member of the Army, Navy, Air Force, or Marine Corps of the United States, or the National Guard, while on duty and acting within the scope and course of employment.

(b) Nothing in this chapter prohibits the sale to, or the purchase, possession, transportation, storage, or use by any person who is a regularly employed and paid officer, employee, or member of a fire department or fire protection or firefighting agency of the federal government, the State of California, a city, county, city and county, district, or other public or municipal corporation or political subdivision of this state, while on duty and acting within the scope and course of employment, of any equipment used by that department or agency in the course of fire suppression.

(Added by Stats. 2010, Ch. 711, Sec. 6. (SB 1080) Effective January 1, 2011. Operative January 1, 2012, by Sec. 10 of Ch. 711.)

ARTICLE 3. Permit and Inspection [18900 - 18910]

(Article 3 added by Stats. 2010, Ch. 711, Sec. 6.)

18900.

(a) Every dealer, manufacturer, importer, and exporter of any destructive device, or any motion picture or television studio using destructive devices in the conduct of its business, shall obtain a permit for the conduct of that business from the Department of Justice.

(b) Any person, firm, or corporation not mentioned in subdivision (a) shall obtain a permit from the Department of Justice in order to possess or transport any destructive device. No permit shall be issued to any person who meets any of the following criteria:

(1) Has been convicted of any felony.

(2) Is addicted to the use of any narcotic drug.

(3) Is prohibited by state or federal law from possessing, receiving, owning, or purchasing a firearm.

(c) An application for a permit shall comply with all of the following:

(1) It shall be filed in writing.

(2) It shall be signed by the applicant if an individual, or by a member or officer qualified to sign if the applicant is a firm or corporation.

(3) It shall state the name, business in which engaged, business address, and a full description of the use to which the destructive devices are to be put.

(d) Applications and permits shall be uniform throughout the state on forms prescribed by the Department of Justice.

(Added by Stats. 2010, Ch. 711, Sec. 6. (SB 1080) Effective January 1, 2011. Operative January 1, 2012, by Sec. 10 of Ch. 711.)

18905.

(a) Each applicant for a permit under this article shall pay at the time of filing the application a fee not to exceed the application processing costs of the Department of Justice.

(b) A permit granted under this article may be renewed one year from the date of issuance, and annually thereafter, upon the filing of a renewal application and the payment of a permit renewal fee not to exceed the application processing costs of the Department of Justice.

(c) After the department establishes fees sufficient in amount to cover processing costs, the amount of the fees shall only increase at a rate not to exceed the legislatively approved cost-of-living adjustment for the department.

(Added by Stats. 2010, Ch. 711, Sec. 6. (SB 1080) Effective January 1, 2011. Operative January 1, 2012, by Sec. 10 of Ch. 711.)

18910.

(a) Except as provided in subdivision (b), the Department of Justice shall, for every person, firm, or corporation to whom a permit is issued under this article, annually conduct an inspection for security and safe storage purposes, and to reconcile the inventory of destructive devices.

(b) A person, firm, or corporation with an inventory of fewer than five devices that require any Department of Justice permit shall be subject to an inspection for security and safe storage purposes, and to reconcile inventory, once every five years, or more frequently if determined by the department.

(Added by Stats. 2010, Ch. 711, Sec. 6. (SB 1080) Effective January 1, 2011. Operative

/ARTICLE 4. Destructive Device Constituting Nuisance [19000- 19000.]

(Article 4 added by Stats. 2010, Ch. 711, Sec. 6.)

19000.

(a) Possession of any destructive device in violation of this chapter is a public nuisance.

(b) The Attorney General or district attorney of any city, county, or city and county may bring an action in the superior court to enjoin the possession of any destructive device.

(c) Any destructive device found to be in violation of this chapter shall be surrendered to the Department of Justice, or to the sheriff or chief of police, if the sheriff or chief of police has elected to perform the services required by this section. The department, sheriff, or chief of police shall destroy the destructive device so as to render it unusable and unrepairable as a destructive device, except upon the filing of a certificate with the department by a judge or district attorney stating that the preservation of the destructive device is necessary to serve the ends of justice.

(Added by Stats. 2010, Ch. 711, Sec. 6. (SB 1080) Effective January 1, 2011. Operative January 1, 2012, by Sec. 10 of Ch. 711.)

CHAPTER 2. Explosive Substance Other Than Fixed Ammunition [19100 - 19190]

(Chapter 2 added by Stats. 2010, Ch. 711, Sec. 6.)

19100.

Except as provided in Chapter 1 (commencing with Section 17700) of Division 2, any person in this state who carries concealed upon the person any explosive substance, other than fixed ammunition, is punishable by imprisonment in a county jail not exceeding one year or imprisonment pursuant to subdivision (h) of Section 1170.

(Amended by Stats. 2012, Ch. 43, Sec. 84. (SB 1023) Effective June 27, 2012.)

19190.

The unlawful concealed carrying upon the person of any explosive substance other than fixed ammunition, as provided in Section 19100, is a nuisance and is subject to Sections 18000 and 18005.

(Added by Stats. 2010, Ch. 711, Sec. 6. (SB 1080) Effective January 1, 2011. Operative January 1, 2012, by Sec. 10 of Ch. 711.)

CHAPTER 2. Explosive Substance Other Than Fixed Ammunition [19100 - 19190]

(Chapter 2 added by Stats. 2010, Ch. 711, Sec. 6.)
19100.
Except as provided in Chapter 1 (commencing with Section 17700) of Division 2, any person in this state who carries concealed upon the person any explosive substance, other than fixed ammunition, is punishable by imprisonment in a county jail not exceeding one year or imprisonment pursuant to subdivision (h) of Section 1170.
(Amended by Stats. 2012, Ch. 43, Sec. 84. (SB 1023) Effective June 27, 2012.)
19190.
The unlawful concealed carrying upon the person of any explosive substance other than fixed ammunition, as provided in Section 19100, is a nuisance and is subject to Sections 18000 and 18005.
(Added by Stats. 2010, Ch. 711, Sec. 6. (SB 1080) Effective January 1, 2011. Operative January 1, 2012, by Sec. 10 of Ch. 711.)

DIVISION 6. LESS LETHAL WEAPONS [19400 - 19405]

(Division 6 added by Stats. 2010, Ch. 711, Sec. 6.)

19400.

A person who is a peace officer or a custodial officer, as defined in Chapter 4.5 (commencing with Section 830) of Title 3 of Part 2, may, if authorized by and under the terms and conditions as are specified by the person's employing agency, purchase, possess, or transport any less lethal weapon or ammunition for any less lethal weapon, for official use in the discharge of the person's duties.

(Added by Stats. 2010, Ch. 711, Sec. 6. (SB 1080) Effective January 1, 2011. Operative January 1, 2012, by Sec. 10 of Ch. 711.)

19405.

Any person who sells a less lethal weapon to a person under the age of 18 years is guilty of a misdemeanor, punishable by imprisonment in the county jail for up to six months or by a fine of not more than one thousand dollars ($1,000), or by both that imprisonment and fine.

(Added by Stats. 2010, Ch. 711, Sec. 6. (SB 1080) Effective January 1, 2011. Operative January 1, 2012, by Sec. 10 of Ch. 711.)

DIVISION 3. BOOBYTRAP [20110- 20110.]

(Division 3 added by Stats. 2010, Ch. 711, Sec. 6.)

20110.

(a) Except as provided in Chapter 1 (commencing with Section 18710) of Division 5 of Title 2, any person who assembles, maintains, places, or causes to be placed a boobytrap device is guilty of a felony punishable by imprisonment pursuant to subdivision (h) of Section 1170 for two, three, or five years.

(b) Possession of any device with the intent to use the device as a boobytrap is punishable by imprisonment pursuant to subdivision (h) of Section 1170, or in a county jail not exceeding one year, or by a fine not exceeding five thousand dollars ($5,000), or by both that fine and imprisonment.
(Amended by Stats. 2012, Ch. 43, Sec. 86. (SB 1023) Effective June 27, 2012.)

DIVISION 4. IMITATION FIREARMS [20150 - 20180]

(Division 4 added by Stats. 2010, Ch. 711, Sec. 6.)

20150.
(a) Any person who changes, alters, removes, or obliterates any coloration or markings that are required by any applicable state or federal law or regulation, for any imitation firearm, or any device described in subdivision (b) of Section 16700, in a way that makes the imitation firearm or device look more like a firearm, is guilty of a misdemeanor.
(b) This section does not apply to a manufacturer, importer, or distributor of imitation firearms.
(c) This section does not apply to lawful use in theatrical productions, including motion pictures, television, and stage productions.
(Added by Stats. 2010, Ch. 711, Sec. 6. (SB 1080) Effective January 1, 2011. Operative January 1, 2012, by Sec. 10 of Ch. 711.)

20155.
Any manufacturer, importer, or distributor of toy, look-alike, or imitation firearms that fails to comply with any applicable federal law or regulation governing the marking of a toy, look-alike, or imitation firearm, is guilty of a misdemeanor. The definition of "imitation firearm" specified in Section 16700 does not apply to this section.
(Amended by Stats. 2018, Ch. 185, Sec. 4. (AB 2176) Effective January 1, 2019.)

20160.
(a) Any imitation firearm manufactured after July 1, 2005, shall, at the time of offer for sale in this state, be accompanied by a conspicuous advisory in writing as part of the packaging, but not necessarily affixed to the imitation firearm, to the effect that the product may be mistaken for a firearm by law enforcement officers or others, that altering the coloration or markings required by state or federal law or regulations so as to make the product look more like a firearm is dangerous, and may be a crime, and that brandishing or displaying the product in public may cause confusion and may be a crime.
(b) Any manufacturer, importer, or distributor that fails to comply with this advisory for any imitation firearm manufactured after July 1, 2005, shall be liable for a civil fine for each action brought by a city attorney or district attorney of not more than one thousand dollars ($1,000) for the first action, five thousand dollars ($5,000) for the second action, and ten thousand dollars ($10,000) for the third action and each subsequent action.
(Added by Stats. 2010, Ch. 711, Sec. 6. (SB 1080) Effective January 1, 2011. Operative January 1, 2012, by Sec. 10 of Ch. 711.)

20165.
(a) Any person who, for commercial purposes, purchases, sells, manufactures, ships, transports, distributes, or receives, by mail order or in any other manner, an imitation firearm, except as authorized by this section, is liable for a civil fine in an action brought by the city attorney or the district attorney of not more than ten thousand dollars ($10,000) for each violation.
(b) The manufacture, purchase, sale, shipping, transport, distribution, or receipt, by mail or in any other manner, of an imitation firearm is authorized if the device is manufactured, purchased, sold, shipped, transported, distributed, or received for any of the following purposes:
(1) Solely for export in interstate or foreign commerce.
(2) Solely for lawful use in theatrical productions, including motion picture, television, and stage productions.
(3) For use in a certified or regulated sporting event or competition.
(4) For use in military or civil defense activities, or ceremonial activities.
(5) For public displays authorized by public or private schools.
(Added by Stats. 2010, Ch. 711, Sec. 6. (SB 1080) Effective January 1, 2011. Operative January 1, 2012, by Sec. 10 of Ch. 711.)

20170.
(a) No person may openly display or expose any imitation firearm in a public place.
(b) As used in this section, "public place" means an area open to the public and includes any of the following:
(1) A street.
(2) A sidewalk.
(3) A bridge.
(4) An alley.
(5) A plaza.
(6) A park.
(7) A driveway.
(8) A front yard.
(9) A parking lot.
(10) An automobile, whether moving or not.
(11) A building open to the general public, including one that serves food or drink, or provides entertainment.
(12) A doorway or entrance to a building or dwelling.
(13) A public school.
(14) A public or private college or university.
(Added by Stats. 2010, Ch. 711, Sec. 6. (SB 1080) Effective January 1, 2011. Operative January 1, 2012, by Sec. 10 of Ch. 711.)

20175.
Section 20170 does not apply in any of the following circumstances:
(a) The imitation firearm is packaged or concealed so that it is not subject to public viewing.
(b) The imitation firearm is displayed or exposed in the course of commerce, including a commercial film or video production, or for service, repair, or restoration of the imitation firearm.
(c) The imitation firearm is used in a theatrical production, a motion picture, video, television, or stage production.
(d) The imitation firearm is used in conjunction with a certified or regulated sporting event or competition.
(e) The imitation firearm is used in conjunction with lawful hunting, or a lawful pest control activity.
(f) The imitation firearm is used or possessed at a certified or regulated public or private shooting range.
(g) The imitation firearm is used at a fair, exhibition, exposition, or other similar activity for which a permit has been obtained from a local or state government.
(h) The imitation firearm is used in a military, civil defense, or civic activity, including a flag ceremony, color guard, parade, award presentation, historical reenactment, or memorial.
(i) The imitation firearm is used for a public display authorized by a public or private school or a display that is part of a museum collection.
(j) The imitation firearm is used in a parade, ceremony, or other similar activity for which a permit has been obtained from a local or state government.
(k) The imitation firearm is displayed on a wall plaque or in a presentation case.
(l) The imitation firearm is used in an area where the discharge of a firearm is lawful.

(m) The entire exterior surface of the imitation firearm is white, bright red, bright orange, bright yellow, bright green, bright blue, bright pink, or bright purple, either singly or as the predominant color in combination with other colors in any pattern, or the entire device is constructed of transparent or translucent material that permits unmistakable observation of the device's complete contents. Merely having an orange tip as provided in federal law and regulations does not satisfy this requirement. The entire surface must be colored or transparent or translucent.
(Added by Stats. 2010, Ch. 711, Sec. 6. (SB 1080) Effective January 1, 2011. Operative January 1, 2012, by Sec. 10 of Ch. 711.)

20180.
(a) Except as provided in subdivision (b), violation of Section 20170 is an infraction punishable by a fine of one hundred dollars ($100) for the first offense, and three hundred dollars ($300) for a second offense.
(b) A third or subsequent violation of Section 20170 is punishable as a misdemeanor.
(c) Nothing in Section 20170, 20175, or this section shall be construed to preclude prosecution for a violation of Section 171b, 171.5, or 626.10.
(Added by Stats. 2010, Ch. 711, Sec. 6. (SB 1080) Effective January 1, 2011. Operative January 1, 2012, by Sec. 10 of Ch. 711.)

DIVISION 5. KNIVES AND SIMILAR WEAPONS [20200 - 21590]

(Division 5 added by Stats. 2010, Ch. 711, Sec. 6.)

CHAPTER 1. General Provisions [20200- 20200.]

(Chapter 1 added by Stats. 2010, Ch. 711, Sec. 6.)

20200.
A knife carried in a sheath that is worn openly suspended from the waist of the wearer is not concealed within the meaning of Section 16140, 16340, 17350, or 21310.
(Added by Stats. 2010, Ch. 711, Sec. 6. (SB 1080) Effective January 1, 2011. Operative January 1, 2012, by Sec. 10 of Ch. 711.)

CHAPTER 2. Disguised or Misleading Appearance [20310 - 20990]

(Chapter 2 added by Stats. 2010, Ch. 711, Sec. 6.)

ARTICLE 1. Air Gauge Knife [20310 - 20390]
(Article 1 added by Stats. 2010, Ch. 711, Sec. 6.)

20310.
Except as provided in Chapter 1 (commencing with Section 17700) of Division 2 of Title 2, any person in this state who manufactures or causes to be manufactured, imports into the state, keeps for sale, or offers or exposes for sale, or who gives, lends, or possesses any air gauge knife is punishable by imprisonment in a county jail not exceeding one year or imprisonment pursuant to subdivision (h) of Section 1170.
(Amended by Stats. 2012, Ch. 43, Sec. 87. (SB 1023) Effective June 27, 2012.)

20390.
Except as provided in Chapter 1 (commencing with Section 17700) of Division 2 of Title 2, any air gauge knife is a nuisance and is subject to Section 18010.
(Added by Stats. 2010, Ch. 711, Sec. 6. (SB 1080) Effective January 1, 2011. Operative Ja ### ARTICLE 2. Belt Buckle Knife [20410 - 20490]
(Article 2 added by Stats. 2010, Ch. 711, Sec. 6.)

20410.
Except as provided in Chapter 1 (commencing with Section 17700) of Division 2 of Title 2, any person in this state who manufactures or causes to be manufactured, imports into the state, keeps for sale, or offers or exposes for sale, or who gives, lends, or possesses any belt buckle knife is punishable by imprisonment in a county jail not exceeding one year or imprisonment pursuant to subdivision (h) of Section 1170.
(Amended by Stats. 2012, Ch. 43, Sec. 88. (SB 1023) Effective June 27, 2012.)

20490.
Except as provided in Chapter 1 (commencing with Section 17700) of Division 2 of Title 2, any belt buckle knife is a nuisance and is subject to Section 18010.
(Added by Stats. 2010, Ch. 711, Sec. 6. (SB 1080) Effective January 1, 2011. Operative January 1, 2012, by Sec. 10 of Ch. 711.)

ARTICLE 3. Cane Sword [20510 - 20590]
(Article 3 added by Stats. 2010, Ch. 711, Sec. 6.)

20510.
Except as provided in Chapter 1 (commencing with Section 17700) of Division 2 of Title 2, any person in this state who manufactures or causes to be manufactured, imports into the state, keeps for sale, or offers or exposes for sale, or who gives, lends, or possesses any cane sword is punishable by imprisonment in a county jail not exceeding one year or imprisonment pursuant to subdivision (h) of Section 1170.
(Amended by Stats. 2012, Ch. 43, Sec. 89. (SB 1023) Effective June 27, 2012.)

20590.
Except as provided in Chapter 1 (commencing with Section 17700) of Division 2 of Title 2, any cane sword is a nuisance and is subject to Section 18010.
(Added by Stats. 2010, Ch. 711, Sec. 6. (SB 1080) Effective January 1, 2011. Operative January 1, 2012, by Sec. 10 of Ch. 711.)

ARTICLE 4. Lipstick Case Knife [20610 - 20690]
(Article 4 added by Stats. 2010, Ch. 711, Sec. 6.)

20610.
Except as provided in Chapter 1 (commencing with Section 17700) of Division 2 of Title 2, any person in this state who manufactures or causes to be manufactured, imports into the state, keeps for sale, or offers or exposes for sale, or who gives, lends, or possesses any lipstick case knife is punishable by imprisonment in a county jail not exceeding one year or imprisonment pursuant to subdivision (h) of Section 1170.
(Amended by Stats. 2012, Ch. 43, Sec. 90. (SB 1023) Effective June 27, 2012.)

20690.
Except as provided in Chapter 1 (commencing with Section 17700) of Division 2 of Title 2, any lipstick case knife is a nuisance and is subject to Section 18010.
(Added by Stats. 2010, Ch. 711, Sec. 6. (SB 1080) Effective January 1, 2011. Operative January 1, 2012, by Sec. 10 of Ch. 711.)

ARTICLE 5. Shobi-zue [20710 - 20790]
(Article 5 added by Stats. 2010, Ch. 711, Sec. 6.)

20710.
Except as provided in Chapter 1 (commencing with Section 17700) of Division 2 of Title 2, any person in this state who manufactures or causes to be manufactured, imports into the state, keeps for sale, or offers or exposes for sale, or who gives, lends, or possesses any shobi-zue is punishable by imprisonment in a county jail not exceeding one year or imprisonment pursuant to subdivision (h) of Section 1170.
(Amended by Stats. 2012, Ch. 43, Sec. 91. (SB 1023) Effective June 27, 2012.)

20790.

Except as provided in Chapter 1 (commencing with Section 17700) of Division 2 of Title 2, any shobi-zue is a nuisance and is subject to Section 18010.
(Added by Stats. 2010, Ch. 711, Sec. 6. (SB 1080) Effective January 1, 2011. Operative January 1, 2012, by Sec. 10 of Ch. 711.)

ARTICLE 7. Writing Pen Knife [20910 - 20990]
(Article 7 added by Stats. 2010, Ch. 711, Sec. 6.)
20910.
Except as provided in Chapter 1 (commencing with Section 17700) of Division 2 of Title 2, any person in this state who manufactures or causes to be manufactured, imports into the state, keeps for sale, or offers or exposes for sale, or who gives, lends, or possesses any writing pen knife is punishable by imprisonment in a county jail not exceeding one year or imprisonment pursuant to subdivision (h) of Section 1170.
(Amended by Stats. 2012, Ch. 43, Sec. 92. (SB 1023) Effective June 27, 2012.)
20990.
Except as provided in Chapter 1 (commencing with Section 17700) of Division 2 of Title 2, any writing pen knife is a nuisance and is subject to Section 18010.
(Added by Stats. 2010, Ch. 711, Sec. 6. (SB 1080) Effective January 1, 2011. Operative January 1, 2012, by Sec. 10 of Ch. 711.)

CHAPTER 3. Ballistic Knife [21110 - 21190]

(Chapter 3 added by Stats. 2010, Ch. 711, Sec. 6.)
21110.
Except as provided in Chapter 1 (commencing with Section 17700) of Division 2 of Title 2, any person in this state who manufactures or causes to be manufactured, imports into the state, keeps for sale, or offers or exposes for sale, or who gives, lends, or possesses any ballistic knife is punishable by imprisonment in a county jail not exceeding one year or imprisonment pursuant to subdivision (h) of Section 1170.
(Amended by Stats. 2012, Ch. 43, Sec. 93. (SB 1023) Effective June 27, 2012.)
21190.
Except as provided in Chapter 1 (commencing with Section 17700) of Division 2 of Title 2, any ballistic knife is a nuisance and is subject to Section 18010.
(Added by Stats. 2010, Ch. 711, Sec. 6. (SB 1080) Effective January 1, 2011. Operative Januar CHAPTER 4. Dirk or Dagger [21310 - 21390]
(Chapter 4 added by Stats. 2010, Ch. 711, Sec. 6.)
21310.
Except as provided in Chapter 1 (commencing with Section 17700) of Division 2 of Title 2, any person in this state who carries concealed upon the person any dirk or dagger is punishable by imprisonment in a county jail not exceeding one year or imprisonment pursuant to subdivision (h) of Section 1170.
(Amended by Stats. 2012, Ch. 43, Sec. 94. (SB 1023) Effective June 27, 2012.)
21390.
The unlawful concealed carrying upon the person of any dirk or dagger, as provided in Section 21310, is a nuisance and is subject to Sections 18000 and 18005.
(Added by Stats. 2010, Ch. 711, Sec. 6. (SB 1080) Effective January 1, 2011. Operative January 1, 2012, by Sec. 10 of Ch. 711.)

CHAPTER 5. Switchblade Knife [21510 - 21590]

(Chapter 5 added by Stats. 2010, Ch. 711, Sec. 6.)
21510.
Every person who does any of the following with a switchblade knife having a blade two or more inches in length is guilty of a misdemeanor:
(a) Possesses the knife in the passenger's or driver's area of any motor vehicle in any public place or place open to the public.
(b) Carries the knife upon the person.
(c) Sells, offers for sale, exposes for sale, loans, transfers, or gives the knife to any other person.
(Added by Stats. 2010, Ch. 711, Sec. 6. (SB 1080) Effective January 1, 2011. Operative January 1, 2012, by Sec. 10 of Ch. 711.)
21590.
The unlawful possession or carrying of any switchblade knife, as provided in Section 21510, is a nuisance and is subject to Sections 18000 and 18005.
(Added by Stats. 2010, Ch. 711, Sec. 6. (SB 1080) Effective January 1, 2011. Operative January 1, 2012, by Sec. 10 of Ch. 711.)

CHAPTER 5. Switchblade Knife [21510 - 21590]

(Chapter 5 added by Stats. 2010, Ch. 711, Sec. 6.)
21510.
Every person who does any of the following with a switchblade knife having a blade two or more inches in length is guilty of a misdemeanor:
(a) Possesses the knife in the passenger's or driver's area of any motor vehicle in any public place or place open to the public.
(b) Carries the knife upon the person.
(c) Sells, offers for sale, exposes for sale, loans, transfers, or gives the knife to any other person.
(Added by Stats. 2010, Ch. 711, Sec. 6. (SB 1080) Effective January 1, 2011. Operative January 1, 2012, by Sec. 10 of Ch. 711.)
21590.
The unlawful possession or carrying of any switchblade knife, as provided in Section 21510, is a nuisance and is subject to Sections 18000 and 18005.
(Added by Stats. 2010, Ch. 711, Sec. 6. (SB 1080) Effective January 1, 2011. Operative January 1, 2012, by Sec. 10 of Ch. 711.)

CHAPTER 2. Metal Knuckles [21810 - 21890]

(Chapter 2 added by Stats. 2010, Ch. 711, Sec. 6.)
21810.
Except as provided in Chapter 1 (commencing with Section 17700) of Division 2 of Title 2, any person in this state who manufactures or causes to be manufactured, imports into the state, keeps for sale, or offers or exposes for sale, or who gives, lends, or possesses any metal knuckles is punishable by imprisonment in a county jail not exceeding one year or imprisonment pursuant to subdivision (h) of Section 1170.
(Amended by Stats. 2012, Ch. 43, Sec. 95. (SB 1023) Effective June 27, 2012.)
21890.
Except as provided in Chapter 1 (commencing with Section 17700) of Division 2 of Title 2, metal knuckles are a nuisance and are subject to Section 18010.

(Added by Stats. 2010, Ch. 711, Sec. 6. (SB 1080) Effective January 1, 2011. Operative January 1, 2012, by Sec. 10 of Ch. 711.)

DIVISION 7. NUNCHAKU [22010 - 22090]

(Division 7 added by Stats. 2010, Ch. 711, Sec. 6.)
22010.
Except as provided in Section 22015 and Chapter 1 (commencing with Section 17700) of Division 2 of Title 2, any person in this state who manufactures or causes to be manufactured, imports into the state, keeps for sale, or offers or exposes for sale, or who gives, lends, or possesses any nunchaku is punishable by imprisonment in a county jail not exceeding one year or imprisonment pursuant to subdivision (h) of Section 1170.
(Amended by Stats. 2012, Ch. 43, Sec. 96. (SB 1023) Effective June 27, 2012.)
22015.
Section 22010 does not apply to either of the following:
(a) The possession of a nunchaku on the premises of a school that holds a regulatory or business license and teaches the arts of self-defense.
(b) The manufacture of a nunchaku for sale to, or the sale of a nunchaku to, a school that holds a regulatory or business license and teaches the arts of self-defense.
(Added by Stats. 2010, Ch. 711, Sec. 6. (SB 1080) Effective January 1, 2011. Operative January 1, 2012, by Sec. 10 of Ch. 711.)
22090.
Except as provided in Section 22015 and in Chapter 1 (commencing with Section 17700) of Division 2 of Title 2, any nunchaku is a nuisance and is subject to Section 18010.
(Added by Stats. 2010, Ch. 711, Sec. 6. (SB 1080) Effective January 1, 2011. Operative January 1, 2012, by Sec. 10 of Ch. 711.)

DIVISION 8. SAPS AND SIMILAR WEAPONS [22210 - 22295]

(Division 8 added by Stats. 2010, Ch. 711, Sec. 6.)
22210.
Except as provided in Section 22215 and Chapter 1 (commencing with Section 17700) of Division 2 of Title 2, any person in this state who manufactures or causes to be manufactured, imports into the state, keeps for sale, or offers or exposes for sale, or who gives, lends, or possesses any leaded cane, or any instrument or weapon of the kind commonly known as a billy, blackjack, sandbag, sandclub, sap, or slungshot, is punishable by imprisonment in a county jail not exceeding one year or imprisonment pursuant to subdivision (h) of Section 1170.
(Amended by Stats. 2012, Ch. 43, Sec. 97. (SB 1023) Effective June 27, 2012.)
22215.
Section 22210 does not apply to the manufacture for, sale to, exposing or keeping for sale to, importation of, or lending of wooden clubs or batons to special police officers or uniformed security guards authorized to carry any wooden club or baton pursuant to Section 22295 by entities that are in the business of selling wooden clubs or batons to special police officers and uniformed security guards when engaging in transactions with those persons.
(Added by Stats. 2010, Ch. 711, Sec. 6. (SB 1080) Effective January 1, 2011. Operative January 1, 2012, by Sec. 10 of Ch. 711.)
22290.
Except as provided in Section 22215 and in Chapter 1 (commencing with Section 17700) of Division 2 of Title 2, any leaded cane or any instrument or weapon of the kind commonly known as a billy, blackjack, sandbag, sandclub, sap, or slungshot is a nuisance and is subject to Section 18010.
(Added by Stats. 2010, Ch. 711, Sec. 6. (SB 1080) Effective January 1, 2011. Operative January 1, 2012, by Sec. 10 of Ch. 711.)
22295.
(a) Nothing in any provision listed in Section 16580 prohibits any police officer, special police officer, peace officer, or law enforcement officer from carrying any wooden club or baton.
(b) Nothing in any provision listed in Section 16580 prohibits a uniformed security guard, regularly employed and compensated by a person engaged in any lawful business, while actually employed and engaged in protecting and preserving property or life within the scope of employment, from carrying any wooden club or baton if the uniformed security guard has satisfactorily completed a course of instruction certified by the Department of Consumer Affairs in the carrying and use of the club or baton. The training institution certified by the Department of Consumer Affairs to present this course, whether public or private, is authorized to charge a fee covering the cost of the training.
(c) The Department of Consumer Affairs, in cooperation with the Commission on Peace Officer Standards and Training, shall develop standards for a course in the carrying and use of a club or baton.
(d) Any uniformed security guard who successfully completes a course of instruction under this section is entitled to receive a permit to carry and use a club or baton within the scope of employment, issued by the Department of Consumer Affairs. The department may authorize a certified training institution to issue permits to carry and use a club or baton. A fee in the amount provided by law shall be charged by the Department of Consumer Affairs to offset the costs incurred by the department in course certification, quality control activities associated with the course, and issuance of the permit.
(e) Any person who has received a permit or certificate that indicates satisfactory completion of a club or baton training course approved by the Commission on Peace Officer Standards and Training prior to January 1, 1983, shall not be required to obtain a club or baton permit or complete a course certified by the Department of Consumer Affairs.
(f) Any person employed as a county sheriff's or police security officer, as defined in Section 831.4, shall not be required to obtain a club or baton permit or to complete a course certified by the Department of Consumer Affairs in the carrying and use of a club or baton, provided that the person completes a course approved by the Commission on Peace Officer Standards and Training in the carrying and use of the club or baton, within 90 days of employment.
(g) Nothing in any provision listed in Section 16580 prohibits an animal control officer, as described in Section 830.9, a humane officer, as described in paragraph (5) of subdivision (h) of Section 14502 of the Corporations Code, or an illegal dumping enforcement officer, as described in Section 830.7, from carrying any wooden club or baton if the animal control officer, humane officer, or illegal dumping enforcement officer has satisfactorily completed the course of instruction certified by the Commission on Peace Officer Standards and Training in the carrying and use of the club or baton. The training institution certified by the Commission on Peace Officer Standards and Training to present this course, whether public or private, is authorized to charge a fee covering the cost of the training.
(Amended by Stats. 2018, Ch. 20, Sec. 2. (AB 2349) Effective January 1, 2019.)

DIVISION 9. SHURIKEN [22410 - 22490]
(Division 9 added by Stats. 2010, Ch. 711, Sec. 6.)
22410.
Except as provided in Chapter 1 (commencing with Section 17700) of Division 2 of Title 2, any person in this state who manufactures or causes to be manufactured, imports into the state, keeps for sale, or offers or exposes for sale, or who gives, lends, or

possesses any shuriken is punishable by imprisonment in a county jail not exceeding one year or imprisonment pursuant to subdivision (h) of Section 1170.
(Amended by Stats. 2012, Ch. 43, Sec. 98. (SB 1023) Effective June 27, 2012.)
22490.
Except as provided in Chapter 1 (commencing with Section 17700) of Division 2 of Title 2, any shuriken is a nuisance and is subject to Section 18010.
(Added by Stats. 2010, Ch. 711, Sec. 6. (SB 1080) Effective January 1, 2011. Operative January 1, 2012, by Sec. 10 of Ch. 711.)

DIVISION 10. STUN GUN [22610 - 22625]

(Division 10 added by Stats. 2010, Ch. 711, Sec. 6.)
22610.
Notwithstanding any other provision of law, any person may purchase, possess, or use a stun gun, subject to the following requirements:
(a) No person convicted of a felony or any crime involving an assault under the laws of the United States, the State of California, or any other state, government, or country, or convicted of misuse of a stun gun under Section 244.5, shall purchase, possess, or use any stun gun.
(b) No person addicted to any narcotic drug shall purchase, possess, or use a stun gun.
(c) (1) No person shall sell or furnish any stun gun to a minor unless the minor is at least 16 years of age and has the written consent of the minor's parent or legal guardian.
(2) Violation of this subdivision shall be a public offense punishable by a fifty-dollar ($50) fine for the first offense. Any subsequent violation of this subdivision is a misdemeanor.
(d) No minor shall possess any stun gun unless the minor is at least 16 years of age and has the written consent of the minor's parent or legal guardian.
(Added by Stats. 2010, Ch. 711, Sec. 6. (SB 1080) Effective January 1, 2011. Operative January 1, 2012, by Sec. 10 of Ch. 711.)
22615.
Each stun gun sold shall contain both of the following:
(a) The name of the manufacturer stamped on the stun gun.
(b) The serial number applied by the manufacturer.
(Added by Stats. 2010, Ch. 711, Sec. 6. (SB 1080) Effective January 1, 2011. Operative January 1, 2012, by Sec. 10 of Ch. 711.)
22620.
Unless otherwise specified, any violation of this division is a misdemeanor.
(Added by Stats. 2010, Ch. 711, Sec. 6. (SB 1080) Effective January 1, 2011. Operative January 1, 2012, by Sec. 10 of Ch. 711.)
22625.
(a) Each stun gun sold in this state shall be accompanied by an instruction booklet.
(b) Violation of this section shall be a public offense punishable by a fifty-dollar ($50) fine for each weapon sold without the booklet.
(Added by Stats. 2010, Ch. 711, Sec. 6. (SB 1080) Effective January 1, 2011. Operative January 1, 2012, by Sec. 10 of Ch. 711.)

DIVISION 11. TEAR GAS AND TEAR GAS WEAPONS [22810 - 23025]

(Division 11 added by Stats. 2010, Ch. 711, Sec. 6.)

CHAPTER 1. General Provisions [22810 - 22840]

(Chapter 1 added by Stats. 2010, Ch. 711, Sec. 6.)
22810.
Notwithstanding any other provision of law, any person may purchase, possess, or use tear gas or any tear gas weapon for the projection or release of tear gas if the tear gas or tear gas weapon is used solely for self-defense purposes, subject to the following requirements:
(a) No person convicted of a felony or any crime involving an assault under the laws of the United States, the State of California, or any other state, government, or country, or convicted of misuse of tear gas under subdivision (g), shall purchase, possess, or use tear gas or any tear gas weapon.
(b) No person addicted to any narcotic drug shall purchase, possess, or use tear gas or any tear gas weapon.
(c) No person shall sell or furnish any tear gas or tear gas weapon to a minor.
(d) No minor shall purchase, possess, or use tear gas or any tear gas weapon.
(e) (1) No person shall purchase, possess, or use any tear gas weapon that expels a projectile, or that expels the tear gas by any method other than an aerosol spray, or that contains more than 2.5 ounces net weight of aerosol spray.
(2) Every tear gas container and tear gas weapon that may be lawfully purchased, possessed, and used pursuant to this section shall have a label that states: "WARNING: The use of this substance or device for any purpose other than self-defense is a crime under the law. The contents are dangerous — use with care."
(3) After January 1, 1984, every tear gas container and tear gas weapon that may be lawfully purchased, possessed, and used pursuant to this section shall have a label that discloses the date on which the useful life of the tear gas weapon expires.
(4) Every tear gas container and tear gas weapon that may be lawfully purchased pursuant to this section shall be accompanied at the time of purchase by printed instructions for use.
(f) Effective March 1, 1994, every tear gas container and tear gas weapon that may be lawfully purchased, possessed, and used pursuant to this section shall be accompanied by an insert including directions for use, first aid information, safety and storage information, and explanation of the legal ramifications of improper use of the tear gas container or tear gas product.
(g) (1) Except as provided in paragraph (2), any person who uses tear gas or any tear gas weapon except in self-defense is guilty of a public offense and is punishable by imprisonment pursuant to subdivision (h) of Section 1170 for 16 months, or two or three years or in a county jail not to exceed one year or by a fine not to exceed one thousand dollars ($1,000), or by both the fine and imprisonment.
(2) If the use is against a peace officer, as defined in Chapter 4.5 (commencing with Section 830) of Title 3 of Part 2, engaged in the performance of official duties and the person committing the offense knows or reasonably should know that the victim is a peace officer, the offense is punishable by imprisonment pursuant to subdivision (h) of Section 1170 for 16 months or two or three years or by a fine of one thousand dollars ($1,000), or by both the fine and imprisonment.
(Amended by Stats. 2011, Ch. 15, Sec. 538. (AB 109) Effective April 4, 2011. Amending action operative October 1, 2011, by Sec. 636 of Ch. 15, as amended by Stats. 2011, Ch. 39, Sec. 68. Section operative January 1, 2012, pursuant to Stats. 2010, Ch. 711, Sec. 10.)
22815.
(a) Notwithstanding subdivision (d) of Section 22810, a minor who has attained the age of 16 years may purchase and possess tear gas or a tear gas weapon pursuant to this division if the minor is accompanied by a parent or guardian, or has the written consent of a parent or guardian.
(b) Notwithstanding subdivision (c) of Section 22810, a person may sell or furnish tear gas or a tear gas weapon to a minor who has attained the age of 16 years and who is accompanied by a parent or guardian, or who presents a statement of consent signed by the minor's parent or guardian.
(c) Any civil liability of a minor arising out of the minor's use of tear gas or a tear gas weapon other than for self-defense is imposed upon the parent, guardian, or other person who authorized the provision of tear gas to a minor by signing a statement of consent or accompanying the minor, as specified in subdivision (b). That parent, guardian, or other person shall be jointly and severally liable with the minor for any damages proximately resulting from the negligent or wrongful act or omission of the minor in the use of the tear gas or a tear gas weapon.
(Amended by Stats. 2018, Ch. 185, Sec. 5. (AB 2176) Effective January 1, 2019.)
22820.
Nothing in this division prohibits any person who is a peace officer, as defined in Chapter 4.5 (commencing with Section 830) of Title 3 of Part 2, from purchasing, possessing, transporting, or using any tear gas or tear gas weapon if the person has satisfactorily completed a course of instruction approved by the Commission on Peace Officer Standards and Training in the use of tear gas.
(Added by Stats. 2010, Ch. 711, Sec. 6. (SB 1080) Effective January 1, 2011. Operative January 1, 2012, by Sec. 10 of Ch. 711.)
22825.
A custodial officer of a county may carry a tear gas weapon pursuant to Section 22820 only while on duty. A custodial officer of a county may carry a tear gas weapon while off duty only in accordance with all other laws.
(Added by Stats. 2010, Ch. 711, Sec. 6. (SB 1080) Effective January 1, 2011. Operative January 1, 2012, by Sec. 10 of Ch. 711.)
22830.
Nothing in this division prohibits any member of the military or naval forces of this state or of the United States or any federal law enforcement officer from purchasing, possessing, or transporting any tear gas or tear gas weapon for official use in the discharge of duties.
(Added by Stats. 2010, Ch. 711, Sec. 6. (SB 1080) Effective January 1, 2011. Operative January 1, 2012, by Sec. 10 of Ch. 711.)
22835.
Notwithstanding any other provision of law, a person holding a license as a private investigator pursuant to Chapter 11.3 (commencing with Section 7512) of Division 3 of the Business and Professions Code, or as a private patrol operator pursuant to Chapter 11.5 (commencing with Section 7580) of Division 3 of the Business and Professions Code, or a uniformed patrolperson employee of a private patrol operator, may purchase, possess, or transport any tear gas weapon, if it is used solely for defensive purposes in the course of the activity for which the license was issued and if the person has satisfactorily completed a course of instruction approved by the Department of Consumer Affairs in the use of tear gas.
(Added by Stats. 2010, Ch. 711, Sec. 6. (SB 1080) Effective January 1, 2011. Operative January 1, 2012, by Sec. 10 of Ch. 711.)
22840.
Nothing in this division authorizes the possession of tear gas or a tear gas weapon in any institution described in Section 4574, or within the grounds belonging or adjacent to any institution described in Section 4574, except where authorized by the person in charge of the institution.
(Added by Stats. 2010, Ch. 711, Sec. 6. (SB 1080) Effective January 1, 2011. Operative January 1, 2012, by Sec. 10 of Ch. 711.)

CHAPTER 2. Unlawful Possession, Sale, or Transportation [22900 - 22910]

(Chapter 2 added by Stats. 2010, Ch. 711, Sec. 6.)
22900.
Any person, firm, or corporation who within this state knowingly sells or offers for sale, possesses, or transports any tear gas or tear gas weapon, except as permitted under the provisions of this division, is guilty of a public offense and upon conviction thereof shall be punishable by imprisonment in the county jail for not exceeding one year or by a fine not to exceed two thousand dollars ($2,000), or by both that fine and imprisonment.
(Added by Stats. 2010, Ch. 711, Sec. 6. (SB 1080) Effective January 1, 2011. Operative January 1, 2012, by Sec. 10 of Ch. 711.)
22905.
Each tear gas weapon sold, transported, or possessed under the authority of this division shall bear the name of the manufacturer and a serial number applied by the manufacturer.
(Added by Stats. 2010, Ch. 711, Sec. 6. (SB 1080) Effective January 1, 2011. Operative January 1, 2012, by Sec. 10 of Ch. 711.)
22910.
(a) Any person who changes, alters, removes, or obliterates the name of the manufacturer, the serial number, or any other mark of identification on any tear gas weapon is guilty of a public offense and, upon conviction, shall be punished by imprisonment pursuant to subdivision (h) of Section 1170 or by a fine of not more than two thousand dollars ($2,000), or by both that fine and imprisonment.
(b) Possession of any such weapon upon which the same shall have been changed, altered, removed, or obliterated, shall be presumptive evidence that such possessor has changed, altered, removed, or obliterated the same.
(Amended by Stats. 2011, Ch. 15, Sec. 539. (AB 109) Effective April 4, 2011. Amending action operative October 1, 2011, by Sec. 636 of Ch. 15, as amended by Stats. 2011, Ch. 39, Sec. 68. Section operative January 1, 2012, pursuant to Stats. 2010, Ch. 711, Sec. 10.)

CHAPTER 3. Permits [23000 - 23025]

(Chapter 3 added by Stats. 2010, Ch. 711, Sec. 6.)
23000.
The Department of Justice may issue a permit for the possession and transportation of tear gas or a tear gas weapon that is not intended or certified for personal self-defense purposes, upon proof that good cause exists for issuance of the permit to the applicant. The permit may also allow the applicant to install, maintain, and operate a protective system involving the use of tear gas or a tear gas weapon in any place that is accurately and completely described in the permit application.
(Added by Stats. 2010, Ch. 711, Sec. 6. (SB 1080) Effective January 1, 2011. Operative January 1, 2012, by Sec. 10 of Ch. 711.)
23005.
(a) An application for a permit shall satisfy all of the following requirements:
(1) It shall be filed in writing.
(2) It shall be signed by the applicant if an individual, or by a member or officer qualified to sign if the applicant is a firm or corporation.

(3) It shall state the applicant's name, business in which engaged, business address, and a full description of the place or vehicle in which the tear gas or tear gas weapon is to be transported, kept, installed, or maintained.

(b) If the tear gas or tear gas weapon is to be used in connection with, or to constitute, a protective system, the application shall also contain the name of the person who is to install the protective system.

(c) Applications and permits shall be uniform throughout the state upon forms prescribed by the Department of Justice.

(Added by Stats. 2010, Ch. 711, Sec. 6. (SB 1080) Effective January 1, 2011. Operative January 1, 2012, by Sec. 10 of Ch. 711.)

23010.

(a) Each applicant for a permit shall pay, at the time of filing the application, a fee determined by the Department of Justice, not to exceed the application processing costs of the Department of Justice.

(b) A permit granted pursuant to this chapter may be renewed one year from the date of issuance, and annually thereafter, upon the filing of a renewal application and the payment of a permit renewal fee, not to exceed the application processing costs of the Department of Justice.

(c) After the department establishes fees sufficient to reimburse the department for processing costs, fees charged shall increase at a rate not to exceed the legislatively approved annual cost-of-living adjustments for the department's budget.

(Added by Stats. 2010, Ch. 711, Sec. 6. (SB 1080) Effective January 1, 2011. Operative January 1, 2012, by Sec. 10 of Ch. 711.)

23015.

(a) Notwithstanding Section 23000, a bank, a savings and loan association, a credit union, or an industrial loan company that maintains more than one office or branch may make a single annual application for a permit.

(b) In addition to the requirements set forth in this chapter, an application under this section shall separately state the business address and a full description of each office or branch in which the tear gas or tear gas weapon is to be kept, installed, or maintained. Any location addition or deletion as to an office or branch shall be reported to the department within 60 days of the change.

(c) A single permit issued under this section shall allow for the possession, operation, and maintenance of tear gas at each office or branch named in the application, including any location change.

(Added by Stats. 2010, Ch. 711, Sec. 6. (SB 1080) Effective January 1, 2011. Operative January 1, 2012, by Sec. 10 of Ch. 711.)

23020.

Every person, firm, or corporation to whom a permit is issued shall either carry the permit upon the person or keep it in the place described in the permit. The permit shall be open to inspection by any peace officer or other person designated by the authority issuing the permit.

(Added by Stats. 2010, Ch. 711, Sec. 6. (SB 1080) Effective January 1, 2011. Operative January 1, 2012, by Sec. 10 of Ch. 711.)

23025.

A permit issued in accordance with this chapter may be revoked or suspended by the issuing authority at any time when it appears that the need for the possession or transportation of the tear gas or tear gas weapon or protective system involving the use thereof, has ceased, or that the holder of the permit has engaged in an unlawful business or occupation or has wrongfully made use of the tear gas or tear gas weapon or the permit issued.

(Added by Stats. 2010, Ch. 711, Sec. 6. (SB 1080) Effective January 1, 2011. Operative January 1, 2012, by Sec. 10 of Ch. 711.)

TITLE 4. FIREARMS [23500 - 34370]

(Title 4 added by Stats. 2010, Ch. 711, Sec. 6.)

DIVISION 1. PRELIMINARY PROVISIONS [23500 - 23520]

(Division 1 added by Stats. 2010, Ch. 711, Sec. 6.)

23500.

The provisions listed in Section 16580 shall be known and may be cited as "The Dangerous Weapons Control Law."

(Added by Stats. 2010, Ch. 711, Sec. 6. (SB 1080) Effective January 1, 2011. Operative January 1, 2012, by Sec. 10 of Ch. 711.)

23505.

If any section, subdivision, paragraph, subparagraph, sentence, clause, or phrase of any provision listed in Section 16580 is for any reason held unconstitutional, that decision does not affect the validity of any other provision listed in Section 16580. The Legislature hereby declares that it would have passed the provisions listed in Section 16580 and each section, subdivision, paragraph, subparagraph, sentence, clause, and phrase of those provisions, irrespective of the fact that any one or more other sections, subdivisions, paragraphs, subparagraphs, sentences, clauses, or phrases be declared unconstitutional.

(Amended by Stats. 2011, Ch. 285, Sec. 25. (AB 1402) Effective January 1, 2012.)

23510.

(a) For purposes of Sections 25400 and 26500, Sections 27500 to 27590, inclusive, Section 28100, Sections 29610 to 29750, inclusive, Sections 29800 to 29905, inclusive, and Section 31615 of this code, and any provision listed in subdivision (a) of Section 16585 of this code, and Sections 8100, 8101, and 8103 of the Welfare and Institutions Code, notwithstanding the fact that the term "any firearm" may be used in those sections, each firearm or the frame or receiver of each firearm constitutes a distinct and separate offense under those sections.

(b) For purposes of Section 25135, notwithstanding the fact that the term "any firearm" may be used in that section, each firearm constitutes a distinct and separate offense under that section.

(Amended by Stats. 2013, Ch. 737, Sec. 6. (AB 500) Effective January 1, 2014.)

23515.

As used in the provisions listed in Section 16580, an offense that involves the violent use of a firearm includes any of the following:

(a) A violation of paragraph (2) or (3) of subdivision (a) of Section 245 or a violation of subdivision (d) of Section 245.

(b) A violation of Section 246.

(c) A violation of paragraph (2) of subdivision (a) of Section 417.

(d) A violation of subdivision (c) of Section 417.

(Added by Stats. 2010, Ch. 711, Sec. 6. (SB 1080) Effective January 1, 2011. Operative January 1, 2012, by Sec. 10 of Ch. 711.)

23520.

Each application that requires any firearms eligibility determination involving the issuance of any license, permit, or certificate pursuant to this part shall include two copies of the applicant's fingerprints on forms prescribed by the Department of Justice. One copy of the fingerprints may be submitted to the United States Federal Bureau of Investigation.

(Added by Stats. 2010, Ch. 711, Sec. 6. (SB 1080) Effective January 1, 2011. Operative January 1, 2012, by Sec. 10 of Ch. 711.)

DIVISION 2. FIREARM SAFETY DEVICES, GUN SAFES, AND RELATED WARNINGS [23620 - 23690]

(Division 2 added by Stats. 2010, Ch. 711, Sec. 6.)

23620.

This division and Sections 16540, 16610, and 16870 shall be known and may be cited as the "Aroner-Scott-Hayden Firearms Safety Act of 1999."

(Added by Stats. 2010, Ch. 711, Sec. 6. (SB 1080) Effective January 1, 2011. Operative January 1, 2012, by Sec. 10 of Ch. 711.)

23625.

The Legislature makes the following findings:

(a) In the years 1987 to 1996, nearly 2,200 children in the United States under the age of 15 years died in unintentional shootings. In 1996 alone, 138 children were shot and killed unintentionally. Thus, more than 11 children every month, or one child every three days, were shot or killed unintentionally in firearms-related incidents.

(b) The United States leads the industrialized world in the rates of children and youth lost to unintentional, firearms-related deaths. A 1997 study from the federal Centers for Disease Control and Prevention reveals that for unintentional firearm-related deaths for children under the age of 15, the rate in the United States was nine times higher than in 25 other industrialized countries combined.

(c) While the number of unintentional deaths from firearms is an unacceptable toll on America's children, nearly eight times that number are treated in U.S. hospital emergency rooms each year for nonfatal unintentional gunshot wounds.

(d) A study of unintentional firearm deaths among children in California found that unintentional gunshot wounds most often involve handguns.

(e) A study in the December 1995 issue of the Archives of Pediatric and Adolescent Medicine found that children as young as three years old are strong enough to fire most commercially available handguns. The study revealed that 25 percent of three to four year olds and 70 percent of five to six year olds had sufficient finger strength to fire 59 (92 percent) of the 64 commonly available handguns referenced in the study.

(f) The Government Accounting Office (GAO), in its March 1991 study, "Accidental Shootings: Many Deaths and Injuries Caused by Firearms Could be Prevented," estimates that 31 percent of accidental deaths caused by firearms might be prevented by the addition of two safety devices: a child-resistant safety device that automatically engages and a device that indicates whether the gun is loaded. According to the study results, of the 107 unintentional firearms-related fatalities the GAO examined for the calendar years 1988 and 1989, 8 percent could have been prevented had the firearm been equipped with a child-resistant safety device. This 8 percent represents instances in which children under the age of six unintentionally shot and killed themselves or other persons.

(g) Currently, firearms are the only products manufactured in the United States that are not subject to minimum safety standards.

(h) A 1997 public opinion poll conducted by the National Opinion Research Center at the University of Chicago in conjunction with the Johns Hopkins Center for Gun Policy and Research found that 74 percent of Americans support safety regulation of the firearms industry.

(i) Some currently available trigger locks and other similar devices are inadequate to prevent the accidental discharge of the firearms to which they are attached, or to prevent children from gaining access to the firearm.

(Added by Stats. 2010, Ch. 711, Sec. 6. (SB 1080) Effective January 1, 2011. Operative January 1, 2012, by Sec. 10 of Ch. 711.)

23630.

(a) This division does not apply to the commerce of any antique firearm.

(b) (1) This division does not apply to the commerce of any firearm intended to be used by a salaried, full-time peace officer, as defined in Chapter 4.5 (commencing with Section 830) of Title 3 of Part 2, for purposes of law enforcement.

(2) Nothing in this division precludes a local government, local agency, or state law enforcement agency from requiring its peace officers to store their firearms in gun safes or attach firearm safety devices to those firearms.

(Added by Stats. 2010, Ch. 711, Sec. 6. (SB 1080) Effective January 1, 2011. Operative January 1, 2012, by Sec. 10 of Ch. 711.)

23635.

(a) Any firearm sold or transferred in this state by a licensed firearms dealer, including a private transfer through a dealer, and any firearm manufactured in this state, shall include or be accompanied by a firearm safety device that is listed on the Department of Justice's roster of approved firearm safety devices and that is identified as appropriate for that firearm by reference to either the manufacturer and model of the firearm, or to the physical characteristics of the firearm that match those listed on the roster for use with the device.

(b) The sale or transfer of a firearm shall be exempt from subdivision (a) if both of the following apply:

(1) The purchaser or transferee owns a gun safe that meets the standards set forth in Section 23650. Gun safes shall not be required to be tested, and therefore may meet the standards without appearing on the Department of Justice roster.

(2) The purchaser or transferee presents an original receipt for purchase of the gun safe, or other proof of purchase or ownership of the gun safe as authorized by the Attorney General, to the firearms dealer. The dealer shall maintain a copy of this receipt or proof of purchase with the dealer's record of sales of firearms.

(c) The sale or transfer of a firearm shall be exempt from subdivision (a) if all of the following apply:

(1) The purchaser or transferee purchases an approved safety device no more than 30 days prior to the day the purchaser or transferee takes possession of the firearm.

(2) The purchaser or transferee presents the approved safety device to the firearms dealer when picking up the firearm.

(3) The purchaser or transferee presents an original receipt to the firearms dealer, which shows the date of purchase, the name, and the model number of the safety device.

(4) The firearms dealer verifies that the requirements in paragraphs (1) to (3), inclusive, have been satisfied.

(5) The firearms dealer maintains a copy of the receipt along with the dealer's record of sales of firearms.

(d) (1) Any long-gun safe commercially sold or transferred in this state, or manufactured in this state for sale in this state, that does not meet the standards for gun safes adopted pursuant to Section 23650 shall be accompanied by the following warning:

"WARNING: This gun safe does not meet the safety standards for gun safes specified in California Penal Code Section 23650. It does not satisfy the requirements of Penal Code Section 23635, which mandates that all firearms sold in California be accompanied by a firearm safety device or proof of ownership, as required by law, of a gun safe that meets the Section 23650 minimum safety standards developed by the California Attorney General."

(2) This warning shall be conspicuously displayed in its entirety on the principal display panel of the gun safe's package, on any descriptive materials that accompany the gun safe, and on a label affixed to the front of the gun safe.

(3) This warning shall be displayed in both English and Spanish, in conspicuous and legible type in contrast by typography, layout, or color with other printed matter on the

package or descriptive materials, in a manner consistent with Part 1500.121 of Title 16 of the Code of Federal Regulations, or successor regulations thereto.

(e) Any firearm sold or transferred in this state by a licensed firearms dealer, including a private transfer through a dealer, and any firearm manufactured in this state, shall be accompanied by warning language or a label as described in Section 23640.

(Added by Stats. 2010, Ch. 711, Sec. 6. (SB 1080) Effective January 1, 2011. Operative January 1, 2012, by Sec. 10 of Ch. 711.)

23640.

(a) (1) The packaging of any firearm and any descriptive materials that accompany any firearm sold or transferred in this state, or delivered for sale in this state, by any licensed manufacturer, or licensed dealer, shall bear a label containing the following warning statement:

WARNING

Firearms must be handled responsibly and securely stored to prevent access by children and other unauthorized users. California has strict laws pertaining to firearms, and you may be fined or imprisoned if you fail to comply with them. Visit the Web site of the California Attorney General at https://oag.ca.gov/firearms for information on firearm laws applicable to you and how you can comply.

Prevent child access by always keeping guns locked away and unloaded when not in use. If you keep a loaded firearm where a child obtains and improperly uses it, you may be fined or sent to prison.

(2) A yellow triangle containing an exclamation mark shall appear immediately before the word "Warning" on the label.

(b) If the firearm is sold or transferred without accompanying packaging, the warning label or notice shall be affixed to the firearm itself by a method to be prescribed by regulation of the Attorney General.

(c) The warning statement required under subdivisions (a) and (b) shall satisfy both of the following requirements:

(1) It shall be displayed in its entirety on the principal display panel of the firearm's package, and on any descriptive materials that accompany the firearm.

(2) It shall be displayed in both English and Spanish, in conspicuous and legible type in contrast by typography, layout, or color with other printed matter on that package or descriptive materials, in a manner consistent with Part 1500.121 of Title 16 of the Code of Federal Regulations, or successor regulations thereto.

(Amended by Stats. 2017, Ch. 825, Sec. 1. (AB 1525) Effective January 1, 2018.)

23645.

(a) Any violation of Section 23635 or Section 23640 is punishable by a fine of one thousand dollars ($1,000).

(b) On a second violation of any of those sections, a licensed firearm manufacturer shall be ineligible to manufacture, or a licensed firearm dealer shall be ineligible to sell, firearms in this state for 30 days, and shall be punished by a fine of one thousand dollars ($1,000).

(c) (1) On a third violation of any of those sections, a firearm manufacturer shall be permanently ineligible to manufacture firearms in this state.

(2) On a third violation of any of those sections, a licensed firearm dealer shall be permanently ineligible to sell firearms in this state.

(Added by Stats. 2010, Ch. 711, Sec. 6. (SB 1080) Effective January 1, 2011. Operative January 1, 2012, by Sec. 10 of Ch. 711.)

23650.

(a) The Attorney General shall develop regulations to implement a minimum safety standard for firearm safety devices and gun safes to significantly reduce the risk of firearm-related injuries to children 17 years of age and younger. The final standard shall do all of the following:

(1) Address the risk of injury from unintentional gunshot wounds.

(2) Address the risk of injury from self-inflicted gunshot wounds by unauthorized users.

(3) Include provisions to ensure that all firearm safety devices and gun safes are reusable and of adequate quality and construction to prevent children and unauthorized users from firing the firearm and to ensure that these devices cannot be readily removed from the firearm or that the firearm cannot be readily removed from the gun safe except by an authorized user utilizing the key, combination, or other method of access intended by the manufacturer of the device.

(4) Include additional provisions as appropriate.

(b) The Attorney General may consult, for the purposes of guidance in development of the standards, test protocols such as those described in Title 16 (commencing with Part 1700) of the Code of Federal Regulations, relating to poison prevention packaging standards. These protocols may be consulted to provide suggestions for potential methods to utilize in developing standards and shall serve as guidance only. The Attorney General shall also give appropriate consideration to the use of devices that are not detachable, but are permanently installed and incorporated into the design of a firearm.

(c) The Attorney General shall commence development of regulations under this section no later than January 1, 2000. The Attorney General shall adopt and issue regulations implementing a final standard no later than January 1, 2001. The Attorney General shall report to the Legislature on these standards by January 1, 2001. The final standard shall be effective January 1, 2002.

(Added by Stats. 2010, Ch. 711, Sec. 6. (SB 1080) Effective January 1, 2011. Operative January 1, 2012, by Sec. 10 of Ch. 711.)

23655.

(a) The Department of Justice shall certify laboratories to verify compliance with standards for firearm safety devices set forth in Section 23650.

(b) The Department of Justice may charge any laboratory that is seeking certification to test firearm safety devices a fee not exceeding the costs of certification, including costs associated with the development and approval of regulations and standards pursuant to Section 23650.

(c) The certified laboratory shall, at the manufacturer's or dealer's expense, test a firearm safety device and submit a copy of the final test report directly to the Department of Justice, along with the firearm safety device. The department shall notify the manufacturer or dealer of its receipt of the final test report and the department's determination as to whether the firearm safety device tested may be sold in this state.

(d) Commencing on July 1, 2001, the Department of Justice shall compile, publish, and maintain a roster listing all of the firearm safety devices that have been tested by a certified testing laboratory, have been determined to meet the department's standards for firearm safety devices, and may be sold in this state.

(e) The roster shall list, for each firearm safety device, the manufacturer, model number, and model name.

(f) The department may randomly retest samples obtained from sources other than directly from the manufacturer of the firearm safety device listed on the roster to ensure compliance with the requirements of this division.

(g) Firearm safety devices used for random sample testing and obtained from sources other than the manufacturer shall be in new, unused condition, and still in the manufacturer's original and unopened package.

(Added by Stats. 2010, Ch. 711, Sec. 6. (SB 1080) Effective January 1, 2011. Operative January 1, 2012, by Sec. 10 of Ch. 711.)

23660.

(a) No person shall keep for commercial sale, offer, or expose for commercial sale, or commercially sell any firearm safety device that is not listed on the roster maintained pursuant to subdivision (d) of Section 23655, or that does not comply with the standards for firearm safety devices adopted pursuant to Section 23650.

(b) No person may distribute as part of an organized firearm safety program, with or without consideration, any firearm safety device that is not listed on the roster maintained pursuant to subdivision (d) of Section 23655, or that does not comply with the standards for firearm safety devices adopted pursuant to Section 23650.

(Added by Stats. 2010, Ch. 711, Sec. 6. (SB 1080) Effective January 1, 2011. Operative January 1, 2012, by Sec. 10 of Ch. 711.)

23665.

(a) No long-gun safe may be manufactured in this state for sale in this state that does not comply with the standards for gun safes adopted pursuant to Section 23650, unless the long-gun safe is labeled by the manufacturer consistent with the requirements of Section 23635.

(b) (1) Any person who keeps for commercial sale, offers, or exposes for commercial sale, or who commercially sells a long-gun safe that does not comply with the standards for gun safes adopted pursuant to Section 23650, and who knows or has reason to know, that the long-gun safe in question does not meet the standards for gun safes adopted pursuant to Section 23650, is in violation of this section, and is punishable as provided in Section 23670, unless the long-gun safe is labeled pursuant to Section 23635.

(2) Any person who keeps for commercial sale, offers, or exposes for commercial sale, or who commercially sells a long-gun safe that does not comply with the standards for gun safes adopted pursuant to Section 23650, and who removes or causes to be removed, from the long-gun safe, the label required pursuant to Section 23635, is in violation of this section, and is punishable as provided in Section 23670.

(Added by Stats. 2010, Ch. 711, Sec. 6. (SB 1080) Effective January 1, 2011. Operative January 1, 2012, by Sec. 10 of Ch. 711.)

23670.

(a) (1) A violation of Section 23660 or 23665 is punishable by a civil fine of up to five hundred dollars ($500).

(2) A second violation of any of those sections, which occurs within five years of the date of a previous offense, is punishable by a civil fine of up to one thousand dollars ($1,000) and, if the violation is committed by a licensed firearms dealer, the dealer shall be ineligible to sell firearms in this state for 30 days.

(3) A third or subsequent violation that occurs within five years of two or more previous offenses is punishable by a civil fine of up to five thousand dollars ($5,000) and, if the violation is committed by a licensed firearms dealer, the firearms dealer shall be permanently ineligible to sell firearms in this state.

(b) The Attorney General, a district attorney, or a city attorney may bring a civil action for a violation of Section 23660 or 23665.

(Added by Stats. 2010, Ch. 711, Sec. 6. (SB 1080) Effective January 1, 2011. Operative January 1, 2012, by Sec. 10 of Ch. 711.)

23675.

Compliance with the requirements set forth in this division does not relieve any person from liability to any other person as may be imposed pursuant to common law, statutory law, or local ordinance.

(Added by Stats. 2010, Ch. 711, Sec. 6. (SB 1080) Effective January 1, 2011. Operative January 1, 2012, by Sec. 10 of Ch. 711.)

23680.

(a) If at any time the Attorney General determines that a gun safe or firearm safety device subject to the provisions of this division and sold after January 1, 2002, does not conform with the standards required by subdivision (a) of Section 23635 or Section 23650, the Attorney General may order the recall and replacement of the gun safe or firearm safety device, or order that the gun safe or firearm safety device be brought into conformity with those requirements.

(b) If the firearm safety device can be separated and reattached to the firearm without damaging the firearm, the licensed manufacturer or licensed firearms dealer shall immediately provide a conforming replacement as instructed by the Attorney General.

(c) If the firearm safety device cannot be separated from the firearm without damaging the firearm, the Attorney General may order the recall and replacement of the firearm.

(Added by Stats. 2010, Ch. 711, Sec. 6. (SB 1080) Effective January 1, 2011. Operative January 1, 2012, by Sec. 10 of Ch. 711.)

23685.

Each lead law enforcement agency investigating an incident shall report to the State Department of Health Services any information obtained that reasonably supports the conclusion that a child 18 years of age or younger suffered an unintentional or self-inflicted gunshot wound inflicted by a firearm that was sold or transferred in this state, or manufactured in this state. The report shall also indicate whether as a result of that incident the child died, suffered serious injury, or was treated for an injury by a medical professional.

(Amended by Stats. 2018, Ch. 185, Sec. 6. (AB 2176) Effective January 1, 2019.)

23690.

(a) (1) The Department of Justice may require each dealer to charge each firearm purchaser or transferee a fee not to exceed one dollar ($1) for each firearm transaction, except that the Department of Justice may increase the fee at a rate not to exceed any increase in the California Consumer Price Index, as compiled and reported by the Department of Industrial Relations, and not to exceed the reasonable cost of regulation to the Department of Justice.

(2) The fee shall be for the purpose of supporting department program costs related to this act, including the establishment, maintenance, and upgrading of related database systems and public rosters.

(b) (1) There is hereby created within the General Fund the Firearm Safety Account.

(2) Revenue from the fee imposed by subdivision (a) shall be deposited into the Firearm Safety Account and shall be available for expenditure by the Department of Justice upon appropriation by the Legislature.

(3) Expenditures from the Firearm Safety Account shall be limited to program expenditures as defined by subdivision (a).

(Amended by Stats. 2016, Ch. 33, Sec. 37. (SB 843) Effective June 27, 2016.)

DIVISION 3. DISGUISED OR MISLEADING APPEARANCE [23800 - 24790]

(Division 3 added by Stats. 2010, Ch. 711, Sec. 6.)

CHAPTER 1. Miscellaneous Provisions [23800-23800.]

(Chapter 1 added by Stats. 2010, Ch. 711, Sec. 6.)

23800.

Any person who, for commercial purposes, purchases, sells, manufactures, ships, transports, distributes, or receives a firearm, where the coloration of the entire exterior surface of the firearm is bright orange or bright green, either singly, in combination, or as the predominant color in combination with other colors in any pattern, is liable for a civil fine in an action brought by the city attorney of the city, or the district attorney for the county, of not more than ten thousand dollars ($10,000).

(Added by Stats. 2010, Ch. 711, Sec. 6. (SB 1080) Effective January 1, 2011. Operative Ja CHAPTER 2. Obliteration of Identification Marks [23900 - 23925]

(Chapter 2 added by Stats. 2010, Ch. 711, Sec. 6.)

23900.

Any person who changes, alters, removes, or obliterates the name of the maker, model, manufacturer's number, or other mark of identification, including any distinguishing number or mark assigned by the Department of Justice, on any pistol, revolver, or any other firearm, without first having secured written permission from the department to make that change, alteration, or removal shall be punished by imprisonment pursuant to subdivision (h) of Section 1170.

(Amended by Stats. 2011, Ch. 15, Sec. 540. (AB 109) Effective April 4, 2011. Amending action operative October 1, 2011, by Sec. 636 of Ch. 15, as amended by Stats. 2011, Ch. 39, Sec. 68. Section operative January 1, 2012, pursuant to Stats. 2010, Ch. 711, Sec. 10.)

23910.

The Department of Justice, upon request, may assign a distinguishing number or mark of identification to any firearm whenever the firearm lacks a manufacturer's number or other mark of identification. Whenever the manufacturer's number or other mark of identification or a distinguishing number or mark assigned by the department has been destroyed or obliterated, the Department of Justice, upon request, shall assign a distinguishing number or mark of identification to any firearm in accordance with Section 29182.

(Amended by Stats. 2016, Ch. 60, Sec. 3. (AB 857) Effective January 1, 2017.)

23915.

(a) Any person may place or stamp on any pistol, revolver, or other firearm any number or identifying indicium, provided the number or identifying indicium does not change, alter, remove, or obliterate the manufacturer's name, number, model, or other mark of identification.

(b) This section does not prohibit restoration by the owner of the name of the maker or model, or of the original manufacturer's number or other mark of identification, when that restoration is authorized by the department.

(c) This section does not prevent any manufacturer from placing in the ordinary course of business the name of the maker, model, manufacturer's number, or other mark of identification upon a new firearm.

(Added by Stats. 2010, Ch. 711, Sec. 6. (SB 1080) Effective January 1, 2011. Operative January 1, 2012, by Sec. 10 of Ch. 711.)

23920.

Except as provided in Section 23925, any person who, with knowledge of any change, alteration, removal, or obliteration described in this section, buys, receives, disposes of, sells, offers for sale, or has in possession any pistol, revolver, or other firearm that has had the name of the maker or model, or the manufacturer's number or other mark of identification, including any distinguishing number or mark assigned by the Department of Justice, changed, altered, removed, or obliterated, is guilty of a misdemeanor.

(Added by Stats. 2010, Ch. 711, Sec. 6. (SB 1080) Effective January 1, 2011. Operative January 1, 2012, by Sec. 10 of Ch. 711.)

23925.

Section 23920 does not apply to any of the following:

(a) The acquisition or possession of a firearm described in Section 23920 by any member of the military forces of this state or of the United States, while on duty and acting within the scope and course of employment.

(b) The acquisition or possession of a firearm described in Section 23920 by any peace officer described in Chapter 4.5 (commencing with Section 830) of Title 3 of Part 2, while on duty and acting within the scope and course of employment.

(c) The acquisition or possession of a firearm described in Section 23920 by any employee of a forensic laboratory, while on duty and acting within the scope and course of employment.

(d) The possession and disposition of a firearm described in Section 23920 by a person who meets all of the following:

(1) The person is not prohibited by state or federal law from possessing, receiving, owning, or purchasing a firearm.

(2) The person possessed the firearm no longer than was necessary to deliver it to a law enforcement agency for that agency's disposition according to law.

(3) If the person is transporting the firearm, the person is transporting it to a law enforcement agency in order to deliver it to the agency for the agency's disposition according to law.

(4) If the person is transporting the firearm to a law enforcement agency, the person has given prior notice to the agency that the person is transporting the firearm to that agency for the agency's disposition according to law.

(5) The firearm is transported in a locked container as defined in Section 16850.

(Added by Stats. 2010, Ch. 711, Sec. 6. (SB 1080) Effective January 1, 2011. Operative January 1, 2012, by Sec. 10 of Ch. 711.)

CHAPTER 3. Camouflaging Firearm Container [24310 - 24390]

(Chapter 3 added by Stats. 2010, Ch. 711, Sec. 6.)

24310.

Except as provided in Chapter 1 (commencing with Section 17700) of Division 2 of Title 2, any person in this state who manufactures or causes to be manufactured, imports into the state, keeps for sale, or offers or exposes for sale, or who gives, lends, or possesses any camouflaging firearm container is punishable by imprisonment in a county jail not exceeding one year or imprisonment pursuant to subdivision (h) of Section 1170.

(Amended by Stats. 2012, Ch. 43, Sec. 99. (SB 1023) Effective June 27, 2012.)

24390.

Except as provided in Chapter 1 (commencing with Section 17700) of Division 2 of Title 2, any camouflaging firearm container is a nuisance and is subject to Section 18010.

(Added by Stats. 2010, Ch. 711, Sec. 6. (SB 1080) Effective January 1, 2011. Operative January 1, 2012, by Sec. 10 of Ch. 711.)

CHAPTER 4. Cane Gun [24410 - 24490]

(Chapter 4 added by Stats. 2010, Ch. 711, Sec. 6.)

24410.

Except as provided in Chapter 1 (commencing with Section 17700) of Division 2 of Title 2, any person in this state who manufactures or causes to be manufactured, imports into the state, keeps for sale, or offers or exposes for sale, or who gives, lends, or possesses any cane gun is punishable by imprisonment in a county jail not exceeding one year or imprisonment pursuant to subdivision (h) of Section 1170.

(Amended by Stats. 2012, Ch. 43, Sec. 100. (SB 1023) Effective June 27, 2012.)

24490.

Except as provided in Chapter 1 (commencing with Section 17700) of Division 2 of Title 2, any cane gun is a nuisance and is subject to Section 18010.

(Added by Stats. 2010, Ch. 711, Sec. 6. (SB 1080) Effective January 1, 2011. Operative January 1, 2012, by Sec. 10 of Ch. 711.)

CHAPTER 5. Firearm Not Immediately Recognizable as a Firearm [24510 - 24590]

(Chapter 5 added by Stats. 2010, Ch. 711, Sec. 6.)

24510.

Except as provided in Chapter 1 (commencing with Section 17700) of Division 2 of Title 2, any person in this state who manufactures or causes to be manufactured, imports into the state, keeps for sale, or offers or exposes for sale, or who gives, lends, or possesses any firearm not immediately recognizable as a firearm is punishable by imprisonment in a county jail not exceeding one year or imprisonment pursuant to subdivision (h) of Section 1170.

(Amended by Stats. 2012, Ch. 43, Sec. 101. (SB 1023) Effective June 27, 2012.)

24590.

Except as provided in Chapter 1 (commencing with Section 17700) of Division 2 of Title 2, any firearm not immediately recognizable as a firearm is a nuisance and is subject to Section 18010.

(Added by Stats. 2010, Ch. 711, Sec. 6. (SB 1080) Effective January 1, 2011. Operative January 1, 2012, by Sec. 10 of Ch. 711.)

CHAPTER 6. Undetectable Firearm and Firearm Detection Equipment [24610 - 24690]

(Chapter 6 added by Stats. 2010, Ch. 711, Sec. 6.)

24610.

Except as provided in Chapter 1 (commencing with Section 17700) of Division 2 of Title 2, any person in this state who manufactures or causes to be manufactured, imports into the state, keeps for sale, or offers or exposes for sale, or who gives, lends, or possesses any undetectable firearm is punishable by imprisonment in a county jail not exceeding one year or imprisonment pursuant to subdivision (h) of Section 1170.

(Amended by Stats. 2012, Ch. 43, Sec. 102. (SB 1023) Effective June 27, 2012.)

24680.

Any firearm detection equipment newly installed in a nonfederal public building in this state shall be of a type identified by either the United States Attorney General, the Secretary of Transportation, or the Secretary of the Treasury, as appropriate, as available state-of-the-art equipment capable of detecting an undetectable firearm, while distinguishing innocuous metal objects likely to be carried on one's person sufficient for reasonable passage of the public.

(Added by Stats. 2010, Ch. 711, Sec. 6. (SB 1080) Effective January 1, 2011. Operative January 1, 2012, by Sec. 10 of Ch. 711.)

24690.

Except as provided in Chapter 1 (commencing with Section 17700) of Division 2 of Title 2, any undetectable firearm is a nuisance and is subject to Section 18010.

(Added by Stats. 2010, Ch. 711, Sec. 6. (SB 1080) Effective January 1, 2011. Operative January 1, 2012, by Sec. 10 of Ch. 711.)

CHAPTER 7. Wallet Gun [24710 - 24790]

(Chapter 7 added by Stats. 2010, Ch. 711, Sec. 6.)

24710.

Except as provided in Chapter 1 (commencing with Section 17700) of Division 2 of Title 2, any person in this state who manufactures or causes to be manufactured, imports into the state, keeps for sale, or offers or exposes for sale, or who gives, lends, or possesses any wallet gun is punishable by imprisonment in a county jail not exceeding one year or imprisonment pursuant to subdivision (h) of Section 1170.

(Amended by Stats. 2012, Ch. 43, Sec. 103. (SB 1023) Effective June 27, 2012.)

24790.

Except as provided in Chapter 1 (commencing with Section 17700) of Division 2 of Title 2, any wallet gun is a nuisance and is subject to Section 18010.

(Added by Stats. 2010, Ch. 711, Sec. 6. (SB 1080) Effective January 1, 2011. Operative January 1, 2012, by Sec. 10 of Ch. 711.)

DIVISION 4. STORAGE OF FIREARMS [25000 - 25225]

(Division 4 added by Stats. 2010, Ch. 711, Sec. 6.)

CHAPTER 1. Preliminary Provisions [25000- 25000.]

(Chapter 1 added by Stats. 2010, Ch. 711, Sec. 6.)

25000.

As used in this division, "child" means a person under 18 years of age.

(Added by Stats. 2010, Ch. 711, Sec. 6. (SB 1080) Effective January 1, 2011. Operative January 1, 2012, by Sec. 10 of Ch. 711.)

CHAPTER 2. Criminal Storage of Firearm [25100 - 25140]

(Chapter 2 added by Stats. 2010, Ch. 711, Sec. 6.)

25100.

(a) Except as provided in Section 25105, a person commits the crime of "criminal storage of a firearm in the first degree" if all of the following conditions are satisfied:

(1) The person keeps any loaded firearm within any premises that are under the person's custody or control.

(2) The person knows or reasonably should know that a child is likely to gain access to the firearm without the permission of the child's parent or legal guardian, or that a person prohibited from possessing a firearm or deadly weapon pursuant to state or federal law is likely to gain access to the firearm.

(3) The child obtains access to the firearm and thereby causes death or great bodily injury to the child or any other person, or the person prohibited from possessing a firearm or deadly weapon pursuant to state or federal law obtains access to the firearm and thereby causes death or great bodily injury to himself or herself or any other person.

(b) Except as provided in Section 25105, a person commits the crime of "criminal storage of a firearm in the second degree" if all of the following conditions are satisfied:

(1) The person keeps any loaded firearm within any premises that are under the person's custody or control.

(2) The person knows or reasonably should know that a child is likely to gain access to the firearm without the permission of the child's parent or legal guardian, or that a person prohibited from possessing a firearm or deadly weapon pursuant to state or federal law is likely to gain access to the firearm.

(3) The child obtains access to the firearm and thereby causes injury, other than great bodily injury, to the child or any other person, or carries the firearm either to a public place or in violation of Section 417, or the person prohibited from possessing a firearm or deadly weapon pursuant to state or federal law obtains access to the firearm and thereby causes injury, other than great bodily injury, to himself or herself or any other person, or carries the firearm either to a public place or in violation of Section 417.

(c) Except as provided in Section 25105, a person commits the crime of "criminal storage of a firearm in the third degree" if the person keeps any loaded firearm within any premises that are under the person's custody or control and negligently stores or leaves a loaded firearm in a location where the person knows, or reasonably should know, that a child is likely to gain access to the firearm without the permission of the child's parent or legal guardian, unless reasonable action is taken by the person to secure the firearm against access by the child.

(Amended by Stats. 2013, Ch. 758, Sec. 1.5. (SB 363) Effective January 1, 2014.)

25105.

Section 25100 does not apply whenever any of the following occurs:

(a) The child obtains the firearm as a result of an illegal entry to any premises by any person.

(b) The firearm is kept in a locked container or in a location that a reasonable person would believe to be secure.

(c) The firearm is carried on the person or within close enough proximity thereto that the individual can readily retrieve and use the firearm as if carried on the person.

(d) The firearm is locked with a locking device, as defined in Section 16860, which has rendered the firearm inoperable.

(e) The person is a peace officer or a member of the Armed Forces or the National Guard and the child obtains the firearm during, or incidental to, the performance of the person's duties.

(f) The child obtains, or obtains and discharges, the firearm in a lawful act of self-defense or defense of another person.

(g) The person who keeps a loaded firearm on premises that are under the person's custody or control has no reasonable expectation, based on objective facts and circumstances, that a child is likely to be present on the premises.

(Amended by Stats. 2011, Ch. 285, Sec. 26. (AB 1402) Effective January 1, 2012.)

25110.

(a) Criminal storage of a firearm in the first degree is punishable by imprisonment pursuant to subdivision (h) of Section 1170 for 16 months, or two or three years, by a fine not exceeding ten thousand dollars ($10,000), or by both that imprisonment and fine; or by imprisonment in a county jail not exceeding one year, by a fine not exceeding one thousand dollars ($1,000), or by both that imprisonment and fine.

(b) Criminal storage of a firearm in the second degree is punishable by imprisonment in a county jail not exceeding one year, by a fine not exceeding one thousand dollars ($1,000), or by both that imprisonment and fine.

(c) Criminal storage of a firearm in the third degree is punishable as a misdemeanor.

(Amended by Stats. 2013, Ch. 730, Sec. 2. (AB 231) Effective January 1, 2014.)

25115.

If a person who allegedly violated Section 25100 is the parent or guardian of a child who is injured or who dies as the result of an accidental shooting, the district attorney shall consider, among other factors, the impact of the injury or death on the person alleged to have violated Section 25100 when deciding whether to prosecute the alleged violation. It is the Legislature's intent that a parent or guardian of a child who is injured or who dies as the result of an accidental shooting shall be prosecuted only in those instances in which the parent or guardian behaved in a grossly negligent manner or where similarly egregious circumstances exist. This section shall not otherwise restrict, in any manner, the factors that a district attorney may consider when deciding whether to prosecute an alleged violation of Section 25100.

(Added by Stats. 2010, Ch. 711, Sec. 6. (SB 1080) Effective January 1, 2011. Operative January 1, 2012, by Sec. 10 of Ch. 711.)

25120.

(a) If a person who allegedly violated Section 25100 is the parent or guardian of a child who was injured or who died as the result of an accidental shooting, no arrest of the person for the alleged violation of Section 25100 shall occur until at least seven days after the date upon which the accidental shooting occurred.

(b) In addition to the limitation stated in subdivision (a), before arresting a person for a violation of Section 25100, a law enforcement officer shall consider the health status of a child who suffered great bodily injury as the result of an accidental shooting, if the person to be arrested is the parent or guardian of the injured child. The intent of this section is to encourage law enforcement officials to delay the arrest of a parent or guardian of a seriously injured child while the child remains on life-support equipment or is in a similarly critical medical condition.

(Added by Stats. 2010, Ch. 711, Sec. 6. (SB 1080) Effective January 1, 2011. Operative January 1, 2012, by Sec. 10 of Ch. 711.)

25125.

(a) The fact that a person who allegedly violated Section 25100 attended a firearm safety training course prior to the purchase of the firearm that was obtained by a child in violation of Section 25100 shall be considered a mitigating factor by a district attorney when deciding whether to prosecute the alleged violation.

(b) In any action or trial commenced under Section 25100, the fact that the person who allegedly violated Section 25100 attended a firearm safety training course prior to the purchase of the firearm that was obtained by a child in violation of Section 25100 is admissible.

(Added by Stats. 2010, Ch. 711, Sec. 6. (SB 1080) Effective January 1, 2011. Operative January 1, 2012, by Sec. 10 of Ch. 711.)

25130.

Every person licensed under Sections 26700 to 26915, inclusive, shall post within the licensed premises the notice required by Section 26835, disclosing the duty imposed by this chapter upon any person who keeps a loaded firearm.

(Added by Stats. 2010, Ch. 711, Sec. 6. (SB 1080) Effective January 1, 2011. Operative January 1, 2012, by Sec. 10 of Ch. 711.)

25135.

(a) A person who is 18 years of age or older, and who is the owner, lessee, renter, or other legal occupant of a residence, who owns a firearm and who knows or has reason to know that another person also residing therein is prohibited by state or federal law from possessing, receiving, owning, or purchasing a firearm shall not keep in that residence any firearm that he or she owns unless one of the following applies:

(1) The firearm is maintained within a locked container.

(2) The firearm is disabled by a firearm safety device.

(3) The firearm is maintained within a locked gun safe.

(4) The firearm is maintained within a locked trunk.

(5) The firearm is locked with a locking device as described in Section 16860, which has rendered the firearm inoperable.

(6) The firearm is carried on the person or within close enough proximity thereto that the individual can readily retrieve and use the firearm as if carried on the person.

(b) A violation of this section is a misdemeanor.

(c) The provisions of this section are cumulative, and do not restrict the application of any other law. However, an act or omission punishable in different ways by different provisions of law shall not be punished under more than one provision.

(Added by Stats. 2013, Ch. 737, Sec. 7. (AB 500) Effective January 1, 2014.)

25140.

(a) Except as otherwise provided in subdivision (b), a person shall, when leaving a handgun in an unattended vehicle, lock the handgun in the vehicle's trunk, lock the handgun in a locked container and place the container out of plain view, lock the handgun in a locked container that is permanently affixed to the vehicle's interior and not in plain view, or lock the handgun in a locked toolbox or utility box.

(b) A peace officer, when leaving a handgun in an unattended vehicle not equipped with a trunk, may, if unable to otherwise comply with subdivision (a), lock the handgun out of plain view within the center utility console of that motor vehicle with a padlock, keylock, combination lock, or other similar locking device.

(c) A violation of subdivision (a) is an infraction punishable by a fine not exceeding one thousand dollars ($1,000).

(d) (1) As used in this section, the following definitions shall apply:

(A) "Locked container" means a secure container that is fully enclosed and locked by a padlock, keylock, combination lock, or similar locking device. The term "locked container" does not include the utility or glove compartment of a motor vehicle.

(B) "Locked toolbox or utility box" means a fully enclosed container that is permanently affixed to the bed of a pickup truck or vehicle that does not contain a trunk, and is locked by a padlock, keylock, combination lock, or other similar locking device.

(C) "Peace officer" means a sworn officer described in Chapter 4.5 (commencing with Section 830) of Title 3 of Part 2, or a sworn federal law enforcement officer, who is authorized to carry a firearm in the course and scope of that officer's duties, while that officer is on duty or off duty.

(D) "Trunk" means the fully enclosed and locked main storage or luggage compartment of a vehicle that is not accessible from the passenger compartment. A trunk does not include the rear of a hatchback, station wagon, or sport utility vehicle, any compartment which has a window, or a toolbox or utility box attached to the bed of a pickup truck.

(E) "Vehicle" has the same meaning as specified in Section 670 of the Vehicle Code.

(2) For purposes of this section, a vehicle is unattended when a person who is lawfully carrying or transporting a handgun in a vehicle is not within close enough proximity to the vehicle to reasonably prevent unauthorized access to the vehicle or its contents.

(3) For purposes of this section, plain view includes any area of the vehicle that is visible by peering through the windows of the vehicle, including windows that are tinted, with or without illumination.

(e) This section does not apply to a peace officer during circumstances requiring immediate aid or action that are within the course of his or her official duties.

(f) This section does not supersede any local ordinance that regulates the storage of handguns in unattended vehicles if the ordinance was in effect before September 26, 2016.

(Amended by Stats. 2018, Ch. 94, Sec. 1. (SB 1382) Effective January 1, 2019.)

CHAPTER 2. Criminal Storage of Firearm [25100 - 25140]

(Chapter 2 added by Stats. 2010, Ch. 711, Sec. 6.)

25100.

(a) Except as provided in Section 25105, a person commits the crime of "criminal storage of a firearm in the first degree" if all of the following conditions are satisfied:

(1) The person keeps any loaded firearm within any premises that are under the person's custody or control.

(2) The person knows or reasonably should know that a child is likely to gain access to the firearm without the permission of the child's parent or legal guardian, or that a person prohibited from possessing a firearm or deadly weapon pursuant to state or federal law is likely to gain access to the firearm.

(3) The child obtains access to the firearm and thereby causes death or great bodily injury to the child or any other person, or the person prohibited from possessing a firearm or deadly weapon pursuant to state or federal law obtains access to the firearm and thereby causes death or great bodily injury to himself or herself or any other person.

(b) Except as provided in Section 25105, a person commits the crime of "criminal storage of a firearm in the second degree" if all of the following conditions are satisfied:

(1) The person keeps any loaded firearm within any premises that are under the person's custody or control.

(2) The person knows or reasonably should know that a child is likely to gain access to the firearm without the permission of the child's parent or legal guardian, or that a person prohibited from possessing a firearm or deadly weapon pursuant to state or federal law is likely to gain access to the firearm.

(3) The child obtains access to the firearm and thereby causes injury, other than great bodily injury, to the child or any other person, or carries the firearm either to a public place or in violation of Section 417, or the person prohibited from possessing a firearm or deadly weapon pursuant to state or federal law obtains access to the firearm and thereby causes injury, other than great bodily injury, to himself or herself or any other person, or carries the firearm either to a public place or in violation of Section 417.

(c) Except as provided in Section 25105, a person commits the crime of "criminal storage of a firearm in the third degree" if the person keeps any loaded firearm within any premises that are under the person's custody or control and negligently stores or leaves a loaded firearm in a location where the person knows, or reasonably should know, that a child is likely to gain access to the firearm without the permission of the child's parent or legal guardian, unless reasonable action is taken by the person to secure the firearm against access by the child.

(Amended by Stats. 2013, Ch. 758, Sec. 1.5. (SB 363) Effective January 1, 2014.)

25105.

Section 25100 does not apply whenever any of the following occurs:

(a) The child obtains the firearm as a result of an illegal entry to any premises by any person.

(b) The firearm is kept in a locked container or in a location that a reasonable person would believe to be secure.

(c) The firearm is carried on the person or within close enough proximity thereto that the individual can readily retrieve and use the firearm as if carried on the person.

(d) The firearm is locked with a locking device, as defined in Section 16860, which has rendered the firearm inoperable.

(e) The person is a peace officer or a member of the Armed Forces or the National Guard and the child obtains the firearm during, or incidental to, the performance of the person's duties.

(f) The child obtains, or obtains and discharges, the firearm in a lawful act of self-defense or defense of another person.

(g) The person who keeps a loaded firearm on premises that are under the person's custody or control has no reasonable expectation, based on objective facts and circumstances, that a child is likely to be present on the premises.

(Amended by Stats. 2011, Ch. 285, Sec. 26. (AB 1402) Effective January 1, 2012.)

25110.

(a) Criminal storage of a firearm in the first degree is punishable by imprisonment pursuant to subdivision (h) of Section 1170 for 16 months, or two or three years, by a fine not exceeding ten thousand dollars ($10,000), or by both that imprisonment and fine; or by imprisonment in a county jail not exceeding one year, by a fine not exceeding one thousand dollars ($1,000), or by both that imprisonment and fine.

(b) Criminal storage of a firearm in the second degree is punishable by imprisonment in a county jail not exceeding one year, by a fine not exceeding one thousand dollars ($1,000), or by both that imprisonment and fine.

(c) Criminal storage of a firearm in the third degree is punishable as a misdemeanor.

(Amended by Stats. 2013, Ch. 730, Sec. 2. (AB 231) Effective January 1, 2014.)
25115.

If a person who allegedly violated Section 25100 is the parent or guardian of a child who is injured or who dies as the result of an accidental shooting, the district attorney shall consider, among other factors, the impact of the injury or death on the person alleged to have violated Section 25100 when deciding whether to prosecute the alleged violation. It is the Legislature's intent that a parent or guardian of a child who is injured or who dies as the result of an accidental shooting shall be prosecuted only in those instances in which the parent or guardian behaved in a grossly negligent manner or where similarly egregious circumstances exist. This section shall not otherwise restrict, in any manner, the factors that a district attorney may consider when deciding whether to prosecute an alleged violation of Section 25100.

(Added by Stats. 2010, Ch. 711, Sec. 6. (SB 1080) Effective January 1, 2011. Operative January 1, 2012, by Sec. 10 of Ch. 711.)
25120.

(a) If a person who allegedly violated Section 25100 is the parent or guardian of a child who was injured or who died as the result of an accidental shooting, no arrest of the person for the alleged violation of Section 25100 shall occur until at least seven days after the date upon which the accidental shooting occurred.

(b) In addition to the limitation stated in subdivision (a), before arresting a person for a violation of Section 25100, a law enforcement officer shall consider the health status of a child who suffered great bodily injury as the result of an accidental shooting, if the person to be arrested is the parent or guardian of the injured child. The intent of this section is to encourage law enforcement officials to delay the arrest of a parent or guardian of a seriously injured child while the child remains on life-support equipment or is in a similarly critical medical condition.

(Added by Stats. 2010, Ch. 711, Sec. 6. (SB 1080) Effective January 1, 2011. Operative January 1, 2012, by Sec. 10 of Ch. 711.)
25125.

(a) The fact that a person who allegedly violated Section 25100 attended a firearm safety training course prior to the purchase of the firearm that was obtained by a child in violation of Section 25100 shall be considered a mitigating factor by a district attorney when deciding whether to prosecute the alleged violation.

(b) In any action or trial commenced under Section 25100, the fact that the person who allegedly violated Section 25100 attended a firearm safety training course prior to the purchase of the firearm that was obtained by a child in violation of Section 25100 is admissible.

(Added by Stats. 2010, Ch. 711, Sec. 6. (SB 1080) Effective January 1, 2011. Operative January 1, 2012, by Sec. 10 of Ch. 711.)
25130.

Every person licensed under Sections 26700 to 26915, inclusive, shall post within the licensed premises the notice required by Section 26835, disclosing the duty imposed by this chapter upon any person who keeps a loaded firearm.

(Added by Stats. 2010, Ch. 711, Sec. 6. (SB 1080) Effective January 1, 2011. Operative January 1, 2012, by Sec. 10 of Ch. 711.)
25135.

(a) A person who is 18 years of age or older, and who is the owner, lessee, renter, or other legal occupant of a residence, who owns a firearm and who knows or has reason to know that another person also residing therein is prohibited by state or federal law from possessing, receiving, owning, or purchasing a firearm shall not keep in that residence any firearm that he or she owns unless one of the following applies:

(1) The firearm is maintained within a locked container.

(2) The firearm is disabled by a firearm safety device.

(3) The firearm is maintained within a locked gun safe.

(4) The firearm is maintained within a locked trunk.

(5) The firearm is locked with a locking device as described in Section 16860, which has rendered the firearm inoperable.

(6) The firearm is carried on the person or within close enough proximity thereto that the individual can readily retrieve and use the firearm as if carried on the person.

(b) A violation of this section is a misdemeanor.

(c) The provisions of this section are cumulative, and do not restrict the application of any other law. However, an act or omission punishable in different ways by different provisions of law shall not be punished under more than one provision.

(Added by Stats. 2013, Ch. 737, Sec. 7. (AB 500) Effective January 1, 2014.)
25140.

(a) Except as otherwise provided in subdivision (b), a person shall, when leaving a handgun in an unattended vehicle, lock the handgun in the vehicle's trunk, lock the handgun in a locked container and place the container out of plain view, lock the handgun in a locked container that is permanently affixed to the vehicle's interior and not in plain view, or lock the handgun in a locked toolbox or utility box.

(b) A peace officer, when leaving a handgun in an unattended vehicle not equipped with a trunk, may, if unable to otherwise comply with subdivision (a), lock the handgun out of plain view within the center utility console of that motor vehicle with a padlock, keylock, combination lock, or other similar locking device.

(c) A violation of subdivision (a) is an infraction punishable by a fine not exceeding one thousand dollars ($1,000).

(d) (1) As used in this section, the following definitions shall apply:

(A) "Locked container" means a secure container that is fully enclosed and locked by a padlock, keylock, combination lock, or similar locking device. The term "locked container" does not include the utility or glove compartment of a motor vehicle.

(B) "Locked toolbox or utility box" means a fully enclosed container that is permanently affixed to the bed of a pickup truck or vehicle that does not contain a trunk, and is locked by a padlock, keylock, combination lock, or other similar locking device.

(C) "Peace officer" means a sworn officer described in Chapter 4.5 (commencing with Section 830) of Title 3 of Part 2, or a sworn federal law enforcement officer, who is authorized to carry a firearm in the course and scope of that officer's duties, while that officer is on duty or off duty.

(D) "Trunk" means the fully enclosed and locked main storage or luggage compartment of a vehicle that is not accessible from the passenger compartment. A trunk does not include the rear of a hatchback, station wagon, or sport utility vehicle, any compartment which has a window, or a toolbox or utility box attached to the bed of a pickup truck.

(E) "Vehicle" has the same meaning as specified in Section 670 of the Vehicle Code.

(2) For purposes of this section, a vehicle is unattended when a person who is lawfully carrying or transporting a handgun in a vehicle is not within close enough proximity to the vehicle to reasonably prevent unauthorized access to the vehicle or its contents.

(3) For purposes of this section, plain view includes any area of the vehicle that is visible by peering through the windows of the vehicle, including windows that are tinted, with or without illumination.

(e) This section does not apply to a peace officer during circumstances requiring immediate aid or action that are within the course of his or her official duties.

(f) This section does not supersede any local ordinance that regulates the storage of handguns in unattended vehicles if the ordinance was in effect before September 26, 2016.

(Amended by Stats. 2018, Ch. 94, Sec. 1. (SB 1382) Effective January 1, 2019.)

DIVISION 4.5. LOST OR STOLEN FIREARMS [25250 - 25275]

(Division 4.5 added November 8, 2016, by initiative Proposition 63, Sec. 4.1.)
25250.

(a) Commencing July 1, 2017, every person shall report the loss or theft of a firearm he or she owns or possesses to a local law enforcement agency in the jurisdiction in which the theft or loss occurred within five days of the time he or she knew or reasonably should have known that the firearm had been stolen or lost.

(b) Every person who has reported a firearm lost or stolen under subdivision (a) shall notify the local law enforcement agency in the jurisdiction in which the theft or loss occurred within five days if the firearm is subsequently recovered by the person.

(c) Notwithstanding subdivision (a), a person shall not be required to report the loss or theft of a firearm that is an antique firearm within the meaning of subdivision (c) of Section 16170.

(Added November 8, 2016, by initiative Proposition 63, Sec. 4.1.)
25255.

Section 25250 shall not apply to the following:

(a) Any law enforcement agency or peace officer acting within the course and scope of his or her employment or official duties if he or she reports the loss or theft to his or her employing agency.

(b) Any United States marshal or member of the Armed Forces of the United States or the National Guard, while engaged in his or her official duties.

(c) Any person who is licensed, pursuant to Chapter 44 (commencing with Section 921) of Title 18 of the United States Code and the regulations issued pursuant thereto, and who reports the theft or loss in accordance with Section 923(g)(6) of Title 18 of the United States Code, or the successor provision thereto, and applicable regulations issued thereto.

(d) Any person whose firearm was lost or stolen prior to July 1, 2017.

(Added November 8, 2016, by initiative Proposition 63, Sec. 4.1.)
25260.

Pursuant to Section 11108.2, every sheriff or police chief shall submit a description of each firearm that has been reported lost or stolen directly into the Department of Justice Automated Firearms System.

(Amended by Stats. 2018, Ch. 864, Sec. 6. (AB 2222) Effective January 1, 2019. Note: This section was added November 8, 2016, by initiative Proposition 63.)
25265.

(a) Every person who violates Section 25250 is, for a first violation, guilty of an infraction, punishable by a fine not to exceed one hundred dollars ($100).

(b) Every person who violates Section 25250 is, for a second violation, guilty of an infraction, punishable by a fine not to exceed one thousand dollars ($1,000).

(c) Every person who violates Section 25250 is, for a third or subsequent violation, guilty of a misdemeanor, punishable by imprisonment in a county jail not exceeding six months, or by a fine not to exceed one thousand dollars ($1,000), or by both that fine and imprisonment.

(Added November 8, 2016, by initiative Proposition 63, Sec. 4.1.)
25270.

Every person reporting a lost or stolen firearm pursuant to Section 25250 shall report the make, model, and serial number of the firearm, if known by the person, and any additional relevant information required by the local law enforcement agency taking the report.

(Added November 8, 2016, by initiative Proposition 63, Sec. 4.1.)
25275.

(a) No person shall report to a local law enforcement agency that a firearm has been lost or stolen, knowing the report to be false. A violation of this section is an infraction, punishable by a fine not exceeding two hundred fifty dollars ($250) for a first offense, and by a fine not exceeding one thousand dollars ($1,000) for a second or subsequent offense.

(b) This section shall not preclude prosecution under any other law.

(Added November 8, 2016, by initiative Proposition 63, Sec. 4.1.)

DIVISION 5. CARRYING FIREARMS [25300 - 26405]

(Division 5 added by Stats. 2010, Ch. 711, Sec. 6.)

CHAPTER 1. Miscellaneous Rules Relating to Carrying Firearms [25300- 25300.]

(Chapter 1 added by Stats. 2010, Ch. 711, Sec. 6.)
25300.

(a) A person commits criminal possession of a firearm when the person carries a firearm in a public place or on any public street while masked so as to hide the person's identity.

(b) Criminal possession of a firearm is punishable by imprisonment pursuant to subdivision (h) of Section 1170 or by imprisonment in a county jail not to exceed one year.

(c) Subdivision (a) does not apply to any of the following:

(1) A peace officer in performance of the officer's duties.

(2) A full-time paid peace officer of another state or the federal government who is carrying out official duties while in this state.

(3) Any person summoned by any of the officers enumerated in paragraph (1) or (2) to assist in making an arrest or preserving the peace while that person is actually engaged in assisting that officer.

(4) The possession of an unloaded firearm or a firearm loaded with blank ammunition by an authorized participant in, or while rehearsing for, a motion picture, television, video production, entertainment event, entertainment activity, or lawfully organized and conducted activity when the participant lawfully uses the firearm as part of that production, event, or activity.

(5) The possession of a firearm by a licensed hunter while actually engaged in lawful hunting, or while going directly to or returning directly from the hunting expedition. *(Amended by Stats. 2011, Ch. 15, Sec. 542. (AB 109) Effective April 4, 2011. Amending action operative October 1, 2011, by Sec. 636 of Ch. 15, as amended by Stats. 2011, Ch. 39, Sec. 68. Section operative January 1, 2012, pursuant to Stats. 2010, Ch. 711, Sec.* **CHAPTER 2. Carrying a Concealed Firearm [25400 - 25700]**
(Chapter 2 added by Stats. 2010, Ch. 711, Sec. 6.)

ARTICLE 1. Crime of Carrying a Concealed Firearm [25400- 25400.]
(Article 1 added by Stats. 2010, Ch. 711, Sec. 6.)
25400.

(a) A person is guilty of carrying a concealed firearm when the person does any of the following:

(1) Carries concealed within any vehicle that is under the person's control or direction any pistol, revolver, or other firearm capable of being concealed upon the person.

(2) Carries concealed upon the person any pistol, revolver, or other firearm capable of being concealed upon the person.

(3) Causes to be carried concealed within any vehicle in which the person is an occupant any pistol, revolver, or other firearm capable of being concealed upon the person.

(b) A firearm carried openly in a belt holster is not concealed within the meaning of this section.

(c) Carrying a concealed firearm in violation of this section is punishable as follows:

(1) If the person previously has been convicted of any felony, or of any crime made punishable by a provision listed in Section 16580, as a felony.

(2) If the firearm is stolen and the person knew or had reasonable cause to believe that it was stolen, as a felony.

(3) If the person is an active participant in a criminal street gang, as defined in subdivision (a) of Section 186.22, under the Street Terrorism Enforcement and Prevention Act (Chapter 11 (commencing with Section 186.20) of Title 7 of Part 1), as a felony.

(4) If the person is not in lawful possession of the firearm or the person is within a class of persons prohibited from possessing or acquiring a firearm pursuant to Chapter 2 (commencing with Section 29800) or Chapter 3 (commencing with Section 29900) of Division 9 of this title, or Section 8100 or 8103 of the Welfare and Institutions Code, as a felony.

(5) If the person has been convicted of a crime against a person or property, or of a narcotics or dangerous drug violation, by imprisonment pursuant to subdivision (h) of Section 1170, or by imprisonment in a county jail not to exceed one year, by a fine not to exceed one thousand dollars ($1,000), or by both that imprisonment and fine.

(6) If both of the following conditions are met, by imprisonment pursuant to subdivision (h) of Section 1170, or by imprisonment in a county jail not to exceed one year, by a fine not to exceed one thousand dollars ($1,000), or by both that fine and imprisonment:

(A) The pistol, revolver, or other firearm capable of being concealed upon the person is loaded, or both it and the unexpended ammunition capable of being discharged from it are in the immediate possession of the person or readily accessible to that person.

(B) The person is not listed with the Department of Justice pursuant to paragraph (1) of subdivision (c) of Section 11106 as the registered owner of that pistol, revolver, or other firearm capable of being concealed upon the person.

(7) In all cases other than those specified in paragraphs (1) to (6), inclusive, by imprisonment in a county jail not to exceed one year, by a fine not to exceed one thousand dollars ($1,000), or by both that imprisonment and fine.

(d) (1) Every person convicted under this section who previously has been convicted of a misdemeanor offense enumerated in Section 23515 shall be punished by imprisonment in a county jail for at least three months and not exceeding six months, or, if granted probation, or if the execution or imposition of sentence is suspended, it shall be a condition thereof that the person be imprisoned in a county jail for at least three months.

(2) Every person convicted under this section who has previously been convicted of any felony, or of any crime made punishable by a provision listed in Section 16580, if probation is granted, or if the execution or imposition of sentence is suspended, it shall be a condition thereof that the person be imprisoned in a county jail for not less than three months.

(e) The court shall apply the three-month minimum sentence as specified in subdivision (d), except in unusual cases where the interests of justice would best be served by granting probation or suspending the imposition or execution of sentence without the minimum imprisonment required in subdivision (d) or by granting probation or suspending the imposition or execution of sentence with conditions other than those set forth in subdivision (d), in which case, the court shall specify on the record and shall enter on the minutes the circumstances indicating that the interests of justice would best be served by that disposition.

(f) A peace officer may arrest a person for a violation of paragraph (6) of subdivision (c) if the peace officer has probable cause to believe that the person is not listed with the Department of Justice pursuant to paragraph (1) of subdivision (c) of Section 11106 as the registered owner of the pistol, revolver, or other firearm capable of being concealed upon the person, and one or more of the conditions in subparagraph (A) of paragraph (6) of subdivision (c) is met.

(Amended by Stats. 2011, Ch. 15, Sec. 543. (AB 109) Effective April 4, 2011. Amending action operative October 1, 2011, by Sec. 636 of Ch. 15, as amended by Stats. 2011, Ch. 39, Sec. 68. Section operative January 1, 2012, pursuant to Stats. 2010, Ch. 711, Sec. 10.)

ARTICLE 2. Peace Officer Exemption [25450 - 25475]
(Article 2 added by Stats. 2010, Ch. 711, Sec. 6.)

25450.

As provided in this article, Section 25400 does not apply to, or affect, any of the following:

(a) Any peace officer, listed in Section 830.1 or 830.2, or subdivision (a) of Section 830.33, whether active or honorably retired.

(b) Any other duly appointed peace officer.

(c) Any honorably retired peace officer listed in subdivision (c) of Section 830.5.

(d) Any other honorably retired peace officer who during the course and scope of his or her appointment as a peace officer was authorized to, and did, carry a firearm.

(e) Any full-time paid peace officer of another state or the federal government who is carrying out official duties while in California.

(f) Any person summoned by any of these officers to assist in making arrests or preserving the peace while the person is actually engaged in assisting that officer.
(Amended by Stats. 2013, Ch. 267, Sec. 1. (AB 703) Effective January 1, 2014.)

25452.

A peace officer and an honorably retired peace officer shall, when leaving a handgun in an unattended vehicle, secure the handgun in the vehicle pursuant to Section 25140.
(Added by Stats. 2016, Ch. 651, Sec. 2. (SB 869) Effective January 1, 2017.)

25455.

(a) Any peace officer described in Section 25450 who has been honorably retired shall be issued an identification certificate by the law enforcement agency from which the officer retired.

(b) The issuing agency may charge a fee necessary to cover any reasonable expenses incurred by the agency in issuing certificates pursuant to this article.

(c) Any officer, except an officer listed in Section 830.1 or 830.2, subdivision (a) of Section 830.33, or subdivision (c) of Section 830.5 who retired prior to January 1, 1981, shall have an endorsement on the identification certificate stating that the issuing agency approves the officer's carrying of a concealed firearm.

(d) An honorably retired peace officer listed in Section 830.1 or 830.2, subdivision (a) of Section 830.33, or subdivision (c) of Section 830.5 who retired prior to January 1, 1981, shall not be required to obtain an endorsement from the issuing agency to carry a concealed firearm.
(Added by Stats. 2010, Ch. 711, Sec. 6. (SB 1080) Effective January 1, 2011. Operative January 1, 2012, by Sec. 10 of Ch. 711.)

25460.

(a) Except as provided in subdivision (b), no endorsement or renewal endorsement issued pursuant to Section 25465 shall be effective unless it is in the format set forth in subdivision (c).

(b) Any peace officer listed in subdivision (f) of Section 830.2 or in subdivision (c) of Section 830.5, who retired between January 2, 1981, and on or before December 31, 1988, and who is authorized to carry a concealed firearm pursuant to this article, shall not be required to have an endorsement in the format set forth in subdivision (c) until the time of the issuance, on or after January 1, 1989, of a renewal endorsement pursuant to Section 25465.

(c) A certificate issued pursuant to Section 25455 for any person who is not listed in Section 830.1 or 830.2, subdivision (a) of Section 830.33, or subdivision (c) of Section 830.5, or for any person retiring after January 1, 1981, shall be in the following format: it shall be on a 2x3 inch card, bear the photograph of the retiree, include the retiree's name, date of birth, the date that the retiree retired, and the name and address of the agency from which the retiree retired, and have stamped on it the endorsement "CCW Approved" and the date the endorsement is to be renewed. A certificate issued pursuant to Section 25455 shall not be valid as identification for the sale, purchase, or transfer of a firearm.
(Added by Stats. 2010, Ch. 711, Sec. 6. (SB 1080) Effective January 1, 2011. Operative January 1, 2012, by Sec. 10 of Ch. 711.)

25465.

Every five years, a retired peace officer, except an officer listed in Section 830.1 or 830.2, subdivision (a) of Section 830.33, or subdivision (c) of Section 830.5 who retired prior to January 1, 1981, shall petition the issuing agency for renewal of the officer's privilege to carry a concealed firearm.
(Added by Stats. 2010, Ch. 711, Sec. 6. (SB 1080) Effective January 1, 2011. Operative January 1, 2012, by Sec. 10 of Ch. 711.)

25470.

(a) The agency from which a peace officer is honorably retired may, upon initial retirement of that peace officer, or at any time subsequent thereto, deny or revoke for good cause the retired officer's privilege to carry a concealed firearm.

(b) A peace officer who is listed in Section 830.1 or 830.2, subdivision (a) of Section 830.33, or subdivision (c) of Section 830.5 who retired prior to January 1, 1981, shall have the privilege to carry a concealed firearm denied or revoked by having the agency from which the officer retired stamp on the officer's identification certificate "No CCW privilege."
(Added by Stats. 2010, Ch. 711, Sec. 6. (SB 1080) Effective January 1, 2011. Operative January 1, 2012, by Sec. 10 of Ch. 711.)

25475.

(a) An honorably retired peace officer who is listed in subdivision (c) of Section 830.5 and authorized to carry a concealed firearm by this article shall meet the training requirements of Section 832 and shall qualify with the firearm at least annually.

(b) The individual retired peace officer shall be responsible for maintaining eligibility to carry a concealed firearm.

(c) The Department of Justice shall provide subsequent arrest notification pursuant to Section 11105.2 regarding honorably retired peace officers listed in subdivision (c) of Section 830.5 to the agency from which the officer has retired.
(Added by Stats. 2010, Ch. 711, Sec. 6. (SB 1080) Effective January 1, 2011. Operative January 1, 2012, by Sec. 10 of Ch. 711.)

ARTICLE 2. Peace Officer Exemption [25450 - 25475]
(Article 2 added by Stats. 2010, Ch. 711, Sec. 6.)

25450.

As provided in this article, Section 25400 does not apply to, or affect, any of the following:

(a) Any peace officer, listed in Section 830.1 or 830.2, or subdivision (a) of Section 830.33, whether active or honorably retired.

(b) Any other duly appointed peace officer.

(c) Any honorably retired peace officer listed in subdivision (c) of Section 830.5.

(d) Any other honorably retired peace officer who during the course and scope of his or her appointment as a peace officer was authorized to, and did, carry a firearm.

(e) Any full-time paid peace officer of another state or the federal government who is carrying out official duties while in California.

(f) Any person summoned by any of these officers to assist in making arrests or preserving the peace while the person is actually engaged in assisting that officer.
(Amended by Stats. 2013, Ch. 267, Sec. 1. (AB 703) Effective January 1, 2014.)

25452.

A peace officer and an honorably retired peace officer shall, when leaving a handgun in an unattended vehicle, secure the handgun in the vehicle pursuant to Section 25140.
(Added by Stats. 2016, Ch. 651, Sec. 2. (SB 869) Effective January 1, 2017.)

25455.

(a) Any peace officer described in Section 25450 who has been honorably retired shall be issued an identification certificate by the law enforcement agency from which the officer retired.

(b) The issuing agency may charge a fee necessary to cover any reasonable expenses incurred by the agency in issuing certificates pursuant to this article.

(c) Any officer, except an officer listed in Section 830.1 or 830.2, subdivision (a) of Section 830.33, or subdivision (c) of Section 830.5 who retired prior to January 1, 1981, shall have an endorsement on the identification certificate stating that the issuing agency approves the officer's carrying of a concealed firearm.

(d) An honorably retired peace officer listed in Section 830.1 or 830.2, subdivision (a) of Section 830.33, or subdivision (c) of Section 830.5 who retired prior to January 1, 1981, shall not be required to obtain an endorsement from the issuing agency to carry a concealed firearm.
(Added by Stats. 2010, Ch. 711, Sec. 6. (SB 1080) Effective January 1, 2011. Operative January 1, 2012, by Sec. 10 of Ch. 711.)

25460.

(a) Except as provided in subdivision (b), no endorsement or renewal endorsement issued pursuant to Section 25465 shall be effective unless it is in the format set forth in subdivision (c).

(b) Any peace officer listed in subdivision (f) of Section 830.2 or in subdivision (c) of Section 830.5, who retired between January 2, 1981, and on or before December 31, 1988, and who is authorized to carry a concealed firearm pursuant to this article, shall not be required to have an endorsement in the format set forth in subdivision (c) until the time of the issuance, on or after January 1, 1989, of a renewal endorsement pursuant to Section 25465.

(c) A certificate issued pursuant to Section 25455 for any person who is not listed in Section 830.1 or 830.2, subdivision (a) of Section 830.33, or subdivision (c) of Section 830.5, or for any person retiring after January 1, 1981, shall be in the following format: it shall be on a 2x3 inch card, bear the photograph of the retiree, include the retiree's name, date of birth, the date that the retiree retired, and the name and address of the agency from which the retiree retired, and have stamped on it the endorsement "CCW Approved" and the date the endorsement is to be renewed. A certificate issued pursuant to Section 25455 shall not be valid as identification for the sale, purchase, or transfer of a firearm.
(Added by Stats. 2010, Ch. 711, Sec. 6. (SB 1080) Effective January 1, 2011. Operative January 1, 2012, by Sec. 10 of Ch. 711.)

25465.

Every five years, a retired peace officer, except an officer listed in Section 830.1 or 830.2, subdivision (a) of Section 830.33, or subdivision (c) of Section 830.5 who retired prior to January 1, 1981, shall petition the issuing agency for renewal of the officer's privilege to carry a concealed firearm.

(Added by Stats. 2010, Ch. 711, Sec. 6. (SB 1080) Effective January 1, 2011. Operative January 1, 2012, by Sec. 10 of Ch. 711.)
25470.
(a) The agency from which a peace officer is honorably retired may, upon initial retirement of that peace officer, or at any time subsequent thereto, deny or revoke for good cause the retired officer's privilege to carry a concealed firearm.
(b) A peace officer who is listed in Section 830.1 or 830.2, subdivision (a) of Section 830.33, or subdivision (c) of Section 830.5 who retired prior to January 1, 1981, shall have the privilege to carry a concealed firearm denied or revoked by having the agency from which the officer retired stamp on the officer's identification certificate "No CCW privilege."
(Added by Stats. 2010, Ch. 711, Sec. 6. (SB 1080) Effective January 1, 2011. Operative January 1, 2012, by Sec. 10 of Ch. 711.)
25475.
(a) An honorably retired peace officer who is listed in subdivision (c) of Section 830.5 and authorized to carry a concealed firearm by this article shall meet the training requirements of Section 832 and shall qualify with the firearm at least annually.
(b) The individual retired peace officer shall be responsible for maintaining eligibility to carry a concealed firearm.
(c) The Department of Justice shall provide subsequent arrest notification pursuant to Section 11105.2 regarding honorably retired peace officers listed in subdivision (c) of Section 830.5 to the agency from which the officer has retired.
(Added by Stats. 2010, Ch. 711, Sec. 6. (SB 1080) Effective January 1, 2011. Operative January 1, 2012, by Sec. 10 of Ch. 711.)

ARTICLE 3. Conditional Exemptions [25505 - 25595]
(Article 3 added by Stats. 2010, Ch. 711, Sec. 6.)
25505.
In order for a firearm to be exempted under this article, while being transported to or from a place, the firearm shall be unloaded and kept in a locked container, and the course of travel shall include only those deviations between authorized locations as are reasonably necessary under the circumstances.
(Added by Stats. 2010, Ch. 711, Sec. 6. (SB 1080) Effective January 1, 2011. Operative January 1, 2012, by Sec. 10 of Ch. 711.)
25510.
Section 25400 does not apply to, or affect, any of the following:
(a) The possession of a firearm by an authorized participant in a motion picture, television, or video production, or an entertainment event, when the participant lawfully uses the firearm as part of that production or event, or while going directly to, or coming directly from, that production or event.
(b) The transportation of a firearm by an authorized employee or agent of a supplier of firearms when going directly to, or coming directly from, a motion picture, television, or video production, or an entertainment event, for the purpose of providing that firearm to an authorized participant to lawfully use as a part of that production or event.
(Added by Stats. 2010, Ch. 711, Sec. 6. (SB 1080) Effective January 1, 2011. Operative January 1, 2012, by Sec. 10 of Ch. 711.)
25515.
Section 25400 does not apply to, or affect, the possession of a firearm in a locked container by a member of any club or organization, organized for the purpose of lawfully collecting and lawfully displaying pistols, revolvers, or other firearms, while the member is at a meeting of the club or organization or while going directly to, and coming directly from, a meeting of the club or organization.
(Added by Stats. 2010, Ch. 711, Sec. 6. (SB 1080) Effective January 1, 2011. Operative January 1, 2012, by Sec. 10 of Ch. 711.)
25520.
Section 25400 does not apply to, or affect, the transportation of a firearm by a participant when going directly to, or coming directly from, a recognized safety or hunter safety class, or a recognized sporting event involving that firearm.
(Added by Stats. 2010, Ch. 711, Sec. 6. (SB 1080) Effective January 1, 2011. Operative January 1, 2012, by Sec. 10 of Ch. 711.)
25525.
(a) Section 25400 does not apply to, or affect, the transportation of a firearm by any citizen of the United States or legal resident over the age of 18 years who resides or is temporarily within this state, and who is not within the excepted classes prescribed by Chapter 2 (commencing with Section 29800) or Chapter 3 (commencing with Section 29900) of Division 9 of this title, or Section 8100 or 8103 of the Welfare and Institutions Code, directly between any of the following places:
(1) The person's place of residence.
(2) The person's place of business.
(3) Private property owned or lawfully possessed by the person.
(b) Section 25400 does not apply to, or affect, the transportation of a firearm by a person listed in subdivision (a) when going directly from the place where that person lawfully received that firearm to that person's place of residence or place of business or to private property owned or lawfully possessed by that person.
(Added by Stats. 2010, Ch. 711, Sec. 6. (SB 1080) Effective January 1, 2011. Operative January 1, 2012, by Sec. 10 of Ch. 711.)
25530.
Section 25400 does not apply to, or affect, the transportation of a firearm by a person when going directly to, or coming directly from, a fixed place of business or private residential property for the purpose of the lawful repair or the lawful sale, loan, or transfer of that firearm.
(Added by Stats. 2010, Ch. 711, Sec. 6. (SB 1080) Effective January 1, 2011. Operative January 1, 2012, by Sec. 10 of Ch. 711.)
25535.
Section 25400 does not apply to, or affect, any of the following:
(a) The transportation of a firearm by a person when going directly to, or coming directly from, a gun show, swap meet, or similar event to which the public is invited, for the purpose of displaying that firearm in a lawful manner.
(b) The transportation of a firearm by a person when going directly to, or coming directly from, a gun show or event, as defined in Section 478.100 of Title 27 of the Code of Federal Regulations, for the purpose of lawfully transferring, selling, or loaning that firearm in accordance with Section 27545.
(Added by Stats. 2010, Ch. 711, Sec. 6. (SB 1080) Effective January 1, 2011. Operative January 1, 2012, by Sec. 10 of Ch. 711.)
25540.
Section 25400 does not apply to, or affect, the transportation of a firearm by a person when going directly to, or coming directly from, a target range, which holds a regulatory or business license, for the purposes of practicing shooting at targets with that firearm at that target range.
(Added by Stats. 2010, Ch. 711, Sec. 6. (SB 1080) Effective January 1, 2011. Operative January 1, 2012, by Sec. 10 of Ch. 711.)
25545.
Section 25400 does not apply to, or affect, the transportation of a firearm by a person when going directly to, or coming directly from, a place designated by a person authorized to issue licenses pursuant to Section 26150, 26155, 26170, or 26215, when done at the request of the issuing agency so that the issuing agency can determine whether or not a license should be issued to that person to carry that firearm.
(Added by Stats. 2010, Ch. 711, Sec. 6. (SB 1080) Effective January 1, 2011. Operative January 1, 2012, by Sec. 10 of Ch. 711.)
25550.

(a) Section 25400 does not apply to, or affect, the transportation of a firearm by a person when going directly to, or coming directly from, a lawful camping activity for the purpose of having that firearm available for lawful personal protection while at the lawful campsite.
(b) This section shall not be construed to override the statutory authority granted to the Department of Parks and Recreation or any other state or local governmental agencies to promulgate rules and regulations governing the administration of parks and campgrounds.
(Added by Stats. 2010, Ch. 711, Sec. 6. (SB 1080) Effective January 1, 2011. Operative January 1, 2012, by Sec. 10 of Ch. 711.)
25555.
Section 25400 does not apply to, or affect, the transportation of a firearm by a person in order to comply with Section 27870, 27875, 27915, 27920, or 27925, as it pertains to that firearm.
(Added by Stats. 2010, Ch. 711, Sec. 6. (SB 1080) Effective January 1, 2011. Operative January 1, 2012, by Sec. 10 of Ch. 711.)
25560.
Section 25400 does not apply to, or affect, the transportation of a firearm by a person in order to utilize Section 28000 as it pertains to that firearm.
(Added by Stats. 2010, Ch. 711, Sec. 6. (SB 1080) Effective January 1, 2011. Operative January 1, 2012, by Sec. 10 of Ch. 711.)
25565.
Section 25400 does not apply to, or affect, the transportation of a firearm by a person in order to sell, deliver, or transfer the firearm as specified in Section 27850 or 31725 to an authorized representative of a city, city and county, county, or state or federal government that is acquiring the weapon as part of an authorized, voluntary program in which the entity is buying or receiving weapons from private individuals.
(Added by Stats. 2010, Ch. 711, Sec. 6. (SB 1080) Effective January 1, 2011. Operative January 1, 2012, by Sec. 10 of Ch. 711.)
25570.
Section 25400 does not apply to, or affect, any of the following:
(a) The transportation of a firearm by a person who finds the firearm, if the person is transporting the firearm in order to comply with Article 1 (commencing with Section 2080) of Chapter 4 of Division 3 of the Civil Code as it pertains to that firearm, and, if the person is transporting the firearm to a law enforcement agency, the person gives prior notice to the law enforcement agency that the person is transporting the firearm to the law enforcement agency.
(b) The transportation of a firearm by a person who finds the firearm and is transporting it to a law enforcement agency for disposition according to law, if the person gives prior notice to the law enforcement agency that the person is transporting the firearm to the law enforcement agency for disposition according to law.
(Added by Stats. 2010, Ch. 711, Sec. 6. (SB 1080) Effective January 1, 2011. Operative January 1, 2012, by Sec. 10 of Ch. 711.)
25575.
Section 25400 does not apply to, or affect, the transportation of a firearm by a person in order to comply with Section 27560 as it pertains to that firearm.
(Added by Stats. 2010, Ch. 711, Sec. 6. (SB 1080) Effective January 1, 2011. Operative January 1, 2012, by Sec. 10 of Ch. 711.)
25580.
Section 25400 does not apply to, or affect, the transportation of a firearm that is a curio or relic, as defined in Section 478.11 of Title 27 of the Code of Federal Regulations, by a person in order to comply with Section 27565 as it pertains to that firearm.
(Added by Stats. 2010, Ch. 711, Sec. 6. (SB 1080) Effective January 1, 2011. Operative January 1, 2012, by Sec. 10 of Ch. 711.)
25585.
Section 25400 does not apply to, or affect, the transportation of a firearm by a person for the purpose of obtaining an identification number or mark assigned to that firearm from the Department of Justice pursuant to Section 23910.
(Added by Stats. 2010, Ch. 711, Sec. 6. (SB 1080) Effective January 1, 2011. Operative January 1, 2012, by Sec. 10 of Ch. 711.)
25590.
Section 25400 does not apply to, or affect, the transportation of a firearm by a person if done directly between any of the places set forth below:
(a) A place where the person may carry that firearm pursuant to an exemption from the prohibition set forth in subdivision (a) of Section 25400.
(b) A place where that person may carry that firearm pursuant to an exemption from the prohibition set forth in subdivision (a) of Section 25850, or a place where the prohibition set forth in subdivision (a) of Section 25850 does not apply.
(c) A place where that person may carry a firearm pursuant to an exemption from the prohibition set forth in subdivision (a) of Section 26350, or a place where the prohibition set forth in subdivision (a) of Section 26350 does not apply.
(Added by Stats. 2011, Ch. 725, Sec. 11. (AB 144) Effective January 1, 2012.)
25595.
This article does not prohibit or limit the otherwise lawful carrying or transportation of any handgun in accordance with the provisions listed in Section 16580.
(Amended by Stats. 2011, Ch. 725, Sec. 12. (AB 144) Effective January 1, 2012.)

ARTICLE 4. Other Exemptions [25600 - 25655]
(Article 4 added by Stats. 2010, Ch. 711, Sec. 6.)
25600.
(a) A violation of Section 25400 is justifiable when a person who possesses a firearm reasonably believes that person is in grave danger because of circumstances forming the basis of a current restraining order issued by a court against another person who has been found to pose a threat to the life or safety of the person who possesses the firearm. This section may not apply when the circumstances involve a mutual restraining order issued pursuant to Division 10 (commencing with Section 6200) of the Family Code absent a factual finding of a specific threat to the person's life or safety. It is not the intent of the Legislature to limit, restrict, or narrow the application of current statutory or judicial authority to apply this or other justifications to a defendant charged with violating Section 25400 or committing another similar offense.
(b) Upon trial for violating Section 25400, the trier of fact shall determine whether the defendant was acting out of a reasonable belief that the defendant was in grave danger.
(Added by Stats. 2010, Ch. 711, Sec. 6. (SB 1080) Effective January 1, 2011. Operative January 1, 2012, by Sec. 10 of Ch. 711.)
25605.
(a) Section 25400 and Chapter 6 (commencing with Section 26350) of Division 5 shall not apply to or affect any citizen of the United States or legal resident over the age of 18 years who resides or is temporarily within this state, and who is not within the excepted classes prescribed by Chapter 2 (commencing with Section 29800) or Chapter 3 (commencing with Section 29900) of Division 9 of this title, or Section 8100 or 8103 of the Welfare and Institutions Code, who carries, either openly or concealed, anywhere within the citizen's or legal resident's place of residence, place of business, or on private property owned or lawfully possessed by the citizen or legal resident, any handgun.
(b) No permit or license to purchase, own, possess, keep, or carry, either openly or concealed, shall be required of any citizen of the United States or legal resident over the age of 18 years who resides or is temporarily within this state, and who is not within the excepted classes prescribed by Chapter 2 (commencing with Section 29800) or Chapter 3 (commencing with Section 29900) of Division 9 of this title, or Section 8100 or 8103 of the Welfare and Institutions Code, to purchase, own, possess, keep, or carry, either openly or concealed, a handgun within the citizen's or legal resident's place of

residence, place of business, or on private property owned or lawfully possessed by the citizen or legal resident.

(c) Nothing in this section shall be construed as affecting the application of Sections 25850 to 26055, inclusive.

(Amended by Stats. 2011, Ch. 725, Sec. 13. (AB 144) Effective January 1, 2012.)

25610.

(a) Section 25400 shall not be construed to prohibit any citizen of the United States over the age of 18 years who resides or is temporarily within this state, and who is not prohibited by state or federal law from possessing, receiving, owning, or purchasing a firearm, from transporting or carrying any pistol, revolver, or other firearm capable of being concealed upon the person, provided that the following applies to the firearm:

(1) The firearm is within a motor vehicle and it is locked in the vehicle's trunk or in a locked container in the vehicle.

(2) The firearm is carried by the person directly to or from any motor vehicle for any lawful purpose and, while carrying the firearm, the firearm is contained within a locked container.

(b) The provisions of this section do not prohibit or limit the otherwise lawful carrying or transportation of any pistol, revolver, or other firearm capable of being concealed upon the person in accordance with the provisions listed in Section 16580.

(Added by Stats. 2010, Ch. 711, Sec. 6. (SB 1080) Effective January 1, 2011. Operative January 1, 2012, by Sec. 10 of Ch. 711.)

25612.

A person shall, when leaving a handgun in an unattended vehicle, secure the handgun in the vehicle pursuant to Section 25140.

(Added by Stats. 2016, Ch. 651, Sec. 3. (SB 869) Effective January 1, 2017.)

25615.

Section 25400 does not apply to, or affect, the possession or transportation of unloaded pistols, revolvers, or other firearms capable of being concealed upon the person as merchandise by a person who is engaged in the business of manufacturing, importing, wholesaling, repairing, or dealing in firearms and who is licensed to engage in that business, or the authorized representative or authorized agent of that person, while engaged in the lawful course of the business.

(Added by Stats. 2010, Ch. 711, Sec. 6. (SB 1080) Effective January 1, 2011. Operative January 1, 2012, by Sec. 10 of Ch. 711.)

25620.

Section 25400 does not apply to, or affect, any member of the Army, Navy, Air Force, Coast Guard, or Marine Corps of the United States, or the National Guard, when on duty, or any organization that is by law authorized to purchase or receive those weapons from the United States or this state.

(Added by Stats. 2010, Ch. 711, Sec. 6. (SB 1080) Effective January 1, 2011. Operative January 1, 2012, by Sec. 10 of Ch. 711.)

25625.

Section 25400 does not apply to, or affect, the carrying of unloaded pistols, revolvers, or other firearms capable of being concealed upon the person by duly authorized military or civil organizations while parading, or the members thereof when going to and from the places of meeting of their respective organizations.

(Added by Stats. 2010, Ch. 711, Sec. 6. (SB 1080) Effective January 1, 2011. Operative January 1, 2012, by Sec. 10 of Ch. 711.)

25630.

Section 25400 does not apply to, or affect, any guard or messenger of any common carrier, bank, or other financial institution, while actually employed in and about the shipment, transportation, or delivery of any money, treasure, bullion, bonds, or other thing of value within this state.

(Added by Stats. 2010, Ch. 711, Sec. 6. (SB 1080) Effective January 1, 2011. Operative January 1, 2012, by Sec. 10 of Ch. 711.)

25635.

Section 25400 does not apply to, or affect, members of any club or organization organized for the purpose of practicing shooting at targets upon established target ranges, whether public or private, while the members are using pistols, revolvers, or other firearms capable of being concealed upon the person upon the target ranges, or transporting these firearms unloaded when going to and from the ranges.

(Added by Stats. 2010, Ch. 711, Sec. 6. (SB 1080) Effective January 1, 2011. Operative January 1, 2012, by Sec. 10 of Ch. 711.)

25640.

Section 25400 does not apply to, or affect, licensed hunters or fishermen carrying pistols, revolvers, or other firearms capable of being concealed upon the person while engaged in hunting or fishing, or transporting those firearms unloaded when going to or returning from the hunting or fishing expedition.

(Added by Stats. 2010, Ch. 711, Sec. 6. (SB 1080) Effective January 1, 2011. Operative January 1, 2012, by Sec. 10 of Ch. 711.)

25645.

Sections 25140 and 25400 do not apply to, or affect, the transportation of unloaded firearms by a person operating a licensed common carrier or an authorized agent or employee thereof when the firearms are transported in conformance with applicable federal law.

(Amended by Stats. 2016, Ch. 651, Sec. 4. (SB 869) Effective January 1, 2017.)

25650.

(a) Upon approval of the sheriff of the county in which the retiree resides, Section 25400 does not apply to, or affect, any honorably retired federal officer or agent of any federal law enforcement agency, including, but not limited to, the Federal Bureau of Investigation, the United States Secret Service, the United States Customs Service, the federal Bureau of Alcohol, Tobacco, Firearms and Explosives, the Federal Bureau of Narcotics, the United States Drug Enforcement Administration, the United States Border Patrol, and any officer or agent of the Internal Revenue Service who was authorized to carry weapons while on duty, who was assigned to duty within the state for a period of not less than one year, or who retired from active service in the state.

(b) A retired federal officer or agent shall provide the sheriff with certification from the agency from which the officer or agent retired certifying that person's service in the state, stating the nature of that person's retirement, and indicating the agency's concurrence that the retired federal officer or agent should be accorded the privilege of carrying a concealed firearm.

(c) Upon that approval, the sheriff shall issue a permit to the retired federal officer or agent indicating that the retiree may carry a concealed firearm in accordance with this section. The permit shall be valid for a period not exceeding five years, shall be carried by the retiree while carrying a concealed firearm, and may be revoked for good cause.

(d) The sheriff of the county in which the retired federal officer or agent resides may require recertification prior to a permit renewal, and may suspend the privilege for cause. The sheriff may charge a fee necessary to cover any reasonable expenses incurred by the county.

(Amended by Stats. 2011, Ch. 296, Sec. 230. (AB 1023) Effective January 1, 2012.)

25655.

Section 25400 does not apply to, or affect, the carrying of a pistol, revolver, or other firearm capable of being concealed upon the person by a person who is authorized to carry that weapon in a concealed manner pursuant to Chapter 4 (commencing with Section 26150).

(Added by Stats. 2010, Ch. 711, Sec. 6. (SB 1080) Effective January 1, 2011. Operative January 1, 2012, by Sec. 10 of Ch. 711.)

ARTICLE 5. Concealed Carrying of Firearm as a Nuisance [25700- 25700.]
(Article 5 added by Stats. 2010, Ch. 711, Sec. 6.)

25700.

(a) The unlawful carrying of any handgun in violation of Section 25400 is a nuisance and is subject to Sections 18000 and 18005.

(b) This section does not apply to any of the following:

(1) Any firearm in the possession of the Department of Fish and Game.

(2) Any firearm that was used in the violation of any provision of the Fish and Game Code or any regulation adopted pursuant thereto.

(3) Any firearm that is forfeited pursuant to Section 5008.6 of the Public Resources Code.

(Added by Stats. 2010, Ch. 711, Sec. 6. (SB 1080) Effective January 1, 2011. Operative January 1, 2012, by Sec. 10 of Ch. 711.)

CHAPTER 3. Carrying a Loaded Firearm [25800 - 26100]

(Chapter 3 added by Stats. 2010, Ch. 711, Sec. 6.)

ARTICLE 1. Armed Criminal Action [25800- 25800.]
(Article 1 added by Stats. 2010, Ch. 711, Sec. 6.)

25800.

(a) Every person who carries a loaded firearm with the intent to commit a felony is guilty of armed criminal action.

(b) Armed criminal action is punishable by imprisonment in a county jail not exceeding one year, or in the state prison.

(Added by Stats. 2010, Ch. 711, Sec. 6. (SB 1080) Effective January 1, 2011. Operative January 1, 2012, by Sec. 10 of Ch. 711.)

ARTICLE 2. Crime of Carrying a Loaded Firearm in Public [25850- 25850.]
(Article 2 added by Stats. 2010, Ch. 711, Sec. 6.)

25850.

(a) A person is guilty of carrying a loaded firearm when the person carries a loaded firearm on the person or in a vehicle while in any public place or on any public street in an incorporated city or in any public place or on any public street in a prohibited area of unincorporated territory.

(b) In order to determine whether or not a firearm is loaded for the purpose of enforcing this section, peace officers are authorized to examine any firearm carried by anyone on the person or in a vehicle while in any public place or on any public street in an incorporated city or prohibited area of an unincorporated territory. Refusal to allow a peace officer to inspect a firearm pursuant to this section constitutes probable cause for arrest for violation of this section.

(c) Carrying a loaded firearm in violation of this section is punishable, as follows:

(1) Where the person previously has been convicted of any felony, or of any crime made punishable by a provision listed in Section 16580, as a felony.

(2) Where the firearm is stolen and the person knew or had reasonable cause to believe that it was stolen, as a felony.

(3) Where the person is an active participant in a criminal street gang, as defined in subdivision (a) of Section 186.22, under the Street Terrorism Enforcement and Prevention Act (Chapter 11 (commencing with Section 186.20) of Title 7 of Part 1), as a felony.

(4) Where the person is not in lawful possession of the firearm, or is within a class of persons prohibited from possessing or acquiring a firearm pursuant to Chapter 2 (commencing with Section 29800) or Chapter 3 (commencing with Section 29900) of Division 9 of this title, or Section 8100 or 8103 of the Welfare and Institutions Code, as a felony.

(5) Where the person has been convicted of a crime against a person or property, or of a narcotics or dangerous drug violation, by imprisonment pursuant to subdivision (h) of Section 1170, or by imprisonment in a county jail not to exceed one year, by a fine not to exceed one thousand dollars ($1,000), or by both that imprisonment and fine.

(6) Where the person is not listed with the Department of Justice pursuant to Section 11106 as the registered owner of the handgun, by imprisonment pursuant to subdivision (h) of Section 1170, or by imprisonment in a county jail not to exceed one year, or by a fine not to exceed one thousand dollars ($1,000), or both that fine and imprisonment.

(7) In all cases other than those specified in paragraphs (1) to (6), inclusive, as a misdemeanor, punishable by imprisonment in a county jail not to exceed one year, by a fine not to exceed one thousand dollars ($1,000), or by both that imprisonment and fine.

(d) (1) Every person convicted under this section who has previously been convicted of an offense enumerated in Section 23515, or of any crime made punishable under a provision listed in Section 16580, shall serve a term of at least three months in a county jail, or, if granted probation or if the execution or imposition of sentence is suspended, it shall be a condition thereof that the person be imprisoned for a period of at least three months.

(2) The court shall apply the three-month minimum sentence except in unusual cases where the interests of justice would best be served by granting probation or suspending the imposition or execution of sentence without the minimum imprisonment required in this section or by granting probation or suspending the imposition or execution of sentence with conditions other than those set forth in this section, in which case, the court shall specify on the record and shall enter on the minutes the circumstances indicating that the interests of justice would best be served by that disposition.

(e) A violation of this section that is punished by imprisonment in a county jail not exceeding one year shall not constitute a conviction of a crime punishable by imprisonment for a term exceeding one year for the purposes of determining federal firearms eligibility under Section 922(g)(1) of Title 18 of the United States Code.

(f) Nothing in this section, or in Article 3 (commencing with Section 25900) or Article 4 (commencing with Section 26000), shall preclude prosecution under Chapter 2 (commencing with Section 29800) or Chapter 3 (commencing with Section 29900) of Division 9 of this title, Section 8100 or 8103 of the Welfare and Institutions Code, or any other law with a greater penalty than this section.

(g) Notwithstanding paragraphs (2) and (3) of subdivision (a) of Section 836, a peace officer may make an arrest without a warrant:

(1) When the person arrested has violated this section, although not in the officer's presence.

(2) Whenever the officer has reasonable cause to believe that the person to be arrested has violated this section, whether or not this section has, in fact, been violated.

(h) A peace officer may arrest a person for a violation of paragraph (6) of subdivision (c), if the peace officer has probable cause to believe that the person is carrying a handgun in violation of this section and that person is not listed with the Department of Justice pursuant to paragraph (1) of subdivision (c) of Section 11106 as the registered owner of that handgun.

(Amended by Stats. 2011, Ch. 15, Sec. 544. (AB 109) Effective April 4, 2011. Amending action operative October 1, 2011, by Sec. 636 of Ch. 15, as amended by Stats. 2011, Ch. 39, Sec. 68. Section operative January 1, 2012, pursuant to Stats. 2010, Ch. 711, Sec. 10.)

ARTICLE 3. Peace Officer Exemption to the Crime of Carrying a Loaded Firearm in Public [25900 - 25925]
(Article 3 added by Stats. 2010, Ch. 711, Sec. 6.)

25900.

As provided in this article, Section 25850 does not apply to any of the following:

(a) Any peace officer, listed in Section 830.1 or 830.2, or subdivision (a) of Section 830.33, whether active or honorably retired.

(b) Any other duly appointed peace officer.

(c) Any honorably retired peace officer listed in subdivision (c) of Section 830.5.

(d) Any other honorably retired peace officer who during the course and scope of his or her appointment as a peace officer was authorized to, and did, carry a firearm.

(e) Any full-time paid peace officer of another state or the federal government who is carrying out official duties while in California.

(f) Any person summoned by any of these officers to assist in making arrests or preserving the peace while the person is actually engaged in assisting that officer.

(Amended by Stats. 2013, Ch. 267, Sec. 2. (AB 703) Effective January 1, 2014.)

25905.

(a) (1) Any peace officer described in Section 25900 who has been honorably retired shall be issued an identification certificate by the law enforcement agency from which the officer has retired.

(2) If the agency from which the officer has retired is no longer providing law enforcement services or the relevant governmental body is dissolved, the agency that subsequently provides law enforcement services for that jurisdiction shall issue the identification certificate to that peace officer. This paragraph shall apply only if the following conditions are met:

(A) The successor agency is in possession of the retired officer's complete personnel records or can otherwise verify the retired officer's honorably retired status.

(B) The retired officer is in compliance with all the requirements of the successor agency for the issuance of a retirement identification card and concealed weapon endorsement.

(b) The issuing agency may charge a fee necessary to cover any reasonable expenses incurred by the agency in issuing certificates pursuant to Sections 25900, 25910, 25925, and this section.

(c) Any officer, except an officer listed in Section 830.1 or 830.2, subdivision (a) of Section 830.33, or subdivision (c) of Section 830.5 who retired prior to January 1, 1981, shall have an endorsement on the identification certificate stating that the issuing agency approves the officer's carrying of a loaded firearm.

(d) An honorably retired peace officer listed in Section 830.1 or 830.2, subdivision (a) of Section 830.33, or subdivision (c) of Section 830.5 who retired prior to January 1, 1981, shall not be required to obtain an endorsement from the issuing agency to carry a loaded firearm.

(Amended by Stats. 2013, Ch. 149, Sec. 1. (SB 303) Effective January 1, 2014.)

25910.

(a) Except as provided in subdivision (b), no endorsement or renewal endorsement issued pursuant to Section 25915 shall be effective unless it is in the format set forth in subdivision (c) of Section 25460.

(b) Any peace officer listed in subdivision (f) of Section 830.2 or in subdivision (c) of Section 830.5, who is retired between January 2, 1981, and on or before December 31, 1988, and who is authorized to carry a loaded firearm pursuant to this article, shall not be required to have an endorsement in the format set forth in subdivision (c) of Section 25460 until the time of the issuance, on or after January 1, 1989, of a renewal endorsement pursuant to Section 25915.

(Added by Stats. 2010, Ch. 711, Sec. 6. (SB 1080) Effective January 1, 2011. Operative January 1, 2012, by Sec. 10 of Ch. 711.)

25915.

Every five years, a retired peace officer, except an officer listed in Section 830.1 or 830.2, subdivision (a) of Section 830.33, or subdivision (c) of Section 830.5 who retired prior to January 1, 1981, shall petition the issuing agency, or a successor agency pursuant to paragraph (2) of subdivision (a) of Section 25905, for renewal of the privilege to carry a loaded firearm.

(Amended by Stats. 2013, Ch. 149, Sec. 2. (SB 303) Effective January 1, 2014.)

25920.

(a) The agency from which a peace officer is honorably retired, or a successor agency pursuant to paragraph (2) of subdivision (a) of Section 25905, may, upon initial retirement of the peace officer, or at any time subsequent thereto, deny or revoke for good cause the retired officer's privilege to carry a loaded firearm.

(b) A peace officer who is listed in Section 830.1 or 830.2, subdivision (a) of Section 830.33, or subdivision (c) of Section 830.5 who is retired prior to January 1, 1981, shall have the privilege to carry a loaded firearm denied or revoked by having the agency from which the officer retired, or a successor agency pursuant to paragraph (2) of subdivision (a) of Section 25905, stamp on the officer's identification certificate "No CCW privilege."

(Amended by Stats. 2013, Ch. 149, Sec. 3. (SB 303) Effective January 1, 2014.)

25925.

(a) An honorably retired peace officer who is listed in subdivision (c) of Section 830.5 and authorized to carry a loaded firearm by this article shall meet the training requirements of Section 832 and shall qualify with the firearm at least annually.

(b) The individual retired peace officer shall be responsible for maintaining eligibility to carry a loaded firearm.

(c) The Department of Justice shall provide subsequent arrest notification pursuant to Section 11105.2 regarding honorably retired peace officers listed in subdivision (c) of Section 830.5 to the agency from which the officer has retired, or a successor agency pursuant to paragraph (2) of subdivision (a) of Section 25905.

(Amended by Stats. 2013, Ch. 149, Sec. 4. (SB 303) Effective January 1, 2014.)

ARTICLE 4. Other Exemptions to the Crime of Carrying a Loaded Firearm in Public [26000 - 26060]

(Article 4 added by Stats. 2010, Ch. 711, Sec. 6.)

26000.

Section 25850 does not apply to members of the military forces of this state or of the United States engaged in the performance of their duties.

(Added by Stats. 2010, Ch. 711, Sec. 6. (SB 1080) Effective January 1, 2011. Operative January 1, 2012, by Sec. 10 of Ch. 711.)

26005.

Section 25850 does not apply to either of the following:

(a) Persons who are using target ranges for the purpose of practice shooting with a firearm.

(b) Members of shooting clubs while hunting on the premises of those clubs.

(Added by Stats. 2010, Ch. 711, Sec. 6. (SB 1080) Effective January 1, 2011. Operative January 1, 2012, by Sec. 10 of Ch. 711.)

26010.

Section 25850 does not apply to the carrying of any handgun by any person as authorized pursuant to Chapter 4 (commencing with Section 26150) of Division 5.

(Added by Stats. 2010, Ch. 711, Sec. 6. (SB 1080) Effective January 1, 2011. Operative January 1, 2012, by Sec. 10 of Ch. 711.)

26015.

Section 25850 does not apply to any armored vehicle guard, as defined in Section 7582.1 of the Business and Professions Code, if either of the following conditions is satisfied:

(a) The guard was hired prior to January 1, 1977, and is acting within the course and scope of employment.

(b) The guard was hired on or after January 1, 1977, has received a firearms qualification card from the Department of Consumer Affairs, and is acting within the course and scope of employment.

(Added by Stats. 2010, Ch. 711, Sec. 6. (SB 1080) Effective January 1, 2011. Operative January 1, 2012, by Sec. 10 of Ch. 711.)

26020.

(a) Upon approval of the sheriff of the county in which the retiree resides, Section 25850 does not apply to any honorably retired federal officer or agent of any federal law enforcement agency, including, but not limited to, the Federal Bureau of Investigation, the United States Secret Service, the United States Customs Service, the federal Bureau of Alcohol, Tobacco, Firearms and Explosives, the Federal Bureau of Narcotics, the United States Drug Enforcement Administration, the United States Border Patrol, and any officer or agent of the Internal Revenue Service who was authorized to carry weapons while on duty, who was assigned to duty within the state for a period of not less than one year, or who retired from active service in the state.

(b) A retired federal officer or agent shall provide the sheriff with certification from the agency from which the officer or agent retired certifying that person's service in the state, stating the nature of that person's retirement, and indicating the agency's concurrence that the retired federal officer or agent should be accorded the privilege of carrying a loaded firearm.

(c) Upon approval, the sheriff shall issue a permit to the retired federal officer or agent indicating that the retiree may carry a loaded firearm in accordance with this section. The permit shall be valid for a period not exceeding five years, shall be carried by the retiree while carrying a loaded firearm, and may be revoked for good cause.

(d) The sheriff of the county in which the retired federal officer or agent resides may require recertification prior to a permit renewal, and may suspend the privilege for cause. The sheriff may charge a fee necessary to cover any reasonable expenses incurred by the county.

(Amended by Stats. 2011, Ch. 296, Sec. 231. (AB 1023) Effective January 1, 2012.)

26025.

Section 25850 does not apply to any of the following who have completed a regular course in firearms training approved by the Commission on Peace Officer Standards and Training:

(a) Patrol special police officers appointed by the police commission of any city, county, or city and county under the express terms of its charter who also, under the express terms of the charter, satisfy all of the following requirements:

(1) They are subject to suspension or dismissal after a hearing on charges duly filed with the commission after a fair and impartial trial.

(2) They are not less than 18 years of age or more than 40 years of age.

(3) They possess physical qualifications prescribed by the commission.

(4) They are designated by the police commission as the owners of a certain beat or territory as may be fixed from time to time by the police commission.

(b) Animal control officers or zookeepers, regularly compensated in that capacity by a governmental agency, when carrying weapons while acting in the course and scope of their employment and when designated by a local ordinance or, if the governmental agency is not authorized to act by ordinance, by a resolution, either individually or by class, to carry the weapons.

(c) Persons who are authorized to carry the weapons pursuant to Section 14502 of the Corporations Code, while actually engaged in the performance of their duties pursuant to that section.

(d) Harbor police officers designated pursuant to Section 663.5 of the Harbors and Navigation Code.

(Added by Stats. 2010, Ch. 711, Sec. 6. (SB 1080) Effective January 1, 2011. Operative January 1, 2012, by Sec. 10 of Ch. 711.)

26030.

(a) Section 25850 does not apply to any of the following who have been issued a certificate pursuant to subdivision (d):

(1) Guards or messengers of common carriers, banks, and other financial institutions, while actually employed in and about the shipment, transportation, or delivery of any money, treasure, bullion, bonds, or other thing of value within this state.

(2) Guards of contract carriers operating armored vehicles pursuant to California Highway Patrol and Public Utilities Commission authority, if they were hired prior to January 1, 1977.

(3) Guards of contract carriers operating armored vehicles pursuant to California Highway Patrol and Public Utilities Commission authority, if they were hired on or after January 1, 1977, and they have completed a course in the carrying and use of firearms that meets the standards prescribed by the Department of Consumer Affairs.

(4) Private investigators licensed pursuant to Chapter 11.3 (commencing with Section 7512) of Division 3 of the Business and Professions Code, while acting within the course and scope of their employment.

(5) Uniformed employees of private investigators licensed pursuant to Chapter 11.3 (commencing with Section 7512) of Division 3 of the Business and Professions Code, while acting within the course and scope of their employment.

(6) Private patrol operators licensed pursuant to Chapter 11.5 (commencing with Section 7580) of Division 3 of the Business and Professions Code, while acting within the course and scope of their employment.

(7) Uniformed employees of private patrol operators licensed pursuant to Chapter 11.5 (commencing with Section 7580) of Division 3 of the Business and Professions Code, while acting within the course and scope of their employment.

(8) Alarm company operators licensed pursuant to Chapter 11.6 (commencing with Section 7590) of Division 3 of the Business and Professions Code, while acting within the course and scope of their employment.

(9) Uniformed security guards or night watch persons employed by any public agency, while acting within the scope and course of their employment.

(10) Uniformed security guards, regularly employed and compensated in that capacity by persons engaged in any lawful business, and uniformed alarm agents employed by an alarm company operator, while actually engaged in protecting and preserving the property of their employers, or on duty or en route to or from their residences or their places of employment, and security guards and alarm agents en route to or from their residences or employer-required range training.

(b) Nothing in paragraph (10) of subdivision (a) shall be construed to prohibit cities and counties from enacting ordinances requiring alarm agents to register their names.

(c) A certificate under this section shall not be required of any person who is a peace officer, who has completed all training required by law for the exercise of the person's power as a peace officer, and who is employed while not on duty as a peace officer.

(d) The Department of Consumer Affairs may issue a certificate to any person referred to in this section, upon notification by the school where the course was completed, that the person has successfully completed a course in the carrying and use of firearms and a course of training in the exercise of the powers of arrest, which meet the standards prescribed by the department pursuant to Section 7583.5 of the Business and Professions Code.

(Added by Stats. 2010, Ch. 711, Sec. 6. (SB 1080) Effective January 1, 2011. Operative January 1, 2012, by Sec. 10 of Ch. 711.)

26035.

Nothing in Section 25850 shall prevent any person engaged in any lawful business, including a nonprofit organization, or any officer, employee, or agent authorized by that person for lawful purposes connected with that business, from having a loaded firearm within the person's place of business, or any person in lawful possession of private property from having a loaded firearm on that property.

(Added by Stats. 2010, Ch. 711, Sec. 6. (SB 1080) Effective January 1, 2011. Operative January 1, 2012, by Sec. 10 of Ch. 711.)

26040.

Nothing in Section 25850 shall prevent any person from carrying a loaded firearm in an area within an incorporated city while engaged in hunting, provided that the hunting at that place and time is not prohibited by the city council.
(Added by Stats. 2010, Ch. 711, Sec. 6. (SB 1080) Effective January 1, 2011. Operative January 1, 2012, by Sec. 10 of Ch. 711.)
26045.
(a) Nothing in Section 25850 is intended to preclude the carrying of any loaded firearm, under circumstances where it would otherwise be lawful, by a person who reasonably believes that any person or the property of any person is in immediate, grave danger and that the carrying of the weapon is necessary for the preservation of that person or property.
(b) A violation of Section 25850 is justifiable when a person who possesses a firearm reasonably believes that person is in grave danger because of circumstances forming the basis of a current restraining order issued by a court against another person who has been found to pose a threat to the life or safety of the person who possesses the firearm. This subdivision may not apply when the circumstances involve a mutual restraining order issued pursuant to Division 10 (commencing with Section 6200) of the Family Code absent a factual finding of a specific threat to the person's life or safety. It is not the intent of the Legislature to limit, restrict, or narrow the application of current statutory or judicial authority to apply this or other justifications to a defendant charged with violating Section 25850 or committing another similar offense. Upon trial for violating Section 25850, the trier of fact shall determine whether the defendant was acting out of a reasonable belief that the defendant was in grave danger.
(c) As used in this section, "immediate" means the brief interval before and after the local law enforcement agency, when reasonably possible, has been notified of the danger and before the arrival of its assistance.
(Amended by Stats. 2018, Ch. 185, Sec. 7. (AB 2176) Effective January 1, 2019.)
26050.
Nothing in Section 25850 is intended to preclude the carrying of a loaded firearm by any person while engaged in the act of making or attempting to make a lawful arrest.
(Added by Stats. 2010, Ch. 711, Sec. 6. (SB 1080) Effective January 1, 2011. Operative January 1, 2012, by Sec. 10 of Ch. 711.)
26055.
Nothing in Section 25850 shall prevent any person from having a loaded weapon, if it is otherwise lawful, at the person's place of residence, including any temporary residence or campsite.
(Added by Stats. 2010, Ch. 711, Sec. 6. (SB 1080) Effective January 1, 2011. Operative January 1, 2012, by Sec. 10 of Ch. 711.)
26060.
Nothing in Section 25850 shall prevent any person from storing aboard any vessel or aircraft any loaded or unloaded rocket, rocket propelled projectile launcher, or similar device designed primarily for emergency or distress signaling purposes, or from possessing that type of a device while in a permitted hunting area or traveling to or from a permitted hunting area and carrying a valid California permit or license to hunt.
(Added by Stats. 2010, Ch. 711, Sec. 6. (SB 1080) Effective January 1, 2011. Operative January 1, 2012, by Sec. 10 of Ch. 711.)

ARTICLE 5. Loaded Firearm in a Motor Vehicle [26100- 26100.]
(Article 5 added by Stats. 2010, Ch. 711, Sec. 6.)
26100.
(a) It is a misdemeanor for a driver of any motor vehicle or the owner of any motor vehicle, whether or not the owner of the vehicle is occupying the vehicle, knowingly to permit any other person to carry into or bring into the vehicle a firearm in violation of Section 25850 of this code or Section 2006 of the Fish and Game Code.
(b) Any driver or owner of any vehicle, whether or not the owner of the vehicle is occupying the vehicle, who knowingly permits any other person to discharge any firearm from the vehicle is punishable by imprisonment in the county jail for not more than one year or in state prison for 16 months or two or three years.
(c) Any person who willfully and maliciously discharges a firearm from a motor vehicle at another person other than an occupant of a motor vehicle is guilty of a felony punishable by imprisonment in state prison for three, five, or seven years.
(d) Except as provided in Section 3002 of the Fish and Game Code, any person who willfully and maliciously discharges a firearm from a motor vehicle is guilty of a public offense punishable by imprisonment in the county jail for not more than one year or in the state prison.
(Added by Stats. 2010, Ch. 711, Sec. 6. (SB 1080) Effective January 1, 2011. Operative January 1, 2012, by Sec. 10 of Ch. 711.)

CHAPTER 4. License to Carry A Pistol, Revolver, or Other Firearm Capable of Being Concealed Upon the Person [26150 - 26225]

(Chapter 4 added by Stats. 2010, Ch. 711, Sec. 6.)
26150.
(a) When a person applies for a license to carry a pistol, revolver, or other firearm capable of being concealed upon the person, the sheriff of a county may issue a license to that person upon proof of all of the following:
(1) The applicant is of good moral character.
(2) Good cause exists for issuance of the license.
(3) The applicant is a resident of the county or a city within the county, or the applicant's principal place of employment or business is in the county or a city within the county and the applicant spends a substantial period of time in that place of employment or business.
(4) The applicant has completed a course of training as described in Section 26165.
(b) The sheriff may issue a license under subdivision (a) in either of the following formats:
(1) A license to carry concealed a pistol, revolver, or other firearm capable of being concealed upon the person.
(2) Where the population of the county is less than 200,000 persons according to the most recent federal decennial census, a license to carry loaded and exposed in only that county a pistol, revolver, or other firearm capable of being concealed upon the person.
(c) (1) Nothing in this chapter shall preclude the sheriff of the county from entering into an agreement with the chief or other head of a municipal police department of a city to process all applications for licenses, renewals of licenses, or amendments to licenses pursuant to this chapter, in lieu of the sheriff.
(2) This subdivision shall only apply to applicants who reside within the city in which the chief or other head of the municipal police department has agreed to process applications for licenses, renewals of licenses, and amendments to licenses, pursuant to this chapter.
(Amended by Stats. 2015, Ch. 785, Sec. 2. (AB 1134) Effective January 1, 2016.)
26155.
(a) When a person applies for a license to carry a pistol, revolver, or other firearm capable of being concealed upon the person, the chief or other head of a municipal police department of any city or city and county may issue a license to that person upon proof of all of the following:
(1) The applicant is of good moral character.

(2) Good cause exists for issuance of the license.
(3) The applicant is a resident of that city.
(4) The applicant has completed a course of training as described in Section 26165.
(b) The chief or other head of a municipal police department may issue a license under subdivision (a) in either of the following formats:
(1) A license to carry concealed a pistol, revolver, or other firearm capable of being concealed upon the person.
(2) Where the population of the county in which the city is located is less than 200,000 persons according to the most recent federal decennial census, a license to carry loaded and exposed in only that county a pistol, revolver, or other firearm capable of being concealed upon the person.
(c) Nothing in this chapter shall preclude the chief or other head of a municipal police department of any city from entering an agreement with the sheriff of the county in which the city is located for the sheriff to process all applications for licenses, renewals of licenses, and amendments to licenses, pursuant to this chapter.
(Added by Stats. 2010, Ch. 711, Sec. 6. (SB 1080) Effective January 1, 2011. Operative January 1, 2012, by Sec. 10 of Ch. 711.)
26160.
Each licensing authority shall publish and make available a written policy summarizing the provisions of Section 26150 and subdivisions (a) and (b) of Section 26155.
(Added by Stats. 2010, Ch. 711, Sec. 6. (SB 1080) Effective January 1, 2011. Operative January 1, 2012, by Sec. 10 of Ch. 711.)
26165.
(a) For new license applicants, the course of training for issuance of a license under Section 26150 or 26155 may be any course acceptable to the licensing authority that meets all of the following criteria:
(1) The course shall be no less than eight hours, but shall not be required to exceed 16 hours in length.
(2) The course shall include instruction on firearm safety, firearm handling, shooting technique, and laws regarding the permissible use of a firearm.
(3) The course shall include live-fire shooting exercises on a firing range and shall include a demonstration by the applicant of safe handling of, and shooting proficiency with, each firearm that the applicant is applying to be licensed to carry.
(b) A licensing authority shall establish, and make available to the public, the standards it uses when issuing licenses with regards to the required live-fire shooting exercises, including, but not limited to, a minimum number of rounds to be fired and minimum passing scores from specified firing distances.
(c) Notwithstanding subdivision (a), the licensing authority may require a community college course certified by the Commission on Peace Officer Standards and Training, up to a maximum of 24 hours, but only if required uniformly of all license applicants without exception.
(d) For license renewal applicants, the course of training may be any course acceptable to the licensing authority, shall be no less than four hours, and shall satisfy the requirements of paragraphs (2) and (3) of subdivision (a). No course of training shall be required for any person certified by the licensing authority as a trainer for purposes of this section, in order for that person to renew a license issued pursuant to this article.
(e) The applicant shall not be required to pay for any training courses prior to the determination of good cause being made pursuant to Section 26202.
(Amended by Stats. 2018, Ch. 752, Sec. 1. (AB 2103) Effective January 1, 2019.)
26170.
(a) Upon proof of all of the following, the sheriff of a county, or the chief or other head of a municipal police department of any city or city and county, may issue to an applicant a license to carry concealed a pistol, revolver, or other firearm capable of being concealed upon the person:
(1) The applicant is of good moral character.
(2) Good cause exists for issuance of the license.
(3) The applicant has been deputized or appointed as a peace officer pursuant to subdivision (a) or (b) of Section 830.6 by that sheriff or that chief of police or other head of a municipal police department.
(b) Direct or indirect fees for the issuance of a license pursuant to this section may be waived.
(c) The fact that an applicant for a license to carry a pistol, revolver, or other firearm capable of being concealed upon the person has been deputized or appointed as a peace officer pursuant to subdivision (a) or (b) of Section 830.6 shall be considered only for the purpose of issuing a license pursuant to this section, and shall not be considered for the purpose of issuing a license pursuant to Section 26150 or 26155.
(Added by Stats. 2010, Ch. 711, Sec. 6. (SB 1080) Effective January 1, 2011. Operative January 1, 2012, by Sec. 10 of Ch. 711.)
26175.
(a) (1) Applications for licenses and applications for amendments to licenses under this article shall be uniform throughout the state, upon forms to be prescribed by the Attorney General.
(2) The Attorney General shall convene a committee composed of one representative of the California State Sheriffs' Association, one representative of the California Police Chiefs Association, and one representative of the Department of Justice to review, and, as deemed appropriate, revise the standard application form for licenses. The committee shall meet for this purpose if two of the committee's members deem that necessary.
(3) (A) The Attorney General shall develop a uniform license that may be used as indicia of proof of licensure throughout the state.
(B) The Attorney General shall approve the use of licenses issued by local agencies that contain all the information required in subdivision (i), including a recent photograph of the applicant, and are deemed to be in substantial compliance with standards developed by the committee described in subparagraph (C), if developed, as they relate to the physical dimensions and general appearance of the licenses. The Attorney General shall retain exemplars of approved licenses and shall maintain a list of agencies issuing local licenses. Approved licenses may be used as indicia of proof of licensure under this chapter in lieu of the uniform license developed by the Attorney General.
(C) A committee composed of two representatives of the California State Sheriffs' Association, two representatives of the California Police Chiefs Association, and one representative of the Department of Justice shall convene to review and revise, as the committee deems appropriate, the design standard for licenses issued by local agencies that may be used as indicia of proof of licensure throughout the state, provided that the design standard meets the requirements of subparagraph (B). The committee shall meet for this purpose if two of the committee's members deem it necessary.
(b) The application shall include a section summarizing the requirements of state law that result in the automatic denial of a license.
(c) The standard application form for licenses described in subdivision (a) shall require information from the applicant, including, but not limited to, the name, occupation, residence, and business address of the applicant, the applicant's age, height, weight, color of eyes and hair, and reason for desiring a license to carry the weapon.
(d) Applications for licenses shall be filed in writing and signed by the applicant.
(e) Applications for amendments to licenses shall be filed in writing and signed by the applicant, and shall state what type of amendment is sought pursuant to Section 26215 and the reason for desiring the amendment.
(f) The forms shall contain a provision whereby the applicant attests to the truth of statements contained in the application.
(g) An applicant shall not be required to complete any additional application or form for a license, or to provide any information other than that necessary to complete the

standard application form described in subdivision (a), except to clarify or interpret information provided by the applicant on the standard application form.

(h) The standard application form described in subdivision (a) is deemed to be a local form expressly exempt from the requirements of the Administrative Procedure Act (Chapter 3.5 (commencing with Section 11340) of Part 1 of Division 3 of Title 2 of the Government Code).

(i) Any license issued upon the application shall set forth the licensee's name, occupation, residence and business address, the licensee's age, height, weight, color of eyes and hair, and the reason for desiring a license to carry the weapon, and shall, in addition, contain a description of the weapon or weapons authorized to be carried, giving the name of the manufacturer, the serial number, and the caliber. The license issued to the licensee may be laminated.

(Amended by Stats. 2016, Ch. 645, Sec. 1. (AB 2510) Effective January 1, 2017.)
26180.
(a) Any person who files an application required by Section 26175 knowing that any statement contained therein is false is guilty of a misdemeanor.

(b) Any person who knowingly makes a false statement on the application regarding any of the following is guilty of a felony:

(1) The denial or revocation of a license, or the denial of an amendment to a license, issued pursuant to this article.

(2) A criminal conviction.

(3) A finding of not guilty by reason of insanity.

(4) The use of a controlled substance.

(5) A dishonorable discharge from military service.

(6) A commitment to a mental institution.

(7) A renunciation of United States citizenship.

(Added by Stats. 2010, Ch. 711, Sec. 6. (SB 1080) Effective January 1, 2011. Operative January 1, 2012, by Sec. 10 of Ch. 711.)
26185.
(a) (1) The fingerprints of each applicant shall be taken and two copies on forms prescribed by the Department of Justice shall be forwarded to the department.

(2) Upon receipt of the fingerprints and the fee as prescribed in Section 26190, the department shall promptly furnish the forwarding licensing authority a report of all data and information pertaining to any applicant of which there is a record in its office, including information as to whether the person is prohibited by state or federal law from possessing, receiving, owning, or purchasing a firearm.

(3) No license shall be issued by any licensing authority until after receipt of the report from the department.

(b) Notwithstanding subdivision (a), if the license applicant has previously applied to the same licensing authority for a license to carry firearms pursuant to this article and the applicant's fingerprints and fee have been previously forwarded to the Department of Justice, as provided by this section, the licensing authority shall note the previous identification numbers and other data that would provide positive identification in the files of the Department of Justice on the copy of any subsequent license submitted to the department in conformance with Section 26225 and no additional application form or fingerprints shall be required.

(c) If the license applicant has a license issued pursuant to this article and the applicant's fingerprints have been previously forwarded to the Department of Justice, as provided in this section, the licensing authority shall note the previous identification numbers and other data that would provide positive identification in the files of the Department of Justice on the copy of any subsequent license submitted to the department in conformance with Section 26225 and no additional fingerprints shall be required.

(Added by Stats. 2010, Ch. 711, Sec. 6. (SB 1080) Effective January 1, 2011. Operative January 1, 2012, by Sec. 10 of Ch. 711.)
26190.
(a) (1) Each applicant for a new license or for the renewal of a license shall pay at the time of filing the application a fee determined by the Department of Justice. The fee shall not exceed the application processing costs of the Department of Justice for the direct costs of furnishing the report required by Section 26185.

(2) After the department establishes fees sufficient to reimburse the department for processing costs, fees charged shall increase at a rate not to exceed the legislatively approved annual cost-of-living adjustments for the department's budget.

(3) The officer receiving the application and the fee shall transmit the fee, with the fingerprints if required, to the Department of Justice.

(b) (1) The licensing authority of any city, city and county, or county may charge an additional fee in an amount equal to the actual costs for processing the application for a new license, including any required notices, excluding fingerprint and training costs, but in no case to exceed one hundred dollars ($100), and shall transmit the additional fee, if any, to the city, city and county, or county treasury.

(2) The first 20 percent of this additional local fee may be collected upon filing of the initial application. The balance of the fee shall be collected only upon issuance of the license.

(c) The licensing authority may charge an additional fee, not to exceed twenty-five dollars ($25), for processing the application for a license renewal, and shall transmit an additional fee, if any, to the city, city and county, or county treasury.

(d) These local fees may be increased at a rate not to exceed any increase in the California Consumer Price Index as compiled and reported by the Department of Industrial Relations.

(e) (1) In the case of an amended license pursuant to Section 26215, the licensing authority of any city, city and county, or county may charge a fee, not to exceed ten dollars ($10), for processing the amended license.

(2) This fee may be increased at a rate not to exceed any increase in the California Consumer Price Index as compiled and reported by the Department of Industrial Relations.

(3) The licensing authority shall transmit the fee to the city, city and county, or county treasury.

(f) (1) If psychological testing on the initial application is required by the licensing authority, the license applicant shall be referred to a licensed psychologist used by the licensing authority for the psychological testing of its own employees. The applicant may be charged for the actual cost of the testing in an amount not to exceed one hundred fifty dollars ($150).

(2) Additional psychological testing of an applicant seeking license renewal shall be required only if there is compelling evidence to indicate that a test is necessary. The cost to the applicant for this additional testing shall not exceed one hundred fifty dollars ($150).

(g) Except as authorized pursuant to this section, no requirement, charge, assessment, fee, or condition that requires the payment of any additional funds by the applicant, or requires the applicant to obtain liability insurance, may be imposed by any licensing authority as a condition of the application for a license.

(Amended by Stats. 2011, Ch. 741, Sec. 2. (SB 610) Effective January 1, 2012.)
26195.
(a) A license under this article shall not be issued if the Department of Justice determines that the person is prohibited by state or federal law from possessing, receiving, owning, or purchasing a firearm.

(b) (1) A license under this article shall be revoked by the local licensing authority if at any time either the local licensing authority is notified by the Department of Justice that a licensee is prohibited by state or federal law from owning or purchasing firearms, or the

local licensing authority determines that the person is prohibited by state or federal law from possessing, receiving, owning, or purchasing a firearm.

(2) If at any time the Department of Justice determines that a licensee is prohibited by state or federal law from possessing, receiving, owning, or purchasing a firearm, the department shall immediately notify the local licensing authority of the determination.

(3) If the local licensing authority revokes the license, the Department of Justice shall be notified of the revocation pursuant to Section 26225. The licensee shall also be immediately notified of the revocation in writing.

(Added by Stats. 2010, Ch. 711, Sec. 6. (SB 1080) Effective January 1, 2011. Operative January 1, 2012, by Sec. 10 of Ch. 711.)
26200.
(a) A license issued pursuant to this article may include any reasonable restrictions or conditions that the issuing authority deems warranted, including restrictions as to the time, place, manner, and circumstances under which the licensee may carry a pistol, revolver, or other firearm capable of being concealed upon the person.

(b) Any restrictions imposed pursuant to subdivision (a) shall be indicated on any license issued.

(Added by Stats. 2010, Ch. 711, Sec. 6. (SB 1080) Effective January 1, 2011. Operative January 1, 2012, by Sec. 10 of Ch. 711.)
26202.
Upon making the determination of good cause pursuant to Section 26150 or 26155, the licensing authority shall give written notice to the applicant of the licensing authority's determination. If the licensing authority determines that good cause exists, the notice shall inform the applicants to proceed with the training requirements specified in Section 26165. If the licensing authority determines that good cause does not exist, the notice shall inform the applicant that the request for a license has been denied and shall state the reason from the department's published policy, described in Section 26160, as to why the determination was made.

(Added by Stats. 2011, Ch. 741, Sec. 3. (SB 610) Effective January 1, 2012.)
26205.
The licensing authority shall give written notice to the applicant indicating if the license under this article is approved or denied. The licensing authority shall give this notice within 90 days of the initial application for a new license or a license renewal, or 30 days after receipt of the applicant's criminal background check from the Department of Justice, whichever is later. If the license is denied, the notice shall state which requirement was not satisfied.

(Amended by Stats. 2011, Ch. 741, Sec. 4. (SB 610) Effective January 1, 2012.)
26210.
(a) When a licensee under this article has a change of address, the license shall be amended to reflect the new address and a new license shall be issued pursuant to subdivision (b) of Section 26215.

(b) The licensee shall notify the licensing authority in writing within 10 days of any change in the licensee's place of residence.

(c) If both of the following conditions are satisfied, a license to carry a concealed handgun may not be revoked solely because the licensee's place of residence has changed to another county:

(1) The licensee has not breached any of the conditions or restrictions set forth in the license.

(2) The licensee has not become prohibited by state or federal law from possessing, receiving, owning, or purchasing a firearm.

(d) Notwithstanding subdivision (c), if a licensee's place of residence was the basis for issuance of a license, any license issued pursuant to Section 26150 or 26155 shall expire 90 days after the licensee moves from the county of issuance.

(e) If the license is one to carry loaded and exposed a pistol, revolver, or other firearm capable of being concealed upon the person, the license shall be revoked immediately upon a change of the licensee's place of residence to another county.

(Added by Stats. 2010, Ch. 711, Sec. 6. (SB 1080) Effective January 1, 2011. Operative January 1, 2012, by Sec. 10 of Ch. 711.)
26215.
(a) A person issued a license pursuant to this article may apply to the licensing authority for an amendment to the license to do one or more of the following:

(1) Add or delete authority to carry a particular pistol, revolver, or other firearm capable of being concealed upon the person.

(2) Authorize the licensee to carry concealed a pistol, revolver, or other firearm capable of being concealed upon the person.

(3) If the population of the county is less than 200,000 persons according to the most recent federal decennial census, authorize the licensee to carry loaded and exposed in only that county a pistol, revolver, or other firearm capable of being concealed upon the person.

(4) Change any restrictions or conditions on the license, including restrictions as to the time, place, manner, and circumstances under which the person may carry a pistol, revolver, or other firearm capable of being concealed upon the person.

(b) If the licensing authority amends the license, a new license shall be issued to the licensee reflecting the amendments.

(c) An amendment to the license does not extend the original expiration date of the license and the license shall be subject to renewal at the same time as if the license had not been amended.

(d) An application to amend a license does not constitute an application for renewal of the license.

(Added by Stats. 2010, Ch. 711, Sec. 6. (SB 1080) Effective January 1, 2011. Operative January 1, 2012, by Sec. 10 of Ch. 711.)
26220.
(a) Except as otherwise provided in this section and in subdivision (c) of Section 26210, a license issued pursuant to Section 26150 or 26155 is valid for any period of time not to exceed two years from the date of the license.

(b) If the licensee's place of employment or business was the basis for issuance of a license pursuant to Section 26150, the license is valid for any period of time not to exceed 90 days from the date of the license. The license shall be valid only in the county in which the license was originally issued. The licensee shall give a copy of this license to the licensing authority of the city, county, or city and county in which the licensee resides. The licensing authority that originally issued the license shall inform the licensee verbally and in writing in at least 16-point type of this obligation to give a copy of the license to the licensing authority of the city, county, or city and county of residence. Any application to renew or extend the validity of, or reissue, the license may be granted only upon the concurrence of the licensing authority that originally issued the license and the licensing authority of the city, county, or city and county in which the licensee resides.

(c) A license issued pursuant to Section 26150 or 26155 is valid for any period of time not to exceed three years from the date of the license if the license is issued to any of the following individuals:

(1) A judge of a California court of record.

(2) A full-time court commissioner of a California court of record.

(3) A judge of a federal court.

(4) A magistrate of a federal court.

(d) A license issued pursuant to Section 26150 or 26155 is valid for any period of time not to exceed four years from the date of the license if the license is issued to a custodial officer who is an employee of the sheriff as provided in Section 831.5, except that the license shall be invalid upon the conclusion of the person's employment pursuant to Section 831.5 if the four-year period has not otherwise expired or any other condition imposed pursuant to this article does not limit the validity of the license to a shorter time period.

(e) A license issued pursuant to Section 26170 to a peace officer appointed pursuant to Section 830.6 is valid for any period of time not to exceed four years from the date of the license, except that the license shall be invalid upon the conclusion of the person's appointment pursuant to Section 830.6 if the four-year period has not otherwise expired or any other condition imposed pursuant to this article does not limit the validity of the license to a shorter time period.

(Added by Stats. 2010, Ch. 711, Sec. 6. (SB 1080) Effective January 1, 2011. Operative January 1, 2012, by Sec. 10 of Ch. 711.)

26225.

(a) A record of the following shall be maintained in the office of the licensing authority:
(1) The denial of a license.
(2) The denial of an amendment to a license.
(3) The issuance of a license.
(4) The amendment of a license.
(5) The revocation of a license.

(b) Copies of each of the following shall be filed immediately by the issuing officer or authority with the Department of Justice:
(1) The denial of a license.
(2) The denial of an amendment to a license.
(3) The issuance of a license.
(4) The amendment of a license.
(5) The revocation of a license.

(c) (1) Commencing on or before January 1, 2000, and annually thereafter, each licensing authority shall submit to the Attorney General the total number of licenses issued to peace officers pursuant to Section 26170, and to judges pursuant to Section 26150 or 26155.
(2) The Attorney General shall collect and record the information submitted pursuant to this subdivision by county and licensing authority.

(Added by Stats. 2010, Ch. 711, Sec. 6. (SB 1080) Effective January 1, 2011. Operative January 1, 2012, by Sec. 10 of Ch. 711.)

CHAPTER 5. Retired Peace Officer Carrying A Concealed and Loaded Firearm [26300 - 26325]

(Chapter 5 added by Stats. 2010, Ch. 711, Sec. 6.)

26300.

(a) Any peace officer listed in Section 830.1 or 830.2 or subdivision (c) of Section 830.5 who retired prior to January 1, 1981, is authorized to carry a concealed and loaded firearm if the agency issued the officer an identification certificate and the certificate has not been stamped as specified in Section 25470.

(b) Any peace officer employed by an agency and listed in Section 830.1 or 830.2 or subdivision (c) of Section 830.5 who retired after January 1, 1981, shall have an endorsement on the officer's identification certificate stating that the issuing agency approves the officer's carrying of a concealed and loaded firearm.

(c) (1) Any peace officer not listed in subdivision (a) or (b) who was authorized to, and did, carry a firearm during the course and scope of his or her appointment as a peace officer shall have an endorsement on the officer's identification certificate stating that the issuing agency approves the officer's carrying of a concealed and loaded firearm.
(2) This subdivision applies to a retired reserve officer if the retired reserve officer satisfies the requirements of paragraph (1), was a level I reserve officer as described in paragraph (1) of subdivision (a) of Section 832.6, and he or she served in the aggregate the minimum amount of time as specified by the retiree's agency's policy as a level I reserve officer, provided that the policy shall not set an aggregate term requirement that is less than 10 years or more than 20 years. Service as a reserve officer, other than a level I reserve officer prior to January 1, 1997, shall not count toward the accrual of time required by this section. A law enforcement agency shall have the discretion to revoke or deny an endorsement issued under this subdivision pursuant to Section 26305.

(Amended by Stats. 2013, Ch. 267, Sec. 3. (AB 703) Effective January 1, 2014.)

26305.

(a) No peace officer who is retired after January 1, 1989, because of a psychological disability shall be issued an endorsement to carry a concealed and loaded firearm pursuant to this article.

(b) A retired peace officer may have the privilege to carry a concealed and loaded firearm revoked or denied by violating any departmental rule, or state or federal law that, if violated by an officer on active duty, would result in that officer's arrest, suspension, or removal from the agency.

(c) An identification certificate authorizing the officer to carry a concealed and loaded firearm or an endorsement on the certificate may be immediately and temporarily revoked by the issuing agency when the conduct of a retired peace officer compromises public safety.

(d) An identification certificate authorizing the officer to carry a concealed and loaded firearm or an endorsement may be permanently revoked or denied by the issuing agency only upon a showing of good cause. Good cause shall be determined at a hearing, as specified in Section 26320.

(Added by Stats. 2010, Ch. 711, Sec. 6. (SB 1080) Effective January 1, 2011. Operative January 1, 2012, by Sec. 10 of Ch. 711.)

26310.

(a) Issuance of an identification certificate authorizing the officer to carry a concealed and loaded firearm or an endorsement may be denied prior to a hearing.

(b) If a hearing is not conducted prior to the denial of an endorsement, a retired peace officer, within 15 days of the denial, shall have the right to request a hearing. A retired peace officer who fails to request a hearing pursuant to this section shall forfeit the right to a hearing.

(Added by Stats. 2010, Ch. 711, Sec. 6. (SB 1080) Effective January 1, 2011. Operative January 1, 2012, by Sec. 10 of Ch. 711.)

26312.

(a) Notice of a temporary revocation shall be effective upon personal service or upon receipt of a notice that was sent by first-class mail, postage prepaid, return receipt requested, to the retiree's last known place of residence.

(b) The retiree shall have 15 days to respond to the notification and request a hearing to determine if the temporary revocation should become permanent.

(c) A retired peace officer who fails to respond to the notice of hearing within the 15-day period shall forfeit the right to a hearing and the authority of the officer to carry a firearm shall be permanently revoked. The retired officer shall immediately return the identification certificate to the issuing agency.

(d) If a hearing is requested, good cause for permanent revocation shall be determined at a hearing, as specified in Section 26320. The hearing shall be held no later than 120 days after the request by the retired officer for a hearing is received.

(e) A retiree may waive the right to a hearing and immediately return the identification certificate to the issuing agency.

(Added by Stats. 2010, Ch. 711, Sec. 6. (SB 1080) Effective January 1, 2011. Operative January 1, 2012, by Sec. 10 of Ch. 711.)

26315.

(a) An identification certificate authorizing the officer to carry a concealed and loaded firearm or an endorsement may be permanently revoked only after a hearing, as specified in Section 26320.

(b) Any retired peace officer whose identification certificate authorizing the officer to carry a concealed and loaded firearm or an endorsement is to be revoked shall receive notice of the hearing. Notice of the hearing shall be served either personally on the retiree or sent by first-class mail, postage prepaid, return receipt requested to the retiree's last known place of residence.

(c) From the date the retiree signs for the notice or upon the date the notice is served personally on the retiree, the retiree shall have 15 days to respond to the notification. A retired peace officer who fails to respond to the notice of the hearing shall forfeit the right to a hearing and the authority of the officer to carry a firearm shall be permanently revoked. The retired officer shall immediately return the identification certificate to the issuing agency.

(d) If a hearing is requested, good cause for permanent revocation shall be determined at the hearing, as specified in Section 26320. The hearing shall be held no later than 120 days after the request by the retired officer for a hearing is received.

(e) The retiree may waive the right to a hearing and immediately return the identification certificate to the issuing agency.

(Added by Stats. 2010, Ch. 711, Sec. 6. (SB 1080) Effective January 1, 2011. Operative January 1, 2012, by Sec. 10 of Ch. 711.)

26320.

(a) Any hearing conducted under this article shall be held before a three-member hearing board. One member of the board shall be selected by the agency and one member shall be selected by the retired peace officer or his or her employee organization. The third member shall be selected jointly by the agency and the retired peace officer or his or her employee organization.

(b) Any decision by the board shall be binding on the agency and the retired peace officer.

(Added by Stats. 2010, Ch. 711, Sec. 6. (SB 1080) Effective January 1, 2011. Operative January 1, 2012, by Sec. 10 of Ch. 711.)

26325.

(a) A retired peace officer, when notified of the revocation of the privilege to carry a concealed and loaded firearm, after the hearing, or upon forfeiting the right to a hearing, shall immediately surrender to the issuing agency the officer's identification certificate.

(b) The issuing agency shall reissue a new identification certificate without an endorsement.

(c) Notwithstanding subdivision (b), if the peace officer retired prior to January 1, 1981, and was at the time of retirement a peace officer listed in Section 830.1 or 830.2 or subdivision (c) of Section 830.5, the issuing agency shall stamp on the identification certificate "No CCW privilege."

(Added by Stats. 2010, Ch. 711, Sec. 6. (SB 1080) Effective January 1, 2011. Operative January 1, 2012, by Sec. 10 of Ch. 711.)

CHAPTER 6. Openly Carrying an Unloaded Handgun [26350 - 26391]

(Chapter 6 added by Stats. 2011, Ch. 725, Sec. 14.)

ARTICLE 1. Crime of Openly Carrying an Unloaded Handgun [26350-26350.]
(Article 1 added by Stats. 2011, Ch. 725, Sec. 14.)

26350.

(a) (1) A person is guilty of openly carrying an unloaded handgun when that person carries upon his or her person an exposed and unloaded handgun outside a vehicle while in or on any of the following:
(A) A public place or public street in an incorporated city or city and county.
(B) A public street in a prohibited area of an unincorporated area of a county or city and county.
(C) A public place in a prohibited area of a county or city and county.
(2) A person is guilty of openly carrying an unloaded handgun when that person carries an exposed and unloaded handgun inside or on a vehicle, whether or not on his or her person, while in or on any of the following:
(A) A public place or public street in an incorporated city or city and county.
(B) A public street in a prohibited area of an unincorporated area of a county or city and county.
(C) A public place in a prohibited area of a county or city and county.

(b) (1) Except as specified in paragraph (2), a violation of this section is a misdemeanor.
(2) A violation of subparagraph (A) of paragraph (1) of subdivision (a) is punishable by imprisonment in a county jail not exceeding one year, or by a fine not to exceed one thousand dollars ($1,000), or by both that fine and imprisonment, if both of the following conditions exist:
(A) The handgun and unexpended ammunition capable of being discharged from that handgun are in the immediate possession of that person.
(B) The person is not in lawful possession of that handgun.

(c) (1) Nothing in this section shall preclude prosecution under Chapter 2 (commencing with Section 29800) or Chapter 3 (commencing with Section 29900) of Division 9, Section 8100 or 8103 of the Welfare and Institutions Code, or any other law with a penalty greater than is set forth in this section.
(2) The provisions of this section are cumulative and shall not be construed as restricting the application of any other law. However, an act or omission punishable in different ways by different provisions of law shall not be punished under more than one provision.

(d) Notwithstanding the fact that the term "an unloaded handgun" is used in this section, each handgun shall constitute a distinct and separate offense under this section.

(Added by Stats. 2011, Ch. 725, Sec. 14. (AB 144) Effective January 1, 2012.)

ARTICLE 2. Exemptions [26361 - 26391]
(Article 2 added by Stats. 2011, Ch. 725, Sec. 14.)

26361.

Section 26350 does not apply to, or affect, the open carrying of an unloaded handgun by any peace officer or any honorably retired peace officer if that officer may carry a concealed firearm pursuant to Article 2 (commencing with Section 25450) of Chapter 2, or a loaded firearm pursuant to Article 3 (commencing with Section 25900) of Chapter 3.

(Added by Stats. 2011, Ch. 725, Sec. 14. (AB 144) Effective January 1, 2012.)

26362.

Section 26350 does not apply to, or affect, the open carrying of an unloaded handgun by any person to the extent that person may openly carry a loaded handgun pursuant to Article 4 (commencing with Section 26000) of Chapter 3.

(Added by Stats. 2011, Ch. 725, Sec. 14. (AB 144) Effective January 1, 2012.)

26363.

Section 26350 does not apply to, or affect, the open carrying of an unloaded handgun as merchandise by a person who is engaged in the business of manufacturing,

importing, wholesaling, repairing, or dealing in firearms and who is licensed to engage in that business, or the authorized representative or authorized agent of that person, while engaged in the lawful course of the business.
(Added by Stats. 2011, Ch. 725, Sec. 14. (AB 144) Effective January 1, 2012.)
26364.
Section 26350 does not apply to, or affect, the open carrying of an unloaded handgun by a duly authorized military or civil organization, or the members thereof, while parading or while rehearsing or practicing parading, when at the meeting place of the organization.
(Added by Stats. 2011, Ch. 725, Sec. 14. (AB 144) Effective January 1, 2012.)
26365.
Paragraph (1) of subdivision (a) of Section 26350 does not apply to, or affect, the open carrying of an unloaded handgun by a member of any club or organization organized for the purpose of practicing shooting at targets upon established target ranges, whether public or private, while the members are using handguns upon the target ranges or incident to the use of a handgun at that target range.
(Added by Stats. 2011, Ch. 725, Sec. 14. (AB 144) Effective January 1, 2012.)
26366.
Section 26350 does not apply to, or affect, the open carrying of an unloaded handgun by a licensed hunter while engaged in hunting or while transporting that handgun when going to or returning from that hunting expedition.
(Added by Stats. 2011, Ch. 725, Sec. 14. (AB 144) Effective January 1, 2012.)
26366.5.
Section 26350 does not apply to, or affect, the open carrying of an unloaded handgun by a licensed hunter while actually engaged in training a dog for the purpose of using the dog in hunting that is not prohibited by law, or while transporting the firearm while going to or returning from that training.
(Added by Stats. 2012, Ch. 700, Sec. 9. (AB 1527) Effective January 1, 2013.)
26367.
Section 26350 does not apply to, or affect, the open carrying of an unloaded handgun incident to transportation of a handgun by a person operating a licensed common carrier, or by an authorized agent or employee thereof, when transported in conformance with applicable federal law.
(Added by Stats. 2011, Ch. 725, Sec. 14. (AB 144) Effective January 1, 2012.)
26368.
Section 26350 does not apply to, or affect, the open carrying of an unloaded handgun by a member of an organization chartered by the Congress of the United States or a nonprofit mutual or public benefit corporation organized and recognized as a nonprofit tax-exempt organization by the Internal Revenue Service while on official parade duty or ceremonial occasions of that organization or while rehearsing or practicing for official parade duty or ceremonial occasions.
(Added by Stats. 2011, Ch. 725, Sec. 14. (AB 144) Effective January 1, 2012.)
26369.
Paragraph (1) of subdivision (a) of Section 26350 does not apply to, or affect, the open carrying of an unloaded handgun within a gun show conducted pursuant to Article 1 (commencing with Section 27200) and Article 2 (commencing with Section 27300) of Chapter 3 of Division 6.
(Added by Stats. 2011, Ch. 725, Sec. 14. (AB 144) Effective January 1, 2012.)
26370.
Section 26350 does not apply to, or affect, the open carrying of an unloaded handgun within a school zone, as defined in Section 626.9, if that carrying is not prohibited by Section 626.9.
(Amended by Stats. 2017, Ch. 779, Sec. 2. (AB 424) Effective January 1, 2018.)
26371.
Section 26350 does not apply to, or affect, the open carrying of an unloaded handgun when in accordance with the provisions of Section 171b.
(Added by Stats. 2011, Ch. 725, Sec. 14. (AB 144) Effective January 1, 2012.)
26372.
Section 26350 does not apply to, or affect, the open carrying of an unloaded handgun by any person while engaged in the act of making or attempting to make a lawful arrest.
(Added by Stats. 2011, Ch. 725, Sec. 14. (AB 144) Effective January 1, 2012.)
26373.
Section 26350 does not apply to, or affect, the open carrying of an unloaded handgun incident to loaning, selling, or transferring that handgun in accordance with Article 1 (commencing with Section 27500) of Chapter 4 of Division 6, or in accordance with any of the exemptions from Section 27545, so long as that handgun is possessed within private property and the possession and carrying is with the permission of the owner or lessee of that private property.
(Added by Stats. 2011, Ch. 725, Sec. 14. (AB 144) Effective January 1, 2012.)
26374.
Section 26350 does not apply to, or affect, the open carrying of an unloaded handgun by a person engaged in firearms-related activities, while on the premises of a fixed place of business that is licensed to conduct and conducts, as a regular course of its business, activities related to the sale, making, repair, transfer, pawn, or the use of firearms, or related to firearms training.
(Added by Stats. 2011, Ch. 725, Sec. 14. (AB 144) Effective January 1, 2012.)
26375.
Section 26350 does not apply to, or affect, the open carrying of an unloaded handgun by an authorized participant in, or an authorized employee or agent of a supplier of firearms for, a motion picture, television or video production, or entertainment event, when the participant lawfully uses the handgun as part of that production or event, as part of rehearsing or practicing for participation in that production or event, or while the participant or authorized employee or agent is at that production or event, or rehearsal or practice for that production or event.
(Added by Stats. 2011, Ch. 725, Sec. 14. (AB 144) Effective January 1, 2012.)
26376.
Paragraph (1) of subdivision (a) of Section 26350 does not apply to, or affect, the open carrying of an unloaded handgun incident to obtaining an identification number or mark assigned for that handgun from the Department of Justice pursuant to Section 23910.
(Added by Stats. 2011, Ch. 725, Sec. 14. (AB 144) Effective January 1, 2012.)
26377.
Paragraph (1) of subdivision (a) of Section 26350 does not apply to, or affect, the open carrying of an unloaded handgun at any established target range, whether public or private, while the person is using the handgun upon the target range.
(Added by Stats. 2011, Ch. 725, Sec. 14. (AB 144) Effective January 1, 2012.)
26378.
Section 26350 does not apply to, or affect, the open carrying of an unloaded handgun by a person when that person is summoned by a peace officer to assist in making arrests or preserving the peace, while the person is actually engaged in assisting that officer.
(Added by Stats. 2011, Ch. 725, Sec. 14. (AB 144) Effective January 1, 2012.)
26379.
Paragraph (1) of subdivision (a) of Section 26350 does not apply to, or affect, the open carrying of an unloaded handgun incident to any of the following:
(a) Complying with Section 27560 or 27565, as it pertains to that handgun.
(b) Section 28000, as it pertains to that handgun.
(c) Section 27850 or 31725, as it pertains to that handgun.
(d) Complying with Section 27870 or 27875, as it pertains to that handgun.
(e) Complying with Section 27915, 27920, or 27925, as it pertains to that handgun.

(Added by Stats. 2011, Ch. 725, Sec. 14. (AB 144) Effective January 1, 2012.)
26380.
Section 26350 does not apply to, or affect, the open carrying of an unloaded handgun incident to, and in the course and scope of, training of or by an individual to become a sworn peace officer as part of a course of study approved by the Commission on Peace Officer Standards and Training.
(Added by Stats. 2011, Ch. 725, Sec. 14. (AB 144) Effective January 1, 2012.)
26381.
Section 26350 does not apply to, or affect, the open carrying of an unloaded handgun incident to, and in the course and scope of, training of or by an individual to become licensed pursuant to Chapter 4 (commencing with Section 26150) as part of a course of study necessary or authorized by the person authorized to issue the license pursuant to that chapter.
(Added by Stats. 2011, Ch. 725, Sec. 14. (AB 144) Effective January 1, 2012.)
26382.
Section 26350 does not apply to, or affect, the open carrying of an unloaded handgun incident to and at the request of a sheriff or chief or other head of a municipal police department.
(Added by Stats. 2011, Ch. 725, Sec. 14. (AB 144) Effective January 1, 2012.)
26383.
Paragraph (1) of subdivision (a) of Section 26350 does not apply to, or affect, the open carrying of an unloaded handgun by a person when done within a place of business, a place of residence, or on private property, if done with the permission of a person who, by virtue of subdivision (a) of Section 25605, may carry openly an unloaded handgun within that place of business, place of residence, or on that private property owned or lawfully possessed by that person.
(Added by Stats. 2011, Ch. 725, Sec. 14. (AB 144) Effective January 1, 2012.)
26384.
Paragraph (1) of subdivision (a) of Section 26350 does not apply to, or affect, the open carrying of an unloaded handgun if all of the following conditions are satisfied:
(a) The open carrying occurs at an auction or similar event of a nonprofit public benefit or mutual benefit corporation, at which firearms are auctioned or otherwise sold to fund the activities of that corporation or the local chapters of that corporation.
(b) The unloaded handgun is to be auctioned or otherwise sold for that nonprofit public benefit or mutual benefit corporation.
(c) The unloaded handgun is to be delivered by a person licensed pursuant to, and operating in accordance with, Sections 26700 to 26915, inclusive.
(Amended by Stats. 2013, Ch. 738, Sec. 1. (AB 538) Effective January 1, 2014.)
26385.
Section 26350 does not apply to, or affect, the open carrying of an unloaded handgun pursuant to paragraph (3) of subdivision (b) of Section 171c.
(Added by Stats. 2011, Ch. 725, Sec. 14. (AB 144) Effective January 1, 2012.)
26386.
Section 26350 does not apply to, or affect, the open carrying of an unloaded handgun pursuant to Section 171d.
(Added by Stats. 2011, Ch. 725, Sec. 14. (AB 144) Effective January 1, 2012.)
26387.
Section 26350 does not apply to, or affect, the open carrying of an unloaded handgun pursuant to subparagraph (F) of paragraph (1) subdivision (c) of Section 171.7.
(Added by Stats. 2011, Ch. 725, Sec. 14. (AB 144) Effective January 1, 2012.)
26388.
Section 26350 does not apply to, or affect, the open carrying of an unloaded handgun on publicly owned land, if the possession and use of a handgun is specifically permitted by the managing agency of the land and the person carrying that handgun is in lawful possession of that handgun.
(Added by Stats. 2011, Ch. 725, Sec. 14. (AB 144) Effective January 1, 2012.)
26389.
Section 26350 does not apply to, or affect, the carrying of an unloaded handgun if the handgun is carried either in the locked trunk of a motor vehicle or in a locked container.
(Added by Stats. 2011, Ch. 725, Sec. 14. (AB 144) Effective January 1, 2012.)
26390.
Section 26350 does not apply to, or affect, the open carrying of an unloaded handgun in any of the following circumstances:
(a) The open carrying of an unloaded handgun that is regulated pursuant to Chapter 1 (commencing with Section 18710) of Division 5 of Title 2 by a person who holds a permit issued pursuant to Article 3 (commencing with Section 18900) of that chapter, if the carrying of that handgun is conducted in accordance with the terms and conditions of the permit.
(b) The open carrying of an unloaded handgun that is regulated pursuant to Chapter 2 (commencing with Section 30500) of Division 10 by a person who holds a permit issued pursuant to Section 31005, if the carrying of that handgun is conducted in accordance with the terms and conditions of the permit.
(c) The open carrying of an unloaded handgun that is regulated pursuant to Chapter 6 (commencing with Section 32610) of Division 10 by a person who holds a permit issued pursuant to Section 32650, if the carrying is conducted in accordance with the terms and conditions of the permit.
(d) The open carrying of an unloaded handgun that is regulated pursuant to Article 2 (commencing with Section 33300) of Chapter 8 of Division 10 by a person who holds a permit issued pursuant to Section 33300, if the carrying of that handgun is conducted in accordance with the terms and conditions of the permit.
(Added by Stats. 2012, Ch. 700, Sec. 10. (AB 1527) Effective January 1, 2013.)
26391.
Section 26350 does not apply to, or affect, the open carrying of an unloaded handgun when done in accordance with the provisions of subdivision (d) of Section 171.5.
(Added by Stats. 2012, Ch. 700, Sec. 11. (AB 1527) Effective January 1, 2013.)

CHAPTER 7. Carrying an Unloaded Firearm That is not a Handgun [26400 - 26405]

(Heading of Chapter 7 amended by Stats. 2017, Ch. 734, Sec. 1.)
ARTICLE 1. Crime of Carrying an Unloaded Firearm that is not a Handgun [26400- 26400.]
(Heading of Article 1 amended by Stats. 2017, Ch. 734, Sec. 2.)
26400.
(a) A person is guilty of carrying an unloaded firearm that is not a handgun when that person carries upon his or her person an unloaded firearm that is not a handgun outside a vehicle while in any of the following areas:
(1) An incorporated city or city and county.
(2) A public place or a public street in a prohibited area of an unincorporated area of a county.
(b) (1) Except as specified in paragraph (2), a violation of this section is a misdemeanor.
(2) A violation of subdivision (a) is punishable by imprisonment in a county jail not exceeding one year, or by a fine not to exceed one thousand dollars ($1,000), or by both that fine and imprisonment, if the firearm and unexpended ammunition capable of

being discharged from that firearm are in the immediate possession of the person and the person is not in lawful possession of that firearm.

(c) (1) Nothing in this section shall preclude prosecution under Chapter 2 (commencing with Section 29800) or Chapter 3 (commencing with Section 29900) of Division 9, Section 8100 or 8103 of the Welfare and Institutions Code, or any other law with a penalty greater than is set forth in this section.

(2) The provisions of this section are cumulative and shall not be construed as restricting the application of any other law. However, an act or omission punishable in different ways by different provisions of law shall not be punished under more than one provision.

(d) Notwithstanding the fact that the term "an unloaded firearm that is not a handgun" is used in this section, each individual firearm shall constitute a distinct and separate offense under this section.

(Amended by Stats. 2017, Ch. 734, Sec. 3. (AB 7) Effective January 1, 2018.)

ARTICLE 2. Exemptions [26405- 26405.]

(Article 2 added by Stats. 2012, Ch. 700, Sec. 12.)

26405.

Section 26400 does not apply to, or affect, the carrying of an unloaded firearm that is not a handgun in any of the following circumstances:

(a) By a person when carried within a place of business, a place of residence, or on private real property, if that person, by virtue of subdivision (a) of Section 25605, may carry a firearm within that place of business, place of residence, or on that private real property owned or lawfully occupied by that person.

(b) By a person when carried within a place of business, a place of residence, or on private real property, if done with the permission of a person who, by virtue of subdivision (a) of Section 25605, may carry a firearm within that place of business, place of residence, or on that private real property owned or lawfully occupied by that person.

(c) When the firearm is either in a locked container or encased and it is being transported directly between places where a person is not prohibited from possessing that firearm and the course of travel shall include only those deviations between authorized locations as are reasonably necessary under the circumstances.

(d) If the person possessing the firearm reasonably believes that he or she is in grave danger because of circumstances forming the basis of a current restraining order issued by a court against another person or persons who has or have been found to pose a threat to his or her life or safety. This subdivision may not apply when the circumstances involve a mutual restraining order issued pursuant to Division 10 (commencing with Section 6200) of the Family Code absent a factual finding of a specific threat to the person's life or safety. Upon a trial for violating Section 26400, the trier of fact shall determine whether the defendant was acting out of a reasonable belief that he or she was in grave danger.

(e) By a peace officer or an honorably retired peace officer if that officer may carry a concealed firearm pursuant to Article 2 (commencing with Section 25450) of Chapter 2, or a loaded firearm pursuant to Article 3 (commencing with Section 25900) of Chapter 3.

(f) By a person to the extent that person may openly carry a loaded firearm that is not a handgun pursuant to Article 4 (commencing with Section 26000) of Chapter 3.

(g) As merchandise by a person who is engaged in the business of manufacturing, importing, wholesaling, repairing, or dealing in firearms and who is licensed to engage in that business, or the authorized representative or authorized agent of that person, while engaged in the lawful course of the business.

(h) By a duly authorized military or civil organization, or the members thereof, while parading or while rehearsing or practicing parading, when at the meeting place of the organization.

(i) By a member of a club or organization organized for the purpose of practicing shooting at targets upon established target ranges, whether public or private, while the members are using firearms that are not handguns upon the target ranges or incident to the use of a firearm that is not a handgun at that target range.

(j) By a licensed hunter while engaged in hunting or while transporting that firearm when going to or returning from that hunting expedition.

(k) Incident to transportation of a handgun by a person operating a licensed common carrier, or by an authorized agent or employee thereof, when transported in conformance with applicable federal law.

(l) By a member of an organization chartered by the Congress of the United States or a nonprofit mutual or public benefit corporation organized and recognized as a nonprofit tax-exempt organization by the Internal Revenue Service while on official parade duty or ceremonial occasions of that organization or while rehearsing or practicing for official parade duty or ceremonial occasions.

(m) Within a gun show conducted pursuant to Article 1 (commencing with Section 27200) and Article 2 (commencing with Section 27300) of Chapter 3 of Division 6.

(n) Within a school zone, as defined in Section 626.9, if that carrying is not prohibited by Section 626.9.

(o) When in accordance with the provisions of Section 171b.

(p) By a person while engaged in the act of making or attempting to make a lawful arrest.

(q) By a person engaged in firearms-related activities, while on the premises of a fixed place of business that is licensed to conduct and conducts, as a regular course of its business, activities related to the sale, making, repair, transfer, pawn, or the use of firearms, or related to firearms training.

(r) By an authorized participant in, or an authorized employee or agent of a supplier of firearms for, a motion picture, television, or video production or entertainment event, when the participant lawfully uses that firearm as part of that production or event, as part of rehearsing or practicing for participation in that production or event, or while the participant or authorized employee or agent is at that production or event, or rehearsal or practice for that production or event.

(s) Incident to obtaining an identification number or mark assigned for that firearm from the Department of Justice pursuant to Section 23910.

(t) At an established public target range while the person is using that firearm upon that target range.

(u) By a person when that person is summoned by a peace officer to assist in making arrests or preserving the peace, while the person is actually engaged in assisting that officer.

(v) Incident to any of the following:

(1) Complying with Section 27560 or 27565, as it pertains to that firearm.

(2) Section 28000, as it pertains to that firearm.

(3) Section 27850 or 31725, as it pertains to that firearm.

(4) Complying with Section 27870 or 27875, as it pertains to that firearm.

(5) Complying with Section 27915, 27920, or 27925, as it pertains to that firearm.

(w) Incident to, and in the course and scope of, training of, or by an individual to become a sworn peace officer as part of a course of study approved by the Commission on Peace Officer Standards and Training.

(x) Incident to, and in the course and scope of, training of, or by an individual to become licensed pursuant to Chapter 4 (commencing with Section 26150) as part of a course of study necessary or authorized by the person authorized to issue the license pursuant to that chapter.

(y) Incident to and at the request of a sheriff, chief, or other head of a municipal police department.

(z) If all of the following conditions are satisfied:

(1) The open carrying occurs at an auction or similar event of a nonprofit public benefit or mutual benefit corporation at which firearms are auctioned or otherwise sold to fund the activities of that corporation or the local chapters of that corporation.

(2) The unloaded firearm that is not a handgun is to be auctioned or otherwise sold for that nonprofit public benefit or mutual benefit corporation.

(3) The unloaded firearm that is not a handgun is to be delivered by a person licensed pursuant to, and operating in accordance with, Sections 26700 to 26915, inclusive.

(aa) Pursuant to paragraph (3) of subdivision (b) of Section 171c.

(ab) Pursuant to Section 171d.

(ac) Pursuant to subparagraph (F) of paragraph (1) of subdivision (c) of Section 171.7.

(ad) On publicly owned land, if the possession and use of an unloaded firearm that is not a handgun is specifically permitted by the managing agency of the land and the person carrying that firearm is in lawful possession of that firearm.

(ae) By any of the following:

(1) The carrying of an unloaded firearm that is not a handgun that is regulated pursuant to Chapter 1 (commencing with Section 18710) of Division 5 of Title 2 by a person who holds a permit issued pursuant to Article 3 (commencing with Section 18900) of that chapter, if the carrying of that firearm is conducted in accordance with the terms and conditions of the permit.

(2) The carrying of an unloaded firearm that is not a handgun that is regulated pursuant to Chapter 2 (commencing with Section 30500) of Division 10 by a person who holds a permit issued pursuant to Section 31005, if the carrying of that firearm is conducted in accordance with the terms and conditions of the permit.

(3) The carrying of an unloaded firearm that is not a handgun that is regulated pursuant to Chapter 6 (commencing with Section 32610) of Division 10 by a person who holds a permit issued pursuant to Section 32650, if the carrying of that firearm is conducted in accordance with the terms and conditions of the permit.

(4) The carrying of an unloaded firearm that is not a handgun that is regulated pursuant to Article 2 (commencing with Section 33300) of Chapter 8 of Division 10 by a person who holds a permit issued pursuant to Section 33300, if the carrying of that firearm is conducted in accordance with the terms and conditions of the permit.

(af) By a licensed hunter while actually engaged in training a dog for the purpose of using the dog in hunting that is not prohibited by law, or while transporting the firearm while going to or returning from that training.

(ag) Pursuant to the provisions of subdivision (d) of Section 171.5.

(ah) By a person who is engaged in the business of manufacturing ammunition and who is licensed to engage in that business, or the authorized representative or authorized agent of that person, while the firearm is being used in the lawful course and scope of the licensee's activities as a person licensed pursuant to Chapter 44 (commencing with Section 921) of Title 18 of the United States Code and regulations issued pursuant thereto.

(ai) On the navigable waters of this state that are held in public trust, if the possession and use of an unloaded firearm that is not a handgun is not prohibited by the managing agency thereof and the person carrying the firearm is in lawful possession of the firearm.

(Amended by Stats. 2017, Ch. 779, Sec. 3. (AB 424) Effective January 1, 2018.)

DIVISION 6. SALE, LEASE, OR TRANSFER OF FIREARMS [26500 - 28490]

(Division 6 added by Stats. 2010, Ch. 711, Sec. 6.)

CHAPTER 1. License Requirement for Sale, Lease, or Transfer of Firearms [26500 - 26620]

(Chapter 1 added by Stats. 2010, Ch. 711, Sec. 6.)

ARTICLE 1. License Requirement and Miscellaneous Exceptions [26500 - 26590]

(Article 1 added by Stats. 2010, Ch. 711, Sec. 6.)

26500.

(a) No person shall sell, lease, or transfer firearms unless the person has been issued a license pursuant to Article 1 (commencing with Section 26700) and Article 2 (commencing with Section 26800) of Chapter 2.

(b) Any person violating this article is guilty of a misdemeanor.

(Added by Stats. 2010, Ch. 711, Sec. 6. (SB 1080) Effective January 1, 2011. Operative January 1, 2012, by Sec. 10 of Ch. 711.)

26505.

Section 26500 does not apply to the sale, lease, or transfer of any firearm by any of the following:

(a) A person acting pursuant to operation of law.

(b) A person acting pursuant to a court order.

(c) A person acting pursuant to the Enforcement of Judgments Law (Title 9 (commencing with Section 680.010) of Part 2 of the Code of Civil Procedure).

(d) A person who liquidates a personal firearm collection to satisfy a court judgment.

(Added by Stats. 2010, Ch. 711, Sec. 6. (SB 1080) Effective January 1, 2011. Operative January 1, 2012, by Sec. 10 of Ch. 711.)

26510.

Section 26500 does not apply to a person acting pursuant to subdivision (f) of Section 186.22a or Section 18000 or 18005.

(Added by Stats. 2010, Ch. 711, Sec. 6. (SB 1080) Effective January 1, 2011. Operative January 1, 2012, by Sec. 10 of Ch. 711.)

26515.

Section 26500 does not apply to the sale, lease, or transfer of a firearm if both of the following conditions are satisfied:

(a) The sale, lease, or transfer is made by a person who obtains title to the firearm by intestate succession or bequest, or as a surviving spouse pursuant to Chapter 1 (commencing with Section 13500) of Part 2 of Division 8 of the Probate Code.

(b) The person disposes of the firearm within 60 days of receipt of the firearm.

(Added by Stats. 2010, Ch. 711, Sec. 6. (SB 1080) Effective January 1, 2011. Operative January 1, 2012, by Sec. 10 of Ch. 711.)

26520.

(a) Section 26500 does not apply to the infrequent sale, lease, or transfer of firearms.

(b) As used in this section, "infrequent" has the meaning provided in Section 16730.

(Added by Stats. 2010, Ch. 711, Sec. 6. (SB 1080) Effective January 1, 2011. Operative January 1, 2012, by Sec. 10 of Ch. 711.)

26525.

(a) Section 26500 does not apply to the sale, lease, or transfer of used firearms, other than handguns, at gun shows or events, as specified in Article 1 (commencing with Section 26700) and Article 2 (commencing with Section 26800) of Chapter 2, by a person other than a licensee or dealer, provided the person has a valid federal firearms license and a current certificate of eligibility issued by the Department of Justice, as specified in Section 26710, and provided all the sales, leases, or transfers fully comply with Section 27545. However, the person shall not engage in the sale, lease, or transfer of used firearms other than handguns at more than 12 gun shows or events in any calendar year and shall not sell, lease, or transfer more than 15 used firearms other than handguns at any single gun show or event. In no event shall the person sell more than 75 used firearms other than handguns in any calendar year.

(b) The Department of Justice shall adopt regulations to administer this program and shall recover the full costs of administration from fees assessed applicants.

(Added by Stats. 2010, Ch. 711, Sec. 6. (SB 1080) Effective January 1, 2011. Operative January 1, 2012, by Sec. 10 of Ch. 711.)

26530.

Section 26500 does not apply to sales, deliveries, or transfers of firearms between or to importers and manufacturers of firearms licensed to engage in that business pursuant to Chapter 44 (commencing with Section 921) of Title 18 of the United States Code and the regulations issued pursuant thereto.

(Added by Stats. 2010, Ch. 711, Sec. 6. (SB 1080) Effective January 1, 2011. Operative January 1, 2012, by Sec. 10 of Ch. 711.)

26535.

Section 26500 does not apply to any sale, delivery, or transfer of firearms that satisfies both of the following conditions:

(a) It is made by an importer or manufacturer licensed pursuant to Chapter 44 (commencing with Section 921) of Title 18 of the United States Code and the regulations issued pursuant thereto.

(b) It is made to a dealer or wholesaler.

(Added by Stats. 2010, Ch. 711, Sec. 6. (SB 1080) Effective January 1, 2011. Operative January 1, 2012, by Sec. 10 of Ch. 711.)

26540.

Section 26500 does not apply to deliveries and transfers of firearms made pursuant to Sections 18000 and 18005, pursuant to Division 4 (commencing with Section 18250) of Title 2, or pursuant to Sections 34005 and 34010.

(Added by Stats. 2010, Ch. 711, Sec. 6. (SB 1080) Effective January 1, 2011. Operative January 1, 2012, by Sec. 10 of Ch. 711.)

26545.

Section 26500 does not apply to the loan of a firearm for the purposes of shooting at targets, if the loan occurs on the premises of a target facility that holds a business or regulatory license or on the premises of any club or organization organized for the purposes of practicing shooting at targets upon established ranges, whether public or private, if the firearm is at all times kept within the premises of the target range or on the premises of the club or organization.

(Added by Stats. 2010, Ch. 711, Sec. 6. (SB 1080) Effective January 1, 2011. Operative January 1, 2012, by Sec. 10 of Ch. 711.)

26550.

Section 26500 does not apply to any sale, delivery, or transfer of firearms that satisfies all of the following requirements:

(a) It is made by a manufacturer, importer, or wholesaler licensed pursuant to Chapter 44 (commencing with Section 921) of Title 18 of the United States Code and the regulations issued pursuant thereto.

(b) It is made to a person who resides outside this state and is licensed pursuant to Chapter 44 (commencing with Section 921) of Title 18 of the United States Code and the regulations issued pursuant thereto.

(c) It is made in accordance with Chapter 44 (commencing with Section 921) of Title 18 of the United States Code and the regulations issued pursuant thereto.

(Added by Stats. 2010, Ch. 711, Sec. 6. (SB 1080) Effective January 1, 2011. Operative January 1, 2012, by Sec. 10 of Ch. 711.)

26555.

Section 26500 does not apply to any sale, delivery, or transfer of firearms that satisfies all of the following requirements:

(a) It is made by a person who resides outside this state and is licensed outside this state pursuant to Chapter 44 (commencing with Section 921) of Title 18 of the United States Code and the regulations issued pursuant thereto.

(b) It is made to a manufacturer, importer, or wholesaler.

(c) It is made in accordance with Chapter 44 (commencing with Section 921) of Title 18 of the United States Code and the regulations issued pursuant thereto.

(Added by Stats. 2010, Ch. 711, Sec. 6. (SB 1080) Effective January 1, 2011. Operative January 1, 2012, by Sec. 10 of Ch. 711.)

26560.

Section 26500 does not apply to any sale, delivery, or transfer of firearms by a wholesaler to a dealer.

(Added by Stats. 2010, Ch. 711, Sec. 6. (SB 1080) Effective January 1, 2011. Operative January 1, 2012, by Sec. 10 of Ch. 711.)

26565.

Section 26500 does not apply to any sale, delivery, or transfer of firearms that satisfies all of the following conditions:

(a) It is made by a person who resides outside this state.

(b) It is made to a person licensed pursuant to Sections 26700 to 26915, inclusive.

(c) It is made in accordance with Chapter 44 (commencing with Section 921) of Title 18 of the United States Code and the regulations issued pursuant thereto.

(Added by Stats. 2010, Ch. 711, Sec. 6. (SB 1080) Effective January 1, 2011. Operative January 1, 2012, by Sec. 10 of Ch. 711.)

26570.

Section 26500 does not apply to any sale, delivery, or transfer of firearms that satisfies all of the following conditions:

(a) It is made by a person who resides outside this state and is licensed pursuant to Chapter 44 (commencing with Section 921) of Title 18 of the United States Code and the regulations issued pursuant thereto.

(b) It is made to a dealer.

(c) It is made in accordance with Chapter 44 (commencing with Section 921) of Title 18 of the United States Code and the regulations issued pursuant thereto.

(Added by Stats. 2010, Ch. 711, Sec. 6. (SB 1080) Effective January 1, 2011. Operative January 1, 2012, by Sec. 10 of Ch. 711.)

26575.

Section 26500 does not apply to the sale, delivery, or transfer of an unloaded firearm by one wholesaler to another wholesaler if that firearm is intended as merchandise in the receiving wholesaler's business.

(Added by Stats. 2010, Ch. 711, Sec. 6. (SB 1080) Effective January 1, 2011. Operative January 1, 2012, by Sec. 10 of Ch. 711.)

26580.

Section 26500 does not apply to the loan of an unloaded firearm or the loan of a firearm loaded with blank cartridges for use solely as a prop for a motion picture, television, or video production or entertainment or theatrical event.

(Added by Stats. 2010, Ch. 711, Sec. 6. (SB 1080) Effective January 1, 2011. Operative January 1, 2012, by Sec. 10 of Ch. 711.)

26585.

Section 26500 does not apply to the delivery of an unloaded firearm that is a curio or relic, as defined in Section 478.11 of Title 27 of the Code of Federal Regulations, if the delivery satisfies all of the following conditions:

(a) It is made by a person licensed as a collector pursuant to Chapter 44 (commencing with Section 921) of Title 18 of the United States Code and the regulations issued pursuant thereto.

(b) It is made by a person with a current certificate of eligibility issued pursuant to Section 26710.

(c) It is made to a dealer.

(Added by Stats. 2010, Ch. 711, Sec. 6. (SB 1080) Effective January 1, 2011. Operative January 1, 2012, by Sec. 10 of Ch. 711.)

26587.

Section 26500 does not apply to either of the following:

(a) A loan of a firearm to a gunsmith for service or repair.

(b) The return of the firearm by the gunsmith.

(Added by Stats. 2010, Ch. 711, Sec. 6. (SB 1080) Effective January 1, 2011. Operative January 1, 2012, by Sec. 10 of Ch. 711.)

26588.

Section 26500 does not apply to any of the following:

(a) The sale, delivery, transfer, or return of a firearm regulated pursuant to Chapter 1 (commencing with Section 18710) of Division 5 of Title 2 by a person who holds a permit issued pursuant to Article 3 (commencing with Section 18900) of that chapter, if the sale, delivery, transfer, or return is conducted in accordance with the terms and conditions of the permit.

(b) The sale, delivery, transfer, or return of a firearm regulated pursuant to Chapter 2 (commencing with Section 30500) of Division 10 by a person who holds a permit issued pursuant to Section 31005, if the sale, delivery, transfer, or return is conducted in accordance with the terms and conditions of the permit.

(c) The sale, delivery, transfer, or return of a firearm regulated pursuant to Chapter 6 (commencing with Section 32610) of Division 10 by a person who holds a permit issued pursuant to Section 32650, if the sale, delivery, transfer, or return is conducted in accordance with the terms and conditions of the permit.

(d) The sale, delivery, transfer, or return of a firearm regulated pursuant to Article 2 (commencing with Section 33300) of Chapter 8 of Division 10 by a person who holds a permit issued pursuant to Section 33300, if the sale, delivery, transfer, or return is conducted in accordance with the terms and conditions of the permit.

(Added by Stats. 2010, Ch. 711, Sec. 6. (SB 1080) Effective January 1, 2011. Operative January 1, 2012, by Sec. 10 of Ch. 711.)

26590.

Section 26500 does not apply to deliveries, transfers, or returns of firearms made by a court or a law enforcement agency pursuant to Chapter 2 (commencing with Section 33850) of Division 11.

(Added by Stats. 2010, Ch. 711, Sec. 6. (SB 1080) Effective January 1, 2011. Operative January 1, 2012, by Sec. 10 of Ch. 711.)

ARTICLE 2. Exceptions Relating to Law Enforcement [26600 - 26625]
 (Article 2 added by Stats. 2010, Ch. 711, Sec. 6.)

26600.

(a) Section 26500 does not apply to any sale, delivery, or transfer of firearms made to an authorized law enforcement representative of any city, county, city and county, or state, or of the federal government, for exclusive use by that governmental agency if, prior to the sale, delivery, or transfer of these firearms, written authorization from the head of the agency authorizing the transaction is presented to the person from whom the purchase, delivery, or transfer is being made.

(b) Proper written authorization is defined as verifiable written certification from the head of the agency by which the purchaser or transferee is employed, identifying the employee as an individual authorized to conduct the transaction, and authorizing the transaction for the exclusive use of the agency by which that person is employed.

(c) Within 10 days of the date a handgun, and commencing January 1, 2014, any firearm, is acquired by the agency, a record of the same shall be entered as an institutional weapon into the Automated Firearms System (AFS) via the California Law Enforcement Telecommunications System (CLETS) by the law enforcement or state agency. Any agency without access to AFS shall arrange with the sheriff of the county in which the agency is located to input this information via this system.

(Amended by Stats. 2011, Ch. 745, Sec. 4. (AB 809) Effective January 1, 2012.)

26605.

Section 26500 does not apply to the loan of a firearm if all of the following conditions are satisfied:

(a) The loan is made by an authorized law enforcement representative of a city, county, or city and county, or of the state or federal government.

(b) The loan is made to a peace officer employed by that agency and authorized to carry a firearm.

(c) The loan is made for the carrying and use of that firearm by that peace officer in the course and scope of the officer's duties.

(Added by Stats. 2010, Ch. 711, Sec. 6. (SB 1080) Effective January 1, 2011. Operative January 1, 2012, by Sec. 10 of Ch. 711.)

26610.

(a) Section 26500 does not apply to the sale, delivery, or transfer of a firearm by a law enforcement agency to a peace officer pursuant to Section 10334 of the Public Contract Code.

(b) Within 10 days of the date that a handgun, and commencing January 1, 2014, any firearm, is sold, delivered, or transferred pursuant to Section 10334 of the Public Contract Code to that peace officer, the name of the officer and the make, model, serial number, and other identifying characteristics of the firearm being sold, delivered, or transferred shall be entered into the Automated Firearms System (AFS) via the California Law Enforcement Telecommunications System (CLETS) by the law enforcement or state agency that sold, delivered, or transferred the firearm, provided, however, that if the firearm is not a handgun and does not have a serial number, identification number, or identification mark assigned to it, that fact shall be noted in AFS. Any agency without access to AFS shall arrange with the sheriff of the county in which the agency is located to input this information via this system.

(Amended by Stats. 2011, Ch. 745, Sec. 5. (AB 809) Effective January 1, 2012.)

26613.

Section 26500 does not apply to the delivery of a firearm by a law enforcement agency to a dealer in order for that dealer to deliver the firearm to the spouse or domestic partner of a peace officer who died in the line of duty if the sale of that firearm to the spouse or domestic partner is made in accordance with subdivision (d) of Section 10334 of the Public Contract Code.

(Added by Stats. 2013, Ch. 16, Sec. 1. (AB 685) Effective January 1, 2014.)

26615.

(a) Section 26500 does not apply to the sale, delivery, or transfer of a firearm by a law enforcement agency to a retiring peace officer who is authorized to carry a firearm pursuant to Chapter 5 (commencing with Section 26300) of Division 5.

(b) Within 10 days of the date that a handgun, and commencing January 1, 2014, any firearm, is sold, delivered, or transferred to that retiring peace officer, the name of the officer and the make, model, serial number, and other identifying characteristics of the firearm being sold, delivered, or transferred shall be entered into the Automated Firearms System (AFS) via the California Law Enforcement Telecommunications System (CLETS) by the law enforcement or state agency that sold, delivered, or transferred the firearm, provided, however, that if the firearm is not a handgun and does not have a serial number, identification number, or identification mark assigned to it, that fact shall be noted in AFS. Any agency without access to AFS shall arrange with the sheriff of the county in which the agency is located to input this information via this system.

(Amended by Stats. 2011, Ch. 745, Sec. 6. (AB 809) Effective January 1, 2012.)

26620.

Section 26500 does not apply to the sale, delivery, or transfer of a firearm when made by an authorized law enforcement representative of a city, county, city and county, or of the state or federal government, if all of the following requirements are met:

(a) The sale, delivery, or transfer is made to one of the following:

(1) A person licensed pursuant to Sections 26700 to 26915, inclusive.
(2) A wholesaler.
(3) A manufacturer or importer of firearms or ammunition licensed to engage in that business pursuant to Chapter 44 (commencing with Section 921) of Title 18 of the United States Code and the regulations issued pursuant thereto.
(b) The sale, delivery, or transfer of the firearm is not subject to the procedures set forth in Section 18000, 18005, 34000, or 34005.
(c) If the authorized law enforcement representative sells, delivers, or transfers a firearm that the governmental agency owns to a person licensed pursuant to Sections 26700 to 26915, inclusive, within 10 days of the date that the firearm is delivered to that licensee pursuant to this section by that agency, the agency has entered a record of the delivery into the Automated Firearms System (AFS) via the California Law Enforcement Telecommunications System (CLETS). Any agency without access to the AFS shall arrange with the sheriff of the county in which the agency is located to input this information via this system.
(Added by Stats. 2013, Ch. 738, Sec. 3. (AB 538) Effective January 1, 2014.)
26625.
Section 26500 does not apply to the loan of a firearm if the loan of the firearm is to a person enrolled in the course of basic training prescribed by the Commission on Peace Officer Standards and Training, or any other course certified by the commission, for purposes of participation in the course.
(Added by Stats. 2017, Ch. 783, Sec. 1. (AB 693) Effective October 14, 2017.)

CHAPTER 2. Issuance, Forfeiture, and Conditions of License to Sell, Lease, or Transfer Firearms at Retail [26700 - 27140]

(Chapter 2 added by Stats. 2010, Ch. 711, Sec. 6.)

ARTICLE 1. License to Sell, Lease, or Transfer Firearms at Retail [26700 - 26725]
(Article 1 added by Stats. 2010, Ch. 711, Sec. 6.)
26700.
As used in this division, and in any other provision listed in Section 16580, "dealer," "licensee," or "person licensed pursuant to Sections 26700 to 26915, inclusive" means a person who satisfies all of the following requirements:
(a) Has a valid federal firearms license.
(b) Has any regulatory or business license, or licenses, required by local government.
(c) Has a valid seller's permit issued by the State Board of Equalization.
(d) Has a certificate of eligibility issued by the Department of Justice pursuant to Section 26710.
(e) Has a license issued in the format prescribed by subdivision (c) of Section 26705.
(f) Is among those recorded in the centralized list specified in Section 26715.
(Added by Stats. 2010, Ch. 711, Sec. 6. (SB 1080) Effective January 1, 2011. Operative January 1, 2012, by Sec. 10 of Ch. 711.)
26705.
(a) The duly constituted licensing authority of a city, county, or a city and county shall accept applications for, and may grant licenses permitting, licensees to sell firearms at retail within the city, county, or city and county. The duly constituted licensing authority shall inform applicants who are denied licenses of the reasons for the denial in writing.
(b) No license shall be granted to any applicant who fails to provide a copy of the applicant's valid federal firearms license, valid seller's permit issued by the State Board of Equalization, and the certificate of eligibility described in Section 26710.
(c) A license granted by the duly constituted licensing authority of any city, county, or city and county, shall be valid for not more than one year from the date of issuance and shall be in one of the following forms:
(1) In the form prescribed by the Attorney General.
(2) A regulatory or business license that states on its face "Valid for Retail Sales of Firearms" and is endorsed by the signature of the issuing authority.
(3) A letter from the duly constituted licensing authority having primary jurisdiction for the applicant's intended business location stating that the jurisdiction does not require any form of regulatory or business license or does not otherwise restrict or regulate the sale of firearms.
(d) Local licensing authorities may assess fees to recover their full costs of processing applications for licenses.
(Added by Stats. 2010, Ch. 711, Sec. 6. (SB 1080) Effective January 1, 2011. Operative January 1, 2012, by Sec. 10 of Ch. 711.)
26710.
(a) A person may request a certificate of eligibility from the Department of Justice.
(b) The Department of Justice shall examine its records and records available to the department in the National Instant Criminal Background Check System in order to determine if the applicant is prohibited by state or federal law from possessing, receiving, owning, or purchasing a firearm.
(c) The department shall issue a certificate to an applicant if the department's records indicate that the applicant is not a person who is prohibited by state or federal law from possessing firearms.
(d) The department shall adopt regulations to administer the certificate of eligibility program and shall recover the full costs of administering the program by imposing fees assessed to applicants who apply for those certificates.
(Added by Stats. 2010, Ch. 711, Sec. 6. (SB 1080) Effective January 1, 2011. Operative January 1, 2012, by Sec. 10 of Ch. 711.)
26715.
(a) Except as otherwise provided in paragraphs (1) and (3) of subdivision (b), the Department of Justice shall keep a centralized list of all persons licensed pursuant to subdivisions (a) to (e), inclusive, of Section 26700.
(b) (1) The department may remove from this list any person who knowingly or with gross negligence violates a provision listed in Section 16575.
(2) The department shall remove from the centralized list any person whose federal firearms license has expired or has been revoked.
(3) Upon removal of a dealer from this list, notification shall be provided to local law enforcement and licensing authorities in the jurisdiction where the dealer's business is located.
(c) Information compiled from the list shall be made available, upon request, for the following purposes only:
(1) For law enforcement purposes.
(2) When the information is requested by a person licensed pursuant to Chapter 44 (commencing with Section 921) of Title 18 of the United States Code for determining the validity of the license for firearm shipments.
(3) When information is requested by a person promoting, sponsoring, operating, or otherwise organizing a show or event as defined in Section 478.100 of Title 27 of the Code of Federal Regulations, or its successor, who possesses a valid certificate of eligibility issued pursuant to Article 1 (commencing with Section 27200) of Chapter 3, if that information is requested by the person to determine the eligibility of a prospective participant in a gun show or event to conduct transactions as a firearms dealer pursuant to subdivision (b) of Section 26805.

(d) Information provided pursuant to subdivision (c) shall be limited to information necessary to corroborate an individual's current license status as being one of the following:
(1) A person licensed pursuant to subdivisions (a) to (e), inclusive, of Section 26700.
(2) A person who is licensed pursuant to Chapter 44 (commencing with Section 921) of Title 18 of the United States Code, and who is not subject to the requirement of being licensed pursuant to subdivisions (a) to (e), inclusive, of Section 26700.
(Added by Stats. 2010, Ch. 711, Sec. 6. (SB 1080) Effective January 1, 2011. Operative January 1, 2012, by Sec. 10 of Ch. 711.)
26720.
(a) The Department of Justice may inspect dealers to ensure compliance with the provisions listed in Section 16575.
(b) The department may assess an annual fee, not to exceed one hundred fifteen dollars ($115), to cover the reasonable cost of maintaining the list described in Section 26715, including the cost of inspections.
(c) Dealers whose place of business is in a jurisdiction that has adopted an inspection program to ensure compliance with firearms law shall be exempt from that portion of the department's fee that relates to the cost of inspections. The applicant is responsible for providing evidence to the department that the jurisdiction in which the business is located has the inspection program.
(Added by Stats. 2010, Ch. 711, Sec. 6. (SB 1080) Effective January 1, 2011. Operative January 1, 2012, by Sec. 10 of Ch. 711.)
26725.
The Department of Justice shall maintain and make available upon request information concerning all of the following:
(a) The number of inspections conducted and the amount of fees collected pursuant to Section 26720.
(b) A listing of exempted jurisdictions, as defined in Section 26720.
(c) The number of dealers removed from the centralized list defined in Section 26715.
(d) The number of dealers found to have violated a provision listed in Section 16575 with knowledge or gross negligence.
(Added by Stats. 2010, Ch. 711, Sec. 6. (SB 1080) Effective January 1, 2011. Operative January 1, 2012, by Sec. 10 of Ch. 711.)

ARTICLE 2. Grounds for Forfeiture of License [26800 - 26915]
(Article 2 added by Stats. 2010, Ch. 711, Sec. 6.)
26800.
A license under this chapter is subject to forfeiture for a breach of any of the prohibitions and requirements of this article, except those stated in the following provisions:
(a) Subdivision (c) of Section 26890.
(b) Subdivision (d) of Section 26890.
(c) Subdivision (b) of Section 26900.
(Added by Stats. 2010, Ch. 711, Sec. 6. (SB 1080) Effective January 1, 2011. Operative January 1, 2012, by Sec. 10 of Ch. 711.)
26805.
(a) Except as provided in subdivisions (b) and (c), the business of a licensee shall be conducted only in the buildings designated in the license.
(b) (1) A person licensed pursuant to Sections 26700 and 26705 may take possession of firearms and commence preparation of registers for the sale, delivery, or transfer of firearms at any gun show or event, as defined in Section 478.100 of Title 27 of the Code of Federal Regulations, or its successor, if the gun show or event is not conducted from any motorized or towed vehicle. A person conducting business pursuant to this subdivision shall be entitled to conduct business as authorized herein at any gun show or event in the state, without regard to the jurisdiction within this state that issued the license pursuant to Sections 26700 and 26705, provided the person complies with all applicable laws, including, but not limited to, the waiting period specified in subdivision (a) of Section 26815, and all applicable local laws, regulations, and fees, if any.
(2) A person conducting business pursuant to this subdivision shall publicly display the person's license issued pursuant to Sections 26700 and 26705, or a facsimile thereof, at any gun show or event, as specified in this subdivision.
(c) (1) A person licensed pursuant to Sections 26700 and 26705 may engage in the sale and transfer of firearms other than handguns, at events specified in Sections 26955, 27655, 27900, and 27905, subject to the prohibitions and restrictions contained in those sections.
(2) A person licensed pursuant to Sections 26700 and 26705 may also accept delivery of firearms other than handguns, outside the building designated in the license, provided the firearm is being donated for the purpose of sale or transfer at an auction or similar event specified in Section 27900.
(d) The firearm may be delivered to the purchaser, transferee, or person being loaned the firearm at one of the following places:
(1) The building designated in the license.
(2) The places specified in subdivision (b) or (c).
(3) The place of residence of, the fixed place of business of, or on private property owned or lawfully possessed by, the purchaser, transferee, or person being loaned the firearm.
(Amended by Stats. 2011, Ch. 745, Sec. 7. (AB 809) Effective January 1, 2012.)
26810.
A person's license under this chapter, or a copy thereof certified by the issuing authority, shall be displayed on the premises where it can easily be seen.
(Added by Stats. 2010, Ch. 711, Sec. 6. (SB 1080) Effective January 1, 2011. Operative January 1, 2012, by Sec. 10 of Ch. 711.)
26815.
No firearm shall be delivered:
(a) Within 10 days of the application to purchase, or, after notice by the department pursuant to Section 28220, within 10 days of the submission to the department of any correction to the application, or within 10 days of the submission to the department of any fee required pursuant to Section 28225, whichever is later.
(b) Unless unloaded and securely wrapped or unloaded and in a locked container.
(c) Unless the purchaser, transferee, or person being loaned the firearm presents clear evidence of the person's identity and age to the dealer.
(d) Whenever the dealer is notified by the Department of Justice that the person is prohibited by state or federal law from processing, owning, purchasing, or receiving a firearm. The dealer shall make available to the person in the prohibited class a prohibited notice and transfer form, provided by the department, stating that the person is prohibited from owning or possessing a firearm, and that the person may obtain from the department the reason for the prohibition.
(Added by Stats. 2010, Ch. 711, Sec. 6. (SB 1080) Effective January 1, 2011. Operative January 1, 2012, by Sec. 10 of Ch. 711.)
26820.
No handgun or imitation handgun, or placard advertising the sale or other transfer thereof, shall be displayed in any part of the premises where it can readily be seen from the outside.
(Amended by Stats. 2011, Ch. 745, Sec. 8. (AB 809) Effective January 1, 2012.)
26825.
A licensee shall agree to and shall act properly and promptly in processing firearms transactions pursuant to Chapter 5 (commencing with Section 28050).
(Added by Stats. 2010, Ch. 711, Sec. 6. (SB 1080) Effective January 1, 2011. Operative January 1, 2012, by Sec. 10 of Ch. 711.)
26830.

A licensee shall comply with all of the following:
(a) Sections 27500 to 27535, inclusive.
(b) Section 27555.
(c) Section 28100.
(d) Article 2 (commencing with Section 28150) of Chapter 6.
(e) Article 3 (commencing with Section 28200) of Chapter 6.
(f) Section 30300.
(Added by Stats. 2010, Ch. 711, Sec. 6. (SB 1080) Effective January 1, 2011. Operative January 1, 2012, by Sec. 10 of Ch. 711.)
26835.
(a) A licensee shall post conspicuously within the licensed premises the following warnings in block letters not less than one inch in height:
(1) "FIREARMS MUST BE HANDLED RESPONSIBLY AND SECURELY STORED TO PREVENT ACCESS BY CHILDREN AND OTHER UNAUTHORIZED USERS. CALIFORNIA HAS STRICT LAWS PERTAINING TO FIREARMS, AND YOU MAY BE FINED OR IMPRISONED IF YOU FAIL TO COMPLY WITH THEM. VISIT THE WEB SITE OF THE CALIFORNIA ATTORNEY GENERAL AT HTTPS://OAG.CA.GOV/FIREARMS FOR INFORMATION ON FIREARM LAWS APPLICABLE TO YOU AND HOW YOU CAN COMPLY."
(2) "IF YOU KEEP A LOADED FIREARM WITHIN ANY PREMISES UNDER YOUR CUSTODY OR CONTROL, AND A PERSON UNDER 18 YEARS OF AGE OBTAINS IT AND USES IT, RESULTING IN INJURY OR DEATH, OR CARRIES IT TO A PUBLIC PLACE, YOU MAY BE GUILTY OF A MISDEMEANOR OR A FELONY UNLESS YOU STORED THE FIREARM IN A LOCKED CONTAINER OR LOCKED THE FIREARM WITH A LOCKING DEVICE, TO KEEP IT FROM TEMPORARILY FUNCTIONING."
(3) "CHILDREN MAY BE UNABLE TO DISTINGUISH FIREARMS FROM TOYS AND MAY OPERATE FIREARMS, CAUSING SEVERE INJURIES OR DEATH. IF YOU KEEP A PISTOL, REVOLVER, OR OTHER FIREARM CAPABLE OF BEING CONCEALED UPON THE PERSON, WITHIN ANY PREMISES UNDER YOUR CUSTODY OR CONTROL, AND A PERSON UNDER 18 YEARS OF AGE GAINS ACCESS TO THE FIREARM, AND CARRIES IT OFF-PREMISES, YOU MAY BE GUILTY OF A MISDEMEANOR, UNLESS YOU STORED THE FIREARM IN A LOCKED CONTAINER, OR LOCKED THE FIREARM WITH A LOCKING DEVICE, TO KEEP IT FROM TEMPORARILY FUNCTIONING."
(4) "YOU MAY BE GUILTY OF A MISDEMEANOR, INCLUDING A SIGNIFICANT FINE OR IMPRISONMENT, IF YOU KEEP A FIREARM WHERE A MINOR IS LIKELY TO ACCESS IT OR IF A MINOR OBTAINS AND IMPROPERLY USES IT, OR CARRIES IT OFF OF THE PREMISES TO A SCHOOL OR SCHOOL-SPONSORED EVENT, UNLESS YOU STORED THE FIREARM IN A LOCKED CONTAINER OR LOCKED THE FIREARM WITH A LOCKING DEVICE."
(5) "IF YOU NEGLIGENTLY STORE OR LEAVE A LOADED FIREARM WITHIN ANY PREMISES UNDER YOUR CUSTODY OR CONTROL, WHERE A PERSON UNDER 18 YEARS OF AGE IS LIKELY TO ACCESS IT, YOU MAY BE GUILTY OF A MISDEMEANOR, INCLUDING A SIGNIFICANT FINE, UNLESS YOU STORED THE FIREARM IN A LOCKED CONTAINER, OR LOCKED THE FIREARM WITH A LOCKING DEVICE."
(6) "DISCHARGING FIREARMS IN POORLY VENTILATED AREAS, CLEANING FIREARMS, OR HANDLING AMMUNITION MAY RESULT IN EXPOSURE TO LEAD, A SUBSTANCE KNOWN TO CAUSE BIRTH DEFECTS, REPRODUCTIVE HARM, AND OTHER SERIOUS PHYSICAL INJURY. HAVE ADEQUATE VENTILATION AT ALL TIMES. WASH HANDS THOROUGHLY AFTER EXPOSURE."
(7) "FEDERAL REGULATIONS PROVIDE THAT IF YOU DO NOT TAKE PHYSICAL POSSESSION OF THE FIREARM THAT YOU ARE ACQUIRING OWNERSHIP OF WITHIN 30 DAYS AFTER YOU COMPLETE THE INITIAL BACKGROUND CHECK PAPERWORK, THEN YOU HAVE TO GO THROUGH THE BACKGROUND CHECK PROCESS A SECOND TIME IN ORDER TO TAKE PHYSICAL POSSESSION OF THAT FIREARM."
(8) "NO PERSON SHALL MAKE AN APPLICATION TO PURCHASE MORE THAN ONE PISTOL, REVOLVER, OR OTHER FIREARM CAPABLE OF BEING CONCEALED UPON THE PERSON WITHIN ANY 30-DAY PERIOD AND NO DELIVERY SHALL BE MADE TO ANY PERSON WHO HAS MADE AN APPLICATION TO PURCHASE MORE THAN ONE PISTOL, REVOLVER, OR OTHER FIREARM CAPABLE OF BEING CONCEALED UPON THE PERSON WITHIN ANY 30-DAY PERIOD."
(9) "IF A FIREARM YOU OWN OR POSSESS IS LOST OR STOLEN, YOU MUST REPORT THE LOSS OR THEFT TO A LOCAL LAW ENFORCEMENT AGENCY WHERE THE LOSS OR THEFT OCCURRED WITHIN FIVE DAYS OF THE TIME YOU KNEW OR REASONABLY SHOULD HAVE KNOWN THAT THE FIREARM HAD BEEN LOST OR STOLEN."
(b) This section shall become operative on January 1, 2019.
(Repealed (in Sec. 2) and added by Stats. 2017, Ch. 825, Sec. 3. (AB 1525) Effective January 1, 2018. Note: This section was amended on November 8, 2016, by initiative Prop. 63.)
26840.
(a) A dealer shall not deliver a firearm unless the person receiving the firearm presents to the dealer a valid firearm safety certificate, or, in the case of a handgun, an unexpired handgun safety certificate. The firearms dealer shall retain a photocopy of the firearm safety certificate as proof of compliance with this requirement.
(b) This section shall become operative on January 1, 2015.
(Repealed (in Sec. 3) and added by Stats. 2013, Ch. 761, Sec. 4. (SB 683) Effective January 1, 2014. Section operative January 1, 2015, by its own provisions.)
26845.
(a) No handgun may be delivered unless the purchaser, transferee, or person being loaned the firearm presents documentation indicating that the person is a California resident.
(b) Satisfactory documentation shall include a utility bill from within the last three months, a residential lease, a property deed, or military permanent duty station orders indicating assignment within this state, or other evidence of residency as permitted by the Department of Justice.
(c) The firearms dealer shall retain a photocopy of the documentation as proof of compliance with this requirement.
(Amended by Stats. 2011, Ch. 745, Sec. 10. (AB 809) Effective January 1, 2012.)
26850.
(a) Except as authorized by the department, no firearms dealer may deliver a handgun unless the recipient performs a safe handling demonstration with that handgun.
(b) The safe handling demonstration shall commence with the handgun unloaded and locked with the firearm safety device with which it is required to be delivered, if applicable. While maintaining muzzle awareness, that is, the firearm is pointed in a safe direction, preferably down at the ground, and trigger discipline, that is, the trigger finger is outside of the trigger guard and along side of the handgun frame, at all times, the handgun recipient shall correctly and safely perform the following:
(1) If the handgun is a semiautomatic pistol, the steps listed in Section 26853.
(2) If the handgun is a double-action revolver, the steps listed in Section 26856.
(3) If the handgun is a single-action revolver, the steps listed in Section 26859.
(c) The recipient shall receive instruction regarding how to render that handgun safe in the event of a jam.
(d) The firearms dealer shall sign and date an affidavit stating that the requirements of subdivisions (a) and (b) have been met. The firearms dealer shall additionally obtain the signature of the handgun purchaser on the same affidavit. The firearms dealer shall retain the original affidavit as proof of compliance with this requirement.
(e) The recipient shall perform the safe handling demonstration for a department-certified instructor.
(f) No demonstration shall be required if the dealer is returning the handgun to the owner of the handgun.

(g) Department-certified instructors who may administer the safe handling demonstration shall meet the requirements set forth in subdivision (b) of Section 31635.
(h) The persons who are exempt from the requirements of subdivision (a) of Section 31615, pursuant to Section 31700, are also exempt from performing the safe handling demonstration.
(Amended by Stats. 2011, Ch. 745, Sec. 11. (AB 809) Effective January 1, 2012.)
26853.
To comply with Section 26850, a safe handling demonstration for a semiautomatic pistol shall include all of the following steps:
(a) Remove the magazine.
(b) Lock the slide back. If the model of firearm does not allow the slide to be locked back, pull the slide back, visually and physically check the chamber to ensure that it is clear.
(c) Visually and physically inspect the chamber, to ensure that the handgun is unloaded.
(d) Remove the firearm safety device, if applicable. If the firearm safety device prevents any of the previous steps, remove the firearm safety device during the appropriate step.
(e) Load one bright orange, red, or other readily identifiable dummy round into the magazine. If no readily identifiable dummy round is available, an empty cartridge casing with an empty primer pocket may be used.
(f) Insert the magazine into the magazine well of the firearm.
(g) Manipulate the slide release or pull back and release the slide.
(h) Remove the magazine.
(i) Visually inspect the chamber to reveal that a round can be chambered with the magazine removed.
(j) Lock the slide back to eject the bright orange, red, or other readily identifiable dummy round. If the handgun is of a model that does not allow the slide to be locked back, pull the slide back and physically check the chamber to ensure that the chamber is clear. If no readily identifiable dummy round is available, an empty cartridge casing with an empty primer pocket may be used.
(k) Apply the safety, if applicable.
(l) Apply the firearm safety device, if applicable. This requirement shall not apply to an Olympic competition pistol if no firearm safety device, other than a cable lock that the department has determined would damage the barrel of the pistol, has been approved for the pistol, and the pistol is either listed in subdivision (b) of Section 32105 or is subject to subdivision (c) of Section 32105.
(Added by Stats. 2010, Ch. 711, Sec. 6. (SB 1080) Effective January 1, 2011. Operative January 1, 2012, by Sec. 10 of Ch. 711.)
26856.
To comply with Section 26850, a safe handling demonstration for a double-action revolver shall include all of the following steps:
(a) Open the cylinder.
(b) Visually and physically inspect each chamber, to ensure that the revolver is unloaded.
(c) Remove the firearm safety device. If the firearm safety device prevents any of the previous steps, remove the firearm safety device during the appropriate step.
(d) While maintaining muzzle awareness and trigger discipline, load one bright orange, red, or other readily identifiable dummy round into a chamber of the cylinder and rotate the cylinder so that the round is in the next-to-fire position. If no readily identifiable dummy round is available, an empty cartridge casing with an empty primer pocket may be used.
(e) Close the cylinder.
(f) Open the cylinder and eject the round.
(g) Visually and physically inspect each chamber to ensure that the revolver is unloaded.
(h) Apply the firearm safety device, if applicable. This requirement shall not apply to an Olympic competition pistol if no firearm safety device, other than a cable lock that the department has determined would damage the barrel of the pistol, has been approved for the pistol, and the pistol is either listed in subdivision (b) of Section 32105 or is subject to subdivision (c) of Section 32105.
(Added by Stats. 2010, Ch. 711, Sec. 6. (SB 1080) Effective January 1, 2011. Operative January 1, 2012, by Sec. 10 of Ch. 711.)
26859.
To comply with Section 26850, a safe handling demonstration for a single-action revolver shall include all of the following steps:
(a) Open the loading gate.
(b) Visually and physically inspect each chamber, to ensure that the revolver is unloaded.
(c) Remove the firearm safety device required to be sold with the handgun. If the firearm safety device prevents any of the previous steps, remove the firearm safety device during the appropriate step.
(d) Load one bright orange, red, or other readily identifiable dummy round into a chamber of the cylinder, close the loading gate and rotate the cylinder so that the round is in the next-to-fire position. If no readily identifiable dummy round is available, an empty cartridge casing with an empty primer pocket may be used.
(e) Open the loading gate and unload the revolver.
(f) Visually and physically inspect each chamber to ensure that the revolver is unloaded.
(g) Apply the firearm safety device, if applicable. This requirement shall not apply to an Olympic competition pistol if no firearm safety device, other than a cable lock that the department has determined would damage the barrel of the pistol, has been approved for the pistol, and the pistol is either listed in subdivision (b) of Section 32105 or is subject to subdivision (c) of Section 32105.
(Added by Stats. 2010, Ch. 711, Sec. 6. (SB 1080) Effective January 1, 2011. Operative January 1, 2012, by Sec. 10 of Ch. 711.)
26860.
(a) Except as authorized by the department, commencing January 1, 2015, a firearms dealer shall not deliver a long gun unless the recipient performs a safe handling demonstration with that long gun.
(b) The department shall, not later than January 1, 2015, adopt regulations establishing a long gun safe handling demonstration that shall include, at a minimum, loading and unloading the long gun.
(c) The firearms dealer shall sign and date an affidavit stating that the requirements of subdivision (a) and the regulations adopted pursuant to subdivision (b) have been met. The firearms dealer shall additionally obtain the signature of the long gun purchaser on the same affidavit. The firearms dealer shall retain the original affidavit as proof of compliance with this section.
(d) The recipient shall perform the safe handling demonstration for a department-certified instructor.
(e) A demonstration is not required if the dealer is returning the long gun to the owner of the long gun.
(f) Department-certified instructors who may administer the safe handling demonstration shall meet the requirements set forth in subdivision (b) of Section 31635.
(g) An individual who is exempt from the requirements of subdivision (a) of Section 31615, pursuant to Section 31700, is also exempt from performing the safe handling demonstration.
(Added by Stats. 2013, Ch. 761, Sec. 5. (SB 683) Effective January 1, 2014.)
26865.
A licensee shall offer to provide the purchaser or transferee of a firearm, or person being loaned a firearm, with a copy of the pamphlet described in Section 34205, and may add the cost of the pamphlet, if any, to the sales price of the firearm.

(Amended by Stats. 2011, Ch. 745, Sec. 12. (AB 809) Effective January 1, 2012.)
26870.
A licensee shall not commit an act of collusion as defined in Section 27550.
(Added by Stats. 2010, Ch. 711, Sec. 6. (SB 1080) Effective January 1, 2011. Operative January 1, 2012, by Sec. 10 of Ch. 711.)
26875.
A licensee shall post conspicuously within the licensed premises a detailed list of each of the following:
(a) All charges required by governmental agencies for processing firearm transfers required by Section 12806, Chapter 5 (commencing with Section 28050), and Article 3 (commencing with Section 28200) of Chapter 6.
(b) All fees that the licensee charges pursuant to Section 12806 and Chapter 5 (commencing with Section 28050).
(Added by Stats. 2010, Ch. 711, Sec. 6. (SB 1080) Effective January 1, 2011. Operative January 1, 2012, by Sec. 10 of Ch. 711.)
26880.
A licensee shall not misstate the amount of fees charged by a governmental agency pursuant to Section 12806, Chapter 5 (commencing with Section 28050), and Article 3 (commencing with Section 28200) of Chapter 6.
(Added by Stats. 2010, Ch. 711, Sec. 6. (SB 1080) Effective January 1, 2011. Operative January 1, 2012, by Sec. 10 of Ch. 711.)
26885.
(a) Except as provided in subdivisions (b) and (c) of Section 26805, all firearms that are in the inventory of a licensee shall be kept within the licensed location.
(b) Within 48 hours of discovery, a licensee shall report the loss or theft of any of the following items to the appropriate law enforcement agency in the city, county, or city and county where the licensee's business premises are located:
(1) Any firearm or ammunition that is merchandise of the licensee.
(2) Any firearm or ammunition that the licensee takes possession of pursuant to Chapter 5 (commencing with Section 28050), or pursuant to Section 30312.
(3) Any firearm or ammunition kept at the licensee's place of business.
(Amended November 8, 2016, by initiative Proposition 63, Sec. 7.1.)
26890.
(a) Except as provided in subdivisions (b) and (c) of Section 26805, any time when the licensee is not open for business, all inventory firearms shall be stored in the licensed location. All firearms shall be secured using one of the following methods as to each particular firearm:
(1) Store the firearm in a secure facility that is a part of, or that constitutes, the licensee's business premises.
(2) Secure the firearm with a hardened steel rod or cable of at least one-eighth inch in diameter through the trigger guard of the firearm. The steel rod or cable shall be secured with a hardened steel lock that has a shackle. The lock and shackle shall be protected or shielded from the use of a boltcutter and the rod or cable shall be anchored in a manner that prevents the removal of the firearm from the premises.
(3) Store the firearm in a locked fireproof safe or vault in the licensee's business premises.
(b) The licensing authority in an unincorporated area of a county or within a city may impose security requirements that are more strict or are at a higher standard than those specified in subdivision (a).
(c) Upon written request from a licensee, the licensing authority may grant an exemption from compliance with the requirements of subdivision (a) if the licensee is unable to comply with those requirements because of local ordinances, covenants, lease conditions, or similar circumstances not under the control of the licensee.
(d) Subdivisions (a) and (b) shall not apply to a licensee organized as a nonprofit public benefit corporation pursuant to Part 2 (commencing with Section 5110) of Division 2 of Title 1 of the Corporations Code, or as a mutual benefit corporation pursuant to Part 3 (commencing with Section 7110) of Division 2 of Title 1 of the Corporations Code, if both of the following conditions are satisfied:
(1) The nonprofit public benefit or mutual benefit corporation obtained the dealer's license solely and exclusively to assist that corporation or local chapters of that corporation in conducting auctions or similar events at which firearms are auctioned off to fund the activities of that corporation or the local chapters of the corporation.
(2) The firearms are not handguns.
(Amended by Stats. 2018, Ch. 185, Sec. 8. (AB 2176) Effective January 1, 2019.)
26895.
Commencing January 1, 1994, a licensee shall, upon the issuance or renewal of a license, submit a copy of it to the Department of Justice.
(Added by Stats. 2010, Ch. 711, Sec. 6. (SB 1080) Effective January 1, 2011. Operative January 1, 2012, by Sec. 10 of Ch. 711.)
26900.
(a) A licensee shall maintain and make available for inspection during business hours to any peace officer, authorized local law enforcement employee, or Department of Justice employee designated by the Attorney General, upon the presentation of proper identification, a firearm transaction record, as defined in Section 16550.
(b) A licensee shall be in compliance with the provisions of subdivision (a) if the licensee maintains and makes available for inspection during business hours to any peace officer, authorized local law enforcement employee, or Department of Justice employee designated by the Attorney General, upon the presentation of proper identification, the bound book containing the same information referred to in Section 478.124a and subdivision (e) of Section 478.125 of Title 27 of the Code of Federal Regulations and the records referred to in subdivision (a) of Section 478.124 of Title 27 of the Code of Federal Regulations.
(Added by Stats. 2010, Ch. 711, Sec. 6. (SB 1080) Effective January 1, 2011. Operative January 1, 2012, by Sec. 10 of Ch. 711.)
26905.
(a) On the date of receipt, a licensee shall report to the Department of Justice, in a format prescribed by the department, the acquisition by the licensee of the ownership of a handgun, and commencing January 1, 2014, of any firearm.
(b) The provisions of this section shall not apply to any of the following transactions:
(1) A transaction subject to the provisions of Sections 26960 and 27660.
(2) The dealer acquired the firearm from a wholesaler.
(3) The dealer acquired the firearm from a person who is licensed as a manufacturer or importer to engage in those activities pursuant to Chapter 44 (commencing with Section 921) of Title 18 of the United States Code and any regulations issued pursuant thereto.
(4) The dealer acquired the firearm from a person who resides outside this state who is licensed pursuant to Chapter 44 (commencing with Section 921) of Title 18 of the United States Code and any regulations issued pursuant thereto.
(5) The dealer is also licensed as a secondhand dealer pursuant to Article 4 (commencing with Section 21625) of Chapter 9 of Division 8 of the Business and Professions Code, acquires a handgun, and, commencing January 1, 2014, any firearm, and reports its acquisition pursuant to Section 21628.2 of the Business and Professions Code.
(Amended by Stats. 2011, Ch. 745, Sec. 14. (AB 809) Effective January 1, 2012.)
26910.
A licensee shall forward, in a format prescribed by the Department of Justice, information as required by the department on any firearm that is not delivered within the time period set forth in Section 478.102(c) of Title 27 of the Code of Federal Regulations.
(Added by Stats. 2010, Ch. 711, Sec. 6. (SB 1080) Effective January 1, 2011. Operative January 1, 2012, by Sec. 10 of Ch. 711.)

26915.
(a) Commencing January 1, 2018, a firearms dealer shall require any agent or employee who handles, sells, or delivers firearms to obtain and provide to the dealer a certificate of eligibility from the Department of Justice pursuant to Section 26710. On the application for the certificate, the agent or employee shall provide the name and California firearms dealer number of the firearms dealer with whom the person is employed.
(b) The department shall notify the firearms dealer in the event that the agent or employee who has a certificate of eligibility is or becomes prohibited from possessing firearms.
(c) If the local jurisdiction requires a background check of the agents or employees of a firearms dealer, the agent or employee shall obtain a certificate of eligibility pursuant to subdivision (a).
(d) (1) Nothing in this section shall be construed to preclude a local jurisdiction from conducting an additional background check pursuant to Section 11105. The local jurisdiction may not charge a fee for the additional criminal history check.
(2) Nothing in this section shall be construed to preclude a local jurisdiction from prohibiting employment based on criminal history that does not appear as part of obtaining a certificate of eligibility.
(e) The licensee shall prohibit any agent who the licensee knows or reasonably should know is within a class of persons prohibited from possessing firearms pursuant to Chapter 2 (commencing with Section 29800) or Chapter 3 (commencing with Section 29900) of Division 9 of this title, or Section 8100 or 8103 of the Welfare and Institutions Code, from coming into contact with any firearm that is not secured and from accessing any key, combination, code, or other means to open any of the locking devices described in subdivision (g).
(f) Nothing in this section shall be construed as preventing a local government from enacting an ordinance imposing additional conditions on licensees with regard to agents or employees.
(g) For purposes of this article, "secured" means a firearm that is made inoperable in one or more of the following ways:
(1) The firearm is inoperable because it is secured by a firearm safety device listed on the department's roster of approved firearm safety devices pursuant to subdivision (d) of Section 23655.
(2) The firearm is stored in a locked gun safe or long-gun safe that meets the standards for department-approved gun safes set forth in Section 23650.
(3) The firearm is stored in a distinct locked room or area in the building that is used to store firearms, which can only be unlocked by a key, a combination, or similar means.
(4) The firearm is secured with a hardened steel rod or cable that is at least one-eighth of an inch in diameter through the trigger guard of the firearm. The steel rod or cable shall be secured with a hardened steel lock that has a shackle. The lock and shackle shall be protected or shielded from the use of a boltcutter and the rod or cable shall be anchored in a manner that prevents the removal of the firearm from the premises.
(Amended November 8, 2016, by initiative Proposition 63, Sec. 7.2.)

ARTICLE 3. Exceptions Extending Only to Waiting Period [26950 - 26970]
(Article 3 added by Stats. 2010, Ch. 711, Sec. 6.)
26950.
(a) The waiting period described in Section 26815 does not apply to the sale, delivery, or transfer of firearms made to any person who satisfies both of the following requirements:
(1) The person is properly identified as a full-time paid peace officer, as defined in Chapter 4.5 (commencing with Section 830) of Title 3 of Part 2.
(2) The officer's employer has authorized the officer to carry firearms while in the performance of duties.
(b) (1) Proper identification is defined as verifiable written certification from the head of the agency by which the purchaser or transferee is employed, identifying the purchaser or transferee as a peace officer who is authorized to carry firearms while in the performance of duties, and authorizing the purchase or transfer.
(2) The certification shall be delivered to the dealer at the time of purchase or transfer and the purchaser or transferee shall identify himself or herself as the person authorized in the certification.
(3) The dealer shall keep the certification with the record of sale.
(4) On the date that the sale, delivery, or transfer is made, the dealer delivering the firearm shall transmit to the Department of Justice an electronic or telephonic report of the transaction as is indicated in Section 28160 or 28165.
(Added by Stats. 2010, Ch. 711, Sec. 6. (SB 1080) Effective January 1, 2011. Operative January 1, 2012, by Sec. 10 of Ch. 711.)
26955.
(a) The waiting period described in Section 26815 does not apply to a dealer who delivers a firearm, other than a handgun, at an auction or similar event described in Section 27900, as authorized by subdivision (c) of Section 26805.
(b) Within two business days of completion of the application to purchase, the dealer shall forward by prepaid mail to the Department of Justice a report of the application as is indicated in Section 28160 or 28165, as applicable.
(c) If the electronic or telephonic transfer of applicant information is used, within two business days of completion of the application to purchase, the dealer delivering the firearm shall transmit to the Department of Justice an electronic or telephonic report of the application as is indicated in Section 28160 or 28165, as applicable.
(Amended by Stats. 2011, Ch. 745, Sec. 15. (AB 809) Effective January 1, 2012.)
26960.
(a) The waiting period described in Section 26815 does not apply to the sale, delivery, or transfer of a handgun, and commencing January 1, 2014, a firearm that is not a handgun, by a dealer in either of the following situations:
(1) The dealer is delivering the firearm to another dealer, the firearm is not intended as merchandise in the receiving dealer's business, and the requirements of subdivisions (b) and (c) are satisfied.
(2) The dealer is delivering the firearm to himself or herself, the firearm is not intended as merchandise in the dealer's business, and the requirements of subdivision (c) are satisfied.
(b) If the dealer is receiving the firearm from another dealer, the dealer receiving the firearm shall present proof to the dealer delivering the firearm that the receiving dealer is licensed pursuant to Article 1 (commencing with Section 26700) and Article 2 (commencing with Section 26800). This shall be done by complying with Section 27555.
(c) (1) Regardless of whether the dealer is selling, delivering, or transferring the firearm to another dealer or to himself or herself, on the date that the application to purchase is completed, the dealer delivering the firearm shall forward by prepaid mail to the Department of Justice a report of the application and the type of information concerning the purchaser or transferee as is indicated in Section 28160.
(2) Where electronic or telephonic transfer of applicant information is used, on the date that the application to purchase is completed, the dealer delivering the firearm shall transmit an electronic or telephonic report of the application and the type of information concerning the purchaser or transferee as is indicated in Section 28160.
(Amended by Stats. 2011, Ch. 745, Sec. 16. (AB 809) Effective January 1, 2012.)
26965.
(a) The waiting period described in Section 26815 does not apply to the sale, delivery, or transfer of a firearm to the holder of a special weapons permit issued by the Department of Justice pursuant to Section 32650 or 33300, pursuant to Article 3 (commencing with Section 18900) of Chapter 1 of Division 5 of Title 2, or pursuant to Article 4 (commencing with Section 32700) of Chapter 6 of Division 10.

(b) On the date that the application to purchase is completed, the dealer delivering the firearm shall transmit to the Department of Justice an electronic or telephonic report of the application as is indicated in Section 28160 or 28165, as applicable.
(Amended by Stats. 2011, Ch. 745, Sec. 17. (AB 809) Effective January 1, 2012.)
26970.
(a) The waiting period described in Section 26815 does not apply to the sale, delivery, loan, or transfer of a firearm if all of the following conditions are satisfied:
(1) The firearm is a curio or relic, as defined in Section 478.11 of Title 27 of the Code of Federal Regulations, or its successor.
(2) The sale, delivery, loan, or transfer is made by a dealer.
(3) The sale, delivery, loan, or transfer is made to a person who is licensed as a collector pursuant to Chapter 44 (commencing with Section 921) of Title 18 of the United States Code and the regulations issued pursuant thereto.
(4) The licensed collector has a current certificate of eligibility issued by the Department of Justice pursuant to Section 26710.
(b) On the date that the sale, delivery, or transfer is made, the dealer delivering the firearm shall transmit to the Department of Justice an electronic or telephonic report of the transaction as is indicated in Section 28160 or 28165.
(Added by Stats. 2010, Ch. 711, Sec. 6. (SB 1080) Effective January 1, 2011. Operative January 1, 2012, by Sec. 10 of Ch. 711.)

ARTICLE 4. Exceptions Extending Only to Grounds for Forfeiture of License [27000 - 27005]
(Article 4 added by Stats. 2010, Ch. 711, Sec. 6.)
27000.
(a) Article 2 (commencing with Section 26800) does not apply to the loan of a firearm if all of the following conditions are satisfied:
(1) The firearm is unloaded.
(2) The loan is made by a dealer.
(3) The loan is made to a person who possesses a valid entertainment firearms permit issued pursuant to Chapter 2 (commencing with Section 29500) of Division 8.
(4) The firearm is loaned solely for use as a prop in a motion picture, television, video, theatrical, or other entertainment production or event.
(b) The dealer shall retain a photocopy of the entertainment firearms permit as proof of compliance with this requirement.
(Added by Stats. 2010, Ch. 711, Sec. 6. (SB 1080) Effective January 1, 2011. Operative January 1, 2012, by Sec. 10 of Ch. 711.)
27005.
(a) Article 2 (commencing with Section 26800) does not apply to the loan of an unloaded firearm to a consultant-evaluator by a person licensed pursuant to Sections 26700 to 26915, inclusive, if the loan does not exceed 45 days from the date of delivery.
(b) At the time of the loan, the consultant-evaluator shall provide the following information, which the dealer shall retain for two years:
(1) A photocopy of a valid, current, government-issued identification to determine the consultant-evaluator's identity, including, but not limited to, a California driver's license, identification card, or passport.
(2) A photocopy of the consultant-evaluator's valid, current certificate of eligibility.
(3) A letter from the person licensed as an importer, manufacturer, or dealer pursuant to Chapter 44 (commencing with Section 921) of Title 18 of the United States Code, with whom the consultant-evaluator has a bona fide business relationship. The letter shall detail the bona fide business purposes for which the firearm is being loaned and confirm that the consultant-evaluator is being loaned the firearm as part of a bona fide business relationship.
(4) The signature of the consultant-evaluator on a form indicating the date the firearm is loaned and the last day the firearm may be returned.
(Added by Stats. 2010, Ch. 711, Sec. 6. (SB 1080) Effective January 1, 2011. Operative January 1, 2012, by Sec. 10 of Ch. 711.)

ARTICLE 5. Exceptions Relating to Law Enforcement [27050 - 27065]
(Article 5 added by Stats. 2010, Ch. 711, Sec. 6.)
27050.
(a) Article 1 (commencing with Section 26700) and Article 2 (commencing with Section 26800) do not apply to any sale, delivery, or transfer of firearms made to an authorized law enforcement representative of any city, county, city and county, or state, or of the federal government, for exclusive use by that governmental agency if, prior to the sale, delivery, or transfer of these firearms, written authorization from the head of the agency authorizing the transaction is presented to the person from whom the purchase, delivery, or transfer is being made.
(b) Proper written authorization is defined as verifiable written certification from the head of the agency by which the purchaser or transferee is employed, identifying the employee as an individual authorized to conduct the transaction, and authorizing the transaction for the exclusive use of the agency by which that person is employed.
(c) Within 10 days of the date a handgun, and commencing January 1, 2014, any firearm, is acquired by the agency, a record of the same shall be entered as an institutional weapon into the Automated Firearms System (AFS) via the California Law Enforcement Telecommunications System (CLETS) by the law enforcement or state agency. Any agency without access to AFS shall arrange with the sheriff of the county in which the agency is located to input this information via this system.
(Amended by Stats. 2011, Ch. 745, Sec. 18. (AB 809) Effective January 1, 2012.)
27055.
Article 1 (commencing with Section 26700) and Article 2 (commencing with Section 26800) do not apply to the loan of a firearm if all of the following conditions are satisfied:
(a) The loan is made by an authorized law enforcement representative of a city, county, or city and county, or of the state or federal government.
(b) The loan is made to a peace officer employed by that agency and authorized to carry a firearm.
(c) The loan is made for the carrying and use of that firearm by that peace officer in the course and scope of the officer's duties.
(Added by Stats. 2010, Ch. 711, Sec. 6. (SB 1080) Effective January 1, 2011. Operative January 1, 2012, by Sec. 10 of Ch. 711.)
27060.
(a) Article 1 (commencing with Section 26700) and Article 2 (commencing with Section 26800) do not apply to the sale, delivery, or transfer of a firearm by a law enforcement agency to a peace officer pursuant to Section 10334 of the Public Contract Code.
(b) Within 10 days of the date that a handgun, and commencing January 1, 2014, any firearm, is sold, delivered, or transferred pursuant to Section 10334 of the Public Contract Code to that peace officer, the name of the officer and the make, model, serial number, and other identifying characteristics of the firearm being sold, delivered, or transferred shall be entered into the Automated Firearms System (AFS) via the California Law Enforcement Telecommunications System (CLETS) by the law enforcement or state agency that sold, delivered, or transferred the firearm, provided, however, that if the firearm is not a handgun and does not have a serial number, identification number, or identification mark assigned to it, that fact shall be noted in AFS. Any agency without access to AFS shall arrange with the sheriff of the county in which the agency is located to input this information via this system.
(Amended by Stats. 2011, Ch. 745, Sec. 19. (AB 809) Effective January 1, 2012.)
27065.

(a) Article 1 (commencing with Section 26700) and Article 2 (commencing with Section 26800) do not apply to the sale, delivery, or transfer of a firearm by a law enforcement agency to a retiring peace officer who is authorized to carry a firearm pursuant to Chapter 5 (commencing with Section 26300) of Division 5.
(b) Within 10 days of the date that a handgun, and commencing January 1, 2014, any firearm, is sold, delivered, or transferred to that retiring peace officer, the name of the officer and the make, model, serial number, and other identifying characteristics of the firearm being sold, delivered, or transferred shall be entered into the Automated Firearms System (AFS) via the California Law Enforcement Telecommunications System (CLETS) by the law enforcement or state agency that sold, delivered, or transferred the firearm, provided, however, that if the firearm is not a handgun and does not have a serial number, identification number, or identification mark assigned to it, that fact shall be noted in AFS. Any agency without access to AFS shall arrange with the sheriff of the county in which the agency is located to input this information via this system.
(Amended by Stats. 2011, Ch. 745, Sec. 20. (AB 809) Effective January 1, 2012.)

ARTICLE 6. Other Exceptions [27100 - 27140]
(Article 6 added by Stats. 2010, Ch. 711, Sec. 6.)
27100.
Article 1 (commencing with Section 26700) and Article 2 (commencing with Section 26800) do not apply to sales, deliveries, or transfers of firearms between or to importers and manufacturers of firearms licensed to engage in that business pursuant to Chapter 44 (commencing with Section 921) of Title 18 of the United States Code and the regulations issued pursuant thereto.
(Added by Stats. 2010, Ch. 711, Sec. 6. (SB 1080) Effective January 1, 2011. Operative January 1, 2012, by Sec. 10 of Ch. 711.)
27105.
Article 1 (commencing with Section 26700) and Article 2 (commencing with Section 26800) do not apply to the delivery of a firearm to a gunsmith for service or repair, or to the return of the firearm to its owner by the gunsmith, or to the delivery of a firearm by a gunsmith to a person licensed pursuant to Chapter 44 (commencing with Section 921) of Title 18 of the United States Code for service or repair and the return of the firearm to the gunsmith.
(Added by Stats. 2010, Ch. 711, Sec. 6. (SB 1080) Effective January 1, 2011. Operative January 1, 2012, by Sec. 10 of Ch. 711.)
27115.
Article 1 (commencing with Section 26700) and Article 2 (commencing with Section 26800) do not apply to the sale, delivery, or transfer of unloaded firearms by a dealer to a person who resides outside this state and is licensed pursuant to Chapter 44 (commencing with Section 921) of Title 18 of the United States Code and the regulations issued pursuant thereto.
(Added by Stats. 2010, Ch. 711, Sec. 6. (SB 1080) Effective January 1, 2011. Operative January 1, 2012, by Sec. 10 of Ch. 711.)
27120.
Article 1 (commencing with Section 26700) and Article 2 (commencing with Section 26800) do not apply to the sale, delivery, or transfer of unloaded firearms to a wholesaler if the firearms are being returned to the wholesaler and are intended as merchandise in the wholesaler's business.
(Added by Stats. 2010, Ch. 711, Sec. 6. (SB 1080) Effective January 1, 2011. Operative January 1, 2012, by Sec. 10 of Ch. 711.)
27125.
Article 1 (commencing with Section 26700) and Article 2 (commencing with Section 26800) do not apply to the sale, delivery, or transfer of firearms if all of the following conditions are satisfied:
(a) The firearms are unloaded.
(b) The sale, delivery, or transfer is made by one dealer to another dealer, upon proof of compliance with the requirements of Section 27555.
(c) The firearms are intended as merchandise in the receiving dealer's business.
(Added by Stats. 2010, Ch. 711, Sec. 6. (SB 1080) Effective January 1, 2011. Operative January 1, 2012, by Sec. 10 of Ch. 711.)
27130.
Until January 1, 2014, Article 1 (commencing with Section 26700) and Article 2 (commencing with Section 26800) do not apply to the sale, delivery, or transfer of an unloaded firearm, other than a handgun, by a dealer to himself or herself.
(Amended by Stats. 2011, Ch. 745, Sec. 22. (AB 809) Effective January 1, 2012.)
27135.
Article 1 (commencing with Section 26700) and Article 2 (commencing with Section 26800) do not apply to the loan of an unloaded firearm by a dealer who also operates a target facility that holds a business or regulatory license on the premises of the building designated in the license or whose building designated in the license is on the premises of any club or organization organized for the purposes of practicing shooting at targets upon established ranges, whether public or private, to a person at that target facility or that club or organization, if the firearm is at all times kept within the premises of the target range or on the premises of the club or organization.
(Added by Stats. 2010, Ch. 711, Sec. 6. (SB 1080) Effective January 1, 2011. Operative January 1, 2012, by Sec. 10 of Ch. 711.)
27140.
Article 1 (commencing with Section 26700) and Article 2 (commencing with Section 26800) do not apply to the sale, delivery, or transfer of a firearm regulated pursuant to any of the following statutes, if the sale, delivery, or transfer of that firearm is conducted in accordance with the applicable provisions of the statute:
(a) Chapter 1 (commencing with Section 18710) of Division 5 of Title 2, relating to destructive devices and explosives.
(b) Section 24410, relating to cane guns, and the exemptions in Chapter 1 (commencing with Section 17700) of Title 2, as they relate to cane guns.
(c) Section 24510, relating to firearms that are not immediately recognizable as firearms, and the exemptions in Chapter 1 (commencing with Section 17700) of Title 2, as they relate to firearms that are not immediately recognizable as firearms.
(d) Sections 24610 and 24680, relating to undetectable firearms, and the exemptions in Chapter 1 (commencing with Section 17700) of Title 2, as they relate to undetectable firearms.
(e) Section 24710, relating to wallet guns, and the exemptions in Chapter 1 (commencing with Section 17700) of Title 2, as they relate to wallet guns.
(f) Chapter 2 (commencing with Section 30500) of Division 10, relating to assault weapons.
(g) Section 31500, relating to unconventional pistols, and the exemptions in Chapter 1 (commencing with Section 17700) of Title 2, as they relate to unconventional pistols.
(h) Sections 33215 to 33225, inclusive, relating to short-barreled rifles and short-barreled shotguns, and the exemptions in Chapter 1 (commencing with Section 17700) of Title 2, as they relate to short-barreled rifles and short-barreled shotguns.
(i) Chapter 6 (commencing with Section 32610) of Division 10, relating to machineguns.
(j) Section 33600, relating to zip guns, and the exemptions in Chapter 1 (commencing with Section 17700) of Title 2, as they relate to zip guns.
(Added by Stats. 2010, Ch. 711, Sec. 6. (SB 1080) Effective January 1, 2011. Operative January 1, 2012, by Sec. 10 of Ch. 711.)

CHAPTER 3. Gun Show or Event [27200 - 27415]

(Chapter 3 added by Stats. 2010, Ch. 711, Sec. 6.)

ARTICLE 1. Gun Show or Event [27200 - 27245]

(Article 1 added by Stats. 2010, Ch. 711, Sec. 6.)

27200.

(a) No person shall produce, promote, sponsor, operate, or otherwise organize a gun show or event, as specified in subdivision (b) of Section 26805, unless that person possesses a valid certificate of eligibility from the Department of Justice.

(b) Unless the department's records indicate that the applicant is a person prohibited from possessing firearms, a certificate of eligibility shall be issued by the Department of Justice to an applicant provided the applicant does all of the following:

(1) Certifies that the applicant is familiar with the provisions of this article and Article 2 (commencing with Section 27300).

(2) Ensures that liability insurance is in effect for the duration of an event or show in an amount of not less than one million dollars ($1,000,000).

(3) Provides an annual list of the gun shows or events that the applicant plans to promote, produce, sponsor, operate, or otherwise organize during the year for which the certificate of eligibility is issued, including the date, time, and location of the gun shows or events.

(c) If during that year the information required by paragraph (3) of subdivision (b) changes, or additional gun shows or events will be promoted, produced, sponsored, operated, or otherwise organized by the applicant, the producer shall notify the Department of Justice no later than 30 days prior to the gun show or event.

(d) The Department of Justice shall adopt regulations to administer the certificate of eligibility program under this section.

(e) The Department of Justice shall recover the full costs of administering the certificate of eligibility program by fees assessed applicants who apply for certificates. A licensed gun show producer shall be assessed an annual fee of eighty-five dollars ($85) by the department.

(f) It is the intent of the Legislature that the certificate of eligibility program established pursuant to this section be incorporated into the certificate of eligibility program established pursuant to Section 26710 to the maximum extent practicable.

(Added by Stats. 2010, Ch. 711, Sec. 6. (SB 1080) Effective January 1, 2011. Operative January 1, 2012, by Sec. 10 of Ch. 711.)

27205.

(a) Before commencement of a gun show or event, the producer thereof shall, upon written request from a law enforcement agency with jurisdiction over the facility, make available to that agency, within 48 hours or a later time specified by the agency, a complete and accurate list of all persons, entities, and organizations that have leased or rented, or are known to the producer to intend to lease or rent, any table, display space, or area at the gun show or event for the purpose of selling, leasing, or transferring firearms.

(b) The producer shall thereafter, upon written request, for every day the gun show or event operates, within 24 hours or a later time specified by the requesting law enforcement agency, make available to that agency an accurate, complete, and current list of the persons, entities, and organizations that have leased or rented, or are known to the producer to intend to lease or rent, any table, display space, or area at the gun show or event for the purpose of selling, leasing, or transferring firearms.

(c) Subdivisions (a) and (b) apply to any person, entity, or organization, regardless of whether that person, entity, or organization participates in the entire gun show or event, or only a portion thereof.

(d) The information that may be requested by the law enforcement agency with jurisdiction over the facility, and that shall be provided by the producer upon request, may include, but is not limited to, the following information relative to a vendor who offers for sale firearms manufactured after December 31, 1898:

(1) The vendor's complete name.

(2) A driver's license or identification card number.

(Added by Stats. 2010, Ch. 711, Sec. 6. (SB 1080) Effective January 1, 2011. Operative January 1, 2012, by Sec. 10 of Ch. 711.)

27210.

(a) The producer and facility's manager of a gun show or event shall prepare an annual event and security plan and schedule that shall include, at a minimum, the following information for each show or event:

(1) The type of show or event, including, but not limited to, antique or general firearms.

(2) The estimated number of vendors offering firearms for sale or display.

(3) The estimated number of attendees.

(4) The number of entrances and exits at the gun show or event site.

(5) The location, dates, and times of the show or event.

(6) The contact person and telephone number for both the producer and the facility.

(7) The number of sworn peace officers employed by the producer or the facility's manager who will be present at the show or event.

(8) The number of nonsworn security personnel employed by the producer or the facility's manager who will be present at the show or event.

(b) The annual event and security plan shall be submitted by either the producer or the facility's manager to the Department of Justice and the law enforcement agency with jurisdiction over the facility.

(c) If significant changes have been made since the annual plan was submitted, the producer shall, not later than 15 days before commencement of the gun show or event, submit to the department, the law enforcement agency with jurisdiction over the facility site, and the facility's manager, a revised event and security plan, including a revised list of vendors that the producer knows, or reasonably should know, will be renting tables, space, or otherwise participating in the gun show or event.

(d) The event and security plan shall be approved by the facility's manager before the event or show, after consultation with the law enforcement agency with jurisdiction over the facility.

(e) A gun show or event shall not commence unless the requirements of subdivisions (b), (c), and (d) are met.

(Amended by Stats. 2015, Ch. 303, Sec. 415. (AB 731) Effective January 1, 2016.)

27215.

The producer of a gun show or event shall be responsible for informing prospective gun show vendors of the requirements of this article and of Article 2 (commencing with Section 27300) that apply to vendors.

(Added by Stats. 2010, Ch. 711, Sec. 6. (SB 1080) Effective January 1, 2011. Operative January 1, 2012, by Sec. 10 of Ch. 711.)

27220.

(a) Within seven calendar days of the commencement of a gun show or event, but not later than noon on Friday for a show or event held on a weekend, the producer shall submit a list of all prospective vendors and designated firearms transfer agents who are licensed firearms dealers to the Department of Justice for the purpose of determining whether these prospective vendors and designated firearms transfer agents possess valid licenses and are thus eligible to participate as licensed dealers at the show or event.

(b) The department shall examine its records and if it determines that a dealer's license is not valid, it shall notify the show or event producer of that fact before the show or event commences.

(Added by Stats. 2010, Ch. 711, Sec. 6. (SB 1080) Effective January 1, 2011. Operative January 1, 2012, by Sec. 10 of Ch. 711.)

27225.

If a licensed firearms dealer fails to cooperate with a producer of a gun show or event, or fails to comply with the applicable requirements of this article or Article 2 (commencing with Section 27300), that person shall not be allowed to participate in that show or event.

(Added by Stats. 2010, Ch. 711, Sec. 6. (SB 1080) Effective January 1, 2011. Operative January 1, 2012, by Sec. 10 of Ch. 711.)

27230.

If a producer fails to comply with Section 27215 or 27220, the gun show or event shall not commence until those requirements are met.

(Added by Stats. 2010, Ch. 711, Sec. 6. (SB 1080) Effective January 1, 2011. Operative January 1, 2012, by Sec. 10 of Ch. 711.)

27235.

Every producer of a gun show or event shall have a written contract with each gun show vendor selling firearms at the show or event.

(Added by Stats. 2010, Ch. 711, Sec. 6. (SB 1080) Effective January 1, 2011. Operative January 1, 2012, by Sec. 10 of Ch. 711.)

27240.

(a) The producer of a gun show or event shall require that signs be posted in a readily visible location at each public entrance to the show containing, but not limited to, the following notices:

(1) This gun show follows all federal, state, and local firearms and weapons laws, without exception.

(2) Any firearm carried onto the premises by any member of the public will be checked, cleared of any ammunition, and secured in a manner that prevents it from being operated, and an identification tag or sticker will be attached to the firearm before the person is allowed admittance to the show.

(3) No member of the public under the age of 18 years shall be admitted to the show unless accompanied by a parent, grandparent, or legal guardian.

(4) All firearms transfers between private parties at the show shall be conducted through a licensed dealer in accordance with applicable state and federal laws.

(5) Persons possessing firearms at this facility must have in their immediate possession government-issued photo identification, and display it upon request to any security officer or any peace officer, as defined in Section 830.

(b) The show producer shall post, in a readily visible location at each entrance to the parking lot at the show, signage that states: "The transfer of firearms on the parking lot of this facility is a crime."

(Added by Stats. 2010, Ch. 711, Sec. 6. (SB 1080) Effective January 1, 2011. Operative January 1, 2012, by Sec. 10 of Ch. 711.)

27245.

(a) A willful failure by a gun show producer to comply with any of the requirements of this article, except for the posting of required signs, shall be a misdemeanor punishable by a fine not to exceed two thousand dollars ($2,000), and shall render the producer ineligible for a gun show producer license for one year from the date of the conviction.

(b) A willful failure of a gun show producer to post signs as required by this article shall be a misdemeanor punishable by a fine not to exceed one thousand dollars ($1,000) for the first offense and not to exceed two thousand dollars ($2,000) for the second or subsequent offense, and with respect to the second or subsequent offense, shall render the producer ineligible for a gun show producer license for one year from the date of the conviction.

(c) Multiple violations charged pursuant to subdivision (a) arising from more than one gun show or event shall be grounds for suspension of a producer's certificate of eligibility pending adjudication of the violations.

(Added by Stats. 2010, Ch. 711, Sec. 6. (SB 1080) Effective January 1, 2011. Operative January 1, 2012, by Sec. 10 of Ch. 711.)

ARTICLE 2. Gun Show Enforcement and Security Act of 2000 [27300 - 27350]

(Article 2 added by Stats. 2010, Ch. 711, Sec. 6.)

27300.

This article shall be known, and may be cited as, the Gun Show Enforcement and Security Act of 2000.

(Added by Stats. 2010, Ch. 711, Sec. 6. (SB 1080) Effective January 1, 2011. Operative January 1, 2012, by Sec. 10 of Ch. 711.)

27305.

All gun show or event vendors shall certify in writing to the producer that they:

(a) Will not display, possess, or offer for sale any firearms, knives, or weapons for which possession or sale is prohibited.

(b) Acknowledge that they are responsible for knowing and complying with all applicable federal, state, and local laws dealing with the possession and transfer of firearms.

(c) Will not engage in activities that incite or encourage hate crimes.

(d) Will process all transfers of firearms through licensed firearms dealers as required by state law.

(e) Will verify that all firearms in their possession at the show or event will be unloaded, and that the firearms will be secured in a manner that prevents them from being operated except for brief periods when the mechanical condition of a firearm is being demonstrated to a prospective buyer.

(f) Have complied with the requirements of Section 27320.

(g) Will not display or possess black powder, or offer it for sale.

(Added by Stats. 2010, Ch. 711, Sec. 6. (SB 1080) Effective January 1, 2011. Operative January 1, 2012, by Sec. 10 of Ch. 711.)

27310.

All firearms transfers at a gun show or event shall be in accordance with applicable state and federal laws.

(Added by Stats. 2010, Ch. 711, Sec. 6. (SB 1080) Effective January 1, 2011. Operative January 1, 2012, by Sec. 10 of Ch. 711.)

27315.

Except for purposes of showing ammunition to a prospective buyer, ammunition at a gun show or event may be displayed only in closed original factory boxes or other closed containers.

(Added by Stats. 2010, Ch. 711, Sec. 6. (SB 1080) Effective January 1, 2011. Operative January 1, 2012, by Sec. 10 of Ch. 711.)

27320.

(a) Before commencement of a gun show or event, each vendor who will offer for sale firearms manufactured after December 31, 1898, shall provide to the producer all of the following information relative to the vendor, the vendor's employees, and other persons, compensated or not, who will be working or otherwise providing services to the public at the vendor's display space:

(1) The person's complete name.

(2) The person's driver's license or state-issued identification card number.

(3) The person's date of birth.

(b) The producer shall keep the information at the onsite headquarters of the show or event for the duration of the show or event, and at the producer's regular place of business for two weeks after the conclusion of the show or event. The producer shall make the information available upon request to any sworn peace officer for purposes of the officer's official law enforcement duties.

(Added by Stats. 2010, Ch. 711, Sec. 6. (SB 1080) Effective January 1, 2011. Operative January 1, 2012, by Sec. 10 of Ch. 711.)

27325.

At any gun show or event, each vendor and each employee of a vendor shall wear a name tag indicating first and last name.

(Added by Stats. 2010, Ch. 711, Sec. 6. (SB 1080) Effective January 1, 2011. Operative January 1, 2012, by Sec. 10 of Ch. 711.)

27330.

No person at a gun show or event, other than security personnel or sworn peace officers, shall possess at the same time both a firearm and ammunition that is designed to be fired in the firearm. Vendors having those items at the show for sale or exhibition are exempt from this prohibition.

(Added by Stats. 2010, Ch. 711, Sec. 6. (SB 1080) Effective January 1, 2011. Operative January 1, 2012, by Sec. 10 of Ch. 711.)

27335.

No member of the public who is under the age of 18 years shall be admitted to, or be permitted to remain at, a gun show or event unless accompanied by a parent or legal guardian. Any member of the public who is under the age of 18 years shall be accompanied by that person's parent, grandparent, or legal guardian while at the show or event.

(Added by Stats. 2010, Ch. 711, Sec. 6. (SB 1080) Effective January 1, 2011. Operative January 1, 2012, by Sec. 10 of Ch. 711.)

27340.

(a) Persons other than show or event security personnel, sworn peace officers, or vendors, who bring firearms onto the gun show or event premises shall sign in ink the tag or sticker that is attached to the firearm prior to being allowed admittance to the show or event, as provided for in subdivision (b).

(b) All firearms carried onto the premises of a gun show or event by members of the public shall be checked, cleared of any ammunition, secured in a manner that prevents them from being operated, and an identification tag or sticker shall be attached to the firearm, prior to the person being allowed admittance to the show. The identification tag or sticker shall state that all firearms transfers between private parties at the show or event shall be conducted through a licensed dealer in accordance with applicable state and federal laws. The person possessing the firearm shall complete the following information on the tag before it is attached to the firearm:

(1) The gun owner's signature.

(2) The gun owner's printed name.

(3) The identification number from the gun owner's government-issued photo identification.

(Added by Stats. 2010, Ch. 711, Sec. 6. (SB 1080) Effective January 1, 2011. Operative January 1, 2012, by Sec. 10 of Ch. 711.)

27345.

Any person who possesses a firearm at a gun show or event shall have government-issued photo identification in immediate possession, and shall display it upon request to any security officer or peace officer.

(Added by Stats. 2010, Ch. 711, Sec. 6. (SB 1080) Effective January 1, 2011. Operative January 1, 2012, by Sec. 10 of Ch. 711.)

27350.

(a) Unless otherwise specified, a first violation of this article is an infraction.

(b) Any second or subsequent violation of this article is a misdemeanor.

(c) Any person who commits an act the person knows to be a violation of this article is guilty of a misdemeanor for a first offense.

(Added by Stats. 2010, Ch. 711, Sec. 6. (SB 1080) Effective January 1, 2011. Operative January 1, 2012, by Sec. 10 of Ch. 711.)

ARTICLE 3. Exceptions Relating to Law Enforcement [27400 - 27415]

(Article 3 added by Stats. 2010, Ch. 711, Sec. 6.)

27400.

(a) Article 1 (commencing with Section 27200) and Article 2 (commencing with Section 27300) do not apply to any sale, delivery, or transfer of firearms made to an authorized law enforcement representative of any city, county, city and county, or state, or of the federal government, for exclusive use by that governmental agency if, prior to the sale, delivery, or transfer of these firearms, written authorization from the head of the agency authorizing the transaction is presented to the person from whom the purchase, delivery, or transfer is being made.

(b) Proper written authorization is defined as verifiable written certification from the head of the agency by which the purchaser or transferee is employed, identifying the employee as an individual authorized to conduct the transaction, and authorizing the transaction for the exclusive use of the agency by which that person is employed.

(c) Within 10 days of the date a handgun, and commencing January 1, 2014, any firearm, is acquired by the agency, a record of the same shall be entered as an institutional weapon into the Automated Firearms System (AFS) via the California Law Enforcement Telecommunications System (CLETS) by the law enforcement or state agency. Any agency without access to AFS shall arrange with the sheriff of the county in which the agency is located to input this information via this system.

(Amended by Stats. 2011, Ch. 745, Sec. 23. (AB 809) Effective January 1, 2012.)

27405.

Article 1 (commencing with Section 27200) and Article 2 (commencing with Section 27300) do not apply to the loan of a firearm if all of the following conditions are satisfied:

(a) The loan is made by an authorized law enforcement representative of a city, county, or city and county, or of the state or federal government.

(b) The loan is made to a peace officer employed by that agency and authorized to carry a firearm.

(c) The loan is made for the carrying and use of that firearm by that peace officer in the course and scope of the officer's duties.

(Added by Stats. 2010, Ch. 711, Sec. 6. (SB 1080) Effective January 1, 2011. Operative January 1, 2012, by Sec. 10 of Ch. 711.)

27410.

(a) Article 1 (commencing with Section 27200) and Article 2 (commencing with Section 27300) do not apply to the sale, delivery, or transfer of a firearm by a law enforcement agency to a peace officer pursuant to Section 10334 of the Public Contract Code.

(b) Within 10 days of the date that a handgun, and commencing January 1, 2014, any firearm, is sold, delivered, or transferred pursuant to Section 10334 of the Public Contract Code to that peace officer, the name of the officer and the make, model, serial number, and other identifying characteristics of the firearm being sold, delivered, or transferred shall be entered into the Automated Firearms System (AFS) via the California Law Enforcement Telecommunications System (CLETS) by the law enforcement or state agency that sold, delivered, or transferred the firearm, provided, however, that if the firearm is not a handgun and does not have a serial number, identification number, or identification mark assigned to it, that fact shall be noted in AFS. Any agency without access to AFS shall arrange with the sheriff of the county in which the agency is located to input this information via this system.

(Amended by Stats. 2011, Ch. 745, Sec. 24. (AB 809) Effective January 1, 2012.)

27415.

(a) Article 1 (commencing with Section 27200) and Article 2 (commencing with Section 27300) do not apply to the sale, delivery, or transfer of a firearm by a law enforcement agency to a retiring peace officer who is authorized to carry a firearm pursuant to Chapter 5 (commencing with Section 26300) of Division 5.

(b) Within 10 days of the date that a handgun, and commencing January 1, 2014, any firearm, is sold, delivered, or transferred to that retiring peace officer, the name of the officer and the make, model, serial number, and other identifying characteristics of the firearm being sold, delivered, or transferred shall be entered into the Automated Firearms System (AFS) via the California Law Enforcement Telecommunications System (CLETS) by the law enforcement or state agency that sold, delivered, or transferred the firearm, provided, however, that if the firearm is not a handgun and does not have a serial number, identification number, or identification mark assigned to it, that fact shall

be noted in AFS. Any agency without access to AFS shall arrange with the sheriff of the county in which the agency is located to input this information via this system.

(Amended by Stats. 2011, Ch. 745, Sec. 25. (AB 809) Effective January 1, 2012.)

CHAPTER 4. Crimes Relating to Sale, Lease, or Transfer of Firearms [27500 - 28000]

(Chapter 4 added by Stats. 2010, Ch. 711, Sec. 6.)

ARTICLE 1. Crimes Relating to Sale, Lease, or Transfer of Firearms [27500 - 27590]

(Article 1 added by Stats. 2010, Ch. 711, Sec. 6.)

27500.

(a) No person, corporation, or firm shall knowingly sell, supply, deliver, or give possession or control of a firearm to any person within any of the classes prohibited by Chapter 2 (commencing with Section 29800) or Chapter 3 (commencing with Section 29900) of Division 9.

(b) No person, corporation, or dealer shall sell, supply, deliver, or give possession or control of a firearm to anyone whom the person, corporation, or dealer has cause to believe is within any of the classes prohibited by Chapter 2 (commencing with Section 29800) or Chapter 3 (commencing with Section 29900) of Division 9 of this title, or Section 8100 or 8103 of the Welfare and Institutions Code.

(Added by Stats. 2010, Ch. 711, Sec. 6. (SB 1080) Effective January 1, 2011. Operative January 1, 2012, by Sec. 10 of Ch. 711.)

27505.

(a) No person, corporation, or firm shall sell, loan, or transfer a firearm to a minor, nor sell a handgun to an individual under 21 years of age.

(b) Subdivision (a) shall not apply to or affect the following circumstances:

(1) The sale of a handgun, if the handgun is an antique firearm and the sale is to a person at least 18 years of age.

(2) The transfer or loan of a firearm, other than a handgun, to a minor by the minor's parent or legal guardian.

(3) The transfer or loan of a firearm, other than a handgun, to a minor by a grandparent who is not the legal guardian of the minor, if the transfer is done with the express permission of the minor's parent or legal guardian.

(4) The loan of a firearm, other than a handgun, to a minor, with the express permission of the minor's parent or legal guardian, if the loan does not exceed 30 days in duration and is for a lawful purpose.

(5) The loan of a handgun to a minor by the minor's parent or legal guardian, if both of the following requirements are satisfied:

(A) The minor is being loaned the firearm for the purposes of engaging in a lawful, recreational sport, including, but not limited to, competitive shooting, or agricultural, ranching, or hunting activity, or a motion picture, television, or video production, or entertainment or theatrical event, the nature of which involves the use of a firearm.

(B) The duration of the loan does not exceed the amount of time that is reasonably necessary to engage in the lawful, recreational sport, including, but not limited to, competitive shooting, or agricultural, ranching, or hunting activity, or a motion picture, television, or video production, or entertainment or theatrical event, the nature of which involves the use of a firearm.

(6) The loan of a handgun to a minor by a person who is not the minor's parent or legal guardian, if all of the following requirements are satisfied:

(A) The minor is accompanied by the minor's parent or legal guardian when the loan is made, or the minor has the written consent of the minor's parent or legal guardian, which is presented at the time of the loan, or earlier.

(B) The minor is being loaned the firearm for the purpose of engaging in a lawful, recreational sport, including, but not limited to, competitive shooting, or agricultural, ranching, or hunting activity, or a motion picture, television, or video production, or entertainment or theatrical event, the nature of which involves the use of a firearm.

(C) The duration of the loan does not exceed the amount of time that is reasonably necessary to engage in the lawful, recreational sport, including, but not limited to, competitive shooting, or agricultural, ranching, or hunting activity, or a motion picture, television, or video production, or entertainment or theatrical event, the nature of which involves the use of a firearm.

(D) The duration of the loan does not, in any event, exceed 10 days.

(Added by Stats. 2010, Ch. 711, Sec. 6. (SB 1080) Effective January 1, 2011. Operative January 1, 2012, by Sec. 10 of Ch. 711.)

27510.

(a) A person licensed under Sections 26700 to 26915, inclusive, shall not sell, supply, deliver, or give possession or control of a firearm to any person under 21 years of age.

(b) (1) Subdivision (a) does not apply to or affect the sale, supplying, delivery, or giving possession or control of a firearm that is not a handgun to a person 18 years of age or older who possesses a valid, unexpired hunting license issued by the Department of Fish and Wildlife.

(2) Subdivision (a) does not apply to or affect the sale, supplying, delivery, or giving possession or control of a firearm that is not a handgun to any of the following persons who are 18 years of age or older:

(A) An active peace officer, as described in Chapter 4.5 (commencing with Section 830) of Title 3 of Part 2, who is authorized to carry a firearm in the course and scope of his or her employment.

(B) An active federal officer or law enforcement agent who is authorized to carry a firearm in the course and scope of his or her employment.

(C) A reserve peace officer, as defined in Section 832.6, who is authorized to carry a firearm in the course and scope of his or her employment as a reserve peace officer.

(D) A person who provides proper identification of his or her active membership in the United States Armed Forces, the National Guard, the Air National Guard, or active reserve components of the United States. For purposes of this subparagraph, proper identification includes an Armed Forces Identification Card or other written documentation certifying that the individual is an active member.

(E) A person who provides proper identification that he or she is an honorably discharged member of the United States Armed Forces, the National Guard, the Air National Guard, or the active reserve components of the United States. For purposes of this subparagraph, proper identification includes an Armed Forces Identification Card or other written documentation certifying that the individual is an honorably discharged member.

(Amended by Stats. 2018, Ch. 894, Sec. 1. (SB 1100) Effective January 1, 2019.)

27515.

No person, corporation, or dealer shall sell, loan, or transfer a firearm to anyone whom the person, corporation, or dealer knows or has cause to believe is not the actual purchaser or transferee of the firearm, or to anyone who is not the one actually being loaned the firearm, if the person, corporation, or dealer has either of the following:

(a) Knowledge that the firearm is to be subsequently sold, loaned, or transferred to avoid the provisions of Section 27540 or 27545.

(b) Knowledge that the firearm is to be subsequently sold, loaned, or transferred to avoid the requirements of any exemption to the provisions of Section 27540 or 27545.

(Added by Stats. 2010, Ch. 711, Sec. 6. (SB 1080) Effective January 1, 2011. Operative January 1, 2012, by Sec. 10 of Ch. 711.)

27520.
No person, corporation, or dealer shall acquire a firearm for the purpose of selling, loaning, or transferring the firearm, if the person, corporation, or dealer has either of the following:
(a) In the case of a dealer, intent to violate Section 27510 or 27540.
(b) In any other case, intent to avoid either of the following:
(1) The provisions of Section 27545.
(2) The requirements of any exemption to the provisions of Section 27545.
(Added by Stats. 2010, Ch. 711, Sec. 6. (SB 1080) Effective January 1, 2011. Operative January 1, 2012, by Sec. 10 of Ch. 711.)
27525.
(a) A dealer shall comply with Section 26905.
(b) A dealer shall comply with Section 26910.
(Added by Stats. 2010, Ch. 711, Sec. 6. (SB 1080) Effective January 1, 2011. Operative January 1, 2012, by Sec. 10 of Ch. 711.)
27530.
No person shall sell or otherwise transfer ownership in a handgun unless the firearm bears either:
(a) The name of the manufacturer, the manufacturer's make or model, and a manufacturer's serial number assigned to that firearm.
(b) The identification number or mark assigned to the firearm by the Department of Justice pursuant to Section 23910.
(Added by Stats. 2010, Ch. 711, Sec. 6. (SB 1080) Effective January 1, 2011. Operative January 1, 2012, by Sec. 10 of Ch. 711.)
27535.
(a) No person shall make an application to purchase more than one handgun within any 30-day period.
(b) Subdivision (a) shall not apply to any of the following:
(1) Any law enforcement agency.
(2) Any agency duly authorized to perform law enforcement duties.
(3) Any state or local correctional facility.
(4) Any private security company licensed to do business in California.
(5) Any person who is properly identified as a full-time paid peace officer, as defined in Chapter 4.5 (commencing with Section 830) of Title 3 of Part 2, and who is authorized to, and does carry a firearm during the course and scope of employment as a peace officer.
(6) Any motion picture, television, or video production company or entertainment or theatrical company whose production by its nature involves the use of a firearm.
(7) Any person who may, pursuant to Article 2 (commencing with Section 27600), Article 3 (commencing with Section 27650), or Article 4 (commencing with Section 27700), claim an exemption from the waiting period set forth in Section 27540.
(8) Any transaction conducted through a licensed firearms dealer pursuant to Chapter 5 (commencing with Section 28050).
(9) Any person who is licensed as a collector pursuant to Chapter 44 (commencing with Section 921) of Title 18 of the United States Code and the regulations issued pursuant thereto, and has a current certificate of eligibility issued by the Department of Justice pursuant to Article 1 (commencing with Section 26700) of Chapter 2.
(10) The exchange of a handgun where the dealer purchased that firearm from the person seeking the exchange within the 30-day period immediately preceding the date of exchange or replacement.
(11) The replacement of a handgun when the person's handgun was lost or stolen, and the person reported that firearm lost or stolen pursuant to Section 25250 prior to the completion of the application to purchase the replacement handgun.
(12) The return of any handgun to its owner.
(13) A community college that is certified by the Commission on Peace Officer Standards and Training to present the law enforcement academy basic course or other commission-certified law enforcement training.
(Amended by Stats. 2018, Ch. 423, Sec. 122. (SB 1494) Effective January 1, 2019.)
27540.
A dealer, whether or not acting pursuant to Chapter 5 (commencing with Section 28050), shall not deliver a firearm to a person, as follows:
(a) Within 10 days of the application to purchase, or, after notice by the department pursuant to Section 28220, within 10 days of the submission to the department of any correction to the application, or within 10 days of the submission to the department of any fee required pursuant to Section 28225, whichever is later.
(b) Unless unloaded and securely wrapped or unloaded and in a locked container.
(c) Unless the purchaser, transferee, or person being loaned the firearm presents clear evidence of the person's identity and age to the dealer.
(d) Whenever the dealer is notified by the Department of Justice that the person is prohibited by state or federal law from possessing, receiving, owning, or purchasing a firearm.
(e) A handgun shall not be delivered unless the purchaser, transferee, or person being loaned the handgun presents a handgun safety certificate. Commencing January 1, 2015, any firearm, including a handgun, shall not be delivered unless the purchaser, transferee, or person being loaned the firearm presents a firearm safety certificate to the dealer, except that in the case of a handgun, an unexpired handgun safety certificate may be presented.
(f) A handgun shall not be delivered whenever the dealer is notified by the Department of Justice that within the preceding 30-day period the purchaser has made another application to purchase a handgun and that the previous application to purchase involved none of the entities specified in subdivision (b) of Section 27535.
(Amended by Stats. 2013, Ch. 761, Sec. 6. (SB 683) Effective January 1, 2014.)
27545.
Where neither party to the transaction holds a dealer's license issued pursuant to Sections 26700 to 26915, inclusive, the parties to the transaction shall complete the sale, loan, or transfer of that firearm through a licensed firearms dealer pursuant to Chapter 5 (commencing with Section 28050).
(Added by Stats. 2010, Ch. 711, Sec. 6. (SB 1080) Effective January 1, 2011. Operative January 1, 2012, by Sec. 10 of Ch. 711.)
27550.
(a) No person may commit an act of collusion relating to Sections 31610 to 31700, inclusive.
(b) For purposes of this section and Section 26870, collusion may be proven by any one of the following factors:
(1) Answering a test applicant's questions during an objective test relating to firearms safety.
(2) Knowingly grading the examination falsely.
(3) Providing an advance copy of the test to an applicant.
(4) Taking or allowing another person to take the basic firearms safety course for one who is the applicant for a basic firearms safety certificate or a handgun safety certificate.
(5) Allowing another to take the objective test for the applicant, purchaser, or transferee.
(6) Using or allowing another to use one's identification, proof of residency, or thumbprint.
(7) Allowing others to give unauthorized assistance during the examination.
(8) Reference to unauthorized materials during the examination and cheating by the applicant.
(9) Providing originals or photocopies of the objective test, or any version thereof, to any person other than as authorized by the department.

(Added by Stats. 2010, Ch. 711, Sec. 6. (SB 1080) Effective January 1, 2011. Operative January 1, 2012, by Sec. 10 of Ch. 711.)
27555.
(a) (1) Commencing July 1, 2008, a person who is licensed pursuant to Chapter 44 (commencing with Section 921) of Title 18 of the United States Code may not sell, deliver, or transfer a firearm to a person in California who is licensed pursuant to Chapter 44 (commencing with Section 921) of Title 18 of the United States Code unless, prior to delivery, the person intending to sell, deliver, or transfer the firearm obtains a verification number via the Internet for the intended sale, delivery, or transfer, from the Department of Justice.
(2) If Internet service is unavailable to either the department or the licensee due to a technical or other malfunction, or a federal firearms licensee who is located outside of California does not possess a computer or have Internet access, alternate means of communication, including facsimile or telephone, shall be made available for a licensee to obtain a verification number in order to comply with this section.
(b) For every verification number request received pursuant to this section, the department shall determine whether the intended recipient is on the centralized list of firearms dealers pursuant to Section 26715, or the centralized list of exempted federal firearms licensees pursuant to Section 28450, or the centralized list of firearms manufacturers pursuant to Section 29060.
(c) (1) If the department finds after the reviews specified in subdivision (b) that the intended recipient is authorized to receive the firearm shipment, the department shall issue to the inquiring party, a unique verification number for the intended sale, delivery, or transfer. One verification number shall be issued for each sale, delivery, or transfer, which may involve multiple firearms.
(2) In addition to the unique verification number, the department may provide to the inquiring party information necessary for determining the eligibility of the intended recipient to receive the firearm.
(3) The person intending to sell, deliver, or transfer the firearm shall provide the unique verification number to the recipient along with the firearm upon delivery, in a manner to be determined by the department.
(d) If the department finds after the reviews specified in subdivision (b) that the intended recipient is not authorized to receive the firearm shipment, the department shall notify the inquiring party that the intended recipient is ineligible to receive the shipment.
(e) The department shall prescribe the manner in which the verification numbers may be requested via the Internet, or by alternate means of communication, such as by facsimile or telephone, including all required enrollment information and procedures.
(Added by Stats. 2010, Ch. 711, Sec. 6. (SB 1080) Effective January 1, 2011. Operative January 1, 2012, by Sec. 10 of Ch. 711.)
27560.
(a) Within 60 days of bringing a handgun, and commencing January 1, 2014, any firearm, into this state, a personal firearm importer shall do one of the following:
(1) Forward by prepaid mail or deliver in person to the Department of Justice, a report prescribed by the department including information concerning that individual and a description of the firearm in question.
(2) Sell or transfer the firearm in accordance with the provisions of Section 27545 or in accordance with the provisions of an exemption from Section 27545.
(3) Sell or transfer the firearm to a dealer licensed pursuant to Article 1 (commencing with Section 26700) and Article 2 (commencing with Section 26800) of Chapter 2.
(4) Sell or transfer the firearm to a sheriff or police department.
(b) If all of the following requirements are satisfied, the personal firearm importer shall have complied with the provisions of this section:
(1) The personal firearm importer sells or transfers the firearm pursuant to Section 27545.
(2) The sale or transfer cannot be completed by the dealer to the purchaser or transferee.
(3) The firearm can be returned to the personal firearm importer.
(c) (1) The provisions of this section are cumulative and shall not be construed as restricting the application of any other law.
(2) However, an act or omission punishable in different ways by this article and different provisions of the Penal Code shall not be punished under more than one provision.
(d) The department shall conduct a public education and notification program regarding this section to ensure a high degree of publicity of the provisions of this section.
(e) As part of the public education and notification program described in this section, the department shall do all of the following:
(1) Work in conjunction with the Department of Motor Vehicles to ensure that any person who is subject to this section is advised of the provisions of this section, and provided with blank copies of the report described in paragraph (1) of subdivision (a), at the time when that person applies for a California driver's license or registers a motor vehicle in accordance with the Vehicle Code.
(2) Make the reports referred to in paragraph (1) of subdivision (a) available to dealers licensed pursuant to Article 1 (commencing with Section 26700) and Article 2 (commencing with Section 26800) of Chapter 2.
(3) Make the reports referred to in paragraph (1) of subdivision (a) available to law enforcement agencies.
(4) Make persons subject to the provisions of this section aware of all of the following:
(A) The report referred to in paragraph (1) of subdivision (a) may be completed at either a law enforcement agency or the licensed premises of a dealer licensed pursuant to Article 1 (commencing with Section 26700) and Article 2 (commencing with Section 26800) of Chapter 2.
(B) It is advisable to do so for the sake of accuracy and completeness of the report.
(C) Before transporting a firearm to a law enforcement agency to comply with subdivision (a), the person should give notice to the law enforcement agency that the person is doing so.
(D) In any event, the handgun should be transported unloaded and in a locked container and a firearm that is not a handgun should be transported unloaded.
(f) Any costs incurred by the department to implement this section shall be absorbed by the department within its existing budget and the fees in the Dealers' Record of Sale Special Account allocated for implementation of subdivisions (d) and (e) of this section pursuant to Section 28235.
(Amended by Stats. 2011, Ch. 745, Sec. 27. (AB 809) Effective January 1, 2012.)
27565.
(a) This section applies in the following circumstances:
(1) A person is licensed as a collector pursuant to Chapter 44 (commencing with Section 921) of Title 18 of the United States Code and the regulations issued pursuant thereto.
(2) The licensed premises of that person are within this state.
(3) The licensed collector acquires, outside of this state, a handgun, and commencing January 1, 2014, any firearm.
(4) The licensed collector takes actual possession of that firearm outside of this state pursuant to the provisions of subsection (j) of Section 923 of Title 18 of the United States Code, as amended by Public Law 104-208, and transports the firearm into this state.
(5) The firearm is a curio or relic, as defined in Section 478.11 of Title 27 of the Code of Federal Regulations.
(b) Within five days of transporting a firearm into this state under the circumstances described in subdivision (a), the licensed collector shall report the acquisition of that firearm to the department in a format prescribed by the department.

(Amended by Stats. 2011, Ch. 745, Sec. 28. (AB 809) Effective January 1, 2012.)

27570.

(a) It is the intent of the Legislature that a violation of Section 27560 or 27565 shall not constitute a "continuing offense" and the statute of limitations for commencing a prosecution for a violation of Section 27560 or 27565 commences on the date that the applicable grace period specified in Section 27560 or 27565 expires.

(b) Sections 27560 and 27565 shall not apply to a person who reports ownership of a handgun after the applicable grace period specified in Section 27560 or 27565 expires if evidence of that violation arises only as the result of the person submitting the report described in Section 27560 or 27565.

(Added by Stats. 2010, Ch. 711, Sec. 6. (SB 1080) Effective January 1, 2011. Operative January 1, 2012, by Sec. 10 of Ch. 711.)

27585.

(a) Commencing January 1, 2015, a resident of this state shall not import into this state, bring into this state, or transport into this state, any firearm that he or she purchased or otherwise obtained on or after January 1, 2015, from outside of this state unless he or she first has that firearm delivered to a dealer in this state for delivery to that resident pursuant to the procedures set forth in Section 27540 and Article 1 (commencing with Section 26700) and Article 2 (commencing with Section 26800) of Chapter 2.

(b) Subdivision (a) does not apply to or affect any of the following:

(1) A licensed collector who is subject to and complies with Section 27565.

(2) A dealer, if the dealer is acting in the course and scope of his or her activities as a dealer.

(3) A wholesaler, if the wholesaler is acting in the course and scope of his or her activities as a wholesaler.

(4) A person licensed as an importer of firearms or ammunition or licensed as a manufacturer of firearms or ammunition, pursuant to Section 921 et seq. of Title 18 of the United States Code and the regulations issued pursuant thereto if the importer or manufacturer is acting in the course and scope of his or her activities as a licensed importer or manufacturer.

(5) A personal firearm importer who is subject to and complies with Section 27560.

(6) A person who complies with subdivision (b) of Section 27875.

(7) A person who complies with subdivision (b), (c), or (d) of Section 27920.

(8) A person who is on the centralized list of exempted federal firearms licensees pursuant to Section 28450 if that person is acting in the course and scope of his or her activities as a licensee.

(9) A firearm regulated pursuant to Chapter 1 (commencing with Section 18710) of Division 5 of Title 2 acquired by a person who holds a permit issued pursuant to Article 3 (commencing with Section 18900) of Chapter 1 of Division 5 of Title 2, if that person is acting within the course and scope of his or her activities as a licensee and in accordance with the terms and conditions of the permit.

(10) A firearm regulated pursuant to Chapter 2 (commencing with Section 30500) of Division 10 acquired by a person who holds a permit issued pursuant to Section 31005, if that person is acting within the course and scope of his or her activities as a licensee and in accordance with the terms and conditions of the permit.

(11) A firearm regulated pursuant to Chapter 6 (commencing with Section 32610) of Division 10 acquired by a person who holds a permit issued pursuant to Section 32650, if that person is acting within the course and scope of his or her activities as a licensee and in accordance with the terms and conditions of the permit.

(12) A firearm regulated pursuant to Article 2 (commencing with Section 33300) of Chapter 8 of Division 10 acquired by a person who holds a permit issued pursuant to Section 33300, if that person is acting within the course and scope of his or her activities as a licensee and in accordance with the terms and conditions of the permit.

(13) The importation of a firearm into the state, bringing a firearm into the state, or transportation of a firearm into the state, that is regulated by any of the following statutes, if the acquisition of that firearm occurred outside of California and is conducted in accordance with the applicable provisions of the following statutes:

(A) Chapter 1 (commencing with Section 18710) of Division 5 of Title 2, relating to destructive devices and explosives.

(B) Section 24410, relating to cane guns.

(C) Section 24510, relating to firearms that are not immediately recognizable as firearms.

(D) Sections 24610 and 24680, relating to undetectable firearms.

(E) Section 24710, relating to wallet guns.

(F) Chapter 2 (commencing with Section 30500) of Division 10, relating to assault weapons.

(G) Section 31500, relating to unconventional pistols.

(H) Sections 33215 to 33225, inclusive, relating to short-barreled rifles and short-barreled shotguns.

(I) Chapter 6 (commencing with Section 32610) of Division 10, relating to machineguns.

(J) Section 33600, relating to zip guns, and the exemptions in Chapter 1 (commencing with Section 17700) of Division 2 of Title 2, as they relate to zip guns.

(c) The provisions of this section are cumulative and do not restrict the application of any other law. However, an act or omission punishable in different ways by this section and different provisions of this code shall not be punished under more than one provision.

(Added by Stats. 2014, Ch. 878, Sec. 4. (AB 1609) Effective January 1, 2015.)

27590.

(a) Except as provided in subdivision (b), (c), or (e), a violation of this article is a misdemeanor.

(b) If any of the following circumstances apply, a violation of this article is punishable by imprisonment pursuant to subdivision (h) of Section 1170 for two, three, or four years.

(1) If the violation is of subdivision (a) of Section 27500.

(2) If the defendant has a prior conviction of violating the provisions, other than Section 27535, Section 27560 involving a firearm that is not a handgun, or Section 27565 involving a firearm that is not a handgun, of this article or former Section 12100 of this code, as Section 12100 read at any time from when it was enacted by Section 3 of Chapter 1386 of the Statutes of 1988 to when it was repealed by Section 18 of Chapter 23 of the Statutes of 1994, or Section 8101 of the Welfare and Institutions Code.

(3) If the defendant has a prior conviction of violating any offense specified in Section 29905 or of a violation of Section 32625 or 33410, or of former Section 12560, as that section read at any time from when it was enacted by Section 4 of Chapter 931 of the Statutes of 1965 to when it was repealed by Section 14 of Chapter 9 of the Statutes of 1990, or of any provision listed in Section 16590.

(4) If the defendant is in a prohibited class described in Chapter 2 (commencing with Section 29800) or Chapter 3 (commencing with Section 29900) of Division 9 of this title, or Section 8100 or 8103 of the Welfare and Institutions Code.

(5) A violation of this article by a person who actively participates in a "criminal street gang" as defined in Section 186.22.

(6) A violation of Section 27510 involving the delivery of any firearm to a person who the dealer knows, or should know, is a minor.

(c) If any of the following circumstances apply, a violation of this article shall be punished by imprisonment in a county jail not exceeding one year or pursuant to subdivision (h) of Section 1170, or by a fine not to exceed one thousand dollars ($1,000), or by both that fine and imprisonment.

(1) A violation of Section 27515, 27520, or subdivision (b) of Section 27500.

(2) A violation of Section 27505 involving the sale, loan, or transfer of a handgun to a minor.

(3) A violation of Section 27510 involving the delivery of a handgun.

(4) A violation of subdivision (a), (c), (d), (e), or (f) of Section 27540 involving a handgun.

(5) A violation of Section 27545 involving a handgun.

(6) A violation of Section 27550.

(7) A violation of Section 27585 involving a handgun.

(d) If both of the following circumstances apply, an additional term of imprisonment pursuant to subdivision (h) of Section 1170 for one, two, or three years shall be imposed in addition and consecutive to the sentence prescribed.

(1) A violation of Section 27510 or subdivision (b) of Section 27500.

(2) The firearm transferred in violation of Section 27510 or subdivision (b) of Section 27500 is used in the subsequent commission of a felony for which a conviction is obtained and the prescribed sentence is imposed.

(e) (1) A first violation of Section 27535 is an infraction punishable by a fine of fifty dollars ($50).

(2) A second violation of Section 27535 is an infraction punishable by a fine of one hundred dollars ($100).

(3) A third or subsequent violation of Section 27535 is a misdemeanor.

(4) For purposes of this subdivision each application to purchase a handgun in violation of Section 27535 shall be deemed a separate offense.

(Amended by Stats. 2014, Ch. 878, Sec. 5. (AB 1609) Effective January 1, 2015.)

ARTICLE 2. Exceptions Relating to Law Enforcement [27600 - 27620]

(Article 2 added by Stats. 2010, Ch. 711, Sec. 6.)

27600.

(a) Article 1 (commencing with Section 27500) does not apply to any sale, delivery, or transfer of firearms made to, or the importation of firearms by, an authorized law enforcement representative of any city, county, city and county, or state, or of the federal government, for exclusive use by that governmental agency if, prior to the sale, delivery, transfer, or importation of these firearms, written authorization from the head of the agency authorizing the transaction is presented to the person from whom the purchase, delivery, or transfer is being made or from whom the firearm is being imported.

(b) Proper written authorization is defined as verifiable written certification from the head of the agency by which the purchaser or transferee is employed, identifying the employee as an individual authorized to conduct the transaction, and authorizing the transaction for the exclusive use of the agency by which that person is employed.

(c) Within 10 days of the date a firearm is acquired by the agency, a record of the same shall be entered as an institutional weapon into the Automated Firearms System (AFS) via the California Law Enforcement Telecommunications System (CLETS) by the law enforcement or state agency. Any agency without access to the AFS shall arrange with the sheriff of the county in which the agency is located to input this information via this system.

(d) Any agency that is the registered owner of an institutional weapon in accordance with subdivision (c) that subsequently destroys that weapon shall enter information that the weapon has been destroyed into the Automated Firearms System (AFS) via the California Law Enforcement Telecommunications System (CLETS) within 10 days of the destruction in accordance with procedures prescribed by the Department of Justice. Any agency without access to the AFS shall arrange with the sheriff of the county in which the agency is located to input this information via this system.

(Amended by Stats. 2014, Ch. 878, Sec. 6. (AB 1609) Effective January 1, 2015.)

27605.

Article 1 (commencing with Section 27500) does not apply to the loan of a firearm if all of the following conditions are satisfied:

(a) The loan is made by an authorized law enforcement representative of a city, county, or city and county, or of the state or federal government.

(b) The loan is made to a peace officer employed by that agency and authorized to carry a firearm.

(c) The loan is made for the carrying and use of that firearm by that peace officer in the course and scope of the officer's duties.

(Added by Stats. 2010, Ch. 711, Sec. 6. (SB 1080) Effective January 1, 2011. Operative January 1, 2012, by Sec. 10 of Ch. 711.)

27610.

(a) Article 1 (commencing with Section 27500) does not apply to the sale, delivery, or transfer of a firearm by a law enforcement agency to a peace officer pursuant to Section 10334 of the Public Contract Code.

(b) Within 10 days of the date that a handgun, and commencing January 1, 2014, any firearm, is sold, delivered, or transferred pursuant to Section 10334 of the Public Contract Code to that peace officer, the name of the officer and the make, model, serial number, and other identifying characteristics of the firearm being sold, delivered, or transferred shall be entered into the Automated Firearms System (AFS) via the California Law Enforcement Telecommunications System (CLETS) by the law enforcement or state agency that sold, delivered, or transferred the firearm, provided, however, that if the firearm is not a handgun and does not have a serial number, identification number, or identification mark assigned to it, that fact shall be noted in AFS. Any agency without access to AFS shall arrange with the sheriff of the county in which the agency is located to input this information via this system.

(Amended by Stats. 2011, Ch. 745, Sec. 31. (AB 809) Effective January 1, 2012.)

27615.

(a) Article 1 (commencing with Section 27500) does not apply to the sale, delivery, or transfer of a firearm by a law enforcement agency to a retiring peace officer who is authorized to carry a firearm pursuant to Chapter 5 (commencing with Section 26300) of Division 5.

(b) Within 10 days of the date that a handgun, and commencing January 1, 2014, any firearm, is sold, delivered, or transferred to that retiring peace officer, the name of the officer and the make, model, serial number, and other identifying characteristics of the firearm being sold, delivered, or transferred shall be entered into the Automated Firearms System (AFS) via the California Law Enforcement Telecommunications System (CLETS) by the law enforcement or state agency that sold, delivered, or transferred the firearm, provided, however, that if the firearm is not a handgun and does not have a serial number, identification number, or identification mark assigned to it, that fact shall be noted in AFS. Any agency without access to AFS shall arrange with the sheriff of the county in which the agency is located to input this information via this system.

(Amended by Stats. 2011, Ch. 745, Sec. 32. (AB 809) Effective January 1, 2012.)

27620.

Section 27545 does not apply to the sale, delivery, or transfer of a firearm when made by an authorized law enforcement representative of a city, county, city and county, or of the state or federal government, if all of the following conditions are met:

(a) The sale, delivery, or transfer is made to one of the following:

(1) A wholesaler.

(2) A manufacturer or importer of firearms or ammunition licensed to engage in that business pursuant to Chapter 44 (commencing with Section 921) of Title 18 of the United States Code and the regulations issued pursuant thereto.

(b) The sale, delivery, or transfer of the firearm is not subject to the procedures set forth in Section 18000, 18005, 34000, or 34005.

(c) Within 10 days of the date that any firearm is delivered pursuant to this section, the governmental agency has entered a record of the delivery into the Automated Firearms System (AFS) via the California Law Enforcement Telecommunications System (CLETS). Any agency without access to the AFS shall arrange with the sheriff of the county in which the agency is located to input this information via this system.

(Added by Stats. 2013, Ch. 738, Sec. 5. (AB 538) Effective January 1, 2014.)

ARTICLE 3. Exceptions Extending Only to Waiting Period [27650 - 27670]

(Article 3 added by Stats. 2010, Ch. 711, Sec. 6.)

27650.

(a) The waiting period described in Section 27540 does not apply to the sale, delivery, or transfer of firearms made to any person who satisfies both of the following requirements:

(1) The person is properly identified as a full-time paid peace officer, as defined in Chapter 4.5 (commencing with Section 830) of Title 3 of Part 2.

(2) The officer's employer has authorized the officer to carry firearms while in the performance of duties.

(b) (1) Proper identification is defined as verifiable written certification from the head of the agency by which the purchaser or transferee is employed, identifying the purchaser or transferee as a peace officer who is authorized to carry firearms while in the performance of duties, and authorizing the purchase or transfer.

(2) The certification shall be delivered to the dealer at the time of purchase or transfer and the purchaser or transferee shall identify himself or herself as the person authorized in the certification.

(3) The dealer shall keep the certification with the record of sale.

(4) On the date that the sale, delivery, or transfer is made, the dealer delivering the firearm shall transmit to the Department of Justice an electronic or telephonic report of the transaction as is indicated in Section 28160 or 28165.

(Added by Stats. 2010, Ch. 711, Sec. 6. (SB 1080) Effective January 1, 2011. Operative January 1, 2012, by Sec. 10 of Ch. 711.)

27655.

(a) The waiting period described in Section 27540 does not apply to a dealer who delivers a firearm, other than a handgun, at an auction or similar event described in Section 27900, as authorized by subdivision (c) of Section 26805.

(b) Within two business days of completion of the application to purchase, the dealer shall forward by prepaid mail to the Department of Justice a report of the application as is indicated in Section 28160 or 28165, as applicable.

(c) If the electronic or telephonic transfer of applicant information is used, within two business days of completion of the application to purchase, the dealer delivering the firearm shall transmit to the Department of Justice an electronic or telephonic report of the application as is indicated in Section 28160 or 28165, as applicable.

(Amended by Stats. 2011, Ch. 745, Sec. 33. (AB 809) Effective January 1, 2012.)

27660.

(a) The waiting period described in Section 27540 does not apply to the sale, delivery, or transfer of a handgun, and commencing January 1, 2014, any firearm, by a dealer in either of the following situations:

(1) The dealer is delivering the firearm to another dealer, the firearm is not intended as merchandise in the receiving dealer's business, and the requirements of subdivisions (b) and (c) are satisfied.

(2) The dealer is delivering the firearm to himself or herself, the firearm is not intended as merchandise in the dealer's business, and the requirements of subdivision (c) are satisfied.

(b) If the dealer is receiving the firearm from another dealer, the dealer receiving the firearm shall present proof to the dealer delivering the firearm that the receiving dealer is licensed pursuant to Article 1 (commencing with Section 26700) and Article 2 (commencing with Section 26800). This shall be done by complying with Section 27555.

(c) (1) Regardless of whether the dealer is selling, delivering, or transferring the firearm to another dealer or to himself or herself, on the date that the application to purchase is completed, the dealer delivering the firearm shall forward by prepaid mail to the Department of Justice a report of the application and the type of information concerning the purchaser or transferee as is indicated in Section 28160.

(2) Where electronic or telephonic transfer of applicant information is used, on the date that the application to purchase is completed, the dealer delivering the firearm shall transmit an electronic or telephonic report of the application and the type of information concerning the purchaser or transferee as is indicated in Section 28160.

(Amended by Stats. 2011, Ch. 745, Sec. 34. (AB 809) Effective January 1, 2012.)

27665.

(a) The waiting period described in Section 27540 does not apply to the sale, delivery, or transfer of a firearm to the holder of a special weapons permit issued by the Department of Justice pursuant to Section 32650 or 33300, pursuant to Article 3 (commencing with Section 18900) of Chapter 1 of Division 5 of Title 2, or pursuant to Article 4 (commencing with Section 32700) of Chapter 6 of Division 10.

(b) On the date that the application to purchase is completed, the dealer delivering the firearm shall transmit to the Department of Justice an electronic or telephonic report of the application as is indicated in Section 28160 or 28165, as applicable.

(Amended by Stats. 2011, Ch. 745, Sec. 35. (AB 809) Effective January 1, 2012.)

27670.

(a) The waiting period described in Section 27540 does not apply to the sale, delivery, loan, or transfer of a firearm if all of the following conditions are satisfied:

(1) The firearm is a curio or relic, as defined in Section 478.11 of Title 27 of the Code of Federal Regulations, or its successor.

(2) The sale, delivery, loan, or transfer is made by a dealer.

(3) The sale, delivery, loan, or transfer is made to a person who is licensed as a collector pursuant to Chapter 44 (commencing with Section 921) of Title 18 of the United States Code and the regulations issued pursuant thereto.

(4) The licensed collector has a current certificate of eligibility issued by the Department of Justice pursuant to Section 26710.

(b) On the date that the sale, delivery, or transfer is made, the dealer delivering the firearm shall transmit to the Department of Justice an electronic or telephonic report of the transaction as is indicated in Section 28160 or 28165.

(Added by Stats. 2010, Ch. 711, Sec. 6. (SB 1080) Effective January 1, 2011. Operative January 1, 2012, by Sec. 10 of Ch. 711.)

ARTICLE 4. Exceptions to Restrictions on Delivery of a Firearm [27700 - 27750]

(Article 4 added by Stats. 2010, Ch. 711, Sec. 6.)

27700.

Section 27540 does not apply to sales, deliveries, or transfers of firearms between or to importers and manufacturers of firearms licensed to engage in that business pursuant to Chapter 44 (commencing with Section 921) of Title 18 of the United States Code and the regulations issued pursuant thereto.

(Added by Stats. 2010, Ch. 711, Sec. 6. (SB 1080) Effective January 1, 2011. Operative January 1, 2012, by Sec. 10 of Ch. 711.)

27705.

Section 27540 does not apply to the delivery of a firearm to a gunsmith for service or repair, or to the return of the firearm to its owner by the gunsmith, or to the delivery of a firearm by a gunsmith to a person licensed pursuant to Chapter 44 (commencing with Section 921) of Title 18 of the United States Code for service or repair and the return of the firearm to the gunsmith.

(Added by Stats. 2010, Ch. 711, Sec. 6. (SB 1080) Effective January 1, 2011. Operative January 1, 2012, by Sec. 10 of Ch. 711.)

27715.

Section 27540 does not apply to the sale, delivery, or transfer of unloaded firearms by a dealer to a person who resides outside this state and is licensed pursuant to Chapter 44 (commencing with Section 921) of Title 18 of the United States Code and the regulations issued pursuant thereto.

(Added by Stats. 2010, Ch. 711, Sec. 6. (SB 1080) Effective January 1, 2011. Operative January 1, 2012, by Sec. 10 of Ch. 711.)

27720.

Section 27540 does not apply to the sale, delivery, or transfer of unloaded firearms to a wholesaler if the firearms are being returned to the wholesaler and are intended as merchandise in the wholesaler's business.

(Added by Stats. 2010, Ch. 711, Sec. 6. (SB 1080) Effective January 1, 2011. Operative January 1, 2012, by Sec. 10 of Ch. 711.)

27725.

Section 27540 does not apply to the sale, delivery, or transfer of firearms if all of the following conditions are satisfied:

(a) The firearms are unloaded.

(b) The sale, delivery, or transfer is made by one dealer to another dealer, upon proof of compliance with the requirements of Section 27555.

(c) The firearms are intended as merchandise in the receiving dealer's business.

(Added by Stats. 2010, Ch. 711, Sec. 6. (SB 1080) Effective January 1, 2011. Operative January 1, 2012, by Sec. 10 of Ch. 711.)

27730.

Until January 1, 2014, Section 27540 does not apply to the sale, delivery, or transfer of an unloaded firearm, other than a handgun, by a dealer to himself or herself.

(Amended by Stats. 2011, Ch. 745, Sec. 37. (AB 809) Effective January 1, 2012.)

27735.

Section 27540 does not apply to the loan of an unloaded firearm by a dealer who also operates a target facility that holds a business or regulatory license on the premises of the building designated in the license or whose building designated in the license is on the premises of any club or organization organized for the purposes of practicing shooting at targets upon established ranges, whether public or private, to a person at that target facility or that club or organization, if the firearm is at all times kept within the premises of the target range or on the premises of the club or organization.

(Added by Stats. 2010, Ch. 711, Sec. 6. (SB 1080) Effective January 1, 2011. Operative January 1, 2012, by Sec. 10 of Ch. 711.)

27740.

Section 27540 does not apply to the sale, delivery, or transfer of a firearm regulated pursuant to any of the following statutes, if the sale, delivery, or transfer of that firearm is conducted in accordance with the applicable provisions of the statute:

(a) Chapter 1 (commencing with Section 18710) of Division 5 of Title 2, relating to destructive devices and explosives.

(b) Section 24410, relating to cane guns, and the exemptions in Chapter 1 (commencing with Section 17700) of Title 2, as they relate to cane guns.

(c) Section 24510, relating to firearms that are not immediately recognizable as firearms, and the exemptions in Chapter 1 (commencing with Section 17700) of Title 2, as they relate to firearms that are not immediately recognizable as firearms.

(d) Sections 24610 and 24680, relating to undetectable firearms, and the exemptions in Chapter 1 (commencing with Section 17700) of Title 2, as they relate to undetectable firearms.

(e) Section 24710, relating to wallet guns, and the exemptions in Chapter 1 (commencing with Section 17700) of Title 2, as they relate to wallet guns.

(f) Chapter 2 (commencing with Section 30500) of Division 10, relating to assault weapons.

(g) Section 31500, relating to unconventional pistols, and the exemptions in Chapter 1 (commencing with Section 17700) of Title 2, as they relate to unconventional pistols.

(h) Sections 33215 to 33225, inclusive, relating to short-barreled rifles and short-barreled shotguns, and the exemptions in Chapter 1 (commencing with Section 17700) of Title 2, as they relate to short-barreled rifles and short-barreled shotguns.

(i) Chapter 6 (commencing with Section 32610) of Division 10, relating to machineguns.

(j) Section 33600, relating to zip guns, and the exemptions in Chapter 1 (commencing with Section 17700) of Title 2, as they relate to zip guns.

(Added by Stats. 2010, Ch. 711, Sec. 6. (SB 1080) Effective January 1, 2011. Operative January 1, 2012, by Sec. 10 of Ch. 711.)

27745.

(a) Section 27540 does not apply to the loan of a firearm if all of the following conditions are satisfied:

(1) The firearm is unloaded.

(2) The loan is made by a dealer.

(3) The loan is made to a person who possesses a valid entertainment firearms permit issued pursuant to Chapter 2 (commencing with Section 29500) of Division 8.

(4) The firearm is loaned solely for use as a prop in a motion picture, television, video, theatrical, or other entertainment production or event.

(b) The dealer shall retain a photocopy of the entertainment firearms permit as proof of compliance with this requirement.

(Added by Stats. 2010, Ch. 711, Sec. 6. (SB 1080) Effective January 1, 2011. Operative January 1, 2012, by Sec. 10 of Ch. 711.)

27750.

(a) Section 27540 does not apply to the loan of an unloaded firearm to a consultant-evaluator by a person licensed pursuant to Sections 26700 to 26915, inclusive, if the loan does not exceed 45 days from the date of delivery.

(b) At the time of the loan, the consultant-evaluator shall provide the following information, which the dealer shall retain for two years:

(1) A photocopy of a valid, current, government-issued identification to determine the consultant-evaluator's identity, including, but not limited to, a California driver's license, identification card, or passport.

(2) A photocopy of the consultant-evaluator's valid, current certificate of eligibility.

(3) A letter from the person licensed as an importer, manufacturer, or dealer pursuant to Chapter 44 (commencing with Section 921) of Title 18 of the United States Code, with whom the consultant-evaluator has a bona fide business relationship. The letter shall detail the bona fide business purposes for which the firearm is being loaned and confirm that the consultant-evaluator is being loaned the firearm as part of a bona fide business relationship.

(4) The signature of the consultant-evaluator on a form indicating the date the firearm is loaned and the last day the firearm may be returned.

(Added by Stats. 2010, Ch. 711, Sec. 6. (SB 1080) Effective January 1, 2011. Operative January 1, 2012, by Sec. 10 of Ch. 711.)

ARTICLE 5. Exceptions to the Requirement of Obtaining a Verification Number [27805 - 27835]

(Article 5 added by Stats. 2010, Ch. 711, Sec. 6.)

27805.

(a) Section 27555 does not apply to the loan of a firearm if all of the following conditions are satisfied:

(1) The firearm is unloaded.

(2) The loan is made by a dealer.

(3) The loan is made to a person who possesses a valid entertainment firearms permit issued pursuant to Chapter 2 (commencing with Section 29500) of Division 8.

(4) The firearm is loaned solely for use as a prop in a motion picture, television, video, theatrical, or other entertainment production or event.

(b) The dealer shall retain a photocopy of the entertainment firearms permit as proof of compliance with this requirement.

(Added by Stats. 2010, Ch. 711, Sec. 6. (SB 1080) Effective January 1, 2011. Operative January 1, 2012, by Sec. 10 of Ch. 711.)

27810.

(a) Section 27555 does not apply to the loan of a firearm if all of the following requirements are satisfied:
(1) The firearm is unloaded.
(2) The loan is made by a person who is not a dealer but is a federal firearms licensee pursuant to Chapter 44 of Title 18 (commencing with Section 921) of the United States Code.
(3) The loan is made to a person who possesses a valid entertainment firearms permit issued pursuant to Chapter 2 (commencing with Section 29500) of Division 8.
(4) The firearm is loaned for use solely as a prop in a motion picture, television, video, theatrical, or other entertainment production or event.
(b) The person loaning the firearm pursuant to this section shall retain a photocopy of the entertainment firearms permit as proof of compliance with this requirement.
(Added by Stats. 2010, Ch. 711, Sec. 6. (SB 1080) Effective January 1, 2011. Operative January 1, 2012, by Sec. 10 of Ch. 711.)
27815.
(a) Section 27555 does not apply to the loan of an unloaded firearm to a consultant-evaluator by a person licensed pursuant to Sections 26700 to 26915, inclusive, if the loan does not exceed 45 days from the date of delivery.
(b) At the time of the loan, the consultant-evaluator shall provide the following information, which the dealer shall retain for two years:
(1) A photocopy of a valid, current, government-issued identification to determine the consultant-evaluator's identity, including, but not limited to, a California driver's license, identification card, or passport.
(2) A photocopy of the consultant-evaluator's valid, current certificate of eligibility.
(3) A letter from the person licensed as an importer, manufacturer, or dealer pursuant to Chapter 44 (commencing with Section 921) of Title 18 of the United States Code, with whom the consultant-evaluator has a bona fide business relationship. The letter shall detail the bona fide business purposes for which the firearm is being loaned and confirm that the consultant-evaluator is being loaned the firearm as part of a bona fide business relationship.
(4) The signature of the consultant-evaluator on a form indicating the date the firearm is loaned and the last day the firearm may be returned.
(Added by Stats. 2010, Ch. 711, Sec. 6. (SB 1080) Effective January 1, 2011. Operative January 1, 2012, by Sec. 10 of Ch. 711.)
27820.
If all of the following requirements are satisfied, Section 27555 does not apply to the sale, loan, or transfer of a firearm:
(a) The sale, loan, or transfer is infrequent, as defined in Section 16730.
(b) The firearm is not a handgun.
(c) The firearm is a curio or relic manufactured at least 50 years prior to the current date but is not a replica, as defined in Section 478.11 of Title 27 of the Code of Federal Regulations, or its successor.
(Added by Stats. 2010, Ch. 711, Sec. 6. (SB 1080) Effective January 1, 2011. Operative January 1, 2012, by Sec. 10 of Ch. 711.)
27825.
Section 27555 does not apply to the delivery of a firearm to a gunsmith for service or repair, or to the return of the firearm to its owner by the gunsmith, or to the delivery of a firearm by a gunsmith to a person licensed pursuant to Chapter 44 (commencing with Section 921) of Title 18 of the United States Code for service or repair and the return of the firearm to the gunsmith.
(Added by Stats. 2010, Ch. 711, Sec. 6. (SB 1080) Effective January 1, 2011. Operative January 1, 2012, by Sec. 10 of Ch. 711.)
27830.
Section 27555 does not apply where the transferor and the transferee are the same person or corporation.
(Added by Stats. 2010, Ch. 711, Sec. 6. (SB 1080) Effective January 1, 2011. Operative January 1, 2012, by Sec. 10 of Ch. 711.)
27835.
Section 27555 does not apply where the transfer is to or from a person who has a valid entertainment firearms permit and the transfer involves the loan or return of a firearm used solely as a prop in a television, film, or theatrical production.
(Added by Stats. 2010, Ch. 711, Sec. 6. (SB 1080) Effective January 1, 2011. Operative January 1, 2012, by Sec. 10 of Ch. 711.)

ARTICLE 6. Exceptions to the Requirement of Using a Dealer for a Private Party Firearms Transaction [27850 - 27970]

(Article 6 added by Stats. 2010, Ch. 711, Sec. 6.)
27850.
(a) Section 27545 does not apply to a sale, delivery, or transfer of firearms if both of the following requirements are satisfied:
(1) The sale, delivery, or transfer is to an authorized representative of a city, city and county, county, or state government, or of the federal government, and is for the governmental entity.
(2) The entity is acquiring the weapon as part of an authorized, voluntary program in which the entity is buying or receiving weapons from private individuals.
(b) Any weapons acquired pursuant to this section shall be disposed of pursuant to the applicable provisions of Section 34000 or Sections 18000 and 18005.
(Added by Stats. 2010, Ch. 711, Sec. 6. (SB 1080) Effective January 1, 2011. Operative January 1, 2012, by Sec. 10 of Ch. 711.)
27855.
Section 27545 does not apply to the sale, delivery, loan, or transfer of a firearm made by an authorized law enforcement representative of a city, county, city and county, or state, or of the federal government, to any public or private nonprofit historical society, museum, or institutional collection, or the purchase or receipt of that firearm by that public or private nonprofit historical society, museum, or institutional collection, if all of the following conditions are met:
(a) The entity receiving the firearm is open to the public.
(b) The firearm prior to delivery is deactivated or rendered inoperable.
(c) The firearm is not subject to any of the following:
(1) Sections 18000 and 18005.
(2) Division 4 (commencing with Section 18250) of Title 2.
(3) Section 34000.
(4) Sections 34005 and 34010.
(d) The firearm is not prohibited by other provisions of law from being sold, delivered, or transferred to the public at large.
(e) Prior to delivery, the entity receiving the firearm submits a written statement to the law enforcement representative stating that the firearm will not be restored to operating condition, and will either remain with that entity, or if subsequently disposed of, will be transferred in accordance with the applicable provisions listed in Section 16575 and, if applicable, with Section 31615.
(f) Within 10 days of the date that the firearm is sold, loaned, delivered, or transferred to that entity, all of the following information shall be reported to the department in a manner prescribed by the department:
(1) The name of the government entity delivering the firearm.
(2) The make, model, serial number, and other identifying characteristics of the firearm.
(3) The name of the person authorized by the entity to take possession of the firearm.
(g) In the event of a change in the status of the designated representative, the entity shall notify the department of a new representative within 30 days.
(Added by Stats. 2010, Ch. 711, Sec. 6. (SB 1080) Effective January 1, 2011. Operative January 1, 2012, by Sec. 10 of Ch. 711.)

27860.
Section 27545 does not apply to the sale, delivery, loan, or transfer of a firearm made by any person other than a representative of an authorized law enforcement agency to any public or private nonprofit historical society, museum, or institutional collection, if all of the following conditions are met:
(a) The entity receiving the firearm is open to the public.
(b) The firearm is deactivated or rendered inoperable prior to delivery.
(c) The firearm is not of a type prohibited from being sold, delivered, or transferred to the public.
(d) Prior to delivery, the entity receiving the firearm submits a written statement to the person selling, loaning, or transferring the firearm stating that the firearm will not be restored to operating condition, and will either remain with that entity, or if subsequently disposed of, will be transferred in accordance with the applicable provisions listed in Section 16575 and, if applicable, with Section 31615.
(e) If title to a handgun, and commencing January 1, 2014, any firearm, is being transferred to the public or private nonprofit historical society, museum, or institutional collection, then the designated representative of that entity shall, within 30 days of taking possession of that firearm, forward by prepaid mail or deliver in person to the Department of Justice, a single report signed by both parties to the transaction, which includes all of the following information:
(1) Information identifying the person representing the public or private historical society, museum, or institutional collection.
(2) Information on how title was obtained and from whom.
(3) A description of the firearm in question.
(4) A copy of the written statement referred to in subdivision (d).
(f) The report forms that are to be completed pursuant to this section shall be provided by the Department of Justice.
(g) In the event of a change in the status of the designated representative, the entity shall notify the department of a new representative within 30 days.
(Amended by Stats. 2011, Ch. 745, Sec. 38. (AB 809) Effective January 1, 2012.)
27865.
Section 27545 does not apply to sales, deliveries, or transfers of firearms between or to importers and manufacturers of firearms licensed to engage in that business pursuant to Chapter 44 (commencing with Section 921) of Title 18 of the United States Code and the regulations issued pursuant thereto.
(Added by Stats. 2010, Ch. 711, Sec. 6. (SB 1080) Effective January 1, 2011. Operative January 1, 2012, by Sec. 10 of Ch. 711.)
27875.
(a) Section 27545 does not apply to the transfer of a firearm by gift, bequest, intestate succession, or other means from one individual to another, if all of the following requirements are met:
(1) The transfer is infrequent, as defined in Section 16730.
(2) The transfer is between members of the same immediate family.
(3) Within 30 days of taking possession of the firearm, the person to whom it is transferred shall submit a report to the Department of Justice, in a manner prescribed by the department, that includes information concerning the individual taking possession of the firearm, how title was obtained and from whom, and a description of the firearm in question. The reports that individuals complete pursuant to this subdivision shall be made available to them in a format prescribed by the department.
(4) Until January 1, 2015, the person taking title to the firearm shall first obtain a valid handgun safety certificate if the firearm is a handgun, and commencing January 1, 2015, a valid firearm safety certificate for any firearm, except that in the case of a handgun, a valid unexpired handgun safety certificate may be used.
(5) The person receiving the firearm is 18 years of age or older.
(b) Subdivision (a) of Section 27585 does not apply to a person who imports a firearm into this state, brings a firearm into this state, or transports a firearm into this state if all of the following requirements are met:
(1) The person acquires ownership of the firearm from an immediate family member by bequest or intestate succession.
(2) The person has obtained a valid firearm safety certificate, except that in the case of a handgun, a valid unexpired handgun safety certificate may be used.
(3) The receipt of any firearm by the individual by bequest or intestate succession is infrequent, as defined in Section 16730.
(4) The person acquiring ownership of the firearm by bequest or intestate succession is 18 years of age or older.
(5) Within 30 days of that person taking possession of the firearm and importing, bringing, or transporting it into this state, the person shall submit a report to the Department of Justice, in a manner prescribed by the department, that includes information concerning the individual taking possession of the firearm, how title was obtained and from whom, and a description of the firearm in question. The reports that individuals complete pursuant to this subdivision shall be made available to them in a format prescribed by the department.
(Amended by Stats. 2014, Ch. 878, Sec. 7. (AB 1609) Effective January 1, 2015.)
27880.
Section 27545 does not apply to the loan of a firearm if all of the following requirements are satisfied:
(a) The loan is to a spouse, registered domestic partner, or any of the following relations, whether by consanguinity, adoption, or steprelation:
(1) Parent.
(2) Child.
(3) Sibling.
(4) Grandparent.
(5) Grandchild.
(b) The loan is infrequent, as defined in Section 16730.
(c) The loan is for any lawful purpose.
(d) The loan does not exceed 30 days in duration.
(e) Until January 1, 2015, if the firearm is a handgun, the individual being loaned the firearm shall have a valid handgun safety certificate. Commencing January 1, 2015, for any firearm, the individual being loaned the firearm shall have a valid firearm safety certificate, except that in the case of a handgun, an unexpired handgun safety certificate may be used.
(f) If the firearm being loaned is a handgun, the handgun is registered to the person making the loan pursuant to Section 11106.
(Amended by Stats. 2016, Ch. 41, Sec. 1. (AB 1511) Effective January 1, 2017.)
27885.
Section 27545 does not apply to the loan of a firearm if all of the following conditions exist:
(a) The person loaning the firearm is at all times within the presence of the person being loaned the firearm.
(b) The loan is for a lawful purpose.
(c) The loan does not exceed three days in duration.
(d) The individual receiving the firearm is not prohibited by state or federal law from possessing, receiving, owning, or purchasing a firearm.
(e) The person loaning the firearm is 18 years of age or older.
(f) The person being loaned the firearm is 18 years of age or older.
(Added by Stats. 2010, Ch. 711, Sec. 6. (SB 1080) Effective January 1, 2011. Operative January 1, 2012, by Sec. 10 of Ch. 711.)
27890.

Section 27545 does not apply to the delivery of a firearm to a gunsmith for service or repair, or to the return of the firearm to its owner by the gunsmith, or to the delivery of a firearm by a gunsmith to a person licensed pursuant to Chapter 44 (commencing with Section 921) of Title 18 of the United States Code for service or repair and the return of the firearm to the gunsmith.
(Added by Stats. 2010, Ch. 711, Sec. 6. (SB 1080) Effective January 1, 2011. Operative January 1, 2012, by Sec. 10 of Ch. 711.)
27895.
Section 27545 does not apply to the sale, delivery, or transfer of firearms if all of the following requirements are satisfied:
(a) The sale, delivery, or transfer is made by a person who resides in this state.
(b) The sale, delivery, or transfer is made to a person who resides outside this state and is licensed pursuant to Chapter 44 (commencing with Section 921) of Title 18 of the United States Code and the regulations issued pursuant thereto.
(c) The sale, delivery, or transfer is in accordance with Chapter 44 (commencing with Section 921) of Title 18 of the United States Code and the regulations issued pursuant thereto.
(Added by Stats. 2010, Ch. 711, Sec. 6. (SB 1080) Effective January 1, 2011. Operative January 1, 2012, by Sec. 10 of Ch. 711.)
27900.
(a) Section 27545 does not apply to the infrequent sale or transfer of a firearm other than a handgun at an auction or similar event conducted by a nonprofit mutual or public benefit corporation organized pursuant to the Corporations Code.
(b) As used in this section, "infrequent" has the meaning provided in Section 16730.
(Added by Stats. 2010, Ch. 711, Sec. 6. (SB 1080) Effective January 1, 2011. Operative January 1, 2012, by Sec. 10 of Ch. 711.)
27905.
Section 27545 does not apply to the transfer of a firearm if all of the following requirements are satisfied:
(a) The firearm is not a handgun.
(b) The firearm is donated for an auction or similar event described in Section 27900.
(c) The firearm is delivered to the nonprofit corporation immediately preceding, or contemporaneous with, the auction or similar event.
(Added by Stats. 2010, Ch. 711, Sec. 6. (SB 1080) Effective January 1, 2011. Operative January 1, 2012, by Sec. 10 of Ch. 711.)
27910.
Section 27545 does not apply to the loan of a firearm to a person 18 years of age or older for the purposes of shooting at targets if the loan occurs on the premises of a target facility that holds a business or regulatory license or on the premises of any club or organization organized for the purposes of practicing shooting at targets upon established ranges, whether public or private, if the firearm is at all times kept within the premises of the target range or on the premises of the club or organization.
(Added by Stats. 2010, Ch. 711, Sec. 6. (SB 1080) Effective January 1, 2011. Operative January 1, 2012, by Sec. 10 of Ch. 711.)
27920.
(a) Section 27545 does not apply to a person who takes title or possession of a firearm by operation of law if the person is not prohibited by state or federal law from possessing, receiving, owning, or purchasing a firearm and all of the following conditions are met:
(1) If the person taking title or possession is neither a levying officer as defined in Section 481.140, 511.060, or 680.260 of the Code of Civil Procedure, nor a person who is receiving that firearm pursuant to subdivision (g), (h), (i), or (j) of Section 16990, the person shall, within 30 days of taking possession, submit a report to the Department of Justice, in a manner prescribed by the department, that includes information concerning the individual taking possession of the firearm, how title or possession was obtained and from whom, and a description of the firearm in question.
(2) If the person taking title or possession is receiving the firearm pursuant to subdivision (g) or (h) of Section 16990, the person shall do both of the following:
(A) Within 30 days of taking possession, submit a report to the Department of Justice, in a manner prescribed by the department, that includes information concerning the individual taking possession of the firearm, how title or possession was obtained and from whom, and a description of the firearm in question.
(B) Until January 1, 2015, prior to taking title or possession of the firearm, the person shall obtain a handgun safety certificate, if the firearm is a handgun. Commencing January 1, 2015, prior to taking title or possession of the firearm, the person shall obtain a valid firearm safety certificate for any firearm, except that in the case of a handgun, a valid unexpired handgun safety certificate may be presented.
(3) Where the person receiving title or possession of the firearm is a person described in subdivision (i) of Section 16990, on the date that the person is delivered the firearm, the name and other information concerning the person taking possession of the firearm, how title or possession of the firearm was obtained and from whom, and a description of the firearm by make, model, serial number, and other identifying characteristics shall be entered into the Automated Firearms System (AFS) via the California Law Enforcement Telecommunications System (CLETS) by the law enforcement or state agency that transferred or delivered the firearm, provided, however, that if the firearm is not a handgun and does not have a serial number, identification number, or identification mark assigned to it, that fact shall be noted in AFS. An agency without access to AFS shall arrange with the sheriff of the county in which the agency is located to input this information via this system.
(4) Where the person receiving title or possession of the firearm is a person described in subdivision (j) of Section 16990, on the date that the person is delivered the firearm, the name and other information concerning the person taking possession of the firearm, how title or possession of the firearm was obtained and from whom, and a description of the firearm by make, model, serial number, and other identifying characteristics shall be entered into the AFS via the CLETS by the law enforcement or state agency that transferred or delivered the firearm, provided, however, that if the firearm is not a handgun and does not have a serial number, identification number, or identification mark assigned to it, that fact shall be noted in AFS. An agency without access to AFS shall arrange with the sheriff of the county in which the agency is located to input this information via this system. In addition, that law enforcement agency shall not deliver the firearm to the person referred to in this subdivision unless, prior to the delivery of the firearm, the person presents proof to the agency that the person is the holder of a valid handgun safety certificate if the firearm is a handgun, and commencing January 1, 2015, a valid firearm safety certificate for any firearm, except that in the case of a handgun, a valid unexpired handgun safety certificate may be presented.
(b) Subdivision (a) of Section 27585 does not apply to a person who imports a firearm into this state, brings a firearm into this state, or transports a firearm into this state if all of the following requirements are met:
(1) The person acquires ownership of the firearm as an executor or administrator of an estate.
(2) If acquisition of the firearm had occurred within this state, the receipt of the firearm by the executor or administrator would be exempt from the provisions of Section 27545 pursuant to paragraph (1) of subdivision (a).
(3) Within 30 days of taking possession of the firearm and importing, bringing, or transporting it into this state, the person shall submit a report to the Department of Justice, in a manner prescribed by the department, that includes information concerning the individual taking possession of the firearm, how title was obtained and from whom, and a description of the firearm in question.

(4) If the executor or administrator subsequently acquires ownership of that firearm in an individual capacity, prior to transferring ownership to himself or herself, he or she shall obtain a valid firearm safety certificate, except that in the case of a handgun, a valid unexpired handgun safety certificate may be used.
(5) The executor or administrator is 18 years of age or older.
(c) Subdivision (a) of Section 27585 does not apply to a person who imports a firearm into this state, brings a firearm into this state, or transports a firearm into this state if all of the following requirements are met:
(1) The person acquires ownership of the firearm by bequest or intestate succession as a surviving spouse or as the surviving registered domestic partner of the decedent who owned that firearm.
(2) If acquisition of the firearm had occurred within this state, the receipt of the firearm by the surviving spouse or registered domestic partner would be exempt from the provisions of Section 27545 pursuant to paragraph (2) of subdivision (a) by virtue of subdivision (h) of Section 16990.
(3) Within 30 days of taking possession of the firearm and importing, bringing, or transporting it into this state, the person shall submit a report to the Department of Justice, in a manner prescribed by the department, that includes information concerning the individual taking possession of the firearm, how title was obtained and from whom, and a description of the firearm in question.
(4) The person has obtained a valid firearm safety certificate, except that in the case of a handgun, a valid unexpired handgun safety certificate may be used.
(d) Subdivision (a) of Section 27585 does not apply to a person who imports a firearm into this state, brings a firearm into this state, or transports a firearm into this state if all of the following requirements are met:
(1) The firearm is imported into this country pursuant to provisions of Section 925(a)(4) of Title 18 of the United States Code.
(2) The person is not subject to the requirements of Section 27560.
(3) The firearm is not a firearm that is prohibited by any provision listed in Section 16590.
(4) The firearm is not an assault weapon.
(5) The firearm is not a machinegun.
(6) The firearm is not a .50 BMG rifle.
(7) The firearm is not a destructive device.
(8) The person is 18 years of age or older.
(9) Within 30 days of that person taking possession of the firearm and importing, bringing, or transporting it into this state, the person shall submit a report to the Department of Justice, in a manner prescribed by the department, that includes information concerning the individual taking possession of the firearm, how title was obtained and from whom, and a description of the firearm in question.
(e) The reports that individuals complete pursuant to this section shall be made available to them in a format prescribed by the Department of Justice.
(Amended by Stats. 2014, Ch. 878, Sec. 8. (AB 1609) Effective January 1, 2015.)
27925.
(a) Section 27545 does not apply to a person who takes possession of a firearm by operation of law in a representative capacity who subsequently transfers ownership of the firearm to himself or herself in an individual capacity.
(b) Until January 1, 2015, in the case of a handgun, the individual shall obtain a handgun safety certificate prior to transferring ownership to himself or herself, or taking possession of a handgun in an individual capacity. Beginning January 1, 2015, the individual shall obtain a firearm safety certificate prior to transferring ownership to himself or herself, or taking possession of a firearm in an individual capacity, except that in the case of a handgun, an unexpired handgun safety certificate may be used.
(Amended by Stats. 2013, Ch. 761, Sec. 10. (SB 683) Effective January 1, 2014.)
27930.
Section 27545 does not apply to deliveries, transfers, or returns of firearms made pursuant to any of the following:
(a) Sections 18000 and 18005.
(b) Division 4 (commencing with Section 18250) of Title 2.
(c) Chapter 2 (commencing with Section 33850) of Division 11.
(d) Sections 34005 and 34010.
(e) Section 29810.
(Amended November 8, 2016, by initiative Proposition 63, Sec. 10.2.)
27935.
Section 27545 does not apply to the sale, delivery, or transfer of unloaded firearms to a wholesaler as merchandise in the wholesaler's business by a manufacturer or importer licensed to engage in that business pursuant to Chapter 44 (commencing with Section 921) of Title 18 of the United States Code and the regulations issued pursuant thereto, or by another wholesaler, if the sale, delivery, or transfer is made in accordance with Chapter 44 (commencing with Section 921) of Title 18 of the United States Code.
(Added by Stats. 2010, Ch. 711, Sec. 6. (SB 1080) Effective January 1, 2011. Operative January 1, 2012, by Sec. 10 of Ch. 711.)
27940.
Section 27545 does not apply to the sale, delivery, or transfer of a firearm regulated pursuant to any of the following statutes, if the sale, delivery, or transfer of that firearm is conducted in accordance with the applicable provisions of the statute:
(a) Chapter 1 (commencing with Section 18710) of Division 5 of Title 2, relating to destructive devices and explosives.
(b) Section 24410, relating to cane guns, and the exemptions in Chapter 1 (commencing with Section 17700) of Title 2, as they relate to cane guns.
(c) Section 24510, relating to firearms that are not immediately recognizable as firearms, and the exemptions in Chapter 1 (commencing with Section 17700) of Title 2, as they relate to firearms that are not immediately recognizable as firearms.
(d) Sections 24610 and 24680, relating to undetectable firearms, and the exemptions in Chapter 1 (commencing with Section 17700) of Title 2, as they relate to undetectable firearms.
(e) Section 24710, relating to wallet guns, and the exemptions in Chapter 1 (commencing with Section 17700) of Title 2, as they relate to wallet guns.
(f) Chapter 2 (commencing with Section 30500) of Division 10, relating to assault weapons.
(g) Section 31500, relating to unconventional pistols, and the exemptions in Chapter 1 (commencing with Section 17700) of Title 2, as they relate to unconventional pistols.
(h) Sections 33215 to 33225, inclusive, relating to short-barreled rifles and short-barreled shotguns, and the exemptions in Chapter 1 (commencing with Section 17700) of Title 2, as they relate to short-barreled rifles and short-barreled shotguns.
(i) Chapter 6 (commencing with Section 32610) of Division 10, relating to machineguns.
(j) Section 33600, relating to zip guns, and the exemptions in Chapter 1 (commencing with Section 17700) of Title 2, as they relate to zip guns.
(Added by Stats. 2010, Ch. 711, Sec. 6. (SB 1080) Effective January 1, 2011. Operative January 1, 2012, by Sec. 10 of Ch. 711.)
27945.
Section 27545 does not apply to or affect the following circumstances:
(a) The transfer or loan of a firearm, other than a handgun, to a minor by the minor's parent or legal guardian.
(b) The transfer or loan of a firearm, other than a handgun, to a minor by a grandparent who is not the legal guardian of the minor, if the transfer is done with the express permission of the minor's parent or legal guardian.

(c) The loan of a firearm, other than a handgun, to a minor, with the express permission of the minor's parent or legal guardian, if the loan does not exceed 30 days in duration and is for a lawful purpose.

(d) The loan of a handgun to a minor by the minor's parent or legal guardian, if both of the following requirements are satisfied:

(1) The minor is being loaned the firearm for the purposes of engaging in a lawful, recreational sport, including, but not limited to, competitive shooting, or agricultural, ranching, or hunting activity, or a motion picture, television, or video production, or entertainment or theatrical event, the nature of which involves the use of a firearm.

(2) The duration of the loan does not exceed the amount of time that is reasonably necessary to engage in the lawful, recreational sport, including, but not limited to, competitive shooting, or agricultural, ranching, or hunting activity, or a motion picture, television, or video production, or entertainment or theatrical event, the nature of which involves the use of a firearm.

(e) The loan of a handgun to a minor by a person who is not the minor's parent or legal guardian, if all of the following requirements are satisfied:

(1) The minor is accompanied by the minor's parent or legal guardian when the loan is made, or the minor has the written consent of the minor's parent or legal guardian, which is presented at the time of the loan, or earlier.

(2) The minor is being loaned the firearm for the purpose of engaging in a lawful, recreational sport, including, but not limited to, competitive shooting, or agricultural, ranching, or hunting activity, or a motion picture, television, or video production, or entertainment or theatrical event, the nature of which involves the use of a firearm.

(3) The duration of the loan does not exceed the amount of time that is reasonably necessary to engage in the lawful, recreational sport, including, but not limited to, competitive shooting, or agricultural, ranching, or hunting activity, or a motion picture, television, or video production, or entertainment or theatrical event, the nature of which involves the use of a firearm.

(4) The duration of the loan does not, in any event, exceed 10 days.

(Added by Stats. 2010, Ch. 711, Sec. 6. (SB 1080) Effective January 1, 2011. Operative January 1, 2012, by Sec. 10 of Ch. 711.)

27950.
Section 27545 does not apply to the loan of a firearm, other than a handgun, to a licensed hunter for use by that hunter for a period of time not to exceed the duration of the hunting season for which the firearm is to be used.

(Added by Stats. 2010, Ch. 711, Sec. 6. (SB 1080) Effective January 1, 2011. Operative January 1, 2012, by Sec. 10 of Ch. 711.)

27955.
Section 27545 does not apply to the loan of a firearm if all of the following requirements are satisfied:

(a) The loan is infrequent, as defined in Section 16730.

(b) The firearm is unloaded.

(c) The loan is made by a person who is neither a dealer nor a federal firearms licensee pursuant to Chapter 44 (commencing with Section 921) of Title 18 of the United States Code.

(d) The loan is made to a person 18 years of age or older.

(e) The loan is for use solely as a prop in a motion picture, television, video, theatrical, or other entertainment production or event.

(Added by Stats. 2010, Ch. 711, Sec. 6. (SB 1080) Effective January 1, 2011. Operative January 1, 2012, by Sec. 10 of Ch. 711.)

27960.
(a) Section 27545 does not apply to the loan of a firearm if all of the following requirements are satisfied:

(1) The firearm is unloaded.

(2) The loan is made by a person who is not a dealer but is a federal firearms licensee pursuant to Chapter 44 (commencing with Section 921) of Title 18 of the United States Code.

(3) The loan is made to a person who possesses a valid entertainment firearms permit issued pursuant to Chapter 2 (commencing with Section 29500) of Division 8.

(4) The firearm is loaned for use solely as a prop in a motion picture, television, video, theatrical, or other entertainment production or event.

(b) The person loaning the firearm pursuant to this section shall retain a photocopy of the entertainment firearms permit as proof of compliance with this requirement.

(Added by Stats. 2010, Ch. 711, Sec. 6. (SB 1080) Effective January 1, 2011. Operative January 1, 2012, by Sec. 10 of Ch. 711.)

27966.
Commencing January 1, 2014, if all of the following requirements are satisfied, Section 27545 shall not apply to the sale, loan, or transfer of a firearm:

(a) The sale, loan, or transfer is infrequent, as defined in Section 16730.

(b) The firearm is not a handgun.

(c) The firearm is a curio or relic, as defined in Section 478.11 of Title 27 of the Code of Federal Regulations, or its successor.

(d) The person receiving the firearm has a current certificate of eligibility issued pursuant to Section 26710.

(e) The person receiving the firearm is licensed as a collector pursuant to Chapter 44 of Title 18 of the United States Code and the regulations issued thereto.

(f) Within 30 days of taking possession of the firearm, the person to whom it is transferred shall forward by prepaid mail, or deliver in person to the Department of Justice, a report that includes information concerning the individual taking possession of the firearm, how title was obtained and from whom, and a description of the firearm in question. The report forms that individuals complete pursuant to this section shall be provided to them by the department.

(Added by Stats. 2011, Ch. 745, Sec. 45. (AB 809) Effective January 1, 2012.)

27970.
Section 27545 does not apply to the loan of a firearm if the loan of the firearm is to a person enrolled in the course of basic training prescribed by the Commission on Peace Officer Standards and Training, or any other course certified by the commission, for purposes of participation in the course.

(Added by Stats. 2017, Ch. 783, Sec. 2. (AB 693) Effective October 14, 2017.)

ARTICLE 7. Report to Department of Justice [28000- 28000.]
(Article 7 added by Stats. 2010, Ch. 711, Sec. 6.)

28000.
A person who is exempt from Section 27545 or is otherwise not required by law to report acquisition, ownership, destruction, or disposal of a firearm, or who moves out of this state with the person's firearm, may report that information to the Department of Justice in a format prescribed by the department.

(Amended by Stats. 2013, Ch. 738, Sec. 6. (AB 538) Effective January 1, 2014.)

CHAPTER 4.1. Registration and Assignment of Firearms by Private Patrol Operators [28010 - 28024]

(Chapter 4.1 added by Stats. 2014, Ch. 423, Sec. 6.)
28010.

(a) The Legislature finds and declares that current practices and statutes authorize the purchase, registration, and ownership of firearms by an individual, but not by a business entity.

(b) It is the intent of the Legislature in enacting this chapter to allow business ownership and registration of firearms in the case of licensed Private Patrol Operators (PPOs) who are actively providing armed private contract security services. It is further the intent of the Legislature to establish procedures whereby a PPO may assign firearms it owns to its employees who are licensed to carry firearms and that assignment of a firearm by a PPO to that employee would not constitute a loan, sale, or transfer of a firearm.

(c) It is the intent of the Legislature to require notification of the Bureau of Security and Investigative Services any time a security guard is listed on the Prohibited Armed Persons File so that the bureau may proceed with appropriate action regarding the licensing of the employee.

(d) For purposes of this chapter, the following definitions apply:

(1) "Bureau" means the Bureau of Security and Investigative Services within the Department of Consumer Affairs.

(2) "Department" means the Department of Justice.

(3) "Director" means the Director of the Department of Consumer Affairs.

(4) "Private patrol operator" or "PPO" means a private patrol operator licensed pursuant to Chapter 11.5 (commencing with Section 7580) of Division 3 of the Business and Professions Code whose license is not suspended, revoked, expired, inactive, delinquent, or canceled.

(5) "Security guard" means a security guard registered pursuant to Chapter 11.5 (commencing with Section 7580) of Division 3 of the Business and Professions Code whose registration is not suspended, revoked, expired, inactive, delinquent, or canceled.

(Added by Stats. 2014, Ch. 423, Sec. 6. (AB 2220) Effective January 1, 2015. Section operative July 1, 2016, pursuant to Section 28024.)

28012.
(a) A PPO may be the registered owner of a firearm if the PPO is registered with the department pursuant to procedures established by the department.

(b) The department shall modify the department's Dealers' Record of Sale (DROS) form to allow a PPO to be listed as the purchaser and registered owner of a firearm. The form shall also require the PPO to identify its type of business formation and to include any tax identification number or other identifying number of the PPO that may be required by the department.

(c) (1) The department shall modify the department's DROS form to require the PPO to designate a "firearms custodian" for the firearm owned by the PPO that is listed in the DROS. A firearms custodian shall possess a valid firearms qualification permit issued by the bureau. A firearms custodian is responsible for the tracking, safekeeping, and inventory of those firearms of the PPO for which the custodian is designated, and shall serve as a point of contact for the department regarding the firearms for which the custodian is designated.

(2) If a firearms custodian is no longer employed by the PPO in that capacity, or otherwise becomes ineligible to be the firearms custodian, the PPO shall notify the department of that fact within seven days in a manner prescribed by the department, and the PPO shall notify the department of the designated replacement firearms custodian within 20 days of the original notice.

(d) A security guard shall possess a valid firearm qualification permit issued by the bureau prior to receiving a firearm from a PPO pursuant to a Certificate of Assignment (COA). A firearm shall be assigned by a PPO to a security guard who is employed to work for the PPO only when that employment requires the security guard to be armed.

(e) (1) (A) The department shall prescribe a "Certificate of Assignment" or "COA." The COA may include fields that are in the DROS form, and shall be used to identify the employee of the PPO who has been assigned a PPO-owned firearm by the PPO pursuant to this chapter.

(B) The COA shall also be used to identify an employee of the PPO who will use his or her own firearm in the course of his or her duties as a security guard. The COA shall not require specific information regarding an employee-owned firearm.

(2) A PPO shall register a PPO-owned firearm acquired prior to July 1, 2016, as a PPO-owned firearm in a manner prescribed by the department prior to filing a COA for that firearm.

(3) Upon the PPO assigning a firearm to an employee who is a security guard, the PPO shall complete the COA and file it with the department in a timely manner as prescribed by the department.

(f) The department shall cause the information contained on the COA to be entered into the Automated Firearms System in a timely manner. Upon termination of the employment assignment that requires the security guard to be armed and the transfer of the firearm from the security guard back to the PPO, the PPO shall complete a COA indicating that the firearm is no longer assigned to the employee and that the firearm is in the possession of the PPO and shall file the COA with the department in a timely manner, as prescribed.

(g) If a security guard becomes listed on the Prohibited Armed Persons File, the department shall immediately notify the bureau of the listing by secured electronic delivery. Upon that notification, the bureau shall take appropriate action regarding the security guard. In addition, the department shall notify the PPO, in the manner the department deems appropriate, that the PPO employee is prohibited from being armed. This chapter does not prohibit the department from also notifying the bureau if a security guard has been arrested and charged with an offense that, upon conviction, would constitute a basis for revocation of a firearms qualification permit or security guard registration.

(Added by Stats. 2014, Ch. 423, Sec. 6. (AB 2220) Effective January 1, 2015. Section operative July 1, 2016, pursuant to Section 28024.)

28014.
The department shall charge a fee not to exceed the reasonable costs to the department for filing and processing a COA, and for the costs incurred in the implementation and administration of this chapter, including, but not limited to, entering information obtained pursuant to this chapter into the Automated Firearms System and other databases as deemed necessary by the department. The fee shall be deposited in the Dealers' Record of Sale Special Account.

(Added by Stats. 2014, Ch. 423, Sec. 6. (AB 2220) Effective January 1, 2015. Section operative July 1, 2016, pursuant to Section 28024.)

28016.
(a) If the PPO ceases to do business, ceases to possess a valid PPO license issued by the bureau that is not suspended, revoked, expired, inactive, delinquent, or canceled, ceases as a business entity, or changes its type of business formation, the PPO shall, within 30 days and unless otherwise prohibited by law, lawfully sell or transfer all PPO-owned firearms.

(b) A PPO shall notify the department of the sale or transfer of a PPO-owned firearm within five business days of the transaction in a manner prescribed by the department. This subdivision shall not apply if the sale or transfer was made to or through a licensed firearms dealer pursuant to Chapter 5 (commencing with Section 28050).

(Added by Stats. 2014, Ch. 423, Sec. 6. (AB 2220) Effective January 1, 2015. Section operative July 1, 2016, pursuant to Section 28024.)

28018.
Notwithstanding any other law, an assignment of a firearm pursuant to this chapter shall not constitute a loan, sale, or transfer of a firearm.

(Added by Stats. 2014, Ch. 423, Sec. 6. (AB 2220) Effective January 1, 2015. Section operative July 1, 2016, pursuant to Section 28024.)

28020.

(a) Within 48 hours of the PPO's request, for any reason, or within 48 hours of separation of employment or revocation of the firearm qualification card, the security guard shall return to the PPO the firearm owned by the PPO and listed on a COA.

(b) The failure of a security guard to comply with subdivision (a) is a misdemeanor.

(c) If a security guard employed by a PPO does not comply with subdivision (a), the PPO shall notify the bureau within seven business days from the date that the security guard was required to return the firearm to the PPO.

(d) This chapter does not limit the right of a security guard to use, possess, or otherwise lawfully carry a firearm owned by that security guard.

(Added by Stats. 2014, Ch. 423, Sec. 6. (AB 2220) Effective January 1, 2015. Section operative July 1, 2016, pursuant to Section 28024.)

28022.

(a) The director, through his or her designee, may assess an administrative fine of up to one thousand dollars ($1,000) against a PPO or a security guard for each willful violation of this chapter. All fines collected pursuant to this chapter shall be deposited in the Private Security Services Fund.

(b) An assessment imposed pursuant to this section may be appealed pursuant to Section 7581.3 of the Business and Professions Code.

(Added by Stats. 2014, Ch. 423, Sec. 6. (AB 2220) Effective January 1, 2015. Section operative July 1, 2016, pursuant to Section 28024.)

28024.

This chapter shall become operative on July 1, 2016.

(Added by Stats. 2014, Ch. 423, Sec. 6. (AB 2220) Effective January 1, 2015. Note: This section prescribes a delayed operative date (July 1, 2016) for Chapter 4.1, commencing with Section 28010.)

CHAPTER 5. Procedure For a Private Party Firearms Transaction [28050 - 28070]

(Chapter 5 added by Stats. 2010, Ch. 711, Sec. 6.)

28050.

(a) A person shall complete any sale, loan, or transfer of a firearm through a person licensed pursuant to Sections 26700 to 26915, inclusive, in accordance with this chapter in order to comply with Section 27545.

(b) The seller or transferor or the person loaning the firearm shall deliver the firearm to the dealer who shall retain possession of that firearm.

(c) The dealer shall then deliver the firearm to the purchaser or transferee or the person being loaned the firearm, if it is not prohibited, in accordance with Section 27540.

(d) If the dealer cannot legally deliver the firearm to the purchaser or transferee or the person being loaned the firearm, the dealer shall forthwith, without waiting for the conclusion of the waiting period described in Sections 26815 and 27540, return the firearm to the transferor or seller or the person loaning the firearm. The dealer shall not return the firearm to the seller or transferor or the person loaning the firearm when to do so would constitute a violation of Section 27500, 27505, 27515, 27520, 27525, 27530, or 27535. If the dealer cannot legally return the firearm to the transferor or seller or the person loaning the firearm, then the dealer shall forthwith deliver the firearm to the sheriff of the county or the chief of police or other head of a municipal police department of any city or city and county, who shall then dispose of the firearm in the manner provided by Sections 18000, 18005, and 34000.

(Added by Stats. 2010, Ch. 711, Sec. 6. (SB 1080) Effective January 1, 2011. Operative January 1, 2012, by Sec. 10 of Ch. 711.)

28055.

(a) For a sale, loan, or transfer conducted pursuant to this chapter, the purchaser or transferee or person being loaned the firearm may be required by the dealer to pay a fee not to exceed ten dollars ($10) per firearm.

(b) No other fee may be charged by the dealer for a sale, loan, or transfer of a firearm conducted pursuant to this chapter, except for the applicable fees that may be charged pursuant to Sections 23690 and 28300 and Article 3 (commencing with Section 28200) of Chapter 6 and forwarded to the Department of Justice, and the fees set forth in Section 31650.

(c) The dealer may not charge any additional fees.

(d) Nothing in these provisions shall prevent a dealer from charging a smaller fee.

(Added by Stats. 2010, Ch. 711, Sec. 6. (SB 1080) Effective January 1, 2011. Operative January 1, 2012, by Sec. 10 of Ch. 711.)

28060.

The Attorney General shall adopt regulations under this chapter to do all of the following:

(a) Allow the seller or transferor or the person loaning the firearm, and the purchaser or transferee or the person being loaned the firearm, to complete a sale, loan, or transfer through a dealer, and to allow those persons and the dealer to preserve the confidentiality of those records and to comply with the requirements of this chapter and all of the following:

(1) Article 1 (commencing with Section 26700) and Article 2 (commencing with Section 26800) of Chapter 2.

(2) Article 1 (commencing with Section 27500) of Chapter 4.

(3) Article 2 (commencing with Section 28150) of Chapter 6.

(4) Article 3 (commencing with Section 28200) of Chapter 6.

(b) Record sufficient information for purposes of Section 11106 in the instance where a firearm is returned to a personal firearm importer because a sale or transfer of that firearm by the personal firearm importer could not be completed.

(c) Ensure that the register or record of electronic transfer shall state all of the following:

(1) The name and address of the seller or transferor of the firearm or the person loaning the firearm.

(2) Whether or not the person is a personal firearm importer.

(3) Any other information required by Article 2 (commencing with Section 28150) of Chapter 6.

(Amended by Stats. 2011, Ch. 745, Sec. 47. (AB 809) Effective January 1, 2012.)

28065.

Notwithstanding any other provision of law, a dealer who does not sell, transfer, or keep an inventory of handguns is not required to process private party transfers of handguns.

(Added by Stats. 2010, Ch. 711, Sec. 6. (SB 1080) Effective January 1, 2011. Operative January 1, 2012, by Sec. 10 of Ch. 711.)

28070.

A violation of this chapter by a dealer is a misdemeanor.

(Added by Stats. 2010, Ch. 711, Sec. 6. (SB 1080) Effective January 1, 2011. Operative January 1, 2012, by Sec. 10 of Ch. 711.)

CHAPTER 6. Recordkeeping, Background Checks, and Fees Relating to Sale, Lease, or Transfer of Firearms [28100 - 28490]

(Chapter 6 added by Stats. 2010, Ch. 711, Sec. 6.)

ARTICLE 1. General Provisions Relating to the Register or the Record of Electronic or Telephonic Transfer [28100 - 28110]

(Article 1 added by Stats. 2010, Ch. 711, Sec. 6.)

28100.

(a) As required by the Department of Justice, every dealer shall keep a register or record of electronic or telephonic transfer in which shall be entered the information prescribed in Article 2 (commencing with Section 28150).

(b) This section shall not apply to any of the following transactions:

(1) The loan of an unloaded firearm by a dealer to a person who possesses a valid entertainment firearms permit issued pursuant to Chapter 2 (commencing with Section 29500) of Division 8, for use solely as a prop in a motion picture, television, video, theatrical, or other entertainment production or event.

(2) The delivery of an unloaded firearm by a dealer to a gunsmith for service or repair.

(3) Until January 1, 2014, the sale, delivery, or transfer of an unloaded firearm, other than a handgun, by a dealer to another dealer, upon proof of compliance with the requirements of Section 27555.

(4) The sale, delivery, or transfer of an unloaded firearm by a dealer who sells, delivers, or transfers the firearm to a person who resides outside this state and is licensed pursuant to Chapter 44 (commencing with Section 921) of Title 18 of the United States Code and any regulations issued pursuant thereto.

(5) The sale, delivery, or transfer of an unloaded firearm by a dealer to a wholesaler if that firearm is being returned to the wholesaler and is intended as merchandise in the wholesaler's business.

(6) The sale, delivery, or transfer of an unloaded firearm by a dealer to another dealer, upon proof of compliance with the requirements of Section 27555, if the firearm is intended as merchandise in the receiving dealer's business.

(7) Until January 1, 2014, the sale, delivery, or transfer of an unloaded firearm, other than a handgun, by a dealer to himself or herself.

(8) The loan of an unloaded firearm by a dealer who also operates a target facility which holds a business or regulatory license on the premises of the building designated in the license or whose building designated in the license is on the premises of any club or organization organized for the purpose of practicing shooting at targets upon established ranges, whether public or private, to a person at that target facility or club or organization, if the firearm is kept at all times within the premises of the target range or on the premises of the club or organization.

(9) The loan of an unloaded firearm by a dealer to a consultant-evaluator, if the loan does not exceed 45 days from the date of delivery of the firearm by the dealer to the consultant-evaluator.

(10) The return of an unloaded firearm to the owner of that firearm by a dealer, if the owner initially delivered the firearm to the dealer for service or repair.

(11) The sale, delivery, or transfer of an unloaded firearm by a dealer to a person licensed as an importer or manufacturer pursuant to Chapter 44 (commencing with Section 921) of Title 18 of the United States Code and any regulations issued pursuant thereto.

(c) A violation of this section is a misdemeanor.

(Amended by Stats. 2011, Ch. 745, Sec. 48. (AB 809) Effective January 1, 2012.)

28105.

(a) (1) The register required by Section 28100 shall be prepared by and obtained from the State Printer.

(2) The State Printer shall furnish the register only to dealers on application, at a cost to be determined by the Department of General Services.

(3) The Department of General Services shall determine the cost for each 100 leaves in quadruplicate, one original and three duplicates for the making of carbon copies.

(4) The original and duplicate copies shall differ in color, and shall be in the form provided by this chapter.

(b) Where the electronic transfer of applicant information is used, the Department of Justice shall develop the standards for all appropriate electronic equipment and telephone numbers to effect the transfer of information to the department.

(Added by Stats. 2010, Ch. 711, Sec. 6. (SB 1080) Effective January 1, 2011. Operative January 1, 2012, by Sec. 10 of Ch. 711.)

28110.

(a) The State Printer upon issuing a register shall forward to the Department of Justice both of the following:

(1) The name and business address of the dealer.

(2) The series and sheet numbers of the register.

(b) The register shall not be transferable.

(c) If the dealer moves the business to a different location, the dealer shall notify the department of that fact in writing within 48 hours.

(Added by Stats. 2010, Ch. 711, Sec. 6. (SB 1080) Effective January 1, 2011. Operative January 1, 2012, by Sec. 10 of Ch. 711.)

ARTICLE 2. Form of the Register or the Record of Electronic Transfer [28150 - 28180]

(Article 2 added by Stats. 2010, Ch. 711, Sec. 6.)

28150.

As used in this article, the following words have the following meanings:

(a) "Purchase" means the purchase, loan, or transfer of a firearm.

(b) "Purchaser" means the purchaser or transferee of a firearm or the person being loaned a firearm.

(c) "Sale" means the sale, loan, or transfer of a firearm.

(Added by Stats. 2010, Ch. 711, Sec. 6. (SB 1080) Effective January 1, 2011. Operative January 1, 2012, by Sec. 10 of Ch. 711.)

28155.

The Department of Justice shall prescribe the form of the register and the record of electronic transfer pursuant to Section 28105.

(Added by Stats. 2010, Ch. 711, Sec. 6. (SB 1080) Effective January 1, 2011. Operative January 1, 2012, by Sec. 10 of Ch. 711.)

28160.

(a) For all firearms, the register or record of electronic transfer shall include all of the following information:

(1) The date and time of sale.

(2) The make of firearm.

(3) Peace officer exemption status pursuant to the provisions listed in subdivision (c) of Section 16585, and the agency name.

(4) Any applicable waiting period exemption information.

(5) California Firearms Dealer number issued pursuant to Article 1 (commencing with Section 26700) of Chapter 2.

(6) For transactions occurring on or after January 1, 2003, the purchaser's handgun safety certificate number issued pursuant to Article 2 (commencing with Section 31610) of Chapter 4 of Division 10 of this title, or pursuant to former Article 8 (commencing with Section 12800) of Chapter 6 of Title 2 of Part 4, as that article read at any time from when it became operative on January 1, 2003, to when it was repealed by the Deadly Weapons Recodification Act of 2010.

(7) Manufacturer's name if stamped on the firearm.

(8) Model name or number, if stamped on the firearm.

(9) Serial number, if applicable.

(10) Other number, if more than one serial number is stamped on the firearm.

(11) Any identification number or mark assigned to the firearm pursuant to Section 23910.
(12) If the firearm is not a handgun and does not have a serial number, identification number, or mark assigned to it, a notation as to that fact.
(13) Caliber.
(14) Type of firearm.
(15) If the firearm is new or used.
(16) Barrel length.
(17) Color of the firearm.
(18) Full name of purchaser.
(19) Purchaser's complete date of birth.
(20) Purchaser's local address.
(21) If current address is temporary, complete permanent address of purchaser.
(22) Identification of purchaser.
(23) Purchaser's place of birth (state or country).
(24) Purchaser's complete telephone number.
(25) Purchaser's occupation.
(26) Purchaser's gender.
(27) Purchaser's physical description.
(28) All legal names and aliases ever used by the purchaser.
(29) Yes or no answer to questions that prohibit purchase, including, but not limited to, conviction of a felony as described in Chapter 2 (commencing with Section 29800) or an offense described in Chapter 3 (commencing with Section 29900) of Division 9 of this title, the purchaser's status as a person described in Section 8100 of the Welfare and Institutions Code, whether the purchaser is a person who has been adjudicated by a court to be a danger to others or found not guilty by reason of insanity, and whether the purchaser is a person who has been found incompetent to stand trial or placed under conservatorship by a court pursuant to Section 8103 of the Welfare and Institutions Code.
(30) Signature of purchaser.
(31) Signature of salesperson, as a witness to the purchaser's signature.
(32) Salesperson's certificate of eligibility number, if the salesperson has obtained a certificate of eligibility.
(33) Name and complete address of the dealer or firm selling the firearm as shown on the dealer's license.
(34) The establishment number, if assigned.
(35) The dealer's complete business telephone number.
(36) Any information required by Chapter 5 (commencing with Section 28050).
(37) Any information required to determine whether subdivision (f) of Section 27540 applies.
(38) A statement of the penalties for signing a fictitious name or address, knowingly furnishing any incorrect information, or knowingly omitting any information required to be provided for the register.
(39) A statement informing the purchaser, after his or her ownership of a firearm, of all of the following:
(A) Upon his or her application, the Department of Justice shall furnish him or her any information reported to the department as it relates to his or her ownership of that firearm.
(B) The purchaser is entitled to file a report of his or her acquisition, disposition, or ownership of a firearm with the department pursuant to Section 28000.
(C) Instructions for accessing the department's Internet Web site for more information.
(40) For transactions on and after January 1, 2015, the purchaser's firearm safety certificate number, except that in the case of a handgun, the number from an unexpired handgun safety certificate may be used.
(b) The purchaser shall provide the purchaser's right thumbprint on the register in a manner prescribed by the department. No exception to this requirement shall be permitted except by regulations adopted by the department.
(c) The firearms dealer shall record on the register or record of electronic transfer the date that the firearm is delivered, together with the firearm dealer's signature indicating delivery of the firearm.
(d) The purchaser shall sign the register or the record of electronic transfer on the date that the firearm is delivered to him or her.
(Amended by Stats. 2013, Ch. 761, Sec. 11.5. (SB 683) Effective January 1, 2014.)
28170.
Where the register is used, the following shall apply:
(a) Dealers shall use ink to complete each document.
(b) The dealer or salesperson making a sale shall ensure that all information is provided legibly. The dealer and salespersons shall be informed that incomplete or illegible information will delay sales.
(c) Each dealer shall be provided instructions regarding the procedure for completion of the form and routing of the form. Dealers shall comply with these instructions, which shall include the information set forth in this section.
(d) One firearm transaction shall be reported on each record of sale document.
(Amended by Stats. 2011, Ch. 745, Sec. 51. (AB 809) Effective January 1, 2012.)
28175.
The dealer or salesperson making a sale shall ensure that all required information has been obtained from the purchaser. The dealer and all salespersons shall be informed that incomplete information will delay sales.
(Added by Stats. 2010, Ch. 711, Sec. 6. (SB 1080) Effective January 1, 2011. Operative January 1, 2012, by Sec. 10 of Ch. 711.)
28180.
(a) The purchaser's name, date of birth, and driver's license or identification number shall be obtained electronically from the magnetic strip on the purchaser's driver's license or identification and shall not be supplied by any other means, except as authorized by the department.
(b) The requirement of subdivision (a) shall not apply in either of the following cases:
(1) The purchaser's identification consists of a military identification card.
(2) Due to technical limitations, the magnetic strip reader is unable to obtain the required information from the purchaser's identification. In those circumstances, the firearms dealer shall obtain a photocopy of the identification as proof of compliance.
(c) In the event that the dealer has reported to the department that the dealer's equipment has failed, information pursuant to this section shall be obtained by an alternative method to be determined by the department.
(Amended by Stats. 2011, Ch. 745, Sec. 52. (AB 809) Effective January 1, 2012.)

ARTICLE 3. Submission of Fees and Firearm Purchaser Information to the Department of Justice [28200 - 28255]
(Article 3 added by Stats. 2010, Ch. 711, Sec. 6.)
28200.
As used in this article, the following words have the following meanings:
(a) "Purchase" means the purchase, loan, or transfer of a firearm.
(b) "Purchaser" means the purchaser or transferee of a firearm or the person being loaned a firearm.
(c) "Sale" means the sale, loan, or transfer of a firearm.
(d) "Seller" means, if the transaction is being conducted pursuant to Chapter 5 (commencing with Section 28050), the person selling, loaning, or transferring the firearm.
(Added by Stats. 2010, Ch. 711, Sec. 6. (SB 1080) Effective January 1, 2011. Operative January 1, 2012, by Sec. 10 of Ch. 711.)
28205.

(a) Until January 1, 1998, the Department of Justice shall determine the method by which a dealer shall submit firearm purchaser information to the department. The information shall be in one of the following formats:
(1) Submission of the register described in Article 2 (commencing with Section 28150).
(2) Electronic or telephonic transfer of the information contained in the register described in Article 2 (commencing with Section 28150).
(b) On or after January 1, 1998, electronic or telephonic transfer, including voice or facsimile transmission, shall be the exclusive means by which purchaser information is transmitted to the department.
(c) On or after January 1, 2003, except as permitted by the department, electronic transfer shall be the exclusive means by which information is transmitted to the department. Telephonic transfer shall not be permitted for information regarding sales of any firearms.
(Added by Stats. 2010, Ch. 711, Sec. 6. (SB 1080) Effective January 1, 2011. Operative January 1, 2012, by Sec. 10 of Ch. 711.)
28210.
(a) (1) Where the register is used, the purchaser of any firearm shall be required to present to the dealer clear evidence of the person's identity and age.
(2) The dealer shall require the purchaser to sign the purchaser's current legal name and affix the purchaser's residence address and date of birth to the register in quadruplicate.
(3) The salesperson shall sign the register in quadruplicate, as a witness to the signature and identification of the purchaser.
(b) Any person furnishing a fictitious name or address, knowingly furnishing any incorrect information, or knowingly omitting any information required to be provided for the register shall be punished as provided in Section 28250.
(c) (1) The original of the register shall be retained by the dealer in consecutive order.
(2) Each book of 50 originals shall become the permanent register of transactions, which shall be retained for not less than three years from the date of the last transaction.
(3) Upon presentation of proper identification, the permanent register of transactions shall be available for inspection by any peace officer, Department of Justice employee designated by the Attorney General, or agent of the federal Bureau of Alcohol, Tobacco, Firearms and Explosives. Until January 1, 2014, no information shall be compiled therefrom regarding the purchasers or other transferees of firearms that are not handguns.
(d) On the date of the application to purchase, two copies of the original sheet of the register shall be placed in the mail, postage prepaid, and properly addressed to the Department of Justice.
(e) (1) A photocopy of the register shall be provided to the purchaser by the dealer at the time of delivery of the firearm and after the dealer notes the date of delivery and the dealer's signature indicating delivery of the firearm, and the purchaser acknowledges the receipt of the firearm.
(2) The requirements of this subdivision apply if a dealer is delivering a firearm pursuant to Section 27540 or Chapter 5 (commencing with Section 28050).
(f) If the transaction is a private party transfer conducted pursuant to Chapter 5 (commencing with Section 28050), a photocopy of the original shall be provided to the seller by the dealer at the time the register is signed by the seller. The dealer shall redact all of the purchaser's personal information, as required pursuant to subdivision (a) of Section 28160 and subdivision (a) of Section 28165, from the seller's copy, and the seller's personal information from the purchaser's copy.
(Amended by Stats. 2013, Ch. 738, Sec. 8. (AB 538) Effective January 1, 2014.)
28215.
(a) (1) Where the electronic or telephonic transfer of applicant information is used, the purchaser shall be required to present to the dealer clear evidence of the person's identity and age.
(2) The dealer shall require the purchaser to sign the purchaser's current legal name to the record of electronic or telephonic transfer.
(3) The salesperson shall sign the record of electronic or telephonic transfer, as a witness to the signature and identification of the purchaser.
(b) Any person furnishing a fictitious name or address, knowingly furnishing any incorrect information, or knowingly omitting any information required to be provided for the electronic or telephonic transfer shall be punished as provided in Section 28250.
(c) (1) The original of each record of electronic or telephonic transfer shall be retained by the dealer in consecutive order.
(2) Each original shall become the permanent record of the transaction, which shall be retained for not less than three years from the date of the last transaction.
(3) Upon presentation of proper identification, the permanent record of the transaction shall be provided for inspection by any peace officer, Department of Justice employee designated by the Attorney General, or agent of the federal Bureau of Alcohol, Tobacco, Firearms and Explosives.
(d) On the date of the application to purchase, the record of applicant information shall be transmitted to the Department of Justice by electronic or telephonic transfer.
(e) (1) A copy of the record of electronic or telephonic transfer shall be provided to the purchaser by the dealer at the time of delivery of the firearm and after the dealer notes the date of delivery and the dealer's signature indicating delivery of the firearm, and the purchaser acknowledges the receipt of the firearm.
(2) The requirements of this subdivision apply if a dealer is delivering a firearm pursuant to Section 27540 or Chapter 5 (commencing with Section 28050).
(f) If the transaction is a private party transfer conducted pursuant to Chapter 5 (commencing with Section 28050), a copy shall be provided to the seller by the dealer at the time the record of electronic or telephonic transfer is signed by the seller. The dealer shall redact all of the purchaser's personal information, as required pursuant to subdivision (a) of Section 28160 and subdivision (a) of Section 28165, from the seller's copy, and the seller's personal information from the purchaser's copy.
(Amended by Stats. 2013, Ch. 738, Sec. 9. (AB 538) Effective January 1, 2014.)
28220.
(a) Upon submission of firearm purchaser information, the Department of Justice shall examine its records, as well as those records that it is authorized to request from the State Department of State Hospitals pursuant to Section 8104 of the Welfare and Institutions Code, in order to determine if the purchaser is a person described in subdivision (a) of Section 27535, or is prohibited by state or federal law from possessing, receiving, owning, or purchasing a firearm.
(b) The Department of Justice shall participate in the National Instant Criminal Background Check System (NICS), as described in subsection (t) of Section 922 of Title 18 of the United States Code, and shall notify the dealer and the chief of the police department of the city or city and county in which the sale was made, or if the sale was made in a district in which there is no municipal police department, the sheriff of the county in which the sale was made, that the purchaser is a person prohibited from acquiring a firearm under federal law.
(c) If the department determines that the purchaser is prohibited by state or federal law from possessing, receiving, owning, or purchasing a firearm or is a person described in subdivision (a) of Section 27535, it shall immediately notify the dealer and the chief of the police department of the city or city and county in which the sale was made, or if the sale was made in a district in which there is no municipal police department, the sheriff of the county in which the sale was made, of that fact.
(d) If the department determines that the copies of the register submitted to it pursuant to subdivision (d) of Section 28210 contain any blank spaces or inaccurate, illegible, or incomplete information, preventing identification of the purchaser or the handgun or

other firearm to be purchased, or if any fee required pursuant to Section 28225 is not submitted by the dealer in conjunction with submission of copies of the register, the department may notify the dealer of that fact. Upon notification by the department, the dealer shall submit corrected copies of the register to the department, or shall submit any fee required pursuant to Section 28225, or both, as appropriate and, if notification by the department is received by the dealer at any time prior to delivery of the firearm to be purchased, the dealer shall withhold delivery until the conclusion of the waiting period described in Sections 26815 and 27540.

(e) If the department determines that the information transmitted to it pursuant to Section 28215 contains inaccurate or incomplete information preventing identification of the purchaser or the handgun or other firearm to be purchased, or if the fee required pursuant to Section 28225 is not transmitted by the dealer in conjunction with transmission of the electronic or telephonic record, the department may notify the dealer of that fact. Upon notification by the department, the dealer shall transmit corrections to the record of electronic or telephonic transfer to the department, or shall transmit any fee required pursuant to Section 28225, or both, as appropriate, and if notification by the department is received by the dealer at any time prior to delivery of the firearm to be purchased, the dealer shall withhold delivery until the conclusion of the waiting period described in Sections 26815 and 27540.

(f) (1) (A) The department shall immediately notify the dealer to delay the transfer of the firearm to the purchaser if the records of the department, or the records available to the department in the National Instant Criminal Background Check System, indicate one of the following:

(i) The purchaser has been taken into custody and placed in a facility for mental health treatment or evaluation and may be a person described in Section 8100 or 8103 of the Welfare and Institutions Code and the department is unable to ascertain whether the purchaser is a person who is prohibited from possessing, receiving, owning, or purchasing a firearm, pursuant to Section 8100 or 8103 of the Welfare and Institutions Code, prior to the conclusion of the waiting period described in Sections 26815 and 27540.

(ii) The purchaser has been arrested for, or charged with, a crime that would make him or her, if convicted, a person who is prohibited by state or federal law from possessing, receiving, owning, or purchasing a firearm, and the department is unable to ascertain whether the purchaser was convicted of that offense prior to the conclusion of the waiting period described in Sections 26815 and 27540.

(iii) The purchaser may be a person described in subdivision (a) of Section 27535, and the department is unable to ascertain whether the purchaser, in fact, is a person described in subdivision (a) of Section 27535, prior to the conclusion of the waiting period described in Sections 26815 and 27540.

(B) The dealer shall provide the purchaser with information about the manner in which he or she may contact the department regarding the delay described in subparagraph (A).

(2) The department shall notify the purchaser by mail regarding the delay and explain the process by which the purchaser may obtain a copy of the criminal or mental health record the department has on file for the purchaser. Upon receipt of that criminal or mental health record, the purchaser shall report any inaccuracies or incompleteness to the department on an approved form.

(3) If the department ascertains the final disposition of the arrest or criminal charge, or the outcome of the mental health treatment or evaluation, or the purchaser's eligibility to purchase a firearm, as described in paragraph (1), after the waiting period described in Sections 26815 and 27540, but within 30 days of the dealer's original submission of the purchaser information to the department pursuant to this section, the department shall do the following:

(A) If the purchaser is not a person described in subdivision (a) of Section 27535, and is not prohibited by state or federal law, including, but not limited to, Section 8100 or 8103 of the Welfare and Institutions Code, from possessing, receiving, owning, or purchasing a firearm, the department shall immediately notify the dealer of that fact and the dealer may then immediately transfer the firearm to the purchaser, upon the dealer's recording on the register or record of electronic transfer the date that the firearm is transferred, the dealer signing the register or record of electronic transfer indicating delivery of the firearm to that purchaser, and the purchaser signing the register or record of electronic transfer acknowledging the receipt of the firearm on the date that the firearm is delivered to him or her.

(B) If the purchaser is a person described in subdivision (a) of Section 27535, or is prohibited by state or federal law, including, but not limited to, Section 8100 or 8103 of the Welfare and Institutions Code, from possessing, receiving, owning, or purchasing a firearm, the department shall immediately notify the dealer and the chief of the police department in the city or city and county in which the sale was made, or if the sale was made in a district in which there is no municipal police department, the sheriff of the county in which the sale was made, of that fact in compliance with subdivision (c) of Section 28220.

(4) If the department is unable to ascertain the final disposition of the arrest or criminal charge, or the outcome of the mental health treatment or evaluation, or the purchaser's eligibility to purchase a firearm, as described in paragraph (1), within 30 days of the dealer's original submission of purchaser information to the department pursuant to this section, the department shall immediately notify the dealer and the dealer may then immediately transfer the firearm to the purchaser, upon the dealer's recording on the register or record of electronic transfer the date that the firearm is transferred, the dealer signing the register or record of electronic transfer indicating delivery of the firearm to that purchaser, and the purchaser signing the register or record of electronic transfer acknowledging the receipt of the firearm on the date that the firearm is delivered to him or her.

(g) Commencing July 1, 2017, upon receipt of information demonstrating that a person is prohibited from possessing a firearm pursuant to federal or state law, the department shall submit the name, date of birth, and physical description of the person to the National Instant Criminal Background Check System Index, Denied Persons Files. The information provided shall remain privileged and confidential, and shall not be disclosed, except for the purpose of enforcing federal or state firearms laws.

(Amended November 8, 2016, by initiative Proposition 63, Sec. 5.1.)
28225.

(a) The Department of Justice may require the dealer to charge each firearm purchaser a fee not to exceed fourteen dollars ($14), except that the fee may be increased at a rate not to exceed any increase in the California Consumer Price Index as compiled and reported by the Department of Industrial Relations.

(b) The fee under subdivision (a) shall be no more than is necessary to fund the following:

(1) The department for the cost of furnishing this information.

(2) The department for the cost of meeting its obligations under paragraph (2) of subdivision (b) of Section 8100 of the Welfare and Institutions Code.

(3) Local mental health facilities for state-mandated local costs resulting from the reporting requirements imposed by Section 8103 of the Welfare and Institutions Code.

(4) The State Department of State Hospitals for the costs resulting from the requirements imposed by Section 8104 of the Welfare and Institutions Code.

(5) Local mental hospitals, sanitariums, and institutions for state-mandated local costs resulting from the reporting requirements imposed by Section 8105 of the Welfare and Institutions Code.

(6) Local law enforcement agencies for state-mandated local costs resulting from the notification requirements set forth in subdivision (a) of Section 6385 of the Family Code.

(7) Local law enforcement agencies for state-mandated local costs resulting from the notification requirements set forth in subdivision (c) of Section 8105 of the Welfare and Institutions Code.

(8) For the actual costs associated with the electronic or telephonic transfer of information pursuant to Section 28215.

(9) The Department of Food and Agriculture for the costs resulting from the notification provisions set forth in Section 5343.5 of the Food and Agricultural Code.

(10) The department for the costs associated with subdivisions (d) and (e) of Section 27560.

(11) The department for the costs associated with funding Department of Justice firearms-related regulatory and enforcement activities related to the sale, purchase, possession, loan, or transfer of firearms pursuant to any provision listed in Section 16580.

(c) The fee established pursuant to this section shall not exceed the sum of the actual processing costs of the department, the estimated reasonable costs of the local mental health facilities for complying with the reporting requirements imposed by paragraph (3) of subdivision (b), the costs of the State Department of State Hospitals for complying with the requirements imposed by paragraph (4) of subdivision (b), the estimated reasonable costs of local mental hospitals, sanitariums, and institutions for complying with the reporting requirements imposed by paragraph (5) of subdivision (b), the estimated reasonable costs of local law enforcement agencies for complying with the notification requirements set forth in subdivision (a) of Section 6385 of the Family Code, the estimated reasonable costs of local law enforcement agencies for complying with the notification requirements set forth in subdivision (c) of Section 8105 of the Welfare and Institutions Code imposed by paragraph (7) of subdivision (b), the estimated reasonable costs of the Department of Food and Agriculture for the costs resulting from the notification provisions set forth in Section 5343.5 of the Food and Agricultural Code, the estimated reasonable costs of the department for the costs associated with subdivisions (d) and (e) of Section 27560, and the estimated reasonable costs of department firearms-related regulatory and enforcement activities related to the sale, purchase, possession, loan, or transfer of firearms pursuant to any provision listed in Section 16580.

(d) Where the electronic or telephonic transfer of applicant information is used, the department shall establish a system to be used for the submission of the fees described in this section to the department.

(Amended by Stats. 2012, Ch. 24, Sec. 57. (AB 1470) Effective June 27, 2012.)
28230.

(a) The Department of Justice may charge a fee sufficient to reimburse it for each of the following but not to exceed fourteen dollars ($14), except that the fee may be increased at a rate not to exceed any increase in the California Consumer Price Index as compiled and reported by the Department of Industrial Relations:

(1) For the actual costs associated with the preparation, sale, processing, and filing of forms or reports required or utilized pursuant to any provision listed in subdivision (a) of Section 16585.

(2) For the actual processing costs associated with the submission of a Dealers' Record of Sale to the department.

(3) For the actual costs associated with the preparation, sale, processing, and filing of reports utilized pursuant to Section 26905, 27565, 27875, 27966, or 28000, paragraph (1) of subdivision (a) of Section 27560, or paragraphs (1) and (2) of subdivision (a) of, and subdivisions (b), (c), and (d) of, Section 27920.

(4) For the actual costs associated with the electronic or telephonic transfer of information pursuant to Section 28215.

(b) If the department charges a fee pursuant to paragraph (2) of subdivision (a), it shall be charged in the same amount to all categories of transaction that are within that paragraph.

(c) Any costs incurred by the Department of Justice to implement this section shall be reimbursed from fees collected and charged pursuant to this section. No fees shall be charged to the dealer pursuant to Section 28225 for implementing this section.

(Amended by Stats. 2014, Ch. 878, Sec. 9. (AB 1609) Effective January 1, 2015.)
28235.

All moneys received by the department pursuant to this article shall be deposited in the Dealers' Record of Sale Special Account of the General Fund, which is hereby created, to be available, upon appropriation by the Legislature, for expenditure by the department to offset the costs incurred pursuant to any of the following:

(a) This article.

(b) Section 18910.

(c) Section 27555.

(d) Subdivisions (d) and (e) of Section 27560.

(e) Chapter 4.1 (commencing with Section 28010).

(f) Article 6 (commencing with Section 28450).

(g) Section 31110.

(h) Section 31115.

(i) Subdivision (a) of Section 32020.

(j) Section 32670.

(k) Section 33320.

(Amended by Stats. 2014, Ch. 423, Sec. 7. (AB 2220) Effective January 1, 2015.)
28240.

(a) Until January 1, 2014, only one fee shall be charged pursuant to this article for a single transaction on the same date for the sale of any number of firearms that are not handguns, or for the taking of possession of those firearms.

(b) Beginning January 1, 2014, only one fee shall be charged pursuant to this article for a single transaction on the same date for taking title or possession of any number of firearms.

(Amended by Stats. 2012, Ch. 691, Sec. 1. (AB 1559) Effective January 1, 2013.)
28245.

Whenever the Department of Justice acts pursuant to this article as it pertains to firearms other than handguns, the department's acts or omissions shall be deemed to be discretionary within the meaning of the Government Claims Act pursuant to Division 3.6 (commencing with Section 810) of Title 1 of the Government Code.

(Amended by Stats. 2012, Ch. 759, Sec. 8. (AB 2690) Effective January 1, 2013.)
28250.

(a) Any person who does any of the following is guilty of a misdemeanor:

(1) Furnishing a fictitious name or address for the register under Section 28210 or the electronic or telephonic transfer under Section 28215.

(2) Knowingly furnishing any incorrect information for the register under Section 28210 or the electronic or telephonic transfer under Section 28215.

(3) Knowingly omitting any information required to be provided for the register under Section 28210 or the electronic or telephonic transfer under Section 28215.

(4) Violating any provision of this article.

(b) Notwithstanding subdivision (a), any person who is prohibited from obtaining a firearm pursuant to Chapter 2 (commencing with Section 29800) or Chapter 3 (commencing with Section 29900) of Division 9 of this title, or Section 8100 or 8103 of the Welfare and Institutions Code, who does any of the following shall be punished by imprisonment in a county jail not exceeding one year or imprisonment pursuant to subdivision (h) of Section 1170 for a term of 8, 12, or 18 months:

(1) Knowingly furnishes a fictitious name or address for the register under Section 28210 or the electronic or telephonic transfer under Section 28215.

(2) Knowingly furnishes any incorrect information for the register under Section 28210 or the electronic or telephonic transfer under Section 28215.

(3) Knowingly omits any information required to be provided for the register under Section 28210 or the electronic or telephonic transfer under Section 28215.
(Amended by Stats. 2011, Ch. 15, Sec. 546. (AB 109) Effective April 4, 2011. Amending action operative October 1, 2011, by Sec. 636 of Ch. 15, as amended by Stats. 2011, Ch. 39, Sec. 68. Section operative January 1, 2012, pursuant to Stats. 2010, Ch. 711, Sec. 10.)

28255.
Commencing January 1, 2014, if after the conclusion of the waiting period described in Sections 26815 and 27540, the individual named in the application as the purchaser of the firearm takes possession of the firearm set forth in the application to purchase, the dealer shall notify the Department of Justice of that fact in a manner and within a time period specified by the department, and with sufficient information to identify the purchaser and the firearm that the purchaser took possession of.
(Added by Stats. 2013, Ch. 737, Sec. 9. (AB 500) Effective January 1, 2014.)

ARTICLE 4. Firearms Safety and Enforcement Special Fund [28300-28300.]
(Article 4 added by Stats. 2010, Ch. 711, Sec. 6.)

28300.
(a) The Firearms Safety and Enforcement Special Fund is hereby established in the State Treasury and shall be administered by the Department of Justice.
(b) The Department of Justice may require firearms dealers to charge each person who obtains a firearm a fee not to exceed five dollars ($5) for each transaction, except that the fee may be increased at a rate not to exceed any increase in the California Consumer Price Index as compiled and reported by the Department of Industrial Relations, and not to exceed the reasonable cost of regulation to the department. Revenues from this fee shall be deposited in the Firearms Safety and Enforcement Special Fund.
(c) Revenue deposited into the Firearms Safety and Enforcement Special Fund shall be available for expenditure by the Department of Justice upon appropriation by the Legislature for the purpose of implementing and enforcing the provisions of Article 2 (commencing with Section 31610) of Chapter 4 of Division 10, enforcing Section 830.95, Title 2 (commencing with Section 12001) of Part 4, Sections 16000 to 16960, inclusive, Sections 16970 to 17230, inclusive, Sections 17240 to 21390, inclusive, and Sections 21590 to 34370, inclusive, and for the establishment, maintenance, and upgrading of equipment and services necessary for firearms dealers to comply with Article 2 (commencing with Section 28150).
(Amended by Stats. 2016, Ch. 33, Sec. 38. (SB 843) Effective June 27, 2016.)

ARTICLE 5. Exceptions Relating to Law Enforcement [28400 - 28415]
(Article 5 added by Stats. 2010, Ch. 711, Sec. 6.)

28400.
(a) Article 1 (commencing with Section 28100), Article 2 (commencing with Section 28150), Article 3 (commencing with Section 28200), and Article 4 (commencing with Section 28300) do not apply to any sale, delivery, or transfer of firearms made to an authorized law enforcement representative of any city, county, city and county, or state, or of the federal government, for exclusive use by that governmental agency if, prior to the sale, delivery, or transfer of these firearms, written authorization from the head of the agency authorizing the transaction is presented to the person from whom the purchase, delivery, or transfer is being made.
(b) Proper written authorization is defined as verifiable written certification from the head of the agency by which the purchaser or transferee is employed, identifying the employee as an individual authorized to conduct the transaction, and authorizing the transaction for the exclusive use of the agency by which that person is employed.
(c) Within 10 days of the date a handgun, and commencing January 1, 2014, any firearm, is acquired by the agency, a record of the same shall be entered as an institutional weapon into the Automated Firearms System (AFS) via the California Law Enforcement Telecommunications System (CLETS) by the law enforcement or state agency. Any agency without access to AFS shall arrange with the sheriff of the county in which the agency is located to input this information via this system.
(Amended by Stats. 2011, Ch. 745, Sec. 59. (AB 809) Effective January 1, 2012.)

28405.
Article 1 (commencing with Section 28100), Article 2 (commencing with Section 28150), Article 3 (commencing with Section 28200), and Article 4 (commencing with Section 28300) do not apply to the loan of a firearm if all of the following conditions are satisfied:
(a) The loan is made by an authorized law enforcement representative of a city, county, or city and county, or of the state or federal government.
(b) The loan is made to a peace officer employed by that agency and authorized to carry a firearm.
(c) The loan is made for the carrying and use of that firearm by that peace officer in the course and scope of the officer's duties.
(Added by Stats. 2010, Ch. 711, Sec. 6. (SB 1080) Effective January 1, 2011. Operative January 1, 2012, by Sec. 10 of Ch. 711.)

28410.
(a) Article 1 (commencing with Section 28100), Article 2 (commencing with Section 28150), Article 3 (commencing with Section 28200), and Article 4 (commencing with Section 28300) do not apply to the sale, delivery, or transfer of a firearm by a law enforcement agency to a peace officer pursuant to Section 10334 of the Public Contract Code.
(b) Within 10 days of the date that a handgun, and commencing January 1, 2014, any firearm, is sold, delivered, or transferred pursuant to Section 10334 of the Public Contract Code to that peace officer, the name of the officer and the make, model, serial number, and other identifying characteristics of the firearm being sold, delivered, or transferred shall be entered into the Automated Firearms System (AFS) via the California Law Enforcement Telecommunications System (CLETS) by the law enforcement or state agency that sold, delivered, or transferred the firearm, provided, however, that if the firearm is not a handgun and does not have a serial number, identification number, or identification mark assigned to it, that fact shall be noted in AFS. Any agency without access to AFS shall arrange with the sheriff of the county in which the agency is located to input this information via this system.
(Amended by Stats. 2011, Ch. 745, Sec. 60. (AB 809) Effective January 1, 2012.)

28415.
(a) Article 1 (commencing with Section 28100), Article 2 (commencing with Section 28150), Article 3 (commencing with Section 28200), and Article 4 (commencing with Section 28300) do not apply to the sale, delivery, or transfer of a firearm by a law enforcement agency to a retiring peace officer who is authorized to carry a firearm pursuant to Chapter 5 (commencing with Section 26300) of Division 5.
(b) Within 10 days of the date that a handgun, and commencing January 1, 2014, any firearm, is sold, delivered, or transferred to that retiring peace officer, the name of the officer and the make, model, serial number, and other identifying characteristics of the firearm being sold, delivered, or transferred shall be entered into the Automated Firearms System (AFS) via the California Law Enforcement Telecommunications System (CLETS) by the law enforcement or state agency that sold, delivered, or transferred the firearm, provided, however, that if the firearm is not a handgun and does not have a serial number, identification number, or identification mark assigned to it, that fact shall be noted in AFS. Any agency without access to AFS shall arrange with the sheriff of the county in which the agency is located to input this information via this system.
(Amended by Stats. 2011, Ch. 745, Sec. 61. (AB 809) Effective January 1, 2012.)

ARTICLE 6. Centralized List of Exempted Federal Firearms Licensees [28450 - 28490]
(Article 6 added by Stats. 2010, Ch. 711, Sec. 6.)

28450.
(a) Commencing January 1, 2008, the Department of Justice shall keep a centralized list of persons who identify themselves as being licensed pursuant to Chapter 44 (commencing with Section 921) of Title 18 of the United States Code as a dealer, importer, or manufacturer of firearms whose licensed premises are within this state and who declare to the department an exemption from the firearms dealer licensing requirements of Section 26500.
(b) The list shall be known as the centralized list of exempted federal firearms licensees.
(c) To qualify for placement on the centralized list, an applicant shall do all of the following:
(1) Possess a valid federal firearms license pursuant to Chapter 44 (commencing with Section 921) of Title 18 of the United States Code as a dealer, importer, or manufacturer of firearms.
(2) Possess a current, valid certificate of eligibility pursuant to Section 26710.
(3) Maintain with the department a signed declaration enumerating the applicant's statutory exemptions from licensing requirements of Section 26500.
(Added by Stats. 2010, Ch. 711, Sec. 6. (SB 1080) Effective January 1, 2011. Operative January 1, 2012, by Sec. 10 of Ch. 711.)

28455.
Any person furnishing a fictitious name, knowingly furnishing any incorrect information, or knowingly omitting any information for the declaration under paragraph (3) of subdivision (c) of Section 28450 shall be guilty of a misdemeanor.
(Added by Stats. 2010, Ch. 711, Sec. 6. (SB 1080) Effective January 1, 2011. Operative January 1, 2012, by Sec. 10 of Ch. 711.)

28460.
(a) Commencing January 1, 2008, the department shall assess an annual fee of one hundred fifteen dollars ($115) to cover its costs of maintaining the centralized list of exempted federal firearms licensees prescribed by Section 28450, conducting inspections in accordance with this article, and for the cost of maintaining the firearm shipment verification number system described in Section 27555.
(b) The department may increase the fee at a rate not to exceed the increase in the California Consumer Price Index as compiled and reported by the Department of Industrial Relations.
(c) The fees collected shall be deposited in the Dealers' Record of Sale Special Account.
(d) A person who satisfies all of the following conditions shall not be charged a fee:
(1) The person is not licensed pursuant to Sections 26700 to 26915, inclusive.
(2) The person has been issued a permit pursuant to Section 31005, 32650, or 33300, or pursuant to Article 3 (commencing with Section 18900) of Chapter 1 of Division 5 of Title 2.
(3) The person is placed on the centralized list of exempted federal firearms licensees.
(Added by Stats. 2010, Ch. 711, Sec. 6. (SB 1080) Effective January 1, 2011. Operative January 1, 2012, by Sec. 10 of Ch. 711.)

28465.
(a) Any person licensed pursuant to Chapter 44 (commencing with Section 921) of Title 18 of the United States Code as a dealer, importer, or manufacturer of firearms whose licensed premises are within this state shall not import or receive firearms from any source unless listed on the centralized list of firearms dealers pursuant to Section 26715, or the centralized list of exempted federal firearms licensees pursuant to Section 28450, or the centralized list of firearms manufacturers pursuant to Section 29060.
(b) A violation of this section is a misdemeanor.
(Added by Stats. 2010, Ch. 711, Sec. 6. (SB 1080) Effective January 1, 2011. Operative January 1, 2012, by Sec. 10 of Ch. 711.)

28470.
(a) All persons on the centralized list of exempted federal firearms licensees prescribed by Section 28450 shall record and keep on file for three years, the verification number that shall accompany firearms received from other federal firearms licensees pursuant to Section 27555.
(b) A violation of this section is cause for immediate removal from the centralized list.
(Added by Stats. 2010, Ch. 711, Sec. 6. (SB 1080) Effective January 1, 2011. Operative January 1, 2012, by Sec. 10 of Ch. 711.)

28475.
Information compiled from the list described in Section 28450 shall be made available for the following purposes:
(a) Requests from local, state, and federal law enforcement agencies and the duly constituted city, county, and city and county licensing authorities.
(b) When the information is requested by a person licensed pursuant to Chapter 44 (commencing with Section 921) of Title 18 of the United States Code for determining the validity of the license for firearm shipments.
(Added by Stats. 2010, Ch. 711, Sec. 6. (SB 1080) Effective January 1, 2011. Operative January 1, 2012, by Sec. 10 of Ch. 711.)

28480.
(a) The department may conduct onsite inspections at the business premises of a person on the centralized list described in Section 28450 to determine compliance with firearms laws pursuant to the provisions listed in Section 16575.
(b) The department shall work in consultation with the federal Bureau of Alcohol, Tobacco, Firearms and Explosives to ensure that licensees are not subject to duplicative inspections.
(c) During the inspection the following firearm records shall be made available for review:
(1) Federal records referred to in subdivision (a) of Section 478.125 of Title 27 of the Code of Federal Regulations and the bound book containing the same information referred to in Section 478.124a and subdivision (e) of Section 478.125 of Title 27 of the Code of Federal Regulations.
(2) Verification numbers issued pursuant to Section 27555.
(3) Any other records requested by the department to determine compliance with the provisions listed in Section 16575.
(Amended by Stats. 2014, Ch. 103, Sec. 10. (AB 1798) Effective January 1, 2015.)

28485.
The department may remove from the centralized list described in Section 28450 any person who violates a provision listed in Section 16575.
(Added by Stats. 2010, Ch. 711, Sec. 6. (SB 1080) Effective January 1, 2011. Operative January 1, 2012, by Sec. 10 of Ch. 711.)

28490.
The department may adopt regulations as necessary to carry out the provisions of this article, Article 1 (commencing with Section 26700) and Article 2 (commencing with Section 26800) of Chapter 2, and Sections 27555 to 27570, inclusive. The department shall work in consultation with the federal Bureau of Alcohol, Tobacco, Firearms and Explosives to ensure that state regulations are not duplicative of federal regulations.
(Amended by Stats. 2014, Ch. 103, Sec. 11. (AB 1798) Effective January 1, 2015.)

DIVISION 7. MANUFACTURE OF FIREARMS [29010 - 29184]
(Division 7 added by Stats. 2010, Ch. 711, Sec. 6.)

CHAPTER 1. License Requirement for Manufacture of Firearms [29010- 29010.]

(Chapter 1 added by Stats. 2010, Ch. 711, Sec. 6.)

29010.

(a) Commencing July 1, 1999, no person, firm, or corporation licensed to manufacture firearms pursuant to Chapter 44 (commencing with Section 921) of Title 18 of the United States Code may manufacture firearms within this state unless that person, firm, or corporation is licensed pursuant to Chapter 2 (commencing with Section 29030).

(b) Subdivision (a) does not apply to a person licensed to manufacture firearms pursuant to Chapter 44 (commencing with Section 921) of Title 18 of the United States Code who manufactures fewer than 100 firearms in a calendar year within this state.

(c) If a person, firm, or corporation required to be licensed pursuant to Chapter 2 (commencing with Section 29030) ceases operations, then the records required pursuant to Section 29130 and subdivision (b) of Section 29115 shall be forwarded to the federal Bureau of Alcohol, Tobacco, Firearms and Explosives within three days of the closure of business.

(d) A violation of this section is a misdemeanor.

(Amended by Stats. 2011, Ch. 296, Sec. 233. (AB 1023) Effective January 1, 2012.)

CHAPTER 2. Issuance, Forfeiture, and Conditions of License to Manufacture Firearms [29030 - 29150]

(Chapter 2 added by Stats. 2010, Ch. 711, Sec. 6.)

ARTICLE 1. Preliminary Provisions [29030- 29030.]

(Article 1 added by Stats. 2010, Ch. 711, Sec. 6.)

29030.

In this chapter, "licensee" means a person, firm, or corporation that satisfies both of the following:

(a) Has a license issued pursuant to subdivision (b) of Section 29050.

(b) Is among those recorded in the centralized list specified in Section 29060.

(Added by Stats. 2010, Ch. 711, Sec. 6. (SB 1080) Effective January 1, 2011. Operative January 1, 2012, by Sec. 10 of Ch. 711.)

ARTICLE 2. Licensing Process [29050 - 29075]

(Article 2 added by Stats. 2010, Ch. 711, Sec. 6.)

29050.

(a) The Department of Justice shall accept applications for, and shall grant licenses permitting, the manufacture of firearms within this state.

(b) No license shall be granted by the department unless and until the applicant presents proof that the applicant has all of the following:

(1) A valid license to manufacture firearms issued pursuant to Chapter 44 (commencing with Section 921) of Title 18 of the United States Code.

(2) Any regulatory or business license required by local government.

(3) A valid seller's permit or resale certificate issued by the State Board of Equalization, if applicable.

(4) A certificate of eligibility issued by the Department of Justice pursuant to Section 26710.

(c) A license granted by the department shall be valid for no more than one year from the date of issuance and shall be in the form prescribed by the Attorney General.

(d) The department shall inform applicants who are denied licenses of the reasons for the denial in writing.

(Added by Stats. 2010, Ch. 711, Sec. 6. (SB 1080) Effective January 1, 2011. Operative January 1, 2012, by Sec. 10 of Ch. 711.)

29055.

(a) The department shall adopt regulations to administer this chapter and Chapter 1 (commencing with Section 29010).

(b) The department shall recover the full costs of administering the program by collecting fees from license applicants. Recoverable costs shall include, but not be limited to, the costs of inspections and maintaining a centralized list of licensed firearm manufacturers.

(c) The fee for licensed manufacturers who produce fewer than 500 firearms in a calendar year within this state shall not exceed two hundred fifty dollars ($250) per year or the actual costs of inspections and maintaining a centralized list of firearm manufacturers and any other duties of the department required pursuant to this chapter and Chapter 1 (commencing with Section 29010), whichever is less.

(Added by Stats. 2010, Ch. 711, Sec. 6. (SB 1080) Effective January 1, 2011. Operative January 1, 2012, by Sec. 10 of Ch. 711.)

29060.

(a) Except as otherwise provided in subdivisions (a) and (b) of Section 20965, the Department of Justice shall maintain a centralized list of all persons licensed pursuant to subdivision (b) of Section 29050.

(b) The centralized list shall be provided annually to each police department and county sheriff within the state.

(Added by Stats. 2010, Ch. 711, Sec. 6. (SB 1080) Effective January 1, 2011. Operative January 1, 2012, by Sec. 10 of Ch. 711.)

29065.

(a) Except as provided in subdivision (b), the license of any licensee who violates this chapter may be revoked.

(b) The license of any licensee who knowingly or with gross negligence violates this chapter or violates this chapter three times shall be revoked, and that person, firm, or corporation shall become permanently ineligible to obtain a license pursuant to this chapter.

(c) Upon the revocation of the license, notification shall be provided to local law enforcement authorities in the jurisdiction where the licensee's business is located and to the federal Bureau of Alcohol, Tobacco, Firearms and Explosives.

(Amended by Stats. 2011, Ch. 296, Sec. 234. (AB 1023) Effective January 1, 2012.)

29070.

(a) The department shall make information concerning the location and name of a licensee available, upon request, for the following purposes only:

(1) Law enforcement.

(2) When the information is requested by a person licensed pursuant to Chapter 44 (commencing with Section 921) of Title 18 of the United States Code for determining the validity of the license for firearm shipments.

(b) Notwithstanding subdivision (a), the department shall make the name and business address of a licensee available to any person upon written request.

(Added by Stats. 2010, Ch. 711, Sec. 6. (SB 1080) Effective January 1, 2011. Operative January 1, 2012, by Sec. 10 of Ch. 711.)

29075.

The Department of Justice shall maintain and make available upon request information concerning all of the following:

(a) The number of inspections conducted and the amount of fees collected pursuant to Section 29055.

(b) The number of licensees removed from the centralized list described in Sections 29060 and 29065.

(c) The number of licensees found to have violated this chapter.

(Added by Stats. 2010, Ch. 711, Sec. 6. (SB 1080) Effective January 1, 2011. Operative January 1, 2012, by Sec. 10 of Ch. 711.)

ARTICLE 3. Prohibitions and Requirements Applicable to Licensee [29100 - 29150]

(Article 3 added by Stats. 2010, Ch. 711, Sec. 6.)

29100.

A licensee shall comply with the prohibitions and requirements described in this article.

(Added by Stats. 2010, Ch. 711, Sec. 6. (SB 1080) Effective January 1, 2011. Operative January 1, 2012, by Sec. 10 of Ch. 711.)

29105.

The business of a licensee shall be conducted only in the buildings designated in the license.

(Added by Stats. 2010, Ch. 711, Sec. 6. (SB 1080) Effective January 1, 2011. Operative January 1, 2012, by Sec. 10 of Ch. 711.)

29110.

A licensee shall display the license or a copy thereof, certified by the department, on the premises where it can easily be seen.

(Added by Stats. 2010, Ch. 711, Sec. 6. (SB 1080) Effective January 1, 2011. Operative January 1, 2012, by Sec. 10 of Ch. 711.)

29115.

(a) Whenever a licensee discovers that a firearm has been stolen or is missing from the licensee's premises, the licensee shall report the loss or theft within 48 hours of the discovery to all of the following:

(1) The Department of Justice, in a manner prescribed by the department.

(2) The federal Bureau of Alcohol, Tobacco, Firearms and Explosives.

(3) The police department in the city or city and county where the building designated in the license is located.

(4) If there is no police department in the city or city and county where the building designated in the license is located, the sheriff of the county where the building designated in the license is located.

(b) For at least 10 years, the licensee shall maintain records of all firearms that are lost or stolen, as prescribed by the Department of Justice.

(Amended by Stats. 2011, Ch. 296, Sec. 235. (AB 1023) Effective January 1, 2012.)

29120.

(a) A licensee shall require that each employee obtain a certificate of eligibility pursuant to Section 26710, which shall be renewed annually, before being allowed to come into contact with any firearm.

(b) A licensee shall prohibit any employee who the licensee knows or reasonably should know is prohibited by state or federal law from possessing, receiving, owning, or purchasing a firearm from coming into contact with any firearm.

(Added by Stats. 2010, Ch. 711, Sec. 6. (SB 1080) Effective January 1, 2011. Operative January 1, 2012, by Sec. 10 of Ch. 711.)

29125.

(a) Each firearm a licensee manufactures in this state shall be identified with a unique serial number stamped onto the firearm utilizing the method of compression stamping.

(b) Licensed manufacturers who produce fewer than 500 firearms in a calendar year within this state may serialize long guns only by utilizing a method of compression stamping or by engraving the serial number onto the firearm.

(c) The licensee shall stamp the serial number onto the firearm within one business day of the time the frame or receiver is manufactured.

(d) The licensee shall not use the same serial number for more than one firearm.

(Added by Stats. 2010, Ch. 711, Sec. 6. (SB 1080) Effective January 1, 2011. Operative January 1, 2012, by Sec. 10 of Ch. 711.)

29130.

(a) A licensee shall record the type, model, caliber, or gauge, and serial number of each firearm manufactured or acquired, and the date of the manufacture or acquisition, within one business day of the manufacture or acquisition.

(b) The licensee shall maintain permanently within the building designated in the license the records required pursuant to subdivision (a).

(c) Backup copies of the records described in subdivision (a), whether electronic or hard copy, shall be made at least once a month. These backup records shall be maintained in a facility separate from the one in which the primary records are stored.

(Added by Stats. 2010, Ch. 711, Sec. 6. (SB 1080) Effective January 1, 2011. Operative January 1, 2012, by Sec. 10 of Ch. 711.)

29135.

(a) A licensee shall allow the department to inspect the building designated in the license to ensure compliance with the requirements of this chapter.

(b) A licensee shall allow any peace officer, authorized law enforcement employee, or Department of Justice employee designated by the Attorney General, upon the presentation of proper identification, to inspect facilities and records during business hours to ensure compliance with the requirements of this chapter.

(Added by Stats. 2010, Ch. 711, Sec. 6. (SB 1080) Effective January 1, 2011. Operative January 1, 2012, by Sec. 10 of Ch. 711.)

29140.

A licensee shall store in a secure facility all firearms manufactured and all barrels for firearms manufactured.

(Added by Stats. 2010, Ch. 711, Sec. 6. (SB 1080) Effective January 1, 2011. Operative January 1, 2012, by Sec. 10 of Ch. 711.)

29141.

Except as otherwise provided in Section 29142, as used in this chapter, "secure facility" means that the facility satisfies all of the following:

(a) The facility is equipped with a burglar alarm with central monitoring.

(b) All perimeter entries to areas in which firearms are stored other than doors, including windows and skylights, are secured with steel window guards or an audible, silent, or sonic alarm to detect entry.

(c) All perimeter doorways are designed in one of the following ways:

(1) A windowless steel security door equipped with both a deadbolt and a doorknob lock.

(2) A windowed metal door equipped with both a deadbolt and a doorknob lock. If the window has an opening of five inches or more measured in any direction, the window is covered with steel bars of at least one-half inch diameter or metal grating of at least nine gauge affixed to the exterior or interior of the door.

(3) A metal grate that is padlocked and affixed to the licensee's premises independent of the door and doorframe.

(4) Hinges and hasps attached to doors by welding, riveting, or bolting with nuts on the inside of the door.

(5) Hinges and hasps installed so that they cannot be removed when the doors are closed and locked.

(d) Heating, ventilating, air-conditioning, and service openings are secured with steel bars, metal grating, or an alarm system.

(e) No perimeter metal grates are capable of being entered by any person.

(f) Steel bars used to satisfy the requirements of this section are not capable of being entered by any person.

(g) Perimeter walls of rooms in which firearms are stored are constructed of concrete or at least 10-gauge expanded steel wire mesh utilized along with typical wood frame and drywall construction. If firearms are not stored in a vault, the facility shall use an exterior security-type door along with a high security, single-key deadbolt, or other door that is more secure. All firearms shall be stored in a separate room away from any general living area or work area. Any door to the storage facility shall be locked while unattended.
(h) Perimeter doorways, including the loading dock area, are locked at all times when not attended by paid employees or contracted employees, including security guards.
(i) Except when a firearm is currently being tested, any ammunition on the premises is removed from all manufactured guns and stored in a separate and locked room, cabinet, or box away from the storage area for the firearms. Ammunition may be stored with a weapon only in a locked safe.
(Added by Stats. 2010, Ch. 711, Sec. 6. (SB 1080) Effective January 1, 2011. Operative January 1, 2012, by Sec. 10 of Ch. 711.)
29142.
(a) For purposes of this chapter, any licensed manufacturer who produces fewer than 500 firearms in a calendar year within this state may maintain a "secure facility" by complying with all of the requirements described in Section 29141, or may design a security plan that is approved by the Department of Justice or the federal Bureau of Alcohol, Tobacco, Firearms and Explosives.
(b) If a security plan is approved by the federal Bureau of Alcohol, Tobacco, Firearms and Explosives, the approved plan, along with proof of approval, shall be filed with the Department of Justice and the local police department. If there is no police department, the filing shall be with the county sheriff's office.
(c) If a security plan is approved by the Department of Justice, the approved plan, along with proof of approval, shall be filed with the local police department. If there is no police department, the filing shall be with the county sheriff's office.
(Amended by Stats. 2011, Ch. 296, Sec. 236. (AB 1023) Effective January 1, 2012.)
29150.
(a) A licensee shall notify the chief of police or other head of the municipal police department in the city or city and county where the building designated in the license is located that the licensee is manufacturing firearms within that city or city and county and the location of the licensed premises.
(b) If there is no police department in the city or city and county where the building designated in the license is located, the licensee shall notify the sheriff of the county where the building designated in the license is located that the licensee is manufacturing firearms within that county and the location of the licensed premises.
(Added by Stats. 2010, Ch. 711, Sec. 6. (SB 1080) Effective January 1, 2011. Operative January 1, 2012, by Sec. 10 of Ch. 711.)

CHAPTER 3. Assembly of Firearms [29180 - 29184]

(Chapter 3 added by Stats. 2016, Ch. 60, Sec. 4.)
29180.
(a) For purposes of this chapter, "manufacturing" or "assembling" a firearm means to fabricate or construct a firearm, or to fit together the component parts of a firearm to construct a firearm.
(b) Commencing July 1, 2018, prior to manufacturing or assembling a firearm, a person manufacturing or assembling the firearm shall do all of the following:
(1) Apply to the Department of Justice for a unique serial number or other mark of identification pursuant to Section 29182.
(2) (A) Within 10 days of manufacturing or assembling a firearm in accordance with paragraph (1), the unique serial number or other mark of identification provided by the department shall be engraved or permanently affixed to the firearm in a manner that meets or exceeds the requirements imposed on licensed importers and licensed manufacturers of firearms pursuant to subsection (i) of Section 923 of Title 18 of the United States Code and regulations issued pursuant thereto.
(B) If the firearm is manufactured or assembled from polymer plastic, 3.7 ounces of material type 17-4 PH stainless steel shall be embedded within the plastic upon fabrication or construction with the unique serial number engraved or otherwise permanently affixed in a manner that meets or exceeds the requirements imposed on licensed importers and licensed manufacturers of firearms pursuant to subsection (i) of Section 923 of Title 18 of the United States Code and regulations issued pursuant thereto.
(3) After the serial number provided by the department is engraved or otherwise permanently affixed to the firearm, the person shall notify the department of that fact in a manner and within a time period specified by the department, and with sufficient information to identify the owner of the firearm, the unique serial number or mark of identification provided by the department, and the firearm in a manner prescribed by the department.
(c) By January 1, 2019, any person who, as of July 1, 2018, owns a firearm that does not bear a serial number assigned to it pursuant to either Section 23910 or Chapter 44 (commencing with Section 921) of Part 1 of Title 18 of the United States Code and the regulations issued pursuant thereto, shall do all of the following:
(1) Apply to the Department of Justice for a unique serial number or other mark of identification pursuant to Section 29182.
(2) Within 10 days of receiving a unique serial number or other mark of identification from the department, the unique serial number or other mark of identification provided by the department shall be engraved or permanently affixed to the firearm in accordance with regulations prescribed by the department pursuant to Section 29182 and in a manner that meets or exceeds the requirements imposed on licensed importers and licensed manufacturers of firearms pursuant to subsection (i) of Section 923 of Title 18 of the United States Code and regulations issued pursuant thereto.
(3) After the serial number provided by the department is engraved or otherwise permanently affixed to the firearm, the person shall notify the department of that fact in a manner and within a time period specified by the department and with sufficient information to identify the owner of the firearm, the unique serial number or mark of identification provided by the department, and the firearm in a manner prescribed by the department.
(d) (1) The sale or transfer of ownership of a firearm manufactured or assembled pursuant to this section is prohibited.
(2) Paragraph (1) does not apply to the transfer, surrender, or sale of a firearm to a law enforcement agency.
(3) Any firearms confiscated by law enforcement that do not bear an engraved serial number or other mark of identification pursuant to subdivision (b) or (c), or a firearm surrendered, transferred, or sold to a law enforcement agency pursuant to paragraph (2) shall be destroyed as provided in Section 18005.
(4) Sections 26500 and 27545, and subdivision (a) of Section 31615, do not apply to the transfer, sale, or surrender of firearms to a law enforcement agency pursuant to paragraph (2).
(e) A new resident to the state shall apply for a unique serial number or other mark of identification pursuant to Section 29182 within 60 days of arrival for any firearm the resident wishes to possess in the state that the resident previously manufactured or assembled or a firearm the resident owns, that does not have a unique serial number or other mark of identification.
(f) A person, corporation, or firm shall not knowingly allow, facilitate, aid, or abet the manufacture or assembling of a firearm pursuant to this section by a person who is within any of the classes identified by Chapter 2 (commencing with Section 29800) or Chapter 3 (commencing with Section 29900) of Division 9 of this code, or Section 8100 or 8103 of the Welfare and Institutions Code.
(g) If the firearm is a handgun, a violation of this section is punishable by imprisonment in a county jail not to exceed one year, or by a fine not to exceed one thousand dollars ($1,000), or by both that fine and imprisonment. For all other firearms, a violation of this section is punishable by imprisonment in a county jail not to exceed six months, or by a fine not to exceed one thousand dollars ($1,000), or by both that fine and imprisonment. Each firearm found to be in violation of this section constitutes a distinct and separate offense. This section does not preclude prosecution under any other law providing for a greater penalty.
(Amended by Stats. 2018, Ch. 780, Sec. 4. (SB 746) Effective January 1, 2019.)
29181.
Section 29180 does not apply to or affect any of the following:
(a) A firearm that has a serial number assigned to it pursuant to either Section 23910 or Chapter 44 (commencing with Section 921) of Part 1 of Title 18 of the United States Code and the regulations issued pursuant thereto.
(b) A firearm made or assembled prior to December 16, 1968, that is not a handgun.
(c) A firearm which was entered into the centralized registry set forth in Section 11106 prior to July 1, 2018, as being owned by a specific individual or entity if that firearm has assigned to it a distinguishing number or mark of identification because the department accepted entry of that firearm into the centralized registry.
(d) A firearm that has a serial number assigned to it pursuant to Chapter 53 of Title 26 of the United States Code and the regulations issued pursuant thereto.
(e) A firearm that is a curio or relic, or an antique firearm, as those terms are defined in Section 479.11 of Title 27 of the Code of Federal Regulations.
(Amended by Stats. 2017, Ch. 561, Sec. 201. (AB 1516) Effective January 1, 2018.)
29182.
(a) (1) The Department of Justice shall accept applications from, and shall grant applications in the form of serial numbers pursuant to Section 23910 to, persons who wish to manufacture or assemble firearms pursuant to subdivision (b) of Section 29180.
(2) The Department of Justice shall accept applications from, and shall grant applications in the form of serial numbers pursuant to Section 23910 to, persons who wish to own a firearm described in subdivision (c) of Section 29180.
(b) An application made pursuant to subdivision (a) shall only be granted by the department if the applicant does all of the following:
(1) For each transaction, completes a firearms eligibility check pursuant to Section 28220 demonstrating that the applicant is not prohibited by state or federal law from possessing, receiving, owning, or purchasing a firearm.
(2) (A) Presents proof of age and identity as specified in Section 16400. Except as provided in subparagraph (B), the applicant shall be 21 years of age or older to obtain a unique serial number or mark of identification for a firearm.
(B) The department shall grant an application to an applicant who is at least 18 years of age, but less than 21 years of age, for a serial number for a firearm that is not a handgun, if that application is made before February 1, 2019.
(3) Provides a description of the firearm that he or she owns or intends to manufacture or assemble, in a manner prescribed by the department.
(4) Has a valid firearm safety certificate or handgun safety certificate.
(c) The department shall inform applicants who are denied an application of the reasons for the denial in writing.
(d) All applications shall be granted or denied within 15 calendar days of the receipt of the application by the department.
(e) (1) This chapter does not authorize a person to manufacture, assemble, or possess a weapon prohibited under Section 16590, an assault weapon as defined in Section 30510 or 30515, a machinegun as defined in Section 16880, a .50 BMG rifle as defined in Section 30530, or a destructive device as defined in Section 16460.
(2) This chapter does not authorize a person, on or after July 1, 2018, to manufacture or assemble an unsafe handgun, as defined in Section 31910.
(f) The department shall adopt regulations to administer this chapter.
(Amended by Stats. 2018, Ch. 894, Sec. 2.5. (SB 1100) Effective January 1, 2019.)
29183.
The Department of Justice may charge an applicant a fee for each distinguishing number or mark it issues in an amount sufficient to reimburse it for the actual costs associated with assigning a distinguishing number or mark to a firearm pursuant to Sections 29180 and 29182 and for conducting a firearms eligibility check pursuant to paragraph (1) of subdivision (b) of Section 29182. All money received pursuant to this section shall be deposited in the Dealers' Record of Sale Special Account of the General Fund, to be available upon appropriation by the Legislature.
(Amended by Stats. 2018, Ch. 780, Sec. 6. (SB 746) Effective January 1, 2019.)
29184.
The Department of Justice shall maintain and make available upon request information concerning both of the following:
(a) The number of serial numbers issued pursuant to Section 29182.
(b) The number of arrests for violations of Section 29180.
(Added by Stats. 2016, Ch. 60, Sec. 4. (AB 857) Effective January 1, 2017.)

DIVISION 8. MISCELLANEOUS RULES RELATING TO FIREARMS GENERALLY [29300 - 29535]

(Division 8 added by Stats. 2010, Ch. 711, Sec. 6.)

CHAPTER 1. Miscellaneous Provisions [29300-29300.]

(Chapter 1 added by Stats. 2010, Ch. 711, Sec. 6.)
29300.
(a) Except as provided in subdivision (c), a firearm of any nature owned or possessed in violation of Chapter 1 (commencing with Section 29610), Chapter 2 (commencing with Section 29800), or Chapter 3 (commencing with Section 29900) of Division 9 of this title, or Chapter 3 (commencing with Section 8100) of Division 5 of the Welfare and Institutions Code, or used in the commission of any misdemeanor as provided in this code, any felony, or an attempt to commit any misdemeanor as provided in this code or any felony, is, upon a conviction of the defendant or upon a juvenile court finding that an offense which would be a misdemeanor or felony if committed by an adult was committed or attempted by the juvenile with the use of a firearm, a nuisance, and is subject to Sections 18000 and 18005.
(b) A finding that the defendant was guilty of the offense but was insane at the time the offense was committed is a conviction for the purposes of this section.
(c) A firearm is not a nuisance pursuant to this section if the firearm owner disposes of the firearm pursuant to Section 29810.
(d) This section does not apply to any of the following:
(1) Any firearm in the possession of the Department of Fish and Game.

(2) Any firearm that was used in the violation of any provision of the Fish and Game Code or any regulation adopted pursuant thereto.
(3) Any firearm that is forfeited pursuant to Section 5008.6 of the Public Resources Code.
(Added by Stats. 2010, Ch. 711, Sec. 6. (SB 1080) Effective January 1, 2011. Operative January 1, 2012, by Sec. 10 of Ch. 711.)

CHAPTER 2. Entertainment Firearms Permit [29500 - 29535]

(Chapter 2 added by Stats. 2010, Ch. 711, Sec. 6.)
29500.
Any person who is at least 21 years of age may apply for an entertainment firearms permit from the Department of Justice. An entertainment firearms permit authorizes the permitholder to possess firearms loaned to the permitholder for use solely as a prop in a motion picture, television, video, theatrical, or other entertainment production or event.
(Added by Stats. 2010, Ch. 711, Sec. 6. (SB 1080) Effective January 1, 2011. Operative January 1, 2012, by Sec. 10 of Ch. 711.)
29505.
(a) Requests for entertainment firearms permits shall be made on application forms prescribed by the Department of Justice that require applicant information, including, but not limited to, the following:
(1) Complete name.
(2) Residential and mailing address.
(3) Telephone number.
(4) Date of birth.
(5) Place of birth.
(6) Country of citizenship and, if other than United States, alien number or admission number.
(7) Valid driver's license number or valid identification card number issued by the California Department of Motor Vehicles.
(8) Social security number.
(9) Signature.
(b) All applications must be submitted with the appropriate fee as specified in Section 29510.
(Added by Stats. 2010, Ch. 711, Sec. 6. (SB 1080) Effective January 1, 2011. Operative January 1, 2012, by Sec. 10 of Ch. 711.)
29510.
(a) The Department of Justice shall recover the full costs of administering the entertainment firearms permit program by assessing the following application fees:
(1) For the initial application: one hundred four dollars ($104). Of this sum, fifty-six dollars ($56) shall be deposited into the Fingerprint Fee Account, and forty-eight dollars ($48) shall be deposited into the Dealers' Record of Sale Special Account.
(2) For each annual renewal application: twenty-nine dollars ($29), which shall be deposited into the Dealers' Record of Sale Special Account.
(b) The department shall annually review and shall adjust the fees specified in subdivision (a), if necessary, to fully fund, but not to exceed the actual costs of, the permit program provided for by this chapter, including enforcement of the program.
(Amended by Stats. 2011, Ch. 285, Sec. 27. (AB 1402) Effective January 1, 2012.)
29515.
(a) Upon receipt of an initial or renewal application submitted as specified in Sections 29505, 29520, and 29525, the department shall examine its records, records the department is authorized to request from the State Department of State Hospitals pursuant to Section 8104 of the Welfare and Institutions Code, and records of the National Instant Criminal Background Check System as described in subsection (t) of Section 922 of Title 18 of the United States Code, in order to determine if the applicant is prohibited from possessing or receiving firearms.
(b) The department shall issue an entertainment firearms permit only if the records indicate that the applicant is not prohibited from possessing or receiving firearms pursuant to any federal, state, or local law.
(Amended by Stats. 2012, Ch. 24, Sec. 58. (AB 1470) Effective June 27, 2012.)
29520.
(a) An initial application for an entertainment firearms permit shall require the submission of fingerprint images and related information in a manner prescribed by the department, for the purpose of obtaining information as to the existence and nature of a record of state or federal level convictions and state or federal level arrests for which the department establishes that the individual was released on bail or on the individual's own recognizance pending trial as needed to determine whether the applicant may be issued the permit. Requests for federal level criminal offender record information received by the Department of Justice pursuant to this chapter shall be forwarded by the department to the Federal Bureau of Investigation.
(b) The Department of Justice shall review the criminal offender record information specified in subdivision (l) of Section 11105 for entertainment firearms permit applicants.
(c) The Department of Justice shall review subsequent arrests, pursuant to Section 11105.2, to determine the continuing validity of the permit as specified in Section 29530 for all entertainment firearms permitholders.
(Added by Stats. 2010, Ch. 711, Sec. 6. (SB 1080) Effective January 1, 2011. Operative January 1, 2012, by Sec. 10 of Ch. 711.)
29525.
Any person who furnishes a fictitious name or address or knowingly furnishes any incorrect information or knowingly omits any information required to be provided on an application for an entertainment firearms permit is guilty of a misdemeanor.
(Added by Stats. 2010, Ch. 711, Sec. 6. (SB 1080) Effective January 1, 2011. Operative January 1, 2012, by Sec. 10 of Ch. 711.)
29530.
(a) An entertainment firearms permit issued by the Department of Justice shall be valid for one year from the date of issuance.
(b) If at any time during that year the permitholder becomes prohibited from possessing or receiving firearms pursuant to any federal, state, or local law, the entertainment firearms permit shall be no longer valid.
(Added by Stats. 2010, Ch. 711, Sec. 6. (SB 1080) Effective January 1, 2011. Operative January 1, 2012, by Sec. 10 of Ch. 711.)
29535.
The implementation of Sections 29500, 29505, 29515, 29520, and 29525, and of subdivision (a) of Section 29510, by the department is exempt from the Administrative Procedure Act (Chapter 3.5 (commencing with Section 11340) of Part 1 of Division 3 of Title 2 of the Government Code).
(Added by Stats. 2010, Ch. 711, Sec. 6. (SB 1080) Effective January 1, 2011. Operative January 1, 2012, by Sec. 10 of Ch. 711.)

DIVISION 9. SPECIAL FIREARM RULES RELATING TO PARTICULAR PERSONS [29610 - 30165]

(Division 9 added by Stats. 2010, Ch. 711, Sec. 6.)

CHAPTER 1. Juvenile [29610 - 29750]

(Chapter 1 added by Stats. 2010, Ch. 711, Sec. 6.)
ARTICLE 1. Possession of Handgun [29610 - 29615]
(Article 1 added by Stats. 2010, Ch. 711, Sec. 6.)
29610.
A minor shall not possess a pistol, revolver, or other firearm capable of being concealed upon the person.
(Added by Stats. 2010, Ch. 711, Sec. 6. (SB 1080) Effective January 1, 2011. Operative January 1, 2012, by Sec. 10 of Ch. 711.)
29615.
Section 29610 shall not apply if one of the following circumstances exists:
(a) The minor is accompanied by a parent or legal guardian, and the minor is actively engaged in, or is in direct transit to or from, a lawful, recreational sport, including, but not limited to, competitive shooting, or agricultural, ranching, or hunting activity, or a motion picture, television, or video production, or entertainment or theatrical event, the nature of which involves this use of a firearm.
(b) The minor is accompanied by a responsible adult, the minor has the prior written consent of a parent or legal guardian, and the minor is actively engaged in, or is in direct transit to or from, a lawful, recreational sport, including, but not limited to, competitive shooting, or agricultural, ranching, or hunting activity, or a motion picture, television, or video production, or entertainment or theatrical event, the nature of which involves the use of a firearm.
(c) The minor is at least 16 years of age, the minor has the prior written consent of a parent or legal guardian, and the minor is actively engaged in, or is in direct transit to or from, a lawful recreational sport, including, but not limited to, competitive shooting, or agricultural, ranching, or hunting activity, or a motion picture, television, or video production, or entertainment or theatrical event, the nature of which involves the use of a firearm.
(d) The minor has the prior written consent of a parent or legal guardian, the minor is on lands owned or lawfully possessed by the parent or legal guardian, and the minor is actively engaged in, or is in direct transit to or from, a lawful, recreational sport, including, but not limited to, competitive shooting, or agricultural, ranching, or hunting activity, or a motion picture, television, or video production, or entertainment or theatrical event, the nature of which involves the use of a firearm.
(Amended by Stats. 2011, Ch. 296, Sec. 238. (AB 1023) Effective January 1, 2012.)
ARTICLE 2. Possession of Live Ammunition [29650 - 29655]
(Article 2 added by Stats. 2010, Ch. 711, Sec. 6.)
29650.
A minor shall not possess live ammunition.
(Added by Stats. 2010, Ch. 711, Sec. 6. (SB 1080) Effective January 1, 2011. Operative January 1, 2012, by Sec. 10 of Ch. 711.)
29655.
Section 29650 shall not apply if one of the following circumstances exists:
(a) The minor has the written consent of a parent or legal guardian to possess live ammunition.
(b) The minor is accompanied by a parent or legal guardian.
(c) The minor is actively engaged in, or is going to or from, a lawful, recreational sport, including, but not limited to, competitive shooting, or agricultural, ranching, or hunting activity, the nature of which involves the use of a firearm.
(Added by Stats. 2010, Ch. 711, Sec. 6. (SB 1080) Effective January 1, 2011. Operative January 1, 2012, by Sec. 10 of Ch. 711.)
ARTICLE 3. Punishment [29700 - 29705]
(Article 3 added by Stats. 2010, Ch. 711, Sec. 6.)
29700.
Every minor who violates this chapter shall be punished as follows:
(a) By imprisonment pursuant to subdivision (h) of Section 1170 or in a county jail if one of the following applies:
(1) The minor has been found guilty previously of violating this chapter.
(2) The minor has been found guilty previously of an offense specified in Section 29905, 32625, or 33410, or an offense specified in any provision listed in Section 16590.
(3) The minor has been found guilty of a violation of Section 29610.
(b) Violations of this chapter other than those violations specified in subdivision (a) shall be punishable as a misdemeanor.
(Amended by Stats. 2011, Ch. 15, Sec. 547. (AB 109) Effective April 4, 2011. Amending action operative October 1, 2011, by Sec. 636 of Ch. 15, as amended by Stats. 2011, Ch. 39, Sec. 68. Section operative January 1, 2012, pursuant to Stats. 2010, Ch. 711, Sec. 10.)
29705.
In a proceeding to enforce this chapter brought pursuant to Article 14 (commencing with Section 601) of Chapter 2 of Part 1 of Division 2 of the Welfare and Institutions Code, the court may require the custodial parent or legal guardian of a minor who violates this chapter to participate in classes on parenting education that meet the requirements established in Section 16507.7 of the Welfare and Institutions Code.
(Added by Stats. 2010, Ch. 711, Sec. 6. (SB 1080) Effective January 1, 2011. Operative January 1, 2012, by Sec. 10 of Ch. 711.)
ARTICLE 4. Legislative Intent [29750- 29750.]
(Article 4 added by Stats. 2010, Ch. 711, Sec. 6.)
29750.
In enacting the amendments to former Sections 12078 and 12101 by Section 10 of Chapter 33 of the Statutes of 1994, First Extraordinary Session, it was not the intent of the Legislature to expand or narrow the application of the then-existing statutory and judicial authority as to the rights of minors to be loaned or to possess live ammunition or a firearm for the purpose of self-defense or the defense of others.
(Added by Stats. 2010, Ch. 711, Sec. 6. (SB 1080) Effective January 1, 2011. Operative January 1, 2012, by Sec. 10 of Ch. 711.)

CHAPTER 2. Person Convicted of Specified Offense, Addicted to Narcotic, or Subject to Court Order [29800 - 29875]

(Chapter 2 added by Stats. 2010, Ch. 711, Sec. 6.)
ARTICLE 1. Prohibitions on Firearm Access [29800 - 29830]
(Article 1 added by Stats. 2010, Ch. 711, Sec. 6.)

29800.

(a) (1) Any person who has been convicted of, or has an outstanding warrant for, a felony under the laws of the United States, the State of California, or any other state, government, or country, or of an offense enumerated in subdivision (a), (b), or (d) of Section 23515, or who is addicted to the use of any narcotic drug, and who owns, purchases, receives, or has in possession or under custody or control any firearm is guilty of a felony.

(2) Any person who has two or more convictions for violating paragraph (2) of subdivision (a) of Section 417 and who owns, purchases, receives, or has in possession or under custody or control any firearm is guilty of a felony.

(b) Notwithstanding subdivision (a), any person who has been convicted of a felony or of an offense enumerated in Section 23515, when that conviction results from certification by the juvenile court for prosecution as an adult in an adult court under Section 707 of the Welfare and Institutions Code, and who owns or has in possession or under custody or control any firearm is guilty of a felony.

(c) Subdivision (a) shall not apply to a person who has been convicted of a felony under the laws of the United States unless either of the following criteria is satisfied:

(1) Conviction of a like offense under California law can only result in imposition of felony punishment.

(2) The defendant was sentenced to a federal correctional facility for more than 30 days, or received a fine of more than one thousand dollars ($1,000), or received both punishments.

(Amended by Stats. 2017, Ch. 17, Sec. 44. (AB 103) Effective June 27, 2017.)

29805.

(a) Except as provided in Section 29855, subdivision (a) of Section 29800, or subdivision (b), any person who has been convicted of, or has an outstanding warrant for, a misdemeanor violation of Section 71, 76, 136.1, 136.5, or 140, subdivision (d) of Section 148, subdivision (f) of Section 148.5, Section 171b, paragraph (1) of subdivision (a) of Section 171c, Section 171d, 186.28, 240, 241, 242, 243, 243.4, 244.5, 245, 245.5, 246.3, 247, 273.5, 273.6, 417, 417.6, 422, 422.6, 626.9, 646.9, 830.95, 17500, 17510, 25300, 25800, 30315, or 32625, subdivision (b) or (d) of Section 26100, or Section 27510, or Section 8100, 8101, or 8103 of the Welfare and Institutions Code, any firearm-related offense pursuant to Sections 871.5 and 1001.5 of the Welfare and Institutions Code, Section 490.2 if the property taken was a firearm, or of the conduct punished in subdivision (c) of Section 27590, and who, within 10 years of the conviction, or if the individual has an outstanding warrant, owns, purchases, receives, or has in possession or under custody or control, any firearm is guilty of a public offense, punishable by imprisonment in a county jail not exceeding one year or in the state prison, by a fine not exceeding one thousand dollars ($1,000), or by both that imprisonment and fine.

(b) Any person who is convicted, on or after January 1, 2019, of a misdemeanor violation of Section 273.5, and who subsequently owns, purchases, receives, or has in possession or under custody or control, any firearm is guilty of a public offense, punishable by imprisonment in a county jail not exceeding one year or in the state prison, by a fine not exceeding one thousand dollars ($1,000), or by both that imprisonment and fine.

(c) The court, on forms prescribed by the Department of Justice, shall notify the department of persons subject to this section. However, the prohibition in this section may be reduced, eliminated, or conditioned as provided in Section 29855 or 29860.

(Amended by Stats. 2018, Ch. 883, Sec. 1. (AB 3129) Effective January 1, 2019. Note: This section was amended on Nov. 8, 2016, by initiative Prop. 63.)

29810.

(a) (1) Upon conviction of any offense that renders a person subject to Section 29800 or Section 29805, the person shall relinquish all firearms he or she owns, possesses, or has under his or her custody or control in the manner provided in this section.

(2) The court shall, upon conviction of a defendant for an offense described in subdivision (a), instruct the defendant that he or she is prohibited from owning, purchasing, receiving, possessing, or having under his or her custody or control, any firearms, ammunition, and ammunition feeding devices, including but not limited to magazines, and shall order the defendant to relinquish all firearms in the manner provided in this section. The court shall also provide the defendant with a Prohibited Persons Relinquishment Form developed by the Department of Justice.

(3) Using the Prohibited Persons Relinquishment Form, the defendant shall name a designee and grant the designee power of attorney for the purpose of transferring or disposing of any firearms. The designee shall be either a local law enforcement agency or a consenting third party who is not prohibited from possessing firearms under state or federal law. The designee shall, within the time periods specified in subdivisions (d) and (e), surrender the firearms to the control of a local law enforcement agency, sell the firearms to a licensed firearms dealer, or transfer the firearms for storage to a firearms dealer pursuant to Section 29830.

(b) The Prohibited Persons Relinquishment Form shall do all of the following:

(1) Inform the defendant that he or she is prohibited from owning, purchasing, receiving, possessing, or having under his or her custody or control, any firearms, ammunition, and ammunition feeding devices, including but not limited to magazines, and that he or she shall relinquish all firearms through a designee within the time periods set forth in subdivision (d) or (e) by surrendering the firearms to the control of a local law enforcement agency, selling the firearms to a licensed firearms dealer, or transferring the firearms for storage to a firearms dealer pursuant to Section 29830.

(2) Inform the defendant that any cohabitant of the defendant who owns firearms must store those firearms in accordance with Section 25135.

(3) Require the defendant to declare any firearms that he or she owned, possessed, or had under his or her custody or control at the time of his or her conviction, and require the defendant to describe the firearms and provide all reasonably available information about the location of the firearms to enable a designee or law enforcement officials to locate the firearms.

(4) Require the defendant to name a designee, if the defendant declares that he or she owned, possessed, or had under his or her custody or control any firearms at the time of his or her conviction, and grant the designee power of attorney for the purpose of transferring or disposing of all firearms.

(5) Require the designee to indicate his or her consent to the designation and, except a designee that is a law enforcement agency, to declare under penalty of perjury that he or she is not prohibited from possessing any firearms under state or federal law.

(6) Require the designee to state the date each firearm was relinquished and the name of the party to whom it was relinquished, and to attach receipts from the law enforcement officer or licensed firearms dealer who took possession of the relinquished firearms.

(7) Inform the defendant and the designee of the obligation to submit the completed Prohibited Persons Relinquishment Form to the assigned probation officer within the time periods specified in subdivisions (d) and (e).

(c) (1) When a defendant is convicted of an offense described in subdivision (a), the court shall immediately assign the matter to a probation officer to investigate whether the Automated Firearms System or other credible information, such as a police report, reveals that the defendant owns, possesses, or has under his or her custody or control any firearms. The assigned probation officer shall receive the Prohibited Persons Relinquishment Form from the defendant or the defendant's designee, as applicable, and ensure that the Automated Firearms System has been properly updated to indicate that the defendant has relinquished those firearms.

(2) Prior to final disposition or sentencing in the case, the assigned probation officer shall report to the court whether the defendant has properly complied with the requirements of this section by relinquishing all firearms identified by the probation officer's investigation or declared by the defendant on the Prohibited Persons Relinquishment Form, and by timely submitting a completed Prohibited Persons Relinquishment Form. The probation officer shall also report to the Department of Justice on a form to be developed by the department whether the Automated Firearms System has been updated to indicate which firearms have been relinquished by the defendant.

(3) Prior to final disposition or sentencing in the case, the court shall make findings concerning whether the probation officer's report indicates that the defendant has relinquished all firearms as required, and whether the court has received a completed Prohibited Persons Relinquishment Form, along with the receipts described in paragraph (1) of subdivision (d) or paragraph (1) of subdivision (e). The court shall ensure that these findings are included in the abstract of judgment. If necessary to avoid a delay in sentencing, the court may make and enter these findings within 14 days of sentencing.

(4) If the court finds probable cause that the defendant has failed to relinquish any firearms as required, the court shall order the search for and removal of any firearms at any location where the judge has probable cause to believe the defendant's firearms are located. The court shall state with specificity the reasons for and scope of the search and seizure authorized by the order.

(5) Failure by a defendant to timely file the completed Prohibited Persons Relinquishment Form with the assigned probation officer shall constitute an infraction punishable by a fine not exceeding one hundred dollars ($100).

(d) The following procedures shall apply to any defendant who is a prohibited person within the meaning of paragraph (1) of subdivision (a) who does not remain in custody at any time within the five-day period following conviction:

(1) The designee shall dispose of any firearms the defendant owns, possesses, or has under his or her custody or control within five days of the conviction by surrendering the firearms to the control of a local law enforcement agency, selling the firearms to a licensed firearms dealer, or transferring the firearms for storage to a firearms dealer pursuant to Section 29830, in accordance with the wishes of the defendant. Any proceeds from the sale of the firearms shall become the property of the defendant. The law enforcement officer or licensed dealer taking possession of any firearms pursuant to this subdivision shall issue a receipt to the designee describing the firearms and listing any serial number or other identification on the firearms at the time of surrender.

(2) If the defendant owns, possesses, or has under his or her custody or control any firearms to relinquish, the defendant's designee shall submit the completed Prohibited Persons Relinquishment Form to the assigned probation officer within five days following the conviction, along with the receipts described in paragraph (1) of subdivision (d) showing the defendant's firearms were surrendered to a local law enforcement agency or sold or transferred to a licensed firearms dealer.

(3) If the defendant does not own, possess, or have under his or her custody or control any firearms to relinquish, he or she shall, within five days following conviction, submit the completed Prohibited Persons Relinquishment Form to the assigned probation officer, with a statement affirming that he or she has no firearms to be relinquished.

(e) The following procedures shall apply to any defendant who is a prohibited person within the meaning of paragraph (1) of subdivision (a) who is in custody at any point within the five-day period following conviction:

(1) The designee shall dispose of any firearms the defendant owns, possesses, or has under his or her custody or control within 14 days of the conviction by surrendering the firearms to the control of a local law enforcement agency, selling the firearms to a licensed firearms dealer, or transferring the firearms for storage to a firearms dealer pursuant to Section 29830, in accordance with the wishes of the defendant. Any proceeds from the sale of the firearms shall become the property of the defendant. The law enforcement officer or licensed dealer taking possession of any firearms pursuant to this subdivision shall issue a receipt to the designee describing the firearms and listing any serial number or other identification on the firearms at the time of surrender.

(2) If the defendant owns, possesses, or has under his or her custody or control any firearms to relinquish, the defendant's designee shall submit the completed Prohibited Persons Relinquishment Form to the assigned probation officer, within 14 days following conviction, along with the receipts described in paragraph (1) of subdivision (e) showing the defendant's firearms were surrendered to a local law enforcement agency or sold or transferred to a licensed firearms dealer.

(3) If the defendant does not own, possess, or have under his or her custody or control any firearms to relinquish, he or she shall, within 14 days following conviction, submit the completed Prohibited Persons Relinquishment Form to the assigned probation officer, with a statement affirming that he or she has no firearms to be relinquished.

(4) If the defendant is released from custody during the 14 days following conviction and a designee has not yet taken temporary possession of each firearm to be relinquished as described above, the defendant shall, within five days following his or her release, relinquish each firearm required to be relinquished pursuant to paragraph (1) of subdivision (d).

(f) For good cause, the court may shorten or enlarge the time periods specified in subdivisions (d) and (e), enlarge the time period specified in paragraph (3) of subdivision (c), or allow an alternative method of relinquishment.

(g) The defendant shall not be subject to prosecution for unlawful possession of any firearms declared on the Prohibited Persons Relinquishment Form if the firearms are relinquished as required.

(h) Any firearms that would otherwise be subject to relinquishment by a defendant under this section, but which are lawfully owned by a cohabitant of the defendant, shall be exempt from relinquishment, provided the defendant is notified that the cohabitant must store the firearm in accordance with Section 25135.

(i) A law enforcement agency shall update the Automated Firearms System to reflect any firearms that were relinquished to the agency pursuant to this section. A law enforcement agency shall retain a firearm that was relinquished to the agency pursuant to this section for 30 days after the date the firearm was relinquished. After the 30-day period has expired, the firearm is subject to destruction, retention, sale or other transfer by the agency, except upon the certificate of a judge of a court of record, or of the district attorney of the county, that the retention of the firearm is necessary or proper to the ends of justice, or if the defendant provides written notice of an intent to appeal a conviction for an offense described in subdivision (a), or if the Automated Firearms System indicates that the firearm was reported lost or stolen by the lawful owner. If the firearm was reported lost or stolen, the firearm shall be restored to the lawful owner, as soon as its use as evidence has been served, upon the lawful owner's identification of the weapon and proof of ownership, and after the law enforcement agency has complied with Chapter 2 (commencing with Section 33850) of Division 11 of Title 4. The agency shall notify the Department of Justice of the disposition of relinquished firearms pursuant to Section 34010.

(j) A city, county, or city and county, or a state agency may adopt a regulation, ordinance, or resolution imposing a charge equal to its administrative costs relating to the seizure, impounding, storage, or release of a firearm pursuant to Section 33880.

(k) This section shall become operative on January 1, 2018.

(Repealed (in Sec. 10.3) and added November 8, 2016, by initiative Proposition 63, Sec. 10.4. Section operative January 1, 2018, by its own provisions.)

29815.

(a) Any person who, as an express condition of probation, is prohibited or restricted from owning, possessing, controlling, receiving, or purchasing a firearm and who owns, purchases, receives, or has in possession or under custody or control, any firearm, but who is not subject to Section 29805 or subdivision (a) of Section 29800, is guilty of a public offense, which shall be punishable by imprisonment in a county jail not exceeding one year or in the state prison, by a fine not exceeding one thousand dollars ($1,000), or by both that imprisonment and fine.

(b) The court, on forms provided by the Department of Justice, shall notify the department of persons subject to this section. The notice shall include a copy of the order of probation and a copy of any minute order or abstract reflecting the order and conditions of probation.

(Added by Stats. 2010, Ch. 711, Sec. 6. (SB 1080) Effective January 1, 2011. Operative January 1, 2012, by Sec. 10 of Ch. 711.)

29820.

(a) This section applies to any person who satisfies both of the following requirements:

(1) The person is alleged to have committed an offense listed in subdivision (b) of Section 707 of the Welfare and Institutions Code, an offense described in subdivision (b) of Section 1203.073, any offense enumerated in Section 29805, or any offense described in Section 25850, subdivision (a) of Section 25400, or subdivision (a) of Section 26100.

(2) The person is subsequently adjudged a ward of the juvenile court within the meaning of Section 602 of the Welfare and Institutions Code because the person committed an offense listed in subdivision (b) of Section 707 of the Welfare and Institutions Code, an offense described in subdivision (b) of Section 1203.073, any offense enumerated in Section 29805, or any offense described in Section 25850, subdivision (a) of Section 25400, or subdivision (a) of Section 26100.

(b) Any person described in subdivision (a) shall not own, or have in possession or under custody or control, any firearm until the age of 30 years.

(c) A violation of this section shall be punishable by imprisonment in a county jail not exceeding one year or in the state prison, by a fine not exceeding one thousand dollars ($1,000), or by both that imprisonment and fine.

(d) The juvenile court, on forms prescribed by the Department of Justice, shall notify the department of persons subject to this section. Notwithstanding any other law, the forms required to be submitted to the department pursuant to this section may be used to determine eligibility to acquire a firearm.

(Added by Stats. 2010, Ch. 711, Sec. 6. (SB 1080) Effective January 1, 2011. Operative January 1, 2012, by Sec. 10 of Ch. 711.)

29825.

(a) Every person who purchases or receives, or attempts to purchase or receive, a firearm knowing that the person is prohibited from doing so by a temporary restraining order or injunction issued pursuant to Section 527.6, 527.8, or 527.85 of the Code of Civil Procedure, a protective order as defined in Section 6218 of the Family Code, a protective order issued pursuant to Section 136.2 or 646.91 of this code, or a protective order issued pursuant to Section 15657.03 of the Welfare and Institutions Code, is guilty of a public offense, which shall be punishable by imprisonment in a county jail not exceeding one year or in the state prison, by a fine not exceeding one thousand dollars ($1,000), or by both that imprisonment and fine.

(b) Every person who owns or possesses a firearm knowing that the person is prohibited from doing so by a temporary restraining order or injunction issued pursuant to Section 527.6, 527.8, or 527.85 of the Code of Civil Procedure, a protective order as defined in Section 6218 of the Family Code, a protective order issued pursuant to Section 136.2 or 646.91 of this code, or a protective order issued pursuant to Section 15657.03 of the Welfare and Institutions Code, is guilty of a public offense, which shall be punishable by imprisonment in a county jail not exceeding one year, by a fine not exceeding one thousand dollars ($1,000), or by both that imprisonment and fine.

(c) If probation is granted upon conviction of a violation of this section, the court shall impose probation consistent with Section 1203.097.

(d) The Judicial Council shall provide notice on all protective orders that the respondent is prohibited from owning, possessing, purchasing, receiving, or attempting to purchase or receive a firearm while the protective order is in effect. The order shall also state that a firearm owned or possessed by the person shall be relinquished to the local law enforcement agency for that jurisdiction, sold to a licensed firearms dealer, or transferred to a licensed firearms dealer pursuant to Section 29830 for the duration of the period that the protective order is in effect, and that proof of surrender or sale shall be filed within a specified time of receipt of the order. The order shall state the penalties for a violation of the prohibition. The order shall also state on its face the expiration date for relinquishment.

(Amended by Stats. 2013, Ch. 739, Sec. 3. (AB 539) Effective January 1, 2014.)

29830.

(a) A person who is prohibited from owning or possessing a firearm or ammunition pursuant to any law, may transfer or cause to be transferred, any firearm or ammunition in his or her possession, or of which he or she is the owner, to a firearms dealer licensed pursuant to Sections 26700 to 26915, inclusive, or may transfer ammunition to an ammunition vendor, licensed pursuant to Sections 30385 to 30395, inclusive, for storage during the duration of the prohibition, if the prohibition on owning or possessing the firearm or ammunition will expire on a specific ascertainable date, whether or not specified in the court order, or pursuant to Section 29800, 29805, or 29810.

(b) A firearms dealer or ammunition vendor who stores a firearm or ammunition pursuant to subdivision (a), may charge the owner a reasonable fee for the storage of the firearm or ammunition.

(c) A firearms dealer or ammunition vendor who stores a firearm or ammunition pursuant to subdivision (a) shall notify the Department of Justice of the date that the firearms dealer or ammunition vendor has taken possession of the firearm or ammunition.

(d) Any firearm that is returned by a dealer to the owner of the firearm pursuant to this section shall be returned in accordance with the procedures set forth in Section 27540 and Article 1 (commencing with Section 26700) and Article 2 (commencing with Section 26800) of Chapter 2 of Division 6.

(e) Any ammunition that is returned by a firearms dealer or ammunition vendor to the owner of the ammunition pursuant to this section shall be returned in accordance with the procedures set forth in Article 4 (commencing with Section 30370) of Chapter 1 of Division 10.

(f) This section shall remain in effect only until July 1, 2020, and as of that date is repealed.

(Amended by Stats. 2018, Ch. 780, Sec. 7. (SB 746) Effective January 1, 2019. Repealed as of July 1, 2020, by its own provisions. See later operative version added by Stats. 2018, Ch. 780.)

29830.

(a) A person who is prohibited from owning or possessing a firearm, ammunition feeding device, or ammunition pursuant to any law, may transfer or cause to be transferred, any firearm, ammunition feeding device, or ammunition in his or her possession, or of which he or she is the owner, to a firearms dealer licensed pursuant to Sections 26700 to 26915, inclusive, or may transfer ammunition to an ammunition vendor, licensed pursuant to Sections 30385 to 30395, inclusive, for storage during the duration of the prohibition, if the prohibition on owning or possessing the firearm, ammunition feeding device, or ammunition will expire on a specific ascertainable date, whether or not specified in the court order, or pursuant to Section 29800, 29805, or 29810.

(b) A firearms dealer or ammunition vendor who stores a firearm, ammunition feeding device, or ammunition pursuant to subdivision (a), may charge the owner a reasonable fee for the storage of the firearm, ammunition feeding device, or ammunition.

(c) A firearms dealer or ammunition vendor who stores a firearm, ammunition feeding device, or ammunition pursuant to subdivision (a) shall notify the Department of Justice of the date that the firearms dealer or ammunition vendor has taken possession of the firearm, ammunition feeding device, or ammunition.

(d) Any firearm that is returned by a dealer to the owner of the firearm pursuant to this section shall be returned in accordance with the procedures set forth in Section 27540 and Article 1 (commencing with Section 26700) and Article 2 (commencing with Section 26800) of Chapter 2 of Division 6.

(e) Any ammunition that is returned by a firearms dealer or ammunition vendor to the owner of the ammunition pursuant to this section shall be returned in accordance with the procedures set forth in Article 4 (commencing with Section 30370) of Chapter 1 of Division 10.

(f) This section shall become operative on July 1, 2020.

(Repealed and added by Stats. 2018, Ch. 780, Sec. 8. (SB 746) Effective January 1, 2019. Section operative July 1, 2020, by its own provisions.)

ARTICLE 2. Exemption or Petition for Relief [29850 - 29865]
(Article 2 added by Stats. 2010, Ch. 711, Sec. 6.)

29850.

(a) A violation of Section 29800, 29805, 29815, or 29820 is justifiable where all of the following conditions are met:

(1) The person found the firearm or took the firearm from a person who was committing a crime against the person who found or took the firearm.

(2) The person possessed the firearm no longer than was necessary to deliver or transport the firearm to a law enforcement agency for that agency's disposition according to law or to a licensed firearms dealer for transfer or for storage pursuant to Section 29830.

(3) If the firearm was transported to a law enforcement agency or to a licensed firearms dealer, it was transported in accordance with subdivision (b) of Section 25570.

(4) If the firearm is being transported to a law enforcement agency or to a licensed firearms dealer, the person transporting the firearm has given prior notice to the law enforcement agency or to the licensed firearms dealer that the person is transporting the firearm to the law enforcement agency or the licensed firearms dealer for disposition according to law.

(b) Upon the trial for violating Section 29800, 29805, 29815, or 29820, the trier of fact shall determine whether the defendant was acting within the provisions of the exemption created by this section. .

(c) The defendant has the burden of proving by a preponderance of the evidence that the defendant comes within the provisions of the exemption created by this section.

(Amended by Stats. 2013, Ch. 739, Sec. 5. (AB 539) Effective January 1, 2014.)

29851.

Sections 29800 and 29805 do not apply to or affect a person who otherwise violates those sections if the person did not have knowledge of the outstanding warrant.

(Added by renumbering Section 29581 by Stats. 2018, Ch. 92, Sec. 169. (SB 1289) Effective January 1, 2019.)

29855.

(a) Any person employed as a peace officer described in Section 830.1, 830.2, 830.31, 830.32, 830.33, or 830.5 whose employment or livelihood is dependent on the ability to legally possess a firearm, who is subject to the prohibition imposed by Section 29805 because of a conviction under Section 273.5, 273.6, or 646.9, may petition the court only once for relief from this prohibition.

(b) The petition shall be filed with the court in which the petitioner was sentenced. If possible, the matter shall be heard before the same judge who sentenced the petitioner.

(c) Upon filing the petition, the clerk of the court shall set the hearing date and shall notify the petitioner and the prosecuting attorney of the date of the hearing.

(d) Upon making each of the following findings, the court may reduce or eliminate the prohibition, impose conditions on reduction or elimination of the prohibition, or otherwise grant relief from the prohibition as the court deems appropriate:

(1) Finds by a preponderance of the evidence that the petitioner is likely to use a firearm in a safe and lawful manner.

(2) Finds that the petitioner is not within a prohibited class as specified in Section 29815, 29820, 29825, or 29900, or subdivision (a) or (b) of Section 29800, and the court is not presented with any credible evidence that the petitioner is a person described in Section 8100 or 8103 of the Welfare and Institutions Code.

(3) Finds that the petitioner does not have a previous conviction under Section 29805, no matter when the prior conviction occurred.

(e) In making its decision, the court shall consider the petitioner's continued employment, the interest of justice, any relevant evidence, and the totality of the circumstances. The court shall require, as a condition of granting relief from the prohibition under Section 29805, that the petitioner agree to participate in counseling as deemed appropriate by the court. Relief from the prohibition shall not relieve any other person or entity from any liability that might otherwise be imposed. It is the intent of the Legislature that courts exercise broad discretion in fashioning appropriate relief under this section in cases in which relief is warranted. However, nothing in this section shall be construed to require courts to grant relief to any particular petitioner. It is the intent of the Legislature to permit persons who were convicted of an offense specified in Section 273.5, 273.6, or 646.9 to seek relief from the prohibition imposed by Section 29805.

(Amended by Stats. 2011, Ch. 296, Sec. 239. (AB 1023) Effective January 1, 2012.)

29860.

(a) Any person who is subject to the prohibition imposed by Section 29805 because of a conviction of an offense prior to that offense being added to Section 29805 may petition the court only once for relief from this prohibition.

(b) The petition shall be filed with the court in which the petitioner was sentenced. If possible, the matter shall be heard before the same judge that sentenced the petitioner.

(c) Upon filing the petition, the clerk of the court shall set the hearing date and notify the petitioner and the prosecuting attorney of the date of the hearing.

(d) Upon making each of the following findings, the court may reduce or eliminate the prohibition, impose conditions on reduction or elimination of the prohibition, or otherwise grant relief from the prohibition as the court deems appropriate:

(1) Finds by a preponderance of the evidence that the petitioner is likely to use a firearm in a safe and lawful manner.

(2) Finds that the petitioner is not within a prohibited class as specified in Section 29815, 29820, 29825, or 29900, or subdivision (a) or (b) of Section 29800, and the court is not presented with any credible evidence that the petitioner is a person described in Section 8100 or 8103 of the Welfare and Institutions Code.

(3) Finds that the petitioner does not have a previous conviction under Section 29805, no matter when the prior conviction occurred.

(e) In making its decision, the court may consider the interest of justice, any relevant evidence, and the totality of the circumstances. It is the intent of the Legislature that courts exercise broad discretion in fashioning appropriate relief under this section in cases in which relief is warranted. However, nothing in this section shall be construed to require courts to grant relief to any particular petitioner.

(Added by Stats. 2010, Ch. 711, Sec. 6. (SB 1080) Effective January 1, 2011. Operative January 1, 2012, by Sec. 10 of Ch. 711.)

29865.

Law enforcement officials who enforce the prohibition specified in Section 29805 against a person who has been granted relief pursuant to Section 29855 or 29860 shall be immune from any liability for false arrest arising from the enforcement of Section 29805 unless the person has in possession a certified copy of the court order that granted the person relief from the prohibition. This immunity from liability shall not relieve any person or entity from any other liability that might otherwise be imposed.

(Added by Stats. 2010, Ch. 711, Sec. 6. (SB 1080) Effective January 1, 2011. Operative January 1, 2012, by Sec. 10 of Ch. 711.)

ARTICLE 3. Miscellaneous Provisions [29875- 29875.]

(Article 3 added by Stats. 2010, Ch. 711, Sec. 6.)

29875.

Subject to available funding, the Attorney General, working with the Judicial Council, the California Alliance Against Domestic Violence, prosecutors, and law enforcement, probation, and parole officers, shall develop a protocol for the implementation of the provisions of Section 12021, as it reads in Section 2 of Chapter 830 of the Statutes of 2002, and as later amended at any time before completion of the protocol. The protocol shall be designed to facilitate the enforcement of restrictions on firearm ownership, including provisions for giving notice to defendants who are restricted, provisions for informing those defendants of the procedures by which defendants shall dispose of firearms when required to do so, provisions explaining how defendants shall provide proof of the lawful disposition of firearms, and provisions explaining how defendants may obtain possession of seized firearms when legally permitted to do so pursuant to any provision of law. The protocol shall be completed on or before January 1, 2005.

(Added by Stats. 2010, Ch. 711, Sec. 6. (SB 1080) Effective January 1, 2011. Operative January 1, 2012, by Sec. 10 of Ch. 711.)

CHAPTER 3. Person Convicted of Violent Offense [29900 - 29905]

(Chapter 3 added by Stats. 2010, Ch. 711, Sec. 6.)

29900.

(a) (1) Notwithstanding subdivision (a) of Section 29800, any person who has been previously convicted of any of the offenses listed in Section 29905 and who owns or has in possession or under custody or control any firearm is guilty of a felony.

(2) A dismissal of an accusatory pleading pursuant to Section 1203.4a involving an offense set forth in Section 29905 does not affect the finding of a previous conviction.

(3) If probation is granted, or if the imposition or execution of sentence is suspended, it shall be a condition of the probation or suspension that the defendant serve at least six months in a county jail.

(b) (1) Any person previously convicted of any of the offenses listed in Section 29905 which conviction results from certification by the juvenile court for prosecution as an adult in adult court under the provisions of Section 707 of the Welfare and Institutions Code, who owns or has in possession or under custody or control any firearm, is guilty of a felony.

(2) If probation is granted, or if the imposition or execution of sentence is suspended, it shall be a condition of the probation or suspension that the defendant serve at least six months in a county jail.

(c) The court shall apply the minimum sentence as specified in subdivisions (a) and (b) except in unusual cases where the interests of justice would best be served by granting probation or suspending the imposition or execution of sentence without the imprisonment required by subdivisions (a) and (b), or by granting probation or suspending the imposition or execution of sentence with conditions other than those set forth in subdivisions (a) and (b), in which case the court shall specify on the record and shall enter on the minutes the circumstances indicating that the interests of justice would best be served by the disposition.

(Added by Stats. 2010, Ch. 711, Sec. 6. (SB 1080) Effective January 1, 2011. Operative January 1, 2012, by Sec. 10 of Ch. 711.)

29905.

(a) As used in this chapter, a violent offense includes any of the following:

(1) Murder or voluntary manslaughter.

(2) Mayhem.

(3) Rape.

(4) Sodomy by force, violence, duress, menace, or threat of great bodily harm.

(5) Oral copulation by force, violence, duress, menace, or threat of great bodily harm.

(6) Lewd acts on a child under the age of 14 years.

(7) Any felony punishable by death or imprisonment in the state prison for life.

(8) Any other felony in which the defendant inflicts great bodily injury on any person, other than an accomplice, that has been charged and proven, or any felony in which the defendant uses a firearm which use has been charged and proven.

(9) Attempted murder.

(10) Assault with intent to commit rape or robbery.

(11) Assault with a deadly weapon or instrument on a peace officer.

(12) Assault by a life prisoner on a noninmate.

(13) Assault with a deadly weapon by an inmate.

(14) Arson.

(15) Exploding a destructive device or any explosive with intent to injure.

(16) Exploding a destructive device or any explosive causing great bodily injury.

(17) Exploding a destructive device or any explosive with intent to murder.

(18) Robbery.

(19) Kidnapping.

(20) Taking of a hostage by an inmate of a state prison.

(21) Attempt to commit a felony punishable by death or imprisonment in the state prison for life.

(22) Any felony in which the defendant personally used a dangerous or deadly weapon.

(23) Escape from a state prison by use of force or violence.

(24) Assault with a deadly weapon or force likely to produce great bodily injury.

(25) Any felony violation of Section 186.22.

(26) Any offense enumerated in subdivision (a), (b), or (d) of Section 23515.

(27) Carjacking.

(28) Any offense enumerated in subdivision (c) of Section 23515 if the person has two or more convictions for violating paragraph (2) of subdivision (a) of Section 417.

(b) As used in this chapter, a violent offense also includes any attempt to commit a crime listed in subdivision (a) other than an assault.

(Added by Stats. 2010, Ch. 711, Sec. 6. (SB 1080) Effective January 1, 2011. Operative January 1, 2012, by Sec. 10 of Ch. 711.)

CHAPTER 4. Prohibited Armed Persons File [30000 - 30020]

(Chapter 4 added by Stats. 2010, Ch. 711, Sec. 6.)

30000.

(a) The Attorney General shall establish and maintain an online database to be known as the Prohibited Armed Persons File. The purpose of the file is to cross-reference persons who have ownership or possession of a firearm on or after January 1, 1996, as indicated by a record in the Consolidated Firearms Information System, and who, subsequent to the date of that ownership or possession of a firearm, fall within a class of persons who are prohibited from owning or possessing a firearm.

(b) The information contained in the Prohibited Armed Persons File shall only be available to those entities specified in, and pursuant to, subdivision (b) or (c) of Section 11105, through the California Law Enforcement Telecommunications System, for the purpose of determining if persons are armed and prohibited from possessing firearms.

(Amended by Stats. 2014, Ch. 182, Sec. 1. (AB 2300) Effective January 1, 2015.)

30005.

The Prohibited Armed Persons File database shall function as follows:

(a) Upon entry into the Automated Criminal History System of a disposition for a conviction of any felony, a conviction for any firearms-prohibiting charge specified in Chapter 2 (commencing with Section 29800), a conviction for an offense described in Chapter 3 (commencing with Section 29900), a firearms prohibition pursuant to Section 8100 or 8103 of the Welfare and Institutions Code, or any firearms possession prohibition identified by the federal National Instant Criminal Background Check System, the Department of Justice shall determine if the subject has an entry in the Consolidated Firearms Information System indicating possession or ownership of a firearm on or after January 1, 1996, or an assault weapon registration, or a .50 BMG rifle registration.

(b) Upon an entry into any department automated information system that is used for the identification of persons who are prohibited by state or federal law from acquiring, owning, or possessing firearms, the department shall determine if the subject has an entry in the Consolidated Firearms Information System indicating ownership or possession of a firearm on or after January 1, 1996, or an assault weapon registration, or a .50 BMG rifle registration.

(c) If the department determines that, pursuant to subdivision (a) or (b), the subject has an entry in the Consolidated Firearms Information System indicating possession or ownership of a firearm on or after January 1, 1996, or an assault weapon registration, or a .50 BMG rifle registration, the following information shall be entered into the Prohibited Armed Persons File:

(1) The subject's name.

(2) The subject's date of birth.

(3) The subject's physical description.

(4) Any other identifying information regarding the subject that is deemed necessary by the Attorney General.

(5) The basis of the firearms possession prohibition.

(6) A description of all firearms owned or possessed by the subject, as reflected by the Consolidated Firearms Information System.

(Amended by Stats. 2014, Ch. 182, Sec. 2. (AB 2300) Effective January 1, 2015.)

30010.

The Attorney General shall provide investigative assistance to local law enforcement agencies to better ensure the investigation of individuals who are armed and prohibited from possessing a firearm.

(Added by Stats. 2010, Ch. 711, Sec. 6. (SB 1080) Effective January 1, 2011. Operative January 1, 2012, by Sec. 10 of Ch. 711.)

30012.

(a) No later than April 1, 2020, and no later than April 1 of each year thereafter, the Department of Justice shall report to the Joint Legislative Budget Committee and the fiscal committees of each house of the Legislature all of the following information for the immediately preceding calendar year:

(1) The total number of individuals in the Armed Prohibited Persons System (APPS) and the number of cases which are active and pending, as follows:

(A) (i) For active cases, the department shall report the status of each case for which the department has initiated an investigation. This information shall include, at a minimum, the number of cases that have not been actively investigated for 12 months or longer, along with a breakdown of the time period that has elapsed since a case was added to the system.

(ii) For purposes of this paragraph, "investigation" means any work conducted by sworn or nonsworn staff to determine whether a prohibited person possesses one or more firearms, whether to remove the person from the database, or whether to shift the person to the pending caseload.

(B) For pending cases, the department shall separately report the number of cases that are unable to be cleared, unable to be located, related to out-of-state individuals, related to only federal firearms prohibitions, and related to incarcerated individuals.

(2) The number of individuals added to the APPS database.

(3) The number of individuals removed from the APPS database, including a breakdown of the basis on which they were removed. At a minimum, this information shall separately report those cases that were removed because the individual is deceased, had prohibitions expire or removed, or had their cases resolved as a result of department firearm seizure activities.

(4) The degree to which the backlog in the APPS has been reduced or eliminated. For purposes of this section, "backlog" means the number of cases for which the department did not initiate an investigation within six months of the case being added to the APPS or has not completed investigatory work within six months of initiating an investigation on the case.

(5) The number of individuals in the APPS before and after the relevant reporting period, including a breakdown of why each individual in the APPS is prohibited from possessing a firearm.

(6) The number of agents and other staff hired for enforcement of the APPS.

(7) The number of firearms recovered due to enforcement of the APPS.

(8) The number of contacts made during the APPS enforcement efforts.

(9) Information regarding task forces or collaboration with local law enforcement on reducing the APPS file or backlog.

(b) For purposes of this section, "Armed Prohibited Persons System" means the "Prohibited Armed Persons File," as described in Section 30000.

(Added by Stats. 2019, Ch. 25, Sec. 52. (SB 94) Effective June 27, 2019.)

30015.

(a) The sum of twenty-four million dollars ($24,000,000) is hereby appropriated from the Dealers' Record of Sale Special Account of the General Fund to the Department of Justice to address the backlog in the Armed Prohibited Persons System (APPS) and the illegal possession of firearms by those prohibited persons.

(b) No later than March 1, 2015, and no later than March 1 each year thereafter, the department shall report to the Joint Legislative Budget Committee all of the following for the immediately preceding calendar year:

(1) The degree to which the backlog in the APPS has been reduced or eliminated.

(2) The number of agents hired for enforcement of the APPS.

(3) The number of people cleared from the APPS.

(4) The number of people added to the APPS.

(5) The number of people in the APPS before and after the relevant reporting period, including a breakdown of why each person in the APPS is prohibited from possessing a firearm.

(6) The number of firearms recovered due to enforcement of the APPS.

(7) The number of contacts made during the APPS enforcement efforts.

(8) Information regarding task forces or collaboration with local law enforcement on reducing the APPS backlog.

(c) (1) The requirement for submitting a report imposed under subdivision (b) is inoperative on March 1, 2019, pursuant to Section 10231.5 of the Government Code.

(2) A report to be submitted pursuant to subdivision (b) shall be submitted in compliance with Section 9795 of the Government Code.

(Added by Stats. 2013, Ch. 2, Sec. 2. (SB 140) Effective May 1, 2013.)

30020.

(a) The Department of Justice shall complete an initial review of a match in the daily queue of the Armed Prohibited Persons System within seven days of the match being

placed in the queue and shall periodically reassess whether the department can complete those reviews more efficiently.
(b) (1) For the purpose of this section, "Armed Prohibited Persons System" means the "Prohibited Armed Persons File," as described in Section 30000.
(2) For the purpose of this section, "match" means the entry into the Automated Criminal History System or into any department automated information system of the name and other information of an individual who may be prohibited from acquiring, owning, or possessing a firearm, and a corresponding record of ownership or possession of a firearm by that individual, as described in Section 30005.
(Added by Stats. 2016, Ch. 638, Sec. 1. (AB 1999) Effective January 1, 2017.)

CHAPTER 5. Firearms Eligibility Check [30105 - 30165]

(Chapter 5 added by Stats. 2010, Ch. 711, Sec. 6.)

ARTICLE 1. Firearms Eligibility Check [30105- 30105.]
(Article 1 added by Stats. 2010, Ch. 711, Sec. 6.)
30105.
(a) An individual may request that the Department of Justice perform a firearms eligibility check for that individual. The applicant requesting the eligibility check shall provide the personal information required by Section 28160 or 28165, as applicable, but not any information regarding any firearm, to the department, in an application specified by the department.
(b) The department shall charge a fee of twenty dollars ($20) for performing the eligibility check authorized by this section, but not to exceed the actual processing costs of the department. After the department establishes fees sufficient to reimburse the department for processing costs, fees charged may increase at a rate not to exceed the legislatively approved cost-of-living adjustment for the department's budget or as otherwise increased through the Budget Act.
(c) An applicant for the eligibility check pursuant to subdivision (a) shall complete the application, have it notarized by any licensed California Notary Public, and submit it by mail to the department.
(d) Upon receipt of a notarized application and fee, the department shall do all of the following:
(1) Examine its records, and the records it is authorized to request from the State Department of State Hospitals pursuant to Section 8104 of the Welfare and Institutions Code, to determine if the purchaser is prohibited by state or federal law from possessing, receiving, owning, or purchasing a firearm.
(2) Notify the applicant by mail of its determination of whether the applicant is prohibited by state or federal law from possessing, receiving, owning, or purchasing a firearm. The department's notification shall state either "eligible to possess firearms as of the date the check was completed" or "ineligible to possess firearms as of the date the check was completed."
(e) If the department determines that the information submitted to it in the application contains any blank spaces, or inaccurate, illegible, or incomplete information, preventing identification of the applicant, or if the required fee is not submitted, the department shall not be required to perform the firearms eligibility check.
(f) The department shall make applications to conduct a firearms eligibility check as described in this section available to licensed firearms dealers and on the department's Internet Web site.
(g) The department shall be immune from any liability arising out of the performance of the firearms eligibility check, or any reliance upon the firearms eligibility check.
(h) Except as provided in Sections 29180 and 29182, a person or agency shall not require or request an individual to obtain a firearms eligibility check or notification of a firearms eligibility check pursuant to this section. A violation of this subdivision is a misdemeanor.
(i) The department shall include on the application specified in subdivision (a) and the notification of eligibility specified in subdivision (d) the following statements:
"No person or agency may require or request an individual to obtain a firearms eligibility check or notification of firearms eligibility check pursuant to Section 30105 of the Penal Code. A violation of these provisions is a misdemeanor."
"If the applicant for a firearms eligibility check purchases, transfers, or receives a firearm through a licensed dealer as required by law, a waiting period and background check are both required."
(Amended by Stats. 2016, Ch. 60, Sec. 5. (AB 857) Effective January 1, 2017.)
ARTICLE 2. Exceptions Relating to Law Enforcement [30150 - 30165]
(Article 2 added by Stats. 2010, Ch. 711, Sec. 6.)
30150.
(a) Section 30105 does not apply to any sale, delivery, or transfer of firearms made to an authorized law enforcement representative of any city, county, city and county, or state, or of the federal government, for exclusive use by that governmental agency if, prior to the sale, delivery, or transfer of these firearms, written authorization from the head of the agency authorizing the transaction is presented to the person from whom the purchase, delivery, or transfer is being made.
(b) Proper written authorization is defined as verifiable written certification from the head of the agency by which the purchaser or transferee is employed, identifying the employee as an individual authorized to conduct the transaction, and authorizing the transaction for the exclusive use of the agency by which that person is employed.
(c) Within 10 days of the date a handgun, and commencing January 1, 2014, any firearm, is acquired by the agency, a record of the same shall be entered as an institutional weapon into the Automated Firearms System (AFS) via the California Law Enforcement Telecommunications System (CLETS) by the law enforcement or state agency. Any agency without access to AFS shall arrange with the sheriff of the county in which the agency is located to input this information via this system.
(Amended by Stats. 2011, Ch. 745, Sec. 63. (AB 809) Effective January 1, 2012.)
30155.
Section 30105 does not apply to the loan of a firearm if all of the following conditions are satisfied:
(a) The loan is made by an authorized law enforcement representative of a city, county, or city and county, or of the state or federal government.
(b) The loan is made to a peace officer employed by that agency and authorized to carry a firearm.
(c) The loan is made for the carrying and use of that firearm by that peace officer in the course and scope of the officer's duties.
(Added by Stats. 2010, Ch. 711, Sec. 6. (SB 1080) Effective January 1, 2011. Operative January 1, 2012, by Sec. 10 of Ch. 711.)
30160.
(a) Section 30105 does not apply to the sale, delivery, or transfer of a firearm by a law enforcement agency to a peace officer pursuant to Section 10334 of the Public Contract Code.
(b) Within 10 days of the date that a handgun, and commencing January 1, 2014, any firearm, is sold, delivered, or transferred pursuant to Section 10334 of the Public Contract Code to that peace officer, the name of the officer and the make, model, serial number, and other identifying characteristics of the firearm being sold, delivered, or transferred shall be entered into the Automated Firearms System (AFS) via the California

Law Enforcement Telecommunications System (CLETS) by the law enforcement or state agency that sold, delivered, or transferred the firearm, provided, however, that if the firearm is not a handgun and does not have a serial number, identification number, or identification mark assigned to it, that fact shall be noted in AFS. Any agency without access to AFS shall arrange with the sheriff of the county in which the agency is located to input this information via this system.
(Amended by Stats. 2011, Ch. 745, Sec. 64. (AB 809) Effective January 1, 2012.)
30165.
(a) Section 30105 does not apply to the sale, delivery, or transfer of a firearm by a law enforcement agency to a retiring peace officer who is authorized to carry a firearm pursuant to Chapter 5 (commencing with Section 26300) of Division 5.
(b) Within 10 days of the date that a handgun, and commencing January 1, 2014, any firearm, is sold, delivered, or transferred to that retiring peace officer, the name of the officer and the make, model, serial number, and other identifying characteristics of the firearm being sold, delivered, or transferred shall be entered into the Automated Firearms System (AFS) via the California Law Enforcement Telecommunications System (CLETS) by the law enforcement or state agency that sold, delivered, or transferred the firearm, provided, however, that if the firearm is not a handgun and does not have a serial number, identification number, or identification mark assigned to it, that fact shall be noted in AFS. Any agency without access to AFS shall arrange with the sheriff of the county in which the agency is located to input this information via this system.
(Amended by Stats. 2011, Ch. 745, Sec. 65. (AB 809) Effective January 1, 2012.)

DIVISION 10. SPECIAL RULES RELATING TO PARTICULAR TYPES OF FIREARMS OR FIREARM EQUIPMENT [30210 - 33690]
(Division 10 added by Stats. 2010, Ch. 711, Sec. 6.)

CHAPTER 1. Ammunition [30210 - 30395]

(Chapter 1 added by Stats. 2010, Ch. 711, Sec. 6.)
ARTICLE 1. Flechette Dart Ammunition or Bullet Containing or Carrying an Explosive Agent [30210 - 30290]
(Article 1 added by Stats. 2010, Ch. 711, Sec. 6.)
30210.
Except as provided in Section 30215 and Chapter 1 (commencing with Section 17700) of Division 2 of Title 2, any person in this state who manufactures or causes to be manufactured, imports into the state, keeps for sale, or offers or exposes for sale, or who gives, lends, or possesses either of the following is punishable by imprisonment in a county jail not exceeding one year or imprisonment pursuant to subdivision (h) of Section 1170:
(a) Any ammunition that contains or consists of any flechette dart.
(b) Any bullet containing or carrying an explosive agent.
(Amended by Stats. 2012, Ch. 43, Sec. 104. (SB 1023) Effective June 27, 2012.)
30215.
Section 30210 does not apply to tracer ammunition manufactured for use in a shotgun.
(Added by Stats. 2010, Ch. 711, Sec. 6. (SB 1080) Effective January 1, 2011. Operative January 1, 2012, by Sec. 10 of Ch. 711.)
30290.
Except as provided in Section 30215 and in Chapter 1 (commencing with Section 17700) of Division 2 of Title 2, any ammunition that contains or consists of any flechette dart, or any bullet containing or carrying an explosive agent, is a nuisance and is subject to Section 18010.
(Added by Stats. 2010, Ch. 711, Sec. 6. (SB 1080) Effective January 1, 2011. Operative January 1, 2012, by Sec. 10 of Ch. 711.)
ARTICLE 2. Other Restrictions Relating to Ammunition [30300 - 30340]
(Article 2 added by Stats. 2010, Ch. 711, Sec. 6.)
30300.
(a) Any person, corporation, or dealer who does any of the following shall be punished by imprisonment in a county jail for a term not to exceed six months, or by a fine not to exceed one thousand dollars ($1,000), or by both the imprisonment and fine:
(1) Sells any ammunition or reloaded ammunition to a person under 18 years of age.
(2) Sells any ammunition or reloaded ammunition designed and intended for use in a handgun to a person under 21 years of age. Where ammunition or reloaded ammunition may be used in both a rifle and a handgun, it may be sold to a person who is at least 18 years of age, but less than 21 years of age, if the vendor reasonably believes that the ammunition is being acquired for use in a rifle and not a handgun.
(3) Supplies, delivers, or gives possession of any ammunition to any minor who the person, corporation, or dealer knows, or using reasonable care should know, is prohibited from possessing that ammunition at that time pursuant to Chapter 1 (commencing with Section 29610) of Division 9 of Title 4 of Part 6.
(b) Proof that a person, corporation, or dealer, or his or her agent or employee, demanded, was shown, and acted in reasonable reliance upon, bona fide evidence of majority and identity shall be a defense to any criminal prosecution under this section.
(Added by Stats. 2010, Ch. 711, Sec. 6. (SB 1080) Effective January 1, 2011. Operative January 1, 2012, by Sec. 10 of Ch. 711.)
30305.
(a) (1) No person prohibited from owning or possessing a firearm under Chapter 2 (commencing with Section 29800) or Chapter 3 (commencing with Section 29900) of Division 9 of this title, or Section 8100 or 8103 of the Welfare and Institutions Code, shall own, possess, or have under custody or control, any ammunition or reloaded ammunition.
(2) A violation of this subdivision is punishable by imprisonment in a county jail not to exceed one year or in the state prison, by a fine not to exceed one thousand dollars ($1,000), or by both the fine and imprisonment.
(b) (1) A person who is not prohibited by subdivision (a) from owning, possessing, or having under the person's custody or control, any ammunition or reloaded ammunition, but who is enjoined from engaging in activity pursuant to an injunction issued pursuant to Section 3479 of the Civil Code against that person as a member of a criminal street gang, as defined in Section 186.22, may not own, possess, or have under the person's custody or control, any ammunition or reloaded ammunition.
(2) A violation of this subdivision is a misdemeanor.
(c) A violation of subdivision (a) or (b) is justifiable where all of the following conditions are met:
(1) The person found the ammunition or reloaded ammunition or took the ammunition or reloaded ammunition from a person who was committing a crime against the person who found or took the ammunition or reloaded ammunition.
(2) The person possessed the ammunition or reloaded ammunition no longer than was necessary to deliver or transport the ammunition or reloaded ammunition to a law enforcement agency for that agency's disposition according to law.
(3) The person is prohibited from possessing any ammunition or reloaded ammunition solely because that person is prohibited from owning or possessing a firearm only by virtue of Chapter 2 (commencing with Section 29800) of Division 9 or ammunition or reloaded ammunition because of subdivision (b).

(d) Upon the trial for violating subdivision (a) or (b), the trier of fact shall determine whether the defendant is subject to the exemption created by subdivision (c). The defendant has the burden of proving by a preponderance of the evidence that the defendant is subject to the exemption provided by subdivision (c).
(Added by Stats. 2010, Ch. 711, Sec. 6. (SB 1080) Effective January 1, 2011. Operative January 1, 2012, by Sec. 10 of Ch. 711.)
30306.
(a) Any person, corporation, firm, or other business enterprise who supplies, delivers, sells, or gives possession or control of, any ammunition to any person who he or she knows or using reasonable care should know is prohibited from owning, possessing, or having under custody or control, any ammunition or reloaded ammunition pursuant to subdivision (a) or (b) of Section 30305, is guilty of a misdemeanor, punishable by imprisonment in a county jail not exceeding one year, or a fine not exceeding one thousand dollars ($1,000), or by both that fine and imprisonment.
(b) Any person, corporation, firm, or other business enterprise who supplies, delivers, sells, or gives possession or control of, any ammunition to any person whom the person, corporation, firm, or other business enterprise knows or has cause to believe is not the actual purchaser or transferee of the ammunition, with knowledge or cause to believe that the ammunition is to be subsequently sold or transferred to a person who is prohibited from owning, possessing, or having under custody or control any ammunition or reloaded ammunition pursuant to subdivision (a) or (b) of Section 30305, is guilty of a misdemeanor, punishable by imprisonment in a county jail not exceeding one year, or a fine not exceeding one thousand dollars ($1,000), or by both that fine and imprisonment.
(c) The provisions of this section are cumulative and shall not be construed as restricting the application of any other law. However, an act or omission punishable in different ways by this section and another provision of law shall not be punished under more than one provision.
(Amended November 8, 2016, by initiative Proposition 63, Sec. 8.5.)
30310.
(a) Unless it is with the written permission of the school district superintendent, the superintendent's designee, or equivalent school authority, no person shall carry ammunition or reloaded ammunition onto school grounds, except sworn law enforcement officers acting within the scope of their duties.
(b) This section shall not apply to any of the following:
(1) A duly appointed peace officer as defined in Chapter 4.5 (commencing with Section 830) of Title 3 of Part 2.
(2) A full-time paid peace officer of another state or the federal government who is carrying out official duties while in California.
(3) Any person summoned by any of these officers to assist in making an arrest or preserving the peace while that person is actually engaged in assisting the officer.
(4) A member of the military forces of this state or of the United States who is engaged in the performance of that person's duties.
(5) An armored vehicle guard, who is engaged in the performance of that person's duties, as defined in subdivision (d) of Section 7582.1 of the Business and Professions Code.
(6) Any peace officer, listed in Section 830.1 or 830.2, or subdivision (a) of Section 830.33, whether active or honorably retired.
(7) Any other duly appointed peace officer.
(8) Any honorably retired peace officer listed in subdivision (c) of Section 830.5.
(9) Any other honorably retired peace officer who during the course and scope of his or her appointment as a peace officer was authorized to, and did, carry a firearm.
(10) (A) A person carrying ammunition or reloaded ammunition onto school grounds that is in a motor vehicle at all times and is within a locked container or within the locked trunk of the vehicle.
(B) For purposes of this paragraph, the term "locked container" has the same meaning as set forth in Section 16850.
(c) A violation of this section is punishable by imprisonment in a county jail for a term not to exceed six months, a fine not to exceed one thousand dollars ($1,000), or both the imprisonment and fine.
(Amended by Stats. 2015, Ch. 766, Sec. 2. (SB 707) Effective January 1, 2016.)
30312.
(a) (1) Commencing January 1, 2018, the sale of ammunition by any party shall be conducted by or processed through a licensed ammunition vendor.
(2) When neither party to an ammunition sale is a licensed ammunition vendor, the seller shall deliver the ammunition to a vendor to process the transaction. The ammunition vendor shall promptly and properly deliver the ammunition to the purchaser, if the sale is not prohibited, as if the ammunition were the vendor's own merchandise. If the ammunition vendor cannot legally deliver the ammunition to the purchaser, the vendor shall forthwith return the ammunition to the seller. The ammunition vendor may charge the purchaser an administrative fee to process the transaction, in an amount to be set by the Department of Justice, in addition to any applicable fees that may be charged pursuant to the provisions of this title.
(b) Commencing January 1, 2018, the sale, delivery, or transfer of ownership of ammunition by any party may only occur in a face-to-face transaction with the seller, deliverer, or transferor, provided, however, that ammunition may be purchased or acquired over the Internet or through other means of remote ordering if a licensed ammunition vendor initially receives the ammunition and processes the transaction in compliance with this section and Article 3 (commencing with Section 30342) of Chapter 1 of Division 10 of Title 4 of this part.
(c) Subdivisions (a) and (b) shall not apply to the sale, delivery, or transfer of ammunition to any of the following:
(1) An authorized law enforcement representative of a city, county, city and county, or state or federal government, if the sale, delivery, or transfer is for exclusive use by that government agency and, prior to the sale, delivery, or transfer of the ammunition, written authorization from the head of the agency employing the purchaser or transferee is obtained, identifying the employee as an individual authorized to conduct the transaction, and authorizing the transaction for the exclusive use of the agency employing the individual.
(2) A sworn peace officer, as defined in Chapter 4.5 (commencing with Section 830) of Title 3 of Part 2, or sworn federal law enforcement officer, who is authorized to carry a firearm in the course and scope of the officer's duties.
(3) An importer or manufacturer of ammunition or firearms who is licensed to engage in business pursuant to Chapter 44 (commencing with Section 921) of Title 18 of the United States Code and the regulations issued pursuant thereto.
(4) A person who is on the centralized list of exempted federal firearms licensees maintained by the Department of Justice pursuant to Article 6 (commencing with Section 28450) of Chapter 6 of Division 6 of this title.
(5) A person whose licensed premises are outside this state and who is licensed as a dealer or collector of firearms pursuant to Chapter 44 (commencing with Section 921) of Title 18 of the United States Code and the regulations issued pursuant thereto.
(6) A person who is licensed as a collector of firearms pursuant to Chapter 44 (commencing with Section 921) of Title 18 of the United States Code and the regulations issued pursuant thereto, whose licensed premises are within this state, and who has a current certificate of eligibility issued by the Department of Justice pursuant to Section 26710.
(7) An ammunition vendor.
(8) A consultant-evaluator.

(9) A person who purchases or receives ammunition at a target facility holding a business or other regulatory license, provided that the ammunition is at all times kept within the facility's premises.
(10) A person who purchases or receives ammunition from a spouse, registered domestic partner, or immediate family member as defined in Section 16720.
(11) A person enrolled in the basic training academy for peace officers or any other course certified by the Commission on Peace Officer Standards and Training, an instructor of the academy or course, or a staff member of the academy or entity providing the course, who is purchasing the ammunition for the purpose of participation or use in the course.
(d) A violation of this section is a misdemeanor.
(Amended by Stats. 2017, Ch. 783, Sec. 3. (AB 693) Effective October 14, 2017. Note: This section was amended on Nov. 8, 2016, by initiative Prop. 63.)
30314.
(a) Commencing January 1, 2018, a resident of this state shall not bring or transport into this state any ammunition that he or she purchased or otherwise obtained from outside of this state unless he or she first has that ammunition delivered to a licensed ammunition vendor for delivery to that resident pursuant to the procedures set forth in Section 30312.
(b) Subdivision (a) does not apply to any of the following:
(1) An ammunition vendor.
(2) A sworn peace officer, as defined in Chapter 4.5 (commencing with Section 830) of Title 3 of Part 2, or sworn federal law enforcement officer, who is authorized to carry a firearm in the course and scope of the officer's duties.
(3) An importer or manufacturer of ammunition or firearms who is licensed to engage in business pursuant to Chapter 44 (commencing with Section 921) of Title 18 of the United States Code and the regulations issued pursuant thereto.
(4) A person who is on the centralized list of exempted federal firearms licensees maintained by the Department of Justice pursuant to Article 6 (commencing with Section 28450) of Chapter 6 of Division 6.
(5) A person who is licensed as a collector of firearms pursuant to Chapter 44 (commencing with Section 921) of Title 18 of the United States Code and the regulations issued pursuant thereto, whose licensed premises are within this state, and who has a current certificate of eligibility issued by the Department of Justice pursuant to Section 26710.
(6) A person who acquired the ammunition from a spouse, registered domestic partner, or immediate family member as defined in Section 16720.
(c) A violation of this section is an infraction for any first time offense, and either an infraction or a misdemeanor for any subsequent offense.
(Added November 8, 2016, by initiative Proposition 63, Sec. 8.7.)
30315.
Any person, firm, or corporation who, within this state knowingly possesses any handgun ammunition designed primarily to penetrate metal or armor is guilty of a public offense and upon conviction thereof shall be punished by imprisonment pursuant to subdivision (h) of Section 1170, or in the county jail for a term not to exceed one year, or by a fine not to exceed five thousand dollars ($5,000), or by both that fine and imprisonment.
(Amended by Stats. 2011, Ch. 15, Sec. 548. (AB 109) Effective April 4, 2011. Amending action operative October 1, 2011, by Sec. 636 of Ch. 15, as amended by Stats. 2011, Ch. 39, Sec. 68. Section operative January 1, 2012, pursuant to Stats. 2010, Ch. 711, Sec. 10.)
30320.
Any person, firm, or corporation who, within this state, manufactures, imports, sells, offers to sell, or knowingly transports any handgun ammunition designed primarily to penetrate metal or armor is guilty of a felony and upon conviction thereof shall be punished by imprisonment in state prison, or by a fine not to exceed five thousand dollars ($5,000), or by both that fine and imprisonment.
(Added by Stats. 2010, Ch. 711, Sec. 6. (SB 1080) Effective January 1, 2011. Operative January 1, 2012, by Sec. 10 of Ch. 711.)
30325.
Nothing in this article shall apply to or affect the possession of handgun ammunition designed primarily to penetrate metal or armor by a person who found the ammunition, if that person is not prohibited from possessing firearms or ammunition pursuant to subdivision (a) of Section 30305, Chapter 2 (commencing with Section 29800) or Chapter 3 (commencing with Section 29900) of Division 9 of this title, or Section 8100 or 8103 of the Welfare and Institutions Code, and the person is transporting the ammunition to a law enforcement agency for disposition according to law.
(Added by Stats. 2010, Ch. 711, Sec. 6. (SB 1080) Effective January 1, 2011. Operative January 1, 2012, by Sec. 10 of Ch. 711.)
30330.
Nothing in this article shall apply to or affect the sale to, purchase by, possession of, or use of any ammunition by any member of the Army, Navy, Air Force, or Marine Corps of the United States, or the National Guard, while on duty and acting within the scope and course of employment, or any police agency or forensic laboratory or any person who is the holder of a valid permit issued pursuant to Article 3 (commencing with Section 18900) of Chapter 1 of Division 5 of Title 2.
(Added by Stats. 2010, Ch. 711, Sec. 6. (SB 1080) Effective January 1, 2011. Operative January 1, 2012, by Sec. 10 of Ch. 711.)
30335.
Nothing in this article shall prohibit the possession, importation, sale, attempted sale, or transport of ammunition from which the propellant has been removed and the primer has been permanently deactivated.
(Added by Stats. 2010, Ch. 711, Sec. 6. (SB 1080) Effective January 1, 2011. Operative January 1, 2012, by Sec. 10 of Ch. 711.)
30340.
Nothing in this article shall prohibit the manufacture of ammunition under contracts approved by agencies of the state or federal government.
(Added by Stats. 2010, Ch. 711, Sec. 6. (SB 1080) Effective January 1, 2011. Operative January 1, 2012, by Sec. 10 of Ch. 711.)

ARTICLE 3. Ammunition Vendors [30342 - 30365]
(Heading of Article 3 amended November 8, 2016, by initiative Proposition 63, Sec. 8.8.)
30342.
(a) Commencing January 1, 2018, a valid ammunition vendor license shall be required for any person, firm, corporation, or other business enterprise to sell more than 500 rounds of ammunition in any 30-day period.
(b) A violation of this section is a misdemeanor.
(Added November 8, 2016, by initiative Proposition 63, Sec. 8.9.)
30345.
A vendor shall comply with all of the conditions, requirements, and prohibitions stated in this article.
(Added by Stats. 2010, Ch. 711, Sec. 6. (SB 1080) Effective January 1, 2011. Operative January 1, 2012, by Sec. 10 of Ch. 711.)
30347.
(a) An ammunition vendor shall require any agent or employee who handles, sells, delivers, or has under his or her custody or control any ammunition, to obtain and provide to the vendor a certificate of eligibility from the Department of Justice issued pursuant to Section 26710. On the application for the certificate, the agent or employee shall provide the name and address of the ammunition vendor with whom the person is

employed, or the name and California firearms dealer number of the ammunition vendor if applicable.

(b) The department shall notify the ammunition vendor in the event that the agent or employee who has a certificate of eligibility is or becomes prohibited from possessing ammunition under subdivision (a) of Section 30305 or federal law.

(c) An ammunition vendor shall not permit any agent or employee who the vendor knows or reasonably should know is a person described in Chapter 2 (commencing with Section 29800) or Chapter 3 (commencing with Section 29900) of Division 9 of this title or Section 8100 or 8103 of the Welfare and Institutions Code to handle, sell, deliver, or have under his or her custody or control, any ammunition in the course and scope of employment.

(Amended November 8, 2016, by initiative Proposition 63, Sec. 8.10.)

30348.

(a) Except as provided in subdivision (b), the sale of ammunition by a licensed vendor shall be conducted at the location specified in the license.

(b) A vendor may sell ammunition at a gun show or event if the gun show or event is not conducted from any motorized or towed vehicle.

(c) For purposes of this section, "gun show or event" means a function sponsored by any national, state, or local organization, devoted to the collection, competitive use, or other sporting use of firearms, or an organization or association that sponsors functions devoted to the collection, competitive use, or other sporting use of firearms in the community.

(d) Sales of ammunition at a gun show or event shall comply with all applicable laws including Sections 30347, 30350, 30352, and 30360.

(Added November 8, 2016, by initiative Proposition 63, Sec. 8.11.)

30350.

An ammunition vendor shall not sell or otherwise transfer ownership of, offer for sale or otherwise offer to transfer ownership of, or display for sale or display for transfer of ownership of any ammunition in a manner that allows that ammunition to be accessible to a purchaser or transferee without the assistance of the vendor or an employee of the vendor.

(Amended November 8, 2016, by initiative Proposition 63, Sec. 8.12.)

30352.

(a) Commencing July 1, 2019, an ammunition vendor shall not sell or otherwise transfer ownership of any ammunition without, at the time of delivery, legibly recording the following information on a form to be prescribed by the Department of Justice:

(1) The date of the sale or other transfer.

(2) The purchaser's or transferee's driver's license or other identification number and the state in which it was issued.

(3) The brand, type, and amount of ammunition sold or otherwise transferred.

(4) The purchaser's or transferee's full name and signature.

(5) The name of the salesperson who processed the sale or other transaction.

(6) The purchaser's or transferee's full residential address and telephone number.

(7) The purchaser's or transferee's date of birth.

(b) Commencing July 1, 2019, an ammunition vendor shall electronically submit to the department the information required by subdivision (a) for all sales and transfers of ownership of ammunition. The department shall retain this information in a database to be known as the Ammunition Purchase Records File. This information shall remain confidential and may be used by the department and those entities specified in, and pursuant to, subdivision (b) or (c) of Section 11105, through the California Law Enforcement Telecommunications System, only for law enforcement purposes. The ammunition vendor shall not use, sell, disclose, or share the information for any other purpose other than the submission required by this subdivision without the express written consent of the purchaser or transferee.

(c) Commencing on July 1, 2019, only those persons listed in this subdivision, or those persons or entities listed in subdivision (e), shall be authorized to purchase ammunition. Prior to delivering any ammunition, an ammunition vendor shall require bona fide evidence of identity to verify that the person who is receiving delivery of the ammunition is a person or entity listed in subdivision (e) or one of the following:

(1) A person authorized to purchase ammunition pursuant to Section 30370.

(2) A person who was approved by the department to receive a firearm from the ammunition vendor, pursuant to Section 28220, if that vendor is a licensed firearms dealer, and the ammunition is delivered to the person in the same transaction as the firearm.

(d) Commencing July 1, 2019, the ammunition vendor shall verify with the department, in a manner prescribed by the department, that the person is authorized to purchase ammunition. If the person is not listed as an authorized ammunition purchaser, the vendor shall deny the sale or transfer.

(e) Subdivisions (a) and (d) shall not apply to sales or other transfers of ownership of ammunition by ammunition vendors to any of the following, if properly identified:

(1) An ammunition vendor.

(2) A person who is on the centralized list of exempted federal firearms licensees maintained by the department pursuant to Article 6 (commencing with Section 28450) of Chapter 6 of Division 6.

(3) A person who purchases or receives ammunition at a target facility holding a business or other regulatory license, provided that the ammunition is at all times kept within the facility's premises.

(4) A gunsmith.

(5) A wholesaler.

(6) A manufacturer or importer of firearms or ammunition licensed pursuant to Chapter 44 (commencing with Section 921) of Title 18 of the United States Code, and the regulations issued pursuant thereto.

(7) An authorized law enforcement representative of a city, county, city and county, or state or federal government, if the sale or other transfer of ownership is for exclusive use by that government agency, and, prior to the sale, delivery, or transfer of the handgun ammunition, written authorization from the head of the agency authorizing the transaction is presented to the person from whom the purchase, delivery, or transfer is being made. Proper written authorization is defined as verifiable written certification from the head of the agency by which the purchaser, transferee, or person otherwise acquiring ownership is employed, identifying the employee as an individual authorized to conduct the transaction, and authorizing the transaction for the exclusive use of the agency by which that individual is employed.

(8) (A) A properly identified sworn peace officer, as defined in Chapter 4.5 (commencing with Section 830) of Title 3 of Part 2, or properly identified sworn federal law enforcement officer, who is authorized to carry a firearm in the course and scope of the officer's duties.

(B) (i) Proper identification is defined as verifiable written certification from the head of the agency by which the purchaser or transferee is employed, identifying the purchaser or transferee as a full-time paid peace officer who is authorized to carry a firearm in the course and scope of the officer's duties.

(ii) The certification shall be delivered to the vendor at the time of purchase or transfer and the purchaser or transferee shall provide bona fide evidence of identity to verify that he or she is the person authorized in the certification.

(iii) The vendor shall keep the certification with the record of sale and submit the certification to the department.

(f) The department is authorized to adopt regulations to implement the provisions of this section.

(Amended (as amended Nov. 8, 2016, by Proposition 63) by Stats. 2016, Ch. 55, Sec. 12. (SB 1235) Effective January 1, 2017.)

30355.

Commencing February 1, 2011, the records required by this article shall be maintained on the premises of the vendor for a period of not less than five years from the date of the recorded transfer.

(Added by Stats. 2010, Ch. 711, Sec. 6. (SB 1080) Effective January 1, 2011. Operative January 1, 2012, by Sec. 10 of Ch. 711.)

30357.

(a) Commencing February 1, 2011, the records referred to in Section 30352 shall be subject to inspection at any time during normal business hours by any peace officer employed by a sheriff, city police department, or district attorney as provided in subdivision (a) of Section 830.1, or employed by the department as provided in subdivision (b) of Section 830.1, provided that the officer is conducting an investigation where access to those records is or may be relevant, is seeking information about persons prohibited from owning a firearm or ammunition, or is engaged in ensuring compliance with the Dangerous Weapons Control Law, as defined in Section 23500, or any other laws pertaining to firearms or ammunition.

(b) The records referred to in Section 30352 shall also be subject to inspection at any time during normal business hours by any other employee of the department, provided that the employee is conducting an investigation where access to those records is or may be relevant, is seeking information about persons prohibited from owning a firearm or ammunition, or is engaged in ensuring compliance with the Dangerous Weapons Control Law, as defined in Section 23500, or any other laws pertaining to firearms or ammunition.

(Added by Stats. 2010, Ch. 711, Sec. 6. (SB 1080) Effective January 1, 2011. Operative January 1, 2012, by Sec. 10 of Ch. 711.)

30360.

Commencing February 1, 2011, a vendor shall not knowingly make a false entry in, fail to make a required entry in, fail to obtain the required thumbprint, or otherwise fail to maintain in the required manner, records prepared in accordance with Section 30352. If the right thumbprint is not available, then the vendor shall have the purchaser or transferee use the left thumb, or any available finger, and shall so indicate on the form.

(Added by Stats. 2010, Ch. 711, Sec. 6. (SB 1080) Effective January 1, 2011. Operative January 1, 2012, by Sec. 10 of Ch. 711.)

30362.

(a) Commencing February 1, 2011, no vendor shall, during any inspection conducted pursuant to this article, refuse to permit a person authorized under Section 30357 to examine any record prepared in accordance with this article.

(b) Commencing February 1, 2011, no vendor shall refuse to permit the use of any record or information by a person authorized under Section 30357.

(Added by Stats. 2010, Ch. 711, Sec. 6. (SB 1080) Effective January 1, 2011. Operative January 1, 2012, by Sec. 10 of Ch. 711.)

30363.

Within 48 hours of discovery, an ammunition vendor shall report the loss or theft of any of the following items to the appropriate law enforcement agency in the city, county, or city and county where the vendor's business premises are located:

(1) Any ammunition that is merchandise of the vendor.

(2) Any ammunition that the vendor takes possession of pursuant to Section 30312.

(3) Any ammunition kept at the vendor's place of business.

(Added November 8, 2016, by initiative Proposition 63, Sec. 8.14.)

30365.

(a) A violation of Section 30352, 30355, 30360, or 30362 is a misdemeanor.

(b) The provisions of this section are cumulative, and shall not be construed as restricting the application of any other law. However, an act or omission punishable in different ways by different provisions of law shall not be punished under more than one provision.

(Added by Stats. 2010, Ch. 711, Sec. 6. (SB 1080) Effective January 1, 2011. Operative January 1, 2012, by Sec. 10 of Ch. 711.)

ARTICLE 4. Ammunition Purchase Authorizations [30370 - 30371]

(Article 4 added November 8, 2016, by initiative Proposition 63, Sec. 8.15.)

30370.

(a) Commencing July 1, 2019, the department shall electronically approve the purchase or transfer of ammunition through a vendor, as defined in Section 16151, except as otherwise specified. This approval shall occur at the time of purchase or transfer, prior to the purchaser or transferee taking possession of the ammunition. Pursuant to the authorization specified in paragraph (1) of subdivision (c) of Section 30352, the following persons are authorized to purchase ammunition:

(1) A purchaser or transferee whose information matches an entry in the Automated Firearms System (AFS) and who is eligible to possess ammunition as specified in subdivision (b).

(2) A purchaser or transferee who has a current certificate of eligibility issued by the department pursuant to Section 26710.

(3) A purchaser or transferee who is not prohibited from purchasing or possessing ammunition in a single ammunition transaction or purchase made pursuant to the procedure developed pursuant to subdivision (c).

(b) To determine if the purchaser or transferee is eligible to purchase or possess ammunition pursuant to paragraph (1) of subdivision (a), the department shall cross-reference the ammunition purchaser's or transferee's name, date of birth, current address, and driver's license or other government identification number, as described in Section 28180, with the information maintained in the AFS. If the purchaser's or transferee's information does not match an AFS entry, the transaction shall be denied. If the purchaser's or transferee's information matches an AFS entry, the department shall determine if the purchaser or transferee falls within a class of persons who are prohibited from owning or possessing ammunition by cross-referencing with the Prohibited Armed Persons File. If the purchaser or transferee is prohibited from owning or possessing a firearm, the transaction shall be denied.

(c) The department shall develop a procedure in which a person who is not prohibited from purchasing or possessing ammunition may be approved for a single ammunition transaction or purchase. The department shall recover the cost of processing and regulatory and enforcement activities related to this section by charging the ammunition transaction or purchase applicant a fee not to exceed the fee charged for the department's Dealers' Record of Sale (DROS) process, as described in Section 28225 and not to exceed the department's reasonable costs.

(d) A vendor is prohibited from providing a purchaser or transferee ammunition without department approval. If a vendor cannot electronically verify a person's eligibility to purchase or possess ammunition via an Internet connection, the department shall provide a telephone line to verify eligibility. This option is available to ammunition vendors who can demonstrate legitimate geographical and telecommunications limitations in submitting the information electronically and who are approved by the department to use the telephone line verification.

(e) The department shall recover the reasonable cost of regulatory and enforcement activities related to this article by charging ammunition purchasers and transferees a per transaction fee not to exceed one dollar ($1), provided, however, that the fee may be increased at a rate not to exceed any increases in the California Consumer Price Index as compiled and reported by the Department of Industrial Relations, not to exceed the reasonable regulatory and enforcement costs.

(f) A fund to be known as the "Ammunition Safety and Enforcement Special Fund" is hereby created within the State Treasury. All fees received pursuant to this section shall be deposited into the Ammunition Safety and Enforcement Special Fund and, notwithstanding Section 13340 of the Government Code, are continuously appropriated for purposes of implementing, operating, and enforcing the ammunition authorization program provided for in this section and Section 30352 and for repaying the start-up loan provided for in Section 30371.

(g) The Department of Justice is authorized to adopt regulations to implement this section.

(Added by Stats. 2016, Ch. 55, Sec. 15. (SB 1235) Effective January 1, 2017. Note: Stats. 2016, Ch. 55, Sec. 16, repealed the prior version of Section 30370, which was added November 8, 2016, by Proposition 63.)

30371.

(a) There is hereby appropriated twenty-five million dollars ($25,000,000) from the General Fund as a loan for the start-up costs of implementing, operating and enforcing the provisions of the ammunition authorization program provided for in Sections 30352 and 30370.

(b) For purposes of repaying the loan, the Controller shall, after disbursing moneys necessary to implement, operate and enforce the ammunition authorization program provided for in Sections 30352 and 30370, transfer all proceeds from fees received by the Ammunition Safety and Enforcement Special Fund up to the amount of the loan provided by this section, including interest at the pooled money investment account rate, to the General Fund.

(Added November 8, 2016, by initiative Proposition 63, Sec. 8.15.)

ARTICLE 5. Ammunition Vendor Licenses [30385 - 30395]
(Article 5 added November 8, 2016, by initiative Proposition 63, Sec. 8.16.)

30385.

(a) The Department of Justice is authorized to issue ammunition vendor licenses pursuant to this article. The department shall, commencing July 1, 2017, commence accepting applications for ammunition vendor licenses. If an application is denied, the department shall inform the applicant of the reason for denial in writing.

(b) The ammunition vendor license shall be issued in a form prescribed by the department and shall be valid for a period of one year. The department may adopt regulations to administer the application and enforcement provisions of this article. The license shall allow the licensee to sell ammunition at the location specified in the license or at a gun show or event as set forth in Section 30348.

(c) (1) In the case of an entity other than a natural person, the department shall issue the license to the entity, but shall require a responsible person to pass the background check pursuant to Section 30395.

(2) For purposes of this article, "responsible person" means a person having the power to direct the management, policies, and practices of the entity as it pertains to ammunition.

(d) Commencing January 1, 2018, a firearms dealer licensed pursuant to Sections 26700 to 26915, inclusive, shall automatically be deemed a licensed ammunition vendor, provided the dealer complies with the requirements of Article 2 (commencing with Section 30300) and Article 3 (commencing with Section 30342).

(Added November 8, 2016, by initiative Proposition 63, Sec. 8.16.)

30390.

(a) The Department of Justice may charge ammunition vendor license applicants a reasonable fee sufficient to reimburse the department for the reasonable, estimated costs of administering the license program, including the enforcement of this program and maintenance of the registry of ammunition vendors.

(b) The fees received by the department pursuant to this article shall be deposited in the Ammunition Vendors Special Account, which is hereby created. Notwithstanding Section 13340 of the Government Code, the revenue in the fund is continuously appropriated for use by the department for the purpose of implementing, administering and enforcing the provisions of this article, and for collecting and maintaining information submitted pursuant to Section 30352.

(c) The revenue in the Firearms Safety and Enforcement Special Fund shall also be available upon appropriation to the department for the purpose of implementing and enforcing the provisions of this article.

(Added November 8, 2016, by initiative Proposition 63, Sec. 8.16.)

30395.

(a) The Department of Justice is authorized to issue ammunition vendor licenses to applicants who the department has determined, either as an individual or a responsible person, are not prohibited from possessing, receiving, owning, or purchasing ammunition under subdivision (a) of Section 30305 or federal law, and who provide a copy of any regulatory or business license required by local government, a valid seller's permit issued by the State Board of Equalization, a federal firearms license if the person is federally licensed, and a certificate of eligibility issued by the department.

(b) The department shall keep a registry of all licensed ammunition vendors. Law enforcement agencies shall be provided access to the registry for law enforcement purposes.

(c) An ammunition vendor license is subject to forfeiture for a breach of any of the prohibitions and requirements of Article 2 (commencing with Section 30300) or Article 3 (commencing with Section 30342).

(Added November 8, 2016, by initiative Proposition 63, Sec. 8.16.)

CHAPTER 2. Assault Weapons and .50 BMG Rifles [30500 - 31115]

(Chapter 2 added by Stats. 2010, Ch. 711, Sec. 6.)

ARTICLE 1. General Provisions [30500 - 30530]
(Article 1 added by Stats. 2010, Ch. 711, Sec. 6.)

30500.

This chapter shall be known as the Roberti-Roos Assault Weapons Control Act of 1989 and the .50 Caliber BMG Regulation Act of 2004.

(Added by Stats. 2010, Ch. 711, Sec. 6. (SB 1080) Effective January 1, 2011. Operative January 1, 2012, by Sec. 10 of Ch. 711.)

30505.

(a) The Legislature hereby finds and declares that the proliferation and use of assault weapons poses a threat to the health, safety, and security of all citizens of this state. The Legislature has restricted the assault weapons specified in Section 30510 based upon finding that each firearm has such a high rate of fire and capacity for firepower that its function as a legitimate sports or recreational firearm is substantially outweighed by the danger that it can be used to kill and injure human beings. It is the intent of the Legislature in enacting this chapter to place restrictions on the use of assault weapons and to establish a registration and permit procedure for their lawful sale and possession. It is not, however, the intent of the Legislature by this chapter to place restrictions on the use of those weapons which are primarily designed and intended for hunting, target practice, or other legitimate sports or recreational activities.

(b) The Legislature hereby finds and declares that the proliferation and use of .50 BMG rifles poses a clear and present terrorist threat to the health, safety, and security of all residents of, and visitors to, this state, based upon findings that those firearms have such a high capacity for long distance and highly destructive firepower that they pose an unacceptable risk to the death and serious injury of human beings, destruction or serious damage of vital public and private buildings, civilian, police and military vehicles, power generation and transmission facilities, petrochemical production and storage facilities, and transportation infrastructure. It is the intent of the Legislature in enacting

this chapter to place restrictions on the use of these rifles and to establish a registration and permit procedure for their lawful sale and possession.

(Added by Stats. 2010, Ch. 711, Sec. 6. (SB 1080) Effective January 1, 2011. Operative January 1, 2012, by Sec. 10 of Ch. 711.)

30510.

As used in this chapter and in Sections 16780, 17000, and 27555, "assault weapon" means the following designated semiautomatic firearms:

(a) All of the following specified rifles:

(1) All AK series including, but not limited to, the models identified as follows:

(A) Made in China AK, AKM, AKS, AK47, AK47S, 56, 56S, 84S, and 86S.

(B) Norinco 56, 56S, 84S, and 86S.

(C) Poly Technologies AKS and AK47.

(D) MAADI AK47 and ARM.

(2) UZI and Galil.

(3) Beretta AR-70.

(4) CETME Sporter.

(5) Colt AR-15 series.

(6) Daewoo K-1, K-2, Max 1, Max 2, AR 100, and AR 110C.

(7) Fabrique Nationale FAL, LAR, FNC, 308 Match, and Sporter.

(8) MAS 223.

(9) HK-91, HK-93, HK-94, and HK-PSG-1.

(10) The following MAC types:

(A) RPB Industries Inc. sM10 and sM11.

(B) SWD Incorporated M11.

(11) SKS with detachable magazine.

(12) SIG AMT, PE-57, SG 550, and SG 551.

(13) Springfield Armory BM59 and SAR-48.

(14) Sterling MK-6.

(15) Steyer AUG.

(16) Valmet M62S, M71S, and M78S.

(17) Armalite AR-180.

(18) Bushmaster Assault Rifle.

(19) Calico M-900.

(20) J&R ENG M-68.

(21) Weaver Arms Nighthawk.

(b) All of the following specified pistols:

(1) UZI.

(2) Encom MP-9 and MP-45.

(3) The following MAC types:

(A) RPB Industries Inc. sM10 and sM11.

(B) SWD Incorporated M-11.

(C) Advance Armament Inc. M-11.

(D) Military Armament Corp. Ingram M-11.

(4) Intratec TEC-9.

(5) Sites Spectre.

(6) Sterling MK-7.

(7) Calico M-950.

(8) Bushmaster Pistol.

(c) All of the following specified shotguns:

(1) Franchi SPAS 12 and LAW 12.

(2) Striker 12.

(3) The Streetsweeper type S/S Inc. SS/12.

(d) Any firearm declared to be an assault weapon by the court pursuant to former Section 12276.5, as it read in Section 3 of Chapter 19 of the Statutes of 1989, Section 1 of Chapter 874 of the Statutes of 1990, or Section 3 of Chapter 954 of the Statutes of 1991, which is specified as an assault weapon in a list promulgated pursuant to former Section 12276.5, as it read in Section 3 of Chapter 954 of the Statutes of 1991.

(e) This section is declaratory of existing law and a clarification of the law and the Legislature's intent which bans the weapons enumerated in this section, the weapons included in the list promulgated by the Attorney General pursuant to former Section 12276.5, as it read in Section 3 of Chapter 954 of the Statutes of 1991, and any other models that are only variations of those weapons with minor differences, regardless of the manufacturer. The Legislature has defined assault weapons as the types, series, and models listed in this section because it was the most effective way to identify and restrict a specific class of semiautomatic weapons.

(f) As used in this section, "series" includes all other models that are only variations, with minor differences, of those models listed in subdivision (a), regardless of the manufacturer.

(Added by Stats. 2010, Ch. 711, Sec. 6. (SB 1080) Effective January 1, 2011. Operative January 1, 2012, by Sec. 10 of Ch. 711.)

30515.

(a) Notwithstanding Section 30510, "assault weapon" also means any of the following:

(1) A semiautomatic, centerfire rifle that does not have a fixed magazine but has any one of the following:

(A) A pistol grip that protrudes conspicuously beneath the action of the weapon.

(B) A thumbhole stock.

(C) A folding or telescoping stock.

(D) A grenade launcher or flare launcher.

(E) A flash suppressor.

(F) A forward pistol grip.

(2) A semiautomatic, centerfire rifle that has a fixed magazine with the capacity to accept more than 10 rounds.

(3) A semiautomatic, centerfire rifle that has an overall length of less than 30 inches.

(4) A semiautomatic pistol that does not have a fixed magazine but has any one of the following:

(A) A threaded barrel, capable of accepting a flash suppressor, forward handgrip, or silencer.

(B) A second handgrip.

(C) A shroud that is attached to, or partially or completely encircles, the barrel that allows the bearer to fire the weapon without burning the bearer's hand, except a slide that encloses the barrel.

(D) The capacity to accept a detachable magazine at some location outside of the pistol grip.

(5) A semiautomatic pistol with a fixed magazine that has the capacity to accept more than 10 rounds.

(6) A semiautomatic shotgun that has both of the following:

(A) A folding or telescoping stock.

(B) A pistol grip that protrudes conspicuously beneath the action of the weapon, thumbhole stock, or vertical handgrip.

(7) A semiautomatic shotgun that has the ability to accept a detachable magazine.

(8) Any shotgun with a revolving cylinder.

(b) For purposes of this section, "fixed magazine" means an ammunition feeding device contained in, or permanently attached to, a firearm in such a manner that the device cannot be removed without disassembly of the firearm action.

(c) The Legislature finds a significant public purpose in exempting from the definition of "assault weapon" pistols that are designed expressly for use in Olympic target shooting events. Therefore, those pistols that are sanctioned by the International Olympic Committee and by USA Shooting, the national governing body for international shooting competition in the United States, and that were used for Olympic target shooting purposes as of January 1, 2001, and that would otherwise fall within the definition of "assault weapon" pursuant to this section are exempt, as provided in subdivision (d).

(d) "Assault weapon" does not include either of the following:

(1) Any antique firearm.

(2) Any of the following pistols, because they are consistent with the significant public purpose expressed in subdivision (c):

MANUFACTURER	MODEL	CALIBER
BENELLI	MP90	.22LR
BENELLI	MP90	.32 S&W LONG
BENELLI	MP95	.22LR
BENELLI	MP95	.32 S&W LONG
HAMMERLI	280	.22LR
HAMMERLI	280	.32 S&W LONG
HAMMERLI	SP20	.22LR
HAMMERLI	SP20	.32 S&W LONG
PARDINI	GPO	.22 SHORT
PARDINI	GP-SCHUMANN	.22 SHORT
PARDINI	HP	.32 S&W LONG
PARDINI	MP	.32 S&W LONG
PARDINI	SP	.22LR
PARDINI	SPE	.22LR
WALTHER	GSP	.22LR
WALTHER	GSP	.32 S&W LONG
WALTHER	OSP	.22 SHORT
WALTHER	OSP-2000	.22 SHORT

(3) The Department of Justice shall create a program that is consistent with the purposes stated in subdivision (c) to exempt new models of competitive pistols that would otherwise fall within the definition of "assault weapon" pursuant to this section from being classified as an assault weapon. The exempt competitive pistols may be based on recommendations by USA Shooting consistent with the regulations contained in the USA Shooting Official Rules or may be based on the recommendation or rules of any other organization that the department deems relevant.

(Amended by Stats. 2016, Ch. 48, Sec. 1. (SB 880) Effective January 1, 2017.)

30520.

(a) The Attorney General shall prepare a description for identification purposes, including a picture or diagram, of each assault weapon listed in Section 30510, and any firearm declared to be an assault weapon pursuant to former Section 12276.5, as it read in Section 3 of Chapter 19 of the Statutes of 1989, Section 1 of Chapter 874 of the Statutes of 1990, or Section 3 of Chapter 954 of the Statutes of 1991, and shall distribute the description to all law enforcement agencies responsible for enforcement of this chapter. Those law enforcement agencies shall make the description available to all agency personnel.

(b) (1) Until January 1, 2007, the Attorney General shall promulgate a list that specifies all firearms designated as assault weapons in former Section 12276, as it read in Section 2 of Chapter 954 of the Statutes of 1991, Section 134 of Chapter 427 of the Statutes of 1992, or Section 19 of Chapter 606 of the Statutes of 1993, or declared to be assault weapons pursuant to former Section 12276.5, as it read in Section 3 of Chapter 19 of the Statutes of 1989, Section 1 of Chapter 874 of the Statutes of 1990, or Section 3 of Chapter 954 of the Statutes of 1991. The Attorney General shall file that list with the Secretary of State for publication in the California Code of Regulations. Any declaration that a specified firearm is an assault weapon shall be implemented by the Attorney General who, within 90 days, shall promulgate an amended list which shall include the specified firearm declared to be an assault weapon. The Attorney General shall file the amended list with the Secretary of State for publication in the California Code of Regulations. Any firearm declared to be an assault weapon prior to January 1, 2007, shall remain on the list filed with the Secretary of State.

(2) Chapter 3.5 (commencing with Section 11340) of Part 1 of Division 3 of Title 2 of the Government Code, pertaining to the adoption of rules and regulations, shall not apply to any list of assault weapons promulgated pursuant to this section.

(c) The Attorney General shall adopt those rules and regulations that may be necessary or proper to carry out the purposes and intent of this chapter.

(Added by Stats. 2010, Ch. 711, Sec. 6. (SB 1080) Effective January 1, 2011. Operative January 1, 2012, by Sec. 10 of Ch. 711.)

30525.

As used in this part, ".50 BMG cartridge" means a cartridge that is designed and intended to be fired from a center fire rifle and that meets all of the following criteria:

(a) It has an overall length of 5.54 inches from the base to the tip of the bullet.

(b) The bullet diameter for the cartridge is from .510 to, and including, .511 inch.

(c) The case base diameter for the cartridge is from .800 inch to, and including, .804 inch.

(d) The cartridge case length is 3.91 inches.

(Added by Stats. 2010, Ch. 711, Sec. 6. (SB 1080) Effective January 1, 2011. Operative January 1, 2012, by Sec. 10 of Ch. 711.)

30530.

(a) As used in this part, ".50 BMG rifle" means a center fire rifle that can fire a .50 BMG cartridge and is not already an assault weapon or a machinegun.

(b) A ".50 BMG rifle" does not include any antique firearm, nor any curio or relic as defined in Section 478.11 of Title 27 of the Code of Federal Regulations.

(Added by Stats. 2010, Ch. 711, Sec. 6. (SB 1080) Effective January 1, 2011. Operative January 1, 2012, by Sec. 10 of Ch. 711.)

ARTICLE 2. Unlawful Acts Relating to Assault Weapons and .50 BMG Rifles [30600 - 30680]

(Article 2 added by Stats. 2010, Ch. 711, Sec. 6.)

30600.

(a) Any person who, within this state, manufactures or causes to be manufactured, distributes, transports, or imports into the state, keeps for sale, or offers or exposes for sale, or who gives or lends any assault weapon or any .50 BMG rifle, except as provided by this chapter, is guilty of a felony, and upon conviction shall be punished by imprisonment pursuant to subdivision (h) of Section 1170 for four, six, or eight years.

(b) In addition and consecutive to the punishment imposed under subdivision (a), any person who transfers, lends, sells, or gives any assault weapon or any .50 BMG rifle to a minor in violation of subdivision (a) shall receive an enhancement of imprisonment pursuant to subdivision (h) of Section 1170 of one year.

(c) Except in the case of a first violation involving not more than two firearms as provided in Sections 30605 and 30610, for purposes of this article, if more than one assault weapon or .50 BMG rifle is involved in any violation of this article, there shall be a distinct and separate offense for each.

(Amended by Stats. 2011, Ch. 15, Sec. 549. (AB 109) Effective April 4, 2011. Amending action operative October 1, 2011, by Sec. 636 of Ch. 15, as amended by Stats. 2011, Ch. 39, Sec. 68. Section operative January 1, 2012, pursuant to Stats. 2010, Ch. 711, Sec. 10.)

30605.

(a) Any person who, within this state, possesses any assault weapon, except as provided in this chapter, shall be punished by imprisonment in a county jail for a period not exceeding one year, or by imprisonment pursuant to subdivision (h) of Section 1170.

(b) Notwithstanding subdivision (a), a first violation of these provisions is punishable by a fine not exceeding five hundred dollars ($500) if the person was found in possession of no more than two firearms in compliance with Section 30945 and the person meets all of the following conditions:

(1) The person proves that he or she lawfully possessed the assault weapon prior to the date it was defined as an assault weapon.

(2) The person has not previously been convicted of a violation of this article.

(3) The person was found to be in possession of the assault weapon within one year following the end of the one-year registration period established pursuant to Section 30900.

(4) The person relinquished the firearm pursuant to Section 31100, in which case the assault weapon shall be destroyed pursuant to Sections 18000 and 18005.

(Amended by Stats. 2011, Ch. 15, Sec. 550. (AB 109) Effective April 4, 2011. Amending action operative October 1, 2011, by Sec. 636 of Ch. 15, as amended by Stats. 2011, Ch. 39, Sec. 68. Section operative January 1, 2012, pursuant to Stats. 2010, Ch. 711, Sec. 10.)

30610.

(a) Any person who, within this state, possesses any .50 BMG rifle, except as provided in this chapter, shall be punished by a fine of one thousand dollars ($1,000), imprisonment in a county jail for a period not to exceed one year, or by both that fine and imprisonment.

(b) Notwithstanding subdivision (a), a first violation of these provisions is punishable by a fine not exceeding five hundred dollars ($500) if the person was found in possession of no more than two firearms in compliance with Section 30905 and the person satisfies all of the following conditions:

(1) The person proves that he or she lawfully possessed the .50 BMG rifle prior to January 1, 2005.

(2) The person has not previously been convicted of a violation of this article.

(3) The person was found to be in possession of the .50 BMG rifle within one year following the end of the .50 BMG rifle registration period established pursuant to Section 30905.

(c) Firearms seized pursuant to this section from persons who meet all of the conditions in paragraphs (1), (2), and (3) of subdivision (b) shall be returned unless the court finds in the interest of public safety, after notice and hearing, that the .50 BMG rifle should be destroyed pursuant to Sections 18000 and 18005. Firearms seized from persons who do not meet the conditions set forth in paragraphs (1), (2), and (3) of subdivision (b) shall be destroyed pursuant to Sections 18000 and 18005.

(Added by Stats. 2010, Ch. 711, Sec. 6. (SB 1080) Effective January 1, 2011. Operative January 1, 2012, by Sec. 10 of Ch. 711.)

30615.

Notwithstanding Section 654 or any other provision of law, any person who commits another crime while violating this article may receive an additional, consecutive punishment of one year for violating this article, in addition and consecutive to the punishment, including enhancements, which is prescribed for the other crime.

(Added by Stats. 2010, Ch. 711, Sec. 6. (SB 1080) Effective January 1, 2011. Operative January 1, 2012, by Sec. 10 of Ch. 711.)

30620.

As used in this chapter, the date a firearm is an assault weapon is the earliest of the following:

(a) The effective date of an amendment to Section 30510 or to former Section 12276 that adds the designation of the specified firearm.

(b) The effective date of the list promulgated pursuant to former Section 12276.5, as that section read in Section 3 of Chapter 954 of the Statutes of 1991, which adds or changes the designation of the specified firearm.

(c) January 1, 2000, which was the operative date of former Section 12276.1, as enacted by Section 7 of Chapter 129 of the Statutes of 1999.

(Added by Stats. 2010, Ch. 711, Sec. 6. (SB 1080) Effective January 1, 2011. Operative January 1, 2012, by Sec. 10 of Ch. 711.)

30625.

Sections 30600, 30605, and 30610 do not apply to the sale of an assault weapon or .50 BMG rifle to, or the purchase, importation, or possession of an assault weapon or a .50 BMG rifle by, the Department of Justice, police departments, sheriffs' offices, marshals' offices, the Department of Corrections and Rehabilitation, the Department of the California Highway Patrol, district attorneys' offices, the Department of Fish and Wildlife, the Department of Parks and Recreation, or the military or naval forces of this state or of the United States, or any federal law enforcement agency for use in the discharge of their official duties.

(Amended by Stats. 2015, Ch. 303, Sec. 416. (AB 731) Effective January 1, 2016.)

30630.

(a) Sections 30605 and 30610 shall not prohibit the possession or use of assault weapons or a .50 BMG rifle by sworn peace officer members of those agencies specified in Section 30625 for law enforcement purposes, whether on or off duty.

(b) (1) Sections 30600, 30605, and 30610 shall not prohibit the sale, delivery, or transfer of an assault weapon or a .50 BMG rifle to, or the possession of an assault weapon or a .50 BMG rifle by, a sworn peace officer member of an agency specified in Section 30625 if the peace officer is authorized by the officer's employer to possess or receive the assault weapon or the .50 BMG rifle. Required authorization is defined as verifiable written certification from the head of the agency, identifying the recipient or possessor of the assault weapon as a peace officer and authorizing that person to receive or possess the specific assault weapon.

(2) For this exemption to apply, in the case of a peace officer who possesses or receives the assault weapon prior to January 1, 2002, the officer shall register the assault weapon on or before April 1, 2002, pursuant to former Section 12285, as it read at any time from when it was enacted by Section 3 of Chapter 19 of the Statutes of 1989, to and including when it was amended by Section 9 of Chapter 129 of the Statutes of 1999. In the case of a peace officer who possesses or receives the assault weapon on or after January 1, 2002, the officer shall, not later than 90 days after possession or receipt, register the assault weapon pursuant to Article 5 (commencing with Section 30900), or pursuant to former Section 12285, as it read at any time from when it was amended by Section 9 of Chapter 129 of the Statutes of 1999 to when it was repealed by the Deadly Weapons Recodification Act of 2010. In the case of a peace officer who possesses or receives a .50 BMG rifle on or before January 1, 2005, the officer shall register the .50 BMG rifle on or before April 30, 2006. In the case of a peace officer who possesses or receives a .50 BMG rifle after January 1, 2005, the officer shall register the .50 BMG rifle not later than one year after possession or receipt.

(3) With the registration, the peace officer shall include a copy of the authorization required pursuant to this subdivision.

(c) Nothing in this article shall be construed to limit or prohibit the sale, delivery, or transfer of an assault weapon or a .50 BMG rifle to, or the possession of an assault weapon or a .50 BMG rifle by, a member of a federal law enforcement agency provided that person is authorized by the employing agency to possess the assault weapon or .50 BMG rifle.

(Added by Stats. 2010, Ch. 711, Sec. 6. (SB 1080) Effective January 1, 2011. Operative January 1, 2012, by Sec. 10 of Ch. 711.)

30635.

Section 30605 shall not apply to the possession of an assault weapon during the 90-day period immediately after the date it was specified as an assault weapon pursuant to former Section 12276.5, as that section read in Section 3 of Chapter 19 of the Statutes of 1989, Section 1 of Chapter 874 of the Statutes of 1990, or Section 3 of Chapter 954 of the Statutes of 1991, or during the one-year period after the date it was defined as an assault weapon pursuant to former Section 12276.1, as that section read at any time from when it was enacted by Section 7 of Chapter 129 of the Statutes of 1999 to when it was repealed by the Deadly Weapons Recodification Act of 2010, if all of the following are applicable:

(a) At the time of the possession in question, the person was eligible under the then-applicable version of former Chapter 2.3 (commencing with Section 12275) of Title 2 of Part 4 to register the particular assault weapon.

(b) The person lawfully possessed the particular assault weapon prior to the date it was specified as an assault weapon pursuant to former Section 12276.5, or prior to the date it was defined as an assault weapon pursuant to former Section 12276.1.

(c) At the time of the possession in question, the person was otherwise in compliance with the then-applicable version of former Chapter 2.3 (commencing with Section 12275) of Title 2 of Part 4.

(Added by Stats. 2010, Ch. 711, Sec. 6. (SB 1080) Effective January 1, 2011. Operative January 1, 2012, by Sec. 10 of Ch. 711.)

30640.

Section 30610 shall not apply to the possession of a .50 BMG rifle, which was not defined or specified as an assault weapon pursuant to the then-applicable version of the former Chapter 2.3 (commencing with Section 12275) of Title 2 of Part 4 that was added to this code by Section 3 of Chapter 19 of the Statutes of 1989, by any person prior to May 1, 2006, if all of the following are applicable:

(a) At the time of the possession in question, the person was eligible under the then-applicable version of former Chapter 2.3 (commencing with Section 12275) of Title 2 of Part 4 to register that .50 BMG rifle.

(b) The person lawfully possessed the .50 BMG rifle prior to January 1, 2005.

(c) At the time of the possession in question, the person was otherwise in compliance with the then-applicable version of former Chapter 2.3 (commencing with Section 12275) of Title 2 of Part 4.

(Added by Stats. 2010, Ch. 711, Sec. 6. (SB 1080) Effective January 1, 2011. Operative January 1, 2012, by Sec. 10 of Ch. 711.)

30645.

Sections 30600, 30605, and 30610 shall not apply to the manufacture by any person who is issued a permit pursuant to Section 31005 of assault weapons or .50 BMG rifles for sale to the following:

(a) Exempt entities listed in Section 30625.

(b) Entities and persons who have been issued permits pursuant to Section 31000 or 31005.

(c) Federal military and law enforcement agencies.

(d) Law enforcement and military agencies of other states.

(e) Foreign governments and agencies approved by the United States State Department.

(f) Entities outside the state who have, in effect, a federal firearms dealer's license solely for the purpose of distribution to an entity listed in subdivisions (c) to (e), inclusive.

(Added by Stats. 2010, Ch. 711, Sec. 6. (SB 1080) Effective January 1, 2011. Operative January 1, 2012, by Sec. 10 of Ch. 711.)

30650.

Sections 30600, 30605, and 30610 shall not apply to the sale of assault weapons or .50 BMG rifles by persons who are issued permits pursuant to Section 31005 to any of the following:

(a) Exempt entities listed in Section 30625.

(b) Entities and persons who have been issued permits pursuant to Section 31000 or 31005.

(c) Federal military and law enforcement agencies.

(d) Law enforcement and military agencies of other states.

(e) Foreign governments and agencies approved by the United States State Department.

(f) Officers described in Section 30630 who are authorized to possess assault weapons or .50 BMG rifles pursuant to Section 30630.

(Added by Stats. 2010, Ch. 711, Sec. 6. (SB 1080) Effective January 1, 2011. Operative January 1, 2012, by Sec. 10 of Ch. 711.)

30655.

(a) Section 30600 shall not apply to a person who is the executor or administrator of an estate that includes an assault weapon or a .50 BMG rifle registered under Article 5 (commencing with Section 30900) or that was possessed pursuant to subdivision (a) of Section 30630 that is disposed of as authorized by the probate court, if the disposition is otherwise permitted by this chapter.

(b) Sections 30605 and 30610 shall not apply to a person who is the executor or administrator of an estate that includes an assault weapon or a .50 BMG rifle registered under Article 5 (commencing with Section 30900) or that was possessed pursuant to subdivision (a) of Section 30630, if the assault weapon or .50 BMG rifle is possessed at a place set forth in subdivision (a) of Section 30945 or as authorized by the probate court.

(Added by Stats. 2010, Ch. 711, Sec. 6. (SB 1080) Effective January 1, 2011. Operative January 1, 2012, by Sec. 10 of Ch. 711.)

30660.

(a) Section 30600 shall not apply to a person who lawfully possesses and has registered an assault weapon or .50 BMG rifle pursuant to this chapter who lends that assault weapon or .50 BMG rifle to another person, if all the following requirements are satisfied:

(1) The person to whom the assault weapon or .50 BMG rifle is lent is 18 years of age or over and is not prohibited by state or federal law from possessing, receiving, owning, or purchasing a firearm.

(2) The person to whom the assault weapon or .50 BMG rifle is lent remains in the presence of the registered possessor of the assault weapon or .50 BMG rifle.

(3) The assault weapon or .50 BMG rifle is possessed at any of the following locations:

(A) While on a target range that holds a regulatory or business license for the purpose of practicing shooting at that target range.

(B) While on the premises of a target range of a public or private club or organization organized for the purpose of practicing shooting at targets.

(C) While attending any exhibition, display, or educational project that is about firearms and that is sponsored by, conducted under the auspices of, or approved by a law enforcement agency or a nationally or state recognized entity that fosters proficiency in, or promotes education about, firearms.

(b) Section 30600 shall not apply to the return of an assault weapon or .50 BMG rifle to the registered possessor, or the lawful possessor, which is lent by that registered or lawful possessor pursuant to subdivision (a).

(c) Sections 30605 and 30610 shall not apply to the possession of an assault weapon or .50 BMG rifle by a person to whom an assault weapon or .50 BMG rifle is lent pursuant to subdivision (a).

(Added by Stats. 2010, Ch. 711, Sec. 6. (SB 1080) Effective January 1, 2011. Operative January 1, 2012, by Sec. 10 of Ch. 711.)

30665.

Sections 30600, 30605, and 30610 shall not apply to the possession and importation of an assault weapon or a .50 BMG rifle into this state by a nonresident if all of the following conditions are met:

(a) The person is attending or going directly to or coming directly from an organized competitive match or league competition that involves the use of an assault weapon or a .50 BMG rifle.

(b) The competition or match is conducted on the premises of one of the following:

(1) A target range that holds a regulatory or business license for the purpose of practicing shooting at that target range.

(2) A target range of a public or private club or organization that is organized for the purpose of practicing shooting at targets.

(c) The match or competition is sponsored by, conducted under the auspices of, or approved by, a law enforcement agency or a nationally or state recognized entity that fosters proficiency in, or promotes education about, firearms.

(d) The assault weapon or .50 BMG rifle is transported in accordance with Section 25610 or Article 3 (commencing with Section 25505) of Chapter 2 of Division 5.

(e) The person is 18 years of age or over and is not in a class of persons prohibited from possessing firearms by virtue of Chapter 2 (commencing with Section 29800) or Chapter 3 (commencing with Section 29900) of Division 9 of this code or Section 8100 or 8103 of the Welfare and Institutions Code.

(Added by Stats. 2010, Ch. 711, Sec. 6. (SB 1080) Effective January 1, 2011. Operative January 1, 2012, by Sec. 10 of Ch. 711.)

30670.

(a) Section 30600 shall not apply to the importation into this state of an assault weapon or a .50 BMG rifle by the registered owner of that assault weapon or a .50 BMG rifle if it is in accordance with the provisions of Section 30945.

(b) Section 30600 shall not apply during the first 180 days of the 2005 calendar year to the importation into this state of a .50 BMG rifle by a person who lawfully possessed that .50 BMG rifle in this state prior to January 1, 2005.

(Added by Stats. 2010, Ch. 711, Sec. 6. (SB 1080) Effective January 1, 2011. Operative January 1, 2012, by Sec. 10 of Ch. 711.)

30675.

(a) Sections 30605 and 30610 shall not apply to any of the following persons:

(1) A person acting in accordance with Section 31000 or 31005.

(2) A person who has a permit to possess an assault weapon or a .50 BMG rifle issued pursuant to Section 31000 or 31005 when that person is acting in accordance with Section 31000 or 31005 or Article 5 (commencing with Section 30900).

(b) Sections 30600, 30605, and 30610 shall not apply to any of the following persons:

(1) A person acting in accordance with Article 5 (commencing with Section 30900).

(2) A person acting in accordance with Section 31000, 31005, 31050, or 31055.

(c) Sections 30605 and 30610 shall not apply to the registered owner of an assault weapon or a .50 BMG rifle possessing that firearm in accordance with Section 30945.

(Added by Stats. 2010, Ch. 711, Sec. 6. (SB 1080) Effective January 1, 2011. Operative January 1, 2012, by Sec. 10 of Ch. 711.)

30680.

Section 30605 does not apply to the possession of an assault weapon by a person who has possessed the assault weapon prior to January 1, 2017, if all of the following are applicable:

(a) Prior to January 1, 2017, the person would have been eligible to register that assault weapon pursuant to subdivision (b) of Section 30900.

(b) The person lawfully possessed that assault weapon prior to January 1, 2017.

(c) The person registers the assault weapon by July 1, 2018, in accordance with subdivision (b) of Section 30900.

(Amended (as added by Stats. 2016, Ch. 40, Sec. 2) by Stats. 2017, Ch. 17, Sec. 47. (AB 103) Effective June 27, 2017. See similar section (added by Stats. 2016, Ch. 48), as amended by Stats. 2017, Ch. 17, Sec. 48.)

30680.

Section 30605 does not apply to the possession of an assault weapon by a person who has possessed the assault weapon prior to January 1, 2017, if all of the following are applicable:

(a) Prior to January 1, 2017, the person was eligible to register that assault weapon pursuant to subdivision (b) of Section 30900.

(b) The person lawfully possessed that assault weapon prior to January 1, 2017.

(c) The person registers the assault weapon by July 1, 2018, in accordance with subdivision (b) of Section 30900.

(Amended (as added by Stats. 2016, Ch. 48, Sec. 2) by Stats. 2017, Ch. 17, Sec. 48. (AB 103) Effective June 27, 2017.)

ARTICLE 3. SKS Rifles [30710 - 30735]
(Article 3 added by Stats. 2010, Ch. 711, Sec. 6.)

30710.

Notwithstanding paragraph (11) of subdivision (a) of Section 30510, an "SKS rifle" under this article means all SKS rifles commonly referred to as "SKS Sporter" versions, manufactured to accept a detachable AK-47 magazine and imported into this state and sold by a licensed gun dealer, or otherwise lawfully possessed in this state by a resident of this state who is not a licensed gun dealer, between January 1, 1992, and December 19, 1997.

(Added by Stats. 2010, Ch. 711, Sec. 6. (SB 1080) Effective January 1, 2011. Operative January 1, 2012, by Sec. 10 of Ch. 711.)

30715.

(a) (1) Any person who, or firm, company, or corporation that operated a retail or other commercial firm, company, or corporation, and manufactured, distributed, transported, imported, possessed, possessed for sale, offered for sale, or transferred, for commercial purpose, an SKS rifle in California between January 1, 1992, and December 19, 1997, shall be immune from criminal prosecution under Article 2 (commencing with Section 30600) or former Section 12280.

(2) The immunity provided in this subdivision shall apply retroactively to any person who, or firm, company, or corporation that, is or was charged by complaint or indictment with a violation of former Section 12280 for conduct related to an SKS rifle, whether or not the case of that person, firm, company, or corporation is final.

(b) (1) Any person who possessed, gave, loaned, or transferred an SKS rifle in California between January 1, 1992, and December 19, 1997, shall be immune from criminal prosecution under Article 2 (commencing with Section 30600) or former Section 12280.

(2) The immunity provided in this subdivision shall apply retroactively to any person who was charged by complaint or indictment with a violation of former Section 12280 for conduct related to an SKS rifle, whether or not the case of that person is final.

(c) Any SKS rifle in the possession of any person who, or firm, company, or corporation that, is described in subdivision (a) or (b), shall not be subject to seizure by law enforcement for violation of Article 2 (commencing with Section 30600) or former Section 12280 prior to January 1, 2000.

(d) Any person, firm, company, or corporation, convicted under former Section 12280 for conduct relating to an SKS rifle, shall be permitted to withdraw a plea of guilty or nolo contendere, or to reopen the case and assert the immunities provided in this article, if the court determines that the allowance of the immunity is in the interests of justice. The court shall interpret this article liberally to the benefit of the defendant.

(e) For purposes of this section, "former Section 12280" refers to former Section 12280, as added by Section 3 of Chapter 19 of the Statutes of 1989 or as subsequently amended.

(Added by Stats. 2010, Ch. 711, Sec. 6. (SB 1080) Effective January 1, 2011. Operative January 1, 2012, by Sec. 10 of Ch. 711.)

30720.

(a) Any person, firm, company, or corporation that is in possession of an SKS rifle shall do one of the following on or before January 1, 2000:

(1) Relinquish the SKS rifle to the Department of Justice pursuant to subdivision (h) of former Section 12281.

(2) Relinquish the SKS rifle to a law enforcement agency pursuant to former Section 12288, as added by Section 3 of Chapter 19 of the Statutes of 1989.

(3) Dispose of the SKS rifle as permitted by former Section 12285, as it read in Section 20 of Chapter 23 of the Statutes of 1994.

(b) Any person who has obtained title to an SKS rifle by bequest or intestate succession shall be required to comply with paragraph (1) or (2) of subdivision (a) unless that person otherwise complies with paragraph (1) of subdivision (b) of former Section 12285, as it read in Section 20 of Chapter 23 of the Statutes of 1994, or as subsequently amended.

(c) Any SKS rifle relinquished to the department pursuant to this section shall be in a manner prescribed by the department.

(Added by Stats. 2010, Ch. 711, Sec. 6. (SB 1080) Effective January 1, 2011. Operative January 1, 2012, by Sec. 10 of Ch. 711.)

30725.

(a) Any person who complies with Section 30720 shall be exempt from the prohibitions set forth in Section 30600 or 30605 for those acts by that person associated with complying with the requirements of Section 30720.

(b) Failure to comply with Section 30720 is a public offense punishable by imprisonment pursuant to subdivision (h) of Section 1170, or in a county jail, not exceeding one year.

(Amended by Stats. 2011, Ch. 15, Sec. 551. (AB 109) Effective April 4, 2011. Amending action operative October 1, 2011, by Sec. 636 of Ch. 15, as amended by Stats. 2011, Ch. 39, Sec. 68. Section operative January 1, 2012, pursuant to Stats. 2010, Ch. 711, Sec. 10.)

30730.

(a) (1) The department shall purchase any SKS rifle relinquished pursuant to Section 30720 from funds appropriated for this purpose by the act amending former Section 12281 in the 1997–98 Regular Session of the Legislature or by subsequent budget acts or other legislation.

(2) The department shall adopt regulations for this purchase program that include, but are not limited to, the manner of delivery, the reimbursement to be paid, and the manner in which persons shall be informed of the state purchase program.

(3) Any person who relinquished possession of an SKS rifle to a law enforcement agency pursuant to any version of former Section 12288 prior to the effective date of the purchase program set forth in paragraph (1) shall be eligible to be reimbursed from the purchase program. The procedures for reimbursement pursuant to this paragraph shall be part of the regulations adopted by the department pursuant to paragraph (2).

(b) In addition to the regulations required pursuant to subdivision (a), emergency regulations for the purchase program described in subdivision (a) shall be adopted pursuant to Chapter 3.5 (commencing with Section 11340) of Part 1 of Division 3 of Title 2 of the Government Code.

(Added by Stats. 2010, Ch. 711, Sec. 6. (SB 1080) Effective January 1, 2011. Operative January 1, 2012, by Sec. 10 of Ch. 711.)

30735.

(a) The Department of Justice shall notify all district attorneys on or before January 31, 1999, of the provisions of former Section 12281.

(b) The department shall identify all criminal prosecutions in the state for conduct related to SKS rifles on or before April 1, 1999. In all cases so identified by the Attorney General, the district attorneys shall inform defense counsel, or the defendant if the defendant is in propria persona, in writing, of the provisions of former Section 12281 on or before May 1, 1999.

(c) Commencing no later than January 1, 1999, the department shall conduct a public education and notification program as described in Section 31115 or in former Section 12289, as added by Section 6 of Chapter 954 of the Statutes of 1991 or as subsequently amended.

(Added by Stats. 2010, Ch. 711, Sec. 6. (SB 1080) Effective January 1, 2011. Operative January 1, 2012, by Sec. 10 of Ch. 711.)

ARTICLE 4. Assault Weapon or .50 BMG Rifle Constituting Nuisance [30800- 30800.]

(Article 4 added by Stats. 2010, Ch. 711, Sec. 6.)

30800.

(a) (1) Except as provided in Article 2 (commencing with Section 30600), possession of any assault weapon or of any .50 BMG rifle in violation of this chapter is a public nuisance, solely for purposes of this section and subdivision (c) of Section 18005.

(2) The Attorney General, any district attorney, or any city attorney, may, in lieu of criminal prosecution, bring a civil action or reach a civil compromise in any superior court to enjoin the possession of the assault weapon or .50 BMG rifle that is a public nuisance.

(b) Upon motion of the Attorney General, district attorney, or city attorney, a superior court may impose a civil fine not to exceed three hundred dollars ($300) for the first assault weapon or .50 BMG rifle deemed a public nuisance pursuant to subdivision (a) and up to one hundred dollars ($100) for each additional assault weapon or .50 BMG rifle deemed a public nuisance pursuant to subdivision (a).

(c) Any assault weapon or .50 BMG rifle deemed a public nuisance under subdivision (a) shall be destroyed in a manner so that it may no longer be used, except upon a finding

by a court, or a declaration from the Department of Justice, district attorney, or city attorney stating that the preservation of the assault weapon or .50 BMG rifle is in the interest of justice.

(d) Upon conviction of any misdemeanor or felony involving the illegal possession or use of an assault weapon, the assault weapon shall be deemed a public nuisance and disposed of pursuant to subdivision (c) of Section 18005.

(Added by Stats. 2010, Ch. 711, Sec. 6. (SB 1080) Effective January 1, 2011. Operative January 1, 2012, by Sec. 10 of Ch. 711.)

ARTICLE 5. Registration of Assault Weapons and .50 BMG Rifles and Related Rules [30900 - 30965]

(Article 5 added by Stats. 2010, Ch. 711, Sec. 6.)

30900.

(a) (1) Any person who, prior to June 1, 1989, lawfully possessed an assault weapon, as defined in former Section 12276, as added by Section 3 of Chapter 19 of the Statutes of 1989, shall register the firearm by January 1, 1991, and any person who lawfully possessed an assault weapon prior to the date it was specified as an assault weapon pursuant to former Section 12276.5, as added by Section 3 of Chapter 19 of the Statutes of 1989 or as amended by Section 1 of Chapter 874 of the Statutes of 1990 or Section 3 of Chapter 954 of the Statutes of 1991, shall register the firearm within 90 days with the Department of Justice pursuant to those procedures that the department may establish.

(2) Except as provided in Section 30600, any person who lawfully possessed an assault weapon prior to the date it was defined as an assault weapon pursuant to former Section 12276.1, as it read in Section 7 of Chapter 129 of the Statutes of 1999, and which was not specified as an assault weapon under former Section 12276, as added by Section 3 of Chapter 19 of the Statutes of 1989 or as amended at any time before January 1, 2001, or former Section 12276.5, as added by Section 3 of Chapter 19 of the Statutes of 1989 or as amended at any time before January 1, 2001, shall register the firearm by January 1, 2001, with the department pursuant to those procedures that the department may establish.

(3) The registration shall contain a description of the firearm that identifies it uniquely, including all identification marks, the full name, address, date of birth, and thumbprint of the owner, and any other information that the department may deem appropriate.

(4) The department may charge a fee for registration of up to twenty dollars ($20) per person but not to exceed the reasonable processing costs of the department. After the department establishes fees sufficient to reimburse the department for processing costs, fees charged shall increase at a rate not to exceed the legislatively approved annual cost-of-living adjustment for the department's budget or as otherwise increased through the Budget Act but not to exceed the reasonable costs of the department. The fees shall be deposited into the Dealers' Record of Sale Special Account.

(b) (1) Any person who, from January 1, 2001, to December 31, 2016, inclusive, lawfully possessed an assault weapon that does not have a fixed magazine, as defined in Section 30515, including those weapons with an ammunition feeding device that can be readily removed from the firearm with the use of a tool, shall register the firearm before July 1, 2018, but not before the effective date of the regulations adopted pursuant to paragraph (5), with the department pursuant to those procedures that the department may establish by regulation pursuant to paragraph (5).

(2) Registrations shall be submitted electronically via the Internet utilizing a public-facing application made available by the department.

(3) The registration shall contain a description of the firearm that identifies it uniquely, including all identification marks, the date the firearm was acquired, the name and address of the individual from whom, or business from which, the firearm was acquired, as well as the registrant's full name, address, telephone number, date of birth, sex, height, weight, eye color, hair color, and California driver's license number or California identification card number.

(4) The department may charge a fee in an amount of up to fifteen dollars ($15) per person but not to exceed the reasonable processing costs of the department. The fee shall be paid by debit or credit card at the time that the electronic registration is submitted to the department. The fee shall be deposited in the Dealers' Record of Sale Special Account to be used for purposes of this section.

(5) The department shall adopt regulations for the purpose of implementing this subdivision. These regulations are exempt from the Administrative Procedure Act (Chapter 3.5 (commencing with Section 11340) of Part 1 of Division 3 of Title 2 of the Government Code).

(Amended by Stats. 2017, Ch. 17, Sec. 49. (AB 103) Effective June 27, 2017.)

30905.

(a) Except as provided in Section 30600, any person who lawfully possesses any .50 BMG rifle prior to January 1, 2005, that is not specified as an assault weapon under former Section 12276, as it reads in Section 19 of Chapter 606 of the Statutes of 1993, or former Section 12276.5, as it reads in Section 3 of Chapter 954 of the Statutes of 1991, or defined as an assault weapon pursuant to former Section 12276.1, as it reads in Section 3 of Chapter 911 of the Statutes of 2002, shall register the .50 BMG rifle with the department no later than April 30, 2006, pursuant to those procedures that the department may establish.

(b) The registration shall contain a description of the firearm that identifies it uniquely, including all identification marks, the full name, address, date of birth, and thumbprint of the owner, and any other information that the department may deem appropriate.

(c) The department may charge a fee for registration of twenty-five dollars ($25) per person to cover the actual processing and public education campaign costs of the department. The fees shall be deposited into the Dealers' Record of Sale Special Account. Data-processing costs associated with modifying the department's data system to accommodate .50 caliber BMG rifles shall not be paid from the Dealers' Record of Sale Special Account.

(Added by Stats. 2010, Ch. 711, Sec. 6. (SB 1080) Effective January 1, 2011. Operative January 1, 2012, by Sec. 10 of Ch. 711.)

30910.

Except as provided in Section 30925, no assault weapon possessed pursuant to this article may be sold or transferred on or after January 1, 1990, to anyone within this state other than to a licensed gun dealer or as provided in Section 31100.

(Added by Stats. 2010, Ch. 711, Sec. 6. (SB 1080) Effective January 1, 2011. Operative January 1, 2012, by Sec. 10 of Ch. 711.)

30915.

Any person who obtains title to an assault weapon registered under this article or that was possessed pursuant to subdivision (a) of Section 30630 by bequest or intestate succession shall, within 90 days, do one or more of the following:

(a) Render the weapon permanently inoperable.

(b) Sell the weapon to a licensed gun dealer.

(c) Obtain a permit from the Department of Justice in the same manner as specified in Article 3 (commencing with Section 32650) of Chapter 6.

(d) Remove the weapon from this state.

(Added by Stats. 2010, Ch. 711, Sec. 6. (SB 1080) Effective January 1, 2011. Operative January 1, 2012, by Sec. 10 of Ch. 711.)

30920.

(a) Any person who lawfully possessed a firearm subsequently declared to be an assault weapon pursuant to former Section 12276.5, as it reads in Section 3 of Chapter 19 of the Statutes of 1989, Section 1 of Chapter 874 of the Statutes of 1990, or Section 3 of Chapter 954 of the Statutes of 1991, or subsequently defined as an assault weapon pursuant to former Section 12276.1, as that section read at any time from when it was enacted by Section 7 of Chapter 129 of the Statutes of 1999 to when it was repealed by the Deadly Weapons Recodification Act of 2010, shall, within 90 days, do one or more of the following:

(1) Render the weapon permanently inoperable.

(2) Sell the weapon to a licensed gun dealer.

(3) Obtain a permit from the Department of Justice in the same manner as specified in Article 3 (commencing with Section 32650) of Chapter 6.

(4) Remove the weapon from this state.

(b) Notwithstanding subdivision (a), a person who lawfully possessed a firearm that was subsequently declared to be an assault weapon pursuant to former Section 12276.5 may alternatively register the firearm within 90 days of the declaration issued pursuant to subdivision (f) of former Section 12276.5, as it reads in Section 3 of Chapter 19 of the Statutes of 1989, Section 1 of Chapter 874 of the Statutes of 1990, or Section 3 of Chapter 954 of the Statutes of 1991.

(Added by Stats. 2010, Ch. 711, Sec. 6. (SB 1080) Effective January 1, 2011. Operative January 1, 2012, by Sec. 10 of Ch. 711.)

30925.

A person moving into this state, otherwise in lawful possession of an assault weapon, shall do one of the following:

(a) Prior to bringing the assault weapon into this state, that person shall first obtain a permit from the Department of Justice in the same manner as specified in Article 3 (commencing with Section 32650) of Chapter 6.

(b) The person shall cause the assault weapon to be delivered to a licensed gun dealer in this state in accordance with Chapter 44 (commencing with Section 921) of Title 18 of the United States Code and the regulations issued pursuant thereto. If the person obtains a permit from the Department of Justice in the same manner as specified in Article 3 (commencing with Section 32650) of Chapter 6, the dealer shall redeliver that assault weapon to the person. If the licensed gun dealer is prohibited from delivering the assault weapon to a person pursuant to this section, the dealer shall possess or dispose of the assault weapon as allowed by this chapter.

(Added by Stats. 2010, Ch. 711, Sec. 6. (SB 1080) Effective January 1, 2011. Operative January 1, 2012, by Sec. 10 of Ch. 711.)

30930.

Except as provided in Section 30940, no .50 BMG rifle possessed pursuant to this article may be sold or transferred on or after January 1, 2005, to anyone within this state other than to a licensed gun dealer or as provided in Section 31100.

(Added by Stats. 2010, Ch. 711, Sec. 6. (SB 1080) Effective January 1, 2011. Operative January 1, 2012, by Sec. 10 of Ch. 711.)

30935.

Any person who obtains title to a .50 BMG rifle registered under this article or that was possessed pursuant to subdivision (a) of Section 30630 by bequest or intestate succession shall, within 180 days of receipt, do one or more of the following:

(a) Render the weapon permanently inoperable.

(b) Sell the weapon to a licensed gun dealer.

(c) Obtain a permit from the Department of Justice in the same manner as specified in Article 3 (commencing with Section 32650) of Chapter 6.

(d) Remove the weapon from this state.

(Added by Stats. 2010, Ch. 711, Sec. 6. (SB 1080) Effective January 1, 2011. Operative January 1, 2012, by Sec. 10 of Ch. 711.)

30940.

A person moving into this state, otherwise in lawful possession of a .50 BMG rifle, shall do one of the following:

(a) Prior to bringing the .50 BMG rifle into this state, that person shall first obtain a permit from the Department of Justice in the same manner as specified in Article 3 (commencing with Section 32650) of Chapter 6.

(b) The person shall cause the .50 BMG rifle to be delivered to a licensed gun dealer in this state in accordance with Chapter 44 (commencing with Section 921) of Title 18 of the United States Code and the regulations issued pursuant thereto. If the person obtains a permit from the Department of Justice in the same manner as specified in Article 3 (commencing with Section 32650) of Chapter 6, the dealer shall redeliver that .50 BMG rifle to the person. If the licensed gun dealer is prohibited from delivering the .50 caliber BMG rifle to a person pursuant to this section, the dealer shall dispose of the .50 BMG rifle as allowed by this chapter.

(Added by Stats. 2010, Ch. 711, Sec. 6. (SB 1080) Effective January 1, 2011. Operative January 1, 2012, by Sec. 10 of Ch. 711.)

30945.

Unless a permit allowing additional uses is first obtained under Section 31000, a person who has registered an assault weapon or registered a .50 BMG rifle under this article may possess it only under any of the following conditions:

(a) At that person's residence, place of business, or other property owned by that person, or on property owned by another with the owner's express permission.

(b) While on the premises of a target range of a public or private club or organization organized for the purpose of practicing shooting at targets.

(c) While on a target range that holds a regulatory or business license for the purpose of practicing shooting at that target range.

(d) While on the premises of a shooting club that is licensed pursuant to the Fish and Game Code.

(e) While attending any exhibition, display, or educational project that is about firearms and that is sponsored by, conducted under the auspices of, or approved by a law enforcement agency or a nationally or state recognized entity that fosters proficiency in, or promotes education about, firearms.

(f) While on publicly owned land, if the possession and use of a firearm described in Section 30510, 30515, 30520, or 30530, is specifically permitted by the managing agency of the land.

(g) While transporting the assault weapon or .50 BMG rifle between any of the places mentioned in this section, or to any licensed gun dealer, for servicing or repair pursuant to Section 31050, if the assault weapon is transported as required by Sections 16850 and 25610.

(Added by Stats. 2010, Ch. 711, Sec. 6. (SB 1080) Effective January 1, 2011. Operative January 1, 2012, by Sec. 10 of Ch. 711.)

30950.

No person who is under the age of 18 years, and no person who is prohibited by state or federal law from possessing, receiving, owning, or purchasing a firearm, may register or possess an assault weapon or .50 BMG rifle.

(Added by Stats. 2010, Ch. 711, Sec. 6. (SB 1080) Effective January 1, 2011. Operative January 1, 2012, by Sec. 10 of Ch. 711.)

30955.

The department's registration procedures shall provide the option of joint registration for any assault weapon or .50 BMG rifle owned by family members residing in the same household.

(Added by Stats. 2010, Ch. 711, Sec. 6. (SB 1080) Effective January 1, 2011. Operative January 1, 2012, by Sec. 10 of Ch. 711.)

30960.

(a) For 90 days following January 1, 1992, a forgiveness period shall exist to allow any person specified in subdivision (b) of former Section 12280, as it reads in Section 4.5 of Chapter 954 of the Statutes of 1991, to register with the Department of Justice any assault weapon that the person lawfully possessed prior to June 1, 1989.

(b) (1) Any person who registers an assault weapon during the 90-day forgiveness period described in subdivision (a), and any person whose registration form was received by the Department of Justice after January 1, 1991, and who was issued a

temporary registration prior to the end of the forgiveness period, shall not be charged with a violation of subdivision (b) of former Section 12280, as added by Section 3 of Chapter 19 of the Statutes of 1989 or as subsequently amended, if law enforcement becomes aware of that violation only as a result of the registration of the assault weapon.

(2) This section shall have no effect upon any person charged prior to January 1, 1992, with a violation of subdivision (b) of former Section 12280 as added by Section 3 of Chapter 19 of the Statutes of 1989 or as subsequently amended, provided that law enforcement was aware of the violation before the weapon was registered.

(Added by Stats. 2010, Ch. 711, Sec. 6. (SB 1080) Effective January 1, 2011. Operative January 1, 2012, by Sec. 10 of Ch. 711.)

30965.

(a) Any person who registered a firearm as an assault weapon pursuant to the provisions of law in effect prior to January 1, 2000, where the assault weapon is thereafter defined as an assault weapon pursuant to Section 30515 or former Section 12276.1, as that section read at any time from when it was enacted by Section 7 of Chapter 129 of the Statutes of 1999 to when it was repealed by the Deadly Weapons Recodification Act of 2010, shall be deemed to have registered the weapon for purposes of this chapter and shall not be required to reregister the weapon pursuant to this article.

(b) Any person who legally registered a firearm as an assault weapon pursuant to the provisions of law in effect prior to January 1, 2005, where the assault weapon is thereafter defined as a .50 caliber BMG rifle pursuant to Section 30530 or former Section 12278, shall be deemed to have registered the weapon for purposes of this chapter and shall not be required to reregister the weapon pursuant to this article.

(Added by Stats. 2010, Ch. 711, Sec. 6. (SB 1080) Effective January 1, 2011. Operative January 1, 2012, by Sec. 10 of Ch. 711.)

ARTICLE 6. Permits for Assault Weapons and .50 BMG Rifles [31000 - 31005]

(Article 6 added by Stats. 2010, Ch. 711, Sec. 6.)

31000.

(a) Any person who lawfully acquired an assault weapon before June 1, 1989, or a .50 BMG rifle before January 1, 2005, and wishes to use it in a manner different than specified in Section 30945 shall first obtain a permit from the Department of Justice in the same manner as specified in Article 3 (commencing with Section 32650) of Chapter 6.

(b) Any person who lawfully acquired an assault weapon between June 1, 1989, and January 1, 1990, and wishes to keep it after January 1, 1990, shall first obtain a permit from the Department of Justice in the same manner as specified in Article 3 (commencing with Section 32650) of Chapter 6.

(c) Any person who wishes to acquire an assault weapon after January 1, 1990, or a .50 BMG rifle after January 1, 2005, shall first obtain a permit from the Department of Justice in the same manner as specified in Article 3 (commencing with Section 32650) of Chapter 6.

(d) On and after January 1, 2014, no partnership, corporation, limited liability company, association, or any other group or entity, regardless of how the entity was created, may be issued a permit to possess an assault weapon or a .50 BMG rifle.

(Amended by Stats. 2014, Ch. 54, Sec. 16. (SB 1461) Effective January 1, 2015.)

31005.

(a) The Department of Justice may, upon a finding of good cause, issue permits for the manufacture or sale of assault weapons or .50 BMG rifles for the sale to, purchase by, or possession of assault weapons or .50 BMG rifles by, any of the following:

(1) The agencies listed in Section 30625, and the officers described in Section 30630.

(2) Entities and persons who have been issued permits pursuant to this section or Section 31000.

(3) Federal law enforcement and military agencies.

(4) Law enforcement and military agencies of other states.

(5) Foreign governments and agencies approved by the United States State Department.

(6) Entities outside the state who have, in effect, a federal firearms dealer's license solely for the purpose of distribution to an entity listed in paragraphs (3) to (5), inclusive.

(b) Application for the permits, the keeping and inspection thereof, and the revocation of permits shall be undertaken in the same manner as specified in Article 3 (commencing with Section 32650) of Chapter 6.

(Added by Stats. 2010, Ch. 711, Sec. 6. (SB 1080) Effective January 1, 2011. Operative January 1, 2012, by Sec. 10 of Ch. 711.)

ARTICLE 7. Licensed Gun Dealers [31050 - 31055]

(Article 7 added by Stats. 2010, Ch. 711, Sec. 6.)

31050.

(a) Any licensed gun dealer may take possession of any assault weapon or .50 BMG rifle for the purposes of servicing or repair from any person to whom it is legally registered or who has been issued a permit to possess it pursuant to this chapter.

(b) Any licensed gun dealer may transfer possession of any assault weapon or .50 BMG rifle received pursuant to subdivision (a), to a gunsmith for purposes of accomplishing service or repair of that weapon. A transfer is permissible only to the following persons:

(1) A gunsmith who is in the dealer's employ.

(2) A gunsmith with whom the dealer has contracted for gunsmithing services.

(c) In order for paragraph (2) of subdivision (b) to apply, the gunsmith receiving the assault weapon or .50 BMG rifle shall hold all of the following:

(1) A dealer's license issued pursuant to Chapter 44 (commencing with Section 921) of Title 18 of the United States Code and the regulations issued pursuant thereto.

(2) Any business license required by a state or local governmental entity.

(Added by Stats. 2010, Ch. 711, Sec. 6. (SB 1080) Effective January 1, 2011. Operative January 1, 2012, by Sec. 10 of Ch. 711.)

31055.

In addition to the uses allowed in Article 5 (commencing with Section 30900), any licensed gun dealer who lawfully possesses an assault weapon or .50 BMG rifle pursuant to Article 5 (commencing with Section 30900) may do any of the following:

(a) Transport the firearm between dealers or out of the state if that person is permitted pursuant to the National Firearms Act. Any transporting allowed by this section or Section 31050 shall be done as required by Sections 16850 and 25610.

(b) Display the firearm at any gun show licensed by a state or local governmental entity.

(c) Sell the firearm to a resident outside the state.

(d) Sell the firearm to a person who has been issued a permit pursuant to Section 31000.

(Added by Stats. 2010, Ch. 711, Sec. 6. (SB 1080) Effective January 1, 2011. Operative January 1, 2012, by Sec. 10 of Ch. 711.)

ARTICLE 8. Miscellaneous Provisions [31100 - 31115]

(Article 8 added by Stats. 2010, Ch. 711, Sec. 6.)

31100.

Any individual may arrange in advance to relinquish an assault weapon or a .50 BMG rifle to a police or sheriff's department. The assault weapon or .50 BMG rifle shall be transported in accordance with Sections 16850 and 25610.

(Added by Stats. 2010, Ch. 711, Sec. 6. (SB 1080) Effective January 1, 2011. Operative January 1, 2012, by Sec. 10 of Ch. 711.)

31105.

(a) No peace officer or dispatcher shall broadcast over a police radio that an individual has registered, or has obtained a permit to possess, an assault weapon or .50 BMG rifle pursuant to this chapter, unless there exists a reason to believe in good faith that one of the following conditions exist:

(1) The individual has engaged, or may be engaged, in criminal conduct.

(2) The police are responding to a call in which the person allegedly committing a criminal violation may gain access to the assault weapon or .50 BMG rifle.

(3) The victim, witness, or person who reported the alleged criminal violation may be using the assault weapon or .50 BMG rifle to hold the person allegedly committing the criminal violation, or may be using the weapon in defense of self or another person.

(b) This section shall not prohibit a peace officer or dispatcher from broadcasting over a police radio that an individual has not registered, or has not obtained a permit to possess, an assault weapon or .50 BMG rifle pursuant to this chapter.

(c) This section does not limit the transmission of an assault weapon or a .50 BMG rifle ownership status via law enforcement computers or any other medium that is legally accessible only to peace officers or other authorized personnel.

(Added by Stats. 2010, Ch. 711, Sec. 6. (SB 1080) Effective January 1, 2011. Operative January 1, 2012, by Sec. 10 of Ch. 711.)

31110.

(a) Except as provided in subdivision (b), the Department of Justice shall, for every person to whom a permit is issued pursuant to this article, annually conduct an inspection for security and safe storage purposes, and to reconcile the inventory of assault weapons.

(b) A person, firm, or corporation with an inventory of fewer than five devices that require any Department of Justice permit shall be subject to an inspection for security and safe storage purposes, and to reconcile inventory, once every five years, or more frequently if determined by the department.

(Amended by Stats. 2013, Ch. 729, Sec. 3. (AB 170) Effective January 1, 2014.)

31115.

(a) The Department of Justice shall conduct a public education and notification program regarding the registration of assault weapons and the definition of the weapons set forth in Section 30515 and former Section 12276.1, as it read at any time from when it was added by Section 7 of Chapter 129 of the Statutes of 1999 to when it was repealed by the Deadly Weapons Recodification Act of 2010.

(b) The public education and notification program shall include outreach to local law enforcement agencies and utilization of public service announcements in a variety of media approaches, to ensure maximum publicity of the limited forgiveness period of the registration requirement specified in subdivision (f) of former Section 12285, as that subdivision read in Section 5 of Chapter 954 of the Statutes of 1991, and the consequences of nonregistration. The department shall develop posters describing gunowners' responsibilities under former Chapter 2.3 (commencing with Section 12275) of Title 2 of Part 4, as that chapter read when the forgiveness period commenced on January 1, 1992, which shall be posted in a conspicuous place in every licensed gun store in the state during the forgiveness period.

(c) For .50 BMG rifles, the department's education campaign shall provide materials to dealers of .50 BMG rifles, and to recognized national associations that specialize in .50 BMG rifles.

(d) Any costs incurred by the Department of Justice to implement this section, which cannot be absorbed by the department, shall be funded from the Dealers' Record of Sale Special Account, as set forth in Section 28235, or former Section 12076 as it read at any time from when it was amended by Section 1.7 of Chapter 954 of the Statutes of 1991 to when it was repealed by Section 12 of Chapter 606 of the Statutes of 1993, or former Section 12076 as it read at any time from when it was enacted by Section 13 of Chapter 606 of the Statutes of 1993 to when it was repealed by the Deadly Weapons Recodification Act of 2010, upon appropriation by the Legislature.

(Added by Stats. 2010, Ch. 711, Sec. 6. (SB 1080) Effective January 1, 2011. Operative January 1, 2012, by Sec. 10 of Ch. 711.)

CHAPTER 3. Body Armor [31310 - 31360]

(Chapter 3 added by Stats. 2010, Ch. 711, Sec. 6.)

31310.

No body armor shall be acquired by the commissioner pursuant to Section 2259.5 of the Vehicle Code unless, pursuant to subdivision (a) of Section 31315, the Department of Justice has certified the body armor.

(Added by Stats. 2010, Ch. 711, Sec. 6. (SB 1080) Effective January 1, 2011. Operative January 1, 2012, by Sec. 10 of Ch. 711.)

31315.

(a) Before any body armor may be purchased for use by state peace officers, the Department of Justice, after consultation with the Department of the California Highway Patrol, shall establish minimum ballistic performance standards, and shall determine that the armor satisfies those standards.

(b) Only body armor that meets state requirements under subdivision (a) for acquisition or purchase shall be eligible for testing for certification under the ballistic performance standards established by the Department of Justice.

(c) Only body armor that is certified as acceptable by the department shall be purchased for use by state peace officers.

(Amended by Stats. 2011, Ch. 296, Sec. 241. (AB 1023) Effective January 1, 2012.)

31320.

(a) Any person engaged in the manufacture or sale of body armor may apply to the Department of Justice for certification that a particular type of body armor manufactured or sold by that person is acceptable.

(b) The applicant shall reimburse the state for any actual expenses incurred by the state in testing and certifying a particular type of body armor.

(Added by Stats. 2010, Ch. 711, Sec. 6. (SB 1080) Effective January 1, 2011. Operative January 1, 2012, by Sec. 10 of Ch. 711.)

31325.

Any application submitted pursuant to Section 31320 shall contain all of the following:

(a) Full written reports of any investigation conducted for the purpose of determining whether the body armor is acceptable.

(b) A full written statement of the design of the body armor.

(c) A full written statement of the methods used in, and the facilities and controls used for, the manufacture of the body armor.

(d) Any samples of the body armor and its components as the Department of Justice may require.

(e) Specimens of the instructions and advertisements used or proposed to be used for the body armor.

(Added by Stats. 2010, Ch. 711, Sec. 6. (SB 1080) Effective January 1, 2011. Operative January 1, 2012, by Sec. 10 of Ch. 711.)

31330.

The Department of Justice, in cooperation with the office of procurement of the Department of General Services, shall establish a schedule for ballistic testing for certification pursuant to subdivision (b) of Section 31315.

(Added by Stats. 2010, Ch. 711, Sec. 6. (SB 1080) Effective January 1, 2011. Operative January 1, 2012, by Sec. 10 of Ch. 711.)

31335.

The Department of Justice shall issue an order refusing to certify a body armor as acceptable if, after due notice to the applicant, the department finds any of the following:

(a) That the body armor does not satisfy the ballistic performance standards established by the department pursuant to subdivision (b) of Section 31315.

(b) That the application contains any misrepresentation of a material fact.

(c) That the application is materially incomplete.

(d) That the applicant has failed to reimburse the state as required by Section 31320.

(Added by Stats. 2010, Ch. 711, Sec. 6. (SB 1080) Effective January 1, 2011. Operative January 1, 2012, by Sec. 10 of Ch. 711.)

31340.

The Department of Justice shall issue an order revoking certification of a body armor if, after due notice to the applicant, the department finds any of the following:

(a) The experience or additional testing show that the body armor does not comply with the department's ballistic performance standards.

(b) The application contains any misrepresentation of a material fact.

(c) The body armor must be retested for certification under new department standards.

(Added by Stats. 2010, Ch. 711, Sec. 6. (SB 1080) Effective January 1, 2011. Operative January 1, 2012, by Sec. 10 of Ch. 711.)

31345.

(a) All purchases of certified body armor under the provisions of this chapter shall be made by the Department of General Services on behalf of an authorized state agency or department. Purchases of body armor shall be based upon written requests submitted by an authorized state agency or department to the Department of General Services.

(b) The Department of General Services shall make certified body armor available to peace officers of the Department of Justice, as defined by Section 830.3, while engaged in law enforcement activities.

(Added by Stats. 2010, Ch. 711, Sec. 6. (SB 1080) Effective January 1, 2011. Operative January 1, 2012, by Sec. 10 of Ch. 711.)

31350.

The Department of General Services shall, pursuant to departmental regulation, after consultation with the Department of the California Highway Patrol, define the term "enforcement activities" for purposes of this chapter, and develop standards regarding what constitutes sufficient wear on body armor to necessitate replacement of the body armor.

(Added by Stats. 2010, Ch. 711, Sec. 6. (SB 1080) Effective January 1, 2011. Operative January 1, 2012, by Sec. 10 of Ch. 711.)

31355.

The Department of Justice shall adopt and promulgate regulations for the fair and efficient enforcement of this chapter.

(Added by Stats. 2010, Ch. 711, Sec. 6. (SB 1080) Effective January 1, 2011. Operative January 1, 2012, by Sec. 10 of Ch. 711.)

31360.

(a) A person who has been convicted of a violent felony under the laws of the United States, the State of California, or any other state, government, or country, who purchases, owns, or possesses body armor, as defined in Section 16288, except as authorized under subdivision (b), is guilty of a felony, punishable by imprisonment in state prison for 16 months, or two or three years.

(b) A person whose employment, livelihood, or safety is dependent on the ability to legally possess and use body armor, who is subject to the prohibition imposed by subdivision (a) due to a prior violent felony conviction, may file a petition for an exception to this prohibition with the chief of police or county sheriff of the jurisdiction in which that person seeks to possess and use the body armor. The chief of police or sheriff may reduce or eliminate the prohibition, impose conditions on reduction or elimination of the prohibition, or otherwise grant relief from the prohibition as the chief of police or sheriff deems appropriate, based on the following:

(1) A finding that the petitioner is likely to use body armor in a safe and lawful manner.

(2) A finding that the petitioner has a reasonable need for this type of protection under the circumstances.

In making its decision, the chief of police or sheriff shall consider the petitioner's continued employment, the interests of justice, any relevant evidence, and the totality of the circumstances. It is the intent of the Legislature that law enforcement officials exercise broad discretion in fashioning appropriate relief under this paragraph in cases in which relief is warranted. However, this paragraph may not be construed to require law enforcement officials to grant relief to any particular petitioner. Relief from this prohibition does not relieve any other person or entity from any liability that might otherwise be imposed.

(c) The chief of police or sheriff shall require, as a condition of granting an exception under subdivision (b), that the petitioner agree to maintain on the petitioner's person a certified copy of the law enforcement official's permission to possess and use body armor, including any conditions or limitations.

(d) Law enforcement officials who enforce the prohibition specified in subdivision (a) against a person who has been granted relief pursuant to subdivision (b), shall be immune from any liability for false arrest arising from the enforcement of this subdivision unless the person has in possession a certified copy of the permission granting the person relief from the prohibition, as required by subdivision (c). This immunity from liability does not relieve any person or entity from any other liability that might otherwise be imposed.

(Amended by Stats. 2012, Ch. 43, Sec. 105. (SB 1023) Effective June 27, 2012.)

CHAPTER 4. Handguns and Firearm Safety [31500 - 32110]

(Heading of Chapter 4 amended by Stats. 2013, Ch. 761, Sec. 12.)

ARTICLE 1. Unconventional Pistol [31500 - 31590]
(Article 1 added by Stats. 2010, Ch. 711, Sec. 6.)

31500.

Except as provided in Chapter 1 (commencing with Section 17700) of Division 2 of Title 2, any person in this state who manufactures or causes to be manufactured, imports into the state, keeps for sale, or offers or exposes for sale, or who gives, lends, or possesses any unconventional pistol is punishable by imprisonment in a county jail not exceeding one year or imprisonment pursuant to subdivision (h) of Section 1170.

(Amended by Stats. 2012, Ch. 43, Sec. 106. (SB 1023) Effective June 27, 2012.)

31590.

Except as provided in Chapter 1 (commencing with Section 17700) of Division 2 of Title 2, any unconventional pistol is a nuisance and is subject to Section 18010.

(Added by Stats. 2010, Ch. 711, Sec. 6. (SB 1080) Effective January 1, 2011. Operative January 1, 2012, by Sec. 10 of Ch. 711.)

ARTICLE 2. Firearm Safety Certificate [31610 - 31670]
(Heading of Article 2 amended by Stats. 2013, Ch. 761, Sec. 13.)

31610.

(a) It is the intent of the Legislature in enacting this article to require that persons who obtain firearms have a basic familiarity with those firearms, including, but not limited to, the safe handling and storage of those firearms. It is not the intent of the Legislature to require a firearm safety certificate for the mere possession of a firearm.

(b) This section shall become operative on January 1, 2015.

(Repealed (in Sec. 14) and added by Stats. 2013, Ch. 761, Sec. 15. (SB 683) Effective January 1, 2014. Section operative January 1, 2015, by its own provisions.)
31615.
(a) A person shall not do either of the following:
(1) Purchase or receive any firearm, except an antique firearm, without a valid firearm safety certificate, except that in the case of a handgun, an unexpired handgun safety certificate may be used.
(2) Sell, deliver, loan, or transfer any firearm, except an antique firearm, to any person who does not have a valid firearm safety certificate, except that in the case of a handgun, an unexpired handgun safety certificate may be used.
(b) Any person who violates subdivision (a) is guilty of a misdemeanor.
(c) The provisions of this section are cumulative, and shall not be construed as restricting the application of any other law. However, an act or omission punishable in different ways by different provisions of this code shall not be punished under more than one provision.
(d) This section shall become operative on January 1, 2015.
(Repealed (in Sec. 16) and added by Stats. 2013, Ch. 761, Sec. 17. (SB 683) Effective January 1, 2014. Section operative January 1, 2015, by its own provisions.)
31620.
(a) A person shall not commit an act of collusion as specified in Section 27550.
(b) Any person who alters, counterfeits, or falsifies a handgun safety certificate, or who uses or attempts to use any altered, counterfeited, or falsified handgun safety certificate to purchase a handgun, is guilty of a misdemeanor.
(c) Commencing January 1, 2015, any person who alters, counterfeits, or falsifies a firearm safety certificate, or who uses or attempts to use any altered, counterfeited, or falsified firearm safety certificate to purchase a firearm, is guilty of a misdemeanor.
(d) The provisions of this section are cumulative and shall not be construed as restricting the application of any other law. However, an act or omission punishable in different ways by this section and different provisions of this code shall not be punished under more than one provision.
(Amended by Stats. 2013, Ch. 761, Sec. 18. (SB 683) Effective January 1, 2014.)
31625.
(a) A certified instructor shall not issue a firearm safety certificate to any person who has not complied with this article. Proof of compliance shall be forwarded to the department by certified instructors as frequently as the department may determine.
(b) A certified instructor shall not issue a firearm safety certificate to any person who is under 18 years of age.
(c) A violation of this section shall be grounds for the department to revoke the instructor's certification to issue firearm safety certificates.
(d) This section shall become operative on January 1, 2015.
(Repealed (in Sec. 19) and added by Stats. 2013, Ch. 761, Sec. 20. (SB 683) Effective January 1, 2014. Section operative January 1, 2015, by its own provisions.)
31630.
(a) The department shall develop an instruction manual in English and in Spanish. The department shall make the instruction manual available to firearm dealers licensed pursuant to Sections 26700 to 26915, inclusive, who shall make it available to the general public. Essential portions of the manual may be included in the pamphlet described in Section 34205.
(b) The department shall develop audiovisual materials in English and in Spanish to be issued to instructors certified by the department.
(c) The department shall solicit input from any reputable association or organization, including any law enforcement association that has as one of its objectives the promotion of firearm safety, in the development of the firearm safety certificate instructional materials.
(d) The instruction manual shall prominently include the following firearm safety warning: Firearms must be handled responsibly and securely stored to prevent access by children and other unauthorized users. California has strict laws pertaining to firearms, and you can be fined or imprisoned if you fail to comply with them. Visit the Web site of the California Attorney General at https://oag.ca.gov/firearms for information on firearm laws applicable to you and how you can comply.
(Amended by Stats. 2018, Ch. 92, Sec. 170. (SB 1289) Effective January 1, 2019.)
31635.
(a) The department shall prescribe a minimum level of skill, knowledge, and competency to be required of all firearm safety certificate instructors.
(b) Department Certified Instructor applicants shall have a certification to provide training from one of the following organizations, as specified, or any entity found by the department to give comparable instruction in firearms safety, or the applicant shall have similar or equivalent training to that provided by the following, as determined by the department:
(1) Department of Consumer Affairs, State of California-Firearm Training Instructor.
(2) Director of Civilian Marksmanship, Instructor or Rangemaster.
(3) Federal Government, Certified Rangemaster or Firearm Instructor.
(4) Federal Law Enforcement Training Center, Firearm Instructor Training Program or Rangemaster.
(5) United States Military, Military Occupational Specialty (MOS) as marksmanship or firearms instructor. Assignment as Range Officer or Safety Officer is not sufficient.
(6) National Rifle Association-Certified Instructor, Law Enforcement Instructor, Rangemaster, or Training Counselor.
(7) Commission on Peace Officer Standards and Training (POST), State of California-Firearm Instructor or Rangemaster.
(8) Authorization from a State of California accredited school to teach a firearm training course.
(c) This section shall become operative on January 1, 2015.
(Repealed (in Sec. 23) and added by Stats. 2013, Ch. 761, Sec. 24. (SB 683) Effective January 1, 2014. Section operative January 1, 2015, by its own provisions.)
31640.
(a) The department shall develop a written objective test, in English and in Spanish, and prescribe its content, form, and manner, to be administered by an instructor certified by the department.
(b) If the person taking the test is unable to read, the test shall be administered orally. If the person taking the test is unable to read English or Spanish, the test may be administered orally by a translator.
(c) The test shall cover, but not be limited to, all of the following:
(1) The laws applicable to carrying and handling firearms, particularly handguns.
(2) The responsibilities of ownership of firearms, particularly handguns.
(3) Current law as it relates to the private sale and transfer of firearms.
(4) Current law as it relates to the permissible use of lethal force.
(5) What constitutes safe firearm storage.
(6) Issues associated with bringing a firearm into the home.
(7) Prevention strategies to address issues associated with bringing firearms into the home.
(d) Commencing January 1, 2019, the test shall require the applicant to be provided with, and acknowledge receipt of, the following warning information:
(1) "Firearms must be handled responsibly and securely stored to prevent access by children and other unauthorized users. California has strict laws pertaining to firearms and you can be fined or imprisoned if you fail to comply with them. Visit the Web site of the California Attorney General at https://oag.ca.gov/firearms for information on firearm laws applicable to you and how you can comply."

(2) "If you decide to sell or give your firearm to someone, you must generally complete a 'Dealer Record of Sale (DROS)' form and conduct the transfer through a licensed firearms dealer. Remember, it is generally a crime to transfer a firearm without first filling out this form. If the police recover a firearm that was involved in a crime, the firearm's previous owner may be prosecuted if he or she did not fill out the DROS form. Please make sure you go to a licensed firearms dealer and fill out that form if you want to sell or give away your firearm."
(e) (1) The department shall update test materials related to this article at least once every five years.
(2) The department shall update the Internet Web site referenced in subdivision (d) regularly to reflect current laws and regulations.
(f) If a dealer licensed pursuant to Sections 26700 to 26915, inclusive, or his or her employee, or where the managing officer or partner is certified as an instructor pursuant to this article, he or she shall also designate a separate room or partitioned area for a person to take the objective test, and maintain adequate supervision to ensure that no acts of collusion occur while the objective test is being administered.
(Amended by Stats. 2018, Ch. 185, Sec. 9. (AB 2176) Effective January 1, 2019.)
31645.
(a) An applicant for a firearm safety certificate shall successfully pass the objective test referred to in Section 31640, with a passing grade of at least 75 percent. Any person receiving a passing grade on the objective test shall immediately be issued a firearm safety certificate by the instructor, provided that, commencing January 1, 2019, the applicant has acknowledged receipt of the firearm safety warning required by subdivision (d) of Section 31640.
(b) An applicant who fails to pass the objective test upon the first attempt shall be offered additional instructional materials by the instructor, such as a videotape or booklet. The person may not retake the objective test under any circumstances until 24 hours have elapsed after the failure to pass the objective test upon the first attempt. The person failing the test on the first attempt shall take another version of the test upon the second attempt. All tests shall be taken from the same instructor except upon permission by the department, which shall be granted only for good cause shown. The instructor shall make himself or herself available to the applicant during regular business hours in order to retake the test.
(Amended by Stats. 2017, Ch. 825, Sec. 6. (AB 1525) Effective January 1, 2018.)
31650.
(a) The certified instructor may charge a fee of twenty-five dollars ($25), fifteen dollars ($15) of which is to be paid to the department pursuant to subdivision (c).
(b) An applicant to renew a firearm safety certificate shall be required to pass the objective test. The certified instructor may charge a fee of twenty-five dollars ($25), fifteen dollars ($15) of which is to be forwarded to the department pursuant to subdivision (c).
(c) The department may charge the certified instructor up to fifteen dollars ($15) for each firearm safety certificate issued by that instructor to cover the department's cost in carrying out and enforcing this article, and enforcing the provisions listed in subdivision (e), as determined annually by the department.
(d) All money received by the department pursuant to this article shall be deposited into the Firearms Safety and Enforcement Special Fund created pursuant to Section 28300.
(e) The department shall conduct enforcement activities, including, but not limited to, law enforcement activities to ensure compliance with the following provisions:
(1) Section 830.95.
(2) Title 2 (commencing with Section 12001) of Part 4.
(3) This part, except Sections 16965, 17235, and 21510.
(f) This section shall become operative on January 1, 2015.
(Repealed (in Sec. 29) and added by Stats. 2013, Ch. 761, Sec. 30. (SB 683) Effective January 1, 2014. Section operative January 1, 2015, by its own provisions.)
31655.
(a) The department shall develop firearm safety certificates to be issued by instructors certified by the department to those persons who have complied with this article.
(b) A firearm safety certificate shall include, but not be limited to, the following information:
(1) A unique firearm safety certificate identification number.
(2) The holder's full name.
(3) The holder's date of birth.
(4) The holder's driver's license or identification number.
(5) The holder's signature.
(6) The signature of the issuing instructor.
(7) The date of issuance.
(c) The firearm safety certificate shall expire five years after the date that it was issued by the certified instructor.
(d) This section shall become operative on January 1, 2015.
(Repealed (in Sec. 31) and added by Stats. 2013, Ch. 761, Sec. 32. (SB 683) Effective January 1, 2014. Section operative January 1, 2015, by its own provisions.)
31660.
(a) In the case of loss or destruction of a firearm safety certificate, the issuing instructor shall issue a duplicate certificate upon request and proof of identification to the certificate holder.
(b) In the case of loss or destruction of a handgun safety certificate, the issuing instructor shall issue a duplicate certificate upon request and proof of identification to the certificate holder, which shall be valid only for the balance of the unexpired term of the original certificate.
(c) The department may authorize the issuing instructor to charge a fee, not to exceed fifteen dollars ($15), for a duplicate certificate. Revenues from this fee shall be deposited in the Firearms Safety and Enforcement Special Fund created pursuant to Section 28300.
(d) This section shall become operative on January 1, 2015.
(Repealed (in Sec. 33) and added by Stats. 2013, Ch. 761, Sec. 34. (SB 683) Effective January 1, 2014. Section operative January 1, 2015, by its own provisions.)
31665.
The department shall be immune from any liability arising from implementing Sections 31630, 31635, 31640, and subdivision (a) of Section 31655.
(Added by Stats. 2010, Ch. 711, Sec. 6. (SB 1080) Effective January 1, 2011. Operative January 1, 2012, by Sec. 10 of Ch. 711.)
31670.
Except for the provisions of former Section 12804, former Article 8 (commencing with Section 12800) of Chapter 6 of Title 2 of Part 4, as added by Section 10 of Chapter 942 of the Statutes of 2001, became operative on January 1, 2003.
(Added by Stats. 2010, Ch. 711, Sec. 6. (SB 1080) Effective January 1, 2011. Operative January 1, 2012, by Sec. 10 of Ch. 711.)

ARTICLE 3. Exceptions to Firearm Safety Certificate Requirement [31700 - 31835]
(Heading of Article 3 amended by Stats. 2013, Ch. 761, Sec. 35.)
31700.
(a) The following persons, properly identified, are exempted from the firearm safety certificate requirement in subdivision (a) of Section 31615:
(1) Any active or honorably retired peace officer, as defined in Chapter 4.5 (commencing with Section 830) of Title 3 of Part 2.
(2) Any active or honorably retired federal officer or law enforcement agent.
(3) Any reserve peace officer, as defined in Section 832.6.

(4) Any person who has successfully completed the course of training specified in Section 832.

(5) A firearms dealer licensed pursuant to Sections 26700 to 26915, inclusive, who is acting in the course and scope of that person's activities as a person licensed pursuant to Sections 26700 to 26915, inclusive.

(6) A federally licensed collector who is acquiring or being loaned a firearm that is a curio or relic, as defined in Section 478.11 of Title 27 of the Code of Federal Regulations, who has a current certificate of eligibility issued by the department pursuant to Section 26710.

(7) A person to whom a firearm is being returned, where the person receiving the firearm is the owner of the firearm.

(8) A family member of a peace officer or deputy sheriff from a local agency who receives a firearm pursuant to Section 50081 of the Government Code.

(9) Any individual who has a valid concealed weapons permit issued pursuant to Chapter 4 (commencing with Section 26150) of Division 5.

(10) An active or honorably retired member of the United States Armed Forces, the National Guard, the Air National Guard, or the active reserve components of the United States, where individuals in those organizations are properly identified. For purposes of this section, proper identification includes the Armed Forces Identification Card or other written documentation certifying that the individual is an active or honorably retired member.

(11) Any person who is authorized to carry loaded firearms pursuant to Section 26025 or 26030.

(12) Persons who are the holders of a special weapons permit issued by the department pursuant to Section 32650 or 33300, pursuant to Article 3 (commencing with Section 18900) of Chapter 1 of Division 5 of Title 2, or pursuant to Article 4 (commencing with Section 32700) of Chapter 6 of this division.

(b) The following persons who take title or possession of a firearm by operation of law in a representative capacity, until or unless they transfer title ownership of the firearm to themselves in a personal capacity, are exempted from the firearm safety certificate requirement in subdivision (a) of Section 31615:

(1) The executor or administrator of an estate.

(2) A secured creditor or an agent or employee thereof when the firearms are possessed as collateral for, or as a result of, a default under a security agreement under the Commercial Code.

(3) A levying officer, as defined in Section 481.140, 511.060, or 680.260 of the Code of Civil Procedure.

(4) A receiver performing the functions of a receiver.

(5) A trustee in bankruptcy performing the duties of a trustee.

(6) An assignee for the benefit of creditors performing the functions of an assignee.

(c) A person, validly identified, who has been issued a valid hunting license that is unexpired or that was issued for the hunting season immediately preceding the calendar year in which the person takes title or possession of a firearm is exempt from the firearm safety certificate requirement in subdivision (a) of Section 31615, except as to handguns.

(d) This section shall become operative on January 1, 2015.

(Amended by Stats. 2018, Ch. 185, Sec. 10. (AB 2176) Effective January 1, 2019.)

31705.

(a) Subdivision (a) of Section 31615 does not apply to any sale, delivery, or transfer of firearms made to an authorized law enforcement representative of any city, county, city and county, or state, or of the federal government, for exclusive use by that governmental agency if, prior to the sale, delivery, or transfer of these firearms, written authorization from the head of the agency authorizing the transaction is presented to the person from whom the purchase, delivery, or transfer is being made.

(b) Proper written authorization is defined as verifiable written certification from the head of the agency by which the purchaser or transferee is employed, identifying the employee as an individual authorized to conduct the transaction, and authorizing the transaction for the exclusive use of the agency by which that person is employed.

(c) Within 10 days of the date a handgun, and commencing January 1, 2014, any firearm, is acquired by the agency, a record of the same shall be entered as an institutional weapon into the Automated Firearms System (AFS) via the California Law Enforcement Telecommunications System (CLETS) by the law enforcement or state agency. Any agency without access to AFS shall arrange with the sheriff of the county in which the agency is located to input this information via this system.

(Amended by Stats. 2011, Ch. 745, Sec. 66. (AB 809) Effective January 1, 2012.)

31710.

Subdivision (a) of Section 31615 does not apply to the loan of a firearm if all of the following conditions are satisfied:

(a) The loan is made by an authorized law enforcement representative of a city, county, or city and county, or of the state or federal government.

(b) The loan is made to a peace officer employed by that agency and authorized to carry a firearm.

(c) The loan is made for the carrying and use of that firearm by that peace officer in the course and scope of the officer's duties.

(Added by Stats. 2010, Ch. 711, Sec. 6. (SB 1080) Effective January 1, 2011. Operative January 1, 2012, by Sec. 10 of Ch. 711.)

31715.

(a) Subdivision (a) of Section 31615 does not apply to the sale, delivery, or transfer of a firearm by a law enforcement agency to a peace officer pursuant to Section 10334 of the Public Contract Code.

(b) Within 10 days of the date that a handgun, and commencing January 1, 2014, any firearm, is sold, delivered, or transferred pursuant to Section 10334 of the Public Contract Code to that peace officer, the name of the officer and the make, model, serial number, and other identifying characteristics of the firearm being sold, delivered, or transferred shall be entered into the Automated Firearms System (AFS) via the California Law Enforcement Telecommunications System (CLETS) by the law enforcement or state agency that sold, delivered, or transferred the firearm, provided, however, that if the firearm is not a handgun and does not have a serial number, identification number, or identification mark assigned to it, that fact shall be noted in AFS. Any agency without access to AFS shall arrange with the sheriff of the county in which the agency is located to input this information via this system.

(Amended by Stats. 2011, Ch. 745, Sec. 67. (AB 809) Effective January 1, 2012.)

31720.

(a) Subdivision (a) of Section 31615 does not apply to the sale, delivery, or transfer of a firearm by a law enforcement agency to a retiring peace officer who is authorized to carry a firearm pursuant to Chapter 5 (commencing with Section 26300) of Division 5.

(b) Within 10 days of the date that a handgun, and commencing January 1, 2014, any firearm, is sold, delivered, or transferred to that retiring peace officer, the name of the officer and the make, model, serial number, and other identifying characteristics of the firearm being sold, delivered, or transferred shall be entered into the Automated Firearms System (AFS) via the California Law Enforcement Telecommunications System (CLETS) by the law enforcement or state agency that sold, delivered, or transferred the firearm, provided, however, that if the firearm is not a handgun and does not have a serial number, identification number, or identification mark assigned to it, that fact shall be noted in AFS. Any agency without access to AFS shall arrange with the sheriff of the county in which the agency is located to input this information via this system.

(Amended by Stats. 2011, Ch. 745, Sec. 68. (AB 809) Effective January 1, 2012.)

31725.

(a) Subdivision (a) of Section 31615 does not apply to a sale, delivery, or transfer of firearms if both of the following requirements are satisfied:

(1) The sale, delivery, or transfer is to an authorized representative of a city, city and county, county, or state government, or of the federal government, and is for the governmental entity.

(2) The entity is acquiring the weapon as part of an authorized, voluntary program in which the entity is buying or receiving weapons from private individuals.

(b) Any weapons acquired pursuant to this section shall be disposed of pursuant to the applicable provisions of Section 34000 or Sections 18000 and 18005.

(Added by Stats. 2010, Ch. 711, Sec. 6. (SB 1080) Effective January 1, 2011. Operative January 1, 2012, by Sec. 10 of Ch. 711.)

31730.

Subdivision (a) of Section 31615 does not apply to the sale, delivery, loan, or transfer of a firearm made by an authorized law enforcement representative of a city, county, city and county, or state, or of the federal government, to any public or private nonprofit historical society, museum, or institutional collection, or the purchase or receipt of that firearm by that public or private nonprofit historical society, museum, or institutional collection, if all of the following conditions are met:

(a) The entity receiving the firearm is open to the public.

(b) The firearm prior to delivery is deactivated or rendered inoperable.

(c) The firearm is not subject to any of the following:

(1) Sections 18000 and 18005.

(2) Division 4 (commencing with Section 18250) of Title 2.

(3) Section 34000.

(4) Sections 34005 and 34010.

(d) The firearm is not prohibited by other provisions of law from being sold, delivered, or transferred to the public at large.

(e) Prior to delivery, the entity receiving the firearm submits a written statement to the law enforcement representative stating that the firearm will not be restored to operating condition, and will either remain with that entity, or if subsequently disposed of, will be transferred in accordance with the applicable provisions listed in Section 16575 and, if applicable, Section 31615.

(f) Within 10 days of the date that the firearm is sold, loaned, delivered, or transferred to that entity, all of the following information shall be reported to the department in a manner prescribed by the department:

(1) The name of the government entity delivering the firearm.

(2) The make, model, serial number, and other identifying characteristics of the firearm.

(3) The name of the person authorized by the entity to take possession of the firearm.

(g) In the event of a change in the status of the designated representative, the entity shall notify the department of a new representative within 30 days.

(Added by Stats. 2010, Ch. 711, Sec. 6. (SB 1080) Effective January 1, 2011. Operative January 1, 2012, by Sec. 10 of Ch. 711.)

31735.

Subdivision (a) of Section 31615 does not apply to the sale, delivery, loan, or transfer of a firearm made by any person other than a representative of an authorized law enforcement agency to any public or private nonprofit historical society, museum, or institutional collection, if all of the following conditions are met:

(a) The entity receiving the firearm is open to the public.

(b) The firearm is deactivated or rendered inoperable prior to delivery.

(c) The firearm is not of a type prohibited from being sold, delivered, or transferred to the public.

(d) Prior to delivery, the entity receiving the firearm submits a written statement to the person selling, loaning, or transferring the firearm stating that the firearm will not be restored to operating condition, and will either remain with that entity, or if subsequently disposed of, will be transferred in accordance with the applicable provisions listed in Section 16575 and, if applicable, with Section 31615.

(e) If title to a handgun, and commencing January 1, 2014, any firearm, is being transferred to the public or private nonprofit historical society, museum, or institutional collection, then the designated representative of that entity shall, within 30 days of taking possession of that firearm, forward by prepaid mail or deliver in person to the Department of Justice, a single report signed by both parties to the transaction, which includes all of the following information:

(1) Information identifying the person representing the public or private historical society, museum, or institutional collection.

(2) Information on how title was obtained and from whom.

(3) A description of the firearm in question.

(4) A copy of the written statement referred to in subdivision (d).

(f) The report forms that are to be completed pursuant to this section shall be provided by the Department of Justice.

(g) In the event of a change in the status of the designated representative, the entity shall notify the department of a new representative within 30 days.

(Amended by Stats. 2011, Ch. 745, Sec. 69. (AB 809) Effective January 1, 2012.)

31740.

Subdivision (a) of Section 31615 does not apply to sales, deliveries, or transfers of firearms between or to importers and manufacturers of firearms licensed to engage in that business pursuant to Chapter 44 (commencing with Section 921) of Title 18 of the United States Code and the regulations issued pursuant thereto.

(Added by Stats. 2010, Ch. 711, Sec. 6. (SB 1080) Effective January 1, 2011. Operative January 1, 2012, by Sec. 10 of Ch. 711.)

31745.

Subdivision (a) of Section 31615 shall not apply to the sale, delivery, or transfer of a handgun to a person licensed pursuant to Sections 26700 to 26915, inclusive, where the licensee is receiving the handgun in the course and scope of the licensee's activities as a person licensed pursuant to Sections 26700 to 26915, inclusive.

(Added by Stats. 2010, Ch. 711, Sec. 6. (SB 1080) Effective January 1, 2011. Operative January 1, 2012, by Sec. 10 of Ch. 711.)

31750.

Subdivision (a) of Section 31615 does not apply to the loan of a firearm if all of the following conditions exist:

(a) The person loaning the firearm is at all times within the presence of the person being loaned the firearm.

(b) The loan is for a lawful purpose.

(c) The loan does not exceed three days in duration.

(d) The individual receiving the firearm is not prohibited by state or federal law from possessing, receiving, owning, or purchasing a firearm.

(e) The person loaning the firearm is 18 years of age or older.

(f) The person being loaned the firearm is 18 years of age or older.

(Added by Stats. 2010, Ch. 711, Sec. 6. (SB 1080) Effective January 1, 2011. Operative January 1, 2012, by Sec. 10 of Ch. 711.)

31755.

Subdivision (a) of Section 31615 does not apply to the delivery of a firearm to a gunsmith for service or repair, or to the return of the firearm to its owner by the gunsmith, or to the delivery of a firearm by a gunsmith to a person licensed pursuant to Chapter 44 (commencing with Section 921) of Title 18 of the United States Code for service or repair and the return of the firearm to the gunsmith.

(Added by Stats. 2010, Ch. 711, Sec. 6. (SB 1080) Effective January 1, 2011. Operative January 1, 2012, by Sec. 10 of Ch. 711.)

31760.

Subdivision (a) of Section 31615 does not apply to the sale, delivery, or transfer of firearms if all of the following requirements are satisfied:
(a) The sale, delivery, or transfer is made by a person who resides in this state.
(b) The sale, delivery, or transfer is made to a person who resides outside this state and is licensed pursuant to Chapter 44 (commencing with Section 921) of Title 18 of the United States Code and the regulations issued pursuant thereto.
(c) The sale, delivery, or transfer is in accordance with Chapter 44 (commencing with Section 921) of Title 18 of the United States Code and the regulations issued pursuant thereto.
(Added by Stats. 2010, Ch. 711, Sec. 6. (SB 1080) Effective January 1, 2011. Operative January 1, 2012, by Sec. 10 of Ch. 711.)
31765.
Subdivision (a) of Section 31615 does not apply to the loan of a firearm to a person 18 years of age or older for the purposes of shooting at targets if the loan occurs on the premises of a target facility that holds a business or regulatory license or on the premises of any club or organization organized for the purposes of practicing shooting at targets upon established ranges, whether public or private, if the firearm is at all times kept within the premises of the target range or on the premises of the club or organization.
(Added by Stats. 2010, Ch. 711, Sec. 6. (SB 1080) Effective January 1, 2011. Operative January 1, 2012, by Sec. 10 of Ch. 711.)
31770.
Subdivision (a) of Section 31615 does not apply to deliveries, transfers, or returns of firearms made pursuant to any of the following:
(a) Sections 18000 and 18005.
(b) Division 4 (commencing with Section 18250) of Title 2.
(c) Chapter 2 (commencing with Section 33850) of Division 11.
(d) Sections 34005 and 34010.
(Added by Stats. 2010, Ch. 711, Sec. 6. (SB 1080) Effective January 1, 2011. Operative January 1, 2012, by Sec. 10 of Ch. 711.)
31780.
Subdivision (a) of Section 31615 does not apply to the sale, delivery, or transfer of unloaded firearms by a dealer to a person who resides outside this state and is licensed pursuant to Chapter 44 (commencing with Section 921) of Title 18 of the United States Code and the regulations issued pursuant thereto.
(Added by Stats. 2010, Ch. 711, Sec. 6. (SB 1080) Effective January 1, 2011. Operative January 1, 2012, by Sec. 10 of Ch. 711.)
31785.
Subdivision (a) of Section 31615 does not apply to the sale, delivery, or transfer of unloaded firearms to a wholesaler if the firearms are being returned to the wholesaler and are intended as merchandise in the wholesaler's business.
(Added by Stats. 2010, Ch. 711, Sec. 6. (SB 1080) Effective January 1, 2011. Operative January 1, 2012, by Sec. 10 of Ch. 711.)
31790.
Subdivision (a) of Section 31615 does not apply to the sale, delivery, or transfer of firearms if all of the following conditions are satisfied:
(a) The firearms are unloaded.
(b) The sale, delivery, or transfer is made by one dealer to another dealer, upon proof of compliance with the requirements of Section 27555.
(c) The firearms are intended as merchandise in the receiving dealer's business.
(Added by Stats. 2010, Ch. 711, Sec. 6. (SB 1080) Effective January 1, 2011. Operative January 1, 2012, by Sec. 10 of Ch. 711.)
31800.
Subdivision (a) of Section 31615 does not apply to the loan of an unloaded firearm by a dealer who also operates a target facility that holds a business or regulatory license on the premises of the building designated in the license or whose building designated in the license is on the premises of any club or organization organized for the purposes of practicing shooting at targets upon established ranges, whether public or private, to a person at that target facility or that club or organization, if the firearm is at all times kept within the premises of the target range or on the premises of the club or organization.
(Added by Stats. 2010, Ch. 711, Sec. 6. (SB 1080) Effective January 1, 2011. Operative January 1, 2012, by Sec. 10 of Ch. 711.)
31805.
Subdivision (a) of Section 31615 does not apply to the sale, delivery, or transfer of unloaded firearms to a wholesaler as merchandise in the wholesaler's business by a manufacturer or importer licensed to engage in that business pursuant to Chapter 44 (commencing with Section 921) of Title 18 of the United States Code and the regulations issued pursuant thereto, or by another wholesaler, if the sale, delivery, or transfer is made in accordance with Chapter 44 (commencing with Section 921) of Title 18 of the United States Code.
(Added by Stats. 2010, Ch. 711, Sec. 6. (SB 1080) Effective January 1, 2011. Operative January 1, 2012, by Sec. 10 of Ch. 711.)
31810.
Subdivision (a) of Section 31615 does not apply to or affect the following circumstances:
(a) The loan of a handgun, and commencing January 1, 2015, any firearm, to a minor by the minor's parent or legal guardian, if both of the following requirements are satisfied:
(1) The minor is being loaned the firearm for the purposes of engaging in a lawful, recreational sport, including, but not limited to, competitive shooting, or agricultural, ranching, or hunting activity or hunting education, or a motion picture, television, or video production, or entertainment or theatrical event, the nature of which involves the use of a firearm.
(2) The duration of the loan does not exceed the amount of time that is reasonably necessary to engage in the lawful, recreational sport, including, but not limited to, competitive shooting, or agricultural, ranching, or hunting activity or hunting education, or a motion picture, television, or video production, or entertainment or theatrical event, the nature of which involves the use of a firearm.
(b) The loan of a handgun, and commencing January 1, 2015, any firearm, to a minor by a person who is not the minor's parent or legal guardian, if all of the following requirements are satisfied:
(1) The minor is accompanied by the minor's parent or legal guardian when the loan is made, or the minor has the written consent of the minor's parent or legal guardian, which is presented at the time of the loan, or earlier.
(2) The minor is being loaned the firearm for the purpose of engaging in a lawful, recreational sport, including, but not limited to, competitive shooting, or agricultural, ranching, or hunting activity or hunting education, or a motion picture, television, or video production, or entertainment or theatrical event, the nature of which involves the use of a firearm.
(3) The duration of the loan does not exceed the amount of time that is reasonably necessary to engage in the lawful, recreational sport, including, but not limited to, competitive shooting, or agricultural, ranching, or hunting activity or hunting education, or a motion picture, television, or video production, or entertainment or theatrical event, the nature of which involves the use of a firearm.
(4) The duration of the loan does not, in any event, exceed 10 days.
(Amended by Stats. 2013, Ch. 761, Sec. 38. (SB 683) Effective January 1, 2014.)
31815.
Subdivision (a) of Section 31615 does not apply to the loan of a firearm if all of the following requirements are satisfied:
(a) The loan is infrequent, as defined in Section 16730.
(b) The firearm is unloaded.
(c) The loan is made by a person who is neither a dealer nor a federal firearms licensee pursuant to Chapter 44 (commencing with Section 921) of Title 18 of the United States Code.
(d) The loan is made to a person 18 years of age or older.
(e) The loan is for use solely as a prop in a motion picture, television, video, theatrical, or other entertainment production or event.
(Added by Stats. 2010, Ch. 711, Sec. 6. (SB 1080) Effective January 1, 2011. Operative January 1, 2012, by Sec. 10 of Ch. 711.)
31820.
(a) Subdivision (a) of Section 31615 does not apply to the loan of a firearm if all of the following requirements are satisfied:
(1) The firearm is unloaded.
(2) The loan is made by a person who is not a dealer but is a federal firearms licensee pursuant to Chapter 44 (commencing with Section 921) of Title 18 of the United States Code.
(3) The loan is made to a person who possesses a valid entertainment firearms permit issued pursuant to Chapter 2 (commencing with Section 29500) of Division 8.
(4) The firearm is loaned for use solely as a prop in a motion picture, television, video, theatrical, or other entertainment production or event.
(b) The person loaning the firearm pursuant to this section shall retain a photocopy of the entertainment firearms permit as proof of compliance with this requirement.
(Added by Stats. 2010, Ch. 711, Sec. 6. (SB 1080) Effective January 1, 2011. Operative January 1, 2012, by Sec. 10 of Ch. 711.)
31825.
(a) Subdivision (a) of Section 31615 does not apply to the loan of a firearm if all of the following conditions are satisfied:
(1) The firearm is unloaded.
(2) The loan is made by a dealer.
(3) The loan is made to a person who possesses a valid entertainment firearms permit issued pursuant to Chapter 2 (commencing with Section 29500) of Division 8.
(4) The firearm is loaned solely for use as a prop in a motion picture, television, video, theatrical, or other entertainment production or event.
(b) The dealer shall retain a photocopy of the entertainment firearms permit as proof of compliance with this requirement.
(Added by Stats. 2010, Ch. 711, Sec. 6. (SB 1080) Effective January 1, 2011. Operative January 1, 2012, by Sec. 10 of Ch. 711.)
31830.
(a) Subdivision (a) of Section 31615 does not apply to the loan of an unloaded firearm to a consultant-evaluator by a person licensed pursuant to Sections 26700 to 26915, inclusive, if the loan does not exceed 45 days from the date of delivery.
(b) At the time of the loan, the consultant-evaluator shall provide the following information, which the dealer shall retain for two years:
(1) A photocopy of a valid, current, government-issued identification to determine the consultant-evaluator's identity, including, but not limited to, a California driver's license, identification card, or passport.
(2) A photocopy of the consultant-evaluator's valid, current certificate of eligibility.
(3) A letter from the person licensed as an importer, manufacturer, or dealer pursuant to Chapter 44 (commencing with Section 921) of Title 18 of the United States Code, with whom the consultant-evaluator has a bona fide business relationship. The letter shall detail the bona fide business purposes for which the firearm is being loaned and confirm that the consultant-evaluator is being loaned the firearm as part of a bona fide business relationship.
(4) The signature of the consultant-evaluator on a form indicating the date the firearm is loaned and the last day the firearm may be returned.
(Added by Stats. 2010, Ch. 711, Sec. 6. (SB 1080) Effective January 1, 2011. Operative January 1, 2012, by Sec. 10 of Ch. 711.)
31835.
Subdivision (a) of Section 31615 does not apply to the delivery, sale, or transfer of firearms when made by authorized law enforcement representatives for cities, counties, cities and counties, or of the state or federal government, if all of the following conditions are met:
(a) The sale, delivery, or transfer is made to one of the persons or entities identified in subdivision (a) of Section 26620.
(b) The sale, delivery, or transfer of the firearm is not subject to the procedures set forth in Section 18000, 18005, 34000, or 34005.
(c) The sale, delivery, or transfer of the firearm follows the procedures set forth in subdivision (c) of Section 26620.
(Added by Stats. 2013, Ch. 738, Sec. 10. (AB 538) Effective January 1, 2014.)

ARTICLE 4. "Unsafe Handgun" and Related Definitions [31900 - 31910]

(Article 4 added by Stats. 2010, Ch. 711, Sec. 6.)
31900.
As used in this part, the "drop safety requirement for handguns" means that at the conclusion of the firing requirements for handguns described in Section 31905, the same certified independent testing laboratory shall subject the same three handguns of the make and model for which certification is sought, to the following test:
(a) A primed case (no powder or projectile) shall be inserted into the chamber. For a pistol, the slide shall be released, allowing it to move forward under the impetus of the recoil spring, and an empty magazine shall be inserted. For both a pistol and a revolver, the weapon shall be placed in a drop fixture capable of dropping the pistol from a drop height of 1m + 1cm (39.4 + 0.4 in.) onto the largest side of a slab of solid concrete having minimum dimensions of 7.5 x 15 x 15 cm (3 x 6 x 6 in.). The drop distance shall be measured from the lowermost portion of the weapon to the top surface of the slab. The weapon shall be dropped from a fixture and not from the hand. The weapon shall be dropped in the condition that it would be in if it were dropped from a hand (cocked with no manual safety applied). If the pistol is designed so that upon leaving the hand a "safety" is automatically applied by the pistol, this feature shall not be defeated. An approved drop fixture is a short piece of string with the weapon attached at one end and the other end held in an air vise until the drop is initiated.
(b) The following six drops shall be performed:
(1) Normal firing position with barrel horizontal.
(2) Upside down with barrel horizontal.
(3) On grip with barrel vertical.
(4) On muzzle with barrel vertical.
(5) On either side with barrel horizontal.
(6) If there is an exposed hammer or striker, on the rearmost point of that device, otherwise on the rearmost point of the weapon.
(c) The primer shall be examined for indentations after each drop. If indentations are present, a fresh primed case shall be used for the next drop.
(d) The handgun shall pass this test if each of the three test guns does not fire the primer.
(Added by Stats. 2010, Ch. 711, Sec. 6. (SB 1080) Effective January 1, 2011. Operative January 1, 2012, by Sec. 10 of Ch. 711.)
31905.
(a) As used in this part, "firing requirement for handguns" means a test in which the manufacturer provides three handguns of the make and model for which certification is sought to an independent testing laboratory certified by the Attorney General pursuant to Section 32010. These handguns may not be refined or modified in any way from

those that would be made available for retail sale if certification is granted. The magazines of a tested pistol shall be identical to those that would be provided with the pistol to a retail customer.

(b) The test shall be conducted as follows:

(1) The laboratory shall fire 600 rounds from each gun, stopping after each series of 50 rounds has been fired for 5 to 10 minutes to allow the weapon to cool, stopping after each series of 100 rounds has been fired to tighten any loose screws and clean the gun in accordance with the manufacturer's instructions, and stopping as needed to refill the empty magazine or cylinder to capacity before continuing.

(2) The ammunition used shall be of the type recommended by the handgun manufacturer in the user manual, or if none is recommended, any standard ammunition of the correct caliber in new condition that is commercially available.

(c) A handgun shall pass this test if each of the three test guns meets both of the following:

(1) Fires the first 20 rounds without a malfunction that is not due to ammunition that fails to detonate.

(2) Fires the full 600 rounds with no more than six malfunctions that are not due to ammunition that fails to detonate and without any crack or breakage of an operating part of the handgun that increases the risk of injury to the user.

(d) If a pistol or revolver fails the requirements of either paragraph (1) or (2) of subdivision (c) due to ammunition that fails to detonate, the pistol or revolver shall be retested from the beginning of the "firing requirement for handguns" test. A new model of the pistol or revolver that failed due to ammunition that fails to detonate may be submitted for the test to replace the pistol or revolver that failed.

(e) As used in this section, "malfunction" means a failure to properly feed, fire, or eject a round, or failure of a pistol to accept or eject the magazine, or failure of a pistol's slide to remain open after the magazine has been expended.

(Added by Stats. 2010, Ch. 711, Sec. 6. (SB 1080) Effective January 1, 2011. Operative January 1, 2012, by Sec. 10 of Ch. 711.)

31910.

As used in this part, "unsafe handgun" means any pistol, revolver, or other firearm capable of being concealed upon the person, for which any of the following is true:

(a) For a revolver:

(1) It does not have a safety device that, either automatically in the case of a double-action firing mechanism, or by manual operation in the case of a single-action firing mechanism, causes the hammer to retract to a point where the firing pin does not rest upon the primer of the cartridge.

(2) It does not meet the firing requirement for handguns.

(3) It does not meet the drop safety requirement for handguns.

(b) For a pistol:

(1) It does not have a positive manually operated safety device, as determined by standards relating to imported guns promulgated by the federal Bureau of Alcohol, Tobacco, Firearms and Explosives.

(2) It does not meet the firing requirement for handguns.

(3) It does not meet the drop safety requirement for handguns.

(4) Commencing January 1, 2006, for a center fire semiautomatic pistol that is not already listed on the roster pursuant to Section 32015, it does not have either a chamber load indicator, or a magazine disconnect mechanism.

(5) Commencing January 1, 2007, for all center fire semiautomatic pistols that are not already listed on the roster pursuant to Section 32015, it does not have both a chamber load indicator and if it has a detachable magazine, a magazine disconnect mechanism.

(6) Commencing January 1, 2006, for all rimfire semiautomatic pistols that are not already listed on the roster pursuant to Section 32015, it does not have a magazine disconnect mechanism, if it has a detachable magazine.

(7) (A) Commencing January 1, 2010, for all semiautomatic pistols that are not already listed on the roster pursuant to Section 32015, it is not designed and equipped with a microscopic array of characters that identify the make, model, and serial number of the pistol, etched or otherwise imprinted in two or more places on the interior surface or internal working parts of the pistol, and that are transferred by imprinting on each cartridge case when the firearm is fired, provided that the Department of Justice certifies that the technology used to create the imprint is available to more than one manufacturer unencumbered by any patent restrictions.

(B) The Attorney General may also approve a method of equal or greater reliability and effectiveness in identifying the specific serial number of a firearm from spent cartridge casings discharged by that firearm than that which is set forth in this paragraph, to be thereafter required as otherwise set forth by this paragraph where the Attorney General certifies that this new method is also unencumbered by any patent restrictions. Approval by the Attorney General shall include notice of that fact via regulations adopted by the Attorney General for purposes of implementing that method for purposes of this paragraph.

(C) The microscopic array of characters required by this section shall not be considered the name of the maker, model, manufacturer's number, or other mark of identification, including any distinguishing number or mark assigned by the Department of Justice, within the meaning of Sections 23900 and 23920.

(Amended by Stats. 2011, Ch. 296, Sec. 242. (AB 1023) Effective January 1, 2012.)

ARTICLE 5. Rules Governing Unsafe Handguns [32000 - 32030]
(Article 5 added by Stats. 2010, Ch. 711, Sec. 6.)

32000.

(a) A person in this state who manufactures or causes to be manufactured, imports into the state for sale, keeps for sale, offers or exposes for sale, gives, or lends an unsafe handgun shall be punished by imprisonment in a county jail not exceeding one year.

(b) This section shall not apply to any of the following:

(1) The manufacture in this state, or importation into this state, of a prototype handgun when the manufacture or importation is for the sole purpose of allowing an independent laboratory certified by the Department of Justice pursuant to Section 32010 to conduct an independent test to determine whether that handgun is prohibited by Sections 31900 to 32110, inclusive, and, if not, allowing the department to add the firearm to the roster of handguns that may be sold in this state pursuant to Section 32015.

(2) The importation or lending of a handgun by employees or authorized agents of entities determining whether the weapon is prohibited by this section.

(3) Firearms listed as curios or relics, as defined in Section 478.11 of Title 27 of the Code of Federal Regulations.

(4) The sale or purchase of a handgun, if the handgun is sold to, or purchased by, the Department of Justice, a police department, a sheriff's official, a marshal's office, the Department of Corrections and Rehabilitation, the Department of the California Highway Patrol, any district attorney's office, any federal law enforcement agency, or the military or naval forces of this state or of the United States for use in the discharge of their official duties. This section does not prohibit the sale to, or purchase by, sworn members of these agencies of a handgun.

(5) The sale, purchase, or delivery of a handgun, if the sale, purchase, or delivery of the handgun is made pursuant to subdivision (d) of Section 10334 of the Public Contract Code.

(6) Subject to the limitations set forth in subdivision (c), the sale or purchase of a handgun, if the handgun is sold to, or purchased by, any of the following entities or sworn members of these entities who have satisfactorily completed the firearms portion of a training course prescribed by the Commission on Peace Officer Standards and Training pursuant to Section 832:

(A) The Department of Parks and Recreation.

(B) The Department of Alcoholic Beverage Control.

(C) The Division of Investigation of the Department of Consumer Affairs.

(D) The Department of Motor Vehicles.

(E) The Fraud Division of the Department of Insurance.

(F) The State Department of State Hospitals.

(G) The Department of Fish and Wildlife.

(H) The State Department of Developmental Services.

(I) The Department of Forestry and Fire Protection.

(J) A county probation department.

(K) The Los Angeles World Airports, as defined in Section 830.15.

(L) A K–12 public school district for use by a school police officer, as described in Section 830.32.

(M) A municipal water district for use by a park ranger, as described in Section 830.34.

(N) A county for use by a welfare fraud investigator or inspector, as described in Section 830.35.

(O) A county for use by the coroner or the deputy coroner, as described in Section 830.35.

(P) The Supreme Court and the courts of appeal for use by marshals of the Supreme Court and bailiffs of the courts of appeal, and coordinators of security for the judicial branch, as described in Section 830.36.

(Q) A fire department or fire protection agency of a county, city, city and county, district, or the state for use by either of the following:

(i) A member of an arson-investigating unit, regularly paid and employed in that capacity pursuant to Section 830.37.

(ii) A member other than a member of an arson-investigating unit, regularly paid and employed in that capacity pursuant to Section 830.37.

(R) The University of California Police Department, or the California State University Police Departments, as described in Section 830.2.

(S) A California Community College police department, as described in Section 830.32.

(T) A harbor or port district or other entity employing peace officers described in subdivision (b) of Section 830.33, the San Diego Unified Port District Harbor Police, and the Harbor Department of the City of Los Angeles.

(c) (1) Notwithstanding Section 26825, a person licensed pursuant to Sections 26700 to 26915, inclusive, shall not process the sale or transfer of an unsafe handgun between a person who has obtained an unsafe handgun pursuant to an exemption specified in paragraph (6) of subdivision (b) and a person who is not exempt from the requirements of this section.

(2) (A) A person who obtains an unsafe handgun pursuant to paragraph (6) of subdivision (b) shall, when leaving the handgun in an unattended vehicle, lock the handgun in the vehicle's trunk, lock the handgun in a locked container and place the container out of plain view, or lock the handgun in a locked container that is permanently affixed to the vehicle's interior and not in plain view.

(B) A violation of subparagraph (A) is an infraction punishable by a fine not exceeding one thousand dollars ($1,000).

(C) For purposes of this paragraph, the following definitions shall apply:

(i) "Vehicle" has the same meaning as defined in Section 670 of the Vehicle Code.

(ii) A vehicle is "unattended" when a person who is lawfully carrying or transporting a handgun in the vehicle is not within close proximity to the vehicle to reasonably prevent unauthorized access to the vehicle or its contents.

(iii) "Locked container" has the same meaning as defined in Section 16850.

(D) Subparagraph (A) does not apply to a peace officer during circumstances requiring immediate aid or action that are within the course of his or her official duties.

(E) This paragraph does not supersede any local ordinance that regulates the storage of handguns in unattended vehicles if the ordinance was in effect before January 1, 2017.

(d) Violations of subdivision (a) are cumulative with respect to each handgun and shall not be construed as restricting the application of any other law. However, an act or omission punishable in different ways by this section and other provisions of law shall not be punished under more than one provision, but the penalty to be imposed shall be determined as set forth in Section 654.

(Amended by Stats. 2018, Ch. 56, Sec. 1. (AB 1872) Effective January 1, 2019.)

32005.

(a) Every person who is licensed as a manufacturer of firearms pursuant to Chapter 44 (commencing with Section 921) of Title 18 of the United States Code and who manufactures firearms in this state shall certify under penalty of perjury and any other remedy provided by law that every model, kind, class, style, or type of pistol, revolver, or other firearm capable of being concealed upon the person that the person manufactures is not an unsafe handgun as prohibited by Sections 31900 to 32110, inclusive.

(b) Every person who imports into the state for sale, keeps for sale, or offers or exposes for sale any firearm shall certify under penalty of perjury and any other remedy provided by law that every model, kind, class, style, or type of pistol, revolver, or other firearm capable of being concealed upon the person that the person imports, keeps, or exposes for sale is not an unsafe handgun as prohibited by Sections 31900 to 32110, inclusive.

(Added by Stats. 2010, Ch. 711, Sec. 6. (SB 1080) Effective January 1, 2011. Operative January 1, 2012, by Sec. 10 of Ch. 711.)

32010.

(a) Any pistol, revolver, or other firearm capable of being concealed upon the person manufactured in this state, imported into the state for sale, kept for sale, or offered or exposed for sale, shall be tested within a reasonable period of time by an independent laboratory certified pursuant to subdivision (b) to determine whether that pistol, revolver, or other firearm capable of being concealed upon the person meets or exceeds the standards defined in Section 31910.

(b) On or before October 1, 2000, the Department of Justice shall certify laboratories to verify compliance with the standards defined in Section 31910. The department may charge a fee to certify a laboratory to test any pistol, revolver, or other firearm capable of being concealed upon the person pursuant to Sections 31900 to 32110, inclusive. The fee shall not exceed the costs of certification.

(c) The certified testing laboratory shall, at the manufacturer's or importer's expense, test the firearm and submit a copy of the final test report directly to the Department of Justice along with a prototype of the weapon to be retained by the department. The department shall notify the manufacturer or importer of its receipt of the final test report and the department's determination as to whether the firearm tested may be sold in this state.

(d) (1) Commencing January 1, 2006, no center-fire semiautomatic pistol may be submitted for testing pursuant to Sections 31900 to 32110, inclusive, if it does not have either a chamber load indicator, or a magazine disconnect mechanism if it has a detachable magazine.

(2) Commencing January 1, 2007, no center-fire semiautomatic pistol may be submitted for testing pursuant to Sections 31900 to 32110, inclusive, if it does not have both a chamber load indicator and a magazine disconnect mechanism.

(3) Commencing January 1, 2006, no rimfire semiautomatic pistol may be submitted for testing pursuant to Sections 31900 to 32110, inclusive, if it has a detachable magazine, and does not have a magazine disconnect mechanism.

(Amended by Stats. 2018, Ch. 185, Sec. 11. (AB 2176) Effective January 1, 2019.)

32015.

(a) On and after January 1, 2001, the Department of Justice shall compile, publish, and thereafter maintain a roster listing all of the handguns that have been tested by a certified testing laboratory, have been determined not to be unsafe handguns, and may be sold in this state pursuant to this part. The roster shall list, for each firearm, the manufacturer, model number, and model name.

(b) (1) The department may charge every person in this state who is licensed as a manufacturer of firearms pursuant to Chapter 44 (commencing with Section 921) of Title 18 of the United States Code, and any person in this state who manufactures or causes to be manufactured, imports into the state for sale, keeps for sale, or offers or exposes for sale any handgun in this state, an annual fee not exceeding the costs of preparing, publishing, and maintaining the roster pursuant to subdivision (a) and the costs of research and development, report analysis, firearms storage, and other program infrastructure costs necessary to implement Sections 31900 to 32110, inclusive. Commencing January 1, 2015, the annual fee shall be paid on January 1, or the next business day, of every year.

(2) Any handgun that is manufactured by a manufacturer who manufactures or causes to be manufactured, imports into the state for sale, keeps for sale, or offers or exposes for sale any handgun in this state, and who fails to pay any fee required pursuant to paragraph (1), may be excluded from the roster.

(3) If a purchaser has initiated a transfer of a handgun that is listed on the roster as not unsafe, and prior to the completion of the transfer, the handgun is removed from the roster of not unsafe handguns because of failure to pay the fee required to keep that handgun listed on the roster, the handgun shall be deliverable to the purchaser if the purchaser is not otherwise prohibited from purchasing or possessing the handgun. However, if a purchaser has initiated a transfer of a handgun that is listed on the roster as not unsafe, and prior to the completion of the transfer, the handgun is removed from the roster pursuant to subdivision (d) of Section 32020, the handgun shall not be deliverable to the purchaser.

(Amended by Stats. 2013, Ch. 758, Sec. 4. (SB 363) Effective January 1, 2014.)
32020.

(a) The Attorney General may annually retest up to 5 percent of the handgun models that are listed on the roster described in subdivision (a) of Section 32015.

(b) The retesting of a handgun model pursuant to subdivision (a) shall conform to the following:

(1) The Attorney General shall obtain from retail or wholesale sources, or both, three samples of the handgun model to be retested.

(2) The Attorney General shall select the certified laboratory to be used for the retesting.

(3) The ammunition used for the retesting shall be of a type recommended by the manufacturer in the user manual for the handgun. If the user manual for the handgun model makes no ammunition recommendation, the Attorney General shall select the ammunition to be used for the retesting. The ammunition shall be of the proper caliber for the handgun, commercially available, and in new condition.

(c) The retest shall be conducted in the same manner as the testing prescribed in Sections 31900 and 31905.

(d) If the handgun model fails retesting, the Attorney General shall remove the handgun model from the roster maintained pursuant to subdivision (a) of Section 32015.

(Added by Stats. 2010, Ch. 711, Sec. 6. (SB 1080) Effective January 1, 2011. Operative January 1, 2012, by Sec. 10 of Ch. 711.)
32025.

A handgun model removed from the roster pursuant to subdivision (d) of Section 32020 may be reinstated on the roster if all of the following are met:

(a) The manufacturer petitions the Attorney General for reinstatement of the handgun model.

(b) The manufacturer pays the Department of Justice for all of the costs related to the reinstatement testing of the handgun model, including the purchase price of the handguns, prior to reinstatement testing.

(c) The reinstatement testing of the handguns shall be in accordance with subdivisions (b) and (c) of Section 32020.

(d) The three handgun samples shall be tested only once for reinstatement. If the sample fails it may not be retested.

(e) If the handgun model successfully passes testing for reinstatement, and if the manufacturer of the handgun is otherwise in compliance with Sections 31900 to 32110, inclusive, the Attorney General shall reinstate the handgun model on the roster maintained pursuant to subdivision (a) of Section 32015.

(f) The manufacturer shall provide the Attorney General with the complete testing history for the handgun model.

(g) Notwithstanding subdivision (a) of Section 32020, the Attorney General may, at any time, further retest any handgun model that has been reinstated to the roster.

(Added by Stats. 2010, Ch. 711, Sec. 6. (SB 1080) Effective January 1, 2011. Operative January 1, 2012, by Sec. 10 of Ch. 711.)
32030.

(a) A firearm shall be deemed to satisfy the requirements of subdivision (a) of Section 32015 if another firearm made by the same manufacturer is already listed and the unlisted firearm differs from the listed firearm only in one or more of the following features:

(1) Finish, including, but not limited to, bluing, chrome-plating, oiling, or engraving.

(2) The material from which the grips are made.

(3) The shape or texture of the grips, so long as the difference in grip shape or texture does not in any way alter the dimensions, material, linkage, or functioning of the magazine well, the barrel, the chamber, or any of the components of the firing mechanism of the firearm.

(4) Any other purely cosmetic feature that does not in any way alter the dimensions, material, linkage, or functioning of the magazine well, the barrel, the chamber, or any of the components of the firing mechanism of the firearm.

(b) Any manufacturer seeking to have a firearm listed under this section shall provide to the Department of Justice all of the following:

(1) The model designation of the listed firearm.

(2) The model designation of each firearm that the manufacturer seeks to have listed under this section.

(3) A statement, under oath, that each unlisted firearm for which listing is sought differs from the listed firearm only in one or more of the ways identified in subdivision (a) and is in all other respects identical to the listed firearm.

(c) The department may, in its discretion and at any time, require a manufacturer to provide to the department any model for which listing is sought under this section, to determine whether the model complies with the requirements of this section.

(Added by Stats. 2010, Ch. 711, Sec. 6. (SB 1080) Effective January 1, 2011. Operative January 1, 2012, by Sec. 10 of Ch. 711.)

ARTICLE 6. Exceptions to Rules Governing Unsafe Handguns [32100 - 32110]

(Article 6 added by Stats. 2010, Ch. 711, Sec. 6.)
32100.

(a) Article 4 (commencing with Section 31900) and Article 5 (commencing with Section 32000) shall not apply to a single-action revolver that has at least a five-cartridge capacity with a barrel length of not less than three inches, and meets any of the following specifications:

(1) Was originally manufactured prior to 1900 and is a curio or relic, as defined in Section 478.11 of Title 27 of the Code of Federal Regulations.

(2) Has an overall length measured parallel to the barrel of at least seven and one-half inches when the handle, frame or receiver, and barrel are assembled.

(3) Has an overall length measured parallel to the barrel of at least seven and one-half inches when the handle, frame or receiver, and barrel are assembled and that is currently approved for importation into the United States pursuant to the provisions of paragraph (3) of subsection (d) of Section 925 of Title 18 of the United States Code.

(b) Article 4 (commencing with Section 31900) and Article 5 (commencing with Section 32000) shall not apply to a single-shot pistol with a break top or bolt action and a barrel length of not less than six inches and that has an overall length of at least 10½ inches when the handle, frame or receiver, and barrel are assembled. However, Article 4 (commencing with Section 31900) and Article 5 (commencing with Section 32000) shall apply to a semiautomatic pistol that has been temporarily or permanently altered so that it will not fire in a semiautomatic mode.

(Amended by Stats. 2014, Ch. 147, Sec. 1. (AB 1964) Effective January 1, 2015.)
32105.

(a) The Legislature finds a significant public purpose in exempting pistols that are designed expressly for use in Olympic target shooting events. Therefore, those pistols that are sanctioned by the International Olympic Committee and by USA Shooting, the national governing body for international shooting competition in the United States, and that were used for Olympic target shooting purposes as of January 1, 2001, and that fall within the definition of "unsafe handgun" pursuant to paragraph (3) of subdivision (b) of Section 31910 shall be exempt, as provided in subdivisions (b) and (c).

(b) Article 4 (commencing with Section 31900) and Article 5 (commencing with Section 32000) shall not apply to any of the following pistols, because they are consistent with the significant public purpose expressed in subdivision (a):

MANUFACTURER	MODEL	CALIBER
ANSCHUTZ	FP	.22LR
BENELLI	MP90	.22LR
BENELLI	MP90	.32 S&W LONG
BENELLI	MP95	.22LR
BENELLI	MP95	.32 S&W LONG
DRULOV	FP	.22LR
GREEN	ELECTROARM	.22LR
HAMMERLI	100	.22LR
HAMMERLI	101	.22LR
HAMMERLI	102	.22LR
HAMMERLI	162	.22LR
HAMMERLI	280	.22LR
HAMMERLI	280	.32 S&W LONG
HAMMERLI	FP10	.22LR
HAMMERLI	MP33	.22LR
HAMMERLI	SP20	.22LR
HAMMERLI	SP20	.32 S&W LONG
MORINI	CM102E	.22LR
MORINI	22M	.22LR
MORINI	32M	.32 S&W LONG
MORINI	CM80	.22LR
PARDINI	GP	.22 SHORT
PARDINI	GPO	.22 SHORT
PARDINI	GP-SCHUMANN	.22 SHORT
PARDINI	HP	.32 S&W LONG
PARDINI	K22	.22LR
PARDINI	MP	.32 S&W LONG
PARDINI	PGP75	.22LR
PARDINI	SP	.22LR
PARDINI	SPE	.22LR

SAKO	FINMASTER	.22LR
STEYR	FP	.22LR
VOSTOK	IZH NO. 1	.22LR
VOSTOK	MU55	.22LR
VOSTOK	TOZ35	.22LR
WALTHER	FP	.22LR
WALTHER	GSP	.22LR
WALTHER	GSP	.32 S&W LONG
WALTHER	OSP	.22 SHORT
WALTHER	OSP-2000	.22 SHORT

(c) The department shall create a program that is consistent with the purpose stated in subdivision (a) to exempt new models of competitive firearms from Article 4 (commencing with Section 31900) and Article 5 (commencing with Section 32000). The exempt competitive firearms may be based on recommendations by USA Shooting consistent with the regulations contained in the USA Shooting Official Rules or may be based on the recommendation or rules of any other organization that the department deems relevant.
(Amended by Stats. 2011, Ch. 296, Sec. 243. (AB 1023) Effective January 1, 2012.)
32110.
Article 4 (commencing with Section 31900) and Article 5 (commencing with Section 32000) shall not apply to any of the following:
(a) The sale, loan, or transfer of any firearm pursuant to Chapter 5 (commencing with Section 28050) of Division 6 in order to comply with Section 27545.
(b) The sale, loan, or transfer of any firearm that is exempt from the provisions of Section 27545 pursuant to any applicable exemption contained in Article 2 (commencing with Section 27600) or Article 6 (commencing with Section 27850) of Chapter 4 of Division 6, if the sale, loan, or transfer complies with the requirements of that applicable exemption to Section 27545.
(c) The sale, loan, or transfer of any firearm as described in paragraph (3) of subdivision (b) of Section 32000.
(d) The delivery of a pistol, revolver, or other firearm capable of being concealed upon the person to a person licensed pursuant to Sections 26700 to 26915, inclusive, for the purposes of the service or repair of that firearm.
(e) The return of a pistol, revolver, or other firearm capable of being concealed upon the person by a person licensed pursuant to Sections 26700 to 26915, inclusive, to its owner where that firearm was initially delivered in the circumstances set forth in subdivision (a), (d), (f), or (i).
(f) The delivery of a pistol, revolver, or other firearm capable of being concealed upon the person to a person licensed pursuant to Sections 26700 to 26915, inclusive, for the purpose of a consignment sale or as collateral for a pawnbroker loan.
(g) The sale, loan, or transfer of any pistol, revolver, or other firearm capable of being concealed upon the person listed as a curio or relic, as defined in Section 478.11 of Title 27 of the Code of Federal Regulations.
(h) The sale, loan, or transfer of any semiautomatic pistol that is to be used solely as a prop during the course of a motion picture, television, or video production by an authorized participant therein in the course of making that production or event or by an authorized employee or agent of the entity producing that production or event.
(i) The delivery of a pistol, revolver, or other firearm capable of being concealed upon the person to a person licensed pursuant to Sections 26700 to 26915, inclusive, where the firearm is being loaned by the licensee to a consultant-evaluator.
(j) The delivery of a pistol, revolver, or other firearm capable of being concealed upon the person by a person licensed pursuant to Sections 26700 to 26915, inclusive, where the firearm is being loaned by the licensee to a consultant-evaluator.
(k) The return of a pistol, revolver, or other firearm capable of being concealed upon the person to a person licensed pursuant to Sections 26700 to 26915, inclusive, where it was initially delivered pursuant to subdivision (j).
(Added by Stats. 2010, Ch. 711, Sec. 6. (SB 1080) Effective January 1, 2011. Operative January 1, 2012, by Sec. 10 of Ch. 711.)

CHAPTER 5. Large-Capacity Magazine [32310 - 32450]

(Chapter 5 added by Stats. 2010, Ch. 711, Sec. 6.)
ARTICLE 1. Rules Governing Large-Capacity Magazines [32310 - 32390]
(Article 1 added by Stats. 2010, Ch. 711, Sec. 6.)
32310.
(a) Except as provided in Article 2 (commencing with Section 32400) of this chapter and in Chapter 1 (commencing with Section 17700) of Division 2 of Title 2, any person in this state who manufactures or causes to be manufactured, imports into the state, keeps for sale, or offers or exposes for sale, or who gives, lends, buys, or receives any large-capacity magazine is punishable by imprisonment in a county jail not exceeding one year or imprisonment pursuant to subdivision (h) of Section 1170.
(b) For purposes of this section, "manufacturing" includes both fabricating a magazine and assembling a magazine from a combination of parts, including, but not limited to, the body, spring, follower, and floor plate or end plate, to be a fully functioning large-capacity magazine.
(c) Except as provided in Article 2 (commencing with Section 32400) of this chapter and in Chapter 1 (commencing with Section 17700) of Division 2 of Title 2, commencing July 1, 2017, any person in this state who possesses any large-capacity magazine, regardless of the date the magazine was acquired, is guilty of an infraction punishable by a fine not to exceed one hundred dollars ($100) per large-capacity magazine, or is guilty of a misdemeanor punishable by a fine not to exceed one hundred dollars ($100) per large-capacity magazine, by imprisonment in a county jail not to exceed one year, or by both that fine and imprisonment.
(d) Any person who may not lawfully possess a large-capacity magazine commencing July 1, 2017 shall, prior to July 1, 2017:
(1) Remove the large-capacity magazine from the state;

(2) Sell the large-capacity magazine to a licensed firearms dealer; or
(3) Surrender the large-capacity magazine to a law enforcement agency for destruction.
(Amended November 8, 2016, by initiative Proposition 63, Sec. 6.1.)
32311.
(a) Except as provided in Article 2 (commencing with Section 32400) of this chapter and in Chapter 1 (commencing with Section 17700) of Division 2 of Title 2, commencing January 1, 2014, any person in this state who knowingly manufactures or causes to be manufactured, imports into the state, keeps for sale, or offers or exposes for sale, or who gives, lends, buys, or receives any large capacity magazine conversion kit is punishable by a fine of not more than one thousand dollars ($1,000) or imprisonment in a county jail not to exceed six months, or by both that fine and imprisonment. This section does not apply to a fully assembled large-capacity magazine, which is governed by Section 32310.
(b) For purposes of this section, a "large capacity magazine conversion kit" is a device or combination of parts of a fully functioning large-capacity magazine, including, but not limited to, the body, spring, follower, and floor plate or end plate, capable of converting an ammunition feeding device into a large-capacity magazine.
(Added by Stats. 2013, Ch. 728, Sec. 2. (AB 48) Effective January 1, 2014.)
32315.
Upon a showing that good cause exists, the Department of Justice may issue permits for the possession, transportation, or sale between a person licensed pursuant to Sections 26700 to 26915, inclusive, and an out-of-state client, of large-capacity magazines.
(Added by Stats. 2010, Ch. 711, Sec. 6. (SB 1080) Effective January 1, 2011. Operative January 1, 2012, by Sec. 10 of Ch. 711.)
32390.
Except as provided in Article 2 (commencing with Section 32400) of this chapter and in Chapter 1 (commencing with Section 17700) of Division 2 of Title 2, any large-capacity magazine is a nuisance and is subject to Section 18010.
(Added by Stats. 2010, Ch. 711, Sec. 6. (SB 1080) Effective January 1, 2011. Operative January 1, 2012, by Sec. 10 of Ch. 711.)

ARTICLE 2. Exceptions Relating Specifically to Large-Capacity Magazines [32400 - 32455]
(Article 2 added by Stats. 2010, Ch. 711, Sec. 6.)
32400.
Section 32310 does not apply to the sale of, giving of, lending of, possession of, importation into this state of, or purchase of, any large-capacity magazine to or by any federal, state, county, city and county, or city agency that is charged with the enforcement of any law, for use by agency employees in the discharge of their official duties, whether on or off duty, and where the use is authorized by the agency and is within the course and scope of their duties.
(Amended November 8, 2016, by initiative Proposition 63, Sec. 6.2.)
32405.
Section 32310 does not apply to the sale to, lending to, transfer to, purchase by, receipt of, possession of, or importation into this state of, a large-capacity magazine by a sworn peace officer, as defined in Chapter 4.5 (commencing with Section 830) of Title 3 of Part 2, or sworn federal law enforcement officer, who is authorized to carry a firearm in the course and scope of that officer's duties.
(Amended November 8, 2016, by initiative Proposition 63, Sec. 6.3.)
32406.
Subdivision (c) of Section 32310 does not apply to an honorably retired sworn peace officer, as defined in Chapter 4.5 (commencing with Section 830) of Title 3 of Part 2, or honorably retired sworn federal law enforcement officer, who was authorized to carry a firearm in the course and scope of that officer's duties. "Honorably retired" shall have the same meaning as provided in Section 16690.
(Added November 8, 2016, by initiative Proposition 63, Sec. 6.4. See same-numbered section added by Stats. 2016, Ch. 58.)
32406.
Subdivisions (b) and (c) of Section 32310 do not apply to the following:
(a) An individual who honorably retired from being a sworn peace officer, as defined in Chapter 4.5 (commencing with Section 830) of Title 3 of Part 2, or an individual who honorably retired from being a sworn federal law enforcement officer, who was authorized to carry a firearm in the course and scope of that officer's duties. For purposes of this section, "honorably retired" has the same meaning as provided in Section 16690.
(b) A federal, state, or local historical society, museum or institutional society, or museum or institutional collection, that is open to the public, provided that the large-capacity magazine is unloaded, properly housed within secured premises, and secured from unauthorized handling.
(c) A person who finds a large-capacity magazine, if the person is not prohibited from possessing firearms or ammunition, and possessed it no longer than necessary to deliver or transport it to the nearest law enforcement agency.
(d) A forensic laboratory, or an authorized agent or employee thereof in the course and scope of his or her authorized activities.
(e) The receipt or disposition of a large-capacity magazine by a trustee of a trust, or an executor or administrator of an estate, including an estate that is subject to probate, that includes a large-capacity magazine.
(f) A person lawfully in possession of a firearm that the person obtained prior to January 1, 2000, if no magazine that holds 10 or fewer rounds of ammunition is compatible with that firearm and the person possesses the large-capacity magazine solely for use with that firearm.
(Added by Stats. 2016, Ch. 58, Sec. 4. (SB 1446) Effective January 1, 2017. See same-numbered section added November 8, 2016, by Proposition 63.)
32410.
Section 32310 does not apply to the sale, purchase, or possession of any large-capacity magazine to or by a person licensed pursuant to Sections 26700 to 26915, inclusive.
(Amended November 8, 2016, by initiative Proposition 63, Sec. 6.5.)
32415.
Section 32310 does not apply to the loan of a lawfully possessed large-capacity magazine between two individuals if all of the following conditions are met:
(a) The person being loaned the large-capacity magazine is not prohibited by Chapter 1 (commencing with Section 29610), Chapter 2 (commencing with Section 29800), or Chapter 3 (commencing with Section 29900) of Division 9 of this title or Section 8100 or 8103 of the Welfare and Institutions Code from possessing firearms or ammunition.
(b) The loan of the large-capacity magazine occurs at a place or location where the possession of the large-capacity magazine is not otherwise prohibited, and the person who lends the large-capacity magazine remains in the accessible vicinity of the person to whom the large-capacity magazine is loaned.
(Added by Stats. 2010, Ch. 711, Sec. 6. (SB 1080) Effective January 1, 2011. Operative January 1, 2012, by Sec. 10 of Ch. 711.)
32425.
Section 32310 does not apply to any of the following:
(a) The lending or giving of any large-capacity magazine to a person licensed pursuant to Sections 26700 to 26915, inclusive, or to a gunsmith, for the purposes of maintenance, repair, or modification of that large-capacity magazine.
(b) The possession of any large-capacity magazine by a person specified in subdivision (a) for the purposes specified in subdivision (a).
(c) The return to its owner of any large-capacity magazine by a person specified in subdivision (a).

(Amended November 8, 2016, by initiative Proposition 63, Sec. 6.7.)
32430.
Section 32310 does not apply to the possession of, importation into this state of, or sale of, any large-capacity magazine by a person who has been issued a permit to engage in those activities pursuant to Section 32315, when those activities are in accordance with the terms and conditions of that permit.
(Amended by Stats. 2016, Ch. 58, Sec. 8. (SB 1446) Effective January 1, 2017.)
32435.
Section 32310 does not apply to any of the following:
(a) The sale of, giving of, lending of, possession of, importation into this state of, or purchase of, any large-capacity magazine, to or by any entity that operates an armored vehicle business pursuant to the laws of this state.
(b) The lending of large-capacity magazines by an entity specified in subdivision (a) to its authorized employees, while in the course and scope of employment for purposes that pertain to the entity's armored vehicle business.
(c) The possession of any large-capacity magazines by the employees of an entity specified in subdivision (a) for purposes that pertain to the entity's armored vehicle business.
(d) The return of those large-capacity magazines to the entity specified in subdivision (a) by those employees specified in subdivision (b).
(Amended November 8, 2016, by initiative Proposition 63, Sec. 6.8.)
32440.
Section 32310 does not apply to any of the following:
(a) The manufacture of a large-capacity magazine for any federal, state, county, city and county, or city agency that is charged with the enforcement of any law, for use by agency employees in the discharge of their official duties, whether on or off duty, and where the use is authorized by the agency and is within the course and scope of their duties.
(b) The manufacture of a large-capacity magazine for use by a sworn peace officer, as defined in Chapter 4.5 (commencing with Section 830) of Title 3 of Part 2, who is authorized to carry a firearm in the course and scope of that officer's duties.
(c) The manufacture of a large-capacity magazine for export or for sale to government agencies or the military pursuant to applicable federal regulations.
(Added by Stats. 2010, Ch. 711, Sec. 6. (SB 1080) Effective January 1, 2011. Operative January 1, 2012, by Sec. 10 of Ch. 711.)
32445.
Section 32310 does not apply to the loan of a large-capacity magazine for use solely as a prop for a motion picture, television, or video production.
(Added by Stats. 2010, Ch. 711, Sec. 6. (SB 1080) Effective January 1, 2011. Operative January 1, 2012, by Sec. 10 of Ch. 711.)
32450.
Section 32310 does not apply to the purchase or possession of a large-capacity magazine by the holder of a special weapons permit issued pursuant to Section 31000, 32650, or 33300, or pursuant to Article 3 (commencing with Section 18900) of Chapter 1 of Division 5 of Title 2, or pursuant to Article 4 (commencing with Section 32700) of Chapter 6 of this division, for any of the following purposes:
(a) For use solely as a prop for a motion picture, television, or video production.
(b) For export pursuant to federal regulations.
(c) For resale to law enforcement agencies, government agencies, or the military, pursuant to applicable federal regulations.
(Amended November 8, 2016, by initiative Proposition 63, Sec. 6.9.)
32455.
Section 32310 does not apply to the sale, gift, or loan of a large-capacity magazine to a person enrolled in the course of basic training prescribed by the Commission on Peace Officer Standards and Training, or any other course certified by the commission, nor to the possession of, or purchase by, the person, for purposes of participation in the course during his or her period of enrollment. Upon completion of the course the large-capacity magazine shall be removed from the state, sold to a licensed firearms dealer, or surrendered to a law enforcement agency, unless another exemption to Section 32310 applies.
(Added by Stats. 2017, Ch. 783, Sec. 4. (AB 693) Effective October 14, 2017.)

CHAPTER 6. Machineguns [32610 - 32750]

(Chapter 6 added by Stats. 2010, Ch. 711, Sec. 6.)
ARTICLE 1. General Provisions [32610- 32610.]
(Article 1 added by Stats. 2010, Ch. 711, Sec. 6.)
32610.
Nothing in this chapter shall affect or apply to any of the following:
(a) The sale to, purchase by, or possession of machineguns by a police department, a sheriff's office, a marshal's office, a district attorney's office, the California Highway Patrol, the Department of Justice, the Department of Corrections for use by the department's Special Emergency Response Teams and Law Enforcement Liaison/Investigations Unit, or the military or naval forces of this state or of the United States for use in the discharge of their official duties, provided, however, that any sale to these entities be transacted by a person who is permitted pursuant to Section 32650 and licensed pursuant to Article 4 (commencing with Section 32700).
(b) The possession of machineguns by regular, salaried, full-time peace officer members of a police department, sheriff's office, marshal's office, district attorney's office, the California Highway Patrol, the Department of Justice, or the Department of Corrections for use by the department's Special Emergency Response Teams and Law Enforcement Liaison/Investigations Unit, when on duty and if the use is within the scope of their duties.
(Added by Stats. 2010, Ch. 711, Sec. 6. (SB 1080) Effective January 1, 2011. Operative January 1, 2012, by Sec. 10 of Ch. 711.)
ARTICLE 2. Unlawful Acts Relating to Machineguns [32625- 32625.]
(Article 2 added by Stats. 2010, Ch. 711, Sec. 6.)
32625.
(a) Any person, firm, or corporation, who within this state possesses or knowingly transports a machinegun, except as authorized by this chapter, is guilty of a public offense and upon conviction thereof shall be punished by imprisonment pursuant to subdivision (h) of Section 1170, or by a fine not to exceed ten thousand dollars ($10,000), or by both that fine and imprisonment.
(b) Any person, firm, or corporation who within this state intentionally converts a firearm into a machinegun, or who sells, or offers for sale, or knowingly manufactures a machinegun, except as authorized by this chapter, is punishable by imprisonment pursuant to subdivision (h) of Section 1170 for four, six, or eight years.
(Amended by Stats. 2011, Ch. 15, Sec. 553. (AB 109) Effective April 4, 2011. Amendment operative October 1, 2011, by Sec. 636 of Ch. 15, as amended by Stats. 2011, Ch. 39, Sec. 68. Section operative January 1, 2012, pursuant to Stats. 2010, Ch. 711, Sec. 10.)
ARTICLE 3. Permits [32650 - 32670]
(Article 3 added by Stats. 2010, Ch. 711, Sec. 6.)
32650.

(a) The Department of Justice may issue permits for the possession, manufacture, and transportation or possession, manufacture, or transportation of machineguns, upon a satisfactory showing that good cause exists for the issuance of the permit to the applicant. No permit shall be issued to a person who is under 18 years of age.
(b) A permit for possession issued pursuant to this section may only be issued to an individual, and may not be issued to a partnership, corporation, limited liability company, association, or any other group or entity, regardless of how that entity was created.
(Amended by Stats. 2013, Ch. 729, Sec. 4. (AB 170) Effective January 1, 2014.)
32655.
(a) An application for a permit under this article shall satisfy all of the following conditions:
(1) It shall be filed in writing.
(2) It shall be signed by the applicant if an individual, or by a member or officer qualified to sign if the applicant is a firm or corporation.
(3) It shall state the applicant's name.
(4) It shall state the business in which the applicant is engaged.
(5) It shall state the applicant's business address.
(6) It shall include a full description of the use to which the firearms are to be put.
(b) Applications and permits shall be uniform throughout the state on forms prescribed by the Department of Justice.
(c) Each applicant for a permit shall pay at the time of filing the application a fee determined by the Department of Justice. The fee shall not exceed the application processing costs of the Department of Justice.
(d) A permit granted pursuant to this article may be renewed one year from the date of issuance, and annually thereafter, upon the filing of a renewal application and the payment of a permit renewal fee, which shall not exceed the application processing costs of the Department of Justice.
(e) After the department establishes fees sufficient to reimburse the department for processing costs, fees charged shall increase at a rate not to exceed the legislatively approved annual cost-of-living adjustments for the department's budget.
(Added by Stats. 2010, Ch. 711, Sec. 6. (SB 1080) Effective January 1, 2011. Operative January 1, 2012, by Sec. 10 of Ch. 711.)
32660.
Every person, firm, or corporation to whom a permit is issued under this article shall keep it on the person or at the place where the firearms are kept. The permit shall be open to inspection by any peace officer or any other person designated by the authority issuing the permit.
(Added by Stats. 2010, Ch. 711, Sec. 6. (SB 1080) Effective January 1, 2011. Operative January 1, 2012, by Sec. 10 of Ch. 711.)
32665.
A permit issued in accordance with this chapter may be revoked by the issuing authority at any time, when it appears that the need for the firearms has ceased or that the holder of the permit has used the firearms for purposes other than those allowed by the permit or that the holder of the permit has not exercised great care in retaining custody of any weapons possessed under the permit.
(Added by Stats. 2010, Ch. 711, Sec. 6. (SB 1080) Effective January 1, 2011. Operative January 1, 2012, by Sec. 10 of Ch. 711.)
32670.
(a) Except as provided in subdivision (b), the Department of Justice shall, for every person, firm, or corporation to whom a permit is issued pursuant to this article, annually conduct an inspection for security and safe storage purposes, and to reconcile the inventory of machineguns.
(b) A person, firm, or corporation with an inventory of fewer than five devices that require any Department of Justice permit shall be subject to an inspection for security and safe storage purposes, and to reconcile inventory, once every five years, or more frequently if determined by the department.
(Added by Stats. 2010, Ch. 711, Sec. 6. (SB 1080) Effective January 1, 2011. Operative January 1, 2012, by Sec. 10 of Ch. 711.)
ARTICLE 5. Machinegun Constituting Nuisance [32750- 32750.]
(Article 5 added by Stats. 2010, Ch. 711, Sec. 6.)
32750.
(a) It shall be a public nuisance to possess any machinegun in violation of this chapter.
(b) The Attorney General, any district attorney, or any city attorney may bring an action before the superior court to enjoin the possession of any machinegun in violation of this chapter.
(c) Any machinegun found to be in violation of this chapter shall be surrendered to the Department of Justice. The department shall destroy the machinegun so as to render it unusable and unrepairable as a machinegun, except upon the filing of a certificate with the department by a judge or district attorney stating that the preservation of the machinegun is necessary to serve the ends of justice.
(Added by Stats. 2010, Ch. 711, Sec. 6. (SB 1080) Effective January 1, 2011. Operative January 1, 2012, by Sec. 10 of Ch. 711.)

CHAPTER 7. Multiburst Trigger Activator [32900 - 32990]

(Chapter 7 added by Stats. 2010, Ch. 711, Sec. 6.)
32900.
Except as provided in Chapter 1 (commencing with Section 17700) of Division 2 of Title 2, any person in this state who manufactures or causes to be manufactured, imports into the state, keeps for sale, or offers or exposes for sale, or who gives, lends, or possesses any multiburst trigger activator is punishable by imprisonment in a county jail not exceeding one year or imprisonment pursuant to subdivision (h) of Section 1170.
(Amended by Stats. 2012, Ch. 43, Sec. 108. (SB 1023) Effective June 27, 2012.)
32990.
Except as provided in Chapter 1 (commencing with Section 17700) of Division 2 of Title 2, any multiburst trigger activator is a nuisance and is subject to Section 18010.
(Added by Stats. 2010, Ch. 711, Sec. 6. (SB 1080) Effective January 1, 2011. Operative January 1, 2012, by Sec. 10 of Ch. 711.)

CHAPTER 8. Short-Barreled Rifle or Short-Barreled Shotgun [33210 - 33320]

(Chapter 8 added by Stats. 2010, Ch. 711, Sec. 6.)
ARTICLE 1. Restrictions Relating to Short-Barreled Rifle or Short-Barreled Shotgun [33210 - 33290]
(Article 1 added by Stats. 2010, Ch. 711, Sec. 6.)
33210.
Except as expressly provided in Sections 33215 to 33225, inclusive, and in Chapter 1 (commencing with Section 17700) of Division 2 of Title 2, and solely in accordance with those provisions, no person may manufacture, import into this state, keep for sale, offer for sale, give, lend, or possess any short-barreled rifle or short-barreled shotgun.

Nothing else in any provision listed in Section 16580 shall be construed as authorizing the manufacture, importation into the state, keeping for sale, offering for sale, or giving, lending, or possession of any short-barreled rifle or short-barreled shotgun.
(Added by Stats. 2010, Ch. 711, Sec. 6. (SB 1080) Effective January 1, 2011. Operative January 1, 2012, by Sec. 10 of Ch. 711.)
33215.
Except as provided in Sections 33220 and 33225 and in Chapter 1 (commencing with Section 17700) of Division 2 of Title 2, any person in this state who manufactures or causes to be manufactured, imports into the state, keeps for sale, or offers or exposes for sale, or who gives, lends, or possesses any short-barreled rifle or short-barreled shotgun is punishable by imprisonment in a county jail not exceeding one year or imprisonment pursuant to subdivision (h) of Section 1170.
(Amended by Stats. 2012, Ch. 43, Sec. 109. (SB 1023) Effective June 27, 2012.)
33220.
Section 33215 does not apply to either of the following:
(a) The sale to, purchase by, or possession of short-barreled rifles or short-barreled shotguns by a police department, sheriff's office, marshal's office, the California Highway Patrol, the Department of Justice, the Department of Corrections and Rehabilitation, or the military or naval forces of this state or of the United States, for use in the discharge of their official duties.
(b) The possession of short-barreled rifles and short-barreled shotguns by peace officer members of a police department, sheriff's office, marshal's office, the California Highway Patrol, the Department of Justice, or the Department of Corrections and Rehabilitation, when on duty and the use is authorized by the agency and is within the course and scope of their duties, and the officers have completed a training course in the use of these weapons certified by the Commission on Peace Officer Standards and Training.
(Added by Stats. 2010, Ch. 711, Sec. 6. (SB 1080) Effective January 1, 2011. Operative January 1, 2012, by Sec. 10 of Ch. 711.)
33225.
Section 33215 does not apply to the manufacture, possession, transportation, or sale of a short-barreled rifle or short-barreled shotgun, when authorized by the Department of Justice pursuant to Article 2 (commencing with Section 33300) and not in violation of federal law.
(Added by Stats. 2010, Ch. 711, Sec. 6. (SB 1080) Effective January 1, 2011. Operative January 1, 2012, by Sec. 10 of Ch. 711.)
33290.
Except as provided in Sections 33220 and 33225 and in Chapter 1 (commencing with Section 17700) of Division 2 of Title 2, any short-barreled rifle or short-barreled shotgun is a nuisance and is subject to Section 18010.
(Added by Stats. 2010, Ch. 711, Sec. 6. (SB 1080) Effective January 1, 2011. Operative January 1, 2012, by Sec. 10 of Ch. 711.)

ARTICLE 2. Permit for Short-Barreled Rifle or Short-Barreled Shotgun [33300 - 33320]

(Article 2 added by Stats. 2010, Ch. 711, Sec. 6.)
33300.
(a) Upon a showing that good cause exists for issuance of a permit to the applicant, and if the Department of Justice finds that issuance of the permit does not endanger the public safety, the department may issue a permit for the manufacture, possession, importation, transportation, or sale of short-barreled rifles or short-barreled shotguns. The permit shall be initially valid for a period of one year, and renewable annually thereafter. No permit shall be issued to a person who is under 18 years of age.
(b) Good cause, for the purposes of this section, shall be limited to only the following:
(1) The permit is sought for the manufacture, possession, importation, or use with blank cartridges, of a short-barreled rifle or short-barreled shotgun, solely as a prop for a motion picture, television, or video production or entertainment event.
(2) The permit is sought for the manufacture of, exposing for sale, keeping for sale, sale of, importation or lending of short-barreled rifles or short-barreled shotguns to the entities listed in Section 33220 by persons who are licensed as dealers or manufacturers under the provisions of Chapter 53 (commencing with Section 5801) of Title 26 of the United States Code, as amended, and the regulations issued pursuant thereto.
(Amended by Stats. 2012, Ch. 691, Sec. 2. (AB 1559) Effective January 1, 2013.)
33305.
(a) An application for a permit under this article shall satisfy all of the following conditions:
(1) It shall be filed in writing.
(2) It shall be signed by the applicant if an individual, or by a member or officer qualified to sign if the applicant is a firm or corporation.
(3) It shall state the applicant's name.
(4) It shall state the business in which the applicant is engaged.
(5) It shall state the applicant's business address.
(6) It shall include a full description of the use to which the short-barreled rifles or short-barreled shotguns are to be put.
(b) Applications and permits shall be uniform throughout the state on forms prescribed by the Department of Justice.
(c) Each applicant for a permit shall pay at the time of filing the application a fee determined by the Department of Justice. The fee shall not exceed the application processing costs of the Department of Justice.
(d) A permit granted pursuant to this article may be renewed one year from the date of issuance, and annually thereafter, upon the filing of a renewal application and the payment of a permit renewal fee, which shall not exceed the application processing costs of the Department of Justice.
(e) After the department establishes fees sufficient to reimburse the department for processing costs, fees charged shall increase at a rate not to exceed the legislatively approved annual cost-of-living adjustments for the department's budget.
(Added by Stats. 2010, Ch. 711, Sec. 6. (SB 1080) Effective January 1, 2011. Operative January 1, 2012, by Sec. 10 of Ch. 711.)
33310.
(a) Every person, firm, or corporation to whom a permit is issued under this article shall keep it on the person or at the place where the short-barreled rifles or short-barreled shotguns are kept. The permit shall be open to inspection by any peace officer or any other person designated by the authority issuing the permit.
(b) Every short-barreled rifle or short-barreled shotgun possessed pursuant to the provisions of this article shall bear a unique identifying number. If a weapon does not bear a unique identifying number, the Department of Justice shall assign a number which shall be placed or stamped on that weapon.
(Added by Stats. 2010, Ch. 711, Sec. 6. (SB 1080) Effective January 1, 2011. Operative January 1, 2012, by Sec. 10 of Ch. 711.)
33315.
A permit issued in accordance with this article may be revoked by the issuing authority at any time, when it appears that the need for the short-barreled rifles or short-barreled shotguns has ceased or that the holder of the permit has used the short-barreled rifles or short-barreled shotguns for purposes other than those allowed by the permit or that the holder of the permit has not exercised great care in retaining custody of any weapons possessed under the permit.
(Added by Stats. 2010, Ch. 711, Sec. 6. (SB 1080) Effective January 1, 2011. Operative January 1, 2012, by Sec. 10 of Ch. 711.)
33320.

(a) Except as provided in subdivision (b), the Department of Justice shall, for every person, firm, or corporation to whom a permit is issued pursuant to this article, annually conduct an inspection for security and safe storage purposes, and to reconcile the inventory of short-barreled rifles and short-barreled shotguns.
(b) A person, firm, or corporation with an inventory of fewer than five devices that require any Department of Justice permit shall be subject to an inspection for security and safe storage purposes, and to reconcile inventory, once every five years, or more frequently if determined by the department.
(Added by Stats. 2010, Ch. 711, Sec. 6. (SB 1080) Effective January 1, 2011. Operative January 1, 2012, by Sec. 10 of Ch. 711.)

CHAPTER 9. Silencers [33410 - 33415]

(Chapter 9 added by Stats. 2010, Ch. 711, Sec. 6.)
33410.
Any person, firm, or corporation who within this state possesses a silencer is guilty of a felony and upon conviction thereof shall be punished by imprisonment pursuant to subdivision (h) of Section 1170 or by a fine not to exceed ten thousand dollars ($10,000), or by both that fine and imprisonment.
(Amended by Stats. 2011, Ch. 15, Sec. 554. (AB 109) Effective April 4, 2011. Amending action operative October 1, 2011, by Sec. 636 of Ch. 15, as amended by Stats. 2011, Ch. 39, Sec. 68. Section operative January 1, 2012, pursuant to Stats. 2010, Ch. 711, Sec. 10.)
33415.
Section 33410 shall not apply to, or affect, any of the following:
(a) The sale to, purchase by, or possession of silencers by agencies listed in Section 830.1, or the military or naval forces of this state or of the United States, for use in the discharge of their official duties.
(b) The possession of silencers by regular, salaried, full-time peace officers who are employed by an agency listed in Section 830.1, or by the military or naval forces of this state or of the United States, when on duty and when the use of silencers is authorized by the agency and is within the course and scope of their duties.
(c) The manufacture, possession, transportation, or sale or other transfer of silencers to an entity described in subdivision (a) by dealers or manufacturers registered under Chapter 53 (commencing with Section 5801) of Title 26 of the United States Code and the regulations issued pursuant thereto.
(Added by Stats. 2010, Ch. 711, Sec. 6. (SB 1080) Effective January 1, 2011. Operative January 1, 2012, by Sec. 10 of Ch. 711.)

CHAPTER 10. Zip Guns [33600 - 33690]

(Chapter 10 added by Stats. 2010, Ch. 711, Sec. 6.)
33600.
Except as provided in Chapter 1 (commencing with Section 17700) of Division 2 of Title 2, any person in this state who manufactures or causes to be manufactured, imports into the state, keeps for sale, or offers or exposes for sale, or who gives, lends, or possesses any zip gun is punishable by imprisonment in a county jail not exceeding one year or imprisonment pursuant to subdivision (h) of Section 1170.
(Amended by Stats. 2012, Ch. 43, Sec. 110. (SB 1023) Effective June 27, 2012.)
33690.
Except as provided in Chapter 1 (commencing with Section 17700) of Division 2 of Title 2, any zip gun is a nuisance and is subject to Section 18010.
(Added by Stats. 2010, Ch. 711, Sec. 6. (SB 1080) Effective January 1, 2011. Operative January 1, 2012, by Sec. 10 of Ch. 711.)

DIVISION 11. FIREARM IN CUSTODY OF COURT OR LAW ENFORCEMENT AGENCY OR SIMILAR SITUATION [33800 - 34010]
(Division 11 added by Stats. 2010, Ch. 711, Sec. 6.)

CHAPTER 1. Procedure for Taking Firearm into Custody [33800- 33800.]

(Chapter 1 added by Stats. 2010, Ch. 711, Sec. 6.)
33800.
(a) When a firearm is taken into custody by a law enforcement officer, the officer shall issue the person who possessed the firearm a receipt describing the firearm, and listing any serial number or other identification on the firearm.
(b) The receipt shall indicate where the firearm may be recovered, any applicable time limit for recovery, and the date after which the owner or possessor may recover the firearm pursuant to Chapter 2 (commencing with Section 33850).
(c) Nothing in this section is intended to displace any existing law regarding the seizure or return of firearms.
(Added by Stats. 2010, Ch. 711, Sec. 6. (SB 1080) Effective January 1, 2011. Operative January 1, 2012, by Sec. 10 of Ch. 711.)

CHAPTER 2. Return or Transfer of Firearm in Custody or Control of Court or Law Enforcement Agency [33850 - 33895]

(Chapter 2 added by Stats. 2010, Ch. 711, Sec. 6.)
33850.
(a) Any person who claims title to any firearm that is in the custody or control of a court or law enforcement agency and who wishes to have the firearm returned shall make application for a determination by the Department of Justice as to whether the applicant is eligible to possess a firearm. The application shall be submitted electronically via the California Firearms Application Reporting System (CFARS) and shall include the following:
(1) The applicant's name, date and place of birth, gender, telephone number, and complete address.
(2) Whether the applicant is a United States citizen. If the applicant is not a United States citizen, the application shall also include the applicant's country of citizenship and the applicant's alien registration or I-94 number.
(3) If the seized property is a firearm, the firearm's make, model, caliber, barrel length, type, country of origin, and serial number, provided, however, that if the firearm is not a

handgun and does not have a serial number, identification number, or identification mark assigned to it, there shall be a place on the application to note that fact.

(4) For residents of California, the applicant's valid California driver's license number or valid California identification card number issued by the Department of Motor Vehicles. For nonresidents of California, a copy of the applicant's military identification with orders indicating that the individual is stationed in California, or a copy of the applicant's valid driver's license from the applicant's state of residence, or a copy of the applicant's state identification card from the applicant's state of residence. Copies of the documents provided by non-California residents shall be notarized.

(5) The name of the court or law enforcement agency holding the firearm.

(6) The signature of the applicant and the date of signature.

(7) Any person furnishing a fictitious name or address or knowingly furnishing any incorrect information or knowingly omitting any information required to be provided for the application, including any notarized information pursuant to paragraph (4), shall be guilty of a misdemeanor.

(b) A person who owns a firearm that is in the custody of a court or law enforcement agency and who does not wish to obtain possession of the firearm, and the firearm is an otherwise legal firearm, and the person otherwise has right to title of the firearm, shall be entitled to sell or transfer title of the firearm to a licensed dealer or a third party that is not prohibited from possessing that firearm. Any sale or transfer to a third party pursuant to this subdivision shall be conducted pursuant to Section 27545.

(c) A person who owns any ammunition that is in the custody of a court or a law enforcement agency and who does not wish to obtain possession of the ammunition, and the ammunition is otherwise legal, shall be entitled to sell or otherwise transfer the ammunition to a licensed firearms dealer or ammunition vendor or a third party that is not prohibited from possessing that ammunition. Any sale or other transfer of ammunition to a third party pursuant to subdivision (b) shall be conducted through an ammunition vendor in accordance with the procedures set forth in Article 4 (commencing with Section 30370) of Chapter 1 of Division 10.

(d) Any person furnishing a fictitious name or address, or knowingly furnishing any incorrect information or knowingly omitting any information required to be provided for the application, including any notarized information pursuant to paragraph (4) of subdivision (a), is punishable as a misdemeanor.

(e) This section shall remain in effect only until July 1, 2020, and as of that date is repealed.

(Amended by Stats. 2018, Ch. 780, Sec. 9. (SB 746) Effective January 1, 2019. Repealed as of July 1, 2020, by its own provisions. See later operative version added by Stats. 2018, Ch. 780.)

33850.

(a) Any person who claims title to any firearm, ammunition feeding device, or ammunition that is in the custody or control of a court or law enforcement agency and who wishes to have the firearm, ammunition feeding device, or ammunition returned shall make application for a determination by the Department of Justice as to whether the applicant is eligible to possess a firearm, ammunition feeding device, or ammunition. The application shall be submitted electronically via the California Firearms Application Reporting System (CFARS) and shall include the following:

(1) The applicant's name, date and place of birth, gender, telephone number, and complete address.

(2) Whether the applicant is a United States citizen. If the applicant is not a United States citizen, the application shall also include the applicant's country of citizenship and the applicant's alien registration or I-94 number.

(3) If the seized property is a firearm, the firearm's make, model, caliber, barrel length, type, country of origin, and serial number, provided, however, that if the firearm is not a handgun and does not have a serial number, identification number, or identification mark assigned to it, there shall be a place on the application to note that fact.

(4) For residents of California, the applicant's valid California driver's license number or valid California identification card number issued by the Department of Motor Vehicles. For nonresidents of California, a copy of the applicant's military identification with orders indicating that the individual is stationed in California, or a copy of the applicant's valid driver's license from the applicant's state of residence, or a copy of the applicant's state identification card from the applicant's state of residence. Copies of the documents provided by non-California residents shall be notarized.

(5) The name of the court or law enforcement agency holding the firearm, ammunition feeding device, or ammunition.

(6) The signature of the applicant and the date of signature.

(7) Any person furnishing a fictitious name or address or knowingly furnishing any incorrect information or knowingly omitting any information required to be provided for the application, including any notarized information pursuant to paragraph (4), shall be guilty of a misdemeanor.

(b) A person who owns a firearm that is in the custody of a court or law enforcement agency and who does not wish to obtain possession of the firearm, and the firearm is an otherwise legal firearm, and the person otherwise has right to title of the firearm, shall be entitled to sell or transfer title of the firearm to a licensed dealer or a third party that is not prohibited from possessing that firearm. Any sale or transfer to a third party pursuant to this subdivision shall be conducted pursuant to Section 27545.

(c) A person who owns an ammunition feeding device or ammunition that is in the custody of a court or a law enforcement agency and who does not wish to obtain possession of the ammunition or ammunition feeding device, and the ammunition feeding device or ammunition is otherwise legal, shall be entitled to sell or otherwise transfer the ammunition feeding device or ammunition to a licensed firearms dealer or ammunition vendor or a third party that is not prohibited from possessing that ammunition feeding device or ammunition. Any sale or other transfer of ammunition to a third party pursuant to subdivision (b) shall be conducted through an ammunition vendor in accordance with the procedures set forth in Article 4 (commencing with Section 30370) of Chapter 1 of Division 10.

(d) Any person furnishing a fictitious name or address, or knowingly furnishing any incorrect information or knowingly omitting any information required to be provided for the application, including any notarized information pursuant to paragraph (4) of subdivision (a), is punishable as a misdemeanor.

(e) This section shall become operative on July 1, 2020.

(Repealed and added by Stats. 2018, Ch. 780, Sec. 10. (SB 746) Effective January 1, 2019. Section operative July 1, 2020, by its own provisions.)

33855.

A law enforcement agency or court that has taken custody of any firearm shall not return the firearm to any individual unless the following requirements are satisfied:

(a) The individual presents to the agency or court notification of a determination by the department pursuant to Section 33865 that the person is eligible to possess firearms.

(b) If the agency or court has direct access to the Automated Firearms System, the agency or court has verified that the firearm is not listed as stolen pursuant to Section 11108.2, and that the firearm has been recorded in the Automated Firearms System in the name of the individual who seeks its return.

(c) If the firearm has been reported lost or stolen pursuant to Section 11108.2, a law enforcement agency shall notify the owner or person entitled to possession pursuant to Section 11108.5. However, that person shall provide proof of eligibility to possess a firearm pursuant to Section 33865.

(d) This section does not prevent the local law enforcement agency from charging the rightful owner or person entitled to possession of the firearm the fees described in Section 33880. However, an individual who is applying for a background check to retrieve a firearm that came into the custody or control of a court or law enforcement

agency pursuant to Section 33850 shall be exempt from the fees in Section 33860, provided that the court or agency determines the firearm was reported stolen to a law enforcement agency prior to the date the firearm came into custody or control of the court or law enforcement agency, or within five business days of the firearm being stolen from its owner. The court or agency shall notify the Department of Justice of this fee exemption in a manner prescribed by the department.

(e) This section shall remain in effect only until July 1, 2020, and as of that date is repealed.

(Amended by Stats. 2018, Ch. 864, Sec. 7.5. (AB 2222) Effective January 1, 2019. Repealed as of July 1, 2020, by its own provisions. See later operative version added by Stats. 2018, Ch. 864.)

33855.

A law enforcement agency or court that has taken custody of any firearm, ammunition feeding device, or ammunition shall not return the firearm, ammunition feeding device, or ammunition to any individual unless all of the following requirements are satisfied:

(a) The individual presents to the agency or court notification of a determination by the department pursuant to Section 33865 that the person is eligible to possess a firearm, ammunition feeding device, or ammunition.

(b) If the seized property is a firearm and the agency or court has direct access to the Automated Firearms System, the agency or court has verified that the firearm is not listed as stolen pursuant to Section 11108.2, and that the firearm has been recorded in the Automated Firearms System in the name of the individual who seeks its return.

(c) If the firearm has been reported lost or stolen pursuant to Section 11108.2, a law enforcement agency shall notify the owner or person entitled to possession pursuant to Section 11108.5. However, that person shall provide proof of eligibility to possess a firearm pursuant to Section 33865.

(d) This section does not prevent the local law enforcement agency from charging the rightful owner or person entitled to possession of the firearm the fees described in Section 33880. However, an individual who is applying for a background check to retrieve a firearm that came into the custody or control of a court or law enforcement agency pursuant to Section 33850 shall be exempt from the fees in Section 33860, provided that the court or agency determines the firearm was reported stolen to a law enforcement agency prior to the date the firearm came into custody or control of the court or law enforcement agency, or within five business days of the firearm being stolen from its owner. The court or agency shall notify the Department of Justice of this fee exemption in a manner prescribed by the department.

(e) This section shall become operative on July 1, 2020.

(Repealed and added by Stats. 2018, Ch. 864, Sec. 7.6. (AB 2222) Effective January 1, 2019. Section operative July 1, 2020, by its own provisions.)

33860.

(a) The Department of Justice shall establish a fee of twenty dollars ($20) per request for return of a firearm, plus a three-dollar ($3) charge for each additional firearm being processed as part of the request to return a firearm, to cover its reasonable costs for processing firearm clearance determinations submitted pursuant to this chapter.

(b) The fees collected pursuant to subdivision (a) shall be deposited into the Dealers' Record of Sale Special Account.

(c) The department shall annually review and shall adjust the fees specified in subdivision (a), if necessary, to fully fund, but not to exceed the reasonable costs of processing applications pursuant to this section.

(d) This section shall remain in effect only until July 1, 2020, and as of that date is repealed.

(Amended by Stats. 2018, Ch. 780, Sec. 13. (SB 746) Effective January 1, 2019. Repealed as of July 1, 2020, by its own provisions. See later operative version added by Stats. 2018, Ch. 780.)

33860.

(a) The Department of Justice shall establish a fee of twenty dollars ($20) per request for return of a firearm, ammunition feeding device, or any quantity of ammunition plus a three-dollar ($3) charge for each additional firearm being processed as part of the request to return a firearm, to cover its reasonable costs for processing applications submitted pursuant to this chapter.

(b) The fees collected pursuant to subdivision (a) shall be deposited into the Dealers' Record of Sale Special Account.

(c) The department shall annually review and shall adjust the fees specified in subdivision (a), if necessary, to fully fund, but not to exceed the reasonable costs of processing applications submitted pursuant to this section.

(d) This section shall become operative on July 1, 2020.

(Repealed and added by Stats. 2018, Ch. 780, Sec. 14. (SB 746) Effective January 1, 2019. Section operative July 1, 2020, by its own provisions.)

33865.

(a) When the Department of Justice receives a completed application pursuant to Section 33850 accompanied by the fee required pursuant to Section 33860, it shall conduct an eligibility check of the applicant to determine whether the applicant is eligible to possess a firearm.

(b) The department shall have 30 days from the date of receipt to complete the background check, unless the background check is delayed by circumstances beyond the control of the department. The applicant may contact the department via the California Firearms Application Reporting System (CFARS) to inquire about the reason for a delay.

(c) If the department determines that the applicant is eligible to possess the firearm, the department shall provide the applicant with written notification that includes the following:

(1) The identity of the applicant.

(2) A statement that the applicant is eligible to possess a firearm.

(3) A description of the firearm by make, model, and serial number, provided, however, that if the firearm is not a handgun and does not have a serial number, identification number, or identification mark assigned to it, that fact shall be noted.

(d) The department shall enter a record of the firearm into the Automated Firearms System (AFS), provided, however, that if the firearm is not a handgun and does not have a serial number, identification number, or identification mark assigned to it, that fact shall be noted in AFS.

(e) If the department denies the application, and the firearm is an otherwise legal firearm, the department shall notify the applicant of the denial and provide a form for the applicant to use to sell or transfer the firearm to a licensed dealer.

(f) If the department denies the application, the applicant shall receive notification via CFARS from the department explaining the reason for the denial and information regarding the appeal process.

(g) This section shall remain in effect only until July 1, 2020, and as of that date is repealed.

(Amended by Stats. 2018, Ch. 780, Sec. 15. (SB 746) Effective January 1, 2019. Repealed as of July 1, 2020, by its own provisions. See later operative version added by Stats. 2018, Ch. 780.)

33865.

(a) When the Department of Justice receives a completed application pursuant to Section 33850 accompanied by the fee required pursuant to Section 33860, it shall conduct an eligibility check of the applicant to determine whether the applicant is eligible to possess a firearm, ammunition feeding device, or ammunition.

(b) The department shall have 30 days from the date of receipt to complete the background check, unless the background check is delayed by circumstances beyond the control of the department. The applicant may contact the department via the

California Firearms Application Reporting System (CFARS) to inquire about the reason for a delay.
(c) If the department determines that the applicant is eligible to possess the firearm, ammunition feeding device, or ammunition, the department shall provide the applicant with written notification that includes the following:
(1) The identity of the applicant.
(2) A statement that the applicant is eligible to possess a firearm, ammunition feeding device, or ammunition.
(3) If applicable, a description of the firearm by make, model, and serial number, provided, however, that if the firearm is not a handgun and does not have a serial number, identification number, or identification mark assigned to it, that fact shall be noted.
(d) The department shall enter a record of the firearm into the Automated Firearms System (AFS), provided, however, that if the firearm is not a handgun and does not have a serial number, identification number, or identification mark assigned to it, that fact shall be noted in AFS.
(e) If the department denies the application, and the firearm is an otherwise legal firearm, the department shall notify the applicant of the denial and provide a form for the applicant to use to sell or transfer the firearm to a licensed dealer.
(f) If the department denies the application, the applicant shall receive notification via CFARS from the department explaining the reason for the denial and information regarding the appeal process.
(g) This section shall become operative on July 1, 2020.
(Repealed and added by Stats. 2018, Ch. 780, Sec. 16. (SB 746) Effective January 1, 2019. Section operative July 1, 2020, by its own provisions.)
33870.
(a) If a law enforcement agency determines that the applicant is the legal owner of any firearm or ammunition deposited with the agency, that the applicant is prohibited from possessing any firearm or ammunition, and that the firearm or ammunition is otherwise legal, the applicant shall be entitled to sell or transfer the firearm or ammunition to a licensed firearms dealer, or licensed ammunition vendor, as applicable. If a law enforcement agency determines that the applicant is prohibited from owning or possessing any firearm or ammunition and the prohibition will expire on a specific ascertainable date, whether or not that date is specified in a court order, the applicant shall be entitled to have the firearm or ammunition stored by a licensed firearms dealer or licensed ammunition vendor, as applicable, for the duration of the prohibition period pursuant to Section 29830.
(b) If the firearm or ammunition has been lost or stolen, it shall be restored to the lawful owner pursuant to Section 11108.5 upon the owner's identification of the property, proof of ownership, and proof of eligibility to possess a firearm or ammunition pursuant to Section 33865.
(c) This section does not prevent the local law enforcement agency from charging the rightful owner of the property the fees described in Section 33880.
(d) This section shall remain in effect only until July 1, 2020, and as of that date is repealed.
(Amended by Stats. 2018, Ch. 780, Sec. 17. (SB 746) Effective January 1, 2019. Repealed as of July 1, 2020, by its own provisions. See later operative version added by Stats. 2018, Ch. 780.)
33870.
(a) If a law enforcement agency determines that the applicant is the legal owner of any firearm, ammunition feeding device, or ammunition deposited with the agency, that the applicant is prohibited from possessing any firearm, ammunition feeding device, or ammunition, and that the firearm, ammunition feeding device, or ammunition is otherwise legal, the applicant shall be entitled to sell or transfer the firearm, ammunition feeding device, or ammunition to a licensed firearms dealer, or licensed ammunition vendor, as applicable. If a law enforcement agency determines that the applicant is prohibited from owning or possessing any firearm, ammunition feeding device, or ammunition and the prohibition will expire on a specific ascertainable date, whether or not that date is specified in a court order, the applicant shall be entitled to have the firearm, ammunition feeding device, or ammunition stored by a licensed firearms dealer or licensed ammunition vendor, as applicable, for the duration of the prohibition period pursuant to Section 29830.
(b) If the firearm, ammunition feeding device, or ammunition has been lost or stolen, it shall be restored to the lawful owner pursuant to Section 11108.5 upon the owner's identification of the property, proof of ownership, and proof of eligibility to possess a firearm, ammunition feeding device, or ammunition pursuant to Section 33865.
(c) This section does not prevent the local law enforcement agency from charging the rightful owner of the property the fees described in Section 33880.
(d) This section shall become operative on July 1, 2020.
(Repealed and added by Stats. 2018, Ch. 780, Sec. 18. (SB 746) Effective January 1, 2019. Section operative July 1, 2020, by its own provisions.)
33875.
(a) Notwithstanding any other law, no law enforcement agency or court shall be required to retain any firearm for more than 180 days after the owner has been notified by the court or law enforcement agency that the property has been made available for return. Any unclaimed firearm may be disposed of after the 180-day period has expired.
(b) This section shall remain in effect only until July 1, 2020, and as of that date is repealed.
(Amended by Stats. 2018, Ch. 780, Sec. 19. (SB 746) Effective January 1, 2019. Repealed as of July 1, 2020, by its own provisions. See later operative version added by Stats. 2018, Ch. 780.)
33875.
(a) Notwithstanding any other law, no law enforcement agency or court shall be required to retain any firearm, ammunition feeding device, or ammunition for more than 180 days after the owner has been notified by the court or law enforcement agency that the property has been made available for return. An unclaimed firearm, ammunition feeding device, or ammunition may be disposed of after the 180-day period has expired.
(b) This section shall become operative on July 1, 2020.
(Repealed and added by Stats. 2018, Ch. 780, Sec. 20. (SB 746) Effective January 1, 2019. Section operative July 1, 2020, by its own provisions.)
33880.
(a) A city, county, or city and county, or a state agency may adopt a regulation, ordinance, or resolution imposing a charge equal to its administrative costs relating to the seizure, impounding, storage, or release of any firearm or ammunition.
(b) The fee under subdivision (a) shall not exceed the actual costs incurred for the expenses directly related to taking possession of any firearm or ammunition, storing it, and surrendering possession of it to a licensed firearms dealer or to the owner.
(c) The administrative costs described in subdivisions (a) and (b) may be waived by the local or state agency upon verifiable proof that the firearm or ammunition was reported stolen at the time it came into the custody or control of the law enforcement agency.
(d) The following apply to any charges imposed for administrative costs pursuant to this section:
(1) The charges shall only be imposed on the person claiming title to the firearm or ammunition.
(2) Any charges shall be collected by the local or state authority only from the person claiming title to the firearm or ammunition.
(3) The charges shall be in addition to any other charges authorized or imposed pursuant to this code.

(4) A charge shall not be imposed for a hearing or appeal relating to the removal, impound, storage, or release of any firearm or ammunition, unless that hearing or appeal was requested in writing by the legal owner of the property. In addition, the charge may be imposed only upon the person requesting that hearing or appeal.
(e) Costs for a hearing or appeal related to the release of any firearm or ammunition shall not be charged to the legal owner who redeems the property, unless the legal owner voluntarily requests the poststorage hearing or appeal. A city, county, city and county, or state agency shall not require a legal owner to request a poststorage hearing as a requirement for release of the firearm or ammunition to the legal owner.
(f) This section shall remain in effect only until July 1, 2020, and as of that date is repealed.
(Amended by Stats. 2018, Ch. 780, Sec. 21. (SB 746) Effective January 1, 2019. Repealed as of July 1, 2020, by its own provisions. See later operative version added by Stats. 2018, Ch. 780.)
33880.
(a) A city, county, or city and county, or a state agency may adopt a regulation, ordinance, or resolution imposing a charge equal to its administrative costs relating to the seizure, impounding, storage, or release of any firearm, ammunition feeding device, or ammunition.
(b) The fee under subdivision (a) shall not exceed the actual costs incurred for the expenses directly related to taking possession of any firearm, ammunition feeding device, or ammunition, storing it, and surrendering possession of it to a licensed firearms dealer or to the owner.
(c) The administrative costs described in subdivisions (a) and (b) may be waived by the local or state agency upon verifiable proof that the firearm, ammunition feeding device, or ammunition was reported stolen at the time it came into the custody or control of the law enforcement agency.
(d) The following apply to any charges imposed for administrative costs pursuant to this section:
(1) The charges shall only be imposed on the person claiming title to the firearm, ammunition feeding device, or ammunition.
(2) Any charges shall be collected by the local or state authority only from the person claiming title to the firearm, ammunition feeding device, or ammunition.
(3) The charges shall be in addition to any other charges authorized or imposed pursuant to this code.
(4) A charge shall not be imposed for a hearing or appeal relating to the removal, impound, storage, or release of any firearm, ammunition feeding device, or ammunition, unless that hearing or appeal was requested in writing by the legal owner of the property. In addition, the charge may be imposed only upon the person requesting that hearing or appeal.
(e) Costs for a hearing or appeal related to the release of any firearm, ammunition feeding device, or ammunition shall not be charged to the legal owner who redeems the property, unless the legal owner voluntarily requests the poststorage hearing or appeal. A city, county, city and county, or state agency shall not require a legal owner to request a poststorage hearing as a requirement for release of the firearm, ammunition feeding device, or ammunition to the legal owner.
(f) This section shall become operative on July 1, 2020.
(Repealed and added by Stats. 2018, Ch. 780, Sec. 22. (SB 746) Effective January 1, 2019. Section operative July 1, 2020, by its own provisions.)
33885.
(a) In a proceeding for the return of any firearm seized and not returned pursuant to this chapter, where the defendant or cross-defendant is a law enforcement agency, the court shall award reasonable attorney's fees to the prevailing party.
(b) This section shall remain in effect only until July 1, 2020, and as of that date is repealed.
(Amended by Stats. 2018, Ch. 780, Sec. 23. (SB 746) Effective January 1, 2019. Repealed as of July 1, 2020, by its own provisions. See later operative version added by Stats. 2018, Ch. 780.)
33885.
(a) In a proceeding for the return of any firearm, ammunition feeding device, or ammunition seized and not returned pursuant to this chapter, where the defendant or cross-defendant is a law enforcement agency, the court shall award reasonable attorney's fees to the prevailing party.
(b) This section shall become operative on July 1, 2020.
(Repealed and added by Stats. 2018, Ch. 780, Sec. 24. (SB 746) Effective January 1, 2019. Section operative July 1, 2020, by its own provisions.)
33895.
(a) Section 27545 does not apply to deliveries, transfers, or returns of firearms made pursuant to this chapter.
(b) This section shall remain in effect only until July 1, 2020, and as of that date is repealed.
(Amended by Stats. 2018, Ch. 780, Sec. 25. (SB 746) Effective January 1, 2019. Repealed as of July 1, 2020, by its own provisions. See later operative version added by Stats. 2018, Ch. 780.)
33895.
(a) Section 27545 does not apply to deliveries, transfers, or returns of firearms made pursuant to this chapter.
(b) Sections 30312 and 30342 do not apply to deliveries or transfers of returns of ammunition or ammunition feeding devices by a court or law enforcement agency made pursuant to this chapter.
(c) This section shall become operative on July 1, 2020.
(Repealed and added by Stats. 2018, Ch. 780, Sec. 26. (SB 746) Effective January 1, 2019. Section operative July 1, 2020, by its own provisions.)

CHAPTER 3. Firearms that are Unclaimed, Abandoned, or Subject to Destruction [34000 - 34010]

(Chapter 3 added by Stats. 2010, Ch. 711, Sec. 6.)
34000.
(a) Notwithstanding any provision of law or of any local ordinance to the contrary, when any firearm is in the possession of any officer of the state, or of a county, city, or city and county, or of any campus of the University of California or the California State University, and the firearm is an exhibit filed in any criminal action or proceeding which is no longer needed or is unclaimed or abandoned property, which has been in the possession of the officer for at least 180 days, the firearm shall be sold, or destroyed, as provided for in Sections 18000 and 18005.
(b) This section does not apply to any firearm in the possession of the Department of Fish and Game, or which was used in the violation of any provision in the Fish and Game Code, or any regulation under that code.
(Added by Stats. 2010, Ch. 711, Sec. 6. (SB 1080) Effective January 1, 2011. Operative January 1, 2012, by Sec. 10 of Ch. 711.)
34005.
(a) (1) An officer having custody of any firearm that may be useful to the California National Guard, the Coast Guard Auxiliary, or to any military or naval agency of the

federal or state government, including, but not limited to, the California State Military Museum and Resource Center, located in Sacramento, and at branch museums located at the California National Guard facilities at Camp Roberts, Camp San Luis Obispo, and Los Alamitos Armed Forces Reserve Center, may, upon the authority of the legislative body of the city, city and county, or county by which the officer is employed and the approval of the Adjutant General, deliver the firearm to the commanding officer of a unit of the California National Guard, the Coast Guard Auxiliary, or any other military agency of the state or federal government, in lieu of destruction as required by any of the provisions listed in Section 16580.

(2) Any state agency, county, municipality, or special purpose district may offer any excess military weapons or equipment, such as historical war equipment like artillery, tanks, or armored vehicles, to the California State Military Museum and Resource Center or any branch museum described in paragraph (1).

(3) The officer delivering a firearm pursuant to this subdivision shall take a receipt for it, which contains a complete description of the firearm, and shall keep the receipt on file in his or her office as a public record.

(b) Any law enforcement agency that has custody of any firearms, or any parts of any firearms, which are subject to destruction as required by any of the provisions listed in Section 16580, may, in lieu of destroying the weapons, retain and use any of them as may be useful in carrying out the official duties of the agency. Alternatively, upon approval of a court, the agency may do either of the following:

(1) Release the weapons to any other law enforcement agency for use in carrying out the official duties of that agency.

(2) Turn over to the criminalistics laboratory of the Department of Justice or the criminalistics laboratory of a police department, sheriff's office, or district attorney's office, any weapons that may be useful in carrying out the official duties of the respective agencies.

(c) (1) Any firearm, or part of any firearm, which, rather than being destroyed, is used for official purposes pursuant to this section, shall be destroyed by the agency using the weapon when it is no longer needed by the agency for use in carrying out its official duties.

(2) Firearms or weaponry donated to the California State Military Museum and Resource Center may be disposed of pursuant to Section 179 of the Military and Veterans Code.

(d) (1) Any law enforcement agency that has custody of any firearms, or any parts of any firearms, which are subject to destruction as required by any of the provisions listed in Section 16580, may, in lieu of destroying the firearms, obtain an order from the superior court directing the release of the firearms to the sheriff.

(2) The sheriff shall enter those weapons into the Automated Firearms System (AFS), via the California Law Enforcement Telecommunications System, with a complete description of each weapon, including the make, type, category, caliber, and serial number of the firearms, and the name of the academy receiving the weapon entered into the AFS miscellaneous field.

(3) The sheriff shall then release the firearms to the basic training academy certified by the Commission on Peace Officer Standards and Training, so that the firearms may be used for instructional purposes in the certified courses. All firearms released to an academy shall be under the care, custody, and control of the particular academy.

(4) Any firearm, or part of any firearm, which is not destroyed, and is used for the purposes authorized by this section, shall be returned to the law enforcement agency that had original custody of the firearm when it is no longer needed by the basic training academy, or when the basic training academy is no longer certified by the commission.

(5) When those firearms are returned, the law enforcement agency to which the firearms are returned, shall on the date of the return, enter into the Automated Firearms System (AFS), via the California Law Enforcement Telecommunications System, a complete description of each weapon, including the make, type, category, caliber, and serial number of the firearms, and the name of the entity returning the firearm.

(Amended by Stats. 2013, Ch. 698, Sec. 1. (SB 759) Effective January 1, 2014.)
34010.
Any law enforcement agency that retains custody of any firearm pursuant to Section 34005, or that destroys a firearm pursuant to Sections 18000 and 18005, shall notify the Department of Justice of the retention or destruction. This notification shall consist of a complete description of each firearm, including the name of the manufacturer or brand name, model, caliber, and serial number.

(Added by Stats. 2010, Ch. 711, Sec. 6. (SB 1080) Effective January 1, 2011. Operative January 1, 2012, by Sec. 10 of Ch. 711.)

DIVISION 12. MISCELLANEOUS DUTIES OF THE DEPARTMENT OF JUSTICE [34200 - 34370]

(Division 12 added by Stats. 2010, Ch. 711, Sec. 6.)

CHAPTER 1. Miscellaneous Reports and Publications [34200 - 34205]

(Chapter 1 added by Stats. 2010, Ch. 711, Sec. 6.)
34200.
The Attorney General shall provide the Legislature on or before April 15 of each year, commencing in 1998, a written report on the specific types of firearms used in the commission of crimes based upon information obtained from state and local crime laboratories. The report shall include all of the following information regarding crimes in which firearms were used:

(a) A description of the relative occurrence of firearms most frequently used in the commission of violent crimes, distinguishing whether the firearms used were handguns, rifles, shotguns, assault weapons, or other related types of weapons.

(b) A description of specific types of firearms that are used in homicides or street gang and drug trafficking crimes.

(c) The frequency with which stolen firearms were used in the commission of the crimes.

(d) The frequency with which fully automatic firearms were used in the commission of the crimes.

(e) Any trends of importance such as those involving specialized ammunition or firearms modifications, such as conversion to a fully automatic weapon, removal of serial number, shortening of barrel, or use of a suppressor.

(Added by Stats. 2010, Ch. 711, Sec. 6. (SB 1080) Effective January 1, 2011. Operative January 1, 2012, by Sec. 10 of Ch. 711.)
34205.
(a) The Department of Justice shall prepare a pamphlet that summarizes California firearms laws as they pertain to persons other than law enforcement officers or members of the armed services.

(b) The pamphlet shall include the following matters:

(1) Lawful possession.
(2) Licensing procedures.
(3) Transportation and use of firearms.
(4) Acquisition of hunting licenses.
(5) The safe handling and use of firearms.
(6) Various methods of safe storage and child proofing of firearms.
(7) The availability of firearms safety programs and devices.
(8) The responsibilities of firearms ownership.

(9) The operation of various types of firearms.
(10) The lawful use of deadly force.

(c) The department shall offer copies of the pamphlet at actual cost to firearms dealers licensed pursuant to Sections 26700 to 26915, inclusive, who shall have copies of the most current version available for sale to retail purchasers or transferees of firearms. The cost of the pamphlet, if any, may be added to the sale price of the firearm. Other interested parties may purchase copies directly from the Department of General Services.

(d) The pamphlet shall declare that it is merely intended to provide a general summary of laws applicable to firearms and is not designed to provide individual guidance for specific areas. Individuals having specific questions shall be directed to contact their local law enforcement agency or private counsel.

(e) The Department of Justice or any other public entity shall be immune from any liability arising from the drafting, publication, or dissemination of the pamphlet or any reliance upon it. All receipts from the sale of these pamphlets shall be deposited as reimbursements to the support appropriation for the Department of Justice.

(Added by Stats. 2010, Ch. 711, Sec. 6. (SB 1080) Effective January 1, 2011. Operative January 1, 2012, by Sec. 10 of Ch. 711.)

CHAPTER 2. Ballistics Identification System [34350 - 34370]

(Chapter 2 added by Stats. 2010, Ch. 711, Sec. 6.)
34350.
(a) The Attorney General shall conduct a study to evaluate ballistics identification systems to determine the feasibility and potential benefits to law enforcement of utilizing a statewide ballistics identification system capable of maintaining a database of ballistic images and information from test fired and sold firearms. The study shall include an evaluation of ballistics identification systems currently used by state and federal law enforcement agencies and the firearms industry. The Attorney General shall consult with law enforcement agencies, firearms industry representatives, private technology providers, and other appropriate parties in conducting the study.

(b) In evaluating ballistics identification systems to determine the feasibility of utilizing a statewide system as required pursuant to subdivision (a), the Attorney General shall consider, at a minimum, the following:

(1) The development of methods by which firearm manufacturers, importers, and dealers may potentially capture ballistic images from firearms prior to sale in California and forward that information to the Attorney General.

(2) The development of methods by which the Attorney General will receive, store, and make available to law enforcement ballistic images submitted by firearm manufacturers, importers, and dealers prior to sale in California.

(3) The potential financial costs to the Attorney General of implementing and operating a statewide ballistics identification system, including the process for receipt of information from firearm manufacturers, importers, and dealers.

(4) The capability of a ballistics identification system maintaining a database of ballistic images and information from test fired firearms for all firearms sold in California.

(5) The compatibility of a ballistics identification system with ballistics identification systems that are currently used by law enforcement agencies in California.

(6) A method to ensure that state and local law enforcement agencies can forward ballistic identification information to the Attorney General for inclusion in a statewide ballistics identification system.

(7) The feasibility and potential benefits to law enforcement of requiring firearm manufacturers, importers, and dealers to provide the Attorney General with ballistic images from any, or a selected number of, test fired firearms prior to the sale of those firearms in California.

(c) The Attorney General shall submit a report to the Legislature with the results of the study not later than June 1, 2001. In the event the report includes a determination that a ballistics identification system and database is feasible and would benefit law enforcement, the report shall also recommend a strategy for implementation.

(Added by Stats. 2010, Ch. 711, Sec. 6. (SB 1080) Effective January 1, 2011. Operative January 1, 2012, by Sec. 10 of Ch. 711.)
34355.
(a) Section 34350 does not apply to any sale, delivery, or transfer of firearms made to an authorized law enforcement representative of any city, county, city and county, or state, or of the federal government, for exclusive use by that governmental agency if, prior to the sale, delivery, or transfer of these firearms, written authorization from the head of the agency authorizing the transaction is presented to the person from whom the purchase, delivery, or transfer is being made.

(b) Proper written authorization is defined as verifiable written certification from the head of the agency by which the purchaser or transferee is employed, identifying the employee as an individual authorized to conduct the transaction, and authorizing the transaction for the exclusive use of the agency by which that person is employed.

(c) Within 10 days of the date a handgun, and commencing January 1, 2014, any firearm, is acquired by the agency, a record of the same shall be entered as an institutional weapon into the Automated Firearms System (AFS) via the California Law Enforcement Telecommunications System (CLETS) by the law enforcement or state agency. Any agency without access to AFS shall arrange with the sheriff of the county in which the agency is located to input this information via this system.

(Amended by Stats. 2011, Ch. 745, Sec. 76. (AB 809) Effective January 1, 2012.)
34360.
Section 34350 does not apply to the loan of a firearm if all of the following conditions are satisfied:

(a) The loan is made by an authorized law enforcement representative of a city, county, or city and county, or of the state or federal government.

(b) The loan is made to a peace officer employed by that agency and authorized to carry a firearm.

(c) The loan is made for the carrying and use of that firearm by that peace officer in the course and scope of the officer's duties.

(Added by Stats. 2010, Ch. 711, Sec. 6. (SB 1080) Effective January 1, 2011. Operative January 1, 2012, by Sec. 10 of Ch. 711.)
34365.
(a) Section 34350 does not apply to the sale, delivery, or transfer of a firearm by a law enforcement agency to a peace officer pursuant to Section 10334 of the Public Contract Code.

(b) Within 10 days of the date that a handgun, and commencing January 1, 2014, any firearm, is sold, delivered, or transferred pursuant to Section 10334 of the Public Contract Code to that peace officer, the name of the officer and the make, model, serial number, and other identifying characteristics of the firearm being sold, delivered, or transferred shall be entered into the Automated Firearms System (AFS) via the California Law Enforcement Telecommunications System (CLETS) by the law enforcement or state agency that sold, delivered, or transferred the firearm, provided, however, that if the firearm is not a handgun and does not have a serial number, identification number, or identification mark assigned to it, that fact shall be noted in AFS. Any agency without access to AFS shall arrange with the sheriff of the county in which the agency is located to input this information via this system.

(Amended by Stats. 2011, Ch. 745, Sec. 77. (AB 809) Effective January 1, 2012.)

34370.

(a) Section 34350 does not apply to the sale, delivery, or transfer of a firearm by a law enforcement agency to a retiring peace officer who is authorized to carry a firearm pursuant to Chapter 5 (commencing with Section 26300) of Division 5.

(b) Within 10 days of the date that a handgun, and commencing January 1, 2014, any firearm, is sold, delivered, or transferred to that retiring peace officer, the name of the officer and the make, model, serial number, and other identifying characteristics of the firearm being sold, delivered, or transferred shall be entered into the Automated Firearms System (AFS) via the California Law Enforcement Telecommunications System (CLETS) by the law enforcement or state agency that sold, delivered, or transferred the firearm, provided, however, that if the firearm is not a handgun and does not have a serial number, identification number, or identification mark assigned to it, that fact shall be noted in AFS. Any agency without access to AFS shall arrange with the sheriff of the county in which the agency is located to input this information via this system.

(Amended by Stats. 2011, Ch. 745, Sec. 78. (AB 809) Effective January 1, 2012.)

Made in the USA
Monee, IL
14 November 2020

47673749R00332